CollegeBoard

D1358709

29.95

The College Board
2009 College
HANDBOOK

The College Board

# College

# HANDBOOK

CollegeBoard

Forty-Sixth Edition

The College Board, New York

**CollegeBoard**

**The College Board: Connecting Students to College Success**

The College Board is a not-for-profit membership association whose mission is to connect students to college success and opportunity. Founded in 1900, the association is composed of more than 5,400 schools, colleges, universities, and other educational organizations. Each year, the College Board serves seven million students and their parents, 23,000 high schools, and 3,500 colleges through major programs and services in college admissions, guidance, assessment, financial aid, enrollment, and teaching and learning. Among its best-known programs are the SAT®, the PSAT/NMSQT®, and the Advanced Placement Program® (AP®). The College Board is committed to the principles of excellence and equity, and that commitment is embodied in all of its programs, services, activities, and concerns.

For further information, visit www.collegeboard.com.

Editorial inquiries concerning this book should be directed to College Planning Services, The College Board, 45 Columbus Avenue, New York, NY 10023-6992; or telephone 212 713-8000.

Copies of this book are available from your local bookseller or may be ordered from College Board Publications, P.O. Box 869010, Plano, TX 75074-0998. The book may also be ordered online through the College Board Store at www.collegeboard.com. The price is $29.95.

Library of Congress Catalog Number: 41-12971

ISBN-13: 978-0-87447-823-5

ISBN-10: 0-87447-823-5

Printed in the United States of America

Distributed by Macmillan

# Contents

# Preface

When the *College Handbook* first appeared in 1941, students and parents had little access to college information of any kind. Now, in this Internet age, many find the amount of available information to be overwhelming.

What's needed is a single, trusted source where the key facts about colleges can be compared and contrasted on a consistent basis. From its inception, the *Handbook* has met this need by providing college-bound students and their advisers with the authoritative, reliable, and up-to-date facts necessary to make informed college decisions.

This edition of the *Handbook* presents facts about 3,845 colleges, universities, and technical schools. To be included, an institution must be accredited by a national or regional accrediting association recognized by the U.S. Department of Education and offer some undergraduate degree programs—at least an associate degree.

Throughout the *Handbook*, information is presented in accordance with the Common Data Set initiative, in which the College Board has taken a leading role. The goal of this collaborative effort with other publishers and college administrators is to provide students with the most accurate, consistently comparable data available.

The college descriptions are based on information supplied by the colleges themselves in response to the College Board's Annual Survey of Colleges 2008. The survey was completed by participating colleges in spring 2008. Several thousand college administrators across the country participated in this effort. Without their continued cooperation, publication of the *Handbook* would not be possible.

A staff of data editors verified the facts to be certain that all descriptions are as complete and accurate as possible. Although the College Board makes every effort to ensure that the information about colleges is correct and up to date, we urge students to confirm facts with the colleges themselves.

The enormous task of data collection, management, and verification was directed by Connie Betterton and Stan Bernstein, with the assistance of Cathy Serico, Andrew Costello, Renée Gernand, Roger Harris, Doris Chow, and Ralph Hockens. Marci Arnold, Mary Anne Blazier, Leah Swaggerty, Stewart Both, Jenny Xie, Christina Latimer, May Cooper, Diana McDermott, and Randy Peery compiled, edited, and verified the data. The Web-based survey tool they used was programmed and maintained by Mike Starinieri, Xuhe Wang, Robert Hargrove, Brenda Levathes, June Ni, and Eugene Hsiang. Enterprise database services for survey data were provided by David Skrobela, Jim Clewley, Alexandre Hulot, and Iyad Lahham.

We thank our readers—you and the many students, parents, and counselors whose comments and suggestions over the years have helped to make this the most widely used college directory in the nation. We welcome your suggestions on how the *Handbook* can continue to meet the ever-changing needs of future generations of college-bound students.

Tom Vanderberg
Senior Editor, College Planning Services

# What's in this book

If you're beginning your college search feeling a bit overwhelmed and intimidated by the sheer number of choices, you're not alone. Just about everyone starts out feeling that way. But even the most daunting job can be easily handled with the right tools and a plan, and the *College Handbook* gives you both.

## Getting Started

The *College Handbook* is the best place to begin your college search, and you will no doubt find yourself returning to this source as your search progresses and evolves. You should not, however, rely on this book exclusively. Take advantage of the other resources available to you—the Internet, campus visits and interviews, college fairs and viewbooks, your school counselor, family and friends—before you make your final decision. Don't be dismayed if you find that you must change directions more than once as you learn about the colleges. This only means that you are learning more about yourself as well.

The *Handbook* is divided into four major sections. The first (where you are now) contains guidance materials to help you plan for college. Four-year college descriptions are in the second section, two-year college descriptions are in the third, and the last section contains tables and indexes. Margin tabs help you to quickly move from section to section.

Although you might be eager to dive right into the college descriptions, it is far better to start your college search with a basic idea of what you want to look for. Take the time to go through the guidance materials in the first section to get on the right track. Read the articles, ranging from college admissions and placement tests to dorm life. The valuable insights you gain will give you confidence as you continue your college search.

Once you can identify your needs and preferences with regard to college size and type and have an idea of what other characteristics are important to you, the indexes at the end of the book will help you locate colleges that fit the bill.

**KNOW THE LINGO**

You'll find sidebars like this throughout the first part of this book highlighting and defining key terms. There's also a comprehensive glossary beginning on page 40.

For a complete explanation of the various index categories, see "Tables and Indexes" beginning on page 7.

The heart and soul of the *Handbook*, of course, are the descriptions of four-year and two-year colleges. These follow standard formats to make it easy to find a particular item of information in any description and to compare one college with another. Read "The College Descriptions" below to see what the descriptions contain and how the information is presented. If you are not sure of the meaning of a term found in the *Handbook* descriptions or guidance materials, check the glossary beginning on page 38.

# The College Descriptions

**The college.** Each description begins with the college's official name—which isn't always the one in popular use. The heading also includes the college's city, state, and Web site address. Most colleges now have Web sites that are invaluable resources in your college search. The designation "CB member" after the college's name indicates that the college is a member of the College Board; the four-digit CB code should be used when requesting that SAT® scores or Advanced Placement Program® (AP®) grades be sent to the college.

**Key facts.** The bulleted list highlights information that you may want to compare across colleges and that you'll need if you decide to apply. This information includes:

- Type of institution (e.g., liberal arts college, university) and whether it has a religious affiliation.

- Whether the campus is urban, suburban, or rural, and whether it is primarily a residential or a commuter campus.

- Total number of undergraduate students; profile of the undergraduate student body (percent part-time, women, minority breakdown, international); total number of graduate students on campus. *Two-year undergraduate data are included under Student Profile.*

- Percent of applicants admitted to the freshman class, which gives you some idea of how competitive the college is. *Four-year colleges only.*

- Admissions requirements for fall 2009: tests, essay, interview (if required of all applicants).

- Percent of students who graduate within six years (most students take more than four years to earn a bachelor's degree). Caveat: This figure is based on students who enrolled as freshmen and remained to graduate; it does not include students who transferred into or out of the college during that period.

**General information.** The date the college was founded, the type of institutional accreditation it has, the number and type of degrees awarded in 2006-07, and whether the college has an ROTC program will give you a sense of the academic life on campus. Whether the college organizes its calendar on a semester, trimester, quarter, or some other schedule indicates the way the college structures its courses.

Pay particular attention to the faculty information. The total number of faculty and its makeup are important to your everyday experience at an institution. Class size information, showing percentages of classes with few or many students, is another indication of a college's learning environment. Colleges were also invited to provide a list of special facilities (from arboretums to zoos) or additional unique information about their institutions in this section.

*For two-year colleges only:* This is where you will find total enrollment figures for both degree-seeking and non-degree-seeking students, and information about partnerships with other schools or organizations.

**Freshman class profile.** (*Four-year colleges*) This provides a snapshot of the college's 2007 freshman class and is presented in tabular format to make it easily accessible. This is the best source of information about whether your own profile fits in with that of students currently attending the college, and whether you'd be comfortable if admitted.

- Number who applied, were admitted, and enrolled.

- Mid-50 percent of enrolled freshmen's SAT/ACT test scores. This is the score range for half the freshman class. (Remember that 25 percent of enrolled freshmen scored below and 25 percent above the reported figures.)

- Information about high school GPA and class rank.

- Percentage who completed the year in good standing and returned as sophomores.

- Percentage who come from out of state, live on campus, are international students, and join fraternities or sororities.

**Student profile.** (*Two-year colleges*) This is similar to the freshman class profile for four-year colleges, but the data presented covers the entire undergraduate student body.

- Percentage enrolled in transfer or vocational programs. Number admitted and enrolled as first-time, first-year students. Percentage who already have a bachelor's degree or higher. Number who transferred from other institutions.

- Percentage of the total undergraduate student body who are part-time students, live on campus, are women, come from out of state, are minorities, and are international students.

**Transfer out.** (*Two-year colleges*)

- Percentage of students in transfer programs who go on to four-year colleges.

- Colleges to which most students transferred in 2007.

**Basis for selection.** This is where you can find the details of a college's admissions policies, including factors the college considers most important in deciding whether or not to offer you admission. If it says "Open admission," that means the college accepts anyone with a high school or GED diploma, space permitting. Special requirements for homeschooled and learning disabled students are also reported here.

**High school preparation.** Almost all colleges listed in the *Handbook* require a high school diploma or its equivalent. Some colleges have very specific requirements in terms of education background and high school courses taken. The required and recommended number of course units that applicants should have taken in high school is listed here. Where a range is given, the lower number represents the required units; the higher number is a recommendation.

**2008-09 annual costs.** You should estimate and anticipate the total annual costs for each college you are considering. In doing so, the elements listed below need to be considered. Unless otherwise noted, the reported figures reflect the costs for the 2008-09 academic year.

- *Tuition/fees* include the cost of instruction and mandated fees for all students. For public colleges, both in-state and out-of-state costs are listed. If the college combines tuition, fees, and room and board expenses, that single figure is given as a comprehensive fee.

- *Room/board* figures are for a student living on campus in a double room with a full meal plan. Single rooms or rooms for three or more could cost a lot more or less than the figure reported here. Many colleges have a range of meal plans with fewer meals per week, which would lower your board cost.

- *Books/supplies* expenses can vary depending on the program you take. Some fields, such as art or architecture, may require more expensive supplies.

- *Personal expenses* include items such as clothing, laundry, entertainment, and furnishings. Personal expenses will vary widely depending on your lifestyle. Transportation costs are not included.

- *Per-credit-hour tuition* (two-year colleges only) is of particular interest to students planning to attend college part-time.

**Financial aid.** This information provides a summary of financial aid awarded for the academic year(s) indicated, and describes financial aid award policies for need-based and non-need-based aid. This information will give you an idea of how first-year and undergraduate student assistance has been awarded and will help you compare financial aid policies among the colleges. You should always contact the admissions or financial aid office for complete information and for answers to any questions you might have regarding eligibility and award policies.

**Application procedures.** This is where you can find out about the college's application procedures and deadlines for both admissions and financial aid.

- *Admissions.* Most colleges require an application fee, noted here, but will waive it for applicants with need. Take note of any "priority dates"—after which qualified applicants are considered on a first-come, first-served basis, and only for as long as slots are available.

- *Financial aid.* Required forms plus priority, closing, notification, and reply dates are listed for fall term financial aid applications. The Free Application for Federal Student Aid (FAFSA) is required by every college offering federal financial aid. If the college requires the CSS/Financial Aid PROFILE® to determine your eligibility for nonfederal funds, it is noted here. "Institutional form" means the college has a form of its own. Pay special attention to priority dates and deadlines; if the college indicates "no deadline" for financial aid, it means it will continue to process requests as long as funds are available. You should always apply as early as possible to obtain the best consideration for financial aid awards.

**Academics.** Many colleges offer a range of special study options that can enrich or enhance your education experience. Special academic programs are listed in this section. Check the glossary for brief descriptions of each of the programs listed.

College policies on granting credit or advanced standing through the College Board's Advanced Placement Program and College-Level Examination Program® (CLEP®), the International Baccalaureate (IB) program, and/or institutional tests are listed next. Most colleges have a maximum number of credit hours by examination that may be counted toward a degree, which is also listed.

Academic support services list the programs the college provides to assist students in succeeding academically. Preadmission summer programs, special counselors, tutoring, learning disabled programs, and study skills assistance are some of the options offered.

**Honors college/program.** If a college has a separate undergraduate honors college or a program with different admissions and academic offerings from those available to regular students, this section will tell you what's available and how to apply.

**Majors.** Only majors leading to a bachelor's degree (for four-year colleges) or an associate degree (for two-year colleges) are included here. They are listed alphabetically by general category. The majors listed here are based on the U.S. Department of Education's Classification of Instructional Programs; colleges were asked to match the majors they offer to this list. Many colleges additionally offer concentrations within a major, which are not reflected here.

**Most popular majors.** This will give you an idea of whether a substantial number of students are completing a major in an area that is of interest to you. This list is based on the percentage of students who were awarded degrees in each of the general categories listed in the 2006-07 academic year.

**Computing on campus.** Whether you bring your own computer to campus, or plan on using college-provided workstations, you'll want to know what technological support the college provides for student use, and whether the college requires you to bring your own PC or laptop. This section lists the number of workstations available for student use and where they're located; whether dorms are wired for high-speed Internet access and/or linked to the campus network; if there is a wireless network; if there's online course registration, an online library, or student Web hosting; and whether commuter students can link to the campus network.

**Student life.** If you attend the college, you will need to know if it requires enrollees to attend freshman orientation, and if it has policies and regulations governing student behavior.

If on-campus housing is available—whether it's in the form of dormitories, apartments, fraternity/sorority housing, or cooperative housing—it will be indicated here. Most dormitories today are coeducational, but many colleges offer single-sex accommodations either in separate buildings or separate floors. Some colleges are now also offering "substance-free" or "wellness" dormitories, whose residents pledge not to use alcohol, tobacco, or any illegal drugs. This section also indicates if on-campus housing is guaranteed for freshmen, or for all four years; and the policies and deadlines for deposits.

Most colleges have provided a selective list of student activities sponsored by the institution. Read the list carefully to see if it reflects the type of student organizations and opportunities of interest to you.

**Athletics.** Intercollegiate and intramural sports available at the college are listed here, along with the team name. Sports offered for men or women only are indicated by (M) or (W). The athletic association to which the college belongs also is indicated. If you're interested in NCAA division offerings, the indexes starting on page 2126 show, sport by sport, the division level a college offers.

**Student services.** This section lists the college's basic range of services for students. Among these are health, personal counseling, services for adult students, student employment services, placement service for graduates, veterans' counseling, and on-campus day care. This section also lists special services/facilities for learning disabled students and those with visual, speech, or hearing impairments.

**Contact.** The last item in each description provides the admissions office's e-mail address, telephone and fax numbers, the name and/or title of the admissions director, and the mailing address of the college office to contact for further information and applications.

# Brief Descriptions

The 448 colleges that did not respond to our Annual Survey of Colleges are described in brief with the following information: name, city, state, college type, accreditation, location, and calendar. Annual costs and financial aid information are provided, if available. The addresses to contact for further information are also listed.

# Tables and Indexes

The tables and indexes in the back of this book are a useful tool to find colleges quickly and zero in on the schools that interest you.

## Early Application and Wait-List Outcomes

If you are considering applying to a college early, the Early Decision and Early Action table on page 2053 shows application deadlines and notification dates for early application programs, as well as the number of students who applied and were admitted last year under those policies.

If you find that you have been placed on a college's wait list for acceptance, consult the wait list table on page 2067. It will give you a sense of your chances, by showing how many students were placed on the wait list last year, how many accepted their place on the list, and how many were eventually admitted from the list.

## College Indexes

You can use the college indexes to quickly find schools that interest you. In most of the indexes, colleges are listed alphabetically by state because, for many students, geographic location is a primary requirement. Colleges that are part of a system are listed alphabetically under the system name.

The following explanation of index terms may help you decide whether a certain type of college or a special program or policy interests you.

### College type

**Liberal arts.** Sometimes known as arts and sciences. The study of liberal arts is intended to develop general knowledge and reasoning ability as opposed to specific preparation for a career. Most liberal arts colleges are privately controlled. They generally don't offer as many majors in the technical or scientific disciplines as comprehensive colleges or universities.

**Upper-division.** Offer the last two years of undergraduate study (junior and senior courses only), usually in specialized programs leading to the bachelor's degree. Students generally transfer to upper-division colleges after completing an associate degree or after finishing their second year of study at a four-year college.

**Specialized.** Concentrate their offerings in one or two specific areas, such as business or engineering. Students who enroll at specialized colleges generally have a precise idea of what they want to study.

**KNOW THE LINGO**

There are so many **types of specialized colleges** that we didn't have room to describe them all here. If you'd like to know more about a specific type of college, see the glossary that begins on page 38.

# Special characteristics

**Colleges for men/women.** Some of these colleges may enroll a few women or men, but their student bodies are predominantly of one sex.

**Colleges with religious affiliations.** Lists each college under the official name of the denomination with which it is affiliated. Student life at some colleges is greatly influenced by the religious affiliation. At other colleges, the affiliation may be historic only, having little influence on college life.

**Historically black colleges.** Identifies historically or predominantly black colleges that are committed to educating African American students. The information was obtained from the National Association for Equal Opportunity in Higher Education and the U.S. government.

**Hispanic-serving colleges.** Identifies colleges where Hispanic students comprise at least 25 percent of the total full-time undergraduate enrollment. The information was obtained from the Hispanic Association of Colleges and Universities (HACU).

**Tribal colleges.** Identifies colleges committed to serving geographically isolated populations of Native Americans. The information was obtained from the Carnegie Classification of Institutions of Higher Education.

# Undergraduate enrollment size

The number of students at a college helps determine its environment.

**Very small.** Fewer than 750 undergraduates.

**Small.** 750 to 1,999 undergraduates.

**Medium to large.** 2,000 to 7,499 undergraduates.

**Large.** 7,500 to 14,999 undergraduates.

**Very large.** 15,000 or more undergraduates.

# Admissions selectivity

**Admit under 50 percent, 50–75 percent, over 75 percent.** Colleges in three categories of selectivity that limit admission to applicants who meet specific requirements.

**Open admissions.** Colleges that admit virtually all applicants with a high school diploma or its equivalent, as long as space is available.

Many public institutions offer open admissions to state residents but have selective admissions requirements for out-of-state students or to selected programs; check the college descriptions to see what applies.

# Admissions/placement policies

**No closing date.** These colleges will accept applications up to the time of registration.

**SAT Subject Test required/recommended.** These two indexes list colleges that require or recommend that applicants take one or more

SAT Subject Tests™ for admission. The college descriptions provide more detailed information.

## Colleges that offer ROTC

The U.S. armed forces offer Reserve Officer's Training Corps programs that prepare candidates for commissions in the Air Force, Army, and Navy (Naval ROTC includes the Marine Corps). These programs are offered either at the colleges listed in the index or at cooperating institutions. ROTC programs may take either two or four years to complete. Use this index, organized by branch of service, to find colleges that offer the ROTC program of interest to you.

## Colleges with NCAA sports

Lists National Collegiate Athletic Association (NCAA) championship sports by division level and the colleges, state by state, that offer them. Also indicates whether each sport is available for men only or for women only. (Crew is an NCAA sport for women only; use the college search on collegeboard.com to find colleges that offer crew for men.) To be an NCAA member, colleges must offer at least four sports and have at least one in each season (fall, winter, and spring).

## Alphabetical index of colleges

Lists the name and state abbreviation for every institution in the *Handbook*. If a name has changed, the old name is cross-referenced to the new name.

**KEEP IN MIND**

The **NCAA sports indexes** only list colleges that offer sports for which the NCAA holds a championship. There are NCAA sports that don't have a championship, such as men's rowing. And remember that many colleges offer sports through a different association (NAIA or NJCAA), or offer intramural play.

# About accreditation

Every college and university in this book is accredited by an agency recognized by the U.S. Department of Education. That means you can trust that any of them will give you an education that meets basic standards for college-level study, that your studies will qualify for federal need-based financial aid and/or federal education tax breaks, and that the degree you will earn at the end of your studies will be recognized by future employers.

# What Is Accreditation?

Accreditation is a voluntary process of peer review and self-regulation. The standards for each accrediting agency are slightly different but, generally, each agency ensures that its members meet basic standards in their administrative procedures, physical facilities, and the quality of their academic programs.

The agencies listed on page 12 are *regional* and *national* agencies that accredit entire institutions. In majors that lead to a professional certification—such as nursing, engineering, or teacher education—there may also be *specialized* agencies that accredit just one program, department, or school at the college. For example, the Accreditation Board for Engineering and Technology (ABET) accredits engineering and engineering technology programs. In addition to guaranteeing the academic quality of programs, these specialized agencies often have a guidance component that helps university students make the transition to professional careers. You can find more information about specialized accrediting agencies in the College Board's *Book of Majors*, or at the Council for Higher Education Accreditation's Web site (www.chea.org).

# What Does Accreditation Mean to Me?

If you attend an accredited college, you can be sure that:

- You will be able to use federal student aid (Title IV money) to help pay for your costs if you qualify based on financial need.

- Your tuition will qualify you for federal income tax deductions and/or credits (if you meet other conditions).

- Academic credits you earn there are eligible to transfer to another accredited college.

- Employers and professional licensing boards will recognize the degree you earn as an academic credential, as will graduate schools and other academic institutions to which you may apply.

You should, however, understand what accreditation *doesn't* mean:

- There's no guarantee that you will receive federal need-based financial aid just by attending any college, even if it's accredited.

- Regional and national accreditation ensures that every academic program at the college meets standards, but that doesn't mean that the quality of every program at the college is equal.

- If you're applying for transfer from one undergraduate institution to another, there's no guarantee that all your credits will count toward the graduation requirements of the college where you plan to finish your degree. If you plan to attend a lower-division college for your first two years of study and then go on to earn a bachelor's degree, be sure to talk to the transfer counselor there before enrolling in courses.

- Similarly, there's no guarantee that graduate schools or employers will see your undergraduate course of study as appropriate preparation for the demands of their program or job requirements.

# REGIONAL
# ACCREDITING ASSOCIATIONS

**Middle States Commission on Higher Education**
3624 Market Street
Philadelphia, PA 19104-2680
www.msche.org

> Delaware, District of Columbia, Maryland, New Jersey, New York, Pennsylvania, Puerto Rico, Virgin Islands

**New England Association
of Schools and Colleges**
209 Burlington Road
Bedford, MA 01730-1433
www.neasc.org

> Connecticut, Maine, Massachusetts, New Hampshire, Rhode Island, Vermont.

**North Central Association
of Colleges and Schools**
30 North LaSalle Street, Suite 2400
Chicago, IL 60602-2504
www.ncahigherlearningcommission.org

> Arizona, Arkansas, Colorado, Illinois, Indiana, Iowa, Kansas, Michigan, Minnesota, Missouri, Nebraska, New Mexico, North Dakota, Ohio, Oklahoma, South Dakota, West Virginia, Wisconsin, Wyoming

**Northwest Association of Accredited Schools**
1510 Robert Street, Suite 103
Boise, ID 83705-5194
www.northwestaccreditation.org

> Alaska, Idaho, Montana, Nevada, Oregon, Utah, Washington

**Southern Association of Colleges and Schools**
1866 Southern Lane
Decatur, GA 30033-4097
www.sacs.org

> Alabama, Florida, Georgia, Kentucky, Louisiana, Mississippi, North Carolina, South Carolina, Tennessee, Texas, Virginia

**Western Association of Schools and Colleges**
Accrediting Commission for Senior Colleges and Universities
985 Atlantic Avenue, Suite 100
Alameda, CA 94501
www.wascweb.org

Accrediting Commission for Community and Junior Colleges
10 Commercial Boulevard, Suite 204
Novato, CA 94949
www.accjc.org

> American Samoa, California, Guam, Hawaii, Trust Territory of the Pacific

**New York Board of Regents**
Office of College and University Evaluation
New York State Education Department
Room 110EB
Albany, NY 12234
www.regents.nysed.gov

# NATIONAL
# ACCREDITING ASSOCIATIONS

**ACICS**  **Accrediting Council for Independent Colleges and Schools**
750 First Street NE, Suite 980
Washington, DC 20002-4241
www.acics.org

**ACCSCT**  **Accrediting Commission of Career Schools/Colleges of Technology**
2101 Wilson Boulevard, Suite 302
Arlington, VA 22201
www.accsct.org

**ABHE**  **Association for Biblical Higher Education**
5575 S. Semoran Boulevard, Suite 26
Orlando, FL 32822-1781
www.abhe.org

**AARTS**  **Association of Advanced Rabbinical and Talmudic Schools**
11 Broadway
New York, NY 10004

**ATS**  **Association of Theological Schools in the United States and Canada**
10 Summit Park Drive
Pittsburgh, PA 15275-1110
www.ats.edu

**DETC**  **Distance Education and Training Council**
1601 18th Street NW
Washington, DC 20009
www.detc.org

# Selecting colleges

There are more than 3,800 accredited colleges in the United States. This book will help you get an idea of the types of colleges you're interested in attending and learn more about colleges that fall into those categories. From there, you can create a list of colleges you would like to learn more about, and start requesting information from them, visiting their Web sites, and (if you can) visiting their campuses. By December of your senior year, you should have your choices narrowed down to a final list of four to eight colleges to which you want to apply.

# Finding Your Fit

Every college is unique in some way. And everybody has different interests, ambitions, and needs. When investigating colleges, you will probably look for different things than your friends, parents, and siblings did when they applied. But there are some "big picture" elements that everyone, including you, should consider.

Colleges fall into broad categories—small and large, liberal arts and professionally oriented, academically selective and open admissions. There are also personal criteria you need to consider, such as whether a college is in your hometown or a thousand miles away.

## Type of Institution

This will give you a sense of how the college organizes its academic departments. Different types of institutions include:

**Liberal arts colleges** offer a broad base of courses in the humanities, social sciences, and natural sciences. Most are private and focus mainly on undergraduate students. Classes tend to be small, and personal attention is available. An education at a liberal arts college will prepare you for a broad range of career and graduate school options.

**Community and junior colleges** offer a degree after the completion of two years of full-time study. They frequently offer technical programs that prepare you for immediate entry into the job market. To learn more about the benefits of attending a community college, read "About Community Colleges" on page 20.

**Agricultural colleges, technical schools, and professional institutes** emphasize preparation for specific careers. Examples include art institutes and music conservatories, Bible colleges, business colleges, schools of health science, seminaries and rabbinical yeshivas, and teachers colleges.

**Universities** are generally bigger than colleges and offer more majors and research facilities. Classes in introductory subjects may have hundreds of students, and some classes may be taught by graduate students.

Most universities are subdivided into colleges or schools. For example, a state university might have a large college of liberal arts, a school of engineering and applied sciences, a small school of nursing, a teachers college, and several graduate schools all on the same campus.

Different universities have different rules for whether you can, for example, take a computer science course offered by the engineering school while enrolled in the liberal arts college. Generally, the different colleges of a university share campus facilities (such as dorms and dining halls) and some research facilities (such as libraries), and a university-wide administration handles admissions, financial aid, and similar services for the various colleges.

# Size of the Student Body and Faculty

Size will affect many of your opportunities and experiences, including:

- the range of academic majors offered;

- the possibilities for extracurricular activities and athletics;

- the amount of personal attention you'll receive from faculty, administrators, and other students; and

- the availability and size of academic facilities such as laboratories, libraries, and art studios.

When considering size, be sure to look beyond the raw number of students attending. For example, perhaps you're considering a large university, but you'll be applying to its much smaller school of health sciences.

Also remember to investigate not just the number of faculty, but also how accessible faculty members are to students. You can get a rough sense of this from the "class size" entry in the *Handbook* descriptions, but if you are already interested in a particular major or department, it really helps to visit the campus and talk to students who are enrolled in that program.

# Location

Do you want to go home frequently, or do you see this as a time to experience a new part of the country? Perhaps you like an urban environment with access to museums, ethnic food, or major league ball games. Or maybe you hope for easy access to the outdoors or the serenity of a small town.

# Academic Quality

The easiest way to measure a school's quality and the satisfaction of its students is to learn the percentage of students who return after the first year and the percentage of entering students who remain to graduate. Comparatively good retention and graduation rates are indicators that responsible academic, social, and financial support systems exist for most students. These figures are reported in the *Handbook* descriptions. On average nationwide, 55 percent of four-year college students graduate from the same institution within six years or less.

One of the best ways to research a college's reputation is by talking to people who are familiar with colleges or the fields that interest you. Ask your parents if anyone they know went to one of the colleges on your short list. Talk to your school counselor—he or she probably knows quite a bit about local colleges and nationally known universities. Talk to your teachers—they might know the academic reputations of departments that relate to their teaching field. You can also research the reputations of colleges on the Internet, but beware—not everyone on the Internet is an expert, and sometimes rumors get passed along as fact.

If you already know what subjects you want to study, research the strengths of those schools or departments at the colleges and universities in which you're interested. One way to do this is to look at their departmental Web sites for the following:

- Are there a lot of courses offered, or just a few?

- Do the courses offered concentrate on one subfield within the major? This is not necessarily a bad thing, but it could tell you that the department is strong in some areas and weak in others.

- Do most of the professors have terminal degrees in their field? Usually the Ph.D. is the terminal degree, but in some fields, it's another graduate degree.

- The Web site may also tell you about research and scholarship that professors are doing, work that undergraduate students are doing, or the careers of recent alumni.

These are general questions that would apply to any department. For questions to ask colleges about a specific major, see the College Board's *Book of Majors*. It contains profiles of undergraduate majors, and each profile has a list of things to look for in a department offering that major.

**GOOD TO KNOW**

If you're still **undecided about your college major**, relax—just pick an academically balanced institution that offers a range of majors and programs, and take courses in subjects you find intriguing. Most colleges offer advising or mentoring to help you find a focus.

# Campus Life

Consider what your college life will be like beyond the classroom. Aim for a balance between academics, activities, and social life. In your research, try to learn the answers to these questions:

- What extracurricular activities, athletics, and special activities are available?
- Does the community around the college offer interesting outlets for students?
- Are students welcomed by the surrounding community?
- Is there a congregation of my faith on campus? Are there student groups based around my ethnic group or national culture?
- Is the college religiously affiliated? If so, how does that affiliation affect student life—for example, is attendance at services required?
- How do fraternities and sororities influence campus life?
- Is housing guaranteed? How are dorms assigned? (For more about housing options, see page 36.)

You can learn the answers to many of these questions by reading the college profiles in this book but, for others, you may have to do more in-depth research, such as visiting the college's Web site or its campus.

## Can I Afford this College?

Today's college price tags make cost an important consideration for most students. At the same time, most colleges work to ensure that academically qualified students from every economic circumstance can find financial aid. Be sure to look beyond the price tag in considering cost. The *Handbook* descriptions give you a general idea of the college's cost and its financial aid packages. For more detailed "cost profiles" of the colleges, and for general advice about financial aid, see the College Board's *Getting Financial Aid*, which is a companion volume to this book.

# Where Can I Get In?

Of course, finding a college that's the right fit for you is only half of the equation. Unless you're applying to a college with an open admissions policy, you also have to convince the admissions reviewers that you really are a good fit.

## What Are Colleges Looking For?

When they review your application, college admissions officers want to see, foremost, "students who have challenged themselves academically," says Martha Pitts, the director of admissions at the University of Oregon. But they don't just want to see good grades; they also want to make sure that candidates will add something positive to the campus community. Mike Sexton,

"Students should look at a school because it's the right fit for them academically, socially, spiritually, and geographically. **Is cost an important part?** Yes. It's a consideration, but only one among many."

—*Bonnie Lee Behm, Director of Financial Assistance, Villanova University*

# Where to Find More Information

Once you've created a list of colleges you'd like to learn more about, you should try to get information from as many sources as possible. Different people will tell you different things about colleges, so the more the merrier!

✔ **Your school counselor** can tell you about colleges and let you know when college fairs or visits from admissions recruiters are coming to your school. He or she may also have a file of college course catalogs, viewbooks, and other literature.

✔ **Visiting admissions staff** who come to your school—either by themselves or as part of a large college fair—can tell you more about the college they represent and its application process.

✔ **College Web sites and guidebooks** offer a wealth of information about majors offered, activities, and life on campus.

✔ **Returning graduates** who went to your school and come home for breaks will probably be eager to tell you all about their experiences.

✔ **Campus visits** are a chance to see the campus and its dorms, libraries, and other facilities in person; talk to admissions officers (whether informally or in an interview); observe classes and talk to students; and much more. Try to visit the campus while classes are in session. For tips on planning a visit, read the articles in the "Find a College" section of www.collegeboard.com, or get *Campus Visits & College Interviews* by Zola Dincin Schneider (College Board, 2002).

the dean of admissions at Lewis & Clark College, puts it this way: He looks at the applications for "a spark that tells us they'll be good roommates, good lab partners, good to have in class."

One thing you should never do is try to guess what the admissions committee is looking for and try to tailor your application to it. Admissions officers read thousands of applications every year, and they can almost instantly tell feigned interest in a college or a false presentation of oneself from the real thing.

## Your transcript is the most important thing

There it is, in large type, but it bears repeating: Your high school transcript is the most important thing for your application success. Colleges want to see that you've challenged yourself academically throughout high school and that you are willing to put academics first for the next two to four years.

Be aware that admissions staff won't just look at the grades on your transcript. They will look at which courses you took, and the grade trend over four years. For example, if you barely passed Intro to Biology as a freshman, but then turned around and got a B in AP Biology as a junior, colleges will consider that a plus. On the other hand, if you've been getting steady C's in English for the last three years, colleges may wonder why you haven't improved.

A related factor that admissions officers look for is an upward trend in the difficulty of your course work. Sexton says he becomes concerned when students "start taking a lighter load senior year. I can see why they would do it sometimes, but for some people, it's going to close doors." Don't feel you need to suffocate yourself with too many courses and extracurriculars, but don't try to cruise through your senior year either.

## Test scores are just part of the picture

Your scores on the SAT or the ACT can be important but, generally, they're not as important as your high school transcript. Most often, admissions officers will use your test scores to supplement your transcript or help them interpret it.

Although grades earned in high school courses are very important, they don't always mean the same thing. An A earned in the same course taught by different teachers in your school may not represent exactly the same amount of work, the same teaching, or the same level of learning. Likewise, an A earned in the same course but in different schools and different parts of the country may not really be the same. That's where standardized tests can help.

If you've already taken the SAT or ACT, look at your scores the same way the admissions committee will look at them—objectively. They don't represent all that you've achieved or will achieve. The scores are one indicator of how far along you are right now in developing the skills you need for college and a career. In deciding where to apply to college, it's helpful to compare your scores to those of the mid-50 percent score range of freshmen who enrolled the previous year in the colleges you're considering. You'll find this information in the section titled "freshman class profile" of each four-year college description. If your scores compare favorably, you're on your way to finding the right match. But if your scores are higher or lower, it's not necessarily a mismatch. Only 50 out of every 100 freshmen had scores in that range, which means 25 had higher scores and 25 had lower scores. You may be well suited for this college in other important ways. You'll be better able to decide after reading the entire college description, visiting the college's Web site, and (if possible) visiting the campus.

## Personality can go a long way

Very few colleges assess applications using just transcripts and test scores. Most will ask for information about your involvement in extracurricular activities, recommendations from your teachers, a recommendation from your counselor, and a brief application essay. Some will ask for an interview as well. A few will ask for recommendations from someone who is not on your school faculty, for example, a minister, employer, or friend.

What all of these application components have in common is that they help admissions officers look "beyond the numbers" and see what kind of person you are, and how you might contribute to their campus community. They won't be the first, or most important, thing the college looks at, but they can

"**The first thing most colleges and universities will consider** will be the high school courses a student chose. Are they challenging? Are they college-prep, honors, or AP courses?"

—*Mary Ellen Anderson, Director of Admissions, Indiana University–Bloomington* help round out your application and may help the admissions committee decide between you and several equally qualified candidates.

Here's a closer look at each of the personal factors colleges usually look at:

**Recommendations.** Recommendations will give the college a sense of your overall attitude toward learning, your character, and the context for the grades on your transcript. Do you have a real passion for mathematics? Did you try really hard and improve over the year to get that "B" in U.S. History? Or could you have been an "A" student if you had taken the class more seriously? For tips on choosing which teachers to ask for recommendations, and how to ask them, see pages 27 and 28.

**Extracurriculars.** Your involvement in extracurricular activities—whether they're sports, a part-time job, volunteering in your community, the school play, the yearbook, or something entirely different—will tell the college about how active you are in your community. From that, they'll have a good picture of your leadership potential and how likely you are to contribute to their own campus community. They'll also have a sense of how much time you spend on nonschool work, which gives them a context for reading your grades. Generally, it's best to dedicate yourself to a few extracurricular activities in which you're really interested. Making minor contributions to 10 different activities doesn't look as impressive as becoming a leader of one club that you're passionate about. Similarly, changing activities every semester makes you look fickle; it's better to show some consistency.

**Essays.** Admissions officers use application essays to learn how creative you are, how well you can write and, sometimes, whether you're truly interested in attending their college. They are the most subjective of all the components of an application, but they are also the one component over which you have total control. For more about how applications are used by admissions officials, and tips on writing your essays, read *The College Application Essay* by Sarah Myers McGinty (College Board, 2004).

**Interviews.** Interviews are rarely required and usually don't carry a great deal of weight in the overall application. If you are asked to come to an interview, you should look at it as an opportunity to put a personal face on your application, tell the college more about yourself, and learn more about whether the college would be a good fit for you. If you are shy, don't worry— no one ever gets rejected by a college because of a bad interview. For more about interviews, including checklists of questions to expect and questions you should ask, read *Campus Visits & College Interviews* by Zola Dincin Schneider (College Board, 2002).

## How "interested" are you?

As college admissions have become more competitive, colleges have begun to weigh an additional factor along with the other parts of the application: "demonstrated interest." What this means is that admissions officials try to determine whether, if they accept you, you will enroll at their college.

**GOOD TO KNOW**

You can use the college descriptions in this *Handbook* to learn their course requirements and what they recommend beyond these requirements. **This is your best indication of whether you can get in:** Do you have the lab science courses and foreign language study they require? Have you settled for the required minimum of history and social sciences, or have you taken their full recommendation? You can also learn about the high school GPAs of last year's entering class, and how those students were ranked in their high schools.

**GOOD TO KNOW**

Your school counselor will send the colleges to which you apply a **profile of your high school**, which will list what courses are offered, describe high school diploma requirements, and generally give admissions officers an overview of the academic program at your school. From this, **colleges will know whether you haven't taken the most rigorous courses available**—or, for that matter, if you've done extremely well despite a gap in your school's academic program.

Interest in a college is not something you should try to fake—if you have to pretend to want to go to a college, you won't be happy going there, so your application is a waste of time. If you really want to go to a college, your interest will show itself naturally, and colleges will be able to tell. That said, here are some things that colleges usually look for when they try to gauge your level of interest:

- Is your application essay customized to their college, or does it seem like a generic essay that you could have sent to any college?

- Did you write the college asking for information about their programs?

- Have you talked to any admissions officers from the college—at your high school, via e-mail, or when visiting the campus?

- If you interview with the college, do you ask basic questions that you could have answered by reading their Web site, or do you ask in-depth questions that show that you've already researched the college?

Like the personal factors, your level of interest in the college isn't nearly as important as the courses you've taken, your grades, or your test scores. But if the admissions committee is trying to decide between you and another equally qualified candidate, it could tip your application one way or the other.

# About Community Colleges

Do you want a quick start to a career path? Do you need to cut the cost of a four-year college degree? Do you want to sharpen your study skills before enrolling at a university? Do you need to attend classes at night or on weekends? Do you want to attend a college close to home?

If you said yes to even one question above, check out your options at a community college (CC). You won't be alone—45 percent of all first-time freshmen go to two-year colleges. One reason: These institutions offer two kinds of learning.

- If your goal is a four-year degree, you can earn a two-year associate degree at a low-cost community college, then transfer to a four-year college as a junior.

- If your goal is career training, you can earn an occupational degree or certificate in two years or less, then start working immediately in many high-demand fields (like health care or computer technology).

## Fit Your Education to Your Needs

A community college offers many advantages in terms of academic preparation for upper-division university work.

**If you need more academic preparation**, a community college can offer a leg up to achieving your goals. New students usually take placement tests in reading, writing, and math. Those who need to build skills can take catch-up courses, then—over time—move into a regular academic program.

**A STUDENT'S STORY**

"I'm getting the basics out of the way at an inexpensive cost," says Samantha Mattioli, a freshman at Westchester Community College in Valhalla, New York. Sam, who is majoring in business management, says, **"I won't have a lot of debt** when I finish my associate degree." That will free up funds for her second degree, in massage therapy—step two toward Sam's goal of running her own massage therapy business.

**If your high school grades aren't the greatest**, but a four-year college is your goal, taking community college courses—and building a record of good grades—can polish your academic record. Then you can transfer. (But don't expect it to be easy—community college courses are no different than four-year college courses.)

**If you're achievement oriented**, community colleges offer challenging honors courses. Honors programs not only stimulate you but also offer mentoring and networking opportunities. They will also make you a strong candidate for transfer to a four-year college.

**If English is your second language**, community colleges have special programs that will help you build your English skills.

# Keep on Track at a Community College

If you go to a community college or junior college, it's important for you to keep your goals in mind as you choose courses.

## PLANNING TO TRANSFER TO A FOUR-YEAR COLLEGE?

✔ Talk to advisers at the community college. Most public CCs offer two-year course plans that fulfill requirements at nearby colleges. To transfer without losing credits, follow those plans!

✔ Talk to advisers at the four-year college you hope to attend, too. They may have inside info.

✔ Make sure you've fulfilled requirements to declare a major at the four-year college—not just the general admissions requirements. For example, Biology 101 at your CC may transfer, but might not be enough preparation for you to take the junior-level courses in the chemistry major.

✔ Don't self-advise! If you're not sure whether a course will transfer, ask. Wrong courses waste your time and money, and that's discouraging.

✔ Keep going. Don't "gap" your education, taking time out between semesters or colleges. Once you begin, keep at it—that's the path to getting your four-year degree.

## TRAINING FOR AN OCCUPATION?

Make sure your degree or certificate can lead to employment.

✔ Talk to advisers at your community college, but don't just accept claims that when you graduate, you'll get a job.

✔ Ask how many students have gone straight from the college to the workforce in recent years, what jobs they got, and with which employers.

✔ Before you enroll, talk to potential employers in the outside world, too.

# Learn on Your Schedule

Many CC students have jobs and family responsibilities. Scheduling classes may be a big challenge. So community colleges tend to offer day, night, and weekend courses. They have pioneered new teaching methods, too. Some offer online courses (distance learning), combine Internet and classroom learning, give interactive TV courses, condense semester courses into a shorter time frame, and more.

# Community College Can Be a Ticket to Hot Job Markets

With two years or less of community college training, you can earn an occupational degree or certificate in

- Fast-growing health fields
- The computer world
- New and emerging fields

A community college may be the best route to many high-demand jobs that require two-year degrees not available at four-year colleges. Look for CC courses in construction technology, culinary arts, law enforcement, and biotechnology. With homeland security in the news, colleges are training many first responders.

Many community colleges also have certificate options that provide intensive training in a specialized field like computer-assisted drafting, food service technology, or paralegal studies. These certificates usually take six months to a year to complete.

## CCs often focus on preparing people to work in local industries.

Do you want work in your area? Look for programs like these in local community colleges:

**Joliet, IL.** Joliet Junior College is nationally known for its agriculture and horticulture programs. Farming is big business in the Midwest, and Joliet grads have job offers waiting. Students learn at a 100-acre college farm and do paid internships for credit.

**Tucson, AZ.** Home to many air-industry businesses, Pima Community College boasts an FAA–certified aviation tech program that prepares students to repair the structure, "airframe," and power plants of commercial jetliners. Pima's job placement record for successful grads of the program is over 95 percent.

Not bad! But also, not the case at every CC or in every field. So research your CC and your local job markets like crazy—just as you'd research a four-year college.

# Applying to colleges

After you've gone through some exploration and preliminary research, it's time to sit down and apply! In order to successfully apply, you'll need to budget and manage your time, follow each college's instructions to a tee and, most important, take a good hard look at yourself and your interests.

## Managing Your Time

Most deadlines for regular admissions applications are due in early January or February, and most early application deadlines are in November. For any application, you'll need to fill out forms and request that your transcript and standardized test scores be sent to the college. For most applications to selective colleges, you'll also need to ask teachers and your counselor for recommendations, write an essay or personal statement, and maybe even schedule an interview with the admissions office. You may also want to take the SAT or ACT or some SAT Subject Tests™ in November or December. Meanwhile, you'll be in the middle of your senior year, with academic, extracurricular, and social commitments all over your calendar.

The first thing you should do once you decide to which colleges you're applying is to make a checklist of all the deadlines and tasks you'll have to accomplish for the applications. Remember to budget time for other people to do things. Teachers won't write recommendations overnight, and testing organizations will need a few weeks to send official score reports to colleges.

For some sample checklists and a college application calendar, read the articles in the "Apply to College" section of www.collegeboard.com. For more help, use the My Organizer feature of the site, which will help you plan and remind you of upcoming deadlines, or read *Get It Together for College: A Planner to Help You Get Organized and Get In* (College Board, 2008).

# JUNIOR YEAR CALENDAR

## THE SUMMER BEFORE

- **Read** interesting books—no matter what you select as a major in college, you'll need a good vocabulary and strong reading comprehension skills. Reading is also one of the best ways to prep for college entrance exams.
- **Get a social security number** if you don't already have one—you'll need it for your college applications.

- **Think about yourself.** What are you curious about—nature and animals? People and places? Math and science? What do you like to do—working with your hands or with computers? Helping people? Being outdoors? Knowing the basics about yourself will help you make the right college choices.
- **Talk to your family and friends** about college and your goals. They know you best and will have good insights.

## SEPTEMBER

- **Meet with your school counselor** to make sure you are taking the courses that colleges look for.
- **Resolve to get the best grades** you can this year. The payoff will be more colleges to choose from, and a better chance for scholarship money.
- **Pick up the *Official Student Guide to the PSAT/NMSQT®*** from your guidance office and take the practice test (you'll take the real test in October).
- Get involved in an **extracurricular activity**.
- Find out if your school will have a **college night**.

## OCTOBER

- Take the **PSAT/NMSQT**.
- Attend a **college fair**.
- Begin looking through the *College Handbook*—**start a preliminary list of colleges** that might interest you.
- Start to **learn about financial aid**. Use the College Board's *Getting Financial Aid* to learn how it works, and the financial aid calculators at **www.collegeboard.com** to estimate how much aid you might receive.

## NOVEMBER

- Begin to **research scholarships**—use the College Board's *Scholarship Handbook* to find out about deadlines and eligibility requirements.
- **Learn about the SAT Reasoning Test™ (SAT®)**. Go to collegeboard.com. Also, pick up the official bulletin at your guidance office.
- If you are planning to major in the arts (drama, music, fine art), ask your teachers about requirements for a **portfolio or audition**.

## DECEMBER

- Review your **PSAT/NMSQT Score Report** with your school counselor. Sign up for your free My College QuickStart™ account on collegeboard.com.
- Spend time over the holidays to **think about what kind of college** you want. Big or small? Far away or close to home? **Make a list** of the college features that are important to you.
- **Begin preparing for the SAT** and/or ACT. Visit the SAT Preparation Center™ on **collegeboard.com**.

## JANUARY

- **Meet with your school counselor** to talk about the colleges in which you are interested, what entrance exams you should take, and when you should take them.
- If English is not your primary language, decide when to take the **TOEFL** test.
- Start thinking about **what you want to study in college**. Use resources like the College Board's *Book of Majors* and My College QuickStart™.
- **Register for the SAT** if you want to take it in **March**.

## FEBRUARY

- Think about which teachers you will ask to write **letters of recommendation**.
- If you're in Advanced Placement Program® (AP®) courses, **register for AP Exams** given in May.
- Ask your counselor or teacher about taking the **SAT Subject Tests™** in the spring. You should take them while course material is still fresh in your mind.

## MARCH

- **Register for the SAT and/or SAT Subject Tests** if you want to take them in **May**.
- **Narrow your college list** to a reasonable number. Explore the colleges' Web sites, read their brochures and catalogues, and talk to your family and friends.
- **Practice the SAT**. Ask your school counselor for the *SAT Preparation Booklet*—it's free and has a full-length practice test; you can also download a free test from **collegeboard.com**.

## APRIL

- **Register for the SAT and/or SAT Subject Tests** if you want to take them in **June**.
- **Plan courses for your senior year.** Make sure you are going to meet the high school course requirements for your top-choice colleges.
- **Plan campus visits.** It's best to go when classes are in session. Start with colleges that are close by.

## MAY

- If you are considering **military academies or ROTC** scholarships, contact your counselor before leaving school for the summer.
- Talk to your counselor about **NCAA requirements** if you want to play Division I or II sports in college.
- Start looking for a **summer job or volunteer work**—the good ones go fast.

# SENIOR YEAR CALENDAR

## THE SUMMER BEFORE

- **Register for the SAT Reasoning Test™ (SAT®) and/or SAT Subject Tests™** if you want to take them in **October or November**.
- If you want to play a NCAA Division I or II sport in college, **register with the NCAA Eligibility Center (www.ncaaclearinghouse.net)**.
- **Visit colleges** on your list. Call ahead for the campus tour schedule.

- Begin working on your **college application essays**.
- Find out about **local scholarships** offered by church groups, civic associations, and businesses in your area.
- **Write a résumé** (accomplishments, activities, and work experiences) to help you later with your college applications.
- **Request college application forms** if you aren't going to apply online.

## SEPTEMBER

- Meet with your school counselor to **finalize your list of colleges**. Be sure your list includes "safety," "reach," and "target" schools.
- **Start a checklist** of all application requirements, deadlines, fees, etc.
- If you can't afford application fees, your counselor can help you request a **fee waiver**.
- Set up **final campus visits and interviews**; attend open houses at colleges that interest you.
- Find out if there will be a **family financial aid night** at your school or elsewhere in your area this fall, and put it on your calendar.

## OCTOBER

- **Register for the SAT and/or SAT Subject Tests** if you want to take them in **December or January**.
- If you are going to apply under an **Early Decision or Early Action** plan, get started now.
- **Ask for letters of recommendation** from your counselor, teachers, coaches, or employers.
- Write **first drafts of your college essays** and ask your parents and teachers to review them.
- If you need to fill out the **CSS/Financial Aid PROFILE®**, you can register on collegeboard.com starting October 1.

## NOVEMBER

- **Finish your application essays**. Proofread them rigorously for mistakes.
- **Apply to colleges with rolling admission** (first-come, first-served) as early as possible. Keep hard copies.
- Make sure your **SAT and/or ACT scores** will be sent by the testing agency to each one of your colleges.
- Give your school counselor the proper **forms to send transcripts** to your colleges at least two weeks in advance.
- **Get PINs for the FAFSA** for both yourself and for one of your parents from **www.pin.ed.gov**.

## DECEMBER

- Try to **wrap up college applications** before winter break. Make copies for yourself and your school counselor.
- If you applied for **Early Decision**, you should have an answer by Dec. 15. If you are denied or deferred, submit applications now to other colleges.
- **Apply for scholarships** in time to meet application deadlines.
- Start gathering what you need to complete the FAFSA. **Visit FAFSA on the Web** for a list of needed documents.
- **Contact the financial aid office** at the colleges on your list to see if they require any **other financial aid forms**.

## JANUARY

- **Submit your FAFSA** as soon as you can. If a college to which you're applying has a financial aid priority date of February 1, use estimates based on your end-of-year pay stubs and last year's tax returns.
- **Submit other financial aid forms** that may be required—such as PROFILE or the college's own forms. Keep copies.
- If a college wants to see your **midyear grades**, give the form to your school counselor.
- If you have any **new honors or accomplishments** that were not in your original application, let your colleges know.

## FEBRUARY

- **Contact your colleges** to confirm that all application materials have been received.
- Correct or update your **Student Aid Report (SAR)** that follows the FAFSA.
- If any **special circumstances** affect your family's financial situation, alert each college's financial aid office.
- **File income tax returns early.** Some colleges want copies of your family's returns before finalizing financial aid offers.
- **Register for AP Exams** you want to take. (If you are homeschooled or your school does not offer AP, you must contact AP Services by March 1.)

## MARCH

- **Admissions decisions start arriving.** Read everything you receive carefully, as some documents may require prompt action on your part.
- **Revisit colleges** that accepted you if it's hard to make a choice.
- **Don't get senioritis!** Colleges want to see strong grades in the second half of your senior year.

## APRIL

- **Carefully compare financial aid award letters** from the colleges that accept you—it might not be clear which is the better offer. If you have questions, contact the college's financial aid office or talk to your school counselor.
- **If you don't get enough aid**, consider your options, which include appealing the award.
- Make a final decision, **accept the aid package, and mail a deposit check** to the college you select before May 1 (the acceptance deadline for most schools).
- **Notify the other colleges** that you won't be attending (so another student can have your spot).

## MAY

- AP Exams are given. Make sure your **AP Grade Report** is sent to your college.
- **Study hard for final exams**. Most admissions offers are contingent on your final grades.
- **Thank everyone** who wrote you recommendations or otherwise helped with your college applications.
- If you plan on playing a Division I or II college sport, have your school counselor send your **final transcript to the NCAA Eligibility Center**.
- **If you weren't accepted** anywhere, don't give up—you still have options. Talk to your school counselor about them.

# Filling Out the Application

A typical application will ask you to provide some personal information; a list of schools you have attended; brief descriptions of your extracurricular activities, jobs, and any academic honors you have earned; and standardized test scores. They will also ask for information about your family and their education background, which colleges may use to determine whether you merit special consideration as a first-generation college student or a "legacy" applicant. Finally, most applications give you the option of affiliating yourself with a race or ethnic group. If you choose to do so, colleges may take that into consideration when reviewing your application; however, your answer won't hurt your chances of admission.

Finally, all applications will ask whether and when you plan to file for financial aid. Checking this box does not mean you have applied for financial aid! It just lets the admissions office know that they should coordinate with the financial aid office later on. For more information on financial aid and how to apply for it, read the articles in the "Pay for College" section of www.collegeboard.com, or get the College Board's *Getting Financial Aid 2009*.

## What Goes with Your Application

Besides the application form, there are several things that need to be included with your application. You will have to send some of them with the form; others will be sent to the college by other people.

### Application fee

The average college application fee is around $25. (Some colleges charge up to $60, while others don't have an application fee at all.) The fee is usually nonrefundable, even if you're not offered admission. Many colleges offer fee waivers for applicants from low-income families. If you need a fee waiver, call the college's admissions office for more information.

### High school transcript

This form is filled out by an official of your high school. If it comes with your admissions materials, you should give it to the guidance office to complete as early as possible. Some colleges send this form directly to your school after receiving your application.

### Admissions test scores

If you need to submit standardized test scores, you must make sure the testing agency itself sends an official score report. Writing your scores on your application or sending a photocopy of your own personal score report will not suffice. When you take the SAT or the ACT, you are entitled to four official score reports, which are sent to the colleges you choose. This service is included in the fee you pay to take either test.

**PLANNING AHEAD**

In addition to the traditional typed or handwritten application, many schools today accept **online applications** (if they do, it will say so in their *Handbook* description). You may also be able to fill out the **Common Application** and send it to several schools—though you should be aware that some Common Application subscribers also require a supplementary form of their own.

**KEEP IN MIND**

**If you apply online**, remember to print your applications and proofread them before you submit them, just as you would with a printed application. Also, be sure to tell your school counselor that you've applied online—your school will still need to send your transcript to the college.

# Letters of recommendation

Some colleges ask you to submit one or more letters of recommendation from a teacher, counselor, or other adult who knows you well. Usually the person writing the letter will send it directly to the college, though sometimes your school counselor will assemble the letters and send them with your transcript.

# Essays short and long

If you're applying to selective colleges, your essay often plays a very important role. Whether you're writing an autobiographical statement or an essay on a specific theme, take the opportunity to express your individuality in a way that sets you apart from other applicants.

Some applications will ask you to attach a separate essay of one or two pages, others will ask you to fill in some one-paragraph short responses directly on the application form, and others will ask for both. Whichever type of question you're answering, give it some thought; draft, revise, and edit your response before putting it with the application; and be sure to type or (if you must) print legibly. (The "fun" fonts that came with your word processor are usually not legible.)

Your parents, school counselors, and teachers may have some helpful insights into things you should talk about in your essays. For tips and strategies on how to approach different types of essay questions, general advice on the writing process, and information about how admissions officers evaluate essays, obtain a copy of Sarah Myers McGinty's *The College Application Essay* (College Board, 2004).

# Interview

An interview is required or recommended by some colleges. Even if it's not required, it's a good idea to set up an interview because it gives you a chance to make a personal connection with someone who will have a voice in deciding whether or not you'll be offered admission. If you're too far away for an on-campus interview, try to arrange to meet with an alumnus in your community.

Try to schedule interviews early in your senior year—if you wait until December you may not have time to make the appointment before the application is due. Also, scheduling an interview late in the year may make the college think that your decision to apply was an afterthought. Many students feel most comfortable scheduling their first interviews with colleges they feel confident about getting into. That way, they can experience interview situations and build their confidence before going to "high stakes" interviews with their "reach" schools.

For tips on preparing for interviews and getting the most out of them, obtain a copy of Zola Dincin Schneider's *Campus Visits & College Interviews* (College Board, 2002), or read the articles in the "Apply to College" section of the College Board Web site.

# How to ask for recommendations

The key to getting a great recommendation is to be a great student. But showing good manners helps.

✔ Be sure to *ask* for a recommendation—don't demand one.

✔ Respect the time constraints of those you're asking for this favor. Mary Lee Hoganson, a former counselor at Homewood-Flossmoor High School in Illinois, says that "teachers should always receive a minimum of two weeks' notice."

✔ Provide teachers and counselors with a deadline for each recommendation that you are requesting, especially noting the earliest deadline.

✔ Offer them a "brag sheet" or résumé reminding them of your accomplishments over the years. They might know your work in their classes very well, but they might not remember that you were also responsible for organizing the school talent show your junior year.

✔ Include addressed and stamped envelopes for each school to which you're applying.

✔ On the application form, waive your right to view recommendation letters. This makes the recommendation more credible in the eyes of the college.

✔ Follow up with your recommendation writers a week or so before your first deadline.

✔ Once you have decided which college to attend, write thank-you notes to everyone who provided a recommendation and tell them where you've decided to go to college. Be sure to do this before you leave high school.

**EXPERT ADVICE**

"Be sure to **ask for recommendations in a way that allows a teacher to decline** comfortably if he or she does not have time to do an adequate job. For example: 'Do you feel you know me well enough, and do you have enough time to write a supportive letter of recommendation?'"

—*Mary Lee Hoganson, former counselor, Homewood-Flossmoor High School, Flossmoor, Illinois*

## Auditions, portfolios, and other supplementary materials

If you're applying for a fine or performing arts program in music, studio art, or graphic design, you may have to document prior work by auditioning on campus or submitting an audiotape, slides, or some other sample of your work to demonstrate your ability. Talk to a teacher or mentor in your subject for advice on both how to assemble a portfolio and which of your pieces to include. Be sure to check the deadlines for auditions—they are often different from the deadlines for applications.

In some cases, a college will ask all students to submit an academic writing sample, either instead of or in addition to a personal statement. You should send a graded essay, presentation, or lab report that you did well on, preferably a copy that has your teacher's comments and the grade you received on it.

# Taking college admissions and placement tests

In your junior or senior year of high school, you will probably have to take a college admissions test to satisfy the admissions requirements at the colleges you are considering.

You may also want to take college-level exams in specific subjects in order to strengthen your application portfolio, place out of introductory college courses, get college credit for your high school work, or all three. At the end of this chapter, you'll find an introduction to the two most widely recognized college credit-by-exam programs.

## College Admissions Tests: Why You Should Take Them

This chapter will give you advice on how to prepare and register for the standardized tests that satisfy the admissions requirements at the colleges you are considering. You may also want to take the college-level exams in specific subjects in order to strengthen your application portfolio, place out of introductory college courses, get college credit for your high school work, or all three.

Some colleges also require one or more SAT Subject Tests in addition to, or instead of, the SAT Reasoning Test™. These requirements are all spelled out in the *Handbook* descriptions for each college.

# The SAT

The SAT Reasoning Test (SAT), owned by the College Board, tests your knowledge of subjects that are necessary for college success: reading, writing, and mathematics. It tells you how well you use the skills and knowledge you have attained in and outside of the classroom—including how you think, solve problems, and communicate. The SAT is an important resource for colleges, and it is one of the best predictors of how well you'll do in college. The SAT is a fair and unbiased test that is geared to all students. Each question goes through a rigorous review to ensure that it's fair in content for all students.

# What Are SAT Subject Tests™?

SAT Subject Tests are one-hour exams offered in 20 subjects that measure your achievement in foreign languages, mathematics, sciences, history, and literature.

If your grades in college-preparatory courses are good, you may want to take one or several of these tests to demonstrate the content mastery you've achieved. The best time to take a Subject Test is after you have completed, or nearly completed, all the courses in that subject. A number of colleges use SAT Subject Test scores for various purposes:

**Admission:** Some colleges require Subject Tests for admission for all students. Others require them only for certain applicants, such as students who were homeschooled in high school. If they do, their *Handbook* descriptions will indicate this in the bulleted list of key facts and in the "Basis for selection" section.

**Placement in honors programs:** A college might require Subject Tests for placement in an honors college or other special program.

**Scholarship awards:** Merit scholarships may be awarded partly on the basis of Subject Test scores. Information about each college's merit scholarships and their requirements is included in the College Board's *Getting Financial Aid 2009*.

**Advanced placement:** Some colleges will allow you to skip introductory courses if your Subject Test score is sufficient.

For help preparing for your test(s), visit the SAT Subject Tests Learning Center on www.collegeboard.com, or get the *The Official Study Guide for all SAT Subject Tests*™, which is available in bookstores and libraries everywhere.

## KNOW THE LINGO

**SAT Reasoning Test**—A measure of the critical thinking skills you'll need for academic success in college. The SAT assesses how well you analyze and solve problems—skills you learned in high school that you'll need in college. It consists of three sections: mathematics, critical reading, and writing. The writing section includes both multiple-choice questions and a short essay.

**SAT Subject Tests**—Tests designed to measure mastery of specific subjects like English, history, mathematics, science, and language. The tests are independent of any particular textbook or method of instruction. Depending on the subject, an SAT Subject Test may include multiple-choice questions, an essay, or (for some foreign language tests) a listening section.

# 2008–2009 SAT® PROGRAM TEST CALENDAR

| Test Dates | Oct. 4* | Nov. 1 | Dec. 6 | Jan. 24* | Mar. 14 | May 2* | June 6 |
|---|---|---|---|---|---|---|---|
| **Registration Deadlines** | | | | | | | |
| Regular | Sept. 9 | Sept. 26 | Nov. 5 | Dec. 26 | Feb. 10 | Mar. 31 | May 5 |
| Late | Sept. 16 | Oct. 10 | Nov. 18 | Jan. 6 | Feb. 24 | Apr. 9 | May 15 |
| **SAT Reasoning Test™** | ■ | ■ | ■ | ■ | ■ | ■ | ■ |
| **SAT Subject Tests™** | | | | | | | |
| Literature | ■ | ■ | ■ | ■ | | ■ | ■ |
| United States (U.S.) History | ■ | ■ | ■ | ■ | | ■ | ■ |
| World History | | | ■ | | | | ■ |
| Mathematics Level 1† | ■ | ■ | ■ | ■ | | ■ | ■ |
| Mathematics Level 2† | ■ | ■ | ■ | ■ | | ■ | ■ |
| Biology E/M (Ecological/Molecular) | ■ | ■ | ■ | ■ | | ■ | ■ |
| Chemistry | ■ | ■ | ■ | ■ | | ■ | ■ |
| Physics | ■ | ■ | ■ | ■ | | ■ | ■ |
| **Languages: Reading Only** | | | | | | | |
| French | ■ | | ■ | ■ | | ■ | |
| German | | | | | | | ■ |
| Modern Hebrew | | | | | | | ■ |
| Italian | | | ■ | | | | |
| Latin | | | ■ | | | | ■ |
| Spanish | ■ | | ■ | ■ | | ■ | ■ |
| **Languages: Reading and Listening** | | | | | | | |
| Chinese | | ■ | | | | | |
| French | | ■ | | | | | |
| German | | ■ | | | | | |
| Japanese | | ■ | | | | | |
| Korean | | ■ | | | | | |
| Spanish | | ■ | | | | | |

*Question-and-Answer Service available.
†Calculator required.
*NOTE:* Sunday test dates follow each Saturday test date for students who cannot test on Saturday because of a religious observance.

## Services for Students with Disabilities

**Students may receive accommodations** (extended time, large print, etc.) on College Board exams if they submit an eligibility form and meet the eligibility requirements. **Students must: 1)** have a disability that requires testing accommodations; **2)** have documentation on file that supports the need for accommodations; **and 3)** receive and use the requested accommodations for school-based tests. (See program material regarding the Guidelines for Documentation, and for exceptions to the above requirements.)

### SSD Contacts
(all College Board programs):

| | |
|---|---|
| Voice | 609 771-7137 |
| TTY | 609 882-4118 |
| Fax | 609 771-7944 |
| E-mail | sat.ssd@ets.org |

www.collegeboard.com/ssd

# Preparing for the SAT

The best way to prepare for a college admissions test is to take as many challenging courses as you can, study hard in all of them, and read as much general literature as you can outside of class. But it also helps to be familiar with the test. Here are some tips on how to do that.

**Take the PSAT/NMSQT®** in the fall of your sophomore and junior years. Taking the test in your sophomore year gives you a head start in preparing for the SAT, and taking the test in your junior year provides you with the opportunity to qualify for National Merit Scholarship Corporation and other scholarship programs. The score report that you receive after the test contains personalized "how to improve" skills advice based on your performance. Use it with your customized SAT study plan in My College QuickStart™ to review PSAT/NMSQT questions you missed and answer SAT practice questions of the same type, prepare for the SAT essay, and review high-level SAT math questions. Then, take advantage of free online resources such as an official SAT practice test, the Official SAT Question of the Day™, and sample questions at www.collegeboard.com.

**Get the *SAT Preparation Booklet*™** for free from your school's guidance office, or go online to www.collegeboard.com to download your own copy.

**Familiarize yourself with all aspects of the test**, such as the question types, the directions for taking the test, and information on how the test is scored. For example, will your score go down if you answer a question wrong, or are you free to guess with no penalty?

**Take a free full-length practice test** that uses official questions. Take it under real conditions—in one sitting, in a quiet place, and without having looked through the questions first.

**If you want** to take additional practice tests or drill for a certain type of question, you don't need to break the bank.

- The College Board publishes *The Official SAT Study Guide*™, which is available in bookstores and libraries everywhere.

- The College Board also offers The Official SAT Online Course™ through its Web site. (The book you're reading gives you a $10 discount on a four-month subscription to the course. See the inside back cover for details.)

**Remember** that your test scores aren't going to be the most important thing in your life, or even on your college application. Don't study for an admissions test at the expense of your high school course work.

# Taking the Test

## When should I take the test?

Many students decide that the end of their junior year is a logical point at which to take a college admissions test for the first time. By then, you've been studying English, math, science, social studies, and other courses for

**PLANNING AHEAD**

**Most students take the SAT in the spring of their junior year** and again in the fall of their senior year. Students who take SAT Subject Tests usually do so either in June of their junior year or in November or December of their senior year.

When you know which test(s) to take, you'll find a schedule of registration and administration dates on page 31. Your school counselor can tell you where the SAT will be administered close to your home and school. You can also find SAT information and preparation tools at **www.collegeboard.com/sat**.

more than 11 years! You've been reading, studying, and taking tests regularly during that time. And if you took the PSAT/NMSQT in October of your junior year, your memory will be fresh from the experience.

## How to register

The best way to register is online. It's fast and easy, and it helps you avoid late fees or missed postmark deadlines. You can even register for next year's tests over the summer. SAT registration may be completed at www.collegeboard.com.

To register for the SAT by mail, complete the paper registration form included with the *SAT Registration Booklet* and send it with your test fee payment. You can get a *Registration Booklet* in your school's guidance office. Registration deadlines are about four and a half weeks before the test date. There are also late registration deadlines, and it's possible to register on a standby basis. Both of these involve an additional fee.

## Should I take an admissions test more than once?

Many students who take a college admissions test the second time improve their scores. If you take a test over and over again, your scores may fluctuate—slightly up one time, down the next, and eventually clustering around the point that represents your "true score."

If you take an admissions test in the spring of your junior year and earn a score that satisfies the requirements at colleges that interest you, you may not need to take the test again. But you may find that you want to reach beyond the requirements for various reasons: to qualify for a scholarship or honors program, perhaps, or just to make your application more competitive.

If you do decide to take an admissions test a second time, here are some tips:

- If you take an admissions test in the spring of your junior year and want to try to improve your scores, take it again in the early fall. The experience of having already taken the test may help to improve your performance the second time.

- If you take the SAT in October, January, or May, you can order the Question-and-Answer Service. This report gives you a copy of your SAT test, the test booklet, your answers and the correct answers, scoring instructions, and information about the questions. Reviewing this information carefully could help you improve your score the next time you take the test.

- Don't worry if your score fluctuates downward the second time you take the test. Many colleges only look at your best score when reviewing your application.

## The ACT

The ACT is another admissions test that measures English, math, science, and reading skills. It is given throughout the year. Consult the ACT Web site for more information.

# Earning College Credit by Examination

Most colleges allow you to place out of introductory courses in subject areas where you have already done college-level work, either in high school or through your own life experiences. For example, you might be able to skip the first year of college Spanish and go straight to intermediate-level courses. In order to demonstrate your knowledge, the college usually requires you to either take a nationally offered standardized test, such as an AP Examination or a CLEP exam, or to take an exam offered by the college on campus. (You often have a choice of doing either—that is, if you haven't taken the AP Spanish Language Exam, you can take the college's Spanish placement test as an alternative.)

If you take an AP or CLEP exam, many colleges also allow you to earn credit based on your exam score. To use the same example as above, you wouldn't just place into second-year Spanish; you would also earn credits toward graduation as if you had taken first-year Spanish there on campus. If you have qualifying scores on enough exams, some colleges will even grant you "sophomore standing," meaning you are treated as a sophomore for academic purposes such as when you get to register for courses. (You still have to obey the college's other rules for freshmen, though, so don't expect to be given a single dorm room and a parking permit just because you have sophomore standing through AP.)

## AP Course Calendar

| | |
|---|---|
| **Spring before starting an AP course** | Well ahead of time, you need to start thinking about what AP courses you might want to take. Discuss your plans with your parents, teachers, and school counselor. |
| **Summer** | Some AP teachers require you to complete work (like reading) during the summer months to prepare for their courses. For example, for AP English you may be given a reading list. Make sure you complete these assignments so that you're up to speed when the class begins. |
| **January** | Talk to your AP teachers and/or AP Coordinator about taking the exams. Contact the disabilities (SSD) coordinator at your school if you will need testing accommodations. |
| **February** | Deadlines for students with disabilities whose eligibility forms require Documentation Review. |
| **March** | Deadlines for homeschooled students and students whose schools do not offer AP to arrange for testing at a nearby school. Deadlines for students with disabilities whose eligibility forms do not require Documentation Review. |
| **May 4–8 and May 11–15, 2009** | Exam dates. |
| **May 21–23, 2009** | Late-testing dates. |
| **June 15, 2009** | Deadline for receipt of requests for grade withholding, grade cancellation, or a change in a college grade report recipient. |
| **July** | AP Grade Reports released to designated colleges, and to students and their high schools. |

# More About the Advanced Placement Program® (AP®)

The AP Program offers a wide range of college-level courses that are taught in high schools by high school teachers; a national exam is given for each subject every May. AP courses give you a chance to do college-level work while still in high school. Research studies have shown that students with AP experience succeed in college at a rate significantly higher than the average student.

In all, there are 37 courses and exams offered in 22 subject areas. Even if an AP course is not offered at your school, you can still take the exam if you make arrangements with your school's AP Coordinator (usually a school counselor or a teacher). If your school doesn't offer AP at all, or you are home-schooled, you can still make arrangements to take an AP Exam at a nearby school that offers AP.

AP courses are challenging—after all, you're doing college-level work in high school! They can also be very rewarding. If you're not sure whether you should take an AP course, talk to your teachers, your school counselor, and your parents. You might also want to obtain a copy of the College Board bilingual publications *The Value of AP Courses and Exams/El Valor de Los Cursos y Exámenes AP*, or *Get with the Program/Avanza con el Programa*. Your school should be able to order copies of these for you and your parents.

# More About the College-Level Examination Program® (CLEP®)

CLEP, as the program is familiarly known, is the most widely accepted college credit-by-examination program in the country. Approximately 2,900 accredited colleges and universities award credit for qualifying scores on CLEP exams.

Unlike AP Exams, CLEP exams do not correspond to courses that you take in high school. Rather, CLEP offers 34 exams in the areas of business, English composition and literature, foreign languages, history and social studies, and science and mathematics. You can take a CLEP exam at any time during your college career, and the exams are offered year-round. You can learn about specific CLEP policies for each exam at every college using College Search on www.collegeboard.com.

All CLEP examinations are administered on the computer. The computer-based CLEP provides you with instant score reports, so you know that day if you will be awarded credit for your performance. To get used to the format of the computer-based test, visit www.collegeboard.com/clep and download the CLEP Sampler. The Sampler gives you a tutorial for taking CLEP on the computer as well as test-taking tips, examination information, and more. Study guides for individual CLEP exams are also available for downloading through collegeboard.com.

# Life on campus

A college isn't just a place where you'll take classes for two or four years. You'll also be spending most of your time there—and, if you're a residential student, you'll even be living there. When you're deciding where to go, academics should come first, but you should also consider how comfortable the campus feels. Some things to take into account are the housing options, local transit, whether the campus feels safe, and the social life of the campus.

## Housing Options

At most colleges, you'll have lots of choices about where to live. You may live in an on-campus dorm, an off-campus house or apartment building, or a fraternity/sorority house. At some colleges, you won't have as many choices your freshman year, but even then you may have a choice of several freshman dorms.

Typically, after you accept an offer of admission, the college's housing office will ask you to submit a form stating your housing preferences. You should use this form not only to state your preference of what dorm in which they will place you, but also to help them find you a roommate who will be compatible. Are you a quiet person? What times do you usually wake up and go to bed? Are you messy or neat? Do you smoke? The housing office will try to find someone whose answers to those questions were similar to your own.

### Living in Dorms

College dormitories have changed a lot over the years. While they were once bare-bones facilities that offered little more than a place to sleep, today most dorms offer a complete living and learning environment. It's not uncommon to find study areas, TV lounges, computer labs, small kitchens, or even fast-food take-out restaurants built into modern dorms. While some dorms are still built on the traditional floor plan of a hallway of double rooms sharing a bathroom, others are based around suites or apartments.

Some colleges offer theme-related residences for both freshmen and upper-classmen. These programs give you the opportunity to live with other students who share similar interests in a field of study, culture, hobby, or personal value. Students in theme residences not only live together, but often they also eat together and participate in social events related around the dorm's theme. Some theme residences will also have a member of the faculty who lives in the dorm and advises its students. Examples of theme residences include:

- *Diversity programs,* where the residents come from a wide variety of cultural backgrounds
- *Honors residences,* where all the students are on merit scholarships
- *Discipline-based residences,* such as a dorm for engineering and science majors
- *Foreign language immersion dorms,* where all the residents study and speak a particular foreign language
- *Substance-free housing* (a.k.a. "wellness" or "positive choice" housing), where all the residents pledge not to drink, smoke, or do drugs

## Roommate issues

Most roommate situations work out OK; often, freshman roommates become good friends. But there are cases when roommates just don't get along.

The best way to avoid this is to communicate with your roommates. At the beginning of the semester, tell them what you expect in terms of when you'll go to bed, when you'll get up in the mornings, when it's OK to have friends visit the room, and whether you'll be able to sleep while they work on their computer. Remember that communication is a two-way street: you should also ask your roommates about their own expectations, and listen to what they tell you.

As the semester goes on, be sure to let your roommates know if something is bothering you. Don't ignore problems or obnoxious behavior—they will only get worse if you don't speak up. Similarly, if your roommate complains about your own habits, try to correct them.

If worse comes to worst, it's not unknown for colleges to reassign roommates in midsemester. But because of space issues, this isn't always possible, and when it is possible, it's not always ideal. You'll probably find yourself living in a new dorm, away from all the friends you've already made. You might also find yourself as the new third roommate who is squeezed into a room that had previously slept two.

# Glossary

Definitions of commonly used terms vary from college to college. Consult specific college catalogs or their Web sites for more detailed information.

**Accelerated study.** A college program of study completed in less time than is usually required, most often by attending classes in the summer or by taking extra courses during the regular academic terms. Completion of a bachelor's degree program in three years is an example of acceleration.

**Accreditation.** Recognition by an accrediting organization or agency that a college meets certain acceptable standards in its education programs, services, and facilities. Regional accreditation applies to a college as a whole and not to any particular programs or courses of study. Accreditation of specific types of schools, such as Bible colleges or trade and technical schools, may also be determined by a national organization. Institutional accreditation by regional accrediting associations and by national accrediting organizations is included in the *Handbook's* descriptions of colleges. See pages 10–12 for more information about accreditation and the names and addresses of the national and regional accrediting associations.

**ACT.** A college entrance examination given at test centers in the United States and other countries on specified dates throughout the year. It includes tests in English, mathematics, reading, and science.

**Advanced placement.** Admission or assignment of a freshman to an advanced course in a certain subject on the basis of evidence that the student has already completed the equivalent of the college's freshman course in that subject.

**Advanced Placement Program (AP).** A program of the College Board that provides high schools with course descriptions of college subjects and AP Exams in those subjects. The AP Program offers 37 exams in 22 subject areas. High schools offer the courses and administer the exams to interested students. Most colleges and universities in the United States accept qualifying AP Exam grades for credit, advanced placement, or both.

**Agricultural college.** A college or university that primarily trains students in the agricultural sciences and agribusiness operations.

**Articulation agreement.** A formal agreement between two higher education institutions, stating specific policies relating to transfer and recognition of academic achievement in order to facilitate the successful transfer of students without duplication of course work.

**Associate degree.** A degree granted by a college or university after the satisfactory completion of the equivalent of a two-year, full-time program of study. In general, the associate of arts (A.A.) or associate of science (A.S.) degree is granted after completing a program of study similar to the first two years of a four-year college curriculum. The associate in applied science (A.A.S.) is awarded by many colleges on completion of technological or vocational programs of study.

**Bachelor's, or baccalaureate, degree.** A degree received after the satisfactory completion of a four- or five-year, full-time program of study (or its part-time equivalent) at a college or university. The bachelor of arts (B.A.), bachelor of science (B.S.), and bachelor of fine arts (B.F.A.) are the most common baccalaureates. Policies concerning their award vary from college to college.

**Bible college.** An undergraduate institution whose program, in addition to a general education in the liberal arts, includes a significant element of Bible study. Most Bible colleges seek to prepare their students for vocational or lay Christian ministry.

**Branch campus.** A part of a college, university, or community college that is geographically separate from the main campus, has its own faculty and administration, and may have separate admissions requirements and degree programs.

**Business college.** A college that primarily prepares students to work in an office or entrepreneurial setting. The curriculum may focus on management, clerical positions, or both.

**Campus.** The physical location of a college or university. Includes classroom buildings, libraries, research facilities, dormitories, dining halls, and administration buildings.

**Calendar.** The system by which an institution divides its year into shorter periods for instruction and awarding credit. The most common calendars are those based on the semester, trimester, quarter, and 4-1-4.

**Candidates Reply Date Agreement (CRDA).** A college subscribing to this College Board–sponsored agreement will not require any applicants offered admission as freshmen to notify the college of their decision to attend (or to accept an offer of financial aid) before May 1 of the year the applicants apply. The purpose of the agreement is to give applicants time to hear from all the colleges to which they have applied before having to make a commitment to any of them.

**CB code.** A four-digit College Board code number that students use to designate colleges or scholarship programs to receive their SAT score reports.

**Certificate.** An award for completing a particular program or course of study, usually given by two-year colleges or vocational or technical schools for nondegree programs of a year or less.

**College.** The generic term for an institution of higher education. Also a term used to designate divisions within a university.

**College-Level Examination Program (CLEP).** A series of examinations in undergraduate college courses that provides students of any age the opportunity to demonstrate college-level achievement, thereby reducing costs and time to degree completion. The examinations, which are sponsored by the College Board, are administered at colleges year-round. All CLEP exams are delivered on computer, providing test-takers instant score results.

**College-preparatory subjects.** A term used to describe subjects required for admission to, or recommended as preparation for, college. It is usually understood to mean subjects from the fields of English, history and social studies, foreign languages, mathematics, science, and the arts.

**College Scholarship Service® (CSS®).** A unit of the College Board that assists postsecondary institutions, state scholarship programs, and private scholarship organizations in the equitable and efficient distribution of student financial aid funds.

**Combined bachelor's/graduate degree.** A program in which students complete a bachelor's degree and a master's degree or first-professional degree in less than the usual amount of time. In most programs, students apply to the graduate program during their first three years of undergraduate study, and begin the graduate program in their fourth year of college. Successful completion results in awarding of both a bachelor's degree and a graduate degree. At some colleges, this option is called a joint degree program.

**Common Application.** The standard application form distributed by the National Association of Secondary School Principals to colleges who are subscribers to the Common Application Group.

**Community/junior college.** A college that offers only the first two years of undergraduate study. Community colleges are public institutions, whereas junior colleges are privately operated on a not-for-profit basis. Both usually offer terminal (or "vocational") programs and transfer programs.

**Consortium.** A group of colleges and universities that share a common geographic location. Consortiums of colleges in the same town often allow students at one institution to take classes at other consortium colleges and use facilities (such as libraries) at the member colleges. Larger consortiums, on the state or regional level, may allow for "visiting semesters" or offer in-state tuition to out-of-state students.

**Cooperative education (co-op).** A program that provides for alternative class attendance and employment in business, industry, or government. Students are typically paid for their work. Under a cooperative plan, five years are normally required to complete a bachelor's degree, but graduates have the advantage of about a year's practical work experience in addition to their studies.

**Cooperative housing.** College-owned, operated, or affiliated housing in which students share room and board expenses and participate in household chores to reduce their living expenses.

**Credit hour.** A unit of measure representing an hour (50 minutes) of instruction over a 15-week period in a semester or trimester system, or over a 10-week period in a quarter system. It is applied toward the total number of hours needed for completing the requirements of a degree, diploma, certificate, or other formal award.

**Credit/placement by examination.** Academic credit or placement out of introductory courses granted by a college to entering students who have demonstrated proficiency in college-level studies through examinations such as those sponsored by the College Board's AP and CLEP programs.

**Cross-registration.** The practice, through agreements between colleges, of permitting students enrolled at one college or university to enroll in courses at another institution without formally applying for admission to the second institution.

**CSS/Financial Aid PROFILE®.** A form and service offered by the College Board, which is used by some colleges, universities, and private scholarship programs to award their own private financial aid funds. Students pay a fee to register for PROFILE and send reports to institutions and programs that use it. Students register with PROFILE on www.collegeboard.com. PROFILE provides a customized application for each registrant, based on the individual's information and the requirements of the colleges and programs from which she or he is seeking aid. Students complete and submit the customized application and supplements, if required, to the College Board for processing and reporting to institutions. The PROFILE is not a federal form and may not be used to apply for federal student aid.

**Culinary school.** A vocational college that primarily prepares students to work as chefs or caterers.

**Deferred admission.** The practice of permitting students to postpone enrollment, usually for one year, after acceptance to the college.

**Degree.** An award given by a college or university certifying that a student has completed a course of study. *See* bachelor's degree, associate degree, graduate degree. *See also* Certificate.

**Distance learning.** An option for earning course credit off campus via cable television, the Internet, satellite classes, videotapes, correspondence courses, or other means. *See also* Virtual university.

**Doctoral degree (doctorate).** *See* Graduate degree.

**Dormitory.** *See* Residence hall.

**Double major.** Any program in which a student concurrently completes the requirements of two majors.

**Dual enrollment.** The practice of students enrolling in college courses while still in high school.

**Early Action (EA).** Students who apply under a college's Early Action plan receive a decision earlier than the standard response date but are not required to accept the admissions offer or to make a deposit prior to May 1. See the Early Decision/Early Action table for a list of colleges that offer Early Action plans, including application deadlines and notification dates.

**Early admission.** The policy of some colleges of admitting certain students who have not completed high school—usually students of exceptional ability who have completed their junior year. These students are enrolled full-time in college.

**Early Decision (ED).** Students who apply under Early Decision make a commitment to enroll at the college if admitted and offered a satisfactory financial aid package. Application deadlines are usually in November or December with a mid-to-late-December notification date. Some colleges have two rounds of Early Decision. See the Early Decision/Early Action table for details.

**Engineering college/institute/school.** An institution of higher education that primarily prepares students for careers as licensed professional engineers or engineering technologists.

**Exchange student program.** Any arrangement that permits a student to study for a semester or more at another college in the United States without extending the amount of time required for a degree.

**External degree program.** A system of study whereby a student earns credit toward a degree through independent study, college courses, proficiency examinations, and personal experience. External degree colleges generally have no campus or classroom facilities.

**FAFSA.** *See* Free Application for Federal Student Aid (FAFSA).

**First-professional degree.** A degree granted upon completion of academic requirements to become licensed in a recognized profession. The programs of study require at least two years of previous college work for entrance, and at least six years of total college work for completion. The medical doctorate (M.D.) is one kind of first-professional degree.

**For-profit college.** A private institution operated by its owners as a profit-making enterprise.

**4-1-4 calendar.** A variation of the semester calendar system, the 4-1-4 calendar consists of two terms of about 16 weeks each, separated by a one-month intersession used for intensive short courses, independent study, off-campus work, or other types of instruction.

**Free Application for Federal Student Aid (FAFSA).** A form completed by all applicants for federal student aid. In many states, completion of the FAFSA is also sufficient to establish eligibility for state-sponsored aid programs. There is no charge to students for completing the FAFSA. The online form may be filed any time after January 1 of the year for which one is seeking aid (e.g., after January 1, 2009, for academic year 2009-10 assistance).

**General Educational Development (GED).** A series of five tests that individuals who did not complete high school may take through their state education system to qualify for a high school equivalency certificate. The tests cover correctness and effectiveness of expression, interpretation of reading materials in the natural sciences and the social sciences, interpretation of literary materials, and general mathematics ability. Many colleges accept satisfactory GED test results in lieu of high school graduation. Some colleges require homeschooled students to take the GED.

**Grade point average (GPA) or ratio.** A system used by many schools for evaluating the overall scholastic performance of students. Grade points are determined by first multiplying the number of hours given for a course by the numerical value of the grade and then dividing the sum of all grade points by the total number of hours carried. The most common system of numerical values for grades is A = 4, B = 3, C = 2, D = 1, and E or F = 0. Also called quality point average or ratio.

**Graduate degree.** A degree pursued after a student has earned a bachelor's degree. The master's degree, which requires one to three years of study, is usually the degree earned after the bachelor's. The doctoral degree requires further study. First-professional degrees are also graduate degrees.

**Health sciences college.** An institution of higher education that primarily prepares students to enter work in a clinic, hospital, or private medical practice.

**Hispanic-serving college.** A college where Hispanic students compose at least 25 percent of the full-time undergraduate enrollment.

**Historically black college.** An institution founded before 1964 whose mission was historically, and remains, the education of African Americans.

**Homeschooled.** For purposes of the application requirements described in the "basis for selection" entries of the college descriptions, this refers to homeschooling during the four years of secondary school (grades 9–12).

**Honors program.** Any special program for very able students that offers the opportunity for education enrichment, independent study, acceleration, or some combination of these.

**Independent student.** For financial aid purposes, a student who is not dependent on financial support from his or her parents. Also called self-supporting student.

**Independent study.** Academic work chosen or designed by the student under an instructor's supervision. This work is usually undertaken outside of the regular classroom structure.

**International Baccalaureate (IB).** A comprehensive and rigorous two-year curriculum (usually taken in the final two years of high school) that is similar to the final year of secondary school in Europe. Some colleges award credit or advanced placement to students who have completed an IB program.

**Internship.** A short-term, supervised work experience, usually related to a student's major field, for which the student earns academic credit. The work can be full- or part-time, on or off campus, paid or unpaid. Student teaching and apprenticeships are examples.

**Intersession term.** A short term offered between semesters. *See also* 4-1-4 calendar.

**Junior college.** *See* Community/junior college.

**Liberal arts.** The study of the humanities (literature, the arts, and philosophy), history, foreign languages, social sciences, mathematics, and natural sciences. Study of the liberal arts and humanities prepares students to develop general knowledge and reasoning ability rather than specific skills.

**Liberal arts/career combination.** A program of study in which a student typically completes three years of study in a liberal arts field followed by two years of professional/technical study (for example, engineering) at the end of which the student is awarded bachelor of arts and bachelor of science degrees. The combination is also referred to as a 3+2 program.

**Liberal arts college.** A college that emphasizes the liberal arts in its core curriculum and academic offerings and does not offer vocational or professional programs.

**Lower division.** The freshman and sophomore years of college study.

**Major.** A student's academic field of specialization. In general, most courses in the major are taken during the junior and senior years.

**Maritime college/institute/academy.** An institution of higher education that prepares students to operate commercial shipping or fishing vessels. Upon graduation, students of most maritime academies are commissioned as officers in the United States Merchant Marine, and simultaneously commissioned as officers in the U.S. Navy Reserve.

**Master's degree.** *See* Graduate degree.

**Military college/institute/academy.** An institution of higher education that prepares students (who are called "cadets" while enrolled) to become active-duty officers in the armed services. The curriculum usually combines a study of the liberal arts, military science, and engineering. Cadets usually participate in military training assignments during the summer term in addition to attending the college in the fall and spring semesters.

**Minor.** Course work that is not as extensive as that in a major but gives students some specialized knowledge of a second field.

**NAIA.** The National Association of Intercollegiate Athletics. NAIA members are mostly small colleges. Championships are offered in 13 sports.

**NCAA.** The National Collegiate Athletics Association. The largest collegiate athletic association, it oversees the most athletic scholarship money. The NCAA governs league play in 23 championship sports.

**NCCAA.** National Christian College Athletic Association. NCCAA sponsors league play among Bible colleges and other Christian-oriented institutions.

**NJCAA.** The National Junior College Athletic Association. NJCAA members are two-year junior or community colleges.

**Need-based financial aid.** Financial aid given to students who have demonstrated financial need, which is calculated by subtracting the student's expected family contribution from a college's total costs. The expected family contribution is derived from a need analysis of the family's overall financial circumstances, using either a Federal Methodology to determine a student's eligibility for federal student aid, or an Institutional Methodology to determine eligibility for nonfederal financial aid.

**Nondegree study.** A college-level course of study that does not lead to a degree. Non-degree study may or may not be part of a program leading to a certificate.

**Nursing college.** An institution of higher education that primarily prepares students to become registered nurses (RNs) or licensed practical nurses (LPNs).

**Open admissions.** The college admissions policy of admitting high school graduates and other adults generally without regard to conventional academic qualifications, such as high school subjects, high school grades, and admissions test scores. Virtually all applicants with high school diplomas or their equivalent are accepted, space permitting.

**Placement by examination.** *See* Credit/placement by examination.

**Private college.** Institutions described in this book as "private" are operated on a not-for-profit basis. They may be independent or church-affiliated. *See also* Proprietary college.

**PROFILE.** *See* CSS/Financial Aid PROFILE.

**Priority date.** The date by which an application, whether for admission, housing, or financial aid, must be received to be given the strongest possible consideration. After that date, applicants are considered on a first-come, first-served basis.

**Proprietary college.** *See* For-profit college.

**PSAT/NMSQT® (Preliminary SAT/National Merit Scholarship Qualifying Test).** A preparatory tool for the SAT that is administered by high schools to sophomores and juniors each year in October. The PSAT/NMSQT serves as the qualifying test for scholarships awarded by the National Merit Scholarship Corporation.

**Public college/university.** An institution that is supported by taxes and other public revenue and governed by a county, state, or federal government agency.

**Quality point average.** *See* Grade point average (GPA) or ratio.

**Quarter.** An academic calendar period of about 12 weeks. Four quarters make up an academic year, but at colleges using the quarter system, students make normal academic progress by attending three quarters each year. In some colleges, students can accelerate their programs by attending all four quarters in one or more years.

**Rabbinical college.** *See* Seminary/rabbinical college.

**Regional accreditation.** *See* Accreditation.

**Regular admission.** Admission during the college's normal calendar for admissions, as opposed to Early Decision or Early Action admissions.

**Reserve Officers Training Corps (ROTC).** Programs conducted by certain colleges in cooperation with the United States Air Force, Army, and Navy. Naval ROTC includes the Marine Corps (the Coast Guard and Merchant Marine do not sponsor ROTC programs). Local recruiting offices of the services themselves can supply detailed information about these programs, as can participating colleges.

**Residence hall.** An on-campus living facility. Also known as a dormitory (or "dorm").

**Residency requirement.** The minimum number of terms that a student must spend taking courses on campus (as opposed to independent study, transfer credits from other colleges, or credit by examination) to be eligible for graduation. Can also refer to the minimum amount of time a student must have lived in-state in order to qualify for the in-state tuition rate at a public college or university.

**Rolling admissions.** An admissions procedure by which the college considers each student's application as soon as all the required credentials, such as school records and test scores, have been received. The college usually notifies an applicant of its decision without delay. At many colleges, rolling admissions allows for early notification and works much like nonbinding Early Action programs.

**Room and board.** The cost of housing and meals for students who reside on campus and/or dine in college-operated meal halls.

**SAT® Question-and-Answer Service.** A service of the College Board that provides students with a copy of their SAT Reasoning Test™, their answers and the correct answers, scoring instructions, and information about the questions. The service is only available for certain test dates.

**SAT®.** The College Board's test of critical reading, writing, and mathematical reasoning abilities, given on specified dates throughout the year at test centers in the United States and other countries. The SAT is required by many colleges and sponsors of financial aid programs, and many colleges use scores on the SAT as criteria for the awarding of merit scholarships.

**SAT Subject Tests™.** College Board tests in specific subjects, given at test centers in the United States and other countries on specified dates throughout the year. Used by colleges not only to help with decisions about admission but also in course placement and exemption of enrolled freshmen.

**Semester.** A period of about 16 weeks. Colleges on a semester system offer two semesters of instruction a year; there may be an additional summer session.

**Semester at sea.** A program for credit, usually for students with majors in oceanography or marine-related fields, in which students live on a ship, frequently a research vessel, for part of a semester. Academic courses are generally taken in conjunction with the sea experience.

**Seminary/rabbinical college.** An institution that prepares its student for professional religious ministry. Most seminaries are graduate-only institutions that offer first-professional degrees in divinity or rabbinical studies. The seminaries described in this book also offer undergraduate programs in philosophy, theology, Bible studies, or other related liberal arts.

**Sophomore standing.** Consideration of a student as a sophomore for academic purposes such as registering for classes and declaring a major. A college may grant incoming freshmen sophomore standing if they have enough credits from AP, CLEP, or IB exams.

**Student Aid Report (SAR).** A report produced by the U.S. Department of Education and sent to students in response to their having filed the Free Application for Federal Student Aid (FAFSA). The SAR contains information the student provided on the FAFSA as well as the federally calculated result, which the financial aid office will use in determining the student's eligibility for a Federal Pell Grant and other federal student aid programs.

**Student-designed major.** An academic program that allows a student to construct a major field of study not formally offered by the college. Often nontraditional and interdisciplinary in nature, the major is developed by the student with the approval of a designated college officer or committee.

**Study abroad.** Any arrangement by which a student completes part of the college program—typically the junior year but sometimes only a semester or a summer—by studying in another country. A college may operate a campus abroad, or it may have a cooperative agreement with some other U.S. college or an institution of the other country.

**Teacher certification.** A college program designed to prepare students to meet the requirements for certification as teachers in elementary and secondary schools.

**Teachers college.** A college that specializes in preparing students to teach in elementary or secondary schools. Most teachers colleges offer a curriculum that combines a study of the liberal arts with the study of pedagogy.

**Technical college/school.** A college that offers a wide variety of vocational programs to students.

**Term.** The shorter period into which colleges divide the school year. *See* Calendar.

**Terminal degree.** The highest degree level attainable in a particular field. For most teaching faculty this is a doctoral degree. In certain fields, however, a master's degree is the highest level.

**Terminal program.** An education program designed to prepare students for immediate employment. These programs usually can be completed in less than four years beyond high school and are available in most community colleges and vocational-technical institutes.

**Transcript.** A copy of a student's official academic record listing all courses taken and grades received.

**Transfer program.** An education program in a two-year college (or a four-year college that offers associate degrees), primarily for students who plan to continue their studies in a four-year college or university.

**Transfer student.** A student who has attended another college for any period, which may be defined by various colleges as any time from a single term up to three years. A transfer student may receive credit for all or some of the courses successfully completed before the transfer.

**Trimester.** An academic calendar period of about 15 weeks. Three trimesters make up one year. Students normally progress by attending two of the trimesters each year and in some colleges can accelerate their programs by attending all three trimesters in one or more years.

**Tuition.** The price of instruction at a college. Tuition may be charged per term or per credit hour.

**Two-year college.** *See* Community/junior college; Upper-division college.

**United Nations semester.** A program in which students take courses at a college in New York City while interning at the United Nations.

**University.** An institution of higher education that is divided into several colleges, schools, or institutes. When applying to a university, students typically have to apply for admission to a specific college, which may have its own admissions requirements. Not all colleges within a university will admit applicants who are high school graduates— some may be for graduate study only, and some may be upper-division colleges. Generally, university students take classes in the college to which they were accepted, but they may be allowed to take some courses offered by other colleges within the university and can use shared facilities such as libraries and laboratories.

**Upper division.** The junior and senior years of study.

**Upper-division college.** A college offering bachelor's degree programs that begin with the junior year. Entering students must have completed their freshman and sophomore years at other colleges.

**Urban semester.** A program for credit in which students spend a semester in a major city and experience the complexities of an urban center through course work, seminars, and/or internships related to their major.

**USCAA.** United States Collegiate Athletic Association. USCAA's members are primarily very small colleges.

**Virtual university.** A degree-granting, accredited institution wherein all courses are delivered by distance learning, with no physical campus.

**Vocational program.** *See* Terminal program.

**Wait list.** A list of students who meet the admissions requirements, but will only be offered a place in the class if space becomes available. See the wait-list table in the back of this book for a list of colleges that placed students on a wait list last year, along with the number of students who were eventually accepted from that list.

**Washington semester.** A program in which students intern with a government agency or department in the Washington, D.C., metropolitan area. Students earn field service credit for their work and frequently take courses at area colleges.

**Weekend college.** A program that allows students to take a complete course of study and attend classes only on weekends. These programs are generally restricted to a few areas of study at a college and require more than the traditional number of years to complete.

**Work-study.** An arrangement by which a student combines employment and college study. The employment may be an integral part of the academic program (as in cooperative education and internships) or simply a means of paying for college (as in the Federal Work-Study Program).

# Four-year colleges

## Alabama

---

### Alabama Agricultural and Mechanical University

**Huntsville, Alabama**
www.aamu.edu

**CB member**
**CB code: 1003**

- Public 4-year university and agricultural college
- Residential campus in small city
- 4,716 degree-seeking undergraduates: 7% part-time, 53% women, 95% African American, 2% international
- 990 degree-seeking graduate students
- 32% of applicants admitted
- SAT or ACT (ACT writing optional) required
- 33% graduate within 6 years

**General.** Founded in 1875. Regionally accredited. Campus located near Redstone Arsenal-Defense Research/Space Research Center. **Degrees:** 559 bachelor's awarded; master's, doctoral offered. **ROTC:** Army. **Location:** 2 miles from downtown, 95 miles from Birmingham. **Calendar:** Semester, extensive summer session. **Full-time faculty:** 319 total; 69% have terminal degrees, 36% women. **Part-time faculty:** 72 total; 68% women. **Special facilities:** State Black archives research center and museum.

**Freshman class profile.** 6,470 applied, 2,059 admitted, 885 enrolled.

| Mid 50% test scores | | Out-of-state: | 40% |
|---|---|---|---|
| ACT composite: | 16-19 | Live on campus: | 91% |
| Return as sophomores: | 83% | | |

**Basis for selection.** 2.0 GPA required. Test scores important, but may be waived dependent upon evaluation of GPA and other achievements. Interview, essay recommended. **Homeschooled:** Must meet Alabama State Department of Education requirements.

**High school preparation.** Required units include English 4, mathematics 4 and science 2.

**2007-2008 Annual costs.** Tuition/fees: $4,930; $9,220 out-of-state. Part-time student required fees are $440. Room/board: $3,592.

**Financial aid.** **Non-need-based:** Scholarships awarded for athletics, minority status.

**Application procedures.** **Admission:** Priority date 5/1; deadline 7/15 (receipt date). $25 fee, may be waived for applicants with need. Application may be submitted online. Admission notification on a rolling basis. **Financial aid:** FAFSA, institutional form required. Applicants notified on a rolling basis; must reply within 2 week(s) of notification.

**Academics.** Bachelor of technical studies available to adult learners in nontraditional fields. **Special study options:** Cooperative education, distance learning, double major, dual enrollment of high school students, exchange student, honors, independent study, internships, study abroad, teacher certification program, Washington semester, weekend college. **Credit/placement by examination:** AP, CLEP, SAT, ACT, institutional tests. 9 credit hours maximum toward bachelor's degree. Scores from DANTES, CLEP, ACE, and similar tests, and work experiences considered for credit toward degree. **Support services:** Learning center, reduced course load, remedial instruction, study skills assistance, tutoring.

**Honors college/program.** Second semester freshmen with ACT score of 20-21 (SAT 1030) may be considered for admission if they have at least 3.5 GPA with a minimum of 12 credit hours completed at the university, and a cumulative high school average of 3.3. The academic program consists of honors core courses.

**Majors. Agriculture:** Economics. **Architecture:** Urban/community planning. **Biology:** General. **Business:** General, accounting, business admin, finance, marketing, office management, public finance. **Communications:** Journalism. **Communications technology:** General, graphic/printing. **Computer sciences:** General. **Education:** General, business, early childhood, elementary, music, physical, school counseling, secondary, special, speech impaired. **Engineering:** Civil, mechanical. **Engineering technology:** Civil. **English:** English lit. **Family/consumer sciences:** General. **Math:** General. **Physical sciences:** Chemistry, physics. **Psychology:** General. **Public administration:** Social work. **Social sciences:** Political science, sociology. **Visual/performing arts:** Art, conducting, music performance.

**Computing on campus.** 928 workstations in dormitories, library, computer center, student center. Dormitories linked to campus network. Commuter students can connect to campus network. Helpline available.

**Student life. Freshman orientation:** Mandatory, $100 fee. Preregistration for classes offered. **Housing:** Guaranteed on-campus for all undergraduates. Single-sex dorms available. $100 deposit, deadline 8/1. **Activities:** Bands, choral groups, dance, drama, literary magazine, music ensembles, radio station, student government, student newspaper, TV station, Christian student organization, honor society, service clubs, NAACP, African-American political club, Baptist student union, Islamic association, Caribbean students association, International Association of Nigerian Students.

**Athletics.** NCAA. **Intercollegiate:** Baseball M, basketball, bowling W, cross-country, football (tackle) M, golf, soccer, softball W, tennis, track and field, volleyball W. **Intramural:** Basketball, football (tackle) M, soccer W, softball, volleyball. **Team name:** Bulldogs.

**Student services.** Adult student services, career counseling, student employment services, health services, personal counseling, placement for graduates, veterans' counselor. **Physically disabled:** Services for visually, speech, hearing impaired.

**Contact.** E-mail: Juan.alexander@aamu.edu
Phone: (256) 372-5245 Toll-free number: (256) 372-5245
Fax: (256) 372-5249
Juan Alexander, Director of Admissions, Alabama Agricultural and Mechanical University, Box 908, Normal, AL 35762

---

### Alabama State University

**Montgomery, Alabama**
www.alasu.edu

**CB member**
**CB code: 1006**

- Public 4-year university
- Residential campus in small city
- 4,589 degree-seeking undergraduates: 9% part-time, 60% women, 98% African American
- 929 degree-seeking graduate students
- 42% of applicants admitted
- Interview required

**General.** Founded in 1867. Regionally accredited. **Degrees:** 508 bachelor's awarded; master's, doctoral, first professional offered. **ROTC:** Army, Air Force. **Location:** 91 miles from Birmingham, 162 miles from Atlanta. **Calendar:** Semester, limited summer session. **Full-time faculty:** 239 total; 65% have terminal degrees, 72% minority, 45% women. **Part-time faculty:** 171 total; 28% have terminal degrees, 82% minority, 60% women. **Special facilities:** Black history collection, E. D. Nixon papers from civil rights movement of 1960's.

**Freshman class profile.** 11,309 applied, 4,781 admitted, 1,366 enrolled.

| Mid 50% test scores | | Rank in top quarter: | 11% |
|---|---|---|---|
| SAT critical reading: | 340-440 | Rank in top tenth: | 3% |
| SAT math: | 340-420 | Return as sophomores: | 55% |
| ACT composite: | 14-17 | Out-of-state: | 39% |
| GPA 3.50 or higher: | 10% | Live on campus: | 71% |
| GPA 3.0-3.49: | 20% | International: | 1% |
| GPA 2.0-2.99: | 69% | | |

**Basis for selection.** School record and GPA very important. All applicants must have minimum 2.20 GPA from accredited high school. Interview and essay recommended. Audition required of music majors. Portfolio recommended for art majors. **Homeschooled:** Transcript of courses and grades required. Applicants must score 20 or above on the ACT. **Learning Disabled:** Must submit appropriate documentation in order to be given special consideration.

**High school preparation.** 16 units required. Required units include English 4, mathematics 3, history 3, science 3, foreign language 1, computer science 1 and visual/performing arts 1.

**2007-2008 Annual costs.** Tuition/fees: $4,508; $8,516 out-of-state. Room/board: $4,150. Books/supplies: $1,000. Personal expenses: $1,380.

**2007-2008 Financial aid. Need-based:** 1,327 full-time freshmen applied for aid; 1,279 were judged to have need; 1,023 of these received aid. Average need met was 73%. Average scholarship/grant was $4,313; average loan $3,477. 43% of total undergraduate aid awarded as scholarships/grants, 57% as loans/jobs. **Non-need-based:** Awarded to 1,497 full-time undergraduates, including 515 freshmen. Scholarships awarded for academics, alumni affiliation, art, athletics, job skills, leadership, minority status, music/drama, ROTC, state residency.

**Application procedures. Admission:** Closing date 7/30 (postmark date). $25 fee, may be waived for applicants with need. Application may be submitted online. Admission notification on a rolling basis beginning on or about 9/1. **Financial aid:** Priority date 4/1; no closing date. FAFSA required. Applicants notified on a rolling basis starting 5/15.

**Academics. Special study options:** Combined bachelor's/graduate degree, cooperative education, cross-registration, double major, honors, independent study, internships, teacher certification program. **Credit/placement by examination:** AP, CLEP, ACT, institutional tests. 45 credit hours maximum toward bachelor's degree. Students must have approval of the academic advisor, department head, dean and vice president for academic affairs prior to taking CLEP exam. **Support services:** Learning center, remedial instruction, study skills assistance, tutoring, writing center.

**Honors college/program.** Minimum requirements are 3.3 GPA and 24 ACT or 1100 SAT. 34 freshmen admitted.

**Majors. Biology:** General, marine. **Business:** Accounting, business admin, finance, marketing. **Communications:** General. **Computer sciences:** Computer science, information systems. **Education:** Early childhood, elementary, music, physical, secondary, special. **English:** English lit. **Health:** Medical records admin. **History:** General. **Math:** General. **Parks/recreation:** Facilities management. **Physical sciences:** Chemistry, physics. **Protective services:** Criminal justice. **Psychology:** General. **Public administration:** Social work. **Social sciences:** Political science, sociology. **Visual/performing arts:** Art, dramatic.

**Most popular majors.** Biology 6%, business/marketing 14%, communications/journalism 6%, computer/information sciences 12%, education 22%, psychology 7%, public administration/social services 9%, security/protective services 8%, visual/performing arts 6%.

**Computing on campus.** 405 workstations in library, computer center. Online course registration, online library, helpline, wireless network available.

**Student life. Freshman orientation:** Mandatory, $55 fee. Preregistration for classes offered. **Housing:** Single-sex dorms, special housing for disabled, substance-free housing available. $200 deposit, deadline 5/31. Housing for nontraditional students available. **Activities:** Bands, campus ministries, choral groups, dance, drama, international student organizations, music ensembles, Model UN, musical theater, radio station, student government, student newspaper, Student Christian Association.

**Athletics.** NCAA. **Intercollegiate:** Baseball M, basketball, bowling W, cross-country, football (tackle) M, golf, soccer W, softball W, tennis, track and field, volleyball W. **Intramural:** Baseball M, basketball, softball, swimming, tennis, track and field, volleyball W. **Team name:** Hornets.

**Student services.** Adult student services, alcohol/substance abuse counseling, career counseling, services for economically disadvantaged, student employment services, financial aid counseling, health services, minority student services, personal counseling, placement for graduates, veterans' counselor. **Physically disabled:** Services for visually impaired. **Learning disabled:** Comprehensive services available.

**Contact.** E-mail: mpettway@alasu.edu
Phone: (334) 229-4291 Toll-free number: (800) 253-5037
Fax: (334) 229-4984
Martha Pettway, Director of Admissions and Recruitment, Alabama State University, PO Box 271, Montgomery, AL 36101-0271

## Amridge University
### Montgomery, Alabama
www.amridgeuniversity.edu          CB code: 7001

- Private 4-year university and seminary college affiliated with Church of Christ
- Commuter campus in small city
- 342 degree-seeking undergraduates: 27% part-time, 52% women
- 379 degree-seeking graduate students

**General.** Founded in 1967. Regionally accredited. **Degrees:** 104 bachelor's awarded; master's, doctoral, first professional offered. **Location:** 100 miles from Birmingham, 150 miles from Atlanta. **Calendar:** Semester, extensive summer session. **Full-time faculty:** 58 total. **Part-time faculty:** 37 total.

**Basis for selection.** Open admission, but selective for some programs. Students admitted under conditional admission must earn a 2.0 during the first 24 semester hours attempted.

**High school preparation.** 15 units recommended.

**2007-2008 Annual costs.** $260 per-credit-hour charge (including required fees) for undergraduates; some courses require additional lab and/or exam fees, which are the responsibility of the student. Books/supplies: $800. Personal expenses: $1,739.

**Financial aid. Non-need-based:** Scholarships awarded for academics, leadership. **Additional information:** Scholarships based on need and grades. Half-tuition scholarship is available for full-time undergraduate students.

**Application procedures. Admission:** No deadline. $50 fee. Application may be submitted online. Admission notification on a rolling basis. **Financial aid:** Priority date 5/1, closing date 6/30. FAFSA, institutional form required. Applicants notified by 6/30; must reply by 8/15 or within 2 week(s) of notification.

**Academics. Special study options:** Accelerated study, distance learning, double major, independent study, internships. Participant in the U.S. Department of Education's Distance Education Demonstration Program and in eArmyU and GoArmyEd initiatives. **Credit/placement by examination:** CLEP. 36 credit hours maximum toward bachelor's degree. **Support services:** Tutoring.

**Majors. Business:** Business admin. **Liberal arts:** Arts/sciences. **Theology:** Bible.

**Most popular majors.** Liberal arts 58%, theological studies 42%.

**Computing on campus.** PC or laptop required. 25 workstations in library, computer center. Online course registration, online library, helpline available.

**Student life. Freshman orientation:** Available. Online orientation available 24 hours a day, seven days a week.

**Student services.** Financial aid counseling, placement for graduates, veterans' counselor.

**Contact.** E-mail: admissions@amridgeuniversity.edu
Phone: (334) 387-7513 Toll-free number: (800) 351-4040 ext. 7513
Fax: (334) 387-3878
Rick Johnson, Director of Enrollment Management, Amridge University, 1200 Taylor Road, Montgomery, AL 36117-3553

## Andrew Jackson University
### Birmingham, Alabama
www.aju.edu          CB code: 3877

- For-profit 4-year virtual liberal arts college
- Very large city
- 200 degree-seeking undergraduates

**General.** Accredited by DETC. **Degrees:** 4 bachelor's, 7 associate awarded; master's offered. **Calendar:** Continuous, extensive summer session. **Part-time faculty:** 46 total.

**Basis for selection.** Open admission. **Homeschooled:** State high school equivalency certificate, letter of recommendation (nonparent) required.

**2007-2008 Annual costs.** Tuition/fees: $5,550. Books/supplies: $1,000.

**Application procedures. Admission:** No deadline. $75 fee. Application may be submitted online. Admission notification on a rolling basis. Must reply by May 1 or within 12 week(s) if notified thereafter.

**Academics. Special study options:** Accelerated study, distance learning, independent study. **Credit/placement by examination:** AP, CLEP. 15 credit hours maximum toward associate degree, 30 toward bachelor's. **Support services:** Reduced course load.

**Majors. Business:** General. **Communications:** General. **Protective services:** Criminal justice.

**Most popular majors.** Business/marketing 11%, public administration/social services 89%.

**Computing on campus.** PC or laptop required.

**Student life. Freshman orientation:** Available.

**Contact.** E-mail: admissions@aju.edu
Phone: (205) 871-9288 Toll-free number: (800) 429-9300
Fax: (205) 871-9294
Tammy Kassner, Director of Student Affairs, Andrew Jackson University, 2919 John Hawkins Parkway, Birmingham, AL 35244

## Athens State University
**Athens, Alabama**
www.athens.edu                                  **CB code: 0706**

▶ Public two-year upper-division business and teachers college
▶ Commuter campus in large town

**General.** Founded in 1822. Regionally accredited. State's only 2-year senior college serving transfers from junior, community, technical colleges and other 4-year accredited institutions. **Degrees:** 814 bachelor's awarded. **Articulation:** Agreements with state schools through the Alabama Articulation and General Studies Committee. **Location:** 14 miles from Decatur, 24 miles from Huntsville. **Calendar:** Semester, extensive summer session. **Full-time faculty:** 64 total; 84% have terminal degrees, 9% minority, 47% women. **Part-time faculty:** 86 total; 12% minority, 54% women. **Class size:** 44% < 20, 44% 20-39, 4% 40-49, 3% 50-99, 5% >100.

**Student profile.** 2,858 degree-seeking undergraduates. 942 applied as first-time-transfer students. 81% transferred from two-year, 19% transferred from four-year institutions.

| | | | |
|---|---|---|---|
| Women: | 68% | Live on campus: | 1% |
| Part-time: | 53% | 25 or older: | 69% |
| Out-of-state: | 6% | | |

**Basis for selection.** College transcript required. Transfer accepted as juniors, seniors.

**2007-2008 Annual costs.** Tuition/fees: $4,050; $7,350 out-of-state. Books/supplies: $800.

**Financial aid. Need-based:** 21% of total undergraduate aid awarded as scholarships/grants, 79% as loans/jobs. **Non-need-based:** Scholarships awarded for academics, alumni affiliation, art, athletics, leadership, minority status.

**Application procedures. Admission:** Rolling admission. $30 fee. Application may be submitted online. **Financial aid:** FAFSA required.

**Academics. Special study options:** Cooperative education, distance learning, double major, dual enrollment of high school students, independent study, study abroad, teacher certification program, weekend college. **Credit/placement by examination:** AP, CLEP.

**Majors. Biology:** General. **Business:** Accounting, business admin, human resources, information resources management. **Computer sciences:** General. **Education:** General, biology, chemistry, early childhood, elementary, English, history, mathematics, middle, physical, physics, science, secondary, social science, social studies, special, trade/industrial. **Engineering technology:** Instrumentation. **English:** English lit. **History:** General. **Interdisciplinary:** Behavioral sciences. **Liberal arts:** Arts/sciences. **Math:** General.

**Philosophy/religion:** Religion. **Physical sciences:** Chemistry, physics. **Protective services:** Criminal justice. **Psychology:** General. **Social sciences:** Political science, sociology. **Visual/performing arts:** Art.

**Most popular majors.** Business/marketing 31%, computer/information sciences 6%, education 34%, interdisciplinary studies 6%, liberal arts 6%.

**Computing on campus.** 341 workstations in library, computer center, student center. Commuter students can connect to campus network. Online library available.

**Student life. Housing:** Coed dorms available. **Activities:** Campus ministries, drama, student government, student newspaper, African-American history association, Centurions, Athenian Hosts/Hostesses, TKE, Tau Kappa Epsilon, Wesley Fellowship Campus Ministries, Pi tau Chi, Pre-Law Society, Council for Exceptional Children.

**Athletics. Team name:** Bears.

**Student services.** Career counseling, student employment services, financial aid counseling, minority student services, placement for graduates, veterans' counselor. **Physically disabled:** Services for visually, speech, hearing impaired.

**Contact.** E-mail: admissions@athens.edu
Phone: (256) 233-8220 Toll-free number: (800) 522-0272
Fax: (256) 233-6565
Necedah Henderson, Coordinator of Admissions, Athens State University, 300 North Beaty Street, Athens, AL 35611

## Auburn University
**Auburn, Alabama**                              **CB member**
www.auburn.edu                                   **CB code: 1005**

▶ Public 4-year university
▶ Commuter campus in large town
▶ 19,794 degree-seeking undergraduates: 8% part-time, 49% women, 9% African American, 2% Asian American, 2% Hispanic American, 1% Native American, 1% international
▶ 4,285 degree-seeking graduate students
▶ 69% of applicants admitted
▶ SAT or ACT (ACT writing optional), application essay required
▶ 63% graduate within 6 years

**General.** Founded in 1856. Regionally accredited. **Degrees:** 3,799 bachelor's awarded; master's, doctoral, first professional offered. **ROTC:** Army, Naval, Air Force. **Location:** 55 miles from Montgomery, 110 miles from Atlanta. **Calendar:** Semester, extensive summer session. **Full-time faculty:** 1,132 total; 17% minority, 29% women. **Part-time faculty:** 154 total; 7% minority, 44% women. **Class size:** 27% < 20, 54% 20-39, 5% 40-49, 9% 50-99, 5% >100. **Special facilities:** Space power institute, electron microscopes, rhizotron, nuclear science center, arboretum, torsatron, center for arts and humanities, sports museum.

**Freshman class profile.** 17,798 applied, 12,291 admitted, 4,191 enrolled.

| Mid 50% test scores | | | |
|---|---|---|---|
| SAT critical reading: | 500-610 | GPA 2.0-2.99: | 8% |
| SAT math: | 520-630 | Rank in top quarter: | 57% |
| ACT composite: | 22-27 | Rank in top tenth: | 27% |
| GPA 3.50 or higher: | 59% | Return as sophomores: | 86% |
| GPA 3.0-3.49: | 33% | Out-of-state: | 41% |

**Basis for selection.** Each student evaluated based on combination of standardized test scores, high school GPA, and additional information required on application.

**High school preparation.** 12 units required; 15 recommended. Required and recommended units include English 4, mathematics 3, social studies 3-4, science 2-3 (laboratory 1) and foreign language 1. Mathematics must include algebra I, algebra II, and either geometry, trigonometry, calculus or analysis. Science must include biology and a physical science.

**2007-2008 Annual costs.** Tuition/fees: $5,834; $16,334 out-of-state. Room/board: $7,466. Books/supplies: $1,100. Personal expenses: $2,350.

**2006-2007 Financial aid. Need-based:** 1,928 full-time freshmen applied for aid; 1,333 were judged to have need; 1,235 of these received aid. Average need met was 43%. Average scholarship/grant was $5,025; average loan $2,897. 36% of total undergraduate aid awarded as scholarships/grants,

64% as loans/jobs. **Non-need-based:** Awarded to 2,276 full-time undergraduates, including 653 freshmen. **Additional information:** State of Alabama has pre-paid college tuition plan for residents.

**Application procedures. Admission:** Closing date 2/1 (postmark date). $25 fee, may be waived for applicants with need. Application may be submitted online. Admission notification 2/1. Admission notification on a rolling basis beginning on or about 10/1. Must reply by 5/1. **Financial aid:** No deadline. FAFSA, institutional form required. Applicants notified on a rolling basis.

**Academics. Special study options:** Accelerated study, cooperative education, distance learning, double major, dual enrollment of high school students, ESL, honors, independent study, internships, liberal arts/career combination, study abroad, teacher certification program. DVM/master's in veterinary specialty, dual option program in education/subject areas. **Credit/placement by examination:** AP, CLEP, SAT, ACT, institutional tests. **Support services:** Learning center, reduced course load, study skills assistance, tutoring, writing center.

**Honors college/program.** Minimum 29 ACT or 1280 SAT (exclusive of Writing) and GPA 3.5 required. 3.4 GPA considered. Approximately 200 freshmen accepted last year.

**Majors. Agriculture:** Animal sciences, aquaculture, economics, horticultural science, poultry, soil science. **Architecture:** Architecture, environmental design, interior. **Biology:** General, bacteriology, biochemistry, botany, entomology, marine, molecular, zoology. **Business:** Accounting, business admin, communications, finance, human resources, international, logistics, managerial economics, marketing, operations. **Communications:** Journalism, public relations, radio/tv. **Computer sciences:** General. **Conservation:** Environmental science, forest sciences, wildlife. **Education:** Adult/continuing, early childhood, elementary, English, foreign languages, health, mathematics, music, physical, science, social science, special, voc/tech. **Engineering:** Aerospace, agricultural, architectural, chemical, civil, computer, electrical, materials, mechanical, software, textile. **English:** English lit. **Family/consumer sciences:** Apparel marketing, family studies, food/nutrition, housing. **Foreign languages:** French, German, Spanish. **Health:** Audiology/speech pathology, communication disorders, health care admin, nursing (RN), premedicine. **History:** General. **Math:** General, applied. **Parks/recreation:** Exercise sciences. **Philosophy/religion:** Philosophy, religion. **Physical sciences:** Chemistry, geology, physics. **Psychology:** General. **Public administration:** General, social work. **Science technology:** Biological. **Social sciences:** Anthropology, criminology, economics, geography, political science, sociology. **Transportation:** Aviation management. **Visual/performing arts:** Design, dramatic, industrial design, studio arts.

**Most popular majors.** Biology 7%, business/marketing 24%, education 11%, engineering/engineering technologies 13%, social sciences 7%.

**Computing on campus.** 600 workstations in dormitories, library, computer center, student center. Dormitories linked to campus network. Commuter students can connect to campus network. Online course registration, online library, helpline, repair service available.

**Student life. Freshman orientation:** Available, $75 fee. Preregistration for classes offered. **Housing:** Coed dorms, single-sex dorms, special housing for disabled, apartments, fraternity/sorority housing, substance-free housing available. Honors housing available. **Activities:** Bands, campus ministries, choral groups, dance, drama, film society, international student organizations, literary magazine, music ensembles, musical theater, opera, radio station, student government, student newspaper, symphony orchestra, TV station, over 300 religious, political, ethnic, and social service organizations.

**Athletics.** NCAA. **Intercollegiate:** Baseball M, basketball, cross-country, diving, equestrian W, football (tackle) M, golf, gymnastics W, soccer W, softball W, swimming, tennis, track and field, volleyball W. **Intramural:** Badminton, basketball, bowling, cheerleading, football (non-tackle), golf, gymnastics, lacrosse, racquetball, rugby, skiing, soccer, softball, swimming, table tennis, tennis, track and field, volleyball, wrestling M. **Team name:** Tigers.

**Student services.** Adult student services, alcohol/substance abuse counseling, career counseling, student employment services, financial aid counseling, health services, minority student services, personal counseling, placement for graduates, veterans' counselor, women's services. **Physically disabled:** Services for visually, speech, hearing impaired.

**Contact.** E-mail: admissions@auburn.edu
Phone: (334) 844-4080 Toll-free number: (800) 282-8769
Fax: (334) 844-6436
Cindy Singley, Director of University Recruitment, Auburn University, Quad Center, Auburn, AL 36849-5111

---

## Auburn University at Montgomery

Montgomery, Alabama
www.aum.edu

CB member
CB code: 1036

- Public 4-year university
- Commuter campus in small city
- 4,134 degree-seeking undergraduates: 33% part-time, 63% women
- 703 degree-seeking graduate students
- 92% of applicants admitted
- SAT or ACT (ACT writing optional) required

**General.** Founded in 1967. Regionally accredited. **Degrees:** 574 bachelor's awarded; master's, doctoral offered. **ROTC:** Army, Air Force. **Location:** 7 miles from downtown. **Calendar:** Semester, extensive summer session. **Full-time faculty:** 200 total; 17% minority, 41% women. **Part-time faculty:** 134 total; 11% minority, 56% women. **Class size:** 47% < 20, 49% 20-39, 2% 40-49, 2% 50-99, less than 1% >100.

**Freshman class profile.** 1,210 applied, 1,110 admitted, 666 enrolled.

| Mid 50% test scores | | | |
|---|---|---|---|
| ACT composite: | 18-22 | Return as sophomores: | 57% |
| | | Live on campus: | 22% |

**Basis for selection.** GPA and ACT/SAT scores considered for admission. Provisional admission may be available for students who do not meet requirements for regular admission. C average after 18 hours of academic courses required for provisional students to become regular students.

**High school preparation.** College-preparatory program recommended. 4 units recommended. Recommended units include English 3, mathematics 2, social studies 2, history 2, science 2 (laboratory 2), foreign language 2 and academic electives 2.

**2007-2008 Annual costs.** Tuition/fees: $5,010; $14,490 out-of-state. Room/board: $4,890. Books/supplies: $800. Personal expenses: $1,890.

**2007-2008 Financial aid. Need-based:** 348 full-time freshmen applied for aid; 270 were judged to have need; 258 of these received aid. Average scholarship/grant was $3,688; average loan $3,243. 31% of total undergraduate aid awarded as scholarships/grants, 69% as loans/jobs. **Non-need-based:** Scholarships awarded for academics, alumni affiliation, art, athletics, job skills, leadership, minority status, music/drama, religious affiliation, ROTC.

**Application procedures. Admission:** No deadline. $25 fee. Application may be submitted online. **Financial aid:** Priority date 3/15; no closing date. FAFSA required. Applicants notified on a rolling basis starting 5/1; must reply within 2 week(s) of notification.

**Academics.** Interdisciplinary Master of Liberal Arts available. **Special study options:** Accelerated study, cooperative education, cross-registration, distance learning, double major, dual enrollment of high school students, ESL, honors, independent study, internships, liberal arts/career combination, study abroad, teacher certification program, weekend college. Joint Ph.D. in public administration with Auburn University; cooperative doctoral program in educational leadership with Auburn University (Ed.D.). **Credit/placement by examination:** AP, CLEP, IB, SAT, ACT, institutional tests. 60 credit hours maximum toward bachelor's degree. **Support services:** Learning center, reduced course load, remedial instruction, tutoring.

**Majors. Biology:** General. **Business:** General, accounting, business admin, finance, human resources, management information systems, managerial economics, marketing. **Communications:** General. **Education:** Elementary, secondary. **English:** English lit. **Foreign languages:** General. **Health:** Nursing (RN). **History:** General. **Liberal arts:** Arts/sciences. **Math:** General. **Physical sciences:** General. **Protective services:** Criminal justice. **Psychology:** General. **Social sciences:** Political science, sociology. **Visual/performing arts:** Art.

**Most popular majors.** Biology 9%, business/marketing 33%, education 14%, health sciences 12%, security/protective services 8%.

**Computing on campus.** 478 workstations in library, computer center, student center. Dormitories wired for high-speed internet access and linked to campus network. Commuter students can connect to campus network. Online course registration, online library, repair service, student web hosting, wireless network available.

**Student life. Freshman orientation:** Mandatory, $50 fee. Preregistration for classes offered. 2 sessions, one hour each, morning and evening. Programs held 2 days before start of each semester. **Policies:** Students are required to conform to all policies and regulations of the university by October registration. **Housing:** Coed dorms, special housing for disabled, apartments available. $100 nonrefundable deposit. **Activities:** Campus ministries, choral groups, dance, drama, film society, international student organizations, literary magazine, musical theater, student government, student newspaper, American Humanics, Caunterbury Society, Disciples of Christ, Circle K, NAACP.

**Athletics.** NAIA. **Intercollegiate:** Baseball M, basketball, soccer, tennis. **Intramural:** Baseball, basketball M, bowling, football (non-tackle), softball, tennis, volleyball. **Team name:** Senators.

**Student services.** Adult student services, career counseling, student employment services, health services, personal counseling, placement for graduates, veterans' counselor. **Physically disabled:** Services for visually, speech, hearing impaired.

**Contact.** E-mail: AdmitMe@mail.aum.edu
Phone: (334) 244-3616 Toll-free number: (800) 227-2649
Fax: (334) 244-3795
Valerie Crawford, Director of Admissions, Auburn University at Montgomery, 7400 East Drive, Room 139 Taylor Center, Montgomery, AL 36124-4023

---

## Birmingham-Southern College
**Birmingham, Alabama**            **CB member**
www.bsc.edu                        **CB code: 1064**

▶ Private 4-year liberal arts college affiliated with United Methodist Church
▶ Residential campus in large city
▶ 1,339 degree-seeking undergraduates: 2% part-time, 51% women, 8% African American, 3% Asian American, 1% Hispanic American, 1% Native American
▶ 50 degree-seeking graduate students
▶ 66% of applicants admitted
▶ SAT or ACT (ACT writing recommended), application essay required
▶ 72% graduate within 6 years; 50% enter graduate study

**General.** Founded in 1856. Regionally accredited. **Degrees:** 281 bachelor's awarded; master's offered. **ROTC:** Army, Air Force. **Location:** 3 miles from downtown. **Calendar:** 4-1-4, limited summer session. **Full-time faculty:** 101 total; 96% have terminal degrees, 2% minority, 44% women. **Part-time faculty:** 33 total; 21% have terminal degrees, 46% women. **Class size:** 73% < 20, 26% 20-39, 1% 40-49. **Special facilities:** Planetarium, southern environmental center and interactive museum, ecoscape garden.

**Freshman class profile.** 2,282 applied, 1,505 admitted, 450 enrolled.

| Mid 50% test scores | | Rank in top tenth: | 27% |
|---|---|---|---|
| SAT critical reading: | 520-640 | End year in good standing: | 95% |
| SAT math: | 520-650 | Return as sophomores: | 84% |
| ACT composite: | 22-28 | Out-of-state: | 33% |
| GPA 3.50 or higher: | 43% | Live on campus: | 93% |
| GPA 3.0-3.49: | 28% | Fraternities: | 61% |
| GPA 2.0-2.99: | 29% | Sororities: | 45% |
| Rank in top quarter: | 55% | | |

**Basis for selection.** High school record most important, followed by test scores, recommendations, and required essay. Interview required for early admission; recommended for borderline applicants. Auditions required for music, theater, dance majors. **Homeschooled:** Interviews recommended.

**High school preparation.** 16 units required. Required and recommended units include English 4, mathematics 4, social studies 2, history 2, science 4 (laboratory 2), foreign language 2 and academic electives 10.

**2007-2008 Annual costs.** Tuition/fees: $24,300. Room/board: $8,378. Books/supplies: $1,000. Personal expenses: $500.

**2007-2008 Financial aid. Need-based:** 305 full-time freshmen applied for aid; 243 were judged to have need; 243 of these received aid. Average need met was 83%. Average scholarship/grant was $6,618; average loan $4,586. 86% of total undergraduate aid awarded as scholarships/grants, 14% as loans/jobs. **Non-need-based:** Awarded to 1,237 full-time undergraduates, including 429 freshmen. Scholarships awarded for academics, alumni affiliation, art, job skills, leadership, minority status, music/drama, religious affiliation, state residency. **Additional information:** Auditions required for music, theater, dance applicants seeking scholarships. Portfolios required for art applicants seeking scholarships, and essays recommended for all applicants seeking scholarships.

**Application procedures. Admission:** Priority date 1/1; no deadline. $40 fee, may be waived for applicants with need. Application may be submitted online. Admission notification on a rolling basis beginning on or about 9/15. Must reply by May 1 or within 3 week(s) if notified thereafter. **Financial aid:** Priority date 3/1; no closing date. FAFSA required. Applicants notified on a rolling basis starting 3/1; must reply by 8/21.

**Academics. Special study options:** Combined bachelor's/graduate degree, cooperative education, cross-registration, double major, dual enrollment of high school students, exchange student, honors, independent study, internships, semester at sea, student-designed major, study abroad, teacher certification program, Washington semester. 4-1-4 in nursing with Vanderbilt; 3-2 in engineering with Washington University, Columbia University, University of Alabama, and Auburn University; 3-2 in environment studies with Duke University. **Credit/placement by examination:** AP, CLEP, IB, SAT, ACT, institutional tests. 64 credit hours maximum toward bachelor's degree. **Support services:** Pre-admission summer program, reduced course load, study skills assistance, tutoring, writing center.

**Majors. Biology:** General. **Business:** General, accounting, finance, international, marketing. **Computer sciences:** General, computer science. **Conservation:** Environmental studies. **Education:** General, art, early childhood, elementary, music, special. **English:** English lit. **Foreign languages:** French, German, Spanish. **History:** General. **Interdisciplinary:** Math/computer science. **Math:** General. **Philosophy/religion:** Philosophy, religion. **Physical sciences:** Chemistry, physics. **Psychology:** General. **Social sciences:** Economics, political science, sociology. **Theology:** Sacred music. **Visual/performing arts:** General, art, art history/conservation, dance, dramatic, drawing, music history, music theory/composition, painting, photography, piano/organ, sculpture, voice/opera.

**Most popular majors.** Biology 20%, business/marketing 20%, education 6%, English 7%, interdisciplinary studies 9%, psychology 6%, social sciences 7%, visual/performing arts 10%.

**Computing on campus.** 252 workstations in dormitories, library, computer center, student center, student center. Dormitories wired for high-speed internet access and linked to campus network. Commuter students can connect to campus network. Online course registration, online library, helpline, student web hosting, wireless network available.

**Student life. Freshman orientation:** Mandatory. Preregistration for classes offered. One day mini-session in June and 4 day session prior to beginning of classes. **Housing:** Guaranteed on-campus for all undergraduates. Single-sex dorms, special housing for disabled, apartments, fraternity/sorority housing, substance-free housing available. $200 nonrefundable deposit, deadline 5/1. Handicapped students accommodated on individual basis. **Activities:** Bands, campus ministries, choral groups, dance, drama, international student organizations, literary magazine, music ensembles, musical theater, opera, student government, student newspaper, Fellowship of Christian Athletes, Young Republicans, Young Democrats, Black Student Union, Allies, Students Offering Support, Conservancy, Wesley Fellowship, Intervarsity Christian Fellowship.

**Athletics.** NCAA. **Intercollegiate:** Baseball M, basketball, cheerleading, cross-country, football (tackle) M, golf, lacrosse, rifle W, soccer, softball W, tennis, track and field, volleyball W. **Intramural:** Basketball, football (non-tackle), racquetball, soccer, softball, table tennis, volleyball, water polo. **Team name:** Panthers.

**Student services.** Alcohol/substance abuse counseling, campus ministries, career counseling, student employment services, financial aid counseling, health services, personal counseling, placement for graduates, veterans' counselor.

**Contact.** E-mail: admission@bsc.edu
Phone: (205) 226-4696 Toll-free number: (800) 523-5793
Fax: (205) 226-3074
Sheri Salmon, Dean for Enrollment Management, Birmingham-Southern College, 900 Arkadelphia Road, Birmingham, AL 35254

---

## Columbia Southern University
**Orange Beach, Alabama**
www.columbiasouthern.edu          **CB code: 3878**

▶ For-profit 4-year virtual business college
▶ Small town
▶ 7,710 degree-seeking undergraduates
▶ 2,300 graduate students

**General.** Accredited by DETC. **Degrees:** 955 bachelor's awarded; master's, doctoral offered. **Location:** 60 miles from Mobile. **Calendar:** Continuous. **Full-time faculty:** 12 total; 50% have terminal degrees, 50% women. **Part-time faculty:** 84 total; 46% have terminal degrees, 44% women.

**Basis for selection.** Open admission.

**2007-2008 Annual costs.** Tuition/fees: $4,770.

**Application procedures. Admission:** No deadline. $25 fee.

**Academics. Credit/placement by examination:** CLEP.

**Majors. Business:** Business admin. **Protective services:** Law enforcement admin.

**Student life. Activities:** Student newspaper.

**Contact.**  E-mail: admissions@columbiasouthern.edu
Phone: (251) 981-3771 ext. 521 Toll-free number: (800) 977-8449 ext. 521
Fax: (251) 981-3815
Tommy Cooley, Director of Admissions, Columbia Southern University, 25326 Canal Road, Orange Beach, AL 36561

## Concordia College
### Selma, Alabama

CB code: 1989

- Private 4-year liberal arts college affiliated with Lutheran Church - Missouri Synod
- Residential campus in large town
- 554 degree-seeking undergraduates
- 94% of applicants admitted

**General.** Founded in 1922. Regionally accredited. **Degrees:** 43 bachelor's, 24 associate awarded. **Location:** 50 miles from Montgomery. **Calendar:** Semester, limited summer session. **Full-time faculty:** 9 total. **Part-time faculty:** 28 total.

**Freshman class profile.** 289 applied, 271 admitted, 156 enrolled.

**Basis for selection.** 2.0 GPA required for unconditional admission. Students who do not fulfill requirements may be admitted on conditional basis.

**High school preparation.** 20 units recommended. Recommended units include English 4, mathematics 2, social studies 3, science 2 and foreign language 1.

**2007-2008 Annual costs.** Tuition/fees: $6,826. Room/board: $3,200. Books/supplies: $400.

**2006-2007 Financial aid.** All financial aid based on need. 98% of total undergraduate aid awarded as scholarships/grants, 2% as loans/jobs.

**Application procedures. Admission:** Priority date 8/1; deadline 8/15. $10 fee, may be waived for applicants with need. Admission notification on a rolling basis beginning on or about 8/15. **Financial aid:** Priority date 4/1, closing date 4/15. FAFSA, institutional form, CSS PROFILE required. Applicants notified on a rolling basis starting 6/15; must reply within 2 week(s) of notification.

**Academics. Special study options:** Independent study, liberal arts/career combination. **Credit/placement by examination:** CLEP, institutional tests. **Support services:** Learning center, pre-admission summer program, reduced course load, remedial instruction, tutoring.

**Majors. Business:** Business admin. **Education:** Early childhood, elementary.

**Most popular majors.** Biology 18%, education 82%.

**Computing on campus.** 30 workstations in library, computer center.

**Student life. Freshman orientation:** Mandatory. Preregistration for classes offered. **Housing:** Single-sex dorms available. **Activities:** Choral groups, drama, music ensembles, student government, student newspaper, Phi Theta Kappa, Gentlemen Care Group Club, Ambassador's Club, American Red Cross Club.

**Athletics. Intercollegiate:** Baseball M, basketball, softball W. **Intramural:** Baseball M, basketball, football (tackle) M, softball, table tennis, tennis, volleyball. **Team name:** Hornets.

**Student services.** Adult student services, career counseling, student employment services, health services, personal counseling, placement for graduates, veterans' counselor.

**Contact.**  Phone: (334) 874-5700
Gwendolyn Stewart, Director of Admissions, Concordia College, 1804 Green Street, Selma, AL 36701

## Faulkner University
### Montgomery, Alabama
www.faulkner.edu

CB code: 1034

- Private 4-year university and liberal arts college affiliated with Church of Christ
- Residential campus in large city
- 2,565 degree-seeking undergraduates
- 59% of applicants admitted
- SAT or ACT (ACT writing optional) required

**General.** Founded in 1942. Regionally accredited. Extension centers in Birmingham, Huntsville, and Mobile offer associate degrees. **Degrees:** 569 bachelor's, 44 associate awarded; master's, first professional offered. **ROTC:** Army, Air Force. **Location:** 5 miles from downtown. **Calendar:** Semester, limited summer session. **Full-time faculty:** 105 total; 67% have terminal degrees, 11% minority, 32% women. **Part-time faculty:** 50 total; 44% have terminal degrees, 14% minority, 40% women. **Class size:** 77% < 20, 18% 20-39, 3% 40-49, 2% 50-99, less than 1% >100.

**Freshman class profile.** 982 applied, 579 admitted, 279 enrolled.

| Mid 50% test scores | | | |
|---|---|---|---|
| SAT critical reading: | 420-520 | GPA 2.0-2.99: | 40% |
| SAT math: | 430-540 | Rank in top quarter: | 14% |
| ACT composite: | 18-22 | Rank in top tenth: | 12% |
| GPA 3.50 or higher: | 31% | Out-of-state: | 33% |
| GPA 3.0-3.49: | 27% | Live on campus: | 58% |
| | | International: | 2% |

**Basis for selection.** Academic record, test scores, and personal or career goals most important. Interview, essay recommended.

**High school preparation.** 15 units required. 9 units from among social sciences, foreign language, mathematics and science required.

**2007-2008 Annual costs.** Tuition/fees: $12,025. Room/board: $6,050. Books/supplies: $1,200. Personal expenses: $1,200.

**2007-2008 Financial aid. Need-based:** 32% of total undergraduate aid awarded as scholarships/grants, 68% as loans/jobs. **Non-need-based:** Scholarships awarded for academics, alumni affiliation, art, athletics, leadership, music/drama, religious affiliation, ROTC, state residency.

**Application procedures. Admission:** Priority date 2/15; no deadline. $10 fee, may be waived for applicants with need. Application may be submitted online. Admission notification on a rolling basis beginning on or about 8/15. **Financial aid:** Priority date 5/1; no closing date. FAFSA, institutional form required. Applicants notified on a rolling basis starting 6/1; must reply within 3 week(s) of notification.

**Academics.** Full-time students required to take 1 Bible course per semester. **Special study options:** Combined bachelor's/graduate degree, cooperative education, cross-registration, distance learning, double major, dual enrollment of high school students, honors, independent study, internships, liberal arts/career combination, study abroad, teacher certification program, weekend college. **Credit/placement by examination:** AP, CLEP, institutional tests. 16 credit hours maximum toward associate degree, 32 toward bachelor's. **Support services:** Learning center, reduced course load, remedial instruction, study skills assistance, tutoring, writing center.

**Majors. Area/ethnic studies:** American. **Biology:** General. **Business:** General, accounting, business admin, human resources, marketing, office management. **Computer sciences:** Information systems. **Education:** General, biology, chemistry, elementary, English, history, mathematics, middle, physical, science, secondary, social studies. **English:** English lit. **Health:** Predental, premedicine, preveterinary. **History:** General. **Interdisciplinary:** Biological/physical sciences. **Legal studies:** Prelaw. **Liberal arts:** Arts/sciences. **Math:** General. **Parks/recreation:** Sports admin. **Philosophy/religion:** Religion. **Protective services:** Criminal justice. **Psychology:** General. **Theology:** Bible, religious ed, theology. **Visual/performing arts:** General, studio arts.

**Computing on campus.** 250 workstations in dormitories, library, computer center, student center. Dormitories wired for high-speed internet access and linked to campus network. Online library, helpline, wireless network available.

**Student life. Freshman orientation:** Mandatory. Preregistration for classes offered. **Policies:** Religious observance required. **Housing:** Guaranteed on-campus for all undergraduates. Single-sex dorms, special housing for disabled, apartments available. $50 nonrefundable deposit. **Activities:** Choral groups, drama, music ensembles, musical theater, student government, student newspaper, minister's club, service organizations, religious organizations.

**Athletics.** NAIA, NCCAA. **Intercollegiate:** Baseball M, basketball M, cheerleading M, cross-country, football (tackle) M, golf M, softball W, volleyball W. **Intramural:** Badminton, basketball, bowling, football (tackle), racquetball, softball, table tennis, tennis, track and field, volleyball. **Team name:** Eagles.

**Student services.** Adult student services, career counseling, student employment services, health services, personal counseling, placement for graduates, veterans' counselor.

**Contact.** E-mail: admissions@faulkner.edu
Phone: (334) 386-7200 Toll-free number: (800) 879-9816
Fax: (334) 386-7137
Keith Mock, Director of Admissions, Faulkner University, 5345 Atlanta Highway, Montgomery, AL 36109-3398

## Heritage Christian University
**Florence, Alabama**
www.hcu.edu                                         CB code: 0805

♦ Private 4-year Bible college affiliated with Church of Christ
♦ Commuter campus in large town
♦ 53 full-time, degree-seeking undergraduates
♦ 71% of applicants admitted

**General.** Founded in 1971. Accredited by ABHE. **Degrees:** 14 bachelor's, 4 associate awarded; master's offered. **Location:** 125 miles from Birmingham, 50 miles from Huntsville. **Calendar:** Semester, limited summer session. **Full-time faculty:** 10 total. **Part-time faculty:** 19 total. **Class size:** 96% < 20, 4% 20-39.

**Freshman class profile.** 7 applied, 5 admitted, 5 enrolled.

Out-of-state:          40%      Live on campus:          10%

**Basis for selection.** Religious affiliation and recommendations very important, school achievement considered. Interview recommended.

**2007-2008 Annual costs.** Tuition/fees: $9,810. Room only: $3,000.

**Application procedures. Admission:** No deadline. $25 fee. Admission notification on a rolling basis. **Financial aid:** Priority date 6/1; no closing date. FAFSA required. Applicants notified on a rolling basis starting 6/1; must reply by 7/28 or within 2 week(s) of notification.

**Academics. Special study options:** Accelerated study, distance learning, dual enrollment of high school students, independent study, internships. **Credit/placement by examination:** AP, CLEP, institutional tests. 24 credit hours maximum toward associate degree, 24 toward bachelor's. **Support services:** Reduced course load, remedial instruction, study skills assistance, tutoring.

**Majors. Theology:** Bible.

**Computing on campus.** 12 workstations in library, computer center. Wireless network available.

**Student life. Freshman orientation:** Mandatory. Preregistration for classes offered. 2 semester hour course. **Housing:** Guaranteed on-campus for freshmen. Single-sex dorms, apartments, substance-free housing available. **Activities:** Student government, Christian service program, mission club.

**Student services.** Career counseling, student employment services, personal counseling, placement for graduates, veterans' counselor.

**Contact.** E-mail: hcu@hcu.edu
Phone: (256) 766-6610 Toll-free number: (800) 367-3565
Fax: (256) 766-9289
Travis Harmon, Director of Enrollment Services, Heritage Christian University, 3625 Helton Drive, Florence, AL 35630

## Herzing College
**Birmingham, Alabama**
www.herzing.edu                                     CB code: 2851

♦ For-profit 4-year business and technical college
♦ Very large city

**General.** Regionally accredited. **Calendar:** Semester.

**Annual costs/financial aid.** $300 to $335 per-credit-hour depending on program and/or course. Need-based financial aid available for full-time students.

**Contact.** Phone: (205) 916-2800
Director of Admissions, 280 West Valley Avenue, Birmingham, AL 35209

## Huntingdon College
**Montgomery, Alabama**                             CB member
www.huntingdon.edu                                  CB code: 1303

♦ Private 4-year liberal arts college affiliated with United Methodist Church
♦ Residential campus in small city
♦ 943 degree-seeking undergraduates: 17% part-time, 49% women
♦ 66% of applicants admitted
♦ SAT or ACT (ACT writing optional) required
♦ 48% graduate within 6 years

**General.** Founded in 1854. Regionally accredited. **Degrees:** 168 bachelor's awarded. **ROTC:** Army, Air Force. **Location:** 90 miles from Birmingham, 180 miles from Atlanta. **Calendar:** Semester, limited summer session. **Full-time faculty:** 44 total; 80% have terminal degrees, 43% women. **Part-time faculty:** 20 total; 35% have terminal degrees, 60% women. **Class size:** 61% < 20, 32% 20-39, 4% 40-49, 2% 50-99, less than 1% >100. **Special facilities:** Recital hall with individual practice studios, ecological center, sports medicine and athletic training facilities, United Methodist Church archives.

**Freshman class profile.** 985 applied, 649 admitted, 256 enrolled.

| Mid 50% test scores | | Rank in top quarter: | 39% |
|---|---|---|---|
| SAT critical reading: | 410-660 | Rank in top tenth: | 16% |
| SAT math: | 420-650 | End year in good standing: | 86% |
| ACT composite: | 18-26 | Return as sophomores: | 60% |
| GPA 3.50 or higher: | 44% | Out-of-state: | 16% |
| GPA 3.0-3.49: | 33% | Fraternities: | 10% |
| GPA 2.0-2.99: | 22% | Sororities: | 24% |

**Basis for selection.** GPA and test scores important. Marginal cases require essay, letters of recommendation, interview and other documentation. Interview, essay recommended. Audition required of music majors; portfolio recommended for art majors. **Learning Disabled:** When a 504 applicant is identified, he/she begins to meet with the Center for Learning Enrichment to assign appropriate academic assistance and services, which take effect upon matriculation.

**High school preparation.** 14 units recommended. Recommended units include English 4, mathematics 3, social studies 3, science 2 (laboratory 2) and foreign language 2. 2 units in humanities recommended.

**2008-2009 Annual costs.** Tuition/fees (projected): $20,020. Room/board: $6,950. Books/supplies: $900. Personal expenses: $1,045.

**2007-2008 Financial aid. Need-based:** Average need met was 80%. Average scholarship/grant was $7,673; average loan $3,782. 83% of total undergraduate aid awarded as scholarships/grants, 17% as loans/jobs. **Non-need-based:** Scholarships awarded for academics, alumni affiliation, art, leadership, music/drama, religious affiliation, ROTC, state residency.

**Application procedures. Admission:** Priority date 12/1; deadline 8/1 (receipt date). $20 fee, may be waived for applicants with need. Application may be submitted online. Admission notification on a rolling basis beginning on or about 9/15. Must reply by 5/1. **Financial aid:** Priority date 4/17; no closing date. FAFSA, institutional form required. Applicants notified on a rolling basis starting 3/1; must reply by 5/1 or within 4 week(s) of notification.

**Academics. Special study options:** Combined bachelor's/graduate degree, cross-registration, double major, honors, independent study, internships, liberal arts/career combination, student-designed major, study abroad, teacher certification program, Washington semester. Dual engineering degree with Auburn University and exchange student program with universities in Korea and Ireland; travel/study opportunities provided to all full-time juniors and seniors within regular educational costs or for nominal additional fees. **Credit/placement by examination:** AP, CLEP, IB, ACT, institutional tests. 30 credit hours maximum toward bachelor's degree. No credit will be granted on the basis of General Examinations taken after the student has entered college. A $25.00 recording fee per awarded credit hour is assessed. **Support services:** Learning center, reduced course load, study skills assistance, tutoring, writing center.

**Majors. Biology:** General, cell/histology. **Business:** General, accounting. **Communications:** General. **Education:** Elementary. **English:** English lit. **Health:** Athletic training. **History:** General. **Math:** General. **Parks/recreation:** Exercise sciences, health/fitness. **Philosophy/religion:** Religion. **Physical sciences:** Chemistry. **Psychology:** General. **Social sciences:** Political science. **Visual/performing arts:** Art, music performance.

**Most popular majors.** Biology 10%, business/marketing 53%, parks/recreation 8%.

**Computing on campus.** PC or laptop required. 13 workstations in library. Dormitories wired for high-speed internet access and linked to campus network. Commuter students can connect to campus network. Online library, repair service, student web hosting, wireless network available.

**Student life. Freshman orientation:** Mandatory. Preregistration for classes offered. **Housing:** Guaranteed on-campus for all undergraduates. Coed dorms, special housing for disabled available. $50 fully refundable deposit, deadline 5/1. Students under age 21 must live on campus unless living with parent in metropolitan area. **Activities:** Bands, campus ministries, choral groups, dance, drama, international student organizations, literary magazine, music ensembles, musical theater, opera, student government, student newspaper, 50 clubs and organizations.

**Athletics.** NCAA. **Intercollegiate:** Baseball M, basketball, cross-country, football (tackle) M, golf M, soccer, softball W, tennis, volleyball W. **Intramural:** Baseball, basketball, football (non-tackle), golf, soccer, softball, tennis, volleyball. **Team name:** Hawks.

**Student services.** Adult student services, campus ministries, career counseling, student employment services, financial aid counseling, health services, placement for graduates. **Physically disabled:** Services for visually, hearing impaired.

**Contact.** E-mail: admiss@huntingdon.edu
Phone: (334) 833-4497 Toll-free number: (800) 763-0313
Fax: (334) 833-4347
Joseph Miller, Director of Admission, Huntingdon College, 1500 East Fairview Avenue, Montgomery, AL 36106-2148

## Huntsville Bible College
Huntsville, Alabama
www.huntsvillebiblecollege.com

▶ Private 4-year Bible college
▶ Small city

**General.** Accredited by ABHE. **Location:** 87 miles from Birmingham, 100 miles from Nashville, Tennessee. **Calendar:** Semester.

**Annual costs/financial aid.** Tuition/fees (2007-2008): $2,330.

**Contact.** Phone: (256) 539-0834
Director of Admissions, 904 Oakwood Avenue, Huntsville, AL 35811

## ITT Technical Institute: Birmingham
Bessemer, Alabama
www.itt-tech.edu                    CB code: 2696

▶ For-profit 4-year technical college
▶ Commuter campus in very large city

**General.** Accredited by ACICS. **Calendar:** Quarter.

**Annual costs/financial aid.** Tuition varies by program, $260-$368 per credit hour.

**Contact.** Phone: (205) 991-5410
Director of Recruitment, 6270 Park South Drive, Bessemer, AL 35022

## Jacksonville State University
Jacksonville, Alabama
www.jsu.edu                         CB code: 1736

▶ Public 4-year university
▶ Commuter campus in small town
▶ 7,391 degree-seeking undergraduates: 22% part-time, 59% women, 26% African American, 1% Asian American, 1% Hispanic American, 1% Native American, 2% international
▶ 1,592 degree-seeking graduate students
▶ 86% of applicants admitted
▶ SAT or ACT (ACT writing optional) required
▶ 38% graduate within 6 years

**General.** Founded in 1883. Regionally accredited. **Degrees:** 1,175 bachelor's awarded; master's offered. **ROTC:** Army. **Location:** 75 miles from Birmingham, 100 miles from Atlanta. **Calendar:** Semester, extensive summer session. **Full-time faculty:** 323 total; 62% have terminal degrees, 10% minority, 46% women. **Part-time faculty:** 135 total; 17% have terminal degrees, 3% minority, 61% women. **Class size:** 45% < 20, 45% 20-39, 5% 40-49, 5% 50-99, less than 1% >100. **Special facilities:** Space observatory, Little River Canyon field school.

**Freshman class profile.** 3,299 applied, 2,853 admitted, 1,302 enrolled.

| Mid 50% test scores | | Rank in top tenth: | 3% |
|---|---|---|---|
| SAT critical reading: | 410-500 | Return as sophomores: | 69% |
| SAT math: | 410-500 | Out-of-state: | 29% |
| ACT composite: | 17-22 | Live on campus: | 60% |
| GPA 3.50 or higher: | 30% | International: | 2% |
| GPA 3.0-3.49: | 40% | Fraternities: | 9% |
| GPA 2.0-2.99: | 26% | Sororities: | 9% |
| Rank in top quarter: | 13% | | |

**Basis for selection.** High school record and test scores very important. ACT score of at least 16 or SAT score of at least 750 (exclusive of Writing) required for conditional admission. ACT score of at least 19 or SAT score of at least 900 (exclusive of Writing) required for unconditional admission. SAT/ACT scores must be submitted by beginning of term.

**High school preparation.** 15 units required. Required units include English 3 and academic electives 4. 8 units required in mathematics, science, foreign language, social studies/history.

**2007-2008 Annual costs.** Tuition/fees: $5,070; $10,140 out-of-state. Room/board: $3,763. Books/supplies: $1,089. Personal expenses: $2,903.

**Financial aid. Non-need-based:** Scholarships awarded for academics, alumni affiliation, art, athletics, music/drama, ROTC.

**Application procedures. Admission:** No deadline. $20 fee. Application may be submitted online. Admission notification on a rolling basis. **Financial aid:** Priority date 3/15; no closing date. FAFSA, institutional form required. Applicants notified on a rolling basis starting 5/15; must reply within 2 week(s) of notification.

**Academics. Special study options:** Accelerated study, combined bachelor's/graduate degree, cooperative education, distance learning, double major, dual enrollment of high school students, ESL, honors, independent study, internships, teacher certification program. **Credit/placement by examination:** AP, CLEP, SAT, ACT, institutional tests. 46 credit hours maximum toward bachelor's degree. Maximum credit hours awarded through CLEP examinations: 31 for general tests, 15 through subject tests. **Support services:** Learning center, pre-admission summer program, remedial instruction, tutoring.

**Majors. Biology:** General. **Business:** Accounting, business admin, finance, managerial economics, marketing. **Communications:** Radio/tv. **Computer sciences:** General. **Education:** Elementary, health, physical, secondary, special. **Engineering technology:** Electrical, manufacturing, occupational safety. **English:** English lit. **Family/consumer sciences:** General. **Foreign languages:** General. **Health:** Nursing (RN). **History:** General. **Liberal arts:** Arts/sciences. **Math:** General. **Parks/recreation:** General. **Physical sciences:** Chemistry, physics. **Protective services:** Criminal justice. **Psychology:** General. **Public administration:** Social work. **Social sciences:** Economics, geography, political science, sociology. **Visual/performing arts:** Art, dramatic.

**Most popular majors.** Business/marketing 16%, education 24%, health sciences 13%, public administration/social services 6%, security/protective services 8%, social sciences 6%.

**Computing on campus.** 330 workstations in library, computer center, student center. Dormitories linked to campus network. Commuter students can connect to campus network. Online course registration, helpline available.

**Student life. Freshman orientation:** Available. $40 fee. Preregistration for classes offered. **Housing:** Coed dorms, single-sex dorms, apartments, fraternity/sorority housing, substance-free housing available. $100 deposit. **Activities:** Bands, choral groups, drama, international student organizations, music ensembles, musical theater, opera, radio station, student government, student newspaper, symphony orchestra, TV station, Panhellenic council, adult learners forum, peer counselors, African American association, book club.

**Athletics.** NCAA. **Intercollegiate:** Baseball M, basketball, cross-country, football (tackle) M, golf, rifle, soccer W, softball W, tennis, track and field, volleyball W. **Intramural:** Basketball, bowling, football (tackle) M, racquetball, rugby M, softball, tennis, track and field, volleyball. **Team name:** Gamecocks.

**Student services.** Career counseling, student employment services, financial aid counseling, health services, minority student services, on-campus daycare, personal counseling, placement for graduates, veterans' counselor. **Physically disabled:** Services for visually, speech, hearing impaired.

**Contact.** E-mail: info@jsucc.jsu.edu
Phone: (256) 782-5268 Toll-free number: (800) 231-5291
Fax: (256) 782-5121
Martha Mitchell, Director of Admissions, Jacksonville State University, 700 Pelham Road North, Jacksonville, AL 36265-1602

## Judson College
### Marion, Alabama
www.judson.edu · · · · · · · · · · · · · · · · CB code: 1349

- Private 4-year liberal arts college for women affiliated with Baptist faith
- Residential campus in small town
- 311 degree-seeking undergraduates: 23% part-time, 96% women, 15% African American, 1% Hispanic American, 1% international
- 80% of applicants admitted
- SAT or ACT (ACT writing optional), interview required
- 54% graduate within 6 years; 22% enter graduate study

**General.** Founded in 1838. Regionally accredited. Men accepted for distance learning program only. **Degrees:** 42 bachelor's awarded. **ROTC:** Army. **Location:** 75 miles from Birmingham and Montgomery. **Calendar:** Semester, limited summer session. **Full-time faculty:** 21 total; 81% have terminal degrees, 43% women. **Part-time faculty:** 15 total; 27% have terminal degrees, 67% women. **Class size:** 86% < 20, 14% 20-39. **Special facilities:** Alabama Women's Hall of Fame, Baptist missionary memorabilia, equestrian facilities.

**Freshman class profile.** 309 applied, 248 admitted, 79 enrolled.

| Mid 50% test scores | | Rank in top quarter: | 55% |
|---|---|---|---|
| SAT math: | 520-640 | Rank in top tenth: | 21% |
| ACT composite: | 19-25 | End year in good standing: | 69% |
| GPA 3.50 or higher: | 34% | Return as sophomores: | 60% |
| GPA 3.0-3.49: | 36% | Out-of-state: | 21% |
| GPA 2.0-2.99: | 30% | Live on campus: | 95% |

**Basis for selection.** Academic record, recommendations, test scores considered. Interview required.

**High school preparation.** 16 units required; 20 recommended. Required and recommended units include English 4, mathematics 2-4, social studies 3-4, history 2, science 2-4, foreign language 2 and academic electives 5.

**2007-2008 Annual costs.** Tuition/fees: $11,120. Room/board: $7,120. Books/supplies: $800. Personal expenses: $1,600.

**2007-2008 Financial aid. Need-based:** Average need met was 86%. Average scholarship/grant was $7,837; average loan $3,982. 67% of total undergraduate aid awarded as scholarships/grants, 33% as loans/jobs. **Non-need-based:** Awarded to 42 full-time undergraduates, including 15 freshmen. Scholarships awarded for academics, art, athletics, leadership, music/drama, religious affiliation, state residency.

**Application procedures. Admission:** Priority date 8/1; no deadline. $32 fee, may be waived for applicants with need. Application may be submitted online. Admission notification on a rolling basis beginning on or about 9/1. **Financial aid:** Priority date 3/1; no closing date. FAFSA, institutional form required. Applicants notified on a rolling basis starting 3/1; must reply within 2 week(s) of notification.

**Academics. Special study options:** Accelerated study, cross-registration, distance learning, double major, dual enrollment of high school students, independent study, internships, student-designed major, study abroad, teacher certification program, Washington semester. **Credit/placement by examination:** AP, CLEP, institutional tests. 30 credit hours maximum toward bachelor's degree. No student may receive more than 30 semester hours of non-attendance credit from all sources, or more than six semester hours in any one department. Maximum permitted from CLEP General Examinations is 15 of 30 hours. **Support services:** Reduced course load, remedial instruction, study skills assistance, tutoring, writing center.

**Majors. Biology:** General. **Business:** Business admin. **Education:** Elementary, English, mathematics, music, science, social science. **English:** English lit. **Foreign languages:** General. **History:** General. **Math:** General. **Philosophy/religion:** Religion. **Physical sciences:** Chemistry. **Protective services:** Law enforcement admin. **Psychology:** General. **Visual/performing arts:** Art.

**Most popular majors.** Biology 17%, education 20%, history 12%, psychology 21%, public administration/social services 10%.

**Computing on campus.** 55 workstations in library, computer center, student center. Dormitories wired for high-speed internet access. Online library, helpline available.

**Student life. Freshman orientation:** Mandatory, $100 fee. Preregistration for classes offered. Orientation includes placement tests, academic registration. **Housing:** Guaranteed on-campus for all undergraduates. Substance-free housing available. $105 nonrefundable deposit. **Activities:** Campus ministries, choral groups, drama, literary magazine, music ensembles, musical theater, student government, student newspaper, students in free enterprise, College Democrats, College Republicans, Psych-Key Club, Cahaba River Society, Judson Ambassadors.

**Athletics.** USCAA. **Intercollegiate:** Basketball W, equestrian W, softball W, tennis W, volleyball W. **Intramural:** Basketball W, equestrian W, field hockey W, softball W, swimming W, table tennis W, tennis W, volleyball W. **Team name:** Lady Eagles.

**Student services.** Adult student services, alcohol/substance abuse counseling, campus ministries, career counseling, student employment services, financial aid counseling, health services, personal counseling.

**Contact.** E-mail: admissions@judson.edu
Phone: (334) 683-5110 Toll-free number: (800) 447-9472
Fax: (334) 683-5282
Charlotte Clements, Vice President for Admissions and Financial Aid, Judson College, 302 Bibb Street, Marion, AL 36756

## Miles College
### Birmingham, Alabama
www.miles.edu · · · · · · · · · · · · · · · · CB code: 1468

- Private 4-year liberal arts college affiliated with Christian Methodist Episcopal Church
- Commuter campus in very large city
- 1,804 degree-seeking undergraduates

**General.** Founded in 1905. Regionally accredited. **Degrees:** 182 bachelor's awarded. **ROTC:** Army, Air Force. **Location:** 6 miles from downtown. **Calendar:** Semester, limited summer session. **Full-time faculty:** 92 total; 33% have terminal degrees, 70% minority, 50% women. **Part-time faculty:** 40 total; 12% have terminal degrees, 100% minority. **Special facilities:** African-American materials center, learning research center.

**Basis for selection.** Open admission, but selective for some programs. Admission to education program based on 2.0 high school GPA, ACT composite score of 16 and recommendations; 3 letters of recommendation required of all.

**High school preparation.** 20 units recommended. Recommended units include English 4, mathematics 4, social studies 4, history 4 and science 4. 4 units mathematics and science recommended, particularly, for natural science applicants.

**2007-2008 Annual costs.** Tuition/fees: $7,051. Room/board: $4,866. Books/supplies: $400. Personal expenses: $1,000.

**2006-2007 Financial aid.** All financial aid based on need. 349 full-time freshmen applied for aid; 325 were judged to have need; 325 of these received aid. Average need met was 10%. Average loan was $2,213. 43% of total undergraduate aid awarded as scholarships/grants, 57% as loans/jobs.

**Application procedures. Admission:** Closing date 7/15. No application fee. Application may be submitted online. Admission notification on a rolling basis. **Financial aid:** Priority date 4/15; no closing date. FAFSA required. Applicants notified on a rolling basis starting 7/15; must reply within 2 week(s) of notification.

**Academics. Special study options:** Cooperative education, cross-registration, double major, dual enrollment of high school students, exchange student, honors, independent study, internships, teacher certification program. **Credit/placement by examination:** CLEP, institutional tests. **Support services:** Reduced course load, remedial instruction, study skills assistance, tutoring, writing center.

**Majors. Biology:** General. **Business:** Accounting, business admin, purchasing. **Communications:** General. **Computer sciences:** General. **Conservation:** Environmental science. **Education:** Elementary, English, instructional media, mathematics, science, secondary, social science, social studies. **English:** English lit. **History:** General. **Math:** General. **Physical sciences:**

Chemistry. **Public administration:** Social work. **Social sciences:** Political science. **Visual/performing arts:** Music pedagogy, music performance.

**Computing on campus.** 150 workstations in dormitories, library, computer center. Commuter students can connect to campus network.

**Student life. Freshman orientation:** Available, $100 fee. Preregistration for classes offered. Week-long program held one week prior to the start of classes. **Policies:** Students must maintain a 2.0 grade point average to participate in student activities that are not co-curricular on campus. **Housing:** Single-sex dorms, apartments, substance-free housing available. $150 non-refundable deposit. **Activities:** Marching band, choral groups, dance, drama, music ensembles, musical theater, radio station, student government, student newspaper, TV station, interdenominational ministerial association.

**Athletics.** NCAA. **Intercollegiate:** Baseball M, basketball, cross-country, football (tackle) M, softball W, volleyball. **Intramural:** Badminton, basketball, softball, tennis, volleyball. **Team name:** Golden Bears.

**Student services.** Adult student services, campus ministries, career counseling, services for economically disadvantaged, student employment services, financial aid counseling, health services, personal counseling, placement for graduates.

**Contact.** E-mail: admissions@miles.edu
Phone: (205) 929-1655 Fax: (205) 923-9292
Christopher Robertson, Director of Admissions and Recruitment, Miles College, 5500 Myron-Massey Boulevard, Fairfield, AL 35064

## Oakwood College
**Huntsville, Alabama**
**www.oakwood.edu**
**CB member**
**CB code: 1586**

- Private 4-year liberal arts college affiliated with Seventh-day Adventists
- Residential campus in small city
- 1,778 degree-seeking undergraduates: 5% part-time, 57% women, 89% African American, 1% Hispanic American, 7% international
- 57% of applicants admitted
- SAT or ACT (ACT writing optional) required

**General.** Founded in 1896. Regionally accredited. **Degrees:** 265 bachelor's, 5 associate awarded. **Location:** 5 miles from Huntsville. **Calendar:** Semester, limited summer session. **Full-time faculty:** 103 total; 60% have terminal degrees, 50% women. **Part-time faculty:** 79 total; 19% have terminal degrees, 54% women. **Class size:** 52% < 20, 39% 20-39, 5% 40-49, 4% 50-99, less than 1% >100.

**Freshman class profile.** 1,492 applied, 856 admitted, 457 enrolled.

| Mid 50% test scores | | | |
|---|---|---|---|
| SAT critical reading: | 410-530 | Rank in top quarter: | 20% |
| SAT math: | 380-500 | Rank in top tenth: | 12% |
| ACT composite: | 15-22 | Out-of-state: | 89% |
| GPA 3.50 or higher: | 25% | Live on campus: | 94% |
| GPA 3.0-3.49: | 24% | International: | 5% |
| GPA 2.0-2.99: | 46% | | |

**Basis for selection.** Applicants with GPA of at least 2.0 considered for acceptance. Special consideration for exceptional applicants. **Home-schooled:** Transcript of courses and grades, letter of recommendation (nonparent) required.

**High school preparation.** 18 units recommended. Recommended units include English 4, mathematics 2, social studies 1, history 1, science 2 (laboratory 1) and foreign language 2. One typing or computer applications recommended.

**2007-2008 Annual costs.** Tuition/fees: $12,668. Room/board: $7,170.

**Financial aid. Non-need-based:** Scholarships awarded for academics, leadership, religious affiliation, state residency.

**Application procedures. Admission:** Priority date 6/30; no deadline. $25 fee, may be waived for applicants with need. Admission notification on a rolling basis beginning on or about 12/1. **Financial aid:** Priority date 3/31; no closing date. FAFSA required. Applicants notified on a rolling basis starting 4/1.

**Academics. Special study options:** Double major, honors, internships, study abroad, teacher certification program. **Credit/placement by examination:** AP, CLEP, SAT, ACT, institutional tests. **Support services:** Learning center, reduced course load, remedial instruction, study skills assistance, tutoring, writing center.

**Majors. Biology:** General, biochemistry, biomedical sciences. **Business:** Accounting, business admin, finance, marketing. **Communications:** General. **Computer sciences:** General, computer science, information technology. **Education:** Biology, business, chemistry, elementary, English, family/consumer sciences, history, mathematics, music, physical, science, social science. **English:** English lit. **Family/consumer sciences:** General, family studies, food/nutrition. **Foreign languages:** French, Spanish. **Health:** Cytotechnology. **History:** General. **Interdisciplinary:** Math/computer science, natural sciences. **Liberal arts:** Arts/sciences. **Math:** General, applied. **Parks/recreation:** Health/fitness. **Philosophy/religion:** Religion. **Physical sciences:** Chemistry. **Psychology:** General. **Public administration:** Social work. **Theology:** Religious ed, theology.

**Most popular majors.** Biology 20%, business/marketing 22%, health sciences 9%, psychology 9%, theological studies 7%.

**Computing on campus.** 300 workstations in dormitories, library. Dormitories wired for high-speed internet access and linked to campus network. Commuter students can connect to campus network. Wireless network available.

**Student life. Freshman orientation:** Mandatory. **Policies:** Students sit on most faculty and administrative committees. Religious observance required. **Housing:** Single-sex dorms, apartments available. **Activities:** Choral groups, music ensembles, radio station, student government, student newspaper, Outreach, NAACP.

**Athletics. Intramural:** Baseball M, basketball, golf, gymnastics, soccer, softball, tennis, volleyball. **Team name:** Ambassadors.

**Student services.** Adult student services, campus ministries, career counseling, student employment services, financial aid counseling, health services, on-campus daycare, personal counseling, placement for graduates, veterans' counselor.

**Contact.** E-mail: admission@oakwood.edu
Phone: (256) 726-7030 Toll-free number: (800) 824-5312
Fax: (256) 726-7154
Jason McCracken, Director of Enrollment Management, Oakwood College, 7000 Adventist Boulevard, NW, Huntsville, AL 35896

## Samford University
**Birmingham, Alabama**
**www.samford.edu**
**CB member**
**CB code: 1302**

- Private 4-year university affiliated with Southern Baptist Convention
- Residential campus in small city
- 2,841 degree-seeking undergraduates: 6% part-time, 64% women, 6% African American, 1% Asian American, 1% Hispanic American
- 1,604 degree-seeking graduate students
- 92% of applicants admitted
- SAT or ACT (ACT writing recommended), application essay required
- 67% graduate within 6 years

**General.** Founded in 1841. Regionally accredited. Students taught to integrate Christian faith with learning and living. **Degrees:** 653 bachelor's, 10 associate awarded; master's, doctoral, first professional offered. **ROTC:** Army, Air Force. **Location:** 6 miles from downtown. **Calendar:** 4-1-4, extensive summer session. **Special facilities:** Computer-assisted journalism laboratory, geographic information system, observatory, global center, planetarium, conservatory.

**Freshman class profile.** 1,810 applied, 1,661 admitted, 713 enrolled.

| Mid 50% test scores | | | |
|---|---|---|---|
| SAT critical reading: | 510-620 | Rank in top quarter: | 59% |
| SAT math: | 490-630 | Rank in top tenth: | 32% |
| ACT composite: | 22-28 | Return as sophomores: | 84% |
| GPA 3.50 or higher: | 63% | Out-of-state: | 34% |
| GPA 3.0-3.49: | 27% | Live on campus: | 96% |
| GPA 2.0-2.99: | 10% | Fraternities: | 38% |
| | | Sororities: | 41% |

**Basis for selection.** High school GPA, courses selected and rigor, test scores, recommendations, essay, academic content and trend of high school grades are important. Interview recommended. Audition required for music majors. Portfolio recommended for art and journalism majors. **Home-schooled:** Statement describing homeschool structure and mission, transcript of courses and grades, letter of recommendation (nonparent) required. Leadership resume, SAT or ACT scores also required.

**High school preparation.** 4 units required. Required and recommended units include English 4, mathematics 3, social studies 2, history 2, science 3 (laboratory 2) and foreign language 2.

**2007-2008 Annual costs.** Tuition/fees: $17,920. Room/board: $6,320. Books/supplies: $1,075. Personal expenses: $3,560.

**2006-2007 Financial aid. Need-based:** 446 full-time freshmen applied for aid; 279 were judged to have need; 276 of these received aid. Average need met was 76%. Average scholarship/grant was $10,682; average loan $2,523. 64% of total undergraduate aid awarded as scholarships/grants, 36% as loans/jobs. **Non-need-based:** Awarded to 849 full-time undergraduates, including 213 freshmen. Scholarships awarded for academics, athletics, leadership, music/drama, religious affiliation, ROTC, state residency. **Additional information:** Consideration for merit scholarships automatically given to students with admission files completed by December 15.

**Application procedures. Admission:** Priority date 3/1; no deadline. $35 fee, may be waived for applicants with need. Application may be submitted online. Admission notification on a rolling basis beginning on or about 11/1. Must reply by May 1 or within 2 week(s) if notified thereafter. **Financial aid:** Priority date 3/1; no closing date. FAFSA required. Applicants notified by 4/1.

**Academics. Special study options:** Accelerated study, combined bachelor's/graduate degree, cooperative education, cross-registration, double major, exchange student, honors, independent study, internships, liberal arts/career combination, study abroad, teacher certification program. Semester offered at Samford London Study Center. **Credit/placement by examination:** AP, CLEP, IB, SAT, ACT, institutional tests. 30 credit hours maximum toward associate degree, 30 toward bachelor's. **Support services:** Learning center, reduced course load, study skills assistance, tutoring, writing center.

**Majors. Area/ethnic studies:** Asian, Latin American. **Biology:** General, biochemistry, marine. **Business:** Accounting, business admin, human resources, international, managerial economics. **Communications:** General, journalism. **Computer sciences:** Computer science. **Conservation:** Environmental science. **Education:** Biology, English, history, multi-level teacher, music, physical, science, social science, speech. **Engineering:** Physics. **English:** English lit. **Family/consumer sciences:** Family studies, human nutrition. **Foreign languages:** General, ancient Greek, classics, French, German, Latin, Spanish. **Health:** Athletic training, nursing (RN), premedicine. **History:** General. **Interdisciplinary:** Classical/archaeology, nutrition sciences, science/society. **Math:** General. **Parks/recreation:** Exercise sciences, health/fitness. **Philosophy/religion:** Philosophy, religion. **Physical sciences:** Chemistry, physics. **Protective services:** Law enforcement admin. **Psychology:** General. **Public administration:** General, community org/advocacy. **Social sciences:** General, cartography, geography, international relations, political science, sociology. **Theology:** Sacred music. **Visual/performing arts:** Art, dramatic, graphic design, interior design, music performance, music theory/composition, musical theater, piano/organ, voice/opera.

**Most popular majors.** Biology 8%, business/marketing 14%, communications/journalism 9%, education 6%, family/consumer sciences 7%, health sciences 13%, social sciences 8%, visual/performing arts 7%.

**Computing on campus.** 504 workstations in library, computer center, student center. Dormitories wired for high-speed internet access and linked to campus network. Commuter students can connect to campus network. Online library, helpline, repair service, wireless network available.

**Student life. Freshman orientation:** Mandatory, $150 fee. Preregistration for classes offered. 4 orientation sessions lasting 1 and a half days in summer; includes students and parents. **Policies:** Student code of values observed. Religious observance required. **Housing:** Guaranteed on-campus for freshmen. Single-sex dorms, special housing for disabled, fraternity/sorority housing, substance-free housing available. $250 nonrefundable deposit, deadline 5/1. **Activities:** Bands, choral groups, dance, drama, literary magazine, music ensembles, musical theater, radio station, student government, student newspaper, symphony orchestra, Amnesty International, Circle K, Habitat for Humanity, Gamma Sigma Sigma, Alpha Phi Omega, College Republicans, international club, Samford Ambassadors, Beta Beta Beta, Ville Crew.

**Athletics.** NCAA. **Intercollegiate:** Baseball M, basketball, cross-country, football (tackle) M, golf, soccer W, softball W, tennis, track and field, volleyball W. **Intramural:** Basketball, bowling, cheerleading, football (non-tackle) M, football (tackle), golf, racquetball, soccer, softball, table tennis, tennis, volleyball, water polo. **Team name:** Bulldogs.

**Student services.** Adult student services, campus ministries, career counseling, student employment services, financial aid counseling, health services, personal counseling, placement for graduates. **Physically disabled:** Services for visually, speech, hearing impaired. **Learning disabled:** Comprehensive services available.

**Contact.** E-mail: admiss@samford.edu
Phone: (205) 726-3673 Toll-free number: (800) 888-7218
Fax: (205) 726-2171
R Kimrey, Dean of Admission, Samford University, 800 Lakeshore Drive, Birmingham, AL 35229

## Selma University
### Selma, Alabama
**CB code: 1792**

- Private 4-year university affiliated with Baptist faith
- Large town

**General.** Founded in 1878. Candidate for regional accreditation. **Location:** 50 miles from Montgomery. **Calendar:** Semester.

**Annual costs/financial aid.** Tuition/fees (2007-2008): $3,550. Books/supplies: $600. Personal expenses: $600.

**Contact.** Phone: (334) 872-2533
Registrar, 1501 Lapsley Street, Selma, AL 36701

## South University
### Montgomery, Alabama
### www.southuniversity.edu
**CB code: 3947**

- For-profit 4-year business and health science college
- Commuter campus in small city
- 504 degree-seeking undergraduates
- SAT or ACT (ACT writing recommended), interview required

**General.** Founded in 1887. Regionally accredited. **Degrees:** 19 bachelor's, 61 associate awarded; master's offered. **Location:** 100 miles from Birmingham, 160 miles from Atlanta. **Calendar:** Quarter, extensive summer session. **Full-time faculty:** 19 total. **Part-time faculty:** 33 total. **Class size:** 69% < 20, 31% 20-39.

**Basis for selection.** High school diploma or GED required. Entrance test most important. CPT (school-administered entrance test) or SAT/ACT required for admission, unless applicant is a transfer student with at least 30 quarter hours and a GPA of at least 2.0.

**2007-2008 Annual costs.** Tuition/fees: $12,570. Books/supplies: $900. Personal expenses: $1,622.

**Financial aid.** All financial aid based on need.

**Application procedures. Admission:** No deadline. $50 fee. Application may be submitted online. Admission notification on a rolling basis. **Financial aid:** No deadline. FAFSA required. Applicants notified on a rolling basis starting 6/1.

**Academics. Special study options:** Distance learning, double major, internships. **Credit/placement by examination:** CLEP, institutional tests. **Support services:** Remedial instruction, study skills assistance, tutoring.

**Majors. Business:** Business admin. **Computer sciences:** Information technology. **Legal studies:** General.

**Computing on campus.** 58 workstations in library, computer center. Online library, repair service, wireless network available.

**Student life. Freshman orientation:** Mandatory. Preregistration for classes offered.

**Student services.** Career counseling, financial aid counseling, personal counseling, placement for graduates, veterans' counselor.

**Contact.** E-mail: apearson@southuniversity.edu
Phone: (334) 395-8800 Fax: (334) 395-8859
Anna Pearson, Director of Admissions, South University, 5355 Vaughn Road, Montgomery, AL 36116-1120

## Southeastern Bible College
### Birmingham, Alabama
### www.sebc.edu
**CB code: 1723**

- Private 4-year Bible college affiliated with nondenominational tradition
- Commuter campus in very large city
- 213 degree-seeking undergraduates: 26% part-time, 40% women, 29% African American
- 96% of applicants admitted
- SAT or ACT (ACT writing optional), application essay required

**General.** Founded in 1935. Accredited by ABHE. **Degrees:** 35 bachelor's, 2 associate awarded. **Location:** 10 miles from downtown. **Calendar:** Semester, limited summer session. **Full-time faculty:** 9 total; 89% have terminal degrees, 22% women. **Part-time faculty:** 20 total; 45% have terminal degrees, 5% minority, 25% women. **Class size:** 81% < 20, 14% 20-39, 4% 50-99.

**Freshman class profile.** 79 applied, 76 admitted, 34 enrolled.

| Mid 50% test scores | | | |
|---|---|---|---|
| SAT critical reading: | 450-610 | GPA 3.0-3.49: | 19% |
| SAT math: | 350-420 | GPA 2.0-2.99: | 44% |
| SAT writing: | 430-590 | Return as sophomores: | 67% |
| ACT composite: | 17-23 | Out-of-state: | 18% |
| GPA 3.50 or higher: | 31% | Live on campus: | 59% |

**Basis for selection.** Minimum 2.0 GPA required; serious commitment to Christian life and service; 2 recommendations important. **Learning Disabled:** Students should meet with equity coordinator if desired.

**High school preparation.** 24 units recommended. Recommended units include English 4, mathematics 4, social studies 4, science 4, computer science .5.

**2007-2008 Annual costs.** Tuition/fees: $10,035. Room only: $2,300.

**2007-2008 Financial aid. Need-based:** 23% of total undergraduate aid awarded as scholarships/grants, 77% as loans/jobs. **Non-need-based:** Scholarships awarded for academics, leadership, music/drama.

**Application procedures. Admission:** Closing date 8/1 (postmark date). $30 fee. Application may be submitted online. Admission notification on a rolling basis. **Financial aid:** Priority date 5/1, closing date 8/15. FAFSA, institutional form required. Applicants notified by 7/15; must reply within 2 week(s) of notification.

**Academics. Special study options:** Double major, dual enrollment of high school students, internships, teacher certification program. **Credit/placement by examination:** AP, CLEP, IB, institutional tests. **Support services:** Reduced course load, study skills assistance.

**Majors. Theology:** Bible. **Other:** Leadership ministries.

**Most popular majors.** Philosophy/religious studies 95%.

**Computing on campus.** 25 workstations in library, computer center. Dormitories wired for high-speed internet access. Online library, wireless network available.

**Student life. Freshman orientation:** Mandatory. Preregistration for classes offered. One-half day on the first day of registration. **Policies:** Religious observance required. **Housing:** Single-sex dorms, substance-free housing available. **Activities:** Choral groups, music ensembles, student government, student missions fellowship.

**Athletics. Intercollegiate:** Basketball. **Team name:** Sabers.

**Student services.** Adult student services, campus ministries, career counseling, student employment services, financial aid counseling, personal counseling, placement for graduates. **Physically disabled:** Services for visually, speech, hearing impaired.

**Contact.** E-mail: info@sebc.edu
Phone: (205) 970-9210 Toll-free number: (800) 749-8878
Fax: (205) 970-9207
Lynn Gannett-Malick, Director of Enrollment Management, Southeastern Bible College, 2545 Valleydale Road, Birmingham, AL 35244-2083

---

## Spring Hill College
Mobile, Alabama
www.shc.edu

**CB member**
**CB code: 1733**

- Private 4-year liberal arts college affiliated with Roman Catholic Church
- Residential campus in large city
- 1,268 degree-seeking undergraduates: 8% part-time, 66% women, 17% African American, 1% Asian American, 6% Hispanic American, 1% Native American, 1% international
- 174 degree-seeking graduate students
- 66% of applicants admitted
- SAT or ACT (ACT writing recommended), application essay required
- 56% graduate within 6 years; 32% enter graduate study

**General.** Founded in 1830. Regionally accredited. **Degrees:** 246 bachelor's awarded; master's offered. **ROTC:** Army, Air Force. **Location:** 140 miles from New Orleans. **Calendar:** Semester, limited summer session. **Full-time faculty:** 80 total; 88% have terminal degrees, 6% minority, 44% women. **Part-time faculty:** 67 total; 28% have terminal degrees, 12% minority, 55% women. **Class size:** 54% < 20, 45% 20-39, 1% 40-49. **Special facilities:** National historic buildings, public radio broadcasting station, 450-acre wooded campus, 18-hole golf course.

**Freshman class profile.** 3,042 applied, 2,003 admitted, 383 enrolled.

| Mid 50% test scores | | | |
|---|---|---|---|
| SAT critical reading: | 490-610 | Rank in top quarter: | 61% |
| SAT math: | 480-570 | Rank in top tenth: | 26% |
| SAT writing: | 490-600 | End year in good standing: | 82% |
| ACT composite: | 21-26 | Return as sophomores: | 79% |
| GPA 3.50 or higher: | 56% | Out-of-state: | 56% |
| GPA 3.0-3.49: | 26% | Live on campus: | 88% |
| GPA 2.0-2.99: | 18% | International: | 1% |

**Basis for selection.** Grades, test scores, and achievements outside the classroom important. Interview recommended; portfolio recommended of art majors. **Homeschooled:** Statement describing homeschool structure and mission, transcript of courses and grades, interview required. Portfolio should include thorough explanation of all coursework, how it was graded, a comprehensive reading list, documentation of any program affiliation, and personal assessments provided by both the student and the primary teacher. Information on any independent research project, community outreach, or unique experience that enriched the home-schooling experience may be included. **Learning Disabled:** SHC has no special admission requirements or procedures for students with learning disabilities.

**High school preparation.** 16 units recommended. Recommended units include English 4, mathematics 3, social studies 2, history 1, science 3 (laboratory 1), foreign language 2 and academic electives 1.

**2008-2009 Annual costs.** Tuition/fees: $24,240. Room/board: $9,260. Books/supplies: $1,300. Personal expenses: $1,250.

**2007-2008 Financial aid. Need-based:** 317 full-time freshmen applied for aid; 265 were judged to have need; 265 of these received aid. Average need met was 84%. Average scholarship/grant was $17,253; average loan $4,188. 74% of total undergraduate aid awarded as scholarships/grants, 26% as loans/jobs. **Non-need-based:** Awarded to 973 full-time undergraduates, including 300 freshmen. Scholarships awarded for academics, alumni affiliation, athletics, job skills, leadership, minority status, state residency.

**Application procedures. Admission:** Priority date 1/15; deadline 7/15 (postmark date). $25 fee, may be waived for applicants with need. Application may be submitted online. Admission notification on a rolling basis beginning on or about 11/1. Must reply by May 1 or within 2 week(s) if notified thereafter. **Financial aid:** Priority date 3/1; no closing date. FAFSA required. Applicants notified on a rolling basis starting 2/15; must reply by 5/1 or within 2 week(s) of notification.

**Academics. Special study options:** Accelerated study, combined bachelor's/graduate degree, distance learning, double major, dual enrollment of high school students, honors, independent study, internships, student-designed major, study abroad, teacher certification program, Washington semester. Marine biology majors take credit courses at the Dauphin Island Sea Laboratory of the Marine Environmental Sciences Consortium; 3-2 engineering with Auburn University, University of Alabama at Birmingham, Marquette University, University of Florida, and Texas A & M University. **Credit/placement by examination:** AP, CLEP, IB, SAT, ACT, institutional tests. 30 credit hours maximum toward bachelor's degree. **Support services:** Remedial instruction, study skills assistance, tutoring.

**Majors. Biology:** General, biochemistry. **Business:** Business admin. **Communications:** General. **Education:** Early childhood, elementary, secondary. **Engineering:** General. **English:** English lit. **Foreign languages:** Spanish. **Health:** Art therapy, nursing (RN). **History:** General. **Interdisciplinary:** Biopsychology. **Liberal arts:** Humanities. **Math:** General. **Philosophy/religion:** Philosophy. **Physical sciences:** Chemistry. **Psychology:** General. **Social sciences:** General, international relations, political science, sociology. **Theology:** Theology. **Visual/performing arts:** Arts management, dramatic, graphic design, studio arts.

**Most popular majors.** Biology 11%, business/marketing 21%, communications/journalism 10%, English 6%, health sciences 6%, psychology 9%, social sciences 7%.

**Computing on campus.** 200 workstations in dormitories, library, computer center, student center. Dormitories wired for high-speed internet access and linked to campus network. Commuter students can connect to campus network. Online course registration, online library, helpline, student web hosting, wireless network available.

**Student life. Freshman orientation:** Mandatory, $250 fee. Preregistration for classes offered. Weekend program held in the summer for students and parents. **Housing:** Guaranteed on-campus for all undergraduates. Coed dorms, single-sex dorms, apartments available. $150 fully refundable deposit, deadline 6/1. **Activities:** Campus ministries, choral groups, dance, drama, literary magazine, student government, student newspaper, Amnesty International, College Democrats, College Republicans, Multicultural student union, NAACP, Students for Justice, Students for Life, Circle K, Sierra Club.

**Athletics.** NAIA. **Intercollegiate:** Baseball M, basketball, cross-country, golf, soccer, softball W, tennis, volleyball W. **Intramural:** Basketball, football (non-tackle), racquetball, soccer, table tennis, volleyball. **Team name:** Badgers.

**Student services.** Adult student services, alcohol/substance abuse counseling, campus ministries, career counseling, student employment services, financial aid counseling, health services, personal counseling, placement for graduates.

**Contact.** E-mail: admit@shc.edu
Phone: (251) 380-3030 Toll-free number: (800) 742-6704
Fax: (251) 460-2186
Steven Pochard, Dean of Admissions and Financial Aid, Spring Hill College, 4000 Dauphin Street, Mobile, AL 36608-1791

## Stillman College

**Tuscaloosa, Alabama**
**www.stillman.edu**

**CB member**
**CB code: 1739**

- Private 4-year liberal arts college affiliated with Presbyterian Church (USA)
- Residential campus in small city
- 915 full-time, degree-seeking undergraduates
- 38% of applicants admitted
- SAT or ACT (ACT writing optional) required

**General.** Founded in 1876. Regionally accredited. **Degrees:** 116 bachelor's awarded. **ROTC:** Army, Naval, Air Force. **Location:** 60 miles from Birmingham. **Calendar:** Semester, limited summer session. **Full-time faculty:** 60 total; 62% have terminal degrees, 63% minority, 52% women. **Part-time faculty:** 10 total. **Class size:** 64% < 20, 24% 20-39, 5% 40-49, 7% 50-99.

**Freshman class profile.** 3,386 applied, 1,282 admitted, 342 enrolled.

| Mid 50% test scores | | GPA 3.0-3.49: | 25% |
|---|---|---|---|
| SAT critical reading: | 310-410 | GPA 2.0-2.99: | 65% |
| SAT math: | 320-430 | Rank in top quarter: | 28% |
| ACT composite: | 15-19 | Rank in top tenth: | 8% |
| GPA 3.50 or higher: | 10% | | |

**Basis for selection.** School achievement record most important. Class rank, test scores, essay, extracurricular activities also important. **Homeschooled:** Students unable to present a high school transcript may enroll upon presentation of satisfactory passing score on GED.

**High school preparation.** 24 units required. Required units include English 4, mathematics 2, social studies 2 and science 1.

**2007-2008 Annual costs.** Tuition/fees: $12,186. Room/board: $5,572.

**2006-2007 Financial aid.** All financial aid based on need. Average need met was 75%. Average scholarship/grant was $5,000; average loan $5,500. 50% of total undergraduate aid awarded as scholarships/grants, 50% as loans/jobs.

**Application procedures. Admission:** Priority date 5/1; no deadline. $50 fee, may be waived for applicants with need. Admission notification on a rolling basis. Admitted applicants must reply within 5 days of notification of acceptance. **Financial aid:** No deadline. FAFSA, institutional form required. Applicants notified on a rolling basis; must reply within 4 week(s) of notification.

**Academics. Special study options:** Combined bachelor's/graduate degree, cooperative education, double major, dual enrollment of high school students, honors, independent study, internships, study abroad, teacher certification program. **Credit/placement by examination:** AP, CLEP, SAT, ACT, institutional tests. 30 credit hours maximum toward bachelor's degree. **Support services:** Learning center, reduced course load, remedial instruction, tutoring, writing center.

**Honors college/program.** Minimum high school average of A-, demonstrated success in arts, SAT of 1075 (exclusive of Writing), or ACT of 23, demonstrated leadership activity, strong performance in sciences, and original essay.

**Majors. Biology:** General. **Business:** Business admin. **Computer sciences:** General. **Education:** Elementary, health. **English:** English lit. **History:** General. **Math:** General. **Visual/performing arts:** Art.

**Computing on campus.** PC or laptop required. 225 workstations in dormitories, library, computer center, student center. Dormitories wired for high-speed internet access and linked to campus network. Commuter students can connect to campus network. Online course registration, online library, helpline, student web hosting, wireless network available.

**Student life. Freshman orientation:** Available, $50 fee. Preregistration for classes offered. **Policies:** Religious observance required. **Housing:** Guaranteed on-campus for freshmen. Single-sex dorms available. $200 nonrefundable deposit, deadline 7/1. **Activities:** Bands, choral groups, drama, music ensembles, radio station, student government, student newspaper, Christian Student Association, Chancellorettes, Chancellors.

**Athletics.** NCAA. **Intercollegiate:** Baseball M, basketball, cross-country, football (tackle) M, softball W, tennis, track and field, volleyball W. **Intramural:** Basketball, softball, track and field W, volleyball. **Team name:** Tigers.

**Student services.** Campus ministries, career counseling, student employment services, financial aid counseling, health services, personal counseling, placement for graduates, veterans' counselor.

**Contact.** E-mail: mfinch@stillman.edu
Phone: (205) 366-8814 Toll-free number: (800) 841-5722
Fax: (205) 366-8941
Monica Finch, Director of Admissions, Stillman College, 3600 Stillman Boulevard, Tuscaloosa, AL 35403

## Talladega College

**Talladega, Alabama**
**www.talladega.edu**

**CB code: 1800**

- Private 4-year liberal arts college affiliated with United Church of Christ
- Residential campus in large town

**General.** Founded in 1867. Regionally accredited. **Location:** 55 miles from Birmingham, 120 miles from Atlanta. **Calendar:** Semester.

**Annual costs/financial aid.** Tuition/fees (2007-2008): $7,348. Room/board: $4,420. Books/supplies: $1,178. Personal expenses: $1,100. Need-based financial aid available to full-time and part-time students.

**Contact.** Phone: (205) 761-6235
Director of Admissions, 627 West Battle Street, Talladega, AL 35160

## Troy University

**Troy, Alabama**
**www.troy.edu**

**CB member**
**CB code: 1738**

- Public 4-year university
- Residential campus in large town
- 21,046 degree-seeking undergraduates: 53% part-time, 56% women, 37% African American, 1% Asian American, 4% Hispanic American, 1% Native American, 2% international
- 7,602 degree-seeking graduate students
- 64% of applicants admitted
- SAT or ACT (ACT writing optional) required
- 48% graduate within 6 years

**General.** Founded in 1887. Regionally accredited. **Degrees:** 2,548 bachelor's, 441 associate awarded; master's offered. **ROTC:** Army, Air Force. **Location:** 50 miles from Montgomery. **Calendar:** Semester, extensive summer session. **Full-time faculty:** 486 total; 14% minority. **Part-time faculty:** 1,119 total; 16% minority. **Class size:** 51% < 20, 42% 20-39, 5% 40-49, 2% 50-99, less than 1% >100. **Special facilities:** Rosa Parks Library and Museum, planetarium, performing arts theatre.

**Freshman class profile.** 5,237 applied, 3,363 admitted, 2,783 enrolled.

| Mid 50% test scores | | | |
|---|---|---|---|
| ACT composite: | 17-22 | Rank in top quarter: | 43% |
| GPA 3.50 or higher: | 25% | End year in good standing: | 67% |
| GPA 3.0-3.49: | 25% | Return as sophomores: | 68% |
| GPA 2.0-2.99: | 43% | Out-of-state: | 35% |
| | | International: | 1% |

**Basis for selection.** A minimum 2.0 GPA and an ACT score of 18 or above are required for first-time freshmen. Audition required of music education majors.

**High school preparation.** 15 units required. Required units include English 3.

**2007-2008 Annual costs.** Tuition/fees: $4,264; $8,428 out-of-state. Room/board: $5,718. Books/supplies: $920. Personal expenses: $2,214.

**2007-2008 Financial aid. Need-based:** 1,178 full-time freshmen applied for aid; 1,178 were judged to have need; 1,178 of these received aid. Average scholarship/grant was $3,493; average loan $3,441. 14% of total undergraduate aid awarded as scholarships/grants, 86% as loans/jobs. **Non-need-based:** Awarded to 3,041 full-time undergraduates, including 826 freshmen. Scholarships awarded for academics, alumni affiliation, art, athletics, leadership, minority status, music/drama, ROTC.

**Application procedures. Admission:** No deadline. $30 fee. Application may be submitted online. Admission notification on a rolling basis. **Financial aid:** Closing date 5/1. FAFSA, institutional form required. Applicants notified on a rolling basis starting 5/1; must reply within 2 week(s) of notification.

**Academics. Special study options:** Distance learning, double major, dual enrollment of high school students, ESL, external degree, honors, independent study, internships, study abroad, teacher certification program, weekend college. **Credit/placement by examination:** AP, CLEP, SAT, ACT, institutional tests. 45 credit hours maximum toward associate degree, 90 toward bachelor's. **Support services:** Learning center, pre-admission summer program, reduced course load, remedial instruction, study skills assistance, tutoring, writing center.

**Majors. Biology:** General, marine. **Business:** General, accounting, business admin, finance, management information systems, marketing. **Communications:** Journalism, radio/tv. **Computer sciences:** General. **Conservation:** Environmental science. **Education:** Early childhood, elementary, multilevel teacher, secondary. **Engineering technology:** Electrical, surveying. **English:** English lit, speech/rhetoric. **Foreign languages:** General. **Health:** Athletic training, nursing (RN). **History:** General. **Liberal arts:** Arts/sciences. **Math:** General. **Parks/recreation:** Sports admin. **Physical sciences:** General, chemistry. **Protective services:** Criminal justice. **Psychology:** General. **Public administration:** Human services, social work. **Social sciences:** General, political science, sociology. **Visual/performing arts:** Art. **Other:** Resources and technology management.

**Most popular majors.** Business/marketing 43%, computer/information sciences 6%, education 8%, psychology 8%, security/protective services 12%.

**Computing on campus.** 1,570 workstations in library, computer center, student center. Online course registration, online library, helpline available.

**Student life. Freshman orientation:** Mandatory, $55 fee. Preregistration for classes offered. 2-day sessions held during summer. During spring and summer terms, new students can attend orientation session prior to registration for classes. **Housing:** Coed dorms, single-sex dorms, apartments, fraternity/sorority housing, substance-free housing available. $100 partly refundable deposit. Substance-abuse-free housing, honor student housing available. **Activities:** Bands, choral groups, dance, drama, music ensembles, musical theater, student government, student newspaper, TV station, Several religious, service, and professional organizations, honor societies, Young Democrats, Young Republicans.

**Athletics.** NCAA. **Intercollegiate:** Baseball M, basketball, cheerleading, cross-country, football (tackle) M, golf, rodeo, soccer W, softball W, tennis, track and field, volleyball W. **Intramural:** Basketball, cross-country, diving, field hockey W, golf, softball, swimming, tennis, track and field, volleyball W. **Team name:** Trojans.

**Student services.** Campus ministries, career counseling, student employment services, financial aid counseling, health services, on-campus daycare, personal counseling, placement for graduates, veterans' counselor, women's services. **Physically disabled:** Services for visually, hearing impaired.

**Contact.** E-mail: bstar@troy.edu
Phone: (334) 670-3179 Toll-free number: (800) 551-9716
Fax: (334) 670-3733
Buddy Starling, Dean of Enrollment Management, Troy University, University Avenue, Adams Administration 111, Troy, AL 36082

## Tuskegee University
Tuskegee, Alabama
www.tuskegee.edu

CB member
CB code: 1813

- Private 4-year university and liberal arts college
- Residential campus in small town
- 2,514 degree-seeking undergraduates: 3% part-time, 55% women
- 422 degree-seeking graduate students
- 58% of applicants admitted
- SAT or ACT (ACT writing optional) required

**General.** Founded in 1881. Regionally accredited. **Degrees:** 323 bachelor's awarded; master's, doctoral, first professional offered. **ROTC:** Army, Air Force. **Location:** 30 miles from Montgomery, 162 miles from Atlanta. **Calendar:** Semester, limited summer session. **Full-time faculty:** 260 total; 76% have terminal degrees, 82% minority, 42% women. **Part-time faculty:** 20 total; 65% have terminal degrees, 70% minority, 35% women. **Class size:** 55% < 20, 27% 20-39, 8% 40-49, 10% 50-99, less than 1% >100. **Special facilities:** George Washington Carver museum, aerospace science and health education center.

**Freshman class profile.** 3,092 applied, 1,800 admitted, 1,590 enrolled.

| Mid 50% test scores | | | |
|---|---|---|---|
| SAT critical reading: | 390-500 | GPA 2.0-2.99: | 49% |
| SAT math: | 380-490 | Rank in top quarter: | 59% |
| ACT composite: | 16-21 | Rank in top tenth: | 20% |
| GPA 3.50 or higher: | 22% | Out-of-state: | 70% |
| GPA 3.0-3.49: | 29% | Live on campus: | 98% |

**Basis for selection.** School achievement record and test scores important. Minimum SAT combined score of 800 (exclusive of Writing) or equivalent ACT required for engineering and nursing applicants, 700 for other applicants. National League for Nursing Guidance Examination required of nursing applicants. Essay recommended; interview recommended for veterinary medicine majors.

**High school preparation.** 16 units required. Required units include English 4, mathematics 3, social studies 3, science 2 and academic electives 4.

**2008-2009 Annual costs.** Tuition/fees (projected): $15,450. Room/board: $7,130. Books/supplies: $949. Personal expenses: $1,596.

**2007-2008 Financial aid. Need-based:** 722 full-time freshmen applied for aid; 613 were judged to have need; 520 of these received aid. Average need met was 81%. Average scholarship/grant was $8,009; average loan $5,725. 37% of total undergraduate aid awarded as scholarships/grants, 63% as loans/jobs. **Non-need-based:** Awarded to 1,397 full-time undergraduates, including 639 freshmen. Scholarships awarded for academics, athletics, ROTC, state residency.

**Application procedures. Admission:** Priority date 5/15; deadline 7/15. $25 fee. Application may be submitted online. Admission notification on a rolling basis beginning on or about 3/1. Must reply by May 1 or within 2 week(s) if notified thereafter. **Financial aid:** Closing date 3/31. FAFSA, institutional form, CSS PROFILE required. Applicants notified on a rolling basis starting 5/15; must reply within 2 week(s) of notification.

**Academics. Special study options:** Combined bachelor's/graduate degree, cooperative education, double major, honors, independent study, internships, liberal arts/career combination, teacher certification program. Engineering program with 2-year colleges. **Credit/placement by examination:** AP, CLEP, SAT, ACT. Credit-by-examination policies determined individually by dean. **Support services:** Learning center, pre-admission summer program, reduced course load, remedial instruction, study skills assistance, tutoring.

**Majors. Agriculture:** Animal sciences, plant sciences, poultry, soil science. **Architecture:** Architecture. **Biology:** General, ecology. **Business:** Accounting, business admin, finance, hospitality admin, management science. **Computer sciences:** General. **Conservation:** General, forestry. **Education:** General, biology, early childhood, elementary, mathematics, mentally handicapped, physical, science, voc/tech. **Engineering:** Aerospace, chemical, electrical, mechanical. **Engineering technology:** Construction. **English:** English lit. **Family/consumer sciences:** Food/nutrition. **Health:** Clinical lab science. **History:** General. **Math:** General. **Physical sciences:** Chemistry, physics. **Psychology:** General. **Public administration:** Social work. **Social sciences:** Economics, political science, sociology.

**Most popular majors.** Agriculture 11%, biology 10%, business/marketing 25%, engineering/engineering technologies 16%, health sciences 6%, history 12%.

**Computing on campus.** 1,000 workstations in dormitories, library, computer center, student center. Dormitories wired for high-speed internet access and linked to campus network. Commuter students can connect to campus network. Online course registration, online library, helpline, repair service, wireless network available.

**Student life.** Freshman orientation: Available. **Housing:** Single-sex dorms, apartments available. $300 deposit. Honors dormitories available. Freshmen and sophomores not living with parents or guardians required to reside on campus. **Activities:** Bands, choral groups, dance, drama, film society, student government, student newspaper.

**Athletics.** NCAA. **Intercollegiate:** Baseball M, basketball, cross-country, football (tackle) M, softball W, tennis, track and field, volleyball W. **Intramural:** Basketball M, rifle. **Team name:** Golden Tigers.

**Student services.** Campus ministries, career counseling, financial aid counseling, health services, on-campus daycare, personal counseling, placement for graduates, veterans' counselor.

**Contact.** E-mail: adm@tuskegee.edu
Phone: (334) 727-8500 Toll-free number: (800) 622-6531
Fax: (334) 724-4402
Robert Laney, Vice President/Director of Admissions and Enrollment Management, Tuskegee University, 102 Old Administration Building, Tuskegee, AL 36088.

## United States Sports Academy
### Daphne, Alabama
### www.ussa.edu

- Private two-year upper-division university
- Large town

**General.** Regionally accredited. **Degrees:** 9 bachelor's awarded; master's, doctoral offered. **Calendar:** Semester. **Full-time faculty:** 10 total. **Part-time faculty:** 20 total.

**Student profile.** 100 degree-seeking undergraduates.

**2007-2008 Annual costs.** Tuition/fees: $8,200.

**Application procedures.** Admission: $50 fee.

**Academics.** Credit/placement by examination: CLEP.

**Majors.** Parks/recreation: Sports admin. **Other:** Sports studies.

**Contact.** E-mail: admissions@ussa.edu
Phone: (251) 626-3303 Toll-free number: (800) 223-2668
Queint Higgins, Registrar, United States Sports Academy, One Academy Drive, Daphne, AL 36526

## University of Alabama
### Tuscaloosa, Alabama
### www.ua.edu
CB member
CB code: 1830

- Public 4-year university
- Residential campus in small city
- 20,910 degree-seeking undergraduates: 8% part-time, 53% women, 11% African American, 1% Asian American, 2% Hispanic American, 1% Native American, 1% international
- 4,268 degree-seeking graduate students
- 64% of applicants admitted
- SAT or ACT (ACT writing optional) required
- 64% graduate within 6 years; 25% enter graduate study

**General.** Founded in 1831. Regionally accredited. Services available for learning impaired students. **Degrees:** 3,131 bachelor's awarded; master's, doctoral, first professional offered. **ROTC:** Army, Air Force. **Location:** 60 miles from Birmingham. **Calendar:** Semester, extensive summer session. **Full-time faculty:** 987 total; 90% have terminal degrees, 15% minority, 39% women. **Part-time faculty:** 288 total; 58% have terminal degrees, 5% minority, 52% women. **Class size:** 43% < 20, 36% 20-39, 5% 40-49, 10% 50-99, 6% >100. **Special facilities:** Museum of natural history, arboretum, marine science laboratory, archeological park, observatory, access to CRAY X-UP/24 supercomputer in Huntsville, simulated coal mine setting, concert hall.

**Freshman class profile.** 14,313 applied, 9,140 admitted, 4,538 enrolled.

| Mid 50% test scores | | Rank in top tenth: | 38% |
|---|---|---|---|
| SAT critical reading: | 490-610 | End year in good standing: | 91% |
| SAT math: | 500-620 | Return as sophomores: | 86% |
| ACT composite: | 21-27 | Out-of-state: | 33% |
| GPA 3.50 or higher: | 46% | Live on campus: | 91% |
| GPA 3.0-3.49: | 31% | International: | 1% |
| GPA 2.0-2.99: | 23% | Fraternities: | 18% |
| Rank in top quarter: | 57% | Sororities: | 22% |

**Basis for selection.** Test scores, high school GPA in academic courses most important. Typically, students with 3.0 GPA and 20 ACT composite or 970 combined SAT (exclusive of Writing) will be admitted. Tests are not required of freshman applicants who are 25 years of age or older. An interview is required by any student that appeals their admission type or reject decision. Audition required for some performance programs. **Homeschooled:** Statement describing homeschool structure and mission, state high school equivalency certificate required. GED required if program is not certified and the student must meet GED admission requirements. Transcript and grades are required for all students. **Learning Disabled:** Documentation concerning disability should be submitted to the Office of Disability Services upon admission.

**High school preparation.** 15 units required. Required units include English 4, mathematics 3, social studies 3, history 1, science 3 (laboratory 2), foreign language 1, computer science 1, visual/performing arts 1 and academic electives 5.

**2007-2008 Annual costs.** Tuition/fees: $5,700; $16,518 out-of-state. Room/board: $5,868. Books/supplies: $950. Personal expenses: $1,952.

**2006-2007 Financial aid.** Need-based: 2,157 full-time freshmen applied for aid; 1,388 were judged to have need; 1,357 of these received aid. Average need met was 66%. Average scholarship/grant was $3,891; average loan $2,714. 33% of total undergraduate aid awarded as scholarships/grants, 67% as loans/jobs. **Non-need-based:** Awarded to 7,313 full-time undergraduates, including 2,237 freshmen. Scholarships awarded for academics, alumni affiliation, art, athletics, leadership, minority status, music/drama, ROTC, state residency.

**Application procedures.** Admission: Priority date 2/1; no deadline. $35 fee, may be waived for applicants with need. Application may be submitted online. Admission notification on a rolling basis beginning on or about 7/1. **Financial aid:** Priority date 3/1; no closing date. FAFSA required. Applicants notified on a rolling basis starting 4/1; must reply within 3 week(s) of notification.

**Academics.** Special study options: Accelerated study, combined bachelor's/graduate degree, cooperative education, cross-registration, distance learning, double major, dual enrollment of high school students, ESL, exchange student, external degree, honors, independent study, internships, liberal arts/career combination, student-designed major, study abroad, teacher certification program, Washington semester, weekend college. **Credit/placement by examination:** AP, CLEP, IB, institutional tests. 45 total semester hours are accepted from: AP; CLEP; placement in English; placement/performance in foreign languages; credit for prior military service; USAFI and DANTES credit. Test scores must be sent directly to the Office of Undergraduate Admissions from the testing agencies. **Support services:** Learning center, pre-admission summer program, remedial instruction, study skills assistance, tutoring, writing center.

**Majors.** **Area/ethnic studies:** American, Asian, Latin American. **Biology:** General, marine, microbiology. **Business:** Accounting, business admin, finance, management information systems, management science, managerial economics, marketing, restaurant/food services. **Communications:** General, advertising, journalism, public relations, radio/tv. **Computer sciences:** General. **Conservation:** Environmental science. **Education:** Early childhood, elementary, music, physical, secondary, special. **Engineering:** Aerospace, chemical, civil, construction, electrical, mechanical, metallurgical. **English:** English lit. **Family/consumer sciences:** General, clothing/textiles, family resources, family studies. **Foreign languages:** General, Spanish. **Health:** Athletic training, audiology/speech pathology, dietetics, facilities admin, health services, nursing (RN). **History:** General. **Interdisciplinary:** Intercultural. **Math:** General. **Philosophy/religion:** Philosophy, religion. **Physical sciences:** Chemistry, geology, physics. **Protective services:** Criminal justice. **Psychology:** General. **Public administration:** Social work. **Social sciences:** Anthropology, geography, international relations, political science, sociology. **Visual/performing arts:** Art history/conservation, dance, dramatic, interior design, studio arts.

**Most popular majors.** Business/marketing 27%, communications/journalism 11%, engineering/engineering technologies 6%, family/consumer sciences 7%, health sciences 10%.

**Computing on campus.** 2,200 workstations in dormitories, library, computer center, student center. Dormitories wired for high-speed internet access and linked to campus network. Commuter students can connect to campus network. Online course registration, online library, helpline, repair service, student web hosting, wireless network available.

**Student life. Freshman orientation:** Mandatory, $115 fee. Preregistration for classes offered. 15 freshman sessions for a day and a half, 4 one day sessions for transfers and a one day combined freshman and transfer students. **Policies:** Academic integrity policies are guided by our Capstone Creed and administered through student honors council. Living/learning program offered. **Housing:** Guaranteed on-campus for freshmen. Coed dorms, single-sex dorms, special housing for disabled, apartments, fraternity/sorority housing, substance-free housing available. $200 partly refundable deposit, deadline 3/1. Apartments for visiting scholars available. **Activities:** Bands, campus ministries, choral groups, dance, drama, film society, international student organizations, literary magazine, music ensembles, musical theater, opera, radio station, student government, student newspaper, symphony orchestra, TV station, College Republicans, College Democrats, NAACP, African American association, Golden Key, National Society of Black Engineers.

**Athletics.** NCAA. **Intercollegiate:** Baseball M, basketball, cheerleading, cross-country, diving, football (tackle) M, golf, gymnastics W, rowing (crew) W, soccer W, softball W, swimming, tennis, track and field, volleyball W. **Intramural:** Badminton, basketball, bowling, football (non-tackle), football (tackle), golf, racquetball, soccer, softball, squash, table tennis, tennis, track and field, volleyball, wrestling W. **Team name:** Crimson Tide.

**Student services.** Adult student services, alcohol/substance abuse counseling, campus ministries, career counseling, services for economically disadvantaged, student employment services, financial aid counseling, health services, legal services, minority student services, on-campus daycare, personal counseling, placement for graduates, veterans' counselor, women's services. **Physically disabled:** Services for visually, speech, hearing impaired.

**Contact.** E-mail: admissions@ua.edu
Phone: (205) 348-5666 Toll-free number: (800) 933-2262
Fax: (205) 348-9046
Mary Spiegel, Executive Director of Undergraduate Admissions, University of Alabama, Box 870132, Tuscaloosa, AL 35487-0132

## University of Alabama at Birmingham
**Birmingham, Alabama**
www.uab.edu

CB member
CB code: 1856

- Public 4-year university
- Commuter campus in very large city
- 10,228 degree-seeking undergraduates: 25% part-time, 60% women, 29% African American, 4% Asian American, 1% Hispanic American, 2% international
- 4,910 degree-seeking graduate students
- 77% of applicants admitted
- SAT or ACT (ACT writing optional) required

**General.** Founded in 1969. Regionally accredited. **Degrees:** 1,814 bachelor's awarded; master's, doctoral, first professional offered. **ROTC:** Army, Air Force. **Location:** Downtown. **Calendar:** Semester, extensive summer session. **Full-time faculty:** 823 total; 87% have terminal degrees, 18% minority, 41% women. **Part-time faculty:** 72 total; 76% have terminal degrees, 12% minority, 36% women. **Class size:** 37% < 20, 41% 20-39, 9% 40-49, 9% 50-99, 4% >100. **Special facilities:** Alabama Museum of Health Sciences.

**Freshman class profile.** 4,398 applied, 3,373 admitted, 1,416 enrolled.

| Mid 50% test scores | | | |
|---|---|---|---|
| ACT composite: | 21-27 | Return as sophomores: | 75% |
| GPA 3.50 or higher: | 52% | Out-of-state: | 8% |
| GPA 3.0-3.49: | 21% | Live on campus: | 59% |
| GPA 2.0-2.99: | 27% | International: | 2% |
| Rank in top quarter: | 56% | Fraternities: | 17% |
| Rank in top tenth: | 30% | Sororities: | 12% |

**Basis for selection.** High school record and test scores most important. Nontraditional students (typically older students) not required to submit standardized test scores for admission. **Homeschooled:** Statement describing homeschool structure and mission required.

**High school preparation.** 17 units required. Required units include English 4, mathematics 3, social studies 3, science 3 (laboratory 2), foreign language 1 and academic electives 3.

**2007-2008 Annual costs.** Tuition/fees: $5,186; $11,546 out-of-state. Room/board: $7,500. Books/supplies: $900. Personal expenses: $1,500.

**2006-2007 Financial aid. Need-based:** 1,172 full-time freshmen applied for aid; 642 were judged to have need; 629 of these received aid.

Average need met was 33%. Average scholarship/grant was $3,232; average loan $2,831. 33% of total undergraduate aid awarded as scholarships/grants, 67% as loans/jobs. **Non-need-based:** Awarded to 3,299 full-time undergraduates, including 868 freshmen. Scholarships awarded for academics, alumni affiliation, art, athletics, leadership, minority status, music/drama, ROTC.

**Application procedures. Admission:** Closing date 3/1 (receipt date). $35 fee, may be waived for applicants with need. Application may be submitted online. Admission notification on a rolling basis beginning on or about 9/1. **Financial aid:** Priority date 4/1; no closing date. FAFSA, institutional form required. Applicants notified on a rolling basis starting 4/1; must reply within 4 week(s) of notification.

**Academics.** Combined bachelors/masters program also available in Biology. **Special study options:** Combined bachelor's/graduate degree, cooperative education, cross-registration, distance learning, double major, dual enrollment of high school students, honors, independent study, internships, student-designed major, study abroad, teacher certification program, weekend college. **Credit/placement by examination:** AP, CLEP, IB, SAT, ACT, institutional tests. 45 credit hours maximum toward bachelor's degree. **Support services:** Reduced course load, remedial instruction, study skills assistance, tutoring.

**Honors college/program.** Additional application required. Maximum of 50 students admitted annually. Honors coursework (combination of interdisciplinary and in-major) substitutes for all core coursework except for math.

**Majors. Area/ethnic studies:** African-American. **Biology:** General. **Business:** Accounting, business admin, finance, management information systems, managerial economics, marketing, sales/distribution. **Communications:** General. **Computer sciences:** General. **Education:** Early childhood, elementary, health, physical, secondary, special. **Engineering:** Biomedical, civil, electrical, materials, mechanical. **English:** English lit. **Foreign languages:** General. **Health:** Clinical lab science, cytotechnology, medical radiologic technology/radiation therapy, medical records admin, nuclear medical technology, nursing (RN), respiratory therapy technology. **History:** General. **Interdisciplinary:** Biological/physical sciences, global studies, natural sciences. **Math:** General. **Philosophy/religion:** Philosophy. **Physical sciences:** Chemistry, physics. **Protective services:** Criminal justice. **Psychology:** General. **Public administration:** Social work. **Social sciences:** Anthropology, political science, sociology. **Visual/performing arts:** Art, dramatic. **Other:** Industrial distribution.

**Most popular majors.** Biology 8%, business/marketing 17%, communications/journalism 7%, education 7%, engineering/engineering technologies 6%, health sciences 21%, psychology 8%.

**Computing on campus.** 400 workstations in library, computer center. Dormitories wired for high-speed internet access and linked to campus network. Commuter students can connect to campus network. Online course registration, helpline, student web hosting, wireless network available.

**Student life. Freshman orientation:** Mandatory, $40 fee. Preregistration for classes offered. 2-day program offered various times between June and August. **Housing:** Coed dorms, single-sex dorms, apartments available. $250 deposit, deadline 5/1. **Activities:** Bands, campus ministries, choral groups, dance, drama, international student organizations, literary magazine, music ensembles, musical theater, opera, radio station, student government, student newspaper, Young Democrats, College Republicans, campus civitan club, veterans student organization, Catholic student association, Muslim student association, Chinese student association, African student association.

**Athletics.** NCAA. **Intercollegiate:** Baseball M, basketball, cross-country W, football (tackle) M, golf, rifle, soccer, softball W, synchronized swimming W, tennis, track and field W, volleyball W. **Intramural:** Badminton, basketball, bowling, football (non-tackle), racquetball, skiing, soccer, softball, squash, swimming, table tennis, tennis, track and field, volleyball, water polo, wrestling M. **Team name:** Blazers.

**Student services.** Adult student services, career counseling, student employment services, financial aid counseling, health services, minority student services, on-campus daycare, personal counseling, placement for graduates, veterans' counselor, women's services. **Physically disabled:** Services for visually, speech, hearing impaired.

**Contact.** E-mail: UndergradAdmit@uab.edu
Phone: (205) 934-8221 Toll-free number: (800) 421-8743
Fax: (205) 975-7114
Chenise Ryan, Director of Admission, University of Alabama at Birmingham, HUC 260, 1530 Third Avenue South, Birmingham, AL 35294-1150

## University of Alabama in Huntsville

**Huntsville, Alabama**
www.uah.edu

CB member
CB code: 1854

- Public 4-year university
- Commuter campus in small city
- 5,562 degree-seeking undergraduates: 24% part-time, 48% women, 15% African American, 3% Asian American, 2% Hispanic American, 2% Native American, 3% international
- 1,378 degree-seeking graduate students
- 88% of applicants admitted
- SAT or ACT (ACT writing recommended) required
- 44% graduate within 6 years

**General.** Founded in 1950. Regionally accredited. **Degrees:** 840 bachelor's awarded; master's, doctoral offered. **ROTC:** Army. **Location:** 100 miles from Birmingham, 100 miles from Nashville, Tennessee. **Calendar:** Semester, extensive summer session. **Full-time faculty:** 289 total; 91% have terminal degrees, 19% minority, 37% women. **Part-time faculty:** 176 total; 35% have terminal degrees, 8% minority, 46% women. **Class size:** 40% < 20, 42% 20-39, 10% 40-49, 7% 50-99, 1% >100. **Special facilities:** Centers for: applied optics, micro-gravity research, robotics, solar research, space plasma, aeronomic research, observatory with vector magnetograph.

**Freshman class profile.** 1,850 applied, 1,628 admitted, 800 enrolled.

| Mid 50% test scores | | | |
|---|---|---|---|
| SAT critical reading: | 490-610 | Rank in top tenth: | 28% |
| SAT math: | 490-620 | End year in good standing: | 89% |
| ACT composite: | 22-27 | Return as sophomores: | 77% |
| GPA 3.50 or higher: | 45% | Out-of-state: | 15% |
| GPA 3.0-3.49: | 27% | Live on campus: | 42% |
| GPA 2.0-2.99: | 27% | International: | 3% |
| Rank in top quarter: | 56% | Fraternities: | 8% |
| | | Sororities: | 7% |

**Basis for selection.** School achievement record and test scores are the most important factors for admission. Conditional admission may be available for applicants with evidence of a serious commitment to academic pursuits who do not meet requirements for regular admission. **Homeschooled:** Official high school record of courses completed should contain the titles of courses in each subject area, beginning with grade nine; record should contain annotation of the general content in the academic courses and the textbooks used; teaching credentials of the home school teacher should also be included with the application for admission.

**High school preparation.** 20 units required. Required units include English 4, mathematics 3, social studies 4, science 3 and academic electives 6.

**2007-2008 Annual costs.** Tuition/fees: $5,216; $11,024 out-of-state. Per-credit-hour rate decreases as number of hours registered increases. Room/board: $5,810. Books/supplies: $942. Personal expenses: $1,729.

**2007-2008 Financial aid. Need-based:** 671 full-time freshmen applied for aid; 315 were judged to have need; 313 of these received aid. Average need met was 68%. Average scholarship/grant was $4,879; average loan $3,600. 38% of total undergraduate aid awarded as scholarships/grants, 62% as loans/jobs. **Non-need-based:** Awarded to 1,151 full-time undergraduates, including 336 freshmen. Scholarships awarded for academics, art, athletics, leadership, minority status, music/drama, ROTC. **Additional information:** Application deadline for institutional scholarships is February 1.

**Application procedures. Admission:** Closing date 8/15. $30 fee, may be waived for applicants with need. Application may be submitted online. Admission notification on a rolling basis. **Financial aid:** Priority date 4/1, closing date 7/31. FAFSA required. Applicants notified on a rolling basis starting 4/1; must reply within 2 week(s) of notification.

**Academics. Special study options:** Accelerated study, combined bachelor's/graduate degree, cooperative education, cross-registration, distance learning, double major, dual enrollment of high school students, ESL, honors, independent study, internships, liberal arts/career combination, study abroad, teacher certification program. 3-2 program in engineering. Research centers employ undergraduate students on campus and in the community. Co-op program with U.S. Army Redstone Arsenal, NASA Marshall Space Flight Center, U.S. Army Missile Command, over 50 Fortune 500 companies. Intensive English Program (IEP) for nonnative speakers of English available prior to enrollment in a degree program. **Credit/placement by examination:** AP, CLEP, IB, SAT, ACT, institutional tests. 32 credit hours maximum toward bachelor's degree. **Support services:** Learning center, reduced course load, remedial instruction, study skills assistance, tutoring, writing center.

**Majors. Biology:** General. **Business:** Accounting, business admin, finance, management information systems, marketing. **Computer sciences:** General. **Education:** Elementary. **Engineering:** Chemical, civil, computer, electrical, industrial, mechanical. **English:** English lit, speech/rhetoric. **Foreign** languages: General. **Health:** Nursing (RN). **History:** General. **Math:** General. **Philosophy/religion:** Philosophy. **Physical sciences:** Chemistry, physics. **Psychology:** General. **Social sciences:** Political science, sociology. **Visual/performing arts:** Art.

**Most popular majors.** Biology 7%, business/marketing 25%, engineering/engineering technologies 23%, health sciences 15%.

**Computing on campus.** 1,153 workstations in dormitories, library, computer center, student center. Dormitories wired for high-speed internet access and linked to campus network. Commuter students can connect to campus network. Online course registration, online library, helpline, wireless network available.

**Student life. Freshman orientation:** Available, $65 fee. Preregistration for classes offered. One 1/2 day residential program for students and parents held during the summer. **Housing:** Coed dorms, special housing for disabled, apartments, fraternity/sorority housing, substance-free housing available. $125 fully refundable deposit, deadline 5/1. Pets allowed in dorm rooms. **Activities:** Bands, campus ministries, choral groups, dance, drama, international student organizations, literary magazine, music ensembles, Model UN, musical theater, student government, student newspaper, symphony orchestra, Black student association, Campus Crusade for Christ, Chinese student & scholar association, College Democrats, College Republicans, Indian students organization, Invisible Children United, National Society of Black Engineers, Reformed University Fellowship.

**Athletics.** NCAA. **Intercollegiate:** Baseball M, basketball, cross-country, ice hockey M, soccer, softball W, tennis, track and field, volleyball W. **Intramural:** Badminton, basketball, football (non-tackle), golf, racquetball, soccer, softball, table tennis, volleyball. **Team name:** Chargers.

**Student services.** Alcohol/substance abuse counseling, campus ministries, career counseling, student employment services, financial aid counseling, health services, minority student services, on-campus daycare, personal counseling, placement for graduates, veterans' counselor. **Physically disabled:** Services for visually, speech, hearing impaired.

**Contact.** E-mail: admitme@uah.edu
Phone: (256) 824-6070 Toll-free number: (800) 824-2255
Fax: (256) 824-6073
John Maxon, Interim Director of Admissions, University of Alabama in Huntsville, UAH Office of Undergraduate Admissions, Huntsville, AL 35899

## University of Mobile

**Mobile, Alabama**
www.umobile.edu

CB code: 1515

- Private 4-year university and liberal arts college affiliated with Baptist faith
- Commuter campus in small city
- 1,346 degree-seeking undergraduates: 15% part-time, 66% women, 22% African American, 1% Hispanic American, 3% Native American, 2% international
- 195 degree-seeking graduate students
- 90% of applicants admitted
- SAT or ACT (ACT writing optional) required

**General.** Founded in 1961. Regionally accredited. **Degrees:** 265 bachelor's, 22 associate awarded; master's offered. **ROTC:** Army, Air Force. **Location:** 12 miles from downtown, 170 miles from New Orleans. **Calendar:** Semester, extensive summer session. **Full-time faculty:** 86 total; 88% have terminal degrees, 4% minority, 51% women. **Part-time faculty:** 64 total; 12% have terminal degrees, 48% women. **Class size:** 65% < 20, 33% 20-39, 1% 40-49, less than 1% 50-99. **Special facilities:** Forest learning center, comprised of 125 acres with nature trails.

**Freshman class profile.** 1,937 applied, 1,738 admitted, 231 enrolled.

| Mid 50% test scores | | | |
|---|---|---|---|
| SAT critical reading: | 500-700 | Rank in top quarter: | 42% |
| SAT math: | 500-650 | Rank in top tenth: | 20% |
| SAT writing: | 450-700 | Out-of-state: | 25% |
| ACT composite: | 22-26 | Live on campus: | 28% |
| | | International: | 3% |

**Basis for selection.** Admission decisions based on test scores, high school record. Interview recommended for nursing majors, audition recommended for music majors, portfolio recommended for art majors. **Homeschooled:** Statement describing homeschool structure and mission required.

**High school preparation.** 22 units recommended. Recommended units include English 4, mathematics 3, social studies 3 and foreign language 2.

**2008-2009 Annual costs.** Tuition/fees: $13,970. Room/board: $7,170. Books/supplies: $500. Personal expenses: $1,000.

**2007-2008 Financial aid. Need-based:** Average need met was 87%. Average scholarship/grant was $1,981; average loan $1,553. 64% of total undergraduate aid awarded as scholarships/grants, 36% as loans/jobs. **Non-need-based:** Scholarships awarded for academics, alumni affiliation, art, athletics, job skills, leadership, minority status, music/drama, religious affiliation, ROTC, state residency.

**Application procedures. Admission:** Priority date 3/31; no deadline. $30 fee. Application may be submitted online. Admission notification on a rolling basis beginning on or about 11/1. Students with 26 or greater ACT may apply for early admission and scholarships. Early applicants invited to attend private luncheon hosted by president; also receive top consideration for scholarship monies. **Financial aid:** Priority date 3/31; no closing date. FAFSA, institutional form required. Applicants notified on a rolling basis; must reply within 2 week(s) of notification.

**Academics. Special study options:** Accelerated study, combined bachelor's/graduate degree, distance learning, double major, honors, independent study, internships, liberal arts/career combination, teacher certification program. **Credit/placement by examination:** AP, CLEP, IB, SAT, ACT, institutional tests. 30 credit hours maximum toward bachelor's degree. **Support services:** Learning center, pre-admission summer program, reduced course load, remedial instruction, study skills assistance, tutoring, writing center.

**Majors. Biology:** General, marine. **Business:** General, accounting, business admin, marketing. **Communications:** General. **Computer sciences:** General. **Education:** Biology, chemistry, early childhood, elementary, English, history, mathematics, music, physical, social studies. **English:** English lit. **Health:** Athletic training, nursing (RN). **History:** General. **Liberal arts:** Humanities. **Math:** General. **Parks/recreation:** Health/fitness. **Philosophy/religion:** Religion. **Psychology:** General. **Social sciences:** General, political science, sociology. **Theology:** Theology. **Visual/performing arts:** General, art, dramatic.

**Most popular majors.** Business/marketing 8%, education 25%, health sciences 12%, interdisciplinary studies 17%, psychology 6%, theological studies 15%.

**Computing on campus.** 110 workstations in library, computer center. Dormitories wired for high-speed internet access. Online library available.

**Student life. Freshman orientation:** Mandatory. Preregistration for classes offered. **Policies:** Religious observance required. **Housing:** Guaranteed on-campus for freshmen. Single-sex dorms, substance-free housing available. $150 nonrefundable deposit. **Activities:** Bands, choral groups, dance, drama, music ensembles, musical theater, opera, student government, student newspaper, symphony orchestra, Ministerial association, Baptist student union, honor societies, academic organizations, Fellowship of Christian Athletes, multicultural club.

**Athletics.** NAIA. **Intercollegiate:** Baseball M, basketball, cross-country, golf, soccer, softball W, tennis W. **Intramural:** Basketball, softball, table tennis, volleyball. **Team name:** Rams.

**Student services.** Adult student services, campus ministries, career counseling, student employment services, financial aid counseling, health services, personal counseling, veterans' counselor.

**Contact.** E-mail: adminfo@umobile.edu
Phone: (251) 442-2287 Toll-free number: (800) 946-7267
Fax: (251) 442-2498
Kim Leousis, Vice President for Enrollment Management, University of Mobile, 5735 College Parkway, Mobile, AL 36613-2842

---

## University of Montevallo

Montevallo, Alabama
www.montevallo.edu

CB member
CB code: 1004

- Public 4-year university and liberal arts college
- Residential campus in small town
- 2,473 degree-seeking undergraduates: 10% part-time, 68% women, 14% African American, 1% Asian American, 2% Hispanic American, 2% international
- 435 graduate students
- 78% of applicants admitted
- SAT or ACT (ACT writing optional) required

**General.** Founded in 1896. Regionally accredited. A National Historic District. **Degrees:** 470 bachelor's awarded; master's offered. **ROTC:** Army, Air Force. **Location:** 30 miles from Birmingham. **Calendar:** Semester, extensive summer session. **Full-time faculty:** 137 total; 90% have terminal degrees, 11% minority, 49% women. **Part-time faculty:** 78 total; 14% have terminal degrees, 3% minority, 63% women. **Class size:** 44% < 20, 51% 20-39, 4% 40-49, 1% 50-99. **Special facilities:** Foreign language laboratory, child development center, mass communication production center, traffic safety center.

**Freshman class profile.** 1,437 applied, 1,120 admitted, 491 enrolled.

| Mid 50% test scores | | | |
|---|---|---|---|
| ACT composite: | 19-24 | Out-of-state: | 3% |
| GPA 3.50 or higher: | 39% | Live on campus: | 63% |
| GPA 3.0-3.49: | 29% | International: | 2% |
| GPA 2.0-2.99: | 32% | Fraternities: | 19% |
| | | Sororities: | 16% |

**Basis for selection.** High school record and test scores essential factors in individual evaluation. Interview recommended. Audition required of music majors; portfolio required of art majors. **Homeschooled:** Transcript of courses and grades required. **Learning Disabled:** Students with disabilities must meet the same admissions requirements as other students. Conditional admission may be an option if standard requirements are not met. Reasonable accommodations will be provided as necessary. Enrolled students needing disability accommodations and services must provide current documentation and make requests through the Services for Students with Disabiltiies Office.

**High school preparation.** 16 units required. Required and recommended units include English 4, mathematics 2-3, social studies 2, history 2, science 2-3, foreign language 2 and academic electives 4.

**2007-2008 Annual costs.** Tuition/fees: $6,080; $11,930 out-of-state. Room/board: $4,214. Books/supplies: $850. Personal expenses: $1,900.

**2007-2008 Financial aid. Need-based:** Average need met was 71%. Average scholarship/grant was $3,936; average loan $2,988. 43% of total undergraduate aid awarded as scholarships/grants, 57% as loans/jobs. **Non-need-based:** Scholarships awarded for academics, art, athletics, job skills, leadership, minority status, music/drama, religious affiliation, ROTC.

**Application procedures. Admission:** Closing date 8/20. $25 fee, may be waived for applicants with need. Application may be submitted online. Admission notification on a rolling basis. **Financial aid:** Priority date 4/1; no closing date. FAFSA required. Applicants notified by 5/10; must reply within 2 week(s) of notification.

**Academics.** Academic support programs available to all first-generation college students from low-income families and students with disabilities. **Special study options:** Accelerated study, combined bachelor's/graduate degree, cross-registration, double major, dual enrollment of high school students, exchange student, honors, independent study, internships, study abroad, teacher certification program. **Credit/placement by examination:** AP, CLEP, institutional tests. 45 credit hours maximum toward bachelor's degree. **Support services:** Learning center, pre-admission summer program, reduced course load, remedial instruction, study skills assistance, tutoring, writing center.

**Majors. Biology:** General. **Business:** Accounting, business admin, finance, management information systems, marketing. **Communications:** Radio/tv. **Education:** Early childhood, elementary. **English:** English lit, speech/rhetoric. **Family/consumer sciences:** General. **Foreign languages:** General. **Health:** Audiology/hearing, speech pathology. **History:** General. **Math:** General. **Parks/recreation:** Health/fitness. **Physical sciences:** Chemistry. **Psychology:** General. **Public administration:** Social work. **Social sciences:** General, political science, sociology. **Visual/performing arts:** Art, dramatic, music pedagogy.

**Most popular majors.** Biology 7%, business/marketing 17%, communications/journalism 7%, education 10%, family/consumer sciences 8%, social sciences 6%, visual/performing arts 12%.

**Computing on campus.** 340 workstations in dormitories, library, computer center. Dormitories wired for high-speed internet access and linked to campus network. Commuter students can connect to campus network. Online course registration, online library, helpline, wireless network available.

**Student life. Freshman orientation:** Mandatory. Preregistration for classes offered. Fall semester freshmen attend one of two preregistration sessions during the summer and return to campus for Freshman Orientation immediately prior to the beginning of Fall semester classes. **Housing:** Guaranteed on-campus for freshmen. Coed dorms, single-sex dorms, apartments available. $100 fully refundable deposit. Several rooms are handicapped accessible. **Activities:** Bands, choral groups, dance, drama, literary magazine, music ensembles, musical theater, student government, student newspaper, TV station, African American Society, Young Republicans, Young Democrats, Baptist campus ministries, campus outreach, Catholic campus ministry, Presbyterian campus ministry, Methodist campus ministry.

**Athletics.** NAIA, NCAA. **Intercollegiate:** Baseball M, basketball, cross-country W, golf, soccer, tennis W, volleyball W. **Intramural:** Basketball, bowling, soccer, softball, volleyball. **Team name:** Falcons.

**Student services.** Adult student services, alcohol/substance abuse counseling, campus ministries, career counseling, student employment services, financial aid counseling, health services, minority student services, personal counseling, placement for graduates, veterans' counselor. **Physically disabled:** Services for visually, speech, hearing impaired.

**Contact.** E-mail: admissions@montevallo.edu
Phone: (205) 665-6030 Toll-free number: (800) 292-4349
Fax: (205) 665-6032
Ira Gurganus, Director of Admissions, University of Montevallo, Station 6030, Montevallo, AL 35115-6030

---

### University of North Alabama

Florence, Alabama
www.una.edu

CB member
CB code: 1735

- Public 4-year university
- Commuter campus in large town
- 5,299 degree-seeking undergraduates: 13% part-time, 56% women, 10% African American, 1% Asian American, 1% Hispanic American, 1% Native American, 9% international
- 1,326 degree-seeking graduate students
- 85% of applicants admitted
- SAT or ACT required
- 55% graduate within 6 years

**General.** Founded in 1830. Regionally accredited. **Degrees:** 866 bachelor's awarded; master's offered. **ROTC:** Army. **Location:** 116 miles from Birmingham. **Calendar:** Semester, extensive summer session. **Full-time faculty:** 230 total; 71% have terminal degrees, 21% minority, 46% women. **Part-time faculty:** 130 total; 8% have terminal degrees, 12% minority, 52% women. **Class size:** 45% <20, 38% 20-39, 12% 40-49, 4% 50-99, less than 1% >100. **Special facilities:** Planetarium-observatory, laboratory school.

**Freshman class profile.** 2,302 applied, 1,947 admitted, 1,023 enrolled.

| Mid 50% test scores | | | |
|---|---|---|---|
| ACT composite: | 18-24 | Rank in top quarter: | 44% |
| GPA 3.50 or higher: | 27% | Return as sophomores: | 68% |
| GPA 3.0-3.49: | 23% | Out-of-state: | 15% |
| GPA 2.0-2.99: | 41% | International: | 17% |

**Basis for selection.** Minimum 18 ACT or 700 SAT (exclusive of Writing), or rank in upper 50 percent of high school class, or minimum 35 on each section of GED, or average of 45 on all GED test sections required. Auditions required of music majors. Interviews recommended for education, nursing, social work, preprofessional programs. Portfolios recommended for art majors.

**High school preparation.** 13 units required. Required units include English 4, mathematics 2, social studies 3, science 2 and foreign language 2.

**2007-2008 Annual costs.** Tuition/fees: $5,093; $9,203 out-of-state. Room/board: $4,460. Books/supplies: $830.

**Financial aid. Non-need-based:** Scholarships awarded for academics, art, athletics, leadership, minority status, music/drama, ROTC, state residency.

**Application procedures. Admission:** Priority date 8/1; no deadline. $25 fee. Application may be submitted online. Admission notification on a rolling basis beginning on or about 6/15. **Financial aid:** Priority date 4/1; no closing date. FAFSA required. Applicants notified on a rolling basis starting 5/31; must reply within 2 week(s) of notification.

**Academics. Special study options:** Accelerated study, cooperative education, distance learning, double major, dual enrollment of high school students, ESL, honors, independent study, internships, student-designed major, teacher certification program, weekend college. **Credit/placement by examination:** AP, CLEP, institutional tests. 34 credit hours maximum toward bachelor's degree. **Support services:** Learning center, pre-admission summer program, reduced course load, remedial instruction, study skills assistance, tutoring.

**Majors. Biology:** General, marine. **Business:** Accounting, business admin, finance, management information systems, managerial economics, marketing. **Computer sciences:** General. **Education:** Elementary, multi-level teacher, secondary. **English:** English lit, speech/rhetoric. **Family/consumer sciences:** General. **Foreign languages:** General. **Health:** Nursing (RN). **History:** General. **Math:** General. **Parks/recreation:** General. **Physical sciences:** Chemistry, geology, physics. **Protective services:** Law enforcement

admin. **Psychology:** General. **Public administration:** Social work. **Social sciences:** Geography, political science, sociology. **Visual/performing arts:** Studio arts.

**Most popular majors.** Business/marketing 29%, education 8%, English 8%, health sciences 16%, social sciences 8%.

**Computing on campus.** 600 workstations in dormitories, library, computer center, student center. Dormitories wired for high-speed internet access and linked to campus network. Commuter students can connect to campus network. Online course registration, online library, helpline available.

**Student life. Freshman orientation:** Mandatory, $25 fee. Preregistration for classes offered. 2-day sessions in June and July include orientation, academic advisement. **Housing:** Coed dorms, single-sex dorms, apartments, fraternity/sorority housing available. $100 deposit. **Activities:** Bands, choral groups, drama, literary magazine, music ensembles, musical theater, radio station, student government, student newspaper, Young Democrats, Young Republicans, Circle-K, Gold Triangle, Black Student Alliance, Christian Student Fellowship.

**Athletics.** NCAA. **Intercollegiate:** Baseball M, basketball, cross-country, football (tackle) M, golf M, soccer W, softball W, tennis, volleyball W. **Intramural:** Badminton, baseball M, basketball, bowling, cross-country, football (tackle) M, golf M, racquetball, softball W, swimming, table tennis, tennis, volleyball. **Team name:** Lions.

**Student services.** Adult student services, alcohol/substance abuse counseling, campus ministries, career counseling, student employment services, financial aid counseling, health services, minority student services, on-campus daycare, personal counseling, placement for graduates, veterans' counselor, women's services. **Physically disabled:** Services for visually, speech, hearing impaired.

**Contact.** E-mail: admissions@una.edu
Phone: (256) 765-4608 Toll-free number: (800) 825-5862
Fax: (256) 765-4329
Kim Mauldin, Director of Admissions, University of North Alabama, One Harrison Plaza, UNA Box 5011, Florence, AL 35632-0001

---

### University of South Alabama

Mobile, Alabama
www.southalabama.edu

CB code: 1880

- Public 4-year university
- Commuter campus in small city
- 10,459 degree-seeking undergraduates: 26% part-time, 60% women, 19% African American, 3% Asian American, 2% Hispanic American, 1% Native American, 5% international
- 3,089 degree-seeking graduate students
- 88% of applicants admitted
- SAT or ACT required
- 37% graduate within 6 years

**General.** Founded in 1963. Regionally accredited. **Degrees:** 1,445 bachelor's awarded; master's, doctoral, first professional offered. **ROTC:** Army, Air Force. **Location:** 10 miles from downtown, 150 miles from New Orleans. **Calendar:** Semester, extensive summer session. **Full-time faculty:** 722 total; 75% have terminal degrees, 38% women. **Part-time faculty:** 297 total; 55% women. **Special facilities:** Sea laboratory.

**Freshman class profile.** 3,089 applied, 2,727 admitted, 1,529 enrolled.

| Mid 50% test scores | | | |
|---|---|---|---|
| SAT critical reading: | 420-560 | Return as sophomores: | 70% |
| SAT math: | 430-540 | International: | 5% |
| ACT composite: | 19-24 | Fraternities: | 10% |
| | | Sororities: | 10% |

**Basis for selection.** School achievement record and test scores important. Auditions required of music majors. **Learning Disabled:** Submit required documentation to special student services office if requesting services.

**High school preparation.** 16 units recommended. Recommended units include English 4, mathematics 3, social studies 2, science 2 and academic electives 2.

**2007-2008 Annual costs.** Tuition/fees: $4,822; $8,842 out-of-state. Room/board: $4,698. Books/supplies: $1,000.

**2006-2007 Financial aid. Need-based:** 21% of total undergraduate aid awarded as scholarships/grants, 79% as loans/jobs. **Non-need-based:** Scholarships awarded for academics, alumni affiliation, art, athletics, minority status, music/drama, ROTC, state residency.

**Application procedures. Admission:** Closing date 8/10. $35 fee. Application must be submitted on paper. Admission notification on a rolling basis. **Financial aid:** Priority date 5/1; no closing date. FAFSA, institutional form required. Applicants notified on a rolling basis starting 5/15.

**Academics.** Students in entry-level programming courses must own a laptop. **Special study options:** Combined bachelor's/graduate degree, cooperative education, distance learning, double major, ESL, honors, independent study, internships, student-designed major, study abroad, teacher certification program, weekend college. **Credit/placement by examination:** AP, CLEP, institutional tests. Maximum of 32 credit hours can be awarded under any combination of AP and CLEP examination credits. **Support services:** Learning center, remedial instruction, study skills assistance, tutoring, writing center.

**Majors. Biology:** General, biomedical sciences. **Business:** General, accounting, business admin, e-commerce, finance, marketing. **Communications:** General. **Computer sciences:** General. **Education:** Early childhood, elementary, health, physical, secondary, special. **Engineering:** Chemical, civil, computer, electrical, mechanical. **English:** English lit. **Foreign languages:** General. **Health:** Audiology/speech pathology, clinical lab science, medical radiologic technology/radiation therapy, nursing (RN), respiratory therapy technology. **History:** General. **Liberal arts:** Arts/sciences. **Math:** Statistics. **Parks/recreation:** General. **Philosophy/religion:** Philosophy. **Physical sciences:** Atmospheric science, chemistry, geology, physics. **Protective services:** Criminal justice. **Psychology:** General. **Social sciences:** Anthropology, geography, political science, sociology. **Visual/performing arts:** Art, dramatic.

**Most popular majors.** Business/marketing 16%, communications/journalism 6%, education 13%, engineering/engineering technologies 6%, health sciences 25%.

**Computing on campus.** 500 workstations in library, computer center, student center. Dormitories wired for high-speed internet access and linked to campus network. Commuter students can connect to campus network. Online course registration, online library, helpline available.

**Student life. Freshman orientation:** Mandatory, $75 fee. **Housing:** Coed dorms, special housing for disabled, apartments, fraternity/sorority housing available. $150 deposit. **Activities:** Bands, choral groups, dance, drama, film society, literary magazine, music ensembles, musical theater, opera, student government, student newspaper, symphony orchestra, TV station.

**Athletics.** NCAA. **Intercollegiate:** Baseball M, basketball, cross-country, golf, soccer W, softball W, tennis, track and field, volleyball W. **Intramural:** Basketball, bowling, football (non-tackle), golf, racquetball, soccer, softball, table tennis, tennis, volleyball, water polo. **Team name:** Jaguars.

**Student services.** Adult student services, alcohol/substance abuse counseling, campus ministries, career counseling, services for economically disadvantaged, student employment services, financial aid counseling, health services, minority student services, personal counseling, placement for graduates, veterans' counselor. **Physically disabled:** Services for visually, speech, hearing impaired.

**Contact.** E-mail: admiss@usouthal.edu
Phone: (251) 460-6141 Toll-free number: (800) 872-5247
Fax: (251) 460-7876
Norma Tanner, Director of Admissions, University of South Alabama, Meisler Hall, Suite 2500, Mobile, AL 36688-0002

---

## University of West Alabama
**Livingston, Alabama**
**www.uwa.edu**
**CB code: 1737**

- Public 4-year university
- Residential campus in small town
- 1,999 degree-seeking undergraduates
- 75% of applicants admitted
- ACT (writing recommended) required

**General.** Founded in 1835. Regionally accredited. **Degrees:** 207 bachelor's, 47 associate awarded; master's offered. **ROTC:** Air Force. **Location:** 60 miles from Tuscaloosa. **Calendar:** Semester, limited summer session. **Full-time faculty:** 94 total; 72% have terminal degrees, 15% minority, 44% women. **Part-time faculty:** 4 total; 25% have terminal degrees, 75% women. **Special facilities:** Nature trail, herbarium, greenhouses, wildflower gardens, bluebird trail.

**Freshman class profile.** 856 applied, 646 admitted, 352 enrolled.

| Mid 50% test scores | | Out-of-state: | 12% |
|---|---|---|---|
| ACT composite: | 15-22 | | |

**Basis for selection.** School achievement record and test scores most important.

**High school preparation.** 15 units required. Required units include English 3, mathematics 3, social studies 3, science 3 and academic electives 3.

**2007-2008 Annual costs.** Tuition/fees: $4,607; $8,713 out-of-state. Room/board: $3,624. Books/supplies: $900. Personal expenses: $1,200.

**Financial aid. Non-need-based:** Scholarships awarded for academics, alumni affiliation, athletics, leadership, music/drama, state residency.

**Application procedures. Admission:** No deadline. $20 fee. Admission notification on a rolling basis. **Financial aid:** Priority date 4/1; no closing date. FAFSA required. Applicants notified on a rolling basis starting 6/1; must reply within 2 week(s) of notification.

**Academics. Special study options:** Accelerated study, cooperative education, distance learning, double major, dual enrollment of high school students, honors, internships, teacher certification program. **Credit/placement by examination:** AP, CLEP, SAT, ACT, institutional tests. 15 credit hours maximum toward associate degree, 30 toward bachelor's. **Support services:** Learning center, reduced course load, remedial instruction, study skills assistance, tutoring, writing center.

**Majors. Biology:** General, marine. **Business:** Accounting, business admin, management information systems. **Conservation:** General. **Education:** Early childhood, elementary, physical, secondary, special. **Engineering technology:** Manufacturing. **English:** English lit. **Health:** Athletic training. **History:** General. **Math:** General. **Physical sciences:** Chemistry. **Psychology:** General. **Social sciences:** Sociology.

**Most popular majors.** Biology 6%, business/marketing 24%, education 27%, engineering/engineering technologies 9%, health sciences 10%, psychology 8%, social sciences 7%.

**Computing on campus.** 310 workstations in dormitories, library, computer center, student center. Dormitories wired for high-speed internet access and linked to campus network. Commuter students can connect to campus network. Online library, helpline, wireless network available.

**Student life. Freshman orientation:** Mandatory, $40 fee. Preregistration for classes offered. **Housing:** Guaranteed on-campus for all undergraduates. Coed dorms, single-sex dorms, apartments, substance-free housing available. $100 deposit. **Activities:** Bands, campus ministries, choral groups, drama, student government, student newspaper, Wesley Foundation, campus outreach, Fellowship of Christian Athletes, student support services club, African-American cultural association.

**Athletics.** NCAA. **Intercollegiate:** Baseball M, basketball, cross-country, football (tackle) M, rodeo, softball W, tennis, volleyball W. **Intramural:** Basketball, softball, table tennis, tennis, volleyball, wrestling M. **Team name:** Tigers.

**Student services.** Career counseling, student employment services, health services, personal counseling, placement for graduates, veterans' counselor. **Physically disabled:** Services for visually, hearing impaired.

**Contact.** Phone: (205) 652-3578 Fax: (205) 652-3708
Richard Hester, Director of Admissions, University of West Alabama, Station 4, Livingston, AL 35470

---

## Virginia College
**Birmingham, Alabama**
**www.vc.edu**
**CB code: 2596**

- For-profit 4-year technical college
- Commuter campus in very large city

**General.** Founded in 1975. Accredited by ACICS. **Calendar:** Quarter.

**Annual costs/financial aid.** Per-credit-hour charge ranges from $285-$385 depending on program and includes fees and books. Personal expenses: $100.

**Contact.** Phone: (205) 802-1200
Director of Admissions, Box 19249, Birmingham, AL 35219

## Virginia College at Huntsville
**Huntsville, Alabama**
www.vc.edu                              **CB code: 3451**

- For-profit 4-year business and technical college
- Small city
- 860 degree-seeking undergraduates

**General.** Accredited by ACICS. **Degrees:** 20 bachelor's, 83 associate awarded. **Calendar:** Continuous. **Full-time faculty:** 25 total. **Part-time faculty:** 65 total.

**Freshman class profile.** 172 applied, 135 admitted, 135 enrolled.

**Basis for selection.** Open admission. Accuplacer used for placement; SAT or ACT if submitted may be substituted for Accuplacer.

**2007-2008 Annual costs.** Tuition is based on a quarterly charge which varies by program. Personal expenses: $2,978.

**Application procedures. Admission:** No deadline. $100 fee. **Financial aid:** No deadline. FAFSA, institutional form required. Applicants notified on a rolling basis.

**Academics. Credit/placement by examination:** CLEP.

**Majors. Protective services:** Law enforcement admin.

**Contact.** Phone: (256) 533-7387
Pat Foster, Vice President of Enrollment, Virginia College at Huntsville, 2800 Bob Wallace Avenue, Huntsville, AL 35805

# Alaska

## Alaska Bible College
### Glennallen, Alaska
### www.akbible.edu
**CB code: 1237**

- Private 4-year Bible college affiliated with nondenominational tradition
- Residential campus in rural community
- 23 degree-seeking undergraduates
- SAT or ACT, application essay, interview required

**General.** Founded in 1966. Accredited by ABHE. **Degrees:** 3 bachelor's, 2 associate awarded. **Location:** 187 miles from Anchorage, 250 miles from Fairbanks. **Calendar:** Semester. **Full-time faculty:** 3 total. **Part-time faculty:** 4 total. **Class size:** 100% < 20. **Special facilities:** Largest theological library collection in Alaska, Alaskan book collection.

**Freshman class profile.** 6 applied, 6 admitted, 5 enrolled.

Out-of-state: 50%  **Live on campus:** 83%

**Basis for selection.** Open admission, but selective for some programs. Applicants considered on a case-by-case basis. References and indications of religious commitment most important, followed by school grade record. Test scores and extracurricular activities also considered. **Homeschooled:** Applicants need to have documentation of high school equivalence.

**High school preparation.** Recommended units include English 4, mathematics 4, social studies 4, history 4, science 4 and foreign language 2.

**2007-2008 Annual costs.** Tuition/fees: $6,500. Room/board: $5,000. Books/supplies: $425. Personal expenses: $1,000.

**Financial aid.** All financial aid based on need.

**Application procedures. Admission:** Closing date 7/1 (postmark date). $35 fee. Application must be submitted on paper. Admission notification on a rolling basis beginning on or about 7/1. Must reply by 7/15. **Financial aid:** Priority date 4/30, closing date 8/1. Institutional form required. Applicants notified on a rolling basis; must reply within 2 week(s) of notification.

**Academics. Special study options:** Double major, dual enrollment of high school students, independent study, internships. **Credit/placement by examination:** AP, CLEP, institutional tests. **Support services:** Remedial instruction, tutoring.

**Majors. Theology:** Bible.

**Computing on campus.** 11 workstations in library, computer center, student center.

**Student life. Freshman orientation:** Mandatory. Preregistration for classes offered. 4-5 day program held immediately before beginning of school year. **Policies:** Religious observance required. **Housing:** Guaranteed on-campus for freshmen. Single-sex dorms, apartments, substance-free housing available. $150 fully refundable deposit, deadline 7/1. **Activities:** Radio station, student government.

**Athletics. Intramural:** Basketball, soccer, volleyball.

**Student services.** Campus ministries, financial aid counseling, health services.

**Contact.** E-mail: info@akbible.edu
Phone: (907) 822-3201 Toll-free number: (800) 478-7884
Fax: (907) 822-5027
Bill Lambert, Director of Admissions, Alaska Bible College, Box 289, Glennallen, AK 99588-0289

## Alaska Pacific University
### Anchorage, Alaska
### www.alaskapacific.edu
**CB code: 4201**

- Private 4-year university and liberal arts college
- Commuter campus in large city

- 452 degree-seeking undergraduates: 39% part-time, 68% women, 6% African American, 2% Asian American, 5% Hispanic American, 16% Native American
- 187 degree-seeking graduate students
- 93% of applicants admitted
- SAT or ACT (ACT writing optional), application essay required
- 36% graduate within 6 years

**General.** Founded in 1957. Regionally accredited. **Degrees:** 85 bachelor's, 5 associate awarded; master's offered. **ROTC:** Air Force. **Calendar:** Differs by program, limited summer session. **Full-time faculty:** 48 total; 4% minority, 52% women. **Part-time faculty:** 66 total; 8% minority, 47% women. **Class size:** 96% < 20, 4% 20-39. **Special facilities:** Climbing wall, walking trails, lake for canoeing and kayaking, Alaskana collection.

**Freshman class profile.** 128 applied, 119 admitted, 43 enrolled.

| Mid 50% test scores | | | |
|---|---|---|---|
| SAT critical reading: | 460-620 | Rank in top quarter: | 63% |
| SAT math: | 450-580 | Rank in top tenth: | 51% |
| ACT composite: | 18-26 | End year in good standing: | 85% |
| GPA 3.50 or higher: | 33% | Return as sophomores: | 43% |
| GPA 3.0-3.49: | 40% | Out-of-state: | 68% |
| GPA 2.0-2.99: | 27% | Live on campus: | 83% |

**Basis for selection.** High school record, level of involvement in school and community activities, test scores, writing samples, recommendations most important. **Learning Disabled:** Documentation verifying the disability condition required.

**High school preparation.** 14 units recommended. Recommended units include English 4, mathematics 3, social studies 1, history 1, science 2 (laboratory 1) and foreign language 2.

**2007-2008 Annual costs.** Tuition/fees: $21,010. Room/board: $7,700. Books/supplies: $1,000. Personal expenses: $2,700.

**2007-2008 Financial aid. Need-based:** 41 full-time freshmen applied for aid; 34 were judged to have need; 34 of these received aid. Average need met was 88%. Average scholarship/grant was $7,495; average loan $3,353. 54% of total undergraduate aid awarded as scholarships/grants, 46% as loans/jobs. **Non-need-based:** Awarded to 217 full-time undergraduates, including 48 freshmen. Scholarships awarded for academics, alumni affiliation, leadership, religious affiliation, state residency.

**Application procedures. Admission:** Priority date 12/1; deadline 8/15. $25 fee, may be waived for applicants with need. Application may be submitted online. Admission notification on a rolling basis beginning on or about 1/15. **Financial aid:** Priority date 4/15; no closing date. FAFSA required. Applicants notified on a rolling basis starting 2/1; must reply within 4 week(s) of notification.

**Academics. Special study options:** Accelerated study, distance learning, double major, independent study, internships, liberal arts/career combination, student-designed major, study abroad, teacher certification program. Eco-League exchange program for Environmental Sciences with Prescott College, Northland College, College of the Atlantic, Antioch College, Green Mountain College. **Credit/placement by examination:** AP, CLEP, IB, institutional tests. 22 credit hours maximum toward associate degree, 45 toward bachelor's. Sophomore standing available through AP and IB examinations by earning equivalent of 32 semester hours. **Support services:** Learning center, reduced course load, remedial instruction, study skills assistance, tutoring, writing center.

**Majors. Biology:** Marine. **Business:** Accounting/business management, business admin. **Conservation:** Environmental science, environmental studies, management/policy. **Education:** Elementary, middle. **Health:** Health care admin. **Liberal arts:** Arts/sciences. **Parks/recreation:** Facilities management. **Psychology:** General. **Public administration:** Human services.

**Most popular majors.** Business/marketing 29%, education 12%, liberal arts 9%, natural resources/environmental science 6%, parks/recreation 25%, psychology 9%.

**Computing on campus.** 60 workstations in dormitories, library, computer center, student center. Dormitories wired for high-speed internet access. Online course registration, online library, helpline, student web hosting, wireless network available.

**Student life. Freshman orientation:** Mandatory. Usually 10 days long, includes outdoor camping events. **Policies:** Student representation on faculty committees and councils stressed. **Housing:** Guaranteed on-campus for freshmen. Coed dorms, cooperative housing, substance-free housing available. $300 deposit, deadline 4/30. **Activities:** Campus ministries, choral groups, drama, international student organizations, literary magazine, music ensembles, student government, student newspaper, art club, business club, environmental club, photgraphy club, psychology club, service club, soccer club, volleyball club.

**Athletics. Team name:** Moose.

**Student services.** Campus ministries, career counseling, student employment services, financial aid counseling, minority student services, personal counseling.

**Contact.** E-mail: admissions@alaskapacific.edu
Phone: (907) 564-8248 Toll-free number: (800) 252-7528
Fax: (907) 564-8317
Michael Warner, Director of Admissions, Alaska Pacific University, 4101 University Drive, Anchorage, AK 99508

---

### Charter College
**Anchorage, Alaska**
www.chartercollege.edu                          **CB code: 3453**

- Private 4-year junior and technical college
- Commuter campus in large city

**General.** Accredited by ACICS. **Calendar:** Continuous.

**Annual costs/financial aid.** Total cost for program resulting in an Associate degree ranges from $21,500 to $30,500; $43,500 to $59,500 for a Bachelor's degree. Costs vary by program and full- or part-time status; includes books and supplies. Books/supplies: $700. Need-based financial aid available to full-time and part-time students.

**Contact.** Phone: (907) 277-1000
Admissions Director, 2221 East Northern Lights Boulevard, Suite 120, Anchorage, AK 99508

---

### University of Alaska Anchorage
**Anchorage, Alaska**                           **CB member**
www.uaa.alaska.edu                              **CB code: 4896**

- Public 4-year university
- Residential campus in large city
- 10,471 degree-seeking undergraduates: 40% part-time, 61% women, 4% African American, 8% Asian American, 5% Hispanic American, 11% Native American, 2% international
- 804 degree-seeking graduate students
- SAT or ACT required

**General.** Founded in 1954. Regionally accredited. **Degrees:** 847 bachelor's, 676 associate awarded; master's offered. **ROTC:** Air Force. **Location:** 3 miles from downtown. **Calendar:** Semester, extensive summer session. **Full-time faculty:** 575 total; 51% have terminal degrees, 13% minority, 52% women. **Part-time faculty:** 658 total; 3% have terminal degrees, 10% minority, 57% women. **Class size:** 57% < 20, 34% 20-39, 5% 40-49, 3% 50-99, less than 1% >100. **Special facilities:** Environment and natural resources institute, film library, center for international business, center for alcohol and addiction studies, center for high latitude health research, institute for circumpolar health, institute for social and economic research.

**Freshman class profile.** 3,115 applied, 2,386 admitted, 1,567 enrolled.

| Mid 50% test scores | | GPA 2.0-2.99: | 43% |
|---|---|---|---|
| SAT critical reading: | 440-580 | Rank in top quarter: | 30% |
| SAT math: | 440-570 | Rank in top tenth: | 11% |
| ACT composite: | 17-24 | Return as sophomores: | 71% |
| GPA 3.50 or higher: | 25% | Out-of-state: | 4% |
| GPA 3.0-3.49: | 29% | | |

**Basis for selection.** Open admission, but selective for some programs. Secondary school record, test scores important; 2.0 high school GPA required. Open admission for non-degree seeking applicants. Interview required of nursing majors; portfolio required of art majors. **Homeschooled:** Transcript of courses and grades required.

**High school preparation.** Recommended units include English 4, mathematics 2, social studies 3, history 1, science 3 and foreign language 1. 1-2 computer science, 1-2 art also recommended. Specific recommendations vary by program.

**2007-2008 Annual costs.** Tuition/fees: $4,400; $13,370 out-of-state. WUE students per-credit-hour charge is $192 for lower-division courses. Room/board: $7,730. Books/supplies: $1,022. Personal expenses: $1,383.

**Financial aid. Non-need-based:** Scholarships awarded for academics, athletics.

**Application procedures. Admission:** Closing date 7/1. $40 fee, may be waived for applicants with need. Application may be submitted online. Admission notification on a rolling basis. Freshman early admit plan allows students to apply early but wait as long as 2 years to enroll. **Financial aid:** Priority date 4/1, closing date 8/1. FAFSA, institutional form required. Applicants notified on a rolling basis starting 3/15; must reply within 4 week(s) of notification.

**Academics.** Many programs to assist nontraditional and/or at-risk students for college success. **Special study options:** Combined bachelor's/graduate degree, cooperative education, cross-registration, distance learning, double major, dual enrollment of high school students, ESL, exchange student, honors, independent study, internships, liberal arts/career combination, semester at sea, student-designed major, study abroad, teacher certification program, Washington semester. **Credit/placement by examination:** AP, CLEP, IB, institutional tests. Credit by examiniation are considered non-resident credit and non-resident credit policies apply. **Support services:** Learning center, reduced course load, remedial instruction, study skills assistance, tutoring, writing center.

**Majors. Biology:** General. **Business:** Accounting, business admin, entrepreneurial studies, finance, hospitality admin, logistics, management information systems, management science, marketing. **Communications:** Journalism. **Computer sciences:** General, computer science. **Education:** Elementary, music, physical. **Engineering:** Civil, electrical. **Engineering technology:** Electrical, surveying. **English:** English lit. **Foreign languages:** General, French, German, Japanese, Russian, Spanish. **Health:** Nursing (RN). **History:** General. **Interdisciplinary:** Biological/physical sciences, math/computer science, natural sciences. **Liberal arts:** Arts/sciences. **Math:** General. **Mechanic/repair:** Aircraft. **Personal/culinary services:** Culinary arts. **Philosophy/religion:** Philosophy. **Physical sciences:** Chemistry. **Psychology:** General. **Public administration:** Human services, social work. **Social sciences:** Anthropology, economics, political science, sociology. **Transportation:** General, air traffic control, airline/commercial pilot, aviation, aviation management. **Visual/performing arts:** General, art, dramatic, music performance, studio arts.

**Most popular majors.** Business/marketing 17%, education 6%, health sciences 19%, psychology 7%, social sciences 6%.

**Computing on campus.** 851 workstations in dormitories, library, computer center, student center. Dormitories wired for high-speed internet access and linked to campus network. Commuter students can connect to campus network. Online course registration, online library, helpline, repair service, student web hosting, wireless network available.

**Student life. Freshman orientation:** Available. Preregistration for classes offered. **Housing:** Coed dorms, special housing for disabled, apartments, substance-free housing available. $200 deposit. Separate floors for: Alaska natives studying engineering, nursing students, honor students, language and cultures, first-year students under age 20, healthy lifestyle, quiet lifestyle, WWAMI program, Far East exchange program. **Activities:** Jazz band, campus ministries, choral groups, dance, drama, international student organizations, literary magazine, music ensembles, radio station, student government, student newspaper, Alaska Native student organization, African American student associations, Baha'i club, College Republicans, Korean Campus Crusade for Christ, Intervarsity Christian Fellowship, disability awareness club, Student Organization Against Racism.

**Athletics.** NCAA. **Intercollegiate:** Basketball, cross-country, gymnastics W, ice hockey M, skiing, track and field, volleyball W. **Intramural:** Basketball, ice hockey, soccer, volleyball. **Team name:** Seawolves.

**Student services.** Adult student services, alcohol/substance abuse counseling, career counseling, services for economically disadvantaged, student employment services, financial aid counseling, health services, legal services, minority student services, on-campus daycare, personal counseling, veterans' counselor. **Physically disabled:** Services for visually, speech, hearing impaired. **Learning disabled:** Comprehensive services available.

**Contact.** E-mail: enroll@uaa.alaska.edu
Phone: (907) 786-1480 Fax: (907) 786-4888
Peggy Byers, Assistant Director of Enrollment Services for Admissions/Recruitment, University of Alaska Anchorage, PO Box 141629, Anchorage, AK 99514-1629

---

### University of Alaska Fairbanks
**Fairbanks, Alaska**                           **CB member**
www.uaf.edu                                     **CB code: 4866**

- Public 4-year university
- Commuter campus in small city

- 4,744 degree-seeking undergraduates: 33% part-time, 57% women, 3% African American, 4% Asian American, 3% Hispanic American, 19% Native American, 2% international
- 1,016 degree-seeking graduate students
- 78% of applicants admitted
- SAT or ACT (ACT writing optional) required
- 31% graduate within 6 years

**General.** Founded in 1917. Regionally accredited. **Degrees:** 464 bachelor's, 210 associate awarded; master's, doctoral offered. **ROTC:** Army. **Location:** 4 miles from downtown. **Calendar:** Semester, limited summer session. **Full-time faculty:** 345 total; 52% have terminal degrees, 21% minority, 40% women. **Part-time faculty:** 729 total; 33% have terminal degrees, 14% minority, 45% women. **Class size:** 66% < 20, 27% 20-39, 3% 40-49, 3% 50-99, less than 1% >100. **Special facilities:** Museum of the north, geophysical institute, bioscience library, institute of arctic biology, arctic region supercomputing center, international arctic research center, boreal forest research range, Alaska native language center, institute of marine sciences, institute of northern engineering, Poker Flat rocketry research range.

**Freshman class profile.** 1,758 applied, 1,373 admitted, 958 enrolled.

| Mid 50% test scores | | | |
|---|---|---|---|
| SAT critical reading: | 450-600 | Rank in top quarter: | 35% |
| SAT math: | 450-590 | Rank in top tenth: | 15% |
| ACT composite: | 18-25 | Return as sophomores: | 72% |
| GPA 3.50 or higher: | 36% | Out-of-state: | 8% |
| GPA 3.0-3.49: | 28% | Live on campus: | 47% |
| GPA 2.0-2.99: | 34% | International: | 1% |

**Basis for selection.** GED not accepted. Minimum 2.0 high school GPA; 2.5 GPA in 16 core classes, for bachelor's degree-seeking students. Open admissions for associate degree applicants over age 18. Some students may be required to take ASSET and/or COMPASS tests for additional course placement. **Learning Disabled:** Contact UAF Disability Services for assistance.

**High school preparation.** 16 units required. Required and recommended units include English 4, mathematics 3, social studies 3, science 3 (laboratory 1), foreign language 2 and academic electives 3. Mathematics should include 3 from algebra, geometry and trigonometry, precalculus or calculus.

**2007-2008 Annual costs.** Tuition/fees: $4,496; $13,466 out-of-state. Estimated course and lab fees: $450 per year. Room/board: $6,640. Books/supplies: $1,300. Personal expenses: $2,250.

**2007-2008 Financial aid. Need-based:** 692 full-time freshmen applied for aid; 319 were judged to have need; 302 of these received aid. Average need met was 74%. Average scholarship/grant was $5,040; average loan $6,712. 29% of total undergraduate aid awarded as scholarships/grants, 71% as loans/jobs. **Non-need-based:** Awarded to 735 full-time undergraduates, including 230 freshmen. Scholarships awarded for academics, art, athletics, leadership, music/drama, ROTC, state residency.

**Application procedures. Admission:** Priority date 2/1; deadline 8/1 (postmark date). $40 fee, may be waived for applicants with need. Application may be submitted online. Admission notification on a rolling basis. **Financial aid:** Priority date 2/15, closing date 7/1. FAFSA required. Applicants notified by 3/1; Applicants notified on a rolling basis starting 3/1; must reply within 2 week(s) of notification.

**Academics.** Student Support Services Program (Federally funded) for students with qualified at-risk status. **Special study options:** Accelerated study, cooperative education, distance learning, double major, dual enrollment of high school students, exchange student, external degree, honors, independent study, internships, semester at sea, student-designed major, study abroad, teacher certification program. Legislative aide intern program, undergraduate research. **Credit/placement by examination:** AP, CLEP, IB, SAT, ACT, institutional tests. 15 credit hours maximum toward associate degree, 30 toward bachelor's. 25% of degree requirements awarded for prior work or life experience. Credit awarded for CEEB Advanced Placement Test scores of 3 or greater CLEP, DANTES-DSST, local credit by exam. **Support services:** Learning center, pre-admission summer program, remedial instruction, study skills assistance, tutoring, writing center.

**Honors college/program.** Minimum composite SAT 1260 (exclusive of Writing) or composite ACT 29 required for incoming freshmen. University GPA greater than 3.5 required for first-semester college sophomores.

**Majors. Area/ethnic studies:** Native American, Russian/Slavic. **Biology:** General. **Business:** Accounting, business admin, managerial economics. **Communications:** General, journalism. **Computer sciences:** Computer science. **Conservation:** General, fisheries, forestry, management/policy, wildlife. **Education:** General, music, physical. **Engineering:** Civil, electrical, geological, geotechnical, industrial, mechanical, mining, petroleum. **English:** English lit, speech/rhetoric. **Foreign languages:** General, Japanese, linguistics, Native American, Russian. **History:** General. **Interdisciplinary:** Biological/physical sciences. **Liberal arts:** Arts/sciences. **Math:** General, applied, statistics. **Philosophy/religion:** Philosophy. **Physical sciences:** Chemistry, geology, physics. **Protective services:** Criminal justice. **Psychology:** General. **Public administration:** Community org/advocacy, social work. **Social sciences:** Anthropology, economics, geography, political science, sociology. **Visual/performing arts:** Art, dramatic, music performance, theater design.

**Most popular majors.** Biology 10%, business/marketing 10%, education 6%, engineering/engineering technologies 9%, natural resources/environmental science 6%, psychology 9%, public administration/social services 7%, social sciences 8%.

**Computing on campus.** 102 workstations in dormitories, library, computer center. Dormitories wired for high-speed internet access and linked to campus network. Commuter students can connect to campus network. Online course registration, online library, helpline, repair service, student web hosting, wireless network available.

**Student life. Freshman orientation:** Mandatory, $30 fee. Preregistration for classes offered. **Policies:** Student organizations must be officially recognized on an annual basis by the UAF Student Activities Office. **Housing:** Coed dorms, special housing for disabled, apartments, substance-free housing available. $260 deposit, deadline 8/1. Alaska Native cultural housing. **Activities:** Bands, campus ministries, choral groups, dance, drama, international student organizations, literary magazine, music ensembles, radio station, student government, student newspaper, symphony orchestra, TV station, American Indian Science and Engineering Society, Black Awareness Student Union, Darwin Society, Japan-Alaska Club, Middle Eastern Dance and Cultural Association, Namaste India, Northern Star Chinese Association, Russian language club, The Gay Club, University Women's Association.

**Athletics.** NCAA. **Intercollegiate:** Basketball, cross-country, ice hockey M, rifle, skiing, swimming W, volleyball W. **Intramural:** Badminton, basketball, bowling, football (non-tackle), ice hockey, lacrosse, racquetball, soccer, softball, swimming, table tennis, tennis, volleyball, water polo. **Team name:** Nanooks.

**Student services.** Alcohol/substance abuse counseling, campus ministries, career counseling, services for economically disadvantaged, student employment services, financial aid counseling, health services, legal services, minority student services, on-campus daycare, personal counseling, placement for graduates, women's services. **Physically disabled:** Services for visually, speech, hearing impaired.

**Contact.** E-mail: admissions@uaf.edu
Phone: (907) 474-7500 Toll-free number: (800) 478-1823
Fax: (907) 474-5379
Tim Stickel, Director of Admissions, University of Alaska Fairbanks, PO Box 757480, Fairbanks, AK 99775-7480

---

## University of Alaska Southeast
**Juneau, Alaska**
www.uas.alaska.edu

CB member
CB code: 4897

- Public 4-year university and liberal arts college
- Commuter campus in large town
- 1,108 degree-seeking undergraduates: 47% part-time, 65% women
- 204 degree-seeking graduate students
- SAT or ACT (ACT writing recommended) required

**General.** Founded in 1972. Regionally accredited. All campuses accessible only by ferry or air. **Degrees:** 108 bachelor's, 83 associate awarded; master's offered. **Location:** Downtown. **Calendar:** Semester, limited summer session. **Full-time faculty:** 107 total; 44% have terminal degrees, 6% minority, 46% women. **Part-time faculty:** 117 total; 3% have terminal degrees, 14% minority, 62% women. **Class size:** 73% < 20, 25% 20-39, less than 1% 40-49, less than 1% 50-99. **Special facilities:** Juneau ice field, Mendenhall glacier, Tongass national forest.

**Freshman class profile.** 298 applied, 150 admitted, 147 enrolled.

| Mid 50% test scores | | | |
|---|---|---|---|
| SAT critical reading: | 490-610 | GPA 2.0-2.99: | 38% |
| SAT math: | 420-560 | Rank in top quarter: | 20% |
| ACT composite: | 21-25 | Rank in top tenth: | 11% |
| GPA 3.50 or higher: | 19% | Return as sophomores: | 55% |
| GPA 3.0-3.49: | 36% | Out-of-state: | 8% |
| | | International: | 1% |

**Basis for selection.** Open admission, but selective for some programs. High school record most important. Students not meeting BA requirements counseled to AA or certificate program with possibility of later transfer to BA program. Some BA programs admit students as pre-majors and upon satisfying prerequisites may be admitted to major. Financial statement and immunization records required of international applicants as well as a statement of educational equivalency written in English. SAT or ACT required for all bachelor degree programs. **Homeschooled:** Student must graduate from an accredited homeschool program, otherwise GED required.

**High school preparation.** Recommended units include English 4, mathematics 2, social studies 3, science 1 (laboratory 1).

**2007-2008 Annual costs.** Tuition/fees: $4,368; $13,338 out-of-state. Tuition reported is for lower division offerings; for upper division, $123 per credit. Room/board: $6,090. Books/supplies: $550. Personal expenses: $1,643.

**2007-2008 Financial aid. Need-based:** 38% of total undergraduate aid awarded as scholarships/grants, 62% as loans/jobs. **Non-need-based:** Scholarships awarded for academics, leadership. **Additional information:** Transfer, continuing, and freshman scholarship deadline March 1.

**Application procedures. Admission:** Priority date 8/1; no deadline. $40 fee, may be waived for applicants with need. Application may be submitted online. Admission notification on a rolling basis. Housing deposit refundable if written letter of cancellation is provided prior to July 1st. **Financial aid:** Priority date 6/1; no closing date. FAFSA required. Applicants notified on a rolling basis starting 2/15; must reply within 3 week(s) of notification.

**Academics. Special study options:** Combined bachelor's/graduate degree, cooperative education, distance learning, dual enrollment of high school students, exchange student, external degree, independent study, internships, study abroad, teacher certification program. **Credit/placement by examination:** AP, CLEP, institutional tests. 15 credit hours maximum toward associate degree, 30 toward bachelor's. **Support services:** Learning center, pre-admission summer program, remedial instruction, study skills assistance, tutoring, writing center.

**Majors. Biology:** General, marine. **Business:** General, accounting, management science, marketing. **Communications:** General. **Computer sciences:** Networking. **Conservation:** Environmental science. **Education:** Elementary. **English:** English lit. **Liberal arts:** Arts/sciences. **Math:** General. **Social sciences:** General, political science. **Visual/performing arts:** Art.

**Most popular majors.** Biology 8%, business/marketing 30%, liberal arts 40%, social sciences 8%.

**Computing on campus.** 225 workstations in dormitories, library, computer center, student center. Dormitories wired for high-speed internet access and linked to campus network. Commuter students can connect to campus network. Online course registration, online library, helpline, repair service, student web hosting, wireless network available.

**Student life. Freshman orientation:** Mandatory, $75 fee. Preregistration for classes offered. 3 day orientation including outdoor experiences. **Housing:** Coed dorms, special housing for disabled, apartments, substance-free housing available. $200 deposit, deadline 4/1. **Activities:** Dance, student government, student newspaper, Global Connections Club, Amnesty International, backcountry skiing club, gay organization, swing dancing club, rock climbing club, English club, Wooch Een Native student organization.

**Athletics. Intramural:** Badminton, basketball, football (non-tackle) M, racquetball, skiing, softball, tennis, volleyball, weight lifting.

**Student services.** Adult student services, alcohol/substance abuse counseling, career counseling, student employment services, financial aid counseling, health services, minority student services, personal counseling, placement for graduates, veterans' counselor. **Physically disabled:** Services for visually, hearing impaired.

**Contact.** E-mail: admissions@uas.alaska.edu
Phone: (907) 796-6100 Toll-free number: (877) 465-4827
Fax: (907) 796-6365
Shontay King, Admissions Director, University of Alaska Southeast, 11120 Glacier Highway, Juneau, AK 99801-8681

# Arizona

## American Indian College of the Assemblies of God

**Phoenix, Arizona**
www.aicag.edu

CB code: 2597

◗ Private 4-year Bible and teachers college affiliated with Assemblies of God

◗ Residential campus in very large city

**General.** Founded in 1957. Regionally accredited. **Location:** 15 miles from downtown. **Calendar:** Semester.

**Annual costs/financial aid.** Tuition/fees (2007-2008): $6,574. Room/board: $4,680. Books/supplies: $500. Personal expenses: $2,570.

**Contact.** Phone: (602) 943-335 ext. 232
Director of Admissions, 10020 North 15th Avenue, Phoenix, AZ 85021-2199

## Arizona State University

**Tempe, Arizona**
www.asu.edu

CB member
CB code: 4007

◗ Public 4-year university

◗ Commuter campus in small city

◗ 38,597 degree-seeking undergraduates: 23% part-time, 49% women, 4% African American, 6% Asian American, 13% Hispanic American, 2% Native American, 3% international

◗ 8,614 degree-seeking graduate students

◗ 95% of applicants admitted

◗ SAT or ACT (ACT writing optional) required

◗ 56% graduate within 6 years

**General.** Founded in 1885. Regionally accredited. **Degrees:** 7,282 bachelor's awarded; master's, doctoral, first professional offered. **ROTC:** Army, Air Force. **Calendar:** Semester, extensive summer session. **Full-time faculty:** 1,748 total; 22% minority, 36% women. **Part-time faculty:** 238 total; 13% minority, 46% women. **Special facilities:** Center for meteorite studies, solar energy research laboratory, center for solid state science, art collections, herbarium, biodesign institute, AZ center for medieval and renaissance studies, global institute of sustainability, upward bound, thermal emission imaging system, North American center for transborder studies, Mars global surveyor TES project, KAET-TV (public television station), institute for computer and information science and engineering, institute for manufacturing enterprise systems.

**Freshman class profile.** 20,290 applied, 19,259 admitted, 7,740 enrolled.

| Mid 50% test scores | | | |
|---|---|---|---|
| SAT critical reading: | 470-600 | Rank in top tenth: | 27% |
| SAT math: | 490-620 | Return as sophomores: | 78% |
| ACT composite: | 20-26 | Out-of-state: | 36% |
| Rank in top quarter: | 52% | International: | 2% |

**Basis for selection.** In-state applicants: rank in top 25% of class, 3.0 GPA, minimum 22 ACT or 1040 SAT (exclusive of writing) required. Out-of-state: 24 ACT or 1110 SAT (exclusive of Writing) required. Additional requirements for some programs. Auditions required of music, dance, theater majors. Portfolios required of graphic design, architecture, environmental design majors.

**High school preparation.** 16 units required. Required units include English 4, mathematics 4, social studies 1, history 1, science 3 (laboratory 3) and foreign language 2. 1 unit American history recommended, 1 fine arts required. 2 of the same foreign languages recommended for College of Liberal Arts and Sciences. 1 each physics and chemistry required for nursing. 4 mathematics, including calculus recommended for engineering.

**2007-2008 Annual costs.** Tuition/fees: $4,971; $17,003 out-of-state. Room/board: $7,320.

**2006-2007 Financial aid. Need-based:** 3,771 full-time freshmen applied for aid; 2,628 were judged to have need; 2,628 of these received aid. Average need met was 61%. Average scholarship/grant was $6,447; average loan $2,665. 52% of total undergraduate aid awarded as scholarships/grants, 48% as loans/jobs. **Non-need-based:** Awarded to 6,340 full-time undergraduates, including 2,164 freshmen. Scholarships awarded for academics, art, athletics, leadership, music/drama, ROTC.

**Application procedures. Admission:** Priority date 2/1; no deadline. $25 fee ($50 out-of-state). Application may be submitted online. Admission notification on a rolling basis. Apply for housing as soon as admitted. **Financial aid:** Priority date 3/1; no closing date. FAFSA required. Applicants notified on a rolling basis.

**Academics. Special study options:** Accelerated study, cooperative education, distance learning, double major, exchange student, honors, independent study, internships, study abroad, teacher certification program. **Credit/placement by examination:** AP, CLEP, IB, SAT, ACT, institutional tests. 60 credit hours maximum toward bachelor's degree. **Support services:** Learning center, study skills assistance, tutoring, writing center.

**Honors college/program.** Rank in top 5% of high school class, 1300 SAT (exclusive of writing) or 29 ACT required. Separate application required. Dual enrollment in college of student's disciplinary major.

**Majors. Architecture:** Architecture, interior, landscape, urban/community planning. **Area/ethnic studies:** African-American, Hispanic-American/Latino/Chicano, Native American, women's. **Biology:** General, biochemistry, biomedical sciences, botany, conservation, microbiology, molecular, zoology. **Business:** Accounting, business admin, construction management, finance, management information systems, marketing, purchasing. **Communications:** General, journalism, radio/tv. **Computer sciences:** Computer science. **Education:** General, art, biology, business, chemistry, drama/dance, early childhood, elementary, English, family/consumer sciences, foreign languages, French, geography, German, history, mathematics, music, physical, physics, secondary, social studies, Spanish, special. **Engineering:** General, aerospace, biomedical, chemical, civil, computer, electrical, industrial, materials, mechanical. **English:** English lit. **Family/consumer sciences:** Family resources. **Foreign languages:** East Asian, French, German, Italian, Russian, Spanish. **Health:** Clinical lab science, communication disorders, music therapy. **History:** General. **Interdisciplinary:** Global studies. **Legal studies:** Prelaw. **Liberal arts:** Arts/sciences, humanities. **Math:** General, computational. **Parks/recreation:** Exercise sciences. **Philosophy/religion:** Philosophy, religion. **Physical sciences:** Chemistry, geology, physics. **Protective services:** Criminal justice. **Psychology:** General. **Social sciences:** Anthropology, economics, geography, political science, sociology. **Visual/performing arts:** Art, dance, dramatic, film/cinema, graphic design, industrial design, music performance, music theory/composition. **Other:** Design and applied arts.

**Most popular majors.** Business/marketing 17%, communications/journalism 10%, education 9%, engineering/engineering technologies 8%, interdisciplinary studies 11%, social sciences 8%, visual/performing arts 7%.

**Computing on campus.** Dormitories wired for high-speed internet access and linked to campus network. Commuter students can connect to campus network. Online course registration, online library, helpline, wireless network available.

**Student life. Freshman orientation:** Available. Preregistration for classes offered. Charge varies by orientation program. **Housing:** Coed dorms, special housing for disabled, apartments, fraternity/sorority housing available. $125 nonrefundable deposit. **Activities:** Bands, campus ministries, choral groups, dance, drama, film society, international student organizations, literary magazine, music ensembles, musical theater, opera, radio station, student government, student newspaper, symphony orchestra, TV station, 579 organizations.

**Athletics.** NCAA. **Intercollegiate:** Baseball M, basketball, cross-country, diving, football (tackle) M, golf, gymnastics W, soccer W, softball W, swimming, tennis, track and field, volleyball W, water polo W, wrestling M. **Intramural:** Basketball, cross-country, football (non-tackle), golf, racquetball, soccer, softball, table tennis, tennis, volleyball. **Team name:** Sun Devils.

**Student services.** Adult student services, career counseling, student employment services, health services, on-campus daycare, personal counseling, placement for graduates, veterans' counselor. **Physically disabled:** Services for visually, speech, hearing impaired.

**Contact.** E-mail: ugradinq@asu.edu
Phone: (480) 965-7788 Fax: (480) 965-3610
Martha Byrd, Dean, Undergraduate Admissions, Arizona State University, Box 870112, Tempe, AZ 85287-0112

## Arizona State University West
**Phoenix, Arizona**
**www.west.asu.edu** CB code: 3882

- Public 4-year university
- Commuter campus in small city
- 5,860 degree-seeking undergraduates: 27% part-time, 64% women, 5% African American, 5% Asian American, 20% Hispanic American, 3% Native American, 1% international
- 1,029 degree-seeking graduate students
- 77% of applicants admitted
- SAT or ACT (ACT writing recommended) required
- 58% graduate within 6 years

**General.** Regionally accredited. **Degrees:** 1,574 bachelor's awarded; master's, doctoral offered. **Calendar:** Semester, limited summer session. **Full-time faculty:** 264 total; 55% women. **Part-time faculty:** 219 total; 66% women. **Class size:** 31% < 20, 52% 20-39, 9% 40-49, 8% 50-99, 1% >100.

**Freshman class profile.** 1,922 applied, 1,485 admitted, 607 enrolled.

| Mid 50% test scores | | | |
|---|---|---|---|
| SAT critical reading: | 450-560 | Rank in top quarter: | 61% |
| SAT math: | 440-570 | Rank in top tenth: | 28% |
| ACT composite: | 19-25 | End year in good standing: | 78% |
| GPA 3.50 or higher: | 45% | Return as sophomores: | 75% |
| GPA 3.0-3.49: | 35% | Out-of-state: | 12% |
| GPA 2.0-2.99: | 19% | Live on campus: | 24% |

**Basis for selection.** Applicant must rank in top quarter of class, have minimum 22 ACT score or 1040 SAT score (exclusive of Writing), and minimum 3.0 GPA. Out-of-state students must have minimum 24 ACT score or 1110 SAT score.

**High school preparation.** 16 units required. Required units include English 4, mathematics 4, social studies 1, history 1, science 3 (laboratory 3) and foreign language 2. One fine arts.

**2007-2008 Annual costs.** Tuition/fees: $4,766; $16,999 out-of-state. Books/supplies: $950. Personal expenses: $1,680.

**2006-2007 Financial aid. Need-based:** 309 full-time freshmen applied for aid; 251 were judged to have need; 251 of these received aid. Average need met was 64%. Average scholarship/grant was $6,307; average loan $2,510. 48% of total undergraduate aid awarded as scholarships/grants, 52% as loans/jobs. **Non-need-based:** Awarded to 395 full-time undergraduates, including 141 freshmen. Scholarships awarded for academics.

**Application procedures. Admission:** Priority date 2/1; no deadline. $25 fee ($50 out-of-state). Application may be submitted online. Admission notification on a rolling basis. **Financial aid:** Priority date 2/1, closing date 3/1. FAFSA required. Applicants notified on a rolling basis starting 3/15; must reply within 4 week(s) of notification.

**Academics. Special study options:** Distance learning, double major, dual enrollment of high school students, honors, independent study, internships, student-designed major, study abroad, teacher certification program. **Credit/placement by examination:** AP, CLEP, IB, SAT, ACT, institutional tests. 60 credit hours maximum toward bachelor's degree. **Support services:** Learning center, study skills assistance, tutoring, writing center.

**Honors college/program.** GPA of 3.8 and above, top 5 percent of high school graduating class, 29 composite ACT score or a 1300 composite SAT score (exclusive of Writing). For transfer students, enter at junior level with a cumulative GPA of 3.5 or better. Freshmen must complete 36 hours of honors coursework and transfer students must complete 18 hours of honors coursework.

**Majors. Area/ethnic studies:** American, women's. **Biology:** General. **Business:** Accounting, international, marketing. **Communications:** General. **Education:** Early childhood, elementary, secondary, special. **English:** English lit. **Foreign languages:** Spanish. **History:** General. **Parks/recreation:** General. **Protective services:** Law enforcement admin. **Psychology:** General. **Public administration:** Social work. **Social sciences:** General, political science, sociology. **Visual/performing arts:** General. **Other:** Ethnic, culture, minority & gender studies.

**Most popular majors.** Business/marketing 25%, communications/journalism 7%, education 24%, psychology 8%, security/protective services 9%, social sciences 6%.

**Computing on campus.** 766 workstations in dormitories, library, computer center. Dormitories wired for high-speed internet access and linked to campus network. Commuter students can connect to campus network. Online course registration, online library, helpline, student web hosting, wireless network available.

**Student life. Freshman orientation:** Mandatory. Preregistration for classes offered. Provides students with the opportunity to meet academic advisors, select and register for classes, investigate financial aid, discover campus resources/services and tour campus. **Housing:** Special housing for disabled, apartments, substance-free housing, available. $275 partly refundable deposit. **Activities:** Drama, literary magazine, student government, student newspaper, Latter-Day Saints student association, Catholic student association, Young Life, College Republicans at ASU's West campus, Asian Student Union, Native American student organization, Black Student Union, Hispanic Honor Society/Latino Students Union, Cancer Awareness Resources Education, Animal Welfare Association.

**Student services.** Career counseling, services for economically disadvantaged, student employment services, financial aid counseling, health services, minority student services, on-campus daycare, personal counseling, veterans' counselor, women's services. **Physically disabled:** Services for visually, speech, hearing impaired.

**Contact.** E-mail: west-info@asu.edu
Phone: (602) 543-8203 Fax: (602) 543-8312
Thomas Cabot, Assistant Dean Enrollment Services, Arizona State University West, PO Box 37100 MC 0250, Phoenix, AZ 85069-7100

## Art Center Design College
**Tucson, Arizona**
**www.theartcenter.edu** CB code: 3037

- For-profit 4-year visual arts college
- Commuter campus in very large city
- 318 degree-seeking undergraduates
- SAT or ACT (ACT writing optional), application essay, interview required

**General. Degrees:** 29 bachelor's awarded. **Calendar:** Trimester, extensive summer session. **Full-time faculty:** 18 total. **Part-time faculty:** 30 total. **Class size:** 100% 20-39.

**Freshman class profile.**

| Mid 50% test scores | | | |
|---|---|---|---|
| SAT critical reading: | 450-530 | SAT math: | 380-470 |
| | | ACT composite: | 17-23 |

**Basis for selection.** Application for admission includes high school transcripts (GED accepted), ACT or SAT scores, essay, interview, career commitment form, and art work for graphic design and animation programs.

**2007-2008 Annual costs.** Tuition/fees: $15,360. Books/supplies: $1,250. Personal expenses: $3,204.

**Financial aid.** All financial aid based on need.

**Application procedures. Admission:** No deadline. $25 fee, may be waived for applicants with need. Application may be submitted online. Admission notification on a rolling basis. **Financial aid:** No deadline. FAFSA required.

**Academics. Special study options:** Double major, independent study, internships. **Credit/placement by examination:** AP, CLEP, SAT, ACT, institutional tests. **Support services:** Learning center, reduced course load, remedial instruction, study skills assistance, tutoring, writing center.

**Majors. Architecture:** Landscape. **Business:** Marketing. **Communications technology:** Animation/special effects. **Visual/performing arts:** Graphic design, illustration, interior design, photography, studio arts. **Other:** Advertising.

**Computing on campus.** Online course registration, wireless network available.

**Student life. Freshman orientation:** Mandatory. Preregistration for classes offered.

**Student services.** Adult student services, career counseling, student employment services, financial aid counseling, personal counseling, placement for graduates, veterans' counselor.

**Contact.** E-mail: inquire@theartcenter.edu
Phone: (520) 325-0123 Toll-free number: (800) 825-8753
Colleen Gimbel-Froebe, Director Admissions and Placement, Art Center Design College, 2525 North Country Club Road, Tucson, AZ 85716

## Art Institute of Phoenix
**Phoenix, Arizona**
**www.artinstitutes.edu/phoenix/**                    CB code: 4003

- For-profit 3-year culinary school and visual arts college
- Commuter campus in very large city
- 1,109 degree-seeking undergraduates
- Application essay, interview required

**General.** Accredited by ACICS. **Degrees:** 204 bachelor's, 39 associate awarded. **Calendar:** Quarter, extensive summer session. **Full-time faculty:** 42 total. **Part-time faculty:** 45 total. **Special facilities:** Culinary labs, video studio, computer labs, editing suites, sound lab.

**Freshman class profile.**

| | | | |
|---|---|---|---|
| Out-of-state: | 31% | Live on campus: | 25% |

**Basis for selection.** High school diploma or GED required; high school GPA considered. TOEFL scores used and required.

**2007-2008 Annual costs.** Tuition/fees: $12,240.

**Application procedures. Admission:** Closing date 10/13 (receipt date). $50 fee. Application may be submitted online. Admission notification on a rolling basis. **Financial aid:** No deadline. FAFSA required.

**Academics. Special study options:** Distance learning, independent study, internships, study abroad. **Credit/placement by examination:** AP, CLEP, IB, SAT, ACT, institutional tests. **Support services:** Learning center, reduced course load, remedial instruction, tutoring.

**Majors. Communications technology:** Animation/special effects. **Computer sciences:** Web page design, webmaster. **Personal/culinary services:** Culinary arts. **Visual/performing arts:** Cinematography, commercial/advertising art, graphic design, interior design.

**Student life. Freshman orientation:** Mandatory. Preregistration for classes offered. **Housing:** Apartments available. **Activities:** Film society.

**Student services.** Adult student services, career counseling, student employment services, financial aid counseling, personal counseling, placement for graduates.

**Contact.** E-mail: aipxadm@aii.edu
Phone: (602) 331-7500 Toll-free number: (800) 474-2479
Fax: (602) 331-5301
Mary Durant, Senior Director of Admissions, Art Institute of Phoenix, 2233 West Dunlap Avenue, Phoenix, AZ 85021-2859

## Art Institute of Tucson
**Tucson, Arizona**
**www.tucsondesigncollege.edu**

- For-profit 4-year liberal arts and technical college
- Residential campus in very large city

**General.** Accredited by ACICS. **Location:** 115 miles from Phoenix. **Calendar:** Quarter.

**Annual costs/financial aid.** Programs are continuous at $250 per credit hour.

**Contact.** Phone: (520) 881-2900
Director of Academics, 1030 North Alvernon Way, Tucson, AZ 85711

## Brown Mackie College: Tucson
**Tucson, Arizona**
**www.chap-col.edu**                    CB code: 3458

- For-profit 4-year career college
- Commuter campus in very large city
- 270 degree-seeking undergraduates
- Interview required

**General.** Accredited by ACICS. **Degrees:** 65 bachelor's, 110 associate awarded. **Calendar:** Continuous. **Full-time faculty:** 20 total. **Part-time faculty:** 5 total; 20% minority, 20% women.

**Basis for selection.** Open admission. **Homeschooled:** State high school equivalency certificate required.

**2007-2008 Annual costs.** Cost of continuous-calendar certificate, associate and bachelor programs is $250 per credit hour.

**Application procedures. Admission:** No deadline. No application fee.

**Academics. Special study options:** Internships. **Credit/placement by examination:** CLEP. **Support services:** Remedial instruction, tutoring.

**Majors. Business:** Accounting, business admin. **Computer sciences:** Computer science.

**Computing on campus.** 200 workstations in library.

**Student services.** Career counseling, financial aid counseling, personal counseling, placement for graduates, veterans' counselor.

**Contact.** Phone: (520) 327-6866
Holly Helscher, President, Brown Mackie College: Tucson, 4585 East Speedway Boulevard, Suite 204, Tucson, AZ 85712

## College of the Humanities and Sciences
**Tempe, Arizona**
**www.chumsci.edu/**

- For-profit 4-year liberal arts college
- Small city

**General.** Accredited by DETC. **Calendar:** Continuous.

**Annual costs/financial aid.** Per-credit-hour charge (tuition only) is $225.

**Contact.** Phone: (877) 248-6724
Registrar, 1105 East Broadway Road, Tempe, AZ 85282

## Collins College
**Tempe, Arizona**
**www.collinscollege.edu**                    CB code: 2174

- For-profit 4-year visual arts and technical college
- Commuter campus in small city

**General.** Founded in 1978. Accredited by ACCSCT. **Location:** 5 miles from Phoenix. **Calendar:** Continuous.

**Annual costs/financial aid.** Tuition/fees (2007-2008): $14,550. Required fees vary by program. Books/supplies: $1,800.

**Contact.** Phone: (480) 966-3000
Vice President of Admissions and Marketing, 1140 South Priest Drive, Tempe, AZ 85281

## DeVry University: Phoenix
**Phoenix, Arizona**
**www.devry.edu**                    CB code: 4277

- For-profit 4-year university
- Commuter campus in large city
- 1,017 degree-seeking undergraduates: 28% part-time, 21% women, 9% African American, 6% Asian American, 19% Hispanic American, 7% Native American, 1% international
- 173 degree-seeking graduate students
- Interview required
- 36% graduate within 6 years

**General.** Founded in 1967. Regionally accredited. **Degrees:** 233 bachelor's, 34 associate awarded; master's offered. **ROTC:** Air Force. **Calendar:** Semester, extensive summer session. **Full-time faculty:** 35 total; 23% women. **Part-time faculty:** 31 total; 36% minority, 26% women.

**Freshman class profile.** 243 enrolled.

| | | | |
|---|---|---|---|
| Return as sophomores: | 52% | Out-of-state: | 12% |

**Basis for selection.** Applicants must have high school diploma or equivalent or a degree from accredited postsecondary institution, demonstrate proficiency in basic college-level skills through SAT or ACT scores or institution-administered placement exams, and be at least 17 years of age on the first day of classes. New students may enter at beginning of any semester. CPT accepted.

**High school preparation.** Required units include mathematics 1.

**2007-2008 Annual costs.** Tuition/fees: $13,220. Books/supplies: $1,300. Personal expenses: $5,082.

**Financial aid.** All financial aid based on need.

**Application procedures. Admission:** No deadline. $50 fee. Application may be submitted online. Admission notification on a rolling basis. **Financial aid:** No deadline. FAFSA required. Applicants notified on a rolling basis.

**Academics. Special study options:** Accelerated study, cooperative education, distance learning, weekend college. **Credit/placement by examination:** CLEP, institutional tests. **Support services:** Learning center, remedial instruction, tutoring.

**Majors. Biology:** Biomedical sciences. **Business:** Business admin, human resources, management information systems, operations. **Computer sciences:** General, game design, information systems, networking, security. **Engineering technology:** General, computer, electrical.

**Most popular majors.** Business/marketing 44%, computer/information sciences 31%, engineering/engineering technologies 25%.

**Computing on campus.** 436 workstations in library, computer center. Online course registration, online library, helpline available.

**Student life. Freshman orientation:** Mandatory. **Housing:** Private apartments, student-plan housing, private rooms. **Activities:** Student government, student newspaper, Institute of Electrical and Electronics Engineers, Campus Crusaders for Christ, travel club, Sigma Beta Delta, computer society, DeVry inventors club, sports compact car club, Tau Alpha Pi, hockey league.

**Athletics. Intramural:** Field hockey M, golf, softball.

**Student services.** Career counseling, student employment services, financial aid counseling, placement for graduates, veterans' counselor. **Physically disabled:** Services for visually, hearing impaired.

**Contact.** E-mail: admissions@phx.devry.edu
Phone: (602) 870-9201 Toll-free number: (800) 528-0250
Fax: (602) 331-1494
Jerry Driskill, Director of Admissions, DeVry University: Phoenix, 2149 West Dunlap Avenue, Phoenix, AZ 85021-2995

---

## Embry-Riddle Aeronautical University: Prescott Campus
Prescott, Arizona
www.embryriddle.edu          CB code: 4305

- Private 4-year university
- Residential campus in large town
- 1,667 degree-seeking undergraduates: 7% part-time, 17% women, 3% African American, 7% Asian American, 8% Hispanic American, 1% Native American, 4% international
- 31 degree-seeking graduate students
- 85% of applicants admitted
- SAT or ACT (ACT writing optional) required
- 50% graduate within 6 years

**General.** Founded in 1978. Regionally accredited. Eastern residential campus in Daytona Beach, Florida. More than 130 continuing education centers located throughout the United States and Europe. **Degrees:** 320 bachelor's awarded; master's offered. **ROTC:** Army, Air Force. **Location:** 100 miles from Phoenix. **Calendar:** Semester, extensive summer session. **Full-time faculty:** 102 total; 69% have terminal degrees, 9% minority, 19% women. **Part-time faculty:** 28 total; 21% have terminal degrees, 7% minority, 39% women. **Class size:** 51% < 20, 44% 20-39, 3% 40-49, 1% 50-99. **Special facilities:** Supersonic wind tunnel, fleet of 40 aircraft, engineering and technical center, aviation safety center.

**Freshman class profile.** 1,288 applied, 1,096 admitted, 400 enrolled.

| Mid 50% test scores | | | |
|---|---|---|---|
| SAT critical reading: | 480-590 | Rank in top tenth: | 21% |
| SAT math: | 510-610 | Return as sophomores: | 76% |
| ACT composite: | 22-28 | Out-of-state: | 85% |
| GPA 3.50 or higher: | 51% | Live on campus: | 96% |
| GPA 3.0-3.49: | 31% | International: | 3% |
| GPA 2.0-2.99: | 18% | Fraternities: | 15% |
| Rank in top quarter: | 52% | Sororities: | 13% |

**Basis for selection.** High school GPA, class rank, test scores most important. Specific requirements vary by degree program. Flight program applicants must pass medical examination for Class I or II Federal Aviation Administration Medical Certificate at least 60 calendar days prior to enrollment. Interview and essay recommended.

**High school preparation.** 16 units required; 18 recommended. Required and recommended units include English 4, mathematics 3-4, social studies 2, history 1, science 2-3 (laboratory 2-3), foreign language 2 and academic electives 4.

**2008-2009 Annual costs.** Tuition/fees: $27,180. Room/board: $7,700. Books/supplies: $1,040. Personal expenses: $1,448.

**2007-2008 Financial aid. Need-based:** 340 full-time freshmen applied for aid; 278 were judged to have need; 278 of these received aid. Average scholarship/grant was $10,344; average loan $4,202. 54% of total undergraduate aid awarded as scholarships/grants, 46% as loans/jobs. **Non-need-based:** Awarded to 63 full-time undergraduates, including 16 freshmen. Scholarships awarded for academics, alumni affiliation, athletics, leadership, ROTC.

**Application procedures. Admission:** Priority date 1/15; no deadline. $50 fee, may be waived for applicants with need. Application may be submitted online. Admission notification on a rolling basis beginning on or about 11/1. Must reply by May 1 or within 2 week(s) if notified thereafter. Application closing date 60 days prior to start of term. Early application encouraged; available facilities limit enrollment in some programs. **Financial aid:** No deadline. FAFSA required. Applicants notified on a rolling basis starting 3/1; must reply within 4 week(s) of notification.

**Academics. Special study options:** Accelerated study, cooperative education, distance learning, double major, dual enrollment of high school students, ESL, exchange student, honors, independent study, internships, student-designed major, study abroad. Flight training. **Credit/placement by examination:** AP, CLEP, IB, SAT, ACT, institutional tests. 15 credit hours maximum toward associate degree, 30 toward bachelor's. **Support services:** Remedial instruction, study skills assistance, tutoring.

**Majors. Engineering:** General, aerospace, computer, electrical, software. **Interdisciplinary:** Science/society. **Physical sciences:** Physics. **Social sciences:** International relations. **Transportation:** Airline/commercial pilot, aviation.

**Most popular majors.** Engineering/engineering technologies 26%, social sciences 11%, visual/performing arts 56%.

**Computing on campus.** 450 workstations in library, computer center, student center. Dormitories linked to campus network. Helpline available.

**Student life. Freshman orientation:** Available. Preregistration for classes offered. **Housing:** Guaranteed on-campus for freshmen. Coed dorms, apartments available. $250 fully refundable deposit, deadline 7/15. **Activities:** Dance, literary magazine, music ensembles, radio station, student government, student newspaper, Rangers (Army ROTC), Student Activities Association, Angel Flight/Silver Wings, Residence Halls Association, Arnold Air Society, Golden Eagles Flight Team, Greeks, Aerobatic Club, Japanese Anime/Manga.

**Athletics.** NAIA. **Intercollegiate:** Soccer, volleyball W, wrestling M. **Intramural:** Basketball, bowling, cross-country, football (non-tackle), golf, racquetball, soccer, softball, swimming, table tennis, tennis, track and field, volleyball, weight lifting. **Team name:** Eagles.

**Student services.** Adult student services, career counseling, student employment services, health services, personal counseling, placement for graduates, veterans' counselor. **Physically disabled:** Services for visually, speech, hearing impaired.

**Contact.** E-mail: pradmit@erau.edu
Phone: (928) 777-6600 Toll-free number: (800) 888-3728
Fax: (928) 777-6606
Bill Thompson, Director of Admissions and Enrollment Management, Embry-Riddle Aeronautical University: Prescott Campus, 3700 North Willow Creek Road, Prescott, AZ 86301-3720

# Grand Canyon University
**Phoenix, Arizona**
www.gcu.edu/clgbrd                         **CB code: 4331**

- For-profit 4-year university
- Commuter campus in very large city
- 4,803 degree-seeking undergraduates: 64% part-time, 71% women, 3% African American, 1% Asian American, 3% Hispanic American, 1% international
- 8,611 graduate students

**General.** Founded in 1949. Regionally accredited. **Degrees:** 683 bachelor's awarded; master's offered. **ROTC:** Army. **Calendar:** Semester, limited summer session. **Full-time faculty:** 52 total. **Part-time faculty:** 346 total. **Class size:** 71% < 20, 29% 20-39. **Special facilities:** Cadaver laboratory.

**Freshman class profile.** 467 enrolled.

**Basis for selection.** Open admission, but selective for some programs. Selective admission to nursing program. **Homeschooled:** Transcript of courses and grades required.

**High school preparation.** Recommended units include English 4, mathematics 4, social studies 2, science 3 (laboratory 1) and foreign language 1.

**2008-2009 Annual costs.** Tuition/fees (projected): $16,030. Books/supplies: $1,680.

**Financial aid. Non-need-based:** Scholarships awarded for academics, athletics, leadership, religious affiliation, ROTC.

**Application procedures. Admission:** No deadline. $100 fee, may be waived for applicants with need. Application may be submitted online. Admission notification on a rolling basis. **Financial aid:** No deadline. FAFSA required. Applicants notified on a rolling basis.

**Academics. Special study options:** Accelerated study, combined bachelor's/graduate degree, cooperative education, distance learning, double major, dual enrollment of high school students, ESL, exchange student, honors, independent study, internships, liberal arts/career combination, study abroad, teacher certification program. **Credit/placement by examination:** AP, CLEP, IB. 30 credit hours maximum toward bachelor's degree. **Support services:** Learning center, reduced course load, remedial instruction, tutoring, writing center.

**Majors. Biology:** General. **Business:** Accounting, business admin, entrepreneurial studies, marketing. **Communications:** General, public relations. **Education:** General, biology, chemistry, elementary, English, mathematics, physical, secondary, special. **English:** English lit. **Health:** Athletic training, nursing (RN). **History:** General. **Parks/recreation:** General, sports admin. **Philosophy/religion:** Religion. **Protective services:** Criminal justice, firefighting. **Psychology:** General. **Social sciences:** Sociology. **Theology:** Bible. **Other:** Medical imaging.

**Most popular majors.** Biology 6%, business/marketing 8%, communications/journalism 8%, education 21%, health sciences 8%, social sciences 6%, visual/performing arts 13%.

**Computing on campus.** 65 workstations in library, computer center. Dormitories wired for high-speed internet access and linked to campus network. Commuter students can connect to campus network. Online course registration, online library, helpline, wireless network available.

**Student life. Freshman orientation:** Available. Preregistration for classes offered. Overview of student life, financial aid, academic advising, and payment options. **Policies:** No alcohol and/or candles are allowed. Smoking allowed outdoors only. **Housing:** Single-sex dorms, apartments, substance-free housing available. **Activities:** Bands, choral groups, drama, literary magazine, music ensembles, musical theater, opera, student government, student newspaper, symphony orchestra, TV station, Baptist Student Union, international student organizations, honors organizations, committee on world awareness, professional clubs, Christ-purposed relationships, ethnic diversity in Christ, wildlife society, student health advocates.

**Athletics.** NCAA. **Intercollegiate:** Baseball M, basketball, cross-country, golf, lacrosse M, soccer, softball W, swimming, tennis W, volleyball W, wrestling M. **Intramural:** Basketball, football (non-tackle), softball, volleyball. **Team name:** Lopes.

**Student services.** Campus ministries, career counseling, student employment services, financial aid counseling, health services, personal counseling, placement for graduates, veterans' counselor. **Physically disabled:** Services for visually, hearing impaired.

**Contact.** E-mail: admissionsonline@gcu.edu
Phone: (888) 261-2393 Toll-free number: (888) 261-2393
Fax: (602) 589-2017
Karilyn VanOosten, Director of Admissions, Grand Canyon University, 3300 West Camelback Road, Phoenix, AZ 85017

# International Import-Export Institute
**Phoenix, Arizona**
www.iiei.edu

- For-profit 4-year virtual university, business and career college
- Commuter campus in very large city
- 50 degree-seeking undergraduates

**General.** Accredited by DETC. **Degrees:** 6 bachelor's awarded. **Calendar:** Semester, extensive summer session. **Part-time faculty:** 60 total.

**Freshman class profile.**

End year in good standing:   94%      Return as sophomores:   91%

**Basis for selection.** Open admission.

**2007-2008 Annual costs.** Three-week courses range in cost from $440-$563; Six-week courses range in cost from $785-$1,045.

**Application procedures. Admission:** No deadline. $50 fee. Application may be submitted online. Admission notification on a rolling basis.

**Academics. Special study options:** Accelerated study. **Credit/placement by examination:** CLEP, IB.

**Computing on campus.** PC or laptop required. Online library, helpline available.

**Student life. Activities:** Student newspaper.

**Contact.** E-mail: iadmissions@expandglobal.com
Phone: (602) 648-5750 Toll-free number: (800) 474-8013
Fax: (62) 648-5755
International Import-Export Institute, 11225 North 28th Drive Suite B201, Phoenix, AZ 85029

# International Institute of the Americas: Mesa
**Mesa, Arizona**
www.iia.edu                              **CB code: 3455**

- Private 4-year branch campus college
- Commuter campus in very large city
- 133 degree-seeking undergraduates
- Interview required

**General.** Accredited by ACICS. Institution has three campuses in Arizona - Phoenix, Mesa, Tucson and one in Albuquerque, New Mexico. **Degrees:** 6 bachelor's, 25 associate awarded. **Location:** 5 miles from Phoenix. **Calendar:** Continuous, extensive summer session. **Full-time faculty:** 8 total; 50% have terminal degrees, 50% women. **Part-time faculty:** 4 total; 25% have terminal degrees, 50% women.

**Basis for selection.** Open admission, but selective for some programs. Selective criteria for some programs.

**2008-2009 Annual costs.** Tuition/fees (projected): $11,400. Tuition and fees may vary by program.

**Financial aid.** All financial aid based on need.

**Application procedures. Admission:** No deadline. $200 fee. Application must be submitted on paper. **Financial aid:** FAFSA, institutional form required.

**Academics. Special study options:** Distance learning. **Credit/placement by examination:** CLEP. **Support services:** Learning center.

**Majors. Business:** Business admin.

**Computing on campus.** Commuter students can connect to campus network. Online library available.

**Student life. Freshman orientation:** Mandatory.

**Student services.** Career counseling, services for economically disadvantaged, financial aid counseling, on-campus daycare, placement for graduates.

**Contact.** E-mail: jpalumbo@iia.edu
Phone: (480) 545-8755 ext. 209 Toll-free number: (888) 744-6340
Fax: (480) 926-1371
John Palumbo, Vice President of Admissions, International Institute of the Americas: Mesa, 925 South Gilbert Road, Suite 201, Mesa, AZ 85204

## International Institute of the Americas: Phoenix

**Phoenix, Arizona**
**www.iia.edu**                                    **CB code: 2188**

- Private 4-year nursing and career college
- Commuter campus in very large city
- 568 degree-seeking undergraduates
- Interview required

**General.** Accredited by ACICS. IIA has four campuses - Phoenix, Mesa, Tucson, AZ and Albuquerque, NM. **Degrees:** 17 bachelor's, 86 associate awarded. **Calendar:** Continuous, extensive summer session. **Full-time faculty:** 19 total; 21% have terminal degrees, 68% women. **Part-time faculty:** 23 total; 17% have terminal degrees, 83% women.

**Basis for selection.** Open admission, but selective for some programs. Selective criteria for some programs.

**2008-2009 Annual costs.** Tuition/fees (projected): $11,400. Tuition and fees may vary by program.

**Financial aid.** All financial aid based on need.

**Application procedures. Admission:** No deadline. $200 fee. Application must be submitted on paper. Admission notification on a rolling basis. **Financial aid:** No deadline. FAFSA, institutional form required.

**Academics. Special study options:** Distance learning. **Credit/placement by examination:** CLEP. **Support services:** Learning center.

**Majors. Business:** Business admin.

**Computing on campus.** 240 workstations in library, computer center. Commuter students can connect to campus network. Online library available.

**Student life. Freshman orientation:** Mandatory.

**Student services.** Career counseling, services for economically disadvantaged, financial aid counseling, on-campus daycare, placement for graduates.

**Contact.** E-mail: jpalumbo@iia.edu
Phone: (602) 242-6265 Toll-free number: (888) 744-6340
Fax: (602) 973-2572
John Palumbo, VP of Admission, International Institute of the Americas: Phoenix, 6049 North 43rd Avenue, Phoenix, AZ 85019

## International Institute of the Americas: Tucson

**Tucson, Arizona**
**www.iia.edu**                                    **CB code: 3454**

- Private 4-year branch campus college
- Commuter campus in very large city
- 292 degree-seeking undergraduates
- Interview required

**General.** Accredited by ACICS. Institution has four campuses; Phoenix, Mesa and Tucson, AZ and Albuquerque, NM. **Degrees:** 5 bachelor's, 43 associate awarded. **Calendar:** Continuous. **Full-time faculty:** 9 total; 22% have terminal degrees, 22% women. **Part-time faculty:** 11 total; 54% women.

**Basis for selection.** Open admission, but selective for some programs. Selective criteria for some programs.

**2008-2009 Annual costs.** Tuition/fees (projected): $11,400. Tuition and fees may vary by program.

**Financial aid.** All financial aid based on need.

**Application procedures. Admission:** No deadline. $200 fee. Application must be submitted on paper. Admission notification on a rolling basis. **Financial aid:** No deadline. FAFSA, institutional form required.

**Academics. Special study options:** Distance learning. **Credit/placement by examination:** CLEP. **Support services:** Learning center.

**Majors. Business:** Business admin.

**Computing on campus.** 240 workstations in library, computer center. Commuter students can connect to campus network. Online library available.

**Student life. Freshman orientation:** Mandatory.

**Student services.** Career counseling, services for economically disadvantaged, financial aid counseling, on-campus daycare, placement for graduates.

**Contact.** E-mail: jpalumbo@iia.edu
Phone: (520) 748-9799 Toll-free number: (888) 744-6340
Fax: (520) 748-9355
John Palumbo, Vice President of Admissions, International Institute of the Americas: Tucson, 5441 East 22nd Street, Suite 125, Tucson, AZ 85711

## ITT Technical Institute: Tempe

**Tempe, Arizona**

- For-profit 4-year technical college
- Commuter campus in small city

**General.** Accredited by ACICS. **Calendar:** Quarter.

**Annual costs/financial aid.** Tuition varies by program, $260-$368 per credit hour.

**Contact.** Phone: (602) 437-7500
Director of Recruitment, 5005 South Wendler Drive, Tempe, AZ 85282

## ITT Technical Institute: Tucson

**Tucson, Arizona**
**www.itt-tech.edu**                                **CB code: 3598**

- For-profit 4-year technical college
- Commuter campus in large city

**General.** Founded in 1984. Accredited by ACICS. **Calendar:** Quarter.

**Annual costs/financial aid.** Tuition varies by program, $260-$368 per credit hour.

**Contact.** Phone: (520) 408-7488
Director of Recruitment, 1455 West River Road, Tucson, AZ 85704

## Midwestern University: Glendale

**Glendale, Arizona**
**www.midwestern.edu**

- Private two-year upper-division university
- Large city

**General.** Regionally accredited. **Degrees:** 19 bachelor's awarded; master's, doctoral, first professional offered. **Location:** 14 miles from Phoenix. **Calendar:** Quarter. **Full-time faculty:** 90 total. **Part-time faculty:** 17 total.

**Student profile.** 26 degree-seeking undergraduates, 1,433 degree-seeking graduate students.

| Women: | 54% | Hispanic American: | 12% |
|---|---|---|---|
| African American: | 4% | Part-time: | 12% |
| Asian American: | 19% | | |

**Basis for selection.** Transfer accepted as juniors, seniors.

**2007-2008 Annual costs.** Tuition/fees: $18,311.

**Application procedures. Admission:** $50 fee.

**Academics.** Academic programs geared towards health professions such as osteopathic medicine and pharmacy. **Credit/placement by examination:** CLEP.

**Majors. Biology:** Biomedical sciences.

**Computing on campus.** 43 workstations in library, student center. Dormitories linked to campus network. Commuter students can connect to campus network. Online library, helpline, wireless network available.

**Contact.** E-mail: admissaz@midwestern.edu
Phone: (623) 572-3215
Heather Kim, Associate Director of Admissions, Midwestern University: Glendale, 19555 North 59th Avenue, Glendale, AZ 85308

## Northcentral University
### Prescott Valley, Arizona
www.ncu.edu                                CB code: 3883

- For-profit 4-year virtual university
- Commuter campus in large town
- 248 degree-seeking undergraduates: 82% part-time, 49% women, 12% African American, 4% Asian American, 9% Hispanic American, 2% Native American
- 5,631 degree-seeking graduate students

**General.** Regionally accredited. All courses and programs are offered via distance education. **Degrees:** 18 bachelor's awarded; master's, doctoral offered. **Calendar:** Continuous, extensive summer session.

**Basis for selection.** Work experience considered.

**2007-2008 Annual costs.** Students pay $250 per semester credit. Books/supplies: $1,200.

**Application procedures. Admission:** No deadline. $50 fee. Application must be submitted online. Admission notification on a rolling basis. **Financial aid:** No deadline. Must reply within 4 week(s) of notification.

**Academics.** Programs are 100 percent online, with one-on-one faculty mentoring and no residency requirement. **Special study options:** Distance learning. **Credit/placement by examination:** AP, CLEP, IB. **Support services:** Reduced course load, writing center.

**Majors. Business:** General, accounting, business admin, e-commerce, international, management science, marketing. **Computer sciences:** General. **Health:** Health care admin. **Protective services:** Law enforcement admin. **Psychology:** General. **Public administration:** General.

**Most popular majors.** Business/marketing 63%, psychology 37%.

**Computing on campus.** Commuter students can connect to campus network. Online course registration, online library, helpline available.

**Student life. Freshman orientation:** Available. Preregistration for classes offered.

**Student services.** Financial aid counseling.

**Contact.** E-mail: info@ncu.edu
Phone: (928) 776-0331 Toll-free number: (866) 776-0331
Fax: (928) 541-7817
Brent Passey, Executive Director of Enrollment, Northcentral University, 10000 East University, Prescott Valley, AZ 86314

## Northern Arizona University
### Flagstaff, Arizona                       CB member
www.nau.edu                                CB code: 4006

- Public 4-year university
- Residential campus in small city
- 15,362 degree-seeking undergraduates: 16% part-time, 60% women, 3% African American, 2% Asian American, 12% Hispanic American, 6% Native American, 2% international
- 5,377 degree-seeking graduate students
- 48% graduate within 6 years

**General.** Founded in 1899. Regionally accredited. **Degrees:** 2,895 bachelor's awarded; master's, doctoral offered. **ROTC:** Army, Air Force. **Location:** 140 miles from Phoenix. **Calendar:** Semester, extensive summer session. **Full-time faculty:** 774 total; 76% have terminal degrees, 13% minority, 45% women. **Part-time faculty:** 726 total; 37% have terminal degrees, 13% minority, 61% women. **Class size:** 39% < 20, 44% 20-39, 7% 40-49, 8% 50-99, 2% >100. **Special facilities:** 400-acre forest, observatory, high altitude training center for athletes.

**Freshman class profile.** 15,486 applied, 11,629 admitted, 3,171 enrolled.

| Mid 50% test scores | | | |
|---|---|---|---|
| SAT critical reading: | 490-590 | GPA 3.0-3.49: | 36% |
| SAT math: | 500-600 | GPA 2.0-2.99: | 19% |
| SAT writing: | 480-570 | Return as sophomores: | 71% |
| ACT composite: | 20-25 | Out-of-state: | 31% |
| GPA 3.50 or higher: | 45% | Live on campus: | 88% |
| | | International: | 1% |

**Basis for selection.** Open admission, but selective for out-of-state students. Cumulative high school GPA of 3.0, class rank in top quarter, ACT composite score of 22 (24 out-of-state) or SAT combined score of 1040 (exclusive of Writing) (1110 out-of-state) required for unconditional admission. Conditional admission if cumulative high school GPA is 2.5 to 2.99, class rank is in upper half, and test scores are lower than those for unconditional admission. Audition required of music, music education majors.

**High school preparation.** Required units include English 4, mathematics 4, social studies 2, history 1, science 3 (laboratory 1) and foreign language 2. Mathematics must include 2 algebra, 1 geometry and 1 year of math after algebra II. One social science must be U.S. history. Other: one fine arts required.

**2007-2008 Annual costs.** Tuition/fees: $4,844; $14,498 out-of-state. Room/board: $6,572. Books/supplies: $830. Personal expenses: $2,148.

**2006-2007 Financial aid. Need-based:** 1,961 full-time freshmen applied for aid; 1,162 were judged to have need; 1,102 of these received aid. Average need met was 68%. Average scholarship/grant was $5,101; average loan $2,666. 44% of total undergraduate aid awarded as scholarships/grants, 56% as loans/jobs. **Non-need-based:** Awarded to 4,713 full-time undergraduates, including 1,381 freshmen. Scholarships awarded for academics, alumni affiliation, art, athletics, leadership, minority status, music/drama, ROTC, state residency.

**Application procedures. Admission:** Priority date 3/1; no deadline. $25 fee. Application may be submitted online. Admission notification on a rolling basis. Applicants encouraged to apply early. **Financial aid:** Priority date 3/1; no closing date. FAFSA required. Applicants notified on a rolling basis starting 3/15.

**Academics. Special study options:** Accelerated study, cooperative education, distance learning, double major, dual enrollment of high school students, ESL, exchange student, honors, independent study, internships, study abroad, teacher certification program. **Credit/placement by examination:** AP, CLEP, IB, SAT, ACT, institutional tests. 30 credit hours maximum toward bachelor's degree. **Support services:** Learning center, pre-admission summer program, reduced course load, remedial instruction, study skills assistance, tutoring, writing center.

**Honors college/program.** New students applying to Honors Program must complete separate application and have either ACT composite score of 29 or higher, SAT combined score of 1290 or higher (exclusive of Writing), or graduation in top five percent of high school class. Students who do not meet criteria can petition for admission to honors program by submitting a completed application and unofficial high school transcript, letter of recommendation, and essay. Transfer students must complete a separate application and have a cumulative grade point average of 3.50 or higher.

**Majors. Area/ethnic studies:** American, Native American, women's. **Biology:** General, animal behavior, aquatic, bacteriology, botany, cell/histology, cellular/molecular, ecology, microbiology, molecular, physiology, wildlife, zoology. **Business:** Accounting, business admin, construction management, fashion, finance, hospitality admin, hotel/motel admin, management information systems, managerial economics, marketing. **Communications:** General, advertising, broadcast journalism, digital media, journalism, public relations, radio/tv. **Computer sciences:** General, computer science. **Conservation:** Environmental science, environmental studies, forest sciences, forestry, wildlife. **Education:** General, art, biology, chemistry, drama/dance, elementary, English, French, German, health, history, mathematics, music, physical, physics, Spanish, special, speech, technology/industrial arts, trade/industrial, voc/tech. **Engineering:** General, civil, computer, electrical, environmental, mechanical, physics. **Engineering technology:** Computer systems, construction. **English:** English lit, speech/rhetoric. **Foreign languages:** General, French, German, Spanish. **Health:** Athletic training, dental hygiene, health care admin, nursing (RN), premedicine, preveterinary. **History:** General. **Interdisciplinary:** Behavioral sciences, biological/physical sciences. **Legal studies:** Prelaw. **Liberal arts:** Arts/sciences, humanities. **Math:** General, probability. **Parks/recreation:** General, exercise sciences, facilities management, health/fitness. **Philosophy/religion:** Philosophy, religion. **Physical sciences:** General, astronomy, astrophysics, chemistry, geochemistry, geology, hydrology, paleontology, physics, planetary, theoretical physics. **Protective services:** Criminal justice, law enforcement admin. **Psychology:** General. **Public administration:** Policy analysis, social work. **Social sciences:** General, anthropology, cartography, economics, geography, international relations, political science, sociology, U.S. government.

**Visual/performing arts:** General, art, art history/conservation, arts management, ceramics, design, dramatic, interior design, metal/jewelry, music history, music performance, painting, photography, printmaking, sculpture, studio arts, voice/opera.

**Most popular majors.** Business/marketing 17%, education 21%, health sciences 6%, liberal arts 9%, social sciences 9%, visual/performing arts 6%.

**Computing on campus.** Dormitories wired for high-speed internet access and linked to campus network. Commuter students can connect to campus network. Online course registration, online library, helpline, repair service, student web hosting, wireless network available.

**Student life. Freshman orientation:** Available, $150 fee. Preregistration for classes offered. **Policies:** Organizations required to register annually, have 12 or more members with cumulative GPA of 2.0 to start club, have constitution and bylaws, be approved by ASNAU Senate and Office of Student Life, and officers must have cumulative GPA of 2.25. **Housing:** Guaranteed on-campus for all undergraduates. Coed dorms, single-sex dorms, special housing for disabled, apartments, fraternity/sorority housing available. $150 partly refundable deposit, deadline 5/1. Honor halls, floors for students 21 years of age and older available. **Activities:** Bands, campus ministries, choral groups, dance, drama, international student organizations, music ensembles, Model UN, radio station, student government, student newspaper, symphony orchestra, TV station, Campus Crusade for Christ, Baptist Student Ministry, Holy Trinity Catholic Newman Center, Hillel at NAU, Episcopal Canterbury Fellowship, Hispanic Honor Society, African students organization, Asian Americans United, Japanese Association.

**Athletics.** NCAA. **Intercollegiate:** Basketball, cross-country, diving W, football (tackle) M, golf W, soccer W, swimming W, tennis, track and field, volleyball W. **Intramural:** Archery, badminton, baseball M, basketball, bowling, cross-country, football (non-tackle), ice hockey M, lacrosse, racquetball, rugby, skiing, soccer, softball, swimming, table tennis, tennis, track and field, volleyball, water polo M. **Team name:** Lumberjacks.

**Student services.** Alcohol/substance abuse counseling, campus ministries, career counseling, student employment services, financial aid counseling, health services, minority student services, personal counseling, placement for graduates, veterans' counselor. **Physically disabled:** Services for visually, speech, hearing impaired.

**Contact.** E-mail: undergraduate.admissions@nau.edu
Phone: (928) 523-5511 Toll-free number: (888) 628-2968
Fax: (928) 523-0226
Paul Orscheln, Director of Admissions, Northern Arizona University, PO Box 4084, Flagstaff, AZ 86011-4084

## Prescott College
**Prescott, Arizona**
www.prescott.edu                               **CB code: 0484**

▶ Private 4-year liberal arts college
▶ Commuter campus in large town
▶ 689 degree-seeking undergraduates: 13% part-time, 59% women, 1% African American, 1% Asian American, 6% Hispanic American, 1% Native American, 1% international
▶ 310 degree-seeking graduate students
▶ 83% of applicants admitted
▶ SAT or ACT (ACT writing optional), application essay required
▶ 52% graduate within 6 years

**General.** Founded in 1966. Regionally accredited. **Degrees:** 224 bachelor's awarded; master's, doctoral offered. **Location:** 100 miles from Phoenix. **Calendar:** Semester, limited summer session. **Full-time faculty:** 34 total; 65% have terminal degrees, 6% minority, 38% women. **Part-time faculty:** 36 total; 19% have terminal degrees, 8% minority, 50% women. **Class size:** 100% < 20. **Special facilities:** Facility for marine studies at Kino Bay, Mexico.

**Freshman class profile.** 252 applied, 209 admitted, 71 enrolled.

| Mid 50% test scores | | Rank in top quarter: | 32% |
|---|---|---|---|
| SAT critical reading: | 510-660 | Rank in top tenth: | 11% |
| SAT math: | 500-610 | End year in good standing: | 83% |
| SAT writing: | 490-600 | Return as sophomores: | 73% |
| ACT composite: | 21-27 | Out-of-state: | 81% |
| GPA 3.50 or higher: | 32% | Live on campus: | 26% |
| GPA 3.0-3.49: | 20% | International: | 1% |
| GPA 2.0-2.99: | 42% | | |

**Basis for selection.** Essay and GPA most important. Letters of recommendation, any personal additions important. College visit, interview recommended. **Homeschooled:** Documentation consistent with requirements in state of residence.

**High school preparation.** 16 units recommended. Recommended units include English 4, mathematics 3, social studies 1, history 2, science 2 and foreign language 3. One arts unit recommended.

**2008-2009 Annual costs.** Tuition/fees: $21,792. Health insurance is required; cost of school-s health insurance is $413 for fall term and $579 for spring term. Room only: $3,400. Books/supplies: $600. Personal expenses: $1,200.

**2007-2008 Financial aid. Need-based:** 34 full-time freshmen applied for aid; 20 were judged to have need; 20 of these received aid. Average need met was 41%. Average scholarship/grant was $4,713; average loan $2,520. 28% of total undergraduate aid awarded as scholarships/grants, 72% as loans/jobs. **Non-need-based:** Awarded to 65 full-time undergraduates, including 25 freshmen. Scholarships awarded for academics, alumni affiliation, minority status, state residency.

**Application procedures. Admission:** Priority date 3/1; deadline 8/15 (postmark date). $25 fee, may be waived for applicants with need. Application may be submitted online. Admission notification on a rolling basis beginning on or about 1/1. Must reply by May 1 or within 4 week(s) if notified thereafter. **Financial aid:** Priority date 4/1; no closing date. FAFSA required. Applicants notified on a rolling basis starting 3/15; must reply within 12 week(s) of notification.

**Academics. Special study options:** Cross-registration, distance learning, double major, exchange student, external degree, independent study, internships, liberal arts/career combination, student-designed major, teacher certification program. Adult degree program designed for working adults to obtain degree on year-round, part-time basis. Master of arts self-study program available. Programs also available at center in Tucson. **Credit/placement by examination:** AP, CLEP, IB, institutional tests. 30 credit hours maximum toward bachelor's degree. **Support services:** Learning center, reduced course load, tutoring.

**Majors. Agriculture:** General, agronomy, food science, plant breeding, soil science. **Architecture:** Environmental design. **Area/ethnic studies:** Latin American, regional, women's. **Biology:** General, botany, conservation, ecology, marine. **Business:** General, accounting, business admin, nonprofit/public, office management. **Communications:** General, journalism, media studies, photojournalism, radio/tv. **Computer sciences:** General, information systems. **Conservation:** General, environmental studies, management/policy, wildlife. **Education:** General, art, bilingual, biology, curriculum, drama/dance, early childhood, early childhood special, elementary, emotionally handicapped, English, foreign languages, history, learning disabled, mathematics, mentally handicapped, multi-level teacher, music, physical, school counseling, science, secondary, social science, social studies, Spanish, special, technology/industrial arts, voc/tech. **English:** British lit, composition, creative writing, English lit. **Family/consumer sciences:** Child development. **Foreign languages:** Comparative lit, Spanish. **Health:** Art therapy, communication disorders, community health services, health care admin, recreational therapy. **History:** General. **Interdisciplinary:** Behavioral sciences, biological/physical sciences, natural sciences, peace/conflict. **Liberal arts:** Arts/sciences, humanities. **Math:** General. **Parks/recreation:** General, facilities management. **Philosophy/religion:** Religion. **Physical sciences:** Geology, planetary. **Psychology:** General, counseling, developmental, environmental, medical, social. **Public administration:** Community org/advocacy, human services, policy analysis. **Social sciences:** General, anthropology, geography, international relations, political science, sociology. **Visual/performing arts:** General, ceramics, cinematography, crafts, dance, dramatic, film/cinema, interior design, painting, photography, play/screenwriting, sculpture, studio arts. **Other:** Adventure education, Agro-Ecology, Alpine geomorphology, Human and organizational development, Rehabilitation/therapeutic professions, Social justice, Somatic psychology.

**Computing on campus.** 50 workstations in dormitories, library, computer center, student center. Dormitories wired for high-speed internet access and linked to campus network. Online library, helpline, student web hosting, wireless network available.

**Student life. Freshman orientation:** Mandatory, $900 fee. 3-week intensive wilderness orientation for freshmen and transfer students. **Housing:** Coed dorms available. $150 fully refundable deposit, deadline 4/15. **Activities:** Dance, drama, film society, literary magazine, radio station, student government, student newspaper, Jewish club, Amnesty International, student union, gay and lesbian group, Center for Peace and Justice, Aztlan Center: Migrant Rights Group, Ripple Project: service learning program.

**Student services.** Adult student services, career counseling, financial aid counseling, personal counseling, placement for graduates, veterans' counselor. **Physically disabled:** Services for visually, speech, hearing impaired.

**Contact.** E-mail: admissions@prescott.edu
Phone: (928) 350-2100 Toll-free number: (877) 350-2100
Fax: (928) 776-5242
Tim Robison, Director of Admissions, Prescott College, 220 Grove Avenue, Prescott, AZ 86301

## Southwestern College
### Phoenix, Arizona
www.swcaz.edu                                      CB code: 4736

- Private 4-year Bible college affiliated with Baptist faith
- Very large city
- 361 degree-seeking undergraduates: 3% African American, 1% Asian American, 2% Hispanic American, 2% Native American, 2% international
- 42% of applicants admitted
- SAT or ACT (ACT writing optional), application essay required

**General.** Founded in 1960. Regionally accredited. **Degrees:** 53 bachelor's awarded. **ROTC:** Naval, Air Force. **Calendar:** Semester, limited summer session. **Full-time faculty:** 10 total. **Part-time faculty:** 37 total.

**Freshman class profile.** 349 applied, 145 admitted, 64 enrolled.

**Basis for selection.** School achievement record and recommendations very important. Written testimony of conversion experience required for admission. **Homeschooled:** Transcript of courses and grades required. Must present ACT or SAT scores for admission.

**High school preparation.** Recommended units include English 4, mathematics 3, social studies 3, science 2 and foreign language 2.

**2007-2008 Annual costs.** Tuition/fees: $13,344. Room/board: $5,046. Books/supplies: $800. Personal expenses: $1,300.

**Financial aid. Non-need-based:** Scholarships awarded for academics, alumni affiliation, leadership, music/drama, religious affiliation.

**Application procedures. Admission:** Priority date 4/30; deadline 8/15. $30 fee, may be waived for applicants with need. Application may be submitted online. Admission notification on a rolling basis. **Financial aid:** Priority date 3/15, closing date 8/31. FAFSA, institutional form required. Applicants notified on a rolling basis.

**Academics.** Off-campus, noncredit Christian internship work required during each semester. **Special study options:** Internships, teacher certification program. **Credit/placement by examination:** AP, CLEP, SAT, ACT. 30 credit hours maximum toward bachelor's degree. **Support services:** Reduced course load, remedial instruction.

**Majors. Education:** Elementary, music, secondary. **Philosophy/religion:** Religion. **Psychology:** Family. **Theology:** Bible, missionary, religious ed, sacred music, theology. **Other:** Behavioral health.

**Computing on campus.** 60 workstations in dormitories, library, computer center. Dormitories wired for high-speed internet access. Online library available.

**Student life. Freshman orientation:** Mandatory. Preregistration for classes offered. **Policies:** Religious observance required. **Housing:** Guaranteed on-campus for all undergraduates. Single-sex dorms, apartments available. $100 nonrefundable deposit, deadline 4/30. **Activities:** Jazz band, choral groups, drama, music ensembles, musical theater, student government, student newspaper, symphony orchestra.

**Athletics.** NCCAA. **Intercollegiate:** Basketball, soccer M, volleyball W. **Intramural:** Football (tackle) M, soccer, table tennis, tennis, volleyball. **Team name:** Eagles.

**Student services.** Student employment services, financial aid counseling, health services, personal counseling, veterans' counselor.

**Contact.** E-mail: admissions@swcaz.edu
Phone: (602) 386-4136 Toll-free number: (800) 247-2697
Fax: (602) 404-2159
Jeanne Crafton, Director of Admissions, Southwestern College, 2625 East Cactus Road, Phoenix, AZ 85032-7042

## University of Advancing Technology
### Tempe, Arizona
www.uat.edu                                        CB code: 3608

- For-profit 4-year university and technical college
- Residential campus in very large city
- 1,195 degree-seeking undergraduates: 8% women, 4% African American, 3% Asian American, 6% Hispanic American, 1% international
- 59 degree-seeking graduate students
- SAT or ACT (ACT writing optional), application essay, interview required

**General.** Founded in 1983. Accredited by ACICS. Bachelor's degree can be earned in 2 2/3 years. **Degrees:** 140 bachelor's, 24 associate awarded; master's offered. **Location:** 7 miles from Phoenix. **Calendar:** Trimester, extensive summer session. **Full-time faculty:** 28 total. **Part-time faculty:** 26 total. **Class size:** 68% < 20, 27% 20-39, 2% 40-49, 3% 50-99. **Special facilities:** Technology lab, motion capture studio, robotics lab, sound and editing studio.

**Freshman class profile.**

| Out-of-state: | 20% | International: | 1% |
|---|---|---|---|

**Basis for selection.** Academic achievements, leadership experience, career aspirations, hobbies and community and extra-curricular involvement considered. Acceptance based on previous education, test scores (ACT/SAT), the student's match with university culture and a passion for technology. SAT or ACT recommended. Test scores are considered during the admissions process, but are not required unless GPA is not satisfactory. **Homeschooled:** Transcript of courses and grades, state high school equivalency certificate required.

**2008-2009 Annual costs.** Tuition/fees: $16,900. Room/board: $8,400. Books/supplies: $1,000. Personal expenses: $2,900.

**Application procedures. Admission:** No deadline. No application fee. Application may be submitted online. Admission notification on a rolling basis. **Financial aid:** Priority date 4/15; no closing date. FAFSA required. Applicants notified on a rolling basis; must reply within 2 week(s) of notification.

**Academics. Special study options:** Accelerated study, distance learning, double major, independent study, internships, student-designed major. **Credit/placement by examination:** AP, CLEP, IB, institutional tests. **Support services:** Learning center, tutoring.

**Majors. Communications technology:** Animation/special effects. **Computer sciences:** Game design, LAN/WAN management, networking, security, web page design, webmaster. **Engineering:** Software. **Engineering technology:** Robotics. **Other:** Computer forensics, Technology management.

**Computing on campus.** 400 workstations in dormitories, library, computer center, student center. Dormitories wired for high-speed internet access and linked to campus network. Commuter students can connect to campus network. Online course registration, online library, helpline, student web hosting, wireless network available.

**Student life. Freshman orientation:** Mandatory. Preregistration for classes offered. **Housing:** Guaranteed on-campus for freshmen. Apartments available. $550 deposit. **Activities:** Dance, film society, student government, student newspaper, Bible Study club.

**Athletics. Intercollegiate:** Fencing.

**Student services.** Career counseling, student employment services, financial aid counseling, personal counseling, placement for graduates.

**Contact.** E-mail: admissions@uat.edu
Phone: (602) 383-8228 Toll-free number: (800) 658-5744
Fax: (602) 383-8222
Chrys Pistillo, Manager of Admissions, Student Services, University of Advancing Technology, 2625 West Baseline Road, Tempe, AZ 85283-1056

## University of Arizona
### Tucson, Arizona                              CB member
www.arizona.edu                                    CB code: 4832

- Public 4-year university
- Residential campus in very large city
- 28,670 degree-seeking undergraduates: 13% part-time, 53% women, 3% African American, 6% Asian American, 16% Hispanic American, 2% Native American, 3% international
- 7,476 degree-seeking graduate students
- 80% of applicants admitted
- 59% graduate within 6 years

**General.** Founded in 1885. Regionally accredited. Sierra Vista campus offers credit-bearing classes in general studies and education. Arizona International College offers liberal arts focus within university setting. **Degrees:** 5,564 bachelor's awarded; master's, doctoral, first professional offered. **ROTC:** Army, Naval, Air Force. **Location:** 111 miles from Phoenix. **Calendar:** Semester, extensive summer session. **Full-time faculty:** 1,408 total; 98% have terminal degrees, 14% minority, 32% women. **Part-time faculty:** 54 total; 98% have terminal degrees, 11% minority, 39% women. **Class size:** 47% < 20, 17% 20-39, 20% 40-49, 8% 50-99, 7% >100. **Special facilities:** Geological museum, state anthropological museum, planetarium, observatory, center for creative photography.

**Freshman class profile.** 21,103 applied, 16,780 admitted, 6,569 enrolled.

| Mid 50% test scores | | | |
|---|---|---|---|
| SAT critical reading: | 490-600 | GPA 2.0-2.99: | 21% |
| SAT math: | 500-630 | Rank in top quarter: | 62% |
| ACT composite: | 20-26 | Rank in top tenth: | 34% |
| GPA 3.50 or higher: | 43% | Return as sophomores: | 80% |
| GPA 3.0-3.49: | 35% | Out-of-state: | 37% |
| | | Live on campus: | 80% |

**Basis for selection.** All applicants: top 25% of class or 3.0 cumulative GPA, SAT score (exclusive of Writing) of 1110 (1040 in-state) or ACT score of 24 (22 in-state) important. Conditional admission may be offered to in-state applicants who meet 1 or more of following: top half of class or 2.5 GPA and no more than 1 deficiency in any 2 required subjects, (deficiency not allowed in both mathematics and science). SAT or ACT recommended. Essays recommended. Auditions required of applied music and all performance majors. Portfolios required for studio art majors. **Homeschooled:** Course work completion information required. **Learning Disabled:** Separate application for fee-based program (SALT).

**High school preparation.** 16 units required. Required units include English 4, mathematics 3, social studies 1, history 1, science 3 (laboratory 3), foreign language 2 and academic electives 1. One unit fine arts required.

**2007-2008 Annual costs.** Tuition/fees: $5,037; $16,271 out-of-state. Room/board: $7,370. Books/supplies: $1,000. Personal expenses: $2,196.

**2006-2007 Financial aid.** **Need-based:** 3,378 full-time freshmen applied for aid; 2,119 were judged to have need; 2,021 of these received aid. Average need met was 64%. Average scholarship/grant was $6,774; average loan $3,042. 53% of total undergraduate aid awarded as scholarships/grants, 47% as loans/jobs. **Non-need-based:** Awarded to 6,289 full-time undergraduates, including 2,388 freshmen. Scholarships awarded for academics, art.

**Application procedures.** **Admission:** Closing date 5/1 (postmark date). $65 fee, may be waived for applicants with need. Application may be submitted online. Admission notification on a rolling basis beginning on or about 11/1. Must reply by May 1 or within 4 week(s) if notified thereafter. **Financial aid:** Priority date 3/1; no closing date. FAFSA required. Applicants notified on a rolling basis starting 4/1; must reply within 3 week(s) of notification.

**Academics.** **Special study options:** Accelerated study, combined bachelor's/graduate degree, cooperative education, cross-registration, distance learning, double major, dual enrollment of high school students, ESL, exchange student, external degree, independent study, internships, liberal arts/career combination, semester at sea, study abroad, teacher certification program, weekend college. **Credit/placement by examination:** AP, CLEP, IB, SAT, ACT, institutional tests. 60 credit hours maximum toward bachelor's degree. **Support services:** Learning center, pre-admission summer program, reduced course load, study skills assistance, tutoring, writing center.

**Majors.** **Agriculture:** General, agronomy, animal sciences, economics, plant sciences, soil science. **Architecture:** Architecture, urban/community planning. **Area/ethnic studies:** East Asian, Hispanic-American/Latino/Chicano, Latin American, Near/Middle Eastern, women's. **Biology:** General, animal physiology, bacteriology, biochemistry, cell/histology, ecology. **Business:** General, accounting, entrepreneurial studies, finance, human resources, management information systems, managerial economics, marketing, operations. **Communications:** General, journalism, radio/tv. **Computer sciences:** General. **Conservation:** General, environmental studies. **Education:** Art, biology, chemistry, drama/dance, elementary, English, family/consumer sciences, foreign languages, French, German, history, kindergarten/preschool, mathematics, music, physical, physics, science, secondary, social science, social studies, Spanish, special, speech. **Engineering:** General, aerospace, agricultural, chemical, civil, computer, electrical, geological, industrial, materials science, mechanical, mining, physics, systems, water resource. **Engineering technology:** Industrial management. **English:** Creative writing, English lit. **Family/consumer sciences:** Consumer economics, family studies. **Foreign languages:** Classics, French, German, Italian, linguistics, Russian, Spanish. **Health:** Clinical lab science, communication disorders, health care admin, nursing (RN), preveterinary, speech pathology. **History:** General. **Interdisciplinary:** Nutrition sciences. **Math:** General. **Philosophy/religion:** Judaic, philosophy, religion. **Physical sciences:** Astronomy, chemistry, geology, hydrology, optics, physics. **Protective services:** Law enforcement admin. **Psychology:** General. **Public administration:** General. **Social sciences:** Anthropology, applied economics, economics, geography, political science, sociology. **Visual/performing arts:** General, art history/conservation, dance, dramatic, music performance, musical theater, studio arts, theater design. **Other:** Applied science, Engineering mathematics.

**Most popular majors.** Biology 8%, business/marketing 13%, communications/journalism 8%, education 9%, engineering/engineering technologies 8%, psychology 7%, social sciences 11%.

**Computing on campus.** 1,950 workstations in dormitories, library, computer center, student center. Dormitories wired for high-speed internet access and linked to campus network. Commuter students can connect to campus network. Online course registration, online library, helpline available.

**Student life.** **Freshman orientation:** Mandatory, $100 fee. Preregistration for classes offered. 2-day program. **Housing:** Coed dorms, single-sex dorms, special housing for disabled, apartments, fraternity/sorority housing available. $250 deposit, deadline 5/1. Special housing for honors students available. **Activities:** Bands, campus ministries, choral groups, dance, drama, international student organizations, literary magazine, music ensembles, Model UN, musical theater, opera, radio station, student government, student newspaper, symphony orchestra, TV station, over 350 clubs and organizations available.

**Athletics.** NCAA. **Intercollegiate:** Baseball M, basketball, cross-country, diving, football (tackle) M, golf, gymnastics W, lacrosse M, soccer W, softball W, swimming, tennis, track and field, volleyball W. **Intramural:** Badminton, basketball, bowling, cross-country, diving, football (non-tackle), golf, racquetball, soccer, softball, swimming, table tennis, tennis, track and field, volleyball. **Team name:** Wildcats.

**Student services.** Adult student services, alcohol/substance abuse counseling, campus ministries, career counseling, services for economically disadvantaged, student employment services, financial aid counseling, health services, legal services, minority student services, personal counseling, placement for graduates, veterans' counselor, women's services. **Physically disabled:** Services for visually, speech, hearing impaired. **Learning disabled:** Comprehensive services available.

**Contact.** E-mail: appinfo@arizona.edu
Phone: (520) 621-3237 Fax: (520) 621-9799
Paul Kohn, Vice President for Enrollment Management, University of Arizona, Robert L. Nugent Building, Tucson, AZ 85721-0040

---

## University of Phoenix
**Phoenix, Arizona**
**www.phoenix.edu**

CB member
CB code: 1024

▸ For-profit 4-year virtual university
▸ Commuter campus in very large city
▸ 246,589 full-time, degree-seeking undergraduates

**General.** Founded in 1976. Regionally accredited. Classes are offered in classroom environment and on-line in 39 states, Puerto Rico, Washington DC, Vancouver, British Columbia, Mexico and Europe. **Degrees:** 27,459 bachelor's, 2,928 associate awarded; master's, doctoral offered. **Calendar:** Continuous, extensive summer session. **Full-time faculty:** 1,076 total. **Part-time faculty:** 19,483 total.

**Basis for selection.** Open admission, but selective for some programs. Undergraduate applicants with fewer than 24 transferable credits must be currently employed, or have the equivalent of one year of full-time work experience and current access to a work environment. Undergraduate applicants entering the University with more than 24 transferable credits must be currently employed, or have current access to a work environment.

**2007-2008 Annual costs.** Tuition/fees: $10,290. Books/supplies: $525.

**Application procedures.** **Admission:** No deadline. $45 fee. Application may be submitted online. Admission notification on a rolling basis. **Financial aid:** No deadline. FAFSA, institutional form required. Applicants notified on a rolling basis.

**Academics.** **Special study options:** Accelerated study, distance learning, independent study, internships, teacher certification program. **Credit/placement by examination:** AP, CLEP, IB. 30 credit hours maximum toward associate degree, 30 toward bachelor's. **Support services:** Remedial instruction, writing center.

**Majors.** **Business:** Accounting, business admin, communications, finance, hospitality admin, management information systems, management science, marketing, retailing. **Computer sciences:** General, database management, networking, programming. **Education:** Elementary. **Health:** Health care admin, health services. **Protective services:** Corrections, criminal justice, law enforcement admin, security management. **Public administration:** General.

**Most popular majors.** Business/marketing 68%, computer/information sciences 19%, health sciences 7%.

**Computing on campus.** Commuter students can connect to campus network. Online library, helpline available.

**Student life. Freshman orientation:** Available.

**Student services.** Adult student services, financial aid counseling, personal counseling.

**Contact.** E-mail: Audra.McQuarie@phoenix.edu
Phone: (480) 317-6151 Toll-free number: (800) 288-7240
Fax: (480) 643-3068
Beth Barilla, Associate Vice President, Student Admissions & Services, University of Phoenix, 4615 East Elwood Street, Phoenix, AZ 85040-1958

---

## Western International University
### Phoenix, Arizona
**www.wintu.edu**                          **CB code: 1316**

- For-profit 4-year university and business college
- Commuter campus in very large city
- 2,050 degree-seeking undergraduates
- 879 graduate students
- 79% of applicants admitted
- 42% graduate within 6 years

**General.** Founded in 1978. Regionally accredited. Adult student body. Portfolio evaluation of relevant experience for course credit. **Degrees:** 376 bachelor's, 20 associate awarded; master's offered. **Calendar:** Semester, extensive summer session. **Part-time faculty:** 400 total.

**Freshman class profile.** 775 applied, 616 admitted, 409 enrolled.

**Basis for selection.** Academic achievement and cumulative GPA very important. Interview and essay recommended.

**High school preparation.** Recommended units include English 4, mathematics 3, social studies 2 and science 2.

**2007-2008 Annual costs.** Per-credit-hour charge $333.

**2006-2007 Financial aid.** All financial aid based on need.

**Application procedures. Admission:** No deadline. $85 fee. Application must be submitted on paper. Admission notification on a rolling basis. **Financial aid:** No deadline. FAFSA, institutional form required. Applicants notified on a rolling basis.

**Academics. Special study options:** Accelerated study, distance learning, double major, dual enrollment of high school students, honors, independent study. **Credit/placement by examination:** AP, CLEP, IB, institutional tests. 24 credit hours maximum toward associate degree, 60 toward bachelor's. Maximum of 60 credits by examination and/or assessment may be counted toward degree; 36 hour residency requirement. **Support services:** Learning center, tutoring, writing center.

**Majors. Business:** General, accounting, business admin, finance, international, management information systems, marketing. **Computer sciences:** General. **Liberal arts:** Arts/sciences.

**Most popular majors.** Business/marketing 76%, computer/information sciences 13%, liberal arts 10%.

**Computing on campus.** PC or laptop required. 195 workstations in library, computer center. Commuter students can connect to campus network. Online course registration, online library, helpline, wireless network available.

**Student life. Freshman orientation:** Mandatory. Preregistration for classes offered. **Policies:** Cultural activities and special seminars/workshops available. **Activities:** International student organizations, student government, Delta Mu Delta, Upsilon Pi Epsilon, Golden Key Honor Societies.

**Student services.** Adult student services, career counseling, financial aid counseling, veterans' counselor.

**Contact.** Phone: (602) 943-2311 Toll-free number: (866) 948-4636
Fax: (602) 371-8637
Jo Arney, Director of University Student Services, Western International University, 9215 North Black Canyon Highway, Phoenix, AZ 85021

# Arkansas

## Arkansas Baptist College
**Little Rock, Arkansas**
www.arkansasbaptist.edu                    **CB code: 7301**

▶ Private 4-year liberal arts college affiliated with American Baptist Churches in the USA

▶ Residential campus in large city

▶ 542 degree-seeking undergraduates: 16% part-time, 28% women

**General.** Founded in 1884. Regionally accredited. **Degrees:** 7 bachelor's, 4 associate awarded. **Calendar:** Semester, limited summer session. **Full-time faculty:** 17 total. **Part-time faculty:** 40 total. **Special facilities:** African american leadership institute, literacy writing center.

**Basis for selection.** Open admission. Academically borderline applicants may be admitted provisionally but must earn 2.0 GPA by end of first semester to continue in good academic standing. **Homeschooled:** Statement describing homeschool structure and mission, interview required.

**High school preparation.** 18 units recommended. Recommended units include English 4, mathematics 4, social studies 1 and science 2. Vocational and agriculture courses also recommended.

**2007-2008 Annual costs.** Tuition/fees: $5,390. Room/board: $8,042. Books/supplies: $700. Personal expenses: $850.

**Financial aid.** All financial aid based on need.

**Application procedures. Admission:** No deadline. $25 fee. Admission notification on a rolling basis beginning on or about 6/30. **Financial aid:** Closing date 5/1. FAFSA required. Applicants notified on a rolling basis starting 6/15.

**Academics. Special study options:** Double major, independent study. **Credit/placement by examination:** CLEP, institutional tests. **Support services:** Remedial instruction, tutoring, writing center.

**Majors. Business:** Business admin. **Education:** Elementary. **Social sciences:** General.

**Student life. Freshman orientation:** Mandatory, $10 fee. Preregistration for classes offered. Held in August and in January each year. **Policies:** Religious observance required. **Housing:** Single-sex dorms available. **Activities:** Choral groups, student government, student newspaper, Baptist Student Union, student teacher organization.

**Athletics.** NJCAA. **Intercollegiate:** Basketball, cheerleading M, football (tackle) M. **Team name:** Buffaloes.

**Student services.** Career counseling, student employment services, health services, on-campus daycare, personal counseling, placement for graduates, veterans' counselor.

**Contact.** E-mail: admissions@arkansasbaptist.edu
Phone: (501) 244-5104 Toll-free number: (866) 920-4222
Vivian Doyne, Director of Enrollment Management, Arkansas Baptist College, 1621 Dr. Martin Luther King Drive, Little Rock, AR 72202

## Arkansas State University
**State University, Arkansas**                    **CB member**
www.astate.edu                                   **CB code: 6011**

▶ Public 4-year university

▶ Commuter campus in small city

▶ 8,791 degree-seeking undergraduates: 17% part-time, 59% women, 18% African American, 1% Asian American, 1% Hispanic American, 1% international

▶ 1,379 degree-seeking graduate students

▶ 80% of applicants admitted

▶ SAT or ACT (ACT writing optional) required

▶ 38% graduate within 6 years; 10% enter graduate study

**General.** Founded in 1909. Regionally accredited. **Degrees:** 1,438 bachelor's, 187 associate awarded; master's, doctoral offered. **ROTC:** Army. **Location:** 70 miles from Memphis. **Calendar:** Semester, extensive summer session. **Full-time faculty:** 459 total; 68% have terminal degrees, 15% minority, 49% women. **Part-time faculty:** 176 total; 7% have terminal degrees, 6% minority, 58% women. **Class size:** 43% < 20, 46% 20-39, 6% 40-49, 4% 50-99, less than 1% >100. **Special facilities:** Environmental ecotoxicology research facility, electron microscope facility, geographic information center facility, museums, equine center, plantation, farmers museum.

**Freshman class profile.** 3,298 applied, 2,634 admitted, 1,733 enrolled.

| Mid 50% test scores | | Return as sophomores: | 69% |
|---|---|---|---|
| ACT composite: | 18-24 | Out-of-state: | 13% |
| GPA 3.50 or higher: | 35% | Live on campus: | 56% |
| GPA 3.0-3.49: | 28% | International: | 1% |
| GPA 2.0-2.99: | 34% | Fraternities: | 16% |
| End year in good standing: | 78% | Sororities: | 13% |

**Basis for selection.** For unconditional admission, must have a minimum of 19 on ACT scores composite, English, math, reading or comparable scores on the SAT, ASSET, or COMPASS and a minimum 2.5 cumulative high school GPA for eight semesters, or 3.75 cumulative high school GPA for six or seven semesters. Students who do not meet the ACT, GPA criteria and state-mandated core for unrestricted admission may seek admission with restrictions if their high school GPA is at least 2.0. Proof of immunization is required. Proof of registration with selective service is required for all males 18 to 25. Students with no ACT or SAT scores may submit ASSET scores. SAT, SAT Subject Tests, ACT scores must be received by first day of classes for fall term admission. Auditions required of music majors; portfolios required of art majors. **Homeschooled:** Must have overall GPA of 2.0. Minimum GED score for restricted admission is 500.

**High school preparation.** 16 units recommended. Recommended units include English 4, mathematics 4, social studies 1, history 2, science 3 (laboratory 3) and foreign language 2.

**2007-2008 Annual costs.** Tuition/fees: $6,010; $13,390 out-of-state. Room/board: $5,060. Books/supplies: $1,000. Personal expenses: $3,055.

**2007-2008 Financial aid. Need-based:** 1,539 full-time freshmen applied for aid; 1,450 were judged to have need; 1,414 of these received aid. Average need met was 68%. Average scholarship/grant was $6,200; average loan $4,200. 58% of total undergraduate aid awarded as scholarships/grants, 42% as loans/jobs. **Non-need-based:** Awarded to 3,715 full-time undergraduates, including 779 freshmen. Scholarships awarded for academics, alumni affiliation, art, athletics, leadership, minority status, music/drama, ROTC, state residency.

**Application procedures. Admission:** Closing date 8/25 (receipt date). $15 fee. Application may be submitted online. Admission notification on a rolling basis. **Financial aid:** Priority date 2/15, closing date 7/1. FAFSA, institutional form required. Applicants notified on a rolling basis starting 6/1; must reply within 2 week(s) of notification.

**Academics.** Of the first 59 hours completed in college, students allowed to repeat courses with final grade of less than C. No more than 18 semester hours of course work may be repeated. **Special study options:** Accelerated study, distance learning, double major, dual enrollment of high school students, exchange student, honors, independent study, internships, study abroad, teacher certification program. **Credit/placement by examination:** AP, CLEP, SAT, ACT, institutional tests. 15 credit hours maximum toward associate degree, 30 toward bachelor's. **Support services:** Reduced course load, remedial instruction, study skills assistance, tutoring.

**Honors college/program.** Students must have a score of 24 or higher on the ACT or a high school GPA of 3.5 or higher.

**Majors. Agriculture:** General, agribusiness operations, animal sciences, plant sciences. **Biology:** General. **Business:** Accounting, business admin, finance, international, managerial economics, marketing, transportation. **Communications:** Digital media, journalism, radio/tv. **Communications technology:** Graphic/printing. **Computer sciences:** General, data processing. **Conservation:** Wildlife. **Education:** Agricultural, art, biology, business, chemistry, early childhood, English, French, health, mathematics, middle, music, physical, physics, social science, Spanish, special, speech. **Engineering:** General. **Engineering technology:** General. **English:** English lit, speech/rhetoric. **Foreign languages:** French, Spanish. **Health:** Athletic training, audiology/speech pathology, clinical lab science, medical radiologic technology/radiation therapy, nursing (RN). **History:** General. **Math:** General. **Parks/recreation:** Exercise sciences, health/fitness, sports admin. **Philosophy/religion:** Philosophy. **Physical sciences:** Chemistry, physics. **Protective services:** Forensics. **Psychology:** General. **Public administration:** Social work. **Social sciences:** Criminology, economics, geography, political science, sociology. **Visual/performing arts:** Art, commercial/advertising art, dramatic, music performance.

**Most popular majors.** Business/marketing 19%, education 19%, health sciences 12%, liberal arts 6%, social sciences 6%.

**Computing on campus.** 510 workstations in dormitories, library, computer center, student center. Dormitories linked to campus network. Commuter students can connect to campus network. Online course registration, helpline, wireless network available.

**Student life. Freshman orientation:** Mandatory. Preregistration for classes offered. All day session held on various dates for students to meet academic advisor, register for classes and learn about the university. **Housing:** Coed dorms, single-sex dorms, apartments, fraternity/sorority housing, substance-free housing available. $100 fully refundable deposit. Honors quarters available. **Activities:** Bands, choral groups, dance, drama, music ensembles, musical theater, opera, radio station, student government, student newspaper, symphony orchestra, TV station, College Democrats, Baptist Student Union, College Republicans Club, Church of Christ Student Center, International Students Association, Islamic Association, Black Student Association, Newman Club, Missionary Baptist Student Fellowship, Wesley Foundation.

**Athletics.** NCAA. **Intercollegiate:** Baseball M, basketball, bowling W, cross-country, football (tackle) M, golf, soccer W, tennis W, track and field, volleyball W. **Intramural:** Archery, badminton, basketball, bowling, golf, racquetball, soccer, softball, table tennis, tennis, volleyball.

**Student services.** Adult student services, career counseling, student employment services, financial aid counseling, health services, minority student services, personal counseling, placement for graduates, veterans' counselor. **Physically disabled:** Services for visually, speech, hearing impaired.

**Contact.**  E-mail: admissions@astate.edu
Phone: (870) 972-3024 Toll-free number: (800) 382-3030
Fax: (870) 972-3406
Tammy Fowler, Director of Admissions, Arkansas State University, PO Box 1630, State University, AR 72467-1630

## Arkansas Tech University
### Russellville, Arkansas
www.atu.edu                                            CB code: 6010

- Public 4-year university and liberal arts college
- Commuter campus in large town
- 6,558 degree-seeking undergraduates: 13% part-time, 53% women, 6% African American, 1% Asian American, 3% Hispanic American, 2% Native American, 3% international
- 538 degree-seeking graduate students
- 91% of applicants admitted
- SAT or ACT (ACT writing optional) required
- 39% graduate within 6 years

**General.** Founded in 1909. Regionally accredited. **Degrees:** 849 bachelor's, 108 associate awarded; master's offered. **ROTC:** Army. **Location:** 75 miles from Little Rock, 85 miles from Fort Smith. **Calendar:** Semester, extensive summer session. **Full-time faculty:** 281 total; 63% have terminal degrees, 8% minority, 47% women. **Part-time faculty:** 126 total; 10% have terminal degrees, 2% minority, 65% women. **Class size:** 35% < 20, 49% 20-39, 8% 40-49, 8% 50-99, less than 1% >100. **Special facilities:** Energy center, observatory, technology center.

**Freshman class profile.** 2,807 applied, 2,556 admitted, 1,627 enrolled.

| Mid 50% test scores | | | |
|---|---|---|---|
| SAT critical reading: | 350-520 | Rank in top tenth: | 19% |
| SAT math: | 430-620 | Return as sophomores: | 66% |
| ACT composite: | 19-26 | Out-of-state: | 4% |
| GPA 3.50 or higher: | 37% | Live on campus: | 61% |
| GPA 3.0-3.49: | 28% | International: | 2% |
| GPA 2.0-2.99: | 33% | Fraternities: | 3% |
| Rank in top quarter: | 44% | Sororities: | 8% |

**Basis for selection.** Secondary school record and standardized test scores are very important; class rank is considered. **Homeschooled:** Documentation of home school completion with a composite ACT of 19 or greater.

**High school preparation.** 21 units required. Required and recommended units include English 4, mathematics 4, social studies 3, history 2, science 3 (laboratory 3), foreign language 2 and academic electives 4.

**2007-2008 Annual costs.** Tuition/fees: $5,120; $9,710 out-of-state. Room/board: $4,422. Books/supplies: $1,320. Personal expenses: $2,390.

**2006-2007 Financial aid. Need-based:** 1,091 full-time freshmen applied for aid; 887 were judged to have need; 873 of these received aid.

Average need met was 36%. Average scholarship/grant was $2,566; average loan $1,005. 50% of total undergraduate aid awarded as scholarships/grants, 50% as loans/jobs. **Non-need-based:** Awarded to 2,260 full-time undergraduates, including 855 freshmen. Scholarships awarded for academics, art, athletics, leadership, minority status, music/drama, ROTC.

**Application procedures. Admission:** No deadline. No application fee. Application may be submitted online. Admission notification on a rolling basis. **Financial aid:** Priority date 4/15; no closing date. FAFSA required. Applicants notified on a rolling basis starting 5/1; must reply within 2 week(s) of notification.

**Academics. Special study options:** Accelerated study, combined bachelor's/graduate degree, cooperative education, distance learning, double major, dual enrollment of high school students, ESL, exchange student, external degree, honors, independent study, internships, student-designed major, study abroad, teacher certification program, weekend college. **Credit/placement by examination:** AP, CLEP, SAT, ACT, institutional tests. 30 credit hours maximum toward associate degree, 30 toward bachelor's. **Support services:** Learning center, reduced course load, remedial instruction, study skills assistance, tutoring.

**Honors college/program.** Minimum GPA of 3.5 and ACT score of 23. Target of 23 students per year. Honors students required to take honors classes throughout their stay at ATU.

**Majors. Agriculture:** Agribusiness operations. **Biology:** General. **Business:** Accounting, business admin, hospitality admin. **Communications:** Journalism. **Computer sciences:** General, information technology, systems analysis. **Conservation:** General. **Education:** Art, biology, business, chemistry, early childhood, elementary, English, foreign languages, mathematics, middle, music, physical, science, social studies, speech. **Engineering:** General, electrical, mechanical, physics. **English:** Creative writing, English lit, speech/rhetoric. **Foreign languages:** General. **Health:** Clinical lab science, medical records admin, nursing (RN). **History:** General. **Interdisciplinary:** Global studies. **Math:** General. **Parks/recreation:** Facilities management. **Physical sciences:** General, chemistry, geology. **Protective services:** Emergency management/homeland security. **Psychology:** General. **Social sciences:** Economics, sociology. **Visual/performing arts:** Art. **Other:** Rehabilitation science.

**Most popular majors.** Business/marketing 12%, education 21%, English 6%, health sciences 11%, history 6%.

**Computing on campus.** 700 workstations in dormitories, library, computer center, student center. Dormitories wired for high-speed internet access and linked to campus network. Commuter students can connect to campus network. Online course registration, helpline, wireless network available.

**Student life. Freshman orientation:** Available. Preregistration for classes offered. **Housing:** Guaranteed on-campus for freshmen. Coed dorms, single-sex dorms, special housing for disabled, apartments, substance-free housing available. $25 nonrefundable deposit. **Activities:** Bands, campus ministries, choral groups, dance, drama, film society, international student organizations, literary magazine, music ensembles, Model UN, musical theater, opera, radio station, student government, student newspaper, symphony orchestra, TV station.

**Athletics.** NCAA. **Intercollegiate:** Baseball M, basketball, cross-country W, football (tackle) M, golf, softball W, tennis W, volleyball W. **Intramural:** Basketball, bowling, cheerleading, cross-country, football (tackle), golf, racquetball, soccer, softball, swimming, table tennis, tennis, volleyball. **Team name:** Wonder Boys, Golden Suns.

**Student services.** Adult student services, alcohol/substance abuse counseling, career counseling, services for economically disadvantaged, student employment services, financial aid counseling, health services, minority student services, personal counseling, placement for graduates, veterans' counselor. **Physically disabled:** Services for visually, speech, hearing impaired.

**Contact.**  E-mail: tech.enroll@atu.edu
Phone: (479) 968-0343 Toll-free number: (800) 582-6953
Fax: (479) 964-0522
Shauna Donnell, Assistant Vice President for Enrollment Management, Arkansas Tech University, Doc Bryan Student Services Building #141, Russellville, AR 72801-2222

## Central Baptist College
### Conway, Arkansas
www.cbc.edu                                            CB code: 0788

- Private 4-year Bible and junior college affiliated with Baptist faith
- Residential campus in large town

♦ 566 degree-seeking undergraduates: 19% part-time, 45% women, 18% African American, 2% Asian American, 2% Hispanic American, 1% Native American, 1% international

♦ 73% of applicants admitted

♦ ACT (writing optional) required

♦ 56% graduate within 6 years

**General.** Founded in 1952. Regionally accredited. **Degrees:** 43 bachelor's, 23 associate awarded. **ROTC:** Army. **Location:** 30 miles from Little Rock. **Calendar:** Semester, limited summer session. **Full-time faculty:** 17 total; 41% have terminal degrees, 29% women. **Part-time faculty:** 37 total; 11% have terminal degrees, 14% minority, 38% women.

**Freshman class profile.** 183 applied, 133 admitted, 115 enrolled.

| Mid 50% test scores | ACT composite: | 17-23 |
|---|---|---|

**Basis for selection.** Religious commitment most important, followed by school achievement record. Interview recommended. **Homeschooled:** Transcript of courses and grades required.

**High school preparation.** 15 units recommended. Recommended units include English 4, mathematics 2, social studies 2 and science 2.

**2007-2008 Annual costs.** Tuition/fees: $9,040. Room/board: $5,000. Books/supplies: $600. Personal expenses: $800.

**Financial aid. Non-need-based:** Scholarships awarded for academics, state residency.

**Application procedures. Admission:** Closing date 8/15 (postmark date). $25 fee, may be waived for applicants with need. Application may be submitted online. Admission notification on a rolling basis. Must reply by 8/15. **Financial aid:** Priority date 7/1, closing date 8/1. FAFSA required. Applicants notified on a rolling basis starting 4/1.

**Academics. Special study options:** Internships. **Credit/placement by examination:** AP, CLEP, ACT, institutional tests. 15 credit hours maximum toward associate degree, 27 toward bachelor's. **Support services:** Learning center, pre-admission summer program, reduced course load, tutoring.

**Majors. Business:** Business admin, marketing, organizational behavior. **Computer sciences:** Data processing. **Public administration:** Social work. **Theology:** Bible, sacred music.

**Most popular majors.** Business/marketing 46%, computer/information sciences 7%, theological studies 28%, visual/performing arts 7%.

**Computing on campus.** Online library available.

**Student life. Freshman orientation:** Mandatory. **Policies:** Religious observance required. **Housing:** Guaranteed on-campus for freshmen. Single-sex dorms, substance-free housing available. $20 deposit, deadline 8/15. **Activities:** Concert band, choral groups, music ensembles, student government, student newspaper, Association of Baptist Students, College Republicans.

**Athletics.** NCCAA. **Intercollegiate:** Baseball M, basketball, softball W, volleyball W. **Intramural:** Badminton, basketball, bowling, softball, table tennis, volleyball. **Team name:** Mustangs.

**Student services.** Career counseling, personal counseling, veterans' counselor.

**Contact.** E-mail: jwilson@cbc.edu
Phone: (501) 329-6872 Toll-free number: (501) 208-6872
Fax: (501) 329-2941
Jonathan Wilson, Director of Admissions, Central Baptist College, 1501 College Avenue, Conway, AR 72034

## Ecclesia College
### Springdale, Arkansas
### www.ecollege.edu

♦ Private 4-year liberal arts college affiliated with interdenominational tradition

♦ Residential campus in large town

♦ 104 degree-seeking undergraduates

♦ ACT (writing optional) required

**General.** Accredited by ABHE. **Degrees:** 14 bachelor's, 1 associate awarded. **Calendar:** Semester, limited summer session. **Part-time faculty:** 33 total; 24% have terminal degrees, 18% women.

**Freshman class profile.** 103 applied, 41 admitted, 41 enrolled.

| Out-of-state: | 25% | Live on campus: | 75% |
|---|---|---|---|

**Basis for selection.** Open admission, but selective for some programs. Recommendations and personal character very important. **Homeschooled:** State high school equivalency certificate required.

**High school preparation.** Recommended units include English 4, mathematics 3, social studies 3, science 3 and foreign language 1.

**2008-2009 Annual costs.** Tuition/fees (projected): $15,090. Full-time students not living on campus may be subject to additional $600 nonresidents fee. Room/board: $5,485. Books/supplies: $500. Personal expenses: $875.

**2006-2007 Financial aid. Need-based:** 44% of total undergraduate aid awarded as scholarships/grants, 56% as loans/jobs. **Non-need-based:** Scholarships awarded for academics, athletics, leadership, music/drama.

**Application procedures. Admission:** Closing date 8/27 (receipt date). $50 fee. Application must be submitted on paper. Admission notification on a rolling basis. **Financial aid:** No deadline. FAFSA required. Applicants notified on a rolling basis starting 7/1.

**Academics. Special study options:** Double major, dual enrollment of high school students, independent study, internships. **Credit/placement by examination:** CLEP, ACT, institutional tests. **Support services:** Remedial instruction, tutoring.

**Majors. Business:** Business admin. **Theology:** Bible, missionary, pastoral counseling, preministerial, religious ed, sacred music, theology, youth ministry. **Other:** Communication ministries.

**Computing on campus.** 15 workstations in library, computer center. Dormitories wired for high-speed internet access. Online library, wireless network available.

**Student life. Freshman orientation:** Mandatory. Preregistration for classes offered. **Policies:** Religious observance required. **Housing:** Single-sex dorms, apartments, substance-free housing available. Pets allowed in dorm rooms. **Activities:** Choral groups, drama, student government.

**Athletics. Intercollegiate:** Baseball M, basketball, golf, track and field. **Team name:** Royals.

**Student services.** Alcohol/substance abuse counseling, campus ministries, career counseling, financial aid counseling, personal counseling, placement for graduates.

**Contact.** E-mail: admissions@ecollege.edu
Phone: (479) 248-7236 ext. 212 Toll-free number: (800) 735-9926
Fax: (479) 248-1455
Titus Hofer, Director of Admissions, Ecclesia College, 9653 Nations Drive, Springdale, AR 72762

## Harding University
### Searcy, Arkansas
### www.harding.edu
**CB code: 6267**

♦ Private 4-year university affiliated with Church of Christ

♦ Residential campus in large town

♦ 4,063 degree-seeking undergraduates: 5% part-time, 55% women, 4% African American, 1% Asian American, 2% Hispanic American, 1% Native American, 5% international

♦ 990 degree-seeking graduate students

♦ 80% of applicants admitted

♦ SAT or ACT (ACT writing optional) required

♦ 60% graduate within 6 years; 24% enter graduate study

**General.** Founded in 1924. Regionally accredited. **Degrees:** 770 bachelor's awarded; master's, doctoral, first professional offered. **ROTC:** Army. **Location:** 50 miles from Little Rock, 105 miles from Memphis. **Calendar:** Semester, extensive summer session. **Full-time faculty:** 226 total; 67% have terminal degrees, 3% minority, 30% women. **Part-time faculty:** 203 total; 31% have terminal degrees, 3% minority, 36% women. **Class size:** 51% < 20, 31% 20-39, 7% 40-49, 11% 50-99.

**Freshman class profile.** 1,768 applied, 1,416 admitted, 965 enrolled.

| Mid 50% test scores | | | |
|---|---|---|---|
| SAT critical reading: | 480-620 | Rank in top tenth: | 27% |
| SAT math: | 480-620 | End year in good standing: | 87% |
| SAT writing: | 450-600 | Return as sophomores: | 80% |
| ACT composite: | 21-28 | Out-of-state: | 75% |
| GPA 3.50 or higher: | 57% | Live on campus: | 96% |
| GPA 3.0-3.49: | 26% | International: | 4% |
| GPA 2.0-2.99: | 15% | Fraternities: | 39% |
| Rank in top quarter: | 54% | Sororities: | 40% |

**Basis for selection.** Test scores, academic record, references, interview important. Selective admission with limited openings, students must apply early. Students are encouraged to take rigorous classes in high school. Audition recommended for music majors, portfolio for art majors.

**High school preparation.** 15 units required. Required and recommended units include English 4, mathematics 3-4, social studies 3-4, science 2-4, foreign language 2 and academic electives 3.

**2007-2008 Annual costs.** Tuition/fees: $12,360. Room/board: $5,578. Books/supplies: $1,200. Personal expenses: $300.

**2006-2007 Financial aid. Need-based:** 670 full-time freshmen applied for aid; 467 were judged to have need; 466 of these received aid. Average need met was 75%. Average scholarship/grant was $6,300; average loan $3,864. 39% of total undergraduate aid awarded as scholarships/grants, 61% as loans/jobs. **Non-need-based:** Awarded to 903 full-time undergraduates, including 306 freshmen. Scholarships awarded for academics, art, athletics, music/drama, religious affiliation, ROTC, state residency. **Additional information:** Music scholarships available, audition required.

**Application procedures. Admission:** No deadline. $35 fee. Application may be submitted online. Admission notification on a rolling basis beginning on or about 5/1. Early application encouraged. **Financial aid:** Priority date 4/1; no closing date. FAFSA, institutional form required. Applicants notified on a rolling basis starting 2/15; must reply within 2 week(s) of notification.

**Academics. Special study options:** Accelerated study, cooperative education, distance learning, double major, dual enrollment of high school students, ESL, honors, independent study, internships, liberal arts/career combination, study abroad, teacher certification program. **Credit/placement by examination:** AP, CLEP, IB, SAT, ACT, institutional tests. 32 credit hours maximum toward bachelor's degree. **Support services:** Learning center, reduced course load, remedial instruction, study skills assistance, tutoring, writing center.

**Honors college/program.** Honors students are eligible with an ACT score of 27 or higher, or SAT of 1200 or higher. There are approximately 175 Honors Students who begin as freshmen each fall. Honors scholars (40 freshmen each fall) must be National Merit finalists or Trustee Scholarship recipients. The Trustee scholarship recipients are selected from a pool of students with an ACT score of 31 or higher, or an SAT of 1330 or higher.

**Majors. Area/ethnic studies:** American. **Biology:** General, biochemistry, Biochemistry/biophysics and molecular biology. **Business:** Accounting, business admin, communications, fashion, human resources, international, marketing, sales/distribution. **Communications:** General, advertising, broadcast journalism, digital media, journalism, public relations. **Computer sciences:** General, computer science, information technology. **Education:** Art, biology, chemistry, early childhood, early childhood special, elementary, English, family/consumer sciences, foreign languages, French, health, mathematics, middle, multi-level teacher, music, physical, science, social studies, Spanish, special, speech. **Engineering:** Computer, electrical, mechanical. **English:** English lit. **Family/consumer sciences:** General. **Foreign languages:** French, Spanish. **Health:** Art therapy, athletic training, clinical lab science, communication disorders, dietetics, health care admin, nursing (RN), predental, premedicine, prepharmacy, preveterinary, speech pathology. **History:** General. **Interdisciplinary:** Global studies. **Legal studies:** Prelaw. **Liberal arts:** Humanities. **Math:** General. **Parks/recreation:** Exercise sciences, sports admin. **Physical sciences:** Chemistry, physics. **Protective services:** Criminal justice. **Psychology:** General. **Public administration:** General, social work. **Social sciences:** General, economics, political science. **Theology:** Bible, missionary, religious ed, theology, youth ministry. **Visual/performing arts:** Art, dramatic, graphic design, interior design, painting, studio arts.

**Most popular majors.** Business/marketing 20%, communications/journalism 6%, education 15%, health sciences 11%, liberal arts 6%, theological studies 6%, visual/performing arts 6%.

**Computing on campus.** 495 workstations in library, computer center, student center. Dormitories wired for high-speed internet access and linked to campus network. Commuter students can connect to campus network.

Online course registration, online library, helpline, repair service, wireless network available.

**Student life. Freshman orientation:** Available, $95 fee. Preregistration for classes offered. Three days of orientation immediately before the start of the fall semester. Includes all activities and meals, plus a t-shirt and academic planner. **Policies:** Religious observance required. **Housing:** Guaranteed on-campus for freshmen. Single-sex dorms, special housing for disabled, apartments, substance-free housing available. $125 fully refundable deposit, deadline 5/1. Approved off-campus housing. **Activities:** Bands, campus ministries, choral groups, drama, international student organizations, music ensembles, radio station, student government, student newspaper, symphony orchestra, TV station, Young Republicans, dactylology club, Good News Singers, Timothy Club, religious mission campaigns, multi-cultural student action committee.

**Athletics.** NCAA. **Intercollegiate:** Baseball M, basketball, cheerleading M, cross-country, football (tackle) M, golf, soccer, tennis, track and field, volleyball W. **Intramural:** Archery M, basketball, cross-country M, football (non-tackle), golf M, racquetball, soccer, softball, swimming, table tennis M, tennis, track and field, volleyball, weight lifting M. **Team name:** Bisons.

**Student services.** Adult student services, campus ministries, career counseling, student employment services, financial aid counseling, health services, minority student services, personal counseling, placement for graduates. **Physically disabled:** Services for visually, speech, hearing impaired.

**Contact.** E-mail: admissions@harding.edu
Phone: (501) 279-4407 Toll-free number: (800) 477-4407
Fax: (501) 279-4129
Glenn Dillard, Assistant Vice President for Enrollment Management,
Harding University, 915 East Market Avenue, Searcy, AR 72149-2255

---

## Henderson State University
**Arkadelphia, Arkansas**
**www.getreddie.com**

**CB member**
**CB code: 6272**

- Public 4-year university and liberal arts college
- Commuter campus in large town
- 3,092 degree-seeking undergraduates: 11% part-time, 54% women, 20% African American, 2% Hispanic American, 1% Native American, 2% international
- 430 degree-seeking graduate students
- 66% of applicants admitted
- SAT or ACT (ACT writing optional) required
- 32% graduate within 6 years

**General.** Founded in 1890. Regionally accredited. **Degrees:** 432 bachelor's awarded; master's offered. **ROTC:** Army. **Location:** 67 miles from Little Rock. **Calendar:** Semester, limited summer session. **Full-time faculty:** 156 total; 69% have terminal degrees, 12% minority, 37% women. **Part-time faculty:** 74 total; 18% have terminal degrees, 5% minority, 70% women. **Class size:** 55% < 20, 38% 20-39, 5% 40-49, 2% 50-99, less than 1% >100. **Special facilities:** Planetarium.

**Freshman class profile.** 2,425 applied, 1,595 admitted, 803 enrolled.

| Mid 50% test scores | | | |
|---|---|---|---|
| SAT critical reading: | 430-580 | Rank in top quarter: | 39% |
| SAT math: | 460-570 | Rank in top tenth: | 16% |
| ACT composite: | 18-25 | Return as sophomores: | 81% |
| GPA 3.50 or higher: | 31% | Out-of-state: | 18% |
| GPA 3.0-3.49: | 31% | Live on campus: | 79% |
| GPA 2.0-2.99: | 36% | International: | 3% |

**Basis for selection.** Applicants must have ACT composite of 19 and minimum 2.5 GPA for unconditional admission. Those not meeting GPA requirement admitted conditionally. Applicants who do not meet minimum test score standards may be admitted through appeal process. Deadline for applying for appeal is July 15. ACT recommended. Test scores must be on file with Admissions prior to registering for classes. Audition recommended for music and theater arts majors. **Homeschooled:** Minimum ACT composite score of 18, transcript required. Completion of college prep curriculum encouraged. **Learning Disabled:** Student Support Disability Services assesses needs of students with learning disabilities.

**High school preparation.** 14 units required; 22 recommended. Required and recommended units include English 4, mathematics 4, social studies 2, history 1 and science 3. Required: 1/2 oral comm, 1/2 fine art, 6 career focus.

**2007-2008 Annual costs.** Tuition/fees: $5,981; $10,601 out-of-state.

**Financial aid. Non-need-based:** Scholarships awarded for academics, alumni affiliation, art, athletics, leadership, minority status, music/drama, state residency.

**Application procedures. Admission:** No deadline. No application fee. Application may be submitted online. Admission notification on a rolling basis beginning on or about 9/1. Application closing date July 15 for applicants with ACT score under 18. **Financial aid:** Priority date 6/1; no closing date. FAFSA required. Applicants notified on a rolling basis starting 4/1; must reply within 2 week(s) of notification.

**Academics. Special study options:** Cross-registration, distance learning, honors, internships, liberal arts/career combination, teacher certification program. **Credit/placement by examination:** AP, CLEP, SAT, ACT, institutional tests. 30 credit hours maximum toward bachelor's degree. **Support services:** Learning center, remedial instruction, study skills assistance, tutoring.

**Honors college/program.** Freshmen must have composite ACT of 26 or higher. Approximately 90 admitted. Sophomores must have cumulative GPA of 3.25 or higher to petition committee for admission.

**Majors. Biology:** General. **Business:** General, accounting, management information systems. **Communications:** Journalism. **Computer sciences:** General. **Education:** Art, biology, business, early childhood, elementary, English, middle, social science. **English:** English lit, speech/rhetoric. **Family/consumer sciences:** General. **Foreign languages:** Spanish. **Health:** Athletic training, clinical lab science, nursing (RN). **History:** General. **Math:** General. **Parks/recreation:** Facilities management. **Physical sciences:** Chemistry, physics. **Psychology:** General. **Public administration:** General, social work. **Social sciences:** Political science, sociology. **Transportation:** Airline/commercial pilot. **Visual/performing arts:** Art, dramatic, music performance.

**Most popular majors.** Business/marketing 16%, education 20%, English 7%, health sciences 8%, psychology 7%, social sciences 6%.

**Computing on campus.** 125 workstations in dormitories, library, computer center, student center. Dormitories linked to campus network. Commuter students can connect to campus network. Helpline available.

**Student life. Freshman orientation:** Mandatory. Preregistration for classes offered. Day-long program for students and parents includes pre-registration, signing up for ID and e-mail address. Program held for week in June, again in July if necessary. **Housing:** Guaranteed on-campus for freshmen. Coed dorms, single-sex dorms, cooperative housing, substance-free housing available. $50 deposit. Special hall for Honors College participants, special floor for freshman interest groups available. On-campus apartments leased by outside firm available. Two residence halls are co-ed. **Activities:** Bands, choral groups, dance, drama, literary magazine, music ensembles, radio station, student government, student newspaper, TV station, College Republicans, Young Democrats, Student Foundation, Heart & Key service organization, several religious organizations.

**Athletics.** NCAA. **Intercollegiate:** Baseball M, basketball, cross-country W, football (tackle) M, golf, softball W, swimming, tennis W, volleyball W. **Intramural:** Soccer M. **Team name:** Reddies.

**Student services.** Career counseling, student employment services, health services, personal counseling, placement for graduates, veterans' counselor. **Physically disabled:** Services for visually, speech, hearing impaired.

**Contact.** E-mail: admissions@hsu.edu
Phone: (870) 230-5028 Toll-free number: (800) 228-7333
Fax: (870) 230-5066
Vikita Hardwrick, Director of Admissions, Henderson State University, 1100 Henderson Street, Arkadelphia, AR 71999-0001

---

## Hendrix College
**Conway, Arkansas**
**www.hendrix.edu**

**CB member**
**CB code: 6273**

- Private 4-year liberal arts college affiliated with United Methodist Church
- Residential campus in small city
- 1,189 degree-seeking undergraduates: 1% part-time, 55% women, 4% African American, 3% Asian American, 3% Hispanic American, 1% Native American, 1% international
- 4 degree-seeking graduate students
- 83% of applicants admitted
- SAT or ACT (ACT writing optional), application essay required
- 66% graduate within 6 years

**General.** Founded in 1876. Regionally accredited. **Degrees:** 203 bachelor's awarded; master's offered. **ROTC:** Army. **Location:** 30 miles from Little Rock. **Calendar:** Semester. **Full-time faculty:** 92 total; 97% have terminal degrees, 11% minority, 36% women. **Part-time faculty:** 40 total; 42% have terminal degrees, 12% minority, 60% women. **Class size:** 65% < 20, 34% 20-39, less than 1% 40-49, less than 1% 50-99. **Special facilities:** Teaching theater, two pipe organs, access to elephant farm for research and volunteer service, arboretum, ring laser, hybrid rocket lab.

**Freshman class profile.** 1,323 applied, 1,094 admitted, 372 enrolled.

| Mid 50% test scores | | Rank in top quarter: | 75% |
|---|---|---|---|
| SAT critical reading: | 570-690 | Rank in top tenth: | 43% |
| SAT math: | 550-660 | End year in good standing: | 88% |
| ACT composite: | 25-31 | Return as sophomores: | 86% |
| GPA 3.50 or higher: | 69% | Out-of-state: | 51% |
| GPA 3.0-3.49: | 22% | Live on campus: | 97% |
| GPA 2.0-2.99: | 9% | International: | 2% |

**Basis for selection.** Academic competence, scholastic potential, motivation, character, and high school leadership important. Interview may be required. **Homeschooled:** Interview required. Portfolio required.

**High school preparation.** 14 units recommended. Recommended units include English 4, mathematics 3, social studies 3, science 2 and foreign language 2.

**2008-2009 Annual costs.** Tuition/fees (projected): $26,080. Room/board: $7,950. Books/supplies: $900. Personal expenses: $1,903.

**2007-2008 Financial aid. Need-based:** 312 full-time freshmen applied for aid; 232 were judged to have need; 232 of these received aid. Average need met was 88%. Average scholarship/grant was $16,387; average loan $4,166. 74% of total undergraduate aid awarded as scholarships/grants, 26% as loans/jobs. **Non-need-based:** Awarded to 698 full-time undergraduates, including 202 freshmen. Scholarships awarded for academics, art, leadership, music/drama, religious affiliation.

**Application procedures. Admission:** Priority date 2/1; deadline 8/1 (postmark date). $40 fee, may be waived for applicants with need. Application may be submitted online. Admission notification on a rolling basis beginning on or about 11/1. Must reply by May 1 or within 4 week(s) if notified thereafter. **Financial aid:** Priority date 2/15; no closing date. FAFSA required. Applicants notified on a rolling basis starting 3/1; must reply by 5/1 or within 2 week(s) of notification.

**Academics. Special study options:** Cooperative education, double major, exchange student, independent study, internships, student-designed major, study abroad, teacher certification program, Washington semester. Hendrix-in-Oxford, Hendrix-in-London, programs with Austria, China, and Japan, American University. **Credit/placement by examination:** AP, CLEP, IB, SAT, ACT, institutional tests. 6 credit hours maximum toward bachelor's degree. **Support services:** Pre-admission summer program, study skills assistance, tutoring, writing center.

**Majors. Area/ethnic studies:** American. **Biology:** General, Biochemistry/biophysics and molecular biology. **Business:** Accounting, managerial economics. **Computer sciences:** Computer science. **Conservation:** Environmental studies. **Education:** Physical. **English:** English lit. **Foreign languages:** French, German, Spanish. **Health:** Health services. **History:** General. **Liberal arts:** Arts/sciences. **Math:** General. **Parks/recreation:** Exercise sciences. **Philosophy/religion:** Philosophy, religion. **Physical sciences:** Chemical physics, chemistry, physics. **Psychology:** General. **Social sciences:** Anthropology, economics, international relations, political science, sociology. **Visual/performing arts:** Art, dramatic. **Other:** Philosophy/religious studies.

**Most popular majors.** Biology 17%, English 6%, history 7%, philosophy/religious studies 7%, psychology 11%, social sciences 19%, visual/performing arts 7%.

**Computing on campus.** 75 workstations in dormitories, library, computer center. Dormitories wired for high-speed internet access and linked to campus network. Commuter students can connect to campus network. Online course registration, helpline, repair service, student web hosting, wireless network available.

**Student life. Freshman orientation:** Mandatory. 7-day program prior to fall term. **Housing:** Guaranteed on-campus for freshmen. Coed dorms, single-sex dorms, special housing for disabled, apartments, substance-free housing available. Language house, small suite-style houses available. **Activities:** Bands, choral groups, dance, drama, literary magazine, music ensembles, musical theater, radio station, student government, student newspaper, symphony orchestra, Students for Black Culture, College Republicans, Young Democrats, environmental group, Amnesty International, BACCHUS, Hendrix Peace Links, religious life council, volunteer action center, Students Promoting the Education of Asian Cultures.

**Athletics.** NCAA. **Intercollegiate:** Baseball M, basketball, cross-country, diving, field hockey, golf, lacrosse, soccer, softball W, swimming, tennis, track and field, volleyball W. **Intramural:** Badminton, basketball, football (non-tackle), racquetball, soccer, softball, tennis, volleyball. **Team name:** Warriors.

**Student services.** Alcohol/substance abuse counseling, campus ministries, career counseling, student employment services, financial aid counseling, health services, minority student services, personal counseling, placement for graduates, veterans' counselor.

**Contact.** E-mail: adm@hendrix.edu
Phone: (501) 450-1362 Toll-free number: (800) 277-9017
Fax: (501) 450-3843
Laura Martin, Director of Admission, Hendrix College, 1600 Washington Avenue, Conway, AR 72032-3080

---

## ITT Technical Institute: Little Rock
**Little Rock, Arkansas**
www.itt-tech.edu                                CB code: 2721

- For-profit 4-year technical college
- Commuter campus in small city

**General.** Accredited by ACICS. **Calendar:** Quarter.

**Annual costs/financial aid.** Tuition varies by program, $260-$368 per credit hour.

**Contact.** Phone: (501) 565-5550
Director of Recruitment, 4520 S. University Avenue, Little Rock, AR 72204

---

## John Brown University
**Siloam Springs, Arkansas**
www.jbu.edu                                     CB code: 6321

- Private 4-year liberal arts college affiliated with interdenominational tradition
- Residential campus in large town
- 1,666 degree-seeking undergraduates: 3% part-time, 53% women
- 353 degree-seeking graduate students
- SAT or ACT (ACT writing optional), application essay required
- 71% graduate within 6 years

**General.** Founded in 1919. Regionally accredited. **Degrees:** 490 bachelor's, 2 associate awarded; master's offered. **ROTC:** Army, Air Force. **Location:** 30 miles from Fayetteville, 75 miles from Tulsa, Oklahoma. **Calendar:** Semester, limited summer session. **Full-time faculty:** 92 total. **Part-time faculty:** 95 total. **Class size:** 51% < 20, 43% 20-39, 6% 40-49. **Special facilities:** Cadaver lab, cathedral, historical cabin.

**Freshman class profile.**

| Mid 50% test scores | | | |
|---|---|---|---|
| SAT critical reading: | 520-650 | GPA 2.0-2.99: | 9% |
| SAT math: | 530-650 | Rank in top quarter: | 67% |
| ACT composite: | 22-29 | Rank in top tenth: | 38% |
| GPA 3.50 or higher: | 69% | Return as sophomores: | 80% |
| GPA 3.0-3.49: | 21% | Out-of-state: | 77% |
|  |  | Live on campus: | 98% |

**Basis for selection.** Test scores, secondary school record, recommendations, essay, interview most important. Special talents, class rank considered. Combined SAT score of 950 (exclusive of Writing), ACT score of 20 or above. Interview recommended. Audition required of music majors; portfolio recommended for art majors. **Homeschooled:** Transcript of courses and grades required.

**High school preparation.** Recommended units include English 4, mathematics 3, social studies 2, history 1, science 2 (laboratory 1) and foreign language 2. 4 units of mathematics, 3 science for science and engineering majors; 2 foreign language recommended for home educated students.

**2007-2008 Annual costs.** Tuition/fees: $17,076. Room/board: $6,220. Books/supplies: $700. Personal expenses: $1,350.

**Financial aid.** **Non-need-based:** Scholarships awarded for academics, alumni affiliation, art, athletics, leadership, music/drama, ROTC.

**Application procedures.** **Admission:** Priority date 5/1; no deadline. $25 fee, may be waived for applicants with need. Application may be submitted online. Admission notification on a rolling basis beginning on or about 12/1. Must reply by May 1 or within 2 week(s) if notified thereafter. **Financial**

---

**aid:** Priority date 3/1; no closing date. FAFSA, institutional form required. Applicants notified on a rolling basis starting 3/1; must reply within 4 week(s) of notification.

**Academics.** **Special study options:** Accelerated study, distance learning, double major, dual enrollment of high school students, ESL, exchange student, honors, independent study, internships, study abroad, teacher certification program, Washington semester. **Credit/placement by examination:** AP, CLEP, IB, SAT, ACT. 15 credit hours maximum toward associate degree, 30 toward bachelor's. **Support services:** Learning center, reduced course load, remedial instruction, study skills assistance, tutoring, writing center.

**Honors college/program.** Selected by admissions office/honors committee, requirements are high school GPA, SAT/ACT score and interview.

**Majors.** **Biology:** General, biochemistry. **Business:** Accounting, business admin, construction management, international, marketing. **Communications:** Broadcast journalism, digital media, journalism, public relations. **Computer sciences:** Computer science. **Conservation:** General. **Education:** Biology, chemistry, early childhood, English, mathematics, middle, music, social studies. **Engineering:** General. **English:** English lit. **Family/consumer sciences:** Family/community services. **Foreign languages:** Spanish. **Health:** Athletic training. **History:** General. **Interdisciplinary:** Global studies. **Math:** General. **Parks/recreation:** Exercise sciences, sports admin. **Physical sciences:** Chemistry. **Psychology:** General. **Social sciences:** Political science. **Theology:** Missionary, sacred music, theology, youth ministry. **Visual/performing arts:** Graphic design, illustration, music performance. **Other:** Leadership and management.

**Most popular majors.** Business/marketing 57%, communications/journalism 7%, visual/performing arts 6%.

**Computing on campus.** 200 workstations in dormitories, library, computer center, student center. Dormitories wired for high-speed internet access and linked to campus network. Commuter students can connect to campus network. Online course registration, online library, helpline, wireless network available.

**Student life.** **Freshman orientation:** Mandatory, $75 fee. Preregistration for classes offered. **Policies:** No alcohol, drugs, or tobacco allowed on campus; all applicants required to sign community covenant each year. Religious observance required. **Housing:** Guaranteed on-campus for freshmen. Coed dorms, single-sex dorms, special housing for disabled, apartments, substance-free housing available. $200 deposit. **Activities:** Pep band, choral groups, drama, music ensembles, musical theater, opera, radio station, student government, student newspaper, council to assist in the unity of student evangelism, Young Republicans, Young Democrats, Young Life, Boys & Girls Club volunteer opportunities.

**Athletics.** NAIA. **Intercollegiate:** Basketball, soccer, swimming W, tennis, volleyball W. **Intramural:** Baseball M, basketball, football (non-tackle), football (tackle) M, racquetball, soccer, softball, tennis, volleyball. **Team name:** Golden Eagles.

**Student services.** Campus ministries, career counseling, student employment services, financial aid counseling, health services, personal counseling, placement for graduates. **Physically disabled:** Services for visually, hearing impaired.

**Contact.** E-mail: jbuinfo@jbu.edu
Phone: (479) 524-7286 Toll-free number: (877) 528-4636
Fax: (479) 524-4196
Don Crandall, Vice President for Enrollment Management, John Brown University, 2000 West University Street, Siloam Springs, AR 72761-2121

---

## Lyon College
**Batesville, Arkansas**                        CB member
www.lyon.edu                                     CB code: 6009

- Private 4-year liberal arts college affiliated with Presbyterian Church (USA)
- Residential campus in small town
- 483 degree-seeking undergraduates: 4% part-time, 54% women, 3% African American, 1% Asian American, 2% Hispanic American, 2% Native American, 2% international
- 69% of applicants admitted
- SAT or ACT (ACT writing optional) required
- 56% graduate within 6 years; 24% enter graduate study

**General.** Founded in 1872. Regionally accredited. **Degrees:** 103 bachelor's awarded. **Location:** 90 miles from Little Rock. **Calendar:** Semester, limited summer session. **Full-time faculty:** 44 total; 89% have terminal degrees, 11% minority, 23% women. **Part-time faculty:** 18 total; 11% have terminal degrees, 6% minority, 78% women. **Class size:** 74% < 20, 26% 20-39. **Special facilities:** Ozark Regional Studies Center.

**Freshman class profile.** 856 applied, 587 admitted, 142 enrolled.

| Mid 50% test scores | | | |
|---|---|---|---|
| SAT critical reading: | 500-590 | Rank in top quarter: | 72% |
| SAT math: | 510-600 | Rank in top tenth: | 30% |
| ACT composite: | 22-27 | End year in good standing: | 87% |
| GPA 3.50 or higher: | 73% | Return as sophomores: | 64% |
| GPA 3.0-3.49: | 18% | Out-of-state: | 30% |
| GPA 2.0-2.99: | 9% | Live on campus: | 93% |
| | | International: | 1% |

**Basis for selection.** High school academic performance and standardized test scores are the most important. Personal essays and letters of recommendation are considered on a case by case basis. Math proficiency and placement are judged with ACT math subscores. Auditions or portfolios required for fine arts.

**High school preparation.** 16 units required; 18 recommended. Required and recommended units include English 4, mathematics 3-4, social studies 1, history 2, science 3-4 (laboratory 2), foreign language 2 and academic electives 1.

**2008-2009 Annual costs.** Tuition/fees: $19,034. Room/board: $6,990. Books/supplies: $1,000. Personal expenses: $1,000.

**2007-2008 Financial aid. Need-based:** 118 full-time freshmen applied for aid; 96 were judged to have need; 96 of these received aid. Average need met was 85%. Average scholarship/grant was $11,863; average loan $3,748. 67% of total undergraduate aid awarded as scholarships/grants, 33% as loans/jobs. **Non-need-based:** Scholarships awarded for academics, art, athletics, leadership, minority status, music/drama, religious affiliation, state residency.

**Application procedures. Admission:** Priority date 1/15; no deadline. $25 fee, may be waived for applicants with need. Application may be submitted online. Admission notification on a rolling basis. Must reply by May 1 or within 2 week(s) if notified thereafter. **Financial aid:** Priority date 3/15; no closing date. FAFSA required. Applicants notified on a rolling basis starting 3/1; must reply by 8/15.

**Academics.** Academic honor code administered by peer-elected student honor council. **Special study options:** Accelerated study, combined bachelor's/graduate degree, cross-registration, double major, dual enrollment of high school students, independent study, internships, student-designed major, study abroad, teacher certification program, Washington semester. **Credit/placement by examination:** AP, CLEP, IB, SAT, ACT, institutional tests. 33 credit hours maximum toward bachelor's degree. **Support services:** Learning center, study skills assistance, tutoring, writing center.

**Majors. Biology:** General, biochemistry. **Business:** Accounting, business admin. **Computer sciences:** Computer science. **Conservation:** Environmental studies. **Education:** Early childhood. **English:** English lit. **Foreign languages:** Spanish. **History:** General. **Math:** General. **Philosophy/religion:** Philosophy, religion. **Physical sciences:** Chemistry. **Psychology:** General. **Social sciences:** Economics, political science. **Visual/performing arts:** Art, dramatic.

**Most popular majors.** Biology 15%, business/marketing 35%, English 9%, history 10%, psychology 10%, social sciences 6%.

**Computing on campus.** 103 workstations in dormitories, library, computer center, student center. Dormitories wired for high-speed internet access and linked to campus network. Commuter students can connect to campus network. Online course registration, online library, helpline, wireless network available.

**Student life. Freshman orientation:** Mandatory. Preregistration for classes offered. **Policies:** Social code administered by peer-elected student social council. **Housing:** Guaranteed on-campus for all undergraduates. Coed dorms, single-sex dorms, apartments, substance-free housing available. $100 fully refundable deposit. Limited college-owned off-campus housing is available. **Activities:** Campus ministries, choral groups, drama, international student organizations, literary magazine, music ensembles, student government, student newspaper, Black students association, Fellowship of Christian Athletes.

**Athletics.** NAIA. **Intercollegiate:** Baseball M, basketball, cheerleading, cross-country, golf, soccer, softball W, tennis, volleyball W. **Intramural:** Badminton, basketball, football (non-tackle), softball, table tennis, tennis, volleyball. **Team name:** Scots (M), Pipers (W).

**Student services.** Campus ministries, career counseling, financial aid counseling, health services, personal counseling, placement for graduates.

**Contact.** E-mail: admissions@lyon.edu
Phone: (870) 307-7250 Toll-free number: (800) 423-2542
Fax: (870) 307-7542
Anne Woodbury, Director of Admission Operations, Lyon College, PO Box 2317, Batesville, AR 72503-2317

## Ouachita Baptist University
### Arkadelphia, Arkansas
**www.obu.edu**  CB code: 6549

- Private 4-year liberal arts college affiliated with Southern Baptist Convention
- Residential campus in large town
- 1,398 degree-seeking undergraduates: 7% African American, 1% Asian American, 2% Hispanic American, 1% Native American, 3% international
- 69% of applicants admitted
- SAT or ACT (ACT writing optional) required
- 66% graduate within 6 years

**General.** Founded in 1886. Regionally accredited. Strong emphasis on global awareness, international study opportunities, missions, and volunteer service. **Degrees:** 264 bachelor's awarded. **ROTC:** Army. **Location:** 65 miles from Little Rock. **Calendar:** Semester, extensive summer session. **Full-time faculty:** 118 total; 72% have terminal degrees, less than 1% minority, 31% women. **Part-time faculty:** 27 total; 7% have terminal degrees, 78% women. **Class size:** 58% < 20, 41% 20-39, less than 1% 40-49, less than 1% 50-99.

**Freshman class profile.** 1,283 applied, 884 admitted, 372 enrolled.

| Mid 50% test scores | | | |
|---|---|---|---|
| SAT critical reading: | 480-630 | Rank in top tenth: | 28% |
| SAT math: | 480-610 | End year in good standing: | 91% |
| ACT composite: | 21-27 | Return as sophomores: | 77% |
| GPA 3.50 or higher: | 59% | Out-of-state: | 47% |
| GPA 3.0-3.49: | 24% | Live on campus: | 99% |
| GPA 2.0-2.99: | 17% | Fraternities: | 30% |
| Rank in top quarter: | 58% | Sororities: | 45% |

**Basis for selection.** Test scores and school achievement record most important. Minimum high school GPA of 2.75 required, ACT score of 20 or higher. Interview recommended. Portfolio recommended for studio art majors.

**High school preparation.** 15 units required; 19 recommended. Required and recommended units include English 4, mathematics 2-3, social studies 1, history 2, science 2-3, foreign language 2 and academic electives 4.

**2008-2009 Annual costs.** Tuition/fees: $18,400. Room/board: $5,530. Books/supplies: $950. Personal expenses: $1,500.

**2007-2008 Financial aid. Need-based:** Average need met was 86%. Average scholarship/grant was $10,681; average loan $3,349. 79% of total undergraduate aid awarded as scholarships/grants, 21% as loans/jobs. **Non-need-based:** Scholarships awarded for academics, alumni affiliation, athletics, job skills, leadership, minority status, music/drama, religious affiliation, ROTC, state residency.

**Application procedures. Admission:** No deadline. $50 fee. Application may be submitted online. Admission notification on a rolling basis. **Financial aid:** Priority date 1/15, closing date 6/1. FAFSA required. Applicants notified on a rolling basis starting 11/1; must reply by 5/1.

**Academics.** Classes in Arkansas Folkways taught at Old Washington State Park. International exchange programs in Australia, Austria, China, Costa Rica, England, France, Germany, Hong Kong, Indonesia, Japan, Morocco, Russia, Scotland, and South Africa. **Special study options:** Cross-registration, distance learning, double major, ESL, exchange student, honors, independent study, internships, study abroad, teacher certification program. **Credit/placement by examination:** AP, CLEP, IB, ACT, institutional tests. 24 credit hours maximum toward bachelor's degree. **Support services:** Learning center, reduced course load, remedial instruction, study skills assistance, tutoring, writing center.

**Majors. Biology:** General. **Business:** Accounting, business admin. **Communications:** Media studies. **Computer sciences:** Computer science. **Education:** General, art, biology, business, chemistry, drama/dance, early childhood, English, foreign languages, French, health, history, mathematics, middle, music, physical, physics, science, secondary, social studies, Spanish, speech. **English:** English lit, speech/rhetoric. **Foreign languages:** French, Russian, Spanish. **Health:** Athletic training, audiology/speech pathology, dietetics, predental, premedicine, prenursing, prepharmacy, preveterinary. **History:** General. **Legal studies:** Prelaw. **Math:** General. **Parks/recreation:** Exercise sciences. **Philosophy/religion:** Philosophy. **Physical sciences:** Chemistry, physics. **Psychology:** General. **Social sciences:** Political science, sociology. **Theology:** Bible, missionary, pastoral counseling, sacred music, theology, youth ministry. **Visual/performing arts:** Dramatic, graphic design, music history, music performance, music theory/composition, piano/organ, studio arts, voice/opera. **Other:** Software engineering.

**Most popular majors.** Business/marketing 14%, communications/journalism 7%, education 8%, health sciences 8%, social sciences 7%, theological studies 14%, visual/performing arts 15%.

**Computing on campus.** 225 workstations in dormitories, library, computer center, student center. Dormitories wired for high-speed internet access and linked to campus network. Commuter students can connect to campus network. Online library, helpline, student web hosting, wireless network available.

**Student life. Freshman orientation:** Mandatory. Preregistration for classes offered. Three-part program: day-long pre-registration and orientation session for students and parents; 3-day weekend program prior to registration with one session for parents; optional 3-day summer retreat. **Policies:** Students under 22 must live in campus housing unless commuting. Only local fraternities and sororities are permitted. Religious observance required. **Housing:** Guaranteed on-campus for all undergraduates. Single-sex dorms, special housing for disabled, apartments, substance-free housing available. $50 fully refundable deposit, deadline 6/1. **Activities:** Bands, campus ministries, choral groups, drama, international student organizations, literary magazine, music ensembles, musical theater, opera, student government, student newspaper, Blue Key, College Republicans, Fellowship of Christian Athletes, Ouachita student foundation, Pew College Society, ROMS, Young Democrats.

**Athletics.** NCAA. **Intercollegiate:** Baseball M, basketball, cross-country W, diving, football (tackle) M, golf M, soccer, softball W, swimming, tennis, volleyball W. **Intramural:** Basketball, cheerleading, football (non-tackle), handball, racquetball, soccer, softball, table tennis, volleyball. **Team name:** Tigers.

**Student services.** Alcohol/substance abuse counseling, campus ministries, career counseling, services for economically disadvantaged, student employment services, financial aid counseling, health services, minority student services, personal counseling, placement for graduates, veterans' counselor. **Physically disabled:** Services for visually, speech, hearing impaired.

**Contact.** E-mail: pittmank@obu.edu
Phone: (870) 245-5110 Toll-free number: (800) 342-5628
Fax: (870) 245-5500
Judy Jones, Director of Admissions/Registrar, Ouachita Baptist University, OBU Box 3776, Arkadelphia, AR 71998-0001

## Philander Smith College

**Little Rock, Arkansas**
www.philander.edu
**CB member**
**CB code: 6578**

- Private 4-year liberal arts college affiliated with United Methodist Church
- Commuter campus in small city
- 561 degree-seeking undergraduates
- 40% of applicants admitted
- SAT or ACT required

**General.** Founded in 1877. Regionally accredited. **Degrees:** 112 bachelor's awarded. **ROTC:** Army. **Calendar:** Semester, limited summer session. **Full-time faculty:** 43 total. **Part-time faculty:** 45 total.

**Freshman class profile.** 2,257 applied, 897 admitted, 138 enrolled.

| Mid 50% test scores | | | |
|---|---|---|---|
| SAT critical reading: | 330-530 | GPA 3.0-3.49: | 29% |
| SAT math: | 340-530 | GPA 2.0-2.99: | 58% |
| SAT writing: | 390-510 | Rank in top quarter: | 33% |
| ACT composite: | 14-20 | Rank in top tenth: | 14% |
| GPA 3.50 or higher: | 9% | Out-of-state: | 27% |

**Basis for selection.** Academic GPA very important followed by standardized test scores and rigor of secondary school record.

**High school preparation.** Recommended units include English 3, mathematics 3, social studies 2, science 3 (laboratory 1) and foreign language 2.

**2007-2008 Annual costs.** Tuition/fees: $8,490. Room/board: $6,356. Books/supplies: $650. Personal expenses: $600.

**2007-2008 Financial aid.** All financial aid based on need. 35% of total undergraduate aid awarded as scholarships/grants, 65% as loans/jobs.

**Application procedures. Admission:** Priority date 3/1; no deadline. $25 fee, may be waived for applicants with need. Admission notification on a rolling basis. **Financial aid:** Priority date 3/1; no closing date. FAFSA, institutional form required. Applicants notified on a rolling basis starting 5/1; must reply within 2 week(s) of notification.

**Academics. Special study options:** Cooperative education, independent study, internships, liberal arts/career combination, study abroad, teacher certification program. **Credit/placement by examination:** AP, CLEP, SAT, ACT. 30 credit hours maximum toward bachelor's degree. **Support services:** Learning center, reduced course load, remedial instruction, tutoring.

**Majors. Biology:** General. **Business:** Administrative services, business admin. **Computer sciences:** Computer science. **Education:** Business. **English:** English lit. **Interdisciplinary:** Math/computer science. **Math:** General. **Philosophy/religion:** Philosophy, religion. **Physical sciences:** Chemistry. **Psychology:** General. **Public administration:** Social work. **Social sciences:** Political science, sociology.

**Computing on campus.** 72 workstations in dormitories, library, computer center. Dormitories wired for high-speed internet access and linked to campus network. Commuter students can connect to campus network. Online library, wireless network available.

**Student life. Freshman orientation:** Mandatory, $75 fee. **Housing:** Single-sex dorms available. $245 nonrefundable deposit, deadline 7/10. **Activities:** Choral groups, drama, student government, student newspaper.

**Athletics. Intercollegiate:** Baseball M, basketball, volleyball W. **Intramural:** Badminton, basketball, tennis. **Team name:** Panthers.

**Student services.** Career counseling, student employment services, health services, personal counseling, veterans' counselor. **Physically disabled:** Services for visually, hearing impaired.

**Contact.** E-mail: admissions@philander.edu
Phone: (501) 370-5221 Toll-free number: (800) 446-6772
Fax: (501) 370-5225
George Gray, Director of Admissions, Philander Smith College, One Trudie Kibbe Reed Drive, Little Rock, AR 72202-3718

## Southern Arkansas University

**Magnolia, Arkansas**
www.saumag.edu
**CB code: 6661**

- Public 4-year university
- Residential campus in large town
- 2,660 degree-seeking undergraduates: 14% part-time, 59% women, 32% African American, 1% Asian American, 1% Hispanic American, 1% Native American, 5% international
- 341 graduate students
- 73% of applicants admitted
- SAT or ACT (ACT writing optional) required
- 35% graduate within 6 years

**General.** Founded in 1909. Regionally accredited. **Degrees:** 331 bachelor's, 80 associate awarded; master's offered. **Location:** 53 miles from Texarkana, Texas, 70 miles from Shreveport, Louisiana. **Calendar:** Semester, extensive summer session. **Full-time faculty:** 152 total; 12% minority, 40% women. **Part-time faculty:** 53 total; 8% minority, 66% women. **Class size:** 55% < 20, 35% 20-39, 6% 40-49, 4% 50-99. **Special facilities:** University farm.

**Freshman class profile.** 1,657 applied, 1,211 admitted, 537 enrolled.

| Mid 50% test scores | | | |
|---|---|---|---|
| SAT critical reading: | 370-500 | Rank in top quarter: | 24% |
| SAT math: | 410-600 | Rank in top tenth: | 9% |
| ACT composite: | 17-23 | Return as sophomores: | 62% |
| GPA 3.50 or higher: | 30% | Out-of-state: | 25% |
| GPA 3.0-3.49: | 30% | Live on campus: | 74% |
| GPA 2.0-2.99: | 35% | International: | 9% |

**Basis for selection.** For unconditional admission, applicants must have ACT of 19 or higher. ACT of 16 to 18 allows conditional admission. TOEFL required for non-native English speakers. Interview required of nursing majors.

**High school preparation.** Recommended units include English 4, mathematics 4, social studies 3, science 3 (laboratory 3) and foreign language 2. 0.5 computer science also recommended.

**2007-2008 Annual costs.** Tuition/fees: $5,224; $7,534 out-of-state. Room/board: $4,100. Books/supplies: $1,000. Personal expenses: $2,000.

**2006-2007 Financial aid. Need-based:** 42% of total undergraduate aid awarded as scholarships/grants, 58% as loans/jobs. **Non-need-based:** Scholarships awarded for academics, alumni affiliation, art, athletics, leadership, minority status, music/drama, state residency.

**Application procedures. Admission:** Closing date 8/30 (receipt date). No application fee. Application may be submitted online. Admission notification on a rolling basis. **Financial aid:** Priority date 7/1; no closing date. FAFSA required. Applicants notified on a rolling basis starting 4/15; must reply within 2 week(s) of notification.

**Academics. Special study options:** Combined bachelor's/graduate degree, cross-registration, distance learning, double major, dual enrollment of high school students, honors, independent study, internships, teacher certification program. **Credit/placement by examination:** AP, CLEP. 15 credit hours maximum toward associate degree, 30 toward bachelor's. **Support services:** Learning center, reduced course load, remedial instruction, tutoring, writing center.

**Honors college/program.** Composite ACT score of 26 or higher.

**Majors. Agriculture:** Business. **Biology:** General. **Business:** General, accounting, business admin, finance, management information systems, marketing, office management, operations. **Communications:** Journalism. **Computer sciences:** General. **Education:** Agricultural, art, biology, business, chemistry, early childhood, elementary, English, mathematics, middle, music, physical, physics, science, social studies, Spanish, speech. **Engineering technology:** Industrial. **English:** English lit. **Foreign languages:** Spanish. **Health:** Athletic training, nursing (RN). **History:** General. **Interdisciplinary:** Biological/physical sciences. **Math:** General. **Parks/recreation:** Exercise sciences. **Physical sciences:** Chemistry. **Protective services:** Criminal justice. **Psychology:** General. **Public administration:** Community org/advocacy, social work. **Social sciences:** General, economics, political science, sociology. **Visual/performing arts:** Art, dramatic, studio arts.

**Most popular majors.** Business/marketing 27%, education 21%, security/protective services 7%.

**Computing on campus.** 202 workstations in dormitories, library, computer center. Dormitories wired for high-speed internet access and linked to campus network. Commuter students can connect to campus network. Online library, helpline, wireless network available.

**Student life. Freshman orientation:** Mandatory, $25 fee. Preregistration for classes offered. **Policies:** Freshmen required to live on campus unless commuting or living with parents. **Housing:** Guaranteed on-campus for all undergraduates. Coed dorms, single-sex dorms, apartments, substance-free housing available. $50 fully refundable deposit. **Activities:** Bands, choral groups, drama, music ensembles, musical theater, radio station, student government, student newspaper, More than 80 student organizations.

**Athletics.** NCAA. **Intercollegiate:** Baseball M, basketball, cross-country, football (tackle) M, golf M, softball W, tennis W, track and field, volleyball W. **Intramural:** Badminton, basketball, football (tackle) M, golf M, softball, table tennis, tennis, volleyball. **Team name:** Muleriders.

**Student services.** Alcohol/substance abuse counseling, career counseling, services for economically disadvantaged, student employment services, financial aid counseling, health services, minority student services, personal counseling, placement for graduates, veterans' counselor, women's services. **Physically disabled:** Services for visually, hearing impaired.

**Contact.** E-mail: sejennings@saumag.edu
Phone: (870) 235-4040 Toll-free number: (800) 332-7286
Fax: (870) 235-4931
Sarah Jennings, Dean of Enrollment Services, Southern Arkansas University, Box 9382, Magnolia, AR 71754-9382

## University of Arkansas
**Fayetteville, Arkansas**
**www.uark.edu**

CB member
CB code: 6866

- Public 4-year university
- Residential campus in small city
- 14,442 degree-seeking undergraduates: 14% part-time, 49% women, 5% African American, 3% Asian American, 3% Hispanic American, 2% Native American, 2% international

- 3,540 degree-seeking graduate students
- 62% of applicants admitted
- SAT or ACT (ACT writing optional) required
- 58% graduate within 6 years

**General.** Founded in 1871. Regionally accredited. Arkansas Center for Space and Planetary Sciences, GENESIS Technology Incubator program provides tech-based companies with research and development support. **Degrees:** 2,382 bachelor's awarded; master's, doctoral, first professional offered. **ROTC:** Army, Air Force. **Location:** 192 miles from Little Rock, 120 miles from Tulsa, Oklahoma. **Calendar:** Semester, limited summer session. **Full-time faculty:** 852 total; 88% have terminal degrees, 12% minority, 35% women. **Part-time faculty:** 78 total; 44% have terminal degrees, 5% minority, 37% women. **Class size:** 34% < 20, 43% 20-39, 7% 40-49, 12% 50-99, 4% >100. **Special facilities:** Arts center, poultry science center, equine pavilion, animal science center.

**Freshman class profile.** 10,132 applied, 6,262 admitted, 2,899 enrolled.

| Mid 50% test scores | | Rank in top tenth: | 32% |
|---|---|---|---|
| SAT critical reading: | 510-630 | Return as sophomores: | 83% |
| SAT math: | 520-650 | Out-of-state: | 33% |
| ACT composite: | 23-29 | Live on campus: | 87% |
| GPA 3.50 or higher: | 61% | International: | 1% |
| GPA 3.0-3.49: | 29% | Fraternities: | 22% |
| GPA 2.0-2.99: | 10% | Sororities: | 32% |
| Rank in top quarter: | 62% | | |

**Basis for selection.** Secondary school record, class rank, test scores, evidence of commitment to success most important. As mandated by state law, those with ACT subscore of 18 or less in English, Mathematics or Reading are assigned developmental coursework or required to take institutional placement test. University policies are more restrictive than the state of Arkansas' policies.

**High school preparation.** 16 units required. Required and recommended units include English 4, mathematics 4, social studies 3, science 3 (laboratory 2), foreign language 2 and academic electives 2. Mathematics must include 1 algebra or 2 applied math, and 2 units chosen from algebra II, geometry, calculus/trigonometry. 2 foreign languages strongly recommended for Arts and Sciences applicants.

**2007-2008 Annual costs.** Tuition/fees: $6,038; $14,492 out-of-state. Room/board: $7,016. Books/supplies: $966. Personal expenses: $1,954.

**2006-2007 Financial aid. Need-based:** 1,560 full-time freshmen applied for aid; 999 were judged to have need; 966 of these received aid. Average need met was 73%. Average scholarship/grant was $4,131; average loan $3,016. 40% of total undergraduate aid awarded as scholarships/grants, 60% as loans/jobs. **Non-need-based:** Awarded to 4,107 full-time undergraduates, including 1,148 freshmen. Scholarships awarded for academics, alumni affiliation, art, athletics, leadership, minority status, music/drama, ROTC, state residency.

**Application procedures. Admission:** Priority date 2/1; deadline 8/15 (receipt date). $40 fee, may be waived for applicants with need. Application may be submitted online. Admission notification on a rolling basis beginning on or about 10/1. **Financial aid:** Priority date 3/15; no closing date. FAFSA required. Applicants notified on a rolling basis starting 4/1; must reply within 4 week(s) of notification.

**Academics. Special study options:** Accelerated study, combined bachelor's/graduate degree, cooperative education, distance learning, double major, dual enrollment of high school students, ESL, honors, independent study, internships, liberal arts/career combination, study abroad, teacher certification program, United Nations semester. **Credit/placement by examination:** AP, CLEP, IB, SAT, ACT, institutional tests. **Support services:** Learning center, reduced course load, remedial instruction, study skills assistance, tutoring, writing center.

**Honors college/program.** Student must be admitted to an honors program in the college of major. Must have a minimum 28 ACT or SAT equivalent and a minimum high school GPA of 3.5. Walton College of Business requires a 28 ACT or SAT equivalent and a minimum high school GPA of 3.75.

**Majors. Agriculture:** Agribusiness operations, agronomy, animal sciences, food science, ornamental horticulture, poultry. **Architecture:** Architecture, landscape. **Area/ethnic studies:** American. **Biology:** General, bacteriology. **Business:** General, accounting, business admin, finance, international, logistics, managerial economics, marketing. **Communications:** General, journalism. **Computer sciences:** General, data processing. **Conservation:** Environmental science. **Education:** Agricultural, elementary, kindergarten/preschool, middle, trade/industrial. **Engineering:** Agricultural, chemical, civil, computer, electrical, industrial, mechanical. **English:** English lit. **Family/consumer sciences:** Clothing/textiles, family studies, food/nutrition, housing. **Foreign languages:** Classics, French, German, Spanish. **Health:** Audiology/speech pathology, nursing (RN). **History:** General. **Math:** General. **Parks/recreation:** General, health/fitness. **Philosophy/religion:** Philosophy. **Physical sciences:** Chemistry, geology, physics. **Protective services:** Criminal justice. **Psychology:** General. **Public administration:** General, social work. **Social sciences:** Anthropology, economics, geography, international relations, political science, sociology. **Visual/performing arts:** Art, dramatic, music performance.

**Most popular majors.** Business/marketing 23%, communications/journalism 7%, education 8%, engineering/engineering technologies 9%, health sciences 6%, social sciences 7%.

**Computing on campus.** 2,270 workstations in dormitories, library, computer center, student center. Dormitories wired for high-speed internet access and linked to campus network. Commuter students can connect to campus network. Online course registration, online library, helpline, repair service, student web hosting, wireless network available.

**Student life. Freshman orientation:** Mandatory, $80 fee. Preregistration for classes offered. 2-day orientation session held in summer for students and parents. **Housing:** Coed dorms, single-sex dorms, apartments, fraternity/sorority housing, substance-free housing available. $235 partly refundable deposit. Honors housing, sophomore and beyond area, suites with private bedrooms, special interest floors, enhanced learning centers, first year experience program area, adaptable housing for disabled students, several residences remain open over holiday and winter breaks. **Activities:** Bands, campus ministries, choral groups, dance, drama, film society, international student organizations, literary magazine, music ensembles, musical theater, opera, radio station, student government, student newspaper, symphony orchestra, TV station, More than 200 organizations available.

**Athletics.** NCAA. **Intercollegiate:** Baseball M, basketball, cheerleading, cross-country, diving W, football (tackle) M, golf, gymnastics W, rowing (crew), soccer W, softball W, swimming W, tennis, track and field, volleyball W. **Intramural:** Badminton, basketball, bowling, golf, handball, judo, racquetball, softball, swimming W, tennis, track and field, volleyball W. **Team name:** Razorbacks.

**Student services.** Adult student services, alcohol/substance abuse counseling, campus ministries, career counseling, student employment services, financial aid counseling, health services, legal services, minority student services, personal counseling, placement for graduates, veterans' counselor. **Physically disabled:** Services for visually, speech, hearing impaired. **Learning disabled:** Comprehensive services available.

**Contact.** E-mail: uofa@uark.edu
Phone: (479) 575-5346 Toll-free number: (800) 377-8632
Fax: (479) 575-7515
Dawn Medley, Director of Admissions, University of Arkansas, 232 Silas Hunt Hall, Fayetteville, AR 72701

## University of Arkansas at Fort Smith
**Fort Smith, Arkansas**                        CB member
www.uafortsmith.edu                         CB code: 6220

- Public 4-year university
- Commuter campus in small city
- 5,833 degree-seeking undergraduates: 30% part-time, 60% women, 4% African American, 4% Asian American, 4% Hispanic American, 5% Native American

**General.** Founded in 1928. Regionally accredited. **Degrees:** 399 bachelor's, 554 associate awarded. **ROTC:** Army, Air Force. **Location:** 150 miles from Little Rock, 120 miles from Tulsa, Oklahoma. **Calendar:** Semester, extensive summer session. **Full-time faculty:** 203 total; 47% have terminal degrees, 7% minority, 48% women. **Part-time faculty:** 162 total; 7% minority, 48% women. **Class size:** 37% < 20, 57% 20-39, 4% 40-49, 1% 50-99.

**Freshman class profile.** 2,776 applied, 1,849 admitted, 1,168 enrolled.

| Mid 50% test scores | | End year in good standing: | 69% |
|---|---|---|---|
| ACT composite: | 19-24 | Return as sophomores: | 68% |
| GPA 3.50 or higher: | 31% | Out-of-state: | 2% |
| GPA 3.0-3.49: | 32% | Live on campus: | 4% |
| GPA 2.0-2.99: | 34% | Fraternities: | 26% |
| Rank in top quarter: | 34% | Sororities: | 24% |
| Rank in top tenth: | 10% | | |

**Basis for selection.** Open admission, but selective for some programs. Special criteria for health career and education programs. Some applicants

required to obtain individual approval of director of admissions and school relations. Conditional enrollment may apply. COMPASS required for placement if ACT/SAT not submitted, or if scores below acceptable minimum (18 on ACT). Interview required of nursing, radiology, surgical technology, paramedic, and dental hygiene majors, as well as teacher education programs. **Homeschooled:** It is required that any private school, home school, or GED student who graduates after May 1, 2002, to have achieved a composite score of 19 on the ACT or the equivalent score on the SAT or COMPASS for unconditional admission to UA Fort Smith. **Learning Disabled:** In order to be considered for accommodations, a student must first submit verification of his or her condition based on Student ADA Services' guidelines and meet with the Student ADA Services coordinator to discuss an accommodation request.

**High school preparation.** 14 units recommended. Recommended units include English 4, mathematics 4, social studies 3, science 3 (laboratory 3).

**2007-2008 Annual costs.** Tuition/fees: $4,060; $8,950 out-of-state. Books/supplies: $1,400. Personal expenses: $1,080.

**2006-2007 Financial aid. Need-based:** 766 full-time freshmen applied for aid; 566 were judged to have need; 546 of these received aid. Average need met was 71%. Average scholarship/grant was $3,447; average loan $2,334. 57% of total undergraduate aid awarded as scholarships/grants, 43% as loans/jobs. **Non-need-based:** Awarded to 1,189 full-time undergraduates, including 552 freshmen. Scholarships awarded for academics, athletics, job skills, leadership, music/drama.

**Application procedures. Admission:** No deadline. No application fee. Application may be submitted online. Admission notification on a rolling basis. Early applications advised for financial aid. **Financial aid:** Priority date 6/15; no closing date. FAFSA required. Applicants notified on a rolling basis starting 3/1; must reply within 4 week(s) of notification.

**Academics. Special study options:** Cooperative education, distance learning, dual enrollment of high school students, external degree, honors, independent study, internships, liberal arts/career combination, study abroad, teacher certification program. Associate of Art through distance learning. **Credit/placement by examination:** AP, CLEP, institutional tests. 30 credit hours maximum toward associate degree, 30 toward bachelor's. Prior work/life experience credits awarded for military transcripts only; maximum 30 hours. **Support services:** Learning center, pre-admission summer program, reduced course load, remedial instruction, study skills assistance, tutoring, writing center.

**Majors. Biology:** General. **Business:** Accounting, business admin. **Computer sciences:** General. **Education:** Biology, chemistry, early childhood, English, history, mathematics, middle, music, Spanish. **English:** English lit, technical writing. **Foreign languages:** Spanish. **Health:** Nursing (RN), radiologic technology/medical imaging. **History:** General. **Interdisciplinary:** Science/society. **Liberal arts:** Arts/sciences. **Math:** General. **Physical sciences:** Chemistry. **Protective services:** Law enforcement admin. **Psychology:** General. **Visual/performing arts:** Graphic design.

**Most popular majors.** Business/marketing 25%, communication technologies 9%, computer/information sciences 6%, education 26%, English 8%, history 7%, psychology 8%.

**Computing on campus.** 590 workstations in dormitories, library, computer center, student center. Dormitories wired for high-speed internet access and linked to campus network. Commuter students can connect to campus network. Online course registration, online library, helpline, wireless network available.

**Student life. Freshman orientation:** Available. Preregistration for classes offered. New students meet their academic advisor; get student I.D.; obtain username and password for email access; learn how to Web register for future terms. **Housing:** Apartments, substance-free housing available. $300 fully refundable deposit. **Activities:** Bands, campus ministries, choral groups, literary magazine, music ensembles, student government, College Democrats, College Republicans, Disabled Students Association, Future Educators Organization, student nurses association, Phi Beta Lambda, OARS, Chi Alpha.

**Athletics.** NJCAA. **Intercollegiate:** Baseball M, basketball, golf, tennis, volleyball W. **Intramural:** Basketball, bowling, football (non-tackle), softball, table tennis, volleyball. **Team name:** Lions.

**Student services.** Adult student services, career counseling, student employment services, financial aid counseling, placement for graduates, veterans' counselor. **Physically disabled:** Services for visually, speech, hearing impaired.

**Contact.** E-mail: information@uafortsmith.edu
Phone: (479) 788-7120 Toll-free number: (888) 512-5466
Fax: (479) 788-7016
Penny Pendleton, Dean, Enrollment Management, University of Arkansas at Fort Smith, PO Box 3649, Fort Smith, AR 72913-3649

## University of Arkansas at Little Rock
Little Rock, Arkansas                           CB member
www.ualr.edu                                    CB code: 6368

- Public 4-year university
- Commuter campus in small city
- 8,908 degree-seeking undergraduates: 38% part-time, 61% women, 30% African American, 2% Asian American, 2% Hispanic American, 1% Native American, 1% international
- 2,432 degree-seeking graduate students
- ACT (writing optional) required

**General.** Founded in 1927. Regionally accredited. **Degrees:** 1,034 bachelor's, 203 associate awarded; master's, doctoral, first professional offered. **ROTC:** Army. **Calendar:** Semester, limited summer session. **Full-time faculty:** 455 total; 42% women. **Part-time faculty:** 369 total. **Special facilities:** Planetarium, observatory, government documents depository.

**Freshman class profile.**

| Mid 50% test scores | | End year in good standing: | 84% |
|---|---|---|---|
| ACT composite: | 17-24 | | |

**Basis for selection.** Unconditional admission based on minimum ACT score of 21 or above, or combined verbal/mathematics SAT score of 990 or above, high school GPA of 2.5 or above, and completion of college preparatory curriculum. Students must meet 2 of 3 basic criteria. All students born after January 1, 1957 required to show Arkansas Certificate of Immunization for Institutions of Higher Education. Interview recommended for academically weak applicants.

**High school preparation.** 15 units required. Required units include English 4, mathematics 3, social studies 3, science 2 (laboratory 2) and foreign language 2. Social studies should include 1 unit each of American history, world history, and civics or American government.

**2007-2008 Annual costs.** Tuition/fees: $5,707; $13,199 out-of-state. Fees vary depending on student's field of study. Room only: $3,100. Books/supplies: $1,000. Personal expenses: $800.

**Application procedures. Admission:** No deadline. No application fee. Admission notification on a rolling basis. **Financial aid:** Closing date 8/1. FAFSA required. Applicants notified on a rolling basis starting 5/1.

**Academics. Special study options:** Accelerated study, cooperative education, distance learning, double major, dual enrollment of high school students, ESL, exchange student, honors, independent study, internships, student-designed major, study abroad, teacher certification program, weekend college. **Credit/placement by examination:** AP, CLEP, ACT, institutional tests. 30 credit hours maximum toward associate degree, 30 toward bachelor's. Credit obtained through examination is recorded as approved hours on the official permanent record without grade or grade points. **Support services:** Learning center, reduced course load, remedial instruction, tutoring, writing center.

**Majors. Biology:** General. **Business:** Accounting, business admin, finance, international, management information systems, managerial economics, marketing. **Communications:** General, advertising, journalism. **Computer sciences:** General, information systems. **Education:** Early childhood, elementary, middle. **Engineering:** Systems. **Engineering technology:** Construction. **English:** English lit, technical writing. **Foreign languages:** French, German, sign language interpretation, Spanish. **Health:** Audiology/speech pathology, environmental health. **History:** General. **Interdisciplinary:** Biological/physical sciences. **Liberal arts:** Arts/sciences. **Math:** General, applied. **Philosophy/religion:** Philosophy. **Physical sciences:** Chemistry, geology, physics. **Protective services:** Criminal justice. **Psychology:** General. **Public administration:** Social work. **Social sciences:** Economics, international relations, political science, sociology. **Visual/performing arts:** Art, art history/conservation, dramatic. **Other:** Applied technology.

**Computing on campus.** 500 workstations in dormitories, library, computer center. Dormitories wired for high-speed internet access and linked to campus network. Commuter students can connect to campus network. Online course registration, online library, wireless network available.

**Student life. Freshman orientation:** Available. **Housing:** Coed dorms available. $100 fully refundable deposit. **Activities:** Bands, choral groups, dance, drama, literary magazine, music ensembles, musical theater, opera, radio station, student government, student newspaper, TV station, Baptist Student Union, University Republicans, Methodist student club, Muslim students association, Young Democrats, Association for Minority Students Education Needs and Development (AMEND), Advocates for People with Disabilities.

**Athletics.** NCAA. **Intercollegiate:** Baseball M, basketball, cross-country, golf, soccer, swimming, tennis, track and field, volleyball W. **Intramural:** Badminton, basketball, bowling, football (tackle) M, golf, softball, swimming, table tennis M, tennis, volleyball. **Team name:** Trojans.

**Student services.** Adult student services, career counseling, student employment services, health services, personal counseling, placement for graduates, veterans' counselor. **Physically disabled:** Services for visually, speech, hearing impaired.

**Contact.** Phone: (501) 569-3127 Toll-free number: (800) 482-8892 Fax: (501) 569-8956
Tammy Harrison, Director of Admissions and Financial Aid, University of Arkansas at Little Rock, 2801 South University Avenue, Little Rock, AR 72204

## University of Arkansas at Monticello
Monticello, Arkansas
www.uamont.edu                                  CB code: 6007

- Public 4-year university and technical college
- Commuter campus in large town
- 2,604 degree-seeking undergraduates: 18% part-time, 59% women, 32% African American, 1% Hispanic American, 1% Native American
- 111 degree-seeking graduate students
- 34% graduate within 6 years

**General.** Founded in 1909. Regionally accredited. **Degrees:** 255 bachelor's, 194 associate awarded; master's offered. **ROTC:** Army. **Location:** 100 miles from Little Rock, 50 miles from Pine Bluff. **Calendar:** Semester, extensive summer session. **Full-time faculty:** 173 total; 47% have terminal degrees, 12% minority, 46% women. **Part-time faculty:** 68 total; 4% have terminal degrees, 6% minority, 71% women. **Class size:** 63% < 20, 31% 20-39, 4% 40-49, 2% 50-99, less than 1% >100. **Special facilities:** Museum of natural history, extensive research forest, planetarium, farm.

**Freshman class profile.** 677 enrolled.

| Mid 50% test scores | | Return as sophomores: | 48% |
|---|---|---|---|
| ACT composite: | 16-22 | Out-of-state: | 13% |
| GPA 3.50 or higher: | 18% | Live on campus: | 45% |
| GPA 3.0-3.49: | 27% | Fraternities: | 10% |
| GPA 2.0-2.99: | 44% | Sororities: | 10% |
| End year in good standing: | 50% | | |

**Basis for selection.** Open admission. **Homeschooled:** Transcript of courses and grades required. ACT or SAT for placement and not for admission.

**High school preparation.** Recommended units include English 4, mathematics 4, social studies 3, science 3 and foreign language 2.

**2007-2008 Annual costs.** Tuition/fees: $4,300; $8,230 out-of-state. Room/board: $3,690. Books/supplies: $800. Personal expenses: $1,980.

**2006-2007 Financial aid. Need-based:** 61% of total undergraduate aid awarded as scholarships/grants, 39% as loans/jobs. **Non-need-based:** Scholarships awarded for academics, athletics, job skills, leadership, music/drama, state residency.

**Application procedures. Admission:** Priority date 8/10; no deadline. No application fee. Application may be submitted online. Admission notification on a rolling basis. **Financial aid:** Priority date 5/1; no closing date. FAFSA, institutional form required. Applicants notified on a rolling basis starting 4/1; must reply within 2 week(s) of notification.

**Academics. Special study options:** Combined bachelor's/graduate degree, cross-registration, distance learning, double major, dual enrollment of high school students, independent study, internships, liberal arts/career combination, study abroad, teacher certification program. **Credit/placement by examination:** AP, CLEP, IB, institutional tests. 9 credit hours maximum toward bachelor's degree. **Support services:** Learning center, pre-admission summer program, reduced course load, remedial instruction, study skills assistance, tutoring, writing center.

**Majors. Agriculture:** Agribusiness operations. **Biology:** General. **Business:** General, accounting, business admin, management information systems. **Communications:** Journalism. **Conservation:** Forestry, wildlife. **Education:** Kindergarten/preschool, middle, music, physical. **Engineering technology:** Surveying. **English:** English lit, speech/rhetoric. **Health:** Nursing (RN). **History:** General. **Interdisciplinary:** Biological/physical sciences. **Math:** General. **Physical sciences:** Chemistry. **Protective services:** Criminal justice. **Psychology:** General. **Public administration:** Social work. **Social sciences:** General, political science. **Visual/performing arts:** Art. **Other:** Applied science.

**Most popular majors.** Business/marketing 24%, education 9%, English 6%, health sciences 15%, psychology 7%, security/protective services 7%.

**Computing on campus.** 400 workstations in dormitories, library, computer center, student center. Dormitories wired for high-speed internet access and linked to campus network. Commuter students can connect to campus network. Online course registration, wireless network available.

**Student life.** **Freshman orientation:** Mandatory. Preregistration for classes offered. One day, beginning of semester. **Housing:** Guaranteed on-campus for all undergraduates. Single-sex dorms, special housing for disabled, apartments, substance-free housing available. $60 fully refundable deposit, deadline 8/15. **Activities:** Bands, choral groups, drama, literary magazine, music ensembles, musical theater, student government, student newspaper, Baptist Student Union, Missionary Baptist Student Fellowship, Wesley Foundation, Christians in Action, Catholic Weevils, Chi Alpha.

**Athletics.** NCAA. **Intercollegiate:** Baseball M, basketball, cross-country, football (tackle) M, golf, rodeo, softball W, tennis W, volleyball W. **Intramural:** Archery, badminton, baseball M, basketball, bowling, boxing M, cross-country, football (tackle) M, golf, handball, racquetball, soccer, softball, swimming, table tennis, tennis, track and field, volleyball. **Team name:** Boll Weevils.

**Student services.** Alcohol/substance abuse counseling, campus ministries, career counseling, student employment services, financial aid counseling, health services, personal counseling, placement for graduates, veterans' counselor. **Physically disabled:** Services for visually, speech, hearing impaired.

**Contact.** E-mail: whitingm@uamont.edu
Phone: (870) 460-1026 Toll-free number: (800) 844-1826
Fax: (870) 460-1926
Mary Whiting, Director of Admissions, University of Arkansas at Monticello, Box 3600, Monticello, AR 71656

## University of Arkansas at Pine Bluff

**Pine Bluff, Arkansas**  CB member
www.uapb.edu  CB code: 6004

- Public 4-year university
- Commuter campus in small city
- 3,048 degree-seeking undergraduates: 12% part-time, 58% women, 96% African American
- 90 degree-seeking graduate students
- 64% of applicants admitted
- SAT or ACT (ACT writing optional) required
- 33% graduate within 6 years

**General.** Founded in 1873. Regionally accredited. **Degrees:** 376 bachelor's awarded; master's offered. **ROTC:** Army. **Location:** 42 miles from Little Rock. **Calendar:** Semester, limited summer session. **Full-time faculty:** 164 total; 65% have terminal degrees, 46% women. **Part-time faculty:** 76 total; 25% have terminal degrees, 50% women. **Class size:** 46% < 20, 45% 20-39, 4% 40-49, 5% 50-99, less than 1% >100. **Special facilities:** 220-acre farm, aquaculture fisheries.

**Freshman class profile.** 2,169 applied, 1,394 admitted, 819 enrolled.

| Mid 50% test scores | | | | |
|---|---|---|---|---|
| SAT critical reading: | 350-440 | Return as sophomores: | | 57% |
| SAT math: | 350-450 | Out-of-state: | | 42% |
| ACT composite: | 14-18 | Live on campus: | | 78% |

**Basis for selection.** Admission credentials for entering freshmen must include formal application, high school transcript, ACT test information and scores (SAT is accepted) and immunization record.

**High school preparation.** 21 units required. Required units include English 4, mathematics 3, social studies 1, history 2, science 3 (laboratory 2), foreign language 2 and academic electives 4.

**2007-2008 Annual costs.** Tuition/fees: $4,499; $8,909 out-of-state. Room/board: $5,972. Books/supplies: $800. Personal expenses: $800.

**Financial aid.** **Non-need-based:** Scholarships awarded for academics, alumni affiliation, art, athletics, leadership, minority status, music/drama, religious affiliation, ROTC, state residency.

**Application procedures.** **Admission:** Priority date 8/1; no deadline. No application fee. Admission notification on a rolling basis. **Financial aid:** Priority date 4/15; no closing date. FAFSA required. Applicants notified on a rolling basis starting 3/1.

**Academics.** **Special study options:** Cooperative education, cross-registration, distance learning, double major, dual enrollment of high school students, honors, internships, study abroad, teacher certification program. **Credit/placement by examination:** AP, CLEP, IB, SAT, ACT. 25 credit hours maximum toward bachelor's degree. **Support services:** Learning center, reduced course load, remedial instruction, study skills assistance, tutoring.

**Majors.** **Biology:** General. **Business:** Accounting, business admin. **Communications:** General. **Computer sciences:** General. **Conservation:** General, fisheries. **Education:** General, agricultural, art, business, early childhood, English, family/consumer sciences, mathematics, middle, physical, science, social science, social studies, special, trade/industrial. **English:** English lit, speech/rhetoric. **Family/consumer sciences:** General, family studies. **Health:** Nursing (RN). **History:** General. **Interdisciplinary:** Gerontology. **Liberal arts:** Arts/sciences. **Math:** General, applied. **Parks/recreation:** General, facilities management. **Physical sciences:** Chemistry, physics. **Protective services:** Criminal justice. **Psychology:** General. **Public administration:** Social work. **Social sciences:** Political science, sociology. **Visual/performing arts:** Art.

**Most popular majors.** Agriculture 7%, biology 6%, business/marketing 16%, education 6%, family/consumer sciences 8%, liberal arts 15%, security/protective services 9%.

**Computing on campus.** 1,000 workstations in dormitories, library, computer center, student center. Dormitories linked to campus network. Commuter students can connect to campus network. Online library, helpline, repair service available.

**Student life.** **Freshman orientation:** Mandatory. Preregistration for classes offered. **Housing:** Single-sex dorms available. $100 deposit. **Activities:** Bands, choral groups, drama, music ensembles, radio station, student government, student newspaper, TV station, Baptist Student Union, political science/pre-law club, Church of God in Christ, Wesley Foundation, criminal justice club.

**Athletics.** NCAA. **Intercollegiate:** Baseball M, basketball, bowling W, cross-country, football (tackle) M, golf, soccer W, softball W, tennis, track and field, volleyball W. **Intramural:** Baseball M, basketball, bowling, cross-country M, football (tackle), golf, gymnastics, handball, racquetball, softball, swimming, table tennis, tennis, volleyball, weight lifting. **Team name:** Golden Lions.

**Student services.** Adult student services, alcohol/substance abuse counseling, campus ministries, career counseling, services for economically disadvantaged, student employment services, financial aid counseling, health services, on-campus daycare, personal counseling, placement for graduates, veterans' counselor.

**Contact.** E-mail: fultone@uapb.edu
Phone: (870) 575-8493 Toll-free number: (800) 264-6585
Fax: (870) 575-4608
Erica Fulton, Registrar, University of Arkansas at Pine Bluff, 1200 North University Drive, Mail Slot 4981, Pine Bluff, AR 71601-2799

## University of Arkansas for Medical Sciences

**Little Rock, Arkansas**
www.uams.edu  CB code: 0424

- Public 4-year university and health science college
- Commuter campus in large city

**General.** Founded in 1876. Regionally accredited. **Location:** One mile from downtown. **Calendar:** Semester.

**Annual costs/financial aid.** In-state students pay $179 per credit hour for the following programs: dental hygiene, diagnostic medical sonography, nuclear medicine imaging sciences and radiologic technology. In-state students pay $170 per credit hour for the following programs: cytotechnology, health information management, medical dosimetry, medical technology, ophthalmic medical technology, radiation therapy, respiratory care and surgical technology. All out-of-state students pay tuition of $411 per credit hour for programs. Emergency medical sciences/paramedic students pay according to program: 4-semester program, $854 tuition; 5-semester program, $683 tuition. Additional required fees vary by program. Books/supplies: $400. Personal expenses: $1,800. Need-based financial aid available to full-time and part-time students.

**Contact.** Phone: (501) 686-5000
4301 West Markham Street, Little Rock, AR 72205

## University of Central Arkansas
**Conway, Arkansas**
www.uca.edu

**CB member**
**CB code: 6012**

- Public 4-year university
- Residential campus in small city
- 9,921 degree-seeking undergraduates: 9% part-time, 58% women, 16% African American, 1% Asian American, 2% Hispanic American, 1% Native American, 4% international
- 1,570 degree-seeking graduate students
- 49% of applicants admitted
- SAT or ACT (ACT writing optional) required
- 54% graduate within 6 years

**General.** Founded in 1907. Regionally accredited. **Degrees:** 1,389 bachelor's, 39 associate awarded; master's, doctoral offered. **ROTC:** Army. **Location:** 30 miles from Little Rock. **Calendar:** Semester, extensive summer session. **Full-time faculty:** 510 total; 69% have terminal degrees, 11% minority, 47% women. **Part-time faculty:** 186 total; 17% have terminal degrees, 30% minority, 64% women. **Class size:** 42% < 20, 45% 20-39, 9% 40-49, 4% 50-99, less than 1% >100. **Special facilities:** Observatory, greenhouse, honors center, visual arts center, nature preserve, 24-hour study center, fitness center, human anatomy lab, herbarium, planetarium.

**Freshman class profile.** 5,780 applied, 2,811 admitted, 1,793 enrolled.

| Mid 50% test scores | | | |
|---|---|---|---|
| ACT composite: | 20-27 | Return as sophomores: | 71% |
| GPA 3.50 or higher: | 40% | Out-of-state: | 6% |
| GPA 3.0-3.49: | 28% | Live on campus: | 99% |
| GPA 2.0-2.99: | 31% | International: | 2% |

**Basis for selection.** Test scores and high school GPA, along with class rank are important. **Learning Disabled:** Eligibility for services determined individually based on documentation of need. Prospective students encouraged to meet with DSS staff.

**High school preparation.** Recommended units include English 4, mathematics 4, social studies 1, history 2, science 3 and academic electives 10.

**2007-2008 Annual costs.** Tuition/fees: $6,062; $10,892 out-of-state. Room/board: $4,600. Books/supplies: $1,000. Personal expenses: $1,899.

**2006-2007 Financial aid. Need-based:** 531 full-time freshmen applied for aid; 520 were judged to have need; 520 of these received aid. Average need met was 51%. Average scholarship/grant was $1,070; average loan $1,195. 44% of total undergraduate aid awarded as scholarships/grants, 56% as loans/jobs. **Non-need-based:** Awarded to 2,157 full-time undergraduates, including 590 freshmen. Scholarships awarded for academics, art, athletics, leadership, minority status, music/drama, ROTC, state residency. **Additional information:** Room and board may be paid monthly.

**Application procedures. Admission:** Priority date 5/1; no deadline. No application fee. Application may be submitted online. Admission notification on a rolling basis. **Financial aid:** Priority date 4/15, closing date 7/1. FAFSA required. Applicants notified on a rolling basis starting 5/4.

**Academics. Special study options:** Accelerated study, combined bachelor's/graduate degree, cooperative education, distance learning, double major, dual enrollment of high school students, ESL, honors, independent study, internships, liberal arts/career combination, study abroad, teacher certification program. 5-year professional programs in physical therapy and occupational therapy. **Credit/placement by examination:** AP, CLEP, IB, SAT, institutional tests. 30 credit hours maximum toward associate degree, 30 toward bachelor's. **Support services:** Learning center, pre-admission summer program, remedial instruction, study skills assistance, tutoring, writing center.

**Honors college/program.** Special honors courses and minor in interdisciplinary studies offered. 28 ACT and 3.5 GPA minimum.

**Majors. Area/ethnic studies:** African-American. **Biology:** General. **Business:** General, accounting, business admin, finance, insurance, management information systems, marketing. **Communications:** Advertising, journalism, public relations. **Computer sciences:** General. **Conservation:** Environmental studies. **Education:** Business, English, family/consumer sciences, kindergarten/preschool, mathematics, middle, physical, science, social studies. **English:** Composition, English lit, speech/rhetoric. **Family/consumer sciences:** General. **Foreign languages:** French, Spanish. **Health:** Athletic training, audiology/speech pathology, clinical lab science, community health services, medical radiologic technology/radiation therapy, nuclear medical technology, nursing (RN), substance abuse counseling. **History:** General. **Interdisciplinary:** Biological/physical sciences, global studies. **Math:** General. **Parks/recreation:** Exercise sciences. **Philosophy/religion:** Philosophy, religion. **Physical sciences:** Chemistry, physics. **Psychology:** General.

**Public administration:** General. **Social sciences:** Economics, geography, political science, sociology. **Visual/performing arts:** Art, cinematography, dramatic, music performance.

**Most popular majors.** Biology 6%, business/marketing 18%, education 12%, English 6%, family/consumer sciences 6%, health sciences 20%, psychology 6%, social sciences 6%.

**Computing on campus.** Dormitories wired for high-speed internet access and linked to campus network. Commuter students can connect to campus network. Online course registration, online library, helpline, repair service, wireless network available.

**Student life. Freshman orientation:** Available. Preregistration for classes offered. **Housing:** Guaranteed on-campus for freshmen. Coed dorms, single-sex dorms, special housing for disabled, apartments, fraternity/sorority housing available. $100 deposit. **Activities:** Bands, campus ministries, choral groups, dance, drama, film society, international student organizations, literary magazine, music ensembles, Model UN, radio station, student government, student newspaper, symphony orchestra, TV station, Baptist Student Union, Methodist Student Union, Newman Club, Young Democrats, College Republicans, Students for Propagation of Black Culture, Association of Baptist Students, Catholic Campus Ministries, International Friends.

**Athletics.** NCAA. **Intercollegiate:** Baseball M, basketball, cheerleading, cross-country, football (tackle) M, golf, soccer, softball W, tennis W, track and field, volleyball W. **Intramural:** Badminton, basketball, bowling, cross-country, football (non-tackle), racquetball, soccer, softball, swimming, table tennis, tennis, track and field, volleyball. **Team name:** Bears.

**Student services.** Alcohol/substance abuse counseling, campus ministries, career counseling, student employment services, financial aid counseling, health services, minority student services, on-campus daycare, personal counseling, placement for graduates, veterans' counselor, women's services. **Physically disabled:** Services for visually, speech, hearing impaired.

**Contact.** E-mail: admissions@uca.edu
Phone: (501) 450-3128 Toll-free number: (800) 243-8245
Fax: (501) 450-5228
Director of Insitutional Research & Admissions, University of Central Arkansas, 201 Donaghey Avenue, Conway, AR 72035

## University of the Ozarks
**Clarksville, Arkansas**
www.ozarks.edu

**CB code: 6111**

- Private 4-year university and liberal arts college affiliated with Presbyterian Church (USA)
- Residential campus in small town
- 612 degree-seeking undergraduates: 3% part-time, 50% women, 5% African American, 1% Asian American, 3% Hispanic American, 3% Native American, 19% international
- 97% of applicants admitted
- SAT or ACT (ACT writing optional), application essay required
- 46% graduate within 6 years

**General.** Founded in 1834. Regionally accredited. **Degrees:** 106 bachelor's awarded. **Location:** 100 miles from Little Rock, 65 miles from Fort Smith. **Calendar:** Semester, limited summer session. **Full-time faculty:** 46 total; 80% have terminal degrees, 30% women. **Part-time faculty:** 23 total; 74% women. **Class size:** 84% < 20, 16% 20-39.

**Freshman class profile.** 656 applied, 635 admitted, 178 enrolled.

| Mid 50% test scores | | | |
|---|---|---|---|
| SAT critical reading: | 420-570 | Rank in top quarter: | 40% |
| SAT math: | 450-590 | Rank in top tenth: | 20% |
| ACT composite: | 19-25 | Return as sophomores: | 67% |
| GPA 3.50 or higher: | 47% | Out-of-state: | 32% |
| GPA 3.0-3.49: | 28% | Live on campus: | 85% |
| GPA 2.0-2.99: | 25% | International: | 15% |

**Basis for selection.** School achievement record and test scores most important. Interview required of those with marginal grades, recommended for all applicants.

**High school preparation.** 16 units recommended. Recommended units include English 4, mathematics 4, social studies 1, history 2, science 3 (laboratory 2) and foreign language 2.

**2007-2008 Annual costs.** Tuition/fees: $16,130. Room/board: $5,475. Books/supplies: $700. Personal expenses: $2,610.

**2007-2008 Financial aid. Need-based:** 133 full-time freshmen applied for aid; 115 were judged to have need; 115 of these received aid. Average need met was 87%. Average scholarship/grant was $12,775; average loan $5,506. 67% of total undergraduate aid awarded as scholarships/grants, 33% as loans/jobs. **Non-need-based:** Awarded to 221 full-time undergraduates, including 54 freshmen. Scholarships awarded for academics, alumni affiliation, art, leadership, minority status, music/drama, religious affiliation. **Additional information:** Walton International Scholarship Program provides full scholarships to selected Central American and Mexican residents.

**Application procedures. Admission:** Priority date 4/1; no deadline. $30 fee, may be waived for applicants with need. Application may be submitted online. Admission notification on a rolling basis beginning on or about 10/1. Must reply by May 1 or within 4 week(s) if notified thereafter. **Financial aid:** Priority date 2/15; no closing date. FAFSA required. Applicants notified on a rolling basis starting 3/15; must reply within 2 week(s) of notification.

**Academics. Special study options:** Cooperative education, double major, dual enrollment of high school students, independent study, internships, liberal arts/career combination, study abroad, teacher certification program. **Credit/placement by examination:** AP, CLEP, SAT, ACT, institutional tests. 30 credit hours maximum toward bachelor's degree. **Support services:** Learning center, remedial instruction, study skills assistance, tutoring.

**Majors. Biology:** General. **Business:** Accounting, business admin, marketing. **Communications:** Broadcast journalism, media studies. **Conservation:** Environmental studies. **Education:** Biology, business, early childhood, elementary, middle, physical, science, special. **English:** English lit. **Health:** Predental, premedicine, prepharmacy, preveterinary. **History:** General. **Legal studies:** Prelaw. **Math:** General. **Parks/recreation:** Health/fitness. **Philosophy/religion:** Philosophy, religion. **Physical sciences:** Chemistry, physics. **Psychology:** General. **Public administration:** General. **Social sciences:** General, political science, sociology. **Visual/performing arts:** General, art, dramatic.

**Most popular majors.** Biology 11%, business/marketing 41%, communications/journalism 6%, education 11%, liberal arts 8%, social sciences 7%.

**Computing on campus.** 150 workstations in dormitories, library, computer center, student center. Dormitories linked to campus network. Commuter students can connect to campus network. Online course registration, helpline available.

**Student life. Freshman orientation:** Mandatory. Preregistration for classes offered. **Housing:** Guaranteed on-campus for freshmen. Coed dorms, single-sex dorms available. $100 partly refundable deposit, deadline 8/15. **Activities:** Choral groups, drama, literary magazine, music ensembles, musical theater, radio station, student government, TV station, Ozarks Area Mission, Alpha & Omega, other religious, ethnic, and social service organizations.

**Athletics.** NCAA. **Intercollegiate:** Baseball M, basketball, cheerleading, cross-country, soccer, softball W, tennis. **Intramural:** Badminton, basketball, bowling, football (non-tackle), racquetball, soccer, softball, tennis, volleyball. **Team name:** Eagles.

**Student services.** Campus ministries, career counseling, student employment services, financial aid counseling, health services, personal counseling, placement for graduates, veterans' counselor. **Learning disabled:** Comprehensive services available.

**Contact.** E-mail: admiss@ozarks.edu
Phone: (479) 979-1227 Toll-free number: (800) 264-8636
Fax: (479) 979-1355
Kim Myrick, Dean of Enrollment, University of the Ozarks, 415 College Avenue, Clarksville, AR 72830

## Williams Baptist College
**Walnut Ridge, Arkansas**
**www.wbcoll.edu**                    CB code: 6658

◆ Private 4-year liberal arts college affiliated with Southern Baptist Convention

◆ Residential campus in small town

◆ 502 degree-seeking undergraduates: 2% part-time, 54% women, 2% African American, 3% Hispanic American, 1% international

◆ 64% of applicants admitted

◆ SAT or ACT (ACT writing optional) required

◆ 46% graduate within 6 years

**General.** Founded in 1941. Regionally accredited. **Degrees:** 104 bachelor's, 4 associate awarded. **ROTC:** Army. **Location:** 30 miles from Jonesboro, 100 miles from Memphis. **Calendar:** Semester, limited summer session. **Full-time faculty:** 29 total; 59% have terminal degrees, 41% women. **Part-time faculty:** 15 total; 7% have terminal degrees, 7% minority, 73% women. **Class size:** 55% < 20, 42% 20-39, 1% 40-49, less than 1% 50-99.

**Freshman class profile.** 481 applied, 309 admitted, 133 enrolled.

| | | | |
|---|---|---|---|
| End year in good standing: | 95% | Live on campus: | 85% |
| Return as sophomores: | 61% | International: | 2% |
| Out-of-state: | 10% | | |

**Basis for selection.** Students must have a 19 composite ACT score and a 2.5 cumulative high school GPA in order to be admitted unconditionally.

**High school preparation.** Recommended units include English 4, mathematics 4, social studies 3, science 3 (laboratory 3) and foreign language 2.

**2007-2008 Annual costs.** Tuition/fees: $10,370. Room/board: $4,700. Books/supplies: $925. Personal expenses: $1,150.

**2006-2007 Financial aid. Need-based:** 120 full-time freshmen applied for aid; 90 were judged to have need; 90 of these received aid. Average scholarship/grant was $2,088; average loan $2,062. 47% of total undergraduate aid awarded as scholarships/grants, 53% as loans/jobs. **Non-need-based:** Awarded to 575 full-time undergraduates, including 159 freshmen. Scholarships awarded for academics, art, athletics, leadership, minority status, music/drama, religious affiliation, state residency. **Additional information:** Art scholarship applicants must submit portfolio.

**Application procedures. Admission:** No deadline. $20 fee. Application may be submitted online. Admission notification on a rolling basis. **Financial aid:** Priority date 5/1; no closing date. FAFSA required. Applicants notified on a rolling basis starting 4/1; must reply within 2 week(s) of notification.

**Academics. Special study options:** Double major, dual enrollment of high school students, independent study, internships, study abroad. **Credit/placement by examination:** AP, CLEP, IB. 30 credit hours maximum toward bachelor's degree. **Support services:** Learning center, reduced course load, remedial instruction, study skills assistance, tutoring.

**Majors. Biology:** General. **Business:** Business admin, finance. **Computer sciences:** General. **Education:** General, art, early childhood, elementary, English, music, physical, secondary, social studies. **English:** English lit. **History:** General. **Psychology:** General. **Theology:** Bible, missionary, religious ed, sacred music, theology, youth ministry. **Visual/performing arts:** Studio arts.

**Most popular majors.** Biology 10%, business/marketing 11%, education 37%, liberal arts 6%, psychology 15%, theological studies 16%.

**Computing on campus.** 70 workstations in library, computer center, student center. Dormitories wired for high-speed internet access and linked to campus network. Online library, wireless network available.

**Student life. Freshman orientation:** Mandatory, $75 fee. 2-day program held at beginning of fall semester. **Policies:** Please see on-line Student Handbook. Religious observance required. **Housing:** Guaranteed on-campus for all undergraduates. Single-sex dorms, apartments available. $75 fully refundable deposit, deadline 5/1. All full-time students under 21 required to live in college housing, unless commuting. **Activities:** Campus ministries, choral groups, drama, international student organizations, student government, Fellowship of Christian Athletes, College Republicans, student activities board, Student Ambassadors.

**Athletics.** NAIA. **Intercollegiate:** Baseball M, basketball, cheerleading, soccer M, softball W, volleyball W. **Intramural:** Baseball M, basketball, football (non-tackle), softball, volleyball. **Team name:** Eagles.

**Student services.** Alcohol/substance abuse counseling, campus ministries, career counseling, financial aid counseling, health services, personal counseling, veterans' counselor.

**Contact.** E-mail: admissions@wbcoll.edu
Phone: (870) 759-4121 Toll-free number: (800) 722-4434
Fax: (870) 886-3924
Angela Flippo, Vice President for Enrollment, Williams Baptist College, PO Box 3665, Walnut Ridge, AR 72476

# California

## Academy of Art University
### San Francisco, California
### www.academyart.edu
**CB code: 1981**

- For-profit 4-year university and visual arts college
- Commuter campus in very large city
- 8,210 degree-seeking undergraduates: 34% part-time, 52% women, 6% African American, 12% Asian American, 9% Hispanic American, 1% Native American, 14% international
- 2,689 degree-seeking graduate students
- 36% graduate within 6 years; 7% enter graduate study

**General.** Founded in 1929. Accredited by ACICS. Equal emphasis on both fine and applied arts. Also accredited by the National Association of Schools of Art and Design. BFA on-campus program Interior Architecture and Design program accredited by CIDA (formerly FIDER). **Degrees:** 659 bachelor's, 67 associate awarded; master's offered. **Calendar:** Semester, extensive summer session. **Full-time faculty:** 171 total; 16% have terminal degrees, 17% minority, 43% women. **Part-time faculty:** 713 total. **Class size:** 79% < 20, 20% 20-39, less than 1% 50-99, less than 1% >100. **Special facilities:** 3 nonprofit galleries, photography darkrooms, Bosch Telecen, green screen stage, interior design resource room, foundry, 50,000-square-foot sculpture center, Final Cut Pro, Media and Avid Express editing stations.

**Freshman class profile.** 3,768 applied, 3,768 admitted, 1,656 enrolled.

| | | | |
|---|---|---|---|
| End year in good standing: | 68% | Live on campus: | 40% |
| Return as sophomores: | 68% | International: | 9% |
| Out-of-state: | 52% | | |

**Basis for selection.** Open admission. Continuing education program offered. Interview recommended, and can be in person or over the phone. **Learning Disabled:** Reasonable accomodations made for students with disabilities.

**High school preparation.** Art and design courses recommended.

**2008-2009 Annual costs.** Tuition/fees (projected): $20,380. Room/board: $13,500. Books/supplies: $1,566. Personal expenses: $2,214.

**2006-2007 Financial aid. Need-based:** 379 full-time freshmen applied for aid; 316 were judged to have need; 312 of these received aid. Average need met was 20%. Average scholarship/grant was $3,957; average loan $2,056. 27% of total undergraduate aid awarded as scholarships/grants, 73% as loans/jobs. **Non-need-based:** Awarded to 98 full-time undergraduates, including 30 freshmen. Scholarships awarded for academics, art. **Additional information:** Numerous summer grant programs available.

**Application procedures. Admission:** No deadline. $100 fee. Application may be submitted online. Admission notification on a rolling basis. Accepted applicants may preregister in mid March. **Financial aid:** Priority date 7/10; no closing date. FAFSA, institutional form required. Applicants notified on a rolling basis.

**Academics. Special study options:** Combined bachelor's/graduate degree, distance learning, dual enrollment of high school students, ESL, honors, independent study, internships, student-designed major, teacher certification program. **Credit/placement by examination:** AP, CLEP, IB. Interview, essay recommended for placement. Portfolio recommended for bachelor of arts applicants. **Support services:** Learning center, pre-admission summer program, reduced course load, remedial instruction, study skills assistance, tutoring, writing center.

**Majors. Communications:** Advertising. **Communications technology:** Animation/special effects, desktop publishing. **Computer sciences:** Web page design. **Visual/performing arts:** Cinematography, commercial photography, commercial/advertising art, design, drawing, fashion design, fiber arts, graphic design, illustration, industrial design, interior design, metal/jewelry, multimedia, painting, photography, printmaking, sculpture, studio arts.

**Most popular majors.** Communication technologies 23%, visual/performing arts 72%.

**Computing on campus.** 800 workstations in dormitories, library, computer center. Dormitories wired for high-speed internet access. Commuter students can connect to campus network. Online course registration, online library, helpline, student web hosting, wireless network available.

**Student life. Freshman orientation:** Mandatory. Preregistration for classes offered. 5-day session week before start of classes. **Housing:** Guaranteed on-campus for freshmen. Coed dorms, single-sex dorms, special housing for disabled, substance-free housing available. $500 deposit. **Activities:** Dance, drama, film society, international student organizations, student government, student newspaper, Chinese society, Circle of Nations.

**Athletics. Intercollegiate:** Baseball M, basketball, cross-country, golf M, soccer, softball W, tennis W, track and field, volleyball M. **Intramural:** Basketball, football (non-tackle), soccer, softball, table tennis, tennis, volleyball. **Team name:** Urban Knights.

**Student services.** Alcohol/substance abuse counseling, career counseling, student employment services, financial aid counseling, personal counseling. **Physically disabled:** Services for visually, hearing impaired.

**Contact.** E-mail: info@academyart.edu
Phone: (415) 274-2200 Toll-free number: (800) 544-2787
Fax: (415) 618-6287
Admissions, Academy of Art University, 79 New Montgomery Street, San Francisco, CA 94105-3410

## Alliant International University
### San Diego, California
### www.alliant.edu
**CB member**
**CB code: 4039**

- Private two-year upper-division university
- Commuter campus in very large city
- 97% of applicants admitted

**General.** Founded in 1952. Regionally accredited. Focuses on preparing students for professional careers in applied social sciences. Students may enter as transfers after 2 years of undergraduate study at San Diego, and as freshmen or transfers at Mexico City. **Degrees:** 73 bachelor's awarded; master's, doctoral offered. **Articulation:** Agreements with Cuyamaca College, Glendale College, Grossmont College, Imperial Valley College, MiraCosta College, Mt. San Antonio College, Mt. San Jacinto College, Palomar College, Pasadena College, Riverside Community College, Saddleback College, San Diego City College, San Diego Mesa College, San Diego Miramar College, Santa Monica College, Southwestern College, Ventura College. **Location:** 16 miles from downtown. **Calendar:** Semester, limited summer session. **Full-time faculty:** 161 total; 100% have terminal degrees, 17% minority, 43% women. **Part-time faculty:** 405 total; 93% have terminal degrees, 12% minority. **Class size:** 100% < 20.

**Student profile.** 179 degree-seeking undergraduates, 3,401 degree-seeking graduate students. 115 applied as first time-transfer students, 111 admitted, 51 enrolled. 45% transferred from two-year, 55% transferred from four-year institutions.

| | | | |
|---|---|---|---|
| Women: | 60% | Part-time: | 22% |
| African American: | 8% | Out-of-state: | 16% |
| Asian American: | 5% | Live on campus: | 38% |
| Hispanic American: | 16% | 25 or older: | 20% |
| International: | 23% | | |

**Basis for selection.** High school transcript, college transcript required. Transfer accepted as sophomores, juniors, seniors.

**2008-2009 Annual costs.** Tuition/fees (projected): $15,210. Books/supplies: $1,260. Personal expenses: $2,214.

**Financial aid. Need-based:** 48% of total undergraduate aid awarded as scholarships/grants, 52% as loans/jobs. **Non-need-based:** Scholarships awarded for academics, alumni affiliation, athletics, leadership.

**Application procedures. Admission:** Priority date 3/2. $45 fee, may be waived for applicants with need. Application may be submitted online. **Financial aid:** FAFSA required.

**Academics. Special study options:** Combined bachelor's/graduate degree, ESL, honors, independent study, internships, liberal arts/career combination, study abroad. **Credit/placement by examination:** AP, CLEP, IB, institutional tests. 27 credit hours maximum toward bachelor's degree.

**Majors. Area/ethnic studies:** Latin American. **Business:** Business admin, hospitality/recreation, international, management information systems, tourism promotion. **Communications:** Journalism. **Conservation:** Environmental studies. **Education:** ESL. **Psychology:** General. **Social sciences:** International relations.

**Most popular majors.** Business/marketing 65%, liberal arts 6%, psychology 15%, social sciences 11%.

**Computing on campus.** 100 workstations in library, computer center. Dormitories wired for high-speed internet access and linked to campus network. Commuter students can connect to campus network. Online library, student web hosting available.

**Student life. Housing:** Guaranteed on-campus for all undergraduates. Coed dorms available. $265 deposit. All dormitories made up of 2-bedroom suites with central living room. **Activities:** International student organizations, Model UN, student government, student newspaper, Indian student association, Latino student organization, Alliant Turk Society.

**Athletics.** NAIA. **Intramural:** Basketball, bowling, soccer, softball, tennis, volleyball.

**Student services.** Adult student services, alcohol/substance abuse counseling, career counseling, student employment services, financial aid counseling, health services, personal counseling, placement for graduates, veterans' counselor, women's services. **Physically disabled:** Services for visually, speech, hearing impaired.

**Contact.** E-mail: admissions3@alliant.edu
Phone: (866) 825-5426 Toll-free number: (866) 825-5426
Fax: (858) 635-4555
Susan Topham, Director of Admissions, Alliant International University, 10455 Pomerado Road, San Diego, CA 92131-1799

## American Jewish University
### Los Angeles, California
### www.ajula.edu
**CB code: 4876**

- Private 4-year university and liberal arts college affiliated with Jewish faith
- Residential campus in very large city
- 107 degree-seeking undergraduates: 55% women, 2% African American, 1% Hispanic American, 6% international
- 127 degree-seeking graduate students
- 71% of applicants admitted
- SAT or ACT (ACT writing recommended), application essay required
- 100% graduate within 6 years; 72% enter graduate study

**General.** Founded in 1947. Regionally accredited. **Degrees:** 26 bachelor's awarded; master's, first professional offered. **Location:** 5 miles from Los Angeles. **Calendar:** Semester. **Full-time faculty:** 19 total; 84% have terminal degrees, 32% women. **Part-time faculty:** 72 total; 31% have terminal degrees, 49% women. **Class size:** 93% < 20, 7% 20-39. **Special facilities:** Sigi Ziering institute, center for Israel studies, Platt & Borstein contemporary art galleries, Whizin center for continuing education, Jewish community documentation center, educational resources center.

**Freshman class profile.** 109 applied, 77 admitted, 32 enrolled.

| Mid 50% test scores | | | |
|---|---|---|---|
| SAT critical reading: | 460-610 | Rank in top quarter: | 35% |
| SAT math: | 470-560 | Rank in top tenth: | 21% |
| SAT writing: | 460-610 | End year in good standing: | 80% |
| GPA 3.50 or higher: | 30% | Return as sophomores: | 86% |
| GPA 3.0-3.49: | 55% | Out-of-state: | 31% |
| GPA 2.0-2.99: | 15% | Live on campus: | 70% |
| | | International: | 13% |

**Basis for selection.** Essay, volunteerism/engagement in community, leadership roles and letters of recommendation are most important, followed by GPA and then standardized test scores. Interview recommended. **Home-schooled:** Transcript of courses and grades, state high school equivalency certificate, letter of recommendation (nonparent) required.

**High school preparation.** 18 units recommended. Recommended units include English 4, mathematics 3, social studies 2, history 2, science 3 (laboratory 2) and foreign language 2.

**2007-2008 Annual costs.** Tuition/fees: $21,340. Room/board: $11,070. Books/supplies: $882. Personal expenses: $1,476.

**2006-2007 Financial aid. Need-based:** 21 full-time freshmen applied for aid; 21 were judged to have need; 21 of these received aid. Average need met was 49%. Average scholarship/grant was $9,328; average loan $3,662. 53% of total undergraduate aid awarded as scholarships/grants, 47% as loans/jobs. **Non-need-based:** Awarded to 9 full-time undergraduates, including 27 freshmen. Scholarships awarded for academics, leadership.

**Application procedures. Admission:** Priority date 1/31; deadline 7/31 (receipt date). $35 fee, may be waived for applicants with need. Application

may be submitted online. Admission notification on a rolling basis beginning on or about 11/1. Must reply by May 1 or within 4 week(s) if notified thereafter. **Financial aid:** Priority date 3/2; no closing date. FAFSA, institutional form required. Applicants notified on a rolling basis starting 3/15; must reply within 3 week(s) of notification.

**Academics.** In addition to majors and general education requirements, students take core curriculum of Jewish and Western Civilization classes. **Special study options:** Accelerated study, combined bachelor's/graduate degree, cross-registration, double major, honors, independent study, internships, student-designed major, study abroad. **Credit/placement by examination:** AP, CLEP, IB, institutional tests. **Support services:** Reduced course load, tutoring.

**Majors. Area/ethnic studies:** Near/Middle Eastern. **Biology:** General, biomedical sciences. **Business:** General. **Communications:** General, broadcast journalism, digital media, journalism, media studies. **English:** English lit, speech/rhetoric. **Foreign languages:** Comparative lit. **Health:** Ethics. **Interdisciplinary:** Biological/physical sciences, natural sciences, peace/conflict. **Legal studies:** Prelaw. **Liberal arts:** Arts/sciences. **Philosophy/religion:** Judaic. **Social sciences:** Political science. **Visual/performing arts:** Dramatic, film/cinema. **Other:** Jewish studies.

**Most popular majors.** Biology 25%, business/marketing 21%, communication technologies 13%, English 8%, philosophy/religious studies 8%, psychology 20%.

**Computing on campus.** 32 workstations in dormitories, library, computer center. Dormitories wired for high-speed internet access and linked to campus network. Commuter students can connect to campus network. Wireless network available.

**Student life. Freshman orientation:** Mandatory. Preregistration for classes offered. Held 1 week prior to start of class; usually lasts 3 days. **Housing:** Guaranteed on-campus for all undergraduates. Coed dorms, apartments available. $100 nonrefundable deposit, deadline 8/15. Kosher meals on campus. Students required to live on campus unless 21 or living with parents. **Activities:** Choral groups, drama, international student organizations, literary magazine, Model UN, musical theater, student government, student newspaper, Hillel: The Foundation for Jewish Life on Campus, Israel Action, political science club, Repair the World service organization.

**Athletics. Team name:** Lions.

**Student services.** Campus ministries, career counseling, student employment services, financial aid counseling, health services, personal counseling, placement for graduates. **Physically disabled:** Services for hearing impaired.

**Contact.** E-mail: admissions@ajula.edu
Phone: (310) 476-9777 ext. 247 Toll-free number: (877) 462-2585
Fax: (310) 471-3657
Matt Davidson, Admissions Director, American Jewish University, 15600 Mulholland Drive, Los Angeles, CA 90077

## Antioch University Los Angeles
### Culver City, California
### www.antiochla.edu
**CB code: 1862**

- Private two-year upper-division branch campus and liberal arts college
- Commuter campus in very large city
- Application essay, interview required

**General.** Founded in 1972. Regionally accredited. **Degrees:** 40 bachelor's awarded; master's offered. **Articulation:** Agreements with UCLA Extension, Santa Monica College, West Los Angeles College, Compton City College. **Location:** 15 miles from Los Angeles. **Calendar:** Quarter, extensive summer session. **Full-time faculty:** 20 total. **Part-time faculty:** 5 total.

**Student profile.** 150 degree-seeking undergraduates.

**Basis for selection.** High school transcript, college transcript, application essay, interview required. Admission decision of full or provisional acceptance made by program chair. Transfer accepted as sophomores, juniors, seniors.

**2007-2008 Annual costs.** Tuition/fees: $15,252. Cost varies with program. Books/supplies: $1,500.

**Application procedures. Admission:** Deadline 8/1. $60 fee, may be waived for applicants with need. Must reply by 8/15. **Financial aid:** FAFSA, institutional form required.

**Academics.** Prior experiential learning credits. **Special study options:** Accelerated study, combined bachelor's/graduate degree, cooperative education, cross-registration, double major, independent study, internships, liberal arts/career combination, student-designed major, study abroad, teacher certification program, weekend college. **Credit/placement by examination:** AP, CLEP. 40 credit hours maximum toward bachelor's degree. DANTES examination scores accepted.

**Majors. Liberal arts:** Arts/sciences.

**Computing on campus.** 12 workstations in computer center. Commuter students can connect to campus network.

**Student life. Activities:** Student government.

**Athletics. Team name:** Radicals.

**Student services.** Adult student services, career counseling, student employment services, financial aid counseling, personal counseling, veterans' counselor. **Physically disabled:** Services for visually, speech, hearing impaired.

**Contact.** E-mail: admissions@antiochla.edu
Phone: (800) 726-8462 Toll-free number: (800) 726-8462
Fax: (310) 822-4824
Judith Magee, Director of Enrollment Management, Antioch University Los Angeles, 400 Corporate Pointe, Culver City, CA 90230-7615

## Antioch University Santa Barbara
**Santa Barbara, California**
**www.antiochsb.edu**                    **CB code: 3071**

- Private two-year upper-division university and liberal arts college
- Commuter campus in small city
- Application essay, interview required

**General.** Founded in 1852. Regionally accredited. **Degrees:** 41 bachelor's awarded; master's, doctoral offered. **Articulation:** Agreements with Santa Barbara City College, University of California: Santa Barbara, Ventura Community College, Cuesta Community College, Allen Hancock Community College. **Location:** Downtown. **Calendar:** Quarter, extensive summer session. **Full-time faculty:** 16 total; 62% women. **Part-time faculty:** 54 total; 54% women.

**Student profile.** 96 degree-seeking undergraduates.

**Basis for selection.** Open admission. High school transcript, college transcript, application essay, interview required. Transfer accepted as juniors, seniors.

**2007-2008 Annual costs.** Tuition/fees: $14,718. Books/supplies: $1,600.

**Financial aid. Need-based:** 18% of total undergraduate aid awarded as scholarships/grants, 82% as loans/jobs.

**Application procedures. Admission:** Rolling admission. $60 fee. Application may be submitted online. **Financial aid:** Priority date 4/1, no deadline. FAFSA, institutional form required.

**Academics. Special study options:** Cross-registration, double major, independent study, internships, liberal arts/career combination, student-designed major, study abroad, teacher certification program, weekend college. **Credit/placement by examination:** AP, CLEP, IB. **Support services:** Remedial instruction.

**Majors. Liberal arts:** Arts/sciences.

**Computing on campus.** 10 workstations in computer center. Online library available.

**Student services.** Adult student services, career counseling, financial aid counseling, personal counseling, veterans' counselor.

**Contact.** E-mail: admissions@antiochsb.edu
Phone: (805) 962-8179 Toll-free number: (866) 562-8462
Fax: (805) 962-4786
Mike Meraz, Director, Marketing and Enrollment Management, Antioch University Santa Barbara, 801 Garden Street, Suite 101, Santa Barbara, CA 93101-1581

## Art Center College of Design
**Pasadena, California**                    **CB member**
**www.artcenter.edu**                    **CB code: 4009**

- Private 4-year visual arts college
- Commuter campus in small city
- 1,500 degree-seeking undergraduates
- SAT or ACT, application essay required

**General.** Founded in 1930. Regionally accredited. **Degrees:** 367 bachelor's awarded; master's offered. **Location:** 15 miles from Los Angeles. **Calendar:** Trimester, extensive summer session. **Full-time faculty:** 65 total. **Part-time faculty:** 340 total. **Class size:** 87% < 20, 12% 20-39, less than 1% 40-49, less than 1% 50-99. **Special facilities:** 3 galleries; state of the art 3-D modelling and industrial design facilities.

**Basis for selection.** Strength of specific portfolio for one major, academic record, standardized test scores. SAT/ACT required only for students applying while still in high school. Interviews recommended for local applicants.

**High school preparation.** Art classes recommended.

**2008-2009 Annual costs.** Tuition/fees: $30,284. Books/supplies: $5,350. Personal expenses: $3,556.

**Financial aid.** All financial aid based on need. **Additional information:** Students may apply for scholarships after they enroll while progressing through the program.

**Application procedures. Admission:** Priority date 3/1; no deadline. $50 fee, may be waived for applicants with need. Admission notification on a rolling basis beginning on or about 1/1. Application 4 to 6 months before fall term recommended. **Financial aid:** Priority date 3/1; no closing date. FAFSA required. Applicants notified on a rolling basis starting 5/15; must reply within 4 week(s) of notification.

**Academics. Special study options:** Cross-registration, independent study, internships, study abroad. **Credit/placement by examination:** AP, CLEP, IB, institutional tests. **Support services:** Tutoring, writing center.

**Majors. Architecture:** Environmental design. **Communications:** Advertising. **Communications technology:** Animation/special effects, graphics. **Visual/performing arts:** Cinematography, commercial photography, commercial/advertising art, graphic design, illustration, industrial design, interior design, painting, photography, sculpture, studio arts.

**Computing on campus.** 250 workstations in library, computer center. Online library, wireless network available.

**Student life. Freshman orientation:** Mandatory. 3-day program including introduction to a mentor and testing. **Activities:** International student organizations, literary magazine, student government, Chroma Contraste, Eco Council, Women in Design, Out Network.

**Student services.** Alcohol/substance abuse counseling, career counseling, student employment services, financial aid counseling, personal counseling, placement for graduates. **Physically disabled:** Services for hearing impaired.

**Contact.** E-mail: admissions@artcenter.edu
Phone: (626) 396-2373 Fax: (626) 795-0578
Kit Baron, Vice President, Admissions, Art Center College of Design, 1700 Lida Street, Pasadena, CA 91103

## Art Institute of California: Orange County
**Santa Ana, California**
**www.artinstitutes.edu/orangecounty/**          **CB code: 3831**

- For-profit 3-year culinary school and visual arts college
- Commuter campus in very large city
- 1,761 degree-seeking undergraduates: 21% part-time, 41% women
- 44% of applicants admitted
- Application essay, interview required

**General.** Accredited by ACICS. **Degrees:** 231 bachelor's, 73 associate awarded. **Location:** 40 miles from Los Angeles, 90 miles from San Diego. **Calendar:** Quarter, extensive summer session. **Full-time faculty:** 53 total. **Part-time faculty:** 121 total. **Special facilities:** 4 professional skills kitchens, 11 computer labs, library, interior design resource center, industrial design workshop, student dining lab.

**Freshman class profile.** 818 applied, 356 admitted, 333 enrolled.

**Basis for selection.** High school record and general appropriateness of educational background to specific program applied for most important. Portfolio, interview also important. Standardized test scores considered if submitted.

**2007-2008 Annual costs.** Typical full-time load 16 credit hours per quarter. Housing costs $2,450-$3,300 per quarter. Culinary lab fee $315 per quarter, online fee $100 per class per quarter. Books/supplies: $1,100. Personal expenses: $2,280.

**Financial aid. Non-need-based:** Scholarships awarded for academics, art, minority status.

**Application procedures. Admission:** No deadline. $50 fee. Application may be submitted online. Admission notification on a rolling basis. **Financial aid:** No deadline. FAFSA required. Applicants notified on a rolling basis; must reply within 2 week(s) of notification.

**Academics. Special study options:** Cooperative education, distance learning, internships. Online courses. **Credit/placement by examination:** CLEP, IB, institutional tests. 3 credit hours maximum toward associate degree, 3 toward bachelor's. **Support services:** Learning center, pre-admission summer program, reduced course load, study skills assistance, tutoring.

**Majors. Communications:** Digital media. **Communications technology:** Animation/special effects. **Computer sciences:** Computer graphics, web page design, webmaster. **Personal/culinary services:** Culinary arts, restaurant/catering. **Visual/performing arts:** Commercial/advertising art, fashion design, graphic design, industrial design, interior design. **Other:** Fashion Marketing and Management.

**Computing on campus.** 312 workstations in library, computer center, student center. Online course registration, online library, helpline, repair service, wireless network available.

**Student life. Freshman orientation:** Mandatory. **Housing:** Special housing for disabled, apartments available. School-sponsored housing available. **Activities:** Film society, student newspaper.

**Student services.** Career counseling, student employment services, financial aid counseling, personal counseling, placement for graduates, veterans' counselor. **Physically disabled:** Services for visually, speech, hearing impaired.

**Contact.** E-mail: aicaocadm@aii.edu
Phone: (888) 549-3055 Toll-free number: (888) 549-3055
Fax: (714) 556-1923
Tim Hansen, Director of Admissions, Art Institute of California: Orange County, 3601 West Sunflower Avenue, Santa Ana, CA 92704-9888

## Art Institute of California: San Diego
**San Diego, California**
**www.artinstitutes.edu/sandiego**     **CB code: 3036**

- For-profit 3-year visual arts college
- Residential campus in very large city
- 2,145 degree-seeking undergraduates
- Application essay, interview required

**General.** Accredited by ACCSCT. **Degrees:** 264 bachelor's, 91 associate awarded. **Calendar:** Quarter. **Full-time faculty:** 62 total. **Part-time faculty:** 63 total. **Special facilities:** Dining lab run by culinary students.

**Basis for selection.** High school record and general appropriateness of educational background to specific program applied for most important. Portfolio, interview, standardized test scores also important. **Learning Disabled:** Students requiring assistance should notify Assistant Director of Admissions.

**2008-2009 Annual costs.** Tuition/fees: $22,272.

**Application procedures. Admission:** No deadline. $50 fee. Application may be submitted online. Admission notification on a rolling basis.

**Academics. Special study options:** Accelerated study, distance learning, internships, study abroad. **Credit/placement by examination:** AP, CLEP. **Support services:** Study skills assistance, tutoring.

**Majors. Communications:** Advertising. **Computer sciences:** Computer graphics, web page design, webmaster. **Visual/performing arts:** Commercial/advertising art, fashion design, graphic design, interior design, multimedia. **Other:** Fashion Marketing and Management.

**Computing on campus.** 300 workstations in computer center.

**Student life. Freshman orientation:** Available. Preregistration for classes offered. **Housing:** Single-sex dorms available. **Activities:** Student government.

**Student services.** Alcohol/substance abuse counseling, career counseling, services for economically disadvantaged, student employment services, financial aid counseling, personal counseling. **Physically disabled:** Services for visually, speech, hearing impaired. **Learning disabled:** Comprehensive services available.

**Contact.** E-mail: aicaadmin@aii.edu
Phone: (800) 275-2422 Toll-free number: (800) 275-2422
Jesus Moreno, Director of Admissions, Art Institute of California: San Diego, 7650 Mission Valley Road, San Diego, CA 92108-4423

## Art Institute of California: San Francisco
**San Francisco, California**
**www.artinstitutes.edu/sanfrancisco**     **CB code: 4421**

- For-profit 4-year visual arts college
- Commuter campus in very large city
- 1,568 degree-seeking undergraduates
- 33% of applicants admitted
- Application essay required

**General.** Founded in 1939. Accredited by ACICS. **Degrees:** 215 bachelor's, 21 associate awarded; master's offered. **Location:** Downtown. **Calendar:** Quarter, extensive summer session. **Full-time faculty:** 35 total. **Part-time faculty:** 87 total. **Special facilities:** Computer-aided fashion design and illustration systems, 2D and 3D animation labs, fashion labs, design library, ZBrush.

**Freshman class profile.** 828 applied, 274 admitted, 250 enrolled.

**Basis for selection.** High school record and general appropriateness of educational background to specific program applied for most important. Portfolio, interview, standardized test scores also important. Interview recommended. Portfolios recommended.

**High school preparation.** Recommended units include English 1, mathematics 1, social studies 1 and history 1. One art class recommended.

**2008-2009 Annual costs.** Tuition/fees (projected): $29,184. Starter kits additional $750-$1,300 estimate for all programs. Standard enrollment generally 16 credits/quarter. Room/board: $10,680. Books/supplies: $1,125.

**Application procedures. Admission:** No deadline. $150 fee. Application may be submitted online. Admission notification on a rolling basis. **Financial aid:** No deadline. FAFSA required. Applicants notified on a rolling basis.

**Academics. Special study options:** Distance learning, honors, internships, study abroad. **Credit/placement by examination:** AP, CLEP, IB. **Support services:** Reduced course load, remedial instruction, study skills assistance, tutoring.

**Majors. Business:** Fashion. **Communications technology:** Animation/special effects. **Computer sciences:** Computer graphics, web page design. **Personal/culinary services:** Chef training, restaurant/catering. **Visual/performing arts:** Commercial/advertising art, fashion design, film/cinema, graphic design, interior design.

**Student life. Freshman orientation:** Mandatory. **Housing:** Coed dorms, apartments available. $300 deposit. **Activities:** Student government, student newspaper, animation club, society of web architects and programmers, fashion salon, graphic design club, game art and design club, anime club, photography club, eco club, student SIGGRAPH chapter, interior design club.

**Student services.** Career counseling, student employment services, financial aid counseling, personal counseling, placement for graduates. **Physically disabled:** Services for hearing impaired.

**Contact.** E-mail: aisfadm@aii.edu
Phone: (415) 865-0198 Toll-free number: (888) 493-3261
Fax: (415) 863-6344
Daniel Chew, Senior Director of Admissions, Art Institute of California: San Francisco, 1170 Market Street, San Francisco, CA 94102

## Azusa Pacific University

**Azusa, California**
www.apu.edu

CB member
CB code: 4596

- Private 4-year university affiliated with interdenominational tradition
- Residential campus in small city
- 4,615 degree-seeking undergraduates: 15% part-time, 63% women
- 3,446 degree-seeking graduate students
- 73% of applicants admitted
- SAT or ACT (ACT writing optional), application essay required
- 67% graduate within 6 years

**General.** Founded in 1899. Regionally accredited. **Degrees:** 1,241 bachelor's awarded; master's, doctoral, first professional offered. **ROTC:** Army. **Location:** 30 miles from Los Angeles. **Calendar:** Semester, limited summer session. **Full-time faculty:** 319 total; 73% have terminal degrees, 23% minority, 46% women. **Part-time faculty:** 32 total; 56% have terminal degrees, 22% minority, 50% women. **Class size:** 64% < 20, 32% 20-39, 2% 40-49, 1% 50-99, less than 1% >100.

**Freshman class profile.** 3,229 applied, 2,370 admitted, 855 enrolled.

| Mid 50% test scores | | | |
|---|---|---|---|
| SAT critical reading: | 480-590 | Rank in top quarter: | 57% |
| SAT math: | 480-590 | Rank in top tenth: | 27% |
| ACT composite: | 21-26 | Return as sophomores: | 80% |
| GPA 3.50 or higher: | 57% | Out-of-state: | 24% |
| GPA 3.0-3.49: | 32% | Live on campus: | 94% |
| GPA 2.0-2.99: | 11% | International: | 4% |

**Basis for selection.** GPA, test scores, references, statement of agreement, essay important. Auditions required for music applicants. Interviews recommended for borderline applicants. **Homeschooled:** SAT or ACT and transcript from organization required.

**High school preparation.** College-preparatory program recommended. Recommended units include English 4, mathematics 3, social studies 1, history 2, science 2 and foreign language 3.

**2007-2008 Annual costs.** Tuition/fees: $25,130. Room/board: $7,518. Books/supplies: $1,314. Personal expenses: $2,088.

**2006-2007 Financial aid. Need-based:** 816 full-time freshmen applied for aid; 535 were judged to have need; 534 of these received aid. Average need met was 72%. Average scholarship/grant was $9,538; average loan $2,492. 73% of total undergraduate aid awarded as scholarships/grants, 27% as loans/jobs. **Non-need-based:** Awarded to 1,291 full-time undergraduates, including 324 freshmen. Scholarships awarded for academics, athletics, leadership, minority status, music/drama, religious affiliation, ROTC.

**Application procedures. Admission:** Priority date 3/1; deadline 6/1 (postmark date). $45 fee, may be waived for applicants with need. Application may be submitted online. Admission notification on a rolling basis. Must reply by 5/1. Students with 3.0 high school GPA or higher and 1000 SAT score or higher can apply at completion of junior year and/or before January 1 for admission consideration. Housing deposit due by move-in date. **Financial aid:** Priority date 3/2, closing date 7/1. FAFSA, institutional form required. Applicants notified on a rolling basis starting 3/1; must reply within 3 week(s) of notification.

**Academics.** More than 20 online masters and credential programs offered for library media teaching. All other online programs are part of individual face to face programs with exception of one course offered completely online. **Special study options:** Accelerated study, cooperative education, distance learning, double major, ESL, exchange student, honors, independent study, internships, study abroad, teacher certification program, urban semester, Washington semester. **Credit/placement by examination:** AP, CLEP, IB, institutional tests. 15 credit hours maximum toward bachelor's degree. Essays required for Analysis and Interpretation of Literature and Freshman College Composition. **Support services:** Learning center, reduced course load, remedial instruction, study skills assistance, tutoring, writing center.

**Majors. Biology:** General, biochemistry. **Business:** General, accounting, business admin, finance, management information systems, marketing. **Communications:** General, broadcast journalism, journalism. **Computer sciences:** General, information systems, web page design. **Education:** General, art, business, elementary, middle, multi-level teacher, physical, secondary. **English:** English lit. **Foreign languages:** Spanish. **Health:** Nurse practitioner, nursing (RN), predental, premedicine. **History:** General. **Liberal arts:** Arts/sciences. **Math:** General. **Philosophy/religion:** Philosophy, religion. **Physical sciences:** General, chemistry, physics. **Psychology:** General. **Public administration:** Social work. **Social sciences:** General, international relations, political science, sociology. **Theology:** Bible, religious ed, sacred music, theology. **Visual/performing arts:** Art, dramatic, music performance, music theory/composition, studio arts.

**Most popular majors.** Business/marketing 23%, communications/journalism 9%, health sciences 7%, liberal arts 18%, philosophy/religious studies 10%, psychology 6%, theological studies 10%, visual/performing arts 6%.

**Computing on campus.** 268 workstations in library, computer center, student center. Dormitories wired for high-speed internet access and linked to campus network. Commuter students can connect to campus network. Online course registration, helpline, repair service, wireless network available.

**Student life. Freshman orientation:** Mandatory. Preregistration for classes offered. Class taken during first semester. **Policies:** Students will refrain from activities which may be spiritually or morally destructive. Religious observance required. **Housing:** Coed dorms, single-sex dorms, apartments available. $250 deposit. **Activities:** Bands, campus ministries, choral groups, drama, international student organizations, music ensembles, musical theater, opera, radio station, student government, student newspaper, symphony orchestra, TV station, minority student association.

**Athletics.** NAIA. **Intercollegiate:** Baseball M, basketball, cross-country, football (tackle) M, soccer, softball W, tennis M, track and field, volleyball W. **Intramural:** Basketball, football (tackle) M, skiing, volleyball. **Team name:** Cougars.

**Student services.** Campus ministries, career counseling, student employment services, financial aid counseling, health services, minority student services, personal counseling, placement for graduates, veterans' counselor. **Physically disabled:** Services for visually, speech, hearing impaired.

**Contact.** E-mail: admissions@apu.edu
Phone: (626) 812-3016 Toll-free number: (800) 825-5278
Fax: (626) 812-3096
Deana Porterfield, Dean of Undergraduate Admissions, Azusa Pacific University, 901 East Alosta Avenue, Azusa, CA 91702-7000

## Bethany University

**Scotts Valley, California**
www.bethany.edu

CB code: 4021

- Private 4-year Bible and liberal arts college affiliated with Assemblies of God
- Residential campus in small town
- 456 degree-seeking undergraduates: 17% part-time, 60% women
- 83 degree-seeking graduate students
- 51% of applicants admitted
- SAT or ACT (ACT writing optional) required
- 40% graduate within 6 years

**General.** Founded in 1919. Regionally accredited. **Degrees:** 90 bachelor's awarded; master's offered. **Location:** 5 miles from Santa Cruz. **Calendar:** Semester, limited summer session. **Full-time faculty:** 25 total; 68% have terminal degrees, 40% women. **Part-time faculty:** 39 total; 59% women. **Class size:** 70% < 20, 25% 20-39, 2% 40-49, 3% 50-99. **Special facilities:** Early childhood learning center.

**Freshman class profile.** 284 applied, 144 admitted, 60 enrolled.

| Mid 50% test scores | | | |
|---|---|---|---|
| SAT critical reading: | 420-550 | Return as sophomores: | 60% |
| SAT math: | 420-530 | Out-of-state: | 17% |
| ACT composite: | 18-22 | Live on campus: | 82% |

**Basis for selection.** Evaluation of academic records, and religious affiliation/commitment very important. Interviews recommended. Auditions recommended for music applicants. **Learning Disabled:** Students with learning disabilities are recommended to contact the Educational Support Services Offices during the admission's process.

**2007-2008 Annual costs.** Tuition/fees: $17,360. Room/board: $6,960. Books/supplies: $1,050. Personal expenses: $2,136.

**Financial aid. Non-need-based:** Scholarships awarded for academics, alumni affiliation, athletics, leadership, minority status, music/drama, religious affiliation.

**Application procedures. Admission:** Closing date 7/31 (postmark date). $35 fee. Application may be submitted online. Admission notification on a rolling basis. **Financial aid:** Priority date 3/2; no closing date. FAFSA, institutional form required. Applicants notified on a rolling basis starting 4/15; must reply within 2 week(s) of notification.

**Academics. Special study options:** Accelerated study, combined bachelor's/ graduate degree, distance learning, double major, external degree, independent study, internships, teacher certification program. **Credit/placement by examination:** AP, CLEP, IB, SAT, ACT. 18 credit hours maximum toward associate degree, 18 toward bachelor's. **Support services:** Learning center, reduced course load, remedial instruction, study skills assistance, tutoring.

**Majors. Business:** General, business admin. **Communications:** General, organizational, public relations. **Education:** Early childhood. **English:** English lit. **Health:** Substance abuse counseling. **Liberal arts:** Arts/sciences. **Psychology:** General. **Social sciences:** General. **Theology:** Bible, missionary, pastoral counseling, sacred music, theology, youth ministry. **Visual/ performing arts:** Dramatic.

**Most popular majors.** Business/marketing 16%, communications/ journalism 7%, education 15%, interdisciplinary studies 8%, psychology 21%, social sciences 13%, theological studies 14%.

**Computing on campus.** 20 workstations in library, computer center, student center. Dormitories wired for high-speed internet access and linked to campus network. Commuter students can connect to campus network. Online course registration, online library, wireless network available.

**Student life. Freshman orientation:** Available, $125 fee. Preregistration for classes offered. 5-day program before beginning of classes. **Policies:** Student ministry opportunities. Religious observance required. **Housing:** Guaranteed on-campus for freshmen. Single-sex dorms, apartments, substance-free housing available. $100 nonrefundable deposit. **Activities:** Concert band, campus ministries, choral groups, drama, international student organizations, music ensembles, musical theater, student government, student newspaper, symphony orchestra.

**Athletics.** NAIA. **Intercollegiate:** Baseball M, basketball M, cheerleading, golf M, soccer, softball W, volleyball W. **Intramural:** Basketball, football (non-tackle). **Team name:** Bruins.

**Student services.** Adult student services, alcohol/substance abuse counseling, campus ministries, career counseling, student employment services, financial aid counseling, health services, on-campus daycare, personal counseling, placement for graduates, veterans' counselor.

**Contact.** E-mail: admissions@fc.bethany.edu
Phone: (831) 438-3800 ext. 3900 Toll-free number: (800) 843-9410
Fax: (831) 461-1621
Rick Podratz, Director of Admission, Bethany University, 800 Bethany Drive, Scotts Valley, CA 95066-2898

---

## Bethesda Christian University
Anaheim, California
www.bcu.edu
CB code: 3895

- Private 4-year university and Bible college affiliated with Christian Church
- Commuter campus in large city
- 254 degree-seeking undergraduates
- Application essay, interview required

**General.** Accredited by ABHE. Extension campus in Seoul, South Korea. **Degrees:** 50 bachelor's awarded; master's, first professional offered. **Location:** 30 miles from Los Angeles. **Calendar:** Semester, limited summer session. **Full-time faculty:** 5 total. **Part-time faculty:** 44 total. **Class size:** 33% < 20, 64% 20-39, 3% 40-49.

**Freshman class profile.** 110 applied, 110 admitted, 80 enrolled.

**Basis for selection.** Open admission. Admissions decision based on religious affiliation, recommendations, essay and interview. Secondary school record also important. If student's TOEFL score 550 or higher or student has graduated from English-speaking high school, ESL placement test not required. Auditions required for music majors. Christian experience essay required.

**2007-2008 Annual costs.** Tuition/fees: $6,420. Books/supplies: $1,000. Personal expenses: $500.

**Financial aid.** All financial aid based on need.

**Application procedures. Admission:** No deadline. $35 fee ($60 out-of-state). Admission notification on a rolling basis. **Financial aid:** Closing date 3/14. FAFSA, institutional form required. Applicants notified on a rolling basis starting 6/30.

**Academics. Special study options:** Combined bachelor's/graduate degree, double major, dual enrollment of high school students, ESL, independent study, liberal arts/career combination. **Credit/placement by examination:** CLEP, IB, institutional tests. **Support services:** Reduced course load.

**Majors. Computer sciences:** Information technology. **Education:** Early childhood. **Foreign languages:** Translation. **Philosophy/religion:** Religion. **Theology:** Bible, missionary, religious ed, sacred music, theology. **Visual/ performing arts:** Conducting, design, fashion design, metal/jewelry, music management, music performance, music theory/composition, piano/organ, stringed instruments, voice/opera.

**Computing on campus.** 50 workstations in dormitories, library, computer center. Dormitories wired for high-speed internet access.

**Student life. Freshman orientation:** Mandatory. Preregistration for classes offered. **Policies:** Religious observance required. **Activities:** Student government.

**Student services.** Campus ministries, financial aid counseling, personal counseling.

**Contact.** E-mail: admission@bcu.edu
Phone: (714) 517-1945 Fax: (714) 517-1948
Jacqueline Ha, Director of Admissions, Bethesda Christian University, 730 North Euclid Street, Anaheim, CA 92801

---

## Biola University
La Mirada, California
www.biola.edu
CB code: 4017

- Private 4-year university and Bible college affiliated with interdenominational tradition
- Residential campus in large town
- 3,550 degree-seeking undergraduates: 3% part-time, 62% women
- 82% of applicants admitted
- SAT or ACT (ACT writing recommended), application essay required

**General.** Founded in 1908. Regionally accredited. Biblically centered Christian institution. **Degrees:** 859 bachelor's awarded; master's, doctoral, first professional offered. **ROTC:** Army, Air Force. **Location:** 22 miles from downtown Los Angeles. **Calendar:** 4-1-4, extensive summer session. **Full-time faculty:** 225 total. **Part-time faculty:** 217 total. **Class size:** 47% < 20, 44% 20-39, 4% 40-49, 3% 50-99, 2% >100. **Special facilities:** Concert hall with pipe organ, electron microscope, recording studio, film studio, MIDI lab for music composition, electronic piano lab, archaeological dig site, recording studio.

**Freshman class profile.** 2,315 applied, 1,891 admitted, 810 enrolled.

| Mid 50% test scores | | | |
|---|---|---|---|
| SAT critical reading: | 500-620 | GPA 3.0-3.49: | 31% |
| SAT math: | 490-620 | GPA 2.0-2.99: | 11% |
| SAT writing: | 500-610 | Rank in top quarter: | 75% |
| ACT composite: | 21-26 | Rank in top tenth: | 43% |
| GPA 3.50 or higher: | 58% | Out-of-state: | 28% |
| | | Live on campus: | 90% |

**Basis for selection.** Christian commitment most important; academic record, personal references, test scores next in importance. School, community, church activities helpful. Out-of-state and ethnic students encouraged to apply. Auditions recommended for music applicants. Portfolios recommended for art applicants. Any body of work recommended for film/tv/ radio applicants. **Homeschooled:** Transcript of courses and grades, letter of recommendation (nonparent) required. Applicants advised to go through accreditation agency. **Learning Disabled:** Student must request the services of the ODS and provide documentation supporting the nature and limitations of a disability.

**High school preparation.** 21 units recommended. Recommended units include English 4, mathematics 3, social studies 3, history 4, science 3 and foreign language 4. 1 algebra and 1 chemistry required of nursing applicants. 2 math, 1 physics, 1 chemistry required of biology applicants. Some deficiencies may be satisfied during freshman year.

**2008-2009 Annual costs.** Tuition/fees: $26,424. Room/board: $7,410. Books/supplies: $1,314. Personal expenses: $2,088.

**2006-2007 Financial aid. Need-based:** Average need met was 68%. Average scholarship/grant was $11,339; average loan $1,796. 57% of total undergraduate aid awarded as scholarships/grants, 43% as loans/jobs. **Non-need-based:** Scholarships awarded for academics, alumni affiliation, art, athletics, leadership, minority status, music/drama, state residency.

**Application procedures. Admission:** Closing date 3/1 (receipt date). $45 fee, may be waived for applicants with need. Application may be submitted online. Admission notification on a rolling basis beginning on or about 4/1. Must reply by 5/1. **Financial aid:** Priority date 1/1; no closing date. FAFSA required. Applicants notified on a rolling basis starting 3/1.

**Academics. Special study options:** Double major, dual enrollment of high school students, ESL, exchange student, honors, internships, New York semester, student-designed major, study abroad, teacher certification program, Washington semester. 3-2 program with Los Angeles College of Chiropractic, 3-2 engineering program with University of Southern California. **Credit/placement by examination:** AP, CLEP, IB, SAT, ACT. Maximum of 32 credits from CLEP, AP, and IB can be counted toward degree. **Support services:** Reduced course load, remedial instruction, study skills assistance, tutoring, writing center.

**Honors college/program.** Admission to Torrey Honors Institute by invitation, after application to the university. Students trained in rigorous discussion group format, learning high-level writing and critical thinking skills.

**Majors. Biology:** General, biochemistry. **Business:** Accounting, business admin, international, management information systems, marketing. **Communications:** General, broadcast journalism, journalism, public relations, radio/tv. **Computer sciences:** Computer science. **Education:** General, elementary, music, physical, secondary. **Engineering:** General. **English:** Creative writing, English lit. **Foreign languages:** Spanish. **Health:** Communication disorders, nursing (RN). **History:** General. **Interdisciplinary:** Intercultural. **Legal studies:** Prelaw. **Liberal arts:** Arts/sciences. **Math:** General. **Philosophy/religion:** Philosophy, religion. **Physical sciences:** Chemistry, physics. **Psychology:** General. **Social sciences:** General, anthropology, sociology. **Theology:** Bible, religious ed, theology. **Visual/performing arts:** Cinematography, commercial/advertising art, dramatic, drawing, music performance, music theory/composition, painting, sculpture, studio arts.

**Most popular majors.** Business/marketing 26%, communications/journalism 11%, education 9%, health sciences 6%, psychology 8%, social sciences 7%, theological studies 14%, visual/performing arts 8%.

**Computing on campus.** 225 workstations in library, computer center. Dormitories wired for high-speed internet access and linked to campus network. Commuter students can connect to campus network. Online course registration, online library, helpline, repair service, student web hosting, wireless network available.

**Student life. Freshman orientation:** Available, $75 fee. Week-long, held week before term begins. Students assigned to core group led by Biola student. **Policies:** All students encouraged to have Christian service assignment. Students adhere to code of conduct. Freshmen and sophomores under 21 required to live on campus unless living with relatives. Religious observance required. **Housing:** Coed dorms, single-sex dorms, special housing for disabled, apartments available. $200 partly refundable deposit, deadline 5/1. Flex-style dorms with building split into floors/wings designated all male or all female available. **Activities:** Bands, choral groups, dance, drama, film society, international student organizations, music ensembles, musical theater, opera, radio station, student government, student newspaper, symphony orchestra, TV station, Student Missionary Union, Korean student association, evangelism team, International Justice Mission, theology club, Society of Christian Philosophy, Tijuana Ministry, Bas Bleu (women's issues), Naturally Diverse.

**Athletics.** NAIA. **Intercollegiate:** Baseball M, basketball, cross-country, soccer, softball W, swimming, tennis, track and field, volleyball W. **Intramural:** Basketball, football (non-tackle), soccer, softball, volleyball. **Team name:** Eagles.

**Student services.** Adult student services, campus ministries, career counseling, student employment services, financial aid counseling, health services, minority student services, personal counseling, placement for graduates, veterans' counselor. **Physically disabled:** Services for speech, hearing impaired.

**Contact.** E-mail: admissions@biola.edu
Phone: (562) 903-4752 Toll-free number: (800) 652-4652
Fax: (562) 903-4709
Greg Vaughan, Director of Enrollment Management, Biola University, 13800 Biola Avenue, La Mirada, CA 90639-0001

---

**Brooks Institute**
**Santa Barbara, California**
**www.brooks.edu**                         CB code: 4228

- For-profit 4-year visual arts college
- Commuter campus in small city
- 1,800 degree-seeking undergraduates
- Application essay, interview required

---

**General.** Founded in 1945. Accredited by ACICS. **Degrees:** 499 bachelor's, 30 associate awarded; master's offered. **Location:** 90 miles from Los Angeles. **Calendar:** Trimester. 6 8-week sessions. Extensive summer session. **Full-time faculty:** 59 total. **Part-time faculty:** 6 total. **Special facilities:** 123,000 square feet of studio space for 40 set-ups, 90 cubicles for black and white enlarging, digital labs in both Santa Barbara and Ventura, design lab for visual communication program.

**Basis for selection.** School achievement record most important. Photographic experience not required for entrance. Advanced standing may be offered to those with 4X5 view camera experience. Evaluation consists of written examination portfolio and review. TOEFL required of students whose first language is not English. Different standards exist based on paper vs. computer scores and for undergraduate and graduate applicants. At time of matriculation, institution will assess English and math proficiencies for students who have not demonstrated proficiency in both at the college level or by receiving minimum standard scores in national tests. Interviews can be conducted via telephone. Interview and photography portfolio required for advanced standing in core courses. **Homeschooled:** GED required if home schooling not recognized by state. **Learning Disabled:** Protocol for students seeking accommodation is mailed to accepted applicants with provisional acceptance letter.

**High school preparation.** Recommended units include English 4, mathematics 2, social studies 1, science 1 and foreign language 2. College preparatory program recommended.

**2007-2008 Annual costs.** Tuition/fees: $17,840.

**Application procedures. Admission:** No deadline. $100 fee. Application may be submitted online. Admission notification on a rolling basis. New undergraduate classes begin in January, March, April, May, July, September, November. New graduate classes begin in January, April, September. Students encouraged to apply at least 6 months in advance. **Financial aid:** Priority date 3/2; no closing date. FAFSA, institutional form required. Applicants notified on a rolling basis starting 5/1.

**Academics. Special study options:** Accelerated study, distance learning, double major, independent study, internships. Upper-division students can apply to participate in documentary courses in foreign countries; upper-division professional photography students can apply for inclusion in annual undersea photography class. **Credit/placement by examination:** CLEP, institutional tests. 54 credit hours maximum toward bachelor's degree. **Support services:** Tutoring.

**Majors. Communications:** Photojournalism. **Visual/performing arts:** Cinematography, graphic design, photography.

**Computing on campus.** 20 workstations in library, computer center. Online library, helpline, wireless network available.

**Student life. Freshman orientation:** Mandatory. Immediately prior to matriculation; normally 2-4 days of activities. **Policies:** Car necessary for travel between campuses and to assignment locations. **Activities:** Student government.

**Student services.** Career counseling, student employment services, financial aid counseling, personal counseling, placement for graduates.

**Contact.** E-mail: admissions@brooks.edu
Phone: (888) 304-3456 Toll-free number: (888) 304-3456
Fax: (805) 565-1386
Michael Jacobsen, Director of Admissions, Brooks Institute, 801 Alston Road, Santa Barbara, CA 93108

---

**Brooks Institute: Ventura**
**Santa Barbara, California**
**www.brooks.edu**

- For-profit 3-year visual arts and career college
- Small city

**General.** Accredited by ACICS. **Location:** Campuses in Ventura and Santa Barbara CA. Santa Barbara is approximately 90 miles north of Los Angeles. Ventura is 30 miles closer to Los Angeles. Both cities are located on Highway 101. **Calendar:** Semester. Alternative schedule of 8 week sessions, 6 per year.

**Annual costs/financial aid.** Tuition/fees (2007-2008): $17,840.

**Contact.** Phone: (805) 966-3888
Vice President of Marketing and Admissions, 801 Alston Road, Santa Barbara, CA

## California Baptist University
### Riverside, California
**CB member**
www.calbaptist.edu
**CB code: 4094**

- Private 4-year university and liberal arts college affiliated with Southern Baptist Convention
- Residential campus in large city
- 2,952 degree-seeking undergraduates: 14% part-time, 64% women
- 801 degree-seeking graduate students
- 72% of applicants admitted
- SAT or ACT (ACT writing optional), application essay required
- 64% graduate within 6 years

**General.** Founded in 1950. Regionally accredited. **Degrees:** 560 bachelor's awarded; master's offered. **ROTC:** Army, Air Force. **Location:** 60 miles from Los Angeles. **Calendar:** Semester. 4-4-1 semester system. Extensive summer session. **Full-time faculty:** 120 total; 65% have terminal degrees, 15% minority, 42% women. **Part-time faculty:** 201 total; 25% have terminal degrees, 27% minority, 42% women. **Class size:** 50% < 20, 38% 20-39, 7% 40-49, 4% 50-99, 1% >100. **Special facilities:** Hymnology collection, performance and recording studios, Nie Wieder! holocaust collection.

**Freshman class profile.** 1,354 applied, 981 admitted, 497 enrolled.

| Mid 50% test scores | | | |
|---|---|---|---|
| SAT critical reading: | 450-550 | Rank in top quarter: | 52% |
| SAT math: | 440-550 | Rank in top tenth: | 21% |
| SAT writing: | 440-550 | End year in good standing: | 85% |
| ACT composite: | 18-23 | Return as sophomores: | 85% |
| GPA 3.50 or higher: | 42% | Out-of-state: | 10% |
| GPA 3.0-3.49: | 34% | Live on campus: | 91% |
| GPA 2.0-2.99: | 24% | International: | 2% |

**Basis for selection.** School achievement record, test scores, essays, recommendations very important. Interviews recommended. Auditions required for music, drama applicants. **Homeschooled:** Transcript of courses and grades, letter of recommendation (nonparent) required.

**High school preparation.** College-preparatory program recommended. 15 units required; 19 recommended. Required and recommended units include English 4, mathematics 3-4, social studies 2, history 2, science 2-3 (laboratory 1-2), foreign language 2-3 and academic electives 3.

**2007-2008 Annual costs.** Tuition/fees: $20,640. Room/board: $7,510. Books/supplies: $1,120. Personal expenses: $1,616.

**Financial aid. Non-need-based:** Scholarships awarded for academics, art, athletics, leadership, music/drama, religious affiliation, ROTC.

**Application procedures. Admission:** Priority date 2/1; no deadline. $45 fee, may be waived for applicants with need. Application may be submitted online. Admission notification on a rolling basis beginning on or about 11/19. **Financial aid:** Priority date 3/2; no closing date. FAFSA required. Applicants notified on a rolling basis starting 3/2; must reply by 5/1 or within 3 week(s) of notification.

**Academics. Special study options:** Accelerated study, distance learning, double major, dual enrollment of high school students, ESL, exchange student, honors, internships, liberal arts/career combination, study abroad, teacher certification program, Washington semester, weekend college. **Credit/placement by examination:** AP, CLEP, IB, SAT, ACT, institutional tests. 30 credit hours maximum toward bachelor's degree. Portfolio course available to assist students in documenting work that may be counted for credit by prior learning experiences. **Support services:** Learning center, reduced course load, remedial instruction, study skills assistance, tutoring, writing center.

**Majors. Biology:** General. **Business:** Accounting, business admin, marketing. **Communications:** General, digital media, journalism. **Education:** General, early childhood, physical. **Engineering:** General, civil, electrical, mechanical. **English:** English lit. **Foreign languages:** Spanish. **Health:** Health services, nursing (RN). **History:** General. **Interdisciplinary:** Behavioral sciences, intercultural. **Liberal arts:** Arts/sciences. **Math:** General. **Parks/recreation:** Exercise sciences. **Philosophy/religion:** Christian, philosophy. **Protective services:** Law enforcement admin, police science. **Psychology:** General. **Social sciences:** Political science, sociology. **Theology:** Bible, missionary. **Visual/performing arts:** Art, graphic design, theater arts management. **Other:** Foundational Mathematics, Interdisciplinary Studies, Organizational Leadership.

**Most popular majors.** Business/marketing 13%, English 6%, interdisciplinary studies 6%, liberal arts 29%, parks/recreation 8%, psychology 9%, security/protective services 7%.

**Computing on campus.** 279 workstations in library, computer center. Dormitories wired for high-speed internet access and linked to campus network. Commuter students can connect to campus network. Online course registration, online library, helpline available.

**Student life. Freshman orientation:** Mandatory, $250 fee. Preregistration for classes offered. Held prior to beginning of semester. **Policies:** Students receiving institutional scholarships required to live in student housing. Religious observance required. **Housing:** Guaranteed on-campus for freshmen. Single-sex dorms, apartments, cooperative housing available. $275 fully refundable deposit, deadline 8/1. **Activities:** Bands, campus ministries, choral groups, drama, international student organizations, music ensembles, musical theater, student government, student newspaper, symphony orchestra, Young Republicans, Young Democrats, Fellowship of Christian Athletes, Black Student Union, Big Brother, Big Sister, active compassion, elderly ministry, homeless ministry.

**Athletics.** NAIA. **Intercollegiate:** Baseball M, basketball, cheerleading, diving, golf, soccer, softball W, swimming, tennis, volleyball, water polo. **Intramural:** Basketball, bowling, football (non-tackle), golf, softball, table tennis, tennis, volleyball. **Team name:** Lancers.

**Student services.** Adult student services, campus ministries, career counseling, student employment services, financial aid counseling, personal counseling, placement for graduates, veterans' counselor.

**Contact.** E-mail: admissions@calbaptist.edu
Phone: (951) 343-4212 Toll-free number: (877) 228-8866
Fax: (951) 343-4525
Allen Johnson, Director, Undergraduate Admissions, California Baptist University, 8432 Magnolia Avenue, Riverside, CA 92504-3297

## California Coast University
### Santa Ana, California
www.calcoast.edu

- For-profit 4-year virtual university
- Large city
- 2,576 degree-seeking undergraduates

**General.** Accredited by DETC. **Degrees:** 159 bachelor's, 6 associate awarded; master's offered. **Calendar:** Continuous. **Part-time faculty:** 26 total.

**Basis for selection.** Open admission.

**2007-2008 Annual costs.** Distance-learning undergraduate program total costs: $6,600 (associate degree) and $13,860 (bachelor's degree); international students pay $7,800 (associate degree) and $16,380 (bachelor's degree) in total costs per program.

**Application procedures. Admission:** No deadline. $75 fee.

**Academics. Special study options:** Accelerated study, cross-registration, distance learning, external degree, honors, independent study. **Credit/placement by examination:** CLEP.

**Majors. Business:** General, business admin. **Health:** Health care admin. **Psychology:** General.

**Student life. Activities:** Student newspaper.

**Contact.** E-mail: admissions@calcoast.edu
Phone: (714) 547-9625
Admissions Director, California Coast University, 700 North Main Street, Santa Ana, CA 92701

## California College of the Arts
### San Francisco, California
**CB member**
www.cca.edu
**CB code: 4031**

- Private 4-year visual arts college
- Residential campus in very large city
- 1,285 degree-seeking undergraduates: 7% part-time, 61% women, 3% African American, 14% Asian American, 10% Hispanic American, 1% Native American, 7% international
- 296 degree-seeking graduate students
- 78% of applicants admitted
- Application essay required
- 120% graduate within 6 years

**General.** Founded in 1907. Regionally accredited. 2 campuses located in San Francisco and Oakland. **Degrees:** 228 bachelor's awarded; master's offered. **Location:** 3 miles from downtown. **Calendar:** Semester, limited summer session. **Full-time faculty:** 65 total; 80% have terminal degrees, 22% minority, 43% women. **Part-time faculty:** 330 total; 62% have terminal degrees, 17% minority, 45% women. **Class size:** 92% < 20, 8% 20-39, less than 1% 50-99. **Special facilities:** Center for Art and Public Life, Materials Resource Center.

**Freshman class profile.** 996 applied, 778 admitted, 187 enrolled.

| Mid 50% test scores | | | |
|---|---|---|---|
| SAT critical reading: | 470-610 | GPA 3.0-3.49: | 46% |
| SAT math: | 450-590 | GPA 2.0-2.99: | 30% |
| SAT writing: | 480-590 | Return as sophomores: | 71% |
| ACT composite: | 18-24 | Out-of-state: | 37% |
| GPA 3.50 or higher: | 24% | Live on campus: | 81% |
| | | International: | 6% |

**Basis for selection.** High school achievement (including art/design activities and interests), GPA, personal essay/statement of purpose, interview, and portfolio very important. SAT or ACT recommended. Test scores are primarily used for placement, but may be considered for admission. SAT or ACT scores with the writing section are highly recommended and are used in English course placement. Portfolio required. Interview not required, but prospective students are invited to meet with an enrollment counselor. **Homeschooled:** Transcript of courses and grades required.

**2008-2009 Annual costs.** Tuition/fees: $31,382. Room only: $6,600. Books/supplies: $1,500. Personal expenses: $2,200.

**Financial aid. Non-need-based:** Scholarships awarded for academics, art. **Additional information:** Application deadline for merit scholarships February 1.

**Application procedures. Admission:** Priority date 2/1; no deadline. $50 fee, may be waived for applicants with need. Application may be submitted online. Admission notification on a rolling basis beginning on or about 1/15. Must reply by May 1 or within 2 week(s) if notified thereafter. Maximum period of postponement is one semester. **Financial aid:** Priority date 3/1; no closing date. FAFSA required. Applicants notified by 4/1; Applicants notified on a rolling basis starting 3/15; must reply by 5/1 or within 3 week(s) of notification.

**Academics. Special study options:** Cross-registration, ESL, exchange student, independent study, internships, student-designed major, study abroad. Community service program, learning disabilities services. **Credit/placement by examination:** AP, CLEP, IB, SAT, ACT, institutional tests. **Support services:** Pre-admission summer program, reduced course load, remedial instruction, study skills assistance, tutoring.

**Majors. Architecture:** Architecture, interior. **English:** Creative writing. **Visual/performing arts:** Art, ceramics, cinematography, commercial/advertising art, crafts, drawing, fashion design, fiber arts, graphic design, illustration, industrial design, interior design, metal/jewelry, painting, photography, printmaking, sculpture, studio arts.

**Most popular majors.** Visual/performing arts 95%.

**Computing on campus.** 251 workstations in dormitories, library, computer center, student center. Dormitories wired for high-speed internet access and linked to campus network. Commuter students can connect to campus network. Online library, helpline, student web hosting, wireless network available.

**Student life. Freshman orientation:** Mandatory. Preregistration for classes offered. Educational and social programs offered week before classes start. **Housing:** Coed dorms, apartments, substance-free housing available. $750 partly refundable deposit, deadline 5/15. First-year community, transfer community, multi-cultural/community service theme halls. **Activities:** International student organizations, literary magazine, student government, student newspaper, Quack (LGBT), Students for Sustainability, Asian student association, salon collective, graduate student alliance, Alliance for Multiculturalism in Architecture, glass league.

**Student services.** Career counseling, student employment services, financial aid counseling, personal counseling, placement for graduates.

**Contact.** E-mail: enroll@cca.edu
Phone: (415) 703-9523 Toll-free number: (800) 447-1278
Fax: (415) 703-9539
Robynne Royster, Director of Undergraduate Admission, California College of the Arts, 1111 Eighth Street, San Francisco, CA 94107-2247

## California College San Diego
San Diego, California
www.cc-sd.edu                    CB code: 3354

- For-profit 4-year business, health science and nursing college
- Very large city
- 550 degree-seeking undergraduates

**General.** Accredited by ACCSCT. **Degrees:** 1 bachelor's, 143 associate awarded. **Calendar:** Continuous. **Full-time faculty:** 12 total. **Part-time faculty:** 22 total.

**Basis for selection.** Open admission.

**2007-2008 Annual costs.** Typical 18-month respiratory care therapist program: $38,600. Costs vary by program.

**Application procedures. Admission:** No deadline.

**Academics. Credit/placement by examination:** CLEP.

**Majors. Business:** Accounting, business admin. **Computer sciences:** Computer science. **Health:** Health care admin, nursing admin, respiratory therapy technology.

**Contact.** Phone: (619) 295-5785 Fax: (619) 295-5762
Randy Wolford, Director of Admissions, California College San Diego, 2820 Camino del Rio South 300, San Diego, CA 92108

## California Design College
Los Angeles, California
www.artinstitutes.edu/cdc              CB code: 3463

- For-profit 4-year visual arts and technical college
- Very large city
- 882 degree-seeking undergraduates: 41% part-time, 77% women
- Application essay, interview required

**General.** Accredited by ACICS. **Degrees:** 19 bachelor's, 27 associate awarded. **Calendar:** Quarter, extensive summer session. **Full-time faculty:** 17 total; 24% have terminal degrees, 53% minority, 65% women. **Part-time faculty:** 64 total; 34% have terminal degrees, 6% minority, 58% women.

**Basis for selection.** Interview, academic transcripts, essay important.

**2008-2009 Annual costs.** Tuition/fees (projected): $20,980. Cost for 7-quarter continuous enrollment associate degree program $52,118; cost for 12-quarter continuous enrollment bachelor's degree program $88,938. Fees vary by program. Room only: $8,685. Books/supplies: $1,692. Personal expenses: $2,520.

**2006-2007 Financial aid. Need-based:** 155 full-time freshmen applied for aid; 155 were judged to have need; 155 of these received aid. Average scholarship/grant was $3,088. 46% of total undergraduate aid awarded as scholarships/grants, 54% as loans/jobs.

**Application procedures. Admission:** No deadline. $50 fee. Application may be submitted online. Admission notification on a rolling basis.

**Academics. Special study options:** Distance learning, honors, independent study, internships, study abroad, weekend college. **Credit/placement by examination:** AP, CLEP, SAT, ACT, institutional tests. **Support services:** Study skills assistance, tutoring.

**Majors. Visual/performing arts:** Fashion design.

**Computing on campus.** 162 workstations in library, computer center. Online library, helpline available.

**Student life. Freshman orientation:** Mandatory. Preregistration for classes offered. **Housing:** $250 fully refundable deposit, deadline 10/2.

**Contact.** E-mail: mromero@aii.edu
Phone: (213) 251-3636 Toll-free number: (877) 468-6232
Fax: (213) 385-3545
Melissa Romero, Director of Admissions, California Design College, 3440 Wilshire Boulevard, 10th Floor, Los Angeles, CA 90010

## California Institute of Integral Studies
San Francisco, California
www.ciis.edu                          CB code: 3609

♦ Private two-year upper-division liberal arts college
♦ Commuter campus in very large city
♦ 73% of applicants admitted
♦ Application essay required

**General.** Regionally accredited. **Degrees:** 40 bachelor's awarded; master's, doctoral offered. **Calendar:** Semester, limited summer session. **Full-time faculty:** 63 total; 100% have terminal degrees, 24% minority, 44% women. **Part-time faculty:** 90 total.

**Student profile.** 56 degree-seeking undergraduates, 1,070 degree-seeking graduate students. 55 applied as first time-transfer students, 40 admitted, 33 enrolled.

| | | | |
|---|---|---|---|
| Women: | 66% | Asian American: | 4% |
| African American: | 9% | Hispanic American: | 7% |

**Basis for selection.** College transcript, application essay required. Transfer accepted as juniors.

**2007-2008 Annual costs.** Tuition/fees: $13,190. Cost quoted for 2 semesters; 3-semester attendance mandatory.

**Application procedures. Admission:** Priority date 7/1. $65 fee, may be waived for applicants with need. Application may be submitted online. Application priority dates differ by program.

**Academics. Special study options:** Distance learning, independent study, internships, weekend college. **Credit/placement by examination:** AP, CLEP. 30 credit hours maximum toward bachelor's degree. **Support services:** Tutoring.

**Majors. Liberal arts:** Arts/sciences, humanities.

**Computing on campus.** 20 workstations in computer center. Commuter students can connect to campus network. Online library, helpline available.

**Student life. Activities:** Student government.

**Student services.** Minority student services, personal counseling, placement for graduates.

**Contact.** E-mail: admissions@ciis.edu
Phone: (415) 575-6150
Pamela Sparkman, Director of Admissions, California Institute of Integral Studies, 1453 Mission Street, San Francisco, CA 94103

## California Institute of Technology
Pasadena, California                    CB member
www.caltech.edu                         CB code: 4034

♦ Private 4-year university
♦ Residential campus in small city
♦ 913 degree-seeking undergraduates: 31% women, 1% African American, 38% Asian American, 5% Hispanic American, 9% international
♦ 1,220 degree-seeking graduate students
♦ 17% of applicants admitted
♦ SAT or ACT (ACT writing optional), SAT Subject Tests, application essay required
♦ 89% graduate within 6 years

**General.** Founded in 1891. Regionally accredited. **Degrees:** 172 bachelor's awarded; master's, doctoral offered. **ROTC:** Army, Air Force. **Location:** 10 miles from downtown Los Angeles. **Calendar:** Quarter. **Full-time faculty:** 291 total; 98% have terminal degrees, 14% minority, 16% women. **Part-time faculty:** 20 total; 65% have terminal degrees, 40% minority, 40% women. **Class size:** 69% < 20, 21% 20-39, 2% 40-49, 4% 50-99, 3% >100. **Special facilities:** Jet propulsion laboratories, observatory, wind and water tunnels, radio observatory, seismological laboratory, marine biological laboratory.

**Freshman class profile.** 3,597 applied, 607 admitted, 231 enrolled.

| Mid 50% test scores | | | |
|---|---|---|---|
| SAT critical reading: | 700-780 | Rank in top tenth: | 99% |
| SAT math: | 770-800 | Return as sophomores: | 98% |
| SAT writing: | 680-770 | Out-of-state: | 64% |
| ACT composite: | 32-35 | Live on campus: | 100% |
| Rank in top quarter: | 100% | International: | 11% |

**Basis for selection.** High school preparation and record (particularly in mathematics and science), test scores, extracurricular activities (science and nonscience-related), counselors' and teachers' recommendations, and demonstrated interest in mathematics and science are major considerations. SAT Subject Test requirements: math level IIC, writing, biology (environmental or molecular), chemistry, or physics.

**High school preparation.** Required and recommended units include English 3-4, mathematics 4, social studies 1, history 1, science 2-4 (laboratory 1).

**2008-2009 Annual costs.** Tuition/fees (projected): $34,515. Room/board: $10,146. Books/supplies: $1,165.

**2006-2007 Financial aid. Need-based:** 173 full-time freshmen applied for aid; 129 were judged to have need; 129 of these received aid. Average need met was 100%. Average scholarship/grant was $22,026; average loan $3,106. 90% of total undergraduate aid awarded as scholarships/grants, 10% as loans/jobs. **Non-need-based:** Awarded to 107 full-time undergraduates, including 15 freshmen. Scholarships awarded for academics.

**Application procedures. Admission:** Closing date 1/1 (postmark date). $60 fee, may be waived for applicants with need. Application may be submitted online. Admission notification 4/1. Must reply by 5/1. **Financial aid:** Closing date 1/15. FAFSA, CSS PROFILE required. Applicants notified by 4/1; must reply by 5/1.

**Academics.** Remedial services not formally offered. Remediation available for students deficient in basic scientific knowledge or technical skills. **Special study options:** Combined bachelor's/graduate degree, cooperative education, cross-registration, double major, ESL, exchange student, independent study, liberal arts/career combination, student-designed major, study abroad. **Credit/placement by examination:** CLEP, institutional tests. **Support services:** Reduced course load, tutoring.

**Majors. Biology:** General. **Business:** Managerial economics. **Computer sciences:** Computer science. **Engineering:** General, chemical, computer, electrical, environmental, materials science, mechanical, physics. **English:** English lit. **History:** General, science/technology. **Interdisciplinary:** Science/society. **Math:** General, applied. **Philosophy/religion:** Philosophy. **Physical sciences:** Astronomy, astrophysics, chemistry, geochemistry, geology, geophysics, physics, planetary. **Social sciences:** General, economics, political science. **Other:** Computational neural systems, Geobiology.

**Most popular majors.** Biology 13%, computer/information sciences 9%, engineering/engineering technologies 31%, mathematics 14%, physical sciences 27%.

**Computing on campus.** 112 workstations in dormitories, library, computer center. Dormitories wired for high-speed internet access and linked to campus network. Commuter students can connect to campus network. Online course registration, online library, helpline, repair service, student web hosting, wireless network available.

**Student life. Freshman orientation:** Mandatory. 3 day camp. **Housing:** Guaranteed on-campus for all undergraduates. Coed dorms, apartments available. Pets allowed in dorm rooms. Single-unit houses available. **Activities:** Bands, choral groups, dance, drama, film society, literary magazine, music ensembles, musical theater, opera, student government, student newspaper, symphony orchestra, Caltech Y, Christian fellowship, Newman Club, Hillel, Amnesty International.

**Athletics.** NCAA. **Intercollegiate:** Baseball M, basketball, cross-country, diving, fencing, soccer M, swimming, tennis, track and field, volleyball W, water polo. **Intramural:** Badminton, baseball M, basketball, cheerleading, cricket M, cross-country, football (tackle) M, soccer, softball, squash, swimming, table tennis, tennis, track and field, volleyball, water polo M. **Team name:** Beavers.

**Student services.** Alcohol/substance abuse counseling, campus ministries, career counseling, student employment services, financial aid counseling, health services, minority student services, on-campus daycare, personal counseling, placement for graduates, women's services. **Physically disabled:** Services for visually, speech, hearing impaired.

Contact. E-mail: ugadmissions@caltech.edu
Phone: (626) 395-6341 Fax: (626) 683-3026
Richard Bischoff, Director of Admissions, California Institute of
Technology, 1200 East California Boulevard, MC 1-94, Pasadena, CA
91125

## California Institute of the Arts

**Valencia, California**     **CB member**
**www.calarts.edu**     **CB code: 4049**

▶ Private 4-year visual arts and performing arts college
▶ Residential campus in small city
▶ 820 degree-seeking undergraduates: 9% African American, 9% Asian American, 12% Hispanic American, 1% Native American, 9% international
▶ 497 graduate students
▶ 32% of applicants admitted
▶ Application essay required
▶ 69% graduate within 6 years

**General.** Founded in 1961. Regionally accredited. Single complex of 6 professional schools: art, critical studies, dance, film/video, music and theater. **Degrees:** 187 bachelor's awarded; master's offered. **Location:** 30 miles from Los Angeles. **Calendar:** Semester. **Full-time faculty:** 156 total; 44% women. **Part-time faculty:** 144 total; 37% women. **Class size:** 79% < 20, 18% 20-39, 1% 40-49, 2% 50-99. **Special facilities:** Art studios, galleries, animation studios, concert halls, 6 theaters.

**Freshman class profile.** 2,914 applied, 940 admitted, 448 enrolled.

| | | | |
|---|---|---|---|
| End year in good standing: | 92% | Live on campus: | 85% |
| Out-of-state: | 48% | International: | 5% |

**Basis for selection.** Admission is talent based, evaluated by faculty via group review. Portfolio required for art/design, film/video, music composition majors, and theater design and production. Auditions required for acting, dance, music majors. Music applicants may submit audio tape recordings in lieu of live audition for some programs. Interview required for directing/performance/production studies majors. **Homeschooled:** Transcript of courses and grades, state high school equivalency certificate, letter of recommendation (nonparent) required.

**2008-2009 Annual costs.** Tuition/fees (projected): $33,435. Books and supplies vary depending on the program. Room/board: $8,530. Books/supplies: $1,500. Personal expenses: $1,991.

**Financial aid. Non-need-based:** Scholarships awarded for academics, art, minority status, music/drama.

**Application procedures. Admission:** Priority date 11/30; deadline 1/4 (receipt date). $70 fee, may be waived for applicants with need. Application must be submitted online. Admission notification on a rolling basis beginning on or about 3/1. Must reply by May 1 or within 2 week(s) if notified thereafter. Some programs remain open after January 4. Please contact the Office of Admissions for more information. **Financial aid:** Priority date 3/2, closing date 3/2. FAFSA required. Applicants notified on a rolling basis starting 4/15; must reply within 3 week(s) of notification.

**Academics.** Numerous special programs that cross traditional lines. **Special study options:** Independent study, internships, student-designed major, study abroad. **Credit/placement by examination:** AP, CLEP, IB, institutional tests. 6 credit hours maximum toward bachelor's degree. **Support services:** Tutoring.

**Majors. Communications technology:** Animation/special effects. **Computer sciences:** Computer graphics. **Visual/performing arts:** General, acting, art, cinematography, commercial/advertising art, dance, dramatic, film/cinema, graphic design, jazz, music performance, music theory/composition, painting, photography, piano/organ, sculpture, stringed instruments, studio arts, theater arts management, theater design, voice/opera.

**Computing on campus.** 40 workstations in library, computer center. Dormitories wired for high-speed internet access. Helpline, wireless network available.

**Student life. Freshman orientation:** Mandatory. Held the week before classes begin each semester. **Housing:** Coed dorms, special housing for disabled, apartments available. $250 nonrefundable deposit, deadline 6/1. **Activities:** Jazz band, dance, drama, film society, literary magazine, music ensembles, opera, radio station, student government, student newspaper, TV station, black student union, Latino student union, GLBT student union, Asian club, political issues club.

**Student services.** Career counseling, student employment services, financial aid counseling, health services, personal counseling, placement for graduates, veterans' counselor. **Physically disabled:** Services for visually, speech, hearing impaired.

Contact. E-mail: admiss@calarts.edu
Phone: (661) 255-1050 ext. 2185 Toll-free number: (800) 545-2787
Fax: (661) 253-7710
Molly Ryan, Director of Admissions, California Institute of the Arts, 24700
McBean Parkway, Valencia, CA 91355

## California Lutheran University

**Thousand Oaks, California**     **CB member**
**www.callutheran.edu**     **CB code: 4088**

▶ Private 4-year university and liberal arts college affiliated with Evangelical Lutheran Church in America
▶ Residential campus in small city
▶ 2,126 degree-seeking undergraduates: 11% part-time, 57% women, 3% African American, 4% Asian American, 15% Hispanic American, 1% Native American, 3% international
▶ 1,225 degree-seeking graduate students
▶ 69% of applicants admitted
▶ SAT or ACT (ACT writing optional), application essay required
▶ 62% graduate within 6 years

**General.** Founded in 1959. Regionally accredited. **Degrees:** 530 bachelor's awarded; master's, doctoral offered. **ROTC:** Army, Air Force. **Location:** 45 miles from Los Angeles. **Calendar:** Semester, limited summer session. **Full-time faculty:** 137 total; 87% have terminal degrees, 18% minority, 45% women. **Part-time faculty:** 149 total; 38% have terminal degrees, 13% minority, 45% women. **Class size:** 68% < 20, 30% 20-39, 2% 40-49, less than 1% 50-99. **Special facilities:** Science facility housing an electronic blackboard, hypermedia computer laboratory, education technology center, television studio with editing room.

**Freshman class profile.** 2,440 applied, 1,678 admitted, 424 enrolled.

| Mid 50% test scores | | GPA 2.0-2.99: | 20% |
|---|---|---|---|
| SAT critical reading: | 480-600 | Rank in top quarter: | 64% |
| SAT math: | 500-610 | Rank in top tenth: | 31% |
| SAT writing: | 460-600 | Return as sophomores: | 75% |
| ACT composite: | 21-26 | Out-of-state: | 27% |
| GPA 3.50 or higher: | 48% | Live on campus: | 87% |
| GPA 3.0-3.49: | 32% | | |

**Basis for selection.** High school achievement record, rank in class, test scores, essay, letters of recommendation very important. Interview recommended. Audition recommended for music, art, and drama majors. **Homeschooled:** Letter of recommendation (nonparent) required. **Learning Disabled:** Once a student with learning disabilities has chosen CLU, meeting with the Accessibility Resource Coordinator recommended.

**High school preparation.** Required units include English 4, mathematics 3, social studies 2, science 3 (laboratory 2) and foreign language 2.

**2008-2009 Annual costs.** Tuition/fees: $27,850. Room/board: $9,650. Books/supplies: $1,399. Personal expenses: $2,176.

**2007-2008 Financial aid. Need-based:** 346 full-time freshmen applied for aid; 263 were judged to have need; 263 of these received aid. Average need met was 80%. Average scholarship/grant was $7,550; average loan $3,466. 69% of total undergraduate aid awarded as scholarships/grants, 31% as loans/jobs. **Non-need-based:** Scholarships awarded for academics, alumni affiliation, art, leadership, minority status, music/drama, religious affiliation, state residency.

**Application procedures. Admission:** Priority date 3/15; deadline 7/1 (postmark date). $45 fee, may be waived for applicants with need. Application may be submitted online. Admission notification on a rolling basis beginning on or about 1/15. Must reply by May 1 or within 2 week(s) if notified thereafter. **Financial aid:** Priority date 3/1; no closing date. FAFSA required. Applicants notified on a rolling basis starting 3/15; must reply within 2 week(s) of notification.

**Academics. Special study options:** Accelerated study, cooperative education, double major, dual enrollment of high school students, exchange student, honors, independent study, internships, New York semester, semester at sea, student-designed major, study abroad, teacher certification program, Washington semester. **Credit/placement by examination:** AP, CLEP, IB, SAT, ACT, institutional tests. 30 credit hours maximum toward bachelor's degree. **Support services:** Learning center, reduced course load, study skills assistance, tutoring, writing center.

**Majors. Biology:** General, biochemistry, molecular. **Business:** General, accounting, business admin, finance, managerial economics, marketing. **Communications:** General, advertising, broadcast journalism, journalism, public relations. **Computer sciences:** General, computer graphics, computer science, information systems, programming. **Conservation:** Environmental science. **Education:** General, art, early childhood, elementary, English, foreign languages, mathematics, middle, music, physical, reading, science, secondary, social science, social studies, special. **Engineering:** Biomedical. **English:** English lit, speech/rhetoric. **Foreign languages:** General, French, German, Spanish. **Health:** Athletic training, predental, premedicine, prepharmacy, preveterinary. **History:** General. **Interdisciplinary:** Biological/physical sciences, math/computer science. **Legal studies:** Prelaw. **Liberal arts:** Arts/sciences. **Math:** General. **Philosophy/religion:** Philosophy, religion. **Physical sciences:** Chemistry, geology, physics. **Protective services:** Police science. **Psychology:** General. **Science technology:** Biological. **Social sciences:** Criminology, economics, international relations, political science, sociology. **Theology:** Religious ed, theology. **Visual/performing arts:** General, art, commercial/advertising art, dramatic.

**Most popular majors.** Biology 6%, business/marketing 32%, communications/journalism 12%, computer/information sciences 6%, psychology 10%, social sciences 15%.

**Computing on campus.** 92 workstations in dormitories, library, computer center, student center. Dormitories wired for high-speed internet access and linked to campus network. Commuter students can connect to campus network. Online library, helpline, wireless network available.

**Student life. Freshman orientation:** Mandatory. Preregistration for classes offered. **Policies:** Alcohol policy - no alcohol on campus except in the chapel for communion, drug free campus. **Housing:** Guaranteed on-campus for freshmen. Coed dorms, special housing for disabled, apartments available. $195 fully refundable deposit, deadline 5/1. On campus houses available. **Activities:** Bands, campus ministries, choral groups, dance, drama, international student organizations, literary magazine, music ensembles, Model UN, musical theater, radio station, student government, student newspaper, symphony orchestra, TV station, Lutheran Church congregation, Circle-K, African American student association, Rotoract, United Students of the World, Latino student union, Habitat for Humanity, Asian American club.

**Athletics.** NCAA. **Intercollegiate:** Baseball M, basketball, cross-country, diving, football (tackle) M, golf M, soccer, softball W, swimming, tennis, track and field, volleyball W, water polo. **Intramural:** Basketball, football (non-tackle), soccer, softball, volleyball, water polo. **Team name:** Kingsmen/Regals.

**Student services.** Adult student services, alcohol/substance abuse counseling, campus ministries, career counseling, services for economically disadvantaged, student employment services, financial aid counseling, health services, minority student services, personal counseling, placement for graduates, veterans' counselor, women's services. **Physically disabled:** Services for visually, hearing impaired. **Learning disabled:** Comprehensive services available.

**Contact.** E-mail: admissions@callutheran.edu
Phone: (805) 493-3135 Toll-free number: (877) 258-3678
Fax: (805) 493-3114
Matthew Ward, Dean of Undergraduate Enrollment, California Lutheran University, 60 West Olsen Road #1350, Thousand Oaks, CA 91360-2787

---

## California Maritime Academy

**Vallejo, California**                          **CB member**
www.csum.edu                                     **CB code: 4035**

- Public 4-year university and maritime college
- Residential campus in small city
- 836 degree-seeking undergraduates
- SAT or ACT required

**General.** Founded in 1929. Regionally accredited. Highest job placement in the California State University system. Not a military school. All students participate in at least one 2-month training cruise around Pacific Ocean geared toward their major. **Degrees:** 148 bachelor's awarded. **ROTC:** Naval. **Location:** 30 miles from San Francisco. **Calendar:** Semester, limited summer session. **Full-time faculty:** 50 total. **Part-time faculty:** 25 total. **Special facilities:** 500-foot training ship, computer-aided radar simulators, bridge simulator, steam simulator.

**Freshman class profile.**

| | | | |
|---|---|---|---|
| Out-of-state: | 17% | Live on campus: | 90% |

**Basis for selection.** Applicants must meet California State University Eligibility Index requirements and have strong grades in mathematics and sciences. All accepted students must pass physical examination. Some students required to take ELM/EPT if test scores are not high enough. Interview recommended; supplemental admission form required.

**High school preparation.** Required and recommended units include English 4, mathematics 3-4, social studies 1, history 1, science 2 (laboratory 2), foreign language 2-3 and academic electives 1. One additional mathematics course recommended for mechanical engineering applicants. Chemistry or physics required. One visual or performing arts elective required.

**2007-2008 Annual costs.** Tuition/fees: $3,728; $13,898 out-of-state. Each student participates in at least one cruise and one internship prior to graduation. Some majors have additional cruise requirements. The cost for a cruise is $3,500. The cost for an internship/co-op is $225. Additionally, each incoming student must purchase a uniform. Prices range from $1,550-$1,680 depending on the major. Room/board: $8,450. Books/supplies: $1,386. Personal expenses: $2,520.

**Financial aid.** All financial aid based on need. **Additional information:** US Maritime Administration provides annual incentive payment of $3,000 per student, with certain conditions. Tuition waiver for children of deceased or disabled California veterans.

**Application procedures. Admission:** Priority date 11/30; no deadline. $55 fee, may be waived for applicants with need. Application may be submitted online. Admission notification on a rolling basis beginning on or about 2/1. Must reply by May 1 or within 2 week(s) if notified thereafter. **Financial aid:** Priority date 3/2; no closing date. FAFSA required. Applicants notified on a rolling basis starting 4/1.

**Academics.** Center for Excellence and Learning provides free tutoring/workshops hosted by professors. **Special study options:** Cooperative education, distance learning, double major, ESL, internships. International training cruise onboard ship "Golden Bear". **Credit/placement by examination:** AP, CLEP. 24 credit hours maximum toward bachelor's degree. **Support services:** Learning center, remedial instruction, tutoring.

**Majors. Business:** Business admin, logistics. **Engineering:** Marine, mechanical. **Engineering technology:** General. **Interdisciplinary:** Global studies. **Social sciences:** Political science. **Other:** Marine transportation.

**Computing on campus.** 85 workstations in dormitories, library, computer center, student center. Dormitories wired for high-speed internet access and linked to campus network. Helpline, repair service available.

**Student life. Freshman orientation:** Mandatory, $200 fee. Preregistration for classes offered. Held last week of August. **Housing:** Guaranteed on-campus for all undergraduates. Coed dorms available. $500 deposit, deadline 7/1. Students required to live on campus except those married or with children. **Activities:** Student government, student newspaper.

**Athletics.** NAIA. **Intercollegiate:** Basketball, rowing (crew), rugby M, sailing, soccer, water polo. **Intramural:** Badminton, baseball M, basketball, boxing M, golf, racquetball, rowing (crew), rugby M, sailing, softball, tennis, volleyball, water polo. **Team name:** Keelhaulers.

**Student services.** Career counseling, student employment services, financial aid counseling, health services, minority student services, personal counseling, placement for graduates, veterans' counselor.

**Contact.** E-mail: admission@csum.edu
Phone: (707) 654-1330 Toll-free number: (800) 561-1945
Fax: (707) 654-1336
Marc McGee, Director of Admissions, California Maritime Academy, 200 Maritime Academy Drive, Vallejo, CA 94590

---

## California National University for Advanced Studies

**Northridge, California**
www.cnuas.edu                                    **CB code: 3894**

- For-profit 4-year virtual business and engineering college
- Small city
- 175 degree-seeking undergraduates

**General.** Accredited by DETC. 100% distance learning university. **Degrees:** 10 bachelor's awarded; master's offered. **Calendar:** Continuous. **Part-time faculty:** 80 total.

**Basis for selection.** Application/portfolio important.

**2007-2008 Annual costs.** Domestic/Canada undergraduate tuition: $270/unit; international undergraduate tuition $300/unit.

**Application procedures. Admission:** No deadline. $75 fee.

**Academics. Special study options:** Distance learning. **Credit/placement by examination:** CLEP.

**Majors. Business:** Business admin. **Computer sciences:** Computer science. **Engineering:** General.

**Contact.** E-mail: cnuadms@mail.cnuas.edu
Phone: (818) 830-2411 Toll-free number: (800) 782-2422
Fax: (818) 830-2418
California National University for Advanced Studies, 8550 Balboa Boulevard, Suite 210, Northridge, CA 91325

---

## California Polytechnic State University: San Luis Obispo

San Luis Obispo, California
www.calpoly.edu

CB member
CB code: 4038

- Public 4-year university
- Residential campus in large town
- 18,728 degree-seeking undergraduates: 5% part-time, 43% women, 1% African American, 11% Asian American, 11% Hispanic American, 1% Native American, 1% international
- 775 degree-seeking graduate students
- 45% of applicants admitted
- SAT or ACT (ACT writing optional) required
- 68% graduate within 6 years

**General.** Founded in 1901. Regionally accredited. **Degrees:** 3,552 bachelor's awarded; master's offered. **ROTC:** Army. **Location:** 200 miles from Los Angeles, 250 miles from San Francisco. **Calendar:** Quarter, extensive summer session. **Full-time faculty:** 786 total; 79% have terminal degrees, 12% minority, 30% women. **Part-time faculty:** 508 total; 32% have terminal degrees, 11% minority, 41% women. **Class size:** 16% < 20, 59% 20-39, 12% 40-49, 10% 50-99, 3% >100. **Special facilities:** Printing press museum, university farm, dairy products technical center, architectural design institute.

**Freshman class profile.** 30,176 applied, 13,520 admitted, 4,369 enrolled.

| Mid 50% test scores | | | |
|---|---|---|---|
| SAT critical reading: | 520-620 | **GPA 2.0-2.99:** | 3% |
| SAT math: | 560-670 | **Rank in top quarter:** | 79% |
| ACT composite: | 23-28 | **Rank in top tenth:** | 42% |
| GPA 3.50 or higher: | 72% | **Return as sophomores:** | 90% |
| GPA 3.0-3.49: | 25% | **Out-of-state:** | 6% |

**Basis for selection.** Course work, high school GPA, test scores most important. Extracurricular activities considered. Portfolio required for art, design majors.

**High school preparation.** 15 units required; 22 recommended. Required and recommended units include English 4-5, mathematics 3-4, social studies 2, history 1, science 3-4 (laboratory 1-2), foreign language 2-3 and visual/performing arts 1. History must be U.S. history/government.

**2007-2008 Annual costs.** Tuition/fees: $4,689; $14,859 out-of-state. Required fees vary by program. Room/board: $8,817. Books/supplies: $1,386. Personal expenses: $2,079.

**2006-2007 Financial aid. Need-based:** 2,447 full-time freshmen applied for aid; 1,158 were judged to have need; 1,053 of these received aid. Average need met was 58%. Average scholarship/grant was $1,765; average loan $2,402. 52% of total undergraduate aid awarded as scholarships/grants, 48% as loans/jobs. **Non-need-based:** Awarded to 929 full-time undergraduates, including 281 freshmen. Scholarships awarded for academics, alumni affiliation, art, athletics, job skills, leadership, music/drama, ROTC, state residency.

**Application procedures. Admission:** Closing date 11/30 (postmark date). $55 fee, may be waived for applicants with need. Application may be submitted online. Admission notification 4/1. Admission notification on a rolling basis. Must reply by 5/1. Housing deposit due on a first come first served basis. **Financial aid:** Priority date 3/1; no closing date. FAFSA required. Applicants notified on a rolling basis starting 4/15; must reply within 8 week(s) of notification.

**Academics. Special study options:** Combined bachelor's/graduate degree, cooperative education, double major, ESL, exchange student, honors, internships, semester at sea, study abroad, teacher certification program. **Credit/placement by examination:** AP, CLEP, SAT, ACT, institutional tests.

45 credit hours maximum toward bachelor's degree. **Support services:** Learning center, pre-admission summer program, reduced course load, remedial instruction, study skills assistance, tutoring, writing center.

**Majors. Agriculture:** Agribusiness operations, agronomy, animal sciences, business, dairy, food science, horticultural science, plant protection, soil science. **Architecture:** Architecture, landscape, urban/community planning. **Biology:** General, biochemistry, microbiology. **Business:** Accounting, construction management, finance, management information systems, marketing. **Communications:** General, journalism. **Communications technology:** Graphics. **Computer sciences:** Computer science. **Conservation:** Forestry. **Education:** Agricultural. **Engineering:** General, aerospace, agricultural, architectural, biomedical, civil, electrical, environmental, industrial, manufacturing, materials, mechanical, software. **English:** English lit. **Family/consumer sciences:** Child development, food/nutrition. **Foreign languages:** General. **History:** General. **Liberal arts:** Arts/sciences. **Math:** General, statistics. **Parks/recreation:** Exercise sciences, facilities management. **Philosophy/religion:** Philosophy. **Physical sciences:** General, chemistry, geology, physics. **Psychology:** General. **Social sciences:** General, economics, political science. **Visual/performing arts:** Art, commercial/advertising art, dramatic. **Other:** Agricultural Science, Art and Design, Comparative Ethnic Studies, Environmental Management & Protection, Industrial Technology.

**Most popular majors.** Agriculture 12%, business/marketing 17%, engineering/engineering technologies 25%.

**Computing on campus.** Dormitories wired for high-speed internet access and linked to campus network. Commuter students can connect to campus network. Online course registration, online library, helpline, student web hosting, wireless network available.

**Student life. Freshman orientation:** Available. Held week prior to start of fall term. **Housing:** Coed dorms, single-sex dorms available. $1,888 fully refundable deposit. Shared, apartment-style housing. **Activities:** Bands, campus ministries, choral groups, dance, drama, international student organizations, literary magazine, music ensembles, Model UN, musical theater, radio station, student government, student newspaper, symphony orchestra, TV station, MECHA, Society of Black Engineers and Scientists, minority engineering program.

**Athletics.** NCAA. **Intercollegiate:** Baseball M, basketball, cross-country, diving, football (tackle) M, golf, soccer, softball W, swimming, tennis, track and field, volleyball W, wrestling M. **Intramural:** Badminton, bowling, equestrian, fencing, field hockey, lacrosse, rugby M, sailing, soccer, triathlon, volleyball, water polo. **Team name:** Mustangs.

**Student services.** Adult student services, alcohol/substance abuse counseling, campus ministries, career counseling, student employment services, health services, minority student services, on-campus daycare, personal counseling, placement for graduates, veterans' counselor, women's services. **Physically disabled:** Services for visually, speech, hearing impaired.

**Contact.** E-mail: admissions@calpoly.edu
Phone: (805) 756-2311 Fax: (805) 756-5400
James Maraviglia, Admissions Officer, California Polytechnic State University: San Luis Obispo, Admissions Office, Cal Poly, San Luis Obispo, CA 93407-0031

---

## California State Polytechnic University: Pomona

Pomona, California
www.csupomona.edu

CB member
CB code: 4082

- Public 4-year university
- Commuter campus in small city
- 19,615 degree-seeking undergraduates: 17% part-time, 43% women, 4% African American, 29% Asian American, 29% Hispanic American, 6% international
- 1,862 degree-seeking graduate students
- 69% of applicants admitted
- SAT or ACT (ACT writing optional) required
- 49% graduate within 6 years

**General.** Founded in 1938. Regionally accredited. **Degrees:** 3,762 bachelor's awarded; master's offered. **ROTC:** Army. **Location:** 30 miles from downtown Los Angeles. **Calendar:** Quarter, extensive summer session. **Full-time faculty:** 602 total; 76% have terminal degrees, 32% minority, 38% women. **Part-time faculty:** 574 total; 32% have terminal degrees, 28% minority, 35% women. **Class size:** 35% < 20, 48% 20-39, 9% 40-49, 7% 50-99, less than 1% >100. **Special facilities:** Electron microscope center, international center, small ruminant center, Arabian horse center, equine research center, land laboratory, ecological reserve, center for regenerative studies, center for community affairs.

**Freshman class profile.** 21,836 applied, 15,021 admitted, 3,620 enrolled.

| Mid 50% test scores | | | |
|---|---|---|---|
| SAT critical reading: | 430-540 | GPA 2.0-2.99: | 28% |
| SAT math: | 460-590 | Return as sophomores: | 80% |
| ACT composite: | 18-23 | Out-of-state: | 1% |
| GPA 3.50 or higher: | 27% | Live on campus: | 30% |
| GPA 3.0-3.49: | 45% | International: | 3% |

**Basis for selection.** High school GPA, courses, and test scores important.

**High school preparation.** 15 units required. Required and recommended units include English 4, mathematics 3-4, social studies 1, history 1, science 2 (laboratory 2), foreign language 2, visual/performing arts 1 and academic electives 1.

**2007-2008 Annual costs.** Tuition/fees: $3,278; $13,448 out-of-state. Room/board: $8,493. Books/supplies: $1,386. Personal expenses: $1,851.

**2007-2008 Financial aid. Need-based:** 2,365 full-time freshmen applied for aid; 1,706 were judged to have need; 1,631 of these received aid. Average need met was 77.3%. Average scholarship/grant was $7,028; average loan $2,964. 59% of total undergraduate aid awarded as scholarships/grants, 41% as loans/jobs. **Non-need-based:** Awarded to 523 full-time undergraduates, including 201 freshmen. Scholarships awarded for academics, alumni affiliation, athletics, leadership, state residency.

**Application procedures. Admission:** Priority date 11/30; deadline 11/30 (postmark date). $55 fee, may be waived for applicants with need. Application may be submitted online. Admission notification on a rolling basis beginning on or about 10/2. Must reply by May 1 or within 3 week(s) if notified thereafter. Applications for first time freshmen accepted October 1 through November 30. **Financial aid:** Priority date 3/2; no closing date. FAFSA required. Applicants notified on a rolling basis starting 4/1.

**Academics. Special study options:** Cooperative education, cross-registration, double major, dual enrollment of high school students, ESL, exchange student, external degree, honors, internships, liberal arts/career combination, study abroad, teacher certification program. Ocean studies institute, desert studies consortium. **Credit/placement by examination:** AP, CLEP, institutional tests. 36 credit hours maximum toward bachelor's degree. **Support services:** Learning center, pre-admission summer program, remedial instruction, study skills assistance, tutoring, writing center.

**Majors. Agriculture:** Agronomy, animal sciences, business, food science, horticultural science, landscaping, ornamental horticulture, plant protection, soil science. **Architecture:** Architecture, landscape, urban/community planning. **Biology:** General, biotechnology, botany, environmental, microbiology, zoology. **Business:** Accounting, business admin, finance, hospitality admin, international, marketing, operations. **Communications:** General. **Computer sciences:** Computer science, information technology. **Engineering:** General, aerospace, chemical, civil, computer, electrical, industrial, manufacturing, materials, mechanical. **Engineering technology:** General, construction, electrical. **English:** English lit. **Family/consumer sciences:** Clothing/textiles. **Foreign languages:** Spanish. **Health:** Dietetics, veterinary technology/assistant. **History:** General. **Interdisciplinary:** Behavioral sciences. **Liberal arts:** Arts/sciences. **Math:** General. **Parks/recreation:** Health/fitness. **Philosophy/religion:** Philosophy. **Physical sciences:** Chemistry, geology, physics. **Psychology:** General. **Social sciences:** General, anthropology, economics, geography, political science, sociology. **Visual/performing arts:** Art, dance, dramatic, graphic design.

**Most popular majors.** Business/marketing 41%, engineering/engineering technologies 16%, liberal arts 6%.

**Computing on campus.** 280 workstations in library, computer center. Dormitories wired for high-speed internet access and linked to campus network. Commuter students can connect to campus network. Online course registration, helpline, student web hosting available.

**Student life. Freshman orientation:** Mandatory, $40 fee. Preregistration for classes offered. One-day orientation. **Housing:** Coed dorms, apartments available. $50 fully refundable deposit. **Activities:** Bands, choral groups, dance, drama, literary magazine, music ensembles, musical theater, opera, student government, student newspaper, symphony orchestra, Campus Crusade for Christ, black student union, Hawaiian club, MECHA, Studies of the World, Newman Club, Hillel, Bahai club, Coptic-Orthodox Christian club.

**Athletics.** NCAA. **Intercollegiate:** Baseball M, basketball, cross-country, soccer, tennis, track and field, volleyball W. **Intramural:** Badminton, basketball, football (non-tackle) M, golf, racquetball, softball, swimming, table tennis, tennis, track and field, volleyball. **Team name:** Broncos.

**Student services.** Adult student services, career counseling, student employment services, health services, on-campus daycare, personal counseling, placement for graduates, veterans' counselor. **Physically disabled:** Services for visually, speech, hearing impaired.

**Contact.** E-mail: admissions@csupomona.edu
Phone: (909) 869-3210 Fax: (909) 869-4529
Scott Duncan, Director of Admissions, California State Polytechnic University: Pomona, 3801 West Temple Avenue, Pomona, CA 91768-4019

## California State University: Bakersfield

Bakersfield, California   CB member
www.csub.edu   CB code: 4110

▶ Public 4-year university and liberal arts college
▶ Commuter campus in small city
▶ 4,991 full-time, degree-seeking undergraduates
▶ 1,166 graduate students
▶ 55% of applicants admitted

**General.** Founded in 1965. Regionally accredited. **Degrees:** 1,291 bachelor's awarded; master's offered. **Location:** 112 miles from Los Angeles. **Calendar:** Quarter, limited summer session. **Full-time faculty:** 330 total. **Part-time faculty:** 185 total. **Class size:** 47% < 20, 44% 20-39, 6% 40-49, 2% 50-99, less than 1% >100. **Special facilities:** 40-acre facility for wild animal care, archaeological information center, center for business and economic research, center for economic education, well-sample repository, center for physiological research.

**Freshman class profile.** 4,295 applied, 2,375 admitted, 870 enrolled.

| Mid 50% test scores | | | |
|---|---|---|---|
| SAT critical reading: | 430-530 | GPA 3.0-3.49: | 43% |
| SAT math: | 440-550 | GPA 2.0-2.99: | 34% |
| ACT composite: | 16-21 | Out-of-state: | 3% |
| GPA 3.50 or higher: | 22% | Live on campus: | 12% |
| | | International: | 3% |

**Basis for selection.** GPA, test scores, and certain honors courses must place applicant in upper third of California high school graduates (upper sixth for out-of-state applicants) using eligibility index table. Minimum test scores slightly higher for out-of-state students. SAT or ACT not required if GPA is above 3.0 (3.6 if out-of-state).

**High school preparation.** Required units include English 4, mathematics 3, history 2, science 2 (laboratory 1), foreign language 2 and academic electives 1. One visual and performing arts required; foreign language must be in same language; math must include algebra, geometry, and intermediate algebra; science must include biology and a physical science.

**2007-2008 Annual costs.** Tuition/fees: $3,708; $13,878 out-of-state. Room/board: $6,537. Books/supplies: $1,386. Personal expenses: $2,520.

**Financial aid.** All financial aid based on need.

**Application procedures. Admission:** Priority date 12/1; no deadline. $55 fee, may be waived for applicants with need. Application may be submitted online. Admission notification on a rolling basis beginning on or about 7/1. **Financial aid:** Priority date 3/2, closing date 4/1. FAFSA required. Applicants notified on a rolling basis; must reply within 2 week(s) of notification.

**Academics.** Most courses are 5 quarter units. Students enrolled in 3 courses are carrying full unit load. **Special study options:** Accelerated study, cooperative education, distance learning, double major, ESL, exchange student, external degree, honors, independent study, internships, liberal arts/career combination, student-designed major, study abroad, teacher certification program. 2+2 at specified locations for liberal studies (teaching) majors. **Credit/placement by examination:** CLEP. Unlimited number of hours of credit by examination may be counted toward degree. **Support services:** Learning center, pre-admission summer program, reduced course load, remedial instruction, study skills assistance, tutoring.

**Majors. Biology:** General. **Business:** Business admin. **Communications:** General. **Computer sciences:** Computer science. **Conservation:** Land use planning. **Education:** Early childhood. **English:** American lit, English lit. **Foreign languages:** Spanish. **Health:** Nursing (RN). **History:** General. **Liberal arts:** Arts/sciences. **Math:** General. **Philosophy/religion:** Philosophy, religion. **Physical sciences:** Chemistry, geology, physics. **Protective services:** Criminal justice. **Psychology:** General. **Public administration:** General. **Social sciences:** Anthropology, criminology, economics, political science, sociology. **Visual/performing arts:** General, art, dramatic.

**Most popular majors.** Business/marketing 15%, liberal arts 27%, psychology 10%, security/protective services 6%, social sciences 7%.

**Computing on campus.** 600 workstations in library, computer center, student center. Dormitories linked to campus network. Commuter students can connect to campus network. Online course registration, online library, helpline, student web hosting available.

**Student life. Freshman orientation:** Available, $15 fee. Preregistration for classes offered. **Housing:** Guaranteed on-campus for all undergraduates. Coed dorms, single-sex dorms available. $50 deposit. **Activities:** Jazz band, choral groups, dance, drama, literary magazine, music ensembles, musical theater, student government, student newspaper, black student union, Movimiento Estudiantil Chicano de Aztlan, Christian union, student nursing association, Circle-K, Latinos United for Education.

**Athletics.** NCAA. **Intercollegiate:** Basketball, cheerleading, cross-country W, golf M, soccer, softball W, swimming, tennis W, track and field, volleyball W, water polo W, wrestling M. **Intramural:** Badminton, basketball, golf, handball, racquetball, soccer, softball, tennis, volleyball. **Team name:** Roadrunners.

**Student services.** Adult student services, alcohol/substance abuse counseling, career counseling, services for economically disadvantaged, student employment services, financial aid counseling, health services, minority student services, on-campus daycare, personal counseling, placement for graduates, veterans' counselor. **Physically disabled:** Services for visually, speech, hearing impaired. **Learning disabled:** Comprehensive services available.

**Contact.** Phone: (661) 654-3036 Toll-free number: (800) 788-2782 Fax: (661) 654-3389
Jacqueline Mimms, Director of Admissions, California State University: Bakersfield, 9001 Stockdale Highway, Bakersfield, CA 93311-1099

## California State University: Channel Islands
**Camarillo, California**
**www.csuci.edu**                                    **CB code: 4128**

- Public 4-year university
- Commuter campus in small city
- 3,289 degree-seeking undergraduates: 19% part-time, 61% women, 3% African American, 7% Asian American, 26% Hispanic American, 1% Native American
- 310 degree-seeking graduate students
- 53% of applicants admitted
- SAT or ACT required

**General.** Regionally accredited. **Degrees:** 576 bachelor's awarded; master's offered. **Calendar:** Semester. **Full-time faculty:** 87 total; 100% have terminal degrees. **Part-time faculty:** 140 total; 100% have terminal degrees.

**Freshman class profile.** 5,562 applied, 2,962 admitted, 526 enrolled.

| Mid 50% test scores | | | |
|---|---|---|---|
| SAT critical reading: | 440-550 | GPA 3.0-3.49: | 40% |
| SAT math: | 440-550 | GPA 2.0-2.99: | 37% |
| ACT composite: | 18-23 | Out-of-state: | 1% |
| GPA 3.50 or higher: | 23% | Live on campus: | 46% |

**High school preparation.** 17 units required. Required units include English 4, mathematics 3, social studies 2, history 2, science 4 (laboratory 2), foreign language 2, visual/performing arts 1 and academic electives 1.

**2007-2008 Annual costs.** Tuition/fees: $3,332; $13,502 out-of-state. Room/board: $10,630. Books/supplies: $1,300. Personal expenses: $2,400.

**2006-2007 Financial aid. Need-based:** 61% of total undergraduate aid awarded as scholarships/grants, 39% as loans/jobs.

**Application procedures. Admission:** $55 fee. Application may be submitted online. Admission notification on a rolling basis.

**Academics. Special study options:** Double major, independent study, study abroad, teacher certification program. **Credit/placement by examination:** AP, CLEP, SAT, ACT. **Support services:** Remedial instruction, tutoring, writing center.

**Majors. Biology:** General, biotechnology. **Business:** General. **Computer sciences:** General. **Conservation:** Environmental science, management/policy. **English:** English lit. **Foreign languages:** Spanish. **History:** General. **Physical sciences:** Chemistry. **Psychology:** General. **Social sciences:** Economics, political science, sociology. **Visual/performing arts:** General, art.

**Most popular majors.** Biology 8%, business/marketing 19%, English 7%, history 6%, liberal arts 23%, psychology 19%, visual/performing arts 8%.

**Computing on campus.** Dormitories wired for high-speed internet access. Commuter students can connect to campus network. Online course registration, online library, helpline, wireless network available.

**Student life. Freshman orientation:** Mandatory, $120 fee. Preregistration for classes offered. Two-day session in July. **Housing:** Coed dorms, substance-free housing available. $1,030 fully refundable deposit, deadline 11/29. **Activities:** Choral groups, student government, student newspaper.

**Student services.** Alcohol/substance abuse counseling, career counseling, services for economically disadvantaged, student employment services, financial aid counseling, health services, personal counseling, women's services. **Physically disabled:** Services for visually, speech, hearing impaired. **Learning disabled:** Comprehensive services available.

**Contact.** E-mail: admissionsandrecords@csuci.edu
Phone: (805) 437-8400
Jane Sweetland, Dean, Enrollment Services, California State University: Channel Islands, One University Drive, Camarillo, CA 93012

## California State University: Chico
**Chico, California**                                 **CB member**
**www.csuchico.edu**                                 **CB code: 4048**

- Public 4-year university and liberal arts college
- Residential campus in small city
- 15,645 degree-seeking undergraduates: 9% part-time, 52% women, 2% African American, 6% Asian American, 12% Hispanic American, 1% Native American, 2% international
- 892 degree-seeking graduate students
- 95% of applicants admitted
- SAT or ACT (ACT writing optional) required
- 54% graduate within 6 years

**General.** Founded in 1887. Regionally accredited. **Degrees:** 2,901 bachelor's awarded; master's offered. **Location:** 90 miles from Sacramento, 175 miles from San Francisco. **Calendar:** Semester, limited summer session. **Full-time faculty:** 560 total; 82% have terminal degrees, 16% minority, 39% women. **Part-time faculty:** 449 total; 26% have terminal degrees, 8% minority, 52% women. **Class size:** 36% < 20, 43% 20-39, 12% 40-49, 7% 50-99, 2% >100. **Special facilities:** 1,000-acre farm, planetarium, instructional media center, biology field station, anthropology museum, intercultural studies center, computer graphics lab, assistive technology center, media prep lab, recording arts studio, hydrotherapy pool, echocardiography system, gas displacement chamber, two ecological preserves with nearly 4,100 acres, forensics lab, archaeology lab and research center.

**Freshman class profile.** 13,857 applied, 13,120 admitted, 2,771 enrolled.

| Mid 50% test scores | | | |
|---|---|---|---|
| SAT critical reading: | 440-550 | Rank in top quarter: | 76% |
| SAT math: | 460-570 | Rank in top tenth: | 35% |
| ACT composite: | 19-24 | End year in good standing: | 75% |
| GPA 3.50 or higher: | 19% | Out-of-state: | 3% |
| GPA 3.0-3.49: | 44% | Live on campus: | 63% |
| GPA 2.0-2.99: | 37% | International: | 3% |

**Basis for selection.** Eligibility index derived from high school GPA and test scores. First-time freshmen applicants rank order based on characteristics of applicant pool. GPA determined from 10th, 11th, and 12th-grade college prep courses only, excluding physical education. Nursing program open only to state residents. Portfolio required of fine arts majors. **Home-schooled:** Transcript of courses and grades required. Must be able to verify completion of required college preparatory subject requirements and meet institutional eligibility index. **Learning Disabled:** Students must meet established admission criteria.

**High school preparation.** 15 units required. Required units include English 4, mathematics 3, social studies 2, science 2 (laboratory 2), foreign language 2 and visual/performing arts 1.

**2007-2008 Annual costs.** Tuition/fees: $3,690; $13,860 out-of-state. Room/board: $9,022. Books/supplies: $1,351. Personal expenses: $2,292.

**2007-2008 Financial aid. Need-based:** 1,634 full-time freshmen applied for aid; 1,135 were judged to have need; 1,103 of these received aid. Average need met was 88%. Average scholarship/grant was $7,387; average loan $3,402. 53% of total undergraduate aid awarded as scholarships/grants,

47% as loans/jobs. **Non-need-based:** Awarded to 3,638 full-time undergraduates, including 1,239 freshmen. Scholarships awarded for academics, art, athletics, leadership, minority status, music/drama, religious affiliation.

**Application procedures. Admission:** Priority date 10/1; deadline 11/30 (postmark date). $55 fee, may be waived for applicants with need. Application may be submitted online. Admission notification 3/1. Admission notification on a rolling basis. Must reply by May 1 or within 2 week(s) if notified thereafter. Applications for the following majors must be made during priority periods of October and August: nursing, media arts, graphic design, recording arts, and interior design. All first time freshmen fall applicants should apply between October 1 and November 30. **Financial aid:** Priority date 3/2; no closing date. FAFSA required. Applicants notified on a rolling basis starting 3/2.

**Academics. Special study options:** Cooperative education, cross-registration, distance learning, double major, dual enrollment of high school students, ESL, exchange student, external degree, honors, independent study, internships, student-designed major, study abroad, teacher certification program. **Credit/placement by examination:** AP, CLEP, IB, SAT, ACT, institutional tests. 30 credit hours maximum toward bachelor's degree. 6 semester hours awarded for each International Baccalaureate higher level exam passed with score of 4 to 7. **Support services:** Learning center, preadmission summer program, reduced course load, remedial instruction, study skills assistance, tutoring, writing center.

**Majors. Agriculture:** Agronomy, animal sciences, business, range science. **Architecture:** Urban/community planning. **Area/ethnic studies:** American, Asian, Latin American, women's. **Biology:** General, biochemistry, botany, ecology, microbiology. **Business:** Accounting, business admin, finance, human resources, management information systems, marketing. **Communications:** Journalism, organizational, public relations, radio/tv. **Computer sciences:** Computer graphics, computer science, information technology. **Conservation:** Environmental science, management/policy. **Education:** Agricultural, art, biology, chemistry, early childhood, English, ESL, French, German, health, instructional media, mathematics, music, physical, science, social science, Spanish. **Engineering:** Civil, computer, mechanical. **Engineering technology:** Construction. **English:** English lit, speech/rhetoric. **Foreign languages:** French, German, linguistics, Spanish. **Health:** Clinical lab science, communication disorders, dietetics, health services, nursing (RN), predental, premedicine, prepharmacy, preveterinary, recreational therapy. **History:** General. **Interdisciplinary:** Accounting/computer science, gerontology, math/computer science. **Legal studies:** Paralegal. **Liberal arts:** Arts/sciences, humanities. **Math:** General, applied, statistics. **Parks/recreation:** General, exercise sciences, facilities management, health/fitness. **Philosophy/religion:** Judaic, philosophy, religion. **Physical sciences:** General, atmospheric science, chemistry, geology, hydrology, physics. **Protective services:** Criminal justice. **Psychology:** General. **Public administration:** General, social work. **Social sciences:** General, anthropology, economics, geography, international economics, international relations, political science, sociology. **Visual/performing arts:** Art, art history/conservation, design, dramatic, graphic design, interior design, music theory/composition, musical theater, piano/organ, studio arts. **Other:** Ecological, Evolutionary and Organismal Biology, Electrical and Computer Engineering, Environmental Economics, Mechatronics, Music Industry and Technology, Supply Chain Management Systems.

**Most popular majors.** Business/marketing 15%, engineering/engineering technologies 8%, English 6%, health sciences 6%, liberal arts 10%, parks/recreation 7%, social sciences 10%, visual/performing arts 9%.

**Computing on campus.** 962 workstations in dormitories, library, student center. Dormitories wired for high-speed internet access and linked to campus network. Commuter students can connect to campus network. Online course registration, online library, helpline, repair service, student web hosting, wireless network available.

**Student life. Freshman orientation:** Available, $50 fee. Preregistration for classes offered. One-day session for students and parents in July. Two-day sessions offered for $90. Mini-orientation offered in August. Online orientation also offered. **Housing:** Coed dorms, special housing for disabled, apartments, fraternity/sorority housing, substance-free housing available. $1,000 fully refundable deposit. Thematic housing available for honors, engineering, minorities in engineering and science, business, math, and natural science. Theme floors include community service, recreational sports, and agricultural. **Activities:** Bands, choral groups, dance, drama, film society, literary magazine, music ensembles, musical theater, opera, radio station, student government, student newspaper, symphony orchestra, over 200 organizations.

**Athletics. NCAA. Intercollegiate:** Baseball M, basketball, cross-country, golf, soccer, softball W, track and field, volleyball W. **Intramural:** Badminton, basketball, bowling, football (non-tackle), soccer, softball, volleyball. **Team name:** Wildcats.

**Student services.** Adult student services, alcohol/substance abuse counseling, career counseling, services for economically disadvantaged, student employment services, financial aid counseling, health services, legal services, minority student services, on-campus daycare, personal counseling, placement for graduates, veterans' counselor, women's services. **Physically disabled:** Services for visually, speech, hearing impaired. **Learning disabled:** Comprehensive services available.

**Contact.** E-mail: info@csuchico.edu
Phone: (530) 898-4428 Toll-free number: (800) 542-4426
Fax: (530) 898-6456
Rocky Raquel, (Interim) Director of Admissions Office, California State University: Chico, 400 West First Street, Chico, CA 95929-0722

---

## California State University: Dominguez Hills

**Carson, California**     **CB member**
**www.csudh.edu**     **CB code: 4098**

- Public 4-year university
- Commuter campus in small city
- 8,409 degree-seeking undergraduates: 36% part-time, 69% women, 29% African American, 8% Asian American, 38% Hispanic American, 2% international
- 2,380 degree-seeking graduate students
- 67% of applicants admitted
- SAT or ACT with writing required
- 33% graduate within 6 years

**General.** Founded in 1960. Regionally accredited. **Degrees:** 1,822 bachelor's awarded; master's offered. **ROTC:** Army, Air Force. **Location:** 13 miles from Los Angeles. **Calendar:** Semester, extensive summer session. **Full-time faculty:** 306 total; 92% have terminal degrees, 30% minority, 48% women. **Part-time faculty:** 582 total; 18% have terminal degrees, 24% minority, 52% women. **Class size:** 28% < 20, 45% 20-39, 14% 40-49, 12% 50-99, less than 1% >100. **Special facilities:** Nature preserve, greenhouse, observatory, urban community research center, Japanese garden and theatre complex.

**Freshman class profile.** 1,846 applied, 1,236 admitted, 995 enrolled.

| | | | |
|---|---|---|---|
| GPA 3.50 or higher: | 11% | Live on campus: | 21% |
| GPA 3.0-3.49: | 36% | International: | 3% |
| GPA 2.0-2.99: | 52% | Fraternities: | 3% |
| End year in good standing: | 56% | Sororities: | 7% |
| Return as sophomores: | 60% | | |

**Basis for selection.** Academic record and test scores are most important. SAT/ACT required of applicants who do not meet minimum requirement based on admissions eligibility index. Interview required of Educational Opportunity Program applicants. **Homeschooled:** Statement describing homeschool structure and mission, transcript of courses and grades, state high school equivalency certificate required. **Learning Disabled:** Student must show proof of learning disability to Office of Disability Services.

**High school preparation.** 15 units required. Required units include English 4, mathematics 3, social studies 2, history 1, science 2 (laboratory 2), foreign language 2, visual/performing arts 1 and academic electives 1.

**2007-2008 Annual costs.** Tuition/fees: $3,377; $13,547 out-of-state. Room/board: $8,690. Books/supplies: $1,300. Personal expenses: $2,300.

**2006-2007 Financial aid. Need-based:** 710 full-time freshmen applied for aid; 426 were judged to have need; 425 of these received aid. Average need met was 76%. Average scholarship/grant was $5,671; average loan $2,320. 65% of total undergraduate aid awarded as scholarships/grants, 35% as loans/jobs. **Non-need-based:** Awarded to 624 full-time undergraduates, including 118 freshmen. Scholarships awarded for academics, alumni affiliation, art, athletics, leadership, music/drama.

**Application procedures. Admission:** Priority date 11/1; no deadline. $55 fee, may be waived for applicants with need. Application may be submitted online. Admission notification on a rolling basis beginning on or about 1/7. **Financial aid:** Priority date 3/2, closing date 4/15. FAFSA required. Applicants notified on a rolling basis starting 2/28; must reply within 4 week(s) of notification.

**Academics. Special study options:** Accelerated study, cross-registration, distance learning, double major, dual enrollment of high school students, external degree, honors, independent study, internships, student-designed major, study abroad, teacher certification program, weekend college. **Credit/placement by examination:** AP, CLEP, IB, SAT, ACT, institutional tests. **Support services:** Learning center, pre-admission summer program, reduced course load, remedial instruction, tutoring, writing center.

**Majors. Area/ethnic studies:** African-American, Hispanic-American/Latino/Chicano. **Biology:** General, biochemistry. **Business:** Business admin, labor relations. **Communications:** General, digital media. **Computer sciences:** Computer science. **Engineering technology:** Quality control. **English:** English lit. **Foreign languages:** Spanish. **Health:** Clinical lab science, health services, nursing (RN). **History:** General. **Interdisciplinary:** Peace/conflict. **Legal studies:** Prelaw. **Liberal arts:** Arts/sciences. **Math:** General. **Parks/recreation:** General, exercise sciences. **Philosophy/religion:** Philosophy. **Physical sciences:** Chemistry, geology, physics. **Protective services:** Law enforcement admin. **Psychology:** General. **Public administration:** General, human services. **Social sciences:** Anthropology, economics, geography, political science, sociology. **Visual/performing arts:** Art, dramatic. **Other:** Interdisciplinary studies.

**Most popular majors.** Business/marketing 20%, communications/journalism 6%, health sciences 10%, liberal arts 21%, psychology 8%, public administration/social services 12%, social sciences 10%.

**Computing on campus.** 256 workstations in library, computer center. Dormitories wired for high-speed internet access and linked to campus network. Commuter students can connect to campus network. Online course registration, online library, helpline, student web hosting, wireless network available.

**Student life. Freshman orientation:** Available, $45 fee. Preregistration for classes offered. Offered eleven times a year to incoming admitted freshmen and transfer students. **Housing:** Special housing for disabled, apartments available. $300 fully refundable deposit. **Activities:** Bands, choral groups, dance, drama, international student organizations, literary magazine, music ensembles, musical theater, radio station, student government, student newspaper, TV station, accounting society, African-American business student association, dance club, literary club, Phi Alpha Delta, political science club, science society, Hispanic Association of natural and social science, campus crusade for christ.

**Athletics.** NCAA. **Intercollegiate:** Baseball M, basketball, cross-country W, golf M, soccer, softball W, track and field W, volleyball W. **Intramural:** Basketball, cross-country, football (non-tackle), golf, soccer, softball, swimming, tennis, track and field, volleyball, water polo, weight lifting. **Team name:** Toros.

**Student services.** Career counseling, services for economically disadvantaged, student employment services, financial aid counseling, health services, on-campus daycare, personal counseling, placement for graduates, veterans' counselor, women's services. **Physically disabled:** Services for visually, speech, hearing impaired.

**Contact,** Phone: (310) 243-3645 Fax: (310) 516-3609
Linda Wise, Acting Director of Admissions, California State University: Dominguez Hills, 1000 East Victoria Street, Carson, CA 90747

## California State University: East Bay

**Hayward, California**  **CB member**
www.csueastbay.edu  **CB code: 4011**

- Public 4-year university
- Commuter campus in small city
- 10,391 degree-seeking undergraduates: 19% part-time, 61% women, 12% African American, 27% Asian American, 14% Hispanic American, 1% Native American, 6% international
- 755 degree-seeking graduate students
- 62% of applicants admitted

**General.** Founded in 1957. Regionally accredited. Branch campus in Concord. **Degrees:** 2,334 bachelor's awarded; master's, doctoral offered. **Location:** 30 miles from San Francisco, 30 miles from San Jose. **Calendar:** Quarter, extensive summer session. **Full-time faculty:** 324 total; 36% minority, 45% women. **Part-time faculty:** 417 total; 24% minority, 55% women. **Class size:** 22% < 20, 49% 20-39, 14% 40-49, 13% 50-99, 2% >100. **Special facilities:** Ecological field station, museum of anthropology, marine laboratory, geology summer field camp.

**Freshman class profile.** 8,832 applied, 5,501 admitted, 3,249 enrolled.

| Mid 50% test scores | | Out-of-state: | 2% |
|---|---|---|---|
| SAT critical reading: | 430-580 | Live on campus: | 32% |
| SAT math: | 450-600 | International: | 6% |
| ACT composite: | 18-24 | | |

**Basis for selection.** Eligibility index based on GPA, test results, and 15 units of subject requirements to yield students in top third of California high school graduates. Out-of-state applicants should be in top sixth of high school class. Test scores not required for residents with high school GPA above 3.0, nonresidents with high school GPA above 3.61.

**High school preparation.** 15 units required. Required units include English 4, mathematics 3, history 2, science 2 (laboratory 2), foreign language 2 and academic electives 1. One visual and performing arts. Math must be algebra, geometry, and intermediate algebra. Science must be biology and a physical science. Foreign language units must be in same language.

**2007-2008 Annual costs.** Tuition/fees: $3,264; $13,434 out-of-state. Quoted freshmen room-only charge is for suite shared by 6 to 8 students. Additional $3200 advance purchase of flexible retail meal credits required. (Standard meal plans not available.). Room only: $5,832. Books/supplies: $1,386. Personal expenses: $2,898.

**2006-2007 Financial aid. Need-based:** 453 full-time freshmen applied for aid; 406 were judged to have need; 390 of these received aid. Average need met was 73%. Average scholarship/grant was $7,497. 65% of total undergraduate aid awarded as scholarships/grants, 35% as loans/jobs.

**Application procedures. Admission:** Closing date 8/31 (postmark date). $55 fee, may be waived for applicants with need. Application may be submitted online. Admission notification on a rolling basis beginning on or about 10/1. **Financial aid:** Priority date 3/2; no closing date. FAFSA required. Applicants notified on a rolling basis; must reply within 3 week(s) of notification.

**Academics. Special study options:** Accelerated study, cooperative education, cross-registration, distance learning, double major, dual enrollment of high school students, ESL, exchange student, honors, independent study, internships, liberal arts/career combination, student-designed major, study abroad, teacher certification program. **Credit/placement by examination:** AP, CLEP, IB, SAT, ACT, institutional tests. 45 credit hours maximum toward bachelor's degree. 45-unit limitation excludes advanced placement. **Support services:** Learning center, pre-admission summer program, reduced course load, remedial instruction, study skills assistance, tutoring.

**Majors. Area/ethnic studies:** African-American, Asian-American, Hispanic-American/Latino/Chicano, Latin American, Native American. **Biology:** General, biochemistry, biomedical sciences. **Business:** General, accounting, business admin, entrepreneurial studies, finance, human resources, management information systems, managerial economics, marketing, purchasing, real estate. **Communications:** General, advertising, broadcast journalism, journalism, public relations. **Computer sciences:** General, computer science, information systems, networking. **Conservation:** General, environmental studies. **Education:** Mathematics, physical, speech. **Engineering:** Software. **Engineering technology:** Industrial management. **English:** American lit, British lit, English lit, speech/rhetoric. **Foreign languages:** French, Spanish. **Health:** Athletic training, audiology/speech pathology, clinical lab technology, environmental health, prenursing, recreational therapy. **History:** General. **Liberal arts:** Arts/sciences. **Math:** General, applied, statistics. **Parks/recreation:** General, exercise sciences, facilities management, health/fitness. **Philosophy/religion:** Philosophy, religion. **Physical sciences:** Chemistry, geology, physics. **Protective services:** Corrections, law enforcement admin. **Psychology:** General. **Public administration:** General, policy analysis, social work. **Social sciences:** Anthropology, archaeology, economics, geography, political science, sociology. **Visual/performing arts:** Art, art history/conservation, arts management, ceramics, commercial/advertising art, dance, dramatic, drawing, painting, photography, printmaking, sculpture, studio arts, theater design.

**Most popular majors.** Business/marketing 33%, health sciences 6%, liberal arts 11%, psychology 6%, social sciences 8%.

**Computing on campus.** 1,062 workstations in dormitories, library, computer center. Dormitories wired for high-speed internet access and linked to campus network. Commuter students can connect to campus network. Online course registration, helpline, student web hosting available.

**Student life. Freshman orientation:** Available, $80 fee. Preregistration for classes offered. 2 day program with overnight lodging on campus optional. **Policies:** Community and campus-based volunteer programs available. **Housing:** Apartments available. $900 deposit, deadline 5/1. Private coeducational dormitory adjacent to campus. **Activities:** Bands, choral groups, dance, drama, literary magazine, music ensembles, musical theater, opera, radio station, student government, student newspaper, symphony orchestra, TV station, 90 campus organizations.

**Athletics.** NAIA, NCAA. **Intercollegiate:** Baseball M, basketball, cross-country, golf, soccer, softball W, swimming W, track and field, volleyball W, water polo W. **Intramural:** Badminton, basketball, golf, gymnastics M, racquetball, soccer, softball, swimming, tennis, volleyball. **Team name:** Pioneers.

**Student services.** Adult student services, career counseling, services for economically disadvantaged, student employment services, financial aid counseling, health services, legal services, minority student services, on-campus daycare, personal counseling, placement for graduates, veterans' counselor. **Physically disabled:** Services for visually, speech, hearing impaired.

**Contact.** E-mail: admissions@csueastbay.edu
Phone: (510) 885-2784 Fax: (510) 885-4059
Gregory Smith, Associate Vice President, Planning and Enrollment
Management, California State University: East Bay, 25800 Carlos Bee
Boulevard, Hayward, CA 94542-3095

## California State University: Fresno

Fresno, California                              CB member
www.csufresno.edu                               CB code: 4312

- Public 4-year university
- Commuter campus in very large city
- 19,191 degree-seeking undergraduates: 19% part-time, 58% women
- 2,266 degree-seeking graduate students
- 69% of applicants admitted
- SAT or ACT (ACT writing optional) required
- 930% graduate within 6 years; 28% enter graduate study

**General.** Founded in 1911. Regionally accredited. Designated as an arboretum in 1978. **Degrees:** 3,354 bachelor's awarded; master's, doctoral offered. **ROTC:** Army, Air Force. **Location:** 217 miles from Los Angeles, 172 miles from Sacramento. **Calendar:** Semester, limited summer session. **Full-time faculty:** 712 total; 74% have terminal degrees, 26% minority, 40% women. **Part-time faculty:** 633 total; 33% have terminal degrees, 18% minority, 49% women. **Class size:** 33% < 20, 45% 20-39, 12% 40-49, 7% 50-99, 2% >100. **Special facilities:** 1,190-acre university farm, strength and conditioning center, planetarium.

**Freshman class profile.** 13,447 applied, 9,253 admitted, 2,637 enrolled.

| Mid 50% test scores | | End year in good standing: | 65% |
|---|---|---|---|
| SAT critical reading: | 380-510 | Return as sophomores: | 79% |
| SAT math: | 410-540 | Out-of-state: | 1% |
| ACT composite: | 16-22 | Live on campus: | 31% |
| GPA 3.50 or higher: | 31% | Fraternities: | 2% |
| GPA 3.0-3.49: | 40% | Sororities: | 2% |
| GPA 2.0-2.99: | 29% | | |

**Basis for selection.** Upper third of California high school graduates based on eligibility index and required college preparatory subjects. Tests recommended, but not required, if student has a high school GPA of 3.0 or higher. **Homeschooled:** Transcript of courses and grades required.

**High school preparation.** 15 units required. Required and recommended units include English 4, mathematics 3, social studies 1, history 1, science 1 (laboratory 1), foreign language 2 and academic electives 3. One visual and performing arts, and 1 US history/government also required.

**2007-2008 Annual costs.** Tuition/fees: $3,299; $13,469 out-of-state. Room/board: $7,053. Books/supplies: $1,072. Personal expenses: $1,638.

**2007-2008 Financial aid. Need-based:** Average need met was 82%. Average scholarship/grant was $7,811; average loan $3,029. 74% of total undergraduate aid awarded as scholarships/grants, 26% as loans/jobs. **Non-need-based:** Scholarships awarded for academics, alumni affiliation, art, athletics, leadership, music/drama, state residency.

**Application procedures. Admission:** Priority date 11/30; deadline 2/1 (receipt date). $55 fee, may be waived for applicants with need. Application may be submitted online. Admission notification on a rolling basis beginning on or about 11/1. Must reply by 5/1. **Financial aid:** Priority date 3/3; no closing date. FAFSA required. Applicants notified on a rolling basis starting 4/1; must reply within 3 week(s) of notification.

**Academics. Special study options:** Accelerated study, combined bachelor's/graduate degree, cooperative education, cross-registration, distance learning, double major, dual enrollment of high school students, ESL, exchange student, honors, independent study, internships, student-designed major, study abroad, teacher certification program. **Credit/placement by examination:** AP, CLEP, IB, institutional tests. 30 credit hours maximum toward bachelor's degree. **Support services:** Learning center, pre-admission summer program, reduced course load, remedial instruction, study skills assistance, tutoring, writing center.

**Honors college/program.** The Smittcamp Family Honors college admits 50 students each year. Prospective students must clearly demonstrate intellectual and creative potential to benefit from honors learning experiences and must have (P)SAT of 1800 (Critical Reading/Math/Writing) or above, be within upper 10 percent of graduating class, or have minimum GPA of 3.6 (through the end of junior year). Once on campus, honors students participate in 2 general education honors courses each semester and an honors colloquium each semester their first two years. They take 3 upper division honors courses during their junior and senior years. Honors students must provide 30 hours of community service their freshmen year. This number changes each year thereafter.

**Majors. Agriculture:** General, agronomy, animal health, animal sciences, business, dairy, food science, horticultural science, plant protection, plant sciences. **Area/ethnic studies:** African-American, women's. **Biology:** General, anatomy, bacteriology, cell/histology, ecology, molecular. **Business:** General, accounting, business admin, finance, human resources, international, management information systems, marketing, real estate. **Communications:** General, journalism, public relations. **Computer sciences:** General, computer science, information systems. **Construction:** Maintenance. **Education:** General, Deaf/hearing impaired, physical. **Engineering:** Civil, computer, electrical, mechanical. **Engineering technology:** Civil, construction, electrical, surveying. **English:** English lit. **Family/consumer sciences:** Child development, food/nutrition. **Foreign languages:** French, linguistics, Spanish. **Health:** Clinical/medical social work, communication disorders, environmental health, health care admin, nursing (RN), occupational health, vocational rehab counseling. **History:** General. **Interdisciplinary:** Natural sciences. **Math:** General. **Parks/recreation:** Exercise sciences, facilities management. **Philosophy/religion:** Philosophy, religion. **Physical sciences:** Chemistry, geology, physics. **Psychology:** General. **Public administration:** General, social work. **Social sciences:** Anthropology, criminology, economics, geography, political science, sociology. **Visual/performing arts:** Art, commercial/advertising art, dance, dramatic, interior design, music theory/composition, theater design.

**Most popular majors.** Business/marketing 17%, communications/journalism 6%, education 10%, English 6%, health sciences 8%, liberal arts 12%, social sciences 8%.

**Computing on campus.** PC or laptop required. 1,500 workstations in dormitories, library, computer center, student center. Dormitories linked to campus network. Commuter students can connect to campus network. Online course registration, online library, helpline, repair service, wireless network available.

**Student life. Freshman orientation:** Available, $45 fee. One day program held during June and July for the fall semester and November and December for the spring semester. **Housing:** Coed dorms, single-sex dorms, apartments, fraternity/sorority housing available. $150 deposit, deadline 4/1. **Activities:** Bands, choral groups, dance, drama, literary magazine, music ensembles, musical theater, radio station, student government, student newspaper, symphony orchestra, TV station, over 250 student organizations including religious and ethnic groups.

**Athletics.** NCAA. **Intercollegiate:** Baseball M, basketball, cross-country, equestrian W, football (tackle) M, golf, soccer W, softball W, tennis, track and field, volleyball W, wrestling M. **Intramural:** Basketball, football (non-tackle), racquetball, soccer, softball, tennis, volleyball. **Team name:** Bulldogs.

**Student services.** Adult student services, career counseling, student employment services, financial aid counseling, health services, minority student services, on-campus daycare, personal counseling, placement for graduates, veterans' counselor, women's services. **Physically disabled:** Services for visually, speech, hearing impaired.

**Contact.** E-mail: vivianf@csufresno.edu
Phone: (559) 278-2261 Fax: (559) 278-4812
Vivian Franco, Director, California State University: Fresno, 5150 North
Maple Avenue, M/S JA 57, Fresno, CA 93740-8026

## California State University: Fullerton

Fullerton, California                           CB member
www.fullerton.edu                               CB code: 4589

- Public 4-year university
- Commuter campus in small city
- 29,788 degree-seeking undergraduates: 24% part-time, 58% women, 4% African American, 22% Asian American, 30% Hispanic American, 1% Native American, 4% international
- 5,362 degree-seeking graduate students
- 61% of applicants admitted
- SAT or ACT (ACT writing recommended) required
- 50% graduate within 6 years

**General.** Founded in 1957. Regionally accredited. **Degrees:** 6,295 bachelor's awarded; master's, doctoral offered. **ROTC:** Army. **Location:** 30 miles from Los Angeles. **Calendar:** Semester, extensive summer session. **Full-time faculty:** 903 total; 76% have terminal degrees, 26% minority, 47% women. **Part-time faculty:** 1,094 total. **Class size:** 27% < 20, 53% 20-39,

11% 40-49, 7% 50-99, 2% >100. **Special facilities:** Wildlife sanctuary, arboretum, desert studies center, twin studies center, center for children who stutter, coastal information center, demographic research center, Institute of Gerontology, center for oral and public history, center for study of religion in American life, center for study of economics of aging.

**Freshman class profile.** 29,812 applied, 18,042 admitted, 4,154 enrolled.

| Mid 50% test scores | | | |
|---|---|---|---|
| SAT critical reading: | 430-530 | Rank in top quarter: | 48% |
| SAT math: | 440-560 | Rank in top tenth: | 14% |
| ACT composite: | 18-23 | End year in good standing: | 77% |
| GPA 3.50 or higher: | 21% | Return as sophomores: | 79% |
| GPA 3.0-3.49: | 46% | Out-of-state: | 1% |
| GPA 2.0-2.99: | 33% | Live on campus: | 7% |
| | | International: | 3% |

**Basis for selection.** Eligibility index consisting of combination of high school GPA and SAT or ACT score. Audition required of music majors.

**High school preparation.** 15 units required; 16 recommended. Required and recommended units include English 4, mathematics 3, social studies 1, history 1, science 2 (laboratory 2), foreign language 2-3, visual/performing arts 1 and academic electives 1. 1 unit U.S. history/government required.

**2007-2008 Annual costs.** Tuition/fees: $3,342; $13,512 out-of-state. Room only: $5,167. Books/supplies: $1,238. Personal expenses: $2,300.

**2006-2007 Financial aid. Need-based:** 2,684 full-time freshmen applied for aid; 1,881 were judged to have need; 1,116 of these received aid. Average need met was 62%. Average scholarship/grant was $6,711; average loan $2,596. 66% of total undergraduate aid awarded as scholarships/grants, 34% as loans/jobs. **Non-need-based:** Awarded to 1,646 full-time undergraduates, including 349 freshmen. Scholarships awarded for academics. **Additional information:** Fee waiver for children of veterans killed in action or with service-connected disability whose annual income is $5,000 or less.

**Application procedures. Admission:** Priority date 10/1; deadline 11/30 (postmark date). $55 fee, may be waived for applicants with need. Application must be submitted online. Admission notification on a rolling basis beginning on or about 1/1. Must reply by 5/15. Reply date given on notification letter. **Financial aid:** Priority date 3/2, closing date 5/23. FAFSA required. Applicants notified by 4/2; Applicants notified on a rolling basis; must reply within 3 week(s) of notification.

**Academics. Special study options:** Cross-registration, distance learning, double major, dual enrollment of high school students, honors, independent study, internships, study abroad, teacher certification program. Service Learning. **Credit/placement by examination:** AP, CLEP, IB, SAT, ACT, institutional tests. 30 credit hours maximum toward bachelor's degree. **Support services:** Learning center, pre-admission summer program, reduced course load, remedial instruction, study skills assistance, tutoring, writing center.

**Majors. Area/ethnic studies:** African-American, American, Asian-American, Central/Eastern European, Hispanic-American/Latino/Chicano, Latin American, women's. **Biology:** General. **Business:** Accounting, business admin, entrepreneurial studies, finance, international, managerial economics, marketing, tourism/travel. **Communications:** General, advertising, journalism, public relations, radio/tv. **Computer sciences:** Computer science, information technology. **Education:** Early childhood, music. **Engineering:** General, civil, computer, electrical, mechanical, operations research, science. **English:** English lit, speech/rhetoric. **Foreign languages:** Comparative lit, French, German, Japanese, linguistics, Spanish. **Health:** Communication disorders, health services, nursing (RN), prenursing. **History:** General. **Liberal arts:** Arts/sciences. **Math:** General, applied, statistics. **Parks/recreation:** Health/fitness. **Philosophy/religion:** Philosophy, religion. **Physical sciences:** Chemistry, geology, physics. **Protective services:** Criminal justice. **Psychology:** General. **Public administration:** General, human services. **Social sciences:** Anthropology, economics, geography, political science, sociology. **Visual/performing arts:** Art, art history/conservation, dance, dramatic, music performance, studio arts.

**Most popular majors.** Business/marketing 25%, communications/journalism 14%, education 7%, psychology 6%, social sciences 6%, visual/performing arts 7%.

**Computing on campus.** 2,000 workstations in dormitories, library, computer center, student center. Dormitories wired for high-speed internet access and linked to campus network. Commuter students can connect to campus network. Online course registration, online library, helpline, repair service, wireless network available.

**Student life. Freshman orientation:** Mandatory. Preregistration for classes offered. **Housing:** Apartments, fraternity/sorority housing available. **Activities:** Bands, choral groups, dance, drama, international student organizations, music ensembles, Model UN, musical theater, radio station, student government, student newspaper, symphony orchestra, Chinese Christian fellowship; Christian student association; disabled student association; Fellowship of Christian Athletes; human services student association; Movimiento Estudiantil Chicano de Atlan (MECHA); New Democratic Movement; Poltical Science Student Association; Asian, Hispanic, and African-American faculty/staff associations.

**Athletics.** NCAA. **Intercollegiate:** Baseball M, basketball, cross-country, fencing, gymnastics W, soccer, softball W, tennis W, track and field, volleyball W, wrestling M. **Intramural:** Badminton, basketball, bowling, football (non-tackle), gymnastics, handball M, racquetball, rugby M, skiing, soccer M, softball, swimming, table tennis, tennis, volleyball, wrestling M. **Team name:** Titans.

**Student services.** Adult student services, career counseling, student employment services, financial aid counseling, health services, legal services, on-campus daycare, personal counseling, placement for graduates, veterans' counselor, women's services. **Physically disabled:** Services for visually, speech, hearing impaired.

**Contact.** E-mail: admissions@fullerton.edu
Phone: (714) 278-2370 Fax: (714) 278-2356
Nancy Dority, Assistant Vice-President of Enrollment Services, California State University: Fullerton, 800 North State College Boulevard, Langsdorf Hall-114, Fullerton, CA 92831-6900

---

## California State University: Long Beach

**Long Beach, California** — CB member
**www.csulb.edu** — CB code: 4389

- Public 4-year university
- Commuter campus in large city
- 30,605 degree-seeking undergraduates: 21% part-time, 60% women, 6% African American, 23% Asian American, 27% Hispanic American, 1% Native American, 5% international
- 4,672 degree-seeking graduate students
- 47% of applicants admitted
- SAT or ACT (ACT writing optional) required
- 47% graduate within 6 years

**General.** Founded in 1949. Regionally accredited. **Degrees:** 6,110 bachelor's awarded; master's offered. **ROTC:** Army. **Location:** 25 miles from Los Angeles. **Calendar:** Semester, extensive summer session. **Full-time faculty:** 982 total; 89% have terminal degrees, 29% minority, 44% women. **Part-time faculty:** 1,281 total; 29% have terminal degrees, 25% minority, 53% women. **Class size:** 25% < 20, 54% 20-39, 11% 40-49, 6% 50-99, 4% >100. **Special facilities:** Japanese garden, performing arts center, media center.

**Freshman class profile.** 45,189 applied, 21,245 admitted, 4,212 enrolled.

| Mid 50% test scores | | | |
|---|---|---|---|
| SAT critical reading: | 440-550 | Rank in top quarter: | 82% |
| SAT math: | 460-580 | End year in good standing: | 87% |
| ACT composite: | 17-23 | Return as sophomores: | 85% |
| GPA 3.50 or higher: | 35% | Out-of-state: | 2% |
| GPA 3.0-3.49: | 49% | Live on campus: | 22% |
| GPA 2.0-2.99: | 16% | International: | 3% |

**Basis for selection.** Admission based on secondary school record and standardized test scores. Audition required of dance, music majors. Portfolio required of art, design majors.

**High school preparation.** 15 units required. Required units include English 4, mathematics 3, social studies 1, history 1, science 2 (laboratory 2), foreign language 2 and academic electives 1. 1 unit fine arts required.

**2007-2008 Annual costs.** Tuition/fees: $3,116; $13,286 out-of-state. Room/board: $7,536. Books/supplies: $1,386. Personal expenses: $1,928.

**2007-2008 Financial aid. Need-based:** Average need met was 81%. Average scholarship/grant was $5,400; average loan $2,862. 62% of total undergraduate aid awarded as scholarships/grants, 38% as loans/jobs. **Non-need-based:** Scholarships awarded for academics, art, athletics, music/drama.

**Application procedures. Admission:** Closing date 11/30 (postmark date). $55 fee, may be waived for applicants with need. Application may be submitted online. Admission notification on a rolling basis beginning on or about 12/1. **Financial aid:** Priority date 3/2; no closing date. FAFSA required. Applicants notified on a rolling basis starting 4/1; must reply within 3 week(s) of notification.

**Academics. Special study options:** Accelerated study, cross-registration, distance learning, double major, dual enrollment of high school students, ESL, honors, independent study, internships, student-designed major, study abroad, teacher certification program, Washington semester. Concurrent enrollment at other CSU campuses. **Credit/placement by examination:** AP, CLEP, IB, SAT, ACT, institutional tests. **Support services:** Learning center, pre-admission summer program, reduced course load, remedial instruction, study skills assistance, tutoring, writing center.

**Majors. Architecture:** Interior. **Area/ethnic studies:** African-American, Hispanic-American/Latino/Chicano, women's. **Biology:** General, bacteriology, biochemistry, botany, cell/histology, molecular. **Business:** General, accounting, fashion, finance, human resources, international, management science, managerial economics, operations, real estate. **Communications:** Broadcast journalism, journalism, public relations. **Computer sciences:** General, computer science, information systems. **Education:** Art, family/consumer sciences, physical. **Engineering:** Aerospace, biomedical, chemical, civil, computer, electrical, materials, mechanical. **Engineering technology:** Civil, construction, electrical, manufacturing. **English:** Composition, creative writing, English lit, speech/rhetoric. **Family/consumer sciences:** General, clothing/textiles, food/nutrition. **Foreign languages:** Classics, comparative lit, French, German, Japanese, Spanish. **Health:** Medical illustrating, medical radiologic technology/radiation therapy, nursing (RN), public health ed. **History:** General. **Liberal arts:** Arts/sciences. **Math:** General, applied, statistics. **Parks/recreation:** Facilities management. **Philosophy/religion:** Philosophy, religion. **Physical sciences:** Chemistry, geology, physics. **Protective services:** Criminal justice. **Psychology:** General. **Public administration:** Social work. **Social sciences:** Anthropology, economics, geography, sociology. **Visual/performing arts:** Art, art history/conservation, ceramics, cinematography, commercial/advertising art, conducting, dance, design, dramatic, drawing, fiber arts, industrial design, interior design, jazz, metal/jewelry, music history, music performance, painting, photography, piano/organ, printmaking, sculpture, studio arts, theater design, voice/opera.

**Most popular majors.** Business/marketing 18%, English 9%, health sciences 7%, liberal arts 7%, social sciences 7%, visual/performing arts 9%.

**Computing on campus.** 1,200 workstations in dormitories, library, computer center. Dormitories linked to campus network. Commuter students can connect to campus network. Online course registration available.

**Student life. Freshman orientation:** Available, $45 fee. One-day pre-semester session. **Housing:** Coed dorms available. **Activities:** Bands, choral groups, dance, drama, film society, literary magazine, music ensembles, musical theater, opera, radio station, student government, student newspaper, symphony orchestra, TV station, more than 150 political, ethnic, and social service organizations.

**Athletics.** NCAA. **Intercollegiate:** Baseball M, basketball, cross-country, golf, soccer W, softball, tennis W, track and field, volleyball, water polo. **Intramural:** Basketball, handball, racquetball, rugby M, soccer, softball, tennis, volleyball. **Team name:** Forty-Niners.

**Student services.** Adult student services, alcohol/substance abuse counseling, campus ministries, career counseling, services for economically disadvantaged, student employment services, financial aid counseling, health services, minority student services, on-campus daycare, personal counseling, placement for graduates, veterans' counselor, women's services. **Physically disabled:** Services for visually, speech, hearing impaired.

**Contact.** E-mail: eslb@csulb.edu
Phone: (562) 985-5471 Fax: (562) 985-4973
Thomas Enders, Assistant Vice President for Enrollment Services, California State University: Long Beach, 1250 Bellflower Boulevard, Long Beach, CA 90840-0106

## California State University: Los Angeles

**Los Angeles, California**  CB member
www.calstatela.edu  CB code: 4399

- Public 4-year university
- Commuter campus in very large city
- 15,727 degree-seeking undergraduates: 26% part-time, 61% women
- 5,324 degree-seeking graduate students
- 63% of applicants admitted
- 30% graduate within 6 years

**General.** Founded in 1947. Regionally accredited. **Degrees:** 3,098 bachelor's awarded; master's, doctoral offered. **ROTC:** Army, Air Force. **Location:** 5 miles from downtown. **Calendar:** Quarter, extensive summer session. **Full-time faculty:** 579 total; 42% minority, 46% women. **Part-time faculty:** 647 total; 40% minority, 46% women. **Class size:** 38% < 20, 46% 20-39, 8% 40-49, 6% 50-99, 2% >100. **Special facilities:** Baroque pipe organ, 4 megavolt Van de Graaff accelerator.

**Freshman class profile.** 20,436 applied, 12,805 admitted, 1,931 enrolled.

| Mid 50% test scores | | | |
|---|---|---|---|
| SAT critical reading: | 380-480 | GPA 2.0-2.99: | 41% |
| SAT math: | 380-490 | Return as sophomores: | 74% |
| ACT composite: | 15-20 | Out-of-state: | 2% |
| GPA 3.50 or higher: | 57% | Live on campus: | 13% |
| | | International: | 6% |

**Basis for selection.** Secondary school record and standardized test scores important. SAT/ACT not required if GPA is 3.0 or above. EPT/ELM required for placement; may be waived based on SAT score. **Homeschooled:** Syllabi and written evaluation of courses completed may be required.

**High school preparation.** 15 units required. Required units include English 4, mathematics 3, social studies 1, history 1, science 2 (laboratory 2), foreign language 2 and academic electives 1. 1 visual and performing arts required.

**2007-2008 Annual costs.** Tuition/fees: $3,332; $13,502 out-of-state. Room only: $3,474. Books/supplies: $1,386. Personal expenses: $2,520.

**Application procedures. Admission:** Closing date 6/15 (postmark date). $55 fee, may be waived for applicants with need. Application may be submitted online. Admission notification on a rolling basis beginning on or about 11/1. **Financial aid:** Priority date 3/1; no closing date. FAFSA required. Applicants notified on a rolling basis starting 4/1; must reply within 3 week(s) of notification.

**Academics. Special study options:** Accelerated study, combined bachelor's/graduate degree, cooperative education, cross-registration, distance learning, double major, dual enrollment of high school students, ESL, exchange student, honors, independent study, internships, student-designed major, study abroad, teacher certification program. **Credit/placement by examination:** AP, CLEP, institutional tests. **Support services:** Learning center, pre-admission summer program, reduced course load, remedial instruction, tutoring.

**Majors. Area/ethnic studies:** African-American, Hispanic-American/Latino/Chicano, Latin American. **Biology:** General, biochemistry, microbiology. **Business:** Business admin. **Communications:** General, radio/tv. **Computer sciences:** General. **Education:** Kindergarten/preschool, physical, technology/industrial arts, trade/industrial. **Engineering:** General, civil, electrical, mechanical. **Engineering technology:** Industrial. **English:** English lit. **Family/consumer sciences:** Food/nutrition. **Foreign languages:** Chinese, French, Japanese, Spanish. **Health:** Communication disorders, nursing (RN). **History:** General. **Interdisciplinary:** Natural sciences. **Liberal arts:** Arts/sciences. **Math:** General. **Philosophy/religion:** Philosophy. **Physical sciences:** Chemistry, geology, physics. **Protective services:** Fire services admin, law enforcement admin. **Psychology:** General. **Public administration:** Social work. **Social sciences:** Anthropology, economics, geography, political science, sociology. **Visual/performing arts:** Art, commercial/advertising art, dramatic, music performance.

**Most popular majors.** Business/marketing 21%, health sciences 27%, psychology 7%, security/protective services 6%, social sciences 7%.

**Computing on campus.** 1,500 workstations in dormitories, library, computer center, student center. Commuter students can connect to campus network. Online library, helpline, repair service, student web hosting, wireless network available.

**Student life. Freshman orientation:** Available, $35 fee. Preregistration for classes offered. **Housing:** Coed dorms, apartments, fraternity/sorority housing available. $100 deposit, deadline 7/2. **Activities:** Jazz band, choral groups, dance, drama, literary magazine, music ensembles, musical theater, opera, student government, student newspaper, symphony orchestra, Chicanos for Creative Medicine, Hispanic business society, society of women engineers, Movimiento Estudiantil Chicanos de Aetlar, Asian student union, black student association, Sisters of the African Star, Vietnamese student association, Latin American society, Chinese American service club.

**Athletics.** NCAA. **Intercollegiate:** Baseball M, basketball, cross-country W, soccer, tennis W, track and field, volleyball W. **Intramural:** Basketball, bowling, gymnastics, handball, judo, racquetball, skiing, soccer, softball, swimming, synchronized swimming, tennis, track and field, volleyball, water polo, wrestling M. **Team name:** Golden Eagles.

**Student services.** Career counseling, student employment services, health services, on-campus daycare, personal counseling, placement for graduates, veterans' counselor. **Physically disabled:** Services for visually, speech, hearing impaired. **Learning disabled:** Comprehensive services available.

**Contact.** E-mail: admission@calstatela.edu
Phone: (323) 343-3901 Fax: (323) 343-3888
Joan Woosley, Director of Admissions and University Registrar, California State University: Los Angeles, 5151 State University Drive SA101, Los Angeles, CA 90032

## California State University: Monterey Bay

Seaside, California     **CB member**
www.csumb.edu     **CB code: 1945**

- Public 4-year liberal arts and teachers college
- Residential campus in large town
- 3,604 degree-seeking undergraduates: 10% part-time, 56% women, 4% African American, 7% Asian American, 28% Hispanic American, 1% Native American, 1% international
- 254 degree-seeking graduate students
- 69% of applicants admitted
- 38% graduate within 6 years

**General.** Founded in 1995. Regionally accredited. Dedicated to serving low-income, adult learner, first-generation, and underrepresented populations. **Degrees:** 598 bachelor's awarded; master's offered. **Location:** 108 miles from San Francisco, 68 miles from San Jose. **Calendar:** Semester, limited summer session. **Full-time faculty:** 105 total; 85% have terminal degrees, 42% minority, 50% women. **Part-time faculty:** 210 total; 23% have terminal degrees, 30% minority, 56% women. **Class size:** 34% < 20, 56% 20-39, 5% 40-49, 5% 50-99, less than 1% >100. **Special facilities:** Watershed facilities to complement earth systems science and policy major, seafloor mapping lab.

**Freshman class profile.** 7,254 applied, 4,996 admitted, 745 enrolled.

| Mid 50% test scores | | | |
|---|---|---|---|
| SAT critical reading: | 430-550 | Rank in top quarter: | 34% |
| SAT math: | 430-550 | Rank in top tenth: | 11% |
| SAT writing: | 430-540 | End year in good standing: | 83% |
| ACT composite: | 18-23 | Return as sophomores: | 67% |
| GPA 3.50 or higher: | 18% | Out-of-state: | 3% |
| GPA 3.0-3.49: | 37% | Live on campus: | 89% |
| GPA 2.0-2.99: | 45% | International: | 1% |

**Basis for selection.** Students must be high school graduates or GED equivalent, complete the 15-unit "a-g" course pattern of college preparatory study with grades of C or better, earn a qualifiable eligibility index. SAT/ACT test scores are not required for those students who earn a GPA of 3.00 or above in high school; 3.61 or above for non-residents. **Homeschooled:** Applicants may be asked to provide supplemental information to document completion of CSU eligibility requirements. **Learning Disabled:** Reviewed case-by-case by Student Disabilities Resources Department.

**High school preparation.** 15 units required. Required units include English 4, mathematics 3, social studies 1, history 1, science 2, foreign language 2, visual/performing arts 1 and academic electives 1. Science lab units must include 1 biological, 1 physical. Language must be the same language both years. History must include U.S. History.

**2007-2008 Annual costs.** Tuition/fees: $3,256; $13,426 out-of-state. Room/board: $9,152. Books/supplies: $1,386. Personal expenses: $2,520.

**Financial aid. Non-need-based:** Scholarships awarded for academics, alumni affiliation, athletics, leadership, state residency.

**Application procedures. Admission:** Closing date 7/15 (postmark date). $55 fee, may be waived for applicants with need. Application may be submitted online. Admission notification on a rolling basis. Must reply by 7/15. Deferral of one semester is permitted. **Financial aid:** Priority date 3/2; no closing date. FAFSA, institutional form required. Applicants notified on a rolling basis starting 2/28.

**Academics. Special study options:** Cross-registration, distance learning, double major, exchange student, independent study, internships, semester at sea, student-designed major, study abroad, teacher certification program. Service Learning. **Credit/placement by examination:** AP, CLEP, IB, SAT, ACT, institutional tests. 30 credit hours maximum toward bachelor's degree. **Support services:** Learning center, reduced course load, remedial instruction, study skills assistance, tutoring, writing center.

**Majors. Biology:** General. **Business:** Business admin. **English:** English lit. **Interdisciplinary:** Global studies. **Liberal arts:** Arts/sciences. **Math:** General. **Psychology:** General. **Other:** Earth systems science & policy, Human communication, Kinesiology, Social and behavioral sciences, Telecommunications, multimedia, and applied computing, Visual and public art, World languages and cultures.

**Most popular majors.** Business/marketing 16%, communications/journalism 8%, computer/information sciences 7%, liberal arts 36%, natural resources/environmental science 6%, public administration/social services 8%, social sciences 11%.

**Computing on campus.** 800 workstations in library, computer center. Dormitories wired for high-speed internet access and linked to campus network. Commuter students can connect to campus network. Online course registration, online library, helpline, student web hosting, wireless network available.

**Student life. Freshman orientation:** Mandatory. **Housing:** Guaranteed on-campus for all undergraduates. Coed dorms, special housing for disabled, apartments, substance-free housing available. $125 fully refundable deposit, deadline 5/1. **Activities:** Bands, campus ministries, choral groups, dance, drama, film society, music ensembles, radio station, student government, student newspaper, Amnesty International, business club, MECHA, Black Students United, baseball club, Raza Unida, art club, photography club, Asian club, sailing club.

**Athletics.** NAIA, NCAA. **Intercollegiate:** Baseball M, basketball, cross-country, golf, sailing, soccer, softball W, volleyball W, water polo. **Intramural:** Basketball, cheerleading, rugby W, sailing, soccer, softball, volleyball. **Team name:** Otters.

**Student services.** Adult student services, alcohol/substance abuse counseling, campus ministries, career counseling, services for economically disadvantaged, student employment services, financial aid counseling, health services, minority student services, on-campus daycare, personal counseling, placement for graduates, veterans' counselor, women's services. **Physically disabled:** Services for visually, speech, hearing impaired.

**Contact.** E-mail: admissions@csumb.edu
Phone: (831) 582-3738 Fax: (831) 582-3783
Ronnie Higgs, AVP, Enrollment Management, California State University: Monterey Bay, 100 Campus Center, Building 47, Seaside, CA 93955-8001

## California State University: Northridge

Northridge, California
www.csun.edu     **CB code: 4707**

- Public 4-year university
- Commuter campus in very large city
- 29,485 degree-seeking undergraduates: 26% part-time, 58% women, 9% African American, 12% Asian American, 29% Hispanic American, 5% international
- 5,962 degree-seeking graduate students
- 69% of applicants admitted
- SAT or ACT required
- 38% graduate within 6 years

**General.** Founded in 1958. Regionally accredited. University center in Ventura. **Degrees:** 5,682 bachelor's awarded; master's offered. **ROTC:** Army, Air Force. **Location:** 20 miles from Los Angeles. **Calendar:** Semester, limited summer session. **Full-time faculty:** 779 total; 31% minority, 43% women. **Part-time faculty:** 1,095 total; 23% minority, 51% women. **Class size:** 15% < 20, 57% 20-39, 16% 40-49, 10% 50-99, 3% >100. **Special facilities:** Anthropology museum, art botanical gardens, urban archives center, observatory, map library, center for the study of cancer and development biology, National Center on Deafness, planetarium.

**Freshman class profile.** 22,756 applied, 15,625 admitted, 4,130 enrolled.

| Mid 50% test scores | | | |
|---|---|---|---|
| SAT critical reading: | 410-520 | Return as sophomores: | 75% |
| SAT math: | 410-540 | Out-of-state: | 2% |
| ACT composite: | 16-21 | International: | 4% |

**Basis for selection.** Index using high school GPA and test scores, and completion of subject requirements. In-state applicants should rank in top third of class; out-of-state in the top sixth. Business administration, economics, engineering, computer science, and physical therapy open to California residents only. Applicants with 3.0 GPA not required to submit test scores. ELM score required for math and English placement. Audition required of music majors.

**High school preparation.** 15 units required. Required units include English 4, mathematics 3, social studies 1, history 1, science 2 (laboratory 2), foreign language 2 and academic electives 1. 1 visual and performing arts.

**2007-2008 Annual costs.** Tuition/fees: $3,300; $13,470 out-of-state. Room/board: $9,350. Books/supplies: $1,350. Personal expenses: $2,520.

**2006-2007 Financial aid. Need-based:** 2,750 full-time freshmen applied for aid; 2,299 were judged to have need; 2,299 of these received aid. Average scholarship/grant was $5,001; average loan $2,434. 62% of total undergraduate aid awarded as scholarships/grants, 38% as loans/jobs. **Non-need-based:** Awarded to 7,726 full-time undergraduates, including 1,804 freshmen. Scholarships awarded for academics, athletics, state residency.

**Application procedures. Admission:** Closing date 11/30. $55 fee, may be waived for applicants with need. Application may be submitted online. Admission notification on a rolling basis beginning on or about 3/1. Must reply by May 1 or within 2 week(s) if notified thereafter. Applications must be completed by November 30 for business administration, economics and physical therapy programs. **Financial aid:** Priority date 3/1; no closing date. FAFSA required. Applicants notified on a rolling basis starting 4/1.

**Academics. Special study options:** Cross-registration, distance learning, double major, dual enrollment of high school students, ESL, exchange student, independent study, internships, student-designed major, study abroad, teacher certification program. **Credit/placement by examination:** AP, CLEP, institutional tests. **Support services:** Learning center, pre-admission summer program, remedial instruction, tutoring.

**Majors. Area/ethnic studies:** African-American, Hispanic-American/Latino/Chicano. **Biology:** General, bacteriology, biochemistry, cell/histology, molecular. **Business:** Banking/financial services, business admin, human resources, management information systems, management science, managerial economics, real estate. **Communications:** Broadcast journalism, journalism. **Computer sciences:** General. **Education:** Art, business, English, family/consumer sciences, foreign languages, health, mathematics, music, physical, social science, social studies, speech impaired. **Engineering:** General, chemical, civil, computer, electrical, materials, mechanical, mechanics. **English:** British lit, creative writing, English lit, speech/rhetoric. **Family/consumer sciences:** General, business, child care, clothing/textiles, family studies, family/community services, food/nutrition, housing. **Foreign languages:** Comparative lit, French, German, linguistics, Spanish. **Health:** Nursing (RN), speech pathology. **History:** General. **Liberal arts:** Arts/sciences. **Math:** General, applied, statistics. **Parks/recreation:** General. **Philosophy/religion:** Philosophy, religion. **Physical sciences:** Chemistry, geology, geophysics, physics, planetary. **Psychology:** General. **Social sciences:** Anthropology, economics, geography, political science, sociology, urban studies. **Visual/performing arts:** Art, art history/conservation, ceramics, commercial/advertising art, crafts, dance, dramatic, drawing, metal/jewelry, music history, music performance, music theory/composition, painting, printmaking, sculpture.

**Most popular majors.** Business/marketing 21%, communications/journalism 7%, English 7%, liberal arts 10%, psychology 9%, social sciences 12%, visual/performing arts 6%.

**Computing on campus.** 723 workstations in library, computer center. Dormitories wired for high-speed internet access and linked to campus network. Commuter students can connect to campus network. Online course registration, online library, helpline, student web hosting, wireless network available.

**Student life. Freshman orientation:** Mandatory. **Housing:** Apartments available. **Activities:** Bands, choral groups, dance, drama, music ensembles, musical theater, radio station, student government, student newspaper, women's center, communities, various clubs and organizations.

**Athletics.** NCAA. **Intercollegiate:** Baseball M, basketball, cross-country, diving, golf, soccer, softball W, swimming, tennis W, track and field, volleyball, water polo W. **Intramural:** Badminton, baseball M, basketball, bowling, cross-country, diving, handball, ice hockey M, racquetball, rugby, sailing, skiing, soccer, softball, swimming, table tennis, tennis, track and field, volleyball. **Team name:** Matadors.

**Student services.** Adult student services, alcohol/substance abuse counseling, career counseling, services for economically disadvantaged, student employment services, financial aid counseling, health services, minority student services, on-campus daycare, personal counseling, placement for graduates, veterans' counselor, women's services. **Physically disabled:** Services for visually, speech, hearing impaired.

**Contact.** E-mail: admissions.records@csun.edu
Phone: (818) 677-3700 Fax: (818) 677-3766
Eric Forbes, Director of Admissions and Records, California State University: Northridge, 18111 Nordhoff Street, Northridge, CA 91328-8207

---

## California State University: Sacramento

Sacramento, California
www.csus.edu

**CB member**
**CB code: 4671**

- Public 4-year university
- Commuter campus in very large city
- 23,724 degree-seeking undergraduates: 24% part-time, 57% women, 7% African American, 19% Asian American, 14% Hispanic American, 1% Native American, 1% international
- 3,651 degree-seeking graduate students
- 67% of applicants admitted
- 39% graduate within 6 years

**General.** Founded in 1947. Regionally accredited. **Degrees:** 4,953 bachelor's awarded; master's, doctoral offered. **ROTC:** Army, Air Force. **Location:** 100 miles from San Francisco. **Calendar:** Semester, extensive summer session. **Full-time faculty:** 834 total; 76% have terminal degrees, 29% minority, 48% women. **Part-time faculty:** 820 total; 28% have terminal degrees, 24% minority, 53% women. **Special facilities:** Aquatic center, anthropology museum, hellenic collection.

**Freshman class profile.** 17,491 applied, 11,658 admitted, 2,466 enrolled.

| Mid 50% test scores | | | |
|---|---|---|---|
| SAT critical reading: | 410-530 | GPA 3.0-3.49: | 43% |
| SAT math: | 430-550 | GPA 2.0-2.99: | 31% |
| ACT composite: | 18-23 | Return as sophomores: | 77% |
| GPA 3.50 or higher: | 25% | Out-of-state: | 1% |
| | | Live on campus: | 26% |

**Basis for selection.** School achievement record, test scores important (GPA weighted 5 times more than test scores). In-state applicants for regular admission normally in top third of class. Test scores not required if high school GPA is 3.0 or higher. ACT or SAT can be used in lieu of placement tests.

**High school preparation.** 15 units required. Required units include English 4, mathematics 3, social studies 1, history 1, science 2 (laboratory 2), foreign language 2, visual/performing arts 1 and academic electives 1. History must be U.S. history/government.

**2007-2008 Annual costs.** Tuition/fees: $3,558; $13,728 out-of-state. Room/board: $10,102. Books/supplies: $1,386. Personal expenses: $2,120.

**2006-2007 Financial aid. Need-based:** 1,471 full-time freshmen applied for aid; 1,139 were judged to have need; 1,014 of these received aid. Average need met was 63%. Average scholarship/grant was $2,123; average loan $2,339. 66% of total undergraduate aid awarded as scholarships/grants, 34% as loans/jobs. **Non-need-based:** Awarded to 866 full-time undergraduates, including 105 freshmen.

**Application procedures. Admission:** Priority date 11/30; deadline 8/1 (receipt date). $55 fee, may be waived for applicants with need. Application may be submitted online. Admission notification on a rolling basis beginning on or about 11/1. Must reply by May 1 or within 2 week(s) if notified thereafter. Early action notification on rolling basis beginning November 1. **Financial aid:** FAFSA required. Applicants notified on a rolling basis starting 4/1; must reply within 4 week(s) of notification.

**Academics. Special study options:** Accelerated study, cooperative education, cross-registration, distance learning, double major, dual enrollment of high school students, ESL, honors, independent study, internships, student-designed major, study abroad, teacher certification program. **Credit/placement by examination:** AP, CLEP, IB, SAT, ACT, institutional tests. SAT/ACT may be used to exempt students from English/math placement tests. **Support services:** Learning center, remedial instruction, study skills assistance, tutoring, writing center.

**Majors. Area/ethnic studies:** Asian. **Biology:** General, cellular/molecular, conservation, microbiology, molecular. **Business:** General, accounting, business admin, finance, human resources, insurance, international, management information systems, marketing, operations, real estate, taxation. **Communications:** General, journalism. **Computer sciences:** General, computer science. **Conservation:** General, environmental studies. **Education:** Early childhood, family/consumer sciences, special. **Engineering:** Civil, computer, electrical, mechanical. **Engineering technology:** Mechanical. **English:** English lit. **Family/consumer sciences:** General, apparel marketing, child development, family studies, food/nutrition. **Foreign languages:** French, Spanish. **Health:** Athletic training, audiology/speech pathology, community health services, health care admin, nursing (RN), occupational health, public health ed. **History:** General. **Interdisciplinary:** Gerontology. **Liberal arts:** Arts/sciences, humanities. **Math:** General. **Parks/recreation:** General, exercise sciences, facilities management, health/fitness. **Philosophy/religion:** Philosophy. **Physical sciences:** General, chemistry, geology, physics. **Protective services:** Criminal justice. **Psychology:** General. **Public administration:** Social work. **Social sciences:** General, anthropology, economics, geography, political science, sociology. **Visual/performing arts:** Art, dance, design, dramatic, graphic design, interior design, music performance, music theory/composition.

**Most popular majors.** Business/marketing 21%, communication technologies 8%, liberal arts 7%, public administration/social services 10%.

**Computing on campus.** 700 workstations in dormitories, library, computer center, student center. Dormitories wired for high-speed internet access and linked to campus network. Commuter students can connect to campus network. Online course registration, helpline, repair service, student web hosting, wireless network available.

**Student life. Freshman orientation:** Available, $60 fee. Preregistration for classes offered. **Housing:** Coed dorms, special housing for disabled, apartments available. Campus affiliated off-campus lofts. **Activities:** Bands, choral groups, dance, drama, international student organizations, music ensembles, musical theater, opera, student government, student newspaper, symphony orchestra, more than 250 clubs, organizations and special interest groups.

**Athletics.** NCAA. **Intercollegiate:** Baseball M, basketball, cheerleading, cross-country, football (tackle) M, golf, gymnastics W, rowing (crew) W, soccer, softball W, tennis, track and field, volleyball W. **Intramural:** Badminton, basketball, bowling, football (tackle) M, golf, handball, ice hockey M, lacrosse M, racquetball, rowing (crew), skiing, soccer, softball, swimming, table tennis, tennis, volleyball, water polo, weight lifting. **Team name:** Hornets.

**Student services.** Adult student services, alcohol/substance abuse counseling, career counseling, services for economically disadvantaged, student employment services, financial aid counseling, health services, legal services, on-campus daycare, personal counseling, placement for graduates, veterans' counselor, women's services. **Physically disabled:** Services for visually, speech, hearing impaired.

**Contact.** E-mail: admissions@csus.edu
Phone: (916) 278-3625 Fax: (916) 278-5603
Emilianio Diaz, Director of Admissions and Outreach, California State University: Sacramento, 6000 J Street, Sacramento, CA 95819-6048

---

## California State University: San Bernardino
**San Bernardino, California** — CB member
www.csusb.edu — CB code: 4099

- Public 4-year university and liberal arts college
- Commuter campus in small city
- 13,311 degree-seeking undergraduates: 17% part-time, 65% women, 12% African American, 8% Asian American, 37% Hispanic American, 1% Native American, 3% international
- 2,385 degree-seeking graduate students
- 61% of applicants admitted
- SAT or ACT (ACT writing optional) required
- 41% graduate within 6 years

**General.** Founded in 1962. Regionally accredited. Palm Desert satellite campus offers day and evening courses in degree and credential programs. **Degrees:** 2,595 bachelor's awarded; master's, doctoral offered. **ROTC:** Army, Air Force. **Location:** 60 miles from Los Angeles. **Calendar:** Quarter, limited summer session. **Full-time faculty:** 450 total; 23% minority, 45% women. **Part-time faculty:** 183 total; 20% minority, 45% women. **Class size:** 30% < 20, 47% 20-39, 8% 40-49, 11% 50-99, 5% >100. **Special facilities:** Animal house, greenhouse, desert studies center.

**Freshman class profile.** 9,987 applied, 6,107 admitted, 1,722 enrolled.

| Mid 50% test scores | | | |
|---|---|---|---|
| SAT critical reading: | 400-510 | Rank in top tenth: | 21% |
| SAT math: | 410-520 | Return as sophomores: | 82% |
| ACT composite: | 16-21 | Out-of-state: | 1% |
| GPA 3.50 or higher: | 23% | Live on campus: | 21% |
| GPA 3.0-3.49: | 44% | International: | 4% |
| GPA 2.0-2.99: | 33% | Fraternities: | 8% |
| Rank in top quarter: | 37% | Sororities: | 6% |

**Basis for selection.** High school GPA and test scores most important. SAT/ACT not required if high school GPA is 3.0 or higher. Entering undergraduates, except those who qualify for exemption, must take CSU entry-level mathematics (ELM) examination and CSU English placement test (EPT) after admission and before they enroll in classes.

**High school preparation.** 15 units required. Required units include English 4, mathematics 3, social studies 1, history 1, science 2 (laboratory 2), foreign language 2 and academic electives 1. One visual and performing arts unit also required. Students with disabilities may substitute alternate courses for specific subject requirements.

**2007-2008 Annual costs.** Tuition/fees: $3,440; $13,610 out-of-state. Room/board: $9,000. Books/supplies: $1,380. Personal expenses: $2,223.

**Application procedures. Admission:** No deadline. $55 fee, may be waived for applicants with need. Admission notification on a rolling basis. Students may apply as late as 3 weeks into quarter. **Financial aid:** Priority date 3/2; no closing date. FAFSA required. Applicants notified on a rolling basis starting 4/1.

**Academics. Special study options:** Accelerated study, cooperative education, cross-registration, distance learning, double major, dual enrollment of high school students, exchange student, honors, independent study, internships, study abroad, teacher certification program. School of Social and Behavioral Sciences offers master's in National Security Studies. **Credit/placement by examination:** AP, CLEP, IB, SAT, ACT, institutional tests. 40 credit hours maximum toward bachelor's degree. **Support services:** Learning center, pre-admission summer program, remedial instruction, tutoring, writing center.

**Majors. Area/ethnic studies:** African-American, American, Hispanic-American/Latino/Chicano. **Biology:** General, biochemistry. **Business:** Accounting, business admin, finance, human resources, international, management information systems, managerial economics, marketing, operations, organizational behavior, real estate. **Communications:** General, radio/tv. **Computer sciences:** Computer science, systems analysis. **Conservation:** Environmental studies. **Education:** Physical, trade/industrial. **English:** Creative writing, English lit. **Family/consumer sciences:** Child development, family studies, food/nutrition. **Foreign languages:** French, Spanish. **Health:** Environmental health, health care admin, nursing (RN), premedicine. **History:** General. **Interdisciplinary:** Museum. **Liberal arts:** Arts/sciences, humanities. **Math:** General. **Parks/recreation:** Exercise sciences. **Philosophy/religion:** Philosophy. **Physical sciences:** Chemistry, geology, physics. **Protective services:** Law enforcement admin. **Psychology:** General. **Public administration:** General, social work. **Social sciences:** General, anthropology, economics, geography, political science, sociology. **Visual/performing arts:** Art, art history/conservation, commercial/advertising art, dramatic, music history, music performance, musicology, studio arts, theater design, theater history.

**Most popular majors.** Business/marketing 23%, liberal arts 17%, psychology 8%, security/protective services 7%, social sciences 9%.

**Computing on campus.** 600 workstations in dormitories, library, computer center, student center. Dormitories wired for high-speed internet access and linked to campus network. Commuter students can connect to campus network. Online course registration, online library available.

**Student life. Freshman orientation:** Available. Preregistration for classes offered. **Housing:** Coed dorms, single-sex dorms, apartments, substance-free housing available. $50 deposit. **Activities:** Jazz band, choral groups, dance, drama, music ensembles, musical theater, radio station, student government, student newspaper, TV station, more than 80 clubs and organizations.

**Athletics.** NCAA. **Intercollegiate:** Baseball M, basketball, cross-country W, golf M, soccer, softball W, swimming, tennis W, volleyball W, water polo. **Intramural:** Basketball, field hockey W, soccer, softball M, volleyball. **Team name:** Coyotes.

**Student services.** Adult student services, career counseling, student employment services, financial aid counseling, health services, legal services, minority student services, on-campus daycare, personal counseling, placement for graduates, veterans' counselor, women's services. **Physically disabled:** Services for visually, speech, hearing impaired.

**Contact.** E-mail: moreinfo@mail.csusb.edu
Phone: (909) 537-5188 Fax: (909) 537-7034
Olivia Rosas, Director of Admissions and Student Recruitment, California State University: San Bernardino, 5500 University Parkway, San Bernardino, CA 92407-2397

---

## California State University: San Marcos
**San Marcos, California** — CB member
www.csusm.edu — CB code: 5677

- Public 4-year university
- Commuter campus in large town
- 7,997 degree-seeking undergraduates: 25% part-time, 61% women
- 581 degree-seeking graduate students
- 77% graduate within 6 years

**General.** Founded in 1989. Regionally accredited. **Degrees:** 1,357 bachelor's awarded; master's offered. **ROTC:** Army, Naval, Air Force. **Location:** 30 miles from San Diego. **Calendar:** Semester, limited summer session. **Full-time faculty:** 205 total; 100% have terminal degrees, 39% minority, 50% women. **Part-time faculty:** 296 total; 18% minority, 56% women. **Class size:** 18% < 20, 60% 20-39, 15% 40-49, 5% 50-99, 2% >100.

## Freshman class profile.

| Mid 50% test scores | | | | |
|---|---|---|---|---|
| SAT critical reading: | 430-530 | GPA 2.0-2.99: | 38% |
| SAT math: | 440-540 | Return as sophomores: | 70% |
| GPA 3.50 or higher: | 17% | Out-of-state: | 1% |
| GPA 3.0-3.49: | 45% | Live on campus: | 39% |
| | | International: | 2% |

**Basis for selection.** Student eligibility index calculated on GPA and test score combination. SAT scores can be used to meet English or math proficiency requirements. **Learning Disabled:** C or better grades in all college preparatory classes -- Minimum GPA-2.0.

**High school preparation.** 15 units required; 16 recommended. Required and recommended units include English 4, mathematics 3-4, social studies 1, history 1, science 2 (laboratory 2), foreign language 2, visual/performing arts 1 and academic electives 1.

**2007-2008 Annual costs.** Tuition/fees: $3,374; $13,544 out-of-state. Room/board: $9,090. Books/supplies: $1,386. Personal expenses: $2,520.

**2006-2007 Financial aid. Need-based:** 99% of total undergraduate aid awarded as scholarships/grants, 1% as loans/jobs. **Non-need-based:** Scholarships awarded for academics, athletics, leadership, state residency.

**Application procedures. Admission:** Closing date 11/30. $55 fee, may be waived for applicants with need. Application may be submitted online. Admission notification on a rolling basis beginning on or about 11/1. Must reply by May 1 or within 3 week(s) if notified thereafter.

**Academics. Special study options:** Cross-registration, distance learning, double major, dual enrollment of high school students, ESL, independent study, internships, student-designed major, study abroad, teacher certification program, weekend college. Evening degree program, Program for Adult College Education (PACE), saturday classes, Air Force ROTC, extended studies, open university, special sessions, including winter. **Credit/placement by examination:** AP, CLEP, IB, institutional tests. 30 credit hours maximum toward bachelor's degree. **Support services:** Learning center, pre-admission summer program, study skills assistance, tutoring, writing center.

**Majors. Area/ethnic studies:** Women's. **Biology:** General. **Business:** Business admin. **Communications:** General. **Computer sciences:** General, computer science. **English:** English lit. **Family/consumer sciences:** Family studies. **Foreign languages:** Spanish. **History:** General. **Liberal arts:** Arts/sciences. **Math:** General. **Physical sciences:** Chemistry. **Psychology:** General. **Social sciences:** General, economics, political science, sociology. **Visual/performing arts:** General.

**Most popular majors.** Business/marketing 27%, communications/journalism 9%, liberal arts 15%, psychology 8%, social sciences 27%.

**Computing on campus.** 1,100 workstations in library, computer center. Commuter students can connect to campus network. Online course registration, helpline, wireless network available.

**Student life. Freshman orientation:** Mandatory, $70 fee. One-day program. **Housing:** Special housing for disabled, apartments available. $50 nonrefundable deposit, deadline 10/1. **Activities:** Choral groups, dance, drama, music ensembles, student newspaper, American Indian Science Engineering Society, Circle K, InterVarsity Christian Fellowship, Latter-day Saints student association, accounting society, Black Men on Campus, College Democrats, pre-health society, student housing asociation.

**Athletics.** NAIA. **Intercollegiate:** Baseball M, cross-country, golf, soccer, softball W, track and field. **Team name:** Cougars.

**Student services.** Adult student services, alcohol/substance abuse counseling, career counseling, services for economically disadvantaged, student employment services, financial aid counseling, health services, on-campus daycare, personal counseling, placement for graduates, veterans' counselor. **Physically disabled:** Services for visually, speech, hearing impaired.

**Contact.** E-mail: apply@csusm.edu
Phone: (760) 750-4848
Nathan Evans, Director of Admissions and Recruitment, California State University: San Marcos, 333 South Twin Oaks Valley Road, San Marcos, CA 92096-0001

## California State University: Stanislaus

**Turlock, California**  CB member
**www.csustan.edu**  CB code: 4713

- Public 4-year business and liberal arts college
- Commuter campus in small city

- 6,883 degree-seeking undergraduates
- 1,748 graduate students

**General.** Founded in 1957. Regionally accredited. **Degrees:** 1,459 bachelor's awarded; master's offered. **Location:** 15 miles from Modesto. **Calendar:** 4-1-4, extensive summer session. **Full-time faculty:** 292 total; 81% have terminal degrees, 22% minority, 46% women. **Part-time faculty:** 219 total; 23% have terminal degrees, 18% minority, 51% women. **Class size:** 38% < 20, 48% 20-39, 7% 40-49, 6% 50-99, 1% >100. **Special facilities:** Observatory, interactive television classrooms, laser laboratory, marine sciences station, greenhouse, mainstage theater, bio-ag eco building.

## Freshman class profile.

| Mid 50% test scores | | | |
|---|---|---|---|
| SAT critical reading: | 410-530 | GPA 3.0-3.49: | 40% |
| SAT math: | 430-540 | GPA 2.0-2.99: | 27% |
| ACT composite: | 17-23 | Out-of-state: | 2% |
| GPA 3.50 or higher: | 33% | Live on campus: | 31% |

**Basis for selection.** High school GPA, courses taken, and test scores. Special consideration for veterans, low-income, and minority applicants. For non-native English speakers, ELPT can be substituted for TOEFL for placement. Exemptions result from scoring well on other specified tests or completion of appropriate courses. Test scores required if high school GPA is less than 3.0. Interview recommended for theatre arts and music majors. Audition recommended for music majors. Portfolio recommended for art majors. **Homeschooled:** Transcript of courses and grades, interview required. Applicant must submit SAT or ACT scores. **Learning Disabled:** Students with diagnosed learning disability or neurological disorder that significantly impairs academic performance in specified area may be eligible for waiver of General Education Breadth (GEB) requirement. Additional coursework required in lieu of GEB. Contact Disabled Student Services or submit documentation of disability.

**High school preparation.** 15 units required. Required units include English 4, mathematics 3, history 2, science 2 (laboratory 2), foreign language 2, visual/performing arts 1 and academic electives 1. History units include history/social studies.

**2007-2008 Annual costs.** Tuition/fees: $3,307; $13,477 out-of-state. Room/board: $8,757. Books/supplies: $1,386. Personal expenses: $2,007.

**Financial aid. Non-need-based:** Scholarships awarded for academics, alumni affiliation, art, athletics, leadership, minority status, music/drama, state residency.

**Application procedures. Admission:** Priority date 11/30; deadline 7/1. $55 fee, may be waived for applicants with need. Application may be submitted online. Admission notification on a rolling basis beginning on or about 1/1. Must reply by May 1 or within 4 week(s) if notified thereafter. **Financial aid:** Priority date 3/2; no closing date. FAFSA required. Applicants notified on a rolling basis starting 3/15; must reply within 3 week(s) of notification.

**Academics. Special study options:** Cooperative education, distance learning, double major, dual enrollment of high school students, ESL, exchange student, honors, independent study, internships, liberal arts/career combination, student-designed major, study abroad, teacher certification program. **Credit/placement by examination:** AP, CLEP, IB, SAT, ACT, institutional tests. 24 credit hours maximum toward bachelor's degree. Credit by examination does not count toward residency requirement. **Support services:** Learning center, pre-admission summer program, reduced course load, remedial instruction, study skills assistance, tutoring, writing center.

**Majors. Agriculture:** General. **Biology:** General. **Business:** Business admin. **Communications:** General. **Computer sciences:** Computer science, information technology. **Education:** Early childhood. **English:** English lit. **Foreign languages:** Spanish. **Health:** Nursing (RN). **History:** General. **Liberal arts:** Arts/sciences. **Math:** General. **Parks/recreation:** Health/fitness. **Philosophy/religion:** Philosophy. **Physical sciences:** General, chemistry, geology, physics. **Protective services:** Criminal justice. **Psychology:** General, cognitive. **Social sciences:** General, anthropology, economics, geography, political science, sociology. **Visual/performing arts:** Art, dramatic, music performance, studio arts.

**Most popular majors.** Business/marketing 18%, liberal arts 25%, psychology 8%, security/protective services 6%, social sciences 13%.

**Computing on campus.** 150 workstations in dormitories, library, computer center, student center. Dormitories wired for high-speed internet access and linked to campus network. Commuter students can connect to campus network. Online course registration, online library, helpline, wireless network available.

**Student life. Freshman orientation:** Available. Preregistration for classes offered. Held year-round. **Housing:** Coed dorms, apartments available. $340 partly refundable deposit. Summer housing available and some housing units can accomodate disabled students. **Activities:** Bands, choral groups, dance, drama, music ensembles, musical theater, opera, radio station, student government, student newspaper, symphony orchestra, Baha'i club, chinese student association, Chi Alpha Christian Fellowship, College Republicans, CSUS Democrats, Hunger Network, MEChA, Rainbow Alliance, Umoja, women's advocacy organization.

**Athletics.** NCAA. **Intercollegiate:** Baseball M, basketball, cross-country, golf M, soccer, softball W, track and field, volleyball W. **Intramural:** Basketball, football (non-tackle) M, soccer M, softball, volleyball. **Team name:** Warriors.

**Student services.** Adult student services, alcohol/substance abuse counseling, career counseling, services for economically disadvantaged, student employment services, financial aid counseling, health services, minority student services, on-campus daycare, personal counseling, placement for graduates, veterans' counselor, women's services. **Physically disabled:** Services for visually, speech, hearing impaired. **Learning disabled:** Comprehensive services available.

**Contact.** E-mail: Outreach_Help_Desk@csustan.edu
Phone: (209) 667-3070 Toll-free number: (800) 300-7420
Fax: (209) 667-3788
Lisa Bernardo, Dean of Admissions, California State University: Stanislaus, 801 West Monte Vista Avenue, Turlock, CA 95382-0256

---

## California University of Management and Sciences
### Anaheim, California
### www.calums.edu

- Private 4-year business and health science college
- Very large city
- 95 degree-seeking undergraduates: 11% part-time, 27% women
- 37 degree-seeking graduate students
- 92% of applicants admitted
- Application essay, interview required

**General.** Regionally accredited; also accredited by ACICS. **Degrees:** 10 bachelor's, 6 associate awarded; master's offered. **Calendar:** Quarter. **Full-time faculty:** 7 total; 86% have terminal degrees, 14% women. **Part-time faculty:** 18 total; 72% have terminal degrees, 11% women.

**Freshman class profile.** 48 applied, 44 admitted, 44 enrolled.

| | | | |
|---|---|---|---|
| End year in good standing: | 100% | Return as sophomores: | 77% |

**Basis for selection.** School record, GPA, interview most important followed by class rank, test scores, essay and recommendations. Completion of high school education is required among applicants for Associate and Bachelor degree programs. TOEFL test scores, EPAT test scores, and Wonderlic Test scores are used for admission purposes. **Homeschooled:** Transcript of courses and grades, interview required.

**2007-2008 Annual costs.** Tuition/fees: $5,790.

**Application procedures. Admission:** Closing date 9/9 (receipt date). $100 fee. Application may be submitted online.

**Academics. Special study options:** Combined bachelor's/graduate degree, ESL, independent study. **Credit/placement by examination:** AP, CLEP, institutional tests. **Support services:** Remedial instruction, tutoring.

**Majors. Business:** Business admin. **Computer sciences:** General.

**Computing on campus.** 20 workstations in computer center. Online library, wireless network available.

**Student life. Freshman orientation:** Mandatory. Preregistration for classes offered.

**Contact.** E-mail: helenk@calums.edu
Phone: (714) 533-3946 Fax: (714) 533-7778
Helen Kim, Director of Admissions, California University of Management and Sciences, 721 North Euclid Streeet, Anaheim, CA 92801

---

## Chapman University
### Orange, California
### www.chapman.edu
**CB member**
**CB code: 4047**

- Private 4-year university and liberal arts college affiliated with Christian Church (Disciples of Christ)
- Residential campus in very large city

- 4,169 degree-seeking undergraduates: 5% part-time, 59% women, 2% African American, 8% Asian American, 10% Hispanic American, 1% Native American, 2% international
- 1,824 degree-seeking graduate students
- 49% of applicants admitted
- SAT or ACT with writing, application essay required
- 67% graduate within 6 years

**General.** Founded in 1861. Regionally accredited. **Degrees:** 898 bachelor's awarded; master's, doctoral, first professional offered. **ROTC:** Army, Air Force. **Location:** 35 miles from Los Angeles, 60 miles from San Diego. **Calendar:** 4-1-4, limited summer session. **Full-time faculty:** 309 total; 90% have terminal degrees, 14% minority, 40% women. **Part-time faculty:** 298 total; 43% women. **Class size:** 36% < 20, 60% 20-39, 2% 40-49, 2% 50-99, less than 1% >100. **Special facilities:** Albert Schweitzer collection of photographs, artifacts, and memorabilia, holocaust memorial library.

**Freshman class profile.** 4,861 applied, 2,399 admitted, 937 enrolled.

| Mid 50% test scores | | Rank in top tenth: | 55% |
|---|---|---|---|
| SAT critical reading: | 550-670 | End year in good standing: | 91% |
| SAT math: | 550-670 | Return as sophomores: | 87% |
| SAT writing: | 560-670 | Out-of-state: | 32% |
| ACT composite: | 25-29 | Live on campus: | 88% |
| GPA 3.50 or higher: | 68% | International: | 3% |
| GPA 3.0-3.49: | 27% | Fraternities: | 12% |
| GPA 2.0-2.99: | 5% | Sororities: | 16% |
| Rank in top quarter: | 91% | | |

**Basis for selection.** Academic course work plus GPA and test scores most important. Recommendations, essay, extracurricular activities also considered. SAT Subject Tests recommended. Interview recommended. Audition required for music, dance, theater majors. Portfolio required for art, film majors. Supplemental application required for film majors. **Homeschooled:** Statement describing homeschool structure and mission, state high school equivalency certificate required.

**High school preparation.** 11 units required; 16 recommended. Required and recommended units include English 2-4, mathematics 2-3, social studies 3-4, science 2-3 (laboratory 1) and foreign language 2-3.

**2008-2009 Annual costs.** Tuition/fees: $34,700. Room/board: $11,315. Books/supplies: $1,100. Personal expenses: $1,500.

**2006-2007 Financial aid. Need-based:** 859 full-time freshmen applied for aid; 529 were judged to have need; 529 of these received aid. Average need met was 100%. Average scholarship/grant was $20,323; average loan $3,522. 76% of total undergraduate aid awarded as scholarships/grants, 24% as loans/jobs. **Non-need-based:** Awarded to 980 full-time undergraduates, including 200 freshmen. Scholarships awarded for academics, alumni affiliation, art, music/drama, religious affiliation, ROTC.

**Application procedures. Admission:** Closing date 1/15 (postmark date). $55 fee, may be waived for applicants with need. Application may be submitted online. Admission notification on a rolling basis beginning on or about 3/1. Must reply by May 1 or within 2 week(s) if notified thereafter. **Financial aid:** Priority date 3/2; no closing date. FAFSA required. Applicants notified on a rolling basis starting 3/15; must reply within 3 week(s) of notification.

**Academics. Special study options:** Distance learning, double major, ESL, exchange student, honors, independent study, internships, liberal arts/career combination, semester at sea, student-designed major, study abroad, teacher certification program, Washington semester. **Credit/placement by examination:** AP, CLEP, IB, SAT, ACT, institutional tests. 32 credit hours maximum toward bachelor's degree. **Support services:** Learning center, reduced course load, remedial instruction, study skills assistance, tutoring, writing center.

**Majors. Biology:** General, biochemistry, exercise physiology, molecular. **Business:** Accounting, business admin, managerial economics, organizational behavior. **Communications:** General, advertising, broadcast journalism. **Computer sciences:** General, computer science. **Education:** Music. **English:** Creative writing, English lit. **Foreign languages:** French, Spanish. **Health:** Athletic training, music therapy, predental, premedicine, preveterinary. **History:** General. **Interdisciplinary:** Peace/conflict. **Liberal arts:** Arts/sciences. **Math:** General. **Philosophy/religion:** Philosophy, religion. **Physical sciences:** Chemistry. **Psychology:** General. **Public administration:** Social work. **Social sciences:** Political science, sociology. **Visual/performing arts:** Art, art history/conservation, cinematography, conducting, dance, dramatic, film/cinema, graphic design, music performance, music theory/composition, play/screenwriting, studio arts, voice/opera.

**Most popular majors.** Business/marketing 23%, communications/journalism 15%, liberal arts 6%, psychology 6%, visual/performing arts 23%.

**Computing on campus.** 453 workstations in dormitories, library, computer center. Dormitories wired for high-speed internet access and linked to campus network. Commuter students can connect to campus network. Online course registration, online library, helpline, repair service, student web hosting, wireless network available.

**Student life. Freshman orientation:** Mandatory, $140 fee. Preregistration for classes offered. 5-day summer program immediately preceding start of semester. **Housing:** Guaranteed on-campus for freshmen. Coed dorms, special housing for disabled, apartments, substance-free housing available. $600 deposit, deadline 5/1. Housing for married, single, and students with dependents available. **Activities:** Bands, campus ministries, choral groups, dance, drama, film society, international student organizations, literary magazine, music ensembles, Model UN, musical theater, opera, radio station, student government, student newspaper, symphony orchestra, Hillel, black student union, Model UN, gay/lesbian/bisexual association, Disciples on Campus, MEChA, Students for Peaceful Empowerment Action and Knowledge, Asian Pacific student association, student organization of Latinos.

**Athletics.** NCAA. **Intercollegiate:** Baseball M, basketball, cross-country, football (tackle) M, golf M, rowing (crew) W, soccer, softball W, swimming W, tennis, track and field W, volleyball W, water polo. **Intramural:** Basketball, soccer, tennis, volleyball. **Team name:** Panthers.

**Student services.** Adult student services, alcohol/substance abuse counseling, campus ministries, career counseling, student employment services, financial aid counseling, health services, on-campus daycare, personal counseling, placement for graduates, veterans' counselor. **Physically disabled:** Services for visually, speech, hearing impaired.

**Contact.** E-mail: admit@chapman.edu
Phone: (714) 997-6711 Toll-free number: (888) 282-7759
Fax: (714) 997-6713
Michael Drummy, Assistant Vice President and Chief Admission Officer, Chapman University, One University Drive, Orange, CA 92866

## Charles R. Drew University of Medicine and Science
### Los Angeles, California
www.cdrewu.edu      CB code: 4982

- Private 4-year university and health science college
- Commuter campus in very large city
- 294 degree-seeking undergraduates
- 263 graduate students
- 27% of applicants admitted
- Application essay, interview required

**General.** Regionally accredited. **Degrees:** 30 bachelor's, 75 associate awarded; master's, first professional offered. **Calendar:** Trimester, limited summer session. **Full-time faculty:** 75 total. **Part-time faculty:** 44 total. **Special facilities:** Biomedical library, basic, clinical and population-based research facilities.

**Freshman class profile.** 300 applied, 80 admitted, 65 enrolled.

| Out-of-state: | 10% | Live on campus: | 5% |
|---|---|---|---|

**Basis for selection.** High school/college transcripts, performance on institutional examination if required by program, essay if required all considered.

**2008-2009 Annual costs.** Tuition/fees (projected): $4,250. Tuition $200/ unit for associate degree programs, $250/unit for bachelor's degree programs, $400/unit for graduate degree programs. Required fees vary by program and enrollment. Room/board: $18,132.

**2007-2008 Financial aid. Need-based:** 46% of total undergraduate aid awarded as scholarships/grants, 54% as loans/jobs.

**Application procedures. Admission:** $35 fee. Application deadlines vary by program.

**Academics.** Pre-admission assessment examinations. Tutoring. College learning skills workshops. Community service learning. Career center. Academic counseling. Computer-assisted instruction. A fully-equipped computer library with a broad variety of computer programs. **Special study options:** Accelerated study, combined bachelor's/graduate degree, cross-registration, distance learning, double major, dual enrollment of high school students, independent study, internships, liberal arts/career combination. **Credit/placement by examination:** AP, CLEP, IB, institutional tests. **Support services:** Learning center, pre-admission summer program, reduced course load, remedial instruction, study skills assistance, tutoring, writing center.

**Majors. Biology:** Biomedical sciences. **Health:** Health services, health services admin, nuclear medical technology, physician assistant, premedicine, radiologic technology/medical imaging, sonography.

**Computing on campus.** 100 workstations in library, computer center, student center. Commuter students can connect to campus network. Online course registration, online library, helpline, wireless network available.

**Student life. Freshman orientation:** Mandatory. Preregistration for classes offered. **Housing:** Off-campus housing available via California State University Dominguez Hills.

**Contact.** E-mail: makaylahall@cdrewu.edu
Phone: (323) 563-5886 Fax: (323) 569-0597
Makayla Hall, Director of Admissions, Charles R. Drew University of Medicine and Science, 1731 East 120th Street, Los Angeles, CA 90059

## Claremont McKenna College
### Claremont, California
www.claremontmckenna.edu      CB member      CB code: 4054

- Private 4-year liberal arts college
- Residential campus in large town
- 1,135 degree-seeking undergraduates: 46% women, 4% African American, 13% Asian American, 13% Hispanic American, 5% international
- 18% of applicants admitted
- SAT or ACT with writing, application essay required
- 89% graduate within 6 years

**General.** Founded in 1946. Regionally accredited. One of a cluster of 5 undergraduate and 2 graduate schools on adjoining campuses. Campuses share facilities. Cross-enrollment available at any of the 5 colleges, which include Claremont McKenna, Harvey Mudd, Pitzer, Pomona, and Scripps. **Degrees:** 284 bachelor's awarded. **ROTC:** Army, Air Force. **Location:** 35 miles from Los Angeles. **Calendar:** Semester. **Full-time faculty:** 112 total; 100% have terminal degrees, 21% minority, 30% women. **Part-time faculty:** 31 total; 81% have terminal degrees, 19% minority, 32% women. **Class size:** 86% < 20, 13% 20-39, 1% 40-49, less than 1% 50-99. **Special facilities:** 11 research institutes, athenaeum (center of intellectual, cultural, and social activities), science center, leadership laboratory.

**Freshman class profile.** 3,778 applied, 671 admitted, 268 enrolled.

| Mid 50% test scores | | Return as sophomores: | 96% |
|---|---|---|---|
| SAT critical reading: | 640-740 | Out-of-state: | 51% |
| SAT math: | 650-740 | Live on campus: | 100% |
| Rank in top quarter: | 98% | International: | 4% |
| Rank in top tenth: | 84% | | |

**Basis for selection.** School achievement record and test scores most important. Extracurricular activities, curriculum, recommendations, essays, interview, and motivation considered. There is also an emphasis on leadership which is examined in the high school career. **Homeschooled:** Interview required. SAT Subject Tests required in 3 subjects (math, English, and one of choice).

**High school preparation.** Required and recommended units include English 4, mathematics 3-4, social studies 1, history 1, science 2-3 (laboratory 2) and foreign language 3. Management-engineering candidates and science majors should have had both physics and chemistry.

**2007-2008 Annual costs.** Tuition/fees: $35,400. Room/board: $11,330. Books/supplies: $900. Personal expenses: $1,000.

**2007-2008 Financial aid. Need-based:** 151 full-time freshmen applied for aid; 129 were judged to have need; 129 of these received aid. Average need met was 100%. Average scholarship/grant was $32,126; average loan $2,624. 92% of total undergraduate aid awarded as scholarships/grants, 8% as loans/jobs. **Non-need-based:** Awarded to 193 full-time undergraduates, including 54 freshmen. Scholarships awarded for academics.

**Application procedures. Admission:** Closing date 1/2 (postmark date). $60 fee, may be waived for applicants with need. Application may be submitted online. Admission notification 4/1. Must reply by 5/1. **Financial aid:** Closing date 2/1. FAFSA, CSS PROFILE required. Applicants notified by 4/1; must reply by 5/1.

**Academics.** Philosophy, Politics and economics (PPE) major patterned after program at Oxford University available to 12-15 new students each year. Students accepted spring of sophomore year. Environment, economics, and politics (EEP) major also offered. **Special study options:** Combined bachelor's/graduate degree, cross-registration, double major, exchange student, independent study, internships, student-designed major, study abroad, Washington semester. **Credit/placement by examination:** AP, CLEP, IB, institutional tests. 16 credit hours maximum toward bachelor's degree. **Support services:** Tutoring, writing center.

**Majors. Area/ethnic studies:** African-American, American, Asian, Asian-American, European, gay/lesbian, Hispanic-American/Latino/Chicano, Latin American, Pacific, regional, South Asian, Southeast Asian, Spanish/Iberian, Western European, women's. **Biology:** General, biochemistry. **Business:** Accounting, accounting/business management, managerial economics. **Communications:** Media studies. **Computer sciences:** Computer science. **Conservation:** Environmental science, environmental studies. **Engineering:** General. **English:** English lit. **Foreign languages:** Chinese, classics, French, German, Italian, Japanese, Russian, Spanish. **Health:** Premedicine. **History:** General. **Interdisciplinary:** Math/computer science, neuroscience. **Legal studies:** General, prelaw. **Math:** General. **Philosophy/religion:** Philosophy, religion. **Physical sciences:** Chemistry, physics. **Psychology:** General. **Social sciences:** Economics, international relations, political science. **Visual/performing arts:** Art, dance, dramatic.

**Most popular majors.** Business/marketing 7%, history 6%, interdisciplinary studies 8%, psychology 9%, social sciences 43%.

**Computing on campus.** 156 workstations in dormitories, library, computer center, student center. Dormitories wired for high-speed internet access and linked to campus network. Commuter students can connect to campus network. Online library, helpline, repair service, student web hosting, wireless network available.

**Student life. Freshman orientation:** Mandatory. 5-day program. Parents invited for first day. **Policies:** Full-time rabbi, priest, and Protestant minister on campus. Also services for Mormon, Islamic, Christian Science, Quaker, and B'hai faiths. **Housing:** Guaranteed on-campus for all undergraduates. Coed dorms, special housing for disabled, apartments, substance-free housing available. $190 fully refundable deposit, deadline 7/1. **Activities:** Choral groups, dance, drama, international student organizations, literary magazine, music ensembles, Model UN, musical theater, radio station, student government, student newspaper, symphony orchestra, TV station, debate/forensics, volunteer service, Young Republicans, Young Democrats, Pan-African Students Association, MECHA, Asian American Student Alliance, religious activities center, intervarsity faith team (Christian nondenominational), Hillel.

**Athletics.** NCAA. **Intercollegiate:** Baseball M, basketball, cross-country, diving, football (tackle) M, golf, lacrosse W, soccer, softball W, swimming, tennis, track and field, volleyball W, water polo. **Intramural:** Archery, badminton, basketball, bowling, fencing, racquetball, rugby, sailing, skiing, soccer, softball, squash, swimming, tennis, track and field, volleyball, water polo, weight lifting. **Team name:** Stags (M), Athenas (W).

**Student services.** Campus ministries, career counseling, student employment services, financial aid counseling, health services, minority student services, personal counseling, placement for graduates, women's services. **Physically disabled:** Services for visually, speech, hearing impaired. **Learning disabled:** Comprehensive services available.

**Contact.** E-mail: admission@claremontmckenna.edu
Phone: (909) 621-8088 Fax: (909) 621-8516
Richard Vos, Vice President and Dean of Admissions and Financial Aid, Claremont McKenna College, 890 Columbia Avenue, Claremont, CA 91711-6425

---

## Cogswell Polytechnical College
**Sunnyvale, California**
www.cogswell.edu
CB code: 4057

- Private 4-year visual arts and engineering college
- Commuter campus in small city
- 230 degree-seeking undergraduates: 52% part-time, 18% women, 3% African American, 11% Asian American, 9% Hispanic American
- 61% of applicants admitted
- Application essay required
- 42% graduate within 6 years

**General.** Founded in 1887. Regionally accredited. Program fusion of art and engineering. **Degrees:** 82 bachelor's awarded. **Location:** 45 miles from San Francisco, 4 miles from San Jose. **Calendar:** Semester, extensive summer session. **Full-time faculty:** 10 total; 60% have terminal degrees, 20% women. **Part-time faculty:** 36 total; 11% have terminal degrees, 28% women. **Class size:** 98% < 20, 2% 20-39. **Special facilities:** Electronic music laboratories, sound/recording studio, video studio, editing studio, computer imaging laboratories, SGI laboratory, MIDI laboratory, sculpture studio, drawing/painting studio, 2D and 3D animation laboratories.

**Freshman class profile.** 41 applied, 25 admitted, 22 enrolled.

| | | | |
|---|---|---|---|
| GPA 3.50 or higher: | 17% | End year in good standing: | 66% |
| GPA 3.0-3.49: | 28% | Return as sophomores: | 83% |
| GPA 2.0-2.99: | 55% | | |

**Basis for selection.** Motivation, 2.7 GPA in academic subjects, test scores most important. Recommendations, art portfolio required for art programs, personal essay. Interview recommended. Portfolio required for all digital art programs. **Homeschooled:** Transcript of courses and grades, state high school equivalency certificate, letter of recommendation (nonparent) required. **Learning Disabled:** Must be documented by medical/psych. professional.

**High school preparation.** 7 units required. Required units include English 3, mathematics 3, science 1, computer science 1 and visual/performing arts 1. 1 algebra, 1 geometry, 1 trigonometry required for engineering program; or 1 algebra, 1 geometry required for art programs.

**2007-2008 Annual costs.** Tuition/fees: $16,548.

**2006-2007 Financial aid. Need-based:** 35% of total undergraduate aid awarded as scholarships/grants, 65% as loans/jobs. **Non-need-based:** Scholarships awarded for academics.

**Application procedures. Admission:** Closing date 3/1 (receipt date). $55 fee, may be waived for applicants with need. Application may be submitted online. Admission notification on a rolling basis. **Financial aid:** Priority date 3/2; no closing date. FAFSA required. Applicants notified on a rolling basis starting 4/30; must reply within 4 week(s) of notification.

**Academics. Special study options:** Distance learning, double major, internships, student-designed major. **Credit/placement by examination:** AP, CLEP, IB, institutional tests. 18 credit hours maximum toward bachelor's degree. **Support services:** Remedial instruction, tutoring.

**Majors. Communications technology:** Animation/special effects. **Engineering:** Electrical, software. **Protective services:** Fire safety technology, fire services admin. **Other:** Digital arts engineering, Digital Audio Technology.

**Most popular majors.** Engineering/engineering technologies 8%, security/protective services 21%, visual/performing arts 70%.

**Computing on campus.** 164 workstations in library, computer center. Online course registration, online library, helpline, wireless network available.

**Student life. Freshman orientation:** Mandatory. Preregistration for classes offered. **Housing:** Apartments available. $300 fully refundable deposit, deadline 7/1. **Activities:** Student government, student newspaper.

**Athletics. Intramural:** Skiing, table tennis.

**Student services.** Alcohol/substance abuse counseling, career counseling, student employment services, financial aid counseling, personal counseling, placement for graduates, veterans' counselor.

**Contact.** E-mail: admissions@cogswell.edu
Phone: (408) 541-0100 Fax: (408) 747-0764
Barb Bloom, Dean of Student Life, Cogswell Polytechnical College, 1175 Bordeaux Drive, Sunnyvale, CA 94089-1299

---

## Coleman College
**San Diego, California**
www.coleman.edu
CB code: 0955

- Private 4-year technical college
- Commuter campus in large city
- 481 degree-seeking undergraduates
- 18 graduate students
- Interview required

**General.** Founded in 1963. Accredited by ACICS. **Degrees:** 82 bachelor's, 135 associate awarded; master's offered. **Calendar:** Continuous. **Full-time faculty:** 95 total. **Part-time faculty:** 40 total.

**Basis for selection.** Open admission, but selective for some programs. Institutional entrance exam important: math, spatial reasoning, and aptitude assessment tested. Test scores recommended for placement and credit. Institutionally administered aptitude test required. Skills test given during interview.

**2007-2008 Annual costs.** Tuition $27,540 for 13-month associate degree program in computer information science. Costs vary depending on program. Books/supplies: $425. Personal expenses: $1,206.

**Financial aid.** All financial aid based on need.

**Application procedures. Admission:** No deadline. $100 fee. Admission notification on a rolling basis. **Financial aid:** Priority date 3/2; no closing date. FAFSA, institutional form required. Applicants notified on a rolling basis.

**Academics.** College uses inverted curriculum with major taken before general curriculum. Vast majority of students are transfers. **Special study options:** Accelerated study, cooperative education, distance learning, double major. **Credit/placement by examination:** AP, CLEP. 26 credit hours maximum toward associate degree, 36 toward bachelor's. **Support services:** Reduced course load, tutoring.

**Majors. Biology:** Bioinformatics. **Business:** Business admin. **Computer sciences:** General. **Engineering:** Computer. **Engineering technology:** Computer. **Visual/performing arts:** Graphic design.

**Most popular majors.** Computer/information sciences 95%.

**Computing on campus.** 365 workstations in library, computer center.

**Student life. Activities:** International student organizations, student government, student newspaper, student activities committee.

**Student services.** Career counseling, personal counseling, placement for graduates, veterans' counselor.

**Contact.** E-mail: admis@coleman.edu
Phone: (858) 499-0202 Toll-free number: (800) 430-2030
Fax: (858) 499-0233
Mike Loreano, Director of Admissions, Coleman College, 8888 Balboa Avenue, San Diego, CA 92123

---

## Columbia College: Hollywood
**Tarzana, California**
www.columbiacollege.edu                    CB code: 1247

- Private 4-year visual arts college
- Commuter campus in very large city
- 314 degree-seeking undergraduates: 8% part-time, 26% women
- 60% graduate within 6 years

**General.** Founded in 1952. Accredited by ACCSCT. **Degrees:** 36 bachelor's, 3 associate awarded. **Location:** 15 miles from downtown Los Angeles. **Calendar:** Quarter, limited summer session. **Full-time faculty:** 3 total; 33% have terminal degrees. **Part-time faculty:** 75 total; 24% have terminal degrees, 29% minority, 28% women. **Class size:** 100% < 20. **Special facilities:** Film and electronic editing facilities, production facilities, dubbing theater, transfer room (video and audio), soundstage, professional shooting sets.

**Freshman class profile.** 127 applied, 116 admitted, 32 enrolled.

| | | | |
|---|---|---|---|
| End year in good standing: | 75% | International: | 7% |
| Out-of-state: | 80% | | |

**Basis for selection.** Open admission, but selective for some programs. References, high school record, and demonstrated interest in film and/or television most important. On-site proficiency tests used to determine reading/mathematics proficiencies. Interview with admission representative recommended. **Homeschooled:** Letter of recommendation (nonparent) required. An essay decribing student's interest and passion in film and/or television required, 500 word minimum. **Learning Disabled:** Documentation required.

**2007-2008 Annual costs.** Tuition/fees: $13,983.

**2007-2008 Financial aid. Need-based:** 47 full-time freshmen applied for aid; 33 were judged to have need; 33 of these received aid. Average need met was 43%. Average scholarship/grant was $3,300; average loan $3,700. 38% of total undergraduate aid awarded as scholarships/grants, 62% as loans/jobs. **Non-need-based:** Awarded to 1 full-time undergraduates, including 1 freshmen. **Additional information:** All financial aid forms due by second week of classes.

**Application procedures. Admission:** Priority date 6/30; deadline 8/15 (receipt date). $50 fee, may be waived for applicants with need. Admission notification on a rolling basis. **Financial aid:** Priority date 2/1; no closing date. FAFSA, institutional form required. Applicants notified on a rolling basis starting 7/15; must reply within 3 week(s) of notification.

**Academics.** Most classes held in afternoon and evening, taught by professionals in motion picture and television/video industries. **Special study options:** Accelerated study, internships. **Credit/placement by examination:** AP, CLEP, institutional tests. **Support services:** Reduced course load, remedial instruction, study skills assistance, tutoring.

**Majors. Communications technology:** General. **Visual/performing arts:** Cinematography, film/cinema.

**Computing on campus.** 24 workstations in dormitories, library, computer center. Dormitories wired for high-speed internet access. Wireless network available.

**Student life. Freshman orientation:** Mandatory, $75 fee. Preregistration for classes offered. **Housing:** Guaranteed on-campus for freshmen. Coed dorms available. $500 fully refundable deposit, deadline 9/1. **Activities:** Film society, student government, student newspaper, TV station.

**Student services.** Adult student services, career counseling, personal counseling, placement for graduates, veterans' counselor.

**Contact.** E-mail: admissions@columbiacollege.edu
Phone: (818) 345-8414 ext. 105 Toll-free number: (800) 785-0585 ext. 105
Fax: (818) 345-9053
Carmen Munoz, Director of Admissions, Columbia College: Hollywood, 18618 Oxnard Street, Tarzana, CA 91356

---

## Concordia University
**Irvine, California**                          CB member
www.cui.edu                                    CB code: 4069

- Private 4-year university and liberal arts college affiliated with Lutheran Church - Missouri Synod
- Residential campus in small city
- 1,203 degree-seeking undergraduates: 3% part-time, 61% women, 4% African American, 4% Asian American, 13% Hispanic American, 1% Native American, 2% international
- 1,019 degree-seeking graduate students
- 67% of applicants admitted
- SAT or ACT (ACT writing recommended) required
- 60% graduate within 6 years

**General.** Founded in 1972. Regionally accredited. **Degrees:** 353 bachelor's awarded; master's offered. **Location:** 40 miles from Los Angeles, 80 miles from San Diego. **Calendar:** Semester, limited summer session. **Full-time faculty:** 91 total; 67% have terminal degrees, 37% women. **Part-time faculty:** 191 total; 24% have terminal degrees, 41% women. **Class size:** 57% < 20, 41% 20-39, 2% 40-49, less than 1% 50-99, less than 1% >100.

**Freshman class profile.** 827 applied, 557 admitted, 227 enrolled.

| Mid 50% test scores | | Rank in top quarter: | 54% |
|---|---|---|---|
| SAT critical reading: | 450-570 | Rank in top tenth: | 20% |
| SAT math: | 450-570 | Return as sophomores: | 73% |
| ACT composite: | 20-24 | Out-of-state: | 26% |
| GPA 3.50 or higher: | 50% | Live on campus: | 93% |
| GPA 3.0-3.49: | 38% | International: | 3% |
| GPA 2.0-2.99: | 12% | | |

**Basis for selection.** Secondary school record, class rank, standardized test scores most important. Recommendations and character/personal qualities also important. Audition required for music majors.

**High school preparation.** 14 units required. Required units include English 4, mathematics 3, social studies 2, science 3 and foreign language 2. Biology, chemistry, algebra I and II, and geometry specifically recommended.

**2007-2008 Annual costs.** Tuition/fees: $22,380. Room/board: $7,480. Books/supplies: $1,300. Personal expenses: $2,320.

**2007-2008 Financial aid. Need-based:** 220 full-time freshmen applied for aid; 163 were judged to have need; 163 of these received aid. Average need met was 76%. Average scholarship/grant was $13,780; average loan $3,325. 75% of total undergraduate aid awarded as scholarships/grants, 25% as loans/jobs. **Non-need-based:** Awarded to 418 full-time undergraduates, including 95 freshmen. Scholarships awarded for academics, alumni affiliation, art, athletics, leadership, music/drama, religious affiliation.

**Application procedures. Admission:** Priority date 3/2; no deadline. $50 fee, may be waived for applicants with need. Application may be submitted online. Admission notification on a rolling basis. Must reply by May 1 or within 4 week(s) if notified thereafter. **Financial aid:** Priority date 3/2, closing date 4/1. FAFSA, institutional form required. Applicants notified on a rolling basis starting 2/1; must reply within 4 week(s) of notification.

**Academics. Special study options:** Accelerated study, combined bachelor's/graduate degree, cross-registration, distance learning, double major, dual enrollment of high school students, ESL, exchange student, honors, independent study, internships, student-designed major, study abroad, teacher certification program. **Credit/placement by examination:** AP, CLEP, IB. 32 credit hours maximum toward bachelor's degree. **Support services:** Learning center, tutoring, writing center.

**Majors. Biology:** General. **Business:** Business admin. **Communications:** Media studies. **Education:** General. **English:** English lit. **Foreign languages:** Biblical. **History:** General. **Interdisciplinary:** Behavioral sciences. **Liberal arts:** Arts/sciences, humanities. **Math:** General. **Parks/recreation:** Exercise sciences. **Physical sciences:** Chemistry. **Psychology:** General. **Social sciences:** Political science. **Theology:** Theology. **Visual/performing arts:** Art, dramatic, film/cinema.

**Most popular majors.** Business/marketing 23%, communications/journalism 7%, education 13%, liberal arts 15%, parks/recreation 7%, social sciences 10%, visual/performing arts 6%.

**Computing on campus.** 48 workstations in dormitories, library, computer center, student center. Dormitories wired for high-speed internet access and linked to campus network. Commuter students can connect to campus network. Online course registration, online library, helpline, wireless network available.

**Student life. Freshman orientation:** Available. Preregistration for classes offered. **Housing:** Guaranteed on-campus for freshmen. Single-sex dorms, special housing for disabled available. $300 deposit, deadline 6/30. **Activities:** Bands, campus ministries, choral groups, dance, drama, film society, literary magazine, music ensembles, musical theater, radio station, student government, student newspaper, Nuestra Voz, improve club, Republican club, math club, sports medicine club, Fellowship of Christian Athletes, ethics club, Cross Cultural Link.

**Athletics.** NAIA. **Intercollegiate:** Baseball M, basketball, cross-country, golf, soccer, softball W, tennis, track and field, volleyball W, water polo M. **Intramural:** Basketball, bowling, football (non-tackle), soccer, softball, table tennis, track and field, volleyball. **Team name:** Eagles.

**Student services.** Adult student services, alcohol/substance abuse counseling, campus ministries, financial aid counseling, health services, minority student services, personal counseling.

**Contact.** E-mail: admission@cui.edu
Phone: (949) 854-8002 ext. 1106 Toll-free number: (800) 229-1200
Fax: (949) 854-6894
Scott Rhodes, Executive Director Admissions, Concordia University, 1530 Concordia West, Irvine, CA 92612-3299

## Design Institute of San Diego
San Diego, California
www.disd.edu                                  CB code: 3492

- For-profit 4-year technical college
- Very large city
- 510 degree-seeking undergraduates
- 84% of applicants admitted
- Application essay, interview required

**General.** Accredited by ACICS. **Degrees:** 69 bachelor's awarded. **Calendar:** Semester. **Full-time faculty:** 6 total. **Part-time faculty:** 59 total.

**Freshman class profile.** 100 applied, 84 admitted, 80 enrolled.

**Basis for selection.** High school/college grades, 2 professional references considered.

**2008-2009 Annual costs.** Tuition/fees: $15,600. Books/supplies: $800. Personal expenses: $4,626.

**Application procedures. Admission:** No deadline. $25 fee. Admission notification on a rolling basis. **Financial aid:** No deadline. Applicants notified on a rolling basis.

**Academics. Credit/placement by examination:** CLEP.

**Majors. Visual/performing arts:** Interior design.

**Contact.** Phone: (858) 566-1200 Toll-free number: (800) 619-4337
Fax: (858) 566-2711
Paula Parrish, Director of Admissions, Design Institute of San Diego, 8555 Commerce Avenue, San Diego, CA 92121

## DeVry University: Fremont
Fremont, California
www.devry.edu                                 CB code: 0520

- For-profit 4-year university
- Commuter campus in small city
- 1,411 degree-seeking undergraduates: 35% part-time, 30% women, 10% African American, 26% Asian American, 18% Hispanic American, 1% Native American
- 162 degree-seeking graduate students
- 35% graduate within 6 years

**General.** Regionally accredited. **Degrees:** 318 bachelor's, 11 associate awarded; master's offered. **Location:** 15 miles from San Jose. **Calendar:** Semester, extensive summer session. **Full-time faculty:** 39 total; 51% minority, 87% women. **Part-time faculty:** 75 total; 31% minority, 67% women.

**Freshman class profile.**

| | | | |
|---|---|---|---|
| Return as sophomores: | 56% | Out-of-state: | 2% |

**Basis for selection.** Applicant must have high school diploma or equivalent, degree from accredited postsecondary institution, pass institutional placement examination, or submit acceptable test scores and be 17 years of age. New students may enter at beginning of any semester. SAT/ACT considered but not required for admission. If applicant chooses not to submit either, must take institution-administered admissions test.

**2007-2008 Annual costs.** Tuition/fees: $14,640. Books/supplies: $1,300. Personal expenses: $5,082.

**2006-2007 Financial aid.** All financial aid based on need.

**Application procedures. Admission:** No deadline. $50 fee. Admission notification on a rolling basis. **Financial aid:** No deadline. FAFSA required. Applicants notified on a rolling basis.

**Academics. Special study options:** Accelerated study, distance learning. **Credit/placement by examination:** CLEP, institutional tests. **Support services:** Learning center, remedial instruction, tutoring.

**Majors. Biology:** Bioinformatics. **Business:** Business admin. **Computer sciences:** Game design, networking, systems analysis. **Engineering technology:** Biomedical, computer, electrical. **Other:** Technical management.

**Most popular majors.** Business/marketing 59%, computer/information sciences 14%, engineering/engineering technologies 27%.

**Computing on campus.** 350 workstations in library, computer center. Online course registration, online library, helpline available.

**Student life. Freshman orientation:** Mandatory. **Housing:** Private apartments, student-plan housing, private rooms available. **Activities:** Institute of Electronic and Electrical Engineers, Hmong Organization on Technology, network communications club, Tau Alpha Pi national honor society for engineering technologies, women's organization, game development, Latino American student organization, Phi Beta Lambda national organization for business majors, chess club, self-defense club.

**Athletics. Intramural:** Soccer.

**Student services.** Career counseling, student employment services, financial aid counseling, placement for graduates, veterans' counselor. **Physically disabled:** Services for visually, hearing impaired.

**Contact.** Phone: (510) 574-1200 Toll-free number: (888) 393-3879
Marc Martin, Director of Admission, DeVry University: Fremont, 6600 Dumbarton Circle, Fremont, CA 94555-3615

## DeVry University: Long Beach
Long Beach, California
www.devry.edu                                 CB code: 2053

- For-profit 4-year university
- Commuter campus in large town

♦ 826 degree-seeking undergraduates: 51% part-time, 32% women, 13% African American, 24% Asian American, 38% Hispanic American
♦ 235 degree-seeking graduate students
♦ Interview required
♦ 35% graduate within 6 years

**General.** Regionally accredited. **Degrees:** 164 bachelor's, 28 associate awarded; master's offered. **Location:** 26 miles from Los Angeles. **Calendar:** Semester, extensive summer session. **Full-time faculty:** 17 total; 29% minority, 12% women. **Part-time faculty:** 66 total; 21% minority, 30% women.

**Freshman class profile.**

Return as sophomores:        46%        International:        1%

**Basis for selection.** Applicant must have high school diploma or equivalent, degree from an accredited postsecondary institution, or submit acceptable test scores and be at least 17 years of age on the first day of classes. New students may enter at beginning of any semester. SAT/ACT considered but not required for admission. If applicant chooses not to submit either, must take institution-administered admissions test.

**2007-2008 Annual costs.** Tuition/fees: $14,010. Books/supplies: $1,300. Personal expenses: $5,082.

**Financial aid.** All financial aid based on need.

**Application procedures. Admission:** No deadline. $50 fee. Application may be submitted online. Admission notification on a rolling basis. **Financial aid:** No deadline. FAFSA required. Applicants notified on a rolling basis.

**Academics. Special study options:** Accelerated study, distance learning. **Credit/placement by examination:** CLEP. **Support services:** Learning center, remedial instruction, tutoring.

**Majors. Biology:** Bioinformatics. **Business:** Business admin, operations. **Computer sciences:** Game design, information technology, networking, systems analysis. **Engineering technology:** Computer, electrical. **Other:** Technical management.

**Most popular majors.** Business/marketing 59%, computer/information sciences 29%, engineering/engineering technologies 13%.

**Computing on campus.** 463 workstations in library, computer center. Online course registration, online library, helpline available.

**Student life. Freshman orientation:** Mandatory. **Housing:** Private apartments, student-plan housing, private rooms available. **Activities:** Associate Student Body Advocates, Society of Hispanic Professional Engineers, Epsilon Delta Pi, United Islands, Tau Alpha Pi, business and accounting association, National Society of Black Engineers (NSBE), Institute of Electronic and Electrical Engineers (IEEE).

**Student services.** Career counseling, student employment services, financial aid counseling, placement for graduates, veterans' counselor. **Physically disabled:** Services for visually, hearing impaired.

**Contact.** Phone: (562) 427-4162 Toll-free number: (800) 597-0444 Elaine Francisco, Director of Admissions, DeVry University: Long Beach, 3880 Kilroy Airport Way, Long Beach, CA 90806

## DeVry University: Pomona
Pomona, California
www.devry.edu
                                         CB code: 4214

♦ For-profit 4-year university
♦ Commuter campus in small city
♦ 1,543 degree-seeking undergraduates: 51% part-time, 28% women, 9% African American, 17% Asian American, 41% Hispanic American, 1% Native American
♦ 172 degree-seeking graduate students
♦ Interview required
♦ 35% graduate within 6 years

**General.** Founded in 1983. Regionally accredited. **Degrees:** 311 bachelor's, 27 associate awarded; master's offered. **Location:** 13 miles from Los Angeles. **Calendar:** Semester, extensive summer session. **Full-time faculty:** 25 total; 40% minority, 16% women. **Part-time faculty:** 59 total; 19% minority, 46% women.

**Freshman class profile.**

Return as sophomores:        49%        Out-of-state:        1%

**Basis for selection.** Applicant must have high school diploma or equivalent, degree from an accredited postsecondary institution, or submit acceptable test scores and be at least 17 years of age on the first day of classes. New students may enter at beginning of any semester. SAT/ACT considered but not required for admission. If applicant chooses not to submit either, must take an institution-administered admissions test.

**2007-2008 Annual costs.** Tuition/fees: $14,020. Books/supplies: $1,300. Personal expenses: $3,152.

**2006-2007 Financial aid.** All financial aid based on need.

**Application procedures. Admission:** No deadline. $50 fee. Application may be submitted online. Admission notification on a rolling basis. **Financial aid:** No deadline. FAFSA required. Applicants notified on a rolling basis.

**Academics. Special study options:** Accelerated study, distance learning. **Credit/placement by examination:** CLEP, institutional tests. **Support services:** Learning center, remedial instruction, tutoring.

**Majors. Business:** General. **Computer sciences:** General, networking. **Engineering technology:** Biomedical, computer, electrical. **Other:** Game and simulation programming, Technical management.

**Most popular majors.** Business/marketing 68%, computer/information sciences 25%, engineering/engineering technologies 7%.

**Computing on campus.** 517 workstations in library, computer center. Online course registration, online library, helpline available.

**Student life. Freshman orientation:** Mandatory. **Housing:** Private apartments, student-plan housing, private rooms available. **Activities:** Gaming association, Institute for Electrical and Electronic Engineers, Living in Truth, National Society of Black Engineers, Phi Beta Lambda, Society of Hispanic Professional Engineers, networking professional association, Toastmasters.

**Student services.** Career counseling, student employment services, financial aid counseling, placement for graduates, veterans' counselor. **Physically disabled:** Services for visually, hearing impaired.

**Contact.** Phone: (909) 622-8866 Jere Thrasher, Director of Admissions, DeVry University: Pomona, 901 Corporate Center Drive, Pomona, CA 91768-2642

## DeVry University: Sherman Oaks
Sherman Oaks, California
www.devry.edu
                                         CB code: 2800

♦ For-profit 4-year university
♦ Commuter campus in large city
♦ 462 degree-seeking undergraduates: 53% part-time, 29% women, 7% African American, 20% Asian American, 32% Hispanic American, 2% Native American, 1% international
♦ 118 degree-seeking graduate students
♦ Interview required
♦ 35% graduate within 6 years

**General.** Regionally accredited. **Degrees:** 134 bachelor's, 17 associate awarded; master's offered. **Location:** 30 miles from Los Angeles. **Calendar:** Semester, extensive summer session. **Full-time faculty:** 10 total; 20% minority, 10% women. **Part-time faculty:** 78 total; 6% minority, 27% women.

**Basis for selection.** Applicant must have high school diploma or equivalent, degree from an accredited postsecondary institution, or submit acceptable test scores and be at least 17 years of age on the first day of classes. New students may enter at beginning of any semester. SAT/ACT tests considered but not required for admission. If applicant chooses not to submit either, must take institution-administered admissions test.

**2007-2008 Annual costs.** Tuition/fees: $14,020. Books/supplies: $1,300. Personal expenses: $5,082.

**2006-2007 Financial aid.** All financial aid based on need.

**Application procedures. Admission:** No deadline. $50 fee. Application may be submitted online. Admission notification on a rolling basis. **Financial aid:** No deadline. FAFSA required. Applicants notified on a rolling basis.

**Academics. Special study options:** Accelerated study, distance learning. **Credit/placement by examination:** CLEP, institutional tests. **Support services:** Learning center, remedial instruction, tutoring.

**Majors. Business:** Business admin. **Computer sciences:** Networking. **Engineering technology:** Computer, electrical. **Other:** Technical management.

**Most popular majors.** Business/marketing 56%, computer/information sciences 29%, engineering/engineering technologies 15%.

**Computing on campus.** 412 workstations in library, computer center. Online course registration, online library, helpline available.

**Student life. Freshman orientation:** Mandatory. **Housing:** Private apartments, student-plan housing, private rooms available. **Activities:** Student government, student newspaper, Institution of Electrical & Electronic Engineers, Society of Hispanic Professional Engineers, Students Under Mass Organization, Progressive Advancement in Life, Diverse National Alliance, bowling club, Omega Sigma Phi, Phi Theta Kappa, Epsilon Delta Pi, Japanese anime club.

**Athletics. Intramural:** Softball.

**Student services.** Career counseling, student employment services, financial aid counseling, placement for graduates, veterans' counselor. **Physically disabled:** Services for visually, hearing impaired.

**Contact.** Phone: (818) 587-6227 Toll-free number: (888) 610-0800 Dewey McGuirk, Director of Admissions, DeVry University: Sherman Oaks, 15301 Ventura Boulevard, D-100, Sherman Oaks, CA 91403

## Dominican School of Philosophy and Theology
**Berkeley, California**
www.dspt.edu                                    CB code: 0877

▶ Private two-year upper-division seminary college affiliated with Roman Catholic Church
▶ Commuter campus in small city
▶ 33% of applicants admitted
▶ Application essay required

**General.** Founded in 1932. Regionally accredited; also accredited by ATS. Part of Graduate Theological Union, a consortium of nine theological schools and ten affiliated institutes sharing a common library and registrar. **Degrees:** 2 bachelor's awarded; master's, first professional offered. **Location:** 10 miles from San Francisco. **Calendar:** Semester, limited summer session. **Full-time faculty:** 13 total. **Part-time faculty:** 8 total. **Class size:** 60% < 20, 40% 20-39.

**Student profile.** 2 degree-seeking undergraduates, 119 graduate students. 3 applied as first time-transfer students, 1 admitted, 1 enrolled. 100% entered as juniors. 100% transferred from four-year institutions.

| Out-of-state: | 100% | Live on campus: | 100% |
|---|---|---|---|

**Basis for selection.** High school transcript, college transcript, application essay required. Admission based on GPA and recommendations. Student must have completed 72 units of general education coursework with at least a 2.3 GPA to enter BA philosophy program. Transfer accepted as juniors, seniors.

**2007-2008 Annual costs.** Tuition/fees: $14,720. Required medical insurance for otherwise uninsured students costs approximately $3.600 per year. Books/supplies: $1,197.

**Financial aid. Non-need-based:** Scholarships awarded for academics.

**Application procedures. Admission:** Priority date 3/15. $40 fee, may be waived for applicants with need. Application may be submitted online. **Financial aid:** Closing date 4/1. FAFSA, institutional form required.

**Academics. Special study options:** Cross-registration, double major, independent study, study abroad. **Credit/placement by examination:** CLEP. **Support services:** Reduced course load.

**Majors. Philosophy/religion:** Philosophy.

**Computing on campus.** 6 workstations in computer center. Online course registration, wireless network available.

**Student life. Housing:** Apartments, cooperative housing available. Limited student housing available near campus in apartment complex. **Activities:** Music ensembles, student government.

**Student services.** Campus ministries, career counseling, student employment services, financial aid counseling, health services, personal counseling, placement for graduates, women's services.

**Contact.** E-mail: admissions@dspt.edu
Phone: (510) 883-2073 Toll-free number: (888) 450-3778
Fax: (510) 849-1372
John Knutsen, Director of Admissions, Dominican School of Philosophy and Theology, 2301 Vine Street, Berkeley, CA 94708

## Dominican University of California
**San Rafael, California**                      CB member
www.dominican.edu                               CB code: 4284

▶ Private 4-year university and liberal arts college affiliated with Roman Catholic heritage
▶ Residential campus in small city
▶ 1,469 degree-seeking undergraduates: 20% part-time, 76% women, 7% African American, 21% Asian American, 16% Hispanic American, 1% Native American, 2% international
▶ 613 degree-seeking graduate students
▶ 56% of applicants admitted
▶ SAT or ACT with writing, application essay required
▶ 54% graduate within 6 years

**General.** Founded in 1890. Regionally accredited. **Degrees:** 275 bachelor's awarded; master's offered. **Location:** 11 miles from San Francisco. **Calendar:** Semester, limited summer session. **Full-time faculty:** 78 total; 73% have terminal degrees, 15% minority, 62% women. **Part-time faculty:** 267 total; 43% have terminal degrees, 6% minority, 60% women. **Class size:** 61% < 20, 35% 20-39, 3% 40-49, less than 1% 50-99.

**Freshman class profile.** 2,586 applied, 1,446 admitted, 297 enrolled.

| Mid 50% test scores | | Rank in top quarter: | 44% |
|---|---|---|---|
| SAT critical reading: | 440-540 | Rank in top tenth: | 16% |
| SAT math: | 450-540 | Return as sophomores: | 74% |
| ACT composite: | 18-24 | Out-of-state: | 9% |
| GPA 3.50 or higher: | 37% | Live on campus: | 88% |
| GPA 3.0-3.49: | 37% | International: | 1% |
| GPA 2.0-2.99: | 26% | | |

**Basis for selection.** School achievement record (2.5 high school GPA), recommendations, test scores, essay, extracurricular activities most important. Class rank and work experience considered. SAT Subject Tests recommended. Interview recommended for borderline applicants. Audition recommended for music majors. Portfolio recommended for art majors.

**High school preparation.** 11 units required. Required units include English 4, mathematics 2, history 1, science 1 (laboratory 1) and foreign language 2.

**2007-2008 Annual costs.** Tuition/fees: $30,570. Room/board: $12,000. Books/supplies: $1,386. Personal expenses: $2,142.

**2006-2007 Financial aid. Need-based:** 199 full-time freshmen applied for aid; 170 were judged to have need; 169 of these received aid. Average need met was 37%. Average scholarship/grant was $17,567; average loan $2,905. 64% of total undergraduate aid awarded as scholarships/grants, 36% as loans/jobs. **Non-need-based:** Awarded to 106 full-time undergraduates, including 31 freshmen. Scholarships awarded for academics, alumni affiliation, athletics, leadership, minority status, music/drama. **Additional information:** 4-year guarantee program.

**Application procedures. Admission:** Priority date 2/1; no deadline. $40 fee, may be waived for applicants with need. Application may be submitted online. Admission notification on a rolling basis beginning on or about 10/15. **Financial aid:** Priority date 3/2; no closing date. FAFSA, institutional form required. Applicants notified on a rolling basis starting 3/15; must reply within 2 week(s) of notification.

**Academics. Special study options:** Accelerated study, combined bachelor's/graduate degree, cross-registration, double major, dual enrollment of high school students, exchange student, honors, independent study, internships, student-designed major, study abroad, teacher certification program, weekend college. Pathways Program (evening/weekend degree program for working adults), semester available at Aquinas College (MI), St. Thomas Aquinas College (NY), Barry University (FL), cross-registration with University of California, Berkeley. **Credit/placement by examination:** AP, CLEP, IB, institutional tests. No more than 30 units can come from one of the following sources: CLEP/Regents College Exams, ACE/PONSI review courses, experiential learning portfolios. No more than 12 units from challenging courses. No more than 38 units from NLN exams. **Support services:** Learning center, study skills assistance, tutoring.

**Majors. Area/ethnic studies:** Women's. **Biology:** General. **Business:** General, business admin, e-commerce, human resources, international. **Communications:** General. **Computer sciences:** Computer graphics. **English:** Composition, creative writing, English lit. **Health:** Nursing (RN). **History:** General. **Liberal arts:** Arts/sciences, humanities. **Philosophy/religion:** Religion. **Psychology:** General. **Social sciences:** Political science. **Visual/performing arts:** Art, art history/conservation, ballet, digital art, music performance.

**Most popular majors.** Biology 8%, business/marketing 17%, health sciences 31%, liberal arts 10%, psychology 17%.

**Computing on campus.** 85 workstations in library, computer center, student center. Dormitories wired for high-speed internet access and linked to campus network. Commuter students can connect to campus network. Helpline, repair service, wireless network available.

**Student life. Freshman orientation:** Available. Preregistration for classes offered. Fall program held week prior to start of classes. **Housing:** Coed dorms, substance-free housing available. $250 fully refundable deposit, deadline 5/1. **Activities:** Jazz band, campus ministries, choral groups, drama, literary magazine, music ensembles, radio station, student government, student newspaper, Republican club, Democratic club, cultural diversity club, Rotaract, various multicultural groups.

**Athletics.** NAIA. **Intercollegiate:** Basketball, golf, lacrosse M, soccer, softball W, tennis, volleyball W. **Team name:** Penguins.

**Student services.** Adult student services, alcohol/substance abuse counseling, campus ministries, career counseling, student employment services, financial aid counseling, health services, personal counseling, placement for graduates. **Physically disabled:** Services for visually impaired.

**Contact.** E-mail: enroll@dominican.edu
Phone: (415) 485-3204 Toll-free number: (888) 323-6763
Fax: (415) 485-3214
Rebecca Finn Kenney, Executive Director of Undergraduate Admissions, Dominican University of California, 50 Acacia Avenue, San Rafael, CA 94901-2298

---

### Ex'pression College for Digital Arts
**Emeryville, California**
**www.expression.edu**

- For-profit 4-year visual arts and technical college
- Small town
- 1,100 full-time, degree-seeking undergraduates

**General.** Accredited by ACCSCT. **Degrees:** 250 bachelor's awarded. **Calendar:** Semester. **Full-time faculty:** 50 total. **Part-time faculty:** 100 total.

**Academics. Credit/placement by examination:** CLEP.

**Majors. Communications technology:** Animation/special effects. **Visual/performing arts:** Graphic design.

**Contact.** Phone: (510) 654-2934 Toll-free number: (877) 833-8800
Brittany Riddell, Director of Admissions, Ex'pression College for Digital Arts, 6601 Shellmound Street, Emeryville, CA 94608

---

### Fresno Pacific University
**Fresno, California**                              CB member
**www.fresno.edu**                            CB code: 4616

- Private 4-year university and liberal arts college affiliated with Mennonite Brethren Church
- Residential campus in large city
- 1,515 degree-seeking undergraduates: 15% part-time, 69% women
- 496 degree-seeking graduate students
- 68% of applicants admitted
- SAT and SAT Subject Tests or ACT (ACT writing optional) required
- 60% graduate within 6 years

**General.** Founded in 1944. Regionally accredited. **Degrees:** 407 bachelor's awarded; master's offered. **Location:** 150 miles from San Francisco. **Calendar:** Semester, limited summer session. **Full-time faculty:** 93 total; 62% have terminal degrees, 10% minority, 33% women. **Part-time faculty:** 262 total; 5% minority, 48% women. **Class size:** 71% < 20, 23% 20-39, 4%

40-49, 2% 50-99, less than 1% >100. **Special facilities:** Center for mennonite brethren studies, center for conflict studies and peacemaking.

**Freshman class profile.** 608 applied, 414 admitted, 184 enrolled.

| Mid 50% test scores | | | |
|---|---|---|---|
| SAT critical reading: | 420-560 | GPA 2.0-2.99: | 20% |
| SAT math: | 440-570 | Rank in top quarter: | 61% |
| SAT writing: | 420-540 | Rank in top tenth: | 27% |
| ACT composite: | 17-24 | Return as sophomores: | 75% |
| GPA 3.50 or higher: | 46% | Out-of-state: | 5% |
| GPA 3.0-3.49: | 34% | Live on campus: | 66% |
| | | International: | 3% |

**Basis for selection.** School achievement record and test scores very important, minimum 3.1 high school GPA. Recommendations, autobiography also considered. Interview recommended for academically weak applicants. Auditions for music, English (with drama emphasis) majors.

**High school preparation.** 13 units required. Required units include English 4, mathematics 3, social studies 2, science 1 (laboratory 1) and foreign language 2. One year of visual or performing arts.

**2007-2008 Annual costs.** Tuition/fees: $21,796. Room/board: $6,600. Books/supplies: $1,314. Personal expenses: $2,088.

**2007-2008 Financial aid. Need-based:** 165 full-time freshmen applied for aid; 150 were judged to have need; 149 of these received aid. Average need met was 71%. Average scholarship/grant was $12,578; average loan $2,539. 57% of total undergraduate aid awarded as scholarships/grants, 43% as loans/jobs. **Non-need-based:** Awarded to 470 full-time undergraduates, including 185 freshmen. Scholarships awarded for academics, athletics, music/drama.

**Application procedures. Admission:** Priority date 12/1; deadline 7/31 (postmark date). $40 fee, may be waived for applicants with need. Application may be submitted online. Admission notification on a rolling basis beginning on or about 12/1. **Financial aid:** Priority date 3/2; no closing date. FAFSA, institutional form required. Applicants notified on a rolling basis starting 3/2; must reply by 7/30 or within 3 week(s) of notification.

**Academics. Special study options:** Accelerated study, distance learning, double major, dual enrollment of high school students, ESL, exchange student, independent study, internships, student-designed major, study abroad, teacher certification program, Washington semester. **Credit/placement by examination:** AP, CLEP, IB. 30 credit hours maximum toward associate degree, 30 toward bachelor's. **Support services:** Learning center, reduced course load, remedial instruction, study skills assistance, tutoring, writing center.

**Majors. Biology:** General. **Business:** General, accounting, business admin, human resources, international, management information systems, marketing, nonprofit/public, organizational behavior. **Communications:** General. **Computer sciences:** Computer science. **Conservation:** Environmental science, environmental studies. **Education:** Biology, business, elementary, English, mathematics, music, physical, science, social science. **English:** Creative writing. **Foreign languages:** Spanish. **Health:** Athletic training, premedicine. **History:** General. **Liberal arts:** Arts/sciences. **Math:** General, applied. **Parks/recreation:** Health/fitness, sports admin. **Philosophy/religion:** Philosophy. **Physical sciences:** Chemistry. **Protective services:** Criminalistics. **Psychology:** General. **Public administration:** Social work. **Social sciences:** General, political science, sociology. **Theology:** Bible. **Visual/performing arts:** Art, dramatic, music performance, music theory/composition.

**Most popular majors.** Business/marketing 38%, education 36%.

**Computing on campus.** 90 workstations in dormitories, library, computer center, student center. Dormitories wired for high-speed internet access and linked to campus network. Commuter students can connect to campus network. Online course registration, helpline, student web hosting, wireless network available.

**Student life. Freshman orientation:** Mandatory. Preregistration for classes offered. 4-day fall orientation, 1-day spring. **Housing:** Single-sex dorms, special housing for disabled, apartments, substance-free housing available. $200 nonrefundable deposit, deadline 6/1. Several college-rented apartments available nearby. Resident freshmen under age 23 required to live on campus. **Activities:** Bands, choral groups, dance, drama, international student organizations, music ensembles, student government, student newspaper, Summer Harvest, Shalom Covenant, Kids Klub, Amigos Unidos, Students In Free Enterprise, student chaplains, Daughters of Christ, Faith Project, social work club.

**Athletics.** NAIA. **Intercollegiate:** Baseball M, basketball, cross-country, soccer, swimming, tennis, track and field, volleyball W, water polo. **Intramural:** Basketball, bowling, football (non-tackle), racquetball, soccer, table tennis, volleyball. **Team name:** Sunbirds.

**Student services.** Adult student services, alcohol/substance abuse counseling, campus ministries, career counseling, student employment services, financial aid counseling, health services, personal counseling. **Physically disabled:** Services for visually, hearing impaired.

**Contact.** E-mail: ugadmis@fresno.edu
Phone: (559) 453-2039 Toll-free number: (800) 660-6089
Fax: (559) 453-2007
Campbell Rina, Director of Undergraduate Admissions, Fresno Pacific University, 1717 South Chestnut Avenue, Fresno, CA 93702-4709

## Golden Gate University
### San Francisco, California
**www.ggu.edu**      **CB code: 4329**

- Private 4-year university
- Commuter campus in very large city
- 492 degree-seeking undergraduates: 78% part-time, 58% women
- 3,020 degree-seeking graduate students

**General.** Founded in 1853. Regionally accredited. Evening and weekend degree programs available in San Francisco, San Jose, Walnut Creek, Sacramento, Monterey Bay, Los Angeles, and Seattle (WA). Program length differs by location. **Degrees:** 178 bachelor's awarded; master's, doctoral, first professional offered. **Calendar:** Trimester, extensive summer session. **Full-time faculty:** 70 total; 29% women. **Part-time faculty:** 757 total; 30% women.

**Basis for selection.** School achievement record most important. Work history or military service factor in determining admission of adult students. SAT recommended. Interviews recommended for undecided major applicants.

**High school preparation.** 14 units recommended. Recommended units include English 4, mathematics 3, social studies 1, history 1, science 2 (laboratory 1) and foreign language 2.

**2008-2009 Annual costs.** Tuition/fees: $16,200.

**Financial aid.** All financial aid based on need.

**Application procedures. Admission:** Priority date 7/1; no deadline. $55 fee. Application may be submitted online. Admission notification on a rolling basis. Students may be admitted up to 1 year (3 trimesters) before they intend to enroll. **Financial aid:** Priority date 1/2; no closing date. FAFSA, institutional form required. Applicants notified on a rolling basis starting 4/1; must reply within 3 week(s) of notification.

**Academics.** Professional degree, certification, and lifelong learning programs in business, law, tax, technology and related professions. **Special study options:** Accelerated study, cooperative education, distance learning, ESL, internships. **Credit/placement by examination:** AP, CLEP, IB, institutional tests. **Support services:** Reduced course load, tutoring, writing center.

**Majors. Business:** Accounting, business admin, finance, human resources, information resources management, international, marketing, operations. **Computer sciences:** Information technology.

**Most popular majors.** Business/marketing 76%, computer/information sciences 21%.

**Computing on campus.** 300 workstations in library, computer center. Commuter students can connect to campus network. Online course registration, online library, wireless network available.

**Student life. Activities:** Student government, student newspaper, Phi Alpha Delta law fraternity, Chi Pi Alpha, Indonesian students organization, Malayan students association, Chinese students club, student government, Indian student association, Korean student association, American Marketing Association, Toastmasters.

**Student services.** Adult student services, career counseling, student employment services, personal counseling, veterans' counselor. **Physically disabled:** Services for visually, speech, hearing impaired.

**Contact.** E-mail: info@ggu.edu
Phone: (415) 442-7800 Fax: (415) 442-7807
Louis Riccardi, Director of Enrollment Services, Golden Gate University, 536 Mission Street, San Francisco, CA 94105-2968

## Harvey Mudd College
### Claremont, California
**www.hmc.edu**      **CB member**
     **CB code: 4341**

- Private 4-year engineering and liberal arts college
- Residential campus in small city
- 737 degree-seeking undergraduates: 33% women, 1% African American, 20% Asian American, 8% Hispanic American, 1% Native American, 4% international
- 28% of applicants admitted
- SAT and SAT Subject Tests or ACT with writing, application essay required
- 84% graduate within 6 years; 40% enter graduate study

**General.** Founded in 1955. Regionally accredited. One of a cluster of 5 undergraduate and 2 graduate schools on adjoining campuses. Campuses share facilities and cross-enrollment is available within the 5 undergraduate colleges, which include Claremont-McKenna, Harvey Mudd, Pitzer, Pomona, and Scripps. **Degrees:** 157 bachelor's awarded. **ROTC:** Army, Air Force. **Location:** 35 miles from Los Angeles. **Calendar:** Semester, limited summer session. **Full-time faculty:** 82 total; 100% have terminal degrees, 23% minority, 28% women. **Class size:** 67% < 20, 26% 20-39, 2% 40-49, 3% 50-99, 3% >100. **Special facilities:** Observatory, biological field station, high performance parallel processor.

**Freshman class profile.** 2,493 applied, 700 admitted, 196 enrolled.

| Mid 50% test scores | | | |
|---|---|---|---|
| SAT critical reading: | 700-770 | Rank in top tenth: | 90% |
| SAT math: | 740-800 | End year in good standing: | 93% |
| SAT writing: | 690-760 | Return as sophomores: | 96% |
| GPA 3.50 or higher: | 100% | Out-of-state: | 63% |
| Rank in top quarter: | 100% | Live on campus: | 100% |
| | | International: | 3% |

**Basis for selection.** School achievement record important, especially in mathematics and science. Test scores, recommendations, school and community activities important, interviews highly recommended. Students who take the SAT or ACT with wrtiting must also submit SAT Subject Tests in Math Level 2 and in another subject of their choice. **Homeschooled:** Portfolio suggested describing texts used, curriculum format, how instruction was given. Recommend lab science and foreign language courses be taken at high school or college.

**High school preparation.** 15 units required. Required and recommended units include English 4, mathematics 4, social studies 1, history 2, science 3 (laboratory 3) and foreign language 2. Calculus, 1 year chemistry, 1 year physics also required.

**2007-2008 Annual costs.** Tuition/fees: $34,891. Room/board: $11,415. Books/supplies: $800. Personal expenses: $900.

**2007-2008 Financial aid. Need-based:** 139 full-time freshmen applied for aid; 115 were judged to have need; 115 of these received aid. Average need met was 100%. Average scholarship/grant was $26,273; average loan $3,455. 84% of total undergraduate aid awarded as scholarships/grants, 16% as loans/jobs. **Non-need-based:** Awarded to 345 full-time undergraduates, including 106 freshmen. Scholarships awarded for academics.

**Application procedures. Admission:** Closing date 1/2 (postmark date). $60 fee, may be waived for applicants with need. Application may be submitted online. Admission notification 4/1. Must reply by May 1 or within 2 week(s) if notified thereafter. **Financial aid:** Closing date 2/1. FAFSA, CSS PROFILE required. Applicants notified by 4/1; must reply by 5/1 or within 2 week(s) of notification.

**Academics.** Course work divided equally between technical core, major, and humanities and social sciences. **Special study options:** Combined bachelor's/graduate degree, cross-registration, double major, exchange student, independent study, internships, liberal arts/career combination, student-designed major, study abroad. Applied engineering, mathematics and computer science clinics, 4+1 BS/MBA with Claremont Graduate University. **Credit/placement by examination:** AP, CLEP, IB, institutional tests. **Support services:** Learning center, pre-admission summer program, reduced course load, study skills assistance, tutoring, writing center.

**Majors. Biology:** General. **Computer sciences:** General. **Engineering:** General. **Interdisciplinary:** Biological/physical sciences. **Math:** General, applied. **Physical sciences:** Chemistry, physics.

**Most popular majors.** Biology 11%, computer/information sciences 14%, engineering/engineering technologies 41%, mathematics 18%, physical sciences 14%.

**Computing on campus.** 360 workstations in dormitories, library, computer center. Dormitories wired for high-speed internet access and linked to

campus network. Commuter students can connect to campus network. On-line course registration, online library, helpline, student web hosting, wire-less network available.

**Student life. Freshman orientation:** Mandatory. 5-day residential intro-duction. **Policies:** Student-directed honor code governs academic and non-academic life on campus. **Housing:** Guaranteed on-campus for freshmen. Coed dorms, special housing for disabled, apartments, substance-free hous-ing available. $150 deposit, deadline 7/1. **Activities:** Bands, choral groups, dance, drama, film society, literary magazine, music ensembles, musical theater, radio station, student government, student newspaper, symphony orchestra, InterVarsity Christian Fellowship, Hillel, Society of Women En-gineers, AIDS Awareness, Asian American student alliance, Korean student union, Muslim student association, Society of Hispanic Engineers, National Society of Black Engineers.

**Athletics.** NCAA. **Intercollegiate:** Baseball M, basketball, cross-country, diving, football (tackle) M, golf M, soccer, softball W, swimming, tennis, track and field, volleyball W, water polo. **Intramural:** Basketball, lacrosse, soccer, softball, tennis, volleyball, water polo. **Team name:** Athenas/Stags.

**Student services.** Alcohol/substance abuse counseling, campus minis-tries, career counseling, student employment services, financial aid counsel-ing, health services, minority student services, personal counseling, place-ment for graduates, women's services.

**Contact.** E-mail: admission@hmc.edu
Phone: (909) 621-8011 Fax: (909) 607-7046
Peter Osgood, Director of Admission, Harvey Mudd College, Kingston Hall, 301 Platt Boulevard, Claremont, CA 91711-5901

## Holy Names University
**Oakland, California**
**www.hnu.edu**
CB code: 4059

- Private 4-year university affiliated with Roman Catholic Church
- Commuter campus in large city
- 656 degree-seeking undergraduates: 23% part-time, 72% women, 29% African American, 13% Asian American, 16% Hispanic American, 1% Native American, 4% international
- 359 degree-seeking graduate students
- 27% of applicants admitted
- SAT or ACT (ACT writing optional), application essay required
- 35% graduate within 6 years

**General.** Founded in 1868. Regionally accredited. **Degrees:** 117 bach-elor's awarded; master's offered. **ROTC:** Army, Air Force. **Location:** 14 miles from San Francisco. **Calendar:** Semester, limited summer session. **Full-time faculty:** 36 total; 78% have terminal degrees, 22% minority, 64% women. **Part-time faculty:** 111 total; 50% have terminal degrees, 22% mi-nority, 62% women. **Class size:** 68% < 20, 31% 20-39, 1% 40-49. **Special facilities:** Folk music collection, learning institute for learning disabled.

**Freshman class profile.** 717 applied, 195 admitted, 139 enrolled.

| Mid 50% test scores | | | |
|---|---|---|---|
| SAT critical reading: | 460-540 | End year in good standing: | 95% |
| SAT math: | 430-530 | Return as sophomores: | 77% |
| ACT composite: | 20-23 | Out-of-state: | 19% |
| GPA 3.50 or higher: | 26% | Live on campus: | 81% |
| GPA 3.0-3.49: | 52% | International: | 6% |
| | | GPA 2.0-2.99: | 22% |

**Basis for selection.** Applicants considered for admission based on over-all strength of high school preparation, SAT or ACT scores, personal essay, letter of recommendation, extracurricular activities and individual talents and achievements. For non-native English speakers, ESL Center proficiency report certifying completion of Level 107 or higher may be substituted for TOEFL. Proficiency exams in theory, sight-singing, dictation and piano are required of all students entering the music program. Exams offered during week prior to beginning of each semester. Music major applicant must also audition for a faculty jury. **Homeschooled:** Transcript of courses and grades, letter of recommendation (nonparent) required. Must submit transcript docu-mentation from primary instructor demonstrating completion of basic credit hours for high school. Transcript should demonstrate academic completion along with short evaluation from primary instructor. May require additional portfolio or performance-based assessments to document competency.

**High school preparation.** 15 units required. Required and recom-mended units include English 4, mathematics 3, history 1, science 1 (labo-ratory 1), foreign language 2-3 and academic electives 3. U.S. history or government required, plus 1 additional year of math, foreign language, or lab science.

**2008-2009 Annual costs.** Tuition/fees: $26,300. Room/board: $8,540. Books/supplies: $1,566. Personal expenses: $2,754.

**Financial aid. Non-need-based:** Scholarships awarded for academics, ath-letics, leadership, music/drama, religious affiliation.

**Application procedures. Admission:** Priority date 3/2; deadline 8/15 (postmark date). $50 fee, may be waived for applicants with need. Applica-tion may be submitted online. Admission notification on a rolling basis beginning on or about 10/1. Must reply by May 1 or within 2 week(s) if notified thereafter. **Financial aid:** Priority date 3/2, closing date 6/30. FAFSA required. Applicants notified on a rolling basis starting 9/1; must reply by 5/1 or within 2 week(s) of notification.

**Academics.** All undergraduate students must satisfy general education requirements. First component is Foundation in Critical Thinking and Com-munication. Remaining components use thematic and disciplinary ap-proaches to learning. **Special study options:** Accelerated study, cross-registration, distance learning, double major, ESL, exchange student, independent study, internships, liberal arts/career combination, student-designed major, study abroad, weekend college. **Credit/placement by ex-amination:** AP, CLEP, IB, institutional tests. 6 credit hours maximum to-ward bachelor's degree. Maximum of 6 credit hours per general exam awarded. **Support services:** Learning center, reduced course load, remedial instruc-tion, study skills assistance, tutoring.

**Majors. Biology:** General. **Business:** Business admin, communications, human resources, marketing. **Communications:** Digital media. **Computer sciences:** Networking. **English:** English lit. **Foreign languages:** Spanish. **Health:** Nursing (RN). **History:** General. **Interdisciplinary:** Biopsychol-ogy. **Liberal arts:** Arts/sciences, humanities. **Philosophy/religion:** Philoso-phy, religion. **Psychology:** General. **Public administration:** Human ser-vices. **Social sciences:** Criminology, international relations, sociology. **Visual/performing arts:** Music pedagogy, music performance.

**Most popular majors.** Business/marketing 24%, health sciences 23%, liberal arts 14%, psychology 10%, social sciences 9%.

**Computing on campus.** 80 workstations in dormitories, library, com-puter center. Dormitories wired for high-speed internet access and linked to campus network. Online library, helpline, student web hosting, wireless net-work available.

**Student life. Freshman orientation:** Mandatory, $50 fee. Preregistration for classes offered. 2-3 day weekend event prior to start of term. **Housing:** Guaranteed on-campus for all undergraduates. Coed dorms, substance-free housing available. $100 fully refundable deposit, deadline 8/18. **Activities:** Choral groups, drama, music ensembles, student government, symphony orchestra, Asian Pacific International, black student union, drama club, speech and debate team, Holy Names Construction, Global Outlook, International Village, Latinos Unidos, Operation Total Anime, Organization of Poetry Appreciation and Learning/Spoken Word.

**Athletics.** NAIA. **Intercollegiate:** Basketball, cross-country, golf M, soc-cer, softball W, volleyball. **Team name:** Hawks.

**Student services.** Adult student services, campus ministries, career coun-seling, student employment services, financial aid counseling, personal coun-seling. **Physically disabled:** Services for visually impaired.

**Contact.** E-mail: admission@hnu.edu
Phone: (510) 436-1351 Toll-free number: (800) 430-1321
Fax: (510) 436-1325
Marcia Nance, Vice President for Enrollment Services, Holy Names University, 3500 Mountain Boulevard, Oakland, CA 94619-1699

## Hope International University
**Fullerton, California**
**www.hiu.edu**
CB code: 4614

- Private 4-year university and liberal arts college affiliated with Independent Christian Churches and Churches of Christ
- Residential campus in small city
- 674 degree-seeking undergraduates: 17% part-time, 60% women
- 271 degree-seeking graduate students
- 71% of applicants admitted
- SAT or ACT (ACT writing optional), application essay required
- 42% graduate within 6 years

**General.** Founded in 1928. Regionally accredited. In addition to the cam-pus in Fullerton, CA, there is an extension site in Corona, CA. **Degrees:** 145 bachelor's, 5 associate awarded; master's offered. **Location:** 35 miles from Los Angeles. **Calendar:** 4-1-4, limited summer session. **Full-time faculty:** 32 total; 62% have terminal degrees, 6% minority, 25% women.

**Part-time faculty:** 142 total; 34% have terminal degrees, 26% minority, 42% women. **Class size:** 68% < 20, 29% 20-39, 2% 40-49, less than 1% 50-99.

**Freshman class profile.** 413 applied, 292 admitted, 130 enrolled.

| Mid 50% test scores | | GPA 2.0-2.99: | 30% |
|---|---|---|---|
| SAT critical reading: | 440-540 | Rank in top quarter: | 37% |
| SAT math: | 420-530 | Rank in top tenth: | 20% |
| SAT writing: | 420-530 | End year in good standing: | 68% |
| ACT composite: | 18-21 | Return as sophomores: | 69% |
| GPA 3.50 or higher: | 37% | Out-of-state: | 28% |
| GPA 3.0-3.49: | 32% | Live on campus: | 84% |

**Basis for selection.** Prior academic achievement, standardized test scores, statement of purpose essays, commitment to the mission of the institution and recommendations are important. Extracurricular activities are also considered along with all other factors bearing on potential success. Interviews recommended for academically borderline applicants. **Homeschooled:** If schooled under the auspices of an organization that can offer transcripts, the university will accept these transcripts and SAT/ACT scores. If not, a GED score and SAT/ACT scores are required in the application process. **Learning Disabled:** All documentation must be recent, within the past three years of enrollment, and must have been completed by an appropriate professional, e.g., State licensed psychologist or school psychologist. Documentation shall include both appropriate tests of learning abilities as well as interview material.

**High school preparation.** 14 units recommended. Recommended units include English 4, mathematics 2, social studies 1, history 1, science 1 (laboratory 1), foreign language 1, computer science 1 and academic electives 3. One half-unit speech and one-half unit computer science or literacy is recommended.

**2008-2009 Annual costs.** Tuition/fees: $21,885. Room/board: $8,230. Books/supplies: $1,386. Personal expenses: $2,520.

**2007-2008 Financial aid. Need-based:** 113 full-time freshmen applied for aid; 93 were judged to have need; 93 of these received aid. Average need met was 83%. Average scholarship/grant was $14,963; average loan $3,605. 72% of total undergraduate aid awarded as scholarships/grants, 28% as loans/jobs. **Non-need-based:** Awarded to 113 full-time undergraduates, including 42 freshmen. Scholarships awarded for academics, alumni affiliation, athletics, leadership, music/drama.

**Application procedures. Admission:** Priority date 7/1; no deadline. $40 fee, may be waived for applicants with need. Application may be submitted online. Admission notification on a rolling basis. **Financial aid:** Priority date 3/2, closing date 3/2. FAFSA, institutional form required. Applicants notified on a rolling basis starting 3/15; must reply within 2 week(s) of notification.

**Academics.** Emphasis on field-based interactive learning combined with direct professional involvement with students. **Special study options:** Accelerated study, combined bachelor's/graduate degree, cooperative education, cross-registration, distance learning, double major, dual enrollment of high school students, ESL, exchange student, external degree, honors, independent study, internships, liberal arts/career combination, semester at sea, student-designed major, study abroad, teacher certification program, Washington semester. **Credit/placement by examination:** AP, CLEP, IB, SAT, institutional tests. 30 credit hours maximum toward bachelor's degree. The amount of credit for examinations depends upon the applicability of the exam(s) to the specific degree program requirements. **Support services:** Reduced course load, remedial instruction, study skills assistance, tutoring.

**Majors. Business:** Business admin. **Education:** Elementary, music, social science. **Family/consumer sciences:** Family studies. **Health:** Athletic training. **Psychology:** General. **Public administration:** Human services. **Social sciences:** General. **Theology:** Bible, missionary, sacred music, theology, youth ministry.

**Most popular majors.** Business/marketing 25%, education 6%, family/consumer sciences 40%, psychology 6%, theological studies 20%.

**Computing on campus.** 53 workstations in dormitories, library, computer center. Dormitories wired for high-speed internet access. Online library, helpline, repair service, wireless network available.

**Student life. Freshman orientation:** Mandatory, $75 fee. Preregistration for classes offered. Fall and spring new student orientation held 3 days before beginning of term. **Policies:** No alcohol permitted, smoking discouraged. Religious observance required. **Housing:** Guaranteed on-campus for freshmen. Single-sex dorms, substance-free housing available. $100 partly refundable deposit, deadline 7/1. Single students required to live on campus until age 21 or reaching junior standing, unless living at home or given special approval. **Activities:** Choral groups, drama, international student organizations, music ensembles, musical theater, student government, student newspaper, school outreach, minority students association, business club.

**Athletics.** NAIA. **Intercollegiate:** Basketball, cheerleading, soccer, softball W, tennis, volleyball. **Intramural:** Badminton, basketball, football (non-tackle) W, soccer, volleyball. **Team name:** Royals.

**Student services.** Adult student services, campus ministries, career counseling, student employment services, financial aid counseling, health services, personal counseling, placement for graduates, veterans' counselor.

**Contact.** E-mail: ug-admissions@hiu.edu
Phone: (714) 879-3901 ext. 2215 Toll-free number: (866) 722-4673
Fax: (714) 681-7423
Butch Ellis, Director of Undergraduate Admissions, Hope International University, 2500 East Nutwood Avenue, Fullerton, CA 92831-3199

---

## Humboldt State University
**Arcata, California**
www.humboldt.edu                                    CB code: 4345

▶ Public 4-year university and liberal arts college
▶ Residential campus in large town
▶ 6,581 degree-seeking undergraduates: 9% part-time, 53% women, 4% African American, 5% Asian American, 11% Hispanic American, 2% Native American
▶ 850 degree-seeking graduate students
▶ 82% of applicants admitted
▶ 42% graduate within 6 years

**General.** Founded in 1913. Regionally accredited. **Degrees:** 1,371 bachelor's awarded; master's offered. **Location:** 275 miles from San Francisco. **Calendar:** Semester, extensive summer session. **Full-time faculty:** 276 total; 84% have terminal degrees, 14% minority, 37% women. **Part-time faculty:** 242 total; 25% have terminal degrees, 18% minority, 58% women. **Class size:** 34% < 20, 46% 20-39, 9% 40-49, 9% 50-99, 2% >100. **Special facilities:** Marine lab, observatory, natural history museum, marsh and wildlife sanctuary, small lakes and ponds, 280-acre sand dune preserve, research vessel, freshwater fish hatchery, small-game animal pen, fungal genetic stock center, 360-acre experimental forest, 170,000 specimen herbarium, center for appropriate technology, energy research center.

**Freshman class profile.** 8,216 applied, 6,768 admitted, 1,051 enrolled.

| Mid 50% test scores | | GPA 2.0-2.99: | 43% |
|---|---|---|---|
| SAT critical reading: | 450-590 | Rank in top quarter: | 39% |
| SAT math: | 450-580 | Rank in top tenth: | 10% |
| SAT writing: | 440-560 | End year in good standing: | 70% |
| ACT composite: | 18-25 | Return as sophomores: | 75% |
| GPA 3.50 or higher: | 22% | Out-of-state: | 17% |
| GPA 3.0-3.49: | 35% | Live on campus: | 82% |

**Basis for selection.** High school GPA and test scores most important. In-state residents with high school GPA of 3.0 or higher or out-of-state applicants with high school GPA over 3.6 do not have to submit test scores for admission. Essay recommended for academically weak, special consideration applicants.

**High school preparation.** 15 units required. Required units include English 4, mathematics 3, social studies 1, history 1, science 2 (laboratory 2), foreign language 2 and academic electives 1.

**2007-2008 Annual costs.** Tuition/fees: $3,843; $14,013 out-of-state. Room/board: $8,522. Books/supplies: $1,314. Personal expenses: $1,860.

**2006-2007 Financial aid. Need-based:** 732 full-time freshmen applied for aid; 516 were judged to have need; 481 of these received aid. Average need met was 69%. Average scholarship/grant was $4,045; average loan $300. 56% of total undergraduate aid awarded as scholarships/grants, 44% as loans/jobs. **Non-need-based:** Awarded to 129 full-time undergraduates, including 31 freshmen. Scholarships awarded for academics.

**Application procedures. Admission:** Priority date 10/1; deadline 8/1. $55 fee, may be waived for applicants with need. Application may be submitted online. Admission notification on a rolling basis beginning on or about 11/15. **Financial aid:** Priority date 3/2; no closing date. FAFSA required. Applicants notified on a rolling basis starting 3/1; must reply within 6 week(s) of notification.

**Academics.** Indian Teacher and Educational Personnel Program, Indian Natural Resources, Sciences and Engineering Program available. **Special study options:** Cooperative education, cross-registration, distance learning, double major, dual enrollment of high school students, ESL, exchange student, honors, independent study, internships, student-designed major, study abroad, teacher certification program. **Credit/placement by examination:**

AP, CLEP, IB, SAT, ACT, institutional tests. 24 credit hours maximum toward bachelor's degree. **Support services:** Learning center, pre-admission summer program, remedial instruction, tutoring, writing center.

**Majors. Agriculture:** Range science. **Area/ethnic studies:** Native American, women's. **Biology:** General, botany, zoology. **Business:** General, business admin. **Communications:** General, journalism. **Computer sciences:** General, information systems. **Conservation:** General, environmental studies, fisheries, forestry, management/policy, wildlife. **Education:** Early childhood, elementary, physical, trade/industrial. **Engineering:** Science. **English:** Composition, English lit. **Foreign languages:** French, German, Spanish. **Health:** Kinesiotherapy, nursing (RN). **History:** General. **Interdisciplinary:** Global studies, intercultural. **Liberal arts:** Arts/sciences. **Math:** General. **Parks/recreation:** Facilities management, health/fitness. **Philosophy/religion:** Philosophy, religion. **Physical sciences:** General, chemistry, geology, oceanography, physics. **Psychology:** General. **Public administration:** Social work. **Social sciences:** General, anthropology, economics, geography, political science, sociology. **Visual/performing arts:** Art, dance, dramatic.

**Most popular majors.** Biology 9%, English 6%, liberal arts 11%, natural resources/environmental science 10%, psychology 6%, social sciences 12%, visual/performing arts 11%.

**Computing on campus.** 770 workstations in dormitories, library, computer center, student center. Dormitories wired for high-speed internet access and linked to campus network. Commuter students can connect to campus network. Online course registration, online library, helpline, student web hosting, wireless network available.

**Student life. Freshman orientation:** Mandatory, $50 fee. Preregistration for classes offered. Student-directed program held June, July and August. **Housing:** Guaranteed on-campus for freshmen. Coed dorms, apartments, fraternity/sorority housing, substance-free housing available. $500 partly refundable deposit, deadline 5/2. Themed residence halls available. **Activities:** Bands, choral groups, dance, drama, film society, literary magazine, music ensembles, musical theater, radio station, student government, student newspaper, symphony orchestra, Newman club, Campus Crusade for Christ, youth educational services, black students union, MECHA, gay, lesbian and bisexual students association, Native American club, Jewish student union, multicultural center, veterans organization.

**Athletics.** NCAA. **Intercollegiate:** Basketball, cross-country, football (tackle) M, rowing (crew) W, soccer, softball W, track and field, volleyball W. **Intramural:** Badminton, basketball, football (tackle) M, soccer, softball, volleyball. **Team name:** Lumberjacks.

**Student services.** Adult student services, career counseling, student employment services, health services, on-campus daycare, personal counseling, placement for graduates, veterans' counselor. **Physically disabled:** Services for visually, speech, hearing impaired.

**Contact.** E-mail: hsuinfo@humboldt.edu
Phone: (707) 826-4402 Toll-free number: (866) 850-9556
Fax: (707) 826-6190
Scott Hagg, Director of Admissions and Student Recruitment, Humboldt State University, Arcata, CA 95521-8299

## Humphreys College
Stockton, California
www.humphreys.edu
CB code: 4346

- Private 4-year business and liberal arts college
- Residential campus in large city
- 666 degree-seeking undergraduates: 41% part-time, 86% women, 17% African American, 12% Asian American, 37% Hispanic American, 1% Native American
- 87 graduate students
- Interview required
- 71% graduate within 6 years; 50% enter graduate study

**General.** Founded in 1896. Regionally accredited. **Degrees:** 61 bachelor's, 38 associate awarded; first professional offered. **Location:** 35 miles from Sacramento. **Calendar:** Quarter, extensive summer session. **Full-time faculty:** 18 total; 17% have terminal degrees, 28% minority, 44% women. **Part-time faculty:** 44 total; 14% have terminal degrees, 46% minority, 41% women. **Class size:** 80% < 20, 20% 20-39.

**Freshman class profile.**

| | | | |
|---|---|---|---|
| End year in good standing: | 91% | Out-of-state: | 3% |
| Return as sophomores: | 62% | Live on campus: | 25% |

**Basis for selection.** Open admission. ACT used for placement only. **Homeschooled:** State high school equivalency certificate required.

**2008-2009 Annual costs.** Tuition/fees (projected): $12,240. School-controlled apartment housing cost quoted, not including utilities. Room only: $3,150. Books/supplies: $522. Personal expenses: $738.

**2007-2008 Financial aid. Need-based:** 39 full-time freshmen applied for aid; 36 were judged to have need; 36 of these received aid. Average need met was 93%. Average scholarship/grant was $4,310; average loan $3,500. 32% of total undergraduate aid awarded as scholarships/grants, 68% as loans/jobs. **Non-need-based:** Scholarships awarded for academics, state residency.

**Application procedures. Admission:** No deadline. $35 fee, may be waived for applicants with need. Application must be submitted on paper. Admission notification on a rolling basis. **Financial aid:** Closing date 6/30. FAFSA required. Applicants notified on a rolling basis; must reply within 2 week(s) of notification.

**Academics. Special study options:** Combined bachelor's/graduate degree, cooperative education, cross-registration, double major, honors, independent study, internships. **Credit/placement by examination:** AP, CLEP, IB, institutional tests. 4 credit hours maximum toward associate degree, 45 toward bachelor's. **Support services:** Learning center, pre-admission summer program, remedial instruction, tutoring, writing center.

**Majors. Business:** General, accounting, administrative services, business admin, office technology, office/clerical. **Computer sciences:** General. **Education:** General. **Health:** Medical secretary. **Legal studies:** Court reporting, legal secretary, paralegal. **Liberal arts:** Arts/sciences. **Public administration:** Community org/advocacy. **Social sciences:** General.

**Computing on campus.** 25 workstations in library, computer center. Wireless network available.

**Student life. Freshman orientation:** Available. Preregistration for classes offered. Held in September. **Housing:** Apartments available. $200 partly refundable deposit, deadline 8/20. **Activities:** Student government, student newspaper, business club.

**Student services.** Career counseling, student employment services, financial aid counseling, on-campus daycare, personal counseling, placement for graduates, veterans' counselor.

**Contact.** E-mail: ugadmission@humphreys.edu
Phone: (209) 478-0800 Fax: (209) 478-8721
Santa Lopez-Minarte, Admissions Director, Humphreys College, 6650 Inglewood Avenue, Stockton, CA 95207-3896

## Interior Designers Institute
Newport Beach, California
www.idi.edu
CB code: 2318

- For-profit 4-year visual arts college
- Large city
- 510 degree-seeking undergraduates

**General.** Accredited by ACCSCT. **Degrees:** 15 bachelor's, 50 associate awarded. **Calendar:** Continuous. **Part-time faculty:** 30 total.

**Basis for selection.** Open admission.

**2007-2008 Annual costs.** 12-week certificate program tuition $1,995. Full year associate and bachelor's degree tuition $14,950. Books/supplies: $1,500.

**Application procedures. Admission:** No deadline. $95 fee. Application must be submitted on paper.

**Academics. Credit/placement by examination:** CLEP.

**Majors. Visual/performing arts:** Interior design.

**Contact.** E-mail: contact@idi.edu
Phone: (949) 675-4451 Fax: (949) 759-0667
Susan Bell, Office Manager, Interior Designers Institute, 1061 Camelback Road, Newport Beach, CA 92660-3228

## International Technological University
Sunnyvale, California
www.itu.edu/

- Private two-year upper-division engineering college
- Commuter campus in small city

**General.** Accredited by ACICS. **Calendar:** Trimester.

**Annual costs/financial aid.** MBA $380 per credit hour; MS engineering $425 per credit hour.

**Contact.** Phone: (408) 331-1014
Registrar, 756 San Aleso Avenue, Sunnyvale, CA 94085

## ITT Technical Institute: Anaheim
**Anaheim, California**
www.itt-tech.edu                                    CB code: 3570

- For-profit 4-year technical college
- Commuter campus in small city

**General.** Founded in 1983. Accredited by ACICS. **Location:** 15 miles from Los Angeles. **Calendar:** Quarter.

**Annual costs/financial aid.** Tuition varies by program, $260-$368 per credit hour.

**Contact.** Phone: (714) 535-3700
Director of Recruitment, 525 North Muller, Anaheim, CA 92801

## ITT Technical Institute: Lathrop
**Lathrop, California**
www.itt-tech.edu                                    CB code: 2720

- For-profit 4-year technical college
- Commuter campus in small town

**General.** Accredited by ACICS. **Calendar:** Quarter.

**Annual costs/financial aid.** Tuition varies by program, $260-$368 per credit hour.

**Contact.** Phone: (209) 858-0077
Director of Recruitment, 16916 South Harlan Road, Lathrop, CA 95330

## ITT Technical Institute: Oxnard
**Oxnard, California**
www.itt-tech.edu                                    CB code: 2744

- For-profit 4-year technical college
- Commuter campus in small city

**General.** Accredited by ACICS. **Location:** 34 miles from Santa Barbara, 52 miles from Los Angeles. **Calendar:** Quarter.

**Annual costs/financial aid.** Tuition varies by program, $260-$368 per credit hour.

**Contact.** Phone: (805) 988-0143
Director of Recruitment, 2051 Solar Drive, Building B, Oxnard, CA 93036

## ITT Technical Institute: Rancho Cordova
**Rancho Cordova, California**
www.itt-tech.edu                                    CB code: 3597

- For-profit 4-year technical college
- Commuter campus in large city

**General.** Founded in 1954. Accredited by ACICS. **Location:** 11 miles from Sacramento, 87 miles from San Francisco. **Calendar:** Quarter.

**Annual costs/financial aid.** Tuition varies by program, $260-$368 per credit hour.

**Contact.** Phone: (916) 366-3900
Director of Recruitment, 10863 Gold Center Drive, Rancho Cordova, CA 95670

## ITT Technical Institute: San Bernardino
**San Bernardino, California**
www.itt-tech.edu                                    CB code: 7103

- For-profit 4-year technical college
- Commuter campus in very large city

**General.** Accredited by ACICS. **Location:** 60 miles from Los Angeles. **Calendar:** Quarter.

**Annual costs/financial aid.** Tuition varies by program, $260-$368 per credit hour.

**Contact.** Phone: (800) 888-3801
Director of Recruitment, 670 East Carnegie Drive, San Bernardino, CA 92408-2800

## ITT Technical Institute: San Diego
**San Diego, California**
www.itt-tech.edu                                    CB code: 0206

- For-profit 4-year technical college
- Commuter campus in very large city

**General.** Founded in 1981. Accredited by ACICS. **Calendar:** Quarter.

**Annual costs/financial aid.** Tuition varies by program, $260-$368 per credit hour.

**Contact.** Phone: (858) 571-8500
Director of Recruitment, 9680 Granite Ridge Drive, San Diego, CA 92123

## ITT Technical Institute: Sylmar
**Sylmar, California**
www.itt-tech.edu                                    CB code: 3571

- For-profit 4-year technical college
- Commuter campus in very large city

**General.** Founded in 1982. Accredited by ACICS. **Calendar:** Quarter.

**Annual costs/financial aid.** Tuition varies by program, $260-$368 per credit hour.

**Contact.** Phone: (818) 364-5151
Director of Recruitment, 12669 Encinitas Avenue, Sylmar, CA 91342-3664

## ITT Technical Institute: Torrance
**Torrance, California**
www.itt-tech.edu                                    CB code: 7104

- For-profit 4-year technical college
- Commuter campus in small city

**General.** Accredited by ACICS. **Calendar:** Quarter.

**Annual costs/financial aid.** Tuition varies by program, $260-$368 per credit hour.

**Contact.** Phone: (310) 380-1555
Director of Recruitment, 20050 South Vermont Avenue, Torrance, CA 90502

## John F. Kennedy University
**Pleasant Hill, California**
www.jfku.edu                                    CB code: 1362

- Private 4-year business and liberal arts college
- Commuter campus in large town
- 236 degree-seeking undergraduates
- 1,330 graduate students
- Application essay, interview required

**General.** Founded in 1964. Regionally accredited. Undergraduate and graduate degree Linking program. **Degrees:** 41 bachelor's awarded; master's, doctoral, first professional offered. **Location:** 35 miles from San Francisco. **Calendar:** Quarter, limited summer session. **Full-time faculty:** 55 total. **Part-time faculty:** 194 total. **Class size:** 81% < 20, 19% 20-39.

**Basis for selection.** For upper-division bachelor's degree completion, transcript, interview required for assessment of qualifications. Students need 45 college units, general education preferred.

**2007-2008 Annual costs.** Tuition/fees: $15,468. Books/supplies: $1,080.

**Financial aid.** All financial aid based on need.

**Application procedures. Admission:** No deadline. $55 fee. Application may be submitted online. Admission notification on a rolling basis. **Financial aid:** Priority date 3/2; no closing date. FAFSA, institutional form required. Applicants notified on a rolling basis; must reply within 4 week(s) of notification.

**Academics. Special study options:** Combined bachelor's/graduate degree, cross-registration, independent study, internships, teacher certification program. **Credit/placement by examination:** AP, CLEP. 105 credit hours maximum toward bachelor's degree. Maximum of 105 units through combination of CLEP, DANTES, 2-year schools, and military training. **Support services:** Study skills assistance, writing center.

**Majors. Business:** Business admin. **Legal studies:** General, paralegal. **Liberal arts:** Arts/sciences. **Psychology:** General. **Visual/performing arts:** Studio arts. **Other:** Philosophy and religion.

**Most popular majors.** Business/marketing 26%, liberal arts 63%, psychology 11%.

**Computing on campus.** 25 workstations in library, computer center. Commuter students can connect to campus network.

**Student life. Activities:** Student government, student newspaper.

**Student services.** Career counseling, student employment services, veterans' counselor. **Physically disabled:** Services for visually, speech, hearing impaired.

**Contact.** E-mail: proginfo@jfku.edu
Phone: (925) 969-3535 Fax: (925) 969-3331
Jen Miller-Hogg, Director of Admissions, John F. Kennedy University, 100 Ellinwood Way, Pleasant Hill, CA 94523-4817

## The King's College and Seminary
**Los Angeles, California**
**www.kingscollege.edu**                    CB code: 3896

- Private 4-year Bible and seminary college affiliated with nondenominational tradition
- Commuter campus in very large city
- 547 degree-seeking undergraduates
- Application essay required

**General.** Accredited by ABHE. Evangelical institution. **Degrees:** 19 bachelor's, 10 associate awarded; master's, doctoral, first professional offered. **ROTC:** Army, Naval, Air Force. **Calendar:** Quarter, limited summer session. **Full-time faculty:** 15 total. **Part-time faculty:** 34 total.

**Basis for selection.** Demonstration of commitment to Christian faith required, essays, references important. Tests recommended, not required. **Homeschooled:** Statement describing homeschool structure and mission, transcript of courses and grades required.

**2007-2008 Annual costs.** Tuition/fees: $7,935. Seminary students pay $185 per credit hour. Books/supplies: $900.

**Financial aid. Non-need-based:** Scholarships awarded for academics, leadership. **Additional information:** Specific scholarships may require specific essays.

**Application procedures. Admission:** No deadline. $45 fee. Application may be submitted online. Admission notification on a rolling basis. **Financial aid:** No deadline. FAFSA required. Applicants notified on a rolling basis.

**Academics. Special study options:** Distance learning, external degree, internships. **Credit/placement by examination:** AP, CLEP, IB, institutional tests. 45 credit hours maximum toward associate degree, 45 toward bachelor's. **Support services:** Reduced course load, remedial instruction, study skills assistance, tutoring.

**Majors. Theology:** Bible.

**Computing on campus.** Online course registration, online library available.

**Student life. Freshman orientation:** Mandatory. Preregistration for classes offered. **Policies:** Drug- and alcohol-free campus. Religious observance required. **Activities:** Student government, C.S. Lewis club, women in ministry group, Delta Epsilon, National Association of Evangelicals.

**Student services.** Campus ministries, career counseling, financial aid counseling, personal counseling, placement for graduates, veterans' counselor, women's services.

**Contact.** E-mail: admissions@kingscollege.edu
Phone: (818) 779-8040 Toll-free number: (888) 779-8040
Fax: (818) 779-8241
Marilyn Chappell, Director of Admissions, The King's College and Seminary, 14800 Sherman Way, Los Angeles, CA 91405-2233

## LA College International
**Los Angeles, California**
**www.lac.edu**                    CB code: 3046

- For-profit 4-year business and technical college
- Commuter campus in very large city
- 120 degree-seeking undergraduates

**General.** Accredited by ACICS. **Degrees:** 9 bachelor's, 16 associate awarded. **Calendar:** Quarter. **Part-time faculty:** 25 total.

**Basis for selection.** Open admission. ATB required if no high school diploma.

**2007-2008 Annual costs.** Tuition/fees: $12,375. Online tuition $325 per credit hour for AA and BS programs in business management. Books/supplies: $210.

**Application procedures. Admission:** No deadline. $35 fee. **Financial aid:** FAFSA, institutional form required.

**Academics. Credit/placement by examination:** CLEP.

**Majors. Business:** Business admin. **Computer sciences:** General.

**Student life. Freshman orientation:** Available. 4 days before start date. **Activities:** Student government.

**Contact.** Phone: (213) 381-3333 Toll-free number: (800) 574-6428
Fax: (213) 383-9369
Shavonne Turner, Admissions Director, LA College International, 3200 Wilshire Boulevard, Suite 400, Los Angeles, CA 90010-1308

## La Sierra University
**Riverside, California**                    CB member
**www.lasierra.edu**                    CB code: 4380

- Private 4-year university affiliated with Seventh-day Adventists
- Residential campus in large city
- 1,422 degree-seeking undergraduates: 10% part-time, 59% women, 8% African American, 25% Asian American, 26% Hispanic American, 11% international
- 274 degree-seeking graduate students
- 45% of applicants admitted
- SAT or ACT (ACT writing optional), application essay required

**General.** Founded in 1922. Regionally accredited. **Degrees:** 208 bachelor's awarded; master's, doctoral, first professional offered. **Location:** 55 miles from Los Angeles. **Calendar:** Quarter, limited summer session. **Full-time faculty:** 96 total; 88% have terminal degrees, 36% minority, 43% women. **Part-time faculty:** 77 total; 23% minority, 44% women. **Class size:** 71% < 20, 23% 20-39, 2% 40-49, 3% 50-99, 1% >100. **Special facilities:** Museum of natural history with large freeze-dried collection (reptiles, mammals, birds), mineral spheres collection, arboretum, observatory, women's resource center.

**Freshman class profile.** 1,307 applied, 593 admitted, 337 enrolled.

| Mid 50% test scores | | | |
|---|---|---|---|
| SAT critical reading: | 420-540 | Rank in top quarter: | 49% |
| SAT math: | 430-550 | Rank in top tenth: | 20% |
| ACT composite: | 17-23 | Return as sophomores: | 61% |
| GPA 3.50 or higher: | 39% | Out-of-state: | 15% |
| GPA 3.0-3.49: | 32% | Live on campus: | 61% |
| GPA 2.0-2.99: | 28% | International: | 10% |

**Basis for selection.** Secondary school record and GPA, test scores, recommendations, and religious affiliation or commitment important.

**High school preparation.** 15 units required. Required and recommended units include English 4, mathematics 3-4, social studies 2, science 2-3 (laboratory 2-3), foreign language 2-3, visual/performing arts 1 and academic electives 1.

**2008-2009 Annual costs.** Tuition/fees (projected): $23,354. Room/board: $6,711. Books/supplies: $1,500. Personal expenses: $2,214.

**2006-2007 Financial aid. Need-based:** 255 full-time freshmen applied for aid; 228 were judged to have need; 226 of these received aid. Average need met was 67%. Average scholarship/grant was $14,617; average loan $2,439. 55% of total undergraduate aid awarded as scholarships/grants, 45% as loans/jobs. **Non-need-based:** Awarded to 422 full-time undergraduates, including 84 freshmen. Scholarships awarded for academics, leadership, music/drama, religious affiliation.

**Application procedures. Admission:** Priority date 2/1; no deadline. $30 fee, may be waived for applicants with need. Application may be submitted online. Admission notification on a rolling basis. **Financial aid:** Priority date 3/2; no closing date. FAFSA required. Applicants notified on a rolling basis starting 4/15; must reply by 9/1.

**Academics. Special study options:** Accelerated study, cross-registration, distance learning, double major, dual enrollment of high school students, ESL, honors, independent study, internships, student-designed major, study abroad, teacher certification program. **Credit/placement by examination:** AP, CLEP, IB, institutional tests. 24 credit hours maximum toward bachelor's degree. **Support services:** Learning center, pre-admission summer program, reduced course load, remedial instruction, study skills assistance, tutoring, writing center.

**Honors college/program.** High school GPA above 3.25 and ACT above 60th percentile. 25 freshmen admitted per year.

**Majors. Biology:** General, biochemistry, biophysics. **Business:** Accounting, business admin, finance. **Communications:** General. **Computer sciences:** Computer science, information systems. **English:** English lit. **Foreign languages:** Spanish. **History:** General. **Interdisciplinary:** Behavioral sciences. **Liberal arts:** Arts/sciences. **Math:** General. **Parks/recreation:** Exercise sciences, health/fitness. **Philosophy/religion:** Religion. **Physical sciences:** Chemistry. **Psychology:** General. **Public administration:** Social work. **Social sciences:** Sociology. **Visual/performing arts:** Art, commercial/advertising art, studio arts.

**Most popular majors.** Biology 19%, business/marketing 25%, liberal arts 15%, parks/recreation 8%, psychology 9%, visual/performing arts 7%.

**Computing on campus.** 135 workstations in dormitories, library, computer center. Dormitories wired for high-speed internet access and linked to campus network. Commuter students can connect to campus network. Online course registration, helpline, wireless network available.

**Student life. Freshman orientation:** Mandatory, $200 fee. Preregistration for classes offered. **Policies:** Smoke- and alcohol-free campus. Religious observance required. **Housing:** Guaranteed on-campus for all undergraduates. Single-sex dorms, apartments, substance-free housing available. $100 fully refundable deposit. Honors residence hall available. **Activities:** Bands, campus ministries, choral groups, drama, international student organizations, literary magazine, music ensembles, student government, student newspaper, symphony orchestra, black student association, Earth Awareness, Amnesty International, Korean club, Ole club, Students in Free Enterprise, South Asia student association.

**Athletics.** NCAA. **Intercollegiate:** Baseball M, basketball, golf M, soccer, softball W, tennis, volleyball W. **Intramural:** Badminton, basketball, football (tackle), softball. **Team name:** Golden Eagles.

**Student services.** Adult student services, campus ministries, career counseling, student employment services, financial aid counseling, health services, personal counseling, placement for graduates, women's services.

**Contact.** E-mail: admissions@lasierra.edu
Phone: (951) 785-2176 Toll-free number: (800) 874-5587
Fax: (951) 785-2477
Faye Swayze, Director of Admissions & Registrar, La Sierra University, 4500 Riverwalk Parkway, Riverside, CA 92515-8247

## Laguna College of Art and Design
**Laguna Beach, California**
www.lagunacollege.edu          CB code: 7248

- Private 4-year visual arts college
- Commuter campus in large town
- 350 degree-seeking undergraduates
- 74% of applicants admitted
- SAT or ACT (ACT writing optional) required

**General.** Founded in 1961. Regionally accredited. **Degrees:** 45 bachelor's awarded; master's offered. **Location:** 50 miles from Los Angeles, 75 miles

from San Diego. **Calendar:** Semester, limited summer session. **Full-time faculty:** 11 total. **Part-time faculty:** 72 total.

**Freshman class profile.** 299 applied, 221 admitted, 65 enrolled.

**Basis for selection.** Selection based on academic record and overall merit of 10-piece portfolio which includes minimum of 4 observational drawings. Application fee waived for online applications. Portfolios required.

**High school preparation.** 14 units recommended. Recommended units include English 2, mathematics 2, social studies 2, history 2, science 2, foreign language 2 and academic electives 2. 3 units of studio art, drawing and painting recommended.

**2008-2009 Annual costs.** Tuition/fees (projected): $20,600. Books/supplies: $1,300. Personal expenses: $2,312.

**Financial aid. Additional information:** Need- and merit-based scholarship deadline March 20.

**Application procedures. Admission:** Priority date 2/2; no deadline. $45 fee, may be waived for applicants with need. Application may be submitted online. Admission notification on a rolling basis. **Financial aid:** No deadline. FAFSA, institutional form required. Applicants notified on a rolling basis; must reply within 2 week(s) of notification.

**Academics. Special study options:** Cooperative education, double major, exchange student, independent study, internships, New York semester, study abroad. **Credit/placement by examination:** CLEP. **Support services:** Pre-admission summer program, reduced course load, remedial instruction, tutoring.

**Majors. Visual/performing arts:** Commercial/advertising art, drawing, painting.

**Computing on campus.** 26 workstations in library, computer center.

**Student life. Policies:** Very strong student government promoting activities on and off campus. Many art-related activities with social gatherings as well. **Activities:** Student government, student newspaper, foreign student organization, cultural diversity organization.

**Student services.** Career counseling, personal counseling, veterans' counselor.

**Contact.** E-mail: admissions@lagunacollege.edu
Phone: (949) 376-6000 Toll-free number: (800) 255-0762
Fax: (949) 376-6009
Mike Rivas, Admissions Director, Laguna College of Art and Design, 2222 Laguna Canyon Road, Laguna Beach, CA 92651-1136

## Life Pacific College
**San Dimas, California**
www.lifepacific.edu          CB code: 4264

- Private 4-year Bible college affiliated with International Church of the Foursquare Gospel
- Residential campus in large town
- 399 degree-seeking undergraduates: 28% part-time, 49% women, 6% African American, 6% Asian American, 14% Hispanic American, 1% Native American
- 81% of applicants admitted
- SAT or ACT with writing, application essay required
- 35% graduate within 6 years

**General.** Founded in 1925. Candidate for regional accreditation; also accredited by ABHE. **Degrees:** 78 bachelor's, 8 associate awarded. **Location:** 30 miles from Los Angeles. **Calendar:** Semester, limited summer session. **Full-time faculty:** 14 total; 29% have terminal degrees, 14% minority, 29% women. **Part-time faculty:** 29 total; 24% have terminal degrees, 17% women. **Class size:** 75% < 20, 20% 20-39, less than 1% 40-49, 5% 50-99.

**Freshman class profile.** 69 applied, 56 admitted, 46 enrolled.

| Mid 50% test scores | | End year in good standing: | 49% |
|---|---|---|---|
| SAT critical reading: | 430-550 | Return as sophomores: | 51% |
| SAT math: | 410-550 | Out-of-state: | 51% |
| SAT writing: | 420-510 | Live on campus: | 93% |
| ACT composite: | 16-20 | | |

**Basis for selection.** Christian character, motivation, and ability to accord with college's program most important. Cumulative GPA in last school attended and SAT or ACT scores also considered. **Homeschooled:** Must present official transcript with graduation date. SAT or ACT required. **Learning Disabled:** LIFE Challenges Program available to students with learning disabilities. Request information.

**2008-2009 Annual costs.** Tuition/fees: $11,450. Room/board: $5,600. Books/supplies: $1,260. Personal expenses: $1,818.

**2007-2008 Financial aid. Non-need-based:** Scholarships awarded for academics, alumni affiliation.

**Application procedures. Admission:** Priority date 4/1; deadline 5/1 (postmark date). $35 fee. Application must be submitted on paper. Admission notification on a rolling basis. **Financial aid:** Closing date 7/1. FAFSA required. Applicants notified on a rolling basis starting 6/1.

**Academics.** Bible studies taught from Charismatic/Pentecostal perspective training leaders for ministry. **Special study options:** Cooperative education, distance learning, dual enrollment of high school students, external degree, independent study, internships, study abroad. **Credit/placement by examination:** AP, CLEP, SAT, ACT, institutional tests. 16 credit hours maximum toward associate degree, 16 toward bachelor's. Credit limited by the number of subjects accepted, course by course basis. **Support services:** Reduced course load, remedial instruction, study skills assistance, writing center.

**Majors. Theology:** Bible, pastoral counseling.

**Computing on campus.** 45 workstations in dormitories, library, computer center, student center. Dormitories wired for high-speed internet access and linked to campus network. Online course registration, online library, helpline, wireless network available.

**Student life. Freshman orientation:** Mandatory, $100 fee. Preregistration for classes offered. One full day (meal provided), includes testing. **Policies:** Religious observance required. **Housing:** Guaranteed on-campus for freshmen. Single-sex dorms, substance-free housing available. $200 nonrefundable deposit, deadline 6/1. **Activities:** Choral groups, dance, drama, film society, music ensembles, student government, learning center (tutoring for junior high and high school).

**Athletics. Team name:** Warriors.

**Student services.** Adult student services, campus ministries, career counseling, student employment services, financial aid counseling, minority student services, personal counseling, placement for graduates, veterans' counselor. **Physically disabled:** Services for speech, hearing impaired.

**Contact.** E-mail: admissions@lifepacific.edu
Phone: (909) 599-5433 ext. 314 Toll-free number: (877) 886-5433
Fax: (909) 706-6690
Aaron Stewart, Recruitment/Admissions Director, Life Pacific College, Attn: Admissions, San Dimas, CA 91773-3203

## Lincoln University
Oakland, California
www.lincolnuca.edu
CB code: 4386

- Private 4-year university and health science college
- Commuter campus in very large city
- 114 degree-seeking undergraduates: 26% Asian American, 57% international
- 205 degree-seeking graduate students
- 96% of applicants admitted

**General.** Founded in 1919. Accredited by ACICS. Institution primarily serves international students. **Degrees:** 5 bachelor's, 3 associate awarded; master's offered. **Location:** 12 miles from San Francisco. **Calendar:** Semester, limited summer session. **Full-time faculty:** 6 total; 50% women. **Part-time faculty:** 27 total; 11% minority, 11% women. **Special facilities:** Language laboratory, media center.

**Freshman class profile.** 25 applied, 24 admitted, 10 enrolled.

**Basis for selection.** High school achievement record most important. Prior to enrollment students take Michigan Test of English Placement. Interview recommended and personal statements encouraged. **Homeschooled:** Transcript of courses and grades, state high school equivalency certificate required.

**2008-2009 Annual costs.** Tuition/fees (projected): $10,150. Tuition for intensive English program $2,560 per 16 weeks. Books/supplies: $600. Personal expenses: $2,520.

**Application procedures. Admission:** No deadline. $75 fee. Admission notification on a rolling basis.

**Academics. Special study options:** Cross-registration, double major, ESL, internships. **Credit/placement by examination:** CLEP. **Support services:** Tutoring.

**Majors. Business:** General, accounting, business admin, international, management science. **Computer sciences:** General.

**Computing on campus.** 30 workstations in library, computer center.

**Student life. Freshman orientation:** Available. Preregistration for classes offered. One hour discussion of procedures, event announcements. Student government provides information on banking, transportation and other related materials. **Housing:** Housing arranged through Universal Student Housing. **Activities:** Student government, student newspaper.

**Student services.** Career counseling, personal counseling.

**Contact.** E-mail: admissions@lincolnuca.edu
Phone: (510) 628-8010 Toll-free number: (888) 810-9998
Fax: (510) 628-8012
Peggy Au, Director of Admissions/Registrar, Lincoln University, 401 15th Street, Oakland, CA 94612

## Loma Linda University
Loma Linda, California
www.llu.edu
CB code: 4062

- Private 3-year health science and nursing college affiliated with Seventh-day Adventists
- Commuter campus in large town
- 1,126 degree-seeking undergraduates: 21% part-time, 72% women
- 2,984 degree-seeking graduate students
- Interview required

**General.** Founded in 1905. Regionally accredited. Two undergraduate schools: School of Allied Health and School of Nursing, offering sophomore, junior, senior year study. All LLU programs require previous college credit. Specific programs are applied to rather than generally to the university. **Degrees:** 280 bachelor's, 198 associate awarded; master's, doctoral, first professional offered. **Location:** 60 miles from Los Angeles, 50 miles from Palm Springs. **Calendar:** Quarter, limited summer session. **Full-time faculty:** 557 total; 64% have terminal degrees, 29% minority, 41% women. **Part-time faculty:** 283 total; 75% have terminal degrees, 39% minority, 38% women.

**Basis for selection.** For undergraduate nursing program applicants, high school algebra I and II or college intermediate algebra and one year of high school physics or college introduction to physics with 2.0 or better required. Minimum GPA of 3.0 on all college course work. Character and personal qualities also important.

**2008-2009 Annual costs.** Tuition/fees: $24,879. Tuition quoted for nursing program. Full-time tuition for dental hygiene program: $22,964 plus $1,530 fees. For allied health program $429 per credit hour; for certificate programs, $322/credit. Application fee may vary by program; tuition may vary by grade level in program. Room only: $2,445. Books/supplies: $1,200. Personal expenses: $1,260.

**2006-2007 Financial aid. Need-based:** 19% of total undergraduate aid awarded as scholarships/grants, 81% as loans/jobs.

**Application procedures. Admission:** No deadline. $60 fee. Application must be submitted online. Notificaion varies by program. Each program is applied to separately and has own requirements and dates. Student must give at least a two-week notice prior to housing entry date in order to receive a full refund; otherwise no refund will be given. **Financial aid:** FAFSA required. Applicants notified on a rolling basis.

**Academics. Special study options:** Combined bachelor's/graduate degree, cross-registration, distance learning, independent study, internships, liberal arts/career combination, study abroad. **Credit/placement by examination:** AP, CLEP.

**Majors. Conservation:** Environmental science. **Health:** Audiology/speech pathology, clinical lab science, cytotechnology, dental hygiene, dietetics, EMT paramedic, health care admin, medical radiologic technology/radiation therapy, medical records admin, nursing (RN). **Physical sciences:** Geology.

**Computing on campus.** Dormitories wired for high-speed internet access and linked to campus network. Commuter students can connect to campus network. Online library, helpline, repair service, wireless network available.

**Student life. Policies:** Students are not allowed to smoke, use alcohol or drugs. Religious observance required. **Housing:** Guaranteed on-campus for all undergraduates. Single-sex dorms, substance-free housing available. $145 fully refundable deposit. **Activities:** Student government, student newspaper, Black Health Professional Student Association, Association of Latin American Students, Social Action Corps, Students for International Mission Service.

**Athletics. Intramural:** Basketball M, football (non-tackle), softball, volleyball.

**Student services.** Alcohol/substance abuse counseling, campus ministries, financial aid counseling, health services, on-campus daycare, personal counseling. **Physically disabled:** Services for hearing impaired.

**Contact.** E-mail: admissions.app@llu.edu
Phone: (909) 651-5029 Toll-free number: (800) 442-4558
Fax: (909) 558-4879
Loma Linda University, Admissions Processing, Loma Linda, CA 92350

## Loyola Marymount University
### Los Angeles, California
### www.lmu.edu

**CB member**
**CB code: 4403**

- Private 4-year university affiliated with Roman Catholic Church
- Residential campus in very large city
- 5,585 degree-seeking undergraduates: 3% part-time, 58% women, 8% African American, 13% Asian American, 20% Hispanic American, 1% Native American, 2% international
- 3,086 degree-seeking graduate students
- 52% of applicants admitted
- SAT or ACT (ACT writing recommended), application essay required
- 75% graduate within 6 years

**General.** Founded in 1911. Regionally accredited. **Degrees:** 1,393 bachelor's awarded; master's, doctoral, first professional offered. **ROTC:** Army, Naval, Air Force. **Location:** 15 miles from downtown. **Calendar:** Semester, extensive summer session. **Full-time faculty:** 485 total; 25% minority, 38% women. **Part-time faculty:** 430 total; 20% minority, 47% women. **Class size:** 46% < 20, 52% 20-39, 1% 40-49, 1% 50-99, less than 1% >100. **Special facilities:** Fine arts complex with recital hall and recording arts facilities; Baja California marine station.

**Freshman class profile.** 8,533 applied, 4,456 admitted, 1,268 enrolled.

| Mid 50% test scores | | | |
|---|---|---|---|
| SAT critical reading: | 520-630 | **GPA 2.0-2.99:** | 7% |
| SAT math: | 530-650 | **Return as sophomores:** | 87% |
| ACT composite: | 23-28 | **Out-of-state:** | 30% |
| GPA 3.50 or higher: | 44% | **Live on campus:** | 94% |
| GPA 3.0-3.49: | 49% | **International:** | 2% |

**Basis for selection.** High school GPA, curriculum, test scores, recommendations, essays, activities important. Interview recommended for early admission, disabled, academically weak applicants. Portfolio required for animation major applicants.

**High school preparation.** 18 units recommended. Recommended units include English 4, mathematics 3, social studies 3, science 2 (laboratory 2), foreign language 3 and academic electives 1. 4 math required of engineering, math, and science majors; physics and chemistry required of engineering and science majors; biology and chemistry required (physics recommended) of biology majors.

**2008-2009 Annual costs.** Tuition/fees: $33,902. Room/board: $11,808. Books/supplies: $1,360. Personal expenses: $2,700.

**2007-2008 Financial aid. Need-based:** 939 full-time freshmen applied for aid; 654 were judged to have need; 630 of these received aid. Average need met was 96%. Average scholarship/grant was $17,301; average loan $4,363. 61% of total undergraduate aid awarded as scholarships/grants, 39% as loans/jobs. **Non-need-based:** Awarded to 1,010 full-time undergraduates, including 360 freshmen. Scholarships awarded for academics, alumni affiliation, athletics, leadership, music/drama.

**Application procedures. Admission:** Priority date 1/15; no deadline. $50 fee, may be waived for applicants with need. Application may be submitted online. Admission notification on a rolling basis beginning on or about 11/1. Must reply by May 1 or within 2 week(s) if notified thereafter. Applicants who desire housing or financial aid should apply by January 15. **Financial aid:** Closing date 3/2. FAFSA, CSS PROFILE required. Applicants notified on a rolling basis starting 3/15; must reply by 5/1 or within 4 week(s) of notification.

**Academics. Special study options:** Cross-registration, distance learning, double major, dual enrollment of high school students, honors, independent study, internships, liberal arts/career combination, semester at sea, study abroad, teacher certification program, Washington semester. Encore Program for adult students. **Credit/placement by examination:** AP, CLEP, IB, institutional tests. **Support services:** Learning center, reduced course load, study skills assistance, tutoring.

**Majors. Area/ethnic studies:** African-American, Asian, European, Hispanic-American/Latino/Chicano, women's. **Biology:** General, biochemistry. **Business:** General, accounting, business admin. **Communications:** General, radio/tv. **Communications technology:** Animation/special effects, recording arts. **Computer sciences:** General. **Engineering:** General, civil, electrical, mechanical, physics. **English:** English lit. **Foreign languages:** Ancient Greek, classics, French, German, Latin, modern Greek, Spanish. **Health:** Art therapy. **History:** General. **Interdisciplinary:** Ancient studies, natural sciences. **Liberal arts:** Arts/sciences, humanities. **Math:** General, applied. **Philosophy/religion:** Philosophy. **Physical sciences:** Chemistry, physics. **Psychology:** General. **Public administration:** General. **Social sciences:** Economics, political science, sociology, urban studies. **Theology:** Theology. **Visual/performing arts:** Art, art history/conservation, cinematography, dance, design, dramatic, film/cinema, play/screenwriting, studio arts.

**Most popular majors.** Biology 6%, business/marketing 31%, communications/journalism 10%, English 6%, psychology 6%, social sciences 10%, visual/performing arts 13%.

**Computing on campus.** 650 workstations in dormitories, library, computer center, student center. Dormitories wired for high-speed internet access and linked to campus network. Commuter students can connect to campus network. Helpline, student web hosting, wireless network available.

**Student life. Freshman orientation:** Available, $165 fee. **Housing:** Guaranteed on-campus for freshmen. Coed dorms, single-sex dorms, special housing for disabled, apartments, cooperative housing, fraternity/sorority housing available. $400 nonrefundable deposit. **Activities:** Pep band, choral groups, dance, drama, film society, literary magazine, music ensembles, musical theater, radio station, student government, student newspaper, TV station, more than 130 student organizations, clubs, and associations.

**Athletics.** NCAA. **Intercollegiate:** Baseball M, basketball, cross-country, golf M, rowing (crew), soccer, softball W, swimming W, tennis, track and field, volleyball W, water polo. **Intramural:** Basketball, football (tackle), soccer, softball, table tennis, tennis, volleyball, water polo. **Team name:** Lions.

**Student services.** Adult student services, alcohol/substance abuse counseling, campus ministries, career counseling, student employment services, financial aid counseling, health services, minority student services, personal counseling, placement for graduates, veterans' counselor. **Physically disabled:** Services for visually, speech, hearing impaired.

**Contact.** E-mail: admissions@lmu.edu
Phone: (310) 338-2750 Toll-free number: (800) 568-4636
Fax: (310) 338-2797
Matthew Fissinger, Director of Admissions, Loyola Marymount University, Admissions, 1 LMU Drive, Los Angeles, CA 90045-8350

## The Master's College
### Santa Clarita, California
### www.masters.edu

**CB code: 4411**

- Private 4-year liberal arts and seminary college affiliated with Christian Church
- Residential campus in small city
- 1,112 degree-seeking undergraduates: 16% part-time, 51% women
- 402 degree-seeking graduate students
- 84% of applicants admitted
- SAT or ACT with writing, application essay required
- 51% graduate within 6 years

**General.** Founded in 1927. Regionally accredited. Branch campus in Israel; very strong overseas summer missions program. **Degrees:** 248 bachelor's awarded; master's, doctoral, first professional offered. **Location:** 40 miles from Los Angeles. **Calendar:** Semester, limited summer session. **Full-time faculty:** 70 total; 81% have terminal degrees, 10% minority, 14% women. **Part-time faculty:** 99 total; 6% minority, 30% women. **Class size:**

77% < 20, 16% 20-39, 2% 40-49, 5% 50-99, less than 1% >100. **Special facilities:** Home economics - family and consumer sciences center.

**Freshman class profile.** 485 applied, 406 admitted, 377 enrolled.

| Mid 50% test scores | | | |
|---|---|---|---|
| SAT critical reading: | 490-630 | Rank in top quarter: | 57% |
| SAT math: | 480-630 | Rank in top tenth: | 35% |
| ACT composite: | 21-29 | End year in good standing: | 85% |
| GPA 3.50 or higher: | 67% | Return as sophomores: | 80% |
| GPA 3.0-3.49: | 22% | Out-of-state: | 35% |
| GPA 2.0-2.99: | 11% | Live on campus: | 90% |
| | | International: | 4% |

**Basis for selection.** School achievement record, references, religious commitment most important. Applications from all individuals who have placed their faith in Jesus Christ as Lord and Savior are welcome. Audition required of music majors. **Homeschooled:** Transcript of courses and grades, letter of recommendation (nonparent) required. **Learning Disabled:** Must speak with human resources department before attending.

**High school preparation.** Required and recommended units include English 4, mathematics 3, history 2, science 2 and academic electives 3.

**2008-2009 Annual costs.** Tuition/fees: $23,120. Room/board: $7,620. Books/supplies: $1,314. Personal expenses: $2,088.

**2006-2007 Financial aid. Need-based:** 139 full-time freshmen applied for aid; 125 were judged to have need; 124 of these received aid. Average need met was 72%. Average scholarship/grant was $12,648; average loan $3,261. 63% of total undergraduate aid awarded as scholarships/grants, 37% as loans/jobs. **Non-need-based:** Awarded to 336 full-time undergraduates, including 84 freshmen. Scholarships awarded for academics, alumni affiliation, art, athletics, leadership, music/drama.

**Application procedures. Admission:** Priority date 3/2; no deadline. $40 fee, may be waived for applicants with need. Application may be submitted online. Admission notification on a rolling basis beginning on or about 3/15. Must reply by May 1 or within 2 week(s) if notified thereafter. **Financial aid:** Priority date 3/2; no closing date. FAFSA, institutional form required. Applicants notified on a rolling basis starting 2/18; must reply by 5/1 or within 2 week(s) of notification.

**Academics.** Students who attend 4 years earn a minor in Biblical Studies upon graduation. **Special study options:** Accelerated study, cooperative education, distance learning, double major, independent study, internships, liberal arts/career combination, study abroad, teacher certification program, Washington semester. Israel semester. **Credit/placement by examination:** AP, CLEP, IB, institutional tests. 32 credit hours maximum toward bachelor's degree. **Support services:** Reduced course load, remedial instruction, study skills assistance, tutoring.

**Majors. Biology:** General, environmental. **Business:** Accounting, actuarial science, business admin, finance, management information systems. **Communications:** Media studies, public relations, radio/tv. **Computer sciences:** General. **Education:** General, elementary, ESL, middle, music, physical, science, secondary. **English:** English lit, speech/rhetoric. **Family/consumer sciences:** General, food/nutrition. **Foreign languages:** Biblical. **Health:** Premedicine. **History:** General. **Interdisciplinary:** Biological/physical sciences, natural sciences. **Legal studies:** Prelaw. **Liberal arts:** Arts/sciences. **Math:** General, applied. **Parks/recreation:** Health/fitness. **Philosophy/religion:** Religion. **Physical sciences:** General. **Social sciences:** Political science, U.S. government. **Theology:** Bible, pastoral counseling, religious ed, sacred music, theology. **Visual/performing arts:** Music management, piano/organ, voice/opera.

**Most popular majors.** Business/marketing 18%, communications/journalism 10%, history 6%, liberal arts 12%, philosophy/religious studies 34%, visual/performing arts 6%.

**Computing on campus.** PC or laptop required. 60 workstations in library, computer center. Dormitories wired for high-speed internet access and linked to campus network. Commuter students can connect to campus network. Online course registration, online library, helpline, repair service, wireless network available.

**Student life. Freshman orientation:** Mandatory. Preregistration for classes offered. 5-day program before start of classes. **Policies:** Emphasis on Godly lifestyle, character and leadership development, service, learning, cross-cultural education. Religious observance required. **Housing:** Single-sex dorms, substance-free housing available. $200 fully refundable deposit, deadline 5/2. **Activities:** Bands, campus ministries, choral groups, drama, music ensembles, opera, student government, symphony orchestra, summer missions, outreach team.

**Athletics.** NAIA, NCCAA. **Intercollegiate:** Baseball M, basketball, cross-country, golf M, soccer, tennis W, volleyball W. **Intramural:** Basketball, football (non-tackle), golf, softball, tennis, volleyball. **Team name:** Mustangs.

**Student services.** Adult student services, campus ministries, career counseling, student employment services, financial aid counseling, health services, personal counseling, placement for graduates, veterans' counselor. **Physically disabled:** Services for visually, speech impaired.

**Contact.** E-mail: enrollment@masters.edu
Phone: (661) 259-3540 ext. 3362 Toll-free
number: (800) 568-6248 ext. 3362 Fax: (661) 288-1037
Hollie Gorsh, Director of Admissions, The Master's College, 21726 Placerita Canyon Road, Santa Clarita, CA 91321-1200

---

## Menlo College
**Atherton, California**
**www.menlo.edu**

CB member
CB code: 4483

- Private 4-year business and liberal arts college
- Residential campus in small city
- 680 degree-seeking undergraduates: 8% part-time, 41% women, 7% African American, 12% Asian American, 14% Hispanic American, 10% international
- 42% of applicants admitted
- SAT or ACT (ACT writing recommended), application essay required

**General.** Founded in 1927. Regionally accredited. **Degrees:** 150 bachelor's awarded. **ROTC:** Army. **Location:** 30 miles from San Francisco, 30 miles from San Jose. **Calendar:** Semester, extensive summer session. **Full-time faculty:** 28 total; 100% have terminal degrees, 4% minority, 39% women. **Part-time faculty:** 55 total; 22% have terminal degrees, 20% minority, 44% women. **Class size:** 69% < 20, 30% 20-39, 1% 50-99.

**Freshman class profile.** 978 applied, 407 admitted, 161 enrolled.

| Mid 50% test scores | | | |
|---|---|---|---|
| SAT critical reading: | 400-510 | GPA 2.0-2.99: | 53% |
| SAT math: | 420-520 | Rank in top quarter: | 26% |
| SAT writing: | 400-440 | Rank in top tenth: | 6% |
| ACT composite: | 15-20 | Out-of-state: | 39% |
| GPA 3.50 or higher: | 15% | Live on campus: | 80% |
| GPA 3.0-3.49: | 31% | International: | 12% |

**Basis for selection.** High school record, test scores (minimum 1000 SAT, exclusive of Writing, or 21 ACT), 1 recommendation, essay, depth of achievement in cocurricular activities considered. **Homeschooled:** Statement describing homeschool structure and mission, transcript of courses and grades, state high school equivalency certificate, letter of recommendation (nonparent) required. **Learning Disabled:** Direct queries to Academic Success Center.

**High school preparation.** 15 units required; 24 recommended. Required and recommended units include English 4, mathematics 3, social studies 3, science 3 and foreign language 2.

**2008-2009 Annual costs.** Tuition/fees: $30,900. Room/board: $11,000. Books/supplies: $1,276. Personal expenses: $2,042.

**2007-2008 Financial aid. Need-based:** 94 full-time freshmen applied for aid; 87 were judged to have need; 87 of these received aid. Average need met was 70%. Average scholarship/grant was $20,020; average loan $2,432. 75% of total undergraduate aid awarded as scholarships/grants, 25% as loans/jobs. **Non-need-based:** Awarded to 199 full-time undergraduates, including 61 freshmen. Scholarships awarded for academics.

**Application procedures. Admission:** Priority date 2/1; no deadline. $40 fee, may be waived for applicants with need. Application may be submitted online. Admission notification on a rolling basis beginning on or about 12/1. Must reply by May 1 or within 4 week(s) if notified thereafter. **Financial aid:** Priority date 3/2, closing date 8/1. FAFSA required. Applicants notified on a rolling basis starting 12/15; must reply by 5/1 or within 2 week(s) of notification.

**Academics.** 21-day Transition to College Program offered to help students not achieving at true academic potential to transition more smoothly to rigors of college academics. Ongoing support and counseling throughout freshman year. **Special study options:** Accelerated study, cooperative education, double major, independent study, internships, student-designed major, study abroad. **Credit/placement by examination:** AP, CLEP, IB, institutional tests. 30 credit hours maximum toward bachelor's degree. **Support services:** Learning center, pre-admission summer program, reduced course load, remedial instruction, study skills assistance, tutoring, writing center.

**Majors. Business:** Business admin. **Communications:** General. **Liberal arts:** Arts/sciences.

**Computing on campus.** 350 workstations in library, computer center. Dormitories wired for high-speed internet access and linked to campus network. Commuter students can connect to campus network. Online course registration, online library, helpline, repair service, wireless network available.

**Student life. Freshman orientation:** Mandatory. Preregistration for classes offered. Weekend before classes begin. Workshops for both parents and students. **Housing:** Guaranteed on-campus for freshmen. Coed dorms, single-sex dorms, special housing for disabled, substance-free housing available. $300 fully refundable deposit, deadline 7/1. **Activities:** Drama, film society, international student organizations, radio station, student government, student newspaper, TV station, International Club, African-American student union, Latino student union, Asia club, Rotaract, Chinese culture research club, women's club, Jewish student organization, Alpha Chi Honor Society, French club.

**Athletics.** NAIA, NCAA. **Intercollegiate:** Baseball M, basketball, cross-country, football (tackle) M, golf M, soccer, softball W, volleyball W, wrestling. **Intramural:** Basketball M. **Team name:** Oaks.

**Student services.** Adult student services, career counseling, student employment services, financial aid counseling, personal counseling, placement for graduates.

**Contact.** E-mail: admissions@menlo.edu
Phone: (650) 543-3753 Toll-free number: (800) 556-3656
Fax: (650) 543-4496
David Placey, Dean of Enrollment Management, Menlo College, 1000 El Camino Real, Atherton, CA 94027

---

## Mills College
**Oakland, California**
**www.mills.edu**

CB member
CB code: 4485

- Private 4-year liberal arts college for women
- Residential campus in large city
- 930 degree-seeking undergraduates: 5% part-time, 100% women, 10% African American, 8% Asian American, 15% Hispanic American, 1% Native American, 2% international
- 430 degree-seeking graduate students
- 64% of applicants admitted
- SAT or ACT (ACT writing optional), application essay required
- 52% graduate within 6 years

**General.** Founded in 1852. Regionally accredited. Men admitted to graduate programs. **Degrees:** 200 bachelor's awarded; master's, doctoral offered. **Location:** 18 miles from San Francisco, 8 miles from Berkeley. **Calendar:** Semester, limited summer session. **Full-time faculty:** 94 total; 87% have terminal degrees, 26% minority, 61% women. **Part-time faculty:** 97 total; 59% have terminal degrees, 23% minority, 73% women. **Class size:** 77% < 20, 20% 20-39, less than 1% 40-49, less than 1% 50-99, less than 1% >100. **Special facilities:** Electronic collaborative learning center, center for contemporary music, children's school (laboratory school for student teachers), women's leadership institute, institute for civic leadership, center for the book.

**Freshman class profile.** 1,098 applied, 707 admitted, 187 enrolled.

| Mid 50% test scores | | Rank in top quarter: | 50% |
|---|---|---|---|
| SAT critical reading: | 520-640 | Rank in top tenth: | 40% |
| SAT math: | 490-610 | End year in good standing: | 89% |
| ACT composite: | 21-27 | Return as sophomores: | 72% |
| GPA 3.50 or higher: | 63% | Out-of-state: | 27% |
| GPA 3.0-3.49: | 30% | Live on campus: | 97% |
| GPA 2.0-2.99: | 7% | | |

**Basis for selection.** Minimum 3.0 GPA required, school achievement record most important. All credentials considered. SAT Subject Tests recommended. Interview recommended. **Homeschooled:** Statement describing homeschool structure and mission, state high school equivalency certificate, letter of recommendation (nonparent) required.

**High school preparation.** Required and recommended units include English 4, mathematics 3-4, social studies 2-4, history 2-4, science 2-4 (laboratory 2), foreign language 2-4, visual/performing arts 2 and academic electives 2.

**2008-2009 Annual costs.** Tuition/fees: $35,190; $35,190 out-of-state. Room/board: $10,550. Books/supplies: $1,300. Personal expenses: $2,000.

**2007-2008 Financial aid. Need-based:** 163 full-time freshmen applied for aid; 140 were judged to have need; 140 of these received aid. Average need met was 88%. Average scholarship/grant was $24,196; average loan $4,487. 71% of total undergraduate aid awarded as scholarships/grants, 29% as loans/jobs. **Non-need-based:** Awarded to 797 full-time undergraduates, including 159 freshmen. Scholarships awarded for academics, leadership, minority status, music/drama.

**Application procedures. Admission:** Priority date 2/1; deadline 8/1 (postmark date). $50 fee, may be waived for applicants with need. Application may be submitted online. Admission notification on a rolling basis beginning on or about 11/1. Must reply by May 1 or within 2 week(s) if notified thereafter. **Financial aid:** Closing date 2/15. FAFSA, institutional form required. Applicants notified on a rolling basis starting 3/1; must reply by 5/1 or within 2 week(s) of notification.

**Academics.** Cooperative bachelor of science in nursing program with Samuel Merritt College; pre-nursing students in this program receive a pre-nursing certificate from Mills upon completion of two years of study. Certificate pre-medicine program available to postbaccalaureate students. BA/MA in Infant Mental Health offered. **Special study options:** Combined bachelor's/graduate degree, cross-registration, double major, exchange student, independent study, internships, student-designed major, study abroad, teacher certification program, Washington semester. **Credit/placement by examination:** AP, CLEP, IB, institutional tests. 8 credit hours maximum toward bachelor's degree. **Support services:** Pre-admission summer program, reduced course load, study skills assistance, tutoring, writing center.

**Majors. Area/ethnic studies:** American, French, Hispanic-American/Latino/Chicano, Latin American, women's. **Biology:** General, biochemistry, molecular biochemistry. **Business:** General, managerial economics. **Computer sciences:** General, computer science. **Conservation:** Environmental science, environmental studies. **Engineering:** General. **English:** British lit, creative writing, English lit. **Family/consumer sciences:** Child development. **Foreign languages:** Comparative lit, French, Spanish. **History:** General, American. **Interdisciplinary:** Biopsychology. **Legal studies:** General. **Liberal arts:** Arts/sciences. **Math:** General. **Philosophy/religion:** Philosophy. **Physical sciences:** Chemistry. **Psychology:** General. **Public administration:** Policy analysis. **Social sciences:** General, anthropology, economics, international relations, political science, sociology, U.S. government. **Visual/performing arts:** Art, art history/conservation, dance, multimedia, studio arts.

**Most popular majors.** Biology 6%, business/marketing 6%, English 15%, history 8%, interdisciplinary studies 9%, psychology 9%, social sciences 7%, visual/performing arts 11%.

**Computing on campus.** 323 workstations in dormitories, library, computer center, student center. Dormitories wired for high-speed internet access and linked to campus network. Commuter students can connect to campus network. Online course registration, online library, helpline, wireless network available.

**Student life. Freshman orientation:** Mandatory. Preregistration for classes offered. 5 days prior to the start of classes. **Housing:** Guaranteed on-campus for all undergraduates. Special housing for disabled, apartments, cooperative housing, substance-free housing available. $150 fully refundable deposit, deadline 6/1. **Activities:** Choral groups, dance, drama, literary magazine, music ensembles, musical theater, opera, student government, student newspaper.

**Athletics.** NCAA. **Intercollegiate:** Cross-country W, rowing (crew) W, soccer W, swimming W, tennis W, volleyball W. **Intramural:** Badminton W, basketball W, cross-country W, equestrian W, fencing W, golf W, sailing W, soccer W, softball W, swimming W, tennis W, track and field W, volleyball W, water polo W. **Team name:** Cyclones.

**Student services.** Adult student services, alcohol/substance abuse counseling, campus ministries, career counseling, services for economically disadvantaged, student employment services, financial aid counseling, health services, minority student services, on-campus daycare, personal counseling, placement for graduates, women's services. **Physically disabled:** Services for visually, speech, hearing impaired.

**Contact.** E-mail: admission@mills.edu
Phone: (510) 430-2135 Toll-free number: (800) 876-4557
Fax: (510) 430-3314
Giulietta Aquino, Dean of Undergraduate Admission, Mills College, 5000 MacArthur Boulevard, Oakland, CA 94613

---

## Monterey Institute of International Studies
**Monterey, California**
**www.miis.edu**

CB code: 4507

- Private two-year upper-division liberal arts college
- Commuter campus in small city

**General.** Founded in 1955. Regionally accredited. **Location:** 130 miles from San Francisco, 60 miles from San Jose. **Calendar:** Semester.

**Annual costs/financial aid.** Tuition/fees (2007-2008): $27,950. Books/supplies: $900. Need-based financial aid available to full-time and part-time students.

**Contact.** Phone: (831) 647-4123
Vice President for Enrollment Management, 460 Pierce Street, Monterey, CA 93940

## Mount St. Mary's College
**Los Angeles, California**     CB member
www.msmc.la.edu     CB code: 4493

- Private 4-year liberal arts college affiliated with Roman Catholic Church
- Residential campus in very large city
- 1,898 degree-seeking undergraduates: 24% part-time, 93% women
- 438 degree-seeking graduate students
- SAT or ACT (ACT writing optional), application essay required

**General.** Founded in 1925. Regionally accredited. Founded by the Sisters of St. Joseph of Carondelet. Men admitted to undergraduate nursing and music programs, graduate division, weekend college and summer division. **Degrees:** 366 bachelor's, 168 associate awarded; master's, doctoral offered. **Location:** 2 miles from Los Angeles. **Calendar:** Semester, limited summer session. **Full-time faculty:** 83 total; 63% have terminal degrees, 12% minority, 81% women. **Part-time faculty:** 235 total; 59% have terminal degrees, 27% minority, 73% women. **Class size:** 65% < 20, 34% 20-39, 1% 40-49, less than 1% 50-99.

### Freshman class profile.

| Mid 50% test scores | | | |
|---|---|---|---|
| SAT critical reading: | 460-540 | GPA 3.0-3.49: | 39% |
| SAT math: | 440-550 | GPA 2.0-2.99: | 14% |
| SAT writing: | 480-560 | Out-of-state: | 5% |
| GPA 3.50 or higher: | 47% | Live on campus: | 76% |

**Basis for selection.** Primary emphasis on school academic record, then test scores, essay, and letters of recommendation. School and community activities also considered. Interview important. Admission requirements considered very competitive in baccalaureate program. Interviews recommended. Auditions recommended of music majors. Portfolios recommended of art majors. **Learning Disabled:** Documentation of learning disability required.

**High school preparation.** 25 units required; 30 recommended. Required and recommended units include English 4, mathematics 3-4, social studies 2-3, history 2-3, science 2-3 (laboratory 2-3), foreign language 2-3 and academic electives 2-3. For associate degree applicants, required courses include algebra, geometry, American history/government, and 3 units English.

**2007-2008 Annual costs.** Tuition/fees: $25,320. Room/board: $9,184. Books/supplies: $648. Personal expenses: $1,170.

**2007-2008 Financial aid. Need-based:** 343 full-time freshmen applied for aid; 323 were judged to have need; 323 of these received aid. Average need met was 75%. Average scholarship/grant was $7,555; average loan $2,844. 73% of total undergraduate aid awarded as scholarships/grants, 27% as loans/jobs. **Non-need-based:** Awarded to 70 full-time undergraduates, including 40 freshmen. Scholarships awarded for academics, alumni affiliation, art, leadership, music/drama.

**Application procedures. Admission:** Priority date 12/1; deadline 2/15. $40 fee, may be waived for applicants with need. Application may be submitted online. Admission notification on a rolling basis. Must reply by May 1 or within 2 week(s) if notified thereafter. **Financial aid:** Priority date 3/1; no closing date. FAFSA, institutional form required. Applicants notified on a rolling basis starting 2/1; must reply by 5/1.

**Academics. Special study options:** Accelerated study, combined bachelor's/graduate degree, cross-registration, double major, exchange student, honors, independent study, internships, student-designed major, study abroad, teacher certification program, United Nations semester, Washington semester, weekend college. **Credit/placement by examination:** AP, CLEP, IB, institutional tests. 24 credit hours maximum toward associate degree, 30 toward bachelor's. **Support services:** Learning center, pre-admission summer program, reduced course load, remedial instruction, study skills assistance, tutoring, writing center.

**Majors. Area/ethnic studies:** American. **Biology:** General, biochemistry. **Business:** General, accounting, business admin, international. **Education:** Elementary, middle, secondary. **English:** English lit. **Foreign languages:** French, Spanish. **Health:** Clinical lab technology, health care admin, nursing (RN), predental, premedicine, preveterinary. **History:** General. **Legal studies:** Prelaw. **Math:** General, applied. **Philosophy/religion:** Philosophy, religion. **Physical sciences:** Chemistry. **Psychology:** General. **Social sciences:** General, political science, sociology. **Theology:** Sacred music. **Visual/performing arts:** Music performance, music theory/composition, studio arts.

**Most popular majors.** Biology 8%, business/marketing 7%, English 7%, health sciences 36%, liberal arts 11%, psychology 7%, social sciences 18%.

**Computing on campus.** 168 workstations in dormitories, library, computer center, student center. Dormitories wired for high-speed internet access and linked to campus network. Commuter students can connect to campus network. Online course registration, helpline, student web hosting, wireless network available.

**Student life. Freshman orientation:** Available. **Policies:** Student resident life largely self-regulated under direction of Residence Council. **Housing:** Guaranteed on-campus for freshmen. Single-sex dorms available. $100 deposit, deadline 5/1. **Activities:** Choral groups, dance, literary magazine, student government, student newspaper, symphony orchestra, campus ministry, volunteer service, ethnic clubs.

**Athletics. Intramural:** Badminton, basketball, football (non-tackle), golf, soccer, swimming, tennis, volleyball. **Team name:** Athenians.

**Student services.** Adult student services, campus ministries, career counseling, student employment services, financial aid counseling, health services, personal counseling, placement for graduates.

**Contact.** E-mail: admissions@msmc.la.edu
Phone: (310) 954-4250 Toll-free number: (800) 999-9893
Fax: (310) 954-4259
Dean Kilgour, Director of Admissions, Mount St. Mary's College, 12001 Chalon Road, Los Angeles, CA 90049

## Mt. Sierra College
**Monrovia, California**
www.mtsierra.edu     CB code: 3090

- For-profit 3-year technical college
- Commuter campus in very large city
- 514 degree-seeking undergraduates
- 85% of applicants admitted

**General.** Accredited by ACCSCT. **Degrees:** 100 bachelor's awarded. **Calendar:** Quarter. **Full-time faculty:** 12 total. **Part-time faculty:** 59 total.

**Freshman class profile.** 66 applied, 56 admitted, 55 enrolled.

**Basis for selection.** Minimum score on CPT exams; non-high school graduates may be admitted on ability-to-benefit. Institutional CPT exams waived if SAT verbal/math scores 560 or higher, or ACT verbal/math scores 20 or higher.

**2007-2008 Annual costs.** Tuition/fees: $14,237. Additional lab fees may apply; varies by program of study. Books/supplies: $2,000.

**Application procedures. Admission:** No deadline. $50 fee. Application may be submitted online. Admission notification on a rolling basis.

**Academics. Special study options:** Accelerated study, distance learning, weekend college. **Credit/placement by examination:** CLEP, IB, institutional tests. **Support services:** Learning center, tutoring, writing center.

**Majors. Business:** Business admin, entrepreneurial studies. **Computer sciences:** General, game design, information technology, networking, security, web page design. **Visual/performing arts:** Digital art, graphic design, multimedia.

**Computing on campus.** PC or laptop required.

**Student life. Freshman orientation:** Available. Held during first week of classes.

**Contact.** E-mail: pazadian@mtsierra.edu
Phone: (626) 873-2144 Toll-free number: (888) 828-8800
Fax: (626) 359-1378
Patrick Azadian, Director of Admissions, Mt. Sierra College, 101 East Huntington Drive, Monrovia, CA 91016

## National Hispanic University

San Jose, California
www.nhu.edu

CB member
CB code: 4593

- Private 4-year university
- Commuter campus in very large city
- 399 degree-seeking undergraduates: 35% part-time, 65% women
- 120 degree-seeking graduate students
- 61% of applicants admitted
- Application essay required

**General.** Regionally accredited. **Degrees:** 19 bachelor's, 3 associate awarded. **ROTC:** Army, Naval. **Calendar:** Semester, limited summer session. **Full-time faculty:** 9 total; 56% have terminal degrees, 33% minority, 22% women. **Part-time faculty:** 64 total; 48% minority, 53% women. **Class size:** 67% < 20, 33% 20-39.

**Freshman class profile.** 205 applied, 126 admitted, 77 enrolled.

**Basis for selection.** High school GPA, transcript, two letters of recommendation, written essay required. **Homeschooled:** State high school equivalency certificate required.

**2008-2009 Annual costs.** Tuition/fees: $6,080. Books/supplies: $1,566. Personal expenses: $2,754.

**2006-2007 Financial aid. Need-based:** 73% of total undergraduate aid awarded as scholarships/grants, 27% as loans/jobs. **Non-need-based:** Scholarships awarded for academics.

**Application procedures. Admission:** No deadline. $50 fee. Application must be submitted on paper. Admission notification on a rolling basis. **Financial aid:** No deadline. FAFSA required.

**Academics. Special study options:** Dual enrollment of high school students, independent study, teacher certification program. **Credit/placement by examination:** CLEP, IB, institutional tests. **Support services:** Learning center, remedial instruction, tutoring, writing center.

**Majors. Business:** Business admin. **Computer sciences:** General. **Liberal arts:** Arts/sciences.

**Most popular majors.** Liberal arts 63%.

**Computing on campus.** 223 workstations in library, computer center, student center. Online library, wireless network available.

**Student life. Freshman orientation:** Mandatory. Preregistration for classes offered. **Activities:** Student government.

**Student services.** Financial aid counseling.

**Contact.** Phone: (408) 273-2772 Fax: (408) 254-1369
Pamela Bustillo, Director of Admissions/Registrar, National Hispanic University, 14271 Story Road, San Jose, CA 95127-3823

## National University

La Jolla, California
www.nu.edu

CB member
CB code: 0470

- Private 4-year university
- Commuter campus in very large city
- 6,675 degree-seeking undergraduates: 67% part-time, 60% women, 11% African American, 9% Asian American, 16% Hispanic American, 1% Native American, 1% international
- 17,840 degree-seeking graduate students
- Interview required
- 54% graduate within 6 years

**General.** Founded in 1971. Regionally accredited. Campuses in 11 major cities throughout California; courses offered both on-site and online. **Degrees:** 966 bachelor's, 84 associate awarded; master's offered. **ROTC:** Army, Naval, Air Force. **Calendar:** Continuous, limited summer session. **Full-time faculty:** 215 total; 79% have terminal degrees, 10% minority, 45% women. **Part-time faculty:** 2,053 total; 27% have terminal degrees, 13% minority, 50% women. **Class size:** 73% < 20, 26% 20-39, less than 1% 40-49, less than 1% 50-99. **Special facilities:** Nursing labs, forensics labs, e-book collection.

**Freshman class profile.** 2,884 admitted, 1,745 enrolled.

| | | | |
|---|---|---|---|
| Return as sophomores: | 100% | **International:** | 2% |
| Out-of-state: | 13% | | |

**Basis for selection.** Open admission, but selective for some programs. Interview, previous business and work experience, academic record considered.

**2007-2008 Annual costs.** Tuition/fees: $9,720. Books/supplies: $1,314. Personal expenses: $1,968.

**2006-2007 Financial aid. Need-based:** 381 full-time freshmen applied for aid; 374 were judged to have need; 179 of these received aid. Average scholarship/grant was $5,176; average loan $8,692. 4% of total undergraduate aid awarded as scholarships/grants, 96% as loans/jobs. **Non-need-based:** Awarded to 1,107 full-time undergraduates, including 179 freshmen.

**Application procedures. Admission:** No deadline. $60 fee. Application may be submitted online. Admission notification on a rolling basis. **Financial aid:** No deadline. FAFSA, institutional form required. Applicants notified on a rolling basis.

**Academics.** Agreements with over 950 public and private schools to place students earning teaching credentials in practicums. **Special study options:** Accelerated study, cross-registration, distance learning, double major, ESL, independent study, internships, liberal arts/career combination, teacher certification program. **Credit/placement by examination:** AP, CLEP, institutional tests. 14 credit hours maximum toward associate degree, 23 toward bachelor's. **Support services:** Learning center, remedial instruction, tutoring, writing center.

**Majors. Area/ethnic studies:** Chinese, Near/Middle Eastern. **Business:** General, accounting, business admin, construction management, hospitality admin, human resources, operations, organizational behavior. **Communications:** Broadcast journalism, digital media, journalism, media studies, radio/tv. **Computer sciences:** General, computer science, game design, information systems, information technology, security, system admin, systems analysis. **Conservation:** Environmental science, management/policy. **Education:** Mathematics. **Engineering:** Construction, systems. **Engineering technology:** Civil drafting. **English:** English lit. **Family/consumer sciences:** Child development. **Foreign languages:** American Sign Language, Arabic, Chinese, Persian. **Health:** Health care admin, licensed practical nurse, preop/surgical nursing. **History:** General. **Interdisciplinary:** Biological/physical sciences, global studies, intercultural. **Legal studies:** General. **Liberal arts:** Arts/sciences. **Math:** General. **Parks/recreation:** Facilities management, sports admin. **Physical sciences:** General, geology. **Protective services:** Criminal justice, law enforcement admin, security services. **Psychology:** General. **Public administration:** General. **Social sciences:** Economics, sociology. **Visual/performing arts:** Multimedia.

**Most popular majors.** Business/marketing 28%, computer/information sciences 12%, interdisciplinary studies 10%, legal studies 13%, liberal arts 11%, psychology 13%.

**Computing on campus.** 3,100 workstations in library, computer center, student center. Commuter students can connect to campus network. Online course registration, online library, helpline, wireless network available.

**Student life. Freshman orientation:** Available. Preregistration for classes offered.

**Student services.** Adult student services, career counseling, services for economically disadvantaged, student employment services, financial aid counseling, minority student services, placement for graduates, veterans' counselor. **Physically disabled:** Services for visually, speech, hearing impaired.

**Contact.** E-mail: advisor@nu.edu
Phone: (800) 628-8648 Toll-free number: (800) 628-8648
Fax: (858) 541-7792
Dominick Giovanniello, Associate Regional Dean - San Diego, National University, 11255 North Torrey Pines Road, La Jolla, CA 92037-1011

## NewSchool of Architecture & Design

San Diego, California
www.newschoolarch.edu

CB code: 2419

- For-profit 5-year visual arts and liberal arts college
- Commuter campus in very large city
- 304 degree-seeking undergraduates
- 98% of applicants admitted
- Interview required

**General.** Founded in 1980. Accredited by ACICS. **Degrees:** 18 bachelor's awarded; master's offered. **Location:** 90 miles from Los Angeles, 17 miles from Tijuana, Mexico. **Calendar:** Quarter, extensive summer session. **Full-time faculty:** 16 total. **Part-time faculty:** 34 total. **Special facilities:** Design clinic.

**Freshman class profile.** 65 applied, 64 admitted, 22 enrolled.

**Basis for selection.** Resume considered if submitted. Portfolio review required.

**2008-2009 Annual costs.** Tuition/fees (projected): $18,945. Books/supplies: $700.

**2006-2007 Financial aid. Need-based:** 19% of total undergraduate aid awarded as scholarships/grants, 81% as loans/jobs. **Non-need-based:** Scholarships awarded for academics.

**Application procedures. Admission:** No deadline. $75 fee, may be waived for applicants with need. Application may be submitted online. Admission notification on a rolling basis. Must reply by May 1 or within 4 week(s) if notified thereafter. **Financial aid:** Priority date 3/2; no closing date. FAFSA required. Applicants notified on a rolling basis.

**Academics. Special study options:** Accelerated study, cooperative education, double major, internships, liberal arts/career combination. Cooperative program available at nearby U.S. International University, where students can take ESL and general education classes. **Credit/placement by examination:** AP, CLEP. **Support services:** Pre-admission summer program, tutoring.

**Majors. Architecture:** Architecture.

**Computing on campus.** 17 workstations in library, computer center.

**Student life. Freshman orientation:** Available. Preregistration for classes offered. Held 1-2 days before start of classes in fall. **Housing:** Some housing through US International University. **Activities:** Literary magazine, student government, student newspaper, American Institute of Architects student chapter.

**Student services.** Career counseling, student employment services, health services, personal counseling, placement for graduates, veterans' counselor.

**Contact.** E-mail: admissions@newschoolarch.edu
Phone: (619) 235-4100. Fax: (619) 235-4651
Reza Garajedaghi, Director of Admissions, NewSchool of Architecture & Design, 1249 F Street, San Diego, CA 92101

---

## Northwestern Polytechnic University
Fremont, California
www.npu.edu                                    CB code: 4335

- Private 4-year business and engineering college
- Commuter campus in small city
- 176 degree-seeking undergraduates
- 832 graduate students
- 84% of applicants admitted

**General.** Accredited by ACICS. **Degrees:** 30 bachelor's awarded; master's, doctoral offered. **Location:** 42 miles from San Francisco, 11 miles from San Jose. **Calendar:** Trimester, extensive summer session. **Full-time faculty:** 17 total. **Part-time faculty:** 55 total.

**Freshman class profile.** 263 applied, 220 admitted, 58 enrolled.

**Basis for selection.** High school record, pre-calculus required. Recommendations and test scores as reference. Interview recommended. English placement exams are given to international students who do not provide standardized English test scores. On-campus English placement exam may replace TOEFL; on-campus freshman exam may replace SAT.

**High school preparation.** Required and recommended units include English 3, mathematics 2, social studies 1 and science 1. 1 math required for business programs.

**2008-2009 Annual costs.** Tuition/fees (projected): $9,140. Books/supplies: $800.

**Financial aid. Additional information:** Work-study, co-op program, internships available. Employment opportunities with local engineering firms help defray costs.

**Application procedures. Admission:** Closing date 8/25 (postmark date). $60 fee. Application may be submitted online. Admission notification on a rolling basis. Must reply by 10/9.

**Academics.** Curricula designed to meet needs of high-tech industries and global businesses. **Special study options:** Cooperative education, ESL. **Credit/placement by examination:** AP, CLEP, institutional tests. 15 credit hours maximum toward bachelor's degree. **Support services:** Learning center, tutoring.

**Majors. Business:** Business admin. **Engineering:** Electrical, software, systems.

**Most popular majors.** Business/marketing 57%, engineering/engineering technologies 43%.

**Computing on campus.** 320 workstations in library, computer center, student center. Dormitories wired for high-speed internet access. Commuter students can connect to campus network. Online library, helpline, repair service, student web hosting, wireless network available.

**Student life. Freshman orientation:** Mandatory. Preregistration for classes offered. One-day program before start of classes. **Policies:** Students required to join student association. **Housing:** Apartments, substance-free housing available. $300 fully refundable deposit, deadline 8/1. **Activities:** Dance, literary magazine, music ensembles, student government, student association, United Nations at Silicon Valley student chapter.

**Athletics. Intercollegiate:** Table tennis. **Intramural:** Table tennis.

**Student services.** Adult student services, career counseling, student employment services, personal counseling, placement for graduates, veterans' counselor.

**Contact.** E-mail: admission@npu.edu
Phone: (510) 657-5913 Fax: (510) 657-8975
Catherine Meng, Director of Admission, Northwestern Polytechnic University, 47671 Westinghouse Drive, Fremont, CA 94539

---

## Notre Dame de Namur University
Belmont, California                            CB member
www.ndnu.edu                                   CB code: 4063

- Private 4-year liberal arts college affiliated with Roman Catholic Church
- Residential campus in large town
- 747 degree-seeking undergraduates: 30% part-time, 67% women, 5% African American, 15% Asian American, 20% Hispanic American, 1% Native American, 3% international
- 516 degree-seeking graduate students
- 99% of applicants admitted
- SAT or ACT with writing, application essay required
- 58% graduate within 6 years

**General.** Founded in 1851. Regionally accredited. **Degrees:** 271 bachelor's awarded; master's offered. **Location:** 24 miles from San Francisco. **Calendar:** Semester, limited summer session. **Full-time faculty:** 58 total; 28% minority, 50% women. **Part-time faculty:** 118 total. **Class size:** 80% < 20, 20% 20-39, less than 1% 40-49.

**Freshman class profile.** 503 applied, 498 admitted, 96 enrolled.

| Mid 50% test scores | | | |
|---|---|---|---|
| SAT critical reading: | 440-540 | GPA 3.0-3.49: | 28% |
| SAT math: | 430-520 | GPA 2.0-2.99: | 57% |
| SAT writing: | 420-540 | Return as sophomores: | 72% |
| ACT composite: | 17-23 | Out-of-state: | 32% |
| GPA 3.50 or higher: | 14% | Live on campus: | 93% |
| | | International: | 2% |

**Basis for selection.** High school record and GPA most important; test scores also important. Essay, recommendation, and school and community activities considered. **Homeschooled:** Statement describing homeschool structure and mission, transcript of courses and grades, state high school equivalency certificate, interview, letter of recommendation (nonparent) required.

**High school preparation.** 15 units required. Required and recommended units include English 4, mathematics 2-3, social studies 2, history 1, science 1-2, foreign language 2-3 and academic electives 3. 3 additional units from fine arts, advanced laboratory science, advanced mathematics, or advanced foreign language also recommended.

**2008-2009 Annual costs.** Tuition/fees (projected): $25,570. Room/board: $10,680. Books/supplies: $1,330. Personal expenses: $3,150.

**Financial aid. Non-need-based:** Scholarships awarded for academics, alumni affiliation, athletics, leadership, music/drama, religious affiliation.

**Application procedures. Admission:** Priority date 2/1; no deadline. $50 fee, may be waived for applicants with need. Application may be submitted online. Admission notification on a rolling basis. Must reply by May 1 or within 3 week(s) if notified thereafter. **Financial aid:** Priority date 3/2; no closing date. FAFSA required. CSS PROFILE accepted but not required. Applicants notified on a rolling basis starting 1/15.

**Academics. Special study options:** Accelerated study, double major, ESL, exchange student, independent study, internships, liberal arts/career combination, student-designed major, study abroad, teacher certification program. **Credit/placement by examination:** AP, CLEP, IB, institutional tests. 30 credit hours maximum toward bachelor's degree. **Support services:** Learning center, reduced course load, remedial instruction, study skills assistance, tutoring, writing center.

**Majors. Biology:** General, biochemistry. **Business:** Business admin. **Communications:** General. **Computer sciences:** General, computer science. **English:** English lit. **Health:** Predental, premedicine, prepharmacy, preveterinary. **History:** General. **Legal studies:** Prelaw. **Liberal arts:** Arts/sciences. **Parks/recreation:** Exercise sciences. **Philosophy/religion:** Philosophy, religion. **Psychology:** General. **Public administration:** Human services. **Social sciences:** General, political science, sociology. **Theology:** Religious ed. **Visual/performing arts:** Art, dramatic, graphic design, music performance, studio arts.

**Most popular majors.** Biology 9%, business/marketing 32%, liberal arts 8%, psychology 11%, public administration/social services 13%, social sciences 10%.

**Computing on campus.** Dormitories wired for high-speed internet access and linked to campus network. Commuter students can connect to campus network. Helpline, student web hosting, wireless network available.

**Student life. Freshman orientation:** Mandatory, $175 fee. Preregistration for classes offered. 1 week preceding opening of classes. **Housing:** Guaranteed on-campus for freshmen. Coed dorms, apartments available. $200 nonrefundable deposit. **Activities:** Campus ministries, choral groups, drama, international student organizations, literary magazine, music ensembles, musical theater, opera, student government, student newspaper, symphony orchestra, Hawaiian club, business/career club, Filipino club, Alianza Latina, Black Student Union, outdoor activities club, Amnesty International, science and medical careers club.

**Athletics.** NCAA. **Intercollegiate:** Basketball, cross-country, golf, lacrosse M, soccer, softball W, tennis W, volleyball W. **Team name:** Argonauts.

**Student services.** Adult student services, alcohol/substance abuse counseling, campus ministries, career counseling, student employment services, financial aid counseling, health services, personal counseling, placement for graduates. **Learning disabled:** Comprehensive services available.

**Contact.** E-mail: admiss@ndnu.edu
Phone: (650) 508-3600 Toll-free number: (800) 263-0545
Fax: (650) 508-3426
Jarrid Whitney, Dean of Enrollment, Notre Dame de Namur University, 1500 Ralston Avenue, Belmont, CA 94002-1908

---

## Occidental College

**Los Angeles, California**      **CB member**
**www.oxy.edu**      **CB code: 4581**

- Private 4-year liberal arts college affiliated with nondenominational tradition
- Residential campus in very large city
- 1,855 degree-seeking undergraduates: 1% part-time, 56% women, 6% African American, 13% Asian American, 15% Hispanic American, 1% Native American, 2% international
- 9 degree-seeking graduate students
- 44% of applicants admitted
- SAT or ACT with writing, application essay required
- 81% graduate within 6 years

**General.** Founded in 1887. Regionally accredited. **Degrees:** 410 bachelor's awarded; master's offered. **ROTC:** Army, Air Force. **Location:** 5 miles from downtown. **Calendar:** Semester. **Full-time faculty:** 156 total; 93% have terminal degrees, 32% minority, 46% women. **Part-time faculty:** 70 total. **Class size:** 64% < 20, 32% 20-39, 3% 40-49, less than 1% 50-99.

**Special facilities:** Film lab, marine biology with scuba access, plasma physics and fluid dynamics labs, ornithology collection, geological collection, astronomical instruments collection, vivarium, greenhouses.

**Freshman class profile.** 5,272 applied, 2,328 admitted, 458 enrolled.

| Mid 50% test scores | | | |
|---|---|---|---|
| SAT critical reading: | 590-700 | Rank in top quarter: | 89% |
| SAT math: | 600-690 | Rank in top tenth: | 57% |
| SAT writing: | 590-690 | End year in good standing: | 95% |
| ACT composite: | 26-30 | Return as sophomores: | 92% |
| GPA 3.50 or higher: | 34% | Out-of-state: | 62% |
| GPA 3.0-3.49: | 34% | Live on campus: | 100% |
| GPA 2.0-2.99: | 32% | International: | 2% |

**Basis for selection.** Primary consideration given to academic credentials and holistic qualities such as intellectual curiosity, out-of-class interests, and personal character. SAT Subject Tests recommended. Interview recommended. **Homeschooled:** Statement describing homeschool structure and mission, transcript of courses and grades, state high school equivalency certificate, letter of recommendation (nonparent) required. At least 2 SAT Subject Tests recommended.

**High school preparation.** 20 units recommended. Recommended units include English 4, mathematics 4, social studies 2, history 2, science 3 (laboratory 2), foreign language 3 and academic electives 2.

**2007-2008 Annual costs.** Tuition/fees: $35,373. Room/board: $10,030. Books/supplies: $914. Personal expenses: $1,300.

**2006-2007 Financial aid. Need-based:** 306 full-time freshmen applied for aid; 234 were judged to have need; 233 of these received aid. Average need met was 100%. Average scholarship/grant was $24,752; average loan $4,591. 77% of total undergraduate aid awarded as scholarships/grants, 23% as loans/jobs. **Non-need-based:** Awarded to 537 full-time undergraduates, including 144 freshmen. Scholarships awarded for academics, leadership.

**Application procedures. Admission:** Closing date 1/10 (postmark date). $50 fee, may be waived for applicants with need. Application may be submitted online. Admission notification 4/1. Must reply by May 1 or within 2 week(s) if notified thereafter. **Financial aid:** Priority date 11/15, closing date 2/1. FAFSA, CSS PROFILE required. Applicants notified by 3/24; must reply by 5/1.

**Academics. Special study options:** Combined bachelor's/graduate degree, cross-registration, double major, exchange student, honors, independent study, internships, student-designed major, study abroad, United Nations semester, Washington semester. **Credit/placement by examination:** AP, CLEP, IB, institutional tests. **Support services:** Learning center, pre-admission summer program, study skills assistance, tutoring, writing center.

**Majors. Area/ethnic studies:** American, Asian, women's. **Biology:** General, biochemistry. **English:** English lit. **Foreign languages:** General, French, Spanish. **History:** General. **Interdisciplinary:** Cognitive science. **Math:** General. **Parks/recreation:** Exercise sciences. **Philosophy/religion:** Philosophy, religion. **Physical sciences:** Chemistry, geology, geophysics, physics. **Psychology:** General. **Social sciences:** Economics, international relations, political science, sociology. **Visual/performing arts:** Art, art history/conservation, dramatic. **Other:** Critical theory and social justice.

**Most popular majors.** Biology 9%, English 9%, history 10%, physical sciences 7%, psychology 8%, social sciences 32%, visual/performing arts 10%.

**Computing on campus.** 300 workstations in dormitories, library, computer center. Dormitories linked to campus network. Commuter students can connect to campus network. Online course registration, online library, helpline, repair service, wireless network available.

**Student life. Freshman orientation:** Mandatory. Preregistration for classes offered. Held 1 week in August prior to start of classes. **Policies:** All residence halls student-run. **Housing:** Guaranteed on-campus for freshmen. Coed dorms, single-sex dorms, fraternity/sorority housing, substance-free housing available. **Activities:** Bands, choral groups, dance, drama, film society, literary magazine, music ensembles, musical theater, radio station, student government, student newspaper, symphony orchestra, more than 100 clubs and organizations.

**Athletics.** NCAA. **Intercollegiate:** Baseball M, basketball, cross-country, diving, football (tackle) M, golf, soccer, softball W, swimming, tennis, track and field, volleyball W, water polo. **Intramural:** Basketball, football (non-tackle), volleyball. **Team name:** Tigers.

**Student services.** Adult student services, alcohol/substance abuse counseling, campus ministries, career counseling, services for economically disadvantaged, student employment services, financial aid counseling, health

services, minority student services, on-campus daycare, personal counseling, women's services. **Physically disabled:** Services for hearing impaired.

**Contact.** E-mail: admission@oxy.edu
Phone: (323) 259-2700 Toll-free number: (800) 825-5262
Fax: (323) 341-4875
Vince Cuseo, Dean of Admission, Occidental College, 1600 Campus Road, Los Angeles, CA 90041

## Otis College of Art and Design
**Los Angeles, California**
www.otis.edu

CB member
CB code: 4394

- Private 4-year visual arts college
- Commuter campus in very large city
- 1,117 degree-seeking undergraduates: 1% part-time, 68% women
- 56 degree-seeking graduate students
- 42% of applicants admitted
- SAT or ACT (ACT writing optional), application essay required
- 49% graduate within 6 years

**General.** Founded in 1918. Regionally accredited. **Degrees:** 216 bachelor's awarded; master's offered. **Calendar:** Semester, limited summer session. **Full-time faculty:** 59 total; 10% have terminal degrees, 15% minority, 61% women. **Part-time faculty:** 212 total; 4% have terminal degrees, 18% minority, 46% women. **Class size:** 78% < 20, 21% 20-39, less than 1% 40-49, less than 1% 50-99. **Special facilities:** Rare art books collection, full foundry and casting facilities, photographic darkroom, fully equipped printmaking studio, fine art book press room, woodworking and metal working shops, toy design department, digital imaging studio.

**Freshman class profile.** 1,113 applied, 473 admitted, 173 enrolled.

| Mid 50% test scores | | | |
|---|---|---|---|
| SAT critical reading: | 430-560 | GPA 3.0-3.49: | 45% |
| SAT math: | 460-570 | GPA 2.0-2.99: | 33% |
| SAT writing: | 430-560 | Return as sophomores: | 85% |
| ACT composite: | 17-21 | Out-of-state: | 32% |
| GPA 3.50 or higher: | 22% | Live on campus: | 58% |
| | | International: | 15% |

**Basis for selection.** Portfolio most important, followed by school achievement record, essay and test scores. Activities, leadership, motivation also considered. Portfolio required. Interview recommended. **Homeschooled:** Documentation that student has solid academic foundation, is socially and intellectually mature, and has passion for the arts.

**High school preparation.** Required and recommended units include English 4, mathematics 3-4, social studies 1-2, history 2-3, science 2-4 (laboratory 1-4) and foreign language 2. Drawing and as much art as possible recommended.

**2008-2009 Annual costs.** Tuition/fees: $30,464. Books/supplies: $1,400. Personal expenses: $1,300.

**2007-2008 Financial aid. Need-based:** 145 full-time freshmen applied for aid; 124 were judged to have need; 124 of these received aid. Average need met was 51%. Average scholarship/grant was $8,864; average loan $3,300. 54% of total undergraduate aid awarded as scholarships/grants, 46% as loans/jobs. **Non-need-based:** Awarded to 237 full-time undergraduates, including 66 freshmen. Scholarships awarded for academics, art.

**Application procedures. Admission:** Priority date 2/15; no deadline. $50 fee, may be waived for applicants with need. Application may be submitted online. Admission notification on a rolling basis beginning on or about 12/15. Must reply by May 1 or within 2 week(s) if notified thereafter. **Financial aid:** Priority date 2/15; no closing date. FAFSA required. Applicants notified by 3/1; Applicants notified on a rolling basis starting 3/1; must reply within 2 week(s) of notification.

**Academics.** Approximately one-third of curriculum consists of liberal arts classes. **Special study options:** Cooperative education, ESL, exchange student, honors, internships, study abroad, teacher certification program. **Credit/placement by examination:** AP, CLEP, IB, institutional tests. **Support services:** Pre-admission summer program, reduced course load, remedial instruction, study skills assistance, tutoring.

**Majors. Architecture:** Architecture, environmental design, interior, landscape. **Communications technology:** Animation/special effects. **Visual/performing arts:** Art, design, fashion design, graphic design, illustration, industrial design, interior design, multimedia, painting, photography, sculpture, studio arts.

**Most popular majors.** Architecture 7%, visual/performing arts 93%.

**Computing on campus.** 350 workstations in library, computer center. Helpline, wireless network available.

**Student life. Freshman orientation:** Mandatory. Orientation held in January and August. **Housing:** Apartments available. $550 nonrefundable deposit, deadline 6/1. Otis sponsored off-campus apartments available. **Activities:** International student organizations, student government, literary organization, Campus Crusade.

**Student services.** Adult student services, alcohol/substance abuse counseling, career counseling, student employment services, financial aid counseling, personal counseling, placement for graduates. **Physically disabled:** Services for hearing impaired.

**Contact.** E-mail: admissions@otis.edu
Phone: (310) 665-6820 Toll-free number: (800) 527-6847
Fax: (310) 665-6821
Marc Meredith, Dean of Admissions, Otis College of Art and Design, 9045 Lincoln Boulevard, Los Angeles, CA 90045-9785

## Pacific Oaks College
**Pasadena, California**
www.pacificoaks.edu

CB code: 0482

- Private two-year upper-division teachers college
- Commuter campus in small city
- 98% of applicants admitted
- Application essay required

**General.** Founded in 1951. Regionally accredited. College and children's school founded by Quaker families as community education center. **Degrees:** 92 bachelor's awarded; master's offered. **Articulation:** Agreements with De Anza College, Glendale City College, College of the Canyons, Pasadena City College, Rio Hondo College, Santa Monica College, Santa Barbara College, East Los Angeles College, El Camino College, Mt. San Antonio College, Citrus College. **Location:** 10 miles from downtown Los Angeles. **Calendar:** Semester, limited summer session. **Full-time faculty:** 21 total; 67% have terminal degrees, 43% minority, 76% women. **Part-time faculty:** 101 total. **Class size:** 72% < 20, 28% 20-39.

**Student profile.** 237 degree-seeking undergraduates, 818 degree-seeking graduate students. 49 applied as first time-transfer students, 48 admitted, 45 enrolled. 87% transferred from two-year, 13% transferred from four-year institutions.

| | | | |
|---|---|---|---|
| Women: | 95% | Native American: | 1% |
| African American: | 11% | Part-time: | 97% |
| Asian American: | 6% | Out-of-state: | 19% |
| Hispanic American: | 40% | 25 or older: | 94% |

**Basis for selection.** College transcript, application essay required. Must have completed equivalent of GED. Transfer accepted as juniors, seniors.

**2007-2008 Annual costs.** Tuition/fees: $23,910. Books/supplies: $924. Personal expenses: $4,000.

**Financial aid.** All financial aid based on need. 17% of total undergraduate aid awarded as scholarships/grants, 83% as loans/jobs.

**Application procedures. Admission:** Priority date 4/15; deadline 6/1. $55 fee, may be waived for applicants with need. Application must be submitted on paper.

**Academics. Special study options:** Accelerated study, distance learning, independent study, internships, teacher certification program, weekend college. **Credit/placement by examination:** CLEP. 30 credit hours maximum toward bachelor's degree. Students age 30-35 without a bachelor's degree may earn credit based on life experience. **Support services:** Learning center, reduced course load, study skills assistance, tutoring, writing center.

**Majors. Family/consumer sciences:** Family studies.

**Computing on campus.** 17 workstations in library, computer center. Online library available.

**Student life. Activities:** Teacher education student association; marriage, family therapy student association.

**Student services.** Adult student services, career counseling, financial aid counseling. **Physically disabled:** Services for visually, speech, hearing impaired.

**Contact.** E-mail: admissions@pacificoaks.edu
Phone: (626) 397-1349 Toll-free number: (800) 684-0900
Fax: (626) 666-1220
Augusta Pickens, Director of Admissions, Pacific Oaks College, 5
Westmoreland Place, Pasadena, CA 91103

## Pacific States University
### Los Angeles, California
www.psuca.edu                    CB code: 3547

- Private 4-year university
- Commuter campus in very large city
- 34 degree-seeking undergraduates: 44% women
- 141 degree-seeking graduate students

**General.** Accredited by ACICS. **Degrees:** 11 bachelor's awarded; master's, doctoral offered. **Location:** 5 miles from downtown. **Calendar:** Quarter, limited summer session. **Full-time faculty:** 6 total; 50% have terminal degrees, 50% minority, 17% women. **Part-time faculty:** 29 total; 38% have terminal degrees, 86% minority, 14% women.

**Freshman class profile.**

| | | | |
|---|---|---|---|
| Live on campus: | 10% | International: | 88% |

**Basis for selection.** Open admission, but selective for some programs. High school diploma and English proficiency required. TOEFL required of students whose native language is not English. **Homeschooled:** Transcript of courses and grades, state high school equivalency certificate required.

**2008-2009 Annual costs.** Tuition/fees (projected): $13,400. Books/supplies: $1,200.

**Financial aid. Non-need-based:** Scholarships awarded for academics.

**Application procedures. Admission:** No deadline. $100 fee. Application must be submitted on paper. Admission notification on a rolling basis. **Financial aid:** No deadline. FAFSA, institutional form required.

**Academics. Special study options:** Combined bachelor's/graduate degree, distance learning, double major, ESL, liberal arts/career combination. **Credit/placement by examination:** CLEP, IB. 8 credit hours maximum toward bachelor's degree.

**Majors. Business:** Accounting, management information systems, marketing. **Computer sciences:** General.

**Computing on campus.** 60 workstations in dormitories, library, computer center. Dormitories wired for high-speed internet access. Online library, wireless network available.

**Student life. Freshman orientation:** Available. Preregistration for classes offered. Held 2 weeks after each quarter starts, lasting 2 hours. **Housing:** Guaranteed on-campus for all undergraduates. Coed dorms, substance-free housing available. **Activities:** Literary magazine, TV station.

**Student services.** Student employment services, financial aid counseling, personal counseling.

**Contact.** E-mail: admissions@psuca.edu
Phone: (323) 731-2383 ext. 11 Toll-free number: (888) 200-0383
Fax: (323) 731-7276
Marina Miller, Assistant Director of Admissions, Pacific States University, 1516 South Western Avenue, Los Angeles, CA 90006

## Pacific Union College
### Angwin, California
www.puc.edu                    CB code: 4600

- Private 4-year liberal arts college affiliated with Seventh-day Adventists
- Residential campus in small town
- 1,358 degree-seeking undergraduates: 13% part-time, 54% women, 3% African American, 26% Asian American, 13% Hispanic American, 7% international
- 1 degree-seeking graduate students
- 75% of applicants admitted
- SAT or ACT (ACT writing recommended) required
- 38% graduate within 6 years

**General.** Founded in 1882. Regionally accredited. **Degrees:** 242 bachelor's, 95 associate awarded; master's offered. **Location:** 30 miles from Napa, 75 miles from San Francisco. **Calendar:** Quarter, limited summer session. **Full-time faculty:** 81 total; 53% have terminal degrees, 24% minority, 41% women. **Part-time faculty:** 10 total; 40% have terminal degrees, 30% minority, 70% women. **Class size:** 66% < 20, 25% 20-39, 5% 40-49, 4% 50-99, less than 1% >100. **Special facilities:** Observatory, airport/flight training, biology museum, Pitcairn Island Study Center, 1500-acre nature preserve.

**Freshman class profile.** 1,706 applied, 1,284 admitted, 272 enrolled.

| Mid 50% test scores | | | |
|---|---|---|---|
| SAT critical reading: | 460-580 | GPA 2.0-2.99: | 29% |
| SAT math: | 440-570 | End year in good standing: | 84% |
| ACT composite: | 17-24 | Return as sophomores: | 73% |
| GPA 3.50 or higher: | 39% | Out-of-state: | 18% |
| GPA 3.0-3.49: | 31% | Live on campus: | 89% |
| | | International: | 6% |

**Basis for selection.** Minimum GPA of 2.3 and acceptable recommendations. **Learning Disabled:** Documentation if available.

**High school preparation.** 8 units required. Required and recommended units include English 4, mathematics 2-3, history 1-2, science 1-3 and foreign language 2. Computer literacy strongly recommended.

**2007-2008 Annual costs.** Tuition/fees: $21,435. Room/board: $5,955. Books/supplies: $1,386. Personal expenses: $2,142.

**Financial aid. Non-need-based:** Scholarships awarded for leadership, religious affiliation.

**Application procedures. Admission:** No deadline. $30 fee, may be waived for applicants with need. Application may be submitted online. Admission notification on a rolling basis beginning on or about 1/15. **Financial aid:** No deadline. FAFSA, institutional form required. Applicants notified on a rolling basis; must reply within 3 week(s) of notification.

**Academics. Special study options:** Combined bachelor's/graduate degree, double major, external degree, honors, independent study, internships, study abroad, teacher certification program. **Credit/placement by examination:** AP, CLEP, IB, SAT, ACT, institutional tests. 24 credit hours maximum toward associate degree, 45 toward bachelor's. **Support services:** Learning center, remedial instruction, study skills assistance, tutoring, writing center.

**Majors. Biology:** General, biochemistry, biophysics. **Business:** General, accounting, business admin, finance, international, management information systems, marketing. **Communications:** General, digital media, journalism, public relations. **Computer sciences:** Computer science. **Education:** Early childhood, elementary, English, mathematics, music, physical. **English:** English lit. **Foreign languages:** French, Spanish. **Health:** Nursing (RN). **History:** General. **Interdisciplinary:** Natural sciences. **Math:** General. **Philosophy/religion:** Religion. **Physical sciences:** Chemistry, physics. **Psychology:** General. **Public administration:** Social work. **Social sciences:** General. **Theology:** Bible, theology. **Transportation:** Aviation. **Visual/performing arts:** Cinematography, commercial/advertising art, music performance, photography, studio arts.

**Most popular majors.** Biology 8%, business/marketing 26%, education 6%, English 7%, health sciences 13%, physical sciences 9%, visual/performing arts 7%.

**Computing on campus.** 178 workstations in dormitories, library. Dormitories wired for high-speed internet access and linked to campus network. Commuter students can connect to campus network. Online course registration, online library, helpline, repair service, wireless network available.

**Student life. Freshman orientation:** Mandatory. Preregistration for classes offered. **Policies:** Religious observance required. **Housing:** Guaranteed on-campus for freshmen. Single-sex dorms, apartments, substance-free housing available. $150 deposit. **Activities:** Bands, choral groups, drama, film society, literary magazine, music ensembles, musical theater, radio station, student government, student newspaper, symphony orchestra, 20 clubs.

**Athletics.** NAIA. **Intercollegiate:** Basketball, cross-country, soccer, volleyball. **Intramural:** Basketball, football (non-tackle) M, softball, volleyball. **Team name:** Pioneers.

**Student services.** Adult student services, alcohol/substance abuse counseling, campus ministries, career counseling, student employment services, financial aid counseling, health services, on-campus daycare, personal counseling, placement for graduates. **Physically disabled:** Services for visually, speech, hearing impaired.

**Contact.** E-mail: enroll@puc.edu
Phone: (707) 965-6336 Toll-free number: (800) 862-7080
Fax: (707) 965-6432
Darren Hagen, Director of Enrollment Services, Pacific Union College, One Angwin Avenue, Angwin, CA 94508

## Patten University
Oakland, California    **CB member**
www.patten.edu    **CB code: 4620**

- Private 4-year university and liberal arts college affiliated with interdenominational tradition
- Residential campus in very large city
- 660 degree-seeking undergraduates
- SAT or ACT (ACT writing optional), application essay, interview required

**General.** Founded in 1944. Regionally accredited. **Degrees:** 36 bachelor's, 22 associate awarded; master's offered. **Location:** 18 miles from San Francisco, 30 miles from San Jose. **Calendar:** Semester, limited summer session. **Full-time faculty:** 20 total. **Part-time faculty:** 120 total.

**Freshman class profile.**

| Mid 50% test scores | | |
|---|---|---|
| SAT critical reading: | 500-610 | ACT composite: 18-25 |
| SAT math: | 460-590 | Out-of-state: 5% |

**Basis for selection.** Christian commitment most important. High school record, interview, essay, test scores, recommendation important.

**High school preparation.** 22 units required. Required units include English 4, mathematics 2, social studies 4, history 2, science 2 (laboratory 1), foreign language 1 and academic electives 6.

**2007-2008 Annual costs.** Tuition/fees: $11,880. Room/board: $6,250. Books/supplies: $550. Personal expenses: $1,100.

**Financial aid. Non-need-based:** Scholarships awarded for academics, athletics, state residency.

**Application procedures. Admission:** Priority date 3/31; deadline 7/31. $35 fee, may be waived for applicants with need. Admission notification on a rolling basis. **Financial aid:** Priority date 3/31; no closing date. FAFSA, institutional form required. Applicants notified on a rolling basis starting 5/31.

**Academics. Special study options:** Accelerated study, double major, dual enrollment of high school students, independent study, teacher certification program, weekend college. **Credit/placement by examination:** AP, CLEP, institutional tests. **Support services:** Learning center, remedial instruction, tutoring, writing center.

**Majors. Business:** Business admin. **Education:** Adult/continuing, early childhood. **Liberal arts:** Arts/sciences. **Philosophy/religion:** Religion. **Psychology:** General. **Theology:** Religious ed, sacred music.

**Computing on campus.** 30 workstations in library, computer center. Dormitories wired for high-speed internet access. Online library, wireless network available.

**Student life. Freshman orientation:** Mandatory. Preregistration for classes offered. 3-day overview held week before start of classes. **Policies:** Christian service program designed to involve students in practical ministry. Religious observance required. **Housing:** Guaranteed on-campus for all undergraduates. Single-sex dorms, apartments available. $150 deposit, deadline 7/31. **Activities:** Concert band, choral groups, drama, music ensembles, student government, student newspaper, symphony orchestra, Community of Faith groups, prison ministry.

**Athletics.** NAIA. **Intercollegiate:** Baseball M, softball W. **Team name:** Lions.

**Student services.** Adult student services, career counseling, student employment services, personal counseling, placement for graduates, veterans' counselor.

**Contact.** E-mail: admissions@patten.edu
Phone: (510) 261-8500 ext. 7764 Toll-free number: (877) 472-8836
Fax: (510) 534-4344
Kim Guerra, Director of Admissions, Patten University, 2433 Coolidge Avenue, Oakland, CA 94601-2699

## Pepperdine University
Malibu, California    **CB member**
www.pepperdine.edu    **CB code: 4630**

- Private 4-year university and liberal arts college affiliated with Church of Christ
- Residential campus in small city
- 3,381 degree-seeking undergraduates: 14% part-time, 56% women, 7% African American, 10% Asian American, 10% Hispanic American, 1% Native American, 6% international
- 4,178 degree-seeking graduate students
- 35% of applicants admitted
- SAT or ACT with writing, application essay required
- 79% graduate within 6 years

**General.** Founded in 1937. Regionally accredited. Education, psychology, business graduate campuses in Los Angeles. Educational centers in Long Beach, Irvine, Encino, West Los Angeles, Westlake Village. 5 campuses in Europe (Germany, England, Italy, Spain, France), 1 in Costa Rica. Education center in Hong-Kong. Part-time, evening, weekend classes for business undergrad programs. **Degrees:** 820 bachelor's awarded; master's, doctoral, first professional offered. **ROTC:** Army, Air Force. **Location:** 14 miles from Santa Monica, 30 miles from Los Angeles. **Calendar:** Semester, limited summer session. **Full-time faculty:** 388 total; 91% have terminal degrees, 12% minority, 36% women. **Part-time faculty:** 290 total; 51% have terminal degrees, 13% minority, 46% women. **Class size:** 68% < 20, 27% 20-39, 2% 40-49, 2% 50-99, 2% >100.

**Freshman class profile.** 6,661 applied, 2,315 admitted, 752 enrolled.

| Mid 50% test scores | | | |
|---|---|---|---|
| SAT critical reading: | 550-670 | GPA 2.0-2.99: | 5% |
| SAT math: | 560-680 | Rank in top quarter: | 74% |
| SAT writing: | 560-670 | Rank in top tenth: | 46% |
| ACT composite: | 24-29 | Return as sophomores: | 88% |
| GPA 3.50 or higher: | 69% | Out-of-state: | 48% |
| GPA 3.0-3.49: | 26% | Live on campus: | 98% |
| | | International: | 5% |

**Basis for selection.** School achievement record and test scores most important. Special talents, school and community activities, letters of recommendation, personal qualities also considered. Audition required for music, theater majors. Portfolio recommended for art majors. **Homeschooled:** Transcript of courses and grades, state high school equivalency certificate required. **Learning Disabled:** Proper documentation from doctor diagnosing learning disability required.

**High school preparation.** 28 units recommended. Recommended units include English 4, mathematics 4, social studies 3, history 3, science 4 (laboratory 3), foreign language 3 and academic electives 3. 1 speech recommended.

**2008-2009 Annual costs.** Tuition/fees: $36,770. Room/board: $10,480. Books/supplies: $1,000. Personal expenses: $700.

**2007-2008 Financial aid. Need-based:** 456 full-time freshmen applied for aid; 270 were judged to have need; 262 of these received aid. Average need met was 85%. Average scholarship/grant was $24,654; average loan $4,769. 74% of total undergraduate aid awarded as scholarships/grants, 26% as loans/jobs. **Non-need-based:** Awarded to 1,074 full-time undergraduates, including 254 freshmen. Scholarships awarded for academics, art, athletics, minority status, music/drama, religious affiliation, ROTC.

**Application procedures. Admission:** Priority date 11/15; deadline 1/15 (postmark date). $65 fee, may be waived for applicants with need. Application must be submitted on paper. Admission notification 4/1. Must reply by 5/1. **Financial aid:** Closing date 2/15. FAFSA, institutional form required. Applicants notified by 4/15; must reply within 2 week(s) of notification.

**Academics.** Great books colloquium, freshman seminars and first year faculty mentor program for all students. **Special study options:** Double major, honors, independent study, internships, student-designed major, study abroad, teacher certification program, Washington semester, weekend college. 3-2 programs in engineering with USC, Washington University, Boston University. **Credit/placement by examination:** AP, CLEP, IB, institutional tests. 32 credit hours maximum toward bachelor's degree. IB credit awarded for higher level exams only: 4 credits for each score of 5 and above; maximum 16. **Support services:** Pre-admission summer program, remedial instruction, tutoring, writing center.

**Majors. Area/ethnic studies:** Asian, European, Latin American. **Biology:** General, biochemistry. **Business:** Accounting, business admin, finance, international, marketing. **Communications:** General, advertising, broadcast journalism, journalism, organizational, public relations, radio/tv. **Computer sciences: General. **Education:** General, chemistry, English, music, physical, speech. **Engineering:** General. **English:** Creative writing, English lit. **Family/consumer sciences:** Food/nutrition. **Foreign languages:** French, German, Spanish. **Health:** Athletic training. **History:** General. **Interdisciplinary:** Global studies, math/computer science, natural sciences, nutrition sciences. **Liberal arts:** Arts/sciences, humanities. **Math:** General. **Parks/recreation:** Exercise sciences, sports admin. **Philosophy/religion:** Philosophy, religion. **Physical sciences:** Chemistry, physics. **Psychology:** General. **Social sciences:** Economics, political science, sociology. **Visual/performing arts:** Acting, art, art history/conservation, dramatic, multimedia, music history, music management, music theory/composition, studio arts, theater design.

**Most popular majors.** Business/marketing 27%, communications/journalism 18%, psychology 7%, social sciences 11%, visual/performing arts 7%.

**Computing on campus.** 292 workstations in dormitories, library, computer center, student center. Dormitories wired for high-speed internet access and linked to campus network. Commuter students can connect to campus network. Online library, helpline, repair service, wireless network available.

**Student life. Freshman orientation:** Mandatory. Orientation held a week before the official start of the Fall semester. **Policies:** Students required to attend weekly convocation. Freshmen and sophomores live on campus or at home with parent or guardian if single and under 21. **Housing:** Guaranteed on-campus for freshmen. Single-sex dorms, special housing for disabled, apartments available. **Activities:** Bands, choral groups, dance, drama, film society, international student organizations, literary magazine, music ensembles, musical theater, opera, radio station, student government, student newspaper, symphony orchestra, TV station, Campus Crusade for Christ, College Republicans, Young Democrats, volunteer center, black student union, Latin student association, Hawaiian club, Korean student association, Japan club.

**Athletics.** NCAA. **Intercollegiate:** Baseball M, basketball, cross-country, golf, soccer W, swimming W, tennis, track and field W, volleyball, water polo M. **Intramural:** Basketball, football (non-tackle), handball, soccer, swimming, tennis, volleyball. **Team name:** Waves.

**Student services.** Alcohol/substance abuse counseling, campus ministries, career counseling, student employment services, financial aid counseling, health services, personal counseling, placement for graduates, veterans' counselor. **Physically disabled:** Services for visually, hearing impaired.

**Contact.** E-mail: admission-seaver@pepperdine.edu
Phone: (310) 506-4392 Fax: (310) 506-4861
Mike Trushke, Director of Admission, Pepperdine University, 24255 Pacific Coast Highway, Malibu, CA 90263-4392

## Pitzer College
Claremont, California
www.pitzer.edu

**CB member**
**CB code:** 4619

- Private 4-year liberal arts college
- Residential campus in large town
- 999 degree-seeking undergraduates: 4% part-time, 59% women, 6% African American, 10% Asian American, 14% Hispanic American, 3% international
- 26% of applicants admitted
- Application essay required
- 72% graduate within 6 years

**General.** Founded in 1963. Regionally accredited. One of a cluster of 5 undergraduate and 2 graduate institutions on adjoining campuses. Campuses share facilities. Cross-enrollment available at any of the 5 colleges, which include Claremont-McKenna, Harvey Mudd, Pitzer, Pomona, and Scripps. Interdisciplinary curriculum with social responsibility requirement, intercultural education objective; no academic departments. **Degrees:** 228 bachelor's awarded. **ROTC:** Army, Air Force. **Location:** 35 miles from Los Angeles. **Calendar:** Semester, limited summer session. **Full-time faculty:** 67 total; 98% have terminal degrees, 33% minority, 48% women. **Part-time faculty:** 24 total; 75% have terminal degrees, 12% minority, 54% women. **Class size:** 67% < 20, 31% 20-39, 2% 40-49. **Special facilities:** Ecology center, nature reserve, arboretum, organic garden, women's studies center, restored arts and crafts home with poetry reading room, 2 art galleries.

**Freshman class profile.** 3,748 applied, 983 admitted, 243 enrolled.

| Mid 50% test scores | | |
|---|---|---|
| SAT critical reading: | 570-680 | |
| SAT math: | 550-650 | |
| GPA 3.50 or higher: | 76% | |
| GPA 3.0-3.49: | 19% | |
| GPA 2.0-2.99: | 5% | |
| Rank in top quarter: | 52% | |
| Rank in top tenth: | 32% | |
| Return as sophomores: | 94% | |
| Out-of-state: | 45% | |
| Live on campus: | 99% | |
| International: | 6% | |

**Basis for selection.** School record, essays (judged for writing ability), 3 recommendations, test scores, leadership, community service, work experience, talent, involvement in sports considered. SAT/ACT not required of students graduating in top 10% of class, or those with an unweighted cumulative GPA of 3.50 or higher in academic subjects. Otherwise, one of the following required: ACT or SAT scores; 2 SAT Subject Tests (one in math); 2 or more AP test scores of at least 4 (one English or English Language and one math or science); 2 International Baccalaureate exams (one English 1A and one math); or one recent junior or senior year graded analytical writing sample from a humanities or social science course and one recent graded exam from an advanced math course. The samples must include the teacher's comments, grades, and the assignment. Interview recommended.

**High school preparation.** 21 units required. Required units include English 4, mathematics 3, social studies 3, history 1, science 3 (laboratory 3), foreign language 3 and visual/performing arts 1.

**2007-2008 Annual costs.** Tuition/fees: $35,912. Room/board: $10,212. Books/supplies: $950. Personal expenses: $1,000.

**2007-2008 Financial aid. Need-based:** 110 full-time freshmen applied for aid; 83 were judged to have need; 83 of these received aid. Average need met was 100%. Average scholarship/grant was $26,794; average loan $3,092. 83% of total undergraduate aid awarded as scholarships/grants, 17% as loans/jobs. **Non-need-based:** Awarded to 53 full-time undergraduates, including 18 freshmen. Scholarships awarded for academics, leadership.

**Application procedures. Admission:** Closing date 1/1 (postmark date). $50 fee, may be waived for applicants with need. Application may be submitted online. Admission notification 4/1. Must reply by 5/1. **Financial aid:** Closing date 2/1. FAFSA, CSS PROFILE required. Applicants notified by 4/1; must reply by 5/1.

**Academics.** Students may take up to one-third of courses at other Claremont campuses and must take 32 courses for graduation. Can create independent study courses and special majors. **Special study options:** Combined bachelor's/graduate degree, cooperative education, cross-registration, double major, ESL, exchange student, honors, independent study, internships, liberal arts/career combination, student-designed major, study abroad, urban semester. New Resources (for students over age 25 and nontraditional students), joint science program, joint BA/DO program. **Credit/placement by examination:** AP, CLEP, IB, institutional tests. **Support services:** Tutoring, writing center.

**Majors. Area/ethnic studies:** African-American, American, Asian, Asian-American, Caribbean, European, Hispanic-American/Latino/Chicano, Latin American, women's. **Biology:** General, biochemistry, biophysics, microbiology. **Business:** Organizational behavior. **Conservation:** Environmental science, environmental studies. **English:** Creative writing, English lit. **Foreign languages:** General, Chinese, classics, French, German, Italian, Japanese, linguistics, Russian, Spanish. **History:** General, American, European. **Interdisciplinary:** Biological/physical sciences, global studies, intercultural, natural sciences, neuroscience, science/society. **Math:** General. **Philosophy/religion:** Philosophy, religion. **Physical sciences:** Chemistry, organic chemistry, physics. **Psychology:** General. **Social sciences:** General, anthropology, economics, international relations, political science, sociology. **Visual/performing arts:** Art, art history/conservation, cinematography, dance, dramatic, film/cinema, studio arts.

**Computing on campus.** 100 workstations in dormitories, library, computer center, student center. Dormitories wired for high-speed internet access and linked to campus network. Commuter students can connect to campus network. Online library, helpline, student web hosting, wireless network available.

**Student life. Freshman orientation:** Mandatory. Held the week prior to start of fall semester. **Policies:** Strong philosophical framework of social responsibility and self-governance. **Housing:** Guaranteed on-campus for freshmen. Coed dorms, special housing for disabled, cooperative housing, substance-free housing available. Theme housing available: hush hall, involvement tower, all female corridors. **Activities:** Choral groups, dance, drama, literary magazine, music ensembles, radio station, student government, student newspaper, symphony orchestra, over 75 social service, religious, political, and ethnic organizations.

**Athletics.** NCAA. **Intercollegiate:** Badminton, baseball M, basketball, cross-country, diving, football (tackle) M, golf, lacrosse, soccer, softball W, swimming, tennis, track and field, volleyball W, water polo. **Intramural:** Archery, badminton, basketball, golf, racquetball, sailing, soccer, softball W, squash, tennis. **Team name:** Sagehens.

**Student services.** Adult student services, alcohol/substance abuse counseling, campus ministries, career counseling, student employment services, financial aid counseling, health services, minority student services, personal counseling, women's services. **Physically disabled:** Services for visually, speech, hearing impaired.

**Contact.** E-mail: admission@pitzer.edu
Phone: (909) 621-8129 Toll-free number: (800) 748-9371
Fax: (909) 621-8770
Arnaldo Rodriguez, Vice President of Admission and Financial Aid, Pitzer College, 1050 North Mills Avenue, Claremont, CA 91711-6101

## Platt College: Ontario
Ontario, California
www.plattcollege.edu                    CB code: 3015

- For-profit 4-year branch campus and technical college
- Commuter campus in small city
- 250 degree-seeking undergraduates
- Application essay, interview required

**General.** Accredited by ACCSCT. Branch of Los Angeles campus. **Degrees:** 36 bachelor's, 37 associate awarded. **Location:** 20 miles from Los Angeles. **Calendar:** Continuous. **Full-time faculty:** 10 total; 40% have terminal degrees, 30% minority. **Part-time faculty:** 25 total; 40% have terminal degrees, 48% minority. **Class size:** 71% < 20, 29% 20-39. **Special facilities:** Motion capture lab.

**Basis for selection.** Students admitted based on interview, high school diploma or GED, entrance test and essay, and completion of the admissions process. Math and English workshops available to students upon entrance if desired or recommended. **Learning Disabled:** Students with learning disabilities may request consideration for extra time to complete entrance test.

**2007-2008 Annual costs.** Annual tuition varies by program: $10,300--$14,230.

**Application procedures. Admission:** No deadline. $75 fee. Application may be submitted online. Admission notification on a rolling basis. **Financial aid:** Priority date 3/2; no closing date. FAFSA, institutional form required. Applicants notified on a rolling basis starting 1/1.

**Academics. Special study options:** Accelerated study, cooperative education, internships. **Credit/placement by examination:** CLEP. 48 credit hours maximum toward associate degree, 48 toward bachelor's. **Support services:** Tutoring.

**Majors. Communications technology:** Animation/special effects, graphics. **Computer sciences:** Computer graphics, web page design. **Legal studies:** Legal secretary, paralegal. **Visual/performing arts:** General, commercial/advertising art, design.

**Computing on campus.** 12 workstations in library.

**Student life. Freshman orientation:** Mandatory. Preregistration for classes offered. Held on first day of classes. **Activities:** Various student clubs and activities available.

**Student services.** Adult student services, career counseling, student employment services, financial aid counseling, placement for graduates.

**Contact.** Phone: (909) 941-9410 Toll-free number: (866) 752-8846
Fax: (909) 941-9660
Admissions Director, Platt College: Ontario, 3700 Inland Empire Boulevard, Ontario, CA 91764

## Platt College: San Diego
San Diego, California
www.platt.edu                    CB code: 3020

- For-profit 4-year visual arts and technical college
- Commuter campus in very large city
- 281 degree-seeking undergraduates: 26% women, 6% African American, 9% Asian American, 19% Hispanic American, 2% international
- Application essay, interview required
- 67% graduate within 6 years

**General.** Accredited by ACCSCT. **Degrees:** 54 bachelor's, 108 associate awarded. **Calendar:** Continuous. **Full-time faculty:** 6 total. **Part-time faculty:** 33 total; 9% have terminal degrees, 15% minority, 54% women. **Class size:** 91% < 20, 9% 20-39.

**Basis for selection.** Open admission, but selective for some programs and for out-of-state students. Aptitude test used to measure academic preparedness to undertake college-level courses; SAT considered in lieu of test.

**2007-2008 Annual costs.** Total program costs range from $16,200 to $28,400, depending on the program chosen. Bachelor degree tuition varies.

**2006-2007 Financial aid. Need-based:** 35% of total undergraduate aid awarded as scholarships/grants, 65% as loans/jobs.

**Application procedures. Admission:** No deadline. No application fee. Application must be submitted on paper. **Financial aid:** Closing date 3/2. FAFSA, institutional form required. Applicants notified on a rolling basis; must reply within 1 week(s) of notification.

**Academics. Special study options:** Accelerated study, internships, liberal arts/career combination. **Credit/placement by examination:** AP, CLEP, institutional tests. **Support services:** Study skills assistance, tutoring.

**Majors. Visual/performing arts:** General, commercial/advertising art.

**Computing on campus.** 200 workstations in library, computer center. Online library available.

**Student life. Freshman orientation:** Mandatory. Preregistration for classes offered.

**Student services.** Career counseling, services for economically disadvantaged, student employment services, financial aid counseling, personal counseling, placement for graduates.

**Contact.** E-mail: info@platt.edu
Phone: (619) 265-0107 Toll-free number: (866) 752-8826
Fax: (619) 308-0570
Craig Hinson, Admissions Director, Platt College: San Diego, 6250 El Cajon Boulevard, San Diego, CA 92115

## Point Loma Nazarene University
San Diego, California                    CB member
www.pointloma.edu                    CB code: 4605

- Private 4-year university and liberal arts college affiliated with Church of the Nazarene
- Residential campus in very large city
- 2,337 degree-seeking undergraduates: 3% part-time, 61% women, 2% African American, 6% Asian American, 11% Hispanic American, 1% Native American
- 583 degree-seeking graduate students
- 73% of applicants admitted
- SAT or ACT (ACT writing recommended), application essay, interview required
- 70% graduate within 6 years

**General.** Founded in 1902. Regionally accredited. **Degrees:** 564 bachelor's awarded; master's offered. **ROTC:** Army, Naval, Air Force. **Location:** 5 miles from downtown. **Calendar:** Semester, limited summer session. **Full-time faculty:** 177 total; 73% have terminal degrees, 10% minority, 40% women. **Class size:** 44% < 20, 44% 20-39, 10% 40-49, 2% 50-99.

**Freshman class profile.** 1,757 applied, 1,291 admitted, 531 enrolled.

| Mid 50% test scores | | | |
|---|---|---|---|
| SAT critical reading: | 510-620 | Rank in top quarter: | 69% |
| SAT math: | 510-620 | Rank in top tenth: | 35% |
| ACT composite: | 21-27 | End year in good standing: | 96% |
| GPA 3.50 or higher: | 70% | Return as sophomores: | 87% |
| GPA 3.0-3.49: | 22% | Out-of-state: | 26% |
| GPA 2.0-2.99: | 8% | Live on campus: | 97% |
| | | International: | 1% |

**Basis for selection.** Moral character, maturity, intellectual ability, and academic achievement important considerations. Preference given to self-directed applicants who appear to share ideals and objectives of college. SAT recommended.

**High school preparation.** 18 units recommended. Recommended units include English 4, mathematics 3, social studies 2, history 2, science 2 (laboratory 2), foreign language 2 and academic electives 1.

**2008-2009 Annual costs.** Tuition/fees: $25,120. Room/board: $8,170. Books/supplies: $1,566. Personal expenses: $2,214.

**2006-2007 Financial aid. Need-based:** 388 full-time freshmen applied for aid; 293 were judged to have need; 291 of these received aid. Average need met was 55%. Average scholarship/grant was $10,664; average loan

$2,256. 62% of total undergraduate aid awarded as scholarships/grants, 38% as loans/jobs. **Non-need-based:** Awarded to 775 full-time undergraduates, including 154 freshmen.

**Application procedures. Admission:** Closing date 3/1 (postmark date). $50 fee, may be waived for applicants with need. Application may be submitted online. Admission notification 4/1. Admission notification on a rolling basis. Must reply by May 1 or within 2 week(s) if notified thereafter. **Financial aid:** Closing date 3/2. FAFSA, institutional form required. Applicants notified on a rolling basis starting 3/1.

**Academics. Special study options:** Double major, honors, independent study, internships, semester at sea, study abroad, teacher certification program, United Nations semester, Washington semester. **Credit/placement by examination:** AP, CLEP, IB, SAT, institutional tests. 32 credit hours maximum toward bachelor's degree. Some restrictions apply in special majors. **Support services:** Learning center, reduced course load, remedial instruction, study skills assistance, tutoring, writing center.

**Majors. Biology:** General, biochemistry. **Business:** Accounting, business admin, communications, management information systems. **Communications:** General, broadcast journalism, journalism, media studies. **Communications technology:** Graphics. **Computer sciences:** Computer science. **Conservation:** Environmental science. **Education:** Art, music. **Engineering:** Physics. **English:** English lit. **Family/consumer sciences:** General, child development, family/community services, food/nutrition. **Foreign languages:** Romance, Spanish. **Health:** Athletic training, dietetics, nursing (RN). **History:** General. **Interdisciplinary:** Global studies. **Liberal arts:** Arts/sciences. **Math:** General. **Parks/recreation:** Exercise sciences, health/fitness. **Philosophy/religion:** Philosophy. **Physical sciences:** Chemistry, physics. **Psychology:** General, industrial. **Public administration:** Social work. **Social sciences:** General, international economic development, political science, sociology. **Theology:** Bible, preministerial, sacred music, youth ministry. **Visual/performing arts:** Art, dramatic, graphic design, music performance, music theory/composition.

**Most popular majors.** Business/marketing 20%, communications/journalism 8%, education 10%, health sciences 11%, psychology 12%, visual/performing arts 7%.

**Computing on campus.** 270 workstations in dormitories, library, computer center, student center. Dormitories wired for high-speed internet access and linked to campus network. Commuter students can connect to campus network. Online course registration, online library, helpline, repair service, wireless network available.

**Student life. Freshman orientation:** Mandatory. **Policies:** Students expected to exercise self-discipline and sound judgment and manage conduct both on and off campus consistent with agreements made upon application and with university catalog and student handbook. Religious observance required. **Housing:** Guaranteed on-campus for freshmen. Single-sex dorms, apartments, substance-free housing available. $425 nonrefundable deposit, deadline 5/1. **Activities:** Bands, campus ministries, choral groups, drama, international student organizations, literary magazine, music ensembles, musical theater, radio station, student government, student newspaper, symphony orchestra, TV station, students for social justice, social work club, College Democrats, College Republicans, Brothers and Sisters United, Association of Latin American Students.

**Athletics.** NAIA. **Intercollegiate:** Baseball M, basketball, cross-country, golf M, soccer, softball W, tennis, track and field, volleyball W. **Intramural:** Badminton, basketball, football (non-tackle), golf, soccer, softball, tennis, track and field, volleyball. **Team name:** Sea Lions.

**Student services.** Campus ministries, career counseling, student employment services, financial aid counseling, health services, minority student services, on-campus daycare, personal counseling, veterans' counselor. **Physically disabled:** Services for visually, hearing impaired.

**Contact.** E-mail: admissions@pointloma.edu
Phone: (619) 849-2273 Toll-free number: (800) 733-7770
Fax: (619) 849-2601
Chip Killingsworth, Director of Undergraduate Admissions, Point Loma Nazarene University, 3900 Lomaland Drive, San Diego, CA 92106-2899

## Pomona College
**Claremont, California**
**www.pomona.edu**

CB member
CB code: 4607

- Private 4-year liberal arts college
- Residential campus in large town
- 1,521 degree-seeking undergraduates: 50% women, 8% African American, 14% Asian American, 11% Hispanic American, 3% international

- 16% of applicants admitted
- SAT and SAT Subject Tests or ACT (ACT writing recommended), application essay required
- 94% graduate within 6 years

**General.** Founded in 1887. Regionally accredited. One of a cluster of 5 undergraduate and 2 graduate schools on adjoining campuses. Campuses share facilities. Cross-enrollment available at any of the 5 colleges, which include Claremont-McKenna, Harvey Mudd, Pitzer, Pomona, and Scripps. Extensive overseas studies. **Degrees:** 381 bachelor's awarded. **ROTC:** Army, Air Force. **Location:** 35 miles from Los Angeles, 20 miles from Pasadena. **Calendar:** Semester. **Full-time faculty:** 184 total; 99% have terminal degrees, 25% minority, 40% women. **Part-time faculty:** 30 total; 33% have terminal degrees, 33% minority, 37% women. **Class size:** 72% < 20, 25% 20-39, 2% 40-49, 1% 50-99. **Special facilities:** Science center, center for modern language and international relations, observatory, biological field station, ecological preserve, botanic garden, social sciences center, Greek theater, multimedia labs.

**Freshman class profile.** 5,908 applied, 964 admitted, 375 enrolled.

| Mid 50% test scores | | | |
|---|---|---|---|
| SAT critical reading: | 690-770 | Rank in top tenth: | 87% |
| SAT math: | 690-760 | Return as sophomores: | 99% |
| SAT writing: | 680-750 | Out-of-state: | 67% |
| ACT composite: | 29-34 | Live on campus: | 100% |
| Rank in top quarter: | 98% | International: | 4% |

**Basis for selection.** School achievement record, test scores, essays, 3 recommendations most important. Special skills in music, art, drama, or athletics; leadership, motivation, and diversity of background also important. Some preference to children of alumni; special consideration for underrepresented groups. School and community activities also considered. Students submitting SAT must also submit 2 SAT Subject Tests in different subject areas. Interview required for early admission applicants, strongly recommended for all applicants. Audition recommended for music, dance, theater majors. Portfolio recommended for studio art majors. **Home-schooled:** SAT and at least 3 SAT Subject Tests required, more recommended. Detailed description of curriculum required.

**High school preparation.** 19 units required. Required and recommended units include English 4, mathematics 3-4, social studies 2, history 3, science 3-4 (laboratory 2-3) and foreign language 2-3. 3-4 laboratory science recommended for science applicants. Mathematics through calculus recommended for all applicants.

**2008-2009 Annual costs.** Tuition/fees: $35,625. Room/board: $12,220. Books/supplies: $850. Personal expenses: $1,000.

**2006-2007 Financial aid.** All financial aid based on need. 249 full-time freshmen applied for aid; 190 were judged to have need; 190 of these received aid. Average need met was 100%. Average scholarship/grant was $29,000; average loan $2,000. 88% of total undergraduate aid awarded as scholarships/grants, 12% as loans/jobs.

**Application procedures. Admission:** Closing date 1/2 (receipt date). $65 fee, may be waived for applicants with need. Application may be submitted online. Admission notification 4/10. Must reply by May 1 or within 1 week(s) if notified thereafter. **Financial aid:** Closing date 2/1. FAFSA, CSS PROFILE required. Applicants notified by 4/10; must reply by 5/1.

**Academics. Special study options:** Combined bachelor's/graduate degree, cross-registration, double major, exchange student, independent study, internships, student-designed major, study abroad, Washington semester. 3-2 program in engineering with California Institute of Technology and Washington University (MO), 4-1 education certification program with Claremont Graduate University. **Credit/placement by examination:** AP, CLEP, IB, SAT, ACT, institutional tests. 2 credit hours maximum toward bachelor's degree. **Support services:** Tutoring, writing center.

**Majors. Area/ethnic studies:** African-American, American, Asian, Asian-American, German, Hispanic-American/Latino/Chicano, Latin American, women's. **Biology:** General, molecular. **Communications:** Media studies. **Computer sciences:** Computer science. **Conservation:** Environmental studies. **English:** English lit. **Foreign languages:** General, Chinese, classics, French, German, Japanese, linguistics, Russian, Spanish. **History:** General. **Interdisciplinary:** Cognitive science, global studies, math/computer science, neuroscience, science/society. **Math:** General. **Philosophy/religion:** Philosophy, religion. **Physical sciences:** Astronomy, chemistry, geology, physics. **Psychology:** General. **Public administration:** Policy analysis. **Social sciences:** General, anthropology, economics, international relations, political science, sociology. **Visual/performing arts:** General, art, art history/conservation, dance, dramatic, studio arts.

**Most popular majors.** Biology 12%, psychology 10%, social sciences 31%.

**Computing on campus.** 180 workstations in dormitories, library, computer center, student center. Dormitories wired for high-speed internet access and linked to campus network. Commuter students can connect to campus network. Online library, helpline, wireless network available.

**Student life. Freshman orientation:** Mandatory. Held immediately prior to fall semester; preorientation adventure available. **Housing:** Guaranteed on-campus for all undergraduates. Coed dorms, substance-free housing available. $500 nonrefundable deposit, deadline 5/1. **Activities:** Bands, campus ministries, choral groups, dance, drama, film society, international student organizations, literary magazine, music ensembles, Model UN, musical theater, radio station, student government, student newspaper, symphony orchestra, TV station, center for religious activities, international peace, Asian students association, Mortar Board (service organization), women's coalition, gay and lesbian student union.

**Athletics.** NCAA. **Intercollegiate:** Baseball M, basketball, cross-country, diving, football (tackle) M, golf, lacrosse W, soccer, softball W, swimming, tennis, track and field, volleyball W, water polo. **Intramural:** Badminton, basketball, equestrian, handball, racquetball, skiing, soccer, softball, squash, table tennis, track and field, volleyball, water polo. **Team name:** Sagehens.

**Student services.** Campus ministries, career counseling, services for economically disadvantaged, student employment services, financial aid counseling, health services, minority student services, personal counseling, placement for graduates. **Physically disabled:** Services for visually, hearing impaired.

**Contact.** E-mail: admissions@pomona.edu
Phone: (909) 621-8134 Fax: (909) 621-8952
Bruce Poch, Vice President and Dean of Admissions, Pomona College, 333 North College Way, Claremont, CA 91711-6312

## Remington College: San Diego
**San Diego, California**
**www.remingtoncollege.edu**                    **CB code: 2574**

- For-profit 4-year university
- Very large city

**General.** Accredited by ACICS. **Calendar:** Quarter.

**Annual costs/financial aid.** Costs of entire programs leading to certificate, associate degree, bachelor's degree range from $13,000 to $36,960; includes books and supplies.

**Contact.** Phone: (619) 686-8600
Admissions Director, 123 Camino de la Reina, Suite 100, North Building, San Diego, CA 92108-3002

## St. Mary's College of California
**Moraga, California**                    **CB member**
**www.stmarys-ca.edu**                    **CB code: 4675**

- Private 4-year liberal arts college affiliated with Roman Catholic Church
- Residential campus in large town
- 2,504 degree-seeking undergraduates: 5% part-time, 61% women, 6% African American, 11% Asian American, 21% Hispanic American, 1% Native American, 2% international
- 1,124 degree-seeking graduate students
- 82% of applicants admitted
- SAT or ACT (ACT writing optional), application essay required
- 67% graduate within 6 years

**General.** Founded in 1863. Regionally accredited. **Degrees:** 718 bachelor's awarded; master's, doctoral offered. **ROTC:** Army, Air Force. **Location:** 20 miles from San Francisco. **Calendar:** 4-1-4. **Full-time faculty:** 196 total; 93% have terminal degrees, 16% minority, 47% women. **Part-time faculty:** 291 total; 69% have terminal degrees, 11% minority, 62% women. **Class size:** 47% < 20, 52% 20-39, less than 1% 40-49. **Special facilities:** Art gallery.

**Freshman class profile.** 3,929 applied, 3,231 admitted, 611 enrolled.

| Mid 50% test scores | | | |
|---|---|---|---|
| SAT critical reading: | 480-590 | GPA 2.0-2.99: | 31% |
| SAT math: | 480-590 | Return as sophomores: | 77% |
| GPA 3.50 or higher: | 34% | Out-of-state: | 15% |
| GPA 3.0-3.49: | 35% | Live on campus: | 93% |
| | | International: | 2% |

**Basis for selection.** School achievement record most important. Interview recommended.

**High school preparation.** 16 units required; 19 recommended. Required and recommended units include English 4, mathematics 3-4, social studies 1, history 1, science 2-3 (laboratory 1), foreign language 2-3 and academic electives 2. One unit each of chemistry, physics, advanced algebra, and trigonometry required for applicants to school of science.

**2008-2009 Annual costs.** Tuition/fees: $33,250. Room/board: $11,680. Books/supplies: $1,224. Personal expenses: $2,286.

**2007-2008 Financial aid. Need-based:** 456 full-time freshmen applied for aid; 391 were judged to have need; 382 of these received aid. Average need met was 64%. Average scholarship/grant was $18,857; average loan $3,787. 71% of total undergraduate aid awarded as scholarships/grants, 29% as loans/jobs. **Non-need-based:** Awarded to 547 full-time undergraduates, including 148 freshmen. Scholarships awarded for academics, alumni affiliation, athletics, leadership.

**Application procedures. Admission:** Priority date 11/15; deadline 2/1 (postmark date). $55 fee, may be waived for applicants with need. Application may be submitted online. Admission notification 3/15. Admission notification on a rolling basis beginning on or about 12/15. Must reply by May 1 or within 2 week(s) if notified thereafter. **Financial aid:** Priority date 2/15; no closing date. FAFSA required. Applicants notified on a rolling basis starting 3/15; must reply by 5/1 or within 2 week(s) of notification.

**Academics. Special study options:** Cross-registration, double major, exchange student, independent study, internships, liberal arts/career combination, student-designed major, study abroad, teacher certification program. 4-year interdisciplinary program with Great Books orientation. **Credit/placement by examination:** AP, CLEP, IB, SAT, institutional tests. 30 credit hours maximum toward bachelor's degree. **Support services:** Learning center, study skills assistance, tutoring, writing center.

**Majors. Area/ethnic studies:** European, Latin American, women's. **Biology:** General, biochemistry. **Business:** General, accounting, business admin, finance, international. **Communications:** General. **English:** English lit. **Foreign languages:** General, classics, French, German, Italian, Japanese, Spanish. **Health:** Health care admin. **History:** General. **Interdisciplinary:** Biopsychology, math/computer science. **Liberal arts:** Arts/sciences. **Math:** General. **Parks/recreation:** Exercise sciences, health/fitness, sports admin. **Philosophy/religion:** Philosophy, religion. **Physical sciences:** Chemistry, physics. **Psychology:** General, developmental, experimental, industrial, social. **Social sciences:** Anthropology, archaeology, economics, political science, sociology. **Visual/performing arts:** General, art, dance, dramatic.

**Most popular majors.** Business/marketing 31%, communications/journalism 10%, liberal arts 8%, psychology 8%, social sciences 12%.

**Computing on campus.** 244 workstations in dormitories, library, computer center. Dormitories wired for high-speed internet access and linked to campus network. Commuter students can connect to campus network. Online course registration, online library, helpline, student web hosting, wireless network available.

**Student life. Freshman orientation:** Mandatory, $250 fee. 4 day and one-half sessions. Freshmen attend 1 session plus 4-day weekend of welcome. **Housing:** Guaranteed on-campus for freshmen. Coed dorms, single-sex dorms, special housing for disabled, apartments available. $350 nonrefundable deposit, deadline 5/1. **Activities:** Bands, campus ministries, choral groups, dance, drama, film society, international student organizations, literary magazine, music ensembles, musical theater, radio station, student government, student newspaper, TV station, Catholic Institute for Lasallian Social Action, Habitat for Humanity, Amnesty International, Lasallian Collegians, Intervarsity Christians, LASA, Black student union, APASA, multicultural club.

**Athletics.** NCAA. **Intercollegiate:** Baseball M, basketball, cross-country, golf M, lacrosse W, rowing (crew) W, soccer, softball W, tennis, volleyball W. **Intramural:** Basketball, bowling, football (non-tackle), golf, lacrosse, rowing (crew), skiing, soccer, softball, table tennis, tennis, volleyball, water polo. **Team name:** Gaels.

**Student services.** Alcohol/substance abuse counseling, campus ministries, career counseling, services for economically disadvantaged, student employment services, financial aid counseling, health services, personal counseling, placement for graduates, veterans' counselor, women's services. **Physically disabled:** Services for visually, speech, hearing impaired.

**Contact.** E-mail: smcadmit@stmarys_ca.edu
Phone: (925) 631-4224 Toll-free number: (800) 800-4762
Fax: (925) 376-7193
Dorothy Jones, Dean of Admissions, St. Mary's College of California, Box 4800, Moraga, CA 94575-4800

## Samuel Merritt College

**Oakland, California**
www.samuelmerritt.edu

**CB member**
**CB code: 4750**

- Private two-year upper-division health science and nursing college
- Commuter campus in large city
- 58% of applicants admitted
- Application essay required

**General.** Founded in 1909. Regionally accredited. Part of Alta Bates Summit Medical Center, a nonprofit, community-based health care organization. Nursing degree offered in partnership with St. Mary's College of California, Holy Names University, and Mills College. **Degrees:** 188 bachelor's awarded; master's, doctoral, first professional offered. **Articulation:** Agreements with Holy Names University, Mills College, Saint Mary's College of California. **ROTC:** Army, Naval, Air Force. **Location:** 15 miles from San Francisco. **Calendar:** Differs by program, limited summer session. **Full-time faculty:** 59 total; 66% have terminal degrees, 19% minority, 71% women. **Part-time faculty:** 113 total; 23% have terminal degrees, 17% minority, 71% women. **Class size:** 10% < 20, 34% 20-39, 48% 40-49, 8% 50-99. **Special facilities:** Nursing resource laboratory, health education center, health science library, anatomy laboratory, therapeutic exercise laboratory, living skills laboratory, human occupations laboratory, health sciences simulation lab.

**Student profile.** 368 degree-seeking undergraduates, 809 degree-seeking graduate students. 235 applied as first time-transfer students, 136 admitted, 106 enrolled. 3% entered as juniors. 100% transferred from two-year institutions.

| | | | |
|---|---|---|---|
| Women: | 88% | Native American: | 1% |
| African American: | 6% | Part-time: | 2% |
| Asian American: | 26% | Live on campus: | 9% |
| Hispanic American: | 10% | 25 or older: | 76% |

**Basis for selection.** College transcript, application essay required. Must have UC transferable college-level coursework in chemistry, anatomy, physiology, multicultural psychology, English (2) and humanities (2). Applicants with fewer than 30 semester hours of transferable credits admitted as freshmen. Letter of recommendation and experience in health care environment required. Transfer accepted as juniors.

**2008-2009 Annual costs.** Tuition/fees (projected): $33,882. Room only: $6,309. Books/supplies: $1,932. Personal expenses: $9,080.

**Financial aid. Need-based:** 320 applied for aid; 316 were judged to have need; 316 of these received aid. Average need met was 63%. 44% of total undergraduate aid awarded as scholarships/grants, 56% as loans/jobs. **Non-need-based:** Awarded to 68 undergraduates. Scholarships awarded for academics, leadership, minority status. **Additional information:** Ongoing private scholarships available. Students eligible to work in Medical Center (associated with college).

**Application procedures. Admission:** Priority date 3/1. $35 fee, may be waived for applicants with need. Application must be submitted on paper. Admission notification 4/1. Must reply by 5/1. **Financial aid:** Priority date 3/1, no deadline. Applicants notified on a rolling basis; must reply within 3 weeks of notification.

**Academics. Special study options:** Accelerated study, combined bachelor's/graduate degree, cooperative education, cross-registration, distance learning, ESL, independent study, internships, liberal arts/career combination. **Credit/placement by examination:** CLEP. 80 credit hours maximum toward bachelor's degree.

**Majors. Health:** Nursing (RN).

**Computing on campus.** 78 workstations in dormitories, library, computer center. Online library, helpline, wireless network available.

**Student life. Housing:** Coed dorms available. $100 fully refundable deposit. **Activities:** Student government, student newspaper, multicultural committee, American Physical Therapy Association, California Nursing Students Association, Christian Fellowship, American Occupational Therapy Association, Chi Eta Phi, gay, lesbian, bisexual and transgender group.

**Student services.** Career counseling, financial aid counseling, health services, personal counseling. **Physically disabled:** Services for visually, speech, hearing impaired.

**Contact.** E-mail: admission@samuelmerritt.edu
Phone: (510) 869-6576 Toll-free number: (800) 607-6377
Fax: (510) 869-6576
Anne Seed, Director of Admissions, Samuel Merritt College, 370 Hawthorne Avenue, Oakland, CA 94609-9954

## San Diego Christian College

**El Cajon, California**
www.sdcc.edu

**CB code: 4150**

- Private 4-year liberal arts college affiliated with nondenominational tradition
- Residential campus in small city
- 469 degree-seeking undergraduates: 10% part-time, 55% women, 7% African American, 5% Asian American, 15% Hispanic American, 2% Native American, 1% international
- 26 degree-seeking graduate students
- 47% of applicants admitted
- SAT or ACT (ACT writing optional), application essay required
- 46% graduate within 6 years

**General.** Founded in 1970. Regionally accredited. **Degrees:** 118 bachelor's awarded. **ROTC:** Army, Air Force. **Location:** 15 miles from downtown San Diego. **Calendar:** Semester, limited summer session. **Full-time faculty:** 32 total; 22% have terminal degrees, 9% minority, 50% women. **Part-time faculty:** 36 total; 6% have terminal degrees, 14% minority, 44% women. **Class size:** 80% < 20, 18% 20-39, 2% 40-49. **Special facilities:** Museum supporting creationist view, aviation school.

**Freshman class profile.** 404 applied, 191 admitted, 85 enrolled.

| Mid 50% test scores | | | |
|---|---|---|---|
| | | **ACT composite:** | 17-21 |
| SAT critical reading: | 430-570 | Return as sophomores: | 51% |
| SAT math: | 400-540 | Out-of-state: | 20% |
| SAT writing: | 430-530 | Live on campus: | 59% |

**Basis for selection.** Academic abilities as indicated by school achievement record and test scores. Personal and spiritual qualities as indicated by essays, recommendations, and interview.

**High school preparation.** 15 units recommended. Recommended units include English 4, mathematics 3, social studies 3, science 3 and foreign language 2.

**2007-2008 Annual costs.** Tuition/fees: $19,070. Room/board: $7,540. Books/supplies: $1,386. Personal expenses: $2,342.

**2007-2008 Financial aid. Need-based:** 55 full-time freshmen applied for aid; 48 were judged to have need; 48 of these received aid. Average need met was 85%. Average scholarship/grant was $6,000; average loan $3,500. 57% of total undergraduate aid awarded as scholarships/grants, 43% as loans/jobs. **Non-need-based:** Awarded to 502 full-time undergraduates, including 91 freshmen. Scholarships awarded for academics, athletics, leadership, music/drama, religious affiliation.

**Application procedures. Admission:** Priority date 7/1; deadline 8/1. $25 fee. Admission notification on a rolling basis. Must reply by May 1 or within 4 week(s) if notified thereafter. **Financial aid:** Priority date 3/2, closing date 7/15. FAFSA, institutional form required. Applicants notified on a rolling basis starting 4/1; must reply by 5/1 or within 4 week(s) of notification.

**Academics. Special study options:** Accelerated study, double major, ESL, independent study, internships, study abroad, teacher certification program. **Credit/placement by examination:** AP, CLEP, IB, institutional tests. 15 credit hours maximum toward bachelor's degree. **Support services:** Learning center, reduced course load, remedial instruction, study skills assistance, tutoring, writing center.

**Majors. Biology:** General. **Business:** Business admin. **Communications:** General. **Education:** General, early childhood, elementary, English, history, mathematics, middle, music, physical, secondary, social science. **English:** English lit. **Family/consumer sciences:** Family studies. **Health:** Athletic training. **History:** General. **Math:** General. **Psychology:** General. **Social sciences:** General. **Theology:** Bible, missionary. **Visual/performing arts:** Dramatic, music performance.

**Computing on campus.** 48 workstations in library, computer center. Dormitories wired for high-speed internet access and linked to campus network. Commuter students can connect to campus network. Online library, helpline, repair service, wireless network available.

**Student life. Freshman orientation:** Mandatory, $70 fee. Preregistration for classes offered. Takes place within 2 weeks of start of classes in fall. **Policies:** Religious observance required. **Housing:** Guaranteed on-campus for all undergraduates. Single-sex dorms, apartments available. $100 deposit, deadline 7/1. **Activities:** Choral groups, music ensembles, student government, student newspaper, missions club, art club, aviator's club, Students in Free Enterprise.

**Athletics.** NAIA, NCCAA. **Intercollegiate:** Basketball, cheerleading W, cross-country, golf M, soccer, volleyball W. **Intramural:** Baseball M, basketball, soccer, softball, tennis, volleyball. **Team name:** Hawks.

**Student services.** Adult student services, campus ministries, career counseling, student employment services, financial aid counseling, health services, personal counseling, placement for graduates.

**Contact.** E-mail: admissions@sdcc.edu
Phone: (619) 588-7747 Toll-free number: (800) 676-2242
Fax: (619) 590-1739
Mitchell FIsk, Vice President of Enrollment, San Diego Christian College, 2100 Greenfield Drive, El Cajon, CA 92019-1157

## San Diego State University
San Diego, California
www.sdsu.edu

CB member
CB code: 4682

- Public 4-year university
- Commuter campus in very large city
- 30,460 degree-seeking undergraduates: 17% part-time, 57% women, 4% African American, 16% Asian American, 23% Hispanic American, 1% Native American, 3% international
- 6,099 degree-seeking graduate students
- 44% of applicants admitted
- SAT or ACT (ACT writing optional) required
- 56% graduate within 6 years

**General.** Founded in 1897. Regionally accredited. Branch campus at Calexico in Imperial Valley. **Degrees:** 6,433 bachelor's awarded; master's, doctoral offered. **ROTC:** Army, Naval, Air Force. **Location:** 8 miles from downtown. **Calendar:** Semester, extensive summer session. **Full-time faculty:** 979 total; 21% minority, 42% women. **Part-time faculty:** 800 total; 22% minority, 54% women. **Class size:** 20% < 20, 49% 20-39, 10% 40-49, 15% 50-99, 5% >100. **Special facilities:** Observatory, electron microscope facility, open-air theater, aquatic center, international student center, American Language Institute, recital hall, field studies stations (off-campus), multimedia interactive fine arts lab.

**Freshman class profile.** 46,718 applied, 20,629 admitted, 5,601 enrolled.

| Mid 50% test scores | | End year in good standing: | 84% |
|---|---|---|---|
| SAT critical reading: | 460-570 | Return as sophomores: | 83% |
| SAT math: | 480-590 | Out-of-state: | 6% |
| ACT composite: | 19-25 | Live on campus: | 57% |
| GPA 3.50 or higher: | 45% | International: | 2% |
| GPA 3.0-3.49: | 46% | Fraternities: | 17% |
| GPA 2.0-2.99: | 9% | Sororities: | 15% |

**Basis for selection.** High school GPA and test scores most important; 20% of those admitted selected using faculty-defined criteria, such as socioeconomic status, special talent, and San Diego and Imperial County residency. **Homeschooled:** Transcript of courses and grades required. In cases where the Lab Science courses are not completed in at a regular high school or community college, we request course descriptions to ensure the lab component meets the CSU requirement for admission.

**High school preparation.** 15 units required. Required and recommended units include English 4, mathematics 3-4, social studies 1, history 1, science 2 (laboratory 2), foreign language 2 and academic electives 1. One visual and performing arts required. History must be U.S. history or U.S. government. Science must be 1 biology, 1 physical science.

**2007-2008 Annual costs.** Tuition/fees: $3,428; $13,598 out-of-state. Room/board: $10,904. Books/supplies: $1,332. Personal expenses: $2,483.

**2007-2008 Financial aid.** **Need-based:** 3,440 full-time freshmen applied for aid; 2,100 were judged to have need; 2,010 of these received aid. Average need met was 67%. Average scholarship/grant was $6,540; average loan $2,350. 52% of total undergraduate aid awarded as scholarships/grants, 48% as loans/jobs. **Non-need-based:** Awarded to 3,200 full-time undergraduates, including 960 freshmen. Scholarships awarded for academics, alumni affiliation, art, athletics, leadership, music/drama, ROTC, state residency.

**Application procedures.** **Admission:** Closing date 11/30 (postmark date). $55 fee, may be waived for applicants with need. Application must be submitted online. Admission notification 3/1. Must reply by 5/1. **Financial aid:** Priority date 3/2; no closing date. FAFSA required. Applicants notified on a rolling basis starting 2/14.

**Academics.** **Special study options:** Cross-registration, distance learning, double major, dual enrollment of high school students, ESL, exchange student, honors, independent study, internships, student-designed major, study abroad, teacher certification program. **Credit/placement by examination:** AP, CLEP, IB, SAT, ACT, institutional tests. 30 credit hours maximum toward bachelor's degree. Must be registered in at least 1 course, matriculated and in good standing. Approval of department chair and dean of college required. Restricted to regular undergraduate courses. Does not count toward 30-unit minimum residency requirement. **Support services:** Preadmission summer program, reduced course load, remedial instruction, tutoring.

**Majors.** **Agriculture:** Business. **Area/ethnic studies:** African-American, American, Asian, Central/Eastern European, European, Hispanic-American/Latino/Chicano, Latin American, Native American, Russian/Slavic, women's. **Biology:** Microbiology. **Business:** General, accounting, business admin, finance, financial planning, hospitality admin, international, marketing, real estate. **Communications:** Advertising, journalism, public relations, radio/tv. **Computer sciences:** General, computer science, information systems, information technology. **Conservation:** General, environmental studies. **Education:** Early childhood, music, trade/industrial. **Engineering:** General, aerospace, civil, computer, electrical, environmental, mechanical. **Engineering technology:** Construction. **English:** English lit, speech/rhetoric. **Family/consumer sciences:** Child development. **Foreign languages:** Classics, comparative lit, French, German, Japanese, linguistics, Russian, Spanish. **Health:** Communication disorders, health services, nursing (RN). **History:** General. **Interdisciplinary:** Gerontology. **Liberal arts:** Arts/sciences, humanities. **Math:** General, applied, statistics. **Parks/recreation:** General, health/fitness. **Philosophy/religion:** Judaic, philosophy, religion. **Physical sciences:** General, astronomy, chemistry, geology, molecular physics, physics, theoretical physics. **Protective services:** Law enforcement admin. **Psychology:** General. **Public administration:** General, social work, **Social sciences:** General, anthropology, economics, geography, international relations, political science, sociology, urban studies. **Visual/performing arts:** Art history/conservation, dance, design, dramatic, graphic design, interior design, music performance, studio arts. **Other:** Dietetics/Food Admin/Nutrition, Evolutionary biology, Modern Jewish Studies, Telecommunications and Film.

**Most popular majors.** Business/marketing 20%, English 6%, liberal arts 6%, psychology 9%, security/protective services 6%, social sciences 12%.

**Computing on campus.** 506 workstations in dormitories, library, computer center, student center. Dormitories wired for high-speed internet access and linked to campus network. Commuter students can connect to campus network. Online course registration, online library, helpline, repair service, wireless network available.

**Student life.** **Freshman orientation:** Mandatory, $55 fee. Preregistration for classes offered. One-day academic orientation in July and August. Student life orientation held in August. **Housing:** Coed dorms, apartments, fraternity/sorority housing available. $800 partly refundable deposit. The Housing and Residential Life Office has a website to assist students and families to find off-campus housing. **Activities:** Bands, campus ministries, choral groups, dance, drama, film society, international student organizations, literary magazine, music ensembles, musical theater, opera, radio station, student government, student newspaper, symphony orchestra, TV station, more than 300 academic, recreational, sports, ethnic, political, honor, and service clubs on campus.

**Athletics.** NCAA. **Intercollegiate:** Baseball M, basketball, cross-country W, diving W, football (tackle) M, golf, rowing (crew) W, soccer, softball W, swimming W, tennis, track and field W, volleyball W, water polo W. **Intramural:** Basketball, bowling, football (non-tackle), golf, racquetball, soccer, softball, tennis, volleyball. **Team name:** Aztecs.

**Student services.** Alcohol/substance abuse counseling, campus ministries, career counseling, services for economically disadvantaged, student employment services, financial aid counseling, health services, on-campus daycare, personal counseling, placement for graduates, veterans' counselor, women's services. **Physically disabled:** Services for visually, speech, hearing impaired. **Learning disabled:** Comprehensive services available.

**Contact.** E-mail: admissions@sdsu.edu
Phone: (619) 594-6336
Beverly Arata, Director of Admissions, San Diego State University, 5500 Campanile Drive, San Diego, CA 92182-7455

## San Francisco Art Institute
San Francisco, California
www.sfai.edu

CB member
CB code: 4036

- Private 4-year visual arts college
- Commuter campus in very large city
- 383 degree-seeking undergraduates
- 32% of applicants admitted
- SAT or ACT with writing, application essay required

**General.** Founded in 1871. Regionally accredited. **Degrees:** 81 bachelor's awarded; master's offered. **Calendar:** Semester, limited summer session. **Full-time faculty:** 48 total. **Part-time faculty:** 99 total. **Class size:** 81% < 20, 17% 20-39, 1% 40-49, less than 1% 50-99. **Special facilities:** EARS XXI high definition research lab, Diego Rivera gallery, Walter & McBean galleries, digital media studio, digital imaging studio, studio production facilities in photography, printmaking, design and technology, and filmmaking, open studio spaces for painting, new genres and sculpture.

**Freshman class profile.** 1,321 applied, 418 admitted, 78 enrolled.

| Mid 50% test scores | | | |
|---|---|---|---|
| | | SAT writing: | 420-570 |
| SAT critical reading: | 490-630 | ACT composite: | 20-25 |
| SAT math: | 450-590 | Live on campus: | 50% |

**Basis for selection.** Admission decisions based on evaluation of portfolio, academic credentials including transcripts and standardized test scores, letters of recommendation, and personal statement. Portfolio of artwork required. Interviews recommended, but not required. **Homeschooled:** State high school equivalency certificate, letter of recommendation (nonparent) required.

**High school preparation.** Strong background in English, humanities, and social sciences as well as extensive high school and extracurricular art education recommended.

**2008-2009 Annual costs.** Tuition/fees (projected): $30,215. Room charges vary for 12-month contract. Room/board: $9,675. Books/supplies: $2,125. Personal expenses: $2,400.

**2007-2008 Financial aid.** **Need-based:** 58% of total undergraduate aid awarded as scholarships/grants, 42% as loans/jobs. **Non-need-based:** Scholarships awarded for academics, art.

**Application procedures.** **Admission:** Priority date 2/15; no deadline. $65 fee, may be waived for applicants with need. Application may be submitted online. Admission notification on a rolling basis. Must reply by May 1 or within 3 week(s) if notified thereafter. **Financial aid:** Priority date 3/1, closing date 5/31. FAFSA required. Applicants notified on a rolling basis starting 4/15; must reply within 3 week(s) of notification.

**Academics.** **Special study options:** Cooperative education, cross-registration, double major, ESL, exchange student, independent study, internships, New York semester, study abroad. **Credit/placement by examination:** AP, CLEP, IB, institutional tests. 20 credit hours maximum toward bachelor's degree. **Support services:** Learning center, remedial instruction, study skills assistance, tutoring, writing center.

**Majors.** **Interdisciplinary:** Museum. **Visual/performing arts:** Art, art history/conservation, ceramics, cinematography, film/cinema, multimedia, painting, photography, printmaking, sculpture, studio arts. **Other:** Urban Studies.

**Computing on campus.** 71 workstations in library, computer center, student center. Wireless network available.

**Student life.** **Freshman orientation:** Mandatory. Preregistration for classes offered. **Housing:** Coed dorms, substance-free housing available. $450 deposit, deadline 6/1. **Activities:** Film society, student government.

**Student services.** Career counseling, student employment services, financial aid counseling, personal counseling, placement for graduates, veterans' counselor. **Physically disabled:** Services for visually, speech, hearing impaired.

**Contact.** E-mail: admissions@sfai.edu
Phone: (415) 749-4500 Toll-free number: (800) 345-7324
Fax: (415) 749-4517
Director of Admissions, San Francisco Art Institute, 800 Chestnut Street, San Francisco, CA 94133-2299

## San Francisco Conservatory of Music
**San Francisco, California**
www.sfcm.edu                CB code: 4744

- Private 4-year music college
- Commuter campus in very large city
- 230 degree-seeking undergraduates
- 160 graduate students
- Application essay required

**General.** Founded in 1917. Regionally accredited. All conservatory students receive extensive performance opportunities, both on campus and in the San Francisco Bay area. **Degrees:** 34 bachelor's awarded; master's offered. **Location:** 3 miles from downtown. **Calendar:** Semester. **Full-time**

faculty: 30 total. **Part-time faculty:** 70 total. **Class size:** 86% < 20, 11% 20-39, 1% 40-49, 1% 50-99. **Special facilities:** Concert performance facility, music library.

**Basis for selection.** Most important criterion is music audition, followed by school achievement record, letters of recommendation, and test scores. Musical needs of institution also influence admission decisions. SAT or ACT recommended. Audition required. **Homeschooled:** Transcript of courses and grades, state high school equivalency certificate, letter of recommendation (nonparent) required. SAT or ACT required.

**High school preparation.** Recommended units include English 3 and foreign language 3.

**2007-2008 Annual costs.** Tuition/fees: $30,054. Books/supplies: $800. Personal expenses: $1,800.

**Financial aid.** All financial aid based on need.

**Application procedures.** **Admission:** Closing date 12/1 (receipt date). $100 fee. Application must be submitted online. Admission notification on a rolling basis beginning on or about 4/1. Must reply by May 1 or within 2 week(s) if notified thereafter. **Financial aid:** Priority date 3/1; no closing date. FAFSA, institutional form required. Applicants notified by 4/1; must reply by 5/1 or within 2 week(s) of notification.

**Academics.** **Special study options:** Independent study. **Credit/placement by examination:** AP, CLEP, institutional tests. 60 credit hours maximum toward bachelor's degree. **Support services:** Remedial instruction, study skills assistance, tutoring.

**Majors.** **Visual/performing arts:** Music performance, music theory/composition, piano/organ, stringed instruments, voice/opera.

**Computing on campus.** 15 workstations in library, computer center. Dormitories wired for high-speed internet access. Wireless network available.

**Student life.** **Freshman orientation:** Mandatory. **Housing:** Coed dorms available. **Activities:** Choral groups, music ensembles, musical theater, opera, student government, symphony orchestra.

**Student services.** Financial aid counseling, health services, personal counseling.

**Contact.** E-mail: admit@sfcm.edu
Phone: (415) 864-7326 Fax: (415) 503-6299
Alexander Brose, Director of Admission, San Francisco Conservatory of Music, 50 Oak Street, San Francisco, CA 94102

## San Francisco State University
**San Francisco, California**            CB member
www.sfsu.edu                  CB code: 4684

- Public 4-year university
- Commuter campus in very large city
- 24,376 degree-seeking undergraduates: 20% part-time, 58% women, 6% African American, 31% Asian American, 16% Hispanic American, 1% Native American, 6% international
- 4,254 degree-seeking graduate students
- 67% of applicants admitted
- 42% graduate within 6 years

**General.** Founded in 1899. Regionally accredited. **Degrees:** 5,564 bachelor's awarded; master's, doctoral offered. **ROTC:** Army, Naval, Air Force. **Location:** 10 miles from downtown. **Calendar:** Semester, limited summer session. **Full-time faculty:** 928 total; 77% have terminal degrees, 36% minority, 48% women. **Part-time faculty:** 917 total; 27% have terminal degrees, 28% minority, 55% women. **Class size:** 21% < 20, 46% 20-39, 12% 40-49, 13% 50-99, 8% >100. **Special facilities:** Access to marine laboratories, environmental studies center, Sierra Nevada field campus, anthropology museum, facility for study of astronomy.

**Freshman class profile.** 27,440 applied, 18,370 admitted, 3,466 enrolled.

| Mid 50% test scores | | | |
|---|---|---|---|
| | | GPA 3.0-3.49: | 42% |
| SAT critical reading: | 440-560 | GPA 2.0-2.99: | 40% |
| SAT math: | 440-560 | Return as sophomores: | 77% |
| SAT writing: | 440-550 | Out-of-state: | 2% |
| ACT composite: | 18-23 | Live on campus: | 46% |
| GPA 3.50 or higher: | 18% | International: | 4% |

**Basis for selection.** School achievement record and score on SAT or ACT most important. Students with GPA over 2.0 may be exempted from SAT/ACT. SAT or ACT scores required if applicant's secondary school GPA is lower than 3.0 for California residents or 3.61 for non-residents. **Home-schooled:** Local school district verification of completion of secondary schooling; SAT or ACT scores.

**High school preparation.** 14 units required. Required and recommended units include English 4, mathematics 3, social studies 1, history 1, science 2 (laboratory 2), foreign language 2, visual/performing arts 1 and academic electives 1.

**2007-2008 Annual costs.** Tuition/fees: $3,456; $13,626 out-of-state. Room/board: $11,500. Books/supplies: $1,400. Personal expenses: $2,718.

**2007-2008 Financial aid.** All financial aid based on need. Average need met was 64%. Average scholarship/grant was $7,098; average loan $2,370. 55% of total undergraduate aid awarded as scholarships/grants, 45% as loans/jobs.

**Application procedures. Admission:** $55 fee, may be waived for applicants with need. Application may be submitted online. Admission notification on a rolling basis beginning on or about 10/15. Must reply by May 1 or within 2 week(s) if notified thereafter. **Financial aid:** Priority date 3/2; no closing date. FAFSA required. Applicants notified on a rolling basis starting 2/1; must reply within 2 week(s) of notification.

**Academics. Special study options:** Cooperative education, cross-registration, distance learning, double major, dual enrollment of high school students, ESL, exchange student, honors, independent study, internships, liberal arts/career combination, student-designed major, study abroad, teacher certification program. **Credit/placement by examination:** AP, CLEP, IB, SAT, ACT, institutional tests. 30 credit hours maximum toward bachelor's degree. **Support services:** Learning center, pre-admission summer program, remedial instruction, study skills assistance, tutoring, writing center.

**Majors. Area/ethnic studies:** African-American, American, Asian-American, Hispanic-American/Latino/Chicano, women's. **Biology:** General, biochemistry, botany, cell/histology, ecology, marine, microbiology, physiology, zoology. **Business:** Accounting, banking/financial services, business admin, e-commerce, finance, hospitality admin, hospitality/recreation, international, labor studies, management science, marketing, restaurant/food services, small business admin. **Communications:** Journalism, radio/tv. **Computer sciences:** General, computer science. **Conservation:** Environmental studies. **Education:** Early childhood. **Engineering:** Civil, computer, electrical, mechanical. **Engineering technology:** Industrial. **English:** English lit, speech/rhetoric, technical writing. **Family/consumer sciences:** General, clothing/textiles. **Foreign languages:** Chinese, classics, comparative lit, French, German, Italian, Japanese, Spanish. **Health:** Clinical lab science, communication disorders, dietetics, nursing (RN), public health ed. **History:** General. **Liberal arts:** Arts/sciences, humanities. **Math:** General, applied, statistics. **Parks/recreation:** Exercise sciences, facilities management. **Philosophy/religion:** Judaic, philosophy. **Physical sciences:** Atmospheric science, chemistry, geology, physics. **Protective services:** Criminal justice. **Psychology:** General. **Public administration:** Social work. **Social sciences:** Anthropology, economics, geography, international relations, political science, sociology, urban studies. **Visual/performing arts:** Art, dance, dramatic, film/cinema, industrial design, interior design, music performance. **Other:** Interdisciplinary Studies, Philosophy and Religion.

**Most popular majors.** Business/marketing 19%, communications/journalism 6%, English 6%, psychology 9%, social sciences 10%, visual/performing arts 10%.

**Computing on campus.** 500 workstations in library, computer center. Dormitories wired for high-speed internet access and linked to campus network. Online course registration, online library, helpline, repair service, student web hosting, wireless network available.

**Student life. Freshman orientation:** Mandatory, $35 fee. Preregistration for classes offered. **Housing:** Coed dorms, special housing for disabled, apartments, substance-free housing available. Theme co-ed housing for science-tech freshmen; women only floors. **Activities:** Bands, choral groups, dance, drama, film society, literary magazine, music ensembles, musical theater, opera, radio station, student government, student newspaper, symphony orchestra, TV station.

**Athletics.** NCAA. **Intercollegiate:** Baseball M, basketball, cross-country, soccer, softball W, track and field W, wrestling M. **Team name:** Gators.

**Student services.** Adult student services, alcohol/substance abuse counseling, career counseling, services for economically disadvantaged, student employment services, financial aid counseling, health services, on-campus daycare, personal counseling, placement for graduates, veterans' counselor. **Physically disabled:** Services for visually, speech, hearing impaired.

**Contact.** E-mail: ugadmit@sfsu.edu
Phone: (415) 338-1113 Fax: (415) 338-7196
John Pliska, Director, Undergraduate Admissions, San Francisco State University, 1600 Holloway Avenue, San Francisco, CA 94132

## San Jose State University
San Jose, California
www.sjsu.edu

**CB member**
**CB code: 4687**

- Public 4-year university and liberal arts college
- Commuter campus in very large city
- 24,390 degree-seeking undergraduates: 23% part-time, 51% women, 6% African American, 35% Asian American, 17% Hispanic American, 4% international
- 7,516 degree-seeking graduate students
- 64% of applicants admitted
- 42% graduate within 6 years

**General.** Founded in 1857. Regionally accredited. **Degrees:** 4,043 bachelor's awarded; master's offered. **ROTC:** Air Force. **Location:** 50 miles from San Francisco. **Calendar:** Semester, limited summer session. **Full-time faculty:** 703 total; 30% minority, 45% women. **Part-time faculty:** 1,220 total; 25% minority, 50% women. **Class size:** 24% < 20, 51% 20-39, 10% 40-49, 12% 50-99, 2% >100. **Special facilities:** Marine laboratory, natural history living museum, nuclear science lab, center for Beethoven studies, Chicano resource center, art metal foundry, deep-sea research ship, electro-acoustic and recording studio.

**Freshman class profile.** 21,555 applied, 13,864 admitted, 3,271 enrolled.

| Mid 50% test scores | | | |
|---|---|---|---|
| SAT critical reading: | 420-540 | GPA 2.0-2.99: | 37% |
| SAT math: | 440-570 | End year in good standing: | 80% |
| ACT composite: | 16-23 | Return as sophomores: | 80% |
| GPA 3.50 or higher: | 20% | Out-of-state: | 2% |
| GPA 3.0-3.49: | 43% | Live on campus: | 46% |

**Basis for selection.** High school record and test scores most important. SAT or ACT required for applicants with less than 3.0 GPA.

**High school preparation.** 15 units required; 17 recommended. Required and recommended units include English 4, mathematics 3-4, history 2, science 2-3 (laboratory 2), foreign language 2, visual/performing arts 1 and academic electives 1. History is 2 units in history/social science.

**2007-2008 Annual costs.** Tuition/fees: $3,632; $13,802 out-of-state. Room/board: $9,505. Books/supplies: $1,386. Personal expenses: $3,672.

**Financial aid.** All financial aid based on need.

**Application procedures. Admission:** Priority date 11/30; deadline 2/1. $55 fee, may be waived for applicants with need. Application must be submitted online. Must reply by May 1 or within 2 week(s) if notified thereafter. **Financial aid:** Priority date 3/2, closing date 6/22. FAFSA required. Applicants notified on a rolling basis starting 4/1; must reply within 2 week(s) of notification.

**Academics. Special study options:** Accelerated study, cooperative education, cross-registration, distance learning, double major, dual enrollment of high school students, ESL, exchange student, honors, independent study, internships, liberal arts/career combination, student-designed major, study abroad, teacher certification program. **Credit/placement by examination:** AP, CLEP.

**Majors. Area/ethnic studies:** African-American. **Biology:** General, biochemistry, conservation, marine, microbiology, molecular, physiology. **Business:** Accounting, business admin, finance, hospitality admin, human resources, international, marketing. **Communications:** Advertising, journalism, public relations, radio/tv. **Computer sciences:** Computer science, information systems, information technology, systems analysis. **Conservation:** Environmental studies. **Education:** Early childhood. **Engineering:** General, aerospace, chemical, civil, computer, electrical, industrial, materials, mechanical, software. **Engineering technology:** Quality control. **English:** English lit, speech/rhetoric. **Foreign languages:** Chinese, French, German, Japanese, linguistics, Spanish. **Health:** Communication disorders, dietetics, health care admin, health services, nursing (RN). **History:** General. **Interdisciplinary:** Accounting/computer science, behavioral sciences, natural sciences. **Liberal arts:** Arts/sciences, humanities. **Math:** General, applied. **Parks/recreation:** General, health/fitness. **Philosophy/religion:** Philosophy, religion. **Physical sciences:** Chemistry, geology, physics. **Protective services:** Criminal justice, forensics. **Psychology:** General. **Public administration:**

Social work. **Social sciences:** General, anthropology, economics, geography, international relations, political science, sociology. **Transportation:** Aviation. **Visual/performing arts:** General, art, art history/conservation, dance, dramatic, graphic design, industrial design, interior design, music performance, studio arts.

**Most popular majors.** Business/marketing 31%, communications/journalism 6%, engineering/engineering technologies 10%, health sciences 7%, social sciences 6%, visual/performing arts 8%.

**Computing on campus.** Dormitories wired for high-speed internet access and linked to campus network. Commuter students can connect to campus network. Online course registration, online library, helpline available.

**Student life. Freshman orientation:** Mandatory. Preregistration for classes offered. Mandatory overnight program for all first-time freshmen. **Housing:** Coed dorms, cooperative housing, fraternity/sorority housing available. **Activities:** Marching band, choral groups, dance, drama, film society, literary magazine, music ensembles, musical theater, radio station, student government, student newspaper.

**Athletics.** NCAA. **Intercollegiate:** Baseball M, basketball, cheerleading, cross-country, diving W, football (tackle) M, golf, gymnastics W, soccer, softball W, swimming W, tennis W, volleyball W, water polo W. **Intramural:** Archery, badminton, baseball M, basketball, bowling, field hockey W, football (non-tackle), lacrosse, racquetball, soccer, softball, swimming, table tennis, tennis, volleyball W, water polo. **Team name:** Spartans.

**Student services.** Adult student services, alcohol/substance abuse counseling, campus ministries, career counseling, services for economically disadvantaged, student employment services, financial aid counseling, health services, legal services, minority student services, on-campus daycare, personal counseling, placement for graduates, veterans' counselor, women's services. **Physically disabled:** Services for visually, speech, hearing impaired.

**Contact.** E-mail: contact@sjsu.edu
Phone: (408) 924-2550
Fernanda Karp, Undergraduate Admissions Manager, San Jose State University, One Washington Square, San Jose, CA 95192-0011

---

## Santa Clara University

Santa Clara, California      **CB member**
www.scu.edu      **CB code: 4851**

- Private 4-year university affiliated with Roman Catholic Church
- Residential campus in small city
- 4,799 degree-seeking undergraduates: 2% part-time, 53% women, 3% African American, 17% Asian American, 13% Hispanic American, 3% international
- 3,227 degree-seeking graduate students
- 61% of applicants admitted
- SAT or ACT (ACT writing optional), application essay required
- 84% graduate within 6 years; 26% enter graduate study

**General.** Founded in 1851. Regionally accredited. **Degrees:** 1,100 bachelor's awarded; master's, doctoral, first professional offered. **ROTC:** Army, Air Force. **Location:** 45 miles from San Francisco, 1 mile from San Jose. **Calendar:** Quarter, limited summer session. **Full-time faculty:** 511 total; 89% have terminal degrees, 18% minority, 42% women. **Part-time faculty:** 268 total; 53% have terminal degrees, 16% minority, 39% women. **Class size:** 36% < 20, 54% 20-39, 9% 40-49, 1% 50-99. **Special facilities:** Historic mission church with artifacts dating from California mission era, applied ethics center, observatory, tennis complex, de Saisset museum.

**Freshman class profile.** 9,459 applied, 5,802 admitted, 1,204 enrolled.

| Mid 50% test scores | | | |
|---|---|---|---|
| SAT critical reading: | 540-650 | Rank in top quarter: | 73% |
| SAT math: | 570-670 | Rank in top tenth: | 36% |
| ACT composite: | 24-29 | End year in good standing: | 95% |
| GPA 3.50 or higher: | 53% | Return as sophomores: | 94% |
| GPA 3.0-3.49: | 40% | Out-of-state: | 42% |
| GPA 2.0-2.99: | 7% | Live on campus: | 94% |
| | | International: | 2% |

**Basis for selection.** GED not accepted. Rigor of high school curriculum and GPA most important, followed by test scores, teacher's recommendation, personal essay, and extracurricular activities. Interviews not recommended. Audition recommended for music, theater arts majors.

**High school preparation.** 15 units required; 19 recommended. Required and recommended units include English 4, mathematics 3-4, social studies 3, science 2-3, foreign language 2-3, visual/performing arts 1 and academic electives 1. Social studies units include history.

**2007-2008 Annual costs.** Tuition/fees: $33,000. Room/board: $10,644. Books/supplies: $1,386. Personal expenses: $2,142.

**2007-2008 Financial aid. Need-based:** Average need met was 72%. Average scholarship/grant was $16,111; average loan $4,398. 79% of total undergraduate aid awarded as scholarships/grants, 21% as loans/jobs. **Non-need-based:** Awarded to 2,035 full-time undergraduates, including 380 freshmen. Scholarships awarded for academics, alumni affiliation, athletics, music/drama, ROTC.

**Application procedures. Admission:** Closing date 1/7 (postmark date). $55 fee, may be waived for applicants with need. Application must be submitted online. Admission notification 4/5. Admission notification on a rolling basis beginning on or about 1/15. Must reply by 5/1. **Financial aid:** Priority date 2/1; no closing date. FAFSA, CSS PROFILE required. Applicants notified by 4/1; must reply by 5/1 or within 2 week(s) of notification.

**Academics. Special study options:** Combined bachelor's/graduate degree, cooperative education, double major, exchange student, honors, independent study, internships, student-designed major, study abroad, teacher certification program, Washington semester. **Credit/placement by examination:** AP, CLEP, IB, institutional tests. No credit by examination awarded to new students. Number of credit hours awarded for International Baccalaureate determined on case-by-case basis. **Support services:** Learning center, reduced course load, study skills assistance, tutoring.

**Majors. Area/ethnic studies:** Women's. **Biology:** General, biochemistry. **Business:** Accounting, accounting/business management, finance, management information systems, managerial economics, marketing, organizational behavior. **Communications:** General. **Conservation:** Environmental science, environmental studies. **Engineering:** General, civil, computer, electrical, mechanical, physics. **English:** English lit. **Foreign languages:** Ancient Greek, classics, French, German, Italian, Latin, Spanish. **History:** General. **Interdisciplinary:** Ancient studies, math/computer science. **Liberal arts:** Arts/sciences. **Math:** General. **Philosophy/religion:** Philosophy, religion. **Physical sciences:** Chemistry, physics. **Psychology:** General. **Social sciences:** Anthropology, economics, political science, sociology. **Visual/performing arts:** Art history/conservation, dramatic, studio arts. **Other:** Combined sciences.

**Most popular majors.** Business/marketing 34%, communications/journalism 9%, engineering/engineering technologies 8%, psychology 8%, social sciences 14%.

**Computing on campus.** 800 workstations in dormitories, library, computer center, student center. Dormitories wired for high-speed internet access and linked to campus network. Commuter students can connect to campus network. Online course registration, online library, helpline, repair service, student web hosting, wireless network available.

**Student life. Freshman orientation:** Mandatory, $285 fee. Preregistration for classes offered. 2-day session in summer and 2-day session on weekend before school starts. Parents attend separate program. **Housing:** Guaranteed on-campus for freshmen. Coed dorms, apartments, substance-free housing available. $250 nonrefundable deposit, deadline 5/1. **Activities:** Bands, choral groups, dance, drama, literary magazine, music ensembles, musical theater, opera, radio station, student government, student newspaper, symphony orchestra, Asian Pacific student union, Ka Mana'o O Hawaii, community action program, Barkada, Community of Portuguese and Brazilians, MECHA, Chinese student association, National Society of Black Engineers, Bronco Christian Fellowship.

**Athletics.** NCAA. **Intercollegiate:** Baseball M, basketball, cross-country, golf, rowing (crew), soccer, softball W, tennis, track and field, volleyball W, water polo. **Intramural:** Badminton, basketball, football (non-tackle), soccer, softball, table tennis, tennis, volleyball. **Team name:** Broncos.

**Student services.** Alcohol/substance abuse counseling, campus ministries, career counseling, student employment services, financial aid counseling, health services, legal services, minority student services, on-campus daycare, personal counseling, placement for graduates, veterans' counselor. **Physically disabled:** Services for visually, speech, hearing impaired.

**Contact.** Phone: (408) 554-4700 Fax: (408) 554-5255
Sandra Hayes, Dean of Undergraduate Admissions, Santa Clara University, 500 El Camino Real, Santa Clara, CA 95053

---

## School of Urban Missions: Oakland

Oakland, California
www.sum.edu

- Private 4-year Bible college affiliated with Assemblies of God
- Residential campus in very large city
- 62 degree-seeking undergraduates: 6% part-time, 48% women, 32% African American, 29% Asian American, 24% Hispanic American

- 75% of applicants admitted
- Application essay, interview required
- 60% graduate within 6 years; 5% enter graduate study

**General.** Regionally accredited; also accredited by ABHE. Extensive hands-on Ministry training with 8 hours per week of ministry. Additional Campus in New Orleans, LA. **Degrees:** 4 associate awarded. **Calendar:** Trimester, limited summer session. **Full-time faculty:** 3 total; 33% have terminal degrees, 67% minority, 33% women. **Part-time faculty:** 6 total; 33% have terminal degrees, 33% minority, 33% women.

**Freshman class profile.** 8 applied, 6 admitted, 5 enrolled.

| | | | |
|---|---|---|---|
| End year in good standing: | 75% | Live on campus: | 75% |
| Return as sophomores: | 70% | | |

**Basis for selection.** Recommendations, interview, character/personal qualities are very important. Academic GPA and application essay are considered. Pastor's recommendation and one general recommendation required. **Homeschooled:** Transcript of courses and grades, state high school equivalency certificate, letter of recommendation (nonparent) required.

**High school preparation.** No academic requirement for high school diploma. Minimum 2.0 GPA preferred.

**2008-2009 Annual costs.** Tuition/fees (projected): $7,180. Room only: $2,400. Books/supplies: $600. Personal expenses: $4,324.

**2006-2007 Financial aid. Need-based:** 33% of total undergraduate aid awarded as scholarships/grants, 67% as loans/jobs. **Non-need-based:** Scholarships awarded for academics, leadership, religious affiliation.

**Application procedures. Admission:** Closing date 7/31 (postmark date). $20 fee. Application may be submitted online. Admission notification 8/15. Admission notification on a rolling basis beginning on or about 1/1. **Financial aid:** No deadline. FAFSA, institutional form required.

**Academics. Special study options:** Distance learning. **Credit/placement by examination:** AP, CLEP. No credit for life experience in the academic courses. Field ministry credits can be considered life experience. **Support services:** Reduced course load, remedial instruction, tutoring.

**Majors. Theology:** Bible.

**Computing on campus.** 15 workstations in dormitories, library, computer center. Dormitories wired for high-speed internet access and linked to campus network. Online library available.

**Student life. Freshman orientation:** Mandatory. Preregistration for classes offered. **Policies:** 2 hours of Christian Service is required per week. Religious observance required. **Housing:** Guaranteed on-campus for all undergraduates. Single-sex dorms, apartments, substance-free housing available. $100 nonrefundable deposit, deadline 8/15. **Activities:** Campus ministries.

**Student services.** Campus ministries, financial aid counseling, health services, personal counseling.

**Contact.** E-mail: sum@sum.edu
Phone: (510) 567-6174 Toll-free number: (888) 567-6174
Fax: (510) 568-1024
Paul Williams, Vice President of Academics, School of Urban Missions: Oakland, 735 105th Avenue, Oakland, CA 94603

---

## Scripps College

Claremont, California
www.scrippscollege.edu

CB member
CB code: 4693

- Private 4-year liberal arts college for women
- Residential campus in large town
- 889 degree-seeking undergraduates: 100% women, 4% African American, 13% Asian American, 8% Hispanic American, 1% Native American, 1% international
- 19 degree-seeking graduate students
- 43% of applicants admitted
- SAT or ACT (ACT writing optional), application essay required
- 80% graduate within 6 years

**General.** Founded in 1926. Regionally accredited. One of cluster of 5 undergraduate and 2 graduate schools on adjoining campuses. Campuses share facilities. Cross-enrollment available at any of the Claremont colleges: Claremont-McKenna, Harvey Mudd, Pitzer, Pomona, and Scripps. **Degrees:** 216 bachelor's awarded. **ROTC:** Army, Air Force. **Location:** 35 miles from Los Angeles. **Calendar:** Semester, limited summer session. **Full-time faculty:** 69 total; 100% have terminal degrees, 19% minority, 52% women. **Part-time faculty:** 27 total; 96% have terminal degrees, 11% minority, 82% women. **Class size:** 75% < 20, 23% 20-39, less than 1% 40-49, less than 1% >100. **Special facilities:** Art slide library, biological field station, humanities museum.

**Freshman class profile.** 1,969 applied, 844 admitted, 227 enrolled.

| Mid 50% test scores | | | |
|---|---|---|---|
| SAT critical reading: | 650-740 | GPA 2.0-2.99: | 1% |
| SAT math: | 630-700 | Rank in top quarter: | 95% |
| SAT writing: | 640-720 | Rank in top tenth: | 72% |
| ACT composite: | 28-31 | End year in good standing: | 100% |
| GPA 3.50 or higher: | 92% | Return as sophomores: | 95% |
| GPA 3.0-3.49: | 7% | Out-of-state: | 59% |
| | | Live on campus: | 100% |

**Basis for selection.** Rigor of high school curriculum, GPA, class rank, aptitude as reflected in standardized testing most important. Essays, recommendations, required graded writing assignment significant. SAT Subject Tests used for placement in language only; institutional language and math exam used for placement. Interviews recommended. Audition recommended for music, dance majors. Portfolio recommended for art majors. **Homeschooled:** Statement describing homeschool structure and mission, transcript of courses and grades, letter of recommendation (nonparent) required. Interview highly recommended. **Learning Disabled:** Documentation of learning disability necessary.

**High school preparation.** 16 units required. Required units include English 4, mathematics 3, social studies 3, science 3 and foreign language 3.

**2007-2008 Annual costs.** Tuition/fees: $35,850. Room/board: $10,800. Books/supplies: $800. Personal expenses: $1,000.

**Financial aid. Non-need-based:** Scholarships awarded for academics, leadership.

**Application procedures. Admission:** Closing date 1/1 (postmark date). $50 fee, may be waived for applicants with need. Admission notification 4/1. Must reply by 5/1. **Financial aid:** Priority date 2/1; no closing date. FAFSA, CSS PROFILE required. Applicants notified by 4/1; must reply by 5/1 or within 2 week(s) of notification.

**Academics.** Almost half of junior class elects to study abroad for semester or year. **Special study options:** Accelerated study, combined bachelor's/graduate degree, cross-registration, double major, exchange student, independent study, internships, New York semester, student-designed major, study abroad, United Nations semester, Washington semester. Post-baccalaureate pre-medical certificate program, humanities internship program, 3-2 engineering. **Credit/placement by examination:** AP, CLEP, IB, institutional tests. 32 credit hours maximum toward bachelor's degree. SAT Subject Tests recommended for placement. **Support services:** Reduced course load, tutoring, writing center.

**Majors. Area/ethnic studies:** African-American, American, Asian, Asian-American, European, French, German, Hispanic-American/Latino/Chicano, Italian, Latin American, Spanish/Iberian, women's. **Biology:** General, biochemistry, molecular. **Business:** Accounting, organizational behavior. **Computer sciences:** Computer science. **Conservation:** Environmental science, environmental studies. **Engineering:** General. **English:** English lit. **Foreign languages:** General, Chinese, classics, French, German, Italian, Japanese, linguistics, Russian, Spanish. **History:** General. **Interdisciplinary:** Biological/physical sciences, neuroscience, science/society. **Legal studies:** General. **Liberal arts:** Humanities. **Math:** General. **Philosophy/religion:** Judaic, philosophy, religion. **Physical sciences:** Chemistry, geology, physics. **Psychology:** General. **Public administration:** Policy analysis. **Social sciences:** Anthropology, economics, political science, sociology. **Visual/performing arts:** Art history/conservation, cinematography, dance, dramatic, studio arts.

**Most popular majors.** Area/ethnic studies 16%, biology 7%, English 8%, interdisciplinary studies 10%, psychology 10%, social sciences 17%, visual/performing arts 16%.

**Computing on campus.** 72 workstations in dormitories, library, computer center. Dormitories wired for high-speed internet access and linked to campus network. Commuter students can connect to campus network. Online library, helpline, repair service, student web hosting, wireless network available.

**Student life. Freshman orientation:** Mandatory. 5-day orientation begins last Thursday in August. **Housing:** Guaranteed on-campus for freshmen. Special housing for disabled, apartments, substance-free housing available. Most sophomores, most juniors and all seniors have single rooms. Off-campus houses available to single students. **Activities:** Choral groups, dance, drama, literary magazine, music ensembles, radio station, student government, student newspaper, symphony orchestra, more than 200 clubs and organizations available.

**Athletics.** NCAA. **Intercollegiate:** Basketball W, cross-country W, diving W, golf W, lacrosse W, soccer W, softball W, swimming W, tennis W, track and field W, volleyball W, water polo W. **Intramural:** Basketball W, soccer W, softball W, volleyball W, water polo W. **Team name:** Athenas.

**Student services.** Adult student services, campus ministries, career counseling, student employment services, financial aid counseling, health services, minority student services, personal counseling, placement for graduates, women's services.

**Contact.** E-mail: admission@scrippscollege.edu
Phone: (909) 621-8149 Toll-free number: (800) 770-1333
Fax: (909) 607-7508
Amy Abrams, Director of Admissions, Scripps College, 1030 Columbia Avenue, Claremont, CA 91711

---

## Silicon Valley University
### San Jose, California
### www.svuca.edu

- Private 4-year business and technical college
- Very large city

**General.** Accredited by ACICS. **Calendar:** Semester.

**Contact.** Phone: (408) 435-8989
6201 San Ignacio, San Jose, CA 95119

---

## Simpson University
### Redding, California
### www.simpsonuniversity.edu          CB code: 4698

- Private 4-year liberal arts college affiliated with Christian and Missionary Alliance
- Residential campus in small city
- 891 degree-seeking undergraduates: 1% part-time, 67% women, 3% African American, 6% Asian American, 6% Hispanic American, 1% Native American, 1% international
- 177 degree-seeking graduate students
- 61% of applicants admitted
- Application essay required
- 47% graduate within 6 years

**General.** Founded in 1921. Regionally accredited. Christ-centered educational community. **Degrees:** 244 bachelor's, 2 associate awarded; master's, first professional offered. **Location:** 170 miles from Sacramento. **Calendar:** Semester, limited summer session. **Full-time faculty:** 44 total; 61% have terminal degrees, 7% minority, 30% women. **Part-time faculty:** 54 total; 39% have terminal degrees, 6% minority, 41% women. **Class size:** 70% < 20, 24% 20-39, 2% 40-49, 3% 50-99.

**Freshman class profile.** 661 applied, 405 admitted, 162 enrolled.

| Mid 50% test scores | | | |
|---|---|---|---|
| SAT critical reading: | 450-570 | GPA 2.0-2.99: | 24% |
| SAT math: | 440-570 | Rank in top quarter: | 56% |
| SAT writing: | 440-570 | Rank in top tenth: | 27% |
| ACT composite: | 21-25 | End year in good standing: | 83% |
| GPA 3.50 or higher: | 53% | Return as sophomores: | 64% |
| GPA 3.0-3.49: | 23% | Out-of-state: | 20% |
| | | Live on campus: | 78% |

**Basis for selection.** Commitment to Jesus Christ as reflected in personal statement and required references, academic achievement, other recommendations, and standardized test scores important. SAT and SAT Subject Tests or ACT recommended. **Homeschooled:** Transcript of courses and grades required.

**High school preparation.** Recommended units include English 4, mathematics 3, social studies 3, science 2 and foreign language 2. College-preparatory program highly recommended; GED required for graduates of nonapproved programs.

**2008-2009 Annual costs.** Tuition/fees: $19,500. Room/board: $6,700. Books/supplies: $1,392. Personal expenses: $1,968.

**2006-2007 Financial aid. Need-based:** 177 full-time freshmen applied for aid; 170 were judged to have need; 170 of these received aid. Average need met was 59%. Average scholarship/grant was $10,406; average loan $3,500. 55% of total undergraduate aid awarded as scholarships/grants, 45% as loans/jobs. **Non-need-based:** Awarded to 810 full-time undergraduates, including 263 freshmen. Scholarships awarded for academics, alumni affiliation, athletics, leadership, minority status, music/drama, religious affiliation, state residency. **Additional information:** Work-study programs available.

**Application procedures. Admission:** No deadline. $40 fee, may be waived for applicants with need. Application may be submitted online. Admission notification on a rolling basis. Must reply by May 1 or within 2 week(s) if notified thereafter. **Financial aid:** Priority date 3/2; no closing date. FAFSA, institutional form required. Applicants notified on a rolling basis starting 3/1; must reply within 4 week(s) of notification.

**Academics.** 34-semester-hour teacher credential program permits students to earn California Clear Credential for grades K-8 (multiple subjects) or for grades 7-12 (single subject). **Special study options:** Accelerated study, combined bachelor's/graduate degree, distance learning, double major, honors, independent study, internships, student-designed major, study abroad, teacher certification program, Washington semester, weekend college. **Credit/ placement by examination:** AP, CLEP, SAT, ACT, institutional tests. 30 credit hours maximum toward bachelor's degree. Credit by examination granted only to enrolled students. Students may take challenge exam for particular course only once. **Support services:** Reduced course load, remedial instruction, study skills assistance, tutoring, writing center.

**Majors. Biology:** General. **Business:** Accounting, business admin, management information systems, organizational behavior. **Communications:** General. **Education:** Elementary, English, mathematics, music, social science. **English:** English lit. **Health:** Health care admin. **History:** General. **Liberal arts:** Arts/sciences. **Math:** General. **Parks/recreation:** General. **Philosophy/ religion:** Christian, religion. **Psychology:** General. **Social sciences:** General. **Theology:** Bible, missionary, pastoral counseling, theology, youth ministry.

**Most popular majors.** Business/marketing 23%, liberal arts 21%, psychology 21%, theological studies 16%.

**Computing on campus.** 50 workstations in dormitories, library, computer center. Dormitories wired for high-speed internet access and linked to campus network. Commuter students can connect to campus network. Online course registration, online library, helpline, repair service, wireless network available.

**Student life. Freshman orientation:** Mandatory. Preregistration for classes offered. Sessions include placement tests. **Policies:** All single undergraduates under 22 required to live on campus. Request for off-campus living must be approved by Vice President for Student Development. Religious observance required. **Housing:** Guaranteed on-campus for all undergraduates. Single-sex dorms, special housing for disabled, apartments, substance-free housing available. $100 fully refundable deposit, deadline 9/1. **Activities:** Jazz band, choral groups, dance, drama, film society, music ensembles, student government, student newspaper, symphony orchestra, Asian fellowship, Hispanic fellowship, summer missions teams, chapel worship team, student senate, spiritual action committee, psychology club, missionary kids association, commuter student association.

**Athletics.** NAIA, NCCAA. **Intercollegiate:** Baseball M, basketball, cross-country, soccer, volleyball W. **Intramural:** Basketball, football (non-tackle), soccer. **Team name:** Red Hawks.

**Student services.** Adult student services, campus ministries, career counseling, student employment services, financial aid counseling, health services, minority student services, personal counseling, veterans' counselor. **Physically disabled:** Services for visually, speech, hearing impaired.

**Contact.** E-mail: admissions@simpsonuniversity.edu
Phone: (530) 226-4606 Toll-free number: (800) 598-2493
Fax: (530) 226-4861
James Herberger, Director of Enrollment Management, Simpson University, 2211 College View Drive, Redding, CA 96003-8606

---

## Soka University of America
### Aliso Viejo, California          CB member
### www.soka.edu          CB code: 4066

- Private 4-year university and liberal arts college
- Residential campus in large town
- 362 degree-seeking undergraduates: 63% women, 3% African American, 22% Asian American, 5% Hispanic American, 48% international
- 6 degree-seeking graduate students
- 54% of applicants admitted
- SAT or ACT with writing, application essay required

**General. Degrees:** 91 bachelor's awarded; master's offered. **Location:** 70 miles from Los Angeles, 75 miles from San Diego. **Calendar:** Semester. **Full-time faculty:** 38 total; 95% have terminal degrees, 32% minority, 45% women. **Part-time faculty:** 17 total; 53% have terminal degrees, 53% minority, 65% women. **Class size:** 100% < 20.

**Freshman class profile.** 378 applied, 205 admitted, 101 enrolled.

| Mid 50% test scores | | | |
|---|---|---|---|
| SAT critical reading: | 460-640 | Rank in top quarter: | 80% |
| SAT math: | 570-680 | Rank in top tenth: | 43% |
| SAT writing: | 490-630 | End year in good standing: | 98% |
| ACT composite: | 23-24 | Return as sophomores: | 85% |
| GPA 3.50 or higher: | 75% | Out-of-state: | 60% |
| GPA 3.0-3.49: | 22% | Live on campus: | 99% |
| GPA 2.0-2.99: | 3% | International: | 32% |

**Basis for selection.** GPA and courses most important. Test scores, essay, recommendations, extracurricular activities also important. **Homeschooled:** State high school equivalency certificate required. Program must be accredited by regional, state, or national agency. **Learning Disabled:** Admission decisions do not consider learning disabilities. Special needs discussed only after student has been admitted and has identified need.

**High school preparation.** 17 units recommended. Recommended units include English 4, mathematics 3, social studies 2, history 2, science 2 (laboratory 2) and foreign language 2.

**2008-2009 Annual costs.** Tuition/fees: $23,434. Room/board: $9,000. Books/supplies: $1,000. Personal expenses: $1,500.

**2007-2008 Financial aid. Need-based:** 101 full-time freshmen applied for aid; 101 were judged to have need; 101 of these received aid. Average need met was 82%. Average scholarship/grant was $8,750; average loan $3,500. 75% of total undergraduate aid awarded as scholarships/grants, 25% as loans/jobs. **Non-need-based:** Awarded to 112 full-time undergraduates, including 34 freshmen. Scholarships awarded for academics.

**Application procedures. Admission:** Closing date 1/15 (postmark date). $45 fee. Application may be submitted online. Admission notification 3/1. Must reply by 5/1. **Financial aid:** Closing date 3/1. FAFSA required. Applicants notified on a rolling basis starting 3/15; must reply within 4 week(s) of notification.

**Academics.** Study abroad required of all students during one semester of their junior year. **Special study options:** ESL, independent study, internships, study abroad. **Credit/placement by examination:** CLEP, institutional tests. **Support services:** Study skills assistance, tutoring, writing center.

**Majors. Liberal arts:** Arts/sciences.

**Computing on campus.** PC or laptop required. 100 workstations in dormitories, library, computer center. Dormitories wired for high-speed internet access and linked to campus network. Commuter students can connect to campus network. Online course registration, online library, helpline, repair service, wireless network available.

**Student life. Freshman orientation:** Mandatory. Preregistration for classes offered. 4-day orientation period before upperclassmen arrive. **Housing:** Guaranteed on-campus for all undergraduates. Coed dorms, substance-free housing available. Students required to live on campus. **Activities:** Jazz band, choral groups, dance, film society, literary magazine, music ensembles, Model UN, student government, student newspaper, Amnesty International, Buena Vista social club, Chinese club, Green Planet, Humanism in Action, orchestra club, Activist Collective, French club.

**Athletics. Intercollegiate:** Cross-country, soccer, swimming, track and field. **Intramural:** Badminton, basketball, racquetball, soccer, tennis, volleyball, weight lifting. **Team name:** Lions.

**Student services.** Alcohol/substance abuse counseling, career counseling, student employment services, financial aid counseling, health services, personal counseling, placement for graduates. **Physically disabled:** Services for visually, hearing impaired.

**Contact.** E-mail: admission@soka.edu
Phone: (949) 480-4150 Toll-free number: (888) 600-7652
Fax: (949) 480-4151
Christopher Brown, Director of Admission and Financial Aid, Soka University of America, 1 University Drive, Aliso Viejo, CA 92656-8081

## Sonoma State University
### Rohnert Park, California
**www.sonoma.edu**                                    **CB code: 4723**

- Public 4-year university and liberal arts college
- Commuter campus in large town
- 7,603 degree-seeking undergraduates: 4% part-time, 62% women
- 651 degree-seeking graduate students
- 73% of applicants admitted
- SAT or ACT (ACT writing optional) required
- 50% graduate within 6 years

**General.** Founded in 1960. Regionally accredited. **Degrees:** 1,674 bachelor's awarded; master's offered. **ROTC:** Army, Naval, Air Force. **Location:** 50 miles from San Francisco, 10 miles from Santa Rosa. **Calendar:** Semester, extensive summer session. **Full-time faculty:** 307 total; 92% have terminal degrees, 15% minority, 46% women. **Part-time faculty:** 350 total; 28% have terminal degrees, 10% minority, 56% women. **Class size:** 37% < 20, 47% 20-39, 8% 40-49, 7% 50-99, 2% >100. **Special facilities:** Observatory, performing arts center, nature preserves, information technology center.

**Freshman class profile.** 10,382 applied, 7,549 admitted, 1,713 enrolled.

| Mid 50% test scores | | | |
|---|---|---|---|
| SAT critical reading: | 450-550 | GPA 2.0-2.99: | 39% |
| SAT math: | 450-560 | End year in good standing: | 85% |
| ACT composite: | 18-23 | Return as sophomores: | 74% |
| GPA 3.50 or higher: | 19% | Out-of-state: | 2% |
| GPA 3.0-3.49: | 42% | Live on campus: | 90% |
| | | International: | 1% |

**Basis for selection.** School GPA and test scores most important. SAT, ACT, SAT Subject Tests must be received before start of term. Audition required of music majors. Portfolio required of art majors. RN required for graduate nursing. **Learning Disabled:** Applicants with disabilities strongly encouraged to complete college preparatory course requirements if at all possible. If applicant judged unable to fulfill specific course requirement because of disability, alternative college preparatory courses may be substituted for specific subject requirements.

**High school preparation.** 15 units required. Required units include English 4, mathematics 3, history 2, science 2 (laboratory 1), foreign language 2, visual/performing arts 1 and academic electives 1. One visual and performing arts, US government required.

**2007-2008 Annual costs.** Tuition/fees: $3,946; $14,116 out-of-state. Room/board: $9,730. Books/supplies: $1,386. Personal expenses: $2,520.

**2006-2007 Financial aid. Need-based:** Average need met was 73%. Average scholarship/grant was $6,853; average loan $2,419. 54% of total undergraduate aid awarded as scholarships/grants, 46% as loans/jobs. **Non-need-based:** Scholarships awarded for academics, alumni affiliation, art, athletics, leadership, minority status, music/drama.

**Application procedures. Admission:** Priority date 11/30; deadline 1/31 (postmark date). $55 fee, may be waived for applicants with need. Application may be submitted online. Admission notification 3/1. Admission notification on a rolling basis beginning on or about 11/1. Must reply by 5/1. **Financial aid:** Priority date 1/31; no closing date. FAFSA required. Applicants notified on a rolling basis starting 3/15; must reply within 2 week(s) of notification.

**Academics. Special study options:** Accelerated study, combined bachelor's/graduate degree, cross-registration, distance learning, double major, dual enrollment of high school students, ESL, exchange student, external degree, honors, independent study, internships, liberal arts/career combination, New York semester, semester at sea, student-designed major, study abroad, teacher certification program, United Nations semester, urban semester, Washington semester. Combined degree programs: bachelor's/MBA; bachelor's/MPA. **Credit/placement by examination:** AP, CLEP, institutional tests. 30 credit hours maximum toward bachelor's degree. **Support services:** Learning center, pre-admission summer program, reduced course load, remedial instruction, study skills assistance, tutoring, writing center.

**Majors. Area/ethnic studies:** African-American, Hispanic-American/Latino/Chicano, women's. **Biology:** General. **Business:** Business admin. **Communications:** General. **Computer sciences:** Computer science, programming. **Conservation:** General, environmental studies. **Engineering:** Computer. **English:** English lit. **Family/consumer sciences:** Family studies. **Foreign languages:** French, German, Spanish. **Health:** Nursing (RN). **History:** General. **Interdisciplinary:** Global studies. **Liberal arts:** Arts/sciences. **Math:** General. **Philosophy/religion:** Philosophy. **Physical sciences:** Chemistry, geology, physics. **Protective services:** Law enforcement admin. **Psychology:** General. **Social sciences:** Anthropology, economics, geography, political science, sociology. **Visual/performing arts:** General, art history/conservation, dramatic, studio arts.

**Most popular majors.** Business/marketing 20%, interdisciplinary studies 9%, liberal arts 9%, psychology 10%, social sciences 17%.

**Computing on campus.** PC or laptop required. 400 workstations in library, computer center. Dormitories wired for high-speed internet access and linked to campus network. Commuter students can connect to campus network. Online course registration, online library, helpline, student web hosting, wireless network available.

**Student life. Freshman orientation:** Available. Preregistration for classes offered. 2-day residential program in June. Parents invited. **Housing:** Guaranteed on-campus for freshmen. Coed dorms, apartments, substance-free housing available. $1,000 partly refundable deposit. Focus learning communities, freshman seminar, healthy living, women in math/science dorms available. **Activities:** Jazz band, choral groups, dance, drama, literary magazine, music ensembles, musical theater, opera, radio station, student government, student newspaper, symphony orchestra, Student Advocates for Education, Model United Nations, College Republicans, Asian Pacific Islander Organization, Raza Native American Council, El Movimiento Estudiantil Chicano/a de Aztlán, InterVarsity Christian Fellowship, Hillel, Best Buddies, Student Ambassadors.

**Athletics. NCAA. Intercollegiate:** Baseball M, basketball, golf, soccer, softball W, tennis, track and field W, volleyball W, water polo W. **Intramural:** Basketball, football (non-tackle), soccer, softball, volleyball. **Team name:** Sea Wolves.

**Student services.** Adult student services, alcohol/substance abuse counseling, career counseling, services for economically disadvantaged, student employment services, financial aid counseling, health services, minority student services, on-campus daycare, personal counseling, placement for graduates, veterans' counselor, women's services. **Physically disabled:** Services for visually, speech, hearing impaired.

**Contact.** Phone: (707) 664-2778 Fax: (707) 664-2060 Gustavo Flores, Director, Admissions, Sonoma State University, 1801 East Cotati Avenue, Rohnert Park, CA 94928

---

## Southern California Institute of Architecture
### Los Angeles, California
www.sciarc.edu      CB code: 1575

- Private 5-year visual arts and technical college
- Commuter campus in very large city
- 256 degree-seeking undergraduates: 30% women, 2% African American, 24% Asian American, 20% Hispanic American, 14% international
- 228 degree-seeking graduate students
- 69% of applicants admitted
- SAT or ACT (ACT writing optional), application essay required

**General.** Founded in 1972. Regionally accredited. **Degrees:** 35 bachelor's awarded; master's offered. **Location:** Downtown. **Calendar:** Semester, limited summer session. **Part-time faculty:** 80 total. **Special facilities:** Media center, architecture gallery, woodshop and modelmaking center, metal fabrication shop, graphics center, darkroom, CNC Milling.

**Freshman class profile.** 145 applied, 100 admitted, 73 enrolled.

| | | | |
|---|---|---|---|
| Return as sophomores: | 88% | **International:** | 19% |
| Out-of-state: | 40% | | |

**Basis for selection.** School achievement record, test scores, portfolio, recommendations, and statement of purpose. Portfolio required.

**High school preparation.** Art design and architecture courses recommended.

**2008-2009 Annual costs.** Tuition/fees: $21,544. International student fee (one-time only) $500. International student mandatory health insurance premium (per year) $822. Books/supplies: $1,400.

**2007-2008 Financial aid. Need-based:** Average scholarship/grant was $3,000; average loan $10,000. **Non-need-based:** Scholarships awarded for academics, state residency.

**Application procedures. Admission:** Closing date 2/1 (postmark date). $60 fee, may be waived for applicants with need. Admission notification on a rolling basis beginning on or about 4/1. **Financial aid:** No deadline. FAFSA, institutional form required. Must reply within 2 week(s) of notification.

**Academics.** Intensive summer session on introduction to architecture offered to graduates and high school students. **Special study options:** Exchange student, internships, study abroad. SCI-Arc study abroad programs in Switzerland and Japan; exchange programs in Japan, Australia, England, Israel, Netherlands, France, Mexico. **Credit/placement by examination:** AP, CLEP, institutional tests. **Support services:** Pre-admission summer program.

**Majors. Architecture:** Architecture.

**Computing on campus.** PC or laptop required. 60 workstations in library, computer center. Commuter students can connect to campus network. Online course registration, helpline, wireless network available.

**Student life. Freshman orientation:** Mandatory. Held right before school begins. **Policies:** Informal weekly gathering of entire school sponsored by student government. **Activities:** Student government, Architects, Designers, and Planners for Social Responsibility, American Institute of Architects student affiliation, Women in Architecture.

**Student services.** Career counseling, financial aid counseling, personal counseling, veterans' counselor. **Physically disabled:** Services for speech, hearing impaired.

**Contact.** E-mail: admissions@sciarc.edu Phone: (213) 613-2200 ext. 320 Fax: (213) 613-2260 JJ Jackman, Director of Admission, Southern California Institute of Architecture, 960 East 3rd Street, Los Angeles, CA 90013

---

## Southern California Institute of Technology
### Anaheim, California
www.scit-scu.edu      CB code: 3034

- For-profit 4-year business and engineering college
- Residential campus in large city
- 370 degree-seeking undergraduates
- Interview required

**General.** Accredited by ACCSCT. **Degrees:** 65 bachelor's, 7 associate awarded. **Calendar:** Quarter, extensive summer session. **Full-time faculty:** 15 total. **Part-time faculty:** 7 total.

**Basis for selection.** Open admission. Wonderlic required. **Homeschooled:** Transcript of courses and grades, interview required.

**2007-2008 Annual costs.** Tuition/fees: $11,185. Tuition and fees quoted for electronic engineering program; required fees cover equipment and book expenses. Costs vary by program. Books/supplies: $2,500.

**Application procedures. Admission:** No deadline. $100 fee. Application must be submitted on paper.

**Academics. Special study options:** Accelerated study, combined bachelor's/graduate degree, cooperative education, double major, ESL, liberal arts/career combination. **Credit/placement by examination:** CLEP. **Support services:** Tutoring.

**Majors. Business:** Business admin. **Engineering:** Electrical.

**Student life. Freshman orientation:** Available. Preregistration for classes offered.

**Student services.** Career counseling, financial aid counseling, placement for graduates.

**Contact.** E-mail: admission@scit-scu.edu Phone: (714) 300-0300 Fax: (714) 300-0310 Jodell Pinesett, Admissions Director, Southern California Institute of Technology, 222 South Harbor Boulevard, Suite 200, Anaheim, CA 92805

---

## Stanford University
### Stanford, California
www.stanford.edu      CB member    CB code: 4704

- Private 4-year university
- Residential campus in small city
- 6,520 degree-seeking undergraduates: 48% women
- 8,186 degree-seeking graduate students
- 10% of applicants admitted

- SAT or ACT with writing, application essay required
- 95% graduate within 6 years; 38% enter graduate study

**General.** Founded in 1885. Regionally accredited. **Degrees:** 1,709 bachelor's awarded; master's, doctoral, first professional offered. **ROTC:** Army, Naval, Air Force. **Location:** 29 miles from San Francisco. **Calendar:** Quarter, extensive summer session. **Full-time faculty:** 1,027 total; 98% have terminal degrees, 17% minority, 24% women. **Part-time faculty:** 21 total; 86% have terminal degrees, 10% women. **Class size:** 74% < 20, 12% 20-39, 3% 40-49, 7% 50-99, 4% >100. **Special facilities:** Linear accelerator, 18 libraries, nature preserve, marine research center, Rodin sculpture garden, two art galleries, observatory, 10 overseas campuses, medical center.

**Freshman class profile.** 23,958 applied, 2,464 admitted, 1,722 enrolled.

| Mid 50% test scores | | | |
|---|---|---|---|
| SAT critical reading: | 660-760 | Rank in top quarter: | 98% |
| SAT math: | 680-790 | Rank in top tenth: | 91% |
| SAT writing: | 660-760 | Return as sophomores: | 98% |
| ACT composite: | 29-33 | Out-of-state: | 56% |
| GPA 3.50 or higher: | 99% | Live on campus: | 100% |
| GPA 3.0-3.49: | 1% | International: | 7% |

**Basis for selection.** School achievement record, test scores, extracurricular activities, teacher and counselor evaluations, and personal qualifications most important. Rigor and variety of academic program very important. Personal qualities also considered. SAT Subject Tests recommended. Arts students may submit supplementary materials for review. Submissions should have previously received significant recognition at regional, state, national or international level. **Homeschooled:** Statement describing homeschool structure and mission required. Standardized test scores important. Subject tests recommended. **Learning Disabled:** Prospective students with disabilities are encouraged to meet with Disability Resource Center staff members.

**High school preparation.** 20 units recommended. Recommended units include English 4, mathematics 4, social studies 2, history 1, science 3 (laboratory 3) and foreign language 3.

**2008-2009 Annual costs.** Tuition/fees: $36,030. Room/board: $11,182. Books/supplies: $1,335. Personal expenses: $1,995.

**2006-2007 Financial aid.** All financial aid based on need. 1,017 full-time freshmen applied for aid; 758 were judged to have need; 750 of these received aid. Average need met was 100%. Average scholarship/grant was $28,829; average loan $1,939. 86% of total undergraduate aid awarded as scholarships/grants, 14% as loans/jobs. **Additional information:** Families with annual incomes of less than $45,000 not expected to contribute to cost of tuition.

**Application procedures. Admission:** Closing date 1/1 (postmark date). $75 fee, may be waived for applicants with need. Application may be submitted online. Admission notification 4/1. Must reply by 5/1. Paper application is available by special permission of the director of admission at Stanford. Early action candidates may not apply to other schools under any type of early action, early decision, or early notification program, but can apply under regular admissions time frame. **Financial aid:** Priority date 2/15; no closing date. FAFSA, CSS PROFILE required. Applicants notified on a rolling basis starting 4/3; must reply by 5/1.

**Academics.** Undergraduate academic offerings stress access to senior faculty from first days on campus through small-group learning experiences and research opportunities. **Special study options:** Distance learning, double major, exchange student, honors, independent study, internships, student-designed major, study abroad, Washington semester. Each year, about 1200 undergraduates pursue research programs. A Summer Research College accommodates about 200 students. About 25 percent of each graduating class earn departmental honors. **Credit/placement by examination:** AP, CLEP, IB, institutional tests. 45 Advanced Placement units allowed. **Support services:** Learning center, pre-admission summer program, study skills assistance, tutoring, writing center.

**Majors. Area/ethnic studies:** African, African-American, American, Asian-American, East Asian, German, Hispanic-American/Latino/Chicano, Native American, women's. **Biology:** General. **Communications:** General. **Computer sciences:** General, computer science. **Conservation:** Environmental science. **Engineering:** General, chemical, civil, electrical, environmental, materials, materials science, mechanical, petroleum. **Engineering technology:** Industrial management. **English:** British lit, composition, English lit. **Foreign languages:** Chinese, classics, comparative lit, French, German, Italian, Japanese, linguistics, Slavic, Spanish. **History:** General. **Interdisciplinary:** Global studies, intercultural, math/computer science, science/society, systems science. **Liberal arts:** Humanities. **Math:** General. **Philosophy/religion:** Philosophy, religion. **Physical sciences:** Chemistry, geology, geophysics, physics. **Psychology:** General. **Public administration:** Policy analysis. **Social sciences:** Anthropology, archaeology, economics, international relations, political science, sociology, urban studies. **Visual/performing arts:** Art, dramatic, studio arts.

**Most popular majors.** Biology 8%, engineering/engineering technologies 15%, interdisciplinary studies 13%, psychology 6%, social sciences 23%.

**Computing on campus.** 1,500 workstations in dormitories, library, computer center, student center. Dormitories wired for high-speed internet access and linked to campus network. Commuter students can connect to campus network. Online course registration, online library, helpline, repair service, student web hosting, wireless network available.

**Student life. Freshman orientation:** Mandatory, $425 fee. 6-day academically oriented program held in late September. **Housing:** Guaranteed on-campus for all undergraduates. Coed dorms, single-sex dorms, special housing for disabled, apartments, cooperative housing, fraternity/sorority housing available. Academic, cross-cultural, language theme, and ethnic theme housing available. **Activities:** Bands, campus ministries, choral groups, dance, drama, film society, international student organizations, literary magazine, music ensembles, Model UN, musical theater, opera, radio station, student government, student newspaper, symphony orchestra, TV station, approximately 600 student groups.

**Athletics.** NCAA. **Intercollegiate:** Baseball M, basketball, cross-country, diving, fencing, field hockey W, football (tackle) M, golf, gymnastics, lacrosse W, rowing (crew), sailing, soccer, softball W, squash W, swimming, synchronized swimming W, tennis, track and field, volleyball, water polo, wrestling M. **Intramural:** Archery, badminton, basketball, bowling, football (non-tackle), handball, soccer, softball, table tennis, tennis, triathlon, volleyball. **Team name:** Cardinal.

**Student services.** Alcohol/substance abuse counseling, campus ministries, career counseling, student employment services, financial aid counseling, health services, legal services, minority student services, on-campus daycare, personal counseling, placement for graduates, women's services. **Physically disabled:** Services for visually, speech, hearing impaired. **Learning disabled:** Comprehensive services available.

**Contact.** E-mail: admission@stanford.edu
Phone: (650) 723-2091 Fax: (650) 723-6050
Richard Shaw, Dean of Undergraduate Admission and Financial Aid, Stanford University, Montag Hall, Stanford, CA 94305-6106

---

## Thomas Aquinas College
### Santa Paula, California
### www.thomasaquinas.edu

**CB member**
**CB code: 4828**

- Private 4-year liberal arts college affiliated with Roman Catholic Church
- Residential campus in rural community
- 360 degree-seeking undergraduates: 49% women, 3% Asian American, 6% Hispanic American, 6% international
- 60% of applicants admitted
- SAT or ACT (ACT writing optional), application essay required
- 78% graduate within 6 years; 20% enter graduate study

**General.** Founded in 1971. Regionally accredited. **Degrees:** 74 bachelor's awarded. **Location:** 6 miles from Santa Paula, 25 miles from Ventura. **Calendar:** Semester. **Full-time faculty:** 29 total; 62% have terminal degrees, 7% women. **Part-time faculty:** 8 total; 75% have terminal degrees, 12% women. **Class size:** 100% < 20.

**Freshman class profile.** 222 applied, 134 admitted, 102 enrolled.

| Mid 50% test scores | | | |
|---|---|---|---|
| SAT critical reading: | 600-740 | Rank in top quarter: | 75% |
| SAT math: | 570-660 | Rank in top tenth: | 75% |
| ACT composite: | 25-29 | End year in good standing: | 97% |
| GPA 3.50 or higher: | 39% | Return as sophomores: | 92% |
| GPA 3.0-3.49: | 55% | Out-of-state: | 39% |
| GPA 2.0-2.99: | 6% | Live on campus: | 100% |
| | | International: | 6% |

**Basis for selection.** Faculty Admission Committee reviews each applicant for evidence of likely success in all parts of 4-year program. Required essays and 3 letters of reference supplement academic records and test scores. Test receipt date is rolling. Interview recommended for early admissions applicants and for those whose academic preparation is uncertain. **Homeschooled:** Applicants not home-schooled through formal programs must provide written records of all studies done from grades 9 through 12.

**High school preparation.** 11 units required; 18 recommended. Required and recommended units include English 4, mathematics 3-4, history 2, science 3 (laboratory 2), foreign language 2 and academic electives 3.

**2008-2009 Annual costs.** Tuition/fees: $21,400. Room/board: $6,950. Books/supplies: $450. Personal expenses: $2,214.

**2007-2008 Financial aid.** All financial aid based on need. 82 full-time freshmen applied for aid; 71 were judged to have need; 71 of these received aid. Average need met was 100%. Average scholarship/grant was $12,148; average loan $2,719. 64% of total undergraduate aid awarded as scholarships/grants, 36% as loans/jobs.

**Application procedures. Admission:** No deadline. No application fee. Application must be submitted on paper. Admission notification on a rolling basis beginning on or about 10/1. Must reply by May 1 or within 1 week(s) if notified thereafter. **Financial aid:** Closing date 3/2. FAFSA, institutional form required. Applicants notified on a rolling basis starting 1/1; must reply by 5/1 or within 2 week(s) of notification.

**Academics.** Great Books curriculum. **Special study options:** Cross-disciplinary curriculum of liberal education through reading and analyzing the "Great Books," with special emphasis on theology, philosophy, math, laboratory science, and literature. **Credit/placement by examination:** CLEP. **Support services:** Tutoring.

**Majors. Liberal arts:** Arts/sciences.

**Computing on campus.** 17 workstations in dormitories, library, student center. Dormitories linked to campus network.

**Student life. Freshman orientation:** Mandatory. Preregistration for classes offered. 2-day program immediately before classes begin. **Housing:** Guaranteed on-campus for all undergraduates. Single-sex dorms, substance-free housing available. **Activities:** Campus ministries, choral groups, dance, drama, literary magazine, music ensembles, musical theater, Legion of Mary, Third Order Dominican, Habitat for Humanity.

**Athletics. Intramural:** Basketball, football (non-tackle) M, football (tackle) M, soccer, softball, table tennis, tennis, volleyball.

**Student services.** Campus ministries, career counseling, financial aid counseling, health services, personal counseling, placement for graduates.

**Contact.** E-mail: admissions@thomasaquinas.edu
Phone: (805) 525-4417 Toll-free number: (800) 634-9797
Fax: (805) 525-9342
Jonathan Daly, Director of Admission, Thomas Aquinas College, 10,000 North Ojai Road, Santa Paula, CA 93060-9621

---

## University of California: Berkeley

| Berkeley, California | CB member |
| --- | --- |
| www.berkeley.edu | CB code: 4833 |

- Public 4-year university
- Residential campus in small city
- 24,636 degree-seeking undergraduates: 3% African American, 42% Asian American, 12% Hispanic American, 1% Native American, 3% international
- 10,317 graduate students
- 23% of applicants admitted
- SAT and SAT Subject Tests or ACT with writing, SAT Subject Tests, application essay required
- 89% graduate within 6 years

**General.** Founded in 1868. Regionally accredited. **Degrees:** 6,629 bachelor's awarded; master's, doctoral, first professional offered. **ROTC:** Army, Naval, Air Force. **Location:** 10 miles from San Francisco. **Calendar:** Semester, extensive summer session. **Class size:** 62% < 20, 21% 20-39, 3% 40-49, 7% 50-99, 7% >100. **Special facilities:** Museums of art, anthropology, archaeology, paleontology and vertebrate zoology, film archive, science museum and research center for K-12 education, botanical garden, libraries of rare books, Western and Latin Americana, seismographic station, herbacia, performing arts facilities.

**Freshman class profile.** 44,149 applied, 10,287 admitted, 4,225 enrolled.

| Mid 50% test scores | | GPA 2.0-2.99: | 1% |
| --- | --- | --- | --- |
| SAT critical reading: | 590-710 | Rank in top quarter: | 100% |
| SAT math: | 620-750 | Rank in top tenth: | 99% |
| SAT writing: | 590-710 | Out-of-state: | 8% |
| GPA 3.50 or higher: | 96% | International: | 3% |
| GPA 3.0-3.49: | 3% | | |

**Basis for selection.** Selection based on thorough review of academic performance; likely contribution to the intellectual and cultural vitality of the campus; diversity in personal background and experience; demonstrated qualities in leadership, motivation, concern for others and community; non-academic achievement in the performing arts, athletics or employment; demonstrated interest in the major. All applicants must complete 2 SAT Subject Tests in different subject areas. If Math SAT Subject Test is taken, must be Level 2. Test scores must meet criteria determined by the applicant's residency and high school GPA.

**High school preparation.** 15 units required; 18 recommended. Required and recommended units include English 4, mathematics 3-4, history 2, (laboratory 2-3), foreign language 2-3, visual/performing arts 1 and academic electives 1. History is 2 units in history/social science.

**2007-2008 Annual costs.** Tuition/fees: $7,164; $26,784 out-of-state. Room/board: $13,848.

**Financial aid. Non-need-based:** Scholarships awarded for academics.

**Application procedures. Admission:** Closing date 11/30. $60 fee, may be waived for applicants with need. Application may be submitted online. Admission notification 3/31. Must reply by 5/1. **Financial aid:** Priority date 3/2, closing date 3/2. FAFSA required. Applicants notified by 4/15.

**Academics.** All students required to pass one American cultures class. **Special study options:** Accelerated study, cross-registration, distance learning, double major, dual enrollment of high school students, ESL, exchange student, honors, independent study, internships, student-designed major, study abroad, teacher certification program. Freshman seminar, undergraduate research apprenticeship, university research expeditions. **Credit/placement by examination:** AP, CLEP, institutional tests. **Support services:** Learning center, pre-admission summer program, reduced course load, study skills assistance, tutoring.

**Majors. Architecture:** Architecture, landscape. **Area/ethnic studies:** African-American, American, Asian, Asian-American, Hispanic-American/Latino/Chicano, Latin American, Native American, Near/Middle Eastern, Southeast Asian, women's. **Biology:** General, botany, cellular/molecular, microbiology, toxicology. **Business:** Business admin. **Communications:** Media studies. **Computer sciences:** Computer science. **Conservation:** General, environmental science, environmental studies, forest management, forestry, management/policy. **Engineering:** Biomedical, chemical, civil, electrical, environmental, geological, manufacturing, materials science, mechanical, nuclear, operations research, physics, science. **English:** English lit, speech/rhetoric. **Foreign languages:** Ancient Greek, Celtic, Chinese, classics, comparative lit, Dutch/Flemish, French, German, Italian, Japanese, Latin, linguistics, Scandinavian, Slavic, Spanish. **History:** General. **Interdisciplinary:** Classical/archaeology, cognitive science, nutrition sciences, peace/conflict. **Legal studies:** General. **Math:** General, applied, statistics. **Philosophy/religion:** Philosophy, religion. **Physical sciences:** General, astrophysics, atmospheric science, chemistry, geology, geophysics, oceanography, physics. **Psychology:** General. **Public administration:** Social work. **Social sciences:** Anthropology, economics, geography, political science, sociology, urban studies. **Visual/performing arts:** Art, art history/conservation, dance, dramatic, film/cinema.

**Most popular majors.** Biology 13%, engineering/engineering technologies 13%, English 6%, social sciences 20%.

**Computing on campus.** Dormitories wired for high-speed internet access and linked to campus network. Commuter students can connect to campus network. Online course registration, online library, helpline, repair service available.

**Student life. Freshman orientation:** Available, $50 fee. Preregistration for classes offered. **Housing:** Guaranteed on-campus for freshmen. Coed dorms, single-sex dorms, special housing for disabled, apartments, cooperative housing, fraternity/sorority housing available. $300 partly refundable deposit, deadline 5/25. Theme program housing. **Activities:** Bands, choral groups, dance, drama, film society, literary magazine, music ensembles, musical theater, radio station, student government, student newspaper, symphony orchestra, TV station, Asian American Christian fellowship, black recruitment and retention center, hiking and outdoor society, Americorps, forensics, Chabad, lesbian and gay alliance, Raza recruitment and retention center, College Democrats, College Republicans.

**Athletics.** NCAA. **Intercollegiate:** Baseball M, basketball, cross-country, diving, field hockey W, football (tackle) M, golf, gymnastics, lacrosse W, rowing (crew), rugby M, soccer, softball W, swimming, tennis, track and field, volleyball W, water polo. **Intramural:** Basketball, bowling, fencing, field hockey M, football (tackle), handball, ice hockey, lacrosse, racquetball, rowing (crew), sailing, skiing, soccer, softball, squash, tennis, volleyball M. **Team name:** Bears.

**Student services.** Adult student services, alcohol/substance abuse counseling, campus ministries, career counseling, services for economically disadvantaged, student employment services, financial aid counseling, health

services, legal services, minority student services, on-campus daycare, personal counseling, placement for graduates, veterans' counselor, women's services. **Physically disabled:** Services for visually, speech, hearing impaired.

**Contact.** Phone: (510) 642-3175
Walter Robinson, Director Undergraduate Admissions, University of California: Berkeley, 110 Sproul Hall, #5800, Berkeley, CA 94720-5800

## University of California: Davis
**Davis, California**                          **CB member**
**www.ucdavis.edu**                            **CB code: 4834**

- Public 4-year university
- Residential campus in small city
- 23,373 degree-seeking undergraduates: 1% part-time, 56% women, 3% African American, 41% Asian American, 12% Hispanic American, 1% Native American, 2% international
- 6,297 degree-seeking graduate students
- 59% of applicants admitted
- SAT or ACT with writing, SAT Subject Tests, application essay required
- 79% graduate within 6 years

**General.** Founded in 1905. Regionally accredited. **Degrees:** 6,015 bachelor's awarded; master's, doctoral, first professional offered. **ROTC:** Army, Naval, Air Force. **Location:** 15 miles from Sacramento, 72 miles from San Francisco. **Calendar:** Quarter, extensive summer session. **Full-time faculty:** 1,600 total. **Part-time faculty:** 300 total. **Class size:** 35% < 20, 33% 20-39, 5% 40-49, 14% 50-99, 13% >100. **Special facilities:** 150-acre arboretum, equestrian center, craft center, marine laboratory, nuclear laboratory, California Regional Primate Research Center, natural reserves, raptor center.

**Freshman class profile.** 35,148 applied, 20,598 admitted, 4,955 enrolled.

| Mid 50% test scores | | Rank in top quarter: | 100% |
|---|---|---|---|
| SAT critical reading: | 490-630 | Rank in top tenth: | 95% |
| SAT math: | 540-660 | Return as sophomores: | 90% |
| SAT writing: | 500-630 | Out-of-state: | 3% |
| GPA 3.50 or higher: | 79% | Live on campus: | 89% |
| GPA 3.0-3.49: | 19% | International: | 2% |
| GPA 2.0-2.99: | 2% | | |

**Basis for selection.** Scholastic achievement most important, followed by school and community activities, academic interests, special circumstances, special achievements and awards. Two SAT Subject Tests in two different subject areas of student's choice required: history/social science, English literature, mathematics (Level 2), laboratory science or language other than English.

**High school preparation.** 15 units required; 18 recommended. Required and recommended units include English 4, mathematics 3-4, social studies 2, science 2-3 (laboratory 2-3), foreign language 2-3, visual/performing arts 1 and academic electives 1. History/social science (social studies above) requirement is one year of U.S. history, or one-half year of U.S. history and one-half year of civics or U.S. government; and one year of world history, cultures and geography. For academic elective ("g" requirement): two semesters chosen from the following areas: visual and performing arts (non-introductory-level courses), history, social science, English, advanced mathematics, laboratory science and language other than English.

**2007-2008 Annual costs.** Tuition/fees: $8,109; $27,729 out-of-state. Students must purchase the Student Health Insurance Plan (SHIP) unless they are able to prove comparable coverage. Room/board: $11,533. Books/supplies: $1,508. Personal expenses: $1,277.

**2006-2007 Financial aid.** All financial aid based on need. 3,289 full-time freshmen applied for aid; 2,263 were judged to have need; 2,129 of these received aid. Average need met was 76%. Average scholarship/grant was $11,037; average loan $4,532. 74% of total undergraduate aid awarded as scholarships/grants, 26% as loans/jobs.

**Application procedures. Admission:** Closing date 11/30. $60 fee, may be waived for applicants with need. Application may be submitted online. Admission notification 3/15. Must reply by 5/1. **Financial aid:** Priority date 3/2; no closing date. FAFSA required. Applicants notified on a rolling basis starting 3/15.

**Academics.** Seventy percent of undergraduates participate in full- and part-time internships. **Special study options:** Accelerated study, cross-registration, double major, dual enrollment of high school students, ESL,

honors, independent study, internships, student-designed major, study abroad, teacher certification program, Washington semester. **Credit/placement by examination:** AP, CLEP. 10 credit hours maximum toward bachelor's degree. **Support services:** Learning center, pre-admission summer program, reduced course load, remedial instruction, study skills assistance, tutoring, writing center.

**Majors. Agriculture:** Agronomy, animal sciences, food science, international, range science, soil science. **Architecture:** Landscape, urban/community planning. **Area/ethnic studies:** African, African-American, American, Asian-American, East Asian, Hispanic-American/Latino/Chicano, Native American, women's. **Biology:** General, biotechnology, botany, cell/histology, entomology, environmental toxicology, exercise physiology, genetics, microbiology, molecular biochemistry, neurobiology/microbiology, zoology. **Communications:** General. **Computer sciences:** Computer science. **Conservation:** General, environmental studies, urban forestry. **Engineering:** Aerospace, biomedical, chemical, civil, computer, electrical, materials, mechanical. **Engineering technology:** Laser/optical. **English:** English lit. **Family/consumer sciences:** Clothing/textiles, family studies. **Foreign languages:** Chinese, comparative lit, French, German, Italian, Japanese, linguistics, Russian, Spanish. **History:** General. **Interdisciplinary:** Classical/archaeology, medieval/Renaissance, natural sciences, nutrition sciences, science/society. **Math:** General, applied, computational, statistics. **Philosophy/religion:** Philosophy, religion. **Physical sciences:** Applied physics, atmospheric science, chemistry, geology, hydrology, physics. **Psychology:** General. **Social sciences:** Anthropology, economics, international relations, political science, sociology. **Visual/performing arts:** Art history/conservation, design, dramatic, film/cinema, studio arts. **Other:** Avian sciences, Computational applied science, Evolution, ecology and biodiversity, Technocultural studies, Wildlife, fish and conservation biology.

**Most popular majors.** Agriculture 7%, biology 19%, engineering/engineering technologies 9%, psychology 10%, social sciences 20%.

**Computing on campus.** 544 workstations in dormitories, library, computer center. Dormitories wired for high-speed internet access and linked to campus network. Commuter students can connect to campus network. On-line course registration, online library, helpline, repair service, wireless network available.

**Student life. Freshman orientation:** Available, $215 fee. Preregistration for classes offered. Summer advising June-August. **Housing:** Coed dorms, single-sex dorms, special housing for disabled, apartments, cooperative housing, substance-free housing available. $450 fully refundable deposit, deadline 6/9. Academic theme, special interest and wellness housing available. **Activities:** Bands, campus ministries, choral groups, dance, drama, film society, international student organizations, literary magazine, music ensembles, musical theater, radio station, student government, student newspaper, symphony orchestra, TV station, 316 student organizations.

**Athletics.** NCAA. **Intercollegiate:** Baseball M, basketball, cross-country, diving, football (tackle) M, golf, gymnastics W, lacrosse, rowing (crew) W, soccer, softball W, swimming, tennis, track and field, volleyball, water polo, wrestling M. **Intramural:** Badminton, basketball, bowling, golf, racquetball, soccer, softball, squash, table tennis, tennis, volleyball, water polo. **Team name:** Aggies.

**Student services.** Adult student services, alcohol/substance abuse counseling, campus ministries, career counseling, services for economically disadvantaged, student employment services, financial aid counseling, health services, legal services, minority student services, on-campus daycare, personal counseling, placement for graduates, veterans' counselor, women's services. **Physically disabled:** Services for visually, speech, hearing impaired. **Learning disabled:** Comprehensive services available.

**Contact.** E-mail: undergraduateadmissions@ucdavis.edu
Phone: (530) 752-2971 Fax: (530) 752-1280
Pamela Burnett, Director of Undergraduate Admissions, University of California: Davis, 178 Mrak Hall, Davis, CA 95616

## University of California: Irvine
**Irvine, California**                          **CB member**
**www.uci.edu**                                **CB code: 4859**

- Public 4-year university
- Residential campus in small city
- 21,696 degree-seeking undergraduates: 2% part-time, 52% women, 2% African American, 51% Asian American, 12% Hispanic American, 3% international
- 4,629 degree-seeking graduate students
- 56% of applicants admitted
- SAT and SAT Subject Tests or ACT with writing, application essay required
- 79% graduate within 6 years

**General.** Founded in 1965. Regionally accredited. **Degrees:** 5,514 bachelor's awarded; master's, doctoral, first professional offered. **ROTC:** Army, Air Force. **Location:** 40 miles from Los Angeles. **Calendar:** Quarter, extensive summer session. **Full-time faculty:** 1,447 total; 91% have terminal degrees, 29% minority, 33% women. **Part-time faculty:** 521 total; 70% have terminal degrees, 25% minority, 44% women. **Class size:** 40% < 20, 35% 20-39, 3% 40-49, 9% 50-99, 12% >100. **Special facilities:** Outdoor laboratory, ecological preserve, freshwater marsh reserve, arboretum, center for art and technology, observatory.

**Freshman class profile.** 39,956 applied, 22,220 admitted, 4,931 enrolled.

| Mid 50% test scores | | Rank in top tenth: | 96% |
|---|---|---|---|
| SAT critical reading: | 510-630 | End year in good standing: | 91% |
| SAT math: | 560-670 | Return as sophomores: | 94% |
| SAT writing: | 520-630 | Out-of-state: | 3% |
| GPA 3.50 or higher: | 94% | Live on campus: | 80% |
| GPA 3.0-3.49: | 5% | International: | 2% |
| GPA 2.0-2.99: | 1% | Fraternities: | 5% |
| Rank in top quarter: | 100% | Sororities: | 7% |

**Basis for selection.** Demonstrated record of academic preparation, educational engagement, talent and skills important. Two SAT Subject Tests required: math and student's choice.

**High school preparation.** 15 units required; 18 recommended. Required and recommended units include English 4, mathematics 3-4, history 2, science 2-3 (laboratory 2-3), foreign language 2-3, visual/performing arts 1 and academic electives 1.

**2007-2008 Annual costs.** Tuition/fees: $7,555; $27,175 out-of-state. Room/board: $10,266. Books/supplies: $1,564. Personal expenses: $1,508.

**2006-2007 Financial aid. Need-based:** 3,603 full-time freshmen applied for aid; 2,308 were judged to have need; 2,114 of these received aid. Average need met was 83%. Average scholarship/grant was $10,038; average loan $5,458. 75% of total undergraduate aid awarded as scholarships/grants, 25% as loans/jobs. **Non-need-based:** Awarded to 1,129 full-time undergraduates, including 218 freshmen. Scholarships awarded for academics, alumni affiliation, art, athletics, music/drama, state residency.

**Application procedures. Admission:** Closing date 11/30. $60 fee, may be waived for applicants with need. Application must be submitted online. Admission notification 3/31. Must reply by 5/1. **Financial aid:** Closing date 3/2. FAFSA required. Applicants notified by 4/1; must reply by 5/1.

**Academics. Special study options:** Accelerated study, combined bachelor's/graduate degree, distance learning, double major, dual enrollment of high school students, ESL, honors, independent study, internships, liberal arts/career combination, semester at sea, study abroad, teacher certification program, Washington semester. **Credit/placement by examination:** AP, CLEP, IB, institutional tests. **Support services:** Learning center, pre-admission summer program, reduced course load, remedial instruction, study skills assistance, tutoring, writing center.

**Majors. Architecture:** Environmental design. **Area/ethnic studies:** African-American, Asian-American, East Asian, European, German, Hispanic-American/Latino/Chicano, women's. **Biology:** General, Biochemistry/biophysics and molecular biology, botany, cell/histology, ecology, genetics. **Communications:** Journalism. **Computer sciences:** General, computer science, information systems. **Engineering:** General, aerospace, biomedical, chemical, civil, computer, electrical, environmental, materials, mechanical. **English:** English lit. **Foreign languages:** Chinese, classics, comparative lit, French, German, Japanese, linguistics, Russian, Spanish. **Health:** Nursing (RN). **History:** General. **Interdisciplinary:** Classical/archaeology, global studies, neuroscience. **Liberal arts:** Humanities. **Math:** General, statistics. **Philosophy/religion:** Philosophy. **Physical sciences:** Chemistry, geology, physics. **Psychology:** General. **Social sciences:** General, anthropology, criminology, economics, political science, sociology. **Visual/performing arts:** Art, art history/conservation, dance, dramatic, film/cinema, music performance, studio arts.

**Most popular majors.** Biology 15%, engineering/engineering technologies 9%, interdisciplinary studies 8%, psychology 12%, social sciences 28%, visual/performing arts 6%.

**Computing on campus.** 1,500 workstations in dormitories, library, computer center, student center. Dormitories wired for high-speed internet access and linked to campus network. Commuter students can connect to campus network. Online course registration, online library, helpline, repair service, student web hosting, wireless network available.

**Student life. Freshman orientation:** Available. Preregistration for classes offered. One or three-day program held during summer. **Housing:** Guaranteed on-campus for freshmen. Coed dorms, single-sex dorms, special housing for disabled, apartments, cooperative housing, fraternity/sorority housing, substance-free housing available. $350 partly refundable deposit. Academic themed houses available. **Activities:** Bands, choral groups, dance, drama, film society, literary magazine, music ensembles, musical theater, opera, radio station, student government, student newspaper, symphony orchestra.

**Athletics.** NCAA. **Intercollegiate:** Baseball M, basketball, cheerleading, cross-country, diving, golf, rowing (crew), sailing, soccer, swimming, tennis, track and field, volleyball, water polo. **Intramural:** Badminton, basketball, bowling, football (non-tackle), golf, racquetball, soccer, softball, swimming, table tennis, tennis, track and field, volleyball, water polo, wrestling. **Team name:** Anteaters.

**Contact.** E-mail: admissions@uci.edu
Phone: (949) 824-6703 Fax: (949) 824-2711
Marguerite Bonous-Hammarth, Director of Admissions, University of California: Irvine, 204 Aldrich Hall, Irvine, CA 92697-1075

## University of California: Los Angeles
**Los Angeles, California**    CB member
www.ucla.edu    CB code: 4837

- Public 4-year university
- Residential campus in very large city
- 25,928 degree-seeking undergraduates: 4% part-time, 55% women, 3% African American, 38% Asian American, 15% Hispanic American, 4% international
- 11,548 degree-seeking graduate students
- 24% of applicants admitted
- SAT or ACT with writing, SAT Subject Tests, application essay required
- 90% graduate within 6 years

**General.** Founded in 1919. Regionally accredited. **Degrees:** 6,990 bachelor's awarded; master's, doctoral, first professional offered. **ROTC:** Army, Naval, Air Force. **Calendar:** Quarter, extensive summer session. **Full-time faculty:** 1,948 total; 98% have terminal degrees, 23% minority, 31% women. **Part-time faculty:** 706 total; 98% have terminal degrees, 24% minority, 43% women. **Class size:** 54% < 20, 22% 20-39, 4% 40-49, 9% 50-99, 10% >100. **Special facilities:** Museums with specialized collections, centers for cancer research, plasma physics research labs, film and television archive, high power auroral simulation observatory, lab for embedded collaborative systems, research centers for molecular and neuroscience, graphic and animation labs, nanoscience research labs and centers, cell mimetic space exploration center, particle beam physics lab, southern California particle center, ranch for ecological studies, ethnomusicology archive.

**Freshman class profile.** 50,755 applied, 11,963 admitted, 4,564 enrolled.

| Mid 50% test scores | | Rank in top quarter: | 100% |
|---|---|---|---|
| SAT critical reading: | 570-690 | Rank in top tenth: | 97% |
| SAT math: | 610-740 | Return as sophomores: | 97% |
| SAT writing: | 580-700 | Out-of-state: | 6% |
| ACT composite: | 24-31 | Live on campus: | 92% |
| GPA 3.50 or higher: | 97% | International: | 3% |
| GPA 3.0-3.49: | 2% | Fraternities: | 11% |
| GPA 2.0-2.99: | 1% | Sororities: | 11% |

**Basis for selection.** GPA, test scores, course work, number of and performance in honors and AP courses most important. Essay considered. Strong senior program important. Extracurricular activities, honors and awards also reviewed. All applicants must take the ACT Plus Writing or the SAT Reasoning Test. In addition, all applicants must take two SAT Subject Tests in two different subject areas. (If a Math SAT Subject Test is chosen by the applicant, he/she must take the Math Level II exam.). Audition required of music, dance, theater majors. Portfolio required of art majors.

**High school preparation.** 15 units required; 18 recommended. Required and recommended units include English 4, mathematics 3-4, history 2, science 2-3 (laboratory 2-3), foreign language 2-3, visual/performing arts 1 and academic electives 1. History is 2 units in history/social science.

**2007-2008 Annual costs.** Tuition/fees: $7,038; $26,658 out-of-state. Room/board: $12,420. Books/supplies: $1,515. Personal expenses: $2,145.

**2006-2007 Financial aid. Need-based:** 2,722 full-time freshmen applied for aid; 2,228 were judged to have need; 2,228 of these received aid. Average need met was 81%. Average scholarship/grant was $12,276; average loan $5,222. 71% of total undergraduate aid awarded as scholarships/grants, 29% as loans/jobs. **Non-need-based:** Awarded to 1,510 full-time undergraduates, including 405 freshmen. Scholarships awarded for academics, alumni affiliation, athletics, ROTC.

**Application procedures. Admission:** Closing date 11/30 (postmark date). $60 fee, may be waived for applicants with need. Application may be submitted online. Admission notification on a rolling basis beginning on or about 3/15. Must reply by May 1 or within 3 week(s) if notified thereafter. **Financial aid:** Priority date 3/2; no closing date. FAFSA required. Applicants notified by 3/15; Applicants notified on a rolling basis starting 3/15; must reply within 3 week(s) of notification.

**Academics. Special study options:** Distance learning, double major, ESL, honors, independent study, internships, liberal arts/career combination, student-designed major, study abroad, Washington semester. **Credit/placement by examination:** AP, CLEP, IB, SAT, institutional tests. **Support services:** Learning center, study skills assistance, tutoring, writing center.

**Majors. Area/ethnic studies:** African-American, Asian, Asian-American, Central/Eastern European, East Asian, European, Hispanic-American/Latino/Chicano, Latin American, Native American, Near/Middle Eastern, Russian/Slavic, Southeast Asian, women's. **Biology:** General, bacteriology, biochemistry, biophysics, biotechnology, botany, cellular/molecular, ecology, immunology, marine, molecular genetics, physiology, systematic. **Business:** Managerial economics. **Computer sciences:** General. **Conservation:** Environmental studies. **Engineering:** Aerospace, agricultural, chemical, civil, computer, electrical, geological, materials, mechanical. **English:** American lit, English lit. **Foreign languages:** African, ancient Greek, Arabic, Chinese, comparative lit, East Asian, French, German, Hebrew, Italian, Japanese, Korean, Latin, linguistics, Portuguese, Romance, Russian, Scandinavian, Slavic, Spanish. **History:** General. **Interdisciplinary:** Classical/archaeology, cognitive science, global studies, neuroscience. **Liberal arts:** Arts/sciences. **Math:** General, applied, computational, statistics. **Philosophy/religion:** Philosophy, religion. **Physical sciences:** Astrophysics, chemistry, geology, geophysics, physics. **Psychology:** General, psychobiology. **Social sciences:** Anthropology, economics, geography, international economic development, international economics, political science, sociology. **Visual/performing arts:** Art, art history/conservation, design, dramatic, film/cinema, music history, musicology.

**Most popular majors.** Biology 14%, engineering/engineering technologies 7%, English 6%, history 8%, psychology 13%, social sciences 26%, visual/performing arts 6%.

**Computing on campus.** Dormitories wired for high-speed internet access and linked to campus network. Commuter students can connect to campus network. Online course registration, online library, helpline, repair service, student web hosting, wireless network available.

**Student life. Freshman orientation:** Available, $340 fee. Preregistration for classes offered. 3-day, 2-night program. **Housing:** Guaranteed on-campus for freshmen. Coed dorms, apartments, cooperative housing, fraternity/sorority housing available. Theme housing available. **Activities:** Bands, campus ministries, choral groups, dance, drama, film society, international student organizations, literary magazine, music ensembles, Model UN, musical theater, opera, radio station, student government, student newspaper, symphony orchestra, TV station.

**Athletics.** NCAA. **Intercollegiate:** Baseball M, basketball, cross-country, diving W, football (tackle) M, golf, gymnastics W, rowing (crew) W, soccer, softball W, swimming W, tennis, track and field, volleyball, water polo. **Intramural:** Badminton, basketball, cross-country, field hockey W, golf, gymnastics, ice hockey, lacrosse, rowing (crew), rugby, sailing, skiing, soccer, softball, squash, swimming, table tennis, tennis, track and field, volleyball, water polo. **Team name:** Bruins.

**Student services.** Alcohol/substance abuse counseling, campus ministries, career counseling, services for economically disadvantaged, student employment services, financial aid counseling, health services, legal services, minority student services, on-campus daycare, personal counseling, placement for graduates, veterans' counselor, women's services. **Physically disabled:** Services for visually, hearing impaired.

**Contact.** E-mail: ugadm@saonet.ucla.edu
Phone: (310) 825-3101 Fax: (310) 206-1206
Vu Tran, Director of Undergraduate Admissions and Relations with Schools, University of California: Los Angeles, 1147 Murphy Hall, Los Angeles, CA 90095-1436

## University of California: Merced
Merced, California
www.ucmerced.edu                           CB code: 4129

- Public 4-year university
- Residential campus in small city
- 1,750 degree-seeking undergraduates: 48% women, 6% African American, 33% Asian American, 29% Hispanic American, 1% Native American, 1% international

- 121 degree-seeking graduate students
- 90% of applicants admitted
- SAT or ACT with writing, SAT Subject Tests, application essay required

**General. Degrees:** 55 bachelor's awarded; master's, doctoral offered. **Location:** 120 miles from San Francisco, 60 miles from Fresno. **Calendar:** Semester, limited summer session. **Full-time faculty:** 118 total; 84% have terminal degrees, 25% minority, 34% women. **Part-time faculty:** 30 total; 43% have terminal degrees, 23% minority, 47% women. **Class size:** 40% < 20, 30% 20-39, 6% 40-49, 15% 50-99, 9% >100. **Special facilities:** Sierra Nevada research institute, research station at Yosemite National Park, Biomedical Sciences research institute, Center for Computational Biology, energy research center.

**Freshman class profile.** 15,094 applied, 13,510 admitted, 669 enrolled.

| Mid 50% test scores | | | |
|---|---|---|---|
| SAT critical reading: | 440-570 | GPA 2.0-2.99: | 7% |
| SAT math: | 480-610 | Rank in top quarter: | 100% |
| SAT writing: | 440-570 | End year in good standing: | 81% |
| GPA 3.50 or higher: | 47% | Return as sophomores: | 80% |
| GPA 3.0-3.49: | 46% | Live on campus: | 85% |
| | | International: | 1% |

**Basis for selection.** Academic record and test scores determine eligibility. **Homeschooled:** If school is not accredited by a regional association, student must meet eligibility by examination alone.

**High school preparation.** 15 units required; 18 recommended. Required and recommended units include English 4, mathematics 3-4, history 2, science 2-3 (laboratory 2-3), foreign language 2-3, visual/performing arts 1 and academic electives 1. History is 2 units in history/social science.

**2007-2008 Annual costs.** Tuition/fees: $7,148; $26,768 out-of-state. Room/board: $10,714. Books/supplies: $1,474. Personal expenses: $1,277.

**Financial aid. Non-need-based:** Scholarships awarded for academics.

**Application procedures. Admission:** Priority date 11/30; deadline 11/30 (postmark date). $60 fee, may be waived for applicants with need. Application may be submitted online. Admission notification 3/31. Must reply by May 1 or within 3 week(s) if notified thereafter. **Financial aid:** Priority date 3/2; no closing date. FAFSA required. Applicants notified on a rolling basis starting 3/2.

**Academics. Special study options:** Accelerated study, distance learning, double major, independent study, internships, study abroad, teacher certification program, Washington semester. Research opportunities and internships at Lawrence Livermore National Laboratories and Yosemite National Park. **Credit/placement by examination:** AP, CLEP, IB, institutional tests. Credit by examination with the approval of the instructor giving the examination and the dean of the school involved. Some courses may not be deemed appropriate for obtaining credit by examination. **Support services:** Learning center, study skills assistance, tutoring, writing center.

**Majors. Biology:** General, molecular. **Business:** Management science. **Engineering:** Biomedical, computer, environmental, materials, mechanical. **English:** English lit. **History:** General. **Interdisciplinary:** Behavioral sciences, intercultural. **Math:** General, applied. **Physical sciences:** Chemistry, geology, physics. **Psychology:** General, cognitive. **Public administration:** Policy analysis. **Social sciences:** Economics. **Other:** World Cultures and History.

**Most popular majors.** Biology 31%, engineering/engineering technologies 13%, psychology 40%.

**Computing on campus.** 62 workstations in dormitories, library, computer center. Dormitories wired for high-speed internet access and linked to campus network. Commuter students can connect to campus network. Online course registration, online library, helpline, wireless network available.

**Student life. Freshman orientation:** Available, $49 fee. Preregistration for classes offered. **Housing:** Coed dorms, special housing for disabled, substance-free housing available. $300 partly refundable deposit, deadline 5/31. **Activities:** Marching band, choral groups, dance, film society, student government, student newspaper, African American student union, liberal activism club, student government advisory committee, Latino students alliance, Filipino student alliance, Circle K International, American Red Cross club, Jewish student union.

**Athletics. Intramural:** Basketball, football (non-tackle), racquetball, soccer, softball, tennis, volleyball. **Team name:** Golden Bobcats.

**Student services.** Alcohol/substance abuse counseling, career counseling, services for economically disadvantaged, student employment services, financial aid counseling, health services, minority student services, personal counseling, veterans' counselor, women's services. **Physically disabled:** Services for visually, hearing impaired. **Learning disabled:** Comprehensive services available.

**Contact.** E-mail: admissions@ucmerced.edu
Phone: (209) 228-4682 Toll-free number: (866) 270-7301
Fax: (209) 228-4244
Encarnacion Ruiz, Director, Admissions and Relations with Schools & Colleges, University of California: Merced, 5200 North Lake Road, Merced, CA 95343-5603

## University of California: Riverside

**Riverside, California**      **CB member**
**www.ucr.edu**      **CB code: 4839**

- Public 4-year university
- Residential campus in large city
- 14,973 degree-seeking undergraduates: 3% part-time, 52% women, 7% African American, 42% Asian American, 26% Hispanic American, 2% international
- 2,146 degree-seeking graduate students
- 87% of applicants admitted
- SAT or ACT with writing, SAT Subject Tests, application essay required
- 64% graduate within 6 years

**General.** Founded in 1954. Regionally accredited. **Degrees:** 3,337 bachelor's awarded; master's, doctoral offered. **ROTC:** Army, Air Force. **Location:** 60 miles from Los Angeles. **Calendar:** Quarter, limited summer session. **Full-time faculty:** 756 total; 98% have terminal degrees, 27% minority, 32% women. **Part-time faculty:** 159 total; 98% have terminal degrees, 24% minority, 49% women. **Class size:** 37% < 20, 38% 20-39, 3% 40-49, 11% 50-99, 11% >100. **Special facilities:** Botanical gardens, air pollution research center, photography museum, 8 nature preserves, citrus research center and agricultural experiment station, institute of geophysics and planetary physics, water resources center, salinity lab.

**Freshman class profile.** 26,866 applied, 23,307 admitted, 3,729 enrolled.

| Mid 50% test scores | | | |
|---|---|---|---|
| SAT critical reading: | 450-560 | GPA 2.0-2.99: | 10% |
| SAT math: | 470-610 | Rank in top quarter: | 100% |
| SAT writing: | 450-560 | Rank in top tenth: | 94% |
| ACT composite: | 18-23 | Return as sophomores: | 83% |
| GPA 3.50 or higher: | 38% | Live on campus: | 71% |
| GPA 3.0-3.49: | 52% | International: | 2% |

**Basis for selection.** Secondary school record, standardized test scores, and completed UC application with essay are used to determine UC eligibility and selection. Freshmen applicants must submit SAT reasoning or ACT plus writing exam. SAT Subject Tests required from 2 different subject areas. Math Subject Test must be Level 2. Portfolio required for home schooled applicants. **Homeschooled:** Transcript of courses and grades required. Portfolio describing subjects studied and methods of study required.

**High school preparation.** 15 units required; 18 recommended. Required and recommended units include English 4, mathematics 3-4, history 2, science 2-3 (laboratory 2-3), foreign language 2-3, visual/performing arts 1 and academic electives 1. One year of elective units from 1 of the following: visual/performing arts (non-introductory), history, English, advanced mathematics, laboratory science, foreign language, social science, arts. 2 social science units must include 1 U.S. history or .5 history and .5 civics, and 1 world history, cultures, or geography.

**2007-2008 Annual costs.** Tuition/fees: $7,355; $26,975 out-of-state. Room/board: $10,800. Books/supplies: $1,700. Personal expenses: $1,700.

**2007-2008 Financial aid. Need-based:** 2,978 full-time freshmen applied for aid; 2,395 were judged to have need; 2,321 of these received aid. Average need met was 88%. Average scholarship/grant was $11,857; average loan $4,889. 70% of total undergraduate aid awarded as scholarships/grants, 30% as loans/jobs. **Non-need-based:** Awarded to 373 full-time undergraduates, including 114 freshmen. Scholarships awarded for academics, alumni affiliation, art, athletics, job skills, leadership, music/drama, religious affiliation, state residency.

**Application procedures. Admission:** Closing date 11/30 (postmark date). $60 fee ($70 out-of-state), may be waived for applicants with need. Application may be submitted online. Admission notification on a rolling basis beginning on or about 2/1. Must reply by May 1 or within 3 week(s) if

notified thereafter. **Financial aid:** Closing date 3/2. FAFSA required. Applicants notified on a rolling basis starting 3/1; must reply by 5/1 or within 3 week(s) of notification.

**Academics. Special study options:** Accelerated study, cooperative education, cross-registration, double major, dual enrollment of high school students, ESL, honors, independent study, internships, liberal arts/career combination, student-designed major, study abroad, teacher certification program, Washington semester. **Credit/placement by examination:** AP, CLEP, IB, SAT, ACT, institutional tests. **Support services:** Learning center, pre-admission summer program, reduced course load, study skills assistance, tutoring, writing center.

**Majors. Area/ethnic studies:** African-American, Asian, Asian-American, German, Hispanic-American/Latino/Chicano, Latin American, Native American, Russian/Slavic, women's. **Biology:** General, biochemistry, botany, entomology. **Business:** Business admin, managerial economics. **Computer sciences:** Computer science, information systems. **Conservation:** Environmental science. **Engineering:** Biomedical, chemical, computer, electrical, environmental, materials science, mechanical. **English:** Creative writing, English lit. **Foreign languages:** General, classics, comparative lit, French, linguistics, Spanish. **History:** General. **Interdisciplinary:** Global studies, neuroscience. **Legal studies:** General. **Liberal arts:** Arts/sciences, humanities. **Math:** General, applied, statistics. **Philosophy/religion:** Philosophy, religion. **Physical sciences:** General, chemistry, geology, geophysics, physics. **Psychology:** General. **Public administration:** General, policy analysis. **Social sciences:** Anthropology, economics, international relations, political science, sociology. **Visual/performing arts:** Art, art history/conservation, dance, dramatic, film/cinema, studio arts. **Other:** Asian Literatures & Cultures, Ethnic studies, History/Law and Society, Multi-/Interdisciplindary Studies, Music and culture, Philosophy/Law and Society, Psychology/Law and Society, Sociology/Law and Society.

**Most popular majors.** Biology 12%, business/marketing 22%, liberal arts 7%, psychology 9%, social sciences 19%.

**Computing on campus.** 1,001 workstations in dormitories, library, computer center, student center. Dormitories wired for high-speed internet access and linked to campus network. Commuter students can connect to campus network. Online course registration, online library, helpline, repair service, student web hosting, wireless network available.

**Student life. Freshman orientation:** Available. 2-day or 1-day summer programs. **Housing:** Guaranteed on-campus for freshmen. Coed dorms, special housing for disabled, apartments available. $250 deposit, deadline 6/1. Theme hall communities available. **Activities:** Bands, choral groups, dance, drama, film society, literary magazine, music ensembles, musical theater, radio station, student government, student newspaper, 250 clubs and organizations available.

**Athletics.** NCAA. **Intercollegiate:** Baseball M, basketball, cross-country, golf, soccer, softball W, tennis, track and field, volleyball W. **Intramural:** Badminton, basketball, bowling, football (non-tackle), golf, racquetball, soccer, softball, squash, table tennis, tennis, volleyball. **Team name:** Highlanders.

**Student services.** Adult student services, alcohol/substance abuse counseling, career counseling, student employment services, financial aid counseling, health services, minority student services, on-campus daycare, personal counseling, placement for graduates, veterans' counselor, women's services. **Physically disabled:** Services for visually, speech, hearing impaired.

**Contact.** E-mail: discover@ucr.edu
Phone: (951) 827-3411 Fax: (951) 827-6344
Merlyn Campos, Associate Director of Undergraduate Admissions, University of California: Riverside, Admissions Office, Riverside, CA 92521

## University of California: San Diego

**La Jolla, California**      **CB member**
**www.ucsd.edu**      **CB code: 4836**

- Public 4-year university
- Residential campus in large town
- 22,048 degree-seeking undergraduates: 52% women
- 5,751 graduate students
- 43% of applicants admitted
- SAT or ACT with writing, SAT Subject Tests, application essay required

**General.** Founded in 1959. Regionally accredited. Includes 6 small undergraduate cluster colleges, each with different housing and general education requirements. **Degrees:** 5,200 bachelor's awarded; master's, doctoral, first professional offered. **Location:** 12 miles from San Diego. **Calendar:** Quarter, extensive summer session. **Full-time faculty:** 1,085 total; 87% have terminal degrees, 20% minority, 21% women. **Part-time faculty:** 184 total; 98% have terminal degrees, 43% women. **Class size:** 47% < 20, 21% 20-39, 5% 40-49, 10% 50-99, 18% >100. **Special facilities:** Aquarium, performing arts centers, student-run co-ops, supercomputer center, nature preserves, electron beam lithography facility, center for music experiment, structural engineering lab.

**Freshman class profile.** 44,959 applied, 19,178 admitted, 4,140 enrolled.

| Mid 50% test scores | | | |
|---|---|---|---|
| SAT critical reading: | 580-700 | Rank in top quarter: | 100% |
| SAT math: | 620-730 | Rank in top tenth: | 99% |
| SAT writing: | 580-700 | Out-of-state: | 3% |
| ACT composite: | 25-31 | Live on campus: | 92% |
| GPA 3.50 or higher: | 96% | Fraternities: | 10% |
| GPA 3.0-3.49: | 4% | Sororities: | 10% |

**Basis for selection.** High school course pattern, GPA, essay and test scores most important. Admission for out-of-state applicants more selective than for residents. All applicants must take 2 SAT Subject Tests in different subject areas. If Math SAT Subject Test is taken, must be Level 2. Interview recommended for music, visual arts, theater majors. Audition recommended for music majors. Portfolio recommended for art majors.

**High school preparation.** 15 units required; 18 recommended. Required and recommended units include English 4, mathematics 3-4, history 2, science 2-3 (laboratory 2-3), foreign language 2-3, visual/performing arts 1 and academic electives 1. History is 2 units in history/social science.

**2007-2008 Annual costs.** Tuition/fees: $7,435; $27,019 out-of-state. Room/board: $10,237. Books/supplies: $1,487. Personal expenses: $1,447.

**2006-2007 Financial aid. Need-based:** 3,264 full-time freshmen applied for aid; 2,246 were judged to have need; 2,113 of these received aid. Average need met was 82%. Average scholarship/grant was $10,233; average loan $4,273. 69% of total undergraduate aid awarded as scholarships/grants, 31% as loans/jobs. **Non-need-based:** Awarded to 700 full-time undergraduates, including 129 freshmen. Scholarships awarded for academics, art, leadership, music/drama.

**Application procedures. Admission:** Closing date 11/30 (receipt date). $60 fee, may be waived for applicants with need. Application must be submitted online. Admission notification 3/31. Must reply by 5/1. **Financial aid:** Priority date 3/2; no closing date. FAFSA required. Applicants notified on a rolling basis starting 3/15; must reply within 3 week(s) of notification.

**Academics. Special study options:** Combined bachelor's/graduate degree, double major, ESL, exchange student, honors, independent study, internships, student-designed major, study abroad, Washington semester. In-depth academic assignments working in small groups or one-to-one with faculty; research programs. **Credit/placement by examination:** AP, CLEP, IB, institutional tests. **Support services:** Learning center, pre-admission summer program, reduced course load, study skills assistance, tutoring, writing center.

**Majors. Architecture:** Urban/community planning. **Area/ethnic studies:** Chinese, German, Italian, Japanese, Latin American, Russian/Slavic, women's. **Biology:** General, animal physiology, bacteriology, biochemistry, bioinformatics, biophysics, biotechnology, cell/histology, ecology, evolutionary, molecular. **Business:** Management science. **Communications:** General, digital media. **Computer sciences:** General, computer science, information systems, systems analysis. **Conservation:** Environmental science, environmental studies. **Engineering:** Aerospace, biomedical, chemical, computer, electrical, mechanical, mechanics, physics, science, structural, systems. **Engineering technology:** Aerospace. **English:** American lit, British lit, composition, English lit. **Family/consumer sciences:** Family studies. **Foreign languages:** General, classics, French, German, Italian, Japanese, linguistics, Russian, Spanish. **History:** General. **Interdisciplinary:** Behavioral sciences, cognitive science, math/computer science, neuroscience. **Math:** General, applied. **Philosophy/religion:** Judaic, philosophy, religion. **Physical sciences:** Chemical physics, chemistry, molecular physics, physics, planetary. **Psychology:** General. **Public administration:** Policy analysis. **Social sciences:** Anthropology, archaeology, economics, political science, sociology, U.S. government, urban studies. **Visual/performing arts:** Art history/conservation, dance, dramatic, studio arts.

**Most popular majors.** Biology 18%, business/marketing 6%, engineering/engineering technologies 15%, psychology 8%, social sciences 20%.

**Computing on campus.** 1,500 workstations in library, computer center, student center. Dormitories wired for high-speed internet access and linked to campus network. Commuter students can connect to campus network. Online course registration, online library, helpline, student web hosting, wireless network available.

**Student life. Freshman orientation:** Mandatory, $125 fee. Preregistration for classes offered. One- to two-day program for freshmen and transfers. **Housing:** Guaranteed on-campus for freshmen. Coed dorms, special housing for disabled, apartments, substance-free housing available. $500 partly refundable deposit, deadline 6/29. Language, cultural interest and international houses available. **Activities:** Pep band, choral groups, dance, drama, film society, international student organizations, literary magazine, music ensembles, musical theater, radio station, student government, student newspaper, TV station, 450 student organizations.

**Athletics.** NCAA. **Intercollegiate:** Baseball M, basketball, cross-country, diving, fencing, golf M, rowing (crew), soccer, softball W, swimming, tennis, track and field, volleyball, water polo. **Intramural:** Basketball, soccer, softball, tennis. **Team name:** Tritons.

**Student services.** Alcohol/substance abuse counseling, career counseling, services for economically disadvantaged, student employment services, financial aid counseling, health services, legal services, minority student services, on-campus daycare, personal counseling, placement for graduates, veterans' counselor, women's services. **Physically disabled:** Services for visually, speech, hearing impaired. **Learning disabled:** Comprehensive services available.

**Contact.** E-mail: admissionsinfo@ucsd.edu
Phone: (858) 534-4831 Fax: (858) 534-5723
Mae Brown, Assistant Vice Chancellor and Director of Admissions / Admissions & Enrollment Services, University of California: San Diego, 9500 Gilman Drive, 0021, La Jolla, CA 92093-0021

## University of California: Santa Barbara

| Santa Barbara, California | CB member |
|---|---|
| www.ucsb.edu | CB code: 4835 |

- Public 4-year university
- Residential campus in small city
- 18,412 degree-seeking undergraduates: 2% part-time, 55% women, 3% African American, 16% Asian American, 19% Hispanic American, 1% Native American, 1% international
- 2,995 degree-seeking graduate students
- 54% of applicants admitted
- SAT and SAT Subject Tests or ACT with writing, application essay required
- 77% graduate within 6 years

**General.** Founded in 1909. Regionally accredited. **Degrees:** 5,442 bachelor's awarded; master's, doctoral offered. **ROTC:** Army. **Location:** 10 miles from downtown, 100 miles from Los Angeles. **Calendar:** Quarter, extensive summer session. **Full-time faculty:** 917 total. **Part-time faculty:** 150 total. **Class size:** 49% < 20, 29% 20-39, 5% 40-49, 9% 50-99, 8% >100. **Special facilities:** Several nature preserves with research facilities, seawater laboratories, robotics laboratory, free electron laser laboratory; institutes for polymers and organic solids, neuroscience research, quantum, nuclear particle astrophysics and cosmology, marine science, theoretical physics.

**Freshman class profile.** 40,933 applied, 22,273 admitted, 4,338 enrolled.

| Mid 50% test scores | | | |
|---|---|---|---|
| SAT critical reading: | 530-650 | Rank in top quarter: | 98% |
| SAT math: | 540-660 | Rank in top tenth: | 96% |
| SAT writing: | 530-650 | End year in good standing: | 88% |
| ACT composite: | 23-29 | Return as sophomores: | 91% |
| GPA 3.50 or higher: | 84% | Out-of-state: | 4% |
| GPA 3.0-3.49: | 16% | Live on campus: | 94% |
| | | International: | 1% |

**Basis for selection.** Eligibility established by high school GPA, course requirement, and SAT scores. Special consideration for disadvantaged students. All applicants must take 2 SAT Subject Tests in different subject areas. If Math SAT Subject Test is taken, must be Level 2. Audition required of music, dance, drama majors. Portfolio required of art majors.

**High school preparation.** Required and recommended units include English 4, mathematics 3-4, history 2, (laboratory 2-3), foreign language 2-3, visual/performing arts 1 and academic electives 1. 2 history/social science units required, including 1 U.S. history or 1/2 of U.S. history and 1/2 civics or American government and 1 world history, cultures, or geography.

**2007-2008 Annual costs.** Tuition/fees: $7,896; $27,516 out-of-state. Room/board: $11,946.

**2006-2007 Financial aid. Need-based:** 3,053 full-time freshmen applied for aid; 2,061 were judged to have need; 1,872 of these received aid. Average need met was 81.3%. Average scholarship/grant was $12,584; average loan $5,398. 72% of total undergraduate aid awarded as scholarships/

grants, 28% as loans/jobs. **Non-need-based:** Awarded to 611 full-time undergraduates, including 128 freshmen. Scholarships awarded for academics, athletics.

**Application procedures. Admission:** Closing date 11/30 (postmark date). $60 fee, may be waived for applicants with need. Application may be submitted online. Admission notification on a rolling basis beginning on or about 3/1. Must reply by 5/1. **Financial aid:** Priority date 3/2, closing date 5/31. FAFSA required. Applicants notified on a rolling basis starting 3/15; must reply within 2 week(s) of notification.

**Academics. Special study options:** Accelerated study, cross-registration, distance learning, double major, dual enrollment of high school students, ESL, exchange student, honors, independent study, internships, student-designed major, study abroad, teacher certification program, Washington semester. Graduate-level classes, off-campus study, freshman seminars, pre-professional programs and advising, academic minors, and undergraduate research, professional studies in school of environmental science and management and school of education. **Credit/placement by examination:** AP, CLEP, institutional tests. **Support services:** Learning center, pre-admission summer program, reduced course load, tutoring.

**Majors. Area/ethnic studies:** African-American, Asian, Hispanic-American/Latino/Chicano, Latin American, women's. **Biology:** General, aquatic, bacteriology, biochemistry, cell/histology, ecology, marine, molecular, pharmacology, zoology. **Business:** Managerial economics. **Communications:** General. **Computer sciences:** General. **Conservation:** Environmental studies. **Engineering:** Chemical, computer, electrical, mechanical. **English:** English lit. **Foreign languages:** Chinese, classics, comparative lit, French, German, Italian, Japanese, linguistics, Portuguese, Russian, Slavic, Spanish. **History:** General. **Interdisciplinary:** Biological/physical sciences, biopsychology, global studies, medieval/Renaissance. **Legal studies:** General. **Math:** General, statistics. **Philosophy/religion:** Philosophy, religion. **Physical sciences:** Chemistry, geology, geophysics, physics. **Psychology:** General. **Social sciences:** Anthropology, economics, geography, political science, sociology. **Visual/performing arts:** General, art, art history/conservation, cinematography, dance, dramatic, film/cinema, studio arts.

**Most popular majors.** Biology 8%, business/marketing 11%, communications/journalism 6%, interdisciplinary studies 8%, psychology 7%, social sciences 18%, visual/performing arts 7%.

**Computing on campus.** Dormitories wired for high-speed internet access.

**Student life. Freshman orientation:** Available. Preregistration for classes offered. Two-day program; includes sessions for parents. **Housing:** Guaranteed on-campus for freshmen. Coed dorms, special housing for disabled, apartments, cooperative housing, fraternity/sorority housing available. **Activities:** Bands, campus ministries, choral groups, dance, drama, film society, international student organizations, literary magazine, music ensembles, Model UN, musical theater, opera, radio station, student government, student newspaper, symphony orchestra, Hillel, Catholic student organization, Democratic and Republican student organizations, El Congreso, Persian student association, Habitat for Humanity.

**Athletics.** NCAA. **Intercollegiate:** Baseball M, basketball, cross-country, golf M, gymnastics, soccer, softball W, swimming, tennis, track and field, volleyball, water polo. **Intramural:** Badminton, basketball, bowling, cross-country, football (non-tackle), golf, gymnastics, racquetball, rowing (crew), soccer, softball, squash, tennis, volleyball, water polo. **Team name:** Gauchos.

**Student services.** Adult student services, alcohol/substance abuse counseling, campus ministries, career counseling, services for economically disadvantaged, student employment services, financial aid counseling, health services, minority student services, on-campus daycare, personal counseling, placement for graduates, veterans' counselor, women's services. **Physically disabled:** Services for visually, speech, hearing impaired. **Learning disabled:** Comprehensive services available.

**Contact.** E-mail: admissions@sa.ucsb.edu
Phone: (805) 893-2881 Fax: (805) 893-2676
Christine Van Gieson, Director of Admissions, University of California: Santa Barbara, 1210 Cheadle Hall, Santa Barbara, CA 93106-2014

## University of California: Santa Cruz

**Santa Cruz, California** — **CB member**
www.ucsc.edu — **CB code: 4860**

- Public 4-year university
- Residential campus in small city
- 14,381 degree-seeking undergraduates: 3% part-time, 54% women, 3% African American, 21% Asian American, 16% Hispanic American, 1% Native American, 1% international

- 1,422 degree-seeking graduate students
- 82% of applicants admitted
- SAT or ACT with writing, SAT Subject Tests, application essay required
- 70% graduate within 6 years

**General.** Founded in 1965. Regionally accredited. **Degrees:** 3,621 bachelor's awarded; master's, doctoral offered. **ROTC:** Army, Naval, Air Force. **Location:** 75 miles from San Francisco, 30 miles from San Jose. **Calendar:** Quarter, limited summer session. **Full-time faculty:** 554 total; 95% have terminal degrees, 21% minority, 34% women. **Part-time faculty:** 237 total; 95% have terminal degrees, 13% minority, 53% women. **Class size:** 39% < 20, 38% 20-39, 4% 40-49, 10% 50-99, 10% >100. **Special facilities:** Observatories, arboretum, agroecology farm, campus preserve, nonlinear science center, music center, bilingual research center, institutes of marine sciences, tectonics, particle physics, center for adaptive optics.

**Freshman class profile.** 24,453 applied, 20,059 admitted, 3,717 enrolled.

| Mid 50% test scores | | | |
|---|---|---|---|
| SAT critical reading: | 500-620 | GPA 2.0-2.99: | 4% |
| SAT math: | 520-630 | Rank in top quarter: | 100% |
| SAT writing: | 500-620 | Rank in top tenth: | 96% |
| ACT composite: | 21-29 | Return as sophomores: | 89% |
| GPA 3.50 or higher: | 48% | Out-of-state: | 3% |
| GPA 3.0-3.49: | 48% | Live on campus: | 99% |
| | | International: | 1% |

**Basis for selection.** Test scores, GPA in required subjects most important. Personal statement very important. All applicants must take 2 SAT Subject Tests in different subject areas. If Math SAT Subject Test is taken, must be Level 2. Audition required for music majors. Portfolio recommended for art majors. **Homeschooled:** Eligibility appraised on basis of entrance examination or previous college-level work. **Learning Disabled:** Any extenuating circumstances should be included in the personal statement.

**High school preparation.** 15 units required; 18 recommended. Required and recommended units include English 4, mathematics 3-4, history 2, science 2-3 (laboratory 2-3), foreign language 2-3, visual/performing arts 1 and academic electives 1. History is 2 units in history/social science. 2 semesters of approved arts courses from single visual and performing arts discipline: dance, drama/theater, music, or visual art. Required elective includes 2 semesters from following areas: visual and performing arts, history, social science, English, advanced mathematics, laboratory science, and language other than English.

**2007-2008 Annual costs.** Tuition/fees: $7,645; $27,229 out-of-state. Room/board: $12,482. Books/supplies: $1,356. Personal expenses: $1,470.

**2006-2007 Financial aid. Need-based:** 2,464 full-time freshmen applied for aid; 1,662 were judged to have need; 1,548 of these received aid. Average need met was 86%. Average scholarship/grant was $11,525; average loan $4,746. 66% of total undergraduate aid awarded as scholarships/grants, 34% as loans/jobs. **Non-need-based:** Awarded to 361 full-time undergraduates, including 67 freshmen. Scholarships awarded for academics, alumni affiliation, art, leadership, music/drama.

**Application procedures. Admission:** Closing date 11/30 (postmark date). $60 fee, may be waived for applicants with need. Application may be submitted online. Admission notification 4/30. Admission notification on a rolling basis beginning on or about 3/15. Must reply by 5/1. **Financial aid:** Closing date 3/2. FAFSA required. Applicants notified on a rolling basis starting 4/1; must reply within 4 week(s) of notification.

**Academics. Special study options:** Combined bachelor's/graduate degree, cooperative education, double major, dual enrollment of high school students, ESL, exchange student, independent study, internships, student-designed major, study abroad, teacher certification program, Washington semester. **Credit/placement by examination:** AP, CLEP, IB, institutional tests. **Support services:** Learning center, reduced course load, remedial instruction, study skills assistance, tutoring, writing center.

**Majors. Agriculture:** Plant sciences. **Area/ethnic studies:** American, German, Italian, women's. **Biology:** General, bioinformatics, cellular/molecular, ecology, marine, molecular biochemistry. **Business:** Managerial economics. **Computer sciences:** General, game design, web page design. **Conservation:** Environmental studies. **Engineering:** Computer, electrical. **English:** English lit. **Foreign languages:** General, classics, linguistics. **History:** General. **Interdisciplinary:** Neuroscience. **Legal studies:** General. **Math:** General. **Philosophy/religion:** Philosophy. **Physical sciences:** Astrophysics, chemistry, geology, physics. **Psychology:** General. **Public administration:** Community org/advocacy. **Social sciences:** Anthropology, economics, political science, sociology. **Visual/performing arts:** Art, art history/conservation, dramatic. **Other:** Area, ethnic, cultural, and gender studies, Biological and biomedical sciences, Computer and information sciences and support services.

**Most popular majors.** Area/ethnic studies 6%, biology 12%, business/marketing 9%, English 7%, psychology 11%, social sciences 17%, visual/performing arts 11%.

**Computing on campus.** 300 workstations in dormitories, library, computer center, student center. Dormitories wired for high-speed internet access and linked to campus network. Commuter students can connect to campus network. Online course registration, online library, helpline, repair service, student web hosting, wireless network available.

**Student life. Freshman orientation:** Available, $105 fee. Preregistration for classes offered. **Policies:** Students may create own organizations. **Housing:** Guaranteed on-campus for freshmen. Coed dorms, single-sex dorms, apartments, cooperative housing, substance-free housing available. $150 partly refundable deposit, deadline 5/1. Theme housing available. **Activities:** Jazz band, choral groups, dance, drama, film society, international student organizations, literary magazine, music ensembles, Model UN, musical theater, opera, radio station, student government, student newspaper, symphony orchestra, TV station, More than 100 student organizations.

**Athletics.** NCAA. **Intercollegiate:** Basketball, cross-country W, diving, golf W, soccer, swimming, tennis, volleyball, water polo. **Intramural:** Basketball, football (non-tackle), soccer, volleyball. **Team name:** Banana Slugs.

**Student services.** Adult student services, alcohol/substance abuse counseling, career counseling, services for economically disadvantaged, student employment services, financial aid counseling, health services, minority student services, on-campus daycare, personal counseling, veterans' counselor, women's services. **Physically disabled:** Services for visually, speech, hearing impaired.

**Contact.** E-mail: admissions@ucsc.edu
Phone: (831) 459-4008 Fax: (831) 459-4452
Michael Mc Cawley, Interim/Acting Director of Admissions and University Registrar, University of California: Santa Cruz, Cook House, 1156 High Street, Santa Cruz, CA 95064

---

## University of La Verne

La Verne, California
www.ulv.edu

**CB member**
**CB code:** 4381

- ◗ Private 4-year university and liberal arts college
- ◗ Commuter campus in large town
- ◗ 1,671 degree-seeking undergraduates: 5% part-time, 64% women, 7% African American, 4% Asian American, 39% Hispanic American, 1% Native American, 1% international
- ◗ 2,187 degree-seeking graduate students
- ◗ 65% of applicants admitted
- ◗ SAT or ACT with writing, application essay required
- ◗ 58% graduate within 6 years

**General.** Founded in 1891. Regionally accredited. Satellite campuses throughout California provide graduate and professional programs to adult students. **Degrees:** 346 bachelor's awarded; master's, doctoral, first professional offered. **ROTC:** Army. **Location:** 35 miles from Los Angeles. **Calendar:** 4-1-4, limited summer session. **Full-time faculty:** 187 total; 81% have terminal degrees, 19% minority, 47% women. **Part-time faculty:** 205 total; 18% minority, 49% women. **Special facilities:** Natural science field station, multiple art galleries.

**Freshman class profile.** 1,538 applied, 993 admitted, 336 enrolled.

| Mid 50% test scores | | | |
|---|---|---|---|
| SAT critical reading: | 440-540 | GPA 2.0-2.99: | 21% |
| SAT math: | 440-540 | Rank in top quarter: | 55% |
| SAT writing: | 430-530 | Rank in top tenth: | 20% |
| ACT composite: | 17-23 | Return as sophomores: | 85% |
| GPA 3.50 or higher: | 36% | Out-of-state: | 5% |
| GPA 3.0-3.49: | 43% | Live on campus: | 62% |
| | | International: | 1% |

**Basis for selection.** Secondary school record, recommendations, standardized test scores, and essay very important; extracurricular activities, character or personal qualities also important. Class rank, interview, special talents or abilities, alumni relationships, volunteer work, work experience may be considered as additional factors. College Board Test of Standard Written English (TSWE) and math department placement exam required. Departmental placement exams required in foreign language. Individual departments may require interview, audition, or portfolio.

**High school preparation.** 14 units required; 19 recommended. Required and recommended units include English 4, mathematics 3-4, social studies 2, history 3, science 2 (laboratory 1-2), foreign language 2 and academic electives 2.

**2008-2009 Annual costs.** Tuition/fees (projected): $26,910. Room/board: $10,460. Books/supplies: $1,566. Personal expenses: $2,379.

**2007-2008 Financial aid. Need-based:** 305 full-time freshmen applied for aid; 276 were judged to have need; 276 of these received aid. Average scholarship/grant was $11,047; average loan $4,668. 72% of total undergraduate aid awarded as scholarships/grants, 28% as loans/jobs. **Non-need-based:** Awarded to 1,278 full-time undergraduates, including 257 freshmen. Scholarships awarded for academics, alumni affiliation, art, leadership, minority status, music/drama, religious affiliation.

**Application procedures. Admission:** Priority date 2/1; no deadline. $50 fee, may be waived for applicants with need. Application must be submitted on paper. Admission notification on a rolling basis beginning on or about 12/1. Must reply by May 1 or within 2 week(s) if notified thereafter. **Financial aid:** Priority date 3/2; no closing date. FAFSA required. Applicants notified on a rolling basis starting 3/2; must reply within 1 week(s) of notification.

**Academics.** Main Campus offers a traditional-age undergraduate program and an accelerated program for adults in school of continuing education. Off-campus centers available for degree-seeking students in selected majors. Current centers in Riverside, Orange, and Ventura counties, San Luis Obispo, San Fernando Valley and Bakersfield. Education programs available at additional sites in California. **Special study options:** Accelerated study, combined bachelor's/graduate degree, distance learning, double major, ESL, exchange student, honors, independent study, internships, liberal arts/career combination, student-designed major, study abroad, teacher certification program, weekend college. **Credit/placement by examination:** AP, CLEP, institutional tests. 21 credit hours maximum toward associate degree, 44 toward bachelor's. **Support services:** Learning center, reduced course load, study skills assistance, tutoring.

**Majors. Biology:** General. **Business:** Accounting, business admin, e-commerce, international, managerial economics. **Communications:** General, journalism, radio/tv. **Computer sciences:** General. **Conservation:** Environmental science. **Education:** General, early childhood, elementary, physical, secondary. **English:** English lit. **Family/consumer sciences:** Child care. **Foreign languages:** Comparative lit, French, German, Spanish. **Health:** Athletic training, health care admin. **History:** General. **Interdisciplinary:** Behavioral sciences, biological/physical sciences, natural sciences. **Legal studies:** General. **Liberal arts:** Arts/sciences. **Math:** General. **Philosophy/religion:** Philosophy, religion. **Physical sciences:** Chemistry, physics. **Psychology:** General. **Public administration:** General. **Social sciences:** General, anthropology, criminology, economics, international relations, political science, sociology. **Visual/performing arts:** Art, art history/conservation, dramatic.

**Most popular majors.** Business/marketing 20%, communications/journalism 13%, liberal arts 14%, psychology 11%, social sciences 14%.

**Computing on campus.** 150 workstations in library, computer center, student center. Dormitories wired for high-speed internet access and linked to campus network. Commuter students can connect to campus network. Online course registration, online library, helpline, student web hosting, wireless network available.

**Student life. Freshman orientation:** Available, $50 fee. Preregistration for classes offered. All-day events for both students and parents. Held primarily in August. **Policies:** Students must be in good academic standing to participate in clubs or organizations, including fraternities/sororities. Freshmen not permitted to join fraternities/sororities. **Housing:** Coed dorms, single-sex dorms, special housing for disabled available. $240 fully refundable deposit, deadline 5/1. **Activities:** Choral groups, drama, international student organizations, literary magazine, Model UN, musical theater, radio station, student government, student newspaper, TV station, African American student alliance, Latino student forum, Brothers Forum, Sisters Circle, Rainbow Alliance.

**Athletics.** NCAA. **Intercollegiate:** Baseball M, basketball, cross-country, diving, football (tackle) M, golf M, soccer, softball W, swimming, tennis, track and field, volleyball W, water polo. **Intramural:** Basketball, soccer, softball, table tennis, volleyball. **Team name:** Leopards.

**Student services.** Adult student services, alcohol/substance abuse counseling, campus ministries, career counseling, services for economically disadvantaged, student employment services, financial aid counseling, health services, minority student services, personal counseling, placement for graduates, veterans' counselor. **Physically disabled:** Services for visually, speech, hearing impaired.

**Contact.** E-mail: admissions@ulv.edu
Phone: (909) 392-2800 Toll-free number: (800) 876-4858
Fax: (909) 392-2714
Ana Liza Zell, Associate Dean of Undergraduate Admissions, University of La Verne, 1950 Third Street, La Verne, CA 91750

# University of Redlands

**Redlands, California**
www.redlands.edu

CB member
CB code: 4848

- Private 4-year university and liberal arts college
- Residential campus in small city
- 2,353 degree-seeking undergraduates: 1% part-time, 57% women, 3% African American, 6% Asian American, 12% Hispanic American, 1% international
- 91 degree-seeking graduate students
- 67% of applicants admitted
- SAT or ACT (ACT writing recommended), application essay required
- 61% graduate within 6 years; 45% enter graduate study

**General.** Founded in 1907. Regionally accredited. **Degrees:** 748 bachelor's awarded; master's, doctoral offered. **ROTC:** Army, Naval, Air Force. **Location:** 65 miles from Los Angeles, 40 miles from Palm Springs. **Calendar:** 4-1-4. **Full-time faculty:** 173 total; 87% have terminal degrees, 16% minority, 51% women. **Part-time faculty:** 162 total; 28% have terminal degrees. **Class size:** 72% < 20, 27% 20-39, less than 1% 40-49, less than 1% 50-99. **Special facilities:** Laboratory of anthropology, geographic information systems laboratory, physics/laser/photonics laboratory, map library.

**Freshman class profile.** 3,607 applied, 2,422 admitted, 607 enrolled.

| Mid 50% test scores | | | |
|---|---|---|---|
| SAT critical reading: | 520-620 | Rank in top quarter: | 70% |
| SAT math: | 540-620 | Rank in top tenth: | 31% |
| ACT composite: | 21-27 | Return as sophomores: | 86% |
| GPA 3.50 or higher: | 58% | Out-of-state: | 39% |
| GPA 3.0-3.49: | 29% | Live on campus: | 94% |
| GPA 2.0-2.99: | 13% | International: | 1% |

**Basis for selection.** Course selection and grades important. Recommendations, test scores, essays, extracurricular activities also considered. Interview required of Johnston Center for Integrated Studies applicants, strongly recommended for others. Audition required of music majors. Portfolio recommended of art (slides only), creative writing majors. **Homeschooled:** Common application home school supplement required.

**High school preparation.** Required and recommended units include English 4, mathematics 3, social studies 2-3, science 2-3 (laboratory 2-3) and foreign language 2-3.

**2007-2008 Annual costs.** Tuition/fees: $30,626. Room/board: $9,728. Books/supplies: $1,400. Personal expenses: $2,932.

**2007-2008 Financial aid. Need-based:** 478 full-time freshmen applied for aid; 382 were judged to have need; 382 of these received aid. Average need met was 85%. Average scholarship/grant was $23,666; average loan $6,545. 69% of total undergraduate aid awarded as scholarships/grants, 31% as loans/jobs. **Non-need-based:** Awarded to 267 full-time undergraduates, including 92 freshmen. Scholarships awarded for academics, art, music/drama.

**Application procedures. Admission:** Priority date 12/15; deadline 4/1 (postmark date). $45 fee, may be waived for applicants with need. Application may be submitted online. Admission notification on a rolling basis beginning on or about 11/1. Must reply by May 1 or within 3 week(s) if notified thereafter. **Financial aid:** Priority date 2/15; no closing date. FAFSA required. Applicants notified on a rolling basis starting 2/28; must reply by 5/1.

**Academics. Special study options:** Cross-registration, double major, exchange student, honors, independent study, internships, liberal arts/career combination, New York semester, student-designed major, study abroad, teacher certification program, United Nations semester, Washington semester. Non-traditional study programs available through Johnston Center for Integrated Studies and schools of business and education. **Credit/placement by examination:** AP, CLEP, IB, institutional tests. 16 credit hours maximum toward bachelor's degree. **Support services:** Learning center, pre-admission summer program, reduced course load, study skills assistance, tutoring, writing center.

**Majors. Area/ethnic studies:** Asian, Latin American, women's. **Biology:** General, biochemistry. **Business:** General, accounting, business admin, management information systems, managerial economics. **Computer sciences:** General. **Conservation:** Environmental science, environmental studies, management/policy. **Education:** Elementary, middle, music, secondary, speech impaired. **English:** British lit, creative writing, English lit. **Foreign languages:** French, German, Spanish. **Health:** Audiology/speech pathology. **History:** General. **Liberal arts:** Arts/sciences. **Math:** General. **Philosophy/religion:** Philosophy, religion. **Physical sciences:** Chemistry, physics. **Psychology:** General. **Social sciences:** Anthropology, economics, international

relations, political science, sociology. **Visual/performing arts:** Art, art history/conservation, dramatic, music history, music performance, music theory/composition.

**Most popular majors.** Business/marketing 17%, history 7%, liberal arts 19%, psychology 8%, social sciences 14%, visual/performing arts 6%.

**Computing on campus.** 655 workstations in dormitories, library, computer center, student center. Dormitories wired for high-speed internet access and linked to campus network. Commuter students can connect to campus network. Online library, helpline, repair service, student web hosting, wireless network available.

**Student life. Freshman orientation:** Mandatory. One full week preceding academic school year. **Housing:** Guaranteed on-campus for freshmen. Coed dorms, single-sex dorms, special housing for disabled, apartments, fraternity/sorority housing, substance-free housing available. **Activities:** Bands, choral groups, dance, drama, literary magazine, music ensembles, musical theater, opera, radio station, student government, student newspaper, symphony orchestra, Associated Students, Intervarsity Christian Fellowship, African American association, Gay, Lesbian, Bisexual student union, women's center, College Republicans, College Democrats, Asian Pacific Islander association, Glenn Wallichs Theater association.

**Athletics.** NCAA. **Intercollegiate:** Baseball M, basketball, cross-country, diving, football (tackle) M, golf, lacrosse W, soccer, softball W, swimming, tennis, track and field, volleyball W, water polo. **Intramural:** Basketball, football (non-tackle), racquetball, soccer, softball, table tennis, tennis, volleyball, water polo. **Team name:** Bulldogs.

**Student services.** Adult student services, alcohol/substance abuse counseling, campus ministries, career counseling, student employment services, financial aid counseling, health services, minority student services, personal counseling, placement for graduates, veterans' counselor, women's services. **Physically disabled:** Services for visually, speech, hearing impaired.

**Contact.** E-mail: admissions@redlands.edu
Phone: (909) 748-8074 Toll-free number: (800) 455-5064
Fax: (909) 335-4089
Paul Driscoll, Dean of Admissions, University of Redlands, 1200 East Colton Avenue, Redlands, CA 92373-0999

# University of San Diego

**San Diego, California**
www.sandiego.edu

CB member
CB code: 4849

- Private 4-year university affiliated with Roman Catholic Church
- Residential campus in very large city
- 4,906 degree-seeking undergraduates: 3% part-time, 58% women, 2% African American, 10% Asian American, 14% Hispanic American, 1% Native American, 2% international
- 2,544 degree-seeking graduate students
- 46% of applicants admitted
- SAT or ACT with writing, application essay required
- 74% graduate within 6 years

**General.** Founded in 1949. Regionally accredited. **Degrees:** 1,183 bachelor's awarded; master's, doctoral, first professional offered. **ROTC:** Army, Naval, Air Force. **Location:** 5 miles from downtown. **Calendar:** 4-1-4, extensive summer session. **Full-time faculty:** 367 total; 95% have terminal degrees, 17% minority, 44% women. **Part-time faculty:** 399 total; 51% have terminal degrees, 14% minority, 54% women. **Class size:** 41% < 20, 55% 20-39, 3% 40-49, less than 1% 50-99.

**Freshman class profile.** 10,048 applied, 4,630 admitted, 1,106 enrolled.

| Mid 50% test scores | | | |
|---|---|---|---|
| | | GPA 2.0-2.99: | 6% |
| SAT critical reading: | 530-630 | Rank in top quarter: | 78% |
| SAT math: | 550-650 | Rank in top tenth: | 43% |
| SAT writing: | 530-660 | Return as sophomores: | 85% |
| ACT composite: | 23-28 | Out-of-state: | 46% |
| GPA 3.50 or higher: | 76% | Live on campus: | 94% |
| GPA 3.0-3.49: | 18% | International: | 2% |

**Basis for selection.** School achievement record, test scores, recommendations, and extracurricular activities important. Out-of-state and international applicants welcome. Advanced Placement English examinations (language or literature) with grade of 4 or 5 may also be used for placement. Audition required of choral scholarship applicants. **Learning Disabled:** Must contact Director of Disability Services.

**High school preparation.** 17 units required; 22 recommended. Required and recommended units include English 4, mathematics 3-4, social studies 3-4, science 3-4 (laboratory 2-3) and foreign language 2-3.

**2008-2009 Annual costs.** Tuition/fees (projected): $34,272. Room/board: $10,960. Books/supplies: $1,380. Personal expenses: $2,142.

**2006-2007 Financial aid. Need-based:** 677 full-time freshmen applied for aid; 495 were judged to have need; 488 of these received aid. Average need met was 73%. Average scholarship/grant was $17,710; average loan $4,845. 69% of total undergraduate aid awarded as scholarships/grants, 31% as loans/jobs. **Non-need-based:** Awarded to 1,794 full-time undergraduates, including 557 freshmen. Scholarships awarded for academics, athletics, leadership, music/drama, religious affiliation, ROTC.

**Application procedures. Admission:** Priority date 1/15; deadline 3/1 (postmark date). $55 fee, may be waived for applicants with need. Application may be submitted online. Admission notification 4/15. Must reply by May 1 or within 2 week(s) if notified thereafter. **Financial aid:** Closing date 3/2. FAFSA required. Applicants notified on a rolling basis starting 3/1; must reply by 5/1 or within 3 week(s) of notification.

**Academics. Special study options:** Combined bachelor's/graduate degree, double major, ESL, honors, independent study, internships, liberal arts/career combination, study abroad, teacher certification program. **Credit/placement by examination:** AP, CLEP, IB, institutional tests. **Support services:** Pre-admission summer program, reduced course load, study skills assistance, tutoring, writing center.

**Majors. Biology:** General, marine. **Business:** Accounting, business admin, finance, managerial economics, marketing. **Communications:** General. **Computer sciences:** Computer science. **Engineering:** Electrical, industrial, mechanical. **English:** English lit. **Foreign languages:** French, Spanish. **Health:** Nursing (RN). **History:** General. **Liberal arts:** Arts/sciences, humanities. **Math:** General. **Philosophy/religion:** Philosophy, religion. **Physical sciences:** Chemistry, physics. **Psychology:** General. **Social sciences:** Anthropology, economics, international relations, political science, sociology, urban studies. **Visual/performing arts:** Art history/conservation, dramatic, studio arts.

**Most popular majors.** Business/marketing 36%, communications/journalism 12%, psychology 10%, social sciences 14%.

**Computing on campus.** 250 workstations in dormitories, library, computer center, student center. Dormitories wired for high-speed internet access and linked to campus network. Commuter students can connect to campus network. Online course registration, helpline, repair service, student web hosting, wireless network available.

**Student life. Freshman orientation:** Mandatory. Preregistration for classes offered. 4-day program that starts at the beginning of the semester. **Housing:** Guaranteed on-campus for all undergraduates. Coed dorms, single-sex dorms, special housing for disabled, apartments, substance-free housing available. $150 partly refundable deposit, deadline 5/1. Freshmen required to live on campus unless living with parents. **Activities:** Bands, campus ministries, choral groups, dance, drama, international student organizations, literary magazine, music ensembles, musical theater, student government, student newspaper, symphony orchestra, TV station, Black student union, Asian student association, Young Democrats, Young Republicans, Hawaiian club, MEChA, Filipino student association, multicultural center.

**Athletics.** NCAA. **Intercollegiate:** Baseball M, basketball, cross-country, diving W, football (tackle) M, golf M, rowing (crew), soccer, softball W, swimming W, tennis, volleyball W. **Intramural:** Badminton, basketball, bowling, cross-country, field hockey, golf, ice hockey M, lacrosse M, rugby M, soccer, softball, swimming, table tennis, tennis, volleyball. **Team name:** Toreros.

**Student services.** Alcohol/substance abuse counseling, campus ministries, career counseling, services for economically disadvantaged, student employment services, financial aid counseling, health services, legal services, on-campus daycare, personal counseling, placement for graduates, veterans' counselor, women's services. **Physically disabled:** Services for visually impaired.

**Contact.** E-mail: admissions@sandiego.edu
Phone: (619) 260-4506 Toll-free number: (800) 248-4873
Fax: (619) 260-6836
Stephen Pultz, Director of Admission, University of San Diego, 5998 Alcala Park, San Diego, CA 92110

---

## University of San Francisco
**San Francisco, California**
www.usfca.edu

CB member
CB code: 4850

- Private 4-year university affiliated with Roman Catholic Church
- Residential campus in very large city

---

- 4,872 degree-seeking undergraduates: 3% part-time, 64% women, 5% African American, 23% Asian American, 14% Hispanic American, 1% Native American, 7% international
- 3,282 degree-seeking graduate students
- 67% of applicants admitted
- SAT or ACT with writing, application essay required
- 65% graduate within 6 years

**General.** Founded in 1855. Regionally accredited. **Degrees:** 1,253 bachelor's awarded; master's, doctoral, first professional offered. **ROTC:** Army, Air Force. **Location:** 3 miles from downtown. **Calendar:** 4-1-4, extensive summer session. **Full-time faculty:** 371 total; 93% have terminal degrees, 20% minority, 46% women. **Part-time faculty:** 526 total; 17% minority, 54% women. **Class size:** 49% < 20, 40% 20-39, 8% 40-49, 2% 50-99, less than 1% >100. **Special facilities:** Rare book room, institute for Chinese western cultural history, electron microscope, separate law library available to all students.

**Freshman class profile.** 7,695 applied, 5,138 admitted, 1,055 enrolled.

| Mid 50% test scores | | | |
|---|---|---|---|
| SAT critical reading: | 510-620 | Rank in top quarter: | 61% |
| SAT math: | 520-620 | Rank in top tenth: | 26% |
| SAT writing: | 510-620 | Return as sophomores: | 82% |
| ACT composite: | 22-27 | Out-of-state: | 29% |
| GPA 3.50 or higher: | 51% | Live on campus: | 90% |
| GPA 3.0-3.49: | 42% | International: | 6% |
| GPA 2.0-2.99: | 7% | Fraternities: | 1% |
| | | Sororities: | 1% |

**Basis for selection.** School achievement record, test scores, class rank, school attended, recommendations, extracurricular activities, alumni relationship, personal essay important. Require TOEFL for non-native speakers of English. Interviews required for nursing students. **Homeschooled:** Statement describing homeschool structure and mission, letter of recommendation (nonparent) required. Statement from parents on curriculum needed if student not evaluated through high school homeschooling program or agency that evaluates home school programs. **Learning Disabled:** After acceptance, students with disabilities must make appointment with Disabilities Specialist in office of Disablity Related Services (DRS) if interested in receiving services and/or accommodations for disability.

**High school preparation.** 20 units required. Required units include English 4, mathematics 3, social studies 3, science 2 (laboratory 2), foreign language 2 and academic electives 6. One chemistry and 1 biology or physics required of nursing and science applicants.

**2008-2009 Annual costs.** Tuition/fees: $33,500. Nursing clinical lab fee, $150 per lab. Nursing clinical lab malpractice insurance, $25 per lab. Room/board: $11,130. Books/supplies: $950. Personal expenses: $2,400.

**Financial aid. Non-need-based:** Scholarships awarded for academics, athletics, ROTC. **Additional information:** Individualized installment plans available.

**Application procedures. Admission:** Priority date 1/15; no deadline. $55 fee, may be waived for applicants with need. Application may be submitted online. Notification begins approximately 4 weeks after all materials submitted including fall grades. Must reply by May 1 or within 2 week(s) if notified thereafter. **Financial aid:** Priority date 2/1; no closing date. FAFSA required. Applicants notified on a rolling basis starting 4/1; must reply within 4 week(s) of notification.

**Academics. Special study options:** Accelerated study, combined bachelor's/graduate degree, cooperative education, cross-registration, distance learning, double major, ESL, exchange student, external degree, honors, independent study, internships, liberal arts/career combination, student-designed major, study abroad, teacher certification program, Washington semester. College of Professional Studies for adult degree-seeking students coming back to school to earn undergraduate bachelor's degree; cooperative work study in Computer Science courses. **Credit/placement by examination:** AP, CLEP, IB, SAT, ACT, institutional tests. 30 credit hours maximum toward bachelor's degree. Credit for experiential learning limited to maximum of 30 undergraduate semester units in College of Professional Studies. **Support services:** Learning center, pre-admission summer program, reduced course load, study skills assistance, tutoring, writing center.

**Majors. Architecture:** Urban/community planning. **Area/ethnic studies:** American. **Biology:** General. **Business:** General, accounting, business admin, entrepreneurial studies, finance, hotel/motel admin, international, marketing, organizational behavior, restaurant/food services. **Communications:** General, media studies. **Computer sciences:** General, information systems. **Conservation:** Environmental science, environmental studies. **English:** English lit. **Foreign languages:** Comparative lit, French, Japanese, Spanish. **Health:** Nursing (RN). **History:** General. **Interdisciplinary:** Global studies. **Liberal arts:** Arts/sciences. **Math:** General. **Parks/recreation:**

Health/fitness. **Philosophy/religion:** Philosophy. **Physical sciences:** Chemistry, physics. **Psychology:** General. **Public administration:** General. **Social sciences:** Economics, international economics, political science, sociology. **Theology:** Theology. **Visual/performing arts:** General, art history/conservation, arts management, commercial/advertising art, studio arts.

**Most popular majors.** Business/marketing 29%, communications/journalism 7%, computer/information sciences 6%, health sciences 8%, psychology 8%, social sciences 14%, visual/performing arts 6%.

**Computing on campus.** 320 workstations in dormitories, library, computer center, student center. Dormitories wired for high-speed internet access and linked to campus network. Commuter students can connect to campus network. Online course registration, online library, helpline, repair service, student web hosting, wireless network available.

**Student life. Freshman orientation:** Mandatory. Preregistration for classes offered. Two-day session including placement tests. **Housing:** Guaranteed on-campus for freshmen. Coed dorms, single-sex dorms, special housing for disabled, apartments available. $300 nonrefundable deposit. Freshman and sophomores under 21 required to live in residence halls unless they have permanent address within 20-mile radius of campus. **Activities:** Pep band, choral groups, dance, drama, international student organizations, literary magazine, music ensembles, musical theater, radio station, student government, student newspaper, TV station, St. Ignatius Institute, People Advocating Cultural Endeavors, Phelan multicultural community.

**Athletics.** NCAA. **Intercollegiate:** Baseball M, basketball, cross-country, golf, rifle, soccer, tennis, track and field, volleyball W. **Intramural:** Basketball, football (non-tackle), racquetball, soccer, softball, swimming, table tennis, tennis, volleyball. **Team name:** Don's.

**Student services.** Adult student services, alcohol/substance abuse counseling, campus ministries, career counseling, student employment services, financial aid counseling, health services, minority student services, personal counseling, placement for graduates. **Physically disabled:** Services for visually, speech, hearing impaired. **Learning disabled:** Comprehensive services available.

**Contact.** E-mail: admissions@usfca.edu
Phone: (415) 422-6563 Toll-free number: (800) 225-5873
Fax: (415) 422-2217
Michael Hughes, Director of Admissions, University of San Francisco, 2130 Fulton Street, San Francisco, CA 94117-1046

---

## University of Southern California

| Los Angeles, California | CB member |
| www.usc.edu | CB code: 4852 |

- Private 4-year university
- Residential campus in very large city
- 16,091 degree-seeking undergraduates: 3% part-time, 50% women, 6% African American, 22% Asian American, 13% Hispanic American, 1% Native American, 9% international
- 16,071 degree-seeking graduate students
- 25% of applicants admitted
- SAT or ACT with writing, application essay required
- 85% graduate within 6 years

**General.** Founded in 1880. Regionally accredited. **Degrees:** 4,676 bachelor's awarded; master's, doctoral, first professional offered. **ROTC:** Army, Naval, Air Force. **Location:** 3 miles from downtown. **Calendar:** Semester, limited summer session. **Full-time faculty:** 1,625 total; 90% have terminal degrees, 23% minority, 34% women. **Part-time faculty:** 1,088 total; 60% have terminal degrees, 26% minority, 38% women. **Class size:** 64% < 20, 19% 20-39, 5% 40-49, 8% 50-99, 4% >100. **Special facilities:** 3 art/architecture galleries, 2 museums, 2 sculpture gardens, marine science center on Santa Catalina Island, integrated media systems center, center for digital arts.

**Freshman class profile.** 33,760 applied, 8,553 admitted, 2,963 enrolled.

| Mid 50% test scores | | | |
|---|---|---|---|
| SAT critical reading: | 620-720 | Rank in top tenth: | 86% |
| SAT math: | 650-740 | End year in good standing: | 96% |
| SAT writing: | 640-720 | Return as sophomores: | 96% |
| ACT composite: | 28-32 | Out-of-state: | 42% |
| GPA 3.50 or higher: | 83% | Live on campus: | 98% |
| GPA 3.0-3.49: | 16% | International: | 7% |
| GPA 2.0-2.99: | 1% | Fraternities: | 16% |
| Rank in top quarter: | 97% | Sororities: | 19% |

**Basis for selection.** GED not accepted. Academic achievement, curriculum and test scores most important. Recommendations, activities, and interviews considered. Tests not required of international applicants attending foreign institutions. Audition required of music and theater majors. Portfolio required of fine arts and architecture majors. **Homeschooled:** In addition to application materials found on Freshman Admission Process site page, students required to submit results from 3 SAT Subject tests (1 must be in math) and must also submit detailed syllabi of courses, names of textbooks, names and applicable credentials of instructors, details of assistance received or curriculum followed through any public or private agency, and any additional information that may be helpful.

**High school preparation.** 16 units required; 20 recommended. Required and recommended units include English 4, mathematics 3-4, social studies 2-3, science 2-3 (laboratory 2-3), foreign language 2-3 and academic electives 3.

**2008-2009 Annual costs.** Tuition/fees (projected): $35,954. Room/board: $10,858. Books/supplies: $750. Personal expenses: $1,600.

**2006-2007 Financial aid. Need-based:** 1,608 full-time freshmen applied for aid; 1,073 were judged to have need; 1,073 of these received aid. Average need met was 100%. Average scholarship/grant was $20,999; average loan $3,816. 77% of total undergraduate aid awarded as scholarships/grants, 23% as loans/jobs. **Non-need-based:** Awarded to 6,183 full-time undergraduates, including 1,400 freshmen. Scholarships awarded for academics, alumni affiliation, art, athletics, leadership, music/drama, ROTC.

**Application procedures. Admission:** Priority date 12/10; deadline 1/10 (postmark date). $65 fee, may be waived for applicants with need. Application may be submitted online. Admission notification 4/1. Must reply by 5/1. **Financial aid:** Priority date 1/22; no closing date. FAFSA, CSS PROFILE required. Applicants notified on a rolling basis starting 3/15; must reply by 5/1.

**Academics. Special study options:** Combined bachelor's/graduate degree, cooperative education, distance learning, double major, ESL, exchange student, honors, independent study, internships, liberal arts/career combination, student-designed major, study abroad, teacher certification program, Washington semester. Learning communities, thematic option, undergraduate research program, freshman seminar program. **Credit/placement by examination:** AP, CLEP, IB, institutional tests. 32 credit hours maximum toward bachelor's degree. **Support services:** Learning center, reduced course load, study skills assistance, tutoring, writing center.

**Majors. Architecture:** Architecture, landscape. **Area/ethnic studies:** African-American, American, Asian-American, East Asian, Hispanic-American/Latino/Chicano, women's. **Biology:** General, biochemistry, biophysics. **Business:** Accounting, business admin, international. **Communications:** General, broadcast journalism, journalism, public relations, radio/tv. **Computer sciences:** Computer science. **Conservation:** Environmental science, environmental studies. **Education:** General, music. **Engineering:** Aerospace, biomedical, chemical, civil, computer, construction, electrical, environmental, industrial, mechanical, petroleum, polymer, structural, systems, water resource. **English:** American lit, creative writing, English lit. **Foreign languages:** Classics, comparative lit, East Asian, French, German, Italian, linguistics, Russian, Spanish. **Health:** Dental hygiene, physician assistant. **History:** General. **Interdisciplinary:** Biopsychology, gerontology, global studies. **Math:** General. **Parks/recreation:** Exercise sciences. **Philosophy/religion:** Ethics, Judaic, philosophy, religion. **Physical sciences:** General, astronomy, chemistry, geology, physics. **Psychology:** General. **Public administration:** General. **Social sciences:** Anthropology, economics, geography, international relations, political science, sociology. **Visual/performing arts:** Acting, art, art history/conservation, dramatic, film/cinema, jazz, music management, music performance, music theory/composition, piano/organ, play/screenwriting, stringed instruments, studio arts, theater arts management, theater design, voice/opera.

**Most popular majors.** Business/marketing 27%, communications/journalism 9%, engineering/engineering technologies 8%, social sciences 13%, visual/performing arts 12%.

**Computing on campus.** 2,700 workstations in dormitories, library, computer center, student center. Dormitories wired for high-speed internet access and linked to campus network. Commuter students can connect to campus network. Online course registration, online library, helpline, repair service, student web hosting, wireless network available.

**Student life. Freshman orientation:** Available, $140 fee. Preregistration for classes offered. Multiple 2-day sessions run all summer. **Policies:** Every incoming student required to take online alcohol education course and pass final exam. **Housing:** Guaranteed on-campus for freshmen. Coed dorms, special housing for disabled, apartments, fraternity/sorority housing, substance-free housing available. $400 fully refundable deposit. African-American, Jewish, Latino, LGBT, multicultural, and Muslim floors; art and architecture, business, cinema, environmental, law, music, occupational therapy, women-in-science-and-engineering, faculty-in-residence programs; residential college; wellness housing. **Activities:** Bands, campus ministries, choral groups,

Four-Year Colleges

dance, drama, film society, international student organizations, literary magazine, music ensembles, Model UN, musical theater, opera, radio station, student government, student newspaper, symphony orchestra, TV station, academic honors assembly, emerging leaders program, minority consortium, religious council, residential community council, student program board, student volunteer center.

**Athletics.** NCAA. **Intercollegiate:** Baseball M, basketball, cross-country, diving, football (tackle) M, golf, rowing (crew) W, soccer W, swimming, tennis, track and field, volleyball, water polo. **Intramural:** Baseball M, basketball, cross-country, football (non-tackle), golf, racquetball, soccer, softball, table tennis, tennis, track and field, volleyball, water polo. **Team name:** Trojans.

**Student services.** Alcohol/substance abuse counseling, campus ministries, career counseling, services for economically disadvantaged, student employment services, financial aid counseling, health services, minority student services, on-campus daycare, personal counseling, placement for graduates, veterans' counselor, women's services. **Physically disabled:** Services for visually, speech, hearing impaired. **Learning disabled:** Comprehensive services available.

**Contact.** E-mail: admitusc@usc.edu
Phone: (213) 740-1111 Fax: (213) 740-1556
L Harrington, Vice Provost/Dean of Admission and Financial Aid,
University of Southern California, Office of Admission, Los Angeles, CA 90089-1158

## University of the Pacific
**Stockton, California**  CB member
www.pacific.edu  CB code: 4065

- Private 4-year university
- Residential campus in large city
- 3,456 degree-seeking undergraduates: 3% part-time, 55% women, 3% African American, 32% Asian American, 10% Hispanic American, 1% Native American, 3% international
- 2,740 degree-seeking graduate students
- 59% of applicants admitted
- SAT or ACT (ACT writing optional), application essay required
- 67% graduate within 6 years

**General.** Founded in 1851. Regionally accredited. School of Dentistry in San Francisco. McGeorge School of Law in Sacramento. **Degrees:** 717 bachelor's awarded; master's, doctoral, first professional offered. **ROTC:** Air Force. **Location:** 80 miles from San Francisco, 40 miles from Sacramento. **Calendar:** Semester, limited summer session. **Full-time faculty:** 426 total; 92% have terminal degrees, 18% minority, 36% women. **Part-time faculty:** 298 total; 61% have terminal degrees, 25% minority, 42% women. **Class size:** 60% < 20, 30% 20-39, 4% 40-49, 5% 50-99, less than 1% >100. **Special facilities:** Recital facilities, center for western studies, housing the John Muir papers, music conservatory.

**Freshman class profile.** 5,894 applied, 3,483 admitted, 766 enrolled.

| Mid 50% test scores | | GPA 2.0-2.99: | 15% |
|---|---|---|---|
| SAT critical reading: | 510-630 | Rank in top quarter: | 70% |
| SAT math: | 540-670 | Rank in top tenth: | 41% |
| SAT writing: | 510-630 | Return as sophomores: | 82% |
| ACT composite: | 23-28 | Out-of-state: | 17% |
| GPA 3.50 or higher: | 53% | Live on campus: | 91% |
| GPA 3.0-3.49: | 32% | International: | 3% |

**Basis for selection.** Secondary school record, standardized test scores, recommendations, essay, extracurricular activities important. SAT Subject Tests recommended. Audition required of music/conservatory majors. **Homeschooled:** Standardized test scores weighted heavily.

**High school preparation.** 16 units required. Required and recommended units include English 4, mathematics 3, social studies 2, history 1, (laboratory 2), foreign language 2 and academic electives 1. 1 fine/performing arts required.

**2008-2009 Annual costs.** Tuition/fees (projected): $30,730. Room/board: $10,185. Books/supplies: $1,566. Personal expenses: $2,214.

**2007-2008 Financial aid. Need-based:** 593 full-time freshmen applied for aid; 488 were judged to have need; 488 of these received aid. Average scholarship/grant was $18,446; average loan $3,341. 72% of total undergraduate aid awarded as scholarships/grants, 28% as loans/jobs. **Non-need-based:** Awarded to 613 full-time undergraduates, including 167 freshmen. Scholarships awarded for academics, athletics, leadership, music/drama, religious affiliation.

**Application procedures. Admission:** Priority date 11/15; deadline 1/5. $60 fee, may be waived for applicants with need. Application may be submitted online. Admission notification on a rolling basis beginning on or about 3/15. Housing deposit refundable if canceled by May 1. **Financial aid:** Priority date 2/15; no closing date. FAFSA required. Applicants notified on a rolling basis starting 3/15.

**Academics. Special study options:** Accelerated study, combined bachelor's/graduate degree, cooperative education, double major, dual enrollment of high school students, ESL, exchange student, honors, independent study, internships, liberal arts/career combination, student-designed major, study abroad, teacher certification program, United Nations semester, Washington semester. Practicum, minors, undergraduate research, combination, ethnic studies, environmental science, gender studies, service learning, thematic minors. **Credit/placement by examination:** AP, CLEP, IB, SAT, ACT, institutional tests. 20 credit hours maximum toward bachelor's degree. **Support services:** Learning center, pre-admission summer program, reduced course load, remedial instruction, tutoring, writing center.

**Majors. Biology:** General, biochemistry. **Business:** Business admin. **Communications:** General. **Computer sciences:** General, computer science, information systems. **Conservation:** Environmental studies. **Education:** General, elementary, multi-level teacher, music, secondary. **Engineering:** General, civil, computer, electrical, mechanical, physics. **Engineering technology:** Industrial management. **English:** English lit. **Foreign languages:** French, German, Japanese, Spanish. **Health:** Dental hygiene, music therapy, speech pathology. **History:** General. **Interdisciplinary:** Biological/physical sciences. **Liberal arts:** Arts/sciences. **Math:** General, applied. **Parks/recreation:** Health/fitness, sports admin. **Philosophy/religion:** Philosophy, religion. **Physical sciences:** Chemistry, geology, physics. **Psychology:** General. **Social sciences:** General, economics, international relations, political science, sociology. **Visual/performing arts:** Art, commercial/advertising art, dramatic, music history, music management, music performance, music theory/composition, piano/organ, studio arts, voice/opera.

**Most popular majors.** Biology 16%, business/marketing 24%, education 7%, engineering/engineering technologies 8%, health sciences 6%, social sciences 8%, visual/performing arts 7%.

**Computing on campus.** 325 workstations in dormitories, library, computer center. Dormitories wired for high-speed internet access and linked to campus network. Commuter students can connect to campus network. Online course registration, online library, helpline, wireless network available.

**Student life. Freshman orientation:** Mandatory, $120 fee. Preregistration for classes offered. Offered in January, June, July & August, 2-4 days each. **Housing:** Guaranteed on-campus for freshmen. Coed dorms, apartments, fraternity/sorority housing, substance-free housing available. $250 fully refundable deposit. Freshmen and sophomores required to live on campus unless living with parents. **Activities:** Bands, campus ministries, choral groups, dance, drama, film society, international student organizations, literary magazine, music ensembles, Model UN, musical theater, opera, radio station, student government, student newspaper, symphony orchestra, 100 student organizations and clubs.

**Athletics.** NCAA. **Intercollegiate:** Baseball M, basketball, cross-country W, field hockey W, golf M, soccer W, softball W, swimming, tennis, volleyball, water polo. **Intramural:** Badminton, basketball, bowling, football (tackle), golf, racquetball, soccer, softball, swimming, tennis, volleyball, water polo. **Team name:** Tigers.

**Student services.** Adult student services, alcohol/substance abuse counseling, campus ministries, career counseling, services for economically disadvantaged, student employment services, financial aid counseling, health services, personal counseling, placement for graduates, veterans' counselor. **Physically disabled:** Services for visually, speech, hearing impaired.

**Contact.** E-mail: admissions@pacific.edu
Phone: (209) 946-2211 Toll-free number: (800) 959-2867
Fax: (209) 946-2413
Rich Toledo, Director of Admissions, University of the Pacific, 3601 Pacific Avenue, Stockton, CA 95211-0197

## University of the West
**Rosemead, California**
www.uwest.edu

- Private 4-year university and liberal arts college affiliated with Buddhism
- Commuter campus in small city
- 64 degree-seeking undergraduates

**General.** WASC-accredited, private, non profit campus, Buddhist founded institution. **Degrees:** 4 bachelor's awarded; master's, doctoral offered. **Calendar:** Semester, limited summer session. **Full-time faculty:** 9 total. **Part-time faculty:** 21 total.

**Basis for selection.** Open admission. SAT scores are not required for admission, however a score does help in consideration for admission and for determination of scholarship awards. **Homeschooled:** Home-schooled applicants are handled on a case-by-case basis.

**2008-2009 Annual costs.** Tuition/fees (projected): $9,135. Tuition is $250 per unit for all non-business courses; $300 per unit for all business courses. Books/supplies: $1,314. Personal expenses: $2,826.

**Application procedures. Admission:** Priority date 3/1; deadline 6/1. $50 fee. Application may be submitted online. Admission notification on a rolling basis. **Financial aid:** No deadline.

**Academics. Special study options:** Combined bachelor's/graduate degree, ESL, exchange student, independent study, internships, study abroad. **Credit/placement by examination:** CLEP, institutional tests. **Support services:** Learning center, remedial instruction, tutoring, writing center.

**Majors. Business:** Accounting, international. **English:** English lit. **History:** General. **Philosophy/religion:** Religion. **Psychology:** General.

**Most popular majors.** Business/marketing 40%, philosophy/religious studies 40%, psychology 8%.

**Computing on campus.** 30 workstations in dormitories, library, computer center. Dormitories wired for high-speed internet access and linked to campus network. Commuter students can connect to campus network. Online course registration, online library, student web hosting, wireless network available.

**Student life. Freshman orientation:** Mandatory. **Housing:** $200 fully refundable deposit.

**Contact.** E-mail: admission@uwest.edu
Phone: (626) 571-8811 ext. 120
Grace Hsiao, Admissions Officer, University of the West, 1409 North Walnut Grove Avenue, Rosemead, CA 91770

---

## Vanguard University of Southern California
**Costa Mesa, California**
**www.vanguard.edu**                    **CB code: 4701**

- Private 4-year university and liberal arts college affiliated with Assemblies of God
- Residential campus in small city
- 1,872 degree-seeking undergraduates: 19% part-time, 63% women, 3% African American, 5% Asian American, 17% Hispanic American, 2% Native American, 1% international
- 299 degree-seeking graduate students
- 82% of applicants admitted
- SAT or ACT (ACT writing optional), application essay required
- 52% graduate within 6 years

**General.** Founded in 1920. Regionally accredited. **Degrees:** 454 bachelor's awarded; master's offered. **ROTC:** Army, Air Force. **Location:** 45 miles from Los Angeles, 70 miles from San Diego. **Calendar:** Semester, limited summer session. **Full-time faculty:** 71 total; 79% have terminal degrees, 13% minority, 41% women. **Part-time faculty:** 11 total; 36% have terminal degrees, 27% minority, 54% women. **Class size:** 65% < 20, 26% 20-39, 3% 40-49, 5% 50-99, less than 1% >100.

**Freshman class profile.** 947 applied, 772 admitted, 370 enrolled.

| Mid 50% test scores | | | |
|---|---|---|---|
| SAT critical reading: | 440-550 | Rank in top quarter: | 49% |
| SAT math: | 420-550 | Rank in top tenth: | 22% |
| ACT composite: | 18-24 | Return as sophomores: | 73% |
| GPA 3.50 or higher: | 42% | Out-of-state: | 24% |
| GPA 3.0-3.49: | 36% | Live on campus: | 98% |
| GPA 2.0-2.99: | 21% | International: | 1% |

**Basis for selection.** Priority given to students with GPA of 2.8 or higher, Christian commitment essay, academic reference, reference from pastor. Applications from Christian students who desire an education that integrates Christian faith with learning and living encouraged. Interview recommended for borderline applicants. Audition recommended for music, theater majors. **Homeschooled:** Statement describing homeschool structure and mission required. Should take GED to qualify for federal financial aid. Must

take ACT or SAT and receive ACT composite minimum of 22 or SAT combined minimum of 1000 (exclusive of Writing) in order to qualify for academic scholarship based on home school GPA.

**High school preparation.** Recommended units include English 4, mathematics 2, social studies 3 and science 2.

**2008-2009 Annual costs.** Tuition/fees: $22,986. Room/board: $7,532. Books/supplies: $1,314. Personal expenses: $2,088.

**2007-2008 Financial aid. Need-based:** 68% of total undergraduate aid awarded as scholarships/grants, 32% as loans/jobs. **Non-need-based:** Scholarships awarded for academics, athletics, music/drama.

**Application procedures. Admission:** Priority date 12/1; no deadline. $45 fee, may be waived for applicants with need. Application may be submitted online. Admission notification on a rolling basis beginning on or about 1/15. Must reply by May 1 or within 3 week(s) if notified thereafter. **Financial aid:** Priority date 3/2; no closing date. FAFSA required. Applicants notified on a rolling basis starting 4/1; must reply within 3 week(s) of notification.

**Academics. Special study options:** Accelerated study, combined bachelor's/graduate degree, double major, liberal arts/career combination, study abroad, teacher certification program, Washington semester. **Credit/placement by examination:** AP, CLEP, IB, SAT, ACT. 24 credit hours maximum toward bachelor's degree. **Support services:** Learning center, reduced course load, study skills assistance, tutoring, writing center.

**Majors. Biology:** General. **Business:** General, accounting, business admin, finance, international, marketing. **Communications:** General, broadcast journalism, digital media. **English:** English lit. **Foreign languages:** Spanish. **Health:** Nursing (RN). **History:** General. **Interdisciplinary:** Biological/physical sciences. **Legal studies:** Prelaw. **Liberal arts:** Arts/sciences. **Math:** General. **Parks/recreation:** Exercise sciences, health/fitness. **Philosophy/religion:** Christian, religion. **Physical sciences:** Chemistry. **Psychology:** General. **Social sciences:** General, anthropology, political science, sociology. **Theology:** Bible, missionary, religious ed, theology, youth ministry. **Visual/performing arts:** Cinematography, dramatic, music history, music performance.

**Most popular majors.** Business/marketing 28%, communications/journalism 11%, education 7%, philosophy/religious studies 9%, psychology 21%, social sciences 8%.

**Computing on campus.** 182 workstations in dormitories, library, computer center. Dormitories wired for high-speed internet access and linked to campus network. Commuter students can connect to campus network. Online course registration, online library, helpline, wireless network available.

**Student life. Freshman orientation:** Mandatory, $70 fee. Preregistration for classes offered. 4-day program prior to first day of fall semester. **Policies:** Students must be in good standing to live on campus. Religious observance required. **Housing:** Guaranteed on-campus for all undergraduates. Coed dorms, single-sex dorms, substance-free housing available. $400 deposit, deadline 7/6. **Activities:** Campus ministries, choral groups, drama, literary magazine, music ensembles, musical theater, radio station, student government, student newspaper, College Republicans, College Democrats, El Puente, Students for Social Action, Habitat for Humanity, Spanish club.

**Athletics.** NAIA. **Intercollegiate:** Baseball M, basketball, cross-country, soccer, softball W, tennis, track and field, volleyball W. **Intramural:** Basketball, football (non-tackle), football (tackle), softball. **Team name:** Lions.

**Student services.** Adult student services, alcohol/substance abuse counseling, campus ministries, career counseling, student employment services, financial aid counseling, health services, minority student services, personal counseling, placement for graduates, veterans' counselor, women's services. **Physically disabled:** Services for visually, hearing impaired.

**Contact.** E-mail: admissions@vanguard.edu
Phone: (714) 556-3610 ext. 3901 Toll-free number: (800) 722-6279
Fax: (714) 966-5471
Amberley Wolf, Director of Undergraduate Admissions, Vanguard University of Southern California, 55 Fair Drive, Costa Mesa, CA 92626-9601

---

## West Coast University
**Los Angeles, California**
**www.westcoastuniversity.com/**        **CB code: 4966**

- For-profit 4-year health science college
- Very large city
- 520 degree-seeking undergraduates

**General.** Accredited by ACICS. **Degrees:** 8 associate awarded. **Calendar:** Semester. **Full-time faculty:** 10 total. **Part-time faculty:** 20 total.

**Basis for selection.** Open admission, but selective for some programs. Academics important.

**2007-2008 Annual costs.** Full program costs: associate's degree $21,346; bachelor's degree $41,737; RN $60,000.

**Application procedures. Admission:** No deadline.

**Academics. Credit/placement by examination:** CLEP.

**Majors. Health:** Health care admin.

**Contact.** Phone: (877) 505-4928
Aaron Perez, Admissions Director, West Coast University, 4021 Rosewood Avenue, Los Angeles, CA 90004

## Western Career College: Emeryville
 • Emeryville, California
www.westerncollege.edu

▶ For-profit 4-year technical college
▶ Commuter campus in small town

**General.** Regionally accredited. **Calendar:** Continuous.

**Annual costs/financial aid.** Need-based financial aid available for full-time students.

**Contact.** Phone: (510) 601-0133
1400 65th Street, Suite 200, Emeryville, CA 94608

## Westmont College
Santa Barbara, California
www.westmont.edu

**CB member**
**CB code: 4950**

▶ Private 4-year liberal arts college affiliated with nondenominational tradition
▶ Residential campus in small city
▶ 1,333 degree-seeking undergraduates: 2% part-time, 61% women, 2% African American, 9% Asian American, 10% Hispanic American, 2% Native American, 1% international
▶ 1 graduate students
▶ 73% of applicants admitted
▶ SAT or ACT with writing, application essay required
▶ 69% graduate within 6 years; 69% enter graduate study

**General.** Founded in 1937. Regionally accredited. **Degrees:** 326 bachelor's awarded. **ROTC:** Army, Air Force. **Location:** 90 miles from Los Angeles. **Calendar:** Semester, limited summer session. **Full-time faculty:** 93 total; 89% have terminal degrees, 11% minority, 31% women. **Part-time faculty:** 43 total; 19% have terminal degrees, 9% minority, 51% women. **Class size:** 62% < 20, 24% 20-39, 10% 40-49, 4% 50-99. **Special facilities:** Arts center with theater, observatory, electronic music lab, physiology lab.

**Freshman class profile.** 1,651 applied, 1,208 admitted, 389 enrolled.

| Mid 50% test scores | | | |
|---|---|---|---|
| SAT critical reading: | 540-650 | Rank in top quarter: | 79% |
| SAT math: | 540-660 | Rank in top tenth: | 45% |
| SAT writing: | 540-650 | End year in good standing: | 96% |
| ACT composite: | 24-28 | Return as sophomores: | 87% |
| GPA 3.50 or higher: | 77% | Out-of-state: | 29% |
| GPA 3.0-3.49: | 21% | Live on campus: | 100% |
| GPA 2.0-2.99: | 2% | International: | 1% |

**Basis for selection.** Personal Christian statement, college preparatory high school curriculum, high school rank, test scores, 1 academic recommendation, and essays important. Personal interview, teacher, pastor, and other recommendations may enhance chances. Test scores must be received by November 1 for Early Action applicants. International applicants must submit TOEFL scores if native language is other than English. Personal interviews recommended. **Homeschooled:** Applicants encouraged. Evaluation based on individual merit as well as high school achievement. Greater emphasis may be given to SAT or ACT scores.

**High school preparation.** 16 units required. Required and recommended units include English 4, mathematics 3, social studies 2, science 3 (laboratory 2), foreign language 2-3 and academic electives 4. Of 3 math credits recommended, 2 algebra, 1 geometry preferred. Applicants should take composition courses at least 1 semester per year.

**2007-2008 Annual costs.** Tuition/fees: $31,212. Room/board: $9,622. Books/supplies: $1,386. Personal expenses: $2,142.

**2007-2008 Financial aid. Need-based:** 299 full-time freshmen applied for aid; 248 were judged to have need; 248 of these received aid. Average need met was 73%. Average scholarship/grant was $17,696; average loan $4,675. 71% of total undergraduate aid awarded as scholarships/grants, 29% as loans/jobs. **Non-need-based:** Awarded to 542 full-time undergraduates, including 140 freshmen. Scholarships awarded for academics, art, athletics, leadership, minority status, music/drama.

**Application procedures. Admission:** Priority date 2/20; no deadline. $50 fee, may be waived for applicants with need. Application may be submitted online. Admission notification on a rolling basis beginning on or about 4/1. Must reply by May 1 or within 2 week(s) if notified thereafter. Candidates not accepted for Early Action may be considered for admission under Regular Decision. This allows time for submission of additional materials that may strengthen overall application. **Financial aid:** Priority date 3/1; no closing date. FAFSA required. Applicants notified by 3/15; Applicants notified on a rolling basis starting 3/15; must reply by 5/1 or within 2 week(s) of notification.

**Academics. Special study options:** Accelerated study, double major, exchange student, honors, independent study, internships, semester at sea, student-designed major, study abroad, teacher certification program, urban semester, Washington semester. Cross-cultural studies in Western and Eastern Europe, England, Africa, East Asia, Egypt; semester study available in San Francisco, Los Angeles, Mexico and at one of 12 other member colleges of the Christian College Consortium. **Credit/placement by examination:** AP, CLEP, IB, SAT, ACT, institutional tests. 32 credit hours maximum toward bachelor's degree. **Support services:** Learning center, study skills assistance, tutoring, writing center.

**Majors. Area/ethnic studies:** European. **Biology:** General. **Business:** General. **Communications:** General. **Computer sciences:** Computer science. **Education:** General. **Engineering:** Physics. **English:** English lit. **Foreign languages:** French, Spanish. **Health:** Predental, premedicine, prenursing, prepharmacy, preveterinary. **History:** General. **Legal studies:** Prelaw. **Math:** General. **Parks/recreation:** Exercise sciences. **Philosophy/religion:** Philosophy, religion. **Physical sciences:** Chemistry, physics. **Psychology:** General. **Social sciences:** General, anthropology, economics, political science, sociology. **Visual/performing arts:** Art, dramatic. **Other:** English and Modern Languages.

**Most popular majors.** Biology 8%, business/marketing 14%, communications/journalism 9%, English 12%, parks/recreation 7%, philosophy/religious studies 9%, social sciences 9%, visual/performing arts 7%.

**Computing on campus.** 100 workstations in library, computer center. Dormitories wired for high-speed internet access and linked to campus network. Commuter students can connect to campus network. Online library, helpline, student web hosting, wireless network available.

**Student life. Freshman orientation:** Mandatory. Preregistration for classes offered. Overnight program in summer. **Policies:** Chapel attendance required on Mondays, Wednesdays, Fridays. Dry, tobacco-free campus. Religious observance required. **Housing:** Guaranteed on-campus for all undergraduates. Coed dorms, single-sex dorms, apartments, substance-free housing available. $500 nonrefundable deposit, deadline 5/1. Coed dorms segregated by floors and/or suites. Men and women do not share hallways and bathrooms. Selected visiting hours for members of opposite sex. **Activities:** Bands, choral groups, dance, drama, film society, literary magazine, music ensembles, musical theater, radio station, student government, student newspaper, symphony orchestra, Amnesty International, Habitat for Humanity, Leadership Development Program, political organizations, Fellowship of Christian Athletes, community service organizations.

**Athletics.** NAIA. **Intercollegiate:** Baseball M, basketball, cross-country, soccer, tennis, track and field, volleyball W. **Intramural:** Badminton, basketball, cross-country, field hockey W, football (non-tackle), golf, lacrosse W, racquetball, soccer, softball, swimming, table tennis, tennis, volleyball, water polo. **Team name:** Warriors.

**Student services.** Alcohol/substance abuse counseling, campus ministries, career counseling, student employment services, financial aid counseling, health services, minority student services, personal counseling, placement for graduates. **Physically disabled:** Services for visually, speech, hearing impaired.

**Contact.** E-mail: admissions@westmont.edu
Phone: (805) 565-6200 Toll-free number: (800) 777-9011
Fax: (805) 565-6234
Joyce Luy, Dean of Admission, Westmont College, 955 La Paz Road, Santa Barbara, CA 93108-1089

## Westwood College: Anaheim
### Anaheim, California
### www.westwood.edu

- For-profit 4-year technical college
- Very large city
- 881 degree-seeking undergraduates
- Interview required

**General.** Accredited by ACCSCT. **Degrees:** 186 bachelor's, 25 associate awarded. **Calendar:** Continuous. **Full-time faculty:** 13 total. **Part-time faculty:** 57 total.

**Basis for selection.** Admissions decisions based on assessment test and interview.

**2007-2008 Annual costs.** Cost of 20-month associate degree program: $12,753. Cost of 34-month bachelor's degree program: $13,392. Costs may vary by specific program.

**Application procedures. Admission:** $25 fee. Admission notification on a rolling basis. **Financial aid:** FAFSA required. Applicants notified on a rolling basis.

**Academics. Credit/placement by examination:** AP, CLEP.

**Majors. Business:** Accounting/finance, business admin, marketing. **Computer sciences:** Networking, security, web page design, webmaster. **Visual/performing arts:** Design.

**Contact.** Phone: (714) 938-6140 ext. 60100 Toll-free number: (877) 650-6050
Wes Camp, Director of Admissions, Westwood College: Anaheim, 1551 South Douglass Road, Anaheim, CA 92806

## Westwood College: Inland Empire
### Upland, California
### www.westwood.edu

- For-profit 3-year business and technical college
- Commuter campus in small city
- 1,000 degree-seeking undergraduates
- Interview required

**General.** Accredited by ACCSCT. **Degrees:** 8 bachelor's, 2 associate awarded. **Location:** 45 miles from Los Angeles, 22 miles from Riverside. **Calendar:** Continuous, extensive summer session. **Full-time faculty:** 15 total. **Part-time faculty:** 70 total. **Class size:** 64% < 20, 36% 20-39.

**Basis for selection.** Interview required, documentation of prior education and proficiency in basic college-level skills required, English language proficiency required for applicants whose native language is not English. SAT or ACT recommended. If SAT or ACT scores are not submitted or do not meet minimum requirements, students must take campus-administered ACCUPLACER placement exam.

**2008-2009 Annual costs.** Tuition/fees (projected): $14,061. Books/supplies: $1,464. Personal expenses: $1,840.

**Financial aid. Non-need-based:** Scholarships awarded for academics.

**Application procedures. Admission:** Priority date 10/15; deadline 10/21 (receipt date). $25 fee. Application may be submitted online. Admission notification on a rolling basis. **Financial aid:** No deadline. FAFSA, institutional form required. Must reply within 1 week(s) of notification.

**Academics. Special study options:** Cooperative education, distance learning, honors, independent study, liberal arts/career combination. Hybrid schedules: combination of both campus and online courses. **Credit/placement by examination:** AP, CLEP, IB, institutional tests. Students may test out of required courses by passing proficiency exams. **Support services:** Learning center, reduced course load, remedial instruction, study skills assistance, tutoring.

**Majors. Business:** E-commerce, marketing. **Communications:** Digital media. **Communications technology:** Animation/special effects. **Computer sciences:** LAN/WAN management, web page design. **Protective services:** Police science. **Visual/performing arts:** Design, interior design.

**Computing on campus.** 50 workstations in library. Online library available.

**Student life. Freshman orientation:** Mandatory. **Activities:** Student government, student newspaper.

**Student services.** Career counseling, services for economically disadvantaged, student employment services, financial aid counseling, placement for graduates, veterans' counselor.

**Contact.** E-mail: laiinternet@westwood.edu
Phone: (909) 931-7550 Toll-free number: (866) 288-9488
Fax: (909) 931-5962
Alma Salazar, Director of Admissions, Westwood College: Inland Empire, 20 West Seventh Street, Upland, CA 91786

## Westwood College: South Bay
### Torrance, California

- For-profit 4-year technical college
- Large city
- 600 degree-seeking undergraduates

**General.** Accredited by ACCSCT. **Degrees:** 61 bachelor's, 13 associate awarded. **Calendar:** Continuous. **Full-time faculty:** 7 total. **Part-time faculty:** 54 total.

**Basis for selection.** High school record and institutional assessment exam most important. Institutional assessment exam required if ACT/SAT not submitted.

**Application procedures. Admission:** No deadline. $100 fee.

**Academics. Credit/placement by examination:** CLEP.

**Majors. Business:** Fashion. **Communications technology:** Animation/special effects, graphics. **Computer sciences:** LAN/WAN management, security. **Protective services:** Criminal justice. **Visual/performing arts:** Interior design.

**Contact.** Phone: (310) 965-0888
Fred Polk, Admissions Director, Westwood College: South Bay, 19700 South Vermont Avenue #100, Long Beach, CA 90502

## Whittier College
### Whittier, California
### www.whittier.edu
**CB member**
**CB code: 4952**

- Private 4-year liberal arts college
- Residential campus in small city
- 1,257 degree-seeking undergraduates: 2% part-time, 55% women, 3% African American, 8% Asian American, 30% Hispanic American, 1% Native American, 2% international
- 623 degree-seeking graduate students
- 67% of applicants admitted
- SAT or ACT with writing, application essay required
- 57% graduate within 6 years

**General.** Founded in 1887. Regionally accredited. Historic affiliation with Quakers. **Degrees:** 285 bachelor's awarded; master's, first professional offered. **ROTC:** Army, Air Force. **Location:** 18 miles from Los Angeles. **Calendar:** 4-1-4, limited summer session. **Full-time faculty:** 87 total; 100% have terminal degrees, 28% minority, 44% women. **Part-time faculty:** 36 total; 42% have terminal degrees, 61% minority, 64% women. **Class size:** 55% < 20, 42% 20-39, 1% 40-49, 1% 50-99. **Special facilities:** Collection of Quaker books and materials, John Greenleaf Whittier collection including manuscripts, letters and furniture, collection of Richard M. Nixon gifts, keck image processing laboratory.

**Freshman class profile.** 2,196 applied, 1,469 admitted, 297 enrolled.

| Mid 50% test scores | | | |
|---|---|---|---|
| SAT critical reading: | 480-600 | Rank in top quarter: | 45% |
| SAT math: | 480-600 | Rank in top tenth: | 34% |
| SAT writing: | 480-590 | Return as sophomores: | 78% |
| ACT composite: | 20-27 | Out-of-state: | 61% |
| GPA 3.50 or higher: | 23% | Live on campus: | 86% |
| GPA 3.0-3.49: | 35% | International: | 4% |
| GPA 2.0-2.99: | 42% | Fraternities: | 11% |
| | | Sororities: | 18% |

**Basis for selection.** GPA, course selection, and class rank most important followed by essays, references, interviews, test scores, activities, and geographic considerations. Interview recommended. **Homeschooled:** Statement describing homeschool structure and mission, transcript of courses and grades, letter of recommendation (nonparent) required.

**High school preparation.** Required and recommended units include English 3-4, mathematics 2-3, social studies 1-2, science 1-2 (laboratory 1) and foreign language 2-3.

**2007-2008 Annual costs.** Tuition/fees: $30,160. Room/board: $8,750. Books/supplies: $800. Personal expenses: $1,700.

**2007-2008 Financial aid. Need-based:** Average need met was 94%. Average scholarship/grant was $15,995; average loan $6,331. 33% of total undergraduate aid awarded as scholarships/grants, 67% as loans/jobs. **Non-need-based:** Scholarships awarded for academics, alumni affiliation, art, leadership, minority status. **Additional information:** Auditions required for talent scholarship applicants in art, music, and theater.

**Application procedures. Admission:** Priority date 2/1; no deadline. $50 fee, may be waived for applicants with need. Application may be submitted online. Admission notification on a rolling basis beginning on or about 12/30. Must reply by May 1 or within 2 week(s) if notified thereafter. **Financial aid:** Priority date 3/1, closing date 6/30. FAFSA, CSS PROFILE required. Applicants notified on a rolling basis starting 2/15; must reply within 2 week(s) of notification.

**Academics. Special study options:** Combined bachelor's/graduate degree, double major, independent study, internships, liberal arts/career combination, semester at sea, student-designed major, study abroad, teacher certification program, Washington semester. **Credit/placement by examination:** AP, CLEP, IB, SAT, institutional tests. 30 credit hours maximum toward bachelor's degree. **Support services:** Learning center, study skills assistance, tutoring, writing center.

**Majors. Area/ethnic studies:** Latin American. **Biology:** General. **Business:** General. **Conservation:** General. **Education:** General, early childhood. **English:** American lit, British lit, English lit. **Foreign languages:** General, comparative lit, French, Spanish. **Health:** Athletic training, predental, premedicine, prepharmacy, preveterinary, recreational therapy. **History:** General. **Legal studies:** Prelaw. **Liberal arts:** Arts/sciences. **Math:** General. **Philosophy/religion:** Philosophy, religion. **Physical sciences:** Chemistry, physics. **Psychology:** General. **Public administration:** Social work. **Social sciences:** Anthropology, international relations, political science, sociology, urban studies. **Visual/performing arts:** Art, art history/conservation, dramatic, music history, theater history.

**Most popular majors.** Biology 11%, business/marketing 15%, parks/recreation 7%, psychology 8%, social sciences 26%, visual/performing arts 6%.

**Computing on campus.** 165 workstations in dormitories, library, computer center. Dormitories wired for high-speed internet access and linked to campus network. Wireless network available.

**Student life. Freshman orientation:** Mandatory, $200 fee. Orientation begins over Labor Day weekend. **Housing:** Guaranteed on-campus for freshmen. Coed dorms, single-sex dorms, substance-free housing available. $100 nonrefundable deposit, deadline 5/1. Multicultural hall, honors floor, living and learning community available. **Activities:** Jazz band, choral groups, dance, drama, international student organizations, literary magazine, music ensembles, musical theater, radio station, student government, student newspaper, national honor societies.

**Athletics.** NCAA. **Intercollegiate:** Baseball M, basketball, cross-country, diving, football (tackle) M, golf, lacrosse, soccer, softball W, swimming, tennis, track and field, volleyball W, water polo. **Intramural:** Basketball, softball, volleyball. **Team name:** Poets.

**Student services.** Career counseling, student employment services, health services, on-campus daycare, personal counseling, placement for graduates.

**Contact.** E-mail: admission@whittier.edu
Phone: (562) 907-4238 Fax: (562) 907-4870
Kieron Miller, Director of Admission, Whittier College, 13406 East Philadelphia Street, Whittier, CA 90608-0634

## William Jessup University
### Rocklin, California
www.jessup.edu                    CB code: 4756

- Private 4-year Bible and liberal arts college affiliated with nondenominational tradition
- Residential campus in small city
- 504 degree-seeking undergraduates: 15% part-time, 59% women, 6% African American, 5% Asian American, 8% Hispanic American, 2% Native American, 1% international
- 6 degree-seeking graduate students
- 57% of applicants admitted

- SAT or ACT (ACT writing recommended), application essay required
- 33% graduate within 6 years

**General.** Founded in 1939. Regionally accredited; also accredited by ABHE. **Degrees:** 121 bachelor's, 2 associate awarded. **Location:** 20 miles from Sacramento. **Calendar:** Semester, limited summer session. **Full-time faculty:** 23 total; 39% have terminal degrees, 4% minority, 48% women. **Part-time faculty:** 89 total; 35% have terminal degrees, 12% minority, 75% women. **Class size:** 75% < 20, 21% 20-39, 2% 40-49, 2% 50-99.

**Freshman class profile.** 146 applied, 83 admitted, 57 enrolled.

| Mid 50% test scores | | | |
|---|---|---|---|
| SAT critical reading: | 480-610 | GPA 2.0-2.99: | 18% |
| SAT math: | 480-590 | Rank in top quarter: | 56% |
| SAT writing: | 470-590 | Rank in top tenth: | 41% |
| ACT composite: | 21-28 | Return as sophomores: | 71% |
| GPA 3.50 or higher: | 56% | Out-of-state: | 4% |
| GPA 3.0-3.49: | 26% | Live on campus: | 81% |
| | | International: | 2% |

**Basis for selection.** Academic records, supporting documents, moral character, willingness to comply with standards and values of university strongly considered. Interview strongly recommended, may be required. Audition required for music scholarship (majors only). **Homeschooled:** Statement describing homeschool structure and mission required. Extra emphasis placed on SAT/ACT; professional/third-party home educators transcript provider preferred over in-home development of transcripts. **Learning Disabled:** Once voluntarily disclosed, student is asked to provide documentation of learning disability and meet with academic support advisor regularly.

**High school preparation.** 17 units required; 24 recommended. Required and recommended units include English 4, mathematics 3-4, social studies 1-2, history 2-3, science 2-3 (laboratory 1-2), foreign language 2-3 and academic electives 2-3. Religion taken for credit at accredited parochial/Christian high school may be given academic consideration.

**2008-2009 Annual costs.** Tuition/fees: $20,480. Room/board: $7,470. Books/supplies: $1,566. Personal expenses: $2,214.

**Financial aid. Non-need-based:** Scholarships awarded for academics, athletics, music/drama.

**Application procedures. Admission:** Priority date 4/1; deadline 8/15 (postmark date). $35 fee, may be waived for applicants with need. Application may be submitted online. Admission notification on a rolling basis beginning on or about 11/15. Must reply by June 1 or within 2 weeks if notified thereafter. $250 confirmation deposit is also housing deposit and refundable until June 1 or within 2 weeks if notified thereafter. **Financial aid:** Priority date 3/2, closing date 8/15. FAFSA required. Applicants notified on a rolling basis starting 3/2; must reply by 6/1 or within 2 week(s) of notification.

**Academics.** All church vocation/ministry-based degrees offer dual major in Bible and Theology. Emphasis placed on pastoral training, missions, youth ministry, and Christian education. **Special study options:** Double major, independent study, internships, study abroad, teacher certification program, Washington semester. Degree completion program for adult: 25 or older or have completed two years of full-time work experience; completion of a minimum of 60 transferable semester hours of credit from an accredited college or post-secondary institution. (A person may be admitted on probation with 47-59 semester hours of credit.); cumulative grade point average of 2.0 (4.0 scale) or higher on all prior academic work; completion of English Composition 1 or higher. **Credit/placement by examination:** AP, CLEP, IB, SAT, ACT, institutional tests. 16 credit hours maximum toward associate degree, 16 toward bachelor's. A maximum of 30 units will be awarded for AP, IB, or CLEP. **Support services:** Reduced course load, study skills assistance, tutoring, writing center.

**Majors. Business:** Business admin. **Education:** Elementary, multi-level teacher. **English:** English lit. **History:** General. **Psychology:** General. **Public administration:** Policy analysis. **Theology:** Missionary, pastoral counseling, religious ed, theology, youth ministry.

**Most popular majors.** Business/marketing 27%, psychology 20%, theological studies 42%, visual/performing arts 7%.

**Computing on campus.** 35 workstations in library, computer center. Dormitories wired for high-speed internet access and linked to campus network. Commuter students can connect to campus network. Online library, helpline, repair service, wireless network available.

**Student life. Freshman orientation:** Mandatory. Preregistration for classes offered. 2-day sessions in late spring and summer. **Policies:** Dry campus. Quiet hours but no curfew. No formal dress code, but appropriate dress recommended. Chapel attendance required. Religious observance required.

**Housing:** Guaranteed on-campus for freshmen. Single-sex dorms, substance-free housing available. **Activities:** Jazz band, campus ministries, choral groups, film society, music ensembles, student government, spiritual formation groups, multicultural fellowship.

**Athletics.** NAIA. **Intercollegiate:** Baseball M, basketball, cross-country, golf M, soccer, softball W, track and field, volleyball W. **Team name:** Warriors.

**Student services.** Campus ministries, career counseling, financial aid counseling, personal counseling. **Physically disabled:** Services for visually, hearing impaired.

**Contact.** E-mail: admissions@jessup.edu
Phone: (916) 577-2222 Toll-free number: (800) 355-7522
Fax: (916) 577-2220
Vance Pascua, Director of Admission, William Jessup University, 333 Sunset Boulevard, Rocklin, CA 95765

## Woodbury University
### Burbank, California
www.woodbury.edu

**CB member**
**CB code: 4955**

- Private 4-year university
- Commuter campus in very large city
- 1,277 degree-seeking undergraduates: 18% part-time, 56% women, 5% African American, 11% Asian American, 32% Hispanic American, 6% international
- 243 degree-seeking graduate students
- 81% of applicants admitted
- SAT or ACT (ACT writing optional), application essay required
- 53% graduate within 6 years

**General.** Founded in 1884. Regionally accredited. **Degrees:** 233 bachelor's awarded; master's offered. **Location:** 15 miles from downtown Los Angeles. **Calendar:** Semester, limited summer session. **Full-time faculty:** 47 total; 79% have terminal degrees, 49% women. **Part-time faculty:** 190 total. **Class size:** 83% < 20, 16% 20-39, less than 1% 40-49. **Special facilities:** Design galleries.

**Freshman class profile.** 486 applied, 393 admitted, 159 enrolled.

| Mid 50% test scores | | | | |
|---|---|---|---|---|
| SAT critical reading: | 410-530 | Out-of-state: | | 10% |
| SAT math: | 420-550 | Live on campus: | | 7% |
| SAT writing: | 410-530 | International: | | 11% |
| Return as sophomores: | 82% | Fraternities: | | 1% |
| | | Sororities: | | 1% |

**Basis for selection.** Primary emphasis placed on applicant's prior academic record and standardized test scores. Interview recommended. **Homeschooled:** State high school equivalency certificate required.

**High school preparation.** College-preparatory program recommended. 15 units recommended. Recommended units include English 4, mathematics 3, social studies 3, history 2, science 3 (laboratory 2) and foreign language 2.

**2007-2008 Annual costs.** Tuition/fees: $25,198. Room/board: $8,660. Books/supplies: $1,386. Personal expenses: $2,142.

**2007-2008 Financial aid.** Need-based: 140 full-time freshmen applied for aid; 129 were judged to have need; 127 of these received aid. Average need met was 59%. Average scholarship/grant was $13,923; average loan $3,367. 54% of total undergraduate aid awarded as scholarships/grants, 46% as loans/jobs. **Non-need-based:** Awarded to 92 full-time undergraduates, including 22 freshmen. Scholarships awarded for academics.

**Application procedures. Admission:** Priority date 3/1; no deadline. $35 fee, may be waived for applicants with need. Application may be submitted online. Admission notification on a rolling basis beginning on or about 11/1. Must reply by May 1 or within 4 week(s) if notified thereafter. **Financial aid:** Priority date 3/2; no closing date. FAFSA, institutional form required. Applicants notified on a rolling basis starting 3/15; must reply by 5/1 or within 2 week(s) of notification.

**Academics.** Combines professional programs in design, architecture, and business with liberal arts components. **Special study options:** Accelerated study, double major, independent study, internships, liberal arts/career combination, student-designed major, study abroad, weekend college. **Credit/placement by examination:** AP, CLEP, IB, institutional tests. Institutional/departmental examinations used for placement or counseling. **Support services:** Learning center, reduced course load, remedial instruction, tutoring.

**Majors. Architecture:** Architecture, interior. **Business:** Accounting, business admin, fashion, marketing, organizational behavior. **Communications:** Media studies. **Computer sciences:** General. **Psychology:** General. **Visual/performing arts:** Commercial/advertising art, fashion design, graphic design. **Other:** Film/video and photographic arts, Politics and history.

**Most popular majors.** Architecture 37%, business/marketing 29%, visual/performing arts 20%.

**Computing on campus.** 135 workstations in library, computer center. Commuter students can connect to campus network. Online course registration, online library, helpline, wireless network available.

**Student life. Freshman orientation:** Mandatory, $75 fee. Preregistration for classes offered. **Housing:** Coed dorms, apartments, substance-free housing available. $150 fully refundable deposit, deadline 5/1. **Activities:** International student organizations, student government, Armenian student association, residence life council.

**Athletics. Intramural:** Basketball, soccer.

**Student services.** Adult student services, alcohol/substance abuse counseling, career counseling, services for economically disadvantaged, student employment services, financial aid counseling, health services, personal counseling, placement for graduates. **Physically disabled:** Services for visually, speech, hearing impaired.

**Contact.** E-mail: admissions@woodbury.edu
Phone: (818) 767-0888 ext. 221 Toll-free number: (800) 784-9663
Fax: (818) 767-7520
Ruth Lorenzana, Director of Admissions, Woodbury University, 7500 Glenoaks Boulevard, Burbank, CA 91510-7846

## World Mission University
### Los Angeles, California
www.wmu.edu

- Private 4-year Bible and seminary college affiliated with Non-Denominational
- Very large city
- 76 degree-seeking undergraduates: 38% part-time, 58% women
- 168 degree-seeking graduate students

**General.** Accredited by ABHE. **Degrees:** 12 bachelor's awarded; master's, first professional offered. **Location:** Downtown. **Calendar:** Semester, limited summer session. **Full-time faculty:** 7 total. **Part-time faculty:** 2 total.

**Basis for selection.** Admissions criteria include sense of calling for Christian ministry, participation in church community, academic performance, test results, recommendations. Audition and additional supplementary application required for music programs. **Homeschooled:** Statement describing homeschool structure and mission, transcript of courses and grades, letter of recommendation (nonparent) required.

**2008-2009 Annual costs.** Tuition/fees (projected): $4,600.

**Application procedures. Admission:** No deadline. $50 fee. Application must be submitted on paper. Admission notification on a rolling basis.

**Academics. Special study options:** Distance learning, dual enrollment of high school students, ESL. **Credit/placement by examination:** CLEP, IB, institutional tests.

**Majors. Theology:** Bible.

**Computing on campus.** Online library, wireless network available.

**Student life. Freshman orientation:** Mandatory.

**Contact.** E-mail: wmuoffice@gmail.com
Phone: (213) 385-2322 Fax: (213) 385-2332
Edmund Rhee, Admissions Director, World Mission University, 500 Shatto Place, Los Angeles, CA 90020

## Yeshiva Ohr Elchonon Chabad/West Coast Talmudical Seminary
### Los Angeles, California

**CB code: 1331**

- Private 4-year rabbinical college for men affiliated with Jewish faith
- Residential campus in very large city

**General.** Founded in 1953. Accredited by AARTS. **Calendar:** Semester.

**Annual costs/financial aid.** Books/supplies: $125. Personal expenses: $100.

**Contact.**   Phone: (323) 937-3763
Director of Admissions, 7215 Waring Avenue, Los Angeles, CA 90046

# Colorado

## Adams State College
**Alamosa, Colorado**
**www.adams.edu**      **CB code: 4001**

▶ Public 4-year liberal arts college
▶ Residential campus in small town
▶ 2,104 degree-seeking undergraduates: 18% part-time, 56% women, 8% African American, 2% Asian American, 28% Hispanic American, 2% Native American
▶ 637 degree-seeking graduate students
▶ 58% of applicants admitted
▶ SAT or ACT (ACT writing optional) required

**General.** Founded in 1921. Regionally accredited. Hispanic-serving institution. **Degrees:** 286 bachelor's, 21 associate awarded; master's offered. **Location:** 225 miles from Denver, 200 miles from Albuquerque, New Mexico. **Calendar:** Semester, limited summer session. **Full-time faculty:** 111 total; 69% have terminal degrees, 18% minority, 42% women. **Part-time faculty:** 73 total; 7% minority, 63% women. **Class size:** 68% < 20, 25% 20-39, 5% 40-49, 2% 50-99, less than 1% >100. **Special facilities:** Observatory, planetarium, natural history museum, geology museum, cross-cultural center.

**Freshman class profile.** 1,928 applied, 1,113 admitted, 541 enrolled.

| Mid 50% test scores | | | |
|---|---|---|---|
| SAT critical reading: | 420-550 | GPA 3.0-3.49: | 30% |
| SAT math: | 420-510 | GPA 2.0-2.99: | 45% |
| SAT writing: | 390-480 | Rank in top quarter: | 20% |
| ACT composite: | 17-22 | Rank in top tenth: | 6% |
| GPA 3.50 or higher: | 20% | Return as sophomores: | 57% |
| | | Out-of-state: | 19% |

**Basis for selection.** Open admissions for associate degree programs only. Bachelor's degree candidates must have either 2.0 high school GPA, or rank in top two-thirds of class with average or above average score on ACT or SAT. Accuplacer tests for math and English required if SAT or ACT not available. Audition required of music majors. Portfolio required of art majors. **Homeschooled:** Transcript of courses and grades required.

**High school preparation.** 15 units recommended. Recommended units include English 4, mathematics 2, social studies 3, history 1, science 2 and foreign language 2. Computer applications: .5 units recommended. Math should include Algebra I and one advanced math course.

**2007-2008 Annual costs.** Tuition/fees: $3,464; $10,808 out-of-state. Room/board: $6,560. Books/supplies: $1,698. Personal expenses: $2,410.

**2006-2007 Financial aid. Need-based:** 452 full-time freshmen applied for aid; 359 were judged to have need; 353 of these received aid. Average need met was 50%. Average scholarship/grant was $3,800; average loan $2,512. 56% of total undergraduate aid awarded as scholarships/grants, 44% as loans/jobs. **Non-need-based:** Awarded to 662 full-time undergraduates, including 244 freshmen. Scholarships awarded for academics, alumni affiliation, art, athletics, leadership, minority status, music/drama, state residency.

**Application procedures. Admission:** Priority date 8/1; no deadline. $20 fee, may be waived for applicants with need. Application may be submitted online. Admission notification on a rolling basis. **Financial aid:** Priority date 3/1, closing date 4/15. FAFSA required. Applicants notified on a rolling basis starting 4/30; must reply within 4 week(s) of notification.

**Academics. Special study options:** Accelerated study, combined bachelor's/graduate degree, distance learning, double major, independent study, internships, study abroad, teacher certification program, weekend college. HIgh School Dual Enrollment. **Credit/placement by examination:** AP, CLEP, IB, SAT, ACT, institutional tests. 30 credit hours maximum toward bachelor's degree. **Support services:** Learning center, reduced course load, remedial instruction, study skills assistance, tutoring, writing center.

**Majors. Agriculture:** Business. **Biology:** General, bacteriology, botany, exercise physiology, zoology. **Business:** General, accounting, business admin, finance, management information systems, marketing, office/clerical, small business admin. **Communications:** General, advertising. **Computer**

**sciences:** General. **Conservation:** Management/policy. **Education:** General, art, biology, business, chemistry, elementary, English, history, mathematics, middle, multi-level teacher, music, physical, science, secondary, social science, social studies, Spanish, speech. **English:** Creative writing, English lit. **Foreign languages:** Spanish. **Health:** Athletic training, health care admin, health services, nursing (RN), predental, premedicine, prenursing, prepharmacy, preveterinary. **History:** General. **Legal studies:** Prelaw. **Liberal arts:** Arts/sciences. **Math:** General. **Parks/recreation:** Exercise sciences, health/fitness. **Physical sciences:** Chemical physics, chemistry, geology, physics. **Psychology:** General. **Social sciences:** General, criminology, economics, sociology. **Visual/performing arts:** Art, ceramics, dramatic, drawing, metal/jewelry, music performance, music theory/composition, painting, photography, printmaking, sculpture, studio arts, voice/opera.

**Most popular majors.** Biology 6%, business/marketing 18%, liberal arts 22%, parks/recreation 7%, psychology 6%, social sciences 14%, visual/performing arts 16%.

**Computing on campus.** 191 workstations in dormitories, library, computer center, student center. Dormitories wired for high-speed internet access and linked to campus network. Commuter students can connect to campus network. Online course registration, online library, helpline, student web hosting, wireless network available.

**Student life. Freshman orientation:** Mandatory. Preregistration for classes offered. Program held weekend before start of fall semester. **Housing:** Guaranteed on-campus for freshmen. Coed dorms, single-sex dorms, apartments, substance-free housing available. $150 partly refundable deposit. Learning community house, freshman interest-group housing, drug and alcohol-free learning community, outdoor adventure community, making the grade community (must maintain 3.5 GPA). **Activities:** Bands, campus ministries, choral groups, dance, drama, literary magazine, music ensembles, Model UN, musical theater, radio station, student government, student newspaper, Circle K, College Republicans, Newman Club, Ski Buffs, Student Ambassadors, Teacher Education Association, Associated Students and Faculty, Phi Beta Lambda.

**Athletics.** NCAA. **Intercollegiate:** Basketball, cross-country, football (tackle) M, golf, soccer W, softball W, track and field, volleyball W, wrestling M. **Intramural:** Basketball, bowling, racquetball, skiing, soccer, softball, swimming, tennis, volleyball, water polo. **Team name:** Grizzlies.

**Student services.** Adult student services, career counseling, student employment services, financial aid counseling, health services, on-campus daycare, personal counseling, placement for graduates, veterans' counselor. **Physically disabled:** Services for visually, hearing impaired.

**Contact.** E-mail: ascadmit@adams.edu
Phone: (719) 587-7712 Toll-free number: (800) 824-6494
Fax: (719) 587-7522
Eric Carpio, Director for Admissions, Adams State College, 208 Edgemont Boulevard, Alamosa, CO 81102

## American Sentinel University
**Aurora, Colorado**
**www.americansentinel.edu**      **CB code: 3806**

▶ For-profit 4-year virtual university
▶ Very large city
▶ 750 degree-seeking undergraduates
▶ 350 graduate students

**General.** Accredited by DETC. **Degrees:** 119 bachelor's awarded; master's offered. **Calendar:** Continuous, extensive summer session. **Full-time faculty:** 5 total. **Part-time faculty:** 70 total.

**Basis for selection.** Open admission.

**2007-2008 Annual costs.** Total maximum cost of a bachelor-s program: $30,000; includes application fee, technology and library fees.

**Application procedures. Admission:** No deadline. $40 fee. Application may be submitted online. Admission notification on a rolling basis.

**Academics. Special study options:** Accelerated study, distance learning, honors, independent study, liberal arts/career combination. **Credit/placement by examination:** AP, CLEP. 45 credit hours maximum toward associate degree, 90 toward bachelor's. **Support services:** Learning center, reduced course load, tutoring.

**Majors. Business:** Business admin, e-commerce, management information systems, marketing. **Computer sciences:** General, computer science, information systems, information technology, system admin.

**Computing on campus.** PC or laptop required.

**Student life. Freshman orientation:** Mandatory. Preregistration for classes offered. **Activities:** Student newspaper.

**Contact.** E-mail: admiss@americansentinel.edu
Phone: (205) 323-6191 Toll-free number: (800) 729-2427
Fax: (205) 328-2229
David Lenhart, Director of Admissions, American Sentinel University, 2101 Magnolia Avenue, Suite 200, Birmingham, AL 35205-2827

## Art Institute of Colorado
**Denver, Colorado**
**www.aic.artinstitutes.edu**                    **CB code: 7150**

- For-profit 4-year visual arts and technical college
- Commuter campus in very large city
- 2,245 degree-seeking undergraduates: 32% part-time, 51% women
- Application essay, interview required

**General.** Founded in 1952. Accredited by ACICS. **Degrees:** 270 bachelor's, 166 associate awarded. **Location:** Downtown. **Calendar:** Quarter, extensive summer session. **Full-time faculty:** 79 total. **Part-time faculty:** 71 total. **Special facilities:** Student-run restaurant at culinary school.

**Basis for selection.** Commitment to career most important; essay, interview important; high school transcript considered with GPA. Portfolio required of advanced standing applicants. **Homeschooled:** Documentation of grades and official gradution date required.

**2008-2009 Annual costs.** Tuition/fees (projected): $21,985. Supply kit $530-$2,155 depending on program. Books/supplies: $2,968.

**Financial aid. Additional information:** Tuition at time of first enrollment guaranteed to students for 4 years providing student maintains continuous attendance and completes program within 150% of program length.

**Application procedures. Admission:** No deadline. $150 fee. Application may be submitted online. Admission notification on a rolling basis. **Financial aid:** No deadline. FAFSA, institutional form required. Applicants notified on a rolling basis.

**Academics. Special study options:** Distance learning, independent study, internships, study abroad. **Credit/placement by examination:** CLEP, IB, institutional tests. 30 credit hours maximum toward associate degree. **Support services:** Learning center, remedial instruction.

**Majors. Business:** Apparel. **Communications technology:** Animation/special effects. **Computer sciences:** Computer graphics, web page design. **Family/consumer sciences:** Food/nutrition, institutional food production. **Personal/culinary services:** Restaurant/catering. **Visual/performing arts:** Cinematography, commercial photography, commercial/advertising art, design, graphic design, industrial design, interior design, multimedia, photography.

**Most popular majors.** Communication technologies 24%, visual/performing arts 72%.

**Computing on campus.** 380 workstations in dormitories, library, computer center. Dormitories wired for high-speed internet access.

**Student life. Freshman orientation:** Mandatory. Preregistration for classes offered. **Housing:** Coed dorms, substance-free housing available. $300 deposit. **Activities:** Student newspaper.

**Student services.** Alcohol/substance abuse counseling, career counseling, student employment services, financial aid counseling, personal counseling, placement for graduates, veterans' counselor. **Physically disabled:** Services for visually, speech, hearing impaired.

**Contact.** E-mail: aicadm@aii.edu
Phone: (303) 837-0825 Toll-free number: (800) 275-2420
Fax: (303) 860-8520
Brian Parker, Director of Admissions, Art Institute of Colorado, 1200 Lincoln Street, Denver, CO 80203

## Aspen University
**Denver, Colorado**
**www.aspen.edu**

- For-profit 4-year virtual business college
- Very large city

- 625 degree-seeking undergraduates
- Application essay required

**General.** Accredited by DETC. **Degrees:** 2 bachelor's awarded; master's offered. **Calendar:** Continuous. **Part-time faculty:** 85 total.

**Basis for selection.** Open admission. Three letters of recommendation required. **Homeschooled:** State high school equivalency certificate required.

**2007-2008 Annual costs.** Tuition/fees: $7,500.

**Application procedures. Admission:** No deadline. $75 fee. Application may be submitted online. Admission notification on a rolling basis.

**Academics. Special study options:** Distance learning. **Credit/placement by examination:** CLEP. **Support services:** Remedial instruction.

**Majors. Business:** Business admin.

**Computing on campus.** PC or laptop required.

**Contact.** E-mail: admissions@aspen.edu
Phone: (303) 333-4224
Amanda Hosking, Director of Admissions, Aspen University, 501 South Cherry Street, Suite 350, Denver, CO 80246

## CollegeAmerica: Colorado Springs
**Colorado Springs, Colorado**
**www.collegeamerica.edu**

- For-profit 4-year technical college
- Commuter campus in large city

**General.** Accredited by ACCSCT. **Calendar:** Continuous.

**Annual costs/financial aid.** Tuition ranges from $260 to $334 per quarter credit depending on program.

**Contact.** Phone: (719) 637-0600
3645 Citadel Drive South, Colorado Springs, CO 80909

## CollegeAmerica: Fort Collins
**Fort Collins, Colorado**
**www.collegeamerica.edu**

- For-profit 4-year business, health science, technical and career college
- Commuter campus in small city
- 135 degree-seeking undergraduates: 74% women

**General.** Accredited by ACCSCT. **Degrees:** 20 bachelor's, 65 associate awarded; master's offered. **Calendar:** Semester, extensive summer session. **Full-time faculty:** 3 total; 100% women. **Part-time faculty:** 10 total; 40% women.

**Basis for selection.** Open admission. **Homeschooled:** Transcript of courses and grades required.

**2007-2008 Annual costs.** Tuition ranges from $260 to $334 per quarter credit depending on program.

**Application procedures. Admission:** No deadline. No application fee. **Financial aid:** No deadline.

**Academics. Special study options:** Accelerated study, combined bachelor's/graduate degree, distance learning. **Credit/placement by examination:** CLEP. **Support services:** Study skills assistance, tutoring.

**Majors. Business:** General, accounting. **Computer sciences:** General. **Health:** Health services.

**Computing on campus.** 50 workstations in library, computer center. Repair service, wireless network available.

**Student life. Freshman orientation:** Mandatory.

**Contact.** Phone: (970) 223-6060 Toll-free number: (800) 622-2894
Kristy McNear, Director of Admissions, CollegeAmerica: Fort Collins, 4601 South Mason, Fort Collins, CO 80525

## Colorado Christian University

Lakewood, Colorado    CB member
www.ccu.edu    CB code: 4659

- Private 4-year university and liberal arts college affiliated with nondenominational tradition
- Residential campus in large city
- 920 degree-seeking undergraduates: 4% part-time, 58% women
- 230 graduate students
- 61% of applicants admitted
- SAT or ACT (ACT writing optional), application essay required

**General.** Founded in 1914. Regionally accredited. Degree completion programs available at Colorado Springs, Grand Junction, Loveland, Denver (multiple locations), and Lakewood campuses. **Degrees:** 135 bachelor's, 15 associate awarded; master's offered. **ROTC:** Army, Air Force. **Location:** 10 miles from Denver. **Calendar:** Semester, limited summer session. **Full-time faculty:** 41 total; 63% have terminal degrees, 5% minority, 44% women. **Class size:** 79% < 20, 18% 20-39, 2% 40-49, 1% 50-99.

**Freshman class profile.** 1,080 applied, 662 admitted, 561 enrolled.

| Mid 50% test scores | | | |
|---|---|---|---|
| SAT critical reading: | 510-630 | GPA 2.0-2.99: | 16% |
| SAT math: | 480-590 | Rank in top quarter: | 47% |
| ACT composite: | 19-25 | Rank in top tenth: | 19% |
| GPA 3.50 or higher: | 59% | Out-of-state: | 45% |
| GPA 3.0-3.49: | 23% | Live on campus: | 91% |

**Basis for selection.** Applicants must show evidence of commitment to Christian faith through written statement. Course selection, GPA, test scores, leadership or service, and motivation important. Interviews encouraged. Audition required of music and theater majors. **Homeschooled:** Transcript of courses and grades required.

**High school preparation.** 19 units recommended. Recommended units include English 4, mathematics 3, social studies 3, history 2, science 2 (laboratory 2) and foreign language 2. Recommend 1 unit of computer science.

**2007-2008 Annual costs.** Tuition/fees: $19,000. Room/board: $7,600. Books/supplies: $1,188. Personal expenses: $1,044.

**2006-2007 Financial aid. Need-based:** 212 full-time freshmen applied for aid; 193 were judged to have need; 187 of these received aid. Average need met was 71%. Average scholarship/grant was $4,000; average loan $2,750. 43% of total undergraduate aid awarded as scholarships/grants, 57% as loans/jobs. **Non-need-based:** Awarded to 651 full-time undergraduates, including 224 freshmen. Scholarships awarded for academics, athletics, leadership, music/drama.

**Application procedures. Admission:** Priority date 3/1; deadline 8/1 (postmark date). $50 fee, may be waived for applicants with need. Application may be submitted online. Admission notification on a rolling basis beginning on or about 11/1. Must reply by May 1 or within 4 week(s) if notified thereafter. **Financial aid:** Priority date 3/15; no closing date. FAFSA required. Applicants notified on a rolling basis starting 4/1; must reply by 5/1 or within 4 week(s) of notification.

**Academics. Special study options:** Accelerated study, cooperative education, distance learning, double major, honors, independent study, internships, semester at sea, student-designed major, study abroad, teacher certification program, urban semester, Washington semester, weekend college. American studies program (Washington, D.C.), host university for Institute for Family Studies; China studies program at various sites in China, Latin American program (Costa Rica), Los Angeles film studies center, Middle East studies (Cairo, Egypt), Oxford honors program (University of Oxford, England), Russian studies program at various sites in Russia, Summer Institute of Journalism (Washington DC). **Credit/placement by examination:** AP, CLEP, IB, ACT, institutional tests. 15 credit hours maximum toward associate degree, 45 toward bachelor's. **Support services:** Learning center, reduced course load, remedial instruction, study skills assistance, tutoring, writing center.

**Majors. Biology:** General. **Business:** Business admin, management information systems, management science. **Communications:** General. **Computer sciences:** General. **Education:** Music. **English:** English lit. **History:** General. **Interdisciplinary:** Biological/physical sciences, global studies. **Liberal arts:** Arts/sciences. **Math:** General. **Parks/recreation:** Health/fitness. **Physical sciences:** Physics. **Psychology:** General. **Social sciences:** General. **Theology:** Bible, youth ministry. **Visual/performing arts:** Music performance, studio arts.

**Most popular majors.** Business/marketing 37%, computer/information sciences 16%, education 14%, psychology 7%, theological studies 6%.

**Computing on campus.** 151 workstations in library, computer center, student center. Dormitories wired for high-speed internet access and linked to campus network. Online course registration, online library, helpline, wireless network available.

**Student life. Freshman orientation:** Mandatory. Preregistration for classes offered. Seminars for students and parents held 4 days prior to beginning of classes. **Policies:** Use of alcoholic beverages, illegal drugs, and tobacco prohibited on campus and at college-sponsored activities. Premarital sexual relationships prohibited. Religious observance required. **Housing:** Guaranteed on-campus for freshmen. Coed dorms, single-sex dorms, special housing for disabled, apartments, substance-free housing available. $150 deposit, deadline 5/1. Theme housing available. **Activities:** Bands, campus ministries, choral groups, drama, literary magazine, music ensembles, musical theater, student government, student newspaper, symphony orchestra, Snappers, Fat Boys, FIRE, West Side, Project CURE, SALT.

**Athletics.** NCAA. **Intercollegiate:** Baseball M, basketball, cross-country, golf, soccer, tennis, volleyball W. **Intramural:** Basketball, football (non-tackle), soccer, softball, table tennis, tennis, volleyball. **Team name:** Cougars.

**Student services.** Campus ministries, career counseling, student employment services, financial aid counseling, health services, personal counseling, veterans' counselor, women's services. **Physically disabled:** Services for visually impaired.

**Contact.** E-mail: admission@ccu.edu
Phone: (303) 963-3200 Toll-free number: (800) 443-2484
Fax: (303) 963-3201
Simeon Turner, Associate Director of Undergraduate Admission, Colorado Christian University, 8787 West Alameda Avenue, Lakewood, CO 80226

## Colorado College

Colorado Springs, Colorado    CB member
www.coloradocollege.edu    CB code: 4072

- Private 4-year liberal arts college
- Residential campus in large city
- 2,034 degree-seeking undergraduates: 54% women, 2% African American, 5% Asian American, 7% Hispanic American, 1% Native American, 2% international
- 20 degree-seeking graduate students
- 32% of applicants admitted
- SAT or ACT (ACT writing optional), application essay required
- 83% graduate within 6 years

**General.** Founded in 1874. Regionally accredited. Mountain cabin located about 35 minutes from campus for class and retreat use. Baca campus in Southern Colorado available for intensive study. **Degrees:** 547 bachelor's awarded; master's offered. **ROTC:** Army. **Location:** 70 miles from Denver. **Calendar:** 8 blocks of 3.5 weeks each. Extensive summer session. **Full-time faculty:** 160 total; 94% have terminal degrees, 18% minority, 41% women. **Part-time faculty:** 26 total. **Class size:** 61% < 20, 39% 20-39, less than 1% 40-49. **Special facilities:** Electronic music studio, telescope dome, multimedia computer lab, press, herbarium, environmental science van equipped for field research, petrographic microscopes, X-ray diffractometer, Fourier transform nuclear magnetic resonance spectrometer, sedimentology lab, metabolic equipment, hydrostatic weighing equipment, cadaver study in sports science, scanning electron microscope, transmission electron microscope.

**Freshman class profile.** 4,826 applied, 1,540 admitted, 524 enrolled.

| Mid 50% test scores | | | |
|---|---|---|---|
| SAT critical reading: | 610-700 | End year in good standing: | 98% |
| SAT math: | 620-690 | Return as sophomores: | 96% |
| SAT writing: | 600-700 | Out-of-state: | 78% |
| ACT composite: | 27-31 | Live on campus: | 96% |
| Rank in top quarter: | 92% | International: | 3% |
| Rank in top tenth: | 60% | Fraternities: | 8% |
| | | Sororities: | 11% |

**Basis for selection.** Personal essays, school achievement record most important. Counselor and teacher recommendations, extracurricular activities and test scores also important. Special talents; geographic, socioeconomic, ethnic diversity considered. Challenging curriculum, including honors/AP/IB courses if available, recommended. Interview optional. **Homeschooled:** Letter of recommendation (nonparent) required. Three letters of recommendation from people outside of the family who have some knowledge of student's academic capabilities and interests. Reading lists, curriculum information, teacher narratives about courses of study, and copies of papers or projects can be used in place of traditional transcript.

**High school preparation.** 16 units required; 20 recommended. Required and recommended units include English 4.

**2007-2008 Annual costs.** Tuition/fees: $33,972. Room/board: $8,498. Books/supplies: $936.

**2007-2008 Financial aid. Need-based:** 236 full-time freshmen applied for aid; 190 were judged to have need; 190 of these received aid. Average need met was 98%. Average scholarship/grant was $27,305; average loan $3,653. 88% of total undergraduate aid awarded as scholarships/grants, 12% as loans/jobs. **Non-need-based:** Awarded to 288 full-time undergraduates, including 74 freshmen. Scholarships awarded for academics, athletics. **Additional information:** Need-based financial aid available only to students enrolled half-time or more.

**Application procedures. Admission:** Closing date 1/15 (postmark date). $50 fee, may be waived for applicants with need. Application may be submitted online. Admission notification 4/1. Must reply by May 1 or within 2 week(s) if notified thereafter. Campus visit recommended. Separate letter requesting early action and explaining reasons for applying early required for early action. **Financial aid:** Closing date 2/15. FAFSA, CSS PROFILE required. Applicants notified by 3/20; must reply by 5/1.

**Academics. Special study options:** Combined bachelor's/graduate degree, double major, ESL, external degree, independent study, internships, liberal arts/career combination, semester at sea, student-designed major, study abroad, teacher certification program, urban semester, Washington semester. Urban studies, urban arts and urban education (Chicago); science semester (Oak Ridge, Tennessee); tropical field research (Costa Rica); wilderness field station (Wisconsin); ACM London-Florence program; study abroad programs in France, Germany, Mexico, Russia, Japan, India, Sweden, the Netherlands, and Wales; ACM program in Tanzania and Zimbabwe. **Credit/placement by examination:** AP, CLEP, IB, institutional tests. 32 credit hours maximum toward bachelor's degree. **Support services:** Learning center, pre-admission summer program, study skills assistance, tutoring, writing center.

**Majors. Area/ethnic studies:** Asian, French, Hispanic-American/Latino/Chicano, regional, Russian/Slavic, women's. **Biology:** General, biochemistry. **Conservation:** Environmental science. **English:** Creative writing, English lit. **Foreign languages:** Classics, comparative lit, French, German, Italian, Russian, Spanish. **History:** General. **Interdisciplinary:** Math/computer science, neuroscience. **Liberal arts:** Arts/sciences. **Math:** General. **Philosophy/religion:** Philosophy, religion. **Physical sciences:** Chemistry, geology, physics. **Psychology:** General. **Social sciences:** Anthropology, econometrics, economics, international economics, political science, sociology. **Visual/performing arts:** Art history/conservation, dance, dramatic, film/cinema, studio arts. **Other:** Classics/History/Politics, Political Economy: American.

**Most popular majors.** Biology 12%, English 7%, history 7%, social sciences 32%, visual/performing arts 8%.

**Computing on campus.** Dormitories wired for high-speed internet access and linked to campus network. Commuter students can connect to campus network. Online course registration, online library, helpline, student web hosting, wireless network available.

**Student life. Freshman orientation:** Mandatory. Preregistration for classes offered. One week program prior to the beginning of fall classes. Parents welcome for first 3 days. Includes service trip. **Housing:** Guaranteed on-campus for all undergraduates. Coed dorms, single-sex dorms, apartments, fraternity/sorority housing, substance-free housing available. $200 nonrefundable deposit, deadline 3/1. Pets allowed in dorm rooms. Themed houses, project-based houses, and language houses. **Activities:** Bands, campus ministries, choral groups, dance, drama, film society, literary magazine, music ensembles, musical theater, radio station, student government, student newspaper, Asian American students union, black student union, Chaverim/Hillel, gay, lesbian, and bisexual alliance, community kitchen, environmental action, Shove Chapel Council, Chicano/Latino organization, victim's assistance team, BreakOut-community service trips.

**Athletics.** NCAA. **Intercollegiate:** Basketball, cross-country, football (tackle) M, ice hockey M, lacrosse, soccer, softball W, swimming, tennis, track and field, volleyball W, water polo W. **Intramural:** Basketball, football (non-tackle), ice hockey, racquetball, soccer, softball, tennis, volleyball. **Team name:** Tigers.

**Student services.** Alcohol/substance abuse counseling, campus ministries, career counseling, student employment services, financial aid counseling, health services, minority student services, on-campus daycare, personal counseling, women's services. **Physically disabled:** Services for visually, speech, hearing impaired.

**Contact.** E-mail: admission@coloradocollege.edu
Phone: (719) 389-6344 Toll-free number: (800) 542-7214
Fax: (719) 389-6816
Roberto Garcia, Director of Admission, Colorado College, 14 East Cache La Poudre, Colorado Springs, CO 80903-9854

---

## Colorado School of Mines
### Golden, Colorado
www.mines.edu

**CB member**
**CB code: 4073**

- Public 4-year university and engineering college
- Residential campus in large town
- 3,300 degree-seeking undergraduates: 18% part-time, 22% women, 2% African American, 5% Asian American, 6% Hispanic American, 1% Native American, 6% international
- 851 degree-seeking graduate students
- 85% of applicants admitted
- SAT or ACT (ACT writing optional) required
- 66% graduate within 6 years; 26% enter graduate study

**General.** Founded in 1874. Regionally accredited. **Degrees:** 563 bachelor's awarded; master's, doctoral offered. **ROTC:** Army, Air Force. **Location:** 20 miles from Denver. **Calendar:** Semester, limited summer session. **Full-time faculty:** 220 total. **Part-time faculty:** 100 total. **Class size:** 43% < 20, 36% 20-39, 12% 40-49, 5% 50-99, 3% >100. **Special facilities:** Geology museum, geophysical observatory, experimental mine.

**Freshman class profile.** 4,188 applied, 3,557 admitted, 787 enrolled.

| Mid 50% test scores | | | |
|---|---|---|---|
| SAT critical reading: | 550-640 | Rank in top tenth: | 53% |
| SAT math: | 620-690 | End year in good standing: | 95% |
| ACT composite: | 26-29 | Return as sophomores: | 86% |
| GPA 3.50 or higher: | 80% | Out-of-state: | 25% |
| GPA 3.0-3.49: | 20% | Live on campus: | 80% |
| Rank in top quarter: | 87% | Fraternities: | 20% |
| | | Sororities: | 20% |

**Basis for selection.** Applicants should rank in top third of class, must complete 16 or more academic units, and submit test scores. Both scores and academic record considered with heavier weight given to academic record. Interview and essay recommended. **Homeschooled:** Transcript of courses and grades required. More weight given to ACT or SAT scores.

**High school preparation.** 16 units required. Required and recommended units include English 4, mathematics 4, social studies 2, science 3, foreign language 2 and academic electives 3. Math units should include 2 algebra, 1 geometry, 1 advanced math (including trigonometry). Science units should include 1 chemistry or physics.

**2007-2008 Annual costs.** Tuition/fees: $10,258; $23,244 out-of-state. Room/board: $7,350. Books/supplies: $1,300. Personal expenses: $1,800.

**2007-2008 Financial aid. Need-based:** 592 full-time freshmen applied for aid; 533 were judged to have need; 533 of these received aid. Average need met was 93%. Average scholarship/grant was $8,350; average loan $5,100. 57% of total undergraduate aid awarded as scholarships/grants, 43% as loans/jobs. **Non-need-based:** Scholarships awarded for academics, alumni affiliation, athletics, music/drama, ROTC, state residency.

**Application procedures. Admission:** Priority date 4/15; deadline 6/1 (postmark date). $45 fee, may be waived for applicants with need. Application may be submitted online. Admission notification on a rolling basis beginning on or about 9/15. Must reply by May 1 or within 4 week(s) if notified thereafter. **Financial aid:** Priority date 3/1; no closing date. FAFSA required. Applicants notified on a rolling basis starting 3/15; must reply by 5/1 or within 2 week(s) of notification.

**Academics. Special study options:** Accelerated study, combined bachelor's/graduate degree, cooperative education, double major, dual enrollment of high school students, ESL, exchange student, honors, independent study, internships, study abroad. **Credit/placement by examination:** AP, CLEP, IB, institutional tests. **Support services:** Pre-admission summer program, reduced course load, remedial instruction, study skills assistance, tutoring, writing center.

**Majors. Computer sciences:** General, computer science. **Engineering:** General, chemical, geological, metallurgical, mining, petroleum, physics. **Interdisciplinary:** Math/computer science. **Math:** Applied. **Physical sciences:** Chemistry, geology, geophysics, physics. **Social sciences:** Economics.

**Most popular majors.** Computer/information sciences 6%, engineering/engineering technologies 77%, physical sciences 11%.

**Computing on campus.** 400 workstations in dormitories, library, computer center, student center. Dormitories wired for high-speed internet access and linked to campus network. Commuter students can connect to campus network. Online course registration, helpline, repair service, wireless network available.

**Student life. Freshman orientation:** Available. Preregistration for classes offered. 2 two-day sessions held during summer; one-day session held at start of fall semester. **Housing:** Guaranteed on-campus for freshmen. Coed dorms, single-sex dorms, apartments, fraternity/sorority housing available. $50 partly refundable deposit, deadline 5/1. **Activities:** Bands, choral groups, drama, literary magazine, music ensembles, student government, student newspaper, symphony orchestra, American Indian Science and Engineering Society, Asian student association, National Society of Black Engineers, Society of Hispanic Professional Engineers, religious clubs, Blue Key, Society of Women Engineers.

**Athletics.** NCAA. **Intercollegiate:** Baseball M, basketball, cross-country, football (tackle) M, golf, soccer, softball W, swimming, track and field, volleyball W, wrestling M. **Intramural:** Badminton, basketball, cross-country, football (non-tackle), handball, racquetball, rugby M, skin diving, soccer, softball, swimming, tennis, track and field, volleyball. **Team name:** Orediggers.

**Student services.** Alcohol/substance abuse counseling, career counseling, student employment services, financial aid counseling, health services, minority student services, personal counseling, placement for graduates, veterans' counselor. **Physically disabled:** Services for visually, hearing impaired.

**Contact.** E-mail: admit@mines.edu
Phone: (303) 273-3220 Toll-free number: (888) 446-9489
Fax: (303) 273-3509
Bruce Goetz, Director of Admissions, Colorado School of Mines, Undergraduate Admissions, Golden, CO 80401

---

## Colorado State University
**Fort Collins, Colorado**
www.welcome.colostate.edu

**CB member**
**CB code: 4075**

- Public 4-year university
- Residential campus in small city
- 20,765 degree-seeking undergraduates: 8% part-time, 52% women, 2% African American, 3% Asian American, 7% Hispanic American, 2% Native American, 2% international
- 4,218 degree-seeking graduate students
- 86% of applicants admitted
- SAT or ACT (ACT writing optional), application essay required
- 64% graduate within 6 years

**General.** Founded in 1870. Regionally accredited. Colorado State University is a Land Grant University. **Degrees:** 4,169 bachelor's awarded; master's, doctoral, first professional offered. **ROTC:** Army, Air Force. **Location:** 60 miles from Denver. **Calendar:** Semester, extensive summer session. **Full-time faculty:** 889 total; 99% have terminal degrees, 12% minority, 30% women. **Part-time faculty:** 34 total; 100% have terminal degrees, 6% minority, 18% women. **Class size:** 37% < 20, 39% 20-39, 7% 40-49, 9% 50-99, 7% >100. **Special facilities:** Concert hall, Bohemian complex with thrust theatre, music hall, art museum, engineering research center, equine center, veterinary teaching hospital, environmental learning center, plant environmental research center.

**Freshman class profile.** 11,727 applied, 10,068 admitted, 4,392 enrolled.

| Mid 50% test scores | | | |
|---|---|---|---|
| SAT critical reading: | 490-610 | Rank in top quarter: | 48% |
| SAT math: | 510-630 | Rank in top tenth: | 19% |
| SAT writing: | 480-590 | Return as sophomores: | 81% |
| ACT composite: | 22-26 | Out-of-state: | 21% |
| GPA 3.50 or higher: | 56% | Live on campus: | 94% |
| GPA 3.0-3.49: | 37% | International: | 1% |
| GPA 2.0-2.99: | 7% | Fraternities: | 3% |
| | | Sororities: | 4% |

**Basis for selection.** Priority consideration given to those with 3.25 GPA and 18 recommended high school credits. Applicants with GPA below 2.5 and/or without the recommended high school units encouraged to apply. The typical entering freshman carries a GPA between 3.2 and 3.8, has an ACT composite between 22-26 and a combined SAT (critical math and reading only) between 1020 and 1220. Essay must be at least 250 words; 1 letter of recommendation required.

**High school preparation.** 15 units required; 18 recommended. Required and recommended units include English 4, mathematics 3-4, social studies 2, history 1, science 3 (laboratory 2), foreign language 2 and academic electives 2. Additional social science or natural science unit required. Engineering majors require 0.5 unit of trigonometry as well as 1 natural science (physics preferred) and 1 chemistry. Individual colleges may have additional requirements.

**2007-2008 Annual costs.** Tuition/fees: $5,419; $18,859 out-of-state. Room/board: $7,382. Books/supplies: $990. Personal expenses: $1,692.

**2006-2007 Financial aid. Need-based:** 2,608 full-time freshmen applied for aid; 1,366 were judged to have need; 1,366 of these received aid. Average need met was 72%. Average scholarship/grant was $7,099; average loan $3,227. 42% of total undergraduate aid awarded as scholarships/grants, 58% as loans/jobs. **Non-need-based:** Awarded to 1,723 full-time undergraduates, including 397 freshmen. Scholarships awarded for academics, art, athletics, leadership, music/drama, ROTC, state residency.

**Application procedures. Admission:** Priority date 2/1; deadline 7/1 (receipt date). $50 fee, may be waived for applicants with need. Application may be submitted online. Admission notification on a rolling basis beginning on or about 9/15. Must reply by May 1 or within 2 week(s) if notified thereafter. Early application (once 6th semester transcript is available) encouraged. **Financial aid:** Priority date 3/1; no closing date. FAFSA required. Applicants notified on a rolling basis starting 3/1.

**Academics. Special study options:** Accelerated study, combined bachelor's/graduate degree, cooperative education, cross-registration, distance learning, double major, dual enrollment of high school students, ESL, exchange student, honors, independent study, internships, liberal arts/career combination, semester at sea, study abroad, teacher certification program. **Credit/placement by examination:** AP, CLEP, IB, SAT, ACT, institutional tests. 30 credit hours maximum toward bachelor's degree. **Support services:** Learning center, study skills assistance, tutoring, writing center.

**Majors. Agriculture:** Agribusiness operations, agronomy, animal sciences, economics, equestrian studies, horticultural science, horticulture, landscaping, range science, soil science. **Architecture:** Landscape. **Biology:** General, biochemistry, biomedical sciences, botany, microbiology, wildlife, zoology. **Business:** Business admin, restaurant/food services. **Communications:** Journalism. **Computer sciences:** General, information systems. **Conservation:** General, forest sciences, management/policy, water/wetlands/marine, wildlife. **Education:** Agricultural. **Engineering:** Chemical, civil, computer, electrical, environmental, mechanical, science. **Engineering technology:** Computer systems. **English:** Creative writing, English lit, speech/rhetoric. **Family/consumer sciences:** General, apparel marketing, family studies, food/nutrition, human nutrition. **Foreign languages:** General. **Health:** Environmental health. **History:** General. **Interdisciplinary:** Natural sciences. **Liberal arts:** Arts/sciences. **Math:** General. **Parks/recreation:** Exercise sciences, facilities management. **Philosophy/religion:** Philosophy. **Physical sciences:** Chemistry, geology, physics. **Protective services:** Fire services admin. **Psychology:** General. **Public administration:** Social work. **Social sciences:** Anthropology, economics, political science, sociology. **Visual/performing arts:** Dramatic, interior design, studio arts.

**Most popular majors.** Agriculture 6%, biology 7%, business/marketing 16%, engineering/engineering technologies 10%, English 7%, family/consumer sciences 9%, parks/recreation 6%, social sciences 9%.

**Computing on campus.** 2,700 workstations in dormitories, library, computer center, student center. Dormitories wired for high-speed internet access and linked to campus network. Commuter students can connect to campus network. Online course registration, online library, helpline, repair service, student web hosting, wireless network available.

**Student life. Freshman orientation:** Available, $90 fee. Preregistration for classes offered. 20 sessions offered from mid-June to mid-July for incoming freshmen, family members, and guests. **Housing:** Guaranteed on-campus for freshmen. Coed dorms, special housing for disabled, apartments, substance-free housing available. $150 partly refundable deposit. Special interest floors, special floors for transfer students available. **Activities:** Bands, campus ministries, choral groups, dance, drama, literary magazine, music ensembles, musical theater, opera, radio station, student government, student newspaper, symphony orchestra, TV station, Asian/American student services, black student services, El Centro student services, Native American student services, Campus Crusade for Christ, CoPIRG, Sierra Club, Habitat for Humanity, Pre Medica.

**Athletics.** NCAA. **Intercollegiate:** Basketball, cross-country, diving W, football (tackle) M, golf, softball W, swimming W, tennis W, track and field, volleyball W, water polo W. **Intramural:** Basketball, bowling, football (non-tackle), golf, racquetball, soccer, softball, volleyball. **Team name:** Rams.

**Student services.** Adult student services, alcohol/substance abuse counseling, campus ministries, career counseling, student employment services, financial aid counseling, health services, legal services, minority student services, on-campus daycare, personal counseling, placement for graduates, veterans' counselor, women's services. **Physically disabled:** Services for visually, speech, hearing impaired.

**Contact.** E-mail: admissions@colostate.edu
Phone: (970) 491-6909 Fax: (970) 491-7799
Mary Ontiveros, Executive Director of Admissions, Colorado State University, Office of Admissions/Colorado State University, Fort Collins, CO 80523-1062

## Colorado State University: Pueblo
### Pueblo, Colorado
### www.colostate-pueblo.edu
**CB code: 4611**

- Public 4-year university
- Commuter campus in small city
- 3,947 degree-seeking undergraduates: 22% part-time, 57% women, 6% African American, 3% Asian American, 25% Hispanic American, 2% Native American, 2% international
- 188 degree-seeking graduate students
- 97% of applicants admitted
- SAT or ACT (ACT writing optional) required
- 35% graduate within 6 years

**General.** Founded in 1933. Regionally accredited. **Degrees:** 762 bachelor's awarded; master's offered. **ROTC:** Army. **Location:** 42 miles from Colorado Springs, 100 miles from Denver. **Calendar:** Semester, extensive summer session. **Full-time faculty:** 155 total; 17% minority, 47% women. **Part-time faculty:** 149 total. **Class size:** 53% < 20, 35% 20-39, 5% 40-49, 7% 50-99, 1% >100. **Special facilities:** 3 electron microscopes, golf course, river trail system, automotive service, ropes course, music amphitheater.

**Freshman class profile.** 1,485 applied, 1,441 admitted, 644 enrolled.

| Mid 50% test scores | | Rank in top quarter: | 8% |
|---|---|---|---|
| SAT critical reading: | 420-530 | Rank in top tenth: | 2% |
| SAT math: | 420-550 | Return as sophomores: | 63% |
| ACT composite: | 18-22 | Out-of-state: | 8% |
| GPA 3.50 or higher: | 25% | Live on campus: | 10% |
| GPA 3.0-3.49: | 31% | Fraternities: | 2% |
| GPA 2.0-2.99: | 42% | Sororities: | 2% |

**Basis for selection.** High school achievement record and test scores most important. Auditions for music, portfolios for art required for scholarships.

**High school preparation.** 15 units required. Required and recommended units include English 4, mathematics 3, social studies 2, history 1, science 3 (laboratory 2), foreign language 2 and academic electives 2.

**2008-2009 Annual costs.** Tuition/fees (projected): $4,557; $14,757 out-of-state. WUE tuition is 44% less than out-of-state rate. Differential tuition charged for business, nursing, computer information systems, and engineering courses at $16 more per-credit-hour. Room/board: $6,300. Books/supplies: $1,698. Personal expenses: $2,998.

**2007-2008 Financial aid. Need-based:** Average need met was 62%. Average scholarship/grant was $5,678; average loan $3,119. 44% of total undergraduate aid awarded as scholarships/grants, 56% as loans/jobs. **Non-need-based:** Scholarships awarded for academics, alumni affiliation, art, athletics, job skills, leadership, minority status, music/drama, ROTC, state residency.

**Application procedures. Admission:** Closing date 8/1 (receipt date). $25 fee, may be waived for applicants with need. Application may be submitted online. Admission notification on a rolling basis beginning on or about 8/1. **Financial aid:** Priority date 3/1; no closing date. FAFSA, institutional form required. Applicants notified on a rolling basis starting 3/15; must reply within 3 week(s) of notification.

**Academics.** Structured first-year program for first-time students. **Special study options:** Accelerated study, combined bachelor's/graduate degree, cooperative education, cross-registration, distance learning, double major, dual enrollment of high school students, ESL, exchange student, external degree, honors, independent study, internships, study abroad, teacher certification program, weekend college. **Credit/placement by examination:** AP, CLEP, IB, SAT, ACT, institutional tests. 30 credit hours maximum toward bachelor's degree. **Support services:** Learning center, reduced course load, remedial instruction, study skills assistance, tutoring, writing center.

**Majors. Biology:** General. **Business:** Accounting, managerial economics. **Communications:** Media studies. **Computer sciences:** Information systems. **Engineering:** General, industrial. **Engineering technology:** Automotive, civil. **English:** English lit. **Foreign languages:** General. **Health:** Nursing (RN). **History:** General. **Liberal arts:** Arts/sciences. **Math:** General. **Parks/recreation:** Exercise sciences. **Physical sciences:** Chemistry, physics. **Psychology:** General. **Public administration:** Social work. **Social sciences:** General, political science, sociology. **Visual/performing arts:** Studio arts. **Other:** Mechatronics.

**Most popular majors.** Biology 6%, business/marketing 16%, communications/journalism 7%, health sciences 11%, liberal arts 6%, parks/recreation 7%, social sciences 17%.

**Computing on campus.** 702 workstations in dormitories, library, computer center, student center. Dormitories wired for high-speed internet access. Commuter students can connect to campus network. Online library, helpline, student web hosting, wireless network available.

**Student life. Freshman orientation:** Mandatory, $50 fee. Preregistration for classes offered. Three hour session held during the summer. **Housing:** Guaranteed on-campus for freshmen. Coed dorms, special housing for disabled, apartments available. $125 partly refundable deposit, deadline 7/1. **Activities:** Bands, campus ministries, choral groups, dance, international student organizations, literary magazine, music ensembles, radio station, student government, student newspaper, symphony orchestra, TV station, Campus Crusade for Christ, Catholic student union, College Republicans, Society of Mexican American Engineers and Scientists, Movimiento Estudiantil Chicano de Aztlan, multicultural center, Tackling Life's Choices.

**Athletics.** NCAA. **Intercollegiate:** Baseball M, basketball, cross-country W, golf, soccer, softball W, tennis, volleyball W. **Intramural:** Basketball, football (non-tackle), golf, handball, racquetball, soccer, softball, table tennis, volleyball. **Team name:** Thunderwolves.

**Student services.** Alcohol/substance abuse counseling, campus ministries, career counseling, student employment services, financial aid counseling, health services, on-campus daycare, personal counseling, placement for graduates, veterans' counselor. **Physically disabled:** Services for visually, speech, hearing impaired.

**Contact.** E-mail: info@colostate-pueblo.edu
Phone: (719) 549-2461 Fax: (719) 549-2419
Joseph Marshall, Director of Admissions and Records, Colorado State University: Pueblo, 2200 Bonforte Boulevard, Pueblo, CO 81001-4901

## Colorado Technical University
### Colorado Springs, Colorado
### www.coloradotech.edu
**CB code: 4133**

- For-profit 4-year university and technical college
- Commuter campus in large city
- 1,500 undergraduates
- 500 graduate students
- Interview required

**General.** Founded in 1965. Regionally accredited. **Degrees:** 200 bachelor's, 70 associate awarded; master's, doctoral offered. **ROTC:** Army. **Location:** 63 miles from Denver. **Calendar:** Quarter, extensive summer session. **Full-time faculty:** 35 total. **Part-time faculty:** 100 total. **Class size:** 69% < 20, 31% 20-39. **Special facilities:** Extensive laboratories and computer facilities.

**Basis for selection.** Secondary school record, test scores, interview important. SAT or ACT recommended.

**2007-2008 Annual costs.** Tuition/fees: $12,540. Lab fees $30 per lab class. Books/supplies: $1,300. Personal expenses: $1,215.

**Financial aid. Non-need-based:** Scholarships awarded for academics, ROTC.

**Application procedures. Admission:** No deadline. $50 fee. Admission notification on a rolling basis. **Financial aid:** No deadline. FAFSA required. Applicants notified on a rolling basis starting 6/30.

**Academics. Special study options:** Accelerated study, cooperative education, distance learning, double major, internships, weekend college. **Credit/placement by examination:** CLEP, institutional tests. 30 credit hours maximum toward associate degree, 60 toward bachelor's. Course challenge test offered. Credit for life experience based on evaluation by faculty. **Support services:** Learning center, reduced course load, remedial instruction, tutoring.

**Majors. Business:** Business admin, e-commerce, human resources, information resources management, logistics, management information systems. **Computer sciences:** General, computer science, information systems, information technology, system admin, systems analysis. **Engineering:** Computer, electrical, software. **Engineering technology:** Electrical.

**Most popular majors.** Business/marketing 34%, computer/information sciences 32%, engineering/engineering technologies 34%.

**Computing on campus.** 154 workstations in library, computer center. Commuter students can connect to campus network. Online library, helpline, wireless network available.

**Student life. Freshman orientation:** Mandatory. Preregistration for classes offered. **Policies:** Students must comply with university's standards of conduct. **Activities:** Student government.

**Student services.** Career counseling, student employment services, financial aid counseling, personal counseling, placement for graduates, veterans' counselor.

**Contact.** E-mail: cosadmissions@coloradotech.edu
Phone: (719) 598-0200 Fax: (719) 598-3740
Beth Braaten, Vice President of Admissions, Colorado Technical University, 4435 North Chestnut Street, Colorado Springs, CO 80907

## DeVry University: Westminster
**Westminster, Colorado**
**www.devry.edu**                    **CB code: 1327**

- For-profit 4-year university
- Commuter campus in very large city
- 596 degree-seeking undergraduates: 51% part-time, 36% women, 7% African American, 4% Asian American, 12% Hispanic American, 1% Native American
- 69 degree-seeking graduate students
- Interview required

**General.** Founded in 1945. Regionally accredited. **Degrees:** 134 bachelor's, 17 associate awarded; master's offered. **Calendar:** Semester, extensive summer session. **Full-time faculty:** 17 total; 12% minority, 24% women. **Part-time faculty:** 18 total; 11% minority, 22% women.

**Freshman class profile.** 94 enrolled.

| Return as sophomores: | 44% | Out-of-state: | 5% |
|---|---|---|---|

**Basis for selection.** Applicants must have high school diploma or equivalent or a degree from an accredited postsecondary institution, demonstrate proficiency in basic college-level skills through SAT or ACT scores or institutional-administered placement exams, and be at least 17 years of age.

**High school preparation.** Math unit must be algebra or higher.

**2007-2008 Annual costs.** Tuition/fees: $14,020. Books/supplies: $1,300. Personal expenses: $5,082.

**Financial aid.** All financial aid based on need.

**Application procedures. Admission:** No deadline. $50 fee. Application may be submitted online. Admission notification on a rolling basis. **Financial aid:** No deadline. FAFSA required. Applicants notified on a rolling basis.

**Academics. Special study options:** Accelerated study, distance learning. **Credit/placement by examination:** CLEP, institutional tests. **Support services:** Learning center, tutoring.

**Majors. Business:** Business admin. **Computer sciences:** Networking, systems analysis. **Engineering:** Software. **Engineering technology:** Computer, electrical. **Other:** Technical management.

**Most popular majors.** Business/marketing 64%, computer/information sciences 16%, engineering/engineering technologies 19%.

**Computing on campus.** 308 workstations in library, computer center. Online course registration, online library, helpline available.

**Student life. Freshman orientation:** Mandatory. **Activities:** Student government, student newspaper.

**Athletics. Intramural:** Basketball, volleyball.

**Student services.** Career counseling, student employment services, financial aid counseling, placement for graduates, veterans' counselor.

**Contact.** E-mail: denver-admissions@den.devry.edu
Phone: (303) 280-7600 Toll-free number: (888) 212-1857
Fax: (303) 280-7606
Rick Rodman, Director of Admissions, DeVry University: Westminster, 1870 West 122 Avenue, Westminster, CO 80234-2010

## Fort Lewis College
**Durango, Colorado**                **CB member**
**www.fortlewis.edu**                **CB code: 4310**

- Public 4-year liberal arts college
- Residential campus in large town

- 3,788 degree-seeking undergraduates: 9% part-time, 47% women, 1% African American, 1% Asian American, 6% Hispanic American, 20% Native American, 1% international
- 72% of applicants admitted
- SAT or ACT (ACT writing optional) required

**General.** Regionally accredited. **Degrees:** 651 bachelor's awarded. **Location:** 220 miles from Albuquerque, New Mexico; 342 miles from Denver. **Calendar:** Semester, extensive summer session. **Full-time faculty:** 176 total; 79% have terminal degrees, 11% minority, 45% women. **Part-time faculty:** 63 total; 16% have terminal degrees, 8% minority, 49% women. **Class size:** 53% < 20, 42% 20-39, 4% 40-49, 2% 50-99. **Special facilities:** Southwest studies center, nuclear magnetic resonance spectrometer, archaeological dig site, community concert hall, separations and spectroscopy lab, mass spectrometer facilities, tissue culture facility, atomic force microscope.

**Freshman class profile.** 3,020 applied, 2,181 admitted, 925 enrolled.

| Mid 50% test scores | | | |
|---|---|---|---|
| SAT critical reading: | 440-570 | GPA 2.0-2.99: | 47% |
| SAT math: | 450-570 | Rank in top quarter: | 25% |
| SAT writing: | 430-540 | Rank in top tenth: | 9% |
| ACT composite: | 19-23 | Return as sophomores: | 57% |
| GPA 3.50 or higher: | 23% | Out-of-state: | 31% |
| GPA 3.0-3.49: | 30% | Live on campus: | 88% |

**Basis for selection.** Colorado Commission on Higher Education index score comprised of high school GPA and test scores utilized as part of admission criteria. Essay recommended. **Homeschooled:** Official copy of high school completion records; minimum score of 1010 SAT (exclusive of Writing), 22 ACT.

**High school preparation.** 15 units recommended. Recommended units include English 4, mathematics 4, social studies 3, science 3, foreign language 2 and academic electives 2.

**2007-2008 Annual costs.** Tuition/fees: $6,464; $14,994 out-of-state. Room/board: $6,876. Books/supplies: $850. Personal expenses: $2,500.

**2006-2007 Financial aid. Need-based:** 595 full-time freshmen applied for aid; 417 were judged to have need; 408 of these received aid. Average need met was 61%. Average scholarship/grant was $3,733; average loan $2,448. 47% of total undergraduate aid awarded as scholarships/grants, 53% as loans/jobs. **Non-need-based:** Awarded to 974 full-time undergraduates, including 352 freshmen. Scholarships awarded for academics, alumni affiliation, art, athletics, leadership, minority status, music/drama, state residency. **Additional information:** Tuition waived for Native Americans of federally recognized tribes; census number and Certificate of Indian Blood must accompany application.

**Application procedures. Admission:** Closing date 8/1 (postmark date). $30 fee, may be waived for applicants with need. Application may be submitted online. Admission notification on a rolling basis beginning on or about 10/15. **Financial aid:** Priority date 2/15; no closing date. FAFSA required. Applicants notified on a rolling basis starting 3/15; must reply within 2 week(s) of notification.

**Academics. Special study options:** Accelerated study, cooperative education, distance learning, double major, dual enrollment of high school students, ESL, exchange student, honors, independent study, internships, liberal arts/career combination, student-designed major, study abroad, teacher certification program. **Credit/placement by examination:** AP, CLEP, IB, SAT, ACT, institutional tests. **Support services:** Learning center, remedial instruction, study skills assistance, tutoring, writing center.

**Majors. Agriculture:** General, business. **Area/ethnic studies:** African, East Asian, Latin American, Native American, regional, women's. **Biology:** General, biochemistry, cellular/molecular, ecology. **Business:** Accounting, business admin, finance, international, management information systems, managerial economics, marketing, operations, tourism/travel. **Communications:** General. **Computer sciences:** General, information systems. **Conservation:** Environmental studies. **Education:** Biology, chemistry, early childhood, elementary, English, multicultural, music, physics, science. **Engineering:** Physics. **English:** English lit. **Foreign languages:** Spanish. **History:** General, American, Asian, European. **Liberal arts:** Humanities. **Math:** General. **Parks/recreation:** General, exercise sciences, sports admin. **Philosophy/religion:** Philosophy. **Physical sciences:** Chemistry, geology, physics. **Psychology:** General. **Social sciences:** Anthropology, criminology, political science, sociology. **Visual/performing arts:** Art, dramatic, music performance, studio arts. **Other:** Engineering managment.

**Most popular majors.** Biology 6%, business/marketing 29%, English 8%, liberal arts 13%, parks/recreation 7%, psychology 7%, social sciences 9%, visual/performing arts 8%.

**Computing on campus.** 672 workstations in dormitories, library, computer center, student center. Dormitories wired for high-speed internet access and linked to campus network. Commuter students can connect to campus network. Online course registration, online library, helpline, repair service, student web hosting, wireless network available.

**Student life. Freshman orientation:** Mandatory, $50 fee. Preregistration for classes offered. **Housing:** Guaranteed on-campus for all undergraduates. Coed dorms, special housing for disabled, apartments available. $100 partly refundable deposit, deadline 7/15. **Activities:** Bands, campus ministries, choral groups, drama, literary magazine, music ensembles, radio station, student government, student newspaper, Newman Club, Circle-K International, international friendship club, business club, American Indian business leaders, American Indian science and engineering society, sociology club, Native American club, Habitat for Humanity.

**Athletics.** NCAA. **Intercollegiate:** Basketball, cross-country, football (tackle) M, golf M, soccer, softball W, volleyball W. **Intramural:** Badminton, basketball, football (tackle), racquetball, soccer, softball, volleyball. **Team name:** Skyhawks.

**Student services.** Adult student services, alcohol/substance abuse counseling, campus ministries, career counseling, services for economically disadvantaged, student employment services, financial aid counseling, health services, legal services, minority student services, on-campus daycare, personal counseling, placement for graduates, veterans' counselor, women's services. **Physically disabled:** Services for visually, speech, hearing impaired.

**Contact.** E-mail: admission@fortlewis.edu
Phone: (970) 247-7184 Fax: (970) 247-7179
Andrew Burns, Director of Admission, Fort Lewis College, 1000 Rim Drive, Durango, CO 81301-3999

## ITT Technical Institute: Thornton
**Thornton, Colorado**
**www.itt-tech.edu**                      **CB code: 3605**

- For-profit 4-year technical college
- Commuter campus in large city

**General.** Founded in 1984. Accredited by ACICS. **Calendar:** Quarter.

**Annual costs/financial aid.** Tuition varies by program, $260-$368 per credit hour.

**Contact.** Phone: (303) 288-4488
Director of Recruitment, 500 East 84th Avenue, Thornton, CO 80229

## Johnson & Wales University: Denver
**Denver, Colorado**
**www.jwu.edu**                      **CB code: 3567**

- Private 4-year university
- Residential campus in large city
- 1,465 degree-seeking undergraduates: 3% part-time, 52% women, 5% African American, 4% Asian American, 11% Hispanic American, 1% Native American, 2% international
- 76% of applicants admitted

**General.** Regionally accredited. **Degrees:** 224 bachelor's, 331 associate awarded. **Calendar:** Quarter, limited summer session. **Full-time faculty:** 46 total. **Part-time faculty:** 28 total. **Class size:** 48% < 20, 42% 20-39, 9% 40-49. **Special facilities:** Community leadership institute.

**Freshman class profile.** 2,217 applied, 1,685 admitted, 363 enrolled.

| Mid 50% test scores | | GPA 3.0-3.49: | 29% |
|---|---|---|---|
| SAT critical reading: | 420-540 | GPA 2.0-2.99: | 44% |
| SAT math: | 440-560 | Live on campus: | 57% |
| GPA 3.50 or higher: | 25% | | |

**Basis for selection.** Academic record important, including secondary school curriculum, GPA, class rank, test scores. Student motivation and interest given strong consideration. SAT or ACT recommended. SAT or ACT required for students entering honors program only.

**High school preparation.** 12 units recommended. Recommended units include English 4, mathematics 3, social studies 2 and science 3.

**2007-2008 Annual costs.** Tuition/fees: $21,717. Weekend meal plan available for $987. Room/board: $8,550. Books/supplies: $900. Personal expenses: $594.

**2007-2008 Financial aid. Need-based:** 299 full-time freshmen applied for aid; 247 were judged to have need; 247 of these received aid. Average need met was 72%. Average scholarship/grant was $7,294; average loan $3,116. 40% of total undergraduate aid awarded as scholarships/grants, 60% as loans/jobs. **Non-need-based:** Awarded to 965 full-time undergraduates, including 280 freshmen. Scholarships awarded for academics, leadership.

**Application procedures. Admission:** No deadline. No application fee. Application may be submitted online. Admission notification on a rolling basis beginning on or about 11/1. **Financial aid:** No deadline. FAFSA required. Applicants notified on a rolling basis starting 3/1; must reply within 2 week(s) of notification.

**Academics. Special study options:** Accelerated study, cooperative education, double major, dual enrollment of high school students, honors, independent study, internships, study abroad. **Credit/placement by examination:** CLEP, institutional tests. **Support services:** Learning center, remedial instruction, study skills assistance, tutoring, writing center.

**Majors. Business:** Accounting, banking/financial services, business admin, entrepreneurial studies, hospitality admin, hotel/motel admin, international, investments/securities, marketing, public finance. **Family/consumer sciences:** Food/nutrition. **Parks/recreation:** Facilities management, sports admin. **Personal/culinary services:** Food service, restaurant/catering. **Protective services:** Law enforcement admin.

**Most popular majors.** Business/marketing 40%, family/consumer sciences 38%, parks/recreation 12%, personal/culinary services 8%.

**Computing on campus.** Dormitories wired for high-speed internet access and linked to campus network. Commuter students can connect to campus network. Online course registration, online library, helpline, repair service, wireless network available.

**Student life. Freshman orientation:** Mandatory, $250 fee. Preregistration for classes offered. **Housing:** Coed dorms available. $300 deposit. **Activities:** Choral groups, dance, literary magazine, student government.

**Athletics.** NAIA. **Intercollegiate:** Basketball, soccer, volleyball M. **Intramural:** Basketball, football (non-tackle), soccer, softball, volleyball. **Team name:** Wildcats.

**Student services.** Adult student services, alcohol/substance abuse counseling, career counseling, student employment services, financial aid counseling, health services, minority student services, personal counseling, placement for graduates. **Physically disabled:** Services for visually, speech, hearing impaired. **Learning disabled:** Comprehensive services available.

**Contact.** E-mail: admissions.den@jwu.edu
Phone: (303) 256-9300 Toll-free number: (877) 598-3368
Kim Ostrowski, Director of Admissions, Johnson & Wales University: Denver, 7150 Montview Boulevard, Denver, CO 80220

## Jones International University
**Centennial, Colorado**
**www.jonesinternational.edu**                      **CB code: 2785**

- For-profit 4-year virtual college
- Large city
- 320 undergraduates
- 1,500 graduate students

**General.** Regionally accredited. Asynchronous learning, 25 student classroom limit, 24/7 technical support. **Degrees:** 137 bachelor's awarded; master's offered. **Calendar:** Continuous. **Full-time faculty:** 5 total. **Part-time faculty:** 90 total. **Special facilities:** Virtual library, online bookstore.

**Basis for selection.** Admissions based on academic record.

**High school preparation.** 16 units recommended. Recommended units include English 4, mathematics 4, social studies 1, history 1, science 3 (laboratory 3) and foreign language 2.

**2007-2008 Annual costs.** Tuition: $1290 per course for bachelor's degrees. $65 technology fee per course. Books are approximately $100 per course.

**Financial aid. Additional information:** Loans available through Sallie Mae and PLATO. Most students have costs reimbursed by employers. GI Bill and VA benefits accepted.

**Application procedures. Admission:** No deadline. $60 fee. Application may be submitted online. Admission notification on a rolling basis. **Financial aid:** FAFSA required.

**Academics. Special study options:** Accelerated study, combined bachelor's/graduate degree, distance learning. **Credit/placement by examination:** CLEP, IB. 60 credit hours maximum toward bachelor's degree.

**Majors. Business:** General, business admin, communications, e-commerce, international, small business admin. **Communications:** General, digital media, journalism, organizational, public relations. **Communications technology:** General. **Computer sciences:** General, computer science, database management, programming, system admin, systems analysis. **Engineering:** Computer.

**Computing on campus.** PC or laptop required.

**Student services.** Career counseling, financial aid counseling.

**Contact.** E-mail: admissions@international.edu
Phone: (303) 784-8247 Toll-free number: (800) 811-5663 ext. 8247
Fax: (303) 799-0966
Thomas Hartman, Director of Admissions and Records/Registrar, Jones International University, 9697 East Mineral Avenue, Centennial, CO 80112

## Mesa State College
### Grand Junction, Colorado
**www.mesastate.edu**  CB code: 4484

▶ Public 4-year community and liberal arts college
▶ Commuter campus in small city
▶ 5,585 degree-seeking undergraduates: 22% part-time, 58% women, 2% African American, 3% Asian American, 9% Hispanic American, 2% Native American
▶ 115 degree-seeking graduate students
▶ 82% of applicants admitted
▶ SAT or ACT (ACT writing optional) required

**General.** Founded in 1925. Regionally accredited. **Degrees:** 588 bachelor's, 154 associate awarded; master's offered. **Location:** 250 miles from Denver, 300 miles from Salt Lake City. **Calendar:** Semester, limited summer session. **Full-time faculty:** 225 total. **Part-time faculty:** 213 total. **Class size:** 56% < 20, 35% 20-39, 4% 40-49, 5% 50-99, less than 1% >100. **Special facilities:** Electron microscope laboratory, herbarium, computer-aided drafting laboratory, technical training facility, environmental restoration laboratory.

**Freshman class profile.** 3,147 applied, 2,582 admitted, 1,315 enrolled.

| Mid 50% test scores | | | |
|---|---|---|---|
| SAT critical reading: | 420-540 | GPA 2.0-2.99: | 47% |
| SAT math: | 420-540 | Rank in top quarter: | 19% |
| ACT composite: | 17-22 | Rank in top tenth: | 6% |
| GPA 3.50 or higher: | 19% | Return as sophomores: | 52% |
| GPA 3.0-3.49: | 28% | Out-of-state: | 11% |
| | | Live on campus: | 51% |

**Basis for selection.** Admission based GPA, ACT/SAT, class rank and satisfaction of HEAR requirements. Open admissions to most technical associates and certificate programs. Audition required of music, music theater, theater majors. Interview recommended for nursing, allied health, teacher certification majors. **Homeschooled:** Statement describing homeschool structure and mission, transcript of courses and grades required.

**High school preparation.** 15 units required. Required and recommended units include English 4, mathematics 3, social studies 3, history 2, science 3 (laboratory 2), foreign language 2 and academic electives 2.

**2007-2008 Annual costs.** Tuition/fees: $4,342; $12,245 out-of-state. Room/board: $8,167. Books/supplies: $1,698. Personal expenses: $1,942.

**2006-2007 Financial aid. Need-based:** 934 full-time freshmen applied for aid; 841 were judged to have need; 841 of these received aid. Average need met was 46%. Average scholarship/grant was $3,903; average loan $2,320. 47% of total undergraduate aid awarded as scholarships/grants, 53% as loans/jobs. **Non-need-based:** Awarded to 881 full-time undergraduates, including 274 freshmen. Scholarships awarded for academics, art, athletics, leadership, minority status, music/drama.

**Application procedures. Admission:** No deadline. $30 fee, may be waived for applicants with need. Application may be submitted online. Admission notification on a rolling basis beginning on or about 9/1. **Financial aid:** Priority date 3/1; no closing date. FAFSA required. Applicants notified on a rolling basis starting 4/1; must reply within 5 week(s) of notification.

**Academics. Special study options:** Accelerated study, combined bachelor's/graduate degree, cooperative education, cross-registration, distance learning, double major, dual enrollment of high school students, ESL, exchange student, honors, independent study, internships, study abroad, teacher certification program. Area vocational school provides training in technical skills. **Credit/placement by examination:** AP, CLEP, IB, SAT, ACT, institutional tests. 12 credit hours maximum toward associate degree, 20 toward bachelor's. **Support services:** Learning center, pre-admission summer program, reduced course load, remedial instruction, study skills assistance, tutoring, writing center.

**Majors. Biology:** General. **Business:** General, accounting, management information systems. **Communications:** Media studies. **Computer sciences:** General. **Conservation:** Environmental science. **English:** English lit. **Foreign languages:** Spanish. **Health:** Athletic training, nursing (RN). **History:** General. **Liberal arts:** Arts/sciences. **Math:** General. **Parks/recreation:** Exercise sciences, sports admin. **Physical sciences:** General. **Protective services:** Criminal justice. **Psychology:** General. **Public administration:** General. **Social sciences:** General, political science, sociology. **Visual/performing arts:** Art, dramatic.

**Most popular majors.** Biology 6%, business/marketing 27%, health sciences 11%, liberal arts 6%, parks/recreation 10%, psychology 7%, social sciences 7%, visual/performing arts 7%.

**Computing on campus.** 525 workstations in dormitories, library, computer center, student center. Dormitories wired for high-speed internet access and linked to campus network. Commuter students can connect to campus network. Online course registration, online library, helpline, student web hosting, wireless network available.

**Student life. Freshman orientation:** Available. Preregistration for classes offered. **Housing:** Coed dorms, special housing for disabled, apartments, substance-free housing available. $150 partly refundable deposit. Pets allowed in dorm rooms. Suite style housing available for sophomores, juniors and seniors. **Activities:** Bands, choral groups, dance, drama, film society, literary magazine, music ensembles, musical theater, radio station, student government, student newspaper, symphony orchestra, TV station, African American college, La Raza, handicapped student organization, Newman Club, Christian fellowship, Latter-Day Saints student association, Baptist student union, Circle-K, Native American council, Polynesian club.

**Athletics.** NCAA. **Intercollegiate:** Baseball M, basketball, cross-country W, football (tackle) M, golf W, soccer, softball W, swimming W, tennis, track and field W, volleyball W, wrestling M. **Intramural:** Badminton, basketball, football (non-tackle), handball, racquetball, skiing, soccer, softball, volleyball. **Team name:** Mavericks.

**Student services.** Adult student services, alcohol/substance abuse counseling, campus ministries, career counseling, services for economically disadvantaged, student employment services, financial aid counseling, health services, minority student services, on-campus daycare, personal counseling, placement for graduates, veterans' counselor. **Physically disabled:** Services for visually, speech, hearing impaired.

**Contact.** E-mail: admissions@mesastate.edu
Phone: (970) 248-1875 Toll-free number: (800) 982-6372
Fax: (970) 248-1973
Rance Larsen, Director of Admissions, Mesa State College, 1100 North Avenue, Grand Junction, CO 81501

## Metropolitan State College of Denver
### Denver, Colorado
**www.mscd.edu**  CB code: 4505

▶ Public 4-year liberal arts college
▶ Commuter campus in very large city
▶ 20,298 degree-seeking undergraduates
▶ SAT or ACT (ACT writing recommended) required

**General.** Founded in 1963. Regionally accredited. Library, student center, physical education facilities, child care center shared with Community College of Denver and University of Colorado at Denver. Degree completion programs offered at off-campus sites in North Glen and Englewood. **Degrees:** 2,510 bachelor's awarded. **ROTC:** Army, Air Force. **Location:** Downtown. **Calendar:** Semester, extensive summer session. **Full-time faculty:** 500 total. **Part-time faculty:** 746 total. **Class size:** 32% < 20, 54% 20-39, 6% 40-49, 8% 50-99, less than 1% >100. **Special facilities:** Art galleries, CAD/CAM laboratory, world indoor airport.

## Freshman class profile.

| Mid 50% test scores | | Rank in top quarter: | 16% |
|---|---|---|---|
| SAT critical reading: | 430-550 | Rank in top tenth: | 3.8% |
| SAT math: | 420-550 | Out-of-state: | 23% |
| ACT composite: | 17-22 | | |

**Basis for selection.** ACT/SAT test results, GPA, and high school class rank important. ACT/SAT not required of those submitting GED. Open admission for applicants 20 years of age and older who are high school graduates, have GED, or have 30 transferable credits from another college.

**High school preparation.** 15 units recommended. Recommended units include English 4, mathematics 3, social studies 2, history 1, science 3 and foreign language 2.

**2007-2008 Annual costs.** Tuition/fees: $3,033; $11,134 out-of-state.

**Financial aid. Non-need-based:** Scholarships awarded for academics, art, athletics, job skills, music/drama, state residency.

**Application procedures. Admission:** Closing date 8/25 (receipt date). $25 fee, may be waived for applicants with need. Application may be submitted online. Admission notification on a rolling basis. **Financial aid:** Priority date 2/15; no closing date. FAFSA required. Applicants notified on a rolling basis starting 3/1.

**Academics. Special study options:** Accelerated study, cooperative education, cross-registration, distance learning, double major, dual enrollment of high school students, external degree, honors, independent study, internships, liberal arts/career combination, student-designed major, study abroad, teacher certification program, Washington semester. **Credit/placement by examination:** AP, CLEP, IB. 64 credit hours maximum toward bachelor's degree. **Support services:** Pre-admission summer program, study skills assistance, tutoring, writing center.

**Majors. Area/ethnic studies:** African-American, Hispanic-American/Latino/Chicano. **Biology:** General. **Business:** Accounting, business admin, finance, hospitality admin, hospitality/recreation, marketing, tourism promotion, tourism/travel. **Communications:** General, broadcast journalism, journalism. **Computer sciences:** General, computer science. **Conservation:** General, environmental studies, land use planning. **Education:** Art, music. **Engineering technology:** Civil, electrical, surveying. **English:** English lit, speech/rhetoric. **Foreign languages:** General, Spanish. **Health:** Health care admin, nursing (RN). **History:** General. **Interdisciplinary:** Behavioral sciences, math/computer science. **Math:** General. **Parks/recreation:** General, exercise sciences. **Philosophy/religion:** Philosophy. **Physical sciences:** Atmospheric science, chemistry, physics. **Protective services:** Criminal justice, law enforcement admin. **Psychology:** General. **Public administration:** Human services, social work. **Social sciences:** Anthropology, economics, political science, sociology. **Transportation:** Air traffic control, aviation, aviation management. **Visual/performing arts:** Art, industrial design, music performance.

**Most popular majors.** Business/marketing 23%, English 9%, interdisciplinary studies 12%, security/protective services 10%, social sciences 9%.

**Computing on campus.** 700 workstations in library, computer center, student center. Commuter students can connect to campus network. Online course registration, online library, helpline, repair service, wireless network available.

**Student life. Freshman orientation:** Mandatory. Preregistration for classes offered. Several sessions held preceding each semester. **Housing:** Off-campus apartments in area. **Activities:** Jazz band, choral groups, dance, drama, literary magazine, music ensembles, musical theater, radio station, student government, student newspaper, approximately 100 student organizations and clubs.

**Athletics.** NCAA. **Intercollegiate:** Baseball M, basketball, cross-country, diving, soccer, swimming, tennis, volleyball W. **Intramural:** Basketball, handball, lacrosse M, racquetball, rugby M, skiing, softball, tennis, volleyball. **Team name:** Roadrunners.

**Student services.** Adult student services, alcohol/substance abuse counseling, campus ministries, career counseling, services for economically disadvantaged, student employment services, financial aid counseling, health services, legal services, on-campus daycare, personal counseling, placement for graduates, veterans' counselor, women's services. **Physically disabled:** Services for visually, speech, hearing impaired. **Learning disabled:** Comprehensive services available.

**Contact.** Phone: (303) 556-3058 Fax: (303) 556-6345
Elena Sandoval-Lucero, Director of Admissions, Metropolitan State College of Denver, Campus Box 16, Denver, CO 80217

## Naropa University
**Boulder, Colorado**
www.naropa.edu

**CB member**
**CB code: 0908**

- Private 4-year liberal arts college
- Commuter campus in small city
- 456 degree-seeking undergraduates: 6% part-time, 63% women, 1% African American, 2% Asian American, 4% Hispanic American, 2% international
- 627 degree-seeking graduate students
- 93% of applicants admitted
- Application essay, interview required
- 46% graduate within 6 years

**General.** Founded in 1974. Regionally accredited. **Degrees:** 129 bachelor's awarded; master's, first professional offered. **Location:** 35 miles from Denver. **Calendar:** Semester, limited summer session. **Full-time faculty:** 51 total; 51% have terminal degrees, 12% minority, 57% women. **Part-time faculty:** 143 total; 31% have terminal degrees, 8% minority, 62% women. **Class size:** 84% < 20, 16% 20-39. **Special facilities:** Meditation halls, maitri rooms, preschool.

**Freshman class profile.** 139 applied, 129 admitted, 69 enrolled.

| Mid 50% test scores | | GPA 3.0-3.49: | 34% |
|---|---|---|---|
| SAT critical reading: | 480-670 | GPA 2.0-2.99: | 42% |
| SAT math: | 460-560 | End year in good standing: | 51% |
| SAT writing: | 470-610 | Return as sophomores: | 56% |
| ACT composite: | 18-25 | Out-of-state: | 74% |
| GPA 3.50 or higher: | 24% | Live on campus: | 96% |

**Basis for selection.** Holistic approach to admissions decisions. Recommendations and interview required. Assessment of academic background, community service, mission and readiness are reviewed. Audition required for BFA.

**High school preparation.** 23 units recommended. Recommended units include English 4, mathematics 3, social studies 3, history 3, science 3 (laboratory 2), foreign language 3 and academic electives 2. Art, dance, theatre and/or creative writing recommended.

**2008-2009 Annual costs.** Tuition/fees: $22,074. Room/board: $7,036. Books/supplies: $686. Personal expenses: $2,998.

**2007-2008 Financial aid.** All financial aid based on need. 48 full-time freshmen applied for aid; 47 were judged to have need; 47 of these received aid. Average need met was 88%. Average scholarship/grant was $13,129; average loan $4,176. 56% of total undergraduate aid awarded as scholarships/grants, 44% as loans/jobs.

**Application procedures. Admission:** Priority date 1/15; no deadline. $50 fee, may be waived for applicants with need. Application may be submitted online. Admission notification on a rolling basis. Must reply by May 1 or within 3 week(s) if notified thereafter. High school students with GED may be admitted early. **Financial aid:** Priority date 3/1; no closing date. FAFSA required. Applicants notified on a rolling basis starting 3/1; must reply within 4 week(s) of notification.

**Academics. Special study options:** Double major, dual enrollment of high school students, independent study, internships, student-designed major, study abroad. **Credit/placement by examination:** AP, CLEP, IB. 30 credit hours maximum toward bachelor's degree. **Support services:** Reduced course load, study skills assistance, tutoring, writing center.

**Majors. Conservation:** Environmental studies. **Education:** Kindergarten/preschool. **English:** English lit. **Interdisciplinary:** Peace/conflict. **Philosophy/religion:** Religion. **Psychology:** General. **Visual/performing arts:** Dramatic, studio arts. **Other:** Interdisciplinary studies, Traditional eastern arts.

**Most popular majors.** English 15%, interdisciplinary studies 14%, parks/recreation 12%, philosophy/religious studies 6%, psychology 31%, visual/performing arts 16%.

**Computing on campus.** 83 workstations in computer center. Online course registration, online library, wireless network available.

**Student life. Freshman orientation:** Mandatory. Preregistration for classes offered. Week-long session in August. One or 2-day orientations offered for parents and families. **Housing:** Guaranteed on-campus for freshmen. Apartments, substance-free housing available. $300 nonrefundable deposit, deadline 7/1. Theme housing. **Activities:** Jazz band, choral groups, dance, drama, literary magazine, music ensembles, student government, diversity awareness working group, student union, gay/lesbian/bi/trans group, poetry coffee houses, volunteer corps, yoga clubs.

**Student services.** Alcohol/substance abuse counseling, campus ministries, career counseling, financial aid counseling, minority student services, personal counseling. **Physically disabled:** Services for visually, hearing impaired.

**Contact.** E-mail: admissions@naropa.edu
Phone: (303) 546-3572 Toll-free number: (800) 772-6951
Fax: (303) 546-3583
Susan Boyle, Dean of Admissions, Naropa University, 2130 Arapahoe Avenue, Boulder, CO 80302-6697

## National American University: Denver
**Denver, Colorado**
**www.national.edu**　　　　　　　　**CB code: 5354**

- For-profit 4-year university and branch campus college
- Commuter campus in very large city
- 165 degree-seeking undergraduates

**General.** Founded in 1941. Regionally accredited. **Degrees:** 21 bachelor's, 5 associate awarded. **Calendar:** Quarter, extensive summer session. **Part-time faculty:** 20 total. **Class size:** 92% < 20, 8% 20-39.

**Basis for selection.** Open admission.

**2007-2008 Annual costs.** Tuition/fees: $12,500. Books/supplies: $1,200.

**Application procedures. Admission:** No deadline. $25 fee. Admission notification on a rolling basis. **Financial aid:** No deadline. Applicants notified on a rolling basis.

**Academics. Special study options:** Accelerated study, cooperative education, distance learning, double major, ESL, external degree, independent study, internships, liberal arts/career combination, weekend college. **Credit/placement by examination:** AP, CLEP, institutional tests. 48 credit hours maximum toward bachelor's degree. **Support services:** Remedial instruction.

**Majors. Business:** Accounting, business admin, management information systems, management science. **Computer sciences:** Applications programming, information systems, LAN/WAN management, system admin. **Health:** Facilities admin, health care admin, health services, health services admin.

**Computing on campus.** Online library available.

**Student life. Activities:** Student government, Phi Beta Lamda (business club), Data Processing Management Association.

**Athletics. Team name:** Mavericks.

**Student services.** Career counseling, placement for graduates.

**Contact.** E-mail: kwalker@national.edu
Phone: (303) 758-6700 Fax: (303) 758-6810
Jaclyn Haack, Senior Admissions Representative, National American University: Denver, 1325 South Colorado Boulevard, Suite 100, Denver, CO 80222-3308

## Nazarene Bible College
**Colorado Springs, Colorado**
**www.nbc.edu**　　　　　　　　**CB code: 0476**

- Private 4-year Bible college affiliated with Church of the Nazarene
- Commuter campus in very large city
- 810 degree-seeking undergraduates
- Application essay required

**General.** Founded in 1964. Accredited by ABHE. **Degrees:** 60 bachelor's, 4 associate awarded. **Location:** 60 miles from Denver. **Calendar:** Trimester, limited summer session. **Full-time faculty:** 14 total. **Part-time faculty:** 65 total.

**Freshman class profile.**

End year in good standing: 100%　　Out-of-state: 96%

**Basis for selection.** Open admission, but selective for some programs. Testimony, 2 recommendations required. **Homeschooled:** Transcript of courses and grades, letter of recommendation (nonparent) required.

**2008-2009 Annual costs.** Tuition/fees (projected): $8,550. Books/supplies: $900.

**Financial aid. Non-need-based:** Scholarships awarded for religious affiliation. **Additional information:** Tuition waiver available to students serving as student body officers.

**Application procedures. Admission:** No deadline. No application fee. Admission notification on a rolling basis beginning on or about 5/1. **Financial aid:** Priority date 6/1; no closing date. FAFSA required. Applicants notified on a rolling basis starting 6/15; must reply within 2 week(s) of notification.

**Academics.** Full programs offered in evening classes. Cater to adult students. Extensive online degree programs offered. Degree competion program offered online and on campus. **Special study options:** Accelerated study, distance learning, double major, internships. **Credit/placement by examination:** CLEP, institutional tests. 12 credit hours maximum toward associate degree, 24 toward bachelor's. **Support services:** Learning center, reduced course load, remedial instruction, tutoring.

**Majors. Theology:** Bible, pastoral counseling, religious ed, sacred music.

**Computing on campus.** 20 workstations in library, computer center. Online library, wireless network available.

**Student life. Freshman orientation:** Mandatory. Preregistration for classes offered. **Policies:** Religious observance required. **Activities:** Concert band, choral groups, music ensembles, student government, Missions in Action Club, Wesley Theological Society.

**Student services.** Campus ministries, career counseling, services for economically disadvantaged, student employment services, financial aid counseling, personal counseling, placement for graduates, women's services. **Physically disabled:** Services for visually, hearing impaired.

**Contact.** E-mail: admissions@nbc.edu
Phone: (719) 884-5000 ext. 5065 Toll-free
number: (800) 873-3873 ext. 5065 Fax: (719) 884-5199
Laurel Matson, Vice President for Enrollment Services, Nazarene Bible College, 1111 Academy Park Loop, Colorado Springs, CO 80910-3717

## Platt College: Aurora
**Aurora, Colorado**
**www.plattcolorado.edu**　　　　　　　　**CB code: 3012**

- For-profit 4-year visual arts and technical college
- Large city
- 165 degree-seeking undergraduates
- Application essay, interview required

**General.** Accredited by ACCSCT. **Degrees:** 29 bachelor's, 12 associate awarded. **Calendar:** Continuous. **Full-time faculty:** 10 total. **Part-time faculty:** 8 total.

**Basis for selection.** Entrance examination, interview, level of interest (assessed during interview) important. Background check, letter of recommendation required for nursing. Institutional entrance examination required. Wonderlic required for graphic arts students. Test of Essential Academic Skills (TEAS) required for nursing students. **Homeschooled:** State high school equivalency certificate required.

**2007-2008 Annual costs.** Visual and Performing Arts: associate program: $34,000; Bachelor's program: $50,107. Nursing program (RN): $68,000. Costs include tuition, registration fee, lab fees, supplies. Cost of books, art kit vary with program.

**Financial aid.** All financial aid based on need.

**Application procedures. Admission:** No deadline. $75 fee. Admission notification on a rolling basis. **Financial aid:** No deadline. FAFSA, institutional form required. Applicants notified on a rolling basis.

**Academics. Credit/placement by examination:** CLEP.

**Majors. Health:** Nursing (RN). **Visual/performing arts:** Commercial/advertising art.

**Contact.** E-mail: admissions@plattcolo.com
Phone: (303) 369-5151
Joni Aaron-Horton, Senior Admissions Coordinator, Platt College: Aurora, 3100 South Parker Road, Aurora, CO 80014

## Regis University
Denver, Colorado
www.regis.edu

CB member
CB code: 4656

- ◗ Private 4-year university and liberal arts college affiliated with Roman Catholic Church
- ◗ Residential campus in very large city
- ◗ 1,623 degree-seeking undergraduates: 3% part-time, 63% women, 2% African American, 5% Asian American, 14% Hispanic American, 1% Native American, 1% international
- ◗ 102 degree-seeking graduate students
- ◗ 58% of applicants admitted
- ◗ SAT or ACT (ACT writing optional), application essay required
- ◗ 57% graduate within 6 years

**General.** Founded in 1877. Regionally accredited. **Degrees:** 315 bachelor's awarded; master's, doctoral offered. **ROTC:** Army, Naval, Air Force. **Location:** 10 miles from downtown. **Calendar:** Semester, limited summer session. **Full-time faculty:** 86 total; 80% have terminal degrees, 13% minority, 45% women. **Part-time faculty:** 30 total; 7% have terminal degrees, 7% minority, 53% women. **Class size:** 66% < 20, 33% 20-39, less than 1% 40-49, less than 1% 50-99. **Special facilities:** War experience study center, Santos collection, recorder music center, arboretum.

**Freshman class profile.** 2,319 applied, 1,345 admitted, 410 enrolled.

| Mid 50% test scores | | | |
|---|---|---|---|
| SAT critical reading: | 480-590 | Rank in top quarter: | 53% |
| SAT math: | 460-570 | Rank in top tenth: | 29% |
| ACT composite: | 20-26 | Return as sophomores: | 83% |
| GPA 3.50 or higher: | 48% | Out-of-state: | 43% |
| GPA 3.0-3.49: | 26% | Live on campus: | 80% |
| GPA 2.0-2.99: | 26% | International: | 1% |

**Basis for selection.** High school record, test scores, recommendations, essay, school and community activities most important. Interview, campus visit recommended. Audition recommended of music majors.

**High school preparation.** 15 units required. Required and recommended units include English 4, mathematics 2, social studies 3, history 2, science 2 (laboratory 1) and foreign language 2.

**2008-2009 Annual costs.** Tuition/fees: $28,700. Room/board: $8,982. Books/supplies: $1,698. Personal expenses: $1,161.

**2006-2007 Financial aid. Need-based:** 401 full-time freshmen applied for aid; 244 were judged to have need; 244 of these received aid. Average scholarship/grant was $11,378; average loan $1,467. 71% of total undergraduate aid awarded as scholarships/grants, 29% as loans/jobs. **Non-need-based:** Awarded to 794 full-time undergraduates, including 299 freshmen. Scholarships awarded for academics, athletics, leadership, minority status, religious affiliation, ROTC, state residency. **Additional information:** Tuition free for any student maintaining the required amount of credit hours who does not graduate in four years.

**Application procedures. Admission:** Priority date 3/1; deadline 8/1 (postmark date). $40 fee, may be waived for applicants with need. Application may be submitted online. Admission notification on a rolling basis beginning on or about 9/1. Must reply by May 1 or within 2 week(s) if notified thereafter. **Financial aid:** Priority date 3/1; no closing date. FAFSA required. Applicants notified on a rolling basis starting 3/15.

**Academics.** School of Professional Studies offers part-time undergraduate, graduate, certificate and corporate education programs to adult students on 6 campuses and online. **Special study options:** Accelerated study, combined bachelor's/graduate degree, cooperative education, cross-registration, distance learning, double major, exchange student, honors, independent study, internships, student-designed major, study abroad, teacher certification program. **Credit/placement by examination:** AP, CLEP, IB, institutional tests. 30 credit hours maximum toward bachelor's degree. Regis, CLEP, DANTES, Challenge exams offered. **Support services:** Learning center, preadmission summer program, reduced course load, remedial instruction, study skills assistance, tutoring, writing center.

**Majors. Area/ethnic studies:** Women's. **Biology:** General, biochemistry. **Business:** General, accounting, business admin. **Communications:** General. **Computer sciences:** General, computer science. **Education:** General, biology, chemistry, elementary, English, history, mathematics, middle, physical, science, secondary, special. **English:** English lit. **Foreign languages:** French, Spanish. **Health:** Medical records admin, predental, premedicine, preveterinary. **History:** General. **Interdisciplinary:** Neuroscience. **Legal studies:** Prelaw. **Liberal arts:** Arts/sciences. **Math:** General. **Philosophy/religion:** Philosophy, religion. **Physical sciences:** Chemistry. **Psychology:**

General. **Social sciences:** Criminology, economics, political science, sociology. **Visual/performing arts:** General.

**Most popular majors.** Biology 10%, business/marketing 28%, communications/journalism 6%, English 6%, interdisciplinary studies 12%, mathematics 6%, social sciences 12%.

**Computing on campus.** 337 workstations in dormitories, library, computer center, student center. Dormitories wired for high-speed internet access and linked to campus network. Commuter students can connect to campus network. Online course registration, online library, helpline, wireless network available.

**Student life. Freshman orientation:** Mandatory, $75 fee. Preregistration for classes offered. Held weekend before classes begin. **Policies:** Freshmen required to live on campus unless residing with parent, guardian or spouse in Denver metropolitan area. **Housing:** Guaranteed on-campus for freshmen. Coed dorms, single-sex dorms, special housing for disabled, apartments, cooperative housing, substance-free housing available. $150 nonrefundable deposit, deadline 5/1. **Activities:** Jazz band, choral groups, dance, drama, literary magazine, music ensembles, musical theater, radio station, student government, student newspaper, peer education, environmental action program, Christian Fellowship, Jewish student group, Asian awareness association, black student alliance, Mi Gente, multicultural awareness committee, Romero House, Young Democrats and Republicans.

**Athletics.** NCAA. **Intercollegiate:** Baseball M, basketball, cross-country, golf, lacrosse W, soccer, softball W, volleyball W. **Intramural:** Basketball, bowling, football (non-tackle), golf M, soccer, softball, tennis, volleyball. **Team name:** Rangers.

**Student services.** Adult student services, alcohol/substance abuse counseling, campus ministries, career counseling, student employment services, financial aid counseling, health services, minority student services, personal counseling, placement for graduates, veterans' counselor. **Physically disabled:** Services for visually, speech, hearing impaired. **Learning disabled:** Comprehensive services available.

**Contact.** E-mail: regisadm@regis.edu
Phone: (303) 458-4900 Toll-free number: (800) 388-2366 ext. 4900
Fax: (303) 964-5534
Victor Davolt, Director of Admissions, Regis College, Regis University, 3333 Regis Boulevard, Mail Code B20, Denver, CO 80221-1099

## Rocky Mountain College of Art & Design
Denver, Colorado
www.rmcad.edu

CB code: 1943

- ◗ For-profit 4-year visual arts college
- ◗ Commuter campus in very large city
- ◗ 496 degree-seeking undergraduates: 13% part-time, 58% women, 2% African American, 2% Asian American, 12% Hispanic American, 1% Native American, 1% international
- ◗ 99% of applicants admitted
- ◗ SAT or ACT with writing, application essay, interview required
- ◗ 44% graduate within 6 years

**General.** Founded in 1963. Regionally accredited. **Degrees:** 115 bachelor's awarded. **Calendar:** Semester, extensive summer session. **Full-time faculty:** 25 total. **Part-time faculty:** 40 total. **Class size:** 88% < 20, 11% 20-39, less than 1% 40-49. **Special facilities:** Fine arts center exhibition space.

**Freshman class profile.** 313 applied, 311 admitted, 129 enrolled.

| Mid 50% test scores | | | |
|---|---|---|---|
| | | ACT composite: | 17-22 |
| SAT critical reading: | 460-550 | Return as sophomores: | 63% |
| SAT math: | 430-560 | Out-of-state: | 38% |
| SAT writing: | 430-560 | International: | 2% |

**Basis for selection.** Applicants must show desire to pursue art career. Portfolio, essay, and recommendations required. Test scores required for all degree candidates. Portfolio and essay required. Interview required of local applicants, recommended for others.

**High school preparation.** Art courses strongly recommended.

**2007-2008 Annual costs.** Tuition/fees: $19,752. Room/board: $8,440.

**Financial aid. Non-need-based:** Scholarships awarded for academics, art, state residency.

**Application procedures. Admission:** No deadline. $50 fee. Application may be submitted online. Admission notification on a rolling basis.

**Financial aid:** Priority date 3/15; no closing date. FAFSA, institutional form required. Applicants notified on a rolling basis starting 4/15; must reply within 2 week(s) of notification.

**Academics. Special study options:** Double major, internships, study abroad. **Credit/placement by examination:** CLEP, SAT, ACT, institutional tests. 64 credit hours maximum toward bachelor's degree. **Support services:** Reduced course load, remedial instruction, study skills assistance, tutoring.

**Majors. Communications technology:** Animation/special effects. **Education:** Art. **Visual/performing arts:** Graphic design, illustration, interior design, painting, sculpture.

**Most popular majors.** Communication technologies 14%, visual/performing arts 81%.

**Computing on campus.** 120 workstations in library, computer center. Online library, helpline, repair service, wireless network available.

**Student life. Freshman orientation:** Mandatory. 2-day program held before start of term. **Activities:** Student government.

**Student services.** Alcohol/substance abuse counseling, career counseling, student employment services, financial aid counseling, personal counseling, placement for graduates, veterans' counselor.

**Contact.** E-mail: admissions@rmcad.edu
Phone: (303) 753-6046 Toll-free number: (800) 888-2787
Fax: (303) 759-4970
Angela Carlson, Director of Marketing and Admissions, Rocky Mountain College of Art & Design, 1600 Pierce Street, Denver, CO 80214

## Teikyo Loretto Heights University
**Denver, Colorado**
www.tlhu.edu                                    CB code: 4878

- Private 4-year business and liberal arts college
- Residential campus in very large city
- 372 degree-seeking undergraduates
- Application essay required

**General.** Accredited by ACICS. Member of the Teikyo University Group of 50 campuses in Asia, Europe, and North America; all students complete part of their studies abroad. **Degrees:** 10 associate awarded; master's offered. **Calendar:** Semester, limited summer session. **Full-time faculty:** 25 total. **Part-time faculty:** 8 total.

**Basis for selection.** High school record, class rank, GPA, recommendations, test scores, and essay most important.

**2007-2008 Annual costs.** Tuition/fees: $14,970. Room/board: $7,300.

**Application procedures. Admission:** No deadline. $50 fee, may be waived for applicants with need. Application may be submitted online. Admission notification on a rolling basis. International students who do not score an appropriate amount on the in-house English placement test must take English classes before attending the Degree Program. **Financial aid:** No deadline. FAFSA required.

**Academics. Special study options:** Combined bachelor's/graduate degree, double major, dual enrollment of high school students, ESL, independent study, internships, liberal arts/career combination, study abroad. **Credit/placement by examination:** AP, CLEP, IB.

**Majors. Business:** International. **Interdisciplinary:** Intercultural.

**Computing on campus.** PC or laptop required. Dormitories wired for high-speed internet access and linked to campus network. Online library available.

**Student life. Freshman orientation:** Available. **Policies:** Students under 21 required to live in dorms; exceptions may be made if living with a family member and for those who live on-campus for 1 year and then meet the waiver requirements to move off-campus. **Housing:** Guaranteed on-campus for all undergraduates. Coed dorms available. $230 nonrefundable deposit.

**Athletics. Team name:** Voyagers.

**Student services.** Career counseling, student employment services, financial aid counseling, placement for graduates.

**Contact.** E-mail: admissions@tlhu.edu
Phone: (303) 937-4280 Fax: (303) 937-4224
Ashley Henderson, Admissions Coordinator, Teikyo Loretto Heights University, 3001 South Federal Boulevard, Denver, CO 80236

## United States Air Force Academy
**USAF Academy, Colorado**                       CB member
www.usafa.edu                                    CB code: 4830

- Public 4-year university and military college
- Residential campus in large city
- 4,467 degree-seeking undergraduates: 19% women, 5% African American, 8% Asian American, 7% Hispanic American, 2% Native American, 1% international
- 17% of applicants admitted
- SAT or ACT with writing, application essay, interview required

**General.** Founded in 1954. Regionally accredited. **Degrees:** 977 bachelor's awarded. **Location:** 8 miles from Colorado Springs, 60 miles from Denver. **Calendar:** Semester, limited summer session. **Full-time faculty:** 563 total; 9% have terminal degrees. **Class size:** 65% < 20, 35% 20-39. **Special facilities:** 2 airfields; tri-sonic wind tunnel; observatory; aeronautics, instrumentation, research and radio-frequency systems laboratories; consolidated educational training facility; meteorology lab; engineering mechanics lab; laser optics center.

**Freshman class profile.** 9,162 applied, 1,600 admitted, 1,287 enrolled.

| Mid 50% test scores | | | |
|---|---|---|---|
| SAT critical reading: | 570-650 | Rank in top quarter: | 83% |
| SAT math: | 600-690 | Rank in top tenth: | 51% |
| SAT writing: | 550-650 | End year in good standing: | 86% |
| ACT composite: | 27-31 | Return as sophomores: | 84% |
| GPA 3.50 or higher: | 82% | Out-of-state: | 95% |
| GPA 3.0-3.49: | 15% | Live on campus: | 100% |
| GPA 2.0-2.99: | 3% | International: | 1% |

**Basis for selection.** Must be a citizen of the United States, unmarried with no dependents, between the ages of 17 and 23, and of good moral character. Legal nomination from member of Congress, US President or Vice President or other selected sources required. Secondary school record, test scores, leadership ability, extracurricular activities, character most important. Satisfactory completion of medical exam and fitness test, and personal interview required.

**High school preparation.** Recommended units include English 4, mathematics 4, social studies 3, history 3, science 4 (laboratory 4) and foreign language 2. One computer science course recommended. English should include college preparatory composition and speech courses. Math should include algebra, geometry, trigonometry, calculus, and functional analysis (if available). Science should include biology, chemistry, physics, computers, and additional science courses. Foreign language instruction should be in a modern language.

**2007-2008 Annual costs.** Tuition, room, board, medical and dental care paid by U.S. Government. Each cadet receives monthly salary to pay for uniforms, supplies and personal expenses. A government loan is advanced to each member of the freshman class.

**Application procedures. Admission:** Closing date 1/31 (postmark date). No application fee. Application may be submitted online. Admission notification on a rolling basis beginning on or about 11/15. Must reply by 5/1. Several stages of application process; begin junior year.

**Academics. Special study options:** Double major, exchange student, honors, study abroad. **Credit/placement by examination:** AP, CLEP, SAT, ACT, institutional tests.

**Majors. Biology:** General. **Business:** Management science. **Computer sciences:** Computer science. **Engineering:** General, aerospace, civil, computer, electrical, environmental, mechanical, mechanics, operations research, systems. **English:** English lit. **History:** General. **Interdisciplinary:** Behavioral sciences, math/computer science. **Legal studies:** General. **Liberal arts:** Humanities. **Physical sciences:** Atmospheric science, chemistry, physics. **Social sciences:** General, economics, geography, political science.

**Most popular majors.** Biology 7%, business/marketing 13%, engineering/engineering technologies 35%, social sciences 21%.

**Computing on campus.** PC or laptop required. Dormitories wired for high-speed internet access and linked to campus network. Online library, helpline, repair service, wireless network available.

**Student life. Freshman orientation:** Available. Three 2-day appointee orientation sessions held in April. **Housing:** Guaranteed on-campus for all undergraduates. Coed dorms available. **Activities:** Pep band, choral groups, drama.

Four-Year Colleges

**Athletics.** NCAA. **Intercollegiate:** Baseball M, basketball, boxing M, cheerleading, cross-country, diving, fencing, football (tackle) M, golf M, gymnastics, ice hockey M, lacrosse M, rifle, soccer, swimming, tennis, track and field, volleyball W, water polo M, wrestling M. **Intramural:** Basketball, boxing M, cross-country, football (non-tackle), racquetball, rugby, soccer, softball, tennis, volleyball. **Team name:** Falcons.

**Student services.** Alcohol/substance abuse counseling, campus ministries, health services, legal services, personal counseling.

**Contact.**  E-mail: rr_webmail@usafa.af.mil
Phone: (719) 333-2520 Toll-free number: (800) 443-9266
Fax: (719) 333-3647
United States Air Force Academy, HQ USAF/RRS, 2304 Cadet Drive, Suite 2300, USAF Academy, CO 80840

---

## University of Colorado at Boulder
**Boulder, Colorado**                                           **CB member**
**www.colorado.edu**                                        **CB code: 4841**

- Public 4-year university
- Residential campus in small city
- 25,521 degree-seeking undergraduates: 7% part-time, 47% women, 2% African American, 6% Asian American, 6% Hispanic American, 1% Native American, 1% international
- 4,914 degree-seeking graduate students
- 82% of applicants admitted
- SAT or ACT (ACT writing optional) required
- 67% graduate within 6 years; 21% enter graduate study

**General.** Founded in 1876. Regionally accredited. **Degrees:** 5,343 bachelor's awarded; master's, doctoral, first professional offered. **ROTC:** Army, Naval, Air Force. **Location:** 30 miles from Denver. **Calendar:** Semester, extensive summer session. **Full-time faculty:** 1,259 total; 91% have terminal degrees, 14% minority, 35% women. **Part-time faculty:** 668 total; 45% have terminal degrees, 10% minority, 49% women. **Class size:** 50% < 20, 30% 20-39, 5% 40-49, 8% 50-99, 7% >100. **Special facilities:** Natural history museum, art museum and galleries, heritage center, observatory, planetarium and science center, electron microscope, outdoor theater, video interactive foreign language laboratory, mountain research station, centrifuge, engineering lab, multipurpose conference center, concert hall, multidisciplinary IT center.

**Freshman class profile.** 19,857 applied, 16,187 admitted, 5,591 enrolled.

| Mid 50% test scores | | | |
|---|---|---|---|
| SAT critical reading: | 520-630 | Rank in top tenth: | 25% |
| SAT math: | 540-650 | End year in good standing: | 87% |
| ACT composite: | 23-28 | Return as sophomores: | 83% |
| GPA 3.50 or higher: | 59% | Out-of-state: | 40% |
| GPA 3.0-3.49: | 35% | Live on campus: | 94% |
| GPA 2.0-2.99: | 6% | International: | 1% |
| Rank in top quarter: | 58% | Fraternities: | 11% |
| | | Sororities: | 12% |

**Basis for selection.** Secondary school record (breadth and rigor of courses, grades, class rank) most important. Tests scores also very important. Personal statement, recommendations, and personal attributes and talents considered. Audition required of music majors.

**High school preparation.** 16 units required. Required units include English 4, mathematics 3, social studies 2, history 1, science 3 (laboratory 2) and foreign language 3. Physics or chemistry with lab; 1 geography, 3 single foreign language required for Colleges of Arts, Sciences and Business. 4 math, 1 physics, 1 chemistry required for College of Engineering. 4 math required for College of Business. 2 single foreign language required for Colleges of Engineering, Music, Architecture and Planning.

**2007-2008 Annual costs.** Tuition/fees: $6,635; $24,797 out-of-state. One-time matriculation fee of $108. Room/board: $9,088. Books/supplies: $1,698. Personal expenses: $2,997.

**2007-2008 Financial aid.** **Need-based:** 4,602 full-time freshmen applied for aid; 2,378 were judged to have need; 2,352 of these received aid. Average need met was 92%. Average scholarship/grant was $5,158; average loan $4,413. 49% of total undergraduate aid awarded as scholarships/grants, 51% as loans/jobs. **Non-need-based:** Awarded to 10,631 full-time undergraduates, including 2,218 freshmen. Scholarships awarded for academics, alumni affiliation, art, athletics, leadership, music/drama, ROTC, state residency.

**Application procedures.** **Admission:** Closing date 1/15 (postmark date). $50 fee, may be waived for applicants with need. Application may be submitted online. Admission notification on a rolling basis beginning on or about 9/1. Must reply by May 1 or within 2 week(s) if notified thereafter. **Financial aid:** Priority date 4/1; no closing date. FAFSA required. Applicants notified on a rolling basis starting 2/1; must reply within 3 week(s) of notification.

**Academics.** Residential Academic Programs in leadership, natural or environmental sciences, humanities and service learning, the arts, honors, American West culture and society, international and global affairs, cultural diversity, business, or engineering available. **Special study options:** Accelerated study, combined bachelor's/graduate degree, cooperative education, cross-registration, distance learning, double major, dual enrollment of high school students, ESL, exchange student, honors, independent study, internships, liberal arts/career combination, semester at sea, student-designed major, study abroad, teacher certification program. **Credit/placement by examination:** AP, CLEP, IB, institutional tests. Policies vary by department. **Support services:** Learning center, pre-admission summer program, reduced course load, study skills assistance, tutoring, writing center.

**Majors.** **Architecture:** Environmental design. **Area/ethnic studies:** Asian, Russian/Slavic, women's. **Biology:** Biochemistry, cellular/molecular, ecology, physiology. **Business:** Accounting, business admin, finance, international, management information systems, marketing, real estate, small business admin. **Communications:** General, journalism. **Computer sciences:** Computer science. **Conservation:** Environmental studies. **Education:** Music. **Engineering:** Aerospace, architectural, chemical, civil, computer, electrical, environmental, mechanical, physics. **English:** English lit. **Foreign languages:** Chinese, classics, French, Germanic, Italian, Japanese, linguistics, Spanish. **Health:** Communication disorders. **History:** General. **Interdisciplinary:** Global studies. **Liberal arts:** Humanities. **Math:** General, applied. **Philosophy/religion:** Philosophy, religion. **Physical sciences:** Astronomy, chemistry, geology, physics. **Psychology:** General. **Social sciences:** Anthropology, economics, geography, political science, sociology. **Visual/performing arts:** Dance, dramatic, film/cinema, music performance, studio arts. **Other:** Chemical & biological engineering, Ethnic studies.

**Most popular majors.** Biology 9%, business/marketing 16%, communications/journalism 9%, engineering/engineering technologies 8%, psychology 9%, social sciences 16%, visual/performing arts 6%.

**Computing on campus.** 1,581 workstations in dormitories, library, computer center, student center. Dormitories wired for high-speed internet access and linked to campus network. Commuter students can connect to campus network. Online course registration, online library, helpline, repair service, student web hosting, wireless network available.

**Student life.** **Freshman orientation:** Mandatory. Preregistration for classes offered. 2-day programs for students and parents held throughout summer, and in January for students entering in the spring. **Policies:** Honor code, lifestyle code of conduct, and 2-strikes disciplinary policy regarding alcohol violations. **Housing:** Guaranteed on-campus for freshmen. Coed dorms, special housing for disabled, apartments, fraternity/sorority housing, substance-free housing available. $250 partly refundable deposit. Residential academic programs within specific dorms. **Activities:** Bands, campus ministries, choral groups, dance, drama, film society, international student organizations, literary magazine, music ensembles, Model UN, musical theater, opera, radio station, student government, student newspaper, symphony orchestra, TV station, student outreach & retention center for equity, multicultural affairs center, volunteer clearing house, victim assistance, disability services, gay lesbian bisexual transgender resource center, ethical and civic engagement institute, College Democrats, College Republicans.

**Athletics.** NCAA. **Intercollegiate:** Basketball, cross-country, football (tackle) M, golf, skiing, soccer W, tennis W, track and field, volleyball W. **Intramural:** Basketball, football (non-tackle), ice hockey, soccer, volleyball, water polo. **Team name:** Colorado Buffaloes.

**Student services.** Adult student services, alcohol/substance abuse counseling, campus ministries, career counseling, services for economically disadvantaged, student employment services, financial aid counseling, health services, legal services, minority student services, on-campus daycare, personal counseling, placement for graduates, veterans' counselor, women's services. **Physically disabled:** Services for visually, speech, hearing impaired.

**Contact.**  E-mail: apply@colorado.edu
Phone: (303) 492-6301 Fax: (303) 492-7115
Kevin McLennan, Director of Admissions, University of Colorado at Boulder, 552 UCB, Boulder, CO 80309-0552

---

## University of Colorado at Colorado Springs
**Colorado Springs, Colorado**
**www.uccs.edu**                                               **CB code: 4874**

- Public 4-year university
- Commuter campus in large city

- 6,181 degree-seeking undergraduates: 21% part-time, 58% women, 4% African American, 5% Asian American, 10% Hispanic American, 1% Native American
- 1,549 degree-seeking graduate students
- 66% of applicants admitted
- SAT or ACT (ACT writing optional) required

**General.** Founded in 1965. Regionally accredited. **Degrees:** 1,225 bachelor's awarded; master's, doctoral offered. **ROTC:** Army. **Location:** 60 miles from Denver. **Calendar:** Semester, limited summer session. **Full-time faculty:** 317 total; 12% minority, 50% women. **Part-time faculty:** 42 total; 10% minority, 57% women. **Class size:** 48% < 20, 32% 20-39, 11% 40-49, 8% 50-99, less than 1% >100.

**Freshman class profile.** 2,741 applied, 1,819 admitted, 850 enrolled.

| Mid 50% test scores | | | |
|---|---|---|---|
| SAT critical reading: | 470-580 | GPA 3.0-3.49: | 37% |
| SAT math: | 470-590 | GPA 2.0-2.99: | 27% |
| SAT writing: | 450-550 | Rank in top quarter: | 42% |
| ACT composite: | 20-25 | Rank in top tenth: | 13% |
| GPA 3.50 or higher: | 36% | Out-of-state: | 24% |

**Basis for selection.** Priority given to applicants who ranked in top 40% of graduating class, scored 1080 SAT (exclusive of Writing) or 24 ACT, 2.8 GPA, and completed all high school course units as required by the college to which they applied. Test of Standard Written English required of liberal arts applicants.

**High school preparation.** 15 units required; 16 recommended. Required and recommended units include English 4, mathematics 3-4, social studies 2-3, history 1, science 3 (laboratory 2), foreign language 2-3 and academic electives 1. Requirements may vary slightly according to college.

**2007-2008 Annual costs.** Tuition/fees: $5,431; $16,381 out-of-state. Room/board: $6,898.

**2006-2007 Financial aid. Need-based:** 574 full-time freshmen applied for aid; 306 were judged to have need; 287 of these received aid. Average need met was 54%. Average scholarship/grant was $5,537; average loan $2,523. 41% of total undergraduate aid awarded as scholarships/grants, 59% as loans/jobs. **Non-need-based:** Awarded to 424 full-time undergraduates, including 134 freshmen. Scholarships awarded for academics, alumni affiliation, athletics, state residency.

**Application procedures. Admission:** Priority date 4/1; deadline 7/1. $50 fee. Application may be submitted online. Admission notification on a rolling basis. **Financial aid:** Priority date 4/1; no closing date. FAFSA required. Applicants notified on a rolling basis starting 4/15.

**Academics. Special study options:** Accelerated study, combined bachelor's/graduate degree, cooperative education, cross-registration, distance learning, double major, dual enrollment of high school students, ESL, exchange student, independent study, internships, liberal arts/career combination, student-designed major, study abroad, teacher certification program. **Credit/placement by examination:** AP, CLEP, IB, institutional tests. 30 credit hours maximum toward bachelor's degree. **Support services:** Learning center, study skills assistance, tutoring, writing center.

**Majors. Biology:** General. **Business:** Accounting, business admin, finance, human resources. **Communications:** General. **Computer sciences:** Computer science. **Education:** Special. **Engineering:** General, computer, electrical, mechanical. **English:** English lit. **Foreign languages:** Spanish. **Health:** Health services, nursing (RN). **History:** General. **Math:** General. **Philosophy/religion:** Philosophy. **Physical sciences:** Chemistry, physics. **Protective services:** Law enforcement admin. **Psychology:** General. **Public administration:** General. **Social sciences:** Anthropology, economics, geography, political science, sociology. **Visual/performing arts:** Studio arts.

**Most popular majors.** Biology 8%, business/marketing 20%, communications/journalism 9%, English 6%, health sciences 13%, psychology 8%, social sciences 15%.

**Computing on campus.** 250 workstations in dormitories, library, computer center. Dormitories wired for high-speed internet access and linked to campus network. Commuter students can connect to campus network. Online course registration, online library, helpline, repair service, wireless network available.

**Student life. Freshman orientation:** Mandatory, $45 fee. One-day sessions throughout summer. **Housing:** Coed dorms, single-sex dorms, special housing for disabled, apartments available. $150 partly refundable deposit. **Activities:** Jazz band, choral groups, dance, drama, film society, literary magazine, music ensembles, musical theater, radio station, student government, student newspaper, advocating women's assistance resources education, counseling honor society, math club, chemistry honor society, black

student union, international student club, Latino student union, Inter-Varsity Christian Fellowship.

**Athletics.** NCAA. **Intercollegiate:** Basketball, cross-country, golf M, soccer M, softball W, track and field, volleyball W. **Intramural:** Basketball, football (non-tackle), soccer, table tennis, volleyball. **Team name:** Mountain Lions.

**Student services.** Adult student services, career counseling, student employment services, financial aid counseling, health services, minority student services, on-campus daycare, personal counseling, veterans' counselor. **Physically disabled:** Services for visually, speech, hearing impaired.

**Contact.** E-mail: admrec@uccs.edu
Phone: (719) 262-3383 Toll-free number: (800) 990-8227 ext. 3383
Fax: (719) 262-3116
Steve Ellis, Director of Admissions, University of Colorado at Colorado Springs, PO Box 7150, Colorado Springs, CO 80933-7150

## University of Colorado at Denver
Denver, Colorado     **CB member**
www.ucdhsc.edu     **CB code: 4875**

- Public 4-year university
- Commuter campus in very large city
- 8,327 degree-seeking undergraduates: 27% part-time, 55% women, 5% African American, 10% Asian American, 12% Hispanic American, 1% Native American, 1% international
- 7,108 degree-seeking graduate students
- 68% of applicants admitted
- SAT or ACT (ACT writing optional), application essay required

**General.** Founded in 1912. Regionally accredited. Library, student center, and classrooms shared with Metropolitan State College and Community College of Denver. **Degrees:** 1,655 bachelor's awarded; master's, doctoral, first professional offered. **ROTC:** Army, Air Force. **Calendar:** Semester, extensive summer session. **Full-time faculty:** 2,249 total; 79% have terminal degrees, 10% minority, 48% women. **Part-time faculty:** 765 total; 41% have terminal degrees, 9% minority, 56% women. **Class size:** 32% < 20, 50% 20-39, 11% 40-49, 5% 50-99, 2% >100. **Special facilities:** Computational math centers, applied psychology center, environmental science center, transportation research center, Fourth World center for study of indigenous law and politics.

**Freshman class profile.** 3,521 applied, 2,380 admitted, 1,062 enrolled.

| Mid 50% test scores | | | |
|---|---|---|---|
| SAT critical reading: | 490-600 | GPA 2.0-2.99: | 27% |
| SAT math: | 490-590 | Rank in top quarter: | 43% |
| ACT composite: | 19-25 | Rank in top tenth: | 17% |
| GPA 3.50 or higher: | 37% | Return as sophomores: | 71% |
| GPA 3.0-3.49: | 36% | Out-of-state: | 5% |
| | | International: | 1% |

**Basis for selection.** Previous academic performance including high school course work and GPA; evidence of academic ability and accomplishments as indicated by test scores; and evidence of maturity, motivation, potential for academic success most important. Audition required of music majors.

**High school preparation.** 15 units required; 18 recommended. Required and recommended units include English 4, mathematics 3, social studies 2, history 1, science 3 (laboratory 2), foreign language 2 and academic electives 1. 4 math required for engineering and business students.

**2007-2008 Annual costs.** Tuition/fees: $5,815; $17,771 out-of-state. Tuition varies by program. One-time matriculation fee of $115 required. Books/supplies: $1,700. Personal expenses: $1,080.

**2006-2007 Financial aid. Need-based:** 507 full-time freshmen applied for aid; 379 were judged to have need; 372 of these received aid. Average need met was 69%. Average scholarship/grant was $4,715; average loan $3,014. 63% of total undergraduate aid awarded as scholarships/grants, 37% as loans/jobs. **Non-need-based:** Awarded to 754 full-time undergraduates, including 146 freshmen. Scholarships awarded for academics, art, leadership, music/drama.

**Application procedures. Admission:** Priority date 7/22; deadline 9/1. $50 fee, may be waived for applicants with need. Application may be submitted online. Admission notification on a rolling basis. **Financial aid:** Closing date 4/1. FAFSA, institutional form required. Applicants notified on a rolling basis starting 5/1.

**Academics.** Learning opportunities through center for internships and cooperative education. **Special study options:** Accelerated study, combined bachelor's/graduate degree, cooperative education, cross-registration, distance learning, double major, ESL, honors, independent study, internships, liberal arts/career combination, student-designed major, study abroad, teacher certification program, weekend college. **Credit/placement by examination:** AP, CLEP, IB, institutional tests. 30 credit hours maximum toward bachelor's degree. **Support services:** Learning center, study skills assistance, tutoring, writing center.

**Majors. Biology:** General, biomedical sciences. **Business:** General. **Communications:** General. **Computer sciences:** General. **Engineering:** Civil, electrical, mechanical. **English:** Composition, English lit. **Foreign languages:** French, Spanish. **Health:** Dental hygiene, nursing (RN). **History:** General. **Interdisciplinary:** Global studies. **Math:** General. **Philosophy/religion:** Philosophy. **Physical sciences:** Chemistry, physics. **Psychology:** General. **Social sciences:** Anthropology, economics, geography, political science, sociology. **Visual/performing arts:** Dramatic, studio arts.

**Most popular majors.** Biology 6%, business/marketing 21%, communications/journalism 7%, engineering/engineering technologies 6%, health sciences 16%, psychology 9%, social sciences 11%, visual/performing arts 8%.

**Computing on campus.** 205 workstations in library, computer center, student center. Dormitories wired for high-speed internet access. Commuter students can connect to campus network. Online course registration, online library, helpline, student web hosting, wireless network available.

**Student life. Freshman orientation:** Mandatory. **Housing:** Coed dorms, substance-free housing available. **Activities:** Jazz band, choral groups, dance, drama, music ensembles, musical theater, student government, student newspaper, more than 60 groups available.

**Athletics. Intramural:** Basketball, racquetball, tennis, volleyball.

**Student services.** Alcohol/substance abuse counseling, career counseling, student employment services, financial aid counseling, health services, legal services, minority student services, on-campus daycare, personal counseling, placement for graduates, veterans' counselor, women's services. **Physically disabled:** Services for visually, speech, hearing impaired.

**Contact.** E-mail: admissions@cudenver.edu
Phone: (303) 556-2704 Fax: (303) 556-4838
Barbara Edwards, Director of Admissions, University of Colorado at Denver, Box 173364, Campus Box 167, Denver, CO 80217-3364

---

## University of Denver

Denver, Colorado
www.du.edu

**CB member**
**CB code: 4842**

- Private 4-year university affiliated with United Methodist Church
- Residential campus in very large city
- 5,260 degree-seeking undergraduates: 9% part-time, 55% women, 3% African American, 5% Asian American, 7% Hispanic American, 1% Native American, 4% international
- 5,230 degree-seeking graduate students
- 74% of applicants admitted
- SAT or ACT (ACT writing optional), application essay required
- 74% graduate within 6 years; 20% enter graduate study

**General.** Founded in 1864. Regionally accredited. **Degrees:** 1,017 bachelor's awarded; master's, doctoral, first professional offered. **ROTC:** Army, Air Force. **Location:** 8 miles from downtown. **Calendar:** Quarter, limited summer session. **Full-time faculty:** 575 total; 91% have terminal degrees, 13% minority, 44% women. **Part-time faculty:** 574 total; 7% minority, 46% women. **Class size:** 62% < 20, 28% 20-39, 6% 40-49, 3% 50-99, less than 1% >100. **Special facilities:** Observatory, high altitude research laboratory, centers for gifted children.

**Freshman class profile.** 5,072 applied, 3,755 admitted, 1,138 enrolled.

| Mid 50% test scores | | | |
|---|---|---|---|
| SAT critical reading: | 530-640 | Rank in top tenth: | 35% |
| SAT math: | 540-650 | Return as sophomores: | 86% |
| ACT composite: | 23-28 | Out-of-state: | 56% |
| GPA 3.50 or higher: | 63% | Live on campus: | 94% |
| GPA 3.0-3.49: | 30% | International: | 5% |
| GPA 2.0-2.99: | 7% | Fraternities: | 26% |
| Rank in top quarter: | 67% | Sororities: | 16% |

**Basis for selection.** High school GPA, test scores and strength of curriculum most important. Interview, academic maturity, contributions to school and community activities, leadership also important; recommendations from

teacher and counselor, personal essay considered. Interview strongly encouraged. Audition required of music majors. Portfolio recommended of art majors. **Homeschooled:** Letter of recommendation (nonparent) required.

**High school preparation.** Recommended units include English 4, mathematics 4, social studies 2, history 2, science 4 (laboratory 2) and foreign language 3.

**2008-2009 Annual costs.** Tuition/fees: $33,810. Room/board: $9,093.

**2006-2007 Financial aid. Need-based:** 669 full-time freshmen applied for aid; 449 were judged to have need; 449 of these received aid. Average need met was 76%. Average scholarship/grant was $18,283; average loan $3,218. 74% of total undergraduate aid awarded as scholarships/grants, 26% as loans/jobs. **Non-need-based:** Awarded to 2,071 full-time undergraduates, including 596 freshmen. Scholarships awarded for academics, art, athletics, leadership, minority status, music/drama, state residency.

**Application procedures. Admission:** Closing date 1/15 (postmark date). $50 fee, may be waived for applicants with need. Application may be submitted online. Admission notification 3/15. Must reply by 5/1. **Financial aid:** Priority date 3/1; no closing date. FAFSA required.

**Academics.** Special 3-week interterm courses available for focused concentration. **Special study options:** Accelerated study, combined bachelor's/graduate degree, cooperative education, distance learning, double major, dual enrollment of high school students, ESL, honors, independent study, internships, liberal arts/career combination, semester at sea, student-designed major, study abroad, teacher certification program, Washington semester, weekend college. **Credit/placement by examination:** AP, CLEP, IB, institutional tests. 45 credit hours maximum toward bachelor's degree. **Support services:** Learning center, pre-admission summer program, tutoring, writing center.

**Majors. Agriculture:** Animal sciences. **Area/ethnic studies:** Asian-American, women's. **Biology:** General, biochemistry, bioinformatics, ecology, molecular. **Business:** General, accounting, business admin, construction management, finance, hospitality admin, international, management information systems, managerial economics, marketing, organizational behavior, real estate, statistics. **Communications:** General, digital media, journalism. **Computer sciences:** Computer science, information technology, systems analysis. **Conservation:** Environmental science. **Engineering:** General, computer, electrical, mechanical. **English:** English lit. **Foreign languages:** French, German, Italian, Russian, Spanish. **History:** General. **Interdisciplinary:** Biological/physical sciences, global studies, science/society. **Legal studies:** General. **Liberal arts:** Arts/sciences. **Math:** General. **Philosophy/religion:** Philosophy, religion. **Physical sciences:** Chemistry, physics. **Psychology:** General. **Public administration:** Policy analysis. **Social sciences:** General, anthropology, criminology, economics, geography, international relations, political science, sociology. **Visual/performing arts:** Art, art history/conservation, dramatic, graphic design, music performance, musicology. **Other:** Computer software and media applications.

**Most popular majors.** Biology 7%, business/marketing 44%, communications/journalism 10%, psychology 7%, social sciences 12%, visual/performing arts 9%.

**Computing on campus.** PC or laptop required. 390 workstations in dormitories, library, computer center, student center. Dormitories wired for high-speed internet access and linked to campus network. Commuter students can connect to campus network. Online course registration, online library, helpline, student web hosting, wireless network available.

**Student life. Freshman orientation:** Available. Preregistration for classes offered. **Housing:** Guaranteed on-campus for freshmen. Coed dorms, apartments, fraternity/sorority housing, substance-free housing available. $200 nonrefundable deposit, deadline 5/1. **Activities:** Bands, campus ministries, choral groups, dance, drama, film society, international student organizations, literary magazine, music ensembles, Model UN, musical theater, opera, radio station, student government, student newspaper, symphony orchestra.

**Athletics.** NCAA. **Intercollegiate:** Basketball, diving, golf, gymnastics W, ice hockey M, lacrosse, skiing, soccer, swimming, tennis, volleyball W. **Intramural:** Basketball, football (non-tackle), ice hockey, racquetball, soccer, softball, table tennis, volleyball. **Team name:** Pioneers.

**Student services.** Campus ministries, career counseling, student employment services, financial aid counseling, health services, minority student services, personal counseling, placement for graduates, veterans' counselor. **Physically disabled:** Services for visually, speech, hearing impaired. **Learning disabled:** Comprehensive services available.

**Contact.** E-mail: admission@du.edu
Phone: (303) 871-2036 Toll-free number: (800) 525-9495
Fax: (303) 871-3301
Thomas Willoughby, Vice Chancellor, Enrollment, University of Denver, 2197 South University Boulevard, Denver, CO 80208

# University of Northern Colorado
## Greeley, Colorado
www.unco.edu      **CB code: 4074**

- Public 4-year university
- Commuter campus in small city
- 10,038 degree-seeking undergraduates: 9% part-time, 61% women, 3% African American, 3% Asian American, 8% Hispanic American, 1% Native American, 1% international
- 1,654 degree-seeking graduate students
- 91% of applicants admitted
- SAT or ACT (ACT writing optional) required
- 49% graduate within 6 years; 3% enter graduate study

**General.** Founded in 1889. Regionally accredited. **Degrees:** 1,997 bachelor's awarded; master's, doctoral offered. **ROTC:** Army, Air Force. **Location:** 50 miles from Denver; 50 miles from Cheyenne, Wyoming. **Calendar:** Semester, limited summer session. **Full-time faculty:** 445 total; 9% minority, 52% women. **Part-time faculty:** 174 total; 9% minority, 58% women. **Class size:** 34% < 20, 51% 20-39, 2% 40-49, 11% 50-99, 1% >100. **Special facilities:** African-American cultural center, Hispanic cultural center, Native American & Asian Pacific cultural center.

**Freshman class profile.** 6,163 applied, 5,600 admitted, 2,272 enrolled.

| Mid 50% test scores | | | |
|---|---|---|---|
| SAT critical reading: | 460-580 | Rank in top quarter: | 32% |
| SAT math: | 460-580 | Rank in top tenth: | 10% |
| SAT writing: | 470-590 | End year in good standing: | 75% |
| ACT composite: | 20-24 | Return as sophomores: | 66% |
| GPA 3.50 or higher: | 31% | Out-of-state: | 10% |
| GPA 3.0-3.49: | 35% | Live on campus: | 92% |
| GPA 2.0-2.99: | 34% | International: | 2% |

**Basis for selection.** Expected 2.9 GPA; 21 ACT or 970 SAT (exclusive of Writing). Higher ACT/SAT score can compensate for lower GPA and higher GPA can compensate for lower test score. Audition required of music majors.

**High school preparation.** 15 units required. Required and recommended units include English 4, mathematics 3, social studies 3, science 3 (laboratory 1). Math should include 2 algebra, additional higher level math unit.

**2007-2008 Annual costs.** Tuition/fees: $4,313; $12,893 out-of-state. Costs reflect student share of tuition after the Colorado College Opportunity Fund. Room/board: $7,292. Books/supplies: $1,135. Personal expenses: $2,897.

**2006-2007 Financial aid. Need-based:** 46% of total undergraduate aid awarded as scholarships/grants, 54% as loans/jobs. **Non-need-based:** Scholarships awarded for academics, athletics, music/drama.

**Application procedures. Admission:** Priority date 8/1; no deadline. $45 fee, may be waived for applicants with need. Application may be submitted online. Admission notification on a rolling basis. **Financial aid:** Priority date 3/1; no closing date. FAFSA required. Applicants notified on a rolling basis starting 4/15; must reply within 4 week(s) of notification.

**Academics. Special study options:** Cooperative education, cross-registration, distance learning, double major, ESL, exchange student, external degree, honors, independent study, internships, semester at sea, student-designed major, study abroad, teacher certification program. **Credit/placement by examination:** AP, CLEP, IB, institutional tests. 30 credit hours maximum toward bachelor's degree. **Support services:** Learning center, reduced course load, remedial instruction, study skills assistance, tutoring, writing center.

**Majors. Area/ethnic studies:** African-American, Hispanic-American/Latino/Chicano. **Biology:** General. **Business:** Business admin. **Communications:** General, journalism. **Education:** Music, special. **English:** English lit. **Family/consumer sciences:** Aging. **Foreign languages:** General, sign language interpretation, Spanish. **Health:** Audiology/hearing, audiology/speech pathology, dietetics, health care admin, health services, nursing (RN), public health ed, speech pathology, vocational rehab counseling. **History:** General. **Math:** General. **Parks/recreation:** Exercise sciences, facilities management. **Philosophy/religion:** Philosophy. **Physical sciences:** Chemistry, geology, physics. **Protective services:** Criminal justice. **Psychology:** General. **Public administration:** Human services. **Social sciences:** General, anthropology, economics, geography, political science, sociology. **Visual/performing arts:** Dramatic, studio arts.

**Most popular majors.** Business/marketing 13%, communications/journalism 8%, health sciences 11%, interdisciplinary studies 14%, parks/recreation 8%, psychology 7%, social sciences 8%, visual/performing arts 8%.

**Computing on campus.** 1,169 workstations in dormitories, library, computer center, student center. Dormitories wired for high-speed internet access and linked to campus network. Commuter students can connect to campus network. Online course registration, online library, helpline, repair service, wireless network available.

**Student life. Freshman orientation:** Available. Preregistration for classes offered. **Housing:** Guaranteed on-campus for all undergraduates. Coed dorms, single-sex dorms, special housing for disabled, apartments, fraternity/sorority housing, substance-free housing available. $250 nonrefundable deposit. **Activities:** Bands, campus ministries, choral groups, dance, drama, film society, literary magazine, music ensembles, musical theater, opera, radio station, student government, student newspaper, symphony orchestra, TV station, African-American student union, Hispanic students organization, international students association, Native American student services, Asian/Pacific American student services.

**Athletics.** NCAA. **Intercollegiate:** Baseball M, basketball, cross-country W, diving W, football (tackle) M, golf, soccer W, softball W, swimming W, tennis, track and field, volleyball W, wrestling M. **Intramural:** Basketball, football (non-tackle), golf, racquetball, soccer, softball, table tennis, tennis, volleyball, water polo. **Team name:** Bears.

**Student services.** Adult student services, alcohol/substance abuse counseling, campus ministries, career counseling, student employment services, financial aid counseling, health services, legal services, minority student services, personal counseling, placement for graduates, veterans' counselor, women's services. **Physically disabled:** Services for visually, speech, hearing impaired.

**Contact.** E-mail: admissions.help@unco.edu
Phone: (970) 351-2881 Toll-free number: (888) 700-4862
Fax: (970) 351-2984
Chris Dowen, Director of Admissions, University of Northern Colorado, Campus Box 10, Greeley, CO 80639

# Western State College of Colorado
## Gunnison, Colorado
www.western.edu      **CB code: 4946**

- Public 4-year liberal arts college
- Residential campus in small town
- 2,400 degree-seeking undergraduates
- SAT or ACT (ACT writing optional) required

**General.** Founded in 1901. Regionally accredited. College-based mountain search and rescue team. **Degrees:** 465 bachelor's awarded. **Location:** 200 miles from Denver. **Calendar:** Semester, limited summer session. **Full-time faculty:** 118 total. **Part-time faculty:** 49 total. **Class size:** 49% < 20, 41% 20-39, 9% 40-49, 1% 50-99, less than 1% >100. **Special facilities:** Botanical gardens, archaeological site, dinosaur reconstruction lab.

**Freshman class profile.** 600 enrolled.

| Mid 50% test scores | | | |
|---|---|---|---|
| | | GPA 2.0-2.99: | 48% |
| SAT critical reading: | 460-560 | Rank in top quarter: | 18% |
| SAT math: | 460-560 | Rank in top tenth: | 7% |
| ACT composite: | 18-23 | Out-of-state: | 35% |
| GPA 3.50 or higher: | 16% | Live on campus: | 94% |
| GPA 3.0-3.49: | 35% | | |

**Basis for selection.** School achievement record, test scores very important; recommendations considered. Essay recommended. Interview recommended for academically weak applicants.

**High school preparation.** Required and recommended units include English 4, mathematics 3-4, social studies 2, history 2, science 3 (laboratory 2) and foreign language 2.

**2007-2008 Annual costs.** Tuition/fees: $3,573; $12,405 out-of-state. Room/board: $7,522. Books/supplies: $950. Personal expenses: $1,226.

**2007-2008 Financial aid. Need-based:** Average need met was 60%. Average scholarship/grant was $3,500; average loan $2,625. **Non-need-based:** Scholarships awarded for academics, alumni affiliation, art, athletics, leadership, music/drama.

**Application procedures. Admission:** Priority date 3/15; deadline 6/1 (postmark date). $30 fee, may be waived for applicants with need. Application may be submitted online. Admission notification on a rolling basis beginning on or about 11/1. Must reply by May 1 or within 2 week(s) if notified thereafter. **Financial aid:** Priority date 4/1; no closing date. FAFSA required. Applicants notified on a rolling basis starting 4/1; must reply within 4 week(s) of notification.

**Academics. Special study options:** Combined bachelor's/graduate degree, cooperative education, double major, dual enrollment of high school students, exchange student, honors, independent study, internships, liberal arts/career combination, semester at sea, study abroad, teacher certification program. **Credit/placement by examination:** AP, CLEP, IB, SAT, ACT, institutional tests. 30 credit hours maximum toward bachelor's degree. **Support services:** Study skills assistance, tutoring, writing center.

**Majors. Biology:** General. **Business:** Accounting, business admin, management information systems, resort management. **Communications:** General. **Conservation:** Environmental studies. **English:** English lit. **Foreign languages:** Spanish. **History:** General. **Legal studies:** Prelaw. **Math:** General. **Parks/recreation:** Exercise sciences. **Physical sciences:** Chemistry, geology. **Protective services:** Criminal justice, police science. **Psychology:** General. **Social sciences:** Anthropology, economics, political science, sociology. **Visual/performing arts:** Art, music management, studio arts. **Other:** Outdoor leadership.

**Computing on campus.** 168 workstations in dormitories, library, student center. Dormitories linked to campus network. Commuter students can connect to campus network. Online course registration available.

**Student life. Freshman orientation:** Available, $65 fee. Preregistration for classes offered. Wilderness-based orientation available. **Housing:** Guaranteed on-campus for freshmen. Coed dorms, single-sex dorms, apartments available. $100 nonrefundable deposit. Theme housing (honors, art, wilderness/outdoor activities) available. **Activities:** Bands, choral groups, dance, drama, literary magazine, music ensembles, radio station, student government, student newspaper, symphony orchestra, TV station, Hillel, black student alliance, Amigos, Campus Crusade, Hui-O-Ka-Aina, lesbian-gay-bisexual alliance, Newman Club, Baptist student union, Christian athletes fellowship, Women's Action Coalition.

**Athletics.** NCAA. **Intercollegiate:** Basketball, cross-country, football (tackle) M, skiing, track and field, volleyball W, wrestling M. **Intramural:** Baseball M, basketball, golf, ice hockey M, lacrosse, rugby, skiing, soccer, softball, swimming, tennis, track and field, volleyball, wrestling M. **Team name:** Mountaineers.

**Student services.** Adult student services, career counseling, health services, on-campus daycare, personal counseling, veterans' counselor. **Physically disabled:** Services for visually, hearing impaired. **Learning disabled:** Comprehensive services available.

**Contact.** E-mail: discover@western.edu
Phone: (970) 943-2119 Toll-free number: (800) 876-5309
Fax: (970) 943-2212
Tim Albers, Director of Admissions, Western State College of Colorado, 600 North Adams Street, Gunnison, CO 81231

---

## Westwood College: Denver North
### Denver, Colorado
**www.westwood.edu**

**CB code: 3948**

- For-profit 3-year technical college
- Commuter campus in very large city

**General.** Founded in 1953. Accredited by ACCSCT. **Location:** 5 miles from downtown. **Calendar:** 5 ten-week terms per year.

**Annual costs/financial aid.** Full-time costs per 10-week term for most programs: $4,251 for tuition. Tuition and fees may vary. Books/supplies: $370. Personal expenses: $2,000. Need-based financial aid available to full-time and part-time students.

**Contact.** Phone: (303) 650-5050
Director of Admissions, 7350 North Broadway, Denver, CO 80221

---

## Westwood College: Denver South
### Denver, Colorado
**www.westwood.edu**

- For-profit 4-year technical college
- Commuter campus in very large city
- 325 degree-seeking undergraduates
- 100% of applicants admitted
- Interview required

**General.** Accredited by ACCSCT. **Degrees:** 76 bachelor's, 34 associate awarded. **Calendar:** Continuous, extensive summer session. **Full-time faculty:** 9 total. **Part-time faculty:** 24 total.

**Freshman class profile.** 110 applied, 110 admitted, 42 enrolled.

**Basis for selection.** Admission based on scores from Accuplacer exam. Non-native English speakers must take ESL course, have TOEFL score of 475, have a HS diploma or GED in the U.S., or proof of completion of an accredited U.S. college program. Accuplacer exam can be waived if student scores 17 on ACT or SAT equivalent.

**2007-2008 Annual costs.** Tuition/fees: $22,275. Tuition and fees may vary by program. Books/supplies: $1,250.

**Application procedures. Admission:** No deadline. $25 fee. Application may be submitted online. Admission notification on a rolling basis. **Financial aid:** No deadline. FAFSA, institutional form required. Applicants notified on a rolling basis; must reply within 2 week(s) of notification.

**Academics. Special study options:** Accelerated study, distance learning, independent study, weekend college. **Credit/placement by examination:** CLEP, institutional tests. 67 credit hours maximum toward associate degree, 135 toward bachelor's. **Support services:** Reduced course load, remedial instruction, study skills assistance, tutoring, writing center.

**Majors. Architecture:** Interior. **Business:** E-commerce, fashion. **Communications technology:** Animation/special effects, desktop publishing, graphics. **Computer sciences:** Computer graphics, LAN/WAN management, networking, security, system admin, web page design, webmaster. **Protective services:** Law enforcement admin. **Visual/performing arts:** Commercial/advertising art, design, graphic design, interior design.

**Computing on campus.** 300 workstations in library, computer center. Commuter students can connect to campus network. Online course registration, online library available.

**Student life. Freshman orientation:** Mandatory. Preregistration for classes offered.

**Student services.** Adult student services, career counseling, student employment services, financial aid counseling, placement for graduates.

**Contact.** Phone: (303) 934-1122 Fax: (303) 934-2583
Michael Rushak, Director of Admissions, Westwood College: Denver South, 3150 South Sheridan Boulevard, Denver, CO 80227-5507

---

## Yeshiva Toras Chaim Talmudical Seminary
### Denver, Colorado

**CB code: 7008**

- Private 4-year rabbinical college for men affiliated with Jewish faith
- Very large city

**General.** Accredited by AARTS. **Calendar:** Trimester.

**Contact.** Phone: (303) 629-8200
1555 Stuart Street PO Box 40067, Denver, CO 80204

# Connecticut

## Albertus Magnus College

**New Haven, Connecticut**
www.albertus.edu

**CB member**
**CB code: 3001**

- Private 4-year liberal arts college affiliated with Roman Catholic Church
- Residential campus in small city
- 1,682 degree-seeking undergraduates: 5% part-time, 68% women, 27% African American, 1% Asian American, 10% Hispanic American
- 336 degree-seeking graduate students
- 82% of applicants admitted
- SAT or ACT (ACT writing optional) required
- 64% graduate within 6 years

**General.** Founded in 1925. Regionally accredited. Majority of students enrolled in adult education and graduate programs. **Degrees:** 441 bachelor's, 154 associate awarded; master's offered. **Location:** 90 miles from New York City. **Calendar:** Semester, limited summer session. **Full-time faculty:** 42 total; 79% have terminal degrees, 43% women. **Part-time faculty:** 16 total; 50% have terminal degrees, 50% women. **Class size:** 75% < 20, 25% 20-39. **Special facilities:** Academic center for science, art and technology.

**Freshman class profile.** 587 applied, 482 admitted, 101 enrolled.

| Mid 50% test scores | | Return as sophomores: | 78% |
|---|---|---|---|
| SAT critical reading: | 490-540 | Out-of-state: | 12% |
| SAT math: | 470-520 | Live on campus: | 56% |
| End year in good standing: | 86% | | |

**Basis for selection.** School achievement record most important. Recommendations, test scores, interview, school and community activities also considered. **Homeschooled:** Letter of recommendation (nonparent) required. GED preferred.

**High school preparation.** 16 units required. Required and recommended units include English 4, mathematics 3, social studies 2, science 2 and foreign language 2.

**2008-2009 Annual costs.** Tuition/fees: $22,724. Room/board: $9,442. Books/supplies: $620. Personal expenses: $940.

**2007-2008 Financial aid. Need-based:** Average need met was 47%. Average scholarship/grant was $9,273; average loan $3,186. 45% of total undergraduate aid awarded as scholarships/grants, 55% as loans/jobs. **Non-need-based:** Scholarships awarded for academics, art, job skills, leadership, music/drama, religious affiliation, state residency.

**Application procedures. Admission:** No deadline. $35 fee, may be waived for applicants with need. Application may be submitted online. Admission notification on a rolling basis beginning on or about 12/1. Must reply by May 1 or within 4 week(s) if notified thereafter. **Financial aid:** Closing date 2/28. FAFSA, institutional form required. Applicants notified on a rolling basis starting 3/1; must reply within 2 week(s) of notification.

**Academics. Special study options:** Accelerated study, double major, honors, independent study, internships, liberal arts/career combination, student-designed major, teacher certification program. **Credit/placement by examination:** AP, CLEP, SAT, institutional tests. 21 credit hours maximum toward associate degree, 45 toward bachelor's. **Support services:** Learning center, reduced course load, study skills assistance, tutoring, writing center.

**Majors. Biology:** General. **Business:** Accounting, business admin, finance, international, management information systems, managerial economics. **Communications:** General, advertising, media studies. **Computer sciences:** Information systems. **Education:** General, art, biology, business, chemistry, English, history, mathematics, middle, science, secondary, social studies, Spanish. **English:** British lit, creative writing, English lit. **Foreign languages:** Spanish. **Health:** Art therapy, premedicine. **History:** General. **Legal studies:** Prelaw. **Liberal arts:** Arts/sciences. **Math:** General. **Philosophy/religion:** Philosophy, religion. **Physical sciences:** Chemistry. **Protective services:** Criminal justice. **Psychology:** General. **Public administration:** Human services, social work. **Social sciences:** General, economics, political science, sociology. **Visual/performing arts:** General, art, art history/conservation, commercial/advertising art, dramatic, photography, studio arts.

**Computing on campus.** 175 workstations in library, computer center, student center. Commuter students can connect to campus network. Repair service, wireless network available.

**Student life. Freshman orientation:** Mandatory. Preregistration for classes offered. **Housing:** Guaranteed on-campus for all undergraduates. Coed dorms, single-sex dorms, substance-free housing available. $400 nonrefundable deposit, deadline 7/1. **Activities:** Campus ministries, choral groups, dance, drama, literary magazine, musical theater, student government, outspoken alliance, multi-cultural student union.

**Athletics.** NCAA. **Intercollegiate:** Baseball M, basketball, cross-country, soccer, softball W, tennis, volleyball W. **Team name:** Falcons.

**Student services.** Adult student services, campus ministries, career counseling, student employment services, financial aid counseling, health services, personal counseling, placement for graduates, veterans' counselor.

**Contact.** E-mail: admissions@albertus.edu
Phone: (203) 773-8501 Toll-free number: (800) 578-9160
Fax: (203) 773-5248
Richard LoLatte, Dean of Admissions and Enrollment Management, Albertus Magnus College, 700 Prospect Street, New Haven, CT 06511-1189

## Briarwood College

**Southington, Connecticut**
www.briarwood.edu

**CB code: 3121**

- For-profit 4-year junior college
- Commuter campus in large town
- 663 degree-seeking undergraduates: 36% part-time, 73% women, 19% African American, 2% Asian American, 11% Hispanic American
- Application essay required

**General.** Founded in 1966. Regionally accredited. **Degrees:** 1 bachelor's, 103 associate awarded. **Location:** 19 miles from Hartford. **Calendar:** Semester, limited summer session. **Full-time faculty:** 25 total. **Part-time faculty:** 60 total.

**Freshman class profile.**

| Out-of-state: | 6% | International: | 1% |
|---|---|---|---|

**Basis for selection.** Open admission, but selective for some programs. 8-hour observation and interview required for Occupational Therapy Assistant program. Interview, essay and 2 letters of recommendation required for Dental Hygiene program. 3 placement tests (English grammar, reading, math) and essay required of all new students.

**High school preparation.** For occupational therapy assistant program, 2 math, 2 science, including 1 biological science, required.

**2007-2008 Annual costs.** Tuition/fees: $17,135. Room only: $3,600. Books/supplies: $1,000. Personal expenses: $2,400.

**Financial aid. Non-need-based:** Scholarships awarded for academics, alumni affiliation, leadership.

**Application procedures. Admission:** No deadline. $25 fee, may be waived for applicants with need. Application may be submitted online. Admission notification on a rolling basis beginning on or about 9/15. **Financial aid:** Priority date 4/30; no closing date. FAFSA required. Applicants notified on a rolling basis starting 3/15; must reply within 2 week(s) of notification.

**Academics. Special study options:** Double major, ESL, independent study, internships, liberal arts/career combination, weekend college. **Credit/placement by examination:** AP, CLEP, institutional tests. 29 credit hours maximum toward associate degree. **Support services:** Learning center, pre-admission summer program, reduced course load, remedial instruction, study skills assistance, tutoring, writing center.

**Majors. Personal/culinary services:** Mortuary science. **Protective services:** Criminal justice.

**Computing on campus.** 66 workstations in library, computer center. Dormitories wired for high-speed internet access.

**Student life. Freshman orientation:** Mandatory. **Housing:** Coed dorms, apartments, substance-free housing available. $100 deposit. Townhouse apartments with kitchens available. **Activities:** Choral groups, radio station, student government, psychology honor society, allied health club.

**Athletics.** NJCAA. **Intramural:** Basketball M.

**Student services.** Career counseling, student employment services, financial aid counseling, health services, personal counseling, placement for graduates, veterans' counselor. **Physically disabled:** Services for visually, hearing impaired.

**Contact.** E-mail: admis@briarwood.edu
Phone: (860) 628-4751 ext. 108 Toll-free number: (800) 952-2444 ext. 108
Fax: (860) 628-6444
Jack LeConche, Dean of Administration, Briarwood College, 2279 Mount Vernon Road, Southington, CT 06489-1057

## Central Connecticut State University

New Britain, Connecticut — CB member
www.ccsu.edu — CB code: 3898

- Public 4-year university
- Commuter campus in small city
- 9,161 degree-seeking undergraduates: 17% part-time, 50% women, 8% African American, 3% Asian American, 6% Hispanic American, 1% international
- 2,068 degree-seeking graduate students
- 61% of applicants admitted
- SAT or ACT with writing, application essay required
- 44% graduate within 6 years

**General.** Founded in 1849. Regionally accredited. **Degrees:** 1,572 bachelor's awarded; master's, doctoral offered. **ROTC:** Army, Air Force. **Location:** 9 miles from Hartford. **Calendar:** Semester, extensive summer session. **Full-time faculty:** 432 total; 70% have terminal degrees, 16% minority, 40% women. **Part-time faculty:** 453 total; 4% have terminal degrees, 6% minority, 44% women. **Class size:** 42% < 20, 56% 20-39, 1% 40-49, 1% 50-99, less than 1% >100. **Special facilities:** Observatory, planetarium.

**Freshman class profile.** 5,665 applied, 3,480 admitted, 1,478 enrolled.

| Mid 50% test scores | | | |
|---|---|---|---|
| SAT critical reading: | 460-540 | End year in good standing: | 72% |
| SAT math: | 460-560 | Return as sophomores: | 79% |
| SAT writing: | 460-540 | Out-of-state: | 7% |
| Rank in top quarter: | 25% | Live on campus: | 56% |
| Rank in top tenth: | 6% | International: | 1% |

**Basis for selection.** High school record, class rank, SAT scores most important. Letters of recommendation, the optional student essay, and resumes of activities to assess applicant's attitude toward future success also considered. School of Business, social work program, communication program, and School of Education programs require acceptance into majors after admission to the university. Interview optional but would be considered. Audition required for music. **Homeschooled:** Statement describing homeschool structure and mission, transcript of courses and grades, state high school equivalency certificate required.

**High school preparation.** 13 units required. Required and recommended units include English 4, mathematics 3, social studies 2, history 1, science 2 (laboratory 1) and foreign language 3. Social science should include US history; mathematics should include algebra I and II and geometry.

**2007-2008 Annual costs.** Tuition/fees: $6,734; $15,454 out-of-state. Room/board: $8,350. Books/supplies: $1,010. Personal expenses: $1,744.

**2006-2007 Financial aid. Need-based:** 923 full-time freshmen applied for aid; 601 were judged to have need; 575 of these received aid. Average need met was 71%. Average scholarship/grant was $3,443; average loan $2,834. 44% of total undergraduate aid awarded as scholarships/grants, 56% as loans/jobs. **Non-need-based:** Awarded to 948 full-time undergraduates, including 221 freshmen. Scholarships awarded for academics, athletics, minority status.

**Application procedures. Admission:** Priority date 10/1; deadline 6/1 (receipt date). $50 fee, may be waived for applicants with need. Application may be submitted online. Admission notification on a rolling basis beginning on or about 12/1. Must reply by May 1 or within 2 week(s) if notified thereafter. **Financial aid:** Priority date 3/1, closing date 9/15. FAFSA required. Applicants notified on a rolling basis starting 3/30; must reply within 2 week(s) of notification.

**Academics. Special study options:** Cooperative education, crossregistration, distance learning, double major, dual enrollment of high school students, ESL, exchange student, honors, independent study, internships, student-designed major, study abroad, teacher certification program. Undergraduates may take graduate classes. **Credit/placement by examination:**

AP, CLEP, IB, institutional tests. 30 credit hours maximum toward bachelor's degree. **Support services:** Learning center, pre-admission summer program, reduced course load, remedial instruction, study skills assistance, tutoring, writing center.

**Honors college/program.** Honor Program provides interdisciplinary, teamtaught approach to general education. Limited scholarships available.

**Majors. Biology:** General, biochemistry, molecular. **Business:** Accounting, business admin, finance, international, management information systems, marketing, organizational behavior, travel services. **Communications:** General. **Computer sciences:** General. **Construction:** General. **Education:** Art, elementary, music, secondary, technology/industrial arts. **Engineering:** Electrical, mechanical. **Engineering technology:** Civil, computer, industrial, manufacturing, mechanical. **English:** English lit. **Foreign languages:** French, German, Italian, Spanish. **Health:** Athletic training, nursing (RN). **History:** General. **Interdisciplinary:** Global studies. **Math:** General. **Philosophy/religion:** Philosophy. **Physical sciences:** Chemistry, geology, physics. **Psychology:** General. **Public administration:** Social work. **Social sciences:** General, anthropology, criminology, economics, geography, political science, sociology. **Visual/performing arts:** Art, design, dramatic.

**Most popular majors.** Business/marketing 29%, education 12%, engineering/engineering technologies 6%, psychology 10%, social sciences 12%.

**Computing on campus.** 875 workstations in dormitories, library, computer center, student center. Dormitories wired for high-speed internet access and linked to campus network. Commuter students can connect to campus network. Online course registration, online library, helpline, repair service, wireless network available.

**Student life. Freshman orientation:** Available, $65 fee. Preregistration for classes offered. One-day orientation, late June and early July. **Housing:** Coed dorms, single-sex dorms available. $250 nonrefundable deposit, deadline 5/1. **Activities:** Bands, campus ministries, choral groups, dance, drama, film society, international student organizations, literary magazine, music ensembles, musical theater, radio station, student government, student newspaper, TV station, Newman Club, Union of Jewish Students, Christian Fellowship, Christian Science Organization, Afro-American and African students, Latin American student association.

**Athletics.** NCAA. **Intercollegiate:** Baseball M, basketball, cross-country, diving W, football (tackle) M, golf, lacrosse W, soccer, softball W, swimming W, track and field, volleyball W. **Intramural:** Badminton, basketball, field hockey W, football (tackle) M, gymnastics W, lacrosse M, rugby, soccer, softball W, tennis, volleyball, water polo M. **Team name:** Blue Devils.

**Student services.** Adult student services, alcohol/substance abuse counseling, campus ministries, career counseling, student employment services, financial aid counseling, health services, minority student services, oncampus daycare, personal counseling, placement for graduates, veterans' counselor, women's services. **Physically disabled:** Services for visually, speech, hearing impaired.

**Contact.** E-mail: admissions@ccsu.edu
Phone: (860) 832-2278 Fax: (860) 832-2295
Richard Bishop, Director of Admissions, Central Connecticut State University, 1615 Stanley Street, New Britain, CT 06050

## Charter Oak State College

New Britain, Connecticut — CB member
www.charteroak.edu — CB code: 0870

- Public 4-year virtual liberal arts college
- Commuter campus in small city
- 1,557 degree-seeking undergraduates: 95% part-time, 60% women

**General.** Founded in 1973. Regionally accredited. **Degrees:** 643 bachelor's, 55 associate awarded. **Location:** 5 miles from Hartford. **Calendar:** Continuous, limited summer session. **Part-time faculty:** 97 total; 40% have terminal degrees, 9% minority, 50% women. **Class size:** 80% < 20, 19% 20-39, less than 1% 40-49.

**Basis for selection.** 9 college-level credits must be completed before enrolling. May be earned through college courses, testing, or ACE/PONSI recommendations for noncollege-sponsored instruction.

**2007-2008 Annual costs.** In-state matriculation fee: $995; out-of-state fees: $1,310. Cost of education varies due to students having the option to take courses at other institutions.

**Financial aid.** All financial aid based on need.

**Application procedures. Admission:** No deadline. $75 fee, may be waived for applicants with need. Application may be submitted online. Admission notification on a rolling basis. **Financial aid:** No deadline. FAFSA, institutional form required. Applicants notified on a rolling basis starting 8/23.

**Academics.** Tutoring and writing center are available online free to students. **Special study options:** Accelerated study, distance learning, dual enrollment of high school students, external degree, independent study, liberal arts/career combination, student-designed major. Students can take courses at any regionally accredited institution. **Credit/placement by examination:** AP, CLEP, institutional tests. 60 credit hours maximum toward associate degree, 120 toward bachelor's. Unlimited number of hours of credit by examination may be counted toward degree. **Support services:** Tutoring, writing center.

**Majors. Liberal arts:** Arts/sciences.

**Most popular majors.** Liberal arts 16%.

**Computing on campus.** Online library, helpline, wireless network available.

**Student life. Activities:** Student government.

**Student services.** Adult student services, financial aid counseling, veterans' counselor.

**Contact.** E-mail: info@charteroak.edu
Phone: (860) 832-3800 Fax: (860) 832-3999
Lori Pendleton, Director of Admission, Charter Oak State College, 55 Paul Manafort Drive, New Britain, CT 06053-2142

---

## Connecticut College

New London, Connecticut

www.conncoll.edu

CB member
CB code: 3284

- Private 4-year liberal arts college
- Residential campus in large town
- 1,746 degree-seeking undergraduates: 1% part-time, 59% women, 4% African American, 4% Asian American, 5% Hispanic American, 4% international
- 12 degree-seeking graduate students
- 35% of applicants admitted
- Application essay required
- 81% graduate within 6 years

**General.** Founded in 1911. Regionally accredited. **Degrees:** 491 bachelor's awarded; master's offered. **Location:** 105 miles from Boston, 124 miles from New York City. **Calendar:** Semester, limited summer session. **Full-time faculty:** 171 total; 91% have terminal degrees, 16% minority, 45% women. **Part-time faculty:** 75 total; 23% have terminal degrees, 9% minority, 52% women. **Special facilities:** 750-acre arboretum, greenhouse, ion accelerator, refracting telescope and observatory, scanning and transmission electron microscopes, nuclear magnetic resonance spectrometer, tunable diode laser spectroscopy laboratory, center for electronic and digital sound, neuroscience and animal behavior laboratories, clinical and social psychology research observation suites.

**Freshman class profile.** 4,742 applied, 1,638 admitted, 492 enrolled.

| Mid 50% test scores | | | |
|---|---|---|---|
| SAT critical reading: | 630-720 | Rank in top tenth: | 60% |
| SAT math: | 610-690 | Return as sophomores: | 90% |
| SAT writing: | 630-720 | Out-of-state: | 85% |
| ACT composite: | 25-29 | Live on campus: | 100% |
| Rank in top quarter: | 93% | International: | 4% |

**Basis for selection.** School achievement record is most important. Recommendations, personal qualities, personal essay, special talents, extracurricular activities are also significant. Either two SAT subject tests or the ACT is required. SAT Reasoning scores are optional and will be considered if an applicant asks us to use them. TOEFL or its equivalent is required for non-native-speaking students. Interview recommended. Audition recommended of those intending a dance or music major. Portfolio recommended of intended art majors. **Homeschooled:** State high school equivalency certificate, letter of recommendation (nonparent) required. Extracurricular activities encouraged.

**2008-2009 Annual costs.** Comprehensive fee: $49,385. Books/supplies: $1,000.

**2007-2008 Financial aid.** All financial aid based on need. 252 full-time freshmen applied for aid; 201 were judged to have need; 201 of these received aid. Average need met was 100%. Average scholarship/grant was $27,364; average loan $3,649. 83% of total undergraduate aid awarded as scholarships/grants, 17% as loans/jobs.

**Application procedures. Admission:** Closing date 1/1 (postmark date). $60 fee, may be waived for applicants with need. Application may be submitted online. Admission notification 3/31. Must reply by 5/1. **Financial aid:** Closing date 2/1. FAFSA, CSS PROFILE required. Applicants notified by 4/1; must reply by 5/1.

**Academics.** Interdisciplinary centers for students to earn a certificate to complement their major(s) available. **Special study options:** Cross-registration, double major, dual enrollment of high school students, exchange student, independent study, internships, student-designed major, study abroad, teacher certification program, Washington semester. 12-college exchange, National Theater Institute, Mystic Seaport Program in American Maritime Studies, Institute for Architecture and Urban Studies, American Academy in Rome, Associated Kyoto Program, cross-registration with U.S. Coast Guard Academy, Trinity College and Wesleyan University, study away-teach away opportunities, specially funded student research opportunities. **Credit/placement by examination:** AP, CLEP, IB, institutional tests. 32 credit hours maximum toward bachelor's degree. Students may use AP credit to repair credit deficiencies that arise from voluntary course withdrawals or failing grades, or to accelerate. **Support services:** Pre-admission summer program, study skills assistance, tutoring, writing center.

**Majors. Architecture:** Architecture. **Area/ethnic studies:** African, American, Chinese, East Asian, German, Hispanic-American/Latino/Chicano, Italian, Japanese, Latin American, Slavic, women's. **Biology:** General, biochemistry, Biochemistry/biophysics and molecular biology, botany, cellular/molecular, molecular. **Computer sciences:** Computer science. **Conservation:** Environmental studies. **Education:** Music, physics. **Engineering:** Physics. **English:** English lit. **Family/consumer sciences:** Family studies. **Foreign languages:** Chinese, classics, French, German, Italian, Japanese, Slavic, Spanish. **History:** General. **Interdisciplinary:** Medieval/Renaissance, neuroscience. **Math:** General. **Philosophy/religion:** Philosophy, religion. **Physical sciences:** Astrophysics, chemistry, physics. **Psychology:** General. **Social sciences:** Anthropology, economics, international relations, political science, sociology, urban studies. **Visual/performing arts:** Art history/conservation, dance, dramatic.

**Most popular majors.** Area/ethnic studies 7%, biology 9%, English 9%, foreign language 7%, psychology 7%, social sciences 24%, visual/performing arts 12%.

**Computing on campus.** 500 workstations in library, computer center, student center. Dormitories wired for high-speed internet access and linked to campus network. Commuter students can connect to campus network. Online course registration, online library, helpline, student web hosting, wireless network available.

**Student life. Freshman orientation:** Mandatory. Preregistration for classes offered. Held week prior to the start of classes. Optional outdoor orientation prior to full orientation. **Policies:** Student-adjudicated social honor code in addition to academic honor code. **Housing:** Guaranteed on-campus for all undergraduates. Coed dorms, special housing for disabled, apartments, cooperative housing, substance-free housing available. $500 nonrefundable deposit, deadline 5/1. Theme dormitories, quiet housing, men's and women's floors within dormitories, living and learning experience available. **Activities:** Bands, campus ministries, choral groups, dance, drama, film society, international student organizations, literary magazine, music ensembles, radio station, student government, student newspaper, symphony orchestra, College Democrats, College Republicans, Hillel, Intervarsity Christian Fellowship, multi-faith student council, Muslim student association, Connecticut College Asian/Asian American student association, Latino American student association, Sexual Orientations United for Liberation, African/African American Student Association.

**Athletics.** NCAA. **Intercollegiate:** Basketball, cross-country, diving, field hockey W, ice hockey, lacrosse, rowing (crew), sailing, soccer, squash, swimming, tennis, track and field, volleyball W, water polo. **Intramural:** Baseball M, basketball, football (non-tackle) M, racquetball, soccer, softball, squash, tennis, volleyball. **Team name:** Camels.

**Student services.** Adult student services, alcohol/substance abuse counseling, campus ministries, career counseling, student employment services, financial aid counseling, health services, minority student services, personal counseling, placement for graduates. **Physically disabled:** Services for visually, speech, hearing impaired. **Learning disabled:** Comprehensive services available.

**Contact.** E-mail: admission@conncoll.edu
Phone: (860) 439-2200 Fax: (860) 439-4301
Martha Merrill, Dean of Admission and Financial Aid, Connecticut College, 270 Mohegan Avenue, New London, CT 06320-4196

# Eastern Connecticut State University
## Willimantic, Connecticut

CB member
CB code: 3966

- Public 4-year university and liberal arts college
- Residential campus in large town
- 4,704 degree-seeking undergraduates: 16% part-time, 55% women, 7% African American, 2% Asian American, 5% Hispanic American, 1% Native American, 1% international
- 289 degree-seeking graduate students
- 58% of applicants admitted
- SAT or ACT (ACT writing optional) required
- 48% graduate within 6 years

**General.** Founded in 1889. Regionally accredited. **Degrees:** 840 bachelor's, 8 associate awarded; master's offered. **ROTC:** Army, Air Force. **Location:** 30 miles from Hartford. **Calendar:** Semester, extensive summer session. **Full-time faculty:** 197 total; 93% have terminal degrees, 26% minority, 42% women. **Part-time faculty:** 209 total; 26% have terminal degrees, 15% minority, 44% women. **Class size:** 39% < 20, 53% 20-39, 8% 40-49, less than 1% 50-99. **Special facilities:** Arboretum, child and family development complex, environmental field laboratory, Free Enterprise Institute, planetarium, Sustainable Energy Institute, 2 electron microscopes, bell carillon.

**Freshman class profile.** 3,740 applied, 2,167 admitted, 880 enrolled.

| Mid 50% test scores | | | |
|---|---|---|---|
| SAT critical reading: | 460-550 | Return as sophomores: | 74% |
| SAT math: | 460-550 | Out-of-state: | 10% |
| Rank in top quarter: | 25% | Live on campus: | 87% |
| Rank in top tenth: | 6% | International: | 1% |

**Basis for selection.** Applicants should be in top half of high school class and recommended by high school. Quality of course work very important; minimum 2.5 GPA in college preparatory program. SAT score also important. Extracurricular activities considered. Interview and essay recommended.

**High school preparation.** Required units include English 4, mathematics 3, social studies 2, history 3, science 2 (laboratory 1) and foreign language 2.

**2007-2008 Annual costs.** Tuition/fees: $6,961; $14,446 out-of-state. Room/board: $8,415. Books/supplies: $1,168. Personal expenses: $2,648.

**2006-2007 Financial aid. Need-based:** 931 full-time freshmen applied for aid; 624 were judged to have need; 485 of these received aid. Average need met was 64%. Average scholarship/grant was $6,079; average loan $2,623. 35% of total undergraduate aid awarded as scholarships/grants, 65% as loans/jobs. **Non-need-based:** Awarded to 514 full-time undergraduates, including 115 freshmen. Scholarships awarded for academics. **Additional information:** Tuition waiver for Veterans and members of National Guard.

**Application procedures. Admission:** Priority date 5/1; no deadline. $50 fee, may be waived for applicants with need. Application may be submitted online. Admission notification on a rolling basis beginning on or about 12/1. Must reply by May 1 or within 2 week(s) if notified thereafter. **Financial aid:** Priority date 3/15; no closing date. FAFSA required. Applicants notified on a rolling basis starting 2/15; must reply within 2 week(s) of notification.

**Academics.** Life Learning Portfolio Class. **Special study options:** Accelerated study, cooperative education, cross-registration, distance learning, double major, dual enrollment of high school students, exchange student, honors, independent study, internships, student-designed major, study abroad, teacher certification program, weekend college. National Student Exchange (NSE). **Credit/placement by examination:** AP, CLEP, institutional tests. 30 credit hours maximum toward associate degree, 60 toward bachelor's. Institutional placement test required for all entering freshmen. **Support services:** Learning center, pre-admission summer program, reduced course load, remedial instruction, study skills assistance, tutoring, writing center.

**Majors. Biology:** General, biochemistry. **Business:** Accounting, business admin, management information systems. **Communications:** General. **Computer sciences:** General. **Conservation:** Environmental science. **Education:** Early childhood, elementary, middle, physical, secondary. **English:** English lit. **Foreign languages:** Spanish. **History:** General. **Math:** General. **Parks/recreation:** Sports admin. **Psychology:** General. **Public administration:** Social work. **Social sciences:** Economics, political science, sociology. **Visual/performing arts:** General, studio arts.

**Most popular majors.** Business/marketing 15%, communications/journalism 8%, English 9%, liberal arts 10%, psychology 13%, social sciences 13%, visual/performing arts 6%.

**Computing on campus.** 637 workstations in dormitories, library, computer center. Dormitories wired for high-speed internet access and linked to campus network. Commuter students can connect to campus network. Online library, helpline, repair service, student web hosting, wireless network available.

**Student life. Freshman orientation:** Mandatory. Preregistration for classes offered. **Policies:** No alcohol permitted on campus; all halls are smoke free; 4 hours per semester community service requirement for all resident students; sign in guest policy for all first year halls from 7pm-12am. **Housing:** Coed dorms, apartments available. $250 nonrefundable deposit, deadline 5/1. **Activities:** Bands, choral groups, dance, drama, international student organizations, literary magazine, music ensembles, musical theater, radio station, student government, student newspaper, TV station, over 60 organizations.

**Athletics.** NCAA. **Intercollegiate:** Baseball M, basketball, cheerleading M, cross-country, field hockey W, lacrosse, soccer, softball W, swimming W, track and field, volleyball W. **Intramural:** Badminton, basketball, bowling, cross-country, football (tackle) M, gymnastics W, racquetball, rugby, skiing, soccer, softball, swimming, tennis, track and field, volleyball, water polo. **Team name:** Warriors.

**Student services.** Adult student services, alcohol/substance abuse counseling, campus ministries, career counseling, services for economically disadvantaged, student employment services, financial aid counseling, health services, minority student services, on-campus daycare, personal counseling, placement for graduates, veterans' counselor, women's services. **Physically disabled:** Services for visually, speech, hearing impaired. **Learning disabled:** Comprehensive services available.

**Contact.** E-mail: admissions@easternct.edu
Phone: (860) 465-5286 Toll-free number: (877) 353-3278
Fax: (860) 465-5544
Kimberly Crone, Director of Admissions and Enrollment Planning, Eastern Connecticut State University, 83 Windham Street, Willimantic, CT 06226-2295

# Fairfield University
## Fairfield, Connecticut
www.fairfield.edu.

CB member
CB code: 3390

- Private 4-year university affiliated with Roman Catholic Church
- Residential campus in small city
- 3,893 degree-seeking undergraduates: 11% part-time, 58% women
- 959 degree-seeking graduate students
- 55% of applicants admitted
- SAT or ACT (ACT writing optional), application essay required
- 81% graduate within 6 years; 20% enter graduate study

**General.** Founded in 1942. Regionally accredited. **Degrees:** 861 bachelor's, 6 associate awarded; master's offered. **ROTC:** Army, Air Force. **Location:** 50 miles from New York City. **Calendar:** Semester, limited summer session. **Full-time faculty:** 239 total; 95% have terminal degrees, 10% minority, 49% women. **Part-time faculty:** 244 total; 39% have terminal degrees, 6% minority, 43% women. **Class size:** 39% < 20, 59% 20-39, less than 1% 40-49, less than 1% 50-99. **Special facilities:** Fine arts center containing 2 theaters, campus ministry center, art galleries, Japanese meditation garden, BEST (Business Experimental, Simulation and Trading) floor in the Dolan School of Business.

**Freshman class profile.** 8,557 applied, 4,686 admitted, 842 enrolled.

| Mid 50% test scores | | | |
|---|---|---|---|
| SAT critical reading: | 530-620 | GPA 2.0-2.99: | 16% |
| SAT math: | 550-640 | Rank in top quarter: | 76% |
| ACT composite: | 23-28 | Rank in top tenth: | 36% |
| GPA 3.50 or higher: | 44% | Return as sophomores: | 88% |
| GPA 3.0-3.49: | 40% | Out-of-state: | 78% |
| | | Live on campus: | 96% |

**Basis for selection.** GED not accepted. School achievement record, test scores, recommendations, school activities, personal statement important. Special consideration given to minority groups, parent/siblings of alumni and students with special talents and/or unique back-grounds. Interview recommended. **Homeschooled:** Statement describing homeschool structure and mission, transcript of courses and grades required.

**High school preparation.** 16 units required; 20 recommended. Required and recommended units include English 4, mathematics 3-4, social studies 2, history 2, science 2-3 (laboratory 2), foreign language 2-4 and academic electives 1. 1 additional mathematics and 2 science recommended for mathematics, business and science. Portfolio highly recommended for music majors, resume for theatre majors.

**2008-2009 Annual costs.** Tuition/fees: $36,075. Room/board: $10,850. Books/supplies: $900. Personal expenses: $1,465.

**2007-2008 Financial aid. Need-based:** 552 full-time freshmen applied for aid; 441 were judged to have need; 438 of these received aid. Average need met was 86%. Average scholarship/grant was $20,313; average loan $4,591. 73% of total undergraduate aid awarded as scholarships/grants, 27% as loans/jobs. **Non-need-based:** Scholarships awarded for academics, alumni affiliation, art, athletics, leadership, music/drama.

**Application procedures. Admission:** Closing date 1/15 (postmark date). $55 fee, may be waived for applicants with need. Application may be submitted online. Admission notification 4/1. Must reply by 5/1. Deadline for those applying for merit scholarships is January 15. **Financial aid:** Priority date 2/15, closing date 2/15. FAFSA, CSS PROFILE required. Applicants notified by 4/1; must reply by 5/1.

**Academics.** Associate's program is a part-time evening program for non-traditional students. **Special study options:** Combined bachelor's/graduate degree, cross-registration, double major, exchange student, honors, independent study, internships, liberal arts/career combination, student-designed major, study abroad, teacher certification program, Washington semester. 3-2 engineering program with University of Connecticut, Rensselaer Polytechnic Institute, Columbia University, and Stevens Institute of Technology. **Credit/placement by examination:** AP, CLEP, IB, institutional tests. 15 credit hours maximum toward bachelor's degree. **Support services:** Study skills assistance, tutoring, writing center.

**Majors. Area/ethnic studies:** American. **Biology:** General. **Business:** Accounting, business admin, finance, management information systems, marketing. **Communications:** General. **Computer sciences:** General. **Education:** Music. **Engineering:** Computer, electrical, mechanical, software. **English:** English lit. **Foreign languages:** French, German, Italian, Spanish. **Health:** Nursing (RN). **History:** General. **Math:** General. **Philosophy/religion:** Philosophy, religion. **Physical sciences:** Chemistry, physics. **Psychology:** General. **Social sciences:** Economics, international relations, political science, sociology. **Visual/performing arts:** General, art history/conservation, dramatic, studio arts. **Other:** New Media Film/Televison/Radio.

**Most popular majors.** Business/marketing 28%, communications/journalism 10%, English 7%, health sciences 9%, psychology 7%, social sciences 16%.

**Computing on campus.** 230 workstations in dormitories, library, computer center, student center. Dormitories wired for high-speed internet access and linked to campus network. Commuter students can connect to campus network. Online course registration, online library, helpline, repair service, student web hosting, wireless network available.

**Student life. Freshman orientation:** Available, $230 fee. Preregistration for classes offered. 2-day program in late June/early July for students and parents. **Policies:** Juniors and seniors may enter lottery to move off-campus. **Housing:** Guaranteed on-campus for all undergraduates. Coed dorms, special housing for disabled, apartments, substance-free housing available. $300 nonrefundable deposit, deadline 5/1. Women in Science theme housing, Sophomore College. **Activities:** Bands, campus ministries, choral groups, dance, drama, film society, international student organizations, literary magazine, music ensembles, Model UN, radio station, student government, student newspaper, symphony orchestra, TV station, AHANA, Peer Education, Appalachian Volunteers, College Democrats, College Republicans, Circle K.

**Athletics.** NCAA. **Intercollegiate:** Baseball M, basketball, cross-country, diving, field hockey W, golf, lacrosse, rowing (crew) W, soccer, softball W, swimming, tennis, volleyball W. **Intramural:** Basketball, football (non-tackle), golf, racquetball, soccer, softball, table tennis, tennis, track and field, volleyball. **Team name:** Stags.

**Student services.** Adult student services, alcohol/substance abuse counseling, campus ministries, career counseling, student employment services, financial aid counseling, health services, minority student services, personal counseling, placement for graduates. **Physically disabled:** Services for visually, hearing impaired.

**Contact.** E-mail: admis@mail.fairfield.edu
Phone: (203) 254-4100 Fax: (203) 254-4199
Karen Pellegrino, Director of Admission, Fairfield University, 1073 North Benson Road, Fairfield, CT 06824-5195

## Holy Apostles College and Seminary
**Cromwell, Connecticut**
www.holyapostles.edu                    **CB code: 0921**

- Private 4-year liberal arts and seminary college affiliated with Roman Catholic Church
- Commuter campus in large town

- 32 degree-seeking undergraduates: 47% part-time, 28% women, 3% African American, 3% Asian American, 12% Hispanic American, 12% international
- 226 degree-seeking graduate students
- 100% of applicants admitted
- SAT, interview required

**General.** Founded in 1956. Regionally accredited. 75% of students are lay students, 25% are seminarians. **Degrees:** 5 bachelor's awarded; master's, first professional offered. **Location:** 13 miles from Hartford. **Calendar:** Semester, limited summer session. **Full-time faculty:** 10 total; 90% have terminal degrees, 10% minority, 30% women. **Part-time faculty:** 16 total; 88% have terminal degrees, 31% women.

**Freshman class profile.** 5 applied, 5 admitted, 5 enrolled.

| | | | |
|---|---|---|---|
| End year in good standing: | 100% | Out-of-state: | 2% |
| Return as sophomores: | 100% | International: | 20% |

**Basis for selection.** Interview, level of interest and recommendations most important. No mandatory minimum SAT score. **Homeschooled:** State high school equivalency certificate required.

**2008-2009 Annual costs.** Tuition/fees (projected): $7,800. Books/supplies: $630. Personal expenses: $580.

**2006-2007 Financial aid.** All financial aid based on need. 2 full-time freshmen applied for aid; 2 were judged to have need; 2 of these received aid. Average loan was $3,500. 7% of total undergraduate aid awarded as scholarships/grants, 93% as loans/jobs.

**Application procedures. Admission:** Priority date 8/15; no deadline. $50 fee, may be waived for applicants with need. Application must be submitted on paper. Admission notification on a rolling basis. Applications accepted up to one week before the beginning of the semester in which the applicant plans to enroll. **Financial aid:** No deadline. FAFSA, institutional form required. Applicants notified on a rolling basis starting 9/15.

**Academics.** 54-credit core curriculum required of all undergraduates. **Special study options:** Distance learning, double major, ESL, independent study. **Credit/placement by examination:** AP, CLEP. 30 credit hours maximum toward bachelor's degree. **Support services:** Reduced course load, remedial instruction, tutoring.

**Majors. Liberal arts:** Humanities. **Philosophy/religion:** Philosophy, religion. **Social sciences:** General.

**Computing on campus.** 10 workstations in library.

**Student life. Freshman orientation:** Available. Preregistration for classes offered. **Activities:** Choral groups, Life League.

**Student services.** Campus ministries, financial aid counseling, personal counseling.

**Contact.** E-mail: registrar@holyapostles.edu
Phone: (860) 632-3033 Toll-free number: (800) 330-7272
Fax: (860) 632-3075
Douglas Mosey, President-Rector, Holy Apostles College and Seminary, 33 Prospect Hill Road, Cromwell, CT 06416-2005

## Lyme Academy College of Fine Arts
**Old Lyme, Connecticut**               **CB member**
www.lymeacademy.edu                    **CB code: 1791**

- Private 4-year visual arts college
- Commuter campus in small town
- 100 degree-seeking undergraduates: 9% part-time, 52% women, 1% Asian American, 3% Hispanic American, 1% Native American
- 1 degree-seeking graduate student
- 91% of applicants admitted
- SAT or ACT (ACT writing recommended), application essay, interview required
- 43% graduate within 6 years

**General.** Founded in 1976. Regionally accredited. **Degrees:** 26 bachelor's awarded. **Location:** 40 miles from Hartford. **Calendar:** Semester, limited summer session. **Full-time faculty:** 7 total; 43% women. **Part-time faculty:** 19 total; 5% have terminal degrees, 32% women. **Class size:** 89% < 20, 11% 20-39. **Special facilities:** Florence Griswold museum.

**Freshman class profile.** 34 applied, 31 admitted, 11 enrolled.

| Mid 50% test scores | | | | |
|---|---|---|---|---|
| SAT critical reading: | 430-570 | | | |
| SAT math: | 410-560 | | | |
| GPA 3.50 or higher: | 18% | | | |
| GPA 3.0-3.49: | 45% | | | |

| | |
|---|---|
| GPA 2.0-2.99: | 37% |
| End year in good standing: | 100% |
| Return as sophomores: | 85% |
| Out-of-state: | 55% |

**Basis for selection.** Admissions based on portfolio, interview, essay, GPA, and SAT/ACT scores. Portfolio, two letters of recommendation required. Campus visit highly recommended. **Homeschooled:** Statement describing homeschool structure and mission, transcript of courses and grades, state high school equivalency certificate, interview, letter of recommendation (nonparent) required.

**2008-2009 Annual costs.** Tuition/fees: $21,480. Books/supplies: $1,000. Personal expenses: $500.

**2007-2008 Financial aid. Need-based:** 11 full-time freshmen applied for aid; 11 were judged to have need; 11 of these received aid. 58% of total undergraduate aid awarded as scholarships/grants, 42% as loans/jobs. **Non-need-based:** Scholarships awarded for academics, art, leadership.

**Application procedures. Admission:** Priority date 3/1; no deadline. $55 fee. Application may be submitted online. Admission notification on a rolling basis beginning on or about 2/15. Must reply by May 1 or within 2 week(s) if notified thereafter. **Financial aid:** Priority date 2/15, closing date 4/15. FAFSA, institutional form required. CSS PROFILE required of all new first year students. Applicants notified on a rolling basis starting 3/1; must reply by 5/1 or within 2 week(s) of notification.

**Academics. Special study options:** Cross-registration, double major, independent study. **Credit/placement by examination:** CLEP, SAT, ACT. **Support services:** Pre-admission summer program, reduced course load, remedial instruction, study skills assistance, writing center.

**Majors. Visual/performing arts:** Painting, sculpture.

**Computing on campus.** 6 workstations in library. Online library available.

**Student life. Freshman orientation:** Mandatory. Preregistration for classes offered. Usually one day before the start of classes in the Fall semester. **Activities:** Literary magazine, student government.

**Athletics. Intramural:** Badminton, basketball, table tennis, volleyball. **Team name:** The Ticks.

**Student services.** Alcohol/substance abuse counseling, career counseling, financial aid counseling, personal counseling, veterans' counselor, women's services.

**Contact.** E-mail: dsigmon@lymeacademy.edu
Phone: (860) 434-5232 ext. 119 Fax: (860) 434-8725
Debbie Sigmon, Director of Admissions, Lyme Academy College of Fine Arts, 84 Lyme Street, Old Lyme, CT 06371

## Mitchell College

New London, Connecticut
www.mitchell.edu

CB member
CB code: 3528

- Private 4-year liberal arts college
- Residential campus in small city
- 868 degree-seeking undergraduates: 13% part-time, 50% women
- Application essay required

**General.** Founded in 1938. Regionally accredited. **Degrees:** 113 bachelor's, 64 associate awarded. **Location:** 100 miles from New York City and Boston. **Calendar:** Semester, limited summer session. **Full-time faculty:** 31 total; 36% have terminal degrees. **Part-time faculty:** 53 total; 9% have terminal degrees. **Special facilities:** Two beaches, dock with sailboat fleet, learning resource center for students with learning disabilities, hiking trails, nature preserve.

**Freshman class profile.**

| Out-of-state: | 45% | Live on campus: | 85% |
|---|---|---|---|

**Basis for selection.** High school achievement, recommendations, interview very important. **Learning Disabled:** Students applying to the Learning Resource Center should submit the following information in order to receive support for a documented learning disability and/or ADHD: 1) Results of a complete psycho educational evaluation. 2) Standardized achievement testing (reading, writing and math). 3) Testing accommodations recommendations made by the professional who completed the evaluation. 4)

A definitive diagnosis of a learning disability or ADHD. All documentation should be less than three years old, and all testing administered by a certified or licensed psychologist.

**High school preparation.** Recommended units include English 4, mathematics 3, social studies 3, history 2, science 3, foreign language 1 and academic electives 4.

**2007-2008 Annual costs.** Tuition/fees: $23,093. Room/board: $10,406. Books/supplies: $900. Personal expenses: $1,050.

**Financial aid. Non-need-based:** Scholarships awarded for academics, alumni affiliation, leadership.

**Application procedures. Admission:** Priority date 4/1; no deadline. $30 fee, may be waived for applicants with need. Application may be submitted online. Admission notification on a rolling basis. Must reply by May 1 or within 2 week(s) if notified thereafter. **Financial aid:** Priority date 3/1; no closing date. FAFSA required. Applicants notified on a rolling basis starting 2/15; must reply within 2 week(s) of notification.

**Academics.** Free professional tutoring in all disciplines. **Special study options:** Dual enrollment of high school students, ESL, internships, student-designed major, teacher certification program. **Credit/placement by examination:** AP, CLEP, institutional tests. 30 credit hours maximum toward associate degree. **Support services:** Learning center, pre-admission summer program, reduced course load, study skills assistance, tutoring, writing center.

**Majors. Biology:** Environmental. **Business:** Accounting/business management, business admin, hospitality admin, small business admin, tourism/travel. **Communications:** Broadcast journalism, digital media, journalism, media studies, organizational, public relations, radio/tv. **Communications technology:** Graphics. **Conservation:** Environmental studies. **Education:** Early childhood, kindergarten/preschool. **Family/consumer sciences:** Child care, family studies. **Health:** Premedicine. **Interdisciplinary:** Behavioral sciences. **Legal studies:** General, prelaw. **Liberal arts:** Arts/sciences. **Parks/recreation:** Sports admin. **Protective services:** Emergency management/homeland security. **Psychology:** General, community, developmental. **Social sciences:** Criminology. **Visual/performing arts:** Graphic design.

**Computing on campus.** 155 workstations in dormitories, library, computer center, student center. Dormitories wired for high-speed internet access and linked to campus network. Commuter students can connect to campus network. Helpline, repair service available.

**Student life. Freshman orientation:** Available. 1-day orientation held in May or August. **Housing:** Guaranteed on-campus for all undergraduates. Coed dorms, single-sex dorms, special housing for disabled, substance-free housing available. $300 nonrefundable deposit, deadline 5/1. **Activities:** Campus ministries, choral groups, dance, drama, international student organizations, student government, student newspaper, multicultural club, Hillel, spirituality club, African American alliance.

**Athletics.** NCAA. **Intercollegiate:** Baseball M, basketball, cross-country, golf, lacrosse M, sailing, soccer, softball W, tennis, volleyball W. **Intramural:** Basketball, sailing, soccer, softball, table tennis, tennis, volleyball. **Team name:** Mariners.

**Student services.** Adult student services, career counseling, services for economically disadvantaged, student employment services, financial aid counseling, health services, minority student services, on-campus daycare, personal counseling, placement for graduates, veterans' counselor. **Physically disabled:** Services for visually, speech, hearing impaired. **Learning disabled:** Comprehensive services available.

**Contact.** E-mail: admissions@mitchell.edu
Phone: (860) 701-5037 Toll-free number: (800) 443-2811
Fax: (860) 444-1209
Kim Hodges, Director of Admission, Mitchell College, 437 Pequot Avenue, New London, CT 06320-4498

## Paier College of Art

Hamden, Connecticut
www.paiercollegeofart.edu

CB code: 3699

- For-profit 4-year visual arts college
- Commuter campus in small city
- 207 degree-seeking undergraduates: 32% part-time, 71% women
- 249 graduate students
- 72% of applicants admitted
- SAT or ACT, interview required
- 77% graduate within 6 years; 30% enter graduate study

**General.** Founded in 1946. Accredited by ACCSCT. **Degrees:** 37 bachelor's, 1 associate awarded. **Location:** 2 miles from New Haven. **Calendar:** Semester. **Full-time faculty:** 9 total; 33% have terminal degrees, 11% women. **Part-time faculty:** 37 total; 38% have terminal degrees, 8% minority, 24% women. **Class size:** 90% < 20, 10% 20-39. **Special facilities:** Extensive image picture reference file.

**Freshman class profile.** 72 applied, 52 admitted, 36 enrolled.

| Mid 50% test scores | | | |
|---|---|---|---|
| SAT critical reading: | 370-530 | Rank in top tenth: | 8% |
| SAT math: | 340-470 | End year in good standing: | 93% |
| Rank in top quarter: | 33% | Return as sophomores: | 93% |

**Basis for selection.** Artistic ability, interest, and potential, as demonstrated in admission interview and portfolio review most important elements. Portfolio of 8 to 10 works of art required; essay recommended.

**High school preparation.** Art classes recommended. All students must pass all state requirements.

**2008-2009 Annual costs.** Tuition/fees: $12,365. Books/supplies: $1,000. Personal expenses: $600.

**2006-2007 Financial aid. Need-based:** 10 full-time freshmen applied for aid; 7 were judged to have need; 7 of these received aid. Average need met was 61%. Average scholarship/grant was $5,557; average loan $3,107. 52% of total undergraduate aid awarded as scholarships/grants, 48% as loans/jobs.

**Application procedures. Admission:** No deadline. $25 fee, may be waived for applicants with need. Application must be submitted on paper. Admission notification on a rolling basis beginning on or about 2/15. **Financial aid:** Priority date 4/15; no closing date. FAFSA required. Applicants notified on a rolling basis starting 6/1; must reply within 3 week(s) of notification.

**Academics.** Academics required for BFA degrees include: 4 art histories, English I and II, 1 requirement each in the humanities, math, physical and social sciences, and 1 academic elective. **Special study options:** Independent study. **Credit/placement by examination:** AP, CLEP, IB, SAT, ACT. 6 credit hours maximum toward associate degree, 12 toward bachelor's. **Support services:** Reduced course load, remedial instruction, study skills assistance, tutoring.

**Majors. Visual/performing arts:** Commercial photography, commercial/advertising art, design, graphic design, illustration, interior design, painting, photography, studio arts.

**Computing on campus.** 65 workstations in library, computer center. Dormitories wired for high-speed internet access.

**Student life. Freshman orientation:** Available. Preregistration for classes offered. Open to incoming students and their parents/guardians. Separate 1-hour library orientation. **Housing:** Affiliation with neighboring Albertus Magnus College provides an option for dormitory housing and student services (library, gym, health center, student dining). **Activities:** Student government.

**Student services.** Career counseling, student employment services, financial aid counseling, personal counseling, placement for graduates, veterans' counselor.

**Contact.** E-mail: paier.admission@snet.net
Phone: (203) 287-3031 Fax: (203) 287-3021
Daniel Paier, Dean of Admissions, Paier College of Art, 20 Gorham Avenue, Hamden, CT 06514-3902

---

## Post University
**Waterbury, Connecticut**
www.post.edu

**CB member**
**CB code: 3698**

- For-profit 4-year university and business college
- Residential campus in small city
- 1,112 degree-seeking undergraduates
- 57 graduate students
- 58% of applicants admitted
- SAT or ACT with writing required

**General.** Founded in 1890. Regionally accredited. **Degrees:** 257 bachelor's, 57 associate awarded; master's offered. **Location:** 32 miles from Hartford, 80 miles from New York City. **Calendar:** Semester, limited summer session. **Full-time faculty:** 28 total; 46% have terminal degrees, 11% minority, 39% women.

**Freshman class profile.** 1,344 applied, 784 admitted, 201 enrolled.

| Mid 50% test scores | | | |
|---|---|---|---|
| SAT critical reading: | 400-550 | GPA 3.0-3.49: | 23% |
| SAT math: | 400-550 | GPA 2.0-2.99: | 70% |
| SAT writing: | 400-500 | Rank in top quarter: | 10% |
| ACT composite: | 19-24 | Rank in top tenth: | 5% |
| GPA 3.50 or higher: | 5% | Out-of-state: | 40% |
| | | Live on campus: | 25% |

**Basis for selection.** Secondary school transcript, interview, and class rank in top half of graduating class most important. Letter of recommendation required. Counselor's recommendation also important. School and community activities and test scores also reviewed and considered. TOEFL also accepted. Interview recommended but not required for admission. **Homeschooled:** Statement describing homeschool structure and mission, transcript of courses and grades, interview, letter of recommendation (nonparent) required.

**High school preparation.** 13 units required. Required and recommended units include English 4, mathematics 3, social studies 1, history 2, science 3 (laboratory 1) and foreign language 2.

**2007-2008 Annual costs.** Tuition/fees: $22,550. Room/board: $8,750. Books/supplies: $1,000. Personal expenses: $1,200.

**Financial aid. Additional information:** Academic merit scholarships available based on GPA and test scores. Renewable contingent upon maintaining specific GPA.

**Application procedures. Admission:** Priority date 3/1; no deadline. $40 fee, may be waived for applicants with need. Application may be submitted online. Admission notification on a rolling basis beginning on or about 12/15. Must reply by May 1 or within 2 week(s) if notified thereafter. **Financial aid:** Priority date 3/15; no closing date. FAFSA required. Applicants notified on a rolling basis starting 4/15; must reply by 5/1 or within 3 week(s) of notification.

**Academics. Special study options:** Accelerated study, cooperative education, cross-registration, distance learning, double major, dual enrollment of high school students, honors, independent study, internships, liberal arts/career combination, student-designed major, study abroad, weekend college. **Credit/placement by examination:** AP, CLEP, institutional tests. 15 credit hours maximum toward associate degree, 30 toward bachelor's. **Support services:** Learning center, pre-admission summer program, reduced course load, remedial instruction, study skills assistance, tutoring, writing center.

**Majors. Agriculture:** Equestrian studies. **Biology:** General. **Business:** General, accounting, business admin, finance, international, marketing. **Computer sciences:** General. **Conservation:** General, environmental studies. **English:** English lit. **Legal studies:** Paralegal, prelaw. **Psychology:** General. **Public administration:** Human services. **Social sciences:** Sociology.

**Computing on campus.** 72 workstations in library, computer center, student center. Dormitories wired for high-speed internet access and linked to campus network. Commuter students can connect to campus network. Online course registration, online library, helpline, wireless network available.

**Student life. Freshman orientation:** Mandatory, $150 fee. Preregistration for classes offered. **Policies:** Student leadership opportunities encouraged and supported throughout student's experience. **Housing:** Guaranteed on-campus for all undergraduates. Coed dorms available. $150 fully refundable deposit, deadline 5/1. **Activities:** Dance, drama, international student organizations, literary magazine, musical theater, student government, Phi Theta Kappa, student ambassadors, peer advisors.

**Athletics.** NCAA. **Intercollegiate:** Baseball M, basketball, cross-country, equestrian, golf, soccer, softball W, tennis, volleyball W. **Intramural:** Baseball M, basketball, racquetball, softball, swimming, tennis, volleyball. **Team name:** Eagles.

**Student services.** Adult student services, alcohol/substance abuse counseling, career counseling, student employment services, financial aid counseling, health services, minority student services, personal counseling, placement for graduates, veterans' counselor. **Physically disabled:** Services for visually impaired.

**Contact.** E-mail: admissions@post.edu
Phone: (203) 596-4520 Toll-free number: (800) 345-2562
Fax: (203) 756-5810
Jay Murray, Director of Admissions, Post University, 800 Country Club Road, Waterbury, CT 06723-2540

# Quinnipiac University
## Hamden, Connecticut
### www.quinnipiac.edu

**CB member**
**CB code: 3712**

- Private 4-year university
- Residential campus in small city
- 5,650 degree-seeking undergraduates: 3% part-time, 62% women, 3% African American, 2% Asian American, 5% Hispanic American, 1% international
- 1,451 degree-seeking graduate students
- 47% of applicants admitted
- SAT or ACT (ACT writing optional), application essay required
- 73% graduate within 6 years; 38% enter graduate study

**General.** Founded in 1929. Regionally accredited. Quinnipiac is located mid-way between New York City and Boston in suburban Connecticut. **Degrees:** 1,312 bachelor's, 4 associate awarded; master's, doctoral, first professional offered. **ROTC:** Army, Air Force. **Location:** 8 miles from New Haven. **Calendar:** Semester, limited summer session. **Full-time faculty:** 281 total; 91% have terminal degrees, 12% minority, 48% women. **Part-time faculty:** 498 total; 8% minority, 55% women. **Class size:** 51% < 20, 48% 20-39, less than 1% 40-49. **Special facilities:** Financial technology center, Quinnipiac Polling Institute, institute for community health education, critical care simulation laboratory, motion analysis lab, Irish Famine museum, Albert Schweitzer Institute.

**Freshman class profile.** 12,060 applied, 5,681 admitted, 1,360 enrolled.

| Mid 50% test scores | | | | |
|---|---|---|---|---|
| SAT critical reading: | 540-610 | Rank in top quarter: | 66% |
| SAT math: | 560-630 | Rank in top tenth: | 25% |
| ACT composite: | 23-27 | End year in good standing: | 93% |
| GPA 3.50 or higher: | 41% | Return as sophomores: | 89% |
| GPA 3.0-3.49: | 48% | Out-of-state: | 75% |
| GPA 2.0-2.99: | 11% | Live on campus: | 95% |

**Basis for selection.** Primary emphasis placed on high school transcript, grades, grade pattern, level of difficulty. Test scores, essay and recommendation(s) also important. Interview recommended, extracurricular activities, evidence of leadership, and employment also considered. Highest SAT (individual scores) or ACT (composite) scores used when reviewing applications. Math and language placement tests as well as a brief essay used for placement during our orientation process. Campus visit recommended for interview, group information session, or open house. **Homeschooled:** Statement describing homeschool structure and mission, transcript of courses and grades, letter of recommendation (nonparent) required. Evaluation of education completed and SAT/ACT scores required.

**High school preparation.** 16 units required. Required and recommended units include English 4, mathematics 3, social studies 2, science 3 (laboratory 2), foreign language 2-3 and academic electives 2. 4 lab science and 4 math are required for students applying to physical therapy, occupational therapy, nursing and physician assistant programs. Physics is highly recommended for the PT applicant.

**2008-2009 Annual costs.** Tuition/fees: $30,900. Room/board: $11,800. Books/supplies: $800. Personal expenses: $900.

**2007-2008 Financial aid. Need-based:** 1,036 full-time freshmen applied for aid; 763 were judged to have need; 760 of these received aid. Average need met was 71%. Average scholarship/grant was $12,861; average loan $3,648. 54% of total undergraduate aid awarded as scholarships/grants, 46% as loans/jobs. **Non-need-based:** Awarded to 1,994 full-time undergraduates, including 596 freshmen. Scholarships awarded for academics, athletics.

**Application procedures. Admission:** Priority date 11/30; deadline 2/1 (postmark date). $45 fee, may be waived for applicants with need. Application may be submitted online. Admission notification on a rolling basis beginning on or about 12/15. Must reply by May 1 or within 2 week(s) if notified thereafter. Students encouraged to apply early in the fall of their senior year in high school. Students applying for Nursing, the 6 1/2 year BS/DPT in Physical Therapy and the 6 year BS/MHS in Physician Assistant programs should file their application for admission by November 1. February 1 is the recommended final deadline for all applications. **Financial aid:** Priority date 3/1; no closing date. FAFSA required. Applicants notified on a rolling basis starting 2/15; must reply by 5/1 or within 2 week(s) of notification.

**Academics.** Incoming students must purchase a university recommended laptop computer. **Special study options:** Combined bachelor's/graduate degree, distance learning, double major, honors, independent study, internships, liberal arts/career combination, semester at sea, student-designed major, study abroad, teacher certification program, Washington semester. **Credit/**

**placement by examination:** AP, CLEP, IB, institutional tests. 32 credit hours maximum toward bachelor's degree. **Support services:** Learning center, tutoring.

**Majors. Biology:** General, biochemistry, biomedical sciences, biotechnology. **Business:** General, accounting, business admin, communications, entrepreneurial studies, finance, human resources, international, international marketing, management information systems, management science, managerial economics, marketing, nonprofit/public, office management. **Communications:** General, advertising, broadcast journalism, digital media, journalism, public relations. **Computer sciences:** General, applications programming, computer graphics, computer science. **Education:** Biology, chemistry, elementary, English, foreign languages, history, mathematics, middle, multi-level teacher, science, secondary, social studies, Spanish. **English:** Composition, English lit. **Foreign languages:** Spanish. **Health:** Athletic training, health care admin, nursing (RN), physician assistant, predental, premedicine, preveterinary, respiratory therapy technology, veterinary technology/assistant. **History:** General. **Interdisciplinary:** Biopsychology, gerontology, math/computer science. **Legal studies:** General, legal secretary, paralegal, prelaw. **Math:** General. **Physical sciences:** Chemistry. **Protective services:** Criminal justice. **Psychology:** General. **Science technology:** Biological. **Social sciences:** General, criminology, economics, political science, sociology. **Visual/performing arts:** Digital art, dramatic. **Other:** Biomedical marketing.

**Most popular majors.** Business/marketing 22%, communications/journalism 17%, health sciences 25%, psychology 8%, social sciences 6%.

**Computing on campus.** PC or laptop required. 400 workstations in library, computer center. Dormitories wired for high-speed internet access and linked to campus network. Commuter students can connect to campus network. Online course registration, online library, helpline, repair service, student web hosting, wireless network available.

**Student life. Freshman orientation:** Mandatory. Preregistration for classes offered. Incoming freshmen attend one of three weekends in June or the two days prior to fall classes. Transfer students attend one day orientation session in June or just prior to the start of fall classes. **Policies:** Resident freshmen may not bring a car to campus. Free shuttle system provided between the campus and shopping areas of Hamden, North Haven and New Haven, as well as the New Haven train station (Amtrak and Metro North). **Housing:** Guaranteed on-campus for freshmen. Coed dorms, apartments, substance-free housing available. $550 partly refundable deposit, deadline 5/1. Housing guaranteed for three years to entering freshmen and two years to incoming transfer students. **Activities:** Pep band, choral groups, dance, drama, literary magazine, radio station, student government, student newspaper, TV station, Hillel, Catholic community, Black Student Union, Latino cultural society, Greenpeace, Amnesty International, SADD, women's center, Asian and Pacific Islander club, Christian Fellowship.

**Athletics.** NCAA. **Intercollegiate:** Baseball M, basketball, cross-country, field hockey W, golf M, ice hockey, lacrosse, soccer, softball W, tennis, track and field, volleyball W. **Intramural:** Archery, badminton, baseball M, basketball, bowling, field hockey W, soccer, softball, table tennis, tennis, volleyball. **Team name:** Bobcats.

**Student services.** Adult student services, alcohol/substance abuse counseling, campus ministries, career counseling, student employment services, financial aid counseling, health services, minority student services, personal counseling, placement for graduates.

**Contact.** E-mail: admissions@quinnipiac.edu
Phone: (203) 582-8600 Toll-free number: (800) 462-1944
Fax: (203) 582-8906
Carla Knowlton, Director of Admisssions, Quinnipiac University, 275 Mount Carmel Avenue, Hamden, CT 06518-1908

# Sacred Heart University
## Fairfield, Connecticut
### www.sacredheart.edu

**CB member**
**CB code: 3780**

- Private 4-year university and liberal arts college affiliated with Roman Catholic Church
- Residential campus in large town
- 4,188 degree-seeking undergraduates: 17% part-time, 61% women, 4% African American, 2% Asian American, 6% Hispanic American, 1% international
- 1,575 degree-seeking graduate students
- 62% of applicants admitted
- SAT or ACT (ACT writing optional), application essay required
- 66% graduate within 6 years; 100% enter graduate study

**General.** Founded in 1963. Regionally accredited. **Degrees:** 779 bachelor's, 39 associate awarded; master's, doctoral offered. **ROTC:** Army. **Location:** 55 miles from New York City. **Calendar:** Semester, extensive summer session. **Full-time faculty:** 199 total; 80% have terminal degrees, 13% minority, 49% women. **Part-time faculty:** 326 total; 28% have terminal degrees, 7% minority, 45% women. **Class size:** 48% < 20, 51% 20-39, less than 1% 40-49. **Special facilities:** Performing arts center, multipurpose communication studios, 36-hole golf course, rehabilitation clinics for occupational and physical therapies, contemporary art gallery.

**Freshman class profile.** 7,532 applied, 4,662 admitted, 956 enrolled.

| Mid 50% test scores | | End year in good standing: | 95% |
|---|---|---|---|
| SAT critical reading: | 490-570 | Return as sophomores: | 76% |
| SAT math: | 500-580 | Out-of-state: | 74% |
| GPA 3.50 or higher: | 40% | Live on campus: | 95% |
| GPA 3.0-3.49: | 37% | International: | 1% |
| GPA 2.0-2.99: | 23% | Fraternities: | 5% |
| Rank in top quarter: | 45% | Sororities: | 7% |
| Rank in top tenth: | 14% | | |

**Basis for selection.** High school record and college preparatory curriculum most important. Interview required for early decision candidates, recommended for all others.

**High school preparation.** 22 units required; 30 recommended. Required and recommended units include English 4, mathematics 3-4, social studies 3-4, history 3-4, science 3-4 (laboratory 1-2), foreign language 2-4 and academic electives 3-4.

**2007-2008 Annual costs.** Tuition/fees: $27,150. Room/board: $10,816. Books/supplies: $700. Personal expenses: $700.

**2007-2008 Financial aid. Need-based:** 807 full-time freshmen applied for aid; 635 were judged to have need; 632 of these received aid. Average need met was 69%. Average scholarship/grant was $10,886; average loan $5,677. 57% of total undergraduate aid awarded as scholarships/grants, 43% as loans/jobs. **Non-need-based:** Awarded to 1,071 full-time undergraduates, including 315 freshmen. Scholarships awarded for academics, alumni affiliation, art, athletics, leadership, minority status, music/drama, ROTC.

**Application procedures. Admission:** Priority date 2/1; no deadline. $50 fee, may be waived for applicants with need. Application may be submitted online. Admission notification on a rolling basis beginning on or about 1/1. Must reply by May 1 or within 2 week(s) if notified thereafter. **Financial aid:** Priority date 2/15; no closing date. FAFSA, CSS PROFILE required. Applicants notified on a rolling basis starting 3/1; must reply within 2 week(s) of notification.

**Academics. Special study options:** Accelerated study, combined bachelor's/graduate degree, cooperative education, cross-registration, distance learning, double major, dual enrollment of high school students, ESL, honors, independent study, internships, liberal arts/career combination, student-designed major, study abroad, teacher certification program, United Nations semester, Washington semester, weekend college. Luxembourg semester, study abroad program in Ireland. **Credit/placement by examination:** AP, CLEP, IB, SAT, ACT, institutional tests. 30 credit hours maximum toward bachelor's degree. **Support services:** Learning center, reduced course load, remedial instruction, study skills assistance, tutoring, writing center.

**Honors college/program.** Holistic review of applicants is conducted. Recommended eligibility requirements include: 3.4 GPA, 1250 combined SAT (exclusive of Writing) with at least a 600 critical reading, rank in top 10% of high school class.

**Majors. Biology:** General, biochemistry. **Business:** General, accounting, finance. **Communications:** General, media studies. **Communications technology:** General. **Computer sciences:** General, computer science, information technology. **Conservation:** General. **English:** English lit. **Foreign languages:** Spanish. **Health:** Athletic training, nursing (RN), preop/surgical nursing. **History:** General. **Liberal arts:** Arts/sciences. **Math:** General. **Parks/recreation:** Sports admin. **Philosophy/religion:** Philosophy, religion. **Physical sciences:** Chemistry. **Protective services:** Law enforcement admin. **Psychology:** General. **Public administration:** Social work. **Social sciences:** Criminology, economics, political science, sociology. **Visual/performing arts:** Art, commercial/advertising art, design.

**Most popular majors.** Business/marketing 32%, health sciences 11%, psychology 21%, security/protective services 6%.

**Computing on campus.** PC or laptop required. 300 workstations in dormitories, library, computer center, student center. Dormitories wired for high-speed internet access and linked to campus network. Commuter students can connect to campus network. Online course registration, online library, helpline, repair service, student web hosting, wireless network available.

**Student life. Freshman orientation:** Mandatory. Preregistration for classes offered. Overnight 2-day program in late spring for both parents and students. **Housing:** Guaranteed on-campus for all undergraduates. Coed dorms, special housing for disabled, apartments, substance-free housing available. $1,500 nonrefundable deposit, deadline 5/1. Living and learning communities available for specific academic programs, wellness floors, honors floors. **Activities:** Bands, campus ministries, choral groups, dance, drama, film society, international student organizations, literary magazine, music ensembles, musical theater, radio station, student government, student newspaper, TV station, La Hispanidad, Habitat for Humanity, Circle K, Best Buddies, Celtic club, Polish club, debate society.

**Athletics.** NCAA. **Intercollegiate:** Baseball M, basketball, bowling, cross-country, equestrian W, fencing, field hockey W, football (tackle) M, golf, ice hockey, lacrosse, rowing (crew) W, soccer, softball W, swimming W, tennis, track and field, volleyball, wrestling M. **Intramural:** Basketball, bowling, cheerleading W, field hockey W, football (non-tackle), golf, skiing, soccer, tennis, volleyball. **Team name:** Pioneers.

**Student services.** Adult student services, alcohol/substance abuse counseling, campus ministries, career counseling, services for economically disadvantaged, student employment services, financial aid counseling, health services, minority student services, personal counseling, placement for graduates, women's services. **Physically disabled:** Services for visually, speech, hearing impaired.

**Contact.** E-mail: enroll@sacredheart.edu
Phone: (203) 371-7880 Fax: (203) 365-7607
Karen Guastelle, Dean of Undergraduate Admissions, Sacred Heart University, 5151 Park Avenue, Fairfield, CT 06825

## St. Joseph College

**West Hartford, Connecticut**
www.sjc.edu

**CB member**
**CB code: 3754**

- Private 4-year liberal arts college for women affiliated with Roman Catholic Church
- Residential campus in small city
- 945 degree-seeking undergraduates: 22% part-time, 99% women, 12% African American, 3% Asian American, 9% Hispanic American
- 575 degree-seeking graduate students
- 83% of applicants admitted
- SAT or ACT (ACT writing optional) required
- 55% graduate within 6 years

**General.** Founded in 1932. Regionally accredited. Men are admitted to the adult undergraduate degree-completion program and the graduate school. **Degrees:** 218 bachelor's awarded; master's offered. **Location:** 3 miles from Hartford. **Calendar:** Semester, limited summer session. **Full-time faculty:** 89 total. **Part-time faculty:** 134 total. **Class size:** 82% < 20, 17% 20-39, less than 1% 40-49, less than 1% 50-99.

**Freshman class profile.** 1,740 applied, 1,446 admitted, 167 enrolled.

| Mid 50% test scores | | Rank in top quarter: | 50% |
|---|---|---|---|
| SAT critical reading: | 430-530 | Rank in top tenth: | 16% |
| SAT math: | 420-530 | Return as sophomores: | 79% |
| GPA 3.50 or higher: | 18% | Out-of-state: | 16% |
| GPA 3.0-3.49: | 45% | Live on campus: | 68% |
| GPA 2.0-2.99: | 35% | International: | 2% |

**Basis for selection.** Rigor of secondary school record, academic GPA, and test scores very important.

**High school preparation.** 16 units required. Required units include English 4, mathematics 3, social studies 3, science 3 and foreign language 3.

**2007-2008 Annual costs.** Tuition/fees: $24,690. Room/board: $11,880. Books/supplies: $100.

**2006-2007 Financial aid. Need-based:** 131 full-time freshmen applied for aid; 121 were judged to have need; 121 of these received aid. Average need met was 70%. Average scholarship/grant was $12,781; average loan $1,870. 52% of total undergraduate aid awarded as scholarships/grants, 48% as loans/jobs. **Non-need-based:** Awarded to 100 full-time undergraduates, including 26 freshmen. Scholarships awarded for academics, state residency.

**Application procedures. Admission:** No deadline. $50 fee, may be waived for applicants with need. Application may be submitted online. Admission notification on a rolling basis. **Financial aid:** Priority date 2/15; no closing date. FAFSA required. Applicants notified on a rolling basis starting 3/1; must reply within 2 week(s) of notification.

Four-Year Colleges

**Academics. Special study options:** Accelerated study, distance learning, double major, honors, independent study, internships, liberal arts/career combination, student-designed major, study abroad, teacher certification program, weekend college. **Credit/placement by examination:** CLEP, institutional tests. **Support services:** Learning center, pre-admission summer program, reduced course load, study skills assistance, tutoring, writing center.

**Majors. Area/ethnic studies:** American, women's. **Biology:** General, biochemistry. **Business:** Accounting, business admin. **Conservation:** Environmental studies. **Education:** Special. **English:** English lit. **Family/consumer sciences:** General, child development, food/nutrition. **Foreign languages:** Spanish. **Health:** Nursing (RN). **History:** General. **Interdisciplinary:** Global studies. **Liberal arts:** Arts/sciences. **Math:** General. **Philosophy/religion:** Philosophy, religion. **Physical sciences:** Chemistry. **Psychology:** General. **Public administration:** Social work. **Social sciences:** Economics, sociology. **Visual/performing arts:** Art history/conservation.

**Most popular majors.** Biology 7%, business/marketing 8%, education 6%, family/consumer sciences 12%, health sciences 28%, psychology 14%, public administration/social services 9%.

**Computing on campus.** Dormitories wired for high-speed internet access and linked to campus network. Online library, helpline available.

**Student life. Freshman orientation:** Available. **Housing:** Special housing for disabled, substance-free housing available. $250 deposit. Single rooms available for nontraditional students. Medical singles with private bathrooms available on a limited basis. **Activities:** Choral groups, dance, drama, literary magazine, music ensembles, opera, student government, student newspaper.

**Athletics.** NCAA. **Intercollegiate:** Basketball W, cross-country W, diving W, lacrosse W, soccer W, softball W, swimming W, tennis W, volleyball W. **Intramural:** Basketball W, soccer W, softball W, tennis W, track and field W, volleyball W. **Team name:** Blue Jays.

**Student services.** Adult student services, alcohol/substance abuse counseling, campus ministries, career counseling, student employment services, financial aid counseling, health services, on-campus daycare, personal counseling, placement for graduates, women's services. **Physically disabled:** Services for hearing impaired.

**Contact.** E-mail: admissions@sjc.edu
Phone: (860) 231-5216 Toll-free number: (866) 442-8752
Nance Wunderly, Director of Admissions, St. Joseph College, 1678 Asylum Avenue, West Hartford, CT 06117

---

## Southern Connecticut State University
New Haven, Connecticut     **CB member**
www.southernct.edu     **CB code: 3662**

- Public 4-year university
- Residential campus in small city
- 8,515 degree-seeking undergraduates: 16% part-time, 62% women, 12% African American, 2% Asian American, 7% Hispanic American, 1% international
- 3,415 degree-seeking graduate students
- 29% of applicants admitted
- SAT or ACT with writing, application essay required
- 38% graduate within 6 years

**General.** Founded in 1893. Regionally accredited. **Degrees:** 1,357 bachelor's awarded; master's, doctoral offered. **ROTC:** Army, Air Force. **Location:** 75 miles from New York City. **Calendar:** Semester, extensive summer session. **Full-time faculty:** 438 total; 83% have terminal degrees, 15% minority, 46% women. **Part-time faculty:** 615 total; 49% have terminal degrees, 10% minority, 55% women. **Class size:** 36% < 20, 57% 20-39, 6% 40-49, less than 1% 50-99, less than 1% >100. **Special facilities:** Planetarium, photonics laboratory, geospatial technology laboratory.

**Freshman class profile.** 6,178 applied, 1,806 admitted, 1,349 enrolled.

| Mid 50% test scores | | | |
|---|---|---|---|
| SAT critical reading: | 420-510 | Return as sophomores: | 72% |
| SAT math: | 410-520 | Out-of-state: | 10% |
| Rank in top quarter: | 24% | Live on campus: | 66% |
| Rank in top tenth: | 5% | Fraternities: | 1% |
| End year in good standing: | 71% | Sororities: | 1% |

**Basis for selection.** School achievement record, test scores most important. Special consideration to culturally disadvantaged students. **Homeschooled:** Statement describing homeschool structure and mission, transcript of courses and grades, letter of recommendation (nonparent) required.

---

**High school preparation.** 16 units required. Required and recommended units include English 4, mathematics 3-4, social studies 2, history 2, science 2 (laboratory 1) and foreign language 2-3. One unit of algebra II required.

**2007-2008 Annual costs.** Tuition/fees: $6,624; $14,110 out-of-state. Out-of-state students pay an additional $1,234 in fees. Room/board: $8,502. Books/supplies: $1,300. Personal expenses: $250.

**2006-2007 Financial aid. Need-based:** 1,289 full-time freshmen applied for aid; 794 were judged to have need; 742 of these received aid. Average need met was 77%. Average scholarship/grant was $5,179; average loan $2,797. 33% of total undergraduate aid awarded as scholarships/grants, 67% as loans/jobs. **Non-need-based:** Awarded to 1,454 full-time undergraduates, including 508 freshmen. Scholarships awarded for academics, alumni affiliation, athletics, ROTC.

**Application procedures. Admission:** Closing date 4/1 (postmark date). $50 fee, may be waived for applicants with need. Application may be submitted online. Admission notification on a rolling basis beginning on or about 12/1. Must reply by May 1 or within 2 week(s) if notified thereafter. **Financial aid:** Closing date 3/9. FAFSA required. Applicants notified on a rolling basis starting 3/9; must reply within 2 week(s) of notification.

**Academics. Special study options:** Accelerated study, cooperative education, cross-registration, distance learning, double major, dual enrollment of high school students, exchange student, external degree, honors, independent study, internships, liberal arts/career combination, student-designed major, study abroad, teacher certification program. **Credit/placement by examination:** AP, CLEP, institutional tests. 30 credit hours maximum toward associate degree, 30 toward bachelor's. **Support services:** Learning center, pre-admission summer program, reduced course load, remedial instruction, study skills assistance, tutoring, writing center.

**Majors. Biology:** General. **Business:** Accounting, business admin, finance, management science, managerial economics, marketing. **Communications:** General, journalism. **Computer sciences:** General. **Education:** General, art, biology, chemistry, elementary, English, history, mathematics, physical, physics, science, secondary, social science, social studies, Spanish. **English:** Composition, English lit. **Foreign languages:** General, French, German, Italian, Spanish. **Health:** Nursing (RN), predental, premedicine, prepharmacy, preveterinary. **History:** General. **Legal studies:** Prelaw. **Liberal arts:** Arts/sciences, library science. **Math:** General. **Parks/recreation:** General, exercise sciences. **Philosophy/religion:** Philosophy. **Physical sciences:** Chemistry, geology, physics. **Psychology:** General. **Public administration:** Social work. **Social sciences:** Geography, political science, sociology. **Visual/performing arts:** Art, art history/conservation, dramatic.

**Most popular majors.** Business/marketing 13%, communications/journalism 9%, education 10%, English 6%, health sciences 9%, liberal arts 9%, psychology 14%, social sciences 8%.

**Computing on campus.** 750 workstations in dormitories, library, computer center, student center. Dormitories wired for high-speed internet access and linked to campus network. Commuter students can connect to campus network. Online course registration, online library, helpline, student web hosting, wireless network available.

**Student life. Freshman orientation:** Mandatory. Preregistration for classes offered. **Housing:** Guaranteed on-campus for all undergraduates. Coed dorms, special housing for disabled, apartments, substance-free housing available. $250 nonrefundable deposit. Students must be 19 or older to live in upperclassmen apartments. **Activities:** Bands, campus ministries, choral groups, drama, literary magazine, music ensembles, radio station, student government, student newspaper, Christian fellowship, Newman Club, Organization of Latin American Students, Black Student Union, People to People, Students for Disability Rights, veterans club.

**Athletics.** NCAA. **Intercollegiate:** Baseball M, basketball, cross-country, field hockey W, football (tackle) M, gymnastics W, lacrosse W, soccer, softball W, swimming, track and field, volleyball M. **Intramural:** Basketball, football (non-tackle), soccer, softball, tennis, volleyball. **Team name:** Owls.

**Student services.** Adult student services, alcohol/substance abuse counseling, campus ministries, career counseling, student employment services, financial aid counseling, health services, personal counseling, placement for graduates, veterans' counselor, women's services. **Physically disabled:** Services for visually, speech, hearing impaired.

**Contact.** Phone: (203) 392-5644 Toll-free number: (888) 500-7278
Fax: (203) 392-5727
James Williams, Admissions and Enrollment Management, Southern Connecticut State University, 131 Farnham Avenue, New Haven, CT 06515-1202

## Trinity College

Hartford, Connecticut
www.trincoll.edu

CB member
CB code: 3899

- Private 4-year liberal arts college
- Residential campus in large city
- 2,243 degree-seeking undergraduates: 2% part-time, 50% women, 6% African American, 5% Asian American, 6% Hispanic American, 4% international
- 136 degree-seeking graduate students
- 34% of applicants admitted
- SAT or ACT (ACT writing recommended), application essay required
- 87% graduate within 6 years; 18% enter graduate study

**General.** Founded in 1823. Regionally accredited. **Degrees:** 514 bachelor's awarded; master's offered. **ROTC:** Army. **Location:** 125 miles from New York City, 100 miles from Boston. **Calendar:** Semester, limited summer session. **Full-time faculty:** 173 total; 92% have terminal degrees, 18% minority, 40% women. **Part-time faculty:** 82 total; 60% have terminal degrees, 10% minority, 42% women. **Class size:** 59% < 20, 33% 20-39, 4% 40-49, 4% 50-99, less than 1% >100. **Special facilities:** Library collections on Native Americans, maritime history, early American texts; nuclear magnetic spectrometer, mass spectrometer, electronic microscope, plasma spectrometer, optical diagnostics and communications laboratory, natural science field station.

**Freshman class profile.** 5,950 applied, 2,037 admitted, 576 enrolled.

| Mid 50% test scores | | | |
|---|---|---|---|
| SAT critical reading: | 600-690 | Rank in top tenth: | 61% |
| SAT math: | 610-690 | End year in good standing: | 86% |
| SAT writing: | 610-700 | Return as sophomores: | 90% |
| ACT composite: | 26-29 | Out-of-state: | 85% |
| Rank in top quarter: | 88% | Live on campus: | 99% |
| | | International: | 5% |

**Basis for selection.** School record and recommendations most important. Test scores used for math and writing placement. SAT Subject Tests recommended. Interview recommended.

**High school preparation.** 16 units required. Required units include English 4, mathematics 3, history 2, science 2 (laboratory 2) and foreign language 3.

**2007-2008 Annual costs.** Tuition/fees: $36,870. One-time $25 transcript fee for new students only. Room/board: $9,420. Books/supplies: $900. Personal expenses: $900.

**2007-2008 Financial aid. Need-based:** 262 full-time freshmen applied for aid; 214 were judged to have need; 214 of these received aid. Average need met was 100%. Average scholarship/grant was $29,793; average loan $3,632. 91% of total undergraduate aid awarded as scholarships/grants, 9% as loans/jobs. **Non-need-based:** Awarded to 240 full-time undergraduates, including 70 freshmen. Scholarships awarded for academics, leadership.

**Application procedures. Admission:** Closing date 1/1 (postmark date). $60 fee, may be waived for applicants with need. Application may be submitted online. Admission notification 4/1. Must reply by May 1 or within 2 week(s) if notified thereafter. **Financial aid:** Priority date 2/1, closing date 3/1. FAFSA, CSS PROFILE required. Applicants notified by 4/1; must reply by 5/1 or within 2 week(s) of notification.

**Academics.** Math Center available. **Special study options:** Accelerated study, combined bachelor's/graduate degree, cross-registration, double major, exchange student, honors, independent study, internships, liberal arts/career combination, New York semester, semester at sea, student-designed major, study abroad, teacher certification program, United Nations semester, urban semester, Washington semester. Community Learning Initiative (courses with community-based components) available. **Credit/placement by examination:** AP, CLEP, IB, SAT, ACT, institutional tests. **Support services:** Study skills assistance, tutoring, writing center.

**Majors. Area/ethnic studies:** African, African-American, American, Asian, gay/lesbian, Latin American, Near/Middle Eastern, Russian/Slavic, women's. **Biology:** General, biochemistry. **Computer sciences:** General, computer science. **Conservation:** Environmental science. **Education:** General. **Engineering:** General, biomedical, electrical, mechanical. **English:** Creative writing, English lit. **Foreign languages:** General, Chinese, classics, comparative lit, French, German, Italian, Japanese, Russian, Spanish. **Health:** Premedicine. **History:** General. **Interdisciplinary:** Neuroscience. **Legal studies:** Prelaw. **Math:** General. **Philosophy/religion:** Judaic, philosophy, religion. **Physical sciences:** Chemistry, physics. **Psychology:** General. **Public administration:** Policy analysis. **Social sciences:** General, anthropology, economics, international relations, political science, sociology, urban studies. **Visual/performing arts:** General, art, art history/conservation, dance, dramatic, film/cinema, studio arts.

**Most popular majors.** Area/ethnic studies 7%, English 7%, foreign language 6%, history 7%, philosophy/religious studies 6%, psychology 7%, social sciences 30%, visual/performing arts 7%.

**Computing on campus.** 327 workstations in library, computer center. Dormitories wired for high-speed internet access and linked to campus network. Commuter students can connect to campus network. Online course registration, online library, helpline, student web hosting, wireless network available.

**Student life. Freshman orientation:** Available. Preregistration for classes offered. 4 days, beginning the Thursday before Labor Day. **Housing:** Guaranteed on-campus for freshmen. Coed dorms, special housing for disabled, apartments, fraternity/sorority housing, substance-free housing available. Community service dorm, quiet dorm, alternative social programming, healthy living theme dorm, cooking units. All dorms are non-smoking. **Activities:** Jazz band, campus ministries, choral groups, dance, drama, film society, international student organizations, literary magazine, Model UN, musical theater, radio station, student government, student newspaper, Asian-American Student Association, Intervarsity Christian Fellowship, Encouraging Respect Of Sexualities, Friends Active in Civic Engagement and Service, Hillel, Imani, La Voz Latina, Promoting Healthy Awareness of the Body, Promoting Respect for Inclusive Diversity in Education, Trinity College Black Women's Organization.

**Athletics.** NCAA. **Intercollegiate:** Baseball M, basketball, cross-country, diving, field hockey W, football (tackle) M, golf M, ice hockey, lacrosse, rowing (crew), soccer, softball W, squash, swimming, tennis, track and field, volleyball W, wrestling M. **Intramural:** Badminton, basketball, football (non-tackle), ice hockey, soccer, softball, squash, tennis, volleyball. **Team name:** Bantams.

**Student services.** Adult student services, alcohol/substance abuse counseling, campus ministries, career counseling, services for economically disadvantaged, student employment services, financial aid counseling, health services, minority student services, on-campus daycare, personal counseling, placement for graduates, women's services.

**Contact.** E-mail: admissions.office@trincoll.edu
Phone: (860) 297-2180 Fax: (860) 297-2287
Larry Dow, Dean of Admissions and Financial Aid, Trinity College, 300 Summit Street, Hartford, CT 06106

## United States Coast Guard Academy

New London, Connecticut
www.uscga.edu

CB member
CB code: 5807

- Public 4-year engineering, military and maritime college
- Residential campus in small city
- 963 degree-seeking undergraduates: 27% women, 3% African American, 4% Asian American, 6% Hispanic American, 1% international
- 27% of applicants admitted
- SAT or ACT with writing, application essay required
- 75% graduate within 6 years

**General.** Founded in 1876. Regionally accredited. Five-year obligatory military service after graduation, serving as commissioned officer in U.S. Coast Guard. **Degrees:** 228 bachelor's awarded. **Location:** 120 miles from New York City, 130 miles from Boston. **Calendar:** Semester, limited summer session. **Full-time faculty:** 105 total; 57% have terminal degrees, 9% minority, 21% women. **Part-time faculty:** 20 total; 90% have terminal degrees, 25% women. **Class size:** 72% < 20, 30% 20-39. **Special facilities:** Museum, research and development center, 295 foot tall ship, ship navigation simulation facilities with bridge simulator, 10,000 gallon circulating water channel, ship model towing tank, observatory with reflector telescope.

**Freshman class profile.** 1,475 applied, 391 admitted, 272 enrolled.

| Mid 50% test scores | | | |
|---|---|---|---|
| SAT critical reading: | 560-660 | Rank in top quarter: | 94% |
| SAT math: | 610-680 | Rank in top tenth: | 59% |
| ACT composite: | 27-30 | End year in good standing: | 96% |
| GPA 3.50 or higher: | 83% | Return as sophomores: | 96% |
| GPA 3.0-3.49: | 14% | Out-of-state: | 93% |
| GPA 2.0-2.99: | 3% | Live on campus: | 100% |
| | | International: | 1% |

**Basis for selection.** Test scores, high school class rank, recommendations, essay, leadership potential as demonstrated by extracurricular activities, athletics, community affairs, and part-time employment considered. Congressional nomination not required. Applicants required to pass medical and physical fitness exams. Interview recommended. **Homeschooled:** AP and SAT Subject Tests recommended. Application should include detailed account of curriculum and course content. Students advised to take courses in math and science at a local college and have professor submit a recommendation. Recommendations from other adults required. Essay should include reasons for undertaking homeschooling, benefits realized, and how experience prepared student to succeed in college.

**High school preparation.** Required units include English 4, mathematics 4, science 3 (laboratory 3). Math units should include algebra, quadratics, plane or coordinate geometry, or equivalent. Calculus and pre-calculus recommended. Sciences should include chemistry and physics.

**2008-2009 Annual costs.** All tuition, room and board paid for by U.S. government. Students make one-time entrance deposit of $3,000 to help defray cost of uniforms, books, supplies and personal computer. All students paid monthly stipend of $734.

**Application procedures. Admission:** Closing date 3/1 (postmark date). No application fee. Application must be submitted online. Admission notification on a rolling basis beginning on or about 12/15. Must reply by May 1 or within 2 week(s) if notified thereafter. Application by 11/01 recommended to allow time to complete essays and supplemental forms, obtain teacher recommendations, and schedule required physical. **Financial aid:** No deadline.

**Academics.** Summers involve introductory and advanced Coast Guard/professional training including opportunities to sail aboard Eagle, fly Coast Guard aircraft, become small arms qualified (rifle and pistol), learn basic shipboard fire fighting and flooding control, and perform actual search and rescue coordination at Coast Guard units. Summer between junior and senior years typically involves piloting and navigation of Coast Guard Cutters and integration into all aspects of operational afloat Coast Guard missions. **Special study options:** Double major, exchange student, honors, independent study, internships. **Credit/placement by examination:** CLEP, institutional tests. **Support services:** Learning center, pre-admission summer program, reduced course load, remedial instruction, study skills assistance, tutoring, writing center.

**Majors. Business:** Business admin. **Engineering:** Civil, electrical, marine, mechanical. **Physical sciences:** Oceanography. **Social sciences:** Political science. **Other:** Operations research.

**Most popular majors.** Biology 14%, business/marketing 20%, engineering/engineering technologies 33%, mathematics 14%, social sciences 19%.

**Computing on campus.** PC or laptop required. 325 workstations in dormitories, library, computer center. Dormitories wired for high-speed internet access and linked to campus network. Online course registration, online library, helpline, repair service, student web hosting, wireless network available.

**Student life. Freshman orientation:** Mandatory. 7-week "swab summer," including one week onboard the Coast Guard Cutter Eagle. **Policies:** Students part of corps of cadets. On-campus residence mandatory. **Housing:** Guaranteed on-campus for all undergraduates. Coed dorms, substance-free housing available. **Activities:** Bands, choral groups, dance, drama, music ensembles, musical theater, student government, student newspaper, Officers Christian Fellowship, multicultural club, Fellowship of Christian Athletes, Big Brothers and Big Sisters, Boy Scouts, Genesis Club.

**Athletics.** NCAA. **Intercollegiate:** Baseball M, basketball, cheerleading M, cross-country, diving, football (tackle) M, rifle, rowing (crew), sailing, soccer, softball W, swimming, tennis M, track and field, volleyball W, wrestling M. **Intramural:** Basketball, football (non-tackle), golf, racquetball, soccer, softball, tennis, volleyball. **Team name:** Bears.

**Student services.** Alcohol/substance abuse counseling, campus ministries, career counseling, health services, legal services, minority student services, on-campus daycare, personal counseling, placement for graduates.

**Contact.** Phone: (860) 444-8500 Toll-free number: (800) 883-8724 Fax: (860) 701-6700
Capt. Susan Bibeau, Director of Admissions, United States Coast Guard Academy, 31 Mohegan Avenue, New London, CT 06320

---

## University of Bridgeport
**Bridgeport, Connecticut**
www.bridgeport.edu

CB. member
CB code: 3914

- Private 4-year university
- Residential campus in small city

---

- 1,791 degree-seeking undergraduates: 32% part-time, 68% women, 33% African American, 3% Asian American, 13% Hispanic American, 14% international
- 2,961 degree-seeking graduate students
- 57% of applicants admitted
- SAT or ACT (ACT writing optional), application essay required
- 48% graduate within 6 years; 50% enter graduate study

**General.** Founded in 1927. Regionally accredited. Off-campus facilities in Stamford and Waterbury. **Degrees:** 273 bachelor's, 31 associate awarded; master's, doctoral, first professional offered. **ROTC:** Army. **Location:** 60 miles from New York City. **Calendar:** Semester, extensive summer session. **Full-time faculty:** 114 total; 79% have terminal degrees, 23% minority, 34% women. **Part-time faculty:** 322 total; 13% minority, 45% women. **Class size:** 71% < 20, 27% 20-39, 1% 40-49, less than 1% 50-99. **Special facilities:** Theater, recital halls, studios, exhibit rooms.

**Freshman class profile.** 4,311 applied, 2,454 admitted, 335 enrolled.

| Mid 50% test scores | | | |
|---|---|---|---|
| SAT critical reading: | 360-490 | Rank in top quarter: | 27% |
| SAT math: | 380-490 | Rank in top tenth: | 6% |
| SAT writing: | 380-480 | Return as sophomores: | 51% |
| ACT composite: | 17-22 | Out-of-state: | 61% |
| GPA 3.50 or higher: | 12% | Live on campus: | 75% |
| GPA 3.0-3.49: | 27% | International: | 12% |
| GPA 2.0-2.99: | 54% | Fraternities: | 1% |
| | | Sororities: | 1% |

**Basis for selection.** School achievement record most important, followed by test scores, activities, trend of grades and curriculum in high school. Audition required of music majors. Portfolio required of fine and applied arts majors. Interview recommended of dental hygiene, basic studies majors.

**High school preparation.** College-preparatory program recommended. 16 units required. Required units include English 4, mathematics 3, social studies 2, science 2 (laboratory 2) and academic electives 5. 4 math required for math, science, computer science and engineering applicants. Chemistry required for dental hygiene.

**2007-2008 Annual costs.** Tuition/fees: $22,860. Room/board: $10,000. Books/supplies: $1,500. Personal expenses: $2,747.

**Financial aid. Non-need-based:** Scholarships awarded for academics, athletics, state residency.

**Application procedures. Admission:** Priority date 4/1; no deadline. $25 fee, may be waived for applicants with need. Application may be submitted online. Admission notification on a rolling basis. Must reply by May 1 or within 2 week(s) if notified thereafter. **Financial aid:** Priority date 4/1; no closing date. FAFSA, institutional form required. Applicants notified on a rolling basis starting 4/1; must reply within 4 week(s) of notification.

**Academics. Special study options:** Accelerated study, combined bachelor's/graduate degree, cooperative education, cross-registration, distance learning, double major, dual enrollment of high school students, ESL, exchange student, honors, independent study, internships, liberal arts/career combination, New York semester, student-designed major, study abroad, teacher certification program, United Nations semester, Washington semester, weekend college. **Credit/placement by examination:** AP, CLEP, IB, SAT, ACT, institutional tests. 30 credit hours maximum toward associate degree, 30 toward bachelor's. **Support services:** Learning center, pre-admission summer program, reduced course load, remedial instruction, study skills assistance, tutoring, writing center.

**Majors. Area/ethnic studies:** East Asian. **Biology:** General. **Business:** General, accounting, fashion, finance, international, labor relations, management information systems, marketing. **Communications:** General, advertising, journalism, media studies, public relations. **Computer sciences:** General. **Engineering:** Computer. **English:** Creative writing, English lit. **Health:** Dental hygiene. **Liberal arts:** Arts/sciences, humanities. **Math:** General. **Philosophy/religion:** Religion. **Physical sciences:** General. **Psychology:** General. **Public administration:** Community org/advocacy. **Social sciences:** General, international relations, political science, sociology. **Visual/performing arts:** Graphic design, illustration, industrial design, interior design.

**Most popular majors.** Business/marketing 22%, health sciences 10%, liberal arts 15%, psychology 7%, public administration/social services 11%, social sciences 12%, visual/performing arts 9%.

**Computing on campus.** 600 workstations in dormitories, library, computer center, student center. Dormitories wired for high-speed internet access and linked to campus network. Commuter students can connect to campus network. Online library, helpline, repair service, student web hosting, wireless network available.

**Student life. Freshman orientation:** Mandatory, $100 fee. Preregistration for classes offered. Placement listing, registration, and orientation held during the summer with final program just prior to class. **Policies:** Student and dormitory governments plan student life activities. **Housing:** Guaranteed on-campus for all undergraduates. Coed dorms, substance-free housing available. $200 deposit, deadline 5/1. Dormitories have special facilities. **Activities:** Choral groups, film society, literary magazine, music ensembles, student government, student newspaper, interfaith center, black student alliance, social service sorority, Newman Center, Hillel, Protestant fellowship, Home Base Community Service Project.

**Athletics.** NCAA. **Intercollegiate:** Baseball M, basketball, cross-country, gymnastics W, soccer, softball W, swimming W, volleyball W. **Intramural:** Basketball, racquetball, soccer, softball, tennis, volleyball. **Team name:** Purple Knights.

**Student services.** Adult student services, alcohol/substance abuse counseling, campus ministries, career counseling, student employment services, financial aid counseling, health services, minority student services, personal counseling, placement for graduates, veterans' counselor. **Physically disabled:** Services for visually, speech, hearing impaired.

**Contact.** E-mail: admit@bridgeport.edu
Phone: (203) 576-4552 Toll-free number: (800) 392-3582
Fax: (203) 576-4941
Barbara Maryak, Associate Vice President of Admissions, University of Bridgeport, 126 Park Avenue, Bridgeport, CT 06604

---

## University of Connecticut

| Storrs, Connecticut | **CB member** |
| --- | --- |
| www.uconn.edu | **CB code: 3915** |

- Public 4-year university
- Residential campus in large town
- 16,036 degree-seeking undergraduates: 3% part-time, 51% women, 5% African American, 7% Asian American, 5% Hispanic American, 1% international
- 6,602 degree-seeking graduate students
- 49% of applicants admitted
- SAT or ACT with writing, application essay required
- 74% graduate within 6 years; 30% enter graduate study

**General.** Founded in 1881. Regionally accredited. Students may take courses at nonresidential campuses in Groton, Hartford, Stamford, Waterbury, and Torrington. **Degrees:** 4,354 bachelor's, 22 associate awarded; master's, doctoral, first professional offered. **ROTC:** Army, Air Force. **Location:** 26 miles from Hartford, 80 miles from Boston. **Calendar:** Semester, extensive summer session. **Full-time faculty:** 1,009 total; 93% have terminal degrees, 19% minority, 34% women. **Part-time faculty:** 331 total; 24% have terminal degrees, 6% minority, 49% women. **Class size:** 44% < 20, 33% 20-39, 7% 40-49, 8% 50-99, 7% >100. **Special facilities:** Museum of natural history, research center, ice hockey/skating rink, dairy bar.

**Freshman class profile.** 21,105 applied, 10,429 admitted, 3,179 enrolled.

| Mid 50% test scores | | Return as sophomores: | 93% |
| --- | --- | --- | --- |
| SAT critical reading: | 530-630 | Out-of-state: | 29% |
| SAT math: | 560-660 | Live on campus: | 97% |
| SAT writing: | 540-640 | International: | 1% |
| ACT composite: | 23-28 | Fraternities: | 6% |
| Rank in top quarter: | 81% | Sororities: | 8% |
| Rank in top tenth: | 40% | | |

**Basis for selection.** Curriculum, grades, rank in class most important, followed by test scores. Particular consideration given to first generation college and/or socio-economically disadvantaged applicants and applicants with special talents. Audition required of music, acting, puppetry majors. Portfolio required for art major. Interview required for design/technical theater and theater studies majors. **Homeschooled:** Statement describing homeschool structure and mission, transcript of courses and grades required. **Learning Disabled:** No special admissions requirements. Students can submit disability documentation to the Center for Students with Disabilities upon admission.

**High school preparation.** 16 units required. Required and recommended units include English 4, mathematics 3, social studies 1, history 1, science 2 (laboratory 2), foreign language 2-3 and academic electives 3. Some programs may require additional units.

**2008-2009 Annual costs.** Tuition/fees: $9,338; $24,050 out-of-state. Incoming out-of-state New England residents pay 175% of in-state tuition rate for programs of study not offered at their home state university. Room/board: $9,300. Books/supplies: $800. Personal expenses: $1,640.

**2007-2008 Financial aid. Need-based:** 2,503 full-time freshmen applied for aid; 1,604 were judged to have need; 1,583 of these received aid. Average need met was 73%. Average scholarship/grant was $6,719; average loan $3,840. 47% of total undergraduate aid awarded as scholarships/grants, 53% as loans/jobs. **Non-need-based:** Awarded to 4,827 full-time undergraduates, including 1,356 freshmen. Scholarships awarded for academics, art, athletics, leadership, minority status, music/drama. **Additional information:** Institution offers variety of need-based financial aid programs. Financial assistance packages may include grants, loans and work-study awards.

**Application procedures. Admission:** Priority date 12/1; deadline 2/1. $70 fee, may be waived for applicants with need. Application may be submitted online. Admission notification on a rolling basis beginning on or about 1/1. Must reply by May 1 or within 2 week(s) if notified thereafter. **Financial aid:** Priority date 3/1; no closing date. FAFSA required. Applicants notified on a rolling basis starting 3/1; must reply within 4 week(s) of notification.

**Academics.** Eurotech Program, 5-year program available combining engineering and the German language, including a 6-month internship in Germany. **Special study options:** Accelerated study, combined bachelor's/graduate degree, cooperative education, distance learning, double major, dual enrollment of high school students, ESL, exchange student, honors, independent study, internships, liberal arts/career combination, New York semester, semester at sea, student-designed major, study abroad, teacher certification program, urban semester, Washington semester. Winter inter-session, summer session, urban semester. **Credit/placement by examination:** AP, CLEP, IB, SAT, ACT, institutional tests. 30 credit hours maximum toward bachelor's degree. **Support services:** Learning center, pre-admission summer program, study skills assistance, tutoring, writing center.

**Majors. Agriculture:** General, agronomy, animal sciences, economics, horticultural science. **Architecture:** Landscape. **Area/ethnic studies:** American, Latin American, Near/Middle Eastern, women's. **Biology:** General, animal physiology, biophysics, cellular/molecular, ecology, marine, pathology. **Business:** General, accounting, actuarial science, business admin, finance, insurance, management information systems, marketing, real estate. **Communications:** General, journalism. **Computer sciences:** Computer science. **Conservation:** General, environmental studies. **Education:** Agricultural, elementary, music, physical, special. **Engineering:** Biomedical, chemical, civil, computer, electrical, environmental, industrial, materials, materials science, mechanical, physics. **English:** English lit. **Family/consumer sciences:** Family studies. **Foreign languages:** Classics, French, German, Italian, linguistics, Spanish. **Health:** Clinical lab science, cytotechnology, dietetics, gene therapy, health care admin, health services, nursing (RN), prepharmacy. **History:** General. **Interdisciplinary:** Cognitive science, nutrition sciences. **Math:** General, applied, statistics. **Parks/recreation:** Facilities management. **Philosophy/religion:** Philosophy. **Physical sciences:** Chemistry, geology, physics. **Psychology:** General, cognitive. **Social sciences:** Anthropology, economics, geography, political science, sociology, urban studies. **Visual/performing arts:** Acting, art history/conservation, dramatic, studio arts, theater design. **Other:** Puppetry.

**Most popular majors.** Biology 7%, business/marketing 14%, communications/journalism 6%, engineering/engineering technologies 7%, health sciences 9%, liberal arts 9%, psychology 8%, social sciences 14%.

**Computing on campus.** 1,318 workstations in dormitories, library, computer center, student center. Dormitories wired for high-speed internet access and linked to campus network. Commuter students can connect to campus network. Online course registration, online library, helpline, repair service, wireless network available.

**Student life. Freshman orientation:** Available, $60 fee. Preregistration for classes offered. 12 two-day sessions extending from late May to early July. **Housing:** Coed dorms, single-sex dorms, special housing for disabled, apartments, fraternity/sorority housing, substance-free housing available. Special interests, honors, foreign languages, substance-free, older-student housing, freshmen year experience housing, global house, Women in Math, Science, and Engineering, and other learning communities. **Activities:** Bands, choral groups, dance, drama, film society, international student organizations, literary magazine, music ensembles, Model UN, musical theater, opera, radio station, student government, student newspaper, symphony orchestra, TV station, over 300 organizations available.

**Athletics.** NCAA. **Intercollegiate:** Baseball M, basketball, cross-country, diving, field hockey W, football (tackle) M, golf M, ice hockey, lacrosse W, rowing (crew) W, soccer, softball W, swimming, tennis, track and field, volleyball W. **Intramural:** Badminton, baseball M, basketball, bowling, cross-country, diving, equestrian, fencing, football (non-tackle), football (tackle) M, ice hockey, lacrosse, racquetball, rowing (crew), rugby, sailing, skiing, soccer, softball, squash, swimming, table tennis, tennis, track and field, volleyball, water polo, weight lifting M. **Team name:** Huskies.

**Student services.** Adult student services, alcohol/substance abuse counseling, campus ministries, career counseling, student employment services, financial aid counseling, health services, minority student services, on-campus daycare, personal counseling, placement for graduates, veterans' counselor, women's services. **Physically disabled:** Services for visually, speech, hearing impaired.

**Contact.** E-mail: beahusky@uconn.edu
Phone: (860) 486-3137 Fax: (860) 486-1476
Lee Melvin, Director of Admission, University of Connecticut, 2131 Hillside Road, Unit 3088, Storrs, CT 06269-3088

---

## University of Hartford
**West Hartford, Connecticut**
www.hartford.edu

CB member
CB code: 3436

- Private 4-year university
- Residential campus in small city
- 5,364 degree-seeking undergraduates: 11% part-time, 52% women
- 1,552 degree-seeking graduate students
- 54% of applicants admitted
- SAT or ACT with writing required
- 55% graduate within 6 years

**General.** Founded in 1877. Regionally accredited. **Degrees:** 1,022 bachelor's, 175 associate awarded; master's, doctoral offered. **ROTC:** Army, Air Force. **Location:** 4 miles from downtown. **Calendar:** Semester, extensive summer session. **Full-time faculty:** 335 total; 79% have terminal degrees, 10% minority, 36% women. **Part-time faculty:** 507 total; 4% minority. **Class size:** 59% < 20, 39% 20-39, less than 1% 40-49, 1% 50-99, less than 1% >100. **Special facilities:** Science center, museum of American political life, engineering applications center, humanities center.

**Freshman class profile.** 11,698 applied, 6,317 admitted, 1,476 enrolled.

| Mid 50% test scores | | Return as sophomores: | 69% |
|---|---|---|---|
| SAT critical reading: | 470-570 | Out-of-state: | 71% |
| SAT math: | 480-590 | Live on campus: | 91% |
| ACT composite: | 20-25 | International: | 3% |

**Basis for selection.** Quality of academic program, school achievement record, class rank important. Test scores secondary. Employment, extracurricular activities, and community service considered. Writing samples and interview also considered. Admission committee can offer admission to alternative program. SAT or ACT can be submitted on a rolling basis. Interview and essay recommended. Audition required of music, dance, acting majors. Portfolio required of art majors.

**High school preparation.** 16 units required. Required and recommended units include English 4, mathematics 2-3, social studies 2, history 2, science 2-3, foreign language 2 and academic electives 4. Physics, chemistry, and 3.5 math (including trigonometry) recommended for engineering and science applicants.

**2008-2009 Annual costs.** Tuition/fees (projected): $28,172. Room/board: $10,876. Books/supplies: $860. Personal expenses: $1,350.

**2006-2007 Financial aid. Need-based:** 1,178 full-time freshmen applied for aid; 1,034 were judged to have need; 1,030 of these received aid. Average need met was 73%. Average scholarship/grant was $13,565; average loan $2,862. 56% of total undergraduate aid awarded as scholarships/grants, 44% as loans/jobs. **Non-need-based:** Awarded to 4,054 full-time undergraduates, including 1,382 freshmen. Scholarships awarded for academics, art, athletics, music/drama.

**Application procedures. Admission:** No deadline. $35 fee, may be waived for applicants with need. Application may be submitted online. Admission notification on a rolling basis beginning on or about 10/1. Must reply by May 1 or within 2 week(s) if notified thereafter. **Financial aid:** Priority date 2/1; no closing date. FAFSA, institutional form required. Applicants notified on a rolling basis starting 3/1; must reply by 5/1.

**Academics. Special study options:** Combined bachelor's/graduate degree, cooperative education, cross-registration, distance learning, double major, dual enrollment of high school students, ESL, exchange student, honors, independent study, internships, liberal arts/career combination, student-designed major, study abroad, teacher certification program, Washington semester. **Credit/placement by examination:** AP, CLEP, SAT, institutional tests. 30 credit hours maximum toward associate degree, 60 toward bachelor's. **Support services:** Learning center, reduced course load, tutoring, writing center.

**Majors. Area/ethnic studies:** Women's. **Biology:** General. **Business:** Accounting, business admin, entrepreneurial studies, finance, insurance, management information systems, marketing. **Communications:** General. **Computer sciences:** General, information systems. **Education:** Early childhood, elementary, music, secondary, special. **Engineering:** General, civil, computer, electrical, mechanical. **Engineering technology:** General, architectural, computer, electrical, environmental, mechanical. **English:** English lit, technical writing. **Foreign languages:** General. **Health:** Clinical lab science, health services, medical radiologic technology/radiation therapy, nursing (RN), respiratory therapy technology. **History:** General. **Legal studies:** General. **Math:** General. **Philosophy/religion:** Judaic, philosophy. **Physical sciences:** Chemistry, physics. **Protective services:** Police science. **Psychology:** General. **Public administration:** Community org/advocacy. **Social sciences:** Economics, international economics, political science, sociology. **Theology:** Sacred music. **Visual/performing arts:** General, acting, art history/conservation, ceramics, cinematography, commercial/advertising art, dance, design, dramatic, drawing, film/cinema, jazz, music history, music management, music performance, music theory/composition, painting, photography, printmaking, sculpture.

**Most popular majors.** Business/marketing 17%, communications/journalism 8%, education 9%, engineering/engineering technologies 12%, health sciences 8%, psychology 7%, visual/performing arts 20%.

**Computing on campus.** 300 workstations in dormitories, library, computer center. Dormitories wired for high-speed internet access and linked to campus network. Commuter students can connect to campus network. Online course registration, online library, helpline, repair service, student web hosting, wireless network available.

**Student life. Freshman orientation:** Mandatory. **Housing:** Guaranteed on-campus for freshmen. Coed dorms, single-sex dorms, special housing for disabled, apartments available. $200 deposit, deadline 2/1. Dormitories with resident faculty members, International residential college, residential college for the arts available. **Activities:** Bands, choral groups, dance, drama, international student organizations, literary magazine, music ensembles, musical theater, opera, radio station, student government, student newspaper, symphony orchestra, TV station, Hillel foundation, Protestant student organization, Newman Club, African American students association, academic department clubs, prelaw and premedical societies, Brothers and Sisters United, Global Friends Association, Malaysian student association, Turkish student association.

**Athletics.** NCAA. **Intercollegiate:** Baseball M, basketball, cross-country, golf, lacrosse M, soccer, softball W, tennis, track and field, volleyball W. **Intramural:** Basketball, football (non-tackle), handball, racquetball, soccer, softball, tennis, volleyball, water polo. **Team name:** Hawks.

**Student services.** Campus ministries, career counseling, student employment services, financial aid counseling, health services, minority student services, personal counseling, placement for graduates, veterans' counselor.

**Contact.** Phone: (860) 768-4296 Fax: (860) 768-4961
Richard Zeiser, Dean of Admission, University of Hartford, Bates House, West Hartford, CT 06117-1599

---

## University of New Haven
**West Haven, Connecticut**
www.newhaven.edu

CB member
CB code: 3663

- Private 4-year university
- Residential campus in small city
- 2,963 degree-seeking undergraduates: 13% part-time, 48% women
- 1,701 degree-seeking graduate students
- 73% of applicants admitted
- SAT or ACT (ACT writing optional), application essay required
- 40% graduate within 6 years

**General.** Founded in 1920. Regionally accredited. **Degrees:** 539 bachelor's, 47 associate awarded; master's offered. **Location:** 3 miles from downtown, 75 miles from New York City. **Calendar:** 4-1-4, limited summer session. **Full-time faculty:** 182 total; 80% have terminal degrees, 15% minority, 23% women. **Part-time faculty:** 317 total; 9% minority, 41% women. **Class size:** 19% < 20, 61% 20-39, 17% 40-49, 2% 50-99, 1% >100. **Special facilities:** Theater, music and sound recording studio, shoreline environmental study preserve, institute of forensic science, learning center for finance and technology.

**Freshman class profile.** 3,155 applied, 2,315 admitted, 705 enrolled.

| Mid 50% test scores | | | |
|---|---|---|---|
| SAT critical reading: | 450-560 | Rank in top tenth: | 14% |
| SAT math: | 450-580 | Return as sophomores: | 79% |
| SAT writing: | 450-560 | Out-of-state: | 52% |
| GPA 3.0-3.49: | 59% | Live on campus: | 89% |
| GPA 2.0-2.99: | 41% | International: | 1% |
| Rank in top quarter: | 40% | Fraternities: | 1% |
| | | Sororities: | 1% |

**Basis for selection.** Academic record, recommendations, test scores, personal essay, advanced placement or honor courses, and extracurricular activities reviewed. **Learning Disabled:** Students required to meet with Disability Services Office to receive accommodations and/or services.

**High school preparation.** Required units include English 4, mathematics 3, social studies 2, science 2 (laboratory 2) and foreign language 2.

**2008-2009 Annual costs.** Tuition/fees (projected): $26,868. Room/board: $10,581. Books/supplies: $800. Personal expenses: $1,000.

**2007-2008 Financial aid. Need-based:** 635 full-time freshmen applied for aid; 568 were judged to have need; 564 of these received aid. Average need met was 73%. Average scholarship/grant was $15,438; average loan $4,514. 74% of total undergraduate aid awarded as scholarships/grants, 26% as loans/jobs. **Non-need-based:** Awarded to 564 full-time undergraduates, including 156 freshmen. Scholarships awarded for academics, athletics.

**Application procedures. Admission:** No deadline. $50 fee, may be waived for applicants with need. Application may be submitted online. Admission notification on a rolling basis beginning on or about 12/1. Must reply by May 1 or within 2 week(s) if notified thereafter. **Financial aid:** Priority date 3/1, closing date 3/1. FAFSA required. Applicants notified on a rolling basis starting 3/15; must reply by 5/1 or within 2 week(s) of notification.

**Academics. Special study options:** Accelerated study, combined bachelor's/graduate degree, cooperative education, distance learning, double major, honors, independent study, internships, study abroad, teacher certification program, weekend college. **Credit/placement by examination:** AP, CLEP, IB, SAT, institutional tests. **Support services:** Learning center, reduced course load, remedial instruction, study skills assistance, tutoring, writing center.

**Majors. Architecture:** Interior. **Biology:** General, ecology, marine. **Business:** Accounting, business admin, finance, hospitality admin, hotel/motel admin, international, managerial economics, marketing. **Communications:** General. **Computer sciences:** General, information systems. **Conservation:** General. **Engineering:** General, chemical, civil, computer, electrical, mechanical. **Engineering technology:** Occupational safety. **English:** English lit. **Health:** Dental hygiene, dietetics. **History:** General. **Interdisciplinary:** Global studies, nutrition sciences. **Legal studies:** General. **Liberal arts:** Arts/sciences. **Math:** General, applied. **Parks/recreation:** Sports admin. **Physical sciences:** Chemistry. **Protective services:** Fire safety technology, firefighting, forensics, law enforcement admin. **Psychology:** General. **Public administration:** General. **Science technology:** Biological. **Social sciences:** Political science. **Visual/performing arts:** Graphic design, interior design, music management, studio arts.

**Most popular majors.** Business/marketing 17%, engineering/engineering technologies 7%, security/protective services 41%, visual/performing arts 11%.

**Computing on campus.** Dormitories wired for high-speed internet access and linked to campus network. Online course registration, helpline available.

**Student life. Freshman orientation:** Available. **Housing:** Coed dorms, apartments available. $200 nonrefundable deposit, deadline 5/1. Living/learning community available for freshmen engineering majors. Some dormitory rooms are handicapped accessible. **Activities:** Bands, campus ministries, choral groups, dance, drama, international student organizations, literary magazine, Model UN, radio station, student government, student newspaper.

**Athletics.** NCAA. **Intercollegiate:** Baseball M, basketball, cross-country, golf M, lacrosse W, soccer, softball W, tennis W, track and field, volleyball W. **Intramural:** Basketball, cricket, football (non-tackle), racquetball, soccer, softball, swimming, table tennis, volleyball. **Team name:** Chargers.

**Student services.** Career counseling, student employment services, financial aid counseling, health services, minority student services, personal counseling, placement for graduates, veterans' counselor, women's services. **Physically disabled:** Services for visually, speech, hearing impaired.

**Contact.** E-mail: adminfo@newhaven.edu
Phone: (203) 932-7319 Toll-free number: (800) 342-5864
Fax: (203) 931-6093
Jane Sangeloty, Director of Undergraduate Admissions, University of New Haven, 300 Boston Post Road, West Haven, CT 06516

## Wesleyan University
**Middletown, Connecticut**
**www.wesleyan.edu**

**CB member**
**CB code: 3959**

- Private 4-year university and liberal arts college
- Residential campus in large town
- 2,787 degree-seeking undergraduates: 50% women, 7% African American, 11% Asian American, 8% Hispanic American, 1% Native American, 6% international
- 293 degree-seeking graduate students
- 27% of applicants admitted
- SAT and SAT Subject Tests or ACT (ACT writing recommended), application essay required
- 93% graduate within 6 years

**General.** Founded in 1831. Regionally accredited. **Degrees:** 735 bachelor's awarded; master's, doctoral offered. **ROTC:** Air Force. **Location:** 15 miles from Hartford, 25 miles from New Haven. **Calendar:** Semester, limited summer session. **Full-time faculty:** 325 total; 92% have terminal degrees, 15% minority, 40% women. **Part-time faculty:** 34 total; 41% have terminal degrees, 26% minority, 53% women. **Class size:** 63% < 20, 29% 20-39, 3% 40-49, 4% 50-99, less than 1% >100. **Special facilities:** 11-building arts center, observatory, science center with electron microscopes and nuclear magnetic resonance spectrometers, film studies center, center for humanities, East Asian studies center, African-American studies center.

**Freshman class profile.** 7,750 applied, 2,123 admitted, 733 enrolled.

| Mid 50% test scores | | | |
|---|---|---|---|
| | | GPA 2.0-2.99: | 2% |
| SAT critical reading: | 650-750 | Rank in top quarter: | 93% |
| SAT math: | 650-740 | Rank in top tenth: | 71% |
| SAT writing: | 650-740 | Return as sophomores: | 94% |
| ACT composite: | 27-32 | Out-of-state: | 92% |
| GPA 3.50 or higher: | 83% | Live on campus: | 100% |
| GPA 3.0-3.49: | 15% | International: | 7% |

**Basis for selection.** High school transcript, class rank, test scores, extracurricular activities, 2 teacher evaluations, personal statement, and other evidence of outstanding accomplishments are considered. 2 SAT Subject Test scores required with SAT score. Interview recommended. **Homeschooled:** Campus interview, statement describing home school structure and mission, transcript of courses and grades, third-party recommendation, and home-school instructor recommendation strongly recommended. Financial aid applicants should be prepared to submit GED.

**High school preparation.** 16 units required; 20 recommended. Required and recommended units include English 4, mathematics 4, social studies 3-4, science 4 (laboratory 3) and foreign language 3-4.

**2007-2008 Annual costs.** Tuition/fees: $37,106. Room/board: $10,130. Books/supplies: $1,155. Personal expenses: $1,155.

**2006-2007 Financial aid.** All financial aid based on need. 397 full-time freshmen applied for aid; 317 were judged to have need; 317 of these received aid. Average need met was 100%. Average scholarship/grant was $26,366; average loan $2,968. 75% of total undergraduate aid awarded as scholarships/grants, 25% as loans/jobs.

**Application procedures. Admission:** Closing date 1/1 (postmark date). $55 fee, may be waived for applicants with need. Application may be submitted online. Admission notification 4/1. Must reply by May 1 or within 2 week(s) if notified thereafter. **Financial aid:** Closing date 2/15. FAFSA, CSS PROFILE required. Applicants notified by 4/1; must reply by 5/1.

**Academics.** Students expected to complete 3 classes in each of following areas before graduation: natural sciences and mathematics, arts and humanities, social and behavioral sciences. **Special study options:** Combined bachelor's/graduate degree, cross-registration, double major, dual enrollment of high school students, exchange student, honors, independent study, semester at sea, student-designed major, study abroad, urban semester, Washington semester. 12-college exchange, semester in environmental science at the Marine Biological Laboratory-Woods Hole, Wesleyan-Trinity-Connecticut College Consortium, 3-2 program in science and engineering, teaching apprentice program. **Credit/placement by examination:** AP, CLEP, IB, institutional tests. 2 credit hours maximum toward bachelor's degree. **Support services:** Reduced course load, tutoring, writing center.

**Majors. Area/ethnic studies:** African-American, American, Central/Eastern European, East Asian, French, gay/lesbian, German, Latin American, Russian/Slavic. **Biology:** General, biochemistry, molecular, molecular biochemistry. **Computer sciences:** General. **Conservation:** Environmental science. **English:** English lit. **Foreign languages:** Chinese, classics, East Asian, French, German, Italian, Japanese, Romance, Russian, Spanish. **History:** General. **Interdisciplinary:** Ancient studies, medieval/Renaissance, neuroscience, science/society. **Liberal arts:** Arts/sciences. **Math:** General. **Philosophy/religion:** Philosophy, religion. **Physical sciences:** Astronomy, chemistry, geology, physics, planetary. **Psychology:** General. **Social sciences:** Anthropology, archaeology, economics, political science, sociology. **Visual/performing arts:** Art history/conservation, dance, dramatic, film/cinema, studio arts.

**Most popular majors.** Area/ethnic studies 13%, English 11%, history 6%, psychology 12%, social sciences 25%, visual/performing arts 12%.

**Computing on campus.** 300 workstations in library, computer center, student center. Dormitories wired for high-speed internet access and linked to campus network. Commuter students can connect to campus network. Online course registration, online library, helpline, repair service, student web hosting, wireless network available.

**Student life. Freshman orientation:** Mandatory. Preregistration for classes offered. Begins one week before start of fall classes. **Housing:** Guaranteed on-campus for all undergraduates. Coed dorms, special housing for disabled, apartments, fraternity/sorority housing, substance-free housing available. 17 residence halls, 25 program houses, 122 woodframe houses. **Activities:** Bands, campus ministries, choral groups, dance, drama, film society, literary magazine, music ensembles, musical theater, radio station, student government, student newspaper, symphony orchestra, more than 230 organizations.

**Athletics.** NCAA. **Intercollegiate:** Baseball M, basketball, cross-country, diving, field hockey W, football (tackle) M, golf M, ice hockey, lacrosse, rowing (crew), soccer, softball W, squash, swimming, tennis, track and field, volleyball W, wrestling M. **Intramural:** Basketball, ice hockey M, soccer, softball, squash, volleyball. **Team name:** Cardinals.

**Student services.** Adult student services, alcohol/substance abuse counseling, campus ministries, career counseling, student employment services, financial aid counseling, health services, minority student services, on-campus daycare, personal counseling, placement for graduates, women's services. **Physically disabled:** Services for visually, speech, hearing impaired.

**Contact.** E-mail: admissions@wesleyan.edu
Phone: (860) 685-3000 Fax: (860) 685-3001
Nancy Meislahn, Dean of Admission and Financial Aid, Wesleyan University, 70 Wyllys Avenue, Middletown, CT 06459-0260

---

## Western Connecticut State University
**Danbury, Connecticut**
www.wcsu.edu                                    CB code: 3350

- Public 4-year university
- Commuter campus in small city
- 5,092 degree-seeking undergraduates: 14% part-time, 55% women, 7% African American, 3% Asian American, 7% Hispanic American
- 573 degree-seeking graduate students
- 58% of applicants admitted
- SAT or ACT with writing required
- 37% graduate within 6 years

**General.** Founded in 1903. Regionally accredited. **Degrees:** 717 bachelor's, 10 associate awarded; master's offered. **ROTC:** Army, Air Force. **Location:** 65 miles from New York City, 50 miles from Hartford. **Calendar:** Semester, extensive summer session. **Full-time faculty:** 212 total; 75% have terminal degrees, 13% minority, 44% women. **Part-time faculty:** 316 total; 4% minority, 42% women. **Class size:** 32% < 20, 62% 20-39, 6% 40-49, less than 1% 50-99. **Special facilities:** Weather station, observatory, nature preserve.

**Freshman class profile.** 4,345 applied, 2,512 admitted, 934 enrolled.

| Mid 50% test scores | | | |
|---|---|---|---|
| SAT critical reading: | 430-540 | Rank in top tenth: | 6% |
| SAT math: | 440-530 | End year in good standing: | 85% |
| SAT writing: | 430-530 | Return as sophomores: | 73% |
| GPA 3.50 or higher: | 13% | Out-of-state: | 10% |
| GPA 3.0-3.49: | 50% | Live on campus: | 55% |
| GPA 2.0-2.99: | 25% | Fraternities: | 8% |
| Rank in top quarter: | 21% | Sororities: | 7% |

**Basis for selection.** Limited freshman class spaces given to students with strongest academic and extracurricular backgrounds, including test results. Essay and interview recommended. Audition required of music majors. Portfolio recommended of graphic design majors. **Homeschooled:** Transcript of courses and grades required. **Learning Disabled:** To receive services or accommodations, students must provide appropriate documentation by contacting the coordinator of disability services.

**High school preparation.** 13 units required. Required and recommended units include English 4, mathematics 3, social studies 1, history 1, science 2 (laboratory 2) and foreign language 2-3. Additional credits in fine arts and computer science recommended. Academic course work in computer science, visual arts, theater, music or dance may be substituted for one of the areas cited above.

**2007-2008 Annual costs.** Tuition/fees: $6,624; $15,344 out-of-state. Room/board: $8,400. Books/supplies: $1,000. Personal expenses: $1,750.

**2007-2008 Financial aid. Need-based:** 671 full-time freshmen applied for aid; 476 were judged to have need; 460 of these received aid. Average need met was 63%. Average scholarship/grant was $2,639; average loan $2,009. 34% of total undergraduate aid awarded as scholarships/grants, 66% as loans/jobs. **Non-need-based:** Awarded to 292 full-time undergraduates, including 92 freshmen. Scholarships awarded for academics.

**Application procedures. Admission:** Priority date 4/1; no deadline. $50 fee, may be waived for applicants with need. Application may be submitted online. Admission notification on a rolling basis beginning on or about 12/1. Must reply by May 1 or within 2 week(s) if notified thereafter. **Financial aid:** Priority date 3/15, closing date 4/15. FAFSA, institutional form required. Applicants notified on a rolling basis starting 3/15; must reply by 5/1 or within 2 week(s) of notification.

**Academics. Special study options:** Accelerated study, cooperative education, cross-registration, distance learning, double major, dual enrollment of high school students, ESL, honors, independent study, internships, student-designed major, study abroad, teacher certification program. Honors Interdisciplinary Bachelor's Degree: a special kind of honors contract major for the highly motivated student to pursue a specialized course of study that examines, in depth, a single theme or idea from the perspective of two or more disciplines. **Credit/placement by examination:** AP, CLEP, IB, SAT, institutional tests. 30 credit hours maximum toward associate degree, 60 toward bachelor's. **Support services:** Learning center, pre-admission summer program, reduced course load, remedial instruction, study skills assistance, tutoring, writing center.

**Majors. Area/ethnic studies:** American. **Biology:** General. **Business:** Accounting, business admin, finance, management information systems, marketing. **Communications:** General. **Computer sciences:** General. **Education:** Elementary, health, music, secondary. **English:** Composition, English lit. **Foreign languages:** Spanish. **Health:** Clinical lab science, community health services, nursing (RN). **History:** General. **Liberal arts:** Arts/sciences. **Math:** General. **Physical sciences:** Atmospheric science, chemistry, geology. **Protective services:** Police science. **Psychology:** General. **Public administration:** Social work. **Social sciences:** General, economics, political science, sociology. **Visual/performing arts:** Art, dramatic, music theory/composition.

**Most popular majors.** Business/marketing 23%, communications/journalism 8%, education 10%, health sciences 6%, psychology 7%, security/protective services 9%, visual/performing arts 7%.

**Computing on campus.** 928 workstations in dormitories, library, computer center, student center. Dormitories wired for high-speed internet access and linked to campus network. Commuter students can connect to campus network. Online course registration, online library, student web hosting, wireless network available.

**Student life. Freshman orientation:** Available. Preregistration for classes offered. 2-day program for students and parents held the weekend before classes start. **Housing:** Guaranteed on-campus for all undergraduates. Coed dorms, single-sex dorms, apartments available. $250 nonrefundable deposit. **Activities:** Bands, campus ministries, choral groups, dance, drama, international student organizations, literary magazine, music ensembles, musical theater, opera, radio station, student government, student newspaper, symphony orchestra, black student alliance, nontraditional student, Habitat for Humanity, Latin American student organizations.

**Athletics.** NCAA. **Intercollegiate:** Baseball M, basketball, field hockey W, football (tackle) M, lacrosse, soccer, softball W, swimming W, tennis, volleyball W. **Intramural:** Basketball M, football (non-tackle) M. **Team name:** Colonials.

**Student services.** Adult student services, alcohol/substance abuse counseling, campus ministries, career counseling, student employment services, financial aid counseling, health services, minority student services, on-campus daycare, personal counseling, placement for graduates, veterans' counselor. **Physically disabled:** Services for visually, speech, hearing impaired.

**Contact.** E-mail: admissions@wcsu.edu
Phone: (203) 837-9000 Toll-free number: (877) 837-9278
Fax: (203) 837-8338
William Hawkins, Enrollment Management Officer, Western Connecticut State University, 181 White Street, Danbury, CT 06810

## Yale University
**New Haven, Connecticut**
www.yale.edu

**CB member**
**CB code: 3987**

- Private 4-year university
- Residential campus in small city
- 5,291 degree-seeking undergraduates: 49% women, 9% African American, 14% Asian American, 8% Hispanic American, 1% Native American, 8% international
- 6,012 degree-seeking graduate students
- 10% of applicants admitted
- SAT and SAT Subject Tests or ACT with writing, application essay required
- 96% graduate within 6 years; 27% enter graduate study

**General.** Founded in 1701. Regionally accredited. **Degrees:** 1,371 bachelor's awarded; master's, doctoral, first professional offered. **ROTC:** Army, Air Force. **Location:** 75 miles from New York City. **Calendar:** Semester, limited summer session. **Full-time faculty:** 1,121 total; 90% have terminal degrees, 18% minority, 32% women. **Part-time faculty:** 438 total; 74% have terminal degrees, 10% minority, 40% women. **Special facilities:** Natural history museum, clean room, wind tunnel, engine testing facility, graphic workstations, robotics labs, crystal growth, nuclear accelerators, nuclear magnetic resonance spectrometers, optical spectroscopy instruments, high-resolution mass spectrometer, x-ray diffraction instruments, electron microscopes, observatories, marine studies field station, Institute for Biospheric Studies, 10,000 acres of forest.

**Freshman class profile.** 19,323 applied, 1,911 admitted, 1,320 enrolled.

| Mid 50% test scores | | | |
|---|---|---|---|
| SAT critical reading: | 700-800 | Return as sophomores: | 99% |
| SAT math: | 700-790 | Out-of-state: | 94% |
| SAT writing: | 700-790 | Live on campus: | 100% |
| ACT composite: | 30-34 | International: | 9% |

**Basis for selection.** First criterion is evidence of ability to do successful academic work. Diversity of interests, background and special talents also sought. Successful candidates usually have done honors work at secondary level, have high SAT scores, and present high degree of accomplishment in one or more nonacademic areas. Interview recommended. **Homeschooled:** Require 2 recommendations from teachers of courses taken outside home, such as community college courses.

**High school preparation.** Students recommended to take richest possible mix of demanding academic offerings.

**2007-2008 Annual costs.** Tuition/fees: $34,530. Room/board: $10,470. Books/supplies: $2,520.

**Financial aid.** All financial aid based on need. **Additional information:** All scholarships based on demonstrated need.

**Application procedures. Admission:** Closing date 12/31 (postmark date). $75 fee, may be waived for applicants with need. Application may be submitted online. Admission notification 4/1. Must reply by 5/1. **Financial aid:** Closing date 3/1. FAFSA, CSS PROFILE required. Applicants notified by 4/1; must reply by 5/1 or within 1 week(s) of notification.

**Academics. Special study options:** Accelerated study, combined bachelor's/graduate degree, double major, ESL, honors, independent study, internships, liberal arts/career combination, student-designed major, study abroad, teacher certification program. **Credit/placement by examination:** AP, CLEP, IB, institutional tests. **Support services:** Study skills assistance, tutoring, writing center.

**Majors. Architecture:** Architecture. **Area/ethnic studies:** African, African-American, American, East Asian, European, Latin American, Russian/Slavic, women's. **Biology:** General, biochemistry, Biochemistry/biophysics and molecular biology, molecular. **Computer sciences:** General. **Engineering:** Biomedical, chemical, electrical, environmental, mechanical, physics, science. **English:** English lit. **Foreign languages:** Ancient Greek, Biblical, Chinese, classics, French, German, Italian, Japanese, Latin, linguistics, Portuguese, Russian, Spanish. **History:** General, science/technology. **Interdisciplinary:** Ancient studies, cognitive science, math/computer science, medieval/Renaissance. **Liberal arts:** Humanities. **Math:** General, applied. **Philosophy/religion:** Judaic, philosophy, religion. **Physical sciences:** Astronomy, astrophysics, chemistry, geology, physics. **Psychology:** General. **Social sciences:** Anthropology, archaeology, economics, political science, sociology. **Visual/performing arts:** Art, art history/conservation, dramatic, film/cinema.

**Most popular majors.** Biology 8%, English 9%, history 14%, interdisciplinary studies 8%, social sciences 26%, visual/performing arts 6%.

**Computing on campus.** 400 workstations in dormitories, library, computer center, student center. Dormitories wired for high-speed internet access and linked to campus network. Commuter students can connect to campus network. Online course registration, online library, helpline, student web hosting, wireless network available.

**Student life. Freshman orientation:** Mandatory. **Housing:** Guaranteed on-campus for freshmen. Coed dorms, special housing for disabled available. **Activities:** Bands, choral groups, dance, drama, film society, literary magazine, music ensembles, musical theater, opera, radio station, student government, student newspaper, symphony orchestra, TV station, over 135 organizations available.

**Athletics.** NCAA. **Intercollegiate:** Baseball M, basketball, cross-country, diving, fencing, field hockey W, football (tackle) M, golf, gymnastics W, ice hockey, lacrosse, rowing (crew), soccer, softball W, squash, swimming, tennis, track and field, volleyball W. **Intramural:** Baseball M, basketball, bowling, cross-country, field hockey W, football (tackle) M, golf, ice hockey, racquetball, rowing (crew), soccer, softball, squash, swimming, table tennis, tennis, volleyball, water polo, wrestling M. **Team name:** Bulldogs.

**Student services.** Alcohol/substance abuse counseling, campus ministries, career counseling, student employment services, financial aid counseling, health services, minority student services, personal counseling, placement for graduates, women's services. **Physically disabled:** Services for visually, speech, hearing impaired.

**Contact.** E-mail: undergraduate.admissions@yale.edu
Phone: (203) 432-9300 Fax: (203) 432-9392
Margit Dahl, Director of Undergraduate Admissions, Yale University, Box 208234, New Haven, CT 06520-8234

# Delaware

## Delaware State University
**Dover, Delaware**
www.desu.edu

**CB member**
**CB code: 5153**

▶ Public 4-year university
▶ Residential campus in large town
▶ 3,374 degree-seeking undergraduates: 11% part-time, 59% women, 77% African American, 1% Asian American, 2% Hispanic American
▶ 382 degree-seeking graduate students
▶ 43% of applicants admitted
▶ SAT or ACT (ACT writing optional) required
▶ 38% graduate within 6 years

**General.** Founded in 1891. Regionally accredited. University has its own fleet of planes. **Degrees:** 404 bachelor's awarded; master's, doctoral offered. **ROTC:** Army, Air Force. **Location:** 46 miles from Wilmington, 100 miles from Washington, DC. **Calendar:** Semester, extensive summer session. **Full-time faculty:** 182 total; 90% have terminal degrees, 38% minority, 37% women. **Part-time faculty:** 154 total; 47% minority, 51% women. **Class size:** 53% < 20, 38% 20-39, 7% 40-49, 2% 50-99. **Special facilities:** Science center, observatory, herbarium.

**Freshman class profile.** 6,503 applied, 2,781 admitted, 806 enrolled.

| Mid 50% test scores | | GPA 2.0-2.99: | 68% |
|---|---|---|---|
| SAT critical reading: | 390-470 | Rank in top quarter: | 17% |
| SAT math: | 380-470 | Rank in top tenth: | 2% |
| ACT composite: | 15-20 | Return as sophomores: | 64% |
| GPA 3.50 or higher: | 10% | Out-of-state: | 77% |
| GPA 3.0-3.49: | 18% | Live on campus: | 88% |

**Basis for selection.** High school curriculum and GPA most important. Test scores only used in conjunction with GPA. Class rank considered. Interviews upon invitation; band students audition for scholarships.

**High school preparation.** 16 units required. Required units include English 4, mathematics 3, social studies 2, science 3 (laboratory 3) and academic electives 4. Math units must include 2 algebra and 1 geometry course.

**2007-2008 Annual costs.** Tuition/fees: $6,146; $13,100 out-of-state. Room/board: $9,006. Books/supplies: $1,500. Personal expenses: $2,000.

**2006-2007 Financial aid.** All financial aid based on need. 760 full-time freshmen applied for aid; 682 were judged to have need; 659 of these received aid. Average need met was 58%. Average scholarship/grant was $2,445; average loan $2,945. 49% of total undergraduate aid awarded as scholarships/grants, 51% as loans/jobs. **Additional information:** Students must file FAFSA by March 17 every year.

**Application procedures. Admission:** Priority date 4/1; no deadline. $25 fee, may be waived for applicants with need. Application may be submitted online. Admission notification on a rolling basis beginning on or about 9/1. **Financial aid:** Priority date 3/1, closing date 7/1. FAFSA required. Applicants notified on a rolling basis starting 4/1; must reply by 8/20.

**Academics. Special study options:** Accelerated study, combined bachelor's/graduate degree, cooperative education, distance learning, double major, dual enrollment of high school students, ESL, exchange student, honors, independent study, internships, semester at sea, study abroad, teacher certification program, weekend college. **Credit/placement by examination:** AP, CLEP, institutional tests. 30 credit hours maximum toward bachelor's degree. **Support services:** Learning center, pre-admission summer program, reduced course load, remedial instruction, study skills assistance, tutoring, writing center.

**Majors. Agriculture:** General, business, plant sciences, soil science. **Biology:** General. **Business:** Accounting, business admin, finance, hospitality admin, nonprofit/public. **Communications:** Media studies. **Computer sciences:** Computer science, data processing. **Conservation:** Fisheries, management/policy, wildlife. **Education:** General, art, biology, business, chemistry, early childhood, elementary, English, French, gifted/talented, health, mathematics, middle, music, physical, physics, science, Spanish, special, trade/industrial. **Engineering:** Aerospace, electrical, geotechnical. **Engineering technology:** Architectural, civil, drafting, electrical, electromechanical, industrial, mechanical. **English:** Composition, English lit. **Family/**

**consumer sciences:** Clothing/textiles, consumer economics, food/nutrition. **Foreign languages:** French, German, Spanish. **Health:** Nursing (RN), prenursing, preveterinary. **History:** General. **Interdisciplinary:** Historic preservation, math/computer science. **Math:** General. **Parks/recreation:** Health/fitness, sports admin. **Philosophy/religion:** Philosophy. **Physical sciences:** Chemistry, forensic chemistry, physics. **Protective services:** Criminal justice, fire safety technology. **Psychology:** General. **Public administration:** Social work. **Science technology:** Biological. **Social sciences:** Criminology, political science, sociology, urban studies. **Transportation:** Aviation, aviation management. **Visual/performing arts:** General, arts management, studio arts. **Other:** Chemical lab technology, Engineering design, Fitness promotions, Natural resources technology, Physics pre-engineering, Political science business administration.

**Most popular majors.** Biology 6%, business/marketing 20%, communications/journalism 10%, education 7%, health sciences 7%, psychology 9%, public administration/social services 10%, social sciences 10%.

**Computing on campus.** 361 workstations in library, computer center, student center. Dormitories wired for high-speed internet access and linked to campus network. Online course registration, online library, helpline, repair service available.

**Student life. Freshman orientation:** Mandatory, $125 fee. Two-day program during June, July and August. **Policies:** First-time, first-year freshmen must submit written request for parking permit. **Housing:** Guaranteed on-campus for freshmen. Coed dorms, single-sex dorms, special housing for disabled, apartments, substance-free housing available. $200 nonrefundable deposit, deadline 4/15. Suite style accommodations available for upper class students and honor students; residence hall available for honors students. **Activities:** Bands, campus ministries, choral groups, dance, drama, international student organizations, music ensembles, musical theater, radio station, student government, student newspaper, TV station, Wesley Foundation, commuters club, NAACP, black studies club, student government association, honor societies, Greek letter organizations, student ambassadors.

**Athletics.** NCAA. **Intercollegiate:** Baseball M, basketball, bowling W, cross-country, equestrian W, football (non-tackle) M, football (tackle) M, soccer W, softball W, tennis, track and field, volleyball W, wrestling M. **Intramural:** Basketball, bowling, rugby, soccer, softball, swimming, table tennis, tennis, track and field, volleyball. **Team name:** Hornets.

**Student services.** Adult student services, alcohol/substance abuse counseling, campus ministries, career counseling, health services, on-campus daycare, personal counseling, placement for graduates, veterans' counselor. **Physically disabled:** Services for visually, speech, hearing impaired.

**Contact.** E-mail: admissions@desu.edu
Phone: (302) 857-6351 Toll-free number: (800) 845-2544
Fax: (302) 857-6352
L. Germaine Scott-Cheatham, Director of Admissions, Delaware State University, 1200 North DuPont Highway, Dover, DE 19901

## Goldey-Beacom College
**Wilmington, Delaware**
www.gbc.edu

**CB member**
**CB code: 5255**

▶ Private 4-year business college
▶ Commuter campus in small city
▶ 874 degree-seeking undergraduates: 31% part-time, 54% women
▶ 334 degree-seeking graduate students
▶ SAT required

**General.** Founded in 1886. Regionally accredited. **Degrees:** 171 bachelor's, 26 associate awarded; master's offered. **Location:** 15 miles from Wilmington, 36 miles from Philadelphia. **Calendar:** Semester, extensive summer session. **Full-time faculty:** 20 total. **Part-time faculty:** 32 total. **Class size:** 33% < 20, 67% 20-39. **Special facilities:** Non-denominational chapel, athletic facilities and fields, fitness center, computer lab.

**Freshman class profile.**

| Out-of-state: | 60% | Live on campus: | 33% |
|---|---|---|---|

**Basis for selection.** Bachelor degree candidates must submit SAT scores and official transcripts from high school(s) and or college(s) attended. High school performance is evaluated. When necessary, interviews are requested. Interview recommended. **Homeschooled:** Statement describing home-school structure and mission, transcript of courses and grades, state high school equivalency certificate, interview required. **Learning Disabled:** Evaluation of diability and submission of documentation regarding disability.

**High school preparation.** 16 units recommended. Recommended units include English 4, mathematics 3 and science 3. 3 math units required for bachelor's degree applicants.

**2008-2009 Annual costs.** Tuition/fees: $16,980. Room only: $4,982. Books/supplies: $800. Personal expenses: $1,068.

**2007-2008 Financial aid.** All financial aid based on need. **Additional information:** Essays required for scholarship applicants.

**Application procedures. Admission:** No deadline. $30 fee, may be waived for applicants with need. Application may be submitted online. Admission notification on a rolling basis. SAT not required but recommended for associate degree applicants for placement and counseling. **Financial aid:** Priority date 4/1; no closing date. FAFSA required. Applicants notified on a rolling basis starting 2/15; must reply within 2 week(s) of notification.

**Academics. Special study options:** Accelerated study, combined bachelor's/graduate degree, cooperative education, cross-registration, double major, honors, independent study, internships, liberal arts/career combination, study abroad. **Credit/placement by examination:** AP, CLEP, IB, SAT, ACT, institutional tests. **Support services:** Learning center, reduced course load, remedial instruction, study skills assistance, tutoring, writing center.

**Majors. Business:** General, accounting, business admin, international, management information systems, management science, marketing. **Computer sciences:** General.

**Most popular majors.** Business/marketing 89%, computer/information sciences 11%.

**Computing on campus.** 200 workstations in dormitories, library, computer center, student center. Dormitories wired for high-speed internet access and linked to campus network. Commuter students can connect to campus network. Online library, wireless network available.

**Student life. Freshman orientation:** Available. Preregistration for classes offered. **Housing:** Guaranteed on-campus for all undergraduates. Coed dorms, special housing for disabled, apartments, fraternity/sorority housing, substance-free housing available. $400 fully refundable deposit, deadline 4/29. Apartment-style residence halls. **Activities:** Choral groups, drama, student government, student newspaper, Christian Fellowship, minority student union, Circle-K, international student association.

**Athletics.** NAIA, NCAA. **Intercollegiate:** Basketball, cross-country, golf M, soccer, softball W, tennis W, track and field, volleyball W. **Intramural:** Baseball M, basketball, soccer, softball W, volleyball. **Team name:** Lightning.

**Student services.** Career counseling, student employment services, financial aid counseling, health services, personal counseling, placement for graduates. **Physically disabled:** Services for visually, speech, hearing impaired.

**Contact.** E-mail: admissions@gbc.edu
Phone: (302) 225-6248 Toll-free number: (302) 225-6248
Fax: (302) 996-5408
Larry Eby, Goldey-Beacom College, 4701 Limestone Road, Wilmington, DE 19808

---

## University of Delaware
**Newark, Delaware**  
**www.udel.edu**  
**CB member**  
**CB code: 5811**

- Public 4-year university
- Residential campus in large town
- 15,318 degree-seeking undergraduates: 5% part-time, 58% women, 5% African American, 4% Asian American, 5% Hispanic American, 1% international
- 3,302 degree-seeking graduate students
- 56% of applicants admitted
- SAT or ACT with writing, application essay required
- 78% graduate within 6 years

**General.** Founded in 1743. Regionally accredited. **Degrees:** 3,416 bachelor's, 162 associate awarded; master's, doctoral offered. **ROTC:** Army, Air Force. **Location:** 12 miles from Wilmington, 30 miles from Philadelphia. **Calendar:** 4-1-4, limited summer session. **Full-time faculty:** 1,167 total; 84% have terminal degrees, 16% minority, 39% women. **Part-time faculty:** 252 total; 40% have terminal degrees, 12% minority, 48% women. **Class size:** 43% < 20, 38% 20-39, 6% 40-49, 10% 50-99, 4% >100. **Special facilities:** Science development center, human performance laboratory, greenhouse, preschool lab, nutrition clinic, engineering research centers, 400-acre

agriculture research complex, center for composites manufacturing and research, apparel design laboratory, simulated hospital rooms for nursing, physical therapy clinic, applied coastal research, Delaware biotechnology institute.

**Freshman class profile.** 20,615 applied, 11,452 admitted, 3,597 enrolled.

| Mid 50% test scores | | | |
|---|---|---|---|
| SAT critical reading: | 540-640 | GPA 2.0-2.99: | 9% |
| SAT math: | 560-670 | Rank in top quarter: | 80% |
| SAT writing: | 540-650 | Rank in top tenth: | 41% |
| ACT composite: | 23-27 | Return as sophomores: | 90% |
| GPA 3.50 or higher: | 62% | Out-of-state: | 70% |
| GPA 3.0-3.49: | 29% | Live on campus: | 91% |
| | | International: | 1% |

**Basis for selection.** High school record, program of study, test scores most important. References, essay, extracurricular accomplishments considered. SAT Subject Tests recommended. Particularly recommended that honors program applicants take SAT Subject Tests. Audition or portfolio required for music or art. **Homeschooled:** Transcript of courses and grades required. Students should provide reading lists for courses they have completed. Sample portfolio of work or sample research paper recommended. Applicants should submit at least 2 SAT Subject Tests of their choice. In lieu of SAT Reasoning Test and SAT Subject Tests, students may submit ACT with Writing score.

**High school preparation.** 18 units required; 22 recommended. Required and recommended units include English 4, mathematics 3-4, social studies 2, history 2, science 3-4 (laboratory 2-3), foreign language 2-4 and academic electives 2. 4 math strongly recommended for engineering, business, science or math applicants. 4 laboratory science strongly recommended for science, nursing, and engineering applicants.

**2007-2008 Annual costs.** Tuition/fees: $8,150; $19,400 out-of-state. Room/board: $7,948. Books/supplies: $800. Personal expenses: $1,500.

**2006-2007 Financial aid.** All financial aid based on need. 2,888 full-time freshmen applied for aid; 1,596 were judged to have need; 1,563 of these received aid. Average need met was 79%. Average scholarship/grant was $5,947; average loan $5,117. 44% of total undergraduate aid awarded as scholarships/grants, 56% as loans/jobs. **Additional information:** December 15 application deadline to receive scholarship consideration. Sibling/parent tuition credit plan. Senior citizen tuition credit for state residents over 60.

**Application procedures. Admission:** Priority date 12/1; deadline 1/15 (postmark date). $70 fee, may be waived for applicants with need. Application may be submitted online. Admission notification 3/15. Must reply by May 1 or within 3 week(s) if notified thereafter. **Financial aid:** Priority date 2/1, closing date 3/15. FAFSA required. Applicants notified on a rolling basis starting 3/15; must reply by 5/1 or within 3 week(s) of notification.

**Academics. Special study options:** Accelerated study, cooperative education, distance learning, double major, dual enrollment of high school students, ESL, honors, independent study, internships, liberal arts/career combination, student-designed major, study abroad, teacher certification program, Washington semester. Research program, minors in 68 disciplines, five-year engineering/liberal arts option. **Credit/placement by examination:** AP, CLEP, IB, SAT, institutional tests. For credit/placement to be awarded for International Baccalaureate, applicant must have taken higher level courses and have minimum score of 4 on exams. **Support services:** Pre-admission summer program, reduced course load, remedial instruction, study skills assistance, tutoring, writing center.

**Honors college/program.** Program emphasizes small classes, undergraduate research, honors housing, special scholarship opportunities. Special application required.

**Majors. Agriculture:** Agribusiness operations, agronomy, animal sciences, business, economics, food science, ornamental horticulture, plant sciences, soil science. **Area/ethnic studies:** Latin American, women's. **Biology:** General, biochemistry, biotechnology, entomology, plant pathology. **Business:** Accounting, business admin, fashion, finance, management information systems, operations. **Communications:** General, journalism. **Computer sciences:** General. **Conservation:** General, management/policy, wildlife. **Education:** General, agricultural, biology, chemistry, early childhood, elementary, English, ESL, family/consumer sciences, foreign languages, French, geography, German, health, history, mathematics, middle, music, physical, physics, psychology, science, secondary, social science, Spanish, special. **Engineering:** Aerospace, agricultural, biomedical, chemical, civil, computer, electrical, environmental, mechanical, operations research. **English:** English lit. **Family/consumer sciences:** General, child care, family studies, family/community services, food/nutrition. **Foreign languages:** General, Biblical, classics, comparative lit, French, German, Italian, Latin, Russian, Spanish. **Health:** Athletic training, clinical lab science, clinical lab technology, nursing (RN), predental, premedicine, prepharmacy, preveterinary. **History:**

General. **Interdisciplinary:** Historic preservation, nutrition sciences. **Legal studies:** Prelaw. **Liberal arts:** Arts/sciences. **Math:** General, statistics. **Parks/recreation:** Exercise sciences, facilities management, health/fitness, sports admin. **Philosophy/religion:** Philosophy. **Physical sciences:** Astronomy, chemistry, geology, geophysics, physics, planetary. **Protective services:** Criminal justice. **Psychology:** General. **Social sciences:** Anthropology, economics, geography, international relations, political science, sociology. **Visual/performing arts:** Art, art history/conservation, commercial/advertising art, fashion design, music performance, music theory/composition, piano/organ, studio arts, theater design, theater history, voice/opera.

**Most popular majors.** Biology 6%, business/marketing 19%, education 10%, engineering/engineering technologies 8%, English 6%, health sciences 6%, social sciences 13%.

**Computing on campus.** 900 workstations in dormitories, library, computer center. Dormitories wired for high-speed internet access and linked to campus network. Commuter students can connect to campus network. Online course registration, online library, helpline, repair service, student web hosting, wireless network available.

**Student life. Freshman orientation:** Mandatory, $65 fee. Preregistration for classes offered. One-day summer program, plus 3-day program before start of classes. **Housing:** Guaranteed on-campus for all undergraduates. Coed dorms, single-sex dorms, special housing for disabled, apartments, fraternity/sorority housing, substance-free housing available. $200 partly refundable deposit, deadline 5/1. Special interest housing including language houses, humanities house, honors hall, music house, international house, farmhouse, and education house available. **Activities:** Bands, campus ministries, choral groups, dance, drama, film society, international student organizations, literary magazine, music ensembles, musical theater, opera, radio station, student government, student newspaper, symphony orchestra, TV station, Black student union; Asian student association; Cosmopolitan Club; Hillel; Hispanic student association; Indian student association; lesbian, gay, bisexual student union; returning adult student association; honorary academic clubs.

**Athletics.** NCAA. **Intercollegiate:** Baseball M, basketball, cheerleading, cross-country, diving, field hockey W, football (tackle) M, golf M, lacrosse, rowing (crew) W, soccer, softball W, swimming, tennis, track and field, volleyball W. **Intramural:** Badminton, basketball, cross-country, fencing, field hockey W, golf, lacrosse, racquetball, soccer, softball, table tennis, tennis, volleyball, water polo M. **Team name:** Fightin' Blue Hens.

**Student services.** Adult student services, alcohol/substance abuse counseling, campus ministries, career counseling, services for economically disadvantaged, student employment services, financial aid counseling, health services, minority student services, personal counseling, placement for graduates, veterans' counselor, women's services. **Physically disabled:** Services for visually, speech, hearing impaired.

**Contact.** E-mail: admissions@udel.edu
Phone: (302) 831-8123 Fax: (302) 831-6905
Lou Hirsh, Director of Admission, University of Delaware, 116 Hullihen Hall, Newark, DE 19716

## Wesley College
**Dover, Delaware**
www.wesley.edu
CB member
CB code: 5894

- Private 4-year liberal arts college affiliated with United Methodist Church
- Residential campus in large town
- 1,808 degree-seeking undergraduates
- SAT or ACT (ACT writing optional) required

**General.** Founded in 1873. Regionally accredited. **Degrees:** 260 bachelor's, 27 associate awarded; master's offered. **ROTC:** Army. **Location:** 75 miles from Philadelphia, 90 miles from Washington, DC. **Calendar:** Semester, limited summer session. **Full-time faculty:** 71 total. **Part-time faculty:** 91 total. **Class size:** 55% < 20, 43% 20-39, less than 1% 40-49, 1% 50-99.

### Freshman class profile.

| Mid 50% test scores | | | |
|---|---|---|---|
| SAT critical reading: | 400-490 | GPA 2.0-2.99: | 58% |
| SAT math: | 400-500 | Rank in top quarter: | 56% |
| SAT writing: | 390-490 | Rank in top tenth: | 24% |
| GPA 3.50 or higher: | 15% | Out-of-state: | 66% |
| GPA 3.0-3.49: | 27% | Live on campus: | 87% |
| | | Sororities: | 6% |

**Basis for selection.** High school performance most important. Campus interview very important. Extracurricular activities important.

**High school preparation.** 20 units recommended. Recommended units include English 4, mathematics 4, social studies 2, history 2, science 4, foreign language 2 and academic electives 2.

**2007-2008 Annual costs.** Tuition/fees: $17,579. Room/board: $7,800. Books/supplies: $1,000. Personal expenses: $750.

**Financial aid.** All financial aid based on need.

**Application procedures. Admission:** Priority date 4/1; no deadline. $25 fee. Application may be submitted online. Admission notification on a rolling basis. Must reply by May 1 or within 4 week(s) if notified thereafter. **Financial aid:** Priority date 2/1; no closing date. FAFSA, institutional form required. Applicants notified on a rolling basis starting 1/1; must reply within 2 week(s) of notification.

**Academics.** Credit requirement for bachelor's degree varies according to program. **Special study options:** Double major, ESL, exchange student, independent study, internships, liberal arts/career combination, study abroad, teacher certification program. **Credit/placement by examination:** AP, CLEP, institutional tests. 15 credit hours maximum toward associate degree, 33 toward bachelor's. **Support services:** Learning center, reduced course load, remedial instruction, study skills assistance, tutoring, writing center.

**Majors. Area/ethnic studies:** American. **Biology:** General. **Business:** Accounting, business admin, sales/distribution. **Communications:** General. **Conservation:** Environmental studies. **Education:** General, elementary, physical. **English:** English lit. **Health:** Clinical lab science, nursing (RN). **History:** General. **Legal studies:** Paralegal. **Liberal arts:** Arts/sciences. **Parks/recreation:** Health/fitness. **Psychology:** General. **Social sciences:** Economics, political science.

**Most popular majors.** Business/marketing 30%, communications/journalism 7%, education 16%, parks/recreation 6%, psychology 16%, social sciences 8%.

**Computing on campus.** 225 workstations in library. Dormitories wired for high-speed internet access and linked to campus network. Commuter students can connect to campus network. Online course registration, online library, helpline, repair service available.

**Student life. Freshman orientation:** Mandatory. Preregistration for classes offered. **Housing:** Coed dorms, single-sex dorms, apartments, substance-free housing available. $175 fully refundable deposit, deadline 5/1. Floors in coed dorms are single-sex. **Activities:** Jazz band, choral groups, drama, literary magazine, music ensembles, student government, student newspaper, TV station, community action, Christian student associations, student activity board, National Coed Community Service Organization, black student union.

**Athletics.** NCAA. **Intercollegiate:** Baseball M, basketball, cheerleading, cross-country, field hockey W, football (tackle) M, golf, lacrosse, soccer, softball W, tennis, volleyball W. **Intramural:** Basketball, cross-country, soccer M, volleyball. **Team name:** Wolverines.

**Student services.** Campus ministries, career counseling, student employment services, financial aid counseling, health services, personal counseling, placement for graduates. **Physically disabled:** Services for speech impaired.

**Contact.** E-mail: admissions@wesley.edu
Phone: (302) 736-2400 Toll-free number: (800) 937-5398
Fax: (302) 736-2400
William Firman, Director of Admissions, Wesley College, 120 North State Street, Dover, DE 19901-3875

## Wilmington University
**New Castle, Delaware**
www.wilmu.edu
CB member
CB code: 5925

- Private 4-year liberal arts college
- Commuter campus in large town
- 4,638 degree-seeking undergraduates

**General.** Founded in 1967. Regionally accredited. Two 7-week sessions within each trimester in addition to regular trimester sessions and weekend modules. **Degrees:** 900 bachelor's, 63 associate awarded; master's, doctoral offered. **ROTC:** Army, Air Force. **Location:** 7 miles from Wilmington. **Calendar:** Trimester, limited summer session. **Full-time faculty:** 82 total. **Part-time faculty:** 880 total. **Class size:** 76% < 20, 24% 20-39.

**Freshman class profile.** 931 applied, 931 admitted, 442 enrolled.

**Basis for selection.** Open admission. Math and English skills testing required of all freshmen. Interview recommended. **Homeschooled:** GED recommended for nonaccredited programs.

**2008-2009 Annual costs.** Tuition/fees: $8,760. Books/supplies: $1,000. Personal expenses: $165.

**Financial aid. Non-need-based:** Scholarships awarded for academics, athletics.

**Application procedures. Admission:** No deadline. $25 fee, may be waived for applicants with need. Admission notification on a rolling basis. **Financial aid:** Priority date 4/30; no closing date. FAFSA required. Applicants notified on a rolling basis starting 8/5; must reply within 2 week(s) of notification.

**Academics.** Mentoring program for all interested incoming freshmen. **Special study options:** Accelerated study, distance learning, double major, independent study, internships, liberal arts/career combination, teacher certification program, weekend college. **Credit/placement by examination:** AP, CLEP, institutional tests. 15 credit hours maximum toward associate degree, 15 toward bachelor's. **Support services:** Learning center, remedial instruction, tutoring, writing center.

**Majors. Business:** Accounting, finance, human resources, information resources management, marketing. **Computer sciences:** General, programming, web page design. **Education:** Early childhood, elementary. **Engineering technology:** Software. **Health:** Preop/surgical nursing. **Interdisciplinary:** Behavioral sciences. **Legal studies:** Prelaw. **Liberal arts:** Arts/sciences. **Protective services:** Criminal justice. **Psychology:** General. **Transportation:** Aviation, aviation management.

**Most popular majors.** Business/marketing 29%, computer/information sciences 12%, education 13%, liberal arts 18%, psychology 11%, social sciences 10%.

**Computing on campus.** 516 workstations in library, computer center.

**Student life. Freshman orientation:** Available. Videotaped orientation distributed to all new students. Two new student orientations offered in the fall. **Policies:** Adherence to student handbook expected. **Activities:** Student government, professional fraternities/organizations, Sigma Theta Tau Nursing Society, Business Professionals of America, Alpha Delta Chi, criminal justice club.

**Athletics.** NCAA. **Intercollegiate:** Baseball M, basketball, cross-country, golf M, lacrosse W, soccer, softball W, volleyball W. **Team name:** Wildcats.

**Student services.** Career counseling, student employment services, financial aid counseling, placement for graduates.

**Contact.** E-mail: inquire@wilmcoll.edu
Phone: (302) 356-4636 Toll-free number: (877) 967-5464
Fax: (302) 328-5902
Christopher Ferguson, Director of Admissions, Wilmington University, 320 Dupont Highway, New Castle, DE 19720

# District of Columbia

## American University
**Washington, District of Columbia**
www.american.edu

CB member
CB code: 5007

- Private 4-year university affiliated with United Methodist Church
- Residential campus in very large city
- 5,824 degree-seeking undergraduates: 3% part-time, 63% women, 5% African American, 5% Asian American, 5% Hispanic American, 6% international
- 5,227 degree-seeking graduate students
- 53% of applicants admitted
- SAT or ACT with writing, application essay required
- 73% graduate within 6 years

**General.** Founded in 1893. Regionally accredited. **Degrees:** 1,428 bachelor's awarded; master's, doctoral, first professional offered. **ROTC:** Army, Air Force. **Location:** 2 miles from downtown. **Calendar:** Semester, extensive summer session. **Full-time faculty:** 559 total; 94% have terminal degrees, 17% minority, 45% women. **Part-time faculty:** 451 total; 10% minority, 48% women. **Class size:** 46% < 20, 46% 20-39, 5% 40-49, 2% 50-99, less than 1% >100. **Special facilities:** Arts center, museum, theater, spiritual life center.

**Freshman class profile.** 15,847 applied, 8,436 admitted, 1,286 enrolled.

| Mid 50% test scores | | | |
|---|---|---|---|
| SAT critical reading: | 590-690 | GPA 2.0-2.99: | 7% |
| SAT math: | 580-670 | Rank in top quarter: | 83% |
| SAT writing: | 580-690 | Rank in top tenth: | 50% |
| ACT composite: | 25-30 | Return as sophomores: | 86% |
| GPA 3.50 or higher: | 58% | Out-of-state: | 89% |
| GPA 3.0-3.49: | 35% | Live on campus: | 99% |
| | | International: | 4% |

**Basis for selection.** High school record, GPA, test scores, writing sample, recommendations very important. Academic interests and demonstrated time commitments outside classroom of interest. Motivation and seriousness of purpose taken into consideration, often revealed in level and rigor of courses taken. Extracurricular activities, class rank, leadership roles considered. SAT Subject Tests recommended. Interview optional, nonevaluative and informational in scope. Audition/interview required of music and music theater majors. **Homeschooled:** Should submit at least 3 SAT Subject Test scores. **Learning Disabled:** Supplementary application, diagnostic reports, and high school transcript required for freshman learning services program.

**High school preparation.** 16 units required; 18 recommended. Required and recommended units include English 4, mathematics 3-4, social studies 2-4, science 3-4 (laboratory 2), foreign language 2-3 and academic electives 3-4.

**2008-2009 Annual costs.** Tuition/fees: $33,283. Room/board: $12,418. Books/supplies: $600. Personal expenses: $1,300.

**2007-2008 Financial aid.** All financial aid based on need. 944 full-time freshmen applied for aid; 577 were judged to have need; 577 of these received aid. Average need met was 48%. Average scholarship/grant was $13,571; average loan $4,252. 60% of total undergraduate aid awarded as scholarships/grants, 40% as loans/jobs. **Additional information:** Early decision applicants must submit estimated AU institutional financial aid application by 11/15 and a FASFA as soon as possible after Jan 1.

**Application procedures. Admission:** Closing date 1/15 (postmark date). $45 fee, may be waived for applicants with need. Application may be submitted online. Admission notification 4/1. Must reply by May 1 or within 4 week(s) if notified thereafter. **Financial aid:** Closing date 2/15. FAFSA, institutional form required. Applicants notified by 4/1; must reply by 5/1 or within 4 week(s) of notification.

**Academics. Special study options:** Accelerated study, combined bachelor's/graduate degree, cooperative education, cross-registration, double major, exchange student, honors, independent study, internships, student-designed major, study abroad, teacher certification program, Washington semester, weekend college. Study abroad program sends students to 48 different countries on 84 different programs including (but not limited to) programs in Peru, Chile, Brazil, London, Rome, Brussels, Copenhagen, Beijing/Hong Kong, Buenos Aires, Paris, Madrid, Madrid and the Mediterranean, Moscow, Prague, Poland, South Africa, Scotland, Turkey, Italy, Canada, Mexico City and Monterey, and Australia/New Zealand. Also offers other study abroad programs such as Alternative Break Programs and specialized programs in School of International Service, KOGOD School of Business, and Washington College of Law. **Credit/placement by examination:** AP, CLEP, IB, institutional tests. 30 credit hours maximum toward bachelor's degree. Credit awarded for some international high school learning programs such as British A Levels or German Arbitur; Advanced Placement, International Baccalaureate higher level tests only. **Support services:** Learning center, pre-admission summer program, reduced course load, study skills assistance, tutoring, writing center.

**Majors. Area/ethnic studies:** American, French, German, Latin American, Russian/Slavic, women's. **Biology:** General, biochemistry, environmental, marine. **Business:** Accounting, business admin, finance, management information systems. **Communications:** Journalism, media studies, public relations, radio/tv. **Communications technology:** Animation/special effects, recording arts. **Computer sciences:** General, computer graphics, computer science. **Conservation:** Environmental studies. **Education:** Elementary, secondary. **English:** English lit. **Foreign languages:** French, German, Russian, Spanish. **Health:** Predental, premedicine, prenursing, prepharmacy, preveterinary. **History:** General. **Interdisciplinary:** Biological/physical sciences, global studies. **Legal studies:** General, prelaw. **Liberal arts:** Arts/sciences. **Math:** General, applied, statistics. **Parks/recreation:** Health/fitness, sports admin. **Philosophy/religion:** Judaic, philosophy. **Physical sciences:** Acoustics, chemistry, physics. **Protective services:** Criminal justice, police science. **Psychology:** General. **Social sciences:** Anthropology, economics, international relations, political science, sociology. **Visual/performing arts:** General, art, art history/conservation, cinematography, design, dramatic, film/cinema, graphic design, multimedia, music history, music performance, music theory/composition, studio arts.

**Most popular majors.** Business/marketing 17%, communications/journalism 13%, social sciences 41%, visual/performing arts 6%.

**Computing on campus.** 650 workstations in dormitories, library, computer center, student center. Dormitories wired for high-speed internet access and linked to campus network. Commuter students can connect to campus network. Online course registration, online library, helpline, repair service, student web hosting, wireless network available.

**Student life. Freshman orientation:** Available, $110 fee. Preregistration for classes offered. Two-day programs in late June and early July. Students take placement exams and meet advisors. Parents may attend. **Policies:** Academic integrity code. **Housing:** Guaranteed on-campus for freshmen. Coed dorms, special housing for disabled, substance-free housing available. $200 nonrefundable deposit, deadline 5/1. Honors floors, wellness floor, and intercultural/international hall available. Housing for handicapped students handled individually; community service floor available. Some single-sex floors in coed dorms. **Activities:** Bands, campus ministries, choral groups, dance, drama, film society, international student organizations, literary magazine, music ensembles, musical theater, opera, radio station, student government, student newspaper, symphony orchestra, TV station, NAACP, political union club (nonpartisan), Amnesty International, Habitat for Humanity, Asian students association, student confederation, concert choir, Hillel, Latin American student organization.

**Athletics.** NCAA. **Intercollegiate:** Basketball, cross-country, diving, field hockey W, lacrosse W, soccer, swimming, track and field, volleyball W, wrestling M. **Intramural:** Basketball, cheerleading W, football (non-tackle), soccer, softball, tennis, volleyball. **Team name:** Eagles.

**Student services.** Adult student services, alcohol/substance abuse counseling, campus ministries, career counseling, student employment services, financial aid counseling, health services, minority student services, on-campus daycare, personal counseling, placement for graduates, veterans' counselor, women's services. **Physically disabled:** Services for visually, speech, hearing impaired.

**Contact.** E-mail: admissions@american.edu
Phone: (202) 885-6000 Fax: (202) 885-6014
Cristan Trahey, Director of Admissions, American University, 4400 Massachusetts Avenue NW, Washington, DC 20016-8001

## Catholic University of America
**Washington, District of Columbia**
www.cua.edu

CB member
CB code: 5104

- Private 4-year university affiliated with Roman Catholic Church
- Residential campus in very large city
- 3,245 degree-seeking undergraduates: 7% part-time, 54% women, 5% African American, 3% Asian American, 6% Hispanic American, 2% international

- 2,964 degree-seeking graduate students
- 80% of applicants admitted
- SAT or ACT with writing, application essay required
- 68% graduate within 6 years; 41% enter graduate study

**General.** Founded in 1887. Regionally accredited. Strong orientation toward service-based activities; internship and study opportunities with Congress, federal agencies, and international embassies. **Degrees:** 611 bachelor's awarded; master's, doctoral, first professional offered. **ROTC:** Army, Naval, Air Force. **Calendar:** Semester, limited summer session. **Full-time faculty:** 347 total; 98% have terminal degrees, 11% minority, 36% women. **Part-time faculty:** 349 total; 1% minority, 45% women. **Class size:** 54% < 20, 36% 20-39, 2% 40-49, 6% 50-99, less than 1% >100. **Special facilities:** Rare book collection, on-campus nuclear reactor, vitreous state laboratory.

**Freshman class profile.** 4,911 applied, 3,930 admitted, 866 enrolled.

| Mid 50% test scores | | | |
|---|---|---|---|
| SAT critical reading: | 520-620 | Rank in top tenth: | 18% |
| SAT math: | 510-610 | Return as sophomores: | 82% |
| ACT composite: | 22-26 | Out-of-state: | 99% |
| GPA 3.50 or higher: | 37% | Live on campus: | 94% |
| GPA 3.0-3.49: | 35% | International: | 1% |
| GPA 2.0-2.99: | 28% | Fraternities: | 1% |
| Rank in top quarter: | 57% | Sororities: | 1% |

**Basis for selection.** School achievement record and test scores most important. Recommendations and extracurricular activities (including leadership and service activities) also important. SAT Subject Tests recommended. Students admitted to School of Arts and Sciences or School of Philosophy asked to submit SAT Subject Test scores in foreign languages for placement purposes. Audition required of music majors. **Homeschooled:** Statement describing homeschool structure and mission, transcript of courses and grades, state high school equivalency certificate, letter of recommendation (nonparent) required. **Learning Disabled:** No special admission requirements or procedures. Matriculated students with learning disabilities asked to submit documentation to Office of Disability Support Services.

**High school preparation.** 17 units recommended. Recommended units include English 4, mathematics 3, social studies 4, science 3 (laboratory 1) and foreign language 2. 1 fine arts or humanities recommended.

**2007-2008 Annual costs.** Tuition/fees: $28,990. Full-time tuition for School of Engineering $27,910. Full-time tuition for School of Architecture $28,330. Part-time tuition for School of Architecture $1,055 per credit hour. Room/board: $10,808.

**2007-2008 Financial aid. Need-based:** 642 full-time freshmen applied for aid; 500 were judged to have need; 500 of these received aid. Average need met was 83%. Average scholarship/grant was $15,520; average loan $7,955. 58% of total undergraduate aid awarded as scholarships/grants, 42% as loans/jobs. **Non-need-based:** Awarded to 1,174 full-time undergraduates, including 325 freshmen. Scholarships awarded for academics, alumni affiliation, leadership, music/drama, religious affiliation, state residency.

**Application procedures. Admission:** Closing date 2/15 (postmark date). $55 fee, may be waived for applicants with need. Application may be submitted online. Admission notification 3/15. Must reply by May 1 or within 2 week(s) if notified thereafter. **Financial aid:** Priority date 3/1; no closing date. FAFSA required. Applicants notified on a rolling basis starting 4/1; must reply by 5/1 or within 2 week(s) of notification.

**Academics.** Students must have 2.0 GPA at end of semester to be in good academic standing. **Special study options:** Accelerated study, combined bachelor's/graduate degree, cross-registration, distance learning, double major, dual enrollment of high school students, ESL, honors, independent study, internships, study abroad, teacher certification program, Washington semester. **Credit/placement by examination:** AP, CLEP, IB, institutional tests. All credit-by-examination awarded on case-by-case basis. No credit by outside examination given to matriculated students. **Support services:** Learning center, pre-admission summer program, reduced course load, study skills assistance, tutoring, writing center.

**Majors. Architecture:** Architecture. **Biology:** General, biochemistry. **Business:** General, accounting, finance, human resources, international finance, management science. **Communications:** General. **Computer sciences:** General. **Education:** General, biology, chemistry, drama/dance, early childhood, elementary, English, ESL, history, mathematics, music, secondary, Spanish. **Engineering:** Biomedical, civil, computer, electrical, mechanical. **English:** English lit. **Foreign languages:** Classics, French, German, Latin, modern Greek, Spanish. **Health:** Clinical lab science, nursing (RN). **History:** General. **Interdisciplinary:** Medieval/Renaissance. **Liberal arts:** Arts/sciences. **Math:** General. **Philosophy/religion:** Philosophy, religion. **Physical sciences:** Chemistry, molecular physics, physics. **Psychology:** General.

**Public administration:** Social work. **Social sciences:** Anthropology, economics, political science, sociology. **Visual/performing arts:** Art, art history/conservation, dramatic, music history, music performance, music theory/composition, piano/organ, voice/opera.

**Most popular majors.** Architecture 11%, business/marketing 6%, communications/journalism 6%, education 7%, engineering/engineering technologies 6%, health sciences 9%, philosophy/religious studies 6%, psychology 6%, social sciences 11%, visual/performing arts 10%.

**Computing on campus.** 500 workstations in dormitories, library, computer center, student center. Dormitories wired for high-speed internet access and linked to campus network. Commuter students can connect to campus network. Online course registration, online library, helpline, repair service, student web hosting, wireless network available.

**Student life. Freshman orientation:** Available. Preregistration for classes offered. Held Thursday-Sunday before start of fall semester. **Housing:** Guaranteed on-campus for freshmen. Coed dorms, single-sex dorms, special housing for disabled, apartments available. Residential college, thematic housing, honors housing available. **Activities:** Jazz band, campus ministries, choral groups, dance, drama, film society, international student organizations, literary magazine, music ensembles, musical theater, opera, radio station, student government, student newspaper, symphony orchestra, Best Buddies, Latin Alliance, College Republicans, College Democrats, Habitat for Humanity, Alpha Phi Omega, NAACP, Filipino Organization of Catholic University Students, Students for Life, Amnesty International.

**Athletics.** NCAA. **Intercollegiate:** Baseball M, basketball, cross-country, field hockey W, football (tackle) M, lacrosse, soccer, softball W, swimming, tennis, track and field, volleyball W. **Intramural:** Basketball, football (tackle), racquetball, soccer, softball, tennis, volleyball. **Team name:** Cardinals.

**Student services.** Adult student services, alcohol/substance abuse counseling, campus ministries, career counseling, student employment services, financial aid counseling, health services, legal services, minority student services, personal counseling, placement for graduates, veterans' counselor. **Physically disabled:** Services for visually, speech, hearing impaired.

**Contact.** E-mail: cua-admissions@cua.edu
Phone: (202) 319-5305 Toll-free number: (800) 673-2772
Fax: (202) 319-6533
Christine Mica, Director of University Admissions, Catholic University of America, 620 Michigan Avenue, NE, Washington, DC 20064

---

## Corcoran College of Art and Design
**Washington, District of Columbia**   CB member
**www.corcoran.edu**   CB code: 5705

- Private 4-year visual arts college
- Commuter campus in very large city
- 337 degree-seeking undergraduates: 14% part-time, 67% women
- 151 degree-seeking graduate students
- 64% of applicants admitted
- SAT or ACT (ACT writing optional) required
- 66% graduate within 6 years; 20% enter graduate study

**General.** Founded in 1890. Regionally accredited. **Degrees:** 67 bachelor's, 7 associate awarded; master's offered. **Calendar:** Semester, limited summer session. **Full-time faculty:** 22 total; 68% have terminal degrees, 4% minority, 54% women. **Part-time faculty:** 147 total; 50% have terminal degrees, 60% women. **Class size:** 98% < 20, 2% 20-39. **Special facilities:** Full partnership to Corcoran Gallery of Art, Student Exhibition space within museum.

**Freshman class profile.** 269 applied, 171 admitted, 58 enrolled.

| Mid 50% test scores | | | |
|---|---|---|---|
| SAT critical reading: | 450-580 | Rank in top quarter: | 50% |
| SAT math: | 400-580 | Rank in top tenth: | 11% |
| SAT writing: | 430-580 | End year in good standing: | 76% |
| ACT composite: | 19-25 | Return as sophomores: | 74% |
| GPA 3.50 or higher: | 28% | Out-of-state: | 88% |
| GPA 3.0-3.49: | 45% | Live on campus: | 72% |
| GPA 2.0-2.99: | 27% | International: | 5% |

**Basis for selection.** School achievement record, art portfolio, interview, and motivation important. Letters of recommendation and personal statement encouraged. School and community activities, test scores considered. Portfolio required (CD may replace original portfolio). Essay recommended. Interview required of applicants within 200 miles. **Homeschooled:** Statement describing homeschool structure and mission, transcript of courses and grades required.

**High school preparation.** Recommended units include English 4, history 4 and visual/performing arts 4. Advanced art courses recommended.

**2007-2008 Annual costs.** Tuition/fees: $26,090. Room only: $9,320. Books/supplies: $2,500. Personal expenses: $1,334.

**Financial aid. Non-need-based:** Scholarships awarded for academics, art.

**Application procedures. Admission:** Priority date 3/1; no deadline. $45 fee, may be waived for applicants with need. Application may be submitted online. Admission notification on a rolling basis. Must reply by May 1 or within 2 week(s) if notified thereafter. **Financial aid:** Priority date 3/15; no closing date. FAFSA, institutional form required. Applicants notified on a rolling basis starting 4/15; must reply by 5/1 or within 2 week(s) of notification.

**Academics. Special study options:** Combined bachelor's/graduate degree, cross-registration, exchange student, internships, New York semester, study abroad. Mobility programs with members of Association of Independent Art Colleges, Washington Consortium Member. **Credit/placement by examination:** AP, CLEP, IB, SAT, ACT. **Support services:** Reduced course load, study skills assistance, tutoring, writing center.

**Majors. Education:** Art. **Visual/performing arts:** General, art, graphic design, interior design, photography, studio arts. **Other:** Drawing and painting.

**Computing on campus.** PC or laptop required. 89 workstations in library, computer center, student center. Dormitories wired for high-speed internet access. Commuter students can connect to campus network. Online library, wireless network available.

**Student life. Freshman orientation:** Mandatory. Preregistration for classes offered. Mandatory session introducing college, museum, faculty, majors, city. **Housing:** Guaranteed on-campus for freshmen. Coed dorms, apartments available. $400 fully refundable deposit, deadline 5/15. **Activities:** Film society, student government.

**Student services.** Alcohol/substance abuse counseling, career counseling, student employment services, financial aid counseling, personal counseling, placement for graduates, veterans' counselor.

**Contact.** E-mail: admissions@corcoran.org
Phone: (202) 639-1814 Toll-free number: (888) 267-2672
Fax: (202) 639-1830
Elizabeth Paladino, Director of Admissions, Corcoran College of Art and Design, 500 17th Street, NW, Washington, DC 20006-4804

## Gallaudet University
**Washington, District of Columbia**
www.gallaudet.edu                                    CB code: 5240

- Private 4-year university and liberal arts college
- Residential campus in very large city
- 1,018 degree-seeking undergraduates
- 553 graduate students
- 69% of applicants admitted
- SAT or ACT (ACT writing optional), application essay required

**General.** Founded in 1857. Regionally accredited. Only liberal arts university in the world designed exclusively for deaf and hard of hearing students. Bilingual (English/American Sign Language), multicultural environment, assistive devices (TTY's or campus phones, closed captioned television and campus films), specially-designed classrooms and dormitories available. **Degrees:** 180 bachelor's awarded; master's, doctoral offered. **Calendar:** Semester, limited summer session. **Full-time faculty:** 235 total. **Class size:** 92% < 20, 8% 20-39. **Special facilities:** Gallaudet Interpreting Services (GIS) provides interpreters for university-related events.

**Freshman class profile.**

| Mid 50% test scores | | ACT composite: | 14-19 |
|---|---|---|---|
| SAT critical reading: | 320-550 | Out-of-state: | 99% |
| SAT math: | 360-520 | | |

**Basis for selection.** Applicants with hearing loss who show evidence of academic ability and motivation considered. Test scores, grades, class rank, essay, recommendation important. Interview recommended. **Learning Disabled:** Untimed tests, psychological evaluations confirming disabilities required.

**High school preparation.** 16 units recommended. Recommended units include English 4, mathematics 4, social studies 4, history 4, science 4 (laboratory 2).

**2007-2008 Annual costs.** Tuition/fees: $10,906. Students from developing countries may apply for reduction in percentage of tuition surcharge. Room/board: $9,030. Books/supplies: $834. Personal expenses: $2,852.

**Financial aid. Non-need-based:** Scholarships awarded for academics. **Additional information:** Institution receives substantial aid from state vocational rehabilitation agencies, supplemented by institutional grants when needed.

**Application procedures. Admission:** No deadline. $50 fee, may be waived for applicants with need. Application may be submitted online. Admission notification on a rolling basis. **Financial aid:** Priority date 7/1; no closing date. FAFSA, institutional form required. Applicants notified on a rolling basis starting 4/1; must reply within 4 week(s) of notification.

**Academics.** Undergraduate degree program open to deaf and hard of hearing students and a limited number of hearing students; visiting and exchange student programs available to any qualified student. **Special study options:** Accelerated study, combined bachelor's/graduate degree, cooperative education, cross-registration, double major, dual enrollment of high school students, ESL, exchange student, honors, independent study, internships, liberal arts/career combination, student-designed major, study abroad, teacher certification program. Experiential programs off-campus including orientation program for employers of deaf students and paraprofessional jobs on campus, programs for interpreter-assisted mainstreaming of students into area colleges such as Georgetown University, George Mason University, Catholic University, Howard University. **Credit/placement by examination:** AP, CLEP, institutional tests. **Support services:** Learning center, pre-admission summer program, reduced course load, remedial instruction, study skills assistance, tutoring, writing center.

**Majors. Biology:** General. **Business:** General, accounting, business admin, entrepreneurial studies, management information systems. **Communications:** General, broadcast journalism. **Computer sciences:** General, computer science, information systems. **Education:** General, art, Deaf/hearing impaired, early childhood, elementary, family/consumer sciences, multiple handicapped, physical, secondary. **English:** British lit, English lit. **Family/consumer sciences:** General, child care, food/nutrition. **Foreign languages:** American Sign Language, French, Spanish. **Health:** Recreational therapy. **History:** General. **Math:** General. **Parks/recreation:** Facilities management. **Philosophy/religion:** Philosophy. **Physical sciences:** Chemistry, physics. **Psychology:** General. **Public administration:** Social work. **Social sciences:** Criminology, economics, political science, sociology. **Visual/performing arts:** General, art history/conservation, commercial/advertising art, dramatic, studio arts.

**Computing on campus.** 352 workstations in dormitories, library, computer center, student center. Dormitories wired for high-speed internet access and linked to campus network. Commuter students can connect to campus network. Online course registration, online library, helpline, repair service, student web hosting, wireless network available.

**Student life. Freshman orientation:** Mandatory. Preregistration for classes offered. Held 1 week before beginning of semester. **Policies:** No alcohol allowed in freshman dorms; no smoking in residence halls. Only full-time students may reside in dorms. **Housing:** Guaranteed on-campus for freshmen. Coed dorms, special housing for disabled, apartments available. $150 deposit, deadline 6/1. All dormitories equipped for deaf and hard of hearing students. **Activities:** Dance, drama, film society, literary magazine, student government, student newspaper, TV station, Asian Pacific association, black deaf student union, Hispanic student association, international student club, literary society.

**Athletics.** NCAA. **Intercollegiate:** Baseball M, basketball, cross-country, football (tackle) M, soccer, softball W, swimming, tennis, track and field, volleyball, wrestling M. **Intramural:** Basketball, football (non-tackle) M, softball, volleyball. **Team name:** Bisons.

**Student services.** Adult student services, alcohol/substance abuse counseling, campus ministries, career counseling, student employment services, health services, minority student services, on-campus daycare, personal counseling, placement for graduates. **Physically disabled:** Services for visually, speech, hearing impaired.

**Contact.** E-mail: admissions@gallaudet.edu
Phone: (202) 651-5750 Toll-free number: (800) 995-0550
Fax: (202) 651-5774
Charity Reedy-Hines, Director of Admissions, Gallaudet University, 800 Florida Avenue, NE, Washington, DC 20002

## George Washington University
**Washington, District of Columbia**                 CB member
www.gwu.edu                                          CB code: 5246

- Private 4-year university
- Residential campus in very large city

- 10,370 degree-seeking undergraduates: 7% part-time, 55% women, 6% African American, 10% Asian American, 6% Hispanic American, 4% international
- 14,377 graduate students
- 37% of applicants admitted
- SAT or ACT (ACT writing recommended), application essay required
- 78% graduate within 6 years

**General.** Founded in 1821. Regionally accredited. **Degrees:** 2,209 bachelor's awarded; master's, doctoral, first professional offered. **ROTC:** Army, Naval, Air Force. **Calendar:** Semester, extensive summer session. **Full-time faculty:** 854 total; 92% have terminal degrees, 19% minority, 36% women. **Part-time faculty:** 1,172 total; 20% have terminal degrees, 15% minority, 42% women. **Class size:** 57% < 20, 26% 20-39, 6% 40-49, 8% 50-99, 3% >100. **Special facilities:** Observatory.

**Freshman class profile.** 19,606 applied, 7,197 admitted, 2,140 enrolled.

| Mid 50% test scores | | | |
|---|---|---|---|
| SAT critical reading: | 600-690 | Rank in top tenth: | 66% |
| SAT math: | 600-690 | Return as sophomores: | 90% |
| SAT writing: | 600-680 | Out-of-state: | 99% |
| ACT composite: | 26-29 | Live on campus: | 99% |
| Rank in top quarter: | 90% | International: | 4% |

**Basis for selection.** GED not accepted. Strong college-preparatory program, 3.0 GPA and class rank in top third important. Teacher and counselor recommendation and personal statement required. SAT Subject Tests recommended. SAT Subject Tests required for applicants to 7-year BA/MD and integrated engineering/MD programs (any math and any science); early admission applicants (any math, student's choice); and recommended for all for admission and placement. Interview recommended for all, required of early admission applicants. Audition required of bachelor of music applicants.

**High school preparation.** Required and recommended units include English 4, mathematics 2-4, social studies 2-4, science 2-4 (laboratory 1) and foreign language 2-4. One physics, 1 chemistry, and additional 1 unit in math required for School of Engineering and Applied Science.

**2008-2009 Annual costs.** Tuition/fees: $40,437. Tuition stays fixed until student graduates, for a maximum of five years. Room/board: $9,920. Books/supplies: $1,000. Personal expenses: $1,350.

**2006-2007 Financial aid. Need-based:** 1,282 full-time freshmen applied for aid; 966 were judged to have need; 910 of these received aid. Average need met was 91%. Average scholarship/grant was $21,246; average loan $5,679. 70% of total undergraduate aid awarded as scholarships/grants, 30% as loans/jobs. **Non-need-based:** Awarded to 3,475 full-time undergraduates, including 734 freshmen. Scholarships awarded for academics, art, athletics, music/drama. **Additional information:** Auditions required for performing arts scholarships.

**Application procedures. Admission:** Closing date 1/10. $65 fee, may be waived for applicants with need. Admission notification 4/1. Admission notification on a rolling basis. Must reply by May 1 or within 2 week(s) if notified thereafter. Applications received after 2/1 reviewed on space-available basis. Supplemental applications required for honors program, 7-year integrated engineering/law program, integrated engineering/MD program. **Financial aid:** Closing date 2/1. FAFSA, CSS PROFILE required. Applicants notified on a rolling basis starting 3/24; must reply by 5/1.

**Academics. Special study options:** Accelerated study, cooperative education, cross-registration, distance learning, double major, dual enrollment of high school students, honors, independent study, internships, liberal arts/career combination, student-designed major, study abroad. 7-year integrated BA/MD liberal arts program, 8-year integrated engineering/JD and engineering/MD programs. **Credit/placement by examination:** AP, CLEP, IB, institutional tests. 30 credit hours maximum toward bachelor's degree. **Support services:** Pre-admission summer program, reduced course load, tutoring.

**Majors. Area/ethnic studies:** American, European, Latin American, Near/Middle Eastern. **Biology:** General, biomedical sciences, biophysics, pharmacology. **Business:** Accounting, business admin, finance, international, management information systems, tourism promotion. **Communications:** General, journalism, political. **Computer sciences:** General, information systems. **Conservation:** General, environmental studies. **Education:** Physical. **Engineering:** General, biomedical, civil, computer, electrical, mechanical. **English:** English lit. **Foreign languages:** General, Arabic, Chinese, classics, French, German, Hebrew, Italian, Japanese, Latin, Portuguese, Romance, Russian, Spanish. **Health:** Audiology/speech pathology, cytotechnology, nuclear medical technology, physician assistant, sonography. **History:** General. **Liberal arts:** Arts/sciences. **Math:** General, applied, statistics. **Parks/recreation:** Exercise sciences. **Philosophy/religion:** Judaic, philosophy, religion. **Physical sciences:** Chemistry, geology, physics. **Protective services:** Criminal

justice, police science. **Psychology:** General. **Public administration:** Human services, policy analysis. **Social sciences:** Anthropology, archaeology, economics, geography, international relations, political science, sociology. **Visual/performing arts:** General, art history/conservation, dance, dramatic, interior design, studio arts, theater history.

**Most popular majors.** Business/marketing 15%, English 6%, health sciences 6%, psychology 7%, social sciences 38%.

**Computing on campus.** 600 workstations in dormitories, library, computer center, student center. Dormitories linked to campus network. Commuter students can connect to campus network. Repair service available.

**Student life. Housing:** Guaranteed on-campus for freshmen. Coed dorms, special housing for disabled, apartments, fraternity/sorority housing available. $800 nonrefundable deposit, deadline 5/1. Residential programs available in politics and values, Roots of Western Civilization, multilingual floors, creative and performing arts floors, healthy living floors available. **Activities:** Bands, choral groups, dance, drama, film society, literary magazine, music ensembles, musical theater, radio station, student government, student newspaper, TV station, religious groups, national political party organizations, ethnic, social action, public affairs groups.

**Athletics.** NCAA. **Intercollegiate:** Baseball M, basketball, cross-country, diving, golf M, gymnastics W, lacrosse W, rowing (crew), soccer, softball W, squash W, swimming, tennis, volleyball W, water polo. **Intramural:** Basketball, football (tackle) M, golf, racquetball, soccer, softball, table tennis, tennis, volleyball. **Team name:** Colonials.

**Student services.** Alcohol/substance abuse counseling, career counseling, student employment services, financial aid counseling, health services, on-campus daycare, personal counseling, placement for graduates, veterans' counselor. **Physically disabled:** Services for visually, speech, hearing impaired.

**Contact.** E-mail: gwadm@gwu.edu
Phone: (202) 994-6040 Toll-free number: (800) 447-3765
Fax: (202) 994-0325
Kathryn Napper, Executive Dean for Undergraduate Admissions, George Washington University, 2121 I Street NW, Suite 201, Washington, DC 20052

## Georgetown University

**Washington, District of Columbia**     **CB member**
www.georgetown.edu     **CB code: 5244**

- Private 4-year university affiliated with Roman Catholic Church
- Residential campus in very large city
- 6,623 degree-seeking undergraduates: 2% part-time, 55% women, 7% African American, 9% Asian American, 7% Hispanic American, 5% international
- 7,604 degree-seeking graduate students
- 21% of applicants admitted
- SAT or ACT (ACT writing optional), application essay, interview required
- 93% graduate within 6 years; 21% enter graduate study

**General.** Founded in 1789. Regionally accredited. **Degrees:** 2,041 bachelor's awarded; master's, doctoral, first professional offered. **ROTC:** Army, Naval, Air Force. **Location:** 1.5 miles from downtown. **Calendar:** Semester, extensive summer session. **Full-time faculty:** 824 total; 89% have terminal degrees, 15% minority, 38% women. **Part-time faculty:** 615 total; 64% have terminal degrees, 8% minority, 35% women. **Special facilities:** Observatory, language learning technology lab with satellite link, library with special collections including archives, rare books, prints, manuscripts dealing with medieval and early modern periods, and American history.

**Freshman class profile.** 16,163 applied, 3,363 admitted, 1,582 enrolled.

| Mid 50% test scores | | | |
|---|---|---|---|
| SAT critical reading: | 650-750 | End year in good standing: | 100% |
| SAT math: | 650-740 | Return as sophomores: | 96% |
| ACT composite: | 29-33 | Out-of-state: | 99% |
| Rank in top quarter: | 96% | Live on campus: | 99% |
| Rank in top tenth: | 90% | International: | 5% |

**Basis for selection.** School academic record most important, in addition to test scores, essays, extracurricular activities, interview, and recommendations. Special consideration given to qualified minorities, athletes, internationals, and alumni relatives. SAT Subject Tests recommended. Interview required unless not possible to assign based on geographic area; portfolio recommended for fine arts majors.

**High school preparation.** Required units include English 4, mathematics 2, social studies 2, history 2, science 1 and foreign language 2. Additional units in science, math, and foreign language recommended for some programs.

**2008-2009 Annual costs.** Tuition/fees: $37,947. Room/board: $12,753. Books/supplies: $1,060. Personal expenses: $1,620.

**2007-2008 Financial aid. Need-based:** 881 full-time freshmen applied for aid; 638 were judged to have need; 632 of these received aid. Average need met was 100%. Average scholarship/grant was $24,371; average loan $1,956. 80% of total undergraduate aid awarded as scholarships/grants, 20% as loans/jobs. **Non-need-based:** Awarded to 228 full-time undergraduates, including 62 freshmen. Scholarships awarded for athletics.

**Application procedures. Admission:** Closing date 1/10 (receipt date). $65 fee, may be waived for applicants with need. Application must be submitted on paper. Admission notification 4/1. Must reply by May 1 or within 2 week(s) if notified thereafter. Early Action plan limits students from applying to binding Early Decision programs. **Financial aid:** Closing date 2/1. FAFSA, CSS PROFILE required. Applicants notified by 4/1; must reply by 5/1 or within 2 week(s) of notification.

**Academics.** Early assurance program to university's medical and law schools. **Special study options:** Combined bachelor's/graduate degree, cross-registration, double major, ESL, honors, independent study, internships, student-designed major, study abroad, Washington semester. **Credit/placement by examination:** AP, CLEP, IB, institutional tests. **Support services:** Learning center, pre-admission summer program, study skills assistance, tutoring, writing center.

**Majors. Area/ethnic studies:** American, women's. **Biology:** General, biochemistry, biomedical sciences. **Business:** Accounting, business admin, finance, international, marketing. **Computer sciences:** Computer science. **English:** English lit. **Foreign languages:** Arabic, Chinese, classics, comparative lit, French, German, Italian, Japanese, linguistics, Portuguese, Russian, Spanish. **Health:** Health care admin, international public health, nursing (RN). **History:** General. **Interdisciplinary:** Biological/physical sciences, medieval/Renaissance, peace/conflict, science/society. **Liberal arts:** Arts/sciences. **Math:** General. **Philosophy/religion:** Philosophy, religion. **Physical sciences:** Chemistry, physics. **Psychology:** General. **Social sciences:** Anthropology, economics, international relations, political science, sociology. **Visual/performing arts:** Art, art history/conservation, studio arts.

**Most popular majors.** Business/marketing 25%, English 8%, foreign language 8%, health sciences 6%, social sciences 32%.

**Computing on campus.** 400 workstations in dormitories, library, computer center. Dormitories wired for high-speed internet access and linked to campus network. Commuter students can connect to campus network. Online course registration, helpline, repair service, wireless network available.

**Student life. Freshman orientation:** Mandatory, $160 fee. Preregistration for classes offered. Student volunteer-led program. **Policies:** Freshmen and sophomores required to live on campus. Upperclass students obtain housing via lottery process. **Housing:** Guaranteed on-campus for freshmen. Coed dorms, special housing for disabled, apartments, substance-free housing available. **Activities:** Bands, choral groups, dance, drama, film society, literary magazine, music ensembles, musical theater, radio station, student government, student newspaper, symphony orchestra, TV station, over 120 student organizations.

**Athletics.** NCAA. **Intercollegiate:** Baseball M, basketball, cross-country, diving, field hockey W, football (tackle) M, golf, lacrosse, rowing (crew), sailing, soccer, softball W, swimming, tennis, track and field, volleyball W. **Intramural:** Basketball, cross-country, football (non-tackle), golf, handball, racquetball, skiing, soccer, softball, squash, table tennis, tennis, volleyball. **Team name:** Hoyas.

**Student services.** Alcohol/substance abuse counseling, campus ministries, career counseling, student employment services, financial aid counseling, health services, minority student services, on-campus daycare, personal counseling, placement for graduates, women's services. **Physically disabled:** Services for visually, hearing impaired.

**Contact.** Phone: (202) 687-3600 Fax: (202) 687-5084
Charles Deacon, Dean of Admissions, Georgetown University, 103 White-Gravenor, Washington, DC 20057-1002

---

## Howard University

**Washington, District of Columbia**

**www.howard.edu**

CB member
CB code: 5297

- Private 4-year university
- Residential campus in very large city

- 6,973 degree-seeking undergraduates: 6% part-time, 66% women, 67% African American, 1% Asian American, 5% international
- 3,131 degree-seeking graduate students
- 54% of applicants admitted
- SAT or ACT with writing required

**General.** Founded in 1867. Regionally accredited. 5 campuses. 25 major research centers and several special programs. **Degrees:** 1,344 bachelor's awarded; master's, doctoral, first professional offered. **ROTC:** Army, Air Force. **Location:** 38 miles from Baltimore, 105 miles from Richmond, Virginia. **Calendar:** Semester, extensive summer session. **Full-time faculty:** 1,068 total; 88% have terminal degrees, 82% minority, 40% women. **Part-time faculty:** 573 total; 77% have terminal degrees, 80% minority, 42% women. **Class size:** 63% < 20, 27% 20-39, 5% 40-49, 4% 50-99, less than 1% >100. **Special facilities:** Research center, including museum and archives, with collections on Africa and persons of African descent; international affairs center.

**Freshman class profile.** 7,603 applied, 4,080 admitted, 1,450 enrolled.

| Mid 50% test scores | | | |
|---|---|---|---|
| SAT critical reading: | 460-660 | GPA 3.0-3.49: | 43% |
| SAT math: | 440-650 | GPA 2.0-2.99: | 33% |
| SAT writing: | 410-650 | Rank in top quarter: | 49% |
| ACT composite: | 20-28 | Rank in top tenth: | 23% |
| GPA 3.50 or higher: | 24% | Out-of-state: | 98% |
| | | Live on campus: | 92% |

**Basis for selection.** High school achievement record, test scores most important. Requirements vary from college to college. SAT Subject Tests recommended. Dental Hygiene Aptitude Test required of dental hygiene applicants. Essay recommended; required of Early Action applicants. Audition required of music, drama majors. Portfolio required of art, architecture majors. Interview recommended for pharmacy and pharmaceutical programs, physician assistant majors. **Homeschooled:** Must have GED.

**High school preparation.** 14 units required; 21 recommended. Required and recommended units include English 4, mathematics 2-3, social studies 2, science 2, foreign language 2 and academic electives 4.

**2008-2009 Annual costs.** Tuition/fees: $15,010. Room/board: $7,436. Books/supplies: $1,300. Personal expenses: $1,800.

**2007-2008 Financial aid.** All financial aid based on need. 1,280 full-time freshmen applied for aid; 1,109 were judged to have need; 767 of these received aid. Average need met was 80%. Average scholarship/grant was $9,431; average loan $5,191. 42% of total undergraduate aid awarded as scholarships/grants, 58% as loans/jobs.

**Application procedures. Admission:** Priority date 11/1; deadline 2/15 (receipt date). $45 fee. Admission notification on a rolling basis beginning on or about 4/15. Must reply by May 1 or within 4 week(s) if notified thereafter. Fall term procedures for applicants does not differ from the spring, however spring term applicants stand a better chance of acceptance. **Financial aid:** Priority date 2/15, closing date 8/15. FAFSA, institutional form required. Applicants notified on a rolling basis starting 4/1; must reply by 8/1 or within 4 week(s) of notification.

**Academics. Special study options:** Accelerated study, combined bachelor's/graduate degree, cooperative education, cross-registration, distance learning, double major, dual enrollment of high school students, exchange student, honors, independent study, internships, student-designed major, study abroad, teacher certification program. **Credit/placement by examination:** AP, CLEP, SAT, ACT, institutional tests. 60 credit hours maximum toward bachelor's degree. **Support services:** Learning center, pre-admission summer program, reduced course load, remedial instruction, study skills assistance, tutoring.

**Majors. Architecture:** Architecture. **Area/ethnic studies:** African, African-American. **Biology:** General. **Business:** Accounting, business admin, fashion, finance, hospitality admin, hospitality/recreation, insurance, international, management information systems, market research. **Communications:** General, broadcast journalism, journalism, radio/tv. **Computer sciences:** Information systems, systems analysis. **Education:** Art, English, health, music, physical. **Engineering:** Chemical, civil, computer, electrical, mechanical, systems. **English:** English lit. **Foreign languages:** Ancient Greek, classics, French, German, modern Greek, Russian, Spanish. **Health:** Clinical lab science, medical radiologic technology/radiation therapy, music therapy, physician assistant, recreational therapy. **History:** General. **Interdisciplinary:** Nutrition sciences. **Math:** General. **Parks/recreation:** General. **Philosophy/religion:** Philosophy. **Physical sciences:** Chemistry, physics. **Psychology:** General. **Social sciences:** Anthropology, economics, political science, sociology. **Visual/performing arts:** General, art, art history/conservation, arts management, conducting, dance, design, interior design, jazz, music history, music management, music theory/composition, piano/organ, theater arts management, theater design, theater history, voice/opera.

**Most popular majors.** Biology 8%, business/marketing 18%, communications/journalism 17%, health sciences 18%, social sciences 8%.

**Computing on campus.** 7,006 workstations in dormitories, library, computer center, student center. Dormitories wired for high-speed internet access and linked to campus network. Commuter students can connect to campus network. Online course registration, online library, helpline, student web hosting, wireless network available.

**Student life. Freshman orientation:** Mandatory. Preregistration for classes offered. **Housing:** Guaranteed on-campus for freshmen. Coed dorms, single-sex dorms, apartments, substance-free housing available. $50 nonrefundable deposit, deadline 4/1. **Activities:** Bands, campus ministries, choral groups, dance, drama, film society, international student organizations, literary magazine, music ensembles, musical theater, opera, radio station, student government, student newspaper, symphony orchestra, TV station, Absalom Jones student association, Adventist committee, Baptist student union, Christian Science organization, Christian Fellowship-Igbimo Otito, Lutheran student organization, Muslim students, Wesley Foundation Methodist Fellowship, William J. Seymour Pentacostal Fellowship, academic honorary societies.

**Athletics.** NCAA. **Intercollegiate:** Baseball M, basketball, bowling, cross-country, diving, football (tackle) M, golf W, gymnastics, lacrosse W, soccer, softball W, swimming, tennis, track and field, volleyball W, wrestling M. **Intramural:** Badminton W, basketball, bowling, soccer W, softball, table tennis. **Team name:** Bison.

**Student services.** Campus ministries, career counseling, student employment services, financial aid counseling, health services, on-campus daycare, personal counseling, placement for graduates, veterans' counselor. **Physically disabled:** Services for visually, speech impaired.

**Contact.** E-mail: admissions@howard.edu
Phone: (202) 806-2700 Toll-free number: (800) 469-2738
Fax: (202) 806-4467
Linda Saunders-Hawkins, Associate Director of Admissions, Howard University, 2400 Sixth Street NW, Washington, DC 20059

## Potomac College
**Washington, District of Columbia**
www.potomac.edu          CB code: 3569

- For-profit 3-year business college
- Commuter campus in very large city
- 580 degree-seeking undergraduates

**General.** Regionally accredited. **Degrees:** 59 bachelor's, 7 associate awarded. **Calendar:** Continuous, extensive summer session. **Full-time faculty:** 8 total. **Part-time faculty:** 30 total.

**Basis for selection.** Open admission.

**2007-2008 Annual costs.** Tuition/fees: $13,480. Books/supplies: $630.

**Application procedures. Admission:** No deadline. $15 fee. Application may be submitted online. Admission notification on a rolling basis beginning on or about 3/31. **Financial aid:** No deadline. FAFSA, institutional form required. Applicants notified on a rolling basis; must reply within 4 week(s) of notification.

**Academics.** Credit earned for work-related research projects. **Special study options:** Accelerated study, independent study, weekend college. **Credit/placement by examination:** CLEP, institutional tests. 30 credit hours maximum toward bachelor's degree. **Support services:** Learning center.

**Majors. Business:** Management science. **Computer sciences:** General.

**Computing on campus.** 23 workstations in library, computer center. Online library available.

**Student life. Freshman orientation:** Mandatory. Preregistration for classes offered. **Activities:** Student government.

**Student services.** Adult student services.

**Contact.** E-mail: admissions@potomac.edu
Phone: (202) 686-0876 Fax: (202) 686-0818
Director of Admissions, Potomac College, 4000 Chesapeake Street NW, Washington, DC 20016

## Southeastern University
**Washington, District of Columbia**
www.seu.edu          CB code: 5622

- Private 4-year business and liberal arts college
- Commuter campus in very large city
- 562 degree-seeking undergraduates
- 239 degree-seeking graduate students
- Application essay required

**General.** Founded in 1879. Regionally accredited. Weekend college degree available for all programs. **Degrees:** 60 bachelor's, 44 associate awarded; master's offered. **Calendar:** Quarter, extensive summer session. **Full-time faculty:** 10 total. **Part-time faculty:** 114 total. **Class size:** 67% < 20, 32% 20-39, 1% 40-49.

**Basis for selection.** Open admission. **Homeschooled:** State high school equivalency certificate required.

**High school preparation.** Recommended units include English 4, mathematics 3, social studies 2 and foreign language 2.

**2007-2008 Annual costs.** Tuition/fees: $12,525. Reduction in fees available for early registration. Online programs: $320 per credit hour. Books/supplies: $1,200. Personal expenses: $1,359.

**Financial aid. Non-need-based:** Scholarships awarded for academics, state residency.

**Application procedures. Admission:** No deadline. $45 fee, may be waived for applicants with need. Application may be submitted online. Admission notification on a rolling basis. **Financial aid:** Closing date 8/15. FAFSA, institutional form required. Applicants notified on a rolling basis; must reply within 2 week(s) of notification.

**Academics. Special study options:** Cross-registration, double major, independent study, internships, weekend college. **Credit/placement by examination:** AP, CLEP, IB, institutional tests. 9 credit hours maximum toward associate degree, 9 toward bachelor's. **Support services:** Learning center, pre-admission summer program, reduced course load, remedial instruction, study skills assistance, tutoring, writing center.

**Majors. Business:** General, accounting, banking/financial services, business admin, management information systems, management science, market research, statistics, tourism/travel. **Computer sciences:** Programming, systems analysis. **Family/consumer sciences:** Child development. **Health:** Health care admin. **Liberal arts:** Arts/sciences. **Protective services:** Police science. **Public administration:** General. **Social sciences:** Economics.

**Most popular majors.** Business/marketing 44%, computer/information sciences 13%, health sciences 9%, liberal arts 15%, public administration/social services 18%.

**Computing on campus.** 137 workstations in library, computer center. Commuter students can connect to campus network. Online course registration available.

**Student life. Freshman orientation:** Mandatory, $255 fee. Preregistration for classes offered. **Activities:** Literary magazine, student government, student newspaper.

**Student services.** Career counseling, student employment services, financial aid counseling, personal counseling, placement for graduates, veterans' counselor. **Physically disabled:** Services for visually, hearing impaired.

**Contact.** E-mail: admissions@admin.seu.edu
Phone: (202) 478-8210 ext. 210 Fax: (202) 488-3172
Dorothy Harris, Dean of Enrollment Management, Southeastern University, 501 I Street SW, Washington, DC 20024

## Strayer University
**Washington, District of Columbia**
www.strayer.edu          CB code: 5632

- For-profit 4-year university and business college
- Commuter campus in very large city

**General.** Founded in 1892. Regionally accredited. **Location:** Downtown. **Calendar:** Quarter.

**Annual costs/financial aid.** Tuition/fees (2007-2008): $12,800. Books/supplies: $1,200.

**Contact.** Phone: (202) 408-2400
1133 15th Sreet NW, Washington, DC 20005

## Trinity Washington University
**Washington, District of Columbia**

**www.trinitydc.edu**

**CB member**

**CB code: 5796**

- Private 4-year liberal arts college for women affiliated with Roman Catholic Church
- Residential campus in very large city
- 1,032 degree-seeking undergraduates
- 75% of applicants admitted
- Application essay required

**General.** Founded in 1897. Regionally accredited. **Degrees:** 130 bachelor's awarded; master's offered. **ROTC:** Army. **Calendar:** Semester, extensive summer session. **Full-time faculty:** 58 total. **Part-time faculty:** 125 total. **Class size:** 70% < 20, 30% 20-39.

**Freshman class profile.** 800 applied, 600 admitted, 260 enrolled.

| | | | |
|---|---|---|---|
| Out-of-state: | 50% | Live on campus: | 53% |

**Basis for selection.** School achievement record, essay, recommendations, interview, school and community activities important. 3.0 GPA preferred. Test scores considered. SAT and SAT Subject Tests or ACT recommended. Interview recommended. **Homeschooled:** Transcript of courses and grades required.

**High school preparation.** 16 units required. Required and recommended units include English 4, mathematics 3-4, social studies 3-4, history 2, science 2-3 (laboratory 1-2) and foreign language 2.

**2008-2009 Annual costs.** Tuition/fees: $18,960. Mandatory health insurance. Room/board: $8,450. Books/supplies: $1,000. Personal expenses: $1,500.

**2007-2008 Financial aid. Need-based:** 57% of total undergraduate aid awarded as scholarships/grants, 43% as loans/jobs. **Non-need-based:** Scholarships awarded for academics, alumni affiliation, leadership.

**Application procedures. Admission:** Priority date 2/1; deadline 9/1 (receipt date). $40 fee, may be waived for applicants with need. Application may be submitted online. Admission notification 9/1. Admission notification on a rolling basis beginning on or about 10/1. Must reply by May 1 or within 3 week(s) if notified thereafter. After August 1, must reply within 1 week. **Financial aid:** Priority date 3/1; no closing date. FAFSA required. Applicants notified on a rolling basis starting 2/1; must reply within 2 week(s) of notification.

**Academics. Special study options:** Accelerated study, cross-registration, distance learning, double major, dual enrollment of high school students, honors, independent study, internships, student-designed major, study abroad, teacher certification program, Washington semester, weekend college. **Credit/placement by examination:** AP, CLEP, institutional tests. **Support services:** Learning center, pre-admission summer program, reduced course load, remedial instruction, tutoring.

**Majors. Biology:** General, biochemistry. **Business:** Business admin. **Communications:** General. **Conservation:** Environmental science. **English:** English lit. **Foreign languages:** General. **History:** General. **Liberal arts:** Arts/sciences. **Math:** General. **Physical sciences:** General, chemistry. **Protective services:** Law enforcement admin. **Psychology:** General. **Public administration:** Human services. **Social sciences:** Economics, international relations, political science, sociology. **Visual/performing arts:** Art history/conservation. **Other:** Languages and cultural studies.

**Most popular majors.** Biology 10%, business/marketing 25%, communications/journalism 15%, English 9%, psychology 50%, social sciences 19%.

**Computing on campus.** 70 workstations in dormitories, library, computer center.

**Student life. Freshman orientation:** Available. Preregistration for classes offered. **Policies:** Student life mostly self-governed. Honor code exists. **Housing:** Guaranteed on-campus for all undergraduates. $100 fully refundable deposit. **Activities:** Choral groups, dance, drama, film society, literary magazine, student government, student newspaper, Young Democrats, Young Republicans, Black Student Alliance, international student association, Inter-American Club, peer ministry.

**Athletics.** NCAA. **Intercollegiate:** Basketball W, lacrosse W, soccer W, tennis W, volleyball W. **Team name:** Tigers.

**Student services.** Adult student services, alcohol/substance abuse counseling, campus ministries, career counseling, student employment services, financial aid counseling, health services, on-campus daycare, personal counseling, placement for graduates, veterans' counselor. **Physically disabled:** Services for visually, speech, hearing impaired.

**Contact.** E-mail: admissions@trinitydc.edu
Phone: (202) 884-9400 Toll-free number: (800) 492-6882
Fax: (202) 884-9229
Kelly Gosnell, Director of Admissions, Trinity Washington University, 125 Michigan Avenue, NE, Washington, DC 20017

## University of the District of Columbia
**Washington, District of Columbia**

**www.udc.edu**

**CB member**

**CB code: 5929**

- Public 4-year university and liberal arts college
- Commuter campus in very large city
- 5,137 degree-seeking undergraduates

**General.** Founded in 1976. Regionally accredited. **Degrees:** 306 bachelor's, 147 associate awarded; master's offered. **ROTC:** Army, Naval, Air Force. **Calendar:** Semester, limited summer session. **Full-time faculty:** 230 total. **Part-time faculty:** 45 total.

**Freshman class profile.**

| | | | |
|---|---|---|---|
| Out-of-state: | 21% | Sororities: | 2% |
| Fraternities: | 1% | | |

**Basis for selection.** Open admission. Special requirements for nursing, art, and music programs. First-time students must take placement test prior to enrollment. Interview recommended for nursing majors. Audition recommended for music majors. Portfolio recommended for art majors.

**High school preparation.** Recommended units include English 4, mathematics 2, social studies 2, history 1, science 2, foreign language 2 and academic electives 3.

**2007-2008 Annual costs.** Tuition/fees: $3,770; $7,070 out-of-state. Books/supplies: $800. Personal expenses: $1,600.

**Financial aid.** All financial aid based on need.

**Application procedures. Admission:** Closing date 6/14 (postmark date). $50 fee, may be waived for applicants with need. Admission notification on a rolling basis. **Financial aid:** Priority date 3/15; no closing date. FAFSA required. Applicants notified on a rolling basis starting 5/1; must reply within 2 week(s) of notification.

**Academics. Special study options:** Cooperative education, cross-registration, double major, dual enrollment of high school students, ESL, honors, independent study, internships, teacher certification program, weekend college. **Credit/placement by examination:** AP, CLEP, IB, institutional tests. **Support services:** Learning center, pre-admission summer program, remedial instruction, tutoring.

**Majors. Architecture:** Architecture, urban/community planning. **Biology:** General. **Business:** Accounting, business admin, finance, office management. **Communications technology:** Graphic/printing. **Computer sciences:** General, computer science. **Conservation:** General. **Education:** Art, business, early childhood, elementary, health, physical. **Engineering:** Civil, electrical, mechanical. **English:** English lit. **Family/consumer sciences:** General, family studies, food/nutrition. **Foreign languages:** French, Spanish. **Health:** Nursing (RN), speech pathology. **History:** General. **Math:** General. **Parks/recreation:** General. **Philosophy/religion:** Philosophy. **Physical sciences:** Chemistry, physics. **Protective services:** Fire services admin. **Psychology:** General. **Public administration:** Social work. **Social sciences:** Anthropology, economics, geography, political science, sociology, urban studies. **Transportation:** Aviation. **Visual/performing arts:** Dramatic, studio arts.

**Most popular majors.** Business/marketing 19%, computer/information sciences 16%, education 6%, health sciences 9%, legal studies 12%, mathematics 14%, visual/performing arts 8%.

**Computing on campus.** 2 workstations in library, computer center. Helpline, repair service available.

**Student life. Freshman orientation:** Mandatory. Preregistration for classes offered. **Activities:** Bands, choral groups, dance, drama, student government, student newspaper, symphony orchestra, TV station.

**Athletics.** NCAA. **Intercollegiate:** Basketball, cross-country, soccer, tennis, track and field, volleyball W. **Intramural:** Basketball, softball, swimming, tennis, volleyball W. **Team name:** Firebirds.

**Student services.** Career counseling, student employment services, health services, personal counseling, placement for graduates, veterans' counselor. **Physically disabled:** Services for visually, speech, hearing impaired.

**Contact.**   Phone: (202) 274-6110 Fax: (202) 274-5552
LaVerne Hill-Flannigan, Director of Enrollment Services, University of the District of Columbia, 4200 Connecticut Avenue NW, Washington, DC 20008

# Florida

## Angley College
**Deland, Florida**
www.angley.edu

- For-profit 4-year business and health science college
- Commuter campus in small city
- 86 degree-seeking undergraduates
- Interview required

**General.** Accredited by ACICS. Child care available at no additional charge; textbook loan program available. **Degrees:** 2 bachelor's, 4 associate awarded. **Location:** 30 miles from Orlando. **Calendar:** Quarter, extensive summer session. **Full-time faculty:** 11 total. **Part-time faculty:** 4 total.

**Basis for selection.** Completion of high school with standard high school diploma, succesful completion of college-administered admission test, and results of interview (in person or via telephone) with admissions officer important. **Homeschooled:** State high school equivalency certificate required.

**2007-2008 Annual costs.** Tuition/fees: $14,625. Books/supplies: $325. Personal expenses: $180.

**Application procedures. Admission:** No deadline. $25 fee. Application may be submitted online. Admission notification on a rolling basis.

**Academics. Special study options:** Accelerated study, cooperative education, double major, ESL, independent study, internships. **Credit/placement by examination:** AP, CLEP, SAT, ACT, institutional tests. 22.5 credit hours maximum toward associate degree, 45 toward bachelor's. **Support services:** Learning center, remedial instruction, study skills assistance, tutoring.

**Majors. Business:** Business admin.

**Computing on campus.** 25 workstations in library, computer center. Online library, wireless network available.

**Student life. Freshman orientation:** Mandatory. Preregistration for classes offered. Held Saturday before each class start; lasts approximately 4 hours. **Activities:** Student government.

**Student services.** Adult student services, alcohol/substance abuse counseling, career counseling, financial aid counseling, on-campus daycare, personal counseling, placement for graduates, veterans' counselor.

**Contact.** E-mail: admissions@angley.edu
Phone: (386) 740-1215 Toll-free number: (866) 639-1215
Fax: (386) 740-2077
Ann Ertel, Director of Admissions, Angley College, 230 North Woodland Boulevard, Suite 310, Deland, FL 32720-4289

## Art Institute of Fort Lauderdale
**Fort Lauderdale, Florida**
www.aifl.edu                                    CB code: 5040

- For-profit 4-year visual arts and technical college
- Commuter campus in large city
- 2,821 degree-seeking undergraduates: 44% part-time, 53% women
- Application essay, interview required

**General.** Founded in 1968. Accredited by ACICS. **Degrees:** 351 bachelor's, 224 associate awarded. **Location:** 25 miles from Miami, 30 miles from West Palm Beach. **Calendar:** Quarter, extensive summer session. **Full-time faculty:** 96 total; 26% have terminal degrees, 12% minority, 46% women. **Part-time faculty:** 59 total; 41% have terminal degrees, 27% minority, 29% women. **Special facilities:** Broadcasting studio, silicon graphics lab, full culinary kitchens.

**Freshman class profile.**

| | | | |
|---|---|---|---|
| Out-of-state: | 20% | Live on campus: | 10% |

**Basis for selection.** Interview, essay important. Portfolio recommended. **Learning Disabled:** Documentation must be submitted if student has special needs to be accommodated.

**High school preparation.** Prefer students with background in chosen major.

**2007-2008 Annual costs.** Tuition/fees: $18,945. Books/supplies: $1,227. Personal expenses: $1,980.

**2006-2007 Financial aid.** All financial aid based on need. 18% of total undergraduate aid awarded as scholarships/grants, 82% as loans/jobs. **Additional information:** Internal scholarships available. Financial planning program allows personalized service to budget and meet college costs through individualized payment plans.

**Application procedures. Admission:** No deadline. $50 fee. Application may be submitted online. Admission notification on a rolling basis. **Financial aid:** No deadline. FAFSA required.

**Academics.** Academic program designed to simulate working environment. After completion of associate degree students may continue to earn a bachelor of science. **Special study options:** ESL, honors, independent study, internships. **Credit/placement by examination:** AP, CLEP, IB. SAT or ACT preferred for placement but ACCUPLACER accepted. **Support services:** Remedial instruction, tutoring, writing center.

**Majors. Architecture:** Interior. **Business:** Fashion. **Communications:** Advertising. **Computer sciences:** Computer graphics, programming, web page design. **Personal/culinary services:** Chef training. **Visual/performing arts:** Cinematography, commercial/advertising art, fashion design, illustration, industrial design, interior design, multimedia.

**Most popular majors.** Architecture 17%, communications/journalism 6%, computer/information sciences 29%, personal/culinary services 7%, visual/performing arts 39%.

**Computing on campus.** Dormitories wired for high-speed internet access and linked to campus network. Online course registration, online library, helpline, repair service, student web hosting, wireless network available.

**Student life. Freshman orientation:** Available. Preregistration for classes offered. Held at the beginning of each quarter. **Housing:** Guaranteed on-campus for all undergraduates. Coed dorms, apartments, substance-free housing available. $275 deposit. **Activities:** International student organizations, radio station, student government, TV station, Industrial Design Society of America, American Society of Interior Design, Gay Straight Alliance, fashion club, comic production club, future video producers and broadcasters.

**Student services.** Alcohol/substance abuse counseling, career counseling, student employment services, financial aid counseling, personal counseling, placement for graduates. **Physically disabled:** Services for hearing impaired.

**Contact.** E-mail: northroe@aii.edu
Phone: (954) 463-3000 ext. 2149 Toll-free number: (800) 275-7603 ext. 2149 Fax: (954) 728-8637
Eileen Northrop, Vice President, Director of Admissions, Art Institute of Fort Lauderdale, 1799 Southeast 17th Street, Fort Lauderdale, FL 33316

## Ave Maria University
**Ave Maria, Florida**
www.avemaria.edu                               CB code: 4249

- Private 4-year university and liberal arts college affiliated with Roman Catholic Church
- Residential campus in small town
- 451 degree-seeking undergraduates
- 56% of applicants admitted
- SAT or ACT with writing, application essay required

**General. Degrees:** 77 bachelor's awarded; master's, doctoral offered. **Location:** 30 miles from Naples. **Calendar:** Semester, limited summer session. **Full-time faculty:** 45 total; 98% have terminal degrees, 11% minority, 16% women. **Part-time faculty:** 10 total; 20% minority. **Class size:** 70% < 20, 29% 20-39, less than 1% 40-49.

**Freshman class profile.** 445 applied, 248 admitted, 138 enrolled.

**Basis for selection.** For regular admission, 2.8 GPA and 1580 SAT or 22 ACT required. Students who do not meet all requirements may attain admission by special recommendation of the Admissions Committee. **Homeschooled:** Transcript of courses and grades, letter of recommendation (nonparent) required.

**High school preparation.** 15 units required; 17 recommended. Required and recommended units include English 3-4, mathematics 3-4, social studies 1, history 1-3, science 3 and foreign language 2.

**2007-2008 Annual costs.** Tuition/fees: $16,255. Room/board: $7,140.

**2007-2008 Financial aid. Need-based:** Average need met was 80%. Average scholarship/grant was $12,923; average loan $3,254. 81% of total undergraduate aid awarded as scholarships/grants, 19% as loans/jobs.

**Application procedures. Admission:** No deadline. No application fee. Application may be submitted online. Admission notification on a rolling basis.

**Academics. Special study options:** Double major, dual enrollment of high school students, internships, study abroad. **Credit/placement by examination:** AP, CLEP, SAT, ACT, institutional tests. **Support services:** Study skills assistance, tutoring, writing center.

**Majors. Biology:** General. **English:** English lit. **Foreign languages:** Classics. **History:** General. **Math:** General. **Philosophy/religion:** Philosophy. **Social sciences:** Economics, political science. **Theology:** Sacred music, theology.

**Computing on campus.** 150 workstations in dormitories, library, computer center, student center. Dormitories wired for high-speed internet access and linked to campus network. Commuter students can connect to campus network. Online library, helpline, wireless network available.

**Student life. Freshman orientation:** Mandatory. Preregistration for classes offered. Three-day program held at beginning of each semester. **Housing:** Guaranteed on-campus for all undergraduates. Single-sex dorms available. **Activities:** Campus ministries, choral groups, dance, drama, film society, international student organizations, Model UN, student government, student newspaper.

**Athletics. Intercollegiate:** Basketball, golf M, soccer. **Intramural:** Basketball, football (non-tackle), soccer, volleyball. **Team name:** Gyrene.

**Student services.** Alcohol/substance abuse counseling, career counseling, student employment services, financial aid counseling, health services, personal counseling. **Physically disabled:** Services for visually impaired.

**Contact.** E-mail: admissions@avemaria.edu
Phone: (239) 280-2556 Toll-free number: (877) 283-8648
Fax: (239) 280-2559
Michael Williams, Associate Director of Admissions, Ave Maria University, 5050 Ave Maria Boulevard, Ave Maria, FL 34142-9505

---

## Baptist College of Florida
### Graceville, Florida
**www.baptistcollege.edu**   **CB code: 7322**

- Private 4-year Bible and teachers college affiliated with Southern Baptist Convention
- Residential campus in small town
- 539 degree-seeking undergraduates: 29% part-time, 36% women, 4% African American, 1% Asian American, 3% Hispanic American, 1% Native American
- 73% of applicants admitted
- SAT or ACT (ACT writing optional), application essay required

**General.** Founded in 1943. Regionally accredited. **Degrees:** 108 bachelor's, 4 associate awarded. **Location:** 90 miles from Tallahassee, 60 miles from Panama City. **Calendar:** Semester, limited summer session. **Full-time faculty:** 26 total; 69% have terminal degrees, 27% women. **Part-time faculty:** 37 total; 57% have terminal degrees, 19% women. **Class size:** 74% < 20, 21% 20-39, 3% 40-49, 2% 50-99.

**Freshman class profile.** 295 applied, 214 admitted, 43 enrolled.

| Mid 50% test scores | | Rank in top tenth: | 10% |
|---|---|---|---|
| ACT composite: | 16-22 | Out-of-state: | 21% |
| Rank in top quarter: | 27% | Live on campus: | 90% |

**Basis for selection.** Applicant must be member in good standing of church affiliated with Southern Baptist Convention or other evangelical body.

---

Special program for non-high school graduates. Recommendations very important. Letter of testimony required. Audition required of music applicants. Interview recommended. **Homeschooled:** Transcript of courses and grades required. Present ACT or SAT test scores no more than 5 years old. Minimum 2.5 GPA, evidence of having earned minimum of 20 units with at least 14 units from fields of English, math, social and natural sciences required.

**High school preparation.** Recommended units include English 4, mathematics 4, social studies 1, history 2 and science 3.

**2007-2008 Annual costs.** Tuition/fees: $7,850. Room/board: $3,736. Books/supplies: $900. Personal expenses: $400.

**Financial aid. Non-need-based:** Scholarships awarded for academics, minority status, music/drama, religious affiliation.

**Application procedures. Admission:** Priority date 6/30; deadline 8/1 (receipt date). $20 fee, may be waived for applicants with need. Application may be submitted online. Admission notification on a rolling basis beginning on or about 9/1. **Financial aid:** Priority date 4/1, closing date 4/15. FAFSA, institutional form required. Applicants notified on a rolling basis starting 6/15; must reply within 4 week(s) of notification.

**Academics. Special study options:** Distance learning, double major, independent study, internships, liberal arts/career combination, teacher certification program, weekend college. **Credit/placement by examination:** AP, CLEP, IB, SAT, ACT, institutional tests. 30 credit hours maximum toward bachelor's degree. **Support services:** Learning center, reduced course load, remedial instruction, study skills assistance, tutoring, writing center.

**Majors. Education:** Elementary, music. **Philosophy/religion:** Religion. **Theology:** Bible, pastoral counseling, religious ed, sacred music, theology.

**Most popular majors.** Education 6%, theological studies 94%.

**Computing on campus.** 25 workstations in library, computer center. Commuter students can connect to campus network. Online course registration, online library, wireless network available.

**Student life. Freshman orientation:** Mandatory. Preregistration for classes offered. Held week before classes begin in fall and spring for 1-2 days depending on major. **Policies:** Religious observance required. **Housing:** Single-sex dorms, apartments available. $100 deposit. **Activities:** Bands, campus ministries, choral groups, drama, music ensembles, radio station, student government, Baptist collegiate ministry, Women of Worth.

**Athletics. Intramural:** Basketball, football (non-tackle), golf, soccer, softball, table tennis, volleyball.

**Student services.** Career counseling, student employment services, financial aid counseling, personal counseling, veterans' counselor. **Physically disabled:** Services for visually, speech, hearing impaired.

**Contact.** E-mail: admissions@baptistcollege.edu
Phone: (850) 263-3261 ext. 460 Toll-free number: (800) 328-2660 ext. 460
Fax: (850) 263-9026
Sandra Richards, Director of Marketing, Baptist College of Florida, 5400 College Drive, Graceville, FL 32440-3306

---

## Barry University
### Miami Shores, Florida
**www.barry.edu**   **CB member**   **CB code: 5053**

- Private 4-year university affiliated with Roman Catholic Church
- Residential campus in large town
- 5,053 degree-seeking undergraduates: 20% part-time, 68% women, 22% African American, 1% Asian American, 29% Hispanic American, 4% international
- 3,507 degree-seeking graduate students
- 57% of applicants admitted
- SAT or ACT (ACT writing optional) required

**General.** Founded in 1940. Regionally accredited. 22 off-campus sites for adult and continuing education and some graduate degrees. Center for Dominican Studies. **Degrees:** 1,401 bachelor's awarded; master's, doctoral, first professional offered. **ROTC:** Army, Air Force. **Location:** 14 miles from Fort Lauderdale, 7 miles from Miami. **Calendar:** Semester, limited summer session. **Full-time faculty:** 340 total; 84% have terminal degrees, 26% minority, 53% women. **Part-time faculty:** 505 total. **Class size:** 68% < 20, 31% 20-39, less than 1% 40-49, less than 1% 50-99, less than 1% >100. **Special facilities:** Human performance laboratory, athletic training room, cell biology/biotechnology lab, classroom of tomorrow, photography facilities, lighting studio, dark room, imaging lab, performing arts center, biomechanics lab.

**Freshman class profile.** 3,315 applied, 1,892 admitted, 474 enrolled.

| Mid 50% test scores | | | |
|---|---|---|---|
| SAT critical reading: | 440-520 | GPA 3.0-3.49: | 36% |
| SAT math: | 420-520 | GPA 2.0-2.99: | 38% |
| ACT composite: | 18-22 | Out-of-state: | 42% |
| GPA 3.50 or higher: | 26% | Live on campus: | 71% |
| | | International: | 7% |

**Basis for selection.** Test scores and school record important. Higher test score, GPA, and course requirements for certain majors. **Homeschooled:** Academic portfolio or GED, transcripts of any traditional high school work, SAT/ACT, copy of home school rules of the state which home school is chartered. **Learning Disabled:** Students must apply directly to comprehensive service program.

**High school preparation.** 12 units recommended. Recommended units include English 4, mathematics 3, social studies 3 and science 3. For nursing program, 1 chemistry, 1 biology, algebra II required. For biology and allied health programs, 2 laboratory science including biology and chemistry, 3.5 mathematics required. For mathematics program, 4 mathematics including algebra, geometry, trigonometry, required. For chemistry program, 3 mathematics, 1 chemistry with lab required.

**2007-2008 Annual costs.** Tuition/fees: $24,500. Room/board: $8,200. Books/supplies: $800. Personal expenses: $1,500.

**2007-2008 Financial aid. Need-based:** 388 full-time freshmen applied for aid; 350 were judged to have need; 348 of these received aid. Average need met was 69%. Average scholarship/grant was $4,602; average loan $5,475. 32% of total undergraduate aid awarded as scholarships/grants, 68% as loans/jobs. **Non-need-based:** Awarded to 3,745 full-time undergraduates, including 465 freshmen. Scholarships awarded for academics, art, athletics, music/drama.

**Application procedures. Admission:** No deadline. $30 fee. Application may be submitted online. Admission notification on a rolling basis beginning on or about 9/8. Students are allowed to postpone enrollment after admissions for up to 1 year. **Financial aid:** No deadline. FAFSA required. Applicants notified on a rolling basis starting 1/25.

**Academics. Special study options:** Accelerated study, combined bachelor's/graduate degree, double major, ESL, honors, internships, study abroad, teacher certification program. **Credit/placement by examination:** AP, CLEP, IB, institutional tests. 30 credit hours maximum toward bachelor's degree. All credit by examination should be completed prior to junior status. **Support services:** Learning center, reduced course load, remedial instruction, study skills assistance, tutoring, writing center.

**Majors. Biology:** General. **Business:** Accounting, business admin, finance, international, marketing. **Communications:** General, advertising, public relations, radio/tv. **Computer sciences:** General, computer science, information technology. **Conservation:** Environmental science, environmental studies. **Education:** Early childhood, elementary, physical, special. **English:** English lit. **Foreign languages:** French, Spanish. **Health:** Athletic training, cardiovascular technology, clinical lab science, cytotechnology, health care admin, nuclear medical technology, nursing (RN), predental, premedicine, prepharmacy, preveterinary, sonography. **History:** General. **Interdisciplinary:** Global studies. **Legal studies:** General, prelaw. **Liberal arts:** Arts/sciences. **Math:** General. **Parks/recreation:** Exercise sciences, health/fitness, sports admin. **Philosophy/religion:** Philosophy. **Physical sciences:** Chemistry. **Psychology:** General. **Public administration:** General, social work. **Social sciences:** Criminology, economics, political science, sociology. **Theology:** Theology. **Visual/performing arts:** Art, dramatic, photography.

**Most popular majors.** Business/marketing 17%, computer/information sciences 9%, education 20%, health sciences 14%, liberal arts 14%, public administration/social services 9%.

**Computing on campus.** 165 workstations in dormitories, library, computer center. Dormitories wired for high-speed internet access and linked to campus network. Commuter students can connect to campus network. Online library, helpline, repair service, wireless network available.

**Student life. Freshman orientation:** Mandatory. Preregistration for classes offered. **Housing:** Coed dorms, single-sex dorms, special housing for disabled available. $200 nonrefundable deposit. **Activities:** Choral groups, dance, drama, literary magazine, music ensembles, musical theater, radio station, student government, student newspaper, TV station, Jamaican association, black student union, Habitat for Humanity, Caribbean student organization, Haitian intercultural association, Jewish/Christian/Muslim interfaith group, Latter-day Saints student association, Best Buddies, Spanish club, Baptist dialogue group.

**Athletics.** NCAA. **Intercollegiate:** Baseball M, basketball, golf, rowing (crew) W, soccer, softball W, tennis, volleyball W. **Intramural:** Basketball, football (non-tackle), golf, skin diving, soccer, softball, volleyball. **Team name:** Buccaneers.

**Student services.** Adult student services, alcohol/substance abuse counseling, campus ministries, career counseling, student employment services, financial aid counseling, health services, personal counseling, placement for graduates. **Physically disabled:** Services for visually, speech, hearing impaired. **Learning disabled:** Comprehensive services available.

**Contact.** E-mail: admissions@mail.barry.edu
Phone: (305) 899-3100 Toll-free number: (800) 695-2279
Fax: (305) 899-2971
Laura Antczak, Director of Undergraduate Admissions, Barry University, 11300 Northeast Second Avenue, Miami Shores, FL 33161-6695

---

## Beacon College
### Leesburg, Florida
**www.beaconcollege.edu**　　　　　　　CB code: 3611

- Private 4-year liberal arts college
- Residential campus in large town
- 117 degree-seeking undergraduates: 40% women, 11% African American, 3% Asian American, 5% Hispanic American
- 63% of applicants admitted
- Application essay, interview required
- 77% graduate within 6 years; 36% enter graduate study

**General.** Regionally accredited. College solely for students with learning disabilities. **Degrees:** 23 bachelor's, 9 associate awarded. **Location:** 50 miles from Orlando. **Calendar:** Semester, limited summer session. **Full-time faculty:** 14 total; 71% have terminal degrees, 7% minority, 50% women. **Part-time faculty:** 3 total. **Class size:** 100% < 20.

**Freshman class profile.** 43 applied, 27 admitted, 17 enrolled.

| End year in good standing: | 83% | Out-of-state: | 74% |
|---|---|---|---|
| Return as sophomores: | 82% | Live on campus: | 100% |

**Basis for selection.** Selective but noncompetitive process. Recommendations, interview, character, level of interest very important; followed by rigor of secondary school record, GPA, test scores, essay, extracurricular activities, ability, volunteer work. Class rank, work experience considered. SAT or ACT recommended. Scores used noncompetitively for informational purposes only. **Homeschooled:** State high school equivalency certificate required. **Learning Disabled:** Students accepted by committee decision based on psychoeducational evaluation documenting learning disability, academic potential, evaluation of high school records, references, and campus interviews with assessments as part of admissions process. Students must provide current psychoeducational report (within 3 years) documenting learning disability as primary handicapping condition, including WAIS score.

**High school preparation.** 12 units required. Required and recommended units include English 4, mathematics 1, social studies 1, history 2-3, science 1-2 and academic electives 3.

**2007-2008 Annual costs.** Tuition/fees: $25,350. Room/board: $7,400. Books/supplies: $750. Personal expenses: $2,565.

**2006-2007 Financial aid.** All financial aid based on need. 12 full-time freshmen applied for aid; 12 were judged to have need; 12 of these received aid. Average need met was 90%. Average scholarship/grant was $15,000. 75% of total undergraduate aid awarded as scholarships/grants, 25% as loans/jobs. **Additional information:** Work-study programs offered based on financial need.

**Application procedures. Admission:** Priority date 5/1; deadline 8/1 (receipt date). $50 fee. Application must be submitted on paper. Admission notification on a rolling basis. Must reply by May 1 or within 2 week(s) if notified thereafter. **Financial aid:** Priority date 4/1; no closing date. FAFSA, institutional form required. Applicants notified on a rolling basis starting 4/1; must reply within 2 week(s) of notification.

**Academics.** Provides remedial coursework in writing, reading, and math. **Special study options:** Double major, independent study, internships, liberal arts/career combination, study abroad. **Credit/placement by examination:** AP, CLEP, institutional tests. **Support services:** Learning center, reduced course load, remedial instruction, study skills assistance, tutoring, writing center.

**Majors. Computer sciences:** General. **Liberal arts:** Arts/sciences. **Public administration:** Human services.

**Most popular majors.** Liberal arts 48%, public administration/social services 52%.

**Computing on campus.** 32 workstations in library, computer center, student center. Dormitories wired for high-speed internet access and linked to campus network. Commuter students can connect to campus network. Online library, helpline, repair service, student web hosting, wireless network available.

**Student life. Freshman orientation:** Mandatory. Preregistration for classes offered. **Housing:** Guaranteed on-campus for all undergraduates. Apartments, substance-free housing available. $750 deposit, deadline 5/1. **Activities:** Dance, literary magazine, student government, student newspaper.

**Athletics. Team name:** Bull Dogs.

**Student services.** Career counseling, student employment services, financial aid counseling, personal counseling, placement for graduates. **Physically disabled:** Services for visually, speech, hearing impaired. **Learning disabled:** Comprehensive services available.

**Contact.** E-mail: admissions@beaconcollege.edu
Phone: (352) 787-7249 Fax: (352) 787-0721
Mary Bruck, Director of Admissions, Beacon College, 105 East Main Street, Leesburg, FL 34748

---

## Bethune-Cookman University

**Daytona Beach, Florida** **CB member**
**www.cookman.edu** **CB code: 5061**

- Private 4-year liberal arts college affiliated with United Methodist Church
- Residential campus in small city
- 3,312 degree-seeking undergraduates: 6% part-time, 59% women, 92% African American, 2% Hispanic American, 2% international
- 39 degree-seeking graduate students
- 72% of applicants admitted
- SAT or ACT (ACT writing optional), application essay required
- 34% graduate within 6 years; 37% enter graduate study

**General.** Founded in 1904. Regionally accredited. **Degrees:** 343 bachelor's awarded; master's offered. **ROTC:** Army, Air Force. **Location:** 60 miles from Orlando. **Calendar:** Semester, limited summer session. **Full-time faculty:** 161 total; 5% have terminal degrees, 58% minority, 50% women. **Part-time faculty:** 28 total; 64% minority, 57% women. **Class size:** 47% < 20, 50% 20-39, 1% 40-49, 1% 50-99. **Special facilities:** Observatory.

**Freshman class profile.** 4,469 applied, 3,205 admitted, 1,102 enrolled.

| Mid 50% test scores | | Rank in top quarter: | 15% |
|---|---|---|---|
| SAT critical reading: | 360-460 | Rank in top tenth: | 5% |
| SAT math: | 360-460 | End year in good standing: | 92% |
| ACT composite: | 14-18 | Return as sophomores: | 76% |
| GPA 3.50 or higher: | 8% | Out-of-state: | 30% |
| GPA 3.0-3.49: | 18% | Live on campus: | 72% |
| GPA 2.0-2.99: | 73% | International: | 2% |

**Basis for selection.** School achievement record most important. Test scores and letters of recommendation important. Interview required of music majors.

**High school preparation.** 19 units required. Required and recommended units include English 4, mathematics 3, social studies 1, history 2, science 3 (laboratory 1), foreign language 2 and academic electives 6. 1 unit computer literacy.

**2008-2009 Annual costs.** Tuition/fees (projected): $12,427. Room/board: $7,378. Books/supplies: $1,000. Personal expenses: $2,800.

**2007-2008 Financial aid.** All financial aid based on need. 60% of total undergraduate aid awarded as scholarships/grants, 40% as loans/jobs.

**Application procedures. Admission:** Priority date 6/30; no deadline. $25 fee, may be waived for applicants with need. Application must be submitted on paper. Admission notification on a rolling basis. **Financial aid:** Priority date 4/1; no closing date. FAFSA required. Applicants notified on a rolling basis starting 4/1; must reply within 3 week(s) of notification.

**Academics. Special study options:** Accelerated study, cooperative education, distance learning, double major, honors, independent study, internships, study abroad, teacher certification program, weekend college. **Credit/placement by examination:** AP, CLEP, IB, SAT, ACT, institutional tests. 30 credit hours maximum toward bachelor's degree. **Support services:** Learning center, reduced course load, remedial instruction, study skills assistance, tutoring, writing center.

**Majors. Biology:** General. **Business:** Accounting, business admin, hotel/motel admin, international. **Communications:** Journalism. **Computer sciences:** Computer science, information systems. **Education:** General, biology, business, chemistry, elementary, English, learning disabled, music, physical, physics, social studies. **Engineering:** Computer. **English:** English lit, speech/rhetoric. **Health:** Nursing (RN). **History:** General. **Interdisciplinary:** Gerontology. **Math:** General. **Philosophy/religion:** Christian. **Physical sciences:** Chemistry, physics. **Protective services:** Law enforcement admin. **Psychology:** General. **Social sciences:** International relations, political science, sociology. **Visual/performing arts:** Music performance.

**Most popular majors.** Business/marketing 15%, communications/journalism 6%, education 26%, health sciences 10%, psychology 13%, social sciences 14%.

**Computing on campus.** 537 workstations in dormitories, library, computer center, student center. Dormitories wired for high-speed internet access and linked to campus network. Commuter students can connect to campus network. Online course registration, online library, helpline, wireless network available.

**Student life. Freshman orientation:** Mandatory. Preregistration for classes offered. One-week program in beginning of fall and spring semster. **Housing:** Guaranteed on-campus for freshmen. Single-sex dorms, substance-free housing available. $200 nonrefundable deposit, deadline 8/15. Scholarship housing for honor students. **Activities:** Bands, choral groups, dance, drama, international student organizations, music ensembles, radio station, student government, student newspaper, YM/YWCA, Religious Life Fellowship, Pre-seminarian club, Greek letter organization, Gamma Sigma Sigma National Service sorority, Kappa Kappa Psi National Band fraternity, Alpha Chi honor sorority, Alpha Kappa Mu honor sorority.

**Athletics.** NCAA. **Intercollegiate:** Baseball M, basketball, bowling W, cross-country, football (tackle) M, golf, softball W, tennis, track and field, volleyball W. **Intramural:** Basketball, football (tackle) M. **Team name:** Wildcats.

**Student services.** Adult student services, campus ministries, career counseling, student employment services, financial aid counseling, health services, personal counseling, placement for graduates, veterans' counselor.

**Contact.** E-mail: admissions@cookman.edu
Phone: (386) 481-2600 Toll-free number: (800) 448-0228
Fax: (386) 481-2601
Les Ferrier, Executive Director of Admissions, Bethune-Cookman University, Dr. Mary McLeod Bethune Boulevard, Daytona Beach, FL 32114-3099

---

## Carlos Albizu University

**Miami, Florida**
**www.albizu.edu** **CB code: 2102**

- Private 4-year university and branch campus college
- Commuter campus in very large city
- 425 degree-seeking undergraduates
- 744 graduate students
- Application essay, interview required

**General.** Founded in 1980. Regionally accredited. **Degrees:** 96 bachelor's awarded; master's, doctoral offered. **Calendar:** Semester, extensive summer session. **Full-time faculty:** 20 total. **Part-time faculty:** 75 total. **Class size:** 39% < 20, 61% 20-39.

**Basis for selection.** Open admission. Minimum 2.0 GPA required. **Homeschooled:** State high school equivalency certificate required.

**2007-2008 Annual costs.** Tuition/fees: $12,468. Reported tuition, fees and per credit hour charge are for bachelor's degree program in business. Other programs individually priced. Books/supplies: $690. Personal expenses: $1,800.

**Financial aid.** All financial aid based on need.

**Application procedures. Admission:** No deadline. $25 fee, may be waived for applicants with need. Application may be submitted online. Admission notification on a rolling basis. **Financial aid:** Priority date 6/1; no closing date. FAFSA, institutional form required. Applicants notified on a rolling basis starting 2/1.

**Academics. Special study options:** Accelerated study, cooperative education, cross-registration, distance learning, double major, dual enrollment of high school students, ESL, honors, independent study, internships, study abroad, teacher certification program, weekend college. **Credit/placement by examination:** CLEP, IB, institutional tests. 12 credit hours maximum toward bachelor's degree. 6 for foreign language, 6 for other foundation courses. **Support services:** Learning center, remedial instruction, study skills assistance, tutoring, writing center.

**Majors. Business:** General. **Education:** Elementary. **Psychology:** General.

**Computing on campus.** 50 workstations in library, computer center, student center. Commuter students can connect to campus network. Online course registration, online library, wireless network available.

**Student life. Freshman orientation:** Mandatory. Preregistration for classes offered. 2 hours, held before each session. **Activities:** Student government, student newspaper.

**Student services.** Adult student services, career counseling, services for economically disadvantaged, student employment services, financial aid counseling, minority student services, placement for graduates.

**Contact.** E-mail: webmaster@albizu.edu
Phone: (305) 593-1223 ext. 137 Toll-free number: (888) 468-6228
Fax: (305) 593-1854
Carlos Alicea, Director of Recruitment and Outreach, Carlos Albizu University, 2173 NW 99th Avenue, Miami, FL 33172

## Chipola Junior College
**Marianna, Florida**
www.chipola.edu
CB code: 5106

- Public 4-year community and junior college
- Commuter campus in small town
- 1,400 degree-seeking undergraduates

**General.** Founded in 1947. Regionally accredited. **Degrees:** 4 bachelor's, 320 associate awarded. **Location:** 70 miles from Tallahassee. **Calendar:** Semester, limited summer session. **Full-time faculty:** 60 total; 17% have terminal degrees, 3% minority, 62% women. **Part-time faculty:** 77 total; 10% minority, 26% women.

**Basis for selection.** Open admission, but selective for some programs.

**High school preparation.** Recommended units include English 4, mathematics 3, social studies 3 and science 3.

**2007-2008 Annual costs.** Tuition/fees: $2,037; $6,001 out-of-state. Books/supplies: $800. Personal expenses: $1,500.

**Financial aid. Non-need-based:** Scholarships awarded for academics, alumni affiliation, art, athletics, job skills, leadership, minority status, music/drama.

**Application procedures. Admission:** Priority date 8/1; no deadline. No application fee. Admission notification on a rolling basis. **Financial aid:** Priority date 5/1; no closing date. FAFSA, institutional form required. Applicants notified on a rolling basis starting 1/2; must reply within 2 week(s) of notification.

**Academics. Special study options:** Accelerated study, cooperative education, distance learning, dual enrollment of high school students, honors, independent study, internships, liberal arts/career combination, teacher certification program. **Credit/placement by examination:** AP, CLEP, IB. 45 credit hours maximum toward associate degree, 45 toward bachelor's. **Support services:** Remedial instruction, study skills assistance, tutoring, writing center.

**Majors. Biology:** General. **Education:** Mathematics, middle, science, secondary. **Math:** General.

**Computing on campus.** 150 workstations in library. Dormitories linked to campus network. Online library available.

**Student life. Freshman orientation:** Mandatory. Preregistration for classes offered. **Housing:** Only men's and women's athletic dorms available. **Activities:** Jazz band, campus ministries, choral groups, dance, drama, musical theater, student government, student newspaper, The Vine (interdenominational organization), Black Student Union.

**Athletics.** NJCAA. **Intercollegiate:** Baseball M, basketball, softball W. **Team name:** Indians.

**Student services.** Career counseling. **Physically disabled:** Services for visually, hearing impaired.

**Contact.** Phone: (850) 526-2761 Fax: (850) 718-2287
Jayne Roberts, Dean of Enrollment Services, Chipola Junior College, 3094 Indian Circle, Marianna, FL 32446

## City College: Fort Lauderdale
**Fort Lauderdale, Florida**
www.citycollege.edu
CB code: 3578

- Private 4-year business and technical college
- Commuter campus in very large city
- 439 degree-seeking undergraduates: 2% part-time, 68% women
- Application essay, interview required

**General.** Accredited by ACICS. **Degrees:** 20 bachelor's, 240 associate awarded. **Calendar:** Quarter. **Full-time faculty:** 14 total. **Part-time faculty:** 46 total.

**Basis for selection.** Open admission, but selective for some programs. **Homeschooled:** Statement describing homeschool structure and mission, transcript of courses and grades required.

**2007-2008 Annual costs.** Tuition/fees: $9,975. Books/supplies: $1,044. Personal expenses: $2,931.

**Application procedures. Admission:** No deadline. $25 fee, may be waived for applicants with need. Admission notification on a rolling basis.

**Academics. Special study options:** Distance learning, independent study, internships. **Credit/placement by examination:** CLEP, IB, institutional tests. 15 credit hours maximum toward associate degree, 30 toward bachelor's. **Support services:** Remedial instruction, tutoring.

**Majors. Business:** Business admin.

**Computing on campus.** 70 workstations in library. Online library available.

**Student life. Freshman orientation:** Mandatory. Preregistration for classes offered.

**Student services.** Adult student services, alcohol/substance abuse counseling, career counseling, student employment services, financial aid counseling, personal counseling, placement for graduates.

**Contact.** Phone: (954) 492-5353 Fax: (954) 491-1965
Ron Lohrmann, Director of Admissions, City College: Fort Lauderdale, 2000 West Commercial Boulevard, Fort Lauderdale, FL 33309

## City College: Miami
**Miami, Florida**
www.citycollege.edu
CB code: 3580

- For-profit 4-year business and health science college
- Large city
- 271 degree-seeking undergraduates

**General.** Accredited by ACICS. **Degrees:** 11 bachelor's, 63 associate awarded. **Calendar:** Continuous. **Full-time faculty:** 4 total. **Part-time faculty:** 25 total.

**Basis for selection.** TABE is required. SAT or ACT considered if submitted.

**2007-2008 Annual costs.** Tuition/fees: $9,900.

**Financial aid.** All financial aid based on need.

**Application procedures. Admission:** No deadline. $25 fee. Admission notification on a rolling basis. **Financial aid:** No deadline. FAFSA, institutional form required. Applicants notified on a rolling basis.

**Academics. Credit/placement by examination:** CLEP.

**Majors. Business:** Business admin.

**Contact.** E-mail: sespath@citycollege.edu
Phone: (305) 666-9242 Fax: (305) 666-9243
Sandy Espath, Director of Admissions, City College: Miami, 9300 South Dadeland Boulevard, Miami, FL 33156

## Clearwater Christian College
**Clearwater, Florida**
www.clearwater.edu
CB code: 5142

- Private 4-year liberal arts college affiliated with nondenominational tradition
- Residential campus in small city

- 575 degree-seeking undergraduates: 2% part-time, 50% women, 3% African American, 2% Asian American, 5% Hispanic American, 1% international
- 93% of applicants admitted
- SAT or ACT, application essay required
- 58% graduate within 6 years; 20% enter graduate study

**General.** Founded in 1966. Regionally accredited. **Degrees:** 139 bachelor's, 3 associate awarded. **ROTC:** Army, Naval, Air Force. **Location:** 20 miles from Tampa, 15 miles from St. Petersburg. **Calendar:** Semester, limited summer session. **Full-time faculty:** 30 total; 67% have terminal degrees, 33% women. **Part-time faculty:** 16 total; 50% have terminal degrees, 38% women. **Class size:** 72% < 20, 18% 20-39, 3% 40-49, 6% 50-99, less than 1% >100.

**Freshman class profile.** 365 applied, 340 admitted, 175 enrolled.

| Mid 50% test scores | | Return as sophomores: | 56% |
|---|---|---|---|
| SAT critical reading: | 450-580 | Out-of-state: | 52% |
| SAT math: | 420-560 | Live on campus: | 95% |
| ACT composite: | 19-25 | International: | 2% |
| Rank in top quarter: | 36% | Fraternities: | 100% |
| Rank in top tenth: | 10% | Sororities: | 100% |

**Basis for selection.** 2.0 GPA, 870 SAT (exclusive of Writing) or 18 ACT, recommendations, Christian testimony important. SAT/ACT scores may be waived for some transfer applicants. Interview recommended. Audition recommended for music majors. **Homeschooled:** Transcript of courses and grades required. GED required if transcript not available; liberal arts/college preparatory program recommended; academic placement testing may be administered.

**High school preparation.** Recommended units include English 4, mathematics 3, social studies 3, science 3 and foreign language 2. Math units should include geometry; English units should emphasize grammar and writing.

**2007-2008 Annual costs.** Tuition/fees: $13,160. Room/board: $5,610. Books/supplies: $850. Personal expenses: $1,750.

**2007-2008 Financial aid. Need-based:** 149 full-time freshmen applied for aid; 120 were judged to have need; 120 of these received aid. Average need met was 62%. Average scholarship/grant was $3,477; average loan $1,866. **Non-need-based:** Scholarships awarded for academics, alumni affiliation, leadership, music/drama, religious affiliation, ROTC. **Additional information:** Special consideration given to children of Christian service workers; need-based scholarships available to first-generation students; scholarships up to $3,000 available to dual-enrolled students.

**Application procedures. Admission:** Closing date 8/1 (receipt date). $35 fee, may be waived for applicants with need. Application may be submitted online. Admission notification on a rolling basis. **Financial aid:** Priority date 3/15; no closing date. FAFSA, institutional form required. Applicants notified on a rolling basis starting 4/15; must reply within 2 week(s) of notification.

**Academics.** All students completing bachelor's degree earn the equivalent of 20-hour minor in Bible. **Special study options:** Distance learning, double major, dual enrollment of high school students, honors, independent study, internships, liberal arts/career combination, student-designed major, study abroad, teacher certification program. **Credit/placement by examination:** AP, CLEP, IB, institutional tests. 24 credit hours maximum toward associate degree, 24 toward bachelor's. **Support services:** Reduced course load, remedial instruction, study skills assistance, tutoring.

**Majors. Biology:** General. **Business:** Accounting, business admin, office management. **Communications:** General. **Education:** Biology, elementary, English, mathematics, music, physical, social studies, special. **English:** English lit. **Health:** Premedicine. **History:** General. **Legal studies:** Prelaw. **Liberal arts:** Arts/sciences. **Math:** General. **Psychology:** General. **Theology:** Bible, religious ed, sacred music, theology.

**Most popular majors.** Biology 9%, business/marketing 18%, education 16%, interdisciplinary studies 7%, liberal arts 16%, theological studies 7%.

**Computing on campus.** 38 workstations in dormitories, library, computer center. Dormitories wired for high-speed internet access and linked to campus network. Commuter students can connect to campus network. Online library, helpline, repair service, wireless network available.

**Student life. Freshman orientation:** Mandatory. Preregistration for classes offered. Two-day program held prior to start of fall semester. **Policies:** Convocation and Christian Life Conference; chapel 4 days per week; evening Bible studies and prayer meetings required of students in the residence halls. Religious observance required. **Housing:** Guaranteed on-campus for all undergraduates. Single-sex dorms, substance-free housing available. $100 deposit. **Activities:** Bands, campus ministries, choral groups, drama, music ensembles, musical theater, student government, student newspaper, symphony orchestra, political club, College Republicans, Fellowship of Preministerial Students, student missionary fellowship, China team, music ministry team, joy club.

**Athletics.** NCCAA. **Intercollegiate:** Baseball M, basketball, golf, soccer, softball W, volleyball W. **Intramural:** Basketball, football (non-tackle) M, soccer, table tennis, tennis, volleyball. **Team name:** Cougars.

**Student services.** Career counseling, student employment services, financial aid counseling, personal counseling, placement for graduates. **Physically disabled:** Services for speech impaired.

**Contact.** E-mail: admissions@clearwater.edu
Phone: (727) 726-1153 ext. 220 Toll-free number: (800) 348-4463
Fax: (727) 726-8597
Keith Hutchison, Director of Admissions and Advising, Clearwater Christian College, 3400 Gulf-to-Bay Boulevard, Clearwater, FL 33759-4595

---

## DeVry University: Miramar
**Miramar, Florida**
**www.devry.edu**                          **CB code: 4134**

- For-profit 4-year university
- Commuter campus in large town
- 886 degree-seeking undergraduates: 50% part-time, 37% women, 36% African American, 2% Asian American, 45% Hispanic American, 5% international
- 137 degree-seeking graduate students
- Interview required

**General. Degrees:** 163 bachelor's, 20 associate awarded; master's offered. **Calendar:** Semester, extensive summer session. **Full-time faculty:** 23 total; 44% minority, 17% women. **Part-time faculty:** 48 total; 35% minority, 31% women.

**Freshman class profile.**

| Return as sophomores: | 56% | International: | 3% |
|---|---|---|---|
| Out-of-state: | 1% | | |

**Basis for selection.** Applicants must have high school diploma or equivalent, or a degree from accredited postsecondary institution, demonstrate proficiency in basic college-level skills through SAT or ACT scores or institution-administered placement exams, and be at least 17 years of age. New students may enter at beginning of any semester. CPT also accepted.

**2007-2008 Annual costs.** Tuition/fees: $14,020. Books/supplies: $1,100. Personal expenses: $1,816.

**Financial aid.** All financial aid based on need.

**Application procedures. Admission:** No deadline. $50 fee. Application may be submitted online. Admission notification on a rolling basis. **Financial aid:** No deadline. FAFSA required. Applicants notified on a rolling basis.

**Academics. Special study options:** Accelerated study, distance learning. **Credit/placement by examination:** CLEP. **Support services:** Learning center, remedial instruction, tutoring.

**Majors. Business:** Business admin, operations. **Computer sciences:** Information systems, LAN/WAN management. **Engineering technology:** Computer, electrical.

**Most popular majors.** Business/marketing 76%, computer/information sciences 14%, engineering/engineering technologies 10%.

**Computing on campus.** Online course registration, online library, helpline available.

**Student life. Activities:** Student government, student newspaper.

**Student services.** Career counseling, student employment services, financial aid counseling, placement for graduates, veterans' counselor. **Physically disabled:** Services for visually, hearing impaired.

**Contact.** E-mail: openhouse@mir.devry.edu
Phone: (954) 499-9700 Toll-free number: (866) 793-3879
Fax: (954) 499-9723
Aaron McCardell, Director of Admission, DeVry University: Miramar, 2300 Southwest 145th Avenue, Miramar, FL 33027

## DeVry University: Orlando
### Orlando, Florida
### www.devry.edu
**CB code: 2881**

- For-profit 4-year university
- Commuter campus in very large city
- 1,249 degree-seeking undergraduates: 48% part-time, 35% women, 27% African American, 3% Asian American, 23% Hispanic American, 2% international
- 158 degree-seeking graduate students
- Interview required

**General.** Regionally accredited. **Degrees:** 216 bachelor's, 21 associate awarded; master's offered. **Calendar:** Semester, extensive summer session. **Full-time faculty:** 26 total; 12% minority, 31% women. **Part-time faculty:** 65 total; 20% minority, 38% women.

**Basis for selection.** Applicants must have high school diploma or equivalent, or degree from an accredited postsecondary institution. New students may enter at the beginning of any semester. SAT or ACT or institution-administered placement examination used to determine proficiency in basic college-level skills.

**High school preparation.** Required units include mathematics 1. Math unit must be algebra or higher.

**2007-2008 Annual costs.** Tuition/fees: $14,020. Books/supplies: $1,300. Personal expenses: $3,152.

**Financial aid.** All financial aid based on need.

**Application procedures. Admission:** No deadline. $50 fee. Application may be submitted online. Admission notification on a rolling basis. **Financial aid:** No deadline. FAFSA required. Applicants notified on a rolling basis starting 7/2.

**Academics. Special study options:** Accelerated study, distance learning. **Credit/placement by examination:** CLEP, institutional tests. **Support services:** Learning center, remedial instruction, tutoring.

**Majors. Business:** Business admin. **Computer sciences:** Game design, information systems, LAN/WAN management, systems analysis. **Engineering technology:** Biomedical, computer, computer systems, electrical.

**Most popular majors.** Business/marketing 70%, computer/information sciences 23%, engineering/engineering technologies 7%.

**Computing on campus.** 303 workstations in library, computer center. Online course registration, online library, helpline available.

**Student life. Freshman orientation:** Mandatory. **Activities:** Student newspaper, student activities council, National Society of Black Engineers, association for IT professionals, chess club, technology forum, Millennia Engineering Students Association.

**Student services.** Career counseling, student employment services, financial aid counseling, placement for graduates, veterans' counselor. **Physically disabled:** Services for visually, hearing impaired.

**Contact.** E-mail: krochford@orl.devry.edu
Phone: (407) 370-3131 Toll-free number: (866) 353-3879
Fax: (407) 370-3198
Jody Wasmer, Director of Admissions, DeVry University: Orlando, 4000 Millennia Boulevard, Orlando, FL 32839-2426

## Eckerd College
### St. Petersburg, Florida
### www.eckerd.edu
**CB member**
**CB code: 5223**

- Private 4-year liberal arts college affiliated with Presbyterian Church (USA)
- Residential campus in large city
- 1,826 degree-seeking undergraduates: 1% part-time, 58% women, 3% African American, 2% Asian American, 4% Hispanic American, 3% international
- 67% of applicants admitted
- SAT or ACT (ACT writing optional), application essay required
- 58% graduate within 6 years

**General.** Founded in 1958. Regionally accredited. **Degrees:** 347 bachelor's awarded. **ROTC:** Army, Air Force. **Location:** 25 miles from Tampa.

**Calendar:** 4-1-4, limited summer session. **Full-time faculty:** 113 total; 95% have terminal degrees, 12% minority, 40% women. **Part-time faculty:** 43 total; 23% have terminal degrees, 21% minority, 51% women. **Class size:** 38% < 20, 58% 20-39, 3% 40-49, 1% 50-99. **Special facilities:** Marine science laboratory, waterfront program.

**Freshman class profile.** 3,118 applied, 2,086 admitted, 539 enrolled.

| Mid 50% test scores | | | |
|---|---|---|---|
| SAT critical reading: | 510-610 | GPA 2.0-2.99: | 25% |
| SAT math: | 500-610 | Rank in top quarter: | 45% |
| SAT writing: | 500-600 | Rank in top tenth: | 17% |
| ACT composite: | 22-27 | Return as sophomores: | 72% |
| GPA 3.50 or higher: | 31% | Out-of-state: | 73% |
| GPA 3.0-3.49: | 44% | Live on campus: | 95% |
| | | International: | 2% |

**Basis for selection.** School achievement record, school/community involvement, essay, student's character, test scores most important. Interview recommended. Audition tapes for music and theater majors accepted, portfolios accepted for art majors. **Homeschooled:** Statement describing homeschool structure and mission, transcript of courses and grades, state high school equivalency certificate, letter of recommendation (nonparent) required. **Learning Disabled:** Students should provide proper documentation for any disability they wish to inform the college about.

**High school preparation.** 18 units required; 22 recommended. Required and recommended units include English 4, mathematics 3-4, social studies 2, history 1-2, science 3-4 (laboratory 2-3), foreign language 2-3 and academic electives 3.

**2008-2009 Annual costs.** Tuition/fees (projected): $30,590. Room/board: $8,754. Books/supplies: $1,000. Personal expenses: $1,400.

**Financial aid. Non-need-based:** Scholarships awarded for academics, art, athletics, leadership, music/drama, religious affiliation.

**Application procedures. Admission:** No deadline. $35 fee, may be waived for applicants with need. Application may be submitted online. Admission notification on a rolling basis beginning on or about 10/1. Must reply by May 1 or within 2 week(s) if notified thereafter. **Financial aid:** Priority date 3/1; no closing date. FAFSA required. Applicants notified on a rolling basis starting 2/1.

**Academics. Special study options:** Accelerated study, combined bachelor's/graduate degree, double major, exchange student, honors, independent study, internships, liberal arts/career combination, semester at sea, student-designed major, study abroad, United Nations semester, Washington semester. Winter term exchange with other 4-1-4 colleges, 3-2 in engineering with Columbia University, Washington University (MO), University of Miami, and Auburn. **Credit/placement by examination:** AP, CLEP, IB, institutional tests. 63 credit hours maximum toward bachelor's degree. **Support services:** Reduced course load, tutoring, writing center.

**Majors. Area/ethnic studies:** American, East Asian, women's. **Biology:** General, biochemistry, environmental, marine. **Business:** Business admin, international, management science. **Communications:** General. **Computer sciences:** General. **Conservation:** Environmental studies. **English:** Creative writing, English lit. **Foreign languages:** General, comparative lit, French, Spanish. **History:** General. **Interdisciplinary:** Global studies. **Liberal arts:** Humanities. **Math:** General. **Philosophy/religion:** Philosophy, religion. **Physical sciences:** Chemistry, physics. **Psychology:** General, developmental. **Social sciences:** Anthropology, economics, international relations, political science, sociology. **Visual/performing arts:** Art history/conservation, dramatic, studio arts.

**Most popular majors.** Biology 15%, business/marketing 21%, foreign language 6%, natural resources/environmental science 10%, social sciences 15%.

**Computing on campus.** 300 workstations in dormitories, library. Dormitories wired for high-speed internet access and linked to campus network. Commuter students can connect to campus network. Online course registration, online library, helpline, repair service, student web hosting, wireless network available.

**Student life. Freshman orientation:** Mandatory. Preregistration for classes offered. Three-week session held in fall. **Housing:** Guaranteed on-campus for all undergraduates. Coed dorms, single-sex dorms, apartments, substance-free housing available. Pets allowed in dorm rooms. **Activities:** Campus ministries, choral groups, drama, film society, international student organizations, literary magazine, music ensembles, Model UN, musical theater, radio station, student government, student newspaper, TV station, Phi Beta Kappa, Afro-American society, search and rescue team, Circle-K, honor societies, Earth society.

**Athletics.** NCAA. **Intercollegiate:** Baseball M, basketball, golf, sailing, soccer, softball W, tennis, volleyball W. **Intramural:** Baseball M, basketball, bowling, sailing, soccer, softball, swimming, table tennis, tennis, volleyball. **Team name:** Tritons.

**Student services.** Adult student services, alcohol/substance abuse counseling, career counseling, student employment services, financial aid counseling, health services, minority student services, personal counseling, placement for graduates, veterans' counselor, women's services.

**Contact.** E-mail: admissions@eckerd.edu
Phone: (727) 864-8331 Toll-free number: (800) 456-9009
Fax: (727) 866-2304
John Sullivan, Dean of Admissions and Financial Aid, Eckerd College, 4200 54th Avenue South, St. Petersburg, FL 33711-4700

## Edison College
**Fort Myers, Florida**  **CB member**
**www.edison.edu**  **CB code: 5191**

- Public 4-year liberal arts college
- Commuter campus in very large city

**General.** Founded in 1961. Regionally accredited. **Location:** 35 miles from Naples, 120 miles from Tampa. **Calendar:** Semester.

**Annual costs/financial aid.** Tuition/fees (2007-2008): $2,091; $7,937 out-of-state. Tuition and fees reported are for associate degree programs; annual tuition and fees for bachelor level program in public safety: $2,301 for in state, $13,447 for out of state. Books/supplies: $626. Personal expenses: $1,060. Need-based financial aid available to full-time and part-time students.

**Contact.** Phone: (239) 489-9121
District Registrar, Box 60210, Fort Myers, FL 33906-6210

## Edward Waters College
**Jacksonville, Florida**
**www.ewc.edu**  **CB code: 5182**

- Private 4-year liberal arts college affiliated with African Methodist Episcopal Church
- Commuter campus in very large city
- 811 degree-seeking undergraduates: 8% part-time, 44% women, 94% African American, 1% Hispanic American, 1% international

**General.** Founded in 1866. Regionally accredited. **Degrees:** 140 bachelor's awarded. **Location:** 150 miles from Orlando; 90 miles from Savannah, Georgia. **Calendar:** Semester, extensive summer session. **Full-time faculty:** 53 total; 53% have terminal degrees, 87% minority, 34% women. **Part-time faculty:** 5 total; 100% minority, 40% women. **Class size:** 71% < 20, 29% 20-39. **Special facilities:** African art collection.

**Freshman class profile.**

| | | | |
|---|---|---|---|
| GPA 3.50 or higher: | 7% | Out-of-state: | 22% |
| GPA 3.0-3.49: | 17% | Live on campus: | 82% |
| GPA 2.0-2.99: | 72% | International: | 1% |
| Return as sophomores: | 53% | | |

**Basis for selection.** Open admission.

**High school preparation.** 13 units recommended. Recommended units include English 4, mathematics 3, social studies 3 and science 3.

**2008-2009 Annual costs.** Tuition/fees (projected): $10,618. Room/board: $6,474. Books/supplies: $500. Personal expenses: $750.

**Application procedures. Admission:** No deadline. $25 fee, may be waived for applicants with need. Admission notification on a rolling basis. Must reply by May 1 or within 4 week(s) if notified thereafter. **Financial aid:** Closing date 4/15. FAFSA required. Applicants notified on a rolling basis starting 5/1; must reply within 2 week(s) of notification.

**Academics. Special study options:** Accelerated study, combined bachelor's/graduate degree, cooperative education, cross-registration, double major, dual enrollment of high school students, independent study, internships, liberal arts/career combination, teacher certification program. **Credit/placement by examination:** AP, CLEP, institutional tests. 30 credit hours maximum toward bachelor's degree. **Support services:** Learning center, pre-admission summer program, remedial instruction, study skills assistance, tutoring.

**Majors. Biology:** General. **Business:** Business admin. **Communications:** General, journalism. **Computer sciences:** Computer science. **Education:** General, mathematics, mentally handicapped, physical, special. **History:** General. **Legal studies:** Prelaw. **Liberal arts:** Arts/sciences. **Math:** General.

**Philosophy/religion:** Religion. **Protective services:** Law enforcement admin. **Psychology:** General. **Public administration:** Social work. **Social sciences:** Sociology.

**Most popular majors.** Business/marketing 52%, education 9%, psychology 9%, security/protective services 11%.

**Computing on campus.** 120 workstations in dormitories, library, computer center. Dormitories wired for high-speed internet access and linked to campus network. Repair service, wireless network available.

**Student life. Freshman orientation:** Mandatory. Preregistration for classes offered. **Policies:** Religious observance required. **Housing:** Guaranteed on-campus for freshmen. Coed dorms, single-sex dorms, substance-free housing available. $100 deposit, deadline 7/31. **Activities:** Bands, campus ministries, choral groups, dance, drama, international student organizations, music ensembles, student government, student newspaper, NAACP, debate club, pre-alumni club.

**Athletics.** NAIA. **Intercollegiate:** Baseball M, basketball, cheerleading, cross-country M, diving W, football (tackle) M, golf, softball W, track and field M, volleyball W. **Intramural:** Table tennis, volleyball. **Team name:** Fighting Tigers.

**Student services.** Adult student services, career counseling, student employment services, financial aid counseling, health services, personal counseling, placement for graduates, veterans' counselor.

**Contact.** E-mail: Admissions@ewc.edu
Phone: (904) 470-8000 Toll-free number: (888) 898-3191
Fax: (904) 470-8041
Lonnie Morris, Director of Admissions, Edward Waters College, 1658 Kings Road, Jacksonville, FL 32209

## Embry-Riddle Aeronautical University
**Daytona Beach, Florida**  **CB member**
**www.embryriddle.edu**  **CB code: 5190**

- Private 4-year university
- Residential campus in small city
- 4,531 degree-seeking undergraduates: 9% part-time, 16% women, 6% African American, 6% Asian American, 8% Hispanic American, 9% international
- 392 degree-seeking graduate students
- 78% of applicants admitted
- SAT or ACT (ACT writing optional) required
- 61% graduate within 6 years; 2% enter graduate study

**General.** Founded in 1926. Regionally accredited. Over 130 teaching centers across United States and Europe. **Degrees:** 818 bachelor's, 1 associate awarded; master's offered. **ROTC:** Army, Naval, Air Force. **Location:** 50 miles from Orlando. **Calendar:** Semester, extensive summer session. **Full-time faculty:** 241 total; 66% have terminal degrees, 13% minority, 20% women. **Part-time faculty:** 86 total; 9% have terminal degrees, 20% minority, 38% women. **Class size:** 24% < 20, 69% 20-39, 6% 40-49, 2% 50-99. **Special facilities:** Airway science simulation lab.

**Freshman class profile.** 3,878 applied, 3,037 admitted, 1,038 enrolled.

| Mid 50% test scores | | | |
|---|---|---|---|
| SAT critical reading: | 470-590 | Rank in top tenth: | 20% |
| SAT math: | 500-630 | Return as sophomores: | 79% |
| ACT composite: | 21-27 | Out-of-state: | 73% |
| GPA 3.50 or higher: | 37% | Live on campus: | 95% |
| GPA 3.0-3.49: | 36% | International: | 8% |
| GPA 2.0-2.99: | 26% | Fraternities: | 12% |
| Rank in top quarter: | 45% | Sororities: | 9% |

**Basis for selection.** High school GPA, rank in class, and test scores important. Specific requirements vary by degree program. Interview and essay recommended.

**High school preparation.** 15 units required; 19 recommended. Required and recommended units include English 4, mathematics 3-4, social studies 2, history 1-2, science 2-3 (laboratory 2), foreign language 1 and academic electives 3.

**2008-2009 Annual costs.** Tuition/fees: $27,540. Room/board: $9,580. Books/supplies: $1,040. Personal expenses: $1,392.

**2007-2008 Financial aid. Need-based:** 781 full-time freshmen applied for aid; 642 were judged to have need; 642 of these received aid. Average

scholarship/grant was $9,374; average loan $4,069. 51% of total undergraduate aid awarded as scholarships/grants, 49% as loans/jobs. **Non-need-based:** Awarded to 127 full-time undergraduates, including 19 freshmen. Scholarships awarded for academics, alumni affiliation, athletics, leadership, ROTC.

**Application procedures. Admission:** No deadline. $50 fee, may be waived for applicants with need. Application may be submitted online. Admission notification on a rolling basis beginning on or about 11/1. Early application encouraged since available facilities limit enrollment in some programs. **Financial aid:** No deadline. FAFSA required. Applicants notified on a rolling basis starting 3/1; must reply within 4 week(s) of notification.

**Academics. Special study options:** Accelerated study, cooperative education, distance learning, double major, dual enrollment of high school students, ESL, honors, independent study, internships, student-designed major, study abroad. **Credit/placement by examination:** AP, CLEP, IB, SAT, ACT, institutional tests. 30 credit hours maximum toward bachelor's degree. **Support services:** Pre-admission summer program, remedial instruction, study skills assistance, tutoring.

**Majors. Business:** Business admin. **Communications:** General. **Computer sciences:** General, computer science. **Engineering:** General, aerospace, civil, computer, electrical, mechanical, physics, software. **Engineering technology:** Aerospace, electrical, occupational safety. **Mechanic/repair:** Aircraft powerplant. **Physical sciences:** Atmospheric science, physics. **Transportation:** Air traffic control, airline/commercial pilot, aviation, aviation management.

**Most popular majors.** Business/marketing 6%, engineering/engineering technologies 31%, trade and industry 56%.

**Computing on campus.** 996 workstations in library, computer center. Dormitories linked to campus network. Commuter students can connect to campus network. Helpline, student web hosting available.

**Student life. Freshman orientation:** Available. Preregistration for classes offered. **Housing:** Guaranteed on-campus for freshmen. Coed dorms available. $250 nonrefundable deposit, deadline 11/1. Special units available in regular coed dorms. **Activities:** Pep band, campus ministries, choral groups, dance, drama, international student organizations, music ensembles, Model UN, radio station, student government, student newspaper, more than 150 clubs and organizations available.

**Athletics.** NAIA. **Intercollegiate:** Baseball M, basketball M, cheerleading, cross-country, golf, soccer, tennis, track and field, volleyball W. **Intramural:** Badminton, basketball, bowling, football (non-tackle), golf, racquetball, soccer, table tennis, volleyball. **Team name:** Eagles.

**Student services.** Alcohol/substance abuse counseling, career counseling, student employment services, financial aid counseling, health services, personal counseling, placement for graduates, veterans' counselor. **Physically disabled:** Services for visually, speech, hearing impaired.

**Contact.** E-mail: dbadmit@erau.edu
Phone: (386) 226-6100 Toll-free number: (800) 862-2416
Fax: (386) 226-7070
Rich Clarke, Director of Admissions, Embry-Riddle Aeronautical University, 600 South Clyde Morris Boulevard, Daytona Beach, FL 32114-3900

## Embry-Riddle Aeronautical University: Worldwide Campus

**Daytona Beach, Florida**
www.embryriddle.edu                    CB code: 5036

- Private 4-year university
- Commuter campus in small city
- 11,569 degree-seeking undergraduates: 82% part-time, 11% women, 9% African American, 3% Asian American, 8% Hispanic American, 1% Native American
- 3,822 degree-seeking graduate students

**General.** Regionally accredited. Campus is network of more than 130 centers and teaching sites in United States and Europe, with virtual presence via distance learning covering every continent. **Degrees:** 2,172 bachelor's, 627 associate awarded; master's offered. **Calendar:** Semester, extensive summer session. **Full-time faculty:** 129 total; 49% have terminal degrees, 6% minority, 22% women. **Part-time faculty:** 2,211 total; 16% have terminal degrees, 15% minority, 20% women.

**Basis for selection.** High school GPA, rank in class, and test scores important. Specific requirements vary by degree program.

**2008-2009 Annual costs.** Per credit hour charges range from $215 to $275.

**2007-2008 Financial aid. Need-based:** 8 full-time freshmen applied for aid; 4 were judged to have need; 4 of these received aid. Average scholarship/grant was $4,126; average loan $3,500. 24% of total undergraduate aid awarded as scholarships/grants, 76% as loans/jobs. **Non-need-based:** Scholarships awarded for academics.

**Application procedures. Admission:** No deadline. $50 fee, may be waived for applicants with need. **Financial aid:** Priority date 4/15; no closing date. FAFSA required. Applicants notified on a rolling basis starting 3/1; must reply within 4 week(s) of notification.

**Academics. Special study options:** Distance learning. **Credit/placement by examination:** AP, CLEP.

**Majors. Business:** Business admin. **Mechanic/repair:** Aircraft powerplant. **Transportation:** Aviation, aviation management.

**Most popular majors.** Business/marketing 13%, trade and industry 87%.

**Contact.** E-mail: ecinfo@erau.edu
Phone: (386) 225-6910 Toll-free number: (800) 522-6787
Fax: (386) 226-6984
Pamela Thomas, Director of Admissions, Embry-Riddle Aeronautical University: Worldwide Campus, 600 South Clyde Morris Boulevard, Daytona Beach, FL 32114-3900

## Everest University: Brandon

**Tampa, Florida**
www.everest.edu                    CB code: 3585

- For-profit 4-year university and business college
- Commuter campus in very large city
- 800 degree-seeking undergraduates
- 50 graduate students

**General.** Accredited by ACICS. **Degrees:** 70 bachelor's, 244 associate awarded; master's offered. **Calendar:** Quarter. **Full-time faculty:** 15 total. **Part-time faculty:** 66 total.

**Basis for selection.** Open admission, but selective for some programs. Special requirements for nursing programs. CPAT required.

**2007-2008 Annual costs.** Tuition/fees: $13,695. Books/supplies: $1,200. Personal expenses: $1,799.

**Financial aid.** All financial aid based on need.

**Application procedures. Admission:** No deadline. $25 fee, may be waived for applicants with need. Admission notification on a rolling basis. **Financial aid:** No deadline. FAFSA, institutional form required. Applicants notified on a rolling basis; must reply within 2 week(s) of notification.

**Academics. Special study options:** Cooperative education, distance learning, ESL. **Credit/placement by examination:** AP, CLEP.

**Majors. Business:** Accounting, business admin, marketing. **Computer sciences:** Information systems. **Legal studies:** Paralegal. **Protective services:** Law enforcement admin.

**Contact.** E-mail: SPointer@cci.edu
Phone: (813) 621-0041 Toll-free number: (877) 338-0068
Fax: (813) 628-0919
Shandretta Pointer, Director of Admissions, Everest University: Brandon, 3924 Coconut Palm Drive, Tampa, FL 33619

## Everest University: Lakeland

**Lakeland, Florida**
www.everest.edu                    CB code: 3584

- For-profit 4-year university and branch campus college
- Small city
- 700 degree-seeking undergraduates

**General.** Accredited by ACICS. **Degrees:** 34 bachelor's, 141 associate awarded. **Calendar:** Quarter, extensive summer session. **Full-time faculty:** 15 total. **Part-time faculty:** 39 total.

Four-Year Colleges

**Basis for selection.** At least one of the following required for admission: ACT of 15; SAT of 700 (exclusive of Writing); passing grade on the university-administered assessment examination.

**2007-2008 Annual costs.** Tuition/fees: $13,695.

**Financial aid.** All financial aid based on need.

**Application procedures. Admission:** No deadline. $25 fee, may be waived for applicants with need. Admission notification on a rolling basis. **Financial aid:** No deadline.

**Academics. Credit/placement by examination:** CLEP.

**Majors. Business:** Accounting, business admin. **Computer sciences:** General. **Protective services:** Criminal justice.

**Student life. Freshman orientation:** Mandatory.

**Contact.** Phone: (863) 686-1444
Stephanie Andrews, Registrar, Everest University: Lakeland, 995 East Memorial Boulevard, Suite 110, Lakeland, FL 33801-1919

## Everest University: North Orlando
Orlando, Florida
www.everest.edu — CB code: 0742

- For-profit 4-year business college
- Commuter campus in very large city

**General.** Founded in 1918. Accredited by ACICS. **Location:** 2 miles from downtown. **Calendar:** Quarter.

**Annual costs/financial aid.** Tuition/fees (2007-2008): $13,695. Books/supplies: $700. Personal expenses: $1,764. Need-based financial aid available to full-time and part-time students.

**Contact.** Phone: (407) 628-5870
Director of Admissions, 5421 Diplomat Circle, Orlando, FL 32810

## Everest University: Pinellas
Clearwater, Florida
www.everest.edu — CB code: 3583

- For-profit 5-year university and business college
- Commuter campus in large city

**General.** Accredited by ACICS. **Location:** 15 miles from Tampa. **Calendar:** Quarter.

**Annual costs/financial aid.** Tuition/fees (2007-2008): $13,695. Books/supplies: $500. Need-based financial aid available to full-time and part-time students.

**Contact.** Phone: (727) 725-2688
Director of Admissions, 2471 McMullen Booth Road, Suite 200, Clearwater, FL 33759

## Everest University: Pompano Beach
Pompano Beach, Florida
www.everest.edu — CB code: 5171

- For-profit 4-year business college
- Small city
- 1,500 degree-seeking undergraduates
- Interview required

**General.** Founded in 1940. Accredited by ACICS. **Degrees:** 150 bachelor's, 180 associate awarded; master's offered. **Location:** 35 miles from Miami. **Calendar:** Quarter, extensive summer session. **Full-time faculty:** 18 total. **Part-time faculty:** 84 total.

**Freshman class profile.**

| | | | |
|---|---|---|---|
| Out-of-state: | 78% | Live on campus: | 40% |

**Basis for selection.** School achievement record, interview considered. School entrance examination required.

**2007-2008 Annual costs.** Tuition/fees: $13,695. Tuition may vary by program. Books/supplies: $600. Personal expenses: $1,584.

**Application procedures. Admission:** No deadline. $25 fee. Admission notification on a rolling basis. **Financial aid:** No deadline. FAFSA, institutional form required. Applicants notified on a rolling basis starting 6/1.

**Academics. Special study options:** Accelerated study, cooperative education, double major, independent study, internships, student-designed major. **Credit/placement by examination:** CLEP, institutional tests. 24 credit hours maximum toward associate degree, 48 toward bachelor's. **Support services:** Learning center, reduced course load, tutoring.

**Majors. Business:** General, accounting, business admin, hospitality admin, international, management information systems, management science, marketing.

**Student life. Housing:** Apartments available. **Activities:** Student government, student newspaper.

**Athletics. Intramural:** Basketball, soccer M, softball, volleyball.

**Student services.** Career counseling, student employment services, personal counseling, placement for graduates, veterans' counselor.

**Contact.** Phone: (954) 783-7339
Fran Heaston, Director of Admissions, Everest University: Pompano Beach, 225 North Federal Highway, Pompano Beach, FL 33062

## Everest University: South Orlando
Orlando, Florida
www.everest.edu — CB code: 3587

- For-profit 4-year university and business college
- Very large city
- 1,900 degree-seeking undergraduates
- Interview required

**General.** Accredited by ACICS. **Calendar:** Quarter, extensive summer session. **Full-time faculty:** 25 total. **Part-time faculty:** 94 total.

**Basis for selection.** 15 ACT or 700 SAT (exclusive of Writing) or passing grade on university-administered assessment exam required. SAT or ACT recommended.

**2007-2008 Annual costs.** Tuition/fees: $13,695. Books/supplies: $800. Personal expenses: $1,764.

**Application procedures. Admission:** No deadline. No application fee. **Financial aid:** No deadline.

**Academics. Credit/placement by examination:** CLEP.

**Majors. Business:** Business admin.

**Contact.** Phone: (407) 851-2525
Annette Cloin, Director of Admissions, Everest University: South Orlando, 9200 Southpark Center Loop, Orlando, FL 32819

## Everest University: Tampa
Tampa, Florida
www.everest.edu — CB code: 0428

- For-profit 4-year university and business college
- Commuter campus in large city
- 1,300 degree-seeking undergraduates
- 80 graduate students

**General.** Founded in 1890. Accredited by ACICS. **Degrees:** 64 bachelor's, 178 associate awarded; master's offered. **Location:** 85 miles from Orlando. **Calendar:** Quarter, extensive summer session. **Full-time faculty:** 20 total. **Part-time faculty:** 61 total.

**Basis for selection.** Open admission.

**2007-2008 Annual costs.** Tuition/fees: $13,695. Cost of tuition may vary with program. Books/supplies: $540. Personal expenses: $1,710.

**Financial aid.** All financial aid based on need.

**Application procedures. Admission:** No deadline. No application fee. Admission notification on a rolling basis. **Financial aid:** No deadline. FAFSA required. Applicants notified on a rolling basis.

**Academics. Special study options:** Accelerated study, distance learning, double major, ESL, independent study, internships. **Credit/placement by examination:** CLEP, institutional tests. **Support services:** Tutoring.

**Majors. Business:** General, accounting, business admin, marketing. **Computer sciences:** General, information systems, programming. **Protective services:** Criminal justice.

**Computing on campus.** 50 workstations in library, computer center.

**Student life. Freshman orientation:** Mandatory. **Activities:** Student newspaper.

**Student services.** Career counseling, student employment services, personal counseling, placement for graduates, veterans' counselor.

**Contact.** Phone: (813) 879-6000 Fax: (813) 871-2483
Donald Broughton, Director of Admissions, Everest University: Tampa, 3319 West Hillsborough Avenue, Tampa, FL 33614

---

## Everglades University
**Boca Raton, Florida**
www.EvergladesUniversity.edu          CB code: 3191

▶ Private 4-year university
▶ Commuter campus in small city

**General.** Accredited by ACCSCT. **Calendar:** Semester.

**Annual costs/financial aid.** Tuition/fees (2007-2008): $14,300. $1,600 education fee for online students. Books/supplies: $1,125. Need-based financial aid available for full-time students.

**Contact.** Phone: (561) 912-1211
Director of Admissions, 5002 T-REX Avenue, Suite 100, Boca Raton, FL 33431

---

## Flagler College
**St. Augustine, Florida**          CB member
www.flagler.edu          CB code: 5235

▶ Private 4-year liberal arts college
▶ Residential campus in large town
▶ 2,537 degree-seeking undergraduates: 3% part-time, 61% women, 1% African American, 1% Asian American, 3% Hispanic American, 1% international
▶ 26% of applicants admitted
▶ SAT or ACT (ACT writing optional), application essay required
▶ 61% graduate within 6 years; 2% enter graduate study

**General.** Founded in 1968. Regionally accredited. Historic St. Augustine Research Institute is a joint partnership of St. Augustine Foundation, Flagler College and the University of Florida. **Degrees:** 520 bachelor's awarded. **Location:** 35 miles from Jacksonville, 50 miles from Daytona Beach. **Calendar:** Semester, limited summer session. **Full-time faculty:** 86 total; 62% have terminal degrees, 5% minority, 41% women. **Part-time faculty:** 94 total; 21% have terminal degrees, 3% minority, 36% women. **Class size:** 37% < 20, 61% 20-39, 1% 40-49, 1% 50-99.

**Freshman class profile.** 2,377 applied, 622 admitted, 472 enrolled.

| Mid 50% test scores | | | |
|---|---|---|---|
| SAT critical reading: | 520-610 | Rank in top quarter: | 50% |
| SAT math: | 510-590 | Rank in top tenth: | 18% |
| SAT writing: | 520-600 | End year in good standing: | 83% |
| ACT composite: | 22-26 | Return as sophomores: | 78% |
| GPA 3.50 or higher: | 27% | Out-of-state: | 35% |
| GPA 3.0-3.49: | 37% | Live on campus: | 92% |
| GPA 2.0-2.99: | 36% | | |

**Basis for selection.** Academic record, including pattern of courses most important, followed by test scores. Extracurricular activities, recommendations, and intended major also considered. Education applicants must score at or above 45th percentile on SAT or ACT. Interview required for early admission applicants; recommended for all others. Admission to Art department based on portfolio.

**High school preparation.** 13 units required; 20 recommended. Required and recommended units include English 4, mathematics 3-4, social studies 2-3, history 1-2, science 2-3 (laboratory 1-2), foreign language 2 and academic electives 1-2.

---

**2008-2009 Annual costs.** Tuition/fees: $13,600. Room/board: $6,900. Books/supplies: $900. Personal expenses: $2,300.

**2007-2008 Financial aid. Need-based:** Average need met was 76%. Average scholarship/grant was $4,529; average loan $3,549. 50% of total undergraduate aid awarded as scholarships/grants, 50% as loans/jobs. **Non-need-based:** Scholarships awarded for academics, art, athletics, job skills, leadership, minority status, music/drama, state residency.

**Application procedures. Admission:** Priority date 1/15; deadline 3/1 (postmark date). $40 fee, may be waived for applicants with need. Application may be submitted online. Admission notification 3/30. Must reply by May 1 or within 3 week(s) if notified thereafter. **Financial aid:** Priority date 4/1; no closing date. FAFSA, institutional form required. Applicants notified on a rolling basis starting 4/1; must reply within 2 week(s) of notification.

**Academics.** Freshmen must earn at least 24 semester hours credit for good academic standing. **Special study options:** Double major, independent study, internships, study abroad, teacher certification program. Deaf education majors work directly with faculty and students at nearby Florida School for the Deaf and Blind. **Credit/placement by examination:** AP, CLEP, IB, SAT, ACT. 30 credit hours maximum toward bachelor's degree. **Support services:** Learning center, reduced course load, study skills assistance, tutoring, writing center.

**Majors. Area/ethnic studies:** Latin American. **Business:** Accounting, business admin. **Communications:** General. **Education:** Art, Deaf/hearing impaired, drama/dance, elementary, English, social science, social studies, special. **English:** English lit. **Foreign languages:** Spanish. **History:** General. **Liberal arts:** Arts/sciences. **Parks/recreation:** Sports admin. **Philosophy/religion:** Philosophy. **Psychology:** General. **Public administration:** General. **Social sciences:** Political science, sociology. **Visual/performing arts:** General, dramatic, studio arts.

**Most popular majors.** Business/marketing 19%, communications/journalism 13%, education 10%, history 6%, psychology 8%, visual/performing arts 13%.

**Computing on campus.** 205 workstations in library, computer center. Dormitories wired for high-speed internet access and linked to campus network. Commuter students can connect to campus network. Online course registration, online library, helpline, student web hosting, wireless network available.

**Student life. Freshman orientation:** Mandatory. Preregistration for classes offered. 3-day program held each semester prior to classes. **Policies:** Male-female interdorm visitation not allowed in residence halls. Alcohol prohibited on campus. No smoking in buildings, including residence halls. **Housing:** Guaranteed on-campus for freshmen. Single-sex dorms available. $200 nonrefundable deposit, deadline 5/1. **Activities:** Choral groups, dance, drama, literary magazine, radio station, student government, student newspaper, TV station, Rotaract, Intervarsity Christian Fellowship, Catholic College Fellowship, Society for Advancement of Management, Students in Free Enterprises, deaf awareness club, sport management club, AIGA, SPIRIT, The Home Team.

**Athletics.** NCAA. **Intercollegiate:** Baseball M, basketball, cross-country, golf, soccer, tennis, ♦volleyball W. **Intramural:** Badminton, basketball, bowling, football (non-tackle), golf, soccer, softball, table tennis, tennis, volleyball, weight lifting. **Team name:** Saints.

**Student services.** Career counseling, student employment services, financial aid counseling, health services, personal counseling, veterans' counselor. **Physically disabled:** Services for visually, speech, hearing impaired.

**Contact.** E-mail: admiss@flagler.edu
Phone: (904) 829-6220 Toll-free number: (800) 304-4208
Fax: (904) 829-6838
Marc Williar, Director of Admissions, Flagler College, 74 King Street, St. Augustine, FL 32084

---

## Florida Agricultural and Mechanical University
**Tallahassee, Florida**          CB member
www.famu.edu          CB code: 5215

▶ Public 4-year university
▶ Residential campus in small city
▶ 9,566 degree-seeking undergraduates: 12% part-time, 58% women, 94% African American, 1% Asian American, 1% Hispanic American, 1% international
▶ 1,996 degree-seeking graduate students
▶ 63% of applicants admitted

- SAT or ACT (ACT writing optional), application essay required
- 41% graduate within 6 years; 34% enter graduate study

**General.** Founded in 1887. Regionally accredited. **Degrees:** 1,329 bachelor's, 63 associate awarded; master's, doctoral, first professional offered. **ROTC:** Army, Naval, Air Force. **Location:** 169 miles from Jacksonville. **Calendar:** Semester, extensive summer session. **Full-time faculty:** 617 total; 72% have terminal degrees, 73% minority, 44% women. **Part-time faculty:** 140 total; 36% have terminal degrees, 68% minority, 40% women. **Class size:** 44% < 20, 39% 20-39, 8% 40-49, 7% 50-99, 2% >100. **Special facilities:** African American archives research center and museum, observatory.

**Freshman class profile.** 5,097 applied, 3,233 admitted, 1,890 enrolled.

| Mid 50% test scores | | | |
|---|---|---|---|
| SAT critical reading: | 440-550 | GPA 2.0-2.99: | 43% |
| SAT math: | 440-550 | End year in good standing: | 94% |
| ACT composite: | 19-22 | Return as sophomores: | 89% |
| GPA 3.50 or higher: | 18% | Out-of-state: | 29% |
| GPA 3.0-3.49: | 38% | Live on campus: | 97% |
| | | International: | 1% |

**Basis for selection.** School achievement record and test scores most important. 2.5 GPA required. Essay required of borderline applicants. Interview recommended for nursing, physical therapy, architecture, pharmacy, engineering majors. Audition required of music majors. Portfolio required of architecture majors. **Homeschooled:** Applicant may be asked to complete GED.

**High school preparation.** 18 units required. Required units include English 4, mathematics 3, social studies 3, science 3 (laboratory 1), foreign language 2 and academic electives 3.

**2007-2008 Annual costs.** Tuition/fees: $3,264; $15,186 out-of-state. Room/board: $5,844. Books/supplies: $800. Personal expenses: $2,400.

**2006-2007 Financial aid. Need-based:** Average need met was 77%. Average scholarship/grant was $6,034; average loan $5,940. 54% of total undergraduate aid awarded as scholarships/grants, 46% as loans/jobs. **Non-need-based:** Scholarships awarded for academics, art, leadership.

**Application procedures. Admission:** Priority date 3/9; deadline 5/9. $20 fee. Admission notification on a rolling basis. **Financial aid:** Priority date 3/1, closing date 6/30. FAFSA required. Applicants notified on a rolling basis starting 3/1; must reply within 2 week(s) of notification.

**Academics. Special study options:** Accelerated study, combined bachelor's/graduate degree, cooperative education, distance learning, double major, dual enrollment of high school students, honors, independent study, internships, study abroad, teacher certification program, weekend college. **Credit/placement by examination:** AP, CLEP, IB. 30 credit hours maximum toward associate degree, 30 toward bachelor's. Student must have passing scores (determined by state) for AP and CLEP exams. **Support services:** Learning center, pre-admission summer program, reduced course load, remedial instruction, study skills assistance, tutoring, writing center.

**Majors. Agriculture:** Agribusiness operations, agronomy, animal sciences, food science, horticultural science, horticulture, landscaping, ornamental horticulture, plant protection. **Architecture:** Architecture. **Area/ethnic studies:** African-American. **Biology:** General. **Business:** Accounting, business admin, managerial economics. **Communications:** Broadcast journalism, journalism, public relations. **Computer sciences:** General. **Conservation:** Environmental science. **Education:** Art, business, early childhood, elementary, English, mathematics, music, physical, science, social studies, trade/industrial. **Engineering:** Agricultural, chemical, civil, electrical, mechanical. **Engineering technology:** Civil, construction, electrical. **English:** English lit. **Foreign languages:** French, Spanish. **Health:** Health care admin, medical records admin, nursing (RN), respiratory therapy technology. **History:** General. **Math:** General. **Philosophy/religion:** Philosophy, religion. **Physical sciences:** Chemistry, physics. **Protective services:** Criminal justice. **Psychology:** General. **Public administration:** Social work. **Social sciences:** Economics, political science, sociology. **Visual/performing arts:** General, commercial/advertising art, dramatic, music performance.

**Most popular majors.** Business/marketing 19%, communications/journalism 6%, education 9%, engineering/engineering technologies 6%, health sciences 13%, psychology 6%, security/protective services 10%, social sciences 9%.

**Computing on campus.** Dormitories wired for high-speed internet access and linked to campus network. Commuter students can connect to campus network. Online course registration, online library, helpline, repair service, wireless network available.

**Student life. Freshman orientation:** Mandatory, $15 fee. Preregistration for classes offered. Five-day session in fall. Cost contingent on whether

student stays on campus. **Housing:** Coed dorms, single-sex dorms, apartments available. $350 partly refundable deposit, deadline 9/10. **Activities:** Bands, choral groups, dance, drama, music ensembles, radio station, student government, student newspaper, symphony orchestra, TV station, religious, honorary and scholastic organizations, marketing club, student social workers.

**Athletics.** NCAA. **Intercollegiate:** Baseball M, basketball, bowling W, cross-country, football (tackle) M, golf, softball W, swimming, tennis, track and field, volleyball W. **Intramural:** Badminton, basketball, bowling, football (tackle) M, gymnastics, racquetball, soccer, softball, table tennis, tennis, track and field, volleyball, weight lifting. **Team name:** Rattlers.

**Student services.** Alcohol/substance abuse counseling, career counseling, student employment services, financial aid counseling, health services, on-campus daycare, personal counseling, placement for graduates, veterans' counselor. **Physically disabled:** Services for visually, hearing impaired.

**Contact.** E-mail: ugrdadmissions@famu.edu
Phone: (850) 599-3796 Fax: (850) 599-3069
Danielle Kennedy-Lamar, Associate Vice President-Director, Florida Agricultural and Mechanical University, FHAC, G-9, Tallahassee, FL 32307-3200

---

## Florida Atlantic University
**Boca Raton, Florida**          CB member
www.fau.edu                      CB code: 5229

- Public 4-year university
- Commuter campus in small city
- 20,525 degree-seeking undergraduates: 40% part-time, 59% women, 18% African American, 5% Asian American, 19% Hispanic American, 3% international
- 3,620 degree-seeking graduate students
- 57% of applicants admitted
- SAT or ACT (ACT writing recommended), application essay required
- 37% graduate within 6 years

**General.** Founded in 1961. Regionally accredited. Courses and degree programs offered at additional sites in Palm Beach, Broward, and St. Lucie counties. **Degrees:** 4,345 bachelor's, 192 associate awarded; master's, doctoral offered. **ROTC:** Army. **Location:** 17 miles from Fort Lauderdale. **Calendar:** Semester, extensive summer session. **Full-time faculty:** 799 total; 87% have terminal degrees, 21% minority, 40% women. **Part-time faculty:** 557 total; 14% minority, 52% women. **Class size:** 35% < 20, 48% 20-39, 5% 40-49, 7% 50-99, 4% >100. **Special facilities:** Environmental center, native fish research center, ocean engineering laboratory, marine research facility, robotics laboratory.

**Freshman class profile.** 11,822 applied, 6,698 admitted, 2,677 enrolled.

| Mid 50% test scores | | | |
|---|---|---|---|
| SAT critical reading: | 460-550 | Rank in top tenth: | 9% |
| SAT math: | 470-560 | End year in good standing: | 78% |
| SAT writing: | 450-540 | Return as sophomores: | 74% |
| ACT composite: | 19-23 | Out-of-state: | 9% |
| GPA 3.50 or higher: | 25% | Live on campus: | 64% |
| GPA 3.0-3.49: | 40% | International: | 2% |
| GPA 2.0-2.99: | 35% | Fraternities: | 1% |
| Rank in top quarter: | 35% | Sororities: | 1% |

**Basis for selection.** Secondary school record, standardized test scores most important. Recommendation, talent, ability also important. Top 20% of state high school graduates guaranteed admission. Audition recommended for theater majors. Portfolio recommended for art majors. **Homeschooled:** State high school equivalency certificate required.

**High school preparation.** 18 units required; 19 recommended. Required and recommended units include English 4, mathematics 3-4, social studies 3, science 3 (laboratory 2) and foreign language 2.

**2007-2008 Annual costs.** Tuition/fees: $3,344; $16,409 out-of-state. Room/board: $8,360. Books/supplies: $724. Personal expenses: $1,458.

**2007-2008 Financial aid. Need-based:** 2,113 full-time freshmen applied for aid; 1,135 were judged to have need; 1,111 of these received aid. Average need met was 97%. Average scholarship/grant was $7,338; average loan $3,165. 60% of total undergraduate aid awarded as scholarships/grants, 40% as loans/jobs. **Non-need-based:** Awarded to 618 full-time undergraduates, including 156 freshmen. Scholarships awarded for academics, athletics, music/drama, state residency.

**Application procedures. Admission:** Closing date 6/1 (receipt date). $30 fee, may be waived for applicants with need. Application may be submitted online. Admission notification on a rolling basis beginning on or about 9/15. **Financial aid:** Priority date 3/1; no closing date. FAFSA required. Applicants notified on a rolling basis starting 4/1; must reply within 3 week(s) of notification.

**Academics. Special study options:** Accelerated study, combined bachelor's/graduate degree, cooperative education, cross-registration, distance learning, double major, dual enrollment of high school students, ESL, honors, independent study, internships, liberal arts/career combination, student-designed major, study abroad, teacher certification program, weekend college. **Credit/placement by examination:** AP, CLEP, IB. 45 credit hours maximum toward bachelor's degree. **Support services:** Learning center, pre-admission summer program, reduced course load, study skills assistance, tutoring, writing center.

**Honors college/program.** Most applicants will have 3.5 GPA, 1280 SAT (exclusive of Writing) or 29 on Enhanced ACT. Exceptional applicants who do not meet these criteria may be admitted on individual basis by Admissions Committee.

**Majors. Architecture:** Architecture, urban/community planning. **Biology:** General. **Business:** Accounting, business admin, finance, hospitality admin, human resources, international, management information systems, marketing, real estate. **Communications:** General, digital media. **Computer sciences:** General. **Education:** Elementary, English, mathematics, music, science, social science, special. **Engineering:** Civil, computer, electrical, mechanical, ocean, surveying. **Engineering technology:** Computer systems. **English:** English lit. **Foreign languages:** French, German, linguistics, Spanish. **Health:** Health care admin, health services, nursing (RN). **History:** General. **Liberal arts:** Arts/sciences. **Math:** General. **Parks/recreation:** Exercise sciences. **Philosophy/religion:** Judaic, philosophy. **Physical sciences:** Chemistry, geology, physics. **Protective services:** Criminal justice. **Psychology:** General, psychobiology, social. **Public administration:** General, social work. **Social sciences:** General, anthropology, economics, geography, political science, sociology. **Visual/performing arts:** Art, dramatic, music management.

**Most popular majors.** Business/marketing 27%, education 10%, health sciences 8%, psychology 6%, security/protective services 6%, social sciences 8%.

**Computing on campus.** 1,000 workstations in dormitories, library, computer center, student center. Dormitories wired for high-speed internet access and linked to campus network. Commuter students can connect to campus network. Online course registration, helpline, repair service, wireless network available.

**Student life. Freshman orientation:** Mandatory, $35 fee. Preregistration for classes offered. Held 2 different dates before semester starts. **Housing:** Guaranteed on-campus for freshmen. Coed dorms, single-sex dorms, apartments available. $200 partly refundable deposit, deadline 8/1. **Activities:** Bands, choral groups, dance, drama, film society, literary magazine, music ensembles, musical theater, opera, radio station, student government, student newspaper, symphony orchestra, TV station, Circle K, College Democrats, College Republicans, B'nai B'rith Hillel, Neumann Club, Christian College Fellowship, Human Rights Organization, European Student Association, NAACP, Peace Finders.

**Athletics. NCAA. Intercollegiate:** Baseball M, basketball, cheerleading, cross-country, football (tackle) M, golf, soccer, softball W, swimming, tennis, track and field W, volleyball W. **Intramural:** Basketball, diving, football (non-tackle), rugby, soccer M, softball, table tennis, volleyball M. **Team name:** Owls.

**Student services.** Adult student services, alcohol/substance abuse counseling, campus ministries, career counseling, student employment services, financial aid counseling, health services, minority student services, on-campus daycare, personal counseling, placement for graduates, veterans' counselor, women's services. **Physically disabled:** Services for visually, speech, hearing impaired. **Learning disabled:** Comprehensive services available.

**Contact.** E-mail: UGAdmissions@fau.edu
Phone: (561) 297-3040 Toll-free number: (800) 299-4328
Fax: (561) 297-2758
Barbara Pletcher, Director of Admissions, Florida Atlantic University, 777 Glades Road, Boca Raton, FL 33431

## Florida Christian College
### Kissimmee, Florida
www.fcc.edu                                              CB code: 2167

- Private 4-year Bible and teachers college affiliated with Christian Churches and Churches of Christ
- Residential campus in small city

- 226 degree-seeking undergraduates: 28% part-time, 42% women, 9% African American, 1% Asian American, 10% Hispanic American
- SAT or ACT (ACT writing optional), application essay required
- 43% graduate within 6 years

**General.** Founded in 1975. Candidate for regional accreditation; also accredited by ABHE. **Degrees:** 52 bachelor's, 9 associate awarded. **Location:** 20 miles from Orlando. **Calendar:** Semester, limited summer session. **Full-time faculty:** 11 total; 100% have terminal degrees, 9% minority, 27% women. **Part-time faculty:** 18 total; 100% have terminal degrees, 6% minority. **Class size:** 79% < 20, 19% 20-39, 1% 40-49, 1% 50-99.

**Freshman class profile.**

| | | | |
|---|---|---|---|
| End year in good standing: | 66% | Out-of-state: | 10% |
| Return as sophomores: | 66% | Live on campus: | 84% |

**Basis for selection.** Autobiographical essays, personal recommendation, and church references required. **Homeschooled:** State high school equivalency certificate, letter of recommendation (nonparent) required.

**2007-2008 Annual costs.** Tuition/fees: $10,200. Room only: $2,400. Books/supplies: $850. Personal expenses: $895.

**Financial aid. Non-need-based:** Scholarships awarded for academics, alumni affiliation, leadership, music/drama, religious affiliation, state residency.

**Application procedures. Admission:** Priority date 7/15; deadline 8/1 (postmark date). $35 fee, may be waived for applicants with need. Application may be submitted online. Admission notification on a rolling basis. **Financial aid:** Priority date 5/1, closing date 7/15. FAFSA, institutional form required. Applicants notified on a rolling basis starting 3/1.

**Academics. Special study options:** Accelerated study, distance learning, dual enrollment of high school students, independent study, internships, student-designed major, teacher certification program. **Credit/placement by examination:** AP, CLEP, IB. 15 credit hours maximum toward associate degree, 30 toward bachelor's. **Support services:** Reduced course load, study skills assistance, tutoring.

**Majors. Education:** Elementary. **Philosophy/religion:** Philosophy, religion. **Theology:** Bible, missionary, pastoral counseling, sacred music, theology.

**Computing on campus.** 8 workstations in library, student center. Dormitories wired for high-speed internet access and linked to campus network. Online course registration, online library, helpline, repair service, student web hosting, wireless network available.

**Student life. Freshman orientation:** Mandatory. **Policies:** Religious observance required. **Housing:** Special housing for disabled, apartments, substance-free housing available. $100 fully refundable deposit, deadline 7/15. **Activities:** Choral groups, drama, music ensembles, student government, student newspaper, Christian service activities, mission group.

**Athletics. NCCAA. Intercollegiate:** Basketball M, volleyball W. **Intramural:** Football (non-tackle), soccer, softball, table tennis. **Team name:** Suns.

**Student services.** Career counseling, financial aid counseling, personal counseling, veterans' counselor. **Physically disabled:** Services for visually impaired.

**Contact.** E-mail: admissions@fcc.edu
Phone: (407) 569-1172 Toll-free number: (877) 468-6322
Fax: (321) 206-2007
Brian Smith, Associate Dean/Registrar, Florida Christian College, 1011 Bill Beck Boulevard, Kissimmee, FL 34744-4402

## Florida College
### Temple Terrace, Florida
www.floridacollege.edu                                   CB code: 5216

- Private 4-year liberal arts college
- Residential campus in large town
- 524 degree-seeking undergraduates: 5% part-time, 54% women, 2% African American, 1% Asian American, 4% Hispanic American, 1% international
- 85% of applicants admitted
- SAT or ACT (ACT writing optional) required

**General.** Founded in 1944. Regionally accredited. **Degrees:** 20 bachelor's, 126 associate awarded. **ROTC:** Army, Air Force. **Location:** 2 miles from Tampa. **Calendar:** Semester, limited summer session. **Full-time faculty:**

31 total; 32% have terminal degrees, 6% minority, 16% women. **Part-time faculty:** 10 total; 30% have terminal degrees, 30% women. **Class size:** 73% < 20, 17% 20-39, 5% 40-49, 4% 50-99.

**Freshman class profile.** 292 applied, 249 admitted, 249 enrolled.

| Mid 50% test scores | | | |
|---|---|---|---|
| | | ACT composite: | 10-26 |
| SAT critical reading: | 430-590 | International: | 1% |
| SAT math: | 460-590 | | |

**Basis for selection.** 2 recommendations, 2.0 high school GPA required. Test scores, moral character important. Interview and essay recommended. Portfolio required for art majors. **Homeschooled:** Must meet high school course minimum requirements, ACT minimum requirements. **Learning Disabled:** Provide voluntary declaration of disability form and documentation.

**High school preparation.** 16 units required. Required and recommended units include English 4, mathematics 3, social studies 2-3, science 2 (laboratory 2) and foreign language 2.

**2007-2008 Annual costs.** Tuition/fees: $11,700. Room/board: $5,640. Books/supplies: $1,200. Personal expenses: $2,000.

**2007-2008 Financial aid. Need-based:** 129 full-time freshmen applied for aid; 129 were judged to have need; 129 of these received aid. Average need met was 86%. Average scholarship/grant was $1,933; average loan $1,686. 51% of total undergraduate aid awarded as scholarships/grants, 49% as loans/jobs. **Non-need-based:** Awarded to 391 full-time undergraduates, including 204 freshmen. Scholarships awarded for academics, athletics, music/drama, state residency. **Additional information:** Music and forensic scholarships available. Audition required for music scholarships.

**Application procedures. Admission:** Priority date 4/1; deadline 8/1. $25 fee. Admission notification on a rolling basis. **Financial aid:** Priority date 4/1, closing date 6/1. FAFSA, institutional form required. Applicants notified on a rolling basis starting 3/1; must reply within 2 week(s) of notification.

**Academics. Special study options:** Cross-registration, independent study, teacher certification program. **Credit/placement by examination:** AP, CLEP, IB, SAT, ACT, institutional tests. 30 credit hours maximum toward associate degree, 30 toward bachelor's. **Support services:** Reduced course load, remedial instruction, study skills assistance, tutoring, writing center.

**Majors. Business:** Business admin. **Education:** Elementary. **Liberal arts:** Arts/sciences. **Theology:** Bible.

**Most popular majors.** Education 9%, liberal arts 56%, philosophy/religious studies 13%, visual/performing arts 22%.

**Computing on campus.** 76 workstations in library, computer center. Dormitories wired for high-speed internet access and linked to campus network. Wireless network available.

**Student life. Freshman orientation:** Mandatory. **Policies:** All campus residents expected to attend Sunday worship services. **Housing:** Guaranteed on-campus for freshmen. Single-sex dorms, substance-free housing available. $150 deposit, deadline 8/1. **Activities:** Bands, choral groups, drama, literary magazine, music ensembles, musical theater, student government, honor society, social clubs.

**Athletics.** USCAA. **Intercollegiate:** Baseball M, basketball M, cheerleading M, soccer, volleyball W. **Intramural:** Basketball, football (non-tackle), soccer, softball, volleyball. **Team name:** Falcons.

**Student services.** Financial aid counseling, health services, personal counseling, veterans' counselor.

**Contact.** E-mail: admission@floridacollege.edu
Phone: (813) 899-6716 Toll-free number: (800) 326-7655
Fax: (813) 899-6772
Matthew Qualls, Director of Admissions, Florida College, 119 North Glen Arven Avenue, Temple Terrace, FL 33617

---

## Florida Gulf Coast University

**Ft. Myers, Florida**
**www.fgcu.edu**

**CB member**
**CB code: 5221**

- Public 4-year university
- Commuter campus in small city
- 7,996 degree-seeking undergraduates: 21% part-time, 60% women, 4% African American, 2% Asian American, 11% Hispanic American, 1% international
- 833 degree-seeking graduate students

- 76% of applicants admitted
- SAT or ACT with writing required

**General.** Regionally accredited. **Degrees:** 1,016 bachelor's, 122 associate awarded; master's offered. **Location:** 100 miles from Tampa, 125 miles from Miami. **Calendar:** Semester, extensive summer session. **Full-time faculty:** 306 total; 79% have terminal degrees, 18% minority, 47% women. **Part-time faculty:** 272 total; 11% minority, 46% women. **Class size:** 31% < 20, 54% 20-39, 8% 40-49, 6% 50-99, 1% >100. **Special facilities:** Natural wetlands, observatory.

**Freshman class profile.** 5,597 applied, 4,273 admitted, 1,902 enrolled.

| Mid 50% test scores | | | |
|---|---|---|---|
| SAT critical reading: | 460-550 | Rank in top tenth: | 15% |
| SAT math: | 470-560 | End year in good standing: | 85% |
| ACT composite: | 20-23 | Return as sophomores: | 76% |
| GPA 3.50 or higher: | 36% | Out-of-state: | 9% |
| GPA 3.0-3.49: | 41% | Live on campus: | 54% |
| GPA 2.0-2.99: | 23% | International: | 1% |
| Rank in top quarter: | 46% | Fraternities: | 5% |
| | | Sororities: | 10% |

**Basis for selection.** Grades in academic units, test scores very important. **Homeschooled:** Transcript of courses and grades required. 1010 SAT (exclusive of Writing) or 21 ACT required.

**High school preparation.** 18 units required. Required units include English 4, mathematics 3, social studies 3, science 3 (laboratory 2), foreign language 2 and academic electives 3.

**2007-2008 Annual costs.** Tuition/fees: $3,656; $16,174 out-of-state. Room/board: $6,860. Books/supplies: $950. Personal expenses: $1,400.

**2006-2007 Financial aid. Need-based:** 1,260 full-time freshmen applied for aid; 569 were judged to have need; 569 of these received aid. Average need met was 64%. Average scholarship/grant was $3,605; average loan $2,688. 45% of total undergraduate aid awarded as scholarships/grants, 55% as loans/jobs. **Non-need-based:** Awarded to 2,244 full-time undergraduates, including 579 freshmen. Scholarships awarded for academics, alumni affiliation, athletics, leadership, minority status, music/drama, religious affiliation, state residency.

**Application procedures. Admission:** Priority date 2/15; deadline 6/2 (postmark date). $30 fee, may be waived for applicants with need. Application may be submitted online. Admission notification on a rolling basis. **Financial aid:** Priority date 3/1, closing date 6/30. FAFSA required. Applicants notified on a rolling basis starting 2/15.

**Academics. Special study options:** Accelerated study, combined bachelor's/graduate degree, cross-registration, distance learning, double major, dual enrollment of high school students, honors, independent study, internships, student-designed major, study abroad, teacher certification program, Washington semester. **Credit/placement by examination:** AP, CLEP, IB, SAT, ACT, institutional tests. 45 credit hours maximum toward bachelor's degree. Credit received from one exam program may not be duplicated by another, nor duplicated through dual enrollment credit. **Support services:** Learning center, reduced course load, remedial instruction, study skills assistance, tutoring, writing center.

**Majors. Biology:** General, biotechnology. **Business:** Accounting, business admin, finance, management information systems, marketing, resort management. **Communications:** Media studies. **Computer sciences:** General. **Conservation:** Environmental studies, water/wetlands/marine. **Education:** Early childhood, elementary, special. **Engineering:** Biomedical, civil, environmental. **English:** English lit. **Foreign languages:** Spanish. **Health:** Athletic training, clinical lab science, community health, health care admin, health services, nursing (RN). **History:** General. **Legal studies:** Paralegal. **Liberal arts:** Arts/sciences. **Math:** General. **Parks/recreation:** Exercise sciences. **Philosophy/religion:** Philosophy. **Physical sciences:** Chemistry. **Protective services:** Criminal justice, criminalistics. **Psychology:** General. **Public administration:** Human services, social work. **Social sciences:** Anthropology, political science, sociology. **Visual/performing arts:** Art, dramatic, music performance.

**Most popular majors.** Business/marketing 26%, education 13%, health sciences 12%, liberal arts 30%.

**Computing on campus.** 302 workstations in dormitories, library, computer center. Dormitories wired for high-speed internet access and linked to campus network. Commuter students can connect to campus network. Online course registration, online library, helpline, student web hosting, wireless network available.

**Student life. Freshman orientation:** Mandatory, $35 fee. Preregistration for classes offered. Two-day summer program prior to fall semester; families invited. **Policies:** Student code of conduct in effect. **Housing:** Coed dorms, special housing for disabled, apartments, substance-free housing available. Honors and other special interest dorms available. **Activities:** Campus ministries, dance, drama, film society, international student organizations, literary magazine, Model UN, student government, student newspaper, College Republicans, College Democrats, Christian Campus Fellowship, Intervarsity Christian Fellowship, Navigators, Colleges Against Cancer, American Association of University Women Student Affiliates, human services student organization.

**Athletics.** NCAA. **Intercollegiate:** Baseball M, basketball, cross-country, golf, softball W, tennis, volleyball W. **Intramural:** Basketball, cross-country, football (non-tackle), soccer, softball, table tennis, tennis, volleyball, water polo. **Team name:** Eagles.

**Student services.** Adult student services, alcohol/substance abuse counseling, career counseling, student employment services, financial aid counseling, health services, minority student services, on-campus daycare, personal counseling, placement for graduates, veterans' counselor, women's services. **Physically disabled:** Services for visually, speech, hearing impaired.

**Contact.** E-mail: admissions@fgcu.edu
Phone: (239) 590-7878 Toll-free number: (888) 889-1095
Fax: (239) 590-7894
Marc Laviolette, Director of Admissions and Records, Florida Gulf Coast University, 10501 FGCU Boulevard South, Ft. Myers, FL 33965-6565

## Florida Hospital College of Health Sciences
Orlando, Florida
www.FHCHS.edu
CB code: 3614

- Private 4-year health science and nursing college affiliated with Seventh-day Adventists
- Commuter campus in large city
- 2,149 degree-seeking undergraduates: 68% part-time, 81% women, 14% African American, 6% Asian American, 13% Hispanic American, 2% international
- Application essay required

**General.** Regionally accredited. Affiliated with Florida Hospital. **Degrees:** 324 bachelor's, 194 associate awarded; master's offered. **Calendar:** Trimester, limited summer session. **Full-time faculty:** 51 total; 82% have terminal degrees, 22% minority, 76% women. **Part-time faculty:** 39 total; 82% have terminal degrees, 28% minority, 54% women. **Class size:** 57% < 20, 32% 20-39, 9% 40-49, 2% 50-99. **Special facilities:** Human patient simulators.

**Freshman class profile.**

| | | | |
|---|---|---|---|
| GPA 3.50 or higher: | 13% | GPA 2.0-2.99: | 48% |
| GPA 3.0-3.49: | 39% | | |

**Basis for selection.** Evidence of graduation with standard high school diploma from regionally accredited school required. 2.5 GPA and satisfactory recommendations required for general college admission. ACT/SAT scores required for advising and placement. Professional program admission requirements vary. Professional programs require essay explaining student's career choice. **Homeschooled:** Curriculums must be regionally accredited. Applicants who have completed non-regionally accredited home school programs may submit passing GED scores or complete 12 hours of credit from regionally accredited college with 2.5 GPA.

**High school preparation.** 21 units recommended. Recommended units include English 4, mathematics 3, social studies 3, history 3, science 3 (laboratory 3) and foreign language 2.

**2007-2008 Annual costs.** Tuition/fees: $7,920. Room only: $3,200. Books/supplies: $1,950. Personal expenses: $1,206.

**Financial aid.** **Non-need-based:** Scholarships awarded for state residency.

**Application procedures.** **Admission:** Closing date 8/4 (postmark date). $20 fee, may be waived for applicants with need. Application may be submitted online. Admission notification on a rolling basis. Students accepted to professional programs have reply dates in order to claim program seat. **Financial aid:** Priority date 4/12; no closing date. FAFSA, institutional form required. Applicants notified on a rolling basis starting 3/1.

**Academics.** **Special study options:** Distance learning, dual enrollment of high school students, independent study. **Credit/placement by examination:** CLEP, SAT, ACT, institutional tests. **Support services:** Learning center, pre-admission summer program, remedial instruction, study skills assistance, tutoring.

**Majors.** **Health:** Health services, nursing (RN), radiologic technology/medical imaging, sonography.

**Computing on campus.** 45 workstations in dormitories, library, computer center. Commuter students can connect to campus network. Online library, repair service, wireless network available.

**Student life.** **Freshman orientation:** Mandatory. One-day program. **Policies:** No-use policy for alcohol, drugs, smoking, and illegal substances. **Housing:** Apartments, substance-free housing available. $200 fully refundable deposit, deadline 8/4. **Activities:** Campus ministries.

**Athletics.** **Intramural:** Basketball, football (non-tackle) M, soccer, volleyball.

**Student services.** Alcohol/substance abuse counseling, career counseling, student employment services, financial aid counseling, health services, personal counseling. **Physically disabled:** Services for visually, speech, hearing impaired.

**Contact.** E-mail: katie.shaw@fhchs.edu
Phone: (407) 303-7742 Toll-free number: (800) 500-7747
Fax: (407) 303-9408
Kaite Shaw, Director of Admissions, Florida Hospital College of Health Sciences, 671 Winyah Drive, Orlando, FL 32803

## Florida Institute of Technology
Melbourne, Florida
CB member
www.fit.edu
CB code: 5080

- Private 4-year university
- Residential campus in small city
- 2,508 degree-seeking undergraduates: 4% part-time, 29% women, 3% African American, 2% Asian American, 6% Hispanic American, 1% Native American, 20% international
- 2,459 degree-seeking graduate students
- 81% of applicants admitted
- SAT or ACT (ACT writing optional) required
- 54% graduate within 6 years; 20% enter graduate study

**General.** Founded in 1958. Regionally accredited. **Degrees:** 483 bachelor's awarded; master's, doctoral offered. **ROTC:** Army. **Location:** 76 miles from Orlando. **Calendar:** Semester, limited summer session. **Full-time faculty:** 224 total; 89% have terminal degrees, 14% minority, 22% women. **Part-time faculty:** 212 total; 58% have terminal degrees, 5% minority, 20% women. **Class size:** 53% < 20, 39% 20-39, 4% 40-49, 3% 50-99. **Special facilities:** Telescope/observatory, botanical gardens, pantherium, medical genetics lab, wind and hurricane impact research lab, microelectronics lab, research vessel delphinus, infectious diseases lab, laser optics and instrumentation lab, robotics and spatial systems lab, synoptic meteorology lab, Vero Beach marine lab.

**Freshman class profile.** 3,027 applied, 2,451 admitted, 681 enrolled.

| Mid 50% test scores | | | |
|---|---|---|---|
| SAT critical reading: | 510-610 | Rank in top tenth: | 27% |
| SAT math: | 530-640 | End year in good standing: | 80% |
| ACT composite: | 22-28 | Return as sophomores: | 75% |
| GPA 3.50 or higher: | 48% | Out-of-state: | 57% |
| GPA 3.0-3.49: | 31% | Live on campus: | 94% |
| GPA 2.0-2.99: | 21% | International: | 19% |
| Rank in top quarter: | 53% | Fraternities: | 20% |
| | | Sororities: | 16% |

**Basis for selection.** Applications reviewed with reference to specific degree programs or for admission to first-year programs in engineering, science and general studies. High school curriculum, GPA, class rank, SAT/ACT, teachers' recommendations, experiential essay, special classes, clubs or teams that involve research projects/opportunities, and advanced problem-solving techniques important. Interview recommended. **Homeschooled:** Transcript of courses and grades required. Self-descriptive 1-page essay, proof of research project participation required. SAT Subject Test strongly recommended (English composition, Math Level II, any sciences related to desired area of study).

**High school preparation.** 16 units required; 22 recommended. Required and recommended units include English 4, mathematics 3-4, social studies 2, history 2, science 3-4 (laboratory 3), foreign language 2, computer science 2 and academic electives 2.

**2007-2008 Annual costs.** Tuition/fees: $28,920. Tuition $26,360 for aeronautics, business, psychology, and humanities programs. Room/board: $7,770. Books/supplies: $2,200.

**2007-2008 Financial aid. Need-based:** Average need met was 85%. Average scholarship/grant was $18,517; average loan $4,320. 61% of total undergraduate aid awarded as scholarships/grants, 39% as loans/jobs. **Non-need-based:** Scholarships awarded for academics, alumni affiliation, athletics, ROTC, state residency.

**Application procedures. Admission:** Priority date 1/15; no deadline. $50 fee, may be waived for applicants with need. Application may be submitted online. Admission notification on a rolling basis beginning on or about 7/1. Must reply by May 1 or within 4 week(s) if notified thereafter. **Financial aid:** Priority date 3/1; no closing date. FAFSA required. Applicants notified on a rolling basis starting 2/15; must reply by 5/1 or within 4 week(s) of notification.

**Academics. Special study options:** Cooperative education, distance learning, double major, dual enrollment of high school students, ESL, independent study, internships, study abroad, teacher certification program. Dual degrees in computer engineering/electrical engineering, chemical engineering/chemistry, molecular/marine biology. **Credit/placement by examination:** AP, CLEP, IB, institutional tests. **Support services:** Learning center, preadmission summer program, remedial instruction, study skills assistance, tutoring.

**Majors. Biology:** General, aquatic, biochemistry, biomedical sciences, ecology, marine, molecular. **Business:** Accounting, business admin, e-commerce, information resources management, international. **Communications:** General. **Computer sciences:** Computer science. **Conservation:** Environmental science. **Education:** Biology, chemistry, computer, mathematics, physics, science. **Engineering:** General, aerospace, chemical, civil, computer, electrical, mechanical, ocean, software. **Interdisciplinary:** Biological/physical sciences. **Liberal arts:** Humanities. **Math:** General, applied. **Physical sciences:** Analytical chemistry, chemistry, hydrology, meteorology, oceanography, physics. **Psychology:** General, forensic. **Transportation:** Aviation, aviation management.

**Most popular majors.** Biology 10%, business/marketing 9%, computer/information sciences 6%, engineering/engineering technologies 39%, physical sciences 8%, psychology 9%, trade and industry 14%.

**Computing on campus.** 400 workstations in library, computer center, student center. Dormitories wired for high-speed internet access and linked to campus network. Commuter students can connect to campus network. Online course registration, online library, helpline, repair service, student web hosting, wireless network available.

**Student life. Freshman orientation:** Mandatory. Preregistration for classes offered. Three-day program in late August. **Policies:** Function in accordance with written constitution and bylaws approved by Dean of Students. **Housing:** Guaranteed on-campus for freshmen. Coed dorms, apartments, substance-free housing available. $200 fully refundable deposit. **Activities:** Pep band, campus ministries, dance, drama, international student organizations, literary magazine, radio station, student government, student newspaper, TV station, Newman Club, Unite, Chinese student association, Saudi student house, National Society of Black Engineers, Society of Women Engineers, Society of Hispanic Professional Engineers, French Connexion, Caribbean students organization.

**Athletics.** NCAA. **Intercollegiate:** Baseball M, basketball, cross-country, golf, rowing (crew) W, soccer, softball W, tennis, volleyball W. **Intramural:** Badminton, basketball, bowling, cricket, football (non-tackle), racquetball, soccer, softball, tennis, volleyball, water polo. **Team name:** Panthers.

**Student services.** Alcohol/substance abuse counseling, career counseling, student employment services, financial aid counseling, health services, personal counseling, veterans' counselor. **Physically disabled:** Services for visually, speech, hearing impaired.

**Contact.** E-mail: admission@fit.edu
Phone: (321) 674-8030 Toll-free number: (800) 888-4348
Fax: (321) 723-9468
Michael Perry, Director, Undergraduate Admissions, Florida Institute of Technology, 150 West University Boulevard, Melbourne, FL 32901-6975

---

## Florida International University
**Miami, Florida**
**www.fiu.edu**

**CB member**
**CB code: 5206**

- Public 4-year university
- Commuter campus in very large city
- 29,584 degree-seeking undergraduates: 37% part-time, 57% women, 13% African American, 4% Asian American, 64% Hispanic American, 4% international
- 6,034 degree-seeking graduate students
- 47% of applicants admitted

- SAT or ACT (ACT writing optional) required
- 49% graduate within 6 years

**General.** Founded in 1965. Regionally accredited. **Degrees:** 5,755 bachelor's, 62 associate awarded; master's, doctoral, first professional offered. **ROTC:** Army, Air Force. **Location:** 10 miles from downtown. **Calendar:** Semester, extensive summer session. **Full-time faculty:** 852 total; 82% have terminal degrees, 34% minority, 36% women. **Part-time faculty:** 736 total; 9% have terminal degrees, 49% minority, 50% women. **Class size:** 26% < 20, 43% 20-39, 12% 40-49, 16% 50-99, 4% >100. **Special facilities:** Nature preserve, museum.

**Freshman class profile.** 14,917 applied, 6,938 admitted, 3,741 enrolled.

| Mid 50% test scores | | | |
|---|---|---|---|
| SAT critical reading: | 500-600 | GPA 3.0-3.49: | 30% |
| SAT math: | 500-590 | GPA 2.0-2.99: | 11% |
| SAT writing: | 490-570 | Return as sophomores: | 87% |
| ACT composite: | 21-25 | Out-of-state: | 5% |
| GPA 3.50 or higher: | 59% | Live on campus: | 23% |
| | | International: | 2% |

**Basis for selection.** 3.0 GPA required Lower GPA considered with higher test score. Audition required of music performance, theater, dance majors. Portfolio required of art and architecture majors. Interview and essay recommended for academically marginal applicants. **Homeschooled:** State high school equivalency certificate required. GED required if state high school equivalency certificate is not available.

**High school preparation.** 18 units required. Required units include English 4, mathematics 3, social studies 3, science 3 (laboratory 2), foreign language 2 and academic electives 3.

**2007-2008 Annual costs.** Tuition/fees: $3,466; $15,865 out-of-state. Room/board: $10,608. Books/supplies: $900. Personal expenses: $2,128.

**Financial aid. Non-need-based:** Scholarships awarded for academics, art, minority status, music/drama, state residency.

**Application procedures. Admission:** Priority date 3/1; no deadline. $30 fee, may be waived for applicants with need. Application may be submitted online. Admission notification on a rolling basis beginning on or about 9/1. **Financial aid:** Priority date 3/1, closing date 5/15. FAFSA required. Must reply within 4 week(s) of notification.

**Academics. Special study options:** Accelerated study, combined bachelor's/graduate degree, cooperative education, distance learning, double major, dual enrollment of high school students, ESL, exchange student, honors, independent study, internships, study abroad, teacher certification program, weekend college. **Credit/placement by examination:** AP, CLEP, IB, SAT, ACT, institutional tests. 45 credit hours maximum toward bachelor's degree. **Support services:** Learning center, pre-admission summer program, study skills assistance, tutoring.

**Honors college/program.** Freshmen must have a 3.5 GPA. Transfer and continuing students must have a 3.3 GPA in all college level work. Students may pursue any major while completing the honors curriculum.

**Majors. Architecture:** Architecture. **Area/ethnic studies:** Asian, women's. **Biology:** General, marine. **Business:** Accounting, business admin, finance, hospitality admin, human resources, insurance, international, management information systems, marketing, real estate, tourism/travel. **Communications:** General. **Computer sciences:** General, information technology. **Conservation:** General. **Education:** Art, elementary, emotionally handicapped, English, family/consumer sciences, foreign languages, health, learning disabled, mathematics, mentally handicapped, music, physical, science, social science, social studies, trade/industrial. **Engineering:** Biomedical, chemical, civil, computer, electrical, mechanical, systems. **Engineering technology:** Construction. **English:** English lit. **Foreign languages:** French, German, Italian, Portuguese, Spanish. **Health:** Health care admin, medical records admin, nursing (RN), orthotics/prosthetics. **History:** General. **Liberal arts:** Arts/sciences. **Math:** General, applied, statistics. **Parks/recreation:** Exercise sciences, facilities management. **Philosophy/religion:** Philosophy, religion. **Physical sciences:** Chemistry, geology, physics. **Protective services:** Criminal justice. **Psychology:** General. **Public administration:** General, social work. **Social sciences:** Economics, geography, international relations, political science, sociology. **Visual/performing arts:** Art history/conservation, dance, dramatic, interior design, studio arts.

**Most popular majors.** Business/marketing 34%, education 6%, engineering/engineering technologies 7%, health sciences 7%, psychology 7%, social sciences 7%.

**Computing on campus.** 1,800 workstations in library, computer center. Dormitories wired for high-speed internet access and linked to campus network. Commuter students can connect to campus network. Online course registration, repair service, wireless network available.

**Student life. Freshman orientation:** Mandatory, $50 fee. **Housing:** Coed dorms, apartments, fraternity/sorority housing available. **Activities:** Bands, choral groups, dance, drama, film society, music ensembles, opera, radio station, student government, student newspaper, symphony orchestra, over 190 clubs available.

**Athletics.** NCAA. **Intercollegiate:** Baseball M, basketball, cross-country, football (tackle) M, golf, soccer, softball W, swimming W, tennis W, track and field, volleyball W. **Intramural:** Basketball, bowling, cross-country, football (tackle) M, golf, lacrosse M, racquetball M, rugby M, sailing, skin diving, soccer, softball, swimming, tennis, volleyball, water polo M. **Team name:** Golden Panthers.

**Student services.** Adult student services, alcohol/substance abuse counseling, campus ministries, career counseling, student employment services, financial aid counseling, health services, minority student services, on-campus daycare, personal counseling, placement for graduates, veterans' counselor. **Physically disabled:** Services for visually, speech, hearing impaired.

**Contact.** E-mail: admiss@fiu.edu
Phone: (305) 348-2363 Fax: (305) 348-3648
Carmen Brown, Director of Admissions, Florida International University, University Park Campus, PC 140, Miami, FL 33199

---

## Florida Memorial University

**Miami Gardens, Florida**          **CB member**
**www.fmuniv.edu**                 **CB code: 5217**

- Private 4-year liberal arts college affiliated with American Baptist Churches in the USA
- Residential campus in very large city
- 1,669 degree-seeking undergraduates: 9% part-time, 62% women
- 81 degree-seeking graduate students
- SAT or ACT with writing, application essay required
- 34% graduate within 6 years

**General.** Founded in 1879. Regionally accredited. 4 branch campuses. **Degrees:** 236 bachelor's awarded; master's offered. **ROTC:** Army. **Location:** 15 miles from downtown Miami. **Calendar:** Semester, limited summer session. **Full-time faculty:** 94 total. **Part-time faculty:** 79 total. **Class size:** 70% < 20, 28% 20-39, 1% 40-49, less than 1% 50-99. **Special facilities:** Black archives, airway science building with simulator and air traffic control tower.

**Freshman class profile.**

| | | | |
|---|---|---|---|
| GPA 3.50 or higher: | 6% | Out-of-state: | 20% |
| GPA 3.0-3.49: | 15% | Live on campus: | 80% |
| GPA 2.0-2.99: | 71% | | |

**Basis for selection.** High school GPA of 2.0 required. School achievement record, test scores, interview, recommendations, alumni affiliation considered. Interview recommended.

**High school preparation.** 15 units recommended. Recommended units include English 4, mathematics 4, social studies 2, science 3 and foreign language 2. College-preparatory program strongly recommended.

**2008-2009 Annual costs.** Tuition/fees: $12,254. Room/board: $5,340. Books/supplies: $1,200. Personal expenses: $3,500.

**Financial aid. Additional information:** Need-based financial aid available to part-time students taking 6 credits or more per semester.

**Application procedures. Admission:** No deadline. $15 fee, may be waived for applicants with need. Application may be submitted online. Admission notification on a rolling basis. **Financial aid:** No deadline. Applicants notified on a rolling basis; must reply within 2 week(s) of notification.

**Academics. Special study options:** Combined bachelor's/graduate degree, cooperative education, double major, dual enrollment of high school students, honors, independent study, internships, liberal arts/career combination, study abroad, teacher certification program, weekend college. **Credit/placement by examination:** AP, CLEP, institutional tests. 30 credit hours maximum toward bachelor's degree. **Support services:** Learning center, pre-admission summer program, remedial instruction, study skills assistance, tutoring, writing center.

**Majors. Biology:** General. **Business:** Accounting, business admin, management information systems. **Computer sciences:** General, computer science. **Education:** Elementary, physical. **English:** English lit. **Health:** Clinical lab science. **Math:** General. **Psychology:** General. **Public administration:** General. **Social sciences:** Sociology. **Transportation:** Aviation.

**Most popular majors.** Biology 9%, business/marketing 17%, computer/information sciences 11%, education 21%, psychology 9%, social sciences 16%.

**Computing on campus.** 300 workstations in dormitories, library, computer center, student center. Dormitories wired for high-speed internet access and linked to campus network. Commuter students can connect to campus network. Online library, helpline, repair service, wireless network available.

**Student life. Freshman orientation:** Mandatory. Preregistration for classes offered. **Housing:** Guaranteed on-campus for freshmen. Single-sex dorms available. **Activities:** Jazz band, choral groups, international student organizations, music ensembles, musical theater, student government, student newspaper, TV station, Christian student union, broadcasting club, Junior NAACP, Toastmasters, Professional Women of Tomorrow.

**Athletics.** NAIA. **Intercollegiate:** Baseball M, basketball, track and field, volleyball W. **Intramural:** Baseball M, basketball, soccer M, softball W, swimming, tennis, volleyball. **Team name:** Figthing lions.

**Student services.** Campus ministries, career counseling, student employment services, health services, minority student services, personal counseling, placement for graduates.

**Contact.** E-mail: admit@fmuniv.edu
Phone: (305) 626-3750 Fax: (305) 623-1462
Peggy Martin, Director of Admissions, Florida Memorial University, 15800 Northwest 42 Avenue, Miami Gardens, FL 33054

---

## Florida Southern College

**Lakeland, Florida**          **CB member**
**www.flsouthern.edu**         **CB code: 5218**

- Private 4-year liberal arts college affiliated with United Methodist Church
- Residential campus in small city
- 1,687 degree-seeking undergraduates: 3% part-time, 60% women, 7% African American, 1% Asian American, 6% Hispanic American, 4% international
- 108 degree-seeking graduate students
- 58% of applicants admitted
- SAT or ACT (ACT writing optional), application essay required
- 54% graduate within 6 years; 27% enter graduate study

**General.** Founded in 1885. Regionally accredited. Campus designed by Frank Lloyd Wright; contains world's largest collection of Wright-designed structures at a single site. **Degrees:** 515 bachelor's awarded; master's offered. **ROTC:** Army, Air Force. **Location:** 30 miles from Tampa, 50 miles from Orlando. **Calendar:** Semester, limited summer session. **Full-time faculty:** 107 total; 82% have terminal degrees, 8% minority, 36% women. **Part-time faculty:** 74 total; 20% have terminal degrees, 11% minority, 40% women. **Class size:** 58% < 20, 39% 20-39, 3% 40-49. **Special facilities:** Planetarium; Frank Lloyd Wright visitor center; nuclear magnetic resonance spectrometer; boathouse for water-skiing, sailing, and kayaking.

**Freshman class profile.** 2,559 applied, 1,490 admitted, 425 enrolled.

| Mid 50% test scores | | | |
|---|---|---|---|
| SAT critical reading: | 480-600 | Rank in top tenth: | 24% |
| SAT math: | 470-600 | End year in good standing: | 85% |
| SAT writing: | 460-570 | Return as sophomores: | 71% |
| ACT composite: | 20-25 | Out-of-state: | 20% |
| GPA 3.50 or higher: | 45% | Live on campus: | 83% |
| GPA 3.0-3.49: | 28% | International: | 4% |
| GPA 2.0-2.99: | 27% | Fraternities: | 18% |
| Rank in top quarter: | 49% | Sororities: | 23% |

**Basis for selection.** School achievement record most important, followed by test scores and recommendations. Character and motivation, extracurricular activities also important. Interview recommended. Audition required for music, audition recommended (required for scholarship consideration) for theater majors. Portfolio recommended (required for scholarship consideration) for art majors. **Homeschooled:** Transcript of courses and grades required.

**High school preparation.** 18 units required. Required and recommended units include English 4, mathematics 3, social studies 3, history 3, science 2 (laboratory 2), foreign language 2 and academic electives 2.

**2007-2008 Annual costs.** Tuition/fees: $21,190. Room/board: $7,500. Books/supplies: $1,150. Personal expenses: $1,050.

**2007-2008 Financial aid. Need-based:** 323 full-time freshmen applied for aid; 265 were judged to have need; 263 of these received aid. Average need met was 78%. Average scholarship/grant was $5,233; average loan $1,885. 68% of total undergraduate aid awarded as scholarships/grants, 32% as loans/jobs. **Non-need-based:** Awarded to 1,664 full-time undergraduates, including 454 freshmen. Scholarships awarded for academics, alumni affiliation, art, athletics, job skills, leadership, music/drama, religious affiliation, ROTC.

**Application procedures. Admission:** Closing date 3/1 (receipt date). $30 fee, may be waived for applicants with need. Application may be submitted online. Admission notification on a rolling basis beginning on or about 1/15. Must reply by May 1 or within 2 week(s) if notified thereafter. Housing deposit refundable only through May 1. **Financial aid:** Priority date 3/1, closing date 7/1. FAFSA, institutional form required. Applicants notified on a rolling basis starting 3/1; must reply within 3 week(s) of notification.

**Academics. Special study options:** Combined bachelor's/graduate degree, double major, dual enrollment of high school students, honors, independent study, internships, liberal arts/career combination, New York semester, student-designed major, study abroad, teacher certification program, United Nations semester, Washington semester. **Credit/placement by examination:** AP, CLEP, IB, SAT, ACT. 60 credit hours maximum toward bachelor's degree. **Support services:** Reduced course load, study skills assistance, tutoring, writing center.

**Majors. Agriculture:** Business, horticultural science, ornamental horticulture, turf management. **Biology:** General, Biochemistry/biophysics and molecular biology, environmental. **Business:** Accounting, business admin, finance, international, management information systems, marketing. **Communications:** Advertising, broadcast journalism, journalism, public relations. **Education:** General, art, early childhood, elementary, music, physical, special. **English:** Composition, English lit. **Foreign languages:** Spanish. **Health:** Athletic training, nursing (RN), predental, preveterinary. **History:** General. **Interdisciplinary:** Math/computer science. **Liberal arts:** Humanities. **Math:** General. **Parks/recreation:** Health/fitness, sports admin. **Philosophy/religion:** Philosophy, religion. **Physical sciences:** Chemistry. **Psychology:** General. **Social sciences:** General, criminology, economics, political science, sociology. **Visual/performing arts:** Art history/conservation, dramatic, graphic design, music management, music theory/composition, studio arts, theater design. **Other:** English: Dramatic Art.

**Most popular majors.** Biology 6%, business/marketing 24%, communications/journalism 9%, education 15%, psychology 6%, social sciences 10%, visual/performing arts 11%.

**Computing on campus.** 376 workstations in dormitories, library, computer center. Dormitories wired for high-speed internet access and linked to campus network. Commuter students can connect to campus network. Online course registration, online library, helpline, wireless network available.

**Student life. Freshman orientation:** Mandatory. Preregistration for classes offered. Four days prior to classes for fall semester. **Housing:** Guaranteed on-campus for all undergraduates. Coed dorms, single-sex dorms, special housing for disabled, apartments, fraternity/sorority housing, substance-free housing available. $500 fully refundable deposit, deadline 5/1. Pets allowed in dorm rooms. Seniors have option to live off-campus independently. Freshmen required to live on campus unless living with relatives. **Activities:** Bands, campus ministries, choral groups, dance, drama, international student organizations, literary magazine, music ensembles, musical theater, opera, student government, student newspaper, symphony orchestra, Wesley Fellowship, community tutorial service organizations, Fellowship of Christian Athletes, All-Campus Fellowship, Upper Room Ministries, Antioch 2, Beyond Campus Ministries, Newman Club, reformed university fellowship.

**Athletics.** NCAA. **Intercollegiate:** Baseball M, basketball, cross-country, golf, soccer, softball W, swimming, tennis, track and field, volleyball W. **Intramural:** Basketball, bowling, football (non-tackle), golf, soccer, softball, swimming, tennis, volleyball. **Team name:** Moccasins.

**Student services.** Adult student services, alcohol/substance abuse counseling, career counseling, student employment services, financial aid counseling, health services, minority student services, personal counseling, placement for graduates.

**Contact.** E-mail: fscadm@flsouthern.edu
Phone: (863) 680-4131 Toll-free number: (800) 274-4131
Fax: (863) 680-4120
Bill Langston, Director of Admission, Florida Southern College, 111 Lake Hollingsworth Drive, Lakeland, FL 33801-5698

## Florida State University
**Tallahassee, Florida**
www.fsu.edu

CB member
CB code: 5219

- Public 4-year university
- Residential campus in small city
- 31,231 degree-seeking undergraduates: 11% part-time, 56% women, 11% African American, 3% Asian American, 11% Hispanic American, 1% Native American
- 8,520 degree-seeking graduate students
- 55% of applicants admitted
- SAT or ACT with writing, application essay required

**General.** Founded in 1851. Regionally accredited. **Degrees:** 7,204 bachelor's, 363 associate awarded; master's, doctoral, first professional offered. **ROTC:** Army, Naval, Air Force. **Location:** 191 miles from Pensacola, 163 miles from Jacksonville. **Calendar:** Semester, extensive summer session. **Full-time faculty:** 1,353 total; 92% have terminal degrees, 15% minority, 36% women. **Part-time faculty:** 340 total; 92% have terminal degrees, 12% minority, 59% women. **Class size:** 39% < 20, 43% 20-39, 6% 40-49, 8% 50-99, 4% >100. **Special facilities:** Marine laboratory/aquarium, institute of molecular biophysics, national high magnetic field laboratory, music research center, accelerator, oceanographic institute, planetarium, reservation, golf course, Middle East center, institute of science and public affairs, center for the advancement of human rights.

**Freshman class profile.** 24,343 applied, 13,415 admitted, 6,133 enrolled.

| Mid 50% test scores | | | |
|---|---|---|---|
| SAT critical reading: | 540-630 | GPA 3.0-3.49: | 32% |
| SAT math: | 550-640 | GPA 2.0-2.99: | 3% |
| SAT writing: | 510-600 | Rank in top quarter: | 64% |
| ACT composite: | 23-28 | Rank in top tenth: | 24% |
| GPA 3.50 or higher: | 65% | Out-of-state: | 12% |
| | | Live on campus: | 58% |

**Basis for selection.** Most Florida residents accepted have B+ average or better in academic subjects and 1100 SAT (exclusive of Writing) or 24 ACT. Highest subscores on SAT/ACT used for admission purposes. Out-of-state students must meet higher standards. Audition required of music, dance, BFA theater majors. Portfolio required of BFA art, interior design majors. Departmental application required for motion picture, television, and recording art programs. **Homeschooled:** Statement describing homeschool structure and mission, transcript of courses and grades required. Must provide detailed course syllabi with complete course description and names of textbooks used.

**High school preparation.** 18 units required; 22 recommended. Required and recommended units include English 4, mathematics 3-4, social studies 1, history 2, science 3-4 (laboratory 2), foreign language 2-4 and academic electives 3. Math courses must be algebra I and above; 2 units of same foreign language required; at least 3 units English with substantial writing requirements; social studies must include history. Additional consideration given for completion of higher level courses (AP, IB, honors, calculus and/or foreign language IV or V) and for completion of 4 or more senior academic courses.

**2007-2008 Annual costs.** Tuition/fees: $3,355; $17,403 out-of-state. Room/board: $8,000.

**2007-2008 Financial aid. Need-based:** 3,771 full-time freshmen applied for aid; 1,855 were judged to have need; 1,855 of these received aid. Average need met was 68%. Average scholarship/grant was $3,467; average loan $2,885. 58% of total undergraduate aid awarded as scholarships/grants, 42% as loans/jobs. **Non-need-based:** Scholarships awarded for academics, athletics, state residency.

**Application procedures. Admission:** Closing date 2/14 (receipt date). $30 fee. Application must be submitted online. Students strongly encouraged to apply early. Those applying before 11/30 who are denied admission are given additional opportunities to improve application standing. **Financial aid:** No deadline. FAFSA required. Applicants notified on a rolling basis starting 3/15.

**Academics.** 2+2 distance learning available in cooperation with selected Florida community colleges includes programs in computer science, interdisciplinary social sciences, and nursing (RN to BSN). **Special study options:** Accelerated study, combined bachelor's/graduate degree, cooperative education, cross-registration, distance learning, double major, dual enrollment of high school students, ESL, honors, independent study, internships, study abroad, teacher certification program. Cooperative programs with Florida Agricultural and Mechanical University and Tallahassee Community College; degree in three years; International year abroad, year-round study abroad in England, Italy, Panama, Spain; summer study abroad in Australia, Brazil,

China, Costa Rica, Croatia, Czech Republic, Ecuador, England, France, Ireland, Italy, Japan, Netherlands, Russia, Switzerland. **Credit/placement by examination:** AP, CLEP, IB, SAT, ACT, institutional tests. 30 credit hours maximum toward associate degree, 45 toward bachelor's. English AP credit not awarded for more than 1 exam. **Support services:** Learning center, reduced course load, study skills assistance, tutoring, writing center.

**Majors. Area/ethnic studies:** American, Asian, Caribbean, Central/Eastern European, Latin American, Russian/Slavic, women's. **Biology:** General, biochemistry, biophysics, marine, zoology. **Business:** Accounting, actuarial science, finance, hospitality admin, human resources, insurance, international, management information systems, marketing, operations, real estate. **Communications:** Advertising, media studies, public relations. **Computer sciences:** General, computer science, information technology. **Conservation:** Environmental science, environmental studies. **Education:** Art, bilingual, early childhood, elementary, emotionally handicapped, English, family/consumer sciences, foreign languages, health, learning disabled, mathematics, mentally handicapped, multicultural, music, physical, physics, science, social science, visually handicapped. **Engineering:** Chemical, civil, computer, electrical, environmental, industrial, materials, mechanical, software. **English:** Creative writing, English lit. **Family/consumer sciences:** General, child development, clothing/textiles, family studies, food/nutrition, merchandising. **Foreign languages:** Ancient Greek, Chinese, classics, French, German, Italian, Japanese, Latin, Russian, Spanish. **Health:** Athletic training, audiology/speech pathology, dietetics, music therapy, nursing (RN), predental, premedicine, prepharmacy, preveterinary, vocational rehab counseling. **History:** General. **Interdisciplinary:** Nutrition sciences. **Legal studies:** Prelaw. **Liberal arts:** Humanities. **Math:** General, applied, computational, statistics. **Parks/recreation:** Exercise sciences, facilities management, health/fitness, sports admin. **Philosophy/religion:** Philosophy, religion. **Physical sciences:** Atmospheric science, chemistry, geology, physics. **Psychology:** General. **Public administration:** Social work. **Social sciences:** General, anthropology, applied economics, criminology, economics, geography, international relations, political science, sociology. **Visual/performing arts:** Acting, art history/conservation, cinematography, dance, dramatic, fashion design, interior design, jazz, music history, music performance, music theory/composition, piano/organ, stringed instruments, studio arts, theater design, voice/opera. **Other:** Computational Biology, Computer Criminology.

**Most popular majors.** Business/marketing 20%, education 7%, family/consumer sciences 10%, security/protective services 6%, social sciences 17%, visual/performing arts 6%.

**Computing on campus.** PC or laptop required. 2,958 workstations in dormitories, library, computer center, student center. Dormitories wired for high-speed internet access and linked to campus network. Commuter students can connect to campus network. Online course registration, online library, helpline, repair service, student web hosting, wireless network available.

**Student life. Freshman orientation:** Mandatory, $25 fee. Preregistration for classes offered. Held during summer. **Housing:** Coed dorms, single-sex dorms, special housing for disabled, apartments, fraternity/sorority housing, substance-free housing available. $225 partly refundable deposit. Honor residences and living and learning communities available. **Activities:** Bands, campus ministries, choral groups, dance, drama, film society, literary magazine, music ensembles, musical theater, opera, radio station, student government, student newspaper, symphony orchestra, TV station, Hillel, Christian student association, Catholic student union, Campus Crusade for Christ, College Democrats, College Republicans, black student union, Hispanic student union, American civil liberties union.

**Athletics.** NCAA. **Intercollegiate:** Baseball M, basketball, cheerleading, cross-country, diving, football (tackle) M, golf, soccer W, softball W, swimming, tennis, track and field, volleyball W. **Intramural:** Basketball, bowling, field hockey, football (non-tackle), golf, racquetball, soccer, softball, swimming, table tennis, tennis, volleyball, wrestling. **Team name:** Seminoles.

**Student services.** Adult student services, alcohol/substance abuse counseling, career counseling, student employment services, financial aid counseling, health services, legal services, minority student services, on-campus daycare, personal counseling, placement for graduates, veterans' counselor, women's services. **Physically disabled:** Services for visually, speech, hearing impaired.

**Contact.** E-mail: admissions@admin.fsu.edu
Phone: (850) 644-6200 Fax: (850) 644-0197
Janice Finney, Director of Admissions, Florida State University, PO Box 3062400, Tallahassee, FL 32306-2400

## Hobe Sound Bible College
**Hobe Sound, Florida**
www.hsbc.edu                                    CB code: 5306

- Private 4-year Bible college affiliated with interdenominational tradition
- Residential campus in small town

- 160 degree-seeking undergraduates
- SAT or ACT (ACT writing optional) required

**General.** Founded in 1960. Accredited by ABHE. **Degrees:** 20 bachelor's, 5 associate awarded. **Location:** 25 miles from West Palm Beach. **Calendar:** 4-1-4, limited summer session. **Full-time faculty:** 25 total. **Part-time faculty:** 10 total.

**Freshman class profile.**

| Mid 50% test scores | | | |
|---|---|---|---|
| SAT critical reading: | 450-680 | SAT math: | 430-570 |
| | | ACT composite: | 14-23 |

**Basis for selection.** Recommendations, essay, religious commitment important. **Homeschooled:** Must submit official transcripts from reputable organizations documenting completion of all academic coursework required for high school diploma.

**2007-2008 Annual costs.** Tuition/fees: $4,650. Room/board: $4,000. Books/supplies: $450. Personal expenses: $2,000.

**Financial aid. Non-need-based:** Scholarships awarded for academics, leadership.

**Application procedures. Admission:** Closing date 8/25. $25 fee, may be waived for applicants with need. Admission notification on a rolling basis beginning on or about 3/1. **Financial aid:** Closing date 8/1. FAFSA required.

**Academics.** Double major required of all students in 4-year programs. All students complete major in Bible as well as major in Christian vocational field. **Special study options:** Distance learning, double major, dual enrollment of high school students, ESL, external degree, internships, teacher certification program. **Credit/placement by examination:** CLEP, institutional tests. **Support services:** Reduced course load, remedial instruction.

**Majors. Education:** Elementary, English, mathematics, music. **Philosophy/religion:** Religion. **Theology:** Bible, missionary, sacred music, theology. **Visual/performing arts:** Music performance, piano/organ. **Other:** Child Evangelism.

**Computing on campus.** 10 workstations in computer center.

**Student life. Freshman orientation:** Mandatory. **Policies:** Religious observance required. **Housing:** Guaranteed on-campus for all undergraduates. Single-sex dorms, apartments available. Unmarried students under 25 required to live in campus dormitories or with parents. **Activities:** Concert band, choral groups, music ensembles, student government, Christian service organizations.

**Athletics. Intramural:** Basketball, football (tackle) M, racquetball, soccer, softball, tennis, volleyball.

**Student services.** Health services, personal counseling.

**Contact.** E-mail: admissions@hsbc.edu
Phone: (772) 546-5534 ext. 1015 Toll-free number: (800) 881-5534
Fax: (772) 545-1422
Judy Fay, Director of Admissions, Hobe Sound Bible College, Box 1065, Hobe Sound, FL 33475

## Hodges University
**Naples, Florida**
www.hodges.edu                                  CB code: 7113

- Private 4-year business college
- Commuter campus in small city
- 1,475 degree-seeking undergraduates: 24% part-time, 68% women, 16% African American, 2% Asian American, 24% Hispanic American
- 212 degree-seeking graduate students
- 79% of applicants admitted

**General.** Founded in 1990. Regionally accredited. **Degrees:** 323 bachelor's, 113 associate awarded; master's offered. **Location:** 110 miles from Miami, 180 miles from Tampa. **Calendar:** Trimester, extensive summer session. **Full-time faculty:** 61 total; 66% have terminal degrees, 8% minority, 33% women. **Part-time faculty:** 53 total; 36% have terminal degrees, 6% minority, 40% women. **Class size:** 81% < 20, 17% 20-39, 1% 40-49, less than 1% 50-99.

**Freshman class profile.** 210 applied, 166 admitted, 156 enrolled.

**Basis for selection.** Essay and interview important; level of interest very important.

**2007-2008 Annual costs.** Tuition/fees: $13,130. Books/supplies: $1,000. Personal expenses: $530.

**2007-2008 Financial aid. Need-based:** 126 full-time freshmen applied for aid; 112 were judged to have need; 112 of these received aid. Average need met was 60%. Average scholarship/grant was $2,300; average loan $2,600. 33% of total undergraduate aid awarded as scholarships/grants, 67% as loans/jobs. **Non-need-based:** Awarded to 659 full-time undergraduates, including 68 freshmen. Scholarships awarded for academics.

**Application procedures. Admission:** No deadline. $20 fee. Application may be submitted online. Admission notification on a rolling basis. **Financial aid:** Priority date 9/7; no closing date. FAFSA required. Applicants notified on a rolling basis starting 7/7.

**Academics. Special study options:** Accelerated study, combined bachelor's/graduate degree, cooperative education, distance learning, double major, ESL, independent study, internships, weekend college. **Credit/placement by examination:** AP, CLEP, IB, institutional tests. **Support services:** Remedial instruction, tutoring.

**Majors. Business:** Accounting, business admin. **Computer sciences:** Information technology. **Health:** Health care admin. **Legal studies:** Paralegal. **Protective services:** Criminal justice.

**Most popular majors.** Business/marketing 44%, computer/information sciences 8%, health sciences 9%, interdisciplinary studies 21%, legal studies 7%, security/protective services 11%.

**Computing on campus.** 500 workstations in library, computer center. Wireless network available.

**Student life. Freshman orientation:** Mandatory. **Activities:** Literary magazine.

**Student services.** Career counseling, financial aid counseling, personal counseling, placement for graduates.

**Contact.** E-mail: admit@internationalcollege.edu
Phone: (239) 513-1122 Toll-free number: (800) 466-8017
Fax: (239) 513-9071
Rita Lampus, Vice President of Student Enrollment Management, Hodges University, 2655 Northbrooke Drive, Naples, FL 34119

## International Academy of Design and Technology: Orlando
**Orlando, Florida**
www.iadt.edu                                   CB code: 4366

◆  For-profit 4-year career college
◆  Very large city
◆  1,038 degree-seeking undergraduates

**General.** Accredited by ACICS. **Degrees:** 29 bachelor's, 115 associate awarded. **Location:** Downtown. **Calendar:** Quarter, extensive summer session. **Full-time faculty:** 12 total. **Part-time faculty:** 78 total.

**Basis for selection.** Open admission.

**Application procedures. Admission:** No deadline. $50 fee. Application may be submitted online. **Financial aid:** No deadline. FAFSA required.

**Academics. Special study options:** Accelerated study. **Credit/placement by examination:** AP, CLEP. **Support services:** Learning center, remedial instruction, tutoring.

**Majors. Business:** Fashion, marketing. **Computer sciences:** Computer graphics, game design, webmaster. **Visual/performing arts:** Interior design.

**Computing on campus.** Online course registration, online library available.

**Student life. Freshman orientation:** Mandatory. Preregistration for classes offered.

**Contact.** Phone: (407) 857-2300
Dave Ritchie, Vice President Admissions and Marketing, International Academy of Design and Technology: Orlando, 5959 Lake Ellenor Drive, Orlando, FL 32809

## International Academy of Design and Technology: Tampa
**Tampa, Florida**
www.academy.edu                                CB code: 7114

◆  For-profit 4-year visual arts and technical college
◆  Commuter campus in very large city
◆  1,985 degree-seeking undergraduates
◆  Interview required

**General.** Accredited by ACICS. **Degrees:** 247 bachelor's, 253 associate awarded. **Calendar:** Quarter, extensive summer session. **Full-time faculty:** 26 total. **Part-time faculty:** 140 total.

**Basis for selection.** Open admission. Essay recommended. **Learning Disabled:** Submit Auxiliary Aid Application.

**2007-2008 Annual costs.** Tuition/fees: $18,780. Books/supplies: $1,800. Personal expenses: $2,015.

**2006-2007 Financial aid. Need-based:** 39% of total undergraduate aid awarded as scholarships/grants, 61% as loans/jobs. **Non-need-based:** Scholarships awarded for academics.

**Application procedures. Admission:** No deadline. $50 fee, may be waived for applicants with need. Admission notification on a rolling basis. **Financial aid:** No deadline. FAFSA required.

**Academics. Special study options:** Accelerated study, cooperative education, internships, study abroad. **Credit/placement by examination:** AP, CLEP, institutional tests. 67 credit hours maximum toward associate degree, 135 toward bachelor's. **Support services:** Learning center, study skills assistance, tutoring.

**Majors. Business:** Merchandising. **Communications technology:** Animation/special effects. **Computer sciences:** Web page design. **Visual/performing arts:** Digital art, fashion design, interior design. **Other:** Recording Arts.

**Computing on campus.** Wireless network available.

**Student life. Freshman orientation:** Mandatory. Preregistration for classes offered.

**Student services.** Adult student services, student employment services, financial aid counseling, placement for graduates, veterans' counselor.

**Contact.** E-mail: admissions@academy.edu
Phone: (813) 881-0007 Toll-free number: (800) 222-3369
Fax: (813) 881-0008
Heidi Demello, Associate Vice President of Admissions and Marketing, International Academy of Design and Technology: Tampa, 5104 Eisenhower Boulevard, Tampa, FL 33634

## ITT Technical Institute: Ft. Lauderdale
**Ft. Lauderdale, Florida**
www.itt-tech.edu                               CB code: 2700

◆  For-profit 4-year technical college
◆  Commuter campus in small city

**General.** Accredited by ACICS. **Calendar:** Quarter.

**Annual costs/financial aid.** Tuition varies by program, $260-$368 per credit hour.

**Contact.** Phone: (954) 476-9300
Director of Recruitment, 3401 South University Drive, Ft. Lauderdale, FL 33328

## ITT Technical Institute: Jacksonville
**Jacksonville, Florida**
www.itt-tech.edu                               CB code: 2716

◆  For-profit 4-year technical college
◆  Commuter campus in very large city

**General.** Accredited by ACICS. **Calendar:** Quarter.

**Annual costs/financial aid.** Tuition varies by program, $260-$368 per credit hour.

**Contact.**  Phone: (904) 573-9100
Director of Recruitment, 6600-10 Youngerman Circle, Jacksonville, FL 32244

## ITT Technical Institute: Lake Mary
Lake Mary, Florida
www.itt-tech.edu

- For-profit 4-year technical college
- Commuter campus in large town

**General.** Accredited by ACICS. **Calendar:** Quarter.

**Annual costs/financial aid.** Tuition varies by program, $260-$368 per credit hour.

**Contact.**  Phone: (407) 660-2900
Director of Recruitment, 1400 International Parkway South, Lake Mary, FL 32746

## ITT Technical Institute: Miami
Miami, Florida
www.itt-tech.edu                    CB code: 2733

- For-profit 4-year technical college
- Commuter campus in large city

**General.** Accredited by ACICS. **Calendar:** Quarter.

**Annual costs/financial aid.** Tuition varies by program, $260-$368 per credit hour.

**Contact.**  Phone: (305) 477-3080
Director of Recruitment, 7955 12th Street, Suite 119, Miami, FL 33126

## ITT Technical Institute: Tampa
Tampa, Florida
www.itt-tech.edu                    CB code: 2145

- For-profit 4-year technical college
- Commuter campus in large city

**General.** Founded in 1981. Accredited by ACICS. **Calendar:** Quarter.

**Annual costs/financial aid.** Tuition varies by program, $260-$368 per credit hour.

**Contact.**  Phone: (813) 885-2244
Director of Recruitment, 4809 Memorial Highway, Tampa, FL 33634

## Jacksonville University
Jacksonville, Florida                    CB member
www.ju.edu                               CB code: 5331

- Private 4-year university and liberal arts college
- Residential campus in very large city
- 2,893 degree-seeking undergraduates: 26% part-time, 59% women, 21% African American, 2% Asian American, 6% Hispanic American, 1% Native American, 2% international
- 378 degree-seeking graduate students
- 40% of applicants admitted
- SAT or ACT (ACT writing optional) required
- 49% graduate within 6 years

**General.** Founded in 1934. Regionally accredited. **Degrees:** 516 bachelor's awarded; master's offered. **ROTC:** Naval. **Calendar:** Semester, limited summer session. **Full-time faculty:** 148 total; 78% have terminal degrees, 7% minority, 47% women. **Part-time faculty:** 82 total; 38% have terminal degrees, 10% minority, 49% women. **Class size:** 57% < 20, 42% 20-39, 1% 40-49, less than 1% 50-99. **Special facilities:** Marine science research vessels, observatory, cybercafe.

**Freshman class profile.** 6,236 applied, 2,513 admitted, 581 enrolled.

| Mid 50% test scores | | | |
|---|---|---|---|
| SAT critical reading: | 440-560 | Return as sophomores: | 65% |
| SAT math: | 450-570 | Out-of-state: | 44% |
| ACT composite: | 18-23 | Live on campus: | 80% |
| GPA 3.50 or higher: | 28% | International: | 1% |
| GPA 3.0-3.49: | 40% | Fraternities: | 21% |
| GPA 2.0-2.99: | 32% | Sororities: | 16% |

**Basis for selection.** GPA and test scores very important, followed by rigor of secondary school record. Audition required of music, dance, theater majors. Portfolio required for art, computer art and design. **Homeschooled:** Transcript of courses and grades, interview, letter of recommendation (non-parent) required. Two letters of recommendation evaluating academic potential from qualified educator or evaluator outside of the homeschool environment, portfolio that includes 2 writing samples of not less than 100 words, bibliography of reading completed and texts used, description of curriculum, and interview required.

**High school preparation.** 13 units required; 16 recommended. Required and recommended units include English 4, mathematics 3-4, social studies 3, science 3 (laboratory 2) and foreign language 2. History units may be included for satisfaction of social studies requirement.

**2007-2008 Annual costs.** Tuition/fees: $22,500. $540 mandatory health insurance fee charged unless proof of other coverage is provided. Room/board: $8,280. Books/supplies: $600. Personal expenses: $600.

**Financial aid. Non-need-based:** Scholarships awarded for academics, art, athletics, job skills, leadership, music/drama, ROTC, state residency.

**Application procedures. Admission:** Priority date 3/1; no deadline. $30 fee, may be waived for applicants with need. Application may be submitted online. Admission notification on a rolling basis beginning on or about 12/15. Must reply by May 1 or within 2 week(s) if notified thereafter. **Financial aid:** Priority date 2/1, closing date 3/15. FAFSA required. Applicants notified on a rolling basis starting 2/1; must reply by 5/1 or within 3 week(s) of notification.

**Academics. Special study options:** Accelerated study, combined bachelor's/graduate degree, cooperative education, distance learning, double major, dual enrollment of high school students, honors, independent study, internships, liberal arts/career combination, semester at sea, student-designed major, study abroad, teacher certification program, Washington semester. Dual degree programs in engineering with Columbia University, Georgia Institute of Technology, University of Florida, University of Miami, Mercer University, Washington University in St. Louis, Stevens Institute of Technology. **Credit/placement by examination:** AP, CLEP, IB, SAT, ACT, institutional tests. 30 credit hours maximum toward associate degree, 30 toward bachelor's. **Support services:** Learning center, remedial instruction, study skills assistance, tutoring, writing center.

**Majors. Biology:** General, marine. **Business:** General, accounting, business admin, finance, international, marketing. **Communications:** General. **Computer sciences:** General. **Education:** General, drama/dance, elementary, music, physical, secondary. **Engineering:** Electrical, mechanical, physics. **English:** English lit. **Foreign languages:** French, Spanish. **Health:** Nursing (RN), predental, premedicine, prenursing, preveterinary. **History:** General. **Legal studies:** Prelaw. **Liberal arts:** Arts/sciences, humanities. **Math:** General. **Parks/recreation:** Exercise sciences. **Philosophy/religion:** Philosophy. **Physical sciences:** Chemistry, physics. **Psychology:** General. **Social sciences:** Economics, geography, political science, sociology. **Theology:** Sacred music. **Transportation:** Airline/commercial pilot, aviation management. **Visual/performing arts:** Art, art history/conservation, dance, design, dramatic, music management, music performance, music theory/composition, studio arts, voice/opera.

**Most popular majors.** Business/marketing 18%, health sciences 34%, social sciences 7%, trade and industry 7%, visual/performing arts 8%.

**Computing on campus.** 400 workstations in dormitories, library, computer center. Dormitories wired for high-speed internet access and linked to campus network. Commuter students can connect to campus network. Online course registration, online library, helpline, wireless network available.

**Student life. Freshman orientation:** Mandatory. Preregistration for classes offered. Spring program available for pre-registration; formal freshmen orientation occurs in the few days preceding first day of class. **Housing:** Guaranteed on-campus for freshmen. Coed dorms, single-sex dorms, special housing for disabled, apartments, fraternity/sorority housing available. $200 deposit, deadline 5/1. **Activities:** Bands, campus ministries, choral groups, dance, drama, literary magazine, music ensembles, musical theater, radio station, student government, student newspaper, TV station, political science society, black student union, Baptist campus ministry, Hillel, Circle-K, Rotaract, Caribbean student group, Dolphin Diversity.

**Athletics.** NCAA. **Intercollegiate:** Baseball M, basketball, cross-country, football (tackle) M, golf, rowing (crew) W, soccer, softball W, tennis, track and field W, volleyball W. **Intramural:** Basketball, bowling, football (non-tackle), soccer, softball, table tennis, tennis, volleyball. **Team name:** Dolphins.

**Student services.** Adult student services, alcohol/substance abuse counseling, career counseling, student employment services, financial aid counseling, health services, minority student services, personal counseling, placement for graduates. **Physically disabled:** Services for visually, speech, hearing impaired.

**Contact.** E-mail: admissions@ju.edu
Phone: (904) 256-7000 Toll-free number: (800) 225-2027
Fax: (904) 256-7012
Lisa Hannasch, Director of First Year Admissions and Enrollment, Jacksonville University, 2800 University Boulevard North, Jacksonville, FL 32211-3394

---

## Johnson & Wales University: North Miami
**North Miami, Florida**
www.jwu.edu                                            CB code: 3441

- Private 4-year university
- Residential campus in large city
- 1,955 degree-seeking undergraduates: 6% part-time, 54% women
- 63% of applicants admitted

**General.** Regionally accredited. **Degrees:** 268 bachelor's, 430 associate awarded. **Calendar:** Quarter, extensive summer session. **Full-time faculty:** 57 total; 35% women. **Part-time faculty:** 23 total; 22% women. **Class size:** 46% < 20, 46% 20-39, 8% 40-49. **Special facilities:** University-operated hotel.

**Freshman class profile.** 5,954 applied, 3,742 admitted, 536 enrolled.

| Mid 50% test scores | | |
|---|---|---|
| SAT critical reading: | 400-500 | |
| SAT math: | 380-500 | |
| GPA 3.50 or higher: | 18% | |

| | |
|---|---|
| GPA 3.0-3.49: | 29% |
| GPA 2.0-2.99: | 50% |
| International: | 5% |

**Basis for selection.** Academic record, secondary school curriculum, GPA, class rank, test scores are important. It is recommended that students submit a personal statement, employment information, letters of recommendation. SAT and ACT required for admission to honors program.

**High school preparation.** 12 units recommended. Recommended units include English 4, mathematics 3, social studies 2 and science 3.

**2007-2008 Annual costs.** Tuition/fees: $21,717. Room/board: $9,600. Books/supplies: $900. Personal expenses: $594.

**2007-2008 Financial aid. Need-based:** Average need met was 69%. Average scholarship/grant was $10,656; average loan $3,368. 47% of total undergraduate aid awarded as scholarships/grants, 53% as loans/jobs. **Non-need-based:** Scholarships awarded for academics, alumni affiliation, job skills, leadership, state residency.

**Application procedures. Admission:** No deadline. No application fee. Application may be submitted online. Admission notification on a rolling basis beginning on or about 10/1. Must reply by May 1 or within 2 week(s) if notified thereafter. **Financial aid:** No deadline. FAFSA required. Applicants notified on a rolling basis starting 3/1; must reply within 2 week(s) of notification.

**Academics. Special study options:** Accelerated study, cooperative education, dual enrollment of high school students, honors, independent study, internships, study abroad, weekend college. **Credit/placement by examination:** CLEP, SAT, ACT, institutional tests. **Support services:** Learning center, pre-admission summer program, reduced course load, remedial instruction, study skills assistance, tutoring, writing center.

**Majors. Business:** Accounting, business admin, hospitality admin, hotel/motel admin, marketing. **Family/consumer sciences:** Institutional food production. **Parks/recreation:** Facilities management, sports admin. **Personal/culinary services:** General, food service, restaurant/catering. **Protective services:** Law enforcement admin.

**Most popular majors.** Business/marketing 50%, family/consumer sciences 20%, parks/recreation 11%, personal/culinary services 7%, security/protective services 12%.

**Computing on campus.** 60 workstations in library, computer center, student center. Dormitories wired for high-speed internet access and linked to campus network. Commuter students can connect to campus network. Online course registration, online library, helpline, repair service, wireless network available.

**Student life. Freshman orientation:** Mandatory, $255 fee. Preregistration for classes offered. **Housing:** Guaranteed on-campus for freshmen. Coed dorms, substance-free housing available. $300 nonrefundable deposit. All housing accessible for disabled students. **Activities:** Dance, drama, student government, student newspaper.

**Athletics.** NAIA. **Intramural:** Basketball M, bowling, football (non-tackle), soccer, softball, volleyball. **Team name:** Wildcats.

**Student services.** Adult student services, alcohol/substance abuse counseling, career counseling, student employment services, financial aid counseling, health services, personal counseling, placement for graduates, veterans' counselor. **Physically disabled:** Services for visually, speech, hearing impaired.

**Contact.** E-mail: admissions.mia@jwu.edu
Phone: (305) 892-7600 Toll-free number: (866) 598-3567
Fax: (305) 892-7020
Jeff Greenip, Director, Johnson & Wales University: North Miami, 1701 Northeast 127th Street, North Miami, FL 33181

---

## Jones College
**Jacksonville, Florida**
www.jones.edu                                          CB code: 5343

- Private 4-year business and teachers college
- Commuter campus in very large city
- 600 degree-seeking undergraduates
- Interview required

**General.** Founded in 1918. Accredited by ACICS. Branch campus in Miami. 2 campuses in Jacksonville. **Degrees:** 88 bachelor's, 35 associate awarded. **Calendar:** Trimester, extensive summer session. **Full-time faculty:** 10 total. **Part-time faculty:** 50 total. **Class size:** 91% < 20, 9% 20-39.

**Basis for selection.** Open admission. **Homeschooled:** State high school equivalency certificate required.

**2008-2009 Annual costs.** Tuition/fees: $8,340. Books/supplies: $1,500. Personal expenses: $4,168.

**Financial aid.** All financial aid based on need.

**Application procedures. Admission:** No deadline. No application fee. Application may be submitted online. Admission notification on a rolling basis. **Financial aid:** No deadline. FAFSA required. Applicants notified on a rolling basis.

**Academics. Special study options:** Accelerated study, distance learning, double major, dual enrollment of high school students, independent study, internships, student-designed major, weekend college. **Credit/placement by examination:** AP, CLEP, institutional tests. 15 credit hours maximum toward associate degree, 15 toward bachelor's. Life experience: 21 hours if in bachelor's degree programs, 9 hours if in associate degree programs. **Support services:** Reduced course load, remedial instruction, study skills assistance, tutoring.

**Majors. Business:** Business admin. **Computer sciences:** General. **Education:** Elementary. **Health:** Medical assistant. **Legal studies:** Paralegal.

**Most popular majors.** Business/marketing 72%, computer/information sciences 11%, health sciences 8%, legal studies 8%.

**Computing on campus.** 166 workstations in library, computer center. Commuter students can connect to campus network. Online library, wireless network available.

**Student life. Freshman orientation:** Mandatory. Preregistration for classes offered. **Activities:** Radio station.

**Student services.** Career counseling, student employment services, financial aid counseling, personal counseling, placement for graduates, veterans' counselor.

**Contact.** E-mail: lvaughn@jones.edu
Phone: (904) 743-1122 ext. 112 Toll-free number: (800) 331-0176 ext. 112
Fax: (904) 743-4446
Linda Vaughn, Director of Admissions, Jones College, 5353 Arlington Expressway, Jacksonville, FL 32211

## Jones College: Miami
**Miami, Florida**
www.jones.edu
CB code: 3444

- Private 4-year business and career college
- Commuter campus in very large city
- 108 degree-seeking undergraduates: 44% part-time, 81% women

**General.** Accredited by ACICS. **Degrees:** 15 bachelor's, 10 associate awarded. **Location:** 30 miles from downtown. **Calendar:** Trimester, extensive summer session. **Part-time faculty:** 25 total. **Class size:** 100% < 20.

**Basis for selection.** Open admission. All students required to take CPAT.

**2008-2009 Annual costs.** Tuition/fees (projected): $8,340. Books/supplies: $750. Personal expenses: $1,700.

**Financial aid.** All financial aid based on need.

**Application procedures. Admission:** No deadline. No application fee. Application may be submitted online. Admission notification on a rolling basis. **Financial aid:** No deadline. FAFSA required. Applicants notified on a rolling basis.

**Academics. Special study options:** Accelerated study, cooperative education, distance learning, double major, dual enrollment of high school students, independent study, internships, weekend college. **Credit/placement by examination:** AP, CLEP, IB, institutional tests. 15 credit hours maximum toward associate degree, 15 toward bachelor's. **Support services:** Learning center, remedial instruction, study skills assistance, tutoring, writing center.

**Majors. Business:** Business admin. **Computer sciences:** General. **Education:** Elementary. **Interdisciplinary:** Accounting/computer science. **Legal studies:** Paralegal.

**Most popular majors.** Business/marketing 44%, interdisciplinary studies 16%, legal studies 19%.

**Computing on campus.** 75 workstations in library, computer center. Online course registration, online library, helpline, wireless network available.

**Student life. Freshman orientation:** Mandatory. Preregistration for classes offered.

**Student services.** Career counseling, student employment services, financial aid counseling, placement for graduates, veterans' counselor.

**Contact.** E-mail: admissions@jones.edu
Phone: (305) 275-9996 Toll-free number: (800) 331-0176
Fax: (305) 275-9571
Linda Vaughn, Director of Admissions, Jones College: Miami, 11430 North Kendall Drive, Suite 200, Miami, FL 33176

## Keiser University
**Ft. Lauderdale, Florida**
www.keiseruniversity.edu
CB code: 7004

- For-profit 4-year business and health science college
- Commuter campus in large city
- 1,524 degree-seeking undergraduates
- SAT or ACT, interview required

**General.** Founded in 1977. Regionally accredited. **Degrees:** 51 bachelor's, 403 associate awarded; master's offered. **Location:** 35 miles from Miami. **Calendar:** Semester, extensive summer session. **Full-time faculty:** 35 total. **Part-time faculty:** 45 total.

**Basis for selection.** Test scores and interview most important. Institutional entrance examination, SAT or ACT required. Minimum scores required: SAT 800 (exclusive of Writing), ACT composite 17, 35-55 on Otis-Lennon evaluation test.

**2007-2008 Annual costs.** Students in business, health services administration, accounting, and computer technology programs pay additional $600 fee per year for lease of computer. Books/supplies: $1,200. Personal expenses: $1,900.

**Application procedures. Admission:** No deadline. $50 fee. Admission notification on a rolling basis. **Financial aid:** No deadline. FAFSA required.

**Academics. Special study options:** Accelerated study. **Credit/placement by examination:** CLEP.

**Majors. Business:** Business admin. **Computer sciences:** Information technology. **Health:** Health care admin, nursing (RN). **Protective services:** Law enforcement admin.

**Student life. Activities:** Student government, student newspaper.

**Athletics. Intercollegiate:** Softball W, volleyball.

**Student services.** Career counseling, student employment services, placement for graduates.

**Contact.** E-mail: admissions-ftl@keisercollege.edu
Phone: (954) 776-4456 Toll-free number: (800) 749-4456
Fax: (954) 771-4894
Lafrawn Mays, Director of Admissions, Keiser University, 1500 Northwest 49th Street, Fort Lauderdale, FL 33309

## Lynn University
**Boca Raton, Florida**
www.lynn.edu
CB member
CB code: 5437

- Private 4-year university
- Residential campus in small city
- 2,144 degree-seeking undergraduates: 10% part-time, 49% women, 4% African American, 1% Asian American, 6% Hispanic American, 13% international
- 366 degree-seeking graduate students
- 68% of applicants admitted
- SAT or ACT (ACT writing recommended), application essay required
- 34% graduate within 6 years

**General.** Founded in 1962. Regionally accredited. **Degrees:** 394 bachelor's awarded; master's offered. **ROTC:** Air Force. **Location:** 20 miles from Fort Lauderdale, 20 miles from Palm Beach. **Calendar:** Semester, extensive summer session. **Full-time faculty:** 103 total; 71% have terminal degrees, 10% minority, 48% women. **Part-time faculty:** 67 total; 36% have terminal degrees, 16% minority, 39% women. **Class size:** 65% < 20, 35% 20-39, less than 1% 50-99. **Special facilities:** University club (private dining room that serves as laboratory for hotel and restaurant management students), flight simulator, conservatory of music.

**Freshman class profile.** 2,647 applied, 1,792 admitted, 522 enrolled.

| Mid 50% test scores | | | |
|---|---|---|---|
| SAT critical reading: | 400-490 | Rank in top quarter: | 9% |
| SAT math: | 410-500 | Rank in top tenth: | 3% |
| ACT composite: | 16-19 | Return as sophomores: | 61% |
| GPA 3.50 or higher: | 8% | Out-of-state: | 78% |
| GPA 3.0-3.49: | 21% | Live on campus: | 87% |
| GPA 2.0-2.99: | 61% | International: | 13% |

**Basis for selection.** School achievement record, high school counselor's recommendation, test scores important; class rank, school and community activities considered. Special consideration given to foreign and minority applicants. Interview and essay recommended. Portfolio recommended for art and graphic design majors. **Learning Disabled:** Submit psychological testing in addition to other admission documents.

**High school preparation.** 16 units required. Required units include English 4, mathematics 4, social studies 2, history 2 and science 4. Mathematics must include algebra I, algebra II, and either geometry, trigonometry, calculus, or analysis. Science must include biology and a physical science.

**2007-2008 Annual costs.** Tuition/fees: $28,490. Room/board: $10,100. Books/supplies: $1,000. Personal expenses: $1,100.

**2007-2008 Financial aid. Need-based:** 338 full-time freshmen applied for aid; 286 were judged to have need; 283 of these received aid. Average need met was 90%. Average scholarship/grant was $26,075; average loan $3,899. 59% of total undergraduate aid awarded as scholarships/grants, 41% as loans/jobs. **Non-need-based:** Awarded to 1,154 full-time undergraduates, including 311 freshmen. Scholarships awarded for academics, athletics, leadership, music/drama, religious affiliation, ROTC, state residency.

**Application procedures. Admission:** No deadline. $50 fee, may be waived for applicants with need. Application may be submitted online. Admission notification on a rolling basis beginning on or about 9/1. Must reply by May 1 or within 2 week(s) if notified thereafter. **Financial aid:** Priority date 3/1; no closing date. FAFSA, institutional form required. Applicants

notified on a rolling basis starting 2/1; must reply within 2 week(s) of notification.

**Academics. Special study options:** Accelerated study, cooperative education, distance learning, double major, dual enrollment of high school students, ESL, honors, independent study, internships, liberal arts/career combination, study abroad, teacher certification program, Washington semester. **Credit/placement by examination:** AP, CLEP, IB, institutional tests. 30 credit hours maximum toward associate degree, 30 toward bachelor's. **Support services:** Learning center, reduced course load, tutoring, writing center.

**Majors. Area/ethnic studies:** American. **Biology:** General. **Business:** Accounting, business admin, fashion, hospitality admin, international, management information systems, management science, marketing, tourism promotion, tourism/travel. **Communications:** Advertising, digital media, journalism, media studies, public relations. **Education:** Early childhood, elementary, multi-level teacher, secondary, special. **English:** English lit. **Health:** Health care admin, premedicine, preop/surgical nursing. **Interdisciplinary:** Behavioral sciences, natural sciences. **Liberal arts:** Arts/sciences. **Parks/recreation:** Facilities management, sports admin. **Protective services:** Emergency management/homeland security, law enforcement admin. **Psychology:** General. **Public administration:** Human services. **Social sciences:** International relations. **Transportation:** Aviation management. **Visual/performing arts:** General, dramatic, graphic design, music performance, stringed instruments.

**Most popular majors.** Business/marketing 50%, communication technologies 14%, psychology 12%, security/protective services 12%, visual/performing arts 6%.

**Computing on campus.** 220 workstations in dormitories, library, computer center. Dormitories wired for high-speed internet access and linked to campus network. Online library, helpline, repair service, wireless network available.

**Student life. Freshman orientation:** Mandatory. **Housing:** Guaranteed on-campus for all undergraduates. Coed dorms, single-sex dorms, special housing for disabled, substance-free housing available. $300 deposit. **Activities:** Choral groups, dance, drama, film society, international student organizations, literary magazine, music ensembles, radio station, student government, student newspaper, symphony orchestra, TV station, Black student union, debate team, gay-straight alliance, Hillel, honors colloquium, hospitality club, Knights of the Roundtable.

**Athletics. NCAA. Intercollegiate:** Baseball M, basketball, cross-country, golf, rowing (crew) M, soccer, softball W, tennis, volleyball W. **Intramural:** Basketball, bowling, cross-country, equestrian, golf, handball, ice hockey, lacrosse, rugby M, soccer, softball, swimming, table tennis, tennis, volleyball, water polo. **Team name:** Fighting Knights.

**Student services.** Adult student services, campus ministries, career counseling, student employment services, health services, personal counseling, placement for graduates, veterans' counselor.

**Contact.** E-mail: admissions@lynn.edu
Phone: (561) 237-7900 Toll-free number: (800) 888-5966 ext. 1
Fax: (561) 237-7100
Juan Tamayo, Director of Admissions, Lynn University, 3601 North Military Trail, Boca Raton, FL 33431-5598

---

## Miami International University of Art and Design
**Miami, Florida**
**www.artinstitutes.edu/miami/**                **CB code: 5327**

- For-profit 3-year visual arts college
- Commuter campus in very large city
- 335 degree-seeking undergraduates
- 305 graduate students
- Application essay, interview required

**General.** Founded in 1965. Regionally accredited. **Degrees:** 203 bachelor's, 96 associate awarded; master's offered. **Location:** 2 miles from downtown. **Calendar:** Quarter, extensive summer session. **Full-time faculty:** 60 total; 7% have terminal degrees, 20% minority, 60% women. **Part-time faculty:** 90 total; 3% have terminal degrees, 31% minority, 41% women. **Class size:** 15% < 20, 81% 20-39, 4% 40-49.

**Freshman class profile.**

| | | | |
|---|---|---|---|
| Out-of-state: | 74% | Live on campus: | 33% |

**Basis for selection.** Keen interest in fashion, merchandising, art, interior design, or related areas. Secondary school record, recommendations, essay important. Portfolio recommended.

**2007-2008 Annual costs.** Tuition/fees: $19,445. Fees vary according to program. Room/board: $2,050. Books/supplies: $1,500. Personal expenses: $1,000.

**Application procedures. Admission:** No deadline. $50 fee. Admission notification on a rolling basis. **Financial aid:** Priority date 7/1; no closing date. FAFSA, CSS PROFILE required. Applicants notified on a rolling basis starting 8/1.

**Academics. Special study options:** Distance learning, ESL, internships, study abroad. **Credit/placement by examination:** AP, CLEP, institutional tests. **Support services:** Learning center, pre-admission summer program, reduced course load, remedial instruction, tutoring.

**Majors. Communications technology:** Animation/special effects. **Visual/performing arts:** General, cinematography.

**Computing on campus.** 87 workstations in library, computer center. Online course registration, online library, wireless network available.

**Student life. Freshman orientation:** Mandatory. Held first week of semester for approximately 4 hours. **Housing:** Coed dorms, single-sex dorms available. **Activities:** Dance, student government, student newspaper.

**Student services.** Career counseling, student employment services, personal counseling, placement for graduates.

**Contact.** E-mail: admissions@aii.edu
Phone: (305) 428-5700 Toll-free number: (800) 225-9023
Fax: (305) 374-5933
Kevin Ryan, Director of Admissions, Miami International University of Art and Design, 1501 Biscayne Boulevard, Suite 100, Miami, FL 33132-1418

---

## New College of Florida
**Sarasota, Florida**                           **CB member**
**www.ncf.edu**                                 **CB code: 5506**

- Public 4-year liberal arts college
- Residential campus in small city
- 767 degree-seeking undergraduates: 61% women, 2% African American, 2% Asian American, 9% Hispanic American, 1% international
- 57% of applicants admitted
- SAT or ACT (ACT writing optional), application essay required
- 57% graduate within 6 years

**General.** Founded in 1960. Regionally accredited. Institution is the Honors College of Florida State University System. Emphasis on individualized learning. **Degrees:** 147 bachelor's awarded. **Location:** 50 miles from Tampa. **Calendar:** 4-1-4. **Full-time faculty:** 69 total; 99% have terminal degrees, 13% minority, 46% women. **Part-time faculty:** 13 total; 77% have terminal degrees, 8% minority, 38% women. **Class size:** 66% < 20, 30% 20-39, 3% 40-49, 1% 50-99. **Special facilities:** High-field nuclear magnetic resonance spectrometer, hardware/software system for brain function analysis, scanning electron microscope, UV-visible and infrared spectrophotometer, inert atmosphere glove box, fine arts center, laboratories for environmental studies, anthropology, psychology, marine biology facility.

**Freshman class profile.** 1,029 applied, 587 admitted, 202 enrolled.

| Mid 50% test scores | | | |
|---|---|---|---|
| SAT critical reading: | 650-750 | GPA 2.0-2.99: | 1% |
| SAT math: | 580-670 | Rank in top quarter: | 81% |
| SAT writing: | 600-690 | Rank in top tenth: | 53% |
| ACT composite: | 26-30 | Return as sophomores: | 87% |
| GPA 3.50 or higher: | 87% | Out-of-state: | 23% |
| GPA 3.0-3.49: | 12% | Live on campus: | 84% |

**Basis for selection.** Challenging courses, strong grades, test scores, recommendations, and writing ability important. Class rank, extracurricular activities considered. Interview recommended; graded analytical paper optional. **Homeschooled:** GED and documentation of required high school credits, either by accredited agency or by program supervisor required. Interview, additional recommendations, additional writing samples, samples of creative work, and/or SAT Subject Tests optional. **Learning Disabled:** Documentaton of disability must be provided.

**High school preparation.** 18 units required; 20 recommended. Required and recommended units include English 4, mathematics 3-4, social

studies 3, science 3 (laboratory 2), foreign language 2 and academic electives 3-5. Advanced courses recommended.

**2007-2008 Annual costs.** Tuition/fees: $3,143; $16,682 out-of-state. Room/board: $6,936. Books/supplies: $800. Personal expenses: $2,600.

**2007-2008 Financial aid. Need-based:** 137 full-time freshmen applied for aid; 79 were judged to have need; 79 of these received aid. Average need met was 95%. Average scholarship/grant was $8,113; average loan $2,603. 66% of total undergraduate aid awarded as scholarships/grants, 34% as loans/jobs. **Non-need-based:** Awarded to 458 full-time undergraduates, including 135 freshmen. Scholarships awarded for academics, state residency.

**Application procedures. Admission:** Priority date 2/15; deadline 4/15 (postmark date). $30 fee, may be waived for applicants with need. Application may be submitted online. Admission notification 4/25. Admission notification on a rolling basis beginning on or about 1/15. Must reply by May 1 or within 4 week(s) if notified thereafter. **Financial aid:** Priority date 2/15; no closing date. FAFSA required. Applicants notified on a rolling basis starting 10/1; must reply by 5/1 or within 4 week(s) of notification.

**Academics.** All students required to complete three 4-week independent study projects, senior thesis, and oral baccalaureate exam before committee of faculty. **Special study options:** Cross-registration, double major, exchange student, honors, independent study, internships, student-designed major, study abroad. **Credit/placement by examination:** AP, CLEP, institutional tests. AP exam scores, IB higher-level exam scores, and CLEP scores at certain levels may be used toward exemptions from Liberal Arts Curriculum requirements. **Support services:** Tutoring, writing center.

**Majors. Area/ethnic studies:** French. **Biology:** General. **Conservation:** Environmental studies. **English:** English lit. **Foreign languages:** General, classics, French, German, Russian, Spanish. **History:** General. **Interdisciplinary:** Global studies, medieval/Renaissance, natural sciences. **Liberal arts:** Arts/sciences, humanities. **Math:** General. **Philosophy/religion:** Philosophy, religion. **Physical sciences:** Chemistry, physics. **Psychology:** General. **Public administration:** Policy analysis. **Social sciences:** General, anthropology, economics, political science, sociology, urban studies. **Visual/performing arts:** Art, art history/conservation, studio arts.

**Computing on campus.** 41 workstations in library, computer center, student center. Dormitories wired for high-speed internet access and linked to campus network. Commuter students can connect to campus network. Online course registration, online library, helpline, student web hosting, wireless network available.

**Student life. Freshman orientation:** Mandatory, $125 fee. Seven-day program. **Housing:** Guaranteed on-campus for freshmen. Coed dorms, special housing for disabled, apartments, substance-free housing available. Specialized housing options may be arranged in response to student interest. **Activities:** Campus ministries, choral groups, dance, drama, film society, literary magazine, music ensembles, musical theater, radio station, student government, student newspaper, Intervarsity Christian Fellowship, multifaith council, Alliance for Peace, College Democrats, Hillel, College Republicans, Feminist Majority Leadership Alliance, PRIDE, Nichiren Buddhist club, ACLU.

**Athletics. Intramural:** Basketball, fencing, football (non-tackle), lacrosse, racquetball, sailing, swimming, table tennis, tennis, volleyball, weight lifting, wrestling.

**Student services.** Alcohol/substance abuse counseling, career counseling, student employment services, financial aid counseling, health services, minority student services, personal counseling, placement for graduates, veterans' counselor, women's services. **Physically disabled:** Services for visually, hearing impaired.

**Contact.** E-mail: admissions@ncf.edu
Phone: (941) 487-5000 Fax: (941) 487-5010
Kathleen Killion, Dean of Admissions and Financial Aid, New College of Florida, 5800 Bay Shore Road, Sarasota, FL 34243-2109

## Northwood University: Florida
**West Palm Beach, Florida**
www.northwood.edu

CB code: 5162

- Private 4-year university and business college
- Residential campus in small city
- 673 degree-seeking undergraduates: 3% part-time, 38% women, 10% African American, 1% Asian American, 10% Hispanic American, 32% international
- 59% of applicants admitted
- SAT or ACT (ACT writing optional), application essay required

**General.** Regionally accredited. Specialty university offering only business degrees in professional management; 3 residential campuses in Michigan, Florida, and Texas; 48 program centers; library center in Maine. **Degrees:** 170 bachelor's, 83 associate awarded. **Location:** 75 miles from Miami. **Calendar:** Quarter, limited summer session. **Full-time faculty:** 18 total; 28% have terminal degrees, 6% minority, 33% women. **Part-time faculty:** 34 total. **Class size:** 53% < 20, 46% 20-39, less than 1% 50-99.

**Freshman class profile.** 811 applied, 479 admitted, 150 enrolled.

| Mid 50% test scores | | | |
|---|---|---|---|
| SAT critical reading: | 400-490 | GPA 2.0-2.99: | 57% |
| SAT math: | 420-510 | Rank in top quarter: | 17% |
| SAT writing: | 400-490 | Rank in top tenth: | 8% |
| ACT composite: | 17-21 | End year in good standing: | 44% |
| GPA 3.50 or higher: | 14% | Return as sophomores: | 55% |
| GPA 3.0-3.49: | 27% | Out-of-state: | 56% |
| | | Live on campus: | 78% |

**Basis for selection.** Minimum GPA of 2.0 and strong interest in business or related field. Test scores considered. Students with lower GPA possibly admitted on probation. Interview recommended. **Homeschooled:** Transcript of courses and grades required.

**2007-2008 Annual costs.** Tuition/fees: $16,455. Room/board: $7,764.

**2007-2008 Financial aid. Need-based:** 89 full-time freshmen applied for aid; 75 were judged to have need; 75 of these received aid. Average need met was 62%. Average scholarship/grant was $7,375; average loan $3,256. 59% of total undergraduate aid awarded as scholarships/grants, 41% as loans/jobs. **Non-need-based:** Awarded to 300 full-time undergraduates, including 97 freshmen. Scholarships awarded for academics, alumni affiliation, athletics, leadership, minority status, state residency.

**Application procedures. Admission:** No deadline. $25 fee, may be waived for applicants with need. Application may be submitted online. Admission notification on a rolling basis beginning on or about 10/1. **Financial aid:** No deadline. FAFSA required. Applicants notified on a rolling basis starting 3/1.

**Academics.** Writing, math and accounting labs available. **Special study options:** Accelerated study, combined bachelor's/graduate degree, distance learning, double major, dual enrollment of high school students, external degree, honors, independent study, internships, study abroad, weekend college. **Credit/placement by examination:** AP, CLEP, IB, SAT, ACT, institutional tests. 12 credit hours maximum toward associate degree, 12 toward bachelor's. **Support services:** Reduced course load, remedial instruction, study skills assistance, tutoring, writing center.

**Majors. Business:** Accounting, banking/financial services, business admin, hotel/motel admin, international, management information systems, marketing, vehicle parts marketing. **Communications:** Advertising. **Computer sciences:** General. **Parks/recreation:** Sports admin.

**Most popular majors.** Business/marketing 92%.

**Computing on campus.** 89 workstations in dormitories, library, computer center, student center. Dormitories wired for high-speed internet access and linked to campus network. Commuter students can connect to campus network. Online course registration, online library, helpline, student web hosting, wireless network available.

**Student life. Freshman orientation:** Mandatory, $125 fee. Preregistration for classes offered. 3-day program in early September. **Policies:** Adheres to all federal and state laws concerning alcohol and drugs. Freshmen and sophomores not living at home must live on campus. **Housing:** Guaranteed on-campus for freshmen. Single-sex dorms, substance-free housing available. $100 nonrefundable deposit, deadline 5/1. **Activities:** International student organizations, student government, residence hall association, ambassador club.

**Athletics.** NAIA. **Intercollegiate:** Baseball M, basketball, golf, soccer, softball W, tennis, volleyball W. **Intramural:** Basketball, bowling, football (non-tackle), racquetball, tennis. **Team name:** Seahawks.

**Student services.** Adult student services, alcohol/substance abuse counseling, career counseling, student employment services, financial aid counseling, health services, personal counseling, placement for graduates. **Physically disabled:** Services for hearing impaired.

**Contact.** E-mail: fladmit@northwood.edu
Phone: (561) 478-5500 Toll-free number: (800) 458-8325
Fax: (561) 640-3328
Jack Letvintchuk, Director of Admissions, Northwood University: Florida, 2600 North Military Trail, West Palm Beach, FL 33409-2911

# Nova Southeastern University

**Fort Lauderdale, Florida**
www.nova.edu

**CB member**
**CB code: 5514**

- Private 4-year university
- Commuter campus in small city
- 5,403 degree-seeking undergraduates: 34% part-time, 73% women, 26% African American, 6% Asian American, 26% Hispanic American, 5% international
- 21,298 degree-seeking graduate students
- 51% of applicants admitted
- SAT or ACT (ACT writing optional) required
- 44% graduate within 6 years

**General.** Founded in 1964. Regionally accredited. Field-based programs offered throughout the nation and in selected international sites. **Degrees:** 1,497 bachelor's, 8 associate awarded; master's, doctoral, first professional offered. **Location:** 10 miles from Fort Lauderdale. **Calendar:** Trimester, limited summer session. **Full-time faculty:** 624 total; 89% have terminal degrees, 21% minority, 45% women. **Part-time faculty:** 992 total; 77% have terminal degrees, 23% minority, 49% women. **Class size:** 76% < 20, 23% 20-39, less than 1% 40-49, less than 1% 50-99. **Special facilities:** Oceanographic center, law center, university school (K-12).

**Freshman class profile.** 2,818 applied, 1,433 admitted, 544 enrolled.

| Mid 50% test scores | | | |
|---|---|---|---|
| SAT critical reading: | 460-540 | GPA 2.0-2.99: | 24% |
| SAT math: | 440-560 | Rank in top quarter: | 47% |
| SAT writing: | 440-540 | Rank in top tenth: | 14% |
| ACT composite: | 19-23 | Return as sophomores: | 60% |
| GPA 3.50 or higher: | 48% | Out-of-state: | 26% |
| GPA 3.0-3.49: | 28% | Live on campus: | 61% |
| | | International: | 2% |

**Basis for selection.** Test scores, GPA important. Career Development Program (adult and evening/weekend) exempt from test score requirement and requires only high school diploma or GED. Interviews and essays recommended. **Homeschooled:** Provide SAT or ACT scores, information about home school program of study pursued and GED score to demonstrate high school equivalence.

**High school preparation.** Required and recommended units include English 4, mathematics 3, social studies 1, history 2, science 3, foreign language 2 and computer science 1.

**2007-2008 Annual costs.** Tuition/fees: $19,500. Room/board: $7,742. Books/supplies: $1,200. Personal expenses: $2,695.

**2006-2007 Financial aid. Need-based:** 52% of total undergraduate aid awarded as scholarships/grants, 48% as loans/jobs. **Non-need-based:** Scholarships awarded for academics, athletics, leadership, music/drama.

**Application procedures. Admission:** No deadline. $50 fee, may be waived for applicants with need. Application may be submitted online. Admission notification on a rolling basis. **Financial aid:** Priority date 4/15; no closing date. FAFSA required. Applicants notified on a rolling basis starting 3/15.

**Academics.** 2 undergraduate programs: college of professional and liberal studies for traditional daytime students, college of career development for adult evening and weekend students. Core curriculum of liberal arts-based courses plus general education required. **Special study options:** Accelerated study, combined bachelor's/graduate degree, cooperative education, distance learning, double major, dual enrollment of high school students, ESL, honors, independent study, internships, study abroad, teacher certification program. Dual admission with NSU graduate/professional programs. **Credit/placement by examination:** AP, CLEP, IB, SAT, ACT, institutional tests. 90 credit hours maximum toward bachelor's degree. **Support services:** Learning center, reduced course load, remedial instruction, study skills assistance, tutoring, writing center.

**Majors. Biology:** General, marine. **Business:** Accounting, business admin, finance, marketing. **Communications:** General. **Computer sciences:** General, computer science. **Conservation:** Environmental science, environmental studies. **Education:** Early childhood, elementary, special. **English:** English lit. **Health:** Athletic training, health services, nursing (RN), premedicine, sonography. **History:** General. **Legal studies:** General, paralegal, prelaw. **Liberal arts:** Arts/sciences, humanities. **Parks/recreation:** Sports admin. **Protective services:** Criminal justice. **Psychology:** General. **Visual/performing arts:** Theater arts management.

**Most popular majors.** Biology 20%, business/marketing 32%, education 11%, health sciences 16%, psychology 10%.

**Computing on campus.** 2,548 workstations in dormitories, library, computer center, student center. Dormitories wired for high-speed internet access and linked to campus network. Commuter students can connect to campus network. Online course registration, online library, helpline, student web hosting, wireless network available.

**Student life. Freshman orientation:** Mandatory. Preregistration for classes offered. Sessions offered 3 times in summer, twice in winter. Summer sessions last 2 days, 1 night. Winter sessions 1 full day with special evening session for evening students. **Housing:** Guaranteed on-campus for freshmen. Coed dorms, special housing for disabled, apartments, substance-free housing available. $500 deposit. **Activities:** Choral groups, drama, international student organizations, literary magazine, radio station, student government, student newspaper, black student association, psychology club, Hillel, pre-med society, Alpha Phi Omega, Salsa, Indian student association, international Muslim association.

**Athletics.** NCAA. **Intercollegiate:** Baseball M, basketball, cheerleading M, cross-country, golf, rowing (crew) W, soccer, softball W, tennis W, volleyball W. **Intramural:** Basketball, football (non-tackle), golf, racquetball, soccer, softball, volleyball. **Team name:** Sharks.

**Student services.** Adult student services, career counseling, student employment services, financial aid counseling, health services, personal counseling, veterans' counselor, women's services. **Physically disabled:** Services for visually, speech, hearing impaired.

**Contact.** E-mail: ncsinfo@nova.edu
Phone: (954) 262-8000 Toll-free number: (800) 338-4723 ext. 8000
Fax: (954) 262-3811
Maria Dillard, Director of Undergraduate Admissions, Nova Southeastern University, 3301 College Avenue, Fort Lauderdale, FL 33314

# Okaloosa-Walton College

**Niceville, Florida**
www.owc.edu

**CB code: 5526**

- Public 4-year business and community college
- Commuter campus in large town
- 4,554 degree-seeking undergraduates

**General.** Founded in 1963. Regionally accredited. Additional teaching centers at Ft. Walton Beach, Eglin Air Force Base, Hurlburt Field, DeFuniak Springs and Crestview. **Degrees:** 26 bachelor's, 787 associate awarded. **ROTC:** Army. **Location:** 55 miles from Pensacola. **Calendar:** Semester, extensive summer session. **Full-time faculty:** 90 total. **Part-time faculty:** 188 total. **Class size:** 3% < 20, 97% 20-39. **Special facilities:** Fine and performing arts center with 2 theaters and 2 art galleries.

**Basis for selection.** Open admission. Applicants without high school diploma may be admitted to credit-bearing certificate programs.

**High school preparation.** Recommended units include English 4, mathematics 3, social studies 3 and science 3.

**2007-2008 Annual costs.** Tuition/fees: $1,763; $6,730 out-of-state. Books/supplies: $974.

**Financial aid. Non-need-based:** Scholarships awarded for academics, art, athletics, leadership, minority status, music/drama.

**Application procedures. Admission:** Priority date 7/25; no deadline. No application fee. Admission notification on a rolling basis. **Financial aid:** Priority date 4/1; no closing date. FAFSA, institutional form required. Applicants notified on a rolling basis starting 2/1; must reply within 2 week(s) of notification.

**Academics. Special study options:** Combined bachelor's/graduate degree, cooperative education, cross-registration, distance learning, dual enrollment of high school students, ESL, independent study, internships, student-designed major. **Credit/placement by examination:** AP, CLEP, institutional tests. 32 credit hours maximum toward associate degree. **Support services:** Learning center, remedial instruction, study skills assistance, tutoring.

**Majors. Health:** Nursing assistant.

**Computing on campus.** 900 workstations in library, computer center. Commuter students can connect to campus network. Online course registration, online library, wireless network available.

**Student life. Freshman orientation:** Mandatory. Preregistration for classes offered. Orientation can be completed online. **Activities:** Bands, campus ministries, choral groups, dance, drama, literary magazine, music ensembles, musical theater, student government, symphony orchestra, Student

Christian Fellowship, African American student association, Circle K, College Republicans, environmental club.

**Athletics.** NJCAA. **Intercollegiate:** Baseball M, basketball, softball W. **Intramural:** Softball, volleyball. **Team name:** Raiders.

**Student services.** Adult student services, career counseling, student employment services, on-campus daycare, personal counseling, placement for graduates, veterans' counselor. **Physically disabled:** Services for visually, speech, hearing impaired.

**Contact.** E-mail: registrar@owc.edu
Phone: (850) 729-5373 Fax: (850) 729-5215
Christine Bishop, Registrar, Okaloosa-Walton College, 100 College Boulevard, Niceville, FL 32578-1295

---

## Palm Beach Atlantic University
### West Palm Beach, Florida
www.pba.edu                                    CB code: 5553

- Private 4-year university and liberal arts college affiliated with nondenominational tradition
- Residential campus in large city
- 2,471 degree-seeking undergraduates: 8% part-time, 62% women, 15% African American, 2% Asian American, 10% Hispanic American, 2% international
- 777 degree-seeking graduate students
- 78% of applicants admitted
- SAT or ACT (ACT writing optional), application essay, interview required
- 51% graduate within 6 years

**General.** Founded in 1968. Regionally accredited. Distinctly Christian university with emphasis on student community service. University offers mission trips around the world, weekly worship services, and student-led prayer groups. **Degrees:** 571 bachelor's, 16 associate awarded; master's, first professional offered. **Location:** 60 miles from Miami, 180 miles from Orlando. **Calendar:** Semester, limited summer session. **Full-time faculty:** 167 total; 75% have terminal degrees, 14% minority, 45% women. **Part-time faculty:** 180 total; 27% have terminal degrees, 17% minority, 48% women. **Class size:** 63% < 20, 34% 20-39, 2% 40-49, 1% 50-99.

**Freshman class profile.** 1,240 applied, 966 admitted, 453 enrolled.

| Mid 50% test scores | | Rank in top quarter: | 46% |
|---|---|---|---|
| SAT critical reading: | 490-590 | Rank in top tenth: | 20% |
| SAT math: | 490-590 | Return as sophomores: | 70% |
| ACT composite: | 21-26 | Out-of-state: | 18% |
| GPA 3.50 or higher: | 54% | Live on campus: | 82% |
| GPA 3.0-3.49: | 32% | International: | 2% |
| GPA 2.0-2.99: | 14% | | |

**Basis for selection.** Secondary school record, recommendations, test scores, interview, autobiographical essay important. Audition required of music, theater and dance majors.

**High school preparation.** 18 units recommended. Recommended units include English 4, mathematics 3, social studies 3 and science 3.

**2007-2008 Annual costs.** Tuition/fees: $20,210. Per-credit-hour charge ranges from $395 to $760 depending on the number of credits. Room/board: $8,086. Books/supplies: $1,200. Personal expenses: $1,500.

**2006-2007 Financial aid. Need-based:** 310 full-time freshmen applied for aid; 254 were judged to have need; 254 of these received aid. Average need met was 18%. Average scholarship/grant was $1,590; average loan $2,371. 45% of total undergraduate aid awarded as scholarships/grants, 55% as loans/jobs. **Non-need-based:** Awarded to 1,842 full-time undergraduates, including 331 freshmen. Scholarships awarded for academics, alumni affiliation, athletics, minority status, music/drama, state residency.

**Application procedures. Admission:** Priority date 2/1; no deadline. $30 fee, may be waived for applicants with need. Application may be submitted online. Admission notification on a rolling basis beginning on or about 12/15. **Financial aid:** Priority date 2/1; no closing date. FAFSA required. Applicants notified on a rolling basis starting 3/1; must reply within 3 week(s) of notification.

**Academics. Special study options:** Accelerated study, combined bachelor's/graduate degree, cooperative education, cross-registration, double major, dual enrollment of high school students, exchange student, honors, independent study, internships, study abroad, teacher certification program, Washington semester. **Credit/placement by examination:** AP, CLEP, IB, SAT, ACT. 32

credit hours maximum toward bachelor's degree. If enrolled in one of undergraduate evening adult programs, aggregate of credit by examination or Professional Education Credit may not exceed 45 semester hours. **Support services:** Study skills assistance, tutoring, writing center.

**Honors college/program.** Students must rank in top 10 percent of the nation according to national test scores.

**Majors. Biology:** General. **Business:** Accounting/finance, business admin, entrepreneurial studies, international, marketing, nonprofit/public. **Communications:** General, broadcast journalism, journalism, organizational, radio/tv. **Education:** General, art, biology, drama/dance, English, history, mathematics, music, physical, social science. **English:** English lit. **Health:** Athletic training, nursing (RN). **History:** General. **Legal studies:** Prelaw. **Math:** General. **Philosophy/religion:** Philosophy, religion. **Psychology:** General. **Social sciences:** Political science. **Theology:** Bible, sacred music, theology. **Visual/performing arts:** General, acting, dance, dramatic, graphic design, music performance, music theory/composition, piano/organ, play/screenwriting, studio arts, voice/opera.

**Most popular majors.** Business/marketing 44%, communications/journalism 9%, health sciences 6%, psychology 8%.

**Computing on campus.** 550 workstations in dormitories, library, computer center, student center. Dormitories wired for high-speed internet access and linked to campus network. Commuter students can connect to campus network. Online course registration, online library, helpline, wireless network available.

**Student life. Freshman orientation:** Mandatory, $40 fee. Preregistration for classes offered. **Policies:** Undergraduate students required to donate 45 hours of community service for each year of attendance. Religious observance required. **Housing:** Guaranteed on-campus for freshmen. Single-sex dorms, substance-free housing available. $200 fully refundable deposit, deadline 5/1. **Activities:** Bands, campus ministries, choral groups, dance, drama, film society, literary magazine, music ensembles, musical theater, radio station, student government, student newspaper, symphony orchestra, TV station, Students in Free Enterprise, Newman club, Kappa Delta Epsilon, Kappa Psi, Lambda Pi Eta, Theta Alpha Kappa, American Society of Health System Pharmacists, American Association of Christian Counselors, Alpha Psi Omega, campus programming association.

**Athletics.** NCAA, NCCAA. **Intercollegiate:** Baseball M, basketball, cheerleading, cross-country, golf, soccer, softball W, tennis, volleyball W. **Intramural:** Basketball, bowling, football (non-tackle), golf, racquetball, soccer, softball, table tennis, volleyball. **Team name:** Sailfish.

**Student services.** Career counseling, student employment services, financial aid counseling, health services, personal counseling, veterans' counselor.

**Contact.** E-mail: admit@pba.edu
Phone: (561) 803-2000 Toll-free number: (888) 468-6722
Fax: (561) 803-2115
Rod Sullivan, Director of Admission, Palm Beach Atlantic University, PO Box 24708, West Palm Beach, FL 33416-4708

---

## Rasmussen College: Ocala
### Ocala, Florida
www.rasmussen.edu                              CB code: 3502

- For-profit 4-year business, health science, nursing and technical college
- Commuter campus in small city
- 500 degree-seeking undergraduates

**General.** Accredited by ACICS. **Degrees:** 14 bachelor's, 77 associate awarded. **Calendar:** Quarter, extensive summer session. **Full-time faculty:** 7 total. **Part-time faculty:** 18 total.

**Basis for selection.** Open admission, but selective for some programs. COMPASS used for placement.

**2007-2008 Annual costs.** Tuition/fees: $10,185. Personal expenses: $2,856.

**Application procedures. Admission:** No deadline. Admission notification on a rolling basis. **Financial aid:** Institutional form required. Applicants notified on a rolling basis; must reply within 1 week(s) of notification.

**Academics. Credit/placement by examination:** CLEP.

**Majors. Business:** Business admin.

**Contact.** E-mail: miguel.ramos@rasmussen.edu
Phone: (352) 629-1941 Fax: (352) 629-0926
Miguel Ramos, Director of Admissions, Rasmussen College: Ocala, 2221
Southwest 19th Avenue Road, Ocala, FL 34471-7051

## Rasmussen College: Pasco County
### Holiday, Florida
www.webstercollege.edu                    CB code: 3503

- For-profit 4-year business college
- Commuter campus in small city

**General.** Accredited by ACICS. **Location:** 30 miles from Tampa. **Calendar:** Quarter.

**Annual costs/financial aid.** Tuition/fees (2007-2008): $12,000. Books/supplies: $203. Personal expenses: $2,448. Need-based financial aid available to full-time and part-time students.

**Contact.** Phone: (727) 942-0069
Director of Admissions, 2127 Grand Boulevard, Holiday, FL 34691

## Remington College: Largo
### Largo, Florida
www.remingtoncollege.edu

- For-profit 4-year technical and career college
- Large city
- 158 degree-seeking undergraduates
- Interview required

**General.** Accredited by ACCSCT. **Degrees:** 1 bachelor's, 51 associate awarded. **Calendar:** Differs by program. Monthly.

**Basis for selection.** Open admission. **Homeschooled:** Transcript of courses and grades required.

**Application procedures. Admission:** No deadline. $50 fee.

**Academics. Credit/placement by examination:** CLEP.

**Majors. Business:** Operations. **Protective services:** Criminal justice.

**Computing on campus.** 75 workstations in library, computer center. Online library, repair service, wireless network available.

**Student services.** Career counseling, financial aid counseling, placement for graduates.

**Contact.** Phone: (727) 532-1999 Fax: (727) 530-7710
Remington College: Largo, 8550 Ulmerton Road, Unit 100, Largo, FL 33771

## Remington College: Tampa
### Tampa, Florida
www.remingtoncollege.edu                    CB code: 0123

- For-profit 4-year technical college
- Commuter campus in very large city
- 261 degree-seeking undergraduates
- Interview required

**General.** Founded in 1948. Accredited by ACCSCT. **Degrees:** 22 bachelor's, 112 associate awarded. **Calendar:** Quarter, extensive summer session. **Full-time faculty:** 12 total. **Part-time faculty:** 16 total.

**Basis for selection.** Open admission. Interview required; recommendations considered; Wonderlic test used.

**2007-2008 Annual costs.** Costs of entire programs leading to certificate, associate degree, bachelor's degree range from $13,000 to $38,880; includes books and supplies. Personal expenses: $1,200.

**Financial aid.** All financial aid based on need.

**Application procedures. Admission:** No deadline. $50 fee. Application may be submitted online. Admission notification on a rolling basis. **Financial aid:** No deadline. FAFSA, institutional form required.

**Academics. Special study options:** Accelerated study, combined bachelor's/graduate degree, distance learning. **Credit/placement by examination:** CLEP. **Support services:** Remedial instruction, tutoring.

**Majors. Protective services:** Law enforcement admin.

**Computing on campus.** 350 workstations in library, computer center. Online library, helpline, repair service, wireless network available.

**Student life. Freshman orientation:** Mandatory. Preregistration for classes offered.

**Student services.** Career counseling, student employment services, financial aid counseling, personal counseling, placement for graduates.

**Contact.** Phone: (813) 935-5700 Toll-free number: (800) 992-4850
Fax: (813) 935-7415
Gary Schwartz, Director of Recruiting, Remington College: Tampa, 2410
East Busch Boulevard, Tampa, FL 33612

## Ringling College of Art and Design
### Sarasota, Florida                    CB member
www.ringling.edu                    CB code: 5573

- Private 4-year visual arts college
- Residential campus in small city
- 1,199 degree-seeking undergraduates: 4% part-time, 54% women, 3% African American, 6% Asian American, 11% Hispanic American, 1% Native American, 5% international
- 73% of applicants admitted
- Application essay required
- 66% graduate within 6 years

**General.** Founded in 1931. Regionally accredited. **Degrees:** 200 bachelor's awarded. **Location:** 50 miles from Tampa. **Calendar:** Semester. **Full-time faculty:** 71 total; 61% have terminal degrees, 4% minority, 31% women. **Part-time faculty:** 65 total; 35% have terminal degrees, 2% minority, 43% women. **Class size:** 64% < 20, 33% 20-39, less than 1% 40-49, 1% 50-99. **Special facilities:** Art library, art gallery.

**Freshman class profile.** 949 applied, 695 admitted, 292 enrolled.

| | | | |
|---|---|---|---|
| GPA 3.50 or higher: | 25% | Out-of-state: | 51% |
| GPA 3.0-3.49: | 33% | Live on campus: | 84% |
| GPA 2.0-2.99: | 42% | International: | 6% |
| End year in good standing: | 81% | Fraternities: | 1% |
| Return as sophomores: | 81% | Sororities: | 1% |

**Basis for selection.** Portfolio, school achievement record, statement of purpose, and recommendations important. Interview recommended. Portfolio required. **Learning Disabled:** Students seeking special accommodations for learning disabilities must provide documentation of disability.

**2007-2008 Annual costs.** Tuition/fees: $25,110. Room/board: $10,000.

**2007-2008 Financial aid.** All financial aid based on need. 212 full-time freshmen applied for aid; 181 were judged to have need; 181 of these received aid. Average need met was 43%. Average scholarship/grant was $6,927; average loan $8,039. 32% of total undergraduate aid awarded as scholarships/grants, 68% as loans/jobs.

**Application procedures. Admission:** Priority date 3/1; no deadline. $40 fee, may be waived for applicants with need. Application may be submitted online. Admission notification on a rolling basis beginning on or about 9/1. **Financial aid:** Priority date 3/1; no closing date. FAFSA required. Applicants notified on a rolling basis starting 4/1; must reply within 2 week(s) of notification.

**Academics. Special study options:** Dual enrollment of high school students, exchange student, independent study, internships, New York semester, study abroad. **Credit/placement by examination:** AP, CLEP, IB. 30 credit hours maximum toward bachelor's degree. **Support services:** Learning center, pre-admission summer program, remedial instruction, study skills assistance, tutoring, writing center.

**Majors. Communications technology:** Animation/special effects. **Visual/performing arts:** Graphic design, illustration, interior design, photography, studio arts.

**Computing on campus.** 650 workstations in dormitories, library, computer center, student center. Dormitories linked to campus network. Commuter students can connect to campus network. Online course registration, helpline available.

**Student life. Freshman orientation:** Mandatory. Held week prior to classes. **Housing:** Single-sex dorms, apartments, substance-free housing available. $100 fully refundable deposit. All housing accommodations are ADA compliant. **Activities:** Campus ministries, dance, international student organizations, literary magazine, student government.

**Athletics. Intramural:** Baseball, basketball, softball, table tennis.

**Student services.** Career counseling, student employment services, financial aid counseling, health services, minority student services, personal counseling, placement for graduates, veterans' counselor, women's services. **Physically disabled:** Services for visually, hearing impaired.

**Contact.** E-mail: admissions@ringling.edu
Phone: (941) 351-5100 Toll-free number: (800) 255-7695
Fax: (941) 359-7517
James Dean, Dean of Admissions, Ringling College of Art and Design, 2700 North Tamiami Trail, Sarasota, FL 34234-5895

---

## Rollins College
### Winter Park, Florida
www.rollins.edu

CB member
CB code: 5572

- Private 4-year liberal arts college
- Residential campus in large town
- 1,778 degree-seeking undergraduates: 58% women, 4% African American, 4% Asian American, 10% Hispanic American, 4% international
- 754 degree-seeking graduate students
- 58% of applicants admitted
- Application essay required
- 68% graduate within 6 years

**General.** Founded in 1885. Regionally accredited. **Degrees:** 400 bachelor's awarded; master's offered. **Location:** 5 miles from Orlando. **Calendar:** Semester, limited summer session. **Full-time faculty:** 193 total; 93% have terminal degrees, 11% minority, 37% women. **Part-time faculty:** 44 total; 46% have terminal degrees, 9% minority, 54% women. **Class size:** 67% <20, 32% 20-39, less than 1% 40-49, less than 1% 50-99. **Special facilities:** 2 theaters, child development center, center for psychology, greenhouse, high tech classrooms.

**Freshman class profile.** 2,900 applied, 1,683 admitted, 525 enrolled.

| Mid 50% test scores | | | | |
|---|---|---|---|---|
| SAT critical reading: | 560-640 | Rank in top quarter: | 75% |
| SAT math: | 560-640 | Rank in top tenth: | 45% |
| ACT composite: | 23-28 | Return as sophomores: | 85% |
| GPA 3.50 or higher: | 35% | Out-of-state: | 50% |
| GPA 3.0-3.49: | 35% | Live on campus: | 93% |
| GPA 2.0-2.99: | 30% | International: | 4% |

**Basis for selection.** School achievement record most important, followed by test scores, activities, essay, recommendations, interview. Audition recommended for music, theater arts majors.

**High school preparation.** 17 units required; 24 recommended. Required and recommended units include English 4, mathematics 3-4, social studies 2-3, history 2-3, science 2-4, foreign language 2-3 and academic electives 2-3.

**2008-2009 Annual costs.** Tuition/fees: $34,520. Room/board: $10,780. Books/supplies: $700. Personal expenses: $2,210.

**2007-2008 Financial aid. Need-based:** 253 full-time freshmen applied for aid; 210 were judged to have need; 210 of these received aid. Average need met was 92%. Average scholarship/grant was $25,245; average loan $4,241. 86% of total undergraduate aid awarded as scholarships/grants, 14% as loans/jobs. **Non-need-based:** Awarded to 404 full-time undergraduates, including 151 freshmen. Scholarships awarded for academics, art, athletics, leadership, music/drama, state residency. **Additional information:** Audition required for theater arts and music scholarship applicants. Portfolio required for art scholarships.

**Application procedures. Admission:** Closing date 2/15 (postmark date). $40 fee, may be waived for applicants with need. Application may be submitted online. Admission notification 4/1. Must reply by May 1 or within 3 week(s) if notified thereafter. **Financial aid:** Closing date 3/1. FAFSA, institutional form required. Applicants notified on a rolling basis starting 3/1.

**Academics.** International business major featuring language training, internships and study abroad available; pre-professional support services. **Special study options:** Accelerated study, combined bachelor's/graduate degree, cross-registration, double major, dual enrollment of high school students, honors, independent study, internships, semester at sea, student-designed major, study abroad, teacher certification program, Washington semester. **Credit/placement by examination:** AP, CLEP, IB, institutional tests. 76 credit hours maximum toward bachelor's degree. **Support services:** Learning center, reduced course load, study skills assistance, tutoring, writing center.

**Honors college/program.** Top 10% of entering freshman class admitted.

**Majors. Area/ethnic studies:** Latin American. **Biology:** General, Biochemistry/biophysics and molecular biology, marine. **Business:** International. **Communications:** Media studies. **Computer sciences:** General. **Conservation:** Environmental studies. **Education:** General. **English:** English lit. **Foreign languages:** Classics, French, Spanish. **History:** General. **Math:** General. **Philosophy/religion:** Philosophy, religion. **Physical sciences:** Chemistry, physics. **Psychology:** General. **Social sciences:** Anthropology, economics, international relations, political science, sociology. **Visual/performing arts:** Art, art history/conservation, dramatic.

**Most popular majors.** Biology 7%, business/marketing 11%, education 7%, English 6%, psychology 13%, social sciences 31%, visual/performing arts 10%.

**Computing on campus.** 205 workstations in dormitories, library, computer center, student center. Dormitories wired for high-speed internet access and linked to campus network. Commuter students can connect to campus network. Online course registration, online library, helpline, repair service, student web hosting, wireless network available.

**Student life. Freshman orientation:** Mandatory. Preregistration for classes offered. Held just prior to fall semester. **Housing:** Guaranteed on-campus for freshmen. Coed dorms, single-sex dorms, special housing for disabled, apartments, fraternity/sorority housing available. $500 nonrefundable deposit, deadline 5/15. Special interest group housing available. **Activities:** Pep band, choral groups, dance, drama, film society, literary magazine, music ensembles, musical theater, radio station, student government, student newspaper, TV station, ally alliance, Muslim student association, Hillel, Rollins, Habitat for Humanity, 5 Stones, cultural action committee, College Republicans, College Democrats, Black Student Union.

**Athletics.** NCAA. **Intercollegiate:** Baseball M, basketball, cross-country, golf, lacrosse, rowing (crew), sailing, skiing, soccer, softball W, swimming, tennis, volleyball W. **Intramural:** Basketball M, football (non-tackle), soccer, softball, table tennis, tennis, volleyball. **Team name:** Tars.

**Student services.** Alcohol/substance abuse counseling, campus ministries, career counseling, student employment services, financial aid counseling, health services, personal counseling, placement for graduates, veterans' counselor. **Physically disabled:** Services for visually, speech, hearing impaired.

**Contact.** E-mail: admission@rollins.edu
Phone: (407) 646-2161 Fax: (407) 646-1502
Mike Lynch, Director of Admission, Rollins College, 1000 Holt Avenue, Winter Park, FL 32789

---

## St. John Vianney College Seminary
### Miami, Florida
www.sjvcs.edu

CB code: 5650

- Private 4-year liberal arts and seminary college for men affiliated with Roman Catholic Church
- Residential campus in very large city
- 62 degree-seeking undergraduates
- 100% of applicants admitted
- Interview required

**General.** Founded in 1959. Regionally accredited. Women students admitted on part-time or full-time basis, by exception. **Degrees:** 21 bachelor's awarded. **Location:** 12 miles from downtown. **Calendar:** Semester, limited summer session. **Full-time faculty:** 7 total. **Part-time faculty:** 12 total. **Class size:** 100% <20.

**Freshman class profile.** 16 applied, 16 admitted, 16 enrolled.

| | | | |
|---|---|---|---|
| Out-of-state: | 2% | Live on campus: | 100% |

**Basis for selection.** Interview, academic record, recommendations required. Those to be formed for priesthood should present evidence of vocation for priesthood and submit psychological and physical evaluations. Applicants referred by home (church) Diocesan Offices of Vocations.

**High school preparation.** 20 units required. Required units include English 4, mathematics 2, social studies 2, history 2, science 2, foreign language 2 and academic electives 6.

**2007-2008 Annual costs.** Tuition/fees: $17,000. Room/board: $9,500. Books/supplies: $600. Personal expenses: $990.

**Application procedures. Admission:** Priority date 6/30; deadline 7/15 (receipt date). No application fee. Admission notification on a rolling basis. **Financial aid:** No deadline. FAFSA required. Applicants notified on a rolling basis.

**Academics.** Fluency in both English and Spanish must be achieved. Students required to take at least 1 course in alternate language each semester. **Special study options:** Cross-registration, ESL, independent study. **Credit/placement by examination:** AP, CLEP, institutional tests. **Support services:** Pre-admission summer program, reduced course load, remedial instruction, study skills assistance, tutoring.

**Majors. Philosophy/religion:** Philosophy.

**Computing on campus.** 12 workstations in library, computer center.

**Student life. Freshman orientation:** Mandatory, $2,000 fee. Preregistration for classes offered. 3 weeks during August. **Policies:** All sophomores and upperclassmen assigned weekly apostolic work at various locations. Religious observance required. **Housing:** Guaranteed on-campus for all undergraduates. **Activities:** Choral groups, drama, music ensembles, student government, student newspaper, apostolic works program.

**Athletics. Intramural:** Baseball M, basketball M, handball M, racquetball M, soccer M, softball M, swimming M, table tennis M, tennis M, volleyball M, weight lifting M.

**Student services.** Adult student services, career counseling, financial aid counseling, health services, personal counseling.

**Contact.** Phone: (305) 223-4561 Fax: (305) 223-0650
Ramon Santos, Academic Dean, St. John Vianney College Seminary, 2900 Southwest 87 Avenue, Miami, FL 33165-3244

---

## St. Leo University

Saint Leo, Florida
www.saintleo.edu

**CB member**
**CB code: 5638**

- Private 4-year university affiliated with Roman Catholic Church
- Residential campus in rural community
- 1,587 degree-seeking undergraduates: 5% part-time, 54% women, 9% African American, 1% Asian American, 10% Hispanic American, 1% Native American, 10% international
- 1,439 degree-seeking graduate students
- 71% of applicants admitted
- SAT or ACT (ACT writing optional), application essay required
- 41% graduate within 6 years

**General.** Founded in 1889. Regionally accredited. **Degrees:** 223 bachelor's, 12 associate awarded; master's offered. **ROTC:** Army, Air Force. **Location:** 25 miles from Tampa. **Calendar:** Semester, limited summer session. **Full-time faculty:** 87 total; 80% have terminal degrees, 8% minority, 34% women. **Part-time faculty:** 52 total; 31% have terminal degrees, 6% minority, 38% women. **Class size:** 47% < 20, 53% 20-39. **Special facilities:** Wetlands nearby for field studies in environmental science, center for Catholic and Jewish studies.

**Freshman class profile.** 2,188 applied, 1,548 admitted, 456 enrolled.

| Mid 50% test scores | | | |
|---|---|---|---|
| SAT critical reading: | 460-540 | Rank in top quarter: | 24% |
| SAT math: | 460-540 | Rank in top tenth: | 7% |
| SAT writing: | 440-520 | End year in good standing: | 77% |
| ACT composite: | 19-23 | Return as sophomores: | 69% |
| GPA 3.50 or higher: | 28% | Out-of-state: | 38% |
| GPA 3.0-3.49: | 35% | Live on campus: | 84% |
| GPA 2.0-2.99: | 37% | International: | 10% |

**Basis for selection.** Test scores, GPA, guidance counselor's recommendation, high school curriculum important. Interview recommended. **Homeschooled:** Transcript of courses and grades, interview, letter of recommendation (nonparent) required. Bibliography of all high school reading material, 2 letters of recommendation, portfolio of sample work required.

**High school preparation.** 16 units recommended. Recommended units include English 4, mathematics 3, social studies 3, science 2, foreign language 2 and academic electives 2. Algebra I and II, geometry strongly recommended. Those planning to study science should complete courses in biology and chemistry.

**2008-2009 Annual costs.** Tuition/fees: $17,150. Room/board: $8,430. Books/supplies: $1,200. Personal expenses: $1,330.

**2007-2008 Financial aid. Need-based:** 400 full-time freshmen applied for aid; 305 were judged to have need; 305 of these received aid. Average need met was 90%. Average scholarship/grant was $11,296; average loan $4,214. 63% of total undergraduate aid awarded as scholarships/grants, 37% as loans/jobs. **Non-need-based:** Awarded to 239 full-time undergraduates, including 64 freshmen. Scholarships awarded for academics, alumni affiliation, athletics, leadership, minority status, music/drama, religious affiliation, state residency.

**Application procedures. Admission:** Priority date 3/1; deadline 8/15 (postmark date). $35 fee, may be waived for applicants with need. Application may be submitted online. Admission notification on a rolling basis beginning on or about 10/15. Must reply by May 1 or within 2 week(s) if notified thereafter. **Financial aid:** Priority date 4/1; no closing date. FAFSA required. Applicants notified on a rolling basis starting 1/31.

**Academics. Special study options:** Combined bachelor's/graduate degree, distance learning, double major, dual enrollment of high school students, honors, independent study, internships, liberal arts/career combination, study abroad, teacher certification program, weekend college. Opportunity to study abroad in Italy, Switzerland, France, Ecuador, Spain, United Kingdom, Ireland, Australia, Germany, and Scotland. **Credit/placement by examination:** AP, CLEP, IB, SAT, ACT, institutional tests. 40 credit hours maximum toward associate degree, 40 toward bachelor's. **Support services:** Learning center, pre-admission summer program, reduced course load, remedial instruction, study skills assistance, tutoring, writing center.

**Honors college/program.** 3.5 GPA and 1160 SAT (exclusive of Writing) or 26 ACT required. Full honors curriculum consists of integrated sequence of 6 courses plus 2 research courses.

**Majors. Biology:** General. **Business:** Accounting, business admin, entrepreneurial studies, hospitality admin, human resources, international, management information systems, management science, marketing. **Communications:** Media studies. **Conservation:** Environmental studies. **Education:** Elementary, middle. **English:** Creative writing, English lit. **Health:** Clinical lab science, facilities admin, health care admin. **History:** General. **Math:** General. **Parks/recreation:** Sports admin. **Protective services:** Criminal justice. **Psychology:** General. **Public administration:** Community org/advocacy, social work. **Social sciences:** International relations, political science, sociology. **Theology:** Theology.

**Most popular majors.** Biology 8%, business/marketing 30%, education 12%, parks/recreation 7%, security/protective services 13%, social sciences 9%.

**Computing on campus.** 1,243 workstations in dormitories, library, student center. Dormitories wired for high-speed internet access and linked to campus network. Commuter students can connect to campus network. Online course registration, online library, helpline, repair service, student web hosting, wireless network available.

**Student life. Freshman orientation:** Mandatory, $300 fee. Preregistration for classes offered. Four-day program in August includes team-building, personal responsibility activities. Advising, testing, introduction to student life in mid-July. **Policies:** Fish aquariums allowed in residence hall rooms. **Housing:** Guaranteed on-campus for all undergraduates. Coed dorms, single-sex dorms, special housing for disabled, apartments, substance-free housing available. $150 nonrefundable deposit, deadline 8/15. Freshmen-only housing available. **Activities:** Concert band, campus ministries, choral groups, dance, drama, film society, literary magazine, music ensembles, musical theater, radio station, student government, student newspaper, TV station, Circle-K, Samaritans, intercultural student association, Saint Leo Ambassadors, Best Buddies, student chaplain program, Pi Sigma Alpha, Brothers and Sisters United, social work club, Latino club.

**Athletics.** NCAA. **Intercollegiate:** Baseball M, basketball, cross-country, golf, lacrosse M, soccer, softball W, swimming, tennis, volleyball W. **Intramural:** Basketball, football (non-tackle), racquetball, soccer, softball, table tennis, tennis, volleyball. **Team name:** Lions.

**Student services.** Adult student services, alcohol/substance abuse counseling, career counseling, student employment services, financial aid counseling, health services, personal counseling. **Physically disabled:** Services for visually impaired.

**Contact.** E-mail: admission@saintleo.edu
Phone: (352) 588-8283 Toll-free number: (800) 334-5532
Fax: (352) 588-8257
Martin Smith, Assistant Vice President of Enrollment, St. Leo University, Office of Admission, Saint Leo, FL 33574-6665

## St. Petersburg College
St. Petersburg, Florida
www.spcollege.edu

CB member
CB code: 5606

- ◆ Public 4-year community college
- ◆ Commuter campus in large city
- ◆ 19,827 degree-seeking undergraduates: 65% part-time, 62% women, 12% African American, 3% Asian American, 6% Hispanic American, 1% international

**General.** Founded in 1927. Regionally accredited. Campuses include Clearwater, Seminole, St. Petersburg, Tarpon Springs. Health education center in Pinellas Park. Criminal justice/computer complex in St. Petersburg. Corporate training and Cisco at the Epicenter. Downtown and midtown centers. **Degrees:** 517 bachelor's, 2,711 associate awarded. **Location:** 20 miles from Tampa. **Calendar:** Semester, extensive summer session. **Full-time faculty:** 316 total; 34% have terminal degrees, 15% minority, 57% women. **Part-time faculty:** 1,419 total; 30% minority, 45% women. **Special facilities:** Observatory, planetarium, firing range, college-operated museums.

**Basis for selection.** Open admission, but selective for some programs. Limited enrollment to health-related programs. Florida CPT required for all degree-seeking students. Interview recommended for allied health applicants. Essay required for B.S. College of Education applicants. **Home-schooled:** Transcript of courses and grades, state high school equivalency certificate required.

**2007-2008 Annual costs.** Tuition/fees: $2,091; $7,558 out-of-state. Books/supplies: $1,100. Personal expenses: $3,080.

**Financial aid. Non-need-based:** Scholarships awarded for academics, art, athletics, minority status, music/drama.

**Application procedures. Admission:** No deadline. $35 fee. Application may be submitted online. Admission notification on a rolling basis. **Financial aid:** Priority date 4/15; no closing date. FAFSA, institutional form required. Applicants notified on a rolling basis starting 5/15; must reply within 2 week(s) of notification.

**Academics. Special study options:** Accelerated study, cooperative education, cross-registration, distance learning, dual enrollment of high school students, ESL, exchange student, honors, independent study, internships, liberal arts/career combination, study abroad, teacher certification program, weekend college. 2-year associate degree program in business and computer science for deaf students. **Credit/placement by examination:** AP, CLEP, IB, institutional tests. 45 credit hours maximum toward associate degree, 45 toward bachelor's. Florida CPT required for placement. **Support services:** Learning center, reduced course load, remedial instruction, study skills assistance, tutoring.

**Majors. Business:** Business admin, finance, international. **Computer sciences:** System admin. **Education:** Biology, business, computer, elementary, mathematics, science, special, technology/industrial arts. **Health:** Critical care nursing, dental hygiene, nursing (RN), orthotics/prosthetics, veterinary technology/assistant. **Legal studies:** Paralegal. **Other:** Security and Protective Services.

**Most popular majors.** Computer/information sciences 19%, education 35%, health sciences 39%.

**Computing on campus.** 4,024 workstations in library, computer center, student center. Commuter students can connect to campus network. Online course registration, online library, helpline, student web hosting, wireless network available.

**Student life. Freshman orientation:** Mandatory. Preregistration for classes offered. **Activities:** Jazz band, choral groups, dance, drama, film society, international student organizations, music ensembles, student government, student newspaper, Phi Theta Kappa, Harambee black culture club, ethics club, math and science Club, American Sign Language club.

**Athletics.** NJCAA. **Intercollegiate:** Baseball M, basketball, softball W, volleyball. **Intramural:** Basketball, bowling, golf, table tennis, tennis, volleyball W, water polo M. **Team name:** Titans.

**Student services.** Career counseling, services for economically disadvantaged, student employment services, financial aid counseling, health services, minority student services, personal counseling, placement for graduates, veterans' counselor, women's services. **Physically disabled:** Services for visually, speech, hearing impaired.

**Contact.** Phone: (727) 341-4792
Susan Fell, St. Petersburg College, Box 13489, St. Petersburg, FL 33733-3489

## Saint Thomas University
Miami Gardens, Florida
www.stu.edu

CB code: 5076

- ◆ Private 4-year university affiliated with Roman Catholic Church
- ◆ Commuter campus in very large city
- ◆ 1,150 degree-seeking undergraduates: 5% part-time, 57% women, 27% African American, 1% Asian American, 47% Hispanic American, 9% international
- ◆ 1,257 degree-seeking graduate students
- ◆ 65% of applicants admitted
- ◆ SAT or ACT (ACT writing optional) required

**General.** Founded in 1961. Regionally accredited. Multilocation institution. Affiliated with Archdiocese of Miami. **Degrees:** 310 bachelor's awarded; master's, doctoral, first professional offered. **Location:** 10 miles from Miami. **Calendar:** Semester, extensive summer session. **Full-time faculty:** 100 total; 91% have terminal degrees, 29% minority, 43% women. **Part-time faculty:** 95 total; 25% have terminal degrees, 54% minority, 42% women. **Class size:** 71% < 20, 28% 20-39, less than 1% 40-49, less than 1% 50-99.

**Freshman class profile.** 610 applied, 399 admitted, 226 enrolled.

| Mid 50% test scores | | | |
|---|---|---|---|
| SAT critical reading: | 400-490 | GPA 2.0-2.99: | 60% |
| SAT math: | 390-490 | Rank in top quarter: | 25% |
| SAT writing: | 400-480 | Rank in top tenth: | 6% |
| ACT composite: | 16-20 | Return as sophomores: | 65% |
| GPA 3.50 or higher: | 12% | Out-of-state: | 14% |
| GPA 3.0-3.49: | 27% | Live on campus: | 31% |
| | | International: | 9% |

**Basis for selection.** High school grades, test scores primary factors. Class rank, interview, school, community activities, recommendations also considered. Interview recommended.

**High school preparation.** 18 units required. Required units include English 4, mathematics 3, social studies 3, science 2 and academic electives 6.

**2007-2008 Annual costs.** Tuition/fees: $19,680. Room/board: $6,206. Books/supplies: $1,000. Personal expenses: $1,870.

**2006-2007 Financial aid. Need-based:** 215 full-time freshmen applied for aid; 194 were judged to have need; 194 of these received aid. Average scholarship/grant was $1,768; average loan $2,280. 71% of total undergraduate aid awarded as scholarships/grants, 29% as loans/jobs. **Non-need-based:** Awarded to 923 full-time undergraduates, including 244 freshmen. Scholarships awarded for academics, athletics, leadership, music/drama, religious affiliation, state residency.

**Application procedures. Admission:** No deadline. $40 fee, may be waived for applicants with need. Application may be submitted online. Admission notification on a rolling basis. Must reply by May 1 or within 2 week(s) if notified thereafter. Applicants needing on-campus housing strongly encouraged to apply before May 15. **Financial aid:** Priority date 4/2; no closing date. FAFSA required. Applicants notified on a rolling basis starting 3/1.

**Academics. Special study options:** Combined bachelor's/graduate degree, distance learning, double major, dual enrollment of high school students, honors, independent study, internships, liberal arts/career combination, teacher certification program. **Credit/placement by examination:** AP, CLEP, SAT, ACT, institutional tests. 45 credit hours maximum toward bachelor's degree. **Support services:** Learning center, pre-admission summer program, reduced course load, remedial instruction, study skills assistance, tutoring, writing center.

**Majors. Biology:** General. **Business:** Accounting, business admin, finance, hospitality admin, international, organizational behavior, tourism/travel. **Communications:** General, media studies. **Computer sciences:** General, computer science. **Conservation:** Environmental studies. **Education:** Elementary, secondary, social studies. **English:** English lit. **Health:** Health care admin, premedicine, preveterinary. **History:** General. **Legal studies:** Prelaw. **Liberal arts:** Arts/sciences. **Parks/recreation:** Sports admin. **Philosophy/**

religion: Religion. **Physical sciences:** Chemistry. **Protective services:** Criminal justice. **Psychology:** General. **Public administration:** Human services. **Social sciences:** Political science. **Theology:** Religious ed.

**Most popular majors.** Business/marketing 51%, education 8%, psychology 11%, security/protective services 6%.

**Computing on campus.** 123 workstations in library, computer center. Dormitories linked to campus network. Online course registration, helpline, wireless network available.

**Student life. Freshman orientation:** Mandatory. **Housing:** Single-sex dorms available. $225 fully refundable deposit. **Activities:** Campus ministries, choral groups, international student organizations, literary magazine, music ensembles, student government, TV station, political action club, Students for Global Preservation, prelaw society, premedicine club, accounting club.

**Athletics.** NAIA. **Intercollegiate:** Baseball M, cross-country, golf, soccer, softball W, tennis, volleyball W. **Intramural:** Golf, soccer M, softball, tennis, volleyball. **Team name:** Bobcats.

**Student services.** Adult student services, alcohol/substance abuse counseling, career counseling, student employment services, financial aid counseling, health services, personal counseling, placement for graduates. **Physically disabled:** Services for visually, hearing impaired.

**Contact.** E-mail: signup@stu.edu
Phone: (305) 628-6546 Toll-free number: (800) 367-9010
Fax: (305) 628-6591
Lydia Amy, Dean, Enrollment Services, Saint Thomas University, 16401 Northwest 37th Avenue, Miami Gardens, FL 33054-6459

## Schiller International University
**Largo, Florida**
**www.schiller.edu**                    **CB code: 0601**

- For-profit 4-year university
- Residential campus in large town
- 81 degree-seeking undergraduates
- Application essay required

**General.** Founded in 1964. Accredited by ACICS. 8 campuses in 6 countries located in or near major urban areas: Dunedin, London, Paris, Madrid, Heidelberg, Strasbourg, Engelberg and Leysin. Students may transfer without loss of credit. **Degrees:** 26 bachelor's, 2 associate awarded; master's offered. **Location:** 20 miles from Tampa. **Calendar:** Semester, extensive summer session. **Full-time faculty:** 2 total. **Part-time faculty:** 45 total. **Special facilities:** University owned and operated hotels.

**Basis for selection.** Open admission. High school diploma or GED required.

**2007-2008 Annual costs.** Tuition/fees: $17,465. Room/board: $7,900. Books/supplies: $1,250. Personal expenses: $2,600.

**Financial aid. Non-need-based:** Scholarships awarded for academics, alumni affiliation, leadership, minority status, state residency. **Additional information:** Special scholarship program for U.S. college students studying abroad at European campuses of Schiller. Work-study available to students taking 2 or more courses.

**Application procedures. Admission:** No deadline. $50 fee. Application must be submitted on paper. Admission notification on a rolling basis. **Financial aid:** Closing date 4/1. FAFSA, institutional form required. Applicants notified on a rolling basis starting 5/1; must reply within 3 week(s) of notification.

**Academics.** Completion of intermediate level of at least one foreign language required for most undergraduate degree programs. **Special study options:** Accelerated study, cooperative education, distance learning, double major, dual enrollment of high school students, ESL, exchange student, independent study, internships, liberal arts/career combination, study abroad, weekend college. **Credit/placement by examination:** AP, CLEP, IB, institutional tests. 16 credit hours maximum toward associate degree, 16 toward bachelor's. **Support services:** Learning center, reduced course load, study skills assistance, tutoring.

**Majors. Area/ethnic studies:** European. **Business:** General, banking/ financial services, business admin, finance, hotel/motel admin, international, international marketing, management information systems, marketing, tourism/travel. **Computer sciences:** Information technology, systems analysis. **Foreign languages:** French, German. **Interdisciplinary:** Global studies. **Psychology:** General. **Social sciences:** International economics, international relations.

**Computing on campus.** 35 workstations in library, computer center, student center. Commuter students can connect to campus network. Online library, repair service, wireless network available.

**Student life. Freshman orientation:** Mandatory. Preregistration for classes offered. 2-day program, 2 days before registration. **Policies:** Alcohol use banned; smoking limited to specific locations. No heating devices allowed. **Housing:** Guaranteed on-campus for freshmen. Coed dorms, substance-free housing available. $400 deposit, deadline 8/5. Students may also live with host families at some campuses. **Activities:** Student government, student newspaper, Model United Nations, Rotaract, Young Skal, honors society, Society for Human Resource Management, student council.

**Athletics. Intramural:** Baseball, basketball, soccer.

**Student services.** Adult student services, career counseling, services for economically disadvantaged, student employment services, financial aid counseling, legal services, personal counseling, placement for graduates.

**Contact.** E-mail: admissions@schiller.edu
Phone: (727) 736-5082 ext. 240 Toll-free number: (800) 336-4133
Fax: (727) 734-0359
Marcus Leibrecht, Associate Director of Admissions, Schiller International University, 300 East Bay Drive, Largo, FL 33770-3716

## South University: West Palm Beach Campus
**West Palm Beach, Florida**
**www.southuniversity.edu**              **CB code: 5321**

- For-profit 4-year business, health science and nursing college
- Commuter campus in large city
- 767 degree-seeking undergraduates
- Application essay, interview required

**General.** Regionally accredited. **Degrees:** 80 bachelor's, 64 associate awarded; master's offered. **Location:** 3 miles from downtown, 29 miles from Fort Lauderdale. **Calendar:** Quarter, extensive summer session. **Full-time faculty:** 21 total. **Part-time faculty:** 40 total.

**Basis for selection.** Test scores most important. Satisfactory score on college-administered entrance exams (CPT), or 660 SAT (exclusive of Writing) or 14 ACT required. Some programs have higher requirements.

**2007-2008 Annual costs.** Tuition/fees: $12,570. Books/supplies: $900. Personal expenses: $1,476.

**Financial aid. Non-need-based:** Scholarships awarded for academics.

**Application procedures. Admission:** No deadline. $25 fee, may be waived for applicants with need. Application may be submitted online. Admission notification on a rolling basis. **Financial aid:** No deadline. FAFSA, institutional form required. Applicants notified on a rolling basis; must reply within 2 week(s) of notification.

**Academics. Special study options:** Accelerated study, double major, dual enrollment of high school students, internships. **Credit/placement by examination:** CLEP, SAT, ACT, institutional tests. No more than 60% of any program requirements may be earned through credits by examinations. **Support services:** Remedial instruction, study skills assistance, tutoring.

**Majors. Business:** Business admin, finance. **Computer sciences:** Information systems. **Health:** Nursing (RN). **Legal studies:** Paralegal.

**Most popular majors.** Business/marketing 25%, health sciences 35%, legal studies 40%.

**Computing on campus.** 75 workstations in library, computer center. Online library available.

**Student life. Freshman orientation:** Mandatory. Preregistration for classes offered. **Activities:** Student government, student newspaper, paralegal club, honor society.

**Student services.** Adult student services, career counseling, student employment services, personal counseling, placement for graduates, veterans' counselor.

**Contact.** E-mail: wpbadmis@southuniversity.edu
Phone: (561) 697-9200 Fax: (561) 697-9944
Lisa Sgherza, Director of Admissions, South University: West Palm Beach Campus, 1760 North Congress Avenue, West Palm Beach, FL 33409-5178

## Southeastern University
### Lakeland, Florida
www.seuniversity.edu  CB code: 5621

- Private 4-year liberal arts and teachers college affiliated with Assemblies of God
- Residential campus in small city
- 2,646 degree-seeking undergraduates: 5% part-time, 59% women, 7% African American, 1% Asian American, 12% Hispanic American
- 124 degree-seeking graduate students
- Application essay required
- 38% graduate within 6 years

**General.** Founded in 1935. Regionally accredited. **Degrees:** 437 bachelor's awarded; master's offered. **ROTC:** Army. **Location:** 40 miles from Tampa, 50 miles from Orlando. **Calendar:** Semester, limited summer session. **Full-time faculty:** 73 total; 60% have terminal degrees, 10% minority, 29% women. **Part-time faculty:** 57 total; 25% have terminal degrees, 9% minority, 46% women. **Class size:** 35% < 20, 42% 20-39, 8% 40-49, 13% 50-99, 1% >100.

**Freshman class profile.** 1,232 applied, 966 admitted, 567 enrolled.

| Mid 50% test scores | | | |
|---|---|---|---|
| SAT critical reading: | 440-570 | GPA 3.0-3.49: | 26% |
| SAT math: | 430-560 | GPA 2.0-2.99: | 22% |
| ACT composite: | 18-24 | Return as sophomores: | 64% |
| GPA 3.50 or higher: | 50% | Out-of-state: | 36% |
| | | Live on campus: | 89% |

**Basis for selection.** Open admission, but selective for some programs. SAT or ACT used for placement in Math, English; also used to determine scholarship eligibility. Accuplacer may be used in lieu of SAT/ACT. Interview recommended for academically weak applicants.

**High school preparation.** Recommended units include English 4, mathematics 4, social studies 4, science 4 and foreign language 2.

**2008-2009 Annual costs.** Tuition/fees (projected): $14,470. Room/board: $7,000. Books/supplies: $900. Personal expenses: $1,000.

**2007-2008 Financial aid. Need-based:** 484 full-time freshmen applied for aid; 382 were judged to have need; 380 of these received aid. Average need met was 22%. Average scholarship/grant was $6,582; average loan $3,369. 49% of total undergraduate aid awarded as scholarships/grants, 51% as loans/jobs. **Non-need-based:** Awarded to 690 full-time undergraduates, including 188 freshmen. Scholarships awarded for academics, leadership, music/drama, state residency.

**Application procedures. Admission:** Closing date 5/1 (postmark date). $40 fee, may be waived for applicants with need. Application may be submitted online. Admission notification on a rolling basis. Must reply by 6/1. **Financial aid:** Priority date 4/15; no closing date. FAFSA, institutional form required. Applicants notified on a rolling basis starting 2/15; must reply within 3 week(s) of notification.

**Academics. Special study options:** Accelerated study, distance learning, double major, dual enrollment of high school students, independent study, internships, study abroad, teacher certification program. **Credit/placement by examination:** AP, CLEP, IB, institutional tests. 45 credit hours maximum toward bachelor's degree. **Support services:** Reduced course load, remedial instruction, study skills assistance, tutoring, writing center.

**Majors. Biology:** General. **Business:** General, accounting, finance, human resources, international, management information systems, marketing, office management. **Communications:** General, journalism, organizational, radio/tv. **Computer sciences:** General. **Education:** General, biology, elementary, English, mathematics, middle, music, science, secondary, social science, special. **English:** English lit. **Health:** Premedicine. **History:** General. **Legal studies:** Prelaw. **Math:** General. **Parks/recreation:** Sports admin. **Philosophy/religion:** Religion. **Protective services:** Law enforcement admin. **Psychology:** General. **Public administration:** Social work. **Theology:** Bible, missionary, preministerial, religious ed, sacred music, youth ministry. **Visual/performing arts:** Dramatic, music performance, piano/organ, theater design, voice/opera. **Other:** Church Leadership.

**Most popular majors.** Business/marketing 28%, communications/journalism 8%, computer/information sciences 11%, psychology 10%, theological studies 29%.

**Computing on campus.** 89 workstations in library, computer center. Dormitories wired for high-speed internet access and linked to campus network. Commuter students can connect to campus network. Online course registration, online library, helpline, wireless network available.

**Student life. Freshman orientation:** Mandatory. Preregistration for classes offered. **Policies:** Religious observance required. **Housing:** Guaranteed on-campus for freshmen. Single-sex dorms, apartments, cooperative housing, substance-free housing available. $200 fully refundable deposit, deadline 6/1. **Activities:** Bands, campus ministries, choral groups, drama, international student organizations, literary magazine, music ensembles, musical theater, opera, radio station, student government, student newspaper, TV station, College Republicans, Habitat for Humanity, international justice mission, social work club, Christian Medical and Dental Association, student missions organization.

**Athletics.** NCCAA. **Intercollegiate:** Baseball M, basketball, cheerleading, golf M, soccer, tennis W, volleyball W. **Intramural:** Basketball, football (non-tackle), soccer, softball, tennis, volleyball. **Team name:** Fire.

**Student services.** Adult student services, career counseling, student employment services, financial aid counseling, health services, personal counseling, placement for graduates.

**Contact.** E-mail: admission@seuniversity.edu
Phone: (863) 667-5018 Toll-free number: (800) 500-8760
Fax: (863) 667-5200
Omar Rashed, Director of Admission, Southeastern University, 1000 Longfellow Boulevard, Lakeland, FL 33801-6034

## Stetson University
### DeLand, Florida
www.stetson.edu  CB member  CB code: 5630

- Private 4-year university
- Residential campus in large town
- 2,219 degree-seeking undergraduates: 4% part-time, 59% women, 5% African American, 2% Asian American, 9% Hispanic American, 3% international
- 1,420 degree-seeking graduate students
- 64% of applicants admitted
- SAT or ACT (ACT writing optional), application essay required
- 67% graduate within 6 years; 48% enter graduate study

**General.** Founded in 1883. Regionally accredited. **Degrees:** 477 bachelor's awarded; master's, first professional offered. **ROTC:** Army. **Location:** 20 miles from Daytona Beach, 40 miles from Orlando. **Calendar:** Semester, limited summer session. **Full-time faculty:** 236 total; 93% have terminal degrees, 10% minority, 42% women. **Part-time faculty:** 124 total; 60% have terminal degrees, 5% minority, 39% women. **Class size:** 59% < 20, 40% 20-39, 1% 40-49, less than 1% 50-99. **Special facilities:** Geological museum, greenhouse with growth chambers, digital arts laboratory.

**Freshman class profile.** 2,948 applied, 1,897 admitted, 558 enrolled.

| Mid 50% test scores | | | |
|---|---|---|---|
| SAT critical reading: | 500-600 | Rank in top quarter: | 74% |
| SAT math: | 480-590 | Rank in top tenth: | 35% |
| SAT writing: | 470-590 | Return as sophomores: | 81% |
| ACT composite: | 21-26 | Out-of-state: | 20% |
| GPA 3.50 or higher: | 64% | Live on campus: | 90% |
| GPA 3.0-3.49: | 24% | International: | 4% |
| GPA 2.0-2.99: | 12% | Fraternities: | 29% |
| | | Sororities: | 27% |

**Basis for selection.** High school record most important, followed by class rank, standardized test scores, and secondary school's recommendation. Extracurricular activities and particular talents or abilities also important. Interview recommended. Audition required of music majors. Portfolio recommended for art majors.

**High school preparation.** 14 units required. Required units include English 4, mathematics 3, social studies 2, science 3 and foreign language 2.

**2008-2009 Annual costs.** Tuition/fees: $30,216. Room/board: $8,436. Books/supplies: $1,000. Personal expenses: $1,620.

**2007-2008 Financial aid. Need-based:** 404 full-time freshmen applied for aid; 331 were judged to have need; 331 of these received aid. Average need met was 87%. Average scholarship/grant was $18,180; average loan $4,787. 71% of total undergraduate aid awarded as scholarships/grants, 29% as loans/jobs. **Non-need-based:** Awarded to 1,090 full-time undergraduates, including 315 freshmen. Scholarships awarded for academics, alumni affiliation, art, athletics, leadership, minority status, music/drama, religious affiliation, ROTC, state residency.

**Application procedures. Admission:** Priority date 3/15; no deadline. $40 fee, may be waived for applicants with need. Application may be submitted online. Admission notification on a rolling basis beginning on or about 12/1. Must reply by May 1 or within 3 week(s) if notified thereafter.

**Financial aid:** Priority date 3/15; no closing date. FAFSA, institutional form required. Applicants notified on a rolling basis.

**Academics. Special study options:** Accelerated study, combined bachelor's/graduate degree, double major, honors, independent study, internships, liberal arts/career combination, student-designed major, study abroad, teacher certification program, Washington semester, weekend college. **Credit/placement by examination:** AP, CLEP, IB, SAT, ACT, institutional tests. **Support services:** Reduced course load, study skills assistance, tutoring, writing center.

**Majors. Area/ethnic studies:** American, Latin American, Russian/Slavic. **Biology:** General, aquatic, biochemistry, molecular. **Business:** Accounting, business admin, entrepreneurial studies, finance, international, management information systems, management science, managerial economics, marketing. **Communications:** General. **Computer sciences:** General, computer science, web page design. **Conservation:** Environmental science. **Education:** Biology, chemistry, elementary, English, foreign languages, French, German, mathematics, music, secondary, social science, Spanish. **English:** English lit. **Foreign languages:** French, German, Spanish. **Health:** Clinical lab science, health services. **History:** General. **Liberal arts:** Humanities. **Math:** General. **Parks/recreation:** Exercise sciences, sports admin. **Philosophy/religion:** Philosophy, religion. **Physical sciences:** Chemistry, physics. **Psychology:** General. **Social sciences:** General, economics, geography, international relations, political science, sociology. **Visual/performing arts:** Art, dramatic, music performance, music theory/composition, piano/organ, stringed instruments, studio arts, voice/opera. **Other:** Music Technology.

**Most popular majors.** Business/marketing 34%, education 8%, psychology 6%, social sciences 8%, visual/performing arts 11%.

**Computing on campus.** 450 workstations in dormitories, library, computer center, student center. Dormitories wired for high-speed internet access and linked to campus network. Commuter students can connect to campus network. Online course registration, online library, helpline, repair service, student web hosting, wireless network available.

**Student life. Freshman orientation:** Mandatory, $100 fee. Preregistration for classes offered. Held 4 days prior to first day of classes. **Housing:** Guaranteed on-campus for all undergraduates. Coed dorms, single-sex dorms, apartments, fraternity/sorority housing, substance-free housing available. $200 nonrefundable deposit. Foreign language houses available. **Activities:** Bands, campus ministries, choral groups, dance, drama, film society, literary magazine, music ensembles, musical theater, opera, radio station, student government, student newspaper, symphony orchestra, Best Buddies, black student association, Caribbean club, Habitat for Humanity, Indian student association, Roots and Shoots, multicultural student council, College Democrats, College Republicans.

**Athletics.** NCAA. **Intercollegiate:** Baseball M, basketball, cross-country, golf, rowing (crew), soccer, softball W, tennis, volleyball W. **Intramural:** Badminton, baseball, basketball, bowling, football (non-tackle), golf, racquetball, soccer, softball, swimming, table tennis, tennis, volleyball, water polo. **Team name:** Hatters.

**Student services.** Career counseling, student employment services, financial aid counseling, health services, minority student services, personal counseling, placement for graduates. **Physically disabled:** Services for visually, speech impaired.

**Contact.** E-mail: admissions@stetson.edu
Phone: (386) 822-7100 Toll-free number: (800) 688-0101
Fax: (386) 822-7112
Deborah Thompson, Vice President for Enrollment Management and Campus Life, Stetson University, Campus Box 8378, DeLand, FL 32723

## Talmudic College of Florida
**Miami Beach, Florida**
**www.talmudicu.edu**　　　　　**CB code: 0514**

▸ Private 4-year rabbinical college for men affiliated with Jewish faith
▸ Very large city

**General.** Founded in 1974. Accredited by AARTS. **Location:** 3 miles from downtown. **Calendar:** Semester.

**Annual costs/financial aid.** Tuition/fees (2007-2008): $10,750. Room/board: $5,000. Books/supplies: $900. Need-based financial aid available to full-time and part-time students.

**Contact.** Phone: (305) 534-0750
Financial Aid Officer, 1910 Alton Road, Miami Beach, FL 33139

## Trinity College of Florida
**Trinity, Florida**
**www.trinitycollege.edu**　　　　　**CB code: 3975**

▸ Private 4-year Bible college affiliated with interdenominational tradition
▸ Commuter campus in small city
▸ 174 degree-seeking undergraduates: 32% part-time, 39% women, 6% African American, 2% Asian American, 7% Hispanic American, 1% international
▸ 69% of applicants admitted
▸ SAT or ACT (ACT writing optional), application essay, interview required
▸ 40% graduate within 6 years; 20% enter graduate study

**General.** Accredited by ABHE. **Degrees:** 36 bachelor's, 1 associate awarded. **Location:** 25 miles from Tampa. **Calendar:** Semester, limited summer session. **Full-time faculty:** 6 total; 83% have terminal degrees, 17% women. **Part-time faculty:** 17 total; 29% have terminal degrees, 29% women. **Class size:** 66% < 20, 34% 20-39.

**Freshman class profile.** 102 applied, 70 admitted, 31 enrolled.

| Mid 50% test scores | | | |
|---|---|---|---|
| SAT critical reading: | 400-640 | GPA 3.0-3.49: | 16% |
| SAT math: | 350-560 | GPA 2.0-2.99: | 68% |
| ACT composite: | 14-20 | End year in good standing: | 58% |
| GPA 3.50 or higher: | 16% | Return as sophomores: | 58% |
| | | Out-of-state: | 10% |

**Basis for selection.** Applicants must provide evidence of Christian character and witness, as well as academic ability largely based upon GPA and SAT/ACT scores.

**High school preparation.** 18 units required. Required units include English 4, mathematics 4, social studies 2, history 2, science 4 and foreign language 2.

**2008-2009 Annual costs.** Tuition/fees: $10,550. Room/board: $5,940. Books/supplies: $790. Personal expenses: $2,485.

**2007-2008 Financial aid.** All financial aid based on need. 29 full-time freshmen applied for aid; 25 were judged to have need; 25 of these received aid. Average need met was 82%. Average scholarship/grant was $3,237; average loan $2,035. 40% of total undergraduate aid awarded as scholarships/grants, 60% as loans/jobs.

**Application procedures. Admission:** Closing date 8/2 (receipt date). $25 fee, may be waived for applicants with need. Application may be submitted online. Admission notification on a rolling basis. **Financial aid:** Priority date 3/15, closing date 8/2. FAFSA, institutional form required. Applicants notified on a rolling basis.

**Academics. Special study options:** Accelerated study, double major, dual enrollment of high school students, honors, independent study, internships, weekend college. **Credit/placement by examination:** AP, CLEP, SAT, ACT, institutional tests. 24 credit hours maximum toward associate degree, 24 toward bachelor's. **Support services:** Reduced course load, remedial instruction, tutoring.

**Majors. Education:** Elementary. **Psychology:** Counseling. **Theology:** Missionary, pastoral counseling, preministerial, theology, youth ministry.

**Most popular majors.** Education 17%, theological studies 83%.

**Computing on campus.** 15 workstations in library, computer center. Dormitories wired for high-speed internet access and linked to campus network. Online library, repair service, wireless network available.

**Student life. Freshman orientation:** Mandatory. Preregistration for classes offered. Held 4 days before classes. **Policies:** Religious observance required. **Housing:** Guaranteed on-campus for all undergraduates. Single-sex dorms, special housing for disabled, apartments, substance-free housing available. $150 fully refundable deposit, deadline 7/1. **Activities:** Choral groups, drama, student government.

**Athletics.** NCCAA. **Intercollegiate:** Basketball, golf, soccer, volleyball W. **Intramural:** Basketball M, softball M, volleyball. **Team name:** Tigers.

**Student services.** Campus ministries, career counseling, financial aid counseling, personal counseling.

**Contact.** E-mail: admissions@trinitycollege.edu
Phone: (727) 569-1411 Toll-free number: (800) 388-0869
Fax: (727) 569-1410
Mark Sawyer, Director of Admissions, Trinity College of Florida, 2430
Welbilt Boulevard, Trinity, FL 34655-4401

## Universidad FLET
Miami, Florida
www.flet.edu

- Private 4-year university and Bible college
- Large city
- 303 degree-seeking undergraduates
- 115 graduate students

**General.** Accredited by DETC. **Degrees:** 31 bachelor's awarded; master's
offered. **Calendar:** Continuous. **Full-time faculty:** 5 total. **Part-time faculty:** 15 total.

**Basis for selection.** Open admission. **Homeschooled:** Letter of recommendation (nonparent) required.

**2007-2008 Annual costs.** Representative tuition plus fees for all programs leading to associate or bachelor's degree: $100 per credit hour. Costs
may vary by program.

**Application procedures. Admission:** No deadline. $20 fee, may be
waived for applicants with need. Application may be submitted online. **Financial aid:** No deadline.

**Academics. Special study options:** Distance learning. **Credit/placement
by examination:** CLEP.

**Majors. Theology:** Bible, theology.

**Student life. Freshman orientation:** Available. Preregistration for classes
offered.

**Contact.** E-mail: admisiones@flet.edu
Phone: (305) 378-8700 Toll-free number: (888) 376-3538
Fax: (305) 232-5832
Janet Ramirez, Director of Admission, Universidad FLET, 14540 SW 136th
Street, Suite 108, Miami, FL 33186

## University of Central Florida
Orlando, Florida                                    CB member
www.ucf.edu                                         CB code: 5233

- Public 4-year university
- Residential campus in very large city
- 41,051 degree-seeking undergraduates: 24% part-time, 54% women,
  9% African American, 5% Asian American, 13% Hispanic American,
  1% international
- 6,461 degree-seeking graduate students
- 50% of applicants admitted
- SAT or ACT with writing required
- 59% graduate within 6 years; 34% enter graduate study

**General.** Founded in 1963. Regionally accredited. **Degrees:** 8,630 bachelor's, 207 associate awarded; master's, doctoral offered. **ROTC:** Army,
Air Force. **Location:** 13 miles from downtown. **Calendar:** Semester, extensive summer session. **Full-time faculty:** 1,193 total; 79% have terminal
degrees, 22% minority, 38% women. **Part-time faculty:** 495 total; 38%
have terminal degrees, 13% minority, 54% women. **Class size:** 26% < 20,
39% 20-39, 9% 40-49, 19% 50-99, 6% >100. **Special facilities:** Solar energy center, simulation and training institute, research/education in optics
and lasers center, space education and research center, biomolecular sciences center, forensic science center, arboretum, observatory.

**Freshman class profile.** 26,312 applied, 13,251 admitted, 6,613 enrolled.

| Mid 50% test scores | | | |
|---|---|---|---|
| SAT critical reading: | 530-620 | Rank in top tenth: | 35% |
| SAT math: | 540-640 | End year in good standing: | 97% |
| SAT writing: | 510-600 | Return as sophomores: | 84% |
| ACT composite: | 23-27 | Out-of-state: | 7% |
| GPA 3.50 or higher: | 65% | Live on campus: | 70% |
| GPA 3.0-3.49: | 32% | International: | 1% |
| GPA 2.0-2.99: | 3% | Fraternities: | 8% |
| Rank in top quarter: | 77% | Sororities: | 6% |

**Basis for selection.** Two-thirds of admission offers made via review of
GPA and standardized test scores. One-third made via review of factors
such as grades, strength of coursework, essays, letters of recommendation,
special talents. Essay recommended. Audition required of music majors.
Portfolio recommended for art majors. **Homeschooled:** Provide detail about
coursework and teaching process.

**High school preparation.** 18 units required. Required units include English 4, mathematics 3, social studies 3, science 3 (laboratory 2), foreign
language 2 and academic electives 3.

**2007-2008 Annual costs.** Tuition/fees: $3,561; $17,763 out-of-state. Room/
board: $8,164. Books/supplies: $924. Personal expenses: $2,210.

**2006-2007 Financial aid. Need-based:** 4,305 full-time freshmen applied for aid; 3,338 were judged to have need; 3,271 of these received aid.
Average need met was 58%. Average scholarship/grant was $3,593; average
loan $2,670. 48% of total undergraduate aid awarded as scholarships/grants,
52% as loans/jobs. **Non-need-based:** Awarded to 10,873 full-time undergraduates, including 3,560 freshmen. Scholarships awarded for academics,
alumni affiliation, athletics, leadership, ROTC, state residency.

**Application procedures. Admission:** Priority date 1/1; deadline 5/1 (postmark date). $30 fee, may be waived for applicants with need. Application
may be submitted online. Admission notification on a rolling basis beginning on or about 10/1. Must reply by May 1 or within 3 week(s) if notified
thereafter. **Financial aid:** Priority date 3/1, closing date 6/30. FAFSA required. Applicants notified on a rolling basis starting 3/15; must reply within
3 week(s) of notification.

**Academics. Special study options:** Accelerated study, combined bachelor's/
graduate degree, cooperative education, distance learning, double major, dual
enrollment of high school students, ESL, honors, independent study, internships, study abroad, teacher certification program. Lead Scholars program.
**Credit/placement by examination:** AP, CLEP, IB, SAT, ACT, institutional
tests. 45 credit hours maximum toward bachelor's degree. **Support services:** Learning center, pre-admission summer program, reduced course load,
study skills assistance, tutoring, writing center.

**Honors college/program.** Requires separate application, admission based
on GPA, test scores, and class rank. Small general and specialized honors
courses, honors building, and residence hall available. Accepts approximately 700 freshmen in the fall.

**Majors. Biology:** General, bacteriology, biotechnology. **Business:** General, accounting, actuarial science, business admin, finance, hospitality admin, management information systems, managerial economics, marketing,
real estate, restaurant/food services, tourism/travel. **Communications:** General, advertising, journalism, media studies, radio/tv. **Computer sciences:**
General, information technology. **Education:** Art, early childhood, elementary, English, foreign languages, mathematics, music, physical, science, social science, special, trade/industrial. **Engineering:** Aerospace, civil, computer, electrical, environmental, industrial, mechanical, science. **Engineering
technology:** General, computer systems, electrical. **English:** English lit. **Foreign languages:** General, French, Spanish. **Health:** Audiology/speech pathology, clinical lab science, health care admin, health services, medical
radiologic technology/radiation therapy, medical records admin, nursing (RN),
predental, premedicine, prepharmacy, preveterinary, respiratory therapy technology. **History:** General. **Legal studies:** Paralegal. **Liberal arts:** Arts/
sciences, humanities. **Math:** General, statistics. **Philosophy/religion:** Philosophy, religion. **Physical sciences:** Chemistry, physics. **Protective services:**
Criminal justice, forensics. **Psychology:** General. **Public administration:**
General, social work. **Social sciences:** General, anthropology, economics,
political science, sociology. **Visual/performing arts:** Art, cinematography,
dramatic, multimedia, music performance, photography, studio arts.

**Most popular majors.** Business/marketing 27%, education 10%, engineering/engineering technologies 8%, health sciences 9%, liberal arts 6%,
psychology 9%.

**Computing on campus.** 3,147 workstations in library, computer center,
student center. Dormitories wired for high-speed internet access and linked
to campus network. Commuter students can connect to campus network.

Online course registration, online library, helpline, repair service, student web hosting, wireless network available.

**Student life. Freshman orientation:** Mandatory, $35 fee. Preregistration for classes offered. Ten sessions offered throughout spring and summer. 2-day event includes financial aid presentation, advising. **Housing:** Coed dorms, single-sex dorms, apartments, fraternity/sorority housing available. $250 nonrefundable deposit, deadline 3/1. Affiliated student residence housing. Students under guidance of university housing resident assistants considered part of on-campus housing. **Activities:** Bands, campus ministries, choral groups, drama, film society, international student organizations, literary magazine, music ensembles, Model UN, musical theater, radio station, student government, student newspaper, symphony orchestra, campus activities board, African American student union, orientation team, Hispanic American student association, Korean student association, Indian student association, Christian student association, Jewish student union.

**Athletics.** NCAA. **Intercollegiate:** Baseball M, basketball, cheerleading, cross-country, football (tackle) M, golf, rowing (crew) W, soccer, softball W, tennis, track and field W, volleyball W. **Intramural:** Badminton, baseball M, basketball, bowling, football (non-tackle), golf, racquetball, soccer, softball, tennis, volleyball, weight lifting, wrestling M. **Team name:** Golden Knights.

**Student services.** Adult student services, alcohol/substance abuse counseling, career counseling, student employment services, financial aid counseling, health services, legal services, minority student services, on-campus daycare, personal counseling, placement for graduates, veterans' counselor, women's services. **Physically disabled:** Services for visually, speech, hearing impaired.

**Contact.** E-mail: admission@mail.ucf.edu
Phone: (407) 823-3000 Fax: (407) 823-5625
Gordon Chavis, Assistant Vice President, University of Central Florida, Box 160111, Orlando, FL 32816-0111

---

## University of Florida
**Gainesville, Florida**
www.ufl.edu

**CB member**
**CB code: 5812**

- Public 4-year university
- Residential campus in small city
- 34,534 degree-seeking undergraduates: 6% part-time, 54% women, 10% African American, 8% Asian American, 14% Hispanic American, 1% international
- 15,715 degree-seeking graduate students
- 42% of applicants admitted
- SAT or ACT with writing, application essay required
- 79% graduate within 6 years

**General.** Founded in 1853. Regionally accredited. **Degrees:** 8,569 bachelor's awarded; master's, doctoral, first professional offered. **Location:** 70 miles from Jacksonville. **Calendar:** Semester, limited summer session. **Full-time faculty:** 2,229 total; 86% have terminal degrees, 17% minority, 30% women. **Part-time faculty:** 82 total; 72% have terminal degrees, 11% minority, 35% women. **Class size:** 39% < 20, 34% 20-39, 7% 40-49, 11% 50-99, 9% >100. **Special facilities:** Natural history museum, astronomical research facility, marine laboratory, wildlife sanctuary, citrus research center, bell carillon, pipe organ, center for performing arts, hyperbaric chamber, microkelvin laboratory, brain institute, engineering and industrial experiment station, art museum, nuclear reactor.

**Freshman class profile.** 24,126 applied, 10,158 admitted, 6,441 enrolled.

| Mid 50% test scores | | | |
|---|---|---|---|
| SAT critical reading: | 560-670 | **GPA 2.0-2.99:** | 1% |
| SAT math: | 580-690 | **Return as sophomores:** | 94% |
| ACT composite: | 25-29 | **Out-of-state:** | 5% |
| GPA 3.50 or higher: | 93% | **Live on campus:** | 77% |
| GPA 3.0-3.49: | 6% | **Fraternities:** | 20% |
| | | **Sororities:** | 21% |

**Basis for selection.** High school grades, academic course selection, SAT/ACT scores, extracurricular activities, awards, honors, recognitions, special talents and recommendations considered. **Homeschooled:** SAT subject test in math (level II-C), foreign language, science and social science required.

**High school preparation.** 18 units required. Required units include English 4, mathematics 3, social studies 3, science 3 (laboratory 2) and foreign language 2. English must include substantial writing. Mathematics must include algebra I and II, and geometry. Foreign language must be 2 units of same language.

**2007-2008 Annual costs.** Tuition/fees: $3,370; $17,150 out-of-state. Room/board: $7,020. Books/supplies: $940. Personal expenses: $3,220.

**2006-2007 Financial aid. Need-based:** 4,145 full-time freshmen applied for aid; 2,621 were judged to have need; 2,613 of these received aid. Average need met was 87%. Average scholarship/grant was $6,197; average loan $3,117. 58% of total undergraduate aid awarded as scholarships/grants, 42% as loans/jobs. **Non-need-based:** Awarded to 28,345 full-time undergraduates, including 6,369 freshmen. Scholarships awarded for academics, art, athletics, leadership, minority status, music/drama, ROTC, state residency.

**Application procedures. Admission:** $30 fee, may be waived for applicants with need. Application must be submitted online. Admission notification on a rolling basis. Must reply by May 1 or within 3 week(s) if notified thereafter. **Financial aid:** Priority date 3/15; no closing date. FAFSA required. Applicants notified on a rolling basis starting 4/1.

**Academics. Special study options:** Accelerated study, cooperative education, cross-registration, distance learning, double major, dual enrollment of high school students, ESL, exchange student, external degree, honors, independent study, internships, liberal arts/career combination, semester at sea, student-designed major, study abroad, teacher certification program, weekend college. **Credit/placement by examination:** AP, CLEP, IB, SAT, ACT, institutional tests. 30 credit hours maximum toward bachelor's degree. **Support services:** Learning center, reduced course load, study skills assistance, tutoring, writing center.

**Majors. Agriculture:** Agronomy, animal sciences, dairy, economics, food science, horticultural science, plant sciences, poultry, soil science. **Architecture:** Architecture, landscape. **Area/ethnic studies:** Asian. **Biology:** Bacteriology, botany, entomology, plant pathology, zoology. **Business:** General, accounting, finance, insurance, management science, marketing, real estate. **Communications:** Advertising, journalism, public relations. **Computer sciences:** General. **Conservation:** Forestry. **Education:** Agricultural, art, elementary, middle, music, special. **Engineering:** Aerospace, agricultural, chemical, civil, computer, electrical, environmental, materials, mechanical, nuclear, science, systems. **Engineering technology:** Construction, surveying. **English:** English lit. **Family/consumer sciences:** Family/community services. **Foreign languages:** Classics, French, German, linguistics, Portuguese, Russian, Spanish. **Health:** Audiology/speech pathology, health services, nursing (RN). **History:** General. **Math:** General, statistics. **Parks/recreation:** Exercise sciences, facilities management. **Philosophy/religion:** Judaic, philosophy, religion. **Physical sciences:** Astronomy, chemistry, geology, physics. **Protective services:** Criminalistics. **Psychology:** General. **Social sciences:** Anthropology, economics, geography, political science, sociology. **Visual/performing arts:** Art history/conservation, dance, dramatic, interior design, studio arts.

**Most popular majors.** Agriculture 6%, business/marketing 17%, engineering/engineering technologies 12%, health sciences 7%, psychology 6%, social sciences 14%.

**Computing on campus.** PC or laptop required. 1,000 workstations in library, computer center, student center. Dormitories wired for high-speed internet access and linked to campus network. Commuter students can connect to campus network. Online course registration, helpline, student web hosting, wireless network available.

**Student life. Freshman orientation:** Mandatory, $42 fee. **Housing:** Coed dorms, special housing for disabled, apartments, fraternity/sorority housing available. $200 partly refundable deposit. Pets allowed in dorm rooms. Undergraduate honor halls, quiet/study floors, faculty-in-residence program, first-year experience program, wellness floor, no-visitation by opposite sex floor available. **Activities:** Bands, choral groups, dance, drama, film society, literary magazine, music ensembles, musical theater, radio station, student government, student newspaper, symphony orchestra, TV station, over 500 student groups on campus.

**Athletics.** NCAA. **Intercollegiate:** Baseball M, basketball, cross-country, diving, football (tackle) M, golf, gymnastics W, soccer W, softball W, swimming, tennis, track and field, volleyball W. **Intramural:** Archery, badminton, basketball, bowling, cross-country, fencing, field hockey W, football (tackle) M, golf, handball, racquetball, sailing, soccer, softball, swimming, tennis, track and field, volleyball. **Team name:** Gators.

**Student services.** Adult student services, alcohol/substance abuse counseling, campus ministries, career counseling, student employment services, health services, legal services, on-campus daycare, personal counseling, placement for graduates, veterans' counselor. **Physically disabled:** Services for visually, speech, hearing impaired.

**Contact.** Phone: (352) 392-1365
Zina Evans, Assistant Provost and Director of Admissions, University of Florida, 201 Criser Hall-PO Box 114000, Gainesville, FL 32611-4000

## University of Miami
### Coral Gables, Florida
**www.miami.edu**

CB member
CB code: 5815

♦ Private 4-year university
♦ Residential campus in small city
♦ 9,997 degree-seeking undergraduates: 5% part-time, 54% women, 8% African American, 5% Asian American, 23% Hispanic American, 6% international
♦ 4,953 degree-seeking graduate students
♦ 38% of applicants admitted
♦ SAT or ACT (ACT writing optional), application essay required
♦ 76% graduate within 6 years

**General.** Founded in 1925. Regionally accredited. **Degrees:** 2,460 bachelor's awarded; master's, doctoral, first professional offered. **ROTC:** Army, Air Force. **Location:** 7 miles from downtown. **Calendar:** Semester, extensive summer session. **Full-time faculty:** 920 total; 86% have terminal degrees, 27% minority, 36% women. **Part-time faculty:** 408 total; 62% have terminal degrees, 30% minority, 43% women. **Class size:** 47% < 20, 41% 20-39, 5% 40-49, 5% 50-99, 2% >100. **Special facilities:** Cinema, observatory, palmetum, marine science research vessels, broadcasting studios, concert hall, arboretum, performing arts theater, film studios, sound stage.

**Freshman class profile.** 19,676 applied, 7,443 admitted, 1,991 enrolled.

| Mid 50% test scores | | | |
|---|---|---|---|
| SAT critical reading: | 580-680 | Rank in top quarter: | 89% |
| SAT math: | 600-690 | Rank in top tenth: | 65% |
| SAT writing: | 560-660 | Return as sophomores: | 90% |
| ACT composite: | 27-31 | Out-of-state: | 57% |
| GPA 3.50 or higher: | 88% | Live on campus: | 84% |
| GPA 3.0-3.49: | 10% | International: | 8% |
| GPA 2.0-2.99: | 2% | Fraternities: | 12% |
| | | Sororities: | 16% |

**Basis for selection.** Secondary school record, test scores, recommendations, essay very important. Math and science SAT Subject Tests required for dual-degree honors programs in medicine. Auditions required for music and theater arts applicants. Portfolio required for art BFA program and architecture. **Homeschooled:** Interview required.

**High school preparation.** 16 units recommended. Recommended units include English 4, mathematics 4, social studies 3, history 2, science 3 (laboratory 2) and foreign language 2.

**2008-2009 Annual costs.** Tuition/fees: $34,834. Room/board: $10,254.

**2007-2008 Financial aid.** **Need-based:** 1,219 full-time freshmen applied for aid; 945 were judged to have need; 945 of these received aid. Average need met was 84%. Average scholarship/grant was $20,226; average loan $4,412. 66% of total undergraduate aid awarded as scholarships/grants, 34% as loans/jobs. **Non-need-based:** Awarded to 3,684 full-time undergraduates, including 898 freshmen. Scholarships awarded for academics, athletics, music/drama, ROTC.

**Application procedures. Admission:** Priority date 11/1; deadline 1/15 (postmark date). $65 fee, may be waived for applicants with need. Application may be submitted online. Admission notification on a rolling basis beginning on or about 12/15. Must reply by May 1 or within 2 week(s) if notified thereafter. **Financial aid:** Priority date 2/1; no closing date. FAFSA required. Applicants notified on a rolling basis starting 3/1.

**Academics. Special study options:** Accelerated study, combined bachelor's/graduate degree, double major, dual enrollment of high school students, ESL, honors, independent study, internships, liberal arts/career combination, student-designed major, study abroad, teacher certification program, Washington semester, weekend college. Learning communities, International Exchange Students Program. **Credit/placement by examination:** AP, CLEP, IB, SAT, institutional tests. 60 credit hours maximum toward bachelor's degree. **Support services:** Learning center, pre-admission summer program, reduced course load, remedial instruction, study skills assistance, tutoring, writing center.

**Majors. Architecture:** Architecture. **Area/ethnic studies:** African-American, American, Latin American, women's. **Biology:** General, bacteriology, biochemistry, biophysics, marine. **Business:** Accounting, business admin, entrepreneurial studies, finance, human resources, international, management science, managerial economics, marketing. **Communications:** General, advertising, broadcast journalism, journalism, media studies, photojournalism, public relations, radio/tv. **Computer sciences:** Computer graphics,

computer science, data processing, information systems, security. **Conservation:** Management/policy. **Education:** Elementary, music, secondary, special. **Engineering:** Aerospace, architectural, biomedical, civil, computer, electrical, environmental, industrial, mechanical, science. **English:** Creative writing, English lit. **Foreign languages:** Classics, French, German, Spanish. **Health:** Athletic training, health services, music therapy, nursing (RN). **History:** General. **Interdisciplinary:** Neuroscience. **Legal studies:** General. **Liberal arts:** Arts/sciences. **Math:** General, applied, probability. **Parks/recreation:** Exercise sciences, sports admin. **Philosophy/religion:** Judaic, philosophy, religion. **Physical sciences:** Chemistry, geology, meteorology, oceanography, physics. **Psychology:** General. **Social sciences:** Anthropology, criminology, economics, geography, international relations, political science, sociology. **Visual/performing arts:** Acting, art, art history/conservation, ceramics, cinematography, design, dramatic, film/cinema, graphic design, jazz, music performance, music theory/composition, painting, photography, piano/organ, printmaking, sculpture, studio arts, theater arts management, theater design, voice/opera. **Other:** Dramatic/Theatre Arts & Stagecraft.

**Computing on campus.** 1,800 workstations in dormitories, library, computer center, student center. Dormitories wired for high-speed internet access and linked to campus network. Commuter students can connect to campus network. Online library, helpline, repair service, student web hosting, wireless network available.

**Student life. Freshman orientation:** Mandatory. Preregistration for classes offered. Three-day program in August. **Policies:** Student initiated and administered honor code designed to protect academic integrity by encouraging consistent ethical behavior among undergraduates. **Housing:** Guaranteed on-campus for all undergraduates. Coed dorms, special housing for disabled, apartments, fraternity/sorority housing, substance-free housing available. $250 nonrefundable deposit, deadline 5/1. Students may live with faculty members and their families in 5 residential colleges. **Activities:** Bands, campus ministries, choral groups, dance, drama, film society, international student organizations, literary magazine, music ensembles, Model UN, musical theater, opera, radio station, student government, student newspaper, symphony orchestra, TV station, 275 clubs and organizations.

**Athletics.** NCAA. **Intercollegiate:** Baseball M, basketball, cheerleading, cross-country, diving W, football (tackle) M, golf W, rowing (crew) W, soccer W, swimming W, tennis, track and field, volleyball W. **Intramural:** Badminton, basketball, football (non-tackle), golf, racquetball, soccer, softball, squash, table tennis, tennis, volleyball, water polo, weight lifting. **Team name:** Hurricanes.

**Student services.** Adult student services, alcohol/substance abuse counseling, career counseling, student employment services, financial aid counseling, health services, minority student services, on-campus daycare, personal counseling, placement for graduates, veterans' counselor, women's services. **Physically disabled:** Services for visually, hearing impaired.

**Contact.** E-mail: admission@miami.edu
Phone: (305) 284-4323 Fax: (305) 284-2507
Edward Gillis, Assistant Vice President for Enrollment Management/Executive Director of Admissions, University of Miami, 132 Ashe Building, Coral Gables, FL 33124-4616

## University of North Florida
### Jacksonville, Florida
**www.unf.edu**

CB member
CB code: 5490

♦ Public 4-year university
♦ Commuter campus in very large city
♦ 14,250 degree-seeking undergraduates: 27% part-time, 57% women, 10% African American, 5% Asian American, 7% Hispanic American, 1% international
♦ 1,644 degree-seeking graduate students
♦ 66% of applicants admitted
♦ SAT or ACT with writing required
♦ 45% graduate within 6 years

**General.** Founded in 1965. Regionally accredited. **Degrees:** 2,561 bachelor's, 409 associate awarded; master's, doctoral offered. **ROTC:** Naval. **Location:** 12 miles from downtown. **Calendar:** Semester, extensive summer session. **Full-time faculty:** 506 total; 94% have terminal degrees, 14% minority, 43% women. **Part-time faculty:** 317 total; 2% have terminal degrees, 14% minority, 60% women. **Class size:** 23% < 20, 53% 20-39, 13% 40-49, 7% 50-99, 5% >100. **Special facilities:** Nature trails, designated bird sanctuary, fine arts center.

**Freshman class profile.** 9,010 applied, 5,985 admitted, 2,297 enrolled.

| Mid 50% test scores | | Rank in top tenth: | 18% |
|---|---|---|---|
| SAT critical reading: | 510-610 | End year in good standing: | 88% |
| SAT math: | 510-610 | Return as sophomores: | 77% |
| ACT composite: | 20-23 | Out-of-state: | 3% |
| GPA 3.50 or higher: | 45% | Live on campus: | 65% |
| GPA 3.0-3.49: | 38% | International: | 1% |
| GPA 2.0-2.99: | 17% | Fraternities: | 36% |
| Rank in top quarter: | 47% | Sororities: | 28% |

**Basis for selection.** SAT or ACT score and high school GPA based on 19 academic units very important. High school academic courses (not including electives) used for calculating GPA. Summer program available for some students who do not meet fall admissions criteria; students admitted on probation. Audition required for music majors. **Homeschooled:** Required to pass all sections of GED.

**High school preparation.** 19 units required. Required units include English 4, mathematics 3, social studies 3, science 3 (laboratory 1), foreign language 2 and academic electives 4.

**2007-2008 Annual costs.** Tuition/fees: $3,491; $15,134 out-of-state. Room/board: $7,011. Books/supplies: $600. Personal expenses: $819.

**Financial aid. Non-need-based:** Scholarships awarded for academics, athletics, leadership, minority status, music/drama, state residency.

**Application procedures. Admission:** Priority date 11/1; deadline 4/1 (receipt date). $30 fee, may be waived for applicants with need. Application may be submitted online. Admission notification on a rolling basis beginning on or about 12/15. Must reply by 7/31. **Financial aid:** Priority date 4/1; no closing date. FAFSA required. Applicants notified on a rolling basis starting 3/15; must reply within 2 week(s) of notification.

**Academics. Special study options:** Accelerated study, combined bachelor's/graduate degree, cooperative education, distance learning, double major, dual enrollment of high school students, ESL, honors, independent study, internships, student-designed major, study abroad, teacher certification program, Washington semester, weekend college. Learning Communities. **Credit/placement by examination:** AP, CLEP, IB, SAT, ACT, institutional tests. 45 credit hours maximum toward bachelor's degree. **Support services:** Learning center, pre-admission summer program, reduced course load, study skills assistance, tutoring, writing center.

**Honors college/program.** Must be in top 10% of graduating class, have 3.75 GPA or higher, 1250 SAT (exclusive of Writing) or 28 ACT. 200 students admitted per year.

**Majors. Biology:** General. **Business:** Accounting, banking/financial services, business admin, finance, international, managerial economics, marketing, transportation. **Communications:** Media studies. **Computer sciences:** General. **Education:** Art, early childhood, elementary, mathematics, middle, music, physical, science, secondary, special, trade/industrial. **Engineering:** Civil, electrical, mechanical. **Engineering technology:** Construction. **English:** English lit. **Foreign languages:** Spanish. **Health:** Athletic training, health services, nursing (RN). **History:** General. **Interdisciplinary:** Biological/physical sciences, global studies. **Liberal arts:** Arts/sciences. **Math:** General, statistics. **Parks/recreation:** Sports admin. **Philosophy/religion:** Philosophy. **Physical sciences:** Chemistry, physics. **Protective services:** Criminal justice. **Psychology:** General. **Social sciences:** Anthropology, economics, political science, sociology. **Visual/performing arts:** Art, jazz, music performance, studio arts.

**Most popular majors.** Business/marketing 21%, communications/journalism 10%, education 11%, health sciences 14%, psychology 9%, social sciences 6%.

**Computing on campus.** 850 workstations in library, computer center, student center. Dormitories wired for high-speed internet access and linked to campus network. Commuter students can connect to campus network. Online course registration, online library, helpline, student web hosting, wireless network available.

**Student life. Freshman orientation:** Mandatory, $35 fee. Preregistration for classes offered. One-and-one-half day program held several times during summer. **Policies:** Students must abide by drug/alcohol policy, student code of conduct, model bill of rights and responsibilities. **Housing:** Coed dorms, special housing for disabled, apartments, fraternity/sorority housing available. $150 partly refundable deposit. Suite style housing available. **Activities:** Bands, campus ministries, choral groups, dance, drama, international student organizations, literary magazine, music ensembles, radio station, student government, student newspaper, TV station, African American student union, Jewish student union, InterVarsity Christian Fellowship, College Republicans, Jeffersonian Society, The New Left, Muslim student association, Filipino student association, Golden Key international honor society.

**Athletics.** NCAA. **Intercollegiate:** Baseball M, basketball, cross-country, diving W, golf M, soccer, softball W, swimming W, tennis, track and field, volleyball W. **Intramural:** Basketball, football (non-tackle), racquetball, soccer, softball, tennis, track and field, volleyball. **Team name:** Ospreys.

**Student services.** Adult student services, alcohol/substance abuse counseling, career counseling, student employment services, financial aid counseling, health services, minority student services, on-campus daycare, personal counseling, placement for graduates, veterans' counselor, women's services. **Physically disabled:** Services for visually, speech, hearing impaired.

**Contact.** E-mail: admissions@unf.edu
Phone: (904) 620-2624 Fax: (904) 620-2414
John Yancey, Director, University of North Florida, 1 UNF Drive, Jacksonville, FL 32224-7699

## University of South Florida

**Tampa, Florida**
**www.usf.edu**

**CB member**
**CB code: 5828**

- Public 4-year university
- Commuter campus in very large city
- 33,998 degree-seeking undergraduates: 28% part-time, 59% women, 13% African American, 6% Asian American, 13% Hispanic American, 1% international
- 8,827 degree-seeking graduate students
- 50% of applicants admitted
- SAT or ACT with writing required

**General.** Founded in 1956. Regionally accredited. Regional campuses in St. Petersburg, Sarasota/Manatee, and Lakeland, plus off-campus sites at a downtown center. **Degrees:** 6,743 bachelor's awarded; master's, doctoral, first professional offered. **ROTC:** Army, Naval, Air Force. **Location:** 10 miles from downtown. **Calendar:** Semester, extensive summer session. **Full-time faculty:** 1,729 total; 86% have terminal degrees, 23% minority, 39% women. **Part-time faculty:** 262 total; 84% have terminal degrees, 18% minority, 42% women. **Class size:** 42% < 20, 43% 20-39, 6% 40-49, 7% 50-99, 2% >100. **Special facilities:** Weather station, botanical garden, anthropology museum.

**Freshman class profile.** 25,216 applied, 12,502 admitted, 4,054 enrolled.

| Mid 50% test scores | | Rank in top tenth: | 27% |
|---|---|---|---|
| SAT critical reading: | 500-600 | End year in good standing: | 82% |
| SAT math: | 510-610 | Return as sophomores: | 81% |
| SAT writing: | 470-570 | Out-of-state: | 4% |
| ACT composite: | 22-26 | Live on campus: | 50% |
| GPA 3.50 or higher: | 70% | International: | 1% |
| GPA 3.0-3.49: | 26% | Fraternities: | 7% |
| GPA 2.0-2.99: | 4% | Sororities: | 6% |
| Rank in top quarter: | 63% | | |

**Basis for selection.** High school GPA and test scores most important. On sliding scale, higher grades compensate for lower test scores. Requirements higher for several degree programs. Audition required of music majors. Portfolio required of art majors.

**High school preparation.** 19 units required. Required units include English 4, mathematics 3, social studies 3, science 3 (laboratory 2), foreign language 2 and academic electives 3. Foreign language units must be in 1 language.

**2007-2008 Annual costs.** Tuition/fees: $3,456; $16,155 out-of-state. Room/board: $7,590. Books/supplies: $800.

**Financial aid. Non-need-based:** Scholarships awarded for academics, alumni affiliation, art, athletics, job skills, leadership, minority status, music/drama, religious affiliation, ROTC, state residency. **Additional information:** Deferred tuition payment plan available for late financial aid recipients.

**Application procedures. Admission:** Priority date 3/1; deadline 4/15 (postmark date). $30 fee, may be waived for applicants with need. Application may be submitted online. Admission notification on a rolling basis beginning on or about 10/1. Must reply by May 1 or within 2 week(s) if notified thereafter. **Financial aid:** Priority date 3/1; no closing date. FAFSA required. Applicants notified on a rolling basis starting 3/15; must reply within 4 week(s) of notification.

**Academics. Special study options:** Accelerated study, combined bachelor's/graduate degree, cooperative education, cross-registration, distance learning, double major, dual enrollment of high school students, exchange student, honors, internships, study abroad, teacher certification program,

Washington semester, weekend college. **Credit/placement by examination:** AP, CLEP, IB, SAT, ACT, institutional tests. **Support services:** Learning center, pre-admission summer program, tutoring.

**Majors. Area/ethnic studies:** African-American, American, women's. **Biology:** General, bacteriology, biomedical sciences. **Business:** General, accounting, business admin, finance, hospitality admin, international, management information systems, managerial economics, marketing. **Communications:** General. **Computer sciences:** General, information systems, information technology. **Conservation:** General. **Education:** General, art, business, drama/dance, early childhood, elementary, emotionally handicapped, English, foreign languages, learning disabled, mathematics, mentally handicapped, music, physical, science, social science, special, trade/industrial. **Engineering:** General, chemical, civil, computer, electrical, manufacturing, mechanical. **English:** English lit, speech/rhetoric. **Foreign languages:** Classics, French, German, Italian, Russian, Spanish. **Health:** Athletic training, audiology/speech pathology, clinical lab science, nursing (RN). **History:** General. **Interdisciplinary:** Biological/physical sciences, gerontology. **Liberal arts:** Arts/sciences, humanities. **Math:** General. **Philosophy/religion:** Philosophy, religion. **Physical sciences:** Chemistry, geology, physics. **Protective services:** Criminal justice. **Psychology:** General. **Public administration:** Social work. **Social sciences:** General, anthropology, criminology, economics, geography, international relations, political science, sociology. **Visual/performing arts:** Art, art history/conservation, dance, dramatic, music performance, studio arts.

**Most popular majors.** Biology 7%, business/marketing 23%, education 10%, engineering/engineering technologies 6%, English 7%, health sciences 6%, psychology 9%, social sciences 16%.

**Computing on campus.** 500 workstations in dormitories, library, computer center, student center. Dormitories wired for high-speed internet access and linked to campus network. Commuter students can connect to campus network. Online course registration, helpline, wireless network available.

**Student life. Freshman orientation:** Mandatory, $35 fee. Preregistration for classes offered. **Housing:** Coed dorms, single-sex dorms, special housing for disabled, apartments, cooperative housing, fraternity/sorority housing, substance-free housing available. $225 partly refundable deposit, deadline 8/1. **Activities:** Bands, campus ministries, choral groups, dance, drama, film society, literary magazine, music ensembles, musical theater, opera, radio station, student government, student newspaper, symphony orchestra, TV station, approximately 300 student organizations available.

**Athletics.** NCAA. **Intercollegiate:** Baseball M, basketball, cross-country, football (tackle) M, golf, sailing, soccer, softball W, tennis, track and field, volleyball W. **Intramural:** Badminton, basketball, bowling, cross-country, fencing, football (tackle) M, golf, handball, ice hockey, lacrosse, racquetball, rugby, sailing, soccer, softball W, swimming, table tennis, tennis, track and field, volleyball, wrestling M. **Team name:** Bulls.

**Student services.** Adult student services, career counseling, student employment services, financial aid counseling, health services, legal services, on-campus daycare, personal counseling, placement for graduates, veterans' counselor. **Physically disabled:** Services for visually, speech, hearing impaired.

**Contact.** E-mail: admissions@admin.usf.edu
Phone: (813) 974-3350 Fax: (813) 974-9689
J. Robert Spatig, Director of Admissions, University of South Florida, 4202 East Fowler Avenue, SVC 1036, Tampa, FL 33620-9951

---

## University of Tampa

Tampa, Florida
www.ut.edu

CB member
CB code: 5819

- Private 4-year university and liberal arts college
- Residential campus in large city
- 4,887 degree-seeking undergraduates: 8% part-time, 60% women, 6% African American, 2% Asian American, 10% Hispanic American, 8% international
- 697 degree-seeking graduate students
- 49% of applicants admitted
- SAT or ACT (ACT writing recommended), application essay required
- 54% graduate within 6 years; 55% enter graduate study

**General.** Founded in 1931. Regionally accredited. **Degrees:** 988 bachelor's, 2 associate awarded; master's offered. **ROTC:** Army, Naval, Air Force. **Location:** 20 miles from St. Petersburg, 70 miles from Orlando. **Calendar:** Semester, extensive summer session. **Full-time faculty:** 225 total; 85% have terminal degrees, 6% minority, 37% women. **Part-time faculty:** 255 total; 31% have terminal degrees, 17% minority, 57% women. **Class size:** 46% < 20, 52% 20-39, 1% 40-49, 1% 50-99. **Special facilities:**

Art and furniture museum, dance studio, art studio, marine science research vessel, marine science research laboratory.

**Freshman class profile.** 7,885 applied, 3,871 admitted, 1,177 enrolled.

| Mid 50% test scores | | | |
|---|---|---|---|
| SAT critical reading: | 490-570 | Rank in top tenth: | 21% |
| SAT math: | 490-580 | End year in good standing: | 81% |
| SAT writing: | 490-570 | Return as sophomores: | 72% |
| ACT composite: | 21-25 | Out-of-state: | 64% |
| GPA 3.50 or higher: | 30% | Live on campus: | 88% |
| GPA 3.0-3.49: | 47% | International: | 8% |
| GPA 2.0-2.99: | 23% | Fraternities: | 13% |
| Rank in top quarter: | 48% | Sororities: | 9% |

**Basis for selection.** Secondary school record, test scores most important. Recommendations, interview, talent/ability, character/personal qualities considered. Interview recommended. Auditions required of music and performing arts majors. Portfolio recommended for art majors. **Learning Disabled:** Dean of Students coordinates assistance for students with disabilities. Student responsible for requesting accommodations each term. Documentation required.

**High school preparation.** 18 units required. Required units include English 4, mathematics 3, social studies 3, science 3 (laboratory 2), foreign language 2 and academic electives 3.

**2007-2008 Annual costs.** Tuition/fees: $20,682. Room/board: $7,616. Books/supplies: $934. Personal expenses: $1,276.

**2007-2008 Financial aid. Need-based:** 795 full-time freshmen applied for aid; 592 were judged to have need; 592 of these received aid. Average need met was 78%. Average scholarship/grant was $7,221; average loan $4,529. 65% of total undergraduate aid awarded as scholarships/grants, 35% as loans/jobs. **Non-need-based:** Awarded to 2,220 full-time undergraduates, including 752 freshmen. Scholarships awarded for academics, alumni affiliation, art, athletics, leadership, music/drama, ROTC, state residency. **Additional information:** Early aid estimator service.

**Application procedures. Admission:** Priority date 11/15; deadline 5/1. $40 fee, may be waived for applicants with need. Application may be submitted online. Admission notification on a rolling basis beginning on or about 10/1. Must reply by May 1 or within 3 week(s) if notified thereafter. **Financial aid:** No deadline. FAFSA required. Applicants notified on a rolling basis starting 2/1; must reply within 3 week(s) of notification.

**Academics. Special study options:** Combined bachelor's/graduate degree, double major, dual enrollment of high school students, exchange student, honors, independent study, internships, liberal arts/career combination, study abroad, teacher certification program, Washington semester, weekend college. **Credit/placement by examination:** AP, CLEP, IB, SAT, ACT, institutional tests. 30 credit hours maximum toward associate degree, 30 toward bachelor's. **Support services:** Learning center, reduced course load, study skills assistance, tutoring, writing center.

**Majors. Biology:** General, biochemistry, marine. **Business:** Accounting, business admin, entrepreneurial studies, finance, international, managerial economics, marketing. **Communications:** General, public relations. **Computer sciences:** General, computer graphics. **Conservation:** Environmental science. **Education:** General, biology, elementary, English, mathematics, music. **English:** Creative writing, English lit. **Foreign languages:** Spanish. **Health:** Athletic training, nursing (RN), predental, premedicine, preveterinary. **History:** General. **Interdisciplinary:** Marine science, math/computer science. **Legal studies:** Prelaw. **Liberal arts:** Arts/sciences. **Math:** General. **Parks/recreation:** Exercise sciences, sports admin. **Physical sciences:** Chemistry, forensic chemistry. **Psychology:** General. **Social sciences:** General, criminology, economics, political science, sociology. **Visual/performing arts:** General, art, cinematography, commercial/advertising art, digital art, film/cinema, graphic design, music performance, music theory/composition. **Other:** Cultural studies, Electronic media, Financial and operations systems.

**Most popular majors.** Biology 7%, business/marketing 27%, communications/journalism 9%, parks/recreation 8%, psychology 6%, social sciences 16%.

**Computing on campus.** 528 workstations in dormitories, library, computer center, student center. Dormitories wired for high-speed internet access and linked to campus network. Commuter students can connect to campus network. Online course registration, online library, helpline, student web hosting, wireless network available.

**Student life. Freshman orientation:** Mandatory, $65 fee. Preregistration for classes offered. **Housing:** Coed dorms, special housing for disabled, apartments, substance-free housing available. $200 fully refundable deposit, deadline 5/1. **Activities:** Bands, choral groups, dance, drama, film society, international student organizations, literary magazine, music ensembles, Model UN, musical theater, radio station, student government, student newspaper, symphony orchestra, TV station, over 120 student organizations.

**Athletics.** NCAA. **Intercollegiate:** Baseball M, basketball, cross-country, golf M, rowing (crew) W, soccer, softball W, swimming, tennis W, track and field, volleyball W. **Intramural:** Basketball, football (non-tackle) W, football (tackle) M, golf, soccer, softball, tennis, volleyball. **Team name:** Spartans.

**Student services.** Adult student services, career counseling, student employment services, financial aid counseling, health services, personal counseling, placement for graduates, veterans' counselor.

**Contact.** E-mail: admissions@ut.edu
Phone: (813) 253-6211 Toll-free number: (888) 646-2738
Fax: (813) 258-7398
Barbara Strickler, Vice President for Enrollment, University of Tampa, 401 West Kennedy Boulevard, Tampa, FL 33606-1490

## University of West Florida

| Pensacola, Florida | CB member |
| uwf.edu | CB code: 5833 |

- Public 4-year university
- Commuter campus in small city
- 8,334 degree-seeking undergraduates: 29% part-time, 61% women, 10% African American, 5% Asian American, 5% Hispanic American, 1% Native American, 1% international
- 1,402 degree-seeking graduate students
- 70% of applicants admitted
- SAT or ACT (ACT writing optional) required
- 42% graduate within 6 years

**General.** Founded in 1963. Regionally accredited. **Degrees:** 1,720 bachelor's, 138 associate awarded; master's, doctoral offered. **ROTC:** Army, Air Force. **Location:** 10 miles from downtown. **Calendar:** Semester, extensive summer session. **Full-time faculty:** 332 total; 84% have terminal degrees, 15% minority, 41% women. **Part-time faculty:** 248 total; 23% have terminal degrees, 8% minority, 55% women. **Class size:** 36% < 20, 46% 20-39, 11% 40-49, 6% 50-99, 1% >100. **Special facilities:** Archaeology museum, nature preserve.

**Freshman class profile.** 3,371 applied, 2,369 admitted, 1,016 enrolled.

| Mid 50% test scores | | | |
|---|---|---|---|
| SAT critical reading: | 470-600 | Rank in top quarter: | 84% |
| SAT math: | 480-580 | Rank in top tenth: | 40% |
| ACT composite: | 21-25 | Return as sophomores: | 71% |
| GPA 3.50 or higher: | 53% | Out-of-state: | 10% |
| GPA 3.0-3.49: | 29% | Live on campus: | 51% |
| GPA 2.0-2.99: | 18% | Fraternities: | 5% |
| | | Sororities: | 5% |

**Basis for selection.** School achievement record, test scores, and school curriculum most important. **Homeschooled:** Transcript of courses and grades required. **Learning Disabled:** If requesting special consideration due to disability, student must provide documentation.

**High school preparation.** 19 units required. Required units include English 4, mathematics 3, social studies 3, science 3 (laboratory 2), foreign language 2 and academic electives 4. 4 academic electives includes courses chosen from list above. Social science includes history, economics, government, psychology, sociology and geography.

**2007-2008 Annual costs.** Tuition/fees: $3,351; $16,233 out-of-state. There is a $10 per course, per semester fee for online courses. Room/board: $7,255. Books/supplies: $1,000. Personal expenses: $2,000.

**2006-2007 Financial aid. Need-based:** 49% of total undergraduate aid awarded as scholarships/grants, 51% as loans/jobs. **Non-need-based:** Scholarships awarded for academics, alumni affiliation, art, athletics, minority status, music/drama, ROTC.

**Application procedures. Admission:** Closing date 6/30 (postmark date). $30 fee, may be waived for applicants with need. Application may be submitted online. Admission notification on a rolling basis beginning on or about 10/1. Must apply by January 1 for scholarship consideration. **Financial aid:** Priority date 3/1; no closing date. FAFSA, institutional form required. Applicants notified on a rolling basis starting 2/1.

**Academics.** Weekend program in nursing (BSN) available. **Special study options:** Cooperative education, distance learning, double major, dual enrollment of high school students, exchange student, honors, independent study, internships, study abroad, teacher certification program. Joint electrical engineering and computer engineering with University of Florida. **Credit/placement by examination:** AP, CLEP, IB, institutional tests. 30 credit hours maximum toward associate degree, 30 toward bachelor's. Up to 60 hours can be accepted, but academic department determines how credit counts toward degree. **Support services:** Learning center, study skills assistance, tutoring, writing center.

**Majors. Biology:** General, marine. **Business:** Accounting, business admin, finance, hospitality admin, management information systems, managerial economics, marketing. **Communications:** Media studies. **Computer sciences:** General, information technology. **Conservation:** Environmental science. **Education:** Art, early childhood, elementary, English, mathematics, mentally handicapped, middle, special, trade/industrial. **Engineering:** Computer, electrical. **Engineering technology:** General. **English:** English lit. **Health:** Community health services, nursing (RN). **History:** General. **Interdisciplinary:** Biological/physical sciences. **Legal studies:** Paralegal. **Liberal arts:** Humanities. **Math:** General. **Parks/recreation:** Health/fitness. **Philosophy/religion:** Philosophy. **Physical sciences:** Chemistry, oceanography, physics. **Protective services:** Criminal justice. **Psychology:** General. **Public administration:** Social work. **Social sciences:** General, anthropology, international relations, political science, sociology. **Visual/performing arts:** Art, dramatic, music performance, studio arts.

**Most popular majors.** Business/marketing 20%, communications/journalism 9%, education 14%, psychology 7%, security/protective services 6%, social sciences 7%.

**Computing on campus.** 200 workstations in dormitories, library, computer center, student center. Dormitories wired for high-speed internet access and linked to campus network. Commuter students can connect to campus network. Online course registration, online library, helpline, wireless network available.

**Student life. Freshman orientation:** Mandatory, $92 fee. Preregistration for classes offered. Two-day programs held throughout summer; includes parents. **Housing:** Coed dorms, apartments, fraternity/sorority housing, substance-free housing available. $225 deposit. **Activities:** Bands, campus ministries, choral groups, dance, drama, international student organizations, music ensembles, musical theater, radio station, student government, student newspaper, symphony orchestra, TV station, black student union, CLOVE, College Republicans.

**Athletics.** NCAA. **Intercollegiate:** Baseball M, basketball, cross-country, golf, soccer, softball W, tennis, track and field, volleyball W. **Intramural:** Badminton, bowling, fencing, football (non-tackle), handball, racquetball, soccer, swimming, table tennis, volleyball, water polo, weight lifting. **Team name:** Argonauts.

**Student services.** Alcohol/substance abuse counseling, career counseling, student employment services, financial aid counseling, health services, minority student services, on-campus daycare, personal counseling, placement for graduates, veterans' counselor. **Physically disabled:** Services for visually, speech, hearing impaired.

**Contact.** E-mail: admissions@uwf.edu
Phone: (850) 474-2230 Toll-free number: (800) 263-1074
Fax: (850) 474-3360
Richard Barth, Director of Admissions, University of West Florida, 11000 University Parkway, Pensacola, FL 32514-5750

## Warner Southern College

| Lake Wales, Florida | |
| www.warner.edu | CB code: 5883 |

- Private 4-year liberal arts college affiliated with Church of God
- Commuter campus in large town
- 1,025 degree-seeking undergraduates: 10% part-time, 61% women, 21% African American, 1% Asian American, 12% Hispanic American, 2% international
- 142 degree-seeking graduate students
- 60% of applicants admitted
- SAT or ACT (ACT writing optional), application essay required

**General.** Founded in 1968. Regionally accredited. Off-site locations including Lakeland Learning Center; Orlando Learning Center; Space Coast Learning Center in Melbourne; teaching sites in Arcadia, Haines City, Port St. Lucie, Titusville and Wauchula. **Degrees:** 290 bachelor's, 24 associate awarded; master's offered. **Location:** 60 miles from Tampa, 55 miles from Orlando. **Calendar:** Semester, limited summer session. **Full-time faculty:** 33 total; 64% have terminal degrees, 9% minority, 33% women. **Part-time faculty:** 106 total; 28% have terminal degrees, 58% women. **Class size:** 72% < 20, 27% 20-39, less than 1% 40-49.

**Freshman class profile.** 452 applied, 271 admitted, 148 enrolled.

| Mid 50% test scores | | | |
|---|---|---|---|
| SAT critical reading: | 360-530 | GPA 2.0-2.99: | 40% |
| SAT math: | 350-540 | Rank in top quarter: | 28% |
| ACT composite: | 14-23 | Rank in top tenth: | 10% |
| GPA 3.50 or higher: | 33% | Out-of-state: | 13% |
| GPA 3.0-3.49: | 27% | Live on campus: | 76% |
| | | International: | 3% |

**Basis for selection.** Two of the following required: 2.25 GPA, top 50% of class, or 18 ACT/870 SAT (exclusive of Writing). ACT Residual test administered to those without scores or with scores too low. Interview recommended. Audition required of music majors. **Homeschooled:** Statement describing homeschool structure and mission, transcript of courses and grades, interview, letter of recommendation (nonparent) required. GED, standardized tests, or portfolio required of applicants without transcripts.

**High school preparation.** Recommended units include English 4, mathematics 3, social studies 1, history 1, science 2, foreign language 2 and academic electives 2.

**2007-2008 Annual costs.** Tuition/fees: $13,860. One-time $50 security deposit for incoming freshmen living on campus. Room/board: $6,381. Books/supplies: $1,000. Personal expenses: $1,792.

**Financial aid. Non-need-based:** Scholarships awarded for academics, alumni affiliation, art, athletics, leadership, music/drama, religious affiliation, state residency.

**Application procedures. Admission:** No deadline. $20 fee, may be waived for applicants with need. Application may be submitted online. Admission notification on a rolling basis beginning on or about 9/15. **Financial aid:** Priority date 5/1; no closing date. FAFSA required. Applicants notified on a rolling basis starting 3/15; must reply within 2 week(s) of notification.

**Academics. Special study options:** Accelerated study, combined bachelor's/graduate degree, distance learning, double major, dual enrollment of high school students, ESL, independent study, internships, study abroad, teacher certification program, Washington semester. Online distance learning opportunities available for those interested in Organizational Management or Church Ministry. **Credit/placement by examination:** AP, CLEP, IB, SAT, ACT, institutional tests. **Support services:** Learning center, remedial instruction, study skills assistance, tutoring.

**Majors. Biology:** General. **Business:** Business admin. **Communications:** General, journalism. **Education:** Elementary, English, music, physical, science, social science, special. **English:** English lit. **History:** General. **Parks/recreation:** Exercise sciences, sports admin. **Psychology:** General. **Public administration:** Social work. **Theology:** Bible, sacred music, theology.

**Computing on campus.** 275 workstations in library, computer center, student center. Dormitories wired for high-speed internet access and linked to campus network. Commuter students can connect to campus network. Online library, helpline, wireless network available.

**Student life. Freshman orientation:** Mandatory. Preregistration for classes offered. Three-day program at start of fall semester. **Policies:** Student lifestyle agreement keeping with the moral and spiritual nature of the institution required. Religious observance required. **Housing:** Guaranteed on-campus for all undergraduates. Single-sex dorms, substance-free housing available. $50 nonrefundable deposit, deadline 8/15. **Activities:** Campus ministries, choral groups, drama, music ensembles, student government, student newspaper, star throwers, missions, Young Americans.

**Athletics.** NAIA. **Intercollegiate:** Baseball M, basketball, cheerleading, cross-country, golf, soccer, softball W, tennis, track and field, volleyball. **Intramural:** Basketball, football (non-tackle), soccer, volleyball W. **Team name:** Royals.

**Student services.** Alcohol/substance abuse counseling, career counseling, student employment services, financial aid counseling, health services, personal counseling, placement for graduates.

**Contact.** E-mail: admission@warner.edu
Phone: (863) 638-7212 Toll-free number: (800) 309-9563
Fax: (863) 638-7290
Jason Roe, Director of Admissions, Warner Southern College, 13895 Highway 27, Lake Wales, FL 33859

## Webber International University
**Babson Park, Florida**
www.webber.edu
CB code: 5893

- Private 4-year university and business college
- Residential campus in rural community

- 535 degree-seeking undergraduates: 11% part-time, 39% women, 23% African American, 1% Asian American, 9% Hispanic American, 15% international
- 60 degree-seeking graduate students
- 57% of applicants admitted
- SAT or ACT (ACT writing recommended) required
- 52% graduate within 6 years

**General.** Founded in 1927. Regionally accredited. **Degrees:** 105 bachelor's, 8 associate awarded; master's offered. **Location:** 50 miles from Orlando, 60 miles from Tampa. **Calendar:** Semester, limited summer session. **Full-time faculty:** 20 total; 70% have terminal degrees, 5% minority, 45% women. **Part-time faculty:** 24 total; 12% have terminal degrees, 12% minority, 38% women. **Class size:** 53% < 20, 47% 20-39. **Special facilities:** Audubon Society nature preserve.

**Freshman class profile.** 407 applied, 230 admitted, 120 enrolled.

| Mid 50% test scores | | | |
|---|---|---|---|
| SAT critical reading: | 380-500 | Rank in top quarter: | 12% |
| SAT math: | 420-520 | Rank in top tenth: | 2% |
| ACT composite: | 16-19 | End year in good standing: | 83% |
| GPA 3.50 or higher: | 25% | Return as sophomores: | 59% |
| GPA 3.0-3.49: | 30% | Out-of-state: | 3% |
| GPA 2.0-2.99: | 45% | Live on campus: | 87% |
| | | International: | 9% |

**Basis for selection.** GPA, standardized test scores very important followed by school record. Interview recommended. **Homeschooled:** Transcript of courses and grades required. Proof of graduation with 2.0 or better. **Learning Disabled:** Documentation of disability required in order to adequately assist student in studies.

**High school preparation.** 15 units recommended. Required and recommended units include English 4, mathematics 2-3, social studies 2, history 2, science 1-3, foreign language 1 and academic electives 4. 2 business courses recommended.

**2008-2009 Annual costs.** Tuition/fees (projected): $16,760. Room/board: $5,960. Books/supplies: $700. Personal expenses: $3,024.

**2007-2008 Financial aid. Need-based:** 105 full-time freshmen applied for aid; 71 were judged to have need; 71 of these received aid. Average need met was 62%. Average scholarship/grant was $12,702; average loan $3,550. 37% of total undergraduate aid awarded as scholarships/grants, 63% as loans/jobs. **Non-need-based:** Scholarships awarded for academics, alumni affiliation, athletics, leadership, state residency.

**Application procedures. Admission:** Priority date 5/1; deadline 8/1 (postmark date). $35 fee, may be waived for applicants with need. Application may be submitted online. Admission notification on a rolling basis beginning on or about 12/1. Must reply by May 1 or within 4 week(s) if notified thereafter. **Financial aid:** Priority date 5/1, closing date 8/1. FAFSA required. Applicants notified on a rolling basis starting 4/1; must reply within 4 week(s) of notification.

**Academics. Special study options:** Combined bachelor's/graduate degree, cooperative education, cross-registration, double major, dual enrollment of high school students, ESL, exchange student, internships, study abroad, weekend college. **Credit/placement by examination:** AP, CLEP, IB, institutional tests. 30 credit hours maximum toward associate degree, 30 toward bachelor's. No more than 6 semester hours credit awarded in each of 5 areas (English, humanities, science, social science, mathematics). **Support services:** Reduced course load, remedial instruction, tutoring.

**Majors. Business:** General, accounting, business admin, finance, hospitality admin, marketing. **Computer sciences:** General. **Legal studies:** Prelaw. **Parks/recreation:** Facilities management.

**Most popular majors.** Business/marketing 80%, parks/recreation 17%.

**Computing on campus.** 92 workstations in library, computer center. Dormitories wired for high-speed internet access. Commuter students can connect to campus network. Online library, helpline available.

**Student life. Freshman orientation:** Mandatory. 5-day program immediately preceding semester opening. **Housing:** Guaranteed on-campus for freshmen. Single-sex dorms available. $205 fully refundable deposit, deadline 8/28. **Activities:** Student government, student newspaper, service clubs, professional development organizations.

**Athletics.** NAIA. **Intercollegiate:** Baseball M, basketball, cross-country, football (tackle) M, golf, soccer, softball W, tennis, track and field, volleyball W. **Intramural:** Basketball, bowling, football (non-tackle), soccer, softball, table tennis, tennis. **Team name:** Warriors.

**Student services.** Adult student services, alcohol/substance abuse counseling, career counseling, student employment services, financial aid counseling, health services, personal counseling, placement for graduates, veterans' counselor, women's services.

**Contact.** E-mail: admissions@webber.edu
Phone: (863) 638-2910 Toll-free number: (800) 741-1844
Fax: (863) 638-1591
Julie Ragans, Director of Admission, Webber International University, 1201 North Scenic Highway, Babson Park, FL 33827-0096

## Yeshiva Gedolah Rabbinical College
### Miami Beach, Florida

▶ Private 4-year rabbinical college for men affiliated with Jewish faith
▶ Very large city

**General.** Accredited by AARTS. **Calendar:** Semester.

**Contact.** Phone: (305) 673-5664
1140 Alton Road, Miami Beach, FL 33139

# Georgia

## Agnes Scott College

Decatur, Georgia
www.agnesscott.edu

CB member
CB code: 5002

- Private 4-year liberal arts college for women affiliated with Presbyterian Church (USA)
- Residential campus in very large city
- 827 degree-seeking undergraduates: 1% part-time, 100% women
- 7 degree-seeking graduate students
- 45% of applicants admitted
- SAT or ACT (ACT writing recommended), application essay required

**General.** Founded in 1889. Regionally accredited. **Degrees:** 161 bachelor's awarded; master's offered. **ROTC:** Army, Air Force. **Location:** 6 miles from downtown Atlanta. **Calendar:** Semester, limited summer session. **Full-time faculty:** 84 total; 18% minority, 60% women. **Class size:** 75% < 20, 25% 20-39. **Special facilities:** Observatory, planetarium, art collection, electron microscope, 30-inch Beck telescope, center for writing and speaking, interactive learning center, multi-media classrooms.

**Freshman class profile.** 1,595 applied, 721 admitted, 218 enrolled.

| Mid 50% test scores | | | |
|---|---|---|---|
| SAT critical reading: | 570-680 | GPA 3.0-3.49: | 25% |
| SAT math: | 520-630 | GPA 2.0-2.99: | 4% |
| SAT writing: | 540-660 | Rank in top quarter: | 70% |
| ACT composite: | 24-29 | Rank in top tenth: | 36% |
| GPA 3.50 or higher: | 71% | Out-of-state: | 50% |
| | | Live on campus: | 96% |

**Basis for selection.** High school record, class rank, test scores, counselor recommendation, personal qualities, and extracurricular activities considered. First-time, first-year applicants are expected to have taken an SAT or ACT test by the December test date. Woodruff Scholars and transfer students must submit their scores by May 1st. Interview recommended. Audition required for music scholarship. **Homeschooled:** Statement describing homeschool structure and mission, interview required. SAT Subject Test scores must be submitted.

**High school preparation.** 16 units recommended. Recommended units include English 4, mathematics 3, social studies 2, history 2, science 2 (laboratory 2) and foreign language 2.

**2008-2009 Annual costs.** Tuition/fees: $29,060. Room/board: $9,850. Books/supplies: $1,000. Personal expenses: $1,000.

**2007-2008 Financial aid. Need-based:** 179 full-time freshmen applied for aid; 154 were judged to have need; 154 of these received aid. Average need met was 99%. Average scholarship/grant was $23,386; average loan $3,262. 80% of total undergraduate aid awarded as scholarships/grants, 20% as loans/jobs. **Non-need-based:** Awarded to 516 full-time undergraduates, including 181 freshmen. Scholarships awarded for academics, leadership, music/drama, religious affiliation, state residency. **Additional information:** Middle Income Assistance Grants available. Auditions required for music scholarship applicants.

**Application procedures. Admission:** Closing date 3/1 (postmark date). $35 fee, may be waived for applicants with need. Application may be submitted online. Admission notification on a rolling basis. Must reply by May 1 or within 2 week(s) if notified thereafter. Scholarship applicants must apply for regular admission by January 15. **Financial aid:** Priority date 2/15, closing date 5/1. FAFSA required. Applicants notified on a rolling basis starting 3/1; must reply by 5/1 or within 2 week(s) of notification.

**Academics.** Global Awareness and Global Connections programs offer opportunities to visit other regions of the world. Internships opportunity guaranteed; over 250 internships and externships available in Atlanta and other cities. Atlanta Semester allows Agnes Scott students to focus on women, leadership and social change. Language Across the Curriculum links foreign languages to other disciplines. Membership in International Student Exchange Program (ISEP) gives students opportunities to study at over 123 universities in 33 countries. **Special study options:** Accelerated study, combined bachelor's/graduate degree, cross-registration, double major, dual enrollment of high school students, exchange student, independent study, internships, semester at sea, student-designed major, study abroad, teacher

certification program, United Nations semester, Washington semester. Woodruff Scholars program for women beyond traditional college age, exchange program with Mills College, Atlanta Semester, exchange program with 123 institutions in 33 countries. **Credit/placement by examination:** AP, CLEP, IB, SAT, ACT, institutional tests. 32 credit hours maximum toward bachelor's degree. **Support services:** Learning center, reduced course load, study skills assistance, tutoring, writing center.

**Majors. Area/ethnic studies:** African, women's. **Biology:** General, biochemistry. **English:** Creative writing, English lit. **Foreign languages:** Classics, French, German, Spanish. **History:** General. **Math:** General. **Philosophy/religion:** Philosophy, religion. **Physical sciences:** Astrophysics, chemistry, physics. **Psychology:** General. **Social sciences:** Anthropology, applied economics, economics, international relations, political science, sociology. **Visual/performing arts:** Art, dance, dramatic, studio arts.

**Most popular majors.** Biology 7%, English 14%, foreign language 9%, history 8%, interdisciplinary studies 7%, psychology 13%, social sciences 25%, visual/performing arts 7%.

**Computing on campus.** 458 workstations in dormitories, library, computer center, student center. Dormitories wired for high-speed internet access and linked to campus network. Commuter students can connect to campus network. Online library, helpline, repair service, wireless network available.

**Student life. Freshman orientation:** Mandatory. Five days prior to the start of semester; includes signing of honor code, breakfast with college president, introduction to Big/Little Sister program. **Housing:** Guaranteed on-campus for all undergraduates. Apartments, substance-free housing available. College-owned houses for nontraditional students, theme houses, CHOICE housing (Choosing Healthy Options in a Community Environment) available. **Activities:** Bands, campus ministries, choral groups, dance, drama, international student organizations, literary magazine, music ensembles, musical theater, student government, student newspaper, symphony orchestra, TV station, religious life council, conservative forum, College Democrats, green Earth organization, Circle-K, African American student group, Asian cultural awareness association, Amnesty International.

**Athletics.** NCAA. **Intercollegiate:** Basketball W, cross-country W, soccer W, softball W, swimming W, tennis W, volleyball W. **Intramural:** Basketball W, cheerleading W, fencing W, field hockey W, football (non-tackle) W, soccer W, swimming W, tennis W, track and field W, volleyball W, weight lifting W. **Team name:** Scotties.

**Student services.** Adult student services, alcohol/substance abuse counseling, career counseling, student employment services, financial aid counseling, health services, minority student services, personal counseling, placement for graduates, women's services. **Physically disabled:** Services for visually, speech, hearing impaired.

**Contact.** E-mail: admission@agnesscott.edu
Phone: (404) 471-6285 Toll-free number: (800) 868-8602
Fax: (404) 471-6414
Stephanie Balmer, Dean of Admission, Agnes Scott College, Office of Admissions, Decatur, GA 30030-3797

## Albany State University

Albany, Georgia
www.asurams.edu

CB member
CB code: 5004

- Public 4-year university and liberal arts college
- Residential campus in small city
- 3,614 degree-seeking undergraduates: 14% part-time, 66% women, 94% African American
- 419 degree-seeking graduate students
- 23% of applicants admitted
- SAT or ACT (ACT writing optional) required
- 41% graduate within 6 years

**General.** Founded in 1903. Regionally accredited. **Degrees:** 396 bachelor's awarded; master's offered. **ROTC:** Army. **Location:** 190 miles from Atlanta. **Calendar:** Semester, limited summer session. **Full-time faculty:** 148 total; 66% have terminal degrees, 75% minority, 46% women. **Part-time faculty:** 98 total; 15% have terminal degrees, 72% minority, 51% women. **Special facilities:** Health and physical education complex.

**Freshman class profile.** 5,910 applied, 1,388 admitted, 593 enrolled.

| Mid 50% test scores | | | |
|---|---|---|---|
| SAT critical reading: | 430-490 | GPA 3.50 or higher: | 11% |
| SAT math: | 420-480 | GPA 3.0-3.49: | 27% |
| SAT writing: | 400-480 | GPA 2.0-2.99: | 61% |
| | | Return as sophomores: | 76% |

**Basis for selection.** Academic record, GPA and test scores very important. **Homeschooled:** Statement describing homeschool structure and mission, transcript of courses and grades required. School must be accredited. **Learning Disabled:** Students with documented disabilities should register with the Office of Counseling, Testing, and Student Disabilities.

**High school preparation.** 16 units required. Required units include English 4, mathematics 4, social studies 1, history 2, science 3 (laboratory 2) and foreign language 2. 2 foreign language in one language.

**2007-2008 Annual costs.** Tuition/fees: $3,470; $12,074 out-of-state. Room/board: $4,914. Books/supplies: $850. Personal expenses: $1,600.

**Financial aid. Non-need-based:** Scholarships awarded for academics, alumni affiliation, art, athletics, music/drama, ROTC.

**Application procedures. Admission:** Priority date 5/1; deadline 7/1. $20 fee, may be waived for applicants with need. Application may be submitted online. Admission notification on a rolling basis. **Financial aid:** Priority date 4/15, closing date 4/30. FAFSA required. Applicants notified on a rolling basis; must reply within 2 week(s) of notification.

**Academics. Special study options:** Cooperative education, cross-registration, distance learning, double major, dual enrollment of high school students, honors, independent study, internships, liberal arts/career combination, study abroad, teacher certification program, weekend college. 3+2 and 2+2 engineering program with Georgia Institute of Technology. **Credit/placement by examination:** CLEP, institutional tests. 45 credit hours maximum toward bachelor's degree. **Support services:** Learning center, remedial instruction, study skills assistance, tutoring, writing center.

**Majors. Biology:** General. **Business:** Accounting, business admin, management information systems, marketing. **Communications:** Journalism. **Computer sciences:** General, information systems. **Education:** Early childhood, elementary, mathematics, middle, music, physical, science, social science, special. **English:** English lit, speech/rhetoric. **Foreign languages:** Spanish. **Health:** Nursing (RN). **History:** General. **Math:** General. **Parks/recreation:** Health/fitness. **Physical sciences:** Chemistry. **Protective services:** Criminal justice. **Psychology:** General. **Public administration:** Social work. **Social sciences:** Political science, sociology. **Visual/performing arts:** Drawing. **Other:** Technology management.

**Computing on campus.** 400 workstations in dormitories, library, computer center, student center. Dormitories wired for high-speed internet access and linked to campus network. Online course registration, online library, helpline available.

**Student life. Freshman orientation:** Mandatory, $120 fee. Preregistration for classes offered. Held in January, May, June and August. **Housing:** Coed dorms, single-sex dorms, special housing for disabled, apartments, substance-free housing available. $150 partly refundable deposit. **Activities:** Bands, choral groups, dance, drama, music ensembles, musical theater, opera, radio station, student government, student newspaper, TV station, NAACP, Habitat for Humanity, history and political science club, HIV/AIDS peer educator, pre-alumni association, Florida Georgia Louis Stokes Alliance for Minority Participation, American Chemical Society, Kappa Kappa Psi band fraternity, Tau Beta Sigma band sorority.

**Athletics.** NCAA. **Intercollegiate:** Baseball M, basketball, cheerleading M, cross-country, football (tackle) M, softball W, tennis W, track and field, volleyball W. **Intramural:** Basketball M, football (tackle) M, track and field. **Team name:** Rams.

**Student services.** Career counseling, student employment services, financial aid counseling, health services, personal counseling, placement for graduates.

**Contact.** E-mail: admissions@asurams.edu
Phone: (229) 430-4646 Toll-free number: (800) 822-7267
Fax: (229) 430-3936
Albany State University, 504 College Drive, Albany, GA 31705-2796

---

## American InterContinental University
**Atlanta, Georgia**     **CB member**
**www.aiubuckhead.com**     **CB code: 2486**

- For-profit 4-year university
- Commuter campus in very large city
- 946 degree-seeking undergraduates
- 92% of applicants admitted
- Application essay, interview required

**General.** Founded in 1977. Regionally accredited. Additional campuses in Dunwoody, Los Angeles, South Florida, London, Dubai, Houston. **Degrees:**

224 bachelor's, 29 associate awarded; master's offered. **Calendar:** Quarter, extensive summer session. **Special facilities:** Sewing labortories, darkroom laboratories, interior design library, video production studios, learning center.

**Freshman class profile.** 256 applied, 236 admitted, 227 enrolled.

**Basis for selection.** Essay, results of personal interview, portfolio, high school GPA and references important. SAT or ACT recommended. Prefer that test scores be received prior to beginning of term since they are used for placement. **Homeschooled:** State high school equivalency certificate required.

**2007-2008 Annual costs.** Tuition/fees: $16,386. Costs vary by program. Room only: $4,800. Books/supplies: $1,500. Personal expenses: $960.

**Application procedures. Admission:** No deadline. $50 fee. Application may be submitted online. Admission notification on a rolling basis. **Financial aid:** Priority date 6/1; no closing date. FAFSA, institutional form required. Applicants notified on a rolling basis.

**Academics. Special study options:** Accelerated study, distance learning, double major, independent study, internships, study abroad. **Credit/placement by examination:** CLEP, IB, institutional tests. **Support services:** Learning center, pre-admission summer program, reduced course load, remedial instruction, study skills assistance, tutoring, writing center.

**Majors. Business:** Business admin, e-commerce, fashion. **Computer sciences:** Information systems. **Visual/performing arts:** Cinematography, commercial/advertising art, fashion design, interior design.

**Computing on campus.** Online library, helpline available.

**Student life. Freshman orientation:** Mandatory. Preregistration for classes offered. **Housing:** Apartments available. **Activities:** Student government, student newspaper, American Society of Interior Designers, fashion association, marketing association, graphic arts association, dressers club, portfolio club, cultural club.

**Student services.** Career counseling, student employment services, health services, personal counseling, placement for graduates, veterans' counselor.

**Contact.** E-mail: info@aiuniv.edu
Phone: (404) 965-5700 Toll-free number: (800) 955-2120
Fax: (404) 965-5701
Mike Betz, Vice President of Admissions, Atlanta Campuses, American InterContinental University, 3330 Peachtree Road, NE, Atlanta, GA 30326-1016

---

## Armstrong Atlantic State University
**Savannah, Georgia**     **CB member**
**www.armstrong.edu**     **CB code: 5012**

- Public 4-year university
- Commuter campus in small city
- 5,997 degree-seeking undergraduates: 34% part-time, 68% women, 22% African American, 2% Asian American, 3% Hispanic American, 4% international
- 777 degree-seeking graduate students
- 60% of applicants admitted
- SAT or ACT with writing required

**General.** Founded in 1935. Regionally accredited. **Degrees:** 768 bachelor's, 88 associate awarded; master's offered. **ROTC:** Army, Naval. **Location:** 250 miles from Atlanta. **Calendar:** Semester, extensive summer session. **Full-time faculty:** 291 total; 53% women. **Part-time faculty:** 200 total; 53% women. **Class size:** 42% < 20, 45% 20-39, 9% 40-49, 3% 50-99, less than 1% >100.

**Freshman class profile.** 2,186 applied, 1,306 admitted, 846 enrolled.

| Mid 50% test scores | | | |
|---|---|---|---|
| SAT critical reading: | 460-550 | GPA 3.0-3.49: | 47% |
| SAT math: | 450-550 | GPA 2.0-2.99: | 37% |
| ACT composite: | 19-22 | Return as sophomores: | 70% |
| GPA 3.50 or higher: | 16% | International: | 4% |

**Basis for selection.** 430 SAT math, 460 SAT verbal and 2.0 GPA required for regular admissions. Conditional admission possible with 1.8 GPA and lower test scores. **Homeschooled:** Applicants who meet all other freshmen admission requirements have option of validating requirements by passing SAT Subject Tests or enrolling in specified freshmen level courses and earning grade of C or higher.

**High school preparation.** Required units include English 4, mathematics 4, social studies 3, science 3 (laboratory 2) and foreign language 2.

**2007-2008 Annual costs.** Tuition/fees: $3,424; $12,028 out-of-state. Room-only housing apartment style for all students. Room only: $5,000. Books/supplies: $1,000.

**2006-2007 Financial aid. Need-based:** Average need met was 85%. Average scholarship/grant was $2,706; average loan $2,368. 37% of total undergraduate aid awarded as scholarships/grants, 63% as loans/jobs. **Non-need-based:** Scholarships awarded for academics, alumni affiliation, art, athletics, leadership, minority status, music/drama, state residency.

**Application procedures. Admission:** Closing date 6/29. $25 fee. Application may be submitted online. Admission notification on a rolling basis beginning on or about 1/1. **Financial aid:** Priority date 3/15; no closing date. FAFSA required. Applicants notified by 4/1; must reply by 4/15 or within 2 week(s) of notification.

**Academics. Special study options:** Combined bachelor's/graduate degree, cooperative education, distance learning, double major, dual enrollment of high school students, honors, independent study, internships, study abroad, teacher certification program, weekend college. **Credit/placement by examination:** AP, CLEP, IB, institutional tests. 30 credit hours maximum toward associate degree, 30 toward bachelor's. **Support services:** Learning center, reduced course load, remedial instruction, study skills assistance, tutoring, writing center.

**Majors. Biology:** General. **Computer sciences:** General, information technology. **Education:** Art, business, early childhood, elementary, English, health, learning disabled, mathematics, middle, music, physical, science, secondary, social science, special, speech impaired. **English:** English lit. **Foreign languages:** Spanish. **Health:** Clinical lab science, communication disorders, dental hygiene, health services, medical radiologic technology/radiation therapy, nuclear medical technology, nursing (RN), respiratory therapy technology, sonography. **History:** General. **Math:** Applied. **Physical sciences:** Chemistry, physics. **Protective services:** Police science. **Psychology:** General. **Social sciences:** Economics, political science. **Visual/performing arts:** Art, dramatic.

**Most popular majors.** Education 18%, health sciences 33%, liberal arts 12%, social sciences 7%.

**Computing on campus.** Dormitories wired for high-speed internet access. Online course registration, online library, helpline, student web hosting, wireless network available.

**Student life. Freshman orientation:** Available, $25 fee. Preregistration for classes offered. One day event prior to registration for spring and fall semesters. **Housing:** Apartments, substance-free housing available. $250 partly refundable deposit. **Activities:** Bands, choral groups, drama, international student organizations, music ensembles, musical theater, student government, student newspaper, symphony orchestra, NAACP, Baptist Student Union, Hispanic outreach and leadership, Cercle Francais, Newman Club, Wesley Foundation, College Democrats, College Republicans.

**Athletics.** NCAA. **Intercollegiate:** Baseball M, basketball, golf, softball W, tennis, volleyball W. **Intramural:** Badminton, basketball, bowling, cheerleading, football (non-tackle), golf, racquetball, soccer, softball, swimming, table tennis, tennis, volleyball. **Team name:** Pirates.

**Student services.** Adult student services, alcohol/substance abuse counseling, career counseling, student employment services, financial aid counseling, health services, minority student services, personal counseling, placement for graduates, veterans' counselor. **Physically disabled:** Services for visually, hearing impaired.

**Contact.** E-mail: adm-info@mail.armstrong.edu
Phone: (912) 927-5277 Toll-free number: (800) 633-2349
Fax: (912) 921-5462
Ana Edwards, Director of Admissions, Armstrong Atlantic State University, 11935 Abercorn Street, Savannah, GA 31419-1997

**General.** Founded in 1949. Regionally accredited. **Degrees:** 253 bachelor's, 173 associate awarded. **Location:** 12 miles from city center. **Calendar:** Quarter, extensive summer session. **Full-time faculty:** 103 total. **Part-time faculty:** 79 total. **Class size:** 47% < 20, 53% 20-39. **Special facilities:** Art gallery; camera video studios; video editing suites; digital audio studio; professional photography studios; traditional darkroom; digital darkroom; digital image capture systems; color-calibrated monitors, scanners, and printers.

**Freshman class profile.** 1,142 applied, 528 admitted, 365 enrolled.

**Out-of-state:** 32% **Live on campus:** 23%

**Basis for selection.** GPA or GED transcript; ACT, SAT, ASSET or COMPASS test scores; essay most important. Applicants for associate degree should have 2.0 GPA; 2.5 GPA for bachelor's degree. Otherwise, test scores or life experience considered. COMPASS test required but can be waived with 500 SAT math and verbal or 21 ACT. Portfolio required for national scholarship competition. **Learning Disabled:** Students with disabilities should submit current documentation of disability to disability services coordinator at least 6 weeks before accommodations will be needed.

**2008-2009 Annual costs.** Tuition/fees: $19,575. Students purchase starting kits for programs; costs vary depending on programs. Some programs require lab fees. Room only: $9,075. Books/supplies: $1,551.

**2006-2007 Financial aid. Need-based:** 31% of total undergraduate aid awarded as scholarships/grants, 69% as loans/jobs. **Non-need-based:** Scholarships awarded for academics, art, state residency.

**Application procedures. Admission:** No deadline. $50 fee. Application may be submitted online. Admission notification on a rolling basis. **Financial aid:** No deadline. FAFSA required. Applicants notified on a rolling basis starting 3/15.

**Academics. Special study options:** Accelerated study, cross-registration, distance learning, dual enrollment of high school students, honors, independent study, internships, study abroad. Academic remediation. **Credit/placement by examination:** CLEP, IB, institutional tests. 24 credit hours maximum toward associate degree, 48 toward bachelor's. **Support services:** Learning center, pre-admission summer program, reduced course load, remedial instruction, study skills assistance, tutoring, writing center.

**Majors. Communications:** Advertising. **Communications technology:** Animation/special effects. **Computer sciences:** Web page design, webmaster. **Personal/culinary services:** Culinary arts, restaurant/catering. **Visual/performing arts:** Cinematography, commercial photography, commercial/advertising art, graphic design, interior design, multimedia.

**Most popular majors.** Visual/performing arts 76%.

**Computing on campus.** 382 workstations in dormitories, library, computer center, student center. Dormitories wired for high-speed internet access. Online course registration, online library, helpline, repair service, student web hosting available.

**Student life. Freshman orientation:** Mandatory. Preregistration for classes offered. Held for 1-2 days the week prior to class start. **Housing:** Guaranteed on-campus for freshmen. Coed dorms, special housing for disabled, apartments available. $250 deposit. Apartment & roommate referral service. **Activities:** Dance, student government, student newspaper, Student Ambassador Program, HAVEN, international student association, student government association.

**Student services.** Adult student services, career counseling, student employment services, financial aid counseling, personal counseling, placement for graduates, veterans' counselor. **Physically disabled:** Services for visually, hearing impaired.

**Contact.** E-mail: aiaadm@aii.edu
Phone: (770) 394-8300 Toll-free number: (800) 275-4242
Fax: (770) 394-0008
Donna Scott, Vice President, Admissions, Art Institute of Atlanta, 6600 Peachtree Dunwoody Road, Atlanta, GA 30328

---

## Art Institute of Atlanta

Atlanta, Georgia **CB member**
www.aia.artinstitutes.edu **CB code: 5429**

- For-profit 4-year visual arts college
- Commuter campus in very large city
- 3,187 degree-seeking undergraduates
- 46% of applicants admitted
- Application essay, interview required

---

## Ashworth University

Norcross, Georgia
www.ashworthuniversity.edu **CB code: 3912**

- For-profit 4-year community college
- Very large city
- 3,200 degree-seeking undergraduates

**General.** Accredited by DETC. **Degrees:** 400 associate awarded; master's offered. **Calendar:** Semester. **Full-time faculty:** 20 total. **Part-time faculty:** 70 total.

**Basis for selection.** Open admission.

**2007-2008 Annual costs.** All-inclusive programs range from $1289 to $2285 per year.

**Academics. Credit/placement by examination:** CLEP.

**Majors. Business:** Business admin, e-commerce, marketing. **Protective services:** Criminal justice.

**Contact.** E-mail: info@ashworthcollege.com
Phone: (770) 729-8400 Toll-free number: (800) 223-4542
Fax: (770) 729-9389
Renee Mason, Registrar, Ashworth University, 430 Technology Parkway, Norcross, GA 30092-3406

---

## Atlanta Christian College
### East Point, Georgia
**www.acc.edu**                      CB code: 5029

- Private 4-year Bible and liberal arts college affiliated with Christian Church
- Residential campus in small city

**General.** Founded in 1937. Regionally accredited. **Location:** 10 miles from Atlanta. **Calendar:** Semester.

**Annual costs/financial aid.** Tuition/fees (2007-2008): $14,120. Room/board: $5,160. Books/supplies: $400. Personal expenses: $500. Need-based financial aid available to full-time and part-time students.

**Contact.** Phone: (404) 669-3202
Admissions Counselor, 2605 Ben Hill Road, East Point, GA 30344

---

## Augusta State University
### Augusta, Georgia                 CB member
**www.aug.edu**                      CB code: 5336

- Public 4-year liberal arts and teachers college
- Commuter campus in small city
- 5,479 degree-seeking undergraduates: 29% part-time, 64% women, 27% African American, 3% Asian American, 3% Hispanic American, 1% international
- 815 degree-seeking graduate students
- 53% of applicants admitted
- SAT or ACT (ACT writing optional) required
- 24% graduate within 6 years

**General.** Founded in 1925. Regionally accredited. **Degrees:** 555 bachelor's, 87 associate awarded; master's offered. **ROTC:** Army. **Location:** 145 miles from Atlanta. **Calendar:** Semester, extensive summer session. **Full-time faculty:** 234 total; 65% have terminal degrees, 15% minority, 51% women. **Part-time faculty:** 168 total; 21% have terminal degrees, 17% minority, 55% women. **Class size:** 42% < 20, 52% 20-39, 6% 40-49, less than 1% 50-99. **Special facilities:** History walk and museum, 18-hole golf course.

**Freshman class profile.** 2,363 applied, 1,243 admitted, 971 enrolled.

| Mid 50% test scores | | | | |
|---|---|---|---|---|
| SAT critical reading: | 440-540 | Return as sophomores: | | 64% |
| SAT math: | 450-540 | Out-of-state: | | 9% |
| ACT composite: | 17-21 | Live on campus: | | 14% |
| GPA 3.50 or higher: | 18% | International: | | 1% |
| GPA 3.0-3.49: | 31% | Fraternities: | | 1% |
| GPA 2.0-2.99: | 50% | Sororities: | | 1% |

**Basis for selection.** 430 SAT verbal or 17 ACT English, and 400 SAT math or 17 ACT math required. SAT Subject Tests required of GED recipients or graduates of non-accredited high schools.

**High school preparation.** 18 units required. Required units include English 4, mathematics 4, social studies 3, science 3, foreign language 2 and academic electives 2.

**2007-2008 Annual costs.** Tuition/fees: $3,404; $12,008 out-of-state. Books/supplies: $1,000. Personal expenses: $1,980.

**2006-2007 Financial aid. Need-based:** 609 full-time freshmen applied for aid; 502 were judged to have need; 467 of these received aid. Average scholarship/grant was $1,667; average loan $1,774. 44% of total undergraduate aid awarded as scholarships/grants, 56% as loans/jobs. **Non-need-based:** Awarded to 1,392 full-time undergraduates, including 322 freshmen. Scholarships awarded for academics, art, athletics, leadership, minority status, music/drama, ROTC, state residency.

**Application procedures. Admission:** Priority date 7/1; no deadline. $20 fee, may be waived for applicants with need. Application must be submitted on paper. Admission notification on a rolling basis. **Financial aid:** Closing date 6/1. FAFSA, institutional form required. Applicants notified on a rolling basis starting 3/1; must reply within 4 week(s) of notification.

**Academics. Special study options:** Cooperative education, cross-registration, distance learning, double major, dual enrollment of high school students, ESL, honors, independent study, internships, study abroad, teacher certification program. Paralegal certificate. **Credit/placement by examination:** AP, CLEP, institutional tests. 30 credit hours maximum toward associate degree, 30 toward bachelor's. **Support services:** Learning center, pre-admission summer program, reduced course load, remedial instruction, study skills assistance, tutoring, writing center.

**Majors. Biology:** General. **Business:** Accounting, business admin, finance, management information systems, marketing. **Communications:** General. **Computer sciences:** General. **Education:** Elementary, mentally handicapped, middle, music, physical, special. **English:** English lit. **Foreign languages:** French, Spanish. **Health:** Clinical lab science. **History:** General. **Math:** General. **Physical sciences:** Chemistry, physics. **Protective services:** Criminal justice. **Psychology:** General. **Public administration:** Social work. **Social sciences:** Political science, sociology. **Visual/performing arts:** Multimedia, music performance.

**Most popular majors.** Biology 6%, business/marketing 27%, communications/journalism 8%, education 17%, psychology 9%, social sciences 9%.

**Computing on campus.** 300 workstations in library, computer center, student center. Commuter students can connect to campus network. Online course registration, online library, helpline, student web hosting, wireless network available.

**Student life. Freshman orientation:** Available. Preregistration for classes offered. **Housing:** Apartments available. **Activities:** Bands, choral groups, drama, international student organizations, literary magazine, radio station, student government, student newspaper, black student union, Los Amigos Hispanos, Le Cercle Francais, Muslim student association, Circle K, chess club, anime club, College Conservatives, Baptist student union.

**Athletics.** NCAA. **Intercollegiate:** Baseball M, basketball, cross-country, golf, softball W, tennis, volleyball W. **Intramural:** Basketball M. **Team name:** Jaguars.

**Student services.** Adult student services, alcohol/substance abuse counseling, career counseling, student employment services, financial aid counseling, minority student services, personal counseling, placement for graduates, veterans' counselor. **Physically disabled:** Services for visually, hearing impaired.

**Contact.** E-mail: admissio@aug.edu
Phone: (706) 737-1632 Toll-free number: (800) 341-4373
Fax: (706) 667-4355
Katherine Sweeney, Registrar and Director of Admissions, Augusta State University, 2500 Walton Way, Augusta, GA 30904-2200

---

## Bauder College
### Atlanta, Georgia
**www.bauder.edu**                   CB code: 5070

- For-profit 4-year career college
- Commuter campus in very large city
- 806 degree-seeking undergraduates: 91% African American, 1% Asian American, 1% Hispanic American, 1% Native American
- Application essay, interview required
- 38% graduate within 6 years

**General.** Founded in 1964. Regionally accredited. Certified as a Pearson VUE Test Center. **Degrees:** 7 bachelor's, 200 associate awarded. **Location:** Downtown. **Calendar:** Quarter, extensive summer session. **Full-time faculty:** 21 total. **Part-time faculty:** 24 total.

**Freshman class profile.**

| | | | |
|---|---|---|---|
| Out-of-state: | 14% | Live on campus: | 50% |

**Basis for selection.** Open admission. Portfolio recommended for interior and fashion design majors. **Homeschooled:** GED recommended.

**2007-2008 Annual costs.** Cost of tuition for design majors in 18-21 month associate degree program is $28,195; books $2,300; $100 administrative fee, $350 student activity fee; $400 technology fee; $250 graduation fee. Tuition only for the associate degree programs varies from $19,580 -$28,195. Tuition for newly instituted bachelor of science in business program is $47,263. Books/supplies: $900. Personal expenses: $1,100.

**Financial aid.** All financial aid based on need.

**Application procedures. Admission:** No deadline. $100 fee. Application must be submitted on paper. Admission notification on a rolling basis. **Financial aid:** No deadline. FAFSA, institutional form required. Applicants notified on a rolling basis starting 7/15.

**Academics. Special study options:** Double major, internships. **Credit/ placement by examination:** AP, CLEP. **Support services:** Reduced course load, remedial instruction, tutoring.

**Majors. Business:** Business admin. **Protective services:** Law enforcement admin.

**Computing on campus.** 38 workstations in library, computer center, student center. Online library, helpline, wireless network available.

**Student life. Freshman orientation:** Mandatory. Preregistration for classes offered. **Housing:** Cooperative housing available. **Activities:** Student government, student newspaper.

**Student services.** Alcohol/substance abuse counseling, career counseling, services for economically disadvantaged, student employment services, financial aid counseling, personal counseling, placement for graduates.

**Contact.** E-mail: admissions@bauder.edu
Phone: (404) 237-7573 Toll-free number: (800) 241-3797
Fax: (404) 237-1619
E. Trey McCray, Director of Admissions, Bauder College, 384 Northyards Boulevard NW, Ste 190, Atlanta, GA 30313

---

## Berry College
Mount Berry, Georgia
www.berry.edu

CB member
CB code: 5059

- Private 4-year liberal arts college
- Residential campus in large town
- 1,719 degree-seeking undergraduates: 1% part-time, 66% women, 3% African American, 2% Asian American, 2% Hispanic American, 2% international
- 111 degree-seeking graduate students
- 70% of applicants admitted
- SAT or ACT (ACT writing recommended) required
- 61% graduate within 6 years

**General.** Founded in 1902. Regionally accredited. **Degrees:** 363 bachelor's awarded; master's offered. **Location:** 65 miles from Atlanta, 65 miles from Chattanooga, Tennessee. **Calendar:** Semester, limited summer session. **Full-time faculty:** 145 total; 83% have terminal degrees, 3% minority, 39% women. **Part-time faculty:** 50 total; 34% have terminal degrees, 2% minority, 44% women. **Class size:** 66% < 20, 33% 20-39, less than 1% 40-49, less than 1% 50-99. **Special facilities:** Museum, waterwheel, wildlife management area and refuge, equine center, dairy and beef cattle research center, on-campus elementary and middle schools, child development center, science center with 60-foot Foucault pendulum.

**Freshman class profile.** 1,813 applied, 1,278 admitted, 537 enrolled.

| Mid 50% test scores | | | |
|---|---|---|---|
| SAT critical reading: | 510-620 | Rank in top quarter: | 65% |
| SAT math: | 510-610 | Rank in top tenth: | 34% |
| ACT composite: | 23-29 | End year in good standing: | 75% |
| GPA 3.50 or higher: | 63% | Return as sophomores: | 76% |
| GPA 3.0-3.49: | 29% | Out-of-state: | 18% |
| GPA 2.0-2.99: | 8% | Live on campus: | 97% |
| | | International: | 1% |

**Basis for selection.** School achievement record and test scores most important. Class rank, recommendations and essays considered. Interview recommended; auditions required of music and theatre majors; portfolio recommended for art majors. **Homeschooled:** Transcript of courses and grades, letter of recommendation (nonparent) required. Must meet or exceed academic profile of previous freshman class. For 2008-2009 applicants: 3.0 GPA, 1100 SAT Critical Reading and Math or 23 ACT Composite.

**High school preparation.** 20 units required. Required units include English 4, mathematics 4, social studies 3, science 3 and foreign language 2. Algebra I, geometry or trigonometry, algebra II and fourth year higher than algebra II required.

**2007-2008 Annual costs.** Tuition/fees: $20,570. Room/board: $7,626. Books/supplies: $900. Personal expenses: $900.

**2007-2008 Financial aid. Need-based:** 446 full-time freshmen applied for aid; 322 were judged to have need; 322 of these received aid. Average need met was 84%. Average scholarship/grant was $13,083; average loan $3,995. 72% of total undergraduate aid awarded as scholarships/grants, 28% as loans/jobs. **Non-need-based:** Awarded to 1,053 full-time undergraduates, including 318 freshmen. Scholarships awarded for academics, art, athletics, minority status, music/drama. **Additional information:** Students are encouraged to work on-campus up to 20 hours per week.

**Application procedures. Admission:** Priority date 2/1; deadline 7/25 (receipt date). $50 fee, may be waived for applicants with need. Application may be submitted online. Admission notification on a rolling basis beginning on or about 11/1. Must reply by May 1 or within 4 week(s) if notified thereafter. **Financial aid:** Priority date 4/1; no closing date. Applicants notified on a rolling basis starting 3/15; must reply by 5/1 or within 4 week(s) of notification.

**Academics. Special study options:** Combined bachelor's/graduate degree, cooperative education, cross-registration, double major, dual enrollment of high school students, honors, independent study, internships, liberal arts/career combination, student-designed major, study abroad, teacher certification program. 3-2 nursing with Emory University, 3-2 engineering with Georgia Institute of Technology. **Credit/placement by examination:** AP, CLEP, IB, institutional tests. **Support services:** Remedial instruction, study skills assistance, tutoring, writing center.

**Majors. Agriculture:** Animal sciences. **Biology:** General, exercise physiology. **Business:** Accounting, finance, marketing. **Communications:** General. **Computer sciences:** Computer science. **Conservation:** Environmental science. **Education:** Early childhood, mathematics, middle, music, physical. **Engineering technology:** General. **English:** English lit. **Foreign languages:** French, German, Spanish. **Health:** Nursing (RN). **History:** General. **Math:** General. **Philosophy/religion:** Religion. **Physical sciences:** Chemistry, physics. **Psychology:** General. **Social sciences:** General, economics, international relations, political science. **Visual/performing arts:** Art, music management, theater arts management.

**Most popular majors.** Biology 7%, business/marketing 15%, communications/journalism 8%, education 11%, physical sciences 7%, psychology 11%, social sciences 11%.

**Computing on campus.** 140 workstations in library, computer center, student center. Dormitories wired for high-speed internet access and linked to campus network. Commuter students can connect to campus network. Online library, helpline, repair service, student web hosting, wireless network available.

**Student life. Freshman orientation:** Mandatory, $90 fee. Preregistration for classes offered. Sessions for students and parents in June, July, or August based on date of prepayment. Additional orientation 4 days prior to start of classes. **Policies:** Limited visitation hours. Dry campus. **Housing:** Guaranteed on-campus for freshmen. Coed dorms, single-sex dorms, apartments, substance-free housing available. $100 fully refundable deposit, deadline 5/1. Special-interest houses for women in math and science available. **Activities:** Bands, campus ministries, choral groups, dance, drama, international student organizations, literary magazine, music ensembles, Model UN, musical theater, student government, student newspaper, symphony orchestra, TV station, Amnesty International, Baptist student union, Wesley Foundation, Catholic student association, Habitat for Humanity, Canterbury club, campus outreach, Presbyterian student fellowship, Young Democrats, Republican club.

**Athletics.** NAIA. **Intercollegiate:** Baseball M, basketball, cheerleading, cross-country, equestrian W, golf, soccer, tennis, track and field, volleyball W. **Intramural:** Badminton, basketball, bowling, cross-country, football (non-tackle), golf, racquetball, soccer, softball, swimming, table tennis, tennis, volleyball, weight lifting. **Team name:** Vikings.

**Student services.** Alcohol/substance abuse counseling, career counseling, student employment services, financial aid counseling, health services, minority student services, on-campus daycare, personal counseling, placement for graduates, veterans' counselor, women's services. **Physically disabled:** Services for visually, hearing impaired.

**Contact.** E-mail: admissions@berry.edu
Phone: (706) 236-2215 Toll-free number: (800) 237-7942
Fax: (706) 290-2178
Timothy Tarpley, Associate Director of Admissions and Financial Aid, Berry College, PO Box 490159, Mount Berry, GA 30149-0159

## Beulah Heights University
### Atlanta, Georgia
www.beulah.org **CB code: 5082**

- Private 5-year university and Bible college affiliated with International Pentecostal Church of Christ
- Commuter campus in very large city
- 611 degree-seeking undergraduates
- 67 graduate students
- Application essay required

**General.** Accredited by ABHE. **Degrees:** 74 bachelor's, 20 associate awarded; master's offered. **Calendar:** Semester, extensive summer session. **Full-time faculty:** 11 total. **Part-time faculty:** 46 total.

**Basis for selection.** Open admission. Applicants must have accepted Christ, although personal denomination not considered. Pastoral and personal references required. Applicants pursuing GED may be accepted prior to completing GED, but must complete GED before college graduation. SAT or ACT recommended.

**2007-2008 Annual costs.** Tuition/fees: $6,530. Room only: $2,250.

**Application procedures. Admission:** No deadline. $35 fee. Admission notification on a rolling basis.

**Academics. Special study options:** Distance learning, double major, ESL, independent study, internships, weekend college. **Credit/placement by examination:** CLEP. **Support services:** Learning center, reduced course load, study skills assistance, tutoring, writing center.

**Majors. Theology:** Bible.

**Computing on campus.** Online course registration, online library available.

**Student life. Freshman orientation:** Mandatory. **Policies:** Religious observance required. **Housing:** Single-sex dorms, apartments, substance-free housing available. **Activities:** Student government.

**Student services.** Campus ministries, personal counseling.

**Contact.** E-mail: admissions@beulah.org
Phone: (404) 627-2681 ext. 104 Toll-free number: (888) 777-2422
Fax: (404) 627-0702
John Dreher, Director of Admissions, Beulah Heights University, 892 Berne Street SE, Atlanta, GA 30316

## Brenau University
### Gainesville, Georgia
www.brenau.edu **CB member**
**CB code: 5066**

- Private 4-year liberal arts college for women
- Residential campus in small city
- 851 degree-seeking undergraduates: 6% part-time, 100% women, 19% African American, 2% Asian American, 3% Hispanic American, 6% international
- 49 degree-seeking graduate students
- 40% of applicants admitted
- SAT or ACT (ACT writing optional) required
- 45% graduate within 6 years

**General.** Founded in 1878. Regionally accredited. Composed of 4 educational units: the Women's College (main campus), the Academy (women's secondary school), the Evening and Weekend College (coeducational), and the Online College. Performing arts and nursing daytime programs are coeducational. Male students may enroll in several Women's College programs through the Evening and Weekend College. **Degrees:** 123 bachelor's awarded; master's offered. **Location:** 45 miles from Atlanta. **Calendar:** Semester, limited summer session. **Full-time faculty:** 70 total; 73% have terminal degrees, 9% minority, 61% women. **Part-time faculty:** 44 total; 27% have terminal degrees, 9% minority, 68% women. **Class size:** 72% <20, 27% 20-39, less than 1% 40-49, less than 1% 50-99. **Special facilities:** Visual arts center, performing arts center, regional history museum, vintage clothing museum.

**Freshman class profile.** 2,687 applied, 1,071 admitted, 226 enrolled.

| Mid 50% test scores | | | |
|---|---|---|---|
| SAT critical reading: | 460-550 | Out-of-state: | 15% |
| SAT math: | 440-540 | Live on campus: | 83% |
| ACT composite: | 19-24 | International: | 3% |
| Return as sophomores: | 62% | Sororities: | 21% |

**Basis for selection.** Course selection most important, followed by GPA and standardized test scores. Admission policies for Evening/Weekend College differ from Women's College. SAT or ACT used for placement into math courses. If student has been out of high school for over 7 years, institutional placement test may be substituted. Auditions required of performing arts majors. **Homeschooled:** Transcript of courses and grades required. Interview required. **Learning Disabled:** Learning disability must be professionally diagnosed.

**High school preparation.** Must meet state of Georgia graduation requirements.

**2007-2008 Annual costs.** Tuition/fees: $17,700. Room/board: $8,950. Books/supplies: $900. Personal expenses: $1,300.

**2007-2008 Financial aid. Need-based:** 186 full-time freshmen applied for aid; 168 were judged to have need; 168 of these received aid. Average need met was 81%. Average scholarship/grant was $14,631; average loan $3,251. 78% of total undergraduate aid awarded as scholarships/grants, 22% as loans/jobs. **Non-need-based:** Awarded to 256 full-time undergraduates, including 73 freshmen. Scholarships awarded for academics, art, athletics, leadership, minority status, music/drama.

**Application procedures. Admission:** No deadline. $35 fee, may be waived for applicants with need. Application may be submitted online. Admission notification on a rolling basis beginning on or about 10/1. **Financial aid:** Priority date 4/1; no closing date. FAFSA required. Applicants notified on a rolling basis starting 3/1.

**Academics.** Leadership curriculum available. **Special study options:** Combined bachelor's/graduate degree, cross-registration, distance learning, double major, dual enrollment of high school students, ESL, exchange student, honors, independent study, internships, student-designed major, study abroad, teacher certification program, weekend college. **Credit/placement by examination:** AP, CLEP, IB, SAT, ACT, institutional tests. 27 credit hours maximum toward bachelor's degree. Total of 27 hours for non-traditional students allowed. **Support services:** Learning center, pre-admission summer program, reduced course load, remedial instruction, study skills assistance, tutoring, writing center.

**Majors. Biology:** General, environmental. **Business:** Accounting, business admin, fashion, marketing. **Communications:** Media studies. **Education:** Art, drama/dance, elementary, mentally handicapped, middle, music, special. **English:** English lit. **Health:** Nursing (RN). **History:** General. **Legal studies:** Prelaw. **Liberal arts:** Arts/sciences. **Psychology:** General. **Social sciences:** International relations. **Visual/performing arts:** Arts management, dance, dramatic, fashion design, graphic design, interior design, music performance, studio arts.

**Most popular majors.** Business/marketing 10%, education 19%, health sciences 23%, psychology 6%, visual/performing arts 28%.

**Computing on campus.** 130 workstations in dormitories, library, computer center, student center. Dormitories wired for high-speed internet access and linked to campus network. Online course registration, online library, helpline, wireless network available.

**Student life. Freshman orientation:** Mandatory. Preregistration for classes offered. **Policies:** Single students under 22 years of age required to live on campus unless living with family or legal guardian; alcohol-free campus; required convocation attendance. **Housing:** Guaranteed on-campus for all undergraduates. Special housing for disabled, apartments, fraternity/sorority housing, substance-free housing available. $350 nonrefundable deposit. **Activities:** Concert band, campus ministries, choral groups, dance, drama, international student organizations, literary magazine, music ensembles, musical theater, opera, radio station, student government, student newspaper, TV station, fellowship association, Fellowship of Christian Athletes, College Republicans, College Democrats, Circle K International, Silhouettes, Eco-Friends, volunteer center, student alumni council, Greek letter service organizations.

**Athletics.** NAIA. **Intercollegiate:** Basketball W, cross-country W, soccer W, softball W, swimming W, tennis W, volleyball W. **Team name:** Golden Tigers.

**Student services.** Alcohol/substance abuse counseling, career counseling, student employment services, financial aid counseling, health services, minority student services, personal counseling, placement for graduates, women's services. **Physically disabled:** Services for visually, speech, hearing impaired. **Learning disabled:** Comprehensive services available.

**Contact.** E-mail: wcadmissions@brenau.edu
Phone: (770) 534-6100 Toll-free number: (800) 252-5119
Fax: (770) 538-4701
Christina White, Associate Vice President of Enrollment Management, Brenau University, 500 Washington Street SE, Gainesville, GA 30501

## Brewton-Parker College
**Mount Vernon, Georgia**
www.bpc.edu

CB member
CB code: 5068

- Private 4-year liberal arts college affiliated with Southern Baptist Convention
- Residential campus in small town
- 1,030 degree-seeking undergraduates: 30% part-time, 62% women, 25% African American, 1% Asian American, 2% Hispanic American, 1% international
- 100% of applicants admitted
- SAT or ACT (ACT writing optional) required

**General.** Founded in 1904. Regionally accredited. **Degrees:** 189 bachelor's, 24 associate awarded. **Location:** 90 miles from Macon and Savannah. **Calendar:** Semester, limited summer session. **Full-time faculty:** 56 total; 64% have terminal degrees, 12% minority, 38% women. **Part-time faculty:** 190 total. **Class size:** 87% < 20, 13% 20-39. **Special facilities:** Living history museum; recital hall, greenhouse, nature trail.

**Freshman class profile.** 387 applied, 387 admitted, 178 enrolled.

| Mid 50% test scores | | Rank in top quarter: | 23% |
|---|---|---|---|
| SAT critical reading: | 400-510 | Rank in top tenth: | 17% |
| SAT math: | 400-520 | Return as sophomores: | 49% |
| SAT writing: | 320-500 | Out-of-state: | 4% |
| ACT composite: | 15-20 | Live on campus: | 46% |

**Basis for selection.** Students evaluated on SAT/ACT scores and high school performance. Not required for non-traditional students. Audition and interview required of music and drama majors.

**High school preparation.** 13 units required. Required units include English 4, mathematics 3, social studies 3 and science 3.

**2007-2008 Annual costs.** Tuition/fees: $14,050. $130 per-credit fee for applied music surcharge. Room/board: $6,070. Books/supplies: $1,000. Personal expenses: $2,000.

**2006-2007 Financial aid. Need-based:** Average scholarship/grant was $8,766; average loan $2,131. 56% of total undergraduate aid awarded as scholarships/grants, 44% as loans/jobs. **Non-need-based:** Scholarships awarded for academics, athletics, music/drama, religious affiliation, state residency.

**Application procedures. Admission:** No deadline. $25 fee. Application may be submitted online. Admission notification on a rolling basis beginning on or about 9/1. **Financial aid:** Priority date 5/1; no closing date. FAFSA required. Applicants notified on a rolling basis starting 2/27; must reply within 2 week(s) of notification.

**Academics. Special study options:** Accelerated study, double major, dual enrollment of high school students, exchange student, external degree, honors, independent study, internships, teacher certification program. **Credit/placement by examination:** AP, CLEP, SAT, ACT. 30 credit hours maximum toward associate degree, 30 toward bachelor's. **Support services:** Learning center, reduced course load, remedial instruction, study skills assistance, tutoring, writing center.

**Majors. Biology:** General. **Business:** Accounting, business admin. **Communications:** General. **Computer sciences:** Information systems. **Education:** General, biology, early childhood, English, history, mathematics, middle, music, physical, science, secondary. **English:** English lit. **Foreign languages:** Spanish. **History:** General. **Legal studies:** Prelaw. **Math:** General. **Parks/recreation:** Health/fitness. **Philosophy/religion:** Religion. **Psychology:** General. **Social sciences:** General, political science, sociology. **Theology:** Theology. **Visual/performing arts:** Music performance.

**Most popular majors.** Business/marketing 15%, education 27%, liberal arts 11%, parks/recreation 9%, philosophy/religious studies 6%, psychology 7%, public administration/social services 7%, social sciences 7%.

**Computing on campus.** 104 workstations in library, computer center. Dormitories wired for high-speed internet access. Online course registration, online library, helpline, wireless network available.

**Student life. Freshman orientation:** Available, $100 fee. Preregistration for classes offered. Held 4 days prior to start of classes. **Policies:** All day students required to live on campus except seniors, students residing with parents, students 22 or older. Religious observance required. **Housing:** Guaranteed on-campus for freshmen. Single-sex dorms available. $100 nonrefundable deposit. **Activities:** Bands, campus ministries, choral groups, drama, film society, literary magazine, music ensembles, musical theater, student government, student newspaper, ministerial association, Fellowship of Christian Athletes, Christian fraternities and sororities, Rotaract, Circle K, student activities council.

**Athletics. NAIA. Intercollegiate:** Baseball M, basketball, cheerleading, soccer, softball W, volleyball W. **Intramural:** Basketball, football (nontackle), softball, table tennis, tennis, volleyball. **Team name:** Barons.

**Student services.** Alcohol/substance abuse counseling, career counseling, student employment services, financial aid counseling, health services, personal counseling, placement for graduates, veterans' counselor. **Physically disabled:** Services for visually, speech, hearing impaired.

**Contact.** E-mail: admissions@bpc.edu
Phone: (912) 583-2241 ext. 265 Toll-free number: (800) 342-1087 ext. 265
Fax: (912) 583-3598
Kenneth Wuerzberger, Director of Admissions, Brewton-Parker College, Brewton-Parker College # 2011, Mount Vernon, GA 30445

## Carver Bible College
**Atlanta, Georgia**
www.carver.edu

- Private 4-year Bible college
- Commuter campus in very large city
- 134 degree-seeking undergraduates

**General.** Accredited by ABHE. **Degrees:** 12 bachelor's, 10 associate awarded. **Calendar:** Semester, limited summer session. **Full-time faculty:** 3 total; 67% have terminal degrees. **Part-time faculty:** 12 total.

**Basis for selection.** Applicants assessed for admittance based on academic record, moral character and personal testimony of faith. Students who cannot meet the general entrance requirements may be given conditional admittance for probationary period.

**2007-2008 Annual costs.** Tuition/fees: $6,000.

**Application procedures. Admission:** No deadline.

**Academics. Special study options:** Distance learning, independent study. **Credit/placement by examination:** CLEP. **Support services:** Learning center.

**Majors. Theology:** Bible.

**Computing on campus.** Wireless network available.

**Student life. Freshman orientation:** Mandatory.

**Contact.** Phone: (404) 527-4520 Fax: (404) 527-4524
Patsy Singh, Director of Admissions, Carver Bible College, 3837 Cascade Road, SW, Atlanta, GA 30313

## Clark Atlanta University
**Atlanta, Georgia**
www.cau.edu

CB member
CB code: 5110

- Private 4-year university affiliated with United Methodist Church
- Commuter campus in very large city
- 3,533 degree-seeking undergraduates: 4% part-time, 73% women, 87% African American, 1% international
- 738 degree-seeking graduate students
- 66% of applicants admitted
- SAT or ACT (ACT writing optional), application essay required
- 44% graduate within 6 years; 26% enter graduate study

**General.** Founded in 1869. Regionally accredited. Member of Atlanta University Center, a consortium of black private education institutions. **Degrees:** 702 bachelor's awarded; master's, doctoral offered. **ROTC:** Army, Naval, Air Force. **Location:** 2 miles from downtown. **Calendar:** Semester, limited summer session. **Full-time faculty:** 230 total; 79% have terminal degrees, 91% minority, 38% women. **Part-time faculty:** 104 total; 7% have terminal degrees, 86% minority, 53% women. **Class size:** 36% < 20, 53%

20-39, 8% 40-49, 2% 50-99, less than 1% >100. **Special facilities:** Exhibition gallery, research center for science and technology.

**Freshman class profile.** 6,829 applied, 4,517 admitted, 1,061 enrolled.

| Mid 50% test scores | | | |
|---|---|---|---|
| SAT critical reading: | 410-490 | GPA 2.0-2.99: | 56% |
| SAT math: | 400-480 | End year in good standing: | 80% |
| ACT composite: | 17-20 | Return as sophomores: | 69% |
| GPA 3.50 or higher: | 14% | Out-of-state: | 77% |
| GPA 3.0-3.49: | 30% | Live on campus: | 55% |
| | | International: | 1% |

**Basis for selection.** Secondary school record most important. Test scores, recommendations, essay also important. Audition recommended for music and drama majors. **Homeschooled:** SAT, SAT Subject Tests or ACT, portfolio required.

**High school preparation.** 18 units required. Required units include English 4, mathematics 3, social studies 3, science 3 (laboratory 1), foreign language 2 and academic electives 3.

**2007-2008 Annual costs.** Tuition/fees: $16,100. Room/board: $7,014. Books/supplies: $1,000. Personal expenses: $2,374.

**2007-2008 Financial aid. Need-based:** Average need met was 11%. Average scholarship/grant was $5,546; average loan $3,442. 25% of total undergraduate aid awarded as scholarships/grants, 75% as loans/jobs. **Non-need-based:** Scholarships awarded for academics, art, athletics, minority status, music/drama, religious affiliation, state residency.

**Application procedures. Admission:** Priority date 3/1; deadline 6/1 (postmark date). $35 fee, may be waived for applicants with need. Application may be submitted online. Admission notification on a rolling basis beginning on or about 1/1. **Financial aid:** Priority date 3/1; no closing date. FAFSA required. Applicants notified on a rolling basis starting 4/1.

**Academics. Special study options:** Accelerated study, combined bachelor's/graduate degree, cooperative education, cross-registration, distance learning, double major, dual enrollment of high school students, exchange student, honors, independent study, internships, study abroad, teacher certification program, Washington semester, weekend college. **Credit/placement by examination:** AP, CLEP, IB, institutional tests. 45 credit hours maximum toward bachelor's degree. **Support services:** Learning center, pre-admission summer program, reduced course load, remedial instruction, study skills assistance, tutoring, writing center.

**Majors. Biology:** General. **Business:** Accounting, business admin, managerial economics. **Computer sciences:** General, computer science. **Education:** General, early childhood. **English:** English lit, speech/rhetoric. **Foreign languages:** French, Spanish. **History:** General. **Math:** General. **Philosophy/religion:** Philosophy, religion. **Physical sciences:** Chemistry, physics. **Protective services:** Criminal justice. **Psychology:** General. **Public administration:** Social work. **Social sciences:** Political science, sociology. **Visual/performing arts:** Art, fashion design, theater history.

**Most popular majors.** Biology 8%, business/marketing 25%, communications/journalism 22%, psychology 12%, visual/performing arts 6%.

**Computing on campus.** 640 workstations in dormitories, library, computer center, student center. Dormitories wired for high-speed internet access and linked to campus network. Commuter students can connect to campus network. Online course registration, online library, helpline, repair service available.

**Student life. Freshman orientation:** Mandatory, $150 fee. Preregistration for classes offered. **Policies:** Drug/alcohol policy, sanctions for violations, policies governing Greek and other student organizations. **Housing:** Guaranteed on-campus for freshmen. Coed dorms, single-sex dorms, special housing for disabled, apartments, substance-free housing available. $300 partly refundable deposit, deadline 6/1. **Activities:** Bands, choral groups, dance, drama, film society, literary magazine, music ensembles, musical theater, radio station, student government, student newspaper, symphony orchestra, TV station, NAACP, pan-Hellenic council, Anointed Students in Fellowship, Campus Crusade for Christ, Christian Fellowship, National Council of Negro Women, Forensic Society, Gamma Sigma Sigma, Caribbean-oriented student organization.

**Athletics.** NCAA. **Intercollegiate:** Baseball M, basketball, cross-country, football (tackle) M, softball W, tennis W, track and field, volleyball W. **Intramural:** Basketball, football (non-tackle), tennis W, track and field. **Team name:** Panthers.

**Student services.** Alcohol/substance abuse counseling, campus ministries, career counseling, student employment services, financial aid counseling, health services, legal services, personal counseling, placement for graduates, veterans' counselor, women's services. **Physically disabled:** Services for visually, speech, hearing impaired.

---

**Contact.** E-mail: cauadmissions@cau.edu
Phone: (404) 880-8784 Toll-free number: (800) 688-3228
Fax: (404) 880-6174
Kevin Williams, Director of Admissions, Clark Atlanta University, 223 James P. Brawley Drive, SW, Atlanta, GA 30314-4391

## Clayton State University
**Morrow, Georgia** — CB member
www.clayton.edu — CB code: 5145

- Public 4-year liberal arts and technical college
- Commuter campus in small city
- 5,985 degree-seeking undergraduates
- 37% of applicants admitted
- SAT or ACT (ACT writing optional) required

**General.** Founded in 1969. Regionally accredited. **Degrees:** 711 bachelor's, 151 associate awarded. **ROTC:** Army, Naval, Air Force. **Location:** 12 miles from Atlanta. **Calendar:** Semester, extensive summer session. **Full-time faculty:** 196 total. **Part-time faculty:** 141 total. **Class size:** 42% < 20, 48% 20-39, 6% 40-49, 4% 50-99, less than 1% >100. **Special facilities:** Concert hall.

**Freshman class profile.** 5,231 applied, 1,951 admitted, 581 enrolled.

| Mid 50% test scores | | | |
|---|---|---|---|
| | | Out-of-state: | 9% |
| SAT critical reading: | 450-530 | Live on campus: | 30% |
| SAT math: | 440-530 | Fraternities: | 8% |
| ACT composite: | 18-21 | Sororities: | 2% |

**Basis for selection.** 17 ACT or 400 SAT math and 430 verbal required. Secondary school record also very important for health sciences, music, teacher education, and business programs. Auditions recommended for music majors. **Homeschooled:** Must validate the completion of a college prep curriculum. SAT tests may be used to do so.

**High school preparation.** 16 units required; 22 recommended. Required and recommended units include English 4, mathematics 4, social studies 3, history 2, science 3-4 (laboratory 3), foreign language 2-3 and academic electives 2. Students not meeting college-preparatory requirements must take remedial classes before entering any program.

**2007-2008 Annual costs.** Tuition/fees: $3,582; $12,186 out-of-state. Books/supplies: $1,000. Personal expenses: $3,440.

**Financial aid. Non-need-based:** Scholarships awarded for academics.

**Application procedures. Admission:** Priority date 2/1; no deadline. $40 fee, may be waived for applicants with need. Application may be submitted online. Admission notification on a rolling basis beginning on or about 1/1. **Financial aid:** Priority date 7/18; no closing date. FAFSA required. Applicants notified on a rolling basis starting 3/12.

**Academics. Special study options:** Cooperative education, cross-registration, distance learning, double major, dual enrollment of high school students, exchange student, honors, independent study, internships, liberal arts/career combination, student-designed major, study abroad, teacher certification program. **Credit/placement by examination:** AP, CLEP, IB, institutional tests. **Support services:** Learning center, reduced course load, remedial instruction, study skills assistance, tutoring.

**Majors. Biology:** General. **Business:** General, accounting, business admin, marketing, office management, operations. **Communications:** General. **Computer sciences:** General, data processing, information systems, programming, systems analysis. **Education:** Middle, music. **Health:** Dental assistant, dental hygiene, facilities admin, health care admin, nursing admin. **History:** General. **Liberal arts:** Arts/sciences. **Protective services:** Criminal justice. **Psychology:** General. **Visual/performing arts:** Music performance, music theory/composition.

**Most popular majors.** Business/marketing 36%, computer/information sciences 15%, health sciences 23%, psychology 11%.

**Computing on campus.** PC or laptop required. Online course registration, online library, helpline, repair service, student web hosting, wireless network available.

**Student life. Freshman orientation:** Mandatory, $40 fee. Preregistration for classes offered. **Housing:** Apartments available. Selection of student housing is responsibility of student and his/her guardians. **Activities:** Jazz band, choral groups, drama, literary magazine, music ensembles, musical theater, opera, student government, student newspaper, Approximately 20 student groups.

**Athletics.** NAIA, NCAA. **Intercollegiate:** Basketball, cross-country, golf M, soccer, tennis W, track and field. **Team name:** Lakers.

**Student services.** Adult student services, alcohol/substance abuse counseling, career counseling, student employment services, financial aid counseling, health services, minority student services, personal counseling, placement for graduates, veterans' counselor. **Physically disabled:** Services for visually, speech, hearing impaired.

**Contact.** E-mail: ccsu-info@mail.clayton.edu
Phone: (770) 961-3500 Fax: (770) 961-3700
Scott Burke, Director of Admissions, Clayton State University, 5900 North Lee Street, Morrow, GA 30260-0285

## Columbus State University
Columbus, Georgia                              CB member
www.colstate.edu                              CB code: 5123

- Public 4-year university and liberal arts college
- Commuter campus in large city
- 6,462 degree-seeking undergraduates: 30% part-time, 61% women, 32% African American, 2% Asian American, 3% Hispanic American, 1% international
- 1,002 degree-seeking graduate students
- 56% of applicants admitted
- SAT or ACT (ACT writing optional) required

**General.** Founded in 1958. Regionally accredited. **Degrees:** 724 bachelor's, 21 associate awarded; master's offered. **ROTC:** Army. **Location:** 100 miles from Atlanta. **Calendar:** Semester, extensive summer session. **Full-time faculty:** 245 total; 78% have terminal degrees, 24% minority, 49% women. **Part-time faculty:** 186 total; 23% have terminal degrees, 16% minority, 50% women. **Class size:** 32% < 20, 57% 20-39, 6% 40-49, 5% 50-99, less than 1% >100. **Special facilities:** Environmental learning center, space science center, performing arts center.

**Freshman class profile.** 3,094 applied, 1,727 admitted, 1,035 enrolled.

| Mid 50% test scores | | End year in good standing: | 89% |
|---|---|---|---|
| SAT critical reading: | 450-560 | Return as sophomores: | 72% |
| SAT math: | 440-550 | Out-of-state: | 8% |
| ACT composite: | 17-22 | Live on campus: | 30% |
| GPA 3.50 or higher: | 21% | Fraternities: | 1% |
| GPA 3.0-3.49: | 32% | Sororities: | 1% |
| GPA 2.0-2.99: | 46% | | |

**Basis for selection.** GED not accepted. 460 SAT Math/19 ACT Math, or 490 SAT Critical Reading/20 ACT English required. Students must be on track to graduate with college preparatory seal. Students with college prep deficiencies will be considered on individual basis. Interviews and auditions required of music majors. Portfolio recommended for art majors. **Home-schooled:** Statement describing homeschool structure and mission, transcript of courses and grades, letter of recommendation (nonparent) required. Must submit combined SAT (exclusive of Writing) score of 1000, official transcripts from any high school and colleges attended, Home School Credit Evaluation Table, letter from primary teacher certifying completion of high school and date of graduation and two letters of recommendation from non-family members.

**High school preparation.** 16 units required. Required units include English 4, mathematics 4, social studies 3, science 3 (laboratory 2) and foreign language 2. Social studies units required include U.S. history and world studies.

**2007-2008 Annual costs.** Tuition/fees: $3,514; $12,118 out-of-state. Room/board: $6,220. Books/supplies: $814. Personal expenses: $1,582.

**2007-2008 Financial aid. Need-based:** 735 full-time freshmen applied for aid; 582 were judged to have need; 448 of these received aid. Average need met was 63%. Average scholarship/grant was $3,359; average loan $2,816. 23% of total undergraduate aid awarded as scholarships/grants, 77% as loans/jobs. **Non-need-based:** Awarded to 3,307 full-time undergraduates, including 714 freshmen. Scholarships awarded for academics, alumni affiliation, art, athletics, job skills, leadership, minority status, music/drama, ROTC.

**Application procedures. Admission:** Priority date 5/1; deadline 7/1 (receipt date). $25 fee, may be waived for applicants with need. Application may be submitted online. Admission notification on a rolling basis beginning on or about 9/1. **Financial aid:** Priority date 5/1; no closing date. FAFSA required. Applicants notified on a rolling basis starting 4/1; must reply within 4 week(s) of notification.

**Academics. Special study options:** Accelerated study, cooperative education, distance learning, double major, dual enrollment of high school students, honors, independent study, internships, liberal arts/career combination, study abroad, teacher certification program. **Credit/placement by examination:** AP, CLEP, IB, institutional tests. 30 credit hours maximum toward associate degree, 60 toward bachelor's. **Support services:** Learning center, reduced course load, remedial instruction, study skills assistance, tutoring, writing center.

**Majors. Biology:** General, biomedical sciences. **Business:** General, accounting, business admin, finance, management information systems, marketing. **Computer sciences:** General. **Education:** Art, drama/dance, early childhood, emotionally handicapped, English, learning disabled, mathematics, mentally handicapped, middle, music, physical, science, secondary, social science, social studies. **English:** English lit, speech/rhetoric. **Foreign languages:** French, Spanish. **Health:** Nursing (RN). **History:** General. **Math:** General. **Parks/recreation:** Exercise sciences. **Physical sciences:** Chemistry, geology. **Protective services:** Criminal justice. **Psychology:** General. **Social sciences:** Political science, sociology. **Visual/performing arts:** Art, dramatic, music performance.

**Most popular majors.** Business/marketing 24%, education 17%, English 6%, health sciences 12%, security/protective services 10%, social sciences 6%, visual/performing arts 6%.

**Computing on campus.** 966 workstations in dormitories, library, computer center, student center. Dormitories wired for high-speed internet access and linked to campus network. Commuter students can connect to campus network. Online course registration, online library, helpline, repair service, wireless network available.

**Student life. Freshman orientation:** Mandatory, $60 fee. Preregistration for classes offered. **Housing:** Coed dorms, single-sex dorms, special housing for disabled, apartments, fraternity/sorority housing, substance-free housing available. $225 deposit, deadline 5/1. Apartments take place of traditional dorms; weekday meals are included in fee. **Activities:** Bands, choral groups, dance, drama, international student organizations, literary magazine, music ensembles, Model UN, musical theater, opera, student government, student newspaper, symphony orchestra, College Republicans, CSU Islamic Association, Freethought Society, Cougars for Christ, CSU Democrats, minority student union, Student Political Awareness, Westminster Fellowship, Baptist student union.

**Athletics.** NCAA. **Intercollegiate:** Baseball M, basketball, cross-country, golf M, soccer W, softball W, tennis. **Intramural:** Badminton, basketball, football (tackle) M, skiing, soccer, softball, table tennis, tennis, volleyball. **Team name:** Cougars.

**Student services.** Adult student services, alcohol/substance abuse counseling, career counseling, student employment services, financial aid counseling, health services, minority student services, personal counseling, placement for graduates, veterans' counselor, women's services. **Physically disabled:** Services for visually, speech, hearing impaired.

**Contact.** E-mail: admissions@colstate.edu
Phone: (706) 568-2035 Toll-free number: (866) 264-2035
Fax: (706) 568-5091
Susan Lovell, Director of Admissions, Columbus State University, 4225 University Avenue, Columbus, GA 31907-5645

## Covenant College
Lookout Mountain, Georgia
www.covenant.edu                              CB code: 6124

- Private 4-year liberal arts college affiliated with Presbyterian Church in America
- Residential campus in small city
- 989 degree-seeking undergraduates: 2% part-time, 56% women, 3% African American, 2% Asian American, 1% Hispanic American, 1% international
- 56 degree-seeking graduate students
- 65% of applicants admitted
- SAT or ACT with writing, application essay required
- 58% graduate within 6 years

**General.** Founded in 1955. Regionally accredited. **Degrees:** 245 bachelor's awarded; master's offered. **Location:** 120 miles from Atlanta, 5 miles from Chattanooga, Tennessee. **Calendar:** Semester, limited summer session. **Full-time faculty:** 65 total; 83% have terminal degrees, 6% minority, 18% women. **Part-time faculty:** 22 total; 32% have terminal degrees, 14% minority, 32% women. **Class size:** 56% < 20, 41% 20-39, 3% 40-49, less than 1% 50-99.

**Freshman class profile.** 939 applied, 610 admitted, 290 enrolled.

| Mid 50% test scores | | GPA 2.0-2.99: | 14% |
|---|---|---|---|
| SAT critical reading: | 510-660 | Rank in top quarter: | 49% |
| SAT math: | 490-630 | Rank in top tenth: | 27% |
| SAT writing: | 500-640 | Return as sophomores: | 78% |
| ACT composite: | 21-28 | Out-of-state: | 77% |
| GPA 3.50 or higher: | 62% | Live on campus: | 98% |
| GPA 3.0-3.49: | 24% | International: | 2% |

**Basis for selection.** 1500 SAT or 21 ACT, 2.5 GPA, academic evaluation, church evaluation, and personal testimony of faith important. Students that do not meet minimum scores may be asked to provide additional information. Auditions required for music and voice majors. **Homeschooled:** Transcript of courses and grades, letter of recommendation (nonparent) required.

**High school preparation.** 16 units required. Required units include English 4, mathematics 3, social studies 2, science 2, foreign language 2 and academic electives 3.

**2007-2008 Annual costs.** Tuition/fees: $22,840. Room/board: $6,490. Books/supplies: $800. Personal expenses: $560.

**2006-2007 Financial aid. Need-based:** 257 full-time freshmen applied for aid; 214 were judged to have need; 214 of these received aid. Average need met was 83%. Average scholarship/grant was $12,617; average loan $4,161. 70% of total undergraduate aid awarded as scholarships/grants, 30% as loans/jobs. **Non-need-based:** Awarded to 297 full-time undergraduates, including 91 freshmen. Scholarships awarded for academics, alumni affiliation, art, athletics, job skills, leadership, minority status, music/drama, religious affiliation, state residency.

**Application procedures. Admission:** Priority date 4/1; no deadline. $45 fee. Application must be submitted on paper. Admission notification on a rolling basis beginning on or about 8/1. Must reply by May 1 or within 3 week(s) if notified thereafter. **Financial aid:** No deadline. FAFSA required. Applicants notified on a rolling basis starting 2/1; must reply within 3 week(s) of notification.

**Academics.** Organizational management program designed for adult students with minimum of 5 years of work experience who have completed at least 2 years of college. Maximum of 32 credit hours given for assessment of life experience learning. All classes held in evenings, with degree completion taking just over 1 year. **Special study options:** Double major, dual enrollment of high school students, exchange student, independent study, internships, student-designed major, study abroad, teacher certification program, Washington semester. Dual engineering degree with Georgia Tech, cooperative program with school of nursing at Emory University and Chattanooga State; bridge program leading to master of nursing science at Vanderbilt University. **Credit/placement by examination:** AP, CLEP, IB, SAT, ACT, institutional tests. 30 credit hours maximum toward associate degree, 30 toward bachelor's. **Support services:** Reduced course load, remedial instruction, study skills assistance, tutoring, writing center.

**Majors. Biology:** General. **Business:** General, business admin. **Computer sciences:** General. **Education:** Elementary, English, history, mathematics, science. **English:** English lit. **History:** General. **Interdisciplinary:** Biological/physical sciences. **Math:** General. **Philosophy/religion:** Philosophy. **Physical sciences:** Chemistry, physics. **Psychology:** General. **Social sciences:** General, sociology. **Theology:** Bible. **Visual/performing arts:** Dramatic, music performance, studio arts. **Other:** Philosophy and religious studies, Physical sciences.

**Most popular majors.** Biology 6%, business/marketing 11%, education 11%, English 11%, history 10%, philosophy/religious studies 6%, psychology 7%, social sciences 14%, visual/performing arts 11%.

**Computing on campus.** 114 workstations in dormitories, library, computer center. Dormitories linked to campus network. Commuter students can connect to campus network. Online library, helpline, repair service, wireless network available.

**Student life. Freshman orientation:** Mandatory, $65 fee. Preregistration for classes offered. One week prior to beginning of classes. **Policies:** Smoking, alcoholic beverages, and drugs prohibited. Students are to use wisdom and Christ-like discretion in the application of Biblical principles to decisions regarding all areas of life such as involvement with various forms of media, all non-college organizations, social interaction (including dance) and physical expression of intimacy in relationships. Religious observance required. **Housing:** Guaranteed on-campus for freshmen. Single-sex dorms, apartments available. $300 nonrefundable deposit. **Activities:** Concert band, campus ministries, choral groups, drama, literary magazine, music ensembles, radio station, student government, student newspaper, Rotaract, Young Life, pre-law club, Psi Chi, Reformed University Fellowship, Evangelism club.

**Athletics. NAIA. Intercollegiate:** Baseball M, basketball, cross-country, golf M, soccer, softball W, volleyball W. **Intramural:** Basketball, football (non-tackle), football (tackle) M, soccer, tennis, volleyball. **Team name:** Scots.

**Student services.** Adult student services, career counseling, student employment services, financial aid counseling, health services, personal counseling, placement for graduates.

**Contact.** E-mail: admissions@covenant.edu
Phone: (706) 419-1148 Toll-free number: (888) 451-2683
Fax: (706) 820-0893
Wallace Anderson, Vice President of Enrollment Management, Covenant College, 14049 Scenic Highway, Lookout Mountain, GA 30750

---

## Dalton State College
**Dalton, Georgia**
www.daltonstate.edu                         CB code: 5167

- Public 4-year liberal arts and teachers college
- Commuter campus in large town
- 4,532 degree-seeking undergraduates: 48% part-time, 62% women
- 51% of applicants admitted

**General.** Founded in 1963. Regionally accredited. **Degrees:** 95 bachelor's, 286 associate awarded. **Location:** 90 miles from Atlanta. **Calendar:** Semester, limited summer session. **Full-time faculty:** 129 total; 56% have terminal degrees, 5% minority, 57% women.

**Freshman class profile.** 1,940 applied, 983 admitted, 826 enrolled.

**Basis for selection.** 1.8 GPA required for transfer associate degree programs. **Homeschooled:** State high school equivalency certificate required.

**High school preparation.** 16 units required. Required units include English 4, mathematics 4, social studies 3, science 3 and foreign language 2.

**2007-2008 Annual costs.** Tuition/fees: $2,088; $7,704 out-of-state.

**2006-2007 Financial aid. Need-based:** 72% of total undergraduate aid awarded as scholarships/grants, 28% as loans/jobs. **Non-need-based:** Scholarships awarded for academics, leadership, minority status, state residency.

**Application procedures. Admission:** No deadline. $25 fee, may be waived for applicants with need. Application may be submitted online. Admission notification on a rolling basis. **Financial aid:** Priority date 7/1; no closing date. FAFSA, institutional form required. Applicants notified on a rolling basis starting 7/1.

**Academics. Special study options:** Cooperative education, double major, dual enrollment of high school students, ESL, external degree, honors, independent study, internships, study abroad, weekend college. **Credit/placement by examination:** CLEP, institutional tests. Credit is awarded only to admitted students and recorded only for those who enroll for credit courses. Credit is awarded only for offered courses. **Support services:** Remedial instruction, study skills assistance, tutoring, writing center.

**Honors college/program.** For early admission, first-time freshmen and early enrollment students need 3.5 GPA, 1100 SAT (exclusive of Writing) with 580 verbal or 24 ACT. Honors essay, 2 letters of recommendation, and interview with honors program director and committee representatives required.

**Majors. Business:** Management information systems, management science, marketing, operations. **Computer sciences:** General. **Education:** Elementary. **Family/consumer sciences:** Work/family studies. **Public administration:** Social work.

**Computing on campus.** 800 workstations in library, computer center, student center. Commuter students can connect to campus network. Online library, helpline available.

**Student life. Freshman orientation:** Mandatory. Preregistration for classes offered. **Activities:** International student organizations, literary magazine, student government, student newspaper, social work club, LPN, Baptist student union, Psychology, black student alliance, Phi The Kappa, Young Democrats, progressive student union.

**Athletics. Intramural:** Badminton, basketball, football (non-tackle) M, softball, table tennis, tennis, volleyball.

**Student services.** Adult student services, career counseling, student employment services, financial aid counseling, personal counseling, placement

for graduates, veterans' counselor. **Physically disabled:** Services for hearing impaired.

**Contact.** Phone: (706) 272-4436 Toll-free number: (800) 829-4436
Fax: (706) 272-2530
Jodi Johnson, Vice President for Enrollment Services, Dalton State College, 650 College Drive, Dalton, GA 30720

## DeVry University: Alpharetta
**Alpharetta, Georgia**
www.devry.edu                                    CB code: 0077

- For-profit 4-year university
- Commuter campus in large town
- 672 degree-seeking undergraduates: 56% part-time, 45% women, 44% African American, 3% Asian American, 4% Hispanic American, 1% international
- 123 degree-seeking graduate students
- Interview required

**General.** Regionally accredited. **Degrees:** 148 bachelor's, 22 associate awarded; master's offered. **Location:** 18 miles from Atlanta. **Calendar:** Semester, extensive summer session. **Full-time faculty:** 29 total; 38% minority, 45% women. **Part-time faculty:** 53 total; 28% minority, 43% women.

**Freshman class profile.**

| | | | |
|---|---|---|---|
| Return as sophomores: | 60% | International: | 1% |
| Out-of-state: | 12% | | |

**Basis for selection.** Applicants must have high school diploma or equivalent, or degree from an accredited postsecondary institution, demonstrate proficiency in basic college-level skills through ACT, SAT, or institution-administered placement examinations, and be at least 17 years of age. New students may enter at the beginning of any semester. SAT/ACT tests are considered but not required for admission. If the applicant chooses not to submit either one, he/she must take a DeVry-administered admissions test.

**2007-2008 Annual costs.** Tuition/fees: $13,220. Books/supplies: $1,300. Personal expenses: $5,082.

**2006-2007 Financial aid.** All financial aid based on need. 36 full-time freshmen applied for aid; 32 were judged to have need; 32 of these received aid. Average need met was 30%. Average scholarship/grant was $3,307; average loan $3,539. 21% of total undergraduate aid awarded as scholarships/grants, 79% as loans/jobs.

**Application procedures. Admission:** No deadline. $50 fee. Application may be submitted online. Admission notification on a rolling basis. **Financial aid:** No deadline. FAFSA required. Applicants notified on a rolling basis.

**Academics. Special study options:** Accelerated study, distance learning. **Credit/placement by examination:** CLEP, institutional tests. **Support services:** Learning center, remedial instruction, tutoring.

**Majors. Business:** Business admin, management information systems, operations. **Communications technology:** General. **Computer sciences:** Game design, information systems, networking, systems analysis. **Engineering:** Software. **Engineering technology:** Computer, electrical.

**Most popular majors.** Business/marketing 67%, computer/information sciences 30%.

**Computing on campus.** 218 workstations in library, computer center. Online course registration, online library, helpline available.

**Student life. Freshman orientation:** Mandatory. **Housing:** Private apartments, student-plan housing, private rooms available. **Activities:** Alpha Sigma Lambda, Toastmasters International, international student organization, National Society of Black Engineers, Alpha Beta Kappa, Delta Pi Chi, Epsilon Delta Pi, Tau Alpha Pi, Future Business Leaders of America.

**Athletics. Intramural:** Basketball, football (non-tackle), softball, volleyball.

**Student services.** Career counseling, student employment services, financial aid counseling, placement for graduates, veterans' counselor. **Physically disabled:** Services for visually, hearing impaired.

**Contact.** E-mail: admissions@devry.edu
Phone: (770) 664-9520 Toll-free number: (800) 346-5420
Fax: (770) 664-8824
Gerry Purcell, Director of Admissions, DeVry University: Alpharetta, 2555 Northwinds Parkway, Alpharetta, GA 30004

## DeVry University: Decatur
**Decatur, Georgia**
www.devry.edu                                    CB code: 5715

- For-profit 4-year university
- Commuter campus in large town
- 2,087 degree-seeking undergraduates: 46% part-time, 50% women, 71% African American, 2% Asian American, 2% Hispanic American, 1% international
- 301 degree-seeking graduate students
- Interview required

**General.** Founded in 1969. Regionally accredited. **Degrees:** 370 bachelor's, 54 associate awarded; master's offered. **Location:** 15 miles from Atlanta. **Calendar:** Semester, extensive summer session. **Full-time faculty:** 42 total; 24% minority, 38% women. **Part-time faculty:** 109 total; 13% minority, 37% women.

**Freshman class profile.** 325 enrolled.

| | | | |
|---|---|---|---|
| Return as sophomores: | 54% | Out-of-state: | 9% |

**Basis for selection.** Applicants must have high school diploma or equivalent, or degree from accredited post-secondary institution, demonstrate proficiency in basic college-level skills through SAT or ACT scores or institution-administered placement examinations, and be at least 17 years of age. New students may enter at beginning of any semester. Applicants may also take a DeVry administered admissions test.

**2007-2008 Annual costs.** Tuition/fees: $13,220. Books/supplies: $1,300. Personal expenses: $5,082.

**Financial aid.** All financial aid based on need.

**Application procedures. Admission:** No deadline. $50 fee. Application may be submitted online. Admission notification on a rolling basis. **Financial aid:** No deadline. FAFSA required. Applicants notified on a rolling basis.

**Academics. Special study options:** Accelerated study, distance learning. **Credit/placement by examination:** CLEP, institutional tests. **Support services:** Learning center, remedial instruction, tutoring.

**Majors. Business:** Business admin, operations. **Computer sciences:** Information systems, networking. **Engineering:** Software. **Engineering technology:** Biomedical, computer, electrical.

**Most popular majors.** Business/marketing 70%, computer/information sciences 20%, engineering/engineering technologies 10%.

**Computing on campus.** 300 workstations in library, computer center. Online course registration, online library, helpline available.

**Student life. Freshman orientation:** Mandatory. **Housing:** Private apartments, student-plan housing, private rooms available. **Activities:** Toastmasters International, National Society of Black Engineers, International Student Organization, Delta Pi Chi, Tau Alpha Pi, Sigma Beta Delta, Alpha Beta Kappa.

**Athletics. Intramural:** Basketball, football (non-tackle), softball, volleyball.

**Student services.** Career counseling, student employment services, financial aid counseling, placement for graduates, veterans' counselor. **Physically disabled:** Services for visually, hearing impaired.

**Contact.** E-mail: dsilva@admin.atl.devry.edu
Phone: (404) 292-2645 Toll-free number: (800) 221-4771
Fax: (404) 292-7011
Barbara Silva, Director of Admissions, DeVry University: Decatur, 250 North Arcadia Avenue, Decatur, GA 30030-2198

## Emmanuel College
**Franklin Springs, Georgia**                    CB member
www.ec.edu                                       CB code: 5184

- Private 4-year liberal arts college affiliated with Pentecostal Holiness Church
- Residential campus in rural community
- 600 degree-seeking undergraduates: 3% part-time, 54% women, 16% African American, 1% Asian American, 4% Hispanic American, 1% international

- 41% of applicants admitted
- SAT or ACT (ACT writing optional) required
- 35% graduate within 6 years

**General.** Founded in 1919. Regionally accredited. **Degrees:** 122 bachelor's, 14 associate awarded. **Location:** 30 miles from Athens, 90 miles from Atlanta. **Calendar:** Semester, limited summer session. **Full-time faculty:** 35 total; 66% have terminal degrees, 3% minority, 37% women. **Part-time faculty:** 36 total; 11% have terminal degrees, 36% women. **Class size:** 72% < 20, 24% 20-39, 4% 40-49, less than 1% 50-99.

**Freshman class profile.** 1,341 applied, 544 admitted, 140 enrolled.

| Mid 50% test scores | | Out-of-state: | 23% |
|---|---|---|---|
| SAT critical reading: | 390-570 | Live on campus: | 43% |
| SAT math: | 400-570 | International: | 1% |
| Return as sophomores: | 60% | | |

**Basis for selection.** High school record and SAT/ACT scores important. Audition required and interview recommended for music majors. **Learning Disabled:** Must submit documentation of disability from professional.

**2008-2009 Annual costs.** Tuition/fees: $12,260. Room/board: $5,584. Books/supplies: $936. Personal expenses: $1,550.

**2007-2008 Financial aid. Need-based:** 121 full-time freshmen applied for aid; 111 were judged to have need; 111 of these received aid. Average need met was 68%. Average scholarship/grant was $6,867; average loan $3,131. 53% of total undergraduate aid awarded as scholarships/grants, 47% as loans/jobs. **Non-need-based:** Awarded to 162 full-time undergraduates, including 41 freshmen. Scholarships awarded for academics, art, athletics, leadership, music/drama, religious affiliation, state residency.

**Application procedures. Admission:** Closing date 8/1 (receipt date). $25 fee, may be waived for applicants with need. Application may be submitted online. Admission notification on a rolling basis beginning on or about 1/1. **Financial aid:** Priority date 5/1, closing date 8/1. FAFSA, institutional form required. Applicants notified on a rolling basis starting 3/1; must reply within 2 week(s) of notification.

**Academics. Special study options:** Dual enrollment of high school students, independent study, internships, teacher certification program. **Credit/placement by examination:** AP, CLEP, institutional tests. 24 credit hours maximum toward associate degree, 24 toward bachelor's. **Support services:** Remedial instruction, study skills assistance, tutoring, writing center.

**Majors. Biology:** General. **Business:** Business admin. **Communications:** General. **Education:** Business, elementary, English, history, mathematics, middle, music. **English:** English lit. **Health:** Premedicine. **History:** General. **Legal studies:** Prelaw. **Math:** General. **Parks/recreation:** Exercise sciences, sports admin. **Psychology:** General. **Theology:** Pastoral counseling, sacred music.

**Most popular majors.** Biology 6%, business/marketing 12%, education 36%, parks/recreation 6%, psychology 9%, theological studies 11%.

**Computing on campus.** 50 workstations in library, computer center. Dormitories wired for high-speed internet access and linked to campus network. Commuter students can connect to campus network. Online course registration, online library, repair service, wireless network available.

**Student life. Freshman orientation:** Mandatory. Preregistration for classes offered. Held first 2 days of semester. **Policies:** Chapel attendance required for all full-time students. Students not living at home must reside in college housing through junior year. Religious observance required. **Housing:** Guaranteed on-campus for all undergraduates. Single-sex dorms, apartments, substance-free housing available. $150 fully refundable deposit, deadline 8/1. **Activities:** Concert band, choral groups, drama, literary magazine, music ensembles, musical theater, student government, student newspaper, ministerial fellowship, missions fellowship, Students in Free Enterprise.

**Athletics.** NAIA, NCCAA. **Intercollegiate:** Baseball M, basketball, soccer, softball W, tennis. **Intramural:** Basketball, soccer, softball, table tennis, tennis, track and field, volleyball. **Team name:** Lions.

**Student services.** Adult student services, campus ministries, career counseling, financial aid counseling, personal counseling, veterans' counselor.

**Contact.** E-mail: admission@ec.edu
Phone: (706) 245-7226 Toll-free number: (800) 860-8800
Fax: (706) 245-4424
Wade Mawdesley, Director of Admissions, Emmanuel College, 181 Spring Street, Franklin Springs, GA 30639-0129

---

## Emory University

**Atlanta, Georgia**
www.emory.edu

CB member
CB code: 5187

- Private 4-year university affiliated with United Methodist Church
- Residential campus in very large city
- 5,094 degree-seeking undergraduates: 56% women, 9% African American, 18% Asian American, 3% Hispanic American, 7% international
- 5,597 degree-seeking graduate students
- 27% of applicants admitted
- SAT or ACT with writing, application essay required
- 88% graduate within 6 years

**General.** Founded in 1836. Regionally accredited. **Degrees:** 1,656 bachelor's, 326 associate awarded; master's, doctoral, first professional offered. **ROTC:** Army, Naval, Air Force. **Location:** 5 miles from downtown. **Calendar:** Semester, limited summer session. **Full-time faculty:** 1,236 total; 99% have terminal degrees, 20% minority, 53% women. **Part-time faculty:** 219 total; 100% have terminal degrees, 11% minority, 53% women. **Class size:** 68% < 20, 23% 20-39, 2% 40-49, 5% 50-99, 2% >100. **Special facilities:** Art and archeology museum, biological field station, primate research center, 185-acre park, planetarium, healthcare facilities.

**Freshman class profile.** 15,366 applied, 4,175 admitted, 1,235 enrolled.

| Mid 50% test scores | | Rank in top quarter: | 95% |
|---|---|---|---|
| SAT critical reading: | 640-730 | Rank in top tenth: | 85% |
| SAT math: | 660-740 | Return as sophomores: | 94% |
| SAT writing: | 640-740 | Out-of-state: | 79% |
| ACT composite: | 29-33 | Live on campus: | 98% |
| GPA 3.50 or higher: | 82% | International: | 10% |
| GPA 3.0-3.49: | 17% | Fraternities: | 33% |
| GPA 2.0-2.99: | 1% | Sororities: | 38% |

**Basis for selection.** GED not accepted. School achievement record, program content and rigor of coursework most important. Test scores, character and maturity important. Diversity of interests, background, and special talents sought. Campus visits or other indications of interest encouraged. **Homeschooled:** 3 SAT Subject Tests required (1 math and 2 of student's choice). Personal interview strongly recommended.

**High school preparation.** 16 units required. Required and recommended units include English 4, mathematics 3-4, social studies 2, history 2, science 2-4 (laboratory 2), foreign language 2-4, visual/performing arts 1 and academic electives 2. At least 2 units required in either social studies or history, including history of a country/region other than the U.S. 4 units math and science, with at least 3 units laboratory science, recommended for students concentrating in science or math.

**2007-2008 Annual costs.** Tuition/fees: $34,336. Room/board: $11,020. Books/supplies: $1,000. Personal expenses: $800.

**Financial aid. Non-need-based:** Scholarships awarded for academics, art, leadership, music/drama, religious affiliation, state residency.

**Application procedures. Admission:** Closing date 1/15 (postmark date). $50 fee, may be waived for applicants with need. Application may be submitted online. Admission notification 4/1. Must reply by May 1 or within 1 week(s) if notified thereafter. **Financial aid:** Priority date 2/15, closing date 4/1. FAFSA, CSS PROFILE required. Applicants notified by 4/15; must reply by 5/1 or within 4 week(s) of notification.

**Academics. Special study options:** Accelerated study, combined bachelor's/graduate degree, cooperative education, cross-registration, double major, dual enrollment of high school students, exchange student, honors, independent study, internships, liberal arts/career combination, study abroad, teacher certification program, Washington semester. 3-2 dual-degree program in engineering with Georgia Institute of Technology. **Credit/placement by examination:** AP, CLEP, IB, institutional tests. **Support services:** Learning center, pre-admission summer program, study skills assistance, tutoring, writing center.

**Majors. Area/ethnic studies:** African, African-American, Asian, Caribbean, Central/Eastern European, French, German, Italian, Latin American, Russian/Slavic, women's. **Biology:** General. **Business:** General, accounting, business admin, finance, management science, marketing. **Communications:** Journalism. **Computer sciences:** Computer science. **Conservation:** Environmental studies. **Education:** General. **English:** Creative writing, English lit. **Foreign languages:** Chinese, classics, comparative lit, French, German, Italian, Japanese, Latin, linguistics, Russian, Spanish. **History:** General. **Interdisciplinary:** Math/computer science, medieval/Renaissance. **Math:**

General. **Philosophy/religion:** Judaic, philosophy, religion. **Physical sciences:** Astronomy, chemistry, physics. **Psychology:** General. **Social sciences:** Anthropology, economics, international relations, political science, sociology. **Visual/performing arts:** Art history/conservation, dance, dramatic, film/cinema.

**Most popular majors.** Biology 7%, business/marketing 14%, interdisciplinary studies 8%, psychology 9%, social sciences 26%.

**Computing on campus.** 700 workstations in dormitories, library, computer center, student center. Dormitories wired for high-speed internet access and linked to campus network. Commuter students can connect to campus network. Online course registration, online library, helpline, repair service, student web hosting, wireless network available.

**Student life. Freshman orientation:** Mandatory. Typically held over 5 days immediately prior to first day of classes. New students receive orientation information by mail in June. **Policies:** Two-year residency requirement. **Housing:** Guaranteed on-campus for all undergraduates. Coed dorms, single-sex dorms, special housing for disabled, apartments, fraternity/sorority housing, substance-free housing available. $200 fully refundable deposit, deadline 5/1. Theme halls available. **Activities:** Bands, campus ministries, choral groups, dance, drama, film society, literary magazine, music ensembles, musical theater, radio station, student government, student newspaper, symphony orchestra, TV station, over 220 student clubs and organizations available.

**Athletics. NCAA. Intercollegiate:** Baseball M, basketball, cross-country, diving, golf M, soccer, softball W, swimming, tennis, track and field, volleyball W. **Intramural:** Badminton, basketball, diving, football (non-tackle), golf, handball, racquetball, soccer, softball, squash, swimming, table tennis, tennis, track and field, volleyball, wrestling. **Team name:** Eagles.

**Student services.** Alcohol/substance abuse counseling, career counseling, student employment services, financial aid counseling, health services, legal services, minority student services, on-campus daycare, personal counseling, placement for graduates, women's services. **Physically disabled:** Services for visually, speech, hearing impaired.

**Contact.** E-mail: admiss@learnlink.emory.edu
Phone: (404) 727-6036 Toll-free number: (800) 727-6036
Fax: (404) 727-4303
Jean Jordan, Dean of Admission, Emory University, 200 Boisfeuillet Jones Center, Atlanta, GA 30322

---

## Fort Valley State University
**Fort Valley, Georgia**
**www.fvsu.edu**

**CB member**
**CB code: 5220**

- Public 4-year liberal arts and teachers college
- Residential campus in small town
- 2,467 degree-seeking undergraduates
- 44% of applicants admitted
- SAT or ACT (ACT writing optional) required

**General.** Founded in 1895. Regionally accredited. 1890 land-grant institution. **Degrees:** 293 bachelor's, 17 associate awarded; master's, first professional offered. **ROTC:** Army. **Location:** 30 miles from Macon. **Calendar:** Semester, limited summer session. **Full-time faculty:** 120 total. **Part-time faculty:** 15 total. **Class size:** 33% < 20, 56% 20-39, 9% 40-49, 2% 50-99.

**Freshman class profile.** 3,539 applied, 1,567 admitted, 696 enrolled.

| Mid 50% test scores | | ACT composite: | 16-22 |
|---|---|---|---|
| SAT critical reading: | 350-550 | Out-of-state: | 6% |
| SAT math: | 330-570 | Live on campus: | 58% |

**Basis for selection.** High school transcript, test scores, physical examination important. Audition recommended for music education majors.

**High school preparation.** 19 units required; 21 recommended. Required and recommended units include English 4, mathematics 3-4, social studies 3-4, science 3-4 and foreign language 2.

**2007-2008 Annual costs.** Tuition/fees: $3,558; $12,162 out-of-state. Room/board: $5,660. Books/supplies: $790. Personal expenses: $1,425.

**Financial aid. Non-need-based:** Scholarships awarded for academics, athletics, ROTC, state residency.

**Application procedures. Admission:** No deadline. $20 fee. Application may be submitted online. Admission notification on a rolling basis. Must reply by May 1 or within 4 week(s) if notified thereafter. **Financial**

**aid:** Priority date 4/1; no closing date. FAFSA, institutional form required. Must reply within 1 week(s) of notification.

**Academics. Special study options:** Cooperative education, double major, dual enrollment of high school students, external degree, honors, independent study, internships, liberal arts/career combination, student-designed major, study abroad, teacher certification program, weekend college. **Credit/placement by examination:** CLEP, institutional tests. 20 credit hours maximum toward associate degree, 45 toward bachelor's. **Support services:** Learning center, reduced course load, remedial instruction, tutoring, writing center.

**Majors. Agriculture:** Animal sciences, economics, farm/ranch, horticultural science, plant sciences. **Biology:** General. **Business:** General, accounting, business admin, marketing, office management. **Communications:** Journalism, public relations. **Computer sciences:** General, information systems. **Education:** Agricultural, elementary, English, family/consumer sciences, foreign languages, French, mathematics, middle, music, physical, secondary. **Engineering:** Agricultural. **Engineering technology:** Electrical. **English:** English lit. **Family/consumer sciences:** General, child care, child development, family studies, food/nutrition. **Health:** Medical assistant, veterinary technology/assistant. **Liberal arts:** Arts/sciences. **Math:** General. **Physical sciences:** Chemistry. **Psychology:** General. **Public administration:** Human services, social work. **Social sciences:** Economics, political science, sociology.

**Most popular majors.** Biology 7%, business/marketing 12%, education 7%, psychology 9%, visual/performing arts 28%.

**Computing on campus.** Dormitories linked to campus network. Commuter students can connect to campus network. Helpline available.

**Student life. Freshman orientation:** Mandatory. Preregistration for classes offered. **Housing:** Single-sex dorms available. $50 deposit. **Activities:** Bands, choral groups, dance, drama, music ensembles, musical theater, student government, student newspaper.

**Athletics. NCAA. Intercollegiate:** Basketball, cross-country, football (tackle) M, softball W, tennis, track and field, volleyball W. **Intramural:** Basketball, softball, swimming, tennis, track and field, volleyball. **Team name:** Wildcats.

**Student services.** Adult student services, career counseling, student employment services, health services, on-campus daycare, personal counseling, placement for graduates, veterans' counselor.

**Contact.** E-mail: admissap@fvsu.edu
Phone: (478) 825-6307 Toll-free number: (877) 462-3878
Fax: (478) 825-6394
Donovan Coley, Director of Admissions, Fort Valley State University, 1005 State University Drive, Fort Valley, GA 31030-4313

---

## Georgia College and State University
**Milledgeville, Georgia**
**www.gcsu.edu**

**CB member**
**CB code: 5252**

- Public 4-year university and liberal arts college
- Residential campus in large town
- 5,292 degree-seeking undergraduates: 9% part-time, 60% women, 6% African American, 1% Asian American, 2% Hispanic American, 2% international
- 829 degree-seeking graduate students
- 59% of applicants admitted
- SAT or ACT with writing, application essay required
- 47% graduate within 6 years

**General.** Founded in 1889. Regionally accredited. Branch campuses in Macon and Warner Robins offering junior, senior, and graduate level options. **Degrees:** 845 bachelor's awarded; master's offered. **ROTC:** Army. **Location:** 95 miles from Atlanta, 30 miles from Macon. **Calendar:** Semester, limited summer session. **Full-time faculty:** 282 total; 73% have terminal degrees, 12% minority, 51% women. **Part-time faculty:** 121 total; 9% minority, 58% women. **Class size:** 34% < 20, 46% 20-39, 13% 40-49, 7% 50-99. **Special facilities:** Art galleries, greenhouse, challenge/ropes course, former Governor's mansion, Flannery O'Connor collection, Georgia education museum and archives.

**Freshman class profile.** 3,442 applied, 2,038 admitted, 1,181 enrolled.

| Mid 50% test scores | | | | |
|---|---|---|---|---|
| SAT critical reading: | 510-590 | GPA 2.0-2.99: | | 22% |
| SAT math: | 510-600 | Return as sophomores: | | 82% |
| ACT composite: | 21-25 | Out-of-state: | | 2% |
| GPA 3.50 or higher: | 31% | Live on campus: | | 99% |
| GPA 3.0-3.49: | 47% | International: | | 1% |
| | | Sororities: | | 22% |

**Basis for selection.** Admission decisions based on total student portfolio and demonstrated potential for contribution to the university and probability for success. Test scores used in academic advising for honors program consideration. Audition required of music and drama. **Homeschooled:** Transcript of courses and grades required. SAT/ACT score equal to or above average score of previous year's entering freshmen class; other documentation may be required. **Learning Disabled:** Students must identify themselves as disabled during admissions process.

**High school preparation.** 16 units required. Required and recommended units include English 4, mathematics 4, social studies 3, science 3 (laboratory 2-3) and foreign language 2-3. Additional courses from the following areas strongly recommended: trigonometry, fine arts and computer technology.

**2007-2008 Annual costs.** Tuition/fees: $5,066; $17,688 out-of-state. Room/board: $7,380. Books/supplies: $900. Personal expenses: $2,084.

**2006-2007 Financial aid. Need-based:** 1,040 full-time freshmen applied for aid; 354 were judged to have need; 352 of these received aid. Average need met was 28%. Average scholarship/grant was $2,751; average loan $2,172. 22% of total undergraduate aid awarded as scholarships/grants, 78% as loans/jobs. **Non-need-based:** Awarded to 1,816 full-time undergraduates, including 411 freshmen. Scholarships awarded for academics, alumni affiliation, art, athletics, job skills, leadership, minority status, music/drama, religious affiliation, ROTC, state residency.

**Application procedures. Admission:** Closing date 4/1 (postmark date). $40 fee. Application may be submitted online. Admission notification on a rolling basis beginning on or about 1/1. Students encouraged to apply early to be considered for admission, university housing, scholarship funding, and financial aid. **Financial aid:** Priority date 3/1; no closing date. FAFSA required. Applicants notified on a rolling basis starting 3/1; must reply within 2 week(s) of notification.

**Academics. Special study options:** Accelerated study, distance learning, double major, ESL, external degree, honors, independent study, internships, liberal arts/career combination, semester at sea, student-designed major, study abroad, teacher certification program, Washington semester. 3-2 engineering program with Georgia Institute of Technology. **Credit/placement by examination:** AP, CLEP, IB, SAT, ACT, institutional tests. 30 credit hours maximum toward bachelor's degree. **Support services:** Learning center, pre-admission summer program, reduced course load, study skills assistance, tutoring, writing center.

**Majors. Biology:** General. **Business:** General, accounting, business admin, international, managerial economics, marketing, office management. **Communications:** Journalism. **Computer sciences:** General. **Conservation:** Environmental science. **Education:** Early childhood, health, middle, music, special. **English:** English lit, speech/rhetoric. **Foreign languages:** French, Spanish. **Health:** Music therapy, nursing (RN). **History:** General. **Liberal arts:** Arts/sciences. **Math:** General. **Parks/recreation:** General. **Philosophy/religion:** Philosophy. **Physical sciences:** Chemistry. **Protective services:** Law enforcement admin. **Psychology:** General. **Social sciences:** Political science, sociology. **Visual/performing arts:** Art, dramatic.

**Most popular majors.** Biology 6%, business/marketing 23%, education 17%, health sciences 10%, psychology 11%.

**Computing on campus.** 180 workstations in dormitories, library, computer center, student center. Dormitories wired for high-speed internet access and linked to campus network. Commuter students can connect to campus network. Online course registration, online library, helpline, wireless network available.

**Student life. Freshman orientation:** Available, $60 fee. Preregistration for classes offered. One-day program. $25 fee for parents/guests. **Policies:** Students who choose student housing must remain in dormitories for full academic year. Meal plan purchase required of all on-campus residents. **Housing:** Guaranteed on-campus for freshmen. Coed dorms, apartments, substance-free housing available. $235 partly refundable deposit, deadline 5/1. Living learning communities available. **Activities:** Bands, campus ministries, choral groups, dance, drama, literary magazine, music ensembles, musical theater, radio station, student government, student newspaper, TV station, Baptist student union, Give Center, Habitat for Humanity, Big Brother/Big Sister, Delta Sigma Theta, black student alliance.

**Athletics.** NCAA. **Intercollegiate:** Archery, baseball M, basketball, cheerleading, cross-country, golf M, soccer W, softball W, tennis. **Intramural:** Basketball, football (non-tackle), golf, racquetball, soccer, softball, table tennis, tennis, volleyball. **Team name:** Bobcats.

**Student services.** Adult student services, career counseling, student employment services, financial aid counseling, health services, minority student services, personal counseling, placement for graduates, veterans' counselor, women's services. **Physically disabled:** Services for visually, hearing impaired.

**Contact.** E-mail: info@gcsu.edu
Phone: (478) 445-2774 Toll-free number: (800) 342-0471
Fax: (478) 445-1914
Mike Augustine, Director, Georgia College and State University, Campus Box 23, Milledgeville, GA 31061-0490

---

## Georgia Institute of Technology
**Atlanta, Georgia**    **CB member**
**www.gatech.edu**    **CB code: 5248**

- Public 4-year university
- Residential campus in very large city
- 12,316 degree-seeking undergraduates: 5% part-time, 30% women, 7% African American, 16% Asian American, 5% Hispanic American, 5% international
- 6,107 degree-seeking graduate students
- 63% of applicants admitted
- SAT or ACT with writing, application essay required
- 78% graduate within 6 years; 30% enter graduate study

**General.** Founded in 1885. Regionally accredited. **Degrees:** 2,543 bachelor's awarded; master's, doctoral offered. **ROTC:** Army, Naval, Air Force. **Calendar:** Semester, extensive summer session. **Full-time faculty:** 863 total; 98% have terminal degrees, 27% minority, 20% women. **Part-time faculty:** 8 total; 88% have terminal degrees, 12% minority, 12% women. **Class size:** 40% < 20, 31% 20-39, 6% 40-49, 16% 50-99, 7% >100. **Special facilities:** Nuclear magnetic resonance spectroscopy center, research institute, ovarian cancer institute, paper museum, mechanical properties research laboratory with scanning electron microscope, virtual factory laboratory.

**Freshman class profile.** 9,664 applied, 6,122 admitted, 2,628 enrolled.

| Mid 50% test scores | | | |
|---|---|---|---|
| SAT critical reading: | 590-690 | Rank in top tenth: | 60% |
| SAT math: | 650-730 | End year in good standing: | 88% |
| SAT writing: | 580-670 | Return as sophomores: | 92% |
| ACT composite: | 27-31 | Out-of-state: | 35% |
| GPA 3.50 or higher: | 83% | Live on campus: | 94% |
| GPA 3.0-3.49: | 17% | International: | 6% |
| Rank in top quarter: | 87% | Fraternities: | 21% |
| | | Sororities: | 30% |

**Basis for selection.** School achievement record and SAT math score most important, followed by SAT verbal score. Activities, leadership, and personal statement required. Test scores accepted through November test dates for competition in President's Scholarship Program; accepted through December test date for admission consideration. **Homeschooled:** If student does not attend home school accredited by one of the approved Council for Higher Education Accreditation organizations, the following must be provided: official documentation of all subjects studied, credit earned per subject, time span of each unit, bibliography of all textbooks used, grades, verification of completion of college preparatory curriculum.

**High school preparation.** 16 units required. Required units include English 4, mathematics 4, social studies 3, science 3 (laboratory 2) and foreign language 2.

**2007-2008 Annual costs.** Tuition/fees: $5,642; $23,366 out-of-state. Room/board: $7,924.

**2007-2008 Financial aid. Need-based:** 1,979 full-time freshmen applied for aid; 865 were judged to have need; 838 of these received aid. Average need met was 55%. Average scholarship/grant was $5,826; average loan $3,546. 55% of total undergraduate aid awarded as scholarships/grants, 45% as loans/jobs. **Non-need-based:** Awarded to 2,427 full-time undergraduates, including 891 freshmen. Scholarships awarded for academics, alumni affiliation, athletics, leadership, state residency.

**Application procedures. Admission:** Closing date 1/15 (postmark date). $50 fee, may be waived for applicants with need. Application may be submitted online. Admission notification 3/15. Must reply by May 1 or within 2 week(s) if notified thereafter. Nonresident applicants advised to apply early. **Financial aid:** Closing date 3/1. FAFSA, institutional form required. Applicants notified on a rolling basis starting 4/1; must reply by 5/1.

**Academics. Special study options:** Accelerated study, combined bachelor's/graduate degree, cooperative education, cross-registration, distance learning, double major, dual enrollment of high school students, ESL, honors, independent study, internships, student-designed major, study abroad. Dual degree program (3-2); Regent's Engineering Transfer Program with 14 colleges in the University System of Georgia; Georgia Tech Regional Engineering Program offers undergraduate and graduate engineering degrees in collaboration with Armstrong Atlantic State University, Georgia Southern University, and Savannah State University. **Credit/placement by examination:** AP, CLEP, IB, SAT, ACT, institutional tests. **Support services:** Learning center, pre-admission summer program, reduced course load, remedial instruction, study skills assistance, tutoring, writing center.

**Majors. Architecture:** Architecture. **Biology:** General, biochemistry. **Business:** Business admin, managerial economics. **Communications:** Digital media. **Computer sciences:** General. **Engineering:** Aerospace, biomedical, chemical, civil, computer, electrical, environmental, industrial, materials, mechanical, nuclear, textile. **History:** Science/technology. **Interdisciplinary:** Global studies, science/society. **Math:** Applied. **Physical sciences:** Chemistry, geology, physics, polymer chemistry. **Psychology:** Industrial. **Public administration:** Policy analysis. **Social sciences:** International relations. **Visual/performing arts:** Industrial design. **Other:** Architecture and related services.

**Most popular majors.** Business/marketing 14%, computer/information sciences 8%, engineering/engineering technologies 58%.

**Computing on campus.** PC or laptop required. 1,996 workstations in dormitories, library, computer center, student center. Dormitories wired for high-speed internet access and linked to campus network. Commuter students can connect to campus network. Online course registration, online library, helpline, student web hosting, wireless network available.

**Student life. Freshman orientation:** Available, $105 fee. Preregistration for classes offered. Two-day program in fall. **Policies:** First-time, first-year students not allowed to have car on campus during first semester. **Housing:** Guaranteed on-campus for freshmen. Coed dorms, single-sex dorms, special housing for disabled, apartments, fraternity/sorority housing, substance-free housing available. $600 partly refundable deposit, deadline 5/1. First year housing guaranteed for freshman and transfer students who submit online application by 5/1. **Activities:** Bands, campus ministries, choral groups, dance, drama, film society, international student organizations, literary magazine, music ensembles, Model UN, musical theater, radio station, student government, student newspaper, symphony orchestra, TV station, Campus Crusade for Christ, Christian Campus Fellowship, Muslim student association, African student association, Asian Christian Fellowship, College Democrats, College Republicans, Bahai Campus Association, Society of Hispanic Professional Engineers.

**Athletics.** NCAA. **Intercollegiate:** Baseball M, basketball, cross-country, diving, football (tackle) M, golf M, softball W, swimming, tennis, track and field, volleyball W. **Intramural:** Basketball, bowling, football (non-tackle), racquetball, soccer, softball, volleyball. **Team name:** Yellow Jackets.

**Student services.** Alcohol/substance abuse counseling, career counseling, student employment services, financial aid counseling, health services, legal services, minority student services, on-campus daycare, personal counseling, placement for graduates, women's services. **Physically disabled:** Services for visually, speech, hearing impaired. **Learning disabled:** Comprehensive services available.

**Contact.** E-mail: admission@gatech.edu
Phone: (404) 894-4154 Fax: (404) 894-9511
Ingrid Hayes, Director of Undergraduate Admissions, Georgia Institute of Technology, Georgia Institute of Technology, Atlanta, GA 30332-0320

---

# Georgia Southern University

**Statesboro, Georgia** — CB member
**www.georgiasouthern.edu** — CB code: 5253

- Public 4-year university
- Residential campus in large town
- 14,157 degree-seeking undergraduates: 7% part-time, 48% women, 22% African American, 1% Asian American, 2% Hispanic American, 1% international
- 1,838 degree-seeking graduate students
- 45% of applicants admitted
- SAT or ACT (ACT writing optional) required
- 45% graduate within 6 years

**General.** Founded in 1906. Regionally accredited. **Degrees:** 2,300 bachelor's awarded; master's, doctoral offered. **ROTC:** Army. **Location:** 50 miles from Savannah, 200 miles from Atlanta. **Calendar:** Semester, extensive

summer session. **Full-time faculty:** 711 total; 81% have terminal degrees, 16% minority, 46% women. **Part-time faculty:** 69 total; 33% have terminal degrees, 3% minority, 55% women. **Class size:** 26% < 20, 54% 20-39, 9% 40-49, 9% 50-99, 2% >100. **Special facilities:** Planetarium, electron microscope, woodland nature preserve, museum, eagle sanctuary, national tick collection, wildlife education center, raptor center, botanical garden, family life center, center for international studies.

**Freshman class profile.** 8,090 applied, 3,669 admitted, 3,058 enrolled.

| Mid 50% test scores | | Rank in top tenth: | 15% |
|---|---|---|---|
| SAT critical reading: | 510-590 | End year in good standing: | 76% |
| SAT math: | 520-590 | Return as sophomores: | 79% |
| ACT composite: | 21-24 | Out-of-state: | 5% |
| GPA 3.50 or higher: | 26% | Live on campus: | 73% |
| GPA 3.0-3.49: | 38% | International: | 1% |
| GPA 2.0-2.99: | 36% | Fraternities: | 5% |
| Rank in top quarter: | 40% | Sororities: | 6% |

**Basis for selection.** GED not accepted. Test scores, high school GPA, and college preparatory curriculum considered. Students may be required to take placement exams. Audition required for music majors. **Homeschooled:** 1100 SAT (exclusive of Writing) or 24 ACT required. **Learning Disabled:** Admissions coordinated through student disability resource center.

**High school preparation.** 16 units required. Required units include English 4, mathematics 4, social studies 3, science 3 (laboratory 2) and foreign language 2.

**2007-2008 Annual costs.** Tuition/fees: $4,082; $12,954 out-of-state. Room/board: $6,860. Books/supplies: $1,200. Personal expenses: $2,800.

**2006-2007 Financial aid. Need-based:** 2,534 full-time freshmen applied for aid; 1,268 were judged to have need; 1,257 of these received aid. Average need met was 65%. Average scholarship/grant was $5,439; average loan $2,487. 47% of total undergraduate aid awarded as scholarships/grants, 53% as loans/jobs. **Non-need-based:** Awarded to 906 full-time undergraduates, including 346 freshmen. Scholarships awarded for academics, alumni affiliation, art, athletics, leadership, minority status, music/drama, ROTC, state residency. **Additional information:** The majority of scholarships available are need-blind.

**Application procedures. Admission:** Closing date 5/1 (postmark date). $30 fee ($30 out-of-state), may be waived for applicants with need. Application may be submitted online. Admission notification on a rolling basis. **Financial aid:** Closing date 4/20. FAFSA required. Applicants notified on a rolling basis starting 4/20.

**Academics. Special study options:** Combined bachelor's/graduate degree, cooperative education, cross-registration, distance learning, double major, dual enrollment of high school students, ESL, external degree, honors, independent study, internships, student-designed major, study abroad, teacher certification program. **Credit/placement by examination:** AP, CLEP, IB, institutional tests. 30 credit hours maximum toward bachelor's degree. For AP exams, more credit hours will be awarded for higher-than-minimum scores. **Support services:** Learning center, pre-admission summer program, reduced course load, remedial instruction, study skills assistance, tutoring, writing center.

**Majors. Biology:** General, pharmacology. **Business:** General, accounting, finance, hotel/motel admin, international, logistics, management information systems, managerial economics, marketing. **Communications:** General, journalism, public relations, radio/tv. **Communications technology:** Graphic/printing. **Computer sciences:** General, information systems. **Conservation:** Forestry. **Education:** Elementary, family/consumer sciences, middle, music, physical, special, technology/industrial arts. **Engineering:** General, civil, computer, electrical, mechanical. **Engineering technology:** Civil, construction, electrical, mechanical. **English:** Composition, English lit, speech/rhetoric. **Family/consumer sciences:** Clothing/textiles, family studies, food/nutrition. **Foreign languages:** French, German, Spanish. **Health:** Athletic training, clinical lab science, nursing (RN), predental, premedicine, prepharmacy, public health ed. **History:** General. **Math:** General. **Parks/recreation:** General, exercise sciences, health/fitness, sports admin. **Philosophy/religion:** Philosophy. **Physical sciences:** Chemistry, geology, physics. **Protective services:** Criminal justice. **Psychology:** General. **Social sciences:** Anthropology, economics, geography, international economic development, international relations, political science, sociology. **Visual/performing arts:** Art, dramatic, interior design, music performance, music theory/composition. **Other:** Industrial production technologies, Pre-veterinary studies.

**Most popular majors.** Business/marketing 25%, communications/journalism 6%, education 13%, engineering/engineering technologies 7%, health sciences 6%, parks/recreation 7%.

**Computing on campus.** 2,385 workstations in dormitories, library, student center. Dormitories wired for high-speed internet access and linked to campus network. Online course registration, online library, helpline, student web hosting, wireless network available.

**Student life. Freshman orientation:** Mandatory, $60 fee. Preregistration for classes offered. Freshman/parent program held for 2 days. $30 fee for first parent; additional fees for guests other than parents. **Housing:** Coed dorms, special housing for disabled, apartments, fraternity/sorority housing, substance-free housing available. $100 partly refundable deposit. **Activities:** Bands, choral groups, dance, drama, film society, literary magazine, music ensembles, musical theater, opera, radio station, student government, student newspaper, symphony orchestra, over 200 clubs and organizations available.

**Athletics.** NCAA. **Intercollegiate:** Baseball M, basketball, cheerleading, cross-country W, diving W, football (tackle) M, golf M, soccer, softball W, swimming W, tennis, track and field W, volleyball W. **Intramural:** Basketball, bowling, football (non-tackle), golf, racquetball, soccer, softball, swimming, table tennis, tennis, volleyball, weight lifting. **Team name:** Eagles.

**Student services.** Adult student services, alcohol/substance abuse counseling, career counseling, services for economically disadvantaged, student employment services, financial aid counseling, health services, legal services, minority student services, on-campus daycare, personal counseling, veterans' counselor, women's services. **Physically disabled:** Services for visually, speech, hearing impaired. **Learning disabled:** Comprehensive services available.

**Contact.** E-mail: admissions@georgiasouthern.edu
Phone: (912) 681-5391 Fax: (912) 871-1156
Susan Davies, Director of Admission, Georgia Southern University, PO Box 8024, Statesboro, GA 30460

---

## Georgia Southwestern State University
**Americus, Georgia**  CB member
**www.gsw.edu**  CB code: 5250

- Public 4-year university and liberal arts college
- Residential campus in large town
- 2,209 degree-seeking undergraduates: 24% part-time, 65% women, 31% African American, 1% Asian American, 1% Hispanic American, 2% international
- 38 degree-seeking graduate students
- 79% of applicants admitted
- SAT or ACT (ACT writing optional) required
- 35% graduate within 6 years

**General.** Founded in 1906. Regionally accredited. **Degrees:** 370 bachelor's, 7 associate awarded; master's offered. **Location:** 135 miles from Atlanta. **Calendar:** Semester, limited summer session. **Full-time faculty:** 92 total; 73% have terminal degrees, 20% minority, 53% women. **Part-time faculty:** 51 total; 28% have terminal degrees, 8% minority, 55% women. **Class size:** 49% < 20, 44% 20-39, 5% 40-49, 2% 50-99. **Special facilities:** Observatory, glass blowing studio, golf course, indoor climbing wall.

**Freshman class profile.** 1,040 applied, 817 admitted, 426 enrolled.

| Mid 50% test scores | | Rank in top tenth: | 19% |
|---|---|---|---|
| SAT critical reading: | 440-530 | Return as sophomores: | 64% |
| SAT math: | 430-530 | Out-of-state: | 7% |
| ACT composite: | 18-21 | Live on campus: | 68% |
| GPA 3.50 or higher: | 31% | International: | 5% |
| GPA 3.0-3.49: | 30% | Fraternities: | 20% |
| GPA 2.0-2.99: | 39% | Sororities: | 16% |
| Rank in top quarter: | 46% | | |

**Basis for selection.** School achievement record, test scores most important. **Homeschooled:** Statement describing homeschool structure and mission, transcript of courses and grades, letter of recommendation (nonparent) required. Must complete home schooled application or submit SAT along with 7 SAT Subject tests or a portfolio outlining work in 5 critical college preparatory areas.

**High school preparation.** 16 units required. Required and recommended units include English 4, mathematics 4, social studies 1, history 2, science 3 (laboratory 2), foreign language 2 and academic electives 2.

**2007-2008 Annual costs.** Tuition/fees: $3,526; $12,130 out-of-state. Room/board: $5,274. Books/supplies: $1,000.

**Financial aid. Non-need-based:** Scholarships awarded for academics, athletics, leadership.

---

**Application procedures. Admission:** Closing date 7/21 (postmark date). $25 fee, may be waived for applicants with need. Application may be submitted online. Admission notification on a rolling basis beginning on or about 8/1. Must reply by May 1 or within 3 week(s) if notified thereafter. **Financial aid:** Priority date 4/1, closing date 6/1. FAFSA, institutional form required. Applicants notified on a rolling basis starting 3/1.

**Academics. Special study options:** Accelerated study, distance learning, double major, dual enrollment of high school students, ESL, honors, independent study, internships, study abroad, teacher certification program. 3+2 program in engineering with Georgia Institute of Technology. **Credit/placement by examination:** AP, CLEP, institutional tests. 45 credit hours maximum toward bachelor's degree. **Support services:** Learning center, reduced course load, remedial instruction, study skills assistance, tutoring.

**Majors. Biology:** General. **Business:** Accounting, business admin, human resources, marketing. **Computer sciences:** General, computer science. **Education:** Elementary, middle, physical, special. **Engineering technology:** Computer. **English:** English lit. **Health:** Nursing (RN). **History:** General. **Math:** General. **Parks/recreation:** Facilities management. **Physical sciences:** Chemistry, geology. **Psychology:** General. **Social sciences:** Political science, sociology. **Visual/performing arts:** Art, dramatic.

**Most popular majors.** Business/marketing 29%, education 28%, health sciences 8%, psychology 11%, social sciences 6%.

**Computing on campus.** 550 workstations in dormitories, library, computer center, student center. Dormitories wired for high-speed internet access and linked to campus network. Commuter students can connect to campus network. Online library, wireless network available.

**Student life. Freshman orientation:** Mandatory, $70 fee. Preregistration for classes offered. 3 sessions in summer; includes parents' program. **Housing:** Guaranteed on-campus for freshmen. Coed dorms, single-sex dorms, fraternity/sorority housing available. $250 deposit. **Activities:** Bands, campus ministries, choral groups, drama, international student organizations, literary magazine, music ensembles, musical theater, student government, student newspaper, TV station, Baptist Student Union, Wesley Foundation, Young Republicans, Young Democrats, SABU, Habitat for Humanity, campus activity board, ZEPHYR recruitment team, College Republicans.

**Athletics.** NCAA. **Intercollegiate:** Baseball M, basketball, cross-country W, golf, soccer, softball W, tennis. **Intramural:** Badminton, basketball, football (non-tackle), racquetball, soccer, table tennis, tennis, volleyball, weight lifting, wrestling M. **Team name:** Hurricanes.

**Student services.** Career counseling, services for economically disadvantaged, student employment services, financial aid counseling, health services, personal counseling, veterans' counselor. **Physically disabled:** Services for visually, speech, hearing impaired.

**Contact.** E-mail: gswapps@canes.gsw.edu
Phone: (229) 928-1273 Toll-free number: (800) 338-0082
Fax: (229) 931-2059
Gaye Hayes, Dean of Students & Admissions Services, Georgia Southwestern State University, 800 Georgia Southwestern State University Drive, Americus, GA 31709-9957

---

## Georgia State University
**Atlanta, Georgia**  CB member
**www.gsu.edu**  CB code: 5251

- Public 4-year university
- Commuter campus in very large city
- 19,282 degree-seeking undergraduates: 25% part-time, 61% women, 29% African American, 11% Asian American, 5% Hispanic American, 3% international
- 6,708 degree-seeking graduate students
- 53% of applicants admitted
- SAT or ACT with writing required
- 47% graduate within 6 years

**General.** Founded in 1913. Regionally accredited. Courses offered at Alpharetta Center and Brookhaven Center. Distance learning and web courses available in College of Health and Human Sciences. **Degrees:** 3,793 bachelor's awarded; master's, doctoral, first professional offered. **ROTC:** Army, Naval, Air Force. **Location:** Downtown. **Calendar:** Semester, extensive summer session. **Full-time faculty:** 1,086 total; 84% have terminal degrees, 21% minority, 45% women. **Part-time faculty:** 416 total. **Class size:** 33% < 20, 40% 20-39, 16% 40-49, 9% 50-99, 3% >100. **Special facilities:** Viral immunology center, writing studio, advanced biotechnology center, Asian studies center, multi-media instructional lab, child development center, performing arts center, language acquisition and research centers, military science leadership lab, music media center, learning disorders center, speech and language center, hearing center.

**Freshman class profile.** 9,775 applied, 5,198 admitted, 2,607 enrolled.

| Mid 50% test scores | | | |
|---|---|---|---|
| SAT critical reading: | 490-590 | Return as sophomores: | 80% |
| SAT math: | 490-590 | Out-of-state: | 4% |
| ACT composite: | 21-25 | Live on campus: | 46% |
| GPA 3.50 or higher: | 29% | International: | 2% |
| GPA 3.0-3.49: | 55% | Fraternities: | 6% |
| GPA 2.0-2.99: | 16% | Sororities: | 7% |

**Basis for selection.** GED not accepted. The minimum test score requirements mandated by the Board of Regents are 430 verbal/critical reading and 400 mathematics on the SAT or 17 English and 17 math on the ACT. Essay recommended. Audition and an interview is required for music majors. A portfolio is required for art majors. **Homeschooled:** Transcript of courses and grades required. 1090 SAT (exclusive of writing) with 430 critical reading and 400 math or 24 ACT with 17 English and math subtests required. SAT Subject Test option available: 520 English Writing, 530 Literature, 500 Math IC or 570 Math IIC, 520 Biology, 540 Chemistry or 590 Physics, 560 American History and Social Studies, and 540 World History.

**High school preparation.** 16 units required. Required units include English 4, mathematics 4, social studies 2, history 1, science 3 (laboratory 2) and foreign language 2. 1 life sciences lab, 1 physical sciences lab plus additional science unit; foreign language units must be same language; math units must be algebra I, geometry, algebra II, and higher.

**2007-2008 Annual costs.** Tuition/fees: $5,484; $18,972 out-of-state. Room only: $5,950. Books/supplies: $1,000. Personal expenses: $2,166.

**2007-2008 Financial aid.** All financial aid based on need. 2,048 full-time freshmen applied for aid; 1,502 were judged to have need; 1,440 of these received aid. Average need met was 28%. Average scholarship/grant was $2,863; average loan $3,249. 47% of total undergraduate aid awarded as scholarships/grants, 53% as loans/jobs.

**Application procedures.** Admission: Priority date 2/1; deadline 3/1 (postmark date). $50 fee, may be waived for applicants with need. Application may be submitted online. Admission notification on a rolling basis beginning on or about 10/1. **Financial aid:** Priority date 4/1, closing date 11/1. FAFSA required. Applicants notified on a rolling basis starting 3/30; must reply within 2 week(s) of notification.

**Academics. Special study options:** Accelerated study, cooperative education, cross-registration, distance learning, double major, dual enrollment of high school students, ESL, honors, independent study, internships, student-designed major, study abroad, teacher certification program. Freshman learning communities. **Credit/placement by examination:** AP, CLEP, IB, institutional tests. 30 credit hours maximum toward bachelor's degree. Some credit awarded for DANTES subject examinations. **Support services:** Learning center, pre-admission summer program, reduced course load, remedial instruction, study skills assistance, tutoring, writing center.

**Honors college/program.** 3.3 GPA and 1800 SAT or 26 ACT required.

**Majors. Area/ethnic studies:** African-American, Asian, regional, women's. **Biology:** General. **Business:** Accounting, actuarial science, business admin, finance, insurance, international, managerial economics, marketing, real estate. **Communications:** General, journalism. **Computer sciences:** General, computer science. **Conservation:** Environmental science. **Education:** Art, early childhood. **English:** English lit. **Family/consumer sciences:** Food/nutrition. **Foreign languages:** General, classics, French, German, Spanish. **Health:** Nursing (RN), respiratory therapy technology. **History:** General. **Interdisciplinary:** Classical/archaeology, gerontology, global studies. **Legal studies:** General. **Math:** General. **Parks/recreation:** Exercise sciences, health/fitness. **Philosophy/religion:** Philosophy, religion. **Physical sciences:** Chemistry, geology, physics. **Protective services:** Criminal justice. **Psychology:** General. **Public administration:** Policy analysis, social work. **Social sciences:** Anthropology, economics, geography, international economics, political science, sociology, urban studies. **Visual/performing arts:** Art, art history/conservation, design, drawing, film/cinema, music management, music performance, theater history.

**Most popular majors.** Biology 6%, business/marketing 32%, psychology 8%, social sciences 14%, visual/performing arts 6%.

**Computing on campus.** 395 workstations in library, computer center. Dormitories wired for high-speed internet access and linked to campus network. Commuter students can connect to campus network. Online course registration, online library, helpline, student web hosting, wireless network available.

**Student life. Freshman orientation:** Mandatory, $56 fee. Preregistration for classes offered. Various summer sessions offered. **Housing:** Coed dorms, special housing for disabled, apartments, substance-free housing available. $525 nonrefundable deposit. **Activities:** Bands, campus ministries, choral groups, dance, drama, film society, literary magazine, music ensembles, radio station, student government, student newspaper, symphony orchestra, TV station, African students association, Amnesty International, Brazillian student association, Bridge Builders, Campus Civitan, Catholic student association, Chinese student union, College Republicans, Christian legal society.

**Athletics.** NCAA. **Intercollegiate:** Baseball M, basketball, cross-country, golf, soccer, softball W, tennis, track and field, volleyball. **Intramural:** Basketball, bowling, football (non-tackle), golf, racquetball, soccer, softball, table tennis, tennis, volleyball. **Team name:** Panthers.

**Student services.** Career counseling, student employment services, financial aid counseling, health services, on-campus daycare, personal counseling, placement for graduates, veterans' counselor. **Physically disabled:** Services for visually, speech, hearing impaired.

**Contact.** E-mail: admissions@gsu.edu
Phone: (404) 413-2500 Fax: (404) 413-2002
Nannette Commander, Director of Admissions, Georgia State University, Box 4009, Atlanta, GA 30302-4009

---

## Herzing College
**Atlanta, Georgia**
www.herzing.edu

CB code: 2342

- For-profit 3-year business and technical college
- Commuter campus in very large city
- 441 degree-seeking undergraduates
- 97% of applicants admitted
- Interview required

**General.** Founded in 1949. Regionally accredited. **Degrees:** 28 bachelor's, 25 associate awarded. **Location:** 120 miles from Birmingham, Alabama; 70 miles from Chattanooga, Tennessee. **Calendar:** Semester, extensive summer session. **Full-time faculty:** 7 total. **Part-time faculty:** 27 total. **Class size:** 84% < 20, 16% 20-39.

**Basis for selection.** Entrance test and evaluation for all applicants.

**2007-2008 Annual costs.** Tuition/fees: $11,100. Costs may vary by program. Tuition includes use of books. Additional charges for technology and engineering programs; surcharge for technology programs.

**Financial aid. Non-need-based:** Scholarships awarded for academics.

**Application procedures. Admission:** No deadline. No application fee. Application may be submitted online. Admission notification on a rolling basis. **Financial aid:** No deadline. FAFSA, institutional form required. Applicants notified on a rolling basis.

**Academics.** Students train on types of equipment used in the field. **Special study options:** Distance learning, independent study, internships, liberal arts/career combination. **Credit/placement by examination:** CLEP, IB, institutional tests. **Support services:** Learning center, study skills assistance, tutoring.

**Majors. Business:** Business admin. **Computer sciences:** Information systems, programming.

**Most popular majors.** Business/marketing 31%, computer/information sciences 41%.

**Computing on campus.** 157 workstations in library, computer center. Online library available.

**Student life. Freshman orientation:** Mandatory. Preregistration for classes offered. Orientation held beginning of each term for 2 hours. **Activities:** Student government.

**Student services.** Career counseling, student employment services, financial aid counseling, personal counseling, placement for graduates, veterans' counselor.

**Contact.** E-mail: info@atl.herzing.edu
Phone: (404) 816-4533 Toll-free number: (800) 573-4533
Fax: (404) 816-5576
Rose White, Director of Admissions, Herzing College, 3393 Peachtree Road NE, Suite 1003, Atlanta, GA 30326

## ITT Technical Institute: Duluth
### Duluth, Georgia

♦ For-profit 4-year technical college
♦ Commuter campus in large town

**General.** Accredited by ACICS. **Calendar:** Quarter.

**Annual costs/financial aid.** Tuition varies by program, $260-$368 per credit hour.

**Contact.** Phone: (866) 489-8818
Director of Recruitment, 10700 Abbotts Bridge Road, Duluth, GA 30097

## Kennesaw State University
### Kennesaw, Georgia
### www.kennesaw.edu

**CB member**
**CB code: 5359**

♦ Public 4-year university
♦ Commuter campus in large town
♦ 18,213 degree-seeking undergraduates: 27% part-time, 61% women, 9% African American, 3% Asian American, 3% Hispanic American, 3% international
♦ 2,209 degree-seeking graduate students
♦ 59% of applicants admitted
♦ SAT or ACT (ACT writing optional) required

**General.** Founded in 1963. Regionally accredited. **Degrees:** 2,505 bachelor's awarded; master's, doctoral offered. **ROTC:** Army, Air Force. **Location:** 20 miles from Atlanta. **Calendar:** Semester, limited summer session. **Full-time faculty:** 716 total; 77% have terminal degrees, 21% minority, 49% women. **Part-time faculty:** 402 total; 33% have terminal degrees, 16% minority, 56% women. **Class size:** 19% < 20, 56% 20-39, 11% 40-49, 13% 50-99, 1% >100. **Special facilities:** Educational technology center, presentation technology department, teacher resource and activity center, 2 art galleries.

**Freshman class profile.** 7,265 applied, 4,290 admitted, 2,493 enrolled.

| Mid 50% test scores | | | |
|---|---|---|---|
| SAT critical reading: | 490-570 | Rank in top quarter: | 53% |
| SAT math: | 490-570 | Rank in top tenth: | 21% |
| SAT writing: | 470-560 | End year in good standing: | 86% |
| ACT composite: | 20-24 | Return as sophomores: | 76% |
| GPA 3.50 or higher: | 25% | Live on campus: | 42% |
| GPA 3.0-3.49: | 40% | International: | 2% |
| GPA 2.0-2.99: | 35% | Fraternities: | 1% |
| | | Sororities: | 1% |

**Basis for selection.** GED not accepted. 2.5 GPA in college prep courses and 490 SAT verbal/460 SAT math or 20 ACT English/19 ACT math required. Applicants with test scores below minimum must take institutional placement exams in appropriate subject areas. Audition required of music majors. Portfolio required of art majors. **Homeschooled:** Students considered based on portfolio, standardized tests scores, extra-curricular activities, and recommendations.

**High school preparation.** 16 units required. Required units include English 4, mathematics 4, social studies 3, science 3 (laboratory 3) and foreign language 2.

**2007-2008 Annual costs.** Tuition/fees: $3,806; $12,678 out-of-state. Room only: $4,990. Books/supplies: $1,000. Personal expenses: $1,464.

**2007-2008 Financial aid. Need-based:** 1,602 full-time freshmen applied for aid; 904 were judged to have need; 894 of these received aid. Average need met was 20%. Average scholarship/grant was $8,135; average loan $2,374. 54% of total undergraduate aid awarded as scholarships/grants, 46% as loans/jobs. **Non-need-based:** Awarded to 4,757 full-time undergraduates, including 1,581 freshmen. Scholarships awarded for academics, alumni affiliation, art, athletics, job skills, leadership, minority status, music/drama, ROTC, state residency.

**Application procedures. Admission:** Closing date 5/16 (receipt date). $40 fee, may be waived for applicants with need. Application may be submitted online. Admission notification on a rolling basis beginning on or about 1/1. **Financial aid:** Priority date 4/1, closing date 7/1. FAFSA required. Applicants notified on a rolling basis starting 5/15.

**Academics. Special study options:** Cooperative education, cross-registration, distance learning, double major, ESL, honors, internships, study abroad, teacher certification program, weekend college. **Credit/placement**

by examination: AP, CLEP, IB, institutional tests. 30 credit hours maximum toward bachelor's degree. **Support services:** Learning center, reduced course load, remedial instruction, study skills assistance, tutoring, writing center.

**Honors college/program.** 3.5 GPA and 1200 SAT (exclusive of Writing) required. Joint enrollment honors program for high school junior and seniors; requires 3.0 GPA, 530 SAT verbal and math (1100 or above exclusive of writing) or 25 ACT, with 24 English and 20 Math subscores.

**Majors. Area/ethnic studies:** African. **Biology:** General, biochemistry, biotechnology. **Business:** Accounting, business admin, finance, international, managerial economics, marketing, operations. **Communications:** General. **Computer sciences:** General, information systems, security. **Education:** Art, biology, elementary, English, mathematics, middle, music, physical, social studies. **English:** English lit. **Foreign languages:** Romance. **Health:** Nursing (RN). **History:** General. **Math:** General. **Parks/recreation:** Exercise sciences, sports admin. **Physical sciences:** Chemistry. **Protective services:** Criminal justice. **Psychology:** General. **Public administration:** Social work. **Social sciences:** Anthropology, cartography, geography, international relations, political science, sociology. **Visual/performing arts:** Art, dramatic, music performance.

**Most popular majors.** Business/marketing 27%; communications/journalism 6%, education 19%, health sciences 8%, psychology 6%, social sciences 6%.

**Computing on campus.** 1,400 workstations in library, computer center, student center. Dormitories wired for high-speed internet access. Commuter students can connect to campus network. Online course registration, online library, helpline, wireless network available.

**Student life. Freshman orientation:** Mandatory, $25 fee. Preregistration for classes offered. Held prior to semester. **Housing:** Apartments available. $350 nonrefundable deposit. **Activities:** Bands, campus ministries, choral groups, dance, drama, international student organizations, literary magazine, music ensembles, Model UN, musical theater, radio station, student government, student newspaper, symphony orchestra, Baptist student union, Student Nurses Association, College Ambassadors, volunteer club, American Marketing Association, African American student alliance, Circle K, Catholic student association.

**Athletics.** NCAA. **Intercollegiate:** Baseball M, basketball, cheerleading M, cross-country, golf, ice hockey M, soccer W, softball W, tennis W, track and field. **Intramural:** Basketball, bowling, soccer, softball, swimming, table tennis, tennis, volleyball, wrestling. **Team name:** Fighting Owls.

**Student services.** Adult student services, alcohol/substance abuse counseling, career counseling, student employment services, financial aid counseling, health services, minority student services, personal counseling, placement for graduates, veterans' counselor. **Physically disabled:** Services for visually, speech, hearing impaired.

**Contact.** E-mail: ksuadmit@kennesaw.edu
Phone: (770) 423-6300 Fax: (770) 423-6541
Joe Head, Dean of University Admissions and Enrollment Services, Kennesaw State University, 1000 Chastain Road, Kennesaw, GA 30144-5591

## LaGrange College
### LaGrange, Georgia
### www.lagrange.edu

**CB member**
**CB code: 5362**

♦ Private 4-year liberal arts college affiliated with United Methodist Church
♦ Residential campus in large town
♦ 989 degree-seeking undergraduates: 8% part-time, 55% women, 21% African American, 2% Asian American, 2% Hispanic American, 1% Native American, 2% international
♦ 93 degree-seeking graduate students
♦ 57% of applicants admitted
♦ SAT or ACT (ACT writing recommended), application essay required
♦ 51% graduate within 6 years

**General.** Founded in 1831. Regionally accredited. **Degrees:** 214 bachelor's, 1 associate awarded; master's offered. **Location:** 70 miles from Atlanta, 45 miles from Columbus. **Calendar:** 4-1-4, limited summer session. **Full-time faculty:** 69 total; 83% have terminal degrees. **Part-time faculty:** 60 total; 33% have terminal degrees. **Class size:** 80% < 20, 18% 20-39, less than 1% 40-49, less than 1% 50-99. **Special facilities:** Performing arts auditorium, natatorium, art center.

**Freshman class profile.** 1,338 applied, 766 admitted, 221 enrolled.

| Mid 50% test scores | | | |
|---|---|---|---|
| SAT critical reading: | 450-550 | Rank in top tenth: | 16% |
| SAT math: | 450-550 | End year in good standing: | 74% |
| ACT composite: | 19-24 | Return as sophomores: | 65% |
| GPA 3.50 or higher: | 41% | Out-of-state: | 13% |
| GPA 3.0-3.49: | 47% | Live on campus: | 88% |
| GPA 2.0-2.99: | 12% | International: | 1% |
| Rank in top quarter: | 33% | Fraternities: | 28% |
| | | Sororities: | 39% |

**Basis for selection.** School achievement record and test scores most important. Interview and recommendations considered. Separate application typically during sophomore year for nursing applicants. Students undergo a writing sample and math placement test prior to registration. **Home-schooled:** Bibliography of high school readings, including textbooks, 2 letters of recommendation, one from outside the home, required. Interview suggested.

**High school preparation.** 14 units required; 16 recommended. Required and recommended units include English 4, mathematics 4, social studies 3, science 3 and foreign language 2.

**2007-2008 Annual costs.** Tuition/fees: $18,500. Room/board: $7,598. Books/supplies: $1,000. Personal expenses: $1,975.

**2006-2007 Financial aid.** **Need-based:** 241 full-time freshmen applied for aid; 203 were judged to have need; 202 of these received aid. Average need met was 86%. Average scholarship/grant was $11,414; average loan $2,631. 64% of total undergraduate aid awarded as scholarships/grants, 36% as loans/jobs. **Non-need-based:** Awarded to 294 full-time undergraduates, including 91 freshmen. Scholarships awarded for academics, art, job skills, leadership, minority status, music/drama, religious affiliation, state residency.

**Application procedures.** **Admission:** Priority date 3/1; no deadline. $30 fee, may be waived for applicants with need. Application may be submitted online. Admission notification on a rolling basis beginning on or about 9/15. Early admission candidates must be highly recommended by counselors and parents. **Financial aid:** Priority date 4/1; no closing date. FAFSA required. Applicants notified on a rolling basis starting 3/15; must reply by 8/15 or within 2 week(s) of notification.

**Academics.** **Special study options:** Accelerated study, combined bachelor's/graduate degree, double major, dual enrollment of high school students, independent study, internships, liberal arts/career combination, student-designed major, study abroad, teacher certification program, Washington semester. **Credit/placement by examination:** AP, CLEP, IB, SAT, institutional tests. 27 credit hours maximum toward bachelor's degree. **Support services:** Study skills assistance, tutoring, writing center.

**Majors.** **Biology:** General, biochemistry. **Business:** Accounting, business admin, organizational behavior. **Computer sciences:** General, computer science. **Education:** Elementary. **English:** English lit. **Foreign languages:** Spanish. **Health:** Nursing (RN). **History:** General. **Math:** General. **Philosophy/religion:** Religion. **Physical sciences:** Chemistry. **Psychology:** General. **Public administration:** Social work. **Social sciences:** Political science, sociology. **Theology:** Religious ed. **Visual/performing arts:** General, dramatic.

**Most popular majors.** Biology 6%, business/marketing 34%, education 6%, health sciences 11%, psychology 8%, public administration/social services 6%, social sciences 6%, visual/performing arts 9%.

**Computing on campus.** 141 workstations in dormitories, library, computer center. Dormitories wired for high-speed internet access and linked to campus network. Commuter students can connect to campus network. Online library, helpline, student web hosting, wireless network available.

**Student life.** **Freshman orientation:** Mandatory. Preregistration for classes offered. Number of 1-day summer orientation sessions available. **Housing:** Guaranteed on-campus for freshmen. Coed dorms, single-sex dorms, apartments, substance-free housing available. $100 fully refundable deposit, deadline 4/9. **Activities:** Choral groups, drama, literary magazine, music ensembles, musical theater, student government, student newspaper, Wesley Fellowship, Baptist Student Union, Circle-K, Rotaract, Interfaith Council, volunteer corps, Habitat for Humanity, Catholic group.

**Athletics.** NCAA. **Intercollegiate:** Baseball M, basketball, cheerleading M, cross-country, football (tackle) M, golf M, soccer, softball W, swimming, tennis, volleyball W. **Intramural:** Basketball, football (tackle) M, softball, volleyball. **Team name:** Panthers.

**Student services.** Adult student services, campus ministries, career counseling, student employment services, financial aid counseling, personal counseling, placement for graduates.

**Contact.** E-mail: admission@lagrange.edu
Phone: (706) 880-8005 Toll-free number: (800) 593-2885
Fax: (706) 880-8010
Dana Paul, Vice President for Enrollment Management, LaGrange College, 601 Broad Street, LaGrange, GA 30240-2999

## Life University
### Marietta, Georgia
### www.life.edu
**CB code: 7006**

- Private 4-year university
- Very large city
- 536 degree-seeking undergraduates: 27% part-time, 49% women, 21% African American, 5% Asian American, 5% Hispanic American, 1% Native American
- 1,368 degree-seeking graduate students
- 30% of applicants admitted
- SAT or ACT with writing required

**General.** Regionally accredited. **Degrees:** 49 bachelor's, 1 associate awarded; master's, first professional offered. **Location:** 10 miles from downtown Atlanta. **Calendar:** Quarter, limited summer session. **Full-time faculty:** 114 total; 87% have terminal degrees, 18% minority, 35% women. **Part-time faculty:** 35 total; 69% have terminal degrees, 20% minority, 54% women. **Class size:** 68% < 20, 25% 20-39, 6% 40-49, 2% 50-99.

**Freshman class profile.** 194 applied, 59 admitted, 28 enrolled.

| Mid 50% test scores | | | |
|---|---|---|---|
| SAT critical reading: | 400-530 | GPA 3.50 or higher: | 10% |
| SAT math: | 380-510 | GPA 3.0-3.49: | 50% |
| SAT writing: | 360-470 | GPA 2.0-2.99: | 40% |
| | | Out-of-state: | 41% |

**Basis for selection.** Standardized test scores and high school record most important. 2.0 GPA and 1430 SAT (including writing) or 18 ACT important. **Homeschooled:** Transcript of courses and grades required. **Learning Disabled:** Letter from doctor required.

**2007-2008 Annual costs.** Tuition/fees: $7,605. Books/supplies: $760.

**2007-2008 Financial aid.** **Need-based:** 23% of total undergraduate aid awarded as scholarships/grants, 77% as loans/jobs.

**Application procedures.** **Admission:** Closing date 9/1 (postmark date). $50 fee, may be waived for applicants with need. Application may be submitted online. Admission notification on a rolling basis. **Financial aid:** Priority date 3/1, closing date 6/15. FAFSA, institutional form required. Applicants notified on a rolling basis starting 5/1.

**Academics.** **Special study options:** Accelerated study, double major, ESL, independent study, internships. **Credit/placement by examination:** AP, CLEP, SAT, ACT. **Support services:** Learning center, reduced course load, remedial instruction, study skills assistance, tutoring, writing center.

**Majors.** **Biology:** General. **Business:** General, management information systems. **Health:** Dietetics. **Interdisciplinary:** Nutrition sciences. **Parks/recreation:** Exercise sciences.

**Most popular majors.** Biology 53%, business/marketing 28%, interdisciplinary studies 17%.

**Computing on campus.** Commuter students can connect to campus network. Online course registration, online library, wireless network available.

**Student life.** **Freshman orientation:** Mandatory. Two-day program usually held on Thursday and Friday before quarter begins. **Housing:** Apartments available. $250 partly refundable deposit. **Activities:** Student government.

**Athletics.** **Intramural:** Basketball, football (tackle), volleyball. **Team name:** Eagles.

**Student services.** Alcohol/substance abuse counseling, financial aid counseling, personal counseling.

**Contact.** E-mail: admissions@life.edu
Phone: (770) 426-2884 Toll-free number: (800) 543-3202
Fax: (770) 426-2895
Deborah Heairlston, Director of New Student Development, Life University, 1269 Barclay Circle, Marietta, GA 30060

## Macon State College
**Macon, Georgia**
www.maconstate.edu

**CB member**
**CB code: 5439**

- Public 4-year business and health science college
- Commuter campus in small city
- 6,234 degree-seeking undergraduates
- 64% of applicants admitted

**General.** Founded in 1968. Regionally accredited. **Degrees:** 330 bachelor's, 375 associate awarded. **Location:** 85 miles from Atlanta. **Calendar:** Semester, extensive summer session. **Full-time faculty:** 198 total. **Part-time faculty:** 108 total. **Class size:** 45% < 20, 51% 20-39, 4% 40-49. **Special facilities:** Botanical gardens.

**Freshman class profile.** 2,432 applied, 1,545 admitted, 1,008 enrolled.

| Mid 50% test scores | | ACT composite: | 15-20 |
|---|---|---|---|
| SAT critical reading: | 400-530 | Out-of-state: | 4% |
| SAT math: | 390-520 | | |

**Basis for selection.** 480 SAT verbal or 21 ACT English, 440 SAT math or 19 ACT math required for uncondional admissions. For early admission applicants or joint high school enrollment applicants, 1010 SAT (exclusive of writing), 530 SAT verbal and 3.0 GPA required. College-preparatory requirements waived for students in career programs and adult applicants. SAT or ACT recommended. Interview required for respiratory therapy, health information technology, health information management, health services administration, and technology programs. **Homeschooled:** Recent GED or home-schooled applicants must submit SAT and provide portfolio indicating courses taken.

**High school preparation.** 16 units required. Required units include English 4, mathematics 4, social studies 1, history 2, science 3 (laboratory 2) and foreign language 2.

**2007-2008 Annual costs.** Tuition/fees: $2,060; $7,676 out-of-state. Books/supplies: $800. Personal expenses: $3,000.

**2006-2007 Financial aid.** All financial aid based on need. 53% of total undergraduate aid awarded as scholarships/grants, 47% as loans/jobs.

**Application procedures. Admission:** Closing date 7/23 (receipt date). $20 fee, may be waived for applicants with need. Application may be submitted online. Admission notification on a rolling basis. **Financial aid:** Priority date 4/1; no closing date. FAFSA required. Applicants notified on a rolling basis starting 4/15; must reply within 2 week(s) of notification.

**Academics. Special study options:** Distance learning, dual enrollment of high school students, honors, internships, liberal arts/career combination, study abroad, teacher certification program. **Credit/placement by examination:** AP, CLEP, IB, institutional tests. 40 credit hours maximum toward associate degree, 40 toward bachelor's. **Support services:** Learning center, pre-admission summer program, reduced course load, remedial instruction, study skills assistance, tutoring, writing center.

**Majors. Business:** Business admin. **Communications:** General. **Computer sciences:** Applications programming, information systems, programming. **Education:** Early childhood. **Health:** Health care admin, health services, medical records admin, nursing (RN). **Public administration:** Human services.

**Most popular majors.** Business/marketing 35%, computer/information sciences 29%, health sciences 19%, public administration/social services 13%.

**Computing on campus.** 150 workstations in library, computer center, student center. Commuter students can connect to campus network. Online course registration, online library, helpline, wireless network available.

**Student life. Freshman orientation:** Available, $25 fee. Preregistration for classes offered. **Activities:** Choral groups, drama, literary magazine, music ensembles, musical theater, student government, student newspaper, TV station, Black Student Unification, Association of Nursing Students, Spanish club, Baptist student union, astronomy club, pre-med club, honors student association, Amnesty International, information technology club.

**Athletics. Intramural:** Basketball, bowling, golf, softball, swimming, table tennis, tennis, volleyball.

**Student services.** Career counseling, student employment services, financial aid counseling, health services, minority student services, personal counseling, veterans' counselor.

**Contact.** E-mail: mscinfo@mail.maconstate.edu
Phone: (478) 471-2800 Toll-free number: (800) 272-7619
Fax: (478) 471-5343
Dee Minter, Associate Vice President for Enrollment Services, Macon State College, 100 College Station Drive, Macon, GA 31206-5145

## Medical College of Georgia
**Augusta, Georgia**
www.mcg.edu

**CB member**
**CB code: 5406**

- Public two-year upper-division health science college
- Commuter campus in large city
- Test scores, application essay required

**General.** Founded in 1828. Regionally accredited. **Degrees:** 325 bachelor's awarded; master's, doctoral, first professional offered. **Location:** 157 miles from Atlanta. **Calendar:** Semester. **Full-time faculty:** 646 total; 88% have terminal degrees, 28% minority, 36% women. **Part-time faculty:** 149 total; 86% have terminal degrees, 13% minority, 44% women. **Special facilities:** 600-bed teaching hospital, over 80 clinics.

**Student profile.** 591 degree-seeking undergraduates, 1,783 degree-seeking graduate students.

| | | | |
|---|---|---|---|
| Women: | 88% | Hispanic American: | 2% |
| African American: | 17% | International: | 1% |
| Asian American: | 4% | Part-time: | 14% |

**Basis for selection.** College transcript, application essay, standardized test scores required. Admission based on GPA, math and science test scores, 3 references, and statement of purpose. SAT or ACT and personal interview required. Minimum of 60 semester hours of transferable prescribed liberal arts courses required. Closing dates and score reports vary by program. Transfer accepted as juniors.

**2007-2008 Annual costs.** Tuition/fees: $5,184; $18,672 out-of-state. Room/board: $1,642.

**Financial aid. Non-need-based:** Scholarships awarded for academics, state residency. **Additional information:** State Hope scholarships only available to Georgia residents.

**Application procedures. Admission:** Rolling admission. $30 fee. **Financial aid:** Priority date 3/31, closing date 5/30. Applicants notified on a rolling basis; must reply within 2 weeks of notification. FAFSA, institutional form required.

**Academics. Special study options:** Combined bachelor's/graduate degree, distance learning, internships, liberal arts/career combination, study abroad. Cooperative program with Augusta State University. **Credit/placement by examination:** AP, CLEP.

**Majors. Health:** Clinical lab technology, dental hygiene, medical radiologic technology/radiation therapy, medical records admin, nursing (RN), physician assistant, preop/surgical nursing, respiratory therapy technology, sonography.

**Computing on campus.** 323 workstations in library, student center. Commuter students can connect to campus network. Online library, wireless network available.

**Student life. Housing:** Coed dorms, apartments, substance-free housing available. **Activities:** Student government, student newspaper, Christian Medical Society, Black Student Medical Alliance.

**Athletics. Intramural:** Badminton, basketball, football (non-tackle), golf, racquetball, soccer, softball, table tennis, volleyball, weight lifting.

**Student services.** Career counseling, student employment services, health services, minority student services, on-campus daycare, personal counseling.

**Contact.** E-mail: underadm@mcg.edu
Phone: (706) 721-2725 Toll-free number: (800) 519-3388
Fax: (706) 721-7279
Carol Nobles, Director of Student Recruitment and Admissions, Medical College of Georgia, Office of Academic Admissions, Room 170 Kelly Building, Augusta, GA 30912-7310

## Mercer University
**Macon, Georgia**
www.mercer.edu

**CB member**
**CB code: 5409**

- Private 4-year university affiliated with Baptist faith
- Residential campus in small city

- 2,245 degree-seeking undergraduates: 2% part-time, 53% women, 17% African American, 7% Asian American, 3% Hispanic American, 2% international
- 2,878 degree-seeking graduate students
- 60% of applicants admitted
- SAT or ACT (ACT writing recommended) required
- 55% graduate within 6 years; 20% enter graduate study

**General.** Founded in 1833. Regionally accredited. Evening and weekend continuing education programs available at 4 regional academic centers and transfer degree programs offered at Atlanta campus. **Degrees:** 972 bachelor's awarded; master's, doctoral, first professional offered. **ROTC:** Army. **Location:** 85 miles from Atlanta. **Calendar:** Semester, extensive summer session. **Full-time faculty:** 352 total; 88% have terminal degrees, 14% minority, 41% women. **Part-time faculty:** 220 total; 41% have terminal degrees, 16% minority, 48% women. **Class size:** 56% < 20, 41% 20-39, 1% 40-49, 2% 50-99, less than 1% >100.

**Freshman class profile.** 4,588 applied, 2,748 admitted, 583 enrolled.

| Mid 50% test scores | | | |
|---|---|---|---|
| SAT critical reading: | 530-640 | Rank in top tenth: | 42% |
| SAT math: | 540-630 | End year in good standing: | 84% |
| SAT writing: | 510-620 | Return as sophomores: | 81% |
| ACT composite: | 23-28 | Out-of-state: | 19% |
| GPA 3.50 or higher: | 69% | Live on campus: | 93% |
| GPA 3.0-3.49: | 22% | International: | 2% |
| GPA 2.0-2.99: | 9% | Fraternities: | 21% |
| Rank in top quarter: | 72% | Sororities: | 22% |

**Basis for selection.** GED not accepted. Admissions based on academic merit. GPA, SAT scores and extracurricular activities important. Interview recommended. Audition recommended for music majors. **Homeschooled:** Minimum SAT of 1100 (exclusive of Writing), certified transcript indicating college-preparatory curriculum including name and title of textbooks used, interview. SAT exams may be substituted for certified transcript. **Learning Disabled:** Documentation from licensed professional required.

**High school preparation.** 16 units required. Required units include English 4, mathematics 4, social studies 1, history 2, science 3 and foreign language 2.

**2007-2008 Annual costs.** Tuition/fees: $26,960. Room/board: $8,015. Books/supplies: $900. Personal expenses: $1,101.

**2007-2008 Financial aid. Need-based:** 519 full-time freshmen applied for aid; 417 were judged to have need; 417 of these received aid. Average need met was 91%. Average scholarship/grant was $19,186; average loan $5,653. 76% of total undergraduate aid awarded as scholarships/grants, 24% as loans/jobs. **Non-need-based:** Awarded to 1,298 full-time undergraduates, including 339 freshmen. Scholarships awarded for academics, art, athletics, job skills, leadership, music/drama, religious affiliation, ROTC, state residency.

**Application procedures. Admission:** Priority date 4/1; deadline 7/1 (postmark date). $50 fee, may be waived for applicants with need. Application may be submitted online. Admission notification on a rolling basis beginning on or about 11/1. Must reply by May 1 or within 4 week(s) if notified thereafter. **Financial aid:** Priority date 4/1; no closing date. FAFSA, institutional form required. Applicants notified on a rolling basis starting 3/15; must reply within 2 week(s) of notification.

**Academics. Special study options:** Accelerated study, combined bachelor's/graduate degree, cooperative education, cross-registration, double major, dual enrollment of high school students, honors, independent study, internships, liberal arts/career combination, student-designed major, study abroad, teacher certification program. Students may satisfy general education requirements by completing either the Great Books Program or the Distributional Program. **Credit/placement by examination:** AP, CLEP, IB, SAT, ACT, institutional tests. 32 credit hours maximum toward bachelor's degree. **Support services:** Learning center, pre-admission summer program, reduced course load, study skills assistance, tutoring, writing center.

**Majors. Area/ethnic studies:** African-American, regional, women's. **Biology:** General, biochemistry. **Business:** General. **Communications:** Journalism, media studies. **Computer sciences:** Computer science, information systems. **Conservation:** Environmental science. **Education:** Elementary, middle, music. **Engineering:** General. **English:** English lit. **Foreign languages:** Classics, French, German, Latin, Spanish. **Health:** Nursing (RN), predental, premedicine. **History:** General. **Liberal arts:** Arts/sciences. **Math:** General. **Philosophy/religion:** Christian, philosophy. **Physical sciences:** Chemistry, physics. **Protective services:** Criminal justice. **Psychology:** General. **Public administration:** Community org/advocacy. **Social sciences:** Economics, international relations, political science, sociology. **Visual/performing arts:** Art, dramatic, music performance.

**Most popular majors.** Biology 7%, business/marketing 24%, engineering/engineering technologies 14%, English 6%, psychology 9%, social sciences 9%, visual/performing arts 6%.

**Computing on campus.** 1,150 workstations in library, computer center, student center. Dormitories wired for high-speed internet access and linked to campus network. Commuter students can connect to campus network. Online course registration, online library, helpline, repair service, wireless network available.

**Student life. Freshman orientation:** Mandatory. Preregistration for classes offered. One-day summer orientation and 4 day program in fall before semester begins. **Policies:** Alcohol not permitted on campus. **Housing:** Guaranteed on-campus for freshmen. Coed dorms, single-sex dorms, special housing for disabled, apartments, fraternity/sorority housing available. **Activities:** Bands, campus ministries, choral groups, dance, drama, film society, international student organizations, literary magazine, music ensembles, opera, radio station, student government, student newspaper, TV station, Baptist student union, Reformed University Fellowship, Habitat for Humanity, black student organization, Catholic Newman center, College Republicans, College Democrats, Hispanic Latino student union, Islamic student organization.

**Athletics.** NCAA. **Intercollegiate:** Baseball M, basketball, cross-country, golf, rifle M, soccer, softball W, tennis, volleyball W. **Intramural:** Basketball, football (non-tackle), soccer, softball, swimming, tennis, volleyball, water polo. **Team name:** Bears.

**Student services.** Adult student services, alcohol/substance abuse counseling, career counseling, services for economically disadvantaged, student employment services, financial aid counseling, health services, minority student services, personal counseling, placement for graduates. **Physically disabled:** Services for visually, speech, hearing impaired.

**Contact.** E-mail: admissions@mercer.edu
Phone: (478) 301-2650 Toll-free number: (800) 840-8577
Fax: (478) 301-2828
Terry Whittum, Senior Vice President, Enrollment Services, Mercer University, 1400 Coleman Avenue, Macon, GA 31207-0001

---

## Morehouse College
### Atlanta, Georgia
www.morehouse.edu

**CB member**
**CB code: 5415**

- Private 4-year liberal arts college for men
- Residential campus in very large city
- 2,810 degree-seeking undergraduates: 5% part-time, 95% African American, 3% international
- 59% of applicants admitted
- SAT or ACT with writing, application essay required
- 57% graduate within 6 years; 34% enter graduate study

**General.** Founded in 1867. Regionally accredited. One of 4 members of Atlanta University Center sharing facilities including library. **Degrees:** 563 bachelor's awarded. **ROTC:** Army, Naval, Air Force. **Calendar:** Semester, limited summer session. **Full-time faculty:** 161 total; 87% have terminal degrees, 80% minority, 36% women. **Part-time faculty:** 75 total. **Class size:** 24% < 20, 69% 20-39, 5% 40-49, 3% 50-99. **Special facilities:** Chapels, meditation room.

**Freshman class profile.** 2,369 applied, 1,399 admitted, 677 enrolled.

| Mid 50% test scores | | | |
|---|---|---|---|
| SAT critical reading: | 480-580 | Rank in top quarter: | 45% |
| SAT math: | 480-590 | Rank in top tenth: | 14% |
| ACT composite: | 20-24 | End year in good standing: | 87% |
| GPA 3.50 or higher: | 28% | Return as sophomores: | 83% |
| GPA 3.0-3.49: | 38% | Out-of-state: | 72% |
| GPA 2.0-2.99: | 33% | Live on campus: | 96% |
| | | International: | 3% |

**Basis for selection.** School academic record most important, followed by test scores, counselor recommendation, school and community activities, and student leadership. Interview recommended.

**High school preparation.** 13 units required; 16 recommended. Required and recommended units include English 4, mathematics 3, social studies 2, science 2 and foreign language 2. 3 additional units may be from any academic discipline.

**2007-2008 Annual costs.** Tuition/fees: $18,678. Room/board: $9,928. Books/supplies: $1,500. Personal expenses: $3,800.

**2006-2007 Financial aid. Need-based:** 676 full-time freshmen applied for aid; 676 were judged to have need; 676 of these received aid. Average

need met was 28%. Average scholarship/grant was $7,484; average loan $2,625. 30% of total undergraduate aid awarded as scholarships/grants, 70% as loans/jobs. **Non-need-based:** Awarded to 2,711 full-time undergraduates, including 567 freshmen. Scholarships awarded for academics, alumni affiliation, art, athletics, leadership, music/drama, ROTC, state residency.

**Application procedures. Admission:** Priority date 11/1; deadline 2/15 (postmark date). $45 fee, may be waived for applicants with need. Application must be submitted on paper. Admission notification on a rolling basis beginning on or about 11/15. Must reply by 5/1. **Financial aid:** Priority date 2/15, closing date 4/1. FAFSA, institutional form, CSS PROFILE required. Must reply by 5/1.

**Academics. Special study options:** Combined bachelor's/graduate degree, cooperative education, cross-registration, double major, dual enrollment of high school students, exchange student, honors, internships, liberal arts/career combination, semester at sea, study abroad. Dual degree program in engineering and architecture with other institutions. **Credit/placement by examination:** AP, CLEP, SAT, ACT, institutional tests. 30 credit hours maximum toward bachelor's degree. **Support services:** Learning center, pre-admission summer program, reduced course load, remedial instruction, study skills assistance, tutoring, writing center.

**Majors. Area/ethnic studies:** African-American. **Biology:** General. **Business:** Business admin. **Computer sciences:** General. **Education:** General. **Engineering:** General. **English:** English lit. **Foreign languages:** French, Spanish. **History:** General. **Math:** General. **Parks/recreation:** Health/fitness. **Philosophy/religion:** Philosophy, religion. **Physical sciences:** Chemistry, physics. **Psychology:** General. **Social sciences:** Economics, international relations, political science, sociology, urban studies. **Visual/performing arts:** Art, dramatic.

**Most popular majors.** Biology 9%, business/marketing 31%, computer/information sciences 6%, psychology 9%, social sciences 15%.

**Computing on campus.** 300 workstations in dormitories, library, computer center. Dormitories wired for high-speed internet access and linked to campus network. Commuter students can connect to campus network. Online course registration, online library, helpline, repair service, wireless network available.

**Student life. Freshman orientation:** Mandatory, $480 fee. Preregistration for classes offered. Held several days before class begins each fall. **Housing:** Guaranteed on-campus for freshmen. Apartments, substance-free housing available. $500 nonrefundable deposit, deadline 6/24. **Activities:** Bands, choral groups, drama, literary magazine, music ensembles, student government, student newspaper, Martin Luther King International Chapel Assistants, international student association, mentoring program, Frederick Douglass Tutorial Program, political science club, New Life Inspirational Gospel Choir, NAACP, Eagle Scout Association.

**Athletics.** NCAA. **Intercollegiate:** Baseball M, basketball M, cross-country M, football (tackle) M, golf M, tennis M, track and field M. **Intramural:** Baseball M, basketball M, football (non-tackle) M, soccer M, softball M, swimming M, table tennis M, tennis M, weight lifting M. **Team name:** Maroon Tigers.

**Student services.** Alcohol/substance abuse counseling, campus ministries, career counseling, student employment services, financial aid counseling, health services, personal counseling, placement for graduates, veterans' counselor. **Physically disabled:** Services for visually, speech, hearing impaired.

**Contact.** E-mail: admissions@morehouse.edu
Phone: (404) 681-2800 ext. 2632 Toll-free number: (800) 851-1254
Fax: (404) 524-5635
Terrance Dixon, Associate Dean of Admissions and Records, Morehouse College, 830 Westview Drive SW, Atlanta, GA 30314

---

## North Georgia College & State University

**Dahlonega, Georgia**
www.ngcsu.edu

**CB member**
**CB code: 5497**

- Public 4-year university and military college
- Commuter campus in small town
- 4,498 degree-seeking undergraduates: 17% part-time, 60% women, 3% African American, 1% Asian American, 3% Hispanic American, 1% international
- 695 graduate students
- 62% of applicants admitted
- SAT or ACT (ACT writing optional) required
- 49% graduate within 6 years

**General.** Founded in 1873. Regionally accredited. 4 years Army ROTC required of all resident male undergraduate students. Military service following graduation not mandatory. **Degrees:** 713 bachelor's, 118 associate awarded; master's, doctoral offered. **ROTC:** Army. **Location:** 70 miles from Atlanta. **Calendar:** Semester, extensive summer session. **Full-time faculty:** 202 total; 65% have terminal degrees, 9% minority, 50% women. **Part-time faculty:** 165 total; 31% have terminal degrees, 11% minority, 58% women. **Class size:** 36% < 20, 56% 20-39, 5% 40-49, 4% 50-99. **Special facilities:** Observatory, rappeling tower, planetarium, nature preserve.

**Freshman class profile.** 2,461 applied, 1,519 admitted, 786 enrolled.

| Mid 50% test scores | | | |
|---|---|---|---|
| SAT critical reading: | 500-580 | GPA 2.0-2.99: | 21% |
| SAT math: | 490-580 | Rank in top quarter: | 53% |
| SAT writing: | 470-570 | Rank in top tenth: | 18% |
| ACT composite: | 20-24 | Return as sophomores: | 75% |
| GPA 3.50 or higher: | 38% | Out-of-state: | 7% |
| GPA 3.0-3.49: | 41% | Live on campus: | 64% |
| | | International: | 1% |

**Basis for selection.** High school academic record, test scores important, disciplinary record considered. Students must provide certification of immunization against communicable diseases. Commuting students must apply for permission to commute. Audition recommended for music majors. Portfolio recommended for art majors. **Homeschooled:** SAT Subject Tests required.

**High school preparation.** 17 units required. Required units include English 4, mathematics 4, social studies 3, science 3 (laboratory 1) and foreign language 2.

**2007-2008 Annual costs.** Tuition/fees: $3,810; $12,414 out-of-state. Room/board: $5,042. Books/supplies: $500. Personal expenses: $1,000.

**Financial aid. Non-need-based:** Scholarships awarded for academics, alumni affiliation, art, athletics, leadership, music/drama, ROTC, state residency.

**Application procedures. Admission:** Closing date 7/1. $25 fee, may be waived for applicants with need. Application may be submitted online. Admission notification on a rolling basis. **Financial aid:** Priority date 5/1; no closing date. FAFSA required. Applicants notified on a rolling basis starting 3/15; must reply within 3 week(s) of notification.

**Academics.** Consortium with Medical College of Georgia and Armstrong Atlantic State University to offer a Doctorate of Physical Therapy. Degree awarded from the Medical College of Georgia. **Special study options:** Combined bachelor's/graduate degree, cooperative education, distance learning, double major, dual enrollment of high school students, external degree, honors, independent study, internships, liberal arts/career combination, study abroad, teacher certification program. Dual degree program in engineering with Georgia Institute of Technology and Clemson University. **Credit/placement by examination:** AP, CLEP, SAT, ACT, institutional tests. 30 credit hours maximum toward associate degree, 30 toward bachelor's. **Support services:** Learning center, pre-admission summer program, reduced course load, remedial instruction, study skills assistance, tutoring, writing center.

**Majors. Biology:** General. **Business:** Accounting, business admin, finance, marketing. **Computer sciences:** General. **Education:** Art, early childhood, middle, music, physical, special. **English:** English lit. **Foreign languages:** French, German, Spanish. **Health:** Athletic training, nursing (RN). **History:** General. **Math:** General. **Parks/recreation:** Health/fitness. **Physical sciences:** Chemistry, physics. **Psychology:** General. **Social sciences:** Political science, sociology.

**Most popular majors.** Biology 7%, business/marketing 24%, education 31%, security/protective services 8%, social sciences 10%.

**Computing on campus.** 470 workstations in dormitories, library, computer center, student center. Dormitories linked to campus network. Commuter students can connect to campus network. Online course registration, online library, helpline, student web hosting available.

**Student life. Freshman orientation:** Available. Preregistration for classes offered. Two and 1/2-day program held 4 times during June, July, August; students stay in residence halls. **Policies:** All male residents must join Corps of Cadets; optional for female residents. **Housing:** Coed dorms, single-sex dorms, apartments available. $250 fully refundable deposit, deadline 5/1. **Activities:** Bands, campus ministries, choral groups, dance, drama, international student organizations, literary magazine, music ensembles, Model UN, student government, student newspaper, Students for Social Awareness, Baptist student union, commuter council, Muslim student association, Newman club, Habitat for Humanity.

**Athletics.** NCAA. **Intercollegiate:** Baseball M, basketball, cheerleading M, cross-country, rifle, soccer, softball W, tennis, track and field. **Intramural:** Basketball, football (non-tackle) W, football (tackle) M, golf, softball W, table tennis, volleyball, water polo. **Team name:** Saints.

**Student services.** Alcohol/substance abuse counseling, career counseling, student employment services, financial aid counseling, health services, minority student services, personal counseling, placement for graduates, veterans' counselor. **Physically disabled:** Services for visually, hearing impaired.

**Contact.** E-mail: admissions@ngcsu.edu
Phone: (706) 864-1800 Toll-free number: (800) 498-9581
Fax: (706) 864-1478
Jennifer Collins, Director of Admissions, North Georgia College & State University, 82 College Circle, Dahlonega, GA 30597

## Oglethorpe University
Atlanta, Georgia
www.oglethorpe.edu

CB member
CB code: 5521

- Private 4-year liberal arts college
- Residential campus in very large city
- 943 degree-seeking undergraduates: 12% part-time, 61% women, 23% African American, 5% Asian American, 3% Hispanic American, 1% Native American, 5% international
- 28 degree-seeking graduate students
- SAT or ACT (ACT writing recommended) required
- 54% graduate within 6 years

**General.** Founded in 1835. Regionally accredited. Campus home to Georgia Shakespeare Festival. **Degrees:** 179 bachelor's awarded; master's offered. **Location:** 10 miles from downtown. **Calendar:** Semester, extensive summer session. **Full-time faculty:** 57 total; 95% have terminal degrees, 10% minority, 33% women. **Part-time faculty:** 45 total; 51% have terminal degrees, 9% minority, 58% women. **Class size:** 77% < 20, 23% 20-39.

**Freshman class profile.** 178 enrolled.

| Mid 50% test scores | | GPA 2.0-2.99: | 20% |
|---|---|---|---|
| SAT critical reading: | 510-640 | Rank in top quarter: | 54% |
| SAT math: | 500-610 | Rank in top tenth: | 23% |
| SAT writing: | 500-610 | Return as sophomores: | 81% |
| ACT composite: | 21-27 | Out-of-state: | 48% |
| GPA 3.50 or higher: | 49% | Live on campus: | 87% |
| GPA 3.0-3.49: | 31% | International: | 7% |

**Basis for selection.** High school GPA and general academic record most important, followed by test scores. Recommendations required. Activities considered. Interview recommended.

**High school preparation.** Required and recommended units include English 4, mathematics 3, social studies 3, science 2 and foreign language 2. Honors, AP, IB recommended where available.

**2008-2009 Annual costs.** Tuition/fees: $25,580. Room/board: $9,500. Books/supplies: $800. Personal expenses: $1,200.

**2007-2008 Financial aid. Need-based:** 138 full-time freshmen applied for aid; 113 were judged to have need; 113 of these received aid. Average need met was 92%. Average scholarship/grant was $20,245; average loan $3,364. 79% of total undergraduate aid awarded as scholarships/grants, 21% as loans/jobs. **Non-need-based:** Awarded to 310 full-time undergraduates, including 74 freshmen. Scholarships awarded for academics, leadership, music/drama.

**Application procedures. Admission:** No deadline. $35 fee, may be waived for applicants with need. Application may be submitted online. Admission notification on a rolling basis beginning on or about 2/1. Must reply by May 1 or within 3 week(s) if notified thereafter. **Financial aid:** Priority date 2/1; no closing date. FAFSA, institutional form required. Applicants notified on a rolling basis starting 4/1; must reply by 5/1 or within 3 week(s) of notification.

**Academics. Special study options:** Accelerated study, cooperative education, cross-registration, double major, dual enrollment of high school students, honors, independent study, internships, liberal arts/career combination, student-designed major, study abroad, Washington semester. Dual engineering degree program with Auburn University, Georgia Institute of Technology, University of Florida, and University of Southern California; dual art degree program with Atlanta College of Art; Urban Leadership Program. **Credit/placement by examination:** AP, CLEP, institutional tests. 30 credit hours maximum toward bachelor's degree. **Support services:** Learning center.

**Majors. Area/ethnic studies:** American. **Biology:** General. **Business:** Accounting, managerial economics, organizational behavior. **Communications:** General. **English:** English lit. **Health:** Clinical lab science, predental, premedicine, prepharmacy, preveterinary. **History:** General.

**Interdisciplinary:** Math/computer science. **Legal studies:** Prelaw. **Liberal arts:** Arts/sciences. **Math:** General. **Philosophy/religion:** Philosophy. **Physical sciences:** Chemistry, physics. **Psychology:** General. **Public administration:** Social work. **Social sciences:** Economics, international relations, political science, sociology. **Visual/performing arts:** Art.

**Most popular majors.** Business/marketing 24%, English 25%, history 7%, liberal arts 6%, psychology 7%, social sciences 12%.

**Computing on campus.** 57 workstations in library, computer center. Dormitories wired for high-speed internet access and linked to campus network. Commuter students can connect to campus network. Helpline, wireless network available.

**Student life. Housing:** Guaranteed on-campus for freshmen. Coed dorms, single-sex dorms, fraternity/sorority housing available. $200 deposit. **Activities:** Choral groups, dance, drama, film society, international student organizations, literary magazine, musical theater, radio station, student government, student newspaper, Catholic student association, black student caucus, christian fellowship, environmentally concerned students, Jewish student union, Students Against Homophobia, APO service organization, Circle K.

**Athletics.** NCAA. **Intercollegiate:** Baseball M, basketball, cross-country, golf, soccer, tennis, track and field, volleyball W. **Intramural:** Badminton, basketball, softball, tennis, volleyball. **Team name:** Stormy Petrels.

**Student services.** Adult student services, career counseling, student employment services, health services, personal counseling, placement for graduates, veterans' counselor. **Physically disabled:** Services for visually impaired.

**Contact.** E-mail: admission@oglethorpe.edu
Phone: (404) 364-8307 Toll-free number: (800) 428-4484
Fax: (404) 364-8500
Dennis Matthews, Associate Dean for Enrollment Management, Oglethorpe University, 4484 Peachtree Road NE, Atlanta, GA 30319-2797

## Paine College
Augusta, Georgia
www.paine.edu

CB member
CB code: 5530

- Private 4-year liberal arts college affiliated with Christian Methodist Episcopal Church and United Methodist Church
- Residential campus in large city
- 908 degree-seeking undergraduates: 6% part-time, 67% women, 97% African American
- 37% of applicants admitted
- SAT or ACT (ACT writing optional), application essay required

**General.** Founded in 1882. Regionally accredited. **Degrees:** 83 bachelor's awarded. **ROTC:** Army. **Location:** 72 miles from Columbia, South Carolina; 150 miles from Atlanta. **Calendar:** Semester, limited summer session. **Full-time faculty:** 76 total; 47% have terminal degrees, 82% minority, 41% women. **Part-time faculty:** 19 total; 32% have terminal degrees, 90% minority, 68% women. **Class size:** 65% < 20, 34% 20-39, less than 1% 40-49.

**Freshman class profile.** 2,961 applied, 1,089 admitted, 259 enrolled.

| Mid 50% test scores | | GPA 3.0-3.49: | 31% |
|---|---|---|---|
| SAT critical reading: | 350-440 | GPA 2.0-2.99: | 48% |
| SAT math: | 350-440 | Return as sophomores: | 60% |
| ACT composite: | 14-18 | Out-of-state: | 28% |
| GPA 3.50 or higher: | 11% | Live on campus: | 88% |

**Basis for selection.** School achievement record, test scores, and recommendations considered. 2.0 GPA required. Interview recommended. Audition required of music majors if applying for scholarship.

**High school preparation.** 16 units recommended. Recommended units include English 4, mathematics 3, social studies 2, history 1, science 3 (laboratory 2) and academic electives 3.

**2007-2008 Annual costs.** Tuition/fees: $10,694. Room/board: $5,216. Books/supplies: $800. Personal expenses: $1,940.

**2007-2008 Financial aid. Need-based:** 242 full-time freshmen applied for aid; 234 were judged to have need; 230 of these received aid. Average need met was 56%. Average scholarship/grant was $6,461; average loan $3,248. 49% of total undergraduate aid awarded as scholarships/grants, 51% as loans/jobs. **Non-need-based:** Awarded to 97 full-time undergraduates, including 19 freshmen. Scholarships awarded for academics, alumni affiliation, athletics, music/drama, religious affiliation, ROTC.

**Application procedures. Admission:** Closing date 8/1 (receipt date). $20 fee, may be waived for applicants with need. Application may be submitted online. Admission notification on a rolling basis. **Financial aid:** Priority date 3/1; no closing date. FAFSA, institutional form required. Applicants notified on a rolling basis starting 5/1; must reply within 2 week(s) of notification.

**Academics. Special study options:** Combined bachelor's/graduate degree, cooperative education, cross-registration, distance learning, dual enrollment of high school students, honors, independent study, internships, liberal arts/career combination, study abroad, teacher certification program. Dual degree in engineering and mathematics with Florida A & M University, Tuskegee University, Tennessee State University. **Credit/placement by examination:** AP, CLEP, SAT, ACT, institutional tests. **Support services:** Learning center, pre-admission summer program, reduced course load, remedial instruction, study skills assistance, tutoring.

**Majors. Biology:** General. **Business:** Accounting, business admin, international, management information systems, marketing. **Communications:** Broadcast journalism, journalism, public relations. **Conservation:** Environmental science. **Education:** Biology, elementary, English, history, mathematics, middle. **English:** English lit. **History:** General. **Interdisciplinary:** Math/computer science. **Math:** General. **Philosophy/religion:** Philosophy, religion. **Physical sciences:** Chemistry. **Psychology:** General, counseling. **Social sciences:** Criminology, sociology. **Visual/performing arts:** Dramatic.

**Most popular majors.** Biology 11%, business/marketing 14%, communications/journalism 11%, mathematics 7%, psychology 18%, social sciences 18%.

**Computing on campus.** 125 workstations in dormitories, library, computer center, student center. Dormitories wired for high-speed internet access and linked to campus network. Commuter students can connect to campus network. Online course registration, online library, repair service, wireless network available.

**Student life. Freshman orientation:** Mandatory, $106 fee. Preregistration for classes offered. Pre-testing and orientation held in June and 1 week at beginning of semester. **Housing:** Single-sex dorms, substance-free housing available. $75 nonrefundable deposit, deadline 8/1. **Activities:** Bands, campus ministries, choral groups, dance, drama, international student organizations, literary magazine, music ensembles, student government, student newspaper, Baptist student union, Methodist student union, NAACP, pre-alumni club, National Pan Hellenic Council, Alpha Kappa Mu honor society.

**Athletics.** NCAA. **Intercollegiate:** Baseball M, basketball, cross-country, golf M, softball W, track and field, volleyball W. **Intramural:** Badminton, baseball M, basketball, cross-country, football (tackle) M, softball, table tennis, tennis, track and field, volleyball, weight lifting. **Team name:** Lions.

**Student services.** Alcohol/substance abuse counseling, career counseling, student employment services, financial aid counseling, health services, personal counseling, placement for graduates, veterans' counselor.

**Contact.** E-mail: tinsleyj@mail.paine.edu
Phone: (706) 824-8320 Toll-free number: (800) 476-7703
Fax: (706) 821-8648
Joseph Tinsley, Director of Admissions, Paine College, 1235 15th Street, Augusta, GA 30901-3182

---

## Piedmont College
**Demorest, Georgia**
www.piedmont.edu

**CB member**
**CB code: 5537**

- Private 4-year liberal arts and teachers college affiliated with United Church of Christ
- Residential campus in rural community
- 1,056 degree-seeking undergraduates: 15% part-time, 67% women, 8% African American, 1% Asian American, 2% Hispanic American
- 1,227 degree-seeking graduate students
- 44% of applicants admitted
- SAT or ACT required
- 49% graduate within 6 years

**General.** Founded in 1897. Regionally accredited. **Degrees:** 276 bachelor's awarded; master's offered. **Location:** 30 miles from Gainesville, 75 miles from Atlanta. **Calendar:** Semester, limited summer session. **Full-time faculty:** 106 total; 74% have terminal degrees, 5% minority, 43% women. **Part-time faculty:** 121 total; 42% have terminal degrees, 6% minority, 52% women. **Class size:** 77% < 20, 23% 20-39, less than 1% 50-99. **Special facilities:** Performing arts and communication center, pipe organ, worship and music center, botanical center.

**Freshman class profile.** 1,293 applied, 575 admitted, 211 enrolled.

| Mid 50% test scores | | | |
|---|---|---|---|
| SAT critical reading: | 450-550 | GPA 2.0-2.99: | 5% |
| SAT math: | 450-560 | Rank in top quarter: | 43% |
| ACT composite: | 18-23 | Rank in top tenth: | 20% |
| GPA 3.50 or higher: | 53% | Return as sophomores: | 70% |
| GPA 3.0-3.49: | 42% | Out-of-state: | 1% |
| | | Live on campus: | 39% |

**Basis for selection.** Test scores and GPA most important. Essay recommended. Interview recommended for academically weak. **Homeschooled:** Transcript or portfolio detailing high school coursework completed, 2 letters of recommendation from sources outside home who have knowledge of student's academic/extracurricular achievements required. Interview with student and family may be required.

**High school preparation.** 21 units recommended. Recommended units include English 4, mathematics 3, social studies 1, history 2, science 3 and foreign language 2.

**2007-2008 Annual costs.** Tuition/fees: $16,500. Room/board: $6,000. Books/supplies: $1,200. Personal expenses: $2,350.

**2007-2008 Financial aid. Need-based:** Average need met was 77%. Average scholarship/grant was $794; average loan $2,841. 38% of total undergraduate aid awarded as scholarships/grants, 62% as loans/jobs. **Non-need-based:** Scholarships awarded for academics, art, leadership, music/drama, religious affiliation, state residency. **Additional information:** College meets 100% of unmet direct financial need for early applicants through grants, scholarships, and loan programs.

**Application procedures. Admission:** Closing date 7/1. No application fee. **Financial aid:** Priority date 5/1; no closing date. FAFSA, institutional form required. Applicants notified on a rolling basis; must reply within 2 week(s) of notification.

**Academics.** Experiential learning credit allows students to document work experience for college credit as appropriate. **Special study options:** Accelerated study, combined bachelor's/graduate degree, distance learning, double major, dual enrollment of high school students, honors, independent study, internships, student-designed major, study abroad, teacher certification program. **Credit/placement by examination:** AP, CLEP. 30 credit hours maximum toward bachelor's degree. **Support services:** Study skills assistance, tutoring.

**Majors. Biology:** General. **Business:** Business admin. **Communications:** Media studies. **Conservation:** Environmental science. **Education:** Biology, chemistry, drama/dance, early childhood, English, history, middle, secondary, special. **English:** English lit. **Foreign languages:** Spanish. **Health:** Nursing (RN). **History:** General. **Interdisciplinary:** Math/computer science. **Math:** General. **Philosophy/religion:** Philosophy, religion. **Physical sciences:** Chemistry. **Protective services:** Criminal justice. **Psychology:** General. **Social sciences:** General, political science, sociology. **Visual/performing arts:** Art, dramatic, studio arts.

**Most popular majors.** Business/marketing 24%, education 30%, health sciences 8%, social sciences 7%.

**Computing on campus.** 225 workstations in dormitories, library, computer center, student center. Dormitories wired for high-speed internet access and linked to campus network. Commuter students can connect to campus network. Online library available.

**Student life. Freshman orientation:** Mandatory. Preregistration for classes offered. Three-day weekend with activities for students, resident assistants, faculty and staff. **Policies:** Unmarried students under 21 must live in dormitories or with blood relatives. **Housing:** Guaranteed on-campus for all undergraduates. Coed dorms, single-sex dorms, special housing for disabled, apartments, substance-free housing available. $100 deposit. **Activities:** Campus ministries, choral groups, drama, film society, music ensembles, radio station, student government, student newspaper, symphony orchestra, TV station, psychology club, Baptist student union, Student Association of Educators, literary society, art club, science club, environmental club, Rotaract, history society.

**Athletics.** NCAA, NCCAA. **Intercollegiate:** Baseball M, basketball, cross-country, golf, soccer, softball W, tennis, volleyball W. **Intramural:** Basketball, football (non-tackle), soccer, softball, table tennis, volleyball. **Team name:** Lions.

**Student services.** Career counseling, financial aid counseling, health services, personal counseling, placement for graduates, veterans' counselor.

**Contact.** E-mail: ugrad@piedmont.edu
Phone: (706) 776-0103 Toll-free number: (800) 277-7020
Fax: (706) 776-6635
Cynthia Peterson, Director of Admissions, Piedmont College, 165 Central Avenue, Demorest, GA 30535-0010

## Reinhardt College
Waleska, Georgia

**CB member**
www.reinhardt.edu
**CB code: 5568**

- Private 4-year business and teachers college affiliated with United Methodist Church
- Commuter campus in rural community
- 971 degree-seeking undergraduates: 9% part-time, 58% women, 9% African American, 1% Asian American, 4% Hispanic American, 1% international
- 20 degree-seeking graduate students
- SAT or ACT required

**General.** Founded in 1883. Regionally accredited. Off-campus centers in Alpharetta and Woodstock. **Degrees:** 207 bachelor's, 12 associate awarded; master's offered. **Location:** 50 miles from Atlanta. **Calendar:** Semester, extensive summer session. **Full-time faculty:** 58 total; 62% have terminal degrees, 5% minority, 50% women. **Class size:** 70% < 20, 30% 20-39. **Special facilities:** Indian history museum, visual arts center, performing arts center.

**Freshman class profile.**

| Mid 50% test scores | | | |
|---|---|---|---|
| SAT critical reading: | 430-530 | GPA 3.0-3.49: | 35% |
| SAT math: | 410-520 | GPA 2.0-2.99: | 54% |
| SAT writing: | 410-520 | Return as sophomores: | 62% |
| GPA 3.50 or higher: | 10% | Out-of-state: | 4% |

**Basis for selection.** School achievement record most important, followed by test scores, recommendations. Interview recommended. Audition required of music majors. Portfolio required of art majors. **Homeschooled:** Transcript of courses and grades, state high school equivalency certificate required. **Learning Disabled:** Recommend that students be counseled by Academic Support Office.

**High school preparation.** 14 units recommended. Recommended units include English 4, mathematics 4, social studies 3, science 3 and foreign language 2.

**2007-2008 Annual costs.** Tuition/fees: $14,970. Room/board: $7,284. Books/supplies: $500.

**Financial aid. Non-need-based:** Scholarships awarded for academics, art, athletics.

**Application procedures. Admission:** No deadline. $25 fee, may be waived for applicants with need. Application may be submitted online. Admission notification on a rolling basis. **Financial aid:** Priority date 5/1; no closing date. Applicants notified on a rolling basis starting 3/15; must reply within 2 week(s) of notification.

**Academics. Special study options:** Accelerated study, combined bachelor's/graduate degree, double major, dual enrollment of high school students, external degree, honors, independent study, internships, study abroad, teacher certification program. **Credit/placement by examination:** AP, CLEP, institutional tests. 15 credit hours maximum toward associate degree, 30 toward bachelor's. **Support services:** Learning center, pre-admission summer program, reduced course load, remedial instruction, study skills assistance, tutoring, writing center.

**Majors. Biology:** General. **Business:** General, accounting, business admin. **Communications:** General. **Computer sciences:** Information systems. **Education:** Biology, early childhood, elementary, English, middle, music, physical. **English:** English lit. **History:** General. **Liberal arts:** Arts/sciences. **Parks/recreation:** Sports admin. **Philosophy/religion:** Religion. **Psychology:** General. **Social sciences:** Sociology. **Visual/performing arts:** Studio arts.

**Most popular majors.** Business/marketing 32%, communications/journalism 9%, education 21%, public administration/social services 10%, social sciences 6%.

**Computing on campus.** 165 workstations in dormitories, library, computer center, student center. Dormitories wired for high-speed internet access and linked to campus network. Commuter students can connect to campus network. Online course registration, online library, helpline, student web hosting, wireless network available.

**Student life. Freshman orientation:** Mandatory, $35 fee. Preregistration for classes offered. 1-2 day program. **Housing:** Guaranteed on-campus for freshmen. Coed dorms, single-sex dorms, apartments, substance-free housing available. $200 fully refundable deposit, deadline 8/15. **Activities:** Bands, choral groups, film society, music ensembles, student government, student newspaper, TV station, Baptist student union, Wesley Foundation, fellowship of Christian athletes, Catholic campus ministry, Reach Out Reinhardt, Phi Theta Kappa, Circle-K.

**Athletics.** NAIA. **Intercollegiate:** Baseball M, basketball, cheerleading, cross-country, golf M, soccer, softball W, tennis. **Intramural:** Basketball, football (non-tackle), soccer, softball, volleyball. **Team name:** Eagles.

**Student services.** Adult student services, alcohol/substance abuse counseling, campus ministries, career counseling, student employment services, financial aid counseling, health services, personal counseling, placement for graduates, veterans' counselor. **Physically disabled:** Services for visually, speech, hearing impaired.

**Contact.** E-mail: admissions@mail.reinhardt.edu
Phone: (770) 720-5526 Toll-free number: (877) 343-4273
Fax: (770) 720-5602
Julie Cook, Director of Admissions, Reinhardt College, 7300 Reinhardt College Circle, Waleska, GA 30183

## Savannah College of Art and Design
Savannah, Georgia

**CB member**
www.scad.edu
**CB code: 5631**

- Private 4-year visual arts and performing arts college
- Commuter campus in small city
- 7,423 degree-seeking undergraduates: 9% part-time, 55% women, 5% African American, 2% Asian American, 3% Hispanic American, 7% international
- 1,443 degree-seeking graduate students
- 54% of applicants admitted
- SAT or ACT (ACT writing optional) required
- 65% graduate within 6 years

**General.** Founded in 1978. Regionally accredited. Additional location in Atlanta. Extensive study abroad program in France at Lacoste School of the Arts. **Degrees:** 1,205 bachelor's awarded; master's offered. **ROTC:** Army. **Location:** 250 miles from Atlanta; 150 miles from Jacksonville, Florida. **Calendar:** Quarter, limited summer session. **Full-time faculty:** 423 total; 75% have terminal degrees, 8% minority, 42% women. **Part-time faculty:** 100 total; 68% have terminal degrees, 4% minority, 40% women. **Class size:** 79% < 20, 21% 20-39. **Special facilities:** Art museums, 2 vintage diners, amphitheater, restored 1943 theater.

**Freshman class profile.** 6,426 applied, 3,460 admitted, 1,603 enrolled.

| Mid 50% test scores | | | |
|---|---|---|---|
| SAT critical reading: | 500-600 | GPA 2.0-2.99: | 23% |
| SAT math: | 480-590 | End year in good standing: | 91% |
| SAT writing: | 480-590 | Return as sophomores: | 80% |
| ACT composite: | 21-26 | Out-of-state: | 81% |
| GPA 3.50 or higher: | 41% | Live on campus: | 92% |
| GPA 3.0-3.49: | 36% | International: | 7% |

**Basis for selection.** Entrance test scores, 3 letters of recommendation, and high school transcript required. Interview, portfolio recommended. Essay recommended for historic preservation, art history, and architectural history programs only. Portfolio or audition required for scholarship consideration. **Homeschooled:** Statement describing homeschool structure and mission, transcript of courses and grades, state high school equivalency certificate required. **Learning Disabled:** Documentation of specific nature of disability required.

**2008-2009 Annual costs.** Tuition/fees (projected): $25,965. A one-time matriculation fee of $500 is required of all students. Room/board: $10,585. Books/supplies: $1,560. Personal expenses: $1,560.

**2007-2008 Financial aid. Need-based:** 1,122 full-time freshmen applied for aid; 887 were judged to have need; 874 of these received aid. Average need met was 11%. Average scholarship/grant was $3,772; average loan $3,409. 24% of total undergraduate aid awarded as scholarships/grants, 76% as loans/jobs. **Non-need-based:** Awarded to 5,081 full-time undergraduates, including 1,311 freshmen. Scholarships awarded for academics, art, athletics, music/drama. **Additional information:** Degree-seeking students may be awarded maximum of one scholarship from college, but may receive additional scholarships from other sources, as well as additional forms of financial aid. Scholarships based on academic achievement are awarded through admission office.

**Application procedures. Admission:** Priority date 4/1; no deadline. $50 fee. Application may be submitted online. Admission notification on a rolling basis. Must reply by May 1 or within 4 week(s) if notified thereafter.

Students encouraged to apply early to gain priority for housing. **Financial aid:** Priority date 2/15; no closing date. FAFSA, institutional form required. Applicants notified on a rolling basis starting 6/1; must reply within 4 week(s) of notification.

**Academics.** Strong fine arts foundation along with strong liberal arts curriculum. **Special study options:** Distance learning, double major, dual enrollment of high school students, ESL, independent study, internships, New York semester, study abroad, teacher certification program. Off-campus programs in Europe and other art centers. Cross registration available at SCAD-Atlanta through membership in ARCHE. Teacher certification in art and drama available through MA in Teaching program. **Credit/placement by examination:** AP, CLEP, IB. 15 credit hours maximum toward bachelor's degree. **Support services:** Learning center, pre-admission summer program, reduced course load, study skills assistance, tutoring, writing center.

**Majors. Architecture:** Architecture, history/criticism. **Communications:** Digital media. **Communications technology:** Animation/special effects, recording arts. **English:** Creative writing. **Interdisciplinary:** Historic preservation. **Visual/performing arts:** Art history/conservation, cinematography, commercial/advertising art, dramatic, fashion design, fiber arts, graphic design, illustration, industrial design, interior design, metal/jewelry, painting, photography, printmaking, sculpture, theater design. **Other:** Furniture design.

**Most popular majors.** Architecture 7%, communication technologies 19%, visual/performing arts 68%.

**Computing on campus.** 3,388 workstations in dormitories, library, computer center, student center. Dormitories wired for high-speed internet access and linked to campus network. Commuter students can connect to campus network. Online course registration, online library, helpline, repair service, student web hosting, wireless network available.

**Student life. Freshman orientation:** Available. Preregistration for classes offered. Two-day program, includes parents; summer options available. **Housing:** Coed dorms, apartments, substance-free housing available. $250 nonrefundable deposit, deadline 6/1. Some apartment-style residence halls with full kitchen facilities available. Students with disabilities accommodated on individual basis. **Activities:** Campus ministries, choral groups, dance, drama, music ensembles, musical theater, radio station, student government, student newspaper, TV station, American Institute of Architecture Students, American Society of Interior Designers, united student forum, inter-club council, student activities council, intercultural student association, Society of Illustrators, art history society, Society for Collegiate Journalists.

**Athletics.** NAIA. **Intercollegiate:** Baseball M, basketball, cheerleading, cross-country, equestrian, golf, lacrosse, soccer, softball W, swimming, tennis, volleyball W. **Intramural:** Basketball, football (non-tackle), lacrosse, rowing (crew), soccer, softball, tennis, volleyball. **Team name:** Bees.

**Student services.** Adult student services, alcohol/substance abuse counseling, career counseling, student employment services, financial aid counseling, health services, personal counseling, placement for graduates. **Physically disabled:** Services for visually, speech, hearing impaired.

**Contact.** E-mail: admission@scad.edu
Phone: (912) 525-5100 Toll-free number: (800) 869-7223
Fax: (912) 525-5986
Pamela Rhame, Vice President for Admission and Communication, Savannah College of Art and Design, PO Box 2072, Savannah, GA 31402-2072

---

## Savannah State University
**Savannah, Georgia**
**www.savstate.edu**

CB member
CB code: 5609

- Public 4-year business and liberal arts college
- Commuter campus in small city
- 2,991 degree-seeking undergraduates: 14% part-time, 57% women, 97% African American
- 128 graduate students
- SAT or ACT (ACT writing optional) required
- 43% graduate within 6 years

**General.** Founded in 1890. Regionally accredited. **Degrees:** 374 bachelor's awarded; master's offered. **ROTC:** Army, Naval. **Location:** 250 miles from Atlanta; 120 miles from Jacksonville, Florida. **Calendar:** Semester, extensive summer session. **Full-time faculty:** 122 total. **Part-time faculty:** 38 total. **Special facilities:** Marine biology dock, college archives, natural estuary.

---

**Freshman class profile.**

| Mid 50% test scores | | |
|---|---|---|
| SAT critical reading: | 400-480 | |
| SAT math: | 400-480 | |
| GPA 3.50 or higher: | 7% | |
| GPA 3.0-3.49: | 23% | |

| | |
|---|---|
| GPA 2.0-2.99: | 69% |
| Return as sophomores: | 72% |
| Out-of-state: | 8% |
| Live on campus: | 50% |

**Basis for selection.** Test scores and high school GPA very important.

**High school preparation.** 15 units required. Required units include English 4, mathematics 3, social studies 3, science 3 and foreign language 2. Students lacking complete college-preparatory requirements admitted on provisional basis.

**2007-2008 Annual costs.** Tuition/fees: $3,486; $12,090 out-of-state. Room/board: $5,348. Books/supplies: $750. Personal expenses: $800.

**Financial aid. Non-need-based:** Scholarships awarded for academics, alumni affiliation, music/drama.

**Application procedures. Admission:** Closing date 7/1. $20 fee, may be waived for applicants with need. Admission notification on a rolling basis beginning on or about 3/1. **Financial aid:** Closing date 4/1. FAFSA required. Applicants notified on a rolling basis starting 4/15; must reply within 2 week(s) of notification.

**Academics. Special study options:** Cooperative education, cross-registration, double major, dual enrollment of high school students, exchange student, honors, independent study, internships. **Credit/placement by examination:** AP, CLEP, institutional tests. 45 credit hours maximum toward associate degree, 45 toward bachelor's. **Support services:** Learning center, remedial instruction, tutoring.

**Majors. Biology:** General. **Business:** Accounting, hospitality/recreation, international, management science. **Communications:** General. **Computer sciences:** General, computer science, information systems. **Education:** Early childhood. **Engineering technology:** Civil, electrical. **English:** English lit. **Health:** Clinical lab science. **History:** General. **Interdisciplinary:** Marine science. **Math:** General. **Parks/recreation:** General. **Physical sciences:** Chemistry. **Public administration:** Social work. **Social sciences:** Political science, sociology. **Visual/performing arts:** Music performance.

**Computing on campus.** 300 workstations in library, computer center. Commuter students can connect to campus network.

**Student life. Freshman orientation:** Available. Preregistration for classes offered. Available during various times leading up to fall semester. Private appointments available upon request. **Housing:** Single-sex dorms, apartments available. $100 deposit. **Activities:** Bands, campus ministries, choral groups, dance, drama, literary magazine, music ensembles, radio station, student government, student newspaper.

**Athletics.** NCAA. **Intercollegiate:** Baseball M, basketball, bowling W, cross-country, football (tackle) M, golf, softball W, tennis W, track and field, volleyball W. **Intramural:** Baseball M, bowling, softball W, table tennis. **Team name:** Tigers.

**Student services.** Student employment services, health services, on-campus daycare, personal counseling, placement for graduates, veterans' counselor.

**Contact.** E-mail: ssvadms@savstate.edu
Phone: (912) 356-2181 Fax: (912) 356-2256
Gwendolyn Moore, Director of Admissions, Savannah State University, State College Branch, Savannah, GA 31404

---

## Shorter College
**Rome, Georgia**
**www.shorter.edu**

CB member
CB code: 5616

- Private 4-year liberal arts college affiliated with Southern Baptist Convention
- Residential campus in large town
- 1,019 degree-seeking undergraduates: 2% part-time, 49% women, 12% African American, 1% Asian American, 3% Hispanic American, 1% Native American, 6% international
- 359 graduate students
- 65% of applicants admitted
- SAT or ACT (ACT writing optional), application essay required
- 47% graduate within 6 years

**General.** Founded in 1873. Regionally accredited. **Degrees:** 171 bachelor's awarded. **Location:** 70 miles from Atlanta; 65 miles from Chattanooga, Tennessee. **Calendar:** Semester, limited summer session. **Full-time faculty:** 71 total; 70% have terminal degrees, 6% minority, 38% women. **Part-time faculty:** 54 total; 11% have terminal degrees, 4% minority, 44% women. **Class size:** 63% < 20, 33% 20-39, 4% 40-49, less than 1% 50-99, less than 1% >100. **Special facilities:** Extensive music collection, microfilm archive of local history.

**Freshman class profile.** 1,131 applied, 731 admitted, 276 enrolled.

| Mid 50% test scores | | | |
|---|---|---|---|
| SAT critical reading: | 440-550 | Rank in top tenth: | 21% |
| SAT math: | 440-550 | End year in good standing: | 76% |
| SAT writing: | 430-540 | Return as sophomores: | 64% |
| ACT composite: | 17-22 | Out-of-state: | 6% |
| GPA 3.50 or higher: | 36% | Live on campus: | 77% |
| GPA 3.0-3.49: | 27% | International: | 4% |
| GPA 2.0-2.99: | 37% | Fraternities: | 5% |
| Rank in top quarter: | 50% | Sororities: | 35% |

**Basis for selection.** High school achievement, curriculum most important. Test scores, essay, counselor recommendation considered. Auditions required of music and drama majors. Portfolios required of art majors. **Homeschooled:** Applicants reviewed according to materials submitted. Interview may be required.

**High school preparation.** 16 units required. Required units include English 4, mathematics 4, history 3, science 3 and foreign language 2. Math units should include 2 algebra, 1 geometry.

**2008-2009 Annual costs.** Tuition/fees: $15,770. Room/board: $7,400. Books/supplies: $1,000. Personal expenses: $4,500.

**2007-2008 Financial aid. Need-based:** 225 full-time freshmen applied for aid; 189 were judged to have need; 189 of these received aid. Average need met was 71%. Average scholarship/grant was $11,103; average loan $3,637. 65% of total undergraduate aid awarded as scholarships/grants, 35% as loans/jobs. **Non-need-based:** Awarded to 724 full-time undergraduates, including 363 freshmen. Scholarships awarded for academics, art, athletics, music/drama, religious affiliation. **Additional information:** Cost is reduced for all in-state students by state tuition equalization grant program. College matches for out-of-state full-time students.

**Application procedures. Admission:** Priority date 3/15; deadline 8/23 (receipt date). $25 fee, may be waived for applicants with need. Application must be submitted on paper. Admission notification on a rolling basis beginning on or about 11/1. Must reply by May 1 or within 2 week(s) if notified thereafter. **Financial aid:** Priority date 4/1; no closing date. FAFSA, institutional form required. Applicants notified on a rolling basis starting 4/1; must reply within 2 week(s) of notification.

**Academics. Special study options:** Cross-registration, double major, dual enrollment of high school students, honors, independent study, internships, student-designed major, study abroad, teacher certification program. Annual extended seacoast field trips in natural science. **Credit/placement by examination:** AP, CLEP, IB, institutional tests. 30 credit hours maximum toward bachelor's degree. **Support services:** Learning center, pre-admission summer program, remedial instruction, study skills assistance, tutoring, writing center.

**Majors. Biology:** General. **Business:** Accounting, business admin, managerial economics. **Communications:** General, public relations. **Computer sciences:** General. **Conservation:** General, environmental studies. **Education:** Art, elementary, mathematics, middle, music. **English:** English lit. **Foreign languages:** French, Spanish. **History:** General. **Interdisciplinary:** Global studies. **Liberal arts:** Arts/sciences. **Math:** General. **Parks/recreation:** Sports admin. **Philosophy/religion:** Religion. **Physical sciences:** Chemistry. **Psychology:** General. **Social sciences:** General, sociology. **Theology:** Sacred music, theology. **Visual/performing arts:** Dramatic, piano/organ, studio arts, voice/opera.

**Most popular majors.** Biology 12%, business/marketing 22%, education 8%, history 6%, psychology 7%, visual/performing arts 13%.

**Computing on campus.** 50 workstations in library, computer center. Dormitories wired for high-speed internet access. Online course registration, helpline, wireless network available.

**Student life. Freshman orientation:** Mandatory, $60 fee. Preregistration for classes offered. Several summer overnight sessions from June to August. Freshmen take placement exams. **Policies:** Religious observance required. **Housing:** Guaranteed on-campus for freshmen. Single-sex dorms, apartments available. $200 deposit, deadline 8/20. **Activities:** Bands, campus ministries, choral groups, dance, drama, film society, international student organizations, literary magazine, music ensembles, Model UN, musical theater, opera, radio station, student government, student newspaper, TV station, Baptist student union, Shorter Relations Society, Fellowship of Christian Athletes.

**Athletics.** NAIA. **Intercollegiate:** Baseball M, basketball, cheerleading, cross-country, football (tackle) M, golf W, soccer, softball W, tennis, track and field, volleyball W. **Intramural:** Basketball, bowling, football (non-tackle), soccer, softball, table tennis, tennis, track and field, volleyball. **Team name:** Hawks.

**Student services.** Adult student services, alcohol/substance abuse counseling, career counseling, student employment services, financial aid counseling, health services, personal counseling, placement for graduates. **Physically disabled:** Services for visually, hearing impaired.

**Contact.** E-mail: admissions@shorter.edu
Phone: (706) 233-7319 Toll-free number: (800) 868-6980
Fax: (706) 233-7224
John Head, Vice President for Enrollment Management, Shorter College, 315 Shorter Avenue, Rome, GA 30165

## South University
Savannah, Georgia
www.southuniversity.edu
CB code: 5157

- For-profit 4-year business and health science college
- Commuter campus in small city
- 4,331 degree-seeking undergraduates
- 370 graduate students
- SAT or ACT, interview required

**General.** Founded in 1899. Regionally accredited. **Degrees:** 89 bachelor's, 63 associate awarded; master's, doctoral, first professional offered. **Location:** 225 miles from Atlanta; 165 miles from Jacksonville, Florida. **Calendar:** Quarter, extensive summer session. **Full-time faculty:** 18 total; 28% have terminal degrees, 17% minority, 56% women. **Part-time faculty:** 43 total; 30% have terminal degrees, 9% minority, 56% women.

**Basis for selection.** Test scores and school achievement record considered. Physician assistant students must have completed 2 years of science-based curriculum. Computerized Placement Test may be submitted in place of test scores for admission. Essays required for physician assistant and physical therapist assistant programs. **Homeschooled:** Letter of recommendation (nonparent) required.

**2007-2008 Annual costs.** Tuition for Business Administration, Legal Studies, Information Technology, Criminal Justice, Healthcare Management, Medical Assisting, Physical Therapist Assistant and Allied Health Programs (pre-professional) is $3,095 per quarter. Tuition for the Bachelor of Science in Nursing Program (Professional Program) is $6,095 per quarter. Tuition for the Physician Assistant Studies bachelor's program is $6,095.00 per quarter and the master-s degree in Physician Assistant Studies is $6,195.00 per quarter. Effective February 2007, cost of the post baccalaureate certificate in paralegal studies is $7895 per program. Tuition for the Doctor of Pharmacy program is $7,995.00 per quarter and tuition for MMSc Anesthesiologist Assistant Program is $6,495. The Master of Arts in Professional Counseling program-s tuition is $5,495 per quarter. Books/supplies: $750.

**Financial aid. Non-need-based:** Scholarships awarded for state residency.

**Application procedures. Admission:** No deadline. $25 fee. Admission notification on a rolling basis. **Financial aid:** No deadline. FAFSA required. Applicants notified on a rolling basis starting 9/1.

**Academics. Special study options:** Accelerated study, combined bachelor's/graduate degree, distance learning, double major, dual enrollment of high school students, independent study, internships, liberal arts/career combination. **Credit/placement by examination:** AP, CLEP, IB, institutional tests. 45 credit hours maximum toward associate degree, 90 toward bachelor's. 60% of total credits, 50% of major credits may be earned by examination. **Support services:** Learning center, reduced course load, remedial instruction, study skills assistance, tutoring.

**Majors. Business:** Accounting, business admin. **Computer sciences:** Information technology. **Health:** Physician assistant. **Legal studies:** General.

**Computing on campus.** 50 workstations in library, computer center. Commuter students can connect to campus network. Online library, helpline, repair service, wireless network available.

**Student life. Freshman orientation:** Mandatory. Preregistration for classes offered. **Housing:** Apartments available.

**Student services.** Career counseling, student employment services, financial aid counseling, personal counseling, placement for graduates, veterans' counselor.

**Contact.** E-mail: mmills@southuniversity.edu
Phone: (912) 201-8100 Toll-free number: (866) 629-2901
Fax: (912) 201-8070
Matthew Mills, Director of Admissions, South University, 709 Mall Boulevard, Savannah, GA 31406

## Southern Polytechnic State University
**Marietta, Georgia**
www.spsu.edu                                    **CB code: 5626**

- Public 4-year university and engineering college
- Commuter campus in small city
- 3,827 degree-seeking undergraduates: 30% part-time, 17% women, 20% African American, 5% Asian American, 4% Hispanic American, 5% international
- 523 graduate students
- 61% of applicants admitted
- SAT or ACT with writing required

**General.** Founded in 1948. Regionally accredited. **Degrees:** 458 bachelor's, 2 associate awarded; master's offered. **ROTC:** Army, Naval, Air Force. **Location:** 15 miles from Atlanta. **Calendar:** Semester, extensive summer session. **Full-time faculty:** 158 total; 64% have terminal degrees, 35% minority, 26% women. **Part-time faculty:** 104 total; 28% have terminal degrees, 28% minority, 36% women. **Class size:** 47% < 20, 48% 20-39, 4% 40-49, 1% 50-99.

**Freshman class profile.** 1,331 applied, 812 admitted, 516 enrolled.

| Mid 50% test scores | | | |
|---|---|---|---|
| SAT critical reading: | 490-570 | Return as sophomores: | 76% |
| SAT math: | 520-610 | Out-of-state: | 2% |
| ACT composite: | 20-24 | Live on campus: | 51% |
| GPA 3.50 or higher: | 30% | International: | 2% |
| GPA 3.0-3.49: | 41% | Fraternities: | 11% |
| GPA 2.0-2.99: | 29% | Sororities: | 6% |

**Basis for selection.** GED not accepted. Test scores, high school units, and GPA important. **Homeschooled:** Porfolio and 1120 SAT (exclusive of Writing) required.

**High school preparation.** 18 units required. Required units include English 4, mathematics 4, social studies 3, science 3 (laboratory 2), foreign language 2 and academic electives 2. Social studies units must include 2 history (1 U.S., 1 world). Foreign Language must include 2 years same language. Math must include 2 algebra, 1 geometry.

**2007-2008 Annual costs.** Tuition/fees: $3,872; $13,590 out-of-state. Room/board: $5,780. Books/supplies: $1,500. Personal expenses: $1,500.

**2007-2008 Financial aid. Need-based:** 394 full-time freshmen applied for aid; 394 were judged to have need; 376 of these received aid. Average need met was 80%. Average scholarship/grant was $2,940; average loan $3,206. 36% of total undergraduate aid awarded as scholarships/grants, 64% as loans/jobs. **Non-need-based:** Scholarships awarded for academics, athletics.

**Application procedures. Admission:** Closing date 8/1 (postmark date). $20 fee, may be waived for applicants with need. Application may be submitted online. Admission notification on a rolling basis. **Financial aid:** Priority date 4/1; no closing date. FAFSA required. Applicants notified on a rolling basis starting 6/1.

**Academics. Special study options:** Cooperative education, cross-registration, distance learning, double major, dual enrollment of high school students, honors, independent study, internships, liberal arts/career combination, study abroad. **Credit/placement by examination:** AP, CLEP, IB, institutional tests. **Support services:** Learning center, reduced course load, study skills assistance, tutoring.

**Majors. Architecture:** Architecture. **Biology:** General. **Business:** Construction management, entrepreneurial studies. **Computer sciences:** Computer science, information technology. **Engineering:** Construction, mechanical, software, systems. **Engineering technology:** General, architectural, civil, computer, electrical, mechanical, surveying, telecommunications. **Math:** General. **Physical sciences:** Chemistry, physics. **Psychology:** General. **Social sciences:** International relations. **Other:** Technical communication; English and professional communication.

**Most popular majors.** Architecture 7%, business/marketing 17%, computer/information sciences 16%, engineering/engineering technologies 48%.

**Computing on campus.** 850 workstations in dormitories, library, computer center, student center. Dormitories wired for high-speed internet access and linked to campus network. Commuter students can connect to campus network. Online course registration, online library, helpline, student web hosting, wireless network available.

**Student life. Freshman orientation:** Mandatory, $60 fee. Preregistration for classes offered. One-and-a-half day program held 2 times prior to beginning of semester. Price includes 1 night in a dorm. **Housing:** Coed dorms, apartments available. $235 partly refundable deposit. Privately-owned apartments are available on campus. **Activities:** Bands, international student organizations, radio station, student government, student newspaper, campus activities board, National Society of Black Engineers, Baptist Student Union, African students association, Bahai Club, Japanese Friendship Society, Muslim student association, Indian Culture Exchange, Chinese Friendship Association, Sexual Acceptance For Everyone, Caribbean student association.

**Athletics.** NAIA. **Intercollegiate:** Baseball M, basketball, soccer M. **Intramural:** Badminton, basketball, football (non-tackle), golf, racquetball, softball, table tennis, tennis, volleyball. **Team name:** Runnin' Hornets.

**Student services.** Alcohol/substance abuse counseling, career counseling, student employment services, financial aid counseling, health services, minority student services, personal counseling, placement for graduates, veterans' counselor. **Physically disabled:** Services for visually, speech, hearing impaired.

**Contact.** E-mail: admiss@spsu.edu
Phone: (678) 915-4188 Toll-free number: (800) 635-3204
Fax: (678) 915-7292
Virginia Head, Director of Admissions, Southern Polytechnic State University, 1100 South Marietta Parkway, Marietta, GA 30060-2896

## Spelman College
**Atlanta, Georgia**                                    **CB member**
www.spelman.edu                                    **CB code: 5628**

- Private 4-year liberal arts college for women
- Residential campus in very large city
- 2,337 degree-seeking undergraduates: 4% part-time, 100% women, 96% African American, 2% international
- 33% of applicants admitted
- SAT or ACT (ACT writing optional), application essay required
- 78% graduate within 6 years

**General.** Founded in 1881. Regionally accredited. One of 6 members of Atlanta University Center sharing facilities, resources, and activities. Students may take courses at the other undergraduate schools in the Atlanta University Consortium. **Degrees:** 437 bachelor's awarded. **ROTC:** Army, Naval, Air Force. **Location:** 2 miles from downtown. **Calendar:** Semester. **Full-time faculty:** 172 total; 83% have terminal degrees, 67% women. **Part-time faculty:** 74 total. **Special facilities:** Women's research and resource center, fine art museum.

**Freshman class profile.** 5,656 applied, 1,866 admitted, 557 enrolled.

| Mid 50% test scores | | | |
|---|---|---|---|
| | | GPA 2.0-2.99: | 8% |
| SAT critical reading: | 500-580 | Rank in top quarter: | 73% |
| SAT math: | 490-570 | Rank in top tenth: | 40% |
| ACT composite: | 21-25 | Return as sophomores: | 88% |
| GPA 3.50 or higher: | 63% | Out-of-state: | 70% |
| GPA 3.0-3.49: | 29% | International: | 6% |

**Basis for selection.** School achievement record, letters of recommendation, test scores, leadership, activities, essay important.

**High school preparation.** 15 units required; 19 recommended. Required and recommended units include English 4, mathematics 3-4, social studies 3-4, history 3, science 3-4 (laboratory 2-3), foreign language 2-4 and academic electives 2. Mathematics units must include algebra and geometry. Must have 2 years of the same foreign language. Social studies units should include 2 years of history.

**2007-2008 Annual costs.** Tuition/fees: $18,615. Room/board: $9,200. Books/supplies: $1,150. Personal expenses: $2,100.

**2006-2007 Financial aid. Need-based:** 523 full-time freshmen applied for aid; 471 were judged to have need; 455 of these received aid. Average need met was 87%. Average scholarship/grant was $3,500; average loan $2,625. 71% of total undergraduate aid awarded as scholarships/grants, 29% as loans/jobs. **Non-need-based:** Awarded to 637 full-time undergraduates,

including 343 freshmen. Scholarships awarded for academics, alumni affiliation, leadership, music/drama, state residency.

**Application procedures. Admission:** Closing date 2/1 (postmark date). $35 fee, may be waived for applicants with need. Application may be submitted online. Admission notification on a rolling basis beginning on or about 12/1. Must reply by 5/1. **Financial aid:** Priority date 3/1; no closing date. FAFSA, institutional form required. Applicants notified on a rolling basis starting 2/15; must reply within 2 week(s) of notification.

**Academics. Special study options:** Cross-registration, double major, dual enrollment of high school students, exchange student, honors, independent study, internships, New York semester, student-designed major, study abroad, teacher certification program, Washington semester. **Credit/placement by examination:** AP, CLEP, IB, institutional tests. 16 credit hours maximum toward bachelor's degree. **Support services:** Learning center, pre-admission summer program, tutoring, writing center.

**Majors. Area/ethnic studies:** Women's. **Biology:** General, biochemistry. **Computer sciences:** General. **Conservation:** Environmental science. **Education:** Early childhood. **Engineering:** General. **English:** English lit. **Family/consumer sciences:** Child care. **Foreign languages:** French, Spanish. **History:** General. **Interdisciplinary:** Biological/physical sciences, global studies. **Math:** General. **Philosophy/religion:** Philosophy, religion. **Physical sciences:** Chemistry, physics. **Psychology:** General. **Public administration:** Human services. **Social sciences:** Economics, political science, sociology. **Visual/performing arts:** Dramatic, studio arts.

**Most popular majors.** Biology 13%, English 12%, psychology 22%, social sciences 25%.

**Computing on campus.** 102 workstations in dormitories, library, computer center, student center. Dormitories wired for high-speed internet access and linked to campus network. Commuter students can connect to campus network. Online library, helpline, repair service, wireless network available.

**Student life. Freshman orientation:** Mandatory. One-week program prior to registration. **Housing:** Guaranteed on-campus for freshmen. $100 deposit, deadline 5/1. **Activities:** Jazz band, choral groups, dance, drama, music ensembles, student government, student newspaper, subject-related clubs, community services office.

**Athletics.** NCAA. **Intercollegiate:** Basketball W, cross-country W, soccer W, softball W, tennis W, track and field W, volleyball W. **Intramural:** Basketball W, bowling W, golf W, soccer W, softball W, swimming W, tennis W, track and field W, volleyball W. **Team name:** Jaguars.

**Student services.** Adult student services, campus ministries, career counseling, student employment services, health services, on-campus daycare, personal counseling, placement for graduates, women's services. **Physically disabled:** Services for visually, speech, hearing impaired.

**Contact.** E-mail: admiss@spelman.edu
Phone: (404) 270-5193 Toll-free number: (800) 982-2411
Fax: (404) 270-5201
Arlene Cash, Vice President, Enrollment Management, Spelman College, 350 Spelman Lane SW, Campus Box 277, Atlanta, GA 30314

## Thomas University
**Thomasville, Georgia**
**www.thomasu.edu**                                    CB code: 5072

- Private 4-year university and liberal arts college
- Commuter campus in large town
- 456 degree-seeking undergraduates: 34% part-time, 73% women, 36% African American, 1% Asian American, 4% Hispanic American, 1% Native American
- 75 degree-seeking graduate students
- 88% graduate within 6 years

**General.** Founded in 1950. Regionally accredited. **Degrees:** 104 bachelor's, 2 associate awarded; master's offered. **Location:** 60 miles from Albany, 35 miles from Tallahassee, Florida. **Calendar:** Semester, extensive summer session. **Full-time faculty:** 41 total; 46% have terminal degrees, 10% minority, 71% women. **Part-time faculty:** 38 total; 13% have terminal degrees, 10% minority, 53% women. **Class size:** 86% < 20, 14% 20-39.

**Freshman class profile.**

| | | | |
|---|---|---|---|
| End year in good standing: | 55% | Out-of-state: | 8% |
| Return as sophomores: | 55% | Live on campus: | 25% |

**Basis for selection.** Open admission, but selective for some programs. Special requirements for nursing program. All students must take the Multiple Assessment Programs & Services examination and successfully complete remedial courses before enrolling in academic courses. **Home-schooled:** Transcript of courses and grades, state high school equivalency certificate required.

**2007-2008 Annual costs.** Tuition/fees: $11,040. Room only: $2,626. Books/supplies: $1,100. Personal expenses: $1,500.

**Financial aid. Non-need-based:** Scholarships awarded for academics, athletics, leadership, state residency.

**Application procedures. Admission:** No deadline. $25 fee. Application may be submitted online. Admission notification on a rolling basis. **Financial aid:** Priority date 5/1; no closing date. FAFSA required. Applicants notified on a rolling basis.

**Academics. Special study options:** Accelerated study, distance learning, dual enrollment of high school students, internships, liberal arts/career combination, teacher certification program. **Credit/placement by examination:** AP, CLEP, institutional tests. 40 credit hours maximum toward associate degree, 40 toward bachelor's. Total of 40 hours applies to credit by examination and prior work/life experience credit combined. **Support services:** Learning center, reduced course load, remedial instruction, study skills assistance, tutoring, writing center.

**Majors. Biology:** General. **Business:** General, accounting, management information systems, marketing. **Education:** Early childhood, elementary, middle, music, secondary. **English:** English lit. **Health:** Nursing (RN), staff services technology. **History:** General. **Liberal arts:** Arts/sciences. **Protective services:** Criminal justice. **Psychology:** General. **Public administration:** Social work. **Social sciences:** General, anthropology.

**Most popular majors.** Business/marketing 12%, education 44%, health sciences 10%, legal studies 11%, social sciences 10%.

**Computing on campus.** 50 workstations in library, computer center. Dormitories wired for high-speed internet access and linked to campus network. Commuter students can connect to campus network. Online course registration, online library, wireless network available.

**Student life. Freshman orientation:** Available. Preregistration for classes offered. Half-day every semester. **Housing:** Guaranteed on-campus for freshmen. Coed dorms, apartments available. $250 deposit, deadline 8/1. **Activities:** Jazz band, choral groups, drama, literary magazine, music ensembles, student government, student newspaper.

**Athletics.** NAIA. **Intercollegiate:** Baseball M, golf, soccer, softball W. **Team name:** Night Hawks.

**Student services.** Adult student services, alcohol/substance abuse counseling, career counseling, student employment services, financial aid counseling, personal counseling, placement for graduates, veterans' counselor. **Physically disabled:** Services for visually, hearing impaired.

**Contact.** E-mail: admissions@thomasu.edu
Phone: (229) 226-1621 ext. 124 Toll-free number: (800) 538-9784 ext. 124
Fax: (229) 227-6919
Micky West, Executive Director for Enrollment Management and Student Affairs, Thomas University, 1501 Millpond Road, Thomasville, GA 31792-7499

## Toccoa Falls College
**Toccoa Falls, Georgia**                              CB member
**www.tfc.edu**                                        CB code: 5799

- Private 4-year Bible and liberal arts college affiliated with Christian and Missionary Alliance
- Residential campus in large town
- 969 degree-seeking undergraduates: 7% part-time, 56% women, 3% African American, 7% Asian American, 2% Hispanic American, 1% international
- 51% of applicants admitted
- SAT or ACT (ACT writing optional), application essay required
- 43% graduate within 6 years

**General.** Founded in 1907. Regionally accredited; also accredited by ABHE. **Degrees:** 135 bachelor's, 8 associate awarded. **Location:** 60 miles from Greenville, South Carolina; 90 miles from Atlanta. **Calendar:** 4-1-4, limited summer session. **Full-time faculty:** 49 total; 59% have terminal degrees, 6% minority, 20% women. **Part-time faculty:** 25 total; 8% have terminal degrees, 8% minority, 32% women. **Class size:** 68% < 20, 23%

20-39, 7% 40-49, 2% 50-99. **Special facilities:** 186-foot waterfall, power house, electric generator built in 1898.

**Freshman class profile.** 1,100 applied, 564 admitted, 228 enrolled.

| Mid 50% test scores | | | |
|---|---|---|---|
| SAT critical reading: | 450-590 | GPA 2.0-2.99: | 20% |
| SAT math: | 420-570 | Rank in top quarter: | 38% |
| ACT composite: | 18-26 | Rank in top tenth: | 12% |
| GPA 3.50 or higher: | 51% | Return as sophomores: | 68% |
| GPA 3.0-3.49: | 29% | Out-of-state: | 43% |
| | | Live on campus: | 83% |

**Basis for selection.** Evidence of Christian commitment, character, capacity and desire to learn considered. Index score calculated by multiplying unweighted GPA by best total standardized test score. Students with score of 48 on GED also considered. Personal statement of Christian faith required.

**High school preparation.** 19 units recommended. Recommended units include English 4, mathematics 3, social studies 3, science 3 and academic electives 6.

**2008-2009 Annual costs.** Tuition/fees: $14,625. Room/board: $5,350. Books/supplies: $908. Personal expenses: $2,270.

**Financial aid. Non-need-based:** Scholarships awarded for academics, alumni affiliation, leadership, music/drama, religious affiliation, state residency.

**Application procedures. Admission:** Priority date 5/1; deadline 8/1 (postmark date). $20 fee, may be waived for applicants with need. Application may be submitted online. Admission notification on a rolling basis beginning on or about 3/1. Must reply by May 1 or within 2 week(s) if notified thereafter. **Financial aid:** Priority date 5/1, closing date 8/1. FAFSA, institutional form required. Applicants notified on a rolling basis starting 3/1; must reply within 2 week(s) of notification.

**Academics.** All students complete at least 30 credit hours of Bible courses (18 credit hours for associate degrees), attend weekly church services and participate in student ministry field assignments. **Special study options:** Distance learning, double major, independent study, internships, teacher certification program. **Credit/placement by examination:** AP, CLEP, SAT, ACT, institutional tests. 30 credit hours maximum toward associate degree, 45 toward bachelor's. **Support services:** Learning center, reduced course load, study skills assistance, tutoring.

**Majors. Biology:** General. **Business:** Business admin. **Communications:** General, media studies. **Education:** Early childhood, English, history, middle, music. **English:** English lit. **Legal studies:** Prelaw. **Philosophy/religion:** Religion. **Psychology:** General. **Theology:** Bible, missionary, pastoral counseling, religious ed, sacred music, youth ministry. **Visual/performing arts:** Music performance.

**Most popular majors.** Business/marketing 7%, communications/journalism 8%, education 11%, psychology 21%, theological studies 41%.

**Computing on campus.** 60 workstations in library, computer center. Dormitories wired for high-speed internet access and linked to campus network. Commuter students can connect to campus network. Online course registration, online library, helpline, student web hosting, wireless network available.

**Student life. Freshman orientation:** Mandatory. Preregistration for classes offered. Held 1 week in fall and throughout spring semester. **Policies:** Over 50 different ministry opportunities. Religious observance required. **Housing:** Guaranteed on-campus for freshmen. Single-sex dorms, apartments, substance-free housing available. $200 fully refundable deposit. Mobile homes available on campus lots for married students. **Activities:** Bands, campus ministries, choral groups, drama, international student organizations, music ensembles, radio station, student government, student newspaper.

**Athletics.** NCCAA. **Intercollegiate:** Baseball M, basketball, cross-country, golf, soccer, volleyball W. **Intramural:** Basketball, football (non-tackle), soccer, softball, volleyball. **Team name:** Eagles.

**Student services.** Career counseling, student employment services, financial aid counseling, health services, personal counseling. **Physically disabled:** Services for visually impaired.

**Contact.** E-mail: admissions@tfc.edu
Phone: (706) 886-6831 ext. 5380 Fax: (706) 282-6012
John Gailer, Director of Admissions, Toccoa Falls College, PO Box 800899, Toccoa Falls, GA 30598-0368

# Truett-McConnell College
**Cleveland, Georgia**
www.truett.edu

CB member
CB code: 5798

▶ Private 4-year liberal arts college affiliated with Southern Baptist Convention
▶ Residential campus in small town
▶ 395 degree-seeking undergraduates
▶ 50% of applicants admitted
▶ SAT or ACT (ACT writing optional) required

**General.** Founded in 1946. Regionally accredited. Associated with Baptist Convention of the State of Georgia. **Degrees:** 6 bachelor's, 35 associate awarded. **Location:** 75 miles from Atlanta, 25 miles from Gainesville. **Calendar:** Semester, limited summer session. **Full-time faculty:** 22 total. **Part-time faculty:** 34 total. **Class size:** 67% < 20, 28% 20-39, 3% 40-49, 2% 50-99.

**Freshman class profile.** 595 applied, 295 admitted, 165 enrolled.

| Mid 50% test scores | | | |
|---|---|---|---|
| SAT critical reading: | 380-490 | GPA 3.0-3.49: | 29% |
| SAT math: | 400-490 | GPA 2.0-2.99: | 50% |
| ACT composite: | 16-20 | Out-of-state: | 2% |
| GPA 3.50 or higher: | 20% | Live on campus: | 86% |

**Basis for selection.** Secondary school record, test scores important. 2.0 GPA in core classes required. 1080 SAT (exclusive of writing) or 15 ACT required. Students with lower scores may apply to academic enrichment program. Audition required of music majors. **Homeschooled:** Transcript of courses and grades required. Letter from local school board stating that student has completed home-school program requirements and placement exams required. **Learning Disabled:** Students may request accommodations upon presentation of appropriate documentation of disability. Determination of reasonable accommodations made on individual basis.

**High school preparation.** Recommended units include English 4, mathematics 3, social studies 3, science 3 and foreign language 2.

**2008-2009 Annual costs.** Tuition/fees: $14,000. Room/board: $5,100. Books/supplies: $1,000. Personal expenses: $1,150.

**Financial aid. Non-need-based:** Scholarships awarded for academics, athletics, music/drama, religious affiliation, state residency. **Additional information:** Installment plan available through AMS.

**Application procedures. Admission:** Closing date 8/1 (receipt date). $25 fee, may be waived for applicants with need. Application may be submitted online. Admission notification on a rolling basis. Must reply by May 1 or within 1 week(s) if notified thereafter. **Financial aid:** Priority date 6/1; no closing date. FAFSA, institutional form required. Applicants notified on a rolling basis starting 4/1; must reply within 2 week(s) of notification.

**Academics. Special study options:** Double major, dual enrollment of high school students, honors, independent study, study abroad. **Credit/placement by examination:** AP, CLEP, SAT, ACT. 30 credit hours maximum toward associate degree, 30 toward bachelor's. **Support services:** Remedial instruction, tutoring.

**Majors. Education:** Early childhood. **Liberal arts:** Humanities. **Philosophy/religion:** Christian.

**Computing on campus.** 47 workstations in library, computer center, student center. Dormitories linked to campus network. Commuter students can connect to campus network.

**Student life. Freshman orientation:** Mandatory. Preregistration for classes offered. Held for one day during July and August. **Policies:** Religious observance required. **Housing:** Single-sex dorms, apartments, substance-free housing available. $100 fully refundable deposit. **Activities:** Bands, choral groups, music ensembles, student government, Baptist Student Union, Phi Theta Kappa, Impact Teams and Majesty, Phi Beta Lambda, Ministerial Association, Student Professional Association of Georgia Educators, Fellowship of Christian Athletes.

**Athletics.** NJCAA. **Intercollegiate:** Baseball M, basketball, cross-country, golf M, soccer, softball W. **Intramural:** Basketball, football (non-tackle), soccer. **Team name:** Bears.

**Student services.** Campus ministries, financial aid counseling, veterans' counselor. **Physically disabled:** Services for visually, speech, hearing impaired.

**Contact.** E-mail: admissions@truett.edu
Phone: (706) 865-2134 Toll-free number: (800) 226-8621
Fax: (706) 865-7615
Mike Davis, Dean of Enrollment Services, Truett-McConnell College, 100
Alumni Drive, Cleveland, GA 30528

## University of Georgia
**Athens, Georgia**  **CB member**
**www.uga.edu**  **CB code: 5813**

- Public 4-year university
- Commuter campus in small city
- 24,971 degree-seeking undergraduates: 7% part-time, 57% women, 6% African American, 6% Asian American, 2% Hispanic American, 1% international
- 7,934 degree-seeking graduate students
- 55% of applicants admitted
- SAT or ACT with writing, application essay required
- 78% graduate within 6 years

**General.** Founded in 1785. Regionally accredited. **Degrees:** 6,203 bachelor's awarded; master's, doctoral, first professional offered. **ROTC:** Army, Air Force. **Location:** 60 miles from of Atlanta. **Calendar:** Semester, extensive summer session. **Full-time faculty:** 1,733 total; 94% have terminal degrees, 26% minority, 33% women. **Part-time faculty:** 441 total; 63% have terminal degrees, 12% minority, 43% women. **Class size:** 38% < 20, 44% 20-39, 7% 40-49, 6% 50-99, 5% >100. **Special facilities:** Botanical garden, golf course.

**Freshman class profile.** 16,871 applied, 9,242 admitted, 4,721 enrolled.

| Mid 50% test scores | | | |
|---|---|---|---|
| SAT critical reading: | 560-660 | Rank in top quarter: | 85% |
| SAT math: | 570-660 | Rank in top tenth: | 51% |
| SAT writing: | 560-640 | Return as sophomores: | 93% |
| ACT composite: | 25-29 | Out-of-state: | 16% |
| GPA 3.50 or higher: | 86% | Live on campus: | 98% |
| GPA 3.0-3.49: | 13% | International: | 1% |
| GPA 2.0-2.99: | 1% | Fraternities: | 27% |
| | | Sororities: | 29% |

**Basis for selection.** GPA in core academic courses, rigor of course selection, and best combination of SAT/ACT scores important. Applications reviewed for conduct issues, recommendations, and satisfactory completion of all courses and completion of required college preparatory courses. Audition required of music majors.

**High school preparation.** 16 units required; 18 recommended. Required and recommended units include English 4, mathematics 4, social studies 3, history 3, science 3 (laboratory 2), foreign language 2-3 and academic electives 1.

**2007-2008 Annual costs.** Tuition/fees: $5,622; $20,726 out-of-state. Room/board: $7,292. Books/supplies: $800.

**2007-2008 Financial aid. Need-based:** 2,960 full-time freshmen applied for aid; 1,449 were judged to have need; 1,439 of these received aid. Average need met was 80%. Average scholarship/grant was $7,492; average loan $2,917. 63% of total undergraduate aid awarded as scholarships/grants, 37% as loans/jobs. **Non-need-based:** Awarded to 2,921 full-time undergraduates, including 763 freshmen. Scholarships awarded for academics, athletics, ROTC, state residency.

**Application procedures. Admission:** Priority date 10/15; deadline 1/15 (postmark date). $50 fee, may be waived for applicants with need. Application may be submitted online. Admission notification on a rolling basis beginning on or about 12/15. Must reply by 5/1. **Financial aid:** Priority date 3/1; no closing date. FAFSA required. Applicants notified on a rolling basis starting 5/15; must reply within 2 week(s) of notification.

**Academics. Special study options:** Accelerated study, combined bachelor's/graduate degree, cooperative education, cross-registration, distance learning, double major, dual enrollment of high school students, exchange student, external degree, honors, independent study, internships, liberal arts/career combination, student-designed major, study abroad, teacher certification program, Washington semester. **Credit/placement by examination:** AP, CLEP, IB, institutional tests. Unlimited number of hours of credit by examination may be counted toward bachelor's degree. **Support services:** Learning center, pre-admission summer program, reduced course load, remedial instruction, study skills assistance, tutoring, writing center.

**Majors. Agriculture:** General, agribusiness operations, animal sciences, communications, dairy, economics, food science, horticulture, landscaping,

poultry, turf management. **Architecture:** Landscape. **Area/ethnic studies:** African-American, Latin American, women's. **Biology:** General, biochemistry, biotechnology, botany, cell/histology, ecology, entomology, genetics, microbiology. **Business:** General, accounting, business admin, fashion, finance, insurance, international, management information systems, managerial economics, marketing, real estate. **Communications:** Advertising, broadcast journalism, journalism, public relations. **Communications technology:** Radio/tv. **Computer sciences:** Computer science. **Conservation:** Environmental studies, fisheries, forestry, wildlife. **Education:** Agricultural, business, English, family/consumer sciences, foreign languages, health, kindergarten/preschool, mathematics, middle, music, physical, sales/marketing, science, social science, social studies, special, technology/industrial arts, voc/tech. **Engineering:** General, agricultural, chemical, computer, environmental. **English:** English lit, speech/rhetoric. **Family/consumer sciences:** Child development, communication, consumer economics, family resources, family studies, food/nutrition, housing. **Foreign languages:** Ancient Greek, Chinese, classics, comparative lit, French, German, Italian, Japanese, Latin, linguistics, Romance, Russian, Spanish. **Health:** Communication disorders, dietetics, environmental health, music therapy, public health ed. **History:** General. **Interdisciplinary:** Biological/physical sciences. **Liberal arts:** Arts/sciences. **Math:** General, statistics. **Parks/recreation:** Sports admin. **Philosophy/religion:** Philosophy, religion. **Physical sciences:** Astronomy, chemistry, geology, physics. **Protective services:** Criminal justice. **Psychology:** General, cognitive, educational. **Public administration:** Social work. **Social sciences:** Anthropology, economics, geography, international relations, political science, sociology. **Visual/performing arts:** Art, art history/conservation, dance, dramatic, film/cinema, music performance, music theory/composition, studio arts. **Other:** Office information system.

**Most popular majors.** Biology 8%, business/marketing 20%, communications/journalism 6%, education 9%, English 7%, family/consumer sciences 6%, psychology 6%, social sciences 10%.

**Computing on campus.** 2,600 workstations in dormitories, library, computer center, student center. Dormitories wired for high-speed internet access and linked to campus network. Commuter students can connect to campus network. Online course registration, online library, helpline, repair service, student web hosting, wireless network available.

**Student life. Freshman orientation:** Mandatory. Preregistration for classes offered. Two-day sessions offered during summer. **Housing:** Guaranteed on-campus for freshmen. Coed dorms, single-sex dorms, special housing for disabled, apartments, fraternity/sorority housing available. $275 nonrefundable deposit, deadline 5/15. Honors and language focused housing available. **Activities:** Bands, campus ministries, choral groups, dance, drama, film society, literary magazine, music ensembles, musical theater, opera, radio station, student government, student newspaper, symphony orchestra, TV station.

**Athletics.** NCAA. **Intercollegiate:** Baseball M, basketball, cross-country, diving, equestrian W, football (tackle) M, golf, gymnastics W, soccer W, softball W, swimming, tennis, track and field, volleyball W. **Intramural:** Basketball, cross-country, football (non-tackle), football (tackle) M, golf, racquetball, soccer, softball, squash, tennis, track and field, volleyball, wrestling M. **Team name:** Bulldogs.

**Student services.** Adult student services, alcohol/substance abuse counseling, career counseling, student employment services, financial aid counseling, health services, legal services, minority student services, on-campus daycare, personal counseling, placement for graduates, veterans' counselor, women's services. **Physically disabled:** Services for visually, speech, hearing impaired. **Learning disabled:** Comprehensive services available.

**Contact.** E-mail: undergrad@admissions.uga.edu
Phone: (706) 542-8776 Fax: (706) 542-1466
Nancy McDuff, Associate Vice President for Admissions and Enrollment Management, University of Georgia, Office of Undergraduate Admissions, Athens, GA 30602-1633

## University of West Georgia
**Carrollton, Georgia**  **CB member**
**www.westga.edu**  **CB code: 5900**

- Public 4-year university
- Commuter campus in large town
- 8,842 degree-seeking undergraduates: 16% part-time, 60% women
- 1,835 graduate students
- 53% of applicants admitted
- SAT or ACT (ACT writing recommended) required
- 36% graduate within 6 years

**General.** Founded in 1906. Regionally accredited. Off-campus sites in Newnan (undergraduate). Advanced Academy of Georgia for academically accelerated high school juniors and seniors. **Degrees:** 1,128 bachelor's awarded;

master's, doctoral, first professional offered. **ROTC:** Army. **Location:** 50 miles from Atlanta. **Calendar:** Semester, extensive summer session. **Full-time faculty:** 415 total; 79% have terminal degrees, 14% minority, 49% women. **Part-time faculty:** 105 total; 37% have terminal degrees, 10% minority, 66% women. **Class size:** 38% < 20, 42% 20-39, 9% 40-49, 7% 50-99, 3% >100. **Special facilities:** Observatory, performing arts center, archaeological laboratory, technology enhanced learning center.

**Freshman class profile.** 5,803 applied, 3,089 admitted, 2,195 enrolled.

| Mid 50% test scores | | | |
|---|---|---|---|
| SAT critical reading: | 460-550 | Return as sophomores: | 73% |
| SAT math: | 450-540 | Out-of-state: | 2% |
| ACT composite: | 18-22 | Live on campus: | 62% |
| GPA 3.50 or higher: | 20% | International: | 2% |
| GPA 3.0-3.49: | 34% | Fraternities: | 9% |
| GPA 2.0-2.99: | 46% | Sororities: | 6% |

**Basis for selection.** GED not accepted. Freshman admission is based on standardized test scores, such as the SAT or ACT, high school GPA in college preparatory subjects, system mandated college preparatory curriculum. **Homeschooled:** SAT scores equal to or greater than the average SAT score of the previous fall freshman class. In addition, applicants must meet required SAT Critical Reading score of 430 and SAT math score of 410. The ACT minimum equivalent scores are English 17 and Math 17. (SAT and ACT scores cannot be mixed in determining admission eligibility.) Must submit academic portfolio booklets detailing all 16 high school college prep courses.

**High school preparation.** 16 units required. Required units include English 4, mathematics 4, social studies 3, science 3 (laboratory 2) and foreign language 2. 1 math higher than algebra II/geometry.

**2007-2008 Annual costs.** Tuition/fees: $3,918; $12,790 out-of-state. Room/board: $5,406. Books/supplies: $1,000.

**2007-2008 Financial aid. Need-based:** Average need met was 65%. Average scholarship/grant was $4,997; average loan $3,196. 42% of total undergraduate aid awarded as scholarships/grants, 58% as loans/jobs. **Non-need-based:** Scholarships awarded for academics, alumni affiliation, art, athletics, leadership, minority status, music/drama, religious affiliation, state residency.

**Application procedures. Admission:** Priority date 5/1; deadline 6/1 (receipt date). $30 fee, may be waived for applicants with need. Application may be submitted online. Admission notification on a rolling basis beginning on or about 9/1. **Financial aid:** Priority date 4/1, closing date 7/7. FAFSA required. Applicants notified by 3/1; Applicants notified on a rolling basis starting 3/1.

**Academics. Special study options:** Accelerated study, cooperative education, distance learning, double major, dual enrollment of high school students, external degree, honors, independent study, internships, study abroad, teacher certification program. **Credit/placement by examination:** AP, CLEP, IB, institutional tests. 30 credit hours maximum toward bachelor's degree. **Support services:** Learning center, pre-admission summer program, reduced course load, remedial instruction, study skills assistance, tutoring, writing center.

**Honors college/program.** Admission to the Honors College is open to entering freshmen who meet two of the following three criteria: (1) a combined SAT score of at least 1200 or the ACT equivalent, (2) a minimum score of 610 on the verbal portion of the SAT or ACT equivalent, or (3) a high school grade point average of 3.5 or higher. The College is also open to any student who has completed 15 or more hours at West Georgia with an overall GPA of 3.2 or higher. To have a realistic chance of completing the Honors College Curriculum, however, students must enter no later than the beginning of their sophomore year. Individual Honors courses are open on a space available basis to any student with a cumulative GPA of 3.2 or higher who has completed 15 or more credit hours. Scores of 4 or 5 in Advanced Placement courses count as West Georgia Honors credit, and students who transfer from other college or university Honors Programs or Colleges may be able to transfer their Honors credit here.

**Majors. Biology:** General. **Business:** Accounting, business admin, finance, management information systems, managerial economics, marketing, real estate. **Communications:** Journalism. **Computer sciences:** General. **Conservation:** Environmental science, environmental studies. **Education:** Biology, business, chemistry, elementary, middle, music, physical, physics, secondary, special. **English:** English lit. **Foreign languages:** French, German, Spanish. **Health:** Nursing (RN), speech pathology. **History:** General. **Math:** General. **Parks/recreation:** Facilities management. **Philosophy/religion:** Philosophy. **Physical sciences:** Chemistry, geology, physics. **Psychology:** General. **Social sciences:** Anthropology, criminology, economics, geography, international economics, international relations, political science, sociology. **Visual/performing arts:** Art, dramatic, music performance, music theory/

composition. **Other:** Earth science/secondary education, Economics/secondary education.

**Most popular majors.** Biology 6%, business/marketing 26%, education 21%, health sciences 8%, psychology 8%, social sciences 8%.

**Computing on campus.** 1,000 workstations in dormitories, library, computer center, student center. Dormitories wired for high-speed internet access and linked to campus network. Online course registration, online library, helpline, repair service, student web hosting, wireless network available.

**Student life. Freshman orientation:** Mandatory, $25 fee. Preregistration for classes offered. **Policies:** All freshmen required to reside on-campus unless married or living with parents, relatives, or legal guardians. **Housing:** Guaranteed on-campus for freshmen. Coed dorms, single-sex dorms, special housing for disabled, apartments, cooperative housing, fraternity/sorority housing available. $250 partly refundable deposit, deadline 7/1. **Activities:** Bands, choral groups, dance, drama, international student organizations, literary magazine, music ensembles, musical theater, opera, radio station, student government, student newspaper, TV station, Baptist Student Union, Catholic Student Life, Muslim student alliance, Latter-Day Saint student association, Jewish student group, Black Students Alliance, Democratic organization, Republican organization.

**Athletics.** NCAA. **Intercollegiate:** Baseball M, basketball, cheerleading, cross-country, football (tackle) M, golf, soccer W, softball W, volleyball W. **Intramural:** Basketball, football (non-tackle), golf, sailing, soccer, softball, table tennis, tennis, track and field, volleyball, weight lifting. **Team name:** Wolves.

**Student services.** Adult student services, career counseling, student employment services, financial aid counseling, health services, minority student services, on-campus daycare, personal counseling, placement for graduates, veterans' counselor. **Physically disabled:** Services for visually, speech, hearing impaired.

**Contact.** E-mail: admiss@westga.edu
Phone: (678) 839-4000 Fax: (678) 839-4747
Bobby Johnson, Director of Admissions, University of West Georgia, 1601 Maple Street, Carrollton, GA 30118

## Valdosta State University
**Valdosta, Georgia**
www.valdosta.edu

**CB member**
**CB code: 5855**

- Public 4-year university
- Commuter campus in small city
- 9,696 degree-seeking undergraduates: 15% part-time, 59% women, 25% African American, 1% Asian American, 2% Hispanic American, 1% international
- 1,485 degree-seeking graduate students
- 63% of applicants admitted
- SAT or ACT (ACT writing optional) required
- 41% graduate within 6 years

**General.** Founded in 1906. Regionally accredited. **Degrees:** 1,449 bachelor's, 60 associate awarded; master's, doctoral offered. **ROTC:** Air Force. **Location:** 235 miles from Atlanta, 138 miles from Jacksonville, Florida. **Calendar:** Semester, extensive summer session. **Full-time faculty:** 438 total; 78% have terminal degrees, 10% minority, 44% women. **Part-time faculty:** 125 total; 19% have terminal degrees, 4% minority, 59% women. **Class size:** 36% < 20, 52% 20-39, 9% 40-49, 2% 50-99, less than 1% >100. **Special facilities:** Planetarium, herbarium, observatory, archives museum, pedestrian mall.

**Freshman class profile.** 5,978 applied, 3,796 admitted, 2,077 enrolled.

| Mid 50% test scores | | | |
|---|---|---|---|
| | | GPA 2.0-2.99: | 44% |
| SAT critical reading: | 470-550 | Return as sophomores: | 71% |
| SAT math: | 460-550 | Out-of-state: | 3% |
| ACT composite: | 20-22 | Live on campus: | 70% |
| GPA 3.50 or higher: | 18% | International: | 2% |
| GPA 3.0-3.49: | 38% | | |

**Basis for selection.** GED not accepted. 440 SAT Verbal, 410 SAT Math or 18 ACT English, 17 ACT Math required. Freshmen Index of 2040 required, based on academic GPA multiplied by 500 added to SAT verbal and math scores. **Homeschooled:** Letter of recommendation (nonparent) required. 1050 SAT (exclusive of Writing) with 440 Verbal/410 Math or 23 ACT with 18 English/17 Math, declaration of intent to homeschool filed with Board of Education, portfolio that demonstrates satisfactory completion of college prep curriculum, letter from primary teacher certifying completion of high school and date of graduation, 2 letters of recommendation from non-family members, certificate of immunization required. **Learning Disabled:** Must meet minimum admission standards; untimed SAT/ACT accepted.

**High school preparation.** 16 units required. Required units include English 4, mathematics 4, social studies 3, science 3 (laboratory 2) and foreign language 2.

**2007-2008 Annual costs.** Tuition/fees: $4,038; $12,910 out-of-state. Room/board: $5,990. Books/supplies: $1,000. Personal expenses: $2,600.

**2006-2007 Financial aid. Need-based:** 1,574 full-time freshmen applied for aid; 1,126 were judged to have need; 1,121 of these received aid. Average need met was 62%. Average scholarship/grant was $5,584; average loan $2,461. 43% of total undergraduate aid awarded as scholarships/grants, 57% as loans/jobs. **Non-need-based:** Awarded to 428 full-time undergraduates, including 164 freshmen. Scholarships awarded for academics, art, athletics, music/drama, ROTC.

**Application procedures. Admission:** Closing date 7/1 (receipt date). $40 fee, may be waived for applicants with need. Application may be submitted online. Admission notification on a rolling basis beginning on or about 8/1. **Financial aid:** Priority date 5/1, closing date 6/15. FAFSA required. Applicants notified on a rolling basis starting 6/1.

**Academics. Special study options:** Cooperative education, distance learning, double major, dual enrollment of high school students, ESL, external degree, honors, independent study, internships, liberal arts/career combination, study abroad, teacher certification program, weekend college. **Credit/placement by examination:** AP, CLEP, IB, SAT, ACT. 30 credit hours maximum toward associate degree, 30 toward bachelor's. **Support services:** Study skills assistance, tutoring, writing center.

**Majors. Biology:** General. **Business:** Accounting, administrative services, business admin, finance, managerial economics, marketing. **Communications:** Media studies. **Computer sciences:** General, information systems. **Conservation:** Environmental science. **Education:** Art, business, early childhood, middle, music, physical, secondary, special, trade/industrial. **English:** English lit, speech/rhetoric. **Foreign languages:** French, sign language interpretation, Spanish. **Health:** Athletic training, nursing (RN), speech pathology. **History:** General. **Legal studies:** Paralegal. **Liberal arts:** Arts/sciences. **Math:** General, applied. **Parks/recreation:** Exercise sciences. **Philosophy/religion:** Philosophy. **Physical sciences:** Astronomy, chemistry, physics. **Protective services:** Criminal justice. **Psychology:** General. **Social sciences:** Political science, sociology. **Visual/performing arts:** General, art, interior design, music performance.

**Most popular majors.** Business/marketing 17%, education 22%, English 7%, health sciences 8%, psychology 6%, social sciences 6%.

**Computing on campus.** 1,600 workstations in library. Dormitories wired for high-speed internet access and linked to campus network. Commuter students can connect to campus network. Online course registration, online library, helpline, repair service, student web hosting, wireless network available.

**Student life. Freshman orientation:** Available, $35 fee. Preregistration for classes offered. One-day programs held in June, July, and August. Sessions for first time freshmen, transfer students, athletes, and international students. **Housing:** Coed dorms, single-sex dorms, special housing for disabled, apartments, substance-free housing available. $300 fully refundable deposit. Wellness, honors floors available. **Activities:** Bands, choral groups, dance, drama, literary magazine, music ensembles, radio station, student government, student newspaper, symphony orchestra, TV station, Black Student League, several religious and social service organizations, outdoor adventure club, Habitat for Humanity.

**Athletics.** NCAA. **Intercollegiate:** Baseball M, basketball, cross-country, football (tackle) M, golf M, softball W, tennis, volleyball W. **Intramural:** Badminton, basketball, bowling, football (non-tackle), golf, racquetball, soccer M, softball, tennis, volleyball, weight lifting. **Team name:** Blazers.

**Student services.** Alcohol/substance abuse counseling, career counseling, student employment services, financial aid counseling, health services, minority student services, personal counseling, placement for graduates, veterans' counselor. **Physically disabled:** Services for visually, speech, hearing impaired. **Learning disabled:** Comprehensive services available.

**Contact.** E-mail: admissions@valdosta.edu
Phone: (229) 333-5791 Toll-free number: (800) 618-1878
Fax: (229) 333-5482
Walter Peacock, Director of Admissions, Valdosta State University, 1500 North Patterson Street, Valdosta, GA 31698

---

# Wesleyan College
### Macon, Georgia
### www.wesleyancollege.edu
**CB member**
**CB code: 5895**

◗ Private 4-year liberal arts college for women affiliated with United Methodist Church
◗ Residential campus in small city
◗ 547 degree-seeking undergraduates: 33% part-time, 100% women
◗ 99 degree-seeking graduate students
◗ 49% of applicants admitted
◗ SAT or ACT (ACT writing optional), application essay required
◗ 56% graduate within 6 years

**General.** Founded in 1836. Regionally accredited. **Degrees:** 78 bachelor's awarded; master's offered. **Location:** 75 miles from Atlanta. **Calendar:** Semester, limited summer session. **Full-time faculty:** 50 total; 98% have terminal degrees, 6% minority, 58% women. **Part-time faculty:** 33 total; 21% have terminal degrees, 73% women. **Class size:** 87% < 20, 13% 20-39, less than 1% 40-49. **Special facilities:** Equestrian facilities, arboretum, lake.

**Freshman class profile.** 617 applied, 302 admitted, 135 enrolled.

| Mid 50% test scores | | | |
|---|---|---|---|
| SAT critical reading: | 490-640 | Rank in top quarter: | 57% |
| SAT math: | 480-580 | Rank in top tenth: | 34% |
| ACT composite: | 19-25 | End year in good standing: | 92% |
| GPA 3.50 or higher: | 53% | Return as sophomores: | 68% |
| GPA 3.0-3.49: | 33% | Out-of-state: | 22% |
| GPA 2.0-2.99: | 13% | Live on campus: | 95% |
| | | International: | 30% |

**Basis for selection.** Admission committee reviews applicants based on academic performance in college preparatory courses, standardized test scores, extra-curricular activities and recommendations. Interview recommended; required for scholarship competitions. Audition required of music or theater students interested in performance arts scholarship. Portfolio required of art majors. **Homeschooled:** Statement describing homeschool structure and mission, transcript of courses and grades, letter of recommendation (nonparent) required. Diplomas issued by parents are recognized. Student may provide biography of high school literature and essay to evaluate exposure and thinking skills. Extra-curricular activities, counselor interviews considered.

**High school preparation.** 15 units required; 22 recommended. Required and recommended units include English 4, mathematics 3-4, social studies 3-4, science 3-4 (laboratory 2-3), foreign language 2-4 and academic electives 2.

**2007-2008 Annual costs.** Tuition/fees: $16,500. Room/board: $7,500. Books/supplies: $1,000. Personal expenses: $1,000.

**Financial aid. Non-need-based:** Scholarships awarded for academics, alumni affiliation, art, job skills, leadership, minority status, music/drama, religious affiliation, state residency. **Additional information:** Fellowships available based on number of hours and cumulative GPA transferred in, with minimum 30 semester or 45 quarter hours and 3.0 GPA required.

**Application procedures. Admission:** Priority date 3/1; deadline 6/1 (postmark date). $30 fee, may be waived for applicants with need. Application may be submitted online. Admission notification on a rolling basis beginning on or about 10/1. Must reply by 7/1. **Financial aid:** Priority date 5/1, closing date 6/3. FAFSA, institutional form required. Applicants notified on a rolling basis starting 3/1; must reply by 5/1 or within 3 week(s) of notification.

**Academics. Special study options:** Accelerated study, cross-registration, double major, dual enrollment of high school students, exchange student, honors, independent study, internships, liberal arts/career combination, student-designed major, study abroad, teacher certification program, weekend college. **Credit/placement by examination:** AP, CLEP, IB, institutional tests. 30 credit hours maximum toward bachelor's degree. **Support services:** Learning center, reduced course load, study skills assistance, tutoring, writing center.

**Majors. Biology:** General. **Business:** Business admin, international. **Communications:** General, advertising. **Computer sciences:** General. **Education:** Early childhood, middle. **English:** English lit. **Foreign languages:** French, Spanish. **History:** General. **Liberal arts:** Arts/sciences. **Math:** General. **Philosophy/religion:** Philosophy, religion. **Physical sciences:** Chemistry, physics. **Psychology:** General. **Social sciences:** General, economics, international relations. **Theology:** Preministerial. **Visual/performing arts:** Art history/conservation, dramatic, studio arts.

**Most popular majors.** Biology 6%, business/marketing 28%, education 11%, English 6%, psychology 10%, visual/performing arts 8%.

**Computing on campus.** PC or laptop required. 20 workstations in library, student center. Dormitories wired for high-speed internet access and linked to campus network. Commuter students can connect to campus network. Online course registration, online library, helpline, repair service, wireless network available.

**Student life. Freshman orientation:** Mandatory. Preregistration for classes offered. Summer orientation held in June and July. Fall orientation held in August prior to start of classes. **Policies:** Students required to live on campus unless married or living with immediate family in the local area. **Housing:** Guaranteed on-campus for all undergraduates. Special housing for disabled, apartments available. $150 deposit, deadline 7/1. **Activities:** Campus ministries, choral groups, dance, drama, international student organizations, literary magazine, music ensembles, Model UN, student government, student newspaper, honor council, Mortar board, Young Democrats, Circle K, College Republicans, Council on Religions Concerns, American Chemical Society, Wesleyan Disciples.

**Athletics.** NCAA. **Intercollegiate:** Basketball W, cross-country W, equestrian W, soccer W, softball W, tennis W. **Intramural:** Basketball W, cross-country W, soccer W, softball W, volleyball W. **Team name:** Pioneers.

**Student services.** Adult student services, alcohol/substance abuse counseling, career counseling, student employment services, financial aid counseling, health services, minority student services, personal counseling, women's services.

**Contact.** E-mail: admission@wesleyancollege.edu
Phone: (478) 757-5206 Toll-free number: (800) 447-6610
Fax: (478) 757-4030
Patricia Gibbs, Vice President for Enrollment and Student Services,
Wesleyan College, 4760 Forsyth Road, Macon, GA 31210-4462

## Westwood College: Atlanta Midtown
### Atlanta, Georgia

- For-profit 3-year technical college
- Commuter campus in very large city

**General.** Accredited by ACICS. **Calendar:** Differs by program.

**Annual costs/financial aid.** Tuition/fees (2007-2008): $13,562.

**Contact.** Phone: (404) 745-9096
Director of Admissions, 1100 Spring Street, Suite 200, Atlanta, GA 30309

## Westwood College: Northlake
### Atlanta, Georgia
### www.westwood.edu

- For-profit 4-year visual arts and technical college
- Very large city

**General.** Accredited by ACICS. **Calendar:** Differs by program.

**Contact.** Phone: (404) 962-2998
2220 Parklake Drive, Suite 175, Atlanta, GA 30345

# Hawaii

## Brigham Young University-Hawaii

Laie, Hawaii
www.byuh.edu

CB member
CB code: 4106

- Private 4-year university and liberal arts college affiliated with Church of Jesus Christ of Latter-day Saints
- Residential campus in small town
- 2,312 degree-seeking undergraduates: 7% part-time, 56% women, 1% African American, 22% Asian American, 2% Hispanic American, 1% Native American, 44% international
- 48% of applicants admitted
- Application essay, interview required
- 47% graduate within 6 years

**General.** Founded in 1955. Regionally accredited. Mission to educate students from Asia and Pacific Rim. **Degrees:** 566 bachelor's, 3 associate awarded. **ROTC:** Army, Air Force. **Location:** 38 miles from Honolulu. **Calendar:** Semester, limited summer session. **Full-time faculty:** 122 total; 80% have terminal degrees, 23% minority, 21% women. **Part-time faculty:** 116 total; 4% have terminal degrees, 47% minority, 64% women. **Class size:** 54% < 20, 40% 20-39, 4% 40-49, 2% 50-99, less than 1% >100. **Special facilities:** Natural history museum, Polynesian Cultural Center, artifact collection housed in library, Institute for Pacific Studies.

**Freshman class profile.** 1,265 applied, 603 admitted, 297 enrolled.

| Mid 50% test scores | | | |
|---|---|---|---|
| SAT critical reading: | 450-570 | GPA 2.0-2.99: | 16% |
| SAT math: | 470-590 | Return as sophomores: | 57% |
| ACT composite: | 20-26 | Out-of-state: | 55% |
| GPA 3.50 or higher: | 47% | Live on campus: | 100% |
| GPA 3.0-3.49: | 37% | International: | 23% |

**Basis for selection.** GED not accepted. Interview, essay, recommendations very important. Test scores also important. 3.0 GPA required for domestic students. ACT recommended. Audition required for music majors. Portfolio required for art majors. Ecclesiastical interviews required for all students. Essays may make difference in admission.

**High school preparation.** Recommended units include English 4, mathematics 2, social studies 3, history 2 and science 2.

**2007-2008 Annual costs.** Tuition/fees: $3,250. 100% higher tuition and per-credit-hour charges for students who are not members of The Church of Jesus Christ of Latter-day Saints. Room/board: $5,364. Books/supplies: $800. Personal expenses: $1,600.

**2006-2007 Financial aid.** **Need-based:** 185 full-time freshmen applied for aid; 171 were judged to have need; 164 of these received aid. Average need met was 75%. Average scholarship/grant was $3,500; average loan $2,280. 30% of total undergraduate aid awarded as scholarships/grants, 70% as loans/jobs. **Non-need-based:** Awarded to 1,209 full-time undergraduates, including 137 freshmen. Scholarships awarded for academics, art, athletics, leadership, music/drama, state residency.

**Application procedures.** **Admission:** Closing date 2/15 (receipt date). $30 fee. Application may be submitted online. Admission notification on a rolling basis beginning on or about 4/1. Must reply by 8/25. **Financial aid:** Closing date 3/15. FAFSA required. Applicants notified by 5/1; must reply by 8/31.

**Academics.** **Special study options:** Cooperative education, double major, ESL, honors, independent study, internships, student-designed major, teacher certification program. **Credit/placement by examination:** AP, CLEP, IB, institutional tests. **Support services:** Learning center, remedial instruction, study skills assistance, tutoring, writing center.

**Majors.** **Area/ethnic studies:** Pacific. **Biology:** General, biochemistry. **Business:** Accounting, hospitality admin, hotel/motel admin, international, tourism/travel. **Computer sciences:** Computer science, information systems. **Education:** Art, biology, business, chemistry, elementary, English, ESL, mathematics, music, physical, physics, science, secondary, social science, special. **English:** English lit. **History:** General. **Interdisciplinary:** Intercultural. **Math:** General. **Parks/recreation:** Exercise sciences, health/fitness.

**Psychology:** General. **Public administration:** Social work. **Science technology:** Biological. **Social sciences:** Political science. **Visual/performing arts:** Art, piano/organ, studio arts, voice/opera.

**Most popular majors.** Business/marketing 24%, computer/information sciences 10%, education 17%, interdisciplinary studies 13%, parks/recreation 6%, public administration/social services 6%, visual/performing arts 6%.

**Computing on campus.** 465 workstations in dormitories, library, computer center, student center. Dormitories wired for high-speed internet access and linked to campus network. Online course registration, online library, helpline, repair service, wireless network available.

**Student life. Freshman orientation:** Mandatory. Preregistration for classes offered. 2 weeks at beginning of semester, includes luau, campus and island tour. **Policies:** Religious observance required. **Housing:** Guaranteed on-campus for freshmen. Single-sex dorms, apartments, substance-free housing available. $50 deposit, deadline 4/30. All first-time, non-local freshmen required to live on campus until sophomore standing achieved. **Activities:** Bands, choral groups, dance, drama, film society, literary magazine, music ensembles, student government, student newspaper, African club, Brasil club, Cambodian club, Fijian club, Filipino club, Hawaiian club, Hong Kong club, Indian club, Japanese club, Korean club.

**Athletics.** NCAA. **Intercollegiate:** Basketball, cross-country, golf M, soccer, softball W, tennis, volleyball W. **Intramural:** Basketball, bowling, cross-country, golf, racquetball, rugby, soccer, softball, swimming, table tennis, tennis, volleyball, water polo M, weight lifting. **Team name:** Seasiders.

**Student services.** Campus ministries, career counseling, student employment services, financial aid counseling, health services, personal counseling, placement for graduates, veterans' counselor, women's services. **Physically disabled:** Services for visually, speech, hearing impaired.

**Contact.** E-mail: admissions@byuh.edu
Phone: (808) 293-3738 Fax: (808) 293-3741
Arapata Meha, Dean of Admissions and Records, Brigham Young University-Hawaii, 55-220 Kulanui Street, #1973, Laie, HI 96762-1294

## Chaminade University of Honolulu

Honolulu, Hawaii
www.chaminade.edu

CB member
CB code: 4105

- Private 4-year university affiliated with Roman Catholic Church
- Commuter campus in large city
- 1,095 degree-seeking undergraduates
- 94% of applicants admitted
- SAT or ACT (ACT writing optional), application essay required

**General.** Founded in 1955. Regionally accredited. Campus shared with St. Louis School. **Degrees:** 350 bachelor's, 165 associate awarded; master's offered. **ROTC:** Army, Air Force. **Location:** 2 miles from Waikiki. **Calendar:** Semester, limited summer session. **Full-time faculty:** 74 total. **Part-time faculty:** 51 total. **Class size:** 63% < 20, 36% 20-39, 1% 40-49. **Special facilities:** Montessori laboratory preschool, observatory, theater.

**Freshman class profile.** 784 applied, 735 admitted, 243 enrolled.

| Mid 50% test scores | | | |
|---|---|---|---|
| SAT critical reading: | 420-510 | ACT composite: | 17-23 |
| SAT math: | 410-520 | Out-of-state: | 57% |
| | | Live on campus: | 65% |

**Basis for selection.** School achievement record, test scores, statement of purpose important. Interview recommended for marginal students.

**High school preparation.** Recommended units include English 4, mathematics 3, social studies 3, science 2 and academic electives 4.

**2008-2009 Annual costs.** Tuition/fees (projected): $15,640. Room/board: $9,800.

**Financial aid.** **Non-need-based:** Scholarships awarded for academics, art, athletics, leadership, religious affiliation, ROTC, state residency. **Additional information:** For students whose eligibility for federal and institutional aid does not meet entire costs, alternative student loans may be secured for eligible applicants.

**Application procedures.** **Admission:** No deadline. $50 fee. Application may be submitted online. Admission notification on a rolling basis. **Financial aid:** Priority date 2/15; no closing date. FAFSA required. Applicants notified on a rolling basis starting 2/15; must reply within 4 week(s) of notification.

**Academics.** **Special study options:** Accelerated study, distance learning, double major, exchange student, independent study, internships, semester at sea, student-designed major, teacher certification program. Accelerated sessions in evening division. **Credit/placement by examination:** AP, CLEP, IB, SAT, ACT, institutional tests. 30 credit hours maximum toward associate degree, 30 toward bachelor's. **Support services:** Learning center, preadmission summer program, remedial instruction, study skills assistance, tutoring.

**Majors.** **Biology:** General. **Business;** Accounting, business admin, marketing. **Communications:** General, broadcast journalism, media studies, public relations. **Computer sciences:** General, computer science. **Conservation:** Environmental studies. **Education:** Early childhood, elementary, secondary. **English:** English lit. **History:** General. **Interdisciplinary:** Behavioral sciences. **Liberal arts:** Arts/sciences. **Philosophy/religion:** Religion. **Protective services:** Criminalistics, forensics. **Psychology:** General. **Social sciences:** General, international relations, political science. **Visual/performing arts:** Interior design.

**Computing on campus.** 96 workstations in dormitories, library, computer center, student center. Dormitories wired for high-speed internet access. Online library, helpline, repair service, wireless network available.

**Student life.** **Freshman orientation:** Mandatory, $140 fee. Preregistration for classes offered. **Housing:** Guaranteed on-campus for freshmen. Coed dorms, single-sex dorms, special housing for disabled, apartments, substance-free housing available. $300 deposit, deadline 5/1. **Activities:** Choral groups, dance, drama, literary magazine, musical theater, student government, student newspaper, Samoan club, Hawaiian club, Rotaract club, accounting club, Black Student Union, Filipino club, CJ Sleuths, communications club.

**Athletics.** NCAA. **Intercollegiate:** Basketball M, cross-country, golf, softball W, tennis, volleyball W, water polo M. **Intramural:** Cheerleading. **Team name:** Silverswords.

**Student services.** Adult student services, alcohol/substance abuse counseling, campus ministries, career counseling, student employment services, financial aid counseling, health services, personal counseling, placement for graduates. **Physically disabled:** Services for visually, speech, hearing impaired.

**Contact.** E-mail: admissions@chaminade.edu
Phone: (808) 735-4735 Toll-free number: (800) 735-3733
Fax: (808) 739-4647
Dan Yoshitake, Associate Director of Admissions, Chaminade University of Honolulu, 3140 Waialae Avenue, Honolulu, HI 96816

---

## Hawaii Pacific University

| Honolulu, Hawaii | CB member |
|---|---|
| www.hpu.edu | CB code: 4352 |

- Private 4-year university and liberal arts college
- Commuter campus in large city
- 6,128 degree-seeking undergraduates: 37% part-time, 62% women
- 1,232 degree-seeking graduate students
- 82% of applicants admitted
- SAT or ACT (ACT writing optional) required
- 37% graduate within 6 years

**General.** Founded in 1965. Regionally accredited. 2 main campuses connected by free shuttle service. Programs offered for military personnel and their dependents and for older students. Satellite campus on 6 military installations on Oahu. Affiliated with the Oceanic Institute. **Degrees:** 1,017 bachelor's, 170 associate awarded; master's offered. **ROTC:** Army, Air Force. **Calendar:** Semester, extensive summer session. **Full-time faculty:** 257 total; 65% have terminal degrees, 25% minority, 49% women. **Part-time faculty:** 335 total; 29% have terminal degrees, 41% minority, 49% women. **Class size:** 52% < 20, 48% 20-39, less than 1% 40-49. **Special facilities:** Research boat, theater.

**Freshman class profile.** 2,948 applied, 2,415 admitted, 695 enrolled.

| Mid 50% test scores | | Rank in top quarter: | 45% |
|---|---|---|---|
| SAT critical reading: | 430-550 | Rank in top tenth: | 20% |
| SAT math: | 420-530 | End year in good standing: | 99% |
| SAT writing: | 420-530 | Return as sophomores: | 69% |
| ACT composite: | 18-24 | Out-of-state: | 42% |
| GPA 3.50 or higher: | 29% | Live on campus: | 24% |
| GPA 3.0-3.49: | 36% | International: | 11% |
| GPA 2.0-2.99: | 34% | | |

**Basis for selection.** Academic record, test scores most important. Interview also important, recommendations considered. Essay recommended. **Homeschooled:** Interview, letter of recommendation (nonparent) required.

**High school preparation.** 14 units recommended. Recommended units include English 4, mathematics 4, social studies 3, history 2, science 2 (laboratory 1) and foreign language 2. Additional science and mathematics required for nursing and marine science.

**2008-2009 Annual costs.** Tuition/fees (projected): $13,080. Room/board: $10,560. Books/supplies: $1,300. Personal expenses: $800.

**2007-2008 Financial aid.** **Need-based:** 485 full-time freshmen applied for aid; 267 were judged to have need; 251 of these received aid. Average need met was 79%. Average scholarship/grant was $4,511; average loan $5,487. 16% of total undergraduate aid awarded as scholarships/grants, 84% as loans/jobs. **Non-need-based:** Awarded to 801 full-time undergraduates, including 179 freshmen. Scholarships awarded for academics, alumni affiliation, athletics, job skills, leadership, music/drama, religious affiliation, ROTC.

**Application procedures.** **Admission:** Priority date 3/1; no deadline. $50 fee, may be waived for applicants with need. Application may be submitted online. Admission notification on a rolling basis. Must reply by May 1 or within 4 week(s) if notified thereafter. **Financial aid:** Priority date 3/1; no closing date. FAFSA required. Applicants notified on a rolling basis starting 4/1; must reply within 3 week(s) of notification.

**Academics.** All students complete core requirements based on following themes: global systems, world cultures, communication skills, research/epistemology, values and choices. **Special study options:** Accelerated study, combined bachelor's/graduate degree, cooperative education, distance learning, double major, dual enrollment of high school students, ESL, honors, independent study, internships, liberal arts/career combination, student-designed major, study abroad, teacher certification program, weekend college. 3-2 engineering program with University of Southern California (CA), Washington University, St. Louis (MO). **Credit/placement by examination:** AP, CLEP, IB, SAT, ACT, institutional tests. 36 credit hours maximum toward associate degree, 36 toward bachelor's. **Support services:** Learning center, pre-admission summer program, reduced course load, remedial instruction, study skills assistance, tutoring.

**Honors college/program.** 3.5 minimum high school GPA, minimum 24 ACT or 1100 SAT, (exclusive of Writing) required. 40-50 admitted and enrolled each fall.

**Majors.** **Biology:** General, marine. **Business:** General, accounting, banking/financial services, business admin, communications, finance, human resources, international, international finance, management information systems, managerial economics, marketing, tourism/travel. **Communications:** General, advertising, journalism, public relations. **Computer sciences:** General, computer science. **Conservation:** General, environmental science, environmental studies. **Education:** ESL. **English:** English lit. **Family/consumer sciences:** Family studies. **Foreign languages:** Comparative lit. **Health:** Nursing (RN), premedicine. **History:** General. **Interdisciplinary:** Behavioral sciences. **Liberal arts:** Arts/sciences. **Math:** Applied. **Physical sciences:** Oceanography. **Protective services:** Law enforcement admin. **Psychology:** General. **Public administration:** General, human services, social work. **Social sciences:** General, anthropology, economics, international relations, political science, sociology.

**Most popular majors.** Business/marketing 37%, communications/journalism 8%, health sciences 24%.

**Computing on campus.** PC or laptop required. 590 workstations in library, computer center, student center. Dormitories wired for high-speed internet access and linked to campus network. Commuter students can connect to campus network. Online course registration, online library, helpline, student web hosting, wireless network available.

**Student life.** **Freshman orientation:** Available, $10 fee. Preregistration for classes offered. Week of activities including on-campus sessions and off-campus activities. In fall, weekend (Friday, Saturday) including above. In spring, day activities that include on-campus sessions in summer. **Housing:** Coed dorms, single-sex dorms, apartments, substance-free housing available. $500 deposit. Homestay program also available. **Activities:** Pep band, choral groups, dance, drama, film society, international student organizations, literary magazine, music ensembles, musical theater, student government, student newspaper, Rotaract, President's Hosts, Christian Fellowship, American marketing association, hiking club, honors societies, computing club, Students In Free Enterprise.

**Athletics.** NCAA. **Intercollegiate:** Baseball M, basketball, cheerleading, cross-country, golf M, softball W, tennis, volleyball W. **Intramural:** Basketball, football (tackle), soccer, softball, table tennis, volleyball. **Team name:** Sea Warriors.

**Student services.** Adult student services, alcohol/substance abuse counseling, campus ministries, career counseling, student employment services, financial aid counseling, personal counseling, placement for graduates, veterans' counselor.

**Contact.** E-mail: admissions@hpu.edu
Phone: (808) 544-0238 Toll-free number: (800) 669-4724
Fax: (808) 544-1136
Sara Sato, Director of Admissions, Hawaii Pacific University, 1164 Bishop Street, Honolulu, HI 96813

## University of Hawaii at Hilo
Hilo, Hawaii    CB member
www.uhh.hawaii.edu    CB code: 4869

- Public 4-year university
- Commuter campus in large town
- 3,144 degree-seeking undergraduates
- 60% of applicants admitted
- SAT or ACT (ACT writing optional) required

**General.** Founded in 1970. Regionally accredited. **Degrees:** 535 bachelor's awarded; master's offered. **Location:** 200 miles from Honolulu. **Calendar:** Semester, limited summer session. **Full-time faculty:** 262 total. **Part-time faculty:** 83 total. **Class size:** 47% < 20, 47% 20-39, 5% 40-49, 1% 50-99. **Special facilities:** Active volcanoes study center, space science center, small business development center, marine education center, 110-acre farm laboratory.

**Freshman class profile.**

| Mid 50% test scores | | | |
|---|---|---|---|
| SAT critical reading: | 440-560 | GPA 2.0-2.99: | 23% |
| SAT math: | 440-600 | Rank in top quarter: | 46% |
| ACT composite: | 17-24 | Rank in top tenth: | 22% |
| GPA 3.50 or higher: | 37% | Out-of-state: | 27% |
| GPA 3.0-3.49: | 40% | Live on campus: | 64% |

**Basis for selection.** High school GPA in academic subjects, SAT/ACT test scores, class rank, and school recommendation considered.

**High school preparation.** 17 units required. Required and recommended units include English 4, mathematics 3, social studies 2, history 2, science 3, foreign language 2 and academic electives 7. 3 mathematics beyond pre-algebra, 7 academic electives not including physical education or ROTC. 4 math and 4 science recommended for science and business majors.

**2007-2008 Annual costs.** Tuition/fees: $3,676; $11,212 out-of-state. Room/board: $6,792. Books/supplies: $1,017. Personal expenses: $1,166.

**Financial aid. Additional information:** Hawaii student incentive grants and tuition waivers (merit and need-based) available to Hawaii residents at participating institutions.

**Application procedures. Admission:** Priority date 3/1; deadline 7/1 (postmark date). $50 fee, may be waived for applicants with need. Application may be submitted online. Admission notification on a rolling basis beginning on or about 10/1. Must reply by May 1 or within 2 week(s) if notified thereafter. **Financial aid:** Priority date 3/1; no closing date. FAFSA required. Applicants notified on a rolling basis starting 4/15; must reply within 2 week(s) of notification.

**Academics. Special study options:** Cross-registration, distance learning, double major, dual enrollment of high school students, exchange student, honors, independent study, internships, student-designed major, study abroad, teacher certification program. Marine sciences and astronomy summer programs. **Credit/placement by examination:** CLEP, IB, institutional tests. 30 credit hours maximum toward bachelor's degree. **Support services:** Learning center, tutoring, writing center.

**Majors. Agriculture:** Agribusiness operations, agronomy, animal sciences, horticultural science, plant protection, soil science. **Area/ethnic studies:** Native American. **Biology:** General, marine. **Business:** General, accounting, business admin, finance, marketing. **Communications:** General. **Computer sciences:** General. **English:** English lit, speech/rhetoric. **Foreign languages:** Japanese, linguistics. **Health:** Premedicine. **History:** General. **Interdisciplinary:** Natural sciences. **Liberal arts:** Arts/sciences. **Math:** General. **Parks/recreation:** Facilities management, health/fitness. **Philosophy/religion:** Philosophy, religion. **Physical sciences:** Astronomy, chemistry, geology, physics. **Psychology:** General. **Public administration:** General. **Social sciences:** Anthropology, economics, geography, political science, sociology. **Visual/performing arts:** Art.

**Most popular majors.** Business/marketing 10%, communication technologies 8%, interdisciplinary studies 7%, physical sciences 6%, psychology 15%, social sciences 17%.

**Computing on campus.** 600 workstations in dormitories, library, computer center, student center. Commuter students can connect to campus network. Online course registration, online library, helpline, repair service available.

**Student life. Freshman orientation:** Available, $25 fee. Preregistration for classes offered. 1-week program before start of classes. **Housing:** Coed dorms, special housing for disabled, apartments available. $20 deposit, deadline 7/15. Student housing units available for mobility-impaired students. **Activities:** Bands, choral groups, dance, drama, literary magazine, music ensembles, musical theater, student government, student newspaper, international student association, Samoan club, Delta Sigma Pi business fraternity, World Hope, Rotoract, Bayanihan club, Bahai Club, Chuukese Student Association, Earth Action, Nihon no kai.

**Athletics.** NCAA. **Intercollegiate:** Baseball M, basketball, cross-country, golf, soccer, softball W, tennis, volleyball W. **Intramural:** Archery, badminton, basketball, bowling, cross-country, golf, softball, table tennis, tennis, volleyball. **Team name:** Vulcans.

**Student services.** Career counseling, services for economically disadvantaged, student employment services, financial aid counseling, health services, minority student services, personal counseling, placement for graduates, women's services. **Physically disabled:** Services for visually, speech, hearing impaired.

**Contact.** E-mail: uhhadm@hawaii.edu
Phone: (808) 974-7414 Toll-free number: (800) 897-4456
Fax: (808) 933-0861
James Cromwell, Director of Admissions, University of Hawaii at Hilo, 200 West Kawili Street, Hilo, HI 96720-4091

## University of Hawaii at Manoa
Honolulu, Hawaii    CB member
www.manoa.hawaii.edu    CB code: 4867

- Public 4-year university
- Commuter campus in very large city
- 13,386 degree-seeking undergraduates: 18% part-time, 55% women
- 5,331 degree-seeking graduate students
- 70% of applicants admitted
- SAT or ACT with writing required
- 51% graduate within 6 years

**General.** Founded in 1907. Regionally accredited. **Degrees:** 2,835 bachelor's awarded; master's, doctoral, first professional offered. **ROTC:** Army, Air Force. **Location:** 3 miles from downtown. **Calendar:** Semester, extensive summer session. **Full-time faculty:** 1,151 total; 98% have terminal degrees, 37% minority, 39% women. **Part-time faculty:** 142 total; 96% have terminal degrees, 42% minority, 48% women. **Class size:** 52% < 20, 35% 20-39, 5% 40-49, 5% 50-99, 3% >100. **Special facilities:** Institute for astronomy, observatories, arboretum, East-West center, Japanese tea house and garden, Hawaiian studies center, Korean studies center.

**Freshman class profile.** 6,136 applied, 4,271 admitted, 1,834 enrolled.

| Mid 50% test scores | | | |
|---|---|---|---|
| SAT critical reading: | 460-570 | Rank in top quarter: | 54% |
| SAT math: | 500-610 | Rank in top tenth: | 24% |
| SAT writing: | 460-560 | Return as sophomores: | 77% |
| ACT composite: | 20-25 | Out-of-state: | 25% |
| GPA 3.50 or higher: | 43% | Live on campus: | 15% |
| GPA 3.0-3.49: | 41% | International: | 2% |
| GPA 2.0-2.99: | 16% | Fraternities: | 1% |
| | | Sororities: | 1% |

**Basis for selection.** School achievement record, test scores, class rank most important. **Homeschooled:** State high school equivalency certificate required. In absence of official transcript from accredited school, students must submit GED results in addition to other requirements.

**High school preparation.** 22 units required. Required and recommended units include English 4, mathematics 3, social studies 3, science 3 (laboratory 1), foreign language 2 and academic electives 4.

**2007-2008 Annual costs.** Tuition/fees: $5,390; $14,654 out-of-state. Room/board: $7,335. Books/supplies: $1,167. Personal expenses: $1,248.

**2006-2007 Financial aid. Need-based:** 1,086 full-time freshmen applied for aid; 545 were judged to have need; 510 of these received aid. Average need met was 68%. Average scholarship/grant was $4,898; average loan $2,535. 45% of total undergraduate aid awarded as scholarships/grants, 55% as loans/jobs. **Non-need-based:** Awarded to 3,454 full-time undergraduates, including 541 freshmen. Scholarships awarded for academics, alumni affiliation, art, athletics, job skills, leadership, minority status, music/drama, religious affiliation, ROTC, state residency. **Additional information:** Hawaii student incentive grants and tuition waivers (merit and need-based) available to Hawaii residents at participating institutions.

**Application procedures. Admission:** Priority date 2/1; deadline 5/1 (receipt date). $50 fee, may be waived for applicants with need. Application may be submitted online. Admission notification on a rolling basis beginning on or about 12/1. Must reply by May 1 or within 2 week(s) if notified thereafter. **Financial aid:** Priority date 3/1; no closing date. FAFSA required. Applicants notified on a rolling basis starting 3/15; must reply within 4 week(s) of notification.

**Academics. Special study options:** Cooperative education, distance learning, double major, ESL, exchange student, honors, independent study, internships, semester at sea, student-designed major, study abroad, teacher certification program. **Credit/placement by examination:** AP, CLEP, IB, SAT, ACT, institutional tests. 30 credit hours maximum toward bachelor's degree. **Support services:** Learning center, pre-admission summer program, remedial instruction, study skills assistance, tutoring, writing center.

**Majors. Agriculture:** Animal sciences, plant protection. **Area/ethnic studies:** American, Asian, Native American. **Biology:** General, botany, marine, microbiology, zoology. **Business:** General, accounting, business admin, finance, human resources, international, management information systems, marketing, tourism/travel. **Communications:** General, journalism. **Computer sciences:** General, computer science. **Conservation:** Environmental science, management/policy. **Education:** Elementary, ESL, secondary. **Engineering:** Agricultural, civil, electrical, mechanical. **English:** English lit. **Family/consumer sciences:** General, clothing/textiles. **Foreign languages:** Chinese, classics, Filipino/Tagalog, French, German, Japanese, Korean, Russian, Spanish. **Health:** Audiology/speech pathology, clinical lab science, dental hygiene, nursing (RN). **History:** General. **Interdisciplinary:** Nutrition sciences. **Liberal arts:** Arts/sciences. **Math:** General. **Parks/recreation:** Exercise sciences. **Philosophy/religion:** Philosophy, religion. **Physical sciences:** Chemistry, geology, meteorology, physics. **Psychology:** General. **Public administration:** Social work. **Social sciences:** Anthropology, economics, geography, political science, sociology. **Visual/performing arts:** Art, dance, dramatic. **Other:** Ethnobotany, Plant and Environmental Biotechnology.

**Most popular majors.** Business/marketing 22%, education 8%, psychology 7%, social sciences 11%.

**Computing on campus.** 1,400 workstations in dormitories, library, computer center. Dormitories wired for high-speed internet access and linked to campus network. Commuter students can connect to campus network. Online course registration, online library, helpline, repair service, student web hosting, wireless network available.

**Student life. Freshman orientation:** Available, $80 fee. Preregistration for classes offered. 2-day program. **Housing:** Guaranteed on-campus for freshmen. Coed dorms, apartments, substance-free housing available. $225 partly refundable deposit, deadline 5/1. Some modified units within student housing facilities available for disabled students. **Activities:** Bands, choral groups, dance, drama, literary magazine, music ensembles, radio station, student government, student newspaper, symphony orchestra, TV station, over 150 registered organizations.

**Athletics.** NCAA. **Intercollegiate:** Baseball M, basketball, cheerleading, cross-country W, diving, football (tackle) M, golf, sailing, soccer W, softball W, swimming, tennis, track and field W, volleyball, water polo W. **Intramural:** Badminton, basketball, cross-country, golf, soccer, softball, table tennis, tennis, track and field W, volleyball, weight lifting. **Team name:** Warriors, Rainbow Warriors, Rainbows, Rainbow Wahine.

**Student services.** Adult student services, alcohol/substance abuse counseling, career counseling, services for economically disadvantaged, student employment services, financial aid counseling, health services, minority student services, on-campus daycare, personal counseling, placement for graduates, veterans' counselor, women's services. **Physically disabled:** Services for visually, speech, hearing impaired.

**Contact.** E-mail: ar-info@hawaii.edu
Phone: (808) 956-8975 Toll-free number: (800) 823-9771
Fax: (808) 956-4148
Jan Heu, Director of Admissions and Records, University of Hawaii at Manoa, 2600 Campus Road, QLC Rm 001, Honolulu, HI 96822

---

## University of Hawaii: West Oahu
**Pearl City, Hawaii**      **CB member**
**www.westoahu.hawaii.edu**      **CB code: 1042**

- Public 4-year liberal arts and teachers college
- Commuter campus in large town

---

- 911 degree-seeking undergraduates: 64% part-time, 69% women, 2% African American, 62% Asian American, 3% Hispanic American
- 68% of applicants admitted

**General.** Founded in 1976. Regionally accredited. **Degrees:** 217 bachelor's awarded. **ROTC:** Army, Air Force. **Location:** 10 miles from Honolulu. **Calendar:** Semester, limited summer session. **Full-time faculty:** 39 total; 95% have terminal degrees, 46% minority, 46% women. **Part-time faculty:** 21 total; 29% minority, 24% women. **Class size:** 50% < 20, 47% 20-39, 2% 40-49.

**Freshman class profile.** 109 applied, 74 admitted, 41 enrolled.

**Basis for selection.** Students with 2.7 high school GPA and 22 credits of required high school coursework will be automatically accepted. **Homeschooled:** State high school equivalency certificate required.

**High school preparation.** 22 units required. Required units include English 4, mathematics 3, social studies 3, science 3 and academic electives 5. Math credits must include Algebra II and Geometry. 4 credits of college prep coursework ( language, fine arts, etc.) also required.

**2007-2008 Annual costs.** Tuition/fees: $3,226; $10,186 out-of-state. Foreign students pay out-of-state tuition rates. However, citizens of an eligible Pacific island district, commonwealth, territory or insular jurisdiction, state or nation which does not provide public institutions that grant baccalaureate degrees may be allowed to pay 150% of the resident tuition. Books/supplies: $1,079. Personal expenses: $1,143.

**2006-2007 Financial aid. Need-based:** 49% of total undergraduate aid awarded as scholarships/grants, 51% as loans/jobs. **Non-need-based:** Scholarships awarded for academics, alumni affiliation, leadership, state residency. **Additional information:** Tuition waivers (merit and need-based) available to Hawaii residents.

**Application procedures. Admission:** Priority date 4/1; deadline 8/1 (postmark date). $50 fee. Application must be submitted on paper. Admission notification on a rolling basis. **Financial aid:** Priority date 4/1; no closing date. FAFSA required.

**Academics. Special study options:** Cross-registration, distance learning, double major, independent study, study abroad, teacher certification program. **Credit/placement by examination:** AP, CLEP, IB, SAT, ACT, institutional tests. 42 credit hours maximum toward bachelor's degree. 21 lower division and 21 upper division credits may be earned through examination. **Support services:** Study skills assistance, tutoring, writing center.

**Majors. Area/ethnic studies:** Pacific. **Business:** Accounting, business admin. **Education:** Early childhood, elementary. **English:** English lit. **History:** General. **Philosophy/religion:** Philosophy. **Protective services:** Law enforcement admin. **Psychology:** General. **Public administration:** General. **Social sciences:** General, anthropology, economics, political science, sociology.

**Most popular majors.** Business/marketing 30%, history 6%, psychology 29%, public administration/social services 17%, social sciences 20%.

**Computing on campus.** 18 workstations in computer center. Commuter students can connect to campus network. Online course registration, online library, helpline, student web hosting, wireless network available.

**Student life. Freshman orientation:** Available. Preregistration for classes offered. **Activities:** Student government, accounting club, anthropology/sociology club, business club, economics club, Hawaiian-Pacific Club; humanities club, political science club, psychology association, students in free enterprise.

**Student services.** Career counseling, student employment services, financial aid counseling, veterans' counselor. **Physically disabled:** Services for visually, hearing impaired.

**Contact.** E-mail: admissions@uhwo.hawaii.edu
Phone: (808) 454-4700 Fax: (808) 453-6075
Robyn Oshiro, Admissions Specialist, University of Hawaii: West Oahu, 96-129 Ala Ike, Pearl City, HI 96782

# Idaho

## Boise Bible College
Boise, Idaho
www.boisebible.edu

CB code: 0891

- Private 4-year Bible college affiliated with nondenominational tradition
- Residential campus in small city
- 167 degree-seeking undergraduates: 10% part-time, 51% women, 2% African American, 2% Asian American, 2% Hispanic American, 1% Native American, 2% international
- 71% of applicants admitted
- SAT or ACT (ACT writing optional), application essay required
- 30% graduate within 6 years

**General.** Founded in 1945. Accredited by ABHE. **Degrees:** 15 bachelor's, 18 associate awarded. **Location:** 4 miles from downtown. **Calendar:** Semester. **Full-time faculty:** 8 total. **Part-time faculty:** 7 total.

**Freshman class profile.** 103 applied, 73 admitted, 50 enrolled.

| Mid 50% test scores | | | |
|---|---|---|---|
| SAT critical reading: | 460-580 | GPA 2.0-2.99: | 33% |
| SAT math: | 430-550 | Rank in top quarter: | 23% |
| ACT composite: | 17-20 | Rank in top tenth: | 3% |
| GPA 3.50 or higher: | 26% | Return as sophomores: | 65% |
| GPA 3.0-3.49: | 39% | International: | 2% |

**Basis for selection.** Christian conduct or ethical code standards based on signed student statement, recommendation of home church minister, 1 employment/school reference, and 1 personal reference required. School achievement important. **Homeschooled:** Transcript of courses and grades required. GED or transcripts from homeschooling agency recommended. Applicants submitting home-prepared transcripts advised to consult admissions office.

**High school preparation.** Recommended units include English 4, mathematics 2, history 2 and foreign language 1.

**2007-2008 Annual costs.** Tuition/fees: $7,776. Room/board: $4,740. Books/supplies: $605. Personal expenses: $1,210.

**Financial aid. Non-need-based:** Scholarships awarded for academics, leadership, music/drama, religious affiliation.

**Application procedures. Admission:** Priority date 5/1; deadline 8/1 (receipt date). $25 fee. Application must be submitted on paper. Admission notification on a rolling basis. Must reply by 6/1. 3 weeks after acceptance date after June 1. **Financial aid:** Priority date 5/1; no closing date. FAFSA, institutional form required. Applicants notified on a rolling basis starting 5/2; must reply by 8/1 or within 2 week(s) of notification.

**Academics. Special study options:** Distance learning, double major, independent study, internships. **Credit/placement by examination:** AP, CLEP, IB, SAT, ACT, institutional tests. ABHE Bible Knowledge Test. **Support services:** Reduced course load, remedial instruction.

**Majors. Theology:** Bible, missionary, pastoral counseling, religious ed, sacred music, theology, youth ministry.

**Computing on campus.** 7 workstations in library, computer center.

**Student life. Freshman orientation:** Mandatory, $50 fee. Preregistration for classes offered. 2 days of training and testing, followed by whitewater boat trip. **Policies:** Religious observance required. **Housing:** Guaranteed on-campus for freshmen. Single-sex dorms available. $150 deposit, deadline 7/1. Trailer hookups for married students. **Activities:** Choral groups, music ensembles, student government, student newspaper, Christian service missions club.

**Athletics. Intramural:** Basketball, football (non-tackle) M, soccer, volleyball. **Team name:** Lions.

**Student services.** Adult student services, career counseling, student employment services, financial aid counseling, health services, personal counseling, placement for graduates, veterans' counselor.

**Contact.** E-mail: boisebible@boisebible.edu
Phone: (208) 376-7731 Toll-free number: (800) 893-7755
Fax: (208) 376-7743
Martin Flaherty, Admissions Director, Boise Bible College, 8695 West Marigold Street, Boise, ID 83714-1220

## Boise State University
Boise, Idaho
www.boisestate.edu

CB member
CB code: 4018

- Public 4-year university and technical college
- Commuter campus in small city
- 16,571 degree-seeking undergraduates: 32% part-time, 54% women, 1% African American, 3% Asian American, 6% Hispanic American, 1% Native American, 1% international
- 1,598 degree-seeking graduate students
- 89% of applicants admitted
- SAT or ACT (ACT writing optional) required

**General.** Founded in 1932. Regionally accredited. **Degrees:** 1,874 bachelor's, 484 associate awarded; master's, doctoral offered. **ROTC:** Army. **Location:** Downtown. **Calendar:** Semester, limited summer session. **Full-time faculty:** 617 total; 91% have terminal degrees, 6% minority, 42% women. **Part-time faculty:** 456 total; 17% have terminal degrees, 6% minority, 48% women. **Class size:** 43% < 20, 44% 20-39, 6% 40-49, 5% 50-99, 2% >100. **Special facilities:** Performing arts center, technology center, natural area and world center for birds of prey research.

**Freshman class profile.** 3,487 applied, 3,104 admitted, 2,665 enrolled.

| Mid 50% test scores | | | |
|---|---|---|---|
| SAT critical reading: | 450-580 | Rank in top tenth: | 11% |
| SAT math: | 460-580 | End year in good standing: | 95% |
| ACT composite: | 19-24 | Return as sophomores: | 64% |
| GPA 3.50 or higher: | 34% | Out-of-state: | 9% |
| GPA 3.0-3.49: | 40% | Live on campus: | 30% |
| GPA 2.0-2.99: | 26% | International: | 1% |
| Rank in top quarter: | 34% | Fraternities: | 1% |
| | | Sororities: | 1% |

**Basis for selection.** Admission based on high school GPA and ACT or SAT score. Applicants without high school diploma or GED may petition for admission. Interview required for vocational-technical, nursing majors. **Homeschooled:** State high school equivalency certificate required.

**High school preparation.** 15 units required. Required and recommended units include English 4, mathematics 3, social studies 3, science 3 and foreign language 1. One unit foreign language, humanities, or fine arts and 1.5 units other college preparatory also recommended.

**2007-2008 Annual costs.** Tuition/fees: $4,410; $12,578 out-of-state. Out-of-state students (undergraduate and graduate) taking less than 8 credit hours pay in-state rate. Room/board: $5,273. Books/supplies: $1,000. Personal expenses: $2,258.

**2007-2008 Financial aid. Need-based:** Average need met was 64%. Average scholarship/grant was $3,640; average loan $3,526. 34% of total undergraduate aid awarded as scholarships/grants, 66% as loans/jobs. **Non-need-based:** Scholarships awarded for academics, athletics, music/drama, ROTC, state residency.

**Application procedures. Admission:** Closing date 7/12 (postmark date). $40 fee. Application may be submitted online. Admission notification on a rolling basis beginning on or about 2/15. Strongly recommended that students apply January-March. **Financial aid:** Priority date 4/1; no closing date. FAFSA required. Applicants notified on a rolling basis starting 6/1; must reply within 2 week(s) of notification.

**Academics.** Basque studies program abroad. **Special study options:** Distance learning, double major, dual enrollment of high school students, exchange student, honors, independent study, internships, student-designed major, study abroad, teacher certification program, weekend college. **Credit/placement by examination:** AP, CLEP, SAT, ACT, institutional tests. 21 credit hours maximum toward associate degree, 42 toward bachelor's. **Support services:** Learning center, pre-admission summer program, reduced course load, remedial instruction, study skills assistance, tutoring.

**Majors. Biology:** General. **Business:** Accounting, construction management, finance, human resources, international, management information systems, managerial economics, market research, marketing, operations. **Communications:** General, journalism. **Computer sciences:** Computer science, information systems. **Education:** General, art, bilingual, business, elementary, music, physical, special. **Engineering:** Civil, electrical, materials science, mechanical. **Engineering technology:** Construction. **English:** American lit, British lit, English lit. **Foreign languages:** French, German, Spanish.

**Health:** Athletic training, environmental health, medical radiologic technology/radiation therapy, medical records admin, nursing (RN), predental, premedicine, preveterinary, respiratory therapy technology. **History:** General. **Liberal arts:** Arts/sciences. **Math:** General, applied. **Parks/recreation:** Exercise sciences, health/fitness. **Philosophy/religion:** Philosophy. **Physical sciences:** Chemistry, geology, geophysics, physics, planetary. **Protective services:** Law enforcement admin. **Psychology:** General. **Public administration:** Social work. **Social sciences:** General, anthropology, economics, political science, sociology. **Visual/performing arts:** Art, commercial/advertising art, dramatic, music management, music performance, music theory/composition.

**Most popular majors.** Business/marketing 24%, communications/journalism 6%, education 9%, health sciences 8%, social sciences 6%, visual/performing arts 6%.

**Computing on campus.** 900 workstations in dormitories, library, computer center. Dormitories wired for high-speed internet access and linked to campus network. Commuter students can connect to campus network. On-line course registration, wireless network available.

**Student life. Freshman orientation:** Mandatory, $75 fee. Preregistration for classes offered. **Housing:** Coed dorms, single-sex dorms, special housing for disabled, apartments, fraternity/sorority housing, substance-free housing available. $75 fully refundable deposit, deadline 7/12. **Activities:** Bands, choral groups, dance, drama, international student organizations, literary magazine, music ensembles, musical theater, radio station, student government, student newspaper, symphony orchestra, TV station, Black Student Union, Native American association, Organization de Estudiantes Latino-Americanos, Latter-day Saints student association, Alternative Mobility Adventure Seekers.

**Athletics.** NCAA. **Intercollegiate:** Basketball, cheerleading, cross-country, football (tackle) M, golf, gymnastics W, rodeo, skiing W, soccer W, swimming W, tennis, track and field, volleyball W, wrestling M. **Intramural:** Baseball M, basketball, bowling, handball, racquetball, soccer M, softball, swimming, tennis, volleyball. **Team name:** Broncos.

**Student services.** Adult student services, career counseling, student employment services, health services, on-campus daycare, personal counseling, placement for graduates, veterans' counselor. **Physically disabled:** Services for visually, speech, hearing impaired.

**Contact.** E-mail: bsuinfo@boisestate.edu
Phone: (208) 426-1156 Toll-free number: (800) 824-7017
Fax: (208) 426-3765
Jenny Cardenas, Director of Admissions, Boise State University, 1910 University Drive, Boise, ID 83725

## Brigham Young University-Idaho
Rexburg, Idaho
www.byui.edu
CB code: 4657

- Private 4-year university affiliated with Church of Jesus Christ of Latter-day Saints
- Residential campus in large town
- 13,155 degree-seeking undergraduates
- ACT (writing optional), application essay required

**General.** Founded in 1888. Regionally accredited. **Degrees:** 2,287 bachelor's, 970 associate awarded. **ROTC:** Army. **Location:** 30 miles from Idaho Falls, 240 miles from Salt Lake City. **Calendar:** Semester, extensive summer session. **Full-time faculty:** 470 total. **Part-time faculty:** 165 total. **Class size:** 28% < 20, 49% 20-39, 8% 40-49, 13% 50-99, 1% >100. **Special facilities:** Observatory, planetarium, livestock center, off-campus outdoor educational facility, leadership and service institute.

**Freshman class profile.**

| Mid 50% test scores | | | |
|---|---|---|---|
| SAT critical reading: | 480-600 | GPA 3.0-3.49: | 40% |
| SAT math: | 490-600 | GPA 2.0-2.99: | 7% |
| ACT composite: | 20-26 | Out-of-state: | 73% |
| GPA 3.50 or higher: | 53% | Live on campus: | 21% |

**Basis for selection.** Religious affiliation, recommendations most important. High school record, test scores, personal essay, extracurricular activities also important. Interview with student's ecclesiastical leader required. Auditions required for music, dance, theater majors. **Homeschooled:** GED required; may be waived for homeschooled students with 24 ACT composite score.

**2007-2008 Annual costs.** Tuition/fees: $3,360. Tuition for students who are not members of The Church of Jesus Christ of Latter-day Saints is $6,120 for academic year. Room/board: $6,300. Books/supplies: $920. Personal expenses: $1,400.

**Financial aid. Non-need-based:** Scholarships awarded for academics, athletics, leadership. **Additional information:** Application deadline for merit scholarships 3/1.

**Application procedures. Admission:** Closing date 2/1 (receipt date). $25 fee. Application may be submitted online. **Financial aid:** Priority date 5/1; no closing date. FAFSA required. Applicants notified on a rolling basis starting 2/1.

**Academics. Special study options:** Accelerated study, distance learning, double major, independent study, internships, student-designed major, study abroad, teacher certification program, urban semester. **Credit/placement by examination:** AP, CLEP, IB, institutional tests. **Support services:** Learning center, reduced course load, remedial instruction, study skills assistance, tutoring, writing center.

**Majors. Agriculture:** Agronomy, animal sciences, horticulture. **Biology:** General, zoology. **Business:** Accounting, business admin. **Communications:** General, advertising, broadcast journalism, journalism, public relations. **Computer sciences:** General, computer science. **Education:** Elementary. **Engineering:** Computer, mechanical. **English:** Composition, English lit. **Health:** Nursing (RN), predental, premedicine, prepharmacy, preveterinary. **History:** General. **Math:** General. **Parks/recreation:** General. **Physical sciences:** Geology, physics. **Psychology:** General. **Social sciences:** Economics, political science, sociology. **Visual/performing arts:** Art, interior design.

**Most popular majors.** Biology 6%, business/marketing 18%, communications/journalism 8%, education 18%, health sciences 9%, liberal arts 9%.

**Computing on campus.** 2,500 workstations in dormitories, library, computer center, student center. Dormitories wired for high-speed internet access and linked to campus network. Commuter students can connect to campus network. Online course registration, online library, helpline, student web hosting, wireless network available.

**Student life. Freshman orientation:** Available. **Policies:** Students encouraged to attend weekly devotional at which noted church leaders speak. Religious observance required. **Housing:** Single-sex dorms, apartments, substance-free housing available. $175 deposit. **Activities:** Bands, choral groups, dance, drama, international student organizations, literary magazine, music ensembles, musical theater, radio station, student government, student newspaper, symphony orchestra, TV station, Lambda Delta Sigma, Sigma Gamma Chi, business club, married student association, outdoor club.

**Athletics. Intramural:** Archery, badminton, baseball, basketball, bowling, cheerleading, cross-country, diving, fencing, field hockey, football (non-tackle), football (tackle), golf, ice hockey, racquetball, skiing, skin diving, soccer, softball, swimming, table tennis, tennis, track and field, volleyball, water polo, wrestling M. **Team name:** Vikings.

**Student services.** Career counseling, student employment services, health services, personal counseling, placement for graduates, veterans' counselor. **Physically disabled:** Services for visually, hearing impaired.

**Contact.** E-mail: admissionser@byui.edu
Phone: (208) 496-1020 Fax: (208) 496-1185
Rob Garrett, Director of Admissions, Brigham Young University-Idaho, 120 Kimball Building, Rexburg, ID 83460-1615

## College of Idaho
Caldwell, Idaho
www.collegeofidaho.edu
CB member
CB code: 4060

- Private 4-year liberal arts college
- Residential campus in large town
- 813 degree-seeking undergraduates: 4% part-time, 61% women, 1% African American, 3% Asian American, 7% Hispanic American, 3% international
- 14 degree-seeking graduate students
- 81% of applicants admitted
- SAT or ACT with writing, application essay required
- 65% graduate within 6 years

**General.** Founded in 1891. Regionally accredited. Founded by Presbyterian Church. **Degrees:** 177 bachelor's awarded; master's offered. **ROTC:** Army. **Location:** 30 miles from Boise. **Calendar:** 13-6-13. **Full-time faculty:** 75 total; 69% have terminal degrees, 4% minority, 36% women. **Part-time faculty:** 31 total; 13% have terminal degrees, 6% minority, 32% women. **Class size:** 74% < 20, 24% 20-39, 1% 40-49, less than 1% 50-99. **Special**

**facilities:** Natural history museum, mineral and gem collection, planetarium, observatory, nuclear magnetic resonance spectrometer, performing and fine arts center, art gallery.

**Freshman class profile.** 911 applied, 738 admitted, 246 enrolled.

| Mid 50% test scores | | | |
|---|---|---|---|
| SAT critical reading: | 490-630 | Rank in top tenth: | 33% |
| SAT math: | 500-630 | End year in good standing: | 82% |
| SAT writing: | 470-620 | Return as sophomores: | 82% |
| ACT composite: | 21-27 | Out-of-state: | 23% |
| GPA 3.50 or higher: | 71% | Live on campus: | 90% |
| GPA 3.0-3.49: | 22% | International: | 5% |
| GPA 2.0-2.99: | 7% | Fraternities: | 12% |
| Rank in top quarter: | 67% | Sororities: | 10% |

**Basis for selection.** Academic record, test scores, extracurricular activities, essay, teacher recommendation important. Interview and essay recommended. Audition required of music, theater majors. Portfolio required of art majors.

**High school preparation.** 15 units required; 20 recommended. Required and recommended units include English 4, mathematics 3-4, social studies 2, history 3, science 2-4, foreign language 4 and academic electives 3.

**2008-2009 Annual costs.** Tuition/fees: $18,990. Room/board: $6,631. Books/supplies: $900. Personal expenses: $700.

**2007-2008 Financial aid. Need-based:** 153 full-time freshmen applied for aid; 101 were judged to have need; 101 of these received aid. Average need met was 78%. Average scholarship/grant was $4,188; average loan $4,615. 76% of total undergraduate aid awarded as scholarships/grants, 24% as loans/jobs. **Non-need-based:** Awarded to 994 full-time undergraduates, including 162 freshmen. Scholarships awarded for academics, alumni affiliation, art, athletics, leadership, minority status, music/drama, religious affiliation, ROTC, state residency.

**Application procedures. Admission:** Closing date 6/1 (postmark date). No application fee. Application may be submitted online. Admission notification on a rolling basis beginning on or about 10/15. Must reply by 5/1. **Financial aid:** Priority date 2/15; no closing date. FAFSA, institutional form required. Applicants notified on a rolling basis starting 1/31; must reply within 3 week(s) of notification.

**Academics.** All freshmen participate in first-year experience course and receive a book to read over summer as preparation. Program for learning-disabled students available through partnership with Lee Pesky Learning Center. **Special study options:** Combined bachelor's/graduate degree, cross-registration, double major, dual enrollment of high school students, exchange student, honors, independent study, internships, liberal arts/career combination, semester at sea, student-designed major, study abroad, teacher certification program, Washington semester. Bachelor's/graduate program in law with University of Idaho, MBA with Gonzaga University (WA), Boise State University, bachelor's/master's degrees in accountancy with University of Idaho, management with Willamette University (OR), natural resources with University of Idaho, economics with University of Idaho, bachelor's in engineering with University of Idaho, Boise State University, Columbia University (NY), Washington University (MO), 5th-year teaching internship, cooperative nursing program with Idaho State University. **Credit/placement by examination:** AP, CLEP, IB, institutional tests. **Support services:** Learning center, reduced course load, remedial instruction, study skills assistance, tutoring, writing center.

**Majors. Biology:** General. **Business:** Accounting, business admin, international. **Conservation:** Environmental studies. **Education:** Physical. **Engineering:** General. **English:** Creative writing, English lit. **Foreign languages:** Spanish. **Health:** Prenursing. **History:** General. **Interdisciplinary:** Math/computer science. **Liberal arts:** Arts/sciences. **Math:** General, applied. **Parks/recreation:** Exercise sciences, health/fitness, sports admin. **Philosophy/religion:** Philosophy, religion. **Physical sciences:** Chemistry. **Psychology:** General. **Social sciences:** Anthropology, economics, international relations, political science, sociology. **Visual/performing arts:** Art, dramatic.

**Most popular majors.** Biology 6%, business/marketing 12%, history 9%, parks/recreation 6%, psychology 11%, social sciences 9%, visual/performing arts 11%.

**Computing on campus.** 276 workstations in dormitories, library, computer center, student center. Dormitories wired for high-speed internet access and linked to campus network. Commuter students can connect to campus network. Online library, helpline, repair service, student web hosting, wireless network available.

**Student life. Freshman orientation:** Mandatory. Preregistration for classes offered. Several 1-day sessions scheduled over the summer for registration,

orientation, and tuition payment; 3-day fall orientation including an overnight stay in the nearby mountains before the start of fall semester. **Policies:** Freshman and sophomores under age 21 must live on campus unless living with parents or relatives. Honor's Code has been implemented for all students. Integrity is valued, expected, and practiced. **Housing:** Guaranteed on-campus for freshmen. Coed dorms, special housing for disabled, apartments, fraternity/sorority housing available. $300 fully refundable deposit, deadline 9/1. Pets allowed in dorm rooms. Honors residence available for students with superior academic records. **Activities:** Bands, campus ministries, choral groups, dance, drama, film society, international student organizations, literary magazine, music ensembles, Model UN, musical theater, opera, radio station, student government, student newspaper, symphony orchestra, Young Democrats, College Republicans, Terra, Intercollegiate Knights, Kiwanis International, progressive student alliance, Philotech, Gay-Straight campus alliance, Fellowship of Christian Athletes.

**Athletics.** NAIA. **Intercollegiate:** Baseball M, basketball, cross-country, golf, skiing, soccer, softball W, swimming, tennis W, track and field, volleyball W. **Intramural:** Badminton, basketball, football (non-tackle), soccer, softball, swimming, table tennis, tennis, volleyball. **Team name:** Coyotes.

**Student services.** Alcohol/substance abuse counseling, campus ministries, career counseling, student employment services, financial aid counseling, health services, minority student services, personal counseling, placement for graduates, women's services. **Physically disabled:** Services for visually, hearing impaired.

**Contact.** E-mail: admission@collegeofidaho.edu
Phone: (208) 459-5305 Toll-free number: (800) 224-3246
Fax: (208) 459-5757
John Klockentager, Vice President of Enrollment, College of Idaho, 2112 Cleveland Boulevard, Caldwell, ID 83605

## Idaho State University
**Pocatello, Idaho**
**www.isu.edu**

**CB member**
**CB code: 4355**

- Public 4-year university
- Commuter campus in small city
- 9,347 degree-seeking undergraduates: 26% part-time, 55% women, 1% African American, 2% Asian American, 5% Hispanic American, 2% Native American, 2% international
- 1,770 degree-seeking graduate students
- 80% of applicants admitted
- SAT or ACT (ACT writing optional) required

**General.** Founded in 1901. Regionally accredited. Designated by State Board of Education as institution specializing in health-related programs. **Degrees:** 1,127 bachelor's, 272 associate awarded; master's, doctoral, first professional offered. **ROTC:** Army. **Location:** 150 miles from Salt Lake City, 230 miles from Boise. **Calendar:** Semester, limited summer session. **Full-time faculty:** 619 total; 57% have terminal degrees, 6% minority, 43% women. **Part-time faculty:** 170 total; 8% have terminal degrees, 4% minority, 56% women. **Class size:** 66% < 20, 28% 20-39, 3% 40-49, 3% 50-99, less than 1% >100. **Special facilities:** Natural history museum, multi-purpose housing/classroom/meeting facility, accelerator center, geographical information systems center, performing arts center.

**Freshman class profile.** 3,713 applied, 2,978 admitted, 1,795 enrolled.

| Mid 50% test scores | | | |
|---|---|---|---|
| SAT critical reading: | 460-600 | Rank in top tenth: | 14% |
| SAT math: | 450-590 | Return as sophomores: | 57% |
| ACT composite: | 18-24 | Out-of-state: | 7% |
| GPA 3.50 or higher: | 37% | Live on campus: | 21% |
| GPA 3.0-3.49: | 29% | International: | 1% |
| GPA 2.0-2.99: | 32% | Fraternities: | 1% |
| Rank in top quarter: | 34% | Sororities: | 1% |

**Basis for selection.** For general admissions, predicted GPA of 2.0 (based on core GPA and test scores). Students not meeting those standards can be admitted through various levels and by petition. TOEFL, IELTS, Compass English, and SAT Critical Reading required for international students. U.S. High School graduates with an "A" or "B" in English and students who completed ELS Language Centers level 112 are exempted. Students from countries where English is the official language can be exempted based on academic performance. ACT preferred. Interview recommended. Audition recommended for music majors. Portfolio recommended for experiential credit-seeking applicants. **Homeschooled:** Students need to complete their GED along with taking the ACT or SAT test.

**High school preparation.** 16 units required. Required and recommended units include English 4, mathematics 3-4, social studies 3, science

3 (laboratory 1) and foreign language 1. Humanities and health also required.

**2007-2008 Annual costs.** Tuition/fees: $4,400; $13,084 out-of-state. $1,046 refundable health insurance. Room/board: $5,346. Books/supplies: $900. Personal expenses: $2,030.

**2006-2007 Financial aid. Need-based:** 762 full-time freshmen applied for aid; 549 were judged to have need; 535 of these received aid. Average need met was 56%. Average scholarship/grant was $2,908; average loan $2,088. 40% of total undergraduate aid awarded as scholarships/grants, 60% as loans/jobs. **Non-need-based:** Awarded to 2,894 full-time undergraduates, including 772 freshmen. Scholarships awarded for academics, alumni affiliation, art, athletics, leadership, minority status, music/drama, ROTC, state residency.

**Application procedures. Admission:** No deadline. $40 fee, may be waived for applicants with need. Application may be submitted online. Admission notification on a rolling basis beginning on or about 3/1. High school students who graduate early may petition admissions committee to enroll full time. **Financial aid:** Priority date 3/1; no closing date. FAFSA required. Applicants notified on a rolling basis starting 4/1.

**Academics. Special study options:** Accelerated study, combined bachelor's/graduate degree, cooperative education, cross-registration, distance learning, double major, dual enrollment of high school students, ESL, exchange student, honors, independent study, internships, liberal arts/career combination, student-designed major, study abroad, teacher certification program, weekend college. **Credit/placement by examination:** AP, CLEP, IB, ACT, institutional tests. 48 credit hours maximum toward bachelor's degree. A student is unable to receive credit by challenge exam for courses already taken, or for courses that are prerequisites to courses already completed. **Support services:** Learning center, remedial instruction, study skills assistance, tutoring, writing center.

**Majors. Area/ethnic studies:** American. **Biology:** General, biochemistry, botany, ecology, microbiology, zoology. **Business:** General, accounting, business admin, finance, human resources, marketing. **Communications:** General, media studies. **Computer sciences:** General, information systems. **Education:** Early childhood, elementary, health, music, physical, secondary, special. **Engineering:** General, civil, electrical, mechanical, nuclear. **Engineering technology:** Surveying. **English:** English lit. **Family/consumer sciences:** General. **Foreign languages:** French, German, sign language interpretation, Spanish. **Health:** Audiology/speech pathology, clinical lab science, dental hygiene, dietetics, health care admin, health services, medical radiologic technology/radiation therapy, nursing (RN). **History:** General. **Math:** General. **Philosophy/religion:** Philosophy. **Physical sciences:** Chemistry, geology, physics. **Psychology:** General. **Public administration:** Social work. **Social sciences:** Anthropology, economics, international relations, political science, sociology. **Visual/performing arts:** Art, dramatic, music performance. **Other:** Measurement & Control Engineering.

**Most popular majors.** Biology 9%, business/marketing 15%, education 16%, health sciences 20%, social sciences 7%.

**Computing on campus.** 507 workstations in dormitories, library, computer center, student center. Dormitories wired for high-speed internet access and linked to campus network. Commuter students can connect to campus network. Online course registration, online library, helpline, repair service, student web hosting, wireless network available.

**Student life. Freshman orientation:** Available, $35 fee. Preregistration for classes offered. **Housing:** Coed dorms, single-sex dorms, special housing for disabled, apartments, fraternity/sorority housing, substance-free housing available. $150 partly refundable deposit, deadline 8/23. Housing modified for disabled available on request, subject to waiting list. Graduate house available. **Activities:** Bands, campus ministries, choral groups, dance, drama, literary magazine, musical theater, radio station, student government, student newspaper, symphony orchestra, TV station, Newman Center, Latter-day Saints Institute, student ambassadors, Young Democrats, Young Republicans, Campus Crusade for Christ, Associated Black Students, Native Americans United, Cooperative Wilderness Handicapped Outdoor Group.

**Athletics.** NCAA. **Intercollegiate:** Basketball, cheerleading, cross-country, football (tackle) M, golf, soccer W, softball W, tennis, track and field, volleyball W. **Intramural:** Badminton, basketball, bowling, fencing, judo, racquetball, soccer, softball, table tennis, tennis, volleyball. **Team name:** Bengals.

**Student services.** Adult student services, alcohol/substance abuse counseling, career counseling, student employment services, financial aid counseling, health services, legal services, minority student services, on-campus daycare, personal counseling, placement for graduates, veterans' counselor, women's services. **Physically disabled:** Services for visually, speech, hearing impaired.

**Contact.** E-mail: info@isu.edu
Phone: (208) 282-2475 Fax: (208) 282-4511
Scott Teichert, Director, Idaho State University, 921 South 8th Stop 8270, Pocatello, ID 83209-8270

## ITT Technical Institute: Boise
**Boise, Idaho**
www.itt-tech.edu                    CB code: 3596

- For-profit 4-year technical college
- Commuter campus in small city

**General.** Founded in 1906. Accredited by ACICS. **Calendar:** Quarter.

**Annual costs/financial aid.** Tuition varies by program, $260-$368 per credit hour.

**Contact.** Phone: (208) 322-8844
Director of Recruitment, 12302 West Explorer Drive, Boise, ID 83713-1529

## Lewis-Clark State College
**Lewiston, Idaho**
www.lcsc.edu                        CB code: 4385

- Public 4-year liberal arts and technical college
- Commuter campus in small city
- 2,944 degree-seeking undergraduates: 23% part-time, 60% women, 1% African American, 1% Asian American, 6% Hispanic American, 4% Native American, 4% international
- 59% of applicants admitted

**General.** Founded in 1893. Regionally accredited. Courses offered at outreach centers (Orofino, Grangeville, Coeur d'Alene, Kamiah, and Lapwai). **Degrees:** 386 bachelor's, 136 associate awarded. **ROTC:** Army, Naval, Air Force. **Location:** 300 miles from Boise, 100 miles from Spokane, Washington. **Calendar:** Semester, limited summer session. **Full-time faculty:** 149 total; 66% have terminal degrees, 5% minority, 51% women. **Part-time faculty:** 9 total; 56% have terminal degrees, 56% women. **Class size:** 63% < 20, 35% 20-39, 1% 40-49, less than 1% 50-99, less than 1% >100. **Special facilities:** Biodiversity museum and collection, geographical information systems center, observatory.

**Freshman class profile.** 1,179 applied, 697 admitted, 556 enrolled.

| Mid 50% test scores | | | |
|---|---|---|---|
| SAT critical reading: | 420-520 | GPA 2.0-2.99: | 42% |
| SAT math: | 440-540 | Rank in top quarter: | 21% |
| ACT composite: | 17-22 | Rank in top tenth: | 5% |
| GPA 3.50 or higher: | 23% | Return as sophomores: | 55% |
| GPA 3.0-3.49: | 31% | Out-of-state: | 19% |
| | | International: | 6% |

**Basis for selection.** High school courses, GPA, test scores considered. Non-native speakers may be required to take ESL classes until they can pass TOEFL. ACT and SAT may be accepted for all students. Students may be asked to take COMPASS test under certain circumstances. **Home-schooled:** Must have predicted college GPA of 2.0 based on ACT or SAT. Must have acceptable performance on 2 testing indicators: GED score of 500 (50 if tested before 2002) or higher, or other standardized diagnostic test such as ACT, SAT, COMPASS, ASSET, or CPT.

**High school preparation.** 15 units required. Required units include English 4, mathematics 3, social studies 2, science 3 (laboratory 2) and academic electives 2. 1 fine arts.

**2007-2008 Annual costs.** Tuition/fees: $4,092; $11,382 out-of-state. Room/board: $4,800. Books/supplies: $1,500. Personal expenses: $5,400.

**2006-2007 Financial aid. Need-based:** 358 full-time freshmen applied for aid; 302 were judged to have need; 290 of these received aid. Average need met was 5%. Average scholarship/grant was $2,966; average loan $2,246. 43% of total undergraduate aid awarded as scholarships/grants, 57% as loans/jobs. **Non-need-based:** Awarded to 636 full-time undergraduates, including 362 freshmen. Scholarships awarded for academics, alumni affiliation, art, athletics, leadership, minority status, music/drama.

**Application procedures. Admission:** Priority date 3/1; no deadline. $35 fee. Application may be submitted online. Admission notification on a rolling basis. **Financial aid:** Priority date 3/1; no closing date. FAFSA required. Applicants notified on a rolling basis starting 4/15; must reply within 2 week(s) of notification.

**Academics.** Communications/speech lab to help students prepare for speeches and presentations. **Special study options:** Accelerated study, cooperative education, distance learning, double major, dual enrollment of high school students, ESL, honors, independent study, internships, student-designed major, study abroad, teacher certification program, weekend college. **Credit/placement by examination:** AP, CLEP, IB, SAT, ACT, institutional tests. 16 credit hours maximum toward associate degree, 32 toward bachelor's. **Support services:** Learning center, reduced course load, remedial instruction, study skills assistance, tutoring, writing center.

**Majors. Biology:** General. **Business:** Accounting technology, administrative services, business admin, hospitality admin, small business admin. **Communications:** General. **Communications technology:** Graphic/printing. **Computer sciences:** General, computer science, webmaster. **Education:** Elementary, English, mathematics, physical, science, social science. **Engineering technology:** Drafting, manufacturing. **English:** Creative writing, English lit. **Family/consumer sciences:** Child development. **Health:** Management/clinical assistant, nursing (RN), office assistant. **Interdisciplinary:** Natural sciences. **Legal studies:** Legal secretary, paralegal. **Math:** General. **Mechanic/repair:** General, auto body, automotive, diesel, electronics/electrical, heating/ac/refrig, industrial electronics. **Parks/recreation:** Exercise sciences. **Physical sciences:** Chemistry. **Production:** Welding. **Protective services:** Corrections, criminal justice, firefighting. **Psychology:** General. **Public administration:** Social work. **Social sciences:** General.

**Most popular majors.** Business/marketing 25%, education 11%, health sciences 19%, public administration/social services 9%, security/protective services 6%.

**Computing on campus.** 455 workstations in dormitories, library, computer center, student center. Dormitories wired for high-speed internet access and linked to campus network. Commuter students can connect to campus network. Online course registration, helpline, student web hosting, wireless network available.

**Student life. Freshman orientation:** Available. Preregistration for classes offered. One-day session held in August. **Housing:** Coed dorms, apartments, substance-free housing available. $100 partly refundable deposit. **Activities:** Jazz band, campus ministries, choral groups, dance, drama, international student organizations, literary magazine, student government, student newspaper, Native American Indian student organization, ambassadors' club, criminal justice society, Idaho student lobby, business students organization, Latter-day Saints student association, College Democrats, College Republicans.

**Athletics.** NAIA. **Intercollegiate:** Baseball M, basketball, cross-country, golf, tennis, track and field W, volleyball W. **Intramural:** Badminton, baseball, basketball, bowling, field hockey, football (non-tackle), golf, lacrosse, racquetball, rugby M, skiing, soccer, softball, table tennis, tennis, volleyball, weight lifting. **Team name:** Warriors.

**Student services.** Adult student services, alcohol/substance abuse counseling, career counseling, services for economically disadvantaged, student employment services, financial aid counseling, health services, minority student services, on-campus daycare, personal counseling, placement for graduates, veterans' counselor, women's services. **Physically disabled:** Services for visually, speech, hearing impaired.

**Contact.** E-mail: admissions@lcsc.edu
Phone: (208) 792-2210 Toll-free number: (800) 933-5272
Fax: (208) 792-2876
Diane Douglas, Registrar/Director of Admissions, Lewis-Clark State College, 500 Eighth Avenue, Lewiston, ID 83501-2698

---

## Northwest Nazarene University
Nampa, Idaho
www.nnu.edu                                           CB code: 4544

- Private 4-year university affiliated with Church of the Nazarene
- Residential campus in small city
- 1,189 degree-seeking undergraduates: 5% part-time, 60% women, 1% African American, 1% Asian American, 2% Hispanic American, 1% Native American, 1% international
- 591 degree-seeking graduate students
- 70% of applicants admitted
- SAT or ACT (ACT writing optional), application essay required

**General.** Founded in 1913. Regionally accredited. **Degrees:** 263 bachelor's awarded; master's offered. **ROTC:** Army, Air Force. **Location:** 18 miles from Boise. **Calendar:** Semester. **Full-time faculty:** 98 total; 68% have terminal degrees, 7% minority, 41% women. **Part-time faculty:** 3 total; 67% have terminal degrees, 67% women. **Class size:** 46% < 20, 40% 20-39, 9% 40-49, 5% 50-99. **Special facilities:** Depository for federal government publications.

### Freshman class profile.

| Mid 50% test scores | | | |
|---|---|---|---|
| SAT critical reading: | 460-610 | GPA 2.0-2.99: | 17% |
| SAT math: | 460-590 | Rank in top quarter: | 47% |
| ACT composite: | 19-26 | Rank in top tenth: | 24% |
| GPA 3.50 or higher: | 60% | Out-of-state: | 54% |
| GPA 3.0-3.49: | 23% | Live on campus: | 89% |
| | | International: | 1% |

**Basis for selection.** For unconditional admission 2 of following criteria must be met: minimum 2.5 high school GPA, class rank in top 50 percent, minimum ACT score of 18. Provisional admission available. Interview recommended for students with provisional admission.

**High school preparation.** Recommended units include English 4, mathematics 3, social studies 3, history 3, science 3 and foreign language 2.

**2008-2009 Annual costs.** Tuition/fees (projected): $21,170. Room/board: $5,520. Books/supplies: $1,000. Personal expenses: $900.

**2007-2008 Financial aid. Need-based:** 204 full-time freshmen applied for aid; 184 were judged to have need; 184 of these received aid. Average need met was 84%. Average scholarship/grant was $7,818; average loan $3,503. 54% of total undergraduate aid awarded as scholarships/grants, 46% as loans/jobs. **Non-need-based:** Scholarships awarded for academics, alumni affiliation, art, athletics, leadership, minority status, music/drama, religious affiliation, ROTC.

**Application procedures. Admission:** Priority date 3/1; deadline 8/15. $25 fee, may be waived for applicants with need. Application may be submitted online. Admission notification on a rolling basis. **Financial aid:** Priority date 3/1; no closing date. FAFSA, institutional form required. Applicants notified on a rolling basis starting 3/1; must reply within 3 week(s) of notification.

**Academics. Special study options:** Accelerated study, combined bachelor's/graduate degree, cooperative education, cross-registration, distance learning, double major, exchange student, honors, independent study, internships, liberal arts/career combination, student-designed major, study abroad, teacher certification program. **Credit/placement by examination:** AP, CLEP, IB, SAT, ACT, institutional tests. 31 credit hours maximum toward bachelor's degree. **Support services:** Learning center, reduced course load, remedial instruction, study skills assistance, tutoring, writing center.

**Majors. Biology:** General, biochemistry, cellular/molecular, ecology. **Business:** Accounting, business admin. **Communications:** General, journalism, media studies. **Computer sciences:** Computer science. **Education:** Art, biology, chemistry, computer, elementary, English, health, history, mathematics, music, physical, physics, psychology, secondary, social science, Spanish. **Engineering:** Aerospace, chemical, civil, electrical, physics. **English:** English lit. **Foreign languages:** Spanish. **Health:** Nursing (RN), physician assistant, predental, premedicine, prepharmacy, preveterinary. **History:** General. **Legal studies:** Prelaw. **Liberal arts:** Arts/sciences. **Math:** General. **Parks/recreation:** General, exercise sciences, health/fitness, sports admin. **Philosophy/religion:** Philosophy, religion. **Physical sciences:** Chemistry, physics. **Psychology:** General, industrial. **Public administration:** Social work. **Social sciences:** General, international relations, political science. **Theology:** Bible, missionary, pastoral counseling, religious ed, sacred music, youth ministry. **Visual/performing arts:** Ceramics, drawing, graphic design, music performance, music theory/composition, painting, piano/organ, printmaking, sculpture, voice/opera. **Other:** Environmental chemistry.

**Computing on campus.** 275 workstations in dormitories, library, computer center, student center. Dormitories wired for high-speed internet access and linked to campus network. Commuter students can connect to campus network. Online library, helpline, repair service, student web hosting, wireless network available.

**Student life. Freshman orientation:** Mandatory. Preregistration for classes offered. **Policies:** All students required to live on campus until senior year or age 21. Religious observance required. **Housing:** Guaranteed on-campus for all undergraduates. Single-sex dorms, apartments available. $50 fully refundable deposit. Some rental units available. **Activities:** Bands, campus ministries, choral groups, drama, international student organizations, literary magazine, music ensembles, musical theater, opera, student government, student newspaper, symphony orchestra, summer ministries, Circle-K, urban ministries club, social work clubs, Angels Ministry, PALS ministry, AIDS ministry, Fellowship of Christian Athletes, multicultural affairs club.

**Athletics.** NCAA. **Intercollegiate:** Baseball M, basketball, cross-country, golf M, soccer W, softball W, track and field, volleyball W. **Intramural:** Basketball, cross-country, football (non-tackle), softball, volleyball. **Team name:** Crusaders.

**Student services.** Adult student services, alcohol/substance abuse counseling, campus ministries, career counseling, student employment services, financial aid counseling, health services, minority student services, personal counseling, placement for graduates. **Physically disabled:** Services for visually, hearing impaired.

**Contact.** E-mail: admissions@nnu.edu
Phone: (208) 467-8496 Toll-free number: (877) 668-4968
Fax: (208) 467-8645
Stacey Berggren, Director of Admissions, Northwest Nazarene University, 623 Holly Street, Nampa, ID 83686-5897

---

## University of Idaho

| Moscow, Idaho | CB member |
| --- | --- |
| www.uidaho.edu | CB code: 4843 |

- Public 4-year university
- Residential campus in large town
- 8,471 degree-seeking undergraduates: 6% part-time, 46% women, 1% African American, 2% Asian American, 5% Hispanic American, 1% Native American, 2% international
- 2,288 degree-seeking graduate students
- 77% of applicants admitted
- SAT or ACT (ACT writing optional) required
- 55% graduate within 6 years

**General.** Founded in 1889. Regionally accredited. Residential land-grant university. **Degrees:** 1,767 bachelor's awarded; master's, doctoral, first professional offered. **ROTC:** Army, Naval, Air Force. **Location:** 85 miles from Spokane, Washington. **Calendar:** Semester, extensive summer session. **Full-time faculty:** 601 total; 75% have terminal degrees, 10% minority, 30% women. **Part-time faculty:** 94 total; 24% have terminal degrees, 4% minority, 49% women. **Class size:** 51% < 20, 36% 20-39, 6% 40-49, 6% 50-99, 1% >100. **Special facilities:** Arboretum, 18-hole golf course, indoor climbing facility.

**Freshman class profile.** 4,577 applied, 3,505 admitted, 1,664 enrolled.

| Mid 50% test scores | | | |
| --- | --- | --- | --- |
| SAT critical reading: | 480-600 | GPA 2.0-2.99: | 24% |
| SAT math: | 480-600 | Rank in top quarter: | 42% |
| SAT writing: | 450-570 | Rank in top tenth: | 18% |
| ACT composite: | 20-25 | Return as sophomores: | 79% |
| GPA 3.50 or higher: | 41% | Out-of-state: | 46% |
| GPA 3.0-3.49: | 35% | International: | 1% |

**Basis for selection.** Applicants must have 3.0 high school GPA, or 2.2 to 3.0 high school GPA with high SAT/ACT scores. Recommendations, essay required of applicants with nonstandard high school diploma and adults long out of high school. **Homeschooled:** Letter of recommendation (nonparent) required. Copy of GED test results, three signed letters of recommendation from individuals who know of and can attest to applicant's academic ability, a written statement from applicant including goals, education and/or professional objective, and explanation of past academic performance.

**High school preparation.** 15 units required. Required units include English 4, mathematics 3, social studies 3, science 3 (laboratory 1), foreign language 1 and academic electives 2. Up to 1 unit of history, literature, philosophy, or fine arts may be substituted for foreign language requirement, but foreign language strongly recommended.

**2007-2008 Annual costs.** Tuition/fees: $4,410; $14,490 out-of-state. Room/board: $6,424. Books/supplies: $1,430. Personal expenses: $2,772.

**2006-2007 Financial aid. Need-based:** 1,238 full-time freshmen applied for aid; 926 were judged to have need; 909 of these received aid. Average need met was 75%. Average scholarship/grant was $3,136; average loan $3,410. 36% of total undergraduate aid awarded as scholarships/grants, 64% as loans/jobs. **Non-need-based:** Awarded to 5,472 full-time undergraduates, including 1,251 freshmen. Scholarships awarded for academics, alumni affiliation, art, athletics, leadership, minority status, music/drama, religious affiliation, ROTC, state residency.

**Application procedures. Admission:** Priority date 2/15; deadline 8/1 (receipt date). $40 fee. Application may be submitted online. Admission notification on a rolling basis. **Financial aid:** Priority date 2/15; no closing date. FAFSA required. Applicants notified on a rolling basis starting 3/30; must reply within 4 week(s) of notification.

**Academics. Special study options:** Accelerated study, combined bachelor's/graduate degree, cooperative education, cross-registration, distance learning, double major, dual enrollment of high school students, ESL, exchange student, honors, independent study, internships, student-designed major, study abroad, teacher certification program. **Credit/placement by examination:**

AP, CLEP, IB, SAT, ACT, institutional tests. 48 credit hours maximum toward bachelor's degree. **Support services:** Learning center, pre-admission summer program, reduced course load, remedial instruction, study skills assistance, tutoring, writing center.

**Majors. Agriculture:** Agronomy, animal sciences, business, dairy, economics, food science, horticultural science, livestock, plant protection, plant sciences, range science, soil science. **Architecture:** Architecture, landscape. **Area/ethnic studies:** American, Latin American. **Biology:** General, bacteriology, biochemistry, molecular. **Business:** Accounting, finance, human resources, management information systems, managerial economics, marketing, operations. **Communications:** General, journalism, public relations, radio/tv. **Computer sciences:** General. **Conservation:** General, environmental science, fisheries, forest resources, forestry, wildlife. **Education:** Agricultural, art, business, early childhood, elementary, English, health, music, physical, secondary, special, technology/industrial arts, trade/industrial, voc/tech. **Engineering:** Agricultural, chemical, civil, computer, electrical, materials science, mechanical, metallurgical. **English:** English lit. **Family/consumer sciences:** Clothing/textiles, family studies, food/nutrition. **Foreign languages:** General, classics, French, German, Latin, Spanish. **Health:** Athletic training, premedicine. **History:** General. **Math:** General, applied. **Parks/recreation:** General. **Philosophy/religion:** Philosophy. **Physical sciences:** Chemistry, geology, physics. **Protective services:** Criminal justice. **Psychology:** General. **Social sciences:** Anthropology, economics, geography, international relations, political science, sociology. **Visual/performing arts:** Art, dance, design, dramatic, interior design, music history, music management, music performance, music theory/composition, musical theater. **Other:** Applied music, Fire ecology and management, Naval science.

**Most popular majors.** Business/marketing 14%, communications/journalism 7%, education 9%, engineering/engineering technologies 10%, natural resources/environmental science 8%, psychology 7%, social sciences 6%.

**Computing on campus.** 492 workstations in dormitories, library, computer center, student center. Dormitories wired for high-speed internet access and linked to campus network. Commuter students can connect to campus network. Online course registration, online library, helpline, repair service, student web hosting, wireless network available.

**Student life. Freshman orientation:** Available. Preregistration for classes offered. **Housing:** Coed dorms, single-sex dorms, special housing for disabled, apartments, fraternity/sorority housing, substance-free housing available. $250 partly refundable deposit. **Activities:** Bands, campus ministries, choral groups, dance, drama, film society, international student organizations, literary magazine, music ensembles, Model UN, musical theater, opera, radio station, student government, student newspaper, symphony orchestra, TV station, Amnesty International, Women of Color Alliance, Environmental Club, War on Hunger, Intervarsity Christian Fellowship, Habitat for Humanity, Sabor de la Raza, Soil Stewards, Society of Professional Journalists.

**Athletics.** NCAA. **Intercollegiate:** Basketball, cross-country, football (tackle) M, golf, soccer W, swimming W, tennis, track and field, volleyball W. **Intramural:** Badminton, basketball, golf, racquetball, rifle, skiing, soccer, softball, table tennis, tennis, wrestling M. **Team name:** Vandals.

**Student services.** Adult student services, alcohol/substance abuse counseling, campus ministries, career counseling, student employment services, financial aid counseling, health services, legal services, minority student services, on-campus daycare, personal counseling, placement for graduates, veterans' counselor, women's services. **Physically disabled:** Services for visually, speech, hearing impaired.

**Contact.** E-mail: admissions@uidaho.edu
Phone: (208) 885-6326 Toll-free number: (888) 884-3246
Fax: (208) 885-9119
Daniel Davenport, Director of Admissions and Student Financial Aid, University of Idaho, PO Box 444264, Moscow, ID 83844-4264

# Illinois

## American Academy of Art
### Chicago, Illinois
### www.aaart.edu
**CB code: 1013**

- For-profit 4-year visual arts college
- Commuter campus in very large city

**General.** Founded in 1923. Accredited by ACCSCT. **Location:** Downtown. **Calendar:** Semester.

**Annual costs/financial aid.** Tuition/fees (2007-2008): $21,680. Books/supplies: $800.

**Contact.** Phone: (312) 461-0600
Director of Admissions, 332 South Michigan Avenue, Suite 300, Chicago, IL 60604-4302

## Argosy University
### Chicago, Illinois
### www.argosy.edu
**CB code: 3922**

- For-profit 4-year university
- Very large city

**General.** Regionally accredited. **Calendar:** Continuous.

**Annual costs/financial aid.** Tuition/fees (2007-2008): $14,000. Costs vary by program.

**Contact.** Phone: (312) 201-0200
Director of Admissions, 350 North New Orleans Street, Chicago, IL 60654

## Augustana College
### Rock Island, Illinois
### www.augustana.edu
**CB member**
**CB code: 1025**

- Private 4-year liberal arts college affiliated with Evangelical Lutheran Church in America
- Residential campus in large city
- 2,518 degree-seeking undergraduates: 1% part-time, 57% women, 2% African American, 2% Asian American, 4% Hispanic American, 1% Native American, 1% international
- 73% of applicants admitted
- 76% graduate within 6 years

**General.** Founded in 1860. Regionally accredited. **Degrees:** 540 bachelor's awarded. **Location:** 165 miles from Chicago. **Calendar:** Quarter, limited summer session. **Full-time faculty:** 173 total; 91% have terminal degrees, 9% minority, 43% women. **Part-time faculty:** 95 total; 22% have terminal degrees, 7% minority, 55% women. **Class size:** 63% < 20, 34% 20-39, 3% 40-49, less than 1% 50-99. **Special facilities:** Educational technology center, planetarium/observatory, map library, geology museum, Swedish immigration research center, research foundation, 500 acres of environmental laboratories, scanning electron mircroscope, high-field NMR, x-ray diffractometer, scanning tunneling microscope, HeliFlux station magnetometer.

**Freshman class profile.** 3,080 applied, 2,257 admitted, 712 enrolled.

| Mid 50% test scores | | Return as sophomores: | 88% |
|---|---|---|---|
| ACT composite: | 23-28 | Out-of-state: | 12% |
| Rank in top quarter: | 63% | Live on campus: | 95% |
| Rank in top tenth: | 34% | | |

**Basis for selection.** GPA, class rank, test scores, high school curriculum most important. Extracurricular activities and essay important. Academic honors and special qualifications also considered. SAT/ACT optional for those who interview and submit graded high school paper. Interview and essay required of freshman honors program applicants, recommended for all applicants. Essay required of academically marginal applicants and for certain departmental programs. Portfolio required of applicants to some art programs. Audition recommended for music and theater majors.

**High school preparation.** 16 units recommended. Recommended units include English 4, mathematics 3, social studies 1, history 1, science 2, foreign language 1 and academic electives 4. Engineering, science, and math majors should have 3 units math (1.5 algebra, 1 plane geometry, .5 trigonometry).

**2007-2008 Annual costs.** Tuition/fees: $26,484. Room/board: $7,233. Books/supplies: $675. Personal expenses: $800.

**2006-2007 Financial aid. Need-based:** 580 full-time freshmen applied for aid; 467 were judged to have need; 466 of these received aid. Average need met was 83%. Average scholarship/grant was $12,891; average loan $3,717. 62% of total undergraduate aid awarded as scholarships/grants, 38% as loans/jobs. **Non-need-based:** Awarded to 1,753 full-time undergraduates, including 531 freshmen. Scholarships awarded for academics, alumni affiliation, art, leadership, music/drama, religious affiliation.

**Application procedures. Admission:** Priority date 2/1; no deadline. $35 fee, may be waived for applicants with need. Application may be submitted online. Admission notification on a rolling basis. **Financial aid:** Priority date 4/1; no closing date. FAFSA, institutional form required. Applicants notified on a rolling basis.

**Academics.** Term-abroad programs in Asia, Europe, and South America. Internship programs in cities throughout United States and in South America, Europe, Asia, Africa, and Australia. Exchange programs with universities in People's Republic of China, Peru, and Sweden. Summer language study programs in Sweden, France, Ecuador and Israel. Team-taught, interdisciplinary honors sequence available. June registration for classes. **Special study options:** Accelerated study, combined bachelor's/graduate degree, cooperative education, double major, honors, independent study, internships, liberal arts/career combination, study abroad, teacher certification program. 3-2 forestry and environmental management program with Duke University, 3-2 landscape architecture program with University of Illinois at Urbana-Champaign, 3-2 engineering program with Washington University (MO), Iowa State University, University of Illinois at Urbana-Champaign, and Purdue University, 3-2 occupational therapy program with Washington University, early selection programs in dentistry with University of Iowa, study abroad programs in Asia, Europe, and South America. **Credit/placement by examination:** AP, CLEP, IB, ACT, institutional tests. More than 18 hours of credit by examination must be approved by the Dean of the College. **Support services:** Learning center, pre-admission summer program, reduced course load, study skills assistance, tutoring, writing center.

**Majors. Area/ethnic studies:** Asian. **Biology:** General. **Business:** General, accounting, business admin, finance, international, management information systems, marketing. **Communications:** General. **Computer sciences:** Computer science. **Conservation:** General. **Education:** General, art, biology, chemistry, elementary, English, foreign languages, French, German, history, mathematics, middle, music, physical, physics, science, secondary, social science, Spanish, speech. **Engineering:** Physics. **English:** English lit, speech/rhetoric. **Foreign languages:** Ancient Greek, classics, French, German, Latin, Scandinavian, Spanish. **Health:** Audiology/speech pathology, predental, premedicine. **History:** General. **Interdisciplinary:** Math/computer science. **Legal studies:** Prelaw. **Liberal arts:** Arts/sciences. **Math:** General. **Philosophy/religion:** Philosophy, religion. **Physical sciences:** Chemistry, geology, physics, planetary. **Psychology:** General. **Public administration:** General. **Social sciences:** Economics, geography, political science, sociology. **Visual/performing arts:** Art, art history/conservation, dramatic, jazz, music performance, piano/organ, studio arts, voice/opera.

**Most popular majors.** Biology 14%, business/marketing 22%, education 6%, English 12%, health sciences 11%, psychology 6%, social sciences 11%.

**Computing on campus.** 500 workstations in dormitories, library, computer center, student center. Dormitories wired for high-speed internet access and linked to campus network. Commuter students can connect to campus network. Online course registration, online library, helpline, repair service, student web hosting, wireless network available.

**Student life. Freshman orientation:** Mandatory, $100 fee. Preregistration for classes offered. Three-day program held before start of fall classes. **Policies:** Students represented on all major faculty/administrative committees and act as observers at Board of Trustees meetings. Student life governed by Bill of Student Rights and code of social conduct. Campus judiciary process includes student participation. Lower-division students not living with parents required to live on campus unless released to live off-campus by student services office. **Housing:** Guaranteed on-campus for all undergraduates. Coed dorms, single-sex dorms, apartments, substance-free housing available. $100 deposit. Theme housing available. **Activities:** Bands, campus ministries, choral groups, dance, drama, international student organizations, literary magazine, music ensembles, musical theater, opera, radio station, student government, student newspaper, symphony orchestra, black student union, Asian student organization, Latinos Unidos, Latin American council, multicultural programming board, feminist forum, Global Affect, Intervarsity Christian Fellowship, Catholic organization, Muslim student association, Viking Volunteers, College Republicans/Democrats, Habitat for Humanity, Amnesty International.

**Athletics.** NCAA. **Intercollegiate:** Baseball M, basketball, cross-country, diving, football (tackle) M, golf, soccer, softball W, swimming, tennis, track and field, volleyball W, wrestling M. **Intramural:** Badminton, basketball, bowling, cross-country, football (non-tackle), golf, handball, racquetball, rowing (crew), skiing, soccer, softball, swimming M, table tennis, tennis, track and field, volleyball, water polo, wrestling M. **Team name:** Vikings.

**Student services.** Alcohol/substance abuse counseling, campus ministries, career counseling, student employment services, financial aid counseling, health services, minority student services, personal counseling, placement for graduates, women's services. **Physically disabled:** Services for visually, speech, hearing impaired.

**Contact.** E-mail: admissions@augustana.edu
Phone: (309) 794-7341 Toll-free number: (800) 798-8100
Fax: (309) 794-7422
W. Kent Barnds, Vice President of Enrollment, Augustana College, 639 38th Street, Rock Island, IL 61201-2296

## Aurora University
**Aurora, Illinois**
www.aurora.edu                    CB code: 1027

- Private 4-year university
- Commuter campus in small city
- 2,065 degree-seeking undergraduates: 14% part-time, 68% women, 10% African American, 3% Asian American, 12% Hispanic American
- 1,747 degree-seeking graduate students
- 73% of applicants admitted
- SAT or ACT (ACT writing optional) required
- 45% graduate within 6 years

**General.** Founded in 1893. Regionally accredited. Additional 200-acre academic campus and conference center in Williams Bay, Wisconsin offering several undergraduate and graduate programs. **Degrees:** 458 bachelor's awarded; master's, doctoral offered. **ROTC:** Army. **Location:** 40 miles from Chicago. **Calendar:** Semester, limited summer session. **Full-time faculty:** 103 total; 81% have terminal degrees, 7% minority, 50% women. **Part-time faculty:** 246 total; 28% have terminal degrees, 13% minority, 55% women. **Class size:** 48% < 20, 52% 20-39. **Special facilities:** Museum of Native American history.

**Freshman class profile.** 1,420 applied, 1,043 admitted, 342 enrolled.

| Mid 50% test scores | | | |
|---|---|---|---|
| SAT critical reading: | 520-600 | Rank in top tenth: | 11% |
| SAT math: | 490-600 | End year in good standing: | 84% |
| ACT composite: | 19-23 | Return as sophomores: | 73% |
| GPA 3.50 or higher: | 26% | Out-of-state: | 9% |
| GPA 3.0-3.49: | 35% | Live on campus: | 66% |
| GPA 2.0-2.99: | 39% | Fraternities: | 1% |
| Rank in top quarter: | 36% | Sororities: | 1% |

**Basis for selection.** School achievement record most important, followed by test scores. Interview and recommendation also considered. Interview and essay recommended. **Homeschooled:** State high school equivalency certificate, interview required.

**High school preparation.** 16 units required. Required units include English 4, mathematics 3, social studies 3, science 3 and academic electives 3.

**2008-2009 Annual costs.** Tuition/fees: $17,500. Course laboratory fees in sciences, photography, nursing, physical education and student teaching. Tuition will vary for several adult degree completion programs. Room/board: $7,250. Books/supplies: $1,000. Personal expenses: $1,200.

**2007-2008 Financial aid. Need-based:** 306 full-time freshmen applied for aid; 255 were judged to have need; 255 of these received aid. Average need met was 88%. Average scholarship/grant was $6,633; average loan $3,287. 53% of total undergraduate aid awarded as scholarships/grants, 47% as loans/jobs. **Non-need-based:** Awarded to 1,672 full-time undergraduates, including 332 freshmen. Scholarships awarded for academics, alumni affiliation, art, music/drama, religious affiliation, ROTC, state residency.

**Application procedures. Admission:** Closing date 5/1 (receipt date). $25 fee, may be waived for applicants with need. Application may be submitted online. Admission notification on a rolling basis beginning on or about 9/1. Must reply by 6/20. Candidates may apply early and have until May 1 to have tuition and housing deposits refunded. **Financial aid:** Priority date 4/15; no closing date. FAFSA required. Applicants notified on a rolling basis starting 3/1; must reply by 5/1 or within 3 week(s) of notification.

**Academics. Special study options:** Accelerated study, cross-registration, double major, honors, independent study, internships, liberal arts/career combination, student-designed major, study abroad, teacher certification program. **Credit/placement by examination:** AP, CLEP, SAT, ACT, institutional tests. 30 credit hours maximum toward bachelor's degree. **Support services:** Learning center, pre-admission summer program, reduced course load, remedial instruction, study skills assistance, tutoring, writing center.

**Majors. Biology:** General. **Business:** General, accounting, management information systems, management science, marketing, operations. **Communications:** General. **Computer sciences:** General, networking. **Education:** Elementary, physical, secondary, special. **English:** English lit. **Foreign languages:** Spanish. **Health:** Clinical lab science, nursing (RN). **History:** General. **Legal studies:** Prelaw. **Liberal arts:** Arts/sciences. **Math:** General. **Parks/recreation:** General. **Philosophy/religion:** Religion. **Protective services:** Criminal justice. **Psychology:** General. **Public administration:** Social work. **Social sciences:** Political science, sociology. **Visual/performing arts:** Art, dramatic.

**Most popular majors.** Business/marketing 22%, education 21%, health sciences 14%, psychology 7%, public administration/social services 6%, security/protective services 6%.

**Computing on campus.** 90 workstations in library, computer center, student center. Dormitories wired for high-speed internet access and linked to campus network. Commuter students can connect to campus network. Online library, helpline, student web hosting, wireless network available.

**Student life. Freshman orientation:** Mandatory. Preregistration for classes offered. Day-long sessions held each summer. **Housing:** Coed dorms, substance-free housing available. $100 fully refundable deposit, deadline 5/1. **Activities:** Choral groups, dance, drama, literary magazine, student government, student newspaper, Black student association, Latin American student organization, Native American club, Students for Wellness, Fellowship of Christian Athletes, Circle K International, Intervarsity Christian Fellowship, political science club, Future Leaders of the World, games club.

**Athletics.** NCAA. **Intercollegiate:** Baseball M, basketball, cross-country, football (tackle) M, golf, soccer, softball W, tennis, track and field, volleyball W. **Intramural:** Basketball, football (non-tackle), volleyball. **Team name:** Spartans.

**Student services.** Adult student services, alcohol/substance abuse counseling, campus ministries, career counseling, student employment services, financial aid counseling, health services, personal counseling, placement for graduates. **Physically disabled:** Services for visually, speech, hearing impaired.

**Contact.** E-mail: admission@aurora.edu
Phone: (630) 844-5533 Toll-free number: (800) 742-5281
Fax: (630) 844-5535
James Lancaster, Director of Freshman Admission, Aurora University, 347 South Gladstone Avenue, Aurora, IL 60506-4892

## Benedictine University
**Lisle, Illinois**
www.ben.edu                      CB code: 1707

- Private 4-year university and liberal arts college affiliated with Roman Catholic Church
- Commuter campus in large town
- 2,883 degree-seeking undergraduates: 32% part-time, 57% women
- 1,355 degree-seeking graduate students
- 79% of applicants admitted
- SAT or ACT (ACT writing optional), application essay required

**General.** Founded in 1887. Regionally accredited. **Degrees:** 483 bachelor's, 41 associate awarded; master's, doctoral offered. **ROTC:** Army. **Location:** 25 miles from Chicago. **Calendar:** Semester, extensive summer session. **Full-time faculty:** 90 total; 90% have terminal degrees, 36% women. **Part-time faculty:** 433 total; 22% have terminal degrees, 48% women. **Class size:** 63% < 20, 34% 20-39, 3% 40-49, less than 1% 50-99. **Special facilities:** Nature museum, Benedictine abbey, arboretum, Fermi nuclear accelerator laboratories, Argonne national laboratories.

**Freshman class profile.** 1,449 applied, 1,150 admitted, 388 enrolled.

| Mid 50% test scores | | | |
|---|---|---|---|
| SAT critical reading: | 460-580 | GPA 2.0-2.99: | 30% |
| SAT math: | 540-610 | Rank in top quarter: | 44% |
| SAT writing: | 390-570 | Rank in top tenth: | 18% |
| ACT composite: | 21-25 | Out-of-state: | 6% |
| GPA 3.50 or higher: | 42% | Live on campus: | 48% |
| GPA 3.0-3.49: | 28% | International: | 1% |

**Basis for selection.** Require rank in top half of class and 21 ACT. Candidates falling below these criteria reviewed by admissions committee. Audition required of musical instrument and voice majors.

**High school preparation.** 16 units required. Required and recommended units include English 4, mathematics 3-4, social studies 3, history 1, science 2-3 (laboratory 1-2) and foreign language 2.

**2007-2008 Annual costs.** Tuition/fees: $21,310. Room/board: $6,955. Books/supplies: $1,200. Personal expenses: $2,150.

**2007-2008 Financial aid. Need-based:** Average scholarship/grant was $6,395; average loan $3,043. 55% of total undergraduate aid awarded as scholarships/grants, 45% as loans/jobs. **Non-need-based:** Scholarships awarded for academics, alumni affiliation, minority status, music/drama, ROTC. **Additional information:** Need-based financial aid available to part-time students who are enrolled at least half-time.

**Application procedures. Admission:** Priority date 8/30; no deadline. $40 fee, may be waived for applicants with need. Application may be submitted online. Admission notification on a rolling basis. Must reply by May 1 or within 2 week(s) if notified thereafter. **Financial aid:** Priority date 4/15; no closing date. FAFSA, institutional form required. Applicants notified on a rolling basis starting 2/15; must reply within 2 week(s) of notification.

**Academics. Special study options:** Accelerated study, combined bachelor's/graduate degree, cross-registration, distance learning, double major, dual enrollment of high school students, honors, independent study, internships, liberal arts/career combination, study abroad, teacher certification program, weekend college. Engineering degree program with Illinois Institute of Technology. **Credit/placement by examination:** AP, CLEP, institutional tests. 30 credit hours maximum toward bachelor's degree. **Support services:** Learning center, study skills assistance, tutoring, writing center.

**Majors. Biology:** General, biochemistry, molecular. **Business:** Accounting, finance, international, managerial economics, marketing, organizational behavior. **Communications:** General, publishing. **Computer sciences:** Computer science, information systems. **Conservation:** Environmental studies. **Education:** Elementary, special. **Engineering:** Science. **English:** English lit. **Foreign languages:** Comparative lit, Spanish. **Health:** Clinical lab science, health care admin, nuclear medical technology, nursing (RN). **History:** General. **Math:** General. **Philosophy/religion:** Philosophy. **Physical sciences:** Chemistry, physics. **Psychology:** General. **Social sciences:** General, economics, political science, sociology. **Visual/performing arts:** Arts management, studio arts.

**Most popular majors.** Biology 6%, business/marketing 34%, communications/journalism 6%, education 9%, health sciences 14%, psychology 9%, social sciences 9%.

**Computing on campus.** 200 workstations in dormitories, library, computer center, student center. Dormitories wired for high-speed internet access and linked to campus network. Commuter students can connect to campus network. Online course registration, online library, helpline, wireless network available.

**Student life. Freshman orientation:** Mandatory, $125 fee. Preregistration for classes offered. **Housing:** Coed dorms, single-sex dorms, apartments, substance-free housing available. $125 deposit. **Activities:** Bands, campus ministries, choral groups, film society, literary magazine, music ensembles, student government, student newspaper, symphony orchestra, TV station, Muslim student association, African-American student union, Knights of Columbus, Mediterranean club, Daughters of Isabella, Students for Life, Relay for Life, Best Buddies, South Asian student association.

**Athletics.** NCAA. **Intercollegiate:** Baseball M, basketball, cross-country, football (tackle) M, golf M, soccer, softball W, swimming, tennis W, track and field, volleyball W. **Intramural:** Basketball, bowling, tennis W. **Team name:** Eagles.

**Student services.** Adult student services, career counseling, student employment services, financial aid counseling, health services, personal counseling, placement for graduates. **Physically disabled:** Services for visually, speech, hearing impaired. **Learning disabled:** Comprehensive services available.

**Contact.** E-mail: admissions@ben.edu
Phone: (630) 829-6300 Toll-free number: (888) 829-6363
Fax: (630) 829-6301
Kari Gibbons, Dean of Enrollment, Benedictine University, 5700 College Road, Lisle, IL 60532

---

## Blackburn College
**Carlinville, Illinois**
**www.blackburn.edu**

CB member
CB code: 1065

- Private 4-year liberal arts college affiliated with Presbyterian Church (USA)
- Residential campus in small town
- 613 degree-seeking undergraduates: 2% part-time, 54% women, 8% African American, 1% Asian American, 1% Hispanic American
- 61% of applicants admitted
- SAT or ACT (ACT writing optional) required

**General.** Founded in 1837. Regionally accredited. **Degrees:** 98 bachelor's awarded. **Location:** 40 miles from Springfield, 60 miles from St. Louis. **Calendar:** Semester, limited summer session. **Full-time faculty:** 33 total; 85% have terminal degrees, 6% minority, 30% women. **Part-time faculty:** 40 total; 12% have terminal degrees, 55% women. **Class size:** 72% < 20, 25% 20-39, 2% 40-49, less than 1% 50-99.

**Freshman class profile.** 969 applied, 595 admitted, 175 enrolled.

| Mid 50% test scores | | | |
|---|---|---|---|
| ACT composite: | 18-24 | Rank in top quarter: | 43% |
| GPA 3.50 or higher: | 47% | Rank in top tenth: | 15% |
| GPA 3.0-3.49: | 25% | Out-of-state: | 9% |
| GPA 2.0-2.99: | 28% | Live on campus: | 87% |

**Basis for selection.** High school academic record, substantiated by test scores, most important. Interview recommended. Audition recommended for music majors. Portfolio recommended for art majors. **Homeschooled:** Statement describing homeschool structure and mission, transcript of courses and grades, state high school equivalency certificate required.

**High school preparation.** 16 units recommended. Recommended units include English 4, mathematics 3, social studies 2, history 2, science 3 and foreign language 2.

**2008-2009 Annual costs.** Tuition/fees (projected): $13,610. All on-campus students participate in a work program which reduces net tuition costs. Room/board: $4,363. Books/supplies: $700. Personal expenses: $800.

**2007-2008 Financial aid. Need-based:** 179 full-time freshmen applied for aid; 159 were judged to have need; 159 of these received aid. Average need met was 88%. Average scholarship/grant was $9,955; average loan $2,004. 63% of total undergraduate aid awarded as scholarships/grants, 37% as loans/jobs. **Non-need-based:** Scholarships awarded for academics, state residency. **Additional information:** Each resident student works 160 hours per semester.

**Application procedures. Admission:** No deadline. No application fee. Application may be submitted online. Admission notification on a rolling basis beginning on or about 10/15. **Financial aid:** Priority date 4/1; no closing date. FAFSA required. Applicants notified on a rolling basis starting 3/1; must reply within 4 week(s) of notification.

**Academics. Special study options:** Accelerated study, cooperative education, double major, dual enrollment of high school students, independent study, internships, student-designed major, study abroad, teacher certification program, Washington semester. British studies semester, Mexico studies semester. **Credit/placement by examination:** AP, CLEP, SAT, ACT, institutional tests. 30 credit hours maximum toward bachelor's degree. **Support services:** Learning center, reduced course load, remedial instruction, study skills assistance, tutoring, writing center.

**Majors. Area/ethnic studies:** Latin American. **Biology:** General, biochemistry, environmental. **Business:** Accounting, marketing. **Communications:** General. **Computer sciences:** Computer science. **Education:** Art, biology, elementary, English, mathematics, physical, social science. **English:** English lit. **Foreign languages:** Spanish. **Health:** Clinical lab science. **History:** General. **Math:** General. **Parks/recreation:** Health/fitness. **Physical sciences:** Chemistry. **Protective services:** Criminal justice. **Psychology:** General. **Public administration:** General. **Social sciences:** Political science. **Visual/performing arts:** Art.

**Most popular majors.** Biology 9%, business/marketing 19%, communications/journalism 12%, education 24%, psychology 8%, security/protective services 7%.

**Computing on campus.** 75 workstations in library, computer center. Dormitories linked to campus network. Helpline available.

**Student life. Freshman orientation:** Mandatory. Preregistration for classes offered. One day summer orientation and two day orientation prior to beginning of fall semester. **Policies:** Participation in student-managed work program required for all resident students. Resident students work 160 hours per semester to reduce costs and gain valuable career skills. Alcohol allowed for students 21 and older. All residence halls are smoke-free. **Housing:** Guaranteed on-campus for all undergraduates. Coed dorms, single-sex dorms, substance-free housing available. $150 fully refundable deposit, deadline 7/31. Quiet study housing available. **Activities:** Concert band, choral groups, drama, literary magazine, student government, student newspaper, Cultural Expressions, Habitat for Humanity chapter, Catacombs, Newman Club, Common Ground, Republican club, health and wellness club, fishing club, Beavers Against Destructive Decisions, psychology club.

**Athletics.** NCAA. **Intercollegiate:** Baseball M, basketball, cross-country, football (tackle) M, golf M, soccer, softball W, tennis W, volleyball W. **Intramural:** Badminton, basketball, racquetball, softball, swimming, table tennis, tennis, volleyball, water polo. **Team name:** Beavers.

**Student services.** Adult student services, alcohol/substance abuse counseling, career counseling, student employment services, financial aid counseling, minority student services, personal counseling, placement for graduates. **Physically disabled:** Services for visually, hearing impaired.

**Contact.** E-mail: jmali@blackburn.edu
Phone: (217) 854-3231 Toll-free number: (800) 233-3550
Fax: (217) 854-3713
John Malin, Dean of Enrollment Management, Blackburn College, 700 College Avenue, Carlinville, IL 62626

## Blessing-Rieman College of Nursing
**Quincy, Illinois**
www.brcn.edu                                    CB code: 0139

- Private 4-year nursing college
- Commuter campus in large town
- 211 degree-seeking undergraduates: 6% part-time, 92% women, 4% African American, 3% Asian American, 1% Hispanic American
- 8 degree-seeking graduate students
- 100% of applicants admitted
- SAT or ACT (ACT writing optional) required
- 59% graduate within 6 years

**General.** Founded in 1891. Regionally accredited. Joint degree programs with Culver-Stockton College (MO) and Quincy University (IL) leading to Bachelor of Science in Nursing degree. General education classes held at partner campus, with nursing classes at B-RCN campus and regional medical center. **Degrees:** 39 bachelor's awarded. **Location:** 120 miles from St. Louis, 100 miles from Springfield. **Calendar:** Semester, limited summer session. **Full-time faculty:** 20 total; 85% have terminal degrees, 100% women. **Part-time faculty:** 7 total; 100% women. **Class size:** 52% < 20, 48% 20-39.

**Freshman class profile.** 24 applied, 24 admitted, 24 enrolled.

| Mid 50% test scores | | End year in good standing: | 64% |
|---|---|---|---|
| ACT composite: | 22-25 | Return as sophomores: | 79% |
| GPA 3.50 or higher: | 30% | Out-of-state: | 39% |
| GPA 3.0-3.49: | 70% | Live on campus: | 82% |

**Basis for selection.** 3.0 GPA and at least 22 ACT composite score required for nursing majors.

**High school preparation.** Required units include English 4, mathematics 2, social studies 3, science 3 (laboratory 2). Biology, chemistry, algebra required.

**2007-2008 Annual costs.** Tuition/fees: $17,775. Tuition and fees are average costs charged to freshman. Partnered with Quincy University and Culver-Stockton College. Freshmen and sophomores pay partnering school's tuition rate. Books/supplies: $1,000. Personal expenses: $1,775.

**Financial aid. Additional information:** Financial aid for freshmen and sophomores administered by Culver-Stockton College and Quincy University.

**Application procedures. Admission:** No deadline. No application fee. Application must be submitted on paper. Admission notification on a rolling basis. **Financial aid:** No deadline. FAFSA required.

**Academics. Special study options:** Accelerated study, combined bachelor's/graduate degree, internships. **Credit/placement by examination:** CLEP, IB, SAT, ACT, institutional tests. **Support services:** Study skills assistance, tutoring.

**Majors. Health:** Nursing (RN).

**Computing on campus.** 25 workstations in dormitories, library, computer center. Dormitories linked to campus network. Online library available.

**Student life. Policies:** Immunization and background check required for sophomore level and up. **Housing:** Guaranteed on-campus for all undergraduates. Coed dorms, single-sex dorms, apartments, substance-free housing available. Men's and women's dormitories available at Culver-Stockton College and Quincy University. **Activities:** Student government, Student Nurses Organization, club and intramural sports, fraternities and sororities available at Culver-Stockton College and Quincy University.

**Student services.** Alcohol/substance abuse counseling, career counseling, student employment services, financial aid counseling, health services, on-campus daycare, personal counseling, placement for graduates.

**Contact.** E-mail: admissions@brcn.edu
Phone: (217) 228-5520 ext. 6949 Toll-free
number: (800) 877-9140 ext. 6949 Fax: (217) 223-4661
Pam Brown, President, Blessing-Rieman College of Nursing, PO Box 7005, Quincy, IL 62305-7005

## Bradley University
**Peoria, Illinois**                             CB member
www.bradley.edu                                  CB code: 1070

- Private 4-year university
- Residential campus in large city
- 5,205 degree-seeking undergraduates: 5% part-time, 55% women, 6% African American, 4% Asian American, 3% Hispanic American, 1% international
- 763 degree-seeking graduate students
- 83% of applicants admitted
- SAT or ACT (ACT writing recommended), application essay required

**General.** Founded in 1897. Regionally accredited. **Degrees:** 1,289 bachelor's awarded; master's, doctoral offered. **ROTC:** Army. **Location:** 157 miles from Chicago, 164 miles from St. Louis. **Calendar:** Semester, limited summer session. **Full-time faculty:** 335 total; 82% have terminal degrees, 13% minority, 35% women. **Part-time faculty:** 217 total; 5% minority, 53% women. **Class size:** 49% < 20, 44% 20-39, 4% 40-49, 3% 50-99, less than 1% >100. **Special facilities:** Global communications center, 2 art galleries.

**Freshman class profile.** 4,612 applied, 3,844 admitted, 1,080 enrolled.

| Mid 50% test scores | | Rank in top tenth: | 28% |
|---|---|---|---|
| SAT critical reading: | 510-610 | End year in good standing: | 95% |
| SAT math: | 530-640 | Return as sophomores: | 89% |
| ACT composite: | 23-27 | Out-of-state: | 13% |
| GPA 3.50 or higher: | 61% | Live on campus: | 93% |
| GPA 3.0-3.49: | 31% | International: | 1% |
| GPA 2.0-2.99: | 8% | Fraternities: | 35% |
| Rank in top quarter: | 65% | Sororities: | 37% |

**Basis for selection.** High school curriculum and achievement, test scores, special talents, co-curricular activities, letters of recommendation, personal statement, educational goals important. Student's academic interest, motivational level, and quality of secondary school education also considered. Interview recommended. Audition required of music majors, recommended for theater majors. Portfolio recommended for art majors. **Homeschooled:** Applicants must submit ACT or SAT score, record of courses taken, grades earned, personal statement, letter of recommendation and record of activities or club memberships. Interview may be required and highly recommended.

**High school preparation.** 16 units required. Required and recommended units include English 4-5, mathematics 3-4, social studies 2-3, science 2-3 (laboratory 2-3) and foreign language 2. Additional requirements for business, science, engineering, music, nursing, and health science majors.

**2007-2008 Annual costs.** Tuition/fees: $21,378. Room/board: $7,050. Personal expenses: $1,500.

**2006-2007 Financial aid. Need-based:** 905 full-time freshmen applied for aid; 686 were judged to have need; 686 of these received aid. Average

need met was 79%. Average scholarship/grant was $11,370; average loan $3,713. 67% of total undergraduate aid awarded as scholarships/grants, 33% as loans/jobs. **Non-need-based:** Awarded to 1,650 full-time undergraduates, including 382 freshmen. Scholarships awarded for academics, alumni affiliation, art; athletics, leadership, music/drama.

**Application procedures. Admission:** Priority date 3/1; deadline 8/1 (postmark date). $35 fee, may be waived for applicants with need. Application may be submitted online. Admission notification on a rolling basis beginning on or about 10/1. Must reply by May 1 or within 2 week(s) if notified thereafter. **Financial aid:** Priority date 3/1; no closing date. FAFSA required. Applicants notified on a rolling basis starting 2/15.

**Academics.** Academic Exploration Program assists undergraduates in choosing major. **Special study options:** Accelerated study, combined bachelor's/graduate degree, cooperative education, double major, honors, independent study, internships, liberal arts/career combination, student-designed major, study abroad, teacher certification program, Washington semester. **Credit/placement by examination:** AP, CLEP, IB, institutional tests. 60 credit hours maximum toward bachelor's degree. **Support services:** Learning center, study skills assistance, tutoring, writing center.

**Majors. Biology:** General, biochemistry, cellular/molecular. **Business:** Accounting, actuarial science, business admin, entrepreneurial studies, finance, human resources, insurance, international, management information systems, managerial economics, marketing, selling, small business admin. **Communications:** General, advertising, digital media, journalism, photojournalism, public relations, radio/tv. **Communications technology:** Animation/special effects. **Computer sciences:** Computer science, information systems. **Conservation:** Environmental science. **Education:** Art, biology, chemistry, drama/dance, early childhood, elementary, English, family/consumer sciences, French, German, history, learning disabled, mathematics, mentally handicapped, music, physics, psychology, science, social science, social studies, Spanish, speech. **Engineering:** Civil, computer, construction, electrical, environmental, industrial, manufacturing, mechanical, physics. **Engineering technology:** Electrical, manufacturing. **English:** English lit. **Family/consumer sciences:** General, merchandising. **Foreign languages:** French, German, Spanish. **Health:** Clinical lab science, dietetics, nursing (RN). **History:** General. **Liberal arts:** Arts/sciences, humanities. **Math:** General. **Philosophy/religion:** Philosophy, religion. **Physical sciences:** Chemistry, geology, physics. **Protective services:** Law enforcement admin. **Psychology:** General. **Public administration:** Social work. **Social sciences:** Economics, international relations, political science, sociology. **Visual/performing arts:** Acting, art, art history/conservation, ceramics, directing/producing, dramatic, drawing, graphic design, music management, music performance, music theory/composition, painting, photography, printmaking, sculpture, studio arts. **Other:** Legal studies in business.

**Most popular majors.** Business/marketing 22%, communications/journalism 10%, education 11%, engineering/engineering technologies 13%, health sciences 10%.

**Computing on campus.** 900 workstations in dormitories, library, computer center. Dormitories wired for high-speed internet access and linked to campus network. Commuter students can connect to campus network. Online course registration, helpline, student web hosting, wireless network available.

**Student life. Freshman orientation:** Mandatory, $115 fee. Preregistration for classes offered. 13 sessions throughout summer. **Housing:** Guaranteed on-campus for freshmen. Coed dorms, single-sex dorms, apartments, fraternity/sorority housing, substance-free housing available. $100 partly refundable deposit, deadline 5/1. **Activities:** Bands, choral groups, dance, drama, film society, literary magazine, music ensembles, musical theater, opera, radio station, student government, student newspaper, symphony orchestra, TV station, Alpha Phi Omega, center for student leadership and public services, Hillel, InterVarsity Christian Fellowship, mock trial, Model UN, Amnesty International, Habitat for Humanity, Beyond Prejudice.

**Athletics.** NCAA. **Intercollegiate:** Baseball M, basketball, cross-country, golf, soccer M, softball W, tennis, track and field W, volleyball W. **Intramural:** Badminton, basketball, bowling, fencing, football (tackle) M, golf, handball, racquetball, soccer, softball, swimming, table tennis, tennis, volleyball, water polo, wrestling M. **Team name:** Braves.

**Student services.** Alcohol/substance abuse counseling, career counseling, student employment services, financial aid counseling, health services, minority student services, personal counseling, placement for graduates, veterans' counselor.

**Contact.** E-mail: admissions@bradley.edu
Phone: (309) 677-1000 Toll-free number: (800) 447-6460
Fax: (309) 677-2797
Rodney San Jose, Director of Admissions, Bradley University, 1501 West Bradley Avenue, Peoria, IL 61625

---

## Chicago State University
Chicago, Illinois
www.csu.edu

CB member
CB code: 1118

- Public 4-year university
- Commuter campus in very large city
- 5,157 degree-seeking undergraduates
- 57% of applicants admitted
- SAT or ACT (ACT writing optional) required

**General.** Founded in 1867. Regionally accredited. **Degrees:** 628 bachelor's awarded; master's offered. **ROTC:** Army. **Location:** 12 miles from downtown. **Calendar:** Semester, limited summer session. **Full-time faculty:** 313 total. **Part-time faculty:** 120 total. **Class size:** 48% < 20, 51% 20-39, less than 1% 40-49, less than 1% 50-99. **Special facilities:** Electron microscopy laboratory, video conference room, center of African heritage and culture.

**Freshman class profile.** 2,303 applied, 1,313 admitted, 448 enrolled.

| | | | |
|---|---|---|---|
| Rank in top quarter: | 35% | Out-of-state: | 6% |
| Rank in top tenth: | 13% | Live on campus: | 23% |

**Basis for selection.** High school GPA, standardized test scores, and subject/units completed.

**High school preparation.** 15 units required. Required units include English 4, mathematics 3, social studies 3, science 3 and academic electives 2. 2 units foreign language, music, vocational education or art.

**2007-2008 Annual costs.** Tuition/fees: $7,730; $13,850 out-of-state. Rates are guaranteed for all four years. Tuition quoted is for first-time freshmen. Room/board: $6,752. Books/supplies: $1,400. Personal expenses: $2,800.

**2006-2007 Financial aid. Need-based:** 52% of total undergraduate aid awarded as scholarships/grants, 48% as loans/jobs. **Non-need-based:** Scholarships awarded for academics, athletics, ROTC, state residency. **Additional information:** Freshmen of outstanding academic ability and talent eligible for Scholars Program full-tuition scholarship.

**Application procedures. Admission:** No deadline. $25 fee, may be waived for applicants with need. Admission notification on a rolling basis. **Financial aid:** Priority date 3/1; no closing date. FAFSA, institutional form required.

**Academics. Special study options:** Cooperative education, distance learning, double major, ESL, honors, independent study, internships, liberal arts/career combination, student-designed major, study abroad, teacher certification program. Programs for mature adults (University Without Walls, individualized curriculum, Board of Governors degree program). **Credit/placement by examination:** AP, CLEP, institutional tests. 60 credit hours maximum toward bachelor's degree. **Support services:** Learning center, remedial instruction, study skills assistance, tutoring, writing center.

**Majors. Area/ethnic studies:** African-American. **Biology:** General, bacteriology, biochemistry, environmental, molecular. **Business:** Accounting, business admin, fashion, finance, management information systems. **Communications:** Broadcast journalism. **Computer sciences:** General, data processing, information systems. **Education:** General, art, biology, business, chemistry, early childhood, elementary, English, health, history, mathematics, mentally handicapped, multi-level teacher, music, physical, secondary, special, technology/industrial arts. **English:** English lit, speech/rhetoric, technical writing. **Foreign languages:** Spanish. **Health:** Medical records admin, nursing (RN). **History:** General. **Math:** General. **Parks/recreation:** Health/fitness. **Physical sciences:** Chemistry, physics. **Psychology:** General. **Social sciences:** Anthropology, economics, geography, political science, sociology. **Visual/performing arts:** Art, commercial/advertising art.

**Most popular majors.** Business/marketing 14%, education 11%, health sciences 9%, liberal arts 30%, psychology 8%.

**Computing on campus.** 156 workstations in dormitories, library, computer center, student center. Dormitories wired for high-speed internet access. Commuter students can connect to campus network. Online course registration, online library available.

**Student life. Freshman orientation:** Mandatory. Preregistration for classes offered. One-day programs in July and August. **Housing:** Coed dorms available. $125 deposit, deadline 8/1. **Activities:** Bands, choral groups, dance, drama, literary magazine, music ensembles, radio station, student government, student newspaper, TV station, 47 clubs and organizations.

**Athletics.** NCAA. **Intercollegiate:** Baseball M, basketball, cross-country, golf, tennis, track and field, volleyball W. **Intramural:** Basketball, gymnastics, swimming, volleyball. **Team name:** Cougars.

**Student services.** Adult student services, alcohol/substance abuse counseling, campus ministries, career counseling, student employment services, financial aid counseling, health services, minority student services, on-campus daycare, personal counseling, placement for graduates, veterans' counselor, women's services.

**Contact.** E-mail: ug-admissions@csu.edu
Phone: (773) 995-2513 Fax: (773) 995-3820
Addie Epps, Director of Admissions, Chicago State University, 9501 South King Drive, Chicago, IL 60628

---

## Columbia College Chicago
**Chicago, Illinois**      **CB member**
**www.colum.edu**      **CB code: 1135**

- Private 4-year visual arts and liberal arts college
- Commuter campus in very large city
- 11,256 degree-seeking undergraduates: 11% part-time, 51% women, 14% African American, 3% Asian American, 9% Hispanic American, 1% international
- 655 degree-seeking graduate students
- Application essay required
- 35% graduate within 6 years

**General.** Founded in 1890. Regionally accredited. **Degrees:** 1,663 bachelor's awarded; master's offered. **Location:** Downtown. **Calendar:** Semester, limited summer session. **Full-time faculty:** 328 total; 17% minority. **Part-time faculty:** 1,267 total; 18% minority. **Class size:** 72% < 20, 26% 20-39, less than 1% 40-49, less than 1% 50-99, less than 1% >100. **Special facilities:** Contemporary photography museum, photography studios, film/video sound stage, dance performance space, theater, audio technology center, psychoacoustic classroom, animation facilities, reverb chamber, book and paper arts center, black music research center, center for arts policy, community media workshop, international Latino cultural center, community arts partnership center.

**Freshman class profile.** 4,535 applied, 4,405 admitted, 2,229 enrolled.

| Mid 50% test scores | | Rank in top tenth: | 6% |
|---|---|---|---|
| ACT composite: | 18-25 | Return as sophomores: | 65% |
| GPA 3.50 or higher: | 19% | Out-of-state: | 23% |
| GPA 3.0-3.49: | 28% | Live on campus: | 59% |
| GPA 2.0-2.99: | 45% | International: | 1% |
| Rank in top quarter: | 21% | | |

**Basis for selection.** Open admission, but selective for some programs. Proof of high school graduation (or earned GED), letter of recommendation, and essay required for placement/counseling. Students with less than 2.0 GPA may be required to attend special summer program. All freshmen take COMPASS placement test on campus. Interview recommended. **Homeschooled:** Transcript of courses and grades required. **Learning Disabled:** Student must have regular earned GED or HS diploma and may have to complete BRIDGE program.

**2007-2008 Annual costs.** Tuition/fees: $17,564. Room/board: $12,018. Books/supplies: $1,346. Personal expenses: $1,760.

**Financial aid. Non-need-based:** Scholarships awarded for academics, art, leadership, music/drama, state residency.

**Application procedures. Admission:** Priority date 6/15; no deadline. $35 fee. Application may be submitted online. Admission notification on a rolling basis. **Financial aid:** Priority date 5/1; no closing date. FAFSA, institutional form required. Applicants notified on a rolling basis.

**Academics. Special study options:** Cooperative education, distance learning, dual enrollment of high school students, ESL, independent study, internships, liberal arts/career combination, student-designed major, study abroad, teacher certification program. **Credit/placement by examination:** AP, CLEP, IB, institutional tests. 62 credit hours maximum toward bachelor's degree. **Support services:** Learning center, pre-admission summer program, reduced course load, remedial instruction, study skills assistance, tutoring, writing center.

**Majors. Architecture:** Interior. **Business:** Business admin, fashion, marketing. **Communications:** Advertising, broadcast journalism, journalism, public relations, radio/tv. **Communications technology:** Animation/special effects, recording arts. **Computer sciences:** Web page design. **Education:** Early childhood, kindergarten/preschool. **English:** Creative writing. **Foreign languages:** Sign language interpretation. **Liberal arts:** Arts/sciences. **Visual/performing arts:** General, acting, art, arts management, cinematography, commercial/advertising art, dance, design, directing/producing, dramatic, fashion design, film/cinema, graphic design, illustration, industrial design, interior design, jazz, multimedia, music management, music performance, photography, play/screenwriting, studio arts, theater design, voice/opera. **Other:** Cultural studies.

**Most popular majors.** Business/marketing 9%, communications/journalism 14%, communication technologies 6%, visual/performing arts 60%.

**Computing on campus.** 851 workstations in dormitories, library, computer center, student center. Dormitories wired for high-speed internet access and linked to campus network. Commuter students can connect to campus network. Online course registration, helpline, wireless network available.

**Student life. Freshman orientation:** Mandatory, $70 fee. Preregistration for classes offered. Provides services aid transition to college life. Parent orientation and parent weekend program available. **Housing:** Coed dorms, substance-free housing available. $500 deposit. Student housing available at nearby colleges and universities. **Activities:** Bands, campus ministries, choral groups, dance, drama, film society, international student organizations, literary magazine, music ensembles, musical theater, radio station, student government, student newspaper, TV station, Association of Black Journalists, Umoja, Black Actor's Guild, Black Ink, Latino Alliance, environmental campus organization, Hillel, Not In Our Name.

**Athletics. Intramural:** Baseball, basketball, lacrosse M, soccer.

**Student services.** Alcohol/substance abuse counseling, career counseling, services for economically disadvantaged, student employment services, financial aid counseling, health services, minority student services, personal counseling, placement for graduates, veterans' counselor. **Physically disabled:** Services for visually, speech, hearing impaired.

**Contact.** E-mail: admissions@colum.edu
Phone: (312) 344-7130 Fax: (312) 344-8024
Murphy Monroe, Executive Director of Admissions, Columbia College Chicago, 600 South Michigan Avenue, Chicago, IL 60605-1996

---

## Concordia University
**River Forest, Illinois**      **CB member**
**www.cuchicago.edu**      **CB code: 1140**

- Private 4-year university and teachers college affiliated with Lutheran Church - Missouri Synod
- Residential campus in large town
- 1,026 degree-seeking undergraduates: 5% part-time, 61% women
- 2,902 degree-seeking graduate students
- 84% of applicants admitted
- ACT (writing optional) required
- 59% graduate within 6 years

**General.** Founded in 1864. Regionally accredited. **Degrees:** 198 bachelor's awarded; master's, doctoral offered. **Location:** 10 miles from Chicago. **Calendar:** Semester, limited summer session. **Full-time faculty:** 104 total. **Part-time faculty:** 250 total. **Class size:** 68% < 20, 31% 20-39, less than 1% 40-49, less than 1% 50-99. **Special facilities:** Early childhood education laboratory school, curriculum center (teacher's resource), human performance laboratory.

**Freshman class profile.** 818 applied, 691 admitted, 231 enrolled.

| Mid 50% test scores | | GPA 2.0-2.99: | 35% |
|---|---|---|---|
| SAT critical reading: | 450-590 | Rank in top quarter: | 45% |
| SAT math: | 480-640 | Rank in top tenth: | 20% |
| ACT composite: | 19-25 | End year in good standing: | 86% |
| GPA 3.50 or higher: | 34% | Return as sophomores: | 70% |
| GPA 3.0-3.49: | 31% | Out-of-state: | 38% |

**Basis for selection.** School achievement record, character reference most important. 2.0 GPA in college preparatory classes and rank in top half of class with 20 ACT or 930 SAT (exclusive of Writing) required. Interview recommended. Essay and interview required for students who do not meet academic admission requirements. **Homeschooled:** Statement describing homeschool structure and mission, transcript of courses and grades required. Syllabus for each course, personal statement or essay describing an important event or individual, certificate of completion from home school (if available), official transcripts of any college work completed required.

**High school preparation.** 15 units required. Required and recommended units include English 4, mathematics 3, social studies 2, history 1, science 2-4 (laboratory 1) and foreign language 2.

**2008-2009 Annual costs.** Tuition/fees: $22,390. Room/board: $7,350. Books/supplies: $600. Personal expenses: $450.

**2006-2007 Financial aid.** **Need-based:** 197 full-time freshmen applied for aid; 174 were judged to have need; 174 of these received aid. Average need met was 77%. Average scholarship/grant was $10,486; average loan $5,843. 58% of total undergraduate aid awarded as scholarships/grants, 42% as loans/jobs. **Non-need-based:** Awarded to 407 full-time undergraduates, including 81 freshmen. Scholarships awarded for academics, alumni affiliation, music/drama, religious affiliation, state residency.

**Application procedures.** **Admission:** No deadline. No application fee. Application may be submitted online. Admission notification on a rolling basis beginning on or about 9/4. **Financial aid:** Priority date 4/1, closing date 8/15. FAFSA required. Applicants notified on a rolling basis; must reply within 4 week(s) of notification.

**Academics.** **Special study options:** Cross-registration, distance learning, double major, exchange student, honors, independent study, internships, study abroad, teacher certification program. Adult degree completion program. **Credit/placement by examination:** AP, CLEP, IB, institutional tests. 12 credit hours maximum toward bachelor's degree. **Support services:** Learning center, reduced course load, study skills assistance, tutoring, writing center.

**Majors.** **Biology:** General. **Business:** General, accounting, business admin, marketing. **Communications:** General, advertising. **Computer sciences:** General, computer science. **Education:** General, biology, chemistry, computer, early childhood, elementary, English, history, multi-level teacher, music, physical, science, secondary, social science, social studies. **English:** English lit. **Foreign languages:** Ancient Greek, Hebrew, Latin. **Health:** Prenursing. **History:** General. **Interdisciplinary:** Natural sciences. **Math:** General. **Parks/recreation:** Exercise sciences. **Philosophy/religion:** Philosophy. **Physical sciences:** Chemistry. **Protective services:** Criminal justice, law enforcement admin, police science. **Psychology:** General. **Public administration:** Social work. **Social sciences:** Geography, political science, sociology. **Theology:** Religious ed, sacred music, theology. **Visual/performing arts:** Art, music performance, music theory/composition.

**Most popular majors.** Business/marketing 22%, education 36%, social sciences 6%, theological studies 10%, visual/performing arts 6%.

**Computing on campus.** 85 workstations in library, computer center, student center. Dormitories wired for high-speed internet access and linked to campus network. Commuter students can connect to campus network. Online course registration, helpline, repair service, student web hosting, wireless network available.

**Student life.** **Freshman orientation:** Mandatory. Preregistration for classes offered. **Housing:** Guaranteed on-campus for freshmen. Coed dorms, single-sex dorms available. $200 deposit, deadline 7/1. **Activities:** Bands, campus ministries, choral groups, drama, literary magazine, music ensembles, musical theater, student government, student newspaper, TV station, minority student alliance, Ambassadors for Christ, sociology/social service club, Fellowship of Christian Athletes, environmental awareness club, Pace Jail Ministries, Latin student union.

**Athletics.** NCAA. **Intercollegiate:** Baseball M, basketball, cross-country, football (tackle) M, soccer, softball W, tennis, track and field, volleyball W. **Intramural:** Badminton, basketball, bowling, cross-country, softball, swimming, tennis, track and field, volleyball. **Team name:** Cougars.

**Student services.** Career counseling, student employment services, financial aid counseling, health services, on-campus daycare, personal counseling, placement for graduates.

**Contact.** E-mail: crfadmis@cuchicago.edu
Phone: (708) 209-3100 Toll-free number: (866) 462-2873
Fax: (708) 209-3473
Kathy Graudin, Director of Admission, Concordia University, 7400 Augusta Street, River Forest, IL 60305-1499

## DePaul University
Chicago, Illinois
www.depaul.edu

CB member
CB code: 1165

- Private 4-year university affiliated with Roman Catholic Church
- Residential campus in very large city
- 14,661 degree-seeking undergraduates: 23% part-time, 56% women, 8% African American, 9% Asian American, 12% Hispanic American, 1% international
- 8,192 degree-seeking graduate students
- 63% of applicants admitted
- SAT or ACT (ACT writing optional) required
- 62% graduate within 6 years

**General.** Founded in 1898. Regionally accredited. Largest Catholic university in the United States. **Degrees:** 2,842 bachelor's awarded; master's, doctoral, first professional offered. **ROTC:** Army. **Location:** Downtown. **Calendar:** Quarter, extensive summer session. **Full-time faculty:** 870 total; 88% have terminal degrees, 20% minority, 43% women. **Part-time faculty:** 924 total; 16% have terminal degrees, 12% minority, 47% women. **Class size:** 42% < 20, 47% 20-39, 10% 40-49, less than 1% 50-99, less than 1% >100.

**Freshman class profile.** 12,468 applied, 7,902 admitted, 2,522 enrolled.

| Mid 50% test scores | | | |
|---|---|---|---|
| SAT critical reading: | 520-630 | Rank in top quarter: | 48% |
| SAT math: | 510-620 | Rank in top tenth: | 20% |
| SAT writing: | 530-620 | End year in good standing: | 91% |
| ACT composite: | 22-27 | Return as sophomores: | 84% |
| GPA 3.50 or higher: | 44% | Out-of-state: | 30% |
| GPA 3.0-3.49: | 35% | Live on campus: | 75% |
| GPA 2.0-2.99: | 21% | International: | 1% |

**Basis for selection.** Secondary school record most important; class rank, recommendations, test scores, essay, extracurricular activities, talent/ability, character, volunteer and work experience important. Interview, alumni/ae relation, geographical location, state residency, religious affiliation, racial or ethnic status considered. Interview required of acting, theater technologies, and recording sound technology majors. Auditions required of music and theater majors. Portfolios required of theater technology and design majors. **Homeschooled:** Transcript of courses and grades required. Official community college transcripts for any courses taken required. Listing of textbooks used, especially in math and science, recommended.

**High school preparation.** 16 units required. Required units include English 4, mathematics 3, social studies 2, science 3 (laboratory 2) and academic electives 4.

**2007-2008 Annual costs.** Tuition/fees: $24,110. Room/board: $9,801. Books/supplies: $900. Personal expenses: $1,656.

**2006-2007 Financial aid.** **Need-based:** 2,102 full-time freshmen applied for aid; 1,572 were judged to have need; 1,520 of these received aid. Average need met was 67%. Average scholarship/grant was $13,038; average loan $3,915. 54% of total undergraduate aid awarded as scholarships/grants, 46% as loans/jobs. **Non-need-based:** Awarded to 2,843 full-time undergraduates, including 872 freshmen. Scholarships awarded for academics, art, athletics, leadership, music/drama, ROTC, state residency.

**Application procedures.** **Admission:** Priority date 2/1; no deadline. $40 fee, may be waived for applicants with need. Application may be submitted online. Admission notification on a rolling basis beginning on or about 3/15. Must reply by May 1 or within 2 week(s) if notified thereafter. Students notified of admission decision within 4-6 weeks after receipt of all required admission materials. Early action applicants receive early financial aid estimates, priority registration, priority housing and priority advising. **Financial aid:** Priority date 2/1, closing date 5/1. FAFSA required. Applicants notified on a rolling basis starting 3/15; must reply by 5/1 or within 4 week(s) of notification.

**Academics.** Honors programs offered in arts and sciences, business. Conservatory program in theater and music provides professional training. **Special study options:** Accelerated study, combined bachelor's/graduate degree, cooperative education, distance learning, double major, dual enrollment of high school students, ESL, honors, independent study, internships, student-designed major, study abroad, teacher certification program, weekend college. **Credit/placement by examination:** AP, CLEP, IB, SAT, ACT, institutional tests. 99 credit hours maximum toward bachelor's degree. Senior year residency requirement excludes CLEP, AP or IB credits. For transfer students, CLEP, IB or AP credits combined with transfer credits from 2-year institutions may total no more than 99 hours, and combined with transfer credits from 4-year institutions may total no more than 132 hours. **Support services:** Learning center, pre-admission summer program, reduced course load, remedial instruction, study skills assistance, tutoring, writing center.

**Majors.** **Area/ethnic studies:** African-American, American, East Asian, Latin American, women's. **Biology:** General. **Business:** General, accounting, banking/financial services, business admin, e-commerce, finance, human resources, management science, managerial economics, operations, organizational behavior, real estate. **Communications:** General. **Computer sciences:** General, applications programming, computer graphics, computer science, information systems, information technology, networking, programming, security, web page design. **Conservation:** Environmental science. **Education:** Art, biology, chemistry, computer, early childhood, elementary, English, French, geography, German, health, history, mathematics, music, physical, physics, secondary, social science, Spanish, special. **English:** English lit. **Foreign languages:** French, German, Italian, Spanish. **Health:** Art therapy, clinical lab science, nursing (RN). **History:** General. **Interdisciplinary:** Biological/physical sciences, math/computer science. **Liberal arts:**

Humanities. **Math:** General. **Parks/recreation:** Health/fitness. **Philosophy/religion:** Islamic, Judaic, philosophy, religion. **Physical sciences:** Chemistry, physics. **Psychology:** General, educational. **Public administration:** Community org/advocacy, policy analysis. **Social sciences:** General, anthropology, economics, geography, international relations, political science, sociology, urban studies. **Visual/performing arts:** Acting, art, art history/conservation, arts management, dramatic, jazz, music management, music performance, music theory/composition, play/screenwriting, theater design, theater history. **Other:** Human computer interaction, Music - recording technology, Scientific data analysis/visualization.

**Most popular majors.** Business/marketing 34%, communications/journalism 9%, computer/information sciences 6%, education 6%, liberal arts 12%, psychology 8%, social sciences 9%.

**Computing on campus.** 1,117 workstations in dormitories, library, computer center, student center. Dormitories wired for high-speed internet access and linked to campus network. Commuter students can connect to campus network. Online course registration, online library, helpline, student web hosting, wireless network available.

**Student life. Freshman orientation:** Mandatory, $170 fee. Preregistration for classes offered. 2 day summer program for students and their families. **Housing:** Coed dorms, apartments, substance-free housing available. $500 fully refundable deposit, deadline 5/1. Theme housing available. **Activities:** Bands, choral groups, dance, drama, film society, music ensembles, Model UN, musical theater, opera, radio station, student government, student newspaper, symphony orchestra, over 70 clubs and organizations.

**Athletics.** NCAA. **Intercollegiate:** Basketball, cross-country, golf M, soccer, softball W, tennis, track and field, volleyball W. **Intramural:** Badminton, basketball, football (non-tackle), racquetball, soccer, softball, table tennis, tennis, volleyball, water polo. **Team name:** Blue Demons.

**Student services.** Adult student services, alcohol/substance abuse counseling, campus ministries, career counseling, services for economically disadvantaged, student employment services, financial aid counseling, health services, legal services, minority student services, personal counseling, placement for graduates, veterans' counselor, women's services. **Physically disabled:** Services for visually, speech, hearing impaired.

**Contact.** E-mail: admitdpu@depaul.edu
Phone: (312) 362-8300 Toll-free number: (800) 433-7285
Fax: (312) 362-5749
Carlene Klaas, Dean of Undergraduate Admissions, DePaul University, 1 East Jackson Boulevard, Chicago, IL 60604-2287

## DeVry University: Addison
**Addison, Illinois**
**www.devry.edu**                                      **CB code: 3204**

- For-profit 4-year university
- Commuter campus in large town
- 1,312 degree-seeking undergraduates: 40% part-time, 27% women, 10% African American, 12% Asian American, 14% Hispanic American, 5% international
- Interview required

**General.** Founded in 1982. Regionally accredited. **Degrees:** 378 bachelor's, 45 associate awarded. **Location:** 20 miles from Chicago. **Calendar:** Semester, extensive summer session. **Full-time faculty:** 46 total; 22% minority, 67% women. **Part-time faculty:** 55 total; 26% minority, 62% women.

**Freshman class profile.** 173 enrolled.

| Return as sophomores: | 48% | International: | 2% |
|---|---|---|---|
| Out-of-state: | 5% | | |

**Basis for selection.** Applicants must have high school diploma or equivalent, or degree from an accredited postsecondary institution and demonstrate proficiency in basic college-level skills through test scores and/or institution-administered placement examinations, and be at least 17 years of age. New students may enter at the beginning of any semester. SAT/ACT tests are considered but not required for admission. If the applicant chooses not to submit either one, he/she must take a DeVry-administered admissions test.

**2007-2008 Annual costs.** Tuition/fees: $13,220. Books/supplies: $1,300. Personal expenses: $5,082.

**Financial aid.** All financial aid based on need.

**Application procedures. Admission:** No deadline. $50 fee. Application may be submitted online. Admission notification on a rolling basis.

**Financial aid:** No deadline. FAFSA required. Applicants notified on a rolling basis.

**Academics. Special study options:** Accelerated study, distance learning. **Credit/placement by examination:** CLEP, institutional tests. **Support services:** Learning center, remedial instruction, tutoring.

**Majors. Business:** Business admin, e-commerce, operations. **Computer sciences:** Information systems, information technology, networking, systems analysis. **Engineering:** Biomedical, electrical, software. **Engineering technology:** Biomedical, computer, electrical.

**Most popular majors.** Business/marketing 55%, computer/information sciences 33%, engineering/engineering technologies 13%.

**Computing on campus.** 548 workstations in library, computer center. Online course registration, online library, helpline available.

**Student life. Freshman orientation:** Mandatory. **Housing:** Private apartments, student-plan housing, private rooms available. **Activities:** International student organizations, literary magazine, student government, student newspaper, Muslim student association, Alpha Sigma Lambda, Christian Fellowship, Chi Pi Alpha, Epsilon Delta Pi, Phi Theta Kappa, Institute of Electrical and Electronics Engineers, computer users group.

**Athletics. Intramural:** Basketball, soccer M, softball, tennis.

**Student services.** Career counseling, student employment services, financial aid counseling, placement for graduates, veterans' counselor. **Physically disabled:** Services for visually, hearing impaired.

**Contact.** Phone: (630) 953-2000 Toll-free number: (800) 346-5420
Fax: (630) 953-1236
Sandra Stack, Director of Admissions, DeVry University: Addison, 1221 North Swift Road, Addison, IL 60101-6106

## DeVry University: Chicago
**Chicago, Illinois**
**www.devry.edu**                                      **CB code: 1171**

- For-profit 4-year university
- Commuter campus in very large city
- 1,791 degree-seeking undergraduates: 45% part-time, 40% women, 37% African American, 6% Asian American, 32% Hispanic American, 1% Native American, 5% international
- Interview required

**General.** Founded in 1931. Regionally accredited. **Degrees:** 321 bachelor's, 170 associate awarded. **Location:** 6 miles from downtown. **Calendar:** Semester, extensive summer session. **Full-time faculty:** 40 total; 22% minority, 28% women. **Part-time faculty:** 53 total; 38% minority, 36% women.

**Freshman class profile.** 266 enrolled.

| Return as sophomores: | 57% | International: | 1% |
|---|---|---|---|
| Out-of-state: | 1% | | |

**Basis for selection.** Applicants must have high school diploma or equivalent, or degree from an accredited postsecondary institution, demonstrate proficiency in basic college-level skills through ACT scores or institution-administered placement examinations, and be at least 17 years of age. New students may enter at beginning of any semester. SAT/ACT tests are considered but not required for admission. If the applicant chooses not to submit either one, he/she must take a DeVry-administered admissions test.

**2007-2008 Annual costs.** Tuition/fees: $13,220. Books/supplies: $965. Personal expenses: $3,152.

**Financial aid.** All financial aid based on need.

**Application procedures. Admission:** No deadline. $50 fee. Application may be submitted online. Admission notification on a rolling basis. **Financial aid:** No deadline. FAFSA required. Applicants notified on a rolling basis.

**Academics. Special study options:** Accelerated study, distance learning. **Credit/placement by examination:** CLEP, institutional tests. **Support services:** Learning center, remedial instruction, tutoring.

**Majors. Business:** General, business admin. **Computer sciences:** Information systems, information technology, networking, systems analysis. **Engineering:** Biomedical, electrical. **Engineering technology:** Biomedical, computer, electrical.

**Most popular majors.** Business/marketing 52%, computer/information sciences 27%, engineering/engineering technologies 22%.

**Computing on campus.** 600 workstations in library, computer center. Online course registration, online library, helpline available.

**Student life. Freshman orientation:** Mandatory. **Housing:** Private apartments, student-plan housing, private rooms available. **Activities:** Student government, student newspaper, Muslim student association, Alpha Beta Gamma, Alpha Chi, Bible club, National Society of Black Engineers, Tau Alpha Pi.

**Student services.** Career counseling, student employment services, financial aid counseling, placement for graduates, veterans' counselor. **Physically disabled:** Services for visually, hearing impaired.

**Contact.** E-mail: admissions2@devry.edu
Phone: (773) 929-6550 Toll-free number: (800) 383-3879
Fax: (773) 697-2710
Christine Hierl, Director of Admissions, DeVry University: Chicago, 3300 North Campbell Avenue, Chicago, IL 60618-5994

## DeVry University: Online
### Oakbrook Terrace, Illinois
### www.devry.edu

- For-profit 4-year virtual college
- Small city
- 8,596 degree-seeking undergraduates: 68% part-time, 49% women, 24% African American, 2% Asian American, 7% Hispanic American, 1% Native American
- 3,512 degree-seeking graduate students
- 34% graduate within 6 years

**General.** Regionally accredited. **Degrees:** 903 bachelor's, 27 associate awarded; master's offered. **Calendar:** Semester. **Part-time faculty:** 3,111 total; 18% minority, 39% women.

**Freshman class profile.** 1,419 enrolled.

| Return as sophomores: | 35% | Out-of-state: | 91% |
|---|---|---|---|

**Basis for selection.** Applicants must have high school diploma or equivalent, or degree from accredited post-secondary institution, demonstrate proficiency in basic college-level skills through SAT or ACT scores or institution-administered placement examinations, and be at least 17 years of age.

**2007-2008 Annual costs.** Books/supplies: $1,300. Personal expenses: $5,082.

**Financial aid. Non-need-based:** Scholarships awarded for academics.

**Application procedures. Admission:** No deadline. $50 fee. Admission notification on a rolling basis. **Financial aid:** No deadline. FAFSA required. Applicants notified on a rolling basis.

**Academics. Special study options:** Accelerated study, distance learning. **Credit/placement by examination:** CLEP.

**Majors. Business:** Accounting/finance, business admin, e-commerce. **Computer sciences:** Networking, systems analysis. **Engineering:** Software.

**Most popular majors.** Business/marketing 91%, computer/information sciences 9%.

**Contact.** DeVry University: Online, One Tower Lane, Oakbrook Terrace, IL 60181

## DeVry University: Tinley Park
### Tinley Park, Illinois
### www.devry.edu
### CB code: 2818

- For-profit 4-year university
- Commuter campus in large town
- 1,059 degree-seeking undergraduates: 40% part-time, 29% women, 34% African American, 2% Asian American, 8% Hispanic American
- 252 degree-seeking graduate students
- Interview required

**General.** Regionally accredited. **Degrees:** 203 bachelor's, 23 associate awarded; master's offered. **Location:** 20 miles from Chicago. **Calendar:** Semester, extensive summer session. **Full-time faculty:** 35 total; 11% minority, 23% women. **Part-time faculty:** 85 total; 73% minority, 35% women.

**Freshman class profile.** 232 enrolled.

| Return as sophomores: | 57% | Out-of-state: | 19% |
|---|---|---|---|

**Basis for selection.** Applicants must have high school diploma or equivalent, or degree from an accredited postsecondary institution and demonstrate proficiency in basic college-level skills through test scores and/or institution-administered placement examinations, and be at least 17 years of age. New students may enter at the beginning of any semester. SAT/ACT tests are considered but not required for admission. If the applicant chooses not to submit either one, he/she must take a DeVry-administered admissions test.

**2007-2008 Annual costs.** Tuition/fees: $13,220. Books/supplies: $1,300. Personal expenses: $5,082.

**Financial aid.** All financial aid based on need.

**Application procedures. Admission:** No deadline. $50 fee. Application may be submitted online. Admission notification on a rolling basis. **Financial aid:** No deadline. FAFSA required. Applicants notified on a rolling basis.

**Academics. Special study options:** Accelerated study, distance learning. **Credit/placement by examination:** CLEP. **Support services:** Learning center, remedial instruction, tutoring.

**Majors. Business:** Business admin, human resources, management information systems. **Communications technology:** General. **Computer sciences:** Game design, information systems, networking, systems analysis. **Engineering:** Biomedical, computer, software. **Engineering technology:** Biomedical, computer, electrical. **Other:** Technical management.

**Most popular majors.** Business/marketing 54%, computer/information sciences 31%, engineering/engineering technologies 15%.

**Computing on campus.** 344 workstations in library, computer center. Online course registration, online library, helpline available.

**Student life. Freshman orientation:** Mandatory. **Housing:** Private apartments, student-plan housing, private rooms available. **Activities:** Student activities association, student leadership group, women in technology.

**Student services.** Career counseling, student employment services, financial aid counseling, placement for graduates, veterans' counselor. **Physically disabled:** Services for visually, hearing impaired.

**Contact.** Phone: (708) 342-3100 Toll-free number: (877) 305-8184
Fax: (708) 342-3505
Bruce Jones, Director of Admissions, DeVry University: Tinley Park, 18624 West Creek Drive, Tinley Park, IL 60477-6243

## Dominican University
### River Forest, Illinois
### www.dom.edu
### CB member
### CB code: 1667

- Private 4-year university and liberal arts college affiliated with Roman Catholic Church
- Residential campus in large town
- 1,531 degree-seeking undergraduates: 10% part-time, 69% women, 7% African American, 3% Asian American, 22% Hispanic American, 2% international
- 1,487 degree-seeking graduate students
- 85% of applicants admitted
- SAT or ACT (ACT writing optional), application essay required
- 61% graduate within 6 years; 42% enter graduate study

**General.** Founded in 1901. Regionally accredited. **Degrees:** 298 bachelor's awarded; master's offered. **Location:** 10 miles from Chicago. **Calendar:** Semester, extensive summer session. **Full-time faculty:** 124 total; 84% have terminal degrees, 15% minority, 57% women. **Part-time faculty:** 226 total; 25% have terminal degrees, 62% women. **Class size:** 67% < 20, 32% 20-39, less than 1% 40-49. **Special facilities:** Food science laboratory.

**Freshman class profile.** 1,265 applied, 1,077 admitted, 367 enrolled.

| Mid 50% test scores | | | |
|---|---|---|---|
| SAT critical reading: | 480-620 | **Rank in top quarter:** | 49% |
| SAT math: | 460-590 | **Rank in top tenth:** | 20% |
| SAT writing: | 480-610 | **End year in good standing:** | 95% |
| ACT composite: | 20-25 | **Return as sophomores:** | 77% |
| GPA 3.50 or higher: | 42% | **Out-of-state:** | 14% |
| GPA 3.0-3.49: | 27% | **Live on campus:** | 66% |
| GPA 2.0-2.99: | 31% | **International:** | 1% |

**Basis for selection.** Rank in upper half of class, 2.75 GPA, have ACT or SAT at or above national average, and 16 units of college prep work required. Interview recommended. **Homeschooled:** Transcript of courses and grades required.

**High school preparation.** 16 units required. Required and recommended units include English 4, mathematics 3, social studies 1, history 2, science 3 (laboratory 2) and foreign language 2. 14 credits must be in English, math, social science, laboratory science, and foreign languages.

**2007-2008 Annual costs.** Tuition/fees: $22,450. Room/board: $7,000. Books/supplies: $1,000. Personal expenses: $900.

**2007-2008 Financial aid. Need-based:** 311 full-time freshmen applied for aid; 286 were judged to have need; 285 of these received aid. Average need met was 85%. Average scholarship/grant was $14,688; average loan $3,249. 74% of total undergraduate aid awarded as scholarships/grants, 26% as loans/jobs. **Non-need-based:** Scholarships awarded for academics, alumni affiliation, leadership.

**Application procedures. Admission:** Priority date 6/1; no deadline. $25 fee, may be waived for applicants with need. Application may be submitted online. Admission notification on a rolling basis beginning on or about 10/1. Must reply by May 1 or within 2 week(s) if notified thereafter. **Financial aid:** Priority date 6/1; no closing date. FAFSA required. Applicants notified on a rolling basis starting 2/15; must reply within 2 week(s) of notification.

**Academics. Special study options:** Accelerated study, combined bachelor's/graduate degree, cross-registration, distance learning, double major, dual enrollment of high school students, ESL, honors, independent study, internships, liberal arts/career combination, study abroad, teacher certification program, Washington semester. 2+2 nursing with Rush University, 5-year BA/BS engineering program with Illinois Institute of Technology, license preparation in gerontology on-campus, 5 year program in occupational therapy with Rush University leading to master's degree. **Credit/placement by examination:** AP, CLEP, IB, institutional tests. 28 credit hours maximum toward bachelor's degree. **Support services:** Learning center, pre-admission summer program, reduced course load, remedial instruction, study skills assistance, tutoring, writing center.

**Majors. Area/ethnic studies:** African-American, American. **Biology:** General, biochemistry. **Business:** Accounting, business admin, communications, fashion, international. **Communications:** General, journalism. **Computer sciences:** General, computer science, information systems. **Conservation:** Environmental science, environmental studies. **Education:** Early childhood. **Engineering:** Architectural, chemical, civil, computer, electrical, mechanical. **English:** English lit, technical writing. **Family/consumer sciences:** Food/nutrition. **Foreign languages:** French, Italian, Spanish. **Health:** Predental, premedicine, prenursing, prepharmacy, preveterinary, substance abuse counseling. **History:** General. **Interdisciplinary:** Gerontology, math/computer science, nutrition sciences. **Math:** General. **Philosophy/religion:** Philosophy. **Physical sciences:** Chemistry. **Psychology:** General. **Social sciences:** General, criminology, economics, international relations, political science, sociology. **Theology:** Theology. **Visual/performing arts:** Art, art history/conservation, commercial/advertising art, dramatic, fashion design, photography, studio arts.

**Most popular majors.** Business/marketing 31%, interdisciplinary studies 6%, psychology 8%, social sciences 16%, visual/performing arts 8%.

**Computing on campus.** 309 workstations in dormitories, library, computer center, student center. Dormitories wired for high-speed internet access and linked to campus network. Commuter students can connect to campus network. Online course registration, online library, helpline, wireless network available.

**Student life. Freshman orientation:** Mandatory. Preregistration for classes offered. Two-day program with overnight on campus. **Housing:** Guaranteed on-campus for freshmen. Coed dorms, substance-free housing available. $100 partly refundable deposit. **Activities:** Campus ministries, choral groups, dance, drama, international student organizations, literary magazine, musical theater, student government, student newspaper, Organization of Latino Americans, social service organization, business club, Italian club, black student union, psychology club, education club, gospel choir.

**Athletics.** NCAA. **Intercollegiate:** Baseball M, basketball, cross-country, soccer, softball W, tennis, volleyball W. **Intramural:** Basketball, bowling, cheerleading, racquetball, soccer, softball W, table tennis, volleyball, water polo. **Team name:** Stars.

**Student services.** Adult student services, alcohol/substance abuse counseling, career counseling, student employment services, financial aid counseling, health services, minority student services, on-campus daycare, personal counseling, placement for graduates, veterans' counselor. **Physically disabled:** Services for visually, hearing impaired.

**Contact.** E-mail: domadmis@dom.edu
Phone: (708) 524-6800 Toll-free number: (800) 828-8475
Fax: (708) 524-6864
Glenn Hamilton, Director of Freshman Admission, Dominican University, 7900 West Division Street, River Forest, IL 60305-1099

## East-West University
### Chicago, Illinois
www.eastwest.edu                    CB code: 0798

- ◆ Private 4-year university
- ◆ Commuter campus in very large city
- ◆ 1,150 degree-seeking undergraduates: 2% part-time, 65% women
- ◆ Interview required

**General.** Founded in 1978. Regionally accredited. **Degrees:** 69 bachelor's, 61 associate awarded. **Calendar:** Quarter, limited summer session. **Full-time faculty:** 14 total; 100% have terminal degrees, 57% minority, 43% women. **Part-time faculty:** 93 total; 100% have terminal degrees, 56% minority, 46% women.

**Freshman class profile.**

| | | | |
|---|---|---|---|
| Out-of-state: | 10% | **International:** | 7% |

**Basis for selection.** Open admission.

**2007-2008 Annual costs.** Tuition/fees: $12,825. Books/supplies: $1,000. Personal expenses: $1,800.

**Financial aid. Non-need-based:** Scholarships awarded for academics. **Additional information:** Foreign students eligible for institutional scholarship.

**Application procedures. Admission:** No deadline. $30 fee, may be waived for applicants with need. Admission notification on a rolling basis. **Financial aid:** No deadline. FAFSA required. Applicants notified on a rolling basis starting 1/4; must reply within 4 week(s) of notification.

**Academics. Special study options:** Cooperative education, double major, ESL, honors, independent study, internships. **Credit/placement by examination:** CLEP, institutional tests. Interview recommended for placement. **Support services:** Tutoring.

**Majors. Business:** Business admin. **Communications:** General. **Computer sciences:** General. **Engineering technology:** Electrical. **Liberal arts:** Arts/sciences. **Math:** General.

**Most popular majors.** Business/marketing 32%, computer/information sciences 11%, engineering/engineering technologies 16%, liberal arts 40%.

**Computing on campus.** 10 workstations in computer center. Online library available.

**Student life. Freshman orientation:** Available. **Activities:** Drama, student government, student newspaper.

**Athletics. Team name:** Phantom.

**Student services.** Career counseling.

**Contact.** E-mail: seeyou@eastwest.edu
Phone: (312) 939-0111 Toll-free number: (877) 398-9376
Fax: (312) 939-0083
William Link, Director of Admissions, East-West University, 816 South Michigan Avenue, Chicago, IL 60605

## Eastern Illinois University
### Charleston, Illinois
www.eiu.edu                    CB code: 1199

- ◆ Public 4-year university and teachers college
- ◆ Residential campus in large town

- 10,152 degree-seeking undergraduates: 9% part-time, 58% women, 9% African American, 1% Asian American, 3% Hispanic American
- 1,671 degree-seeking graduate students
- 71% of applicants admitted
- SAT or ACT (ACT writing optional) required
- 61% graduate within 6 years

**General.** Founded in 1895. Regionally accredited. Off-campus sites in Arlington Heights, Bridgeview, Carterville, Centralia, Champaign, Danville, Effingham, Olney, River Grove, Mattoon, Robinson and Vandalia. **Degrees:** 2,259 bachelor's awarded; master's offered. **ROTC:** Army. **Location:** 180 miles from Chicago, 135 miles from St. Louis. **Calendar:** Semester, limited summer session. **Full-time faculty:** 660 total; 66% have terminal degrees, 10% minority, 46% women. **Part-time faculty:** 106 total; 9% have terminal degrees, 7% minority, 64% women. **Class size:** 32% < 20, 58% 20-39, 6% 40-49, 2% 50-99, 1% >100. **Special facilities:** Arts center, greenhouse, electron microscope, observatory.

**Freshman class profile.** 7,149 applied, 5,071 admitted, 1,647 enrolled.

| Mid 50% test scores | | | |
|---|---|---|---|
| ACT composite: | 19-23 | Return as sophomores: | 82% |
| GPA 3.50 or higher: | 22% | Out-of-state: | 1% |
| GPA 3.0-3.49: | 30% | Live on campus: | 97% |
| GPA 2.0-2.99: | 48% | International: | 1% |
| Rank in top quarter: | 29% | Fraternities: | 11% |
| Rank in top tenth: | 10% | Sororities: | 15% |

**Basis for selection.** Applicants must be in top quarter of class with 18 ACT, in top half of class with 19 ACT, or be in upper three-quarters of class with 22 ACT. Gateway admissions program for students with at least 14 ACT and 2.0 GPA. Audition required of music majors. **Homeschooled:** GED requirement may be waived with acceptable ACT score for students who present transcript of all courses completed with grades listed for each class.

**High school preparation.** 15 units required. Required and recommended units include English 4, mathematics 3, social studies 3, science 3 (laboratory 3), foreign language 2 and academic electives 2. Significant science lab experience required.

**2007-2008 Annual costs.** Tuition/fees: $7,990; $19,654 out-of-state. New students have a guaranteed tuition rate for 4 years. Room/board: $7,124. Books/supplies: $120. Personal expenses: $1,500.

**2007-2008 Financial aid.** **Need-based:** 1,409 full-time freshmen applied for aid; 864 were judged to have need; 829 of these received aid. Average need met was 75%. Average scholarship/grant was $2,651; average loan $3,016. 44% of total undergraduate aid awarded as scholarships/grants, 56% as loans/jobs. **Non-need-based:** Awarded to 1,632 full-time undergraduates, including 379 freshmen. Scholarships awarded for academics, art, athletics, leadership, music/drama, ROTC.

**Application procedures.** **Admission:** No deadline. $30 fee, may be waived for applicants with need. Application may be submitted online. Admission notification on a rolling basis. Consult university for possible early cut-off date. **Financial aid:** Priority date 3/1; no closing date. FAFSA required. Applicants notified on a rolling basis starting 3/1; must reply within 2 week(s) of notification.

**Academics.** **Special study options:** Distance learning, double major, dual enrollment of high school students, exchange student, honors, independent study, internships, study abroad, teacher certification program. Cooperative program in engineering with University of Illinois. **Credit/placement by examination:** AP, CLEP, ACT, institutional tests. **Support services:** Learning center, reduced course load, study skills assistance, tutoring, writing center.

**Majors.** **Area/ethnic studies:** African-American. **Biology:** General. **Business:** Accounting, business admin, finance, management science, marketing. **Communications:** Journalism. **Education:** Early childhood, elementary, health, physical, science, social science, special, voc/tech. **Engineering:** General. **Engineering technology:** Industrial. **English:** English lit, speech/rhetoric. **Family/consumer sciences:** General. **Foreign languages:** General. **Health:** Clinical lab science, communication disorders. **History:** General. **Interdisciplinary:** Math/computer science. **Liberal arts:** Arts/sciences. **Math:** General. **Parks/recreation:** Facilities management. **Philosophy/religion:** Philosophy. **Physical sciences:** Chemistry, geology, physics. **Psychology:** General. **Social sciences:** Economics, geography, political science, sociology. **Visual/performing arts:** Art, dramatic.

**Most popular majors.** Business/marketing 13%, education 26%, English 10%, family/consumer sciences 7%, liberal arts 8%, psychology 6%, social sciences 7%.

**Computing on campus.** 909 workstations in dormitories, library, computer center. Dormitories wired for high-speed internet access and linked to campus network. Commuter students can connect to campus network. Online course registration, helpline, student web hosting, wireless network available.

**Student life.** **Freshman orientation:** Mandatory. Preregistration for classes offered. All day sessions held on various dates from May-August. **Housing:** Guaranteed on-campus for freshmen. Coed dorms, single-sex dorms, special housing for disabled, apartments, fraternity/sorority housing, substance-free housing available. $50 partly refundable deposit. Quiet study floors available. **Activities:** Bands, choral groups, dance, drama, literary magazine, music ensembles, musical theater, radio station, student government, student newspaper, symphony orchestra, TV station, College Democrats, Republicans, Christian Campus Fellowship, Newman Catholic center, Wesley Foundation, unity gospel choir, black student union, Epsilon Sigma Alpha, Blue Crew.

**Athletics.** NCAA. **Intercollegiate:** Baseball M, basketball, cross-country, diving, football (tackle) M, golf, rugby W, soccer, softball W, swimming, tennis, track and field, volleyball W. **Intramural:** Badminton, basketball, bowling, football (non-tackle), racquetball, soccer, softball, table tennis, tennis, volleyball, weight lifting. **Team name:** Panthers.

**Student services.** Adult student services, alcohol/substance abuse counseling, career counseling, services for economically disadvantaged, student employment services, health services, legal services, minority student services, personal counseling, placement for graduates, veterans' counselor, women's services. **Physically disabled:** Services for visually, speech, hearing impaired.

**Contact.** E-mail: admissions@eiu.edu
Phone: (217) 581-2223 Toll-free number: (877) 581-2348
Fax: (217) 581-7060
Brenda Major, Director of Admissions, Eastern Illinois University, 600 Lincoln Avenue, Charleston, IL 61920-3011

---

## Elmhurst College
**Elmhurst, Illinois**
www.elmhurst.edu

**CB member**
**CB code: 1204**

- Private 4-year liberal arts college affiliated with United Church of Christ
- Commuter campus in large town
- 2,808 degree-seeking undergraduates: 9% part-time, 64% women
- 143 degree-seeking graduate students
- SAT or ACT (ACT writing optional) required

**General.** Founded in 1871. Regionally accredited. **Degrees:** 690 bachelor's awarded; master's offered. **ROTC:** Army, Air Force. **Location:** 15 miles from Chicago. **Calendar:** 4-1-4, limited summer session. **Full-time faculty:** 121 total; 85% have terminal degrees, 8% minority, 47% women. **Part-time faculty:** 192 total; 23% have terminal degrees, 7% minority, 50% women. **Class size:** 60% < 20, 40% 20-39, less than 1% 40-49, less than 1% 50-99. **Special facilities:** 2 nuclear accelerators, 4 electron microscopes, collection of Impressionist art, computer science and technology center, media center, sound studio, greenhouse.

**Freshman class profile.** 508 enrolled.

| Mid 50% test scores | | | |
|---|---|---|---|
| SAT critical reading: | 470-630 | Out-of-state: | 12% |
| SAT math: | 480-620 | Live on campus: | 61% |
| SAT writing: | 480-630 | International: | 1% |
| ACT composite: | 22-26 | Fraternities: | 17% |
| | | Sororities: | 20% |

**Basis for selection.** School achievement record, including grades and course levels, most important, followed by test scores. Applicants should rank in top half of class. Activities and counselor recommendations also important. Interview and essay recommended for all applicants, required of academically marginal applicants. Audition required of music majors. Portfolio recommended for art majors. **Homeschooled:** Interview strongly recommended.

**High school preparation.** 16 units required; 21 recommended. Required and recommended units include English 4, mathematics 2-3, social studies 2-3, history 1-2, science 2-3 (laboratory 2-3), foreign language 1-2 and academic electives 4. Chemistry required for nursing applicants. 3 mathematics required for most business administration and computer-related specialties applicants.

**2007-2008 Annual costs.** Tuition/fees: $24,760. Room/board: $8,064. Books/supplies: $1,000. Personal expenses: $1,200.

**2006-2007 Financial aid. Need-based:** 413 full-time freshmen applied for aid; 345 were judged to have need; 345 of these received aid. Average need met was 90%. Average scholarship/grant was $8,509; average loan $3,007. 78% of total undergraduate aid awarded as scholarships/grants, 22% as loans/jobs. **Non-need-based:** Awarded to 811 full-time undergraduates, including 201 freshmen. Scholarships awarded for academics, alumni affiliation, art, minority status, music/drama, religious affiliation, state residency. **Additional information:** Must be admitted to the college by 1/15 to be considered for scholarships.

**Application procedures. Admission:** Priority date 4/15; no deadline. No application fee. Application may be submitted online. Admission notification on a rolling basis beginning on or about 11/1. Must reply by May 1 or within 2 week(s) if notified thereafter. **Financial aid:** Priority date 4/15; no closing date. FAFSA required. Applicants notified on a rolling basis starting 2/21; must reply within 3 week(s) of notification.

**Academics. Special study options:** Accelerated study, cooperative education, double major, dual enrollment of high school students, honors, independent study, internships, liberal arts/career combination, study abroad, teacher certification program, Washington semester. 3+2 engineering with Illinois Institute of Technology, University of Illinois at Urbana-Champaign, and Washington University (MO). **Credit/placement by examination:** AP, CLEP, IB, institutional tests. 48 credit hours maximum toward bachelor's degree. **Support services:** Learning center, pre-admission summer program, reduced course load, study skills assistance, tutoring.

**Majors. Area/ethnic studies:** American. **Biology:** General. **Business:** Accounting, business admin, finance, international, logistics, marketing. **Communications:** General. **Computer sciences:** Computer science, information systems. **Conservation:** Management/policy. **Education:** General, agricultural, art, biology, chemistry, early childhood, elementary, English, French, German, history, kindergarten/preschool, mathematics, music, physical, physics, secondary, Spanish, special. **English:** English lit. **Foreign languages:** French, German, Spanish. **Health:** Nursing (RN), predental, premedicine, prepharmacy, preveterinary, speech pathology. **History:** General. **Legal studies:** Prelaw. **Liberal arts:** Arts/sciences. **Math:** General. **Parks/recreation:** Exercise sciences, health/fitness, sports admin. **Philosophy/religion:** Philosophy. **Physical sciences:** Chemistry, physics. **Psychology:** General. **Social sciences:** Criminology, economics, geography, political science, sociology, urban studies. **Theology:** Preministerial, theology. **Visual/performing arts:** Art, dramatic, music management.

**Most popular majors.** Business/marketing 22%, communications/journalism 6%, education 18%, English 6%, health sciences 12%, psychology 7%, social sciences 6%, visual/performing arts 6%.

**Computing on campus.** 440 workstations in library, computer center, student center. Dormitories wired for high-speed internet access and linked to campus network. Commuter students can connect to campus network. Online library, helpline, repair service, wireless network available.

**Student life. Freshman orientation:** Mandatory. Three-day program held immediately prior to term. **Policies:** Each residence hall is self-governing. **Housing:** Coed dorms, apartments available. $150 deposit, deadline 4/1. **Activities:** Bands, campus ministries, choral groups, drama, literary magazine, music ensembles, musical theater, radio station, student government, student newspaper, over 90 organizations.

**Athletics.** NCAA. **Intercollegiate:** Baseball M, basketball, bowling W, cross-country, football (tackle) M, golf, soccer, softball W, tennis, track and field, volleyball W, wrestling M. **Intramural:** Basketball, football (tackle) M, golf, racquetball, softball, volleyball. **Team name:** Blue Jays.

**Student services.** Adult student services, career counseling, student employment services, financial aid counseling, health services, minority student services, on-campus daycare, personal counseling, placement for graduates.

**Contact.** E-mail: admit@elmhurst.edu
Phone: (630) 617-3400 Toll-free number: (800) 697-1871
Fax: (630) 617-5501
Stephanie Levenson, Director of Admission, Elmhurst College, 190 South Prospect Avenue, Elmhurst, IL 60126-3296

---

## Eureka College

**Eureka, Illinois**
www.eureka.edu

**CB member**
**CB code: 1206**

- Private 4-year liberal arts college affiliated with Christian Church (Disciples of Christ)
- Residential campus in small town
- 685 degree-seeking undergraduates
- 73% of applicants admitted
- SAT or ACT (ACT writing recommended) required

---

**General.** Founded in 1855. Regionally accredited. **Degrees:** 133 bachelor's awarded. **Location:** 140 miles from Chicago. **Calendar:** Semester, limited summer session. **Full-time faculty:** 43 total. **Part-time faculty:** 24 total. **Class size:** 64% < 20, 36% 20-39. **Special facilities:** Ronald Reagan Museum, peace garden, lilac arboretum, labyrinth, fitness center.

**Freshman class profile.** 762 applied, 553 admitted, 123 enrolled.

| Mid 50% test scores | | Rank in top tenth: | 23% |
|---|---|---|---|
| ACT composite: | 19-27 | Out-of-state: | 4% |
| Rank in top quarter: | 56% | Live on campus: | 90% |

**Basis for selection.** Class rank, high school GPA, ACT scores, and high school curriculum most important. Recommendations and interviews also important. Audition required for music and drama scholarships. Portfolio required for art scholarship. **Homeschooled:** Interview required.

**High school preparation.** 14 units recommended. Recommended units include English 4, mathematics 3, social studies 3, science 2 and foreign language 2.

**2007-2008 Annual costs.** Tuition/fees: $15,270. Room/board: $6,720. Books/supplies: $1,000. Personal expenses: $510.

**Financial aid. Non-need-based:** Scholarships awarded for academics, alumni affiliation, art, leadership, music/drama, religious affiliation.

**Application procedures. Admission:** Priority date 5/1; deadline 8/10 (postmark date). No application fee. Application may be submitted online. Admission notification on a rolling basis. Must reply by May 1 or within 3 week(s) if notified thereafter. **Financial aid:** Priority date 4/15; no closing date. FAFSA required. Applicants notified on a rolling basis starting 2/15; must reply by 5/1 or within 3 week(s) of notification.

**Academics. Special study options:** Cooperative education, double major, dual enrollment of high school students, honors, independent study, internships, liberal arts/career combination, student-designed major, study abroad, teacher certification program, Washington semester. Students who began as freshmen, have a record of leadership and service, and hold a 3.5 GPA at the end of their sophomore year qualify for a mentorship paid for by the college. **Credit/placement by examination:** AP, CLEP, institutional tests. **Support services:** Learning center, reduced course load, remedial instruction, study skills assistance, tutoring, writing center.

**Honors college/program.** Admitted by invitation, includes advanced and special classes, advanced general education requirements along with thesis preparation and presentation, honors seminars on special topics.

**Majors. Biology:** General, environmental. **Business:** General, accounting, business admin, finance, management information systems, marketing. **Communications:** General, media studies, public relations. **Computer sciences:** General, computer science. **Education:** General, elementary, middle, multilevel teacher, secondary, special. **Engineering:** General. **English:** Composition, creative writing, English lit. **Health:** Predental, premedicine, prenursing, preveterinary. **History:** General. **Interdisciplinary:** Math/computer science. **Legal studies:** Prelaw. **Liberal arts:** Arts/sciences. **Math:** General. **Philosophy/religion:** Philosophy, religion. **Physical sciences:** Chemistry. **Protective services:** Law enforcement admin. **Psychology:** General. **Social sciences:** Political science. **Visual/performing arts:** Art, arts management, dramatic, music performance. **Other:** Leadership.

**Computing on campus.** 50 workstations in dormitories, library, computer center, student center. Dormitories wired for high-speed internet access and linked to campus network. Commuter students can connect to campus network. Online library, helpline, repair service available.

**Student life. Freshman orientation:** Mandatory. Preregistration for classes offered. Orientation for new students held at start of school year. **Policies:** All single students under 24 not living with parents required to live on campus. **Housing:** Guaranteed on-campus for all undergraduates. Coed dorms, single-sex dorms, special housing for disabled, fraternity/sorority housing, substance-free housing available. $150 fully refundable deposit, deadline 8/14. **Activities:** Bands, choral groups, dance, drama, film society, literary magazine, music ensembles, musical theater, student government, student newspaper, Disciples on Campus, PRIDE, Young Republicans, Campus Democrats, Catholic Salve Regina Newman Center, Campus Crusade for Christ, Black student union, Habitat for Humanity, Student Foundation, International Healthcare Development Program.

**Athletics.** NCAA. **Intercollegiate:** Baseball M, basketball, cross-country, diving, football (tackle) M, golf, soccer, softball W, swimming, tennis, track and field, volleyball W. **Intramural:** Badminton, basketball, bowling, football (non-tackle), golf, softball, swimming, table tennis, tennis, volleyball. **Team name:** Red Devils.

**Student services.** Adult student services, alcohol/substance abuse counseling, campus ministries, career counseling, student employment services,

financial aid counseling, health services, personal counseling, placement for graduates.

**Contact.** E-mail: admissions@eureka.edu
Phone: (309) 467-6350 Toll-free number: (888) 438-7352
Fax: (309) 467-6576
Kurt Krile, Dean of Admissions and Financial Aid, Eureka College, 300 East College Avenue, Eureka, IL 61530-1500

## Governors State University
**University Park, Illinois**
**www.govst.edu**                         CB code: 0807

- Public two-year upper-division university
- Commuter campus in large town

**General.** Founded in 1969. Regionally accredited. **Degrees:** 908 bachelor's awarded; master's, doctoral offered. **Articulation:** Agreements with Prairie State College, Joliet Junior College, Kankakee CC, Moraine Valley CC, South Suburban College of Cook County, College of DuPage, Morton College, City Colleges of Chicago, Waubonsee CC, Triton College, Parkland College, College of Lake County, Illinois Valley College, Ivy Tech State College (IN). **ROTC:** Army, Air Force. **Location:** 30 miles from Chicago. **Calendar:** Trimester, extensive summer session. **Full-time faculty:** 202 total. **Part-time faculty:** 201 total. **Special facilities:** 750-acre campus, nature trails, 6 lakes, sculpture park, prairie restoration.

**Student profile.** 2,370 degree-seeking undergraduates, 2,591 degree-seeking graduate students. 63% transferred from two-year, 37% transferred from four-year institutions.

| | | | |
|---|---|---|---|
| Women: | 71% | Part-time: | 63% |
| African American: | 36% | Out-of-state: | 3% |
| Asian American: | 1% | 25 or older: | 61% |
| Hispanic American: | 7% | | |

**Basis for selection.** College transcript required. Minimum 60 semester hours or associate degree required. Additional special criteria for selected undergraduate majors. Applicants notified of decisions on rolling basis. Special admissions for applicants not meeting stated requirements available by petition. Institutional examinations required of nursing applicants. ACT/PEP required of nursing applicants from diploma program. Transfer accepted as juniors, seniors.

**2007-2008 Annual costs.** Tuition/fees: $5,966; $16,706 out-of-state. Books/supplies: $700. Personal expenses: $800.

**Financial aid.** **Non-need-based:** Scholarships awarded for academics, ROTC, state residency.

**Application procedures.** **Admission:** Priority date 6/1. $50 fee, may be waived for applicants with need. Application may be submitted online. **Financial aid:** No aid for second bachelor's or second master's degree. FAFSA required.

**Academics.** **Special study options:** Distance learning, dual enrollment of high school students, external degree, honors, independent study, internships, student-designed major, study abroad, teacher certification program, weekend college. Dual enrollment with several community colleges. **Credit/placement by examination:** AP, CLEP. 60 credit hours maximum toward bachelor's degree.

**Majors.** **Biology:** General. **Business:** Accounting, business admin, finance, human resources, international, international marketing, management information systems. **Communications:** General, broadcast journalism, journalism. **Computer sciences:** General, computer science. **Education:** Biology, chemistry, early childhood, elementary, English, mathematics. **English:** English lit. **Health:** Health care admin, preop/surgical nursing, speech pathology. **Liberal arts:** Arts/sciences. **Math:** General. **Physical sciences:** Chemistry. **Protective services:** Criminal justice. **Psychology:** General. **Public administration:** General, social work. **Social sciences:** General. **Visual/performing arts:** Art, art history/conservation.

**Computing on campus.** 280 workstations in library, computer center, student center. Commuter students can connect to campus network. Online library, helpline available.

**Student life.** **Activities:** Choral groups, film society, international student organizations, literary magazine, student government, student newspaper, TV station, veterans organization, Union of African Peoples, naturalist club, 30-plus cocurricular professional service organizations.

**Athletics.** **Intramural:** Badminton, basketball, handball, racquetball, skiing, soccer, softball, table tennis, volleyball.

**Student services.** Career counseling, student employment services, financial aid counseling, minority student services, on-campus daycare, personal counseling, placement for graduates, veterans' counselor. **Physically disabled:** Services for visually, speech, hearing impaired.

**Contact.** Phone: (708) 534-4490 Fax: (708) 534-1640
Director of Admissions, Governors State University, One University Parkway, University Park, IL 60466

## Greenville College
**Greenville, Illinois**
**www.greenville.edu**                        CB code: 1256

- Private 4-year liberal arts college affiliated with Free Methodist Church of North America
- Residential campus in small town
- 1,353 degree-seeking undergraduates: 2% part-time, 54% women, 7% African American, 1% Asian American, 2% Hispanic American, 1% Native American, 1% international
- 151 degree-seeking graduate students
- 81% of applicants admitted
- SAT or ACT (ACT writing optional), application essay required
- 54% graduate within 6 years

**General.** Founded in 1892. Regionally accredited. Academic and Christian values emphasized. **Degrees:** 334 bachelor's awarded; master's offered. **Location:** 50 miles from St. Louis, 190 miles from Indianapolis. **Calendar:** 4-1-4, limited summer session. **Full-time faculty:** 59 total; 71% have terminal degrees, 7% minority, 30% women. **Part-time faculty:** 83 total; 51% women. **Class size:** 60% < 20, 29% 20-39, 4% 40-49, 7% 50-99, less than 1% >100. **Special facilities:** Sculpture collection, Frank Lloyd Wright architectural drawings, 140 acre field station and nature preserve, observatory, environmental education center.

**Freshman class profile.** 942 applied, 760 admitted, 307 enrolled.

| Mid 50% test scores | | | |
|---|---|---|---|
| SAT critical reading: | 430-590 | Rank in top quarter: | 39% |
| SAT math: | 440-580 | Rank in top tenth: | 15% |
| SAT writing: | 430-570 | End year in good standing: | 83% |
| ACT composite: | 20-26 | Return as sophomores: | 73% |
| GPA 3.50 or higher: | 38% | Out-of-state: | 42% |
| GPA 3.0-3.49: | 30% | Live on campus: | 96% |
| GPA 2.0-2.99: | 31% | International: | 1% |

**Basis for selection.** Secondary school record, class rank, standardized test scores, essay, character/personal qualities, and religious affiliation or commitment all very important. Recommendations, extracurricular activities, talent/ability and alumni/ae relation considered. Interview required of academically weak applicants. Audition recommended for music majors. **Homeschooled:** Transcript of courses and grades required.

**High school preparation.** 11 units recommended. Recommended units include English 4, mathematics 2, history 1, science 1 (laboratory 1) and foreign language 2. Math recommendation includes algebra and geometry.

**2008-2009 Annual costs.** Tuition/fees: $19,428. Room/board: $6,568. Books/supplies: $900. Personal expenses: $1,572.

**2006-2007 Financial aid.** **Need-based:** 276 full-time freshmen applied for aid; 244 were judged to have need; 244 of these received aid. Average need met was 81%. Average scholarship/grant was $11,664; average loan $3,336. 66% of total undergraduate aid awarded as scholarships/grants, 34% as loans/jobs. **Non-need-based:** Awarded to 228 full-time undergraduates, including 68 freshmen. Scholarships awarded for academics, alumni affiliation, art, leadership, minority status, music/drama, religious affiliation, state residency.

**Application procedures.** **Admission:** Closing date 8/15. $25 fee, may be waived for applicants with need. Application may be submitted online. Admission notification on a rolling basis beginning on or about 10/15. Housing deposit is not refundable after May 1st. **Financial aid:** Priority date 5/1; no closing date. FAFSA required. Applicants notified on a rolling basis starting 3/15; must reply within 3 week(s) of notification.

**Academics.** **Special study options:** Accelerated study, cooperative education, cross-registration, double major, external degree, honors, independent study, internships, liberal arts/career combination, semester at sea, student-designed major, study abroad, teacher certification program, urban semester, Washington semester. **Credit/placement by examination:** AP, CLEP, IB, SAT, ACT, institutional tests. 32 credit hours maximum toward bachelor's degree. **Support services:** Learning center, reduced course load, remedial instruction, study skills assistance, tutoring.

**Majors. Biology:** General, environmental. **Business:** Accounting, business admin, management information systems, marketing, organizational behavior. **Communications:** Media studies, public relations. **Computer sciences:** General. **Education:** Biology, chemistry, early childhood, elementary, English, history, mathematics, music, physical, physics, Spanish, special. **English:** English lit, speech/rhetoric. **Foreign languages:** Spanish. **Health:** Predental, premedicine, prenursing, preveterinary. **History:** General. **Interdisciplinary:** Global studies. **Liberal arts:** Arts/sciences. **Math:** General. **Parks/recreation:** General, exercise sciences, sports admin. **Philosophy/religion:** Philosophy, religion. **Physical sciences:** Chemistry, physics. **Protective services:** Law enforcement admin. **Psychology:** General. **Public administration:** Social work. **Social sciences:** Sociology. **Theology:** Pastoral counseling, youth ministry. **Visual/performing arts:** Art, dramatic, music management.

**Most popular majors.** Biology 6%, business/marketing 39%, education 26%.

**Computing on campus.** 100 workstations in library, computer center. Dormitories wired for high-speed internet access and linked to campus network. Commuter students can connect to campus network. Online library, helpline, repair service, wireless network available.

**Student life. Freshman orientation:** Mandatory. Preregistration for classes offered. Service project conducted over orientation weekend. **Policies:** Signed statements of Christian values and academic honesty requested. Required chapel. All single students not living at home must live in college housing. Religious observance required. **Housing:** Guaranteed on-campus for all undergraduates. Single-sex dorms, apartments, substance-free housing available. $200 deposit. Upper division students may live in college-owned houses. **Activities:** Bands, campus ministries, choral groups, drama, music ensembles, musical theater, radio station, student government, student newspaper, Habitat for Humanity, Fellowship of Christian Athletes, campus activities board, student outreach, Agape music festival, Circle K, E-cafe, Mosaic, Young Republicans, Big Brother/Big Sister.

**Athletics.** NCAA, NCCAA. **Intercollegiate:** Baseball M, basketball, cross-country, football (tackle) M, soccer, softball W, tennis, track and field, volleyball W. **Intramural:** Badminton, basketball, football (non-tackle), soccer, softball, table tennis, tennis, volleyball. **Team name:** Panthers.

**Student services.** Adult student services, career counseling, student employment services, financial aid counseling, personal counseling, placement for graduates.

**Contact.** E-mail: admissions@greenville.edu
Phone: (618) 664-7100 Toll-free number: (800) 345-4440
Fax: (618) 664-9841
Michael Ritter, Dean of Admissions, Greenville College, 315 East College Avenue, Greenville, IL 62246-0159

## Harrington College of Design
**Chicago, Illinois**
www.harringtoncollege.com                  **CB code: 0940**

- For-profit 4-year visual arts college
- Commuter campus in very large city

**General.** Founded in 1931. Accredited by ACICS. **Location:** Downtown. **Calendar:** Semester.

**Annual costs/financial aid.** Tuition/fees (2007-2008): $18,760. Required fees vary depending on a program. Books/supplies: $850. Personal expenses: $2,500. Need-based financial aid available to full-time and part-time students.

**Contact.** Phone: (312) 939-4975
Vice President of Admissions, 200 West Madison Avenue, Chicago, IL 60606

## Hebrew Theological College
**Skokie, Illinois**
www.htc.edu                  **CB code: 0817**

- Private 4-year rabbinical college
- Residential campus in small city

**General.** Regionally accredited. **Calendar:** Semester.

**Annual costs/financial aid.** Tuition/fees (2007-2008): $16,935. Room/board: $8,035.

**Contact.** Phone: (847) 982-2500
7135 North Carpenter Road, Skokie, IL 60077

## Illinois College
**Jacksonville, Illinois**                  **CB member**
www.ic.edu                  **CB code: 1315**

- Private 4-year liberal arts college affiliated with United Church of Christ and Presbyterian Church (USA)
- Residential campus in large town
- 990 degree-seeking undergraduates: 1% part-time, 52% women, 3% African American, 1% Asian American, 1% Hispanic American, 1% Native American, 2% international
- 1,014 graduate students
- 91% of applicants admitted
- SAT or ACT (ACT writing optional) required
- 59% graduate within 6 years; 33% enter graduate study

**General.** Founded in 1829. Regionally accredited. New England style quad and architecture. **Degrees:** 233 bachelor's awarded. **Location:** 30 miles from Springfield, 90 miles from St. Louis. **Calendar:** Semester, limited summer session. **Full-time faculty:** 72 total; 81% have terminal degrees, 10% minority, 42% women. **Part-time faculty:** 17 total; 59% have terminal degrees, 6% minority, 47% women. **Class size:** 62% < 20, 35% 20-39, 1% 40-49, 2% 50-99. **Special facilities:** Biology station, observatory.

**Freshman class profile.** 917 applied, 838 admitted, 260 enrolled.

| Mid 50% test scores | | | |
|---|---|---|---|
| SAT critical reading: | 510-580 | GPA 2.0-2.99: | 29% |
| SAT math: | 490-640 | Rank in top quarter: | 46% |
| SAT writing: | 460-630 | Rank in top tenth: | 21% |
| ACT composite: | 21-26 | Return as sophomores: | 80% |
| GPA 3.50 or higher: | 37% | Out-of-state: | 7% |
| GPA 3.0-3.49: | 34% | Live on campus: | 91% |

**Basis for selection.** Test scores, rank in top half of class, 1 letter of recommendation from teacher, 1 letter of recommendation from guidance counselor. Interview recommended. Essay considered. **Homeschooled:** Transcript of courses and grades, letter of recommendation (nonparent) required.

**High school preparation.** 15 units required. Required and recommended units include English 3-4, mathematics 1-3, social studies 1, history 1-2, science 1-2, foreign language 2 and academic electives 3.

**2007-2008 Annual costs.** Tuition/fees: $18,800. Room/board: $6,970. Books/supplies: $1,000. Personal expenses: $1,000.

**2007-2008 Financial aid. Need-based:** Average need met was 91%. Average scholarship/grant was $8,174; average loan $4,361. 67% of total undergraduate aid awarded as scholarships/grants, 33% as loans/jobs. **Non-need-based:** Scholarships awarded for academics, art, leadership, minority status, music/drama.

**Application procedures. Admission:** Priority date 3/15; deadline 8/15 (postmark date). No application fee. Admission notification on a rolling basis beginning on or about 10/15. **Financial aid:** Priority date 3/1; no closing date. FAFSA required. Applicants notified on a rolling basis starting 3/1; must reply within 2 week(s) of notification.

**Academics. Special study options:** Combined bachelor's/graduate degree, double major, dual enrollment of high school students, independent study, internships, liberal arts/career combination, student-designed major, study abroad, teacher certification program, Washington semester. Intercultural exchange program with Ritsumeikan University, Japan. **Credit/placement by examination:** AP, CLEP, IB, ACT, institutional tests. 84 credit hours maximum toward bachelor's degree. **Support services:** Reduced course load, tutoring, writing center.

**Majors. Biology:** General. **Business:** General, accounting, finance, management information systems. **Computer sciences:** General. **Conservation:** Environmental science. **Education:** Early childhood, elementary, physical. **Engineering:** General. **English:** English lit, speech/rhetoric. **Foreign languages:** French, German, Spanish. **Health:** Clinical lab science, cytotechnology. **History:** General. **Math:** General. **Parks/recreation:** Sports admin. **Philosophy/religion:** Philosophy, religion. **Physical sciences:** Chemistry, physics. **Psychology:** General. **Social sciences:** Economics, international relations, political science, sociology. **Visual/performing arts:** General, art.

**Most popular majors.** Biology 16%, business/marketing 13%, education 18%, English 6%, interdisciplinary studies 10%, psychology 7%, social sciences 13%.

**Computing on campus.** 125 workstations in library, computer center. Dormitories wired for high-speed internet access and linked to campus network. Commuter students can connect to campus network. Online course registration, online library, helpline, repair service, student web hosting, wireless network available.

**Student life. Freshman orientation:** Mandatory. Preregistration for classes offered. Overnight orientation program; four 2-day summer sessions available. **Policies:** Student representation on faculty committees. **Housing:** Guaranteed on-campus for all undergraduates. Coed dorms, single-sex dorms available. $100 fully refundable deposit, deadline 5/1. German, Spanish houses available. **Activities:** Bands, choral groups, drama, literary magazine, music ensembles, musical theater, student government, student newspaper, symphony orchestra, TV station, Young Republicans, Young Democrats, Alpha Phi Omega, men's and women's literary societies, international club, model United Nations, debate club, Action Jacksonville.

**Athletics.** NCAA. **Intercollegiate:** Baseball M, basketball, cheerleading, cross-country, football (tackle) M, golf, soccer, softball W, tennis, track and field, volleyball W. **Intramural:** Basketball, cricket, football (non-tackle) M, handball, racquetball, softball, volleyball. **Team name:** Blueboys, Lady Blues.

**Student services.** Alcohol/substance abuse counseling, campus ministries, career counseling, student employment services, financial aid counseling, health services, personal counseling, placement for graduates. **Physically disabled:** Services for visually, hearing impaired.

**Contact.** E-mail: admissions@ic.edu
Phone: (217) 245-3030 Toll-free number: (866) 464-5265
Fax: (217) 245-3034
Barb Lundberg, Vice President for Enrollment, Illinois College, 1101 West College Avenue, Jacksonville, IL 62650

## Illinois Institute of Art: Chicago
### Chicago, Illinois
### www.ilic.artinstitutes.edu
**CB code: 2908**

- For-profit 4-year visual arts college
- Commuter campus in very large city
- 3,000 degree-seeking undergraduates
- Application essay required

**General.** Founded in 1916. Accredited by ACCSCT. Branch campus at Woodfield in Schaumburg. **Degrees:** 380 bachelor's, 81 associate awarded. **Calendar:** Semester. **Full-time faculty:** 66 total. **Part-time faculty:** 70 total. **Special facilities:** Computer graphics laboratories, exhibit galleries, incentive studio.

### Freshman class profile.

| Mid 50% test scores | | | |
|---|---|---|---|
| | | SAT writing: | 410-490 |
| SAT critical reading: | 410-490 | ACT composite: | 16-22 |
| SAT math: | 420-490 | Out-of-state: | 20% |

**Basis for selection.** Secondary school record, interview, and personal statement most important. Portfolio required for advertising design, illustration, photography, fashion design, fashion illustration majors.

**High school preparation.** Recommended units include English 4, mathematics 3, social studies 2, science 3 and foreign language 1. Recommend art, interior design, drafting, fashion.

**2007-2008 Annual costs.** Tuition/fees: $20,784. Room/board: $6,570. Books/supplies: $1,000.

**Application procedures. Admission:** No deadline. $150 fee. Admission notification on a rolling basis. SAT or ACT scores recommended for placement and evaluation. **Financial aid:** Priority date 5/1; no closing date. FAFSA required. Applicants notified on a rolling basis.

**Academics. Special study options:** Accelerated study, cooperative education, internships. **Credit/placement by examination:** CLEP. **Support services:** Reduced course load.

**Majors. Business:** Fashion. **Communications:** Advertising. **Visual/performing arts:** Commercial/advertising art, fashion design, interior design.

**Computing on campus.** 25 workstations in computer center.

**Student life. Activities:** Student newspaper, Student Positive Action Committee.

**Student services.** Student employment services, placement for graduates, veterans' counselor.

**Contact.** E-mail: antonj@aii.edu
Phone: (312) 280-3500 Toll-free number: (800) 351-3450
Janice Anton, V.P., Director of Admissions, Illinois Institute of Art: Chicago, 350 North Orleans Street, Chicago, IL 60654

## Illinois Institute of Art: Schaumburg
### Schaumburg, Illinois
### www.ilis.aii.edu
**CB code: 3043**

- For-profit 3-year visual arts college
- Commuter campus in small city
- 1,268 degree-seeking undergraduates
- Application essay, interview required

**General.** Accredited by ACCSCT. **Degrees:** 247 bachelor's, 1 associate awarded. **Location:** 26 miles from Chicago. **Calendar:** Continuous, extensive summer session. **Full-time faculty:** 37 total. **Part-time faculty:** 48 total. **Special facilities:** Motion capture studio, lighting lab, sound lab, green room.

**Basis for selection.** Open admission, but selective for some programs. Essay and interview most important. SAT or ACT recommended.

**2007-2008 Annual costs.** Tuition/fees: $20,784. Room/board: $6,570. Books/supplies: $987. Personal expenses: $1,788.

**Financial aid. Non-need-based:** Scholarships awarded for academics, art. **Additional information:** Merit scholarships based on GPA; talent-based scholarships.

**Application procedures. Admission:** No deadline. $50 fee. Application may be submitted online. Admission notification on a rolling basis. **Financial aid:** Priority date 3/1; no closing date. FAFSA required.

**Academics. Special study options:** Accelerated study, internships, liberal arts/career combination. **Credit/placement by examination:** CLEP. **Support services:** Learning center, pre-admission summer program, reduced course load, remedial instruction, study skills assistance, tutoring.

**Majors. Visual/performing arts:** General, art, commercial/advertising art, design, interior design, multimedia.

**Student life. Freshman orientation:** Mandatory. Held the week before school begins. **Housing:** Single-sex dorms available. $200 deposit. Dormitory-style living in college-leased apartments. **Activities:** Jazz band, student government, student newspaper.

**Student services.** Adult student services, career counseling, student employment services, financial aid counseling, personal counseling, placement for graduates, veterans' counselor.

**Contact.** Phone: (847) 619-3450 Toll-free number: (800) 314-3450
Fax: (847) 619-3064
Phyllis Mack, Director of Admissions, Illinois Institute of Art: Schaumburg, 1000 North Plaza Drive, Schaumburg, IL 60173

## Illinois Institute of Technology
### Chicago, Illinois
### www.iit.edu
**CB member**
**CB code: 1318**

- Private 4-year university and engineering college
- Commuter campus in very large city
- 2,479 degree-seeking undergraduates: 6% part-time, 26% women, 4% African American, 14% Asian American, 7% Hispanic American, 16% international
- 4,547 degree-seeking graduate students
- 56% of applicants admitted
- Application essay required
- 67% graduate within 6 years; 32% enter graduate study

**General.** Founded in 1890. Regionally accredited. **Degrees:** 422 bachelor's awarded; master's, doctoral, first professional offered. **ROTC:** Army, Naval, Air Force. **Location:** 3 miles from downtown. **Calendar:** Semester, extensive summer session. **Full-time faculty:** 359 total; 90% have terminal degrees, 21% minority, 20% women. **Part-time faculty:** 300 total; 24% women. **Class size:** 58% < 20, 34% 20-39, 4% 40-49, 2% 50-99, less than 1% >100. **Special facilities:** Over 20 engineering, design, scientific, medical research centers.

**Freshman class profile.** 4,383 applied, 2,474 admitted, 521 enrolled.

| Mid 50% test scores | | | |
|---|---|---|---|
| SAT critical reading: | 540-670 | Rank in top tenth: | 43% |
| SAT math: | 620-710 | End year in good standing: | 93% |
| SAT writing: | 530-640 | Return as sophomores: | 86% |
| ACT composite: | 25-30 | Out-of-state: | 25% |
| GPA 3.50 or higher: | 72% | Live on campus: | 77% |
| GPA 3.0-3.49: | 22% | International: | 15% |
| GPA 2.0-2.99: | 6% | Fraternities: | 19% |
| Rank in top quarter: | 72% | Sororities: | 10% |

**Basis for selection.** Academic performance, strength of curriculum, test scores, counselor recommendations and essay most important. Class rank and interview, extracurricular activities, alumni relationship, volunteer and work experience also considered. Interview recommended. Portfolio optional for first-year freshmen entering the College of Architecture. **Homeschooled:** Statement describing homeschool structure and mission, letter of recommendation (nonparent) required.

**High school preparation.** 15 units required; 21 recommended. Required and recommended units include English 4, mathematics 4, social studies 2, history 2, science 3 (laboratory 2), foreign language 2, computer science 1 and visual/performing arts 1. Computer, technology and other courses recommended, but not required.

**2007-2008 Annual costs.** Tuition/fees: $25,746. Tuition and fees cover unlimited number of courses during academic year and include library and computer usage fees. Room/board: $8,618.

**2006-2007 Financial aid. Need-based:** 401 full-time freshmen applied for aid; 341 were judged to have need; 341 of these received aid. Average need met was 87%. Average scholarship/grant was $14,593; average loan $3,118. 71% of total undergraduate aid awarded as scholarships/grants, 29% as loans/jobs. **Non-need-based:** Awarded to 1,048 full-time undergraduates, including 236 freshmen. Scholarships awarded for academics, alumni affiliation, athletics, leadership, minority status, ROTC.

**Application procedures. Admission:** Priority date 12/1; deadline 8/1. No application fee. Application may be submitted online. Admission notification on a rolling basis. Must reply by May 1 or within 2 week(s) if notified thereafter. $300 enrollment deposit is required. **Financial aid:** Priority date 4/15; no closing date. FAFSA required. Applicants notified on a rolling basis starting 3/1; must reply by 5/1 or within 2 week(s) of notification.

**Academics. Special study options:** Combined bachelor's/graduate degree, cooperative education, cross-registration, distance learning, double major, ESL, independent study, liberal arts/career combination, study abroad, teacher certification program. Joint enrollment at 2 institutions for 2 degrees. **Credit/placement by examination:** AP, CLEP, IB, SAT, ACT, institutional tests. 18 credit hours maximum toward bachelor's degree. No limit for advanced placement credit. **Support services:** Learning center, study skills assistance, tutoring, writing center.

**Majors. Architecture:** Architecture. **Biology:** General, biochemistry, Biochemistry/biophysics and molecular biology. **Business:** Business admin. **Communications:** Journalism. **Computer sciences:** General, computer science, information technology. **Engineering:** Aerospace, architectural, biomedical, chemical, civil, computer, electrical, materials, mechanical. **Engineering technology:** Industrial management. **Liberal arts:** Arts/sciences. **Math:** Applied. **Physical sciences:** Chemistry, physics. **Psychology:** General. **Social sciences:** Political science.

**Most popular majors.** Architecture 13%, biology 6%, business/marketing 8%, computer/information sciences 10%, engineering/engineering technologies 55%.

**Computing on campus.** 500 workstations in dormitories, library, computer center, student center. Dormitories wired for high-speed internet access and linked to campus network. Online course registration, online library, helpline, student web hosting, wireless network available.

**Student life. Freshman orientation:** Available, $150 fee. Preregistration for classes offered. Five summer sessions; strongly recommended. Welcome Week held prior to start of classes. **Policies:** Student organizations register each semester, are nondiscriminatory and prohibit hazing. **Housing:** Coed dorms, single-sex dorms, special housing for disabled, apartments, fraternity/sorority housing available. **Activities:** Concert band, campus ministries, choral groups, dance, drama, film society, international student organizations, literary magazine, music ensembles, musical theater, radio station, student government, student newspaper, TV station, Red Cross club, Engineers Without Borders, greek council, Haiti Outreach, Intervarsity Christian Fellowship, Latinos Involved in Further Education, National Society of Black Engineers, Society of Women Engineers, union board.

**Athletics.** NAIA. **Intercollegiate:** Baseball M, basketball, cross-country, diving, soccer, swimming, volleyball W. **Intramural:** Badminton, basketball, football (non-tackle), racquetball, table tennis, volleyball. **Team name:** Scarlet Hawks.

**Student services.** Alcohol/substance abuse counseling, career counseling, student employment services, financial aid counseling, health services, legal services, minority student services, personal counseling, placement for graduates, women's services. **Physically disabled:** Services for visually, hearing impaired.

**Contact.** E-mail: admission@iit.edu
Phone: (312) 567-3025 Toll-free number: (800) 448-2329
Fax: (312) 567-6939
Gerald Doyle, Associate Vice President, Undergraduate Admission, Illinois Institute of Technology, 10 West 33rd Street, Chicago, IL 60616

## Illinois State University

| | |
|---|---|
| Normal, Illinois | **CB member** |
| www.ilstu.edu | **CB code: 1319** |

- Public 4-year university
- Residential campus in small city
- 17,637 degree-seeking undergraduates: 6% part-time, 57% women, 6% African American, 2% Asian American, 4% Hispanic American, 1% international
- 2,286 degree-seeking graduate students
- 67% of applicants admitted
- SAT or ACT (ACT writing optional), application essay required
- 65% graduate within 6 years

**General.** Founded in 1857. Regionally accredited. **Degrees:** 4,306 bachelor's awarded; master's, doctoral offered. **ROTC:** Army. **Location:** 132 miles from Chicago, 168 miles from St. Louis. **Calendar:** Semester, limited summer session. **Full-time faculty:** 843 total; 82% have terminal degrees, 12% minority, 45% women. **Part-time faculty:** 293 total; 32% have terminal degrees, 6% minority, 56% women. **Class size:** 31% < 20, 54% 20-39, 3% 40-49, 7% 50-99, 4% >100. **Special facilities:** 310-acre farm, planetarium, museum of nations, laboratory school.

**Freshman class profile.** 12,550 applied, 8,461 admitted, 3,145 enrolled.

| Mid 50% test scores | | | |
|---|---|---|---|
| ACT composite: | 22-26 | Rank in top tenth: | 11% |
| GPA 3.50 or higher: | 40% | Return as sophomores: | 83.3% |
| GPA 3.0-3.49: | 41% | Out-of-state: | 1% |
| GPA 2.0-2.99: | 19% | Live on campus: | 97% |
| Rank in top quarter: | 37% | Fraternities: | 15% |
| | | Sororities: | 17% |

**Basis for selection.** School achievement record and test scores most important. Interview required of special admission applicants. Audition recommended for music majors. Portfolio recommended for art majors.

**High school preparation.** College-preparatory program required. 15 units required. Required units include English 4, mathematics 3, social studies 2, science 2 (laboratory 2), foreign language 2 and academic electives 2. 2 units required in foreign language and/or fine arts, 2 units in social studies and/or history. Electives may include fundamentals of computing or vocational education courses.

**2007-2008 Annual costs.** Tuition/fees: $9,019; $16,339 out-of-state. Room/board: $6,848. Books/supplies: $888. Personal expenses: $2,209.

**2007-2008 Financial aid. Need-based:** 2,376 full-time freshmen applied for aid; 1,637 were judged to have need; 1,432 of these received aid. Average need met was 78%. Average scholarship/grant was $8,318; average loan $5,179. 51% of total undergraduate aid awarded as scholarships/grants, 49% as loans/jobs. **Non-need-based:** Awarded to 2,586 full-time undergraduates, including 773 freshmen. Scholarships awarded for academics, art, athletics, music/drama.

**Application procedures. Admission:** Priority date 11/15; deadline 3/1 (receipt date). $40 fee, may be waived for applicants with need. Application may be submitted online. Admission notification on a rolling basis beginning on or about 9/1. **Financial aid:** Priority date 3/1; no closing date. FAFSA required. Applicants notified on a rolling basis starting 4/1; must reply within 2 week(s) of notification.

**Academics. Special study options:** Accelerated study, combined bachelor's/graduate degree, cooperative education, distance learning, double major, dual enrollment of high school students, ESL, exchange student, honors, independent study, internships, student-designed major, study abroad, teacher certification program, Washington semester. **Credit/placement by examination:** AP, CLEP, SAT, ACT, institutional tests. 26 credit hours maximum toward bachelor's degree. **Support services:** Learning center, preadmission summer program, tutoring.

**Majors. Agriculture:** Agribusiness operations. **Biology:** General, biochemistry. **Business:** Accounting, business admin, finance, insurance, international, management science, marketing. **Communications:** Journalism, public relations. **Computer sciences:** Computer science, information technology, networking. **Education:** Business, early childhood, elementary, health, middle, music, physical, social studies, special, technology/industrial arts. **Engineering technology:** Industrial. **English:** Speech/rhetoric. **Family/consumer sciences:** General. **Foreign languages:** French, German, Spanish. **Health:** Athletic training, audiology/speech pathology, clinical lab science, environmental health, medical records admin, nursing (RN), occupational health. **History:** General. **Liberal arts:** Arts/sciences. **Math:** General. **Parks/recreation:** Exercise sciences, facilities management. **Philosophy/religion:** Philosophy. **Physical sciences:** Chemistry, geology, physics. **Protective services:** Criminal justice. **Psychology:** General. **Public administration:** Social work. **Social sciences:** Anthropology, economics, geography, political science, sociology. **Visual/performing arts:** Art, dramatic, music history, music performance, studio arts.

**Most popular majors.** Business/marketing 17%, communications/journalism 6%, education 20%, health sciences 7%, social sciences 8%.

**Computing on campus.** PC or laptop required. 2,530 workstations in dormitories, library, computer center, student center. Dormitories wired for high-speed internet access and linked to campus network. Commuter students can connect to campus network. Online course registration, helpline, student web hosting, wireless network available.

**Student life. Freshman orientation:** Mandatory, $50 fee. Preregistration for classes offered. Consists of 12 sessions (2 days each), held each week from mid-June to end of July. Students meet with advisers, register, and take placement exams. **Housing:** Guaranteed on-campus for freshmen. Coed dorms, single-sex dorms, special housing for disabled, apartments, fraternity/sorority housing, substance-free housing available. $150 deposit. **Activities:** Bands, choral groups, dance, drama, film society, literary magazine, music ensembles, musical theater, radio station, student government, student newspaper, symphony orchestra, TV station, 250 student organizations.

**Athletics.** NCAA. **Intercollegiate:** Baseball M, basketball, cross-country, diving W, football (tackle) M, golf, gymnastics W, soccer W, softball W, swimming W, tennis, track and field, volleyball W. **Intramural:** Badminton, basketball, football (tackle), golf, racquetball, soccer, softball, volleyball. **Team name:** Redbirds.

**Student services.** Adult student services, alcohol/substance abuse counseling, career counseling, student employment services, financial aid counseling, health services, legal services, minority student services, on-campus daycare, personal counseling, placement for graduates, veterans' counselor. **Physically disabled:** Services for visually, speech, hearing impaired.

**Contact.** E-mail: admissions@ilstu.edu
Phone: (309) 438-2181 Toll-free number: (800) 366-2478
Fax: (309) 438-3932
Molly Arnold, Director of Admissions, Illinois State University, Campus Box 2200, Normal, IL 61790-2200

---

## Illinois Wesleyan University
**Bloomington, Illinois**
www.iwu.edu

**CB member**
**CB code: 1320**

- Private 4-year university and liberal arts college
- Residential campus in small city
- 2,088 degree-seeking undergraduates: 58% women, 5% African American, 4% Asian American, 3% Hispanic American, 2% international
- 56% of applicants admitted
- SAT or ACT (ACT writing optional), application essay required
- 82% graduate within 6 years

**General.** Founded in 1850. Regionally accredited. **Degrees:** 511 bachelor's awarded. **ROTC:** Army. **Location:** 125 miles from Chicago, 165 miles from St. Louis. **Calendar:** 4-4-1 (2 semesters plus May Term). **Full-time faculty:** 161 total; 93% have terminal degrees, 12% minority, 40% women. **Part-time faculty:** 70 total; 44% have terminal degrees, 11% minority, 60% women. **Class size:** 65% < 20, 33% 20-39, less than 1% 40-49, less than 1% 50-99, less than 1% >100. **Special facilities:** Observatory, natural sciences research labs, computerized music lab, social science research lab, visual anthropology lab, student-managed real-dollar investment portfolio program, nursing lab, lab theatre producing original works by undergraduates, Action Research Center (supporting community-based student research for academic credit).

**Freshman class profile.** 3,017 applied, 1,696 admitted, 538 enrolled.

| Mid 50% test scores | | | |
|---|---|---|---|
| SAT critical reading: | 540-680 | Return as sophomores: | 92% |
| SAT math: | 590-690 | Out-of-state: | 12% |
| ACT composite: | 26-30 | Live on campus: | 100% |
| Rank in top quarter: | 76% | International: | 3% |
| Rank in top tenth: | 45% | Fraternities: | 38% |
| | | Sororities: | 32% |

**Basis for selection.** Test scores, class rank, high school record, and essay or personal statement most important. Interview strongly recommended. Audition required for bachelor of music or BFA in theater or music theater. Portfolio review required for BFA in art. **Homeschooled:** Transcript of courses and grades required. **Learning Disabled:** Students welcome to submit information on learning disabilities as part of application review process.

**High school preparation.** 15 units recommended. Recommended units include English 4, mathematics 3, social studies 2, science 3 (laboratory 2) and foreign language 3. Biology and chemistry are required for admission to nursing and biology.

**2008-2009 Annual costs.** Tuition/fees: $32,434. Room/board: $7,350. Books/supplies: $780. Personal expenses: $650.

**2007-2008 Financial aid. Need-based:** 412 full-time freshmen applied for aid; 305 were judged to have need; 305 of these received aid. Average need met was 93%. Average scholarship/grant was $16,880; average loan $4,099. 71% of total undergraduate aid awarded as scholarships/grants, 29% as loans/jobs. **Non-need-based:** Awarded to 860 full-time undergraduates, including 239 freshmen. Scholarships awarded for academics, art, music/drama.

**Application procedures. Admission:** Priority date 11/1; no deadline. No application fee. Application may be submitted online. Admission notification on a rolling basis beginning on or about 12/15. Must reply by May 1 or within 3 week(s) if notified thereafter. **Financial aid:** Closing date 3/1. FAFSA, institutional form, CSS PROFILE required. Applicants notified on a rolling basis starting 2/15; must reply by 5/1 or within 3 week(s) of notification.

**Academics.** Optional 3-week May Term provides opportunities for students to pursue experimental courses, travel courses, interships, or independent research projects. Fall Term in London and Spring Term in Madrid led by Illinois Wesleyan faculty members where students may earn General Education credit during these terms. **Special study options:** Combined bachelor's/graduate degree, double major, exchange student, honors, independent study, internships, New York semester, student-designed major, study abroad, teacher certification program, United Nations semester, urban semester, Washington semester. 3-2 cooperative program in engineering with Washington University, Case Western Reserve University, and Northwestern University; 3-2 program in forestry and environmental management with Duke University; 3-2 program in occupational therapy with Washington University, 2-2 program in engineering with the University of Illinois, and a non-guaranteed cooperative program in engineering with Dartmouth College. **Credit/placement by examination:** AP, CLEP, IB, institutional tests. 32 credit hours maximum toward bachelor's degree. Limit of 16 hours (equivalent to four courses) may count toward general education credit. Up to 16 additional hours (equivalent to four courses) can be awarded as elective credit. **Support services:** Reduced course load, study skills assistance, tutoring, writing center.

**Majors. Area/ethnic studies:** African, American, Asian, Central/Eastern European, Latin American, Western European, women's. **Biology:** General. **Business:** Accounting, business admin, insurance, international. **Computer sciences:** General. **Conservation:** Environmental studies. **Education:** General, biology, chemistry, elementary, English, French, history, mathematics, music, physics, Spanish. **English:** English lit. **Foreign languages:** Classics, French, German, Spanish. **Health:** Nursing (RN). **History:** General. **Math:** General. **Philosophy/religion:** Philosophy, religion. **Physical sciences:** Chemistry, physics. **Psychology:** General. **Social sciences:** Anthropology, economics, political science, sociology. **Visual/performing arts:** Acting, art, dramatic, music performance, music theory/composition, musical theater, piano/organ, stringed instruments, theater design, voice/opera.

**Most popular majors.** Biology 11%, business/marketing 19%, English 7%, foreign language 6%, psychology 8%, social sciences 10%, visual/performing arts 12%.

**Computing on campus.** 400 workstations in dormitories, library, computer center, student center. Dormitories wired for high-speed internet access and linked to campus network. Commuter students can connect to campus network. Online course registration, online library, helpline, repair service, student web hosting, wireless network available.

**Student life. Freshman orientation:** Mandatory. Preregistration for classes offered. Orientation for parents held in June. New student orientation held

5-6 days prior to start of classes. **Policies:** No smoking permitted in residence halls. Beer and wine permitted in designated areas for students of legal age. **Housing:** Guaranteed on-campus for freshmen. Coed dorms, special housing for disabled, apartments, fraternity/sorority housing, substance-free housing available. Theme housing available. **Activities:** Bands, campus ministries, choral groups, dance, drama, film society, literary magazine, music ensembles, Model UN, musical theater, opera, radio station, student government, student newspaper, symphony orchestra, TV station, black student union, InterVarsity Christian Fellowship, Alpha Phi Omega, Council of Latin American Student Enrichment, Habitat for Humanity, several environmental concerns organizations, Amnesty International, Pan-Asian student association, College Democrats, College Republicans.

**Athletics.** NCAA. **Intercollegiate:** Baseball M, basketball, cross-country, diving, football (tackle) M, golf, soccer, softball W, swimming, tennis, track and field, volleyball W. **Intramural:** Badminton, basketball, football (non-tackle), golf, soccer, softball, tennis, volleyball. **Team name:** Titans.

**Student services.** Alcohol/substance abuse counseling, career counseling, student employment services, financial aid counseling, health services, minority student services, personal counseling, placement for graduates. **Physically disabled:** Services for visually, speech, hearing impaired.

**Contact.** E-mail: iwuadmit@iwu.edu
Phone: (309) 556-3031 Toll-free number: (800) 332-2498
Fax: (309) 556-3820
Tony Bankston, Dean of Admissions, Illinois Wesleyan University, PO Box 2900, Bloomington, IL 61702-2900

---

## International Academy of Design and Technology: Chicago
**Chicago, Illinois**
www.iadtchicago.edu     CB code: 3363

- For-profit 4-year visual arts and technical college
- Commuter campus in very large city
- 2,091 degree-seeking undergraduates
- Interview required

**General.** Founded in 1977. Accredited by ACICS. **Degrees:** 319 bachelor's, 67 associate awarded. **Location:** Downtown. **Calendar:** Quarter, extensive summer session. **Full-time faculty:** 12 total. **Part-time faculty:** 136 total. **Class size:** 53% < 20, 44% 20-39, 3% 40-49.

**Freshman class profile.** 784 applied, 784 admitted, 328 enrolled.

**Basis for selection.** Open admission. Students must meet with an admissions representative and go through an interview process. **Homeschooled:** Transcript of courses and grades required. Should be registered with state or accrediting agency.

**2007-2008 Annual costs.** Tuition/fees: $17,250. Books/supplies: $1,800. Personal expenses: $1,596.

**2006-2007 Financial aid.** All financial aid based on need. 36% of total undergraduate aid awarded as scholarships/grants, 64% as loans/jobs. **Additional information:** College work study programs available to day and evening students.

**Application procedures. Admission:** No deadline. $50 fee. Application may be submitted online. Admission notification on a rolling basis. **Financial aid:** No deadline. FAFSA required. Applicants notified on a rolling basis.

**Academics. Special study options:** Distance learning, independent study, internships, study abroad, weekend college. **Credit/placement by examination:** AP, CLEP, IB, institutional tests. 40 credit hours maximum toward associate degree, 100 toward bachelor's. **Support services:** Learning center, reduced course load, remedial instruction, study skills assistance, tutoring.

**Majors. Business:** Fashion. **Communications technology:** Animation/special effects. **Computer sciences:** Computer forensics, game design, information technology. **Visual/performing arts:** Commercial/advertising art, fashion design, graphic design, interior design.

**Most popular majors.** Business/marketing 31%, communication technologies 14%, visual/performing arts 53%.

**Computing on campus.** 386 workstations in library, computer center, student center. Online course registration, online library, wireless network available.

---

**Student life. Freshman orientation:** Mandatory. **Activities:** Student newspaper, Fashion Council, merchandising management club, information technology club, video and animation club, Omega Pi Delta, International Interior Design Association, graphic design club, international club, chess club, movie club.

**Student services.** Adult student services, career counseling, student employment services, financial aid counseling, personal counseling, placement for graduates, veterans' counselor. **Physically disabled:** Services for visually impaired.

**Contact.** Phone: (312) 980-9200 Toll-free number: (877) 222-3369
Fax: (312) 541-3929
Cecily Arroyo, Assistant Vice President of Marketing and Admissions, International Academy of Design and Technology: Chicago, One North State Street, Suite 500, Chicago, IL 60602

---

## International Academy of Design and Technology: Schaumburg
**Schaumburg, Illinois**
www.iadtschaumburg.com

- For-profit 4-year visual arts and technical college
- Commuter campus in small city
- 246 degree-seeking undergraduates

**General.** Accredited by ACICS. **Degrees:** 20 bachelor's, 4 associate awarded. **Calendar:** Quarter. **Full-time faculty:** 3 total. **Part-time faculty:** 27 total.

**Freshman class profile.** 79 enrolled.

**Basis for selection.** Open admission.

**2007-2008 Annual costs.** Tuition/fees: $15,000. Bachelor's degree program is $58,800 plus books and fees. Books/supplies: $1,200.

**2006-2007 Financial aid. Need-based:** 22% of total undergraduate aid awarded as scholarships/grants, 78% as loans/jobs.

**Academics. Credit/placement by examination:** CLEP.

**Majors. Communications technology:** Animation/special effects. **Computer sciences:** Web page design. **Visual/performing arts:** Fashion design, interior design.

**Contact.** Phone: (847) 969-2800 Fax: (847) 969-0599
Kelly Stegmeyer, Director of Admissions, International Academy of Design and Technology: Schaumburg, 915 National Parkway, Schaumburg, IL 60173

---

## ITT Technical Institute: Burr Ridge
**Burr Ridge, Illinois**
www.itt-tech.edu     CB code: 2698

- For-profit 4-year technical college
- Commuter campus in small town

**General.** Accredited by ACICS. **Calendar:** Quarter.

**Annual costs/financial aid.** Tuition varies by program, $260-$368 per credit hour.

**Contact.** Phone: (630) 455-6470
Director of Recruitment, 7040 High Grove Boulevard, Burr Ridge, IL 60527

---

## ITT Technical Institute: Mount Prospect
**Mount Prospect, Illinois**
www.itt-tech.edu     CB code: 4271

- For-profit 4-year technical college
- Commuter campus in small city

**General.** Founded in 1986. Accredited by ACICS. **Location:** 20 miles from Chicago. **Calendar:** Quarter.

**Annual costs/financial aid.** Tuition varies by program, $260-$368 per credit hour.

**Contact.** Phone: (847) 375-8800
Director of Recruitment, 1401 Feehanville Drive, Mount Prospect, IL
60056

## Judson University
### Elgin, Illinois
www.judsonu.edu                                    CB code: 1351

- Private 4-year university and liberal arts college affiliated with
  American Baptist Churches in the USA
- Residential campus in small city
- 1,165 degree-seeking undergraduates
- 75% of applicants admitted
- ACT (writing optional), application essay required

**General.** Founded in 1963. Regionally accredited. **Degrees:** 343 bachelor's awarded; master's offered. **ROTC:** Army, Naval, Air Force. **Location:** 40 miles from Chicago. **Calendar:** Semester, limited summer session.
**Full-time faculty:** 61 total. **Part-time faculty:** 57 total. **Class size:** 66%
< 20, 32% 20-39, less than 1% 40-49, 2% 50-99. **Special facilities:** Green academic center.

**Freshman class profile.** 645 applied, 482 admitted, 170 enrolled.

| Mid 50% test scores | | GPA 2.0-2.99: | 17% |
|---|---|---|---|
| SAT critical reading: | 460-600 | Rank in top quarter: | 42% |
| SAT math: | 470-600 | Rank in top tenth: | 16% |
| ACT composite: | 20-25 | Out-of-state: | 39% |
| GPA 3.50 or higher: | 50% | Live on campus: | 83% |
| GPA 3.0-3.49: | 32% | | |

**Basis for selection.** School achievement record and test scores important. Counselor's reference considered. Audition recommended for performing arts majors. Portfolio recommended for art majors. Essay required for architecture majors. **Homeschooled:** Transcript of courses and grades required.

**High school preparation.** Recommended units include English 4, mathematics 3, social studies 2, science 2 (laboratory 2).

**2007-2008 Annual costs.** Tuition/fees: $20,420. Room/board: $7,200.
Books/supplies: $1,000. Personal expenses: $1,000.

**Financial aid. Non-need-based:** Scholarships awarded for academics, alumni affiliation, art, athletics, music/drama.

**Application procedures. Admission:** No deadline. $35 fee, may be waived for applicants with need. Application may be submitted online. Admission notification on a rolling basis beginning on or about 7/1. **Financial aid:** Priority date 3/1, closing date 8/1. FAFSA required. Applicants notified on a rolling basis starting 3/1; must reply within 4 week(s) of notification.

**Academics. Special study options:** Accelerated study, combined bachelor's/graduate degree, distance learning, double major, honors, independent study, internships, study abroad, teacher certification program, urban semester, Washington semester. **Credit/placement by examination:** AP, CLEP, ACT, institutional tests. 30 credit hours maximum toward bachelor's degree. **Support services:** Learning center, reduced course load, remedial instruction, study skills assistance, tutoring.

**Majors. Architecture:** Architecture. **Biology:** General, biochemistry. **Business:** Accounting, business admin, human resources, management information systems. **Communications:** General, media studies. **Computer sciences:** Computer graphics, information technology, web page design, webmaster. **Conservation:** Environmental studies. **Education:** Art, early childhood, elementary, music, physical, secondary. **English:** English lit, speech/rhetoric. **History:** General. **Math:** General. **Parks/recreation:** Sports admin. **Physical sciences:** Chemistry. **Protective services:** Criminal justice. **Psychology:** General. **Public administration:** Human services. **Social sciences:** Sociology. **Theology:** Bible, sacred music, youth ministry. **Visual/performing arts:** Art, graphic design, music performance, studio arts. **Other:** Management and leadership, Science/Mathematics general.

**Most popular majors.** Business/marketing 41%, education 13%, psychology 8%, public administration/social services 14%, security/protective services 7%, theological studies 6%.

**Computing on campus.** 200 workstations in dormitories, library, computer center, student center. Dormitories wired for high-speed internet access and linked to campus network. Online course registration, online library, helpline, wireless network available.

**Student life. Freshman orientation:** Mandatory. Preregistration for classes offered. **Policies:** Chapel services held 3 mornings a week. **Housing:** Guaranteed on-campus for all undergraduates. Coed dorms, single-sex dorms, special housing for disabled, apartments, substance-free housing available. $400 deposit, deadline 6/1. **Activities:** Concert band, campus ministries, choral groups, drama, music ensembles, student government, student newspaper, symphony orchestra.

**Athletics.** NAIA, NCCAA. **Intercollegiate:** Baseball M, basketball, cross-country, soccer, softball W, tennis, volleyball W. **Intramural:** Badminton, basketball, racquetball, soccer, softball, table tennis, tennis, volleyball. **Team name:** Eagles.

**Student services.** Adult student services, career counseling, student employment services, financial aid counseling, health services, personal counseling, placement for graduates.

**Contact.** E-mail: admissions@judsonu.edu
Phone: (847) 628-2510 Toll-free number: (800) 879-5376
Fax: (847) 628-2526
William Dean, Director of Admissions, Judson University, 1151 North State Street, Elgin, IL 60123-1404

## Kendall College
### Chicago, Illinois
www.kendall.edu                                    CB code: 1366

- Private 4-year culinary school, business and teachers college affiliated with United Methodist Church
- Commuter campus in very large city

**General.** Founded in 1934. Regionally accredited. **Calendar:** Quarter.

**Annual costs/financial aid.** Tuition costs range from $7,200 to $21,450 per academic year. Required fees: $675. Room/board: $10,050. Books/supplies: $500. Need-based financial aid available to full-time and part-time students.

**Contact.** Phone: (312) 752-2020
Vice President of Admissions, 900 North Branch Street North, Chicago, IL 60622-4278

## Knox College
### Galesburg, Illinois
www.knox.edu                      CB member
                                  CB code: 1372

- Private 4-year liberal arts college
- Residential campus in large town
- 1,353 degree-seeking undergraduates: 58% women, 4% African American, 7% Asian American, 5% Hispanic American, 1% Native American, 6% international
- 61% of applicants admitted
- Application essay required
- 72% graduate within 6 years; 99% enter graduate study

**General.** Founded in 1837. Regionally accredited. **Degrees:** 255 bachelor's awarded. **Location:** 180 miles from Chicago, 200 miles from St. Louis. **Calendar:** Trimester. **Full-time faculty:** 98 total; 92% have terminal degrees, 13% minority, 39% women. **Part-time faculty:** 40 total; 42% have terminal degrees, 12% minority, 60% women. **Class size:** 67% < 20, 31% 20-39, 1% 40-49, less than 1% 50-99. **Special facilities:** Electron microscope, greenhouse, studio and large-scale production theaters, 760-acre biological field station, ceramics, sculpture, painting, and printmaking studios.

**Freshman class profile.** 2,419 applied, 1,479 admitted, 307 enrolled.

| Mid 50% test scores | | Rank in top tenth: | 40% |
|---|---|---|---|
| SAT critical reading: | 610-710 | End year in good standing: | 90% |
| SAT math: | 580-670 | Return as sophomores: | 91% |
| SAT writing: | 590-690 | Out-of-state: | 51% |
| ACT composite: | 27-31 | Live on campus: | 96% |
| Rank in top quarter: | 75% | International: | 6% |

**Basis for selection.** Course of study, grades, essay, and recommendations most important. Class rank, extracurricular activities, special skills, talents and personal qualities, and interview also considered. Preference given to students who have taken advantage of academic opportunities offered by high school (honors, Advanced Placement, International Baccalaureate and/or college level courses) if available. SAT or ACT submission optional for most applicants. Scores considered if submitted. Applicants from secondary schools that do not provide grades are asked to submit test scores. Interview strongly recommended. **Homeschooled:** Statement describing homeschool structure and mission, transcript of courses and grades, state high school equivalency certificate required. Applicants should provide detailed documentation of coursework completed, including course syllabi as appropriate. SAT/ACT scores required.

**High school preparation.** 15 units required; 18 recommended. Required and recommended units include English 4, mathematics 4, social studies 2, history 2, science 3 (laboratory 2) and foreign language 3.

**2008-2009 Annual costs.** Tuition/fees (projected): $30,507. Room/board: $6,726. Books/supplies: $900. Personal expenses: $600.

**2007-2008 Financial aid. Need-based:** 263 full-time freshmen applied for aid; 221 were judged to have need; 221 of these received aid. Average need met was 95%. Average scholarship/grant was $17,969; average loan $5,078. 75% of total undergraduate aid awarded as scholarships/grants, 25% as loans/jobs. **Non-need-based:** Awarded to 493 full-time undergraduates, including 106 freshmen. Scholarships awarded for academics, art, music/drama.

**Application procedures. Admission:** Closing date 2/1 (postmark date). $40 fee, may be waived for applicants with need. Application may be submitted online. Admission notification 3/31. Must reply by May 1 or within 2 week(s) if notified thereafter. **Financial aid:** Priority date 2/1; no closing date. FAFSA, institutional form required. Applicants notified on a rolling basis starting 3/15; must reply by 5/1 or within 2 week(s) of notification.

**Academics.** Academic work conducted under honor system, placing primary responsibility for academic honesty on student. Examinations not proctored. **Special study options:** Combined bachelor's/graduate degree, double major, dual enrollment of high school students, honors, independent study, internships, liberal arts/career combination, student-designed major, study abroad, teacher certification program, urban semester, Washington semester. Extensive overseas study centers with more than 30 international and off-campus study programs. Significant independent research opportunities with funding for projects. Repertory theater, psychology, and Green Oaks (environmental) terms. **Credit/placement by examination:** AP, CLEP, IB, SAT, ACT, institutional tests. 9 credit hours maximum toward bachelor's degree. Up to 25% of 36 required Knox credits may be obtained through examination. **Support services:** Learning center, reduced course load, study skills assistance, tutoring, writing center.

**Majors. Area/ethnic studies:** African-American, American, Asian, women's. **Biology:** General, biochemistry. **Computer sciences:** Computer science. **Conservation:** Environmental studies. **Education:** General, social science. **English:** Creative writing, English lit. **Foreign languages:** General, classics, French, German, Spanish. **History:** General. **Interdisciplinary:** Global studies, neuroscience. **Math:** General, applied. **Philosophy/religion:** Philosophy. **Physical sciences:** Chemistry, physics. **Psychology:** General. **Social sciences:** Anthropology, economics, international relations, political science, sociology. **Visual/performing arts:** Art history/conservation, dramatic, studio arts.

**Most popular majors.** Biology 6%, education 8%, English 16%, foreign language 7%, physical sciences 6%, social sciences 27%.

**Computing on campus.** 335 workstations in library, computer center, student center. Dormitories wired for high-speed internet access and linked to campus network. Commuter students can connect to campus network. Online course registration, online library, helpline, student web hosting, wireless network available.

**Student life. Freshman orientation:** Mandatory. Preregistration for classes offered. 1 week before beginning of fall term. Additional orientation held for international students. **Policies:** Students actively engaged in college governance. All students requred to live on campus. **Housing:** Coed dorms, single-sex dorms, apartments, fraternity/sorority housing, substance-free housing available. $200 nonrefundable deposit, deadline 5/1. **Activities:** Bands, choral groups, dance, drama, literary magazine, music ensembles, radio station, student government, student newspaper, symphony orchestra, InterVarsity Christian Fellowship, Amnesty International, Latin American Concerns, Allied Blacks for Liberty and Equality, Lo Nuestro (Hispanic student group), Habitat for Humanity, Common Ground (environmental group).

**Athletics.** NCAA. **Intercollegiate:** Baseball M, basketball, cross-country, diving, football (tackle) M, golf, soccer, softball W, swimming, tennis, track and field, volleyball W, wrestling M. **Intramural:** Basketball, football (tackle), soccer, softball, volleyball. **Team name:** Prairie Fire.

**Student services.** Alcohol/substance abuse counseling, career counseling, services for economically disadvantaged, student employment services, financial aid counseling, health services, minority student services, personal counseling. **Physically disabled:** Services for visually, hearing impaired.

**Contact.** E-mail: admission@knox.edu
Phone: (309) 341-7100 Toll-free number: (800) 678-5669
Fax: (309) 341-7070
Paul Steenis, Dean of Admission, Knox College, Knox College - Campus Box 148, Galesburg, IL 61401-4999

## Lake Forest College
**Lake Forest, Illinois**  CB member
**www.lakeforest.edu**  CB code: 1392

- Private 4-year liberal arts college affiliated with Presbyterian Church (USA)
- Residential campus in large town
- 1,408 degree-seeking undergraduates: 1% part-time, 59% women, 4% African American, 5% Asian American, 6% Hispanic American, 8% international
- 20 degree-seeking graduate students
- 61% of applicants admitted
- Application essay required
- 69% graduate within 6 years

**General.** Founded in 1857. Regionally accredited. **Degrees:** 298 bachelor's awarded; master's offered. **Location:** 30 miles from Chicago. **Calendar:** Semester, limited summer session. **Full-time faculty:** 90 total; 94% have terminal degrees, 13% minority, 39% women. **Part-time faculty:** 67 total; 52% have terminal degrees, 6% minority, 61% women. **Class size:** 63% < 20, 36% 20-39, 2% 40-49. **Special facilities:** Electron microscope, NMR spectrometer, neutron howitzer, multimedia language laboratory, electronic music studio.

**Freshman class profile.** 2,201 applied, 1,346 admitted, 356 enrolled.

| Mid 50% test scores | | | |
|---|---|---|---|
| SAT critical reading: | 560-660 | Rank in top quarter: | 56% |
| SAT math: | 540-660 | Rank in top tenth: | 35% |
| SAT writing: | 540-640 | End year in good standing: | 92% |
| ACT composite: | 24-29 | Return as sophomores: | 82% |
| GPA 3.50 or higher: | 52% | Out-of-state: | 65% |
| GPA 3.0-3.49: | 34% | Live on campus: | 91% |
| GPA 2.0-2.99: | 14% | International: | 10% |

**Basis for selection.** Secondary school curriculum and record most important, followed by school and community activities, essay. Recommendations considered carefully. Copy of graded paper required. ACT/SAT optional except for applicants to the highest academic scholarships. Interview required for merit scholarships in leadership and science and for students who do not submit test scores, recommended for all. Audition required for theater and music scholarships. Portfolio required for art, foreign language and writing scholarships. **Homeschooled:** SAT/ACT required.

**High school preparation.** 19 units required; 23 recommended. Required and recommended units include English 4, mathematics 3-4, social studies 2, history 2, science 3-4 (laboratory 3-4), foreign language 2-4 and academic electives 3.

**2007-2008 Annual costs.** Tuition/fees: $30,964. Room/board: $7,326. Books/supplies: $800. Personal expenses: $410.

**2007-2008 Financial aid. Need-based:** 235 full-time freshmen applied for aid; 189 were judged to have need; 188 of these received aid. Average need met was 88%. Average scholarship/grant was $20,096; average loan $4,444. 75% of total undergraduate aid awarded as scholarships/grants, 25% as loans/jobs. **Non-need-based:** Awarded to 586 full-time undergraduates, including 150 freshmen. Scholarships awarded for academics, alumni affiliation, art, leadership, music/drama.

**Application procedures. Admission:** Priority date 2/15; no deadline. $40 fee, may be waived for applicants with need. Application may be submitted online. Must reply by May 1 or within 3 week(s) if notified thereafter. **Financial aid:** Priority date 2/15; no closing date. FAFSA required. Applicants notified on a rolling basis starting 2/15; must reply by 5/1 or within 3 week(s) of notification.

**Academics.** In freshman studies program students select 1 of 4 fall courses from designated set, usually 25 to 30, with class size limit of 12 students. Faculty member teaching course serves as student's academic adviser. **Special study options:** Double major, honors, independent study, internships, liberal arts/career combination, semester at sea, student-designed major, study abroad, teacher certification program, urban semester, Washington semester. International internship program in Paris and Santiago, Chile; 3-2 engineering program with Washington University. **Credit/placement by examination:** AP, CLEP, IB, institutional tests. **Support services:** Learning center, study skills assistance, tutoring, writing center.

**Majors. Area/ethnic studies:** American, Asian, Latin American. **Biology:** General. **Business:** General. **Communications:** General. **Computer sciences:** Computer science. **Conservation:** Environmental studies. **Education:** General. **English:** English lit. **Foreign languages:** French, Spanish. **History:** General. **Math:** General. **Philosophy/religion:** Philosophy. **Physical sciences:** Chemistry, physics. **Psychology:** General. **Social sciences:** Anthropology, economics, international relations, political science, sociology. **Visual/performing arts:** Art, theater history.

**Most popular majors.** Biology 6%, business/marketing 11%, communications/journalism 14%, English 8%, psychology 7%, social sciences 24%, visual/performing arts 7%.

**Computing on campus.** 200 workstations in library, computer center, student center. Dormitories wired for high-speed internet access and linked to campus network. Commuter students can connect to campus network. Online library, helpline, repair service, student web hosting, wireless network available.

**Student life. Freshman orientation:** Mandatory, $100 fee. Preregistration for classes offered. **Housing:** Guaranteed on-campus for freshmen. Coed dorms, single-sex dorms, substance-free housing available. $300 nonrefundable deposit, deadline 5/1. **Activities:** Jazz band, choral groups, dance, drama, film society, literary magazine, music ensembles, musical theater, radio station, student government, student newspaper, Christian Fellowship, Interfaith Council, Amnesty International, League for Environmental Awareness and Protection, United Black Association, Women's Issues Table, Latinos Unidos, Asian interest group, diversity advocates (ALLY), anti-racism group (STAR), Hillel.

**Athletics.** NCAA. **Intercollegiate:** Basketball, cross-country, diving, football (tackle) M, handball, ice hockey, soccer, softball W, swimming, tennis, volleyball W. **Intramural:** Basketball, football (non-tackle), racquetball, soccer, softball, tennis, volleyball. **Team name:** Foresters.

**Student services.** Adult student services, alcohol/substance abuse counseling, career counseling, student employment services, financial aid counseling, health services, minority student services, personal counseling, placement for graduates, veterans' counselor, women's services. **Physically disabled:** Services for visually, hearing impaired.

**Contact.** E-mail: admissions@lakeforest.edu
Phone: (847) 735-5000 Toll-free number: (800) 828-4751
Fax: (847) 735-6271
William Motzer, Vice President for Admissions and Career Services, Lake Forest College, 555 North Sheridan Road, Lake Forest, IL 60045-2399

## Lakeview College of Nursing
**Danville, Illinois**
www.lakeviewcol.edu
CB code: 0149

- Private two-year upper-division nursing college
- Commuter campus in large town
- 72% of applicants admitted
- Application essay required

**General.** Founded in 1894. Regionally accredited. **Degrees:** 142 bachelor's awarded. **Articulation:** Agreements with Danville Area Community College, Eastern Illinois University. **Location:** 35 miles from Urbana-Champaign, 130 miles from Chicago. **Calendar:** Semester, limited summer session. **Full-time faculty:** 20 total. **Part-time faculty:** 8 total. **Special facilities:** Free clinic, nature preserve.

**Student profile.** 252 degree-seeking undergraduates. 171 applied as first time-transfer students, 123 admitted, 78 enrolled.

| Out-of-state: | 2% | 25 or older: | 83% |
|---|---|---|---|

**Basis for selection.** Open admission. High school transcript, college transcript, application essay required. Based on interview, references, and transcripts. Applicant must have completed 33 credit hours of general course work with 2.5 GPA prior to admission. Transfer accepted as sophomores, juniors.

**2007-2008 Annual costs.** Tuition/fees: $10,950. Books/supplies: $582.

**Financial aid.** All financial aid based on need.

**Application procedures. Admission:** Rolling admission. $100 fee. Application must be submitted on paper. National League for Nursing examinations used to determine advanced placement for entering students who already have RN degree. **Financial aid:** Priority date 4/15, no deadline. FAFSA, institutional form required.

**Academics.** BS in nursing requires total of 125 credit hours. 95% of entering students complete degree in 5 years or less. **Special study options:** Distance learning, honors, independent study. **Credit/placement by examination:** CLEP. **Support services:** Reduced course load, study skills assistance, tutoring.

**Majors. Health:** Nursing (RN).

**Computing on campus.** 12 workstations in library, computer center.

**Student life. Activities:** Student government, student newspaper, Illinois Student Nurses Association, National Student Nurses Association.

**Student services.** Adult student services, career counseling, financial aid counseling, health services, personal counseling, veterans' counselor.

**Contact.** E-mail: admissions@lakeviewcol.edu
Phone: (217) 554-6899 Fax: (217) 477-2970
Connie Young, Registrar, Lakeview College of Nursing, 903 North Logan Avenue, Danville, IL 61832

## Lewis University
**Romeoville, Illinois**
www.lewisu.edu
CB member
CB code: 1404

- Private 4-year university affiliated with Roman Catholic Church
- Residential campus in large town
- 3,822 degree-seeking undergraduates: 23% part-time, 61% women, 11% African American, 4% Asian American, 11% Hispanic American, 3% international
- 1,479 degree-seeking graduate students
- 68% of applicants admitted
- SAT or ACT (ACT writing optional) required
- 53% graduate within 6 years

**General.** Founded in 1932. Regionally accredited. Sponsored by De La Salle Christian Brothers. **Degrees:** 853 bachelor's, 6 associate awarded; master's, doctoral offered. **ROTC:** Army, Air Force. **Location:** 30 miles from Chicago. **Calendar:** Semester, extensive summer session. **Full-time faculty:** 176 total; 65% have terminal degrees, 10% minority, 52% women. **Part-time faculty:** 363 total; 10% have terminal degrees, 13% minority, 47% women. **Class size:** 64% < 20, 34% 20-39, 1% 40-49. **Special facilities:** Campus airport, aeronautical training center, all digital radio station.

**Freshman class profile.** 2,654 applied, 1,795 admitted, 636 enrolled.

| Mid 50% test scores | | Rank in top tenth: | 14% |
|---|---|---|---|
| SAT critical reading: | 460-570 | Return as sophomores: | 77% |
| SAT math: | 480-580 | Out-of-state: | 8% |
| ACT composite: | 19-24 | Live on campus: | 61% |
| GPA 3.50 or higher: | 32% | International: | 2% |
| GPA 3.0-3.49: | 29% | Fraternities: | 7% |
| GPA 2.0-2.99: | 39% | Sororities: | 14% |
| Rank in top quarter: | 36% | | |

**Basis for selection.** Applicants must graduate from approved high school with 2.0 GPA. Class rank and ACT/SAT scores must indicate strong likelihood of success in university studies. 20 ACT required for admission to nursing program. Interview recommended. **Homeschooled:** Statement describing homeschool structure and mission required.

**High school preparation.** 18 units required. Required and recommended units include English 4, mathematics 3, social studies 2, history 1, science 2 (laboratory 1), foreign language 2 and academic electives 3. 1 year chemistry and 2 years math at 2.0 level or above strongly recommended for nursing applicants.

**2008-2009 Annual costs.** Tuition/fees: $21,990. Room/board: $8,000. Books/supplies: $1,000. Personal expenses: $1,320.

**2007-2008 Financial aid. Need-based:** Average need met was 77%. Average scholarship/grant was $7,694; average loan $4,846. 74% of total undergraduate aid awarded as scholarships/grants, 26% as loans/jobs. **Non-need-based:** Scholarships awarded for academics, alumni affiliation, art, athletics, job skills, music/drama, religious affiliation, ROTC.

**Application procedures. Admission:** Priority date 3/1; no deadline. $40 fee, may be waived for applicants with need. Application may be submitted online. Admission notification on a rolling basis beginning on or about 10/1. Must reply by May 1 or within 2 week(s) if notified thereafter. **Financial aid:** Closing date 5/1. FAFSA required. Applicants notified on a rolling basis starting 2/1; must reply by 5/1 or within 2 week(s) of notification.

**Academics.** Accelerated degree completion program available to students 24 years and older. **Special study options:** Accelerated study, combined bachelor's/graduate degree, distance learning, double major, dual enrollment of high school students, ESL, exchange student, honors, independent study, internships, liberal arts/career combination, student-designed major, study abroad, teacher certification program. **Credit/placement by examination:** AP, CLEP, institutional tests. 60 credit hours maximum toward bachelor's degree. **Support services:** Learning center, pre-admission summer program, reduced course load, remedial instruction, study skills assistance, tutoring, writing center.

**Majors. Area/ethnic studies:** American. **Biology:** General, biochemistry, environmental. **Business:** General, accounting, business admin, finance, human resources, international, management information systems, management science, managerial economics, marketing. **Communications:** General, broadcast journalism, digital media, journalism, public relations, radio/tv. **Communications technology:** General, radio/tv. **Computer sciences:** General, computer graphics, computer science, information systems. **Conservation:** General. **Education:** General, elementary, special. **English:** Composition, creative writing, English lit, speech/rhetoric. **Health:** Athletic training, chiropractic assistant, health care admin, health services, nursing (RN), pharmacy assistant, predental, premedicine, prenursing, prepharmacy, preveterinary. **History:** General. **Interdisciplinary:** Global studies. **Legal studies:** Prelaw. **Liberal arts:** Arts/sciences. **Math:** General. **Mechanic/repair:** Aircraft, avionics. **Parks/recreation:** Sports admin. **Philosophy/religion:** Philosophy, religion. **Physical sciences:** Chemistry, physics. **Protective services:** Correctional facilities, criminal justice, forensics, law enforcement admin, police science, security services. **Psychology:** General. **Public administration:** General, community org/advocacy, human services, social work. **Social sciences:** Economics, political science, sociology. **Transportation:** Air traffic control, airline/commercial pilot, aviation, aviation management. **Visual/performing arts:** Art, commercial/advertising art, dramatic, drawing, graphic design, illustration, music management, painting, studio arts, theater arts management. **Other:** Aviation security.

**Most popular majors.** Business/marketing 22%, education 8%, health sciences 20%, psychology 6%, security/protective services 13%, trade and industry 7%.

**Computing on campus.** 350 workstations in library, computer center. Dormitories wired for high-speed internet access and linked to campus network. Commuter students can connect to campus network. Online course registration, online library, helpline, wireless network available.

**Student life. Freshman orientation:** Mandatory, $80 fee. Preregistration for classes offered. Two-day program includes transition seminars, assessment, and academic advising. Summer/winter orientations (overnight optional) available, includes parent orientations and welcome weekend before first day of classes. **Housing:** Guaranteed on-campus for all undergraduates. Coed dorms available. $100 nonrefundable deposit, deadline 5/1. Handicapped accessibility available in most residence halls. **Activities:** Bands, campus ministries, choral groups, dance, drama, international student organizations, literary magazine, music ensembles, musical theater, radio station, student government, student newspaper, TV station, Fellowship of Justice, black student union, Latin American student organization, InterFratority Council, National Panhellenic Council, American Association of Airport Executives, Coffey Aviation student organization, student nurses association, Teachers of Tomorrow.

**Athletics.** NCAA. **Intercollegiate:** Baseball M, basketball, cheerleading, cross-country, golf, soccer, softball W, swimming, tennis, track and field, volleyball. **Intramural:** Basketball, bowling, field hockey, football (nontackle), golf, handball, racquetball, soccer, softball, table tennis, tennis, volleyball. **Team name:** Flyers.

**Student services.** Adult student services, alcohol/substance abuse counseling, career counseling, student employment services, financial aid counseling, health services, minority student services, personal counseling, placement for graduates, veterans' counselor.

**Contact.** E-mail: admissions@lewisu.edu
Phone: (815) 836-5250 Toll-free number: (800) 897-9000
Fax: (815) 836-5002
Andrew Sison, Dean of Admission, Lewis University, One University Parkway, Romeoville, IL 60446-2200

---

## Lexington College
### Chicago, Illinois
### www.lexingtoncollege.edu  CB code: 3843

- Private 4-year hospitality management college for women affiliated with Roman Catholic Church
- Commuter campus in very large city

---

- 57 degree-seeking undergraduates: 25% African American, 4% Asian American, 18% Hispanic American, 2% Native American, 5% international
- 47% of applicants admitted
- SAT or ACT, application essay required

**General.** Founded in 1977. Regionally accredited. **Degrees:** 2 bachelor's, 2 associate awarded. **Location:** Downtown. **Calendar:** Semester. **Full-time faculty:** 4 total; 100% have terminal degrees, 100% minority, 100% women. **Part-time faculty:** 13 total; 100% have terminal degrees, 77% minority, 77% women. **Class size:** 100% < 20. **Special facilities:** Culinary demonstration laboratory, computer laboratory.

**Freshman class profile.** 64 applied, 30 admitted, 8 enrolled.

| Mid 50% test scores | | Return as sophomores: | 85% |
|---|---|---|---|
| ACT composite: | 19-25 | Out-of-state: | 8% |
| End year in good standing: | 85% | | |

**Basis for selection.** School achievement record, essay, and interview most important. Work experience considered. **Homeschooled:** Letter of recommendation (nonparent) required. Must submit GED with scores.

**High school preparation.** 10 units recommended. Recommended units include English 4, mathematics 2, social studies 2 and science 2.

**2007-2008 Annual costs.** Tuition/fees: $20,550. Room/board: $8,000. Books/supplies: $750. Personal expenses: $400.

**Financial aid.** All financial aid based on need. **Additional information:** Work-study is available.

**Application procedures. Admission:** No deadline. $30 fee, may be waived for applicants with need. Admission notification on a rolling basis. **Financial aid:** Priority date 5/15; no closing date. FAFSA required. Applicants notified on a rolling basis starting 7/1; must reply within 2 week(s) of notification.

**Academics. Special study options:** Cooperative education, independent study, internships, study abroad. **Credit/placement by examination:** AP, CLEP, institutional tests. **Support services:** Remedial instruction, study skills assistance, tutoring.

**Majors. Business:** Business admin, hotel/motel admin, restaurant/food services. **Family/consumer sciences:** Institutional food production.

**Computing on campus.** 30 workstations in library, computer center. Online library, wireless network available.

**Student life. Freshman orientation:** Mandatory. Preregistration for classes offered. 2-day program before classes begin. **Activities:** Student government, student newspaper, campus ministry.

**Student services.** Campus ministries, career counseling, student employment services, financial aid counseling, personal counseling, placement for graduates.

**Contact.** E-mail: admissions@lexingtoncollege.edu
Phone: (312) 226-6294 Toll-free number: (866) 647-3093
Fax: (312) 226-6405
Cynthia Selling, Director of Enrollment and Communication, Lexington College, 310 South Peoria Street, Suite 512, Chicago, IL 60607-3534

---

## Lincoln Christian College and Seminary
### Lincoln, Illinois
### www.lccs.edu  CB code: 1405

- Private 4-year Bible and seminary college affiliated with Church of Christ
- Residential campus in large town
- 636 degree-seeking undergraduates: 5% African American, 2% Hispanic American
- 348 graduate students
- 84% of applicants admitted
- SAT or ACT with writing, application essay required
- 53% graduate within 6 years; 10% enter graduate study

**General.** Founded in 1944. Regionally accredited; also accredited by ABHE, ATS. **Degrees:** 109 bachelor's, 4 associate awarded; master's, doctoral, first professional offered. **Location:** 30 miles from Springfield. **Calendar:** Semester, limited summer session. **Full-time faculty:** 44 total; 46% have terminal degrees, 4% minority, 18% women. **Part-time faculty:** 49 total; 10% have terminal degrees, 2% minority, 47% women.

**Freshman class profile.** 195 applied, 164 admitted, 107 enrolled.

| Mid 50% test scores | | Rank in top tenth: | 19% |
|---|---|---|---|
| ACT composite: | 19-25 | End year in good standing: | 65% |
| GPA 3.50 or higher: | 43% | Return as sophomores: | 66% |
| GPA 3.0-3.49: | 29% | Out-of-state: | 40% |
| GPA 2.0-2.99: | 28% | Live on campus: | 90% |
| Rank in top quarter: | 45% | | |

**Basis for selection.** Recommendation of applicant's church leaders as to suitability for church-related vocations very important. High school record (core courses) and ACT scores also considered. Subscores of writing and English and application essay also important. Interview recommended. Audition required of music majors. **Homeschooled:** Transcript of courses and grades, interview, letter of recommendation (nonparent) required. List of involvement outside of education/academics required. **Learning Disabled:** Students with learning disabilities usually recommended to academic resource center.

**High school preparation.** 17 units recommended. Recommended units include English 4, mathematics 3, social studies 3, history 3, science 2 and foreign language 2.

**2008-2009 Annual costs.** Tuition/fees: $11,790. Room/board: $5,355. Books/supplies: $600. Personal expenses: $1,700.

**Financial aid. Non-need-based:** Scholarships awarded for academics.

**Application procedures. Admission:** No deadline. $25 fee, may be waived for applicants with need. Application may be submitted online. Admission notification on a rolling basis. **Financial aid:** Priority date 8/10; no closing date. FAFSA, institutional form required. Applicants notified on a rolling basis starting 3/1; must reply within 2 week(s) of notification.

**Academics. Special study options:** Distance learning, double major, honors, independent study, internships, study abroad, teacher certification program, weekend college. Teacher preparatory program through University of Illinois at Springfield, Illinois State University, and Greenville College. **Credit/placement by examination:** AP, CLEP, ACT, institutional tests. **Support services:** Learning center, reduced course load, remedial instruction, study skills assistance, tutoring, writing center.

**Majors. Business:** Business admin. **Communications:** Media studies. **Education:** Early childhood, secondary. **Family/consumer sciences:** Family/community services. **Philosophy/religion:** Religion. **Theology:** Bible, missionary, religious ed, sacred music, theology, youth ministry.

**Most popular majors.** Business/marketing 12%, education 14%, family/consumer sciences 6%, theological studies 68%.

**Computing on campus.** 51 workstations in library, computer center, student center. Dormitories wired for high-speed internet access and linked to campus network. Commuter students can connect to campus network. Online course registration, online library, helpline, wireless network available.

**Student life. Freshman orientation:** Mandatory, $250 fee. Preregistration for classes offered. **Policies:** Religious observance required. **Housing:** Guaranteed on-campus for all undergraduates. Single-sex dorms, apartments, substance-free housing available. $150 fully refundable deposit, deadline 8/10. **Activities:** Campus ministries, choral groups, drama, international student organizations, music ensembles, musical theater, student government, student newspaper, volunteer groups in local health care institutions, missions interest groups, Christian service and outreach groups.

**Athletics.** NCCAA. **Intercollegiate:** Baseball M, basketball, soccer M, softball W, volleyball W. **Intramural:** Badminton W, basketball M, football (tackle), soccer, volleyball. **Team name:** Preachers.

**Student services.** Adult student services, student employment services, financial aid counseling, health services, personal counseling. **Physically disabled:** Services for visually, hearing impaired. **Learning disabled:** Comprehensive services available.

**Contact.** E-mail: coladmis@lccs.edu
Phone: (217) 732-3168 ext. 2251 Toll-free number: (888) 522-5228
Fax: (217) 732-4199
Jonathan Nimrod, Vice President of Enrollment Management, Lincoln Christian College and Seminary, 100 Campus View Drive, Lincoln, IL 62656-2167

---

## Loyola University Chicago

**Chicago, Illinois**
**www.luc.edu**
**CB member**
**CB code: 1412**

- Private 4-year university affiliated with Roman Catholic Church
- Residential campus in very large city
- 9,365 degree-seeking undergraduates: 5% part-time, 65% women, 5% African American, 12% Asian American, 10% Hispanic American, 1% international
- 5,428 degree-seeking graduate students
- 73% of applicants admitted
- SAT or ACT (ACT writing optional) required
- 65% graduate within 6 years

**General.** Founded in 1870. Regionally accredited. Extensive degree program for returning adults. Lake Shore and Water Tower campuses in Chicago, and medical center campus in suburbs. **Degrees:** 2,169 bachelor's awarded; master's, doctoral, first professional offered. **ROTC:** Army, Naval, Air Force. **Calendar:** Semester, extensive summer session. **Full-time faculty:** 582 total; 11% minority, 44% women. **Part-time faculty:** 749 total; 12% minority, 55% women. **Class size:** 33% < 20, 44% 20-39, 12% 40-49, 9% 50-99, 2% >100. **Special facilities:** Gallery of medieval and renaissance art, job resource center for nursing, seismograph station, electron microscope, theater, art museum, language resource center.

**Freshman class profile.** 17,357 applied, 12,723 admitted, 2,035 enrolled.

| Mid 50% test scores | | Rank in top quarter: | 69% |
|---|---|---|---|
| SAT critical reading: | 540-640 | Rank in top tenth: | 33% |
| SAT math: | 520-640 | End year in good standing: | 94% |
| SAT writing: | 510-630 | Return as sophomores: | 84% |
| ACT composite: | 23-28 | Out-of-state: | 41% |
| GPA 3.50 or higher: | 62% | Live on campus: | 87% |
| GPA 3.0-3.49: | 35% | Fraternities: | 7% |
| GPA 2.0-2.99: | 3% | Sororities: | 7% |

**Basis for selection.** GPA, test scores, and rigor of high school curriculum important. Interview recommended. Essay required for honors program applicants.

**High school preparation.** 15 units required; 20 recommended. Required and recommended units include English 4, mathematics 3-4, social studies 2, history 1-2, science 3, foreign language 2 and academic electives 3. Additional requirements for certain majors.

**2008-2009 Annual costs.** Tuition/fees (projected): $29,486. Room/board: $10,490. Books/supplies: $1,200. Personal expenses: $1,600.

**2006-2007 Financial aid. Need-based:** 1,825 full-time freshmen applied for aid; 1,538 were judged to have need; 1,532 of these received aid. Average need met was 78%. Average scholarship/grant was $14,896; average loan $3,041. 59% of total undergraduate aid awarded as scholarships/grants, 41% as loans/jobs. **Non-need-based:** Awarded to 1,482 full-time undergraduates, including 482 freshmen. Scholarships awarded for academics, athletics, leadership, music/drama, religious affiliation.

**Application procedures. Admission:** Priority date 4/1; no deadline. $25 fee, may be waived for applicants with need. Application may be submitted online. Admission notification on a rolling basis beginning on or about 10/1. Must reply by May 1 or within 2 week(s) if notified thereafter. Honors program applicants must apply by March 1. **Financial aid:** Priority date 3/1; no closing date. FAFSA required. Applicants notified on a rolling basis starting 2/15; must reply within 3 week(s) of notification.

**Academics. Special study options:** Accelerated study, combined bachelor's/graduate degree, double major, dual enrollment of high school students, exchange student, honors, independent study, internships, study abroad, teacher certification program, Washington semester. School of professional studies offers part-time evening programs leading to bachelor's degrees; cooperative programs with Erikson Institute for Early Education and St. Joseph's Seminary; study abroad in Italy and Mexico available. **Credit/placement by examination:** AP, CLEP, IB, SAT, ACT, institutional tests. 64 credit hours maximum toward bachelor's degree. **Support services:** Learning center, pre-admission summer program, reduced course load, study skills assistance, tutoring, writing center.

**Majors. Area/ethnic studies:** Women's. **Biology:** General, bioinformatics. **Business:** Accounting, finance, human resources, international, management information systems, managerial economics, marketing, operations, organizational behavior. **Communications:** General, advertising, journalism, media studies. **Computer sciences:** General, security. **Conservation:** Environmental science. **Education:** Bilingual, elementary, mathematics, secondary, special. **English:** English lit. **Foreign languages:** Ancient Greek, classics, French, German, Italian, Latin, Spanish. **Health:** Clinical nutrition, health care admin, nursing (RN). **History:** General. **Interdisciplinary:** Math/computer science. **Math:** General, statistics. **Parks/recreation:** Sports admin. **Philosophy/religion:** Philosophy. **Physical sciences:** Chemistry, physics. **Protective services:** Criminal justice, forensics. **Psychology:** General. **Public administration:** Human services, social work. **Social sciences:** Anthropology, international relations, political science, sociology. **Theology:** Religious ed, theology. **Visual/performing arts:** Dramatic, studio arts. **Other:** International cinema and video.

**Most popular majors.** Biology 10%, business/marketing 21%, communications/journalism 6%, health sciences 8%, psychology 10%, social sciences 14%.

**Computing on campus.** 696 workstations in library, computer center, student center. Dormitories wired for high-speed internet access and linked to campus network. Commuter students can connect to campus network. Online course registration, online library, helpline, repair service, student web hosting, wireless network available.

**Student life. Freshman orientation:** Mandatory, $250 fee. Preregistration for classes offered. 2-day orientation program at Lake Shore campus. **Housing:** Guaranteed on-campus for freshmen. Coed dorms, special housing for disabled, apartments, substance-free housing available. $250 nonrefundable deposit, deadline 5/1. 24-hour quiet facility available. **Activities:** Bands, choral groups, drama, film society, literary magazine, music ensembles, musical theater, radio station, student government, student newspaper, over 125 clubs and organizations.

**Athletics.** NCAA. **Intercollegiate:** Basketball, cross-country, golf, soccer, softball W, track and field, volleyball. **Intramural:** Badminton, basketball, cross-country, football (non-tackle), golf, racquetball, soccer, table tennis, tennis, volleyball. **Team name:** Ramblers.

**Student services.** Adult student services, alcohol/substance abuse counseling, campus ministries, career counseling, student employment services, financial aid counseling, health services, minority student services, on-campus daycare, personal counseling, placement for graduates, veterans' counselor. **Physically disabled:** Services for visually, speech, hearing impaired.

**Contact.** E-mail: admission@luc.edu
Phone: (312) 915-6500 Toll-free number: (800) 262-2373
Fax: (312) 915-7216
April Hansen, Director of Admissions, Loyola University Chicago, 820 North Michigan Avenue, Chicago, IL 60611-9810

---

## MacMurray College

**Jacksonville, Illinois**
**www.mac.edu**

**CB member**
**CB code: 1435**

- Private 4-year liberal arts college affiliated with United Methodist Church
- Residential campus in large town
- 634 degree-seeking undergraduates
- 61% of applicants admitted
- SAT or ACT required

**General.** Founded in 1846. Regionally accredited. **Degrees:** 124 bachelor's, 1 associate awarded. **Location:** 30 miles from Springfield. **Calendar:** Semester, limited summer session. **Full-time faculty:** 35 total. **Part-time faculty:** 38 total. **Class size:** 59% < 20, 39% 20-39, 2% 40-49, 1% 50-99.

**Freshman class profile.** 813 applied, 494 admitted, 125 enrolled.

| Mid 50% test scores | | Rank in top quarter: | 18% |
|---|---|---|---|
| SAT critical reading: | 350-410 | Rank in top tenth: | 8% |
| SAT math: | 390-420 | Out-of-state: | 13% |
| ACT composite: | 16-22 | Live on campus: | 86% |
| GPA 3.50 or higher: | 17% | Fraternities: | 5% |
| GPA 3.0-3.49: | 27% | Sororities: | 20% |
| GPA 2.0-2.99: | 49% | | |

**Basis for selection.** 23 ACT, class ranking in top 25%, or 20 ACT and class ranking in top 50% important. Applicants with 20-22 ACT and in lower 50% of class, or 17-19 ACT (with no subtest score below 16) and 2.0 GPA reviewed by faculty admission committee. 20 ACT required for nursing applicants. SAT results (equivalent to ACT cutoffs) considered. Participation in school, community, and church activities, and recommendations important. Interview recommended for academically deficient applicants. Audition recommended for music scholarship. Portfolio recommended for art scholarship.

**High school preparation.** 17 units recommended. Recommended units include English 4, mathematics 3, social studies 2, history 3, science 3 (laboratory 2) and foreign language 2.

**2007-2008 Annual costs.** Tuition/fees: $16,850. Room/board: $6,395. Books/supplies: $775. Personal expenses: $555.

**Financial aid. Non-need-based:** Scholarships awarded for academics, alumni affiliation, art, leadership, music/drama, religious affiliation. **Additional information:** Merit scholarships for accepted, enrolled freshman based on academic record. Need-based program meets 100% of direct tuition charges after family contribution and financial aid.

**Application procedures. Admission:** Priority date 5/1; no deadline. No application fee. Application may be submitted online. Admission notification on a rolling basis beginning on or about 9/1. **Financial aid:** Priority date 5/1; no closing date. FAFSA required. Applicants notified on a rolling basis starting 2/1; must reply within 2 week(s) of notification.

**Academics. Special study options:** Accelerated study, combined bachelor's/graduate degree, cooperative education, cross-registration, double major, dual enrollment of high school students, exchange student, independent study, internships, liberal arts/career combination, study abroad, teacher certification program, Washington semester. 3-2 programs in engineering with Washington University (MO) and Columbia University (NY). **Credit/placement by examination:** AP, CLEP, IB, institutional tests. 32 credit hours maximum toward bachelor's degree. **Support services:** Learning center, reduced course load, remedial instruction, study skills assistance, tutoring, writing center.

**Majors. Biology:** General. **Business:** Accounting, business admin, finance, management information systems. **Communications:** Journalism. **Computer sciences:** General, computer science. **Education:** Biology, Deaf/hearing impaired, elementary, emotionally handicapped, English, history, learning disabled, mathematics, music, physical, secondary, Spanish, special. **Engineering:** General. **English:** English lit. **Foreign languages:** French, sign language interpretation, Spanish. **Health:** Predental, premedicine, preveterinary. **History:** General. **Math:** General. **Parks/recreation:** Sports admin. **Philosophy/religion:** Philosophy, religion. **Physical sciences:** Chemistry, physics. **Psychology:** General. **Public administration:** Social work. **Social sciences:** International relations, political science. **Visual/performing arts:** Art, dramatic. **Other:** Student personnel services.

**Most popular majors.** Business/marketing 16%, education 22%, health sciences 11%, psychology 6%, security/protective services 9%.

**Computing on campus.** 75 workstations in dormitories, library, computer center. Dormitories wired for high-speed internet access and linked to campus network. Online library available.

**Student life. Freshman orientation:** Mandatory. Preregistration for classes offered. 2-day acclimation to campus life prior to start of classes. **Housing:** Guaranteed on-campus for all undergraduates. Coed dorms, single-sex dorms, special housing for disabled, substance-free housing available. $150 deposit. **Activities:** Choral groups, dance, drama, literary magazine, music ensembles, musical theater, student government, student newspaper, NAACP, Alpha Phi Omega, Circle-K, Holy Fools, Newman Club.

**Athletics.** NCAA. **Intercollegiate:** Baseball M, basketball, cross-country, football (tackle) M, golf, soccer, softball W, tennis, volleyball W, wrestling M. **Intramural:** Basketball, cheerleading, cross-country, soccer, table tennis, volleyball. **Team name:** Highlanders.

**Student services.** Alcohol/substance abuse counseling, campus ministries, career counseling, student employment services, financial aid counseling, health services, personal counseling, placement for graduates. **Physically disabled:** Services for visually, hearing impaired.

**Contact.** E-mail: admissions@mac.edu
Phone: (217) 479-7056 Toll-free number: (800) 252-7485
Fax: (217) 291-0702
Robert LaVerrriere, Director of Enrollment Services, MacMurray College, 447 East College Avenue, Jacksonville, IL 62650-2590

---

## McKendree University

**Lebanon, Illinois**
**www.mckendree.edu**

**CB code: 1456**

- Private 4-year university and liberal arts college affiliated with United Methodist Church
- Residential campus in small town
- 2,363 degree-seeking undergraduates: 29% part-time, 56% women, 13% African American, 1% Asian American, 2% Hispanic American, 2% international

- 835 degree-seeking graduate students
- 71% of applicants admitted
- SAT or ACT (ACT writing optional), application essay required
- 61% graduate within 6 years; 35% enter graduate study

**General.** Founded in 1828. Regionally accredited. **Degrees:** 468 bachelor's, 24 associate awarded; master's offered. **ROTC:** Army, Air Force. **Location:** 12 miles from Belleville, 23 miles from St. Louis. **Calendar:** Semester, limited summer session. **Full-time faculty:** 95 total; 77% have terminal degrees, 7% minority, 56% women. **Part-time faculty:** 243 total. **Class size:** 72% < 20, 28% 20-39. **Special facilities:** Networked faculty and classroom buildings, fine arts center with theatre.

**Freshman class profile.** 1,097 applied, 778 admitted, 305 enrolled.

| Mid 50% test scores | | Rank in top quarter: | 49% |
|---|---|---|---|
| SAT critical reading: | 400-450 | Rank in top tenth: | 22% |
| SAT math: | 530-600 | End year in good standing: | 85% |
| SAT writing: | 450-490 | Return as sophomores: | 71% |
| ACT composite: | 20-25 | Out-of-state: | 11% |
| GPA 3.50 or higher: | 44% | Live on campus: | 82% |
| GPA 3.0-3.49: | 26% | International: | 4% |
| GPA 2.0-2.99: | 30% | | |

**Basis for selection.** Holistic approach to admissions; variety of criteria considered including GPA, rigor of secondary school record, standardized test scores; and interview (when possible). RN required of Nursing Completion Program applicants. Interviews recommended. Audition required of music majors and minors. Portfolio recommended for art majors. **Homeschooled:** Statement describing homeschool structure and mission, letter of recommendation (nonparent) required. Applicants must submit description of courses studied, 3 letters of recommendation (not including that of parents).

**High school preparation.** 14 units recommended. Recommended units include English 4, mathematics 3, social studies 2, history 1, science 3 and foreign language 1.

**2008-2009 Annual costs.** Tuition/fees: $21,270. Room/board: $8,220. Books/supplies: $1,000. Personal expenses: $600.

**2007-2008 Financial aid. Need-based:** Average need met was 85%. Average scholarship/grant was $14,548; average loan $2,898. 72% of total undergraduate aid awarded as scholarships/grants, 28% as loans/jobs. **Non-need-based:** Scholarships awarded for academics, alumni affiliation, art, athletics, leadership, minority status, music/drama, religious affiliation.

**Application procedures. Admission:** No deadline. $40 fee, may be waived for applicants with need. Application may be submitted online. Admission notification on a rolling basis beginning on or about 9/15. **Financial aid:** Priority date 5/31; no closing date. FAFSA required. Applicants notified on a rolling basis starting 3/1; must reply within 4 week(s) of notification.

**Academics. Special study options:** Accelerated study, combined bachelor's/graduate degree, cooperative education, double major, external degree, honors, independent study, internships, liberal arts/career combination, student-designed major, study abroad, teacher certification program. 3-2 and 3-3 occupational therapy program with Washington University. **Credit/placement by examination:** AP, CLEP, IB, SAT, ACT, institutional tests. 36 credit hours maximum toward associate degree, 64 toward bachelor's. **Support services:** Learning center, reduced course load, remedial instruction, study skills assistance, tutoring, writing center.

**Honors college/program.** 3.6 GPA, 27 ACT, top 10% of class required; approximately 20 freshmen admitted.

**Majors. Biology:** General. **Business:** Accounting, business admin, management science, marketing. **Communications:** General. **Computer sciences:** General, computer science, information systems, information technology. **Education:** General, art, business, elementary, health, history, music, physical, science. **English:** English lit, speech/rhetoric. **Health:** Athletic training, nursing (RN). **History:** General. **Liberal arts:** Arts/sciences. **Math:** General. **Philosophy/religion:** Philosophy, religion. **Physical sciences:** Chemistry. **Psychology:** General. **Social sciences:** General, economics, international relations, political science, sociology. **Visual/performing arts:** Studio arts.

**Most popular majors.** Business/marketing 37%, computer/information sciences 10%, education 11%, health sciences 10%, psychology 6%.

**Computing on campus.** 220 workstations in library, computer center, student center. Dormitories wired for high-speed internet access and linked to campus network. Commuter students can connect to campus network. Online course registration, online library, helpline, repair service, student web hosting, wireless network available.

**Student life. Freshman orientation:** Mandatory, $50 fee. Preregistration for classes offered. Three day program held weekend before start of classes. **Policies:** Students are required to live on campus unless 21 years of age, of senior class standing, married, commuting from the home of a parent or legal guardian, or a veteran with at least two years active military duty. **Housing:** Guaranteed on-campus for all undergraduates. Coed dorms, special housing for disabled, apartments, substance-free housing available. $200 nonrefundable deposit. **Activities:** Bands, campus ministries, choral groups, dance, drama, film society, international student organizations, literary magazine, music ensembles, Model UN, musical theater, radio station, student government, student newspaper, Campus Christian Fellowship, Students Against Social Injustice, black student organization, service organizations, resident hall association, Intergreek Council, Community Service Fellows.

**Athletics.** NAIA. **Intercollegiate:** Baseball M, basketball, bowling, cheerleading, cross-country, football (tackle) M, golf, ice hockey, soccer, softball W, tennis, track and field, volleyball W, wrestling M. **Intramural:** Basketball, football (non-tackle), softball, volleyball. **Team name:** Bearcats.

**Student services.** Adult student services, alcohol/substance abuse counseling, career counseling, student employment services, financial aid counseling, health services, minority student services, personal counseling, placement for graduates, veterans' counselor. **Physically disabled:** Services for visually, speech, hearing impaired.

**Contact.** E-mail: inquiry@mckendree.edu
Phone: (618) 537-6831 Toll-free number: (800) 232-7228 ext. 6831
Fax: (618) 537-6496
Chris Hall, Vice President for Admission and Financial Aid, McKendree University, 701 College Road, Lebanon, IL 62254

## Midstate College
**Peoria, Illinois**
**www.midstate.edu**

CB code: 3329

- For-profit 4-year business college
- Commuter campus in small city
- 560 degree-seeking undergraduates: 58% part-time, 80% women, 22% African American, 1% Asian American
- Application essay, interview required

**General.** Founded in 1888. Regionally accredited. **Degrees:** 6 bachelor's, 78 associate awarded. **Location:** 165 miles from Chicago. **Calendar:** Quarter, extensive summer session. **Full-time faculty:** 25 total; 12% have terminal degrees, 8% minority, 64% women. **Part-time faculty:** 38 total; 8% minority, 55% women.

**Freshman class profile.** 48 applied, 37 admitted, 37 enrolled.

**Basis for selection.** Open admission, but selective for some programs. Rigorous secondary school program and quality of application essay and interview important. Extracurricular acitivities, character and relationships to alumae considered. Entrance exam, including writing sample, and math placement tests administered to all applicants. Necessity for remedial support determined from results.

**2007-2008 Annual costs.** Tuition/fees: $11,250. Fees vary according to program.

**Financial aid. Additional information:** Work-study program available.

**Application procedures. Admission:** No deadline. $25 fee. Application may be submitted online. Admission notification on a rolling basis. **Financial aid:** No deadline. FAFSA, institutional form required. Applicants notified on a rolling basis; must reply within 4 week(s) of notification.

**Academics. Special study options:** Distance learning, double major, dual enrollment of high school students, internships. **Credit/placement by examination:** AP, CLEP, institutional tests. 24 credit hours maximum toward associate degree, 46 toward bachelor's. **Support services:** Learning center, reduced course load, remedial instruction, study skills assistance, tutoring.

**Majors. Business:** Accounting, business admin. **Computer sciences:** Information systems. **Health:** Medical records technology. **Legal studies:** Court reporting.

**Computing on campus.** 92 workstations in library, computer center. Commuter students can connect to campus network. Online library, helpline, repair service, wireless network available.

**Student life. Freshman orientation:** Mandatory. Preregistration for classes offered. Held first day of each quarter and at mid-term for the miniterm. **Activities:** Student government.

**Student services.** Career counseling, student employment services, financial aid counseling, personal counseling, placement for graduates, veterans' counselor.

**Contact.** E-mail: admissions@midstate.edu
Phone: (309) 692-4092 Toll-free number: (800) 251-4299
Fax: (309) 692-3893
Jessica Hancock, Director of Admissions, Midstate College, 411 West Northmoor Road, Peoria, IL 61614-3558

---

## Millikin University
**Decatur, Illinois**  **CB member**
**www.millikin.edu**  **CB code: 1470**

- Private 4-year university affiliated with Presbyterian Church (USA)
- Residential campus in small city
- 2,295 degree-seeking undergraduates: 5% part-time, 60% women
- 41 degree-seeking graduate students
- 68% of applicants admitted
- SAT or ACT (ACT writing optional) required
- 68% graduate within 6 years; 23% enter graduate study

**General.** Founded in 1901. Regionally accredited. **Degrees:** 612 bachelor's awarded; master's offered. **Location:** 180 miles from Chicago, 120 miles from St. Louis. **Calendar:** Semester, limited summer session. **Full-time faculty:** 155 total; 81% have terminal degrees, 8% minority, 48% women. **Part-time faculty:** 129 total; 20% have terminal degrees, 8% minority, 58% women. **Class size:** 66% < 20, 31% 20-39, 1% 40-49, 2% 50-99, less than 1% >100. **Special facilities:** Porcelain, glass and decorative arts museum, 32-track recording studio, computer imaging center, greenhouse, observatory, performance center, 24-hour computer labs, videoconferencing classroom, proscenium theatre, science center, 3-D arts buildng, student-run art gallery, student-owned and operated publishing company, student-operated record label.

**Freshman class profile.** 2,656 applied, 1,798 admitted, 477 enrolled.

| Mid 50% test scores | | Rank in top tenth: | 17% |
|---|---|---|---|
| SAT critical reading: | 470-630 | End year in good standing: | 85% |
| SAT math: | 490-650 | Return as sophomores: | 75% |
| SAT writing: | 450-620 | Out-of-state: | 15% |
| ACT composite: | 20-25 | Live on campus: | 86% |
| Rank in top quarter: | 44% | International: | 1% |

**Basis for selection.** School achievement record most important. Class rank, GPA, recommendation, test scores important. Applicant should rank in top half of class. Character references considered. Interview recommended. Audition required of music, music/theater majors. Portfolio required of art majors.

**High school preparation.** 16 units required. Required and recommended units include English 4, mathematics 3, social studies 2, history 2, science 3 and foreign language 2.

**2007-2008 Annual costs.** Tuition/fees: $23,945. Room/board: $7,210. Books/supplies: $1,000. Personal expenses: $1,250.

**2006-2007 Financial aid. Need-based:** 446 full-time freshmen applied for aid; 373 were judged to have need; 372 of these received aid. Average need met was 87%. Average scholarship/grant was $6,540; average loan $3,486. 66% of total undergraduate aid awarded as scholarships/grants, 34% as loans/jobs. **Non-need-based:** Awarded to 1,688 full-time undergraduates, including 445 freshmen. Scholarships awarded for academics, alumni affiliation, art, leadership, minority status, music/drama.

**Application procedures. Admission:** Priority date 5/1; no deadline. No application fee. Application may be submitted online. Admission notification on a rolling basis beginning on or about 9/15. **Financial aid:** Priority date 3/15; no closing date. FAFSA required. Applicants notified on a rolling basis starting 3/15; must reply by 5/1 or within 4 week(s) of notification.

**Academics.** Small business consulting and accelerated adult education available. **Special study options:** Accelerated study, combined bachelor's/graduate degree, double major, exchange student, honors, independent study, internships, student-designed major, study abroad, teacher certification program, United Nations semester, urban semester, Washington semester. **Credit/placement by examination:** AP, CLEP, IB, ACT, institutional tests. 30 credit hours maximum toward bachelor's degree. To receive CLEP credit student must not have attended secondary school in the past 3 years; CLEP credit cannot count in the major and may not be used if the equivalent course has been attempted. **Support services:** Learning center, reduced course load, study skills assistance, tutoring, writing center.

**Majors. Biology:** General, molecular. **Business:** Accounting, business admin, entrepreneurial studies, finance, international, management information systems, marketing. **Communications:** General. **Computer sciences:** Computer science. **Education:** Art, biology, chemistry, early childhood, elementary, English, mathematics, music, physical, social science. **English:** Creative writing, English lit. **Foreign languages:** Spanish. **Health:** Art therapy, athletic training, nursing (RN), predental, premedicine, prepharmacy, preveterinary. **History:** General. **Legal studies:** Prelaw. **Math:** Applied. **Parks/recreation:** Sports admin. **Philosophy/religion:** Philosophy. **Physical sciences:** Chemistry, physics. **Protective services:** Law enforcement admin. **Psychology:** General. **Public administration:** Human services. **Social sciences:** International relations, political science, sociology. **Visual/performing arts:** Arts management, commercial/advertising art, dramatic, music performance, musical theater, piano/organ, theater design, voice/opera. **Other:** Management and organizational leadership, Multi-Interdiscipinary studies.

**Most popular majors.** Business/marketing 24%, education 17%, health sciences 9%, visual/performing arts 14%.

**Computing on campus.** 198 workstations in dormitories, library, computer center, student center. Dormitories wired for high-speed internet access and linked to campus network. Commuter students can connect to campus network. Online course registration, online library, helpline, student web hosting, wireless network available.

**Student life. Freshman orientation:** Mandatory, $100 fee. Held 5 days before beginning of classes. **Housing:** Guaranteed on-campus for freshmen. Coed dorms, single-sex dorms, special housing for disabled, apartments, fraternity/sorority housing, substance-free housing available. $150 fully refundable deposit, deadline 5/1. Learning communities available. **Activities:** Bands, campus ministries, choral groups, dance, drama, film society, literary magazine, music ensembles, musical theater, opera, radio station, student government, student newspaper, symphony orchestra, black student union, Latino student association, Amnesty International, Multicultural Voices of Praise, Multicultural Affairs Roundtable, Young Republicans, Hand-in-Hand, Up 'til Dawn.

**Athletics.** NCAA. **Intercollegiate:** Baseball M, basketball, cheerleading, cross-country, football (tackle) M, golf, soccer, softball W, swimming, tennis W, track and field, volleyball W, wrestling M. **Intramural:** Basketball, bowling, football (non-tackle), soccer, softball, table tennis, volleyball. **Team name:** Big Blue.

**Student services.** Adult student services, alcohol/substance abuse counseling, career counseling, services for economically disadvantaged, student employment services, financial aid counseling, health services, minority student services, personal counseling, placement for graduates, women's services. **Physically disabled:** Services for visually, speech impaired.

**Contact.** E-mail: admis@millikin.edu
Phone: (217) 424-6210 Toll-free number: (800) 373-7733
Fax: (217) 425-4669
Stacey Hubbard, Dean of Admission and Financial Aid, Millikin University, 1184 West Main Street, Decatur, IL 62522-2084

---

## Monmouth College
**Monmouth, Illinois**  **CB member**
**www.monm.edu**  **CB code: 1484**

- Private 4-year liberal arts college affiliated with Presbyterian Church (USA)
- Residential campus in large town
- 1,331 degree-seeking undergraduates: 1% part-time, 55% women, 5% African American, 1% Asian American, 4% Hispanic American, 1% Native American, 1% international
- 78% of applicants admitted
- SAT or ACT (ACT writing optional) required
- 59% graduate within 6 years

**General.** Founded in 1853. Regionally accredited. **Degrees:** 295 bachelor's awarded. **ROTC:** Army. **Location:** 180 miles from Chicago, 60 miles from Peoria. **Calendar:** Semester. **Full-time faculty:** 91 total; 77% have terminal degrees, 9% minority, 40% women. **Part-time faculty:** 42 total; 12% have terminal degrees, 7% minority, 60% women. **Class size:** 53% < 20, 45% 20-39, 1% 40-49, less than 1% 50-99. **Special facilities:** Ecological field station, biology field station, nature preserve, art and antiquities collection, collection of letters by U.S. First Ladies, government documents repository.

**Freshman class profile.** 1,660 applied, 1,293 admitted, 321 enrolled.

| Mid 50% test scores | | Rank in top tenth: | 13% |
|---|---|---|---|
| SAT critical reading: | 550-580 | End year in good standing: | 66% |
| SAT math: | 560-580 | Return as sophomores: | 68% |
| ACT composite: | 20-26 | Out-of-state: | 10% |
| GPA 3.50 or higher: | 30% | Live on campus: | 93% |
| GPA 3.0-3.49: | 40% | Fraternities: | 18% |
| GPA 2.0-2.99: | 30% | Sororities: | 17% |
| Rank in top quarter: | 37% | | |

**Basis for selection.** School achievement record most important, followed by recommendations of counselor and teacher, test scores, and interview. Interview and essay recommended.

**High school preparation.** 14 units required; 20 recommended. Required and recommended units include English 4, mathematics 3-4, social studies 2-3, history 1-2, science 2-4 (laboratory 1-2) and foreign language 2-3.

**2008-2009 Annual costs.** Tuition/fees: $24,000. Room/board: $7,000. Books/supplies: $650. Personal expenses: $400.

**2007-2008 Financial aid. Need-based:** 385 full-time freshmen applied for aid; 331 were judged to have need; 331 of these received aid. Average need met was 90%. Average scholarship/grant was $15,150; average loan $2,715. 78% of total undergraduate aid awarded as scholarships/grants, 22% as loans/jobs. **Non-need-based:** Awarded to 455 full-time undergraduates, including 127 freshmen. Scholarships awarded for academics, art, music/drama, ROTC.

**Application procedures. Admission:** Priority date 4/1; no deadline. No application fee. Application may be submitted online. Admission notification on a rolling basis beginning on or about 9/1. **Financial aid:** Priority date 3/1; no closing date. FAFSA required. Applicants notified on a rolling basis starting 3/1; must reply by 8/31.

**Academics. Special study options:** Combined bachelor's/graduate degree, double major, honors, independent study, internships, liberal arts/career combination, student-designed major, study abroad, teacher certification program, urban semester, Washington semester. Off-campus programs in cooperation with Associated Colleges of the Midwest, institutional off-campus programs. **Credit/placement by examination:** AP, CLEP, IB, institutional tests. 5 credit hours maximum toward bachelor's degree. **Support services:** Learning center, study skills assistance, tutoring, writing center.

**Majors. Biology:** General, biochemistry. **Business:** Accounting, business admin, international, management information systems, managerial economics. **Communications:** General, public relations. **Computer sciences:** General, computer science. **Conservation:** General, environmental science. **Education:** General, art, elementary, history, multi-level teacher, music, physical, science, secondary, social studies. **Engineering:** General. **English:** English lit, speech/rhetoric. **Foreign languages:** Ancient Greek, classics, French, Latin, Spanish. **History:** General. **Interdisciplinary:** Biopsychology. **Legal studies:** Prelaw. **Liberal arts:** Arts/sciences. **Math:** General. **Physical sciences:** Chemistry, physics. **Psychology:** General. **Social sciences:** Economics, international relations, political science, sociology. **Visual/performing arts:** Art, studio arts.

**Most popular majors.** Biology 7%, business/marketing 28%, education 19%, English 7%, history 7%.

**Computing on campus.** 300 workstations in dormitories, library, computer center, student center. Dormitories wired for high-speed internet access and linked to campus network. Online course registration, online library, helpline, student web hosting, wireless network available.

**Student life. Freshman orientation:** Mandatory, $110 fee. Preregistration for classes offered. **Housing:** Guaranteed on-campus for all undergraduates. Coed dorms, single-sex dorms, special housing for disabled, apartments, cooperative housing, fraternity/sorority housing, substance-free housing available. $150 deposit, deadline 5/1. Theme housing available. **Activities:** Bands, campus ministries, choral groups, dance, drama, film society, literary magazine, music ensembles, radio station, student government, student newspaper, symphony orchestra, TV station, Coalition for Ethnic Awareness, Christian fellowship groups, interdenominational religious group, College Republicans, College Democrats, Students Organized for Service.

**Athletics.** NCAA. **Intercollegiate:** Baseball M, basketball, cheerleading, cross-country, football (tackle) M, golf, soccer, softball W, swimming, tennis, track and field, volleyball W. **Intramural:** Badminton, basketball, cross-country, golf, soccer, softball, swimming, tennis, track and field, volleyball, weight lifting. **Team name:** Fighting Scots.

**Student services.** Alcohol/substance abuse counseling, career counseling, student employment services, financial aid counseling, health services, minority student services, personal counseling, placement for graduates.

**Contact.** E-mail: admit@monm.edu
Phone: (309) 457-2131 Toll-free number: (800) 747-2687
Fax: (309) 457-2141
Christine Johnston, Dean of Admission, Monmouth College, 700 East Broadway, Monmouth, IL 61462-9989

## Moody Bible Institute
### Chicago, Illinois
www.moody.edu                          CB code: 1486

- Private 4-year Bible college affiliated with interdenominational tradition
- Residential campus in very large city
- 2,840 degree-seeking undergraduates
- SAT or ACT with writing, application essay required

**General.** Founded in 1886. Regionally accredited; also accredited by ABHE. **Degrees:** 441 bachelor's, 21 associate awarded; master's, first professional offered. **Location:** Downtown. **Calendar:** Semester, limited summer session. **Full-time faculty:** 75 total. **Part-time faculty:** 80 total.

**Freshman class profile.**

| Out-of-state: | 81% | Live on campus: | 98% |
|---|---|---|---|

**Basis for selection.** Rank in top half of graduating class and/or high school GPA above 2.3. Applicants must have been Christians for at least 1 year. Membership in Evangelical Protestant Church and recommendation from church leadership required. Interview recommended. Audition required of music majors. **Homeschooled:** ACT plus GED or SAT required.

**High school preparation.** 12 units recommended.

**2007-2008 Annual costs.** Undergraduate students in the BA and BMus programs on main campus are not charged tuition. Undergraduate students taking courses through distance learning programs (ABS, BSBS) and in BSMAT (Bachelor of Science in Missionary Aviation) program pay tuition of $199 per credit hour. Books/supplies: $600. Personal expenses: $500.

**Financial aid.** All financial aid based on need. **Additional information:** Aid available to upperclassmen is based on private and not federal/state sources.

**Application procedures. Admission:** Priority date 12/1; deadline 3/1 (postmark date). $35 fee, may be waived for applicants with need. Admission notification 4/1. Must reply by May 1 or within 6 week(s) if notified thereafter. **Financial aid:** No deadline.

**Academics. Special study options:** Distance learning, double major, dual enrollment of high school students, external degree, independent study, internships, study abroad, teacher certification program. Exchange program with International Christian College, Scotland; European Bible Institute, France; Belfast Bible College, Ireland; Spanish Bible Institute, Barcelona, Spain. **Credit/placement by examination:** AP, CLEP, IB, institutional tests. 9 credit hours maximum toward associate degree, 12 toward bachelor's. **Support services:** Learning center, pre-admission summer program, reduced course load, study skills assistance, tutoring.

**Majors. Communications:** General. **Education:** General, ESL. **Foreign languages:** Ancient Greek, Hebrew, linguistics. **Mechanic/repair:** Aircraft. **Philosophy/religion:** Judaic, religion. **Theology:** Bible, missionary, religious ed, sacred music, theology. **Visual/performing arts:** Music performance, music theory/composition, piano/organ, voice/opera.

**Computing on campus.** 40 workstations in library, computer center. Dormitories linked to campus network. Commuter students can connect to campus network. Repair service available.

**Student life. Freshman orientation:** Mandatory. **Policies:** Religious observance required. **Housing:** Guaranteed on-campus for all undergraduates. Single-sex dorms, apartments available. $100 deposit, deadline 5/1. **Activities:** Concert band, choral groups, drama, music ensembles, radio station, student government, student newspaper, symphony orchestra, Student Missionary Fellowship, Gospel Teams, Afro Awareness Fellowship, International Student Fellowship, Big Brother/Big Sister Program, pre-aviation club, married students fellowship, residence activities council, Hispanic Student Fellowship.

**Athletics.** NCCAA. **Intercollegiate:** Basketball, soccer M, volleyball. **Intramural:** Badminton, basketball, cross-country, football (non-tackle) M, racquetball, soccer, swimming, table tennis, volleyball, water polo. **Team name:** Archers.

**Student services.** Career counseling, student employment services, health services, minority student services, on-campus daycare, personal counseling, placement for graduates, veterans' counselor. **Physically disabled:** Services for visually impaired. **Learning disabled:** Comprehensive services available.

**Contact.** E-mail: admissions@moody.edu
Phone: (312) 329-4400 Toll-free number: (800) 967-4624
Fax: (312) 329-8987
Annette Moy, Dean of Enrollment Management, Moody Bible Institute, 820 North La Salle Boulevard, Chicago, IL 60610

## National University of Health Sciences
**Lombard, Illinois**
www.nuhs.edu                                   CB code: 1567

- Private 4-year university and health science college
- Commuter campus in large town
- 210 degree-seeking undergraduates
- 463 graduate students

**General.** Regionally accredited. **Degrees:** 53 bachelor's, 59 associate awarded; master's, first professional offered. **Location:** 20 miles from Chicago. **Calendar:** Trimester, extensive summer session. **Full-time faculty:** 41 total; 93% have terminal degrees, 22% women. **Part-time faculty:** 12 total; 100% have terminal degrees, 25% women. **Special facilities:** Learning resource center, medical library, onsite clinic.

**Basis for selection.** Associate degree and certificate programs require 2.0 GPA or GED; bachelor's completion program in biomedical science requires minimum of 60 semester hours of prerequisite courses. Must be 18 years of age and of good moral character. Applicants to BS degree completion program may be considered for conditional acceptance as a non-degree student for one semester to determine academic eligibility.

**2007-2008 Annual costs.** $16,997 represents average tuition cost for academic year 2007-2008 ($8,498 per trimester). Room only charge ranges from $2,974 to $6,522 for academic year. Room only: $3,694.

**Financial aid. Additional information:** Massage Therapy certificate program is eligible for Title IV financial aid. Program is half-time and qualifies for half-time and less-than-half-time Pell grants, federal work-study, FSEOG, federal Perkins grants, and prorated federal Stafford loans.

**Academics.** College of Professional Studies offers doctor of chiropractic, with a doctor of naturopathy, and master's degrees in acupuncture and Oriental Medicine. Primary undergraduate enrollment is in certificate programs in massage therapy and chiropractic assistance. Accelerated prerequisite program available for students needing to complete science entrance requirements. Bachelor of science completion program available. **Special study options:** Internships. **Credit/placement by examination:** CLEP. **Support services:** Learning center, tutoring.

**Majors. Biology:** Biomedical sciences.

**Computing on campus.** 75 workstations in library, computer center. Online course registration, helpline, student web hosting, wireless network available.

**Student life. Freshman orientation:** Mandatory. Preregistration for classes offered. **Policies:** Must be 21 to live on campus. **Housing:** Coed dorms available. Pets allowed in dorm rooms. **Activities:** Student government, student newspaper, student chiropractic organizations, professional sororities and fraternities, christian chiropractic association.

**Athletics. Intramural:** Basketball, golf, soccer, softball, tennis, volleyball.

**Student services.** Financial aid counseling, health services.

**Contact.** E-mail: admissions@nuhs.edu
Phone: (630) 889-6566 Toll-free number: (800) 826-6285
Fax: (630) 889-6554
Victoria Sweeney, Director of Communications and Enrollment Services, National University of Health Sciences, 200 East Roosevelt Road, Lombard, IL 60148-4583

## National-Louis University
**Chicago, Illinois**                          CB member
www.nl.edu                                     CB code: 1551

- Private 4-year university and teachers college
- Commuter campus in small city

- 1,850 degree-seeking undergraduates
- 97% of applicants admitted
- SAT or ACT required

**General.** Founded in 1886. Regionally accredited. Additional in-state locations in Evanston, Wheeling, Lisle and Elgin. Field programs available on and off campus. Out-of-state campuses located in Milwaukee/Beloit, McLean, Washington DC, and Tampa. **Degrees:** 797 bachelor's awarded; master's, doctoral offered. **Location:** 10 miles from Chicago. **Calendar:** Quarter, limited summer session. **Full-time faculty:** 254 total. **Part-time faculty:** 508 total. **Class size:** 91% < 20, 8% 20-39, less than 1% 40-49. **Special facilities:** Elementary demonstration school for practice teaching and observation.

**Freshman class profile.** 33 applied, 32 admitted, 9 enrolled.

**Basis for selection.** Applicants should rank in top half of high school class, score 19 ACT, 750 SAT (exclusive of Writing) and submit 2 letters of recommendation from counselors or teachers. Interview and essay recommended.

**High school preparation.** Recommended units include English 4, mathematics 3, social studies 3, science 2 (laboratory 1) and foreign language 2. One unit U.S. government or U.S. history recommended.

**2007-2008 Annual costs.** Tuition/fees: $17,925. Books/supplies: $992. Personal expenses: $1,305.

**Financial aid. Non-need-based:** Scholarships awarded for academics.

**Application procedures. Admission:** No deadline. $40 fee, may be waived for applicants with need. Application may be submitted online. Admission notification on a rolling basis. **Financial aid:** Priority date 4/15; no closing date. FAFSA, institutional form required. Applicants notified on a rolling basis starting 5/1; must reply within 2 week(s) of notification.

**Academics.** Degree-completion programs available in allied health leadership, management, and applied behavioral science. Field classes offered evenings/weekends. **Special study options:** Accelerated study, combined bachelor's/graduate degree, distance learning, double major, dual enrollment of high school students, ESL, honors, independent study, internships, liberal arts/career combination, teacher certification program. **Credit/placement by examination:** AP, CLEP. 132 credit hours maximum toward bachelor's degree. **Support services:** Learning center, pre-admission summer program, reduced course load, remedial instruction, tutoring.

**Majors. Biology:** General. **Business:** Accounting, business admin. **Computer sciences:** Information systems. **Education:** Early childhood, elementary. **English:** English lit. **Health:** Clinical lab science, health care admin, medical radiologic technology/radiation therapy, respiratory therapy technology, substance abuse counseling. **Interdisciplinary:** Behavioral sciences, biological/physical sciences. **Liberal arts:** Arts/sciences. **Math:** General, applied. **Psychology:** General. **Public administration:** Human services. **Social sciences:** General, anthropology, economics. **Visual/performing arts:** Dramatic, studio arts.

**Most popular majors.** Business/marketing 50%, education 10%, health sciences 9%, interdisciplinary studies 24%.

**Computing on campus.** 500 workstations in library, computer center. Commuter students can connect to campus network. Online course registration, online library, helpline, repair service available.

**Student life. Freshman orientation:** Available. **Housing:** Coed dorms available. $50 deposit, deadline 7/30. **Activities:** Drama, musical theater, student government, student newspaper, Chinese club, Polish club, educational club, social science club, school psychology club, drama club, educational honorary society.

**Student services.** Adult student services, career counseling, student employment services, health services, personal counseling, placement for graduates. **Physically disabled:** Services for visually, speech, hearing impaired.

**Contact.** E-mail: nluinfo@wheeling1.nl.edu
Phone: (847) 475-1100 ext. 5151 Toll-free number: (800) 443-5522
Fax: (847) 256-1057
Patricia Petillo, Director of Recruitment and Admissions Response, National-Louis University, 122 South Michigan Avenue, Chicago, IL 60603

## North Central College
**Naperville, Illinois**                       CB member
www.northcentralcollege.edu                    CB code: 1555

- Private 4-year liberal arts college affiliated with United Methodist Church
- Residential campus in small city

♦ 2,142 degree-seeking undergraduates: 6% part-time, 58% women, 3% African American, 3% Asian American, 4% Hispanic American, 1% international

♦ 287 degree-seeking graduate students

♦ 69% of applicants admitted

♦ SAT or ACT (ACT writing optional) required

♦ 66% graduate within 6 years

**General.** Founded in 1861. Regionally accredited. **Degrees:** 506 bachelor's awarded; master's offered. **ROTC:** Army, Air Force. **Location:** 25 miles from Chicago. **Calendar:** Quarter, limited summer session. **Full-time faculty:** 113 total; 88% have terminal degrees, 9% minority, 46% women. **Part-time faculty:** 113 total; 32% have terminal degrees, 6% minority, 53% women. **Class size:** 44% < 20, 55% 20-39, less than 1% 40-49. **Special facilities:** Accelerator laboratory, Argonne laboratory, arboretum.

**Freshman class profile.** 2,234 applied, 1,552 admitted, 422 enrolled.

| Mid 50% test scores | | | |
|---|---|---|---|
| SAT critical reading: | 550-670 | GPA 3.0-3.49: | 29% |
| SAT math: | 510-650 | GPA 2.0-2.99: | 16% |
| SAT writing: | 510-650 | End year in good standing: | 86% |
| ACT composite: | 22-27 | Return as sophomores: | 80% |
| GPA 3.50 or higher: | 55% | Out-of-state: | 11% |
| | | Live on campus: | 77% |

**Basis for selection.** Academic record, SAT or ACT scores, and personal character all considered important. Interview and essay recommended for marginal students. **Homeschooled:** Interview required. Review of the student's portfolio and curriculum, writing sample, interview with the Director of Freshman Admission, interview with a faculty member may be required. **Learning Disabled:** Students who self-identify are referred to the academic support center.

**High school preparation.** 16 units required; 19 recommended. Required and recommended units include English 4, mathematics 3, social studies 2, history 1, science 3 (laboratory 1-3), foreign language 3 and academic electives 3.

**2008-2009 Annual costs.** Tuition/fees: $25,938. Room/board: $8,217. Books/supplies: $1,002. Personal expenses: $1,182.

**2007-2008 Financial aid. Need-based:** 362 full-time freshmen applied for aid; 301 were judged to have need; 301 of these received aid. Average need met was 84%. Average scholarship/grant was $15,724; average loan $2,799. 71% of total undergraduate aid awarded as scholarships/grants, 29% as loans/jobs. **Non-need-based:** Awarded to 605 full-time undergraduates, including 128 freshmen. Scholarships awarded for academics, art, leadership, minority status, music/drama, religious affiliation, ROTC, state residency.

**Application procedures. Admission:** Priority date 4/15; no deadline. $25 fee, may be waived for applicants with need. Application may be submitted online. Admission notification on a rolling basis beginning on or about 10/1. Must reply by May 1 or within 4 week(s) if notified thereafter. **Financial aid:** No deadline. FAFSA, institutional form required. Applicants notified on a rolling basis starting 3/1; must reply within 4 week(s) of notification.

**Academics. Special study options:** Accelerated study, combined bachelor's/graduate degree, cross-registration, double major, dual enrollment of high school students, ESL, exchange student, honors, independent study, internships, New York semester, student-designed major, study abroad, teacher certification program, United Nations semester, urban semester, Washington semester. Independent study project grants; 3-2 engineering program with Universities of Illinois at Urbana-Champaign and Minnesota; 5-year bachelor's/master's degree programs. **Credit/placement by examination:** AP, CLEP, IB, SAT, ACT, institutional tests. 28 credit hours maximum toward bachelor's degree. Students must be tested or otherwise assessed in order for experiential credit to be awarded. **Support services:** Pre-admission summer program, reduced course load, remedial instruction, study skills assistance, tutoring, writing center.

**Majors. Area/ethnic studies:** East Asian. **Biology:** General, biochemistry. **Business:** Accounting, actuarial science, business admin, finance, human resources, international, management information systems, marketing, small business admin. **Communications:** General, journalism, organizational, radio/tv. **Communications technology:** Animation/special effects. **Computer sciences:** General. **Education:** General, art, elementary, music, physical. **English:** Creative writing, English lit. **Foreign languages:** Classics, French, German, Japanese, Spanish. **Health:** Athletic training, medical radiologic technology/radiation therapy, nuclear medical technology. **History:** General. **Interdisciplinary:** Biological/physical sciences, global studies. **Liberal arts:** Arts/sciences, humanities. **Math:** General, applied. **Parks/recreation:** Exercise sciences, health/fitness, sports admin. **Philosophy/religion:** Philosophy, religion. **Physical sciences:** Chemistry, physics. **Psychology:** General. **Social sciences:** General, anthropology, economics,

political science, sociology. **Visual/performing arts:** Art, dramatic, jazz, musical theater. **Other:** Interactive media, Interactive media: graphic arts.

**Most popular majors.** Business/marketing 27%, communications/journalism 9%, education 11%, psychology 7%, social sciences 13%.

**Computing on campus.** 325 workstations in dormitories, library, computer center, student center. Dormitories wired for high-speed internet access and linked to campus network. Commuter students can connect to campus network. Online library, helpline, repair service, student web hosting, wireless network available.

**Student life. Freshman orientation:** Available, $125 fee. Three orientations held in June, one in August. Session also held the week before beginning of term. **Housing:** Guaranteed on-campus for all undergraduates. Coed dorms, single-sex dorms, special housing for disabled, substance-free housing available. $100 fully refundable deposit, deadline 5/1. **Activities:** Bands, campus ministries, choral groups, dance, drama, international student organizations, literary magazine, music ensembles, Model UN, musical theater, opera, radio station, student government, student newspaper, United Methodist student organization, black student organization, Fellowship of Christian Athletes, Raza Unida, Cardinals in Action, NCC Green, commuter student organization, Students in Free Enterprise.

**Athletics.** NCAA. **Intercollegiate:** Baseball M, basketball, cross-country, football (tackle) M, golf, soccer, softball W, swimming, tennis, track and field, volleyball W, wrestling M. **Intramural:** Basketball, bowling, cheerleading, football (tackle) M, golf, softball, table tennis, volleyball. **Team name:** Cardinals.

**Student services.** Adult student services, alcohol/substance abuse counseling, career counseling, student employment services, financial aid counseling, health services, minority student services, personal counseling, placement for graduates. **Physically disabled:** Services for visually, hearing impaired.

**Contact.** E-mail: admissions@noctrl.edu
Phone: (630) 637-5800 Toll-free number: (800) 411-1861
Fax: (630) 637-5819
Martin Sauer, Dean of Admissions and Financial Aid, North Central College, PO Box 3063, Naperville, IL 60566-7063

## North Park University

Chicago, Illinois
www.northpark.edu

**CB member**
**CB code: 1556**

♦ Private 4-year university and liberal arts college affiliated with Evangelical Covenant Church

♦ Residential campus in very large city

♦ 2,160 degree-seeking undergraduates: 18% part-time, 63% women, 9% African American, 7% Asian American, 9% Hispanic American, 4% international

♦ 797 degree-seeking graduate students

♦ 68% of applicants admitted

♦ SAT or ACT (ACT writing recommended), application essay required

♦ 54% graduate within 6 years

**General.** Founded in 1891. Regionally accredited. Mid-sized Christian liberal arts institution located in a major urban environment offering multicultural educational experience. **Degrees:** 379 bachelor's awarded; master's, doctoral, first professional offered. **ROTC:** Air Force. **Location:** 8 miles from downtown. **Calendar:** Semester, limited summer session. **Full-time faculty:** 131 total; 86% have terminal degrees, 18% minority, 47% women. **Part-time faculty:** 147 total; 16% minority, 51% women. **Class size:** 47% < 20, 48% 20-39, 3% 40-49, 2% 50-99, less than 1% >100.

**Freshman class profile.** 1,452 applied, 984 admitted, 373 enrolled.

| Mid 50% test scores | | | |
|---|---|---|---|
| SAT critical reading: | 500-630 | Rank in top quarter: | 36% |
| SAT math: | 480-600 | Rank in top tenth: | 17% |
| ACT composite: | 20-25 | End year in good standing: | 71% |
| GPA 3.50 or higher: | 31% | Return as sophomores: | 77% |
| GPA 3.0-3.49: | 34% | Out-of-state: | 43% |
| GPA 2.0-2.99: | 34% | Live on campus: | 77% |
| | | International: | 2% |

**Basis for selection.** Admission based on achievement record, class rank, test scores, recommendations, and community involvement. Interview required for some applicants. All students who visit campus are interviewed. **Homeschooled:** Transcript of courses and grades, letter of recommendation (nonparent) required. **Learning Disabled:** Students should contact office of academic advising.

**High school preparation.** Recommended units include English 4, mathematics 3, social studies 1, history 1, science 3 and foreign language 2.

**2008-2009 Annual costs.** Tuition/fees: $17,600. Room/board: $7,520. Books/supplies: $950. Personal expenses: $1,350.

**2006-2007 Financial aid. Need-based:** 319 full-time freshmen applied for aid; 249 were judged to have need; 249 of these received aid. Average need met was 74%. Average scholarship/grant was $7,186; average loan $2,331. 64% of total undergraduate aid awarded as scholarships/grants, 36% as loans/jobs. **Non-need-based:** Scholarships awarded for academics, art, music/drama, religious affiliation.

**Application procedures. Admission:** Priority date 4/1; deadline 7/1 (receipt date). $40 fee, may be waived for applicants with need. Application may be submitted online. Admission notification on a rolling basis beginning on or about 9/15. Must reply by May 1 or within 4 week(s) if notified thereafter. **Financial aid:** Priority date 5/1, closing date 8/1. FAFSA required. Applicants notified on a rolling basis starting 10/1; must reply by 5/1 or within 3 week(s) of notification.

**Academics.** Intensive summer ESL program. **Special study options:** Accelerated study, combined bachelor's/graduate degree, distance learning, double major, ESL, exchange student, honors, independent study, internships, liberal arts/career combination, student-designed major, study abroad, teacher certification program, Washington semester. **Credit/placement by examination:** AP, CLEP, IB, SAT, ACT, institutional tests. 60 credit hours maximum toward bachelor's degree. **Support services:** Learning center, pre-admission summer program, reduced course load, remedial instruction, study skills assistance, tutoring, writing center.

**Majors. Biology:** General. **Business:** General, business admin, organizational behavior. **Communications:** General, advertising. **Computer sciences:** General. **Education:** Early childhood, elementary, middle, multi-level teacher. **English:** English lit. **Foreign languages:** French, Scandinavian, Spanish. **Health:** Clinical lab science, nursing (RN), predental, premedicine, prepharmacy, preveterinary. **History:** General. **Liberal arts:** Arts/sciences. **Math:** General. **Philosophy/religion:** Christian, philosophy, religion. **Physical sciences:** Chemistry, physics. **Psychology:** General. **Social sciences:** General, political science, sociology. **Theology:** Bible, youth ministry. **Visual/performing arts:** Art, commercial/advertising art, music performance.

**Most popular majors.** Business/marketing 19%, communication technologies 7%, education 6%, health sciences 16%, philosophy/religious studies 6%, psychology 7%, social sciences 6%.

**Computing on campus.** 100 workstations in dormitories, library, computer center, student center. Dormitories wired for high-speed internet access and linked to campus network. Commuter students can connect to campus network. Online course registration, online library, helpline, wireless network available.

**Student life. Freshman orientation:** Mandatory. Preregistration for classes offered. Begins 5 days before start of classes. **Policies:** Dry and smoke-free campus. Visiting hours in residence halls for persons of opposite sex. **Housing:** Guaranteed on-campus for freshmen. Single-sex dorms, apartments available. $250 nonrefundable deposit, deadline 5/1. **Activities:** Bands, campus ministries, choral groups, drama, literary magazine, music ensembles, musical theater, opera, student government, student newspaper, symphony orchestra, Gospel teams, black student association, Latino student association, Korean student association, Catholic association, Middle Eastern student association.

**Athletics.** NCAA. **Intercollegiate:** Baseball M, basketball, cross-country, football (tackle) M, golf, rowing (crew) W, soccer, softball W, track and field, volleyball W. **Intramural:** Basketball, cheerleading W, football (non-tackle), soccer, tennis, volleyball. **Team name:** Vikings.

**Student services.** Adult student services, alcohol/substance abuse counseling, career counseling, services for economically disadvantaged, student employment services, financial aid counseling, health services, minority student services, personal counseling, placement for graduates.

**Contact.** E-mail: admission@northpark.edu
Phone: (773) 244-5500 Toll-free number: (800) 888-6728
Fax: (773) 244-5243
Shari Clemens, Director, Undergraduate Admission, North Park University, 3225 West Foster Avenue, Chicago, IL 60625-4895

---

**Northeastern Illinois University**

**Chicago, Illinois**
**www.neiu.edu**

**CB member**
**CB code: 1090**

- Public 4-year university
- Commuter campus in very large city

---

- 8,891 degree-seeking undergraduates: 44% part-time, 60% women, 10% African American, 11% Asian American, 30% Hispanic American, 1% international
- 2,004 degree-seeking graduate students
- 68% of applicants admitted
- SAT or ACT (ACT writing optional) required

**General.** Founded in 1961. Regionally accredited. Two extension centers serving Hispanic and African-American communities. **Degrees:** 1,367 bachelor's awarded; master's offered. **ROTC:** Army, Air Force. **Calendar:** Semester, limited summer session. **Full-time faculty:** 411 total; 72% have terminal degrees, 25% minority, 48% women. **Part-time faculty:** 291 total; 23% have terminal degrees, 26% minority, 45% women. **Class size:** 44% < 20, 50% 20-39, 3% 40-49, 2% 50-99, less than 1% >100.

**Freshman class profile.** 3,601 applied, 2,465 admitted, 957 enrolled.

| Mid 50% test scores | | |
|---|---|---|
| ACT composite: | 16-21 | |
| GPA 3.0-3.49: | 40% | |
| GPA 2.0-2.99: | 52% | |

| | |
|---|---|
| Rank in top quarter: | 17% |
| Rank in top tenth: | 7% |
| Return as sophomores: | 66% |
| Out-of-state: | 1% |

**Basis for selection.** Rank in top half of graduating class or 19 ACT/equivalent SAT required. Audition recommended for dance and music majors. Portfolio recommended for art majors.

**High school preparation.** 15 units required. Required units include English 4, mathematics 3, social studies 3 and science 3. 2 additional units in fine arts, music, art, foreign languages, or vocational education. (Only 1 vocational education course accepted.).

**2008-2009 Annual costs.** Tuition/fees: $8,016; $14,616 out-of-state. Books/supplies: $1,650. Personal expenses: $3,798.

**2007-2008 Financial aid. Need-based:** 635 full-time freshmen applied for aid; 467 were judged to have need; 455 of these received aid. Average need met was 57%. Average scholarship/grant was $6,631; average loan $3,006. 75% of total undergraduate aid awarded as scholarships/grants, 25% as loans/jobs. **Non-need-based:** Awarded to 323 full-time undergraduates, including 40 freshmen. Scholarships awarded for academics, art, leadership, music/drama.

**Application procedures. Admission:** Closing date 7/1 (receipt date). $25 fee, may be waived for applicants with need. Application may be submitted online. Admission notification on a rolling basis beginning on or about 9/1. **Financial aid:** Priority date 2/28; no closing date. FAFSA, institutional form required. Applicants notified on a rolling basis starting 4/1; must reply within 3 week(s) of notification.

**Academics. Special study options:** Cooperative education, distance learning, double major, dual enrollment of high school students, exchange student, honors, independent study, student-designed major, study abroad, teacher certification program. **Credit/placement by examination:** AP, CLEP, IB, ACT, institutional tests. 30 credit hours maximum toward bachelor's degree. **Support services:** Learning center, pre-admission summer program, remedial instruction, study skills assistance, tutoring, writing center.

**Majors. Area/ethnic studies:** Women's. **Biology:** General. **Business:** General, accounting, business admin, finance, marketing. **Computer sciences:** Computer science. **Conservation:** Environmental studies. **Education:** Bilingual, early childhood, elementary, physical, special. **English:** English lit, speech/rhetoric. **Foreign languages:** French, linguistics, Spanish. **Health:** Community health services. **History:** General. **Liberal arts:** Arts/sciences. **Math:** General. **Philosophy/religion:** Philosophy. **Physical sciences:** Chemistry, geology, physics. **Protective services:** Criminal justice. **Psychology:** General. **Public administration:** Social work. **Social sciences:** General, anthropology, economics, geography, political science, sociology. **Visual/performing arts:** Art.

**Most popular majors.** Business/marketing 19%, education 18%, English 8%, liberal arts 14%, security/protective services 8%, social sciences 7%.

**Computing on campus.** 315 workstations in library, computer center, student center. Commuter students can connect to campus network. Online course registration, helpline, wireless network available.

**Student life. Freshman orientation:** Available. **Activities:** Bands, choral groups, dance, drama, literary magazine, music ensembles, opera, radio station, student government, student newspaper, symphony orchestra, Muslim student association, black heritage club, politics club, Chimexla student union, Indian student association, university bible association, program board, Union of Puerto Rican Students, Hillel, outdoor adventure club.

**Athletics. Intramural:** Badminton, basketball, cross-country, racquetball, soccer, softball, table tennis, tennis, volleyball, weight lifting. **Team name:** Eagles.

**Student services.** Adult student services, career counseling, student employment services, financial aid counseling, health services, minority student services, on-campus daycare, personal counseling, placement for graduates, veterans' counselor, women's services. **Physically disabled:** Services for visually, speech impaired.

**Contact.** E-mail: admerc@neiu.edu
Phone: (773) 442-4000 Fax: (773) 442-4020
Janice Harring-Hendon, Director of Admissions and Records, Northeastern Illinois University, 5500 North St. Louis Avenue, Chicago, IL 60625

## Northern Illinois University
**DeKalb, Illinois**
www.niu.edu

**CB member**
**CB code: 1559**

- Public 4-year university
- Residential campus in large town
- 18,915 degree-seeking undergraduates: 10% part-time, 52% women, 12% African American, 5% Asian American, 7% Hispanic American, 1% international
- 5,236 degree-seeking graduate students
- 61% of applicants admitted
- SAT or ACT required
- 48% graduate within 6 years

**General.** Founded in 1895. Regionally accredited. Classes also held at Loredo Taft Field campus in Oregon. **Degrees:** 3,756 bachelor's awarded; master's, doctoral, first professional offered. **ROTC:** Army. **Location:** 65 miles from Chicago. **Calendar:** Semester, extensive summer session. **Full-time faculty:** 908 total; 82% have terminal degrees, 13% minority, 45% women. **Part-time faculty:** 272 total; 37% have terminal degrees, 6% minority, 56% women. **Class size:** 37% < 20, 47% 20-39, 4% 40-49, 9% 50-99, 3% >100.

**Freshman class profile.** 16,769 applied, 10,274 admitted, 3,013 enrolled.

| Mid 50% test scores | | | |
|---|---|---|---|
| ACT composite: | 19-24 | End year in good standing: | 87% |
| Rank in top quarter: | 33% | Return as sophomores: | 79% |
| Rank in top tenth: | 9% | Out-of-state: | 3% |
| | | Live on campus: | 92% |

**Basis for selection.** 19 ACT required of applicants who rank in top half of class, 23 ACT required of applicants in top two-thirds of class or with high school equivalency certificate. Interview required of CHANCE program applicants. Audition required of music majors. Portfolio recommended for art majors.

**High school preparation.** 15 units required. Required and recommended units include English 4, mathematics 2-4, social studies 2-3, history 1, science 2-4 (laboratory 1-2) and foreign language 1-2. One unit of art, film, music, theater, or foreign language required. Mathematics must include algebra and/or geometry. Social sciences must include US history or a combination of US history and government.

**2007-2008 Annual costs.** Tuition/fees: $7,889; $14,039 out-of-state. Room/board: $8,200. Books/supplies: $700. Personal expenses: $1,584.

**2007-2008 Financial aid. Need-based:** Average scholarship/grant was $8,288; average loan $3,386. 52% of total undergraduate aid awarded as scholarships/grants, 48% as loans/jobs. **Non-need-based:** Scholarships awarded for academics, athletics, ROTC.

**Application procedures. Admission:** Priority date 3/1; deadline 8/1. No application fee. Application may be submitted online. Admission notification on a rolling basis. **Financial aid:** Priority date 3/1; no closing date. FAFSA, institutional form required. Applicants notified on a rolling basis starting 4/15.

**Academics. Special study options:** Cooperative education, distance learning, double major, dual enrollment of high school students, honors, independent study, internships, student-designed major, study abroad, teacher certification program. **Credit/placement by examination:** AP, CLEP, institutional tests. Credit by examination not awarded for courses that are prerequisites for courses for which the student already has credit or is currently enrolled. **Support services:** Tutoring.

**Majors. Biology:** General. **Business:** General, accounting, finance, marketing, operations. **Communications:** General, journalism. **Computer sciences:** General, computer science. **Education:** General, art, elementary, family/consumer sciences, health, physical, special. **Engineering:** Electrical, industrial, mechanical. **Engineering technology:** Industrial. **English:** English lit. **Family/consumer sciences:** Clothing/textiles, family studies, food/nutrition. **Foreign languages:** French, German, Russian, Spanish. **Health:** Clinical lab

science, communication disorders, nursing (RN), public health nursing. **History:** General. **Liberal arts:** Arts/sciences. **Math:** General, applied, computational, probability. **Philosophy/religion:** Philosophy. **Physical sciences:** Atmospheric science, chemistry, geology, physics. **Psychology:** General. **Social sciences:** Anthropology, economics, geography, political science, sociology. **Visual/performing arts:** Art, art history/conservation, dramatic, studio arts.

**Most popular majors.** Business/marketing 20%, communications/journalism 8%, education 11%, engineering/engineering technologies 6%, health sciences 10%, social sciences 12%.

**Computing on campus.** 550 workstations in dormitories, library, computer center, student center. Commuter students can connect to campus network. Helpline available.

**Student life. Freshman orientation:** Mandatory, $60 fee. **Housing:** Guaranteed on-campus for freshmen. Coed dorms, special housing for disabled, apartments, fraternity/sorority housing available. $150 deposit. Quiet and alcohol-free lifestyle floors, 21 and over student floors, honors floors available. **Activities:** Bands, campus ministries, choral groups, dance, drama, film society, opera, radio station, student government, student newspaper, symphony orchestra, TV station, numerous organizations available.

**Athletics.** NCAA. **Intercollegiate:** Baseball M, basketball, cross-country W, football (tackle) M, golf, gymnastics W, soccer, softball W, swimming, tennis, track and field W, volleyball W, wrestling M. **Intramural:** Badminton, baseball M, basketball, football (tackle) M, golf, ice hockey M, racquetball, sailing, soccer, softball, table tennis, tennis, volleyball, wrestling M. **Team name:** Huskies.

**Student services.** Career counseling, student employment services, health services, legal services, minority student services, on-campus daycare, personal counseling, placement for graduates, veterans' counselor, women's services. **Physically disabled:** Services for visually, speech, hearing impaired.

**Contact.** E-mail: admission-info@niu.edu
Phone: (815) 753-0446 Toll-free number: (800) 892-3050
Fax: (815) 753-8312
Robert Burk, Director of Admissions, Northern Illinois University, DeKalb, IL 60115-2854

## Northwestern University
**Evanston, Illinois**
www.northwestern.edu

**CB member**
**CB code: 1565**

- Private 4-year university
- Residential campus in small city
- 8,176 degree-seeking undergraduates: 1% part-time, 53% women, 6% African American, 17% Asian American, 7% Hispanic American, 5% international
- 9,646 degree-seeking graduate students
- 27% of applicants admitted
- SAT or ACT with writing, application essay required
- 93% graduate within 6 years

**General.** Founded in 1851. Regionally accredited. **Degrees:** 2,089 bachelor's awarded; master's, doctoral, first professional offered. **ROTC:** Army, Naval, Air Force. **Location:** 12 miles from Chicago. **Calendar:** Quarter, limited summer session. **Full-time faculty:** 1,010 total; 100% have terminal degrees, 17% minority, 28% women. **Part-time faculty:** 132 total; 100% have terminal degrees, 6% minority, 47% women. **Class size:** 75% < 20, 14% 20-39, 3% 40-49, 5% 50-99, 3% >100. **Special facilities:** Fine-arts complex, dance center, observatory, engineering design center, tennis center.

**Freshman class profile.** 21,930 applied, 5,872 admitted, 1,981 enrolled.

| Mid 50% test scores | | | |
|---|---|---|---|
| SAT critical reading: | 670-750 | Return as sophomores: | 96% |
| SAT math: | 680-770 | Out-of-state: | 75% |
| SAT writing: | 660-750 | Live on campus: | 99% |
| ACT composite: | 30-34 | International: | 5% |
| Rank in top quarter: | 97% | Fraternities: | 25% |
| Rank in top tenth: | 85% | Sororities: | 34% |

**Basis for selection.** Academic record, essays, test scores, activity record, school recommendations important. SAT Subject Tests recommended. SAT Subject Tests in Math Level 2 and Chemistry required of all applicants for Honors Program in Medical Education. Applicants to Integrated Science Program must take SAT Subject Tests in Chemistry or Physics, Math Level

2, plus second science. Audition required for music majors. **Home-schooled:** 3 SAT Subject Tests required. Math Level 1 or 2 for students who plan to study sciences or engineering, Math Level 2 preferable, plus two other SAT Subject Tests of applicant's choice from different subject areas are required.

**High school preparation.** 16 units recommended. Recommended units include English 4, mathematics 3, social studies 2, science 2 (laboratory 2), foreign language 2 and academic electives 1. 4 units of mathematics recommended for engineering applicants. Applicants typically have 20 academic high school units.

**2007-2008 Annual costs.** Tuition/fees: $35,429. Room/board: $10,776. Books/supplies: $1,548. Personal expenses: $1,626.

**2007-2008 Financial aid.** All financial aid based on need. 1,031 full-time freshmen applied for aid; 845 were judged to have need; 845 of these received aid. Average need met was 100%. Average scholarship/grant was $25,228; average loan $3,633. 78% of total undergraduate aid awarded as scholarships/grants, 22% as loans/jobs.

**Application procedures. Admission:** Closing date 1/1 (postmark date). $65 fee, may be waived for applicants with need. Application may be submitted online. Admission notification 4/15. Must reply by May 1 or within 2 week(s) if notified thereafter. **Financial aid:** Closing date 2/15. FAFSA, CSS PROFILE required. Applicants notified by 4/15; must reply by 5/1 or within 2 week(s) of notification.

**Academics.** University awards 1 unit of credit for each course; 45-48 units required for graduation. **Special study options:** Accelerated study, combined bachelor's/graduate degree, cooperative education, double major, honors, independent study, internships, liberal arts/career combination, student-designed major, study abroad, teacher certification program. 3-year integrated science program; 4-year mathematical methods in social sciences bachelor's program; honors programs in undergraduate research engineering, engineering and management, medical education; 7-year BA/MD program resulting in both an undergraduate degree and MD. **Credit/placement by examination:** AP, CLEP, IB, institutional tests. **Support services:** Study skills assistance, tutoring, writing center.

**Majors. Area/ethnic studies:** African-American, American, Asian, European, women's. **Biology:** General, ecology. **Business:** Organizational behavior. **Communications:** General, broadcast journalism, journalism, radio/tv. **Computer sciences:** General, computer science, information systems. **Conservation:** Environmental science, environmental studies. **Education:** General, foundations, learning disabled, mathematics, music, secondary. **Engineering:** General, biomedical, chemical, civil, computer, electrical, environmental, industrial, manufacturing, materials, materials science, mechanical, science. **English:** Creative writing, English lit. **Foreign languages:** Classics, comparative lit, French, German, Italian, linguistics, Slavic, Spanish. **Health:** Communication disorders, premedicine. **History:** General. **Interdisciplinary:** Biological/physical sciences, neuroscience, science/society. **Legal studies:** General. **Liberal arts:** Arts/sciences. **Math:** General, applied, statistics. **Philosophy/religion:** Philosophy, religion. **Physical sciences:** Chemistry, geology, physics. **Psychology:** General, cognitive, community. **Public administration:** Community org/advocacy, policy analysis. **Social sciences:** Anthropology, economics, geography, international relations, political science, sociology, urban studies. **Visual/performing arts:** General, art, art history/conservation, dance, dramatic, jazz, music performance, music theory/composition, musicology, piano/organ, stringed instruments, theater history, voice/opera.

**Most popular majors.** Communications/journalism 18%, engineering/engineering technologies 14%, psychology 8%, social sciences 20%, visual/performing arts 12%.

**Computing on campus.** 678 workstations in dormitories, library, computer center, student center. Dormitories wired for high-speed internet access and linked to campus network. Commuter students can connect to campus network. Online course registration, online library, helpline, repair service, student web hosting, wireless network available.

**Student life. Freshman orientation:** Mandatory. Held for 5 days prior to start of classes. **Housing:** Guaranteed on-campus for freshmen. Coed dorms, single-sex dorms, fraternity/sorority housing, substance-free housing available. $200 nonrefundable deposit, deadline 5/25. Residential colleges devoted to particular themes and 2 nonthematic residential colleges available. **Activities:** Bands, campus ministries, choral groups, dance, drama, film society, international student organizations, literary magazine, music ensembles, musical theater, opera, radio station, student government, student newspaper, symphony orchestra, TV station, over 300 organizations.

**Athletics.** NCAA. **Intercollegiate:** Baseball M, basketball, cheerleading, cross-country W, diving, fencing W, field hockey W, football (tackle), golf, ice hockey, lacrosse W, soccer, softball, swimming, tennis, volleyball, wrestling M. **Intramural:** Basketball, football (non-tackle), ice hockey, racquetball, soccer, softball, table tennis, tennis, volleyball. **Team name:** Wildcats.

**Student services.** Adult student services, alcohol/substance abuse counseling, career counseling, student employment services, financial aid counseling, health services, minority student services, personal counseling, placement for graduates, women's services. **Physically disabled:** Services for visually, speech, hearing impaired.

**Contact.** E-mail: ug-admission@northwestern.edu
Phone: (847) 491-7271
Christopher Watson, Dean of Undergraduate Admissions, Northwestern University, 1801 Hinman Avenue, Evanston, IL 60204-3060

## Olivet Nazarene University
**Bourbonnais, Illinois**
**www.olivet.edu**

**CB member**
**CB code: 1596**

- Private 4-year university and liberal arts college affiliated with Church of the Nazarene
- Residential campus in small city
- 3,190 degree-seeking undergraduates: 16% part-time, 62% women, 10% African American, 2% Asian American, 4% Hispanic American, 1% international
- 1,355 degree-seeking graduate students
- 80% of applicants admitted
- ACT (writing optional) required
- 57% graduate within 6 years

**General.** Founded in 1907. Regionally accredited. Evangelical liberal arts institution emphasizing Christian values. **Degrees:** 525 bachelor's, 86 associate awarded; master's, doctoral offered. **ROTC:** Army. **Location:** 60 miles from Chicago. **Calendar:** Semester, extensive summer session. **Full-time faculty:** 106 total. **Part-time faculty:** 193 total. **Class size:** 33% < 20, 46% 20-39, 10% 40-49, 11% 50-99. **Special facilities:** Planetarium, observatory, science museum, distance learning classroom.

**Freshman class profile.** 2,454 applied, 1,964 admitted, 712 enrolled.

| Mid 50% test scores | | | |
|---|---|---|---|
| ACT composite: | 19-26 | Out-of-state: | 52% |
| Return as sophomores: | 75% | Live on campus: | 90% |

**Basis for selection.** Minimum 2.0 GPA in college-preparatory subjects, ranking in top three-quarters of class, ACT of 18, 2 recommendations required. Interview recommended. Audition required of music majors. Portfolios required for art scholarship applicants. **Homeschooled:** ACT required.

**High school preparation.** 15 units required. Required and recommended units include English 4, mathematics 3, social studies 4, history 2, science 3 and foreign language 2.

**2008-2009 Annual costs.** Tuition/fees: $21,590. Room/board: $6,400. Books/supplies: $1,000. Personal expenses: $400.

**Financial aid. Non-need-based:** Scholarships awarded for academics, art, athletics, leadership, music/drama, religious affiliation, ROTC, state residency.

**Application procedures. Admission:** Closing date 5/15 (postmark date). $25 fee, may be waived for applicants with need. Application may be submitted online. Admission notification on a rolling basis. **Financial aid:** Priority date 3/1; no closing date. FAFSA, institutional form required. Applicants notified on a rolling basis starting 1/15; must reply within 2 week(s) of notification.

**Academics. Special study options:** Accelerated study, distance learning, double major, honors, independent study, internships, liberal arts/career combination, student-designed major, study abroad, teacher certification program, Washington semester. Council of Christian Colleges and Universities study programs, adult studies degree program. **Credit/placement by examination:** AP, CLEP, IB, ACT, institutional tests. **Support services:** Learning center, pre-admission summer program, reduced course load, remedial instruction, tutoring.

**Majors. Biology:** General, zoology. **Business:** General, accounting, business admin, fashion, finance, international, marketing. **Communications:** General, broadcast journalism, journalism. **Computer sciences:** General, computer science, information systems, programming. **Conservation:** Environmental studies. **Education:** Art, biology, chemistry, early childhood, elementary, English, family/consumer sciences, foreign languages, health, history, mathematics, music, physical, science, secondary, social science, social studies, Spanish. **Engineering:** General. **English:** English lit. **Family/consumer sciences:** General, family/community services, housing. **Foreign languages:** General, Spanish. **Health:** Athletic training. **History:** General. **Interdisciplinary:** Biological/physical sciences. **Liberal arts:** Arts/

sciences. **Math:** General. **Parks/recreation:** Exercise sciences, sports admin. **Philosophy/religion:** Religion. **Physical sciences:** Chemistry, geology. **Protective services:** Criminal justice. **Psychology:** General. **Public administration:** Policy analysis, social work. **Social sciences:** General, economics, political science, sociology. **Theology:** Bible, religious ed, sacred music, theology. **Visual/performing arts:** Art, music performance, piano/organ, voice/opera.

**Computing on campus.** 125 workstations in library, computer center, student center. Dormitories wired for high-speed internet access and linked to campus network. Commuter students can connect to campus network. Online library, helpline, repair service, student web hosting, wireless network available.

**Student life. Freshman orientation:** Mandatory. Preregistration for classes offered. 3-day program held on second and third weekends in June. Comprehensive for students and parents. **Policies:** Chapel convocations held twice weekly. Religious observance required. **Housing:** Guaranteed on-campus for all undergraduates. Single-sex dorms, special housing for disabled, apartments available. **Activities:** Bands, choral groups, drama, international student organizations, literary magazine, music ensembles, musical theater, radio station, student government, student newspaper, symphony orchestra, social service clubs, spiritual life groups.

**Athletics.** NAIA, NCCAA. **Intercollegiate:** Baseball M, basketball, cheerleading, cross-country, football (tackle) M, golf M, soccer, softball W, tennis, track and field, volleyball W. **Intramural:** Badminton, basketball, bowling, cross-country, football (non-tackle) W, golf, handball, racquetball, soccer, softball, table tennis, tennis, track and field, volleyball. **Team name:** Tigers.

**Student services.** Adult student services, alcohol/substance abuse counseling, campus ministries, career counseling, services for economically disadvantaged, student employment services, financial aid counseling, health services, personal counseling, placement for graduates, veterans' counselor.

**Contact.** E-mail: admissions@olivet.edu
Phone: (815) 939-5203 Toll-free number: (800) 648-1463
Fax: (815) 939-5069
Susan Wolff, Director of Admissions, Olivet Nazarene University, One University Avenue, Bourbonnais, IL 60914

---

## Principia College
### Elsah, Illinois
### www.prin.edu
**CB member**
**CB code: 1630**

- Private 4-year liberal arts college affiliated with First Church of Christ, Scientist (Christian Science)
- Residential campus in rural community
- 500 degree-seeking undergraduates
- 92% of applicants admitted
- SAT or ACT with writing, application essay required

**General.** Founded in 1910. Regionally accredited. All faculty, staff, and students are Christian Scientists. **Degrees:** 143 bachelor's awarded. **Location:** 35 miles from St. Louis. **Calendar:** Quarter. **Full-time faculty:** 55 total. **Part-time faculty:** 11 total. **Class size:** 94% < 20, 6% 20-39. **Special facilities:** School of Nations museum, astronomical observatory telescope, media center, tropical aviary, on-site mammoth excavation, Christian Science practitioner's office, athletic center with natatorium, 3,069-pipe organ, 39 bronze bell carillon.

### Freshman class profile.

| Mid 50% test scores | | | |
|---|---|---|---|
| SAT critical reading: | 510-640 | GPA 2.0-2.99: | 31% |
| SAT math: | 490-630 | Rank in top quarter: | 63% |
| ACT composite: | 22-29 | Rank in top tenth: | 38% |
| GPA 3.50 or higher: | 51% | Out-of-state: | 90% |
| GPA 3.0-3.49: | 17% | Live on campus: | 100% |

**Basis for selection.** School achievement record and essay or personal statement most important. Applicant must be practicing Christian Scientist. Test scores important. Foreign language SAT Subject Test required for placement purposes. Interview recommended. Portfolio recommended for art majors. **Homeschooled:** Must submit curricula program from accredited high school or accepted agency, plus GED.

**High school preparation.** 16 units required; 20 recommended. Required and recommended units include English 4, mathematics 3, social studies 2, history 1-2, science 2-3 (laboratory 2), foreign language 2-3 and academic electives 2.

**2007-2008 Annual costs.** Tuition/fees: $22,080. Room/board: $8,145. Books/supplies: $900. Personal expenses: $750.

---

**Financial aid. Non-need-based:** Scholarships awarded for academics, alumni affiliation. **Additional information:** Need-based tuition reduction work plan combines job with grant.

**Application procedures. Admission:** Priority date 11/15; deadline 3/1 (postmark date). No application fee. Application may be submitted online. Admission notification on a rolling basis beginning on or about 10/15. Must reply by May 1 or within 2 week(s) if notified thereafter. Admissions, scholarship, and financial aid decisions will be given by 12/1 to those who complete all three applications by 11/15. **Financial aid:** Closing date 3/1. Institutional form, CSS PROFILE required. Applicants notified by 4/1.

**Academics.** First year experience and pre-fall writing program for all students. Emphasis on character education, interdisciplinary curriculum, and individual skill development. Principia abroad and internship programs available. **Special study options:** Double major, independent study, internships, liberal arts/career combination, student-designed major, study abroad, teacher certification program. 3-2 engineering with Washington University, University of Southern California, Southern Illinois University at Edwardsville. **Credit/placement by examination:** AP, CLEP, IB, institutional tests. **Support services:** Learning center, study skills assistance, tutoring, writing center.

**Majors. Biology:** General. **Business:** Business admin. **Communications:** Media studies. **Computer sciences:** General, computer science. **Conservation:** General. **Education:** Elementary. **Engineering:** Science. **English:** English lit. **Foreign languages:** General, French, German, Spanish. **History:** General. **Interdisciplinary:** Global studies. **Liberal arts:** Arts/sciences, humanities. **Math:** General. **Parks/recreation:** Sports admin. **Philosophy/religion:** Philosophy, religion. **Physical sciences:** Chemistry, physics. **Social sciences:** General, anthropology, economics, political science, sociology. **Visual/performing arts:** Art history/conservation, dramatic, studio arts.

**Most popular majors.** Biology 6%, business/marketing 10%, computer/information sciences 7%, liberal arts 8%, visual/performing arts 14%.

**Computing on campus.** 250 workstations in dormitories, library, computer center, student center. Dormitories wired for high-speed internet access and linked to campus network. Online course registration, online library, helpline, student web hosting available.

**Student life. Freshman orientation:** Mandatory. Preregistration for classes offered. Pre-fall writing and orientation program immediately precedes start of classes. **Policies:** Students required to comply with standards of Christian Science. No alcoholic beverages, smoking, drugs. High moral standards and behavior expected. Standards maintained regarding abstinence from premarital sex or homosexual activity. Religious observance required. **Housing:** Guaranteed on-campus for all undergraduates. Single-sex dorms, apartments, substance-free housing available. $100 deposit, deadline 5/1. Housing with single-sex wings, 8 person cottages for nontraditional students, and theme houses available. **Activities:** Jazz band, choral groups, dance, drama, music ensembles, musical theater, radio station, student government, student newspaper, TV station, Christian Science Organization, black student union, Latin American student organization, student volunteer program, public affairs conference.

**Athletics.** NCAA. **Intercollegiate:** Baseball M, basketball, cross-country, diving, football (tackle) M, golf M, soccer, swimming, tennis, track and field, volleyball W. **Intramural:** Basketball, soccer, softball, volleyball W. **Team name:** Panthers.

**Student services.** Adult student services, career counseling, student employment services, financial aid counseling, health services, on-campus daycare, personal counseling.

**Contact.** E-mail: collegeadmissions@principia.edu
Phone: (618) 374-5181 Toll-free number: (800) 277-4648 ext. 2802
Fax: (618) 374-4000
Becky Barthelmess, Director of Admissions, Principia College, One Maybeck Place, Elsah, IL 62028-9799

---

## Quincy University
### Quincy, Illinois
### www.quincy.edu
**CB code: 1645**

- Private 4-year university and liberal arts college affiliated with Roman Catholic Church
- Residential campus in large town
- 982 degree-seeking undergraduates: 7% part-time, 58% women, 7% African American, 1% Asian American, 3% Hispanic American, 1% international
- 181 degree-seeking graduate students
- 96% of applicants admitted

◗ SAT or ACT (ACT writing optional), application essay required
◗ 48% graduate within 6 years; 29% enter graduate study

**General.** Founded in 1860. Regionally accredited. **Degrees:** 230 bachelor's, 1 associate awarded; master's offered. **Location:** 280 miles from Chicago, 120 miles from St. Louis. **Calendar:** Semester, limited summer session. **Full-time faculty:** 51 total; 78% have terminal degrees, 6% minority, 33% women. **Part-time faculty:** 84 total; 21% have terminal degrees, 63% women. **Class size:** 70% < 20, 29% 20-39, less than 1% 40-49. **Special facilities:** College-operated national public radio station.

**Freshman class profile.** 726 applied, 695 admitted, 234 enrolled.

| Mid 50% test scores | | | |
|---|---|---|---|
| SAT critical reading: | 440-570 | Rank in top tenth: | 9% |
| SAT math: | 440-590 | End year in good standing: | 84% |
| ACT composite: | 18-24 | Return as sophomores: | 72% |
| GPA 3.50 or higher: | 34% | Out-of-state: | 32% |
| GPA 3.0-3.49: | 25% | Live on campus: | 77% |
| GPA 2.0-2.99: | 40% | Fraternities: | 8% |
| Rank in top quarter: | 31% | Sororities: | 10% |

**Basis for selection.** School achievement record and test scores most important. Applicants for BS in nursing must have 22 ACT and 3.0 GPA. All applicants must submit letter of recommendation and personal statement. Audition required of music majors. Portfolio recommended for art majors. **Homeschooled:** Transcript of courses and grades, letter of recommendation (nonparent) required. **Learning Disabled:** Must submit documentation of disability.

**High school preparation.** 16 units recommended. Required and recommended units include English 4, mathematics 3, social studies 4, science 3 and foreign language 2.

**2008-2009 Annual costs.** Tuition/fees: $20,790. Room/board: $7,900. Books/supplies: $1,250. Personal expenses: $1,450.

**2007-2008 Financial aid. Need-based:** 220 full-time freshmen applied for aid; 186 were judged to have need; 186 of these received aid. Average need met was 82%. Average scholarship/grant was $16,971; average loan $3,734. 68% of total undergraduate aid awarded as scholarships/grants, 32% as loans/jobs. **Non-need-based:** Awarded to 196 full-time undergraduates, including 63 freshmen. Scholarships awarded for academics, alumni affiliation, art, athletics, music/drama.

**Application procedures. Admission:** No deadline. $25 fee, may be waived for applicants with need. Application may be submitted online. Admission notification on a rolling basis. **Financial aid:** Priority date 4/15; no closing date. FAFSA required. Applicants notified on a rolling basis starting 2/15; must reply by 5/1 or within 2 week(s) of notification.

**Academics.** Associate's degrees are offered in all majors by arrangement with institution. **Special study options:** Accelerated study, distance learning, double major, dual enrollment of high school students, ESL, honors, independent study, internships, liberal arts/career combination, student-designed major, study abroad, teacher certification program. 3-2 in engineering with Washington University; 3-1 in medical technology with various hospitals. **Credit/placement by examination:** AP, CLEP, IB, institutional tests. 40 credit hours maximum toward bachelor's degree. Combined total of 40 semester hours of credit from nontraditional sources accepted toward degree. **Support services:** Learning center, pre-admission summer program, reduced course load, remedial instruction, study skills assistance, tutoring, writing center.

**Majors. Biology:** General. **Business:** Accounting, business admin, finance, marketing. **Communications:** General, broadcast journalism, journalism. **Computer sciences:** Computer science, information systems. **Education:** Elementary, music, physical, special. **English:** English lit. **Foreign languages:** Translation. **Health:** Clinical lab science, nursing (RN). **History:** General. **Liberal arts:** Arts/sciences, humanities. **Math:** General. **Parks/recreation:** Sports admin. **Physical sciences:** Chemistry. **Protective services:** Criminal justice. **Psychology:** General. **Public administration:** Human services, social work. **Social sciences:** Political science. **Theology:** Theology. **Transportation:** Airline/commercial pilot, aviation management. **Visual/performing arts:** Art, graphic design. **Other:** Theology/Philosophy.

**Most popular majors.** Business/marketing 25%, education 14%, health sciences 12%, liberal arts 6%, parks/recreation 6%, psychology 6%.

**Computing on campus.** 200 workstations in dormitories, library, computer center, student center. Dormitories wired for high-speed internet access and linked to campus network. Commuter students can connect to campus network. Online course registration, online library, helpline, student web hosting, wireless network available.

**Student life. Freshman orientation:** Mandatory, $100 fee. Preregistration for classes offered. Academic year begins with 1-2 week registration and advisement program and 1-week social program. **Housing:** Guaranteed on-campus for all undergraduates. Coed dorms, single-sex dorms, apartments, fraternity/sorority housing available. $150 deposit. **Activities:** Bands, campus ministries, choral groups, dance, drama, film society, international student organizations, literary magazine, music ensembles, musical theater, opera, radio station, student government, student newspaper, symphony orchestra, TV station, Circle-K, Black Student Perspective, entrepreneur club, student volunteer services, BACCHUS, inter-cultural exchange, Needs of Our World, Amnesty International.

**Athletics.** NAIA, NCAA. **Intercollegiate:** Baseball M, basketball, football (tackle) M, golf, soccer, softball W, tennis, volleyball. **Intramural:** Basketball, bowling, football (non-tackle), racquetball, softball, volleyball. **Team name:** Hawks.

**Student services.** Alcohol/substance abuse counseling, career counseling, student employment services, financial aid counseling, health services, minority student services, personal counseling, placement for graduates. **Physically disabled:** Services for visually, hearing impaired.

**Contact.** E-mail: admissions@quincy.edu
Phone: (217) 228-5210 Toll-free number: (800) 688-4295
Fax: (217) 228-5479
Syndi Peck, Director of Admissions, Quincy University, 1800 College Avenue, Quincy, IL 62301-2699

## Robert Morris College: Chicago

**Chicago, Illinois**
www.robertmorris.edu

**CB member**
**CB code: 1670**

◗ Private 4-year university
◗ Commuter campus in very large city
◗ 4,535 degree-seeking undergraduates: 5% part-time, 62% women, 34% African American, 3% Asian American, 23% Hispanic American, 1% international
◗ 261 degree-seeking graduate students
◗ 81% of applicants admitted
◗ 71% graduate within 6 years

**General.** Founded in 1913. Regionally accredited. Branch campuses in DuPage, Lake County, Bensenville, Orland Park, Peoria, and Springfield. **Degrees:** 930 bachelor's, 1,127 associate awarded; master's offered. **ROTC:** Army. **Location:** Downtown. **Calendar:** 5 10-week sessions. Extensive summer session. **Full-time faculty:** 124 total; 24% have terminal degrees, 27% minority, 51% women. **Part-time faculty:** 202 total; 14% have terminal degrees, 23% minority, 46% women. **Class size:** 42% < 20, 52% 20-39, 5% 40-49, 1% 50-99, less than 1% >100.

**Freshman class profile.** 3,075 applied, 2,493 admitted, 1,042 enrolled.

| | | | |
|---|---|---|---|
| GPA 3.50 or higher: | 7% | End year in good standing: | 60% |
| GPA 3.0-3.49: | 19% | Return as sophomores: | 59% |
| GPA 2.0-2.99: | 58% | Out-of-state: | 4% |
| Rank in top quarter: | 20% | Live on campus: | 7% |
| Rank in top tenth: | 5% | International: | 1% |

**Basis for selection.** Applicants must submit high school transcript or equivalent GED for review. Secondary school record, class rank, GPA and interview most important. Standardized test scores, extra curricular activities and level of interest considered. Strongly recommend meeting with admissions counselor and campus visit. **Homeschooled:** Transcript of courses and grades, state high school equivalency certificate required. Must submit curriculum documentation, and state certification. In addition, student must take a nationally normed standardized examination demonstrating an acceptable achievement level.

**2008-2009 Annual costs.** Tuition/fees (projected): $18,000. Lab fees vary by program. Books/supplies: $1,350. Personal expenses: $1,417.

**2006-2007 Financial aid. Need-based:** 1,306 full-time freshmen applied for aid; 1,281 were judged to have need; 1,239 of these received aid. Average need met was 39%. Average scholarship/grant was $8,352; average loan $4,171. 47% of total undergraduate aid awarded as scholarships/grants, 53% as loans/jobs. **Non-need-based:** Awarded to 266 full-time undergraduates, including 34 freshmen. Scholarships awarded for academics, art, athletics, state residency.

**Application procedures. Admission:** No deadline. $30 fee, may be waived for applicants with need. Application may be submitted online. Admission notification on a rolling basis. **Financial aid:** No deadline. FAFSA required. Applicants notified on a rolling basis.

**Academics. Special study options:** Accelerated study, combined bachelor's/graduate degree, dual enrollment of high school students, honors, independent study, internships, study abroad. **Credit/placement by examination:** AP, CLEP, institutional tests. 36 credit hours maximum toward associate degree, 36 toward bachelor's. **Support services:** Learning center, study skills assistance, tutoring, writing center.

**Majors. Business:** Business admin. **Computer sciences:** Information technology. **Visual/performing arts:** Graphic design.

**Most popular majors.** Business/marketing 81%, computer/information sciences 10%, visual/performing arts 9%.

**Computing on campus.** 1,792 workstations in library, computer center, student center. Online library, helpline, repair service, wireless network available.

**Student life. Freshman orientation:** Mandatory. Held 1-4 weeks prior to commencement of classes. Students required to attend one 2 1/2-hour session. **Policies:** Students required to comply with college dress and attendance policies. **Housing:** Guaranteed on-campus for all undergraduates. Coed dorms, substance-free housing available. $300 fully refundable deposit, deadline 5/1. **Activities:** Dance, drama, literary magazine, student newspaper.

**Athletics.** NAIA, USCAA. **Intercollegiate:** Baseball M, basketball, bowling, cross-country, golf, ice hockey, lacrosse W, soccer, softball W, tennis W, track and field W, volleyball W. **Team name:** Eagles.

**Student services.** Adult student services, career counseling, services for economically disadvantaged, student employment services, financial aid counseling, personal counseling, placement for graduates, veterans' counselor. **Physically disabled:** Services for visually, hearing impaired.

**Contact.** E-mail: ais@robertmorris.edu
Phone: (312) 935-4400 Toll-free number: (800) 762-5960
Fax: (312) 935-4440
Catherine Lockwood, Vice President of Undergraduate Enrollment, Robert Morris College: Chicago, 401 South State Street, Chicago, IL 60605

---

## Rockford College
**Rockford, Illinois**
**www.rockford.edu**

**CB member**
**CB code: 1665**

- Private 4-year liberal arts college
- Residential campus in small city
- 862 degree-seeking undergraduates: 13% part-time, 63% women, 7% African American, 2% Asian American, 6% Hispanic American
- 266 degree-seeking graduate students
- SAT or ACT (ACT writing optional) required
- 44% graduate within 6 years

**General.** Founded in 1847. Regionally accredited. **Degrees:** 184 bachelor's awarded; master's offered. **Location:** 90 miles from Chicago. **Calendar:** Semester, limited summer session. **Full-time faculty:** 66 total; 77% have terminal degrees, 3% minority, 38% women. **Part-time faculty:** 84 total; 11% minority, 62% women. **Class size:** 75% < 20, 23% 20-39, 1% 40-49. **Special facilities:** Black box theatre, nursing lab, center for civic engagement, prairie conservation area, center for ethics and entrepreneurship.

**Freshman class profile.** 116 enrolled.

| Mid 50% test scores | | Rank in top tenth: | 13% |
|---|---|---|---|
| ACT composite: | 18-24 | End year in good standing: | 84% |
| GPA 3.50 or higher: | 28% | Return as sophomores: | 57% |
| GPA 3.0-3.49: | 28% | Out-of-state: | 18% |
| GPA 2.0-2.99: | 41% | Live on campus: | 69% |
| Rank in top quarter: | 34% | | |

**Basis for selection.** School achievement record and test scores most important. Recommendations and activities also considered. Auditions required of theater arts and musical theater performance majors. Personal statements required of students who fall below standard admission criteria.

**High school preparation.** 15 units required. Required units include English 4, mathematics 3, social studies 3, science 3 (laboratory 3) and academic electives 2.

**2008-2009 Annual costs.** Tuition/fees: $23,500. Room/board: $6,750. Books/supplies: $1,500. Personal expenses: $2,250.

**2006-2007 Financial aid. Need-based:** 86 full-time freshmen applied for aid; 78 were judged to have need; 78 of these received aid. Average

need met was 69%. Average scholarship/grant was $13,400; average loan $2,356. 49% of total undergraduate aid awarded as scholarships/grants, 51% as loans/jobs. **Non-need-based:** Awarded to 145 full-time undergraduates, including 18 freshmen. Scholarships awarded for academics, alumni affiliation, leadership, minority status, music/drama, state residency.

**Application procedures. Admission:** Closing date 8/15 (postmark date). $35 fee, may be waived for applicants with need. Application may be submitted online. Admission notification on a rolling basis beginning on or about 9/15. **Financial aid:** Priority date 3/1; no closing date. FAFSA required. Applicants notified on a rolling basis starting 3/15; must reply within 4 week(s) of notification.

**Academics.** Study abroad program at Regent's College (London) and community-based service learning programs available. **Special study options:** Accelerated study, distance learning, double major, ESL, exchange student, honors, independent study, internships, study abroad, teacher certification program, United Nations semester, Washington semester. Tutorial classes, special studies courses. **Credit/placement by examination:** AP, CLEP, SAT, ACT, institutional tests. 64 credit hours maximum toward bachelor's degree. **Support services:** Learning center, reduced course load, remedial instruction, study skills assistance, tutoring, writing center.

**Majors. Biology:** General, biochemistry. **Business:** Accounting, business admin. **Computer sciences:** Computer science. **Education:** General, elementary, physical. **English:** English lit. **Foreign languages:** Classics, French, German, Latin, Romance, Spanish. **Health:** Nursing (RN), predental, premedicine, prepharmacy, preveterinary. **History:** General. **Legal studies:** Prelaw. **Liberal arts:** Humanities. **Math:** General. **Philosophy/religion:** Philosophy. **Physical sciences:** Chemistry. **Psychology:** General. **Social sciences:** General, anthropology, economics, international relations, political science, sociology. **Visual/performing arts:** Art, art history/conservation, dramatic, musical theater. **Other:** Management studies, Science and mathematics.

**Most popular majors.** Business/marketing 21%, education 30%, health sciences 14%, psychology 10%, social sciences 10%.

**Computing on campus.** 75 workstations in library, computer center. Dormitories wired for high-speed internet access and linked to campus network. Commuter students can connect to campus network. Helpline, repair service, wireless network available.

**Student life. Freshman orientation:** Mandatory. Preregistration for classes offered. Held 4 days prior to start of classes. **Housing:** Coed dorms, special housing for disabled, substance-free housing available. $100 nonrefundable deposit. Special housing available for first-year students. **Activities:** Campus ministries, choral groups, dance, drama, international student organizations, literary magazine, music ensembles, Model UN, musical theater, opera, student government, Cross Roads/Intervarsity, gay/straight alliance, multicultural club, Muslim student organization, nursing student organization, Peace Jam, psychology society, Rotaract, Spanish club.

**Athletics.** NCAA. **Intercollegiate:** Baseball M, basketball, cross-country, football (tackle) M, golf M, soccer, softball W, tennis, track and field, volleyball W. **Team name:** Regents.

**Student services.** Adult student services, alcohol/substance abuse counseling, career counseling, student employment services, financial aid counseling, health services, personal counseling, placement for graduates. **Physically disabled:** Services for visually, speech, hearing impaired.

**Contact.** E-mail: rcadmissions@rockford.edu
Phone: (815) 226-4050 Toll-free number: (800) 892-2984
Fax: (815) 226-2822
Jennifer Nordstrom, Associate Vice President for Undergraduate Admission and Strategic Marketing, Rockford College, 5050 East State Street, Rockford, IL 61108-2393

---

## Roosevelt University
**Chicago, Illinois**
**www.roosevelt.edu**

**CB member**
**CB code: 1666**

- Private 4-year university
- Commuter campus in very large city
- 3,861 degree-seeking undergraduates: 43% part-time, 66% women, 22% African American, 5% Asian American, 11% Hispanic American, 3% international
- 3,135 degree-seeking graduate students
- 43% of applicants admitted
- SAT or ACT, application essay required
- 37% graduate within 6 years

**General.** Founded in 1945. Regionally accredited. **Degrees:** 989 bachelor's awarded; master's, doctoral offered. **Location:** Downtown. **Calendar:** Semester, extensive summer session. **Full-time faculty:** 216 total; 87% have terminal degrees, 12% minority, 40% women. **Part-time faculty:** 415 total; 46% women. **Class size:** 67% < 20, 32% 20-39, 1% 40-49, less than 1% 50-99.

**Freshman class profile.** 2,100 applied, 902 admitted, 292 enrolled.

| Mid 50% test scores | | | |
|---|---|---|---|
| SAT critical reading: | 510-630 | **Rank in top quarter:** | 7% |
| SAT math: | 450-610 | **Rank in top tenth:** | 2% |
| ACT composite: | 20-25 | **Out-of-state:** | 29% |
| GPA 3.50 or higher: | 31% | **Live on campus:** | 61% |
| GPA 3.0-3.49: | 25% | **International:** | 4% |
| GPA 2.0-2.99: | 42% | **Fraternities:** | 1% |
| | | **Sororities:** | 8% |

**Basis for selection.** Recent secondary school performance most crucial. Required essays and recommended interviews can be used to communicate special circumstances. Placement evaluation required for all admitted, degree-seeking undergraduate students. Institutional examination accepted in lieu of SAT or ACT for those applicants out of secondary school at least 5 years. Interview recommended for early admission and borderline applicants. Audition required of music and theater majors. Portfolio recommended for art and theater majors.

**High school preparation.** 15 units required; 19 recommended. Required and recommended units include English 4, mathematics 3-4, social studies 2, history 1-2, science 3 (laboratory 2), foreign language 2 and academic electives 2. Extensive work in English, history, mathematics, foreign language, and science recommended.

**2007-2008 Annual costs.** Tuition/fees: $16,930. Tuition for Chicago College of the Performing Arts is $23,750 per year. Room/board: $10,572. Books/supplies: $1,200. Personal expenses: $2,300.

**Financial aid. Non-need-based:** Scholarships awarded for academics, alumni affiliation, leadership, minority status, music/drama, state residency.

**Application procedures. Admission:** Priority date 8/15; deadline 9/1. $25 fee, may be waived for applicants with need. Admission notification on a rolling basis beginning on or about 10/15. **Financial aid:** Priority date 4/1; no closing date. FAFSA, institutional form required. Applicants notified on a rolling basis starting 3/15; must reply within 2 week(s) of notification.

**Academics. Special study options:** Accelerated study, combined bachelor's/graduate degree, distance learning, double major, dual enrollment of high school students, ESL, honors, independent study, internships, student-designed major, study abroad, teacher certification program. Early admission agreement with John Marshall Law School. **Credit/placement by examination:** AP, CLEP, ACT, institutional tests. 30 credit hours maximum toward bachelor's degree. **Support services:** Learning center, pre-admission summer program, reduced course load, remedial instruction, tutoring.

**Majors. Area/ethnic studies:** African-American, American, women's. **Biology:** General. **Business:** General, accounting, actuarial science, business admin, communications, finance, hospitality admin, human resources, insurance, international, labor relations, management science, managerial economics, marketing, tourism/travel. **Communications:** General, journalism, public relations. **Computer sciences:** General, computer science, information systems. **Conservation:** Environmental studies. **Education:** Biology, chemistry, early childhood, elementary, English, French, history, mathematics, multi-level teacher, music, secondary, social science, Spanish. **Engineering technology:** Electrical. **English:** English lit, speech/rhetoric. **Foreign languages:** General, comparative lit, Spanish. **Health:** Clinical lab technology, health care admin, health services, nuclear medical technology, predental, premedicine, prepharmacy, preveterinary. **History:** General. **Interdisciplinary:** Gerontology, math/computer science. **Legal studies:** General, prelaw. **Liberal arts:** Arts/sciences. **Math:** General, statistics. **Philosophy/religion:** Philosophy. **Physical sciences:** Chemistry, physics. **Protective services:** Criminal justice. **Psychology:** General. **Public administration:** Social work. **Social sciences:** General, criminology, economics, geography, international relations, political science, sociology, urban studies. **Visual/performing arts:** General, art history/conservation, arts management, conducting, dramatic, jazz, music history, music management, music performance, music theory/composition, piano/organ, voice/opera.

**Most popular majors.** Business/marketing 35%, communications/journalism 6%, personal/culinary services 8%, psychology 13%, social sciences 7%, visual/performing arts 8%.

**Computing on campus.** 180 workstations in library, computer center. Commuter students can connect to campus network. Helpline available.

**Student life. Freshman orientation:** Available. **Housing:** Guaranteed on-campus for all undergraduates. Coed dorms available. $250 deposit, deadline 8/1. High-rise residence hall in cooperation with University Center of Chicago available. **Activities:** Dance, international student organizations, literary magazine, radio station, student government, student newspaper, Christian Bible groups, theater club, Black student union, Hispanic organization, residence hall council, Asociacion de Latinos Unidos.

**Athletics. Intramural:** Badminton, basketball, table tennis.

**Student services.** Adult student services, career counseling, student employment services, personal counseling, placement for graduates, veterans' counselor. **Physically disabled:** Services for visually, hearing impaired.

**Contact.** E-mail: applyru@roosevelt.edu
Toll-free number: (877) 277-5978 Fax: (312) 341-3523
Gwen Kanelos, Assistant Vice President of Enrollment Services, Roosevelt University, 430 South Michigan Avenue, Chicago, IL 60605-1394

## Rosalind Franklin University of Medicine and Science
**North Chicago, Illinois**
**www.rosalindfranklin.edu**          **CB code: 0768**

◆ Private two-year upper-division university and health science college
◆ Commuter campus in large town
◆ Application essay required

**General.** Founded in 1912. Regionally accredited. **Degrees:** 7 bachelor's awarded; master's, doctoral, first professional offered. **Location:** 40 miles from Chicago. **Calendar:** Quarter, limited summer session. **Full-time faculty:** 144 total. **Part-time faculty:** 51 total. **Special facilities:** 14 fully equipped patient examination rooms, anatomy lab.

**Student profile.** 4 degree-seeking undergraduates. 100% entered as juniors. 78% transferred from two-year, 22% transferred from four-year institutions.

**Basis for selection.** College transcript, application essay required. Undergraduate education must be completed in an accredited college or university, with at least a "C" in required courses. Proficiency in written and spoken English required. Transfer accepted as juniors.

**2007-2008 Annual costs.** Tuition/fees: $14,803. Full-time tuition rate is for bachelor's degree program in Medical Technology. Books/supplies: $300.

**Financial aid.** All financial aid based on need. **Additional information:** Financial aid application deadline 60 days prior to program start.

**Application procedures. Admission:** Deadline 7/1. $20 fee, may be waived for applicants with need. Application must be submitted on paper. **Financial aid:** FAFSA, institutional form required.

**Academics. Special study options:** Accelerated study, cooperative education, cross-registration, distance learning, double major, dual enrollment of high school students, internships. **Credit/placement by examination:** AP, CLEP, institutional tests. **Support services:** Learning center, reduced course load, study skills assistance, tutoring.

**Majors. Health:** Clinical lab technology.

**Computing on campus.** 106 workstations in library, computer center, student center. Dormitories wired for high-speed internet access and linked to campus network. Commuter students can connect to campus network. Helpline, repair service, wireless network available.

**Student life. Housing:** Apartments available. $500 deposit. Limited on-campus housing available. **Activities:** Choral groups, literary magazine, student government, student newspaper, Asian Pacific American medical student association, Adolescent Substance Abuse Prevention, Christian Medical Association, Hillel, internal health/medicine interest groups, Lesbian, Gay, Bisexual and Transgendered People in Medicine, Middle Eastern medical student association, South Asian Medical Association, Salud Ofrecida A Latinos.

**Student services.** Alcohol/substance abuse counseling, career counseling, financial aid counseling, health services, minority student services, personal counseling, placement for graduates, veterans' counselor.

**Contact.** E-mail: grad.admissions@rosalindfranklin.edu
Phone: (847) 578-3209
Maryann DeCaire, Vice President for Enrollment Services, Rosalind Franklin University of Medicine and Science, 3333 Green Bay Road, North Chicago, IL 60064-3095

## Rush University
Chicago, Illinois
www.rushu.rush.edu
CB code: 3262

- Private two-year upper-division health science and nursing college
- Commuter campus in very large city
- 47% of applicants admitted
- Application essay required

**General.** Founded in 1971. Regionally accredited. Educational component of Rush University Medical Center. Students use clinical and laboratory facilities of the medical center, affiliated hospitals, and community health centers. Based on teacher-practitioner model. **Degrees:** 148 bachelor's awarded; master's, doctoral, first professional offered. **Articulation:** Agreements with College of DuPage, Triton College, Parkland College, Moraine Valley Community College, Oakton Community College, William Rainey Harper College, Kankakee Community College. **Location:** 2 miles from the downtown. **Calendar:** Quarter, limited summer session. **Full-time faculty:** 450 total. **Part-time faculty:** 350 total. **Class size:** 37% < 20, 36% 20-39, 27% 50-99.

**Student profile.** 244 degree-seeking undergraduates, 1,325 degree-seeking graduate students. 310 applied as first time-transfer students, 146 admitted, 97 enrolled. 100% entered as juniors.

| | | | |
|---|---|---|---|
| Women: | 91% | Live on campus: | 20% |
| Part-time: | 6% | 25 or older: | 65% |
| Out-of-state: | 15% | | |

**Basis for selection.** College transcript, application essay required. Admission based on GPA and letters of recommendation. Application closing dates: nursing April 1, clinical lab sciences/medical technology June 1, perfusion technology, March 1. Transfer accepted as juniors.

**2007-2008 Annual costs.** Tuition/fees: $20,058. Tuition costs vary by program. Room only: $8,406. Books/supplies: $700. Personal expenses: $1,220.

**Financial aid. Need-based:** 176 applied for aid; 167 were judged to have need; 160 of these received aid. Average need met was 55%. 36% of total undergraduate aid awarded as scholarships/grants, 64% as loans/jobs. **Non-need-based:** Awarded to 23 undergraduates.

**Application procedures. Admission:** Rolling admission. $50 fee, may be waived for applicants with need. Application may be submitted online. **Financial aid:** Priority date 5/1, no deadline. Applicants notified on a rolling basis starting 4/1; must reply within 3 weeks of notification. FAFSA, institutional form required.

**Academics. Special study options:** Accelerated study, combined bachelor's/graduate degree, distance learning, liberal arts/career combination. Registered nurse completion program. **Credit/placement by examination:** AP, CLEP, institutional tests. 45 credit hours maximum toward bachelor's degree.

**Majors. Health:** Clinical lab science, nursing (RN), perfusion technology.

**Computing on campus.** 140 workstations in library, computer center, student center. Commuter students can connect to campus network. Online library, helpline, wireless network available.

**Student life. Policies:** Funds available for official student groups. **Housing:** Apartments available. $200 deposit. **Activities:** Student government, student newspaper, Christian Fellowship, rape victim advocate program, medical technicians club, National Student Nurses' Association chapter, Lesbian/Gay/Bisexual/Allies, Health Science Students for Choice.

**Student services.** Alcohol/substance abuse counseling, career counseling, student employment services, financial aid counseling, health services, on-campus daycare, personal counseling, veterans' counselor.

**Contact.** E-mail: Rush_Admissions@rush.edu
Phone: (312) 942-7100 Fax: (312) 942-2219
Hicela Woods, Director of College Admission Services, Rush University, College Admissions, Chicago, IL 60612

## Saint Anthony College of Nursing
Rockford, Illinois
www.sacn.edu
CB code: 3923

- Private two-year upper-division nursing college affiliated with Roman Catholic Church
- Commuter campus in small city

**General.** Regionally accredited. **Location:** 90 miles from Chicago. **Calendar:** Semester.

**Annual costs/financial aid.** Tuition/fees (2007-2008): $17,332. Required fees vary from $112-$262. Books/supplies: $1,500. Personal expenses: $1,785. Need-based financial aid available to full-time and part-time students.

**Contact.** Phone: (815) 227-2141
Assistant Dean for Admissions and Student Affairs, 5658 East State Street, Rockford, IL 61108-2468

## St. Augustine College
Chicago, Illinois
www.staugustinecollege.edu
CB code: 0697

- Private 4-year liberal arts college affiliated with Episcopal Church
- Commuter campus in very large city

**General.** Founded in 1980. Regionally accredited. **Calendar:** Semester.

**Annual costs/financial aid.** Tuition/fees (2007-2008): $9,090. Cost includes tuition, fees, books.

**Contact.** Phone: (773) 878-8756
Assistant Dean of Admissions and Records, 1345 West Argyle, Chicago, IL 60640-3501

## St. Francis Medical Center College of Nursing
Peoria, Illinois
www.sfmccon.edu
CB code: 1756

- Private two-year upper-division nursing college affiliated with Roman Catholic Church
- Commuter campus in small city
- 53% of applicants admitted
- Application essay required

**General.** Founded in 1905. Regionally accredited. Located at large medical center. National League of Nursing accredited. NCA accredited. Offers experience at Tazewell County, Fulton County, Peoria City/County Health Departments, Human Service Center and various other community agencies. **Degrees:** 93 bachelor's awarded; master's offered. **Location:** 180 miles from Chicago, 160 miles from St. Louis. **Calendar:** Semester, limited summer session. **Full-time faculty:** 29 total; 24% have terminal degrees, 100% women. **Part-time faculty:** 13 total; 92% women. **Class size:** 7% < 20, 50% 20-39, 36% 40-49, 7% 50-99.

**Student profile.** 329 degree-seeking undergraduates, 105 degree-seeking graduate students. 170 applied as first time-transfer students, 90 admitted, 82 enrolled. 100% entered as juniors. 92% transferred from two-year, 8% transferred from four-year institutions.

| | | | |
|---|---|---|---|
| Women: | 90% | Hispanic American: | 2% |
| African American: | 5% | Part-time: | 16% |
| Asian American: | 2% | 25 or older: | 51% |

**Basis for selection.** High school transcript, college transcript, application essay required. Enrollment depends on satisfactory completion of 62 semester hours of a specified prenursing curriculum. Applications may be submitted after satisfactory completion of 30 semester hours of required prenursing courses. Must include 8 semester hours of physical/life sciences. Require minimum cumulative GPA of 2.50. Transfer accepted as juniors.

**2008-2009 Annual costs.** Tuition/fees: $13,910. Room only: $2,000. Books/supplies: $1,230. Personal expenses: $2,700.

**Financial aid. Need-based:** 231 applied for aid; 159 were judged to have need; 159 of these received aid. Average need met was 79%. 52% of total undergraduate aid awarded as scholarships/grants, 48% as loans/jobs. **Non-need-based:** Awarded to 74 undergraduates. Scholarships awarded for academics, alumni affiliation. **Additional information:** Modified Education Employment Program available to full-time students on a limited basis. Tuition waiver program for hospital employees available.

**Application procedures. Admission:** Deadline 9/1. $50 fee. Application must be submitted on paper. **Financial aid:** No deadline. Applicants notified on a rolling basis starting 5/15; must reply within 2 weeks of notification. FAFSA, institutional form required.

**Academics. Special study options:** Distance learning. **Credit/placement by examination:** CLEP.

**Majors. Health:** Nursing (RN).

**Computing on campus.** 31 workstations in library, computer center. Dormitories linked to campus network. Commuter students can connect to campus network. Online library, helpline, repair service available.

**Student life. Housing:** Guaranteed on-campus for all undergraduates. Coed dorms, substance-free housing available. **Activities:** Student government, Christian Fellowship, Student Nurses' Association, student senate.

**Student services.** Adult student services, financial aid counseling, health services, personal counseling.

**Contact.** E-mail: janice.farquharson@osfhealthcare.org
Phone: (309) 655-2245 Fax: (309) 624-8973
Janice Farquharson, Director of Admissions and Recruitment, St. Francis Medical Center College of Nursing, 511 NE Greenleaf Street, Peoria, IL 61603-3783

## St. John's College
### Springfield, Illinois
### www.st-johns.org/education/schools/nursing

- Private two-year upper-division nursing college affiliated with Roman Catholic Church
- Commuter campus in small city

**General. Degrees:** 28 bachelor's awarded. **Location:** 220 miles from Chicago, 100 miles from St. Louis. **Calendar:** Semester. **Full-time faculty:** 11 total. **Part-time faculty:** 1 total.

**Student profile.** 69 degree-seeking undergraduates.

**2008-2009 Annual costs.** Tuition/fees (projected): $12,068. Books/supplies: $1,644. Personal expenses: $1,854.

**Financial aid. Need-based:** 59% of total undergraduate aid awarded as scholarships/grants, 41% as loans/jobs.

**Academics. Credit/placement by examination:** CLEP.

**Majors. Health:** Nursing (RN).

**Contact.** E-mail: college@st-johns.org
Phone: (217) 525-5628
Linda Quigley, Admissions Director, St. John's College, 729 East Carpenter Street, Springfield, IL 62702

## St. Xavier University
### Chicago, Illinois
### www.sxu.edu
**CB member**
**CB code: 1708**

- Private 4-year university affiliated with Roman Catholic Church
- Commuter campus in very large city
- 3,251 degree-seeking undergraduates: 21% part-time, 71% women, 18% African American, 3% Asian American, 14% Hispanic American, 1% international
- 2,316 degree-seeking graduate students
- 77% of applicants admitted
- SAT or ACT (ACT writing optional) required

**General.** Founded in 1847. Regionally accredited. Affiliated with Sisters of Mercy. **Degrees:** 726 bachelor's awarded; master's offered. **ROTC:** Air Force. **Location:** 20 miles from downtown. **Calendar:** Semester, limited summer session. **Full-time faculty:** 186 total. **Part-time faculty:** 216 total. **Special facilities:** Music performance studio, reading clinic, speech clinic, learning disabilities clinic, mathematics laboratory.

**Freshman class profile.** 2,289 applied, 1,754 admitted, 515 enrolled.

| Mid 50% test scores | | Return as sophomores: | 75% |
|---|---|---|---|
| SAT critical reading: | 480-590 | Out-of-state: | 12% |
| SAT math: | 430-560 | Live on campus: | 59% |
| ACT composite: | 20-24 | | |

**Basis for selection.** GPA, test scores most important. Counselor recommendation, class rank considered. Interview recommended for borderline applicants. Audition required of music majors.

**High school preparation.** 16 units recommended. Recommended units include English 4, mathematics 3, foreign language 2 and academic electives 3. 4 units of science and social studies combined.

**2007-2008 Annual costs.** Tuition/fees: $21,236. Room/board: $7,626. Books/supplies: $900. Personal expenses: $986.

**Financial aid. Non-need-based:** Scholarships awarded for academics, athletics, music/drama.

**Application procedures. Admission:** No deadline. $25 fee, may be waived for applicants with need. Application may be submitted online. Admission notification on a rolling basis. Must reply by May 1 or within 4 week(s) if notified thereafter. **Financial aid:** Priority date 3/1; no closing date. FAFSA required. Applicants notified on a rolling basis starting 2/1; must reply by 5/1 or within 2 week(s) of notification.

**Academics. Special study options:** Accelerated study, combined bachelor's/graduate degree, cooperative education, distance learning, dual enrollment of high school students, ESL, external degree, honors, independent study, internships, liberal arts/career combination, student-designed major, study abroad, teacher certification program. **Credit/placement by examination:** AP, CLEP, institutional tests. 27 credit hours maximum toward bachelor's degree. **Support services:** Learning center, pre-admission summer program, reduced course load, remedial instruction, study skills assistance, tutoring, writing center.

**Majors. Biology:** General, botany. **Business:** General, accounting, actuarial science, international. **Communications:** General. **Computer sciences:** General, computer science. **Education:** General, art, biology, history, mathematics, music, secondary, social science, Spanish. **English:** English lit. **Foreign languages:** Spanish. **Health:** Nursing (RN), premedicine, prepharmacy, preveterinary, speech pathology. **History:** General. **Interdisciplinary:** Biological/physical sciences. **Legal studies:** Prelaw. **Liberal arts:** Arts/sciences. **Math:** General. **Philosophy/religion:** Philosophy, religion. **Physical sciences:** Chemistry. **Protective services:** Criminal justice. **Psychology:** General. **Social sciences:** General, international relations, political science, sociology. **Theology:** Theology. **Visual/performing arts:** Studio arts, voice/opera.

**Most popular majors.** Business/marketing 23%, education 19%, health sciences 19%, liberal arts 9%, psychology 6%.

**Computing on campus.** 306 workstations in dormitories, library, computer center, student center. Dormitories wired for high-speed internet access and linked to campus network. Commuter students can connect to campus network. Online course registration, helpline, student web hosting, wireless network available.

**Student life. Freshman orientation:** Mandatory. Preregistration for classes offered. Two-day overnight orientation held in summer. **Housing:** Coed dorms available. $100 nonrefundable deposit, deadline 5/1. **Activities:** Bands, campus ministries, choral groups, film society, international student organizations, literary magazine, music ensembles, radio station, student government, student newspaper, symphony orchestra, black student organization, Hispanic student organization, student activities board, student nurses association, Muslim student association, Celtic Connection, campus ministry, Fellowship of Christian Athletes, Xi Delta.

**Athletics.** NAIA. **Intercollegiate:** Baseball M, basketball, cross-country, football (tackle) M, soccer, softball W, volleyball W. **Intramural:** Basketball M, bowling, volleyball. **Team name:** Cougars.

**Student services.** Adult student services, alcohol/substance abuse counseling, career counseling, services for economically disadvantaged, student employment services, financial aid counseling, health services, on-campus daycare, personal counseling, placement for graduates. **Physically disabled:** Services for speech impaired.

**Contact.** E-mail: admissions@sxu.edu
Phone: (773) 298-3050 Toll-free number: (800) 462-9288
Fax: (773) 298-3076
Beth Gierach, Associate Vice President of Enrollment Services, St. Xavier University, 3700 West 103rd Street, Chicago, IL 60655

## School of the Art Institute of Chicago
### Chicago, Illinois
### www.saic.edu
**CB member**
**CB code: 1713**

- Private 4-year visual arts college
- Commuter campus in very large city
- 2,330 degree-seeking undergraduates: 6% part-time, 64% women, 3% African American, 11% Asian American, 8% Hispanic American, 1% Native American, 18% international

- 602 graduate students
- 80% of applicants admitted
- SAT or ACT (ACT writing optional), application essay required
- 54% graduate within 6 years

**General.** Founded in 1866. Regionally accredited. **Degrees:** 425 bachelor's awarded; master's offered. **Location:** Downtown. **Calendar:** Semester, extensive summer session. **Full-time faculty:** 134 total; 87% have terminal degrees, 16% minority, 43% women. **Part-time faculty:** 493 total; 49% women. **Class size:** 87% < 20, 11% 20-39, 2% 40-49, less than 1% >100. **Special facilities:** Film center, video data bank, gallery, project space, student union galleries, poetry center, fashion resource center, artists' book collection, visiting artists' program, Roger Brown study collection, architecture library.

**Freshman class profile.** 1,739 applied, 1,392 admitted, 452 enrolled.

| | | | |
|---|---|---|---|
| Return as sophomores: | 74% | Live on campus: | 85% |
| Out-of-state: | 81% | International: | 17% |

**Basis for selection.** Portfolio most important; statement of purpose, 500 SAT verbal or 20 ACT English, academic credentials, and recommendations also considered. Interview recommended. Portfolio required. **Learning Disabled:** With proper documentation, admissions' academic review offered.

**High school preparation.** Advanced-level study of art recommended.

**2007-2008 Annual costs.** Tuition/fees: $31,040. Students will be required to purchase a laptop through SAIC. Costs range from $2,000 to $2,200. Room only: $8,900. Books/supplies: $2,340. Personal expenses: $2,460.

**Financial aid. Non-need-based:** Scholarships awarded for academics, art.

**Application procedures. Admission:** Priority date 1/2; deadline 6/1 (postmark date). $65 fee, may be waived for applicants with need. Application must be submitted online. Admission notification on a rolling basis beginning on or about 10/1. **Financial aid:** Priority date 3/15; no closing date. FAFSA required. Applicants notified on a rolling basis starting 3/1.

**Academics.** Interdisciplinary curriculum allows students to personalize education or concentrate on single discipline. **Special study options:** Cooperative education, double major, ESL, exchange student, independent study, internships, New York semester, student-designed major, study abroad, teacher certification program. Credit/no-credit grading system, 6 credit off-campus study requirement. **Credit/placement by examination:** AP, CLEP, IB. 18 credit hours maximum toward bachelor's degree. DANTES scores accepted. **Support services:** Learning center, pre-admission summer program, reduced course load, remedial instruction, study skills assistance, tutoring.

**Majors. Architecture:** Interior. **Communications:** Digital media. **Communications technology:** Recording arts. **Education:** Art. **English:** Creative writing. **Visual/performing arts:** General, art, art history/conservation, ceramics, cinematography, design, digital art, drawing, fashion design, fiber arts, graphic design, industrial design, interior design, multimedia, painting, photography, printmaking, sculpture, studio arts. **Other:** Sonic art.

**Computing on campus.** PC or laptop required. 430 workstations in dormitories, library, computer center. Dormitories wired for high-speed internet access and linked to campus network. Commuter students can connect to campus network. Online library, helpline, student web hosting, wireless network available.

**Student life. Freshman orientation:** Mandatory, $50 fee. Preregistration for classes offered. Held 4 days prior to beginning of class. First day open to parents, family and friends. **Housing:** Coed dorms, special housing for disabled, substance-free housing available. $550 nonrefundable deposit. **Activities:** Campus ministries, dance, drama, film society, international student organizations, literary magazine, radio station, student government, student newspaper, TV station, Agape, creative writing guild, Korean student association, Student Organization for the Advancement of Philosophy, Students for Sexual Diversity, Taiwanese student organization, Veggies Unite!, yoga group.

**Student services.** Alcohol/substance abuse counseling, career counseling, student employment services, financial aid counseling, health services, minority student services, personal counseling, veterans' counselor. **Physically disabled:** Services for visually, speech, hearing impaired.

**Contact.** E-mail: admiss@saic.edu
Phone: (312) 629-6100 Toll-free number: (800) 232-7242
Fax: (312) 629-6101
Scott Ramon, Director, Undergraduate Admissions, School of the Art Institute of Chicago, 36 South Wabash Avenue, Chicago, IL 60603

---

## Shimer College
### Chicago, Illinois
www.shimer.edu                                CB code: 1717

- Private 4-year liberal arts college
- Residential campus in very large city
- 76 degree-seeking undergraduates: 12% African American, 4% Asian American, 4% Hispanic American, 3% international
- 14 graduate students
- 69% of applicants admitted
- Application essay, interview required
- 43% graduate within 6 years

**General.** Founded in 1853. Regionally accredited. **Degrees:** 17 bachelor's awarded. **Calendar:** Semester. **Full-time faculty:** 12 total; 8% minority, 25% women. **Part-time faculty:** 4 total; 25% have terminal degrees, 25% women.

**Freshman class profile.** 45 applied, 31 admitted, 13 enrolled.

| | | | |
|---|---|---|---|
| GPA 3.50 or higher: | 42% | Return as sophomores: | 66% |
| GPA 3.0-3.49: | 37% | Out-of-state: | 31% |
| GPA 2.0-2.99: | 21% | Live on campus: | 62% |

**Basis for selection.** Essays and interviews most important. Test scores, GPA, recommendations, motivation, maturity considered. Demonstrated writing skills and interest in and enthusiasm about Shimer's Great Books curriculum and discussion method important. Early entrants and other applicants who do not have high school diplomas may be required to submit GED; applicants without high school diplomas who are too young to take GED may be required to complete additional approved testing in order to comply with financial aid regulations.

**High school preparation.** 21 units recommended. Recommended units include English 4, mathematics 3, social studies 3, history 2, science 3 (laboratory 1), foreign language 3 and visual/performing arts 1.

**2007-2008 Annual costs.** Tuition/fees: $24,890. Required fee figure includes cost of books for core curriculum required of all undergraduates. Room/board: $8,830. Books/supplies: $1,400. Personal expenses: $1,020.

**2006-2007 Financial aid. Need-based:** 7 full-time freshmen applied for aid; 7 were judged to have need; 7 of these received aid. Average need met was 33%. Average scholarship/grant was $7,361; average loan $6,366. 51% of total undergraduate aid awarded as scholarships/grants, 49% as loans/jobs. **Non-need-based:** Awarded to 8 full-time undergraduates, including 1 freshmen. Scholarships awarded for academics, alumni affiliation, music/drama.

**Application procedures. Admission:** No deadline. $25 fee, may be waived for applicants with need. Application may be submitted online. Admission notification on a rolling basis beginning on or about 9/15. Must reply by May 1 or within 3 week(s) if notified thereafter. **Financial aid:** No deadline. FAFSA, institutional form required. Applicants notified on a rolling basis starting 4/1; must reply by 5/1 or within 3 week(s) of notification.

**Academics.** Classes are all discussion-based with fewer than 12 students per class; curriculum based on Great Books of Western Culture, using original sources rather than text books. **Special study options:** Combined bachelor's/graduate degree, cross-registration, double major, independent study, internships, study abroad, weekend college. One-on-one tutorials with faculty member for in-depth study; accelerated BA to JD program. **Credit/placement by examination:** CLEP, institutional tests. **Support services:** Reduced course load, study skills assistance, tutoring, writing center.

**Majors. Interdisciplinary:** Natural sciences. **Liberal arts:** Arts/sciences, humanities. **Social sciences:** General.

**Computing on campus.** 25 workstations in dormitories, computer center. Dormitories wired for high-speed internet access and linked to campus network. Commuter students can connect to campus network. Helpline, wireless network available.

**Student life. Freshman orientation:** Mandatory. Held 3-4 days prior to start of classes. Includes demonstration class, placement exams. **Housing:** Guaranteed on-campus for freshmen. Coed dorms, single-sex dorms, apartments, substance-free housing available. $300 partly refundable deposit, deadline 5/1. Pets allowed in dorm rooms. **Activities:** Campus ministries, choral groups, drama, literary magazine, music ensembles, radio station, student government, student newspaper.

**Athletics. Intramural:** Basketball, football (non-tackle), softball, volleyball.

**Student services.** Adult student services, alcohol/substance abuse counseling, career counseling, student employment services, financial aid counseling, health services, personal counseling, placement for graduates.

**Contact.** E-mail: admissions@shimer.edu
Phone: (312) 235-3505 Toll-free number: (800) 215-7173
Fax: (312) 235-3501
Elaine Vincent, Director of Admission, Shimer College, 3424 South State Street, Chicago, IL 60616

## Southern Illinois University Carbondale
**Carbondale, Illinois**　　　　　　　　**CB member**
**www.siuc.edu**　　　　　　　　**CB code: 1726**

- Public 4-year university
- Residential campus in large town
- 16,125 degree-seeking undergraduates: 10% part-time, 43% women, 18% African American, 2% Asian American, 4% Hispanic American, 1% international
- 4,298 degree-seeking graduate students
- 71% of applicants admitted
- SAT or ACT (ACT writing optional) required
- 46% graduate within 6 years; 44% enter graduate study

**General.** Founded in 1869. Regionally accredited. Active production schedule in several theaters includes contemporary works, musicals, operas, original plays by faculty and students, and world drama from major periods in theater history. **Degrees:** 4,328 bachelor's, 68 associate awarded; master's, doctoral, first professional offered. **ROTC:** Army, Air Force. **Location:** 100 miles from St. Louis. **Calendar:** Semester, extensive summer session. **Full-time faculty:** 915 total; 83% have terminal degrees, 16% minority, 36% women. **Part-time faculty:** 147 total; 58% have terminal degrees, 8% minority, 40% women. **Class size:** 45% < 20, 46% 20-39, 4% 40-49, 4% 50-99, 1% >100. **Special facilities:** University press, coal research center, materials technology center, outdoor education laboratory, university farms, center for study of crime, electron microscopy center, cooperative wildlife research laboratory, cooperative fisheries research laboratory, vivarium, airport training facility, laboratory theatre, child development laboratory, center for archaeological investigations, small business incubator, public policy institute, dental and medical clinics, environmental center.

**Freshman class profile.** 9,807 applied, 6,941 admitted, 2,636 enrolled.

| Mid 50% test scores | | Rank in top quarter: | 28% |
|---|---|---|---|
| SAT critical reading: | 440-540 | Rank in top tenth: | 9% |
| SAT math: | 460-550 | Return as sophomores: | 70% |
| SAT writing: | 420-540 | International: | 1% |
| ACT composite: | 19-24 | | |

**Basis for selection.** High school class rank and ACT scores most important. **Homeschooled:** Transcript of courses and grades required.

**High school preparation.** 15 units required. Required units include English 4, mathematics 3, social studies 3, science 3 (laboratory 3) and academic electives 2.

**2007-2008 Annual costs.** Tuition/fees: $8,899; $18,421 out-of-state. Room/board: $6,666. Books/supplies: $900. Personal expenses: $1,218.

**2007-2008 Financial aid.** **Need-based:** 2,136 full-time freshmen applied for aid; 1,672 were judged to have need; 1,651 of these received aid. Average need met was 97%. Average scholarship/grant was $7,282; average loan $3,869. 53% of total undergraduate aid awarded as scholarships/grants, 47% as loans/jobs. **Non-need-based:** Awarded to 4,856 full-time undergraduates, including 1,015 freshmen. Scholarships awarded for academics, alumni affiliation, art, athletics, job skills, leadership, minority status, music/drama, ROTC, state residency. **Additional information:** Need-based financial aid available to part-time students enrolled in minimum of 6 semester hours.

**Application procedures.** **Admission:** Priority date 5/1; no deadline. $30 fee, may be waived for applicants with need. Application may be submitted online. Admission notification on a rolling basis beginning on or about 9/1. Must reply by May 1 or within 6 week(s) if notified thereafter. **Financial aid:** Priority date 4/1; no closing date. FAFSA required. Applicants notified on a rolling basis starting 3/23; must reply within 3 week(s) of notification.

**Academics.** **Special study options:** Cooperative education, distance learning, double major, ESL, honors, independent study, internships, student-designed major, study abroad, teacher certification program, Washington semester. After core curriculum is completed, remaining coursework for Workforce Education and Development degree offered on weekends. **Credit/placement by examination:** AP, CLEP, IB, ACT, institutional tests. 15 credit hours maximum toward associate degree, 30 toward bachelor's. Credit by

proficiency exams available. **Support services:** Learning center, pre-admission summer program, remedial instruction, study skills assistance, tutoring, writing center.

**Majors.** **Agriculture:** General, animal sciences, economics, plant sciences. **Architecture:** Architecture. **Biology:** General, botany, microbiology, physiology, zoology. **Business:** Accounting, business admin, finance, management science, managerial economics, marketing. **Communications:** Journalism, radio/tv. **Computer sciences:** Computer science, information systems. **Conservation:** Forestry. **Education:** Early childhood, elementary, health, physical, special, trade/industrial. **Engineering:** Civil, computer, electrical, mechanical, mining. **Engineering technology:** General, automotive, electrical, industrial. **English:** English lit, speech/rhetoric. **Family/consumer sciences:** Clothing/textiles, food/nutrition. **Foreign languages:** Classics, French, German, linguistics, Russian, Spanish. **Health:** Communication disorders, dental hygiene, health care admin, medical radiologic technology/radiation therapy, physician assistant. **History:** General. **Legal studies:** Paralegal. **Liberal arts:** Arts/sciences. **Math:** General. **Mechanic/repair:** Avionics. **Parks/recreation:** General. **Personal/culinary services:** Mortuary science. **Philosophy/religion:** Philosophy. **Physical sciences:** Chemistry, geology, physics. **Protective services:** Fire services admin, law enforcement admin. **Psychology:** General. **Public administration:** Social work. **Social sciences:** General, anthropology, economics, geography, political science, sociology. **Transportation:** Aviation management. **Visual/performing arts:** Art, cinematography, design, dramatic, interior design, studio arts. **Other:** Foreign languages and international trade, Rehabilitation services, Technical Resource Management.

**Most popular majors.** Business/marketing 9%, education 22%, engineering/engineering technologies 12%, health sciences 8%.

**Computing on campus.** 1,776 workstations in dormitories, library, computer center, student center. Dormitories wired for high-speed internet access and linked to campus network. Commuter students can connect to campus network. Online course registration, online library, helpline, student web hosting, wireless network available.

**Student life.** **Freshman orientation:** Mandatory, $75 fee. Preregistration for classes offered. Several 1-day seminars offered April through July. **Housing:** Guaranteed on-campus for freshmen. Coed dorms, single-sex dorms, special housing for disabled, apartments, fraternity/sorority housing, substance-free housing available. $650 partly refundable deposit, deadline 6/1. **Activities:** Bands, campus ministries, choral groups, dance, drama, film society, international student organizations, literary magazine, music ensembles, musical theater, opera, radio station, student government, student newspaper, symphony orchestra, TV station, over 400 student organizations.

**Athletics.** NCAA. **Intercollegiate:** Baseball M, basketball, cheerleading, cross-country, diving, football (tackle) M, golf, softball W, swimming, tennis, track and field, volleyball W. **Intramural:** Badminton, basketball, cricket, cross-country, football (non-tackle), golf, handball, racquetball, soccer, softball, squash, table tennis, tennis, triathlon, volleyball, water polo, wrestling M. **Team name:** Salukis.

**Student services.** Adult student services, alcohol/substance abuse counseling, career counseling, services for economically disadvantaged, student employment services, financial aid counseling, health services, legal services, minority student services, on-campus daycare, personal counseling, placement for graduates, veterans' counselor, women's services. **Physically disabled:** Services for visually, speech, hearing impaired. **Learning disabled:** Comprehensive services available.

**Contact.** E-mail: admrec@siu.edu
Phone: (618) 453-4381 Fax: (618) 453-3250
Jim Carl, Director, Admissions, Southern Illinois University Carbondale, Mailcode 4701, Carbondale, IL 62901-4701

## Southern Illinois University Edwardsville
**Edwardsville, Illinois**　　　　　　　　**CB member**
**www.siue.edu**　　　　　　　　**CB code: 1759**

- Public 4-year university
- Commuter campus in very large city
- 10,843 degree-seeking undergraduates: 15% part-time, 54% women, 10% African American, 2% Asian American, 2% Hispanic American, 1% international
- 2,273 degree-seeking graduate students
- 84% of applicants admitted
- 46% graduate within 6 years; 30% enter graduate study

**General.** Founded in 1957. Regionally accredited. **Degrees:** 2,134 bachelor's awarded; master's, first professional offered. **ROTC:** Army, Air Force. **Location:** 18 miles from St. Louis. **Calendar:** Semester, extensive summer session. **Full-time faculty:** 592 total; 81% have terminal degrees, 12% minority, 46% women. **Part-time faculty:** 281 total; 12% minority, 43% women. **Class size:** 35% < 20, 42% 20-39, 10% 40-49, 12% 50-99, less than 1% >100. **Special facilities:** Museum collections, arboretum, greenhouse, engineering labs, on-campus clinical facility for nursing instruction, observatory, an applied research and technology park, corn-to-ethanol research center, biotechnology laboratory incubator, pharmaceutical care lab.

**Freshman class profile.** 5,658 applied, 4,752 admitted, 1,860 enrolled.

| Mid 50% test scores | | | |
|---|---|---|---|
| ACT composite: | 20-25 | Return as sophomores: | 72% |
| Rank in top quarter: | 45% | Out-of-state: | 9% |
| Rank in top tenth: | 17% | Live on campus: | 70% |

**Basis for selection.** Students admitted with 2.5 GPA and 21 ACT (970-1000 SAT, exclusive of Writing), or with rank in top 25% of class. Applicants who do not meet these requirement subject to additional review. SAT or ACT recommended. Audition recommended for music majors; portfolio recommended for art majors.

**High school preparation.** 15 units required. Required and recommended units include English 4, mathematics 3, social studies 3, science 3 (laboratory 3), foreign language 2 and academic electives 2. 2 years of foreign language, music, dance, theater, art, or vocational education (1 year maximum) electives required. 2 years of 1 foreign language and 1 year of music and/or art recommended. 1 year of chemistry and 1 year of biology required. At least 2 years of history or government required.

**2007-2008 Annual costs.** Tuition/fees: $7,033; $14,874 out-of-state. Required fees include book rental. Room/board: $6,750. Books/supplies: $696. Personal expenses: $1,506.

**Financial aid.** All financial aid based on need.

**Application procedures. Admission:** Priority date 12/1; deadline 5/1 (postmark date). $30 fee, may be waived for applicants with need. Application may be submitted online. Admission notification on a rolling basis beginning on or about 9/1. Application and all official documents required to be on file 3 weeks before beginning of term. **Financial aid:** Priority date 3/1, closing date 6/1. FAFSA required. Applicants notified on a rolling basis starting 3/15; must reply within 4 week(s) of notification.

**Academics.** Senior project required. **Special study options:** Accelerated study, combined bachelor's/graduate degree, cooperative education, cross-registration, distance learning, double major, ESL, honors, independent study, internships, student-designed major, study abroad, teacher certification program, weekend college. **Credit/placement by examination:** AP, CLEP, institutional tests. 32 credit hours maximum toward bachelor's degree. Placement tests required for some students in reading, writing and/or math; determination based on test scores and GPA. **Support services:** Learning center, pre-admission summer program, reduced course load, remedial instruction, study skills assistance, tutoring, writing center.

**Majors. Biology:** General. **Business:** Accounting, business admin, management information systems, managerial economics. **Communications:** Media studies. **Computer sciences:** General, computer science. **Education:** Early childhood, elementary, health, science, special. **Engineering:** Civil, computer, electrical, industrial, manufacturing, mechanical. **Engineering technology:** Construction. **English:** English lit, speech/rhetoric. **Foreign languages:** General. **Health:** Audiology/speech pathology, nursing (RN). **History:** General. **Liberal arts:** Arts/sciences. **Math:** General. **Parks/recreation:** Health/fitness. **Philosophy/religion:** Philosophy. **Physical sciences:** Chemistry, physics. **Protective services:** Criminal justice. **Psychology:** General. **Public administration:** Social work. **Social sciences:** Anthropology, economics, geography, political science, sociology. **Visual/performing arts:** Art, dance, dramatic, studio arts.

**Most popular majors.** Biology 7%, business/marketing 22%, education 10%, engineering/engineering technologies 7%, English 6%, health sciences 9%, psychology 6%, social sciences 7%.

**Computing on campus.** 600 workstations in dormitories, library, computer center, student center. Dormitories linked to campus network. Commuter students can connect to campus network. Online course registration, online library, helpline available.

**Student life. Freshman orientation:** Available. Preregistration for classes offered. Offer summer pre-entry advisement and registration program in addition to freshman orientation. **Housing:** Coed dorms, special housing for disabled, apartments, fraternity/sorority housing, substance-free housing available. $300 deposit, deadline 5/1. Focused-interest communities. **Activities:** Bands, campus ministries, choral groups, dance, drama, film society, literary magazine, music ensembles, musical theater, opera, radio station, student government, student newspaper, symphony orchestra, TV station, 170 organizations and honor societies available.

**Athletics.** NCAA. **Intercollegiate:** Baseball M, basketball, cross-country, golf, soccer, softball W, tennis, track and field, volleyball W, wrestling M. **Intramural:** Badminton, basketball, bowling, fencing, football (non-tackle), golf, racquetball, soccer, softball, table tennis, tennis, volleyball, water polo. **Team name:** Cougars.

**Student services.** Alcohol/substance abuse counseling, career counseling, services for economically disadvantaged, student employment services, financial aid counseling, health services, legal services, on-campus daycare, personal counseling, placement for graduates, veterans' counselor. **Physically disabled:** Services for visually, speech, hearing impaired. **Learning disabled:** Comprehensive services available.

**Contact.** E-mail: admissions@siue.edu
Phone: (618) 650-3705 Toll-free number: (800) 447-7483
Fax: (618) 650-5013
Todd Burrell, Director of Admissions, Southern Illinois University Edwardsville, Campus Box 1600, Rendleman Hall, Rm 2120, Edwardsville, IL 62026-1600

## Telshe Yeshiva-Chicago
### Chicago, Illinois

CB code: 7009

- Private 4-year rabbinical college for men affiliated with Jewish faith
- Very large city

**General.** Accredited by AARTS. **Calendar:** Continuous.

**Annual costs/financial aid.** Comprehensive fee (2007-2008): $11,000.

**Contact.** Phone: (773) 463-7738
Director of Admissions, 3535 West Foster Avenue, Chicago, IL 60625

## Trinity Christian College
### Palos Heights, Illinois
### www.trnty.edu

CB code: 1820

- Private 4-year liberal arts college affiliated with Reformed (unaffiliated)
- Residential campus in very large city
- 1,217 degree-seeking undergraduates: 16% part-time, 69% women, 9% African American, 2% Asian American, 6% Hispanic American, 2% international
- 89% of applicants admitted
- SAT or ACT (ACT writing recommended), application essay, interview required
- 60% graduate within 6 years; 8% enter graduate study

**General.** Founded in 1959. Regionally accredited. **Degrees:** 288 bachelor's awarded. **Location:** 20 miles from Chicago. **Calendar:** Semester, limited summer session. **Full-time faculty:** 74 total; 64% have terminal degrees, 15% minority, 42% women. **Part-time faculty:** 79 total; 8% have terminal degrees, 9% minority, 43% women. **Class size:** 58% < 20, 37% 20-39, 5% 40-49, less than 1% 50-99. **Special facilities:** Dutch heritage center archives.

**Freshman class profile.** 574 applied, 510 admitted, 240 enrolled.

| Mid 50% test scores | | | |
|---|---|---|---|
| SAT critical reading: | 480-600 | Rank in top quarter: | 32% |
| SAT math: | 450-610 | Rank in top tenth: | 12% |
| ACT composite: | 19-26 | End year in good standing: | 85% |
| GPA 3.50 or higher: | 36% | Return as sophomores: | 71% |
| GPA 3.0-3.49: | 30% | Out-of-state: | 47% |
| GPA 2.0-2.99: | 33% | Live on campus: | 90% |
| | | International: | 2% |

**Basis for selection.** 3.0 GPA with 2.0 GPA in English and math, and 22 ACT or 950 SAT (exclusive of Writing) required. ACT recommended. Statement of religious faith recommended.

**High school preparation.** 16 units required; 18 recommended. Required and recommended units include English 3-4, mathematics 3-4, social studies 2-3, history 2, science 2-3 and foreign language 2. One 3-year major in mathematics, science, or social studies, and 2 2-year minors in mathematics, science, social studies, or foreign language recommended.

**2007-2008 Annual costs.** Tuition/fees: $19,241. Room/board: $7,120. Books/supplies: $1,000. Personal expenses: $1,365.

**2007-2008 Financial aid. Need-based:** 231 full-time freshmen applied for aid; 223 were judged to have need; 223 of these received aid. Average

need met was 51%. Average scholarship/grant was $7,053; average loan $4,305. 51% of total undergraduate aid awarded as scholarships/grants, 49% as loans/jobs. **Non-need-based:** Scholarships awarded for academics, alumni affiliation, art, athletics, leadership, minority status, music/drama, religious affiliation. **Additional information:** High school transcripts and ACT or SAT scores required for merit scholarships.

**Application procedures. Admission:** No deadline. $20 fee, may be waived for applicants with need. Application may be submitted online. Admission notification on a rolling basis beginning on or about 9/1. Must reply by May 1 or within 2 week(s) if notified thereafter. **Financial aid:** Priority date 2/15, closing date 4/15. FAFSA, institutional form required. Applicants notified on a rolling basis starting 4/1; must reply by 5/1 or within 2 week(s) of notification.

**Academics. Special study options:** Cooperative education, double major, honors, independent study, internships, liberal arts/career combination, study abroad, teacher certification program, urban semester, Washington semester. **Credit/placement by examination:** AP, CLEP, IB, SAT, ACT, institutional tests. 30 credit hours maximum toward bachelor's degree. **Support services:** Learning center, pre-admission summer program, reduced course load, remedial instruction, study skills assistance, tutoring, writing center.

**Honors college/program.** Must have 28 ACT, be in top 10% of high school class, and have 3.5 high school GPA. 13-19 semester hours of unique courses. Approximately 15 freshmen admitted each year.

**Majors. Biology:** General. **Business:** General, accounting, communications, management information systems. **Communications:** General. **Computer sciences:** Computer science, information systems. **Education:** General, art, biology, business, chemistry, elementary, English, history, mathematics, music, physical, science, Spanish, special. **English:** English lit. **Foreign languages:** Spanish. **Health:** Nursing (RN). **History:** General. **Math:** General. **Parks/recreation:** Exercise sciences, health/fitness. **Philosophy/religion:** Philosophy. **Physical sciences:** Chemistry. **Psychology:** General. **Public administration:** Social work. **Social sciences:** Political science, sociology. **Theology:** Theology. **Visual/performing arts:** Art, music performance, studio arts. **Other:** Church and ministry leadership, Sport and leisure studies.

**Most popular majors.** Business/marketing 20%, education 38%, health sciences 12%.

**Computing on campus.** 140 workstations in dormitories, library, computer center. Dormitories wired for high-speed internet access and linked to campus network. Commuter students can connect to campus network. Helpline, wireless network available.

**Student life. Freshman orientation:** Mandatory, $195 fee. Preregistration for classes offered. Two-day program in early July and 2-week program in late August. **Housing:** Guaranteed on-campus for freshmen. Coed dorms, substance-free housing available. $75 fully refundable deposit, deadline 9/1. **Activities:** Bands, campus ministries, choral groups, dance, drama, literary magazine, music ensembles, student government, student newspaper, religious drama club, theology club, pro-life, Bread for the World, Inter-Varsity Fellowship, Big Brother/Big Sister, Association for Public Justice, PACE literacy program in Cook County Jail.

**Athletics.** NAIA, NCCAA. **Intercollegiate:** Baseball M, basketball, cross-country, soccer, softball W, track and field, volleyball W. **Intramural:** Basketball, racquetball, soccer, volleyball. **Team name:** Trolls.

**Student services.** Adult student services, alcohol/substance abuse counseling, career counseling, student employment services, financial aid counseling, minority student services, personal counseling, placement for graduates, veterans' counselor. **Physically disabled:** Services for visually, speech, hearing impaired.

**Contact.** E-mail: admissions@trnty.edu
Phone: (708) 239-4708 Toll-free number: (866) 874-6463
Fax: (708) 239-4826
Jeremy Klyn, Director of Admissions, Trinity Christian College, 6601 West College Drive, Palos Heights, IL 60463

## Trinity College of Nursing and Health Sciences
**Rock Island, Illinois**
www.trinitycollegeqc.edu                                    CB code: 2555

- Private 4-year nursing college
- Commuter campus in very large city
- 225 degree-seeking undergraduates
- SAT or ACT (ACT writing recommended) required

**General.** Affiliated with Trinity Medical Center and the Iowa Health System. **Degrees:** 16 bachelor's, 47 associate awarded. **Calendar:** Semester, limited summer session. **Full-time faculty:** 15 total; 100% women. **Part-time faculty:** 9 total; 100% women.

**Freshman class profile.**

| | | | |
|---|---|---|---|
| GPA 3.50 or higher: | 25% | GPA 2.0-2.99: | 25% |
| GPA 3.0-3.49: | 50% | | |

**Basis for selection.** Requirements vary by program. **Homeschooled:** Transcript of courses and grades required.

**High school preparation.** Required units include English 4, mathematics 3, social studies 3, science 3 (laboratory 1).

**2008-2009 Annual costs.** Tuition/fees: $11,105. Students are required to have a uniform, and other health equipment.

**Application procedures. Admission:** Closing date 12/15 (postmark date). $50 fee, may be waived for applicants with need. Application may be submitted online. Admission notification on a rolling basis beginning on or about 12/1.

**Academics. Special study options:** Accelerated study, combined bachelor's/graduate degree, cooperative education, distance learning. **Credit/placement by examination:** CLEP, ACT. **Support services:** Study skills assistance, tutoring.

**Majors. Health:** Nursing (RN).

**Computing on campus.** 15 workstations in computer center. Wireless network available.

**Student life. Freshman orientation:** Mandatory, $10 fee. Preregistration for classes offered. **Activities:** Student government.

**Student services.** Career counseling, financial aid counseling, minority student services, on-campus daycare, personal counseling. **Learning disabled:** Comprehensive services available.

**Contact.** Phone: (309) 779-7710 Fax: (309) 779-7748
Cara Banks, Registrar, Trinity College of Nursing and Health Sciences, 2122 25th Avenue, Rock Island, IL 61201

## Trinity International University
**Deerfield, Illinois**                                CB member
www.tiu.edu                                              CB code: 1810

- Private 4-year university and liberal arts college affiliated with Evangelical Free Church of America
- Residential campus in large town
- 1,048 degree-seeking undergraduates: 15% part-time, 55% women, 16% African American, 3% Asian American, 4% Hispanic American, 1% Native American, 2% international
- 1,430 degree-seeking graduate students
- 96% of applicants admitted
- SAT or ACT (ACT writing optional), application essay required
- 47% graduate within 6 years; 32% enter graduate study

**General.** Founded in 1897. Regionally accredited. Off-campus programs available through Christian College Consortium. **Degrees:** 191 bachelor's awarded; master's, doctoral, first professional offered. **Location:** 25 miles from Chicago. **Calendar:** Semester, limited summer session. **Full-time faculty:** 91 total; 85% have terminal degrees, 11% minority, 26% women. **Part-time faculty:** 294 total; 54% have terminal degrees, 21% minority, 33% women. **Class size:** 56% < 20, 34% 20-39, 7% 40-49, 2% 50-99. **Special facilities:** Seminary facilities.

**Freshman class profile.** 408 applied, 393 admitted, 166 enrolled.

| Mid 50% test scores | | | |
|---|---|---|---|
| SAT critical reading: | 480-630 | Rank in top quarter: | 41% |
| SAT math: | 460-590 | Rank in top tenth: | 17% |
| ACT composite: | 20-25 | Return as sophomores: | 78% |
| GPA 3.50 or higher: | 35% | Out-of-state: | 40% |
| GPA 3.0-3.49: | 29% | Live on campus: | 96% |
| GPA 2.0-2.99: | 35% | International: | 4% |

**Basis for selection.** School achievement record, test scores, recommendations, evidence of Christian commitment, essays most important. Interview recommended for borderline applicants. **Homeschooled:** Transcript of courses and grades required.

**High school preparation.** 15 units required. Required units include English 3, mathematics 2, social studies 2, science 2 (laboratory 1), foreign language 2 and academic electives 3.

**2008-2009 Annual costs.** Tuition/fees: $21,930. Room/board: $7,270. Books/supplies: $1,080. Personal expenses: $1,130.

**2007-2008 Financial aid. Need-based:** 164 full-time freshmen applied for aid; 149 were judged to have need; 149 of these received aid. Average need met was 90%. Average scholarship/grant was $8,442; average loan $4,157. 59% of total undergraduate aid awarded as scholarships/grants, 41% as loans/jobs. **Non-need-based:** Scholarships awarded for academics, alumni affiliation, athletics, minority status, music/drama, religious affiliation.

**Application procedures. Admission:** No deadline. $25 fee, may be waived for applicants with need. Application may be submitted online. Admission notification on a rolling basis beginning on or about 9/1. **Financial aid:** Priority date 4/1; no closing date. FAFSA required. Applicants notified on a rolling basis starting 2/15; must reply within 4 week(s) of notification.

**Academics. Special study options:** Accelerated study, cooperative education, cross-registration, distance learning, double major, dual enrollment of high school students, exchange student, honors, independent study, internships, liberal arts/career combination, student-designed major, study abroad, teacher certification program, urban semester, Washington semester. REACH (for nontraditional students with previous college credit), graduate courses available to undergraduates with junior or senior standing. **Credit/placement by examination:** AP, CLEP, IB, SAT, ACT, institutional tests. Permission and approval by department chair required. May not be used to satisfy senior residency requirement. **Support services:** Learning center, remedial instruction, study skills assistance, tutoring, writing center.

**Majors. Biology:** General. **Business:** General, accounting, human resources, management science, marketing, nonprofit/public, organizational behavior, training/development. **Communications:** General. **Education:** Biology, elementary, English, history, mathematics, music, physical, secondary. **English:** English lit. **Health:** Athletic training, premedicine. **History:** General. **Legal studies:** Prelaw. **Liberal arts:** Humanities. **Math:** General. **Parks/recreation:** Health/fitness. **Philosophy/religion:** Philosophy. **Physical sciences:** Chemistry. **Psychology:** General. **Social sciences:** General. **Theology:** Bible, pastoral counseling, preministerial, religious ed, sacred music, theology, youth ministry. **Visual/performing arts:** Music pedagogy, music performance, music theory/composition, piano/organ, voice/opera.

**Most popular majors.** Business/marketing 17%, education 18%, liberal arts 14%, psychology 8%, theological studies 24%.

**Computing on campus.** 100 workstations in library, computer center, student center. Dormitories wired for high-speed internet access and linked to campus network. Commuter students can connect to campus network. Online course registration, online library, helpline, repair service, student web hosting, wireless network available.

**Student life. Freshman orientation:** Mandatory, $30 fee. Preregistration for classes offered. Orientation held the week before classes each fall and spring. Generally lasts entire week. **Policies:** Community expectations, general patterns of Christian lifestyle, policy on drug and alcohol abuse. Religious observance required. **Housing:** Guaranteed on-campus for freshmen. Single-sex dorms, special housing for disabled, apartments, substance-free housing available. $50 deposit. **Activities:** Bands, choral groups, dance, drama, international student organizations, literary magazine, music ensembles, musical theater, opera, student government, student newspaper, symphony orchestra, Association of Believers for Black America, Global Christian Movement, Kappa Tau, Discipleship Cabinet, FAT Thursdays, Chapel Cabinet, Kids on Kampus, Wives Fellowship, Men's Ministry.

**Athletics.** NAIA, NCCAA. **Intercollegiate:** Baseball M, basketball, football (tackle) M, soccer, softball W, volleyball W. **Intramural:** Baseball M, basketball, bowling, football (non-tackle) M, racquetball, rugby M, soccer, softball, volleyball. **Team name:** Trojans.

**Student services.** Alcohol/substance abuse counseling, campus ministries, career counseling, student employment services, financial aid counseling, health services, minority student services, on-campus daycare, personal counseling, placement for graduates. **Physically disabled:** Services for visually impaired.

**Contact.** E-mail: tcadmissions@tiu.edu
Phone: (847) 317-7000 Toll-free number: (800) 822-3225
Fax: (847) 317-8097
Aaron Mahl, Director of Admissions, Trinity International University, 2065 Half Day Road, Deerfield, IL 60015

## University of Chicago
**Chicago, Illinois**
www.uchicago.edu
CB member
CB code: 1832

- Private 4-year university and liberal arts college
- Residential campus in very large city
- 4,898 degree-seeking undergraduates: 1% part-time, 50% women, 5% African American, 13% Asian American, 8% Hispanic American, 8% international
- 7,141 degree-seeking graduate students
- 35% of applicants admitted
- SAT or ACT (ACT writing optional), application essay required
- 90% graduate within 6 years

**General.** Founded in 1891. Regionally accredited. **Degrees:** 1,157 bachelor's awarded; master's, doctoral, first professional offered. **ROTC:** Army, Air Force. **Location:** 7 miles from Chicago. **Calendar:** Quarter, extensive summer session. **Full-time faculty:** 1,084 total; 100% have terminal degrees, 17% minority, 28% women. **Part-time faculty:** 591 total; 68% have terminal degrees, 12% minority, 34% women. **Class size:** 72% < 20, 21% 20-39, 2% 40-49, 3% 50-99, less than 1% >100. **Special facilities:** Oriental Institute, Argonne National Laboratory, library of sciences, Fermi National Accelerator Laboratory, film studies center, National Opinion Research Center, observatory.

**Freshman class profile.** 10,362 applied, 3,597 admitted, 1,300 enrolled.

| Mid 50% test scores | | | |
|---|---|---|---|
| SAT critical reading: | 670-770 | GPA 2.0-2.99: | 2% |
| SAT math: | 660-760 | Rank in top quarter: | 98% |
| ACT composite: | 28-33 | Rank in top tenth: | 83% |
| GPA 3.50 or higher: | 95% | Return as sophomores: | 98% |
| GPA 3.0-3.49: | 3% | Out-of-state: | 78% |
| | | International: | 10% |

**Basis for selection.** Secondary school record, recommendations, essay very important, as are talent/ability and character/personal qualities. Interview recommended.

**High school preparation.** Recommended units include English 4, mathematics 4, social studies 2, history 2, science 4 and foreign language 3.

**2007-2008 Annual costs.** Tuition/fees: $35,868. Room/board: $11,139. Books/supplies: $1,050. Personal expenses: $1,919.

**2007-2008 Financial aid. Need-based:** 849 full-time freshmen applied for aid; 620 were judged to have need; 620 of these received aid. Average need met was 100%. Average scholarship/grant was $28,485; average loan $4,777. 80% of total undergraduate aid awarded as scholarships/grants, 20% as loans/jobs. **Non-need-based:** Awarded to 561 full-time undergraduates, including 169 freshmen. Scholarships awarded for academics, leadership.

**Application procedures. Admission:** Closing date 1/2 (postmark date). $60 fee, may be waived for applicants with need. Application may be submitted online. Admission notification 4/1. Must reply by 5/1. **Financial aid:** Closing date 2/1. FAFSA, institutional form, CSS PROFILE required. Applicants notified by 4/15; must reply by 5/1.

**Academics. Special study options:** Combined bachelor's/graduate degree, cross-registration, double major, dual enrollment of high school students, ESL, exchange student, independent study, internships, student-designed major, study abroad, teacher certification program, Washington semester. **Credit/placement by examination:** AP, CLEP, IB, institutional tests. **Support services:** Study skills assistance, tutoring.

**Majors. Area/ethnic studies:** African, African-American, German, Latin American, Near/Middle Eastern, Russian/Slavic, Slavic, South Asian. **Biology:** General, biochemistry. **Computer sciences:** General. **Conservation:** Environmental studies. **English:** English lit. **Foreign languages:** Ancient Greek, Arabic, Biblical, classics, comparative lit, East Asian, French, German, Hebrew, Italian, Latin, linguistics, Portuguese, Russian, Scandinavian, Slavic, South Asian, Spanish. **History:** General. **Liberal arts:** Arts/sciences. **Math:** General, applied, statistics. **Philosophy/religion:** Judaic, philosophy, religion. **Physical sciences:** Chemistry, geophysics, physics. **Psychology:** General. **Public administration:** Policy analysis. **Social sciences:** Anthropology, economics, geography, international relations, political science, sociology. **Visual/performing arts:** General, art history/conservation, film/cinema.

**Most popular majors.** Biology 10%, English 6%, foreign language 7%, history 6%, mathematics 8%, physical sciences 7%, social sciences 35%.

**Computing on campus.** 1,000 workstations in dormitories, library, computer center, student center. Dormitories wired for high-speed internet access and linked to campus network. Commuter students can connect to campus network. Online course registration, online library, helpline, repair service, student web hosting, wireless network available.

**Student life. Freshman orientation:** Mandatory, $510 fee. Held 10 days before classes begin in the fall. **Housing:** Guaranteed on-campus for all undergraduates. Coed dorms, apartments, fraternity/sorority housing available. **Activities:** Bands, campus ministries, choral groups, dance, drama, film society, international student organizations, literary magazine, music ensembles, Model UN, musical theater, radio station, student government, student newspaper, symphony orchestra, over 500 organizations.

**Athletics.** NCAA. **Intercollegiate:** Baseball M, basketball, cross-country, football (tackle) M, soccer, softball W, swimming, tennis, track and field, volleyball W, wrestling M. **Intramural:** Archery, badminton, basketball, cross-country, fencing, handball, racquetball, soccer, softball, swimming, table tennis, tennis, track and field, volleyball. **Team name:** Maroons.

**Student services.** Adult student services, alcohol/substance abuse counseling, campus ministries, career counseling, services for economically disadvantaged, student employment services, financial aid counseling, health services, minority student services, personal counseling, placement for graduates, veterans' counselor, women's services. **Physically disabled:** Services for visually, hearing impaired.

**Contact.** E-mail: questions@phoenix.uchicago.edu
Phone: (773) 702-8650 Fax: (773) 702-4199
Theodore O'Neill, Dean of Admissions, University of Chicago, 1101 East 58th Street, Chicago, IL 60637

---

## University of Illinois at Chicago

| **Chicago, Illinois** | **CB member** |
|---|---|
| **www.uic.edu** | **CB code: 1851** |

- Public 4-year university
- Commuter campus in very large city
- 15,565 degree-seeking undergraduates: 8% part-time, 53% women, 9% African American, 23% Asian American, 16% Hispanic American, 1% international
- 9,229 degree-seeking graduate students
- 64% of applicants admitted
- SAT or ACT (ACT writing recommended), application essay required
- 50% graduate within 6 years

**General.** Founded in 1946. Regionally accredited. Medical, dental, nursing and pharmacy colleges, and medical center within university complex. **Degrees:** 3,286 bachelor's awarded; master's, doctoral, first professional offered. **ROTC:** Army, Naval, Air Force. **Location:** One mile from downtown. **Calendar:** Semester, limited summer session. **Full-time faculty:** 1,163 total; 78% have terminal degrees, 24% minority, 43% women. **Part-time faculty:** 363 total; 57% have terminal degrees, 15% minority, 47% women. **Class size:** 37% < 20, 37% 20-39, 7% 40-49, 10% 50-99, 9% >100. **Special facilities:** Jane Addams' Hull House museum, prairie preserve, health sciences center, software technologies research facility.

**Freshman class profile.** 13,595 applied, 8,686 admitted, 3,291 enrolled.

| Mid 50% test scores | | Out-of-state: | 2% |
|---|---|---|---|
| ACT composite: | 21-26 | Live on campus: | 47% |
| Rank in top quarter: | 58% | International: | 1% |
| Rank in top tenth: | 23% | Fraternities: | 1% |
| End year in good standing: | 72% | Sororities: | 1% |
| Return as sophomores: | 79% | | |

**Basis for selection.** Class rank, GPA, and test scores most important. High school course selection and personal statement strongly considered. Auditions required of music and theater majors. Portfolio required of art majors. **Homeschooled:** Transcript of courses and grades required. **Learning Disabled:** Students may add learning disability information to personal essay.

**High school preparation.** 16 units required. Required and recommended units include English 4, mathematics 3-4, social studies 3, science 3 (laboratory 3), foreign language 2-4 and academic electives 1. Additional course requirements vary with college and program.

**2007-2008 Annual costs.** Tuition/fees: $9,744; $22,134 out-of-state. Room/board: $8,118. Books/supplies: $1,200. Personal expenses: $2,400.

**2006-2007 Financial aid. Need-based:** 2,249 full-time freshmen applied for aid; 1,666 were judged to have need; 1,608 of these received aid. Average need met was 85%. Average scholarship/grant was $9,416; average loan $3,360. 67% of total undergraduate aid awarded as scholarships/grants, 33% as loans/jobs. **Non-need-based:** Awarded to 2,997 full-time undergraduates, including 458 freshmen. Scholarships awarded for academics, art, athletics, music/drama, ROTC.

**Application procedures. Admission:** Closing date 1/15 (postmark date). $40 fee, may be waived for applicants with need. Application may be submitted online. Admission notification on a rolling basis. Must reply by May 1 or within 2 week(s) if notified thereafter. **Financial aid:** Priority date 3/1; no closing date. FAFSA required. Applicants notified on a rolling basis starting 3/15; must reply by 5/1 or within 2 week(s) of notification.

**Academics. Special study options:** Accelerated study, combined bachelor's/graduate degree, cooperative education, distance learning, double major, dual enrollment of high school students, exchange student, honors, independent study, internships, student-designed major, study abroad, teacher certification program. Concurrent registration at another campus of University of Illinois. **Credit/placement by examination:** AP, CLEP, IB, ACT, institutional tests. 30 credit hours maximum toward bachelor's degree. **Support services:** Learning center, pre-admission summer program, remedial instruction, study skills assistance, tutoring, writing center.

**Majors. Area/ethnic studies:** African-American, German, Latin American. **Biology:** General, biochemistry. **Business:** Accounting, entrepreneurial studies, finance, management science, marketing. **Communications:** General. **Computer sciences:** Computer science, information systems. **Education:** Art, biology, chemistry, elementary, English, French, German, history, mathematics, physics, Spanish. **Engineering:** Biomedical, chemical, civil, computer, electrical, industrial, mechanical, physics. **Engineering technology:** Industrial management. **English:** English lit. **Foreign languages:** Classics, French, German, Italian, Polish, Russian, Spanish. **Health:** Dietetics, medical records admin, nursing (RN), predental. **History:** General. **Interdisciplinary:** Classical/archaeology, math/computer science, neuroscience. **Liberal arts:** Arts/sciences. **Math:** General, statistics. **Parks/recreation:** Exercise sciences. **Philosophy/religion:** Philosophy. **Physical sciences:** Chemistry, geology, physics. **Protective services:** Criminal justice. **Psychology:** General. **Public administration:** Social work. **Social sciences:** Anthropology, economics, political science, sociology, urban studies. **Visual/performing arts:** Art history/conservation, cinematography, dramatic, graphic design, photography, studio arts. **Other:** Gender and women's studies, Performance.

**Most popular majors.** Biology 12%, business/marketing 17%, engineering/engineering technologies 9%, health sciences 8%, psychology 12%, social sciences 9%.

**Computing on campus.** 1,100 workstations in dormitories, library, computer center, student center. Dormitories wired for high-speed internet access and linked to campus network. Commuter students can connect to campus network. Online course registration, online library, helpline, student web hosting, wireless network available.

**Student life. Freshman orientation:** Mandatory, $99 fee. Preregistration for classes offered. Two-day, overnight offered 12 times from early June to mid-August. **Housing:** Coed dorms, special housing for disabled, apartments available. $150 partly refundable deposit, deadline 4/1. Honors floors, men's floors, women's floors, apartment program for married or single students with children, Presidential Award House, special interest floors available. **Activities:** Bands, campus ministries, choral groups, dance, drama, literary magazine, music ensembles, musical theater, radio station, student government, student newspaper, over 200 student groups available.

**Athletics.** NCAA. **Intercollegiate:** Baseball M, basketball, cheerleading, cross-country, diving, gymnastics, soccer M, softball W, swimming, tennis, track and field, volleyball W. **Intramural:** Badminton, basketball, bowling, cross-country, football (non-tackle), racquetball, soccer, softball, table tennis, tennis, volleyball. **Team name:** Flames.

**Student services.** Adult student services, alcohol/substance abuse counseling, career counseling, services for economically disadvantaged, student employment services, financial aid counseling, health services, legal services, minority student services, on-campus daycare, personal counseling, placement for graduates, veterans' counselor, women's services. **Physically disabled:** Services for visually, speech, hearing impaired.

**Contact.** E-mail: uicadmit@uic.edu
Phone: (312) 996-4350 Fax: (312) 413-7628
Thomas Glenn, Executive Director Admissions and Records, University of Illinois at Chicago, PO Box 5220, Chicago, IL 60680-5220

## University of Illinois at Urbana-Champaign
Champaign, Illinois                                    **CB member**
www.illinois.edu                                       **CB code: 1836**

- Public 4-year university
- Residential campus in small city
- 30,395 degree-seeking undergraduates: 2% part-time, 47% women, 7% African American, 13% Asian American, 7% Hispanic American, 5% international
- 10,849 degree-seeking graduate students
- 71% of applicants admitted
- SAT or ACT with writing, application essay required
- 82% graduate within 6 years; 26% enter graduate study

**General.** Founded in 1867. Regionally accredited. **Degrees:** 7,035 bachelor's awarded; master's, doctoral, first professional offered. **ROTC:** Army, Naval, Air Force. **Location:** 130 miles from Chicago, 180 miles from St. Louis. **Calendar:** Semester, extensive summer session. **Full-time faculty:** 1,974 total; 92% have terminal degrees, 23% minority, 30% women. **Part-time faculty:** 66 total; 97% have terminal degrees, 18% minority, 18% women. **Class size:** 38% < 20, 38% 20-39, 5% 40-49, 10% 50-99, 9% >100. **Special facilities:** Natural history museum, museum of world history and culture, performing and visual arts centers, 37 public libraries, engineering library, agricultural library, rare book and manuscript library, chemistry library, institute of genomic biology, institute for advanced science and technology, computer science center, national center for supercomputing applications, arboretum, observatory, hiking trails, Japanese house and gardens.

**Freshman class profile.** 21,645 applied, 15,361 admitted, 6,948 enrolled.

| Mid 50% test scores | | | |
|---|---|---|---|
| SAT critical reading: | 540-670 | Return as sophomores: | 93% |
| SAT math: | 630-740 | Out-of-state: | 5% |
| ACT composite: | 26-31 | Live on campus: | 99% |
| Rank in top quarter: | 89% | International: | 6% |
| Rank in top tenth: | 55% | Fraternities: | 20% |
| | | Sororities: | 24% |

**Basis for selection.** High school course work, personal essay, class rank, SAT/ACT test scores most important. Audition required of dance, music, theater (performance) majors. Professional interest statement required of all applicants. **Homeschooled:** The more information about the home school environment/coursework descriptions the better; applicants should contact admissions office early in high school career with any questions or concerns. **Learning Disabled:** Recommended that students with learning disabilities address disability and any accommodations they receive in required personal statement section.

**High school preparation.** 15 units required. Required units include English 4, mathematics 3, social studies 2, science 2 (laboratory 2), foreign language 2 and academic electives 2. Specific subject requirements vary with college and program.

**2007-2008 Annual costs.** Tuition/fees: $11,130; $25,216 out-of-state. Freshman costs reflect guaranteed tuition plan figures; tuition rate is guaranteed for 4 years. Room/board: $8,196. Books/supplies: $1,200. Personal expenses: $2,624.

**2006-2007 Financial aid. Need-based:** 4,959 full-time freshmen applied for aid; 3,204 were judged to have need; 3,036 of these received aid. Average need met was 71%. Average scholarship/grant was $8,821; average loan $3,715. 53% of total undergraduate aid awarded as scholarships/grants, 47% as loans/jobs. **Non-need-based:** Awarded to 9,480 full-time undergraduates, including 2,298 freshmen. Scholarships awarded for academics, alumni affiliation, art, athletics, leadership, music/drama, ROTC, state residency.

**Application procedures. Admission:** Priority date 11/10; deadline 1/2 (postmark date). $40 fee, may be waived for applicants with need. Application may be submitted online. Notification by 12/14 and 2/15. Must reply by May 1 or within 2 week(s) if notified thereafter. **Financial aid:** Priority date 3/15; no closing date. FAFSA required.

**Academics.** Students generally declare a major upon enrollment. Students without a declared major may apply for the general curriculum option in the Division of General Studies. **Special study options:** Accelerated study, combined bachelor's/graduate degree, cooperative education, cross-registration, distance learning, double major, dual enrollment of high school students, ESL, exchange student, honors, independent study, internships, liberal arts/career combination, semester at sea, student-designed major, study abroad, teacher certification program, Washington semester. Honors program, campus honors, Illinois Leadership & Entrepreneurial programs. **Credit/placement by examination:** AP, CLEP, IB, SAT, ACT, institutional tests. Unlimited credit hours may be counted toward a degree. **Support services:** Learning center, pre-admission summer program, reduced course load, remedial instruction, study skills assistance, tutoring, writing center.

**Majors. Agriculture:** Agronomy, animal husbandry, animal sciences, business, communications, economics, education services, farm/ranch, food processing, food science, horticultural science, horticulture, international, mechanization, ornamental horticulture. **Architecture:** Architecture, landscape, urban/community planning. **Area/ethnic studies:** East Asian, Latin American, Russian/Slavic, women's. **Biology:** General, biochemistry, biophysics, biotechnology, botany, cell/histology, cellular/molecular, entomology, microbiology, physiology, plant molecular. **Business:** General, accounting, accounting/business management, actuarial science, auditing, banking/financial services, business admin, entrepreneurial studies, finance, financial planning, hospitality admin, human resources, insurance, logistics, management information systems, management science, market research, marketing, operations, organizational behavior, purchasing, real estate, sales/distribution. **Communications:** General, advertising, broadcast journalism, journalism, media studies, organizational. **Computer sciences:** General, computer science, programming, security. **Conservation:** General, environmental science, forest sciences, management/policy, urban forestry, wildlife. **Education:** Agricultural, art, biology, chemistry, early childhood, early childhood special, elementary, English, foreign languages, French, German, history, kindergarten/preschool, Latin, mathematics, multi-level teacher, multiple handicapped, music, physical, physics, science, secondary, social science, social studies, Spanish, special. **Engineering:** General, aerospace, agricultural, biomedical, ceramic, chemical, civil, computer, computer hardware, construction, electrical, environmental, geotechnical, industrial, manufacturing, materials, materials science, mechanical, mechanics, metallurgical, nuclear, operations research, physics, polymer, software, structural, transportation, water resource. **English:** Composition, English lit, speech/rhetoric. **Family/consumer sciences:** Child development, consumer economics, family studies, human nutrition. **Foreign languages:** Classics, comparative lit, East Asian, French, German, Hebrew, Italian, linguistics, Portuguese, Russian, Spanish. **Health:** Athletic training, audiology/hearing, audiology/speech pathology, community health, dietetics, environmental health, health services admin, preveterinary, vocational rehab counseling. **History:** General. **Interdisciplinary:** Global studies, math/computer science, science/society. **Legal studies:** Prelaw. **Liberal arts:** Arts/sciences, humanities. **Math:** General, computational, statistics. **Parks/recreation:** General, exercise sciences, sports admin. **Philosophy/religion:** Philosophy, religion. **Physical sciences:** Astronomy, atmospheric science, chemistry, geology, physics. **Psychology:** General. **Social sciences:** Anthropology, economics, geography, political science, sociology. **Transportation:** Airline/commercial pilot, aviation management. **Visual/performing arts:** Acting, art history/conservation, crafts, dance, directing/producing, dramatic, film/cinema, graphic design, jazz, music history, music performance, music theory/composition, painting, photography, sculpture, studio arts, theater history, voice/opera. **Other:** Biological and biomedical sciences, Human sciences business services, Plant protection and integrated pest management.

**Most popular majors.** Biology 8%, business/marketing 15%, engineering/engineering technologies 14%, English 7%, psychology 7%, social sciences 10%.

**Computing on campus.** 4,420 workstations in dormitories, library, computer center, student center. Dormitories wired for high-speed internet access and linked to campus network. Commuter students can connect to campus network. Online course registration, online library, helpline, repair service, student web hosting, wireless network available.

**Student life. Freshman orientation:** Mandatory, $96 fee. Preregistration for classes offered. One-day program, held May 29 to July 11. **Policies:** Freshmen required to live on campus unless over 21 years, married, or living with parents. **Housing:** Guaranteed on-campus for freshmen. Coed dorms, single-sex dorms, special housing for disabled, apartments, cooperative housing, fraternity/sorority housing, substance-free housing available. $200 fully refundable deposit, deadline 5/1. Living/learning communities available. **Activities:** Bands, campus ministries, choral groups, dance, drama, film society, international student organizations, literary magazine, music ensembles, Model UN, musical theater, opera, radio station, student government, student newspaper, symphony orchestra, TV station, more than 1,000 registered student organizations.

**Athletics.** NCAA. **Intercollegiate:** Baseball M, basketball, cheerleading, cross-country, diving W, football (tackle) M, golf, gymnastics, soccer W, softball W, swimming W, tennis, track and field, volleyball W, wrestling M. **Intramural:** Badminton, basketball, cross-country, diving, football (non-tackle), football (tackle) M, golf, racquetball, soccer, softball W, tennis, volleyball, wrestling M. **Team name:** Illini.

**Student services.** Alcohol/substance abuse counseling, career counseling, services for economically disadvantaged, student employment services, financial aid counseling, health services, legal services, minority student services, on-campus daycare, personal counseling, placement for graduates, veterans' counselor, women's services. **Physically disabled:** Services for visually, speech, hearing impaired. **Learning disabled:** Comprehensive services available.

**Contact.** E-mail: ugradadmissioins@uiuc.edu
Phone: (217) 333-0302 Fax: (217) 244-4614
Stacey Kostell, Director of Undergraduate Admissions, University of Illinois at Urbana-Champaign, 901 West Illinois, Urbana, IL 61801-3028

---

## University of Illinois: Springfield

Springfield, Illinois   **CB member**
www.uis.edu   **CB code: 0834**

- Public 4-year university and liberal arts college
- Commuter campus in small city
- 2,696 degree-seeking undergraduates: 38% part-time, 56% women, 11% African American, 3% Asian American, 3% Hispanic American, 1% Native American, 1% international
- 1,741 degree-seeking graduate students
- 62% of applicants admitted
- SAT or ACT (ACT writing recommended) required
- 56% graduate within 6 years

**General.** Founded in 1969. Regionally accredited. Third campus of University of Illinois system with emphasis on public affairs and a liberal arts mission. **Degrees:** 612 bachelor's awarded; master's, doctoral offered. **Location:** 95 miles from St. Louis, 200 miles from Chicago. **Calendar:** Semester, extensive summer session. **Full-time faculty:** 204 total; 92% have terminal degrees, 20% minority, 43% women. **Part-time faculty:** 138 total; 26% have terminal degrees, 12% minority, 48% women. **Class size:** 59% < 20, 39% 20-39, 2% 40-49, less than 1% 50-99. **Special facilities:** Observatory, studio theatre.

**Freshman class profile.** 1,112 applied, 685 admitted, 261 enrolled.

| Mid 50% test scores | | | |
|---|---|---|---|
| ACT composite: | 20-25 | Rank in top tenth: | 11% |
| GPA 3.50 or higher: | 33% | End year in good standing: | 72% |
| GPA 3.0-3.49: | 30% | Return as sophomores: | 72% |
| GPA 2.0-2.99: | 37% | Out-of-state: | 2% |
| Rank in top quarter: | 36% | Live on campus: | 75% |
| | | International: | 2% |

**Basis for selection.** GPA, rank, record, completion of college-prepatory program, recommendations, admission test scores, and formal demonstration of competencies all fully considered. Personal or telephone interview may be required.

**High school preparation.** Required units include English 4, mathematics 3, social studies 3, science 3 and foreign language 2. Fine arts can be substituted for the foreign language.

**2007-2008 Annual costs.** Tuition/fees: $7,826; $16,976 out-of-state. Freshman costs reflect guaranteed tuition plan figures; tuition rate is guaranteed for 4 years. Room/board: $8,446.

**2006-2007 Financial aid. Need-based:** 222 full-time freshmen applied for aid; 135 were judged to have need; 135 of these received aid. Average need met was 75%. Average scholarship/grant was $6,271; average loan $2,407. 47% of total undergraduate aid awarded as scholarships/grants, 53% as loans/jobs. **Non-need-based:** Awarded to 620 full-time undergraduates, including 189 freshmen. Scholarships awarded for academics, alumni affiliation, art, athletics, job skills, leadership, minority status, music/drama, state residency.

**Application procedures. Admission:** Priority date 3/15; no deadline. $40 fee, may be waived for applicants with need. Application may be submitted online. Admission notification on a rolling basis beginning on or about 9/15. Notification reply accepted until class is filled. **Financial aid:** Priority date 4/1, closing date 11/15. FAFSA required. Applicants notified on a rolling basis starting 1/1; must reply within 3 week(s) of notification.

**Academics. Special study options:** Distance learning, double major, ESL, honors, independent study, internships, study abroad, teacher certification program. **Credit/placement by examination:** AP, CLEP, IB, ACT, institutional tests. 30 credit hours maximum toward bachelor's degree. **Support services:** Learning center, reduced course load, study skills assistance, tutoring, writing center.

**Majors. Biology:** General. **Business:** Accounting, business admin. **Communications:** Media studies. **Computer sciences:** Computer science. **English:** English lit. **Health:** Clinical lab science. **History:** General. **Legal studies:** General. **Liberal arts:** Arts/sciences. **Math:** General. **Philosophy/religion:** Philosophy. **Physical sciences:** Chemistry. **Protective services:** Criminal justice. **Psychology:** General. **Public administration:** Social work. **Social sciences:** Economics, political science. **Visual/performing arts:** Studio arts.

**Most popular majors.** Business/marketing 21%, communications/journalism 7%, computer/information sciences 7%, liberal arts 11%, psychology 13%, public administration/social services 8%, security/protective services 7%, social sciences 6%.

**Computing on campus.** 420 workstations in dormitories, library, computer center, student center. Dormitories wired for high-speed internet access and linked to campus network. Commuter students can connect to campus network. Online course registration, online library, helpline, student web hosting, wireless network available.

**Student life. Freshman orientation:** Mandatory. **Housing:** Guaranteed on-campus for freshmen. Coed dorms, special housing for disabled, apartments, substance-free housing available. $150 deposit. Family housing available. **Activities:** Bands, campus ministries, choral groups, dance, drama, film society, international student organizations, music ensembles, Model UN, student government, student newspaper, Christian student fellowship, ACLU, Indian student organization, Habitat for Humanity, Living Word Bible Study, College Democrats, College Republicans, Queer Straight Alliance.

**Athletics.** NAIA. **Intercollegiate:** Basketball, cheerleading M, golf, soccer M, softball W, tennis, volleyball W. **Intramural:** Badminton, basketball, bowling, fencing, football (non-tackle), golf, handball, racquetball, skiing, soccer, softball, tennis, volleyball. **Team name:** Prairie Stars.

**Student services.** Alcohol/substance abuse counseling, career counseling, student employment services, financial aid counseling, health services, minority student services, on-campus daycare, personal counseling, women's services. **Physically disabled:** Services for visually, speech, hearing impaired.

**Contact.** E-mail: admissions@uis.edu
Phone: (217) 206-4847 Toll-free number: (888) 977-4847
Fax: (217) 206-6620
Lori Giordano, Assoc. Director of Admissions, University of Illinois: Springfield, One University Plaza, MS UHB 1080, Springfield, IL 62703

---

## University of St. Francis

Joliet, Illinois
www.stfrancis.edu   **CB code: 1130**

- Private 4-year university and liberal arts college affiliated with Roman Catholic Church
- Commuter campus in small city
- 1,282 degree-seeking undergraduates: 5% part-time, 69% women, 10% African American, 5% Asian American, 8% Hispanic American, 1% international
- 802 degree-seeking graduate students
- 67% of applicants admitted
- SAT or ACT (ACT writing optional) required
- 62% graduate within 6 years; 17% enter graduate study

**General.** Founded in 1920. Regionally accredited. Affiliated with Argonne National Laboratories, Morton Arboretum, Will County Forest Preserve, Midewin Tallgrass Prairie, Shedd Aquarium. **Degrees:** 308 bachelor's awarded; master's offered. **Location:** 35 miles from Chicago. **Calendar:** Semester, extensive summer session. **Full-time faculty:** 78 total; 64% have terminal degrees, 6% minority, 58% women. **Part-time faculty:** 149 total; 26% have terminal degrees, 7% minority, 56% women. **Class size:** 67% < 20, 33% 20-39. **Special facilities:** Performing arts center, greenhouse, health and wellness center.

**Freshman class profile.** 766 applied, 510 admitted, 198 enrolled.

| Mid 50% test scores | | | |
|---|---|---|---|
| ACT composite: | 20-25 | Rank in top tenth: | 14% |
| GPA 3.50 or higher: | 25% | End year in good standing: | 88% |
| GPA 3.0-3.49: | 43% | Return as sophomores: | 74% |
| GPA 2.0-2.99: | 32% | Out-of-state: | 8% |
| Rank in top quarter: | 45% | Live on campus: | 56% |
| | | International: | 1% |

**Basis for selection.** High school GPA and rank, test scores important. Essay and letters of recommendation required and interview recommended for students who do not meet our admissions requirements.

**High school preparation.** 16 units required. Required and recommended units include English 4, mathematics 2, social studies 2, science 2 (laboratory 1), foreign language 1 and academic electives 3. 3 units required from 2 areas: language, music or arts, or computer science.

**2007-2008 Annual costs.** Tuition/fees: $20,830. Room/board: $7,610. Books/supplies: $800. Personal expenses: $1,000.

**2007-2008 Financial aid. Need-based:** 184 full-time freshmen applied for aid; 151 were judged to have need; 151 of these received aid. Average need met was 82%. Average scholarship/grant was $7,988; average loan $3,876. 69% of total undergraduate aid awarded as scholarships/grants, 31% as loans/jobs. **Non-need-based:** Awarded to 1,182 full-time undergraduates, including 189 freshmen. Scholarships awarded for academics, alumni affiliation, art, athletics, leadership, music/drama, religious affiliation, state residency.

**Application procedures. Admission:** Priority date 5/1; deadline 8/1 (receipt date). $30 fee, may be waived for applicants with need. Application may be submitted online. Admission notification on a rolling basis beginning on or about 9/1. **Financial aid:** Priority date 3/15; no closing date. FAFSA, institutional form required. Applicants notified on a rolling basis starting 2/15.

**Academics. Special study options:** Accelerated study, combined bachelor's/graduate degree, distance learning, double major, honors, independent study, internships, student-designed major, study abroad, teacher certification program, Washington semester. **Credit/placement by examination:** AP, CLEP, IB, SAT, ACT, institutional tests. 33 credit hours maximum toward bachelor's degree. **Support services:** Learning center, pre-admission summer program, reduced course load, remedial instruction, study skills assistance, tutoring, writing center.

**Majors. Biology:** General. **Business:** General, accounting, actuarial science, business admin, finance, human resources, management science, marketing, organizational behavior. **Communications:** Advertising, broadcast journalism, media studies, public relations, radio/tv. **Computer sciences:** Computer science, information technology, webmaster. **Conservation:** Environmental science. **Education:** Elementary, English, mathematics, music, science, social studies, special. **English:** English lit. **Health:** Clinical lab science, health care admin, medical radiologic technology/radiation therapy, nuclear medical technology, nursing (RN), predental, premedicine, preveterinary, radiologic technology/medical imaging, recreational therapy. **History:** General. **Interdisciplinary:** Math/computer science. **Liberal arts:** Arts/sciences. **Math:** General. **Parks/recreation:** Facilities management. **Psychology:** General. **Public administration:** Social work. **Social sciences:** Political science. **Theology:** Theology. **Visual/performing arts:** General, music performance.

**Most popular majors.** Business/marketing 11%, education 24%, health sciences 31%.

**Computing on campus.** 365 workstations in dormitories, library, computer center, student center. Dormitories wired for high-speed internet access and linked to campus network. Commuter students can connect to campus network. Online course registration, online library, helpline, wireless network available.

**Student life. Freshman orientation:** Mandatory, $120 fee. **Policies:** Visitation between 9am and 2am each day. Marian Hall is alcohol-free. All Halls close during major breaks (fall break, winter break, spring break) unless special permission is received to remain in the hall at those times. **Housing:** Guaranteed on-campus for freshmen. Coed dorms, apartments, substance-free housing available. $50 fully refundable deposit, deadline 5/1. **Activities:** Campus ministries, choral groups, dance, drama, literary magazine, music ensembles, musical theater, radio station, student government, student newspaper, symphony orchestra, TV station, social work club, black student association, student business association, Association of Republican Students, Council for Environmental and Social Awareness, Council for Social Activism, Unidos Vamos Alcanzar, student nurses association.

**Athletics. NAIA. Intercollegiate:** Baseball M, basketball, cheerleading M, cross-country, football (tackle) M, golf, soccer, softball W, tennis, track and field, volleyball W. **Intramural:** Basketball, bowling, volleyball. **Team name:** Saints.

**Student services.** Adult student services, career counseling, student employment services, financial aid counseling, health services, minority student services, personal counseling, placement for graduates. **Physically disabled:** Services for visually, speech, hearing impaired.

**Contact.** E-mail: admissions@stfrancis.edu
Phone: (815) 740-5037 Toll-free number: (800) 735-7500
Fax: (815) 740-5032
Meghan Connolly, Director Undergraduate Admissions, University of St. Francis, 500 Wilcox Street, Joliet, IL 60435

## VanderCook College of Music
**Chicago, Illinois**
www.vandercook.edu                    CB code: 1872

- Private 4-year music and teachers college
- Residential campus in very large city

- 116 degree-seeking undergraduates: 1% part-time, 46% women, 16% African American, 7% Asian American, 14% Hispanic American, 1% international
- 69 degree-seeking graduate students
- 98% of applicants admitted
- Application essay, interview required
- 58% graduate within 6 years

**General.** Founded in 1909. Regionally accredited. Access to student services at Illinois Institute of Technology. **Degrees:** 16 bachelor's awarded; master's offered. **Location:** Central Chicago. **Calendar:** Semester. **Full-time faculty:** 13 total; 46% have terminal degrees, 15% minority, 69% women. **Part-time faculty:** 17 total; 18% have terminal degrees, 6% minority, 29% women. **Class size:** 64% < 20, 30% 20-39, 1% 50-99, 4% >100. **Special facilities:** MIDI/electronic music laboratory, library with music education collection.

**Freshman class profile.** 44 applied, 43 admitted, 26 enrolled.

| Mid 50% test scores | | | |
|---|---|---|---|
| SAT critical reading: | 450-560 | Rank in top tenth: | 20% |
| SAT writing: | 510-600 | Return as sophomores: | 89% |
| ACT composite: | 19-27 | Out-of-state: | 12% |
| Rank in top quarter: | 40% | Live on campus: | 54% |

**Basis for selection.** Academic credentials, SAT or ACT scores and recommendations are weighed along with student's musical audition and interview. Institutional test required. Audition required. **Homeschooled:** Should obtain experience performing with a concert band or chorus.

**High school preparation.** 15 units recommended. Recommended units include English 3, mathematics 2, social studies 3, science 2, foreign language 2 and academic electives 3. Art may be substituted for foreign language.

**2007-2008 Annual costs.** Tuition/fees: $18,800. Room/board: $8,800. Books/supplies: $1,620. Personal expenses: $2,000.

**Financial aid. Non-need-based:** Scholarships awarded for academics, alumni affiliation, leadership, minority status, music/drama, state residency. **Additional information:** Musical talent considered for partial tuition waiver.

**Application procedures. Admission:** Priority date 4/1; no deadline. $35 fee. Admission notification on a rolling basis. **Financial aid:** Priority date 3/1, closing date 4/30. FAFSA required. Applicants notified on a rolling basis starting 5/15; must reply within 2 week(s) of notification.

**Academics. Special study options:** Teacher certification program. **Credit/placement by examination:** AP, CLEP, SAT, ACT, institutional tests.

**Majors. Education:** Music.

**Computing on campus.** 10 workstations in dormitories, library, computer center, student center.

**Student life. Freshman orientation:** Mandatory. **Policies:** Student life focuses around musical activities at VanderCook and on the Illinois Institue of Technology campus. **Housing:** Guaranteed on-campus for all undergraduates. Coed dorms, apartments, fraternity/sorority housing available. $100 deposit. Apartments for single students 23 and older available. **Activities:** Bands, choral groups, music ensembles, musical theater.

**Student services.** Career counseling, student employment services, health services, personal counseling, placement for graduates.

**Contact.** E-mail: admissions@vandercook.edu
Phone: (312) 225-6288 ext. 230 Fax: (312) 225-5211
Amy Lenting, Director of Recruiting and Retention, VanderCook College of Music, 3140 South Federal Street, Chicago, IL 60616-3731

## West Suburban College of Nursing
**Oak Park, Illinois**
www.wscn.edu                    CB code: 1927

- Private two-year upper-division nursing college affiliated with Roman Catholic Church
- Commuter campus in very large city
- Test scores, application essay required

**General.** Founded in 1982. Regionally accredited. Facilities located in West Suburban Medical Center. **Degrees:** 75 bachelor's awarded; master's offered. **Location:** 10 miles from downtown Chicago. **Calendar:** Semester, limited summer session. **Full-time faculty:** 18 total. **Part-time faculty:** 8

total. **Class size:** 20% < 20, 23% 20-39, 26% 40-49, 31% 50-99. **Special facilities:** In-hospital location, health sciences library, nursing clinical skills laboratory.

**Student profile.** 212 degree-seeking undergraduates, 17 degree-seeking graduate students.

| Women: | 85% | Part-time: | 25% |

**Basis for selection.** College transcript, application essay, standardized test scores required. Natural and behavioral science grades are more heavily weighted. Recommendation and essay required. Must have science GPA of 2.75 cum/4.0. Satisfactory score on TEAS. Transfer accepted as juniors, seniors.

**2007-2008 Annual costs.** Tuition/fees: $20,270. 16 month fast track nursing program available for $28,185. Books/supplies: $400. Personal expenses: $600.

**Financial aid. Need-based:** 31% of total undergraduate aid awarded as scholarships/grants, 69% as loans/jobs. **Non-need-based:** Scholarships awarded for academics, alumni affiliation.

**Application procedures. Admission:** $30 fee. Application may be submitted online. **Financial aid:** No deadline. Applicants notified on a rolling basis; must reply within 3 weeks of notification. FAFSA required.

**Academics. Special study options:** Accelerated study, independent study. Evening and weekend BS completion program for registered nurses. **Credit/ placement by examination:** CLEP.

**Majors. Health:** Nursing (RN).

**Computing on campus.** 10 workstations in library, computer center. Online library, wireless network available.

**Student life. Activities:** Student government.

**Student services.** Career counseling, health services.

**Contact.** E-mail: wsadmis@wscn.edu
Phone: (708) 763-6530 Fax: (708) 763-1531
Cindy Valdez, Director of Admissions and Records/Registrar, West Suburban College of Nursing, Three Erie Court, Oak Park, IL 60302

## Western Illinois University
**Macomb, Illinois**
**www.wiu.edu**                          **CB code: 1900**

- Public 4-year university
- Residential campus in large town
- 11,145 degree-seeking undergraduates: 9% part-time, 47% women, 7% African American, 1% Asian American, 5% Hispanic American, 1% international
- 2,078 degree-seeking graduate students
- 68% of applicants admitted
- SAT or ACT (ACT writing optional) required
- 57% graduate within 6 years

**General.** Founded in 1899. Regionally accredited. **Degrees:** 3,080 bachelor's awarded; master's, doctoral offered. **ROTC:** Army. **Location:** 83 miles from Rock Island, 78 miles from Peoria. **Calendar:** Semester, limited summer session. **Full-time faculty:** 656 total; 72% have terminal degrees, 10% minority, 41% women. **Part-time faculty:** 89 total; 17% have terminal degrees, 2% minority, 45% women. **Class size:** 34% < 20, 51% 20-39, 8% 40-49, 5% 50-99, 2% >100. **Special facilities:** Geology museum.

**Freshman class profile.** 8,201 applied, 5,592 admitted, 1,955 enrolled.

| Mid 50% test scores | | Rank in top tenth: | 6% |
|---|---|---|---|
| ACT composite: | 18-23 | End year in good standing: | 86% |
| GPA 3.50 or higher: | 18% | Return as sophomores: | 72% |
| GPA 3.0-3.49: | 30% | Out-of-state: | 2% |
| GPA 2.0-2.99: | 52% | Live on campus: | 93% |
| Rank in top quarter: | 22% | International: | 1% |

**Basis for selection.** Standardized test scores, class rank very important. Audition required for music majors. **Homeschooled:** Transcript of courses and grades required.

**High school preparation.** 15 units recommended. Recommended units include English 4, mathematics 3, social studies 3, science 3 and academic electives 2. 2 units of art, film, foreign language, music, speech, theater, journalism, religion, philosophy or vocational education also recommended.

**2007-2008 Annual costs.** Tuition/fees: $8,079; $11,027 out-of-state. Residents of nearby counties in Iowa and Missouri pay in-state tuition during first year. Incoming freshmen guaranteed the first year tuition rate for their entire 4 years, provided they are continually enrolled. Room/board: $6,898. Books/supplies: $1,150. Personal expenses: $3,476.

**Financial aid. Non-need-based:** Scholarships awarded for academics, alumni affiliation, art, athletics, leadership, minority status, music/drama, ROTC.

**Application procedures. Admission:** Priority date 5/15; no deadline. $30 fee. Application may be submitted online. Admission notification on a rolling basis. **Financial aid:** Priority date 2/15; no closing date. FAFSA required. Applicants notified on a rolling basis starting 1/15.

**Academics. Special study options:** Distance learning, double major, dual enrollment of high school students, ESL, external degree, honors, independent study, internships, student-designed major, study abroad, teacher certification program, weekend college. **Credit/placement by examination:** AP, CLEP, IB. 30 credit hours maximum toward bachelor's degree. **Support services:** Remedial instruction, study skills assistance, tutoring, writing center.

**Honors college/program.** 28 ACT or upper 10% of class and 24 ACT.

**Majors. Agriculture:** General. **Area/ethnic studies:** African-American, women's. **Biology:** General. **Business:** Accounting, business admin, construction management, finance, human resources, logistics, management information systems, managerial economics, marketing. **Communications:** General, journalism, radio/tv. **Communications technology:** Graphic/printing. **Computer sciences:** General, networking. **Education:** Bilingual, elementary, health, instructional media, special. **Engineering technology:** Industrial, manufacturing. **English:** English lit. **Family/consumer sciences:** General. **Foreign languages:** French, Spanish. **Health:** Clinical lab science, communication disorders, health care admin. **History:** General. **Liberal arts:** Arts/sciences. **Math:** General. **Parks/recreation:** Exercise sciences, facilities management. **Philosophy/religion:** Philosophy. **Physical sciences:** Chemistry, geology, meteorology, physics. **Protective services:** Emergency management/ homeland security, law enforcement admin. **Psychology:** General. **Public administration:** Social work. **Social sciences:** Economics, geography, political science, sociology. **Visual/performing arts:** Art, dramatic, music performance, musical theater, studio arts. **Other:** Forensic chemistry, Interdisciplinary studies.

**Most popular majors.** Business/marketing 15%, communications/ journalism 7%, education 10%, liberal arts 8%, parks/recreation 8%, security/ protective services 16%, social sciences 6%.

**Computing on campus.** 1,000 workstations in dormitories, library, computer center. Dormitories wired for high-speed internet access and linked to campus network. Commuter students can connect to campus network. Online course registration, online library, helpline, wireless network available.

**Student life. Freshman orientation:** Mandatory. Preregistration for classes offered. Held week prior to beginning of classes. **Housing:** Guaranteed on-campus for all undergraduates. Coed dorms, single-sex dorms, apartments, fraternity/sorority housing, substance-free housing available. $100 partly refundable deposit. **Activities:** Bands, choral groups, dance, drama, music ensembles, musical theater, radio station, student government, student newspaper, symphony orchestra, TV station, 67 special-interest organizations, 5 service organizations, 14 religious organizations, 32 national honorary and professional fraternities.

**Athletics.** NCAA. **Intercollegiate:** Baseball M, basketball, cheerleading, cross-country, diving, football (tackle) M, golf, soccer, softball W, swimming, tennis, track and field, volleyball W. **Intramural:** Badminton, basketball, bowling, cross-country, football (non-tackle), football (tackle) M, golf, handball, lacrosse M, racquetball, rugby, skin diving, soccer, softball, swimming, table tennis; tennis, volleyball, water polo. **Team name:** Leathernecks (men), Westerwinds (women).

**Student services.** Adult student services, alcohol/substance abuse counseling, career counseling, student employment services, financial aid counseling, health services, legal services, minority student services, on-campus daycare, personal counseling, placement for graduates, veterans' counselor, women's services. **Physically disabled:** Services for visually, speech, hearing impaired.

**Contact.** E-mail: wiuadm@wiu.edu
Phone: (309) 298-3157 Toll-free number: (877) 742-5948
Fax: (309) 298-3111
Eric Campbell, Director of Admissions, Western Illinois University, One University Circle, Macomb, IL 61455-1390

## Western Illinois University: Quad Cities
### Moline, Illinois
### www.wiu.edu/qc

- Public two-year upper-division university and branch campus college
- Commuter campus in large city

**General.** Regionally accredited. **Degrees:** 2,455 bachelor's awarded; master's, doctoral offered. **Articulation:** Agreement with Illinois Articulation Initiative. **Calendar:** Semester, extensive summer session. **Full-time faculty:** 34 total. **Part-time faculty:** 25 total.

**Student profile.** 655 degree-seeking undergraduates, 640 degree-seeking graduate students. 77% transferred from two-year, 23% transferred from four-year institutions.

| | | | |
|---|---|---|---|
| Women: | 62% | Part-time: | 54% |
| African American: | 5% | Out-of-state: | 34% |
| Hispanic American: | 6% | 25 or older: | 85% |
| Native American: | 1% | | |

**Basis for selection.** College transcript required. Transfer accepted as sophomores, juniors, seniors.

**2007-2008 Annual costs.** Tuition/fees: $6,436; $9,384 out-of-state. Room/board: $6,898. Books/supplies: $1,150.

**Financial aid.** **Non-need-based:** Scholarships awarded for academics.

**Application procedures.** **Admission:** Rolling admission. $30 fee. Application may be submitted online. **Financial aid:** Priority date 2/1, no deadline. Applicants notified on a rolling basis.

**Academics.** 9 upper-division undergraduate programs, 7 certificate programs, 16 graduate programs, education specialist and educational doctorate programs offered. **Special study options:** Distance learning, double major, independent study, internships, teacher certification program, weekend college. **Credit/placement by examination:** AP, CLEP, IB. 30 credit hours maximum toward bachelor's degree.

**Majors. Business:** Accounting, business admin, management information systems, marketing. **Education:** Elementary. **Engineering:** Manufacturing. **Liberal arts:** Arts/sciences. **Parks/recreation:** Facilities management. **Protective services:** Law enforcement admin.

**Computing on campus.** 71 workstations in library. Online library, wireless network available.

**Contact.**  E-mail: wiu-qc@wiu.edu
Phone: (309) 762-9481 Fax: (309) 762-6989
Curtis Williams, Assistant Director of Admissions, Western Illinois University: Quad Cities, 3561 60th Street, Moline, IL 61265

## Westwood College: Chicago Loop
### Chicago, Illinois
### www.westwood.edu

- For-profit 4-year technical college
- Commuter campus in very large city
- 830 undergraduates
- 77% of applicants admitted

**General.** Accredited by ACICS. **Degrees:** 71 bachelor's, 16 associate awarded. **Location:** Downtown. **Calendar:** Continuous. **Full-time faculty:** 15 total. Part-time faculty: 63 total.

**Basis for selection.** Admission based on interview, applicant's level of interest and test scores. SAT or ACT recommended.

**High school preparation.** 4 units required.

**2007-2008 Annual costs.** $4,251 per term; 5 terms per year.

**Application procedures.** **Admission:** Priority date 8/6; deadline 8/9. $25 fee. **Financial aid:** No deadline.

**Academics.** **Special study options:** Independent study, internships. **Credit/placement by examination:** CLEP, SAT, ACT, institutional tests.

**Majors. Business:** Marketing. **Communications technology:** Animation/special effects. **Computer sciences:** Security. **Protective services:** Police science. **Visual/performing arts:** Design.

**Contact.**  Phone: (312) 739-0850 Toll-free number: (800) 281-2978
Fax: (312) 739-1004
Jeff Hill, Director of Admissions, Westwood College: Chicago Loop, 17 North State Street, Suite 300, Chicago, IL 60602

## Westwood College: DuPage
### Woodridge, Illinois
### www.westwood.edu
**CB code: 5096**

- For-profit 4-year technical college
- Commuter campus in large city
- 634 degree-seeking undergraduates: 13% part-time, 31% women
- Interview required

**General.** Accredited by ACICS. **Degrees:** 67 bachelor's, 34 associate awarded. **Location:** 20 miles from downtown Chicago. **Calendar:** Quarter. **Full-time faculty:** 6 total; 33% women. **Part-time faculty:** 49 total; 10% have terminal degrees, 16% minority, 37% women.

**Basis for selection.** Successful completion of Accuplacer test required prior to admission; SAT/ACT scores may be used in lieu of Accuplacer. SAT or ACT recommended.

**2008-2009 Annual costs.** Expenses vary by program; however, average cost for academic year is $14,867, which includes tuition, fees and books.

**2006-2007 Financial aid.** **Need-based:** 38% of total undergraduate aid awarded as scholarships/grants, 62% as loans/jobs.

**Application procedures.** **Admission:** No deadline. $100 fee. Application may be submitted online.

**Academics.** **Special study options:** Accelerated study, independent study. **Credit/placement by examination:** CLEP, institutional tests.

**Majors. Business:** Business admin. **Computer sciences:** Game design, security, webmaster. **Construction:** Site management. **Protective services:** Criminal justice. **Visual/performing arts:** Interior design.

**Student life. Activities:** Student government.

**Contact.**  Phone: (630) 434-8244 Toll-free number: (866) 721-7646
Fax: (630) 434-8255
Scott Kawall, Director of Admissions, Westwood College: DuPage, 7155 Janes Avenue, Woodridge, IL 60517

## Westwood College: O'Hare Airport
### Chicago, Illinois
### www.westwood.edu

- For-profit 4-year technical and career college
- Commuter campus in very large city
- 519 degree-seeking undergraduates
- 71% of applicants admitted
- Application essay, interview required

**General.** Accredited by ACICS. **Degrees:** 79 bachelor's, 5 associate awarded. **Calendar:** Continuous, extensive summer session. **Full-time faculty:** 7 total; 43% women. **Part-time faculty:** 31 total; 26% women. **Special facilities:** Graphic design finishing room, information systems security laboratory, interior design resource room, medical assisting laboratory, computer assisted drawing and design laboratory, game software design laboratory, animation and visual communication laboratory.

**Freshman class profile.** 700 applied, 500 admitted, 350 enrolled.

**Basis for selection.** Placement test and letter of intent required. Assessment given to all students; passing score required for admission to college programs.

**2007-2008 Annual costs.** Tuition/fees: $13,902. Books/supplies: $300. Personal expenses: $400.

**Application procedures.** **Admission:** No deadline. $25 fee. Application must be submitted on paper. **Financial aid:** Priority date 3/1, closing date 6/30. FAFSA, institutional form required.

**Academics.** **Special study options:** Accelerated study, cooperative education, distance learning, double major, independent study, internships, liberal arts/career combination, study abroad. **Credit/placement by examination:** AP, CLEP, institutional tests. **Support services:** Tutoring.

**Majors. Architecture:** Environmental design, interior, urban/community planning. **Business:** Marketing. **Communications technology:** Animation/special effects. **Computer sciences:** General, information technology. **Construction:** Site management. **Health:** Facilities admin, office admin. **Legal studies:** General, legal secretary, prelaw. **Protective services:** Correctional facilities, corrections, criminal justice, criminalistics, forensics, juvenile corrections, law enforcement admin, police science, security management, security services. **Public administration:** General, community org/advocacy, human services, policy analysis. **Social sciences:** Criminology. **Visual/performing arts:** Design, graphic design, interior design.

**Computing on campus.** Online library available.

**Student life. Freshman orientation:** Available. Preregistration for classes offered. **Housing:** Substance-free housing available. **Activities:** Student government, student newspaper.

**Student services.** Adult student services, alcohol/substance abuse counseling, career counseling, student employment services, financial aid counseling, personal counseling, placement for graduates, veterans' counselor.

**Contact.** Phone: (773) 380-6800 Toll-free number: (877) 877-8857 Fax: (773) 714-0828
Hamed Shibli, Director of Admissions, Westwood College: O'Hare Airport, 8501 West Higgins Road, Chicago, IL 60631

## Westwood College: River Oaks
**Calumet City, Illinois**
**www.westwood.edu**

- For-profit 4-year career college
- Commuter campus in very large city
- 625 degree-seeking undergraduates
- 61% of applicants admitted

**General.** Accredited by ACICS. **Degrees:** 66 bachelor's, 13 associate awarded. **Calendar:** Continuous, limited summer session. **Full-time faculty:** 10 total. **Part-time faculty:** 35 total.

**Basis for selection.** Must pass institutional admissions test.

**2007-2008 Annual costs.** Associate degree program $34,072; bachelor's degree $66,054. Costs include tuition, fees, and books for the entire program.

**Application procedures. Admission:** No deadline.

**Academics. Credit/placement by examination:** CLEP.

**Contact.** Phone: (708) 832-1988
Westwood College: River Oaks, 80 River Oaks Center, Suite D-49, Calumet City, IL 60409

## Wheaton College
**Wheaton, Illinois**                                                    **CB member**
**www.wheaton.edu**                                                **CB code: 1905**

- Private 4-year liberal arts college affiliated with nondenominational tradition
- Residential campus in small city
- 2,357 degree-seeking undergraduates: 3% part-time, 51% women, 3% African American, 7% Asian American, 4% Hispanic American, 1% international
- 424 degree-seeking graduate students
- 55% of applicants admitted
- SAT or ACT with writing, application essay required
- 86% graduate within 6 years; 32% enter graduate study

**General.** Founded in 1860. Regionally accredited. **Degrees:** 581 bachelor's awarded; master's, doctoral offered. **ROTC:** Army, Air Force. **Location:** 25 miles from Chicago. **Calendar:** Semester, limited summer session. **Full-time faculty:** 194 total; 93% have terminal degrees, 9% minority, 28% women. **Part-time faculty:** 105 total; 33% have terminal degrees, 9% minority, 50% women. **Class size:** 53% < 20, 39% 20-39, 7% 40-49, 1% 50-99, less than 1% >100. **Special facilities:** Billy Graham museum, science station, Christian residential camp, collection of books and papers of 7 British authors, center for applied Christian ethics.

**Freshman class profile.** 2,160 applied, 1,192 admitted, 583 enrolled.

| Mid 50% test scores | | | |
|---|---|---|---|
| SAT critical reading: | 630-720 | GPA 2.0-2.99: | 1% |
| SAT math: | 610-700 | Rank in top quarter: | 88% |
| SAT writing: | 610-710 | Rank in top tenth: | 56% |
| ACT composite: | 27-31 | Return as sophomores: | 96% |
| GPA 3.50 or higher: | 83% | Out-of-state: | 81% |
| GPA 3.0-3.49: | 16% | Live on campus: | 100% |
| | | International: | 1% |

**Basis for selection.** Evidence of a vital Christian experience, moral character, personal integrity, social concern, academic ability, and desire for a liberal arts education as defined by the college are most important. Interview recommended. Audition required of music majors. **Homeschooled:** Statement describing homeschool structure and mission required. Applicants advised to take the ACT to satisfy the "Ability to Benefit" requirements. **Learning Disabled:** Personal interview required. Student must contact Registrar to request services or equipment and provide documentation/diagnosis of disability.

**High school preparation.** 18 units required. Required and recommended units include English 4, mathematics 4, social studies 4, science 4 and foreign language 3.

**2008-2009 Annual costs.** Tuition/fees: $25,500. Room/board: $7,618. Books/supplies: $768. Personal expenses: $1,936.

**2007-2008 Financial aid. Need-based:** 435 full-time freshmen applied for aid; 295 were judged to have need; 289 of these received aid. Average need met was 84%. Average scholarship/grant was $15,172; average loan $4,740. 68% of total undergraduate aid awarded as scholarships/grants, 32% as loans/jobs. **Non-need-based:** Awarded to 856 full-time undergraduates, including 227 freshmen. Scholarships awarded for academics, alumni affiliation, art, minority status, music/drama.

**Application procedures. Admission:** Closing date 1/10 (receipt date). $50 fee, may be waived for applicants with need. Application may be submitted online. Admission notification 4/1. Must reply by May 1 or within 3 week(s) if notified thereafter. **Financial aid:** Priority date 2/15; no closing date. FAFSA, institutional form required. Applicants notified on a rolling basis starting 3/1.

**Academics. Special study options:** Combined bachelor's/graduate degree, cross-registration, exchange student, independent study, internships, liberal arts/career combination, student-designed major, study abroad, teacher certification program, urban semester, Washington semester. **Credit/placement by examination:** AP, CLEP, IB, institutional tests. 76 credit hours maximum toward bachelor's degree. **Support services:** Study skills assistance, writing center.

**Majors. Biology:** General. **Business:** Managerial economics. **Communications:** General. **Computer sciences:** Computer science. **Conservation:** Environmental studies. **Education:** Elementary, music, secondary. **Engineering:** General. **English:** English lit. **Foreign languages:** Classics, French, German, Spanish. **Health:** Health services, nursing (RN). **History:** General. **Math:** General. **Philosophy/religion:** Philosophy. **Physical sciences:** Chemistry, geology, physics. **Psychology:** General. **Social sciences:** Anthropology, archaeology, economics, international relations, political science, sociology. **Theology:** Bible, religious ed. **Visual/performing arts:** Art, music history, music performance, music theory/composition.

**Most popular majors.** Business/marketing 8%, education 7%, English 9%, psychology 8%, social sciences 15%, theological studies 10%, visual/performing arts 7%.

**Computing on campus.** 125 workstations in dormitories, library, computer center, student center. Dormitories wired for high-speed internet access and linked to campus network. Commuter students can connect to campus network. Online library, helpline, wireless network available.

**Student life. Freshman orientation:** Mandatory. Preregistration for classes offered. Four-day program during the week before classes begin. **Policies:** All college and college-related functions are alcohol and tobacco free. Religious observance required. **Housing:** Guaranteed on-campus for freshmen. Single-sex dorms, special housing for disabled, apartments, cooperative housing, substance-free housing available. **Activities:** Bands, campus ministries, choral groups, drama, film society, international student organizations, literary magazine, music ensembles, Model UN, musical theater, opera, radio station, student government, student newspaper, symphony orchestra, TV station, Christian Service Council, Student Missionary Project, Youth Hostel Ministries, World Christian Fellowship, Students for Biblical Equality, Amnesty International, Earthkeepers, Jonathan Blanchard Society, Unidad Christiana, Koinonia.

**Athletics.** NCAA. **Intercollegiate:** Baseball M, basketball, cross-country, football (tackle) M, golf, soccer, softball W, swimming, tennis, track and field, volleyball W, water polo W, wrestling M. **Intramural:** Badminton, basketball, bowling, football (non-tackle) M, soccer, softball M, tennis, volleyball, water polo. **Team name:** Thunder.

**Student services.** Career counseling, student employment services, financial aid counseling, health services, minority student services, personal counseling, placement for graduates, veterans' counselor. **Physically disabled:** Services for visually, speech, hearing impaired.

**Contact.** E-mail: admissions@wheaton.edu
Phone: (630) 752-5005 Toll-free number: (800) 222-2419
Fax: (630) 752-5285
Shawn Leftwich, Director of Undergraduate Admissions, Wheaton College,
501 College Avenue, Wheaton, IL 60187-5593

# Indiana

## American Conservatory of Music

Hammond, Indiana
www.americanconservatory.edu          CB code: 1014

- Private 4-year music and seminary college affiliated with Orthodox Church
- Commuter campus in very large city

**General.** Founded in 1886. **Location:** 25 miles from downtown. **Calendar:** Semester.

**Annual costs/financial aid.** Annual full-time cost ranges from $10,000-$18,000 depending on teacher. Books/supplies: $500. Personal expenses: $1,200.

**Contact.** Phone: (219) 931-6000
Admissions Director, 252 Wildwood Road, Hammond, IN 46324

## Anderson University

Anderson, Indiana                    CB member
www.anderson.edu                     CB code: 1016

- Private 4-year liberal arts college affiliated with Church of God
- Residential campus in small city
- 2,131 degree-seeking undergraduates: 9% part-time, 56% women, 6% African American, 1% Asian American, 1% Hispanic American, 2% international
- 559 degree-seeking graduate students
- 67% of applicants admitted
- SAT or ACT with writing required
- 54% graduate within 6 years; 17% enter graduate study

**General.** Founded in 1917. Regionally accredited. **Degrees:** 439 bachelor's, 2 associate awarded; master's, doctoral, first professional offered. **Location:** 45 miles from Indianapolis. **Calendar:** Semester, limited summer session. **Full-time faculty:** 143 total; 66% have terminal degrees, 4% minority, 45% women. **Part-time faculty:** 182 total; 12% have terminal degrees, 9% minority, 46% women. **Class size:** 60% < 20, 33% 20-39, 5% 40-49, 2% 50-99, less than 1% >100. **Special facilities:** Religious art collection, museum of Bible and Near Eastern studies, glass studio, wellness center.

**Freshman class profile.** 2,081 applied, 1,393 admitted, 486 enrolled.

| Mid 50% test scores | | Rank in top quarter: | 45% |
|---|---|---|---|
| SAT critical reading: | 450-570 | Rank in top tenth: | 20% |
| SAT math: | 450-580 | End year in good standing: | 83% |
| ACT composite: | 20-26 | Return as sophomores: | 73% |
| GPA 3.50 or higher: | 40% | Out-of-state: | 33% |
| GPA 3.0-3.49: | 28% | Live on campus: | 91% |
| GPA 2.0-2.99: | 30% | International: | 1% |

**Basis for selection.** GED not accepted. Rank in top half of class, test scores, reference important. School, church, and community activities also considered. Additional requirements for entry into nursing, athletic training, and educational programs. Essay recommended. Interview required of academically weak applicants. Audition required of music majors. Portfolio recommended for art majors. **Homeschooled:** Interview may be required.

**High school preparation.** 17 units required; 30 recommended. Required and recommended units include English 4, mathematics 3-4, social studies 1-2, history 1-2, science 3-4 (laboratory 3-4), foreign language 2-3, computer science 1, visual/performing arts 1 and academic electives 5.

**2007-2008 Annual costs.** Tuition/fees: $20,976. Room/board: $6,770. Books/supplies: $950. Personal expenses: $1,500.

**Financial aid. Non-need-based:** Scholarships awarded for academics, leadership, minority status, music/drama, state residency.

**Application procedures. Admission:** Priority date 1/15; deadline 7/1. $25 fee, may be waived for applicants with need. Application may be submitted online. Admission notification on a rolling basis beginning on or about 9/1. Must reply by May 1 or within 2 week(s) if notified thereafter. **Financial aid:** Priority date 3/1; no closing date. FAFSA required. Applicants notified on a rolling basis starting 3/1.

**Academics. Special study options:** Accelerated study, combined bachelor's/graduate degree, cross-registration, double major, honors, independent study, internships, student-designed major, study abroad, teacher certification program, urban semester. **Credit/placement by examination:** AP, CLEP, IB, SAT, ACT, institutional tests. 30 credit hours maximum toward bachelor's degree. **Support services:** Learning center, pre-admission summer program, reduced course load, tutoring.

**Majors. Biology:** General, biochemistry. **Business:** Accounting, business admin, finance, managerial economics, marketing, organizational behavior. **Communications:** Media studies. **Computer sciences:** Computer science, information systems. **Education:** General, art, biology, chemistry, drama/dance, elementary, English, French, mathematics, music, physical, physics, social studies, Spanish. **English:** English lit. **Family/consumer sciences:** Family systems. **Foreign languages:** French, Spanish. **Health:** Athletic training, nursing (RN). **History:** General. **Interdisciplinary:** Math/computer science. **Legal studies:** Prelaw. **Math:** General. **Parks/recreation:** Exercise sciences. **Philosophy/religion:** Philosophy, religion. **Physical sciences:** Chemistry, physics. **Protective services:** Criminal justice. **Psychology:** General. **Public administration:** Social work. **Social sciences:** Political science, sociology. **Theology:** Bible, sacred music, theology. **Visual/performing arts:** Design, dramatic, music management, music performance, studio arts, voice/opera.

**Most popular majors.** Business/marketing 23%, education 16%, health sciences 9%, visual/performing arts 7%.

**Computing on campus.** 225 workstations in dormitories, library, computer center, student center. Dormitories linked to campus network. Commuter students can connect to campus network. Wireless network available.

**Student life. Freshman orientation:** Mandatory. Preregistration for classes offered. **Policies:** Religious observance required. **Housing:** Coed dorms, single-sex dorms, apartments, substance-free housing available. $100 non-refundable deposit, deadline 5/1. **Activities:** Bands, campus ministries, choral groups, dance, drama, international student organizations, literary magazine, music ensembles, Model UN, musical theater, opera, radio station, student government, student newspaper, symphony orchestra, multicultural student union, Religious Life Council, business club, women's clubs, men's clubs, international student association.

**Athletics.** NCAA. **Intercollegiate:** Baseball M, basketball, cross-country, football (tackle) M, golf, soccer, softball W, tennis, track and field, volleyball W. **Intramural:** Basketball, rugby M, softball, swimming, tennis, volleyball. **Team name:** Ravens.

**Student services.** Adult student services, campus ministries, career counseling, student employment services, health services, minority student services, personal counseling, placement for graduates, veterans' counselor. **Physically disabled:** Services for visually, speech impaired.

**Contact.** E-mail: info@anderson.edu
Phone: (765) 641-4080 Toll-free number: (800) 428-6414
Fax: (765) 641-4091
Jim King, Director of Admissions, Anderson University, 1100 East Fifth Street, Anderson, IN 46012-3495

## Ball State University

Muncie, Indiana                      CB member
www.bsu.edu                          CB code: 1051

- Public 4-year university
- Residential campus in small city
- 16,422 degree-seeking undergraduates: 6% part-time, 52% women, 7% African American, 1% Asian American, 2% Hispanic American
- 2,836 degree-seeking graduate students
- 72% of applicants admitted
- 57% graduate within 6 years

**General.** Founded in 1918. Regionally accredited. **Degrees:** 3,576 bachelor's, 392 associate awarded; master's, doctoral offered. **ROTC:** Army. **Location:** 56 miles from Indianapolis. **Calendar:** Semester, extensive summer session. **Full-time faculty:** 917 total; 76% have terminal degrees, 12% minority, 42% women. **Part-time faculty:** 249 total; 22% have terminal degrees, 5% minority, 51% women. **Class size:** 36% < 20, 47% 20-39, 7% 40-49, 6% 50-99, 3% >100. **Special facilities:** Planetarium, nature preserves, wellness institute, art museum, media design center.

**Freshman class profile.** 13,198 applied, 9,502 admitted, 3,773 enrolled.

| Mid 50% test scores | | | |
|---|---|---|---|
| SAT critical reading: | 470-570 | Rank in top tenth: | 15% |
| SAT math: | 470-580 | Return as sophomores: | 77% |
| SAT writing: | 460-560 | Out-of-state: | 9% |
| ACT composite: | 19-24 | Live on campus: | 89% |
| Rank in top quarter: | 43% | Fraternities: | 9% |
| | | Sororities: | 9% |

**Basis for selection.** Curriculum, GPA, test scores most important; academic index calculated by BSU admissions. Credentials of non-traditional students (age 23 or older) evaluated for admission on individual basis. Personal statement required of all non-traditional students. Test for placement required for transfers and non-traditional freshmen. Interview and essay recommended; audition required of music and theater majors; portfolio recommended for art and architecture majors.

**High school preparation.** Required and recommended units include English 4, mathematics 3, social studies 3, science 3 (laboratory 2) and foreign language 3.

**2007-2008 Annual costs.** Tuition/fees: $7,148; $18,216 out-of-state. Room/board: $7,240. Books/supplies: $930. Personal expenses: $1,500.

**2007-2008 Financial aid.** Need-based: 3,172 full-time freshmen applied for aid; 2,271 were judged to have need; 2,252 of these received aid. Average net met was 66%. Average scholarship/grant was $5,646; average loan $3,584. 52% of total undergraduate aid awarded as scholarships/grants, 48% as loans/jobs. Non-need-based: Awarded to 5,708 full-time undergraduates, including 1,855 freshmen. Scholarships awarded for academics, athletics, leadership, minority status, music/drama, ROTC, state residency.

**Application procedures.** Admission: Priority date 3/1; deadline 8/15. $25 fee, may be waived for applicants with need. Application may be submitted online. Admission notification on a rolling basis. Must reply by May 1 or within 2 week(s) if notified thereafter. Financial aid: Priority date 3/10; no closing date. FAFSA required. Applicants notified on a rolling basis starting 4/1.

**Academics.** Minimum credit hours in major for associate degree range from 30 to 45; for bachelor's, 45 to 65. All undergraduates must meet writing competency requirement. Special study options: Accelerated study, combined bachelor's/graduate degree, cooperative education, distance learning, double major, dual enrollment of high school students, ESL, exchange student, honors, independent study, internships, liberal arts/career combination, student-designed major, study abroad, teacher certification program, Washington semester, weekend college. Credit/placement by examination: AP, CLEP, IB, SAT, ACT, institutional tests. 15 credit hours maximum toward associate degree, 63 toward bachelor's. Support services: Learning center, pre-admission summer program, reduced course load, study skills assistance, tutoring, writing center.

**Honors college/program.** Separate curriculum, undergraduate research fellowships and study abroad programs; 310 freshmen students were admitted in Fall 2007.

**Majors. Architecture:** Architecture, environmental design, landscape, urban/community planning. **Area/ethnic studies:** Women's. **Biology:** General. **Business:** General, accounting, actuarial science, business admin, entrepreneurial studies, finance, human resources, management information systems, managerial economics, marketing, office management, operations. **Communications:** Journalism, radio/tv. **Computer sciences:** General. **Conservation:** General. **Education:** Business, elementary, health, kindergarten/preschool, multiple handicapped, physical, science, technology/industrial arts. **Engineering:** General. **Engineering technology:** Industrial. **English:** English lit, speech/rhetoric. **Family/consumer sciences:** General. **Foreign languages:** Classics, French, German, Japanese, Latin, Spanish. **Health:** Audiology/speech pathology, clinical lab science, dietetics, nursing (RN), predental, premedicine, respiratory therapy technology. **History:** General. **Liberal arts:** Arts/sciences. **Math:** General. **Philosophy/religion:** Philosophy, religion. **Physical sciences:** Chemistry, geology, physics. **Protective services:** Criminal justice. **Psychology:** General. **Public administration:** Social work. **Social sciences:** General, anthropology, economics, geography, political science, sociology, urban studies. **Visual/performing arts:** Art, dance, dramatic. **Other:** Graphic arts management, Vocation, family, and consumer science.

**Most popular majors.** Business/marketing 14%, communications/journalism 11%, education 15%, health sciences 6%, liberal arts 11%.

**Computing on campus.** 1,450 workstations in dormitories, library, computer center, student center. Dormitories wired for high-speed internet access and linked to campus network. Commuter students can connect to campus network. Online library, helpline, repair service, student web hosting, wireless network available.

**Student life. Freshman orientation:** Mandatory. Preregistration for classes offered. 2-day program. **Housing:** Guaranteed on-campus for freshmen. Coed dorms, single-sex dorms, special housing for disabled, apartments, substance-free housing available. $125 fully refundable deposit. Freshmen and sophomore transfer students required to live on campus unless living with parents or guardian, or 21 years of age or older. **Activities:** Bands, campus ministries, choral groups, dance, drama, film society, international student organizations, literary magazine, music ensembles, musical theater, radio station, student government, student newspaper, symphony orchestra, TV station, over 300 student organizations.

**Athletics.** NCAA. **Intercollegiate:** Baseball M, basketball, cheerleading, cross-country, diving, equestrian, field hockey W, football (tackle) M, golf, gymnastics W, soccer W, softball W, swimming, tennis, track and field, volleyball. **Intramural:** Badminton, baseball M, basketball, bowling, football (non-tackle), golf, lacrosse, racquetball, rugby, soccer, softball, swimming, table tennis, tennis, track and field, volleyball. **Team name:** Cardinals.

**Student services.** Adult student services, alcohol/substance abuse counseling, career counseling, student employment services, financial aid counseling, health services, legal services, minority student services, on-campus daycare, personal counseling, placement for graduates, veterans' counselor, women's services. **Physically disabled:** Services for visually, speech, hearing impaired.

**Contact.** E-mail: askus@bsu.edu
Phone: (765) 285-8300 Toll-free number: (800) 482-4278
Fax: (765) 285-1632
Tom Taylor, Vice President of Enrollment, Marketing and Communications, Ball State University, 2000 University Avenue, Muncie, IN 47306-1022

## Bethel College
**Mishawaka, Indiana**
**www.bethelcollege.edu** — CB code: 1079

- Private 4-year liberal arts college affiliated with Missionary Church
- Commuter campus in large town
- 2,099 degree-seeking undergraduates: 45% part-time, 34% women, 12% African American, 1% Asian American, 3% Hispanic American, 1% Native American, 2% international
- 193 degree-seeking graduate students
- 86% of applicants admitted
- SAT or ACT (ACT writing optional) required
- 64% graduate within 6 years

**General.** Founded in 1947. Regionally accredited. **Degrees:** 380 bachelor's, 22 associate awarded; master's offered. **ROTC:** Army, Naval, Air Force. **Location:** 140 miles from Indianapolis, 90 miles from Chicago. **Calendar:** Semester, limited summer session. **Full-time faculty:** 94 total; 7% minority, 44% women. **Part-time faculty:** 104 total; 10% minority, 55% women. **Class size:** 75% < 20, 22% 20-39, 2% 40-49, 1% 50-99.

**Freshman class profile.** 657 applied, 565 admitted, 280 enrolled.

| Mid 50% test scores | | | |
|---|---|---|---|
| SAT critical reading: | 430-570 | GPA 2.0-2.99: | 32% |
| SAT math: | 430-570 | Rank in top quarter: | 56% |
| SAT writing: | 420-570 | Rank in top tenth: | 30% |
| ACT composite: | 18-26 | Return as sophomores: | 76% |
| GPA 3.50 or higher: | 41% | Out-of-state: | 32% |
| GPA 3.0-3.49: | 26% | Live on campus: | 75% |
| | | International: | 2% |

**Basis for selection.** School achievement record, test scores, character recommendations, personal statement important. Interview recommended. Audition required of music majors and scholarship candidates. Portfolio recommended for returning adults, fine arts majors.

**High school preparation.** 17 units recommended. Recommended units include English 4, mathematics 3, social studies 1, history 2, science 1 (laboratory 1); foreign language 2 and academic electives 3.

**2007-2008 Annual costs.** Tuition/fees: $18,006. All first-time, full-time students must pay a one-time fee of $600. Room/board: $5,630. Books/supplies: $600. Personal expenses: $700.

**2007-2008 Financial aid.** Need-based: 200 full-time freshmen applied for aid; 179 were judged to have need; 179 of these received aid. Average need met was 41%. Average scholarship/grant was $7,770; average loan $3,360. 43% of total undergraduate aid awarded as scholarships/grants, 57% as loans/jobs. Non-need-based: Awarded to 1,057 full-time undergraduates, including 245 freshmen. Scholarships awarded for academics, art, athletics, job skills, leadership, minority status, music/drama, religious affiliation, ROTC, state residency.

**Application procedures. Admission:** Priority date 12/1; deadline 8/15 (receipt date). $25 fee, may be waived for applicants with need. Application may be submitted online. Admission notification on a rolling basis beginning on or about 10/1. Must reply by 5/1. **Financial aid:** Priority date 3/1; no closing date. FAFSA required. Applicants notified by 4/15; must reply within 3 week(s) of notification.

**Academics. Special study options:** Accelerated study, cross-registration, double major, ESL, exchange student, independent study, internships, student-designed major, study abroad, teacher certification program, urban semester, Washington semester. **Credit/placement by examination:** AP, CLEP, IB, SAT, ACT, institutional tests. 20 credit hours maximum toward bachelor's degree. **Support services:** Learning center, reduced course load, remedial instruction, study skills assistance, tutoring.

**Majors. Biology:** General. **Business:** Accounting, business admin, human resources. **Communications:** General. **Computer sciences:** Information systems. **Conservation:** General. **Education:** Business, elementary, English, mathematics, music, physical, science, social studies. **Engineering:** General. **English:** English lit. **Foreign languages:** Sign language interpretation. **Health:** Nursing (RN), predental, premedicine. **History:** General. **Liberal arts:** Arts/sciences. **Math:** General. **Parks/recreation:** Facilities management. **Philosophy/religion:** Philosophy, religion. **Physical sciences:** Chemistry. **Psychology:** General. **Public administration:** Human services. **Social sciences:** General, international relations, sociology. **Theology:** Bible, sacred music, theology. **Visual/performing arts:** Art, design, dramatic.

**Most popular majors.** Business/marketing 31%, education 13%, health sciences 10%, liberal arts 10%, theological studies 12%.

**Computing on campus.** 215 workstations in dormitories, library, computer center.

**Student life. Freshman orientation:** Mandatory. **Policies:** Religious observance required. **Housing:** Single-sex dorms, special housing for disabled available. $200 fully refundable deposit, deadline 5/1. **Activities:** Bands, choral groups, drama, music ensembles, musical theater, opera, radio station, student government, student newspaper, symphony orchestra, Fellowship of Christian Athletes, ministerial association, interest clubs.

**Athletics.** NAIA, NCCAA. **Intercollegiate:** Baseball M, basketball, cross-country, golf M, soccer M, softball W, tennis, track and field, volleyball W. **Intramural:** Basketball M, football (tackle) M, soccer, table tennis, volleyball. **Team name:** Pilots.

**Student services.** Adult student services, campus ministries, career counseling, student employment services, financial aid counseling, health services, minority student services, personal counseling, placement for graduates. **Physically disabled:** Services for hearing impaired.

**Contact.** E-mail: admissions@bethelcollege.edu
Phone: (574) 257-3339 Fax: (574) 257-3335
Randy Beachy, Director of Admissions, Bethel College, 1001 West McKinley Avenue, Mishawaka, IN 46545

---

## Butler University
**Indianapolis, Indiana**
www.butler.edu

CB member
CB code: 1073

- Private 4-year university
- Residential campus in very large city
- 3,593 degree-seeking undergraduates: 1% part-time, 61% women, 3% African American, 2% Asian American, 2% Hispanic American, 3% international
- 760 degree-seeking graduate students
- 76% of applicants admitted
- SAT or ACT with writing, application essay required
- 74% graduate within 6 years; 22% enter graduate study

**General.** Founded in 1855. Regionally accredited. **Degrees:** 742 bachelor's awarded; master's, first professional offered. **ROTC:** Army, Air Force. **Location:** 5 miles from downtown. **Calendar:** Semester, limited summer session. **Full-time faculty:** 302 total; 82% have terminal degrees, 11% minority, 44% women. **Part-time faculty:** 165 total; 21% have terminal degrees, 5% minority, 44% women. **Class size:** 57% <20, 38% 20-39, 1% 40-49, 3% 50-99, less than 1% >100. **Special facilities:** Observatory, planetarium, herbarium, performing arts auditorium, canal, nature preserve.

**Freshman class profile.** 5,265 applied, 3,987 admitted, 988 enrolled.

| Mid 50% test scores | | | |
|---|---|---|---|
| SAT critical reading: | 520-630 | Rank in top quarter: | 79% |
| SAT math: | 530-650 | Rank in top tenth: | 48% |
| SAT writing: | 520-610 | End year in good standing: | 97% |
| ACT composite: | 24-29 | Return as sophomores: | 86% |
| GPA 3.50 or higher: | 71% | Out-of-state: | 43% |
| GPA 3.0-3.49: | 21% | Live on campus: | 95% |
| GPA 2.0-2.99: | 8% | International: | 3% |

**Basis for selection.** Test scores, high school record most important. Recommendations, activities considered. Audition required of dance, drama, music, and media arts majors. **Homeschooled:** Statement describing home-school structure and mission, transcript of courses and grades, letter of recommendation (nonparent) required.

**High school preparation.** College-preparatory program required. 16 units required. Required units include English 4, mathematics 3, history 2, science 3, foreign language 2 and academic electives 2. 4 mathematics units for business administration majors.

**2007-2008 Annual costs.** Tuition/fees: $26,806. Room/board: $8,960. Books/supplies: $800. Personal expenses: $1,450.

**2007-2008 Financial aid. Need-based:** 919 full-time freshmen applied for aid; 621 were judged to have need; 621 of these received aid. Average scholarship/grant was $15,733; average loan $3,976. 66% of total undergraduate aid awarded as scholarships/grants, 34% as loans/jobs. **Non-need-based:** Scholarships awarded for academics, athletics, music/drama.

**Application procedures. Admission:** Priority date 12/1; deadline 3/1 (postmark date). $35 fee, may be waived for applicants with need. Application may be submitted online. Admission notification on a rolling basis beginning on or about 12/20. Must reply by May 1 or within 2 week(s) if notified thereafter. **Financial aid:** Priority date 3/1; no closing date. FAFSA required. Applicants notified on a rolling basis starting 3/15; must reply within 3 week(s) of notification.

**Academics. Special study options:** Combined bachelor's/graduate degree, cross-registration, double major, dual enrollment of high school students, exchange student, honors, independent study, internships, student-designed major, study abroad, teacher certification program, Washington semester. Dual-degree engineering program with Purdue University; cooperative program in Business. **Credit/placement by examination:** AP, CLEP, IB, SAT, ACT, institutional tests. **Support services:** Learning center, reduced course load, study skills assistance, tutoring, writing center.

**Majors. Biology:** General. **Business:** Accounting, actuarial science, finance, international, marketing. **Communications:** General, journalism, radio/tv. **Communications technology:** Recording arts. **Computer sciences:** General, information systems. **Education:** Early childhood, elementary, kindergarten/preschool, middle, music, secondary. **Engineering:** Physics. **English:** Creative writing, English lit, speech/rhetoric. **Foreign languages:** French, German, Latin, modern Greek, Spanish. **Health:** Communication disorders, physician assistant. **History:** General. **Interdisciplinary:** Science/society. **Liberal arts:** Arts/sciences. **Math:** General. **Philosophy/religion:** Philosophy, religion. **Physical sciences:** Chemistry, physics. **Protective services:** Criminal justice. **Psychology:** General. **Social sciences:** Anthropology, criminology, economics, international relations, political science, sociology, urban studies. **Visual/performing arts:** Arts management, dance, dramatic, music management, music pedagogy, music performance, music theory/composition, piano/organ, stringed instruments, voice/opera. **Other:** Pharmacy.

**Most popular majors.** Business/marketing 15%, communications/journalism 7%, education 10%, health sciences 20%, social sciences 8%, visual/performing arts 8%.

**Computing on campus.** 430 workstations in dormitories, library, computer center, student center. Dormitories wired for high-speed internet access and linked to campus network. Commuter students can connect to campus network. Online course registration, helpline, wireless network available.

**Student life. Freshman orientation:** Mandatory, $100 fee. Preregistration for classes offered. 3-day program held in August. Early registration for Fall classes held March through June. **Housing:** Guaranteed on-campus for all undergraduates. Coed dorms, single-sex dorms, apartments, fraternity/sorority housing, substance-free housing available. $100 fully refundable deposit, deadline 5/1. Service learning housing for women. **Activities:** Bands, choral groups, dance, drama, literary magazine, music ensembles, opera, student government, student newspaper, symphony orchestra, TV station, volunteer center, Black Student Union, Campus Crusade for Christ, YMCA, College Republicans, Mortar Board, academic honoraries, Alpha Phi Omega.

**Athletics.** NCAA. **Intercollegiate:** Baseball M, basketball, cross-country, football (tackle) M, golf, soccer, softball W, swimming W, tennis, track and field, volleyball W. **Intramural:** Badminton, baseball M, basketball, bowling, football (tackle) M, golf, soccer, softball, swimming, table tennis, tennis, track and field, volleyball, weight lifting. **Team name:** Bulldogs.

**Student services.** Alcohol/substance abuse counseling, career counseling, student employment services, financial aid counseling, health services, minority student services, on-campus daycare, personal counseling, placement for graduates. **Physically disabled:** Services for visually, speech impaired.

**Contact.**  E-mail: admission@butler.edu
Phone: (317) 940-8100 Toll-free number: (888) 940-8100
Fax: (317) 940-8150
Scott McIntyre, Director of Admissions, Butler University, 4600 Sunset Avenue, Indianapolis, IN 46208

---

## Calumet College of St. Joseph
### Whiting, Indiana
**www.ccsj.edu**  **CB code: 1776**

- Private 4-year liberal arts college affiliated with Roman Catholic Church
- Commuter campus in small city
- 1,025 degree-seeking undergraduates: 57% part-time, 54% women
- 178 degree-seeking graduate students
- 47% of applicants admitted
- Application essay required

**General.** Founded in 1951. Regionally accredited. **Degrees:** 311 bachelor's, 15 associate awarded; master's offered. **Location:** 20 miles from Chicago. **Calendar:** Semester, limited summer session. **Full-time faculty:** 29 total; 69% have terminal degrees, 14% minority, 31% women. **Part-time faculty:** 3 total; 33% have terminal degrees, 33% women. **Class size:** 70% < 20, 22% 20-39, 8% 40-49.

**Freshman class profile.** 291 applied, 138 admitted, 96 enrolled.

| | | | |
|---|---|---|---|
| GPA 3.50 or higher: | 10% | Rank in top quarter: | 25% |
| GPA 3.0-3.49: | 20% | Rank in top tenth: | 8% |
| GPA 2.0-2.99: | 50% | | |

**Basis for selection.** High school record most important. ACT/COMPASS Assessment Test required for all applicants, top half of class, minimum 2.0 GPA. For placement testing, we use the Compass testing through ACT to place our students in their courses. We also have students write an essay to place them in their English courses as part of the placement exam. SAT or ACT recommended. Interview recommended. **Homeschooled:** State high school equivalency certificate required.

**High school preparation.** 15 units recommended. Recommended units include English 4, mathematics 3, social studies 3, science 2 (laboratory 1) and foreign language 1.

**2007-2008 Annual costs.** Tuition/fees: $11,650. Books/supplies: $1,500. Personal expenses: $1,080.

**2006-2007 Financial aid. Need-based:** 87 full-time freshmen applied for aid; 69 were judged to have need; 69 of these received aid. Average need met was 76%. Average scholarship/grant was $9,625; average loan $2,334. 48% of total undergraduate aid awarded as scholarships/grants, 52% as loans/jobs. **Non-need-based:** Awarded to 541 full-time undergraduates, including 126 freshmen. Scholarships awarded for academics, alumni affiliation, religious affiliation. **Additional information:** Immediate computerized estimate of financial aid eligibility available to students applying in person.

**Application procedures. Admission:** No deadline. No application fee. Application may be submitted online. Admission notification on a rolling basis. **Financial aid:** Priority date 3/1; no closing date. FAFSA required. Applicants notified on a rolling basis; must reply within 2 week(s) of notification.

**Academics. Special study options:** Accelerated study, cooperative education, double major, dual enrollment of high school students, ESL, honors, independent study, internships, liberal arts/career combination, student-designed major, teacher certification program, weekend college. **Credit/placement by examination:** AP, CLEP, institutional tests. 30 credit hours maximum toward associate degree, 60 toward bachelor's. **Support services:** Learning center, reduced course load, remedial instruction, study skills assistance, tutoring, writing center.

**Majors. Business:** General, accounting, business admin, organizational behavior. **Communications:** General, media studies. **Computer sciences:** General. **Education:** General, elementary, science, secondary. **English:** English

lit. **Health:** Health care admin. **Legal studies:** Paralegal. **Liberal arts:** Arts/sciences. **Philosophy/religion:** Religion. **Protective services:** Police science. **Psychology:** General. **Public administration:** Human services. **Social sciences:** General. **Visual/performing arts:** Studio arts.

**Computing on campus.** 72 workstations in library, computer center. Online library, wireless network available.

**Student life. Freshman orientation:** Mandatory. Preregistration for classes offered. Held one week before classes begin, followed up by mentoring program. **Activities:** Choral groups, dance, drama, literary magazine, student government, student newspaper, Los Amigos, Black student organization, criminal justice club, media and fine arts club, creative writing club, paralegal studies club, booster club, human services club, educators club.

**Athletics.** NAIA. **Intercollegiate:** Baseball M, basketball, bowling, cross-country, golf, soccer, softball W, tennis, volleyball. **Team name:** Crimson Wave.

**Student services.** Campus ministries, career counseling, student employment services, financial aid counseling, on-campus daycare, personal counseling, placement for graduates, veterans' counselor.

**Contact.**  E-mail: admissions@ccsj.edu
Phone: (219) 473-4215 Toll-free number: (877) 700-9100
Fax: (219) 473-4259
Chuck Walz, Director of Admissions/Financial Aid, Calumet College of St. Joseph, 2400 New York Avenue, Whiting, IN 46394-2195

---

## DePauw University
### Greencastle, Indiana
**www.depauw.edu**  **CB member**  **CB code: 1166**

- Private 4-year music and liberal arts college affiliated with United Methodist Church
- Residential campus in small town
- 2,350 degree-seeking undergraduates: 56% women, 6% African American, 3% Asian American, 3% Hispanic American, 2% international
- 69% of applicants admitted
- SAT or ACT with writing, application essay required
- 82% graduate within 6 years

**General.** Founded in 1837. Regionally accredited. **Degrees:** 496 bachelor's awarded. **ROTC:** Army, Air Force. **Location:** 45 miles from Indianapolis. **Calendar:** 4-1-4. **Full-time faculty:** 231 total; 17% minority, 42% women. **Part-time faculty:** 57 total; 9% minority, 42% women. **Class size:** 67% < 20, 33% 20-39. **Special facilities:** Nature park and arboretum, ethnographic museums, closed circuit tv studio facilities, music instructional technology studio, digital media laboratory, visual resources library with digital image collection, digital video studio, observatory, two theaters, two music concert halls, concert pipe organ.

**Freshman class profile.** 3,624 applied, 2,505 admitted, 664 enrolled.

| Mid 50% test scores | | | |
|---|---|---|---|
| SAT critical reading: | 560-660 | GPA 2.0-2.99: | 4% |
| SAT math: | 570-660 | Rank in top quarter: | 83% |
| SAT writing: | 550-650 | Rank in top tenth: | 50% |
| ACT composite: | 25-29 | Return as sophomores: | 87% |
| GPA 3.50 or higher: | 66% | Out-of-state: | 56% |
| GPA 3.0-3.49: | 30% | Live on campus: | 100% |
| | | International: | 5% |

**Basis for selection.** Academic achievement and preparation, demonstrated verbal and quantitative skills, evidence of continuing commitment to learning most important. TOEFL recommended for international students. Interview strongly recommended. Audition required for school of music candidates. **Homeschooled:** Transcript of courses and grades, interview required.

**High school preparation.** 32 units recommended. Recommended units include English 4, mathematics 4, social studies 3, history 3, science 4 (laboratory 2), foreign language 3 and academic electives 10.

**2008-2009 Annual costs.** Tuition/fees: $31,825. Room/board: $8,400. Books/supplies: $700. Personal expenses: $1,000.

**Financial aid. Non-need-based:** Scholarships awarded for academics, alumni affiliation, leadership, minority status, music/drama, ROTC.

**Application procedures. Admission:** Closing date 2/1 (postmark date). $40 fee, may be waived for applicants with need. Application may be submitted online. Admission notification 4/1. Must reply by 5/1. **Financial aid:**

Priority date 2/15; no closing date. FAFSA, institutional form required. Applicants notified by 3/27; must reply by 5/1.

**Academics.** Demonstrated competence in writing, quantitative reasoning, and oral communication required of all students. Seminar, thesis, project, or comprehensive examination in major also required. More than 700 students participate in off-campus winter term programs; 40% study off-campus. **Special study options:** Combined bachelor's/graduate degree, double major, dual enrollment of high school students, exchange student, honors, independent study, internships, New York semester, student-designed major, study abroad, teacher certification program, urban semester, Washington semester. **Credit/placement by examination:** AP, CLEP, IB, SAT, ACT, institutional tests. 32 credit hours maximum toward bachelor's degree. **Support services:** Learning center, study skills assistance, tutoring, writing center.

**Majors. Area/ethnic studies:** African-American, East Asian, Russian/ Slavic, women's. **Biology:** General, biochemistry. **Communications:** Media studies. **Computer sciences:** Computer science. **Conservation:** Environmental science. **Education:** Elementary, music, physical. **English:** Composition, English lit. **Foreign languages:** Ancient Greek, classics, French, German, Latin, Romance, Spanish. **Health:** Athletic training. **History:** General. **Interdisciplinary:** Peace/conflict. **Math:** General. **Parks/recreation:** Exercise sciences. **Philosophy/religion:** Philosophy, religion. **Physical sciences:** Chemistry, geology, physics. **Psychology:** General. **Social sciences:** Anthropology, economics, political science, sociology. **Visual/performing arts:** Art history/conservation, dramatic, film/cinema, music management, music performance, music theory/composition, studio arts.

**Most popular majors.** Biology 12%, communications/journalism 9%, English 10%, foreign language 9%, social sciences 22%, visual/performing arts 6%.

**Computing on campus.** PC or laptop required. 413 workstations in dormitories, library, computer center, student center. Dormitories wired for high-speed internet access and linked to campus network. Commuter students can connect to campus network. Online course registration, online library, helpline, repair service, student web hosting, wireless network available.

**Student life. Freshman orientation:** Mandatory. Preregistration for classes offered. 4-day program in August. **Housing:** Guaranteed on-campus for all undergraduates. Coed dorms, apartments, fraternity/sorority housing, substance-free housing available. $400 nonrefundable deposit, deadline 5/1. **Activities:** Bands, choral groups, dance, drama, film society, literary magazine, music ensembles, musical theater, opera, radio station, student government, student newspaper, symphony orchestra, TV station, Association of African American Students, international students association, Union Board, Coalition for Women's Concerns, College Republicans, College Democrats, Habitat for Humanity, JC Christian Fellowship, United DePauw, Committee for Latino Concerns.

**Athletics.** NCAA. **Intercollegiate:** Baseball M, basketball, cross-country, diving, field hockey W, football (tackle) M, golf, soccer, softball W, swimming, tennis, track and field, volleyball W. **Intramural:** Badminton, basketball, bowling, football (non-tackle), golf M, racquetball, soccer, softball, table tennis, tennis, volleyball. **Team name:** Tigers.

**Student services.** Alcohol/substance abuse counseling, campus ministries, career counseling, student employment services, financial aid counseling, health services, minority student services, on-campus daycare, personal counseling, placement for graduates, women's services. **Physically disabled:** Services for visually, hearing impaired.

**Contact.** E-mail: admission@depauw.edu
Phone: (765) 658-4006 Toll-free number: (800) 447-2495
Fax: (765) 658-4007
Stefanie Niles, Vice President for Admission and Financial Aid, DePauw University, 101 East Seminary Street, Greencastle, IN 46135-1611

## DeVry University: Indianapolis
**Indianapolis, Indiana**
**www.devry.edu**

- For-profit 4-year university
- Commuter campus in very large city
- 185 degree-seeking undergraduates: 74% part-time, 56% women, 39% African American, 2% Asian American, 2% Hispanic American, 1% Native American, 1% international
- 105 degree-seeking graduate students

**General. Degrees:** 15 bachelor's awarded; master's offered. **Calendar:** Semester. **Part-time faculty:** 11 total; 82% minority, 46% women.

**Freshman class profile.** 27 enrolled.

**Basis for selection.** Interview and GPA important; standardized test scores considered.

**2007-2008 Annual costs.** Tuition/fees: $13,020. Books/supplies: $1,300. Personal expenses: $5,082.

**Financial aid. Non-need-based:** Scholarships awarded for academics.

**Application procedures. Admission:** No deadline. $50 fee. Admission notification on a rolling basis. **Financial aid:** No deadline. FAFSA required.

**Academics. Special study options:** Accelerated study, distance learning. **Credit/placement by examination:** CLEP.

**Majors. Business:** Business admin. **Computer sciences:** Security.

**Most popular majors.** Business/marketing 93%, computer/information sciences 7%.

**Student life. Housing:** Private apartments, student-plan housing, private rooms.

**Contact.** Phone: (866) 513-3879
DeVry University: Indianapolis, 9100 Keystone Crossing, Suite 350, Indianapolis, IN 46240

## Earlham College
**Richmond, Indiana**              **CB member**
**www.earlham.edu**               **CB code: 1195**

- Private 4-year liberal arts and seminary college affiliated with Society of Friends (Quaker)
- Residential campus in large town
- 1,156 degree-seeking undergraduates: 1% part-time, 55% women, 6% African American, 2% Asian American, 3% Hispanic American, 10% international
- 141 degree-seeking graduate students
- 69% of applicants admitted
- SAT or ACT with writing, application essay required
- 75% graduate within 6 years; 15% enter graduate study

**General.** Founded in 1847. Regionally accredited; also accredited by ATS. **Degrees:** 282 bachelor's awarded; master's, first professional offered. **Location:** 70 miles from Indianapolis, 45 miles from Dayton, Ohio. **Calendar:** Semester. **Full-time faculty:** 97 total; 96% have terminal degrees, 23% minority, 45% women. **Part-time faculty:** 7 total; 43% have terminal degrees, 29% women. **Class size:** 69% < 20, 26% 20-39, 3% 40-49, 3% 50-99. **Special facilities:** Natural history museum, observatory, planetarium, herbarium, working farm, biological field stations.

**Freshman class profile.** 1,748 applied, 1,204 admitted, 301 enrolled.

| Mid 50% test scores | | | |
|---|---|---|---|
| SAT critical reading: | 570-690 | Rank in top quarter: | 62% |
| SAT math: | 550-650 | Rank in top tenth: | 31% |
| ACT composite: | 24-29 | End year in good standing: | 87% |
| GPA 3.50 or higher: | 50% | Return as sophomores: | 84% |
| GPA 3.0-3.49: | 38% | Out-of-state: | 81% |
| GPA 2.0-2.99: | 12% | Live on campus: | 98% |
| | | International: | 10% |

**Basis for selection.** Combination of GPA, quality of high school program, SAT or ACT scores, recommendations, essay, and extracurricular activities important. Interview preferred. **Homeschooled:** Statement describing homeschool structure and mission, interview, letter of recommendation (nonparent) required. Portfolio or other evidence of learning, test scores, and essay.

**High school preparation.** 15 units required; 20 recommended. Required and recommended units include English 4, mathematics 3-4, social studies 2-3, history 1, science 3-4 (laboratory 2), foreign language 2-4 and visual/performing arts 1.

**2008-2009 Annual costs.** Tuition/fees: $34,030. Room/board: $6,814. Books/supplies: $850. Personal expenses: $1,000.

**2006-2007 Financial aid. Need-based:** 214 full-time freshmen applied for aid; 189 were judged to have need; 187 of these received aid. Average need met was 95%. Average scholarship/grant was $15,897; average loan $3,733. 76% of total undergraduate aid awarded as scholarships/grants, 24% as loans/jobs. **Non-need-based:** Awarded to 644 full-time undergraduates, including 165 freshmen. Scholarships awarded for academics, minority status, religious affiliation.

**Application procedures. Admission:** Closing date 2/15 (postmark date). $30 fee, may be waived for applicants with need. Application may be submitted online. Admission notification 3/15. Must reply by May 1 or within 2 week(s) if notified thereafter. **Financial aid:** Closing date 3/1. FAFSA, institutional form required. Applicants notified on a rolling basis starting 2/15; must reply by 5/1.

**Academics. Special study options:** Accelerated study, cross-registration, double major, ESL, independent study, internships, New York semester, student-designed major, study abroad, urban semester. Teacher certification at Master's level only. **Credit/placement by examination:** AP, CLEP, IB, institutional tests. 18 credit hours maximum toward bachelor's degree. **Support services:** Learning center, pre-admission summer program, study skills assistance, tutoring, writing center.

**Majors. Area/ethnic studies:** African-American, Japanese, Latin American, women's. **Biology:** General, biochemistry. **Business:** Business admin. **Computer sciences:** General. **Conservation:** Environmental studies. **English:** English lit. **Foreign languages:** Classics, comparative lit, French, German, Spanish. **Health:** Premedicine. **History:** General. **Interdisciplinary:** Peace/conflict. **Math:** General. **Philosophy/religion:** Philosophy, religion. **Physical sciences:** Chemistry, physics. **Psychology:** General, psychobiology. **Social sciences:** Economics, political science, sociology. **Visual/performing arts:** Art, dramatic. **Other:** Geosciences, International Studies.

**Most popular majors.** Area/ethnic studies 8%, biology 10%, foreign language 8%, interdisciplinary studies 14%, physical sciences 6%, psychology 8%, social sciences 14%, visual/performing arts 11%.

**Computing on campus.** 164 workstations in library, computer center. Dormitories wired for high-speed internet access and linked to campus network. Commuter students can connect to campus network. Online library, helpline, repair service, student web hosting, wireless network available.

**Student life. Freshman orientation:** Mandatory. Preregistration for classes offered. 5-day program held just prior to beginning of fall semester. **Policies:** Community and academic honor codes exist. **Housing:** Guaranteed on-campus for all undergraduates. Coed dorms, special housing for disabled, apartments, cooperative housing, substance-free housing available. 27 college-owned off-campus language and special interest houses (e.g. Japan House, German House, Peace House, Living/Learning House) available to upperclassmen. Single sex halls in some co-ed dorms. **Activities:** Bands, campus ministries, choral groups, dance, drama, film society, international student organizations, literary magazine, music ensembles, Model UN, musical theater, radio station, student government, student newspaper, symphony orchestra, Fellowship of Christian Athletes, Earlham Young Friends, Jewish Students' Union, Black Leadership Action Coalition, Black Men United, Bahai Club, Sociedad de Estudiantes Latinos, Committee for Justice in Middle East, Volunteer Exchange, Action Against Rape.

**Athletics.** NCAA. **Intercollegiate:** Baseball M, basketball, cross-country, field hockey W, football (tackle) M, soccer, tennis, track and field, volleyball W. **Intramural:** Basketball, football (non-tackle) M, racquetball, soccer, triathlon. **Team name:** Quakers.

**Student services.** Campus ministries, career counseling, student employment services, financial aid counseling, health services, minority student services, on-campus daycare, personal counseling, placement for graduates, women's services. **Physically disabled:** Services for visually, speech, hearing impaired.

**Contact.** E-mail: admission@earlham.edu
Phone: (765) 983-1600 Toll-free number: (800) 327-5426
Fax: (765) 983-1560
Jeff Rickey, Dean of Admissions and Financial Aid, Earlham College, 801 National Road West, Richmond, IN 47374-4095

---

## Franklin College

| Franklin, Indiana | CB member |
|---|---|
| www.franklincollege.edu | CB code: 1228 |

- Private 4-year liberal arts college affiliated with American Baptist Churches in the USA
- Residential campus in large town
- 1,130 degree-seeking undergraduates: 10% part-time, 49% women, 3% African American, 1% Asian American, 1% Hispanic American
- 66% of applicants admitted
- SAT or ACT with writing, application essay required

**General.** Founded in 1834. Regionally accredited. **Degrees:** 219 bachelor's awarded. **ROTC:** Army. **Location:** 20 miles from Indianapolis. **Calendar:** 4-1-4, limited summer session. **Full-time faculty:** 65 total; 86% have terminal degrees, 5% minority, 38% women. **Part-time faculty:** 48 total; 19% have terminal degrees, 2% minority, 48% women. **Class size:** 66% < 20, 34% 20-39.

**Freshman class profile.** 1,517 applied, 1,008 admitted, 391 enrolled.

| Mid 50% test scores | | | |
|---|---|---|---|
| SAT critical reading: | 430-550 | GPA 2.0-2.99: | 28% |
| SAT math: | 450-530 | Rank in top quarter: | 31% |
| SAT writing: | 430-530 | Rank in top tenth: | 13% |
| ACT composite: | 18-23 | Live on campus: | 89% |
| GPA 3.50 or higher: | 40% | Fraternities: | 13% |
| GPA 3.0-3.49: | 31% | Sororities: | 26% |

**Basis for selection.** Class rank, test scores, essay and counselor recommendations important. Extracurricular activities considered. Interview recommended for all. **Homeschooled:** Transcript of courses and grades, interview, letter of recommendation (nonparent) required. Submit research paper(s), art work, community service projects, educational trip or programs, writing samples, other pertinent documents. Formal interview on campus required. **Learning Disabled:** Students with learning disabilities asked to schedule meeting with Director of Academic Support Services.

**High school preparation.** Required and recommended units include English 4, mathematics 4, social studies 3, science 2 and foreign language 2.

**2008-2009 Annual costs.** Tuition/fees (projected): $21,325. Room/board: $6,390.

**2006-2007 Financial aid.** All financial aid based on need. 271 full-time freshmen applied for aid; 238 were judged to have need; 237 of these received aid. Average need met was 84%. Average scholarship/grant was $13,576; average loan $3,519. 73% of total undergraduate aid awarded as scholarships/grants, 27% as loans/jobs.

**Application procedures. Admission:** Priority date 1/15; no deadline. $30 fee, may be waived for applicants with need. Application may be submitted online. Admission notification on a rolling basis beginning on or about 9/1. **Financial aid:** Priority date 3/1, closing date 3/1. FAFSA, institutional form required. Applicants notified by 4/1; must reply by 5/1 or within 4 week(s) of notification.

**Academics. Special study options:** Cross-registration, double major, dual enrollment of high school students, exchange student, independent study, internships, semester at sea, study abroad, teacher certification program, United Nations semester, Washington semester. **Credit/placement by examination:** AP, CLEP, SAT, ACT, institutional tests. 30 credit hours maximum toward bachelor's degree. **Support services:** Learning center, remedial instruction, study skills assistance, tutoring, writing center.

**Majors. Area/ethnic studies:** American, Canadian. **Biology:** General. **Business:** General, accounting. **Communications:** Journalism. **Computer sciences:** General, computer science. **Education:** Biology, chemistry, elementary, English, French, mathematics, physical, Spanish. **English:** English lit. **Foreign languages:** French, Spanish. **Health:** Athletic training. **History:** General. **Math:** General. **Parks/recreation:** General. **Philosophy/religion:** Philosophy, religion. **Physical sciences:** Chemistry. **Psychology:** General. **Social sciences:** Economics, political science, sociology. **Visual/performing arts:** Dramatic.

**Most popular majors.** Biology 11%, business/marketing 12%, communications/journalism 18%, education 18%, foreign language 6%, psychology 6%, social science 12%.

**Computing on campus.** 250 workstations in dormitories, library, student center. Dormitories wired for high-speed internet access and linked to campus network. Online course registration, online library, helpline, repair service, wireless network available.

**Student life. Freshman orientation:** Mandatory, $50 fee. Preregistration for classes offered. Orientation for all students held 4 days prior to start of classes. **Policies:** All students must live on campus until senior year unless living with family. **Housing:** Guaranteed on-campus for all undergraduates. Coed dorms, single-sex dorms, special housing for disabled, fraternity/sorority housing, substance-free housing available. $100 deposit, deadline 5/1. **Activities:** Pep band, choral groups, dance, drama, literary magazine, musical theater, radio station, student government, student newspaper, student association for the support of multiculturalism, Habitat for Humanity, college mentors for kids, Fellowship of Christian Athletes, ODK Leadership, international club.

**Athletics.** NCAA. **Intercollegiate:** Baseball M, basketball, cheerleading M, cross-country, football (tackle) M, golf, soccer, softball W, tennis, track and field, volleyball W. **Intramural:** Basketball, football (non-tackle), racquetball, softball, volleyball. **Team name:** Grizzlies.

**Student services.** Alcohol/substance abuse counseling, campus ministries, career counseling, student employment services, financial aid counseling, health services, minority student services, personal counseling, placement for graduates, veterans' counselor, women's services.

**Contact.** E-mail: admissions@franklincollege.edu
Phone: (317) 738-8062 Toll-free number: (800) 852-0232
Fax: (317) 738-8274
Jacqueline Acosta, Director of Admissions, Franklin College, 101 Branigin Boulevard, Franklin, IN 46131-2623

---

## Goshen College
### Goshen, Indiana
**www.goshen.edu**                           CB code: 1251

- Private 4-year liberal arts college affiliated with Mennonite Church
- Residential campus in large town
- 955 degree-seeking undergraduates: 8% part-time, 60% women, 3% African American, 2% Asian American, 6% Hispanic American, 6% international
- 16 degree-seeking graduate students
- 73% of applicants admitted
- SAT or ACT (ACT writing optional), application essay required
- 61% graduate within 6 years

**General.** Founded in 1894. Regionally accredited. 1150 acre environmental study facility located 30 miles from campus. **Degrees:** 236 bachelor's awarded; master's offered. **Location:** 25 miles from South Bend, 120 miles from Chicago. **Calendar:** Semester, limited summer session. **Full-time faculty:** 70 total; 63% have terminal degrees, 3% minority, 49% women. **Part-time faculty:** 43 total; 37% have terminal degrees, 12% minority, 56% women. **Class size:** 60% < 20, 35% 20-39, 2% 40-49, 4% 50-99. **Special facilities:** Concert hall, X-ray precision laboratory, electron microscope, marine biology laboratory in Florida Keys, historical library and archives, laboratory kindergarten and child care center, media production studio, nature preserve, student-run coffee shop.

**Freshman class profile.** 621 applied, 454 admitted, 202 enrolled.

| Mid 50% test scores | | Rank in top quarter: | 61% |
|---|---|---|---|
| SAT critical reading: | 510-640 | Rank in top tenth: | 31% |
| SAT math: | 500-650 | End year in good standing: | 95% |
| SAT writing: | 480-630 | Return as sophomores: | 84% |
| ACT composite: | 22-28 | Out-of-state: | 52% |
| GPA 3.50 or higher: | 56% | Live on campus: | 84% |
| GPA 3.0-3.49: | 32% | International: | 4% |
| GPA 2.0-2.99: | 12% | | |

**Basis for selection.** Admission review required for low GPA, class rank and/or test scores. Nursing and education programs require college GPA of 2.5 for entrance and continuation. Minimum score of TOEFL 550 if student does not have at least two years of high school in U.S. and English is not first language. Tests not required if out of high school five (+) years. Interview recommended. **Homeschooled:** Transcript of courses and grades required. **Learning Disabled:** Documentation of disability and special requirements dated within last 3 years required. Exit interview with high school special needs counselor, if working with one, required.

**High school preparation.** 12 units required; 16 recommended. Required and recommended units include English 4, mathematics 2-3, social studies 2, history 2, science 2-3 and foreign language 2.

**2008-2009 Annual costs.** Tuition/fees: $22,300. Room/board: $7,400. Books/supplies: $800. Personal expenses: $1,100.

**2006-2007 Financial aid. Need-based:** 206 full-time freshmen applied for aid; 160 were judged to have need; 160 of these received aid. Average need met was 84%. Average scholarship/grant was $12,612; average loan $3,832. 74% of total undergraduate aid awarded as scholarships/grants, 26% as loans/jobs. **Non-need-based:** Awarded to 640 full-time undergraduates, including 180 freshmen. Scholarships awarded for academics, art, athletics, leadership, music/drama.

**Application procedures. Admission:** Priority date 2/1; deadline 8/1 (postmark date). $25 fee, may be waived for applicants with need. Application may be submitted online. Admission notification on a rolling basis beginning on or about 9/15. Must reply by May 1 or within 2 week(s) if notified thereafter. **Financial aid:** Priority date 2/1; no closing date. FAFSA, institutional form required. Applicants notified by 3/1; must reply by 5/1 or within 2 week(s) of notification.

**Academics.** Practicum and senior seminar course required in all majors. International education through on-campus courses or study abroad required. Study abroad incorporates language study, academic and cultural learning and service. Students live in homes of country where studying for one semester. **Special study options:** Combined bachelor's/graduate degree, cross-registration, double major, dual enrollment of high school students, independent study, internships, liberal arts/career combination, student-designed major, study abroad, teacher certification program, urban semester, Washington semester. Adult degree completion program (one evening per week, concentrated study). **Credit/placement by examination:** AP, CLEP, IB, SAT, ACT, institutional tests. **Support services:** Learning center, reduced course load, remedial instruction, study skills assistance, tutoring, writing center.

**Majors. Biology:** General, molecular. **Business:** Accounting, business admin. **Computer sciences:** Computer science, information systems. **Conservation:** Environmental science. **Education:** General, art, biology, business, chemistry, elementary, English, ESL, mathematics, music, physical, physics, science, secondary, social studies, Spanish, special. **English:** English lit. **Foreign languages:** American Sign Language, sign language interpretation, Spanish. **Health:** Nursing (RN). **History:** General. **Interdisciplinary:** Peace/conflict. **Math:** General, applied. **Parks/recreation:** Health/fitness. **Physical sciences:** Chemistry, physics. **Psychology:** General. **Public administration:** Social work. **Social sciences:** Sociology. **Theology:** Sacred music, youth ministry. **Visual/performing arts:** Art, dramatic. **Other:** Bible and religion, Journalism education, Music business/technology.

**Most popular majors.** Biology 9%, business/marketing 19%, health sciences 23%, visual/performing arts 8%.

**Computing on campus.** 130 workstations in dormitories, library, computer center, student center. Dormitories wired for high-speed internet access and linked to campus network. Commuter students can connect to campus network. Online library, helpline, student web hosting, wireless network available.

**Student life. Freshman orientation:** Mandatory. Preregistration for classes offered. 1 of 3 possible days during May, June and July, plus 3 days prior to fall semester in August. **Policies:** No smoking and no drinking alcoholic beverages on campus. **Housing:** Guaranteed on-campus for all undergraduates. Coed dorms, single-sex dorms, special housing for disabled, apartments, substance-free housing available. $200 nonrefundable deposit, deadline 5/1. **Activities:** Bands, campus ministries, choral groups, drama, film society, international student organizations, music ensembles, musical theater, opera, radio station, student government, student newspaper, symphony orchestra, Black student union, Latino student union, women's association, Third Culture Support Group, Catholic student group, environmental concerns club, Peace (Pax) club, Fellowship of Christian Athletes.

**Athletics.** NAIA. **Intercollegiate:** Baseball M, basketball, cross-country, golf M, soccer, softball W, tennis, track and field, volleyball W. **Intramural:** Badminton, basketball, ice hockey M, racquetball, soccer, softball, table tennis, volleyball. **Team name:** Maple Leafs.

**Student services.** Adult student services, alcohol/substance abuse counseling, campus ministries, career counseling, student employment services, financial aid counseling, health services, minority student services, on-campus daycare, personal counseling, placement for graduates, women's services. **Physically disabled:** Services for visually, speech, hearing impaired.

**Contact.** E-mail: admission@goshen.edu
Phone: (574) 535-7535 Toll-free number: (800) 348-7422
Fax: (574) 535-7609
Lynn Jackson, Executive Director of Enrollment Services, Goshen College, 1700 South Main Street, Goshen, IN 46526

---

## Grace College
### Winona Lake, Indiana
**www.grace.edu**                           CB code: 1252

- Private 4-year liberal arts college affiliated with Brethren Church
- Residential campus in large town
- 1,146 degree-seeking undergraduates: 6% part-time, 48% women, 12% African American, 1% Asian American, 2% Hispanic American, 1% Native American, 1% international
- 177 graduate students
- 56% of applicants admitted
- SAT or ACT (ACT writing recommended) required
- 57% graduate within 6 years

**General.** Founded in 1948. Regionally accredited. **Degrees:** 210 bachelor's, 75 associate awarded; master's, doctoral, first professional offered.

**Location:** 36 miles from Fort Wayne. **Calendar:** Semester, limited summer session. **Full-time faculty:** 48 total; 67% have terminal degrees, 6% minority, 21% women. **Part-time faculty:** 91 total; 16% have terminal degrees, 4% minority, 34% women. **Class size:** 63% < 20, 31% 20-39, 3% 40-49, 4% 50-99, less than 1% >100. **Special facilities:** Creation science center, Winona history museum.

**Freshman class profile.** 1,536 applied, 865 admitted, 235 enrolled.

| Mid 50% test scores | | Rank in top quarter: | 59% |
|---|---|---|---|
| SAT critical reading: | 460-490 | Rank in top tenth: | 29% |
| SAT math: | 460-590 | Return as sophomores: | 79% |
| ACT composite: | 21-28 | Out-of-state: | 58% |
| GPA 3.50 or higher: | 60% | Live on campus: | 79% |
| GPA 3.0-3.49: | 25% | International: | 1% |
| GPA 2.0-2.99: | 15% | | |

**Basis for selection.** References, religious affiliation/commitment, high school class rank, test scores most important. Interview recommended for music and art majors. Audition recommended for music majors. Portfolio recommended for art majors. **Homeschooled:** Must take ACT or SAT.

**High school preparation.** Required and recommended units include English 3-4, mathematics 2-4, social studies 2-3, history 2-3, science 2-3 (laboratory 2-3) and foreign language 2-4.

**2008-2009 Annual costs.** Tuition/fees: $20,376. Room/board: $6,648. Books/supplies: $800. Personal expenses: $800.

**2007-2008 Financial aid. Need-based:** 78% of total undergraduate aid awarded as scholarships/grants, 22% as loans/jobs. **Non-need-based:** Scholarships awarded for academics, art, athletics, leadership, music/drama.

**Application procedures. Admission:** Priority date 12/1; deadline 3/1 (postmark date). $20 fee, may be waived for applicants with need. Application may be submitted online. Admission notification on a rolling basis beginning on or about 9/15. Must reply by May 1 or within 2 week(s) if notified thereafter. **Financial aid:** Closing date 3/10. FAFSA required. Applicants notified on a rolling basis starting 3/1; must reply by 5/1.

**Academics. Special study options:** Combined bachelor's/graduate degree, cooperative education, cross-registration, distance learning, double major, dual enrollment of high school students, exchange student, honors, independent study, internships, liberal arts/career combination, study abroad, teacher certification program. **Credit/placement by examination:** AP, CLEP, IB, SAT, ACT, institutional tests. 30 credit hours maximum toward associate degree, 30 toward bachelor's. **Support services:** Learning center, reduced course load, remedial instruction, study skills assistance, tutoring, writing center.

**Majors. Biology:** General. **Business:** General, accounting, administrative services, business admin, finance, international, management information systems, marketing. **Communications:** General, journalism. **Computer sciences:** Information technology. **Education:** Art, business, elementary, English, French, German, mathematics, music, physical, science, social studies, Spanish, special. **English:** English lit. **Foreign languages:** General, French, German, Spanish. **History:** General. **Math:** General, statistics. **Parks/recreation:** Health/fitness, sports admin. **Physical sciences:** General. **Protective services:** Criminal justice. **Psychology:** General. **Public administration:** Social work. **Social sciences:** Sociology. **Theology:** Bible, youth ministry. **Visual/performing arts:** Drawing, graphic design, illustration, music performance. **Other:** Journalism education, Social studies, non-teaching.

**Most popular majors.** Business/marketing 25%, education 25%, psychology 17%, theological studies 6%, visual/performing arts 7%.

**Computing on campus.** 160 workstations in dormitories, library, computer center, student center. Dormitories wired for high-speed internet access and linked to campus network. Commuter students can connect to campus network. Online course registration, helpline, wireless network available.

**Student life. Freshman orientation:** Mandatory. Preregistration for classes offered. Weekend in the beginning of the fall semester in late August and at the beginning of the spring semester in early January. **Policies:** Students are to refrain from the use of alcoholic beverages, illegal drugs, tobacco, sexual misconduct, coarse or obscene language or any other conduct inconsistent with the goals and traditions of the college. Further, students are to abstain from morally degrading media and literature. Religious observance required. **Housing:** Guaranteed on-campus for all undergraduates. Single-sex dorms, apartments, substance-free housing available. $200 deposit, deadline 5/1. **Activities:** Bands, choral groups, drama, music ensembles, musical theater, opera, student government, student newspaper, symphony orchestra, 20 Christian clubs and organizations.

**Athletics.** NAIA, NCCAA. **Intercollegiate:** Baseball M, basketball, cross-country, golf M, soccer, softball W, tennis, track and field, volleyball W.

**Intramural:** Badminton, basketball, soccer, softball, volleyball. **Team name:** Lancers.

**Student services.** Campus ministries, career counseling, student employment services, health services, personal counseling, placement for graduates, veterans' counselor.

**Contact.** E-mail: admissions@grace.edu
Phone: (574) 372-5100 ext. 6008 Toll-free
number: (800) 544-7223 ext. 6008 Fax: (574) 372-5120
Grace College, 200 Seminary Drive, Winona Lake, IN 46590

---

## Hanover College

**Hanover, Indiana**
**www.hanover.edu**

**CB member**
**CB code: 1290**

- Private 4-year liberal arts college affiliated with Presbyterian Church (USA)
- Residential campus in rural community
- 916 degree-seeking undergraduates: 53% women, 1% African American, 2% Asian American, 1% Hispanic American, 1% Native American, 3% international
- 66% of applicants admitted
- SAT or ACT with writing, application essay required
- 59% graduate within 6 years; 23% enter graduate study

**General.** Founded in 1827. Regionally accredited. **Degrees:** 203 bachelor's awarded. **Location:** 85 miles from Indianapolis, 40 miles from Louisville, Kentucky. **Calendar:** 4-1-4. 4-4-1. **Full-time faculty:** 89 total; 10% minority, 44% women. **Part-time faculty:** 8 total; 75% have terminal degrees, 12% minority, 38% women. **Class size:** 88% < 20, 12% 20-39, less than 1% 40-49. **Special facilities:** Geology museum, observatory, nearby wildlife refuge, state park.

**Freshman class profile.** 1,894 applied, 1,247 admitted, 231 enrolled.

| Mid 50% test scores | | Rank in top quarter: | 77% |
|---|---|---|---|
| SAT critical reading: | 510-630 | Rank in top tenth: | 39% |
| SAT math: | 520-630 | End year in good standing: | 95% |
| SAT writing: | 490-610 | Return as sophomores: | 77% |
| ACT composite: | 22-28 | Out-of-state: | 30% |
| GPA 3.50 or higher: | 68% | Live on campus: | 97% |
| GPA 3.0-3.49: | 29% | International: | 3% |
| GPA 2.0-2.99: | 3% | | |

**Basis for selection.** GED not accepted. Selection of and performance in academic courses most important. Interview recommended.

**High school preparation.** 18 units required; 25 recommended. Required and recommended units include English 4, mathematics 3-4, social studies 2-3, history 2-3, science 3-4 (laboratory 2-3), foreign language 2-4 and academic electives 2-3.

**2008-2009 Annual costs.** Tuition/fees: $25,220. Room/board: $7,500. Books/supplies: $900. Personal expenses: $900.

**2007-2008 Financial aid. Need-based:** 199 full-time freshmen applied for aid; 165 were judged to have need; 165 of these received aid. Average need met was 91%. Average scholarship/grant was $17,868; average loan $2,501. 83% of total undergraduate aid awarded as scholarships/grants, 17% as loans/jobs. **Non-need-based:** Awarded to 414 full-time undergraduates, including 101 freshmen. Scholarships awarded for academics, alumni affiliation, music/drama, religious affiliation, state residency. **Additional information:** Academic Honors Diploma Scholarship is a grant program committed to meeting 100% of Indiana student's demonstrated need. Available to Indiana students who graduate with an Academic Honors Diploma (AHD), have completed their application for admission by January 15, and file a complete and valid FAFSA by March 10.

**Application procedures. Admission:** Closing date 3/1 (postmark date). $35 fee, may be waived for applicants with need. Application may be submitted online. Admission notification on a rolling basis beginning on or about 1/15. Must reply by May 1 or within 2 week(s) if notified thereafter. **Financial aid:** Priority date 3/10; no closing date. FAFSA required. Applicants notified on a rolling basis starting 3/1; must reply by 5/1.

**Academics.** Students take only one course in the 4-week spring term. **Special study options:** Double major, dual enrollment of high school students, independent study, internships, student-designed major, study abroad, teacher certification program, Washington semester. Philadelphia Center, Washington Center internships, Center for Business Preparation. **Credit/placement by examination:** AP, CLEP, IB, institutional tests. **Support services:** Learning center, reduced course load, study skills assistance, tutoring, writing center.

**Majors.** **Area/ethnic studies:** Latin American. **Biology:** General. **Communications:** General. **Computer sciences:** General. **Education:** Elementary. **English:** English lit. **Foreign languages:** Classics, French, German, Spanish. **History:** General. **Interdisciplinary:** Medieval/Renaissance. **Math:** General. **Parks/recreation:** Exercise sciences. **Philosophy/religion:** Philosophy. **Physical sciences:** Chemistry, geology, physics. **Psychology:** General. **Social sciences:** Anthropology, economics, political science, sociology. **Theology:** Theology. **Visual/performing arts:** Art history/conservation, dramatic, studio arts.

**Most popular majors.** Biology 7%, business/marketing 9%, communications/journalism 6%, English 9%, mathematics 7%, physical sciences 6%, psychology 8%, social sciences 22%.

**Computing on campus.** 195 workstations in library, computer center, student center. Dormitories wired for high-speed internet access and linked to campus network. Commuter students can connect to campus network. Online course registration, online library, helpline, student web hosting, wireless network available.

**Student life.** **Freshman orientation:** Available. Preregistration for classes offered. 5 one-day orientation sessions in March, April, May, June, and August that include registering for fall courses. Freshmen orientation starts 1 week before classes begin. **Housing:** Guaranteed on-campus for freshmen. Coed dorms, single-sex dorms, apartments, fraternity/sorority housing, substance-free housing available. $250 fully refundable deposit, deadline 5/1. Theme housing available. **Activities:** Bands, campus ministries, choral groups, dance, drama, film society, international student organizations, literary magazine, music ensembles, musical theater, radio station, student government, student newspaper, symphony orchestra, TV station, Campus Fellowship, political and social service organizations, international club, academic clubs, Christian Life, Love Out Loud.

**Athletics.** NCAA. **Intercollegiate:** Baseball M, basketball, cross-country, football (tackle) M, golf, soccer, softball W, tennis, track and field, volleyball W. **Intramural:** Basketball, football (non-tackle) W, football (tackle) M, racquetball, soccer, softball, volleyball. **Team name:** Panthers.

**Student services.** Alcohol/substance abuse counseling, campus ministries, career counseling, student employment services, financial aid counseling, health services, personal counseling, placement for graduates.

**Contact.** E-mail: admission@hanover.edu
Phone: (812) 866-7021 Toll-free number: (800) 213-2178
Fax: (812) 866-7098
William Preble, Dean of Admission and Financial Assistance, Hanover College, PO Box 108, Hanover, IN 47243-0108

## Holy Cross College
**Notre Dame, Indiana**     **CB member**
www.hcc-nd.edu     **CB code: 1309**

- Private 4-year liberal arts college affiliated with Roman Catholic Church
- Residential campus in small city
- 481 degree-seeking undergraduates
- SAT or ACT (ACT writing optional), application essay required

**General.** Founded in 1966. Regionally accredited. **Degrees:** 14 bachelor's, 38 associate awarded. **ROTC:** Army, Air Force. **Location:** One mile from South Bend, 80 miles from Chicago. **Calendar:** Semester, limited summer session. **Full-time faculty:** 24 total. **Part-time faculty:** 21 total.

### Freshman class profile.

| Mid 50% test scores | | | |
|---|---|---|---|
| SAT critical reading: | 470-590 | Out-of-state: | 49% |
| SAT math: | 430-470 | Live on campus: | 49% |

**Basis for selection.** School achievement and student's perception of value of program for future plans most important. Interview recommended.

**High school preparation.** Required and recommended units include English 4, mathematics 3-4, social studies 2-4, science 2-4 and foreign language 2.

**2007-2008 Annual costs.** Tuition/fees: $15,660. Room/board: $8,250. Books/supplies: $500.

**Financial aid.** **Non-need-based:** Scholarships awarded for academics, leadership.

**Application procedures.** **Admission:** Priority date 7/1; deadline 8/15. $50 fee, may be waived for applicants with need. Application may be submitted online. Admission notification on a rolling basis. **Financial aid:** Priority date 3/1; no closing date. FAFSA required. Applicants notified on a rolling basis starting 5/1; must reply within 2 week(s) of notification.

**Academics.** **Special study options:** Accelerated study, cross-registration, ESL, honors, study abroad. **Credit/placement by examination:** AP, CLEP, SAT, ACT, institutional tests. 30 credit hours maximum toward associate degree. **Support services:** Learning center, pre-admission summer program, reduced course load, remedial instruction, study skills assistance, tutoring, writing center.

**Majors.** **Liberal arts:** Arts/sciences.

**Computing on campus.** 32 workstations in computer center, student center. Dormitories wired for high-speed internet access and linked to campus network. Commuter students can connect to campus network. Online library, repair service, wireless network available.

**Student life.** **Freshman orientation:** Mandatory. Preregistration for classes offered. **Housing:** Coed dorms, single-sex dorms, special housing for disabled, apartments available. $500 deposit, deadline 8/15. **Activities:** Marching band, choral groups, drama, literary magazine, music ensembles, student government, student newspaper, campus ministry, student advisory committee, Flip Side.

**Athletics.** NAIA. **Intercollegiate:** Cross-country M. **Intramural:** Basketball, cheerleading, football (non-tackle), football (tackle) M, golf, lacrosse M, soccer, volleyball. **Team name:** Saints.

**Student services.** Alcohol/substance abuse counseling, campus ministries, career counseling, financial aid counseling, health services, personal counseling.

**Contact.** E-mail: admissions@hcc-nd.edu
Phone: (574) 239-8400 Fax: (574) 239-8323
Vincent Duke, Director of Admissions, Holy Cross College, 54515 State Road 933N, Notre Dame, IN 46556-0308

## Huntington University
**Huntington, Indiana**
www.huntington.edu     **CB code: 1304**

- Private 4-year university and liberal arts college affiliated with United Brethren in Christ
- Residential campus in large town
- 866 degree-seeking undergraduates: 3% part-time, 54% women, 1% Asian American, 1% Hispanic American, 4% international
- 229 degree-seeking graduate students
- 86% of applicants admitted
- SAT or ACT with writing, application essay required
- 59% graduate within 6 years; 10% enter graduate study

**General.** Founded in 1897. Regionally accredited. **Degrees:** 177 bachelor's, 1 associate awarded; master's offered. **Location:** 20 miles from Fort Wayne. **Calendar:** 4-1-4, limited summer session. **Full-time faculty:** 58 total; 76% have terminal degrees, 3% minority, 36% women. **Part-time faculty:** 35 total; 20% have terminal degrees, 43% women. **Class size:** 75% < 20, 22% 20-39, 4% 40-49. **Special facilities:** Nature preserve, greenhouse, disc golf course.

**Freshman class profile.** 797 applied, 685 admitted, 247 enrolled.

| Mid 50% test scores | | End year in good standing: | 93% |
|---|---|---|---|
| SAT critical reading: | 460-630 | Return as sophomores: | 72% |
| SAT math: | 440-620 | Out-of-state: | 43% |
| ACT composite: | 21-29 | Live on campus: | 90% |
| GPA 3.50 or higher: | 39% | International: | 2% |
| GPA 3.0-3.49: | 46% | Sororities: | 1% |
| GPA 2.0-2.99: | 15% | | |

**Basis for selection.** Class rank in top half, satisfactory test scores, GPA of 2.3 most important. Selected students with SAT score of 860 (exclusive of Writing) or more, GPA of 2.0, or rank in top 50% of class may be admitted on minimum load. Interview recommended. Audition required of music majors. Portfolio required for art scholarships. Essay required for presidential scholarships.

**High school preparation.** Required and recommended units include English 4, mathematics 3, social studies 2, history 2, science 2 (laboratory 1), foreign language 2, computer science 1 and visual/performing arts 2.

**2007-2008 Annual costs.** Tuition/fees: $19,430. Room/board: $6,730. Books/supplies: $800. Personal expenses: $1,200.

**2007-2008 Financial aid. Need-based:** 218 full-time freshmen applied for aid; 185 were judged to have need; 185 of these received aid. Average need met was 79%. Average scholarship/grant was $12,311; average loan $4,086. 62% of total undergraduate aid awarded as scholarships/grants, 38% as loans/jobs. **Non-need-based:** Scholarships awarded for academics, alumni affiliation, art, athletics, leadership, music/drama, religious affiliation. **Additional information:** Students may lock in their tuition rate for all four years.

**Application procedures. Admission:** Priority date 3/1; deadline 8/1 (receipt date). $20 fee, may be waived for applicants with need. Application may be submitted online. Admission notification on a rolling basis beginning on or about 10/1. Education majors must apply separately to the Education Department before entering those major classes. Performance grants also require a separate application process for those majoring in music, theatre, art, and communication. **Financial aid:** Priority date 3/1; no closing date. FAFSA required. Applicants notified on a rolling basis starting 3/1; must reply by 5/1 or within 2 week(s) of notification.

**Academics. Special study options:** Double major, independent study, internships, liberal arts/career combination, study abroad, teacher certification program, Washington semester. **Credit/placement by examination:** AP, CLEP, SAT, ACT, institutional tests. 38 credit hours maximum toward bachelor's degree. **Support services:** Learning center, pre-admission summer program, reduced course load, remedial instruction, study skills assistance, tutoring, writing center.

**Majors. Biology:** General. **Business:** General, accounting, accounting/finance, business admin, entrepreneurial studies, managerial economics, nonprofit/public, small business admin. **Communications:** General, broadcast journalism, digital media, journalism, public relations, radio/tv. **Computer sciences:** General, computer science. **Conservation:** Environmental science. **Education:** General, art, biology, business, chemistry, elementary, English, mathematics, music, physical, science, secondary, social studies, Spanish, special. **English:** English lit, speech/rhetoric. **Foreign languages:** Spanish. **Health:** Nursing (RN), premedicine. **History:** General. **Interdisciplinary:** Math/computer science. **Legal studies:** Prelaw. **Math:** General. **Parks/recreation:** Exercise sciences, facilities management, sports admin. **Philosophy/religion:** Philosophy, religion. **Physical sciences:** Chemistry. **Psychology:** General. **Public administration:** Social work. **Social sciences:** Sociology. **Theology:** Bible, missionary, religious ed, sacred music, youth ministry. **Visual/performing arts:** Art, dramatic, film/cinema, graphic design, music management, music performance, piano/organ, studio arts, theater arts management, theater design, voice/opera.

**Most popular majors.** Business/marketing 23%, communications/journalism 6%, education 27%, parks/recreation 7%, psychology 7%, theological studies 11%, visual/performing arts 8%.

**Computing on campus.** 164 workstations in dormitories, library, computer center, student center. Dormitories wired for high-speed internet access and linked to campus network. Commuter students can connect to campus network. Online library, helpline, student web hosting, wireless network available.

**Student life. Freshman orientation:** Mandatory. 3-day orientation held immediately before first semester. **Policies:** No social dancing. Chapel/convocation attendance required 2 out of 4 weekly programs. Use of alcohol, drugs, tobacco prohibited. Religious observance required. **Housing:** Guaranteed on-campus for all undergraduates. Single-sex dorms, apartments, substance-free housing available. $100 partly refundable deposit, deadline 8/15. College-owned houses available. **Activities:** Bands, choral groups, dance, drama, film society, literary magazine, music ensembles, musical theater, opera, radio station, student government, student newspaper, TV station, minority student fellowship, Collegians for Life, international club, Joe Mertz Center for Volunteer Service.

**Athletics.** NAIA, NCCAA. **Intercollegiate:** Baseball M, basketball, cross-country, golf M, soccer, softball W, tennis, track and field, volleyball W. **Intramural:** Basketball, football (non-tackle), racquetball, softball, volleyball. **Team name:** Foresters.

**Student services.** Adult student services, alcohol/substance abuse counseling, campus ministries, career counseling, student employment services, financial aid counseling, health services, minority student services, on-campus daycare, personal counseling, placement for graduates, women's services. **Physically disabled:** Services for visually, speech, hearing impaired.

**Contact.** E-mail: admissions@huntington.edu
Phone: (260) 359-4000 Toll-free number: (800) 642-6493
Fax: (260) 358-3699
Jeffrey Berggren, Vice President of Enrollment Management & Marketing, Huntington University, 2303 College Avenue, Huntington, IN 46750-1237

## Indiana Institute of Technology
**Fort Wayne, Indiana**   **CB member**
www.indianatech.edu   **CB code: 1323**

- Private 4-year business and engineering college
- Residential campus in large city
- 3,026 degree-seeking undergraduates: 40% part-time, 53% women, 20% African American, 1% Asian American, 2% Hispanic American
- 344 degree-seeking graduate students
- 65% of applicants admitted
- SAT or ACT (ACT writing optional) required

**General.** Founded in 1930. Regionally accredited. ABET accreditation for electrical engineering and mechanical engineering. **Degrees:** 398 bachelor's, 172 associate awarded; master's offered. **Location:** 120 miles from Indianapolis. **Calendar:** Semester, limited summer session. **Full-time faculty:** 34 total; 24% have terminal degrees, 6% minority, 29% women. **Part-time faculty:** 241 total; 5% have terminal degrees, 6% minority, 36% women. **Class size:** 87% < 20, 13% 20-39, less than 1% 50-99. **Special facilities:** Computer-aided design center, amphitheater, movie theater.

**Freshman class profile.** 1,743 applied, 1,129 admitted, 347 enrolled.

| Mid 50% test scores | | | |
|---|---|---|---|
| SAT critical reading: | 400-520 | Rank in top tenth: | 10% |
| SAT math: | 410-530 | End year in good standing: | 69% |
| ACT composite: | 17-22 | Return as sophomores: | 60% |
| GPA 3.50 or higher: | 14% | Out-of-state: | 37% |
| GPA 3.0-3.49: | 27% | Live on campus: | 63% |
| GPA 2.0-2.99: | 53% | International: | 1% |
| Rank in top quarter: | 28% | Fraternities: | 4% |

**Basis for selection.** GPA and test scores most important. Interview recommended.

**High school preparation.** Required and recommended units include English 4, mathematics 2-4, science 2-3 and academic electives 7. Engineering and computer science majors require 13.5 units including 4 English; 3.5 mathematics; 2 physical science; 4 history, social studies, or language.

**2007-2008 Annual costs.** Tuition/fees: $19,480. Room/board: $7,300. Personal expenses: $3,000.

**Financial aid. Non-need-based:** Scholarships awarded for academics, alumni affiliation, athletics, leadership, minority status, music/drama, state residency.

**Application procedures. Admission:** No deadline. $50 fee, may be waived for applicants with need. Application may be submitted online. Admission notification on a rolling basis beginning on or about 10/15. **Financial aid:** Closing date 3/10. FAFSA, institutional form required. Applicants notified on a rolling basis starting 2/2; must reply within 2 week(s) of notification.

**Academics. Special study options:** Accelerated study, combined bachelor's/graduate degree, cross-registration, distance learning, double major, dual enrollment of high school students, external degree, independent study, internships, student-designed major. **Credit/placement by examination:** AP, CLEP, IB, SAT, ACT, institutional tests. 45 credit hours maximum toward associate degree, 90 toward bachelor's. **Support services:** Learning center, reduced course load, remedial instruction, study skills assistance, tutoring.

**Majors. Business:** General, accounting, business admin, human resources, management information systems, marketing, operations. **Communications:** General. **Computer sciences:** General, computer science, information systems, networking, security. **Education:** Elementary, physical. **Engineering:** Biomedical, computer, electrical, industrial, mechanical, software. **Health:** Recreational therapy. **Parks/recreation:** Facilities management, sports admin. **Protective services:** Criminal justice, law enforcement admin. **Psychology:** General. **Public administration:** Human services. **Other:** Internet technologies, Organizational leadership.

**Most popular majors.** Business/marketing 87%.

**Computing on campus.** PC or laptop required. 270 workstations in library, computer center. Dormitories wired for high-speed internet access and linked to campus network. Commuter students can connect to campus network. Online library, helpline, repair service, student web hosting, wireless network available.

**Student life. Freshman orientation:** Mandatory. Preregistration for classes offered. 1-day program. **Housing:** Guaranteed on-campus for freshmen. Coed dorms, apartments, fraternity/sorority housing available. $350 deposit. **Activities:** Bands, campus ministries, choral groups, dance, student government, student newspaper, Student Board, Black Student Association, Nova Society, Society for Women Engineers, American Society of Mechanical Engineers, Society for Human Resource Management, Society of Automotive Engineering, Institute of Electrical and Electronics Engineers, Society for Manufacturing Engineers.

**Athletics.** NAIA. **Intercollegiate:** Baseball M, basketball, cross-country, golf, soccer, softball W, tennis, track and field, volleyball W. **Intramural:** Badminton, basketball, bowling, soccer, softball, volleyball. **Team name:** Warriors.

**Student services.** Adult student services, campus ministries, career counseling, student employment services, financial aid counseling, personal counseling, placement for graduates, veterans' counselor.

**Contact.** E-mail: admissions@indianatech.edu
Phone: (260) 422-5561 ext. 2205 Toll-free
number: (800) 937-2448 ext. 2205 Fax: (260) 422-7696
Allison Carnahan, Vice President of Enrollment Management, Indiana
Institute of Technology, 1600 East Washington Boulevard, Fort Wayne, IN
46803-1297

---

## Indiana State University
**Terre Haute, Indiana**
**www.indstate.edu**

**CB member**
**CB code: 1322**

- Public 4-year university
- Residential campus in small city
- 8,303 degree-seeking undergraduates: 13% part-time, 51% women, 13% African American, 1% Asian American, 1% Hispanic American, 1% international
- 2,013 degree-seeking graduate students
- 70% of applicants admitted
- SAT or ACT with writing required
- 41% graduate within 6 years

**General.** Founded in 1865. Regionally accredited. **Degrees:** 1,415 bachelor's, 119 associate awarded; master's, doctoral offered. **ROTC:** Army, Air Force. **Location:** 70 miles from Indianapolis. **Calendar:** Semester, extensive summer session. **Full-time faculty:** 446 total; 80% have terminal degrees, 12% minority, 40% women. **Part-time faculty:** 194 total; 18% have terminal degrees, 7% minority, 55% women. **Class size:** 49% < 20, 38% 20-39, 8% 40-49, 4% 50-99, less than 1% >100. **Special facilities:** Observatory, museum, flight simulator.

**Freshman class profile.** 6,428 applied, 4,520 admitted, 1,852 enrolled.

| Mid 50% test scores | | | |
|---|---|---|---|
| SAT critical reading: | 410-520 | Rank in top tenth: | 11% |
| SAT math: | 420-530 | End year in good standing: | 66% |
| SAT writing: | 400-500 | Return as sophomores: | 69% |
| ACT composite: | 17-22 | Out-of-state: | 10% |
| GPA 3.50 or higher: | 20% | Live on campus: | 70% |
| GPA 3.0-3.49: | 31% | International: | 1% |
| GPA 2.0-2.99: | 48% | Fraternities: | 9% |
| Rank in top quarter: | 29% | Sororities: | 12% |

**Basis for selection.** Students who rank in top 50% of high school class usually admitted. High school curriculum, GPA, test scores, class rank, type of high school, and interview all considered. Interview required of some scholarship applicants, recommended for applicants below 50th percentile of high school graduating class. Essay recommended. Audition required of music majors. Portfolio recommended for art majors.

**High school preparation.** 20 units recommended. Recommended units include English 4, mathematics 3, social studies 2, history 1, science 3 (laboratory 3), foreign language 1 and academic electives 1. 3 or more units recommended in career area. 1 in health & safety/physical education recommended.

**2008-2009 Annual costs.** Tuition/fees (projected): $7,148; $15,402 out-of-state. Books/supplies: $1,170. Personal expenses: $1,832.

**2006-2007 Financial aid.** All financial aid based on need. 1,453 full-time freshmen applied for aid; 1,166 were judged to have need; 1,131 of these received aid. Average need met was 75%. Average scholarship/grant was $5,398; average loan $2,508. 53% of total undergraduate aid awarded as scholarships/grants, 47% as loans/jobs. **Additional information:** Financial aid application deadline March 1 for Indiana residents applying for state grant.

**Application procedures. Admission:** Priority date 7/1; deadline 8/15. $25 fee, may be waived for applicants with need. Application may be submitted online. Admission notification on a rolling basis. Must reply by 5/1. **Financial aid:** Priority date 3/1; no closing date. FAFSA required. Applicants notified on a rolling basis starting 4/15.

**Academics. Special study options:** Accelerated study, cooperative education, distance learning, double major, dual enrollment of high school students, ESL, honors, independent study, internships, study abroad, teacher certification program. **Credit/placement by examination:** AP, CLEP, SAT, ACT, institutional tests. 31 credit hours maximum toward bachelor's degree. **Support services:** Learning center, pre-admission summer program, study skills assistance, tutoring, writing center.

**Majors. Architecture:** Interior. **Area/ethnic studies:** African-American. **Biology:** General. **Business:** Accounting, business admin, finance, human resources, insurance, management information systems, marketing, office management, operations. **Communications:** General. **Computer sciences:** General, information technology. **Education:** Elementary, physical, science, special, trade/industrial. **Engineering technology:** Architectural, automotive, computer, electrical, electromechanical, industrial, manufacturing, mechanical, occupational safety, robotics. **English:** English lit. **Family/consumer sciences:** General, clothing/textiles, family studies, food/nutrition. **Foreign languages:** French, German, linguistics, Spanish. **Health:** Athletic training, clinical lab science, community health services, environmental health, nursing (RN). **History:** General. **Liberal arts:** Arts/sciences. **Math:** General. **Parks/recreation:** Facilities management. **Philosophy/religion:** Philosophy. **Physical sciences:** Chemistry, geology, physics. **Psychology:** General. **Public administration:** Social work. **Social sciences:** Anthropology, criminology, economics, geography, political science, sociology. **Transportation:** Airline/commercial pilot, aviation management. **Visual/performing arts:** Art, dramatic, music performance, studio arts.

**Most popular majors.** Business/marketing 18%, communications/journalism 6%, education 13%, engineering/engineering technologies 8%, health sciences 8%, social sciences 10%.

**Computing on campus.** PC or laptop required. 467 workstations in library, computer center, student center. Dormitories wired for high-speed internet access and linked to campus network. Commuter students can connect to campus network. Online course registration, online library, helpline, repair service, student web hosting, wireless network available.

**Student life. Freshman orientation:** Mandatory. Preregistration for classes offered. One-day program includes registration, question and answer sessions, placement testing, campus tour, and meeting with advisers. Parents encouraged to attend. **Housing:** Guaranteed on-campus for freshmen. Coed dorms, single-sex dorms, special housing for disabled, apartments, fraternity/sorority housing, substance-free housing available. Apartments for students with dependent children. **Activities:** Bands, choral groups, dance, drama, film society, literary magazine, music ensembles, musical theater, radio station, student government, student newspaper, symphony orchestra, over 170 student organizations available.

**Athletics.** NCAA. **Intercollegiate:** Baseball M, basketball, cross-country, football (tackle) M, golf W, soccer W, softball W, tennis, track and field, volleyball W. **Intramural:** Badminton, basketball, bowling, football (non-tackle), soccer, softball, swimming, table tennis, tennis, track and field, volleyball. **Team name:** Sycamores.

**Student services.** Adult student services, campus ministries, career counseling, student employment services, financial aid counseling, health services, minority student services, on-campus daycare, personal counseling, placement for graduates, women's services. **Physically disabled:** Services for visually, speech, hearing impaired.

**Contact.** E-mail: admissions@indstate.edu
Phone: (812) 237-2121 Toll-free number: (800) 468-6478
Fax: (812) 237-8023
Richard Toomey, Director, Indiana State University, Office of Admissions, Erickson 114, Terre Haute, IN 47809-9989

---

## Indiana University Bloomington
**Bloomington, Indiana**
**www.iub.edu**

**CB member**
**CB code: 1324**

- Public 4-year university
- Residential campus in small city
- 29,734 degree-seeking undergraduates: 3% part-time, 51% women, 4% African American, 4% Asian American, 2% Hispanic American, 5% international
- 8,162 degree-seeking graduate students
- 70% of applicants admitted

▶ SAT or ACT with writing required
▶ 72% graduate within 6 years

**General.** Founded in 1820. Regionally accredited. Big Ten research university. **Degrees:** 6,181 bachelor's, 59 associate awarded; master's, doctoral, first professional offered. **ROTC:** Army, Air Force. **Location:** 50 miles from Indianapolis. **Calendar:** Semester, extensive summer session. **Full-time faculty:** 1,943 total; 76% have terminal degrees, 16% minority, 37% women. **Part-time faculty:** 366 total; 27% have terminal degrees, 7% minority, 51% women. **Special facilities:** Cyclotron, 2 observatories, museum of anthropology, history, and folklore, rare book library, outdoor educational center, center for excellence in education, garden and nature center, arboretum, CAVE Automated Virtual Environment.

**Freshman class profile.** 29,059 applied, 20,282 admitted, 7,197 enrolled.

| Mid 50% test scores | | Rank in top tenth: | 31% |
|---|---|---|---|
| SAT critical reading: | 510-620 | Return as sophomores: | 89% |
| SAT math: | 520-640 | Out-of-state: | 39% |
| ACT composite: | 23-28 | Live on campus: | 98% |
| Rank in top quarter: | 68% | International: | 3% |

**Basis for selection.** Strength of student's college preparatory program, senior year program, grade trends in academic program, class rank, if provided, and SAT or ACT test scores important. SAT Subject Tests recommended. Campus visit encouraged. Audition required for majority of music majors. **Learning Disabled:** Current and comprehensive documentation of disability required to receive services.

**High school preparation.** 14 units required; 19 recommended. Required and recommended units include English 4, mathematics 3-4, social studies 2-3, science 1-3 (laboratory 1), foreign language 3 and academic electives 4. Indiana students are expected to complete Core 40 state mandated requirements. Non-Indiana students are expected to complete a minimum of 32 semesters in required areas.

**2007-2008 Annual costs.** Tuition/fees: $7,837; $22,316 out-of-state. Room/board: $6,676. Books/supplies: $758. Personal expenses: $2,256.

**2006-2007 Financial aid. Need-based:** 4,786 full-time freshmen applied for aid; 3,010 were judged to have need; 2,907 of these received aid. Average need met was 66%. Average scholarship/grant was $7,213; average loan $2,869. 49% of total undergraduate aid awarded as scholarships/grants, 51% as loans/jobs. **Non-need-based:** Awarded to 6,965 full-time undergraduates, including 2,239 freshmen. Scholarships awarded for academics, art, athletics, leadership, minority status, music/drama, religious affiliation, ROTC. **Additional information:** Majority of institutional gift aid merit-based. Some need-based grants go to merit winners with financial need.

**Application procedures. Admission:** Priority date 4/1; no deadline. $50 fee, may be waived for applicants with need. Application may be submitted online. Admission notification on a rolling basis. Must reply by May 1 or within 3 week(s) if notified thereafter. **Financial aid:** Priority date 3/1; no closing date. FAFSA required. Applicants notified on a rolling basis starting 4/1.

**Academics. Special study options:** Accelerated study, combined bachelor's/graduate degree, cooperative education, distance learning, double major, dual enrollment of high school students, ESL, external degree, honors, independent study, internships, liberal arts/career combination, semester at sea, student-designed major, study abroad, teacher certification program, United Nations semester, Washington semester. **Credit/placement by examination:** AP, CLEP, IB, SAT, ACT, institutional tests. **Support services:** Learning center, pre-admission summer program, reduced course load, remedial instruction, study skills assistance, tutoring, writing center.

**Honors college/program.** Top 5 percent of high school graduating class or minimum 1350 SAT or 31 ACT. Qualified students will receive application to Honors College Scholarship automatically. Completed applications reviewed by faculty panel. Honors College participants complete at least 3 approved honors courses during first 4 semesters on campus.

**Majors. Area/ethnic studies:** African-American, East Asian, women's. **Biology:** General, bacteriology, biochemistry. **Business:** General, accounting, business admin, finance, labor relations. **Communications:** General, digital media, journalism. **Communications technology:** Recording arts. **Computer sciences:** General. **Conservation:** General, environmental science. **Education:** General, art, biology, chemistry, early childhood, elementary, English, French, German, health, Latin, mathematics, multi-level teacher, music, physical, physics, science, secondary, social studies, Spanish, special, speech. **English:** Composition, English lit. **Family/consumer sciences:** Clothing/textiles. **Foreign languages:** General, African, ancient Greek, comparative lit, East Asian, French, German, Italian, Latin, linguistics, Portuguese, Slavic, Spanish. **Health:** Audiology/hearing, audiology/speech pathology, cytotechnology, dental hygiene, health care admin, medical radiologic technology/radiation therapy, medical records technology, nuclear medical

technology, nursing (RN), respiratory therapy technology, sonography. **History:** General. **Interdisciplinary:** Science/society, systems science. **Liberal arts:** Arts/sciences. **Math:** General. **Parks/recreation:** General, facilities management. **Philosophy/religion:** Judaic, philosophy, religion. **Physical sciences:** Astronomy, astrophysics, chemistry, geology, physics. **Protective services:** Criminal justice. **Psychology:** General. **Public administration:** General. **Social sciences:** General, anthropology, economics, geography, political science, sociology. **Visual/performing arts:** General, art history/conservation, commercial/advertising art, conducting, dance, dramatic, interior design, jazz, music performance, music theory/composition, piano/organ, studio arts, voice/opera.

**Most popular majors.** Biology 6%, business/marketing 19%, communications/journalism 10%, education 17%, public administration/social services 6%, social sciences 7%, visual/performing arts 6%.

**Computing on campus.** 2,262 workstations in dormitories, library, computer center, student center. Dormitories wired for high-speed internet access and linked to campus network. Commuter students can connect to campus network. Online course registration, helpline, repair service, student web hosting, wireless network available.

**Student life. Freshman orientation:** Mandatory, $112 fee. Preregistration for classes offered. 2-day program held between June 14 and July 20. **Housing:** Guaranteed on-campus for freshmen. Coed dorms, single-sex dorms, special housing for disabled, apartments, cooperative housing, fraternity/sorority housing, substance-free housing available. $200 deposit. Residential language houses, living/learning centers, wellness center, African-American living/learning center, honors college floors, first-year academic interest group housing available. **Activities:** Bands, choral groups, dance, drama, literary magazine, music ensembles, musical theater, opera, radio station, student government, student newspaper, symphony orchestra, TV station, College Democrats, College Republicans, Young Americans for Freedom, Black Student Union, Latinos Unidos, Asian-American Association, Alpha Phi Omega, Volunteers Student Bureau, College Mentors for Kids, Golden Key.

**Athletics.** NCAA. **Intercollegiate:** Baseball M, basketball, cross-country, diving, field hockey W, football (tackle) M, golf, rowing (crew) W, soccer, softball W, swimming, tennis, track and field, volleyball W, water polo W, wrestling M. **Intramural:** Archery, badminton, basketball, bowling, cross-country, diving, equestrian, fencing, field hockey W, gymnastics, handball, ice hockey M, lacrosse, racquetball, rifle, rowing (crew), rugby, sailing, skiing, skin diving, soccer, softball, squash, swimming, table tennis, tennis, track and field, volleyball, water polo, wrestling M. **Team name:** Hoosiers.

**Student services.** Adult student services, alcohol/substance abuse counseling, campus ministries, career counseling, services for economically disadvantaged, student employment services, financial aid counseling, health services, legal services, minority student services, on-campus daycare, personal counseling, placement for graduates, veterans' counselor, women's services. **Physically disabled:** Services for visually, speech, hearing impaired.

**Contact.** E-mail: iuadmit@indiana.edu
Phone: (812) 855-0661 Fax: (812) 855-5102
Mary Ellen Anderson, Director of Undergraduate Admissions, Indiana University Bloomington, 300 North Jordan Avenue, Bloomington, IN 47405

## Indiana University East
**Richmond, Indiana**
www.iue.edu                                      CB code: 1194

▶ Public 4-year university and branch campus college
▶ Commuter campus in large town
▶ 1,974 degree-seeking undergraduates: 37% part-time, 68% women, 4% African American, 2% Hispanic American
▶ 42 graduate students

**General.** Founded in 1971. Regionally accredited. **Degrees:** 246 bachelor's, 81 associate awarded. **Location:** 70 miles from Indianapolis. **Calendar:** Semester, extensive summer session. **Full-time faculty:** 81 total; 53% have terminal degrees, 9% minority, 60% women. **Part-time faculty:** 110 total; 16% have terminal degrees, 4% minority, 52% women.

**Freshman class profile.** 547 applied, 449 admitted, 326 enrolled.

| Mid 50% test scores | | Rank in top quarter: | 28% |
|---|---|---|---|
| SAT critical reading: | 400-500 | Rank in top tenth: | 8% |
| SAT math: | 400-510 | Return as sophomores: | 60% |
| ACT composite: | 18-22 | Out-of-state: | 13% |

**Basis for selection.** Open admission, but selective for some programs. Additional admission criteria for nursing program. Traditional students (3 years or less after high school graduation) required to take SAT or ACT for placement. May attend 1 semester while waiting to take test. Interview recommended. **Homeschooled:** Must graduate from national accredited home school program or take GED.

**High school preparation.** 14 units required; 16 recommended. Required and recommended units include English 4, mathematics 3, social studies 2, science 1 (laboratory 1) and academic electives 4. 4 units in some combination of additional mathematics, laboratory science, social science, computer science, and other courses of college preparatory nature. Foreign language strongly recommended.

**2007-2008 Annual costs.** Tuition/fees: $5,292; $12,831 out-of-state. Books/supplies: $930. Personal expenses: $1,380.

**2006-2007 Financial aid. Need-based:** 221 full-time freshmen applied for aid; 178 were judged to have need; 170 of these received aid. Average need met was 59%. Average scholarship/grant was $4,700; average loan $2,156. 45% of total undergraduate aid awarded as scholarships/grants, 55% as loans/jobs. **Non-need-based:** Awarded to 66 full-time undergraduates, including 20 freshmen. Scholarships awarded for academics, alumni affiliation, leadership.

**Application procedures. Admission:** No deadline. $25 fee, may be waived for applicants with need. Application may be submitted online. Admission notification on a rolling basis. **Financial aid:** Priority date 3/1; no closing date. FAFSA, institutional form required. Applicants notified on a rolling basis starting 5/1; must reply within 2 week(s) of notification.

**Academics. Special study options:** Cooperative education, cross-registration, distance learning, double major, dual enrollment of high school students, external degree, independent study, internships, teacher certification program, weekend college. State-wide technology program with Purdue University. **Credit/placement by examination:** AP, CLEP, institutional tests. **Support services:** Remedial instruction, study skills assistance, tutoring, writing center.

**Majors. Biology:** General. **Business:** Accounting, business admin, management information systems, marketing. **Communications:** General. **Education:** Elementary, secondary. **English:** English lit. **Health:** Nursing (RN). **Interdisciplinary:** Biological/physical sciences, natural sciences. **Liberal arts:** Humanities. **Protective services:** Criminal justice. **Psychology:** General. **Public administration:** Social work. **Social sciences:** Sociology.

**Most popular majors.** Education 10%, health sciences 18%, liberal arts 20%, philosophy/religious studies 27%, public administration/social services 8%.

**Computing on campus.** 120 workstations in library, computer center.

**Student life. Freshman orientation:** Mandatory. Preregistration for classes offered. **Activities:** Drama, student government, student newspaper, TV station.

**Athletics. Intramural:** Basketball, softball, volleyball. **Team name:** Pioneers.

**Student services.** Adult student services, career counseling, student employment services, financial aid counseling, health services, on-campus daycare, personal counseling, placement for graduates. **Physically disabled:** Services for visually, speech, hearing impaired.

**Contact.** E-mail: eaadmit@indiana.edu
Phone: (765) 973-8208 Toll-free number: (800) 959-3278
Fax: (765) 973-8288
Molly Vanderpool, Director of Admissions, Indiana University East, 2325 Chester Boulevard, Richmond, IN 47374-1289

## Indiana University Kokomo
**Kokomo, Indiana**
www.iuk.edu                                   **CB code: 1337**

- Public 4-year university
- Commuter campus in large town
- 2,387 degree-seeking undergraduates: 42% part-time, 71% women, 4% African American, 1% Asian American, 2% Hispanic American, 1% Native American
- 86 degree-seeking graduate students
- 83% of applicants admitted
- SAT or ACT with writing required

**General.** Founded in 1945. Regionally accredited. **Degrees:** 277 bachelor's, 205 associate awarded; master's offered. **ROTC:** Army. **Location:** 50 miles from Indianapolis. **Calendar:** Semester, limited summer session.

**Full-time faculty:** 94 total; 65% have terminal degrees, 15% minority, 57% women. **Part-time faculty:** 68 total; 3% have terminal degrees, 3% minority, 54% women. **Special facilities:** Observatory.

**Freshman class profile.** 725 applied, 605 admitted, 435 enrolled.

| Mid 50% test scores | | | |
|---|---|---|---|
| SAT critical reading: | 420-510 | Rank in top quarter: | 23% |
| SAT math: | 430-530 | Rank in top tenth: | 5% |
| ACT composite: | 16-23 | Return as sophomores: | 53% |

**Basis for selection.** Test scores, class rank, course work important; 2 out of 3 should be met for admission. In-state applicants should be in top half of graduating class (top third for out-of-state applicants).

**High school preparation.** 14 units required. Required and recommended units include English 4, mathematics 3, social studies 2, history 2, science 1 and foreign language 2.

**2007-2008 Annual costs.** Tuition/fees: $5,325; $12,861 out-of-state. Books/supplies: $840. Personal expenses: $1,338.

**2006-2007 Financial aid. Need-based:** 287 full-time freshmen applied for aid; 206 were judged to have need; 185 of these received aid. Average need met was 58%. Average scholarship/grant was $4,658; average loan $2,278. 43% of total undergraduate aid awarded as scholarships/grants, 57% as loans/jobs. **Non-need-based:** Awarded to 126 full-time undergraduates, including 49 freshmen. Scholarships awarded for academics.

**Application procedures. Admission:** Priority date 8/3; no deadline. $30 fee, may be waived for applicants with need. Application must be submitted on paper. Admission notification on a rolling basis. **Financial aid:** Closing date 3/1. FAFSA, institutional form required. Applicants notified on a rolling basis starting 5/1; must reply within 4 week(s) of notification.

**Academics. Special study options:** Accelerated study, cross-registration, distance learning, double major, dual enrollment of high school students, external degree, honors, independent study, internships, study abroad, teacher certification program. **Credit/placement by examination:** AP, CLEP, SAT, ACT, institutional tests. **Support services:** Learning center, reduced course load, remedial instruction, tutoring.

**Majors. Biology:** General. **Business:** General, accounting, business admin, labor relations, marketing. **Communications:** General. **Computer sciences:** General. **Education:** Elementary. **English:** English lit. **Health:** Nursing (RN). **Interdisciplinary:** Behavioral sciences, biological/physical sciences, gerontology. **Liberal arts:** Humanities. **Math:** General. **Physical sciences:** Chemistry. **Protective services:** Criminal justice. **Psychology:** General. **Public administration:** General. **Social sciences:** General, sociology.

**Most popular majors.** Business/marketing 15%, education 13%, health sciences 26%, liberal arts 21%, security/protective services 7%.

**Computing on campus.** 100 workstations in library, computer center, student center. Online course registration, helpline available.

**Student life. Freshman orientation:** Available, $26 fee. Preregistration for classes offered. **Activities:** Choral groups, drama, music ensembles, student government, student newspaper.

**Athletics. Intramural:** Basketball M, soccer, softball, volleyball.

**Student services.** Adult student services, career counseling, student employment services, financial aid counseling, minority student services, on-campus daycare, personal counseling, placement for graduates, veterans' counselor. **Physically disabled:** Services for visually, hearing impaired.

**Contact.** E-mail: iuadmis@iuk.edu
Phone: (765) 455-9217 Toll-free number: (888) 875-4485
Fax: (765) 455-9537
Reeta Piirala-Skoglund, Assistant Director of Admissions, Indiana University Kokomo, Box 9003, KC 230A, Kokomo, IN 46904-9003

## Indiana University Northwest
**Gary, Indiana**
www.iun.edu                                   **CB code: 1338**

- Public 4-year university
- Commuter campus in small city
- 3,965 degree-seeking undergraduates: 39% part-time, 70% women, 22% African American, 2% Asian American, 12% Hispanic American
- 453 degree-seeking graduate students
- 78% of applicants admitted

- ♦ SAT or ACT with writing required
- ♦ 32% graduate within 6 years

**General.** Founded in 1948. Regionally accredited. **Degrees:** 411 bachelor's, 279 associate awarded; master's offered. **ROTC:** Army. **Location:** 35 miles from Chicago. **Calendar:** Semester, limited summer session. **Full-time faculty:** 186 total; 72% have terminal degrees, 23% minority, 52% women. **Part-time faculty:** 167 total; 21% have terminal degrees, 18% minority, 55% women.

**Freshman class profile.** 1,379 applied, 1,077 admitted, 719 enrolled.

| Mid 50% test scores | | | |
|---|---|---|---|
| SAT critical reading: | 400-510 | Rank in top quarter: | 21% |
| SAT math: | 390-510 | Rank in top tenth: | 7% |
| ACT composite: | 16-20 | Return as sophomores: | 62% |
| | | Out-of-state: | 2% |

**Basis for selection.** School achievement record and test scores most important. Applicants should be in top half of class and have 2.0 high school GPA or better.

**High school preparation.** 16 units required. Required and recommended units include English 4, mathematics 3, social studies 2, science 1 (laboratory 1), foreign language 2 and academic electives 4.

**2007-2008 Annual costs.** Tuition/fees: $5,398. Books/supplies: $864. Personal expenses: $3,076.

**2006-2007 Financial aid. Need-based:** 486 full-time freshmen applied for aid; 378 were judged to have need; 346 of these received aid. Average need met was 50%. Average scholarship/grant was $4,778; average loan $2,306. 41% of total undergraduate aid awarded as scholarships/grants, 59% as loans/jobs. **Non-need-based:** Awarded to 146 full-time undergraduates, including 40 freshmen. Scholarships awarded for academics, athletics.

**Application procedures. Admission:** Priority date 8/1; no deadline. $25 fee, may be waived for applicants with need. Admission notification on a rolling basis. **Financial aid:** Priority date 3/1; no closing date. FAFSA, institutional form required. Applicants notified on a rolling basis starting 5/1; must reply within 2 week(s) of notification.

**Academics. Special study options:** Accelerated study, cooperative education, distance learning, double major, dual enrollment of high school students, external degree, independent study, internships, liberal arts/career combination, student-designed major, study abroad, teacher certification program, Washington semester, weekend college. **Credit/placement by examination:** AP, CLEP, institutional tests. **Support services:** Learning center, pre-admission summer program, reduced course load, remedial instruction, tutoring.

**Majors. Area/ethnic studies:** African-American. **Biology:** General. **Business:** General, actuarial science, labor relations. **Communications:** General. **Computer sciences:** Data processing. **Education:** Elementary, English, mathematics, secondary, social studies, Spanish. **English:** English lit. **Foreign languages:** French, Spanish. **Health:** Health care admin, medical records admin, nursing (RN). **History:** General. **Math:** General. **Philosophy/religion:** Philosophy. **Physical sciences:** Chemistry, geology. **Protective services:** Criminal justice. **Psychology:** General. **Public administration:** General. **Social sciences:** Economics, political science, sociology. **Visual/performing arts:** Art, dramatic.

**Most popular majors.** Business/marketing 13%, education 11%, health sciences 20%, liberal arts 17%, psychology 7%, security/protective services 12%.

**Computing on campus.** 170 workstations in library, computer center, student center. Commuter students can connect to campus network. Online course registration, helpline available.

**Student life. Freshman orientation:** Available. Preregistration for classes offered. **Activities:** Choral groups, drama, literary magazine, student government, student newspaper, Christian Student Fellowship, Young Republicans, Young Democrats, Women with a Challenge, Student Guide Services, Black Student Union.

**Athletics.** NAIA. **Intercollegiate:** Basketball, golf, volleyball W. **Intramural:** Baseball M, basketball M, bowling, cheerleading W, golf. **Team name:** Red Hawks.

**Student services.** Adult student services, career counseling, student employment services, financial aid counseling, on-campus daycare, personal counseling, placement for graduates, veterans' counselor, women's services. **Physically disabled:** Services for visually impaired.

**Contact.** E-mail: admit@iun.edu
Phone: (219) 980-6991 Toll-free number: (800) 968-7486
Fax: (219) 981-4219
Linda Templeton, Director of Admissions, Indiana University Northwest, 3400 Broadway, Gary, IN 46408

## Indiana University South Bend
### South Bend, Indiana
### www.iusb.edu
CB code: 1339

- ♦ Public 4-year university
- ♦ Commuter campus in small city
- ♦ 5,718 degree-seeking undergraduates: 36% part-time, 63% women, 7% African American, 1% Asian American, 4% Hispanic American, 2% international
- ♦ 769 degree-seeking graduate students
- ♦ 83% of applicants admitted
- ♦ SAT or ACT required

**General.** Founded in 1922. Regionally accredited. Off-campus course offerings in Elkhart, Warsaw, Plymouth. **Degrees:** 532 bachelor's, 186 associate awarded; master's offered. **ROTC:** Army, Naval, Air Force. **Location:** 90 miles from Chicago. **Calendar:** Semester, limited summer session. **Full-time faculty:** 277 total; 68% have terminal degrees, 18% minority, 50% women. **Part-time faculty:** 274 total; 20% have terminal degrees, 7% minority, 56% women.

**Freshman class profile.** 1,905 applied, 1,588 admitted, 1,068 enrolled.

| Mid 50% test scores | | | |
|---|---|---|---|
| SAT critical reading: | 410-520 | Rank in top tenth: | 6% |
| SAT math: | 420-530 | Return as sophomores: | 63% |
| ACT composite: | 17-23 | Out-of-state: | 2% |
| Rank in top quarter: | 24% | International: | 1% |

**Basis for selection.** Rank in top half of class important. Core 40 completion with "C" or higher. Interview recommended for academically weak applicants or those with unusual circumstances. Audition required of music majors. Portfolios required for some art majors. **Homeschooled:** Applicants to degree-seeking programs must meet institution's requirement for college-prep courses.

**High school preparation.** 13 units required. Required and recommended units include English 4, mathematics 3, social studies 2, science 1 (laboratory 1) and foreign language 2. Strong preparation in mathematics and sciences recommended.

**2007-2008 Annual costs.** Tuition/fees: $5,491; $13,918 out-of-state. Books/supplies: $976. Personal expenses: $1,604.

**2006-2007 Financial aid. Need-based:** 635 full-time freshmen applied for aid; 479 were judged to have need; 442 of these received aid. Average need met was 51%. Average scholarship/grant was $4,450; average loan $2,097. 44% of total undergraduate aid awarded as scholarships/grants, 56% as loans/jobs. **Non-need-based:** Awarded to 183 full-time undergraduates, including 30 freshmen. Scholarships awarded for academics, athletics.

**Application procedures. Admission:** Priority date 7/1; no deadline. $47 fee, may be waived for applicants with need. Application may be submitted online. Admission notification on a rolling basis. **Financial aid:** Closing date 3/1. FAFSA, institutional form required. Applicants notified on a rolling basis starting 5/1.

**Academics.** Most allied health programs must be completed at Indianapolis campus. **Special study options:** Accelerated study, cross-registration, distance learning, double major, ESL, external degree, honors, internships, liberal arts/career combination, study abroad, teacher certification program, weekend college. Electrical, mechanical engineering, computer technology with Purdue University on Indiana University South Bend campus; Northern Indiana Consortium for Education (NICE) - IUSB is one of 6 member institutions sharing library resources, faculty expertise, and academic strengths. **Credit/placement by examination:** AP, CLEP, IB, institutional tests. 90 credit hours maximum toward bachelor's degree. **Support services:** Learning center, pre-admission summer program, reduced course load, remedial instruction, tutoring, writing center.

**Majors. Area/ethnic studies:** Women's. **Biology:** General. **Business:** General, actuarial science, business admin, finance, labor relations, labor studies, marketing. **Communications:** Media studies. **Computer sciences:** General. **Education:** Biology, chemistry, elementary, mathematics, music, physics, science, secondary, social studies, Spanish, special. **English:** Composition, English lit, speech/rhetoric. **Foreign languages:** French, German, Spanish.

**Health:** Health care admin, nursing (RN). **History:** General. **Math:** General, applied. **Philosophy/religion:** Philosophy. **Physical sciences:** Chemistry, physics. **Protective services:** Criminal justice. **Psychology:** General. **Public administration:** General. **Social sciences:** Economics, political science, sociology. **Visual/performing arts:** Art, dramatic, music performance, studio arts.

**Most popular majors.** Business/marketing 19%, education 7%, health sciences 14%, liberal arts 19%, security/protective services 7%, visual/performing arts 6%.

**Computing on campus.** 325 workstations in library, computer center. Commuter students can connect to campus network. Online library, helpline available.

**Student life. Freshman orientation:** Available, $30 fee. Preregistration for classes offered. Two and a half hour sessions held in May, June, July and August. **Housing:** Some housing for athletes and visiting scholars. **Activities:** Jazz band, campus ministries, choral groups, drama, film society, international student organizations, literary magazine, music ensembles, musical theater, opera, student government, student newspaper, symphony orchestra, student educational association, black student union, student council for exceptional children, Latino student union, Asian student union, women's student union, Habitat for Humanity, departmental clubs.

**Athletics.** NAIA. **Intercollegiate:** Basketball. **Intramural:** Badminton, basketball, bowling, football (tackle), racquetball, softball, table tennis, tennis, volleyball. **Team name:** Titans.

**Student services.** Adult student services, campus ministries, career counseling, student employment services, on-campus daycare, personal counseling, placement for graduates, veterans' counselor. **Physically disabled:** Services for visually, speech, hearing impaired.

**Contact.** E-mail: admissio@iusb.edu
Phone: (574) 520-4480 Fax: (574) 520-4834
Jeff Johnston, Director Recruitment/Admissions, Indiana University South Bend, 1700 Mishawaka Avenue, South Bend, IN 46634-7111

## Indiana University Southeast

| New Albany, Indiana | CB member |
| --- | --- |
| www.ius.edu | CB code: 1314 |

- Public 4-year university
- Commuter campus in large town
- 5,167 degree-seeking undergraduates: 36% part-time, 61% women, 5% African American, 1% Asian American, 2% Hispanic American
- 590 degree-seeking graduate students
- 89% of applicants admitted
- SAT or ACT with writing required

**General.** Founded in 1941. Regionally accredited. **Degrees:** 672 bachelor's, 148 associate awarded; master's offered. **ROTC:** Army, Air Force. **Location:** 10 miles from Louisville. **Calendar:** Semester, limited summer session. **Full-time faculty:** 192 total; 73% have terminal degrees, 13% minority, 46% women. **Part-time faculty:** 243 total; 19% have terminal degrees, 10% minority, 49% women. **Special facilities:** Cultural and community center.

**Freshman class profile.** 1,431 applied, 1,273 admitted, 882 enrolled.

| Mid 50% test scores | | Rank in top quarter: | 27% |
| --- | --- | --- | --- |
| SAT critical reading: | 420-530 | Rank in top tenth: | 7% |
| SAT math: | 420-520 | Return as sophomores: | 62% |
| ACT composite: | 18-22 | Out-of-state: | 16% |

**Basis for selection.** Rank in top half of class for in-state applicants. Interview recommended.

**High school preparation.** 14 units required; 19 recommended. Required and recommended units include English 4, mathematics 3-4, social studies 2, history 1, science 1-2 (laboratory 1-2), foreign language 2 and academic electives 4.

**2007-2008 Annual costs.** Tuition/fees: $5,376; $12,913 out-of-state. Books/supplies: $770. Personal expenses: $1,800.

**2006-2007 Financial aid. Need-based:** 564 full-time freshmen applied for aid; 414 were judged to have need; 381 of these received aid. Average need met was 54%. Average scholarship/grant was $4,474; average loan $2,265. 41% of total undergraduate aid awarded as scholarships/grants, 59% as loans/jobs. **Non-need-based:** Awarded to 258 full-time undergraduates, including 82 freshmen. Scholarships awarded for academics, art, athletics, leadership, minority status, music/drama.

**Application procedures. Admission:** Priority date 7/15; no deadline. $30 fee, may be waived for applicants with need. Application may be submitted online. Admission notification on a rolling basis. **Financial aid:** Priority date 3/1; no closing date. FAFSA required. Applicants notified on a rolling basis starting 5/1; must reply within 3 week(s) of notification.

**Academics. Special study options:** Accelerated study, cross-registration, double major, dual enrollment of high school students, external degree, independent study, internships, student-designed major, study abroad, teacher certification program, weekend college. Member of Metroversity consortium of institutions of higher education in Louisville area. **Credit/placement by examination:** AP, CLEP, IB, institutional tests. **Support services:** Reduced course load, remedial instruction, study skills assistance, tutoring, writing center.

**Majors. Biology:** General. **Business:** General, accounting, accounting technology, labor relations. **Communications:** General, journalism. **Computer sciences:** General. **Education:** General, biology, elementary, English, mathematics, science, secondary, social studies, special. **English:** English lit. **Foreign languages:** French, German, Spanish. **Health:** Clinical lab science, nursing (RN). **History:** General. **Math:** General. **Philosophy/religion:** Philosophy. **Physical sciences:** Chemistry, physics. **Psychology:** General. **Social sciences:** Economics, geography, international relations, political science, sociology. **Visual/performing arts:** Art, studio arts.

**Most popular majors.** Business/marketing 19%, education 16%, health sciences 7%, liberal arts 23%, social sciences 6%.

**Computing on campus.** 165 workstations in library, computer center, student center. Commuter students can connect to campus network. Online course registration, online library, helpline, student web hosting, wireless network available.

**Student life. Freshman orientation:** Mandatory. Preregistration for classes offered. One-day summer program. **Activities:** Concert band, choral groups, drama, literary magazine, music ensembles, student government, student newspaper, symphony orchestra, Christian fellowship, Students for World Peace, multicultural student union.

**Athletics.** NAIA. **Intercollegiate:** Baseball M, basketball, cross-country, tennis, volleyball W. **Intramural:** Basketball, bowling, softball, tennis, volleyball. **Team name:** Grenadier.

**Student services.** Adult student services, alcohol/substance abuse counseling, campus ministries, career counseling, student employment services, financial aid counseling, minority student services, on-campus daycare, personal counseling, placement for graduates, veterans' counselor. **Physically disabled:** Services for visually, speech, hearing impaired.

**Contact.** E-mail: admissions@ius.edu
Phone: (812) 941-2212 Toll-free number: (800) 852-8835
Fax: (812) 941-2595
Anne Skuce, Assistant Vice Chancellor for Enrollment Management, Indiana University Southeast, 4201 Grant Line Road, New Albany, IN 47150-6405

## Indiana University-Purdue University Fort Wayne

| Fort Wayne, Indiana | CB member |
| --- | --- |
| www.ipfw.edu | CB code: 1336 |

- Public 4-year university and branch campus college
- Commuter campus in large city
- 10,659 degree-seeking undergraduates: 31% part-time, 56% women, 5% African American, 2% Asian American, 3% Hispanic American, 1% international
- 681 degree-seeking graduate students
- 97% of applicants admitted
- SAT or ACT (ACT writing optional) required
- 22% graduate within 6 years; 25% enter graduate study

**General.** Founded in 1964. Regionally accredited. Degrees awarded through Indiana University or Purdue University, depending on course of study. **Degrees:** 995 bachelor's, 479 associate awarded; master's offered. **Location:** 110 miles from Indianapolis. **Calendar:** Semester, limited summer session. **Full-time faculty:** 383 total; 86% have terminal degrees, 15% minority, 40% women. **Part-time faculty:** 415 total; 10% have terminal degrees, 8% minority, 54% women. **Class size:** 46% < 20, 46% 20-39, 4% 40-49, 3% 50-99, less than 1% >100. **Special facilities:** Lake biological research station.

**Freshman class profile.** 3,103 applied, 3,012 admitted, 2,044 enrolled.

| Mid 50% test scores | | | |
|---|---|---|---|
| SAT critical reading: | 420-530 | Rank in top quarter: | 30% |
| SAT math: | 430-550 | Rank in top tenth: | 9% |
| SAT writing: | 410-520 | End year in good standing: | 95% |
| ACT composite: | 18-23 | Return as sophomores: | 60% |
| GPA 3.50 or higher: | 25% | Out-of-state: | 10% |
| GPA 3.0-3.49: | 31% | Live on campus: | 20% |
| GPA 2.0-2.99: | 41% | International: | 1% |

**Basis for selection.** In-state applicants should rank in top half of high school class, out-of-state in top third. Test scores important. TOEFL or Michigan Test may be used to assess English proficiency. Audition required of music majors. Portfolio required of visual arts majors. **Homeschooled:** Transcript of courses and grades required.

**High school preparation.** 20 units required. Required units include English 4, mathematics 3, social studies 3, science 3, foreign language 2 and academic electives 5. Additional requirements vary by program.

**2007-2008 Annual costs.** Tuition/fees: $6,312; $14,666 out-of-state. Room only: $5,140. Books/supplies: $1,250. Personal expenses: $1,642.

**2006-2007 Financial aid. Need-based:** 1,369 full-time freshmen applied for aid; 1,063 were judged to have need; 985 of these received aid. Average need met was 45%. Average scholarship/grant was $4,428; average loan $2,264. 35% of total undergraduate aid awarded as scholarships/grants, 65% as loans/jobs. **Non-need-based:** Awarded to 1,128 full-time undergraduates, including 361 freshmen. Scholarships awarded for academics, athletics, state residency.

**Application procedures. Admission:** Closing date 8/1. $30 fee, may be waived for applicants with need. Application may be submitted online. Admission notification on a rolling basis beginning on or about 11/1. **Financial aid:** Priority date 3/10; no closing date. FAFSA required. Applicants notified on a rolling basis starting 5/15; must reply within 3 week(s) of notification.

**Academics. Special study options:** Accelerated study, cooperative education, distance learning, double major, ESL, exchange student, honors, independent study, internships, liberal arts/career combination, student-designed major, study abroad, teacher certification program, Washington semester, weekend college. **Credit/placement by examination:** AP, CLEP, IB, institutional tests. Hours of credit awarded by examination varies by program. **Support services:** Learning center, pre-admission summer program, remedial instruction, study skills assistance, tutoring, writing center.

**Majors. Area/ethnic studies:** Women's. **Biology:** General. **Business:** Accounting, business admin, finance, hospitality admin, labor studies, managerial economics, marketing, operations. **Communications:** General, media studies, organizational. **Computer sciences:** Computer science, information systems. **Education:** Art, biology, chemistry, elementary, English, French, German, history, mathematics, music, physics, science, secondary, social studies, Spanish, speech. **Engineering:** Civil, computer, electrical, mechanical. **Engineering technology:** Computer, construction, electrical, industrial, mechanical. **English:** British lit, composition, English lit, technical writing. **Foreign languages:** French, German, Spanish. **Health:** Audiology/hearing, clinical lab science, clinical lab technology, community health services, health care admin, health services admin, mental health services, music therapy, nursing (RN), predental, premedicine, preveterinary, substance abuse counseling. **History:** General. **Interdisciplinary:** Math/computer science. **Math:** General, computational, statistics. **Philosophy/religion:** Philosophy. **Physical sciences:** Chemistry, geology, physics. **Protective services:** Law enforcement admin. **Psychology:** General. **Public administration:** General, policy analysis. **Social sciences:** Anthropology, economics, political science, sociology. **Visual/performing arts:** Commercial/advertising art, crafts, dramatic, drawing, graphic design, interior design, painting, photography, piano/organ, printmaking, sculpture, studio arts, voice/opera.

**Most popular majors.** Business/marketing 19%, education 13%, engineering/engineering technologies 8%, liberal arts 17%, psychology 6%, public administration/social services 6%.

**Computing on campus.** 472 workstations in dormitories, library, computer center, student center. Dormitories wired for high-speed internet access and linked to campus network. Commuter students can connect to campus network. Online course registration, online library, helpline, repair service, student web hosting, wireless network available.

**Student life. Freshman orientation:** Mandatory, $25 fee. Preregistration for classes offered. 4-hour program; 10-12 dates between June and August. **Housing:** Apartments, substance-free housing available. $150 fully refundable deposit. **Activities:** Bands, choral groups, dance, drama, international student organizations, literary magazine, music ensembles, musical theater, opera, student government, student newspaper, symphony orchestra, TV station, Black Collegian Caucus, Hispanos Unidos, InterVarsity Christian Fellowship, Graduate Business Council.

**Athletics.** NCAA. **Intercollegiate:** Baseball M, basketball, cross-country, golf, soccer, softball W, tennis, track and field W, volleyball. **Intramural:** Badminton, basketball, football (non-tackle), football (tackle) M, golf, racquetball, soccer, tennis, volleyball. **Team name:** Mastodons.

**Student services.** Adult student services, alcohol/substance abuse counseling, campus ministries, career counseling, student employment services, financial aid counseling, health services, minority student services, on-campus daycare, personal counseling, placement for graduates, veterans' counselor, women's services. **Physically disabled:** Services for visually, speech, hearing impaired.

**Contact.** E-mail: ASK@ipfw.edu
Phone: (260) 481-6812 Toll-free number: (800) 324-4739
Fax: (260) 481-6880
Carol Isaacs, Director of Admissions, Indiana University-Purdue University Fort Wayne, 2101 East Coliseum Boulevard, Fort Wayne, IN 46805-1499

---

## Indiana University-Purdue University Indianapolis

| Indianapolis, Indiana | CB member |
|---|---|
| www.iupui.edu | CB code: 1325 |

- Public 4-year university
- Commuter campus in very large city
- 20,136 degree-seeking undergraduates: 29% part-time, 59% women, 10% African American, 3% Asian American, 3% Hispanic American, 2% international
- 7,858 degree-seeking graduate students
- 71% of applicants admitted
- SAT or ACT with writing required
- 32% graduate within 6 years

**General.** Founded in 1969. Regionally accredited. **Degrees:** 2,866 bachelor's, 474 associate awarded; master's, doctoral, first professional offered. **ROTC:** Army, Naval, Air Force. **Calendar:** Semester, extensive summer session. **Full-time faculty:** 2,205 total; 82% have terminal degrees, 20% minority, 37% women. **Part-time faculty:** 956 total; 25% have terminal degrees, 12% minority, 52% women.

**Freshman class profile.** 7,958 applied, 5,616 admitted, 2,949 enrolled.

| Mid 50% test scores | | | |
|---|---|---|---|
| SAT critical reading: | 430-540 | Return as sophomores: | 66% |
| SAT math: | 440-560 | Out-of-state: | 3% |
| ACT composite: | 18-23 | Live on campus: | 14% |
| Rank in top quarter: | 40% | International: | 4% |
| Rank in top tenth: | 14% | Fraternities: | 1% |
| | | Sororities: | 1% |

**Basis for selection.** Course curriculum, grades, trend in grades, and test scores are the factors used. Portfolio recommended for some art applicants.

**High school preparation.** 21 units required; 26 recommended. Required and recommended units include English 4, mathematics 3-4, social studies 2, history 2, science 3-4 (laboratory 3), foreign language 3 and academic electives 4. Additional mathematics and science units required for science, engineering and nursing programs. 4 additional units required in some combination of foreign language, laboratory science, mathematics, social science, or computer science. Courses that develop writing composition skills strongly recommended.

**2007-2008 Annual costs.** Tuition/fees: $6,851; $18,905 out-of-state. Room/board: $5,100. Books/supplies: $672. Personal expenses: $2,600.

**2006-2007 Financial aid. Need-based:** 2,128 full-time freshmen applied for aid; 1,686 were judged to have need; 1,615 of these received aid. Average need met was 52%. Average scholarship/grant was $5,690; average loan $2,371. 40% of total undergraduate aid awarded as scholarships/grants, 60% as loans/jobs. **Non-need-based:** Awarded to 1,345 full-time undergraduates, including 375 freshmen. Scholarships awarded for academics, ROTC.

**Application procedures. Admission:** Closing date 5/1. $50 fee. Application may be submitted online. Admission notification on a rolling basis. Application deadlines for nursing and allied health programs range from October 15 to February 1. **Financial aid:** Priority date 3/1; no closing date. FAFSA required. Applicants notified on a rolling basis starting 4/1.

**Academics. Special study options:** Accelerated study, cooperative education, cross-registration, distance learning, double major, dual enrollment of high school students, ESL, external degree, honors, independent study, internships, liberal arts/career combination, student-designed major, study abroad, teacher certification program, weekend college. **Credit/placement by examination:** AP, CLEP, IB, institutional tests. Policy varies by school. **Support services:** Learning center, reduced course load, remedial instruction, tutoring, writing center.

**Majors. Biology:** General. **Business:** General, accounting, finance, human resources, international, labor relations, labor studies, management information systems, market research, nonprofit/public, tourism/travel. **Communications:** General, advertising, journalism, public relations. **Computer sciences:** General, computer graphics, information systems, system admin, web page design, webmaster. **Conservation:** Environmental science. **Education:** Art, biology, chemistry, elementary, English, ESL, French, German, health occupations, mathematics, physical, physics, secondary, social studies, Spanish, speech. **Engineering:** General, biomedical, computer, electrical, mechanical. **Engineering technology:** Computer, computer hardware, computer systems, construction, electrical, mechanical, robotics, software. **English:** English lit. **Foreign languages:** American Sign Language, French, German, Spanish. **Health:** Clinical lab science, cytotechnology, dental hygiene, medical informatics, medical radiologic technology/radiation therapy, medical records admin, nuclear medical technology, nursing (RN), predental, premedicine, prenursing, prepharmacy, preveterinary, radiologic technology/medical imaging, respiratory therapy assistant. **History:** General. **Legal studies:** Prelaw. **Liberal arts:** Arts/sciences. **Math:** General. **Parks/recreation:** Exercise sciences. **Philosophy/religion:** Philosophy, religion. **Physical sciences:** Chemistry, geology, physics. **Protective services:** Criminal justice, forensics. **Psychology:** General. **Public administration:** General, social work. **Social sciences:** Anthropology, economics, geography, political science, sociology. **Visual/performing arts:** Art, art history/conservation, ceramics, design, interior design, painting, photography, printmaking, sculpture, studio arts.

**Most popular majors.** Business/marketing 15%, education 11%, engineering/engineering technologies 8%, health sciences 14%, liberal arts 15%.

**Computing on campus.** 750 workstations in library, computer center, student center. Dormitories wired for high-speed internet access and linked to campus network. Commuter students can connect to campus network. Online course registration, helpline, repair service, wireless network available.

**Student life. Freshman orientation:** Mandatory, $100 fee. Preregistration for classes offered. **Policies:** Smoking policy, code of conduct. **Housing:** Coed dorms, apartments available. $100 deposit. **Activities:** Bands, choral groups, dance, drama, literary magazine, music ensembles, student government, student newspaper, Black Student Union, international affairs club.

**Athletics.** NCAA. **Intercollegiate:** Basketball, cheerleading, cross-country, diving, golf, soccer, softball W, swimming, tennis, volleyball W. **Intramural:** Basketball, football (non-tackle), golf, ice hockey, racquetball, soccer, softball, tennis, volleyball. **Team name:** Jaguars.

**Student services.** Adult student services, campus ministries, career counseling, student employment services, financial aid counseling, health services, minority student services, on-campus daycare, personal counseling, placement for graduates, veterans' counselor, women's services. **Physically disabled:** Services for visually, speech, hearing impaired. **Learning disabled:** Comprehensive services available.

**Contact.** E-mail: apply@iupui.edu
Phone: (317) 274-4591 Fax: (317) 278-1862
Chris Foley, Director of Admissions, Indiana University-Purdue University Indianapolis, 425 North University Boulevard, Cavanaugh Hall R129, Indianapolis, IN 46202-5143

## Indiana Wesleyan University
**Marion, Indiana**
**www.indwes.edu**          **CB code: 1446**

- Private 4-year university and liberal arts college affiliated with Wesleyan Church
- Residential campus in large town
- 2,881 degree-seeking undergraduates: 3% part-time, 63% women, 1% African American, 1% Asian American, 2% Hispanic American
- 81% of applicants admitted
- SAT or ACT (ACT writing recommended), application essay required
- 74% graduate within 6 years

**General.** Founded in 1920. Regionally accredited. Education centers in Indianapolis, Fort Wayne, Columbus (IN), Kokomo (IN), Merrillville (IN), Shelbyville (IN), Cleveland, Cincinnati, Lexington, Louisville and Dayton. **Degrees:** 522 bachelor's, 8 associate awarded; master's, doctoral offered.

**ROTC:** Army. **Location:** 65 miles from Indianapolis. **Calendar:** Semester, limited summer session. **Full-time faculty:** 152 total; 56% have terminal degrees, 7% minority, 37% women. **Part-time faculty:** 97 total; 13% have terminal degrees, 5% minority, 52% women. **Class size:** 59% < 20, 32% 20-39, 5% 40-49, 3% 50-99, 1% >100. **Special facilities:** History museum, nature preserve, museum of European oil paintings, photograph collection.

**Freshman class profile.** 2,261 applied, 1,838 admitted, 747 enrolled.

| Mid 50% test scores | | Rank in top quarter: | 58% |
|---|---|---|---|
| SAT critical reading: | 480-600 | Rank in top tenth: | 27% |
| SAT math: | 480-600 | End year in good standing: | 98% |
| ACT composite: | 21-27 | Return as sophomores: | 82% |
| GPA 3.50 or higher: | 59% | Out-of-state: | 46% |
| GPA 3.0-3.49: | 26% | Live on campus: | 78% |
| GPA 2.0-2.99: | 15% | | |

**Basis for selection.** High school record, class rank, and test scores most important. Recommendations required. Standardized tests and insitutional tests used to assist students in selecting classes appropriate to their preparation, designated scores determine placement in Math and English. Audition recommended for music majors. Portfolio recommended for art majors. **Homeschooled:** Transcript of courses and grades, letter of recommendation (nonparent) required. Transcript must have the GPA on a 4.0 scale. Recommendation from a pastor required.

**High school preparation.** 20 units recommended. Recommended units include English 4, mathematics 3, social studies 3, science 3, foreign language 2 and academic electives 5. 1 Health/PE.

**2008-2009 Annual costs.** Tuition/fees: $19,376. Required fees vary by program but are minimal. Room/board: $6,564. Books/supplies: $800. Personal expenses: $800.

**2007-2008 Financial aid. Need-based:** 718 full-time freshmen applied for aid; 639 were judged to have need; 639 of these received aid. Average need met was 79%. Average scholarship/grant was $12,667; average loan $3,127. 63% of total undergraduate aid awarded as scholarships/grants, 37% as loans/jobs. **Non-need-based:** Awarded to 1,104 full-time undergraduates, including 324 freshmen. Scholarships awarded for academics, alumni affiliation, art, athletics, music/drama, ROTC.

**Application procedures. Admission:** Priority date 12/1; deadline 8/1 (receipt date). $25 fee, may be waived for applicants with need. Application may be submitted online. Admission notification on a rolling basis beginning on or about 10/1. **Financial aid:** Closing date 3/1. FAFSA required. Applicants notified by 4/1.

**Academics. Special study options:** Accelerated study, cross-registration, distance learning, dual enrollment of high school students, honors, independent study, internships, liberal arts/career combination, student-designed major, study abroad, teacher certification program. **Credit/placement by examination:** AP, CLEP, IB, SAT, ACT, institutional tests. Students must complete at least 30 hours in residence. **Support services:** Learning center, reduced course load, remedial instruction, study skills assistance, tutoring, writing center.

**Honors college/program.** Applicant must possess at least a combined score of 1250 on the SAT (Math/Critical Reading) or 28 on the ACT, hold at least a 3.6 high school G.P.A. or class rank in the top 10 percent, and desire to participate in an interdisciplinary community of committed learners.

**Majors. Biology:** General, Biochemistry/biophysics and molecular biology. **Business:** Accounting, business admin, finance, management information systems, managerial economics, marketing. **Communications:** General, journalism, media studies, public relations. **Computer sciences:** General, applications programming, computer graphics, computer science, web page design, webmaster. **Education:** Art, business, elementary, English, mathematics, middle, music, physical, science, secondary, social studies. **English:** Creative writing, English lit. **Foreign languages:** Spanish. **Health:** Athletic training, nursing (RN), predental, premedicine, prepharmacy, preveterinary, substance abuse counseling. **History:** General. **Legal studies:** Prelaw. **Math:** General. **Parks/recreation:** Exercise sciences, facilities management, health/fitness, sports admin. **Philosophy/religion:** Philosophy, religion. **Physical sciences:** Chemistry. **Protective services:** Criminal justice. **Psychology:** General. **Public administration:** Social work. **Social sciences:** General, criminology, economics, international relations, political science, urban studies. **Theology:** Bible, religious ed, sacred music, theology. **Visual/performing arts:** Ceramics, dramatic, drawing, graphic design, illustration, interior design, music performance, music theory/composition, painting, photography, printmaking, studio arts.

**Most popular majors.** Business/marketing 13%, computer/information sciences 6%, education 17%, health sciences 17%, psychology 6.3%, theological studies 13%.

**Computing on campus.** 591 workstations in dormitories, library, computer center, student center. Dormitories wired for high-speed internet access and linked to campus network. Commuter students can connect to campus network. Online library, helpline, repair service, student web hosting, wireless network available.

**Student life. Freshman orientation:** Mandatory. Preregistration for classes offered. Held the weekend before school begins. **Policies:** No alcohol allowed on campus, students attend chapel services three times weekly. Religious observance required. **Housing:** Guaranteed on-campus for all undergraduates. Single-sex dorms, special housing for disabled, apartments, substance-free housing available. $100 fully refundable deposit, deadline 8/15. **Activities:** Bands, campus ministries, choral groups, drama, film society, international student organizations, literary magazine, music ensembles, musical theater, opera, radio station, student government, student newspaper, symphony orchestra, TV station, World Christian Fellowship, Fellowship of Christian Athletes, Habitat for Humanity, Young Republicans, College Libertarians, IWU Democrats.

**Athletics.** NAIA, NCCAA. **Intercollegiate:** Baseball M, basketball, cross-country, golf M, soccer, softball W, tennis, track and field, volleyball W. **Intramural:** Badminton, basketball, bowling, football (non-tackle), golf, racquetball, soccer, softball, swimming, table tennis, tennis, volleyball, water polo, weight lifting. **Team name:** Wildcats.

**Student services.** Adult student services, alcohol/substance abuse counseling, campus ministries, career counseling, services for economically disadvantaged, student employment services, financial aid counseling, health services, minority student services, personal counseling, placement for graduates. **Physically disabled:** Services for visually, speech, hearing impaired. **Learning disabled:** Comprehensive services available.

**Contact.** E-mail: admissions@indwes.edu
Phone: (765) 677-2138 Toll-free number: (800) 332-6901
Fax: (765) 677-2333
Daniel Solms, Director of Admissions, Indiana Wesleyan University, 4201 South Washington Street, Marion, IN 46953-4999

---

## International Business College
**Fort Wayne, Indiana**

CB code: 1330

- For-profit 4-year business and community college
- Small city
- 620 degree-seeking undergraduates

**General.** Founded in 1889. Accredited by ACICS. Branch campus located in Indianapolis. **Degrees:** 68 bachelor's, 196 associate awarded. **Location:** 4 miles from downtown. **Calendar:** Semester, extensive summer session. **Full-time faculty:** 13 total. **Part-time faculty:** 40 total.

**Freshman class profile.**

| | | | |
|---|---|---|---|
| Out-of-state: | 30% | Live on campus: | 40% |

**Basis for selection.** Open admission, but selective for some programs. School achievement record and personal interview most important. Recommendations important.

**2007-2008 Annual costs.** Tuition varies by program. Medical assisting program $600 per semester. Books/supplies: $900.

**Application procedures. Admission:** No deadline. $50 fee. Admission notification on a rolling basis. **Financial aid:** Closing date 5/1. Applicants notified by 9/15.

**Academics. Special study options:** Independent study, internships. **Credit/placement by examination:** CLEP. **Support services:** Tutoring.

**Majors. Business:** General.

**Computing on campus.** 146 workstations in library, computer center.

**Student life. Freshman orientation:** Available. **Housing:** Coed dorms, single-sex dorms available. **Activities:** Student government, accounting club, secretarial club.

**Student services.** Career counseling, student employment services, personal counseling, placement for graduates.

**Contact.** Phone: (260) 459-4500 Toll-free number: (800) 589-6363
Fax: (260) 436-1896
Steve Kinzer, Director of Admissions, International Business College, 5699 Coventry Lane, Fort Wayne, IN 46804

---

## ITT Technical Institute: Fort Wayne
**Fort Wayne, Indiana**
www.itt-tech.edu

CB code: 0650

- For-profit 4-year technical college
- Commuter campus in large city

**General.** Founded in 1967. Accredited by ACICS. **Location:** 122 miles from Indianapolis. **Calendar:** Quarter.

**Annual costs/financial aid.** Tuition varies by program, $260-$368 per credit hour.

**Contact.** Phone: (260) 484-4107
Director of Recruitment, 2810 Dupont Commerce Court, Fort Wayne, IN 46825

---

## ITT Technical Institute: Indianapolis
**Indianapolis, Indiana**
www.itt-tech.edu

CB code: 0640

- For-profit 4-year technical college
- Commuter campus in very large city

**General.** Founded in 1956. Accredited by ACICS. **Location:** 10 miles from downtown. **Calendar:** Quarter.

**Annual costs/financial aid.** Tuition varies by program, $260-$368 per credit hour.

**Contact.** Phone: (317) 875-8640
Director of Recruitment, 9511 Angola Court, Indianapolis, IN 46268-1119

---

## Manchester College
**North Manchester, Indiana**
www.manchester.edu

CB member
CB code: 1440

- Private 4-year liberal arts college affiliated with Church of the Brethren
- Residential campus in small town
- 1,011 degree-seeking undergraduates: 1% part-time, 50% women, 4% African American, 1% Asian American, 2% Hispanic American, 1% Native American, 4% international
- 73% of applicants admitted
- SAT or ACT with writing required
- 55% graduate within 6 years

**General.** Founded in 1889. Regionally accredited. **Degrees:** 188 bachelor's, 3 associate awarded; master's offered. **Location:** 35 miles from Fort Wayne, 100 miles from Indianapolis. **Calendar:** 4-1-4, limited summer session. **Full-time faculty:** 70 total; 89% have terminal degrees, 6% minority, 46% women. **Part-time faculty:** 18 total; 44% have terminal degrees, 39% women. **Class size:** 60% < 20, 35% 20-39, 4% 40-49, 1% 50-99. **Special facilities:** Observatory, 100-acre environmental studies and retreat center.

**Freshman class profile.** 1,636 applied, 1,202 admitted, 317 enrolled.

| Mid 50% test scores | | | |
|---|---|---|---|
| SAT critical reading: | 440-550 | Rank in top quarter: | 48% |
| SAT math: | 460-580 | Rank in top tenth: | 21% |
| SAT writing: | 420-550 | Out-of-state: | 11% |
| ACT composite: | 19-24 | Live on campus: | 95% |
| | | International: | 3% |

**Basis for selection.** School achievement record most important, with emphasis on college-preparatory courses, followed by SAT or ACT scores, class rank, recommendations. Interview recommended. Essay recommended for academically borderline applicants. Audition recommended for music majors. **Homeschooled:** Provide full information in detailed cover letter with application. **Learning Disabled:** School reviews ability to meet student needs.

**High school preparation.** 14 units required; 17 recommended. Required and recommended units include English 4, mathematics 2-3, social studies 2, history 1-2, science 2-3 (laboratory 2-3), foreign language 2 and academic electives 1-2.

**2008-2009 Annual costs.** Tuition/fees: $22,700. Health insurance and other fees as required. Room/board: $8,100. Books/supplies: $1,000. Personal expenses: $900.

**2007-2008 Financial aid. Need-based:** Average need met was 91%. Average scholarship/grant was $15,776; average loan $5,277. 69% of total undergraduate aid awarded as scholarships/grants, 31% as loans/jobs. **Non-need-based:** Scholarships awarded for academics, alumni affiliation, minority status, music/drama, religious affiliation. **Additional information:** Students are automatically considered for all scholarship programs.

**Application procedures. Admission:** Priority date 5/1; no deadline. $25 fee, may be waived for applicants with need. Application may be submitted online. Admission notification on a rolling basis beginning on or about 9/1. Must reply by May 1 or within 2 week(s) if notified thereafter. **Financial aid:** Priority date 3/1; no closing date. FAFSA required. Applicants notified on a rolling basis starting 2/15; must reply within 2 week(s) of notification.

**Academics.** Students are required to earn 2 credits in Values, Ideas and the Arts. **Special study options:** Accelerated study, cross-registration, double major, dual enrollment of high school students, exchange student, honors, independent study, internships, liberal arts/career combination, student-designed major, study abroad, teacher certification program, urban semester. Medical technology programs with area hospitals, 3-2 engineering dual-degree program with Washington University (MO) and others, 2-2 nursing program with Goshen College. **Credit/placement by examination:** AP, CLEP, IB, SAT, ACT, institutional tests. First year students take college proficiency tests to place out of the first year of modern language. Unlimited credit hours by examination may be counted toward associate or bachelor's degree. **Support services:** Learning center, reduced course load, study skills assistance, tutoring, writing center.

**Majors. Area/ethnic studies:** Women's. **Biology:** General, biochemistry. **Business:** General, accounting, banking/financial services, business admin, marketing, nonprofit/public. **Communications:** General, broadcast journalism, journalism. **Computer sciences:** General, computer science. **Conservation:** General, environmental studies. **Education:** General, biology, chemistry, elementary, English, foreign languages, French, German, health, history, mathematics, mentally handicapped, middle, multi-level teacher, music, physical, physics, science, secondary, social science, social studies, Spanish, special. **Engineering:** Science. **English:** English lit. **Foreign languages:** General, French, German, Spanish. **Health:** Clinical lab science, predental, premedicine, prepharmacy, preveterinary. **History:** General. **Interdisciplinary:** Global studies, math/computer science, peace/conflict. **Legal studies:** Prelaw. **Liberal arts:** Arts/sciences. **Math:** General. **Philosophy/religion:** Philosophy, religion. **Physical sciences:** Chemistry, physics. **Psychology:** General. **Public administration:** Social work. **Social sciences:** General, economics, political science, sociology. **Theology:** Sacred music. **Visual/performing arts:** Art, music performance.

**Most popular majors.** Business/marketing 17%, education 29%, health sciences 8%, psychology 7%, social sciences 7%.

**Computing on campus.** 165 workstations in dormitories, library, computer center. Dormitories wired for high-speed internet access and linked to campus network. Helpline, student web hosting available.

**Student life. Freshman orientation:** Mandatory, $125 fee. Preregistration for classes offered. 3 days prior to start of fall classes. **Policies:** Significant student involvement in governance, programming, activities, and administrative services such as security, health, and residence hall management. **Housing:** Guaranteed on-campus for freshmen. Coed dorms, single-sex dorms, special housing for disabled, apartments, substance-free housing available. All students over 21 may live off-campus. Other students required to live on-campus unless living with family. **Activities:** Bands, campus ministries, choral groups, dance, drama, international student organizations, literary magazine, music ensembles, Model UN, radio station, student government, student newspaper, symphony orchestra, political clubs, Black Student Union, Hispanos Unidos, Habitat for Humanity, volunteer corps, Intercollegiate Ministries, Amnesty International, Manchester Environmental Club.

**Athletics.** NCAA. **Intercollegiate:** Baseball M, basketball, cross-country, football (tackle) M, golf, soccer, softball W, tennis, track and field, volleyball W, wrestling M. **Intramural:** Badminton, basketball, bowling, cross-country, golf, racquetball, soccer, softball, swimming, table tennis, tennis, track and field, volleyball, wrestling M. **Team name:** Spartans.

**Student services.** Campus ministries, career counseling, student employment services, financial aid counseling, health services, minority student services, personal counseling, placement for graduates, veterans' counselor. **Physically disabled:** Services for visually, hearing impaired.

**Contact.** E-mail: admitinfo@manchester.edu
Phone: (260) 982-5055 Toll-free number: (800) 852-3648
Fax: (260) 982-5239
Stuart Jones, Dean of Enrollment, Manchester College, 604 East College Avenue, North Manchester, IN 46962-0365

---

## Marian College
**Indianapolis, Indiana** — CB member
**www.marian.edu** — CB code: 1442

- Private 4-year liberal arts college affiliated with Roman Catholic Church
- Residential campus in very large city
- 1,906 degree-seeking undergraduates: 26% part-time, 68% women
- 18 degree-seeking graduate students
- 62% of applicants admitted
- SAT or ACT with writing required
- 52% graduate within 6 years

**General.** Founded in 1851. Regionally accredited. **Degrees:** 280 bachelor's, 93 associate awarded; master's offered. **ROTC:** Army. **Location:** 4 miles from downtown. **Calendar:** Semester, limited summer session. **Full-time faculty:** 80 total; 44% have terminal degrees, 6% minority, 52% women. **Part-time faculty:** 76 total; 20% have terminal degrees, 4% minority, 53% women. **Class size:** 69% < 20, 27% 20-39, 2% 40-49, 2% 50-99. **Special facilities:** Archives (materials on development of education in Archdiocese), 35 acre wetlands biology/ecology laboratory, Allison and Wheeler-Stokely mansions, Japanese tea house and garden, undergraduate seminary.

**Freshman class profile.** 1,376 applied, 851 admitted, 308 enrolled.

| Mid 50% test scores | | | |
|---|---|---|---|
| SAT critical reading: | 440-550 | GPA 2.0-2.99: | 32% |
| SAT math: | 430-610 | Rank in top quarter: | 36% |
| ACT composite: | 19-25 | Rank in top tenth: | 13% |
| GPA 3.50 or higher: | 34% | Return as sophomores: | 76% |
| GPA 3.0-3.49: | 32% | Out-of-state: | 12% |
| | | Live on campus: | 77% |

**Basis for selection.** School achievement record, test scores, recommendations important. TOEFL required for nonnative speakers of English. Interview recommended. Essay recommended for academically weak applicants. **Homeschooled:** Transcript of courses and grades, letter of recommendation (nonparent) required.

**High school preparation.** 20 units required. Required and recommended units include English 4, mathematics 2-3, social studies 2, science 2-3 (laboratory 2), foreign language 1-2 and academic electives 9.

**2007-2008 Annual costs.** Tuition/fees: $20,800. Room/board: $7,400. Books/supplies: $700. Personal expenses: $900.

**2006-2007 Financial aid. Need-based:** 251 full-time freshmen applied for aid; 232 were judged to have need; 232 of these received aid. Average need met was 88%. Average scholarship/grant was $9,414; average loan $3,486. 67% of total undergraduate aid awarded as scholarships/grants, 33% as loans/jobs. **Non-need-based:** Awarded to 1,085 full-time undergraduates, including 210 freshmen. Scholarships awarded for academics, alumni affiliation, art, athletics, leadership, music/drama, religious affiliation.

**Application procedures. Admission:** Priority date 5/1; deadline 8/1. $20 fee, may be waived for applicants with need. Application may be submitted online. Admission notification on a rolling basis beginning on or about 9/15. Must reply by May 1 or within 3 week(s) if notified thereafter. **Financial aid:** Closing date 3/10. FAFSA, institutional form required. Applicants notified on a rolling basis starting 3/15; must reply within 3 week(s) of notification.

**Academics. Special study options:** Accelerated study, cooperative education, cross-registration, double major, dual enrollment of high school students, honors, independent study, internships, liberal arts/career combination, study abroad, teacher certification program. **Credit/placement by examination:** AP, CLEP, IB, SAT, ACT, institutional tests. 30 credit hours maximum toward associate degree, 60 toward bachelor's. **Support services:** Learning center, reduced course load, remedial instruction, study skills assistance, tutoring, writing center.

**Majors. Biology:** General. **Business:** General, accounting, finance, management information systems, marketing. **Communications:** General. **Education:** Elementary, physical. **English:** English lit. **Foreign languages:** French, Spanish. **Health:** Nursing (RN). **History:** General. **Math:** General. **Parks/recreation:** Sports admin. **Philosophy/religion:** Philosophy. **Physical sciences:** Chemistry. **Psychology:** General. **Social sciences:** Economics, political science, sociology. **Theology:** Religious ed, theology. **Visual/performing arts:** Art, art history/conservation, commercial/advertising art.

**Most popular majors.** Business/marketing 46%, education 6%, health sciences 20%.

**Computing on campus.** 225 workstations in dormitories, library, computer center, student center. Dormitories wired for high-speed internet access and linked to campus network. Online library, helpline, wireless network available.

**Student life. Freshman orientation:** Mandatory. Preregistration for classes offered. Held weekend prior to start of school. Community service project required. **Policies:** Drinking under the age of 21 on campus prohibited. **Housing:** Guaranteed on-campus for freshmen. Coed dorms, single-sex dorms, apartments, substance-free housing available. $125 deposit, deadline 6/1. College-owned apartments for students 21 or older, voluntary spiritual living community, nonsmoking areas, suite-style rooms, singles available. **Activities:** Bands, choral groups, dance, drama, literary magazine, music ensembles, musical theater, student government, student newspaper, campus ministry, service organization, Campus America Life League, BACCHUS, Project Earth, community ministries, Union for Black Identity, Fellowship of Christian Athletes, student association, Campus Crusade for Christ.

**Athletics.** NAIA. **Intercollegiate:** Baseball M, basketball, cheerleading, cross-country, football (tackle) M, golf, soccer, softball W, tennis, track and field, volleyball W. **Intramural:** Basketball, fencing, football (non-tackle), handball, racquetball, softball, table tennis, tennis, volleyball. **Team name:** Knights.

**Student services.** Adult student services, alcohol/substance abuse counseling, campus ministries, career counseling, student employment services, financial aid counseling, health services, personal counseling, placement for graduates. **Physically disabled:** Services for visually, hearing impaired.

**Contact.** E-mail: admissions@marian.edu
Phone: (317) 955-6300 Toll-free number: (800) 772-7264
Fax: (317) 955-6401
Luann Brames, Director of Enrollment, Marian College, 3200 Cold Spring Road, Indianapolis, IN 46222-1997

## Martin University
### Indianapolis, Indiana
### www.martin.edu
**CB code: 1379**

- Private 4-year university and liberal arts college
- Commuter campus in very large city
- 615 degree-seeking undergraduates
- Interview required

**General.** Founded in 1977. Regionally accredited. **Degrees:** 62 bachelor's awarded; master's offered. **Calendar:** Semester, extensive summer session. **Full-time faculty:** 26 total. **Part-time faculty:** 10 total.

**Basis for selection.** Open admission. Essay important and recommendations considered.

**2007-2008 Annual costs.** Tuition/fees: $13,520. Books/supplies: $820. Personal expenses: $1,114.

**Application procedures. Admission:** Priority date 3/1; no deadline. $25 fee, may be waived for applicants with need. Application must be submitted on paper. Admission notification on a rolling basis. **Financial aid:** Priority date 5/1; no closing date. FAFSA required. Applicants notified on a rolling basis starting 6/1; must reply within 2 week(s) of notification.

**Academics. Special study options:** Accelerated study, cross-registration, double major, internships, liberal arts/career combination, student-designed major. **Credit/placement by examination:** CLEP. **Support services:** Learning center, remedial instruction, tutoring.

**Majors. Area/ethnic studies:** African, African-American. **Biology:** General. **Business:** General, accounting, insurance. **Communications:** General. **Communications technology:** General. **Conservation:** Environmental science. **Education:** Adult/continuing, early childhood. **English:** Composition, English lit. **Foreign languages:** Spanish. **Health:** Genetic counseling. **History:** General. **Liberal arts:** Arts/sciences. **Math:** General. **Philosophy/religion:** Religion. **Psychology:** General. **Social sciences:** General, political science, sociology. **Theology:** Religious ed. **Visual/performing arts:** Music performance, piano/organ, studio arts.

**Most popular majors.** Biology 8%, business/marketing 29%, family/consumer sciences 8%, legal studies 17%, philosophy/religious studies 13%.

**Computing on campus.** 14 workstations in computer center.

**Student life. Activities:** Choral groups, dance, drama, music ensembles, opera, student government, student newspaper, GIFT of Brightwood.

**Student services.** Adult student services, career counseling, student employment services, health services, personal counseling, placement for graduates, veterans' counselor.

**Contact.** Phone: (317) 543-3238 Fax: (317) 543-3257
Charlesetta Staley, Director of Admissions, Martin University, 2171 Avondale Place, Indianapolis, IN 46218

## Oakland City University
### Oakland City, Indiana
### www.oak.edu
**CB code: 1585**

- Private 4-year university and liberal arts college affiliated with Baptist General Conference
- Commuter campus in small town
- 1,492 degree-seeking undergraduates: 11% part-time, 53% women, 11% African American, 1% Asian American, 1% Hispanic American, 2% international
- 263 graduate students
- 63% graduate within 6 years

**General.** Founded in 1885. Regionally accredited. Branches in Bedford and at Branchville Training Center. Accelerated degrees offered at several off-campus sites (National Guard bases and civilian locations), Rockville Training Center, Madison Correctional Facility, NewCastle Correctional Facility, Miami Correctional Center, and Indiana Women's Prison. **Degrees:** 302 bachelor's, 184 associate awarded; master's, doctoral, first professional offered. **Location:** 30 miles from Evansville. **Calendar:** Semester, limited summer session. **Full-time faculty:** 43 total. **Part-time faculty:** 85 total. **Class size:** 81% < 20, 19% 20-39, less than 1% 40-49.

**Freshman class profile.** 620 applied, 349 admitted, 349 enrolled.

| Mid 50% test scores | | | |
|---|---|---|---|
| SAT critical reading: | 400-510 | GPA 3.0-3.49: | 31% |
| SAT math: | 420-530 | GPA 2.0-2.99: | 27% |
| SAT writing: | 400-500 | Rank in top quarter: | 16% |
| ACT composite: | 17-23 | Rank in top tenth: | 9% |
| GPA 3.50 or higher: | 30% | Return as sophomores: | 72% |
| | | Out-of-state: | 10% |

**Basis for selection.** Open admission, but selective for some programs. High school GPA of 2.5 and SAT or ACT test scores most important. Recommendations considered. Interview and essay recommended. **Homeschooled:** Transcript of courses and grades required.

**High school preparation.** 12 units recommended. Recommended units include English 4, mathematics 3, social studies 2 and science 3.

**2007-2008 Annual costs.** Tuition/fees: $14,820. Room/board: $5,900. Books/supplies: $1,500. Personal expenses: $1,500.

**2007-2008 Financial aid. Need-based:** 70% of total undergraduate aid awarded as scholarships/grants, 30% as loans/jobs. **Non-need-based:** Scholarships awarded for academics, alumni affiliation, art, athletics, minority status, music/drama, religious affiliation.

**Application procedures. Admission:** Closing date 9/8 (receipt date). $35 fee, may be waived for applicants with need. Application may be submitted online. Admission notification on a rolling basis. **Financial aid:** Closing date 3/1. FAFSA required. Applicants notified on a rolling basis starting 5/1.

**Academics. Special study options:** Accelerated study, combined bachelor's/graduate degree, cooperative education, distance learning, double major, dual enrollment of high school students, external degree, honors, independent study, internships, liberal arts/career combination, teacher certification program. Combined bachelor's/graduate degree: M.S. in Management. **Credit/placement by examination:** AP, CLEP, IB, institutional tests. 16 credit hours maximum toward associate degree, 32 toward bachelor's. **Support services:** Learning center, pre-admission summer program, reduced course load, remedial instruction, tutoring.

**Majors. Biology:** General. **Business:** General, accounting, business admin, human resources, management information systems, organizational behavior. **Computer sciences:** General. **Education:** Art, biology, business, early childhood, elementary, English, health, history, mathematics, music, physical, reading, science, social science, social studies, special, voc/tech. **English:** English lit. **History:** General. **Liberal arts:** Arts/sciences, humanities. **Math:** Applied. **Parks/recreation:** Health/fitness. **Philosophy/religion:** Religion. **Protective services:** Criminal justice. **Psychology:** General. **Social sciences:** General, sociology. **Visual/performing arts:** Art, graphic design, industrial design, music performance.

**Most popular majors.** Business/marketing 59%, education 15%, liberal arts 7%.

**Computing on campus.** 92 workstations in library, computer center, student center. Dormitories wired for high-speed internet access and linked to campus network. Commuter students can connect to campus network. Online library, wireless network available.

**Student life. Freshman orientation:** Mandatory, $75 fee. Preregistration for classes offered. One day immediately before each semester. **Housing:** Guaranteed on-campus for all undergraduates. Single-sex dorms, apartments, substance-free housing available. $100 fully refundable deposit, deadline 7/22. **Activities:** Pep band, choral groups, drama, music ensembles, student government, student newspaper, mental health assistance group, Circle-K, Student Christian Association, Fellowship of Christian Athletes, Theologs, student education association.

**Athletics.** NCAA, NCCAA. **Intercollegiate:** Baseball M, basketball, cheerleading M, cross-country, golf, soccer, softball W, tennis, volleyball W. **Intramural:** Basketball, bowling, football (non-tackle), softball, table tennis, tennis, volleyball. **Team name:** Oaks.

**Student services.** Adult student services, campus ministries, career counseling, services for economically disadvantaged, student employment services, financial aid counseling, personal counseling, placement for graduates, veterans' counselor.

**Contact.** E-mail: ocuadmit@oak.edu
Phone: (812) 749-4781 ext. 222 Toll-free number: (800) 737-5125
Fax: (812) 749-1433
Brian Baker, Director of Admissions, Oakland City University, 138 North Lucretia Street, Oakland City, IN 47660

---

### Purdue University
**West Lafayette, Indiana**  **CB member**
**www.purdue.edu**  **CB code: 1631**

- Public 4-year university
- Residential campus in small city
- 30,952 degree-seeking undergraduates: 4% part-time, 42% women, 4% African American, 6% Asian American, 3% Hispanic American, 7% international
- 7,740 degree-seeking graduate students
- 79% of applicants admitted
- SAT or ACT with writing required
- 71% graduate within 6 years

**General.** Founded in 1869. Regionally accredited. **Degrees:** 5,839 bachelor's, 458 associate awarded; master's, doctoral, first professional offered. **ROTC:** Army, Naval, Air Force. **Location:** 65 miles from Indianapolis. **Calendar:** Semester, limited summer session. **Full-time faculty:** 2,097 total; 80% have terminal degrees, 18% minority, 29% women. **Part-time faculty:** 290 total; 33% have terminal degrees, 8% minority, 53% women. **Class size:** 34% < 20, 40% 20-39, 6% 40-49, 11% 50-99, 9% >100. **Special facilities:** Linear accelerator, horticultural park, concert hall, 3 theaters, outdoor concert facility, 2 professional golf courses, on-campus airport.

**Freshman class profile.** 25,929 applied, 20,429 admitted, 6,888 enrolled.

| Mid 50% test scores | | | |
|---|---|---|---|
| SAT critical reading: | 490-610 | GPA 2.0-2.99: | 11% |
| SAT math: | 530-660 | Rank in top quarter: | 63% |
| ACT composite: | 23-28 | Rank in top tenth: | 31% |
| GPA 3.50 or higher: | 56% | Return as sophomores: | 85% |
| GPA 3.0-3.49: | 33% | Out-of-state: | 29% |
| | | International: | 6% |

**Basis for selection.** Rigor of high school curriculum, standardized test scores and high school GPA most important. Class rank also important. Interview is required for veterinary medicine, veterinary technology and pharmacy applicants.

**High school preparation.** Required and recommended units include English 4, mathematics 3, science 2-3 (laboratory 2-3) and foreign language 2. 2 units in history or social science recommended.

**2007-2008 Annual costs.** Tuition/fees: $7,416; $22,224 out-of-state. Engineering students pay additional $628 fee per year. Management students pay additional $978 fee per year. Room/board: $7,962. Books/supplies: $1,050. Personal expenses: $1,690.

**2007-2008 Financial aid. Need-based:** 4,821 full-time freshmen applied for aid; 2,994 were judged to have need; 2,984 of these received aid. Average need met was 93%. Average scholarship/grant was $10,988; average loan $3,490. 53% of total undergraduate aid awarded as scholarships/grants, 47% as loans/jobs. **Non-need-based:** Awarded to 5,914 full-time

undergraduates, including 2,017 freshmen. Scholarships awarded for academics, athletics, leadership, music/drama, ROTC, state residency. **Additional information:** Cooperative work for credit available in many programs.

**Application procedures. Admission:** Priority date 3/1; no deadline. $30 fee, may be waived for applicants with need. Application may be submitted online. Admission notification on a rolling basis beginning on or about 9/15. Must reply by May 1 or within 3 week(s) if notified thereafter. November 15 deadline for flight technology program and deadine for veterinary technology program. December 1 preferential deadline for pre-pharmacy, health sciences and nursing. **Financial aid:** Priority date 3/1; no closing date. FAFSA required. Applicants notified by 4/15.

**Academics.** Minimal number of courses outside major allowed on pass/fail basis, not to exceed 20 percent of total credit hours required. **Special study options:** Accelerated study, combined bachelor's/graduate degree, cooperative education, cross-registration, distance learning, double major, dual enrollment of high school students, exchange student, honors, independent study, internships, liberal arts/career combination, study abroad, teacher certification program, weekend college. **Credit/placement by examination:** AP, CLEP, IB, SAT, ACT, institutional tests. **Support services:** Learning center, pre-admission summer program, reduced course load, remedial instruction, study skills assistance, tutoring, writing center.

**Majors. Agriculture:** General, agronomy, animal sciences, communications, economics, farm/ranch, food science, horticultural science, horticulture, mechanization, production, products processing. **Architecture:** Landscape. **Area/ethnic studies:** African-American, Asian, French, German, Japanese, women's. **Biology:** General, biochemistry, Biochemistry/biophysics and molecular biology, botany, cellular/molecular, entomology, microbiology, molecular, plant genetics, zoology. **Business:** Accounting, accounting/business management, accounting/finance, actuarial science, business admin, fashion, financial planning, hospitality admin, hotel/motel admin, human resources, marketing, operations, tourism/travel. **Communications:** General, advertising, broadcast journalism, journalism, public relations. **Computer sciences:** General, computer graphics, computer science, networking. **Conservation:** General, environmental science, fisheries, forestry, wildlife. **Education:** General, agricultural, art, biology, chemistry, early childhood, early childhood special, elementary, family/consumer sciences, foreign languages, French, German, health, kindergarten/preschool, mathematics, multi-level teacher, physical, physics, secondary, social studies, Spanish, technology/industrial arts. **Engineering:** Aerospace, agricultural, biomedical, chemical, civil, computer, construction, electrical, industrial, materials, mechanical, nuclear, surveying. **Engineering technology:** Aerospace, architectural, computer, construction, electrical, industrial, industrial management, manufacturing, mechanical, mechanical drafting, robotics, surveying. **English:** Creative writing, English lit. **Family/consumer sciences:** General, clothing/textiles, family studies, family/community services, food/nutrition. **Foreign languages:** General, classics, Japanese, Russian, Spanish. **Health:** Athletic training, audiology/hearing, audiology/speech pathology, clinical lab science, dietetic technician, health services, nursing (RN), occupational health, predental, premedicine, speech pathology, veterinary technology/assistant. **History:** General. **Interdisciplinary:** Biological/physical sciences, nutrition sciences. **Liberal arts:** Arts/sciences, humanities. **Math:** General, applied, statistics. **Parks/recreation:** Exercise sciences, health/fitness. **Philosophy/religion:** Philosophy, religion. **Physical sciences:** Atmospheric science, chemistry, geology, meteorology, physics. **Protective services:** Law enforcement admin. **Psychology:** General. **Public administration:** Social work. **Social sciences:** General, anthropology, political science, sociology. **Transportation:** Air traffic control, airline/commercial pilot, aviation, aviation management. **Visual/performing arts:** General, acting, art, art history/conservation, design, dramatic, fashion design, film/cinema, interior design, photography, studio arts.

**Most popular majors.** Business/marketing 15%, education 6%, engineering/engineering technologies 28%, family/consumer sciences 6%, health sciences 7%.

**Computing on campus.** 1,986 workstations in dormitories, library, computer center. Dormitories wired for high-speed internet access and linked to campus network. Commuter students can connect to campus network. Online library, wireless network available.

**Student life. Freshman orientation:** Available, $300 fee. Preregistration for classes offered. Held the week before classes. **Policies:** Nondiscrimination, antiharassment, antihazing policies; bill of students' rights. **Housing:** Coed dorms, single-sex dorms, special housing for disabled, apartments, cooperative housing, fraternity/sorority housing, substance-free housing available. $75 nonrefundable deposit, deadline 3/1. **Activities:** Bands, choral groups, dance, drama, literary magazine, music ensembles, musical theater, radio station, student government, student newspaper, symphony orchestra, TV station, Over 750 religious, political, ethnic, academic, hobby and social service organizations.

**Athletics.** NCAA. **Intercollegiate:** Baseball M, basketball, cross-country, diving, football (tackle) M, golf, soccer W, softball W, swimming, tennis, track and field, volleyball W, wrestling M. **Intramural:** Badminton, basketball, cross-country, football (non-tackle), golf, racquetball, soccer, softball, swimming, table tennis, tennis, track and field, volleyball. **Team name:** Boilermakers.

**Student services.** Adult student services, alcohol/substance abuse counseling, campus ministries, career counseling, services for economically disadvantaged, student employment services, financial aid counseling, health services, legal services, minority student services, on-campus daycare, personal counseling, placement for graduates, veterans' counselor, women's services. **Physically disabled:** Services for visually, speech, hearing impaired.

**Contact.** E-mail: admissions@purdue.edu
Phone: (765) 494-1776 Fax: (765) 494-0544
Pamela Horne, Dean of Admissions, Purdue University, 475 Stadium Mall Drive, West Lafayette, IN 47907-2050

---

## Purdue University Calumet
### Hammond, Indiana
**CB member**
### www.calumet.purdue.edu
**CB code: 1638**

- Public 4-year university and branch campus college
- Commuter campus in small city
- 8,097 degree-seeking undergraduates: 34% part-time, 56% women, 18% African American, 1% Asian American, 14% Hispanic American, 3% international
- 714 degree-seeking graduate students
- 79% of applicants admitted
- SAT or ACT with writing required

**General.** Founded in 1943. Regionally accredited. **Degrees:** 793 bachelor's, 257 associate awarded; master's offered. **ROTC:** Army. **Location:** 20 miles from Chicago. **Calendar:** Semester, extensive summer session. **Full-time faculty:** 302 total; 64% have terminal degrees, 17% minority, 47% women. **Part-time faculty:** 224 total; 11% have terminal degrees, 12% minority, 58% women. **Class size:** 24% < 20, 66% 20-39, 6% 40-49, 4% 50-99, less than 1% >100.

**Freshman class profile.** 3,007 applied, 2,367 admitted, 1,452 enrolled.

| Mid 50% test scores | | | |
|---|---|---|---|
| SAT critical reading: | 400-510 | GPA 2.0-2.99: | 55% |
| SAT math: | 390-510 | Rank in top quarter: | 21% |
| SAT writing: | 380-480 | Rank in top tenth: | 6% |
| GPA 3.50 or higher: | 13% | Return as sophomores: | 62% |
| GPA 3.0-3.49: | 16% | Out-of-state: | 12% |

**Basis for selection.** A combination of class rank, grade average in subjects related to degree objectives, trends in achievement throughout high school, satisfactory high school subject matter requirements, strength of college preparatory program, and standardized test results. Graduation from high school with a minimum of 15 units of credit is required. Beginning applicants who have graduated high school within the last year must take SAT/ACT. Those who have been out of high school more than 1 year must take appropriate placement tests offered through school Skills Assessment and Development Center. Individuals transferring from non-Purdue school may be required to take math and/or English placement tests. **Homeschooled:** Transcript of courses and grades required.

**High school preparation.** 14 units recommended. Recommended units include English 4, mathematics 2, social studies 1, history 1, science 2 and foreign language 2. Course requirements vary according to program.

**2007-2008 Annual costs.** Tuition/fees: $5,807; $12,797 out-of-state. Books/supplies: $1,050.

**2006-2007 Financial aid. Need-based:** 834 full-time freshmen applied for aid; 613 were judged to have need; 548 of these received aid. Average need met was 19%. Average scholarship/grant was $2,648; average loan $1,405. 38% of total undergraduate aid awarded as scholarships/grants, 62% as loans/jobs. **Non-need-based:** Awarded to 667 full-time undergraduates, including 154 freshmen. Scholarships awarded for academics, alumni affiliation, athletics, minority status, state residency.

**Application procedures. Admission:** No deadline. No application fee. Application may be submitted online. Admission notification on a rolling basis. **Financial aid:** Priority date 3/10, closing date 6/30. FAFSA required. Applicants notified on a rolling basis starting 5/1; must reply within 2 week(s) of notification.

**Academics. Special study options:** Combined bachelor's/graduate degree, cooperative education, distance learning, double major, dual enrollment of high school students, ESL, honors, independent study, internships,

study abroad, teacher certification program. **Credit/placement by examination:** AP, CLEP, SAT, ACT, institutional tests. **Support services:** Learning center, reduced course load, remedial instruction, study skills assistance, tutoring, writing center.

**Honors college/program.** Minimum high school GPA of 3.5/4.0, ACT score of 27 or higher, or a 1200 SAT (verbal + math) or higher. Current students should have a cumulative GPA of at least 3.5. Must maintain a cumulative GPA of 3.5/4.0. Factors taken into consideration include outstanding academic achievement, strength of academic program, ACT or SAT scores, demonstrated leadership, creativity, community involvement, essay, and letter(s) of recommendation.

**Majors. Biology:** General. **Business:** General, accounting, business admin, entrepreneurial studies, finance, human resources, retailing, small business admin. **Communications:** General, broadcast journalism, journalism, public relations. **Computer sciences:** General, computer graphics, computer science, database management, information systems, networking, programming. **Education:** General, biology, chemistry, early childhood, elementary, English, French, multi-level teacher, physics, science, secondary, social science, social studies, special. **Engineering:** General, computer, electrical, mechanical, mechanics, software. **Engineering technology:** Construction, electrical, industrial management. **English:** American lit, composition, English lit. **Foreign languages:** General, French, Spanish. **Health:** Clinical lab science, nursing (RN), premedicine, preop/surgical nursing, prepharmacy, preveterinary. **History:** General. **Interdisciplinary:** Gerontology, math/computer science. **Legal studies:** Prelaw. **Math:** General, applied. **Philosophy/religion:** Philosophy. **Physical sciences:** Chemistry, physics. **Protective services:** Law enforcement admin. **Psychology:** General. **Social sciences:** Political science, sociology.

**Most popular majors.** Business/marketing 26%, communications/journalism 6%, computer/information sciences 7%, education 7%, engineering/engineering technologies 14%, social sciences 10%.

**Computing on campus.** 1,500 workstations in library, computer center, student center. Dormitories wired for high-speed internet access and linked to campus network. Commuter students can connect to campus network. Online course registration, online library, helpline, wireless network available.

**Student life. Freshman orientation:** Mandatory. Preregistration for classes offered. **Housing:** Apartments, substance-free housing available. **Activities:** Choral groups, dance, drama, international student organizations, literary magazine, musical theater, radio station, student government, student newspaper, TV station, Black Student Union, Los Latinos, Society of Professional Hispanic Engineers, InterVarsity Christian Fellowship, Muslim Student Association, New Life Ministries, National Society of Black Engineers, Purdue Indian Students Association, Korean Student Organization, Social Justice Club.

**Athletics.** NAIA. **Intercollegiate:** Basketball, cheerleading. **Intramural:** Basketball, bowling, golf, racquetball, sailing, soccer, softball, table tennis, volleyball, weight lifting. **Team name:** Peregrines.

**Student services.** Adult student services, career counseling, student employment services, financial aid counseling, health services, on-campus daycare, personal counseling, placement for graduates, veterans' counselor. **Physically disabled:** Services for visually, speech, hearing impaired.

**Contact.** E-mail: adms@calumet.purdue.edu
Phone: (219) 989-2213 Toll-free number: (800) 447-76383 ext. 2213
Fax: (219) 989-2775
Paul McGuinness, Director of Admissions, Purdue University Calumet, 2200 169th Street, Hammond, IN 46323-2094

---

## Purdue University North Central
### Westville, Indiana
**CB member**
### www.pnc.edu
**CB code: 1640**

- Public 4-year branch campus college
- Commuter campus in rural community
- 3,512 degree-seeking undergraduates: 35% part-time, 58% women
- 90 degree-seeking graduate students
- 87% of applicants admitted

**General.** Founded in 1943. Regionally accredited. **Degrees:** 257 bachelor's, 306 associate awarded; master's offered. **Location:** 10 miles from Michigan City, 13 miles from Laporte. **Calendar:** Semester, limited summer session. **Full-time faculty:** 110 total; 58% have terminal degrees, 18% minority, 44% women. **Part-time faculty:** 175 total; 13% have terminal degrees, 5% minority, 49% women. **Class size:** 62% < 20, 35% 20-39, 1% 40-49, 2% 50-99, less than 1% >100.

**Freshman class profile.** 1,330 applied, 1,152 admitted, 842 enrolled.

| Mid 50% test scores | | | |
|---|---|---|---|
| SAT critical reading: | 410-510 | GPA 2.0-2.99: | 53% |
| SAT math: | 410-520 | Rank in top quarter: | 19% |
| ACT composite: | 18-21 | Rank in top tenth: | 4% |
| GPA 3.50 or higher: | 11% | Return as sophomores: | 53% |
| GPA 3.0-3.49: | 29% | Out-of-state: | 2% |

**Basis for selection.** Class rank and test scores important. Admission requirements are reduced for community college division. SAT or ACT recommended. Interview recommended for academically weak applicants.

**High school preparation.** 17 units required. Required and recommended units include English 4, mathematics 3, social studies 1, history 1, science 2-3 (laboratory 2-3) and academic electives 5.

**2007-2008 Annual costs.** Tuition/fees: $5,817; $13,593 out-of-state. Books/supplies: $1,749. Personal expenses: $1,616.

**2007-2008 Financial aid.** All financial aid based on need. Average need met was 60%. Average scholarship/grant was $4,958; average loan $2,970. 53% of total undergraduate aid awarded as scholarships/grants, 47% as loans/jobs.

**Application procedures. Admission:** Priority date 8/1; no deadline. No application fee. Application may be submitted online. Admission notification on a rolling basis beginning on or about 8/1. **Financial aid:** Priority date 3/10, closing date 6/30. FAFSA required. Applicants notified on a rolling basis starting 5/31; must reply within 2 week(s) of notification.

**Academics. Special study options:** Combined bachelor's/graduate degree, distance learning, dual enrollment of high school students, independent study, internships, teacher certification program, weekend college. **Credit/placement by examination:** CLEP, institutional tests. **Support services:** Learning center, reduced course load, remedial instruction, tutoring.

**Majors. Biology:** General. **Business:** General, accounting, human resources, labor relations, operations. **Communications:** General. **Computer sciences:** Applications programming, data processing. **Education:** Elementary. **Engineering technology:** General, electrical, mechanical. **English:** English lit. **Health:** Nursing (RN). **Liberal arts:** Arts/sciences.

**Most popular majors.** Business/marketing 33%, education 8%, engineering/engineering technologies 13%, interdisciplinary studies 8%, liberal arts 24%.

**Computing on campus.** 240 workstations in library, computer center.

**Student life. Freshman orientation:** Available. **Activities:** Campus ministries, drama, literary magazine, student government, student newspaper, Campus Crusade for Christ, computer club, photography club, accounting club, student cultural society, Students in Fall Enterprise.

**Athletics. Intercollegiate:** Baseball M, basketball M, cross-country M. **Intramural:** Basketball, bowling, cross-country, football (tackle) M, golf, skiing, softball, table tennis, tennis, volleyball. **Team name:** Panthers.

**Student services.** Career counseling, student employment services, on-campus daycare, personal counseling, placement for graduates. **Physically disabled:** Services for visually, hearing impaired.

**Contact.** E-mail: admissions@pnc.edu
Phone: (219) 785-5505 Toll-free number: (800) 782-1231
Fax: (219) 785-5538
Anthony Cardenas, Director of Admissions, Purdue University North Central, 1401 South US Highway 421, Westville, IN 46391-9528

---

## Rose-Hulman Institute of Technology

**Terre Haute, Indiana**
**www.rose-hulman.edu**

**CB member**
**CB code: 1668**

- Private 4-year engineering college
- Residential campus in small city
- 1,821 degree-seeking undergraduates: 21% women, 2% African American, 5% Asian American, 2% Hispanic American, 2% international
- 107 degree-seeking graduate students
- 70% of applicants admitted
- SAT or ACT (ACT writing optional) required
- 83% graduate within 6 years; 20% enter graduate study

**General.** Founded in 1874. Regionally accredited. **Degrees:** 418 bachelor's awarded; master's offered. **ROTC:** Army, Air Force. **Location:** 73 miles from Indianapolis. **Calendar:** Quarter, limited summer session. **Full-time faculty:** 158 total; 99% have terminal degrees, 10% minority, 22% women. **Part-time faculty:** 8 total; 75% have terminal degrees, 25% women. **Class size:** 40% < 20, 60% 20-39, less than 1% 40-49. **Special facilities:** Advanced learning center, observatory, center for technological research with industry.

**Freshman class profile.** 3,088 applied, 2,152 admitted, 474 enrolled.

| Mid 50% test scores | | | |
|---|---|---|---|
| SAT critical reading: | 560-680 | End year in good standing: | 85% |
| SAT math: | 630-710 | Return as sophomores: | 91% |
| SAT writing: | 550-650 | Out-of-state: | 58% |
| ACT composite: | 27-31 | Live on campus: | 99% |
| Rank in top quarter: | 92% | International: | 1% |
| Rank in top tenth: | 59% | Fraternities: | 35% |
| | | Sororities: | 29% |

**Basis for selection.** GED not accepted. Primary consideration given to school achievement record and subjects taken. Applicants must rank in top quarter of graduating class. Test scores also very important. Recommendations important. Extracurricular and leadership activities, alumni ties considered. Interviews, although not required, can be determining factor. **Home-schooled:** Statement describing homeschool structure and mission, transcript of courses and grades, letter of recommendation (nonparent) required. Lab courses must have been taken at high school or community college.

**High school preparation.** College-preparatory program required. 16 units required. Required and recommended units include English 4, mathematics 4-5, social studies 2, science 2-3 (laboratory 2) and academic electives 4.

**2008-2009 Annual costs.** Tuition/fees: $32,826. Purchase of laptop computer (approximately $2,900) required of freshmen. Room/board: $8,868. Books/supplies: $1,500. Personal expenses: $1,500.

**2007-2008 Financial aid. Need-based:** 417 full-time freshmen applied for aid; 335 were judged to have need; 335 of these received aid. Average need met was 88%. Average scholarship/grant was $17,652; average loan $14,434. 47% of total undergraduate aid awarded as scholarships/grants, 53% as loans/jobs. **Non-need-based:** Awarded to 545 full-time undergraduates, including 128 freshmen. Scholarships awarded for academics, minority status, ROTC.

**Application procedures. Admission:** Priority date 12/1; deadline 3/1 (postmark date). $40 fee, may be waived for applicants with need. Application may be submitted online. Admission notification on a rolling basis beginning on or about 10/1. Must reply by 5/1. **Financial aid:** Priority date 3/1; no closing date. FAFSA required. Applicants notified on a rolling basis starting 3/10.

**Academics.** Area minor programs in science, engineering, humanities and social sciences. Additional certificate and interdisciplinary programs available in imaging systems, German technical translation, consulting engineering, and management studies. **Special study options:** Accelerated study, cooperative education, cross-registration, double major, independent study, study abroad. **Credit/placement by examination:** AP, CLEP, IB, institutional tests. **Support services:** Learning center, reduced course load, study skills assistance, tutoring, writing center.

**Majors. Biology:** General. **Computer sciences:** Computer science. **Engineering:** Biomedical, chemical, civil, computer, electrical, mechanical, physics, software. **Math:** General. **Physical sciences:** Chemistry, physics. **Social sciences:** Economics. **Other:** Optical Engineering.

**Most popular majors.** Computer/information sciences 9%, engineering/engineering technologies 79%.

**Computing on campus.** PC or laptop required. 20 workstations in library. Dormitories wired for high-speed internet access and linked to campus network. Commuter students can connect to campus network. Online course registration, online library, helpline, repair service, student web hosting, wireless network available.

**Student life. Freshman orientation:** Mandatory. **Housing:** Guaranteed on-campus for freshmen. Coed dorms, single-sex dorms, apartments, fraternity/sorority housing available. $75 fully refundable deposit, deadline 6/15. **Activities:** Bands, campus ministries, choral groups, dance, drama, international student organizations, literary magazine, music ensembles, musical theater, radio station, student government, student newspaper, Inter-Varsity Christian Fellowship, Circle K, National Society of Black Engineers, Spanish club, student activities board, Society of Woman Engineers, Alpha Phi Omega Service Fraternity, Catholic campus ministry.

**Athletics. NCAA. Intercollegiate:** Baseball M, basketball, cheerleading M, cross-country, diving, football (tackle) M, golf, rifle, soccer, softball W, swimming, tennis, track and field, volleyball W, wrestling M. **Intramural:** Basketball, cross-country, football (non-tackle), golf, racquetball, soccer, softball, tennis, volleyball. **Team name:** Fightin' Engineers.

**Student services.** Alcohol/substance abuse counseling, campus ministries, career counseling, student employment services, financial aid counseling, health services, personal counseling, placement for graduates.

**Contact.** E-mail: admissions@rose-hulman.edu
Phone: (812) 877-8213 Toll-free number: (800) 248-7448
Fax: (812) 877-8941
James Goecker, Dean of Admissions and Financial Aid, Rose-Hulman Institute of Technology, Office of Admissions, Terre Haute, IN 47803-3999

---

## Saint Joseph's College
Rensselaer, Indiana
www.saintjoe.edu

CB member
CB code: 1697

- Private 4-year liberal arts college affiliated with Roman Catholic Church
- Residential campus in small town
- 1,051 degree-seeking undergraduates: 3% part-time, 59% women, 8% African American, 4% Hispanic American, 1% international
- 75% of applicants admitted
- SAT or ACT (ACT writing optional) required
- 57% graduate within 6 years; 19% enter graduate study

**General.** Founded in 1889. Regionally accredited. **Degrees:** 203 bachelor's, 1 associate awarded; master's offered. **Location:** 80 miles from Chicago, 90 miles from Indianapolis. **Calendar:** Semester, limited summer session. **Full-time faculty:** 59 total; 81% have terminal degrees, 7% minority, 39% women. **Part-time faculty:** 30 total; 47% have terminal degrees, 3% minority, 57% women. **Class size:** 77% < 20, 20% 20-39, 1% 40-49, 1% 50-99.

**Freshman class profile.** 1,321 applied, 991 admitted, 286 enrolled.

| Mid 50% test scores | | | |
|---|---|---|---|
| SAT critical reading: | 420-530 | Rank in top quarter: | 33% |
| SAT math: | 440-560 | Rank in top tenth: | 13% |
| ACT composite: | 19-24 | End year in good standing: | 88% |
| GPA 3.50 or higher: | 28% | Return as sophomores: | 67% |
| GPA 3.0-3.49: | 24% | Out-of-state: | 37% |
| GPA 2.0-2.99: | 45% | Live on campus: | 94% |

**Basis for selection.** For applicants with requirement deficiencies, admissions decision may be deferred until additional requirements (which may include an interview, recommendations, further course work, or an essay) are evaluated. Limited number of these applicants will be admitted under the Freshman Academic Support Program. **Homeschooled:** Statement describing homeschool structure and mission, transcript of courses and grades required. **Learning Disabled:** Documentation of learning disability not considered in application process. After admission, documentation of learning disability must be submitted to Director of Counseling Services in order to receive academic accommodations.

**High school preparation.** 15 units recommended. Recommended units include English 4, mathematics 3, social studies 3, science 3 (laboratory 2) and foreign language 2. 10 recommended units must be from English, foreign language, social studies, mathematics, and natural science. 3 units distributed among social studies, history, and academic electives.

**2008-2009 Annual costs.** Tuition/fees: $23,180. Room/board: $7,170. Books/supplies: $800. Personal expenses: $670.

**2006-2007 Financial aid. Need-based:** 231 full-time freshmen applied for aid; 201 were judged to have need; 201 of these received aid. Average need met was 76%. Average scholarship/grant was $13,285; average loan $3,157. 63% of total undergraduate aid awarded as scholarships/grants, 37% as loans/jobs. **Non-need-based:** Awarded to 308 full-time undergraduates, including 79 freshmen. Scholarships awarded for academics, alumni affiliation, athletics, minority status, music/drama.

**Application procedures. Admission:** Priority date 12/1; no deadline. $25 fee, may be waived for applicants with need. Application may be submitted online. Admission notification on a rolling basis beginning on or about 12/1. Must reply by May 1 or within 2 week(s) if notified thereafter. **Financial aid:** Priority date 3/1; no closing date. FAFSA required. Applicants notified on a rolling basis starting 3/1; must reply by 5/1 or within 2 week(s) of notification.

**Academics.** Core program is a sequence of 10 interdisciplinary courses and seeks to integrate Christian humanism with critical appraisal of human condition. **Special study options:** Accelerated study, cross-registration, double major, dual enrollment of high school students, honors, independent study, internships, liberal arts/career combination, student-designed major, study abroad, teacher certification program, Washington semester. **Credit/**

**placement by examination:** AP, CLEP, institutional tests. Current policy is being reevaluated. **Support services:** Learning center, reduced course load, study skills assistance, tutoring.

**Majors. Biology:** General, biochemistry. **Business:** General, accounting, management information systems. **Communications:** Media studies. **Computer sciences:** General. **Education:** Art, elementary, physical, secondary. **English:** Creative writing, English lit. **Health:** Clinical lab science, nursing (RN), predental, premedicine, preveterinary. **History:** General. **Legal studies:** Prelaw. **Math:** General. **Parks/recreation:** Health/fitness. **Philosophy/religion:** Philosophy. **Physical sciences:** Chemistry. **Protective services:** Criminal justice. **Psychology:** General. **Public administration:** Social work. **Social sciences:** Economics, international relations, political science, sociology. **Theology:** Pastoral counseling. **Visual/performing arts:** Directing/producing, music history, music management, studio arts. **Other:** Religion/philosophy.

**Most popular majors.** Biology 8%, business/marketing 21%, education 17%, health sciences 7%, security/protective services 9%, visual/performing arts 8%.

**Computing on campus.** 69 workstations in library, computer center, student center. Dormitories wired for high-speed internet access and linked to campus network. Helpline, student web hosting, wireless network available.

**Student life. Freshman orientation:** Mandatory. Preregistration for classes offered. One day optional early registrations in June and July; 4-day required orientation in August. **Policies:** Core curriculum is interdisciplinary sequence of general education courses spread over 8 semesters. **Housing:** Guaranteed on-campus for all undergraduates. Coed dorms, single-sex dorms, special housing for disabled, apartments, substance-free housing available. $200 nonrefundable deposit, deadline 5/1. Special dormitories available for non-traditional full-time students. **Activities:** Bands, choral groups, dance, drama, film society, literary magazine, music ensembles, musical theater, radio station, student government, student newspaper, TV station, Gallagher Charitable Society, Habitat for Humanity, Kairos Team, College Republicans, College Democrats, Peer Ministry, Right to Life, Volunteer Corps, Diversity Coalition, St. Thomas Aquinas Catholic Society.

**Athletics.** NCAA. **Intercollegiate:** Baseball M, basketball, cross-country, football (tackle) M, golf, soccer, softball W, tennis, track and field, volleyball W. **Intramural:** Basketball, football (non-tackle), soccer, softball, volleyball. **Team name:** Pumas.

**Student services.** Campus ministries, career counseling, financial aid counseling, health services, personal counseling, placement for graduates.

**Contact.** E-mail: admissions@saintjoe.edu
Phone: (219) 866-6170 Toll-free number: (800) 447-8781
Fax: (219) 866-6122
Karen Raftus, Director of Admissions, Saint Joseph's College, Box 890, Rensselaer, IN 47978

---

## St. Mary-of-the-Woods College
St. Mary-of-the-Woods, Indiana
www.smwc.edu

CB member
CB code: 1704

- Private 4-year liberal arts college for women affiliated with Roman Catholic Church
- Residential campus in rural community
- 1,279 degree-seeking undergraduates: 68% part-time, 96% women, 2% African American, 1% Hispanic American, 1% Native American
- 158 degree-seeking graduate students
- 82% of applicants admitted
- Application essay required
- 51% graduate within 6 years

**General.** Founded in 1840. Regionally accredited. The traditional campus program is open to women only. The external degree (distance education) undergraduate program is now open to men as well as to women. Graduate programs are open to women and men. **Degrees:** 162 bachelor's, 5 associate awarded; master's offered. **ROTC:** Army, Air Force. **Location:** 4 miles from Terre Haute, 70 miles from Indianapolis. **Calendar:** Semester, limited summer session. **Full-time faculty:** 64 total; 55% have terminal degrees, 6% minority, 67% women. **Part-time faculty:** 2 total; 50% have terminal degrees, 100% women. **Class size:** 95% < 20, 5% 20-39. **Special facilities:** Equine indoor and outdoor arenas, wildlife habitat restoration areas.

**Freshman class profile.** 200 applied, 163 admitted, 85 enrolled.

| Mid 50% test scores | | | |
|---|---|---|---|
| SAT critical reading: | 460-560 | GPA 3.0-3.49: | 26% |
| SAT math: | 420-540 | GPA 2.0-2.99: | 22% |
| SAT writing: | 410-530 | Return as sophomores: | 82% |
| ACT composite: | 20-27 | Out-of-state: | 20% |
| GPA 3.50 or higher: | 51% | Live on campus: | 70% |

**Basis for selection.** School achievement record, test scores most important. Recommendations, evaluation of potential for college success considered. Interview recommended. Audition required of music majors. Portfolio required of art and journalism majors. **Learning Disabled:** Meeting with Learning Resource Coordinator strongly recommended.

**High school preparation.** 13 units required; 16 recommended. Required and recommended units include English 4, mathematics 3, social studies 3, science 3 (laboratory 3) and foreign language 2.

**2007-2008 Annual costs.** Tuition/fees: $20,180. Room/board: $7,380. Books/supplies: $1,500. Personal expenses: $1,000.

**2006-2007 Financial aid. Need-based:** 72 full-time freshmen applied for aid; 66 were judged to have need; 66 of these received aid. Average need met was 85%. Average scholarship/grant was $16,817; average loan $3,145. 67% of total undergraduate aid awarded as scholarships/grants, 33% as loans/jobs. **Non-need-based:** Awarded to 98 full-time undergraduates, including 25 freshmen. Scholarships awarded for academics, alumni affiliation, art, athletics, leadership, minority status, music/drama, state residency. **Additional information:** Portfolio or audition required of applicants who wish to be considered for Creative Arts Scholarship.

**Application procedures. Admission:** Closing date 8/15 (receipt date). $30 fee, may be waived for applicants with need. Application may be submitted online. Admission notification on a rolling basis beginning on or about 9/1. Must reply by 5/1. **Financial aid:** Priority date 3/1; no closing date. FAFSA required. Applicants notified on a rolling basis starting 12/1; must reply within 6 week(s) of notification.

**Academics.** Distance education program available in over 20 majors. **Special study options:** Accelerated study, cross-registration, distance learning, double major, external degree, independent study, internships, student-designed major, study abroad, teacher certification program, weekend college. Woods' External Degree Program: students throughout country visit campus 1 or 2 days twice a year and do course work at home. Exchange program with Providence University in Taiwan. Agreement with Regent's College, London. **Credit/placement by examination:** AP, CLEP, IB, institutional tests. 30 credit hours maximum toward associate degree, 60 toward bachelor's. We follow ACE guidelines for the awarding of credit by testing. **Support services:** Learning center, reduced course load, study skills assistance, tutoring, writing center.

**Majors. Agriculture:** Animal husbandry, equestrian studies, equine science. **Biology:** General. **Business:** General, accounting, business admin, communications, e-commerce, human resources, marketing, nonprofit/public. **Communications:** Journalism, media studies, public relations. **Communications technology:** General, graphics. **Computer sciences:** General, web page design. **Education:** General, art, biology, early childhood, elementary, English, foreign languages, kindergarten/preschool, mathematics, music, science, secondary, social science, social studies, Spanish, special. **English:** Creative writing, English lit, technical writing. **Family/consumer sciences:** Aging, family studies. **Health:** Music therapy, predental, premedicine, prepharmacy, preveterinary. **Interdisciplinary:** Biological/physical sciences. **Legal studies:** Paralegal, prelaw. **Liberal arts:** Arts/sciences, humanities. **Math:** General. **Psychology:** General. **Public administration:** Human services. **Social sciences:** General, criminology. **Theology:** Theology. **Visual/performing arts:** Art, design, dramatic, graphic design, music performance, photography. **Other:** Women and theatre.

**Most popular majors.** Agriculture 7%, biology 7%, business/marketing 8%, education 31%, legal studies 7%, liberal arts 7%, psychology 7%, public administration/social services 7%, visual/performing arts 9%.

**Computing on campus.** 90 workstations in dormitories, library, computer center, student center. Dormitories wired for high-speed internet access and linked to campus network. Commuter students can connect to campus network. Online library, helpline, wireless network available.

**Student life. Freshman orientation:** Mandatory. Preregistration for classes offered. First 3 days of fall semester. Requires service component. **Policies:** All students whose families do not live in a contiguous county must live on-campus all four years. **Housing:** Guaranteed on-campus for all undergraduates. Substance-free housing available. $100 fully refundable deposit. **Activities:** Bands, campus ministries, choral groups, dance, drama, literary magazine, music ensembles, musical theater, student government, student newspaper, symphony orchestra, Habitat for Humanity, literacy volunteers,

environmentalist activities, peace and justice committee, arts and issues committee, Race-for-the-Cure, United Way.

**Athletics.** USCAA. **Intercollegiate:** Basketball W, equestrian W, soccer W, softball W. **Team name:** Pomeroys.

**Student services.** Adult student services, alcohol/substance abuse counseling, campus ministries, career counseling, student employment services, financial aid counseling, health services, on-campus daycare, personal counseling, placement for graduates. **Physically disabled:** Services for visually, hearing impaired.

**Contact.** E-mail: smwcadms@smwc.edu
Phone: (812) 535-5106 Toll-free number: (800) 926-7692
Fax: (812) 535-5010
Jill Blunk, Director of Admission, St. Mary-of-the-Woods College, Guerin Hall, SMWC, St. Mary of the Woods, IN 47876

---

## Saint Mary's College

Notre Dame, Indiana
www.saintmarys.edu

**CB member**
**CB code:** 1702

- Private 4-year liberal arts college for women affiliated with Roman Catholic Church
- Residential campus in small city
- 1,591 degree-seeking undergraduates: 2% part-time, 100% women, 1% African American, 2% Asian American, 5% Hispanic American
- 81% of applicants admitted
- SAT or ACT (ACT writing optional), application essay required
- 75% graduate within 6 years; 21% enter graduate study

**General.** Founded in 1844. Regionally accredited. College has campus in Rome, Italy and sponsors programs in Ireland, India, Spain, France and Australia. Summer European study tour. Co-exchange enrollment with the University of Notre Dame. Volunteer service opportunities in the United States and abroad. **Degrees:** 349 bachelor's awarded. **ROTC:** Army, Naval, Air Force. **Location:** One mile from South Bend. **Calendar:** Semester, limited summer session. **Full-time faculty:** 137 total; 88% have terminal degrees, 10% minority, 66% women. **Part-time faculty:** 81 total; 24% have terminal degrees, 5% minority, 69% women. **Class size:** 61% < 20, 37% 20-39, less than 1% 40-49, 1% 50-99. **Special facilities:** Nature trail, performing arts center, greenhouse.

**Freshman class profile.** 1,281 applied, 1,041 admitted, 479 enrolled.

| Mid 50% test scores | | | |
|---|---|---|---|
| SAT critical reading: | 510-620 | GPA 2.0-2.99: | 2% |
| SAT math: | 510-620 | Rank in top quarter: | 65% |
| SAT writing: | 520-630 | Rank in top tenth: | 32% |
| ACT composite: | 22-27 | End year in good standing: | 96% |
| GPA 3.50 or higher: | 70% | Return as sophomores: | 86% |
| GPA 3.0-3.49: | 28% | Out-of-state: | 74% |
| | | Live on campus: | 99% |

**Basis for selection.** School achievement record, high school transcript, GPA, class rank, test scores, and activities important. Essay and school recommendations considered. Students must submit at least one writing component; ACT with Writing required if applicant is not also taking SAT (with mandatory Writing); ACT with Writing recommended even if applicant is also taking SAT. Interview recommended. Audition recommended for music majors. Portfolio recommended for art majors. **Homeschooled:** Students are encouraged to apply. Candidate should contact the Admission Office for details.

**High school preparation.** 16 units required. Required and recommended units include English 4, mathematics 3-4, social studies 2, science 2-4 (laboratory 2), foreign language 2-4 and academic electives 4. Science and nursing programs require more science and mathematics. All students must take an additional 4 units distributed among English, math, science, foreign language, and social studies.

**2007-2008 Annual costs.** Tuition/fees: $26,875. Room/board: $8,675. Books/supplies: $1,150. Personal expenses: $1,350.

**2007-2008 Financial aid. Need-based:** 461 full-time freshmen applied for aid; 317 were judged to have need; 314 of these received aid. Average need met was 84%. Average scholarship/grant was $14,699; average loan $4,059. 66% of total undergraduate aid awarded as scholarships/grants, 34% as loans/jobs. **Non-need-based:** Awarded to 562 full-time undergraduates, including 256 freshmen. Scholarships awarded for academics, art.

**Application procedures. Admission:** Priority date 3/1; no deadline. $30 fee, may be waived for applicants with need. Application may be submitted online. Admission notification on a rolling basis beginning on or about 12/

15. $200 housing deposit refunded if letter sent in by May 1. Housing deposit nonrefundable for early decision. **Financial aid:** Priority date 3/1; no closing date. FAFSA, CSS PROFILE required. Applicants notified on a rolling basis starting 12/15; must reply by 5/1.

**Academics.** Department of Religious Studies coordinated with Department of Theology at University of Notre Dame. After first year, student can take courses in either department. **Special study options:** Accelerated study, cooperative education, cross-registration, double major, exchange student, independent study, internships, liberal arts/career combination, student-designed major, study abroad, teacher certification program, Washington semester. **Credit/placement by examination:** AP, CLEP, IB, institutional tests. 30 credit hours maximum toward bachelor's degree. **Support services:** Reduced course load, tutoring, writing center.

**Majors. Biology:** General. **Business:** Accounting, business admin, management information systems. **Communications:** General. **Education:** Elementary. **English:** British lit, creative writing. **Foreign languages:** French, Spanish. **Health:** Cytotechnology, nursing (RN). **History:** General. **Interdisciplinary:** Math/computer science. **Liberal arts:** Humanities. **Math:** General, applied, statistics. **Philosophy/religion:** Philosophy, religion. **Physical sciences:** Chemistry. **Psychology:** General. **Public administration:** Social work. **Social sciences:** Economics, political science, sociology. **Visual/performing arts:** Art, dramatic, studio arts.

**Most popular majors.** Biology 7%, business/marketing 12%, communications/journalism 8%, education 10%, English 7%, health sciences 10%, psychology 6%, social sciences 8%, visual/performing arts 7%.

**Computing on campus.** 209 workstations in dormitories, library, computer center, student center. Dormitories wired for high-speed internet access and linked to campus network. Commuter students can connect to campus network. Online course registration, online library, helpline, repair service, student web hosting, wireless network available.

**Student life. Freshman orientation:** Mandatory. Preregistration for classes offered. Held during weekend prior to beginning of fall semester. Preorientation sessions held for fall admits during summer months. **Policies:** Educational judicial system guaranteeing certain due process rights to all students involved in discipline situation; student judicial board provides opportunity for peer review system. **Housing:** Guaranteed on-campus for all undergraduates. Apartments available. $200 fully refundable deposit. **Activities:** Marching band, choral groups, dance, drama, literary magazine, music ensembles, musical theater, opera, radio station, student government, student newspaper, TV station, neighborhood study help program, Community of International Lay Apostolate, Urban Plunge community program, Circle-K, World Hunger Coalition, Student Alliance for Women's Colleges, Right to Life, Women for the Environment, Sisters of Nefertiti, Fuerza y Union Entre las Razas.

**Athletics.** NCAA. **Intercollegiate:** Basketball W, cross-country W, diving W, golf W, soccer W, softball W, swimming W, tennis W, volleyball W. **Intramural:** Soccer W, softball W, tennis W, volleyball W. **Team name:** Belles.

**Student services.** Adult student services, campus ministries, career counseling, student employment services, financial aid counseling, health services, minority student services, on-campus daycare, personal counseling, placement for graduates. **Physically disabled:** Services for visually, hearing impaired.

**Contact.** E-mail: admission@saintmarys.edu
Phone: (574) 284-4587 Toll-free number: (800) 551-7621
Fax: (574) 284-4841
Mona Bowe, Director of Admissions, Saint Mary's College, Notre Dame, IN 46556-5001

---

## Taylor University
**Upland, Indiana**
www.taylor.edu

CB member
CB code: 1802

- Private 4-year university and liberal arts college affiliated with interdenominational tradition
- Residential campus in small town
- 1,858 degree-seeking undergraduates: 2% part-time, 55% women, 2% African American, 2% Asian American, 2% Hispanic American, 2% international
- 91% of applicants admitted
- SAT or ACT (ACT writing recommended), application essay, interview required
- 76% graduate within 6 years; 19% enter graduate study

**General.** Founded in 1846. Regionally accredited. Christ-centered, covenant community committed to service. **Degrees:** 426 bachelor's, 4 associate awarded. **Location:** 20 miles from Muncie, 70 miles from Indianapolis. **Calendar:** 4-1-4, limited summer session. **Full-time faculty:** 122 total; 84% have terminal degrees, 5% minority, 25% women. **Part-time faculty:** 65 total; 17% have terminal degrees, 3% minority, 62% women. **Class size:** 55% < 20, 36% 20-39, 5% 40-49, 2% 50-99, 1% >100. **Special facilities:** Arboretum, environmental studies laboratory, NASA-approved clean room, particle accelerator, NASA project space research equipment, C.S. Lewis Collection of original manuscripts.

**Freshman class profile.** 1,393 applied, 1,269 admitted, 474 enrolled.

| Mid 50% test scores | | | |
|---|---|---|---|
| SAT critical reading: | 520-670 | Rank in top tenth: | 38% |
| SAT math: | 520-670 | End year in good standing: | 94% |
| SAT writing: | 510-640 | Return as sophomores: | 87% |
| ACT composite: | 23-30 | Out-of-state: | 72% |
| Rank in top quarter: | 68% | Live on campus: | 99% |
| | | International: | 1% |

**Basis for selection.** High school transcript, test scores important. Recommend rank in top 25% of graduating class with GPA of 3.3 and SAT combined score of 1000 (exclusive of Writing). Essay and personal statement required. Recommendations from applicant's pastor and counselor required. Cocurricular activities considered. Audition required of music majors. Portfolio recommended for art majors.

**High school preparation.** 15 units required. Required and recommended units include English 4, mathematics 3-4, social studies 2-3, science 3-4 (laboratory 3-4), foreign language 2 and academic electives 3.

**2008-2009 Annual costs.** Tuition/fees (projected): $24,474. Reduced rates for high school students during academic year. Room/board: $6,352. Books/supplies: $900.

**2007-2008 Financial aid. Need-based:** 373 full-time freshmen applied for aid; 309 were judged to have need; 309 of these received aid. Average need met was 77%. Average scholarship/grant was $12,526; average loan $4,514. 65% of total undergraduate aid awarded as scholarships/grants, 35% as loans/jobs. **Non-need-based:** Awarded to 566 full-time undergraduates, including 142 freshmen. Scholarships awarded for academics, alumni affiliation, art, athletics, leadership, minority status, music/drama, religious affiliation, state residency.

**Application procedures. Admission:** No deadline. $25 fee, may be waived for applicants with need. Application may be submitted online. Admission notification on a rolling basis beginning on or about 10/1. Must reply by May 1 or within 2 week(s) if notified thereafter. **Financial aid:** Closing date 3/10. FAFSA required. Applicants notified on a rolling basis starting 3/1; must reply by 5/1.

**Academics. Special study options:** Combined bachelor's/graduate degree, cooperative education, distance learning, double major, dual enrollment of high school students, exchange student, honors, independent study, internships, semester at sea, student-designed major, study abroad, teacher certification program, urban semester, Washington semester. **Credit/placement by examination:** AP, CLEP, institutional tests. 30 credit hours maximum toward associate degree, 30 toward bachelor's. **Support services:** Learning center, remedial instruction, study skills assistance, tutoring, writing center.

**Majors. Biology:** General. **Business:** Accounting, business admin, finance, financial planning, human resources, international, management science, managerial economics, marketing. **Communications:** General, broadcast journalism, journalism, media studies. **Computer sciences:** General, computer graphics, computer science. **Conservation:** Environmental science. **Education:** Art, biology, chemistry, elementary, English, French, history, mathematics, music, physical, physics, science, social science, social studies, Spanish. **Engineering:** Computer, environmental, physics. **English:** English lit. **Foreign languages:** French, Spanish. **History:** General. **Interdisciplinary:** Biological/physical sciences, math/computer science. **Math:** General. **Parks/recreation:** Exercise sciences, health/fitness, sports admin. **Philosophy/religion:** Philosophy. **Physical sciences:** General, chemistry, physics. **Psychology:** General. **Public administration:** Social work. **Social sciences:** General, economics, geography, political science, sociology. **Theology:** Bible, youth ministry. **Visual/performing arts:** Art, dramatic, music management, music performance.

**Most popular majors.** Business/marketing 16%, education 21%, psychology 10%, theological studies 8%.

**Computing on campus.** 228 workstations in library, computer center. Dormitories wired for high-speed internet access and linked to campus network. Commuter students can connect to campus network. Online course registration, online library, helpline, repair service, student web hosting, wireless network available.

**Student life. Freshman orientation:** Available. Preregistration for classes offered. **Policies:** Students and faculty sign Life Together Covenant explaining expectations and responsibilities of living in Christian community where faith is integrated with academic progress. Religious observance required. **Housing:** Guaranteed on-campus for freshmen. Single-sex dorms, apartments, substance-free housing available. $200 deposit, deadline 5/1. Some off-campus apartments available to upperclassmen with special permission. **Activities:** Bands, choral groups, drama, film society, literary magazine, music ensembles, musical theater, opera, radio station, student government, student newspaper, symphony orchestra, TV station, missions service program, multicultural society, Missionary Kids Organizations, community outreach, Campus Life/Young Life, international student society, Habitat for Humanity, ReaLife Inner City Children's Ministry, high school youth conference, Acting on AIDS.

**Athletics.** NAIA, NCCAA. **Intercollegiate:** Baseball M, basketball, cross-country, football (tackle) M, golf M, soccer, softball W, tennis, track and field, volleyball W. **Intramural:** Badminton, basketball, football (non-tackle), golf, racquetball, soccer, softball, table tennis, tennis, volleyball. **Team name:** Trojans.

**Student services.** Campus ministries, career counseling, student employment services, financial aid counseling, health services, minority student services, personal counseling, placement for graduates. **Physically disabled:** Services for visually, speech, hearing impaired.

**Contact.** E-mail: admissions@tayloru.edu
Phone: (765) 998-5511 Toll-free number: (800) 882-3456
Fax: (765) 998-4925
Stephen Mortland, Dean of Enrollment Management, Taylor University, 236 West Reade Avenue, Upland, IN 46989-1001

---

## Taylor University Fort Wayne
### Fort Wayne, Indiana
www.fw.taylor.edu                              CB code: 1227

- Private 4-year university and liberal arts college affiliated with Christian Church
- Residential campus in large city
- 363 degree-seeking undergraduates: 18% part-time, 62% women
- 68% of applicants admitted
- SAT or ACT (ACT writing recommended), application essay required
- 49% graduate within 6 years

**General.** Regionally accredited. **Degrees:** 68 bachelor's, 6 associate awarded. **Calendar:** 4-1-4, limited summer session. **Full-time faculty:** 19 total; 58% have terminal degrees, 5% minority, 47% women. **Part-time faculty:** 21 total; 19% have terminal degrees, 48% women. **Class size:** 72% < 20, 25% 20-39, less than 1% 40-49, 2% 50-99.

**Freshman class profile.** 321 applied, 219 admitted, 80 enrolled.

| Mid 50% test scores | | | |
|---|---|---|---|
| SAT critical reading: | 450-580 | Rank in top quarter: | 37% |
| SAT math: | 430-590 | Rank in top tenth: | 20% |
| SAT writing: | 430-580 | End year in good standing: | 64% |
| ACT composite: | 21-27 | Return as sophomores: | 59% |
| GPA 3.50 or higher: | 45% | Out-of-state: | 33% |
| GPA 3.0-3.49: | 30% | Live on campus: | 95% |
| GPA 2.0-2.99: | 21% | | |

**Basis for selection.** High school record and religious affiliation most important.

**High school preparation.** 14 units required; 16 recommended. Required and recommended units include English 4, mathematics 3, social studies 2, history 2, science 3 and foreign language 2. Recommend 2 units of fine arts.

**2007-2008 Annual costs.** Tuition/fees: $20,074. Room/board: $5,390. Books/supplies: $900. Personal expenses: $1,700.

**2007-2008 Financial aid. Need-based:** 75 full-time freshmen applied for aid; 67 were judged to have need; 67 of these received aid. Average need met was 84%. Average scholarship/grant was $14,119; average loan $4,625. 67% of total undergraduate aid awarded as scholarships/grants, 33% as loans/jobs. **Non-need-based:** Awarded to 65 full-time undergraduates, including 18 freshmen. Scholarships awarded for academics, alumni affiliation, athletics, leadership, music/drama.

**Application procedures. Admission:** No deadline. $20 fee, may be waived for applicants with need. Application may be submitted online. Admission notification on a rolling basis. Must reply by May 1 or within 2 week(s) if notified thereafter. **Financial aid:** Priority date 3/1; no closing

date. Institutional form required. Applicants notified on a rolling basis starting 2/15; must reply by 5/1 or within 2 week(s) of notification.

**Academics. Special study options:** Accelerated study, combined bachelor's/graduate degree, cooperative education, cross-registration, distance learning, double major, dual enrollment of high school students, ESL, exchange student, external degree, independent study, internships, liberal arts/career combination, student-designed major, study abroad, teacher certification program. **Credit/placement by examination:** AP, CLEP, SAT, ACT, institutional tests. 30 credit hours maximum toward bachelor's degree. **Support services:** Learning center, reduced course load, remedial instruction, study skills assistance, tutoring, writing center.

**Majors. Business:** Business admin, marketing. **Education:** Elementary. **English:** Creative writing, English lit. **Health:** Health care admin. **Interdisciplinary:** Intercultural. **Protective services:** Criminal justice. **Public administration:** Social work. **Theology:** Bible, missionary, pastoral counseling, religious ed, youth ministry.

**Computing on campus.** 69 workstations in dormitories, library, computer center, student center. Dormitories wired for high-speed internet access and linked to campus network. Commuter students can connect to campus network. Online library, helpline, wireless network available.

**Student life. Freshman orientation:** Mandatory. Preregistration for classes offered. Held the weekend before classes start. **Policies:** Religious observance required. **Housing:** Guaranteed on-campus for freshmen. Coed dorms, single-sex dorms, apartments, substance-free housing available. $50 fully refundable deposit. **Activities:** Jazz band, choral groups, drama, music ensembles, student government, student newspaper, world outreach, student organization, multicultural activities council, student activities council, adult fellowship, prayer council, dorm council, theatre organization, Sanctity of Life organization.

**Athletics.** USCAA. **Intercollegiate:** Basketball, soccer M, volleyball W. **Intramural:** Basketball, football (non-tackle), table tennis, volleyball. **Team name:** Falcons.

**Student services.** Adult student services, alcohol/substance abuse counseling, campus ministries, career counseling, services for economically disadvantaged, student employment services, financial aid counseling, health services, personal counseling, placement for graduates. **Physically disabled:** Services for visually, speech, hearing impaired.

**Contact.** E-mail: admissions@fw.taylor.edu
Phone: (260) 744-8689 Toll-free number: (800) 233-3922
Fax: (260) 744-8850
Palmer Muntz, Associate Vice President for Enrollment Management, Taylor University Fort Wayne, 1025 West Rudisill Boulevard, Fort Wayne, IN 46807

---

## Tri-State University
### Angola, Indiana
www.tristate.edu                 CB member / CB code: 1811

- Private 4-year university and engineering college
- Residential campus in small town
- 1,265 degree-seeking undergraduates: 6% part-time, 31% women
- 9 degree-seeking graduate students
- 74% of applicants admitted
- SAT or ACT (ACT writing optional) required
- 51% graduate within 6 years; 35% enter graduate study

**General.** Founded in 1884. Regionally accredited. **Degrees:** 186 bachelor's, 38 associate awarded; master's offered. **ROTC:** Air Force. **Location:** 40 miles from Fort Wayne, 80 miles from Toledo, Ohio. **Calendar:** Semester, limited summer session. **Full-time faculty:** 69 total; 65% have terminal degrees, 4% minority, 25% women. **Part-time faculty:** 30 total; 17% have terminal degrees, 3% minority, 30% women. **Class size:** 60% < 20, 40% 20-39. **Special facilities:** Educational media resource center, golf course.

**Freshman class profile.** 2,250 applied, 1,657 admitted, 417 enrolled.

| Mid 50% test scores | | | |
|---|---|---|---|
| SAT critical reading: | 440-550 | Rank in top quarter: | 46% |
| SAT math: | 490-620 | Rank in top tenth: | 20% |
| ACT composite: | 20-25 | Return as sophomores: | 66% |
| GPA 3.50 or higher: | 37% | Out-of-state: | 38% |
| GPA 3.0-3.49: | 35% | Live on campus: | 87% |
| GPA 2.0-2.99: | 27% | Fraternities: | 5% |
| | | Sororities: | 1% |

**Basis for selection.** School achievement, class rank, test scores, school and community activities, and recommendations important. Interview and essay recommended. **Homeschooled:** Statement describing homeschool structure and mission, transcript of courses and grades required. **Learning Disabled:** Must submit a clinical evaluation of the learning disability (completed within the last five years prior to enrollment).

**High school preparation.** 18 units required. Required units include English 4, mathematics 3, social studies 3, science 3 (laboratory 2) and academic electives 3. 3 1/2 years of mathematics, physics, and chemistry required for engineering, mathematics and computer science majors.

**2007-2008 Annual costs.** Tuition/fees: $22,250. Room/board: $6,500. Books/supplies: $1,200. Personal expenses: $3,500.

**2007-2008 Financial aid. Need-based:** 415 full-time freshmen applied for aid; 290 were judged to have need; 290 of these received aid. Average scholarship/grant was $4,477; average loan $3,449. 56% of total undergraduate aid awarded as scholarships/grants, 44% as loans/jobs. **Non-need-based:** Awarded to 1,169 full-time undergraduates, including 415 freshmen. Scholarships awarded for academics, alumni affiliation, music/drama, ROTC.

**Application procedures. Admission:** Priority date 6/1; deadline 8/1. No application fee. Application must be submitted online. Admission notification 8/1. Admission notification on a rolling basis beginning on or about 9/15. Must reply by 5/1. **Financial aid:** Priority date 3/10, closing date 3/10. FAFSA required. Applicants notified by 2/1; Applicants notified on a rolling basis starting 2/1; must reply by 5/1 or within 2 week(s) of notification.

**Academics. Special study options:** Combined bachelor's/graduate degree, cooperative education, distance learning, double major, dual enrollment of high school students, ESL, honors, internships, study abroad, teacher certification program. **Credit/placement by examination:** AP, CLEP, IB, institutional tests. **Support services:** Learning center, reduced course load, remedial instruction, study skills assistance, tutoring, writing center.

**Majors. Biology:** General. **Business:** Accounting, business admin, entrepreneurial studies, finance, management information systems, operations. **Communications:** General. **Computer sciences:** General, computer science. **Education:** Elementary, English, health, mathematics, middle, physical, science, social studies. **Engineering:** Chemical, civil, electrical, mechanical. **Engineering technology:** Drafting, industrial management. **English:** English lit. **Health:** Premedicine. **Math:** General. **Parks/recreation:** Health/fitness, sports admin. **Physical sciences:** Chemistry. **Protective services:** Criminal justice, forensics. **Psychology:** General. **Social sciences:** General.

**Most popular majors.** Business/marketing 21%, education 18%, engineering/engineering technologies 36%, security/protective services 9%.

**Computing on campus.** 150 workstations in dormitories, library, computer center, student center. Dormitories wired for high-speed internet access and linked to campus network. Commuter students can connect to campus network. Online library, helpline, wireless network available.

**Student life. Freshman orientation:** Mandatory. Preregistration for classes offered. 3 days at the start of the fall semester. **Housing:** Guaranteed on-campus for freshmen. Coed dorms, single-sex dorms, apartments available. $150 nonrefundable deposit, deadline 5/1. Honors housing; independent fraternity/sorority housing available. **Activities:** Bands, choral groups, dance, drama, music ensembles, radio station, student government, student newspaper, Circle K, Newman Fellowship, InterVarsity Christian Fellowship, international student association, multicultural student association, Students Against Destructive Decisions, Habitat for Humanity.

**Athletics.** NCAA. **Intercollegiate:** Baseball M, basketball, cross-country, football (tackle) M, golf, lacrosse, soccer, softball W, tennis, track and field, volleyball W, wrestling M. **Intramural:** Badminton, basketball, cheerleading W, football (non-tackle) M, golf, handball, racquetball, softball, table tennis, volleyball. **Team name:** Thunder.

**Student services.** Alcohol/substance abuse counseling, campus ministries, career counseling, student employment services, financial aid counseling, personal counseling, placement for graduates, veterans' counselor.

**Contact.** E-mail: admit@tristate.edu
Phone: (260) 665-4100 Toll-free number: (800) 347-4878
Fax: (260) 665-4578
Scott Goplin, Dean of Admission, Tri-State University, One University Avenue, Angola, IN 46703

---

## University of Evansville
Evansville, Indiana
www.evansville.edu

CB member
CB code: 1208

- Private 4-year university and liberal arts college affiliated with United Methodist Church
- Residential campus in small city

- 2,539 degree-seeking undergraduates: 5% part-time, 59% women, 3% African American, 1% Asian American, 2% Hispanic American, 6% international
- 113 degree-seeking graduate students
- 89% of applicants admitted
- SAT or ACT with writing required
- 62% graduate within 6 years; 20% enter graduate study

**General.** Founded in 1854. Regionally accredited. **Degrees:** 549 bachelor's, 9 associate awarded; master's, doctoral offered. **Location:** 180 miles from Indianapolis, 170 miles from St. Louis. **Calendar:** Semester, limited summer session. **Full-time faculty:** 177 total; 86% have terminal degrees, 7% minority, 34% women. **Part-time faculty:** 52 total; 38% have terminal degrees, 58% women. **Class size:** 51% < 20, 43% 20-39, 5% 40-49, 1% 50-99.

**Freshman class profile.** 2,863 applied, 2,537 admitted, 652 enrolled.

| Mid 50% test scores | | | |
|---|---|---|---|
| SAT critical reading: | 500-620 | Rank in top tenth: | 36% |
| SAT math: | 510-640 | End year in good standing: | 96% |
| SAT writing: | 500-600 | Return as sophomores: | 84% |
| ACT composite: | 22-28 | Out-of-state: | 40% |
| GPA 3.50 or higher: | 66% | Live on campus: | 85% |
| GPA 3.0-3.49: | 23% | International: | 5% |
| GPA 2.0-2.99: | 11% | Fraternities: | 29% |
| Rank in top quarter: | 69% | Sororities: | 20% |

**Basis for selection.** Weighted GPA calculated using academic courses only. Extracurricular activities important. Interview recommended. Audition required of music and theater majors. **Homeschooled:** Letter of recommendation (nonparent) required. **Learning Disabled:** Students requesting accommodations must provide documentation of the disability and the significant impact of the disability on academic functioning.

**High school preparation.** 11 units required; 15 recommended. Required and recommended units include English 4, mathematics 3-4, social studies 1, history 1, science 2-3 (laboratory 2) and foreign language 2. One or more years of physics, additional chemistry and math, and 2 or more years of a foreign language recommended for engineering programs.

**2008-2009 Annual costs.** Tuition/fees: $25,845. Room/board: $8,170. Books/supplies: $1,000. Personal expenses: $900.

**2007-2008 Financial aid. Need-based:** 570 full-time freshmen applied for aid; 487 were judged to have need; 487 of these received aid. Average need met was 89%. Average scholarship/grant was $18,368; average loan $3,915. 77% of total undergraduate aid awarded as scholarships/grants, 23% as loans/jobs. **Non-need-based:** Awarded to 2,058 full-time undergraduates, including 598 freshmen. Scholarships awarded for academics, alumni affiliation, art, athletics, leadership, minority status, music/drama, religious affiliation. **Additional information:** Early financial planning service allows prospective students to get free estimate of available aid.

**Application procedures. Admission:** Priority date 12/1; deadline 2/1 (postmark date). $35 fee, may be waived for applicants with need. Application may be submitted online. Admission notification 12/15. Admission notification on a rolling basis. Must reply by May 1 or within 2 week(s) if notified thereafter. **Financial aid:** Priority date 3/10; no closing date. FAFSA required. Applicants notified on a rolling basis starting 3/24; must reply by 5/1.

**Academics. Special study options:** Accelerated study, cooperative education, double major, dual enrollment of high school students, ESL, external degree, honors, independent study, internships, semester at sea, student-designed major, study abroad, teacher certification program, Washington semester. Italian archeological excavation program, British campus at Harlaxton College, British Parliament internship, American University semester study, US Pentagon internship, undergraduate research program. **Credit/placement by examination:** AP, CLEP, IB, SAT, ACT, institutional tests. 6 credit hours maximum toward associate degree, 6 toward bachelor's. **Support services:** Learning center, pre-admission summer program, study skills assistance, tutoring, writing center.

**Majors. Biology:** General, biochemistry. **Business:** Accounting, business admin, finance, international, management information systems, managerial economics, marketing. **Computer sciences:** General, computer support specialist. **Conservation:** Environmental science, environmental studies. **Education:** General, art, biology, chemistry, drama/dance, elementary, English, French, German, mathematics, music, physical, physics, social science, social studies, Spanish, special. **Engineering:** Civil, computer, electrical, mechanical. **English:** Composition, creative writing, English lit. **Foreign languages:** Classics, French, German, Spanish. **Health:** Athletic training, clinical lab science, health care admin, music therapy, nursing (RN), predental, premedicine, prepharmacy, preveterinary. **History:** General. **Interdisciplinary:** Cognitive science, neuroscience. **Liberal arts:** Arts/sciences. **Math:** General. **Parks/recreation:** Exercise sciences, sports admin. **Philosophy/religion:** Philosophy. **Physical sciences:** Chemistry, physics. **Psychology:** General. **Social sciences:** Archaeology, economics, international relations, political science, sociology. **Theology:** Bible, theology. **Visual/performing arts:** Art, art history/conservation, design, dramatic, graphic design, music management, music performance, theater arts management. **Other:** Communication and media studies, Legal professions.

**Most popular majors.** Business/marketing 9%, education 11%, engineering/engineering technologies 9%, health sciences 11%, liberal arts 6%, parks/recreation 8%, social sciences 7%, visual/performing arts 12%.

**Computing on campus.** 300 workstations in dormitories, library, student center. Dormitories wired for high-speed internet access and linked to campus network. Commuter students can connect to campus network. Online library, helpline, student web hosting, wireless network available.

**Student life. Freshman orientation:** Mandatory. Preregistration for classes offered. 2 programs available: one in summer includes testing, advising, and registration; another 3 1/2 day program held prior to beginning of semester. **Housing:** Guaranteed on-campus for freshmen. Coed dorms, single-sex dorms, apartments, fraternity/sorority housing, substance-free housing available. $100 partly refundable deposit, deadline 5/1. Honors program housing, global living and learning community. **Activities:** Bands, campus ministries, choral groups, dance, drama, film society, international student organizations, literary magazine, music ensembles, musical theater, opera, radio station, student government, student newspaper, symphony orchestra, Black Student Union, Hillel, Kappa Chi (service), Amnesty International, Habitat for Humanity, Circle K, College Democrats, College Republicans.

**Athletics.** NCAA. **Intercollegiate:** Baseball M, basketball, cross-country, diving, golf, soccer, softball W, swimming, tennis W, volleyball W. **Intramural:** Badminton, basketball, bowling, cross-country, diving, football (nontackle), golf, racquetball, soccer, softball, swimming, table tennis, tennis, volleyball. **Team name:** Purple Aces.

**Student services.** Adult student services, alcohol/substance abuse counseling, campus ministries, career counseling, student employment services, financial aid counseling, health services, minority student services, personal counseling, placement for graduates, veterans' counselor. **Physically disabled:** Services for visually impaired.

**Contact.** E-mail: admission@evansville.edu
Phone: (812) 488-2468 Toll-free number: (800) 423-8633 ext. 2468
Fax: (812) 488-4076
Don Vos, Dean of Admission, University of Evansville, 1800 Lincoln Avenue, Evansville, IN 47722

---

## University of Indianapolis
**Indianapolis, Indiana**
www.uindy.edu

CB member
CB code: 1321

- Private 4-year university and liberal arts college affiliated with United Methodist Church
- Residential campus in very large city
- 3,474 degree-seeking undergraduates: 24% part-time, 67% women, 10% African American, 1% Asian American, 2% Hispanic American, 5% international
- 1,034 degree-seeking graduate students
- 82% of applicants admitted
- SAT or ACT (ACT writing optional) required
- 52% graduate within 6 years

**General.** Founded in 1902. Regionally accredited. **Degrees:** 545 bachelor's, 65 associate awarded; master's, doctoral offered. **ROTC:** Army. **Location:** 5 miles from downtown. **Calendar:** Semester, limited summer session. **Full-time faculty:** 197 total. **Class size:** 65% < 20, 33% 20-39, less than 1% 40-49, less than 1% 50-99. **Special facilities:** Observatory, fine arts center.

**Freshman class profile.** 3,192 applied, 2,611 admitted, 743 enrolled.

| Mid 50% test scores | | | |
|---|---|---|---|
| SAT critical reading: | 440-560 | GPA 2.0-2.99: | 26% |
| SAT math: | 450-580 | Rank in top quarter: | 55% |
| SAT writing: | 420-550 | Rank in top tenth: | 26% |
| ACT composite: | 19-25 | Return as sophomores: | 74% |
| GPA 3.50 or higher: | 42% | Out-of-state: | 10% |
| GPA 3.0-3.49: | 32% | Live on campus: | 70% |

**Basis for selection.** Recommendations, GPA, SAT/ACT scores, class rank important. Involvements and extracurricular activities considered. Essay recommended. Interview recommended for borderline applicants. Audition required of music majors. Portfolio recommended for art majors. **Homeschooled:** Transcript of courses and grades required. **Learning Disabled:** Students with learning disabilities may apply to the BUILD program through separate application process.

**High school preparation.** 15 units required; 18 recommended. Required and recommended units include English 4, mathematics 3-4, social studies 1, history 1, science 2-3 (laboratory 1-2), foreign language 2 and academic electives 1-3.

**2007-2008 Annual costs.** Tuition/fees: $19,730. Room/board: $7,560. Books/supplies: $850. Personal expenses: $1,460.

**Financial aid. Non-need-based:** Scholarships awarded for academics, alumni affiliation, art, athletics, job skills, leadership, music/drama, religious affiliation, state residency.

**Application procedures. Admission:** No deadline. $25 fee, may be waived for applicants with need. Application may be submitted online. Admission notification on a rolling basis beginning on or about 9/1. Must reply by May 1 or within 2 week(s) if notified thereafter. **Financial aid:** Priority date 3/10; no closing date. FAFSA, institutional form required. Applicants notified by 4/15; Applicants notified on a rolling basis starting 3/1; must reply within 3 week(s) of notification.

**Academics. Special study options:** Accelerated study, combined bachelor's/graduate degree, cross-registration, double major, dual enrollment of high school students, ESL, honors, independent study, internships, liberal arts/career combination, student-designed major, study abroad, teacher certification program. Baccalaureate for University of Indianapolis Learning Disabled (BUILD). **Credit/placement by examination:** AP, CLEP, IB, SAT, ACT, institutional tests. 3 to 8 hours awarded for International Baccalaureate based on scores. **Support services:** Learning center, pre-admission summer program, reduced course load, remedial instruction, study skills assistance, tutoring, writing center.

**Majors. Biology:** General, cell/histology. **Business:** Accounting, business admin, international, management information systems, managerial economics, marketing, tourism/travel. **Communications:** General. **Computer sciences:** General, computer science, information systems. **Education:** General, art, biology, business, chemistry, elementary, English, foreign languages, French, history, mathematics, music, physical, physics, science, secondary, social studies, Spanish, speech. **English:** English lit. **Foreign languages:** French, German, Spanish. **Health:** Art therapy, athletic training, clinical lab technology, nursing (RN), respiratory therapy technology. **History:** General. **Math:** General. **Parks/recreation:** Exercise sciences, sports admin. **Philosophy/religion:** Philosophy, religion. **Physical sciences:** Chemistry, geology, physics. **Protective services:** Law enforcement admin. **Psychology:** General. **Public administration:** Social work. **Social sciences:** Anthropology, archaeology, economics, international relations, political science, sociology. **Visual/performing arts:** Art, commercial/advertising art, design, dramatic, music performance.

**Most popular majors.** Business/marketing 20%, education 13%, health sciences 18%, liberal arts 8%, psychology 8%.

**Computing on campus.** 222 workstations in library, computer center. Dormitories wired for high-speed internet access and linked to campus network. Commuter students can connect to campus network. Online library, helpline, wireless network available.

**Student life. Freshman orientation:** Mandatory, $40 fee. Preregistration for classes offered. Student attends one of 6 summer registration programs. **Housing:** Coed dorms, single-sex dorms, apartments, substance-free housing available. $50 partly refundable deposit, deadline 5/1. **Activities:** Bands, choral groups, dance, drama, literary magazine, music ensembles, musical theater, opera, radio station, student government, student newspaper, TV station, Young Democrats, Young Republicans, Fellowship of Christian Athletes, Circle-K, social service, honorary societies.

**Athletics.** NCAA. **Intercollegiate:** Baseball M, basketball, cross-country, diving, football (tackle) M, golf, soccer, softball W, swimming, tennis, track and field, volleyball W, wrestling M. **Intramural:** Basketball, football (nontackle) M, soccer, softball, volleyball. **Team name:** Greyhounds.

**Student services.** Adult student services, campus ministries, career counseling, student employment services, health services, personal counseling, placement for graduates, veterans' counselor. **Physically disabled:** Services for visually, speech, hearing impaired. **Learning disabled:** Comprehensive services available.

**Contact.** E-mail: admissions@uindy.edu
Phone: (317) 788-3216 Toll-free number: (800) 232-8634
Fax: (317) 788-3300
Ron Wilks, Director of Admissions, University of Indianapolis, 1400 East Hanna Avenue, Indianapolis, IN 46227-3697

## University of Notre Dame
### Notre Dame, Indiana
www.nd.edu

CB member
CB code: 1841

- Private 4-year university affiliated with Roman Catholic Church
- Residential campus in small city
- 8,369 degree-seeking undergraduates: 47% women, 4% African American, 7% Asian American, 9% Hispanic American, 1% Native American, 3% international
- 3,213 degree-seeking graduate students
- 24% of applicants admitted
- SAT or ACT (ACT writing optional), application essay required
- 95% graduate within 6 years; 29% enter graduate study

**General.** Founded in 1842. Regionally accredited. Notre Dame Study Centers in Washington, DC; Dublin, Ireland; London, England; Rome, Italy; and Jerusalem; as well as several other countries. **Degrees:** 2,073 bachelor's awarded; master's, doctoral, first professional offered. **ROTC:** Army, Naval, Air Force. **Location:** 90 miles from Chicago. **Calendar:** Semester, extensive summer session. **Special facilities:** Germ-free research facility, radiation laboratory, nature preserve for biological research, wind-tunnel research facility, art museum.

**Freshman class profile.** 14,503 applied, 3,549 admitted, 1,991 enrolled.

| Mid 50% test scores | | | |
|---|---|---|---|
| SAT critical reading: | 640-750 | Rank in top tenth: | 87% |
| SAT math: | 660-760 | Return as sophomores: | 97% |
| SAT writing: | 630-720 | Out-of-state: | 89% |
| ACT composite: | 31-34 | Live on campus: | 100% |
| Rank in top quarter: | 97% | International: | 3% |

**Basis for selection.** GED not accepted. Demonstrated academic achievement and test scores most important. Essay, teacher recommendations, extracurricular activities, and personal statement also important. Three SAT Subject Tests required for home schooled students. Audition recommended for music majors. Portfolio recommended for art majors.

**High school preparation.** 16 units required; 20 recommended. Required and recommended units include English 4, mathematics 3-4, history 2-4, science 2-4 (laboratory 2), foreign language 2-4 and academic electives 2. Pre-calculus or calculus, chemistry and physics recommended for architecture, engineering and science programs. Social studies requirement should include history.

**2008-2009 Annual costs.** Tuition/fees: $36,847. Room/board: $9,828. Books/supplies: $850. Personal expenses: $900.

**2007-2008 Financial aid.** **Need-based:** 1,386 full-time freshmen applied for aid; 933 were judged to have need; 933 of these received aid. Average need met was 100%. Average scholarship/grant was $24,124; average loan $3,291. 76% of total undergraduate aid awarded as scholarships/grants, 24% as loans/jobs. **Non-need-based:** Awarded to 3,096 full-time undergraduates, including 790 freshmen. Scholarships awarded for athletics, job skills, ROTC.

**Application procedures.** **Admission:** Closing date 12/31 (postmark date). $65 fee, may be waived for applicants with need. Application may be submitted online. Admission notification 4/10. Must reply by May 1 or within 2 week(s) if notified thereafter. **Financial aid:** Priority date 2/15, closing date 2/15. FAFSA, CSS PROFILE required. Applicants notified by 4/1; must reply by 5/1.

**Academics.** **Special study options:** Accelerated study, cross-registration, distance learning, double major, exchange student, honors, independent study, internships, liberal arts/career combination, student-designed major, study abroad, Washington semester. Teacher certification available only through cross-registration with St. Mary's College; triple majors, quadruple majors, triple degrees, double majors within dual degrees. **Credit/placement by examination:** AP, CLEP, IB, institutional tests. Students with HL score of 6 or 7 eligible to receive credit in anthropology, biology, chemistry, English, French, German, Greek, American history, Latin, mathematics, music, physics, psychology, and Spanish. **Support services:** Learning center, study skills assistance, tutoring, writing center.

**Majors.** **Architecture:** Architecture. **Area/ethnic studies:** African-American, American. **Biology:** General, biochemistry. **Business:** General, accounting, finance, management information systems, marketing. **Computer sciences:** General. **Conservation:** Environmental science. **Education:** Science. **Engineering:** Aerospace, chemical, civil, computer, electrical, environmental, mechanical. **English:** English lit. **Foreign languages:** Ancient Greek, Arabic, Chinese, classics, French, German, Italian, Japanese, Romance, Russian, Spanish. **Health:** Premedicine. **History:** General. **Interdisciplinary:** Biological/physical sciences, medieval/Renaissance. **Liberal arts:** Arts/sciences. **Math:** General. **Philosophy/religion:** Philosophy, religion. **Physical sciences:** Chemistry, physics. **Psychology:** General. **Social sciences:** Anthropology, economics, political science, sociology. **Theology:** Theology. **Visual/performing arts:** Art history/conservation, design, dramatic, studio arts.

**Most popular majors.** Business/marketing 21%, engineering/engineering technologies 8%, foreign language 6%, health sciences 8%, psychology 6%, social sciences 18%.

**Computing on campus.** 221 workstations in dormitories, library, computer center, student center. Dormitories linked to campus network. Commuter students can connect to campus network. Online course registration, helpline, repair service, wireless network available.

**Student life.** **Freshman orientation:** Mandatory. Preregistration for classes offered. **Housing:** Guaranteed on-campus for freshmen. Single-sex dorms available. $50 deposit, deadline 5/1. Requests for ground level housing or housing suitable for a disabled student will be honored. **Activities:** Bands, choral groups, dance, drama, film society, literary magazine, music ensembles, musical theater, opera, radio station, student government, student newspaper, symphony orchestra, more than 260 clubs and organizations available.

**Athletics.** NCAA. **Intercollegiate:** Baseball M, basketball, cross-country, diving, fencing, football (tackle) M, golf, ice hockey M, lacrosse, rowing (crew) W, soccer, softball W, swimming, tennis, track and field, volleyball W. **Intramural:** Badminton, baseball M, basketball, cross-country, football (non-tackle), football (tackle) M, golf, ice hockey, racquetball, soccer, softball, table tennis, tennis. **Team name:** Fighting Irish.

**Student services.** Alcohol/substance abuse counseling, campus ministries, career counseling, student employment services, health services, minority student services, on-campus daycare, personal counseling, placement for graduates, women's services. **Physically disabled:** Services for visually, hearing impaired.

**Contact.** E-mail: admissions@nd.edu
Phone: (574) 631-7505 Fax: (574) 631-8865
Daniel Saracino, Director of Admissions, University of Notre Dame, 220 Main Building, Notre Dame, IN 46556

## University of St. Francis
### Fort Wayne, Indiana
www.sf.edu

CB code: 1693

- Private 4-year university and liberal arts college affiliated with Roman Catholic Church
- Commuter campus in small city
- 1,789 degree-seeking undergraduates: 18% part-time, 69% women, 5% African American, 1% Asian American, 2% Hispanic American
- 286 degree-seeking graduate students
- SAT or ACT (ACT writing optional) required

**General.** Founded in 1890. Regionally accredited. **Degrees:** 183 bachelor's, 153 associate awarded; master's offered. **Location:** 150 miles from Chicago. **Calendar:** Semester, limited summer session. **Full-time faculty:** 101 total; 44% have terminal degrees, 7% minority, 61% women. **Part-time faculty:** 122 total; 17% have terminal degrees, 5% minority, 61% women. **Class size:** 62% < 20, 33% 20-39, 4% 40-49, 1% 50-99. **Special facilities:** Planetarium, nature preserve.

**Freshman class profile.**

| Mid 50% test scores | | | |
|---|---|---|---|
| SAT critical reading: | 420-530 | GPA 3.50 or higher: | 29% |
| SAT math: | 440-560 | GPA 3.0-3.49: | 33% |
| SAT writing: | 410-530 | GPA 2.0-2.99: | 37% |
| ACT composite: | 19-24 | Rank in top quarter: | 33% |
| | | Rank in top tenth: | 11% |

**Basis for selection.** School achievement record, rank in top half of class, and test scores most important. Additional requirements for health care majors, education majors. Admission procedures may vary among schools within the university. Essay and portfolio recommended. Interview recommended for underprepared applicants. **Homeschooled:** State high school equivalency certificate, letter of recommendation (nonparent) required. Bibliography of books read, extracurricular activities.

**High school preparation.** 20 units required; 26 recommended. Required and recommended units include English 4, mathematics 2-3, social studies 2-3, history 1, science 2-3 and academic electives 1-4.

**2007-2008 Annual costs.** Tuition/fees: $19,570. Room/board: $6,006. Books/supplies: $1,000. Personal expenses: $1,100.

**2006-2007 Financial aid. Need-based:** 357 full-time freshmen applied for aid; 304 were judged to have need; 302 of these received aid. Average need met was 77%. Average scholarship/grant was $11,396; average loan $2,388. 56% of total undergraduate aid awarded as scholarships/grants, 44% as loans/jobs. **Non-need-based:** Awarded to 466 full-time undergraduates, including 138 freshmen. Scholarships awarded for academics, alumni affiliation, art, athletics, music/drama.

**Application procedures. Admission:** Priority date 8/1; no deadline. $20 fee, may be waived for applicants with need. Application may be submitted online. Admission notification on a rolling basis beginning on or about 8/1. **Financial aid:** Priority date 3/10; no closing date. FAFSA required. Applicants notified on a rolling basis starting 3/1.

**Academics. Special study options:** Combined bachelor's/graduate degree, cross-registration, double major, dual enrollment of high school students, exchange student, honors, independent study, internships, liberal arts/career combination, teacher certification program. **Credit/placement by examination:** AP, CLEP, SAT, ACT, institutional tests. 16 credit hours maximum toward associate degree, 32 toward bachelor's. **Support services:** Learning center, reduced course load, remedial instruction, study skills assistance, tutoring, writing center.

**Majors. Business:** Accounting, business admin, human resources. **Communications:** General, public relations. **Conservation:** General, environmental studies. **Education:** Art, business, chemistry, elementary, English, health, science, social studies, special. **English:** English lit. **Health:** Clinical lab science, nursing (RN), physician assistant, predental, premedicine, prepharmacy. **History:** General. **Legal studies:** Prelaw. **Liberal arts:** Arts/sciences. **Math:** General. **Philosophy/religion:** Philosophy. **Psychology:** General. **Public administration:** Social work. **Social sciences:** Political science, sociology. **Theology:** Theology. **Visual/performing arts:** Art, commercial/advertising art, graphic design, studio arts. **Other:** American studies, Music technology, Social welfare.

**Most popular majors.** Business/marketing 21%, education 18%, health sciences 21%, liberal arts 7%, visual/performing arts 13%.

**Computing on campus.** 404 workstations in dormitories, library, computer center, student center. Dormitories wired for high-speed internet access and linked to campus network. Commuter students can connect to campus network. Online course registration, online library, helpline, repair service, wireless network available.

**Student life. Freshman orientation:** Mandatory, $32 fee. 3-day program during weekend prior to beginning of classes. **Policies:** No alcohol allowed in residence halls, no smoking in campus buildings. **Housing:** Guaranteed on-campus for freshmen. Coed dorms, apartments available. $200 deposit. Full-time students under 21 not living at home or with adult relatives must live in residence halls. **Activities:** Bands, campus ministries, choral groups, dance, drama, film society, student government, student newspaper, Educators in Action, student nursing association, peer ministers, Fellowship of Christian Athletes.

**Athletics.** NAIA. **Intercollegiate:** Baseball M, basketball, cheerleading, cross-country, football (tackle) M, golf, soccer, softball W, tennis W, track and field, volleyball W. **Intramural:** Basketball, bowling, volleyball. **Team name:** Cougars.

**Student services.** Adult student services, campus ministries, career counseling, student employment services, financial aid counseling, health services, personal counseling, placement for graduates. **Physically disabled:** Services for visually, hearing impaired.

**Contact.** E-mail: admiss@sf.edu
Phone: (260) 434-3279 Toll-free number: (800) 729-4732
Fax: (260) 434-7590
Ron Schumacher, Vice President, Enrollment Management, University of St. Francis, 2701 Spring Street, Fort Wayne, IN 46808

## University of Southern Indiana
**Evansville, Indiana**
www.usi.edu
CB code: 1335

- Public 4-year university and liberal arts college
- Commuter campus in small city

- 9,008 degree-seeking undergraduates: 16% part-time, 59% women, 5% African American, 1% Asian American, 1% Hispanic American, 1% international
- 613 degree-seeking graduate students
- 90% of applicants admitted
- SAT or ACT (ACT writing recommended) required
- 35% graduate within 6 years

**General.** Founded in 1965. Regionally accredited. Credit courses offered at various off-campus sites in Evansville and surrounding areas. **Degrees:** 1,154 bachelor's, 172 associate awarded; master's offered. **ROTC:** Army. **Location:** 150 miles from Indianapolis. **Calendar:** Semester, limited summer session. **Full-time faculty:** 322 total; 61% have terminal degrees, 6% minority, 53% women. **Part-time faculty:** 289 total; 17% have terminal degrees, 4% minority, 54% women. **Class size:** 36% < 20, 54% 20-39, 5% 40-49, 4% 50-99, 1% >100. **Special facilities:** Restored historic town managed by university.

**Freshman class profile.** 4,934 applied, 4,457 admitted, 2,136 enrolled.

| Mid 50% test scores | | | |
|---|---|---|---|
| SAT critical reading: | 410-520 | Rank in top quarter: | 28% |
| SAT math: | 420-530 | Rank in top tenth: | 10% |
| SAT writing: | 410-510 | Return as sophomores: | 63% |
| ACT composite: | 17-23 | Out-of-state: | 5% |
| GPA 3.50 or higher: | 21% | Live on campus: | 61% |
| GPA 3.0-3.49: | 27% | International: | 2% |
| GPA 2.0-2.99: | 47% | Fraternities: | 1% |
| | | Sororities: | 2% |

**Basis for selection.** 2.0 GPA for out-of-state applicants. Combined SAT score of 900 (exclusive of Writing) for applicants to health programs. Students accepted at 1 of 3 levels based on academic record and test scores. Placement test administered prior to registration. SAT/ACT used to place students at 1 of 3 levels within institution. **Homeschooled:** Transcript of courses and grades required.

**High school preparation.** 18 units recommended. Recommended units include English 4, mathematics 4, social studies 2, history 2, science 3, foreign language 2 and academic electives 2. 2 units computer and/or art recommended.

**2008-2009 Annual costs.** Tuition/fees (projected): $5,219; $12,154 out-of-state. Room/board: $6,542. Books/supplies: $900. Personal expenses: $2,474.

**2007-2008 Financial aid. Need-based:** 1,809 full-time freshmen applied for aid; 1,257 were judged to have need; 1,224 of these received aid. Average need met was 73%. Average scholarship/grant was $2,688; average loan $3,155. 46% of total undergraduate aid awarded as scholarships/grants, 54% as loans/jobs. **Non-need-based:** Awarded to 1,875 full-time undergraduates, including 556 freshmen. Scholarships awarded for academics, alumni affiliation, art, athletics, job skills, leadership, music/drama, state residency.

**Application procedures. Admission:** Closing date 8/15 (receipt date). $25 fee, may be waived for applicants with need. Application may be submitted online. Admission notification on a rolling basis beginning on or about 7/1. Applicants accepted through first week of classes, but encouraged to apply by August 15 for fall and January 1 for spring. **Financial aid:** Closing date 3/1. FAFSA, institutional form required. Applicants notified on a rolling basis starting 4/15.

**Academics. Special study options:** Combined bachelor's/graduate degree, cooperative education, distance learning, double major, dual enrollment of high school students, ESL, honors, independent study, internships, study abroad, teacher certification program. **Credit/placement by examination:** AP, CLEP, SAT, ACT, institutional tests. 96 credit hours maximum toward bachelor's degree. **Support services:** Learning center, reduced course load, remedial instruction, study skills assistance, tutoring, writing center.

**Majors. Biology:** General, biophysics. **Business:** General, accounting, business admin, entrepreneurial studies, finance, marketing, office management. **Communications:** Advertising, journalism, media studies, radio/tv. **Computer sciences:** General, data processing. **Education:** Business, early childhood, elementary, physical. **Engineering:** General. **English:** English lit. **Foreign languages:** French, German, Spanish. **Health:** Dental hygiene, nursing (RN). **History:** General. **Interdisciplinary:** Biological/physical sciences, nutrition sciences. **Liberal arts:** Arts/sciences. **Math:** General. **Parks/recreation:** Exercise sciences. **Philosophy/religion:** Philosophy. **Physical sciences:** Chemistry, geology. **Psychology:** General. **Public administration:** Social work. **Social sciences:** General, economics, international relations, political science, sociology. **Visual/performing arts:** Art, dramatic.

**Most popular majors.** Business/marketing 22%, communications/journalism 10%, education 16%, health sciences 17%, social sciences 7%.

**Computing on campus.** 306 workstations in dormitories, library, computer center, student center. Dormitories linked to campus network. Commuter students can connect to campus network. Online course registration, helpline, wireless network available.

**Student life. Freshman orientation:** Mandatory, $65 fee. Preregistration for classes offered. 2-day program (parent participation). Lunch and dinner included first day. **Housing:** Coed dorms, special housing for disabled, apartments, fraternity/sorority housing, substance-free housing available. $200 deposit, deadline 3/1. **Activities:** Jazz band, campus ministries, choral groups, dance, drama, international student organizations, literary magazine, Model UN, radio station, student government, student newspaper, Black Student Union, Habitat for Humanity, Kappa Chi (Christian Service Fraternity), Baptist Student Ministry, Newman Catholic Student Organization, Collegiate Democrats, Collegiate Republicans.

**Athletics.** NCAA. **Intercollegiate:** Baseball M, basketball, cheerleading, cross-country, golf, soccer, softball W, tennis, track and field, volleyball W. **Intramural:** Badminton, basketball, bowling, cross-country, football (non-tackle), golf, soccer, softball, swimming, table tennis, tennis, volleyball. **Team name:** Screaming Eagles.

**Student services.** Adult student services, campus ministries, career counseling, student employment services, financial aid counseling, health services, minority student services, on-campus daycare, personal counseling, placement for graduates, veterans' counselor. **Physically disabled:** Services for visually, speech, hearing impaired.

**Contact.** E-mail: enroll@usi.edu
Phone: (812) 464-1765 Toll-free number: (800) 467-1965
Fax: (812) 465-7154
Eric Otto, Director of Admission, University of Southern Indiana, 8600 University Boulevard, Evansville, IN 47712

---

## Valparaiso University

**Valparaiso, Indiana**
**www.valpo.edu**

**CB member**
**CB code: 1874**

- Private 4-year university affiliated with Lutheran Church
- Residential campus in large town
- 2,834 degree-seeking undergraduates: 4% part-time, 52% women, 4% African American, 1% Asian American, 4% Hispanic American, 3% international
- 910 degree-seeking graduate students
- 90% of applicants admitted
- SAT or ACT (ACT writing recommended), application essay required
- 77% graduate within 6 years; 23% enter graduate study

**General.** Founded in 1859. Regionally accredited. **Degrees:** 691 bachelor's, 5 associate awarded; master's, first professional offered. **ROTC:** Army, Air Force. **Location:** 55 miles from Chicago. **Calendar:** Semester, limited summer session. **Full-time faculty:** 254 total; 91% have terminal degrees, 10% minority, 34% women. **Part-time faculty:** 123 total; 58% have terminal degrees, 9% minority, 54% women. **Class size:** 54% < 20, 38% 20-39, 4% 40-49, 3% 50-99, less than 1% >100. **Special facilities:** Electron microscope, observatory, storm chasing equipment, weather station, Doppler Radar facility, planetarium, center for learning and information resources, virtual nursing learning center, scientific visualization laboratory.

**Freshman class profile.** 3,475 applied, 3,134 admitted, 715 enrolled.

| Mid 50% test scores | | | |
|---|---|---|---|
| SAT critical reading: | 490-610 | Rank in top tenth: | 28% |
| SAT math: | 500-640 | End year in good standing: | 89% |
| SAT writing: | 480-610 | Return as sophomores: | 85% |
| ACT composite: | 22-28 | Out-of-state: | 65% |
| GPA 3.50 or higher: | 44% | Live on campus: | 91% |
| GPA 3.0-3.49: | 33% | International: | 2% |
| GPA 2.0-2.99: | 23% | Fraternities: | 27% |
| Rank in top quarter: | 60% | Sororities: | 22% |

**Basis for selection.** High school record most important. Test scores next in importance, followed by recommendations and activities. Nature of high school program considered. Interview recommended. Audition required of music majors. Portfolio recommended for art majors. **Homeschooled:** Transcript of courses and grades required. SAT/ACT scores directly from testing center. Specify primary educator. Course description list or reading list required. **Learning Disabled:** Student should submit suitable documentation to the Disability Support Services Office following admission into the University in order to determine eligibility of services.

**High school preparation.** 16 units required; 19 recommended. Required and recommended units include English 4, mathematics 3-4, social studies 1, history 2, science 2-3 (laboratory 2-3), foreign language 2 and academic electives 3.

**2008-2009 Annual costs.** Tuition/fees: $26,950. College of engineering sophomores, juniors, and seniors pay an additional fee of $700. Nursing lab and test fee is $525 at the beginning of sophomore year. Room/board: $7,620. Books/supplies: $1,200. Personal expenses: $890.

**2007-2008 Financial aid. Need-based:** 656 full-time freshmen applied for aid; 546 were judged to have need; 546 of these received aid. Average need met was 84%. Average scholarship/grant was $16,502; average loan $5,441. 73% of total undergraduate aid awarded as scholarships/grants, 27% as loans/jobs. **Non-need-based:** Awarded to 970 full-time undergraduates, including 236 freshmen. Scholarships awarded for academics, alumni affiliation, art, athletics, leadership, music/drama, religious affiliation, ROTC. **Additional information:** Financial assistance based on need, academic record, talent, etc., available through university.

**Application procedures. Admission:** Priority date 1/15; deadline 8/15 (receipt date). $30 fee, may be waived for applicants with need. Application may be submitted online. Admission notification on a rolling basis beginning on or about 10/1. Must reply by May 1 or within 4 week(s) if notified thereafter. **Financial aid:** Priority date 3/1; no closing date. FAFSA required. Applicants notified on a rolling basis starting 3/1; must reply by 5/1.

**Academics. Special study options:** Accelerated study, combined bachelor's/graduate degree, cooperative education, cross-registration, distance learning, double major, ESL, exchange student, honors, independent study, internships, liberal arts/career combination, student-designed major, study abroad, teacher certification program, United Nations semester, urban semester, Washington semester. **Credit/placement by examination:** AP, CLEP, IB, institutional tests. **Support services:** Learning center, reduced course load, study skills assistance, tutoring, writing center.

**Honors college/program.** Approximately 80 students enroll per year in Christ College, the Honors College. Must demonstrate academic excellence in high school, intellectual curiosity, and leadership skills. Program integrates history, literature, philosophy, religion, and art.

**Majors. Area/ethnic studies:** American, East Asian. **Biology:** General, biochemistry. **Business:** Accounting, actuarial science, finance, international, management science, marketing. **Communications:** General, journalism, media studies, organizational, public relations, radio/tv. **Computer sciences:** Computer science. **Conservation:** Environmental science. **Education:** Art, biology, chemistry, drama/dance, elementary, English, foreign languages, French, geography, German, history, mathematics, middle, music, physical, physics, psychology, science, secondary, social science, Spanish. **Engineering:** Civil, computer, electrical, mechanical. **English:** Creative writing, English lit, technical writing. **Foreign languages:** Classics, French, German, Spanish. **Health:** Nursing (RN). **History:** General. **Liberal arts:** Humanities. **Math:** General. **Parks/recreation:** Exercise sciences, health/fitness, sports admin. **Philosophy/religion:** Philosophy. **Physical sciences:** Atmospheric science, chemistry, geology, physics. **Psychology:** General. **Public administration:** Social work. **Social sciences:** General, criminology, economics, geography, international economics, international relations, political science, sociology. **Theology:** Theology, youth ministry. **Visual/performing arts:** Art, dramatic, music management, music performance, music theory/composition, piano/organ, voice/opera. **Other:** Church music, Economics/computer analysis, Geoscience, Information/decision sciences, Multi-/Interdisciplinary studies.

**Most popular majors.** Business/marketing 14%, education 7%, engineering/engineering technologies 9%, health sciences 8%, physical sciences 8%, social sciences 10%.

**Computing on campus.** 901 workstations in dormitories, library, computer center, student center. Dormitories wired for high-speed internet access and linked to campus network. Commuter students can connect to campus network. Online course registration, helpline, student web hosting, wireless network available.

**Student life. Freshman orientation:** Available, $90 fee. Preregistration for classes offered. Overnight program held in June. **Housing:** Guaranteed on-campus for all undergraduates. Coed dorms, single-sex dorms, apartments, fraternity/sorority housing, substance-free housing available. $100 fully refundable deposit, deadline 5/1. Residence hall for German language students. **Activities:** Bands, campus ministries, choral groups, dance, drama, film society, international student organizations, literary magazine, music ensembles, musical theater, radio station, student government, student newspaper, symphony orchestra, Alpha Phi Omega, InterVarsity Christian Fellowship, St. Teresa of Avila, Black Student Organization, Habitat for Humanity, Asian American Association, Latinos in Valparaiso for Excellence, College Democrats.

**Athletics.** NCAA. **Intercollegiate:** Baseball M, basketball, cross-country, diving, football (tackle) M, soccer, softball W, swimming, tennis, track and field, volleyball W. **Intramural:** Badminton, basketball, bowling, football (non-tackle), golf, racquetball, soccer, softball, swimming, table tennis, tennis, volleyball. **Team name:** Crusaders.

**Student services.** Adult student services, alcohol/substance abuse counseling, campus ministries, career counseling, student employment services,

financial aid counseling, health services, legal services, minority student services, personal counseling, placement for graduates. **Physically disabled:** Services for visually impaired.

**Contact.** E-mail: undergrad.admissions@valpo.edu
Phone: (219) 464-5011 Toll-free number: (888) 468-2576
Fax: (219) 464-6898
David Fevig, Director of Admission, Valparaiso University, Kretzmann Hall, 1700 Chapel Drive, Valparaiso, IN 46383-6493

## Wabash College
**Crawfordsville, Indiana**
**www.wabash.edu**

**CB member**
**CB code: 1895**

- Private 4-year liberal arts college for men
- Residential campus in large town
- 910 degree-seeking undergraduates: 6% African American, 2% Asian American, 5% Hispanic American, 5% international
- 47% of applicants admitted
- SAT or ACT (ACT writing optional), application essay required
- 71% graduate within 6 years; 31% enter graduate study

**General.** Founded in 1832. Regionally accredited. **Degrees:** 160 bachelor's awarded. **Location:** 45 miles from Indianapolis, 125 miles from Chicago. **Calendar:** Semester. **Full-time faculty:** 86 total; 98% have terminal degrees, 10% minority, 22% women. **Part-time faculty:** 5 total; 80% have terminal degrees, 20% women. **Class size:** 73% < 20, 23% 20-39, 2% 40-49, 1% 50-99, less than 1% >100. **Special facilities:** Biology field station, center for teaching and learning in theology and religion, qualitative and quantitative skills center, electron microscope, parallel computer, nature preserve, archival center.

**Freshman class profile.** 1,419 applied, 670 admitted, 250 enrolled.

| Mid 50% test scores | | | |
|---|---|---|---|
| SAT critical reading: | 520-630 | Rank in top quarter: | 70% |
| SAT math: | 540-660 | Rank in top tenth: | 37% |
| SAT writing: | 500-610 | End year in good standing: | 93% |
| ACT composite: | 21-27 | Return as sophomores: | 89% |
| GPA 3.50 or higher: | 59% | Out-of-state: | 27% |
| GPA 3.0-3.49: | 31% | Live on campus: | 99% |
| GPA 2.0-2.99: | 10% | International: | 4% |
| | | Fraternities: | 66% |

**Basis for selection.** Class rank, school achievement, recommendation, essay and test scores important. Interview recommended. Character and personal qualities considered. TOEFL required of non-native speakers of English. **Homeschooled:** Case-by-case basis. **Learning Disabled:** All students considered on an individual basis.

**High school preparation.** 17 units recommended. Recommended units include English 4, mathematics 4, social studies 2, science 2 (laboratory 2), foreign language 2 and academic electives 3.

**2008-2009 Annual costs.** Tuition/fees: $27,950. Room/board: $7,900. Books/supplies: $900. Personal expenses: $1,500.

**2007-2008 Financial aid. Need-based:** 224 full-time freshmen applied for aid; 186 were judged to have need; 186 of these received aid. Average need met was 100%. Average scholarship/grant was $18,094; average loan $4,878. 72% of total undergraduate aid awarded as scholarships/grants, 28% as loans/jobs. **Non-need-based:** Awarded to 314 full-time undergraduates, including 82 freshmen. Scholarships awarded for academics, art, leadership, music/drama, state residency.

**Application procedures. Admission:** Priority date 12/15; no deadline. $40 fee, may be waived for applicants with need. Application may be submitted online. Admission notification on a rolling basis beginning on or about 12/15. Must reply by May 1 or within 2 week(s) if notified thereafter. **Financial aid:** Priority date 2/15, closing date 3/1. FAFSA, CSS PROFILE required. Applicants notified by 4/1; must reply by 5/1 or within 2 week(s) of notification.

**Academics. Special study options:** Combined bachelor's/graduate degree, double major, independent study, internships, liberal arts/career combination, New York semester, semester at sea, student-designed major, study abroad, teacher certification program, United Nations semester, urban semester, Washington semester. Cooperative law program with Columbia University (NY), International and Domestic Study Program of Great Lakes Colleges Association, 3-2 engineering program with Columbia University and Washington University. **Credit/placement by examination:** AP, CLEP, institutional tests. AP credit not given solely based on AP exam scores. Scores used in conjunction with in-house exams and subsequent coursework. **Support services:** Learning center, study skills assistance, tutoring, writing center.

**Majors. Biology:** General. **English:** English lit, speech/rhetoric. **Foreign languages:** Ancient Greek, classics, French, German, Latin, Spanish. **History:** General. **Liberal arts:** Arts/sciences. **Math:** General. **Philosophy/religion:** Philosophy, religion. **Physical sciences:** Chemistry, physics. **Psychology:** General. **Social sciences:** Economics, political science. **Visual/performing arts:** Art, dramatic.

**Most popular majors.** Biology 9%, English 16%, history 13%, philosophy/religious studies 10%, physical sciences 7%, psychology 13%, social sciences 14%, visual/performing arts 8%.

**Computing on campus.** 360 workstations in dormitories, library, computer center, student center. Dormitories wired for high-speed internet access and linked to campus network. Commuter students can connect to campus network. Online library, helpline, repair service, student web hosting, wireless network available.

**Student life. Freshman orientation:** Mandatory. Preregistration for classes offered. 5-day program orients students to library and computer resources, the Gentleman's Rule, and includes all class members in community service projects. **Policies:** The Gentleman's Rule is the college's only rule. **Housing:** Guaranteed on-campus for all undergraduates. Apartments, cooperative housing, fraternity/sorority housing, substance-free housing available. $150 nonrefundable deposit, deadline 7/1. Limited wheelchair accessibility available. **Activities:** Bands, choral groups, drama, film society, literary magazine, music ensembles, musical theater, radio station, student government, student newspaper, symphony orchestra, Malcolm X Institute for Black Studies, political groups, Newman Center, Alpha Phi Omega, Fellowship of Christian Athletes, Muslim student association, Wabash Christian Fellowship, model U.N., Pre-Law Society, moot court competition, Sphinx Club.

**Athletics.** NCAA. **Intercollegiate:** Baseball M, basketball M, cross-country M, diving M, football (tackle) M, golf M, soccer M, swimming M, tennis M, track and field M, wrestling M. **Intramural:** Badminton M, basketball M, bowling M, cross-country M, diving M, football (non-tackle) M, golf M, handball M, racquetball M, soccer M, softball M, swimming M, table tennis M, tennis M, track and field M, volleyball M, wrestling M. **Team name:** Little Giants.

**Student services.** Alcohol/substance abuse counseling, campus ministries, career counseling, student employment services, financial aid counseling, health services, minority student services, personal counseling, placement for graduates. **Physically disabled:** Services for visually impaired.

**Contact.** E-mail: admissions@wabash.edu
Phone: (765) 361-6225 Toll-free number: (800) 345-5385
Fax: (765) 361-6437
Steven Klein, Dean of Admissions, Wabash College, PO Box 352, Crawfordsville, IN 47933

# Iowa

## Allen College
### Waterloo, Iowa
www.allencollege.edu

CB code: 3610

- Private 4-year health science and nursing college
- Commuter campus in small city
- 377 degree-seeking undergraduates: 12% part-time, 96% women
- 80 degree-seeking graduate students
- 76% of applicants admitted
- SAT or ACT (ACT writing optional) required
- 55% graduate within 6 years; 10% enter graduate study

**General.** Regionally accredited. **Degrees:** 87 bachelor's, 15 associate awarded; master's offered. **ROTC:** Army. **Calendar:** Semester, limited summer session. **Full-time faculty:** 27 total; 22% have terminal degrees, 4% minority, 100% women. **Part-time faculty:** 5 total; 100% women. **Class size:** 56% < 20, 30% 20-39, 6% 40-49, 8% 50-99.

**Freshman class profile.** 88 applied, 67 admitted, 45 enrolled.

| Mid 50% test scores | | | |
|---|---|---|---|
| ACT composite: | 20-24 | Rank in top quarter: | 67% |
| GPA 3.50 or higher: | 68% | Rank in top tenth: | 27% |
| GPA 3.0-3.49: | 32% | Return as sophomores: | 94% |
| | | Live on campus: | 47% |

**Basis for selection.** Secondary school record, class rank, test scores important; recommendations, essay (when required) considered. **Home-schooled:** Complete ACT.

**High school preparation.** 4 units required. Required units include English 4, mathematics 3, social studies 3, science 3 (laboratory 2).

**2008-2009 Annual costs.** Tuition/fees (projected): $14,895. Room/board: $6,178. Books/supplies: $891. Personal expenses: $2,724.

**2006-2007 Financial aid.** **Need-based:** 26 full-time freshmen applied for aid; 24 were judged to have need; 24 of these received aid. Average need met was 49%. Average scholarship/grant was $5,348; average loan $2,186. 32% of total undergraduate aid awarded as scholarships/grants, 68% as loans/jobs. **Non-need-based:** Awarded to 12 full-time undergraduates, including 5 freshmen. Scholarships awarded for academics, leadership, minority status, ROTC.

**Application procedures.** **Admission:** Priority date 3/1; deadline 8/1 (receipt date). $50 fee, may be waived for applicants with need. Application may be submitted online. Admission notification on a rolling basis. Must reply by May 1 or within 4 week(s) if notified thereafter. **Financial aid:** Priority date 6/1; no closing date. FAFSA, institutional form required. Applicants notified on a rolling basis starting 4/1; must reply within 2 week(s) of notification.

**Academics.** **Special study options:** Accelerated study, combined bachelor's/graduate degree, cooperative education, distance learning, external degree, honors, independent study, internships, liberal arts/career combination. **Credit/placement by examination:** AP, CLEP, IB. **Support services:** Learning center, study skills assistance, tutoring, writing center.

**Majors.** **Health:** Nursing (RN).

**Computing on campus.** 29 workstations in dormitories, library, computer center. Dormitories wired for high-speed internet access. Online library, helpline, wireless network available.

**Student life.** **Freshman orientation:** Mandatory. Includes registration, assessment testing, and completion of mandatory health career training. **Housing:** Coed dorms, single-sex dorms, special housing for disabled, apartments, cooperative housing, substance-free housing available. $200 nonrefundable deposit. On-campus suite housing available and dorm-style housing is offered at cooperating institutions. **Activities:** Student government, student newspaper.

**Student services.** Alcohol/substance abuse counseling, campus ministries, career counseling, financial aid counseling, health services, on-campus daycare, personal counseling, placement for graduates, women's services. **Physically disabled:** Services for visually, speech, hearing impaired.

**Contact.** E-mail: AllenCollegeAdmissions@ihs.org
Phone: (319) 226-2000 Fax: (319) 226-2051
Michelle Koehn, Admissions Counselor, Allen College, 1825 Logan Avenue, Waterloo, IA 50703

## Ashford University
### Clinton, Iowa
www.ashford.edu

CB code: 6418

- For-profit 4-year university
- Commuter campus in large town
- 9,805 degree-seeking undergraduates: 1% part-time, 77% women, 23% African American, 2% Asian American, 7% Hispanic American, 1% Native American
- 702 degree-seeking graduate students
- 39% graduate within 6 years

**General.** Founded in 1918. Regionally accredited. **Degrees:** 307 bachelor's, 5 associate awarded; master's offered. **Location:** 35 miles from Davenport, 138 miles from Chicago. **Calendar:** Semester, limited summer session. **Full-time faculty:** 36 total; 36% minority, 39% women. **Part-time faculty:** 232 total; 28% minority, 62% women. **Class size:** 71% < 20, 29% 20-39. **Special facilities:** Restored prairie land adjacent to campus.

**Freshman class profile.**

| | | | |
|---|---|---|---|
| GPA 3.50 or higher: | 17% | Rank in top tenth: | 5% |
| GPA 3.0-3.49: | 22% | Return as sophomores: | 41% |
| GPA 2.0-2.99: | 53% | International: | 1% |
| Rank in top quarter: | 21% | | |

**Basis for selection.** High school record, GPA, class rank, test scores all considered. Applicants not meeting selection criteria may be admitted conditionally. Interview required for teacher education majors. Audition recommended for fine arts. Portfolio recommended for art majors. Essay recommended for academically weak applicants.

**High school preparation.** 20 units recommended. Recommended units include English 4, mathematics 3, social studies 3, history 3, science 3 (laboratory 2) and foreign language 2.

**2007-2008 Annual costs.** Tuition/fees: $15,890. Room/board: $5,800. Books/supplies: $600. Personal expenses: $600.

**2007-2008 Financial aid.** **Need-based:** 46% of total undergraduate aid awarded as scholarships/grants, 54% as loans/jobs. **Non-need-based:** Scholarships awarded for academics, art, athletics, music/drama.

**Application procedures.** **Admission:** No deadline. $20 fee, may be waived for applicants with need. Application may be submitted online. Admission notification on a rolling basis beginning on or about 9/1. **Financial aid:** Priority date 3/1; no closing date. FAFSA, institutional form required. Applicants notified on a rolling basis starting 2/15; must reply within 2 week(s) of notification.

**Academics.** Liberal arts program has interdisciplinary approach. Freshmen take a freshman experience course that teaches them effective study habits, time management, adjustment to college, and an introduction to Franciscanism. **Special study options:** Accelerated study, combined bachelor's/graduate degree, distance learning, double major, dual enrollment of high school students, external degree, honors, independent study, internships, student-designed major, teacher certification program. Off campus study, senior capstone or culminating academic experience, student designed major summer school. **Credit/placement by examination:** AP, CLEP, institutional tests. 32 credit hours maximum toward associate degree, 32 toward bachelor's. Awards credit for CLEP exams in accordance with the American Council on Education (ACE) designated passing score and recommended credit. **Support services:** Learning center, reduced course load, remedial instruction, tutoring.

**Majors.** **Biology:** General. **Business:** General, accounting, business admin, communications, finance, human resources, marketing. **Communications:** General. **Computer sciences:** General. **Conservation:** Environmental studies. **Education:** Biology, chemistry, early childhood, elementary, English, history, mathematics, middle, music, reading, science, secondary, social science, social studies. **English:** English lit. **Health:** Cytotechnology, health care admin, premedicine. **Interdisciplinary:** Math/computer science. **Legal studies:** Prelaw. **Liberal arts:** Arts/sciences. **Psychology:** General. **Social sciences:** General. **Visual/performing arts:** Graphic design, studio arts.

**Most popular majors.** Business/marketing 66%, psychology 15%.

**Computing on campus.** PC or laptop required. 109 workstations in dormitories, library, computer center. Dormitories wired for high-speed internet access and linked to campus network. Online library, helpline, repair service, wireless network available.

**Student life. Freshman orientation:** Mandatory. Preregistration for classes offered. 2-day orientation program held in the summer prior to beginning of fall classes. **Housing:** Guaranteed on-campus for all undergraduates. Coed dorms, single-sex dorms available. $125 deposit. **Activities:** Choral groups, drama, music ensembles, musical theater, student government, student newspaper, Christian Fellowship club, Hispanic American Leadership Organization, Circle K, Black Student Union, State Iowa Education Association.

**Athletics.** NAIA. **Intercollegiate:** Baseball M, basketball, cross-country, golf M, soccer, softball W, track and field, volleyball W. **Intramural:** Basketball, bowling, football (non-tackle), swimming, volleyball. **Team name:** Saints.

**Student services.** Adult student services, campus ministries, career counseling, student employment services, financial aid counseling, minority student services, on-campus daycare, placement for graduates.

**Contact.** E-mail: admissns@ashford.edu
Phone: (563) 242-4153 Toll-free number: (800) 242-4153
Fax: (563) 243-6102
Waunita Sullivan, Director of Enrollment, Ashford University, 400 North Bluff Boulevard, Clinton, IA 52733-2967

---

## Briar Cliff University
**Sioux City, Iowa**
**www.briarcliff.edu**                                    **CB code: 6046**

- Private 4-year liberal arts college affiliated with Roman Catholic Church
- Residential campus in small city
- 1,074 degree-seeking undergraduates: 11% part-time, 55% women, 4% African American, 2% Asian American, 6% Hispanic American
- 34 degree-seeking graduate students
- 71% of applicants admitted
- ACT (writing optional) required
- 45% graduate within 6 years; 15% enter graduate study

**General.** Founded in 1930. Regionally accredited. **Degrees:** 234 bachelor's, 1 associate awarded; master's offered. **Location:** 90 miles from Omaha, Nebraska. **Calendar:** Trimester, limited summer session. **Full-time faculty:** 58 total; 59% have terminal degrees, 5% minority, 50% women. **Part-time faculty:** 42 total; 12% have terminal degrees, 64% women. **Class size:** 67% < 20, 30% 20-39, 2% 40-49, less than 1% 50-99. **Special facilities:** Prairie nature preserve, human anatomy/cadaver laboratory, integrated media lab, nursing simulation lab, entrepreneurship lab, music lab.

**Freshman class profile.** 1,434 applied, 1,013 admitted, 255 enrolled.

| Mid 50% test scores | | | |
|---|---|---|---|
| SAT critical reading: | 410-510 | **GPA 2.0-2.99:** | 36% |
| SAT math: | 460-550 | **Rank in top quarter:** | 29% |
| SAT writing: | 350-460 | **Rank in top tenth:** | 10% |
| ACT composite: | 19-23 | **End year in good standing:** | 81% |
| **GPA 3.50 or higher:** | 34% | **Return as sophomores:** | 63% |
| **GPA 3.0-3.49:** | 30% | **Out-of-state:** | 49% |
| | | **Live on campus:** | 94% |

**Basis for selection.** 2.0 GPA and 18 ACT required for full acceptance. Students not meeting requirement may be accepted conditionally or may appeal admission decision if not accepted. Interview and essay recommended. **Homeschooled:** A transcript of high school work should be obtained from the school district where the student resides full time. **Learning Disabled:** Students should submit official documentation directly to Student Support Services office.

**High school preparation.** 16 units recommended. Recommended units include English 4, mathematics 3, social studies 3, science 3, foreign language 2 and academic electives 1.

**2008-2009 Annual costs.** Tuition/fees: $21,510. Room/board: $6,411. Books/supplies: $825. Personal expenses: $1,935.

**2006-2007 Financial aid. Need-based:** 250 full-time freshmen applied for aid; 200 were judged to have need; 200 of these received aid. Average need met was 92%. Average scholarship/grant was $6,400; average loan $3,800. 53% of total undergraduate aid awarded as scholarships/grants, 47% as loans/jobs. **Non-need-based:** Awarded to 1,068 full-time undergraduates, including 297 freshmen. Scholarships awarded for academics, alumni affiliation, art, athletics, leadership, music/drama, religious affiliation, state

residency. **Additional information:** 97% of Briar Cliff's student body receive some sort of aid.

**Application procedures. Admission:** Priority date 4/1; no deadline. $20 fee, may be waived for applicants with need. Application may be submitted online. Admission notification on a rolling basis beginning on or about 6/1. **Financial aid:** Priority date 3/15; no closing date. FAFSA required. Applicants notified on a rolling basis starting 3/15; must reply by 5/1 or within 2 week(s) of notification.

**Academics. Special study options:** Accelerated study, cross-registration, distance learning, double major, honors, independent study, internships, liberal arts/career combination, student-designed major, study abroad, teacher certification program, urban semester, Washington semester, weekend college. Radiologic technology 1-2-1 program, medical technology 3-1 program. **Credit/placement by examination:** AP, CLEP, IB, ACT, institutional tests. 45 credit hours maximum toward bachelor's degree. Examinations must be taken before student enters last 30 hours of study. **Support services:** Learning center, pre-admission summer program, reduced course load, remedial instruction, study skills assistance, tutoring, writing center.

**Majors. Biology:** General. **Business:** Accounting, business admin, human resources, management information systems. **Communications:** Digital media, media studies. **Communications technology:** Graphics. **Computer sciences:** General, computer science. **Conservation:** Environmental science. **Education:** General, art, biology, chemistry, elementary, English, history, mathematics, music, physical, reading, science, secondary, social science. **English:** Composition, creative writing, English lit. **Foreign languages:** Spanish. **Health:** Clinical lab science, medical radiologic technology/radiation therapy, nursing (RN). **History:** General. **Interdisciplinary:** Biological/physical sciences. **Math:** General. **Parks/recreation:** Exercise sciences, health/fitness, sports admin. **Physical sciences:** Chemistry. **Protective services:** Law enforcement admin. **Psychology:** General. **Public administration:** Social work. **Social sciences:** Political science, sociology. **Theology:** Theology. **Visual/performing arts:** Art, dramatic, film/cinema, graphic design.

**Most popular majors.** Business/marketing 24%, education 12%, health sciences 24%, parks/recreation 9%.

**Computing on campus.** 112 workstations in dormitories, library, computer center, student center. Dormitories wired for high-speed internet access and linked to campus network. Commuter students can connect to campus network. Online library, helpline, repair service, student web hosting, wireless network available.

**Student life. Freshman orientation:** Mandatory, $95 fee. Preregistration for classes offered. Freshman orientation begins when the students move onto campus, prior to the beginning of classes. **Housing:** Guaranteed on-campus for freshmen. Coed dorms available. $150 deposit. **Activities:** Jazz band, campus ministries, choral groups, dance, drama, literary magazine, music ensembles, musical theater, opera, radio station, student government, student newspaper, Best Buddies, BCCares, Champions of Characters Council of Athletes, College Democrats, College Republicans, criminal justice club, departmental clubs, ethnic relations club, mentors in violence prevention.

**Athletics.** NAIA. **Intercollegiate:** Baseball M, basketball, cheerleading M, cross-country, football (tackle) M, golf, soccer, softball W, tennis W, track and field, volleyball W, wrestling M. **Intramural:** Badminton, basketball, bowling, cross-country, football (non-tackle) M, golf, handball, racquetball, soccer, softball, table tennis, tennis, track and field, volleyball. **Team name:** Chargers.

**Student services.** Career counseling, services for economically disadvantaged, student employment services, financial aid counseling, health services, personal counseling, placement for graduates. **Physically disabled:** Services for visually impaired.

**Contact.** E-mail: admissions@briarcliff.edu
Phone: (712) 279-5200 Toll-free number: (800) 662-3303 ext. 5200
Fax: (712) 279-1632
Sharisue Wilcoxon, Vice President for Enrollment Management, Briar Cliff University, 3303 Rebecca Street, Sioux City, IA 51104-0100

---

## Buena Vista University
**Storm Lake, Iowa**
**www.bvu.edu**                                    **CB code: 6047**

- Private 4-year liberal arts college affiliated with Presbyterian Church (USA)
- Residential campus in large town
- 1,022 degree-seeking undergraduates: 53% women, 4% African American, 1% Asian American, 3% Hispanic American, 1% international

- 94 degree-seeking graduate students
- 74% of applicants admitted
- SAT or ACT (ACT writing optional) required
- 54% graduate within 6 years; 17% enter graduate study

**General.** Founded in 1891. Regionally accredited. 14 branch campuses throughout Iowa provide educational opportunities for nontraditional students. **Degrees:** 777 bachelor's awarded; master's offered. **Location:** 150 miles from Des Moines, 80 miles from Sioux City. **Calendar:** 4-1-4, limited summer session. **Full-time faculty:** 84 total; 71% have terminal degrees, 4% minority, 45% women. **Part-time faculty:** 31 total; 10% have terminal degrees, 6% minority, 55% women. **Class size:** 72% < 20, 27% 20-39, 1% 40-49. **Special facilities:** Multimedia production facilities, underground buildings, information technology center, digitally-controlled acoustic music practice rooms.

**Freshman class profile.** 1,163 applied, 866 admitted, 228 enrolled.

| Mid 50% test scores | | Rank in top tenth: | 17% |
|---|---|---|---|
| ACT composite: | 19-24 | Return as sophomores: | 71% |
| GPA 3.50 or higher: | 37% | Out-of-state: | 25% |
| GPA 3.0-3.49: | 42% | Live on campus: | 100% |
| GPA 2.0-2.99: | 21% | International: | 2% |
| Rank in top quarter: | 40% | | |

**Basis for selection.** High school GPA and curriculum, rank in class, standardized test scores, interview, school and community activities important. Essay recommended.

**High school preparation.** College-preparatory program recommended. 15 units required. Required and recommended units include English 4, mathematics 4, social studies 2, history 2, science 2-4, foreign language 2 and computer science 1.

**2007-2008 Annual costs.** Tuition/fees: $23,842. Room/board: $6,712. Books/supplies: $1,000. Personal expenses: $1,500.

**2007-2008 Financial aid. Need-based:** Average need met was 93%. Average scholarship/grant was $9,007; average loan $4,884. 62% of total undergraduate aid awarded as scholarships/grants, 38% as loans/jobs. **Non-need-based:** Scholarships awarded for academics, art, minority status, music/drama, religious affiliation. **Additional information:** Portfolio required of art scholarship applicants, audition required of music and drama scholarship applicants.

**Application procedures. Admission:** No deadline. No application fee. Application may be submitted online. Admission notification on a rolling basis. **Financial aid:** Priority date 6/1; no closing date. FAFSA required. Applicants notified on a rolling basis starting 2/20.

**Academics.** Students must earn credit by attending the Academic and Cultural Events Series, featuring lectures by national and international leaders and performances by world-famous classical performing groups and artists. **Special study options:** Combined bachelor's/graduate degree, distance learning, double major, dual enrollment of high school students, ESL, exchange student, external degree, honors, independent study, internships, student-designed major, study abroad, teacher certification program, Washington semester. Rollins Fellows (competitive international internships). **Credit/placement by examination:** AP, CLEP, IB, institutional tests. 20 credit hours maximum toward bachelor's degree. **Support services:** Learning center, reduced course load, remedial instruction, study skills assistance, tutoring, writing center.

**Majors. Biology:** General. **Business:** Accounting, banking/financial services, entrepreneurial studies, human resources, international, management information systems, managerial economics, marketing. **Communications:** General, media studies, organizational. **Computer sciences:** Computer science. **Conservation:** Environmental science. **Education:** Art, biology, business, chemistry, computer, elementary, English, history, mathematics, multilevel teacher, music, physical, physics, psychology, reading, science, secondary, social science, Spanish, special, speech. **English:** English lit. **Foreign languages:** Spanish. **Health:** Athletic training, premedicine. **History:** General. **Interdisciplinary:** Biological/physical sciences. **Math:** General. **Parks/recreation:** Exercise sciences, sports admin. **Philosophy/religion:** Philosophy. **Physical sciences:** Chemistry, physics. **Protective services:** Criminal justice. **Psychology:** General. **Public administration:** General, social work. **Social sciences:** General, political science, sociology. **Visual/performing arts:** Art, arts management, commercial/advertising art, music performance, theater history.

**Most popular majors.** Business/marketing 31%, education 15%, interdisciplinary studies 14%, psychology 12%, security/protective services 8%.

**Computing on campus.** 400 workstations in dormitories, library, computer center, student center. Dormitories wired for high-speed internet access and linked to campus network. Commuter students can connect to campus network. Online course registration, online library, helpline, repair service, wireless network available.

**Student life. Freshman orientation:** Mandatory. Preregistration for classes offered. 2-day orientation offered during summer. **Housing:** Guaranteed on-campus for all undergraduates. Coed dorms, single-sex dorms, substance-free housing available. $150 deposit. **Activities:** Bands, campus ministries, choral groups, drama, international student organizations, music ensembles, musical theater, radio station, student government, student newspaper, TV station, Circle-K, Students Concerned about Tomorrow's Environment, intervarsity multicultural club, international club, Fellowship of Christian Athletes, College Democrats, College Republicans, Reshaping Our Campus Community.

**Athletics.** NCAA. **Intercollegiate:** Baseball M, basketball, cross-country, football (tackle) M, golf, soccer, softball W, tennis, track and field, volleyball W, wrestling M. **Intramural:** Basketball, football (non-tackle) M, handball, racquetball, soccer, softball, table tennis, volleyball. **Team name:** Beavers.

**Student services.** Adult student services, alcohol/substance abuse counseling, campus ministries, career counseling, student employment services, financial aid counseling, health services, minority student services, personal counseling, placement for graduates, veterans' counselor. **Physically disabled:** Services for visually, speech, hearing impaired.

**Contact.** E-mail: admissions@bvu.edu
Phone: (712) 749-2235 Toll-free number: (800) 383-9600
Fax: (712) 749-2037
Alan Coheley, Vice President, Enrollment Management, Buena Vista University, 610 West Fourth Street, Storm Lake, IA 50588

## Central College
Pella, Iowa
www.central.edu

**CB member**
**CB code: 6087**

- Private 4-year liberal arts college affiliated with Reformed Church in America
- Residential campus in large town
- 1,452 degree-seeking undergraduates: 2% part-time, 52% women
- 79% of applicants admitted
- SAT or ACT (ACT writing optional) required
- 71% graduate within 6 years

**General.** Founded in 1853. Regionally accredited. **Degrees:** 314 bachelor's awarded. **Location:** 45 miles from Des Moines. **Calendar:** Semester, limited summer session. **Full-time faculty:** 98 total; 84% have terminal degrees, 9% minority, 41% women. **Part-time faculty:** 43 total; 37% have terminal degrees, 44% women. **Class size:** 63% < 20, 34% 20-39, 2% 40-49, 1% 50-99. **Special facilities:** Glass-blowing studio, cross-cultural study center, center for communication and theater.

**Freshman class profile.** 1,919 applied, 1,522 admitted, 424 enrolled.

| Mid 50% test scores | | Return as sophomores: | 82% |
|---|---|---|---|
| SAT critical reading: | 410-640 | Out-of-state: | 25% |
| SAT math: | 450-650 | Live on campus: | 100% |
| ACT composite: | 19-29 | International: | 1% |
| GPA 3.50 or higher: | 52% | Fraternities: | 15% |
| GPA 3.0-3.49: | 33% | Sororities: | 9% |
| GPA 2.0-2.99: | 15% | | |

**Basis for selection.** High school curriculum, GPA, class rank, test scores important. Recommendations, school and community activities, alumni affiliation also considered. Interview and essay recommended. Audition recommended for music and theater majors. Portfolio recommended for art majors. **Homeschooled:** Transcript of courses and grades required. **Learning Disabled:** Special assistance for students with physical and learning disabilities.

**High school preparation.** 15 units recommended. Required and recommended units include English 4, mathematics 2-3, social studies 3, science 2-3 (laboratory 2) and foreign language 2.

**2007-2008 Annual costs.** Tuition/fees: $22,510. Costs provided are for main campus only. International location costs may vary by program location. Room/board: $7,624. Books/supplies: $750. Personal expenses: $1,500.

**2007-2008 Financial aid. Need-based:** 397 full-time freshmen applied for aid; 344 were judged to have need; 344 of these received aid. Average need met was 83%. Average scholarship/grant was $15,042; average loan $3,765. 65% of total undergraduate aid awarded as scholarships/grants, 35% as loans/jobs. **Non-need-based:** Awarded to 417 full-time undergraduates, including 119 freshmen. Scholarships awarded for academics, alumni affiliation, art, leadership, minority status, music/drama, religious affiliation, state residency. **Additional information:** Institutional parent loan program and interest-earning, tuition prepayment savings account available. Auditions required for music and theater scholarships, portfolios required for art scholarships. Monthly payment plan available.

**Application procedures. Admission:** No deadline. $25 fee, may be waived for applicants with need. Application may be submitted online. Admission notification on a rolling basis. **Financial aid:** Priority date 3/15; no closing date. FAFSA required. Applicants notified on a rolling basis starting 3/15; must reply by 5/1 or within 2 week(s) of notification.

**Academics. Special study options:** Combined bachelor's/graduate degree, cooperative education, cross-registration, double major, dual enrollment of high school students, honors, independent study, internships, liberal arts/career combination, student-designed major, study abroad, teacher certification program, urban semester, Washington semester. Chicago semester, study centers in France, Austria, Spain, England, Wales, Mexico, China, and the Netherlands. More than 40% of students spend a semester or year outside the United States. **Credit/placement by examination:** AP, CLEP, IB, institutional tests. **Support services:** Learning center, reduced course load, study skills assistance, tutoring, writing center.

**Majors. Biology:** General. **Business:** Accounting, business admin, international. **Communications:** General. **Computer sciences:** General, information systems. **Conservation:** Environmental studies. **Education:** Elementary, music. **English:** English lit. **Foreign languages:** French, German, linguistics, Spanish. **History:** General. **Interdisciplinary:** Global studies, math/computer science, natural sciences. **Math:** General. **Parks/recreation:** Exercise sciences. **Philosophy/religion:** Philosophy, religion. **Physical sciences:** Chemistry, physics. **Psychology:** General. **Social sciences:** General, anthropology, economics, political science, sociology. **Visual/performing arts:** Art, dramatic.

**Most popular majors.** Biology 6%, business/marketing 12%, communications/journalism 6%, education 10%, foreign language 8%, parks/recreation 12%, psychology 6%, social sciences 10%.

**Computing on campus.** 256 workstations in dormitories, library, computer center, student center. Dormitories wired for high-speed internet access and linked to campus network. Commuter students can connect to campus network. Online library, helpline, repair service, student web hosting, wireless network available.

**Student life. Freshman orientation:** Mandatory. Preregistration for classes offered. Held weekends in June. **Housing:** Guaranteed on-campus for all undergraduates. Coed dorms, single-sex dorms, apartments, fraternity/sorority housing available. $200 fully refundable deposit, deadline 5/1. 24 town houses, each housing 16 to 32 students, available to juniors and seniors. French, German, and Spanish houses available to language majors. **Activities:** Bands, choral groups, drama, literary magazine, music ensembles, musical theater, radio station, student government, student newspaper, symphony orchestra, Young Democrats, Young Republicans, Fellowship of Christian Athletes, Inter-Varsity Christian Fellowship, Alcohol Awareness Committee, Coalition for a Multicultural Campus, Circle-K, Amnesty International, Students Against Apartheid, Students Concerned About the Environment.

**Athletics.** NCAA. **Intercollegiate:** Baseball M, basketball, cross-country, football (tackle) M, golf, soccer, softball W, tennis, track and field, volleyball W, wrestling M. **Intramural:** Basketball, racquetball, rugby, softball, volleyball. **Team name:** Dutch.

**Student services.** Alcohol/substance abuse counseling, campus ministries, career counseling, services for economically disadvantaged, student employment services, financial aid counseling, health services, minority student services, personal counseling, placement for graduates, veterans' counselor. **Physically disabled:** Services for visually, speech, hearing impaired. **Learning disabled:** Comprehensive services available.

**Contact.** E-mail: admissions@central.edu
Phone: (641) 628-5286 Toll-free number: (877) 462-3687
Fax: (641) 628-5316
Carol Williamson, Dean of Admission, Central College, 812 University Street, Pella, IA 50219-1999

---

## Clarke College
**Dubuque, Iowa**
**www.clarke.edu**                                    **CB code: 6099**

- Private 4-year liberal arts college affiliated with Roman Catholic Church
- Residential campus in small city
- 1,008 degree-seeking undergraduates: 12% part-time, 71% women
- 208 graduate students

---

- 62% of applicants admitted
- SAT or ACT (ACT writing optional) required

**General.** Founded in 1843. Regionally accredited. **Degrees:** 195 bachelor's, 1 associate awarded; master's, doctoral offered. **ROTC:** Army. **Location:** 150 miles from Chicago. **Calendar:** Semester, limited summer session. **Full-time faculty:** 74 total. **Part-time faculty:** 66 total. **Class size:** 71% < 20, 28% 20-39, less than 1% 40-49. **Special facilities:** Planetarium, art and communications laboratory, writing center, art slide library, computerized mathematics laboratory, nursing laboratory, human gross anatomy laboratory with A.D.A.M. software.

**Freshman class profile.** 1,020 applied, 636 admitted, 188 enrolled.

| Mid 50% test scores | | | |
|---|---|---|---|
| SAT critical reading: | 480-550 | GPA 3.0-3.49: | 32% |
| SAT math: | 460-640 | GPA 2.0-2.99: | 21% |
| SAT writing: | 510-560 | Rank in top quarter: | 45% |
| ACT composite: | 20-25 | Rank in top tenth: | 17% |
| GPA 3.50 or higher: | 45% | Out-of-state: | 47% |
| | | Live on campus: | 84% |

**Basis for selection.** High school record of primary importance. Particular attention paid to grades on college preparatory course work and test scores. Interview required of the academically weak. Auditions required of music and drama majors. Portfolio required of art majors.

**High school preparation.** 21 units required. Required and recommended units include English 4, mathematics 3-4, social studies 3, science 3-4 (laboratory 2), foreign language 2 and academic electives 4. 4 college preparatory math and science, including 3 lab, required for physical therapy program.

**2008-2009 Annual costs.** Tuition/fees: $22,378. Room/board: $6,574. Books/supplies: $700. Personal expenses: $700.

**2007-2008 Financial aid. Need-based:** 68% of total undergraduate aid awarded as scholarships/grants, 32% as loans/jobs. **Non-need-based:** Scholarships awarded for academics, alumni affiliation, art, athletics, leadership, music/drama, religious affiliation, state residency. **Additional information:** Reduced tuition for family members of BVMs.

**Application procedures. Admission:** No deadline. $25 fee, may be waived for applicants with need. Application may be submitted online. Admission notification on a rolling basis beginning on or about 1/15. Must reply by May 1 or within 3 week(s) if notified thereafter. **Financial aid:** Priority date 4/15; no closing date. FAFSA required. Applicants notified on a rolling basis starting 3/15; must reply by 5/1 or within 2 week(s) of notification.

**Academics. Special study options:** Accelerated study, combined bachelor's/graduate degree, cooperative education, cross-registration, distance learning, double major, ESL, honors, independent study, internships, liberal arts/career combination, student-designed major, study abroad, teacher certification program. **Credit/placement by examination:** AP, CLEP, IB, SAT, ACT, institutional tests. 15 credit hours maximum toward associate degree, 30 toward bachelor's. Students applying for prior learning assessment (PLA) credit must be 24 years of age or older. Maximum of 30 credits granted for PLA, CLEP or DANTES within 5-year period. If more than 15 PLA credits are awarded based on portfolio evaluation, additional credit up to 30 hours must be matched by regular college credit. PLA does not count toward the 30 hour residency requirement and is awarded only after 5 hours in degree program are completed. Guidelines may vary by department. **Support services:** Learning center, reduced course load, study skills assistance, tutoring, writing center.

**Majors. Biology:** General, biochemistry, bioinformatics. **Business:** Accounting, business admin. **Communications:** General. **Computer sciences:** General, computer science. **Education:** Elementary, music, physical. **English:** English lit. **Foreign languages:** Spanish. **Health:** Predental, premedicine, prepharmacy, preveterinary. **History:** General. **Math:** General. **Parks/recreation:** Exercise sciences, sports admin. **Philosophy/religion:** Philosophy, religion. **Physical sciences:** Chemistry. **Psychology:** General. **Public administration:** Social work. **Visual/performing arts:** Art, art history/conservation, dramatic, studio arts.

**Most popular majors.** Business/marketing 22%, education 13%, health sciences 25%, psychology 6%, public administration/social services 6%, visual/performing arts 19%.

**Computing on campus.** 237 workstations in dormitories, library, computer center, student center. Dormitories wired for high-speed internet access and linked to campus network. Commuter students can connect to campus network. Online course registration, online library, wireless network available.

**Student life. Freshman orientation:** Available. Preregistration for classes offered. **Housing:** Guaranteed on-campus for freshmen. Coed dorms, single-sex dorms, apartments, substance-free housing available. $100 fully refundable deposit, deadline 7/15. **Activities:** Jazz band, choral groups, drama, literary magazine, music ensembles, radio station, student government, student newspaper, Amnesty International, peace and justice, peer ministry program, minority student organization, Walden Society (political discussion group).

**Athletics.** NAIA. **Intercollegiate:** Baseball M, basketball, cheerleading M, cross-country, golf, soccer, softball W, tennis, track and field, volleyball. **Intramural:** Basketball, bowling, football (non-tackle), softball, table tennis, tennis, volleyball. **Team name:** Crusaders.

**Student services.** Adult student services, alcohol/substance abuse counseling, campus ministries, career counseling, student employment services, financial aid counseling, health services, minority student services, personal counseling. **Physically disabled:** Services for visually, hearing impaired.

**Contact.** E-mail: admissions@clarke.edu
Phone: (563) 588-6316 Toll-free number: (800) 383-2345
Fax: (563) 588-6789
Andy Schroeder, Director of Admission, Clarke College, 1550 Clarke Drive, Dubuque, IA 52001-3198

## Coe College
**Cedar Rapids, Iowa**
www.coe.edu

**CB member**
**CB code: 6101**

- Private 4-year liberal arts college affiliated with Presbyterian Church (USA)
- Residential campus in small city
- 1,298 degree-seeking undergraduates
- 18 graduate students
- 64% of applicants admitted
- SAT or ACT (ACT writing optional), application essay required

**General.** Founded in 1851. Regionally accredited. **Degrees:** 292 bachelor's awarded; master's offered. **ROTC:** Army, Air Force. **Location:** 230 miles from Chicago, 300 miles from Minneapolis-St. Paul. **Calendar:** Semester, limited summer session. **Full-time faculty:** 78 total. **Part-time faculty:** 43 total. **Special facilities:** Bird museum, infrared spectrometer, analytical physiology units, music library, wilderness field station.

**Freshman class profile.** 1,890 applied, 1,209 admitted, 342 enrolled.

| Mid 50% test scores | | | |
|---|---|---|---|
| SAT critical reading: | 530-630 | GPA 3.0-3.49: | 26% |
| SAT math: | 570-670 | GPA 2.0-2.99: | 2% |
| SAT writing: | 510-620 | Rank in top quarter: | 67% |
| ACT composite: | 23-28 | Rank in top tenth: | 30% |
| GPA 3.50 or higher: | 72% | Live on campus: | 97% |
| | | Fraternities: | 17% |

**Basis for selection.** School achievement record and test scores most important. Recommendations and school activities also important. Interview and community activities considered. **Homeschooled:** GED, test scores, and portfolio required. **Learning Disabled:** Submission of disability assessment required.

**High school preparation.** 18 units recommended. Recommended units include English 4, mathematics 3, social studies 3, science 3 (laboratory 1), foreign language 2 and academic electives 2.

**2007-2008 Annual costs.** Tuition/fees: $26,390. Cost per course for part-time students (fewer than 3.0 course credits) is $3,200. Room/board: $6,600. Books/supplies: $600. Personal expenses: $1,100.

**Financial aid.** **Non-need-based:** Scholarships awarded for academics, alumni affiliation, art, leadership, music/drama, ROTC.

**Application procedures.** **Admission:** Priority date 12/10; deadline 3/1 (postmark date). $30 fee, may be waived for applicants with need. Application may be submitted online. Admission notification 3/15. Must reply by May 1 or within 2 week(s) if notified thereafter. **Financial aid:** Priority date 3/1; no closing date. FAFSA required. Applicants notified on a rolling basis starting 3/15; must reply by 5/1 or within 2 week(s) of notification.

**Academics.** Writing emphasis courses required. Semester practicum required for all students. **Special study options:** Accelerated study, combined bachelor's/graduate degree, cross-registration, double major, dual enrollment of high school students, ESL, exchange student, honors, independent study, internships, New York semester, student-designed major, study abroad, teacher certification program, urban semester, Washington semester. Oak Ridge science semester; research program at the Coe College wilderness field station- Minnesota Superior National Forest; tropical field research in Costa Rica; travel abroad to England, Hong Kong, India, Italy, Japan, Russia, Latin America, Czech Republic, Tanzania, Germany, Sweden, Spain, France, Korea, Thailand, Ireland. **Credit/placement by examination:** AP,

CLEP, IB, institutional tests. **Support services:** Pre-admission summer program, reduced course load, study skills assistance, tutoring, writing center.

**Majors.** **Area/ethnic studies:** African-American, American, Asian, French, German, Spanish/Iberian. **Biology:** General, biochemistry, molecular. **Business:** Accounting, business admin. **Communications:** General, public relations. **Computer sciences:** Computer science. **Conservation:** Environmental science. **Education:** General, art, elementary, middle, music, physical, science, secondary. **English:** Creative writing, English lit, speech/rhetoric. **Foreign languages:** Classics, French, German, Spanish. **Health:** Athletic training, nursing (RN), predental, premedicine, preveterinary. **History:** General. **Interdisciplinary:** Accounting/computer science, biological/physical sciences, math/computer science. **Legal studies:** Prelaw. **Math:** General. **Parks/recreation:** Health/fitness. **Philosophy/religion:** Philosophy, religion. **Physical sciences:** General, chemistry, physics. **Psychology:** General. **Social sciences:** Economics, political science, sociology. **Visual/performing arts:** Acting, art, ceramics, directing/producing, dramatic, music performance, music theory/composition, painting, photography, studio arts, theater design.

**Computing on campus.** Dormitories wired for high-speed internet access and linked to campus network. Commuter students can connect to campus network. Online course registration, online library, helpline, student web hosting, wireless network available.

**Student life.** **Freshman orientation:** Mandatory, $75 fee. 4-5 day program. **Policies:** Students must live on campus unless residing with relatives or granted off-campus permission by Department of Residence Life. **Housing:** Guaranteed on-campus for all undergraduates. Coed dorms, single-sex dorms, apartments, fraternity/sorority housing, substance-free housing available. $200 nonrefundable deposit, deadline 5/1. **Activities:** Bands, campus ministries, choral groups, drama, international student organizations, literary magazine, music ensembles, radio station, student government, student newspaper, symphony orchestra, black self-education organization, Friends club, Egalitarians Supporting the Advancement of Women, Christian Fellowship, College Republicans, Habitat for Humanity, green club, College Democrats, Fellowship of Christian Athletes.

**Athletics.** NCAA. **Intercollegiate:** Baseball M, basketball, cheerleading M, cross-country, diving, football (tackle) M, golf, soccer, softball W, swimming, tennis, track and field, volleyball W, wrestling M. **Intramural:** Badminton, basketball, football (non-tackle) M, racquetball, soccer, softball, squash, table tennis, tennis, volleyball, wrestling M. **Team name:** Kohawks.

**Student services.** Adult student services, alcohol/substance abuse counseling, career counseling, student employment services, financial aid counseling, health services, minority student services, personal counseling, placement for graduates.

**Contact.** E-mail: admission@coe.edu
Phone: (319) 399-8500 Toll-free number: (877) 225-5263
Fax: (319) 399-8816
John Grundig, Dean of Admission, Coe College, 1220 First Avenue NE, Cedar Rapids, IA 52402

## Cornell College
**Mount Vernon, Iowa**
www.cornellcollege.edu

**CB member**
**CB code: 6119**

- Private 4-year liberal arts college affiliated with United Methodist Church
- Residential campus in small town
- 1,075 degree-seeking undergraduates: 1% part-time, 51% women, 3% African American, 2% Asian American, 3% Hispanic American, 1% Native American, 3% international
- 45% of applicants admitted
- SAT or ACT (ACT writing optional), application essay required
- 64% graduate within 6 years

**General.** Founded in 1853. Regionally accredited. **Degrees:** 300 bachelor's awarded. **Location:** 15 miles from Cedar Rapids, 20 miles from Iowa City. **Calendar:** Nine terms of 3 and 1/2 weeks, one course per term. **Full-time faculty:** 83 total; 95% have terminal degrees, 7% minority, 48% women. **Part-time faculty:** 14 total; 64% have terminal degrees, 21% minority, 64% women. **Class size:** 67% < 20, 33% 20-39. **Special facilities:** Canadian/Minnesota border wilderness station, geology museum.

**Freshman class profile.** 2,659 applied, 1,209 admitted, 316 enrolled.

| Mid 50% test scores | | Rank in top quarter: | 51% |
|---|---|---|---|
| SAT critical reading: | 540-680 | Rank in top tenth: | 25% |
| SAT math: | 530-650 | End year in good standing: | 96% |
| ACT composite: | 24-29 | Return as sophomores: | 85% |
| GPA 3.50 or higher: | 55% | Out-of-state: | 78% |
| GPA 3.0-3.49: | 28% | Live on campus: | 99% |
| GPA 2.0-2.99: | 16% | International: | 2% |

**Basis for selection.** Academic record, statement of purpose, interview weighed on individual basis. Test scores often secondary. Interviews are recommended but not required. **Homeschooled:** Applicants asked to provide as many documents pertaining to their education as possible. **Learning Disabled:** Must have recent documentation of disability from offical source if student requires special arrangements in academic setting.

**High school preparation.** 15 units recommended. Recommended units include English 4, mathematics 3, social studies 3, science 3 and foreign language 2. As many advanced, honors, and/or AP courses as possible recommended.

**2007-2008 Annual costs.** Tuition/fees: $26,280. Room/board: $6,970. Books/supplies: $720. Personal expenses: $540.

**2007-2008 Financial aid. Need-based:** 270 full-time freshmen applied for aid; 214 were judged to have need; 214 of these received aid. Average need met was 93%. Average scholarship/grant was $10,815; average loan $3,370. 79% of total undergraduate aid awarded as scholarships/grants, 21% as loans/jobs. **Non-need-based:** Awarded to 877 full-time undergraduates, including 238 freshmen. Scholarships awarded for academics, art, leadership, minority status, music/drama, religious affiliation, state residency. **Additional information:** Portfolio required for art scholarship applicants. Audition required for music scholarship applicants.

**Application procedures. Admission:** Priority date 2/1; deadline 3/1 (postmark date). $30 fee, may be waived for applicants with need. Application may be submitted online. Must reply by May 1 or within 2 week(s) if notified thereafter. **Financial aid:** Closing date 3/1. FAFSA, institutional form required. Applicants notified on a rolling basis starting 3/1; must reply by 5/1 or within 2 week(s) of notification.

**Academics. Special study options:** Accelerated study, combined bachelor's/graduate degree, double major, ESL, exchange student, independent study, internships, liberal arts/career combination, semester at sea, student-designed major, study abroad, teacher certification program, urban semester, Washington semester. **Credit/placement by examination:** AP, CLEP, IB, institutional tests. **Support services:** Learning center, study skills assistance, tutoring, writing center.

**Majors. Area/ethnic studies:** Latin American, Russian/Slavic, women's. **Biology:** General, Biochemistry/biophysics and molecular biology. **Computer sciences:** Computer science. **Conservation:** Environmental studies. **Education:** General, art, biology, chemistry, elementary, English, French, German, history, mathematics, middle, music, physical, physics, science, secondary, social science, social studies, Spanish. **English:** English lit. **Foreign languages:** General, classics, French, German, Russian, Spanish. **History:** General. **Math:** General. **Parks/recreation:** Health/fitness. **Philosophy/religion:** Philosophy, religion. **Physical sciences:** Chemistry, geology, physics. **Psychology:** General. **Social sciences:** Economics, international relations, political science, sociology. **Visual/performing arts:** Art, dramatic, music performance. **Other:** Ethnic studies, Medieval and early modern studies, Sociology and anthropology.

**Most popular majors.** Biology 10%, education 7%, English 6%, interdisciplinary studies 6%, philosophy/religious studies 7%, psychology 9%, social sciences 18%, visual/performing arts 10%.

**Computing on campus.** 181 workstations in library, computer center, student center. Dormitories wired for high-speed internet access and linked to campus network. Commuter students can connect to campus network. Online library, helpline, repair service, student web hosting, wireless network available.

**Student life. Freshman orientation:** Mandatory. Five-day orientation held before fall classes begin. **Housing:** Guaranteed on-campus for freshmen. Coed dorms, single-sex dorms, apartments, substance-free housing available. $300 fully refundable deposit, deadline 5/1. First-year halls or first year only floors available. **Activities:** Bands, campus ministries, choral groups, dance, drama, international student organizations, literary magazine, music ensembles, musical theater, opera, radio station, student government, student newspaper, symphony orchestra, Alpha Phi Omega, alumni student association, fellowship of Christian athletes, Black Awareness Cultural Organization, women's action group, Young Democrats, College Republicans, Habitat for Humanity, women's social groups, men's social groups, lunch buddies/youth mentoring.

**Athletics.** NCAA. **Intercollegiate:** Baseball M, basketball, cross-country, football (tackle) M, golf, soccer, softball W, tennis, track and field, volleyball W, wrestling M. **Intramural:** Badminton, basketball, bowling, football (non-tackle), lacrosse, racquetball, soccer, softball, table tennis, track and field, volleyball. **Team name:** Rams.

**Student services.** Adult student services, alcohol/substance abuse counseling, career counseling, student employment services, financial aid counseling, health services, minority student services, personal counseling, women's services.

**Contact.** E-mail: admissions@cornellcollege.edu
Phone: (319) 895-4477 Toll-free number: (800) 747-1112
Fax: (319) 895-4451
Jonathan Stroud, Vice President for Enrollment/Dean of Admissions and Financial Aid, Cornell College, 600 First Street SW, Mount Vernon, IA 52314-1098

---

## Divine Word College
**Epworth, Iowa**
www.dwci.edu                          CB code: 6174

- Private 4-year liberal arts and seminary college for men affiliated with Roman Catholic Church
- Rural community
- 49 degree-seeking undergraduates
- 89% of applicants admitted
- Application essay, interview required

**General.** Founded in 1912. Regionally accredited. **Degrees:** 4 bachelor's awarded. **Location:** 15 miles from Dubuque. **Calendar:** Semester. **Full-time faculty:** 22 total. **Part-time faculty:** 3 total.

**Freshman class profile.** 9 applied, 8 admitted, 8 enrolled.

| Mid 50% test scores | | SAT math: | 520-570 |
|---|---|---|---|
| SAT critical reading: | 520-620 | | |

**Basis for selection.** Interview and religious commitment most important. School achievement record, test scores, recommendations, and school and community activities also considered. Minnesota Multiphasic Personality Inventory (MMPI) used for admission and counseling. SAT or ACT writing component considered if submitted.

**High school preparation.** 16 units required. Required and recommended units include mathematics 3, social studies 3, science 3 and foreign language 2. 1 performing arts recommended.

**2007-2008 Annual costs.** Tuition/fees: $10,100. Room/board: $2,550. Books/supplies: $500.

**Application procedures. Admission:** Closing date 7/15. $25 fee, may be waived for applicants with need. Admission notification on a rolling basis beginning on or about 1/1. **Financial aid:** Priority date 8/31; no closing date. Applicants notified on a rolling basis starting 8/1.

**Academics. Special study options:** Double major, dual enrollment of high school students, independent study, study abroad. **Credit/placement by examination:** AP, CLEP, institutional tests. **Support services:** Reduced course load, remedial instruction, tutoring.

**Majors. Interdisciplinary:** Intercultural. **Philosophy/religion:** Philosophy.

**Computing on campus.** 26 workstations in computer center.

**Student life. Policies:** Religious observance required. **Housing:** All students live in dormitories on campus. **Activities:** Campus ministries, choral groups, student government, Vietnamese student organization, Sudanese student organization, Social Justice Committee, Right to Life Committee.

**Athletics. Intramural:** Basketball M, soccer M, swimming M, table tennis M, tennis M, volleyball M.

**Student services.** Career counseling, health services, personal counseling.

**Contact.** E-mail: svdvocations@dwci.edu
Phone: (563) 876-3332
Len Uhal, Vice President for Recruitment and Admissions, Divine Word College, 102 Jacoby Drive SW, Epworth, IA 52045

## Dordt College
**Sioux Center, Iowa**
www.dordt.edu
**CB code: 6171**

- Private 4-year liberal arts college affiliated with Christian Reformed Church
- Residential campus in small town
- 1,263 degree-seeking undergraduates: 4% part-time, 50% women, 1% Hispanic American, 17% international
- 64 graduate students
- 88% of applicants admitted
- SAT or ACT (ACT writing optional) required
- 71% graduate within 6 years; 15% enter graduate study

**General.** Founded in 1955. Regionally accredited. **Degrees:** 259 bachelor's, 21 associate awarded; master's offered. **Location:** 45 miles from Sioux City; 55 miles from Sioux Falls, South Dakota. **Calendar:** Semester. **Full-time faculty:** 70 total; 97% have terminal degrees, 9% minority, 29% women. **Part-time faculty:** 25 total; 28% have terminal degrees, 56% women. **Class size:** 63% < 20, 26% 20-39, 6% 40-49, 4% 50-99, less than 1% >100. **Special facilities:** Farm, biotechnology research facility.

**Freshman class profile.** 905 applied, 794 admitted, 396 enrolled.

| Mid 50% test scores | | | |
|---|---|---|---|
| SAT critical reading: | 480-630 | GPA 2.0-2.99: | 18% |
| SAT math: | 500-640 | Rank in top quarter: | 48% |
| SAT writing: | 450-610 | Rank in top tenth: | 30% |
| ACT composite: | 21-27 | Out-of-state: | 65% |
| GPA 3.50 or higher: | 49% | Live on campus: | 95% |
| GPA 3.0-3.49: | 32% | International: | 19% |

**Basis for selection.** School achievement record, high school GPA, test scores, religious affiliation or commitment important. Interview recommended for academically borderline applicants. **Homeschooled:** Must submit certified GPA. **Learning Disabled:** Copies of prior testing and interview with learning disabilities advisor required.

**High school preparation.** 17 units required; 25 recommended. Required and recommended units include English 3-4, mathematics 2-3, social studies 1, history 2, science 2-4, foreign language 2-3 and academic electives 6. 10 units must be in social science, English, foreign language, natural science, or math. Math must include algebra, geometry.

**2008-2009 Annual costs.** Tuition/fees: $21,040. Room/board: $5,720. Books/supplies: $780. Personal expenses: $2,000.

**2006-2007 Financial aid. Need-based:** 341 full-time freshmen applied for aid; 296 were judged to have need; 296 of these received aid. Average need met was 86%. Average scholarship/grant was $10,287; average loan $5,160. 55% of total undergraduate aid awarded as scholarships/grants, 45% as loans/jobs. **Non-need-based:** Awarded to 306 full-time undergraduates, including 90 freshmen. Scholarships awarded for academics, alumni affiliation, art, athletics, job skills, leadership, minority status, music/drama, religious affiliation, state residency.

**Application procedures. Admission:** Closing date 7/31. $25 fee, may be waived for applicants with need. Application may be submitted online. Admission notification on a rolling basis beginning on or about 10/1. Must reply by May 1 or within 1 week(s) if notified thereafter. Applicants with high school GPA under 2.25 considered on individual basis, may be admitted on probation. **Financial aid:** Priority date 4/1; no closing date. FAFSA, institutional form required. Applicants notified on a rolling basis starting 3/15; must reply within 3 week(s) of notification.

**Academics. Special study options:** Combined bachelor's/graduate degree, distance learning, double major, ESL, honors, independent study, internships, liberal arts/career combination, student-designed major, study abroad, teacher certification program, urban semester, Washington semester. Iowa Legislative Intern program; China, England, Costa Rica, Russia, Latin America, Netherlands, and Germany semesters; Los Angeles-Film Institute semester, Chicago Metro semester, American Studies semester. **Credit/placement by examination:** AP, CLEP, IB, SAT, ACT, institutional tests. Registrar makes determination on case-by-case basis. **Support services:** Learning center, reduced course load, remedial instruction, study skills assistance, tutoring.

**Majors. Agriculture:** Agribusiness operations, animal sciences, business, plant sciences. **Biology:** General. **Business:** General, accounting, accounting/business management, information resources management, marketing. **Communications:** General, broadcast journalism, journalism, media studies, public relations. **Communications technology:** General, graphics. **Computer sciences:** General, computer science, information systems, LAN/WAN management, system admin. **Conservation:** General, environmental studies. **Education:** General, art, biology, business, chemistry, drama/dance, elementary, English, foreign languages, health, history, mathematics, middle, music, physical, physics, reading, science, secondary, social science, social studies, Spanish, special, speech. **Engineering:** General, agricultural, biomedical, civil, computer, electrical, mechanical. **English:** Composition, English lit, speech/rhetoric. **Foreign languages:** Dutch/Flemish, Spanish. **Health:** Athletic training, clinical lab science, clinical lab technology, health services, nursing (RN), predental, premedicine, prepharmacy, preveterinary. **History:** General. **Legal studies:** Prelaw. **Liberal arts:** Arts/sciences. **Math:** General. **Parks/recreation:** General, exercise sciences, health/fitness. **Philosophy/religion:** Philosophy, religion. **Physical sciences:** General, chemistry, physics. **Protective services:** Police science. **Psychology:** General. **Public administration:** General, social work. **Social sciences:** General, political science. **Theology:** Missionary, sacred music, theology, youth ministry. **Visual/performing arts:** Art, commercial/advertising art, design, dramatic, piano/organ, stringed instruments, voice/opera.

**Most popular majors.** Agriculture 6%, business/marketing 18%, education 16%, engineering/engineering technologies 8%, visual/performing arts 7%.

**Computing on campus.** 200 workstations in dormitories, library, computer center, student center. Dormitories wired for high-speed internet access and linked to campus network. Commuter students can connect to campus network. Online course registration, online library, helpline, wireless network available.

**Student life. Freshman orientation:** Mandatory. Preregistration for classes offered. 3 days prior to the beginning of classes. **Policies:** Religious observance required. **Housing:** Guaranteed on-campus for all undergraduates. Single-sex dorms, special housing for disabled, apartments, substance-free housing available. $100 deposit, deadline 6/1. **Activities:** Bands, choral groups, dance, drama, film society, literary magazine, music ensembles, musical theater, opera, radio station, student government, student newspaper, symphony orchestra, 50 clubs and student organizations.

**Athletics.** NAIA. **Intercollegiate:** Baseball M, basketball, cross-country, football (tackle) M, golf M, ice hockey M, soccer, softball W, tennis, track and field, volleyball W. **Intramural:** Badminton, basketball, bowling, cross-country, field hockey W, golf, racquetball, soccer, softball, swimming, tennis, volleyball. **Team name:** Defenders.

**Student services.** Adult student services, alcohol/substance abuse counseling, campus ministries, career counseling, student employment services, financial aid counseling, health services, minority student services, personal counseling, placement for graduates, veterans' counselor. **Physically disabled:** Services for visually, speech, hearing impaired. **Learning disabled:** Comprehensive services available.

**Contact.** E-mail: admission@dordt.edu
Phone: (712) 722-6080 Toll-free number: (800) 343-6738
Fax: (712) 722-1198
Quentin Van Essen, Executive Director of Admissions, Dordt College, 498 Fourth Avenue, NE, Sioux Center, IA 51250

## Drake University
**Des Moines, Iowa**
www.drake.edu
**CB member**
**CB code: 6168**

- Private 4-year university
- Residential campus in large city
- 3,362 degree-seeking undergraduates: 5% part-time, 57% women, 3% African American, 5% Asian American, 2% Hispanic American, 7% international
- 2,026 degree-seeking graduate students
- 78% of applicants admitted
- SAT or ACT (ACT writing optional), application essay required
- 77% graduate within 6 years

**General.** Founded in 1881. Regionally accredited. **Degrees:** 699 bachelor's awarded; master's, doctoral, first professional offered. **ROTC:** Army. **Location:** 243 miles from Minneapolis-St. Paul, 150 miles from Omaha, Nebraska. **Calendar:** Semester, extensive summer session. **Full-time faculty:** 257 total; 95% have terminal degrees, 12% minority, 46% women. **Part-time faculty:** 177 total. **Class size:** 47% < 20, 35% 20-39, 10% 40-49, 4% 50-99, 4% >100. **Special facilities:** Observatory, green house.

**Freshman class profile.** 4,712 applied, 3,692 admitted, 924 enrolled.

| Mid 50% test scores | | | |
|---|---|---|---|
| SAT critical reading: | 520-630 | Rank in top tenth: | 37% |
| SAT math: | 550-660 | Return as sophomores: | 86% |
| ACT composite: | 24-29 | Out-of-state: | 70% |
| GPA 3.50 or higher: | 68% | Live on campus: | 97% |
| GPA 3.0-3.49: | 25% | International: | 3% |
| GPA 2.0-2.99: | 7% | Fraternities: | 22% |
| Rank in top quarter: | 69% | Sororities: | 31% |

**Basis for selection.** High school academic record, test scores, extracurricular activities, counselor recommendation, and essay important. Comprehensive review completed and each item in student's file considered. Interview recommended for all, required for some. Audition required of music and theater majors. Portfolio recommended for art majors.

**High school preparation.** 16 units recommended. Recommended units include English 4, mathematics 3, social studies 4, science 2 and foreign language 2.

**2008-2009 Annual costs.** Tuition/fees: $24,872. Room/board: $7,410. Books/supplies: $900. Personal expenses: $1,500.

**2007-2008 Financial aid. Need-based:** 744 full-time freshmen applied for aid; 565 were judged to have need; 565 of these received aid. Average need met was 89%. Average scholarship/grant was $13,469; average loan $5,462. 60% of total undergraduate aid awarded as scholarships/grants, 40% as loans/jobs. **Non-need-based:** Awarded to 1,553 full-time undergraduates, including 488 freshmen. Scholarships awarded for academics, alumni affiliation, art, athletics, music/drama, ROTC, state residency.

**Application procedures. Admission:** Priority date 3/1; no deadline. $25 fee, may be waived for applicants with need. Application may be submitted online. Admission notification on a rolling basis beginning on or about 10/1. **Financial aid:** Priority date 3/1; no closing date. FAFSA required. Applicants notified on a rolling basis starting 3/1.

**Academics.** Peer support through academic departments and residence halls offered. **Special study options:** Accelerated study, combined bachelor's/graduate degree, cooperative education, distance learning, double major, dual enrollment of high school students, ESL, honors, independent study, internships, liberal arts/career combination, semester at sea, student-designed major, study abroad, teacher certification program, Washington semester. **Credit/placement by examination:** AP, CLEP, IB, institutional tests. 66 credit hours maximum toward bachelor's degree. **Support services:** Study skills assistance, tutoring, writing center.

**Majors. Biology:** General, biochemistry, cellular/molecular, pharmacology. **Business:** General, accounting, actuarial science, finance, international, management information systems, management science, managerial economics, marketing. **Communications:** General, advertising, broadcast journalism, journalism, media studies, public relations, radio/tv. **Computer sciences:** General, computer science, information technology. **Conservation:** Environmental science, management/policy. **Education:** Curriculum, elementary, mathematics, music, secondary. **English:** Composition, English lit, speech/rhetoric. **Health:** Health services, pharmaceutical sciences. **History:** General. **Interdisciplinary:** Neuroscience. **Legal studies:** General. **Math:** General. **Philosophy/religion:** Ethics, philosophy, religion. **Physical sciences:** Astronomy, chemistry, physics. **Psychology:** General. **Social sciences:** General, anthropology, economics, international relations, political science, sociology. **Visual/performing arts:** Acting, art history/conservation, commercial/advertising art, directing/producing, dramatic, drawing, music management, music performance, painting, printmaking, sculpture, theater design.

**Most popular majors.** Biology 7%, business/marketing 32%, communications/journalism 15%, education 9%, English 6%, social sciences 7%, visual/performing arts 7%.

**Computing on campus.** 1,000 workstations in dormitories, library, computer center, student center. Dormitories wired for high-speed internet access and linked to campus network. Commuter students can connect to campus network. Online course registration, online library, helpline, repair service, student web hosting, wireless network available.

**Student life. Freshman orientation:** Available, $90 fee. Preregistration for classes offered. Four 1-1/2 day sessions; all held in June, includes parents. **Policies:** Student leaders must maintain 2.0 GPA. Students must live on campus the first 2 years following high school. **Housing:** Guaranteed on-campus for freshmen. Coed dorms, special housing for disabled, apartments, fraternity/sorority housing, substance-free housing available. $100 nonrefundable deposit, deadline 5/1. **Activities:** Bands, campus ministries, choral groups, dance, drama, international student organizations, literary magazine, music ensembles, Model UN, musical theater, radio station, student government, student newspaper, TV station, Coalition of Black Students,

Best Buddies, College Republicans, College Democrats, La Fuerza Latina, Alpha Phi Omega, South Asian student association, Rainbow Union, Drake Hillel.

**Athletics.** NCAA. **Intercollegiate:** Basketball, cheerleading, cross-country, football (tackle) M, golf, rowing (crew) W, soccer, softball W, tennis, track and field, volleyball W. **Intramural:** Badminton, basketball, football (non-tackle), football (tackle) M, golf, racquetball, soccer, swimming, tennis, volleyball. **Team name:** Bulldogs.

**Student services.** Career counseling, student employment services, financial aid counseling, health services, legal services, personal counseling, placement for graduates. **Physically disabled:** Services for visually, speech, hearing impaired.

**Contact.** E-mail: admission@drake.edu
Phone: (515) 271-3181 Toll-free number: (800) 443-7253
Fax: (515) 271-2831
Laura Linn, Director of Admission, Drake University, 2507 University Avenue, Des Moines, IA 50311-4505

---

## Emmaus Bible College

Dubuque, Iowa
www.emmaus.edu

CB code: 1215

- Private 4-year Bible college affiliated with Brethren Church
- Residential campus in small city
- 235 degree-seeking undergraduates
- SAT or ACT (ACT writing optional), application essay required

**General.** Founded in 1942. Accredited by ABHE. **Degrees:** 27 bachelor's, 17 associate awarded. **Location:** 90 miles from Waterloo, 150 miles from Chicago. **Calendar:** Semester. **Full-time faculty:** 17 total. **Part-time faculty:** 14 total. **Class size:** 75% < 20, 14% 20-39, 4% 40-49, 7% 50-99.

**Freshman class profile.**

| Mid 50% test scores | | | |
|---|---|---|---|
| SAT critical reading: | 490-660 | ACT composite: | 16-26 |
| SAT math: | 490-640 | Out-of-state: | 75% |
| | | Live on campus: | 99% |

**Basis for selection.** Recommendations and essay most important. GPA also important. All high school students admitted, but some may be placed on academic probation. Interview recommended. **Homeschooled:** Transcript of courses and grades required.

**2007-2008 Annual costs.** Tuition/fees: $10,118. Room/board: $4,782. Books/supplies: $450. Personal expenses: $850.

**Financial aid. Non-need-based:** Scholarships awarded for academics, music/drama.

**Application procedures. Admission:** Priority date 7/1; no deadline. $25 fee. Admission notification on a rolling basis. Must reply by May 1 or within 2 week(s) if notified thereafter. **Financial aid:** Priority date 5/15, closing date 7/1. FAFSA, institutional form required. Applicants notified on a rolling basis starting 3/1; must reply within 2 week(s) of notification.

**Academics. Special study options:** Combined bachelor's/graduate degree, distance learning, double major, ESL, internships, teacher certification program. **Credit/placement by examination:** AP, CLEP, IB, SAT, ACT, institutional tests. 18 credit hours maximum toward bachelor's degree. **Support services:** Study skills assistance, tutoring.

**Majors. Computer sciences:** General. **Education:** Elementary. **Theology:** Bible, missionary, theology, youth ministry.

**Most popular majors.** Computer/information sciences 10%, education 20%, theological studies 43%.

**Computing on campus.** 60 workstations in library, computer center, student center. Dormitories wired for high-speed internet access and linked to campus network. Online library available.

**Student life. Freshman orientation:** Mandatory. 4 days immediately preceding first day of class. **Policies:** No smoking, alcohol consumption, dancing. **Housing:** Guaranteed on-campus for all undergraduates. Single-sex dorms available. $400 deposit, deadline 7/1. **Activities:** Choral groups, drama, radio station, student government.

**Athletics.** NCCAA. **Intercollegiate:** Basketball. **Intramural:** Badminton, basketball, cross-country, football (non-tackle), golf, handball, racquetball, soccer, softball, table tennis, tennis, volleyball. **Team name:** Eagles.

**Student services.** Career counseling, student employment services, financial aid counseling, health services, personal counseling, veterans' counselor.

**Contact.** Phone: (563) 588-8000 ext. 1310 Fax: (563) 588-1216
Steven Witter, Director of Admissions, Emmaus Bible College, 2570 Asbury Road, Dubuque, IA 52001

## Faith Baptist Bible College and Theological Seminary
**Ankeny, Iowa**
**www.faith.edu**　　　　　　　　　　　　**CB code: 6214**

⬥ Private 4-year Bible and seminary college affiliated with General Association of Regular Baptist Churches
⬥ Residential campus in large town
⬥ 320 degree-seeking undergraduates: 11% part-time, 52% women, 1% African American, 1% Asian American, 2% Hispanic American
⬥ 56 degree-seeking graduate students
⬥ 86% of applicants admitted
⬥ SAT or ACT (ACT writing optional), application essay required
⬥ 43% graduate within 6 years; 28% enter graduate study

**General.** Founded in 1921. Regionally accredited; also accredited by ABHE. **Degrees:** 44 bachelor's, 13 associate awarded; master's, first professional offered. **Location:** 6 miles from Des Moines. **Calendar:** Semester, limited summer session. **Full-time faculty:** 20 total; 70% have terminal degrees, 10% minority, 15% women. **Part-time faculty:** 15 total; 40% have terminal degrees, 7% minority, 33% women. **Class size:** 71% < 20, 13% 20-39, 5% 40-49, 7% 50-99, 3% >100.

**Freshman class profile.** 146 applied, 126 admitted, 96 enrolled.

| Mid 50% test scores | | | |
|---|---|---|---|
| SAT critical reading: | 450-500 | GPA 2.0-2.99: | 25% |
| SAT math: | 410-500 | Rank in top quarter: | 41% |
| SAT writing: | 420-450 | Rank in top tenth: | 18% |
| ACT composite: | 18-21 | Return as sophomores: | 78% |
| GPA 3.50 or higher: | 53% | Out-of-state: | 53% |
| GPA 3.0-3.49: | 22% | Live on campus: | 95% |

**Basis for selection.** Recommendations, church affiliation, character qualities important. Interview recommended for borderline applicants. **Homeschooled:** Transcript of courses and grades required. Validation by third-party testing recommended, such as SAT, ACT, GED. **Learning Disabled:** Request for accommodation must be submitted.

**2008-2009 Annual costs.** Tuition/fees: $12,706. Room/board: $5,010.

**Financial aid. Non-need-based:** Scholarships awarded for academics, leadership, music/drama.

**Application procedures. Admission:** Priority date 6/1; deadline 8/1 (postmark date). $25 fee; may be waived for applicants with need. Application must be submitted on paper. Admission notification on a rolling basis. **Financial aid:** Priority date 4/1; no closing date. FAFSA required. Applicants notified on a rolling basis starting 3/15.

**Academics. Special study options:** Double major, internships, liberal arts/career combination, study abroad, teacher certification program. **Credit/placement by examination:** AP, CLEP, institutional tests. 6 credit hours maximum toward associate degree, 12 toward bachelor's. **Support services:** Learning center, reduced course load, remedial instruction, study skills assistance, tutoring.

**Majors. Education:** Elementary, English, middle, music, secondary. **Theology:** Bible, missionary, religious ed, sacred music, theology.

**Most popular majors.** Education 39%, philosophy/religious studies 36%, theological studies 23%.

**Computing on campus.** 46 workstations in dormitories, library, computer center. Dormitories wired for high-speed internet access and linked to campus network. Repair service, wireless network available.

**Student life. Freshman orientation:** Mandatory. Preregistration for classes offered. Held weekend before classes start in fall. **Policies:** All single students under the age of 26 and not living at home must live in the residence halls. Religious observance required. **Housing:** Guaranteed on-campus for freshmen. Single-sex dorms, special housing for disabled, apartments available. $200 deposit, deadline 6/1. **Activities:** Bands, choral groups, drama,

music ensembles, student government, student missionary fellowship, missionary kids fellowship, missions ambassadors, student association, Future Christian Teachers Association, ladies fellowship.

**Athletics.** NCCAA. **Intercollegiate:** Basketball, soccer, volleyball W. **Intramural:** Basketball, football (tackle). **Team name:** Eagles.

**Student services.** Career counseling, financial aid counseling, health services, personal counseling, placement for graduates, veterans' counselor.

**Contact.** E-mail: admissions@faith.edu
Phone: (515) 964-0601 ext. 233 Toll-free number: (888) 324-8448
Fax: (515) 964-1638
Timothy Nilius, Vice President Enrollment/Constituency Services, Faith Baptist Bible College and Theological Seminary, 1900 NW Fourth Street, Ankeny, IA 50023

## Graceland University
**Lamoni, Iowa**
**www.graceland.edu**　　　　　　　　　　**CB code: 6249**

⬥ Private 4-year university and liberal arts college affiliated with Community of Christ
⬥ Residential campus in rural community
⬥ 1,480 degree-seeking undergraduates: 5% African American, 3% Asian American, 3% Hispanic American, 9% international
⬥ 768 degree-seeking graduate students
⬥ 54% of applicants admitted
⬥ SAT or ACT (ACT writing optional) required
⬥ 47% graduate within 6 years; 9% enter graduate study

**General.** Founded in 1895. Regionally accredited. Campus in Independence, Missouri. Evening and weekend programs offered at Indian Hills Community College in Centerville, North Central Missouri College in Trenton, Missouri. **Degrees:** 451 bachelor's awarded; master's offered. **Location:** 75 miles from Des Moines, 110 miles from Kansas City. **Calendar:** 4-1-4, limited summer session. **Full-time faculty:** 92 total; 61% have terminal degrees, 6% minority, 51% women. **Part-time faculty:** 19 total; 5% minority, 63% women. **Class size:** 66% < 20, 29% 20-39, 4% 40-49, 2% 50-99. **Special facilities:** Electron microscope, communications network, international health center, center for study of Korean War.

**Freshman class profile.** 1,026 applied, 550 admitted, 272 enrolled.

| Mid 50% test scores | | | |
|---|---|---|---|
| SAT critical reading: | 400-540 | Rank in top quarter: | 21% |
| SAT math: | 400-540 | Rank in top tenth: | 12% |
| SAT writing: | 410-530 | End year in good standing: | 88% |
| ACT composite: | 18-24 | Return as sophomores: | 71% |
| GPA 3.50 or higher: | 33% | Out-of-state: | 80% |
| GPA 3.0-3.49: | 29% | Live on campus: | 98% |
| GPA 2.0-2.99: | 36% | International: | 15% |

**Basis for selection.** Rank in upper 50% of class, 2.5 GPA, 21 ACT or 960 SAT (exclusive of Writing) important. Interview required of applicants who do not meet admissions requirements, recommended for others. Portfolio recommended of art majors. Auditions required for music, theater and athletic performance areas. **Homeschooled:** Certificate of completion of home study program recognized by home state required.

**High school preparation.** 16 units recommended. Recommended units include English 3, mathematics 2, social studies 2, science 2, foreign language 2 and academic electives 5.

**2007-2008 Annual costs.** Tuition/fees: $17,900. Room/board: $6,000. Books/supplies: $1,000. Personal expenses: $1,500.

**2007-2008 Financial aid. Need-based:** Average need met was 92%. Average scholarship/grant was $14,957; average loan $4,944. 57% of total undergraduate aid awarded as scholarships/grants, 43% as loans/jobs. **Non-need-based:** Scholarships awarded for academics, alumni affiliation, art, athletics, job skills, leadership, music/drama, religious affiliation.

**Application procedures. Admission:** No deadline. $50 fee, may be waived for applicants with need. Application may be submitted online. Admission notification on a rolling basis. Applicants who do not meet admissions criteria may be considered individually. If accepted, they will be required to take developmental courses. Some applicants may be requested to test for Chance Program prior to being considered for acceptance. **Financial aid:** Priority date 3/1; no closing date. FAFSA required. Applicants notified on a rolling basis starting 3/1; must reply within 2 week(s) of notification.

**Academics.** Distance Learning programs delivered to online cohorts and at multiple off-campus locations. Nursing program delivered through online study and on-campus residency sessions, and available only to individuals licensed as registered nurses in the U.S. **Special study options:** Accelerated study, combined bachelor's/graduate degree, distance learning, double major, dual enrollment of high school students, ESL, external degree, honors, independent study, internships, liberal arts/career combination, student-designed major, study abroad, teacher certification program. Accelerated program for nursing only. **Credit/placement by examination:** AP, CLEP, IB, SAT, ACT, institutional tests. 30 credit hours maximum toward bachelor's degree. Credit by standardized examinations is awarded based on American Council on Education recommendations. **Support services:** Learning center, reduced course load, remedial instruction, study skills assistance, tutoring, writing center.

**Majors. Biology:** General. **Business:** Accounting, business admin, international. **Communications technology:** Desktop publishing. **Computer sciences:** General, computer science, information systems. **Education:** Elementary. **English:** Composition, speech/rhetoric. **Family/consumer sciences:** Food/nutrition. **Foreign languages:** General, comparative lit, German, Spanish. **Health:** Athletic training, clinical lab science, nursing (RN). **History:** General. **Liberal arts:** Arts/sciences. **Math:** General. **Parks/recreation:** General, health/fitness, sports admin. **Philosophy/religion:** Religion. **Physical sciences:** Chemistry. **Protective services:** Criminal justice. **Psychology:** General. **Public administration:** Human services. **Social sciences:** General, economics, sociology. **Visual/performing arts:** General, commercial/advertising art, dramatic, studio arts.

**Most popular majors.** Business/marketing 25%, education 22%, health sciences 25%, liberal arts 8%.

**Computing on campus.** 106 workstations in dormitories, library, computer center, student center. Dormitories wired for high-speed internet access and linked to campus network. Commuter students can connect to campus network. Online library, helpline, student web hosting, wireless network available.

**Student life. Freshman orientation:** Mandatory. Preregistration for classes offered. Early orientation sessions in spring and summer (1 day each). Additional 2-3 day orientation at beginning of semester. **Policies:** No tobacco, alcohol, or drug use on campus. Students required to live on campus through sophomore year unless married or living with relatives. **Housing:** Guaranteed on-campus for all undergraduates. Single-sex dorms, special housing for disabled, apartments, substance-free housing available. $200 partly refundable deposit, deadline 6/1. **Activities:** Bands, choral groups, drama, music ensembles, musical theater, radio station, student government, student newspaper, symphony orchestra, Religious Life Program, social service projects, peace organization, Amnesty International, OASIS, Students for Free Enterprise, Habitat for Humanity, Young Republicans, Young Democrats.

**Athletics.** NAIA. **Intercollegiate:** Baseball M, basketball, cross-country, football (tackle) M, golf, soccer, softball W, tennis, track and field, volleyball. **Intramural:** Badminton, baseball M, basketball, cross-country, football (non-tackle), golf, handball, racquetball, soccer, softball, swimming, table tennis, tennis, track and field, volleyball. **Team name:** Yellowjackets.

**Student services.** Adult student services, alcohol/substance abuse counseling, campus ministries, career counseling, student employment services, financial aid counseling, health services, minority student services, personal counseling, placement for graduates, veterans' counselor. **Physically disabled:** Services for visually impaired.

**Contact.** E-mail: admissions@graceland.edu
Phone: (641) 784-5196 Toll-free number: (866) 472-2352
Fax: (641) 784-5480
Greg Sutherland, Vice President for Enrollment and Dean of Admissions, Graceland University, One University Place, Lamoni, IA 50140

---

## Grand View College
**Des Moines, Iowa**      **CB member**
**www.gvc.edu**      **CB code: 6251**

- Private 4-year liberal arts college affiliated with Evangelical Lutheran Church in America
- Commuter campus in large city
- 1,680 degree-seeking undergraduates: 20% part-time, 69% women, 5% African American, 2% Asian American, 2% Hispanic American, 1% international
- 98% of applicants admitted
- SAT or ACT (ACT writing recommended) required
- 38% graduate within 6 years

---

**General.** Founded in 1896. Regionally accredited. **Degrees:** 366 bachelor's, 2 associate awarded. **ROTC:** Army, Air Force. **Location:** 200 miles from Kansas City, Missouri, 250 miles from Minneapolis-St. Paul. **Calendar:** Semester, extensive summer session. **Full-time faculty:** 88 total; 59% have terminal degrees, 6% minority, 62% women. **Part-time faculty:** 86 total; 30% have terminal degrees, 1% minority, 55% women. **Class size:** 70% < 20, 30% 20-39, less than 1% 40-49.

**Freshman class profile.** 399 applied, 390 admitted, 171 enrolled.

| Mid 50% test scores | | | |
|---|---|---|---|
| SAT critical reading: | 410-540 | GPA 2.0-2.99: | 38% |
| SAT math: | 420-530 | Rank in top quarter: | 37% |
| SAT writing: | 440-520 | Rank in top tenth: | 12% |
| ACT composite: | 18-23 | Return as sophomores: | 67% |
| GPA 3.50 or higher: | 28% | Out-of-state: | 9% |
| GPA 3.0-3.49: | 32% | Live on campus: | 73% |
| | | International: | 3% |

**Basis for selection.** Admissions based on individualized evaluation of applicant's secondary school record and SAT or ACT score.

**High school preparation.** 15 units recommended. Recommended units include English 4, mathematics 3, social studies 3, science 3 and foreign language 2.

**2008-2009 Annual costs.** Tuition/fees (projected): $18,554. Room/board: $6,164. Books/supplies: $900. Personal expenses: $2,150.

**2007-2008 Financial aid. Need-based:** 157 full-time freshmen applied for aid; 137 were judged to have need; 137 of these received aid. Average need met was 92%. Average scholarship/grant was $14,486; average loan $3,688. 54% of total undergraduate aid awarded as scholarships/grants, 46% as loans/jobs. **Non-need-based:** Awarded to 341 full-time undergraduates, including 53 freshmen. Scholarships awarded for academics, alumni affiliation, art, athletics, leadership, music/drama, religious affiliation.

**Application procedures. Admission:** Closing date 8/15 (receipt date). $35 fee, may be waived for applicants with need. Application may be submitted online. Admission notification on a rolling basis beginning on or about 9/15. **Financial aid:** Priority date 3/1; no closing date. FAFSA required. Applicants notified on a rolling basis starting 3/1; must reply by 5/1 or within 4 week(s) of notification.

**Academics.** College emphasizes integration of liberal arts core with career-related majors. Internships are a primary focus in many majors. **Special study options:** Accelerated study, combined bachelor's/graduate degree, co-operative education, cross-registration, distance learning, double major, dual enrollment of high school students, honors, independent study, internships, liberal arts/career combination, student-designed major, study abroad, teacher certification program, Washington semester, weekend college. **Credit/placement by examination:** AP, CLEP, IB, ACT, institutional tests. 32 credit hours maximum toward bachelor's degree. ACT PEP credit accepted, DANTES accepted. **Support services:** Learning center, reduced course load, remedial instruction, study skills assistance, tutoring, writing center.

**Majors. Agriculture:** Business. **Biology:** General. **Business:** General, accounting, entrepreneurial studies, finance, hospitality admin, human resources, marketing, real estate. **Communications:** Broadcast journalism, journalism, media studies, public relations, radio/tv. **Communications technology:** Graphics. **Computer sciences:** General, information technology, programming. **Education:** Elementary, secondary. **English:** English lit. **Health:** Health services, nursing (RN), premedicine, prepharmacy. **History:** General. **Legal studies:** Paralegal, prelaw. **Liberal arts:** Arts/sciences. **Math:** Applied. **Parks/recreation:** Health/fitness, sports admin. **Philosophy/religion:** Religion. **Protective services:** Criminal justice. **Psychology:** General. **Public administration:** Human services. **Social sciences:** General, political science. **Visual/performing arts:** Dramatic, graphic design, studio arts.

**Most popular majors.** Business/marketing 17%, education 11%, health sciences 23%, liberal arts 7%, visual/performing arts 7%.

**Computing on campus.** Dormitories wired for high-speed internet access and linked to campus network. Commuter students can connect to campus network. Online library, helpline, student web hosting, wireless network available.

**Student life. Freshman orientation:** Mandatory. Preregistration for classes offered. Program includes low ropes course at nearby camp. 3 day program just before start of fall semester. **Housing:** Coed dorms, apartments available. College owned on-campus houses available. **Activities:** Choral groups, dance, drama, literary magazine, music ensembles, radio station, student government, student newspaper, TV station, Concerned Black Students, student political awareness alliance, art club, Key Club, environmental club, human services club, education club, nursing club, Habitat for Humanity, College Republicans.

**Athletics.** NAIA. **Intercollegiate:** Baseball M, basketball, cross-country, golf, soccer, softball W, track and field, volleyball W. **Intramural:** Badminton, basketball, cheerleading W, football (non-tackle), soccer, softball, swimming, table tennis, tennis, track and field, volleyball. **Team name:** Vikings.

**Student services.** Adult student services, alcohol/substance abuse counseling, campus ministries, career counseling, student employment services, financial aid counseling, health services, minority student services, personal counseling, placement for graduates, veterans' counselor. **Physically disabled:** Services for visually, speech, hearing impaired.

**Contact.** E-mail: admissions@gvc.edu
Phone: (515) 263-2810 Toll-free number: (800) 444-6083
Fax: (515) 263-2974
Diane Johnson, Director of Admissions, Grand View College, 1200 Grandview Avenue, Des Moines, IA 50316-1599

## Grinnell College
**Grinnell, Iowa**
**www.grinnell.edu**

**CB member**
**CB code: 6252**

- Private 4-year liberal arts college
- Residential campus in small town
- 1,623 degree-seeking undergraduates: 53% women, 5% African American, 7% Asian American, 5% Hispanic American, 11% international
- 50% of applicants admitted
- SAT or ACT (ACT writing optional), application essay required
- 87% graduate within 6 years; 65% enter graduate study

**General.** Founded in 1846. Regionally accredited. **Degrees:** 351 bachelor's awarded. **Location:** 55 miles from Des Moines. **Calendar:** Semester, limited summer session. **Full-time faculty:** 165 total; 94% have terminal degrees, 17% minority, 46% women. **Part-time faculty:** 33 total; 48% have terminal degrees, 12% minority, 46% women. **Class size:** 60% < 20, 39% 20-39, less than 1% 40-49. **Special facilities:** 365-acre environmental research area, research telescope, 2 theaters.

**Freshman class profile.** 3,077 applied, 1,534 admitted, 427 enrolled.

| Mid 50% test scores | | End year in good standing: | 100% |
|---|---|---|---|
| SAT critical reading: | 610-750 | Return as sophomores: | 94% |
| SAT math: | 620-740 | Out-of-state: | 88% |
| ACT composite: | 29-33 | Live on campus: | 100% |
| Rank in top quarter: | 93% | International: | 13% |
| Rank in top tenth: | 66% | | |

**Basis for selection.** Scholastic ability plus extracurricular pursuits, accomplishments most important. Curiosity, motivation, and persistence are stressed. Interview recommended. **Homeschooled:** Copy of curriculum, writing sample, interview, letter of reference required. SAT Subject Tests strongly recommended.

**High school preparation.** 20 units recommended. Recommended units include English 4, mathematics 4, social studies 4, science 4 (laboratory 3) and foreign language 4.

**2008-2009 Annual costs.** Tuition/fees: $35,428. Room/board: $8,272. Books/supplies: $750. Personal expenses: $600.

**2007-2008 Financial aid. Need-based:** 330 full-time freshmen applied for aid; 267 were judged to have need; 267 of these received aid. Average need met was 100%. Average scholarship/grant was $24,252; average loan $4,842. 81% of total undergraduate aid awarded as scholarships/grants, 19% as loans/jobs. **Non-need-based:** Awarded to 614 full-time undergraduates, including 135 freshmen. Scholarships awarded for academics. **Additional information:** Students may apply financial aid to off-campus study programs.

**Application procedures. Admission:** Closing date 1/20 (postmark date). $30 fee, may be waived for applicants with need. Application may be submitted online. Admission notification 4/1. Must reply by 5/1. **Financial aid:** Closing date 2/1. FAFSA, institutional form required. Applicants notified by 4/1; must reply by 5/1.

**Academics.** Internships available in public agencies, private organizations, and corporations. **Special study options:** Accelerated study, double major, independent study, internships, liberal arts/career combination, student-designed major, study abroad, teacher certification program, urban semester, Washington semester. **Credit/placement by examination:** AP, CLEP, IB, institutional tests. **Support services:** Reduced course load, study skills assistance, tutoring, writing center.

**Majors. Area/ethnic studies:** African-American, American, East Asian, Latin American, Russian/Slavic, Western European, women's. **Biology:** General, biochemistry. **Computer sciences:** Computer science. **English:** English lit. **Foreign languages:** Chinese, classics, French, German, Japanese, Russian, Spanish. **History:** General. **Interdisciplinary:** Biological/physical sciences. **Math:** General. **Philosophy/religion:** Philosophy, religion. **Physical sciences:** Chemistry, physics. **Psychology:** General. **Social sciences:** Anthropology, economics, political science, sociology. **Visual/performing arts:** Art, dramatic.

**Most popular majors.** Biology 11%, foreign language 12%, history 7%, mathematics 7%, philosophy/religious studies 6%, psychology 8%, social sciences 26%, visual/performing arts 11%.

**Computing on campus.** 205 workstations in dormitories, library, computer center, student center. Dormitories wired for high-speed internet access and linked to campus network. Online library, helpline, student web hosting, wireless network available.

**Student life. Freshman orientation:** Mandatory. 4-day program. **Housing:** Guaranteed on-campus for all undergraduates. Coed dorms, cooperative housing, substance-free housing available. $200 nonrefundable deposit, deadline 5/1. All residence halls and college-owned off-campus houses self-governing: residents decide how their individual hall will operate and share responsibility for budget, quiet hours, social policy, regulations. **Activities:** Bands, choral groups, dance, drama, film society, literary magazine, music ensembles, musical theater, radio station, student government, student newspaper, symphony orchestra, Muslim prayer group, Chalutzim, Friends silent meeting, Concerned Black Students, Asian Students in Alliance, Student Organization of Latino/as, Campus Democrats, College Republicans, Palestinian solidarity group, Alternative Break (intensive volunteer experience).

**Athletics.** NCAA. **Intercollegiate:** Baseball M, basketball, cross-country, diving, football (tackle) M, golf, soccer, softball W, swimming, tennis, track and field, volleyball W. **Intramural:** Badminton, basketball, football (non-tackle), racquetball, soccer, softball, tennis, volleyball. **Team name:** Pioneers.

**Student services.** Alcohol/substance abuse counseling, campus ministries, career counseling, financial aid counseling, health services, minority student services, personal counseling, placement for graduates, veterans' counselor. **Physically disabled:** Services for visually, hearing impaired.

**Contact.** E-mail: askgrin@grinnell.edu
Phone: (641) 269-3600 Toll-free number: (800) 247-0113
Fax: (641) 269-4800
Seth Allen, Dean of Admission and Financial Aid, Grinnell College, 1103 Park Street, Grinnell, IA 50112-1690

## Hamilton Technical College
**Davenport, Iowa**
**www.hamiltontechcollege.com**

**CB code: 1588**

- For-profit 3-year technical college
- Commuter campus in small city
- 158 degree-seeking undergraduates
- Interview required

**General.** Founded in 1969. Accredited by ACCSCT. **Degrees:** 57 bachelor's, 145 associate awarded. **Location:** 190 miles from Des Moines, 175 miles from Chicago. **Calendar:** Semester. **Full-time faculty:** 15 total. **Part-time faculty:** 1 total.

**Basis for selection.** Open admission. Pseudoisochromatic Color Plates and Wonderlic required for placement.

**2007-2008 Annual costs.** Medical assistant diploma program tuition: $7,800. Tuition varies by program.

**Application procedures. Admission:** No deadline. $25 fee. Admission notification on a rolling basis. **Financial aid:** No deadline. FAFSA, institutional form required. Applicants notified on a rolling basis.

**Academics. Credit/placement by examination:** CLEP. 35 credit hours maximum toward associate degree, 60 toward bachelor's. **Support services:** Tutoring.

**Majors. Engineering technology:** Electrical.

**Student services.** Career counseling, placement for graduates.

**Contact.** E-mail: cnelson@hamiltontechcollege.com
Phone: (563) 386-3570 Fax: (563) 386-6756
Chad Nelson, Admissions Director, Hamilton Technical College, 1011 East 53rd Street, Davenport, IA 52807

## Iowa State University

**Ames, Iowa**
**www.iastate.edu**

**CB member**
**CB code: 6306**

- Public 4-year university
- Residential campus in small city
- 20,613 degree-seeking undergraduates: 5% part-time, 43% women, 3% African American, 3% Asian American, 3% Hispanic American, 3% international
- 5,156 degree-seeking graduate students
- 89% of applicants admitted
- SAT or ACT (ACT writing optional) required
- 66% graduate within 6 years; 18% enter graduate study

**General.** Founded in 1858. Regionally accredited. **Degrees:** 4,269 bachelor's awarded; master's, doctoral, first professional offered. **ROTC:** Army, Naval, Air Force. **Location:** 30 miles from Des Moines. **Calendar:** Semester, extensive summer session. **Full-time faculty:** 1,346 total; 93% have terminal degrees, 19% minority, 30% women. **Part-time faculty:** 238 total; 68% have terminal degrees, 13% minority, 50% women. **Class size:** 35% < 20, 40% 20-39, 7% 40-49, 10% 50-99, 8% >100. **Special facilities:** Observatory, nature preserve, research park, molecular biology building, computation center, center for designing foods, Department of Energy laboratory, virtual reality applications center, crop utilization center, transportation research and education center, sustainable environmental technologies center, gardens, field-oriented lakeside research facility.

**Freshman class profile.** 11,058 applied, 9,832 admitted, 4,347 enrolled.

| Mid 50% test scores | | | |
|---|---|---|---|
| SAT critical reading: | 510-640 | Rank in top tenth: | 26% |
| SAT math: | 530-680 | Return as sophomores: | 85% |
| ACT composite: | 22-27 | Out-of-state: | 29% |
| GPA 3.50 or higher: | 53% | Live on campus: | 89% |
| GPA 3.0-3.49: | 31% | International: | 3% |
| GPA 2.0-2.99: | 16% | Fraternities: | 14% |
| Rank in top quarter: | 58% | Sororities: | 17% |

**Basis for selection.** Rank in top half of graduating class and completion of prescribed set of college-preparatory high school courses. Test scores considered as alternative criteria to class rank in some instances. Level of difficulty of courses also considered. **Homeschooled:** Emphasis placed on standardized examinations.

**High school preparation.** 12 units required; 19 recommended. Required and recommended units include English 4, mathematics 3-4, social studies 2-4, science 3-4 (laboratory 2-3) and foreign language 2-3. 2 foreign language and 3 social studies required for the College of Liberal Arts & Sciences.

**2007-2008 Annual costs.** Tuition/fees: $6,161; $16,919 out-of-state. Additional tuition of $1,558 for junior and senior engineering students; additional $211 in fees for engineering and for computer science programs; additional $40 in fees for business program. Room/board: $6,645. Books/supplies: $978. Personal expenses: $2,783.

**2007-2008 Financial aid.** **Need-based:** 3,275 full-time freshmen applied for aid; 2,084 were judged to have need; 2,050 of these received aid. Average need met was 84%. Average scholarship/grant was $5,728; average loan $3,551. 40% of total undergraduate aid awarded as scholarships/grants, 60% as loans/jobs. **Non-need-based:** Awarded to 11,524 full-time undergraduates, including 2,564 freshmen. Scholarships awarded for academics, art, athletics, leadership, minority status, music/drama, ROTC, state residency. **Additional information:** Short-term loan program available to meet unplanned needs. Financial counseling clinic provides budget and credit education assistance.

**Application procedures. Admission:** Closing date 7/1. $30 fee. Application may be submitted online. Admission notification on a rolling basis. Must reply by May 1 or within 2 week(s) if notified thereafter. **Financial aid:** Priority date 3/1; no closing date. FAFSA required. Applicants notified on a rolling basis starting 4/1.

**Academics.** Classes offered over the Internet, by videotape, at distant locations through the state's fiber-optic communication network, and at off-campus locations taught face-to-face by the university's professors. **Special study options:** Accelerated study, combined bachelor's/graduate degree, cooperative education, cross-registration, distance learning, double major, dual enrollment of high school students, ESL, exchange student, external degree, honors, independent study, internships, liberal arts/career combination, student-designed major, study abroad, teacher certification program, Washington

semester, weekend college. National Collegiate Honors Council Honors Semester. Combined bachelor's/graduate programs include: landscape architecture, agriculture and biosystems engineering, biochemistry and biophysics, electrical and computer engineering, civil and construction engineering, chemical engineering, food science and human nutrition, material science engineering, zoology and genetics. **Credit/placement by examination:** AP, CLEP, IB, SAT, ACT, institutional tests. No limit on number of hours of credit by examination that may be counted toward degree. **Support services:** Learning center, pre-admission summer program, reduced course load, remedial instruction, study skills assistance, tutoring, writing center.

**Majors. Agriculture:** Agribusiness operations, agronomy, animal sciences, dairy, education services, farm/ranch, horticulture, international, mechanization, plant protection, plant sciences. **Architecture:** Architecture, landscape, urban/community planning. **Area/ethnic studies:** Russian/Slavic, women's. **Biology:** General, biochemistry, biophysics, entomology, genetics, microbiology. **Business:** General, accounting, finance, hospitality admin, international, logistics, management information systems, managerial economics, marketing, operations, statistics. **Communications:** General, advertising, journalism. **Computer sciences:** General. **Conservation:** Environmental science, environmental studies, forestry. **Education:** General, agricultural, early childhood, elementary, family/consumer sciences, health, kindergarten/preschool, music, technology/industrial arts, trade/industrial. **Engineering:** General, aerospace, agricultural, chemical, civil, computer, construction, electrical, industrial, materials, materials science, mechanical, software. **English:** English lit, speech/rhetoric, technical writing. **Family/consumer sciences:** General, apparel marketing, clothing/textiles, family resources, family/community services, housing, human nutrition, textile manufacture. **Foreign languages:** French, German, linguistics, Russian, Spanish. **Health:** Dietetics, medical illustrating, premedicine, preveterinary. **History:** General. **Liberal arts:** Arts/sciences. **Math:** General, statistics. **Parks/recreation:** Exercise sciences. **Philosophy/religion:** Philosophy, religion. **Physical sciences:** Chemistry, geology, physics, planetary. **Psychology:** General. **Social sciences:** Anthropology, economics, international relations, political science, sociology. **Visual/performing arts:** General, art, commercial/advertising art, design, fashion design, graphic design, interior design.

**Most popular majors.** Agriculture 8%, biology 6%, business/marketing 23%, education 6%, engineering/engineering technologies 17%, visual/performing arts 6%.

**Computing on campus.** 2,400 workstations in dormitories, library, computer center, student center. Dormitories wired for high-speed internet access and linked to campus network. Commuter students can connect to campus network. Online course registration, online library, helpline, repair service, wireless network available.

**Student life. Freshman orientation:** Available. Preregistration for classes offered. Two-day, overnight program. **Housing:** Guaranteed on-campus for all undergraduates. Coed dorms, single-sex dorms, special housing for disabled, apartments, fraternity/sorority housing, substance-free housing available. $135 partly refundable deposit, deadline 5/1. Learning communities, family, quiet, non-smoking, alcohol-free, adult housing available. **Activities:** Bands, campus ministries, choral groups, dance, drama, film society, literary magazine, music ensembles, musical theater, opera, radio station, student government, student newspaper, symphony orchestra, TV station, more than 500 clubs and organizations.

**Athletics.** NCAA. **Intercollegiate:** Basketball, cross-country, football (tackle) M, golf, gymnastics W, soccer W, softball W, swimming W, tennis W, track and field, volleyball W, wrestling M. **Intramural:** Badminton, basketball, bowling, boxing M, cross-country, diving, golf, handball, ice hockey, racquetball, skiing, soccer, softball, squash, swimming, table tennis, tennis, volleyball, water polo, weight lifting, wrestling. **Team name:** Cyclones.

**Student services.** Adult student services, alcohol/substance abuse counseling, career counseling, student employment services, financial aid counseling, health services, legal services, minority student services, on-campus daycare, personal counseling, placement for graduates, veterans' counselor, women's services. **Physically disabled:** Services for visually, speech, hearing impaired. **Learning disabled:** Comprehensive services available.

**Contact.** E-mail: admissions@iastate.edu
Phone: (515) 294-5836 Toll-free number: (800) 262-3810
Fax: (515) 294-2592
Marc Harding, Director of Admissions, Iowa State University, 100 Alumni Hall, Ames, IA 50011-2011

## Iowa Wesleyan College

**Mount Pleasant, Iowa**
**www.iwc.edu**

**CB member**
**CB code: 6308**

- Private 4-year liberal arts college affiliated with United Methodist Church
- Residential campus in small town

- 833 degree-seeking undergraduates: 24% part-time, 61% women
- 60% of applicants admitted
- SAT or ACT (ACT writing optional) required

**General.** Founded in 1842. Regionally accredited. **Degrees:** 150 bachelor's awarded. **Location:** 47 miles from Iowa City, 25 miles from Burlington. **Calendar:** Semester, limited summer session. **Full-time faculty:** 47 total; 49% have terminal degrees, 4% minority, 43% women. **Part-time faculty:** 42 total; 7% have terminal degrees, 67% women. **Class size:** 86% < 20, 14% 20-39. **Special facilities:** Public interest institute.

**Freshman class profile.** 796 applied, 478 admitted, 127 enrolled.

| | | | |
|---|---|---|---|
| Out-of-state: | 61% | **Fraternities:** | 3% |
| Live on campus: | 91% | **Sororities:** | 8% |

**Basis for selection.** Upper 50% class rank preferred. Automatic acceptance: 2.5 GPA and 19 ACT. Audition recommended for music majors. Portfolio recommended for art, creative programs majors. Essay recommended for applicants who do not meet regular admission requirements. **Homeschooled:** Transcript of courses and grades required. GED or portfolio may be substituted for high school transcript requirement.

**High school preparation.** 16 units recommended. Recommended units include English 4, mathematics 3, social studies 3, science 2 (laboratory 2) and academic electives 4.

**2007-2008 Annual costs.** Tuition/fees: $18,870. Room/board: $5,880. Books/supplies: $800.

**Financial aid. Non-need-based:** Scholarships awarded for academics, art, athletics, music/drama.

**Application procedures. Admission:** Priority date 4/1; no deadline. No application fee. Application may be submitted online. Admission notification on a rolling basis beginning on or about 8/15. Must reply by May 1 or within 2 week(s) if notified thereafter. **Financial aid:** Priority date 4/1; no closing date. FAFSA required. Applicants notified on a rolling basis starting 3/1; must reply within 2 week(s) of notification.

**Academics. Special study options:** Combined bachelor's/graduate degree, cross-registration, distance learning, double major, dual enrollment of high school students, exchange student, independent study, internships, liberal arts/career combination, student-designed major, study abroad, teacher certification program, Washington semester. **Credit/placement by examination:** AP, CLEP, IB, institutional tests. 30 credit hours maximum toward bachelor's degree. **Support services:** Learning center, reduced course load, study skills assistance, tutoring, writing center.

**Majors. Biology:** General. **Business:** General, accounting, business admin, human resources. **Communications:** General, broadcast journalism, journalism. **Computer sciences:** General, computer science. **Conservation:** Forestry. **Education:** General, art, biology, chemistry, early childhood, elementary, English, health, mathematics, middle, music, physical, secondary. **Engineering:** General. **English:** English lit. **Health:** Environmental health, nursing (RN), predental, premedicine, prepharmacy, preveterinary. **History:** General. **Legal studies:** Prelaw. **Liberal arts:** Library science. **Math:** General. **Parks/recreation:** Exercise sciences, health/fitness, sports admin. **Philosophy/religion:** Christian, philosophy, religion. **Physical sciences:** Chemistry. **Protective services:** Criminal justice. **Psychology:** General. **Social sciences:** Sociology. **Visual/performing arts:** Design, studio arts. **Other:** Church leadership.

**Most popular majors.** Business/marketing 23%, education 32%, health sciences 10%, parks/recreation 6%, psychology 10%.

**Computing on campus.** 90 workstations in dormitories, library, computer center. Dormitories wired for high-speed internet access and linked to campus network. Commuter students can connect to campus network. Online library, repair service available.

**Student life. Freshman orientation:** Mandatory. Preregistration for classes offered. Three-day program held weekend before classes begin. **Housing:** Guaranteed on-campus for all undergraduates. Coed dorms, single-sex dorms, substance-free housing available. $100 deposit, deadline 8/20. Pets allowed in dorm rooms. **Activities:** Bands, campus ministries, choral groups, dance, drama, international student organizations, literary magazine, music ensembles, radio station, student government, student newspaper, symphony orchestra, black awareness organization, Fellowship of Christian Athletics, Bacchus, Unidad.

**Athletics.** NAIA. **Intercollegiate:** Baseball M, basketball, football (tackle) M, golf, soccer, softball W, track and field, volleyball W. **Intramural:** Badminton, basketball, bowling, football (non-tackle), softball, table tennis, tennis, volleyball. **Team name:** Tigers.

**Student services.** Adult student services, alcohol/substance abuse counseling, career counseling, student employment services, financial aid counseling, health services, personal counseling, placement for graduates.

**Contact.** E-mail: admit@iwc.edu
Phone: (319) 385-6231 Toll-free number: (800) 582-2383 ext. 6231
Fax: (319) 385-6240
Mark Petty, Dean of Admissions, Iowa Wesleyan College, 601 North Main Street, Mount Pleasant, IA 52641-1398

## Kaplan University: Cedar Falls
**Cedar Falls, Iowa**
**www.ju-cedarfalls.com**

- For-profit 4-year university and branch campus college
- Commuter campus in small city
- 478 degree-seeking undergraduates
- Application essay, interview required

**General. Degrees:** 56 bachelor's, 138 associate awarded. **Location:** 120 miles from Des Moines. **Calendar:** Continuous, extensive summer session. **Full-time faculty:** 15 total; 7% minority, 73% women. **Part-time faculty:** 26 total; 15% have terminal degrees, 15% minority, 58% women. **Class size:** 64% < 20, 33% 20-39, 3% 40-49.

**Basis for selection.** Open admission, but selective for some programs. Entrance test required for most programs. 2-year degree, ACT with a score of 17+, SAT score of 830+ (exclusive of writing) will be accepted in place of school-administered entrance exam.

**2007-2008 Annual costs.** Tuition/fees: $11,250. Costs may vary by program.

**Financial aid.** All financial aid based on need.

**Application procedures. Admission:** No deadline. $20 fee. Application must be submitted on paper. Admission notification on a rolling basis. **Financial aid:** No deadline. FAFSA, institutional form required. Applicants notified on a rolling basis.

**Academics. Special study options:** Cooperative education, distance learning. **Credit/placement by examination:** AP, CLEP, institutional tests. 32 credit hours maximum toward associate degree. **Support services:** Learning center, tutoring.

**Majors. Business:** Business admin.

**Student life. Freshman orientation:** Available.

**Student services.** Student employment services, financial aid counseling, placement for graduates.

**Contact.** E-mail: admissions@hamiltoncf.com
Phone: (319) 277-0220 Toll-free number: (800) 728-1220
Fax: (319) 243-2961
Jill Lines, Director, Admissions, Kaplan University: Cedar Falls, 7009 Nordic Drive, Cedar Falls, IA 50613

## Kaplan University: Cedar Rapids
**Cedar Rapids, Iowa**
**www.KU-CedarRapids.com**        **CB code: 3384**

- For-profit 4-year university and Bible college
- Commuter campus in small city
- 542 degree-seeking undergraduates
- Application essay, interview required

**General.** Regionally accredited. **Degrees:** 49 bachelor's, 181 associate awarded. **Calendar:** Differs by program, extensive summer session. **Full-time faculty:** 15 total; 7% have terminal degrees, 7% minority, 67% women. **Part-time faculty:** 29 total; 10% have terminal degrees, 3% minority, 62% women. **Class size:** 49% < 20, 51% 20-39.

**Basis for selection.** Open admission, but selective for some programs. All students must take WonderLic test on campus during initial interview. **Homeschooled:** State high school equivalency certificate required.

**2007-2008 Annual costs.** Tuition/fees: $13,532.

**Financial aid. Non-need-based:** Scholarships awarded for academics.

**Application procedures. Admission:** No deadline. No application fee. Application must be submitted on paper. Admission notification on a rolling basis. **Financial aid:** Priority date 6/30; no closing date. FAFSA, institutional form required. Applicants notified on a rolling basis.

**Academics. Special study options:** Accelerated study, distance learning, honors, independent study, internships. **Credit/placement by examination:** AP, CLEP, institutional tests. Combined credit by examination and for life/work experiences shall not exceed 25% of program requirements. **Support services:** Learning center, remedial instruction, tutoring.

**Majors. Business:** Business admin.

**Most popular majors.** Business/marketing 39%, health sciences 61%.

**Computing on campus.** 207 workstations in library. Commuter students can connect to campus network. Online library available.

**Student life. Freshman orientation:** Mandatory.

**Student services.** Adult student services, career counseling, student employment services, financial aid counseling, placement for graduates. **Physically disabled:** Services for visually, hearing impaired.

**Contact.** E-mail: nidonahue@hamiltonia.edu
Phone: (319) 363-0481 Toll-free number: (800) 728-0481
Fax: (319) 363-3812
Niki Donahue, Director of Admissions, Kaplan University: Cedar Rapids, 3165 Edgewood Parkway, SW, Cedar Rapids, IA 52404

## Kaplan University: Davenport
**Davenport, Iowa**
www.kaplan.edu/ku                    **CB code: 5848**

- For-profit 4-year university
- Residential campus in large city
- 32,669 degree-seeking undergraduates
- Interview required

**General.** Founded in 1937. Regionally accredited. **Degrees:** 1,561 bachelor's, 2,189 associate awarded; master's offered. **Location:** 165 miles from Des Moines, 180 miles from Chicago. **Calendar:** Quarter, extensive summer session. **Full-time faculty:** 64 total. **Part-time faculty:** 1,002 total.

**Basis for selection.** Open admission.

**2007-2008 Annual costs.** Tuition/fees: $13,680. Tuition figure includes books.

**Financial aid. Non-need-based:** Scholarships awarded for academics.

**Application procedures. Admission:** No deadline. $25 fee. Application may be submitted online. Admission notification on a rolling basis. **Financial aid:** Priority date 5/15; no closing date. FAFSA, institutional form required. Applicants notified on a rolling basis starting 3/4; must reply by 6/15 or within 2 week(s) of notification.

**Academics. Special study options:** Distance learning, double major, internships. **Credit/placement by examination:** CLEP, institutional tests. 22 credit hours maximum toward associate degree, 45 toward bachelor's. Up to 25% of all credit in a particular program can be earned through examination. **Support services:** Learning center, reduced course load, remedial instruction, study skills assistance, tutoring.

**Majors. Business:** General, business admin, management information systems. **Computer sciences:** Information technology. **Legal studies:** Paralegal. **Protective services:** Criminal justice.

**Most popular majors.** Business/marketing 56%, computer/information sciences 6%, legal studies 13%, security/protective services 24%.

**Computing on campus.** 121 workstations in library, student center. Online course registration, online library, helpline, student web hosting, wireless network available.

**Student life. Freshman orientation:** Available. **Activities:** Student government, student newspaper.

**Student services.** Career counseling, student employment services, financial aid counseling, personal counseling, placement for graduates.

**Contact.** E-mail: rhoffmann@kucampus.edu
Phone: (563) 355-3500 Toll-free number: (800) 747-1035
Fax: (563) 355-1320
Robert Hoffmann, Director of Admissions, Kaplan University: Davenport, 1801 East Kimberly Road, Suite 1, Davenport, IA 52807-2095

## Kaplan University: Des Moines
**Urbandale, Iowa**
www.KU-DesMoines.com                    **CB code: 3388**

- For-profit 4-year university
- Commuter campus in large city
- 710 degree-seeking undergraduates
- 2,166 graduate students
- Interview required

**General.** Regionally accredited. **Degrees:** 34 bachelor's, 179 associate awarded. **Location:** 4 miles from Des Moines. **Calendar:** Continuous, extensive summer session. **Full-time faculty:** 20 total. **Part-time faculty:** 40 total.

**Basis for selection.** Open admission, but selective for some programs.

**2007-2008 Annual costs.** Tuition/fees: $13,482. Tuition includes books and fees. Personal expenses: $1,500.

**Financial aid.** All financial aid based on need.

**Application procedures. Admission:** No deadline. $25 fee, may be waived for applicants with need. Application must be submitted on paper. Admission notification on a rolling basis. **Financial aid:** Priority date 6/30; no closing date. FAFSA, institutional form required.

**Academics. Special study options:** Accelerated study, distance learning, independent study, internships, liberal arts/career combination. **Credit/placement by examination:** AP, CLEP, institutional tests. 32 credit hours maximum toward associate degree, 32 toward bachelor's. **Support services:** Learning center, remedial instruction, study skills assistance, tutoring.

**Majors. Business:** Accounting, business admin. **Computer sciences:** Information technology.

**Computing on campus.** 195 workstations in library, computer center. Commuter students can connect to campus network. Online library, repair service available.

**Student life. Freshman orientation:** Mandatory. Preregistration for classes offered. **Activities:** Student government, student newspaper.

**Student services.** Adult student services, career counseling, student employment services, financial aid counseling, placement for graduates.

**Contact.** Phone: (515) 727-2100 Toll-free number: (800) 383-0253
Fax: (515) 727-2115
Bob Pilardi, Director of Admissions, Kaplan University: Des Moines, 4655 121st Street, Urbandale, IA 50323

## Kaplan University: Mason City
**Mason City, Iowa**
www.ku-masoncity.com                    **CB code: 6289**

- For-profit 4-year branch campus college
- Commuter campus in large town
- 296 degree-seeking undergraduates
- Interview required

**General.** Regionally accredited; also accredited by ACICS. **Degrees:** 26 bachelor's, 150 associate awarded. **Location:** 127 miles from Des Moines. **Calendar:** Quarter, limited summer session. **Full-time faculty:** 12 total; 75% women. **Part-time faculty:** 19 total; 21% have terminal degrees, 5% minority, 74% women. **Class size:** 92% < 20, 8% 20-39.

**Freshman class profile.** 36 applied, 36 admitted, 13 enrolled.

**Basis for selection.** Open admission. **Homeschooled:** GED required.

**2007-2008 Annual costs.** Yearly tuition and fees range from $12,000 to $13,500 (including books) depending on program. Personal expenses: $1,809.

**Financial aid. Non-need-based:** Scholarships awarded for academics.

**Application procedures. Admission:** No deadline. $20 fee. Application must be submitted on paper. Admission notification on a rolling basis. **Financial aid:** Closing date 6/1. FAFSA required. Applicants notified on a rolling basis.

**Academics. Special study options:** Accelerated study, combined bachelor's/graduate degree, distance learning, dual enrollment of high school students, independent study, internships, student-designed major, study abroad, teacher certification program. **Credit/placement by examination:** CLEP. **Support services:** Learning center, study skills assistance, tutoring.

**Majors. Business:** Accounting, business admin. **Computer sciences:** General. **Protective services:** Law enforcement admin.

**Computing on campus.** Commuter students can connect to campus network. Online library, helpline, repair service, wireless network available.

**Student life. Freshman orientation:** Mandatory. Preregistration for classes offered. **Activities:** Student government.

**Student services.** Adult student services, student employment services, financial aid counseling, placement for graduates. **Physically disabled:** Services for hearing impaired.

**Contact.** Phone: (641) 423-2530 Toll-free number: (800) 274-2530
Fax: (641) 423-7512
Marcy Pischel, Director of Admissions, Kaplan University: Mason City, 2570 Fourth Street, SW, Mason City, IA 50401

## Loras College
### Dubuque, Iowa
### www.loras.edu
**CB code: 6370**

▶ Private 4-year liberal arts college affiliated with Roman Catholic Church
▶ Residential campus in small city
▶ 1,500 degree-seeking undergraduates: 3% part-time, 48% women, 1% African American, 1% Asian American, 2% Hispanic American, 3% international
▶ 53 degree-seeking graduate students
▶ 74% of applicants admitted
▶ SAT or ACT (ACT writing optional) required
▶ 63% graduate within 6 years; 18% enter graduate study

**General.** Founded in 1839. Regionally accredited. **Degrees:** 360 bachelor's awarded; master's offered. **ROTC:** Army. **Location:** 180 miles from Chicago. **Calendar:** Semester, extensive summer session. **Full-time faculty:** 122 total; 89% have terminal degrees, 5% minority, 38% women. **Part-time faculty:** 44 total; 4% minority, 61% women. **Class size:** 59% < 20, 41% 20-39, less than 1% 40-49. **Special facilities:** Planetarium, observatory, residential arts complex.

**Freshman class profile.** 1,490 applied, 1,109 admitted, 376 enrolled.

| Mid 50% test scores | | Rank in top tenth: | 11% |
|---|---|---|---|
| ACT composite: | 20-25 | End year in good standing: | 84% |
| GPA 3.50 or higher: | 39% | Return as sophomores: | 79% |
| GPA 3.0-3.49: | 36% | Out-of-state: | 50% |
| GPA 2.0-2.99: | 25% | Live on campus: | 96% |
| Rank in top quarter: | 30% | International: | 3% |

**Basis for selection.** High school academic record and test scores most important. Interview and essay recommended. **Homeschooled:** Considered by admissions committee on individual basis. **Learning Disabled:** All students applying for the enhanced learning disabilities program must have materials submitted by the required date. All files are reviewed by the learning disabilities program.

**High school preparation.** 16 units recommended. Recommended units include English 4, mathematics 3, social studies 3, history 3 and science 3.

**2008-2009 Annual costs.** Tuition/fees (projected): $24,440. Room/board: $6,500. Books/supplies: $1,100.

**2007-2008 Financial aid. Need-based:** 353 full-time freshmen applied for aid; 339 were judged to have need; 339 of these received aid. Average scholarship/grant was $8,447; average loan $3,658. 73% of total undergraduate aid awarded as scholarships/grants, 27% as loans/jobs. **Non-need-based:** Awarded to 1,402 full-time undergraduates, including 300 freshmen. Scholarships awarded for academics, alumni affiliation, leadership, minority status, music/drama. **Additional information:** Audition or portfolio recommended for music and art financial aid applicants.

**Application procedures. Admission:** No deadline. $25 fee, may be waived for applicants with need. Application may be submitted online. Admission notification on a rolling basis. Must reply by May 1 or within 2 week(s) if notified thereafter. **Financial aid:** Priority date 4/15; no closing date. FAFSA required. Applicants notified on a rolling basis starting 3/1; must reply within 3 week(s) of notification.

**Academics. Special study options:** Cooperative education, cross-registration, double major, dual enrollment of high school students, exchange student, honors, independent study, internships, student-designed major, study abroad, teacher certification program, urban semester, Washington semester. **Credit/placement by examination:** AP, CLEP, IB. **Support services:** Learning center, reduced course load, remedial instruction, study skills assistance, tutoring, writing center.

**Majors. Biology:** General, biochemistry. **Business:** General, accounting, business admin, finance, management information systems, marketing. **Communications:** Journalism, media studies, public relations. **Computer sciences:** Computer science. **Education:** General, art, early childhood, elementary, emotionally handicapped, mentally handicapped, multi-level teacher, physical, secondary, special. **Engineering:** Electrical, physics. **English:** Creative writing, English lit. **Foreign languages:** Spanish. **Health:** Athletic training. **History:** General. **Legal studies:** Prelaw. **Liberal arts:** Arts/sciences. **Math:** General. **Parks/recreation:** Exercise sciences. **Philosophy/religion:** Philosophy, religion. **Physical sciences:** General, chemistry. **Protective services:** Criminal justice. **Psychology:** General. **Public administration:** Social work. **Social sciences:** Economics, international relations, political science, sociology. **Visual/performing arts:** General.

**Most popular majors.** Business/marketing 24%, communications/journalism 6%, education 20%, English 7%, security/protective services 6%, social sciences 10%.

**Computing on campus.** PC or laptop required. 20 workstations in library, computer center, student center. Dormitories wired for high-speed internet access and linked to campus network. Commuter students can connect to campus network. Online course registration, online library, helpline, repair service, student web hosting, wireless network available.

**Student life. Freshman orientation:** Mandatory. Preregistration for classes offered. Held from early June through the start of fall term. **Housing:** Guaranteed on-campus for freshmen. Coed dorms, apartments available. $100 fully refundable deposit. **Activities:** Bands, choral groups, dance, drama, film society, international student organizations, literary magazine, music ensembles, musical theater, radio station, student government, student newspaper, TV station, Peace and Justice, African Hispanic Asian Native American, Amnesty International, environmental action forum, fellowship of Christian athletes.

**Athletics.** NCAA. **Intercollegiate:** Baseball M, basketball, cross-country, diving, football (tackle) M, golf, soccer, softball W, swimming, tennis W, track and field, volleyball W, wrestling M. **Intramural:** Badminton, baseball M, basketball, bowling, cheerleading, cross-country, diving, football (non-tackle), golf, handball, racquetball, soccer, softball, swimming, table tennis, tennis, track and field, volleyball, water polo, weight lifting, wrestling M. **Team name:** Duhawks.

**Student services.** Adult student services, alcohol/substance abuse counseling, campus ministries, career counseling, student employment services, financial aid counseling, health services, minority student services, personal counseling, placement for graduates, veterans' counselor. **Physically disabled:** Services for visually, speech, hearing impaired. **Learning disabled:** Comprehensive services available.

**Contact.** E-mail: adms@loras.edu
Phone: (563) 588-7236 Toll-free number: (800) 245-6727
Fax: (563) 588-7119
Sharon Lyons, Director of Admissions, Loras College, 1450 Alta Vista Street, Dubuque, IA 52004-0178

## Luther College
### Decorah, Iowa
### www.luther.edu
**CB member**
**CB code: 6375**

▶ Private 4-year liberal arts college affiliated with Evangelical Lutheran Church in America
▶ Residential campus in small town
▶ 2,405 degree-seeking undergraduates: 57% women, 1% African American, 2% Asian American, 2% Hispanic American, 4% international
▶ 83% of applicants admitted
▶ SAT or ACT (ACT writing optional), application essay required
▶ 74% graduate within 6 years; 21% enter graduate study

**General.** Founded in 1861. Regionally accredited. **Degrees:** 566 bachelor's awarded. **Location:** 70 miles from Rochester, Minnesota, 50 miles from LaCrosse, Wisconsin. **Calendar:** 4-1-4, limited summer session. **Full-time faculty:** 177 total; 90% have terminal degrees, 3% minority, 38% women. **Part-time faculty:** 74 total; 27% have terminal degrees, 3% minority, 62% women. **Class size:** 56% < 20, 39% 20-39, 2% 40-49, 2% 50-99, less than 1% >100. **Special facilities:** Planetarium, Norwegian-American museum, extensive biology field study areas, cadaver laboratory.

**Freshman class profile.** 2,054 applied, 1,696 admitted, 659 enrolled.

| Mid 50% test scores | | Rank in top quarter: | 60% |
|---|---|---|---|
| SAT critical reading: | 480-670 | Rank in top tenth: | 29% |
| SAT math: | 540-650 | End year in good standing: | 91% |
| SAT writing: | 500-650 | Return as sophomores: | 86% |
| ACT composite: | 22-28 | Out-of-state: | 67% |
| GPA 3.50 or higher: | 62% | Live on campus: | 99% |
| GPA 3.0-3.49: | 25% | International: | 5% |
| GPA 2.0-2.99: | 13% | | |

**Basis for selection.** Rigor of high school curriculum most important, followed by test scores and teacher recommendation(s). Applicants should rank in top half of high school class. Audition recommended for music scholarships. Portfolio recommended for art majors. Interview recommended for borderline students. **Homeschooled:** If graduate of non-diploma-granting organization, evidence of preparation for college required. Must provide at least 2 of the following: home school transcript listing all courses; detailed portfolio of high school work completed; bibliography of major books read, with brief essay on one of the selected works; additional reference letter completed by an educator assessing the applicant's academic preparation; scores from any AP exams and/or GED test results.

**High school preparation.** 14 units recommended. Recommended units include English 4, mathematics 3, social studies 3, science 2 (laboratory 1) and foreign language 2.

**2008-2009 Annual costs.** Tuition/fees: $31,707. Room/board: $5,040. Books/supplies: $910. Personal expenses: $1,510.

**2007-2008 Financial aid. Need-based:** 550 full-time freshmen applied for aid; 463 were judged to have need; 463 of these received aid. Average need met was 93%. Average scholarship/grant was $15,913; average loan $5,224. 72% of total undergraduate aid awarded as scholarships/grants, 28% as loans/jobs. **Non-need-based:** Awarded to 440 full-time undergraduates, including 167 freshmen. Scholarships awarded for academics, alumni affiliation, art, minority status, music/drama.

**Application procedures. Admission:** No deadline. $25 fee, may be waived for applicants with need. Application may be submitted online. Admission notification on a rolling basis beginning on or about 11/1. Must reply by May 1 or within 4 week(s) if notified thereafter. **Financial aid:** Priority date 3/1; no closing date. FAFSA, institutional form required. Applicants notified on a rolling basis starting 3/1; must reply by 5/1 or within 4 week(s) of notification.

**Academics. Special study options:** Combined bachelor's/graduate degree, double major, dual enrollment of high school students, honors, independent study, internships, student-designed major, study abroad, teacher certification program, Washington semester. **Credit/placement by examination:** AP, CLEP, IB, institutional tests. No limit, but must satisfy Luther's residency requirement. **Support services:** Learning center, reduced course load, remedial instruction, study skills assistance, tutoring, writing center.

**Majors. Area/ethnic studies:** African-American, Scandinavian, women's. **Biology:** General. **Business:** Accounting, business admin, management information systems. **Communications:** Media studies. **Computer sciences:** Computer science. **Conservation:** Environmental studies. **Education:** Elementary, health, physical. **English:** English lit. **Foreign languages:** Ancient Greek, Biblical, classics, French, German, Latin, Spanish. **Health:** Nursing (RN). **History:** General. **Math:** General, statistics. **Parks/recreation:** Health/fitness, sports admin. **Philosophy/religion:** Philosophy, religion. **Physical sciences:** Chemistry, physics. **Psychology:** General. **Public administration:** Social work. **Social sciences:** Anthropology, economics, political science, sociology. **Visual/performing arts:** Art, dramatic.

**Most popular majors.** Biology 11%, business/marketing 12%, education 6%, health sciences 7%, social sciences 11%, visual/performing arts 12%.

**Computing on campus.** 500 workstations in dormitories, library, computer center, student center. Dormitories wired for high-speed internet access and linked to campus network. Commuter students can connect to campus network. Online course registration, online library, helpline, student web hosting, wireless network available.

**Student life. Freshman orientation:** Mandatory. Preregistration for classes offered. Held before classes begin at the start of semester. **Housing:** Guaranteed on-campus for all undergraduates. Coed dorms, special housing for

disabled, apartments, substance-free housing available. Clusters, quiet floors, honors floor, chemical-free/wellness floor options available. **Activities:** Bands, campus ministries, choral groups, dance, drama, film society, international student organizations, literary magazine, music ensembles, Model UN, musical theater, radio station, student government, student newspaper, symphony orchestra, various religious and political clubs, black student union, Asian student association, Hispanic/Latino student association, Phi Beta Kappa, Amnesty International.

**Athletics.** NCAA. **Intercollegiate:** Baseball M, basketball, cheerleading, cross-country, diving, football (tackle) M, golf, soccer, softball W, swimming, tennis, track and field, volleyball W, wrestling M. **Intramural:** Archery, badminton, basketball, bowling, football (non-tackle), golf, handball, racquetball, rugby, skiing, soccer, softball, table tennis, tennis, track and field, volleyball, water polo. **Team name:** The Norse.

**Student services.** Alcohol/substance abuse counseling, career counseling, student employment services, financial aid counseling, health services, minority student services, personal counseling, placement for graduates. **Physically disabled:** Services for visually, hearing impaired.

**Contact.** E-mail: admissions@luther.edu
Phone: (563) 387-1287 Toll-free number: (800) 458-8437
Fax: (563) 387-2159
Scot Schaeffer, Vice President for Enrollment Management, Luther College, 700 College Drive, Decorah, IA 52101-1042

## Maharishi University of Management
**Fairfield, Iowa**
**www.mum.edu** CB code: 4497

- Private 4-year university and liberal arts college
- Residential campus in small town
- 199 degree-seeking undergraduates: 5% part-time, 43% women, 2% African American, 4% Asian American, 7% Hispanic American, 17% international
- 733 degree-seeking graduate students
- Application essay required
- 46% graduate within 6 years

**General.** Founded in 1971. Regionally accredited. Many campus buildings are built according to Vedic system of architecture. **Degrees:** 42 bachelor's awarded; master's, doctoral offered. **Location:** 60 miles from Iowa City, 110 miles from Des Moines. **Calendar:** Semester, limited summer session. **Full-time faculty:** 52 total; 98% have terminal degrees, 14% minority, 21% women. **Special facilities:** Scanning electron microscope, two large domes for transcendental meditation, greenhouses, college prep-school, indoor rock-climbing wall, student center with sustainable features.

**Freshman class profile.** 45 enrolled.

| Live on campus: | 78% | International: | 20% |
|---|---|---|---|

**Basis for selection.** Academics, grades, academic test scores, recommendations, high school and college transcripts, advanced placement tests, extracurricular activities, work experience, interview with admissions officer, and essay important. SAT or ACT recommended. Students encouraged to visit campus for 4-day weekend. **Homeschooled:** Must supply a detailed record of courses and objectives. Home school certification required.

**High school preparation.** 15 units recommended. Recommended units include English 4, mathematics 3, social studies 3, science 3 and foreign language 2.

**2007-2008 Annual costs.** Tuition/fees: $24,430. Room/board: $6,000. Books/supplies: $800. Personal expenses: $1,500.

**2006-2007 Financial aid. Need-based:** 42 full-time freshmen applied for aid; 40 were judged to have need; 40 of these received aid. Average need met was 89%. Average scholarship/grant was $15,138; average loan $6,625. 36% of total undergraduate aid awarded as scholarships/grants, 64% as loans/jobs. **Additional information:** Students may earn scholarships through volunteer staff program.

**Application procedures. Admission:** No deadline. $30 fee. Application must be submitted online. Admission notification on a rolling basis. **Financial aid:** Priority date 7/15, closing date 7/30. FAFSA required. Applicants notified on a rolling basis starting 3/1; must reply within 4 week(s) of notification.

**Academics.** Provides consciousness-based education and incorporates group practice of the Maharishi Transcendental Meditation technique into a traditional academic program. Curriculum is taught one course at a time in a four-week block system. **Special study options:** Double major, exchange student, honors, independent study, internships, liberal arts/career combination, study abroad, teacher certification program. A course is offered in the U.S. or abroad, the course of study linked to the geographic locale, e.g. ancient culture in Greece, or media, communications and the creative arts in L.A.; innovative modular block system in which students study one subject per month, 10 subjects per year. **Credit/placement by examination:** AP, CLEP, IB, institutional tests. 12 credit hours maximum toward bachelor's degree. **Support services:** Study skills assistance.

**Majors. Business:** Business admin. **Computer sciences:** Computer science. **Education:** Elementary, secondary. **English:** English lit. **Math:** General. **Visual/performing arts:** Studio arts. **Other:** Physiology and health, Sustainable living.

**Most popular majors.** Biology 6%, business/marketing 12%, computer/information sciences 6%, liberal arts 35%, mathematics 6%, natural resources/environmental science 18%, visual/performing arts 15%.

**Computing on campus.** 400 workstations in library, computer center, student center. Dormitories wired for high-speed internet access and linked to campus network. Commuter students can connect to campus network. Online library, helpline available.

**Student life. Freshman orientation:** Mandatory. One day, first day of class. **Policies:** Daily practice of transcendental meditation by all students, faculty, and staff. Smoking, alcohol and drugs not permitted on campus. Organic, vegetarian food served in dining halls. **Housing:** Guaranteed on-campus for all undergraduates. Single-sex dorms, special housing for disabled, apartments, substance-free housing available. $100 fully refundable deposit. Family housing, quiet dorms available. **Activities:** Choral groups, dance, drama, international student organizations, music ensembles, musical theater, radio station, student government, student newspaper, many clubs and activities available.

**Athletics. Team name:** Flyers.

**Student services.** Career counseling, financial aid counseling, health services, on-campus daycare, personal counseling, placement for graduates.

**Contact.** E-mail: admissions@mum.edu
Phone: (641) 472-1110 Toll-free number: (800) 369-6480
Fax: (641) 472-1179
Barbara Rainbow, Associate Dean of Admissions, Maharishi University of Management, 1000 North Fourth Street, Fairfield, IA 52557

## Mercy College of Health Sciences
**Des Moines, Iowa**
**www.mchs.edu**                                     CB code: 2803

- Private 4-year health science college affiliated with Roman Catholic Church
- Commuter campus in large city
- 680 degree-seeking undergraduates: 38% part-time, 91% women
- 80% of applicants admitted
- SAT or ACT (ACT writing optional) required

**General.** Regionally accredited. **Degrees:** 29 bachelor's, 172 associate awarded. **Calendar:** Semester, limited summer session. **Full-time faculty:** 36 total; 14% have terminal degrees, 6% minority, 89% women. **Part-time faculty:** 6 total; 83% women. **Class size:** 100% 50-99.

**Freshman class profile.** 528 applied, 425 admitted, 227 enrolled.

| Mid 50% test scores | ACT composite: | 19-23 |
|---|---|---|

**Basis for selection.** Admission decisions based primarily on secondary school record and standardized test scores. Recommendations and interview also important.

**2007-2008 Annual costs.** Tuition/fees: $12,600. Books/supplies: $1,200.

**2006-2007 Financial aid. Need-based:** 15% of total undergraduate aid awarded as scholarships/grants, 85% as loans/jobs. **Non-need-based:** Scholarships awarded for academics.

**Application procedures. Admission:** Closing date 7/20 (postmark date). $25 fee, may be waived for applicants with need. Application may be submitted online. Admission notification on a rolling basis. **Financial aid:** Closing date 7/1. FAFSA required. Applicants notified on a rolling basis; must reply by 1/1 or within 2 week(s) of notification.

**Academics. Special study options:** Accelerated study, combined bachelor's/graduate degree. **Credit/placement by examination:** AP, CLEP, institutional tests. 24 credit hours maximum toward associate degree, 24 toward

bachelor's. **Support services:** Study skills assistance, tutoring, writing center.

**Majors. Health:** Health care admin, nursing (RN), preop/surgical nursing.

**Computing on campus.** 49 workstations in library, computer center. Commuter students can connect to campus network. Online library available.

**Student life. Freshman orientation:** Mandatory. Preregistration for classes offered. Orientation and registration sessions last one day and are held at various times before the beginning of each term. **Activities:** Student government.

**Student services.** Alcohol/substance abuse counseling, career counseling, student employment services, financial aid counseling, minority student services, personal counseling.

**Contact.** E-mail: admissions@mchs.edu
Phone: (515) 643-6725 Toll-free number: (800) 637-2994 ext. 33180
Sara Hill, Admissions Counselor, Mercy College of Health Sciences, 928 Sixth Avenue, Des Moines, IA 50309

## Morningside College
**Sioux City, Iowa**
**www.morningside.edu**                              CB code: 6415

- Private 4-year liberal arts college affiliated with United Methodist Church
- Residential campus in small city
- 1,181 degree-seeking undergraduates: 3% part-time, 54% women, 1% African American, 2% Asian American, 3% Hispanic American, 1% Native American, 1% international
- 313 degree-seeking graduate students
- 79% of applicants admitted
- SAT or ACT (ACT writing optional) required
- 42% graduate within 6 years; 11% enter graduate study

**General.** Founded in 1894. Regionally accredited. All full-time students receive notebook computers. **Degrees:** 216 bachelor's awarded; master's offered. **Location:** 90 miles from Omaha, Nebraska, 90 miles from Sioux Falls, South Dakota. **Calendar:** Semester, limited summer session. **Full-time faculty:** 70 total; 79% have terminal degrees, 3% minority, 46% women. **Part-time faculty:** 80 total; 5% minority, 68% women. **Class size:** 50% < 20, 47% 20-39, 2% 40-49, less than 1% 50-99. **Special facilities:** Biology research station.

**Freshman class profile.** 1,375 applied, 1,090 admitted, 290 enrolled.

| Mid 50% test scores | | End year in good standing: | 83% |
|---|---|---|---|
| ACT composite: | 20-25 | Return as sophomores: | 77% |
| GPA 3.50 or higher: | 41% | Out-of-state: | 36% |
| GPA 3.0-3.49: | 41% | Live on campus: | 91% |
| GPA 2.0-2.99: | 18% | International: | 1% |
| Rank in top quarter: | 45% | Fraternities: | 5% |
| Rank in top tenth: | 16% | Sororities: | 3% |

**Basis for selection.** Students with 20 ACT/1410 SAT and either rank in top half of class or have 2.5 GPA meet academic standards for admission. Interview recommended. Audition or audition tape recommended for music majors and theater applicants. Portfolio recommended for art majors. **Homeschooled:** Transcript of courses and grades required. In lieu of transcript, Home School Credit Evaluation form from Office of Admissions accepted. **Learning Disabled:** Students who want to participate in learning disability program must go through separate admissions process which includes application, teacher recommendations, and recent documentation.

**High school preparation.** 10 units recommended. Recommended units include English 3, mathematics 2, social studies 3 and science 2. Math or science majors should have 4 units math and science.

**2007-2008 Annual costs.** Tuition/fees: $20,010. Room/board: $6,166. Books/supplies: $800. Personal expenses: $1,500.

**2007-2008 Financial aid. Need-based:** 287 full-time freshmen applied for aid; 263 were judged to have need; 263 of these received aid. Average need met was 85%. Average scholarship/grant was $13,644; average loan $3,806. 63% of total undergraduate aid awarded as scholarships/grants, 37% as loans/jobs. **Non-need-based:** Awarded to 809 full-time undergraduates, including 208 freshmen. Scholarships awarded for academics, alumni affiliation, art, athletics, job skills, leadership, music/drama, religious affiliation, ROTC, state residency.

**Application procedures. Admission:** Priority date 8/15; no deadline. $25 fee, may be waived for applicants with need. Application may be submitted online. Admission notification on a rolling basis. **Financial aid:** Priority date 3/1; no closing date. FAFSA required. Applicants notified on a rolling basis starting 3/31.

**Academics. Special study options:** Distance learning, double major, dual enrollment of high school students, ESL, honors, independent study, internships, liberal arts/career combination, student-designed major, study abroad, teacher certification program, United Nations semester, Washington semester. **Credit/placement by examination:** AP, CLEP, IB, institutional tests. 32 credit hours maximum toward bachelor's degree. Maximum 12 hours may be used for general studies core requirements. **Support services:** Learning center, reduced course load, remedial instruction, study skills assistance, tutoring.

**Majors. Biology:** General. **Business:** Accounting, business admin, communications, finance, human resources, international, marketing. **Communications:** Advertising, media studies. **Computer sciences:** Programming. **Education:** Art, biology, chemistry, elementary, English, history, mathematics, music, physics, science, Spanish, special. **Engineering:** Mechanics, physics. **English:** English lit. **Foreign languages:** Spanish. **Health:** Clinical lab science, nursing (RN). **History:** General, American, European. **Interdisciplinary:** Biopsychology. **Math:** General. **Philosophy/religion:** Philosophy, religion. **Physical sciences:** Chemistry, physics. **Psychology:** General, counseling, industrial. **Social sciences:** International relations, political science. **Visual/performing arts:** Dramatic, graphic design, music performance, photography, studio arts.

**Most popular majors.** Biology 6%, business/marketing 26%, education 20%, health sciences 7%, psychology 7%, visual/performing arts 9%.

**Computing on campus.** PC or laptop required. Dormitories wired for high-speed internet access and linked to campus network. Commuter students can connect to campus network. Online library, helpline, repair service, student web hosting, wireless network available.

**Student life. Freshman orientation:** Mandatory. Preregistration for classes offered. Held 4 days before school begins. **Housing:** Guaranteed on-campus for freshmen. Coed dorms, apartments, fraternity/sorority housing available. $100 fully refundable deposit. Apartments for adult non-traditional students available. **Activities:** Bands, campus ministries, choral groups, dance, drama, literary magazine, music ensembles, musical theater, radio station, student government, student newspaper, symphony orchestra, TV station, civic union, Project Hope, Fellowship of Christian Athletes, peace and justice club, mission trips, Cross by Color, Spanish club.

**Athletics.** NAIA. **Intercollegiate:** Baseball M, basketball, cross-country, football (tackle) M, golf, soccer, softball W, swimming, tennis, track and field, volleyball W. **Intramural:** Basketball, bowling, football (non-tackle), golf, soccer, softball, swimming, tennis, track and field, volleyball. **Team name:** Mustangs.

**Student services.** Alcohol/substance abuse counseling, career counseling, student employment services, financial aid counseling, health services, minority student services, personal counseling, placement for graduates, veterans' counselor. **Physically disabled:** Services for visually, speech, hearing impaired. **Learning disabled:** Comprehensive services available.

**Contact.** E-mail: mscadm@morningside.edu
Phone: (712) 274-5000 ext. 5511 Toll-free
number: (800) 831-0806 ext. 5511 Fax: (712) 274-5101
Amy Williams, Co-Director of Admissions, Morningside College, 1501 Morningside Avenue, Sioux City, IA 51106

---

## Mount Mercy College
**Cedar Rapids, Iowa**
**www.mtmercy.edu**                      CB code: 6417

- Private 4-year liberal arts college affiliated with Roman Catholic Church
- Commuter campus in small city
- 1,480 degree-seeking undergraduates: 37% part-time, 72% women
- 72% of applicants admitted
- SAT or ACT (ACT writing optional), application essay required
- 58% graduate within 6 years; 11% enter graduate study

**General.** Founded in 1928. Regionally accredited. **Degrees:** 352 bachelor's awarded. **Location:** 220 miles from Chicago. **Calendar:** 4-1-4, limited summer session. **Full-time faculty:** 78 total; 56% have terminal degrees, 5% minority, 64% women. **Part-time faculty:** 78 total; 17% have terminal degrees, 68% women. **Class size:** 75% < 20, 23% 20-39, 2% 40-49, less than 1% 50-99. **Special facilities:** Campus buildings connected by tunnel system.

**Freshman class profile.** 457 applied, 328 admitted, 140 enrolled.

| Mid 50% test scores | | Rank in top tenth: | 16% |
|---|---|---|---|
| ACT composite: | 20-24 | End year in good standing: | 100% |
| GPA 3.50 or higher: | 48% | Return as sophomores: | 70% |
| GPA 3.0-3.49: | 37% | Out-of-state: | 10% |
| GPA 2.0-2.99: | 15% | Live on campus: | 83% |
| Rank in top quarter: | 39% | International: | 1% |

**Basis for selection.** Minimum criteria for acceptance: 2.5 GPA, class rank in top half of class, 20 ACT. **Homeschooled:** Transcript of courses and grades, letter of recommendation (nonparent) required. Submit records of studies or detailed account of subjects and materials.

**High school preparation.** Recommended units include English 4, mathematics 3, social studies 3, history 3, science 3 (laboratory 1) and foreign language 2.

**2007-2008 Annual costs.** Tuition/fees: $20,070. Room/board: $6,270. Books/supplies: $910. Personal expenses: $1,726.

**2007-2008 Financial aid. Need-based:** 130 full-time freshmen applied for aid; 106 were judged to have need; 106 of these received aid. Average need met was 82%. Average scholarship/grant was $16,233; average loan $6,257. 64% of total undergraduate aid awarded as scholarships/grants, 36% as loans/jobs. **Non-need-based:** Awarded to 756 full-time undergraduates, including 124 freshmen. Scholarships awarded for academics, art, leadership, music/drama.

**Application procedures. Admission:** Closing date 8/15 (receipt date). $20 fee, may be waived for applicants with need. Application may be submitted online. Admission notification on a rolling basis. Must reply by May 1 or within 2 week(s) if notified thereafter. **Financial aid:** Priority date 3/1; no closing date. FAFSA required. Applicants notified on a rolling basis starting 3/15; must reply by 5/1 or within 3 week(s) of notification.

**Academics. Special study options:** Accelerated study, cross-registration, double major, dual enrollment of high school students, honors, independent study, internships, liberal arts/career combination, study abroad, teacher certification program. **Credit/placement by examination:** AP, CLEP, ACT, institutional tests. 60 credit hours maximum toward bachelor's degree. **Support services:** Learning center, remedial instruction, study skills assistance, tutoring, writing center.

**Majors. Biology:** General. **Business:** General, accounting, business admin, management information systems, marketing. **Communications:** Digital media, journalism, media studies, public relations. **Computer sciences:** Computer science. **Conservation:** General. **Education:** Elementary, secondary. **English:** English lit, speech/rhetoric. **Health:** Clinical lab science, clinical lab technology, health care admin, nursing (RN). **History:** General. **Legal studies:** Prelaw. **Math:** General. **Philosophy/religion:** Philosophy, religion. **Protective services:** Law enforcement admin. **Psychology:** General. **Public administration:** Social work. **Social sciences:** Political science, sociology, urban studies. **Visual/performing arts:** Art, commercial/advertising art. **Other:** Health care systems, Multi/Interdisciplinary.

**Most popular majors.** Business/marketing 36%, education 11%, health sciences 18%, security/protective services 6%.

**Computing on campus.** 135 workstations in dormitories, library, computer center. Dormitories wired for high-speed internet access and linked to campus network. Commuter students can connect to campus network. Online library, helpline, wireless network available.

**Student life. Freshman orientation:** Available. Preregistration for classes offered. 4-day orientation held prior to start of fall term; 3 one-day orientation/registration sessions in the spring and summer. **Housing:** Guaranteed on-campus for freshmen. Coed dorms, apartments, substance-free housing available. $50 nonrefundable deposit, deadline 8/15. **Activities:** Choral groups, drama, literary magazine, musical theater, student government, student newspaper, activities and planning board, College Pastoral Council, art club, investments club, drama club, gaming club, Bacchus, women's organization, Students in Free Enterprise, Mustang Adventure Team.

**Athletics.** NAIA. **Intercollegiate:** Baseball M, basketball, cheerleading M, cross-country, golf, soccer, softball W, track and field, volleyball W. **Intramural:** Basketball, football (non-tackle) M, racquetball, soccer, softball, table tennis, tennis, volleyball. **Team name:** Mustangs.

**Student services.** Adult student services, alcohol/substance abuse counseling, campus ministries, career counseling, student employment services, financial aid counseling, health services, personal counseling, placement for graduates, veterans' counselor. **Physically disabled:** Services for visually, speech, hearing impaired.

**Contact.** E-mail: admission@mtmercy.edu
Phone: (319) 368-6460 Toll-free number: (800) 248-4504
Fax: (319) 363-5270
Philip Adams, Vice President for Enrollment and Student Services, Mount
Mercy College, 1330 Elmhurst Drive NE, Cedar Rapids, IA 52402-4797

## Northwestern College
### Orange City, Iowa
**www.nwciowa.edu**                     **CB code: 6490**

- Private 4-year liberal arts college affiliated with Reformed Church in America
- Residential campus in small town
- 1,269 degree-seeking undergraduates: 1% part-time, 61% women, 1% African American, 1% Asian American, 1% Hispanic American, 3% international
- 79% of applicants admitted
- SAT or ACT (ACT writing optional) required
- 61% graduate within 6 years

**General.** Founded in 1882. Regionally accredited. **Degrees:** 236 bachelor's awarded. **Location:** 40 miles from Sioux City; 75 miles from Sioux Falls, South Dakota. **Calendar:** Semester, limited summer session. **Full-time faculty:** 82 total; 77% have terminal degrees, 2% minority, 35% women. **Part-time faculty:** 46 total; 4% have terminal degrees, 61% women. **Class size:** 60% < 20, 37% 20-39, 1% 40-49, 1% 50-99. **Special facilities:** Natural prairie restoration project.

**Freshman class profile.** 1,311 applied, 1,034 admitted, 324 enrolled.

| Mid 50% test scores | | | |
|---|---|---|---|
| ACT composite: | 22-27 | Return as sophomores: | 76% |
| Rank in top quarter: | 56% | Out-of-state: | 51% |
| Rank in top tenth: | 31% | Live on campus: | 97% |
| | | International: | 2% |

**Basis for selection.** Top half of class and test scores above 50th percentile most important. Recommendations also important. Must have 2.0 GPA to be considered. Interview and essay recommended. Audition recommended for theater, music majors. Portfolio recommended for art majors. **Homeschooled:** Transcript of courses and grades required. **Learning Disabled:** Students provide documentation to the Director of Academic Support upon admittance.

**High school preparation.** 16 units recommended. Recommended units include English 4, mathematics 3, social studies 3, science 3 and foreign language 3.

**2007-2008 Annual costs.** Tuition/fees: $21,648. 1-4 credits, $420 per credit hour; 5-8 credits, $620 per credit hour; 9-11 credits, $820 per credit hour. Room/board: $6,302. Books/supplies: $900. Personal expenses: $2,026.

**Financial aid. Non-need-based:** Scholarships awarded for academics, art, athletics, music/drama, religious affiliation, state residency.

**Application procedures. Admission:** Priority date 6/2; no deadline. $25 fee, may be waived for applicants with need. Application may be submitted online. Admission notification on a rolling basis beginning on or about 10/1. Must reply by May 1 or within 3 week(s) if notified thereafter. **Financial aid:** Priority date 4/1, closing date 6/30. FAFSA required. Applicants notified on a rolling basis starting 3/15; must reply within 3 week(s) of notification.

**Academics. Special study options:** Double major, ESL, honors, independent study, internships, liberal arts/career combination, student-designed major, study abroad, teacher certification program, Washington semester. American Studies Program (Washington, D.C.), AuSable Institute of Environmental Studies Program (Michigan), Los Angeles Film Studies Semester, Chicago Metropolitan Studies Program (Chicago), China Studies Program (Xiaman, China), Middle East Studies Program (Cairo, Egypt), Oxford Summer Program (Oxford, England), Russian Studies Program, Contemporary Music Center (Martha's Vineyard, MA), Latin American Studies Program (Costa Rica), Oxford Honours Programme (England), Trinity Christian College: Semester in Spain, Creation Care Study Program, and Summer Institute of Journalism (Washington, DC). **Credit/placement by examination:** AP, CLEP, IB, SAT, ACT, institutional tests. 18 credit hours maximum toward bachelor's degree. **Support services:** Learning center, reduced course load, remedial instruction, study skills assistance, tutoring, writing center.

**Majors. Agriculture:** Business. **Biology:** General. **Business:** Accounting, actuarial science, business admin, finance, human resources, managerial economics, marketing. **Communications:** Digital media, journalism, public relations. **Computer sciences:** General, computer science. **Conservation:** General. **Education:** General, elementary. **English:** Creative writing, English

lit. **Foreign languages:** Spanish. **Health:** Athletic training, clinical lab technology, nursing (RN). **History:** General. **Liberal arts:** Arts/sciences. **Math:** General. **Parks/recreation:** Exercise sciences, health/fitness. **Philosophy/religion:** Philosophy, religion. **Physical sciences:** Chemistry. **Psychology:** General. **Public administration:** Social work. **Social sciences:** Economics, political science, sociology. **Theology:** Religious ed. **Visual/performing arts:** Art, dramatic.

**Most popular majors.** Biology 7%, business/marketing 23%, education 22%, psychology 6%, social sciences 6%, visual/performing arts 8%.

**Computing on campus.** 250 workstations in dormitories, library, computer center, student center. Dormitories linked to campus network. Commuter students can connect to campus network. Online course registration, online library, helpline, repair service, wireless network available.

**Student life. Freshman orientation:** Available. Preregistration for classes offered. One-day orientation program in late May. **Policies:** Use of alcohol prohibited on campus. Resident living required for all students unless granted commuting status or living with parents. Religious observance required. **Housing:** Guaranteed on-campus for all undergraduates. Single-sex dorms, special housing for disabled, apartments available. $100 fully refundable deposit, deadline 8/1. **Activities:** Bands, campus ministries, choral groups, dance, drama, international student organizations, literary magazine, music ensembles, student government, student newspaper, symphony orchestra, TV station, student activities council, Fellowship of Christian Athletes, College Republicans, Campus Democrats, Phi Beta Lambda, Sigma Tau, Spanish club, education club.

**Athletics.** NAIA. **Intercollegiate:** Baseball M, basketball, cross-country, football (tackle) M, golf, soccer, softball W, track and field, volleyball W, wrestling M. **Intramural:** Badminton, basketball, bowling, football (non-tackle), golf, racquetball, soccer, softball, table tennis, tennis, volleyball. **Team name:** Red Raiders.

**Student services.** Alcohol/substance abuse counseling, career counseling, student employment services, financial aid counseling, health services, personal counseling, placement for graduates, veterans' counselor. **Physically disabled:** Services for visually, speech, hearing impaired.

**Contact.** E-mail: admissions@nwciowa.edu
Phone: (712) 707-7130 Toll-free number: (800) 747-4757
Fax: (712) 707-7164
Mark Bloemendaal, Director of Admissions, Northwestern College, 101 Seventh Street, SW, Orange City, IA 51041

## St. Ambrose University
### Davenport, Iowa
**www.sau.edu**                     **CB code: 6617**

- Private 4-year university and liberal arts college affiliated with Roman Catholic Church
- Residential campus in small city
- 2,779 degree-seeking undergraduates: 16% part-time, 62% women, 3% African American, 1% Asian American, 3% Hispanic American, 1% Native American, 1% international
- 951 degree-seeking graduate students
- 70% of applicants admitted
- SAT or ACT with writing required
- 61% graduate within 6 years

**General.** Founded in 1882. Regionally accredited. **Degrees:** 560 bachelor's awarded; master's, doctoral offered. **Location:** 180 miles from Des Moines, 175 miles from Chicago. **Calendar:** 4-1-4, extensive summer session. **Full-time faculty:** 169 total; 75% have terminal degrees, 8% minority, 45% women. **Part-time faculty:** 166 total; 19% have terminal degrees, 7% minority, 51% women. **Class size:** 57% < 20, 43% 20-39, less than 1% 40-49. **Special facilities:** Transmission electron microscope, cable television channel, observatory, national prairie garden, radio station.

**Freshman class profile.** 2,145 applied, 1,491 admitted, 510 enrolled.

| Mid 50% test scores | | | |
|---|---|---|---|
| ACT composite: | 19-24 | Rank in top tenth: | 22% |
| GPA 3.50 or higher: | 32% | End year in good standing: | 88% |
| GPA 3.0-3.49: | 31% | Return as sophomores: | 79% |
| GPA 2.0-2.99: | 37% | Out-of-state: | 65% |
| Rank in top quarter: | 41% | Live on campus: | 94% |

**Basis for selection.** Minimum 2.5 GPA and 20 ACT/950 SAT (exclusive of Writing) or 18-19 ACT/870-950 SAT and rank in top half of class required. Interview recommended. Portfolio required for art majors. **Home-schooled:** Students who do not have a high school diploma required to score 50 on GED with 18 ACT or 860 SAT (exclusive of Writing).

**High school preparation.** 18 units recommended. Recommended units include English 4, mathematics 3, social studies 1, history 1, science 2 (laboratory 2), foreign language 1 and academic electives 4.

**2008-2009 Annual costs.** Tuition/fees: $21,610. Room/board: $7,825. Books/supplies: $1,000. Personal expenses: $1,125.

**2007-2008 Financial aid. Need-based:** 508 full-time freshmen applied for aid; 370 were judged to have need; 369 of these received aid. Average need met was 29%. Average scholarship/grant was $10,522; average loan $3,816. 49% of total undergraduate aid awarded as scholarships/grants, 51% as loans/jobs. **Non-need-based:** Awarded to 1,313 full-time undergraduates, including 369 freshmen. Scholarships awarded for academics, alumni affiliation, art, athletics, job skills, music/drama. **Additional information:** Iowa applicants must apply for financial aid by July 1. Audition required for music, drama scholarship applicants.

**Application procedures. Admission:** No deadline. $25 fee, may be waived for applicants with need. Application may be submitted online. Admission notification on a rolling basis beginning on or about 10/1. Must reply by May 1 or within 2 week(s) if notified thereafter. **Financial aid:** Priority date 3/15; no closing date. FAFSA required. Applicants notified on a rolling basis starting 2/1; must reply within 2 week(s) of notification.

**Academics. Special study options:** Accelerated study, combined bachelor's/graduate degree, cooperative education, distance learning, double major, independent study, internships, liberal arts/career combination, student-designed major, study abroad, teacher certification program. Service learning program in which students work as volunteers for community and earn 1-3 semester hours credit, license preparation for occupational therapy on campus, accounting majors volunteer to work on income tax forms for low income families on campus. **Credit/placement by examination:** AP, CLEP, IB, SAT, ACT, institutional tests. 60 credit hours maximum toward bachelor's degree. **Support services:** Learning center, pre-admission summer program, reduced course load, remedial instruction, study skills assistance, tutoring, writing center.

**Majors. Biology:** General. **Business:** General, accounting, business admin, finance, international, management science, marketing, organizational behavior. **Communications:** General, advertising, broadcast journalism, journalism, media studies, public relations, radio/tv. **Computer sciences:** General, computer science, information systems, LAN/WAN management, security, systems analysis. **Education:** General, art, biology, business, chemistry, early childhood, elementary, English, foreign languages, French, German, health, history, mathematics, music, physical, physics, psychology, science, secondary, social science, Spanish. **Engineering:** Industrial, physics. **English:** English lit, speech/rhetoric. **Foreign languages:** French, German, Spanish. **Health:** Nursing (RN). **History:** General. **Interdisciplinary:** Biological/physical sciences, natural sciences, neuroscience. **Math:** General. **Parks/recreation:** Exercise sciences, health/fitness, sports admin. **Philosophy/religion:** Philosophy. **Physical sciences:** Chemistry, physics. **Protective services:** Criminal justice, criminalistics. **Psychology:** General, forensic. **Public administration:** General. **Social sciences:** Economics, political science, sociology. **Visual/performing arts:** Commercial/advertising art, dramatic, graphic design, multimedia, studio arts, theater arts management.

**Most popular majors.** Biology 6%, business/marketing 29%, communications/journalism 6%, education 11%, health sciences 8%, psychology 11%.

**Computing on campus.** 190 workstations in library, computer center, student center. Dormitories wired for high-speed internet access and linked to campus network. Commuter students can connect to campus network. Online course registration, online library, helpline, wireless network available.

**Student life. Freshman orientation:** Mandatory. Preregistration for classes offered. Held 2 days per month in April, June, August. **Policies:** Campus smoke-free in all buildings. **Housing:** Guaranteed on-campus for freshmen. Coed dorms, single-sex dorms, special housing for disabled, apartments, substance-free housing available. $250 partly refundable deposit, deadline 5/1. Townhouses for seniors, houses for juniors and seniors available. **Activities:** Bands, campus ministries, choral groups, dance, drama, literary magazine, music ensembles, musical theater, opera, radio station, student government, student newspaper, symphony orchestra, TV station, Fellowship of Christian Athletes, black student union, philosophy club, Young Republicans, Young Democrats, veterans club, art club, music club, psychology club, multicultural club.

**Athletics.** NAIA. **Intercollegiate:** Baseball M, basketball, cheerleading, cross-country, football (tackle) M, golf, soccer, softball W, tennis, track and field, volleyball. **Intramural:** Badminton, basketball, bowling, football (non-tackle), golf, handball, racquetball, softball, tennis, triathlon, volleyball. **Team name:** Fighting Bees.

**Student services.** Adult student services, alcohol/substance abuse counseling, career counseling, student employment services, financial aid counseling, health services, minority student services, on-campus daycare, personal counseling, placement for graduates, veterans' counselor, women's services. **Physically disabled:** Services for visually, speech, hearing impaired.

**Contact.** E-mail: admit@sau.edu
Phone: (563) 333-6300 Toll-free number: (800) 383-2627
Fax: (563) 333-6243
Meg Halligan, Director of Admissions, St. Ambrose University, 518 West Locust Street, Davenport, IA 52803-2898

## Simpson College

**Indianola, Iowa**     **CB member**
**www.simpson.edu**     **CB code: 6650**

- Private 4-year liberal arts college affiliated with United Methodist Church
- Residential campus in large town
- 1,910 degree-seeking undergraduates: 21% part-time, 58% women, 2% African American, 1% Asian American, 2% Hispanic American, 1% international
- 22 degree-seeking graduate students
- 88% of applicants admitted
- SAT or ACT (ACT writing optional) required
- 65% graduate within 6 years; 15% enter graduate study

**General.** Founded in 1860. Regionally accredited. **Degrees:** 415 bachelor's awarded; master's offered. **Location:** 12 miles from Des Moines. **Calendar:** 4-4-1. Extensive summer session. **Full-time faculty:** 97 total; 88% have terminal degrees, 5% minority, 39% women. **Part-time faculty:** 109 total; 88% have terminal degrees, 7% minority, 37% women. **Class size:** 66% < 20, 32% 20-39, 2% 40-49, less than 1% 50-99. **Special facilities:** Antebellum-era collection, cadaver laboratory, Iowa history center, urban studies institute.

**Freshman class profile.** 1,346 applied, 1,180 admitted, 385 enrolled.

| Mid 50% test scores | | | |
|---|---|---|---|
| ACT composite: | 22-27 | Out-of-state: | 16% |
| Rank in top quarter: | 59% | Live on campus: | 97% |
| Rank in top tenth: | 25% | International: | 1% |
| End year in good standing: | 91% | Fraternities: | 18% |
| Return as sophomores: | 82% | Sororities: | 21% |

**Basis for selection.** High school academic record, including college preparatory courses taken and grades received in those courses, class rank, and ACT/SAT scores most important. Recommendations also considered. Interview recommended. Audition recommended for music, drama majors. Portfolio recommended for art majors. Auditions and portfolios required for scholarships in music, theater, or art. **Homeschooled:** Letter of recommendation (nonparent) required. Must submit GED or high school diploma and transcripts with description of course content. **Learning Disabled:** Documentation of disability needed in order to ensure the college can provide adequate facilities.

**High school preparation.** 16 units recommended. Recommended units include English 4, mathematics 3, social studies 3, science 3 (laboratory 3) and foreign language 3.

**2008-2009 Annual costs.** Tuition/fees: $24,771. Room/board: $6,988. Books/supplies: $900. Personal expenses: $1,300.

**2007-2008 Financial aid. Need-based:** 385 full-time freshmen applied for aid; 339 were judged to have need; 339 of these received aid. Average need met was 89%. Average scholarship/grant was $16,149; average loan $3,650. 71% of total undergraduate aid awarded as scholarships/grants, 29% as loans/jobs. **Non-need-based:** Awarded to 355 full-time undergraduates, including 94 freshmen. Scholarships awarded for academics, alumni affiliation, art, leadership, minority status, music/drama, religious affiliation, state residency. **Additional information:** Music and theater scholarships based on audition. Art scholarships based on portfolio.

**Application procedures. Admission:** Priority date 5/1; no deadline. No application fee. Application may be submitted online. Admission notification on a rolling basis. Reply date determined by date student receives financial aid package. **Financial aid:** Priority date 4/1; no closing date. FAFSA required. Applicants notified on a rolling basis starting 3/12; must reply by 5/1 or within 3 week(s) of notification.

**Academics. Special study options:** Accelerated study, combined bachelor's/graduate degree, double major, honors, independent study, internships, liberal arts/career combination, New York semester, study abroad, teacher certification program, United Nations semester, Washington semester. 3-2 and 4-2 engineering program with Washington University in St. Louis, Iowa State University, and Institute of Technology, University of Minnesota, Minneapolis. **Credit/placement by examination:** AP, CLEP, IB, ACT, institutional tests. 24 credit hours maximum toward bachelor's degree. **Support services:** Learning center, reduced course load, study skills assistance, tutoring, writing center.

**Majors. Biology:** General, biochemistry. **Business:** Accounting, business admin, international, managerial economics, marketing. **Communications:** General, journalism, media studies. **Computer sciences:** Computer science, information systems. **Conservation:** Environmental science. **Education:** General, early childhood, elementary, middle, music, physical. **Engineering:** General. **English:** English lit. **Foreign languages:** French, German, Spanish. **Health:** Athletic training, predental, premedicine, prepharmacy, preveterinary. **History:** General. **Legal studies:** Prelaw. **Liberal arts:** Arts/sciences. **Math:** General. **Parks/recreation:** Health/fitness, sports admin. **Philosophy/religion:** Philosophy, religion. **Physical sciences:** Chemistry, physics. **Protective services:** Criminal justice, forensics. **Psychology:** General. **Social sciences:** Economics, international relations, political science, sociology. **Theology:** Preministerial. **Visual/performing arts:** Art, dramatic, music performance.

**Most popular majors.** Biology 8%, business/marketing 31%, communications/journalism 7%, education 10%, liberal arts 7%, social sciences 9%.

**Computing on campus.** 314 workstations in dormitories, library, computer center, student center. Dormitories wired for high-speed internet access and linked to campus network. Commuter students can connect to campus network. Online library, repair service, wireless network available.

**Student life. Freshman orientation:** Mandatory. Preregistration for classes offered. 4 one-day summer registration programs in June with orientation the first week students are on campus. **Housing:** Guaranteed on-campus for all undergraduates. Coed dorms, single-sex dorms, apartments, fraternity/sorority housing, substance-free housing available. $200 fully refundable deposit. Theme housing available. **Activities:** Bands, choral groups, dance, drama, literary magazine, music ensembles, musical theater, opera, radio station, student government, student newspaper, Religious Life Community, Interfaith Fellowship, Multicultural Student Alliance, Alpha Phi Omega, College Democrats, College Republicans, Fellowship of Christian Athletes, Students Embracing Responsible Volunteer Experiences, Habitat for Humanity, Amnesty International.

**Athletics.** NCAA. **Intercollegiate:** Baseball M, basketball, cheerleading, cross-country, football (tackle) M, golf, soccer, softball W, swimming W, tennis, track and field, volleyball W, wrestling M. **Intramural:** Badminton, basketball, football (non-tackle), golf, racquetball, soccer, softball, swimming, table tennis, tennis, volleyball, weight lifting. **Team name:** Storm.

**Student services.** Adult student services, campus ministries, career counseling, student employment services, financial aid counseling, health services, minority student services, personal counseling, placement for graduates. **Physically disabled:** Services for visually, speech, hearing impaired.

**Contact.** E-mail: admiss@simpson.edu
Phone: (515) 961-1624 Toll-free number: (800) 362-2454
Fax: (515) 961-1870
Deborah Tierney, Vice President for Enrollment, Simpson College, 701 North C Street, Indianola, IA 50125

---

## University of Dubuque

| Dubuque, Iowa | CB member |
|---|---|
| www.dbq.edu | CB code: 6869 |

- Private 4-year university and seminary college affiliated with Presbyterian Church (USA)
- Residential campus in small city
- 1,240 degree-seeking undergraduates
- 70% of applicants admitted
- SAT or ACT (ACT writing optional), application essay required

**General.** Founded in 1852. Regionally accredited. **Degrees:** 188 bachelor's awarded; master's, doctoral, first professional offered. **ROTC:** Army. **Location:** 180 miles from Chicago. **Calendar:** Semester, limited summer session. **Full-time faculty:** 75 total. **Part-time faculty:** 62 total. **Class size:** 59% < 20, 40% 20-39, less than 1% 40-49, less than 1% 50-99. **Special facilities:** Floating laboratory on Mississippi River, curriculum laboratory

for teachers, aviation operations center, studio laboratory for animation program, wetland area management, science center.

**Freshman class profile.**

| Mid 50% test scores | | | |
|---|---|---|---|
| SAT critical reading: | 410-500 | Rank in top quarter: | 23% |
| SAT math: | 410-530 | Rank in top tenth: | 5% |
| ACT composite: | 17-22 | Out-of-state: | 60% |
| GPA 3.50 or higher: | 20% | Live on campus: | 71% |
| GPA 3.0-3.49: | 30% | Fraternities: | 18% |
| GPA 2.0-2.99: | 50% | Sororities: | 14% |

**Basis for selection.** 18 ACT, 860 SAT (exclusive of writing), rank in top half of class most important. 2.0 GPA in college preparatory classes also considered. Recommendations required. **Learning Disabled:** Students must request assistance.

**High school preparation.** 10 units required; 15 recommended. Required and recommended units include English 4, mathematics 2-3, social studies 2-3, science 2-3 and foreign language 2.

**2007-2008 Annual costs.** Tuition/fees: $19,180. Room/board: $6,520. Books/supplies: $750.

**Financial aid. Non-need-based:** Scholarships awarded for academics, alumni affiliation, music/drama, ROTC.

**Application procedures. Admission:** No deadline. $25 fee, may be waived for applicants with need. Application may be submitted online. Admission notification on a rolling basis beginning on or about 8/15. Must reply by May 1 or within 3 week(s) if notified thereafter. **Financial aid:** Priority date 4/1; no closing date. FAFSA required. Applicants notified on a rolling basis starting 3/1; must reply within 3 week(s) of notification.

**Academics. Special study options:** Combined bachelor's/graduate degree, cooperative education, cross-registration, double major, dual enrollment of high school students, independent study, internships, liberal arts/career combination, study abroad, teacher certification program, urban semester. Undergraduate students may take graduate courses. **Credit/placement by examination:** AP, CLEP, IB, SAT, ACT, institutional tests. 24 credit hours maximum toward associate degree, 24 toward bachelor's. **Support services:** Learning center, reduced course load, remedial instruction, study skills assistance, tutoring, writing center.

**Majors. Biology:** General, ecology. **Business:** Accounting, business admin. **Communications:** General. **Computer sciences:** General, computer graphics. **Conservation:** General, environmental science. **Education:** Elementary, physical. **English:** English lit, speech/rhetoric. **Health:** Nursing (RN). **Parks/recreation:** General. **Philosophy/religion:** Philosophy, religion. **Physical sciences:** Planetary. **Protective services:** Criminal justice. **Psychology:** General. **Social sciences:** Sociology. **Transportation:** Aviation, aviation management, flight instructor. **Visual/performing arts:** Commercial/advertising art, graphic design.

**Computing on campus.** 200 workstations in dormitories, library, computer center, student center. Dormitories wired for high-speed internet access and linked to campus network. Commuter students can connect to campus network. Online course registration, online library, helpline, student web hosting available.

**Student life. Freshman orientation:** Mandatory, $60 fee. Preregistration for classes offered. Held 4 days prior to beginning of class. **Policies:** Students required to live on-campus through junior year or until they reach 21 years of age or if living with parents within 50 miles of campus. **Housing:** Guaranteed on-campus for freshmen. Coed dorms, special housing for disabled, apartments, substance-free housing available. $200 fully refundable deposit, deadline 6/1. Houses and townhouses available. **Activities:** Pep band, campus ministries, choral groups, dance, drama, film society, international student organizations, music ensembles, student government, student newspaper, social service organizations, service fraternity, environmental group, student activities board, College Republicans, College Democrats.

**Athletics.** NCAA. **Intercollegiate:** Baseball M, basketball, cross-country, football (tackle) M, golf, soccer, softball W, tennis, track and field, volleyball W, wrestling M. **Intramural:** Archery, badminton, baseball M, basketball, bowling, cheerleading, football (non-tackle) M, golf, racquetball, soccer, softball, table tennis, tennis, volleyball. **Team name:** Spartans.

**Student services.** Alcohol/substance abuse counseling, career counseling, student employment services, financial aid counseling, health services, minority student services, personal counseling, placement for graduates, veterans' counselor.

**Contact.** E-mail: admssns@dbq.edu
Phone: (563) 589-3200 Toll-free number: (800) 722-5583
Fax: (563) 589-3690
Jesse James, Dean of Admission, University of Dubuque, 2000 University
Avenue, Dubuque, IA 52001-5099

## University of Iowa
### Iowa City, Iowa
**www.uiowa.edu**

**CB member**
**CB code: 6681**

- Public 4-year university
- Residential campus in small city
- 20,207 degree-seeking undergraduates: 8% part-time, 52% women
- 8,210 graduate students
- 83% of applicants admitted
- SAT or ACT (ACT writing optional) required
- 66% graduate within 6 years

**General.** Founded in 1847. Regionally accredited. **Degrees:** 4,219 bachelor's awarded; master's, doctoral, first professional offered. **ROTC:** Army, Air Force. **Location:** 20 miles from Cedar Rapids, 110 miles from Des Moines. **Calendar:** Semester, extensive summer session. **Full-time faculty:** 1,559 total; 97% have terminal degrees, 17% minority, 29% women. **Part-time faculty:** 96 total; 95% have terminal degrees, 6% minority, 27% women. **Class size:** 51% < 20, 35% 20-39, 4% 40-49, 5% 50-99, 4% >100. **Special facilities:** Field campus, accelerator, observatory, natural history museum, driving simulator.

**Freshman class profile.** 14,678 applied, 12,209 admitted, 4,287 enrolled.

| Mid 50% test scores | | Rank in top quarter: | 54% |
|---|---|---|---|
| SAT critical reading: | 520-650 | Rank in top tenth: | 23% |
| SAT math: | 550-670 | Return as sophomores: | 83% |
| ACT composite: | 23-27 | Out-of-state: | 43% |
| GPA 3.50 or higher: | 58% | Live on campus: | 94% |
| GPA 3.0-3.49: | 35% | International: | 1% |
| GPA 2.0-2.99: | 7% | | |

**Basis for selection.** For in-state applicants, rank in top half of class or acceptable admission index score. For nonresidents, rank in top 30% or acceptable admission index score. Regent Admission Index (RAI) score of 245 for state residents; 255 for non-residents. ACT or SAT, class rank, GPA and number of completed high school core courses determine RAI score. Audition required of music, dance majors. **Homeschooled:** Personal essay describing homeschool experience strongly recommended and required in certain circumstances.

**High school preparation.** 15 units required. Required and recommended units include English 4, mathematics 3-4, social studies 3, science 3 and foreign language 2-4. Math units must include 2 algebra, 1 geometry; engineering majors require fourth unit of higher math. Science units must include 2 of the following: biology, chemistry, and physics. Engineering requires 1 unit chemistry and 1 unit physics. Engineering majors require only 2 units social studies.

**2007-2008 Annual costs.** Tuition/fees: $6,293; $19,465 out-of-state. Room/board: $6,685. Books/supplies: $960. Personal expenses: $2,480.

**2006-2007 Financial aid.** **Need-based:** 2,983 full-time freshmen applied for aid; 1,983 were judged to have need; 1,884 of these received aid. Average need met was 99%. Average scholarship/grant was $4,529; average loan $2,845. 46% of total undergraduate aid awarded as scholarships/grants, 54% as loans/jobs. **Non-need-based:** Awarded to 5,624 full-time undergraduates, including 1,834 freshmen. Scholarships awarded for academics, alumni affiliation, art, athletics, leadership, minority status, music/drama, ROTC, state residency.

**Application procedures.** **Admission:** Priority date 2/1; deadline 4/1 (postmark date). $40 fee, may be waived for applicants with need. Application may be submitted online. Admission notification on a rolling basis beginning on or about 9/15. Must reply by 5/1. **Financial aid:** Priority date 1/1; no closing date. FAFSA, institutional form required. Applicants notified on a rolling basis starting 3/1.

**Academics.** Distance learning programs available via several options; bachelor of liberal studies degree may be earned with distance education course work. **Special study options:** Accelerated study, combined bachelor's/graduate degree, cooperative education, distance learning, double major, dual enrollment of high school students, ESL, exchange student, external degree, honors, independent study, internships, New York semester, semester at sea, student-designed major, study abroad, teacher certification program, Washington semester. **Credit/placement by examination:** AP, CLEP, IB, SAT,

ACT, institutional tests. 30 credit hours maximum toward bachelor's degree. **Support services:** Learning center, pre-admission summer program, reduced course load, remedial instruction, study skills assistance, tutoring, writing center.

**Majors.** **Area/ethnic studies:** African, African-American, American, Asian, Russian/Slavic, women's. **Biology:** General, biochemistry, microbiology. **Business:** Accounting, actuarial science, business admin, finance, human resources, labor relations, management information systems, management science, managerial economics, marketing. **Communications:** General, journalism, media studies. **Computer sciences:** General, computer science. **Conservation:** Environmental science, environmental studies. **Education:** Elementary. **Engineering:** General, biomedical, chemical, civil, electrical, industrial, mechanical. **English:** English lit, speech/rhetoric. **Foreign languages:** Ancient Greek, Chinese, classics, comparative lit, French, German, Italian, Japanese, Latin, linguistics, Portuguese, Russian, Sanskrit, Spanish. **Health:** Athletic training, audiology/hearing, clinical lab science, music therapy, nuclear medical technology, nursing (RN), predental, premedicine, prenursing, prepharmacy, preveterinary, radiologic technology/medical imaging, recreational therapy. **History:** General. **Interdisciplinary:** Ancient studies, global studies. **Legal studies:** Prelaw. **Liberal arts:** Arts/sciences. **Math:** General, applied, statistics. **Parks/recreation:** General, exercise sciences, facilities management, sports admin. **Philosophy/religion:** Philosophy, religion. **Physical sciences:** Astronomy, chemistry, geology, physics. **Psychology:** General. **Public administration:** Social work. **Social sciences:** Anthropology, economics, geography, political science, sociology. **Visual/performing arts:** Art, art history/conservation, arts management, ceramics, cinematography, dance, dramatic, drawing, film/cinema, jazz, metal/jewelry, music management, music performance, music theory/composition, painting, photography, piano/organ, printmaking, sculpture, stringed instruments, studio arts, voice/opera.

**Most popular majors.** Business/marketing 19%, communications/journalism 12%, health sciences 7%, psychology 8%, social sciences 10%, visual/performing arts 7%.

**Computing on campus.** 1,100 workstations in dormitories, library, computer center, student center. Dormitories wired for high-speed internet access and linked to campus network. Commuter students can connect to campus network. Online course registration, helpline, repair service, student web hosting, wireless network available.

**Student life.** **Freshman orientation:** Mandatory, $175 fee. Preregistration for classes offered. Two-day summer program. **Housing:** Coed dorms, special housing for disabled, apartments, fraternity/sorority housing, substance-free housing available. $120 partly refundable deposit, deadline 2/18. International, freshman and transfer honors, leadership and service, quiet houses, some major specific housing also available. **Activities:** Bands, campus ministries, choral groups, dance, drama, film society, international student organizations, literary magazine, music ensembles, musical theater, opera, radio station, student government, student newspaper, symphony orchestra, College Republicans, University Democrats, American Indian student association, Hispanic Society, black student union, Amnesty International, gay/lesbian/bisexual/transgendered and allied union, honor societies, Habitat for Humanity, writer's club.

**Athletics.** NCAA. **Intercollegiate:** Baseball M, basketball, cheerleading, cross-country, diving, field hockey W, football (tackle) M, golf, gymnastics, rowing (crew) W, soccer W, softball W, swimming, tennis, track and field, volleyball W, wrestling M. **Intramural:** Badminton, basketball, bowling, football (non-tackle), golf, racquetball, soccer, softball, table tennis, tennis, volleyball, wrestling. **Team name:** Hawkeyes.

**Student services.** Adult student services, alcohol/substance abuse counseling, career counseling, services for economically disadvantaged, student employment services, financial aid counseling, health services, legal services, minority student services, on-campus daycare, personal counseling, placement for graduates, veterans' counselor, women's services. **Physically disabled:** Services for visually, speech, hearing impaired.

**Contact.** E-mail: admissions@uiowa.edu
Phone: (319) 335-3847 Toll-free number: (800) 553-4692
Fax: (319) 335-1535
Michael Barron, Assistant Provost for Enrollment Services, University of Iowa, 107 Calvin Hall, Iowa City, IA 52242-1396

## University of Northern Iowa
### Cedar Falls, Iowa
**www.uni.edu**

**CB code: 6307**

- Public 4-year university
- Residential campus in small city
- 10,756 degree-seeking undergraduates: 9% part-time, 57% women, 3% African American, 1% Asian American, 2% Hispanic American, 2% international

- 1,402 degree-seeking graduate students
- 80% of applicants admitted
- SAT or ACT (ACT writing optional) required
- 65% graduate within 6 years

**General.** Founded in 1876. Regionally accredited. **Degrees:** 2,259 bachelor's awarded; master's, doctoral offered. **ROTC:** Army. **Location:** 63 miles from Cedar Rapids. **Calendar:** Semester, limited summer session. **Full-time faculty:** 621 total; 71% have terminal degrees, 11% minority, 44% women. **Part-time faculty:** 190 total; 30% have terminal degrees, 4% minority, 54% women. **Class size:** 35% < 20, 50% 20-39, 8% 40-49, 6% 50-99, 2% >100. **Special facilities:** Performing arts center, center for energy and environmental education, NASA teacher resource center, observatory, natural preserve, wellness and recreation center.

**Freshman class profile.** 4,722 applied, 3,759 admitted, 1,991 enrolled.

| Mid 50% test scores | | |
|---|---|---|
| SAT critical reading: | 410-620 | |
| SAT math: | 450-630 | |
| ACT composite: | 21-26 | |
| GPA 3.50 or higher: | 50% | |
| GPA 3.0-3.49: | 36% | |
| GPA 2.0-2.99: | 14% | |
| Rank in top quarter: | 49% | |
| Rank in top tenth: | 19% | |
| End year in good standing: | 95% | |
| Return as sophomores: | 82% | |
| Out-of-state: | 5% | |
| Live on campus: | 91% | |
| International: | 1% | |
| Fraternities: | 6% | |
| Sororities: | 4% | |

**Basis for selection.** Rank in top half of class, completion of high school curriculum requirements most important factors for admission. In the absence of class rank, standardized test scores may carry greater weight in the admissions process. Audition required of music majors. Interview may be recommended for borderline applicants who do not meet admission requirements. **Homeschooled:** Statement describing homeschool structure and mission, transcript of courses and grades required.

**High school preparation.** 15 units required. Required and recommended units include English 4, mathematics 3, social studies 3, science 3 (laboratory 1), foreign language 2 and academic electives 2. English units must include 1 composition. Math[ ]units must include algebra, geometry and advanced algebra. 2 electives required in subjects listed above and/or fine arts.

**2007-2008 Annual costs.** Tuition/fees: $6,190; $14,282 out-of-state. Room/board: $6,268. Books/supplies: $966. Personal expenses: $2,445.

**2007-2008 Financial aid. Need-based:** 1,699 full-time freshmen applied for aid; 1,156 were judged to have need; 1,114 of these received aid. Average need met was 74%. Average scholarship/grant was $3,727; average loan $3,534. 30% of total undergraduate aid awarded as scholarships/grants, 70% as loans/jobs. **Non-need-based:** Awarded to 3,235 full-time undergraduates, including 1,320 freshmen. Scholarships awarded for academics, alumni affiliation, art, athletics, leadership, minority status, music/drama, ROTC, state residency.

**Application procedures. Admission:** Closing date 8/15 (postmark date). $40 fee. Application may be submitted online. Admission notification on a rolling basis beginning on or about 9/1. **Financial aid:** No deadline. FAFSA required. Applicants notified on a rolling basis starting 3/1.

**Academics.** 15 master's degrees, 2 undergraduate degrees available through distance learning within Iowa. Coursework delivered through Iowa Communications Network (ICN) and World Wide Web. Many programs also have on-campus components. Bachelor of Liberal Studies (BLS) degree is external undergraduate degree completion program available to Iowan and non-resident students. **Special study options:** Accelerated study, combined bachelor's/graduate degree, cooperative education, distance learning, double major, dual enrollment of high school students, ESL, exchange student, external degree, honors, independent study, internships, liberal arts/career combination, student-designed major, study abroad, teacher certification program, Washington semester, weekend college. Combined bachelors/masters degree programs (BA/MA, BS/MS, BA/MS); undergraduate dual degree majors; undergraduate and graduate certificates. **Credit/placement by examination:** AP, CLEP, IB, ACT, institutional tests. 32 credit hours maximum toward bachelor's degree. A maximum of 32 semester hours of credit earned by examination is applicable toward degree requirements. This includes credit earned by examination of other colleges and universities. **Support services:** Learning center, pre-admission summer program, reduced course load, remedial instruction, study skills assistance, tutoring, writing center.

**Majors. Area/ethnic studies:** American, Asian, European, Latin American, Russian/Slavic. **Biology:** General, biochemistry, bioinformatics, biomedical sciences, biotechnology, ecology, microbiology. **Business:** Accounting, actuarial science, business admin, construction management, finance, management information systems, marketing, real estate. **Communications:** General, digital media, organizational, public relations. **Communications technology:** Graphics. **Computer sciences:** General, computer science, networking. **Conservation:** Environmental science. **Education:** Business,

elementary, ESL, foreign languages, health, kindergarten/preschool, middle, music, physical, reading, science, social science, speech, technology/industrial arts. **Engineering:** Physics. **Engineering technology:** Electromechanical, industrial, manufacturing. **English:** English lit, speech/rhetoric. **Family/consumer sciences:** Clothing/textiles, family/community services. **Foreign languages:** General, French, German, Russian, Spanish. **Health:** Athletic training, speech pathology. **History:** General. **Interdisciplinary:** Biological/physical sciences, gerontology. **Liberal arts:** Arts/sciences, humanities. **Math:** General, applied. **Parks/recreation:** General, health/fitness. **Philosophy/religion:** Philosophy, religion. **Physical sciences:** Chemistry, geology, physics. **Psychology:** General. **Public administration:** General, social work. **Social sciences:** Anthropology, applied economics, criminology, econometrics, economics, geography, political science, sociology. **Visual/performing arts:** Acting, art, art history/conservation, dramatic, interior design, music performance, music theory/composition, studio arts, theater design.

**Most popular majors.** Business/marketing 22%, communications/journalism 6%, education 17%, social sciences 6%, visual/performing arts 6%.

**Computing on campus.** 1,900 workstations in dormitories, library, computer center, student center. Dormitories wired for high-speed internet access and linked to campus network. Commuter students can connect to campus network. Online course registration, online library, helpline, student web hosting, wireless network available.

**Student life. Freshman orientation:** Available, $125 fee. Preregistration for classes offered. Ten 2-day sessions in summer and immediately preceding beginning of semesters. **Housing:** Guaranteed on-campus for freshmen. Coed dorms, single-sex dorms, apartments, fraternity/sorority housing, substance-free housing available. $200 deposit. Facilities accessible by persons with disabilities. **Activities:** Bands, campus ministries, choral groups, dance, drama, international student organizations, literary magazine, music ensembles, musical theater, opera, radio station, student government, student newspaper, symphony orchestra, Amnesty International, Asian American student union, black student union, Campus Crusade for Christ, Catholic student association, College Republicans, conservation club, Fellowship of Christian Athletes, Habitat for Humanity, Democrat club.

**Athletics.** NCAA. **Intercollegiate:** Baseball M, basketball, cross-country, diving W, football (tackle) M, golf, soccer W, softball W, swimming W, tennis W, track and field, volleyball W, wrestling M. **Intramural:** Badminton, basketball, bowling, cheerleading, cross-country, football (non-tackle), football (tackle) M, golf, racquetball, rowing (crew), soccer, softball, swimming, table tennis, tennis, track and field, volleyball, weight lifting, wrestling M. **Team name:** Panthers.

**Student services.** Adult student services, alcohol/substance abuse counseling, career counseling, student employment services, financial aid counseling, health services, minority student services, on-campus daycare, personal counseling, placement for graduates, veterans' counselor. **Physically disabled:** Services for visually, speech, hearing impaired.

**Contact.** E-mail: admissions@uni.edu
Phone: (319) 273-2281 Toll-free number: (800) 772-2037
Fax: (319) 273-2885
Philip Patton, Director of Admissions, University of Northern Iowa, Towers 130, Cedar Falls, IA 50614-0018

---

## Upper Iowa University
**Fayette, Iowa**
**www.uiu.edu**                                          CB code: 6885

- Private 4-year university
- Residential campus in rural community
- 745 degree-seeking undergraduates
- 62% of applicants admitted
- SAT or ACT (ACT writing recommended) required

**General.** Founded in 1857. Regionally accredited. 2 consecutive 8-week terms equal one semester. **Degrees:** 1,077 bachelor's, 36 associate awarded; master's offered. **Location:** 50 miles from Waterloo, 70 miles from Cedar Rapids. **Calendar:** Semester, limited summer session. **Full-time faculty:** 35 total. **Part-time faculty:** 2 total. **Special facilities:** Electron microscope lab, greenhouse, television and media lab with computer animation suite.

**Freshman class profile.** 1,005 applied, 625 admitted, 164 enrolled.

| Mid 50% test scores | | ACT composite: | 17-22 |
|---|---|---|---|
| SAT critical reading: | 400-460 | Out-of-state: | 45% |
| SAT math: | 410-530 | | |

**Basis for selection.** 2.0 GPA, 16 ACT, 760 SAT (exclusive of Writing) important. Early application recommended because of limited enrollment policy. Interview recommended for academically weak applicants. Portfolio recommended for art majors. **Homeschooled:** Letters of recommendation strongly encouraged. GED or proof of completed coursework required.

**High school preparation.** 14 units recommended. Recommended units include English 4, mathematics 3, social studies 2, history 1, science 3 (laboratory 1).

**2007-2008 Annual costs.** Tuition/fees: $19,625. Room/board: $6,075. Books/supplies: $1,400. Personal expenses: $1,600.

**Financial aid.** **Non-need-based:** Scholarships awarded for academics.

**Application procedures.** **Admission:** No deadline. $15 fee. Application may be submitted online. Admission notification on a rolling basis. **Financial aid:** Priority date 6/1; no closing date. FAFSA required. Applicants notified on a rolling basis starting 4/1.

**Academics.** **Special study options:** Accelerated study, combined bachelor's/graduate degree, cooperative education, double major, dual enrollment of high school students, exchange student, external degree, independent study, internships, liberal arts/career combination, student-designed major, study abroad, teacher certification program. **Credit/placement by examination:** AP, CLEP, IB, institutional tests. 30 credit hours maximum toward bachelor's degree. **Support services:** Learning center, tutoring.

**Majors.** **Area/ethnic studies:** American. **Biology:** General. **Business:** General, accounting, business admin, management information systems. **Communications:** General. **Conservation:** General, environmental science, forestry, management/policy. **Education:** General, biology, chemistry, early childhood, elementary, health, history, kindergarten/preschool, middle, physical, reading, science, secondary, social science, social studies, special. **English:** English lit. **Health:** Athletic training, facilities admin, health care admin, physical therapy assistant, predental, premedicine, prepharmacy, preveterinary. **Legal studies:** Prelaw. **Math:** General. **Parks/recreation:** Facilities management, health/fitness. **Personal/culinary services:** Mortuary science. **Physical sciences:** Chemistry. **Protective services:** Criminal justice. **Psychology:** General. **Public administration:** Human services. **Social sciences:** General, criminology, sociology. **Visual/performing arts:** Art, arts management, commercial/advertising art, studio arts.

**Computing on campus.** 3 workstations in dormitories, library, computer center, student center. Dormitories wired for high-speed internet access.

**Student life.** **Freshman orientation:** Mandatory. Preregistration for classes offered. Held during summer, includes financial aid counseling. **Housing:** Guaranteed on-campus for all undergraduates. Coed dorms, single-sex dorms available. $100 deposit. **Activities:** Campus ministries, drama, student government, student newspaper, various organizations available.

**Athletics.** NCAA. **Intercollegiate:** Baseball M, basketball, cheerleading, cross-country, football (tackle) M, golf, soccer, softball W, tennis, track and field, volleyball W, wrestling M. **Intramural:** Badminton, basketball, softball, table tennis, volleyball. **Team name:** Peacocks.

**Student services.** Career counseling, student employment services, financial aid counseling, health services, personal counseling, placement for graduates.

**Contact.** E-mail: admission@uiu.edu
Phone: (563) 425-5281 Toll-free number: (800) 553-4150 ext. 2
Fax: (563) 425-5323
Jobyna Johnston, Director of Admission, Upper Iowa University, Parker Fox Hall, Fayette, IA 52142

---

### Vennard College
**University Park, Iowa**
www.vennard.edu                                **CB code: 6094**

- Private 4-year Bible college affiliated with interdenominational tradition
- Residential campus in large town
- 70 degree-seeking undergraduates: 4% part-time, 47% women, 4% international
- 55% of applicants admitted
- SAT or ACT (ACT writing optional) required

**General.** Founded in 1910. Regionally accredited; also accredited by ABHE. Dedicated to education in basic Christian doctrine and to preparing students for service in church-related ministries, or as lay persons in a Christian context. **Degrees:** 11 bachelor's, 2 associate awarded. **Location:** 65 miles from Des Moines. **Calendar:** Semester, limited summer session. **Full-time faculty:** 4 total. **Part-time faculty:** 8 total. **Class size:** 77% < 20, 23% 20-39.

**Freshman class profile.** 33 applied, 18 admitted, 11 enrolled.

| Mid 50% test scores | | Rank in top tenth: | 12% |
|---|---|---|---|
| ACT composite: | 19-24 | End year in good standing: | 95% |
| GPA 3.50 or higher: | 20% | Return as sophomores: | 100% |
| GPA 3.0-3.49: | 60% | Out-of-state: | 100% |
| GPA 2.0-2.99: | 20% | Live on campus: | 100% |
| Rank in top quarter: | 12% | International: | 9% |

**Basis for selection.** Statement of Christian experience and recommendation of pastor important. GPA in core academic courses and national test scores used to evaluate ability to succeed academically. Character references carefully considered. Minimum ACT score and GPA flexible, depending on other factors as considered by admissions office and academic departments. **Homeschooled:** Students without official high school transcript must take ASSET test to be eligible for financial aid. Homeschool code required if the state of the homeschooler requires one. **Learning Disabled:** Provide certification of learning disability and recommended learning aid strategies.

**2007-2008 Annual costs.** Tuition/fees: $9,750. Room/board: $4,950. Books/supplies: $500. Personal expenses: $1,390.

**2006-2007 Financial aid.** **Need-based:** 46% of total undergraduate aid awarded as scholarships/grants, 54% as loans/jobs. **Non-need-based:** Scholarships awarded for religious affiliation. **Additional information:** Institutional aid award available (sum of financial need grant and academic scholarship); FAFSA required. New students must have ACT/SAT score and GPA from high school; transfer students must have a GPA based on transcript from at least 24 credit hours from previous college.

**Application procedures.** **Admission:** No deadline. $20 fee, may be waived for applicants with need. Application may be submitted online. Admission notification on a rolling basis. **Financial aid:** Priority date 7/1; no closing date. FAFSA required. Applicants notified on a rolling basis starting 8/29; must reply within 8 week(s) of notification.

**Academics.** All students choose double major, one of which must be Bible. Individualized tutoring available. **Special study options:** Combined bachelor's/graduate degree, distance learning, double major, dual enrollment of high school students, independent study, internships, student-designed major. **Credit/placement by examination:** AP, CLEP, IB, SAT, ACT, institutional tests. 18 credit hours maximum toward associate degree, 18 toward bachelor's. Placement out of courses that are requirements of major will need the permission of program coordinator. **Support services:** Learning center, reduced course load, remedial instruction, study skills assistance, tutoring.

**Majors.** **Business:** Human resources. **Psychology:** General. **Theology:** Missionary, pastoral counseling, religious ed, theology, youth ministry.

**Most popular majors.** Business/marketing 11%, interdisciplinary studies 22%, psychology 11%, theological studies 55%.

**Computing on campus.** 20 workstations in library, computer center. Dormitories wired for high-speed internet access and linked to campus network. Online library, repair service, wireless network available.

**Student life.** **Freshman orientation:** Mandatory. Preregistration for classes offered. Held 2-3 days before classes begin; includes placement tests. **Policies:** College emphasizes social life disciplines as they relate to Christian life. Religious observance required. **Housing:** Guaranteed on-campus for freshmen. Single-sex dorms, apartments, substance-free housing available. $100 fully refundable deposit. Single students over 25 may petition for permission to live off campus. **Activities:** Campus ministries, choral groups, music ensembles, student government, World Christian Fellowship, Ministerial Association.

**Athletics.** NCCAA. **Intercollegiate:** Basketball, cross-country M, soccer M, volleyball W. **Intramural:** Basketball, table tennis, tennis, volleyball. **Team name:** Cougars.

**Student services.** Financial aid counseling, personal counseling.

**Contact.** E-mail: admiss@vennard.edu
Phone: (641) 673-8391 ext. 106 Toll-free number: (800) 686-8365
Fax: (641) 673-8365
Jeff Anderson, Director of Admissions, Vennard College, Box 29, University Park, IA 52595-0029

## Waldorf College

**Forest City, Iowa**
www.waldorf.edu

CB member
CB code: 6925

- Private 4-year liberal arts college affiliated with Evangelical Lutheran Church in America
- Residential campus in small town
- 566 degree-seeking undergraduates
- 53% of applicants admitted
- SAT or ACT (ACT writing optional) required

**General.** Founded in 1903. Regionally accredited. **Degrees:** 130 bachelor's, 10 associate awarded. **Location:** 125 miles from Des Moines. **Calendar:** Semester, limited summer session. **Full-time faculty:** 44 total; 59% have terminal degrees, 41% women. **Part-time faculty:** 17 total. **Class size:** 67% < 20, 33% 20-39. **Special facilities:** Multimedia lab for video, digital editing and communications.

**Freshman class profile.** 691 applied, 364 admitted, 141 enrolled.

| Mid 50% test scores | | Rank in top quarter: | 27% |
|---|---|---|---|
| ACT composite: | 18-26 | Rank in top tenth: | 9% |
| GPA 3.50 or higher: | 27% | Out-of-state: | 42% |
| GPA 3.0-3.49: | 28% | Live on campus: | 90% |
| GPA 2.0-2.99: | 42% | | |

**Basis for selection.** School record and test scores most important, recommendations important, class rank and interview (when administered) considered. Interview recommended. Audition and portfolio recommended for music, theater majors. **Learning Disabled:** Interview during campus visit required.

**High school preparation.** 16 units recommended. Recommended units include English 4, mathematics 3, social studies 4, science 3 and foreign language 2.

**2008-2009 Annual costs.** Tuition/fees (projected): $19,504. Room/board: $5,921. Books/supplies: $950. Personal expenses: $1,650.

**Financial aid. Non-need-based:** Scholarships awarded for academics, alumni affiliation, athletics, job skills, leadership, music/drama, religious affiliation, state residency.

**Application procedures. Admission:** No deadline. No application fee. Application may be submitted online. Admission notification on a rolling basis beginning on or about 10/7. **Financial aid:** Priority date 3/1; no closing date. FAFSA, institutional form required. Applicants notified on a rolling basis starting 3/1; must reply within 2 week(s) of notification.

**Academics.** Internships required in all baccalaureate programs. **Special study options:** Accelerated study, combined bachelor's/graduate degree, double major, dual enrollment of high school students, ESL, honors, independent study, internships, liberal arts/career combination, study abroad, teacher certification program. **Credit/placement by examination:** AP, CLEP, IB, SAT, ACT, institutional tests. 8 credit hours maximum toward associate degree, 8 toward bachelor's. **Support services:** Learning center, reduced course load, remedial instruction, study skills assistance, tutoring, writing center.

**Majors. Biology:** General. **Business:** General, business admin, finance, marketing. **Communications:** Broadcast journalism, journalism, media studies, radio/tv. **Communications technology:** General. **Computer sciences:** General, information systems. **Education:** Drama/dance, elementary, English, history, middle, multi-level teacher, music, secondary, social studies. **English:** British lit, composition, creative writing, English lit. **Family/consumer sciences:** Food/nutrition. **History:** General. **Legal studies:** Pre-law. **Liberal arts:** Arts/sciences, humanities. **Psychology:** General. **Social sciences:** General, political science. **Visual/performing arts:** General, arts management, dramatic, music management, music performance, piano/organ, theater arts management, voice/opera.

**Most popular majors.** Business/marketing 32%, communications/journalism 11%, education 22%, health sciences 10%, history 8%.

**Computing on campus.** PC or laptop required. Dormitories wired for high-speed internet access and linked to campus network. Online library, helpline, repair service, wireless network available.

**Student life. Freshman orientation:** Mandatory. Preregistration for classes offered. Held 2 days prior to the start of school. **Policies:** No alcohol on campus. **Housing:** Guaranteed on-campus for all undergraduates. Coed dorms, single-sex dorms, special housing for disabled, substance-free housing available. $100 fully refundable deposit, deadline 9/8. **Activities:** Bands, choral groups, drama, literary magazine, music ensembles, musical theater, radio station, student government, student newspaper, TV station, Lutheran youth encounter, fellowship of Christian athletes, science club, student senate, youth ministry, culture club, Amnesty International, social warriors activities team, awareness ambassadors.

**Athletics.** NAIA. **Intercollegiate:** Baseball M, basketball, cheerleading M, football (tackle) M, golf, soccer, softball W, volleyball W, wrestling M. **Intramural:** Badminton, basketball, racquetball, rugby W, skiing, soccer, softball, table tennis, volleyball, weight lifting. **Team name:** Warriors.

**Student services.** Alcohol/substance abuse counseling, campus ministries, career counseling, student employment services, financial aid counseling, health services, minority student services, personal counseling, placement for graduates, veterans' counselor. **Physically disabled:** Services for visually, speech, hearing impaired.

**Contact.** E-mail: admissions@waldorf.edu
Phone: (641) 585-8112 Toll-free number: (800) 292-1903
Fax: (641) 585-8125
Linda Hoopes, Vice President of Admissions, Waldorf College, 106 South Sixth Street, Forest City, IA 50436-1713

## Wartburg College

**Waverly, Iowa**
www.wartburg.edu

CB code: 6926

- Private 4-year liberal arts college affiliated with Evangelical Lutheran Church in America
- Residential campus in small town
- 1,764 degree-seeking undergraduates: 2% part-time, 52% women, 3% African American, 2% Asian American, 2% Hispanic American, 6% international
- 84% of applicants admitted
- SAT or ACT (ACT writing optional) required
- 62% graduate within 6 years; 21% enter graduate study

**General.** Founded in 1852. Regionally accredited. **Degrees:** 406 bachelor's awarded. **Location:** 15 miles from Waterloo-Cedar Falls. **Calendar:** 4-4-1. Limited summer session. **Full-time faculty:** 107 total; 84% have terminal degrees, 4% minority, 44% women. **Part-time faculty:** 56 total; 16% have terminal degrees, 4% minority, 59% women. **Class size:** 41% < 20, 51% 20-39, 4% 40-49, 4% 50-99, less than 1% >100. **Special facilities:** Sports and wellness center, planetarium/observatory, prairie preserve, fine arts center, journalism laboratory, mathematics simulation laboratory, institute for leadership education, international museum, music laboratory, science center, center for community engagement.

**Freshman class profile.** 1,982 applied, 1,656 admitted, 545 enrolled.

| Mid 50% test scores | | Rank in top quarter: | 59% |
|---|---|---|---|
| SAT critical reading: | 480-610 | Rank in top tenth: | 31% |
| SAT math: | 510-630 | End year in good standing: | 97% |
| SAT writing: | 510-640 | Return as sophomores: | 81% |
| ACT composite: | 21-26 | Out-of-state: | 23% |
| GPA 3.50 or higher: | 61% | Live on campus: | 99% |
| GPA 3.0-3.49: | 25% | International: | 6% |
| GPA 2.0-2.99: | 14% | | |

**Basis for selection.** Class rank, GPA, courses taken, test scores, recommendations important. Students with 18 ACT or below or who rank in lower half of high school class are reviewed by admission and scholarship committee for final decision. Interview recommended. Audition recommended for music majors. Portfolio recommended for art majors. **Learning Disabled:** Documentation of disability required.

**High school preparation.** 15 units recommended. Recommended units include English 4, mathematics 3, social studies 2, science 3, foreign language 2 and computer science 1.

**2007-2008 Annual costs.** Tuition/fees: $24,300. Room/board: $6,985. Books/supplies: $900.

**2006-2007 Financial aid. Need-based:** 463 full-time freshmen applied for aid; 402 were judged to have need; 402 of these received aid. Average need met was 90%. Average scholarship/grant was $14,629; average loan $4,680. 70% of total undergraduate aid awarded as scholarships/grants, 30% as loans/jobs. **Non-need-based:** Awarded to 529 full-time undergraduates, including 174 freshmen. Scholarships awarded for academics, alumni affiliation, music/drama, religious affiliation.

**Application procedures. Admission:** Priority date 5/1; no deadline. No application fee. Admission notification on a rolling basis beginning on or about 9/1. **Financial aid:** Priority date 3/1; no closing date. FAFSA required. Applicants notified on a rolling basis starting 3/1; must reply within 2 week(s) of notification.

**Academics. Special study options:** Accelerated study, double major, dual enrollment of high school students, honors, independent study, internships, student-designed major, study abroad, teacher certification program, urban semester, Washington semester. Wartburg West urban academic internship experience in Denver, CO; Washington Center Academic Internship Program; cultural immersions in U.S. and around the world; Leadership Certificate Program; 3-2 engineering agreements; deferred admission program with the University of Iowa College of Dentistry, community-based learning courses and first-year seminars. **Credit/placement by examination:** AP, CLEP, SAT, ACT, institutional tests. **Support services:** Learning center, reduced course load, remedial instruction, study skills assistance, tutoring, writing center.

**Majors. Biology:** General, biochemistry. **Business:** Accounting, business admin, finance, international, marketing. **Communications:** General, broadcast journalism, journalism, public relations. **Computer sciences:** General, information systems. **Education:** Art, elementary, history, music, physical. **Engineering:** Science. **English:** Composition, English lit, speech/rhetoric. **Foreign languages:** French, German, Spanish. **Health:** Clinical lab science, music therapy. **History:** General. **Math:** General. **Parks/recreation:** Sports admin. **Philosophy/religion:** Philosophy, religion. **Physical sciences:** Chemistry, physics. **Psychology:** General. **Public administration:** Social work. **Social sciences:** Economics, international relations, political science, sociology. **Theology:** Pastoral counseling, religious ed, sacred music. **Visual/performing arts:** Art, commercial/advertising art, dramatic, music performance, music theory/composition.

**Most popular majors.** Biology 11%, business/marketing 18%, communications/journalism 10%, education 13%, mathematics 6%, parks/recreation 7%, social sciences 6%.

**Computing on campus.** 250 workstations in dormitories, library, computer center, student center. Dormitories wired for high-speed internet access and linked to campus network. Commuter students can connect to campus network. Online course registration, online library, helpline, wireless network available.

**Student life. Freshman orientation:** Mandatory, $150 fee. Preregistration for classes offered. Two-day program in summer; continues in fall for 1 week. **Policies:** Students actively assist in residential-life design and food-service planning. **Housing:** Guaranteed on-campus for freshmen. Coed dorms, single-sex dorms, apartments available. $100 deposit, deadline 5/1. Townhomes for single senior students available. **Activities:** Bands, campus ministries, choral groups, dance, drama, film society, international student organizations, literary magazine, music ensembles, musical theater, opera, radio station, student government, student newspaper, symphony orchestra, TV station, Campus Crusade for Christ, Young Democrats, Young Republicans, cultural awareness center/organization, Habitat for Humanity, peace and justice club, Fellowship of Christian Athletes, volunteer action center.

**Athletics.** NCAA. **Intercollegiate:** Baseball M, basketball, cross-country, football (tackle) M, golf, soccer, softball W, tennis, track and field, volleyball W, wrestling M. **Intramural:** Badminton, basketball, football (non-tackle), golf, racquetball, softball, tennis, volleyball. **Team name:** Knights.

**Student services.** Alcohol/substance abuse counseling, career counseling, student employment services, financial aid counseling, health services, minority student services, personal counseling.

**Contact.** E-mail: admissions@wartburg.edu
Phone: (319) 352-8264 Toll-free number: (800) 772-2085
Fax: (319) 352-8579
Todd Coleman, Assistant Vice President for Admissions and Alumni/Parent Programs, Wartburg College, 100 Wartburg Boulevard, PO Box 1003, Waverly, IA 50677-0903

## William Penn University
Oskaloosa, Iowa
www.wmpenn.edu                          CB code: 6943

- Private 4-year liberal arts college affiliated with Society of Friends (Quaker)
- Residential campus in large town
- 1,833 degree-seeking undergraduates
- 53% of applicants admitted
- SAT or ACT (ACT writing optional) required
- 48% graduate within 6 years

**General.** Founded in 1873. Regionally accredited. **Degrees:** 336 bachelor's, 121 associate awarded. **Location:** 60 miles from Des Moines. **Calendar:** Semester, limited summer session. **Full-time faculty:** 44 total; 46%

have terminal degrees, 9% minority, 43% women. **Part-time faculty:** 138 total; 2% have terminal degrees, 4% minority, 46% women. **Class size:** 64% < 20, 35% 20-39, 2% 50-99. **Special facilities:** Middle Eastern art collection, prairie wildlife preservation area.

**Freshman class profile.** 783 applied, 414 admitted, 192 enrolled.

| Mid 50% test scores | | | |
|---|---|---|---|
| SAT critical reading: | 360-460 | SAT writing: | 340-480 |
| SAT math: | 330-480 | ACT composite: | 17-20 |
| | | End year in good standing: | 58% |

**Basis for selection.** Class rank, test scores, high school GPA important. Extracurricular activities, alumni relationship, recommendation, personal essay considered. Interview and essay recommended for academically marginal applicants. Audition recommended for music grants.

**High school preparation.** 15 units required. Required and recommended units include English 4, mathematics 2, social studies 2, history 2, science 2 and academic electives 3.

**2007-2008 Annual costs.** Tuition/fees: $16,880. Room/board: $5,042. Books/supplies: $800. Personal expenses: $900.

**Financial aid. Non-need-based:** Scholarships awarded for academics, alumni affiliation, athletics, leadership, music/drama, religious affiliation.

**Application procedures. Admission:** No deadline. $20 fee, may be waived for applicants with need. Application may be submitted online. Admission notification on a rolling basis beginning on or about 11/1. **Financial aid:** Priority date 7/1; no closing date. FAFSA required. Applicants notified on a rolling basis starting 1/1; must reply within 2 week(s) of notification.

**Academics.** College for Working Adults (CWA) degree program; Leadership core curriculum replaces general education requirements. **Special study options:** Accelerated study, distance learning, double major, dual enrollment of high school students, independent study, internships, liberal arts/career combination, study abroad, teacher certification program. 3-2 engineering program offered with Iowa State University. **Credit/placement by examination:** AP, CLEP, IB, SAT, ACT, institutional tests. 32 credit hours maximum toward bachelor's degree. **Support services:** Learning center, reduced course load, remedial instruction, study skills assistance, tutoring, writing center.

**Majors. Biology:** General. **Business:** Accounting, business admin. **Communications:** General, journalism, public relations. **Computer sciences:** General. **Education:** General, biology, business, chemistry, driver/safety, elementary, English, ESL, health, history, mathematics, physical, physics, science, secondary, social science, social studies, special, technology/industrial arts, trade/industrial. **Engineering:** Mechanical. **English:** English lit. **History:** General, American. **Interdisciplinary:** Biological/physical sciences. **Legal studies:** Prelaw. **Liberal arts:** Arts/sciences. **Math:** General. **Parks/recreation:** Health/fitness, sports admin. **Protective services:** Criminal justice. **Psychology:** General. **Public administration:** Human services. **Social sciences:** General, political science, sociology. **Visual/performing arts:** General.

**Most popular majors.** Business/marketing 63%, education 11%, health sciences 8%.

**Computing on campus.** 85 workstations in dormitories, library, computer center, student center. Dormitories wired for high-speed internet access and linked to campus network. Commuter students can connect to campus network. Online library, helpline, repair service, wireless network available.

**Student life. Freshman orientation:** Mandatory. Preregistration for classes offered. Three-day orientation activities before classes begin in fall. **Housing:** Guaranteed on-campus for freshmen. Coed dorms, single-sex dorms, special housing for disabled, apartments, substance-free housing available. $100 partly refundable deposit, deadline 8/1. **Activities:** Bands, campus ministries, choral groups, dance, drama, literary magazine, music ensembles, musical theater, radio station, student government, student newspaper, Fellowship of Christian Athletes, Students for Minority Interests, international relations club, honor societies, computer club, various religious activity groups.

**Athletics.** NAIA. **Intercollegiate:** Baseball M, basketball, cheerleading M, cross-country, football (tackle) M, golf M, soccer, softball W, track and field, volleyball W, wrestling M. **Intramural:** Basketball, bowling, football (non-tackle) M, softball, table tennis, tennis, volleyball. **Team name:** Lady Statesmen, Statesmen.

**Student services.** Adult student services, alcohol/substance abuse counseling, career counseling, student employment services, financial aid counseling, personal counseling, placement for graduates, veterans' counselor. **Physically disabled:** Services for visually, hearing impaired.

**Contact.**   E-mail: admissions@wmpenn.edu
Phone: (641) 673-1012 Toll-free number: (800) 779-7366
Fax: (641) 673-2113
John Ottosson, Vice President for Enrollment Management, William Penn
University, 201 Trueblood Avenue, Oskaloosa, IA 52577

# Kansas

**Majors. Biology:** General, molecular, wildlife. **Business:** General, accounting, international. **Communications:** General, media studies. **Computer sciences:** Computer science, information systems, web page design. **Education:** Art, elementary, middle, music, secondary. **English:** English lit. **Foreign languages:** French, German, Spanish. **History:** General. **Interdisciplinary:** Global studies. **Math:** General. **Parks/recreation:** Exercise sciences, health/fitness, sports admin. **Philosophy/religion:** Philosophy, religion. **Physical sciences:** Chemistry, physics. **Psychology:** General. **Social sciences:** Economics, political science, sociology. **Visual/performing arts:** Art history/conservation, dramatic, studio arts.

**Most popular majors.** Biology 8%, business/marketing 30%, communications/journalism 6%, education 13%, parks/recreation 7%, psychology 7%.

**Computing on campus.** 222 workstations in dormitories, library, computer center. Dormitories wired for high-speed internet access and linked to campus network. Online library, helpline, repair service, student web hosting, wireless network available.

**Student life. Freshman orientation:** Available. Preregistration for classes offered. 2-day program in summer and 4-day program prior to start of fall term. **Policies:** Students required to live in campus or Greek housing unless granted permission to live off-campus. Freshmen not allowed to live in Greek housing. **Housing:** Guaranteed on-campus for freshmen. Coed dorms, single-sex dorms, special housing for disabled, apartments, fraternity/sorority housing available. $100 deposit. **Activities:** Bands, choral groups, dance, drama, international student organizations, literary magazine, music ensembles, radio station, student government, student newspaper, TV station, Mungano (minority student organization), Fellowship of Christian Athletes, Parmentors, Ambassadors, Earth We Are, College Republicans, Young Democrats, Bacchus.

**Athletics.** NAIA. **Intercollegiate:** Baseball M, basketball, cheerleading, cross-country, football (tackle) M, golf, soccer, softball W, tennis, track and field, volleyball W. **Intramural:** Basketball, football (non-tackle), softball, table tennis, volleyball. **Team name:** Wildcats.

**Student services.** Alcohol/substance abuse counseling, campus ministries, career counseling, student employment services, financial aid counseling, health services, minority student services, personal counseling, placement for graduates, veterans' counselor, women's services. **Physically disabled:** Services for visually, hearing impaired.

**Contact.** E-mail: admissions@bakeru.edu
Phone: (785) 594-8307 Toll-free number: (800) 873-4282
Fax: (785) 594-8372
Daniel McKinney, Director of Admissions, Baker University, 618 Eighth Street, Baldwin City, KS 66006-0065

---

## Baker University
**Baldwin City, Kansas**
www.bakeru.edu

CB member
CB code: 6031

- Private 4-year liberal arts and teachers college affiliated with United Methodist Church
- Residential campus in small town
- 911 degree-seeking undergraduates: 1% part-time, 54% women, 8% African American, 1% Asian American, 3% Hispanic American, 1% international
- 63% of applicants admitted
- SAT or ACT (ACT writing optional) required
- 56% graduate within 6 years

**General.** Founded in 1858. Regionally accredited. Additional campus locations include Overland Park, Topeka, Wichita, and Lee's Summit in Missouri. **Degrees:** 179 bachelor's awarded. **ROTC:** Army, Air Force. **Location:** 15 miles from Lawrence, 35 miles from Kansas City, Missouri. **Calendar:** 4-1-4, limited summer session. **Full-time faculty:** 70 total; 80% have terminal degrees, 47% women. **Part-time faculty:** 55 total; 16% have terminal degrees, 47% women. **Class size:** 71% < 20, 25% 20-39, 3% 40-49, less than 1% 50-99. **Special facilities:** Wetlands, old castle museum, bible collections, retail art gallery.

**Freshman class profile.** 1,141 applied, 716 admitted, 250 enrolled.

| Mid 50% test scores | | | |
|---|---|---|---|
| SAT critical reading: | 470-610 | Rank in top tenth: | 22% |
| SAT math: | 460-600 | Return as sophomores: | 78% |
| ACT composite: | 20-25 | Out-of-state: | 35% |
| GPA 3.50 or higher: | 58% | Live on campus: | 87% |
| GPA 3.0-3.49: | 30% | International: | 1% |
| GPA 2.0-2.99: | 12% | Fraternities: | 35% |
| Rank in top quarter: | 49% | Sororities: | 42% |

**Basis for selection.** Strong core curriculum during high school very important. GPA, class rank, course selection, ACT or SAT, and recommendation from high school core teacher or guidance counselor important. Involvement in school, community and church activities considered. Interview and essay recommended. Audition recommended for music and theater majors. Portfolio recommended for art majors. **Homeschooled:** Letter of recommendation (nonparent) required.

**High school preparation.** 17 units recommended. Recommended units include English 4, mathematics 3, social studies 3, science 3 (laboratory 1) and foreign language 2. One fine arts and one computing course recommended.

**2007-2008 Annual costs.** Tuition/fees: $18,830. Room/board: $6,150. Books/supplies: $1,200. Personal expenses: $1,400.

**2007-2008 Financial aid. Need-based:** Average need met was 85%. Average scholarship/grant was $6,358; average loan $4,136. 53% of total undergraduate aid awarded as scholarships/grants, 47% as loans/jobs. **Non-need-based:** Scholarships awarded for academics, alumni affiliation, art, athletics, leadership, music/drama, religious affiliation, ROTC.

**Application procedures. Admission:** No deadline. No application fee. Application may be submitted online. Admission notification on a rolling basis. **Financial aid:** Priority date 3/1; no closing date. FAFSA, institutional form required. Applicants notified on a rolling basis starting 3/1; must reply by 5/1 or within 6 week(s) of notification.

**Academics.** Liberal arts core consisting of nine hours stressing critical thinking skills, strong writing ability, and application of these skills to various academic disciplines required. **Special study options:** Accelerated study, double major, honors, independent study, internships, liberal arts/career combination, student-designed major, study abroad, teacher certification program. **Credit/placement by examination:** AP, CLEP, IB, SAT, ACT. **Support services:** Learning center, reduced course load, study skills assistance, tutoring, writing center.

---

## Barclay College
**Haviland, Kansas**
www.barclaycollege.edu

CB code: 6228

- Private 4-year Bible college affiliated with Evangelical Friends Alliance and Friends United Meeting
- Residential campus in rural community
- 114 degree-seeking undergraduates: 10% part-time, 49% women
- 124 graduate students
- 86% of applicants admitted
- ACT (writing optional), application essay, interview required

**General.** Founded in 1917. Accredited by ABHE. **Degrees:** 15 bachelor's, 2 associate awarded. **Location:** 100 miles from Wichita, 65 miles from Dodge City. **Calendar:** Semester, limited summer session. **Full-time faculty:** 6 total; 33% have terminal degrees, 17% minority, 33% women. **Part-time faculty:** 11 total; 18% have terminal degrees, 27% women. **Class size:** 81% < 20, 19% 20-39.

**Freshman class profile.** 49 applied, 42 admitted, 37 enrolled.

| Mid 50% test scores | | | |
|---|---|---|---|
| | | ACT composite: | 15-21 |
| SAT critical reading: | 480-680 | Out-of-state: | 38% |
| SAT math: | 480-640 | Live on campus: | 100% |
| SAT writing: | 450-570 | International: | 3% |

**Basis for selection.** Personal references and commitment to Christian vocation important. Committee reviews file and conducts phone interview. Audition recommended for music majors.

**2007-2008 Annual costs.** Tuition/fees: $12,300. Room/board: $6,000. Books/supplies: $1,000. Personal expenses: $1,000.

**2007-2008 Financial aid. Need-based:** 72% of total undergraduate aid awarded as scholarships/grants, 28% as loans/jobs. **Non-need-based:** Scholarships awarded for academics, alumni affiliation, leadership, music/drama, state residency.

**Application procedures. Admission:** Closing date 9/1. $25 fee, may be waived for applicants with need. Application may be submitted online. Admission notification on a rolling basis. **Financial aid:** Priority date 5/31, closing date 7/15. FAFSA, institutional form required. Applicants notified on a rolling basis starting 1/1; must reply within 4 week(s) of notification.

**Academics.** Each student has Bible major in addition to individually chosen major. Emphasis on practicums and internships. **Special study options:** Distance learning, double major, independent study, internships, liberal arts/career combination, teacher certification program. Cooperative classes with Pratt Community College. **Credit/placement by examination:** AP, CLEP, IB, SAT, ACT, institutional tests. 15 credit hours maximum toward associate degree, 30 toward bachelor's. **Support services:** Remedial instruction, study skills assistance, tutoring.

**Majors. Business:** General, business admin. **Education:** Elementary. **Philosophy/religion:** Religion. **Psychology:** General. **Theology:** Bible, missionary, pastoral counseling, sacred music, theology, youth ministry.

**Most popular majors.** Business/marketing 20%, education 27%, psychology 13%, theological studies 40%.

**Computing on campus.** 18 workstations in library, computer center. Dormitories wired for high-speed internet access and linked to campus network. Commuter students can connect to campus network. Online course registration, online library, repair service, wireless network available.

**Student life. Freshman orientation:** Mandatory. Preregistration for classes offered. **Policies:** Christian and social work required. Religious observance required. **Housing:** Guaranteed on-campus for freshmen. Single-sex dorms, substance-free housing available. $50 deposit. **Activities:** Jazz band, choral groups, drama, music ensembles, student government.

**Athletics. Intercollegiate:** Basketball, cheerleading M, golf, soccer M, tennis, volleyball W. **Intramural:** Baseball, basketball, bowling, softball, volleyball. **Team name:** Bears.

**Student services.** Campus ministries, career counseling, student employment services, financial aid counseling, health services, personal counseling, placement for graduates.

**Contact.** E-mail: admissions@barclaycollege.edu
Phone: (620) 862-5252 ext. 21 Toll-free number: (800) 862-0226
Fax: (620) 862-5242
Justin Kendall, Director of Admissions, Barclay College, 607 North Kingman, Haviland, KS 67059

---

## Benedictine College
**Atchison, Kansas**
www.benedictine.edu
**CB member**
**CB code: 6056**

- Private 4-year liberal arts college affiliated with Roman Catholic Church
- Residential campus in large town
- 1,306 degree-seeking undergraduates: 1% part-time, 52% women, 5% African American, 1% Asian American, 6% Hispanic American, 3% international
- 80 degree-seeking graduate students
- 68% of applicants admitted
- SAT or ACT (ACT writing optional) required
- 50% graduate within 6 years

**General. Founded** in 1858. Regionally accredited. Affiliated with Benedictine monastic order. Institution offers additional associate degree and bachelors degree programs in Hong Kong. **Degrees:** 206 bachelor's awarded; master's offered. **ROTC:** Army. **Location:** 45 miles from Kansas City, Missouri. **Calendar:** Semester, limited summer session. **Full-time faculty:** 70 total; 74% have terminal degrees, 7% minority, 26% women. **Part-time faculty:** 38 total; 40% have terminal degrees, 3% minority, 60% women. **Class size:** 63% < 20, 35% 20-39, 1% 40-49, less than 1% 50-99. **Special facilities:** Biological research area, high-tech classrooms, 2 performing arts theaters.

**Freshman class profile.** 1,505 applied, 1,020 admitted, 365 enrolled.

| Mid 50% test scores | | | |
|---|---|---|---|
| SAT critical reading: | 470-600 | Rank in top quarter: | 15% |
| SAT math: | 460-570 | Rank in top tenth: | 5% |
| ACT composite: | 20-26 | End year in good standing: | 75% |
| GPA 3.50 or higher: | 46% | Return as sophomores: | 74% |
| GPA 3.0-3.49: | 27% | Out-of-state: | 73% |
| GPA 2.0-2.99: | 26% | Live on campus: | 98% |

**Basis for selection.** Applicant must satisfy 2 of following requirements: GPA above 2.0, rank in top half of class, requisite ACT or SAT scores. Recommendations and interview considered. Interview recommended for academically weak applicants.

**High school preparation.** Required and recommended units include English 4, mathematics 3-4, social studies 2, history 2, science 2-4 and foreign language 2-4.

**2007-2008 Annual costs.** Tuition/fees: $17,700. Room/board: $6,478. Books/supplies: $2,400. Personal expenses: $2,800.

**2007-2008 Financial aid. Need-based:** 39% of total undergraduate aid awarded as scholarships/grants, 61% as loans/jobs. **Non-need-based:** Scholarships awarded for academics, alumni affiliation, art, athletics, job skills, leadership, minority status, music/drama, religious affiliation, ROTC.

**Application procedures. Admission:** No deadline. $25 fee, may be waived for applicants with need. Application may be submitted online. Admission notification on a rolling basis. Must reply by May 1 or within 4 week(s) if notified thereafter. **Financial aid:** Priority date 3/15; no closing date. FAFSA required. Applicants notified on a rolling basis starting 2/1; must reply within 2 week(s) of notification.

**Academics. Special study options:** Combined bachelor's/graduate degree, cooperative education, double major, dual enrollment of high school students, ESL, exchange student, independent study, internships, liberal arts/career combination, student-designed major, study abroad, teacher certification program. **Credit/placement by examination:** AP, CLEP, IB, institutional tests. 30 credit hours maximum toward associate degree, 30 toward bachelor's. **Support services:** Learning center, reduced course load, remedial instruction, study skills assistance, tutoring.

**Majors. Biology:** General, biochemistry. **Business:** Accounting, business admin, finance, international. **Communications:** Media studies. **Computer sciences:** Computer science. **Education:** Elementary, music, physical, special. **English:** English lit. **Foreign languages:** French, Spanish. **Health:** Athletic training. **History:** General. **Interdisciplinary:** Natural sciences. **Liberal arts:** Arts/sciences. **Math:** General. **Philosophy/religion:** Philosophy, religion. **Physical sciences:** Astronomy, chemistry, physics. **Psychology:** General. **Social sciences:** General, economics, political science, sociology. **Theology:** Youth ministry. **Visual/performing arts:** Dramatic, music management, theater arts management.

**Most popular majors.** Biology 6%, business/marketing 25%, communications/journalism 7%, education 18%, psychology 9%, theological studies 8%.

**Computing on campus.** 83 workstations in dormitories, library, computer center. Dormitories wired for high-speed internet access and linked to campus network. Helpline, repair service, wireless network available.

**Student life. Freshman orientation:** Mandatory. Preregistration for classes offered. Weekend program before classes commence. **Housing:** Guaranteed on-campus for freshmen. Coed dorms, single-sex dorms available. $100 deposit. Off-campus college-owned housing available. **Activities:** Bands, campus ministries, choral groups, dance, drama, literary magazine, music ensembles, musical theater, student government, student newspaper, symphony orchestra, Ravens Respect Life, Young Democrats, Young Republicans, Knights of Columbus, hunger coalition, Fellowship of Catholic University Students, Students in Free Enterprise, Black Student Union, Amnesty International.

**Athletics.** NAIA. **Intercollegiate:** Baseball M, basketball, cheerleading, cross-country, football (tackle) M, golf, soccer, softball W, tennis, track and field, volleyball W. **Intramural:** Baseball M, basketball, handball, racquetball, soccer, softball, table tennis, tennis, volleyball. **Team name:** Ravens.

**Student services.** Alcohol/substance abuse counseling, campus ministries, career counseling, student employment services, financial aid counseling, health services, personal counseling, placement for graduates, veterans' counselor. **Physically disabled:** Services for visually, speech, hearing impaired.

**Contact.** E-mail: bcadmiss@benedictine.edu
Phone: (913) 360-7476 Toll-free number: (800) 467-5340
Fax: (913) 367-5462
Pete Helgesen, Dean of Enrollment Management, Benedictine College, 1020 North Second Street, Atchison, KS 66002-1499

## Bethany College
### Lindsborg, Kansas
### www.bethanylb.edu                    CB code: 6034

- Private 4-year liberal arts college affiliated with Evangelical Lutheran Church in America
- Residential campus in small town
- 520 degree-seeking undergraduates: 2% part-time, 49% women, 10% African American, 1% Asian American, 6% Hispanic American, 1% Native American, 3% international
- 537 graduate students
- 61% of applicants admitted
- SAT or ACT (ACT writing optional) required
- 54% graduate within 6 years; 20% enter graduate study

**General.** Founded in 1881. Regionally accredited. **Degrees:** 101 bachelor's awarded. **Location:** 20 miles from Salina, 60 miles from Wichita. **Calendar:** 4-1-4, limited summer session. **Full-time faculty:** 43 total; 70% have terminal degrees, 2% minority, 35% women. **Part-time faculty:** 44 total; 25% have terminal degrees, 46% women. **Class size:** 82% < 20, 16% 20-39, 1% 40-49, less than 1% 50-99.

**Freshman class profile.** 632 applied, 388 admitted, 128 enrolled.

| Mid 50% test scores | | | |
|---|---|---|---|
| SAT critical reading: | 370-480 | Rank in top tenth: | 18% |
| SAT math: | 380-520 | End year in good standing: | 75% |
| SAT writing: | 370-480 | Return as sophomores: | 61% |
| ACT composite: | 20-25 | Out-of-state: | 43% |
| GPA 3.50 or higher: | 41% | Live on campus: | 95% |
| GPA 3.0-3.49: | 34% | International: | 3% |
| GPA 2.0-2.99: | 25% | Fraternities: | 2% |
| Rank in top quarter: | 45% | Sororities: | 1% |

**Basis for selection.** High school GPA, course selection, trends in grades, class rank, standardized test scores very important. Interview, letters of recommendation, leadership, curriculum, involvement considered. Interview and essay recommended for some. Audition required of music and theater majors. Portfolio required of art majors.

**High school preparation.** College-preparatory program recommended. Recommended units include English 4, mathematics 3, social studies 3, science 3 (laboratory 2) and foreign language 2.

**2008-2009 Annual costs.** Tuition/fees (projected): $18,124. Room/board: $5,650. Books/supplies: $1,000. Personal expenses: $1,900.

**2007-2008 Financial aid. Need-based:** 126 full-time freshmen applied for aid; 111 were judged to have need; 111 of these received aid. Average need met was 100%. Average scholarship/grant was $6,462; average loan $5,265. 52% of total undergraduate aid awarded as scholarships/grants, 48% as loans/jobs. **Non-need-based:** Awarded to 163 full-time undergraduates, including 52 freshmen. Scholarships awarded for academics, alumni affiliation, art, athletics, leadership, music/drama, religious affiliation. **Additional information:** State financial aid deadline March 15.

**Application procedures. Admission:** Priority date 2/1; deadline 6/15 (postmark date). $20 fee, may be waived for applicants with need. Application may be submitted online. Admission notification on a rolling basis. **Financial aid:** Priority date 3/15; no closing date. FAFSA required. Applicants notified on a rolling basis starting 2/1; must reply within 3 week(s) of notification.

**Academics. Special study options:** Accelerated study, combined bachelor's/graduate degree, cross-registration, double major, dual enrollment of high school students, exchange student, honors, independent study, internships, liberal arts/career combination, student-designed major, study abroad, teacher certification program, urban semester, Washington semester. Special education program with Associated Colleges of Central Kansas. **Credit/placement by examination:** AP, CLEP, IB, institutional tests. 32 credit hours maximum toward bachelor's degree. **Support services:** Learning center, reduced course load, study skills assistance, tutoring, writing center.

**Majors. Biology:** General. **Business:** Accounting, business admin, finance, managerial economics, marketing. **Communications:** General. **Education:**

General, art, biology, business, chemistry, elementary, English, history, mathematics, music, physical, secondary, social science. **English:** English lit, speech/rhetoric. **Health:** Art therapy, athletic training. **History:** General. **Liberal arts:** Arts/sciences. **Math:** General. **Parks/recreation:** Facilities management, sports admin. **Philosophy/religion:** Christian. **Physical sciences:** Chemistry. **Protective services:** Criminal justice, police science. **Psychology:** General. **Public administration:** Social work. **Social sciences:** General, economics, sociology. **Visual/performing arts:** Art, music performance.

**Most popular majors.** Biology 10%, business/marketing 27%, education 25%, visual/performing arts 11%.

**Computing on campus.** 40 workstations in library, computer center. Dormitories wired for high-speed internet access and linked to campus network. Commuter students can connect to campus network. Online library available.

**Student life. Freshman orientation:** Mandatory. Preregistration for classes offered. 3 days of activities; planned and organized by returning students. **Policies:** No alcohol allowed on campus. **Housing:** Coed dorms, single-sex dorms, substance-free housing available. $100 deposit, deadline 8/1. Full-time students required to live on campus until age 21 or special consideration given. Special interest housing available. **Activities:** Bands, campus ministries, choral groups, dance, drama, international student organizations, music ensembles, musical theater, student government, student newspaper, symphony orchestra, SOAR (Student Outreach or Active Response), Blue Key, Gold Key, Alpha Omega (men's Christian fellowship), Bethany youth ministry program, Bread for the World, departmental organizations, honorary societies.

**Athletics.** NAIA. **Intercollegiate:** Baseball M, basketball, cross-country, football (tackle) M, golf M, soccer, softball W, tennis, track and field, volleyball W. **Intramural:** Basketball, football (non-tackle), racquetball, soccer, softball, table tennis, volleyball, weight lifting. **Team name:** Swedes.

**Student services.** Alcohol/substance abuse counseling, campus ministries, career counseling, student employment services, financial aid counseling, health services, minority student services, personal counseling, placement for graduates, veterans' counselor.

**Contact.** E-mail: admissions@bethanylb.edu
Phone: (785) 227-3380 ext. 8113 Toll-free number: (800) 826-2281
Fax: (785) 227-8993
Tricia Hawk, Dean of Admissions and Financial Aid, Bethany College, 335 East Swensson, Lindsborg, KS 67456-1897

## Bethel College
### North Newton, Kansas
### www.bethelks.edu                    CB code: 6037

- Private 4-year liberal arts college affiliated with Mennonite Church
- Residential campus in large town
- 541 degree-seeking undergraduates: 5% part-time, 50% women, 6% African American, 2% Asian American, 4% Hispanic American, 1% Native American, 11% international
- 75% of applicants admitted
- SAT or ACT (ACT writing optional) required
- 51% graduate within 6 years

**General.** Founded in 1887. Regionally accredited. **Degrees:** 120 bachelor's awarded. **Location:** 25 miles from Wichita. **Calendar:** 4-1-4, limited summer session. **Full-time faculty:** 49 total; 57% have terminal degrees, 47% women. **Part-time faculty:** 22 total; 32% have terminal degrees, 9% minority, 64% women. **Class size:** 65% < 20, 28% 20-39, 2% 40-49, 4% 50-99, less than 1% >100. **Special facilities:** Natural history museum, 80-acre natural history field laboratory, institute for peace and conflict resolution, Mennonite library and archives, observatory, conservatory.

**Freshman class profile.** 411 applied, 310 admitted, 108 enrolled.

| Mid 50% test scores | | | |
|---|---|---|---|
| SAT critical reading: | 450-540 | Rank in top quarter: | 43% |
| SAT math: | 440-560 | Rank in top tenth: | 17% |
| ACT composite: | 20-27 | End year in good standing: | 86% |
| GPA 3.50 or higher: | 50% | Return as sophomores: | 72% |
| GPA 3.0-3.49: | 34% | Out-of-state: | 26% |
| GPA 2.0-2.99: | 15% | Live on campus: | 92% |
| | | International: | 6% |

**Basis for selection.** Automatic admission generally given to students with high school GPA of 2.5 and ACT score of at least 19 or SAT of at least

890 (exclusive of Writing). Essay recommended for academically weak applicants. Audition recommended for drama and music majors. Portfolio recommended for art majors. **Homeschooled:** Evaluative transcript or GED score. ACT or SAT score is also required.

**High school preparation.** College-preparatory program recommended. 18 units recommended. Recommended units include English 4, mathematics 4, social studies 3, history 1, science 3, foreign language 2 and computer science 1.

**2007-2008 Annual costs.** Tuition/fees: $17,800. Room/board: $6,400.

**2006-2007 Financial aid. Need-based:** 97 full-time freshmen applied for aid; 97 were judged to have need; 97 of these received aid. Average need met was 97%. Average scholarship/grant was $3,805; average loan $3,717. 33% of total undergraduate aid awarded as scholarships/grants, 67% as loans/jobs. **Non-need-based:** Awarded to 661 full-time undergraduates, including 170 freshmen. Scholarships awarded for academics, alumni affiliation, art, athletics, minority status, music/drama, religious affiliation, state residency.

**Application procedures. Admission:** No deadline. $20 fee, may be waived for applicants with need. Application may be submitted online. Admission notification on a rolling basis beginning on or about 9/1. **Financial aid:** No deadline. FAFSA required. Applicants notified on a rolling basis starting 2/1; must reply within 2 week(s) of notification.

**Academics.** Curriculum founded on general education program in liberal arts and sciences. Distinctive elements include peace, justice and conflict studies, collaborative inquiry seminary, convocation, and cross-cultural learning requirements and senior capstone course focusing on basic issues of faith and life. **Special study options:** Cross-registration, double major, dual enrollment of high school students, independent study, internships, liberal arts/career combination, study abroad, teacher certification program, urban semester, Washington semester. **Credit/placement by examination:** AP, CLEP, IB, SAT, ACT, institutional tests. **Support services:** Learning center, study skills assistance, tutoring.

**Majors. Biology:** General. **Business:** General. **Communications:** Media studies. **Computer sciences:** Computer science. **Education:** Elementary. **English:** English lit. **Foreign languages:** German, Spanish. **Health:** Athletic training, nursing (RN). **History:** General. **Interdisciplinary:** Natural sciences. **Math:** General. **Parks/recreation:** Health/fitness. **Philosophy/religion:** Religion. **Physical sciences:** Chemistry, physics. **Psychology:** General. **Public administration:** Social work. **Visual/performing arts:** Studio arts.

**Most popular majors.** Business/marketing 9%, education 8%, health sciences 34%, physical sciences 6%, psychology 7%, visual/performing arts 6%.

**Computing on campus.** 56 workstations in library, computer center. Dormitories wired for high-speed internet access and linked to campus network. Commuter students can connect to campus network. Helpline, repair service, student web hosting, wireless network available.

**Student life. Freshman orientation:** Mandatory. Preregistration for classes offered. Held the Wednesday through Sunday before classes begin. **Policies:** Chapel services voluntary. 2 weekly convocations required and credited as part of general education. **Housing:** Guaranteed on-campus for all undergraduates. Coed dorms, special housing for disabled, apartments, substance-free housing available. **Activities:** Bands, campus ministries, choral groups, dance, drama, international student organizations, literary magazine, music ensembles, musical theater, opera, radio station, student government, student newspaper, symphony orchestra, Student Community Action Network for voluntary services, peace club, Bethel Christian Fellowship, service corps-disaster response, Fellowship of Christian Athletes, Amnesty International, environmental action club, Catholic student organization.

**Athletics.** NAIA. **Intercollegiate:** Basketball, cross-country, football (tackle) M, golf, soccer, tennis, track and field, volleyball W. **Intramural:** Badminton, basketball, bowling, football (non-tackle), golf, racquetball, softball, table tennis, tennis, volleyball. **Team name:** Threshers.

**Student services.** Alcohol/substance abuse counseling, campus ministries, career counseling, student employment services, financial aid counseling, health services, minority student services, personal counseling. **Physically disabled:** Services for visually, hearing impaired.

**Contact.** E-mail: admissions@bethelks.edu
Phone: (316) 284-5230 Toll-free number: (800) 522-1887 ext. 230
Fax: (316) 284-5870
Allan Bartel, Director of Admissions and Enrollment, Bethel College, 300 East 27th Street, North Newton, KS 67117-0531

# Central Christian College of Kansas
**McPherson, Kansas**
**www.centralchristian.edu**                     CB code: 6088

- Private 4-year liberal arts college affiliated with Free Methodist Church of North America
- Residential campus in large town
- 307 degree-seeking undergraduates: 47% women, 13% African American, 1% Asian American, 5% Hispanic American, 2% Native American, 3% international
- 49% of applicants admitted

**General.** Founded in 1884. Regionally accredited. **Degrees:** 46 bachelor's, 34 associate awarded. **Location:** 55 miles from Wichita. **Calendar:** 4-1-4. **Full-time faculty:** 19 total; 10% have terminal degrees, 21% women. **Part-time faculty:** 18 total; 11% have terminal degrees, 39% women. **Class size:** 76% < 20, 18% 20-39, 2% 40-49, 4% 50-99.

**Freshman class profile.** 551 applied, 268 admitted, 89 enrolled.

| | | | |
|---|---|---|---|
| GPA 3.50 or higher: | 37% | End year in good standing: | 88% |
| GPA 3.0-3.49: | 40% | Return as sophomores: | 52% |
| GPA 2.0-2.99: | 21% | Out-of-state: | 35% |
| Rank in top quarter: | 27% | Live on campus: | 99% |
| Rank in top tenth: | 10% | International: | 5% |

**Basis for selection.** Secondary school record, recommendations very important; test scores important. SAT or ACT recommended. SAT/ACT required for applicants with GPA lower than 2.5. Interview and essay recommended. **Homeschooled:** Transcript of courses and grades, letter of recommendation (nonparent) required. Transcript required. **Learning Disabled:** Provide Individualized Education Program (IEP).

**High school preparation.** 22 units required. Required units include English 4, mathematics 2, social studies 2, history 1, science 2 (laboratory 1). 1 computer technology recommended.

**2008-2009 Annual costs.** Tuition/fees (projected): $16,000. Room/board: $5,500. Books/supplies: $1,000. Personal expenses: $1,000.

**2007-2008 Financial aid. Need-based:** 74 full-time freshmen applied for aid; 66 were judged to have need; 66 of these received aid. Average need met was 78%. Average scholarship/grant was $4,354; average loan $4,472. 37% of total undergraduate aid awarded as scholarships/grants, 63% as loans/jobs. **Non-need-based:** Awarded to 411 full-time undergraduates, including 139 freshmen. Scholarships awarded for academics, alumni affiliation, athletics, leadership, music/drama, religious affiliation.

**Application procedures. Admission:** Closing date 7/1 (receipt date). $20 fee, may be waived for applicants with need. Application may be submitted online. Admission notification on a rolling basis. **Financial aid:** Priority date 3/1; no closing date. FAFSA required. Applicants notified on a rolling basis starting 3/1; must reply within 4 week(s) of notification.

**Academics. Special study options:** Cooperative education, cross-registration, double major, dual enrollment of high school students, independent study, internships, liberal arts/career combination, student-designed major, urban semester, Washington semester. **Credit/placement by examination:** AP, CLEP, IB, SAT, ACT. 30 credit hours maximum toward associate degree, 30 toward bachelor's. **Support services:** Learning center, reduced course load, remedial instruction, study skills assistance, tutoring.

**Majors. Biology:** General, exercise physiology. **Business:** General, accounting, accounting/business management, business admin, managerial economics, office management, small business admin. **Communications:** General, media studies. **English:** English lit, speech/rhetoric. **Health:** Athletic training, health services. **History:** General. **Interdisciplinary:** Accounting/computer science, natural sciences. **Liberal arts:** Arts/sciences. **Math:** General. **Parks/recreation:** Exercise sciences, facilities management, sports admin. **Philosophy/religion:** Religion. **Physical sciences:** Chemistry. **Protective services:** Law enforcement admin, police science, security management. **Psychology:** General. **Social sciences:** General. **Theology:** Bible, missionary, pastoral counseling, sacred music, theology, youth ministry. **Visual/performing arts:** General, dramatic, music performance, music theory/composition, piano/organ.

**Most popular majors.** Business/marketing 15%, health sciences 11%, liberal arts 24%, natural resources/environmental science 9%, psychology 9%, social sciences 11%, theological studies 13%.

**Computing on campus.** 30 workstations in library, computer center, student center. Dormitories wired for high-speed internet access. Commuter students can connect to campus network. Online course registration, online library, helpline, repair service, wireless network available.

**Student life. Freshman orientation:** Mandatory. Preregistration for classes offered. Fall semester first seven weeks. Interterm and spring 1-2 days. **Policies:** Students must sign a life-style covenant. Alcohol, smoking, drugs not allowed on campus. **Housing:** Guaranteed on-campus for all undergraduates. Coed dorms, single-sex dorms, apartments, substance-free housing available. $150 fully refundable deposit, deadline 8/1. Students 23 years of age or older can live off campus. **Activities:** Bands, campus ministries, choral groups, drama, literary magazine, music ensembles, musical theater, radio station, student government, student newspaper, symphony orchestra, Christian service organization, Flying Tigers, prison ministries, performing arts club, Share teams, C.O.L.O.R.S., PBL, student activities council.

**Athletics.** NAIA. **Intercollegiate:** Baseball M, basketball, cheerleading, cross-country, golf, soccer, softball W, tennis, volleyball W. **Intramural:** Badminton, basketball, bowling, football (non-tackle) M, golf, soccer, softball, table tennis, tennis, volleyball. **Team name:** Tigers.

**Student services.** Adult student services, campus ministries, career counseling, student employment services, financial aid counseling, health services, personal counseling, placement for graduates. **Physically disabled:** Services for visually, speech impaired.

**Contact.** E-mail: admissions@centralchristian.edu
Phone: (620) 241-0723 ext. 337 Toll-free number: (800) 835-0078 ext. 337
Fax: (620) 241-6032
J. Ferrell, Dean of Enrollment, Central Christian College of Kansas, 1200 South Main, McPherson, KS 67460-5740

---

## Emporia State University
**Emporia, Kansas**
**www.emporia.edu**                                   **CB code: 6335**

- Public 4-year university and teachers college
- Commuter campus in large town
- 4,240 degree-seeking undergraduates: 10% part-time, 61% women, 4% African American, 1% Asian American, 4% Hispanic American, 1% Native American, 5% international
- 1,675 degree-seeking graduate students
- 87% of applicants admitted
- SAT or ACT (ACT writing optional) required
- 45% graduate within 6 years; 19% enter graduate study

**General.** Founded in 1863. Regionally accredited. **Degrees:** 771 bachelor's awarded; master's, doctoral offered. **Location:** 50 miles from Topeka, 77 miles from Wichita. **Calendar:** Semester, extensive summer session. **Full-time faculty:** 258 total; 83% have terminal degrees, 9% minority, 43% women. **Part-time faculty:** 5 total; 40% have terminal degrees, 60% women. **Class size:** 46% < 20, 40% 20-39, 9% 40-49, 6% 50-99, less than 1% >100. **Special facilities:** Planetarium, natural history reserve, natural history museum, National Teachers Hall of Fame, Great Plains study center.

**Freshman class profile.** 1,605 applied, 1,389 admitted, 766 enrolled.

| Mid 50% test scores | | Out-of-state: | 8% |
|---|---|---|---|
| ACT composite: | 19-24 | Live on campus: | 90% |
| End year in good standing: | 76% | International: | 2% |
| Return as sophomores: | 71% | | |

**Basis for selection.** Applicants must have one of following: minimum ACT score of 21, rank in top third of high school class, minimum 2.0 GPA in Kansas Core Curriculum for in-state students, or 2.5 GPA for out-of-state students. Limited number of students who do not meet qualifications may be admitted through 10% exceptions window. ACT scores must be received by end of first semester of study. **Homeschooled:** GED must be submitted.

**High school preparation.** College-preparatory program recommended. Required units include English 4, mathematics 3, social studies 3, science 3 and academic electives 1. 1 computer technology recommended. These units required for students who do not have minimum ACT score of 21, or in top 1/3 of high school class.

**2007-2008 Annual costs.** Tuition/fees: $3,926; $11,976 out-of-state. Room/board: $5,582. Books/supplies: $900. Personal expenses: $2,650.

**2006-2007 Financial aid. Need-based:** 682 full-time freshmen applied for aid; 423 were judged to have need; 423 of these received aid. Average need met was 70%. Average scholarship/grant was $2,068; average loan $2,530. 38% of total undergraduate aid awarded as scholarships/grants, 62% as loans/jobs. **Non-need-based:** Awarded to 1,695 full-time undergraduates, including 492 freshmen. Scholarships awarded for academics, alumni affiliation, art, athletics, job skills, leadership, minority status, music/drama, religious affiliation, state residency. **Additional information:** Institution's own payment plan is available.

**Application procedures. Admission:** No deadline. $30 fee, may be waived for applicants with need. Application may be submitted online. Admission notification on a rolling basis. Must reply by May 1 or within 2 week(s) if notified thereafter. **Financial aid:** Priority date 3/15; no closing date. FAFSA required. Applicants notified on a rolling basis starting 2/2; must reply within 2 week(s) of notification.

**Academics. Special study options:** Distance learning, double major, dual enrollment of high school students, ESL, honors, independent study, internships, student-designed major, study abroad, teacher certification program. Career development center and programs, continuing education courses, evening program, interdisciplinary or interdepartmental courses of study, learning assistance programs, pass-fail grading option, service members' opportunity college, summer sessions, tutorial program, trio programs. **Credit/placement by examination:** AP, CLEP, IB, ACT, institutional tests. 30 credit hours maximum toward bachelor's degree. **Support services:** Remedial instruction, writing center.

**Majors. Biology:** General, Biochemistry/biophysics and molecular biology. **Business:** Accounting, business admin, human resources, marketing. **Communications:** General. **Computer sciences:** General, information systems, security. **Education:** Elementary, music, secondary. **English:** English lit. **Foreign languages:** General. **Health:** Athletic training, nursing (RN), public health ed, vocational rehab counseling. **History:** General. **Liberal arts:** Arts/sciences. **Math:** General. **Parks/recreation:** General. **Physical sciences:** General, chemistry, geology, physics. **Psychology:** General. **Social sciences:** General, economics, political science, sociology. **Visual/performing arts:** Art, dramatic. **Other:** Crime and Delinquencies Studies, Information Resources Studies.

**Most popular majors.** Business/marketing 22%, education 31%, health sciences 7%, social sciences 8%, visual/performing arts 6%.

**Computing on campus.** 410 workstations in dormitories, library, computer center, student center. Dormitories wired for high-speed internet access and linked to campus network. Commuter students can connect to campus network. Online library, helpline, student web hosting, wireless network available.

**Student life. Freshman orientation:** Available, $35 fee. Preregistration for classes offered. One-day program for students and parents; held during summer and prior to start of classes. **Housing:** Guaranteed on-campus for freshmen. Coed dorms, special housing for disabled, apartments, fraternity/sorority housing, substance-free housing available. $145 partly refundable deposit, deadline 7/1. **Activities:** Bands, campus ministries, choral groups, dance, drama, film society, international student organizations, literary magazine, music ensembles, musical theater, opera, student government, student newspaper, symphony orchestra, Black Student Union, Hispanic American leadership organization, Catholic Campus Community, Christian student center, Black women's network, Muslim student association, Fellowship of Christian Athletes, Arabic language club, East Asian club, Campus Crusade for Christ.

**Athletics.** NCAA. **Intercollegiate:** Baseball M, basketball, cheerleading, cross-country, football (tackle) M, soccer W, softball W, tennis, track and field, volleyball W. **Intramural:** Badminton, basketball, football (non-tackle), softball, table tennis, tennis, volleyball. **Team name:** Hornets.

**Student services.** Adult student services, alcohol/substance abuse counseling, campus ministries, career counseling, services for economically disadvantaged, student employment services, financial aid counseling, health services, legal services, minority student services, on-campus daycare, personal counseling, placement for graduates, veterans' counselor, women's services. **Physically disabled:** Services for visually, speech, hearing impaired.

**Contact.** E-mail: go2esu@emporia.edu
Phone: (620) 341-5465 Toll-free number: (877) 468-6378
Fax: (620) 341-5599
Laura Eddy, Director of Admisions, Emporia State University, 1200 Commercial, Campus Box 4034, Emporia, KS 66801-5087

---

## Fort Hays State University
**Hays, Kansas**                                      **CB member**
**www.fhsu.edu**                                      **CB code: 6218**

- Public 4-year university
- Commuter campus in large town
- 7,926 degree-seeking undergraduates: 48% part-time, 51% women, 2% African American, 1% Asian American, 3% Hispanic American, 30% international
- 1,029 degree-seeking graduate students
- 88% of applicants admitted

◆ SAT or ACT with writing required
◆ 48% graduate within 6 years

**General.** Founded in 1902. Regionally accredited. **Degrees:** 7 associate awarded; master's offered. **Location:** 170 miles from Wichita, 270 miles from Kansas City. **Calendar:** Semester, extensive summer session. **Full-time faculty:** 268 total; 67% have terminal degrees, 6% minority, 40% women. **Part-time faculty:** 135 total; 22% have terminal degrees, 2% minority, 57% women. **Class size:** 50% < 20, 41% 20-39, 5% 40-49, 3% 50-99, less than 1% >100. **Special facilities:** Observatory, paleontology, natural history, archeology, history, geology, botanical-zoological museums.

**Freshman class profile.** 1,477 applied, 1,301 admitted, 802 enrolled.

| Mid 50% test scores | | | |
|---|---|---|---|
| ACT composite: | 18-24 | Return as sophomores: | 66% |
| GPA 3.50 or higher: | 41% | Out-of-state: | 15% |
| GPA 3.0-3.49: | 31% | Live on campus: | 69% |
| GPA 2.0-2.99: | 26% | International: | 1% |
| Rank in top quarter: | 31% | Fraternities: | 4% |
| Rank in top tenth: | 10% | Sororities: | 3% |

**Basis for selection.** One of following required: minimum ACT composite score of 21, rank in top third of high school class, or minimum 2.0 GPA on Kansas pre-college curriculum (2.5 GPA for out-of-state students). Audition recommended for music majors.

**High school preparation.** 14 units recommended. Recommended units include English 4, mathematics 3, social studies 2, history 1, science 3 and computer science 1.

**2007-2008 Annual costs.** Tuition/fees: $3,355; $10,543 out-of-state. Room/board: $5,878. Books/supplies: $800. Personal expenses: $2,082.

**2006-2007 Financial aid. Need-based:** 533 full-time freshmen applied for aid; 416 were judged to have need; 412 of these received aid. Average need met was 66%. Average scholarship/grant was $3,882; average loan $2,278. 33% of total undergraduate aid awarded as scholarships/grants, 67% as loans/jobs. **Non-need-based:** Awarded to 1,444 full-time undergraduates, including 393 freshmen. Scholarships awarded for academics, art, athletics, leadership, minority status, music/drama.

**Application procedures. Admission:** No deadline. $30 fee. Application may be submitted online. Admission notification on a rolling basis. **Financial aid:** Priority date 3/15; no closing date. FAFSA required. Applicants notified on a rolling basis starting 3/15; must reply within 2 week(s) of notification.

**Academics. Special study options:** Distance learning, double major, dual enrollment of high school students, ESL, exchange student, external degree, honors, independent study, internships, liberal arts/career combination, student-designed major, study abroad, teacher certification program, United Nations semester. **Credit/placement by examination:** AP, CLEP, ACT, institutional tests. **Support services:** Learning center, pre-admission summer program, reduced course load, remedial instruction, study skills assistance, tutoring, writing center.

**Majors. Agriculture:** Business. **Biology:** General. **Business:** General, accounting, business admin, market research, marketing, office management. **Communications:** General. **Computer sciences:** General. **Education:** Business, elementary, music, physical, technology/industrial arts, trade/industrial. **English:** English lit. **Foreign languages:** General. **Health:** Physical therapy assistant, sonography. **History:** General. **Interdisciplinary:** Biological/physical sciences. **Math:** General. **Philosophy/religion:** Philosophy. **Physical sciences:** Chemistry, geology, physics. **Protective services:** Criminal justice. **Psychology:** General. **Public administration:** Social work. **Social sciences:** Economics, political science, sociology. **Visual/performing arts:** Art.

**Most popular majors.** Business/marketing 11%, education 11%, health sciences 7%, liberal arts 47%.

**Computing on campus.** 1,400 workstations in dormitories, library, computer center, student center. Dormitories linked to campus network. Commuter students can connect to campus network. Online course registration, helpline available.

**Student life. Freshman orientation:** Mandatory, $25 fee. Preregistration for classes offered. 3-day program before start of classes; includes skills training. **Housing:** Guaranteed on-campus for freshmen. Coed dorms, single-sex dorms, apartments, fraternity/sorority housing available. $35 nonrefundable deposit. **Activities:** Bands, campus ministries, choral groups, dance, drama, international student organizations, literary magazine, music ensembles, musical theater, opera, radio station, student government, student newspaper, symphony orchestra, TV station, Campus Crusade for Christ,

Disciples of the Catholic Campus Center, Black Student Union, Hispanic American leadership organization, Young Republicans, Young Democrats.

**Athletics.** NCAA. **Intercollegiate:** Baseball M, basketball, cross-country, football (tackle) M, golf, gymnastics W, rodeo, softball W, tennis, track and field, volleyball W, wrestling M. **Intramural:** Archery, badminton, baseball M, basketball, bowling, cross-country, diving, fencing, field hockey W, gymnastics W, racquetball, soccer, softball, swimming, table tennis, tennis, track and field, volleyball, water polo, wrestling M.

**Student services.** Adult student services, career counseling, student employment services, financial aid counseling, health services, on-campus daycare, personal counseling, placement for graduates, veterans' counselor. **Physically disabled:** Services for visually, speech, hearing impaired.

**Contact.** E-mail: tigers@fshu.edu
Phone: (785) 628-5666 Toll-free number: (800) 628-3478
Fax: (785) 432-0248
Roger Schieferecke, Director of Admissions Counseling, Fort Hays State University, 600 Park Street, Hays, KS 67601

---

## Friends University
### Wichita, Kansas
**www.friends.edu**        CB code: 6224

◆ Private 4-year business and liberal arts college affiliated with nondenominational tradition
◆ Commuter campus in large city
◆ 1,354 degree-seeking undergraduates
◆ 858 graduate students
◆ SAT or ACT (ACT writing optional) required

**General.** Founded in 1898. Regionally accredited. **Degrees:** 537 bachelor's, 39 associate awarded; master's offered. **Location:** 1 mile from downtown. **Calendar:** Semester, limited summer session. **Full-time faculty:** 80 total. **Part-time faculty:** 155 total. **Special facilities:** Art center, observatory, Quaker collection.

**Freshman class profile.**

| Mid 50% test scores | | | |
|---|---|---|---|
| | | SAT math: | 420-620 |
| SAT critical reading: | 400-570 | ACT composite: | 18-24 |

**Basis for selection.** ACT score multiplied by GPA must equal 45 or above for admission. Those with score between 20 and 29 admitted provisionally. Audition required of music majors. Portfolio recommended for art majors.

**High school preparation.** 11 units required. Required units include English 4, social studies 2 and science 2.

**2008-2009 Annual costs.** Tuition/fees (projected): $18,320. Room/board: $5,450. Books/supplies: $1,000. Personal expenses: $1,642.

**Financial aid. Non-need-based:** Scholarships awarded for academics, alumni affiliation, art, athletics, leadership, music/drama. **Additional information:** Scholarships for clergy/family of clergy available.

**Application procedures. Admission:** No deadline. $45 fee, may be waived for applicants with need. Admission notification on a rolling basis. **Financial aid:** Priority date 3/15; no closing date. FAFSA, institutional form required. Applicants notified on a rolling basis; must reply within 3 week(s) of notification.

**Academics. Special study options:** Cross-registration, double major, dual enrollment of high school students, external degree, honors, independent study, liberal arts/career combination, student-designed major, study abroad, teacher certification program. Degree completion program for working adults. **Credit/placement by examination:** CLEP, IB. 60 credit hours maximum toward bachelor's degree. **Support services:** Reduced course load, study skills assistance, tutoring, writing center.

**Majors. Biology:** General. **Business:** Accounting, business admin, human resources, international, management information systems. **Communications:** General. **Computer sciences:** General. **Education:** Art, early childhood, elementary, English, mathematics, middle, music, physical, science, secondary, social science, Spanish. **English:** English lit. **Foreign languages:** Spanish. **Health:** Health care admin, medical radiologic technology/radiation therapy. **History:** General. **Liberal arts:** Arts/sciences. **Math:** General. **Parks/recreation:** Facilities management, health/fitness. **Physical sciences:** Chemistry. **Psychology:** General. **Social sciences:** Political science, sociology. **Theology:** Youth ministry. **Visual/performing arts:** Art, dance, dramatic, music performance.

**Computing on campus.** 142 workstations in dormitories, library, computer center. Dormitories linked to campus network. Commuter students can connect to campus network.

**Student life. Freshman orientation:** Mandatory. Preregistration for classes offered. **Housing:** Coed dorms, apartments available. $100 deposit. **Activities:** Bands, choral groups, dance, drama, literary magazine, music ensembles, musical theater, opera, student government, student newspaper, symphony orchestra.

**Athletics.** NAIA. **Intercollegiate:** Baseball M, basketball, cheerleading M, cross-country, football (tackle) M, golf M, soccer, softball W, tennis, track and field, volleyball W. **Intramural:** Basketball, bowling, racquetball, soccer, softball, table tennis, volleyball. **Team name:** Falcons.

**Student services.** Adult student services, career counseling, student employment services, health services, personal counseling, placement for graduates, veterans' counselor. **Physically disabled:** Services for visually, speech, hearing impaired.

**Contact.** E-mail: learn@friends.edu
Phone: (316) 295-5100 Toll-free number: (800) 577-2233
Fax: (316) 295-5101
Marla Sexson, Director of Undergraduate Admissions, Friends University, 2100 University, Wichita, KS 67213

---

### Haskell Indian Nations University
**Lawrence, Kansas**
**www.haskell.edu**                                    **CB code: 0919**

- Public 4-year university
- Residential campus in small city
- 889 degree-seeking undergraduates
- SAT or ACT (ACT writing optional) required

**General.** Founded in 1884. Regionally accredited. Federally owned and operated college provides educational benefits to North American Indians who are under jurisdiction of Bureau of Indian Affairs. Students receive tuition, books, and some college housing. **Degrees:** 50 bachelor's, 106 associate awarded. **ROTC:** Air Force. **Location:** 38 miles from Kansas City, Missouri. **Calendar:** Semester, limited summer session. **Full-time faculty:** 45 total. **Part-time faculty:** 15 total. **Special facilities:** Wetlands south of campus.

**Freshman class profile.**

| Mid 50% test scores | | Out-of-state: | 90% |
|---|---|---|---|
| ACT composite: | 15-19 | Live on campus: | 90% |

**Basis for selection.** For bachelor's programs, secondary school record, class rank important; recommendations, test scores considered. Associate degree programs are open admission. Students must be certified by Bureau of Indian Affairs as member of federally-recognized tribe or quarter degree descendant of tribal member. SAT/ACT scores not used in admission decisions for associate programs. **Learning Disabled:** Must provide IEP from high school and test scores not more than 2 years old.

**2007-2008 Annual costs.** Haskell does not charge tuition. On-campus students pay $440 (includes room/board and required fees) for academic year; off-campus students pay $248 (required fees) for academic year. Books/supplies: $220.

**Financial aid. Additional information:** Some personal expenses may be offset by Bureau of Indian Affairs grants. Most students qualify for only minimum Pell grant.

**Application procedures. Admission:** Closing date 6/30 (postmark date). $10 fee, may be waived for applicants with need. Admission notification on a rolling basis beginning on or about 3/10. **Financial aid:** Priority date 5/15; no closing date. FAFSA required. Applicants notified on a rolling basis starting 3/15; must reply within 9 week(s) of notification.

**Academics. Special study options:** Cooperative education, independent study, internships. **Credit/placement by examination:** CLEP. 10 credit hours maximum toward associate degree. **Support services:** Learning center, reduced course load, remedial instruction, tutoring, writing center.

**Majors. Area/ethnic studies:** Native American. **Business:** Business admin. **Conservation:** General. **Education:** General, elementary.

**Computing on campus.** 45 workstations in dormitories, library, computer center, student center.

**Student life. Freshman orientation:** Mandatory. Preregistration for classes offered. 3 days preceding start of classes. **Housing:** Coed dorms, single-sex dorms available. $35 deposit. **Activities:** Choral groups, drama, student government, student newspaper, Native American clubs, Phi Beta Lambda (service organization), Baptist Student Union, LIGHT House (Lutheran organization), Catholic Center.

**Athletics.** NAIA. **Intercollegiate:** Basketball, cross-country, football (tackle) M, golf M, track and field, volleyball. **Intramural:** Basketball, bowling, racquetball, softball, volleyball, wrestling M. **Team name:** Indians.

**Student services.** Adult student services, alcohol/substance abuse counseling, career counseling, student employment services, financial aid counseling, health services, personal counseling, placement for graduates, veterans' counselor, women's services.

**Contact.** Phone: (785) 749-8454 Fax: (913) 749-8429
Ellen Allen, Director of Admissions and Records, Haskell Indian Nations University, 155 Indian Avenue #5031, Lawrence, KS 66046-4800

---

### Kansas State University
**Manhattan, Kansas**                                  **CB member**
**www.ksu.edu**                                        **CB code: 6334**

- Public 4-year university and technical college
- Commuter campus in large town
- 18,235 degree-seeking undergraduates: 11% part-time, 48% women, 3% African American, 1% Asian American, 3% Hispanic American, 1% Native American, 2% international
- 3,503 degree-seeking graduate students
- 95% of applicants admitted
- 57% graduate within 6 years

**General.** Founded in 1863. Regionally accredited. Additional campus at Salina. Off-campus site at Fort Riley army base. **Degrees:** 3,581 bachelor's, 82 associate awarded; master's, doctoral, first professional offered. **ROTC:** Army, Air Force. **Location:** 120 miles from Kansas City, Missouri. **Calendar:** Semester, extensive summer session. **Full-time faculty:** 940 total; 84% have terminal degrees, 19% minority, 34% women. **Part-time faculty:** 159 total; 54% have terminal degrees, 10% minority, 53% women. **Class size:** 52% < 20, 32% 20-39, 7% 40-49, 5% 50-99, 4% >100. **Special facilities:** Nuclear reactor, prairie for biological research, laser laboratory, cancer research center.

**Freshman class profile.** 6,658 applied, 6,338 admitted, 3,182 enrolled.

| Mid 50% test scores | | Out-of-state: | 13% |
|---|---|---|---|
| ACT composite: | 21-28 | International: | 3% |
| Rank in top quarter: | 62% | Fraternities: | 20% |
| Return as sophomores: | 79% | Sororities: | 20% |

**Basis for selection.** One of following required: minimum ACT score of 21, rank in top third of high school class, or minimum 2.0 GPA on Kansas pre-college curriculum (2.5 GPA for out-of-state students). SAT or ACT recommended. Audition recommended for music and theater majors. Portfolio recommended for art and architecture majors.

**High school preparation.** 14 units recommended. Recommended units include English 4, mathematics 3, social studies 2, history 1.5 and science 3. One unit of technology recommended.

**2007-2008 Annual costs.** Tuition/fees: $6,235; $15,970 out-of-state. Room/board: $6,084. Books/supplies: $1,100. Personal expenses: $3,376.

**2006-2007 Financial aid. Need-based:** 2,595 full-time freshmen applied for aid; 1,789 were judged to have need; 1,720 of these received aid. Average need met was 83%. Average scholarship/grant was $4,152; average loan $2,898. 36% of total undergraduate aid awarded as scholarships/grants, 64% as loans/jobs. **Non-need-based:** Awarded to 4,797 full-time undergraduates, including 1,680 freshmen. Scholarships awarded for academics, alumni affiliation, art, athletics, leadership, music/drama, ROTC, state residency.

**Application procedures. Admission:** No deadline. $30 fee, may be waived for applicants with need. Application may be submitted online. Admission notification on a rolling basis. **Financial aid:** Priority date 3/1; no closing date. FAFSA required. Applicants notified on a rolling basis starting 4/1; must reply within 2 week(s) of notification.

**Academics. Special study options:** Accelerated study, cooperative education, distance learning, double major, ESL, exchange student, honors, independent study, internships, study abroad, teacher certification program. **Credit/placement by examination:** AP, CLEP, IB, SAT, ACT. 10 credit hours maximum toward associate degree, 20 toward bachelor's. PEP, DANTES exams accepted for credit. **Support services:** Learning center, pre-admission summer program, reduced course load, remedial instruction, study skills assistance, tutoring, writing center.

**Majors. Agriculture:** Agronomy, animal sciences, business, communications, economics, food science, horticultural science. **Architecture:** Architecture, interior, landscape. **Biology:** General, biochemistry, microbiology, wildlife. **Business:** General, accounting, business admin, finance. **Communications:** General, journalism, media studies. **Computer sciences:** General, information systems, networking. **Education:** Agricultural, art, elementary, family/consumer sciences, music, secondary. **Engineering:** Agricultural, architectural, chemical, civil, computer, electrical, industrial, manufacturing, mechanical. **Engineering technology:** General, industrial management. **English:** English lit. **Family/consumer sciences:** General, child development, clothing/textiles, communication, family studies, human nutrition. **Foreign languages:** General. **Health:** Athletic training, communication disorders, dietetics, preveterinary. **History:** General. **Liberal arts:** Humanities. **Math:** General, statistics. **Mechanic/repair:** Aircraft. **Parks/recreation:** Exercise sciences, facilities management. **Philosophy/religion:** Philosophy. **Physical sciences:** General, chemistry, geology, physics. **Psychology:** General. **Public administration:** Social work. **Social sciences:** General, anthropology, economics, geography, political science, sociology. **Transportation:** Airline/commercial pilot, aviation management. **Visual/performing arts:** Dramatic, interior design, music performance, studio arts.

**Most popular majors.** Agriculture 11%, business/marketing 18%, education 9%, engineering/engineering technologies 12%, family/consumer sciences 6%, social sciences 10%.

**Computing on campus.** 547 workstations in dormitories, library, computer center. Dormitories linked to campus network. Commuter students can connect to campus network. Online course registration, helpline, repair service available.

**Student life. Freshman orientation:** Available, $25 fee. **Housing:** Coed dorms, single-sex dorms, apartments, cooperative housing, fraternity/sorority housing available. $25 deposit. **Activities:** Bands, campus ministries, choral groups, dance, drama, international student organizations, music ensembles, musical theater, radio station, student government, student newspaper, symphony orchestra, TV station, 340 religious, political, ethnic, and social service clubs and organizations available.

**Athletics. NCAA. Intercollegiate:** Baseball M, basketball, cross-country, equestrian W, football (tackle) M, golf, rowing (crew) W, tennis W, track and field, volleyball W. **Intramural:** Badminton, basketball, bowling, cross-country, golf, handball, soccer, softball, squash, swimming, table tennis, tennis, track and field, volleyball, water polo, wrestling M. **Team name:** Wildcats.

**Student services.** Adult student services, career counseling, student employment services, health services, on-campus daycare, personal counseling, placement for graduates, veterans' counselor. **Physically disabled:** Services for visually, speech, hearing impaired.

**Contact.** E-mail: kstate@ksu.edu
Phone: (785) 532-6250 Fax: (785) 532-6393
Larry Moeder, Director of Admissions, Kansas State University, 119 Anderson Hall, Manhattan, KS 66506

---

## Kansas Wesleyan University
**Salina, Kansas**
**www.kwu.edu**　　　　　　　　**CB code: 6337**

- Private 4-year liberal arts college affiliated with United Methodist Church
- Residential campus in large town
- 802 degree-seeking undergraduates
- SAT or ACT (ACT writing optional) required

**General.** Founded in 1886. Regionally accredited. **Degrees:** 138 bachelor's, 1 associate awarded; master's offered. **Location:** 90 miles from Wichita, 180 miles from Kansas City. **Calendar:** Semester, limited summer session. **Full-time faculty:** 43 total. **Part-time faculty:** 25 total. **Class size:** 66% < 20, 26% 20-39, 6% 40-49, 1% 50-99, less than 1% >100. **Special facilities:** Observatory with 16-inch Cassegrain telescope.

**Freshman class profile.**

| Mid 50% test scores | | ACT composite: | 20-24 |
|---|---|---|---|
| SAT critical reading: | 420-520 | Out-of-state: | 32% |
| SAT math: | 500-590 | Live on campus: | 67% |
| SAT writing: | 420-520 | | |

**Basis for selection.** Applicant must have ACT composite score of 18 or SAT combined score of 850 (exclusive of Writing) and high school GPA of 2.5 or rank in top half of class. Interview recommended for academically weak applicants. Audition recommended for music majors. Portfolio recommended for art majors.

**2007-2008 Annual costs.** Tuition/fees: $17,400. $200 per-credit-hour charge for 1-5 credit hours; $1,800 per semester for 6-8 credit hours; $3,600 per semester for 9-11 credit hours. Room/board: $6,000. Books/supplies: $800. Personal expenses: $500.

**Financial aid. Non-need-based:** Scholarships awarded for academics, alumni affiliation, art, athletics, music/drama, state residency. **Additional information:** Awards available for residence hall students: minimum $7,000 for 3.0 GPA plus ACT score of 22 or SAT of 950 (exclusive of Writing); minimum $8,000 for 3.5 GPA plus ACT score of 22 or SAT score of 1030 (exclusive of Writing); minimum $9,000 for 3.75 GPA plus ACT score of 25 or SAT score of 1140 (exclusive of Writing). Application deadline March 15.

**Application procedures. Admission:** No deadline. $20 fee. Admission notification on a rolling basis. **Financial aid:** Closing date 3/15. FAFSA required. Applicants notified on a rolling basis starting 1/1; must reply by 8/1 or within 3 week(s) of notification.

**Academics. Special study options:** Accelerated study, cross-registration, double major, ESL, independent study, internships, liberal arts/career combination, student-designed major, teacher certification program. **Credit/placement by examination:** AP, CLEP, institutional tests. 30 credit hours maximum toward bachelor's degree. **Support services:** Learning center, reduced course load, remedial instruction, tutoring, writing center.

**Majors. Biology:** General. **Business:** General, accounting. **Communications:** General, public relations. **Computer sciences:** General, computer science. **Education:** Art, elementary, English, secondary. **English:** English lit, speech/rhetoric. **Foreign languages:** General, German, Spanish. **Health:** Preop/surgical nursing. **History:** General. **Math:** General. **Parks/recreation:** Health/fitness. **Philosophy/religion:** Religion. **Physical sciences:** Chemistry, physics. **Protective services:** Criminal justice. **Psychology:** General. **Social sciences:** Sociology. **Theology:** Religious ed. **Visual/performing arts:** Arts management, dramatic, music performance, studio arts.

**Most popular majors.** Business/marketing 32%, education 9%, health sciences 9%, parks/recreation 7%, physical sciences 7%, social sciences 7%.

**Computing on campus.** 50 workstations in library, computer center. Dormitories wired for high-speed internet access and linked to campus network. Online library available.

**Student life. Freshman orientation:** Available. Preregistration for classes offered. **Housing:** Guaranteed on-campus for freshmen. Single-sex dorms, apartments available. $100 deposit. **Activities:** Jazz band, choral groups, dance, drama, literary magazine, music ensembles, musical theater, radio station, student government, student newspaper, Fellowship of Christian Athletes, Religious Life Committee.

**Athletics. NAIA. Intercollegiate:** Baseball M, basketball, cross-country, football (tackle) M, golf, soccer, softball W, tennis, track and field, volleyball W. **Intramural:** Basketball, softball, volleyball, weight lifting. **Team name:** Coyotes.

**Student services.** Adult student services, career counseling, student employment services, financial aid counseling, personal counseling, placement for graduates, veterans' counselor. **Physically disabled:** Services for visually impaired.

**Contact.** E-mail: admissions@kwu.edu
Phone: (785) 827-5541 ext. 1285 Toll-free number: (800) 874-1154
Fax: (785) 827-0927
Jim Allen, Director of Admissions, Kansas Wesleyan University, 100 East Claflin Avenue, Salina, KS 67401-6196

---

## Manhattan Christian College
**Manhattan, Kansas**
**www.mccks.edu**　　　　　　　　**CB code: 6392**

- Private 4-year Bible college affiliated with Christian Church
- Residential campus in large town
- 380 degree-seeking undergraduates
- SAT or ACT (ACT writing optional), application essay required

**General.** Founded in 1927. Regionally accredited; also accredited by ABHE. Students have access to Kansas State University library and facilities at student rates. **Degrees:** 65 bachelor's, 5 associate awarded. **ROTC:** Army, Air Force. **Location:** 130 miles from Kansas City. **Calendar:** Semester, limited summer session. **Full-time faculty:** 12 total. **Part-time faculty:** 20 total.

## Freshman class profile.

Out-of-state: 38%  Live on campus: 98%

**Basis for selection.** High school record, test scores, recommendations important. Character recommendations required. Interview recommended. Audition required for music majors.

**High school preparation.** Recommended units include English 4, mathematics 2 and science 2.

**2007-2008 Annual costs.** Tuition/fees: $10,412. Additional $6 required fee per-credit-hour, up to $72; $140 per-credit-hour charge for part-time, non-degree-seeking students. Part time non-degree and/or audit at $170 per-credit-hour. Room/board: $6,400. Books/supplies: $1,150. Personal expenses: $1,067.

**Financial aid. Non-need-based:** Scholarships awarded for academics, leadership.

**Application procedures. Admission:** Priority date 4/1; deadline 7/1 (postmark date). $25 fee, may be waived for applicants with need. Admission notification on a rolling basis beginning on or about 10/15. **Financial aid:** Priority date 4/1; no closing date. FAFSA required. Applicants notified on a rolling basis starting 5/1; must reply within 2 week(s) of notification.

**Academics. Special study options:** Combined bachelor's/graduate degree, double major, dual enrollment of high school students, internships, liberal arts/career combination. Dual degree program with Kansas State University. **Credit/placement by examination:** CLEP, institutional tests, 36 credit hours maximum toward bachelor's degree. **Support services:** Reduced course load, tutoring.

**Majors. Business:** Business admin. **Philosophy/religion:** Religion. **Theology:** Bible, missionary, pastoral counseling, religious ed, theology.

**Computing on campus.** 12 workstations in library, computer center.

**Student life. Freshman orientation:** Mandatory. Preregistration for classes offered. 3-day program held before start of classes. **Policies:** Religious observance required. **Housing:** Guaranteed on-campus for freshmen. Single-sex dorms, apartments available. $125 deposit, deadline 6/1. **Activities:** Bands, choral groups, drama, music ensembles, student government.

**Athletics.** NCCAA. **Intercollegiate:** Basketball, soccer, volleyball W. **Intramural:** Softball. **Team name:** Crusaders.

**Student services.** Career counseling, student employment services, health services, personal counseling, placement for graduates. **Physically disabled:** Services for speech impaired.

**Contact.** E-mail: admit@mccks.edu
Phone: (785) 539-3571 Toll-free number: (877) 246-4622
Fax: (785) 776-9251
Eric Ingmire, Director of Admissions, Manhattan Christian College, 1415 Anderson Avenue, Manhattan, KS 66502

---

### McPherson College
**McPherson, Kansas**
**www.mcpherson.edu**          CB code: 6404

- Private 4-year liberal arts college affiliated with Church of the Brethren
- Residential campus in large town
- 531 degree-seeking undergraduates: 6% part-time, 40% women, 8% African American, 1% Asian American, 7% Hispanic American, 2% Native American
- 80% of applicants admitted
- SAT or ACT (ACT writing optional) required
- 35% graduate within 6 years

**General.** Founded in 1887. Regionally accredited. **Degrees:** 96 bachelor's awarded. **Location:** 60 miles from Wichita. **Calendar:** 4-1-4, limited summer session. **Full-time faculty:** 39 total; 72% have terminal degrees, 8% minority, 28% women. **Part-time faculty:** 14 total; 50% have terminal degrees, 36% women. **Class size:** 70% < 20, 29% 20-39, less than 1% 40-49.

---

**Freshman class profile.** 466 applied, 374 admitted, 136 enrolled.

| Mid 50% test scores | | |
|---|---|---|
| SAT critical reading: | 420-560 | |
| SAT math: | 460-570 | |
| ACT composite: | 19-24 | |
| GPA 3.50 or higher: | 44% | |
| GPA 3.0-3.49: | 30% | |

| | | |
|---|---|---|
| GPA 2.0-2.99: | 25% |
| Rank in top quarter: | 38% |
| Rank in top tenth: | 14% |
| Return as sophomores: | 66% |
| Out-of-state: | 64% |
| Live on campus: | 93% |

**Basis for selection.** Satisfactory high school performance or completion of GED, corresponding standardized test scores, and appropriate personal qualities. Portfolio required for auto restoration program.

**2008-2009 Annual costs.** Tuition/fees (projected): $17,200. Room/board: $6,500.

**2007-2008 Financial aid. Need-based:** 130 full-time freshmen applied for aid; 109 were judged to have need; 109 of these received aid. Average need met was 87%. Average scholarship/grant was $5,016; average loan $5,416. 43% of total undergraduate aid awarded as scholarships/grants, 57% as loans/jobs. **Non-need-based:** Awarded to 484 full-time undergraduates, including 133 freshmen. Scholarships awarded for academics, alumni affiliation, art, athletics, music/drama, religious affiliation, state residency.

**Application procedures. Admission:** Priority date 3/1; no deadline. $25 fee, may be waived for applicants with need. Application may be submitted online. Admission notification on a rolling basis. Must reply by May 1 or within 4 week(s) if notified thereafter. **Financial aid:** Priority date 3/1; no closing date. FAFSA required. Applicants notified on a rolling basis starting 3/1; must reply within 3 week(s) of notification.

**Academics. Special study options:** Combined bachelor's/graduate degree, cross-registration, double major, dual enrollment of high school students, ESL, independent study, internships, student-designed major, study abroad, teacher certification program, urban semester. Only degree program in antique auto restoration in United States. **Credit/placement by examination:** AP, CLEP, IB, institutional tests. **Support services:** Learning center, reduced course load, remedial instruction, study skills assistance, tutoring, writing center.

**Majors. Biology:** General. **Business:** Accounting, business admin, finance, international. **Communications:** General. **Conservation:** Environmental studies. **Education:** General, art, biology, business, chemistry, computer, early childhood, elementary, English, foreign languages, history, mathematics, middle, music, physical, science, social studies, Spanish, special, speech, technology/industrial arts. **English:** English lit. **Foreign languages:** General, Spanish. **Health:** Predental, premedicine, prepharmacy, preveterinary. **History:** General. **Legal studies:** Prelaw. **Liberal arts:** Arts/sciences. **Math:** General. **Mechanic/repair:** Automotive. **Parks/recreation:** Health/fitness. **Physical sciences:** Chemistry. **Psychology:** General. **Social sciences:** Sociology. **Visual/performing arts:** Art, dramatic, music performance.

**Most popular majors.** Biology 6%, business/marketing 22%, education 8%, engineering/engineering technologies 22%, parks/recreation 10%, psychology 6%, social sciences 6%, visual/performing arts 11%.

**Computing on campus.** 72 workstations in dormitories, library, computer center, student center. Dormitories wired for high-speed internet access and linked to campus network. Commuter students can connect to campus network. Online library, helpline, wireless network available.

**Student life. Freshman orientation:** Mandatory. Preregistration for classes offered. **Policies:** No alcohol permitted on campus. Unmarried students under 23 years old are required to live in residence halls. **Housing:** Guaranteed on-campus for all undergraduates. Coed dorms, single-sex dorms, special housing for disabled available. $150 nonrefundable deposit, deadline 5/1. **Activities:** Bands, choral groups, dance, drama, music ensembles, musical theater, student government, student newspaper, 28 clubs and organizations available.

**Athletics.** NAIA. **Intercollegiate:** Basketball, cheerleading, cross-country, football (tackle) M, softball W, track and field, volleyball W. **Intramural:** Badminton, basketball, football (non-tackle), football (tackle) M, handball, racquetball, soccer, softball, table tennis, volleyball. **Team name:** Bulldogs.

**Student services.** Adult student services, campus ministries, career counseling, student employment services, financial aid counseling, health services, personal counseling, placement for graduates. **Physically disabled:** Services for hearing impaired.

**Contact.** E-mail: admiss@mcpherson.edu
Phone: (620) 241-0731 ext. 1270 Toll-free number: (800) 695-7402
Fax: (620) 241-8443
Dave Barrett, Director of Admission, McPherson College, 1600 East Euclid Street, McPherson, KS 67460-1402

## MidAmerica Nazarene University
### Olathe, Kansas
www.mnu.edu      CB code: 6437

- Private 4-year university and liberal arts college affiliated with Church of the Nazarene
- Residential campus in small city
- 1,283 degree-seeking undergraduates: 11% part-time, 56% women, 8% African American, 1% Asian American, 4% Hispanic American, 1% Native American, 2% international
- 358 degree-seeking graduate students
- 79% of applicants admitted
- SAT or ACT (ACT writing optional) required
- 51% graduate within 6 years

**General.** Founded in 1966. Regionally accredited. **Degrees:** 353 bachelor's, 1 associate awarded; master's offered. **ROTC:** Army, Air Force. **Location:** 19 miles from Kansas City. **Calendar:** Semester, limited summer session. **Full-time faculty:** 86 total; 44% have terminal degrees. **Part-time faculty:** 97 total. **Class size:** 62% < 20, 27% 20-39, 5% 40-49, 6% 50-99.

### Freshman class profile.

| Mid 50% test scores | | | |
|---|---|---|---|
| SAT critical reading: | 360-590 | Rank in top quarter: | 40% |
| SAT math: | 420-560 | Rank in top tenth: | 20% |
| ACT composite: | 20-26 | End year in good standing: | 87% |
| GPA 3.50 or higher: | 50% | Return as sophomores: | 71% |
| GPA 3.0-3.49: | 22% | Out-of-state: | 48% |
| GPA 2.0-2.99: | 26% | Live on campus: | 91% |
| | | International: | 1% |

**Basis for selection.** Secondary school record, class rank, test scores, moral principles important. Nursing, elementary education, secondary education programs have higher standards for admission. Interview recommended for music, nursing, elementary and secondary education programs. Audition recommended for music majors. **Homeschooled:** Transcript of courses and grades, letter of recommendation (nonparent) required.

**High school preparation.** 14 units recommended. Recommended units include English 4, mathematics 3, social studies 3, science 3 and foreign language 1.

**2008-2009 Annual costs.** Tuition/fees (projected): $18,216. Room/board: $6,180. Books/supplies: $1,300. Personal expenses: $2,500.

**2007-2008 Financial aid. Need-based:** 196 full-time freshmen applied for aid; 176 were judged to have need; 176 of these received aid. Average need met was 73%. Average scholarship/grant was $3,911; average loan $4,679. 57% of total undergraduate aid awarded as scholarships/grants, 43% as loans/jobs. **Non-need-based:** Scholarships awarded for academics, art, athletics, leadership, minority status, music/drama, religious affiliation, ROTC, state residency.

**Application procedures. Admission:** Priority date 3/1; deadline 8/1 (postmark date). $25 fee. Application may be submitted online. Admission notification on a rolling basis. **Financial aid:** Priority date 3/1; no closing date. FAFSA, institutional form required. Applicants notified on a rolling basis starting 2/1; must reply within 2 week(s) of notification.

**Academics.** Adults 25 and older may earn bachelor's degree through evening division. **Special study options:** Accelerated study, cross-registration, distance learning, double major, dual enrollment of high school students, independent study, internships, study abroad, teacher certification program, Washington semester. Dual degree program in vocational agriculture with Kansas State University. **Credit/placement by examination:** AP, CLEP, IB, SAT, ACT, institutional tests. 34 credit hours maximum toward associate degree, 34 toward bachelor's. **Support services:** Learning center, reduced course load, remedial instruction, study skills assistance, tutoring.

**Majors. Biology:** General. **Business:** General, accounting, business admin, communications, human resources. **Communications:** General, media studies, public relations. **Computer sciences:** General, computer science, information systems. **Education:** Biology, business, elementary, English, foreign languages, health, mathematics, middle, music, physical, secondary, social studies, Spanish. **English:** English lit. **Foreign languages:** Spanish. **Health:** Athletic training, nursing (RN). **History:** General. **Math:** General. **Parks/recreation:** Exercise sciences, sports admin. **Philosophy/religion:** Religion. **Physical sciences:** Chemistry, physics. **Protective services:** Law enforcement admin. **Psychology:** General. **Social sciences:** General, sociology, urban studies. **Theology:** Missionary, religious ed, sacred music, youth ministry. **Visual/performing arts:** General, music performance, voice/opera.

**Most popular majors.** Business/marketing 53%, education 7%, health sciences 9%.

**Computing on campus.** 90 workstations in dormitories, library, computer center. Dormitories wired for high-speed internet access and linked to campus network. Commuter students can connect to campus network. Online course registration, online library, helpline, student web hosting, wireless network available.

**Student life. Freshman orientation:** Available, $44 fee. Preregistration for classes offered. Program concentrates on essential study skills, time management, value of liberal arts learning, career development aids, proficiency assessment. **Policies:** Religious observance required. **Housing:** Guaranteed on-campus for freshmen. Single-sex dorms, special housing for disabled, apartments, substance-free housing available. $100 deposit, deadline 8/21. **Activities:** Bands, choral groups, drama, music ensembles, radio station, student government, student newspaper, TV station, Circle K, College Republicans, gospel station, Fellowship of Christian Athletes, multicultural student asociation, BYTE (computer science) club, Psych Incorporated (psychology honors club), medical careers club, covenant groups.

**Athletics.** NAIA. **Intercollegiate:** Baseball M, basketball, cheerleading, cross-country, football (tackle) M, soccer, softball W, track and field, volleyball W. **Intramural:** Basketball, bowling, football (non-tackle), football (tackle), golf, soccer, softball, table tennis, tennis, track and field, volleyball. **Team name:** Pioneers.

**Student services.** Campus ministries, career counseling, student employment services, financial aid counseling, health services, personal counseling, placement for graduates, veterans' counselor. **Physically disabled:** Services for visually, speech, hearing impaired.

**Contact.** E-mail: admissions@mnu.edu
Phone: (913) 791-3380 Toll-free number: (800) 800-8887
Fax: (913) 791-3481
Brigit Mattox, Associate Director of Admissions, MidAmerica Nazarene University, 2030 East College Way, Olathe, KS 66062-1899

## Newman University
### Wichita, Kansas
www.newmanu.edu      CB code: 6615

- Private 4-year university and liberal arts college affiliated with Roman Catholic Church
- Commuter campus in large city
- 1,116 degree-seeking undergraduates: 15% part-time, 64% women, 6% African American, 4% Asian American, 8% Hispanic American, 2% Native American, 6% international
- 380 degree-seeking graduate students
- 63% of applicants admitted
- SAT and SAT Subject Tests or ACT (ACT writing optional) required
- 45% graduate within 6 years

**General.** Founded in 1933. Regionally accredited. The university is a sponsored ministry of the Adorers of the Blood of Christ. **Degrees:** 245 bachelor's, 63 associate awarded; master's offered. **Location:** 160 miles from Oklahoma City, 180 miles from Kansas City. **Calendar:** Semester, limited summer session. **Full-time faculty:** 76 total; 53% have terminal degrees, 50% women. **Part-time faculty:** 70 total. **Class size:** 72% < 20, 26% 20-39, 2% 40-49, less than 1% 50-99. **Special facilities:** Photography laboratory, cadaver laboratory.

**Freshman class profile.** 592 applied, 375 admitted, 136 enrolled.

| Mid 50% test scores | | | |
|---|---|---|---|
| SAT critical reading: | 400-600 | GPA 2.0-2.99: | 19% |
| SAT math: | 460-630 | Rank in top quarter: | 49% |
| SAT writing: | 460-590 | End year in good standing: | 91% |
| ACT composite: | 19-26 | Return as sophomores: | 59% |
| GPA 3.50 or higher: | 48% | Out-of-state: | 27% |
| GPA 3.0-3.49: | 33% | Live on campus: | 71% |
| | | International: | 10% |

**Basis for selection.** Minimum GPA 2.0, minimum ACT composite score of 18, or SAT score of 1290 (including Writing). Caliber of high school curriculum important. Portfolio recommended for art majors. **Learning Disabled:** Applicants should submit medical evaluation and recommendation.

**High school preparation.** Recommended units include English 4, mathematics 3, social studies 3 and science 3.

**2007-2008 Annual costs.** Tuition/fees: $17,988. Room/board: $5,442. Books/supplies: $904. Personal expenses: $4,495.

**2007-2008 Financial aid. Need-based:** Average need met was 67%. Average scholarship/grant was $4,255; average loan $2,250. 31% of total undergraduate aid awarded as scholarships/grants, 69% as loans/jobs. **Non-need-based:** Scholarships awarded for academics, alumni affiliation, art, athletics, leadership, music/drama, religious affiliation.

**Application procedures. Admission:** No deadline. $20 fee, may be waived for applicants with need. Application may be submitted online. Admission notification on a rolling basis. **Financial aid:** Priority date 3/1; no closing date. FAFSA, institutional form required. Applicants notified on a rolling basis starting 2/1.

**Academics. Special study options:** Cooperative education, cross-registration, distance learning, double major, dual enrollment of high school students, independent study, internships, liberal arts/career combination, student-designed major, study abroad, teacher certification program. **Credit/placement by examination:** AP, CLEP, IB, institutional tests. 30 credit hours maximum toward bachelor's degree. **Support services:** Learning center, study skills assistance, tutoring, writing center.

**Majors. Biology:** General. **Business:** Accounting, business admin, management information systems, marketing. **Communications:** Media studies. **Computer sciences:** Information systems. **Education:** General, elementary, middle, secondary. **English:** English lit. **Health:** Nursing (RN), sonography. **History:** General. **Liberal arts:** Arts/sciences. **Math:** General. **Physical sciences:** Chemistry. **Protective services:** Law enforcement admin. **Psychology:** General. **Social sciences:** Sociology. **Theology:** Pastoral counseling. **Visual/performing arts:** Art. **Other:** Counseling.

**Most popular majors.** Biology 7%, business/marketing 16%, education 28%, health sciences 25%, psychology 6%.

**Computing on campus.** 90 workstations in dormitories, library, computer center, student center. Dormitories wired for high-speed internet access and linked to campus network. Commuter students can connect to campus network. Online library, helpline, repair service, wireless network available.

**Student life. Freshman orientation:** Mandatory, $10 fee. Preregistration for classes offered. 2-day program prior to fall term. **Housing:** Guaranteed on-campus for freshmen. Coed dorms, apartments, substance-free housing available. $100 fully refundable deposit. Freshmen required to live in college housing for first 2 years if not living with parents. **Activities:** Choral groups, drama, literary magazine, student government, student newspaper, Koinonia, service scholars, Newman Club, international club, Peer Educators, Kansas Catholic College Student Convention, campus ministries, peer ministers.

**Athletics.** NAIA. **Intercollegiate:** Baseball M, basketball, bowling, cross-country, golf, soccer, softball W, tennis, volleyball W, wrestling M. **Intramural:** Baseball M, basketball, football (tackle), table tennis, volleyball, weight lifting. **Team name:** Jets.

**Student services.** Adult student services, campus ministries, career counseling, student employment services, financial aid counseling, on-campus daycare, personal counseling, placement for graduates. **Physically disabled:** Services for visually, speech, hearing impaired.

**Contact.** E-mail: admissions@newmanu.edu
Phone: (316) 942-4291 ext. 2144 Toll-free number: (877) 639-6268
Fax: (316) 942-4483
John Clayton, Dean of Admissions, Newman University, 3100 McCormick, Wichita, KS 67213-2097

## Ottawa University

Ottawa, Kansas **CB member**
www.ottawa.edu **CB code: 6547**

♦ Private 4-year liberal arts college affiliated with American Baptist Churches in the USA
♦ Residential campus in large town
♦ 484 degree-seeking undergraduates
♦ 65% of applicants admitted
♦ SAT or ACT (ACT writing optional) required

**General.** Founded in 1865. Regionally accredited. Degree completion programs in Overland Park, KS; Phoenix, AZ; Milwaukee, WI; Jeffersonville, IN and Pacific Rim countries. Master's programs in Overland Park, KS, Phoenix, AZ, and Milwaukee, WI. **Degrees:** 75 bachelor's awarded. **Location:** 45 miles from Kansas City. **Calendar:** Semester, limited summer session. **Full-time faculty:** 25 total. **Part-time faculty:** 10 total. **Class size:** 63% < 20, 35% 20-39, 2% 40-49, less than 1% 50-99.

### Freshman class profile.

| Mid 50% test scores | | | |
|---|---|---|---|
| SAT critical reading: | 420-490 | GPA 3.0-3.49: | 37% |
| SAT math: | 450-520 | GPA 2.0-2.99: | 25% |
| SAT writing: | 400-470 | Rank in top quarter: | 39% |
| ACT composite: | 18-24 | Rank in top tenth: | 17% |
| GPA 3.50 or higher: | 38% | Out-of-state: | 53% |
| | | Live on campus: | 99% |

**Basis for selection.** Rank in top half of class, 2.5 GPA, test scores important. Personal recommendation, school and community achievements, interview, special talents considered. Audition recommended for music and drama majors. Portfolio recommended for art majors. **Homeschooled:** Transcript of courses and grades required. Must take ACT or SAT. Require a sample of most recent written work/portfolio.

**High school preparation.** Recommended units include English 4, mathematics 3, social studies 1, history 2, science 3 (laboratory 2) and foreign language 1.

**2007-2008 Annual costs.** Tuition/fees: $17,350. Room/board: $5,930. Books/supplies: $1,100. Personal expenses: $1,600.

**Financial aid. Non-need-based:** Scholarships awarded for academics, alumni affiliation, athletics, music/drama, religious affiliation.

**Application procedures. Admission:** Priority date 6/1; no deadline. $15 fee, may be waived for applicants with need. Application may be submitted online. Admission notification on a rolling basis. **Financial aid:** Priority date 3/15; no closing date. FAFSA required. Applicants notified on a rolling basis starting 2/1; must reply within 4 week(s) of notification.

**Academics. Special study options:** Distance learning, double major, dual enrollment of high school students, internships, liberal arts/career combination, student-designed major, study abroad, teacher certification program. **Credit/placement by examination:** AP, CLEP, IB. **Support services:** Learning center, reduced course load, study skills assistance, tutoring.

**Majors. Biology:** General. **Business:** Accounting/business management, business admin, management information systems. **Communications:** General. **Computer sciences:** Information technology. **Education:** Art, elementary, English, mathematics, music, physical. **English:** English lit. **History:** General. **Math:** General. **Parks/recreation:** Health/fitness. **Philosophy/religion:** Religion. **Psychology:** General. **Public administration:** Human services. **Social sciences:** Political science, sociology. **Visual/performing arts:** Art, dramatic.

**Most popular majors.** Biology 10%, business/marketing 24%, communications/journalism 10%, education 11%, health sciences 10%, mathematics 6%, social sciences 14%.

**Computing on campus.** 71 workstations in dormitories, library, computer center. Dormitories wired for high-speed internet access and linked to campus network. Commuter students can connect to campus network. Online course registration, online library, helpline available.

**Student life. Freshman orientation:** Mandatory. Preregistration for classes offered. **Housing:** Guaranteed on-campus for freshmen. Coed dorms, single-sex dorms available. $150 fully refundable deposit, deadline 6/1. Pets allowed in dorm rooms. **Activities:** Jazz band, choral groups, drama, music ensembles, radio station, student government, student newspaper, symphony orchestra, Christian Faith in Action, voluntary service organization, Whole Earth club, Fellowship of Christian Athletes, student activities force, Cognoscenti (literary group), Amnesty International.

**Athletics.** NAIA. **Intercollegiate:** Baseball M, basketball, cross-country, football (tackle) M, golf M, soccer, softball W, track and field, volleyball W. **Intramural:** Badminton, basketball, bowling, golf, handball, racquetball, soccer, softball, table tennis, tennis, track and field, volleyball. **Team name:** Braves.

**Student services.** Alcohol/substance abuse counseling, campus ministries, career counseling, student employment services, financial aid counseling, health services, personal counseling, placement for graduates.

**Contact.** E-mail: admiss@ottawa.edu
Phone: (785) 242-5200 ext. 5421 Toll-free number: (800) 755-5200 ext. 5421 Fax: (785) 242-1008
Roger Kugler, Director of Admissions, Ottawa University, 1001 South Cedar Street, #17, Ottawa, KS 66067-3399

## Pittsburg State University

Pittsburg, Kansas
www.pittstate.edu **CB code: 6336**

♦ Public 4-year university
♦ Residential campus in large town

- 5,824 degree-seeking undergraduates: 8% part-time, 48% women, 3% African American, 1% Asian American, 2% Hispanic American, 2% Native American, 5% international
- 1,215 graduate students
- 88% of applicants admitted
- ACT (writing optional) required
- 50% graduate within 6 years

**General.** Founded in 1903. Regionally accredited. Centers in Kansas City and Wichita. **Degrees:** 1,107 bachelor's, 28 associate awarded; master's offered. **ROTC:** Army. **Location:** 120 miles from Kansas City. **Calendar:** Semester, limited summer session. **Full-time faculty:** 301 total; 70% have terminal degrees, 7% minority, 39% women. **Part-time faculty:** 107 total; 13% have terminal degrees, 6% minority, 54% women. **Class size:** 59% < 20, 33% 20-39, 3% 40-49, 5% 50-99, less than 1% >100. **Special facilities:** Planetarium, observatory, field biology reserve, nature reach, herbarium, technology center, gorilla village, mammal collection, greenhouse, polymer research lab, broadcasting lab, cadaver lab.

**Freshman class profile.** 2,197 applied, 1,923 admitted, 1,027 enrolled.

| Mid 50% test scores | | Rank in top tenth: | 20% |
|---|---|---|---|
| ACT composite: | 19-24 | Return as sophomores: | 75% |
| GPA 3.50 or higher: | 37% | Out-of-state: | 25% |
| GPA 3.0-3.49: | 32% | Live on campus: | 70% |
| GPA 2.0-2.99: | 28% | Fraternities: | 7% |
| Rank in top quarter: | 39% | Sororities: | 7% |

**Basis for selection.** Kansas residents must have one of following: minimum ACT score of 21, or rank in top 1/3 of high school graduating class, or minimum 2.0 GPA in Kansas precollege curriculum. Out-of-state students must have a minimum 2.5 GPA in the precollege curriculum or one of the other qualifications listed above. **Homeschooled:** GED, record of course content and completion required.

**High school preparation.** College-preparatory program recommended. 14 units recommended. Recommended units include English 4, mathematics 3, social studies 3 and science 3. 1 computer technology required.

**2007-2008 Annual costs.** Tuition/fees: $4,060; $11,866 out-of-state. Room/board: $5,088. Books/supplies: $1,000. Personal expenses: $2,100.

**2007-2008 Financial aid.** **Need-based:** 836 full-time freshmen applied for aid; 596 were judged to have need; 563 of these received aid. Average need met was 86%. Average scholarship/grant was $4,046; average loan $3,402. 47% of total undergraduate aid awarded as scholarships/grants, 53% as loans/jobs. **Non-need-based:** Awarded to 1,304 full-time undergraduates, including 392 freshmen. Scholarships awarded for academics, alumni affiliation, art, athletics, leadership, music/drama, ROTC.

**Application procedures.** **Admission:** No deadline. $30 fee. Application may be submitted online. Admission notification on a rolling basis. **Financial aid:** Priority date 3/1; no closing date. FAFSA, institutional form required. Applicants notified on a rolling basis; must reply within 2 week(s) of notification.

**Academics.** **Special study options:** Accelerated study, combined bachelor's/graduate degree, cooperative education, distance learning, double major, dual enrollment of high school students, ESL, exchange student, external degree, honors, independent study, internships, liberal arts/career combination, student-designed major, study abroad, teacher certification program. **Credit/placement by examination:** AP, CLEP, IB, ACT, institutional tests. 24 credit hours maximum toward bachelor's degree. **Support services:** Learning center, tutoring, writing center.

**Honors college/program.** Separate application required. Criteria for selection include minimum 28 ACT score, minimum 3.5 GPA, recommendations, record of participation in academic and other extracurricular activities.

**Majors. Biology:** General, biochemistry, cellular/molecular, plant physiology. **Business:** Accounting, actuarial science, business admin, construction management, fashion, finance, international, managerial economics, marketing. **Communications:** General, advertising, journalism, photojournalism, public relations, radio/tv. **Computer sciences:** General, computer science. **Education:** Art, biology, chemistry, early childhood, elementary, English, family/consumer sciences, French, mathematics, music, physical, physics, psychology, social studies, Spanish, technology/industrial arts, voc/tech. **Engineering technology:** Construction, electrical, manufacturing, mechanical, plastics. **English:** Creative writing, English lit, technical writing. **Family/consumer sciences:** General, child development. **Foreign languages:** French, Spanish. **Health:** Clinical lab science, nursing (RN), predental, premedicine, prepharmacy, preveterinary, recreational therapy. **History:** General. **Legal studies:** Prelaw. **Math:** General. **Mechanic/repair:** Automotive, diesel. **Parks/recreation:** General, facilities management. **Physical sciences:** Chemistry, physics, polymer chemistry. **Psychology:** General, counseling. **Public**

**administration:** Social work. **Social sciences:** Geography, international relations, political science, sociology. **Visual/performing arts:** Art, ceramics, commercial/advertising art, graphic design, interior design, music performance, painting. **Other:** Automotive service management, Communication education, Community, corporate & hospital wellness, Environmental chemistry, Family & individual management, Graphics & imaging technologies, Information assurance and computer security, Justice studies, News editorial, Plant molecular biology, Pre- civil engineering, Pre-optometry, Technology management, Theater, Wood technology.

**Most popular majors.** Biology 6%, business/marketing 16%, communications/journalism 6%, education 12%, health sciences 6%, trade and industry 10%.

**Computing on campus.** 425 workstations in library, computer center, student center. Dormitories wired for high-speed internet access and linked to campus network. Commuter students can connect to campus network. Online course registration, online library, repair service, wireless network available.

**Student life. Freshman orientation:** Mandatory, $20 fee. Eight individual sessions are offered and last approximately eight hours each. **Housing:** Guaranteed on-campus for freshmen. Coed dorms, special housing for disabled, apartments, substance-free housing available. $145 partly refundable deposit. **Activities:** Bands, campus ministries, choral groups, dance, drama, film society, international student organizations, literary magazine, music ensembles, musical theater, opera, radio station, student government, student newspaper, symphony orchestra, TV station, Over 160 clubs and organizations available.

**Athletics.** NCAA. **Intercollegiate:** Baseball M, basketball, cross-country, football (tackle) M, golf M, softball W, track and field, volleyball W. **Intramural:** Basketball, football (non-tackle), racquetball, softball, tennis, volleyball. **Team name:** Gorillas.

**Student services.** Alcohol/substance abuse counseling, campus ministries, career counseling, student employment services, financial aid counseling, health services, legal services, minority student services, personal counseling, placement for graduates, veterans' counselor. **Physically disabled:** Services for visually, speech, hearing impaired.

**Contact.** E-mail: psuadmit@pittstate.edu
Phone: (620) 235-4251 Toll-free number: (800) 854-7488
Fax: (620) 235-6003
Melinda Roelfs, Director of Admission & Enrollment Services, Pittsburg State University, 1701 South Broadway, Pittsburg, KS 66762

## Southwestern College
**Winfield, Kansas**
**www.sckans.edu**        **CB code: 6670**

- Private 4-year liberal arts college affiliated with United Methodist Church
- Residential campus in large town
- 1,415 degree-seeking undergraduates: 60% part-time, 46% women, 10% African American, 1% Asian American, 5% Hispanic American, 2% Native American, 1% international
- 155 degree-seeking graduate students
- 91% of applicants admitted
- SAT or ACT (ACT writing optional), application essay required
- 45% graduate within 6 years

**General.** Founded in 1885. Regionally accredited. Laptop computers issued to all full-time students enrolled at main campus. **Degrees:** 452 bachelor's awarded; master's offered. **Location:** 40 miles from Wichita. **Calendar:** Semester, limited summer session. **Full-time faculty:** 48 total; 58% have terminal degrees, 19% minority, 31% women. **Part-time faculty:** 153 total; 2% have terminal degrees, 51% minority, 42% women. **Class size:** 80% < 20, 18% 20-39, 1% 40-49, less than 1% 50-99. **Special facilities:** Biological field station.

**Freshman class profile.** 329 applied, 300 admitted, 138 enrolled.

| Mid 50% test scores | | Rank in top tenth: | 16% |
|---|---|---|---|
| SAT math: | 430-560 | Return as sophomores: | 65% |
| ACT composite: | 19-25 | Out-of-state: | 46% |
| GPA 3.50 or higher: | 47% | Live on campus: | 98% |
| GPA 3.0-3.49: | 28% | International: | 4% |
| GPA 2.0-2.99: | 25% | Fraternities: | 2% |
| Rank in top quarter: | 40% | Sororities: | 4% |

**Basis for selection.** School achievement record, test scores and personal essay statement most important. Portfolio required. Interview recommended for nursing majors. Audition required for music and drama majors.

**High school preparation.** 13.5 units required. Required units include English 4, mathematics 3, social studies 2.5, history 1, science 2 (laboratory 1). Computer or communication unit may be substituted for foreign language.

**2007-2008 Annual costs.** Tuition/fees: $17,820. Room/board: $5,622. Books/supplies: $600. Personal expenses: $5,069.

**2007-2008 Financial aid. Need-based:** 124 full-time freshmen applied for aid; 109 were judged to have need; 109 of these received aid. Average need met was 84%. Average scholarship/grant was $12,073; average loan $4,782. 69% of total undergraduate aid awarded as scholarships/grants, 31% as loans/jobs. **Non-need-based:** Awarded to 218 full-time undergraduates, including 58 freshmen. Scholarships awarded for academics, alumni affiliation, athletics, leadership, minority status, music/drama, religious affiliation. **Additional information:** Academic and activity grants available.

**Application procedures. Admission:** Closing date 8/25 (receipt date). $20 fee, may be waived for applicants with need. Application may be submitted online. Admission notification on a rolling basis beginning on or about 9/15. Must reply by May 1 or within 3 week(s) if notified thereafter. **Financial aid:** Priority date 4/1, closing date 8/15. FAFSA, institutional form required. Applicants notified on a rolling basis starting 2/1; must reply within 2 week(s) of notification.

**Academics. Special study options:** Accelerated study, distance learning, double major, honors, independent study, internships, student-designed major, study abroad, teacher certification program, urban semester, Washington semester. **Credit/placement by examination:** AP, CLEP, ACT, institutional tests. 30 credit hours maximum toward bachelor's degree. **Support services:** Learning center, reduced course load, remedial instruction, study skills assistance, tutoring.

**Majors. Biology:** General, biochemistry, marine. **Business:** Accounting, business admin, communications, entrepreneurial studies, finance, management information systems, management science, marketing, nonprofit/public, operations, training/development. **Communications:** General, digital media, radio/tv. **Computer sciences:** General, computer science, programming, web page design. **Education:** General, business, drama/dance, early childhood, elementary, English, foreign languages, mathematics, music, physical, science, secondary, speech. **Engineering:** Physics. **Engineering technology:** Computer systems, manufacturing. **English:** English lit. **Health:** Athletic training, nursing (RN). **History:** General. **Liberal arts:** Arts/sciences. **Math:** General. **Parks/recreation:** Health/fitness, sports admin. **Philosophy/religion:** Philosophy, religion. **Physical sciences:** Chemistry, physics. **Protective services:** Criminal justice, security services. **Psychology:** General. **Theology:** Pastoral counseling. **Visual/performing arts:** Dramatic, film/cinema.

**Most popular majors.** Biology 7%, business/marketing 57%, computer/information sciences 8%, security/protective services 8%.

**Computing on campus.** PC or laptop required. 50 workstations in dormitories, library, computer center, student center. Dormitories wired for high-speed internet access and linked to campus network. Commuter students can connect to campus network. Online library, helpline, repair service, student web hosting, wireless network available.

**Student life. Freshman orientation:** Mandatory. Preregistration for classes offered. Three-day orientation held before upperclassmen arrive on campus. Includes laptop distribution and training, community service project. **Policies:** Drug and alcohol-free campus. **Housing:** Guaranteed on-campus for freshmen. Coed dorms, single-sex dorms, special housing for disabled, apartments available. $100 deposit. **Activities:** Bands, choral groups, dance, drama, literary magazine, music ensembles, musical theater, radio station, student government, student newspaper, symphony orchestra, TV station, Black Student Union, Campus Council on Ministries, Sharp Ambassadors, Student Activities Association, Business Students Association, Fellowship of Christian Athletes, Discipleship Southwestern, Leadership Southwestern, outreach teams, SC Association of Nursing Students.

**Athletics.** NAIA. **Intercollegiate:** Basketball, cheerleading, cross-country, football (tackle) M, golf, soccer, softball W, tennis, track and field, volleyball W. **Intramural:** Basketball, bowling, softball, swimming, tennis, volleyball. **Team name:** Moundbuilders.

**Student services.** Adult student services, alcohol/substance abuse counseling, campus ministries, career counseling, student employment services, financial aid counseling, health services, minority student services, on-campus daycare, personal counseling, placement for graduates. **Physically disabled:** Services for visually, hearing impaired.

**Contact.** E-mail: scadmit@sckans.edu
Phone: (620) 229-6236 Toll-free number: (800) 846-1543 ext. 6236
Fax: (620) 229-6344
Todd Moore, Director of Admission, Southwestern College, 100 College Street, Winfield, KS 67156

# Sterling College
### Sterling, Kansas
**www.sterling.edu**   CB code: 6684

- Private 4-year liberal arts college affiliated with Presbyterian Church (USA)
- Residential campus in rural community
- 569 degree-seeking undergraduates: 4% part-time, 44% women, 11% African American, 1% Asian American, 7% Hispanic American, 2% Native American, 1% international
- 58% of applicants admitted
- SAT or ACT (ACT writing optional), application essay required
- 51% graduate within 6 years

**General.** Founded in 1887. Regionally accredited. Christian values of faith and service stressed. Partnerships with Habitat for Humanity and Americorp. **Degrees:** 74 bachelor's awarded. **Location:** 20 miles from Hutchinson, 70 miles from Wichita. **Calendar:** 4-1-4, limited summer session. **Full-time faculty:** 39 total; 38% have terminal degrees, 8% minority, 28% women. **Part-time faculty:** 14 total; 7% have terminal degrees, 50% women. **Class size:** 74% < 20, 23% 20-39, 3% 40-49, less than 1% 50-99.

**Freshman class profile.** 804 applied, 466 admitted, 165 enrolled.

| Mid 50% test scores | | | |
|---|---|---|---|
| SAT critical reading: | 420-490 | GPA 2.0-2.99: | 35% |
| SAT math: | 420-510 | Rank in top quarter: | 32% |
| SAT writing: | 410-490 | Rank in top tenth: | 14% |
| ACT composite: | 18-23 | Return as sophomores: | 52% |
| GPA 3.50 or higher: | 30% | Out-of-state: | 54% |
| GPA 3.0-3.49: | 34% | Live on campus: | 97% |
| | | International: | 1% |

**Basis for selection.** High school record, test scores, recommendations from school counselor and pastor important; commitment to Christian values and service also important. Interview recommended. Audition required of performing arts majors. Portfolio recommended for art majors. **Home-schooled:** Transcript of courses and grades required. State certification strongly recommended for athletic eligibility. **Learning Disabled:** Must provide official documentation with recommended accommodations.

**High school preparation.** 18 units recommended. Recommended units include English 4, mathematics 3, social studies 1, history 2, science 3 (laboratory 2), foreign language 2, computer science 1 and academic electives 1. Physical education recommended.

**2008-2009 Annual costs.** Tuition/fees: $16,700. $335 per credit hour charge for 1 to 6 credits. Room/board: $6,230. Books/supplies: $600. Personal expenses: $700.

**2006-2007 Financial aid. Need-based:** 86 full-time freshmen applied for aid; 68 were judged to have need; 68 of these received aid. Average need met was 77%. Average scholarship/grant was $8,551; average loan $2,988. 70% of total undergraduate aid awarded as scholarships/grants, 30% as loans/jobs. **Non-need-based:** Awarded to 63 full-time undergraduates, including 24 freshmen. Scholarships awarded for academics, alumni affiliation, art, athletics, leadership, minority status, music/drama, religious affiliation, state residency.

**Application procedures. Admission:** Priority date 3/1; no deadline. $25 fee, may be waived for applicants with need. Application may be submitted online. Admission notification on a rolling basis beginning on or about 9/15. **Financial aid:** Priority date 4/1; no closing date. FAFSA required. Applicants notified on a rolling basis starting 1/1; must reply within 3 week(s) of notification.

**Academics. Special study options:** Double major, dual enrollment of high school students, external degree, honors, independent study, internships, liberal arts/career combination, student-designed major, study abroad, teacher certification program, Washington semester. **Credit/placement by examination:** AP, CLEP, SAT, ACT, institutional tests. **Support services:** Learning center, reduced course load, remedial instruction, study skills assistance, tutoring.

**Majors. Biology:** General. **Business:** Business admin. **Communications:** General. **Computer sciences:** General. **Education:** Elementary, mathematics, music. **English:** English lit. **Health:** Athletic training. **History:** General. **Math:** General. **Parks/recreation:** Health/fitness. **Physical sciences:** Chemistry. **Psychology:** General. **Theology:** Religious ed. **Visual/performing arts:** Art, dramatic.

**Most popular majors.** Business/marketing 13%, communications/journalism 9%, education 18%, mathematics 6%, psychology 6%, theological studies 8%, visual/performing arts 20%.

**Computing on campus.** 120 workstations in dormitories, library, computer center, student center. Dormitories wired for high-speed internet access and linked to campus network. Online library, wireless network available.

**Student life. Freshman orientation:** Mandatory. Preregistration for classes offered. 3-day program prior to start of fall classes; includes service project. **Policies:** Prohibition of alcohol and tobacco products. Religious observance required. **Housing:** Guaranteed on-campus for all undergraduates. Single-sex dorms, substance-free housing available. $100 partly refundable deposit, deadline 8/1. All students under age 23 required to live in campus dormitories unless married or with dependents, living at home with parents, 5th-year senior, or by special circumstances. **Activities:** Bands, choral groups, drama, literary magazine, music ensembles, musical theater, radio station, student government, student newspaper, TV station, Future Science Professionals Asso., Alpha Phi Omega, Fellowship of Christian Athletes, behavioral science club, Habitat for Humanity, Chi Beta Sigma (business), P.E.A.C.E. club, Pi Kappa Delta, Catholic Student Association.

**Athletics.** NAIA. **Intercollegiate:** Baseball M, basketball, cross-country, football (tackle) M, golf, soccer, softball W, track and field, volleyball W. **Intramural:** Basketball, bowling, football (non-tackle), softball, table tennis, volleyball. **Team name:** Warriors.

**Student services.** Campus ministries, career counseling, student employment services, financial aid counseling, health services, personal counseling.

**Contact.** E-mail: admissions@sterling.edu
Phone: (620) 278-4275 Toll-free number: (800) 346-1017
Fax: (620) 278-4416
Dennis Dutton, Vice President for Enrollment Services, Sterling College, 125 West Cooper, Sterling, KS 67579

## Tabor College
### Hillsboro, Kansas
www.tabor.edu

CB code: 6815

- Private 4-year liberal arts college affiliated with Mennonite Brethren Church
- Residential campus in small town
- 561 degree-seeking undergraduates: 17% part-time, 50% women
- SAT or ACT (ACT writing optional), application essay required
- 46% graduate within 6 years; 15% enter graduate study

**General.** Founded in 1908. Regionally accredited. Off-campus site in Wichita offers adult degree completion program and graduate studies. **Degrees:** 137 bachelor's, 1 associate awarded; master's offered. **Location:** 50 miles from Wichita. **Calendar:** 4-1-4, limited summer session. **Full-time faculty:** 33 total; 73% have terminal degrees, 6% minority, 39% women. **Part-time faculty:** 48 total; 15% have terminal degrees, 4% minority, 50% women. **Class size:** 71% < 20, 23% 20-39, 4% 40-49, 2% 50-99.

### Freshman class profile.

| Mid 50% test scores | | GPA 2.0-2.99: | 21% |
|---|---|---|---|
| SAT critical reading: | 440-580 | Rank in top quarter: | 39% |
| SAT math: | 450-600 | Rank in top tenth: | 18% |
| ACT composite: | 19-26 | Return as sophomores: | 65% |
| GPA 3.50 or higher: | 49% | Out-of-state: | 43% |
| GPA 3.0-3.49: | 29% | Live on campus: | 99% |

**Basis for selection.** Life values and objectives, desire for Christian growth and personal interviews are important. Students must score a minimum of 18 on ACT and have ACT GPA (4.0 scale) product of 45 or above to be considered for admission. Audition recommended for music or drama. **Learning Disabled:** Must provide IEPs if special accommodations requested.

**High school preparation.** 17 units recommended. Recommended units include English 4, mathematics 3, social studies 2, history 2, science 3 and foreign language 1. 2 units of fine arts are also recommended.

**2007-2008 Annual costs.** Tuition/fees: $17,650. Room/board: $6,250. Books/supplies: $700. Personal expenses: $3,000.

**2007-2008 Financial aid. Need-based:** 120 full-time freshmen applied for aid; 99 were judged to have need; 99 of these received aid. Average need met was 79%. Average scholarship/grant was $4,103; average loan $5,567. 28% of total undergraduate aid awarded as scholarships/grants, 72% as loans/jobs. **Non-need-based:** Awarded to 680 full-time undergraduates, including 189 freshmen. Scholarships awarded for academics, alumni affiliation, athletics, music/drama, religious affiliation, state residency.

**Application procedures. Admission:** Priority date 4/4; no deadline. $30 fee, may be waived for applicants with need. Application may be submitted online. Admission notification on a rolling basis beginning on or about 9/1. **Financial aid:** Priority date 3/1, closing date 8/30. FAFSA required. Applicants notified on a rolling basis starting 3/15; must reply within 4 week(s) of notification.

**Academics. Special study options:** Accelerated study, combined bachelor's/graduate degree, cross-registration, distance learning, double major, dual enrollment of high school students, exchange student, honors, independent study, internships, student-designed major, study abroad, teacher certification program, Washington semester. **Credit/placement by examination:** AP, CLEP, IB, SAT, ACT. 30 credit hours maximum toward bachelor's degree. **Support services:** Learning center, reduced course load, remedial instruction, study skills assistance, tutoring, writing center.

**Majors. Biology:** General, biochemistry. **Business:** Accounting/business management, administrative services, business admin, marketing, office management. **Communications:** General, journalism, organizational, public relations. **Computer sciences:** Computer science, system admin. **Conservation:** Environmental studies. **Education:** General, biology, business, chemistry, developmentally delayed, elementary, emotionally handicapped, English, health, history, kindergarten/preschool, learning disabled, mathematics, mentally handicapped, middle, multi-level teacher, multiple handicapped, music, physical, science, secondary, social science, social studies, special. **English:** English lit. **Health:** Athletic training, clinical lab technology, predental, premedicine, preop/surgical nursing, prepharmacy, preveterinary. **History:** General. **Interdisciplinary:** Biological/physical sciences, math/computer science, natural sciences. **Legal studies:** Prelaw. **Liberal arts:** Humanities. **Math:** General. **Parks/recreation:** General, health/fitness, sports admin. **Philosophy/religion:** Philosophy, religion. **Physical sciences:** Chemistry. **Psychology:** General. **Social sciences:** General, sociology. **Theology:** Bible, theology, youth ministry. **Visual/performing arts:** Commercial/advertising art. **Other:** Social Welfare.

**Most popular majors.** Business/marketing 21%, education 15%, health sciences 14%, parks/recreation 6%, social sciences 8%, theological studies 10%.

**Computing on campus.** 58 workstations in library, computer center, student center. Dormitories wired for high-speed internet access and linked to campus network. Commuter students can connect to campus network. Online library, wireless network available.

**Student life. Freshman orientation:** Mandatory. Preregistration for classes offered. 3-day program prior to fall semester; includes service day. **Policies:** Students required to live on campus until age 23. Religious observance required. **Housing:** Guaranteed on-campus for freshmen. Single-sex dorms, special housing for disabled, substance-free housing available. $125 fully refundable deposit. **Activities:** Bands, campus ministries, choral groups, dance, drama, international student organizations, music ensembles, musical theater, student government, student newspaper, science club, student music association, Christian student organizations, multicultural student union, international student union, English society, student education association, Fellowship of Christian Athletes.

**Athletics.** NAIA. **Intercollegiate:** Baseball M, basketball, cheerleading, cross-country, football (tackle) M, soccer, softball W, tennis, track and field, volleyball W. **Intramural:** Basketball, football (non-tackle), racquetball, soccer, table tennis, tennis, track and field, volleyball. **Team name:** Blue Jays.

**Student services.** Campus ministries, career counseling, student employment services, financial aid counseling, minority student services, personal counseling, placement for graduates. **Physically disabled:** Services for visually, hearing impaired.

**Contact.** E-mail: admissions@tabor.edu
Phone: (620) 947-3121 ext. 1723 Toll-free number: (800) 822-6799
Fax: (620) 947-6276
Rusty Allen, Vice President of Enrollment Management, Tabor College, 400 South Jefferson, Hillsboro, KS 67063-1799

## University of Kansas
### Lawrence, Kansas
www.ku.edu

CB member
CB code: 6871

- Public 4-year university
- Commuter campus in small city
- 19,943 degree-seeking undergraduates: 10% part-time, 49% women, 4% African American, 4% Asian American, 4% Hispanic American, 1% Native American, 3% international
- 6,044 graduate students
- 92% of applicants admitted
- SAT or ACT (ACT writing optional) required
- 59% graduate within 6 years; 28% enter graduate study

**General.** Founded in 1866. Regionally accredited. **Degrees:** 3,679 bachelor's awarded; master's, doctoral, first professional offered. **ROTC:** Army, Naval, Air Force. **Location:** 40 miles from Kansas City. **Calendar:** Semester, extensive summer session. **Full-time faculty:** 1,009 total; 97% have terminal degrees, 17% minority, 32% women. **Part-time faculty:** 76 total; 88% have terminal degrees, 4% minority, 22% women. **Class size:** 40% < 20, 42% 20-39, 6% 40-49, 6% 50-99, 6% >100. **Special facilities:** 12 libraries including art, engineering, science, music, government documents and maps, rare books, manuscripts, and regional collections; art and natural history museums, space technology center, observatory, Institute for Life Span Studies, performing arts center and organ recital hall, Kansas Ecological Reserves, design lab, flight research lab, radar systems and remote sensing lab, film studio, Center for the Humanities, multicultural resource center, Dole Institute of Politics.

**Freshman class profile.** 10,367 applied, 9,554 admitted, 4,084 enrolled.

| Mid 50% test scores | | | |
|---|---|---|---|
| **ACT composite:** | 22-27 | **Rank in top tenth:** | 27% |
| **GPA 3.50 or higher:** | 50% | **Return as sophomores:** | 81% |
| **GPA 3.0-3.49:** | 31% | **Out-of-state:** | 28% |
| **GPA 2.0-2.99:** | 19% | **Live on campus:** | 58% |
| **Rank in top quarter:** | 59% | **International:** | 3% |

**Basis for selection.** Admission to College of Liberal Arts and Sciences requires one of following for in-state students: minimum ACT score of 21 or SAT score of 980 (exclusive of Writing), rank in top third of high school class, or completion of required college preparatory curriculum with 2.0 GPA. For out-of-state students: minimum test scores are 24 on ACT or 1090 on SAT (exclusive of Writing); minimum GPA 2.5 on college preparatory curriculum; rank in top third of high school class. Admission policies for other colleges within university may vary. Audition required for music performance, music education, music therapy majors. **Homeschooled:** Admission based on test scores.

**High school preparation.** 14 units required; 17 recommended. Required and recommended units include English 4, mathematics 3-4, social studies 3, science 3, foreign language 2 and academic electives 1. One computer technology unit required, 1 science unit must be chemistry or physics. 4 units mathematics recommended for mathematics, engineering and architecture majors. Social studies units include history.

**2007-2008 Annual costs.** Tuition/fees: $7,146; $17,556 out-of-state. Room/board: $6,144. Books/supplies: $750. Personal expenses: $2,182.

**2006-2007 Financial aid. Need-based:** 3,222 full-time freshmen applied for aid; 1,547 were judged to have need; 1,468 of these received aid. Average need met was 60%. Average scholarship/grant was $3,974; average loan $2,257. 42% of total undergraduate aid awarded as scholarships/grants, 58% as loans/jobs. **Non-need-based:** Awarded to 4,451 full-time undergraduates, including 1,636 freshmen. Scholarships awarded for academics, alumni affiliation, art, athletics, leadership, minority status, music/drama, ROTC, state residency. **Additional information:** Work study available weekdays.

**Application procedures. Admission:** Priority date 1/15; deadline 4/1 (receipt date). $30 fee. Application may be submitted online. Admission notification on a rolling basis beginning on or about 9/1. Must reply by May 1 or within 2 week(s) if notified thereafter. **Financial aid:** Priority date 3/1; no closing date. FAFSA required. Applicants notified on a rolling basis starting 4/1; must reply within 2 week(s) of notification.

**Academics. Special study options:** Accelerated study, combined bachelor's/graduate degree, cooperative education, distance learning, double major, dual enrollment of high school students, ESL, honors, independent study, internships, study abroad, teacher certification program, Washington semester. **Credit/placement by examination:** AP, CLEP, IB, SAT, ACT, institutional tests. **Support services:** Learning center, remedial instruction, study skills assistance, tutoring, writing center.

**Honors college/program.** Students accepted into any school or college may also be accepted into the honors program.

**Majors. Architecture:** History/criticism. **Area/ethnic studies:** African, American, European, Latin American, Russian/Slavic, women's. **Biology:** General, biochemistry, microbiology, molecular. **Business:** General, accounting, business admin, finance, logistics, management information systems, marketing. **Communications:** Journalism. **Computer sciences:** General. **Conservation:** Environmental studies. **Education:** Art, biology, chemistry, early childhood, elementary, English, foreign languages, history, mathematics, middle, music, physical, physics, science, secondary, social studies. **Engineering:** Aerospace, architectural, chemical, civil, computer, electrical, mechanical, petroleum, physics. **English:** English lit, speech/rhetoric. **Foreign languages:** Classics, East Asian, French, Germanic, linguistics, Slavic, Spanish. **Health:** Athletic training, communication disorders, community health

services, music therapy. **History:** General. **Interdisciplinary:** Ancient studies, behavioral sciences. **Liberal arts:** Arts/sciences, humanities. **Math:** General. **Parks/recreation:** Health/fitness. **Philosophy/religion:** Philosophy, religion. **Physical sciences:** Astronomy, atmospheric science, chemistry, geology, physics. **Psychology:** General, developmental. **Public administration:** General, social work. **Social sciences:** Anthropology, economics, geography, international relations, political science, sociology. **Visual/performing arts:** Art history/conservation, ceramics, commercial/advertising art, dance, design, dramatic, fiber arts, graphic design, illustration, industrial design, interior design, metal/jewelry, music performance, music theory/composition, musicology, painting, piano/organ, printmaking, sculpture, stringed instruments, studio arts, theater design, voice/opera. **Other:** Ecology and Evolutionary Biology.

**Most popular majors.** Biology 7%, business/marketing 13%, communications/journalism 8%, English 10%, health sciences 6%, psychology 7%, social sciences 10%, visual/performing arts 8%.

**Computing on campus.** 1,500 workstations in dormitories, library, computer center. Dormitories wired for high-speed internet access and linked to campus network. Commuter students can connect to campus network. Online course registration, online library, helpline, student web hosting, wireless network available.

**Student life. Freshman orientation:** Available, $55 fee. Preregistration for classes offered. One-day program throughout summer; several 2 day programs available. Additional charges for parent participation and 2 day program. **Policies:** No alcohol permitted on campus, no smoking in any buildings. Parking by permit only. **Housing:** Coed dorms, single-sex dorms, apartments, cooperative housing, fraternity/sorority housing, substance-free housing available. $35 nonrefundable deposit, deadline 2/15. Scholarship halls available to students with high scholastic achievement and financial need. **Activities:** Bands, choral groups, dance, drama, international student organizations, literary magazine, music ensembles, musical theater, opera, radio station, student government, student newspaper, symphony orchestra, TV station, over 400 student organizations and activities available.

**Athletics.** NCAA. **Intercollegiate:** Baseball M, basketball, cross-country, football (tackle) M, golf, rowing (crew) W, soccer W, softball W, swimming W, tennis W, track and field, volleyball W. **Intramural:** Basketball, bowling, golf, racquetball, soccer, softball, table tennis, tennis, volleyball. **Team name:** Jayhawks.

**Student services.** Adult student services, alcohol/substance abuse counseling, career counseling, services for economically disadvantaged, student employment services, financial aid counseling, health services, legal services, minority student services, on-campus daycare, personal counseling, placement for graduates, veterans' counselor, women's services. **Physically disabled:** Services for visually, speech, hearing impaired.

**Contact.** E-mail: adm@ku.edu
Phone: (785) 864-3911 Fax: (785) 864-5017
Lisa Pinamonti Kress, Director of Admissions and Scholarships, University of Kansas, 1502 Iowa Street, Lawrence, KS 66045-7576

---

## University of Kansas Medical Center
**Kansas City, Kansas**
www.kumc.edu                                    CB code: 0414

♦ Public two-year upper-division university and health science college
♦ Commuter campus in small city

**General.** Founded in 1905. Regionally accredited. **Degrees:** 248 bachelor's awarded; master's, doctoral, first professional offered. **Location:** Downtown. **Calendar:** Semester, limited summer session. **Full-time faculty:** 262 total; 77% have terminal degrees, 20% minority, 56% women. **Part-time faculty:** 43 total; 54% have terminal degrees, 7% minority, 65% women. **Class size:** 68% < 20, 19% 20-39, 7% 50-99, 6% >100.

**Student profile.** 512 degree-seeking undergraduates, 1,608 degree-seeking graduate students. 149 applied as first time-transfer students.

| | | | |
|---|---|---|---|
| **Women:** | 88% | **International:** | 1% |
| **African American:** | 5% | **Part-time:** | 22% |
| **Asian American:** | 5% | **Out-of-state:** | 17% |
| **Hispanic American:** | 3% | **25 or older:** | 35% |
| **Native American:** | 1% | | |

**Basis for selection.** College transcript required. Admissions regulations, policies and application closing dates vary by degree program. Transfer accepted as juniors, seniors.

**2007-2008 Annual costs.** Tuition/fees: $6,194; $15,701 out-of-state. Annual tuition for medical students: $22,486 (residents) and $39,877 (nonresidents); required fees are $332. Books/supplies: $1,440.

**Financial aid. Need-based:** 328 applied for aid; 302 were judged to have need; 296 of these received aid. Average need met was 34%. 45% of total undergraduate aid awarded as scholarships/grants, 55% as loans/jobs. **Non-need-based:** Awarded to 189 undergraduates. Scholarships awarded for academics, leadership, minority status, state residency.

**Application procedures. Admission:** $60 fee. Admissions deadlines vary by school and program. **Financial aid:** Priority date 2/14, no deadline. Applicants notified on a rolling basis starting 4/1.

**Academics.** Assessment and reading skills screened. Assistance offered in reviewing APA-style papers. **Special study options:** Combined bachelor's/graduate degree, distance learning, honors, independent study, internships. BS/MOT in occupational therapy. **Credit/placement by examination:** CLEP.

**Majors. Health:** Clinical lab science, cytotechnology, medical records admin, nursing (RN), respiratory therapy technology.

**Computing on campus.** 71 workstations in library, computer center, student center. Commuter students can connect to campus network. Helpline, student web hosting, wireless network available.

**Student life. Activities:** Literary magazine, student government, allied health student senate, graduate student council, medical student assembly, association of undergraduate nurses, Latino Midwest medical student association, American medical women's association, Students for Women's Wellness, Lifewatch Bible Study (Christian medical/dental society), Students Educating and Advocating for Diversity.

**Athletics. Intramural:** Basketball, racquetball, soccer, softball, volleyball.

**Student services.** Campus ministries, financial aid counseling, health services, legal services, personal counseling. **Physically disabled:** Services for visually, speech, hearing impaired.

**Contact.** E-mail: kumcregistrar@kumc.edu
Phone: (913) 588-7055 Fax: (913) 588-4697
University of Kansas Medical Center, 3901 Rainbow Boulevard, Kansas City, KS 66160-7116

## University of St. Mary
**Leavenworth, Kansas**
www.stmary.edu
CB code: 6630

- Private 4-year university affiliated with Roman Catholic Church
- Residential campus in large town
- 475 degree-seeking undergraduates: 14% part-time, 60% women, 12% African American, 1% Asian American, 8% Hispanic American, 1% Native American
- 286 degree-seeking graduate students
- 61% of applicants admitted
- SAT or ACT (ACT writing optional) required
- 32% graduate within 6 years

**General.** Founded in 1923. Regionally accredited. **Degrees:** 87 bachelor's awarded; master's offered. **ROTC:** Army, Air Force. **Location:** 26 miles from Kansas City. **Calendar:** Semester, limited summer session. **Full-time faculty:** 43 total; 46% have terminal degrees, 7% minority, 51% women. **Part-time faculty:** 59 total; 14% have terminal degrees, 5% minority, 51% women. **Class size:** 80% < 20, 19% 20-39, 1% 50-99. **Special facilities:** Sacred Scripture and History of the Catholic Church in Kansas collections in library.

**Freshman class profile.** 442 applied, 270 admitted, 66 enrolled.

| Mid 50% test scores | | Rank in top quarter: | 40% |
|---|---|---|---|
| SAT critical reading: | 420-570 | Rank in top tenth: | 16% |
| SAT math: | 420-590 | End year in good standing: | 65% |
| ACT composite: | 19-25 | Return as sophomores: | 61% |
| GPA 3.50 or higher: | 51% | Out-of-state: | 39% |
| GPA 3.0-3.49: | 22% | Live on campus: | 79% |
| GPA 2.0-2.99: | 26% | | |

**Basis for selection.** Minimum 2.5 high school GPA, 18 ACT, 870 SAT (exclusive of Writing) required. Applicants below required GPA or ACT/SAT may be considered for admission. Portfolio recommended for fine and applied arts majors. **Homeschooled:** ACT or SAT recommended.

**High school preparation.** 12 units required; 24 recommended. Required and recommended units include English 4, mathematics 2-4, social studies 2, history 2-4, science 2-4 (laboratory 2), foreign language 2 and academic electives 2. 1-2 computer programming recommended.

**2008-2009 Annual costs.** Tuition/fees (projected): $18,120. Room/board: $6,400. Books/supplies: $1,000. Personal expenses: $1,732.

**2007-2008 Financial aid. Need-based:** 66 full-time freshmen applied for aid; 51 were judged to have need; 51 of these received aid. Average need met was 47%. Average scholarship/grant was $7,434; average loan $3,814. 51% of total undergraduate aid awarded as scholarships/grants, 49% as loans/jobs. **Non-need-based:** Awarded to 262 full-time undergraduates, including 41 freshmen. Scholarships awarded for academics, art, athletics, leadership, music/drama. **Additional information:** Essays may be required for scholarship applicants. Auditions recommended for music and drama scholarship applicants. Portfolio reviews for art award applicants.

**Application procedures. Admission:** No deadline. $25 fee. Application may be submitted online. Admission notification on a rolling basis. Must reply by May 1 or within 4 week(s) if notified thereafter. **Financial aid:** Priority date 4/1; no closing date. FAFSA required. Applicants notified on a rolling basis starting 2/8; must reply within 2 week(s) of notification.

**Academics. Special study options:** Accelerated study, distance learning, double major, dual enrollment of high school students, exchange student, honors, independent study, internships, student-designed major, study abroad, teacher certification program. Degree completion programs. **Credit/placement by examination:** AP, CLEP, IB, SAT, ACT, institutional tests. 30 credit hours maximum toward bachelor's degree. **Support services:** Learning center, remedial instruction, study skills assistance, tutoring.

**Majors. Biology:** General. **Business:** General, accounting, business admin, international. **Communications:** General. **Computer sciences:** Information technology. **Education:** Elementary. **English:** English lit. **Family/consumer sciences:** Child development. **Health:** Nursing (RN). **History:** General. **Liberal arts:** Arts/sciences. **Math:** General. **Parks/recreation:** Sports admin. **Physical sciences:** Chemistry. **Psychology:** General. **Social sciences:** Political science, sociology. **Theology:** Pastoral counseling, theology. **Visual/performing arts:** Art, dramatic.

**Most popular majors.** Business/marketing 27%, computer/information sciences 7%, education 6%, parks/recreation 6%, psychology 16%, social sciences 14%.

**Computing on campus.** 95 workstations in dormitories, library, computer center. Dormitories wired for high-speed internet access and linked to campus network. Helpline, student web hosting, wireless network available.

**Student life. Freshman orientation:** Mandatory. Preregistration for classes offered. 3-day program at beginning of fall semester. **Housing:** Guaranteed on-campus for freshmen. Coed dorms available. $100 deposit. **Activities:** Bands, campus ministries, choral groups, drama, international student organizations, literary magazine, music ensembles, musical theater, opera, student government, student newspaper, Bacchus, Aristotle Club, Amnesty International, Students in Free Enterprise, Young Democrats, Campus Republicans.

**Athletics. NAIA. Intercollegiate:** Baseball M, basketball, football (tackle) M, soccer, softball W, volleyball W. **Intramural:** Basketball, bowling, racquetball, softball, table tennis, volleyball. **Team name:** Spires.

**Student services.** Adult student services, alcohol/substance abuse counseling, campus ministries, career counseling, student employment services, financial aid counseling, health services, on-campus daycare, personal counseling, placement for graduates, veterans' counselor.

**Contact.** E-mail: admiss@stmary.edu
Phone: (913) 758-6118 Toll-free number: (800) 752-7043
Fax: (913) 758-6140
Jessica Goffinet, Director of Admissions, University of St. Mary, 4100 South Fourth Street Trafficway, Leavenworth, KS 66048

## Washburn University
**Topeka, Kansas**
www.washburn.edu
CB code: 6928

- Public 4-year university
- Commuter campus in small city
- 5,675 degree-seeking undergraduates: 29% part-time, 61% women
- 881 degree-seeking graduate students
- 54% graduate within 6 years

**General.** Founded in 1865. Regionally accredited. **Degrees:** 725 bachelor's, 122 associate awarded; master's, first professional offered. **ROTC:** Army, Naval, Air Force. **Location:** 60 miles from Kansas City. **Calendar:** Semester, extensive summer session. **Full-time faculty:** 262 total; 84% have terminal degrees, 13% minority, 48% women. **Part-time faculty:** 265 total; 42% have terminal degrees, 8% minority, 50% women. **Class size:** 47%

< 20, 45% 20-39, 6% 40-49, 2% 50-99. **Special facilities:** Concert hall, observatory, planetarium, 30-acre natural study and research area.

**Freshman class profile.** 1,549 applied, 1,523 admitted, 793 enrolled.

| Mid 50% test scores | | End year in good standing: | 59% |
|---|---|---|---|
| ACT composite: | 19-25 | Return as sophomores: | 61% |
| GPA 3.50 or higher: | 42% | Out-of-state: | 8% |
| GPA 3.0-3.49: | 29% | Live on campus: | 40% |
| GPA 2.0-2.99: | 26% | Fraternities: | 4% |
| Rank in top quarter: | 37% | Sororities: | 4% |
| Rank in top tenth: | 14% | | |

**Basis for selection.** Open admission, but selective for some programs. Special requirements for health science programs, nursing, school of business, and education. ACT or ASSET required of all students for placement purposes.

**High school preparation.** Recommended units include English 4, mathematics 3, social studies 3, history 1, science 3 and foreign language 2. 1 unit computer technology recommended.

**2007-2008 Annual costs.** Tuition/fees: $5,636; $12,686 out-of-state. Room/board: $5,281. Books/supplies: $1,462. Personal expenses: $2,486.

**2007-2008 Financial aid. Need-based:** 591 full-time freshmen applied for aid; 405 were judged to have need; 405 of these received aid. Average need met was 40%. Average scholarship/grant was $3,464; average loan $3,391. 36% of total undergraduate aid awarded as scholarships/grants, 64% as loans/jobs. **Non-need-based:** Awarded to 2,031 full-time undergraduates, including 330 freshmen. Scholarships awarded for academics, alumni affiliation, art, athletics, job skills, leadership, minority status, music/drama, religious affiliation, ROTC, state residency.

**Application procedures. Admission:** Priority date 7/1; deadline 8/1. $20 fee. Application may be submitted online. Admission notification on a rolling basis beginning on or about 9/1. **Financial aid:** Priority date 2/15; no closing date. FAFSA required. Applicants notified on a rolling basis starting 3/15; must reply within 4 week(s) of notification.

**Academics. Special study options:** Cooperative education, cross-registration, distance learning, double major, dual enrollment of high school students, ESL, honors, independent study, internships, liberal arts/career combination, student-designed major, study abroad, teacher certification program. **Credit/placement by examination:** AP, CLEP, institutional tests. 40 credit hours maximum toward bachelor's degree. **Support services:** Learning center, remedial instruction, study skills assistance, tutoring, writing center.

**Majors. Biology:** General, biochemistry. **Business:** General, accounting, business admin, finance, managerial economics, marketing. **Communications:** General, media studies. **Computer sciences:** General, systems analysis. **Education:** General, art, early childhood, elementary, English, foreign languages, health, mathematics, music, physical, science, secondary, social science, social studies. **English:** English lit, speech/rhetoric. **Foreign languages:** French, German, Spanish. **Health:** Athletic training, clinical lab technology, health services, nursing (RN), predental, premedicine, prepharmacy, preveterinary, sonography, substance abuse counseling. **History:** General. **Interdisciplinary:** Gerontology. **Legal studies:** Paralegal, prelaw. **Liberal arts:** Arts/sciences. **Math:** General. **Parks/recreation:** Exercise sciences, health/fitness, sports admin. **Philosophy/religion:** Philosophy, religion. **Physical sciences:** General, chemistry, physics. **Protective services:** Corrections, criminal justice, forensics, law enforcement admin, police science, security services. **Psychology:** General. **Public administration:** General, social work. **Social sciences:** Anthropology, economics, political science, sociology. **Visual/performing arts:** General, art, art history/conservation, dramatic, music performance, studio arts.

**Most popular majors.** Business/marketing 25%, communications/journalism 6%, education 6%, health sciences 20%, security/protective services 10%, visual/performing arts 6%.

**Computing on campus.** 1,200 workstations in dormitories, library, computer center, student center. Dormitories wired for high-speed internet access and linked to campus network. Commuter students can connect to campus network. Online course registration, online library, helpline, student web hosting, wireless network available.

**Student life. Freshman orientation:** Available. Preregistration for classes offered. Half-day session in summer for pre-registration; 3-day session prior to start of classes. **Housing:** Coed dorms, apartments, fraternity/sorority housing, substance-free housing available. $200 partly refundable deposit. Special interest housing available. **Activities:** Bands, choral groups, dance, drama, film society, international student organizations, literary magazine, music ensembles, musical theater, student government, student newspaper, symphony orchestra, TV station, College Republicans, Young Democrats,

Learning in the Community, Campus Crusade for Christ, Circle K, Project Equal, Fellowship of Christian Athletes, Hispanic American Leadership Organization, Black Men and Women of Today.

**Athletics. NCAA. Intercollegiate:** Baseball M, basketball, cheerleading, football (tackle) M, golf M, soccer W, softball W, tennis, volleyball W. **Intramural:** Badminton, basketball, football (non-tackle), golf, soccer, softball, table tennis, tennis, volleyball. **Team name:** Ichabods.

**Student services.** Adult student services, alcohol/substance abuse counseling, career counseling, services for economically disadvantaged, student employment services, financial aid counseling, health services, minority student services, personal counseling, placement for graduates, veterans' counselor. **Physically disabled:** Services for visually, hearing impaired.

**Contact.** E-mail: admissions@washburn.edu
Phone: (785) 670-1030 Toll-free number: (800) 332-0291
Fax: (785) 670-1113
Kirk Haskins, Director of Admissions, Washburn University, 1700 Southwest College, Morgan 114, Topeka, KS 66621

---

## Wichita State University
### Wichita, Kansas
**www.wichita.edu**        **CB code: 6884**

- Public 4-year university
- Commuter campus in large city
- 10,261 degree-seeking undergraduates: 29% part-time, 56% women, 6% African American, 6% Asian American, 5% Hispanic American, 1% Native American, 5% international
- 2,660 degree-seeking graduate students
- 85% of applicants admitted
- 41% graduate within 6 years

**General.** Founded in 1895. Regionally accredited. **Degrees:** 1,756 bachelor's, 84 associate awarded; master's, doctoral offered. **Calendar:** Semester, extensive summer session. **Full-time faculty:** 476 total; 78% have terminal degrees, 13% minority, 40% women. **Part-time faculty:** 51 total; 47% have terminal degrees, 16% minority, 49% women. **Class size:** 48% < 20, 37% 20-39, 5% 40-49, 8% 50-99, 2% >100. **Special facilities:** Sculpture garden, wind tunnels, Marcusson pipe organ, flow-visualization water tunnel, National Aviation Research Institute, observatory.

**Freshman class profile.** 2,997 applied, 2,548 admitted, 1,352 enrolled.

| Mid 50% test scores | | Rank in top tenth: | 19% |
|---|---|---|---|
| SAT critical reading: | 430-600 | End year in good standing: | 74% |
| SAT math: | 470-620 | Return as sophomores: | 67% |
| ACT composite: | 20-25 | Out-of-state: | 6% |
| GPA 3.50 or higher: | 43% | Live on campus: | 29% |
| GPA 3.0-3.49: | 32% | International: | 4% |
| GPA 2.0-2.99: | 24% | Fraternities: | 12% |
| Rank in top quarter: | 47% | Sororities: | 7% |

**Basis for selection.** In-state criteria: 21 ACT or greater, rank in top 1/3 of high school class, or minimum 2.00 GPA in pre-college curriculum. Some academic colleges within WSU require a higher GPA for admission. Out-of-state criteria: varies by college. **Homeschooled:** State high school equivalency certificate required. ACT required.

**High school preparation.** 14 units required. Required units include English 4, mathematics 3, social studies 3 and science 3. One computer technology required.

**2007-2008 Annual costs.** Tuition/fees: $4,804; $12,151 out-of-state. Room/board: $5,580. Books/supplies: $800. Personal expenses: $1,570.

**2006-2007 Financial aid. Need-based:** 1,069 full-time freshmen applied for aid; 570 were judged to have need; 546 of these received aid. Average need met was 47%. Average scholarship/grant was $3,178; average loan $2,268. 29% of total undergraduate aid awarded as scholarships/grants, 71% as loans/jobs. **Non-need-based:** Awarded to 1,699 full-time undergraduates, including 699 freshmen. Scholarships awarded for academics, alumni affiliation, art, athletics, leadership, music/drama. **Additional information:** Top freshman applicants admitted by October 1 invited to university scholarship competition.

**Application procedures. Admission:** No deadline. $30 fee. Application may be submitted online. Admission notification on a rolling basis. **Financial aid:** Priority date 3/1; no closing date. FAFSA required. Applicants notified on a rolling basis starting 3/15; must reply within 2 week(s) of notification.

**Academics.** 24-hour study room with Internet access. All library databases and other software maintained for student use. **Special study options:** Accelerated study, combined bachelor's/graduate degree, cooperative education, distance learning, double major, dual enrollment of high school students, ESL, exchange student, honors, independent study, internships, liberal arts/career combination, study abroad, teacher certification program, Washington semester. Peace Corps returnee program. **Credit/placement by examination:** AP, CLEP, IB, SAT, ACT, institutional tests. 30 credit hours maximum toward associate degree, 60 toward bachelor's. **Support services:** Learning center, pre-admission summer program, reduced course load, remedial instruction, study skills assistance, tutoring, writing center.

**Majors. Area/ethnic studies:** Women's. **Biology:** General. **Business:** Accounting, business admin, finance, human resources, international, management information systems, marketing. **Communications:** General. **Computer sciences:** General. **Education:** Art, elementary, music, physical, secondary. **Engineering:** Aerospace, computer, electrical, industrial, manufacturing, mechanical. **English:** English lit. **Foreign languages:** French, Latin, Spanish. **Health:** Athletic training, audiology/speech pathology, dental hygiene, health care admin, physician assistant, staff services technology. **History:** General. **Interdisciplinary:** Gerontology. **Liberal arts:** Arts/sciences. **Math:** General. **Parks/recreation:** Exercise sciences, sports admin. **Philosophy/religion:** Philosophy. **Physical sciences:** Chemistry, geology, physics. **Protective services:** Criminal justice. **Psychology:** General. **Public administration:** Social work. **Social sciences:** Anthropology, economics, political science, sociology. **Visual/performing arts:** General, art, art history/conservation, commercial/advertising art, dramatic, studio arts.

**Most popular majors.** Business/marketing 22%, education 8%, engineering/engineering technologies 9%, health sciences 11%, psychology 6%, security/protective services 6%.

**Computing on campus.** 1,500 workstations in dormitories, library, computer center, student center. Dormitories wired for high-speed internet access and linked to campus network. Commuter students can connect to campus network. Online course registration, online library, helpline, wireless network available.

**Student life. Freshman orientation:** Mandatory, $10 fee. Preregistration for classes offered. Held prior to fall semester. **Housing:** Guaranteed on-campus for freshmen. Coed dorms, special housing for disabled, apartments, fraternity/sorority housing, substance-free housing available. **Activities:** Bands, choral groups, dance, drama, film society, international student organizations, literary magazine, music ensembles, Model UN, musical theater, opera, radio station, student government, student newspaper, symphony orchestra, TV station, Campus Crusade for Christ, College Republicans, Chinese student friendship association, Black Student Union, Hispanic American leadership association, Students in Free Enterprise, Association of Hindu Students.

**Athletics.** NCAA. **Intercollegiate:** Baseball M, basketball, cheerleading, cross-country, golf, softball W, tennis, track and field, volleyball W. **Intramural:** Badminton, basketball, football (non-tackle), golf, racquetball, rowing (crew), soccer, softball, swimming, table tennis, tennis, volleyball. **Team name:** Shockers.

**Student services.** Adult student services, alcohol/substance abuse counseling, campus ministries, career counseling, services for economically disadvantaged, student employment services, financial aid counseling, health services, minority student services, on-campus daycare, personal counseling, placement for graduates, veterans' counselor. **Physically disabled:** Services for visually, speech, hearing impaired.

**Contact.** E-mail: admissions@wichita.edu
Phone: (316) 978-3085 Toll-free number: (800) 362-2594
Fax: (316) 978-3174
Bobby Gandu, Director of Admissions, Wichita State University, 1845 Fairmount Box 124, Wichita, KS 67260-0124

# Kentucky

## Alice Lloyd College
**Pippa Passes, Kentucky**
**www.alc.edu**                    **CB code: 1098**

- Private 4-year liberal arts college
- Residential campus in rural community
- 607 degree-seeking undergraduates: 2% part-time, 51% women, 1% African American
- 45% of applicants admitted
- SAT or ACT (ACT writing optional) required

**General.** Founded in 1923. Regionally accredited. **Degrees:** 95 bachelor's awarded. **Location:** 150 miles from Lexington, 100 miles from Huntington, West Virginia. **Calendar:** Semester. **Full-time faculty:** 29 total; 59% have terminal degrees, 10% minority, 41% women. **Part-time faculty:** 13 total; 15% have terminal degrees, 69% women. **Class size:** 41% < 20, 54% 20-39, 5% 40-49. **Special facilities:** Appalachian history collection, photographic archives.

**Freshman class profile.** 1,254 applied, 562 admitted, 177 enrolled.

| Mid 50% test scores | | GPA 2.0-2.99: | 23% |
|---|---|---|---|
| SAT critical reading: | 440-590 | Rank in top quarter: | 58% |
| SAT math: | 480-570 | Rank in top tenth: | 21% |
| SAT writing: | 430-530 | End year in good standing: | 96% |
| ACT composite: | 17-23 | Return as sophomores: | 63% |
| GPA 3.50 or higher: | 42% | Out-of-state: | 21% |
| GPA 3.0-3.49: | 33% | Live on campus: | 91% |

**Basis for selection.** High school record and test scores important. Essay and interview recommended. **Homeschooled:** Transcript of courses and grades, letter of recommendation (nonparent) required. Interview highly recommended.

**High school preparation.** 12 units required. Required units include English 4, mathematics 3, social studies 2 and science 3.

**2007-2008 Annual costs.** Tuition/fees: $8,250. Guaranteed tuition for students from 108-county central Appalachian service area in Kentucky, West Virginia, Virginia, Tennessee, and Ohio. Room/board: $4,050. Books/supplies: $850. Personal expenses: $1,300.

**2006-2007 Financial aid. Need-based:** 201 full-time freshmen applied for aid; 173 were judged to have need; 173 of these received aid. Average need met was 73%. Average scholarship/grant was $6,331; average loan $276. 75% of total undergraduate aid awarded as scholarships/grants, 25% as loans/jobs. **Non-need-based:** Awarded to 219 full-time undergraduates, including 67 freshmen. Scholarships awarded for athletics, minority status, state residency. **Additional information:** All students receive financial aid through student work program. No student denied admission because of inability to pay. All full-time students required to work minimum of 10 hours per week.

**Application procedures. Admission:** Priority date 5/1; no deadline. No application fee. Application may be submitted online. Admission notification on a rolling basis beginning on or about 9/1. **Financial aid:** Priority date 3/15; no closing date. FAFSA required. Applicants notified on a rolling basis starting 4/1; must reply within 6 week(s) of notification.

**Academics.** Scholarships for graduate work following graduation. **Special study options:** Double major, independent study, internships, liberal arts/career combination, student-designed major, study abroad, teacher certification program, Washington semester. **Credit/placement by examination:** AP, CLEP, IB, SAT, ACT, institutional tests. 30 credit hours maximum toward bachelor's degree. Limited number of hours of credit by examination may be counted toward degree, decided on individual basis. **Support services:** Reduced course load, remedial instruction, study skills assistance, tutoring, writing center.

**Majors. Biology:** General. **Business:** Business admin. **Education:** Biology, elementary, English, mathematics, middle, physical, science, secondary, social studies. **English:** English lit. **History:** General. **Interdisciplinary:** Biological/physical sciences. **Parks/recreation:** General. **Social sciences:** General.

**Most popular majors.** Biology 26%, business/marketing 18%, education 23%, English 6%, history 10%, social sciences 11%.

**Computing on campus.** 80 workstations in library, computer center. Dormitories wired for high-speed internet access and linked to campus network. Online library, helpline, repair service, wireless network available.

**Student life. Freshman orientation:** Mandatory. Preregistration for classes offered. Held 3 days before start of first semester. **Policies:** Zero tolerance of on-campus alcohol and/or drug usage or possession. **Housing:** Guaranteed on-campus for all undergraduates. Single-sex dorms available. $50 deposit, deadline 5/15. **Activities:** Choral groups, drama, radio station, student government, student newspaper, Students for Christ, Baptist student union, cultural diversity club, children's outreach club, community service volunteers, Circle K.

**Athletics.** NAIA. **Intercollegiate:** Baseball M, basketball, cheerleading M, cross-country, softball W. **Intramural:** Basketball, bowling, football (nontackle), golf, racquetball, soccer, softball, swimming, table tennis, tennis, volleyball, weight lifting. **Team name:** Eagles.

**Student services.** Alcohol/substance abuse counseling, career counseling, student employment services, financial aid counseling, health services, on-campus daycare, personal counseling, placement for graduates, veterans' counselor.

**Contact.** E-mail: admissions@alc.edu
Phone: (606) 368-6036 Toll-free number: (888) 280-4252
Fax: (606) 368-6215
Bryan Swafford, Director of Admissions, Alice Lloyd College, 100 Purpose Road, Pippa Passes, KY 41844

## Asbury College
**Wilmore, Kentucky**                    **CB member**
**www.asbury.edu**                    **CB code: 1019**

- Private 4-year liberal arts college affiliated with interdenominational tradition
- Residential campus in small town
- 1,252 degree-seeking undergraduates: 2% part-time, 57% women, 2% African American, 1% Asian American, 2% Hispanic American, 1% international
- 62 degree-seeking graduate students
- 62% of applicants admitted
- SAT or ACT (ACT writing optional), application essay required
- 64% graduate within 6 years

**General.** Founded in 1890. Regionally accredited. **Degrees:** 231 bachelor's awarded; master's offered. **ROTC:** Army, Air Force. **Location:** 20 miles from Lexington. **Calendar:** Semester, limited summer session. **Full-time faculty:** 79 total; 76% have terminal degrees, 2% minority, 30% women. **Part-time faculty:** 60 total; 23% have terminal degrees, 8% minority, 43% women. **Class size:** 57% < 20, 39% 20-39, 3% 40-49.

**Freshman class profile.** 1,364 applied, 848 admitted, 318 enrolled.

| Mid 50% test scores | | Rank in top quarter: | 54% |
|---|---|---|---|
| SAT critical reading: | 530-660 | Rank in top tenth: | 31% |
| SAT math: | 510-640 | Return as sophomores: | 87% |
| ACT composite: | 22-28 | Out-of-state: | 60% |
| GPA 3.50 or higher: | 62% | Live on campus: | 94% |
| GPA 3.0-3.49: | 24% | International: | 1% |
| GPA 2.0-2.99: | 14% | | |

**Basis for selection.** Careful consideration given to academic records, test scores, application essays, references, and ability to benefit. Probationary acceptance possible if GPA below 2.5. ACT required prior to admission to education department; both ACT and SAT required for presidential level scholarships. Interview recommended for music majors, academically weak applicants, scholarship applicants. Audition required for music majors. Portfolio recommended for art majors. **Homeschooled:** Transcript of courses and grades, state high school equivalency certificate required.

**High school preparation.** 15 units recommended. Recommended units include English 4, mathematics 3, social studies 1, history 1, science 2 (laboratory 2) and foreign language 2.

**2008-2009 Annual costs.** Tuition/fees: $22,413. Room/board: $5,414. Books/supplies: $770. Personal expenses: $1,170.

**2007-2008 Financial aid. Need-based:** 283 full-time freshmen applied for aid; 219 were judged to have need; 219 of these received aid. Average need met was 84%. Average scholarship/grant was $10,398; average loan

$3,088. 59% of total undergraduate aid awarded as scholarships/grants, 41% as loans/jobs. **Non-need-based:** Scholarships awarded for academics, alumni affiliation, athletics, leadership, minority status, music/drama, religious affiliation, ROTC.

**Application procedures. Admission:** No deadline. $30 fee, may be waived for applicants with need. Application may be submitted online. Admission notification on a rolling basis. Confirmation of intention to enroll requires $200 pre-tuition deposit within 30 days of admission notification. **Financial aid:** Priority date 3/1; no closing date. Institutional form required. Applicants notified on a rolling basis starting 1/31; must reply within 4 week(s) of notification.

**Academics. Special study options:** Double major, ESL, internships, study abroad, teacher certification program, Washington semester. Exchange program with colleges in Christian College Consortium, 3-2 programs in engineering with the University of Kentucky. **Credit/placement by examination:** AP, CLEP, IB, SAT, ACT, institutional tests. **Support services:** Remedial instruction, study skills assistance, tutoring, writing center.

**Majors. Agriculture:** Equestrian studies. **Biology:** General, biochemistry. **Business:** General, accounting. **Communications:** Journalism. **Communications technology:** Radio/tv. **Education:** Art, elementary, middle, music, physical. **English:** Creative writing, English lit, speech/rhetoric. **Foreign languages:** Biblical, French, Spanish. **Health:** Health services, hypnotherapy. **History:** General. **Math:** General, computational. **Parks/recreation:** Facilities management, health/fitness, sports admin. **Philosophy/religion:** Philosophy. **Physical sciences:** General, chemistry. **Psychology:** General. **Public administration:** Social work. **Social sciences:** General, sociology. **Theology:** Bible, missionary, religious ed, youth ministry. **Visual/performing arts:** Dramatic, music management, studio arts. **Other:** Mathematics, financial.

**Most popular majors.** Business/marketing 8%, communication technologies 15%, education 10%, English 9%, psychology 9%, theological studies 10%, visual/performing arts 7%.

**Computing on campus.** 200 workstations in dormitories, library, computer center, student center. Dormitories wired for high-speed internet access and linked to campus network. Commuter students can connect to campus network. Online library, helpline, repair service available.

**Student life. Freshman orientation:** Mandatory. Preregistration for classes offered. Held weekend before fall semester begins. **Policies:** Christian values stressed. Religious observance required. **Housing:** Guaranteed on-campus for freshmen. Single-sex dorms, special housing for disabled, apartments available. **Activities:** Bands, choral groups, drama, literary magazine, music ensembles, musical theater, opera, radio station, student government, student newspaper, symphony orchestra, TV station, Christian service association, student fellowships, Impact, Asburians for Life, ministerial association, outdoors club.

**Athletics.** NAIA, NCCAA. **Intercollegiate:** Baseball M, basketball, cross-country, diving, soccer, swimming, tennis, volleyball W. **Intramural:** Basketball, football (non-tackle), golf, racquetball, soccer, softball, volleyball. **Team name:** Eagles.

**Student services.** Campus ministries, career counseling, student employment services, health services, minority student services, personal counseling, placement for graduates, veterans' counselor.

**Contact.** E-mail: admissions@asbury.edu
Phone: (859) 858-3511 ext. 2142 Toll-free number: (800) 888-1818
Fax: (859) 858-3921
Ronald Anderson, Director of Admissions, Asbury College, One Macklem Drive, Wilmore, KY 40390-1198

## Beckfield College
**Florence, Kentucky**
www.beckfield.edu
**CB code: 3404**

▶ For-profit 4-year business, health science and nursing college
▶ Commuter campus in large town
▶ 575 degree-seeking undergraduates
▶ Interview required

**General.** Accredited by ACICS. **Degrees:** 65 associate awarded. **Location:** 10 miles from Cincinnati. **Calendar:** Quarter, extensive summer session. **Full-time faculty:** 17 total. **Part-time faculty:** 25 total. **Class size:** 100% < 20.

**Basis for selection.** Open admission, but selective for some programs. Nursing program requires qualifying ACT or SAT scores. **Homeschooled:**

Transcript of courses and grades required. Accredited home study course will be considered for admission.

**2007-2008 Annual costs.** Tuition/fees: $10,990. Fees vary by program. Books/supplies: $1,200.

**2006-2007 Financial aid.** All financial aid based on need. **Additional information:** Deadline for filing of financial aid forms is end of first week of classes.

**Application procedures. Admission:** No deadline. $150 fee. Application must be submitted on paper. Admission notification on a rolling basis. **Financial aid:** FAFSA required. Applicants notified on a rolling basis.

**Academics. Special study options:** Combined bachelor's/graduate degree, independent study, internships. **Credit/placement by examination:** CLEP, IB, institutional tests. **Support services:** Reduced course load, remedial instruction, study skills assistance, tutoring.

**Majors. Business:** Business admin. **Health:** Nursing (RN). **Legal studies:** Paralegal. **Protective services:** Law enforcement admin.

**Computing on campus.** 90 workstations in library, computer center. Online library, wireless network available.

**Student life. Freshman orientation:** Mandatory. Preregistration for classes offered. Held for half day 3 days before beginning of quarter.

**Student services.** Alcohol/substance abuse counseling, career counseling, student employment services, financial aid counseling, personal counseling, placement for graduates, veterans' counselor.

**Contact.** E-mail: lboerger@beckfield.edu
Phone: (859) 795-4947 Fax: (859) 371-5096
Leah Boerger, Director of Admissions, Beckfield College, 16 Spiral Drive, Florence, KY 41042

## Bellarmine University
**Louisville, Kentucky**
www.bellarmine.edu
**CB member**
**CB code: 1056**

▶ Private 4-year university and liberal arts college affiliated with Roman Catholic Church
▶ Commuter campus in very large city
▶ 2,032 degree-seeking undergraduates: 7% part-time, 65% women, 3% African American, 2% Asian American, 2% Hispanic American, 2% international
▶ 658 degree-seeking graduate students
▶ 63% of applicants admitted
▶ SAT or ACT (ACT writing optional), application essay required
▶ 65% graduate within 6 years; 31% enter graduate study

**General.** Founded in 1950. Regionally accredited. **Degrees:** 484 bachelor's awarded; master's, doctoral offered. **ROTC:** Army, Air Force. **Location:** 7 miles from downtown, 100 miles from Cincinnati. **Calendar:** Semester, extensive summer session. **Full-time faculty:** 129 total; 80% have terminal degrees, 5% minority, 49% women. **Part-time faculty:** 147 total; 34% have terminal degrees, 4% minority, 54% women. **Class size:** 59% < 20, 38% 20-39, 2% 40-49, less than 1% 50-99.

**Freshman class profile.** 3,481 applied, 2,187 admitted, 569 enrolled.

| Mid 50% test scores | | | |
|---|---|---|---|
| SAT critical reading: | 500-620 | Rank in top quarter: | 50% |
| SAT math: | 510-610 | Rank in top tenth: | 22% |
| ACT composite: | 22-27 | End year in good standing: | 82% |
| GPA 3.50 or higher: | 52% | Return as sophomores: | 77% |
| GPA 3.0-3.49: | 33% | Out-of-state: | 32% |
| GPA 2.0-2.99: | 15% | Live on campus: | 70% |
| | | International: | 1% |

**Basis for selection.** Minimum 2.5 GPA, college preparatory curriculum, 21 ACT or 1000 SAT (exclusive of Writing), strong high school recommendation, submission of acceptable essay (if requested). Applicants not meeting requirements may be admitted on strength of each criterion. School activities also considered. Interview recommended. Audition required of music majors. Portfolio recommended for art majors.

**High school preparation.** 20 units required; 24 recommended. Required and recommended units include English 4, mathematics 3-4, social studies 2-3, science 3-4 (laboratory 1), foreign language 2 and academic electives 6-7.

**2008-2009 Annual costs.** Tuition/fees: $28,030. Room/board: $8,406.

**2007-2008 Financial aid. Need-based:** 499 full-time freshmen applied for aid; 446 were judged to have need; 446 of these received aid. Average need met was 77%. Average scholarship/grant was $17,918; average loan $3,490. 79% of total undergraduate aid awarded as scholarships/grants, 21% as loans/jobs. **Non-need-based:** Awarded to 726 full-time undergraduates, including 144 freshmen. Scholarships awarded for academics, alumni affiliation, art, athletics, leadership, minority status, music/drama, religious affiliation, ROTC, state residency.

**Application procedures. Admission:** Priority date 2/1; no deadline. $25 fee, may be waived for applicants with need. Application may be submitted online. Admission notification on a rolling basis beginning on or about 10/1. Must reply by May 1 or within 3 week(s) if notified thereafter. **Financial aid:** Priority date 3/1; no closing date. FAFSA required. Applicants notified on a rolling basis starting 3/15; must reply by 5/1 or within 3 week(s) of notification.

**Academics. Special study options:** Accelerated study, combined bachelor's/graduate degree, cross-registration, double major, dual enrollment of high school students, honors, independent study, internships, liberal arts/career combination, semester at sea, study abroad, teacher certification program, Washington semester. **Credit/placement by examination:** AP, CLEP, IB, institutional tests. **Support services:** Learning center, reduced course load, study skills assistance, tutoring.

**Majors. Biology:** General, biochemistry. **Business:** Accounting, actuarial science, business admin. **Communications:** General. **Computer sciences:** General, computer science. **Education:** General, elementary, middle, secondary, special. **Engineering:** Computer. **English:** English lit. **Foreign languages:** General. **Health:** Clinical lab science, cytotechnology, nursing (RN), predental, premedicine, prenursing, prepharmacy, respiratory therapy technology. **History:** General. **Liberal arts:** Arts/sciences. **Math:** General. **Philosophy/religion:** Philosophy. **Physical sciences:** Chemistry. **Protective services:** Law enforcement admin. **Psychology:** General. **Social sciences:** Economics, political science, sociology. **Theology:** Theology. **Visual/performing arts:** Art, arts management.

**Most popular majors.** Biology 9%, business/marketing 14%, communications/journalism 7%, education 10%, health sciences 27%, liberal arts 6%, psychology 6%.

**Computing on campus.** 600 workstations in dormitories, library, computer center, student center. Dormitories wired for high-speed internet access and linked to campus network. Commuter students can connect to campus network. Online course registration, helpline, repair service, wireless network available.

**Student life. Freshman orientation:** Mandatory, $200 fee. Preregistration for classes offered. Off-campus 3-day session held in August before classes begin. **Housing:** Guaranteed on-campus for freshmen. Coed dorms, single-sex dorms, special housing for disabled, substance-free housing available. $200 fully refundable deposit, deadline 5/1. Suites available to upperclassmen. **Activities:** Bands, campus ministries, choral groups, dance, drama, literary magazine, music ensembles, musical theater, opera, radio station, student government, student newspaper, symphony orchestra, Catholic students association, Fellowship of Christian Athletes, Hillel, Highland community ministries, Habitat for Humanity.

**Athletics.** NCAA. **Intercollegiate:** Baseball M, basketball, cross-country, field hockey W, golf, lacrosse M, soccer, softball W, tennis, track and field, volleyball W. **Intramural:** Basketball, cheerleading, football (non-tackle) M, golf, soccer, softball, swimming, tennis, volleyball. **Team name:** Knights.

**Student services.** Adult student services, campus ministries, career counseling, student employment services, financial aid counseling, health services, personal counseling, placement for graduates. **Physically disabled:** Services for visually, hearing impaired.

**Contact.** E-mail: admissions@bellarmine.edu
Phone: (502) 452-8131 Toll-free number: (800) 274-4723 ext. 8131
Fax: (502) 452-8002
Timothy Sturgeon, Dean of Admissions, Bellarmine University, 2001 Newburg Road, Louisville, KY 40205

## Berea College

**Berea, Kentucky**
**www.berea.edu**

**CB member**
**CB code: 1060**

▶ Private 4-year liberal arts college
▶ Residential campus in small town
▶ 1,528 degree-seeking undergraduates: 60% women, 18% African American, 2% Asian American, 2% Hispanic American, 1% Native American, 7% international
▶ 29% of applicants admitted

▶ SAT or ACT (ACT writing optional), application essay, interview required
▶ 63% graduate within 6 years

**General.** Founded in 1855. Regionally accredited. **Degrees:** 332 bachelor's awarded. **Location:** 40 miles from Lexington, 100 miles from Louisville. **Calendar:** 4-1-4, limited summer session. **Full-time faculty:** 128 total; 89% have terminal degrees, 13% minority, 42% women. **Part-time faculty:** 43 total; 7% minority, 54% women. **Class size:** 69% < 20, 31% 20-39, less than 1% 50-99. **Special facilities:** Geology museum, planetarium with observatory, Ecovillage, Appalachian artifacts and exhibit studio.

**Freshman class profile.** 2,083 applied, 597 admitted, 421 enrolled.

| Mid 50% test scores | | GPA 2.0-2.99: | 13% |
|---|---|---|---|
| SAT critical reading: | 480-590 | Rank in top quarter: | 67% |
| SAT math: | 480-600 | Rank in top tenth: | 26% |
| SAT writing: | 470-560 | Return as sophomores: | 83% |
| ACT composite: | 21-25 | Out-of-state: | 51% |
| GPA 3.50 or higher: | 46% | Live on campus: | 97% |
| GPA 3.0-3.49: | 41% | International: | 5% |

**Basis for selection.** Rank in top half of class, recommendations, essays, interviews, test scores, involvement in community and school activities important. Financial need absolute prerequisite for admission. **Homeschooled:** If transcript not available, list of homeschooled courses and titles of textbooks used required.

**High school preparation.** 13 units recommended. Recommended units include English 4, mathematics 3, social studies 1, history 1, science 2 (laboratory 2) and foreign language 2.

**2007-2008 Annual costs.** All students receive 4-year full-tuition scholarship. Students and families expected to pay toward room/board and fees if possible. Room/board costs are $5,492 and fees are $776 for the academic year, but most students receive aid and pay $1,500 per academic year on average. Students required to earn portion of expenses by working minimum of 10 hours per week on campus. Value of full-time tuition for 2007/2008: $23,400. Books/supplies: $750. Personal expenses: $1,350.

**2007-2008 Financial aid.** All financial aid based on need. 421 full-time freshmen applied for aid; 421 were judged to have need; 421 of these received aid. Average need met was 94%. Average scholarship/grant was $27,733; average loan $138. 92% of total undergraduate aid awarded as scholarships/grants, 8% as loans/jobs.

**Application procedures. Admission:** Closing date 4/30. No application fee. Application may be submitted online. Admission notification on a rolling basis beginning on or about 12/20. Must reply by 5/1. **Financial aid:** Priority date 4/1; no closing date. FAFSA required. Applicants notified on a rolling basis starting 5/1.

**Academics.** All students are provided with a laptop computer that becomes their property upon graduation. **Special study options:** Combined bachelor's/graduate degree, double major, exchange student, honors, independent study, internships, student-designed major, study abroad, teacher certification program. 3-2 engineering program with Washington University (MO) and University of Kentucky. **Credit/placement by examination:** AP, CLEP, SAT, ACT, institutional tests. Unlimited number of credit hours may be counted toward degree. **Support services:** Learning center, remedial instruction, study skills assistance, tutoring, writing center.

**Majors. Agriculture:** General, agribusiness operations. **Area/ethnic studies:** African-American, women's. **Biology:** General, cellular/molecular. **Business:** General, accounting, business admin, finance, marketing. **Communications:** General. **Education:** General, art, business, elementary, family/consumer sciences, kindergarten/preschool, middle, music, physical, secondary, social science, social studies, technology/industrial arts. **Engineering technology:** Manufacturing. **English:** British lit, creative writing, English lit. **Family/consumer sciences:** Child development, family studies. **Foreign languages:** French, German, Latin, Spanish. **Health:** Dietetics, nursing (RN). **History:** General. **Math:** General. **Parks/recreation:** Exercise sciences, health/fitness. **Philosophy/religion:** Christian, philosophy, religion. **Physical sciences:** Chemistry, physics. **Psychology:** General. **Social sciences:** Economics, political science, sociology. **Visual/performing arts:** Art, art history, conservation, dramatic, music performance, piano/organ, studio arts, voice/opera.

**Most popular majors.** Biology 6%, business/marketing 10%, engineering/engineering technologies 10%, family/consumer sciences 6%, social sciences 9%, visual/performing arts 8%.

**Computing on campus.** Dormitories wired for high-speed internet access and linked to campus network. Online course registration, online library, helpline, repair service, wireless network available.

**Student life. Freshman orientation:** Mandatory. Preregistration for classes offered. Held during the summer for a long weekend; week-long session before classes begin. **Housing:** Guaranteed on-campus for all undergraduates. Single-sex dorms, apartments, substance-free housing available. Apartments for single parent students; 9 small houses which hold 9-12 upperclassmen; Ecovillage. **Activities:** Bands, campus ministries, choral groups, dance, drama, international student organizations, literary magazine, music ensembles, student government, student newspaper, religious organizations, People Who Care, Students for Appalachia, Habitat for Humanity, Cosmopolitan Club.

**Athletics.** NAIA. **Intercollegiate:** Baseball M, basketball, cross-country, diving, golf M, soccer, softball W, swimming, tennis, track and field, volleyball W. **Intramural:** Basketball, football (non-tackle), racquetball, soccer, softball, volleyball. **Team name:** Mountaineers.

**Student services.** Adult student services, alcohol/substance abuse counseling, campus ministries, career counseling, services for economically disadvantaged, student employment services, financial aid counseling, health services, minority student services, on-campus daycare, personal counseling, placement for graduates, veterans' counselor, women's services. **Physically disabled:** Services for visually, speech, hearing impaired.

**Contact.** E-mail: admissions@berea.edu
Phone: (859) 985-3500 Toll-free number: (800) 326-5948
Fax: (859) 985-3512
Joe Bagnoli, Director of Admissions, Berea College, CPO 2220, Berea, KY 40404

---

## Brescia University
**Owensboro, Kentucky**
www.brescia.edu                         CB code: 1071

- Private 4-year university and liberal arts college affiliated with Roman Catholic Church
- Residential campus in small city
- 426 degree-seeking undergraduates
- 77% of applicants admitted
- SAT or ACT (ACT writing optional), application essay required

**General.** Founded in 1950. Regionally accredited. Weekend college for nontraditional students. Lay ministry formation program nationally accredited. **Degrees:** 100 bachelor's, 11 associate awarded; master's offered. **Location:** 120 miles from Louisville; 120 miles from Nashville, Tennessee. **Calendar:** Semester, limited summer session. **Full-time faculty:** 40 total. **Part-time faculty:** 29 total. **Class size:** 84% < 20, 16% 20-39. **Special facilities:** Observatory, greenhouse.

**Freshman class profile.** 358 applied, 274 admitted, 95 enrolled.

| Mid 50% test scores | | | |
|---|---|---|---|
| SAT critical reading: | 330-540 | GPA 3.0-3.49: | 33% |
| SAT math: | 380-520 | GPA 2.0-2.99: | 24% |
| ACT composite: | 18-24 | Out-of-state: | 13% |
| GPA 3.50 or higher: | 43% | Live on campus: | 83% |

**Basis for selection.** Students admitted based on high school grades and ACT/SAT scores. **Homeschooled:** Transcript of courses and grades required.

**High school preparation.** 17 units recommended. Recommended units include English 4, mathematics 3, social studies 2, history 2, science 2, foreign language 2 and academic electives 2. 2 units in fine arts, 2 units in computer science also recommended.

**2008-2009 Annual costs.** Tuition/fees (projected): $15,440. Room/board: $7,000. Books/supplies: $1,000. Personal expenses: $1,800.

**2006-2007 Financial aid. Need-based:** 59% of total undergraduate aid awarded as scholarships/grants, 41% as loans/jobs. **Non-need-based:** Scholarships awarded for academics, alumni affiliation, art, athletics, minority status, music/drama, religious affiliation, state residency.

**Application procedures. Admission:** No deadline. $25 fee, may be waived for applicants with need. Application may be submitted online. Admission notification on a rolling basis beginning on or about 9/1. **Financial aid:** Priority date 8/1, closing date 8/23. FAFSA required. Applicants notified on a rolling basis starting 3/1; must reply within 3 week(s) of notification.

**Academics. Special study options:** Combined bachelor's/graduate degree, cross-registration, distance learning, double major, ESL, exchange student, honors, independent study, internships, liberal arts/career combination, student-designed major, teacher certification program, weekend college.

---

**Credit/placement by examination:** AP, CLEP, IB, SAT, ACT, institutional tests. 18 credit hours maximum toward associate degree, 36 toward bachelor's. **Support services:** Reduced course load, remedial instruction, study skills assistance, tutoring.

**Majors. Biology:** General. **Business:** General, accounting, business admin. **Computer sciences:** General. **Education:** Art, elementary, middle, secondary, social studies, Spanish, special. **English:** English lit. **Foreign languages:** Spanish. **Health:** Audiology/speech pathology, clinical lab science, health care admin. **History:** General. **Interdisciplinary:** Biological/physical sciences, math/computer science. **Liberal arts:** Arts/sciences. **Math:** Applied. **Philosophy/religion:** Religion. **Physical sciences:** Chemistry. **Psychology:** General. **Public administration:** Social work. **Social sciences:** General, political science, sociology. **Theology:** Pastoral counseling, theology. **Visual/performing arts:** Art, commercial/advertising art.

**Most popular majors.** Biology 11%, business/marketing 25%, education 17%, liberal arts 9%, public administration/social services 12%.

**Computing on campus.** 67 workstations in library, computer center, student center. Dormitories wired for high-speed internet access and linked to campus network. Commuter students can connect to campus network. Online library available.

**Student life. Freshman orientation:** Available, $100 fee. Preregistration for classes offered. Activities begin on Sunday prior to classes through Tuesday. **Housing:** Guaranteed on-campus for freshmen. Coed dorms, single-sex dorms, special housing for disabled available. $100 fully refundable deposit, deadline 8/23. Shared apartment houses available. **Activities:** Choral groups, dance, drama, international student organizations, literary magazine, student government, student newspaper, Christian student union, social work association, Council for Exceptional Children, campus ministry.

**Athletics.** NAIA. **Intercollegiate:** Baseball M, basketball, golf, soccer, softball W, tennis W, volleyball W. **Intramural:** Basketball, racquetball, table tennis, volleyball. **Team name:** Bearcats.

**Student services.** Adult student services, alcohol/substance abuse counseling, campus ministries, career counseling, services for economically disadvantaged, student employment services, financial aid counseling, personal counseling, placement for graduates, veterans' counselor, women's services. **Physically disabled:** Services for speech impaired.

**Contact.** E-mail: admissions@brescia.edu
Phone: (270) 686-4241 Toll-free number: (877) 273-7242
Fax: (270) 686-4314
Chris Houk, Dean of Enrollment, Brescia University, 717 Frederica Street, Owensboro, KY 42301-3023

---

## Campbellsville University
**Campbellsville, Kentucky**                     CB member
www.campbellsville.edu                            CB code: 1097

- Private 4-year university affiliated with Baptist faith
- Residential campus in large town
- 1,549 degree-seeking undergraduates: 7% part-time, 53% women, 8% African American, 1% Asian American, 1% Hispanic American, 5% international
- 375 degree-seeking graduate students
- 62% of applicants admitted
- SAT or ACT (ACT writing optional) required
- 42% graduate within 6 years

**General.** Founded in 1906. Regionally accredited. Affiliated with Kentucky Baptist Convention. **Degrees:** 207 bachelor's, 8 associate awarded; master's offered. **ROTC:** Army. **Location:** 80 miles from Louisville, 140 miles from Nashville, Tennessee. **Calendar:** Semester, extensive summer session. **Full-time faculty:** 98 total; 63% have terminal degrees, 7% minority, 50% women. **Part-time faculty:** 162 total; 6% minority, 54% women. **Class size:** 75% < 20, 25% 20-39, less than 1% 40-49. **Special facilities:** Educational and research woodland, American Civil War institute, fine arts center with computer-enhanced practice room with acoustical adjustment system.

**Freshman class profile.** 1,511 applied, 944 admitted, 374 enrolled.

| Mid 50% test scores | | | |
|---|---|---|---|
| SAT critical reading: | 400-560 | Rank in top quarter: | 38% |
| SAT math: | 470-610 | Rank in top tenth: | 17% |
| ACT composite: | 18-24 | End year in good standing: | 78% |
| GPA 3.50 or higher: | 39% | Return as sophomores: | 68% |
| GPA 3.0-3.49: | 28% | Out-of-state: | 16% |
| GPA 2.0-2.99: | 32% | Live on campus: | 73% |
| | | International: | 4% |

**Basis for selection.** Achievement in strong high school program and satisfactory ACT or SAT scores most important. Special consideration for entry to basic skills program may be given to other highly motivated and potentially successful applicants. Interview and essay recommended.

**High school preparation.** 21 units recommended. Recommended units include English 4, mathematics 3, social studies 2, history 2, science 3 (laboratory 1), foreign language 1 and academic electives 6. At least 2 units in the arts recommended for academic elective.

**2007-2008 Annual costs.** Tuition/fees: $17,260. Room/board: $6,230. Books/supplies: $800. Personal expenses: $1,330.

**2006-2007 Financial aid. Need-based:** 279 full-time freshmen applied for aid; 250 were judged to have need; 250 of these received aid. Average need met was 73%. Average scholarship/grant was $11,616; average loan $2,150. 69% of total undergraduate aid awarded as scholarships/grants, 31% as loans/jobs. **Non-need-based:** Awarded to 376 full-time undergraduates, including 93 freshmen. **Additional information:** Matching scholarships available for students whose church contributes $200 annually. Performance grants available to members of marching band.

**Application procedures. Admission:** Priority date 4/15; no deadline. $20 fee, may be waived for applicants with need. Application may be submitted online. Admission notification on a rolling basis beginning on or about 1/2. **Financial aid:** Priority date 4/1; no closing date. FAFSA required. Applicants notified on a rolling basis starting 5/15.

**Academics. Special study options:** Cooperative education, distance learning, double major, dual enrollment of high school students, ESL, exchange student, honors, independent study, internships, study abroad, teacher certification program, Washington semester, London semester. **Credit/placement by examination:** AP, CLEP, institutional tests. 32 credit hours maximum toward bachelor's degree. Institutional/departmental examinations given in some areas. **Support services:** Learning center, preadmission summer program, reduced course load, remedial instruction, study skills assistance, tutoring, writing center.

**Majors. Biology:** General. **Business:** General, accounting, business admin, marketing, office management. **Communications:** General, broadcast journalism, journalism, public relations. **Computer sciences:** General. **Education:** General, art, biology, chemistry, early childhood, elementary, English, health, history; mathematics, middle, music, physical, physics, reading, science, secondary, social science, social studies. **English:** English lit. **Health:** Athletic training, predental, premedicine, prepharmacy, preveterinary. **History:** General. **Legal studies:** Prelaw. **Math:** General. **Parks/recreation:** General, exercise sciences, health/fitness. **Philosophy/religion:** Religion. **Physical sciences:** Chemistry, physics. **Protective services:** Law enforcement admin. **Psychology:** General. **Public administration:** Social work. **Social sciences:** General, economics, political science, sociology. **Theology:** Bible, religious ed, sacred music. **Visual/performing arts:** Art, conducting, dramatic, music performance, music theory/composition, piano/organ, studio arts, voice/opera.

**Most popular majors.** Business/marketing 25%, education 15%, psychology 12%, social sciences 6%, theological studies 12%, visual/performing arts 6%.

**Computing on campus.** 175 workstations in dormitories, library, computer center, student center. Dormitories wired for high-speed internet access and linked to campus network. Online course registration, online library available.

**Student life. Freshman orientation:** Mandatory. Preregistration for classes offered. Held in June and July. **Policies:** Religious observance required. **Housing:** Guaranteed on-campus for all undergraduates. Single-sex dorms, apartments, substance-free housing available. $100 deposit, deadline 7/1. **Activities:** Bands, choral groups, dance, drama, literary magazine, music ensembles, musical theater, opera, radio station, student government, student newspaper, symphony orchestra, TV station, Baptist student union, Young Republicans, Young Democrats, Student Foundation, Fellowship of Christian Athletes, student ambassadors, African American leadership league, world community club.

**Athletics.** NAIA. **Intercollegiate:** Baseball M, basketball, cross-country, football (tackle) M, golf, soccer, softball W, tennis, track and field, volleyball W, wrestling M. **Intramural:** Basketball, racquetball, soccer, softball, table tennis, tennis, volleyball. **Team name:** Tigers.

**Student services.** Adult student services, alcohol/substance abuse counseling, campus ministries, career counseling, student employment services, financial aid counseling, health services, personal counseling, placement for graduates, veterans' counselor.

**Contact.** E-mail: admissions@campbellsville.edu
Phone: (270) 789-5220 Toll-free number: (800) 264-6014
Fax: (270) 789-5071
David Walters, Vice President for Admissions, Campbellsville University, 1 University Drive, Campbellsville, KY 42718-2799

---

## Centre College
**Danville, Kentucky**
www.centre.edu

**CB member**
**CB code: 1109**

- Private 4-year liberal arts college affiliated with Presbyterian Church (USA)
- Residential campus in large town
- 1,184 degree-seeking undergraduates: 54% women, 3% African American, 2% Asian American, 2% Hispanic American, 2% international
- 61% of applicants admitted
- SAT or ACT (ACT writing optional), application essay required
- 73% graduate within 6 years

**General.** Founded in 1819. Regionally accredited. **Degrees:** 231 bachelor's awarded. **ROTC:** Army, Air Force. **Location:** 35 miles from Lexington, 85 miles from Louisville. **Calendar:** 4-1-4. **Full-time faculty:** 102 total; 97% have terminal degrees, 6% minority, 34% women. **Part-time faculty:** 23 total; 65% have terminal degrees, 17% minority, 48% women. **Class size:** 50% < 20, 50% 20-39, less than 1% 40-49. **Special facilities:** Performing arts center, visual arts center, physical science center.

**Freshman class profile.** 2,159 applied, 1,312 admitted, 316 enrolled.

| Mid 50% test scores | | | |
|---|---|---|---|
| SAT critical reading: | 570-690 | Rank in top quarter: | 84% |
| SAT math: | 570-650 | Rank in top tenth: | 58% |
| ACT composite: | 26-30 | Return as sophomores: | 94% |
| GPA 3.50 or higher: | 65% | Out-of-state: | 43% |
| GPA 3.0-3.49: | 24% | Live on campus: | 99% |
| GPA 2.0-2.99: | 11% | International: | 2% |

**Basis for selection.** Achievement and quality of high school program most important. Recommendations, test scores, academic and nonacademic interests, experiences considered. Interview recommended.

**High school preparation.** 14 units required; 24 recommended. Required and recommended units include English 4, mathematics 4, history 2, science 2-4 (laboratory 2-3) and foreign language 2. 1 fine arts recommended.

**2007-2008 Annual costs.** Comprehensive fee: $35,000. Reduced comprehensive fee may be available if student is approved to live off-campus by dean of students. Books/supplies: $900. Personal expenses: $800.

**2007-2008 Financial aid. Need-based:** 247 full-time freshmen applied for aid; 183 were judged to have need; 183 of these received aid. Average need met was 89%. Average scholarship/grant was $19,673; average loan $3,585. 83% of total undergraduate aid awarded as scholarships/grants, 17% as loans/jobs. **Non-need-based:** Awarded to 446 full-time undergraduates, including 116 freshmen. Scholarships awarded for academics, alumni affiliation, music/drama, ROTC.

**Application procedures. Admission:** Closing date 2/1 (postmark date). $40 fee, may be waived for applicants with need. Application may be submitted online. Admission notification 3/15. Must reply by May 1 or within 2 week(s) if notified thereafter. **Financial aid:** Closing date 3/1. FAFSA, institutional form required. Applicants notified by 3/25; must reply by 5/1 or within 2 week(s) of notification.

**Academics.** Unusual courses and off-campus study options offered during 3-week winter term. Sites in England, France, Mexico, Japan, and Ireland; other winter-term international locations vary. **Special study options:** Cross-registration, double major, honors, independent study, internships, liberal arts/career combination, student-designed major, study abroad, teacher certification program, Washington semester. Science semester at Oak Ridge National Laboratories, Tennessee, and 5 other national science laboratories; 3-2 engineering program with Columbia University (NY), Washington University (MO), Vanderbilt University (TN), and University of Kentucky. **Credit/placement by examination:** AP, CLEP, IB, SAT, ACT, institutional tests. **Support services:** Reduced course load, tutoring, writing center.

**Majors. Biology:** General, biochemistry, molecular. **Computer sciences:** Computer science. **Education:** Elementary. **English:** English lit. **Foreign languages:** Classics, French, German, Spanish. **History:** General. **Math:** General. **Philosophy/religion:** Philosophy, religion. **Physical sciences:** Chemical physics, chemistry, physics. **Psychology:** General. **Social sciences:** Anthropology, economics, international relations, political science, sociology. **Visual/performing arts:** Art, dramatic.

**Most popular majors.** Biology 9%, English 11%, foreign language 12%, history 9%, philosophy/religious studies 7%, psychology 8%, social sciences 24%, visual/performing arts 7%.

**Computing on campus.** 170 workstations in dormitories, library, computer center, student center. Dormitories wired for high-speed internet access and linked to campus network. Online course registration, helpline, repair service, wireless network available.

**Student life. Freshman orientation:** Mandatory. Preregistration for classes offered. Held at beginning of fall term. **Housing:** Guaranteed on-campus for all undergraduates. Coed dorms, single-sex dorms, special housing for disabled, apartments, fraternity/sorority housing, substance-free housing available. Fraternity/sorority housing for officers, theme residence halls. **Activities:** Bands, campus ministries, choral groups, dance, drama, film society, international student organizations, literary magazine, music ensembles, musical theater, student government, student newspaper, symphony orchestra, TV station, volunteer services, diversity student union, Fellowship of Christian Athletes, Centre Christian Fellowship, College Life, Centrecycle, LIFT (tutoring and mentoring for at-risk elementary students).

**Athletics.** NCAA. **Intercollegiate:** Baseball M, basketball, cross-country, diving, field hockey W, football (tackle) M, golf, soccer, softball W, swimming, tennis, track and field, volleyball W. **Intramural:** Badminton, basketball, bowling, cross-country, fencing, field hockey W, football (tackle), golf, racquetball, rugby M, soccer, softball, swimming, table tennis, tennis, track and field, volleyball, wrestling M. **Team name:** Colonels.

**Student services.** Alcohol/substance abuse counseling, campus ministries, career counseling, student employment services, financial aid counseling, health services, minority student services, personal counseling, placement for graduates. **Physically disabled:** Services for visually, hearing impaired.

**Contact.** E-mail: admission@centre.edu
Phone: (859) 238-5350 Toll-free number: (800) 423-6236
Fax: (859) 238-5373
Bob Nesmith, Director of Admission, Centre College, 600 West Walnut Street, Danville, KY 40422-1394

---

## Clear Creek Baptist Bible College
**Pineville, Kentucky**
www.ccbbc.edu
CB code: 5975

- Private 4-year Bible college affiliated with Southern Baptist Convention
- Residential campus in small town
- 169 degree-seeking undergraduates: 20% part-time, 20% women, 1% African American, 1% Hispanic American
- Application essay, interview required
- 48% graduate within 6 years; 31% enter graduate study

**General.** Founded in 1926. Regionally accredited; also accredited by ABHE. Adult family Bible college affiliated with Kentucky Baptist Convention that trains individuals for ministry in local church. Prefer students to be at least 21 years of age. **Degrees:** 26 bachelor's, 7 associate awarded. **Location:** 110 miles from Lexington, 76 miles from Knoxville, Tennessee. **Calendar:** Semester, limited summer session. **Full-time faculty:** 6 total. **Part-time faculty:** 17 total. **Class size:** 79% < 20, 21% 20-39. **Special facilities:** Family life center, hiking/walking trails, campus thrift store.

**Freshman class profile.** 14 applied, 14 admitted, 13 enrolled.

| | | | |
|---|---|---|---|
| End year in good standing: | 83% | Out-of-state: | 54% |
| Return as sophomores: | 71% | | |

**Basis for selection.** Open admission. Applicants must demonstrate a clear call to the gospel ministry. Audition required for music minor. **Home-schooled:** Transcript of courses and grades required.

**2007-2008 Annual costs.** Tuition/fees: $5,322. Room and board fee given for single student. Married student housing fees vary from $160 to $325 per month. Room/board: $3,750. Personal expenses: $1,600.

**2006-2007 Financial aid. Need-based:** 21 full-time freshmen applied for aid; 17 were judged to have need; 17 of these received aid. Average need met was 49%. Average scholarship/grant was $3,411. 95% of total undergraduate aid awarded as scholarships/grants, 5% as loans/jobs. **Non-need-based:** Awarded to 67 full-time undergraduates, including 18 freshmen. Scholarships awarded for academics.

**Application procedures. Admission:** Priority date 7/15; deadline 8/2 (receipt date). $40 fee. Application may be submitted online. Admission notification on a rolling basis. **Financial aid:** Priority date 6/30; no closing date. FAFSA, institutional form required. Applicants notified on a rolling basis; must reply by 8/1.

**Academics. Special study options:** Cross-registration, distance learning, double major, dual enrollment of high school students, independent study. **Credit/placement by examination:** CLEP, institutional tests. **Support services:** Reduced course load, remedial instruction, study skills assistance, tutoring.

**Majors. Theology:** Bible.

**Computing on campus.** 12 workstations in library, computer center. Dormitories wired for high-speed internet access and linked to campus network. Online course registration, online library, wireless network available.

**Student life. Freshman orientation:** Available. Preregistration for classes offered. Four-day program held week of registration. **Policies:** Dress code; no tobacco, alcohol, or drugs on campus. Religious observance required. **Housing:** Single-sex dorms, apartments, substance-free housing available. $50 nonrefundable deposit, deadline 7/25. Cottages, family housing available. **Activities:** Campus ministries, choral groups, drama, music ensembles, radio station, student government, student newspaper, women's missionary union, Brotherhood, Young Disciples, Acteens, Royal Ambassadors, Girls in Action, Mission Friends.

**Athletics. Intramural:** Basketball, football (non-tackle) M, softball, swimming, table tennis, tennis, volleyball.

**Student services.** Campus ministries, career counseling, student employment services, financial aid counseling, health services, on-campus daycare, personal counseling, placement for graduates, veterans' counselor.

**Contact.** E-mail: ccbbc@ccbbc.edu
Phone: (606) 337-3196 Toll-free number: (866) 340-3196
Fax: (606) 337-2372
Billy Howell, Director of Admissions, Clear Creek Baptist Bible College, 300 Clear Creek Road, Pineville, KY 40977-9754

---

## Eastern Kentucky University
**Richmond, Kentucky**
www.eku.edu
CB member
CB code: 1200

- Public 4-year university
- Residential campus in large town
- 12,996 degree-seeking undergraduates: 16% part-time, 59% women
- 1,830 degree-seeking graduate students
- 69% of applicants admitted
- SAT or ACT (ACT writing optional) required
- 37% graduate within 6 years

**General.** Founded in 1906. Regionally accredited. Courses offered at additional sites in Corbin, Danville, Manchester, Lancaster, London, Somerset and Barbourville. **Degrees:** 1,979 bachelor's, 210 associate awarded; master's offered. **ROTC:** Army. **Location:** 28 miles from Lexington, 110 miles from Cincinnati. **Calendar:** Semester, extensive summer session. **Full-time faculty:** 584 total; 66% have terminal degrees, 9% minority, 47% women. **Part-time faculty:** 455 total; 18% have terminal degrees, 5% minority, 56% women. **Class size:** 48% < 20, 44% 20-39, 4% 40-49, 3% 50-99, 1% >100. **Special facilities:** Planetarium, nature preserves, law enforcement facilities, music library.

**Freshman class profile.** 6,928 applied, 4,781 admitted, 2,493 enrolled.

| Mid 50% test scores | | | |
|---|---|---|---|
| SAT math: | 440-550 | Live on campus: | 69% |
| ACT composite: | 18-23 | International: | 1% |
| Return as sophomores: | 62% | Fraternities: | 13% |
| Out-of-state: | 17% | Sororities: | 8% |

**Basis for selection.** Out-of-state applicants must rank in top half of graduating class or have 21 ACT or 890 SAT (exclusive of Writing). Resident applicants must have completed specified high school curriculum. Applicants without college preparatory courses subject to remediation. ACT only required for placement for in-state applicants. Interview recommended. Audition recommended for music majors. Portfolio recommended for art and graphic art majors. **Homeschooled:** Transcript of courses and grades required.

**High school preparation.** 25 units required. Required units include English 4, mathematics 3, social studies 3, science 3 (laboratory 1), foreign language 2 and academic electives 7. Art, drama, music, and computer science also recommended.

**2007-2008 Annual costs.** Tuition/fees: $5,682; $15,382 out-of-state. Targeted out-of-state tuition: $8,884. Room/board: $5,479. Books/supplies: $800. Personal expenses: $1,550.

**Financial aid. Non-need-based:** Scholarships awarded for academics, alumni affiliation, art, athletics, job skills, leadership, minority status, music/drama, ROTC.

**Application procedures. Admission:** Closing date 8/1. $30 fee, may be waived for applicants with need. Application may be submitted online. Admission notification on a rolling basis beginning on or about 8/1. **Financial aid:** Priority date 3/15; no closing date. FAFSA required. Applicants notified on a rolling basis starting 4/1.

**Academics. Special study options:** Cooperative education, distance learning, double major, ESL, honors, independent study, internships, liberal arts/career combination, student-designed major, study abroad, teacher certification program. **Credit/placement by examination:** AP, CLEP, SAT, ACT, institutional tests. 30 credit hours maximum toward associate degree, 65 toward bachelor's. **Support services:** Learning center, pre-admission summer program, reduced course load, remedial instruction, study skills assistance, tutoring, writing center.

**Majors. Agriculture:** Ornamental horticulture, turf management. **Area/ethnic studies:** Canadian. **Biology:** General, bacteriology, ecology. **Business:** General, accounting, business admin, fashion, finance, insurance, management information systems, managerial economics, marketing, office management. **Communications:** General, broadcast journalism, journalism, public relations. **Computer sciences:** General, computer science. **Conservation:** Management/policy, wildlife. **Education:** Art, biology, business, Deaf/hearing impaired, elementary, family/consumer sciences, geography, mathematics, middle, music, physical, science, Spanish, special, speech impaired, technology/industrial arts, trade/industrial. **Engineering:** Science. **Engineering technology:** Architectural, manufacturing, water quality. **English:** English lit, speech/rhetoric. **Family/consumer sciences:** Family studies, food/nutrition, housing. **Foreign languages:** General, French, German, sign language interpretation, Spanish. **Health:** Clinical lab assistant, clinical lab science, clinical lab technology, EMT paramedic, health care admin, medical assistant, medical records admin, medical records technology, nursing (RN), predental, premedicine, preop/surgical nursing, prepharmacy. **History:** General. **Legal studies:** Paralegal. **Liberal arts:** Arts/sciences. **Math:** General, statistics. **Parks/recreation:** General, facilities management. **Philosophy/religion:** Philosophy. **Physical sciences:** Chemistry, geology, physics. **Protective services:** Corrections, fire safety technology, forensics, police science, security services. **Psychology:** General. **Public administration:** Social work. **Social sciences:** Anthropology, economics, geography, political science, sociology. **Transportation:** Aviation. **Visual/performing arts:** Art, ceramics, dramatic, drawing, interior design, painting, printmaking, sculpture, studio arts.

**Most popular majors.** Business/marketing 11%, education 13%, health sciences 15%, security/protective services 15%.

**Computing on campus.** 250 workstations in dormitories, library, computer center, student center. Dormitories wired for high-speed internet access and linked to campus network. Commuter students can connect to campus network. Online course registration, online library, helpline, wireless network available.

**Student life. Freshman orientation:** Mandatory. Preregistration for classes offered. Registration and campus tour. **Policies:** Students required to live on campus until age 21 unless living with parent or guardian. **Housing:** Guaranteed on-campus for freshmen. Coed dorms, single-sex dorms, apartments, fraternity/sorority housing available. $100 fully refundable deposit. **Activities:** Bands, choral groups, dance, drama, literary magazine, music ensembles, musical theater, radio station, student government, student newspaper, symphony orchestra, 160 religious, political, ethnic, social service, and special interest organizations.

**Athletics.** NCAA. **Intercollegiate:** Baseball M, basketball, cheerleading, cross-country, football (tackle) M, golf, soccer W, softball W, swimming, tennis, track and field, volleyball W. **Intramural:** Basketball, football (tackle) M, golf, racquetball, softball, tennis, volleyball. **Team name:** Colonels.

**Student services.** Alcohol/substance abuse counseling, campus ministries, career counseling, student employment services, financial aid counseling, health services, personal counseling, placement for graduates, veterans' counselor. **Physically disabled:** Services for visually, speech, hearing impaired.

**Contact.** E-mail: admissions@eku.edu
Phone: (859) 622-2106 Toll-free number: (800) 465-9191
Fax: (859) 622-8024
Steve Byrn, Director of Admissions, Eastern Kentucky University, SSB CPO 54, 521 Lancaster Avenue, Richmond, KY 40475-3102

## Georgetown College
**Georgetown, Kentucky**
**www.georgetowncollege.edu**    **CB code: 1249**

- Private 4-year liberal arts college affiliated with Southern Baptist Convention
- Residential campus in large town
- 1,335 degree-seeking undergraduates: 2% part-time, 57% women, 4% African American, 1% Asian American, 1% Hispanic American, 1% international
- 512 degree-seeking graduate students
- 84% of applicants admitted
- SAT or ACT (ACT writing optional) required
- 61% graduate within 6 years

**General.** Founded in 1829. Regionally accredited. **Degrees:** 247 bachelor's awarded; master's offered. **ROTC:** Army, Air Force. **Location:** 12 miles from Lexington, 60 miles from Louisville. **Calendar:** Semester, limited summer session. **Full-time faculty:** 111 total; 93% have terminal degrees, 6% minority, 43% women. **Part-time faculty:** 42 total; 7% minority, 43% women. **Class size:** 61% < 20, 39% 20-39, less than 1% 40-49. **Special facilities:** Planetarium, Foucault pendulum, fine arts building.

**Freshman class profile.** 1,454 applied, 1,227 admitted, 368 enrolled.

| Mid 50% test scores | | | |
|---|---|---|---|
| SAT critical reading: | 500-590 | Rank in top tenth: | 39% |
| SAT math: | 490-610 | Return as sophomores: | 79% |
| ACT composite: | 21-26 | Out-of-state: | 14% |
| GPA 3.50 or higher: | 61% | Live on campus: | 98% |
| GPA 3.0-3.49: | 22% | International: | 1% |
| GPA 2.0-2.99: | 17% | Fraternities: | 22% |
| Rank in top quarter: | 66% | Sororities: | 43% |

**Basis for selection.** School achievement record, test scores, and rank in top half of class most important. Interview recommended for academically weak or special needs applicants. Audition recommended for music and communication arts majors. Portfolio recommended for art majors.

**High school preparation.** 20 units recommended. Recommended units include English 4, mathematics 3, social studies 2, science 3 and foreign language 2.

**2007-2008 Annual costs.** Tuition/fees: $22,360. Room/board: $6,380. Books/supplies: $1,050. Personal expenses: $1,000.

**2007-2008 Financial aid. Need-based:** 326 full-time freshmen applied for aid; 277 were judged to have need; 277 of these received aid. Average need met was 90%. Average scholarship/grant was $18,787; average loan $3,823. 80% of total undergraduate aid awarded as scholarships/grants, 20% as loans/jobs. **Non-need-based:** Awarded to 822 full-time undergraduates, including 180 freshmen. Scholarships awarded for academics, alumni affiliation, art, athletics, leadership, minority status, music/drama, religious affiliation, ROTC, state residency.

**Application procedures. Admission:** Priority date 5/1; deadline 8/1 (postmark date). $30 fee, may be waived for applicants with need. Application may be submitted online. Admission notification on a rolling basis beginning on or about 10/1. Must reply by May 1 or within 4 week(s) if notified thereafter. **Financial aid:** Priority date 2/15, closing date 8/1. FAFSA, institutional form required. Applicants notified on a rolling basis starting 3/1; must reply by 5/1.

**Academics. Special study options:** Accelerated study, cooperative education, double major, dual enrollment of high school students, honors, independent study, internships, liberal arts/career combination, student-designed major, study abroad, teacher certification program. 3-2 nursing program with University of Kentucky. **Credit/placement by examination:** AP, CLEP, IB, SAT, ACT, institutional tests. **Support services:** Study skills assistance, tutoring, writing center.

**Majors. Area/ethnic studies:** American, European. **Biology:** General, ecology. **Business:** General, accounting. **Communications:** Media studies. **Computer sciences:** General. **Education:** Elementary, middle, music. **English:** English lit. **Foreign languages:** French, German, Spanish. **Health:** Athletic training, predental, prepharmacy, preveterinary. **History:** General. **Liberal arts:** Arts/sciences. **Math:** General. **Parks/recreation:** Exercise sciences, health/fitness. **Philosophy/religion:** Philosophy, religion. **Physical sciences:** Chemistry, physics. **Psychology:** General. **Social sciences:** Economics, political science, sociology. **Visual/performing arts:** Dramatic, studio arts.

**Most popular majors.** Biology 9%, business/marketing 13%, communications/journalism 10%, education 9%, parks/recreation 8%, philosophy/religious studies 6%, psychology 14%, social sciences 9%, visual/performing arts 6%.

**Computing on campus.** 115 workstations in library, computer center, student center. Dormitories wired for high-speed internet access and linked to campus network. Commuter students can connect to campus network. Online course registration, online library, helpline, repair service, wireless network available.

**Student life. Freshman orientation:** Mandatory, $100 fee. Preregistration for classes offered. Five-day orientation held prior to beginning of fall semester. **Policies:** Academic honor code enforced. **Housing:** Single-sex dorms, fraternity/sorority housing available. $200 deposit, deadline 5/1. Most students housed in minidorms of fewer than 80 students each. New apartments available for seniors. **Activities:** Bands, campus ministries, choral groups, dance, drama, literary magazine, music ensembles, musical theater, radio station, student government, student newspaper, Baptist student union, Fellowship of Christian Athletes, union of black leaders, United Nations of Georgetown.

**Athletics.** NAIA. **Intercollegiate:** Baseball M, basketball, cheerleading M, cross-country, football (tackle) M, golf, soccer, softball W, tennis, track and field, volleyball W. **Intramural:** Basketball, equestrian, football (non-tackle), golf, racquetball, soccer, softball, table tennis, tennis, volleyball. **Team name:** Tigers.

**Student services.** Alcohol/substance abuse counseling, campus ministries, career counseling, student employment services, financial aid counseling, health services, minority student services, personal counseling, placement for graduates.

**Contact.** E-mail: admissions@georgetowncollege.edu
Phone: (502) 863-8009 Toll-free number: (800) 788-9985
Fax: (502) 868-7733
Johnnie Johnson, Director of Admissions, Georgetown College, 400 East College Street, Georgetown, KY 40324

## ITT Technical Institute: Louisville
**Louisville, Kentucky**
www.itt-tech.edu                          **CB code: 2728**

- For-profit 4-year technical college
- Large city

**General.** Accredited by ACICS. **Calendar:** Quarter.

**Annual costs/financial aid.** Tuition varies by program, $260-$368 per credit hour.

**Contact.** Phone: (502) 327-7424
Director of Recruitment, 10509 Timberwood Circle, Louisville, KY 40223

## Kentucky Christian University
**Grayson, Kentucky**
www.kcu.edu                               **CB code: 1377**

- Private 4-year Bible and liberal arts college affiliated with Christian Church/Church of Christ
- Residential campus in small town
- 570 degree-seeking undergraduates; 3% part-time, 50% women, 6% African American, 1% Hispanic American, 3% international
- 19 degree-seeking graduate students
- 66% of applicants admitted
- SAT or ACT (ACT writing optional), application essay required
- 44% graduate within 6 years

**General.** Founded in 1919. Regionally accredited. **Degrees:** 84 bachelor's awarded; master's offered. **ROTC:** Army. **Location:** 25 miles from Ashland, 100 miles from Lexington. **Calendar:** Semester, limited summer session. **Full-time faculty:** 34 total; 74% have terminal degrees, 38% women. **Part-time faculty:** 24 total; 8% have terminal degrees, 50% women. **Class size:** 74% < 20, 19% 20-39, 4% 40-49, 3% 50-99.

**Freshman class profile.** 443 applied, 292 admitted, 176 enrolled.

| Mid 50% test scores | | | |
|---|---|---|---|
| SAT critical reading: | 380-500 | Rank in top quarter: | 23% |
| SAT math: | 440-550 | Rank in top tenth: | 11% |
| ACT composite: | 17-22 | Return as sophomores: | 68% |
| GPA 3.50 or higher: | 26% | Out-of-state: | 46% |
| GPA 3.0-3.49: | 28% | Live on campus: | 91% |
| GPA 2.0-2.99: | 43% | International: | 7% |

**Basis for selection.** High school grades, rank in class, ACT or SAT test scores, personal references, and religious commitment given equal weight. Interview recommended for academically weak. **Learning Disabled:** Students with special needs should contact KCU's Director of Campus Counseling to make arrangements for special accommodations.

**2008-2009 Annual costs.** Tuition/fees: $12,120. Room/board: $5,298.

**2007-2008 Financial aid. Need-based:** 157 full-time freshmen applied for aid; 141 were judged to have need; 141 of these received aid. Average need met was 62%. Average scholarship/grant was $5,051; average loan $3,471. 46% of total undergraduate aid awarded as scholarships/grants, 54% as loans/jobs. **Non-need-based:** Awarded to 548 full-time undergraduates, including 176 freshmen. Scholarships awarded for academics, alumni affiliation, leadership, minority status, music/drama, religious affiliation.

**Application procedures. Admission:** No deadline. $30 fee. Application may be submitted online. Admission notification on a rolling basis. **Financial aid:** Priority date 3/1; no closing date. FAFSA required. Applicants notified on a rolling basis starting 3/15; must reply within 2 week(s) of notification.

**Academics.** All students required to major in Bible as a second degree. **Special study options:** Distance learning, double major, dual enrollment of high school students, independent study, internships, liberal arts/career combination, study abroad, teacher certification program. **Credit/placement by examination:** AP, CLEP, IB, ACT. **Support services:** Reduced course load, remedial instruction, tutoring.

**Majors. Business:** Business admin. **Education:** Elementary, English, middle, music, secondary, social studies. **English:** English lit. **Health:** Nursing (RN). **History:** General. **Interdisciplinary:** Intercultural. **Liberal arts:** Humanities. **Psychology:** Counseling. **Public administration:** Social work. **Theology:** Bible, missionary, pastoral counseling, religious ed, sacred music, theology, youth ministry. **Visual/performing arts:** Music management, music performance. **Other:** University Studies.

**Most popular majors.** Business/marketing 8%, education 19%, health sciences 17%, interdisciplinary studies 11%, liberal arts 6%, theological studies 29%.

**Computing on campus.** 50 workstations in library, computer center, student center. Dormitories wired for high-speed internet access and linked to campus network. Commuter students can connect to campus network. Online library, helpline, repair service, wireless network available.

**Student life. Freshman orientation:** Mandatory. Preregistration for classes offered. **Policies:** All students under 26 not living with parents must live in on-campus housing. Religious observance required. **Housing:** Guaranteed on-campus for all undergraduates. Single-sex dorms, special housing for disabled, apartments available. $100 nonrefundable deposit. **Activities:** Bands, campus ministries, choral groups, drama, music ensembles, student government, Global Mission Awareness, Pi Chi Delta, Collegiate Music Educators National Conference, Herodotus Society, Laos Protos, American Association of Christian Counselors, Students in Free Enterprise.

**Athletics.** NCCAA. **Intercollegiate:** Basketball, cheerleading M, cross-country, football (tackle) M, soccer, volleyball W. **Intramural:** Basketball, football (non-tackle) M, soccer, softball, table tennis, volleyball. **Team name:** Knights.

**Student services.** Campus ministries, financial aid counseling, health services, minority student services, personal counseling, women's services. **Physically disabled:** Services for visually, hearing impaired.

**Contact.** E-mail: sdeakins@kcu.edu
Phone: (606) 474-3266 Toll-free number: (800) 522-3181
Fax: (606) 474-3155
Sandra Deakins, Vice President of Enrollment Management, Kentucky Christian University, 100 Academic Parkway, Grayson, KY 41143-2205

## Kentucky Mountain Bible College
**Vancleve, Kentucky**
www.kmbc.edu                              **CB code: 1384**

- Private 4-year Bible college affiliated with Kentucky Mountain Holiness Association
- Residential campus in small town

♦ 59 degree-seeking undergraduates: 17% part-time, 41% women
♦ 66 graduate students
♦ 49% of applicants admitted
♦ ACT (writing optional), application essay required
♦ 45% graduate within 6 years; 18% enter graduate study

**General.** Founded in 1931. Accredited by ABHE. **Degrees:** 9 bachelor's, 7 associate awarded. **Location:** 75 miles from Lexington. **Calendar:** Semester. **Full-time faculty:** 6 total; 17% have terminal degrees, 33% women. **Part-time faculty:** 11 total; 46% women. **Class size:** 88% < 20, 12% 20-39.

**Freshman class profile.** 37 applied, 18 admitted, 11 enrolled.

| | | | |
|---|---|---|---|
| GPA 3.50 or higher: | 50% | Return as sophomores: | 68% |
| GPA 2.0-2.99: | 50% | Out-of-state: | 55% |
| Rank in top quarter: | 50% | Live on campus: | 100% |
| End year in good standing: | 90% | | |

**Basis for selection.** All students must have C average or above and provide 2 recommendations. 15 ACT required. Provisional admission granted. Interview recommended.

**High school preparation.** 18 units required. Required and recommended units include English 4, mathematics 2, history 2 and science 2. A total of 10 units in English, math, science or language required out of 18 units.

**2008-2009 Annual costs.** Tuition/fees: $5,940. Room/board: $3,700. Books/supplies: $400. Personal expenses: $250.

**2007-2008 Financial aid.** **Need-based:** 7 full-time freshmen applied for aid; 7 were judged to have need; 7 of these received aid. Average scholarship/grant was $1,700; average loan $3,500. 54% of total undergraduate aid awarded as scholarships/grants, 46% as loans/jobs. **Non-need-based:** Awarded to 27 full-time undergraduates, including 9 freshmen. Scholarships awarded for academics, job skills, leadership, music/drama.

**Application procedures.** **Admission:** Priority date 6/1; no deadline. $25 fee, may be waived for applicants with need. Application may be submitted online. Admission notification on a rolling basis. **Financial aid:** Priority date 4/1, closing date 6/30. FAFSA, institutional form required. Applicants notified on a rolling basis starting 3/15; must reply by 7/1.

**Academics.** **Special study options:** Independent study, internships, teacher certification program. **Credit/placement by examination:** AP, CLEP, ACT. **Support services:** Reduced course load, remedial instruction, study skills assistance, tutoring.

**Majors. Communications:** General. **Education:** Elementary. **Theology:** Missionary, religious ed, sacred music, theology.

**Most popular majors.** Theological studies 50%.

**Computing on campus.** 12 workstations in library, computer center. Wireless network available.

**Student life. Freshman orientation:** Mandatory. Preregistration for classes offered. Two-day program, includes Bible-knowledge testing. **Policies:** Religious observance required. **Housing:** Guaranteed on-campus for all undergraduates. Single-sex dorms, apartments, substance-free housing available. **Activities:** Campus ministries, choral groups, drama, radio station, student government, student newspaper, missionary student involvement group, student council, class organizations.

**Athletics. Intramural:** Basketball M, volleyball W.

**Student services.** Financial aid counseling, personal counseling.

**Contact.** E-mail: kmbc@kmbc.edu
Phone: (606) 693-5000 ext. 130 Toll-free number: (800) 879-5622 ext. 130
Fax: (606) 693-4884
David Lorimer, Chief Admissions Counselor, Kentucky Mountain Bible College, Box 10, Vancleve, KY 41385-0010

---

## Kentucky State University
**Frankfort, Kentucky**
www.kysu.edu

**CB member**
**CB code: 1368**

♦ Public 4-year university and liberal arts college
♦ Residential campus in large town
♦ 2,201 degree-seeking undergraduates: 15% part-time, 58% women, 66% African American, 1% Asian American, 1% international

♦ 168 degree-seeking graduate students
♦ 40% of applicants admitted
♦ SAT or ACT (ACT writing optional) required

**General.** Founded in 1886. Regionally accredited. **Degrees:** 193 bachelor's, 50 associate awarded; master's offered. **ROTC:** Army, Air Force. **Location:** 50 miles from Louisville, 25 miles from Lexington. **Calendar:** Semester, limited summer session. **Full-time faculty:** 146 total; 64% have terminal degrees, 36% minority, 39% women. **Part-time faculty:** 50 total; 36% have terminal degrees, 26% minority, 48% women. **Class size:** 65% < 20, 34% 20-39, less than 1% 40-49, less than 1% 50-99, less than 1% >100. **Special facilities:** Land grant institution.

**Freshman class profile.** 6,262 applied, 2,500 admitted, 678 enrolled.

| Mid 50% test scores | | GPA 3.0-3.49: | 20% |
|---|---|---|---|
| SAT critical reading: | 370-470 | GPA 2.0-2.99: | 61% |
| SAT math: | 360-450 | Return as sophomores: | 63% |
| SAT writing: | 330-440 | Out-of-state: | 57% |
| ACT composite: | 15-19 | Live on campus: | 78% |
| GPA 3.50 or higher: | 6% | | |

**Basis for selection.** Unconditional admission for graduates of accredited high schools meeting Pre-College Curriculum (PCC) requirements established by Kentucky Council on Higher Education and having admission index of 430. Interview recommended for nursing majors and applicants to College of Leadership Studies. Audition recommended for music majors. Portfolio recommended for art majors. Essay required of applicants to College of Leadership Studies.

**High school preparation.** 22 units required. Required units include English 4, mathematics 3, social studies 3, history 1, science 3, foreign language 2, computer science 1 and academic electives 7.

**2007-2008 Annual costs.** Tuition/fees: $5,320; $12,490 out-of-state. Room/board: $6,340.

**2007-2008 Financial aid.** **Need-based:** Average scholarship/grant was $2,084; average loan $3,078. 45% of total undergraduate aid awarded as scholarships/grants, 55% as loans/jobs. **Non-need-based:** Awarded to 151 full-time undergraduates, including 41 freshmen. Scholarships awarded for academics, alumni affiliation, art, athletics, music/drama.

**Application procedures.** **Admission:** No deadline. $30 fee, may be waived for applicants with need. Application may be submitted online. Admission notification on a rolling basis. **Financial aid:** Priority date 4/15, closing date 6/30. FAFSA required.

**Academics.** **Special study options:** Combined bachelor's/graduate degree, cooperative education, distance learning, double major, ESL, honors, independent study, internships, liberal arts/career combination, student-designed major, study abroad, teacher certification program. **Credit/placement by examination:** AP, CLEP, SAT, ACT, institutional tests. 16 credit hours maximum toward associate degree, 32 toward bachelor's. **Support services:** Learning center, pre-admission summer program, reduced course load, remedial instruction, study skills assistance, tutoring, writing center.

**Majors. Biology:** General. **Business:** General. **Computer sciences:** General, webmaster. **Education:** Elementary, physical. **English:** English lit. **Family/consumer sciences:** Family studies. **Health:** Nursing (RN). **Liberal arts:** Arts/sciences. **Math:** General. **Physical sciences:** Chemistry. **Protective services:** Criminal justice. **Psychology:** General. **Public administration:** General, social work. **Social sciences:** General, political science. **Visual/performing arts:** Studio arts. **Other:** Mass Communication and Journalism.

**Most popular majors.** Biology 6%, business/marketing 15%, computer/information sciences 7%, education 13%, psychology 8%, public administration/social services 12%, security/protective services 9%.

**Computing on campus.** 306 workstations in dormitories, library, computer center, student center. Dormitories wired for high-speed internet access and linked to campus network. Commuter students can connect to campus network. Online library, helpline, repair service, wireless network available.

**Student life. Freshman orientation:** Available. **Housing:** Guaranteed on-campus for freshmen. Single-sex dorms available. $300 deposit. **Activities:** Bands, choral groups, dance, drama, music ensembles, musical theater, opera, student government, student newspaper, symphony orchestra, Alpha Phi Omega, Wesley Club, Baptist student union, Circle-K, international student association, NAACP, optimist club.

**Athletics.** NCAA. **Intercollegiate:** Baseball M, basketball, cross-country, football (tackle) M, golf M, softball W, track and field, volleyball W. **Intramural:** Basketball, football (tackle) M, softball W, track and field, volleyball. **Team name:** Thoroughbreds.

**Student services.** Adult student services, career counseling, student employment services, financial aid counseling, health services, personal counseling, placement for graduates, veterans' counselor. **Physically disabled:** Services for visually, hearing impaired.

**Contact.** E-mail: admissions@kysu.edu
Phone: (502) 597-6813 Toll-free number: (877) 367-5978
Fax: (502) 597-5814
James Burrell, Director of Admissions, Kentucky State University, 400 East Main Street, ASB 312, Frankfort, KY 40601

## Kentucky Wesleyan College
**Owensboro, Kentucky**
**www.kwc.edu**
CB member
CB code: 1369

- Private 4-year liberal arts college affiliated with United Methodist Church
- Residential campus in small city
- 919 degree-seeking undergraduates: 2% part-time, 47% women
- 78% of applicants admitted
- SAT or ACT (ACT writing optional) required
- 42% graduate within 6 years; 26% enter graduate study

**General.** Founded in 1858. Regionally accredited. **Degrees:** 121 bachelor's awarded. **ROTC:** Army. **Location:** 116 miles from Louisville, 120 miles from Nashville, Tennessee. **Calendar:** Semester, limited summer session. **Full-time faculty:** 42 total; 88% have terminal degrees, 5% minority, 36% women. **Part-time faculty:** 58 total; 19% have terminal degrees, 7% minority, 50% women. **Class size:** 69% < 20, 30% 20-39, less than 1% 40-49. **Special facilities:** Center for the sciences, center for the arts, fully computerized writing workshop, center for business studies.

**Freshman class profile.** 1,397 applied, 1,085 admitted, 281 enrolled.

| Mid 50% test scores | | Rank in top quarter: | 34% |
|---|---|---|---|
| SAT critical reading: | 400-480 | Rank in top tenth: | 15% |
| SAT math: | 420-540 | End year in good standing: | 80% |
| SAT writing: | 400-460 | Return as sophomores: | 54% |
| ACT composite: | 19-24 | Out-of-state: | 24% |
| GPA 3.50 or higher: | 29% | Live on campus: | 76% |
| GPA 3.0-3.49: | 29% | Fraternities: | 14% |
| GPA 2.0-2.99: | 41% | Sororities: | 23% |

**Basis for selection.** Secondary school record very important. Test scores, GPA, class rank, and school activities important. Interview recommended.

**High school preparation.** 13 units required. Required and recommended units include English 4, mathematics 3, social studies 3, science 3 and foreign language 2.

**2007-2008 Annual costs.** Tuition/fees: $14,520. Room/board: $5,950. Books/supplies: $1,200. Personal expenses: $2,000.

**2006-2007 Financial aid. Need-based:** 331 full-time freshmen applied for aid; 295 were judged to have need; 289 of these received aid. Average need met was 68%. Average scholarship/grant was $10,283; average loan $2,634. 77% of total undergraduate aid awarded as scholarships/grants, 23% as loans/jobs. **Non-need-based:** Awarded to 257 full-time undergraduates, including 94 freshmen. Scholarships awarded for academics, alumni affiliation, art, athletics, leadership, music/drama, religious affiliation, state residency.

**Application procedures. Admission:** No deadline. No application fee. Application may be submitted online. Admission notification on a rolling basis. **Financial aid:** Closing date 3/15. FAFSA required. Applicants notified on a rolling basis starting 2/15; must reply within 2 week(s) of notification.

**Academics.** Co-curricular leadership program available. **Special study options:** Distance learning, double major, independent study, internships, liberal arts/career combination, student-designed major, study abroad, teacher certification program. **Credit/placement by examination:** AP, CLEP, IB, SAT, ACT, institutional tests. 42 credit hours maximum toward bachelor's degree. International Baccalaureate Diploma credit will be awarded for advanced course scores of 6 or 7, with up to 10 hours of credit awarded. **Support services:** Learning center, reduced course load, remedial instruction, study skills assistance, tutoring, writing center.

**Majors. Biology:** General, zoology. **Business:** General, accounting, business admin. **Communications:** General. **Computer sciences:** General. **Education:** Art, biology, chemistry, elementary, English, mathematics, middle, physical, social studies, Spanish. **English:** English lit. **Foreign languages:** Spanish. **History:** General. **Math:** General. **Parks/recreation:** Sports admin. **Philosophy/religion:** Religion. **Physical sciences:** Chemistry, physics.

**Protective services:** Criminal justice. **Psychology:** General. **Public administration:** Human services. **Social sciences:** Political science, sociology. **Visual/performing arts:** Art, studio arts.

**Most popular majors.** Business/marketing 14%, communications/journalism 10%, education 15%, physical sciences 7%, psychology 10%, security/protective services 12%.

**Computing on campus.** Dormitories wired for high-speed internet access and linked to campus network. Commuter students can connect to campus network. Online course registration, online library, helpline, repair service, wireless network available.

**Student life. Freshman orientation:** Mandatory, $125 fee. Preregistration for classes offered. **Housing:** Guaranteed on-campus for freshmen. Coed dorms, single-sex dorms, special housing for disabled, fraternity/sorority housing, substance-free housing available. $100 fully refundable deposit, deadline 5/1. **Activities:** Bands, campus ministries, choral groups, dance, drama, literary magazine, music ensembles, radio station, student government, student newspaper, student activities programming board, Baptist Student Union, United Methodist Student Fellowship, Brothers and Sisters in Christ, criminal justice association, Kentucky Wesleyan Singers, College Republicans, Young Democrats.

**Athletics.** NCAA. **Intercollegiate:** Baseball M, basketball, cheerleading, cross-country, football (tackle) M, golf, soccer, softball W, tennis W, volleyball W. **Intramural:** Basketball, bowling, football (non-tackle), golf, racquetball, soccer, softball, table tennis, tennis, volleyball. **Team name:** Panthers.

**Student services.** Alcohol/substance abuse counseling, campus ministries, career counseling, student employment services, financial aid counseling, health services, on-campus daycare, personal counseling, placement for graduates, veterans' counselor.

**Contact.** E-mail: admitme@kwc.edu
Phone: (270) 852-3120 Toll-free number: (800) 999-0592
Fax: (270) 852-3133
Clayton Daniels, Dean of Admissions and Finanancial Aid, Kentucky Wesleyan College, 3000 Frederica Street, Owensboro, KY 42301

## Lindsey Wilson College
**Columbia, Kentucky**
**www.lindsey.edu**
CB code: 1409

- Private 4-year liberal arts college affiliated with United Methodist Church
- Residential campus in small town
- 1,562 degree-seeking undergraduates: 5% part-time, 66% women, 7% African American, 1% Hispanic American, 5% international
- 272 graduate students

**General.** Founded in 1903. Regionally accredited. **Degrees:** 253 bachelor's, 41 associate awarded; master's offered. **Location:** 100 miles from Louisville. **Calendar:** Semester, limited summer session. **Full-time faculty:** 70 total; 83% have terminal degrees, 3% minority, 47% women. **Part-time faculty:** 45 total.

**Freshman class profile.** 1,496 applied, 1,184 admitted, 364 enrolled.

| GPA 3.50 or higher: | 28% | Return as sophomores: | 54% |
|---|---|---|---|
| GPA 3.0-3.49: | 25% | Out-of-state: | 5% |
| GPA 2.0-2.99: | 42% | Live on campus: | 69% |
| End year in good standing: | 68% | | |

**Basis for selection.** Open admission, but selective for some programs. Special requirements for education and human services programs. ACCUPLACER or ACT required for placement. Interview recommended.

**2007-2008 Annual costs.** Tuition/fees: $15,806. Room/board: $6,540. Books/supplies: $700. Personal expenses: $800.

**Financial aid.** All financial aid based on need.

**Application procedures. Admission:** Priority date 6/1; no deadline. No application fee. Application may be submitted online. Admission notification on a rolling basis beginning on or about 1/1. **Financial aid:** Priority date 4/15; no closing date. FAFSA, institutional form required. Applicants notified on a rolling basis starting 5/1; must reply within 2 week(s) of notification.

**Academics. Special study options:** Dual enrollment of high school students, independent study, internships, student-designed major, study abroad, teacher certification program, weekend college. On-campus and extension evening program for associate degree in business management and computer science, weekend extension program in human services. **Credit/placement by examination:** AP, CLEP. 16 credit hours maximum toward associate degree, 32 toward bachelor's. **Support services:** Learning center, reduced course load, remedial instruction, study skills assistance, tutoring, writing center.

**Majors. Area/ethnic studies:** American. **Biology:** General. **Business:** Business admin. **Communications:** General, journalism. **Education:** Art, biology, elementary, English, mathematics, middle, physical, secondary, social science. **English:** English lit. **History:** General. **Legal studies:** Prelaw. **Liberal arts:** Humanities. **Math:** General. **Parks/recreation:** Health/fitness. **Philosophy/religion:** Christian. **Protective services:** Criminal justice. **Psychology:** General. **Social sciences:** General. **Visual/performing arts:** Studio arts.

**Most popular majors.** Biology 6%, business/marketing 13%, communications/journalism 7%, education 7%, public administration/social services 47%.

**Computing on campus.** 100 workstations in library, computer center. Dormitories wired for high-speed internet access and linked to campus network. Commuter students can connect to campus network. Online course registration, online library, wireless network available.

**Student life. Freshman orientation:** Available. Preregistration for classes offered. **Policies:** All students not living with family must live in campus housing. **Housing:** Single-sex dorms, apartments, substance-free housing available. $40 deposit. **Activities:** Pep band, choral groups, drama, literary magazine, music ensembles, student government, student newspaper, Christian student organizations, Student Ambassadors, black student union, Students in Free Enterprise, Raider Republicans, international student association.

**Athletics.** NAIA. **Intercollegiate:** Baseball M, basketball, bowling, cross-country, golf, soccer, softball W, tennis, track and field, volleyball W. **Intramural:** Basketball, football (tackle), softball, table tennis, tennis, volleyball. **Team name:** Blue Raiders.

**Student services.** Alcohol/substance abuse counseling, campus ministries, career counseling, student employment services, financial aid counseling, health services, personal counseling, placement for graduates. **Physically disabled:** Services for visually impaired.

**Contact.** E-mail: admissions@lindsey.edu
Phone: (270) 384-8100 Toll-free number: (800) 264-0138
Fax: (270) 384-8591
Traci Pooler, Dean of Admissions, Lindsey Wilson College, 210 Lindsey Wilson Street, Columbia, KY 42728

## Mid-Continent University
**Mayfield, Kentucky**
**www.midcontinent.edu**                 CB code: 0254

- Private 4-year Bible and liberal arts college affiliated with Southern Baptist Convention
- Commuter campus in large town
- 1,541 degree-seeking undergraduates: 14% part-time, 61% women, 13% African American, 1% Hispanic American, 3% international
- 83% of applicants admitted
- SAT or ACT (ACT writing optional), application essay required

**General.** Founded in 1949. Regionally accredited. **Degrees:** 186 bachelor's, 101 associate awarded. **Location:** 20 miles from Paducah, 125 miles from Nashville, Tennessee. **Calendar:** Semester, limited summer session. **Full-time faculty:** 27 total; 48% have terminal degrees, 30% minority, 15% women. **Part-time faculty:** 71 total; 7% have terminal degrees, 4% minority, 45% women. **Class size:** 100% 20-39.

**Freshman class profile.** 463 applied, 382 admitted, 200 enrolled.

| Mid 50% test scores | | | |
|---|---|---|---|
| SAT critical reading: | 370-490 | GPA 3.0-3.49: | 26% |
| SAT math: | 380-580 | GPA 2.0-2.99: | 52% |
| SAT writing: | 320-490 | Rank in top quarter: | 34% |
| ACT composite: | 16-22 | Rank in top tenth: | 10% |
| GPA 3.50 or higher: | 16% | Out-of-state: | 16% |
| | | International: | 8% |

**Basis for selection.** Secondary school record and standardized test scores most important. Entering students tested in mathematics and English. **Homeschooled:** Statement describing homeschool structure and mission, transcript of courses and grades, letter of recommendation (nonparent) required.

**High school preparation.** Required units include English 4, mathematics 2, social studies 2, science 2 and foreign language 1.

**2007-2008 Annual costs.** Tuition/fees: $12,050. Room/board: $6,000. Books/supplies: $1,350. Personal expenses: $2,000.

**2006-2007 Financial aid. Need-based:** 124 full-time freshmen applied for aid; 114 were judged to have need; 114 of these received aid. Average need met was 61%. Average scholarship/grant was $6,619; average loan $2,022. 52% of total undergraduate aid awarded as scholarships/grants, 48% as loans/jobs. **Non-need-based:** Awarded to 129 full-time undergraduates, including 28 freshmen. Scholarships awarded for academics.

**Application procedures. Admission:** Priority date 8/1; no deadline. $20 fee, may be waived for applicants with need. Application may be submitted online. Admission notification on a rolling basis. **Financial aid:** Priority date 3/15, closing date 5/30. FAFSA, institutional form required. Applicants notified on a rolling basis starting 4/1.

**Academics.** Bachelor of ministry degree offered after 36 hours above earned baccalaureate degree from regionally accredited institution. Accelerated programs in organizational leadership for adult learners available. **Special study options:** Accelerated study, combined bachelor's/graduate degree, cooperative education, double major, dual enrollment of high school students, independent study, study abroad, teacher certification program. **Credit/placement by examination:** CLEP, SAT, ACT, institutional tests. 30 credit hours maximum toward bachelor's degree. **Support services:** Remedial instruction, tutoring.

**Majors. Business:** Business admin, organizational behavior. **Education:** Elementary. **English:** English lit. **Philosophy/religion:** Christian. **Psychology:** General, counseling. **Social sciences:** General. **Theology:** Bible, missionary, religious ed.

**Most popular majors.** Business/marketing 80%, theological studies 9%.

**Computing on campus.** 24 workstations in dormitories, library, computer center. Dormitories wired for high-speed internet access. Online library available.

**Student life. Freshman orientation:** Mandatory. Preregistration for classes offered. 2-3 day orientation process at beginning of academic year. **Policies:** Religious observance required. **Housing:** Single-sex dorms available. $200 deposit, deadline 8/1. **Activities:** Student government, student newspaper, Baptist Student Union, Fellowship of Christian Athletes, psychology club, international student association.

**Athletics.** NAIA, NCCAA. **Intercollegiate:** Baseball M, basketball M, soccer M, softball W. **Team name:** Lady Cougars, Cougars.

**Student services.** Campus ministries, career counseling, financial aid counseling, personal counseling, veterans' counselor. **Physically disabled:** Services for visually impaired.

**Contact.** E-mail: admissions@midcontinent.edu
Phone: (270) 247-8521 ext. 238 Toll-free number: (866) 894-8878
Fax: (270) 247-3115
Smith Smith, Director of Admissions, Mid-Continent University, 99 Powell Road East, Mayfield, KY 42066-0357

## Midway College
**Midway, Kentucky**                      CB member
**www.midway.edu**                        CB code: 1467

- Private 4-year liberal arts college for women affiliated with Christian Church (Disciples of Christ)
- Commuter campus in small town
- 1,395 degree-seeking undergraduates: 26% part-time, 91% women, 7% African American, 1% Hispanic American
- SAT or ACT required

**General.** Founded in 1847. Regionally accredited. Men admitted to evening and weekend programs in nursing, business administration, computer information systems, healthcare managment, human resource management, sport management. **Degrees:** 240 bachelor's, 53 associate awarded; master's offered. **ROTC:** Army. **Location:** 12 miles from Lexington, 60 miles from Louisville. **Calendar:** Semester, limited summer session. **Full-time faculty:** 41 total; 46% have terminal degrees, 39% women. **Part-time faculty:** 101 total; 15% have terminal degrees, 72% women. **Class size:** 79% < 20, 19% 20-39, 2% 40-49. **Special facilities:** Equine science center, riding arena, campus farm.

**Freshman class profile.** 456 applied, 323 admitted, 202 enrolled.

| Mid 50% test scores | | | |
|---|---|---|---|
| SAT critical reading: | 420-560 | GPA 2.0-2.99: | 28% |
| SAT math: | 400-560 | Rank in top quarter: | 35% |
| ACT composite: | 18-22 | Rank in top tenth: | 12% |
| GPA 3.50 or higher: | 37% | Out-of-state: | 11% |
| GPA 3.0-3.49: | 31% | Live on campus: | 40% |

**Basis for selection.** Open admission, but selective for some programs. High school record and test scores important. Essay and letters of recommendation encouraged. More competitive requirements established for certain programs such as biology, education, nursing. Interview required for majors in nursing; also required of academically weak. Essay recommended for students who are conditionally admitted.

**High school preparation.** 15 units required. Required and recommended units include English 4, mathematics 3, social studies 1, history 1 and science 2. Specific college-preparatory program required for some majors.

**2007-2008 Annual costs.** Tuition/fees: $15,750. Room/board: $6,400. Books/supplies: $1,200. Personal expenses: $1,000.

**2007-2008 Financial aid. Need-based:** Average need met was 74%. Average scholarship/grant was $10,212; average loan $3,912. 54% of total undergraduate aid awarded as scholarships/grants, 46% as loans/jobs. **Non-need-based:** Scholarships awarded for academics, alumni affiliation, art, athletics, leadership, minority status, religious affiliation. **Additional information:** Audition required of applicants for music scholarships. Portfolio required for art scholarships.

**Application procedures. Admission:** Priority date 4/1; no deadline. $25 fee, may be waived for applicants with need. Application may be submitted online. Admission notification on a rolling basis. Must reply by May 1 or within 4 week(s) if notified thereafter. **Financial aid:** Priority date 4/1, closing date 8/1. FAFSA, institutional form required. Applicants notified on a rolling basis; must reply within 4 week(s) of notification.

**Academics. Special study options:** Accelerated study, cooperative education, distance learning, double major, dual enrollment of high school students, independent study, internships, liberal arts/career combination, study abroad, teacher certification program. Evening business program. **Credit/placement by examination:** AP, CLEP, IB, institutional tests. 12 credit hours maximum toward associate degree, 12 toward bachelor's. **Support services:** Learning center, reduced course load, remedial instruction, tutoring, writing center.

**Majors. Agriculture:** Equestrian studies. **Biology:** General. **Business:** General, organizational behavior. **Computer sciences:** General. **Conservation:** Environmental science. **Education:** Elementary, multi-level teacher, secondary, special. **English:** English lit. **Health:** Health care admin, nursing (RN). **Interdisciplinary:** Intercultural. **Math:** General. **Parks/recreation:** Sports admin. **Psychology:** General.

**Most popular majors.** Agriculture 9%, business/marketing 32%, education 46%, health sciences 7%.

**Computing on campus.** 60 workstations in dormitories, library, computer center, student center. Dormitories wired for high-speed internet access and linked to campus network. Commuter students can connect to campus network. Online course registration, online library, helpline available.

**Student life. Freshman orientation:** Mandatory. Preregistration for classes offered. 2-3 day orientation prior to start of term. **Policies:** All students under 21, unmarried, and not living at home required to live in campus housing. **Housing:** Guaranteed on-campus for all undergraduates. Special housing for disabled, substance-free housing available. $25 deposit, deadline 5/1. **Activities:** Choral groups, international student organizations, student government, vespers committee, Baptist Student Union, Disciples on Campus, Ruth Slack Roach Scholars.

**Athletics.** NAIA. **Intercollegiate:** Basketball W, cross-country W, equestrian W, soccer W, softball W, tennis W, volleyball W. **Team name:** Eagles.

**Student services.** Adult student services, campus ministries, career counseling, student employment services, financial aid counseling, health services, personal counseling, placement for graduates.

**Contact.** E-mail: admissions@midway.edu
Phone: (859) 846-5347 Toll-free number: (800) 755-0031
Fax: (859) 846-5787
Jim Wombles, Chief Enrollment Officer, Midway College, 512 East Stephens Street, Midway, KY 40347-1120

## Morehead State University
**Morehead, Kentucky**
**www.moreheadstate.edu**                    **CB code: 1487**

- Public 4-year university
- Residential campus in small town
- 6,863 degree-seeking undergraduates: 16% part-time, 60% women, 3% African American, 1% Hispanic American
- 1,169 degree-seeking graduate students
- 71% of applicants admitted
- SAT or ACT (ACT writing optional) required
- 43% graduate within 6 years

**General.** Founded in 1922. Regionally accredited. **Degrees:** 1,081 bachelor's, 127 associate awarded; master's offered. **ROTC:** Army. **Location:** 65 miles from Lexington; 70 miles from Huntington, West Virginia. **Calendar:** Semester, extensive summer session. **Full-time faculty:** 379 total; 66% have terminal degrees, 13% minority, 46% women. **Part-time faculty:** 137 total; 3% minority, 56% women. **Class size:** 54% < 20, 38% 20-39, 5% 40-49, 3% 50-99. **Special facilities:** Planetarium, agriculture complex, outdoor learning center at Cave Run, Kentucky folk art center, space science center, space tracking radio telescope.

**Freshman class profile.** 5,257 applied, 3,740 admitted, 1,409 enrolled.

| Mid 50% test scores | | | |
|---|---|---|---|
| SAT critical reading: | 420-520 | Rank in top quarter: | 41% |
| SAT math: | 420-550 | Rank in top tenth: | 18% |
| ACT composite: | 18-24 | Out-of-state: | 19% |
| GPA 3.50 or higher: | 40% | Live on campus: | 72% |
| GPA 3.0-3.49: | 26% | Fraternities: | 14% |
| GPA 2.0-2.99: | 31% | Sororities: | 9% |

**Basis for selection.** Test scores and GPA used to calculate index to determine admission. Status and review of pre-college curriculum important. Interview recommended for applicants to specialized allied health programs. Audition recommended for music majors. **Homeschooled:** Statement describing homeschool structure and mission, transcript of courses and grades, interview, letter of recommendation (nonparent) required.

**High school preparation.** 22 units required. Required units include English 4, mathematics 3, social studies 3, science 3 (laboratory 1), foreign language 2, computer science 1, visual/performing arts 1 and academic electives 7. 1 unit history and appreciation of fine arts recommended.

**2007-2008 Annual costs.** Tuition/fees: $5,280; $13,340 out-of-state. Room/board: $5,470. Books/supplies: $500. Personal expenses: $800.

**Financial aid. Non-need-based:** Scholarships awarded for academics, alumni affiliation, art, athletics, leadership, minority status, music/drama, ROTC, state residency.

**Application procedures. Admission:** No deadline. No application fee. Application may be submitted online. Admission notification on a rolling basis. **Financial aid:** Priority date 3/15; no closing date. FAFSA, institutional form required. Applicants notified on a rolling basis.

**Academics.** 2-year transfer programs in prechiropractic, predentistry, preengineering, preforestry, prelaw, premedicine, preoptometry, prepharmacy, prephysical therapy, preveterinary medicine offered. **Special study options:** Accelerated study, cooperative education, cross-registration, distance learning, double major, dual enrollment of high school students, exchange student, honors, independent study, internships, student-designed major, study abroad, teacher certification program, Washington semester, weekend college. **Credit/placement by examination:** AP, CLEP, SAT, ACT, institutional tests. 16 credit hours maximum toward associate degree, 32 toward bachelor's. **Support services:** Learning center, pre-admission summer program, remedial instruction, study skills assistance, tutoring, writing center.

**Majors. Agriculture:** General. **Biology:** General, ecology. **Business:** Accounting, business admin, finance, management information systems, managerial economics, marketing, real estate. **Communications:** General. **Computer sciences:** General. **Education:** Business, early childhood, elementary, family/consumer sciences, health, middle, physical, special. **Engineering technology:** Manufacturing. **English:** English lit, speech/rhetoric. **Family/consumer sciences:** Work/family studies. **Foreign languages:** French, Spanish. **Health:** Medical radiologic technology/radiation therapy, nursing (RN). **History:** General. **Legal studies:** Paralegal. **Math:** General. **Parks/recreation:** Exercise sciences. **Philosophy/religion:** Philosophy. **Physical sciences:** Chemistry, geology, physics. **Psychology:** General. **Public administration:** Social work. **Social sciences:** General, geography, political science, sociology. **Visual/performing arts:** Dramatic, studio arts.

**Most popular majors.** Business/marketing 13%, education 14%, liberal arts 11%, public administration/social services 6%, social sciences 8%, visual/performing arts 6%.

**Computing on campus.** 1,000 workstations in dormitories, library, computer center, student center. Dormitories wired for high-speed internet access and linked to campus network. Commuter students can connect to campus network. Online library, helpline, student web hosting, wireless network available.

**Student life.** Freshman orientation: Available. Preregistration for classes offered. Offered several times in June and July. **Housing:** Coed dorms, single-sex dorms, special housing for disabled, apartments, fraternity/sorority housing available. $100 fully refundable deposit. Limited housing available at agriculture complex for agriculture science students. Housing for handicapped students and private rooms available. **Activities:** Bands, choral groups, dance, drama, literary magazine, music ensembles, musical theater, opera, radio station, student government, student newspaper, symphony orchestra, TV station, seven religious organizations, Young Democrats, Young Republicans, several service organizations.

**Athletics.** NCAA. **Intercollegiate:** Baseball M, basketball, cross-country, football (tackle) M, golf M, rifle, soccer W, softball W, tennis, track and field, volleyball W. **Intramural:** Archery, badminton, basketball, bowling, football (tackle), golf, racquetball, soccer M, softball, swimming, table tennis, tennis, track and field, volleyball. **Team name:** Eagles.

**Student services.** Adult student services, alcohol/substance abuse counseling, career counseling, services for economically disadvantaged, student employment services, financial aid counseling, health services, minority student services, on-campus daycare, personal counseling, placement for graduates, veterans' counselor. **Physically disabled:** Services for visually, hearing impaired.

**Contact.** E-mail: admissions@moreheadstate.edu
Phone: (606) 783-2000 Toll-free number: (800) 585-6781
Fax: (606) 783-5038
Jeffrey Liles, Assistant Vice President of Enrollment Services, Morehead State University, 100 Admissions Center, Morehead, KY 40351

---

## Murray State University
**Murray, Kentucky**  **CB member**
www.murraystate.edu  **CB code: 1494**

- Public 4-year university
- Residential campus in large town
- 7,749 degree-seeking undergraduates: 11% part-time, 58% women, 6% African American, 1% Asian American, 1% Hispanic American, 1% international
- 1,541 degree-seeking graduate students
- 85% of applicants admitted
- ACT (writing recommended) required
- 51% graduate within 6 years

**General.** Founded in 1922. Regionally accredited. **Degrees:** 1,550 bachelor's, 19 associate awarded; master's offered. **ROTC:** Army. **Location:** 115 miles from Nashville, Tennessee. **Calendar:** Semester, limited summer session. **Full-time faculty:** 396 total. **Part-time faculty:** 194 total. **Class size:** 54% < 20, 34% 20-39, 8% 40-49, 3% 50-99, less than 1% >100. **Special facilities:** Biological research station, aquatic wildlife area, veterinary diagnostic research center, center of excellence for reservoir research, NASA-related technology transfer station, 2 farms, archaeological research and excavation site, West Kentucky regional museum, state center of excellence for telecommunication systems management.

**Freshman class profile.** 3,108 applied, 2,636 admitted, 1,339 enrolled.

| Mid 50% test scores | | End year in good standing: | 87% |
|---|---|---|---|
| ACT composite: | 21-26 | Return as sophomores: | 75% |
| GPA 3.50 or higher: | 54% | Out-of-state: | 32% |
| GPA 3.0-3.49: | 38% | Live on campus: | 81% |
| GPA 2.0-2.99: | 8% | International: | 1% |
| Rank in top quarter: | 55% | Fraternities: | 12% |
| Rank in top tenth: | 25% | Sororities: | 10% |

**Basis for selection.** Selective admission to nursing, business and social work programs. Students must rank in the top half of graduating class or have cumulative GPA of 3.0 or above, ACT score of 18 or above and complete precollege curriculum. Interview recommended for art, music, nursing majors. Auditions recommended for music majors. Portfolio recommended for art majors. **Homeschooled:** Transcript of courses and grades required. Students may be asked to verify lab experience and provide GED if ACT score is less than average. **Learning Disabled:** Contact office for students with learning disabilities.

**High school preparation.** 22 units required. Required and recommended units include English 4, mathematics 3-4, social studies 3, science 3-4 (laboratory 1), foreign language 2 and academic electives 5. 1 art appreciation required. Social sciences must include U.S. history and world civilization. 1 arts and 1 computer science recommended. Math must include 3 algebra I and above. Sciences must include biology and chemistry or physics.

**2007-2008 Annual costs.** Tuition/fees: $5,418; $14,718 out-of-state. Room/board: $5,818. Books/supplies: $700. Personal expenses: $790.

**2007-2008 Financial aid.** Need-based: Average need met was 92%. Average scholarship/grant was $2,590; average loan $1,855. 46% of total undergraduate aid awarded as scholarships/grants, 54% as loans/jobs. **Non-need-based:** Scholarships awarded for academics, alumni affiliation, art, athletics, job skills, leadership, minority status, music/drama, ROTC, state residency. **Additional information:** Tuition discount for children and grandchildren of out-of-state alumni. Regional tuition for students from certain counties in Illinois, Tennessee, Missouri, and Indiana.

**Application procedures.** Admission: Closing date 8/1 (postmark date). $30 fee, may be waived for applicants with need. Application may be submitted online. Admission notification on a rolling basis. **Financial aid:** Priority date 4/1; no closing date. FAFSA, institutional form required. Applicants notified on a rolling basis starting 4/15.

**Academics.** Special study options: Combined bachelor's/graduate degree, cooperative education, cross-registration, distance learning, double major, dual enrollment of high school students, ESL, exchange student, external degree, honors, independent study, internships, liberal arts/career combination, semester at sea, study abroad, teacher certification program, weekend college. Cooperative center for study in Britain, Kentucky Institute for International Studies, national and international student exchange. **Credit/placement by examination:** AP, CLEP, ACT, institutional tests. 96 credit hours maximum toward bachelor's degree. **Support services:** Learning center, pre-admission summer program, reduced course load, remedial instruction, study skills assistance, tutoring, writing center.

**Honors college/program.** Based on standardized test scores, GPA, evidence of creative and leadership abilities as displayed in extracurricular interests and activities, and faculty recommendation.

**Majors.** Agriculture: General. Biology: General. Business: General, accounting, business admin, finance, international, management information systems, marketing. Communications: Advertising, journalism, organizational, public relations, radio/tv. Communications technology: Desktop publishing, printing management. Computer sciences: General, information systems. Conservation: Wildlife. Education: Art, early childhood, elementary, health, middle, music, special. Engineering: Electrical, physics. Engineering technology: Civil, drafting, electromechanical, manufacturing, occupational safety, water quality. English: English lit. Family/consumer sciences: Food/nutrition. Foreign languages: French, German, Spanish. Health: Audiology/speech pathology, nursing (RN), veterinary technology/assistant. History: General. Liberal arts: Arts/sciences. Math: General. Parks/recreation: Exercise sciences, facilities management, health/fitness. Philosophy/religion: Philosophy. Physical sciences: Chemistry, geology, physics. Protective services: Criminal justice. Psychology: General. Public administration: Social work. Social sciences: Economics, international relations, political science, sociology. Visual/performing arts: Dramatic, studio arts. Other: Music Business.

**Most popular majors.** Business/marketing 14%, communications/journalism 9%, education 17%, engineering/engineering technologies 7%, health sciences 10%, liberal arts 7%.

**Computing on campus.** 1,800 workstations in dormitories, library, computer center, student center. Dormitories wired for high-speed internet access and linked to campus network. Commuter students can connect to campus network. Online course registration, online library, helpline, repair service, student web hosting, wireless network available.

**Student life.** Freshman orientation: Available, $125 fee. Preregistration for classes offered. The $125 fee is for the entire family for the two-day orientation and a $75 fee is charged for the entire family attending the one-day orientation. **Housing:** Guaranteed on-campus for freshmen. Coed dorms, single-sex dorms, special housing for disabled, apartments, fraternity/sorority housing, substance-free housing available. $75 deposit, deadline 3/1. **Activities:** Bands, campus ministries, choral groups, dance, drama, film society, international student organizations, literary magazine, music ensembles, musical theater, opera, radio station, student government, student newspaper, symphony orchestra, TV station, Rotaract, Young Democrats, Young Republicans, black student council, Newman center, Baptist student center, Chi Alpha, Christian Fellowship, Wesley Foundation.

**Athletics.** NCAA. **Intercollegiate:** Baseball M, basketball, bowling M, cheerleading, cross-country, equestrian, football (tackle) M, golf, rifle, rodeo, rowing (crew) W, soccer W, tennis, track and field W, volleyball W.

**Intramural:** Basketball, football (non-tackle), golf, racquetball, soccer, softball, tennis, volleyball. **Team name:** Racers.

**Student services.** Adult student services, alcohol/substance abuse counseling, campus ministries, career counseling, services for economically disadvantaged, student employment services, financial aid counseling, health services, legal services, minority student services, on-campus daycare, personal counseling, placement for graduates, veterans' counselor, women's services. **Physically disabled:** Services for visually, hearing impaired. **Learning disabled:** Comprehensive services available.

**Contact.** E-mail: admissions@murraystate.edu
Phone: (270) 809-3741 Toll-free number: (800) 272-4678
Fax: (270) 809-3780
Mary Smith, Director of Admission Services, Murray State University, 113 Sparks Hall, Murray, KY 42071

## Northern Kentucky University
### Highland Heights, Kentucky
www.nku.edu

CB member
CB code: 1574

- Public 4-year university
- Commuter campus in large city
- 12,058 degree-seeking undergraduates: 23% part-time, 58% women, 5% African American, 1% Asian American, 1% Hispanic American, 1% international
- 1,893 degree-seeking graduate students
- 78% of applicants admitted
- SAT or ACT (ACT writing optional) required
- 40% graduate within 6 years

**General.** Founded in 1968. Regionally accredited. **Degrees:** 1,624 bachelor's, 258 associate awarded; master's, first professional offered. **ROTC:** Army, Air Force. **Location:** 7 miles from Cincinnati. **Calendar:** Semester, extensive summer session. **Full-time faculty:** 601 total; 12% minority, 51% women. **Part-time faculty:** 633 total; 10% minority, 55% women. **Class size:** 38% < 20, 52% 20-39, 7% 40-49, 2% 50-99, less than 1% >100. **Special facilities:** Anthropology museum, biology museum, geology exhibit, wildlife exhibit, cadaver lab.

**Freshman class profile.** 4,752 applied, 3,707 admitted, 2,004 enrolled.

| Mid 50% test scores | | | |
|---|---|---|---|
| SAT critical reading: | 440-550 | Return as sophomores: | 68% |
| SAT math: | 450-550 | Out-of-state: | 31% |
| ACT composite: | 19-23 | Live on campus: | 10% |
| GPA 3.50 or higher: | 29% | International: | 1% |
| GPA 3.0-3.49: | 29% | Fraternities: | 4% |
| GPA 2.0-2.99: | 38% | Sororities: | 5% |

**Basis for selection.** Requirements vary by program. General college preparatory programs required for placement, recommended for admission. SAT/ACT scores required for admission to selective programs. **Home-schooled:** Transcript of courses and grades required.

**High school preparation.** 22 units required. Required units include English 4, mathematics 3, social studies 3, history 1, science 3 (laboratory 1), foreign language 2, computer science 1, visual/performing arts 1 and academic electives 5. Chemistry and biology required for nursing program. Computer science recommended for all. 1 history and appreciation of visual, performing arts required.

**2007-2008 Annual costs.** Tuition/fees: $5,952; $10,776 out-of-state. Room/board: $6,000. Books/supplies: $800. Personal expenses: $2,749.

**Financial aid. Non-need-based:** Scholarships awarded for academics, alumni affiliation, art, athletics, job skills, leadership, minority status, music/drama, state residency.

**Application procedures. Admission:** Priority date 5/1; deadline 8/1 (postmark date). $40 fee, may be waived for applicants with need. Application may be submitted online. Admission notification on a rolling basis beginning on or about 10/1. **Financial aid:** Priority date 3/1; no closing date. FAFSA required. Applicants notified on a rolling basis starting 4/1; must reply within 3 week(s) of notification.

**Academics. Special study options:** Accelerated study, cooperative education, cross-registration, distance learning, double major, dual enrollment of high school students, exchange student, honors, independent study, internships, liberal arts/career combination, study abroad, teacher certification program, weekend college. Introductory-level courses and some graduate-level courses and business seminars available at University College Campus in Covington; Summer NKU Academy gives remediation for denied students.

**Credit/placement by examination:** AP, CLEP, SAT, ACT, institutional tests. 16 credit hours maximum toward associate degree, 32 toward bachelor's. Credit may be awarded for military, vocational, and National Occupational Competency Testing Institute exams. **Support services:** Learning center, pre-admission summer program, reduced course load, remedial instruction, tutoring, writing center.

**Majors. Biology:** General. **Business:** General, accounting, business admin, entrepreneurial studies, finance, labor relations, management information systems, managerial economics, marketing, organizational behavior. **Communications:** Broadcast journalism, journalism, public relations, radio/tv. **Computer sciences:** General, information systems, information technology. **Conservation:** Environmental science. **Education:** Business, elementary, kindergarten/preschool, middle, physical. **Engineering technology:** Architectural, computer, electrical, industrial. **English:** English lit, speech/rhetoric. **Foreign languages:** French, German, Spanish. **Health:** Athletic training, health services, mental health services, nursing (RN). **History:** General. **Liberal arts:** Arts/sciences. **Math:** General. **Parks/recreation:** Sports admin. **Philosophy/religion:** Philosophy. **Physical sciences:** Chemistry, geology, physics. **Protective services:** Criminal justice. **Psychology:** General. **Public administration:** Social work. **Social sciences:** General, anthropology, geography, international relations, political science, sociology. **Visual/performing arts:** Commercial/advertising art, dramatic, studio arts.

**Most popular majors.** Business/marketing 24%, communications/journalism 6%, education 11%, English 6%, health sciences 10%, social sciences 6%.

**Computing on campus.** 1,500 workstations in dormitories, library, computer center, student center. Dormitories wired for high-speed internet access and linked to campus network. Commuter students can connect to campus network. Online course registration, online library, helpline, repair service, student web hosting, wireless network available.

**Student life. Freshman orientation:** Mandatory, $75 fee. Preregistration for classes offered. All-day program held 12 times a year. **Policies:** Student organizations required to register annually and attend student organization orientation session annually. **Housing:** Coed dorms, single-sex dorms, special housing for disabled, apartments, cooperative housing, substance-free housing available. $200 nonrefundable deposit, deadline 5/1. One-third of all college housing accessible to handicapped. **Activities:** Bands, campus ministries, choral groups, dance, drama, international student organizations, literary magazine, music ensembles, Model UN, musical theater, opera, radio station, student government, student newspaper, symphony orchestra, TV station, College Democrats, College Republicans, Black United Students, Christian student fellowship, Circle K, freshman service leadership committee, Latino student union, NAACP.

**Athletics.** NCAA. **Intercollegiate:** Baseball M, basketball, cross-country, golf, soccer, softball W, tennis, volleyball W. **Intramural:** Badminton, basketball, bowling, football (non-tackle), racquetball, soccer, softball, table tennis, tennis, volleyball. **Team name:** Norse.

**Student services.** Adult student services, alcohol/substance abuse counseling, campus ministries, career counseling, services for economically disadvantaged, student employment services, financial aid counseling, health services, legal services, minority student services, on-campus daycare, personal counseling, placement for graduates, women's services. **Physically disabled:** Services for visually, speech, hearing impaired.

**Contact.** E-mail: admitnku@nku.edu
Phone: (859) 572-5220 Toll-free number: (800) 637-9948
Fax: (859) 572-6665
Melissa Gorbandt, Director of Admissions - Outreach, Northern Kentucky University, Administrative Center 401, Northern Kentucky University, Highland Heights, KY 41099

## Pikeville College
### Pikeville, Kentucky
www.pc.edu

CB member
CB code: 1625

- Private 4-year liberal arts college affiliated with Presbyterian Church (USA)
- Residential campus in small town
- 791 degree-seeking undergraduates: 9% part-time; 52% women, 9% African American, 1% Asian American, 1% Hispanic American, 1% international
- 306 graduate students

**General.** Founded in 1889. Regionally accredited. **Degrees:** 125 bachelor's, 26 associate awarded; first professional offered. **Location:** 150 miles from Lexington, 140 miles from Charleston, West Virginia. **Calendar:** Semester, limited summer session. **Full-time faculty:** 61 total; 51% have terminal degrees, 52% women. **Part-time faculty:** 13 total; 15% have terminal degrees, 69% women. **Class size:** 60% < 20, 39% 20-39, less than 1% 40-49.

**Freshman class profile.** 1,042 applied, 1,042 admitted, 234 enrolled.

| Mid 50% test scores | | End year in good standing: | 55% |
|---|---|---|---|
| ACT composite: | 17-23 | Return as sophomores: | 49% |
| GPA 3.50 or higher: | 41% | Out-of-state: | 26% |
| GPA 3.0-3.49: | 22% | Live on campus: | 66% |
| GPA 2.0-2.99: | 35% | | |

**Basis for selection.** Open admission, but selective for some programs. 19 ACT required for nursing, 21 ACT required for education majors.

**High school preparation.** 13 units recommended. Recommended units include English 4, mathematics 3, social studies 2, history 1 and science 3.

**2007-2008 Annual costs.** Tuition/fees: $13,750. Room/board: $5,250. Books/supplies: $2,000. Personal expenses: $2,000.

**2007-2008 Financial aid.** All financial aid based on need. 230 full-time freshmen applied for aid; 228 were judged to have need; 228 of these received aid. Average need met was 84%. Average scholarship/grant was $12,036; average loan $2,482. 68% of total undergraduate aid awarded as scholarships/grants, 32% as loans/jobs.

**Application procedures.** Admission: Priority date 3/15; deadline 8/15 (receipt date). No application fee. Admission notification on a rolling basis beginning on or about 9/15. Financial aid: Priority date 3/15; no closing date. FAFSA, institutional form required. Applicants notified on a rolling basis starting 1/15; must reply by 5/1 or within 2 week(s) of notification.

**Academics.** Special study options: Double major, independent study, internships, liberal arts/career combination, student-designed major, study abroad, teacher certification program, Washington semester. **Credit/placement by examination:** AP, CLEP. 15 credit hours maximum toward associate degree, 15 toward bachelor's. **Support services:** Learning center, reduced course load, remedial instruction, study skills assistance, tutoring, writing center.

**Majors.** Biology: General. Business: Business admin. **Communications:** General. **Computer sciences:** General. **Education:** Elementary, middle. **English:** English lit. **History:** General. **Math:** General. **Philosophy/religion:** Religion. **Physical sciences:** Chemistry. **Protective services:** Criminal justice. **Psychology:** General. **Public administration:** Social work. **Social sciences:** General, sociology. **Visual/performing arts:** Art.

**Most popular majors.** Biology 10%, business/marketing 23%, communications/journalism 9%, education 14%, history 8%, psychology 14%, security/protective services 7%.

**Computing on campus.** 162 workstations in library, computer center. Dormitories wired for high-speed internet access and linked to campus network. Commuter students can connect to campus network. Online library, student web hosting, wireless network available.

**Student life.** Freshman orientation: Mandatory. Preregistration for classes offered. Held first 3 days before start of classes. **Policies:** No alcohol allowed on campus. **Housing:** Guaranteed on-campus for freshmen. Coed dorms, single-sex dorms, apartments available. $50 nonrefundable deposit, deadline 5/30. **Activities:** Bands, choral groups, dance, drama, student government, student newspaper, academic team, Appalachian Association for Justice, Baptist student union, Blessed Unity of God, Fellowship of Christian Athletes, Lambda Sigma society, Phi Beta Lambda, Psi Chi, Sigma Tau Delta, Young Republicans club.

**Athletics.** NAIA. Intercollegiate: Baseball M, basketball, bowling, cheerleading, cross-country, football (tackle) M, golf, soccer, softball W, tennis, track and field, volleyball W. **Intramural:** Basketball, bowling, football (non-tackle), softball, tennis, volleyball. **Team name:** Bears.

**Student services.** Campus ministries, career counseling, student employment services, financial aid counseling, health services, personal counseling, veterans' counselor.

**Contact.** E-mail: wewantyou@pc.edu
Phone: (606) 218-5251 Toll-free number: (866) 232-7700
Fax: (606) 218-5255
Melinda Lynch, Dean, Enrollment Management, Pikeville College, 147 Sycamore Street, Pikeville, KY 41501-1194

## St. Catharine College
### St. Catharine, Kentucky
**www.sccky.edu**     **CB code: 1690**

- Private 4-year health science and liberal arts college affiliated with Roman Catholic Church
- Commuter campus in large town
- 548 degree-seeking undergraduates

**General.** Founded in 1931. Regionally accredited. **Degrees:** 11 bachelor's, 102 associate awarded. **Location:** 60 miles from Louisville and Lexington. **Calendar:** Semester, limited summer session. **Full-time faculty:** 42 total. **Part-time faculty:** 18 total.

**Freshman class profile.** 488 applied, 433 admitted, 169 enrolled.

**Basis for selection.** Open admission. Assessment tests in mathematics, English and reading administered upon admission for course placement or remediation.

**2007-2008 Annual costs.** Tuition/fees: $12,008. Higher tuition applies for health science program. Room/board: $6,300. Books/supplies: $700. Personal expenses: $1,080.

**Financial aid.** All financial aid based on need.

**Application procedures.** Admission: No deadline. $15 fee, may be waived for applicants with need. Application must be submitted on paper. Admission notification on a rolling basis. **Financial aid:** Priority date 3/15; no closing date. FAFSA, institutional form required. Applicants notified on a rolling basis; must reply by 8/15.

**Academics.** Special study options: Dual enrollment of high school students, independent study, internships, weekend college. **Credit/placement by examination:** AP, CLEP, institutional tests. 35 credit hours maximum toward associate degree. **Support services:** Learning center, reduced course load, remedial instruction, tutoring.

**Majors.** Business: Business admin. **Health:** Health services, sonography.

**Computing on campus.** 33 workstations in library, computer center. Dormitories wired for high-speed internet access. Online library available.

**Student life.** Freshman orientation: Mandatory, $15 fee. Preregistration for classes offered. 1-day program before start of classes. Semester-long orientation course. **Housing:** Single-sex dorms available. $25 deposit, deadline 8/15. **Activities:** Pep band, campus ministries, choral groups, literary magazine, student government, Phi Theta Kappa, Christian athletics club, African American club, art club, Students Above Traditional Age, student ambassadors, Students in Free Enterprise.

**Athletics.** NJCAA. Intercollegiate: Baseball M, basketball, golf, soccer, softball W. **Team name:** Patriots.

**Student services.** Campus ministries, career counseling, financial aid counseling, on-campus daycare, personal counseling, veterans' counselor.

**Contact.** E-mail: twiley@sccky.edu
Phone: (859) 336-5082 ext. 1259 Toll-free number: (800) 599-2000 ext. 1259 Fax: (859) 336-5031
Toni Wiley, Director of Admissions, St. Catharine College, 2735 Bardstown Road, St. Catharine, KY 40061

## Spalding University
### Louisville, Kentucky
**www.spalding.edu**     **CB member**   **CB code: 1552**

- Private 4-year university affiliated with Roman Catholic Church
- Commuter campus in large city

**General.** Founded in 1814. Regionally accredited. **Location:** One mile from downtown. **Calendar:** Continuous.

**Annual costs/financial aid.** Tuition/fees (2007-2008): $17,100. Room/board: $4,560. Books/supplies: $700. Need-based financial aid available to full-time and part-time students.

**Contact.** Phone: (502) 585-7111
Director of Admissions, 851 South Fourth Street, Louisville, KY 40203

## Sullivan University
**Louisville, Kentucky**
www.sullivan.edu

CB code: 0811

- For-profit 4-year university
- Commuter campus in large city
- 4,201 undergraduates
- 337 graduate students
- Interview required

**General.** Founded in 1962. Regionally accredited. **Degrees:** 360 bachelor's, 395 associate awarded; master's offered. **Location:** 110 miles from Indianapolis, 110 miles from Cincinnati. **Calendar:** Quarter, extensive summer session. **Full-time faculty:** 109 total; 32% have terminal degrees. **Part-time faculty:** 122 total; 34% have terminal degrees. **Special facilities:** University-operated fine dining restaurant.

**Freshman class profile.**

Out-of-state: 17%     **Live on campus:** 19%

**Basis for selection.** Test scores, interview, high school record important. CPAT required for placement if no ACT or SAT scores are available.

**2007-2008 Annual costs.** Tuition, fees and per-credit-hour charges vary by program. Tuition costs range from $14,400 to $15,570 per academic year. Room only: $4,320. Books/supplies: $1,200. Personal expenses: $1,305.

**Financial aid.** All financial aid based on need.

**Application procedures. Admission:** No deadline. $100 fee. Application may be submitted online. Admission notification on a rolling basis. **Financial aid:** No deadline. FAFSA required. Applicants notified on a rolling basis starting 1/2.

**Academics.** Day classes meet Monday to Thursday; special program on Friday for additional help. Night/Weekend classes meet Monday through Sunday; many graduate and undergraduate classes are offered online. **Special study options:** Accelerated study, distance learning, double major, independent study, internships, weekend college. **Credit/placement by examination:** CLEP, IB, SAT, ACT, institutional tests. **Support services:** Reduced course load, remedial instruction, study skills assistance, tutoring.

**Majors. Business:** Accounting, business admin, tourism promotion. **Computer sciences:** General, applications programming. **Legal studies:** Paralegal. **Personal/culinary services:** Culinary arts.

**Computing on campus.** 252 workstations in library, computer center. Commuter students can connect to campus network. Online course registration, online library, helpline available.

**Student life. Freshman orientation:** Mandatory. One and two day orientations held at the beginning of each quarter. **Housing:** Apartments, substance-free housing available. $95 nonrefundable deposit, deadline 9/30. Housing for freshmen under 21 who live outside a 75-mile radius from Louisville. **Activities:** Student newspaper, student activities committee, travel club, Culinary Salon Competition Team, Student Paralegal Association, International Association of Administrative Professionals, Rotarac.

**Athletics. Intramural:** Basketball, bowling, softball, volleyball.

**Student services.** Career counseling, student employment services, financial aid counseling, personal counseling, placement for graduates, veterans' counselor.

**Contact.** E-mail: admissions@sullivan.edu
Phone: (502) 456-6505 Toll-free number: (800) 844-1354
Fax: (502) 456-0040
Terri Thomas, Director of Admissions, Sullivan University, 3101 Bardstown Road, Louisville, KY 40205

## Thomas More College
**Crestview Hills, Kentucky**
www.thomasmore.edu

CB member
CB code: 1876

- Private 4-year liberal arts college affiliated with Roman Catholic Church
- Commuter campus in small town
- 1,293 degree-seeking undergraduates: 10% part-time, 52% women, 5% African American, 1% Hispanic American, 1% Native American
- 106 degree-seeking graduate students
- 83% of applicants admitted

- SAT or ACT (ACT writing optional) required
- 43% graduate within 6 years; 80% enter graduate study

**General.** Founded in 1921. Regionally accredited. Tiered tuition guarantees 3% increase per year. **Degrees:** 243 bachelor's, 57 associate awarded; master's offered. **ROTC:** Army, Air Force. **Location:** 8 miles from Cincinnati. **Calendar:** Semester, limited summer session. **Full-time faculty:** 71 total; 69% have terminal degrees, 6% minority, 45% women. **Part-time faculty:** 64 total. **Class size:** 75% < 20, 24% 20-39, 1% 40-49. **Special facilities:** Biology field station, observatory.

**Freshman class profile.** 990 applied, 821 admitted, 278 enrolled.

| Mid 50% test scores | | | |
|---|---|---|---|
| SAT critical reading: | 440-550 | GPA 2.0-2.99: | 27% |
| SAT math: | 450-580 | Rank in top quarter: | 34% |
| ACT composite: | 18-25 | Rank in top tenth: | 13% |
| GPA 3.50 or higher: | 44% | Return as sophomores: | 74% |
| GPA 3.0-3.49: | 27% | Out-of-state: | 37% |
| | | Live on campus: | 49% |

**Basis for selection.** Rank in top half of graduating class, 2.0 GPA (college-preparatory curriculum), and 20 ACT with at least 20 English score, or 1010 SAT (exclusive of writing) with at least 530 verbal score important. Test scores required prior to registration. Interview recommended. Essay recommended for special admissions. **Learning Disabled:** Need to submit legal documentation of disabilities.

**High school preparation.** 15 units required. Required and recommended units include English 4, mathematics 3, social studies 3, science 3 (laboratory 1), foreign language 2 and academic electives 2. Art appreciation and computer literacy recommended.

**2007-2008 Annual costs.** Tuition/fees: $21,220. Tiered tuition guarantees 3% increase per year. Room/board: $6,250. Books/supplies: $1,000. Personal expenses: $2,200.

**2006-2007 Financial aid. Need-based:** 134 full-time freshmen applied for aid; 134 were judged to have need; 134 of these received aid. Average need met was 72%. Average scholarship/grant was $7,549; average loan $84. 48% of total undergraduate aid awarded as scholarships/grants, 52% as loans/jobs. **Non-need-based:** Awarded to 884 full-time undergraduates, including 143 freshmen. Scholarships awarded for academics, alumni affiliation, art, job skills, leadership, minority status, music/drama, religious affiliation, ROTC, state residency.

**Application procedures. Admission:** Priority date 3/15; deadline 8/15 (postmark date). $25 fee, may be waived for applicants with need. Application may be submitted online. Admission notification on a rolling basis. **Financial aid:** Priority date 3/15; no closing date. FAFSA, institutional form required. Applicants notified on a rolling basis; must reply by 5/1.

**Academics. Special study options:** Accelerated study, cooperative education, cross-registration, double major, dual enrollment of high school students, honors, independent study, internships, liberal arts/career combination, student-designed major, study abroad, teacher certification program, weekend college. **Credit/placement by examination:** AP, CLEP, IB, SAT, ACT, institutional tests. 30 credit hours maximum toward associate degree, 60 toward bachelor's. **Support services:** Learning center, pre-admission summer program, reduced course load, remedial instruction, study skills assistance, tutoring, writing center.

**Majors. Area/ethnic studies:** Latin American. **Biology:** General. **Business:** General, accounting. **Communications:** General. **Computer sciences:** General. **Conservation:** Environmental science. **Education:** General, art, biology, business, chemistry, computer, elementary, English, mathematics, middle, physics, science, secondary, social studies. **English:** English lit, speech/rhetoric. **Health:** Clinical lab science, nursing (RN), predental, premedicine, prepharmacy, preveterinary. **History:** General. **Liberal arts:** Arts/sciences, humanities. **Math:** General. **Parks/recreation:** Sports admin. **Philosophy/religion:** Philosophy, religion. **Physical sciences:** Chemistry, physics. **Protective services:** Forensics, law enforcement admin. **Psychology:** General. **Social sciences:** Economics, international relations, political science, sociology. **Visual/performing arts:** General, dramatic, studio arts.

**Most popular majors.** Biology 7%, business/marketing 54%, education 6%.

**Computing on campus.** 175 workstations in dormitories, library, computer center, student center. Dormitories wired for high-speed internet access and linked to campus network. Commuter students can connect to campus network. Online course registration, online library, helpline, student web hosting, wireless network available.

**Student life. Freshman orientation:** Mandatory, $125 fee. Preregistration for classes offered. Two-day program held at beginning of fall semester in August. **Housing:** Guaranteed on-campus for all undergraduates. Coed dorms, single-sex dorms available. $200 partly refundable deposit, deadline 8/15. **Activities:** Campus ministries, choral groups, drama, international student organizations, literary magazine, student government, student activities board, residence hall government association, African American Society, deans council, service learning, Habitat for Humanity, business society, social issues commune.

**Athletics.** NCAA. **Intercollegiate:** Baseball M, basketball, cross-country, football (tackle) M, golf, soccer, softball W, tennis, volleyball W. **Intramural:** Basketball, football (non-tackle), golf, racquetball, softball, volleyball. **Team name:** Saints.

**Student services.** Adult student services, alcohol/substance abuse counseling, campus ministries, career counseling, student employment services, financial aid counseling, health services, minority student services, personal counseling, placement for graduates, veterans' counselor. **Physically disabled:** Services for visually, speech, hearing impaired.

**Contact.** E-mail: admissions@thomasmore.edu
Phone: (859) 344-3332 Toll-free number: (800) 825-4557
Fax: (859) 344-3444
Director of Admissions, Thomas More College, 333 Thomas More Parkway, Crestview Hills, KY 41017-3495

---

## Transylvania University
**Lexington, Kentucky**
**www.transy.edu**
**CB member**
**CB code: 1808**

- Private 4-year liberal arts college affiliated with Christian Church (Disciples of Christ)
- Residential campus in large city
- 1,149 degree-seeking undergraduates
- 80% of applicants admitted
- SAT or ACT (ACT writing optional), application essay required
- 71% graduate within 6 years; 29% enter graduate study

**General.** Founded in 1780. Regionally accredited. **Degrees:** 230 bachelor's awarded. **ROTC:** Army, Air Force. **Location:** 80 miles from Louisville, 80 miles from Cincinnati. **Calendar:** 4-1-4. 4-4-1. Limited summer session. **Full-time faculty:** 86 total. **Part-time faculty:** 15 total. **Class size:** 62% < 20, 36% 20-39, 1% 40-49. **Special facilities:** Museum of early scientific apparatus, special library collections of early medical and scientific works and Kentucky books.

**Freshman class profile.** 1,365 applied, 1,095 admitted, 335 enrolled.

| Mid 50% test scores | | | |
|---|---|---|---|
| SAT critical reading: | 530-640 | Rank in top quarter: | 73% |
| SAT math: | 530-650 | Rank in top tenth: | 41% |
| SAT writing: | 510-640 | End year in good standing: | 81% |
| ACT composite: | 23-29 | Return as sophomores: | 78% |
| GPA 3.50 or higher: | 78% | Out-of-state: | 18% |
| GPA 3.0-3.49: | 19% | Live on campus: | 96% |
| GPA 2.0-2.99: | 3% | Fraternities: | 50% |
| | | Sororities: | 50% |

**Basis for selection.** Rigor of high school curriculum, high school grade point average, and standardized test scores are most important. Recommendations, essay, and extracurricular activities are important as are excellence of character and high personal goals. Interview recommended. Audition required for music scholarship applicants. Portfolio required for art scholarship applicants. **Learning Disabled:** Meet with coordinator of disability services.

**High school preparation.** 12 units required; 16 recommended. Required and recommended units include English 4, mathematics 3-4, social studies 2, history 1, science 3-4 (laboratory 2), foreign language 2 and academic electives 1. Broad high school curriculum important to allow full participation in required liberal arts course work. Solid background in English highly recommended.

**2008-2009 Annual costs.** Tuition/fees: $23,810. Room/board: $7,450. Books/supplies: $750. Personal expenses: $1,250.

**2007-2008 Financial aid. Need-based:** 239 full-time freshmen applied for aid; 205 were judged to have need; 204 of these received aid. Average need met was 86%. Average scholarship/grant was $14,935; average loan $3,338. **Non-need-based:** Awarded to 489 full-time undergraduates, including 111 freshmen. Scholarships awarded for academics, art, leadership, minority status, music/drama, religious affiliation, ROTC, state residency. **Additional information:** Auditions and portfolios required for music and art scholarships respectively. Essays required for other scholarship programs. Applications for William T. Young scholarships must be received by December 1.

**Application procedures. Admission:** Priority date 12/1; deadline 2/1 (postmark date). $30 fee, may be waived for applicants with need. Application may be submitted online. Admission notification 3/1. Must reply by May 1 or within 4 week(s) if notified thereafter. **Financial aid:** Priority date 3/1; no closing date. FAFSA required. Applicants notified on a rolling basis starting 3/15; must reply by 5/1 or within 2 week(s) of notification.

**Academics. Special study options:** Combined bachelor's/graduate degree, double major, independent study, internships, liberal arts/career combination, student-designed major, study abroad, teacher certification program, Washington semester. **Credit/placement by examination:** AP, CLEP, IB, institutional tests. No limit to AP credit. **Support services:** Learning center, study skills assistance, tutoring, writing center.

**Majors. Biology:** General. **Business:** General, accounting. **Computer sciences:** General. **Education:** Elementary, middle, music, physical. **English:** English lit. **Foreign languages:** Classics, French, Spanish. **History:** General. **Liberal arts:** Arts/sciences. **Math:** General. **Parks/recreation:** Exercise sciences. **Philosophy/religion:** Philosophy, religion. **Physical sciences:** Chemistry, physics. **Psychology:** General. **Social sciences:** Anthropology, economics, political science, sociology. **Visual/performing arts:** Dramatic, music performance, studio arts.

**Most popular majors.** Biology 11%, business/marketing 20%, history 7%, parks/recreation 9%, psychology 11%, social sciences 14%, visual/performing arts 6%.

**Computing on campus.** 250 workstations in dormitories, library, computer center, student center. Dormitories wired for high-speed internet access and linked to campus network. Commuter students can connect to campus network. Online library, helpline, student web hosting, wireless network available.

**Student life. Freshman orientation:** Mandatory. Preregistration for classes offered. One-day summer event; 4-day program before classes begin. **Housing:** Guaranteed on-campus for freshmen. Coed dorms, single-sex dorms, special housing for disabled, apartments, substance-free housing available. $125 nonrefundable deposit, deadline 5/1. Efficiency apartment option for upperclassmen; two units with facilities for disabled students available. **Activities:** Bands, choral groups, dance, drama, literary magazine, music ensembles, musical theater, opera, radio station, student government, student newspaper, diversity action council, College Democrats, College Republicans, Alternative Spring Break, Campus Crusade, student activities board, student alumni association, Disciples on Campus.

**Athletics.** NCAA. **Intercollegiate:** Baseball M, basketball, cross-country, diving, field hockey W, golf, soccer, softball W, swimming, tennis, volleyball W. **Intramural:** Badminton, basketball, bowling, cross-country, football (non-tackle), football (tackle), golf, handball, racquetball, soccer, softball, swimming, table tennis, tennis, volleyball. **Team name:** Pioneers.

**Student services.** Alcohol/substance abuse counseling, campus ministries, career counseling, student employment services, financial aid counseling, health services, minority student services, personal counseling, veterans' counselor. **Physically disabled:** Services for visually, hearing impaired.

**Contact.** E-mail: admissions@transy.edu
Phone: (859) 233-8242 Toll-free number: (800) 872-6798
Fax: (859) 281-3649
Brad Goan, Director of Admissions, Transylvania University, 300 North Broadway, Lexington, KY 40508-1797

---

## Union College
**Barbourville, Kentucky**
**www.unionky.edu**
**CB code: 1825**

- Private 4-year liberal arts and teachers college affiliated with United Methodist Church
- Residential campus in small town
- 694 degree-seeking undergraduates: 7% part-time, 47% women, 9% African American, 2% Hispanic American, 1% Native American, 5% international
- 663 degree-seeking graduate students
- 70% of applicants admitted
- SAT or ACT (ACT writing recommended) required

**General.** Founded in 1879. Regionally accredited. **Degrees:** 98 bachelor's awarded; master's offered. **ROTC:** Army. **Location:** 107 miles from Lexington, 107 miles from Knoxville, Tennessee. **Calendar:** Semester, extensive summer session. **Full-time faculty:** 55 total; 69% have terminal degrees, 13% minority, 46% women. **Part-time faculty:** 41 total; 37% have terminal degrees, 7% minority, 46% women. **Class size:** 79% < 20, 18% 20-39, 1% 40-49, less than 1% 50-99.

**Freshman class profile.** 701 applied, 493 admitted, 160 enrolled.

| Mid 50% test scores | | | |
|---|---|---|---|
| SAT critical reading: | 360-460 | GPA 2.0-2.99: | 43% |
| SAT math: | 360-500 | Return as sophomores: | 50% |
| ACT composite: | 17-21 | Out-of-state: | 21% |
| GPA 3.50 or higher: | 23% | Live on campus: | 73% |
| GPA 3.0-3.49: | 30% | International: | 8% |

**Basis for selection.** School achievement record, course work, class rank, SAT or ACT scores important. ACT preferred for all, required for teacher education program. Interview recommended. **Homeschooled:** Statement describing homeschool structure and mission, transcript of courses and grades, letter of recommendation (nonparent) required. **Learning Disabled:** Students must provide documentation to coordinator of special program to receive necessary accommodations.

**High school preparation.** Recommended units include English 4, mathematics 3, social studies 2, science 2 (laboratory 2) and foreign language 2.

**2008-2009 Annual costs.** Tuition/fees: $16,820. Room/board: $5,250.

**2007-2008 Financial aid. Need-based:** 141 full-time freshmen applied for aid; 134 were judged to have need; 134 of these received aid. Average need met was 82%. Average scholarship/grant was $12,165; average loan $5,050. 60% of total undergraduate aid awarded as scholarships/grants, 40% as loans/jobs. **Non-need-based:** Awarded to 112 full-time undergraduates, including 32 freshmen. Scholarships awarded for academics, athletics, leadership, minority status, music/drama, religious affiliation, state residency.

**Application procedures. Admission:** No deadline. $10 fee, may be waived for applicants with need. Application may be submitted online. Admission notification on a rolling basis. **Financial aid:** Priority date 3/15; no closing date. FAFSA required. Applicants notified on a rolling basis starting 3/1; must reply within 2 week(s) of notification.

**Academics. Special study options:** Combined bachelor's/graduate degree, cooperative education, double major, dual enrollment of high school students, exchange student, honors, independent study, internships, student-designed major, study abroad, teacher certification program. **Credit/placement by examination:** AP, CLEP, ACT, institutional tests. 30 credit hours maximum toward bachelor's degree. **Support services:** Learning center, remedial instruction, study skills assistance, tutoring, writing center.

**Majors. Biology:** General. **Business:** Accounting, business admin. **Communications:** General. **Education:** Elementary, health, middle, physical, science, social studies, special. **English:** English lit. **History:** General. **Math:** General. **Parks/recreation:** Facilities management, sports admin. **Philosophy/religion:** Religion. **Physical sciences:** Chemistry. **Protective services:** Law enforcement admin. **Psychology:** General. **Social sciences:** Sociology. **Theology:** Religious ed.

**Most popular majors.** Business/marketing 29%, education 21%, parks/recreation 6%, psychology 9%, security/protective services 10%, social sciences 8%.

**Computing on campus.** 117 workstations in dormitories, library, computer center, student center. Dormitories wired for high-speed internet access and linked to campus network. Commuter students can connect to campus network. Online course registration, online library, helpline, wireless network available.

**Student life. Freshman orientation:** Mandatory. Preregistration for classes offered. **Housing:** Guaranteed on-campus for freshmen. Single-sex dorms, apartments, substance-free housing available. $50 fully refundable deposit. Private rooms occasionally available to upperclassmen. **Activities:** Pep band, choral groups, drama, literary magazine, student government, student newspaper, Fellowship of Christian Athletes, Appalachian wilderness club, Baptist student union, Methodist student organizations, Newman club, student ambassadors, science society, philosophy society.

**Athletics. NAIA. Intercollegiate:** Baseball M, basketball, bowling, cross-country, football (tackle) M, golf, soccer, softball W, swimming, tennis, volleyball W. **Intramural:** Basketball, football (non-tackle), soccer, softball, table tennis, tennis, volleyball. **Team name:** Bulldogs.

**Student services.** Alcohol/substance abuse counseling, campus ministries, career counseling, services for economically disadvantaged, financial aid counseling, health services, personal counseling, placement for graduates. **Physically disabled:** Services for visually, hearing impaired.

**Contact.** E-mail: enrollme@unionky.edu
Phone: (606) 546-1229 Toll-free number: (800) 489-8646
Fax: (606) 546-1667
Jerry Jackson, Dean of Enrollment Management, Union College, 310 College Street, Box 005, Barbourville, KY 40906

---

## University of Kentucky
**Lexington, Kentucky**
www.uky.edu

CB member
CB code: 1837

- Public 4-year university
- Commuter campus in large city
- 18,424 degree-seeking undergraduates
- 77% of applicants admitted
- SAT or ACT (ACT writing optional) required

**General.** Founded in 1865. Regionally accredited. **Degrees:** 3,613 bachelor's awarded; master's, doctoral, first professional offered. **ROTC:** Army, Air Force. **Location:** 80 miles from Louisville, 90 miles from Cincinnati. **Calendar:** Semester, limited summer session. **Full-time faculty:** 1,269 total. **Part-time faculty:** 440 total. **Class size:** 23% < 20, 53% 20-39, 6% 40-49, 11% 50-99, 7% >100. **Special facilities:** Center for the arts, Van de Graaff accelerator, equine research center, center for the humanities.

**Freshman class profile.** 10,619 applied, 8,172 admitted, 3,865 enrolled.

| Mid 50% test scores | | | |
|---|---|---|---|
| SAT critical reading: | 500-620 | GPA 3.0-3.49: | 24% |
| SAT math: | 500-630 | GPA 2.0-2.99: | 14% |
| ACT composite: | 22-27 | Rank in top quarter: | 50% |
| GPA 3.50 or higher: | 62% | Rank in top tenth: | 23% |
| | | Out-of-state: | 20% |

**Basis for selection.** Test scores and GPA should indicate potential for academic success. Required course work and extracurricular activities also considered. Students out of high school 2 years or more with no college credit admitted on probationary basis. Audition required of music majors. **Homeschooled:** List of textbooks, attendance record and 2 letters of recommendation from persons outside family required.

**High school preparation.** 22 units required. Required and recommended units include English 4, mathematics 3-4, social studies 3, science 3-4, foreign language 2 and academic electives 5. 1 fine or performing arts, .5 health, .5 physical education required.

**2007-2008 Annual costs.** Tuition/fees: $7,096; $14,896 out-of-state. Tuition charges include fees. Upper division tuition $7,302, in-state; $15,094, out-of-state. Room/board: $5,809. Books/supplies: $600. Personal expenses: $1,148.

**Financial aid. Non-need-based:** Scholarships awarded for academics, alumni affiliation, art, athletics, job skills, leadership, minority status, music/drama, ROTC, state residency.

**Application procedures. Admission:** Closing date 2/15 (postmark date). $40 fee, may be waived for applicants with need. Application may be submitted online. Admission notification on a rolling basis beginning on or about 10/1. Reply by 05/01 preferred. **Financial aid:** Priority date 2/15; no closing date. FAFSA required. Applicants notified on a rolling basis starting 4/1; must reply within 3 week(s) of notification.

**Academics. Special study options:** Accelerated study, combined bachelor's/graduate degree, cooperative education, distance learning, double major, ESL, exchange student, honors, independent study, internships, study abroad, teacher certification program, weekend college. **Credit/placement by examination:** AP, CLEP, IB, SAT, ACT, institutional tests. Students who receive Advanced Placement credit for a course may apply this credit the same way credit earned by passing a course is applied. **Support services:** Learning center, reduced course load, remedial instruction, tutoring, writing center.

**Majors. Agriculture:** Agronomy, animal sciences, communications, economics, education services, food science. **Architecture:** Architecture, landscape. **Area/ethnic studies:** Latin American. **Biology:** General. **Business:** General, accounting, finance, hospitality admin, management science, managerial economics, marketing. **Communications:** General, advertising, journalism, radio/tv. **Computer sciences:** General. **Conservation:** General, forest sciences. **Education:** Art, early childhood, elementary, health, mathematics, middle, music, physical, science, special. **Engineering:** Agricultural, chemical, civil, electrical, materials, mechanical, mining. **English:** English lit. **Family/consumer sciences:** General, food/nutrition. **Foreign languages:** Classics, French, German, linguistics, Russian, Spanish. **Health:** Audiology/speech pathology, clinical lab science, health care admin. **History:** General. **Math:** General. **Philosophy/religion:** Philosophy. **Physical sciences:** Chemistry, geology, physics. **Psychology:** General. **Public administration:** Social work. **Social sciences:** General, anthropology, economics, geography, political science, sociology. **Visual/performing arts:** Art history/conservation, arts management, dramatic, interior design, music history, music performance.

**Most popular majors.** Agriculture 6%, biology 6%, business/marketing 17%, communications/journalism 11%, education 8%, engineering/engineering technologies 7%, psychology 6%, social sciences 10%.

**Computing on campus.** 810 workstations in dormitories, library, computer center, student center. Dormitories wired for high-speed internet access and linked to campus network. Commuter students can connect to campus network. Online course registration, online library, helpline, wireless network available.

**Student life. Freshman orientation:** Mandatory, $40 fee. Preregistration for classes offered. $20 additional charge per guest. **Housing:** Coed dorms, single-sex dorms, special housing for disabled, apartments, fraternity/sorority housing available. $300 deposit, deadline 6/1. **Activities:** Bands, choral groups, dance, drama, literary magazine, music ensembles, musical theater, opera, radio station, student government, student newspaper, symphony orchestra, More than 300 organizations.

**Athletics.** NCAA. **Intercollegiate:** Baseball M, basketball, cross-country, diving, football (tackle) M, golf, gymnastics W, rifle, soccer, softball W, swimming, tennis, track and field, volleyball W. **Intramural:** Archery, badminton, basketball, bowling, cross-country, fencing, field hockey W, football (non-tackle), golf, handball, ice hockey M, lacrosse, racquetball, rugby M, skiing, soccer, softball, squash, swimming, table tennis, tennis, track and field, volleyball, wrestling M. **Team name:** Wildcats.

**Student services.** Adult student services, career counseling, student employment services, health services, on-campus daycare, personal counseling, placement for graduates, veterans' counselor. **Physically disabled:** Services for visually, speech, hearing impaired.

**Contact.** E-mail: admisso@uky.edu
Phone: (859) 257-2000 Toll-free number: (800) 432-0967
Fax: (859) 257-3823
Don Witt, Director of Admissions, University of Kentucky, 100 W.D. Funkhouser Building, Lexington, KY 40506-0054

---

## University of Louisville

| Louisville, Kentucky | CB member |
|---|---|
| www.louisville.edu | CB code: 1838 |

- Public 4-year university
- Commuter campus in very large city
- 14,101 degree-seeking undergraduates: 18% part-time, 52% women, 12% African American, 3% Asian American, 2% Hispanic American, 1% international
- 5,227 degree-seeking graduate students
- 70% of applicants admitted
- SAT or ACT (ACT writing optional) required
- 43% graduate within 6 years

**General.** Founded in 1798. Regionally accredited. **Degrees:** 2,328 bachelor's, 22 associate awarded; master's, doctoral, first professional offered. **ROTC:** Army, Air Force. **Location:** 92 miles from Cincinnati, 110 miles from Indianapolis. **Calendar:** Semester, extensive summer session. **Full-time faculty:** 861 total; 88% have terminal degrees, 18% minority, 40% women. **Part-time faculty:** 506 total; 39% have terminal degrees, 12% minority, 45% women. **Class size:** 28% < 20, 53% 20-39, 8% 40-49, 8% 50-99, 4% >100. **Special facilities:** Planetarium, computer-aided engineering building with robotics laboratory, rapid prototype facility with Sinterstation 2000 system.

**Freshman class profile.** 7,280 applied, 5,109 admitted, 2,569 enrolled.

| Mid 50% test scores | | Rank in top tenth: | 24% |
|---|---|---|---|
| SAT critical reading: | 490-610 | Return as sophomores: | 78% |
| SAT math: | 500-640 | Out-of-state: | 16% |
| ACT composite: | 21-27 | Live on campus: | 66% |
| GPA 3.50 or higher: | 53% | International: | 1% |
| GPA 3.0-3.49: | 30% | Fraternities: | 8% |
| GPA 2.0-2.99: | 16% | Sororities: | 5% |
| Rank in top quarter: | 49% | | |

**Basis for selection.** High school grades, curriculum, class rank and test scores very important. Rank in top half of graduating class. Partnership with local community college for those not meeting unit admission requirements. Diagnostic testing/interview option for those failing to meet minimum. Freshmen must have completed state precollege curriculum. SAT/ACT score reports must be received by registration before the first day of class. **Homeschooled:** Transcript of courses and grades required.

**High school preparation.** Required and recommended units include English 4, mathematics 3-4, social studies 3, science 3-4 (laboratory 1), foreign language 2-3, visual/performing arts 1 and academic electives 5. History requirement included in social studies, 5 electives must be rigorous.

**2007-2008 Annual costs.** Tuition/fees: $6,940; $17,734 out-of-state. Room/board: $5,722.

**2007-2008 Financial aid. Need-based:** 1,818 full-time freshmen applied for aid; 1,469 were judged to have need; 1,462 of these received aid. Average need met was 63%. Average scholarship/grant was $7,352; average loan $3,342. 52% of total undergraduate aid awarded as scholarships/grants, 48% as loans/jobs. **Non-need-based:** Awarded to 2,488 full-time undergraduates, including 783 freshmen. Scholarships awarded for academics, art, athletics, leadership, minority status, music/drama, ROTC.

**Application procedures. Admission:** Priority date 2/15; deadline 8/25 (receipt date). $40 fee, may be waived for applicants with need. Application may be submitted online. Admission notification on a rolling basis. Must reply by 5/1. **Financial aid:** Priority date 3/15; no closing date. FAFSA required. Applicants notified on a rolling basis starting 4/1; must reply by 5/1.

**Academics. Special study options:** Accelerated study, combined bachelor's/graduate degree, cooperative education, distance learning, double major, dual enrollment of high school students, ESL, honors, independent study, internships, student-designed major, study abroad, teacher certification program. **Credit/placement by examination:** AP, CLEP, IB, SAT, ACT, institutional tests. 24 credit hours maximum toward bachelor's degree. Candidates for the nursing program may apply no more than 37 semester hours of CLEP credit toward the bachelor's degree. **Support services:** Learning center, preadmission summer program, reduced course load, remedial instruction, tutoring.

**Majors. Area/ethnic studies:** African-American, women's. **Biology:** General. **Business:** Accounting, business admin, finance, management information systems, managerial economics, marketing. **Communications:** General. **Education:** Elementary, music, trade/industrial. **Engineering:** General, biomedical, chemical, civil, computer, electrical, industrial, mechanical. **English:** English lit. **Foreign languages:** French, Spanish. **Health:** Dental hygiene, music therapy, nursing (RN). **History:** General. **Liberal arts:** Arts/sciences, humanities. **Math:** General. **Parks/recreation:** Health/fitness, sports admin. **Philosophy/religion:** Philosophy. **Physical sciences:** Chemistry, physics. **Protective services:** Law enforcement admin. **Psychology:** General. **Social sciences:** Anthropology, economics, geography, political science, sociology. **Visual/performing arts:** Art history/conservation, dramatic, studio arts. **Other:** Equine Business, Science - Medical and Dental.

**Most popular majors.** Business/marketing 19%, communications/journalism 7%, engineering/engineering technologies 8%, health sciences 8%, parks/recreation 6%, psychology 8%, security/protective services 6%, social sciences 9%.

**Computing on campus.** 327 workstations in dormitories, library, computer center, student center. Dormitories wired for high-speed internet access and linked to campus network. Commuter students can connect to campus network. Online course registration, online library, helpline, repair service, student web hosting, wireless network available.

**Student life. Freshman orientation:** Mandatory, $125 fee. Preregistration for classes offered. **Housing:** Coed dorms, special housing for disabled, apartments, fraternity/sorority housing, substance-free housing available. $200 fully refundable deposit. Special residence hall floors with in-house computer facilities for honors students, coed suites available. **Activities:** Bands, choral groups, drama, film society, literary magazine, music ensembles, musical theater, opera, radio station, student government, student newspaper, symphony orchestra, Alpha Phi Omega, College Democrats, College Republicans, UNICEF, Common Ground, L-Raisers, Baptist Student Union, Debate Society, Rho Lambda Honor Society, The Redshirt Company.

**Athletics.** NCAA. **Intercollegiate:** Baseball M, basketball, cross-country, diving, field hockey W, football (tackle) M, golf, soccer, softball W, swimming, tennis, track and field, volleyball W. **Intramural:** Badminton, basketball, bowling, cheerleading, football (non-tackle) M, golf, racquetball, soccer, swimming, table tennis, tennis, track and field, volleyball. **Team name:** Cardinals.

**Student services.** Alcohol/substance abuse counseling, campus ministries, career counseling, student employment services, financial aid counseling, health services, legal services, minority student services, personal counseling, placement for graduates, women's services. **Physically disabled:** Services for visually, speech, hearing impaired.

**Contact.** E-mail: admitme@gwise.louisville.edu
Phone: (502) 852-6531 Toll-free number: (800) 334-8635 ext. 6531
Fax: (502) 852-4776
Jenny Sawyer, Director of Admissions, University of Louisville, 2211 South Brook Street, Louisville, KY 40292

## University of the Cumberlands
**Williamsburg, Kentucky**     **CB member**
www.ucumberlands.edu     **CB code: 1145**

- Private 4-year liberal arts college affiliated with Baptist faith
- Residential campus in small town
- 1,463 degree-seeking undergraduates: 3% part-time, 50% women, 8% African American, 1% Asian American, 3% Hispanic American, 1% Native American, 4% international
- 334 degree-seeking graduate students
- 45% of applicants admitted
- SAT or ACT (ACT writing optional) required
- 41% graduate within 6 years

**General.** Founded in 1889. Regionally accredited. **Degrees:** 240 bachelor's awarded; master's offered. **ROTC:** Army. **Location:** 100 miles from Lexington, 65 miles from Knoxville, Tennessee. **Calendar:** Semester, limited summer session. **Full-time faculty:** 85 total; 67% have terminal degrees, 5% minority, 32% women. **Part-time faculty:** 44 total; 43% have terminal degrees, 57% women. **Class size:** 52% < 20, 41% 20-39, 6% 40-49, 1% 50-99, less than 1% >100. **Special facilities:** Life science museum, greenhouse, conference center and inn.

**Freshman class profile.** 1,192 applied, 532 admitted, 483 enrolled.

| Mid 50% test scores | | | |
|---|---|---|---|
| SAT critical reading: | 410-570 | Rank in top quarter: | 38% |
| SAT math: | 410-560 | Rank in top tenth: | 17% |
| ACT composite: | 19-24 | End year in good standing: | 83% |
| GPA 3.50 or higher: | 45% | Return as sophomores: | 61% |
| GPA 3.0-3.49: | 29% | Out-of-state: | 35% |
| GPA 2.0-2.99: | 26% | Live on campus: | 83% |
| | | International: | 5% |

**Basis for selection.** School achievement and activities, test scores important. **Homeschooled:** Must have GED or high school transcript.

**High school preparation.** Required and recommended units include English 4, mathematics 3, social studies 1-2 and science 2-3.

**2008-2009 Annual costs.** Tuition/fees: $14,658. Room/board: $6,626. Books/supplies: $1,000. Personal expenses: $1,800.

**2007-2008 Financial aid. Need-based:** 442 full-time freshmen applied for aid; 405 were judged to have need; 405 of these received aid. Average need met was 94%. Average scholarship/grant was $8,958; average loan $3,116. 69% of total undergraduate aid awarded as scholarships/grants, 31% as loans/jobs. **Non-need-based:** Awarded to 1,821 full-time undergraduates, including 651 freshmen. Scholarships awarded for academics, alumni affiliation, art, athletics, leadership, music/drama, religious affiliation, ROTC, state residency.

**Application procedures. Admission:** Priority date 3/1; deadline 8/15 (receipt date). $30 fee, may be waived for applicants with need. Application may be submitted online. Admission notification 8/15. Admission notification on a rolling basis. Must reply by May 1 or within 2 week(s) if notified thereafter. **Financial aid:** Priority date 3/1; no closing date. FAFSA required. Applicants notified on a rolling basis starting 4/1; must reply within 2 week(s) of notification.

**Academics.** All students encouraged to take advantage of individualized or computerized tutoring assistance. **Special study options:** Accelerated study, cooperative education, distance learning, double major, ESL, honors, independent study, internships, liberal arts/career combination, student-designed major, study abroad, teacher certification program. **Credit/placement by examination:** AP, CLEP, IB, SAT, ACT, institutional tests. 30 credit hours maximum toward bachelor's degree. **Support services:** Learning center, reduced course load, remedial instruction, study skills assistance, tutoring, writing center.

**Majors. Biology:** General. **Business:** General, accounting, management information systems, organizational behavior. **Communications:** General. **Education:** Art, computer, elementary, health, middle, music, physical, social studies, special. **English:** English lit, speech/rhetoric. **Health:** Community health services. **History:** General. **Math:** General. **Parks/recreation:** Health/fitness, sports admin. **Philosophy/religion:** Philosophy, religion. **Physical sciences:** Chemistry, physics. **Psychology:** General. **Public administration:** Social work. **Social sciences:** Political science. **Theology:** Religious ed. **Visual/performing arts:** Dramatic, studio arts. **Other:** Communication Teacher Education, History & Government.

**Most popular majors.** Biology 10%, business/marketing 18%, communications/journalism 6%, education 13%, health sciences 8%, parks/recreation 7%, psychology 6%.

**Computing on campus.** 300 workstations in dormitories, library, computer center, student center. Dormitories wired for high-speed internet access and linked to campus network. Commuter students can connect to campus network. Online library, helpline, wireless network available.

**Student life. Freshman orientation:** Mandatory. Preregistration for classes offered. One-day session in summer. **Policies:** All students required to complete 40-hour community service project. Religious observance required. **Housing:** Guaranteed on-campus for all undergraduates. Single-sex dorms, substance-free housing available. $125 partly refundable deposit, deadline 8/15. **Activities:** Bands, campus ministries, choral groups, dance, drama, music ensembles, musical theater, radio station, student government, student newspaper, TV station, Baptist Student Union, Fellowship of Christian Athletes, Appalachian Ministries, Mountain Outreach.

**Athletics.** NAIA. **Intercollegiate:** Baseball M, basketball, cheerleading, cross-country, football (non-tackle) M, football (tackle) M, golf, judo, soccer, softball W, swimming, tennis, track and field, volleyball W, wrestling. **Intramural:** Basketball, football (non-tackle), golf, soccer, softball, table tennis, volleyball, water polo. **Team name:** Patriots.

**Student services.** Alcohol/substance abuse counseling, campus ministries, career counseling, student employment services, financial aid counseling, health services, personal counseling, placement for graduates, veterans' counselor, women's services.

**Contact.** E-mail: admiss@ucumberlands.edu
Phone: (606) 539-4241 Toll-free number: (800) 343-1609
Fax: (606) 539-4303
Erica Harris, Director of Admissions, University of the Cumberlands, 6178 College Station Drive, Williamsburg, KY 40769

## Western Kentucky University
**Bowling Green, Kentucky**
www.wku.edu     **CB code: 1901**

- Public 4-year university
- Commuter campus in small city
- 15,502 degree-seeking undergraduates: 15% part-time, 58% women, 10% African American, 1% Asian American, 1% Hispanic American, 1% international
- 2,098 degree-seeking graduate students
- SAT or ACT (ACT writing optional) required
- 49% graduate within 6 years

**General.** Founded in 1906. Regionally accredited. Branch campus located in Glasgow offering general education, nursing, and elementary education programs. Upper division and graduate courses also offered at branch campuses in Owensboro and Fort Knox/Elizabethtown area. **Degrees:** 2,336 bachelor's, 255 associate awarded; master's, doctoral offered. **ROTC:** Army, Air Force. **Location:** 110 miles from Louisville; 65 miles from Nashville, Tennessee. **Calendar:** Semester, limited summer session. **Full-time faculty:** 723 total; 71% have terminal degrees, 12% minority, 46% women. **Part-time faculty:** 423 total; 16% have terminal degrees, 4% minority, 52% women. **Class size:** 43% < 20, 44% 20-39, 9% 40-49, 5% 50-99, less than 1% >100. **Special facilities:** University farm, planetarium.

**Freshman class profile.** 6,846 applied, 6,515 admitted, 3,115 enrolled.

| Mid 50% test scores | | | |
|---|---|---|---|
| SAT critical reading: | 430-530 | Rank in top tenth: | 17% |
| SAT math: | 410-520 | End year in good standing: | 75% |
| ACT composite: | 18-24 | Return as sophomores: | 73% |
| GPA 3.50 or higher: | 35% | Out-of-state: | 16% |
| GPA 3.0-3.49: | 29% | Live on campus: | 73% |
| GPA 2.0-2.99: | 32% | International: | 1% |
| Rank in top quarter: | 40% | Fraternities: | 10% |
| | | Sororities: | 8% |

**Basis for selection.** Open admission, but selective for some programs.

**High school preparation.** 22 units required. Required units include English 4, mathematics 3, social studies 3, science 3 (laboratory 1) and foreign language 2. 0.5 credits required in health, physical education, history, performing arts.

**2007-2008 Annual costs.** Tuition/fees: $6,416; $15,470 out-of-state. Room/board: $5,964. Books/supplies: $800. Personal expenses: $1,600.

**2006-2007 Financial aid. Need-based:** 2,491 full-time freshmen applied for aid; 1,827 were judged to have need; 1,799 of these received aid. Average need met was 30%. Average scholarship/grant was $4,321; average loan $2,322. 49% of total undergraduate aid awarded as scholarships/grants, 51% as loans/jobs. **Non-need-based:** Awarded to 5,736 full-time undergraduates, including 1,917 freshmen. Scholarships awarded for academics, alumni affiliation, art, athletics, job skills, leadership, minority status, music/drama, religious affiliation, ROTC, state residency.

**Application procedures. Admission:** Closing date 8/1 (postmark date). $35 fee, may be waived for applicants with need. Application may be submitted online. Admission notification on a rolling basis. **Financial aid:** Priority date 4/1; no closing date. FAFSA required. Applicants notified on a rolling basis starting 3/1.

**Academics. Special study options:** Cooperative education, distance learning, double major, dual enrollment of high school students, ESL, exchange student, external degree, honors, independent study, internships, New York semester, student-designed major, study abroad, teacher certification program, Washington semester. **Credit/placement by examination:** AP, CLEP, IB, institutional tests. Unlimited number of hours of credit by examination may be counted toward degree. **Support services:** Learning center, pre-admission summer program, reduced course load, remedial instruction, study skills assistance, tutoring, writing center.

**Majors. Agriculture:** General. **Biology:** General, biochemistry, molecular genetics. **Business:** Accounting, business admin, finance, hospitality admin, management information systems, managerial economics, marketing. **Communications:** General, advertising, journalism, organizational, political, public relations, radio/tv. **Computer sciences:** General, information technology. **Education:** Art, business, elementary, family/consumer sciences, middle, physical, special, speech impaired, trade/industrial. **Engineering:** Civil, electrical, mechanical. **Engineering technology:** Civil, environmental, industrial. **English:** English lit. **Family/consumer sciences:** Clothing/textiles, food/nutrition, housing. **Foreign languages:** French, German, Spanish. **Health:** Clinical lab science, community health services, dental hygiene, health care admin, health services, nursing (RN). **History:** General. **Math:** General. **Parks/recreation:** Facilities management. **Philosophy/religion:** Philosophy, religion. **Physical sciences:** Chemistry, geology, physics. **Psychology:** General. **Public administration:** Social work. **Social sciences:** General, anthropology, cartography, economics, geography, political science, sociology. **Visual/performing arts:** General, commercial/advertising art, dance, dramatic, studio arts.

**Most popular majors.** Business/marketing 16%, communications/journalism 12%, education 18%, liberal arts 7%, social sciences 9%.

**Computing on campus.** 1,350 workstations in dormitories, library, computer center, student center. Dormitories wired for high-speed internet access and linked to campus network. Commuter students can connect to campus network. Online course registration, online library, helpline, student web hosting, wireless network available.

**Student life. Freshman orientation:** Mandatory, $45 fee. Preregistration for classes offered. **Housing:** Guaranteed on-campus for freshmen. Coed dorms, single-sex dorms, special housing for disabled, fraternity/sorority housing, substance-free housing available. $150 deposit, deadline 3/31. Learning communities, themed living options-honors, health and fitness, leadership, development, academic enhancement, diversity housing available. **Activities:** Bands, campus ministries, choral groups, dance, drama, film society, international student organizations, literary magazine, music ensembles, musical theater, opera, radio station, student government, student newspaper, symphony orchestra, TV station, Amnesty International, Habitat for Humanity, College Republicans, College Democrats, Campus Crusade, Women in Transition, NAACP, Black Student Alliance, Green Party, mock trial club.

**Athletics.** NCAA. **Intercollegiate:** Baseball M, basketball, cross-country, diving, football (tackle) M, golf, rifle, soccer, softball W, swimming, tennis, track and field, volleyball W. **Intramural:** Archery, badminton, basketball, bowling, equestrian, football (non-tackle), golf, handball, racquetball, soccer, softball, swimming, table tennis, triathlon, volleyball, water polo, wrestling M. **Team name:** Hilltoppers.

**Student services.** Adult student services, alcohol/substance abuse counseling, campus ministries, career counseling, services for economically disadvantaged, student employment services, financial aid counseling, health services, minority student services, on-campus daycare, personal counseling, placement for graduates, veterans' counselor, women's services. **Physically disabled:** Services for visually, speech, hearing impaired.

**Contact.** E-mail: admission@wku.edu
Phone: (270) 745-2551 Toll-free number: (800) 495-8463
Fax: (270) 745-6133
Scott Gordon, Director of Admission and Academic Services, Western Kentucky University, 1906 College Heights Boulevard, Bowling Green, KY 42101

# Louisiana

## Centenary College of Louisiana
**Shreveport, Louisiana**
www.centenary.edu

**CB member**
**CB code: 6082**

- Private 4-year liberal arts college affiliated with United Methodist Church
- Residential campus in small city
- 845 degree-seeking undergraduates
- 62% of applicants admitted
- SAT or ACT (ACT writing optional) required

**General.** Founded in 1825. Regionally accredited. **Degrees:** 169 bachelor's awarded; master's offered. **Location:** 325 miles from New Orleans, 189 miles from Dallas. **Calendar:** Semester, extensive summer session. **Full-time faculty:** 73 total. **Part-time faculty:** 51 total. **Class size:** 67% < 20, 32% 20-39, less than 1% 40-49. **Special facilities:** Amphitheater, playhouse, music library, archives, Jack London collection.

**Freshman class profile.** 1,125 applied, 698 admitted, 199 enrolled.

| Mid 50% test scores | | Rank in top quarter: | 67% |
|---|---|---|---|
| SAT critical reading: | 500-620 | Rank in top tenth: | 37% |
| SAT math: | 510-620 | Out-of-state: | 45% |
| ACT composite: | 22-28 | | |

**Basis for selection.** Academic achievement record, high school GPA, test scores, essay, letters of recommendation, interview recommended. Extracurricular activities and leadership ability considered. Audition required of music, theater, dance majors. Portfolio recommended for art majors. **Homeschooled:** Transcript of courses and grades required.

**High school preparation.** 15 units recommended. Recommended units include English 4, mathematics 3, social studies 3, science 3 (laboratory 2) and foreign language 2.

**2007-2008 Annual costs.** Tuition/fees: $20,950. Room/board: $7,050.

**Financial aid. Non-need-based:** Scholarships awarded for academics, art, athletics, leadership, music/drama, religious affiliation, state residency.

**Application procedures. Admission:** Priority date 2/15; deadline 8/1 (postmark date). $30 fee, may be waived for applicants with need. Application may be submitted online. Admission notification on a rolling basis beginning on or about 11/15. Must reply by May 1 or within 3 week(s) if notified thereafter. **Financial aid:** Priority date 2/15; no closing date. FAFSA, institutional form required. Applicants notified on a rolling basis starting 2/15; must reply by 5/1.

**Academics. Special study options:** Combined bachelor's/graduate degree, cross-registration, double major, dual enrollment of high school students, exchange student, honors, independent study, internships, liberal arts/career combination, student-designed major, study abroad, teacher certification program, Washington semester. Oak Ridge National Laboratory semester, 3-2 engineering program, 3-2 communication disorders program. **Credit/placement by examination:** AP, CLEP, IB, institutional tests. 40 credit hours maximum toward bachelor's degree. Credit awarded only when the student has not already attempted to earn credit in a college classroom at or below the level of the subject covered by the exam. **Support services:** Learning center, reduced course load, study skills assistance, tutoring, writing center.

**Majors. Biology:** General, biochemistry, biophysics. **Business:** Accounting, accounting/business management, accounting/finance, business admin, finance, managerial economics. **Communications:** General, digital media, media studies. **Conservation:** Environmental science. **Education:** Art, biology, chemistry, drama/dance, elementary, English, foreign languages, French, German, health, history, mathematics, middle, multi-level teacher, music, physical, physical, science, secondary, social studies, Spanish. **English:** English lit. **Foreign languages:** General, classics, French, German, Latin, Spanish. **Health:** Predental, premedicine, prepharmacy, preveterinary, speech pathology. **History:** General. **Interdisciplinary:** Neuroscience. **Legal studies:** Prelaw. **Liberal arts:** Arts/sciences. **Math:** General. **Parks/recreation:** Exercise sciences, health/fitness. **Philosophy/religion:** Philosophy, religion. **Physical sciences:** Chemistry, geology, physics. **Psychology:** General. **Social sciences:** Applied economics, economics, political science, sociology.

**Theology:** Sacred music. **Visual/performing arts:** General, art, cinematography, dance, dramatic, music performance, music theory/composition, painting, piano/organ, sculpture, studio arts, theater design, voice/opera.

**Most popular majors.** Biology 18%, business/marketing 23%, communications/journalism 12%, psychology 6%, social sciences 10%, visual/performing arts 6%.

**Computing on campus.** 250 workstations in dormitories, library, computer center. Dormitories linked to campus network. Commuter students can connect to campus network. Online course registration, student web hosting, wireless network available.

**Student life. Freshman orientation:** Mandatory, $100 fee. 4 days prior to beginning of fall classes. **Policies:** Students participate on enrollment management committee, academic affairs committee, student/faculty discipline and other college-wide committees. **Housing:** Guaranteed on-campus for all undergraduates. Coed dorms, single-sex dorms, fraternity/sorority housing available. $200 partly refundable deposit, deadline 7/1. All students 21 years of age or below who are not local residents required to live in college housing. **Activities:** Bands, choral groups, dance, drama, film society, music ensembles, musical theater, opera, radio station, student government, student newspaper, symphony orchestra, church careers institute, United Methodist student movement, Baptist Collegiate Ministry, Canterbury House, Fellowship of Christian Athletes, student government association, Young Democrats, Young Republicans, students for diversity, tutoring service.

**Athletics.** NCAA. **Intercollegiate:** Baseball M, basketball, cross-country, golf, gymnastics W, soccer, softball W, swimming, tennis, volleyball W. **Intramural:** Archery, badminton, basketball, bowling, football (non-tackle), golf, lacrosse M, racquetball, rowing (crew), soccer, softball, table tennis, tennis, volleyball. **Team name:** Gents/Ladies.

**Student services.** Alcohol/substance abuse counseling, campus ministries, career counseling, financial aid counseling, health services, personal counseling, veterans' counselor. **Physically disabled:** Services for visually impaired.

**Contact.** E-mail: tcrowley@centenary.edu
Phone: (318) 869-5131 Toll-free number: (800) 234-4448
Fax: (318) 869-5005
Tim Crowley, Director of Admissions, Centenary College of Louisiana, Box 41188, Shreveport, LA 71134-1188

## Dillard University
**New Orleans, Louisiana**
www.dillard.edu

**CB member**
**CB code: 6164**

- Private 4-year university and liberal arts college affiliated with United Church of Christ and United Methodist Church
- Residential campus in very large city
- 956 degree-seeking undergraduates
- 46% of applicants admitted
- SAT or ACT with writing, application essay required

**General.** Founded in 1869. Regionally accredited. **Degrees:** 180 bachelor's awarded. **ROTC:** Army, Naval, Air Force. **Calendar:** Semester, limited summer session. **Full-time faculty:** 101 total. **Part-time faculty:** 31 total. **Class size:** 60% < 20, 34% 20-39, 5% 40-49, 1% 50-99, less than 1% >100.

**Freshman class profile.** 2,831 applied, 1,300 admitted, 175 enrolled.

| Mid 50% test scores | | Rank in top quarter: | 44% |
|---|---|---|---|
| SAT critical reading: | 350-460 | Rank in top tenth: | 2% |
| SAT math: | 330-450 | Out-of-state: | 46% |
| ACT composite: | 16-20 | | |

**Basis for selection.** Preference to applicants in top 25% of class, 2.5 minimum GPA. Test scores, class rank, participation in extracurricular activities and community projects considered. Interview recommended. **Homeschooled:** Recommended that student apply for state diploma.

**High school preparation.** 19 units required. Required and recommended units include English 4, mathematics 3, social studies 3, science 3, foreign language 2 and academic electives 6.

**2007-2008 Annual costs.** Tuition/fees: $12,240. Room/board: $7,900. Books/supplies: $1,000. Personal expenses: $1,533.

**Financial aid.** All financial aid based on need.

**Application procedures. Admission:** Priority date 12/1; deadline 7/1 (postmark date). $30 fee, may be waived for applicants with need. Application may be submitted online. Admission notification on a rolling basis. Must reply by May 1 or within 2 week(s) if notified thereafter. **Financial aid:** Priority date 12/1, closing date 5/1. FAFSA, institutional form required. Applicants notified on a rolling basis starting 3/1; must reply by 5/1 or within 2 week(s) of notification.

**Academics. Special study options:** Combined bachelor's/graduate degree, double major, dual enrollment of high school students, honors, independent study, internships, liberal arts/career combination, study abroad, teacher certification program. **Credit/placement by examination:** AP, CLEP, IB, institutional tests. 20 credit hours maximum toward bachelor's degree. **Support services:** Learning center, pre-admission summer program, reduced course load, remedial instruction, tutoring.

**Majors. Area/ethnic studies:** African, Japanese. **Biology:** General. **Business:** Accounting, business admin, finance. **Communications:** General. **Computer sciences:** Computer science. **Education:** Brain injured, early childhood, early childhood special, elementary, physical, secondary, special. **English:** English lit. **Foreign languages:** General, French, German, Japanese, Spanish. **Health:** Nursing (RN), premedicine, public health ed. **History:** General. **Math:** General. **Physical sciences:** Chemistry, physics. **Psychology:** General. **Public administration:** Social work. **Social sciences:** Criminology, economics, political science, sociology, urban studies. **Visual/performing arts:** Art, arts management, dramatic, music management.

**Computing on campus.** 400 workstations in dormitories, library, computer center. Dormitories wired for high-speed internet access and linked to campus network. Commuter students can connect to campus network. Online library, helpline, repair service available.

**Student life. Freshman orientation:** Mandatory, $200 fee. Preregistration for classes offered. **Housing:** Guaranteed on-campus for freshmen. Coed dorms, single-sex dorms, special housing for disabled, apartments, substance-free housing available. $300 deposit, deadline 5/1. **Activities:** Jazz band, choral groups, dance, drama, music ensembles, musical theater, radio station, student government, student newspaper, service sororities and fraternities, honor societies, religious groups, NAACP, Santa Filomena, Young Republicans, Baptist Student Union.

**Athletics.** NAIA. **Intercollegiate:** Basketball, cross-country, tennis, volleyball W. **Intramural:** Basketball, football (non-tackle), football (tackle) M, soccer, softball, swimming, table tennis, tennis, track and field, volleyball. **Team name:** Blue Devils.

**Student services.** Campus ministries, career counseling, student employment services, financial aid counseling, health services, personal counseling, placement for graduates.

**Contact.** E-mail: admission@dillard.edu
Phone: (504) 816-4670 Toll-free number: (800) 216-6637
Fax: (504) 816-4895
Meredith Reed, Director of Admissions, Dillard University, 2601 Gentilly Boulevard, New Orleans, LA 70122-3097

---

## Grambling State University
Grambling, Louisiana
www.gram.edu                                    CB code: 6250

- Public 4-year university
- Residential campus in small town
- 4,747 degree-seeking undergraduates: 8% part-time, 55% women, 88% African American, 1% Asian American, 7% international
- 388 degree-seeking graduate students
- 40% graduate within 6 years

**General.** Founded in 1901. Regionally accredited. **Degrees:** 517 bachelor's, 36 associate awarded; master's, doctoral offered. **ROTC:** Army. **Location:** 35 miles from Monroe, 65 miles from Shreveport. **Calendar:** Semester, limited summer session. **Full-time faculty:** 249 total; 61% have terminal degrees, 76% minority, 48% women. **Part-time faculty:** 39 total; 15% have terminal degrees, 67% minority, 54% women. **Class size:** 35% < 20, 54% 20-39, 8% 40-49, 3% 50-99, less than 1% >100.

**Freshman class profile.** 5,957 applied, 1,793 admitted, 1,211 enrolled.

| Mid 50% test scores | | | |
|---|---|---|---|
| SAT critical reading: | 360-450 | Rank in top quarter: | 19% |
| SAT math: | 360-450 | Rank in top tenth: | 6% |
| ACT composite: | 15-18 | End year in good standing: | 67% |
| GPA 3.50 or higher: | 7% | Return as sophomores: | 60% |
| GPA 3.0-3.49: | 22% | Out-of-state: | 46% |
| GPA 2.0-2.99: | 64% | International: | 3% |

**Basis for selection.** Open admission, but selective for out-of-state students. GED not accepted. Students are admitted on conditions of a "B" average; 24 on ACT; and, high school recommendation. Louisiana high school students must have minimum composite ACT of 16 (SAT 760). Out-of-state high school students must have a minimum composite ACT of 17 (SAT 810). Louisiana high school students graduating after 2003 do not have to submit high school transcripts. Out-of-state high school students must submit a final official (sealed) transcript and have earned a minimum cumulative 2.0 GPA (4.0 scale). Proof of immunization and medical history should be submitted. **Homeschooled:** State high school equivalency certificate required.

**High school preparation.** 14.5 units recommended. Recommended units include English 4, mathematics 3, history 3, science 2, foreign language 1, computer science .5 and visual/performing arts 1. One fine arts and .5 computer science units recommended.

**2007-2008 Annual costs.** Tuition/fees: $3,622; $8,972 out-of-state. Room/board: $5,072. Books/supplies: $1,200. Personal expenses: $2,514.

**2006-2007 Financial aid. Need-based:** 1,145 full-time freshmen applied for aid; 1,058 were judged to have need; 1,053 of these received aid. Average need met was 90%. Average scholarship/grant was $3,077; average loan $2,357. 40% of total undergraduate aid awarded as scholarships/grants, 60% as loans/jobs. **Non-need-based:** Awarded to 1,295 full-time undergraduates, including 289 freshmen. Scholarships awarded for academics, alumni affiliation, art, athletics, job skills, leadership, minority status, music/drama, religious affiliation, ROTC, state residency.

**Application procedures. Admission:** Priority date 4/1; deadline 6/1 (receipt date). $20 fee, may be waived for applicants with need. Application may be submitted online. Admission notification on a rolling basis. **Financial aid:** Priority date 4/1, closing date 6/1. FAFSA required. Applicants notified on a rolling basis starting 3/1; must reply within 2 week(s) of notification.

**Academics. Special study options:** Cooperative education, cross-registration, distance learning, double major, exchange student, honors, independent study, internships, study abroad, teacher certification program. **Credit/placement by examination:** AP, CLEP, institutional tests. 30 credit hours maximum toward associate degree, 30 toward bachelor's. Credit by means of Subject CLEP Examinations is limited to 30 semester hours. Whether or not this credit is applicable to a student's program will be determined by those responsible for their academic program. **Support services:** Learning center, reduced course load, remedial instruction, study skills assistance, tutoring, writing center.

**Honors college/program.** Requires minimum ACT score of 25 or SAT equivalent and 3.5 GPA.

**Majors. Biology:** General. **Business:** Accounting, business admin, hotel/motel admin, managerial economics, marketing. **Communications:** Media studies. **Computer sciences:** Computer science, information systems. **Education:** Art, biology, business, early childhood, elementary, English, French, mathematics, middle, music, physical, physics, social studies, special. **Engineering technology:** Drafting, electrical. **English:** English lit. **Foreign languages:** French, Spanish. **Health:** Nursing (RN). **History:** General. **Legal studies:** Paralegal, prelaw. **Math:** General. **Parks/recreation:** General. **Physical sciences:** Chemistry, physics. **Protective services:** Criminal justice. **Psychology:** General. **Public administration:** Social work. **Social sciences:** Political science, sociology. **Visual/performing arts:** Art, dramatic, music performance.

**Most popular majors.** Biology 6%, business/marketing 23%, communications/journalism 7%, computer/information sciences 11%, education 8%, health sciences 12%, security/protective services 11%.

**Computing on campus.** 200 workstations in library, computer center, student center. Dormitories wired for high-speed internet access and linked to campus network. Commuter students can connect to campus network. Online course registration, online library, helpline, wireless network available.

**Student life. Freshman orientation:** Mandatory. Preregistration for classes offered. **Housing:** Single-sex dorms, apartments, substance-free housing available. $50 fully refundable deposit, deadline 7/15. **Activities:** Bands, choral groups, dance, drama, music ensembles, opera, radio station, student government, student newspaper, symphony orchestra, Bayou Boyz social organization, Favrot student union, College Democrats, Ladies of Essence, NAACP, Bayou Girlz.

**Athletics.** NCAA. **Intercollegiate:** Baseball M, basketball, bowling W, cross-country, football (tackle) M, golf, soccer W, softball W, tennis, track and field, volleyball W. **Intramural:** Badminton, baseball M, basketball, bowling, cross-country, golf, gymnastics M, softball W, swimming, tennis, track and field, volleyball. **Team name:** Tigers.

**Student services.** Career counseling, student employment services, financial aid counseling, health services, personal counseling, placement for graduates, veterans' counselor. **Physically disabled:** Services for visually, speech, hearing impaired.

**Contact.** E-mail: admissions@gram.edu
Phone: (318) 274-6183 Toll-free number: (888) 863-3655
Fax: (318) 274-3292
Annie Moss, Director of Admissions and Recruitment, Grambling State University, 403 Main Street, GSU Box 4200, Grambling, LA 71245

---

## Herzing College
### Kenner, Louisiana
### www.herzing.edu
CB code: 3430

- For-profit 4-year branch campus and technical college
- Commuter campus in very large city

**General.** Regionally accredited. **Location:** 10 miles from downtown New Orleans. **Calendar:** Semester.

**Annual costs/financial aid.** Tuition costs vary by program, $315-$375 per credit hour.

**Contact.** Phone: (504) 733-0074
Director of Admissions, 2400 Veterans Boulevard, Suite 410, Kenner, LA 70062

---

## ITT Technical Institute: St. Rose
### St. Rose, Louisiana
### www.itt-tech.edu
CB code: 2766

- For-profit 4-year technical college
- Commuter campus in small town

**General.** Accredited by ACICS. **Calendar:** Quarter.

**Annual costs/financial aid.** Tuition varies by program, $260-$368 per credit hour.

**Contact.** Phone: (504) 463-0338
Director of Recruitment, 140 James Drive East, St. Rose, LA 70087

---

## Louisiana College
### Pineville, Louisiana
### www.lacollege.edu
CB code: 6371

- Private 4-year liberal arts college affiliated with Southern Baptist Convention
- Residential campus in small city
- 1,056 degree-seeking undergraduates
- 78% of applicants admitted
- SAT or ACT (ACT writing optional) required
- 46% graduate within 6 years

**General.** Founded in 1906. Regionally accredited. **Degrees:** 159 bachelor's awarded. **ROTC:** Army. **Calendar:** Semester, limited summer session. **Full-time faculty:** 62 total; 66% have terminal degrees, 3% minority, 42% women. **Part-time faculty:** 34 total; 12% have terminal degrees, 44% women. **Class size:** 70% < 20, 26% 20-39, 3% 40-49, less than 1% 50-99.

**Freshman class profile.** 549 applied, 429 admitted, 247 enrolled.

| Mid 50% test scores | | | |
|---|---|---|---|
| SAT writing: | | | 400-600 |
| SAT critical reading: | 430-600 | ACT composite: | 17-24 |
| SAT math: | 420-600 | | |

**Basis for selection.** 20 ACT (930 SAT) and 2.0 GPA or 17 ACT (810 SAT), 2.0 GPA and rank in the upper 50% of graduating class. Interview

required of nursing, respiratory care majors. Portfolio recommended for art majors.

**High school preparation.** 17 units required. Required units include English 4, mathematics 3, social studies 3, science 3 (laboratory 2) and academic electives 4.

**2007-2008 Annual costs.** Tuition/fees: $11,490. Room/board: $4,256. Books/supplies: $535. Personal expenses: $1,040.

**Financial aid. Non-need-based:** Scholarships awarded for academics, art, leadership, music/drama, ROTC.

**Application procedures. Admission:** Closing date 8/15. $25 fee, may be waived for applicants with need. Application may be submitted online. Admission notification on a rolling basis. Must reply by May 1 or within 2 week(s) if notified thereafter. **Financial aid:** Priority date 3/31; no closing date. FAFSA, institutional form required. Applicants notified on a rolling basis starting 3/1; must reply by 5/1 or within 2 week(s) of notification.

**Academics. Special study options:** Double major, dual enrollment of high school students, independent study, internships, liberal arts/career combination, student-designed major, study abroad, teacher certification program. **Credit/placement by examination:** AP, CLEP, institutional tests. 30 credit hours maximum toward bachelor's degree. **Support services:** Preadmission summer program, reduced course load, remedial instruction, tutoring.

**Majors. Biology:** General. **Business:** General, accounting, business admin, finance, marketing. **Communications:** General, journalism, media studies. **Computer sciences:** Webmaster. **Education:** General, art, business, elementary, English, foreign languages, French, health, mathematics, middle, music, physical, physically handicapped, science, secondary, social studies, Spanish. **English:** English lit. **Foreign languages:** General, French. **Health:** Athletic training, clinical lab technology, nursing (RN), predental, premedicine, prepharmacy, preveterinary. **History:** General. **Interdisciplinary:** Biological/physical sciences. **Legal studies:** Prelaw. **Math:** General. **Parks/recreation:** Health/fitness. **Philosophy/religion:** Religion. **Physical sciences:** Chemistry. **Protective services:** Law enforcement admin. **Psychology:** General. **Public administration:** General, social work. **Social sciences:** General, economics, political science, sociology. **Theology:** Religious ed, sacred music. **Visual/performing arts:** Commercial/advertising art, dramatic, music pedagogy, music performance, piano/organ, studio arts, voice/opera.

**Most popular majors.** Biology 10%, business/marketing 7%, communications/journalism 6%, education 11%, health sciences 15%, history 8%, public administration/social services 7%, social sciences 9%, visual/performing arts 7%.

**Computing on campus.** 242 workstations in library, computer center, student center. Dormitories linked to campus network.

**Student life. Freshman orientation:** Mandatory. Preregistration for classes offered. **Policies:** Religious observance required. **Housing:** Guaranteed on-campus for all undergraduates. Single-sex dorms, apartments, substance-free housing available. $75 deposit, deadline 8/1. **Activities:** Bands, campus ministries, choral groups, drama, international student organizations, literary magazine, music ensembles, musical theater, opera, radio station, student government, student newspaper, Lamda Chi Beta, Delta Xi Omega, Sigma Theta, Kappa Tau Beta, Union Board, church vocation fellowship, Fellowship of Christian Athletes, Jacob's Society.

**Athletics.** NCAA, NCCAA. **Intercollegiate:** Baseball M, basketball, cheerleading, cross-country, football (tackle) M, golf M, soccer, softball W, tennis W. **Intramural:** Badminton, basketball, bowling, golf, softball, swimming, table tennis, tennis, volleyball. **Team name:** Wildcats.

**Student services.** Campus ministries, career counseling, student employment services, financial aid counseling, health services, personal counseling, placement for graduates. **Physically disabled:** Services for visually impaired.

**Contact.** E-mail: admissions@lacollege.edu
Phone: (318) 487-7259 Toll-free number: (800) 487-1906
Fax: (318) 487-7550
Byron McGee, Director of Enrollment Management and Admissions, Louisiana College, LC Box 566, Pineville, LA 71359

---

## Louisiana State University and Agricultural and Mechanical College
### Baton Rouge, Louisiana
### www.lsu.edu
CB member
CB code: 6373

- Public 4-year university and agricultural college
- Commuter campus in large city

- 23,063 degree-seeking undergraduates: 6% part-time, 51% women, 9% African American, 3% Asian American, 3% Hispanic American, 2% international
- 4,994 degree-seeking graduate students
- 73% of applicants admitted
- SAT or ACT required
- 60% graduate within 6 years

**General.** Founded in 1860. Regionally accredited. **Degrees:** 4,617 bachelor's awarded; master's, doctoral, first professional offered. **ROTC:** Army, Naval, Air Force. **Location:** 80 miles from New Orleans. **Calendar:** Semester, extensive summer session. **Full-time faculty:** 1,267 total; 85% have terminal degrees, 14% minority, 34% women. **Part-time faculty:** 170 total; 57% have terminal degrees, 5% minority, 42% women. **Class size:** 35% < 20, 40% 20-39, 7% 40-49, 10% 50-99, 8% >100. **Special facilities:** Mycological herbarium, lichenological herbarium, natural science museum, geoscience museum, rural life museum, Anglo-American art museum, Civil War center, biomedical research center, coastal ecology center, center for advanced microstructures and devices.

**Freshman class profile.** 11,452 applied, 8,332 admitted, 4,596 enrolled.

| Mid 50% test scores | | | |
|---|---|---|---|
| SAT critical reading: | 520-640 | Rank in top quarter: | 55% |
| SAT math: | 550-650 | Rank in top tenth: | 27% |
| SAT writing: | 490-620 | End year in good standing: | 88% |
| ACT composite: | 23-28 | Return as sophomores: | 85% |
| GPA 3.50 or higher: | 55% | Out-of-state: | 17% |
| GPA 3.0-3.49: | 38% | Live on campus: | 66% |
| GPA 2.0-2.99: | 7% | International: | 1% |

**Basis for selection.** Sliding scale admissions criteria include number of academic units earned, GPA on those units, ACT or SAT scores. Students must also meet minimum Board of Regents Master Plan requirements. Applicants not meeting course units and/or grades or test score requirements may be considered by admissions committee. Out-of-state students must score at least 17 ACT or 830 SAT (exclusive of Writing). ACT/SAT writing component required for scholarship and honors college consideration. Audition required for MDA majors. Portfolio required for Art and Landscape Architecture majors. **Homeschooled:** Statement describing homeschool structure and mission, transcript of courses and grades required. Students with ACT score below 26 will be reviewed by admission committee. **Learning Disabled:** Students with learning disabilities who do not meet regular admission requirements may appeal to admission committee and submit documentation explaining positions.

**High school preparation.** 18 units required. Required units include English 4, mathematics 3, social studies 1, history 2, science 3, foreign language 2, academic electives 2.5. Computer literacy (.5 units) also required. Specific courses required in some subject areas.

**2007-2008 Annual costs.** Tuition/fees: $4,543; $12,843 out-of-state. Room/board: $6,852. Books/supplies: $1,500. Personal expenses: $1,692.

**2006-2007 Financial aid. Need-based:** 2,645 full-time freshmen applied for aid; 1,533 were judged to have need; 1,533 of these received aid. Average need met was 68%. Average scholarship/grant was $6,791; average loan $2,723. 53% of total undergraduate aid awarded as scholarships/grants, 47% as loans/jobs. **Non-need-based:** Awarded to 3,975 full-time undergraduates, including 1,317 freshmen. Scholarships awarded for academics, alumni affiliation, art, athletics, leadership, music/drama, ROTC, state residency.

**Application procedures. Admission:** Priority date 11/15; deadline 4/15 (receipt date). $40 fee, may be waived for applicants with need. Application must be submitted online. Admission notification on a rolling basis. **Financial aid:** No deadline. FAFSA, institutional form required. Applicants notified on a rolling basis starting 3/1; must reply within 3 week(s) of notification.

**Academics. Special study options:** Accelerated study, cooperative education, cross-registration, distance learning, double major, dual enrollment of high school students, ESL, exchange student, honors, independent study, internships, student-designed major, study abroad, teacher certification program. **Credit/placement by examination:** AP, CLEP, IB, SAT, ACT, institutional tests. 30 credit hours maximum toward bachelor's degree. **Support services:** Learning center, study skills assistance, tutoring, writing center.

**Honors college/program.** Minimum 30 ACT with 30 English, or 29 ACT with 31 English; or 1320 SAT (exclusive of Writing) with 660 verbal. 3.5 high school GPA required. Essay required.

**Majors. Agriculture:** Animal sciences, business, food science, plant sciences. **Architecture:** Architecture, interior, landscape. **Area/ethnic studies:** Women's. **Biology:** General, biochemistry, microbiology. **Business:** Accounting, business admin, construction management, fashion, finance,

international, management science, managerial economics, marketing. **Communications:** Media studies. **Computer sciences:** Computer science. **Conservation:** Environmental science, forest management, management/policy. **Education:** Adult/continuing, early childhood, elementary, music, physical, secondary. **Engineering:** Biomedical, chemical, civil, computer, electrical, environmental, industrial, mechanical, petroleum. **English:** English lit, speech/rhetoric. **Family/consumer sciences:** General. **Foreign languages:** French, German, Latin, Spanish. **Health:** Audiology/speech pathology, dietetics. **History:** General. **Interdisciplinary:** Global studies. **Liberal arts:** Arts/sciences. **Math:** General. **Philosophy/religion:** Philosophy. **Physical sciences:** Chemistry, geology, oceanography, physics. **Psychology:** General. **Social sciences:** Anthropology, economics, geography, political science, sociology. **Visual/performing arts:** Dramatic, music performance, studio arts.

**Most popular majors.** Biology 8%, business/marketing 19%, education 10%, engineering/engineering technologies 7%, English 6%, liberal arts 9%, social sciences 8%.

**Computing on campus.** 1,500 workstations in dormitories, library, student center. Dormitories wired for high-speed internet access and linked to campus network. Commuter students can connect to campus network. Online course registration, online library, helpline, student web hosting, wireless network available.

**Student life. Freshman orientation:** Mandatory, $76 fee. Preregistration for classes offered. Held in June, July, and August; testing held in spring. **Housing:** Coed dorms, single-sex dorms, special housing for disabled, apartments, fraternity/sorority housing available. $150 partly refundable deposit. **Activities:** Bands, campus ministries, choral groups, dance, drama, film society, literary magazine, music ensembles, musical theater, opera, radio station, student government, student newspaper, symphony orchestra, TV station, various religious, professional, honorary, political, service, and special interest organizations.

**Athletics.** NCAA. **Intercollegiate:** Baseball M, basketball, cross-country, football (tackle) M, golf, gymnastics W, soccer W, softball W, swimming, tennis, track and field, volleyball W. **Intramural:** Badminton, basketball, football (non-tackle), racquetball, soccer, softball, table tennis, tennis, volleyball. **Team name:** Tigers.

**Student services.** Adult student services, alcohol/substance abuse counseling, career counseling, student employment services, financial aid counseling, health services, minority student services, on-campus daycare, personal counseling, placement for graduates, veterans' counselor, women's services. **Physically disabled:** Services for visually, speech, hearing impaired.

**Contact.** E-mail: admissions@lsu.edu
Phone: (225) 578-1175 Fax: (225) 578-4433
Mary Parker, Executive Director of Undergraduate Admissions & Student Aid, Louisiana State University and Agricultural and Mechanical College, 1146 Pleasant Halll, Baton Rouge, LA 70803-2750

---

## Louisiana State University at Alexandria
**Alexandria, Louisiana**
www.lsua.edu                                    CB code: 1632

- Public 4-year university
- Commuter campus in small city
- 2,405 degree-seeking undergraduates

**General.** Founded in 1959. Regionally accredited. **Degrees:** 156 bachelor's, 181 associate awarded. **ROTC:** Army. **Location:** 10 miles from downtown. **Calendar:** Semester, extensive summer session. **Full-time faculty:** 111 total. **Part-time faculty:** 65 total. **Class size:** 42% < 20, 50% 20-39, 4% 40-49, 3% 50-99.

**Basis for selection.** Open admission. ACT scores used to determine placement in math and English courses. **Homeschooled:** Applicants must submit transcript of high school level work with graduation date and ACT scores.

**High school preparation.** 16.5 units recommended. Recommended units include English 4, mathematics 3, social studies 3, science 3, foreign language 2, academic electives 1.5. .5 units in computer studies and 1 unit in fine arts survey recommended.

**2007-2008 Annual costs.** Tuition/fees: $3,158; $5,619 out-of-state. On-campus housing (double-occupancy) $510 per month; meal plan $529 per 160 meals. Books/supplies: $690. Personal expenses: $1,342.

**Financial aid. Non-need-based:** Scholarships awarded for academics, state residency.

**Application procedures. Admission:** Priority date 8/1; no deadline. $20 fee. Admission notification on a rolling basis. **Financial aid:** Priority date 4/1; no closing date. FAFSA, institutional form required. Applicants notified on a rolling basis starting 4/20; must reply within 3 week(s) of notification.

**Academics. Special study options:** Distance learning, dual enrollment of high school students. **Credit/placement by examination:** AP, CLEP, institutional tests. Credit by examination limited to one-fourth number of hours required for degree. **Support services:** Learning center, pre-admission summer program, remedial instruction, study skills assistance, tutoring, writing center.

**Majors. Biology:** General. **Education:** General. **Liberal arts:** Arts/sciences. **Psychology:** General.

**Most popular majors.** Education 24%, liberal arts 74%.

**Computing on campus.** 163 workstations in library, computer center, student center. Commuter students can connect to campus network.

**Student life. Freshman orientation:** Mandatory. Preregistration for classes offered. **Housing:** Apartments available. **Activities:** Choral groups, drama, literary magazine, student government, student newspaper, Baptist Ministry, Catholic student organization, Apostolic Student Fellowship, Canterbury Club, College Republicans, College Democrats, international student organization, nontraditional student organization, Identity, Circle K.

**Athletics. Intramural:** Basketball, cross-country, football (non-tackle) M, soccer, softball, tennis, volleyball. **Team name:** Generals.

**Student services.** Adult student services, campus ministries, career counseling, student employment services, financial aid counseling, minority student services, on-campus daycare, personal counseling, placement for graduates, veterans' counselor.

**Contact.** E-mail: generalinfo@lsua.edu
Phone: (318) 473-6417 Toll-free number: (888) 473-6417
Fax: (318) 473-6418
Teresa Seymour, Registrar, Louisiana State University at Alexandria, 8100 Highway 71 South, Alexandria, LA 71302-9121

---

### Louisiana State University Health Sciences Center
**New Orleans, Louisiana**
**www.lsuhsc.edu**　　　　　　　　　　**CB code: 1192**

▶ Public two-year upper-division health science and nursing college
▶ Commuter campus in large city
▶ Interview required

**General.** Founded in 1931. Regionally accredited. **Degrees:** 227 bachelor's, 4 associate awarded; master's, doctoral, first professional offered. **Articulation:** Agreement with University of New Orleans. **Calendar:** Differs by program, limited summer session. **Part-time faculty:** 9 total.

**Student profile.** 572 degree-seeking undergraduates.

| | | | |
|---|---|---|---|
| Out-of-state: | 1% | 25 or older: | 28% |
| Live on campus: | 20% | | |

**Basis for selection.** College transcript, interview required. Application closing, notification, and response dates vary by program. Transfer accepted as sophomores, juniors, seniors.

**2007-2008 Annual costs.** Tuition/fees: $3,978; $7,110 out-of-state. Room only: $2,210.

**Financial aid. Non-need-based:** Scholarships awarded for academics.

**Application procedures. Admission:** $50 fee. **Financial aid:** FAFSA, institutional form required.

**Academics. Special study options:** Cross-registration, double major, honors, independent study, internships. **Credit/placement by examination:** CLEP.

**Majors. Health:** Cardiovascular technology, clinical lab science, dental hygiene, dental lab technology, nursing (RN), vocational rehab counseling.

**Computing on campus.** 227 workstations in dormitories, library, computer center, student center. Dormitories wired for high-speed internet access and linked to campus network. Commuter students can connect to campus network. Online library, helpline, repair service, wireless network available.

**Student life. Housing:** Coed dorms, apartments, substance-free housing available. **Activities:** Choral groups, student government.

**Student services.** Alcohol/substance abuse counseling, career counseling, financial aid counseling, health services, personal counseling. **Physically disabled:** Services for visually, speech, hearing impaired.

**Contact.** Phone: (504) 568-4808
Louisiana State University Health Sciences Center, 433 Bolivar Street, New Orleans, LA 70112-2223

---

### Louisiana State University in Shreveport
**Shreveport, Louisiana**
**www.lsus.edu**　　　　　　　　　　**CB code: 6355**

▶ Public 4-year university
▶ Commuter campus in large city
▶ 3,211 degree-seeking undergraduates
▶ 404 graduate students
▶ 76% of applicants admitted
▶ ACT (writing optional) required

**General.** Founded in 1965. Regionally accredited. **Degrees:** 461 bachelor's awarded; master's offered. **ROTC:** Army. **Location:** 180 miles from Dallas. **Calendar:** Semester, extensive summer session. **Full-time faculty:** 160 total. **Part-time faculty:** 100 total. **Class size:** 40% < 20, 44% 20-39, 10% 40-49, 6% 50-99. **Special facilities:** Life science museum, pioneer heritage center.

**Freshman class profile.** 796 applied, 605 admitted, 425 enrolled.

| Mid 50% test scores | | | |
|---|---|---|---|
| | | GPA 3.0-3.49: | 29% |
| SAT critical reading: | 480-570 | GPA 2.0-2.99: | 37% |
| SAT math: | 420-530 | End year in good standing: | 87% |
| ACT composite: | 20-24 | Return as sophomores: | 60% |
| GPA 3.50 or higher: | 33% | Out-of-state: | 6% |

**Basis for selection.** Completion of Regents high school core curriculum (currently TOPS core curriculum) of 16.5 course units one of the following required: 2.0 GPA, high school rank in top 50% of class, or 20 ACT. No more than 1 developmental course necessary if ACT English score of 18 or greater, or ACT mathematics score of 18 or greater. For early admission, principal's recommendation, 29 ACT, 15 specific high school units, 3.0 GPA required. Regardless of age, students who have accumulated at least 12 term hours of non-developmental college credit may transfer to LSUS if they meet all transfer requirements. **Homeschooled:** GED required.

**High school preparation.** Recommended units include English 4, mathematics 3, social studies 3, science 3, foreign language 2, computer science 1 and visual/performing arts 1.

**2007-2008 Annual costs.** Tuition/fees: $3,521; $7,847 out-of-state. Books/supplies: $702. Personal expenses: $1,365.

**Application procedures. Admission:** Closing date 7/15. $10 fee. Application must be submitted on paper. Admission notification on a rolling basis. **Financial aid:** No deadline. Applicants notified on a rolling basis.

**Academics. Special study options:** Combined bachelor's/graduate degree, cooperative education, distance learning, double major, dual enrollment of high school students, internships, study abroad, teacher certification program, Washington semester. Cooperative education program with Southern University at Shreveport. **Credit/placement by examination:** AP, CLEP, ACT, institutional tests. 62 credit hours maximum toward bachelor's degree. **Support services:** Learning center, remedial instruction, study skills assistance, tutoring, writing center.

**Majors. Biology:** General, biochemistry. **Business:** Accounting, banking/financial services, business admin, financial planning, managerial economics, marketing. **Communications:** Journalism. **Computer sciences:** Computer science. **Conservation:** Environmental science. **Education:** Art, biology, chemistry, early childhood, elementary, English, French, mathematics, physical, physics, science, social studies, special. **English:** English lit, speech/rhetoric. **Foreign languages:** French, Spanish. **History:** General. **Liberal arts:** Arts/sciences. **Math:** General. **Parks/recreation:** Health/fitness. **Physical sciences:** Chemistry, physics. **Protective services:** Criminal justice. **Psychology:** General. **Social sciences:** Geography, political science, sociology. **Visual/performing arts:** Art.

**Most popular majors.** Biology 9%, business/marketing 31%, education 16%, liberal arts 20%, psychology 8%, social sciences 6%.

**Computing on campus.** 250 workstations in library, computer center, student center. Commuter students can connect to campus network. Online course registration, online library, helpline, student web hosting, wireless network available.

**Student life. Freshman orientation:** Mandatory. Preregistration for classes offered. **Housing:** Guaranteed on-campus for all undergraduates. Apartments available. Pets allowed in dorm rooms. **Activities:** Jazz band, dance, literary magazine, radio station, student government, student newspaper, Baptist student union, College Republicans, government and law society, Catholic student union, Rotaract, foreign language club, psychology club, black student association.

**Athletics.** NAIA. **Intercollegiate:** Baseball M. **Intramural:** Badminton, basketball, football (non-tackle), golf, racquetball, soccer, softball, swimming, table tennis, tennis, track and field, volleyball. **Team name:** Pilots.

**Student services.** Career counseling, student employment services, financial aid counseling, minority student services, personal counseling, placement for graduates, veterans' counselor. **Physically disabled:** Services for visually, speech, hearing impaired.

**Contact.** E-mail: admissions@pilot.lsus.edu
Phone: (318) 797-5061 Toll-free number: (800) 229-5957
Fax: (318) 797-5286
Mickey Diez, Dean of Enrollment Services & Registrar, Louisiana State University in Shreveport, One University Place, Shreveport, LA 71115-2399

---

## Louisiana Tech University

**Ruston, Louisiana**                    **CB member**
**www.latech.edu**                       **CB code: 6372**

◆  Public 4-year university
◆  Commuter campus in large town
◆  8,375 undergraduates
◆  SAT or ACT (ACT writing optional) required

**General.** Founded in 1894. Regionally accredited. **Degrees:** 1,380 bachelor's, 86 associate awarded; master's, doctoral offered. **ROTC:** Army, Naval. **Location:** 70 miles from Shreveport, 30 miles from Monroe. **Calendar:** Quarter, extensive summer session. **Full-time faculty:** 394 total. **Part-time faculty:** 105 total. **Class size:** 37% < 20, 42% 20-39, 11% 40-49, 8% 50-99, 2% >100. **Special facilities:** Natural history museum, on-campus lab school, arboretum, planetarium, rehabilitation science and biomedical engineering center, micromanufacturing institute, water resource center.

### Freshman class profile.

| Mid 50% test scores | | | Fraternities: | 9% |
|---|---|---|---|---|
| ACT composite: | 20-25 | | Sororities: | 17% |
| Out-of-state: | 14% | | | |

**Basis for selection.** High school record, test scores most important. Special talents, school and community activities, recommendations considered. To be admitted, applicant must need no more than one remedial course. Admission deadline for scholarship consideration is January 2 for the following fall term. **Homeschooled:** Applicants must have an overall high school GPA of 2.5, ACT of at least 23, or SAT of at least 1060 (exclusive of Writing).

**High school preparation.** Required units include English 4, mathematics 3, social studies 3, science 3, academic electives 4.5. 2 algebra required. Social studies must include 1 U.S. history. 4.5 units of electives from foreign language, sciences, math, social studies, speech, advanced fine arts, or computer literacy required. Prefer English courses that emphasize grammar, composition, and literature.

**2007-2008 Annual costs.** Tuition/fees: $4,428; $10,893 out-of-state. Room/board: $4,470. Books/supplies: $660. Personal expenses: $1,440.

**Financial aid. Non-need-based:** Scholarships awarded for academics, art, athletics, leadership, music/drama, ROTC.

**Application procedures. Admission:** Priority date 8/1; no deadline. $20 fee, may be waived for applicants with need. Admission notification on a rolling basis beginning on or about 6/1. **Financial aid:** Priority date 4/15; no closing date. FAFSA, institutional form required. Applicants notified on a rolling basis starting 3/18; must reply within 4 week(s) of notification.

**Academics. Special study options:** Combined bachelor's/graduate degree, cooperative education, cross-registration, distance learning, double major, dual enrollment of high school students, ESL, honors, independent study, internships, liberal arts/career combination, study abroad, teacher certification program. Cooperative programs with Grambling State University. **Credit/placement by examination:** AP, CLEP, institutional tests. 30 credit hours

maximum toward associate degree, 30 toward bachelor's. **Support services:** Remedial instruction, study skills assistance, tutoring.

**Majors. Agriculture:** Animal sciences, business. **Architecture:** Architecture, interior. **Biology:** General. **Business:** Accounting, business admin, finance, human resources, management information systems, management science, managerial economics, marketing. **Communications:** Journalism. **Computer sciences:** Computer science. **Conservation:** General, forest resources, forestry. **Education:** Art, early childhood, elementary, French, music, physical, secondary, special, speech impaired. **Engineering:** Biomedical, chemical, civil, electrical, mechanical. **Engineering technology:** Civil, electrical. **English:** English lit, speech/rhetoric. **Family/consumer sciences:** Family studies. **Foreign languages:** French, Spanish. **Health:** Audiology/speech pathology, clinical lab science, medical records admin. **History:** General. **Liberal arts:** Arts/sciences. **Math:** General. **Parks/recreation:** Health/fitness. **Physical sciences:** Chemistry, geology, physics. **Psychology:** General. **Social sciences:** Geography, political science, sociology. **Transportation:** Aviation, aviation management. **Visual/performing arts:** Art, commercial/advertising art, music performance, photography. **Other:** Nanosystems engineering.

**Computing on campus.** 1,800 workstations in dormitories, library, computer center. Dormitories linked to campus network.

**Student life. Freshman orientation:** Available, $55 fee. Preregistration for classes offered. 4 sessions offered during the summer. **Housing:** Guaranteed on-campus for freshmen. Single-sex dorms, special housing for disabled, apartments available. $50 deposit, deadline 7/15. **Activities:** Bands, choral groups, dance, drama, music ensembles, musical theater, radio station, student government, student newspaper, Wesley Foundation, Baptist student union, Union Board, College Republicans, Campus Crusade for Christ, international student association, NAACP, Circle K, Angel Flight.

**Athletics.** NCAA. **Intercollegiate:** Baseball M, basketball, bowling W, cross-country, football (tackle) M, golf M, soccer W, softball W, tennis W, track and field, volleyball W. **Intramural:** Badminton, basketball, bowling, golf M, racquetball, soccer, softball, tennis, volleyball. **Team name:** Bulldogs (M), Lady Techsters (W).

**Student services.** Campus ministries, career counseling, student employment services, financial aid counseling, health services, legal services, minority student services, personal counseling, placement for graduates, veterans' counselor, women's services. **Physically disabled:** Services for speech impaired.

**Contact.** E-mail: bulldog@latech.edu
Phone: (318) 257-3036 Toll-free number: (800) 528-3241
Fax: (318) 257-2499
Jan Albritton, Director of Admissions, College of Basic and Career Studies, Louisiana Tech University, Box 3178, Ruston, LA 71272

---

## Loyola University New Orleans

**New Orleans, Louisiana**              **CB member**
**www.loyno.edu**                       **CB code: 6374**

◆  Private 4-year university and liberal arts college affiliated with Roman Catholic Church
◆  Residential campus in large city
◆  2,591 degree-seeking undergraduates: 10% part-time, 59% women, 12% African American, 4% Asian American, 12% Hispanic American, 1% Native American, 3% international
◆  1,680 degree-seeking graduate students
◆  61% of applicants admitted
◆  SAT or ACT with writing, application essay required
◆  63% graduate within 6 years; 62% enter graduate study

**General.** Founded in 1912. Regionally accredited. **Degrees:** 824 bachelor's awarded; master's, first professional offered. **ROTC:** Army, Naval, Air Force. **Calendar:** Semester, limited summer session. **Full-time faculty:** 258 total; 91% have terminal degrees, 10% minority, 42% women. **Part-time faculty:** 148 total; 48% have terminal degrees, 8% minority, 42% women. **Class size:** 54% < 20, 43% 20-39, 3% 40-49, less than 1% 50-99. **Special facilities:** Humanities lab with Perseus Project and TLG TV, multimedia classrooms, 24-hour microcomputer labs, computer science lab, graphics lab, visual arts lab, ad club/communications lab, RATHE business computer lab, multi-media training center.

**Freshman class profile.** 2,980 applied, 1,832 admitted, 503 enrolled.

| Mid 50% test scores | | Rank in top tenth: | 27% |
|---|---|---|---|
| SAT critical reading: | 550-690 | End year in good standing: | 90% |
| SAT math: | 530-630 | Return as sophomores: | 78% |
| ACT composite: | 23-28 | Out-of-state: | 52% |
| GPA 3.50 or higher: | 51% | Live on campus: | 74% |
| GPA 3.0-3.49: | 32% | International: | 2% |
| GPA 2.0-2.99: | 17% | Fraternities: | 19% |
| Rank in top quarter: | 54% | Sororities: | 21% |

**Basis for selection.** Freshman admission based on credentials submitted by student for admissions portfolio. High school performance, test scores, counselor/teacher evaluation, personal essay, extracurricular activity, community involvement and work experience all considered. Interview recommended. Audition required for music, theater arts and dance majors. Portfolio required for visual arts program applicants. **Homeschooled:** Require proof of high school graduation or its equivalent.

**High school preparation.** 10 units required; 15 recommended. Required and recommended units include English 4, mathematics 2-3, social studies 2-3 and science 2-3.

**2008-2009 Annual costs.** Tuition/fees: $28,044. Room/board: $9,394. Books/supplies: $1,000. Personal expenses: $1,424.

**2007-2008 Financial aid. Need-based:** 382 full-time freshmen applied for aid; 325 were judged to have need; 325 of these received aid. Average need met was 84%. Average scholarship/grant was $20,127; average loan $3,361. 76% of total undergraduate aid awarded as scholarships/grants, 24% as loans/jobs. **Non-need-based:** Awarded to 1,996 full-time undergraduates, including 452 freshmen. Scholarships awarded for academics, alumni affiliation, art, minority status, ROTC.

**Application procedures. Admission:** Priority date 1/15; no deadline. $20 fee, may be waived for applicants with need. Application may be submitted online. Admission notification on a rolling basis beginning on or about 11/1. Must reply by May 1 or within 2 week(s) if notified thereafter. **Financial aid:** Priority date 2/15, closing date 6/1. FAFSA required. Applicants notified on a rolling basis starting 3/1; must reply by 5/1 or within 2 week(s) of notification.

**Academics. Special study options:** Accelerated study, combined bachelor's/graduate degree, cross-registration, distance learning, double major, dual enrollment of high school students, exchange student, external degree, honors, independent study, internships, liberal arts/career combination, student-designed major, study abroad, Washington semester. Weekend and evening courses. **Credit/placement by examination:** AP, CLEP, IB, SAT, ACT, institutional tests. 30 credit hours maximum toward bachelor's degree. At least 25% of semester credit hours required for degree must be earned through instruction offered by Loyola. Unless special permission granted by the dean for the student to pursue coursework elsewhere, the last 30 credit hours must be completed at Loyola. Although transfer students are required to complete at least 15 credit hours in their major while at Loyola, additional hours are normally required. **Support services:** Learning center, pre-admission summer program, reduced course load, remedial instruction, study skills assistance, tutoring, writing center.

**Majors. Biology:** General. **Business:** Accounting, finance, international, managerial economics, marketing. **Communications:** General. **Education:** Music. **English:** Creative writing, English lit. **Foreign languages:** Ancient Greek, French, German, Spanish. **Health:** Music therapy, nursing (RN), predental, premedicine, preveterinary. **History:** General. **Liberal arts:** Arts/sciences. **Math:** General. **Philosophy/religion:** Philosophy, religion. **Physical sciences:** Chemistry, physics. **Protective services:** Criminal justice, forensics. **Psychology:** General. **Social sciences:** General, political science, sociology. **Visual/performing arts:** General, art, commercial/advertising art, dramatic, jazz, music management, music performance, studio arts. **Other:** Chemistry PreMed, Psychology, Pre-Med.

**Most popular majors.** Business/marketing 19%, communications/journalism 17%, English 6%, psychology 9%, social sciences 8%, visual/performing arts 11%.

**Computing on campus.** 510 workstations in dormitories, library, computer center, student center. Dormitories wired for high-speed internet access and linked to campus network. Commuter students can connect to campus network. Online course registration, online library, helpline, repair service, student web hosting, wireless network available.

**Student life. Freshman orientation:** Mandatory, $150 fee. Preregistration for classes offered. Held the weekend before classes begin. **Housing:** Guaranteed on-campus for freshmen. Coed dorms, special housing for disabled, apartments, substance-free housing available. $100 nonrefundable deposit, deadline 5/1. Honors floors available. Counselors live in each hall to provide spiritual/counseling assistance. **Activities:** Bands, campus ministries, choral groups, dance, drama, film society, international student organizations, literary magazine, music ensembles, Model UN, musical theater, opera, radio station, student government, student newspaper, symphony orchestra, Black student union, community action program, Muslim students association, Asian student organization, Student Democrats, gay/lesbian outreach, university programming board, Big Brothers/Big Sisters.

**Athletics.** NAIA. **Intercollegiate:** Baseball M, basketball, cross-country, track and field, volleyball W. **Intramural:** Basketball, golf, racquetball, soccer, softball, swimming, volleyball, weight lifting. **Team name:** Wolfpack.

**Student services.** Adult student services, alcohol/substance abuse counseling, campus ministries, career counseling, student employment services, financial aid counseling, health services, on-campus daycare, personal counseling, placement for graduates, women's services. **Physically disabled:** Services for visually, speech, hearing impaired.

**Contact.** E-mail: admit@loyno.edu
Phone: (504) 865-3240 Toll-free number: (800) 456-9652
Fax: (504) 865-3383
Lori Zawistowski, Dean of Admissions, Loyola University New Orleans, 6363 St. Charles Avenue, New Orleans, LA 70118-6195

## McNeese State University
**Lake Charles, Louisiana**
**www.mcneese.edu**                    **CB code: 6403**

- Public 4-year university
- Commuter campus in small city
- 7,041 degree-seeking undergraduates: 17% part-time, 61% women, 19% African American, 1% Asian American, 1% Hispanic American, 1% Native American, 3% international
- 839 degree-seeking graduate students
- SAT or ACT (ACT writing optional) required

**General.** Founded in 1939. Regionally accredited. **Degrees:** 1,043 bachelor's, 138 associate awarded; master's offered. **Location:** 193 miles from New Orleans, 124 miles from Houston. **Calendar:** Semester, extensive summer session. **Full-time faculty:** 316 total; 66% have terminal degrees, 15% minority, 45% women. **Part-time faculty:** 98 total; 22% have terminal degrees, 7% minority, 57% women. **Special facilities:** Environmental research center, planetarium, vertebrate museum, farm, community health care clinic.

**Freshman class profile.**

| GPA 3.50 or higher: | 32% | Rank in top tenth: | 14% |
|---|---|---|---|
| GPA 3.0-3.49: | 31% | Return as sophomores: | 64% |
| GPA 2.0-2.99: | 34% | Out-of-state: | 7% |
| Rank in top quarter: | 35% | International: | 3% |

**Basis for selection.** Applicants must complete Louisiana Board of Regents high school core curriculum and have 18 ACT English or math score (450 SAT verbal or 430 math). Applicants also must have either 2.0 GPA, 20 ACT, or rank in top 50% of graduating class. Audition required of music majors. Essay and interview required for Honors College. **Homeschooled:** 23 ACT (1060 SAT).

**High school preparation.** 16.5 units recommended. Recommended units include English 4, mathematics 3, social studies 3, science 3 and foreign language 2. 1 fine arts, 0.5 computer science, computer literacy or business computer applications.

**2007-2008 Annual costs.** Tuition/fees: $3,233; $9,299 out-of-state. Room/board: $5,840. Books/supplies: $1,000. Personal expenses: $2,250.

**Financial aid. Non-need-based:** Scholarships awarded for academics, alumni affiliation, art, athletics, leadership, minority status, music/drama, state residency. **Additional information:** Books may be charged and paid in 2 installments during semester.

**Application procedures. Admission:** Priority date 7/15; no deadline. $20 fee. Application may be submitted online. Admission notification on a rolling basis beginning on or about 3/15. **Financial aid:** Priority date 5/1; no closing date. FAFSA, institutional form required. Applicants notified on a rolling basis starting 4/15; must reply within 2 week(s) of notification.

**Academics. Special study options:** Accelerated study, cooperative education, distance learning, double major, dual enrollment of high school students, ESL, honors, independent study, internships, study abroad, teacher certification program. **Credit/placement by examination:** AP, CLEP, ACT, institutional tests. 24 credit hours maximum toward associate degree, 45 toward bachelor's. **Support services:** Learning center, remedial instruction, tutoring, writing center.

**Honors college/program.** 25 freshmen admitted. Requirements include: 27 ACT, 3.4 GPA, essay, interview, and 3 recommendations.

**Majors. Agriculture:** General. **Biology:** General. **Business:** Accounting, business admin, finance, marketing. **Communications:** Media studies. **Computer sciences:** Computer science. **Conservation:** Environmental science, wildlife. **Education:** Agricultural, art, biology, business, chemistry, early childhood, elementary, English, family/consumer sciences, foreign languages, mathematics, music, physical, social studies, special, speech. **Engineering:** General. **Engineering technology:** General. **English:** English lit, speech/rhetoric. **Family/consumer sciences:** General. **Foreign languages:** French, Spanish. **Health:** Clinical lab science, nursing (RN), radiologic technology/medical imaging. **History:** General. **Liberal arts:** Arts/sciences. **Math:** General. **Parks/recreation:** Exercise sciences. **Physical sciences:** Chemistry, physics. **Protective services:** Criminal justice. **Psychology:** General. **Social sciences:** Political science, sociology. **Visual/performing arts:** Art, dramatic, music performance. **Other:** Environmental science education.

**Most popular majors.** Business/marketing 19%, education 11%, health sciences 15%, liberal arts 19%.

**Computing on campus.** 450 workstations in dormitories, library, computer center, student center. Dormitories wired for high-speed internet access and linked to campus network. Commuter students can connect to campus network. Online course registration, online library, helpline, student web hosting, wireless network available.

**Student life. Freshman orientation:** Mandatory, $10 fee. Preregistration for classes offered. Four 2-day programs offered in late May, June and mid-July. **Housing:** Coed dorms, apartments, fraternity/sorority housing available. $175 deposit. **Activities:** Bands, choral groups, dance, drama, literary magazine, music ensembles, musical theater, opera, student government, student newspaper, symphony orchestra, 93 organizations.

**Athletics.** NCAA. **Intercollegiate:** Baseball M, basketball, cheerleading, cross-country, football (tackle) M, golf, rodeo, soccer W, softball W, tennis W, track and field, volleyball W. **Intramural:** Badminton, basketball, bowling, football (non-tackle), golf, handball, racquetball, softball, table tennis, tennis, volleyball, water polo. **Team name:** Cowboys.

**Student services.** Adult student services, alcohol/substance abuse counseling, campus ministries, career counseling, student employment services, financial aid counseling, health services, minority student services, personal counseling, placement for graduates, veterans' counselor. **Physically disabled:** Services for visually, speech, hearing impaired.

**Contact.** E-mail: info@mcneese.edu
Phone: (337) 475-5356 Toll-free number: (800) 622-3352
Fax: (337) 475-5151
Kara Smith, Director of Admissions, McNeese State University, Box 91740 MSU, Lake Charles, LA 70609-1740

---

### New Orleans Baptist Theological Seminary: Leavell College
**New Orleans, Louisiana**
**www.nobts.edu**                              CB code: 5034

- Private 4-year Bible and seminary college affiliated with Southern Baptist Convention
- Very large city

**General.** Regionally accredited. **Calendar:** Semester.

**Annual costs/financial aid.** Tuition/fees (2007-2008): $4,257. Tuition reported for Southern Baptist students. Other Baptist and non-Baptist students pay tuition at a slightly higher rate. Room: $1,710. Books/supplies: $500.

**Contact.** Phone: (504) 282-4455
Registrar and Director of Admissions, 3939 Gentilly Boulevard, New Orleans, LA 70126-4858

---

### Nicholls State University
**Thibodaux, Louisiana**
**www.nicholls.edu**                           CB code: 6221

- Public 4-year university
- Commuter campus in large town

---

- 6,118 degree-seeking undergraduates: 20% part-time, 62% women, 18% African American, 1% Asian American, 2% Hispanic American, 2% Native American, 1% international
- 278 degree-seeking graduate students
- 84% of applicants admitted
- SAT or ACT (ACT writing optional) required
- 26% graduate within 6 years

**General.** Founded in 1948. Regionally accredited. **Degrees:** 724 bachelor's, 166 associate awarded; master's offered. **Location:** 60 miles from New Orleans, 75 miles from Baton Rouge. **Calendar:** Semester, extensive summer session. **Full-time faculty:** 288 total; 55% have terminal degrees, 10% minority, 50% women. **Class size:** 48% < 20, 35% 20-39, 7% 40-49, 8% 50-99, 1% >100. **Special facilities:** Marine research facility, culinary institute, center for women and government, marine biology laboratory, center for study of dyslexia, center for economic education, small business development center, center for traditional boat building, economic council.

**Freshman class profile.** 2,129 applied, 1,787 admitted, 1,202 enrolled.

| Mid 50% test scores | | End year in good standing: | 60% |
|---|---|---|---|
| ACT composite: | 19-23 | Return as sophomores: | 66% |
| GPA 3.50 or higher: | 30% | Out-of-state: | 3% |
| GPA 3.0-3.49: | 32% | Live on campus: | 35% |
| GPA 2.0-2.99: | 36% | International: | 1% |
| Rank in top quarter: | 43% | Fraternities: | 12% |
| Rank in top tenth: | 17% | Sororities: | 7% |

**Basis for selection.** Must meet the Board of Regents Core (TOPS Core) requirement, 2.0 GPA, and meet at least one of the following: 20 ACT or rank in the top half of graduating class.

**High school preparation.** 16.5 units required. Required units include English 4, mathematics 3, social studies 1, history 2, science 3, foreign language 2, academic electives 1.5.

**2007-2008 Annual costs.** Tuition/fees: $3,595; $9,043 out-of-state. Room/board: $4,556. Books/supplies: $1,200. Personal expenses: $1,692.

**2006-2007 Financial aid. Need-based:** 965 full-time freshmen applied for aid; 506 were judged to have need; 500 of these received aid. Average need met was 78%. Average scholarship/grant was $2,160; average loan $2,149. 58% of total undergraduate aid awarded as scholarships/grants, 42% as loans/jobs. **Non-need-based:** Awarded to 903 full-time undergraduates, including 331 freshmen. Scholarships awarded for academics, athletics, state residency.

**Application procedures. Admission:** Priority date 8/15; no deadline. $20 fee ($30 out-of-state). Application may be submitted online. Admission notification on a rolling basis beginning on or about 9/1. **Financial aid:** Priority date 4/17; no closing date. FAFSA, institutional form required. Applicants notified on a rolling basis; must reply within 2 week(s) of notification.

**Academics. Special study options:** Cooperative education, cross-registration, distance learning, dual enrollment of high school students, exchange student, honors, independent study, internships, study abroad, teacher certification program. **Credit/placement by examination:** AP, CLEP, SAT, ACT, institutional tests. 15 credit hours maximum toward associate degree, 30 toward bachelor's. **Support services:** Learning center, pre-admission summer program, reduced course load, remedial instruction, study skills assistance, tutoring, writing center.

**Majors. Agriculture:** Business. **Biology:** General. **Business:** Accounting, business admin, finance, management information systems, marketing. **Communications:** Media studies. **Computer sciences:** Computer science. **Education:** Art, business, early childhood, elementary, English, French, mathematics, middle, music, physical, science, social studies. **Engineering technology:** Mechanical, petroleum, surveying. **English:** English lit. **Family/consumer sciences:** General. **Foreign languages:** French. **Health:** Audiology/speech pathology, dietetics, health services, nursing (RN). **History:** General. **Math:** General. **Personal/culinary services:** Chef training. **Physical sciences:** Chemistry. **Psychology:** General. **Social sciences:** Political science, sociology. **Visual/performing arts:** Art.

**Most popular majors.** Business/marketing 23%, education 11%, health sciences 20%, liberal arts 10%.

**Computing on campus.** 285 workstations in dormitories, library, computer center. Dormitories wired for high-speed internet access and linked to campus network. Commuter students can connect to campus network. Online course registration, online library, wireless network available.

**Student life. Freshman orientation:** Mandatory, $50 fee. Preregistration for classes offered. **Housing:** Guaranteed on-campus for all undergraduates. Coed dorms, single-sex dorms, special housing for disabled, apartments, substance-free housing available. $200 partly refundable deposit, deadline 8/15. **Activities:** Bands, choral groups, dance, drama, film society, international student organizations, literary magazine, music ensembles, musical theater, radio station, student government, student newspaper, TV station, Baptist student union, Circle K, Young Democrats, Support for Older and Returning Students, Order of Athena, Young Republicans, UNITE, Newman Club, Muslim student association.

**Athletics.** NCAA. **Intercollegiate:** Baseball M, basketball, cross-country, football (tackle) M, golf, soccer W, softball W, tennis, track and field W, volleyball W. **Intramural:** Basketball, football (non-tackle), softball, volleyball. **Team name:** Colonels.

**Student services.** Adult student services, alcohol/substance abuse counseling, campus ministries, career counseling, services for economically disadvantaged, student employment services, financial aid counseling, health services, legal services, minority student services, personal counseling, placement for graduates, veterans' counselor, women's services. **Physically disabled:** Services for visually, speech, hearing impaired. **Learning disabled:** Comprehensive services available.

**Contact.** E-mail: nicholls@nicholls.edu
Phone: (985) 448-4507 Toll-free number: (877) 642-4655
Fax: (985) 448-4929
Becky Durocher, Director of Admissions, Nicholls State University, PO Box 2004-NSU, Thibodaux, LA 70310

---

## Northwestern State University

| Natchitoches, Louisiana | CB member |
| www.nsula.edu | CB code: 6492 |

- Public 4-year university
- Commuter campus in large town
- 7,677 degree-seeking undergraduates: 27% part-time, 68% women, 29% African American, 1% Asian American, 2% Hispanic American, 2% Native American, 1% international
- 865 degree-seeking graduate students
- 82% of applicants admitted
- SAT or ACT (ACT writing optional) required
- 40% graduate within 6 years

**General.** Founded in 1884. Regionally accredited. Additional campuses in Shreveport, Leesville, and Alexandria as well as off-campus sites. **Degrees:** 1,052 bachelor's, 373 associate awarded; master's offered. **ROTC:** Army, Air Force. **Location:** 75 miles from Shreveport, 57 miles from Alexandria. **Calendar:** Semester, extensive summer session. **Full-time faculty:** 320 total; 59% have terminal degrees, 8% minority, 52% women. **Part-time faculty:** 289 total; 25% have terminal degrees, 11% minority, 57% women. **Class size:** 47% < 20, 36% 20-39, 8% 40-49, 9% 50-99, less than 1% >100. **Special facilities:** Regional folklife center, Creole heritage center, Southern studies institute, heritage resources laboratory, national center for preservation technology and training.

**Freshman class profile.** 2,872 applied, 2,366 admitted, 1,339 enrolled.

| Mid 50% test scores | | Rank in top quarter: | 36% |
|---|---|---|---|
| SAT critical reading: | 440-560 | Rank in top tenth: | 12% |
| SAT math: | 430-550 | End year in good standing: | 88% |
| ACT composite: | 18-23 | Return as sophomores: | 66% |
| GPA 3.50 or higher: | 27% | Out-of-state: | 8% |
| GPA 3.0-3.49: | 34% | Live on campus: | 56% |
| GPA 2.0-2.99: | 38% | | |

**Basis for selection.** Applicants must have completed the 17.5 unit college preparatory program, need no more than one developmental class, and must have one of the following: 20 on ACT (or SAT equivalent), 2.0 high school GPA, or be in top 50% of graduating class. Out-of-state and homeschooled students admitted based on ACT/SAT scores. Students 21 and older and Louisiana Scholars' College have own admission criteria. Exceptions on case-by-case basis. Students 25 or older are not required to have an ACT/SAT score. The COMPASS test can be used for admission/placement for some students.

**High school preparation.** 17.5 units required. Required units include English 4, mathematics 3, social studies 1, history 2, science 3 (laboratory 3), foreign language 2, computer science .5 and visual/performing arts 1. Additional unit of math or science.

**2007-2008 Annual costs.** Tuition/fees: $3,528; $9,606 out-of-state. Room/board: $5,850.

**2006-2007 Financial aid.** **Need-based:** 1,082 full-time freshmen applied for aid; 939 were judged to have need; 914 of these received aid.

Average need met was 50%. Average scholarship/grant was $3,657; average loan $3,970. 44% of total undergraduate aid awarded as scholarships/grants, 56% as loans/jobs. **Non-need-based:** Awarded to 2,730 full-time undergraduates, including 686 freshmen. Scholarships awarded for academics, alumni affiliation, art, athletics, job skills, leadership, minority status, music/drama, religious affiliation, ROTC, state residency.

**Application procedures. Admission:** Closing date 7/6 (receipt date). $20 fee. Application may be submitted online. Admission notification on a rolling basis. Applications may be submitted after fall deadline but consideration is not guaranteed. **Financial aid:** Priority date 5/1; no closing date. FAFSA, institutional form required. Applicants notified on a rolling basis starting 5/1; must reply within 4 week(s) of notification.

**Academics. Special study options:** Cooperative education, distance learning, double major, dual enrollment of high school students, honors, independent study, internships, study abroad, teacher certification program. **Credit/placement by examination:** AP, CLEP, SAT, ACT, institutional tests. 30 credit hours maximum toward associate degree, 62 toward bachelor's. Maximum semester hours of credit by examination may not exceed half the number of credits required for degree. **Support services:** Learning center, preadmission summer program, reduced course load, remedial instruction, study skills assistance, tutoring, writing center.

**Honors college/program.** Student must have ACT 25 or above, or SAT 1130 (exclusive of Writing) or above; must score 20 or higher on each of their subscores on ACT or 480 or higher on SAT verbal and SAT math; and must have 3.0 high school GPA in the Louisiana core curriculum or 3.0 college GPA.

**Majors. Biology:** General. **Business:** Accounting, business admin, hospitality admin. **Communications:** Journalism. **Computer sciences:** Information systems. **Education:** Biology, business, chemistry, early childhood, elementary, English, family/consumer sciences, mathematics, middle, music, physical, physics, social studies, speech. **Engineering technology:** Electrical, industrial. **English:** English lit. **Family/consumer sciences:** General. **Health:** Nursing (RN), radiologic technology/medical imaging, substance abuse counseling. **History:** General. **Interdisciplinary:** Cultural resource management. **Liberal arts:** Arts/sciences. **Math:** General. **Parks/recreation:** Health/fitness. **Physical sciences:** Chemistry, physics. **Protective services:** Criminal justice. **Psychology:** General. **Public administration:** Social work. **Social sciences:** Anthropology, political science, sociology. **Visual/performing arts:** Dramatic, music performance, studio arts.

**Most popular majors.** Biology 6%, business/marketing 14%, education 8%, health sciences 19%, liberal arts 12%, psychology 11%.

**Computing on campus.** Dormitories linked to campus network. Commuter students can connect to campus network. Online course registration, online library, helpline, student web hosting, wireless network available.

**Student life. Freshman orientation:** Available, $80 fee. Preregistration for classes offered. One- to 2-day program held 6 times during the summer; includes program for parents. **Housing:** Coed dorms, special housing for disabled, apartments, fraternity/sorority housing, substance-free housing available. $75 nonrefundable deposit, deadline 3/1. Theme housing and privately-owned housing available on campus. **Activities:** Bands, campus ministries, choral groups, dance, drama, international student organizations, literary magazine, music ensembles, musical theater, opera, radio station, student government, student newspaper, symphony orchestra, TV station, Catholic Student Organization, Fellowship of Christian Athletes, The Foundation (a Wesley Westminster Ministry), Latter-day Saints Institute, Blue Key Honor Society, Purple Jackets, College Republicans, College Democrats, African-American caucus.

**Athletics.** NCAA. **Intercollegiate:** Baseball M, basketball, cross-country, football (tackle) M, soccer W, softball W, tennis W, track and field, volleyball W. **Intramural:** Badminton, baseball, basketball, bowling, football (non-tackle), golf, racquetball, soccer, softball, table tennis, tennis, volleyball. **Team name:** Demons.

**Student services.** Adult student services, alcohol/substance abuse counseling, campus ministries, career counseling, services for economically disadvantaged, student employment services, financial aid counseling, health services, minority student services, personal counseling, placement for graduates, veterans' counselor. **Physically disabled:** Services for visually, speech, hearing impaired. **Learning disabled:** Comprehensive services available.

**Contact.** E-mail: admissions@nsula.edu
Phone: (318) 357-4078 Toll-free number: (800) 767-8115
Fax: (318) 357-4660
Andrea Maley, Director of Admissions, Northwestern State University, Roy Hall, Room 209, Natchitoches, LA 71497

## Our Lady of Holy Cross College
New Orleans, Louisiana
www.olhcc.edu                    CB code: 6002

- Private 4-year liberal arts college affiliated with Roman Catholic Church
- Commuter campus in very large city

**General.** Founded in 1916. Regionally accredited. **Location:** 3 miles from downtown. **Calendar:** Semester.

**Annual costs/financial aid.** Tuition/fees (2007-2008): $9,200. Books/supplies: $700. Personal expenses: $1,264. Need-based financial aid available to full-time and part-time students.

**Contact.** Phone: (504) 394-7744 ext. 175
Vice President for Enrollment Services, 4123 Woodland Drive, New Orleans, LA 70131-7399

## Our Lady of the Lake College
Baton Rouge, Louisiana
www.ololcollege.edu              CB code: 3928

- Private 4-year health science and nursing college affiliated with Roman Catholic Church
- Commuter campus in large city
- 1,936 degree-seeking undergraduates: 67% part-time, 83% women, 23% African American, 3% Asian American, 2% Hispanic American, 1% Native American
- 150 degree-seeking graduate students
- 78% of applicants admitted
- ACT (writing optional) required

**General.** Regionally accredited. **Degrees:** 93 bachelor's, 223 associate awarded; master's offered. **ROTC:** Air Force. **Calendar:** Semester, extensive summer session. **Full-time faculty:** 63 total. **Part-time faculty:** 60 total. **Class size:** 57% < 20, 38% 20-39, 2% 40-49, 2% 50-99.

**Freshman class profile.** 299 applied, 233 admitted, 138 enrolled.

| Mid 50% test scores | | GPA 3.0-3.49: | 50% |
|---|---|---|---|
| ACT composite: | 19-22 | GPA 2.0-2.99: | 30% |
| GPA 3.50 or higher: | 20% | | |

**Basis for selection.** High school record and test scores important. **Homeschooled:** State high school equivalency certificate required.

**High school preparation.** Required and recommended units include English 4, mathematics 3, social studies 3, science 3 (laboratory 3), foreign language 2 and academic electives 2.

**2008-2009 Annual costs.** Tuition/fees: $9,217. Books/supplies: $1,500. Personal expenses: $1,710.

**2006-2007 Financial aid. Need-based:** 2 full-time freshmen applied for aid; 2 were judged to have need; 2 of these received aid. Average loan was $2,625. 39% of total undergraduate aid awarded as scholarships/grants, 61% as loans/jobs.

**Application procedures. Admission:** Priority date 2/1; deadline 7/1 (receipt date). $35 fee. Application may be submitted online. Admission notification on a rolling basis. **Financial aid:** Closing date 3/1. FAFSA, institutional form required.

**Academics. Special study options:** Accelerated study, combined bachelor's/graduate degree, cross-registration, distance learning, liberal arts/career combination. **Credit/placement by examination:** CLEP, ACT, institutional tests. 15 credit hours maximum toward associate degree, 30 toward bachelor's. **Support services:** Learning center, reduced course load, study skills assistance, tutoring.

**Majors. Biology:** General, biomedical sciences. **Health:** Clinical lab science, facilities admin, health care admin, health services, health services admin, nursing (RN), premedicine. **Liberal arts:** Humanities. **Psychology:** General.

**Most popular majors.** Health sciences 98%.

**Computing on campus.** 150 workstations in library. Commuter students can connect to campus network. Online library, helpline, wireless network available.

**Student life. Freshman orientation:** Mandatory. Preregistration for classes offered. One-day program held the week before classes begin. **Policies:** Smoke-free campus. **Activities:** Student government, student newspaper, American College of Healthcare Executives, Beta Epsilon Fraternity of Radiologic Technology Students, Beta Sigma Mu (Human Medicine), Christian student fellowship, clinical laboratory scientist association, cultural arts association, Epsilon Mu Theta, mathematics and science association, Phi Theta Alpha.

**Student services.** Adult student services, campus ministries, career counseling, financial aid counseling.

**Contact.** E-mail: admission@ololcollege.edu
Phone: (225) 768-1700 Toll-free number: (877) 242-3509
Fax: (225) 768-1726
Rebecca Cannon, Director of Admissions, Our Lady of the Lake College, 7434 Perkins Road, Baton Rouge, LA 70808

## St. Joseph Seminary College
St. Benedict, Louisiana
www.sjasc.edu                    CB code: 6689

- Private 4-year liberal arts and seminary college for men affiliated with Roman Catholic Church
- Residential campus in rural community
- 77 degree-seeking undergraduates: 4% African American, 6% Asian American, 14% Hispanic American, 1% Native American
- 100% of applicants admitted
- ACT (writing optional) required

**General.** Founded in 1891. Regionally accredited. Non-seminarian, non-degree-seeking students may attend part-time. **Degrees:** 15 bachelor's awarded. **Location:** 40 miles from New Orleans. **Calendar:** Semester. **Full-time faculty:** 15 total. **Part-time faculty:** 20 total. **Class size:** 88% < 20, 12% 20-39. **Special facilities:** 1,200 acres of forest, Romanesque abbey church.

**Freshman class profile.** 8 applied, 8 admitted, 8 enrolled.

| End year in good standing: | 8% | Out-of-state: | 10% |
|---|---|---|---|
| Return as sophomores: | 15% | Live on campus: | 100% |

**Basis for selection.** Recommendation by diocesan bishop, academic standing, and test scores required. Michigan test used for placement and proficiency. Interview recommended.

**High school preparation.** 17 units recommended. Recommended units include English 4, mathematics 3, social studies 1, history 1, science 2, foreign language 2 and academic electives 7. Second foreign language recommended.

**2007-2008 Annual costs.** Tuition/fees: $12,215. Room/board: $10,000. Books/supplies: $1,000. Personal expenses: $1,387.

**Financial aid. Non-need-based:** Scholarships awarded for academics, leadership.

**Application procedures. Admission:** No deadline. No application fee. Admission notification on a rolling basis. **Financial aid:** Priority date 3/15; no closing date. FAFSA required. Applicants notified on a rolling basis starting 7/1; must reply within 4 week(s) of notification.

**Academics. Special study options:** ESL. **Credit/placement by examination:** AP, CLEP, IB. 24 credit hours maximum toward bachelor's degree. **Support services:** Reduced course load, remedial instruction, tutoring.

**Majors. Liberal arts:** Arts/sciences.

**Computing on campus.** 14 workstations in library, computer center. Repair service available.

**Student life. Freshman orientation:** Mandatory. Preregistration for classes offered. **Housing:** Guaranteed on-campus for all undergraduates. All students live on campus. **Activities:** Choral groups, drama, music ensembles, musical theater, student government, community, religious, social service activities.

**Athletics. Intramural:** Baseball M, basketball M, handball M, racquetball M, soccer M, softball M, squash M, swimming M, table tennis M, tennis M, volleyball M. **Team name:** Ravens.

**Student services.** Career counseling, health services, personal counseling, veterans' counselor.

**Contact.** E-mail: acdean@sjasc.edu
Phone: (985) 867-2248 ext. 2248 Fax: (985) 867-2270
George Binder, Registrar, St. Joseph Seminary College, 75376 River Road, St. Benedict, LA 70457-9990

## School of Urban Missions: New Orleans
### New Orleans, Louisiana
### www.sum.edu

- Private 4-year Bible college affiliated with Assemblies of God, Church of God in Christ
- Commuter campus in very large city
- 20 degree-seeking undergraduates: 100% part-time, 50% women
- 62% of applicants admitted
- Application essay, interview required
- 68% graduate within 6 years; 10% enter graduate study

**General.** Accredited by ABHE. Additional campus in Oakland, California. **Degrees:** 1 associate awarded. **Location:** 2 miles from New Orleans. **Calendar:** Trimester, limited summer session. **Full-time faculty:** 1 total; 100% have terminal degrees. **Part-time faculty:** 4 total; 25% minority, 25% women. **Class size:** 100% < 20.

**Freshman class profile.** 8 applied, 5 admitted, 5 enrolled.

| End year in good standing: | 70% | Return as sophomores: | 70% |
|---|---|---|---|

**Basis for selection.** Phone interview and personal written testimony of call to ministry and salvation required. SAT or ACT recommended. **Homeschooled:** State high school equivalency certificate required.

**2008-2009 Annual costs.** Tuition/fees (projected): $7,105. Room only: $2,400. Books/supplies: $600. Personal expenses: $4,324.

**2006-2007 Financial aid. Need-based:** 33% of total undergraduate aid awarded as scholarships/grants, 67% as loans/jobs. **Non-need-based:** Scholarships awarded for academics, leadership, religious affiliation.

**Application procedures. Admission:** Closing date 7/31 (postmark date). $20 fee. Application may be submitted online. Admission notification 8/15. Admission notification on a rolling basis beginning on or about 1/1. **Financial aid:** No deadline. FAFSA, institutional form required.

**Academics.** Each trimester students do 80 hours of ministry. **Special study options:** Accelerated study, distance learning, internships. Cohort system at various locations for non-traditional students. **Credit/placement by examination:** AP, CLEP, SAT, ACT. **Support services:** Remedial instruction, tutoring.

**Majors. Theology:** Missionary. **Other:** Church planting.

**Computing on campus.** 20 workstations in library, computer center. Dormitories wired for high-speed internet access and linked to campus network. Online library, wireless network available.

**Student life. Freshman orientation:** Mandatory. Preregistration for classes offered. **Policies:** Morning devotions and chapel attendance required; full-time students required to participate in practicum ministries. Religious observance required. **Housing:** Guaranteed on-campus for all undergraduates. Single-sex dorms, substance-free housing available. $100 nonrefundable deposit, deadline 8/1. **Activities:** Student government, Assemblies of God, Church of God in Christ, Full Gospel Baptist.

**Student services.** Adult student services, campus ministries, career counseling, financial aid counseling, health services, personal counseling, placement for graduates, veterans' counselor.

**Contact.** E-mail: sum@sum.edu
Phone: (504) 362-6364 Toll-free number: (800) 385-6364
Fax: (504) 362-4895
Dave Wallace, Admissions Director, School of Urban Missions: New Orleans, 511 Westbank Expressway, Gretna, LA 70053-3677

## Southeastern Louisiana University
### Hammond, Louisiana
### www.selu.edu                                     CB code: 6656

- Public 4-year university
- Commuter campus in large town
- 12,796 degree-seeking undergraduates: 18% African American, 1% Asian American, 2% Hispanic American, 1% international
- 1,504 graduate students

- 88% of applicants admitted
- SAT or ACT (ACT writing optional) required
- 29% graduate within 6 years

**General.** Founded in 1925. Regionally accredited. **Degrees:** 1,740 bachelor's, 77 associate awarded; master's, doctoral offered. **ROTC:** Army. **Location:** 55 miles from New Orleans, 40 miles from Baton Rouge. **Calendar:** Semester, extensive summer session. **Full-time faculty:** 525 total; 59% have terminal degrees, 12% minority, 56% women. **Part-time faculty:** 156 total; 30% have terminal degrees, 12% minority, 58% women. **Class size:** 32% < 20, 54% 20-39, 6% 40-49, 7% 50-99, 1% >100. **Special facilities:** Environmental research station, social science research center, maritime museum, contemporary art gallery, performing arts theatre.

**Freshman class profile.** 3,603 applied, 3,173 admitted, 1,573 enrolled.

| Mid 50% test scores | | Rank in top tenth: | 9% |
|---|---|---|---|
| ACT composite: | 18-22 | End year in good standing: | 63% |
| GPA 3.50 or higher: | 21% | Return as sophomores: | 62% |
| GPA 3.0-3.49: | 31% | Out-of-state: | 2% |
| GPA 2.0-2.99: | 47% | Live on campus: | 43% |
| Rank in top quarter: | 27% | | |

**Basis for selection.** In-state students must meet the following criteria: completion of Regents high school core curriculum; ACT score of at least 20, or high school rank in upper 50% of graduating class, or high school GPA of 2.0; have no more than 1 developmental course requirement. Out-of-state students must have no more than 1 developmental course requirement and meet same criteria as in-state students or meet all of following criteria: ACT composite of at least 20, high school rank in upper 50% of class, high school GPA of 2.0; or ACT of at least 23. Audition recommended for music majors. **Homeschooled:** Must have GED and minimum of 23 on ACT, and have no more than one developmental course requirement. **Learning Disabled:** No special requirements or procedures.

**High school preparation.** 16.5 units required. Required units include English 4, mathematics 3, social studies 3, science 3, foreign language 2, computer science .5 and visual/performing arts 1.

**2007-2008 Annual costs.** Tuition/fees: $3,561; $9,561 out-of-state. Room/board: $5,990.

**2006-2007 Financial aid. Need-based:** 2,215 full-time freshmen applied for aid; 1,434 were judged to have need; 1,350 of these received aid. Average scholarship/grant was $4,028; average loan $2,715. 42% of total undergraduate aid awarded as scholarships/grants, 58% as loans/jobs. **Non-need-based:** Awarded to 3,175 full-time undergraduates, including 1,026 freshmen. Scholarships awarded for academics, alumni affiliation, art, athletics, job skills, leadership, music/drama, state residency.

**Application procedures. Admission:** Closing date 8/1 (postmark date). $20 fee. Application may be submitted online. Admission notification on a rolling basis beginning on or about 9/1. **Financial aid:** Priority date 5/1; no closing date. FAFSA, institutional form required. Applicants notified on a rolling basis starting 3/1; must reply within 2 week(s) of notification.

**Academics. Special study options:** Accelerated study, cross-registration, distance learning, double major, ESL, honors, independent study, internships, liberal arts/career combination, study abroad, teacher certification program. **Credit/placement by examination:** AP, CLEP, SAT, ACT, institutional tests. 30 credit hours maximum toward bachelor's degree. Maximum of 60 hours through all types of nontraditional educational experiences, i.e., advanced placement credit, correspondence courses, and military service credits. **Support services:** Learning center, remedial instruction, study skills assistance, tutoring, writing center.

**Majors. Agriculture:** Horticultural science. **Biology:** General. **Business:** Accounting, business admin, finance, marketing. **Communications:** General. **Computer sciences:** Computer science. **Education:** Art, computer, early childhood, elementary, English, family/consumer sciences, French, mathematics, middle, music, physical, science, social studies, Spanish, special, speech. **Engineering technology:** Industrial, occupational safety. **English:** English lit. **Family/consumer sciences:** General. **Foreign languages:** French, Spanish. **Health:** Athletic training, audiology/speech pathology, nursing (RN), public health ed. **History:** General. **Liberal arts:** Arts/sciences. **Math:** General. **Physical sciences:** Chemistry, physics. **Protective services:** Criminal justice. **Psychology:** General. **Public administration:** Social work. **Social sciences:** Political science, sociology. **Visual/performing arts:** Art, arts management, music performance.

**Most popular majors.** Business/marketing 31%, education 11%, health sciences 11%, liberal arts 14%.

**Computing on campus.** 879 workstations in library, computer center, student center. Dormitories wired for high-speed internet access and linked to campus network. Commuter students can connect to campus network.

Online course registration, online library, helpline, repair service, student web hosting, wireless network available.

**Student life. Freshman orientation:** Mandatory, $75 fee. Preregistration for classes offered. Students may take orientation either during summer or at beginning of first semester. Must pay room and board for summer session. **Policies:** Freshmen and sophomores must live on campus. **Housing:** Coed dorms, single-sex dorms, apartments, fraternity/sorority housing, substance-free housing available. $150 nonrefundable deposit, deadline 6/15. **Activities:** Bands, campus ministries, choral groups, dance, drama, film society, literary magazine, music ensembles, musical theater, opera, radio station, student government, student newspaper, symphony orchestra, TV station, Gospel Choir, Baptist Collegiate Ministries, student government association, international student organization, press club, Wesley Foundation, campus activities board, Black Student Union, campus outreach, resident halls association.

**Athletics.** NCAA. **Intercollegiate:** Baseball M, basketball, cheerleading, cross-country, football (tackle) M, golf M, soccer W, softball W, tennis, track and field, volleyball W. **Intramural:** Basketball, football (non-tackle), racquetball, soccer, softball, volleyball, weight lifting. **Team name:** Lions, Lady Lions.

**Student services.** Adult student services, alcohol/substance abuse counseling, career counseling, services for economically disadvantaged, student employment services, financial aid counseling, health services, minority student services, personal counseling, placement for graduates, veterans' counselor. **Physically disabled:** Services for visually, speech, hearing impaired.

**Contact.** E-mail: admissions@selu.edu
Phone: (985) 549-2066 Toll-free number: (800) 222-7358
Fax: (985) 549-5632
Director of Admissions, Southeastern Louisiana University, SLU 10752, Hammond, LA 70402

---

## Southern University and Agricultural and Mechanical College
**Baton Rouge, Louisiana**
www.subr.edu                    CB code: 6663

- Public 4-year university
- Commuter campus in large city
- 6,830 degree-seeking undergraduates: 11% part-time, 61% women, 95% African American, 2% international
- 1,155 degree-seeking graduate students
- 59% of applicants admitted
- SAT or ACT (ACT writing optional) required
- 30% graduate within 6 years; 16% enter graduate study

**General.** Founded in 1880. Regionally accredited. **Degrees:** 829 bachelor's, 2 associate awarded; master's, doctoral offered. **ROTC:** Army, Naval, Air Force. **Location:** 80 miles from New Orleans. **Calendar:** Semester, extensive summer session. **Full-time faculty:** 405 total; 66% have terminal degrees, 85% minority, 47% women. **Part-time faculty:** 141 total; 43% have terminal degrees, 86% minority, 57% women. **Class size:** 40% < 20, 45% 20-39, 9% 40-49, 5% 50-99, 2% >100. **Special facilities:** Experimental (laboratory) farm, outdoor learning resource center (nature trail), meat processing plant, Black heritage museum.

**Freshman class profile.** 2,096 applied, 1,229 admitted, 1,121 enrolled.

| Mid 50% test scores | | Rank in top quarter: | 13% |
|---|---|---|---|
| SAT math: | 380-460 | Rank in top tenth: | 3% |
| ACT composite: | 15-18 | Return as sophomores: | 65% |
| GPA 3.50 or higher: | 8% | Out-of-state: | 22% |
| GPA 3.0-3.49: | 24% | Live on campus: | 81% |
| GPA 2.0-2.99: | 66% | International: | 4% |

**Basis for selection.** ACT score of 20 or better (SAT of 940 or better) or high school GPA of 2.0 or better or rank in top 50% of graduation class and require no more than 1 remedial course by having minimum ACT English and Math subscore of 18 (SAT Verbal score of 450 or Math score of 430) as well as 16.5-unit core class requirements. Auditions required for music program. **Homeschooled:** Must meet requirements and submit satisfactory grades and an ACT composite score of 20 or higher (SAT of 940). The records of these students will be evaluated carefully by the Admissions Committee.

**High school preparation.** 16.5 units required. Required units include English 4, mathematics 3, social studies 2, history 1, science 3 and foreign language 2. .5 computer literacy, 1 fine arts required.

**2007-2008 Annual costs.** Tuition/fees: $3,666; $9,458 out-of-state. Room/board: $6,504. Books/supplies: $1,200. Personal expenses: $1,692.

---

**2006-2007 Financial aid. Need-based:** 1,078 full-time freshmen applied for aid; 1,018 were judged to have need; 1,008 of these received aid. Average need met was 89%. Average scholarship/grant was $3,436; average loan $2,399. 35% of total undergraduate aid awarded as scholarships/grants, 65% as loans/jobs. **Non-need-based:** Awarded to 2,431 full-time undergraduates, including 514 freshmen. Scholarships awarded for academics, athletics, ROTC, state residency.

**Application procedures. Admission:** Closing date 7/1 (postmark date). $20 fee. Application may be submitted online. Admission notification on a rolling basis. **Financial aid:** Priority date 1/31, closing date 3/30. FAFSA required. Applicants notified on a rolling basis starting 5/1; must reply within 3 week(s) of notification.

**Academics. Special study options:** Combined bachelor's/graduate degree, cooperative education, cross-registration, distance learning, double major, dual enrollment of high school students, exchange student, honors, independent study, internships, liberal arts/career combination, study abroad, teacher certification program, weekend college. **Credit/placement by examination:** AP, CLEP, SAT, ACT, institutional tests. 30 credit hours maximum toward bachelor's degree. **Support services:** Learning center, pre-admission summer program, reduced course load, remedial instruction, study skills assistance, tutoring, writing center.

**Honors college/program.** Must have ACT composite score of 23 (SAT score of 1070 or above, exclusive of Writing) and GPA of 3.0.

**Majors. Agriculture:** Animal sciences, economics. **Architecture:** Architecture. **Biology:** General. **Business:** Accounting, business admin, e-commerce, finance, managerial economics, marketing. **Communications:** Media studies. **Computer sciences:** Computer science. **Conservation:** Urban forestry. **Education:** Agricultural, art, biology, chemistry, computer, early childhood, elementary, English, French, mathematics, middle, music, physical, physics, science, secondary, social studies, Spanish, special. **Engineering:** Civil, electrical, mechanical. **Engineering technology:** Electrical. **English:** English lit, speech/rhetoric. **Family/consumer sciences:** General. **Foreign languages:** French, Spanish. **Health:** Audiology/speech pathology, nursing (RN), recreational therapy, vocational rehab counseling. **History:** General. **Math:** General. **Physical sciences:** Chemistry, physics. **Protective services:** Criminal justice. **Psychology:** General. **Public administration:** Social work. **Social sciences:** Political science, sociology. **Visual/performing arts:** Dramatic, music performance, studio arts.

**Most popular majors.** Business/marketing 15%, communications/journalism 6%, education 7%, engineering/engineering technologies 8%, family/consumer sciences 6%, health sciences 15%, psychology 7%, security/protective services 8%, social sciences 6%.

**Computing on campus.** 1,500 workstations in library, computer center. Dormitories wired for high-speed internet access and linked to campus network. Commuter students can connect to campus network. Online course registration, online library, helpline, wireless network available.

**Student life. Freshman orientation:** Mandatory. Preregistration for classes offered. 2-day program during registration. **Housing:** Guaranteed on-campus for freshmen. Single-sex dorms, special housing for disabled, substance-free housing available. $50 fully refundable deposit, deadline 12/30. **Activities:** Bands, campus ministries, choral groups, dance, drama, literary magazine, music ensembles, musical theater, student government, student newspaper, Catholic student club, Committed to Christ student organization, Love Alive Christian Fellowship, Muslim student organization, Nation of Islam student organization, Sigma Omega Delta social service organization, College Democrats, College Republicans, Collegiate 100 Black Men.

**Athletics.** NCAA. **Intercollegiate:** Baseball M, basketball, bowling W, cross-country, football (non-tackle) M, football (tackle) M, golf, soccer W, softball W, tennis, track and field, volleyball W. **Intramural:** Football (non-tackle), golf, swimming, volleyball, weight lifting. **Team name:** Jaguars.

**Student services.** Career counseling, student employment services, financial aid counseling, health services, personal counseling, placement for graduates, veterans' counselor. **Physically disabled:** Services for visually, speech, hearing impaired.

**Contact.** E-mail: admit@subr.edu
Phone: (225) 771-2430 Toll-free number: (800) 256-1531
Fax: (225) 771-2500
Tracie Abraham, Director, Southern University and Agricultural and Mechanical College, T.H. Harris Hall, Baton Rouge, LA 70813

---

## Southern University at New Orleans
**New Orleans, Louisiana**
www.suno.edu                    CB code: 1647

- Public 4-year university
- Commuter campus in large city

- 2,139 degree-seeking undergraduates: 95% African American, 1% Asian American, 1% Hispanic American, 1% international
- 503 graduate students

**General.** Founded in 1959. Regionally accredited. Part of Southern University System. **Degrees:** 287 bachelor's, 10 associate awarded; master's offered. **ROTC:** Army, Naval, Air Force. **Location:** Downtown. **Calendar:** Semester, limited summer session. **Full-time faculty:** 88 total. **Part-time faculty:** 23 total. **Class size:** 49% < 20, 47% 20-39, 3% 40-49, less than 1% 50-99, less than 1% >100.

**Freshman class profile.**

| Out-of-state: | 1% | International: | 3% |
|---|---|---|---|

**Basis for selection.** Open admission. ACT required by state law for placement.

**High school preparation.** 16 units recommended. Recommended units include English 4, mathematics 3, social studies 3, science 3 (laboratory 2) and foreign language 1.

**2007-2008 Annual costs.** Tuition/fees: $3,002; $6,742 out-of-state. Books/supplies: $1,000. Personal expenses: $6,000.

**Financial aid.** All financial aid based on need.

**Application procedures. Admission:** Closing date 7/1. $5 fee ($15 out-of-state). Application may be submitted online. Admission notification on a rolling basis. **Financial aid:** Closing date 4/1. FAFSA required. Applicants notified by 5/15; must reply within 1 week(s) of notification.

**Academics. Special study options:** Combined bachelor's/graduate degree, cooperative education, cross-registration, distance learning, double major, dual enrollment of high school students, internships, teacher certification program, weekend college. **Credit/placement by examination:** CLEP. 30 credit hours maximum toward bachelor's degree. **Support services:** Reduced course load, remedial instruction, study skills assistance, tutoring, writing center.

**Majors. Biology:** General. **Business:** Entrepreneurial studies, management information systems. **Education:** Early childhood, elementary. **English:** English lit. **Family/consumer sciences:** Family studies. **Health:** Medical records admin, substance abuse counseling. **Physical sciences:** Physics. **Protective services:** Criminal justice. **Psychology:** General. **Public administration:** General, social work. **Social sciences:** Sociology.

**Most popular majors.** Biology 6%, business/marketing 18%, computer/information sciences 9%, liberal arts 15%, psychology 13%, public administration/social services 9%, security/protective services 13%.

**Computing on campus.** 60 workstations in library, computer center. Online library, helpline, wireless network available.

**Student life. Freshman orientation:** Available. Preregistration for classes offered. **Housing:** Substance-free housing available. **Activities:** Student government.

**Athletics.** NAIA. **Intercollegiate:** Basketball, cross-country. **Team name:** Knights.

**Student services.** Campus ministries, career counseling, student employment services, financial aid counseling, health services, personal counseling, placement for graduates. **Physically disabled:** Services for visually, speech, hearing impaired.

**Contact.** Phone: (504) 286-5000 ext. 5314 Fax: (504) 284-5481 Rene Gill Pratt, Director of Recruitment, Admissions, & Retention, Southern University at New Orleans, 6801 Press Drive, New Orleans, LA 70126

---

## Southwest University
Kenner, Louisiana
www.southwest.edu

- For-profit 4-year virtual university
- Very large city
- 490 degree-seeking undergraduates

**General.** Accredited by DETC. **Degrees:** 32 bachelor's awarded; master's offered. **Calendar:** Continuous. **Full-time faculty:** 6 total. **Part-time faculty:** 40 total.

**Basis for selection.** Open admission.

**2007-2008 Annual costs.** Tuition/fees: $5,150. Graduate tuition $250 per credit hour.

**Application procedures. Admission:** No deadline. $50 fee. Application may be submitted online. Admission notification on a rolling basis.

**Academics. Special study options:** Accelerated study, distance learning, double major, liberal arts/career combination. **Credit/placement by examination:** CLEP.

**Majors. Protective services:** Law enforcement admin.

**Computing on campus.** Online library available.

**Student services.** Adult student services, veterans' counselor.

**Contact.** E-mail: admissions@southwest.edu
Phone: (800) 433-5923 Fax: (504) 468-3213
Lydia Ocmand, Director of Admissions, Southwest University, 2200 Veterans Boulevard, Kenner, LA 70062

---

## Tulane University
New Orleans, Louisiana
www.tulane.edu
CB member
CB code: 6832

- Private 4-year university
- Residential campus in very large city
- 6,408 degree-seeking undergraduates: 21% part-time, 54% women
- 4,070 graduate students
- 44% of applicants admitted
- SAT or ACT with writing, application essay required

**General.** Founded in 1834. Regionally accredited. **Degrees:** 2,020 bachelor's, 37 associate awarded; master's, doctoral, first professional offered. **ROTC:** Army, Naval, Air Force. **Location:** 4 miles from downtown. **Calendar:** Semester, limited summer session. **Full-time faculty:** 835 total; 90% have terminal degrees, 20% minority, 33% women. **Part-time faculty:** 545 total; 44% have terminal degrees, 13% minority, 41% women. **Special facilities:** Jazz archive, Louisiana collection of historical materials, Southeastern architecture archive, center for research on women, political economy institute, center for Latin American studies, middle American research institute, center for bioenvironmental research, performing arts center, Amistad research center.

**Freshman class profile.** 16,967 applied, 7,526 admitted, 1,328 enrolled.

| Mid 50% test scores | | | |
|---|---|---|---|
| SAT critical reading: | 600-690 | GPA 3.0-3.49: | 40% |
| SAT math: | 590-680 | GPA 2.0-2.99: | 16% |
| SAT writing: | 600-690 | Rank in top quarter: | 80% |
| ACT composite: | 27-31 | Rank in top tenth: | 50% |
| GPA 3.50 or higher: | 44% | Out-of-state: | 80% |
| | | Live on campus: | 96% |

**Basis for selection.** High school achievement record most important, followed by test scores, recommendation, personal qualities; special consideration for children of alumni and minority applicants. Candidates should be in top third of graduating class with at least 3.5 GPA. Audition recommended for music majors. Portfolio recommended for architecture, art majors. **Homeschooled:** State high school equivalency certificate, letter of recommendation (nonparent) required. SAT Subject Tests required.

**High school preparation.** Recommended units include English 4, mathematics 4, social studies 3, science 4 (laboratory 4), foreign language 3 and academic electives 3. Chemistry and physics recommended for science or engineering majors.

**2007-2008 Annual costs.** Tuition/fees: $36,610. Room/board: $8,649. Books/supplies: $900. Personal expenses: $930.

**2006-2007 Financial aid. Need-based:** 593 full-time freshmen applied for aid; 437 were judged to have need; 437 of these received aid. Average need met was 95%. Average scholarship/grant was $22,761; average loan $4,027. 76% of total undergraduate aid awarded as scholarships/grants, 24% as loans/jobs. **Non-need-based:** Awarded to 2,384 full-time undergraduates, including 456 freshmen. Scholarships awarded for academics, athletics, leadership, state residency. **Additional information:** Application deadline for merit scholarships December 1.

**Application procedures. Admission:** Priority date 11/1; deadline 1/15 (postmark date). No application fee. Application may be submitted online. Admission notification 4/1. Admission notification on a rolling basis. Must reply by May 1 or within 2 week(s) if notified thereafter. **Financial aid:**

Priority date 1/15, closing date 2/1. FAFSA, CSS PROFILE required. Applicants notified on a rolling basis starting 2/1; must reply by 5/1 or within 2 week(s) of notification.

**Academics. Special study options:** Accelerated study, combined bachelor's/graduate degree, cross-registration, distance learning, double major, ESL, exchange student, honors, independent study, internships, liberal arts/career combination, student-designed major, study abroad, teacher certification program, Washington semester. **Credit/placement by examination:** AP, CLEP, IB, institutional tests. **Support services:** Learning center, study skills assistance, tutoring, writing center.

**Majors. Architecture:** Architecture. **Area/ethnic studies:** African, American, Asian, German, Latin American, Russian/Slavic, women's. **Biology:** General, biochemistry, cell/histology, ecology, evolutionary, molecular. **Business:** General, accounting, business admin, finance, management information systems, marketing. **Communications:** Media studies. **Conservation:** Environmental science, environmental studies. **Engineering:** Biomedical, chemical. **English:** English lit. **Foreign languages:** Classics, French, German, Italian, linguistics, modern Greek, Portuguese, Russian, Spanish. **History:** General. **Interdisciplinary:** Medieval/Renaissance, neuroscience. **Legal studies:** General. **Math:** General. **Philosophy/religion:** Judaic, philosophy. **Physical sciences:** Chemistry, geology, physics. **Psychology:** General. **Social sciences:** Anthropology, economics, international economics, political science, sociology, urban studies. **Visual/performing arts:** Art, art history/conservation, dance, dramatic, multimedia, music performance, music theory/composition, musical theater, studio arts, theater history. **Other:** Earth sciences, Legal studies in business, Mathematical economics, Urban studies.

**Most popular majors.** Biology 6%, business/marketing 25%, engineering/engineering technologies 6%, health sciences 6%, history 6%, liberal arts 11%, psychology 7%.

**Computing on campus.** Dormitories wired for high-speed internet access and linked to campus network. Commuter students can connect to campus network. Online course registration, online library, helpline, repair service, student web hosting, wireless network available.

**Student life. Freshman orientation:** Mandatory, $400 fee. Preregistration for classes offered. **Policies:** Alcohol policy. **Housing:** Guaranteed on-campus for freshmen. Coed dorms, single-sex dorms, special housing for disabled, apartments, substance-free housing available. $150 nonrefundable deposit, deadline 5/1. Honors program residence hall, language floors, women in science, healthy lifestyle, engineering and technology, performing and creative arts, pre-med and pre-law special living floors, quiet-study floors, and international living floors available. **Activities:** Bands, choral groups, dance, drama, film society, literary magazine, music ensembles, musical theater, radio station, student government, student newspaper, symphony orchestra, TV station, Hillel, Episcopal Center, Inter-Varsity Christian Fellowship, Catholic Center, Baptist Student Union, African-American Congress, Latin American students association, Amnesty International.

**Athletics.** NCAA. **Intercollegiate:** Baseball M, basketball, cross-country, diving W, field hockey, football (tackle) M, golf, soccer W, swimming W, tennis, track and field, volleyball W. **Intramural:** Badminton, basketball, bowling, cross-country M, football (tackle) M, golf, handball M, racquetball, soccer, softball, swimming, table tennis M, tennis, track and field M, volleyball, wrestling M. **Team name:** Green Wave.

**Student services.** Alcohol/substance abuse counseling, campus ministries, career counseling, student employment services, financial aid counseling, health services, legal services, minority student services, personal counseling, women's services. **Physically disabled:** Services for visually, speech, hearing impaired.

**Contact.** E-mail: undergrad.admission@tulane.edu
Phone: (504) 865-5731 Toll-free number: (800) 873-9283
Fax: (504) 862-8715
Earl Retif, Vice President for Enrollment Management and University Registrar, Tulane University, 6823 St. Charles Avenue, New Orleans, LA 70118-5680

---

## University of Louisiana at Lafayette
**Lafayette, Louisiana**
www.louisiana.edu

**CB member**
**CB code: 6672**

- Public 4-year university
- Commuter campus in small city
- 14,449 degree-seeking undergraduates: 13% part-time, 57% women, 19% African American, 2% Asian American, 2% Hispanic American, 2% international
- 1,284 degree-seeking graduate students
- 70% of applicants admitted

- SAT or ACT (ACT writing optional) required
- 41% graduate within 6 years

**General.** Founded in 1898. Regionally accredited. **Degrees:** 2,047 bachelor's awarded; master's, doctoral offered. **ROTC:** Army. **Location:** 130 miles from New Orleans, 200 miles from Houston. **Calendar:** Semester, extensive summer session. **Full-time faculty:** 577 total; 74% have terminal degrees, 14% minority, 42% women. **Part-time faculty:** 166 total; 23% have terminal degrees, 8% minority, 51% women. **Class size:** 29% < 20, 49% 20-39, 13% 40-49, 6% 50-99, 3% >100. **Special facilities:** 2 nuclear accelerators, 2 electron microscopes, CAD/CAM laboratory, Acadiana folklore archives, confocal microscope, atomic force microscope, Louisiana Emersive Technology Center, on campus restaurant and hotel (which include instructional facilities), nursery school laboratory, 600-acre sustainable farm, television production studio, marine research facility.

**Freshman class profile.** 7,203 applied, 5,059 admitted, 2,763 enrolled.

| Mid 50% test scores | | End year in good standing: | 77% |
|---|---|---|---|
| ACT composite: | 20-24 | Return as sophomores: | 75% |
| GPA 3.50 or higher: | 29% | Out-of-state: | 3% |
| GPA 3.0-3.49: | 36% | Live on campus: | 26% |
| GPA 2.0-2.99: | 35% | International: | 1% |
| Rank in top quarter: | 39% | Sororities: | 6% |
| Rank in top tenth: | 14% | | |

**Basis for selection.** 2.0 high school GPA, state's Board of Regents core courses, and 18 ACT in English or math required; and either 23 ACT, 2.5 high school GPA, or rank in top 25% of graduating class. Audition required of music majors. Portfolio required of art, architecture majors. Essays required for some applicants.

**High school preparation.** Required units include English 4, mathematics 4, social studies 2, history 1, science 3, academic electives 4.5. Suggested electives: .5 unit computer science, 1 unit fine arts, 1 unit speech.

**2007-2008 Annual costs.** Tuition/fees: $3,430; $9,612 out-of-state. Room/board: $3,820. Books/supplies: $1,000. Personal expenses: $1,631.

**Financial aid.** All financial aid based on need.

**Application procedures. Admission:** Priority date 7/15; no deadline. $25 fee. Application may be submitted online. Admission notification on a rolling basis. **Financial aid:** Priority date 5/1; no closing date. FAFSA, institutional form required. Applicants notified on a rolling basis starting 4/1; must reply within 2 week(s) of notification.

**Academics. Special study options:** Accelerated study, cooperative education, cross-registration, distance learning, double major, dual enrollment of high school students, ESL, exchange student, honors, independent study, internships, student-designed major, study abroad, teacher certification program, Washington semester. **Credit/placement by examination:** AP, CLEP, SAT, ACT, institutional tests. 30 credit hours maximum toward bachelor's degree. **Support services:** Learning center, reduced course load, remedial instruction, study skills assistance, tutoring, writing center.

**Majors. Agriculture:** General. **Architecture:** Architecture, interior. **Biology:** General, conservation, microbiology. **Business:** Accounting, business admin, fashion, finance, hospitality admin, insurance, management information systems, managerial economics, marketing. **Communications:** General, media studies, public relations. **Computer sciences:** Computer science. **Conservation:** Land use planning, management/policy. **Education:** Agricultural, art, biology, business, chemistry, early childhood, early childhood special, elementary, English, family/consumer sciences, French, German, mathematics, middle, music, physical, physics, science, secondary, social studies, Spanish, special, speech, technology/industrial arts. **Engineering:** Chemical, civil, computer, electrical, mechanical, petroleum. **Engineering technology:** Industrial. **Family/consumer sciences:** Family studies. **Foreign languages:** General. **Health:** Athletic training, audiology/speech pathology, dental hygiene, dietetics, medical records admin, nursing (RN). **History:** General. **Math:** General. **Philosophy/religion:** Philosophy. **Physical sciences:** Chemistry, geology, physics. **Protective services:** Criminal justice. **Psychology:** General. **Social sciences:** Anthropology, political science, sociology. **Visual/performing arts:** General, art, industrial design, music performance. **Other:** Earth science education grades 6-12.

**Most popular majors.** Business/marketing 22%, education 12%, engineering/engineering technologies 8%, health sciences 11%, liberal arts 13%.

**Computing on campus.** 2,000 workstations in dormitories, library, computer center, student center. Commuter students can connect to campus network. Online course registration, online library, helpline, wireless network available.

**Student life. Freshman orientation:** Mandatory, $75 fee. Preregistration for classes offered. **Housing:** Single-sex dorms, special housing for disabled, apartments, fraternity/sorority housing, substance-free housing available. $50 deposit, deadline 6/15. **Activities:** Bands, campus ministries, choral groups, dance, drama, film society, international student organizations, literary magazine, music ensembles, musical theater, opera, radio station, student government, student newspaper, Young Republicans, Young Democrats, Omega Phi Alpha, Afro-American student groups.

**Athletics.** NCAA. **Intercollegiate:** Baseball M, basketball, cheerleading, cross-country, football (tackle) M, golf M, soccer W, softball W, tennis, track and field, volleyball W. **Intramural:** Basketball, football (non-tackle), racquetball, soccer, softball, tennis, volleyball, water polo. **Team name:** Ragin' Cajuns.

**Student services.** Adult student services, career counseling, student employment services, financial aid counseling, health services, minority student services, on-campus daycare, personal counseling, placement for graduates, veterans' counselor. **Physically disabled:** Services for visually, speech, hearing impaired.

**Contact.** E-mail: enroll@louisiana.edu
Phone: (337) 482-6553 Toll-free number: (800) 752-6553
Fax: (337) 482-1112
Leroy Broussard, Director of Admissions, University of Louisiana at Lafayette, Box 41210, Lafayette, LA 70504-1210

## University of Louisiana at Monroe
**Monroe, Louisiana**
**www.ulm.edu**      **CB code: 6482**

- Public 4-year university
- Commuter campus in small city
- 7,262 degree-seeking undergraduates: 19% part-time, 63% women, 26% African American, 2% Asian American, 1% Hispanic American, 1% international
- 1,056 degree-seeking graduate students
- 83% of applicants admitted
- SAT or ACT (ACT writing optional) required

**General.** Founded in 1931. Regionally accredited. **Degrees:** 877 bachelor's, 59 associate awarded; master's, doctoral, first professional offered. **ROTC:** Army, Air Force. **Location:** 90 miles from Shreveport, 120 miles from Jackson, Mississippi. **Calendar:** Semester, extensive summer session. **Full-time faculty:** 373 total. **Part-time faculty:** 170 total. **Special facilities:** National Public Radio station, Louisiana state cancer tumor registry archives, regional small business development center, weather research center, museum of natural history, flight simulator.

**Freshman class profile.** 2,628 applied, 2,176 admitted, 1,379 enrolled.

| Mid 50% test scores | | Return as sophomores: | 66% |
|---|---|---|---|
| SAT critical reading: | 500-550 | Out-of-state: | 7% |
| SAT math: | 390-480 | Live on campus: | 49% |
| ACT composite: | 19-23 | International: | 1% |

**Basis for selection.** Students who do not meet defined criteria evaluated on other evidence of academic promise for admittance by exception. Only limited number of students will be granted admittance by exception. **Homeschooled:** Must submit official transcript of grades and official proof of graduation or original diploma to admissions office.

**High school preparation.** 16.5 units required. Required units include English 4, mathematics 3, social studies 1, history 2, science 3, foreign language 2, computer science .5 and visual/performing arts 1.

**2007-2008 Annual costs.** Tuition/fees: $3,607; $9,559 out-of-state. Room/board: $5,500. Books/supplies: $500.

**Financial aid. Non-need-based:** Scholarships awarded for academics, alumni affiliation, art, athletics, job skills, leadership, minority status, music/drama, religious affiliation, ROTC, state residency.

**Application procedures. Admission:** Priority date 4/1; no deadline. $20 fee, may be waived for applicants with need. Application may be submitted online. Admission notification on a rolling basis. **Financial aid:** Priority date 4/1; no closing date. FAFSA required. Applicants notified on a rolling basis starting 6/1; must reply within 2 week(s) of notification.

**Academics.** Credit hours toward graduation may be earned through examination, military service, correspondence and extension courses taken through accredited extension divisions of other colleges and universities. **Special study options:** Accelerated study, combined bachelor's/graduate degree, cooperative education, distance learning, double major, dual enrollment of high school students, ESL, honors, independent study, internships, study abroad, teacher certification program. Evening college. **Credit/placement by examination:** AP, CLEP, SAT, ACT, institutional tests. 22 credit hours maximum toward associate degree, 43 toward bachelor's. Maximum of one-third of credits required for degree may be earned through examination,

military experience, and correspondence courses. **Support services:** Learning center, reduced course load, remedial instruction, study skills assistance, tutoring, writing center.

**Majors. Agriculture:** Business. **Biology:** General, toxicology. **Business:** Accounting, business admin, entrepreneurial studies, finance, insurance, management information systems, managerial economics, marketing. **Communications:** Media studies. **Computer sciences:** Computer science. **Education:** Art, biology, chemistry, elementary, English, family/consumer sciences, French, mathematics, music, physical, physics, social studies, Spanish, speech. **Engineering technology:** Construction. **English:** English lit, speech/rhetoric. **Family/consumer sciences:** General. **Foreign languages:** French, Spanish. **Health:** Audiology/speech pathology, clinical lab science, dental hygiene, nursing (RN), radiologic technology/medical imaging. **History:** General. **Math:** General. **Physical sciences:** Atmospheric science, chemistry. **Protective services:** Criminal justice. **Psychology:** General. **Public administration:** Social work. **Social sciences:** Political science, sociology. **Transportation:** Airline/commercial pilot. **Visual/performing arts:** Music performance, studio arts.

**Most popular majors.** Business/marketing 19%, education 9%, health sciences 21%, liberal arts 16%, psychology 6%.

**Computing on campus.** Dormitories wired for high-speed internet access and linked to campus network. Commuter students can connect to campus network. Online course registration, online library, helpline, repair service, student web hosting, wireless network available.

**Student life. Freshman orientation:** Mandatory. Preregistration for classes offered. 5 regular sessions plus one computer PREP session. **Housing:** Coed dorms, single-sex dorms, apartments, fraternity/sorority housing, substance-free housing available. **Activities:** Bands, choral groups, dance, drama, literary magazine, music ensembles, musical theater, opera, radio station, student government, student newspaper, symphony orchestra.

**Athletics.** NCAA. **Intercollegiate:** Baseball M, basketball, cheerleading, cross-country, football (tackle) M, golf, soccer W, softball W, swimming, tennis W, track and field, volleyball W. **Intramural:** Archery, badminton, basketball, bowling, cross-country, football (non-tackle), golf, racquetball, rodeo, soccer, softball, swimming, tennis, track and field, volleyball, weight lifting. **Team name:** Warhawks.

**Student services.** Adult student services, alcohol/substance abuse counseling, campus ministries, career counseling, student employment services, financial aid counseling, health services, on-campus daycare, personal counseling, placement for graduates, veterans' counselor. **Physically disabled:** Services for visually, speech, hearing impaired.

**Contact.** E-mail: self@ulm.edu
Phone: (318) 342-5430 Toll-free number: (800) 372-5127
Fax: (318) 342-1915
Lisa Miller, Director of Recruitment and Admissions, University of Louisiana at Monroe, 700 University Avenue, Monroe, LA 71209-1160

## University of New Orleans
**New Orleans, Louisiana**      **CB member**
**www.uno.edu**      **CB code: 6379**

- Public 4-year university
- Commuter campus in very large city
- 8,653 degree-seeking undergraduates: 25% part-time, 53% women, 20% African American, 6% Asian American, 7% Hispanic American, 1% Native American, 3% international
- 2,710 degree-seeking graduate students
- 81% of applicants admitted
- SAT or ACT (ACT writing optional) required
- 24% graduate within 6 years

**General.** Founded in 1956. Regionally accredited. **Degrees:** 1,368 bachelor's awarded; master's, doctoral offered. **ROTC:** Army, Naval, Air Force. **Calendar:** Semester, extensive summer session. **Full-time faculty:** 457 total; 66% have terminal degrees, 18% minority, 42% women. **Part-time faculty:** 221 total; 34% have terminal degrees, 14% minority, 39% women. **Class size:** 41% < 20, 40% 20-39, 8% 40-49, 6% 50-99, 3% >100.

**Freshman class profile.** 1,767 applied, 1,430 admitted, 1,119 enrolled.

| Mid 50% test scores | | | |
|---|---|---|---|
| SAT critical reading: | 470-610 | Rank in top quarter: | 33% |
| SAT math: | 480-620 | Rank in top tenth: | 12% |
| SAT writing: | 460-590 | Return as sophomores: | 69% |
| ACT composite: | 20-24 | Out-of-state: | 5% |
| GPA 3.50 or higher: | 19% | Live on campus: | 16% |
| GPA 3.0-3.49: | 32% | International: | 3% |
| GPA 2.0-2.99: | 48% | Fraternities: | 1% |
| | | Sororities: | 2% |

**Basis for selection.** Students who graduate from state-approved high schools must complete Louisiana Board of Regents core curriculum and require no more than 1 developmental/remedial course and 1 of following: ACT composite score of 23 or greater (SAT equivalent), high school cumulative GPA of 2.5 or greater with ACT (SAT equivalent) of 18 or greater on English and/or Math subscores, or high school graduation rank in top 25 percent of class. Audition required of music majors. Portfolio required of fine arts/studio majors. **Homeschooled:** Students who do not meet the core curriculum must satisfy all of following: ACT composite of 23 or greater (SAT equivalent), high school cumulative GPA of 2.5 or greater and high school graduation rank in top 25%. If these not met, student must have composite ACT score of 26 or greater (SAT equivalent) and require no more than 1 remedial/developmental course.

**High school preparation.** 17 units required. Required units include English 4, mathematics 3, social studies 1, history 2, science 3, foreign language 2 and visual/performing arts 1. 1 unit for additional math or science, 0.5 unit for computer science.

**2007-2008 Annual costs.** Tuition/fees: $3,984; $11,028 out-of-state. Room/board: $5,240. Books/supplies: $1,200. Personal expenses: $2,667.

**2007-2008 Financial aid. Need-based:** 914 full-time freshmen applied for aid; 688 were judged to have need; 469 of these received aid. Average need met was 68%. Average scholarship/grant was $5,059; average loan $3,066. 47% of total undergraduate aid awarded as scholarships/grants, 53% as loans/jobs. **Non-need-based:** Awarded to 1,117 full-time undergraduates, including 336 freshmen. Scholarships awarded for academics, athletics. **Additional information:** Students in good academic and financial standing eligible to participate in Extended Payment Plan option.

**Application procedures. Admission:** Priority date 7/1; deadline 8/20 (receipt date). $40 fee. Application may be submitted online. Admission notification on a rolling basis beginning on or about 10/1. **Financial aid:** Priority date 6/30; no closing date. FAFSA, institutional form required. Applicants notified on a rolling basis starting 4/20; must reply within 4 week(s) of notification.

**Academics. Special study options:** Cooperative education, cross-registration, distance learning, double major, dual enrollment of high school students, ESL, exchange student, honors, independent study, internships, student-designed major, study abroad, teacher certification program, Washington semester, weekend college. **Credit/placement by examination:** AP, CLEP, IB, SAT, ACT, institutional tests. 32 credit hours maximum toward bachelor's degree. **Support services:** Learning center, remedial instruction, tutoring.

**Majors. Area/ethnic studies:** Women's. **Biology:** General. **Business:** Accounting, business admin, entrepreneurial studies, finance, hospitality admin, management information systems, managerial economics, marketing. **Communications:** General. **Computer sciences:** Computer science. **Conservation:** Environmental studies. **Education:** Biology, chemistry, early childhood, elementary, English, mathematics, middle, physical, social studies. **Engineering:** Civil, electrical, marine, mechanical. **English:** English lit. **Foreign languages:** French, Spanish. **Health:** Clinical lab science. **History:** General. **Interdisciplinary:** Global studies. **Math:** General. **Parks/recreation:** Health/fitness. **Philosophy/religion:** Philosophy. **Physical sciences:** Chemistry, geology, physics. **Psychology:** General. **Social sciences:** Anthropology, economics, geography, political science, sociology, urban studies. **Visual/performing arts:** Art history/conservation, studio arts. **Other:** Earth science education.

**Most popular majors.** Business/marketing 34%, communications/journalism 8%, education 6%, engineering/engineering technologies 8%, liberal arts 8%, psychology 8%, social sciences 6%.

**Computing on campus.** Dormitories wired for high-speed internet access and linked to campus network. Commuter students can connect to campus network. Online course registration, online library, helpline, wireless network available.

**Student life. Freshman orientation:** Mandatory, $40 fee. Preregistration for classes offered. **Housing:** Coed dorms, special housing for disabled, apartments available. Apartment referral and roommate locator services available. **Activities:** Bands, campus ministries, choral groups, dance, drama, film society, international student organizations, literary magazine, music

ensembles, musical theater, opera, radio station, student government, student newspaper, African student organization, Circle K, Latin American student association, Muslim student association, National Society of Minorities in Hospitality, Pakistani students association, Progressive Black Student Union, Rainbow Alliance, UNO Filmmakers.

**Athletics.** NCAA. **Intercollegiate:** Baseball M, basketball, golf M, swimming W, volleyball W. **Intramural:** Basketball, football (non-tackle), soccer, softball, table tennis, tennis, volleyball. **Team name:** Privateers.

**Student services.** Adult student services, alcohol/substance abuse counseling, campus ministries, career counseling, student employment services, financial aid counseling, health services, legal services, minority student services, on-campus daycare, personal counseling, placement for graduates, veterans' counselor, women's services. **Physically disabled:** Services for visually, speech, hearing impaired.

**Contact.** E-mail: admissions@uno.edu
Phone: (504) 280-6595 Toll-free number: (800) 256-5866
Fax: (504) 280-5522
Andy Benoit, Director of Admissions Office, University of New Orleans, Administration Building Room 103, New Orleans, LA 70148

---

## Xavier University of Louisiana
**New Orleans, Louisiana** — CB member
**www.xula.edu** — CB code: 6975

- Private 4-year university affiliated with Roman Catholic Church
- Commuter campus in very large city
- 2,316 degree-seeking undergraduates: 3% part-time, 72% women, 75% African American, 7% Asian American, 1% Hispanic American, 3% international
- 765 degree-seeking graduate students
- 59% of applicants admitted
- SAT or ACT (ACT writing optional) required
- 38% graduate within 6 years

**General.** Founded in 1915. Regionally accredited. **Degrees:** 347 bachelor's awarded; master's, first professional offered. **ROTC:** Army, Naval, Air Force. **Location:** One mile from downtown. **Calendar:** Semester, limited summer session. **Full-time faculty:** 189 total; 48% minority, 46% women. **Part-time faculty:** 26 total; 50% women. **Class size:** 48% < 20, 36% 20-39, 4% 40-49, 5% 50-99, 7% >100.

**Freshman class profile.** 3,074 applied, 1,821 admitted, 664 enrolled.

| Mid 50% test scores | | | |
|---|---|---|---|
| SAT critical reading: | 400-520 | GPA 2.0-2.99: | 34% |
| SAT math: | 400-560 | Rank in top quarter: | 49% |
| SAT writing: | 410-510 | Rank in top tenth: | 25% |
| ACT composite: | 18-23 | Return as sophomores: | 83% |
| GPA 3.50 or higher: | 35% | Out-of-state: | 42% |
| GPA 3.0-3.49: | 27% | Live on campus: | 56% |
| | | International: | 2% |

**Basis for selection.** High school record or GED scores, standardized test results, and recommendation from counselor important. Interview recommended for academically weak. Audition required for music majors. Portfolio required for art majors.

**High school preparation.** Required and recommended units include English 4, mathematics 2-4, social studies 1, history 1, science 1-3, foreign language 1 and academic electives 8. Math must include 1 algebra.

**2007-2008 Annual costs.** Tuition/fees: $14,700. Room/board: $6,600. Books/supplies: $1,200. Personal expenses: $1,692.

**2006-2007 Financial aid. Need-based:** 423 full-time freshmen applied for aid; 379 were judged to have need; 374 of these received aid. Average need met was 52%. Average scholarship/grant was $6,629; average loan $2,852. 53% of total undergraduate aid awarded as scholarships/grants, 47% as loans/jobs. **Non-need-based:** Awarded to 1,214 full-time undergraduates, including 272 freshmen.

**Application procedures. Admission:** Priority date 3/1; deadline 7/1 (postmark date). $25 fee, may be waived for applicants with need. Application may be submitted online. Must reply by May 1 or within 2 week(s) if notified thereafter. **Financial aid:** Priority date 1/1; no closing date. FAFSA required. Applicants notified on a rolling basis starting 4/1; must reply within 2 week(s) of notification.

**Academics. Special study options:** Accelerated study, combined bachelor's/graduate degree, cooperative education, cross-registration, double major, dual enrollment of high school students, exchange student, honors, independent study, internships, study abroad, teacher certification program. **Credit/**

**placement by examination:** AP, CLEP, SAT, ACT, institutional tests. 30 credit hours maximum toward bachelor's degree. **Support services:** Learning center, pre-admission summer program, reduced course load, remedial instruction, study skills assistance, tutoring, writing center.

**Majors. Biology:** General, biochemistry, microbiology. **Business:** Accounting, business admin, finance, management science, marketing. **Communications:** Media studies. **Computer sciences:** General, computer science. **Education:** General, art, biology, chemistry, early childhood, elementary, English, foreign languages, French, history, mathematics, multi-level teacher, music, physical, science, social studies, Spanish, special. **Engineering:** Computer. **English:** English lit. **Foreign languages:** French, Spanish. **Health:** Predental, premedicine, prepharmacy, preveterinary, speech pathology. **History:** General. **Legal studies:** Prelaw. **Math:** General, statistics. **Parks/recreation:** Health/fitness. **Philosophy/religion:** Philosophy. **Physical sciences:** Chemistry, physics. **Psychology:** General. **Social sciences:** Political science, sociology. **Theology:** Theology. **Visual/performing arts:** Art, music performance, piano/organ, stringed instruments, voice/opera.

**Most popular majors.** Biology 42%, business/marketing 9%, physical sciences 13%, psychology 14%, social sciences 7%.

**Computing on campus.** 350 workstations in dormitories, library, computer center. Dormitories wired for high-speed internet access and linked to campus network. Commuter students can connect to campus network. Online course registration, online library, helpline available.

**Student life. Freshman orientation:** Mandatory. Preregistration for classes offered. One-week program. **Policies:** All recognized student organizations must perform 2 community service activities per semester. **Housing:** Coed dorms, single-sex dorms, special housing for disabled, substance-free housing available. $100 deposit. **Activities:** Concert band, campus ministries, choral groups, drama, international student organizations, literary magazine, music ensembles, opera, student government, student newspaper, symphony orchestra, TV station, over 30 organizations.

**Athletics.** NAIA. **Intercollegiate:** Basketball, cross-country, tennis, volleyball W. **Intramural:** Basketball, cheerleading, football (non-tackle), softball, swimming, table tennis, tennis, track and field, volleyball. **Team name:** Gold Rush.

**Student services.** Adult student services, alcohol/substance abuse counseling, campus ministries, career counseling, student employment services, financial aid counseling, health services, personal counseling, placement for graduates, veterans' counselor, women's services. **Physically disabled:** Services for visually, speech, hearing impaired.

**Contact.** E-mail: apply@xula.edu
Phone: (504) 520-7388 Toll-free number: (877) 928-4378
Fax: (504) 520-7941
Winston Brown, Dean of Admissions, Xavier University of Louisiana, 1 Drexel Drive, New Orleans, LA 70125-1098

# Maine

## Bates College

**Lewiston, Maine**
**www.bates.edu**

**CB member**
**CB code: 3076**

- Private 4-year liberal arts college
- Residential campus in large town
- 1,660 degree-seeking undergraduates: 52% women, 3% African American, 6% Asian American, 2% Hispanic American, 5% international
- 30% of applicants admitted
- Application essay required
- 89% graduate within 6 years

**General.** Founded in 1855. Regionally accredited. **Degrees:** 464 bachelor's awarded. **Location:** 35 miles from Portland. **Calendar:** 4-4-1 semester system. **Full-time faculty:** 162 total; 93% have terminal degrees, 14% minority, 46% women. **Part-time faculty:** 27 total; 63% have terminal degrees, 11% minority, 59% women. **Class size:** 63% < 20, 28% 20-39, 4% 40-49, 5% 50-99. **Special facilities:** Mountain seacoast conservation area, Edmund S. Muskie Archives, art museum, observatory.

**Freshman class profile.** 4,434 applied, 1,312 admitted, 445 enrolled.

| Mid 50% test scores | | | |
|---|---|---|---|
| SAT critical reading: | 640-710 | Return as sophomores: | 93% |
| SAT math: | 630-700 | Out-of-state: | 91% |
| Rank in top quarter: | 86% | Live on campus: | 100% |
| Rank in top tenth: | 55% | International: | 6% |

**Basis for selection.** GED not accepted. School achievement record, recommendations, special talents, leadership, essay, interview all important. Submission of standardized test scores is optional for admission. Interviews are strongly recommended.

**High school preparation.** 17 units required; 23 recommended. Required and recommended units include English 4, mathematics 3-4, social studies 3-4, science 3-4 (laboratory 2-3) and foreign language 2-4. History included in social studies requirement.

**2007-2008 Annual costs.** Comprehensive fee: $46,800. Books/supplies: $1,150.

**2007-2008 Financial aid.** All financial aid based on need. 203 full-time freshmen applied for aid; 203 were judged to have need; 191 of these received aid. Average need-met was 100%. Average scholarship/grant was $30,057; average loan $3,704. 86% of total undergraduate aid awarded as scholarships/grants, 14% as loans/jobs. **Additional information:** Priority date for filing required financial aid forms for early decision students is 11/15.

**Application procedures. Admission:** Closing date 1/1 (postmark date). $60 fee, may be waived for applicants with need. Application may be submitted online. Admission notification 3/31. Must reply by 5/1. **Financial aid:** Closing date 2/1. FAFSA, CSS PROFILE required. Applicants notified by 4/1; must reply by 5/1.

**Academics. Special study options:** Accelerated study, combined bachelor's/graduate degree, cooperative education, double major, honors, independent study, internships, liberal arts/career combination, semester at sea, student-designed major, study abroad, teacher certification program, urban semester, Washington semester. Marine studies program at Mystic Seaport, liberal arts-engineering dual degree program with 5 universities. **Credit/placement by examination:** AP, CLEP, IB, institutional tests. **Support services:** Reduced course load, study skills assistance, tutoring, writing center.

**Majors. Area/ethnic studies:** African-American, American, East Asian, women's. **Biology:** General, biochemistry. **Conservation:** Environmental studies. **Engineering:** General. **English:** English lit, speech/rhetoric. **Foreign languages:** Chinese, French, German, Japanese, Russian, Spanish. **History:** General. **Interdisciplinary:** Ancient studies, neuroscience. **Math:** General. **Philosophy/religion:** Philosophy, religion. **Physical sciences:** Chemistry, geology, physics. **Psychology:** General. **Social sciences:** Anthropology, economics, political science, sociology. **Visual/performing arts:** Art, dramatic.

**Most popular majors.** Biology 11%, English 10%, history 7%, philosophy/religious studies 6%, psychology 10%, social sciences 27%, visual/performing arts 7%.

**Computing on campus.** 415 workstations in dormitories, library, computer center. Dormitories wired for high-speed internet access and linked to campus network. Commuter students can connect to campus network. Online course registration, helpline, repair service, student web hosting, wireless network available.

**Student life. Freshman orientation:** Mandatory. Preregistration for classes offered. Held 5 days prior to start of classes. **Housing:** Guaranteed on-campus for all undergraduates. Coed dorms, single-sex dorms, substance-free housing available. $300 nonrefundable deposit, deadline 5/1. Quiet study house, chemical-free houses, theme houses. **Activities:** Bands, campus ministries, choral groups, dance, drama, film society, international student organizations, literary magazine, music ensembles, radio station, student government, student newspaper, symphony orchestra, Africana Club, Amandla!, Bates Christian Fellowship, Bates Democrats, Bates Hindu Awareness group, College Republicans, Hillel, International Club, Latinos Unidos, Mushahada Club, Sangai Asia, Student Diversity Coalition, Women of Color.

**Athletics.** NCAA. **Intercollegiate:** Baseball M, basketball, cross-country, diving, field hockey W, football (tackle) M, golf, lacrosse, rowing (crew), skiing, soccer, softball W, squash, swimming, tennis, track and field, volleyball W. **Intramural:** Badminton, baseball M, basketball, football (tackle), golf, handball, ice hockey, lacrosse, racquetball, rugby, sailing, soccer, softball, squash, table tennis, tennis, volleyball. **Team name:** Bobcats.

**Student services.** Alcohol/substance abuse counseling, campus ministries, career counseling, student employment services, financial aid counseling, health services, minority student services, personal counseling, placement for graduates, women's services. **Physically disabled:** Services for visually, hearing impaired.

**Contact.** E-mail: admissions@bates.edu
Phone: (207) 786-6000 Fax: (207) 786-6025
Wylie Mitchell, Dean of Admissions, Bates College, 23 Campus Avenue, Lindholm House, Lewiston, ME 04240-9917

## Bowdoin College

**Brunswick, Maine**
**www.bowdoin.edu**

**CB member**
**CB code: 3089**

- Private 4-year liberal arts college
- Residential campus in large town
- 1,710 degree-seeking undergraduates: 52% women, 6% African American, 13% Asian American, 7% Hispanic American, 1% Native American, 3% international
- 19% of applicants admitted
- Application essay required
- 89% graduate within 6 years; 15% enter graduate study

**General.** Founded in 1794. Regionally accredited. **Degrees:** 452 bachelor's awarded. **Location:** 25 miles from Portland, 120 miles from Boston. **Calendar:** Semester. **Full-time faculty:** 166 total; 96% have terminal degrees, 11% minority, 47% women. **Part-time faculty:** 33 total; 67% have terminal degrees, 12% minority, 48% women. **Class size:** 64% < 20, 27% 20-39, 6% 40-49, 3% 50-99. **Special facilities:** Arctic museum, arctic studies center, coastal marine biology and ornithology research facility, scientific station, farm, center for learning and teaching, 2 theaters, visual arts center, hall of music, environmental studies center, outdoor leadership center, community service resource center, African-American center, women's resource center, educational research and development program, career planning center, boathouse, electronic classroom, recital hall, nature trails, language media center, recording studio, crafts center, ceramic studio and photography darkroom.

**Freshman class profile.** 5,961 applied, 1,130 admitted, 476 enrolled.

| Mid 50% test scores | | | |
|---|---|---|---|
| SAT critical reading: | 650-740 | Rank in top tenth: | 89% |
| SAT math: | 650-730 | Return as sophomores: | 99% |
| SAT writing: | 650-730 | Out-of-state: | 88% |
| ACT composite: | 29-33 | Live on campus: | 100% |
| Rank in top quarter: | 99% | International: | 3% |

**Basis for selection.** GED not accepted. Academic record, level of challenge represented in the candidate's course work, counselor/teacher recommendations, interview, quality of application and essay, character and personal qualities, extracurricular activities, talents and abilities, and overall academic potential most important. Test scores considered, but not required.

Motivation of candidate also considered. Interview recommended. Candidates with unusual talent in music, theater or visual arts encouraged to complete Arts Supplement when applying for admission. Audition recommended for music majors. Portfolio recommended for art majors. **Homeschooled:** Applicants applying from systems providing written evaluations rather than grades are required to submit either SAT or ACT-plus-SAT-Subject Test results. SAT Subject Tests should include Math Level 1 or Math Level 2 and one science. Personal interview strongly recommended.

**High school preparation.** 20 units recommended. Recommended units include English 4, mathematics 4, social studies 4, science 4 (laboratory 3) and foreign language 4. Arts, music and computer science or computer literacy recommended.

**2007-2008 Annual costs.** Tuition/fees: $36,370. Room/board: $9,890. Books/supplies: $800. Personal expenses: $1,200.

**2006-2007 Financial aid. Need-based:** 251 full-time freshmen applied for aid; 197 were judged to have need; 197 of these received aid. Average need met was 100%. Average scholarship/grant was $26,293; average loan $3,326. 86% of total undergraduate aid awarded as scholarships/grants, 14% as loans/jobs. **Non-need-based:** Awarded to 70 full-time undergraduates, including 17 freshmen. Scholarships awarded for academics, leadership. **Additional information:** Regardless of financial circumstances, students admitted will receive money they need to attend. International students for regular admission must submit their financial aid applications by January 1st.

**Application procedures. Admission:** Closing date 1/1 (receipt date). $60 fee, may be waived for applicants with need. Application may be submitted online. Admission notification on a rolling basis beginning on or about 4/5. Must reply by May 1 or within 1 week(s) if notified thereafter. Re-enrollment deposit of $400 due by April 1st for returning students. Deposit goes towards following year's expenses. **Financial aid:** Closing date 2/15. FAFSA, CSS PROFILE required. Applicants notified by 4/5; must reply by 5/1 or within 1 week(s) of notification.

**Academics.** Most students pursue independent scholarly research, working closely with a faculty advisor, through an independent study or honors project. About half of the student body studies abroad for one or 2 semesters, usually during the junior year. First-year seminars are limited to 16 first-year students and emphasize college-level reading and writing. Interdisciplinary and self-designed majors are available. **Special study options:** Accelerated study, combined bachelor's/graduate degree, double major, exchange student, independent study, liberal arts/career combination, semester at sea, student-designed major, study abroad, teacher certification program, Washington semester. 3-2 or 4-2 engineering degree programs with California Institute of Technology, Dartmouth College, Columbia University or University of Maine, Orono, 3-3 legal studies program with Columbia University Law School, first-year seminars, summer research fellowships, service-learning courses, The Writing Project, Quantitative Skills Program, Legal Studies Advisory Group, Health Professions Advising, ESL Writing Tutor. **Credit/placement by examination:** AP, CLEP, IB, institutional tests. **Support services:** Learning center, reduced course load, study skills assistance, tutoring, writing center.

**Majors. Area/ethnic studies:** African, Asian, Central/Eastern European, Latin American, women's. **Biology:** General, biochemistry. **Computer sciences:** Computer science. **Conservation:** Environmental studies. **English:** English lit. **Foreign languages:** Classics, French, German, Romance, Russian, Spanish. **History:** General. **Interdisciplinary:** Ancient studies, classical/archaeology, math/computer science, neuroscience. **Math:** General. **Philosophy/religion:** Philosophy, religion. **Physical sciences:** Chemical physics, chemistry, geochemistry, geology, geophysics, physics. **Psychology:** General. **Social sciences:** Anthropology, archaeology, econometrics, economics, political science, sociology. **Visual/performing arts:** Art history/conservation, studio arts, theater history.

**Most popular majors.** Biology 7%, English 6%, foreign language 9%, history 8%, social sciences 33%, visual/performing arts 9%.

**Computing on campus.** 450 workstations in dormitories, library, computer center, student center. Dormitories wired for high-speed internet access and linked to campus network. Commuter students can connect to campus network. Online library, helpline, repair service, student web hosting, wireless network available.

**Student life. Freshman orientation:** Mandatory. 4-5 day program at the end of August, just before the start of classes. Pre-orientation outing trips offered over 4 nights prior to formal orientation; separate charge depending on the trip. **Policies:** Honor code, social code, judicial authority, drug and alcohol policies, policies on sexual misconduct, smoking, illegal drugs, discrimination, information technology use, residential life. **Housing:** Guaranteed on-campus for freshmen. Coed dorms, special housing for disabled, apartments, substance-free housing available. Three small college houses and 8 college system houses available. **Activities:** Bands, choral groups,

dance, drama, film society, international student organizations, literary magazine, music ensembles, musical theater, radio station, student government, student newspaper, symphony orchestra, TV station, African-American society, Asian student organization, Latin American student organization, Hillel, Catholic student union, Christian fellowship, community service council, Evergreens, Democrats, Republicans.

**Athletics.** NCAA. **Intercollegiate:** Baseball M, basketball, cross-country, diving, field hockey W, football (tackle) M, golf, ice hockey, lacrosse, rugby W, sailing, skiing, soccer, softball W, squash, swimming, tennis, track and field, volleyball W. **Intramural:** Badminton, basketball, cricket, cross-country, field hockey, football (non-tackle), ice hockey, rugby, soccer, softball, squash, tennis, volleyball, water polo. **Team name:** Polar Bears.

**Student services.** Alcohol/substance abuse counseling, career counseling, student employment services, health services, minority student services, on-campus daycare, personal counseling, placement for graduates, women's services. **Physically disabled:** Services for visually, speech, hearing impaired.

**Contact.** E-mail: admissions@bowdoin.edu
Phone: (207) 725-3100 Fax: (207) 725-3101
William Shain, Dean of Admissions and Student Aid, Bowdoin College, 5000 College Station, Brunswick, ME 04011-8441

---

## Colby College
**Waterville, Maine**
www.colby.edu

**CB member**
**CB code: 3280**

- Private 4-year liberal arts college
- Residential campus in large town
- 1,867 degree-seeking undergraduates: 55% women, 2% African American, 8% Asian American, 3% Hispanic American, 6% international
- 32% of applicants admitted
- SAT or ACT (ACT writing recommended), application essay required
- 87% graduate within 6 years; 18% enter graduate study

**General.** Founded in 1813. Regionally accredited. Off-campus facilities available for teaching and research in biology, ecology, geology. **Degrees:** 470 bachelor's awarded. **ROTC:** Army. **Location:** 180 miles from Boston, 75 miles from Portland. **Calendar:** 4-1-4. **Full-time faculty:** 159 total; 96% have terminal degrees, 13% minority, 45% women. **Part-time faculty:** 69 total; 55% have terminal degrees, 6% minority, 49% women. **Class size:** 61% < 20, 31% 20-39, 4% 40-49, 4% 50-99. **Special facilities:** Public art museum, astronomical observatory, arboretum, research greenhouses, kettlehole research bog, professional blacksmith's forge, woodworking shop, crew rowing center, technical climbing wall, Nordic ski trails, synthetic turf field, community radio station, scanning and transmission electron microscopes, laser flash photolysis, 400 MHz NMR, x-ray diffractometer, spectrophotometers, chromatographs, electrophoresis, microcalorimeters, piezometers (groundwater monitoring wells).

**Freshman class profile.** 4,679 applied, 1,488 admitted, 467 enrolled.

| Mid 50% test scores | | | | |
|---|---|---|---|---|
| SAT critical reading: | 640-720 | Rank in top tenth: | 60% |
| SAT math: | 640-720 | End year in good standing: | 98% |
| SAT writing: | 630-710 | Return as sophomores: | 94% |
| ACT composite: | 28-31 | Out-of-state: | 92% |
| Rank in top quarter: | 90% | Live on campus: | 100% |
| | | International: | 6% |

**Basis for selection.** School record and personal qualities very important. Test scores, recommendations, potential contribution to college life, essay, interview, important. Social, economic, racial, geographic diversity considered.

**High school preparation.** College-preparatory program recommended. 16 units recommended. Recommended units include English 4, mathematics 3, social studies 2, science 2 (laboratory 2), foreign language 3 and academic electives 2. Social studies units recommended could include history courses.

**2008-2009 Annual costs.** Comprehensive fee: $48,520. Books/supplies: $700. Personal expenses: $900.

**2006-2007 Financial aid.** All financial aid based on need. 219 full-time freshmen applied for aid; 190 were judged to have need; 190 of these received aid. Average need met was 100%. Average scholarship/grant was $28,110; average loan $3,555. 89% of total undergraduate aid awarded as scholarships/grants, 11% as loans/jobs.

**Application procedures. Admission:** Closing date 1/1 (postmark date). $65 fee, may be waived for applicants with need. Application may be submitted online. Admission notification 4/1. Must reply by 5/1. **Financial aid:** Closing date 2/1. FAFSA, CSS PROFILE required. Applicants notified by 4/1; must reply by 5/1.

**Academics. Special study options:** Combined bachelor's/graduate degree, cross-registration, double major, exchange student, honors, independent study, internships, semester at sea, student-designed major, study abroad, teacher certification program, Washington semester. Numerous research, service learning, and intership opportunities through the Goldfarb Center for Public Affairs; summer research assistantships; course exchange programs with Bowdoin College, Bates College, Thomas College; stipends to enable student internships; coordinated 3-2 engineering program with Dartmouth; Idea Network of Biomedical Research Excellence (partnerships with Jackson Labs, Mt. Desert Island Biological Labs, and other colleges). **Credit/placement by examination:** AP, CLEP, IB, institutional tests. 12 credit hours maximum toward bachelor's degree. When appropriate, distribution requirements, as well as certain requirements for the major, may be absolved by examination without course enrollment at the discretion of the department concerned. Matriculated students may earn credit by examination in 100- or 200-level courses to a maximum of 12 hours. Departmental examinations or external examinations approved by the department may be used, with credit given for the equivalent of at least C-level work. The cost of each examination is paid by the student. The college will exempt students from the language requirement for attaining before entrance a score of 64 in a SAT Subject Test in a foreign language or for attaining a score of 64 in Colby's placement test during first-year orientation; in either case, no academic credit will be granted. **Support services:** Tutoring, writing center.

**Majors. Area/ethnic studies:** African-American, American, East Asian, Latin American, Russian/Slavic, women's. **Biology:** General, biochemistry, cell/histology, environmental, molecular, molecular biochemistry, neurobiology/physiology. **Computer sciences:** Computer science. **Conservation:** Environmental science, environmental studies. **English:** Creative writing, English lit. **Foreign languages:** Classics, French, German, Spanish. **History:** General. **Interdisciplinary:** Biological/physical sciences, classical/archaeology, math/computer science, neuroscience, science/society. **Math:** General. **Philosophy/religion:** Philosophy, religion. **Physical sciences:** Chemistry, geology, physics. **Psychology:** General. **Social sciences:** Anthropology, econometrics, economics, international relations, political science, sociology. **Visual/performing arts:** Art, art history/conservation, dramatic, studio arts. **Other:** Administration Science, Classical Civilization: English, International Studies.

**Most popular majors.** Area/ethnic studies 10%, biology 7%, English 11%, foreign language 7%, history 8%, physical sciences 6%, social sciences 24%, visual/performing arts 7%.

**Computing on campus.** 350 workstations in library, computer center. Dormitories wired for high-speed internet access and linked to campus network. Commuter students can connect to campus network. Online course registration, online library, helpline, repair service, student web hosting, wireless network available.

**Student life. Freshman orientation:** Mandatory. Preregistration for classes offered. 4-day optional outdoor component ($175); 3-day on-campus component follows, both held the week before classes begin. **Policies:** Students participate in forming policies and governing social and community activities through student government and serving on official college committees up to and including the Board of Trustees. **Housing:** Guaranteed on-campus for all undergraduates. Coed dorms, substance-free housing available. Senior apartments, quiet dormitories, interest housing, chemical-free halls available. **Activities:** Bands, choral groups, dance, drama, film society, literary magazine, music ensembles, musical theater, radio station, student government, student newspaper, symphony orchestra, Black and Hispanic student group, environmental coalition, social service and political organizations, volunteer center, international club, five a capella groups, Amnesty International, women's group, outing club, Habitat for Humanity.

**Athletics.** NCAA. **Intercollegiate:** Baseball M, basketball, cross-country, diving, field hockey W, football (tackle) M, golf, ice hockey, lacrosse, rowing (crew), skiing, soccer, softball W, squash, swimming, tennis, track and field, volleyball W. **Intramural:** Badminton, basketball, football (nontackle), ice hockey, sailing, soccer, softball, squash, table tennis, volleyball, weight lifting. **Team name:** White Mules.

**Student services.** Alcohol/substance abuse counseling, campus ministries, career counseling, student employment services, financial aid counseling, health services, minority student services, personal counseling, placement for graduates, women's services. **Physically disabled:** Services for visually, hearing impaired.

**Contact.** E-mail: admissions@colby.edu
Phone: (800) 723-3032 Toll-free number: (800) 723-3032
Fax: (207) 859-4828
Parker Beverage, Dean of Admissions and Financial Aid, Colby College, 4800 Mayflower Hill, Waterville, ME 04901-8848

## College of the Atlantic
**Bar Harbor, Maine**
www.coa.edu                                    **CB code: 3305**

- Private 4-year liberal arts college
- Residential campus in small town
- 327 degree-seeking undergraduates: 3% part-time, 64% women, 1% Asian American, 1% Hispanic American, 13% international
- 8 degree-seeking graduate students
- 77% of applicants admitted
- Application essay required
- 56% graduate within 6 years; 15% enter graduate study

**General.** Founded in 1969. Regionally accredited. **Degrees:** 68 bachelor's awarded; master's offered. **Location:** 300 miles from Boston, 50 miles from Bangor. **Calendar:** Three 10-week terms. Limited summer session. **Full-time faculty:** 26 total; 85% have terminal degrees, 8% minority, 35% women. **Part-time faculty:** 15 total; 40% have terminal degrees, 47% women. **Class size:** 96% < 20, 4% 20-39. **Special facilities:** Natural history museum, herbarium, greenhouse, pier, research boat, organic farm, island research stations.

**Freshman class profile.** 305 applied, 235 admitted, 84 enrolled.

| Mid 50% test scores | | | |
|---|---|---|---|
| SAT critical reading: | 590-690 | GPA 2.0-2.99: | 14% |
| SAT math: | 540-640 | Rank in top quarter: | 52% |
| SAT writing: | 570-670 | Rank in top tenth: | 33% |
| ACT composite: | 24-30 | Return as sophomores: | 85% |
| GPA 3.50 or higher: | 61% | Out-of-state: | 79% |
| GPA 3.0-3.49: | 25% | Live on campus: | 94% |
| | | International: | 13% |

**Basis for selection.** Academic ability, motivation, intellectual enthusiasm, independence, creativity, and commitment to ecological concerns and to goals and philosophies of college as demonstrated by high school record, recommendations, and interview important. **Homeschooled:** Thorough outline of topics covered, books read, homework completed, the evaluation process used in assessing work and the progress made over the years required. Standardized test scores recommended. **Learning Disabled:** Meeting with dean of academic services recommended.

**High school preparation.** 15 units required; 19 recommended. Required and recommended units include English 4, mathematics 3-4, social studies 2, history 2, science 2-3 (laboratory 2), foreign language 2 and academic electives 1.

**2007-2008 Annual costs.** Tuition/fees: $29,970. Room/board: $8,190. Books/supplies: $600. Personal expenses: $420.

**2007-2008 Financial aid.** All financial aid based on need. 71 full-time freshmen applied for aid; 68 were judged to have need; 68 of these received aid. Average need met was 97%. Average scholarship/grant was $22,654; average loan $3,341. 80% of total undergraduate aid awarded as scholarships/grants, 20% as loans/jobs.

**Application procedures. Admission:** Closing date 2/15 (postmark date). $45 fee, may be waived for applicants with need. Application may be submitted online. Admission notification 4/1. Must reply by May 1 or within 2 week(s) if notified thereafter. **Financial aid:** Closing date 2/15. FAFSA, institutional form required. Applicants notified by 4/1; must reply by 5/1.

**Academics.** Interdisciplinary curriculum consists of problem-solving course work, seminars, independent study, tutorials, specialized skill courses, and supervised internships away from college. **Special study options:** Independent study, internships, semester at sea, student-designed major, study abroad, teacher certification program. Winter Term program in Yucatan, Mexico. Consortium agreement (Eco-League) with five other colleges for student exchanges (Alaska Pacific University, Antioch College, Green Mountain College, Northland College, Prescott College); as well as academic partnerships with Olin College of Engineering, SALT Institute for Documentary Studies, National Outdoor Leadership School, The Landing School of Boat Design, and Sea Education Association. **Credit/placement by examination:** AP, CLEP, IB. 30 credit hours maximum toward bachelor's degree. **Support services:** Reduced course load, remedial instruction, study skills assistance, tutoring, writing center.

**Majors. Biology:** Ecology.

**Computing on campus.** 50 workstations in library, computer center. Dormitories wired for high-speed internet access and linked to campus network. Online library, helpline, student web hosting, wireless network available.

**Student life. Freshman orientation:** Mandatory, $120 fee. Preregistration for classes offered. Three days on campus with optional 6-day outdoor adventure trips available. **Policies:** Students participate in developing college policy and operate student activities fund. **Housing:** Guaranteed on-campus for freshmen. Coed dorms, special housing for disabled, substance-free housing available. $150 nonrefundable deposit, deadline 5/1. **Activities:** Choral groups, dance, drama, literary magazine, music ensembles, student government, student newspaper, Students for a Free Tibet, SustainUs, outing club, life-drawing club, student drama club.

**Athletics. Intramural:** Badminton, cricket, ice hockey, sailing, soccer, softball, table tennis, volleyball, water polo.

**Student services.** Alcohol/substance abuse counseling, career counseling, student employment services, financial aid counseling, health services, minority student services, personal counseling, placement for graduates. **Physically disabled:** Services for visually, hearing impaired.

**Contact.** E-mail: inquiry@coa.edu
Phone: (207) 288-5015 ext. 230 Toll-free number: (800) 528-0025
Fax: (207) 288-4126
Sarah Baker, Director of Admission, College of the Atlantic, 105 Eden Street, Bar Harbor, ME 04609

---

## Husson College
### Bangor, Maine
**www.husson.edu**

CB member
CB code: 3440

- Private 4-year business and health science college
- Residential campus in large town
- 1,855 degree-seeking undergraduates: 18% part-time, 58% women, 4% African American, 2% Asian American, 1% Hispanic American, 1% Native American, 1% international
- 263 degree-seeking graduate students
- 91% of applicants admitted
- SAT or ACT with writing, application essay required

**General.** Founded in 1898. Regionally accredited. **Degrees:** 315 bachelor's, 39 associate awarded; master's, doctoral offered. **ROTC:** Army, Naval. **Location:** 125 miles from Portland. **Calendar:** Semester, extensive summer session. **Full-time faculty:** 64 total; 70% have terminal degrees, 8% minority, 67% women. **Part-time faculty:** 6 total; 67% women. **Class size:** 42% < 20, 49% 20-39, 7% 40-49, 2% 50-99. **Special facilities:** Center for family business.

**Freshman class profile.** 1,175 applied, 1,066 admitted, 464 enrolled.

| Mid 50% test scores | | | |
|---|---|---|---|
| SAT critical reading: | 400-500 | Rank in top quarter: | 32% |
| SAT math: | 400-510 | Rank in top tenth: | 11% |
| SAT writing: | 390-500 | End year in good standing: | 69% |
| ACT composite: | 17-22 | Out-of-state: | 14% |
| GPA 3.50 or higher: | 34% | Live on campus: | 61% |
| GPA 3.0-3.49: | 31% | | |

| | |
|---|---|
| GPA 2.0-2.99: | 30% |

**Basis for selection.** Class rank and school achievement record most important. Counselor recommendations considered. Test scores important for nursing applicants and occupational and physical therapy applicants. Test scores are used only for placement purposes for business and humanities school applicants. SAT recommended but not required for 2-year program and undeclared majors. Interview recommended. **Homeschooled:** GED required for financial aid to be awarded. **Learning Disabled:** School must be apprised of special accommodation needs at time of payment of tuition deposit.

**High school preparation.** Recommended units include English 4, mathematics 3, social studies 1, history 1, science 3 (laboratory 2).

**2008-2009 Annual costs.** Tuition/fees (projected): $12,750. Room/board: $6,790. Books/supplies: $930. Personal expenses: $1,030.

**2007-2008 Financial aid. Need-based:** Average need met was 70%. Average scholarship/grant was $8,601; average loan $3,069. 50% of total undergraduate aid awarded as scholarships/grants, 50% as loans/jobs. **Non-need-based:** Scholarships awarded for academics, leadership.

**Application procedures. Admission:** Priority date 3/1; deadline 9/1 (postmark date). $25 fee, may be waived for applicants with need. Application must be submitted on paper. Admission notification on a rolling basis beginning on or about 12/1. Must reply by May 1 or within 2 week(s) if notified thereafter. **Financial aid:** Priority date 4/15; no closing date. FAFSA required. Applicants notified on a rolling basis starting 4/1; must reply by 5/1 or within 2 week(s) of notification.

**Academics.** Strong liberal arts core within business programs. **Special study options:** Combined bachelor's/graduate degree, cooperative education, double major, independent study, internships, liberal arts/career combination, student-designed major, teacher certification program, weekend college. **Credit/placement by examination:** AP, CLEP, IB, SAT, ACT, institutional tests. 30 credit hours maximum toward bachelor's degree. **Support services:** Learning center, pre-admission summer program, reduced course load, remedial instruction, study skills assistance, tutoring, writing center.

**Majors. Biology:** General. **Business:** General, accounting, accounting/business management, banking/financial services, business admin, entrepreneurial studies, finance, hospitality admin, hospitality/recreation, hotel/motel admin, international, international marketing, management information systems, managerial economics, market research, marketing, public finance, sales/distribution, small business admin. **Computer sciences:** Applications programming, programming, systems analysis. **Education:** Biology, elementary, English, physical, secondary. **English:** English lit. **Health:** Nursing (RN), prepharmacy. **Legal studies:** Paralegal. **Liberal arts:** Arts/sciences. **Parks/recreation:** Facilities management, health/fitness, sports admin. **Physical sciences:** Chemistry. **Protective services:** Criminal justice, law enforcement admin. **Psychology:** General, clinical. **Social sciences:** Criminology.

**Most popular majors.** Business/marketing 54%, education 6%, health sciences 17%, legal studies 11%, psychology 6%.

**Computing on campus.** 115 workstations in library, computer center, student center. Dormitories wired for high-speed internet access and linked to campus network. Commuter students can connect to campus network. Online course registration, online library, helpline, student web hosting, wireless network available.

**Student life. Freshman orientation:** Mandatory, $75 fee. Preregistration for classes offered. 2 days of meetings with faculty, staff, administration; departmental orientation and activities for students and parents. **Housing:** Guaranteed on-campus for all undergraduates. Coed dorms, fraternity/sorority housing, substance-free housing available. **Activities:** Bands, drama, literary magazine, radio station, student government, student newspaper, international club, campus crusade for Christ, Chi Alpha, political clubs.

**Athletics.** NCAA. **Intercollegiate:** Baseball M, basketball, field hockey W, football (tackle) M, golf M, lacrosse, soccer, softball W, swimming W, volleyball W. **Intramural:** Basketball, football (non-tackle) M, ice hockey, lacrosse, soccer, swimming W, tennis, volleyball. **Team name:** Eagles.

**Student services.** Adult student services, alcohol/substance abuse counseling, campus ministries, career counseling, student employment services, financial aid counseling, health services, personal counseling, placement for graduates, veterans' counselor.

**Contact.** E-mail: admit@husson.edu
Phone: (207) 941-7100 Toll-free number: (800) 448-7766
Fax: (207) 941-7935
Jane Goodwin, Director of Admissions, Husson College, One College Circle, Bangor, ME 04401

---

## Maine College of Art
### Portland, Maine
**www.meca.edu**

CB member
CB code: 3701

- Private 4-year visual arts college
- Commuter campus in small city
- 343 degree-seeking undergraduates; 1% African American, 1% Asian American, 1% Hispanic American, 1% Native American
- 29 graduate students
- 82% of applicants admitted
- SAT or ACT (ACT writing optional), application essay required

**General.** Founded in 1882. Regionally accredited. Personal studio space with 24-hour access for all juniors and seniors. **Degrees:** 82 bachelor's awarded; master's offered. **Location:** 100 miles from Boston. **Calendar:** Semester. **Full-time faculty:** 30 total; 33% have terminal degrees, 47% women. **Part-time faculty:** 40 total; 48% women. **Class size:** 80% < 20, 19% 20-39, less than 1% 50-99. **Special facilities:** 2 art galleries, large visual arts library.

**Freshman class profile.** 322 applied, 263 admitted, 83 enrolled.

| Mid 50% test scores | | GPA 2.0-2.99: | 43% |
|---|---|---|---|
| SAT critical reading: | 430-530 | Rank in top quarter: | 32% |
| SAT math: | 400-490 | Rank in top tenth: | 9% |
| SAT writing: | 420-520 | Out-of-state: | 58% |
| ACT composite: | 18-23 | Live on campus: | 73% |
| GPA 3.50 or higher: | 18% | International: | 1% |
| GPA 3.0-3.49: | 34% | | |

**Basis for selection.** Decision based on interview and portfolio in conjunction with high school achievement record; essay, recommendations important, test scores considered. Interview recommended. Portfolio required. **Homeschooled:** Transcript of courses and grades, state high school equivalency certificate required. Show evidence through the State Certification of Completion of high school program or GED. **Learning Disabled:** Submit proper documentation to Director of Student Affairs (once admitted) and request specific accommodations.

**High school preparation.** 27 units recommended. Recommended units include English 4, mathematics 3, social studies 4, history 4, science 3, foreign language 2 and academic electives 3. 4 units of art strongly recommended.

**2007-2008 Annual costs.** Tuition/fees: $26,090. Studio fees vary per class. Room/board: $9,090. Books/supplies: $2,100. Personal expenses: $1,200.

**2007-2008 Financial aid. Need-based:** Average need met was 57%. Average scholarship/grant was $9,807; average loan $3,725. 56% of total undergraduate aid awarded as scholarships/grants, 44% as loans/jobs. **Non-need-based:** Scholarships awarded for academics, art.

**Application procedures. Admission:** Priority date 2/1; no deadline. $40 fee, may be waived for applicants with need. Application may be submitted online. Admission notification on a rolling basis beginning on or about 1/2. Students strongly encouraged to reply by May 1 or within 3 weeks if notified thereafter. **Financial aid:** Priority date 3/1; no closing date. FAFSA required. Applicants notified on a rolling basis starting 2/15; must reply within 2 week(s) of notification.

**Academics.** 1- to 2-year foundation program in drawing, color, and 2- and 3-dimensional design, followed by transitional year, and final 2 years in major. **Special study options:** Combined bachelor's/graduate degree, cross-registration, double major, exchange student, independent study, internships, liberal arts/career combination, student-designed major, study abroad, teacher certification program. Mobility program with 36 AICAD (Associated Independent Colleges of Art and Design) across the country and in Canada, cross-registration program with 4 other colleges and universities in the greater Portland area; special exchange program with Hanoi Fine Arts College, Vietnam; BFA credit available through Provincetown, MA Fine Arts Work Center. **Credit/placement by examination:** AP, CLEP. **Support services:** Learning center, study skills assistance, tutoring, writing center.

**Majors. Visual/performing arts:** Art, art history/conservation, ceramics, graphic design, illustration, metal/jewelry, painting, photography, printmaking, sculpture, studio arts.

**Computing on campus.** 57 workstations in library, computer center, student center. Dormitories wired for high-speed internet access. Online library, helpline, student web hosting available.

**Student life. Freshman orientation:** Mandatory. Preregistration for classes offered. **Housing:** Coed dorms, apartments, substance-free housing available. $500 partly refundable deposit. **Activities:** Film society, student government, student newspaper, student representative association, ski and snowboard club, outdoor group, bowling club, movie club, peer mentor scholarships, international student union.

**Student services.** Adult student services, alcohol/substance abuse counseling, career counseling, student employment services, financial aid counseling, health services, minority student services, personal counseling.

**Contact.** E-mail: admissions@meca.edu
Toll-free number: (800) 699-1509 Fax: (207) 871-1349
Karen Townsend, Director of Admissions, Maine College of Art, 522 Congress Street, Portland, ME 04101

## Maine Maritime Academy
**Castine, Maine**
**www.mainemaritime.edu**　　　　　　　CB code: 3505

▶ Public 4-year business, engineering and maritime college
▶ Residential campus in rural community
▶ 883 degree-seeking undergraduates: 2% part-time, 16% women

▶ 18 degree-seeking graduate students
▶ 62% of applicants admitted
▶ SAT or ACT with writing required
▶ 70% graduate within 6 years; 10% enter graduate study

**General.** Founded in 1941. Regionally accredited. **Degrees:** 170 bachelor's, 11 associate awarded; master's offered. **ROTC:** Army, Naval. **Location:** 38 miles from Bangor. **Calendar:** Semester, limited summer session. **Full-time faculty:** 69 total; 33% have terminal degrees, 4% minority, 26% women. **Part-time faculty:** 21 total; 52% women. **Special facilities:** 500-foot training ship, 40-foot marine research vessel, 80-foot ocean going tugboat and barge, two-masted arctic schooner, steam and diesel engine laboratories, power plant simulatiors, bridge simulator, planetarium, ocean classrooms.

**Freshman class profile.** 811 applied, 503 admitted, 301 enrolled.

| Mid 50% test scores | | End year in good standing: | 90% |
|---|---|---|---|
| SAT critical reading: | 440-550 | Return as sophomores: | 85% |
| SAT math: | 470-580 | Out-of-state: | 31% |
| ACT composite: | 18-23 | Live on campus: | 95% |

**Basis for selection.** High school academic record followed by SAT/ACT test scores are the most important. Interview, school and community activities, work ethic, and recommendations are also considered. Interview and personal statement are highly recommended. **Homeschooled:** Transcript of courses and grades, letter of recommendation (nonparent) required. ACT/SAT scores and possibly have transcripts/course records evaluated by Maine Department of Education.

**High school preparation.** Required and recommended units include English 4, mathematics 4, science 2-3 (laboratory 2) and foreign language 2. 1 unit computer literacy recommended.

**2007-2008 Annual costs.** Tuition/fees: $8,705; $12,205 out-of-district; $15,305 out-of-state. Fee of $2,400 for U.S. Coast Guard licensing programs. Room/board: $7,400. Books/supplies: $1,000. Personal expenses: $800.

**Financial aid. Non-need-based:** Scholarships awarded for academics, leadership, ROTC, state residency.

**Application procedures. Admission:** Priority date 5/31; deadline 7/1 (receipt date). $15 fee, may be waived for applicants with need. Application may be submitted online. Admission notification on a rolling basis beginning on or about 1/1. Must reply by 5/1. **Financial aid:** Priority date 4/15; no closing date. FAFSA, institutional form required. Applicants notified on a rolling basis starting 3/1; must reply within 4 week(s) of notification.

**Academics. Special study options:** Cooperative education, internships, liberal arts/career combination, semester at sea, student-designed major, study abroad, teacher certification program. 2-month training cruise for USCG unlimited license majors. **Credit/placement by examination:** AP, CLEP, institutional tests. **Support services:** Study skills assistance, tutoring, writing center.

**Majors. Biology:** Marine. **Business:** General, business admin, entrepreneurial studies, international, logistics. **Engineering:** Marine, systems. **Engineering technology:** General. **Physical sciences:** Oceanography. **Transportation:** Maritime/Merchant Marine.

**Most popular majors.** Biology 8%, business/marketing 8%, engineering/engineering technologies 64%, trade and industry 20%.

**Computing on campus.** PC or laptop required. 40 workstations in dormitories, library. Dormitories wired for high-speed internet access and linked to campus network. Commuter students can connect to campus network. Online library, helpline, repair service, wireless network available.

**Student life. Freshman orientation:** Mandatory. Preregistration for classes offered. 8 days immediately preceding start of fall semester. **Policies:** Regimental lifestyle optional for the 2-year program and those majoring in power engineering, ocean studies, international business, and small vessel operations. Regiment is mandatory for United States Coast Guard unlimited license programs (marine transportation and marine engineering). No military obligation. **Housing:** Guaranteed on-campus for all undergraduates. Coed dorms, apartments, substance-free housing available. $200 nonrefundable deposit, deadline 8/15. Students required to live on-campus unless married, over age 23, or have completed 2 or more years of active military service or 6 semesters of study. **Activities:** Bands, choral groups, drama, music ensembles, student government, student newspaper, Alpha Phi Omega, other service organizations.

**Athletics.** NCAA. **Intercollegiate:** Basketball, cross-country, football (tackle) M, golf M, lacrosse M, sailing, soccer, softball W, volleyball W. **Intramural:** Basketball, golf, handball, ice hockey M, racquetball, rifle, rugby M, sailing, skiing, soccer, softball, squash, tennis, volleyball, water polo. **Team name:** Mariners.

**Student services.** Alcohol/substance abuse counseling, career counseling, student employment services, financial aid counseling, health services, personal counseling, placement for graduates, veterans' counselor, women's services.

**Contact.** E-mail: admissions@mma.edu
Phone: (207) 326-2206 Toll-free number: (800) 227-8465
Fax: (207) 326-2515
Jeffrey Wright, Director of Admissions, Maine Maritime Academy, 66 Pleasant Street, Castine, ME 04420

---

## New England School of Communications
### Bangor, Maine
**www.nescom.edu**                                          **CB code: 3101**

- Private 4-year college of communications
- Residential campus in small city
- 393 degree-seeking undergraduates: 5% part-time, 24% women, 2% African American, 1% Asian American, 3% Hispanic American, 1% Native American
- 66% of applicants admitted
- Application essay, interview required

**General.** Accredited by ACCSCT. **Degrees:** 41 bachelor's, 23 associate awarded. **ROTC:** Army. **Location:** 250 miles from Boston. **Calendar:** Semester, limited summer session. **Full-time faculty:** 11 total; 36% have terminal degrees, 9% women. **Part-time faculty:** 46 total; 24% have terminal degrees, 2% minority, 30% women. **Class size:** 40% < 20, 52% 20-39, 3% 40-49, 5% 50-99. **Special facilities:** Television studio, television station, sound recording studio, digital photography lab, mobile production studio.

**Freshman class profile.** 354 applied, 235 admitted, 142 enrolled.

| | | | |
|---|---|---|---|
| Out-of-state: | 23% | Sororities: | 2% |
| Live on campus: | 69% | | |

**Basis for selection.** Interview and Placement Test most important. High school record and essay also important. SAT or ACT recommended. Timed scholastic placement exam, audio reading required for on-air candidates. **Homeschooled:** State high school equivalency certificate, interview, letter of recommendation (nonparent) required. Require GED score if homeschooling is not through an accredited curriculum-based program. **Learning Disabled:** Students requiring additional placement test time must provide professional evaluation documentation requesting extra time prior to interview date.

**High school preparation.** Recommended units include English 4, mathematics 2, social studies 1, history 2, science 2, foreign language 2, computer science 1 and visual/performing arts 1. Recommend additional computer, public speaking, creative arts coursework.

**2008-2009 Annual costs.** Tuition/fees (projected): $10,680. Additional cost of $160 for FireWire hard drive. Room/board: $6,725. Books/supplies: $1,050. Personal expenses: $150.

**Financial aid. Non-need-based:** Scholarships awarded for academics, leadership.

**Application procedures. Admission:** Priority date 4/1; no deadline. $15 fee, may be waived for applicants with need. Application may be submitted online. Admission notification on a rolling basis. **Financial aid:** Priority date 4/15; no closing date. FAFSA, institutional form required. Applicants notified on a rolling basis starting 2/1; must reply by 8/15.

**Academics. Special study options:** Cross-registration, double major, internships, liberal arts/career combination, student-designed major. **Credit/placement by examination:** AP, CLEP, institutional tests. 6 credit hours maximum toward associate degree, 15 toward bachelor's. **Support services:** Reduced course load, study skills assistance, tutoring, writing center.

**Majors. Communications:** Advertising, broadcast journalism, digital media, photojournalism, public relations, radio/tv. **Communications technology:** General, photo/film/video, radio/tv, recording arts. **Computer sciences:** Web page design. **Visual/performing arts:** Acting, cinematography, directing/producing, theater design.

**Computing on campus.** 195 workstations in dormitories, library, computer center, student center. Dormitories wired for high-speed internet access and linked to campus network. Commuter students can connect to campus network. Online library, helpline, wireless network available.

**Student life. Freshman orientation:** Mandatory. Preregistration for classes offered. 3 days before start of fall session. Spring orientation held the Monday before classes start. **Housing:** Guaranteed on-campus for freshmen. Coed dorms, fraternity/sorority housing, substance-free housing available. $50 nonrefundable deposit, deadline 7/1. **Activities:** Pep band, campus ministries, choral groups, drama, international student organizations, literary magazine, music ensembles, musical theater, radio station, student government, student newspaper, TV station, Crusade for Christ, Diversity Club, Habitat for Humanity.

**Athletics. Intramural:** Baseball, basketball, cheerleading, diving, field hockey, football (non-tackle), skiing, soccer, softball, swimming, table tennis, tennis, volleyball, water polo.

**Student services.** Adult student services, alcohol/substance abuse counseling, campus ministries, career counseling, student employment services, financial aid counseling, health services, personal counseling, placement for graduates, veterans' counselor.

**Contact.** E-mail: info@nescom.edu
Phone: (207) 941-7176 Toll-free number: (888) 877-1876 ext. 1093
Fax: (207) 947-3987
Louise Grant, Director of Admissions, New England School of Communications, One College Circle, Bangor, ME 04401

---

## St. Joseph's College
### Standish, Maine
**www.sjcme.edu**                    **CB member**
                                     **CB code: 3755**

- Private 4-year liberal arts college affiliated with Roman Catholic Church
- Residential campus in small town
- 1,071 degree-seeking undergraduates: 1% part-time, 66% women, 2% African American, 1% Asian American, 1% Hispanic American
- 80% of applicants admitted
- SAT or ACT (ACT writing recommended), application essay required
- 60% graduate within 6 years

**General.** Founded in 1912. Regionally accredited. **Degrees:** 186 bachelor's awarded. **ROTC:** Army. **Location:** 18 miles from Portland, 120 miles from Boston. **Calendar:** Semester, limited summer session. **Full-time faculty:** 68 total; 85% have terminal degrees, 2% minority, 52% women. **Part-time faculty:** 61 total; 30% have terminal degrees, 61% women. **Class size:** 60% < 20, 36% 20-39, 2% 40-49, 1% 50-99. **Special facilities:** Telescope, observatory.

**Freshman class profile.** 1,301 applied, 1,046 admitted, 321 enrolled.

| Mid 50% test scores | | | |
|---|---|---|---|
| SAT critical reading: | 430-530 | Return as sophomores: | 77% |
| SAT math: | 420-530 | Out-of-state: | 44% |
| | | Live on campus: | 93% |

**Basis for selection.** School record, class rank, test scores, recommendations, essays, extracurricular activities all considered. Interview optional, but recommended.

**High school preparation.** 16 units recommended. Recommended units include English 4, mathematics 3, social studies 2, history 2, science 2 (laboratory 2) and foreign language 2. Laboratory biology and laboratory chemistry required of nursing and science applicants. For any intended major, transcripts from candidates for admission should include 16 or more college-preparatory courses.

**2007-2008 Annual costs.** Tuition/fees: $23,300. Room/board: $9,600. Books/supplies: $900. Personal expenses: $1,200.

**2007-2008 Financial aid. Need-based:** 295 full-time freshmen applied for aid; 257 were judged to have need; 257 of these received aid. Average need met was 84%. Average scholarship/grant was $13,038; average loan $4,434. 62% of total undergraduate aid awarded as scholarships/grants, 38% as loans/jobs. **Non-need-based:** Awarded to 202 full-time undergraduates, including 101 freshmen. Scholarships awarded for academics, leadership.

**Application procedures. Admission:** Priority date 3/1; no deadline. $50 fee, may be waived for applicants with need. Application may be submitted online. Admission notification on a rolling basis beginning on or about 12/15. Must reply by May 1 or within 3 week(s) if notified thereafter. **Financial aid:** Priority date 3/1; no closing date. FAFSA, institutional form required. Applicants notified on a rolling basis starting 3/1; must reply within 3 week(s) of notification.

**Academics.** College belongs to Greater Portland Alliance, a 5-college consortium with cross registration. **Special study options:** Combined bachelor's/

graduate degree, cooperative education, cross-registration, distance learning, double major, honors, independent study, internships, liberal arts/career combination, semester at sea, student-designed major, study abroad, teacher certification program, Washington semester. **Credit/placement by examination:** AP, CLEP, SAT, ACT, institutional tests. 30 credit hours maximum toward bachelor's degree. **Support services:** Study skills assistance, tutoring, writing center.

**Majors. Biology:** General. **Business:** Accounting, business admin, finance, human resources, international, marketing. **Communications:** Digital media, journalism, public relations. **Conservation:** Environmental science, environmental studies. **Education:** Biology, elementary, English, history, mathematics, physical. **English:** English lit. **Health:** Nursing (RN). **History:** General. **Interdisciplinary:** Marine science. **Math:** General. **Parks/recreation:** Exercise sciences, sports admin. **Philosophy/religion:** Philosophy. **Physical sciences:** Chemistry. **Protective services:** Criminal justice. **Psychology:** General. **Social sciences:** General, political science, sociology. **Theology:** Theology.

**Most popular majors.** Biology 6%, business/marketing 20%, communications/journalism 8%, education 13%, health sciences 21%, parks/recreation 6%, social sciences 6%.

**Computing on campus.** 102 workstations in library, computer center, student center. Dormitories wired for high-speed internet access and linked to campus network. Commuter students can connect to campus network. Helpline, repair service, wireless network available.

**Student life. Freshman orientation:** Available, $50 fee. Preregistration for classes offered. 2-day session in June or July. **Policies:** Mass available daily on campus. **Housing:** Guaranteed on-campus for all undergraduates. Coed dorms, single-sex dorms, substance-free housing available. $100 deposit, deadline 5/1. **Activities:** Choral groups, dance, drama, literary magazine, radio station, student government, student newspaper, Habitat for Humanity, High Adventure, Superkids, business club, campus ministry, culture and heritage club, interhall council, student nurses association.

**Athletics.** NCAA. **Intercollegiate:** Baseball M, basketball, cross-country, field hockey W, golf M, lacrosse, soccer, softball W, swimming, volleyball W. **Intramural:** Basketball, football (non-tackle), soccer, softball, swimming, volleyball. **Team name:** Monks.

**Student services.** Alcohol/substance abuse counseling, campus ministries, career counseling, student employment services, financial aid counseling, health services, personal counseling, placement for graduates, veterans' counselor. **Physically disabled:** Services for visually, speech, hearing impaired. **Learning disabled:** Comprehensive services available.

**Contact.** E-mail: admission@sjcme.edu
Phone: (207) 893-7746 Toll-free number: (800) 338-7057
Fax: (207) 893-7862
Vincent Kloskowski, Dean of Admission, St. Joseph's College, 278 Whites Bridge Road, Standish, ME 04084-5263

---

## Thomas College

**Waterville, Maine**
www.thomas.edu

**CB member**
**CB code: 3903**

- Private 4-year business and liberal arts college
- Residential campus in large town
- 739 degree-seeking undergraduates: 14% part-time, 49% women, 2% African American, 1% Asian American, 1% Hispanic American
- 210 degree-seeking graduate students
- 81% of applicants admitted
- SAT or ACT (ACT writing optional), application essay required
- 52% graduate within 6 years

**General.** Founded in 1894. Regionally accredited. Evening division (undergraduate and graduate) on trimester system. **Degrees:** 108 bachelor's, 10 associate awarded; master's offered. **Location:** 75 miles from Portland. **Calendar:** Semester, limited summer session. **Full-time faculty:** 21 total; 52% have terminal degrees, 38% women. **Part-time faculty:** 60 total; 77% have terminal degrees, 40% women. **Class size:** 53% < 20, 47% 20-39.

**Freshman class profile.** 668 applied, 543 admitted, 247 enrolled.

| Mid 50% test scores | | | |
|---|---|---|---|
| SAT critical reading: | 400-500 | GPA 2.0-2.99: | 50% |
| SAT math: | 390-510 | Rank in top quarter: | 19% |
| SAT writing: | 380-500 | Rank in top tenth: | 7% |
| ACT composite: | 13-22 | Return as sophomores: | 63% |
| GPA 3.50 or higher: | 10% | Out-of-state: | 22% |
| GPA 3.0-3.49: | 32% | Live on campus: | 70% |

**Basis for selection.** Academic transcripts most important. Letters of recommendation and SAT and/or TOEFL Exam scores are also important. Recommend minimum 2.0 overall GPA, rank in top half of class. Test scores required of bachelor's degree candidates, not required for associate degree candidates. Interview recommended. **Homeschooled:** Transcript of courses and grades, state high school equivalency certificate, letter of recommendation (nonparent) required.

**High school preparation.** 16 units recommended. Recommended units include English 4, mathematics 3, social studies 2, history 2, science 3 and foreign language 2.

**2007-2008 Annual costs.** Tuition/fees: $19,100. Room/board: $7,390. Books/supplies: $800. Personal expenses: $1,000.

**2007-2008 Financial aid. Need-based:** 214 full-time freshmen applied for aid; 209 were judged to have need; 209 of these received aid. Average need met was 85%. Average scholarship/grant was $12,369; average loan $4,173. 69% of total undergraduate aid awarded as scholarships/grants, 31% as loans/jobs. **Non-need-based:** Awarded to 122 full-time undergraduates, including 70 freshmen. Scholarships awarded for academics, leadership, state residency.

**Application procedures. Admission:** No deadline. $50 fee, may be waived for applicants with need. Application may be submitted online. Admission notification on a rolling basis beginning on or about 12/1. Must reply by May 1 or within 4 week(s) if notified thereafter. **Financial aid:** Priority date 2/15; no closing date. FAFSA required. Applicants notified on a rolling basis starting 3/15; must reply within 2 week(s) of notification.

**Academics. Special study options:** Combined bachelor's/graduate degree, cross-registration, double major, internships, study abroad, teacher certification program. New England/Quebec Student Exchange Program; Ecole de Gestion et de Commerce in Nante, France. **Credit/placement by examination:** AP, CLEP. 15 credit hours maximum toward associate degree, 15 toward bachelor's. **Support services:** Learning center, reduced course load, study skills assistance, tutoring.

**Majors. Business:** Accounting, business admin, finance, hospitality admin, human resources, international, management information systems, marketing. **Communications:** General. **Computer sciences:** General, computer science, information systems. **Education:** Elementary. **Engineering:** Software. **Legal studies:** Prelaw. **Parks/recreation:** Sports admin. **Protective services:** Criminal justice, law enforcement admin. **Psychology:** General. **Social sciences:** Political science.

**Most popular majors.** Business/marketing 50%, computer/information sciences 16%, parks/recreation 10%, psychology 8%, security/protective services 14%.

**Computing on campus.** 120 workstations in dormitories, library, computer center, student center. Dormitories wired for high-speed internet access and linked to campus network. Commuter students can connect to campus network. Online course registration, online library, helpline, student web hosting, wireless network available.

**Student life. Freshman orientation:** Mandatory. Preregistration for classes offered. One credit pass/fail for first year students. **Housing:** Guaranteed on-campus for freshmen. Coed dorms, substance-free housing available. $200 nonrefundable deposit, deadline 5/1. **Activities:** Choral groups, dance, drama, student government, student newspaper, Diversity Coalition, Fellowship Group; Habitat for Humanity.

**Athletics.** NCAA. **Intercollegiate:** Baseball M, basketball, field hockey W, golf M, lacrosse, soccer, softball W, tennis M, volleyball W. **Intramural:** Basketball, bowling, football (non-tackle), soccer, softball, table tennis, tennis, volleyball, weight lifting. **Team name:** Terriers.

**Student services.** Alcohol/substance abuse counseling, campus ministries, career counseling, student employment services, financial aid counseling, health services, personal counseling, placement for graduates, veterans' counselor.

**Contact.** E-mail: admiss@thomas.edu
Phone: (207) 859-1101 Toll-free number: (800) 339-7001
Fax: (207) 859-1114
Wendy Martin, Director of Admissions, Thomas College, 180 West River Road, Waterville, ME 04901

## Unity College
**Unity, Maine**
**www.unity.edu**
CB code: 3925

- Private 4-year liberal arts college
- Residential campus in rural community
- 552 degree-seeking undergraduates: 3% part-time, 41% women, 1% African American, 1% Asian American, 1% Hispanic American, 1% Native American
- 78% of applicants admitted
- Application essay required
- 40% graduate within 6 years; 7% enter graduate study

**General.** Founded in 1965. Regionally accredited. **Degrees:** 96 bachelor's, 4 associate awarded. **ROTC:** Army. **Location:** 20 miles from Waterville. **Calendar:** Semester, limited summer session. **Full-time faculty:** 36 total; 92% have terminal degrees, 6% minority, 33% women. **Part-time faculty:** 24 total; 75% have terminal degrees, 8% minority, 62% women. **Class size:** 64% <20, 35% 20-39, less than 1% 40-49, less than 1% 50-99. **Special facilities:** Wetlands research area.

**Freshman class profile.** 563 applied, 437 admitted, 177 enrolled.

| | | | |
|---|---|---|---|
| End year in good standing: | 85% | Out-of-state: | 65% |
| Return as sophomores: | 55% | Live on campus: | 90% |

**Basis for selection.** High school transcripts, interviews, recommendations and essay most important. Test scores not required but highly recommended. SAT or ACT recommended. **Homeschooled:** Informative portfolio.

**High school preparation.** 18 units recommended. Required and recommended units include English 4, mathematics 4, social studies 3, history 3, science 3 (laboratory 3) and foreign language 2.

**2007-2008 Annual costs.** Tuition/fees: $19,620. Room/board: $7,310. Books/supplies: $450. Personal expenses: $800.

**2007-2008 Financial aid. Need-based:** Average need met was 78%. Average scholarship/grant was $11,541; average loan $4,644. 56% of total undergraduate aid awarded as scholarships/grants, 44% as loans/jobs. **Non-need-based:** Scholarships awarded for academics, leadership, minority status.

**Application procedures. Admission:** Priority date 7/1; no deadline. $25 fee, may be waived for applicants with need. Application may be submitted online. Admission notification on a rolling basis. **Financial aid:** Priority date 3/1; no closing date. FAFSA required. Applicants notified on a rolling basis starting 2/15.

**Academics. Special study options:** Accelerated study, combined bachelor's/graduate degree, cooperative education, double major, independent study, internships, semester at sea, student-designed major, study abroad, teacher certification program, Washington semester. **Credit/placement by examination:** AP, CLEP, IB, institutional tests. 15 credit hours maximum toward associate degree, 15 toward bachelor's. **Support services:** Learning center, reduced course load, remedial instruction, study skills assistance, tutoring, writing center.

**Majors. Agriculture:** Aquaculture, ornamental horticulture. **Biology:** Ecology, environmental, marine, wildlife. **Conservation:** Environmental science, environmental studies, forestry, management/policy, wildlife. **Health:** Recreational therapy. **Liberal arts:** Arts/sciences. **Parks/recreation:** General, facilities management. **Social sciences:** General.

**Most popular majors.** Biology 27%, education 9%, health sciences 7%, natural resources/environmental science 34%, parks/recreation 13%.

**Computing on campus.** 80 workstations in dormitories, library, computer center, student center. Dormitories wired for high-speed internet access and linked to campus network. Commuter students can connect to campus network. Online library, wireless network available.

**Student life. Freshman orientation:** Mandatory, $100 fee. Preregistration for classes offered. A 5-day outdoor wilderness-based program. **Housing:** Guaranteed on-campus for all undergraduates. Coed dorms, single-sex

dorms available. **Activities:** Drama, radio station, student government, student newspaper, fire-fighting crew, photography club, Environmental Awareness, recycling, community service.

**Athletics. Intercollegiate:** Basketball, cross-country, soccer, volleyball W. **Intramural:** Baseball M, basketball, cross-country, lacrosse M, soccer, softball, volleyball. **Team name:** Rams.

**Student services.** Alcohol/substance abuse counseling, campus ministries, career counseling, student employment services, financial aid counseling, health services, personal counseling, placement for graduates, veterans' counselor.

**Contact.** E-mail: admissions@unity.edu
Phone: (207) 948-3131 ext. 231 Toll-free number: (800) 624-1024
Fax: (207) 948-2928
Kay Fiedler, Director of Admission, Unity College, P.O. 532, Unity, ME 04988-0532

## University of Maine
**Orono, Maine**
**www.umaine.edu**
CB member
CB code: 3916

- Public 4-year university
- Residential campus in large town
- 8,777 degree-seeking undergraduates: 11% part-time, 50% women, 1% African American, 1% Asian American, 1% Hispanic American, 2% Native American, 2% international
- 1,755 degree-seeking graduate students
- 77% of applicants admitted
- SAT or ACT (ACT writing optional), application essay required
- 59% graduate within 6 years

**General.** Founded in 1865. Regionally accredited. **Degrees:** 1,681 bachelor's awarded; master's, doctoral offered. **ROTC:** Army, Naval. **Location:** 12 miles from Bangor. **Calendar:** Semester, extensive summer session. **Full-time faculty:** 506 total; 84% have terminal degrees, 7% minority, 33% women. **Part-time faculty:** 305 total; 30% have terminal degrees, 4% minority, 53% women. **Class size:** 43% <20, 36% 20-39, 7% 40-49, 9% 50-99, 4% >100. **Special facilities:** Advanced manufacturing center, machine tool lab, laboratory for surface science and technology, planetarium, anthropology museum, woodland preserve, botanical garden, arts center, observatory, environmental research facility, performing arts hall, Canadian-American center, Franco-American center, digital media lab, farm museum, marine lab, aquatic production facility, climbing wall.

**Freshman class profile.** 6,958 applied, 5,387 admitted, 1,914 enrolled.

| Mid 50% test scores | | | |
|---|---|---|---|
| SAT critical reading: | 480-580 | GPA 2.0-2.99: | 21% |
| SAT math: | 480-600 | Rank in top quarter: | 52% |
| SAT writing: | 470-570 | Rank in top tenth: | 21% |
| ACT composite: | 19-25 | Out-of-state: | 17% |
| GPA 3.50 or higher: | 29% | Live on campus: | 88% |
| GPA 3.0-3.49: | 50% | International: | 2% |

**Basis for selection.** Strong emphasis on grades earned, GPA, and class rank (if available). Academic requirements for admission vary by program. Interview recommended. Audition required of music majors. Portfolio recommended for art majors. **Homeschooled:** Statement describing homeschool structure and mission, transcript of courses and grades, state high school equivalency certificate, letter of recommendation (nonparent) required. GED requirement may be waived if thorough records submitted.

**High school preparation.** 17 units required; 21 recommended. Required and recommended units include English 4, mathematics 3-4, social studies 2, history 1, science 2-4 (laboratory 2-3), foreign language 2 and academic electives 4. 1 unit physical education required of all College of Education candidates.

**2007-2008 Annual costs.** Tuition/fees: $8,330; $20,540 out-of-state. New England Regional Student Program tuition is 150% of public in-district tuition. Room/board: $7,484. Books/supplies: $700. Personal expenses: $1,100.

**2007-2008 Financial aid. Need-based:** Average need met was 87%. Average scholarship/grant was $6,288; average loan $4,024. 46% of total undergraduate aid awarded as scholarships/grants, 54% as loans/jobs. **Non-need-based:** Scholarships awarded for academics, alumni affiliation, art, athletics, job skills, leadership, minority status, music/drama, religious affiliation, ROTC, state residency. **Additional information:** Financial aid is available for students entering in the spring.

**Application procedures. Admission:** Priority date 3/1; no deadline. $40 fee, may be waived for applicants with need. Application may be submitted online. Admission notification on a rolling basis beginning on or about 1/31. Must reply by May 1 or within 2 week(s) if notified thereafter. **Financial aid:** Priority date 3/1; no closing date. FAFSA required. Applicants notified on a rolling basis starting 3/15; must reply by 5/1 or within 2 week(s) of notification.

**Academics. Special study options:** Accelerated study, combined bachelor's/graduate degree, cooperative education, distance learning, double major, ESL, exchange student, honors, independent study, internships, liberal arts/career combination, semester at sea, study abroad, teacher certification program. **Credit/placement by examination:** AP, CLEP, IB, institutional tests. Duplicate credit may not be granted. Each department may develop or adopt examinations other than CLEP examinations for the purpose of granting credit for specific courses. **Support services:** Reduced course load, remedial instruction, study skills assistance, tutoring.

**Honors college/program.** Admission for first-time and transfer students based on test scores and high school record.

**Majors. Agriculture:** Animal sciences, business, economics, food science, greenhouse operations, horticultural science, landscaping, nursery operations, ornamental horticulture, plant sciences, soil science, turf management. **Architecture:** Landscape. **Area/ethnic studies:** Women's. **Biology:** General, bacteriology, biochemistry, biomedical sciences, botany, cell/histology, ecology, entomology, marine, molecular, pathology, zoology. **Business:** General, accounting, business admin, finance, labor relations, management information systems, managerial economics. **Communications:** General, journalism. **Computer sciences:** General. **Conservation:** Environmental studies, forest resources, forestry, management/policy, wildlife, wood science. **Education:** General, art, biology, chemistry, elementary, English, foreign languages, French, history, mathematics, music, physical, science, secondary, social studies, Spanish. **Engineering:** General, agricultural, chemical, civil, computer, electrical, forest, mechanical, physics, systems. **Engineering technology:** Civil, electrical, surveying. **English:** English lit, speech/rhetoric. **Family/consumer sciences:** Family/community services, food/nutrition. **Foreign languages:** General, French, German, Latin, Spanish. **Health:** Audiology/speech pathology, clinical lab science, communication disorders, nursing (RN). **History:** General. **Interdisciplinary:** Biological/physical sciences, natural sciences. **Liberal arts:** Arts/sciences. **Math:** General. **Parks/recreation:** Facilities management. **Philosophy/religion:** Philosophy. **Physical sciences:** Chemistry, geology, oceanography, physics. **Psychology:** General. **Public administration:** General, social work. **Social sciences:** Anthropology, economics, international relations, political science, sociology. **Visual/performing arts:** Art history/conservation, dramatic, music performance, studio arts.

**Most popular majors.** Business/marketing 13%, communications/journalism 6%, education 12%, engineering/engineering technologies 13%, health sciences 7%, psychology 6%, social sciences 7%.

**Computing on campus.** 500 workstations in library, computer center, student center. Dormitories wired for high-speed internet access and linked to campus network. Commuter students can connect to campus network. Online course registration, online library, helpline, repair service, student web hosting, wireless network available.

**Student life. Freshman orientation:** Available. Preregistration for classes offered. 2-day events in June, parents invited; 4-day welcome program in fall; additional adventure orientations available. **Housing:** Guaranteed on-campus for freshmen. Coed dorms, special housing for disabled, apartments, fraternity/sorority housing, substance-free housing available. Academic grouping wings, substance-free and quiet areas, honors housing, men-only sections, women-only sections available. **Activities:** Bands, choral groups, dance, drama, film society, music ensembles, musical theater, opera, radio station, student government, student newspaper, symphony orchestra, TV station, InterVarsity Christian Fellowship, Campus Crusade for Christ, Catholic Student Association, Hillel, Maine Christian Association, Muslim student organization, Newman Center.

**Athletics. NCAA. Intercollegiate:** Baseball M, basketball, cross-country, diving, field hockey W, football (tackle) M, ice hockey, soccer, softball, swimming, track and field, volleyball W. **Intramural:** Badminton, basketball, cross-country, diving, field hockey W, football (non-tackle) M, golf, racquetball, skiing, soccer, softball, squash, swimming, table tennis, tennis, track and field, triathlon, volleyball, water polo. **Team name:** Black Bears.

**Student services.** Adult student services, alcohol/substance abuse counseling, campus ministries, career counseling, services for economically disadvantaged, student employment services, financial aid counseling, health services, legal services, minority student services, on-campus daycare, personal counseling, placement for graduates, veterans' counselor, women's services. **Physically disabled:** Services for visually, speech, hearing impaired.

**Contact.** E-mail: um-admit@maine.edu
Phone: (207) 581-1561 Toll-free number: (877) 486-2364
Fax: (207) 581-1213
Sharon Oliver, Director of Admissions, University of Maine, 5713 Chadbourne Hall, Orono, ME 04469-5713

---

### University of Maine at Augusta
**Augusta, Maine**
**www.uma.edu**

**CB member**
**CB code: 3929**

- Public 4-year university
- Commuter campus in large town
- 4,207 degree-seeking undergraduates: 65% part-time, 76% women, 1% African American, 1% Hispanic American, 3% Native American

**General.** Founded in 1965. Regionally accredited. Additional centers in Rockland, Brunswick, Rumford, Saco, Sanford, Ellsworth, East Millinocket; additional campuses in Bangor. **Degrees:** 357 bachelor's, 285 associate awarded. **ROTC:** Army, Naval, Air Force. **Location:** 65 miles from Portland, 75 miles from Bangor. **Calendar:** Semester, extensive summer session. **Full-time faculty:** 104 total; 39% have terminal degrees, 52% women. **Part-time faculty:** 114 total; 48% women. **Class size:** 67% < 20, 30% 20-39, 2% 40-49, 1% 50-99. **Special facilities:** Holocaust center.

**Freshman class profile.** 2,649 applied, 2,002 admitted, 1,282 enrolled.

**Basis for selection.** Open admission, but selective for some programs. High school achievement record and test scores considered for admission to allied health and bachelor's degree programs. Talent/ability assessed for admission to music programs. TOEFL is requested of non-native English speakers. Interviews required of dental hygiene and medical laboratory technology majors. Audition required of music majors. **Homeschooled:** Transcript of courses and grades required. Documentation of high school completion required of all.

**High school preparation.** Recommended units include English 4, mathematics 2, social studies 2, history 2, science 2 (laboratory 2). Applicants to health science programs must have biology, chemistry, and Algebra II. Business administration and public administration applicants must have Algebra II and geometry.

**2007-2008 Annual costs.** Tuition/fees: $5,985; $13,395 out-of-state. New England Regional Student Program tuition is 150% of public in-district tuition. Books/supplies: $910.

**2007-2008 Financial aid. Need-based:** 256 full-time freshmen applied for aid; 220 were judged to have need; 212 of these received aid. Average need met was 68%. Average scholarship/grant was $4,698; average loan $3,376. 53% of total undergraduate aid awarded as scholarships/grants, 47% as loans/jobs. **Non-need-based:** Awarded to 157 full-time undergraduates, including 27 freshmen. Scholarships awarded for academics, athletics, leadership, music/drama, state residency.

**Application procedures. Admission:** Priority date 6/15; deadline 8/30 (receipt date). $40 fee, may be waived for applicants with need. Application may be submitted online. Admission notification on a rolling basis. Must reply by May 1 or within 2 week(s) if notified thereafter. **Financial aid:** Priority date 3/1; no closing date. FAFSA required. Applicants notified on a rolling basis starting 3/15; must reply within 2 week(s) of notification.

**Academics. Special study options:** Combined bachelor's/graduate degree, cross-registration, distance learning, double major, dual enrollment of high school students, honors, independent study, internships, liberal arts/career combination, student-designed major, study abroad. **Credit/placement by examination:** AP, CLEP, institutional tests. 45 credit hours maximum toward associate degree, 90 toward bachelor's. **Support services:** Reduced course load, remedial instruction, study skills assistance, tutoring.

**Majors. Architecture:** Technology. **Biology:** General. **Business:** Accounting, business admin, financial planning. **Computer sciences:** General. **English:** English lit. **Health:** Dental hygiene. **Liberal arts:** Library science. **Protective services:** Law enforcement admin. **Public administration:** General. **Social sciences:** General. **Visual/performing arts:** Studio arts.

**Most popular majors.** Business/marketing 18%, health sciences 30%, liberal arts 9%, library sciences 11%, security/protective services 6%, social sciences 8%, visual/performing arts 8%.

**Computing on campus.** 191 workstations in library, computer center. Commuter students can connect to campus network. Online course registration, wireless network available.

**Student life. Freshman orientation:** Available. Preregistration for classes offered. One-day program held 1 week prior to start of each semester and mid-summer. **Activities:** Bands, music ensembles, student government, student newspaper, art and architectural student association, Gay Lesbian Bisexual Transgender friends and associates, student government association, honors English program, english society, student nursing association, Pi Alpha Alpha, international student club, college republicans, mental health and human services club, campus crusade.

**Athletics.** USCAA. **Intercollegiate:** Basketball, soccer W. **Intramural:** Basketball, racquetball, soccer, volleyball. **Team name:** Moose.

**Student services.** Adult student services, alcohol/substance abuse counseling, career counseling, financial aid counseling, personal counseling. **Physically disabled:** Services for visually, hearing impaired.

**Contact.** E-mail: umaadm@maine.edu
Phone: (207) 621-3465 Toll-free number: (877) 862-1234
Fax: (207) 621-3333
Jonathan Henry, Director of Admissions and Dean of Enrollment,
University of Maine at Augusta, 46 University Drive, Augusta, ME 04330

---

## University of Maine at Farmington
**Farmington, Maine**
www.farmington.edu

CB member
CB code: 3506

- Public 4-year liberal arts and teachers college
- Residential campus in small town
- 2,137 degree-seeking undergraduates: 5% part-time, 67% women, 1% African American, 1% Asian American, 1% Hispanic American, 1% Native American
- 71% of applicants admitted
- Application essay required
- 61% graduate within 6 years

**General.** Founded in 1863. Regionally accredited. **Degrees:** 475 bachelor's awarded. **Location:** 38 miles from Augusta, 80 miles from Portland. **Calendar:** Semester, extensive summer session. **Full-time faculty:** 128 total; 88% have terminal degrees, 5% minority, 52% women. **Part-time faculty:** 47 total; 43% have terminal degrees, 60% women. **Class size:** 70% < 20, 30% 20-39, less than 1% 50-99. **Special facilities:** Archaeology research center, campus-wide wireless laptop network, 24/7 computer center, on-site nursery school, day care center teaching labs, multi-media graphics lab, observatory.

**Freshman class profile.** 1,817 applied, 1,298 admitted, 489 enrolled.

| Mid 50% test scores | | | |
|---|---|---|---|
| SAT critical reading: | 440-560 | GPA 2.0-2.99: | 48% |
| SAT math: | 430-550 | Rank in top quarter: | 41% |
| SAT writing: | 440-560 | Rank in top tenth: | 11% |
| GPA 3.50 or higher: | 4% | Return as sophomores: | 75% |
| GPA 3.0-3.49: | 48% | Out-of-state: | 18% |
| | | Live on campus: | 89% |

**Basis for selection.** School achievement record and recommendation most important. School and community activities, interviews and personal essay also important. On campus placement tests required for those below SAT 490 Verbal, 450 Math. Interview recommended. 13-15 page writing sample required for Creative Writing BFA. **Homeschooled:** Transcript of courses and grades, state high school equivalency certificate required. **Learning Disabled:** Students may submit disclosure of learning disability to learning center after admission.

**High school preparation.** 19 units recommended. Required and recommended units include English 4, mathematics 3-4, social studies 2-3, science 2-3 (laboratory 2-3), foreign language 2-3 and academic electives 3. Algebra I and II and geometry required. Two years of same foreign language required. General college preparatory program required for all except those admitted to Liberal Studies Bridge.

**2007-2008 Annual costs.** Tuition/fees: $7,157; $14,837 out-of-state. New England Regional Student Program tuition and fees: $10,677. Room/board: $6,722. Books/supplies: $560. Personal expenses: $2,122.

**Financial aid.** **Non-need-based:** Scholarships awarded for academics, leadership, minority status, state residency. **Additional information:** FAFSA must arrive at Federal processor by 3/1.

**Application procedures.** **Admission:** No deadline. $40 fee, may be waived for applicants with need. Application may be submitted online. Admission notification on a rolling basis beginning on or about 12/15. Must reply by May 1 or within 3 week(s) if notified thereafter. Housing deposit is refundable in full if requested by May 1. **Financial aid:** Priority date 3/1; no closing date. FAFSA required. Applicants notified on a rolling basis starting 3/15; must reply within 2 week(s) of notification.

**Academics.** Interdisciplinary first year seminar. **Special study options:** Accelerated study, cross-registration, distance learning, double major, dual enrollment of high school students, exchange student, honors, independent study, internships, liberal arts/career combination, semester at sea, student-designed major, study abroad, teacher certification program. **Credit/placement by examination:** AP, CLEP, IB, SAT, institutional tests. **Support services:** Learning center, pre-admission summer program, reduced course load, remedial instruction, study skills assistance, tutoring, writing center.

**Majors.** **Area/ethnic studies:** Women's. **Biology:** General. **Business:** Managerial economics. **Computer sciences:** Computer science. **Conservation:** Environmental science, land use planning. **Education:** Biology, early childhood, early childhood special, elementary, English, health, kindergarten/preschool, mathematics, science, secondary, social science, special. **English:** Creative writing, English lit. **Health:** Community health, public health ed. **History:** General. **Interdisciplinary:** Global studies. **Math:** General. **Physical sciences:** Geochemistry, geology. **Psychology:** General. **Social sciences:** Anthropology, geography, political science. **Visual/performing arts:** Art, arts management, dramatic, music management, theater arts management. **Other:** Interdisciplinary Studies, Philosophy and Religious Studies, Rehabilitation Administration and Rehabilitation services.

**Most popular majors.** Business/marketing 6%, education 41%, English 12%, health sciences 9%, interdisciplinary studies 12%, psychology 8%.

**Computing on campus.** 180 workstations in library, computer center, student center. Dormitories wired for high-speed internet access and linked to campus network. Commuter students can connect to campus network. Online course registration, online library, helpline, wireless network available.

**Student life.** **Freshman orientation:** Available, $175 fee. Preregistration for classes offered. Held immmediately before classes; includes outdoor activities and community service. **Housing:** Guaranteed on-campus for freshmen. Coed dorms, single-sex dorms, special housing for disabled, substance-free housing available. Housing for students maintaining certain GPA, medical single rooms, quiet floors, wellness community, independent living environment housing available. **Activities:** Concert band, choral groups, dance, drama, literary magazine, music ensembles, radio station, student government, student newspaper, symphony orchestra, Justice Uniting Students Together, student environmental and political awareness club, Amnesty International, Inter-Varsity Christian Fellowship, student alcohol educators, student admissions club, Alpha Phi Omega, literary guild, Newman Club, student-run entertainment board.

**Athletics.** NCAA. **Intercollegiate:** Baseball M, basketball, cross-country, field hockey W, golf, soccer, softball W, volleyball W. **Intramural:** Basketball, football (non-tackle), soccer, softball, swimming, tennis, volleyball. **Team name:** Beavers.

**Student services.** Alcohol/substance abuse counseling, career counseling, services for economically disadvantaged, student employment services, financial aid counseling, health services, on-campus daycare, personal counseling, placement for graduates, veterans' counselor, women's services. **Physically disabled:** Services for visually, hearing impaired.

**Contact.** E-mail: umfadmit@maine.edu
Phone: (207) 778-7050 Fax: (207) 778-8182
Brandon Lagana, Director of Admission, University of Maine at Farmington, 246 Main Street, Farmington, ME 04938

---

## University of Maine at Fort Kent
**Fort Kent, Maine**
www.umfk.maine.edu

CB member
CB code: 3393

- Public 4-year university
- Commuter campus in small town
- 917 degree-seeking undergraduates: 20% part-time, 64% women, 1% African American, 1% Hispanic American, 1% Native American, 30% international
- Application essay required
- 32% graduate within 6 years

**General.** Founded in 1878. Regionally accredited. Bilingual Franco-American region. **Degrees:** 267 bachelor's, 38 associate awarded. **Location:** 200 miles from Bangor, 21 miles from Edmundston, Canada. **Calendar:** Semester, limited summer session. **Full-time faculty:** 40 total. **Part-time faculty:** 45 total. **Special facilities:** 16-acre biological park, Acadian Archives, interactive television site, Northern Maine Center for Rural Health Science.

**Freshman class profile.**

| | | | |
|---|---|---|---|
| GPA 3.50 or higher: | 6% | Rank in top tenth: | 5% |
| GPA 3.0-3.49: | 29% | Return as sophomores: | 66% |
| GPA 2.0-2.99: | 57% | International: | 15% |
| Rank in top quarter: | 20% | | |

**Basis for selection.** Open admission, but selective for some programs. High school courses and achievement record most important. Recommendations considered. SAT, ACT scores, or on-campus placement exams required. Interview recommended.

**High school preparation.** 16 units required. Required and recommended units include English 4, mathematics 2, social studies 2, science 2 and foreign language 2. Biology and chemistry required for nursing and environmental studies.

**2007-2008 Annual costs.** Tuition/fees: $5,790; $13,440 out-of-state. New England Regional tuition is 150% of public in-district tuition. Room/board: $6,285. Books/supplies: $1,000. Personal expenses: $1,000.

**Financial aid.** **Non-need-based:** Scholarships awarded for academics.

**Application procedures. Admission:** No deadline. $40 fee, may be waived for applicants with need. Application may be submitted online. Admission notification on a rolling basis. Must reply by May 1 or within 4 week(s) if notified thereafter. **Financial aid:** Priority date 3/1; no closing date. FAFSA required. Applicants notified on a rolling basis starting 3/15; must reply within 2 week(s) of notification.

**Academics. Special study options:** Accelerated study, cooperative education, cross-registration, distance learning, double major, dual enrollment of high school students, honors, independent study, internships, liberal arts/career combination, student-designed major, study abroad, teacher certification program. **Credit/placement by examination:** AP, CLEP, IB, institutional tests. 30 credit hours maximum toward associate degree, 90 toward bachelor's. **Support services:** Learning center, pre-admission summer program, reduced course load, remedial instruction, tutoring.

**Majors. Area/ethnic studies:** Canadian. **Biology:** General. **Business:** General, business admin, e-commerce, management information systems. **Computer sciences:** General, information technology, programming, systems analysis. **Conservation:** Environmental science, management/policy. **Education:** General, business, elementary, English, multi-level teacher, music, science, secondary, social studies. **English:** American lit, British lit, English lit. **Foreign languages:** General, comparative lit, French. **Health:** Nursing (RN), predental, premedicine, prepharmacy, preveterinary. **Interdisciplinary:** Math/computer science. **Legal studies:** Prelaw. **Liberal arts:** Arts/sciences. **Psychology:** General. **Public administration:** Social work. **Social sciences:** General, sociology. **Other:** Public Safety Administration.

**Most popular majors.** Education 75%, health sciences 9%, social sciences 6%.

**Computing on campus.** 100 workstations in dormitories, library, computer center. Dormitories linked to campus network. Commuter students can connect to campus network. Online course registration, repair service, student web hosting, wireless network available.

**Student life. Freshman orientation:** Mandatory. Preregistration for classes offered. 3-day social and educational orientation, including workshops. **Housing:** Coed dorms available. $100 deposit. **Activities:** Jazz band, choral groups, dance, drama, music ensembles, musical theater, student government, Christian Fellowship, Newman Club.

**Athletics.** NAIA. **Intercollegiate:** Basketball, skiing, soccer. **Intramural:** Baseball M, basketball, cross-country, golf, ice hockey M, racquetball, skiing, soccer, softball, table tennis, tennis, volleyball, weight lifting. **Team name:** Bengals.

**Student services.** Adult student services, career counseling, financial aid counseling, health services, personal counseling, placement for graduates, veterans' counselor.

**Contact.** E-mail: umfkadm@maine.edu
Phone: (207) 834-7600 Toll-free number: (888) 879-8635
Fax: (207) 834-7609
Jill Cairns, Director of Admissions, University of Maine at Fort Kent, 23 University Drive, Fort Kent, ME 04743

---

## University of Maine at Machias
**Machias, Maine**
www.umm.maine.edu

**CB member**
**CB code: 3956**

- Public 4-year university and liberal arts college
- Commuter campus in rural community

---

- 554 degree-seeking undergraduates: 22% part-time, 65% women, 1% African American, 1% Asian American, 2% Hispanic American, 4% Native American, 4% international
- 92% of applicants admitted
- SAT or ACT (ACT writing optional), application essay required

**General.** Founded in 1909. Regionally accredited. **Degrees:** 72 bachelor's awarded. **Location:** 85 miles from Bangor, 65 miles from Bar Harbor. **Calendar:** Semester, limited summer session. **Full-time faculty:** 40 total. **Part-time faculty:** 60 total. **Class size:** 70% < 20, 30% 20-39. **Special facilities:** Institute for applied marine research and education, mariculture student research facility, greenhouse, GIS lab, early childhood center, field station, international park, sail loft.

**Freshman class profile.** 381 applied, 349 admitted, 110 enrolled.

| Mid 50% test scores | | | |
|---|---|---|---|
| SAT critical reading: | 440-530 | Rank in top quarter: | 24% |
| SAT math: | 400-530 | Rank in top tenth: | 13% |
| ACT composite: | 15-25 | Return as sophomores: | 73% |
| GPA 3.50 or higher: | 16% | Out-of-state: | 25% |
| GPA 3.0-3.49: | 48% | Live on campus: | 67% |
| GPA 2.0-2.99: | 36% | International: | 1% |

**Basis for selection.** Applicants should rank in top half of class and have a B average. Recommendations and test scores are important. Essay and outstanding nonacademic achievement (extracurricular, community, military, life, or work) considered. SAT/ACT not required of applicants for associate of science degree. Test score for fall-term admission must be received before first day of classes. Interview recommended. **Homeschooled:** Statement describing homeschool structure and mission, transcript of courses and grades required. Records of all completed coursework plus documentation verifying proficiency in coursework (such as examples of writing, math skills). Portfolio beneficial for some coursework. Standardized test scores required; campus visit with interview important. **Learning Disabled:** Students evaluated on results of required college preparatory work. Documentation of disability important if seeking assistance from Student Resource Center.

**High school preparation.** 11 units required. Required and recommended units include English 4, mathematics 3, social studies 2, science 2 (laboratory 2), foreign language 2 and academic electives 3. Social studies may include history. Computer applications, fine arts also recommended.

**2007-2008 Annual costs.** Tuition/fees: $5,770; $14,800 out-of-state. New England Regional Student Program tuition is 150% of public in-district tuition. Room/board: $6,270. Books/supplies: $800. Personal expenses: $1,600.

**Financial aid.** **Non-need-based:** Scholarships awarded for academics, alumni affiliation, art, job skills, leadership, minority status, music/drama, state residency.

**Application procedures. Admission:** Closing date 8/15 (receipt date). $40 fee, may be waived for applicants with need. Application may be submitted online. Admission notification on a rolling basis. Must reply by May 1 or within 2 week(s) if notified thereafter. **Financial aid:** Priority date 3/1; no closing date. FAFSA required. Applicants notified on a rolling basis starting 2/15; must reply within 2 week(s) of notification.

**Academics.** Internships and/or cooperative education program available in business studies, recreation management, biology, environmental studies, and behavioral science. **Special study options:** Cooperative education, distance learning, double major, dual enrollment of high school students, honors, independent study, internships, student-designed major, study abroad, teacher certification program. **Credit/placement by examination:** AP, CLEP, SAT, ACT, institutional tests. **Support services:** Learning center, reduced course load, remedial instruction, study skills assistance, tutoring, writing center.

**Majors. Biology:** General, ecology, marine. **Business:** General, accounting, business admin, hospitality admin, hospitality/recreation, marketing, office management, office/clerical, tourism promotion, tourism/travel. **Conservation:** General, environmental studies. **Education:** Business, elementary, middle, secondary. **English:** English lit. **Health:** Mental health services. **History:** General. **Interdisciplinary:** Behavioral sciences. **Liberal arts:** Arts/sciences. **Parks/recreation:** General, facilities management. **Psychology:** General. **Public administration:** Human services. **Visual/performing arts:** General.

**Most popular majors.** Biology 8%, business/marketing 17%, education 14%, English 7%, interdisciplinary studies 18%, liberal arts 7%, natural resources/environmental science 8%, parks/recreation 14%.

**Computing on campus.** 117 workstations in dormitories, library, computer center. Dormitories wired for high-speed internet access and linked to

campus network. Commuter students can connect to campus network. On-line course registration, online library, helpline, repair service, wireless network available.

**Student life. Freshman orientation:** Available. Preregistration for classes offered. Orientation in June, August, and January. **Policies:** Students over 21 may drink in their rooms. Firearms must be stored in safe in Resident Director's office. **Housing:** Guaranteed on-campus for all undergraduates. Coed dorms, substance-free housing available. $100 deposit. Pets allowed in dorm rooms. **Activities:** Concert band, choral groups, dance, drama, literary magazine, music ensembles, musical theater, radio station, student government, Newman Club, Students of Service.

**Athletics.** NAIA. **Intercollegiate:** Basketball, cross-country, soccer, volleyball W. **Intramural:** Basketball, cheerleading W, fencing, football (non-tackle), soccer, softball W, water polo. **Team name:** Clippers.

**Student services.** Career counseling, student employment services, financial aid counseling, health services, on-campus daycare, personal counseling, placement for graduates, veterans' counselor.

**Contact.** E-mail: ummadmissions@maine.edu
Phone: (207) 255-1318 Toll-free number: (888) 468-6866
Fax: (207) 255-1363
Stewart Bennett, Director of Admissions, University of Maine at Machias, 9 O'Brien Avenue, Machias, ME 04654

## University of Maine at Presque Isle
Presque Isle, Maine | CB member
www.umpi.maine.edu | CB code: 3008

- Public 4-year university
- Commuter campus in small town

**General.** Founded in 1903. Regionally accredited. **Location:** 165 miles from Bangor. **Calendar:** Semester.

**Annual costs/financial aid.** Tuition/fees (2007-2008): $5,740; $13,420 out-of-state. Room/board: $5,980. Books/supplies: $800. Personal expenses: $1,100. Need-based financial aid available to full-time and part-time students.

**Contact.** Phone: (207) 768-9532
Director of Admissions, 181 Main Street, Presque Isle, ME 04769

## University of New England
Biddeford, Maine | CB member
www.une.edu | CB code: 3751

- Private 4-year university
- Residential campus in small city
- 1,985 degree-seeking undergraduates: 5% part-time, 73% women, 1% African American, 2% Asian American, 1% Hispanic American
- 1,544 degree-seeking graduate students
- 76% of applicants admitted
- SAT or ACT (ACT writing optional) required
- 64% graduate within 6 years

**General.** Founded in 1831. Regionally accredited. **Degrees:** 233 bachelor's, 100 associate awarded; master's, first professional offered. **ROTC:** Army. **Location:** 15 miles from Portland. **Calendar:** Semester, limited summer session. **Full-time faculty:** 171 total; 86% have terminal degrees, 5% minority, 47% women. **Part-time faculty:** 147 total; 4% minority, 53% women. **Class size:** 42% < 20, 48% 20-39, 4% 40-49, 5% 50-99, less than 1% >100. **Special facilities:** Maine Women Writers collection, osteopathic center, performance enhancement and evaluation center, marine science education and research center.

**Freshman class profile.** 2,904 applied, 2,203 admitted, 594 enrolled.

| Mid 50% test scores | | | |
|---|---|---|---|
| SAT critical reading: | 480-570 | Rank in top quarter: | 49% |
| SAT math: | 490-590 | Rank in top tenth: | 15% |
| GPA 3.50 or higher: | 32% | Return as sophomores: | 77% |
| GPA 3.0-3.49: | 34% | Out-of-state: | 69% |
| GPA 2.0-2.99: | 33% | Live on campus: | 94% |

**Basis for selection.** School achievement record most important. Test scores, school, community activities considered. Exposure to health careers recommended if seeking admission to health science majors. Rigor of curriculum considered. Essay recommended. Interview required for nursing

program, recommended for all, strongly recommended for academically weaker students. **Homeschooled:** Statement describing homeschool structure and mission, transcript of courses and grades required. **Learning Disabled:** Contact the Director of Disability Services.

**High school preparation.** 16 units required; 20 recommended. Required and recommended units include English 4, mathematics 3-4, social studies 1-2, history 1-2, science 2-3 (laboratory 2-3), foreign language 2 and academic electives 2-4.

**2007-2008 Annual costs.** Tuition/fees: $25,290. Room/board: $9,860. Books/supplies: $1,000. Personal expenses: $1,000.

**2006-2007 Financial aid. Need-based:** 453 full-time freshmen applied for aid; 407 were judged to have need; 407 of these received aid. Average need met was 86%. Average scholarship/grant was $12,817; average loan $9,154. 52% of total undergraduate aid awarded as scholarships/grants, 48% as loans/jobs. **Non-need-based:** Awarded to 342 full-time undergraduates, including 100 freshmen. Scholarships awarded for academics, alumni affiliation, leadership.

**Application procedures. Admission:** Priority date 12/1; deadline 2/15 (postmark date). $40 fee, may be waived for applicants with need. Application may be submitted online. Admission notification on a rolling basis beginning on or about 12/15. Must reply by May 1 or within 4 week(s) if notified thereafter. **Financial aid:** Priority date 5/1; no closing date. FAFSA required. Applicants notified on a rolling basis starting 2/1.

**Academics. Special study options:** Combined bachelor's/graduate degree, cooperative education, cross-registration, distance learning, double major, dual enrollment of high school students, honors, independent study, internships, liberal arts/career combination, student-designed major, study abroad, teacher certification program. **Credit/placement by examination:** AP, CLEP, IB, SAT, ACT, institutional tests. **Support services:** Learning center, reduced course load, remedial instruction, study skills assistance, tutoring, writing center.

**Majors. Agriculture:** Aquaculture. **Biology:** General, biochemistry, marine. **Business:** Business admin. **Conservation:** Environmental science, environmental studies. **Education:** General, art, elementary. **English:** English lit. **Health:** Athletic training, clinical lab technology, dental hygiene, health services admin, nursing (RN). **History:** General. **Liberal arts:** Arts/sciences. **Math:** General. **Parks/recreation:** Exercise sciences, sports admin. **Physical sciences:** Chemistry. **Psychology:** General, psychobiology, social. **Social sciences:** Political science, sociology.

**Most popular majors.** Biology 35%, health sciences 31%, parks/recreation 6%, psychology 15%.

**Computing on campus.** 170 workstations in dormitories, library, computer center, student center. Dormitories wired for high-speed internet access and linked to campus network. Commuter students can connect to campus network. Online course registration, online library, helpline, student web hosting, wireless network available.

**Student life. Freshman orientation:** Mandatory. Preregistration for classes offered. **Housing:** Guaranteed on-campus for freshmen. Coed dorms, single-sex dorms, substance-free housing available. $200 partly refundable deposit, deadline 5/1. **Activities:** Literary magazine, student government, Earth's E.C.O., Rotoract, Marine Animal Stranding Helpline, Make A Wish, EMS, Campus Diversity Club, Intervarsity Christian Fellowship, Cross Seekers, Habitat for Humanity, College Democrats.

**Athletics.** NCAA. **Intercollegiate:** Basketball, cross-country, field hockey W, golf M, lacrosse, soccer, softball W, swimming W, volleyball W. **Intramural:** Basketball, gymnastics, racquetball, soccer, softball, table tennis, volleyball W, water polo. **Team name:** Nor-easters.

**Student services.** Adult student services, alcohol/substance abuse counseling, campus ministries, career counseling, student employment services, financial aid counseling, health services, minority student services, personal counseling, veterans' counselor.

**Contact.** E-mail: admissions@une.edu
Phone: (207) 283-0170 ext. 2297 Toll-free number: (800) 477-4863
Fax: (207) 602-5900
Robert Pecchia, Associate Dean of Admissions, University of New England, Hills Beach Road, Biddeford, ME 04005

## University of Southern Maine
Gorham, Maine | CB member
www.usm.maine.edu | CB code: 3691

- Public 4-year university and liberal arts college
- Commuter campus in small city

- 6,603 degree-seeking undergraduates: 29% part-time, 58% women, 2% African American, 2% Asian American, 1% Hispanic American, 1% Native American
- 1,755 degree-seeking graduate students
- 80% of applicants admitted
- SAT or ACT with writing, application essay required
- 31% graduate within 6 years

**General.** Founded in 1878. Regionally accredited. **Degrees:** 1,181 bachelor's, 12 associate awarded; master's, doctoral, first professional offered. **ROTC:** Army, Air Force. **Location:** 110 miles from Boston. **Calendar:** Semester, extensive summer session. **Full-time faculty:** 408 total; 5% minority, 43% women. **Part-time faculty:** 302 total; 1% minority, 53% women. **Class size:** 51% < 20, 41% 20-39, 5% 40-49, 3% 50-99, less than 1% >100. **Special facilities:** Planetarium, cartographic collection, olympic-sized ice arena.

**Freshman class profile.** 4,016 applied, 3,220 admitted, 979 enrolled.

| Mid 50% test scores | | | |
|---|---|---|---|
| SAT critical reading: | 440-550 | GPA 2.0-2.99: | 63% |
| SAT math: | 430-540 | Rank in top quarter: | 33% |
| SAT writing: | 440-540 | Rank in top tenth: | 10% |
| ACT composite: | 20-25 | Return as sophomores: | 67% |
| GPA 3.50 or higher: | 23% | Out-of-state: | 18% |
| GPA 3.0-3.49: | 14% | Live on campus: | 67% |

**Basis for selection.** Level and content of academic program with performance or achievement record, class rank, and standardized test scores most important. Counselor recommendation, essay, and experience outside classroom also important. Interview recommended for all. Audition required of music majors. **Homeschooled:** Transcript of courses and grades, letter of recommendation (nonparent) required. SAT or ACT, annual assessment of courses, and GED required for financial aid purposes. **Learning Disabled:** Must be otherwise qualified to be admitted, may be asked to provide documentation.

**High school preparation.** 16 units required. Required and recommended units include English 4, mathematics 3-4, social studies 2-3, history 2-3, science 2-3 (laboratory 2-3) and foreign language 2-3. 3 lab sciences for science majors. Math, business and electrical engineering majors require 4 years of math.

**2007-2008 Annual costs.** Tuition/fees: $6,670; $17,140 out-of-state. New England Regional Student Program tuition is 150% of public in-district tuition. Room/board: $7,724. Books/supplies: $900. Personal expenses: $2,000.

**2007-2008 Financial aid. Need-based:** Average need met was 61%. Average scholarship/grant was $4,449; average loan $3,857. 42% of total undergraduate aid awarded as scholarships/grants, 58% as loans/jobs. **Non-need-based:** Scholarships awarded for academics, music/drama.

**Application procedures. Admission:** Priority date 2/15; no deadline. $40 fee, may be waived for applicants with need. Application may be submitted online. Admission notification on a rolling basis beginning on or about 1/1. Must reply by May 1 or within 2 week(s) if notified thereafter. **Financial aid:** Priority date 2/15; no closing date. FAFSA required. Applicants notified on a rolling basis starting 3/15; must reply by 5/1 or within 2 week(s) of notification.

**Academics. Special study options:** Accelerated study, combined bachelor's/graduate degree, cooperative education, cross-registration, distance learning, double major, ESL, exchange student, honors, independent study, internships, liberal arts/career combination, semester at sea, student-designed major, study abroad, teacher certification program, Washington semester, weekend college. Preengineering program with University of Maine at Orono, living/learning scholars program, Greater Portland Alliance - cross registration with University of New England, St. Joseph's (Maine), Southern Maine Technical College, and Maine College of Art. **Credit/placement by examination:** AP, CLEP, IB, institutional tests. No numerical limit. Students must meet all course requirements and 30 credit residency for BA/BS and 15 credit residency for AA/AS degrees. **Support services:** Learning center, reduced course load, remedial instruction, study skills assistance, tutoring, writing center.

**Honors college/program.** Honors application required. Several course options available. Interdisciplinary curriculum with small seminar classes.

**Majors. Area/ethnic studies:** French, German, Hispanic-American/Latino/Chicano, Russian/Slavic, women's. **Biology:** General, biotechnology. **Business:** General, accounting, accounting/finance, business admin, finance, management information systems, marketing, organizational behavior. **Communications:** General, media studies. **Computer sciences:** General, applications programming, computer science, programming. **Conservation:** Environmental science, environmental studies. **Construction:** Site management. **Education:** Art, elementary, mathematics, music, technology/

industrial arts, voc/tech. **Engineering:** Electrical, mechanical. **Engineering technology:** Electrical, manufacturing. **English:** Composition, English lit. **Foreign languages:** General, classics, French, linguistics. **Health:** Athletic training, environmental health, medical radiologic technology/radiation therapy, nursing (RN), pediatric nursing, predental, premedicine, preop/surgical nursing, preveterinary, psychiatric nursing, recreational therapy. **History:** General. **Interdisciplinary:** Behavioral sciences, global studies, math/computer science, natural sciences. **Legal studies:** Prelaw. **Liberal arts:** Arts/sciences, humanities. **Math:** General. **Parks/recreation:** General, exercise sciences. **Philosophy/religion:** Philosophy. **Physical sciences:** Chemistry, geology, physics. **Psychology:** General. **Public administration:** Social work. **Social sciences:** General, anthropology, criminology, economics, geography, international relations, political science, sociology. **Visual/performing arts:** General, acting, art, art history/conservation, arts management, directing/producing, dramatic, drawing, jazz, music performance, painting, piano/organ, sculpture, stringed instruments, studio arts, theater arts management, voice/opera. **Other:** Environmental Saftey and Health.

**Most popular majors.** Business/marketing 17%, communications/journalism 8%, health sciences 15%, psychology 6%, social sciences 19%.

**Computing on campus.** 410 workstations in dormitories, library, computer center, student center. Dormitories wired for high-speed internet access and linked to campus network. Commuter students can connect to campus network. Online course registration, helpline, repair service, wireless network available.

**Student life. Freshman orientation:** Mandatory, $150 fee. Preregistration for classes offered. Sessions in summer and autumn. **Policies:** Smoking is not allowed within 50 feet of any dormitory. **Housing:** Coed dorms, special housing for disabled, apartments, fraternity/sorority housing, substance-free housing available. $75 deposit, deadline 5/1. Substance-free floor, 24 hour quiet floor, living/learning communities, community service, health-fitness, outdoor recreation housing available. **Activities:** Bands, choral groups, dance, drama, literary magazine, music ensembles, musical theater, opera, radio station, student government, student newspaper, symphony orchestra, TV station, Amnesty International, American Indian student association, Environmental Coalition, College Republicans, Alliance of Sexual Diversity, Women's Forum, Bahai Association, international students association, ethnic student association.

**Athletics.** NCAA. **Intercollegiate:** Baseball M, basketball, cheerleading, cross-country, field hockey W, golf, ice hockey, lacrosse, soccer, softball W, tennis, track and field, volleyball W, wrestling M. **Intramural:** Basketball, cheerleading W, football (non-tackle), football (tackle) M, ice hockey, lacrosse, racquetball, rugby, sailing, skiing, soccer, softball, squash, table tennis, tennis, volleyball, weight lifting. **Team name:** Huskies.

**Student services.** Adult student services, alcohol/substance abuse counseling, campus ministries, career counseling, services for economically disadvantaged, student employment services, financial aid counseling, health services, legal services, minority student services, on-campus daycare, personal counseling, placement for graduates, veterans' counselor, women's services. **Physically disabled:** Services for visually, speech, hearing impaired.

**Contact.** E-mail: usmadm@usm.maine.edu
Phone: (207) 780-5670 Toll-free number: (800) 800-4876 ext. 5670
Fax: (207) 780-5640
Scott Steinberg, Director of Undergraduate Admission, University of Southern Maine, 37 College Avenue, Gorham, ME 04038

# Maryland

## Baltimore Hebrew University
**Baltimore, Maryland**
**www.bhu.edu**                                    CB code: 2165

▶  Private 4-year university and teachers college
▶  Commuter campus in very large city
▶  4 degree-seeking undergraduates
▶  Application essay, interview required

**General.** Founded in 1919. Regionally accredited. Easy access to regional Jewish community. University population consists primarily of graduate students. **Degrees:** 1 bachelor's awarded; master's, doctoral offered. **Calendar:** Semester, extensive summer session. **Full-time faculty:** 8 total. **Part-time faculty:** 4 total.

**Basis for selection.** Dean reviews high school record, Jewish communal activity and conducts personal interview. Students must have completed 60 hours of undergraduate credit at an accredited insitution before applying.

**2008-2009 Annual costs.** Tuition/fees (projected): $11,250. Books/supplies: $400. Personal expenses: $1,300.

**2006-2007 Financial aid. Need-based:** 34% of total undergraduate aid awarded as scholarships/grants, 66% as loans/jobs. **Non-need-based:** Scholarships awarded for academics.

**Application procedures. Admission:** Closing date 6/1. $50 fee. Admission notification on a rolling basis beginning on or about 5/1. **Financial aid:** Priority date 4/15, closing date 6/1. FAFSA required. Applicants notified on a rolling basis starting 7/15; must reply by 9/9.

**Academics.** University-operated Judaic/Hebraic library. **Special study options:** Cross-registration, dual enrollment of high school students. **Credit/placement by examination:** CLEP, IB, institutional tests. 12 credit hours maximum toward bachelor's degree.

**Majors. Foreign languages:** Hebrew. **Other:** Jewish studies.

**Computing on campus.** 12 workstations in library, computer center.

**Student services.** Career counseling, financial aid counseling, veterans' counselor. **Physically disabled:** Services for hearing impaired.

**Contact.** E-mail: lkott@bhu.edu
Phone: (410) 578-6970 Toll-free number: (888) 248-7420
Fax: (410) 578-6940
Laurie Kott, Director of Admissions and Recruitment, Baltimore Hebrew University, 5800 Park Heights Avenue, Baltimore, MD 21215

## Baltimore International College
**Baltimore, Maryland**
**www.bic.edu**                                    CB code: 5086

▶  Private 4-year culinary school and business college
▶  Commuter campus in very large city
▶  478 degree-seeking undergraduates: 4% part-time, 48% women
▶  12 degree-seeking graduate students
▶  72% of applicants admitted
▶  39% graduate within 6 years

**General.** Founded in 1972. Regionally accredited. **Degrees:** 31 bachelor's, 117 associate awarded; master's offered. **Location:** Downtown. **Calendar:** Semester, limited summer session. **Full-time faculty:** 15 total. **Part-time faculty:** 20 total. **Class size:** 46% < 20, 52% 20-39, 2% 40-49. **Special facilities:** Culinary arts center.

**Freshman class profile.** 284 applied, 205 admitted, 183 enrolled.

Out-of-state:                 18%     **Live on campus:**          23%

**Basis for selection.** Institutional placement evaluation most important. School achievement record, interview, test scores, and recommendations

also important. SAT or ACT recommended. Interview recommended. **Homeschooled:** Must be an accredited home school program or approved by the local school district.

**2007-2008 Annual costs.** Fees shown are for culinary school and include use of computer, culinary supplies, upgrading and maintenance of kitchen equipment and facilities. Day students provided one full meal daily. Business program students pay lower fees. Books/supplies: $1,500.

**2006-2007 Financial aid. Need-based:** 597 full-time freshmen applied for aid; 563 were judged to have need; 563 of these received aid. Average need met was 66%. Average scholarship/grant was $6,102; average loan $7,500. 53% of total undergraduate aid awarded as scholarships/grants, 47% as loans/jobs. **Non-need-based:** Scholarships awarded for academics, alumni affiliation, job skills, leadership, state residency.

**Application procedures. Admission:** No deadline. $40 fee. Application may be submitted online. Admission notification on a rolling basis. **Financial aid:** Priority date 3/1; no closing date. FAFSA, institutional form required. Applicants notified on a rolling basis; must reply within 2 week(s) of notification.

**Academics. Special study options:** Accelerated study, cooperative education, double major, honors, internships, liberal arts/career combination, study abroad. Honors program available at the Virginia Park campus in Ireland. **Credit/placement by examination:** AP, CLEP, institutional tests. 15 credit hours maximum toward associate degree, 15 toward bachelor's. **Support services:** Remedial instruction, study skills assistance, tutoring.

**Majors. Personal/culinary services:** Restaurant/catering.

**Computing on campus.** 45 workstations in dormitories, library, computer center.

**Student life. Freshman orientation:** Mandatory. Preregistration for classes offered. One-day program held approximately a week before first day of classes. **Policies:** Freshmen under 21, single, with permanent residence more than 50 miles from campus required to live on campus. **Housing:** Guaranteed on-campus for freshmen. Coed dorms, substance-free housing available. $100 deposit. **Activities:** Student government, American Culinary Federation.

**Athletics. Team name:** Wolfhounds.

**Student services.** Alcohol/substance abuse counseling, career counseling, services for economically disadvantaged, student employment services, financial aid counseling, health services, minority student services, personal counseling, placement for graduates, veterans' counselor, women's services.

**Contact.** E-mail: admissions@bic.edu
Phone: (410) 752-4710 ext. 120 Toll-free number: (800) 624-9926 ext. 120
Fax: (410) 752-3730
Barbara Catka, Director of Admissions, Baltimore International College, 17 Commerce Street, Baltimore, MD 21202-3230

## Bowie State University
**Bowie, Maryland**                                CB member
**www.bowiestate.edu**                             CB code: 5401

▶  Public 4-year university
▶  Commuter campus in small city
▶  4,179 degree-seeking undergraduates: 14% part-time, 63% women, 90% African American, 1% Asian American, 2% Hispanic American, 1% international
▶  1,121 degree-seeking graduate students
▶  43% of applicants admitted
▶  SAT or ACT (ACT writing optional) required

**General.** Founded in 1865. Regionally accredited. Limited courses offered at off-site locations. **Degrees:** 621 bachelor's awarded; master's, doctoral offered. **ROTC:** Army, Air Force. **Location:** 25 miles from Baltimore, 20 miles from Washington, DC. **Calendar:** Semester, limited summer session. **Full-time faculty:** 212 total; 71% have terminal degrees, 78% minority, 47% women. **Part-time faculty:** 144 total; 42% have terminal degrees, 84% minority, 44% women. **Special facilities:** NASA operations and control center, art gallery, green house, super computer center(limited access).

**Freshman class profile.** 6,445 applied, 2,796 admitted, 1,473 enrolled.

**Basis for selection.** School achievement record in college-preparatory curriculum, test scores, minimum GPA of 2.0, counselor/school recommendation important. Audition required for music program. Portfolio required for art program. Praxis I required for education program. **Homeschooled:**

Statement describing homeschool structure and mission required. Any questions please call Don Kiah at (301) 860-3427.

**High school preparation.** Required units include English 4, mathematics 3, social studies 1, history 2, science 3 and foreign language 2.

**2007-2008 Annual costs.** Tuition/fees: $5,939; $15,629 out-of-state. Room/board: $6,105. Books/supplies: $1,338. Personal expenses: $1,804.

**2007-2008 Financial aid. Need-based:** 470 full-time freshmen applied for aid; 462 were judged to have need; 450 of these received aid. Average need met was 44%. Average scholarship/grant was $5,537; average loan $3,131. 62% of total undergraduate aid awarded as scholarships/grants, 38% as loans/jobs. **Non-need-based:** Scholarships awarded for academics, alumni affiliation, art, athletics, leadership, music/drama, ROTC, state residency.

**Application procedures. Admission:** No deadline. $40 fee, may be waived for applicants with need. Application may be submitted online. Admission notification on a rolling basis. **Financial aid:** Closing date 3/1. FAFSA required. Applicants notified on a rolling basis starting 4/1; must reply within 2 week(s) of notification.

**Academics.** For more information please contact Monica Turner at (301) 860-3296. **Special study options:** Combined bachelor's/graduate degree, cooperative education, cross-registration, distance learning, double major, dual enrollment of high school students, exchange student, honors, independent study, internships, liberal arts/career combination, study abroad, teacher certification program. Dual degree programs in engineering and dentistry with cooperating universities. **Credit/placement by examination:** AP, CLEP, institutional tests. 60 credit hours maximum toward bachelor's degree. Interested parties please call Doris Gillard at (301) 860-3113. **Support services:** Learning center, pre-admission summer program, reduced course load, remedial instruction, tutoring, writing center.

**Honors college/program.** Interested parties please contact Monica Gross at (301) 860-4090.

**Majors. Biology:** General. **Business:** Business admin. **Communications technology:** Radio/tv. **Computer sciences:** Computer science. **Education:** Elementary, kindergarten/preschool, science. **English:** English lit. **Family/consumer sciences:** Child development. **Health:** Nursing (RN). **History:** General. **Math:** General. **Psychology:** General. **Public administration:** Social work. **Social sciences:** Sociology. **Visual/performing arts:** Art, dramatic. **Other:** Technology.

**Most popular majors.** Business/marketing 18%, communication technologies 13%, computer/information sciences 7%, education 7%, health sciences 8%, psychology 11%, social sciences 23%.

**Computing on campus.** 150 workstations in dormitories, library, computer center. Dormitories wired for high-speed internet access and linked to campus network. Commuter students can connect to campus network. Online course registration, online library, helpline, repair service, wireless network available.

**Student life. Freshman orientation:** Mandatory, $75 fee. Preregistration for classes offered. One-day session in the 2nd or 3rd week of August. **Policies:** Zero tolerance policy for illegal substance use and violence. **Housing:** Coed dorms, single-sex dorms, apartments, substance-free housing available. $150 fully refundable deposit. **Activities:** Bands, campus ministries, choral groups, dance, drama, international student organizations, music ensembles, musical theater, radio station, student government, student newspaper, TV station, NAACP, greater Washington urban league chapter, commuter senate.

**Athletics.** NCAA. **Intercollegiate:** Basketball, bowling W, cross-country, football (tackle) M, softball W, tennis W, track and field, volleyball W. **Intramural:** Baseball, basketball, football (non-tackle), golf, gymnastics, racquetball, soccer, softball, swimming, table tennis, tennis, volleyball, weight lifting. **Team name:** Bulldogs.

**Student services.** Adult student services, alcohol/substance abuse counseling, campus ministries, career counseling, student employment services, financial aid counseling, health services, personal counseling, placement for graduates, veterans' counselor. **Physically disabled:** Services for visually, hearing impaired.

**Contact.** E-mail: dkiah@bowiestate.edu
Phone: (301) 860-3415 Fax: (301) 860-3438
Don Kiah, Assistant Vice President, Enrollment Management, Bowie State University, 14000 Jericho Park Road, Bowie, MD 20715

---

## Capitol College
**Laurel, Maryland**
www.capitol-college.edu
CB code: 5101

- Private 4-year business and engineering college
- Commuter campus in large town

---

- 360 degree-seeking undergraduates
- SAT or ACT (ACT writing optional), application essay required

**General.** Founded in 1964. Regionally accredited. **Degrees:** 51 bachelor's, 3 associate awarded; master's offered. **ROTC:** Army. **Location:** 19 miles from Washington, DC, 22 miles from Baltimore. **Calendar:** Semester, limited summer session. **Full-time faculty:** 20 total. **Part-time faculty:** 60 total. **Special facilities:** Video lab, interactive computer classrooms, two engineering labs, telecommunications lab.

**Freshman class profile.**

| Mid 50% test scores | | | |
|---|---|---|---|
| | | SAT math: | 390-470 |
| SAT critical reading: | 400-480 | Live on campus: | 20% |

**Basis for selection.** Academic preparation, school record and test scores most important. Mathematics foundation necessary for successful completion of programs. Interview and essay recommended.

**High school preparation.** 20 units required. Required and recommended units include English 4, mathematics 3-4, social studies 2, history 2, science 1-3 (laboratory 1-2) and academic electives 2-3. Mathematic units include algebra I, geometry, algebra II/trigonometry. Calculus recommended for advanced standing.

**2007-2008 Annual costs.** Tuition/fees: $19,404. Room only: $4,358. Books/supplies: $800. Personal expenses: $1,900.

**Financial aid. Non-need-based:** Scholarships awarded for academics, alumni affiliation, leadership, minority status.

**Application procedures. Admission:** Priority date 5/1; no deadline. $25 fee may be waived for applicants with need. Application may be submitted online. Admission notification on a rolling basis beginning on or about 3/1. Must reply by May 1 or within 3 week(s) if notified thereafter. **Financial aid:** Priority date 2/1; no closing date. FAFSA, institutional form required. Applicants notified on a rolling basis starting 6/3; must reply by 5/1 or within 3 week(s) of notification.

**Academics. Special study options:** Combined bachelor's/graduate degree, cooperative education, distance learning, double major, independent study, liberal arts/career combination, weekend college. **Credit/placement by examination:** AP, CLEP, institutional tests. **Support services:** Learning center, pre-admission summer program, reduced course load, remedial instruction, tutoring.

**Majors. Business:** Business admin. **Computer sciences:** Computer science. **Engineering:** Computer, electrical, software. **Engineering technology:** Aerospace, electrical, telecommunications. **Other:** Information assurance.

**Most popular majors.** Business/marketing 12%, computer/information sciences 29%, engineering/engineering technologies 59%.

**Computing on campus.** 60 workstations in library, computer center. Dormitories wired for high-speed internet access and linked to campus network. Helpline, wireless network available.

**Student life. Freshman orientation:** Mandatory. **Housing:** Coed dorms available. $200 deposit, deadline 5/1. **Activities:** Literary magazine, radio station, student government, student newspaper, computer club, chess club, robotics club, music club, drama club, Society of Black Engineers, Society of Women Engineers.

**Athletics. Intramural:** Basketball M, boxing M, fencing M, golf M, soccer M, softball M, table tennis, tennis, track and field, volleyball, water polo.

**Student services.** Adult student services, career counseling, student employment services, personal counseling, placement for graduates, veterans' counselor.

**Contact.** E-mail: admissions@capitol-college.edu
Phone: (301) 369-2800 Toll-free number: (800) 950-1992
Fax: (301) 953-1442
Tony Miller, Director of Admissions, Capitol College, 11301 Springfield Road, Laurel, MD 20708

---

## College of Notre Dame of Maryland
**Baltimore, Maryland**
www.ndm.edu
CB member
CB code: 5114

- Private 4-year liberal arts college for women affiliated with Roman Catholic Church
- Residential campus in very large city

- 1,476 degree-seeking undergraduates
- 59% of applicants admitted
- SAT or ACT (ACT writing recommended), application essay required

**General.** Founded in 1873. Regionally accredited. Men admitted only to undergraduate and graduate weekend college programs. **Degrees:** 360 bachelor's awarded; master's offered. **ROTC:** Army. **Location:** 5 miles from Baltimore, 37 miles from Washington, DC. **Calendar:** Semester, limited summer session. **Full-time faculty:** 77 total. **Part-time faculty:** 10 total. **Class size:** 78% < 20, 22% 20-39. **Special facilities:** Planetarium, photography laboratories, tv and radio studios.

**Freshman class profile.** 552 applied, 326 admitted, 106 enrolled.

| Mid 50% test scores | | GPA 2.0-2.99: | 27% |
|---|---|---|---|
| SAT critical reading: | 470-600 | Rank in top quarter: | 40% |
| SAT math: | 440-550 | Rank in top tenth: | 23% |
| GPA 3.50 or higher: | 37% | Out-of-state: | 14% |
| GPA 3.0-3.49: | 36% | Live on campus: | 66% |

**Basis for selection.** Careful evaluation of academic record, high school curriculum, test scores, recommendations, personal abilities/talents and goals, intellectual potential and eagerness to learn and be challenged. Students should take SAT by January of senior year. Interview and campus visit highly recommended; visits required for scholarship consideration. Audition recommended for music majors. Portfolio recommended for art, writing majors. **Homeschooled:** Transcript or GED required. **Learning Disabled:** Students with learning disabilities should self-report during admissions process.

**High school preparation.** 18 units required. Required units include English 4, mathematics 3, social studies 2, science 2 (laboratory 2), foreign language 3 and academic electives 4.

**2007-2008 Annual costs.** Tuition/fees: $24,500. Room/board: $8,600. Books/supplies: $800. Personal expenses: $800.

**Financial aid. Non-need-based:** Scholarships awarded for academics, alumni affiliation, art, leadership, music/drama, ROTC. **Additional information:** Maximum consideration for financial aid if application received by February 15. Auditions and portfolios in areas of art, music and writing considered for scholarships.

**Application procedures. Admission:** Priority date 2/15; no deadline. $45 fee, may be waived for applicants with need. Application may be submitted online. Admission notification on a rolling basis beginning on or about 10/1. Must reply by May 1 or within 2 week(s) if notified thereafter. **Financial aid:** Priority date 2/15; no closing date. FAFSA required. Applicants notified on a rolling basis starting 3/15; must reply by 5/1 or within 2 week(s) of notification.

**Academics. Special study options:** Accelerated study, combined bachelor's/graduate degree, cross-registration, double major, dual enrollment of high school students, ESL, honors, independent study, internships, liberal arts/career combination, student-designed major, study abroad, teacher certification program, weekend college. 3-2 programs in engineering and nursing with Johns Hopkins University; academic consortium with seven local colleges and universities. **Credit/placement by examination:** AP, CLEP, IB, institutional tests. 30 credit hours maximum toward bachelor's degree. AP, CLEP and IB credits are posted upon admissions to college. Students should send testing information with their admissions application or prior to start of their first semester. **Support services:** Reduced course load, study skills assistance, writing center.

**Majors. Biology:** General. **Business:** General, finance, international, nonprofit/public. **Communications:** General. **Computer sciences:** General, computer science. **Education:** Early childhood, elementary, secondary, special. **Engineering:** General. **English:** English lit. **Foreign languages:** General, classics, French, Spanish. **Health:** Medical radiologic technology/radiation therapy. **History:** General. **Interdisciplinary:** Biopsychology. **Legal studies:** Prelaw. **Liberal arts:** Arts/sciences. **Math:** General. **Philosophy/religion:** Philosophy, religion. **Physical sciences:** Chemistry, physics. **Psychology:** General. **Public administration:** Community org/advocacy. **Social sciences:** Criminology, economics, international relations, political science. **Visual/performing arts:** Art, art history/conservation, photography, studio arts.

**Most popular majors.** Biology 7%, business/marketing 21%, communications/journalism 8%, education 14%, health sciences 7%, interdisciplinary studies 6%, liberal arts 11%.

**Computing on campus.** 80 workstations in dormitories, library, computer center, student center. Dormitories wired for high-speed internet access and linked to campus network. Commuter students can connect to campus network. Online library, helpline, repair service, wireless network available.

**Student life. Freshman orientation:** Mandatory. Preregistration for classes offered. 2-day program in June; 4-day program prior to start of school in late August/early September. **Policies:** Must abide by honor code. **Housing:** Guaranteed on-campus for all undergraduates. Substance-free housing available. $200 deposit, deadline 5/1. **Activities:** Campus ministries, choral groups, dance, drama, film society, international student organizations, literary magazine, music ensembles, musical theater, radio station, student government, student newspaper, TV station, community service organization, Hispanic society, black student organization, inter-organizational council.

**Athletics.** NCAA. **Intercollegiate:** Basketball W, field hockey W, lacrosse W, soccer W, swimming W, tennis W, volleyball W. **Intramural:** Basketball W, cross-country W, field hockey W, lacrosse W, soccer W, softball W. **Team name:** Gators.

**Student services.** Adult student services, alcohol/substance abuse counseling, campus ministries, career counseling, student employment services, financial aid counseling, health services, personal counseling, placement for graduates, veterans' counselor.

**Contact.** E-mail: admiss@ndm.edu
Phone: (410) 532-5330 Toll-free number: (800) 435-0200
Fax: (410) 532-6287
Director of Admissions, College of Notre Dame of Maryland, 4701 North Charles Street, Baltimore, MD 21210

---

## Columbia Union College
**Takoma Park, Maryland**
www.cuc.edu                                    **CB code: 5890**

- Private 4-year liberal arts college affiliated with Seventh-day Adventists
- Residential campus in large town
- 876 degree-seeking undergraduates: 26% part-time, 62% women
- 75 degree-seeking graduate students
- 49% of applicants admitted
- SAT or ACT with writing required

**General.** Founded in 1904. Regionally accredited. **Degrees:** 179 bachelor's, 6 associate awarded; master's offered. **Location:** 1 mile from Washington, DC. **Calendar:** Semester, limited summer session. **Full-time faculty:** 51 total; 41% have terminal degrees, 29% minority, 43% women. **Part-time faculty:** 2 total; 100% have terminal degrees. **Class size:** 81% < 20, 17% 20-39, less than 1% 40-49, less than 1% 50-99.

**Freshman class profile.** 1,019 applied, 496 admitted, 124 enrolled.

| Mid 50% test scores | | GPA 3.50 or higher: | 27% |
|---|---|---|---|
| SAT critical reading: | 390-500 | GPA 3.0-3.49: | 28% |
| SAT math: | 380-480 | GPA 2.0-2.99: | 45% |
| ACT composite: | 15-22 | Out-of-state: | 54% |

**Basis for selection.** High school GPA of 2.5, school achievement record, test scores very important; recommendations considered. Audition required of music majors. **Homeschooled:** Transcript of courses and grades required. Recognized high school diploma or GED required. **Learning Disabled:** Students must provide written documentation of disabilities and submit written request for all needed services for review by the Disabilities Coordinator three months before registration. All forms may be obtained from Center for Learning Resources.

**High school preparation.** 16 units required. Required units include English 4, mathematics 2, history 2, science 2 (laboratory 2) and academic electives 4. One unit of computer science also recommended.

**2008-2009 Annual costs.** Tuition/fees: $19,350. Room/board: $6,559. Books/supplies: $1,100.

**Financial aid. Non-need-based:** Scholarships awarded for academics, athletics, leadership, music/drama, state residency.

**Application procedures. Admission:** Closing date 8/1 (postmark date). $25 fee, may be waived for applicants with need. Application may be submitted online. Admission notification on a rolling basis. Must reply by 8/15. **Financial aid:** Closing date 3/31. FAFSA required. Applicants notified on a rolling basis starting 5/31; must reply within 4 week(s) of notification.

**Academics. Special study options:** Accelerated study, combined bachelor's/graduate degree, cooperative education, cross-registration, distance learning, double major, ESL, external degree, honors, independent study, internships, liberal arts/career combination, student-designed major, study abroad, teacher certification program, Washington semester. Adult evening program. **Credit/placement by examination:** AP, CLEP, SAT, ACT, institutional tests. 12 credit hours maximum toward associate degree, 24 toward bachelor's.

CLEP business exams not accepted for traditional business majors. **Support services:** Learning center, reduced course load, remedial instruction, study skills assistance, tutoring, writing center.

**Majors. Biology:** General, biochemistry. **Business:** Accounting, business admin, marketing, organizational behavior. **Communications:** General, broadcast journalism, journalism. **Computer sciences:** General, computer science, information systems. **Education:** General, elementary, English, mathematics, music, physical, science, secondary. **English:** English lit. **Health:** Health care admin, nursing (RN), predental, premedicine, prepharmacy, preveterinary. **History:** General. **Legal studies:** Prelaw. **Liberal arts:** Arts/sciences. **Math:** General. **Parks/recreation:** Health/fitness, sports admin. **Philosophy/religion:** Religion. **Physical sciences:** Chemistry. **Psychology:** General, counseling. **Social sciences:** Political science. **Theology:** Religious ed, theology. **Visual/performing arts:** Music performance. **Other:** Health/Fitness Management, Philosophy and Religion.

**Computing on campus.** 60 workstations in dormitories, library, computer center, student center. Dormitories wired for high-speed internet access and linked to campus network. Commuter students can connect to campus network. Online library, wireless network available.

**Student life. Freshman orientation:** Mandatory, $150 fee. Preregistration for classes offered. **Policies:** Attendance required at weekly chapel service. Resident students required to attend dormitory worships. Religious observance required. **Housing:** Guaranteed on-campus for freshmen. Single-sex dorms, apartments, substance-free housing available. $200 fully refundable deposit, deadline 8/15. **Activities:** Bands, campus ministries, choral groups, international student organizations, literary magazine, music ensembles, musical theater, opera, radio station, student government, student newspaper, symphony orchestra, Humanitas, Loaves and Fishes, Shepherd's Hands (puppet ministry), Teach-a-Kid, Youth-to-Youth (drug prevention), student mission club.

**Athletics. NCAA. Intercollegiate:** Baseball M, basketball, cross-country, soccer, softball W, track and field. **Intramural:** Basketball M, soccer M, volleyball M. **Team name:** Pioneers.

**Student services.** Adult student services, campus ministries, career counseling, student employment services, financial aid counseling, health services, personal counseling, placement for graduates, veterans' counselor.

**Contact.** E-mail: enroll@cuc.edu
Phone: (301) 891-4080 Toll-free number: (800) 835-4212
Fax: (301) 891-4230
Emile John, Director of Admissions, Columbia Union College, 7600 Flower Avenue, Takoma Park, MD 20912

---

## Coppin State University

**Baltimore, Maryland**      **CB member**
**www.coppin.edu**      **CB code: 5122**

- Public 4-year nursing and liberal arts college
- Commuter campus in very large city
- 3,151 degree-seeking undergraduates: 22% part-time, 79% women, 86% African American, 4% international
- 388 degree-seeking graduate students
- 36% of applicants admitted
- SAT or ACT (ACT writing optional) required

**General.** Founded in 1900. Regionally accredited. Manages Rosemont Elementary School; educational corridor between Coppin and selected elementary, middle, and high schools; mentorship program with elementary students. **Degrees:** 376 bachelor's awarded; master's offered. **ROTC:** Army. **Location:** 50 miles from Washington, DC. **Calendar:** Semester, extensive summer session. **Full-time faculty:** 145 total; 52% have terminal degrees, 55% women. **Part-time faculty:** 161 total; 26% have terminal degrees, 53% women.

**Freshman class profile.** 5,593 applied, 1,988 admitted, 590 enrolled.

| Mid 50% test scores | | Return as sophomores: | 60% |
|---|---|---|---|
| SAT critical reading: | 390-460 | Out-of-state: | 17% |
| SAT math: | 380-450 | International: | 2% |

**Basis for selection.** Minimum GPA of 2.5 and predictive index based on test scores and school achievement record. Essay recommended. Interview recommended for nursing majors. Portfolio recommended for art majors. **Homeschooled:** Location must be certified by Maryland Department of Education.

**High school preparation.** 16 units required. Required units include English 4, mathematics 3, social studies 3, science 2 (laboratory 2) and foreign

---

language 2. 2 years of advanced tech program courses can be substituted for foreign language requirement.

**2007-2008 Annual costs.** Tuition/fees: $4,980; $12,753 out-of-state. Room/board: $6,799. Books/supplies: $700. Personal expenses: $3,085.

**2007-2008 Financial aid. Need-based:** 51% of total undergraduate aid awarded as scholarships/grants, 49% as loans/jobs. **Non-need-based:** Scholarships awarded for academics, alumni affiliation, athletics, ROTC, state residency. **Additional information:** Funds allocated by State of Maryland for minority students enrolled for at least 6 credits who are Maryland residents and U.S. citizens (Other Race Grant).

**Application procedures. Admission:** Closing date 7/15. $35 fee, may be waived for applicants with need. Application may be submitted online. Admission notification on a rolling basis beginning on or about 3/15. **Financial aid:** Priority date 3/1; no closing date. FAFSA required. Applicants notified on a rolling basis starting 4/15; must reply within 2 week(s) of notification.

**Academics. Special study options:** Accelerated study, combined bachelor's/graduate degree, cooperative education, distance learning, double major, dual enrollment of high school students, external degree, honors, independent study, internships, liberal arts/career combination, study abroad, teacher certification program, weekend college. 3-2 programs in engineering, pharmacy, dentistry, physical therapy. **Credit/placement by examination:** AP, CLEP, IB, SAT, institutional tests. 30 credit hours maximum toward bachelor's degree. **Support services:** Learning center, pre-admission summer program, remedial instruction, study skills assistance, tutoring, writing center.

**Majors. Biology:** General. **Business:** Management science. **Computer sciences:** Computer science. **Education:** Biology, chemistry, early childhood, elementary, mathematics, secondary, special. **English:** English lit. **Health:** Medical records admin, nursing (RN). **History:** General. **Liberal arts:** Arts/sciences. **Math:** General. **Parks/recreation:** Sports admin. **Physical sciences:** Chemistry. **Protective services:** Criminal justice. **Psychology:** General. **Public administration:** Social work. **Social sciences:** General, political science, sociology. **Visual/performing arts:** Art. **Other:** Rehabilitation and Therapeutic Professions.

**Most popular majors.** Business/marketing 11%, education 7%, health sciences 18%, liberal arts 12%, psychology 13%, public administration/social services 6%, security/protective services 12%.

**Computing on campus.** 371 workstations in dormitories, library, computer center, student center. Dormitories wired for high-speed internet access and linked to campus network. Commuter students can connect to campus network. Online course registration, online library, helpline, repair service, student web hosting, wireless network available.

**Student life. Freshman orientation:** Mandatory. Preregistration for classes offered. **Housing:** Coed dorms, special housing for disabled, substance-free housing available. $150 deposit. **Activities:** Campus ministries, choral groups, dance, drama, film society, international student organizations, music ensembles, radio station, student government, student newspaper, TV station, criminal justice club, gospel choir, history club, psychology club, Thurgood Marshall club, social work association.

**Athletics. NCAA. Intercollegiate:** Baseball M, basketball, bowling W, cheerleading M, cross-country, golf W, softball W, tennis, track and field, volleyball W. **Intramural:** Basketball, football (non-tackle), softball, tennis, volleyball. **Team name:** Eagles.

**Student services.** Adult student services, alcohol/substance abuse counseling, career counseling, services for economically disadvantaged, student employment services, financial aid counseling, health services, minority student services, personal counseling, placement for graduates, veterans' counselor, women's services. **Physically disabled:** Services for visually, hearing impaired.

**Contact.** E-mail: admissions@coppin.edu
Phone: (410) 951-3600 Toll-free number: (800) 635-3674
Fax: (410) 523-7351
Michelle Gross, Director of Admissions, Coppin State University, 2500 West North Avenue, Baltimore, MD 21216

---

## DeVry University: Bethesda

**Bethesda, Maryland**
**www.devry.edu**

- For-profit 4-year university
- Commuter campus in small city

- 45 degree-seeking undergraduates: 71% part-time, 40% women, 49% African American, 27% Hispanic American, 2% international
- 54 degree-seeking graduate students

**General. Degrees:** 4 bachelor's awarded; master's offered. **Calendar:** Semester. **Full-time faculty:** 1 total. **Part-time faculty:** 3 total; 67% minority, 67% women.

**Freshman class profile.**

| | | | |
|---|---|---|---|
| Return as sophomores: | 57% | Out-of-state: | 13% |

**Basis for selection.** Interview important.

**2007-2008 Annual costs.** Tuition/fees: $14,440. Books/supplies: $1,300. Personal expenses: $5,082.

**Financial aid. Non-need-based:** Scholarships awarded for academics.

**Application procedures. Admission:** No deadline. $50 fee. Admission notification on a rolling basis. **Financial aid:** No deadline. FAFSA required. Applicants notified on a rolling basis.

**Academics. Special study options:** Accelerated study, distance learning. **Credit/placement by examination:** CLEP.

**Majors. Business:** Business admin. **Computer sciences:** General.

**Contact.** Phone: (301) 652-8477 Fax: (301) 652-8577
DeVry University: Bethesda, 4550 Montgomery Avenue, Suite 100 N, Bethesda, MD 20814

---

## Frostburg State University

**Frostburg, Maryland** — CB member
www.frostburg.edu — CB code: 5402

- Public 4-year university and teachers college
- Residential campus in small town
- 4,268 degree-seeking undergraduates: 5% part-time, 49% women, 20% African American, 2% Asian American, 2% Hispanic American
- 605 degree-seeking graduate students
- 63% of applicants admitted
- SAT or ACT (ACT writing optional) required
- 51% graduate within 6 years

**General.** Founded in 1898. Regionally accredited. Center in Hagerstown offers upper-division undergraduate and graduate courses. **Degrees:** 796 bachelor's awarded; master's offered. **Location:** 150 miles from Baltimore. **Calendar:** Semester, limited summer session. **Full-time faculty:** 233 total; 85% have terminal degrees, 12% minority, 37% women. **Part-time faculty:** 111 total; 15% have terminal degrees, 4% minority, 52% women. **Class size:** 46% < 20, 48% 20-39, 3% 40-49, 3% 50-99. **Special facilities:** Planetarium, arboretum, electron microscope, exploratorium.

**Freshman class profile.** 4,199 applied, 2,634 admitted, 1,074 enrolled.

| Mid 50% test scores | | | |
|---|---|---|---|
| SAT critical reading: | 430-530 | GPA 3.0-3.49: | 31% |
| SAT math: | 430-540 | GPA 2.0-2.99: | 50% |
| SAT writing: | 420-520 | Return as sophomores: | 68% |
| ACT composite: | 17-22 | Out-of-state: | 9% |
| GPA 3.50 or higher: | 19% | Live on campus: | 69% |

**Basis for selection.** High school record and SAT scores most important. Interview recommended. Audition required of music majors. Portfolio required of art majors.

**High school preparation.** 15 units required. Required units include English 4, mathematics 3, social studies 3, science 3 (laboratory 2) and foreign language 2.

**2007-2008 Annual costs.** Tuition/fees: $6,550; $16,162 out-of-state. Room/board: $6,746. Books/supplies: $750. Personal expenses: $900.

**Financial aid. Non-need-based:** Scholarships awarded for academics, leadership, minority status.

**Application procedures. Admission:** Priority date 6/1; no deadline. $30 fee, may be waived for applicants with need. Application may be submitted online. Admission notification on a rolling basis beginning on or about 11/1. Must reply by May 1 or within 4 week(s) if notified thereafter. **Financial aid:** Priority date 3/1; no closing date. FAFSA required. Applicants notified on a rolling basis starting 3/15; must reply within 3 week(s) of notification.

**Academics. Special study options:** Accelerated study, combined bachelor's/graduate degree, cross-registration, distance learning, double major, dual enrollment of high school students, honors, independent study, internships, liberal arts/career combination, study abroad, teacher certification program, weekend college. International student exchange program, dual degree program, combined bachelor's program. **Credit/placement by examination:** AP, CLEP, IB, institutional tests. 30 credit hours maximum toward bachelor's degree. **Support services:** Learning center, reduced course load, remedial instruction, tutoring, writing center.

**Majors. Architecture:** Urban/community planning. **Biology:** General. **Business:** Accounting, business admin. **Communications:** General. **Computer sciences:** General. **Conservation:** General, environmental studies, fisheries, wildlife. **Education:** Early childhood, elementary, English, mathematics, music, physical, social science. **English:** English lit, speech/rhetoric. **Foreign languages:** General. **Health:** Predental, premedicine, prenursing, prepharmacy, preveterinary. **History:** General. **Liberal arts:** Arts/sciences. **Math:** General. **Parks/recreation:** General, exercise sciences, health/fitness, sports admin. **Philosophy/religion:** Philosophy. **Physical sciences:** Chemistry, physics. **Protective services:** Law enforcement admin, police science. **Psychology:** General. **Public administration:** Social work. **Social sciences:** General, economics, geography, international relations, political science, sociology. **Visual/performing arts:** General, commercial/advertising art, dramatic, studio arts. **Other:** Ethnobotany.

**Most popular majors.** Business/marketing 17%, education 11%, liberal arts 9%, psychology 8%, social sciences 9%, visual/performing arts 7%.

**Computing on campus.** 668 workstations in dormitories, library, computer center, student center. Dormitories wired for high-speed internet access and linked to campus network. Commuter students can connect to campus network. Online course registration, online library, helpline, wireless network available.

**Student life. Freshman orientation:** Mandatory. **Housing:** Coed dorms, single-sex dorms, special housing for disabled, substance-free housing available. $100 deposit. Special interest housing. **Activities:** Bands, choral groups, dance, drama, literary magazine, music ensembles, musical theater, radio station, student government, student newspaper, symphony orchestra, TV station, social, religious, political, and ethnic organizations.

**Athletics. NCAA. Intercollegiate:** Baseball M, basketball, cross-country, diving, field hockey W, football (tackle) M, golf, lacrosse W, soccer, softball W, swimming, tennis, track and field, volleyball W. **Intramural:** Basketball, field hockey, football (tackle), golf, lacrosse, racquetball, rugby M, soccer, softball, table tennis, tennis, volleyball, weight lifting, wrestling M. **Team name:** Bobcats.

**Student services.** Campus ministries, career counseling, student employment services, health services, minority student services, on-campus daycare, personal counseling, placement for graduates, veterans' counselor. **Physically disabled:** Services for visually, speech, hearing impaired.

**Contact.** E-mail: fsuadmissions@frostburg.edu
Phone: (301) 687-4201 Fax: (301) 687-7074
Trish Gregory, Director of Admissions, Frostburg State University, 101 Braddock Road, Frostburg, MD 21532-1099

---

## Goucher College

**Baltimore, Maryland** — CB member
www.goucher.edu — CB code: 5257

- Private 4-year liberal arts college
- Residential campus in small city
- 1,462 degree-seeking undergraduates: 2% part-time, 67% women, 5% African American, 3% Asian American, 3% Hispanic American
- 538 degree-seeking graduate students
- 66% of applicants admitted
- Application essay required
- 67% graduate within 6 years

**General.** Founded in 1885. Regionally accredited. Students required to study abroad and are given a voucher of at least $1,200 to help offset travel expenses. **Degrees:** 305 bachelor's awarded; master's offered. **ROTC:** Army. **Location:** 8 miles from Baltimore. **Calendar:** Semester. **Full-time faculty:** 128 total; 87% have terminal degrees, 16% minority, 62% women. **Part-time faculty:** 94 total; 38% have terminal degrees, 22% minority, 63% women. **Class size:** 75% < 20, 23% 20-39, less than 1% 40-49, 1% 50-99, less than 1% >100. **Special facilities:** Politics center, dance studio, pilates studio, computerized scientific visualization lab, nuclear magnetic resonance spectrometer, black box theater.

**Freshman class profile.** 3,563 applied, 2,361 admitted, 399 enrolled.

| Mid 50% test scores | | Rank in top quarter: | 59% |
|---|---|---|---|
| SAT critical reading: | 540-670 | Rank in top tenth: | 17% |
| SAT math: | 510-620 | Return as sophomores: | 78% |
| SAT writing: | 540-650 | Out-of-state: | 77% |
| GPA 3.50 or higher: | 27% | Live on campus: | 97% |
| GPA 3.0-3.49: | 40% | International: | 1% |
| GPA 2.0-2.99: | 33% | | |

**Basis for selection.** Record in traditional college-preparatory program, secondary school record, and recommendations most important. Interview recommended. **Homeschooled:** Statement describing homeschool structure and mission, transcript of courses and grades, state high school equivalency certificate, letter of recommendation (nonparent) required.

**High school preparation.** 16 units required; 20 recommended. Required and recommended units include English 4, mathematics 3-4, social studies 3, science 2-3, foreign language 2-4 and academic electives 2.

**2007-2008 Annual costs.** Tuition/fees: $31,082. Room/board: $9,477. Books/supplies: $800. Personal expenses: $800.

**2007-2008 Financial aid. Need-based:** 291 full-time freshmen applied for aid; 237 were judged to have need; 234 of these received aid. Average need met was 79%. Average scholarship/grant was $19,682; average loan $3,751. 76% of total undergraduate aid awarded as scholarships/grants, 24% as loans/jobs. **Non-need-based:** Awarded to 486 full-time undergraduates, including 123 freshmen. Scholarships awarded for academics, art, leadership, music/drama.

**Application procedures. Admission:** Closing date 2/1 (postmark date). $40 fee, may be waived for applicants with need. Application may be submitted online. Admission notification 4/1. Must reply by 5/1. **Financial aid:** Closing date 2/15. FAFSA, CSS PROFILE required. Applicants notified on a rolling basis starting 4/1; must reply by 5/1 or within 2 week(s) of notification.

**Academics. Special study options:** Cross-registration, distance learning, double major, dual enrollment of high school students, independent study, internships, student-designed major, study abroad, teacher certification program, Washington semester. Teachers Institute, post-baccalaureate premedical program, master's level distance learning, 3-2 engineering program with Johns Hopkins University, 4-1 BA/MA with Monterey Institute of International Studies. Study abroad programs at the Sorbonne in Paris, University of Salamanca in Spain, Hebrew University in Israel, Russian Summer Institute at Odessa State University in Moscow, Oxford University in England, Glasgow School of Art in Scotland, Honduras Institute of Marine Studies in Roatan, University of East Anglia in England, Middlesex University in London, Syracuse University in Florence, Denmark International Study Program Copenhagen. **Credit/placement by examination:** AP, CLEP, IB, SAT, ACT, institutional tests. 30 credit hours maximum toward bachelor's degree. **Support services:** Learning center, reduced course load, study skills assistance, tutoring, writing center.

**Majors. Area/ethnic studies:** American, women's. **Biology:** General. **Business:** Business admin. **Communications:** Media studies. **Computer sciences:** Computer science. **Education:** Elementary, special. **English:** English lit. **Foreign languages:** French, Russian, Spanish. **History:** General. **Interdisciplinary:** Peace/conflict. **Math:** General. **Philosophy/religion:** Philosophy, religion. **Physical sciences:** Chemistry, physics. **Psychology:** General. **Social sciences:** Economics, international relations, political science, sociology. **Visual/performing arts:** Art, dance, dramatic. **Other:** Multi-interdisciplinary studies.

**Most popular majors.** Biology 7%, business/marketing 7%, communications/journalism 8%, English 8%, psychology 18%, social sciences 13%, visual/performing arts 17%.

**Computing on campus.** 140 workstations in library, computer center, student center. Dormitories wired for high-speed internet access. Commuter students can connect to campus network. Online library, helpline, repair service, wireless network available.

**Student life. Freshman orientation:** Available. Preregistration for classes offered. **Housing:** Guaranteed on-campus for freshmen. Coed dorms, single-sex dorms, special housing for disabled, apartments, substance-free housing available. $100 fully refundable deposit, deadline 5/15. Healthy living dorm, language house, first year house available. **Activities:** Jazz band, choral groups, dance, drama, film society, international student organizations, literary magazine, music ensembles, opera, radio station, student government, student newspaper, symphony orchestra, TV station, African alliance, community action program, bisexual gay and lesbian alliance, Hillel, Christian fellowship, Amnesty International, environmental organization, Jubilate Deo.

**Athletics.** NCAA. **Intercollegiate:** Basketball, cross-country, equestrian, field hockey W, lacrosse, soccer, swimming, tennis, track and field, volleyball W. **Intramural:** Football (tackle), racquetball, soccer, softball, squash, tennis, volleyball, water polo, weight lifting. **Team name:** Gophers.

**Student services.** Adult student services, campus ministries, career counseling, student employment services, health services, minority student services, personal counseling, placement for graduates. **Physically disabled:** Services for visually, hearing impaired.

**Contact.** E-mail: admissions@goucher.edu
Phone: (410) 337-6100 Toll-free number: (800) 468-2437
Fax: (410) 337-6354
Carlton Surbeck, Director of Admissions, Goucher College, 1021 Dulaney Valley Road, Baltimore, MD 21204-2753

## Griggs University
### Silver Spring, Maryland
www.griggs.edu

- Private 4-year virtual Bible college affiliated with Seventh-day Adventists
- Small city
- 750 degree-seeking undergraduates
- Application essay required

**General.** Accredited by DETC. **Degrees:** 25 bachelor's, 13 associate awarded; master's offered. **Location:** 30 miles from Washington, DC. **Calendar:** Semester. **Part-time faculty:** 60 total.

**Basis for selection.** Minimum secondary school grade average of 2.00 required. SAT or ACT recommended. **Homeschooled:** Statement describing homeschool structure and mission required.

**High school preparation.** 21 units required; 24 recommended. Required and recommended units include English 4, mathematics 3-4, social studies 1-2, history 2, science 3-4 (laboratory 2-3), foreign language 2, computer science 1, visual/performing arts 1 and academic electives 2-3.

**2007-2008 Annual costs.** Tuition/fees: $8,540.

**Application procedures. Admission:** No deadline. $50 fee, may be waived for applicants with need. Application may be submitted online. Admission notification on a rolling basis. **Financial aid:** No deadline. Institutional form required.

**Academics. Special study options:** Cross-registration, distance learning, dual enrollment of high school students, independent study, student-designed major, study abroad. **Credit/placement by examination:** AP, CLEP, IB, SAT, ACT, institutional tests. 12 credit hours maximum toward associate degree, 24 toward bachelor's. **Support services:** Reduced course load, remedial instruction, tutoring.

**Majors. Business:** Business admin. **Philosophy/religion:** Religion. **Theology:** Bible, religious ed.

**Computing on campus.** PC or laptop required.

**Contact.** Phone: (301) 680-6570
Alayne Thorpe, Vice President for Education, Griggs University, 12501 Old Columbia Pike, Silver Spring, MD 20904-6600

## Hood College
### Frederick, Maryland
www.hood.edu

**CB member**
**CB code: 5296**

- Private 4-year liberal arts college
- Residential campus in small city
- 1,380 degree-seeking undergraduates: 9% part-time, 71% women, 9% African American, 3% Asian American, 3% Hispanic American, 2% international
- 931 degree-seeking graduate students
- 71% of applicants admitted
- SAT or ACT (ACT writing optional) required
- 73% graduate within 6 years

**General.** Founded in 1893. Regionally accredited. **Degrees:** 246 bachelor's awarded; master's offered. **ROTC:** Army. **Location:** 52 miles from Baltimore, 52 miles from Washington, DC. **Calendar:** Semester, limited summer session. **Full-time faculty:** 81 total; 96% have terminal degrees, 16% minority, 54% women. **Part-time faculty:** 171 total; 39% have terminal degrees, 2% minority, 52% women. **Class size:** 59% < 20, 40% 20-39, less than 1% 40-49, less than 1% 50-99. **Special facilities:** Psychology and preschool laboratories, observatory.

**Freshman class profile.** 1,718 applied, 1,218 admitted, 295 enrolled.

| Mid 50% test scores | | | |
|---|---|---|---|
| SAT critical reading: | 490-610 | Rank in top quarter: | 51% |
| SAT math: | 490-590 | Rank in top tenth: | 22% |
| SAT writing: | 490-590 | End year in good standing: | 82% |
| ACT composite: | 20-26 | Return as sophomores: | 76% |
| GPA 3.50 or higher: | 53% | Out-of-state: | 26% |
| GPA 3.0-3.49: | 32% | Live on campus: | 79% |
| GPA 2.0-2.99: | 15% | International: | 2% |

**Basis for selection.** High school record, class rank, test scores important. Recommendations; contributions to school, family and community; essay considered. Interview recommended; essay required of some. **Homeschooled:** Must interview and present bibliography of all reading materials used; two recommendations; partial portfolio of work.

**High school preparation.** 16 units required. Required units include English 4, mathematics 3, social studies 1, history 2, science 3 (laboratory 2), foreign language 2 and academic electives 1.

**2007-2008 Annual costs.** Tuition/fees: $25,076. Room/board: $8,542. Books/supplies: $800. Personal expenses: $700.

**2007-2008 Financial aid. Need-based:** 258 full-time freshmen applied for aid; 201 were judged to have need; 201 of these received aid. Average need met was 89%. Average scholarship/grant was $17,225; average loan $4,048. 78% of total undergraduate aid awarded as scholarships/grants, 22% as loans/jobs. **Non-need-based:** Awarded to 494 full-time undergraduates, including 140 freshmen. Scholarships awarded for academics, alumni affiliation, music/drama, ROTC.

**Application procedures. Admission:** Priority date 2/15; no deadline. $35 fee, may be waived for applicants with need. Application may be submitted online. Admission notification on a rolling basis beginning on or about 10/15. Must reply by May 1 or within 2 week(s) if notified thereafter. Early Action closing dates of 10/1, 11/1 and 12/1. Applications received after February 1 considered on a space available basis. **Financial aid:** Priority date 2/15; no closing date. FAFSA required. Applicants notified on a rolling basis starting 3/1; must reply by 5/1 or within 3 week(s) of notification.

**Academics.** Students in all fields may earn academic credits for internships. Opportunities available for students to earn degree in 3 years, 2 degrees in 4 years, or bachelor's and master's in 5 years. **Special study options:** Accelerated study, combined bachelor's/graduate degree, double major, dual enrollment of high school students, honors, independent study, internships, liberal arts/career combination, student-designed major, study abroad, teacher certification program, Washington semester. **Credit/placement by examination:** AP, CLEP, IB, SAT, institutional tests. 30 credit hours maximum toward bachelor's degree. **Support services:** Learning center, reduced course load, remedial instruction, study skills assistance, tutoring, writing center.

**Majors. Area/ethnic studies:** Latin American. **Biology:** General, biochemistry. **Business:** Business admin. **Communications:** General. **Computer sciences:** Computer science. **Conservation:** Environmental science. **Education:** Early childhood, special. **English:** English lit. **Foreign languages:** French, German, Spanish. **History:** General. **Legal studies:** General. **Math:** General. **Philosophy/religion:** Philosophy, religion. **Physical sciences:** Chemistry. **Psychology:** General. **Public administration:** Social work. **Social sciences:** Economics, political science, sociology. **Visual/performing arts:** Art. **Other:** Art and archaeology, French/German.

**Most popular majors.** Biology 9%, business/marketing 14%, communications/journalism 7%, education 9%, history 9%, psychology 11%, social sciences 7%.

**Computing on campus.** 252 workstations in dormitories, library, computer center, student center. Dormitories wired for high-speed internet access and linked to campus network. Commuter students can connect to campus network. Online course registration, online library, helpline, wireless network available.

**Student life. Freshman orientation:** Mandatory. Preregistration for classes offered. 4 days prior to start of classes. **Policies:** Students responsible for governing themselves through honor code. **Housing:** Guaranteed on-campus for all undergraduates. Coed dorms, single-sex dorms, special housing for disabled available. $250 fully refundable deposit, deadline 5/1. Language (French, German, Spanish), special interest housing available. **Activities:** Jazz band, campus ministries, choral groups, dance, drama, film society, international student organizations, literary magazine, music ensembles, Model UN, musical theater, radio station, student government, student newspaper, symphony orchestra, Black student union, Circle K, La Union Latina, Best Buddies, intervarsity christian fellowship, College Democrats, Jewish student union, College Republicans, For Goodness Sake.

**Athletics.** NCAA. **Intercollegiate:** Basketball, cross-country, field hockey W, golf, lacrosse, soccer, softball W, swimming, tennis, track and field, volleyball W. **Intramural:** Basketball, football (tackle) M, soccer, table tennis, volleyball W. **Team name:** Blazers.

**Student services.** Adult student services, alcohol/substance abuse counseling, campus ministries, career counseling, student employment services, financial aid counseling, health services, minority student services, personal counseling, placement for graduates, veterans' counselor, women's services. **Physically disabled:** Services for visually, speech, hearing impaired.

**Contact.** E-mail: admissions@hood.edu
Phone: (301) 696-3400 Toll-free number: (800) 922-1599
Fax: (301) 696-3819
David Adams, Director of Admissions, Hood College, 401 Rosemont Avenue, Frederick, MD 21701-8575

## ITT Technical Institute: Owings Mill
**Owings Mills, Maryland**

- For-profit 4-year business and technical college
- Large town

**General.** Accredited by ACICS. **Calendar:** Quarter.

**Contact.** 11301 Red Run Boulevard, Owings Mills, MD 21117

## Johns Hopkins University
**Baltimore, Maryland**
www.jhu.edu

**CB member**
**CB code: 5332**

- Private 4-year university
- Residential campus in very large city
- 4,578 degree-seeking undergraduates: 1% part-time, 48% women, 6% African American, 25% Asian American, 7% Hispanic American, 1% Native American, 5% international
- 1,623 degree-seeking graduate students
- 24% of applicants admitted
- SAT or ACT with writing, application essay required
- 91% graduate within 6 years; 38% enter graduate study

**General.** Founded in 1876. Regionally accredited. Centers in Bologna and Florence, Italy, and Nanjing, China. **Degrees:** 1,464 bachelor's awarded; master's, doctoral, first professional offered. **ROTC:** Army, Air Force. **Location:** 4 miles from downtown. **Calendar:** 4-1-4, limited summer session. **Full-time faculty:** 451 total; 94% have terminal degrees, 12% minority, 25% women. **Part-time faculty:** 74 total; 8% minority, 31% women. **Class size:** 65% < 20, 20% 20-39, 4% 40-49, 6% 50-99, 5% >100. **Special facilities:** Space telescope science institute.

**Freshman class profile.** 14,848 applied, 3,603 admitted, 1,206 enrolled.

| Mid 50% test scores | | | |
|---|---|---|---|
| SAT critical reading: | 630-730 | Rank in top quarter: | 97% |
| SAT math: | 660-770 | Rank in top tenth: | 82% |
| SAT writing: | 630-730 | Return as sophomores: | 97% |
| ACT composite: | 28-33 | Out-of-state: | 87% |
| GPA 3.50 or higher: | 77% | Live on campus: | 99% |
| GPA 3.0-3.49: | 21% | International: | 6% |
| GPA 2.0-2.99: | 2% | Fraternities: | 28% |
| | | Sororities: | 23% |

**Basis for selection.** School achievement record most important, with emphasis on course grades related to applicant's major field of academic interest. Test scores important. Intellectual interests and accomplishments, recommendations, personal character, extracurricular activities also significant. Students wishing to enroll in the biomedical engineering major (BME) must indicate BME as their first-choice major. Students are admitted specifically into the BME major based on evaluation of credentials and space availability. SAT Subject Tests recommended. Early Decision applicants should have test scores in by November 1. Recommend 3 SAT Subject Tests. SAT Math Level 2 recommended for students applying to school of engineering. Interview recommended. Audition required of applicants to dual-degree program with Peabody Institute. **Homeschooled:** Statement describing home-school structure and mission, transcript of courses and grades, letter of recommendation (nonparent) required. Secondary school report must include summary of program, complete transcript with course descriptions, bibliography of textbooks, description of evaluation methods, and actual grades or evaluations.

**High school preparation.** Recommended units include English 4, mathematics 4, social studies 2, history 2, science 4 and foreign language 4. 4 combined units recommended for social studies and history.

**2008-2009 Annual costs.** Tuition/fees: $38,200. Room/board: $11,578. Books/supplies: $1,000. Personal expenses: $1,000.

**2007-2008 Financial aid. Need-based:** 783 full-time freshmen applied for aid; 585 were judged to have need; 585 of these received aid. Average need met was 89%. Average scholarship/grant was $26,290; average loan $3,481. 81% of total undergraduate aid awarded as scholarships/grants, 19% as loans/jobs. **Non-need-based:** Awarded to 389 full-time undergraduates, including 98 freshmen. Scholarships awarded for academics, athletics, leadership, ROTC, state residency. **Additional information:** Selected students receive aid packages without loan expectation, grants to full need. Private merit aid does not reduce Hopkins grant.

**Application procedures. Admission:** Closing date 1/1 (postmark date). $70 fee, may be waived for applicants with need. Application may be submitted online. Admission notification 4/1. Must reply by May 1 or within 2 week(s) if notified thereafter. **Financial aid:** Closing date 3/1. FAFSA, CSS PROFILE required. Applicants notified by 4/1; must reply by 5/1 or within 2 week(s) of notification.

**Academics. Special study options:** Combined bachelor's/graduate degree, cross-registration, double major, dual enrollment of high school students, independent study, internships, student-designed major, study abroad, Washington semester. Combined bachelor's/master's programs. **Credit/placement by examination:** AP, CLEP, IB, institutional tests. **Support services:** Pre-admission summer program, reduced course load, study skills assistance, tutoring, writing center.

**Majors. Area/ethnic studies:** African-American, East Asian, Latin American, Near/Middle Eastern. **Biology:** General, biophysics, cell/histology, molecular. **Computer sciences:** General. **Engineering:** General, biomedical, chemical, civil, computer, electrical, environmental, materials, materials science, mechanical, mechanics. **English:** Creative writing, English lit. **Foreign languages:** Classics, French, German, Italian, Spanish. **History:** General, science/technology. **Interdisciplinary:** Behavioral sciences, cognitive science, neuroscience. **Liberal arts:** Arts/sciences. **Math:** General, statistics. **Philosophy/religion:** Philosophy. **Physical sciences:** Astronomy, chemistry, geology, physics. **Psychology:** General. **Public administration:** Policy analysis. **Social sciences:** General, anthropology, economics, geography, international relations, political science, sociology. **Visual/performing arts:** Art history/conservation, film/cinema. **Other:** Film and media studies.

**Most popular majors.** Biology 6%, engineering/engineering technologies 17%, health sciences 25%, interdisciplinary studies 6%, social sciences 15%.

**Computing on campus.** 140 workstations in dormitories, library, computer center. Dormitories wired for high-speed internet access and linked to campus network. Commuter students can connect to campus network. Online course registration, online library, helpline, repair service, student web hosting, wireless network available.

**Student life. Freshman orientation:** Mandatory. Preregistration for classes offered. 5-day extensive program held 1 week prior to start of fall semester. **Policies:** Freshmen and sophomores required to live on campus unless they live with a parent or legal guardian within commuting distance. **Housing:** Guaranteed on-campus for freshmen. Coed dorms, single-sex dorms, special housing for disabled, apartments, fraternity/sorority housing, substance-free available. $200 nonrefundable deposit, deadline 5/25. Substance-free and vacation housing floors available. Specific spaces accessible or modified for disabled students. **Activities:** Bands, campus ministries, choral groups, dance, drama, film society, literary magazine, music ensembles, Model UN, musical theater, radio station, student government, student newspaper, symphony orchestra, Jewish Student Association, Catholic Community, Christian Fellowship, Black Student Union, Organizacion Latina Estudiantil, Chinese Student Association, emergency response organization, senior citizens community outreach program, College Democrats, College Republicans.

**Athletics.** NCAA. **Intercollegiate:** Baseball M, basketball, cross-country, diving, fencing, field hockey W, football (tackle) M, lacrosse, rowing (crew), soccer, swimming, tennis, track and field, volleyball W, water polo M, wrestling M. **Intramural:** Basketball, football (non-tackle), soccer, volleyball. **Team name:** Blue Jays.

**Student services.** Alcohol/substance abuse counseling, campus ministries, career counseling, student employment services, financial aid counseling, health services, minority student services, personal counseling, placement for graduates. **Physically disabled:** Services for visually, speech, hearing impaired.

**Contact.** E-mail: gotojhu@jhu.edu
Phone: (410) 516-8171 Fax: (410) 516-6025
John Latting, Dean of Undergraduate Admissions, Johns Hopkins University, 3400 North Charles Street, Mason Hall, Baltimore, MD 21218

## Johns Hopkins University: Peabody Conservatory of Music
**Baltimore, Maryland**
www.peabody.jhu.edu                          CB code: 5532

- Private 4-year music college
- Residential campus in very large city
- 318 degree-seeking undergraduates: 2% part-time, 50% women
- 348 degree-seeking graduate students
- 54% of applicants admitted
- SAT or ACT required
- 82% graduate within 6 years

**General.** Founded in 1857. Regionally accredited. **Degrees:** 76 bachelor's awarded; master's, doctoral offered. **Location:** 36 miles from Washington, DC. **Calendar:** Semester. **Full-time faculty:** 70 total. **Part-time faculty:** 80 total. **Special facilities:** Concert halls.

**Freshman class profile.** 724 applied, 391 admitted, 58 enrolled.

| | | | |
|---|---|---|---|
| End year in good standing: | 94% | Live on campus: | 100% |
| Return as sophomores: | 90% | | |

**Basis for selection.** Audition most important; secondary school record, test scores also important. Interview recommended. Audition required.

**2008-2009 Annual costs.** Tuition/fees: $34,060. Room/board: $10,200. Books/supplies: $625. Personal expenses: $1,000.

**Financial aid. Non-need-based:** Scholarships awarded for academics, music/drama.

**Application procedures. Admission:** Priority date 11/15; deadline 4/1 (postmark date). $100 fee, may be waived for applicants with need. Application may be submitted online. Admission notification 4/1. Must reply by 5/1. Must apply by December 15 for guarantee of scholarship consideration. **Financial aid:** Closing date 2/1. FAFSA, institutional form required. Applicants notified by 4/7; must reply by 5/1 or within 2 week(s) of notification.

**Academics. Special study options:** Cross-registration, double major, internships, teacher certification program. **Credit/placement by examination:** AP, CLEP, IB, institutional tests. 8 credit hours maximum toward bachelor's degree. **Support services:** Remedial instruction, tutoring.

**Majors. Communications technology:** Recording arts. **Education:** Music. **Visual/performing arts:** Music performance, music theory/composition, piano/organ, voice/opera.

**Most popular majors.** Education 7%, visual/performing arts 93%.

**Computing on campus.** 28 workstations in dormitories, library, computer center. Dormitories linked to campus network. Commuter students can connect to campus network. Online library, helpline, repair service, wireless network available.

**Student life. Freshman orientation:** Available. **Housing:** Guaranteed on-campus for freshmen. Coed dorms, single-sex dorms available. $250 partly refundable deposit, deadline 1/7. **Activities:** Bands, choral groups, music ensembles, opera, student government, symphony orchestra.

**Student services.** Alcohol/substance abuse counseling, career counseling, student employment services, financial aid counseling, health services, personal counseling, placement for graduates. **Physically disabled:** Services for visually, speech, hearing impaired.

**Contact.** Phone: (410) 659-8110 Toll-free number: (800) 368-2521
David Lane, Director of Admissions, Johns Hopkins University: Peabody Conservatory of Music, One East Mount Vernon Place, Baltimore, MD 21202

## Loyola College in Maryland
**Baltimore, Maryland**                       CB member
www.loyola.edu                                CB code: 5370

- Private 4-year business and liberal arts college affiliated with Roman Catholic Church
- Residential campus in very large city
- 3,542 degree-seeking undergraduates: 58% women, 5% African American, 3% Asian American, 3% Hispanic American, 1% international

- 2,361 degree-seeking graduate students
- 60% of applicants admitted
- SAT or ACT (ACT writing optional) required
- 83% graduate within 6 years

**General.** Founded in 1852. Regionally accredited. **Degrees:** 833 bachelor's awarded; master's, doctoral offered. **ROTC:** Army, Air Force. **Location:** 38 miles from Washington, DC, 103 miles from Philadelphia. **Calendar:** Semester, extensive summer session. **Full-time faculty:** 319 total; 82% have terminal degrees, 8% minority, 45% women. **Part-time faculty:** 219 total; 8% have terminal degrees, 5% minority, 40% women. **Class size:** 54% < 20, 46% 20-39, less than 1% 40-49, less than 1% 50-99, less than 1% >100.

**Freshman class profile.** 8,594 applied, 5,138 admitted, 983 enrolled.

| Mid 50% test scores | | | |
|---|---|---|---|
| SAT critical reading: | 560-650 | Rank in top quarter: | 75% |
| SAT math: | 560-660 | Rank in top tenth: | 37% |
| ACT composite: | 24-29 | Return as sophomores: | 91% |
| GPA 3.50 or higher: | 59% | Out-of-state: | 82% |
| GPA 3.0-3.49: | 36% | Live on campus: | 98% |
| GPA 2.0-2.99: | 5% | International: | 1% |

**Basis for selection.** Test scores, school record, academic qualifications most important. Extracurricular activities, recommendations, personal background, class rank also considered. Mid-year senior grades and additional SAT scores required for borderline applicants. Interview and essay recommended.

**High school preparation.** 16 units required; 19 recommended. Required and recommended units include English 4, mathematics 4, social studies 4, history 4, science 4 and foreign language 4.

**2007-2008 Annual costs.** Tuition/fees: $34,250. Food services are available on an a la carte basis. Room only: $7,350. Books/supplies: $930. Personal expenses: $1,050.

**2007-2008 Financial aid. Need-based:** Average need met was 98%. Average scholarship/grant was $16,470; average loan $5,730. 77% of total undergraduate aid awarded as scholarships/grants, 23% as loans/jobs. **Non-need-based:** Scholarships awarded for academics, athletics, minority status, ROTC.

**Application procedures. Admission:** Closing date 2/1. $50 fee, may be waived for applicants with need. Admission notification 4/1. Must reply by 5/1. **Financial aid:** Closing date 2/15. FAFSA, CSS PROFILE required. Applicants notified by 4/1; must reply by 5/1.

**Academics.** Service learning courses available. **Special study options:** Accelerated study, cross-registration, double major, honors, independent study, internships, liberal arts/career combination, study abroad, teacher certification program. **Credit/placement by examination:** AP, CLEP, IB, institutional tests. 30 credit hours maximum toward bachelor's degree. **Support services:** Learning center, remedial instruction, study skills assistance, tutoring.

**Majors. Biology:** General. **Business:** General, accounting. **Communications:** General. **Computer sciences:** General. **Education:** Elementary. **Engineering:** General, electrical. **English:** Creative writing, English lit. **Foreign languages:** Classics, French, German, Latin, Spanish. **Health:** Speech pathology. **History:** General. **Math:** Applied. **Philosophy/religion:** Philosophy, religion. **Physical sciences:** Chemistry, physics. **Psychology:** General. **Social sciences:** Economics, political science, sociology. **Visual/performing arts:** Art.

**Most popular majors.** Business/marketing 32%, communications/journalism 15%, psychology 8%, social sciences 9%.

**Computing on campus.** 292 workstations in dormitories, library, computer center, student center. Dormitories wired for high-speed internet access and linked to campus network. Commuter students can connect to campus network. Helpline, student web hosting available.

**Student life. Freshman orientation:** Mandatory, $125 fee. Preregistration for classes offered. Must attend 1 of 4 programs offered in summer; parents invited to attend. **Housing:** Guaranteed on-campus for freshmen. Coed dorms, apartments, substance-free housing available. $500 partly refundable deposit, deadline 5/1. Honors housing and special interest housing (community service, leadership, wellness) available. **Activities:** Bands, campus ministries, choral groups, dance, drama, international student organizations, literary magazine, music ensembles, musical theater, radio station, student government, student newspaper, TV station, black student association, College Republicans, Korean students association, Circle K, Amnesty International, young feminist, Jewish students association, College Democrats, evergreens for life.

**Athletics.** NCAA. **Intercollegiate:** Basketball, cross-country, diving, golf M, lacrosse, rowing (crew), soccer, swimming, tennis, track and field, volleyball W. **Intramural:** Baseball M, basketball, football (non-tackle), lacrosse, racquetball, rifle, soccer M, softball, squash, tennis, volleyball. **Team name:** Greyhounds.

**Student services.** Alcohol/substance abuse counseling, campus ministries, career counseling, student employment services, financial aid counseling, health services, minority student services, personal counseling, placement for graduates. **Physically disabled:** Services for visually, speech, hearing impaired.

**Contact.** E-mail: admissions@loyola.edu
Phone: (410) 617-5012 Toll-free number: (800) 221-9107
Fax: (410) 617-2176
Elena Hicks, Director of Undergraduate Admission, Loyola College in Maryland, 4501 North Charles Street, Baltimore, MD 21210-2699

---

## Maryland Institute College of Art
**Baltimore, Maryland**   CB member
**www.mica.edu**   CB code: 5399

- Private 4-year visual arts college
- Residential campus in very large city
- 1,668 degree-seeking undergraduates: 1% part-time, 66% women, 4% African American, 10% Asian American, 4% Hispanic American, 4% international
- 227 degree-seeking graduate students
- 37% of applicants admitted
- SAT or ACT (ACT writing optional), application essay required
- 70% graduate within 6 years; 23% enter graduate study

**General.** Founded in 1826. Regionally accredited. **Degrees:** 312 bachelor's awarded; master's offered. **ROTC:** Army. **Location:** 180 miles from New York City, 50 miles from Washington, DC. **Calendar:** Semester, extensive summer session. **Full-time faculty:** 130 total; 82% have terminal degrees, 14% minority, 50% women. **Part-time faculty:** 174 total; 82% have terminal degrees, 14% minority, 50% women. **Class size:** 78% < 20, 21% 20-39, less than 1% 50-99. **Special facilities:** Nature library, slide library with over 250,000 slides, graphics laboratory, independent studios, art galleries, digital print studio.

**Freshman class profile.** 2,602 applied, 964 admitted, 400 enrolled.

| Mid 50% test scores | | | |
|---|---|---|---|
| SAT critical reading: | 530-660 | Return as sophomores: | 84% |
| SAT math: | 500-620 | Out-of-state: | 81% |
| SAT writing: | 490-630 | Live on campus: | 88% |
| End year in good standing: | 98% | International: | 3% |

**Basis for selection.** Emphasis placed on artistic ability as demonstrated in the portfolio, academic achievement, test scores, GPA, and level of coursework. Essays, recommendations, interview, and extra-curricular activities also considered. Portfolio of 12-20 pieces of artwork must be submitted with application. Interview recommended. **Learning Disabled:** Students with documented learning disabilities not required to submit SAT or ACT test scores.

**High school preparation.** 24 units required. Required and recommended units include English 4, mathematics 2-3, social studies 4, history 3-4, science 2-3 (laboratory 1) and academic electives 6. 2 studio art required, 4 studio art recommended, 1 art history recommended.

**2007-2008 Annual costs.** Tuition/fees: $30,680. Room/board: $8,390. Books/supplies: $1,400. Personal expenses: $600.

**Financial aid. Non-need-based:** Scholarships awarded for academics, art.

**Application procedures. Admission:** Closing date 2/15 (receipt date). $50 fee, may be waived for applicants with need. Application must be submitted on paper. Admission notification 3/15. Must reply by 5/1. **Financial aid:** Closing date 3/1. FAFSA, institutional form required. Applicants notified by 4/13; must reply by 5/1.

**Academics.** One-third of course work in liberal arts and two-thirds in studio art required for graduation. Minors available in academic subjects. Independent studio and study requirement sometimes met by job internships. Foundation program required in the first year. **Special study options:** Accelerated study, combined bachelor's/graduate degree, cross-registration, distance learning, double major, dual enrollment of high school students, exchange student, independent study, internships, New York semester, student-designed major, study abroad, teacher certification program. Cooperative exchange programs with Johns Hopkins University, Goucher College, Peabody Conservatory of Music, University of Baltimore, Loyola College, Notre Dame College, University of Maryland Baltimore County, Morgan State University, Baltimore Hebrew College and Towson University; 5-year BFA/MA; 5-year BFA/MAT. **Credit/placement by examination:** AP, CLEP, IB, institutional tests. 15 credit hours maximum toward bachelor's degree. **Support services:** Learning center, reduced course load, remedial instruction, study skills assistance, tutoring, writing center.

**Majors. Education:** Art. **Visual/performing arts:** Art history/conservation, ceramics, drawing, fiber arts, graphic design, illustration, interior design, multimedia, painting, photography, printmaking, sculpture. **Other:** Video.

**Most popular majors.** Education 6%, visual/performing arts 94%.

**Computing on campus.** 440 workstations in dormitories, library, computer center, student center. Dormitories wired for high-speed internet access and linked to campus network. Commuter students can connect to campus network. Helpline, student web hosting, wireless network available.

**Student life. Freshman orientation:** Mandatory, $125 fee. Preregistration for classes offered. **Housing:** Guaranteed on-campus for freshmen. Coed dorms, special housing for disabled, apartments available. $650 deposit, deadline 5/1. **Activities:** Choral groups, dance, drama, film society, international student organizations, literary magazine, student government, Asian student alliance, Black student union, Koinonia, Korean-American student association, Bahá'í association, Mission in Christian Artists, Jewish student union, student voice association.

**Student services.** Career counseling, student employment services, financial aid counseling, health services, minority student services, personal counseling, placement for graduates.

**Contact.** E-mail: admissions@mica.edu
Phone: (410) 225-2222 Fax: (410) 225-2337
Theresa Bedoya, Vice President and Dean of Admission and Financial Aid, Maryland Institute College of Art, 1300 Mount Royal Avenue, Baltimore, MD 21217-4134

---

## McDaniel College

**Westminster, Maryland**
www.mcdaniel.edu

**CB member**
**CB code: 5898**

- Private 4-year liberal arts college
- Residential campus in large town
- 1,687 degree-seeking undergraduates: 1% part-time, 56% women, 5% African American, 3% Asian American, 2% Hispanic American, 1% Native American
- 1,469 degree-seeking graduate students
- 73% of applicants admitted
- Application essay required
- 72% graduate within 6 years; 98% enter graduate study

**General.** Founded in 1867. Regionally accredited. **Degrees:** 407 bachelor's awarded; master's offered. **ROTC:** Army. **Location:** 30 miles from Baltimore, 60 miles from Washington, DC. **Calendar:** 4-1-4, limited summer session. **Full-time faculty:** 130 total; 88% have terminal degrees, 10% minority, 51% women. **Part-time faculty:** 221 total; 34% have terminal degrees, 6% minority, 51% women. **Class size:** 64% < 20, 36% 20-39, less than 1% 40-49, less than 1% 50-99. **Special facilities:** 9-hole golf course, film/video production laboratory, photography studio, audiology laboratory, human performance laboratory, graphics laboratory, physics observatory.

**Freshman class profile.** 2,742 applied, 2,007 admitted, 436 enrolled.

| Mid 50% test scores | | | |
|---|---|---|---|
| SAT critical reading: | 500-610 | Rank in top quarter: | 61% |
| SAT math: | 500-630 | Rank in top tenth: | 28% |
| ACT composite: | 21-25 | End year in good standing: | 90% |
| GPA 3.50 or higher: | 55% | Return as sophomores: | 84% |
| GPA 3.0-3.49: | 30% | Out-of-state: | 34% |
| GPA 2.0-2.99: | 15% | Live on campus: | 93% |

**Basis for selection.** Rigor of course work completed and academic performance test scores, writing skills, personal and academic accomplishments, recommendations by counselors and teachers, leadership and participation in non-academic activities. Test score optional for first year students who are in the top 10% of their class or who have a 3.5 cumulative GPA if their high school does not rank. Academic recommendations required. Interview recommended. **Homeschooled:** Statement describing homeschool structure and mission, transcript of courses and grades, letter of recommendation

(nonparent) required. Must submit documentation used to satisfy your state graduation requirement.

**High school preparation.** 16 units required; 19 recommended. Required and recommended units include English 4, mathematics 3-4, social studies 3, science 3-4 (laboratory 3) and foreign language 3-4.

**2008-2009 Annual costs.** Tuition/fees: $30,780. Room/board: $6,150. Books/supplies: $1,200.

**2007-2008 Financial aid. Need-based:** 364 full-time freshmen applied for aid; 310 were judged to have need; 310 of these received aid. Average need met was 96%. Average scholarship/grant was $11,286; average loan $4,500. 82% of total undergraduate aid awarded as scholarships/grants, 18% as loans/jobs. **Non-need-based:** Awarded to 484 full-time undergraduates, including 94 freshmen. Scholarships awarded for academics, ROTC, state residency.

**Application procedures. Admission:** Closing date 2/1 (postmark date). $50 fee, may be waived for applicants with need. Application may be submitted online. Admission notification 4/1. Must reply by May 1 or within 2 week(s) if notified thereafter. **Financial aid:** Priority date 3/1; no closing date. FAFSA, institutional form required. Applicants notified on a rolling basis starting 2/15; must reply by 5/1 or within 2 week(s) of notification.

**Academics.** January term offered as a two-credit period of concentrated study. May include travel, classroom study or independent study. **Special study options:** Cross-registration, double major, dual enrollment of high school students, honors, independent study, internships, New York semester, semester at sea, student-designed major, study abroad, teacher certification program, United Nations semester, Washington semester. 3-2 program in engineering with University of Maryland, 3-2 program in forestry with Duke University. **Credit/placement by examination:** AP, CLEP, IB, SAT, ACT, institutional tests. 32 credit hours maximum toward bachelor's degree. **Support services:** Learning center, reduced course load, remedial instruction, study skills assistance, tutoring, writing center.

**Majors. Biology:** General, biochemistry, environmental. **Business:** Business admin. **Communications:** General. **Computer sciences:** General. **Conservation:** Environmental science. **English:** English lit. **Foreign languages:** French, German, Spanish. **History:** General. **Math:** General. **Parks/recreation:** Exercise sciences. **Philosophy/religion:** Philosophy, religion. **Physical sciences:** Chemistry, physics. **Psychology:** General. **Public administration:** Social work. **Social sciences:** Economics, political science, sociology. **Visual/performing arts:** Art, art history/conservation, dramatic.

**Most popular majors.** Biology 7%, business/marketing 11%, communications/journalism 11%, English 10%, psychology 12%, social sciences 15%, visual/performing arts 10%.

**Computing on campus.** 175 workstations in library, computer center. Dormitories wired for high-speed internet access and linked to campus network. Commuter students can connect to campus network. Online course registration, helpline, wireless network available.

**Student life. Freshman orientation:** Mandatory. Preregistration for classes offered. 5-day program. **Housing:** Guaranteed on-campus for freshmen. Coed dorms, single-sex dorms, apartments, fraternity/sorority housing, substance-free housing available. Honors, language houses, community service groups, single-family homes available. **Activities:** Bands, campus ministries, choral groups, dance, drama, literary magazine, music ensembles, musical theater, radio station, student government, student newspaper, TV station, Jewish student union, Christian fellowship, Circle K, ecology club, Black student union, multicultural student association, German club, French club, Spanish club.

**Athletics.** NCAA. **Intercollegiate:** Baseball M, basketball, cross-country, field hockey W, football (tackle) M, golf, lacrosse, soccer, softball W, swimming, tennis, track and field, volleyball W, wrestling M. **Intramural:** Badminton, basketball, football (tackle) M, golf, racquetball, soccer, softball, swimming, table tennis, tennis, volleyball, weight lifting. **Team name:** The Green Terror.

**Student services.** Career counseling, student employment services, financial aid counseling, health services, minority student services, personal counseling. **Physically disabled:** Services for visually, hearing impaired. **Learning disabled:** Comprehensive services available.

**Contact.** E-mail: admissions@mcdaniel.edu
Phone: (410) 857-2230 Toll-free number: (800) 638-5005
Fax: (410) 857-2757
Florence Hines, Vice President for Enrollment Management and Dean of Admissions, McDaniel College, Two College Hill, Westminster, MD 21157-4390

## Morgan State University
**Baltimore, Maryland**
www.morgan.edu

**CB member**
**CB code: 5416**

▶ Public 4-year university and liberal arts college
▶ Commuter campus in large city
▶ 5,959 degree-seeking undergraduates
▶ 34% of applicants admitted
▶ SAT or ACT with writing required
▶ 34% graduate within 6 years

**General.** Founded in 1867. Regionally accredited. **Degrees:** 821 bachelor's awarded; master's, doctoral offered. **ROTC:** Army. **Location:** 45 miles from Washington, DC, 100 miles from Philadelphia. **Calendar:** Semester, limited summer session. **Full-time faculty:** 319 total; 78% have terminal degrees, 79% minority, 39% women. **Part-time faculty:** 217 total; 80% minority, 39% women. **Special facilities:** Historical and government documents collections, special collections of African American history, super computer, engineering complex.

**Freshman class profile.** 11,804 applied, 3,977 admitted, 1,342 enrolled.

| Mid 50% test scores | | Out-of-state: | 33% |
|---|---|---|---|
| SAT critical reading: | 400-490 | Live on campus: | 76% |
| SAT math: | 400-500 | | |

**Basis for selection.** School achievement record and test scores most important. 820 SAT (exclusive of Writing) with 2.5 high school GPA or 900 SAT (exclusive of Writing) with 2.0 high school GPA, principal's recommendation, and parents' consent form (for minors) required. Interview and essay recommended. Audition recommended for music majors. **Homeschooled:** State high school equivalency certificate required. Need state-recognized diploma. **Learning Disabled:** Students with learning disability must provide documentation and take untimed SAT with assistance from counseling center.

**High school preparation.** 13 units recommended. Recommended units include English 4, mathematics 4, social studies 2, history 2, science 2 and foreign language 1.

**2007-2008 Annual costs.** Tuition/fees: $6,318; $14,438 out-of-state. Room/board: $7,650. Books/supplies: $721. Personal expenses: $2,369.

**Application procedures. Admission:** Priority date 4/15; no deadline. $25 fee, may be waived for applicants with need. Application may be submitted online. Admission notification on a rolling basis. Must reply by May 1 or within 2 week(s) if notified thereafter. **Financial aid:** Priority date 4/1; no closing date. FAFSA required. Applicants notified on a rolling basis starting 6/1; must reply within 2 week(s) of notification.

**Academics. Special study options:** Cooperative education, cross-registration, distance learning, double major, dual enrollment of high school students, honors, independent study, internships, liberal arts/career combination, teacher certification program, weekend college. Fulbright Program. **Credit/placement by examination:** AP, CLEP, institutional tests. 46 credit hours maximum toward bachelor's degree. Proficiency tests in general education requirements. **Support services:** Learning center, pre-admission summer program, reduced course load, remedial instruction, study skills assistance, tutoring, writing center.

**Majors. Architecture:** Architecture, environmental design. **Biology:** General. **Business:** Accounting, business admin, finance, hospitality admin, marketing. **Computer sciences:** Computer science, information systems, networking. **Education:** Elementary, health, physical. **Engineering:** Civil, electrical, industrial, physics. **English:** English lit, speech/rhetoric. **Family/consumer sciences:** Food/nutrition. **Health:** Staff services technology. **History:** General. **Math:** General. **Physical sciences:** Chemistry, physics. **Psychology:** General. **Social sciences:** Economics, political science, sociology. **Visual/performing arts:** Dramatic, studio arts.

**Computing on campus.** Dormitories wired for high-speed internet access and linked to campus network. Commuter students can connect to campus network. Online course registration, online library, helpline, repair service, student web hosting, wireless network available.

**Student life. Freshman orientation:** Mandatory. Preregistration for classes offered. Held twice during summer for 5 days. **Housing:** Coed dorms, single-sex dorms, special housing for disabled, substance-free housing available. **Activities:** Bands, choral groups, dance, drama, film society, music ensembles, musical theater, radio station, student government, student newspaper, TV station, Council on Religious Life.

**Athletics.** NCAA. **Intercollegiate:** Basketball, bowling W, cheerleading M, cross-country, football (tackle) M, softball W, tennis, track and field, volleyball W. **Intramural:** Basketball, cross-country, handball, racquetball, rifle, soccer, softball, swimming, table tennis, tennis, track and field, volleyball. **Team name:** Bears.

**Student services.** Alcohol/substance abuse counseling, career counseling, student employment services, health services, on-campus daycare, personal counseling, placement for graduates, veterans' counselor. **Physically disabled:** Services for visually, speech, hearing impaired.

**Contact.** E-mail: admissions@morgan.edu
Phone: (443) 885-3000 Toll-free number: (800) 332-6674
Fax: (443) 885-8260
Edwin Johnson, Director of Admissions and Recruitment, Morgan State University, 1700 East Cold Spring Lane, Baltimore, MD 21251

## Mount St. Mary's University
**Emmitsburg, Maryland**
www.msmary.edu

**CB member**
**CB code: 5421**

▶ Private 4-year university and liberal arts college affiliated with Roman Catholic Church
▶ Residential campus in rural community
▶ 1,681 degree-seeking undergraduates: 8% part-time, 60% women, 6% African American, 3% Asian American, 5% Hispanic American, 1% international
▶ 476 degree-seeking graduate students
▶ 84% of applicants admitted
▶ SAT or ACT (ACT writing optional) required
▶ 66% graduate within 6 years; 39% enter graduate study

**General.** Founded in 1808. Regionally accredited. **Degrees:** 371 bachelor's awarded; master's, first professional offered. **ROTC:** Army. **Location:** 65 miles from Washington, DC, 50 miles from Baltimore. **Calendar:** Semester, limited summer session. **Full-time faculty:** 118 total; 92% have terminal degrees, 4% minority, 39% women. **Part-time faculty:** 73 total; 10% have terminal degrees, 3% minority, 51% women. **Class size:** 52% < 20, 47% 20-39, less than 1% 40-49, less than 1% 50-99. **Special facilities:** 300 acre recreation area.

**Freshman class profile.** 2,549 applied, 2,141 admitted, 449 enrolled.

| Mid 50% test scores | | Rank in top tenth: | 19% |
|---|---|---|---|
| SAT critical reading: | 480-590 | End year in good standing: | 91% |
| SAT math: | 480-580 | Return as sophomores: | 77% |
| GPA 3.50 or higher: | 29% | Out-of-state: | 48% |
| GPA 3.0-3.49: | 32% | Live on campus: | 95% |
| GPA 2.0-2.99: | 39% | International: | 1% |
| Rank in top quarter: | 49% | | |

**Basis for selection.** High school record most important followed by standardized test scores, character, extracurricular activities. Interview and essay recommended. Auditions and/or portfolios are recommended for VPA majors, but not required. **Homeschooled:** Statement describing homeschool structure and mission, letter of recommendation (nonparent) required.

**High school preparation.** College-preparatory program required. 16 units required. Required units include English 4, mathematics 3, social studies 3, science 3 (laboratory 2), foreign language 2 and academic electives 1.

**2008-2009 Annual costs.** Tuition/fees: $27,560. Room/board: $9,520. Books/supplies: $1,000. Personal expenses: $600.

**2007-2008 Financial aid. Need-based:** 380 full-time freshmen applied for aid; 311 were judged to have need; 310 of these received aid. Average need met was 76%. Average scholarship/grant was $13,800; average loan $4,393. 69% of total undergraduate aid awarded as scholarships/grants, 31% as loans/jobs. **Non-need-based:** Awarded to 861 full-time undergraduates, including 247 freshmen. Scholarships awarded for academics, art, athletics, minority status, music/drama, ROTC.

**Application procedures. Admission:** No deadline. $35 fee, may be waived for applicants with need. Application may be submitted online. Admission notification on a rolling basis beginning on or about 12/1. Must reply by May 1 or within 2 week(s) if notified thereafter. **Financial aid:** Closing date 3/1. FAFSA, institutional form required. Applicants notified on a rolling basis starting 2/1; must reply by 5/1.

**Academics.** Liberal arts core curriculum integrated over 4 years includes: western civilization (clustered with literature and art courses), American experience, philosophy, theology, ethics, non-western cultures, mathematical science, foreign language, social science, written and oral communication. Undergraduate professional studies programs in business and criminal justice in an accelerated format offered off-campus; open to adult students only. **Special study options:** Accelerated study, combined bachelor's/graduate degree, cross-registration, double major, dual enrollment of high school students, honors, independent study, internships, liberal arts/career combination, student-designed major, study abroad, teacher certification program, Washington semester, weekend college. 3-2 with Johns Hopkins University (BS Biology, BS Nursing), 3-3 with Sacred Heart University (BS in Biology, MS in Physical Therapy), 4-2 with Sacred Heart University (BS in Biology, MS in Occupational Therapy). **Credit/placement by examination:** AP, CLEP, IB, SAT, ACT, institutional tests. 30 credit hours maximum toward bachelor's degree. **Support services:** Learning center, reduced course load, remedial instruction, study skills assistance, tutoring, writing center.

**Majors. Biology:** General, biochemistry. **Business:** General, accounting, information resources management. **Communications:** General. **Computer sciences:** General. **Conservation:** Environmental studies. **Education:** Elementary. **English:** English lit. **Foreign languages:** French, German, Spanish. **History:** General. **Math:** General. **Parks/recreation:** Sports admin. **Philosophy/religion:** Philosophy. **Physical sciences:** Chemistry. **Protective services:** Criminal justice. **Psychology:** General. **Social sciences:** General, economics, international relations, political science, sociology. **Theology:** Theology. **Visual/performing arts:** General.

**Most popular majors.** Business/marketing 34%, communications/journalism 6%, education 11%, security/protective services 6%, social sciences 12%.

**Computing on campus.** 150 workstations in library, computer center. Dormitories wired for high-speed internet access and linked to campus network. Commuter students can connect to campus network. Online course registration, helpline, repair service, student web hosting, wireless network available.

**Student life. Freshman orientation:** Mandatory. Preregistration for classes offered. 3-day weekend in August and choice of 1 of 2 weekends in June for pre-registration. **Housing:** Guaranteed on-campus for all undergraduates. Coed dorms, special housing for disabled, apartments, substance-free housing available. Theme houses available. **Activities:** Bands, campus ministries, choral groups, dance, drama, international student organizations, literary magazine, music ensembles, musical theater, radio station, student government, student newspaper, TV station, College Democrats, College Republicans, Amnesty International, Circle K, Heritage, commuter student association, Habitat for Humanity, students for life.

**Athletics.** NCAA. **Intercollegiate:** Baseball M, basketball, cross-country, golf, lacrosse, soccer, softball W, swimming W, tennis, track and field. **Intramural:** Basketball, field hockey W, football (non-tackle) M, racquetball, skiing, soccer, softball, swimming, tennis, volleyball. **Team name:** Mountaineers.

**Student services.** Adult student services, alcohol/substance abuse counseling, campus ministries, career counseling, student employment services, financial aid counseling, health services, minority student services, personal counseling, placement for graduates. **Physically disabled:** Services for visually, hearing impaired.

**Contact.** E-mail: admissions@msmary.edu
Phone: (301) 447-5214 Toll-free number: (800) 448-4347
Fax: (301) 447-5860
Stephen Neitz, Dean of Admissions and Enrollment Management, Mount St. Mary's University, 16300 Old Emmitsburg Road, Emmitsburg, MD 21727

## National Labor College
### Silver Spring, Maryland
www.georgemeany.org                    CB code: 3930

▶ Private 4-year liberal arts college
▶ Small city
▶ 280 degree-seeking undergraduates

**General.** Regionally accredited. **Degrees:** 76 bachelor's awarded. **Calendar:** Trimester. **Full-time faculty:** 12 total. **Part-time faculty:** 6 total.

**2007-2008 Annual costs.** $158 per-credit-hour for union members affiliated with the AFL-CIO. $210 per-credit-hour for union members not affiliated with the AFL-CIO. $1031 per-credit-hour for non-union members.

**Application procedures. Admission:** No deadline. $50 fee. Admission notification on a rolling basis.

**Academics. Credit/placement by examination:** CLEP.

**Majors. Business:** Labor relations, labor studies. **Health:** Occupational health. **Other:** Union leadership and administration.

**Contact.** Phone: (301) 431-6400 Fax: (301) 431-5411
Eve Dauer, Registrar, National Labor College, 10000 New Hampshire Avenue, Silver Spring, MD 20904

## Ner Israel Rabbinical College
### Baltimore, Maryland
CB code: 0839

▶ Private 4-year rabbinical college for men affiliated with Jewish faith
▶ Very large city
▶ 369 degree-seeking undergraduates
▶ 205 degree-seeking graduate students
▶ 62% of applicants admitted
▶ Interview required

**General.** Accredited by AARTS. **Degrees:** 67 bachelor's awarded; master's, doctoral, first professional offered. **Calendar:** Semester. **Full-time faculty:** 23 total.

**Freshman class profile.** 93 applied, 58 admitted, 50 enrolled.

**Basis for selection.** Interview, character, religious affiliation most important. High school record and recommendations also important. **Home-schooled:** Transcript of courses and grades, state high school equivalency certificate, interview, letter of recommendation (nonparent) required.

**2008-2009 Annual costs.** Tuition/fees (projected): $8,500. Room/board: $6,500.

**Application procedures. Admission:** No deadline. $50 fee. Admission notification on a rolling basis. **Financial aid:** Closing date 3/1.

**Academics. Special study options:** Study abroad. **Credit/placement by examination:** CLEP, institutional tests.

**Majors. Theology:** Talmudic.

**Student life. Policies:** Religious observance required.

**Contact.** Phone: (410) 484-7200
Rabbi Beryl Weisbord, Admissions Director, Ner Israel Rabbinical College, 400 Mount Wilson Lane, Baltimore, MD 21208

## St. John's College
### Annapolis, Maryland
www.stjohnscollege.edu          CB member     CB code: 5598

▶ Private 4-year liberal arts college
▶ Residential campus in large town
▶ 481 degree-seeking undergraduates: 47% women, 1% African American, 3% Asian American, 3% Hispanic American
▶ 82 degree-seeking graduate students
▶ 81% of applicants admitted
▶ Application essay required
▶ 75% graduate within 6 years; 19% enter graduate study

**General.** Founded in 1784. Regionally accredited. Second campus in Santa Fe, New Mexico. Students may transfer between campuses. **Degrees:** 103 bachelor's awarded; master's offered. **Location:** 35 miles from Washington, DC, 30 miles from Baltimore. **Calendar:** Semester. **Full-time faculty:** 72 total; 82% have terminal degrees, 4% minority, 25% women. **Part-time faculty:** 7 total; 29% have terminal degrees, 29% women. **Class size:** 94% < 20, 5% 20-39, less than 1% >100. **Special facilities:** Planetarium, boathouse, observatory.

**Freshman class profile.** 441 applied, 356 admitted, 143 enrolled.

| Mid 50% test scores | | End year in good standing: | 93% |
|---|---|---|---|
| SAT critical reading: | 650-760 | Return as sophomores: | 80% |
| SAT math: | 580-680 | Out-of-state: | 82% |
| Rank in top quarter: | 58% | Live on campus: | 100% |
| Rank in top tenth: | 28% | International: | 1% |

**Basis for selection.** One optional and 3 required essays most important. School achievement record and teacher recommendations important. 2-day campus visit and interview recommended. Standardized tests required for

Four-Year Colleges

homeschooled and international students. **Homeschooled:** Statement describing homeschool structure and mission, letter of recommendation (nonparent) required. Must submit results of PSAT, SAT, or ACT if high school diploma will not be earned.

**High school preparation.** 5 units required. Required and recommended units include English 4, mathematics 3-4, social studies 2, history 2, science 3 (laboratory 3) and foreign language 2-4.

**2008-2009 Annual costs.** Tuition/fees: $39,154. Room/board: $9,284. Books/supplies: $280. Personal expenses: $750.

**2007-2008 Financial aid.** All financial aid based on need. 111 full-time freshmen applied for aid; 89 were judged to have need; 89 of these received aid. Average need met was 71%. Average scholarship/grant was $25,640; average loan $4,270. 73% of total undergraduate aid awarded as scholarships/grants, 27% as loans/jobs.

**Application procedures. Admission:** Priority date 3/1; no deadline. No application fee. Application may be submitted online. Admission notification on a rolling basis. Must reply by May 1 or within 2 week(s) if notified thereafter. Early application encouraged as class generally fills by first week in May. **Financial aid:** Priority date 2/15; no closing date. FAFSA, CSS PROFILE required. Applicants notified on a rolling basis starting 1/15; must reply by 5/1.

**Academics. Special study options:** Internships. **Credit/placement by examination:** CLEP. **Support services:** Tutoring, writing center.

**Majors. Area/ethnic studies:** Western European. **Liberal arts:** Arts/sciences, humanities.

**Computing on campus.** 20 workstations in library, computer center. Dormitories wired for high-speed internet access and linked to campus network. Commuter students can connect to campus network.

**Student life. Freshman orientation:** Mandatory. 2-day program, after registration and prior to start of classes. **Policies:** Freshmen required to live in dormitories. **Housing:** Guaranteed on-campus for freshmen. Coed dorms, substance-free housing available. **Activities:** Choral groups, dance, drama, film society, literary magazine, music ensembles, musical theater, student government, student newspaper, Political Forum, Project Politae (campus community service organization), Pink Triangle Society, Christian Fellowship, Jewish Students Society, Student Committee on Instruction, Environmental Club, Amnesty International, Delegate Council.

**Athletics. Intramural:** Badminton, basketball, boxing M, fencing, handball, racquetball, rowing (crew), sailing, soccer, softball, squash, table tennis, tennis, track and field, volleyball.

**Student services.** Alcohol/substance abuse counseling, career counseling, student employment services, financial aid counseling, health services, personal counseling, placement for graduates, women's services.

**Contact.** E-mail: admissions@sjca.edu
Phone: (410) 626-2522 Toll-free number: (800) 727-9238
Fax: (410) 269-7916
John Christensen, Director of Admissions, St. John's College, PO Box 2800, Annapolis, MD 21404

## St. Mary's College of Maryland

**St. Mary's City, Maryland**     **CB member**
**www.smcm.edu**     **CB code: 5601**

- Public 4-year liberal arts college
- Residential campus in rural community
- 1,922 degree-seeking undergraduates: 2% part-time, 57% women, 8% African American, 4% Asian American, 5% Hispanic American, 1% Native American, 2% international
- 22 degree-seeking graduate students
- 55% of applicants admitted
- SAT or ACT (ACT writing optional), application essay required
- 83% graduate within 6 years; 35% enter graduate study

**General.** Founded in 1840. Regionally accredited. Opportunities for participating in colonial and archaeological research. Designated a Public Honors College. **Degrees:** 435 bachelor's awarded; master's offered. **Location:** 70 miles from Washington, DC. **Calendar:** Semester, limited summer session. **Full-time faculty:** 138 total; 97% have terminal degrees, 17% minority, 47% women. **Part-time faculty:** 75 total; 48% have terminal degrees, 8% minority, 51% women. **Class size:** 64% < 20, 33% 20-39, less than 1% 40-49, 2% 50-99. **Special facilities:** Archaeological site of Historic St. Mary's

City, electron microscope, marine research vessel, fresh and salt water research facilities.

**Freshman class profile.** 2,351 applied, 1,288 admitted, 464 enrolled.

| Mid 50% test scores | | | |
|---|---|---|---|
| SAT critical reading: | 570-670 | Rank in top quarter: | 76% |
| SAT math: | 560-660 | Rank in top tenth: | 42% |
| SAT writing: | 560-670 | Return as sophomores: | 88% |
| GPA 3.50 or higher: | 51% | Out-of-state: | 18% |
| GPA 3.0-3.49: | 38% | Live on campus: | 98% |
| GPA 2.0-2.99: | 11% | International: | 2% |

**Basis for selection.** High school record, SAT or ACT scores, recommendations by counselors/teachers, co-curricular resume, and essay most important. Interview recommended for admissions. **Homeschooled:** Transcript of courses and grades, state high school equivalency certificate required.

**High school preparation.** 20 units required; 24 recommended. Required and recommended units include English 4, mathematics 3-4, social studies 2, history 1-2, science 3 (laboratory 2), foreign language 2-4 and academic electives 3.

**2008-2009 Annual costs.** Tuition/fees: $12,604; $23,454 out-of-state. Room/board: $9,225. Books/supplies: $1,000. Personal expenses: $1,800.

**2006-2007 Financial aid. Need-based:** 302 full-time freshmen applied for aid; 194 were judged to have need; 194 of these received aid. Average need met was 59%. Average scholarship/grant was $3,500; average loan $2,625. 68% of total undergraduate aid awarded as scholarships/grants, 32% as loans/jobs. **Non-need-based:** Awarded to 777 full-time undergraduates, including 221 freshmen. Scholarships awarded for academics, alumni affiliation.

**Application procedures. Admission:** Closing date 1/15 (postmark date). $40 fee, may be waived for applicants with need. Application may be submitted online. Admission notification 4/1. Must reply by May 1 or within 2 week(s) if notified thereafter. **Financial aid:** Closing date 3/1. FAFSA required. Applicants notified by 4/1; must reply by 5/1.

**Academics. Special study options:** Double major, dual enrollment of high school students, exchange student, honors, independent study, internships, student-designed major, study abroad, teacher certification program. International study programs in China, England, France, Germany, the Gambia, Japan, Italy, Thailand, and other countries; archaeological field school at historic St. Mary's City; pre-engineering 3-2 program with University of Maryland School of Engineering. **Credit/placement by examination:** AP, CLEP, IB, SAT, institutional tests. 45 credit hours maximum toward bachelor's degree. **Support services:** Reduced course load, study skills assistance, tutoring, writing center.

**Majors. Biology:** General, biochemistry. **Computer sciences:** General. **English:** English lit. **Foreign languages:** General. **History:** General. **Interdisciplinary:** Biological/physical sciences. **Math:** General. **Philosophy/religion:** Philosophy, religion. **Physical sciences:** Chemistry, physics. **Psychology:** General. **Public administration:** Policy analysis. **Social sciences:** Anthropology, economics, political science, sociology. **Visual/performing arts:** Art, dramatic.

**Most popular majors.** Biology 12%, English 13%, history 9%, psychology 14%, social sciences 27%.

**Computing on campus.** 325 workstations in dormitories, library, computer center, student center. Dormitories wired for high-speed internet access and linked to campus network. Commuter students can connect to campus network. Online course registration, online library, helpline, student web hosting, wireless network available.

**Student life. Freshman orientation:** Mandatory, $100 fee. Preregistration for classes offered. Offered in July; additional program in August. **Housing:** Guaranteed on-campus for all undergraduates. Coed dorms, single-sex dorms, special housing for disabled, apartments, substance-free housing available. $300 nonrefundable deposit, deadline 5/1. Townhouses and apartments available. **Activities:** Jazz band, choral groups, dance, drama, international student organizations, literary magazine, music ensembles, musical theater, radio station, student government, student newspaper, symphony orchestra, TV station, Black student union, College Republicans, College Democrats, Amnesty International, For Goodness Sake, Hillel, Habitat for Humanity, Student Environmental Action Coalition, Intervarsity Christian Fellowship, St. Mary's Triangle and Rainbow Society.

**Athletics. NCAA. Intercollegiate:** Baseball M, basketball, field hockey W, lacrosse, sailing, soccer, swimming, tennis, volleyball W. **Intramural:** Basketball, cross-country, football (non-tackle), soccer, softball. **Team name:** Seahawks.

**Student services.** Alcohol/substance abuse counseling, career counseling, student employment services, financial aid counseling, health services, minority student services, personal counseling, placement for graduates, veterans' counselor, women's services. **Physically disabled:** Services for visually, hearing impaired.

**Contact.** E-mail: admissions@smcm.edu
Phone: (240) 895-5000 Toll-free number: (800) 492-7181
Fax: (240) 895-5001
Richard Edgar, Director of Admissions, St. Mary's College of Maryland, 18952 East Fisher Road, St. Mary's City, MD 20686-3001

## Salisbury University
**Salisbury, Maryland**
www.salisbury.edu

**CB member**
**CB code: 5403**

- Public 4-year university and liberal arts college
- Residential campus in large town
- 6,726 degree-seeking undergraduates: 6% part-time, 55% women, 11% African American, 3% Asian American, 2% Hispanic American, 1% Native American, 1% international
- 513 degree-seeking graduate students
- 56% of applicants admitted
- 70% graduate within 6 years; 7% enter graduate study

**General.** Founded in 1925. Regionally accredited. **Degrees:** 1,439 bachelor's awarded; master's offered. **ROTC:** Army. **Location:** 110 miles from Baltimore and Washington, DC. **Calendar:** 4-1-4, extensive summer session. **Full-time faculty:** 363 total; 82% have terminal degrees, 14% minority, 44% women. **Part-time faculty:** 168 total; 10% have terminal degrees, 7% minority, 67% women. **Class size:** 30% < 20, 62% 20-39, 5% 40-49, 2% 50-99, less than 1% >100. **Special facilities:** Arboretum, research center for Delmarva history and culture, center for conflict resolution, small business development center network.

**Freshman class profile.** 6,593 applied, 3,684 admitted, 1,150 enrolled.

| Mid 50% test scores | | | |
|---|---|---|---|
| SAT critical reading: | 510-590 | GPA 2.0-2.99: | 14% |
| SAT math: | 520-610 | Rank in top quarter: | 61% |
| SAT writing: | 520-590 | Rank in top tenth: | 23% |
| ACT composite: | 20-24 | End year in good standing: | 82% |
| GPA 3.50 or higher: | 53% | Return as sophomores: | 81% |
| GPA 3.0-3.49: | 33% | Out-of-state: | 18% |
| | | Live on campus: | 83% |

**Basis for selection.** Rigor of secondary school recording, including level of courses, depth of subjects, GPA most important. Activities, leadership roles, artistic or athletic talents, ability to contribute to a culturally diverse community also important. SAT/ACT scores optional for applicants with high school GPA of 3.5 or higher. Essay recommended.

**High school preparation.** 15 units required; 21 recommended. Required and recommended units include English 4, mathematics 3-4, social studies 3, science 3-4 (laboratory 2-3), foreign language 2-3 and academic electives 3.

**2007-2008 Annual costs.** Tuition/fees: $6,412; $14,500 out-of-state. Room/board: $7,604. Books/supplies: $1,000. Personal expenses: $2,650.

**2006-2007 Financial aid. Need-based:** 808 full-time freshmen applied for aid; 463 were judged to have need; 431 of these received aid. Average need met was 63%. Average scholarship/grant was $6,324; average loan $2,463. 44% of total undergraduate aid awarded as scholarships/grants, 56% as loans/jobs. **Non-need-based:** Awarded to 940 full-time undergraduates, including 202 freshmen. Scholarships awarded for academics, alumni affiliation, art, leadership, music/drama, state residency. **Additional information:** Job opportunities provided for almost 30% of full-time undergraduate students. Students can expect to earn $1500 per academic year by working 10 to 15 hours per week.

**Application procedures. Admission:** Closing date 12/1. $45 fee, may be waived for applicants with need. Application must be submitted online. Admission notification 3/15. Must reply by 5/1. **Financial aid:** Priority date 3/1, closing date 12/31. FAFSA required. Applicants notified by 3/15; Applicants notified on a rolling basis starting 3/15; must reply by 5/1 or within 2 week(s) of notification.

**Academics. Special study options:** Accelerated study, combined bachelor's/graduate degree, cooperative education, cross-registration, distance learning, double major, dual enrollment of high school students, ESL, exchange student, external degree, honors, independent study, internships, liberal arts/career combination, student-designed major, study abroad, teacher certification program, Washington semester. **Credit/placement by examination:** AP, CLEP, IB, institutional tests. 60 credit hours maximum toward bachelor's

degree. **Support services:** Learning center, study skills assistance, tutoring, writing center.

**Majors. Biology:** General. **Business:** Accounting, business admin, finance, marketing. **Communications:** General. **Computer sciences:** General, information systems. **Conservation:** Environmental science. **Education:** Early childhood, elementary, health, physical. **English:** English lit. **Foreign languages:** French, Spanish. **Health:** Athletic training, clinical lab science, environmental health, nursing (RN), respiratory therapy technology. **History:** General. **Interdisciplinary:** Global studies, peace/conflict. **Liberal arts:** Arts/sciences. **Math:** General. **Parks/recreation:** Exercise sciences. **Philosophy/religion:** Philosophy. **Physical sciences:** Chemistry, physics. **Psychology:** General. **Public administration:** Social work. **Social sciences:** Economics, geography, political science, sociology. **Visual/performing arts:** Art, dramatic, studio arts.

**Most popular majors.** Biology 6%, business/marketing 19%, communications/journalism 10%, education 14%, health sciences 8%.

**Computing on campus.** 325 workstations in library, computer center, student center. Dormitories wired for high-speed internet access and linked to campus network. Commuter students can connect to campus network. Online course registration, online library, helpline, repair service, student web hosting, wireless network available.

**Student life. Freshman orientation:** Mandatory. Preregistration for classes offered. Orientation fee varies per program. **Policies:** Class attendance policies vary by instructor. Hazing and smoking is prohibited. **Housing:** Coed dorms, single-sex dorms, apartments, substance-free housing available. $250 deposit. Affiliated off-campus apartments, quiet/study housing available. World living/learning option-community of international and American students. **Activities:** Bands, campus ministries, choral groups, dance, drama, film society, international student organizations, literary magazine, music ensembles, musical theater, radio station, student government, student newspaper, symphony orchestra, TV station, Campus Crusade for Christ, Christian fellowship, reformed university fellowship, Muslim student organization, junior gospel choir, Union of African-Americans, NAACP, African American historical & philosophical society.

**Athletics.** NCAA. **Intercollegiate:** Baseball M, basketball, cross-country, field hockey W, football (tackle) M, lacrosse, soccer, softball W, swimming, tennis, track and field, volleyball W. **Intramural:** Basketball, cross-country, football (non-tackle), golf, ice hockey M, lacrosse, racquetball, soccer, softball, tennis, volleyball, water polo. **Team name:** Seagulls.

**Student services.** Alcohol/substance abuse counseling, career counseling, student employment services, financial aid counseling, health services, minority student services, personal counseling, veterans' counselor. **Physically disabled:** Services for visually, speech, hearing impaired.

**Contact.** E-mail: admissions@salisbury.edu
Phone: (410) 543-6161 Toll-free number: (888) 543-0148
Fax: (410) 546-6016
Laura Thorpe, Director of Admissions, Salisbury University, 1200 Camden Avenue, Salisbury, MD 21801-6862

## Sojourner-Douglass College
**Baltimore, Maryland**
www.sdc.edu

**CB code: 0504**

- Private 4-year liberal arts college
- Very large city
- 1,246 degree-seeking undergraduates: 32% part-time, 88% women
- 78 degree-seeking graduate students
- Interview required

**General.** Founded in 1980. Regionally accredited. Campus in the Bahamas. **Degrees:** 172 bachelor's awarded; master's offered. **Location:** Downtown. **Calendar:** Semester. **Full-time faculty:** 60 total. **Part-time faculty:** 150 total. **Special facilities:** Learning resource center, writing lab.

**Basis for selection.** Essay, interview, and extracurricular activities important. Institutional placement tests used for all programs.

**2007-2008 Annual costs.** Tuition/fees: $7,478. Books/supplies: $800. Personal expenses: $2,800.

**Application procedures. Admission:** No deadline. $25 fee, may be waived for applicants with need. Admission notification on a rolling basis. **Financial aid:** Priority date 3/1; no closing date. FAFSA, institutional form required. Applicants notified on a rolling basis; must reply within 2 week(s) of notification.

**Academics. Special study options:** Accelerated study, cooperative education, honors, independent study, internships. **Credit/placement by examination:** CLEP. **Support services:** Learning center, remedial instruction, tutoring.

**Majors. Business:** Business admin, hospitality admin, management information systems. **Health:** Health care admin. **Interdisciplinary:** Gerontology. **Public administration:** Social work. **Social sciences:** General.

**Most popular majors.** Business/marketing 26%, education 11%, psychology 19%, public administration/social services 45%.

**Computing on campus.** 100 workstations in computer center.

**Student life. Freshman orientation:** Available. Held the Saturday before classes start in the fall. **Activities:** Student government, student newspaper, Phi Beta Sigma, Zeta Phi Beta, Sigma Beta Delta honor society, student government association, Association for the Study of African American Life and History.

**Student services.** Career counseling, on-campus daycare, personal counseling.

**Contact.** Phone: (410) 276-0306 ext. 248 Fax: (410) 675-1811
Diana Samuels, Coordinator of Admissions, Sojourner-Douglass College, 500 North Caroline Street, Baltimore, MD 21205

---

## Towson University

**Towson, Maryland**
**www.towson.edu**

**CB member**
**CB code: 5404**

- Public 4-year university
- Commuter campus in large city
- 15,488 degree-seeking undergraduates: 10% part-time, 60% women, 11% African American, 4% Asian American, 2% Hispanic American, 3% international
- 2,927 degree-seeking graduate students
- 60% of applicants admitted
- SAT or ACT with writing required
- 66% graduate within 6 years

**General.** Founded in 1866. Regionally accredited. **Degrees:** 3,120 bachelor's awarded; master's, doctoral offered. **ROTC:** Army, Air Force. **Location:** 1.5 miles from Baltimore. **Calendar:** Semester, extensive summer session. **Full-time faculty:** 728 total; 77% have terminal degrees, 16% minority, 52% women. **Part-time faculty:** 647 total; 29% have terminal degrees, 11% minority, 54% women. **Class size:** 35% < 20, 59% 20-39, 5% 40-49, 1% 50-99, less than 1% >100. **Special facilities:** Planetarium, Asian art collection, concert hall, greenhouse, herbarium, observatory, animal museum.

**Freshman class profile.** 15,464 applied, 9,223 admitted, 2,665 enrolled.

| Mid 50% test scores | | | |
|---|---|---|---|
| SAT critical reading: | 490-580 | Rank in top quarter: | 44% |
| SAT math: | 500-590 | Rank in top tenth: | 18% |
| SAT writing: | 500-580 | Return as sophomores: | 82% |
| ACT composite: | 20-24 | Out-of-state: | 30% |
| GPA 3.50 or higher: | 46% | Live on campus: | 80% |
| GPA 3.0-3.49: | 48% | International: | 1% |
| GPA 2.0-2.99: | 6% | Fraternities: | 9% |
| | | Sororities: | 10% |

**Basis for selection.** High school record, test scores important; class rank, recommendations, essay considered. Interview and essay recommended. Audition required of music, dance majors. **Homeschooled:** Writing samples, 3 letters of recommendation, course-work summary required.

**High school preparation.** 21 units required. Required and recommended units include English 4, mathematics 3-4, social studies 3, science 3 (laboratory 2-3), foreign language 2-4 and academic electives 6.

**2007-2008 Annual costs.** Tuition/fees: $7,234; $17,174 out-of-state. Room/board: $8,169. Books/supplies: $948. Personal expenses: $1,846.

**2007-2008 Financial aid. Need-based:** 1,942 full-time freshmen applied for aid; 1,222 were judged to have need; 1,166 of these received aid. Average need met was 69%. Average scholarship/grant was $7,295; average loan $3,346. 59% of total undergraduate aid awarded as scholarships/grants, 41% as loans/jobs. **Non-need-based:** Awarded to 3,364 full-time undergraduates, including 871 freshmen. Scholarships awarded for academics, athletics, job skills, music/drama.

**Application procedures. Admission:** Priority date 12/1; deadline 2/15 (postmark date). $45 fee, may be waived for applicants with need. Application may be submitted online. Admission notification on a rolling basis beginning on or about 10/1. Must reply by May 1 or within 2 week(s) if notified thereafter. **Financial aid:** Priority date 1/31; no closing date. FAFSA required. Applicants notified on a rolling basis starting 3/21; must reply within 2 week(s) of notification.

**Academics. Special study options:** Combined bachelor's/graduate degree, cooperative education, cross-registration, distance learning, double major, dual enrollment of high school students, ESL, exchange student, honors, independent study, internships, liberal arts/career combination, student-designed major, study abroad, teacher certification program. 3-2 engineering with University of Maryland, College Park. **Credit/placement by examination:** AP, CLEP, IB, SAT, ACT, institutional tests. 45 credit hours maximum toward bachelor's degree. Portfolio reviews, oral exams, demonstrations or written reports/papers considered for credit. **Support services:** Learning center, remedial instruction, study skills assistance, tutoring, writing center.

**Honors college/program.** Students need to meet two criteria: unweighted GPA of 3.60 or greater on a 4.00 scale and score of 1800 or greater on the SAT R (guaranteed admission). If meet only one, a more comprehensive review of course selection, HS curriculum, and written and comprenhensive skills take place.

**Majors. Area/ethnic studies:** American, women's. **Biology:** General, Biochemistry/biophysics and molecular biology, ecology. **Business:** Accounting, business admin. **Communications:** General, journalism, media studies. **Communications technology:** Radio/tv. **Computer sciences:** General, computer science. **Conservation:** Environmental studies. **Education:** Art, early childhood, elementary, music, physical, special. **English:** English lit. **Family/consumer sciences:** Family systems. **Foreign languages:** General. **Health:** Athletic training, audiology/speech pathology, health care admin, health services, nursing (RN), substance abuse counseling. **History:** General. **Interdisciplinary:** Biological/physical sciences, gerontology. **Legal studies:** General. **Math:** General. **Parks/recreation:** Exercise sciences, sports admin. **Philosophy/religion:** Philosophy, religion. **Physical sciences:** Chemistry, geology, physics, planetary. **Protective services:** Forensics. **Psychology:** General. **Social sciences:** General, economics, geography, international relations, political science, sociology, urban studies. **Visual/performing arts:** Art, dance, dramatic, studio arts.

**Most popular majors.** Business/marketing 18%, communications/journalism 8%, education 14%, health sciences 9%, psychology 8%, social sciences 11%.

**Computing on campus.** 1,200 workstations in dormitories, library, computer center, student center. Dormitories wired for high-speed internet access and linked to campus network. Commuter students can connect to campus network. Online course registration, online library, helpline, student web hosting, wireless network available.

**Student life. Freshman orientation:** Mandatory. Preregistration for classes offered. **Policies:** Students play active role in university governance. **Housing:** Guaranteed on-campus for freshmen. Coed dorms, special housing for disabled, apartments, substance-free housing available. $225 nonrefundable deposit, deadline 5/1. Honors hall, alcohol free floors, academic emphasis floors, non-traditional age area, non-smoking floors, leadership floor, special quiet floors available. **Activities:** Bands, campus ministries, choral groups, dance, drama, international student organizations, literary magazine, music ensembles, musical theater, radio station, student government, student newspaper, symphony orchestra, TV station, Black student union, Jewish student association, Circle K, student ambassadors, Newman Club, Campus Crusades, Hillel, sisterhood.

**Athletics.** NCAA. **Intercollegiate:** Baseball M, basketball, cheerleading, cross-country, diving, field hockey W, football (tackle) M, golf M, gymnastics W, lacrosse, soccer, softball W, swimming, tennis, track and field, volleyball W. **Intramural:** Basketball, cross-country, football (non-tackle), lacrosse, racquetball, soccer, softball, tennis, triathlon, volleyball. **Team name:** Tigers.

**Student services.** Adult student services, alcohol/substance abuse counseling, campus ministries, career counseling, student employment services, financial aid counseling, health services, minority student services, on-campus daycare, personal counseling, placement for graduates, veterans' counselor, women's services. **Physically disabled:** Services for visually, speech, hearing impaired.

**Contact.** E-mail: admissions@towson.edu
Phone: (410) 704-2113 Toll-free number: (888) 486-9766
Fax: (410) 704-3030
Louise Shulack, Director of Undergraduate Admissions, Towson University, 8000 York Road, Towson, MD 21252-0001

# United States Naval Academy

**Annapolis, Maryland** — CB member
**www.usna.edu** — CB code: 5809

- Public 4-year military college
- Residential campus in large town
- 4,443 degree-seeking undergraduates: 21% women, 4% African American, 3% Asian American, 10% Hispanic American, 1% Native American, 1% international
- 12% of applicants admitted
- SAT or ACT (ACT writing optional), application essay, interview required
- 83% graduate within 6 years; 3% enter graduate study

**General.** Founded in 1845. Regionally accredited. Military environment and organization under student leadership with military officer supervision. Professional training at US bases and with units of fleet during summer months. Graduates receive B.S. degree with a major in one of 21 disciplines, plus commission as Ensign in US Navy or Second Lieutenant in US Marine Corps. **Degrees:** 1,037 bachelor's awarded. **Location:** 30 miles from Baltimore, 35 miles from Washington, DC. **Calendar:** Semester, limited summer session. **Full-time faculty:** 525 total; 64% have terminal degrees, 9% minority, 22% women. **Class size:** 61% < 20, 39% 20-39. **Special facilities:** Observatory, planetarium, satellite dish, oceanographic research vessel, weather station, towing tanks, propulsion laboratory, transsonic and hypersonic sound tunnels, museum.

**Freshman class profile.** 12,003 applied, 1,419 admitted, 1,202 enrolled.

| Mid 50% test scores | | | |
|---|---|---|---|
| SAT critical reading: | 560-660 | End year in good standing: | 97% |
| SAT math: | 600-690 | Return as sophomores: | 97% |
| Rank in top quarter: | 81% | Out-of-state: | 95% |
| Rank in top tenth: | 56% | Live on campus: | 100% |
| | | International: | 1% |

**Basis for selection.** Test scores, school achievement record, interview, recommendations of school officials, participation in sports, school, and community activities important. Rank in top 40% of class usually required. Successful candidate must be qualified medically, pass a candidate physical fitness assessment, and be nominated by an official source.

**High school preparation.** Recommended units include English 4, mathematics 4, history 2, science 2 (laboratory 2) and foreign language 2. Familiarity with the use of personal computers, including the Windows operating system, word processing, spreadsheets, and the Internet required.

**2008-2009 Annual costs.** First-year students pay one-time fee of $2,500 upon entering the Naval Academy for initial outfitting of uniforms and other supplies. Tuition, room and board, and medical and dental care provided by United States government. Each midshipman receives monthly salary of about $895 to cover costs of books, supplies, uniforms, laundry, and equipment, including microcomputer. Books/supplies: $1,000.

**Financial aid. Additional information:** The United States Naval Academy does not charge tuition, room, or board; therefore no financial aid is required by students.

**Application procedures. Admission:** Closing date 1/31 (receipt date). No application fee. Application must be submitted online. Admission notification on a rolling basis beginning on or about 9/1. Must reply by May 1 or within 2 week(s) if notified thereafter. Nomination essential prior to consideration for appointment. Nominating authorities include President, Vice President, Secretary of Navy, members of Congress, delegates to Congress, governors of United States Territories, and resident commissioner of Puerto Rico. Applicants for presidential appointments limited by law to sons and daughters of career military personnel, active or retired. Applicants encouraged to apply to the Academy and nominating authority by May one year prior to desired admission.

**Academics. Special study options:** Double major, honors, independent study, study abroad. Qualified students have opportunities to begin work in senior year towards a Master's degree at local graduate schools. Selected midshipmen can also engage in research with thesis, or work towards honors in their majors. **Credit/placement by examination:** AP, CLEP, institutional tests. Midshipmen take local examinations after admission for placement. AP Exam scores also used for validation of some courses. **Support services:** Learning center, remedial instruction, study skills assistance, tutoring, writing center.

**Majors. Computer sciences:** General, information technology. **Engineering:** General, aerospace, electrical, marine, mechanical, ocean, systems. **English:** English lit. **Foreign languages:** Arabic, Chinese. **History:** General.

**Math:** General. **Physical sciences:** General, chemistry, oceanography, physics. **Social sciences:** Econometrics, economics, political science.

**Most popular majors.** Computer/information sciences 6%, engineering/engineering technologies 37%, English 7%, history 9%, social sciences 29%.

**Computing on campus.** PC or laptop required. Dormitories wired for high-speed internet access and linked to campus network. Online course registration, helpline, repair service available.

**Student life. Freshman orientation:** Mandatory. All freshmen (plebes) report in late June for approximately 6 weeks of military indoctrination. **Policies:** The Naval Academy has an Honor Concept administered by the Brigade of Midshipmen. **Housing:** Guaranteed on-campus for all undergraduates. Coed dorms, substance-free housing available. Midshipmen must live in dormitory on campus all four years. **Activities:** Bands, choral groups, drama, film society, literary magazine, music ensembles, musical theater, radio station, student newspaper, Fellowship of Christian Athletes, Black Studies Club, Midshipmen Action Group, Officers' Christian Fellowship, Foreign Affairs Conference, Women's Professional Association.

**Athletics. NCAA. Intercollegiate:** Baseball M, basketball, cross-country, diving, football (tackle) M, golf M, gymnastics M, lacrosse, rifle, rowing (crew), sailing, soccer, squash M, swimming, tennis M, track and field, volleyball W, water polo M, wrestling M. **Intramural:** Basketball, boxing, cross-country, football (non-tackle), golf, handball, judo, racquetball, sailing, soccer, softball, swimming, volleyball, weight lifting, wrestling. **Team name:** Midshipmen.

**Student services.** Alcohol/substance abuse counseling, campus ministries, career counseling, health services, legal services, minority student services, personal counseling, placement for graduates, women's services.

**Contact.** E-mail: webmail@usna.edu
Phone: (410) 293-4361 Toll-free number: (888) 249-7707
Fax: (410) 293-1815
Dean of Admissions, United States Naval Academy, 117 Decatur Road, Annapolis, MD 21402-5018

# University of Baltimore

**Baltimore, Maryland** — CB member
**www.ubalt.edu** — CB code: 5810

- Public 4-year business and liberal arts college
- Commuter campus in very large city
- 2,364 degree-seeking undergraduates
- 3,003 graduate students
- 34% of applicants admitted
- SAT or ACT (ACT writing optional), application essay required

**General.** Founded in 1925. Regionally accredited. **Degrees:** 507 bachelor's awarded; master's, doctoral, first professional offered. **ROTC:** Army. **Location:** Downtown. **Calendar:** Semester, limited summer session. **Full-time faculty:** 166 total. **Part-time faculty:** 186 total. **Special facilities:** Graphics laboratory, business center, interactive video network.

**Freshman class profile.** 862 applied, 293 admitted, 151 enrolled.

| | | | |
|---|---|---|---|
| GPA 3.50 or higher: | 24% | Out-of-state: | 1% |
| GPA 3.0-3.49: | 40% | International: | 1% |
| GPA 2.0-2.99: | 36% | | |

**Basis for selection.** Application: Required items include application, high school transcript, standardized test scores (ACT/SAT) and personal essay.

**High school preparation.** 21 units required. Required units include English 4, mathematics 3, social studies 3 and science 3.

**2007-2008 Annual costs.** Tuition/fees: $6,934; $19,716 out-of-state. Books/supplies: $730.

**Financial aid. Additional information:** Full need met for dependent students only.

**Application procedures. Admission:** Closing date 2/15 (postmark date). $45 fee, may be waived for applicants with need. Application may be submitted online. Must reply by 5/1. **Financial aid:** No deadline. FAFSA, institutional form required. Applicants notified on a rolling basis.

**Academics.** All undergraduate students take 9 hours in an upper-level core curriculum in a general humanities-based general education. **Special study options:** Accelerated study, combined bachelor's/graduate degree, cooperative education, cross-registration, distance learning, dual enrollment of high school students, exchange student, honors, independent study, internships, student-designed major, study abroad, weekend college. **Credit/placement by examination:** AP, CLEP, IB, institutional tests. 30 credit hours maximum toward bachelor's degree. **Support services:** Learning center, reduced course load, remedial instruction, study skills assistance, tutoring, writing center.

**Majors. Business:** General, accounting, business admin, human resources, international, management information systems, managerial economics, marketing. **Communications:** General. **Computer sciences:** General. **English:** English lit. **Health:** Health care admin. **History:** General. **Legal studies:** Prelaw. **Liberal arts:** Arts/sciences. **Protective services:** Criminal justice, forensics. **Psychology:** General. **Public administration:** Human services. **Social sciences:** Political science.

**Most popular majors.** Business/marketing 47%, communications/journalism 6%, health sciences 9%, legal studies 6%, liberal arts 8%, social sciences 17%.

**Computing on campus.** 155 workstations in library, computer center, student center. Commuter students can connect to campus network. Online library, helpline, wireless network available.

**Student life. Freshman orientation:** Available. **Activities:** International student organizations, literary magazine, student government, student newspaper, black student association, Project Hunger, domestic violence advocacy program.

**Athletics. Intramural:** Badminton, basketball, golf, judo, racquetball, rowing (crew), skiing, soccer W, table tennis, tennis, volleyball.

**Student services.** Career counseling, student employment services, health services, personal counseling, placement for graduates, veterans' counselor. **Physically disabled:** Services for visually, speech, hearing impaired.

**Contact.** E-mail: admissions@ubalt.edu
Phone: (410) 837-4777 Toll-free number: (877) 277-5982
Fax: (410) 837-4793
Dawn Griffith, Director of Undergraduate Admissions, University of Baltimore, 1420 North Charles Street, Baltimore, MD 21201-5779

## University of Maryland: Baltimore
Baltimore, Maryland
www.umaryland.edu                                    CB code: 0527

- Public two-year upper-division university and health science college
- Commuter campus in very large city
- 44% of applicants admitted

**General.** Founded in 1807. Regionally accredited. **Degrees:** 354 bachelor's awarded; master's, doctoral, first professional offered. **Articulation:** Agreements with all Maryland community colleges. **Calendar:** 4-1-4, limited summer session. **Full-time faculty:** 1,265 total; 83% have terminal degrees, 26% minority, 40% women. **Part-time faculty:** 227 total; 81% have terminal degrees, 20% minority, 46% women. **Special facilities:** Dental, medical, pharmacy and nursing museums; law library, health sciences library, center for health policy and health services research, center for research on aging, center for vaccine development, biotechnology institute, center for health and homeland security.

**Student profile.** 803 degree-seeking undergraduates, 4,925 degree-seeking graduate students. 874 applied as first time-transfer students, 382 admitted, 286 enrolled. 55% transferred from two-year, 45% transferred from four-year institutions.

| | | | |
|---|---|---|---|
| Women: | 86% | International: | 5% |
| African American: | 28% | Part-time: | 31% |
| Asian American: | 12% | Out-of-state: | 13% |
| Hispanic American: | 3% | 25 or older: | 55% |

**Basis for selection.** College transcript required. Undergraduate deadlines range from February 1 to August 15 (nursing, dental hygiene, medical technology). Transfer accepted as juniors, seniors.

**2007-2008 Annual costs.** Tuition/fees: $7,689; $20,261 out-of-state. Books/supplies: $1,955. Personal expenses: $2,765.

**Financial aid. Need-based:** 33% of total undergraduate aid awarded as scholarships/grants, 67% as loans/jobs. **Additional information:** Maryland state deadline 3/1.

**Application procedures. Admission:** $50 fee. Application may be submitted online. Admission process, fees, and dates differ among undergraduate programs (nursing, dental hygiene, medical technology). **Financial aid:** FAFSA required.

**Academics. Special study options:** Distance learning, double major. **Credit/placement by examination:** CLEP, institutional tests. 30 credit hours maximum toward bachelor's degree.

**Majors. Health:** Clinical lab science, dental hygiene, nursing (RN).

**Computing on campus.** 100 workstations in library, computer center, student center. Dormitories wired for high-speed internet access and linked to campus network. Commuter students can connect to campus network. Online library, helpline, wireless network available.

**Student life. Housing:** Apartments available. **Activities:** International student organizations, student government, Newman Center, African-American student association, Community Volunteer Program.

**Athletics. Intramural:** Badminton, basketball, football (non-tackle), golf, racquetball, soccer, softball, squash, tennis, volleyball.

**Student services.** Alcohol/substance abuse counseling, career counseling, services for economically disadvantaged, student employment services, financial aid counseling, health services, minority student services, on-campus daycare, personal counseling, placement for graduates, women's services. **Physically disabled:** Services for visually, speech, hearing impaired.

**Contact.** E-mail: gradinfo@umaryland.edu
Phone: (410) 706-7480 Fax: (410) 706-4053
Thomas Day, Director of Records and Registration, University of Maryland: Baltimore, 660 West Redwood Street, Room 021, Baltimore, MD 21201

## University of Maryland: Baltimore County
Baltimore, Maryland                                  CB member
www.umbc.edu                                         CB code: 5835

- Public 4-year university
- Residential campus in large city
- 9,304 degree-seeking undergraduates: 15% part-time, 46% women, 16% African American, 21% Asian American, 4% Hispanic American, 1% Native American, 4% international
- 2,262 degree-seeking graduate students
- 69% of applicants admitted
- SAT or ACT (ACT writing recommended), application essay required
- 56% graduate within 6 years

**General.** Founded in 1963. Regionally accredited. **Degrees:** 1,914 bachelor's awarded; master's, doctoral offered. **ROTC:** Army. **Location:** 5 miles from Baltimore, 35 miles from Washington, DC. **Calendar:** 4-1-4, extensive summer session. **Full-time faculty:** 473 total; 88% have terminal degrees, 15% minority, 41% women. **Part-time faculty:** 273 total; 33% have terminal degrees, 19% minority, 46% women. **Class size:** 43% < 20, 36% 20-39, 9% 40-49, 9% 50-99, 4% >100. **Special facilities:** Research telescope, greenhouse, research spectrometers, nuclear magnetic resonance machines, electron microscope facility, computer art laboratory, healthcare informatics laboratory.

**Freshman class profile.** 5,836 applied, 4,024 admitted, 1,437 enrolled.

| Mid 50% test scores | | Rank in top quarter: | 59% |
|---|---|---|---|
| SAT critical reading: | 520-640 | Rank in top tenth: | 28% |
| SAT math: | 560-660 | End year in good standing: | 80% |
| SAT writing: | 520-630 | Return as sophomores: | 85% |
| ACT composite: | 22-27 | Out-of-state: | 9% |
| GPA 3.50 or higher: | 58% | Live on campus: | 72% |
| GPA 3.0-3.49: | 29% | International: | 4% |
| GPA 2.0-2.99: | 13% | | |

**Basis for selection.** High school record, test scores important. Audition required for music, dance, theater majors. Portfolio required for visual arts majors.

**High school preparation.** Required and recommended units include English 4, mathematics 3, social studies 3, science 3-4 and foreign language 2. Algebra I and II, and geometry required.

**2007-2008 Annual costs.** Tuition/fees: $8,717; $17,449 out-of-state. Room/board: $8,658.

**2006-2007 Financial aid. Need-based:** 992 full-time freshmen applied for aid; 647 were judged to have need; 647 of these received aid. Average need met was 87%. Average scholarship/grant was $8,642; average loan $3,037. 63% of total undergraduate aid awarded as scholarships/grants, 37%

as loans/jobs. **Non-need-based:** Awarded to 1,450 full-time undergraduates, including 516 freshmen. Scholarships awarded for academics, alumni affiliation, art, athletics, music/drama.

**Application procedures. Admission:** Priority date 11/1; deadline 2/1 (postmark date). $50 fee, may be waived for applicants with need. Application may be submitted online. Admission notification on a rolling basis beginning on or about 2/1. Must reply by May 1 or within 2 week(s) if notified thereafter. **Financial aid:** Priority date 2/14; no closing date. FAFSA required. Applicants notified on a rolling basis starting 4/1; must reply within 2 week(s) of notification.

**Academics. Special study options:** Combined bachelor's/graduate degree, cooperative education, cross-registration, distance learning, double major, dual enrollment of high school students, ESL, honors, independent study, internships, liberal arts/career combination, semester at sea, student-designed major, study abroad, teacher certification program. **Credit/placement by examination:** AP, CLEP, IB, institutional tests. 60 credit hours maximum toward bachelor's degree. **Support services:** Learning center, remedial instruction, study skills assistance, tutoring, writing center.

**Honors college/program.** Minimum 1300 SAT (exclusive of Writing) and 3.5 GPA required. Approximately 140 students accepted each year, with average SAT of 1300 (exclusive of Writing) and 3.81 GPA. Each semester 40-50 courses offered along with non-curricular activities.

**Majors. Area/ethnic studies:** African-American, American. **Biology:** General, Biochemistry/biophysics and molecular biology, bioinformatics. **Communications:** Media studies. **Computer sciences:** General, information systems. **Conservation:** Environmental science, environmental studies. **Education:** Physics. **Engineering:** General, chemical, computer, mechanical. **English:** English lit. **Foreign languages:** General, linguistics. **Health:** EMT paramedic, health services. **History:** General. **Interdisciplinary:** Ancient studies. **Math:** General, statistics. **Philosophy/religion:** Philosophy. **Physical sciences:** Chemistry, physics. **Psychology:** General. **Public administration:** Social work. **Social sciences:** Anthropology, economics, geography, political science, sociology. **Visual/performing arts:** General, acting, dance, dramatic. **Other:** Gender Studies, Physics Education.

**Most popular majors.** Biology 15%, communication technologies 18%, engineering/engineering technologies 6%, psychology 12%, social sciences 16%, visual/performing arts 8%.

**Computing on campus.** 1,100 workstations in dormitories, library, computer center, student center. Dormitories wired for high-speed internet access and linked to campus network. Commuter students can connect to campus network. Online course registration, online library, helpline, repair service, student web hosting, wireless network available.

**Student life. Freshman orientation:** Mandatory, $125 fee. Preregistration for classes offered. Held June and July. Separate program for honors college students. **Housing:** Guaranteed on-campus for freshmen. Coed dorms, special housing for disabled, apartments, substance-free housing available. $100 nonrefundable deposit, deadline 5/1. Living-learning communities: Center for Women and Information Technology; Emergency Health Services; Exploratory Majors; Honors College; Humanities Floor; Intercultural Living Exchange; Shriver Living Learning Center; Visual and Performing Arts Floor; Women Involved in Learning and Leadership. **Activities:** Bands, choral groups, dance, drama, film society, international student organization, literary magazine, music ensembles, Model UN, musical theater, radio station, student government, student newspaper, symphony orchestra, Black student union, Chinese student association, Jewish student association, Korean club, gay and lesbian organization, progressive action committee, Christian Fellowship, women's union.

**Athletics.** NCAA. **Intercollegiate:** Baseball M, basketball, cheerleading, cross-country, diving, lacrosse, soccer, softball W, swimming, tennis, track and field, volleyball W. **Intramural:** Basketball, football (non-tackle), handball, lacrosse, soccer, softball, tennis, volleyball, weight lifting. **Team name:** Retrievers.

**Student services.** Adult student services, alcohol/substance abuse counseling, campus ministries, career counseling, services for economically disadvantaged, student employment services, financial aid counseling, health services, minority student services, on-campus daycare, personal counseling, placement for graduates, veterans' counselor, women's services. **Physically disabled:** Services for visually, hearing impaired.

**Contact.** E-mail: admissions@umbc.edu
Phone: (410) 455-2291 Toll-free number: (800) 862-2482
Fax: (410) 455-1094
Dale Bittinger, Director of Admissions, University of Maryland: Baltimore County, 1000 Hilltop Circle, Baltimore, MD 21250

## University of Maryland: College Park
**College Park, Maryland**  CB member
**www.maryland.edu**  CB code: 5814

- Public 4-year university
- Commuter campus in large town
- 25,251 degree-seeking undergraduates: 6% part-time, 48% women, 13% African American, 14% Asian American, 6% Hispanic American, 2% international
- 9,577 degree-seeking graduate students
- 47% of applicants admitted
- SAT or ACT with writing, application essay required
- 80% graduate within 6 years

**General.** Founded in 1856. Regionally accredited. Research and internship opportunities at Smithsonian Institution, National Institutes for Health, NASA, US Capitol, White House, FBI, Department of Agriculture, other federal agencies. **Degrees:** 6,107 bachelor's awarded; master's, doctoral, first professional offered. **ROTC:** Army, Naval, Air Force. **Location:** 30 miles from Baltimore, 3 miles from Washington, DC. **Calendar:** Semester, extensive summer session. **Full-time faculty:** 1,568 total; 92% have terminal degrees, 19% minority, 33% women. **Part-time faculty:** 617 total; 57% have terminal degrees, 11% minority, 40% women. **Class size:** 33% < 20, 45% 20-39, 7% 40-49, 8% 50-99, 7% >100. **Special facilities:** National Archives II, astronomy observatory, engineering wind tunnel, space systems lab, nuclear reactor, performing arts center, center for young children, agricultural biotechnology, superconductivity research, institute for systems research, fire and rescue institute.

**Freshman class profile.** 24,172 applied, 11,370 admitted, 4,236 enrolled.

| Mid 50% test scores | | Rank in top tenth: | 56% |
|---|---|---|---|
| SAT critical reading: | 570-680 | Return as sophomores: | 93% |
| SAT math: | 600-700 | Out-of-state: | 35% |
| GPA 3.50 or higher: | 82% | Live on campus: | 93% |
| GPA 3.0-3.49: | 15% | Fraternities: | 13% |
| GPA 2.0-2.99: | 3% | Sororities: | 17% |
| Rank in top quarter: | 89% | | |

**Basis for selection.** Academic record, rigor of the high school academic program, standardized admission test scores, class rank (if available), essay, extracurricular activities, counselor recommendation, and other letters of recommendation reviewed. Test scores submitted after 2/01 will be considered based on space-availability. ACT with or without Writing component accepted when SAT Writing has been submitted. Audition required of music majors. Portfolio recommended for architecture majors. **Homeschooled:** Statement describing homeschool structure and mission, transcript of courses and grades required. Transcript should include description of course work, books used, method of evaluation and actual grades or evaluation. Letter of recommendation required and must be from academic professional.

**High school preparation.** 17 units required; 18 recommended. Required and recommended units include English 4, mathematics 3-4, social studies 3, science 3 (laboratory 2) and foreign language 2. Algebra I and II, plane geometry required. Social studies units should include history.

**2007-2008 Annual costs.** Tuition/fees: $7,969; $22,208 out-of-state. Room/board: $8,854. Books/supplies: $1,025. Personal expenses: $2,268.

**Financial aid. Non-need-based:** Scholarships awarded for academics, art, athletics, music/drama. **Additional information:** Prepaid tuition plans available through state.

**Application procedures. Admission:** Priority date 12/1; deadline 1/20 (receipt date). $55 fee, may be waived for applicants with need. Application may be submitted online. Admission notification 4/1. Must reply by May 1 or within 4 week(s) if notified thereafter. **Financial aid:** Priority date 2/15; no closing date, FAFSA required. Applicants notified on a rolling basis starting 4/1.

**Academics. Special study options:** Accelerated study, combined bachelor's/graduate degree, cooperative education, cross-registration, distance learning, double major, dual enrollment of high school students, ESL, exchange student, external degree, honors, independent study, internships, semester at sea, student-designed major, study abroad, teacher certification program. Living/learning programs: Gemstone program, Honors Humanities, First Year Learning Communities, CIVICUS program, College Park Scholars, Beyond the Classroom, Global Communities, Language House, Jiminez-Porter Writers House, University Honors (the Honors program), Hinman CEOs. **Credit/placement by examination:** AP, CLEP, IB, SAT, ACT, institutional tests.

60 credit hours maximum toward bachelor's degree. **Support services:** Learning center, pre-admission summer program, reduced course load, remedial instruction, study skills assistance, tutoring, writing center.

**Majors. Agriculture:** General, animal sciences, economics, food science. **Architecture:** Architecture, landscape. **Area/ethnic studies:** African-American, American, Russian/Slavic, women's. **Biology:** General, biochemistry, ecology, microbiology. **Business:** General, accounting, finance, international, logistics, management science, marketing. **Communications:** General, journalism. **Computer sciences:** General, information systems. **Conservation:** General. **Education:** Art, elementary, English, foreign languages, health, kindergarten/preschool, mathematics, music, physical, science, social studies, special. **Engineering:** General, aerospace, agricultural, chemical, civil, computer, electrical, materials, mechanical. **English:** English lit. **Family/consumer sciences:** Family/community services, food/nutrition. **Foreign languages:** Chinese, classics, French, German, Italian, Japanese, linguistics, Romance, Russian, Spanish. **Health:** Communication disorders, dietetics, predental, preveterinary. **History:** General. **Legal studies:** Prelaw. **Math:** General. **Parks/recreation:** Exercise sciences. **Philosophy/religion:** Judaic, philosophy. **Physical sciences:** General, astronomy, chemistry, geology, physics. **Psychology:** General. **Social sciences:** Anthropology, criminology, economics, geography, political science, sociology. **Visual/performing arts:** Art history/conservation, dance, dramatic, music performance, studio arts. **Other:** Individual studies.

**Most popular majors.** Biology 9%, business/marketing 16%, communications/journalism 6%, education 6%, engineering/engineering technologies 9%, social sciences 21%.

**Computing on campus.** 1,800 workstations in dormitories, library, computer center, student center. Dormitories wired for high-speed internet access and linked to campus network. Commuter students can connect to campus network. Online course registration, online library, helpline, student web hosting, wireless network available.

**Student life. Freshman orientation:** Mandatory, $145 fee. Preregistration for classes offered. 2-day program. **Housing:** Guaranteed on-campus for freshmen. Coed dorms, single-sex dorms, special housing for disabled, apartments, fraternity/sorority housing, substance-free housing available. **Activities:** Bands, campus ministries, choral groups, dance, drama, film society, international student organizations, literary magazine, music ensembles, musical theater, opera, radio station, student government, student newspaper, symphony orchestra, TV station, Black student union, Asian American student union, Latino student union, Native American student union, Alpha Phi Omega, Habitat for Humanity.

**Athletics.** NCAA. **Intercollegiate:** Baseball M, basketball, cheerleading M, cross-country, equestrian, field hockey W, football (tackle) M, golf, gymnastics W, lacrosse, soccer, softball W, swimming, tennis, track and field, volleyball W, water polo W, wrestling M. **Intramural:** Badminton, basketball, football (non-tackle), golf, ice hockey W, racquetball, soccer, softball, table tennis, tennis, track and field, volleyball, wrestling M. **Team name:** Terrapins.

**Student services.** Adult student services, alcohol/substance abuse counseling, campus ministries, career counseling, services for economically disadvantaged, student employment services, financial aid counseling, health services, legal services, minority student services, on-campus daycare, personal counseling, placement for graduates, veterans' counselor, women's services. **Physically disabled:** Services for visually, speech, hearing impaired.

**Contact.** E-mail: um-admit@uga.umd.edu
Phone: (301) 314-8385 Toll-free number: (800) 422-5867
Fax: (301) 314-9693
Barbara Gill, Director of Undergraduate Admissions, University of Maryland: College Park, Mitchell Building, College Park, MD 20742-5235

---

## University of Maryland: Eastern Shore

**Princess Anne, Maryland**  **CB member**
**www.umes.edu**  **CB code: 5400**

- Public 4-year university
- Residential campus in rural community
- 3,539 degree-seeking undergraduates: 7% part-time, 61% women, 83% African American, 1% Asian American, 1% Hispanic American, 3% international
- 471 degree-seeking graduate students
- 58% of applicants admitted
- SAT or ACT (ACT writing optional), application essay required
- 33% graduate within 6 years; 23% enter graduate study

**General.** Founded in 1886. Regionally accredited. **Degrees:** 436 bachelor's awarded; master's, doctoral offered. **Location:** 12 miles from Salisbury. **Calendar:** Semester, extensive summer session. **Full-time faculty:** 169 total; 65% have terminal degrees, 60% minority, 42% women. **Part-time faculty:** 108 total; 10% have terminal degrees, 44% minority, 59% women. **Class size:** 57% < 20, 37% 20-39, 2% 40-49, 3% 50-99, less than 1% >100. **Special facilities:** Arts and technology center, performing arts center, hydroponic greenhouse, education center.

**Freshman class profile.** 3,651 applied, 2,116 admitted, 891 enrolled.

| Mid 50% test scores | | | |
|---|---|---|---|
| SAT critical reading: | 370-460 | GPA 3.0-3.49: | 22% |
| SAT math: | 350-450 | GPA 2.0-2.99: | 71% |
| SAT writing: | 370-460 | Return as sophomores: | 65% |
| ACT composite: | 14-18 | Out-of-state: | 24% |
| GPA 3.50 or higher: | 7% | Live on campus: | 60% |
| | | International: | 2% |

**Basis for selection.** School record, class rank, and test scores most important. Interview recommended for honors program and physical therapy applicants. Audition required for music majors.

**High school preparation.** 20 units required. Required units include English 4, mathematics 3, social studies 3, science 2, foreign language 2 and academic electives 6.

**2007-2008 Annual costs.** Tuition/fees: $5,988; $12,555 out-of-state. Room/board: $6,580. Books/supplies: $1,400. Personal expenses: $1,400.

**Financial aid. Non-need-based:** Scholarships awarded for academics, alumni affiliation, art, athletics, leadership, music/drama, ROTC, state residency.

**Application procedures. Admission:** Priority date 3/1; deadline 7/15. $25 fee, may be waived for applicants with need. Application may be submitted online. Admission notification on a rolling basis. **Financial aid:** Priority date 3/1, closing date 4/1. FAFSA required. Applicants notified on a rolling basis starting 4/15.

**Academics.** The doctoral program in organizational leadership is a weekend program to meet scheduling needs of its students who are mostly full-time employees. The Library opens in the evenings. **Special study options:** Accelerated study, cooperative education, cross-registration, distance learning, double major, dual enrollment of high school students, exchange student, honors, independent study, internships, liberal arts/career combination, New York semester, study abroad, teacher certification program. **Credit/placement by examination:** AP, CLEP, IB, institutional tests. 60 credit hours maximum toward bachelor's degree. **Support services:** Learning center, pre-admission summer program, reduced course load, remedial instruction, study skills assistance, tutoring, writing center.

**Majors. Agriculture:** General, business, poultry. **Architecture:** Architecture. **Area/ethnic studies:** African-American. **Biology:** General, ecology. **Business:** General, accounting, business admin, hotel/motel admin. **Computer sciences:** General. **Conservation:** Forestry. **Construction:** General. **Education:** General, agricultural, art, business, English, family/consumer sciences, mathematics, music, physical, science, social studies, special, technology/industrial arts. **Engineering:** General. **Engineering technology:** General, civil. **English:** English lit. **Family/consumer sciences:** General. **Health:** Physician assistant. **History:** General. **Liberal arts:** Arts/sciences. **Math:** General. **Parks/recreation:** Exercise sciences. **Physical sciences:** Chemistry. **Protective services:** Police science. **Social sciences:** Sociology. **Transportation:** Aviation. **Visual/performing arts:** Commercial/advertising art. **Other:** Rehabilitation services.

**Most popular majors.** Biology 8%, business/marketing 23%, education 6%, English 6%, health sciences 10%, public administration/social services 18%, social sciences 6%.

**Computing on campus.** 739 workstations in dormitories, library, computer center. Dormitories wired for high-speed internet access and linked to campus network. Commuter students can connect to campus network. Online library, helpline, wireless network available.

**Student life. Freshman orientation:** Mandatory, $100 fee. Preregistration for classes offered. 2 day program in the Fall. **Housing:** Coed dorms, single-sex dorms, apartments, substance-free housing available. $300 partly refundable deposit, deadline 5/1. **Activities:** Bands, campus ministries, choral groups, dance, drama, international student organizations, music ensembles, radio station, student government, student newspaper, NAACP, Students for Progressive Action, Phenomenal Women, Rotaract club, College Democrats of America, Students in Free Enterprise, For Sisters Only, National Student Business League.

**Athletics.** NCAA. **Intercollegiate:** Baseball M, basketball, bowling W, cheerleading M, cross-country, golf M, softball W, tennis, track and field, volleyball W. **Intramural:** Basketball, bowling, football (non-tackle) M, soccer, softball W, swimming, table tennis, volleyball. **Team name:** Hawks.

**Student services.** Adult student services, career counseling, student employment services, financial aid counseling, health services, on-campus daycare, personal counseling, placement for graduates, veterans' counselor. **Physically disabled:** Services for speech, hearing impaired.

**Contact.** E-mail: umesadmissions@umes.edu
Phone: (410) 651-6410 Fax: (410) 651-7922
Tyrone Young, Director of Admissions and Recruitment, University of Maryland: Eastern Shore, Bird Hall, Princess Anne, MD 21853

## University of Maryland: University College
**Adelphi, Maryland**
www.umuc.edu                                    CB code: 0551

◆  Public 4-year university
◆  Commuter campus in large town
◆  19,893 degree-seeking undergraduates: 85% part-time, 58% women, 31% African American, 4% Asian American, 5% Hispanic American, 1% Native American, 2% international
◆  10,017 degree-seeking graduate students

**General.** Founded in 1947. Regionally accredited. Courses held at over 20 locations throughout Maryland, Virginia and Washington, D.C. Associate degree programs available only to active military personnel. Offers BA/BS program with 12 other universities through National University Degree Consortium. Courses offered at more than 120 locations in Europe and Asia. **Degrees:** 2,809 bachelor's, 169 associate awarded; master's, doctoral offered. **Location:** 9 miles from Washington, DC. **Calendar:** Semester, extensive summer session. **Full-time faculty:** 237 total; 76% have terminal degrees, 13% minority, 47% women. **Part-time faculty:** 1,378 total; 66% have terminal degrees, 16% minority, 41% women. **Class size:** 66% < 20, 33% 20-39, 1% 40-49.

**Freshman class profile.** 2,889 applied, 2,889 admitted, 901 enrolled.

Out-of-state:              44%        International:              3%

**Basis for selection.** Open admission.

**2007-2008 Annual costs.** Tuition/fees: $5,670; $11,334 out-of-state. Books/supplies: $1,362. Personal expenses: $4,090.

**2006-2007 Financial aid. Need-based:** 131 full-time freshmen applied for aid; 125 were judged to have need; 76 of these received aid. Average need met was 15%. Average scholarship/grant was $2,475; average loan $2,562. 29% of total undergraduate aid awarded as scholarships/grants, 71% as loans/jobs. **Non-need-based:** Awarded to 344 full-time undergraduates, including 8 freshmen. Scholarships awarded for academics, leadership.

**Application procedures. Admission:** No deadline. $50 fee. Application may be submitted online. Admission notification on a rolling basis. **Financial aid:** Priority date 6/1; no closing date. FAFSA, institutional form required. Applicants notified on a rolling basis starting 5/1; must reply within 2 week(s) of notification.

**Academics.** Degree programs offered primarily for adults attending part-time. No traditional freshman class. **Special study options:** Accelerated study, cooperative education, cross-registration, distance learning, double major, dual enrollment of high school students, external degree, teacher certification program, weekend college. **Credit/placement by examination:** AP, CLEP, IB, institutional tests. 30 credit hours maximum toward associate degree, 60 toward bachelor's. **Support services:** Tutoring, writing center.

**Majors. Area/ethnic studies:** Asian. **Business:** Accounting, business admin, human resources, marketing. **Communications:** General. **Computer sciences:** General, computer science, information systems. **Conservation:** General. **English:** English lit. **History:** General. **Liberal arts:** Arts/sciences. **Psychology:** General. **Social sciences:** General, criminology.

**Most popular majors.** Business/marketing 36%, computer/information sciences 23%, interdisciplinary studies 12%, psychology 7%.

**Computing on campus.** Commuter students can connect to campus network. Online course registration, online library, helpline, student web hosting, wireless network available.

**Student life. Freshman orientation:** Available.

**Student services.** Adult student services, career counseling, veterans' counselor. **Physically disabled:** Services for visually, hearing impaired.

**Contact.** E-mail: admissions@umuc.edu
Phone: (301) 985-7000 Toll-free number: (800) 888-8682
Fax: (301) 985-7364
Jessica Sadaka, Director of Admissions, University of Maryland: University College, 3501 University Boulevard East, Adelphi, MD 20783-8010

## Villa Julie College
**Stevenson, Maryland**                          **CB member**
www.vjc.edu                                      **CB code: 5856**

◆  Private 4-year liberal arts college
◆  Residential campus in very large city
◆  3,047 degree-seeking undergraduates: 16% part-time, 71% women, 15% African American, 3% Asian American, 1% Hispanic American, 1% international
◆  228 degree-seeking graduate students
◆  82% of applicants admitted
◆  SAT or ACT (ACT writing optional), application essay required
◆  61% graduate within 6 years

**General.** Founded in 1947. Regionally accredited. **Degrees:** 553 bachelor's, 3 associate awarded; master's offered. **ROTC:** Army. **Location:** 8 miles from Baltimore. **Calendar:** Semester, limited summer session. **Full-time faculty:** 112 total; 69% have terminal degrees, 11% minority, 57% women. **Part-time faculty:** 274 total; 33% have terminal degrees, 9% minority, 53% women. **Class size:** 67% < 20, 33% 20-39, less than 1% 40-49.

**Freshman class profile.** 2,461 applied, 2,028 admitted, 605 enrolled.

| Mid 50% test scores | | | |
|---|---|---|---|
| SAT critical reading: | 450-550 | GPA 2.0-2.99: | 24% |
| SAT math: | 430-550 | Rank in top quarter: | 45% |
| SAT writing: | 450-550 | Rank in top tenth: | 20% |
| ACT composite: | 18-23 | Return as sophomores: | 83% |
| GPA 3.50 or higher: | 42% | Out-of-state: | 9% |
| GPA 3.0-3.49: | 34% | Live on campus: | 68% |

**Basis for selection.** High school record and test scores most important. Optional interview, recommendations, essay, extracurricular activities also important. Admissions after March 1st priority deadline on space available basis. Interviews are recommended but not required.

**High school preparation.** 17 units required. Required and recommended units include English 4, mathematics 3, social studies 2, history 1, science 3 (laboratory 2), foreign language 2 and academic electives 4.

**2008-2009 Annual costs.** Tuition/fees: $19,200. Room/board: $9,506. Books/supplies: $1,500. Personal expenses: $2,070.

**2007-2008 Financial aid. Need-based:** 523 full-time freshmen applied for aid; 414 were judged to have need; 413 of these received aid. Average need met was 75%. Average scholarship/grant was $12,227; average loan $2,513. 73% of total undergraduate aid awarded as scholarships/grants, 27% as loans/jobs. **Non-need-based:** Awarded to 861 full-time undergraduates, including 265 freshmen. Scholarships awarded for academics, art, leadership, music/drama, ROTC. **Additional information:** Cooperative Education Program allows students to work in their field of study with area corporations.

**Application procedures. Admission:** Priority date 3/1; no deadline. $25 fee, may be waived for applicants with need. Application may be submitted online. Admission notification on a rolling basis beginning on or about 12/1. Must reply by May 1 or within 2 week(s) if notified thereafter. **Financial aid:** Priority date 2/15; no closing date. FAFSA required. Applicants notified on a rolling basis starting 3/15; must reply by 5/1 or within 2 week(s) of notification.

**Academics.** Advanced technology programs, forensic science program and forensic studies programs offered. Cooperative education program available to third- and fourth-year students. Career Architecture, a program for personal and professional development, is integrated into all programs. **Special study options:** Accelerated study, combined bachelor's/graduate degree, cooperative education, cross-registration, distance learning, double major, dual enrollment of high school students, honors, independent study, internships, liberal arts/career combination, student-designed major, study abroad, teacher certification program, Washington semester, weekend college. **Credit/placement by examination:** AP, CLEP, IB, SAT, ACT, institutional tests. 15 credit hours maximum toward associate degree, 30 toward bachelor's. **Support services:** Learning center, pre-admission summer program, reduced course load, remedial instruction, study skills assistance, tutoring, writing center.

**Majors. Biology:** General. **Business:** Accounting, business admin, communications, management information systems. **Communications technology:** General. **Computer sciences:** General, information systems. **Education:** Early childhood, elementary, kindergarten/preschool. **English:** English lit. **Family/consumer sciences:** Family/community services. **Health:** Clinical lab science, nursing (RN). **History:** Public archives. **Interdisciplinary:** Biological/physical sciences. **Legal studies:** Paralegal, prelaw. **Liberal arts:** Arts/sciences. **Math:** Applied. **Physical sciences:** Chemistry. **Psychology:** General. **Science technology:** Biological. **Visual/performing arts:** General, design.

**Most popular majors.** Business/marketing 22%, computer/information sciences 6%, education 9%, health sciences 22%, interdisciplinary studies 7%, legal studies 7%, visual/performing arts 11%.

**Computing on campus.** 550 workstations in library, computer center, student center. Dormitories wired for high-speed internet access and linked to campus network. Commuter students can connect to campus network. Online course registration, online library, helpline, repair service, wireless network available.

**Student life. Freshman orientation:** Mandatory. Preregistration for classes offered. Full-day program, conducted by major, normally held during third week of June. Freshmen also attend second orientation in August, prior to start of fall semester. **Housing:** Apartments, substance-free housing available. $200 fully refundable deposit, deadline 3/12. Suite style housing (2 bedrooms, share bath) accommodations made for students with disabilities. **Activities:** Bands, choral groups, dance, drama, international student organizations, literary magazine, music ensembles, student government, student newspaper, symphony orchestra, Black Student Union, Service Corps, Campus Crusade for Christ, Extreme Acts, Reformed University Fellowship, Angus Dei.

**Athletics.** NCAA. **Intercollegiate:** Baseball M, basketball, cheerleading, cross-country, field hockey W, golf, lacrosse, soccer, softball W, tennis, track and field, volleyball. **Intramural:** Badminton, basketball, fencing, football (tackle) M, sailing, skiing, soccer, table tennis, tennis, track and field, volleyball. **Team name:** Mustangs.

**Student services.** Adult student services, alcohol/substance abuse counseling, career counseling, student employment services, financial aid counseling, health services, personal counseling, placement for graduates, veterans' counselor.

**Contact.** E-mail: admissions@mail.vjc.edu
Phone: (410) 486-7001 Toll-free number: (877) 468-6852
Fax: (443) 352-4440
Mark Hergan, Vice President for Enrollment Management, Villa Julie College, 1525 Greenspring Valley Road, Stevenson, MD 21153-0641

## Washington Bible College
**Lanham, Maryland**
www.bible.edu                                      CB code: 5884

▶ Private 4-year Bible and seminary college affiliated with nondenominational tradition
▶ Commuter campus in large town
▶ 242 degree-seeking undergraduates
▶ SAT or ACT (ACT writing optional), application essay required

**General.** Founded in 1938. Regionally accredited; also accredited by ABHE. Main Campus in Lanham, MD. Branch sites in Baltimore, MD and in Springfield, VA. **Degrees:** 42 bachelor's, 7 associate awarded; master's offered. **Location:** 10 miles from Washington, DC. **Calendar:** Semester, limited summer session. **Full-time faculty:** 9 total. **Part-time faculty:** 16 total.

**Freshman class profile.** 29 enrolled.

| Mid 50% test scores | | Out-of-state: | 31% |
|---|---|---|---|
| SAT critical reading: | 420-580 | Live on campus: | 68% |
| SAT math: | 410-550 | | |

**Basis for selection.** Student's spiritual qualifications most important, followed by academic achievement, test scores, essay, recommendations. 2 references required. Interview recommended. Audition required of music majors.

**High school preparation.** 15 units recommended. Recommended units include English 4, mathematics 2, social studies 2, science 2 and academic electives 5. Typing recommended.

**2007-2008 Annual costs.** Tuition/fees: $11,810. Room/board: $6,450. Books/supplies: $500. Personal expenses: $1,300.

**Financial aid. Non-need-based:** Scholarships awarded for academics, leadership, music/drama, state residency.

**Application procedures. Admission:** Closing date 8/1 (receipt date). $35 fee, may be waived for applicants with need. Application may be submitted online. Admission notification on a rolling basis. Campus visit suggested. Deadline for housing deposit 30 days after acceptance. **Financial aid:** Closing date 3/1. FAFSA, institutional form required. Applicants notified on a rolling basis starting 7/1; must reply within 2 week(s) of notification.

**Academics.** All students major in Bible; other areas may be studied for concentrations. **Special study options:** Double major, ESL, independent study, internships, study abroad, teacher certification program. **Credit/placement by examination:** AP, CLEP, SAT, ACT, institutional tests. 15 credit hours maximum toward bachelor's degree. **Support services:** Reduced course load, tutoring, writing center.

**Majors. Education:** General, early childhood, elementary, multi-level teacher, music, physical, school counseling. **Family/consumer sciences:** Work/family studies. **Psychology:** Counseling. **Theology:** Bible, missionary, pastoral counseling, preministerial, religious ed, sacred music, theology, youth ministry. **Visual/performing arts:** Music performance, piano/organ; voice/opera.

**Computing on campus.** 10 workstations in library, student center. Dormitories wired for high-speed internet access and linked to campus network. Commuter students can connect to campus network. Online library, helpline, wireless network available.

**Student life. Freshman orientation:** Mandatory. 2-day spring and summer programs. **Policies:** Religious observance required. **Housing:** Guaranteed on-campus for freshmen. Single-sex dorms, apartments, substance-free housing available. $100 nonrefundable deposit, deadline 6/1. **Activities:** Choral groups, drama, music ensembles, student government, student newspaper, Student Missions Fellowship, Fellowship of Christian Athletes.

**Athletics.** NCCAA. **Intercollegiate:** Basketball, soccer M, volleyball W. **Intramural:** Basketball M, cheerleading M, football (tackle) M, racquetball, soccer M, table tennis, volleyball, weight lifting. **Team name:** Cougars.

**Student services.** Career counseling, student employment services, financial aid counseling, health services, personal counseling, placement for graduates, veterans' counselor.

**Contact.** E-mail: admissions@bible.edu
Phone: (301) 552-1400 ext. 1212 Toll-free
number: (877) 793-7227 ext. 1212 Fax: (301) 552-2775
Gerard Davis, Director of College Admissions, Washington Bible College, 6511 Princess Garden Parkway, Lanham, MD 20706-3599

## Washington College
**Chestertown, Maryland**                          CB member
www.washcoll.edu                                   CB code: 5888

▶ Private 4-year liberal arts college
▶ Residential campus in small town
▶ 1,162 degree-seeking undergraduates: 1% part-time, 60% women
▶ 47 degree-seeking graduate students
▶ 64% of applicants admitted
▶ SAT or ACT (ACT writing optional), application essay required

**General.** Founded in 1782. Regionally accredited. **Degrees:** 339 bachelor's awarded; master's offered. **Location:** 70 miles from Baltimore, 75 miles from Washington, DC. **Calendar:** Semester, limited summer session. **Full-time faculty:** 95 total; 50% have terminal degrees, 13% minority, 41% women. **Part-time faculty:** 56 total; 48% have terminal degrees, 9% minority, 45% women. **Class size:** 69% < 20, 29% 20-39, 1% 40-49, less than 1% 50-99. **Special facilities:** Center for the study of the American experience, center for the environment and society.

**Freshman class profile.** 2,167 applied, 1,377 admitted, 324 enrolled.

| Mid 50% test scores | | GPA 2.0-2.99: | 20% |
|---|---|---|---|
| SAT critical reading: | 510-620 | Rank in top quarter: | 61% |
| SAT math: | 510-610 | Rank in top tenth: | 29% |
| ACT composite: | 20-25 | Out-of-state: | 49% |
| GPA 3.50 or higher: | 48% | Live on campus: | 100% |
| GPA 3.0-3.49: | 32% | | |

**Basis for selection.** High school program and grades, class rank, test scores, recommendations important, extracurricular activities considered. Interview recommended.

**High school preparation.** 16 units required; 20 recommended. Required and recommended units include English 4, mathematics 3-4, social studies 2-4, science 3-4 (laboratory 2-3) and foreign language 2-4.

**2007-2008 Annual costs.** Tuition/fees: $32,160. Room/board: $6,790.

**2006-2007 Financial aid. Need-based:** 77% of total undergraduate aid awarded as scholarships/grants, 23% as loans/jobs. **Non-need-based:** Scholarships awarded for academics.

**Application procedures. Admission:** Priority date 2/15; deadline 3/1 (postmark date). $45 fee, may be waived for applicants with need. Application may be submitted online. Admission notification on a rolling basis beginning on or about 1/15. Must reply by May 1 or within 2 week(s) if notified thereafter. Applicants applying after February 15 and no later than May 30 may be wait-listed. **Financial aid:** Priority date 2/15; no closing date. FAFSA, institutional form required. Applicants notified on a rolling basis starting 3/15; must reply by 5/1.

**Academics. Special study options:** Combined bachelor's/graduate degree, double major, exchange student, independent study, internships, liberal arts/career combination, student-designed major, study abroad, teacher certification program, Washington semester. **Credit/placement by examination:** AP, CLEP, IB, institutional tests. **Support services:** Learning center, reduced course load, study skills assistance, tutoring, writing center.

**Majors. Area/ethnic studies:** American. **Biology:** General. **Business:** General. **Computer sciences:** Computer science. **Conservation:** Environmental studies. **Education:** General. **English:** English lit. **Foreign languages:** French, German, Spanish. **History:** General. **Interdisciplinary:** Math/computer science, neuroscience. **Liberal arts:** Arts/sciences, humanities. **Philosophy/religion:** Philosophy. **Physical sciences:** Chemistry, physics. **Psychology:** General. **Social sciences:** Anthropology, economics, international relations, political science, sociology. **Visual/performing arts:** Art, dramatic.

**Most popular majors.** Biology 8%, business/marketing 18%, English 10%, history 6%, psychology 11%, public administration/social services 6%, social sciences 6%, visual/performing arts 10%.

**Computing on campus.** 200 workstations in dormitories, library, computer center, student center. Dormitories wired for high-speed internet access and linked to campus network. Commuter students can connect to campus network. Online course registration, online library, helpline, repair service, student web hosting, wireless network available.

**Student life. Freshman orientation:** Mandatory. Preregistration for classes offered. **Housing:** Guaranteed on-campus for freshmen. Coed dorms, single-sex dorms, special housing for disabled, fraternity/sorority housing available. $200 nonrefundable deposit, deadline 6/1. Creative arts dorm, special interest housing for writers, language majors, international studies majors, science/math majors, community service and leadership available. **Activities:** Concert band, choral groups, dance, drama, literary magazine, music ensembles, student government, student newspaper, College Republicans, Christian Fellowship, Amnesty International, International Relations Club, Hillel, Black Student Alliance, Cleopatra's Daughters, College Democrats, Best Buddies, EROS, Newman Club, Canterbury Club.

**Athletics.** NCAA. **Intercollegiate:** Baseball M, basketball, field hockey W, lacrosse, rowing (crew), sailing, soccer, softball W, swimming, tennis, volleyball W. **Intramural:** Basketball, fencing, golf M, ice hockey M, racquetball, rugby, sailing, soccer, softball, squash, tennis, volleyball. **Team name:** Shoremen/Shorewomen.

**Student services.** Adult student services, alcohol/substance abuse counseling, career counseling, student employment services, financial aid counseling, health services, minority student services, personal counseling, placement for graduates, veterans' counselor. **Physically disabled:** Services for hearing impaired.

**Contact.** E-mail: adm.off@washcoll.edu
Phone: (410) 778-7700 Toll-free number: (800) 442-1782
Fax: (410) 778-7287
Kevin Coveney, Vice President for Admissions, Washington College, 300 Washington Avenue, Chestertown, MD 21620-1197

## Yeshiva College of the Nations Capital
### Silver Spring, Maryland

- Private 4-year rabbinical college for men affiliated with Jewish faith
- Residential campus in small city
- 57 degree-seeking undergraduates

**General.** Accredited by AARTS. **Degrees:** 7 bachelor's awarded. **Calendar:** Continuous. **Full-time faculty:** 6 total.

**2007-2008 Annual costs.** Tuition/fees: $9,000. Room/board: $7,000.

**Academics. Credit/placement by examination:** CLEP.

**Majors. Philosophy/religion:** Judaic. **Theology:** Talmudic.

**Contact.** Phone: (301) 593-2534
David Hyatt, Academic Dean, Yeshiva College of the Nations Capital, 1216 Arcola Avenue, Silver Spring, MD 20902

# Massachusetts

## American International College
### Springfield, Massachusetts
www.aic.edu

CB member
CB code: 3002

- Private 4-year liberal arts college
- Residential campus in small city
- 1,510 degree-seeking undergraduates: 8% part-time, 61% women, 27% African American, 3% Asian American, 9% Hispanic American, 1% Native American, 3% international
- 992 degree-seeking graduate students
- 80% of applicants admitted
- SAT or ACT (ACT writing recommended) required
- 47% graduate within 6 years; 59% enter graduate study

**General.** Founded in 1885. Regionally accredited. **Degrees:** 295 bachelor's, 5 associate awarded; master's, doctoral offered. **ROTC:** Army, Air Force. **Location:** 90 miles from Boston, 27 miles from Hartford, Connecticut. **Calendar:** Semester, extensive summer session. **Full-time faculty:** 80 total; 68% have terminal degrees, 8% minority, 58% women. **Part-time faculty:** 165 total; 33% have terminal degrees, 9% minority, 48% women. **Class size:** 42% < 20, 51% 20-39, 4% 40-49, 3% 50-99, less than 1% >100. **Special facilities:** Cultural arts center, performing arts center, anatomical laboratory.

**Freshman class profile.** 1,588 applied, 1,270 admitted, 370 enrolled.

| Mid 50% test scores | | Rank in top quarter: | 25% |
|---|---|---|---|
| SAT critical reading: | 410-560 | Rank in top tenth: | 15% |
| SAT math: | 420-570 | End year in good standing: | 87% |
| ACT composite: | 17-23 | Return as sophomores: | 64% |
| GPA 3.50 or higher: | 10% | Out-of-state: | 44% |
| GPA 3.0-3.49: | 56% | Live on campus: | 64% |
| GPA 2.0-2.99: | 31% | International: | 3% |

**Basis for selection.** Must have satisfied school's graduation requirements except for one course in English and one course in Social Studies. Must have unqualified approval of school counselor or principal and must possess strong academic skills and maturity necessary for success in college. Essay or personal statement recommended. **Homeschooled:** Statement describing homeschool structure and mission, transcript of courses and grades, interview, letter of recommendation (nonparent) required. **Learning Disabled:** Wechsler Adult Intelligence Scale, interview, diagnostic documentation recommended.

**High school preparation.** 16 units required. Required and recommended units include English 4, mathematics 2-3, social studies 1, history 2, science 2 (laboratory 1), foreign language 1-2 and academic electives 4.

**2007-2008 Annual costs.** Tuition/fees: $22,500. Room/board: $9,742. Books/supplies: $1,000. Personal expenses: $1,200.

**2007-2008 Financial aid. Need-based:** Average need met was 75%. Average scholarship/grant was $16,347; average loan $3,426. 61% of total undergraduate aid awarded as scholarships/grants, 39% as loans/jobs. **Non-need-based:** Scholarships awarded for academics, alumni affiliation, athletics, leadership, state residency.

**Application procedures. Admission:** Priority date 7/1; no deadline. $25 fee, may be waived for applicants with need. Application may be submitted online. Admission notification on a rolling basis beginning on or about 12/15. Must reply by May 1 or within 2 week(s) if notified thereafter. **Financial aid:** Priority date 5/1; no closing date. FAFSA required. Applicants notified on a rolling basis starting 3/15; must reply by 5/1 or within 2 week(s) of notification.

**Academics. Special study options:** Accelerated study, combined bachelor's/graduate degree, cross-registration, distance learning, double major, dual enrollment of high school students, ESL, honors, independent study, internships, liberal arts/career combination, study abroad, teacher certification program, Washington semester, weekend college. **Credit/placement by examination:** AP, CLEP, IB, institutional tests. 30 credit hours maximum toward bachelor's degree. **Support services:** Learning center, reduced course load, remedial instruction, study skills assistance, tutoring, writing center.

**Majors. Area/ethnic studies:** American. **Biology:** General, biochemistry. **Business:** General, accounting, business admin, finance, international, management science, managerial economics, marketing. **Communications:** Advertising, broadcast journalism, journalism, media studies, public relations, radio/tv. **Computer sciences:** Computer science, information systems. **Education:** Early childhood, elementary, middle, secondary, special. **English:** English lit. **Health:** Nursing (RN), predental, premedicine, preveterinary. **History:** General. **Interdisciplinary:** Accounting/computer science, biological/physical sciences, math/computer science. **Legal studies:** Prelaw. **Liberal arts:** Arts/sciences. **Math:** General. **Parks/recreation:** General, sports admin. **Physical sciences:** Chemistry. **Protective services:** Criminal justice, law enforcement admin, police science. **Psychology:** General. **Public administration:** General. **Social sciences:** Criminology, economics, international relations, political science, sociology.

**Most popular majors.** Business/marketing 21%, health sciences 22%, interdisciplinary studies 8%, liberal arts 7%, psychology 9%, security/protective services 10%.

**Computing on campus.** 100 workstations in dormitories, library, computer center, student center. Dormitories wired for high-speed internet access and linked to campus network. Commuter students can connect to campus network. Online library, helpline, wireless network available.

**Student life. Freshman orientation:** Available. Preregistration for classes offered. Three-day program in early September prior to start of Fall term. **Housing:** Guaranteed on-campus for all undergraduates. Coed dorms, single-sex dorms, apartments, substance-free housing available. $100 fully refundable deposit, deadline 7/1. **Activities:** Pep band, choral groups, dance, drama, international student organizations, literary magazine, musical theater, radio station, student government, student newspaper, Model Congress, student government, minority student organization, Partners, Best Buddies.

**Athletics.** NCAA. **Intercollegiate:** Baseball M, basketball, cheerleading, cross-country, field hockey W, football (tackle) M, golf M; ice hockey M, lacrosse, soccer, softball W, tennis, track and field, volleyball W, wrestling M. **Intramural:** Basketball, football (non-tackle) M, skiing, soccer, softball, swimming, volleyball. **Team name:** Yellow Jackets.

**Student services.** Adult student services, alcohol/substance abuse counseling, campus ministries, career counseling, services for economically disadvantaged, student employment services, financial aid counseling, health services, minority student services, personal counseling, placement for graduates, veterans' counselor, women's services. **Physically disabled:** Services for visually impaired. **Learning disabled:** Comprehensive services available.

**Contact.** E-mail: inquiry@aic.edu
Phone: (413) 205-3201 Toll-free number: (800) 242-3142
Fax: (413) 205-3051
Peter Miller, Vice President for Admission Services, American International College, 1000 State Street, Springfield, MA 01109

## Amherst College
### Amherst, Massachusetts
www.amherst.edu

CB member
CB code: 3003

- Private 4-year liberal arts college
- Residential campus in large town
- 1,683 degree-seeking undergraduates: 10% African American, 12% Asian American, 9% Hispanic American, 7% international
- 18% of applicants admitted
- SAT and SAT Subject Tests or ACT (ACT writing recommended), application essay required
- 96% graduate within 6 years

**General.** Founded in 1821. Regionally accredited. **Degrees:** 409 bachelor's awarded. **ROTC:** Air Force. **Location:** 90 miles from Boston, 150 miles from New York City. **Calendar:** Semester. **Full-time faculty:** 195 total; 93% have terminal degrees, 19% minority, 38% women. **Part-time faculty:** 17 total; 59% have terminal degrees, 18% minority, 41% women. **Class size:** 75% < 20, 19% 20-39, 3% 40-49, 3% 50-99, less than 1% >100. **Special facilities:** Recital hall, observatory, planetarium, center for Russian culture, Dickinson homestead, natural history museum, fine arts museum, center for community engagement.

**Freshman class profile.** 6,680 applied, 1,175 admitted, 474 enrolled.

| Mid 50% test scores | | | |
|---|---|---|---|
| SAT critical reading: | 670-770 | **Rank in top tenth:** | 85% |
| SAT math: | 660-760 | **Return as sophomores:** | 96% |
| SAT writing: | 670-760 | **Out-of-state:** | 90% |
| ACT composite: | 29-34 | **Live on campus:** | 100% |
| **Rank in top quarter:** | 95% | **International:** | 8% |

**Basis for selection.** Grades, test scores, essays, recommendations, independent work, quality of individual's secondary school program, achievements outside of classroom most important.

**High school preparation.** Recommended units include English 4, mathematics 4, social studies 2, history 2, science 3 (laboratory 1) and foreign language 4.

**2007-2008 Annual costs.** Tuition/fees: $36,232. Health Insurance (waivable): $950. Room/board: $9,420. Books/supplies: $1,000. Personal expenses: $1,700.

**2007-2008 Financial aid.** All financial aid based on need. 300 full-time freshmen applied for aid; 241 were judged to have need; 241 of these received aid. Average need met was 100%. Average scholarship/grant was $34,777; average loan $2,756. 92% of total undergraduate aid awarded as scholarships/grants, 8% as loans/jobs.

**Application procedures. Admission:** Closing date 1/1 (postmark date). $55 fee, may be waived for applicants with need. Application may be submitted online. Admission notification 4/1. Must reply by 5/1. **Financial aid:** Priority date 2/15; no closing date. FAFSA, CSS PROFILE required. Applicants notified by 4/1; must reply by 5/1.

**Academics.** First-year students must choose 1 seminar from range of 20 special topics, often interdisciplinary. No core curriculum, no distribution requirements. Students select major at end of sophomore year. **Special study options:** Cross-registration, double major, exchange student, honors, independent study, internships, student-designed major, study abroad, teacher certification program. Member of 5-college consortium. **Credit/placement by examination:** AP, CLEP, IB, institutional tests. **Support services:** Study skills assistance, tutoring, writing center.

**Majors. Area/ethnic studies:** African, African-American, American, Asian, Central/Eastern European, European, Western European, women's. **Biology:** General. **Computer sciences:** Computer science. **English:** English lit. **Foreign languages:** Ancient Greek, classics, French, German, Latin, Russian, Spanish. **History:** General. **Interdisciplinary:** Math/computer science, neuroscience. **Legal studies:** General. **Math:** General. **Philosophy/religion:** Philosophy, religion. **Physical sciences:** Astronomy, chemistry, geology, physics. **Psychology:** General. **Social sciences:** Anthropology, economics, political science, sociology. **Visual/performing arts:** Dance, dramatic, studio arts.

**Most popular majors.** Area/ethnic studies 8%, English 9%, foreign language 13%, psychology 10%, social sciences 22%, visual/performing arts 9%.

**Computing on campus.** 230 workstations in library, computer center, student center. Dormitories wired for high-speed internet access and linked to campus network. Commuter students can connect to campus network. Helpline, repair service, wireless network available.

**Student life. Freshman orientation:** Mandatory. Eight-day orientation with events planned by student groups and cultural organizations. **Housing:** Guaranteed on-campus for all undergraduates. Coed dorms, cooperative housing, substance-free housing available. Language and other theme houses available including French/Spanish, Russian/German, Latino, African American, health and wellness house, and arts house. Men's and women's floors available to all students. **Activities:** Jazz band, choral groups, dance, drama, film society, international student organizations, literary magazine, music ensembles, Model UN, musical theater, opera, radio station, student government, student newspaper, symphony orchestra, Hillel, Boltwood House (service), Christian association, Newman Club, Black Student Union, Association of Asian Students, Cambodian family tutoring, LaCausa, Amherst Christian Fellowship, Korean American students association.

**Athletics.** NCAA. **Intercollegiate:** Baseball M, basketball, cross-country, diving, field hockey W, football (tackle) M, golf, ice hockey, lacrosse, soccer, softball W, squash, swimming, tennis, track and field, volleyball W. **Intramural:** Badminton, basketball, football (non-tackle), golf, ice hockey, soccer, softball, squash, table tennis, tennis, volleyball. **Team name:** Lord Jeffs.

**Student services.** Alcohol/substance abuse counseling, campus ministries, career counseling, services for economically disadvantaged, student employment services, financial aid counseling, health services, minority student services, personal counseling, placement for graduates, women's services. **Physically disabled:** Services for visually, speech, hearing impaired.

**Contact.** E-mail: admission@amherst.edu
Phone: (413) 542-2328 Fax: (413) 542-2040
Katie Fretwell, Director of Admission, Amherst College, PO Box 5000, Amherst, MA 01002-5000

---

## Anna Maria College
**Paxton, Massachusetts** — CB member
www.annamaria.edu — CB code: 3005

- Private 4-year liberal arts college affiliated with Roman Catholic Church
- Residential campus in small town
- 882 degree-seeking undergraduates: 20% part-time, 56% women, 5% African American, 1% Asian American, 4% Hispanic American
- 329 degree-seeking graduate students
- 89% of applicants admitted
- SAT or ACT (ACT writing optional) required
- 55% graduate within 6 years

**General.** Founded in 1946. Regionally accredited. **Degrees:** 157 bachelor's awarded; master's offered. **ROTC:** Air Force. **Location:** 8 miles from Worcester, 40 miles from Boston. **Calendar:** Semester, limited summer session. **Full-time faculty:** 45 total; 51% have terminal degrees, 2% minority, 69% women. **Part-time faculty:** 120 total; less than 1% minority, 36% women. **Class size:** 79% < 20, 21% 20-39. **Special facilities:** Arts building, nature trail.

**Freshman class profile.** 876 applied, 778 admitted, 264 enrolled.

| Mid 50% test scores | | | |
|---|---|---|---|
| SAT critical reading: | 380-480 | **GPA 2.0-2.99:** | 62% |
| SAT math: | 370-480 | **Rank in top quarter:** | 7% |
| ACT composite: | 16-19 | **Return as sophomores:** | 64% |
| **GPA 3.50 or higher:** | 4% | **Out-of-state:** | 14% |
| **GPA 3.0-3.49:** | 19% | **Live on campus:** | 70% |

**Basis for selection.** High school record most important, followed by test scores, recommendations, school and community activities, interview. Audition required of music majors; portfolio required of art majors, essays required of nursing and transfer students.

**High school preparation.** 19 units required. Required units include English 4, mathematics 3, social studies 2, history 2, science 3 (laboratory 1), foreign language 2 and academic electives 4.

**2007-2008 Annual costs.** Tuition/fees: $24,617. Annual tuition for music program: $25,504. Room/board: $8,915. Books/supplies: $800. Personal expenses: $1,700.

**2007-2008 Financial aid. Need-based:** 238 full-time freshmen applied for aid; 214 were judged to have need; 214 of these received aid. Average need met was 67%. Average scholarship/grant was $10,288; average loan $4,210. 60% of total undergraduate aid awarded as scholarships/grants, 40% as loans/jobs. **Non-need-based:** Awarded to 650 full-time undergraduates, including 243 freshmen. Scholarships awarded for academics, alumni affiliation, music/drama, religious affiliation, state residency.

**Application procedures. Admission:** Priority date 3/1; no deadline. $40 fee, may be waived for applicants with need. Application may be submitted online. Admission notification on a rolling basis beginning on or about 12/1. Must reply by May 1 or within 2 week(s) if notified thereafter. **Financial aid:** Priority date 3/1; no closing date. FAFSA required. Applicants notified on a rolling basis starting 4/1; must reply within 4 week(s) of notification.

**Academics. Special study options:** Accelerated study, combined bachelor's/graduate degree, cooperative education, cross-registration, double major, independent study, internships, liberal arts/career combination, student-designed major, study abroad, teacher certification program, Washington semester. Member of 13-college Worcester Consortium. **Credit/placement by examination:** AP, CLEP, institutional tests. 30 credit hours maximum toward bachelor's degree. **Support services:** Learning center, reduced course load, remedial instruction, study skills assistance, tutoring, writing center.

**Majors. Business:** Business admin, management information systems. **Computer sciences:** General. **Conservation:** Environmental science. **Education:** Art, English, history, kindergarten/preschool, music. **English:** English lit. **Foreign languages:** Spanish. **Health:** Art therapy, health services, music therapy, nursing (RN). **History:** General. **Legal studies:** Paralegal. **Liberal arts:** Arts/sciences. **Parks/recreation:** Sports admin. **Protective services:** Criminal justice, firefighting. **Psychology:** General. **Public**

**administration:** Policy analysis, social work. **Social sciences:** Political science, sociology. **Theology:** Theology. **Visual/performing arts:** Art, graphic design, music performance. **Other:** Media Communications, Social Sciences, Other.

**Most popular majors.** Business/marketing 7%, health sciences 15%, liberal arts 7%, psychology 8%, public administration/social services 14%, security/protective services 32%, visual/performing arts 7%.

**Computing on campus.** 91 workstations in dormitories, library, computer center, student center. Dormitories wired for high-speed internet access and linked to campus network. Online library, wireless network available.

**Student life. Freshman orientation:** Mandatory. Preregistration for classes offered. **Housing:** Guaranteed on-campus for freshmen. Coed dorms, special housing for disabled, substance-free housing available. $300 fully refundable deposit, deadline 5/1. **Activities:** Bands, campus ministries, choral groups, dance, drama, music ensembles, musical theater, student government, Society for Peace and Justice, social action club.

**Athletics.** NCAA. **Intercollegiate:** Baseball M, basketball, cross-country M, field hockey W, golf M, soccer, softball W, volleyball W. **Intramural:** Basketball M, football (non-tackle) M, volleyball. **Team name:** Amcats.

**Student services.** Alcohol/substance abuse counseling, campus ministries, career counseling, student employment services, financial aid counseling, health services, minority student services, personal counseling, placement for graduates. **Physically disabled:** Services for visually, speech, hearing impaired.

**Contact.** E-mail: admission@annamaria.edu
Phone: (508) 849-3360 Toll-free number: (800) 344-4586 ext. 360
Fax: (508) 849-3362
Tim Donahue, Director of Admission, Anna Maria College, 50 Sunset Lane, Box O, Paxton, MA 01612-1198

---

## Art Institute of Boston at Lesley University
**Boston, Massachusetts**
**www.aiboston.edu** **CB code: 3777**

- Private 4-year visual arts college
- Residential campus in very large city

**General.** Regionally accredited. **Location:** Downtown. **Calendar:** Semester.

**Annual costs/financial aid.** Tuition/fees (2007-2008): $23,925. Room/board: $11,100. Personal expenses: $1,975. Need-based financial aid available to full-time and part-time students.

**Contact.** Phone: (617) 585-6710
Director of Operations, 700 Beacon Street, Boston, MA 02215-2598

---

## Assumption College
**Worcester, Massachusetts** **CB member**
**www.assumption.edu** **CB code: 3009**

- Private 4-year liberal arts college affiliated with Roman Catholic Church
- Residential campus in small city
- 2,172 degree-seeking undergraduates: 59% women, 2% African American, 1% Asian American, 3% Hispanic American
- 391 degree-seeking graduate students
- 67% of applicants admitted
- SAT or ACT (ACT writing optional), application essay required
- 68% graduate within 6 years; 22% enter graduate study

**General.** Founded in 1904. Regionally accredited. Students may register for courses at 11 area colleges. Volunteer programs available: comprehensive 2-week programs in Mexico and Puerto Rico, 1-week spring break programs in various locations. **Degrees:** 453 bachelor's awarded; master's offered. **ROTC:** Army, Air Force. **Location:** 45 miles from Boston. **Calendar:** Semester, limited summer session. **Full-time faculty:** 151 total; 89% have terminal degrees, 4% minority, 41% women. **Part-time faculty:** 72 total; 61% have terminal degrees, 11% minority, 49% women. **Class size:** 47% < 20, 53% 20-39, less than 1% 40-49. **Special facilities:** French institute (academic research center for study of Francophone questions).

---

**Freshman class profile.** 3,899 applied, 2,625 admitted, 598 enrolled.

| Mid 50% test scores | | | |
|---|---|---|---|
| SAT critical reading: | 490-570 | Rank in top quarter: | 35% |
| SAT math: | 490-570 | Rank in top tenth: | 12% |
| ACT composite: | 20-24 | End year in good standing: | 83% |
| GPA 3.50 or higher: | 29% | Return as sophomores: | 83% |
| GPA 3.0-3.49: | 69% | Out-of-state: | 33% |
| GPA 2.0-2.99: | 2% | Live on campus: | 97% |

**Basis for selection.** School achievement most important, followed by class rank in top 40%, test scores, extracurricular activities, interview, recommendations. **Homeschooled:** Statement describing homeschool structure and mission, letter of recommendation (nonparent) required.

**High school preparation.** 18 units required. Required units include English 4, mathematics 3, history 2, science 2, foreign language 2 and academic electives 5.

**2007-2008 Annual costs.** Tuition/fees: $27,485. Room/board: $9,492. Books/supplies: $850. Personal expenses: $1,000.

**2007-2008 Financial aid. Need-based:** 509 full-time freshmen applied for aid; 443 were judged to have need; 443 of these received aid. Average need met was 74%. Average scholarship/grant was $14,322; average loan $3,957. 68% of total undergraduate aid awarded as scholarships/grants, 32% as loans/jobs. **Non-need-based:** Awarded to 627 full-time undergraduates, including 178 freshmen. Scholarships awarded for academics, athletics.

**Application procedures. Admission:** Closing date 2/15 (postmark date). $50 fee, may be waived for applicants with need. Application may be submitted online. Admission notification 5/1. Admission notification on a rolling basis. Must reply by May 1 or within 2 week(s) if notified thereafter. **Financial aid:** Closing date 2/1. FAFSA required. Applicants notified on a rolling basis starting 2/16; must reply by 5/1.

**Academics. Special study options:** Combined bachelor's/graduate degree, cross-registration, double major, honors, independent study, internships, semester at sea, student-designed major, study abroad, teacher certification program, Washington semester. Worcester Consortium gerontology studies program; 3-2 engineering program (BA/BS) with Worcester Polytechnic Institute. **Credit/placement by examination:** AP, CLEP, IB, SAT, institutional tests. **Support services:** Learning center, study skills assistance, tutoring, writing center.

**Majors. Area/ethnic studies:** Latin American. **Biology:** General. **Business:** Accounting, business admin, international, marketing. **Communications:** Organizational. **Computer sciences:** General. **Conservation:** Environmental science. **English:** English lit. **Foreign languages:** General, classics, French, Italian, Spanish. **History:** General. **Interdisciplinary:** Global studies. **Math:** General. **Philosophy/religion:** Philosophy. **Physical sciences:** Chemistry. **Psychology:** General. **Social sciences:** Economics, political science, sociology. **Theology:** Theology. **Visual/performing arts:** General. **Other:** Human Services and Rehabilitation Studies.

**Most popular majors.** Biology 10%, business/marketing 23%, communications/journalism 13%, English 8%, health sciences 9%, psychology 10%, social sciences 10%.

**Computing on campus.** 275 workstations in dormitories, library, computer center, student center. Dormitories wired for high-speed internet access and linked to campus network. Commuter students can connect to campus network. Online course registration, online library, helpline, repair service, student web hosting, wireless network available.

**Student life. Freshman orientation:** Mandatory, $265 fee. Preregistration for classes offered. Two-day program in June includes choosing rooms and testing. **Housing:** Guaranteed on-campus for all undergraduates. Coed dorms, single-sex dorms, special housing for disabled, substance-free housing available. Freshman dorms, substance-free dorms, living/learning center available. **Activities:** Bands, campus ministries, choral groups, drama, film society, literary magazine, musical theater, student government, student newspaper, TV station, ALANA Network, College Democrats, College Republicans, student volunteer organization, Students Advocating Change, student health network, service program.

**Athletics.** NCAA. **Intercollegiate:** Baseball M, basketball, cross-country, field hockey W, football (tackle) M, golf M, ice hockey M, lacrosse, rowing (crew) W, soccer, softball W, tennis, track and field, volleyball W. **Intramural:** Basketball, football (non-tackle) M, golf, ice hockey, racquetball, soccer, softball, volleyball. **Team name:** Greyhounds.

**Student services.** Alcohol/substance abuse counseling, campus ministries, career counseling, student employment services, financial aid counseling, health services, minority student services, personal counseling, placement for graduates. **Physically disabled:** Services for visually, speech, hearing impaired.

**Contact.** E-mail: admiss@assumption.edu
Phone: (508) 767-7285 Toll-free number: (888) 882-7786
Fax: (508) 799-4412
Evan Lipp, Vice President for Enrollment Management, Assumption
College, 500 Salisbury Street, Worcester, MA 01609-1296

## Atlantic Union College
**South Lancaster, Massachusetts**
www.auc.edu                                    CB code: 3010

- Private 4-year liberal arts college affiliated with Seventh-day Adventists
- Residential campus in small town
- 469 degree-seeking undergraduates: 13% part-time, 63% women, 47% African American, 3% Asian American, 17% Hispanic American
- 1 degree-seeking graduate students
- 43% of applicants admitted
- SAT or ACT with writing required

**General.** Founded in 1882. Regionally accredited. **Degrees:** 94 bachelor's, 37 associate awarded; master's offered. **Location:** 45 miles from Boston. **Calendar:** Semester, limited summer session. **Full-time faculty:** 35 total. **Part-time faculty:** 26 total. **Special facilities:** Music conservatory.

**Freshman class profile.** 456 applied, 198 admitted, 56 enrolled.

| Mid 50% test scores | | | |
|---|---|---|---|
| SAT math: | 350-450 | GPA 3.50 or higher: | 9% |
| ACT composite: | 16-21 | GPA 3.0-3.49: | 33% |
| | | GPA 2.0-2.99: | 58% |

**Basis for selection.** School achievement record, interview, recommendations, test scores important. Interview recommended for non-Seventh-day Adventists. Audition required of music majors. Portfolio recommended for art majors. **Homeschooled:** Transcript of courses and grades required. Transcript from accredited high school or GED test score required.

**High school preparation.** 14 units required. Required and recommended units include English 4, mathematics 3, social studies 2, science 2 (laboratory 1) and foreign language 2. One unit computer science also required.

**2008-2009 Annual costs.** Tuition/fees: $16,570. Additional fees for nursing program. Room/board: $5,000. Books/supplies: $1,000. Personal expenses: $2,300.

**2007-2008 Financial aid. Need-based:** Average need met was 41%. Average scholarship/grant was $4,226; average loan $3,846. 41% of total undergraduate aid awarded as scholarships/grants, 59% as loans/jobs. **Non-need-based:** Scholarships awarded for academics, alumni affiliation, leadership, music/drama, religious affiliation.

**Application procedures. Admission:** Closing date 8/1. $25 fee, may be waived for applicants with need. Application may be submitted online. Admission notification on a rolling basis. **Financial aid:** Priority date 4/1; no closing date. FAFSA required. Applicants notified on a rolling basis starting 3/1; must reply by 9/12 or within 2 week(s) of notification.

**Academics.** External degree program of directed independent study for those 25 and over. Master of education program available summer session only. **Special study options:** Accelerated study, cooperative education, cross-registration, distance learning, double major, dual enrollment of high school students, ESL, external degree, honors, independent study, internships, liberal arts/career combination, study abroad, teacher certification program. **Credit/placement by examination:** AP, CLEP, IB, institutional tests. 32 credit hours maximum toward bachelor's degree. **Support services:** Learning center, reduced course load, remedial instruction, tutoring, writing center.

**Majors. Biology:** General. **Business:** Accounting, business admin. **Computer sciences:** General, computer science. **Education:** Early childhood, elementary, secondary. **English:** English lit. **Foreign languages:** French, Spanish. **Health:** Nursing (RN). **History:** General. **Liberal arts:** Arts/sciences. **Math:** General. **Philosophy/religion:** Religion. **Psychology:** General. **Public administration:** Social work. **Theology:** Theology. **Visual/performing arts:** Interior design, music history, studio arts.

**Computing on campus.** 84 workstations in dormitories, library, computer center. Dormitories linked to campus network.

**Student life. Freshman orientation:** Mandatory, $150 fee. Preregistration for classes offered. Program held one week before official registration. **Policies:** Religious observance required. **Housing:** Single-sex dorms, apartments available. $350 deposit. **Activities:** Concert band, choral groups, drama,

music ensembles, student government, student newspaper, symphony orchestra, campus community outreach, Big Brother, Adopt-A-Grandparent.

**Athletics. Intramural:** Cross-country, golf, gymnastics, racquetball, sailing, skiing, skin diving, softball, swimming, tennis, track and field, volleyball.

**Student services.** Campus ministries, career counseling, student employment services, financial aid counseling, health services, personal counseling, placement for graduates.

**Contact.** E-mail: rosita.lashley@auc.edu
Phone: (978) 368-2235 Toll-free number: (800) 282-2030
Fax: (978) 368-2015
Rosita Lashley, Director of Admissions, Atlantic Union College, Main Street, South Lancaster, MA 01561

## Babson College
**Babson Park, Massachusetts**                 CB member
www.babson.edu                                 CB code: 3075

- Private 4-year business college
- Residential campus in large town
- 1,799 degree-seeking undergraduates: 41% women, 4% African American, 11% Asian American, 8% Hispanic American, 18% international
- 1,622 degree-seeking graduate students
- 38% of applicants admitted
- SAT or ACT with writing, application essay required
- 89% graduate within 6 years

**General.** Founded in 1919. Regionally accredited. **Degrees:** 423 bachelor's awarded; master's offered. **ROTC:** Army, Naval, Air Force. **Location:** 14 miles from Boston. **Calendar:** Semester, limited summer session. **Full-time faculty:** 150 total; 90% have terminal degrees, 14% minority, 33% women. **Part-time faculty:** 89 total; 40% have terminal degrees, 7% minority, 29% women. **Class size:** 19% < 20, 64% 20-39, 13% 40-49, 4% 50-99. **Special facilities:** Student-run businesses, entrepreneurship center, women's center.

**Freshman class profile.** 3,530 applied, 1,324 admitted, 453 enrolled.

| Mid 50% test scores | | | |
|---|---|---|---|
| SAT critical reading: | 560-640 | Out-of-state: | 58% |
| SAT math: | 590-680 | Live on campus: | 90% |
| SAT writing: | 570-650 | International: | 18% |
| ACT composite: | 25-29 | Fraternities: | 17% |
| Return as sophomores: | 93% | Sororities: | 16% |

**Basis for selection.** Academic performance and level of course work (college preparation, honors, Advanced Placement) most important, followed by academic motivation, including interest in learning and willingness to challenge oneself; test scores; writing ability; involvement in cocurricular activities and/or work experience; leadership, creativity, enthusiasm. SAT Subject Tests recommended. **Homeschooled:** Statement describing homeschool structure and mission, transcript of courses and grades, state high school equivalency certificate, letter of recommendation (nonparent) required. Provide information about completed courses, schooling, testing, and diploma requirements.

**High school preparation.** 20 units required. Required and recommended units include English 4, mathematics 4, social studies 2, history 2, science 4 (laboratory 3) and foreign language 4. Pre-calculus strongly recommended.

**2008-2009 Annual costs.** Tuition/fees: $36,096. Room/board: $12,020. Books/supplies: $1,000.

**2007-2008 Financial aid. Need-based:** 244 full-time freshmen applied for aid; 200 were judged to have need; 200 of these received aid. Average need met was 96%. Average scholarship/grant was $24,774; average loan $3,215. 84% of total undergraduate aid awarded as scholarships/grants, 16% as loans/jobs. **Non-need-based:** Awarded to 246 full-time undergraduates, including 57 freshmen. Scholarships awarded for academics, leadership.

**Application procedures. Admission:** Priority date 11/15; deadline 1/15 (postmark date). $65 fee, may be waived for applicants with need. Application may be submitted online. Admission notification 4/1. Must reply by 5/1. **Financial aid:** Closing date 2/15. FAFSA, CSS PROFILE required. Applicants notified by 4/1; must reply by 5/1.

**Academics. Special study options:** Accelerated study, combined bachelor's/graduate degree, cross-registration, exchange student, honors, independent study, internships, liberal arts/career combination, semester at sea, student-designed major, study abroad. **Credit/placement by examination:** AP, CLEP, IB, institutional tests. 64 credit hours maximum toward bachelor's degree. **Support services:** Reduced course load, study skills assistance, tutoring, writing center.

**Majors. Business:** General, accounting, accounting/business management, accounting/finance, auditing, business admin, communications, entrepreneurial studies, finance, international, international finance, international marketing, investments/securities, management information systems, management science, managerial economics, marketing, office management, operations, sales/distribution, small business admin, statistics. **Communications:** Advertising. **Computer sciences:** General, information systems. **Legal studies:** Prelaw.

**Computing on campus.** PC or laptop required. 290 workstations in dormitories, library, computer center, student center. Dormitories wired for high-speed internet access and linked to campus network. Commuter students can connect to campus network. Online course registration, online library, helpline, repair service, wireless network available.

**Student life. Freshman orientation:** Mandatory. Preregistration for classes offered. 3-day program preceding the start of classes. **Policies:** First-year students required to live on campus unless commuting from home (must live within 25-mile radius of campus). **Housing:** Guaranteed on-campus for all undergraduates. Coed dorms, single-sex dorms, special housing for disabled, fraternity/sorority housing, substance-free housing available. $500 partly refundable deposit, deadline 5/1. Cultural, nontraditional, suite style, single-sex floors, wings for women available. **Activities:** Jazz band, campus ministries, choral groups, dance, drama, film society, international student organizations, literary magazine, music ensembles, musical theater, radio station, student government, student newspaper, symphony orchestra, 60 student-run organizations.

**Athletics.** NCAA. **Intercollegiate:** Baseball M, basketball, cross-country, diving, field hockey W, golf M, ice hockey M, lacrosse, skiing, soccer, softball W, swimming, tennis, track and field, volleyball W. **Intramural:** Basketball, football (non-tackle), ice hockey, racquetball, soccer, softball, squash, tennis, volleyball, water polo. **Team name:** Beavers.

**Student services.** Alcohol/substance abuse counseling, campus ministries, career counseling, student employment services, financial aid counseling, health services, minority student services, personal counseling, placement for graduates. **Physically disabled:** Services for visually, speech, hearing impaired.

**Contact.** E-mail: ugradadmission@babson.edu
Phone: (781) 239-5522 Toll-free number: (800) 488-3696
Fax: (781) 239-4135
Grant Gosselin, Dean of Undergraduate Admission, Babson College, 231 Forest Street, Babson Park, MA 02457-0310

---

## Bard College at Simon's Rock
**Great Barrington, Massachusetts**
www.simons-rock.edu

CB member
CB code: 3795

- Private 4-year liberal arts college
- Residential campus in small town
- 408 degree-seeking undergraduates: 1% part-time, 58% women
- Application essay required
- 96% graduate within 6 years

**General.** Founded in 1964. Regionally accredited. Specifically intended to provide motivated students with the opportunity to begin college in a residential environment after completing the 10th or 11th grade. **Degrees:** 109 bachelor's, 36 associate awarded. **Location:** 22 miles from Pittsfield, 135 miles from Boston. **Calendar:** Semester. **Full-time faculty:** 43 total; 91% have terminal degrees, 14% minority, 35% women. **Part-time faculty:** 27 total; 59% have terminal degrees, 11% minority, 44% women. **Class size:** 98% < 20, 2% 20-39. **Special facilities:** Visual and performing arts center, environmental research center.

**Freshman class profile.**

| Mid 50% test scores | | | |
|---|---|---|---|
| SAT critical reading: | 560-690 | Rank in top quarter: | 82% |
| SAT math: | 530-680 | Rank in top tenth: | 60% |
| ACT composite: | 25-30 | End year in good standing: | 86% |
| GPA 3.50 or higher: | 55% | Return as sophomores: | 82% |
| GPA 3.0-3.49: | 18% | Out-of-state: | 79% |
| GPA 2.0-2.99: | 27% | Live on campus: | 81% |

**Basis for selection.** School achievement record, essays, recommendations (counselor and teacher), interview most important. Institutional testing

used for math and foreign language placement. SAT or ACT recommended. Standardized tests are optional for most students but will be considered if submitted. Students in home school or ungraded academic settings should submit test scores. Campus visit with interview recommended. **Homeschooled:** Statement describing homeschool structure and mission required.

**High school preparation.** 15 units recommended. Recommended units include English 2, mathematics 2, social studies 2, history 2, science 2 (laboratory 1), foreign language 2 and academic electives 2. Applicants who have completed 10th or 11th grade should have 2 or 3 years college-preparatory curriculum respectively.

**2007-2008 Annual costs.** Tuition/fees: $36,550. Annual health services fee of $580. Room/board: $9,730. Books/supplies: $1,000. Personal expenses: $225.

**Financial aid. Non-need-based:** Scholarships awarded for academics, alumni affiliation, leadership, state residency.

**Application procedures. Admission:** Priority date 4/15; deadline 5/31 (postmark date). $50 fee, may be waived for applicants with need. Application must be submitted on paper. Admission notification on a rolling basis beginning on or about 1/15. Must reply by May 1 or within 2 week(s) if notified thereafter. **Financial aid:** Priority date 4/15; no closing date. FAFSA, CSS PROFILE required. Applicants notified on a rolling basis starting 4/15; must reply within 2 week(s) of notification.

**Academics.** Upper-class students may take courses at Bard College. **Special study options:** Combined bachelor's/graduate degree, cooperative education, cross-registration, dual enrollment of high school students, exchange student, independent study, internships, student-designed major, study abroad. Globalization and International Affairs, undergraduate summer research fellows program with Rockefeller University, International Human Rights Exchange, 3/2 engineering program with Columbia University. **Credit/placement by examination:** AP, CLEP, institutional tests. 10 credit hours maximum toward associate degree, 10 toward bachelor's. Credit for Advanced Placement determined by individual divisions. **Support services:** Learning center, reduced course load, study skills assistance, tutoring, writing center.

**Majors. Area/ethnic studies:** African, African-American, Asian, Central/Eastern European, Chinese, East Asian, French, German, Spanish/Iberian, women's. **Biology:** General, ecology. **Communications technology:** Photo/film/video. **Computer sciences:** Computer science. **Conservation:** Environmental science, environmental studies. **Engineering:** General. **English:** British lit, creative writing, English lit. **Foreign languages:** General, Arabic, Chinese, comparative lit, French, German, Germanic, Latin, linguistics, Spanish. **History:** American. **Interdisciplinary:** Math/computer science. **Legal studies:** General. **Liberal arts:** Arts/sciences. **Math:** General, analysis. **Philosophy/religion:** Philosophy. **Physical sciences:** Chemistry, physics. **Psychology:** General. **Social sciences:** General, anthropology, political science, sociology. **Visual/performing arts:** General, acting, art history/conservation, ceramics, cinematography, dance, dramatic, drawing, music history, music performance, music theory/composition, painting, photography, play/screenwriting, printmaking, sculpture, studio arts, theater history.

**Most popular majors.** Area/ethnic studies 10%, biology 8%, English 8%, interdisciplinary studies 8%, legal studies 8%, visual/performing arts 27%.

**Computing on campus.** 50 workstations in dormitories, library, student center. Dormitories wired for high-speed internet access and linked to campus network. Commuter students can connect to campus network. Online library, helpline, repair service, student web hosting, wireless network available.

**Student life. Freshman orientation:** Mandatory, $500 fee. Preregistration for classes offered. One-week writing and thinking workshop prior to start of semester. **Policies:** No alcohol, illegal drugs or weapons allowed on campus. **Housing:** Guaranteed on-campus for freshmen. Coed dorms, single-sex dorms, special housing for disabled, apartments, substance-free housing available. **Activities:** Jazz band, choral groups, dance, drama, film society, literary magazine, music ensembles, radio station, student government, student newspaper, black student union, Latino student union, international students club, Amnesty International, Bible study group, Jew Crew, conservative club, Democrats, Pagan club.

**Athletics. Intercollegiate:** Basketball, cricket, cross-country, fencing, field hockey W, racquetball, soccer, softball, swimming. **Intramural:** Archery, basketball, cricket, cross-country, fencing, field hockey W, racquetball, skiing, soccer, softball, squash, swimming. **Team name:** Llamas.

**Student services.** Alcohol/substance abuse counseling, career counseling, student employment services, financial aid counseling, health services, minority student services, personal counseling, placement for graduates, women's services.

**Contact.** E-mail: admit@simons-rock.edu
Phone: (413) 528-7312 Toll-free number: (800) 235-7186
Fax: (413) 541-0081
Mary Davidson, Dean of Admission and Student Affairs, Bard College at Simon's Rock, 84 Alford Road, Great Barrington, MA 01230-1990

## Bay Path College
### Longmeadow, Massachusetts
**www.baypath.edu**   CB code: 3078

- Private 4-year business college for women
- Residential campus in large town
- 1,322 degree-seeking undergraduates: 22% part-time, 100% women, 11% African American, 1% Asian American, 11% Hispanic American, 1% international
- 266 degree-seeking graduate students
- 76% of applicants admitted
- SAT or ACT (ACT writing recommended) required
- 43% graduate within 6 years

**General.** Founded in 1897. Regionally accredited. Member of 8-college consortium. **Degrees:** 288 bachelor's, 68 associate awarded; master's offered. **ROTC:** Army, Air Force. **Location:** 5 miles from Springfield, 23 miles from Hartford, Connecticut. **Calendar:** Semester, limited summer session. **Full-time faculty:** 46 total; 56% have terminal degrees, 4% minority, 72% women. **Part-time faculty:** 106 total; 36% have terminal degrees, 5% minority, 62% women. **Class size:** 75% < 20, 24% 20-39, less than 1% 40-49. **Special facilities:** Academic development center, on-campus preschool, occupational therapy laboratory, business hall, career development center.

**Freshman class profile.** 644 applied, 492 admitted, 153 enrolled.

| Mid 50% test scores | | | |
|---|---|---|---|
| SAT critical reading: | 450-550 | Rank in top quarter: | 46% |
| SAT math: | 430-520 | Rank in top tenth: | 15% |
| SAT writing: | 450-550 | End year in good standing: | 62% |
| ACT composite: | 18-21 | Return as sophomores: | 62% |
| GPA 3.50 or higher: | 32% | Out-of-state: | 51% |
| GPA 3.0-3.49: | 41% | Live on campus: | 78% |
| GPA 2.0-2.99: | 27% | International: | 1% |

**Basis for selection.** Admission based on applicant's high school transcript and performance, class rank, grade point average, SAT or ACT and/or TOEFL scores, letters of recommendation, and essay. Interview and essay or personal statement is recommended. **Homeschooled:** Statement describing homeschool structure and mission, transcript of courses and grades, letter of recommendation (nonparent) required. Submit certificate from town or Board of Education for proof of completion of educational plan.

**High school preparation.** 15 units required; 17 recommended. Required and recommended units include English 4, mathematics 3-4, social studies 2, history 1-2, science 2-3 (laboratory 2) and foreign language 2.

**2008-2009 Annual costs.** Tuition/fees: $23,840. Room/board: $9,750. Books/supplies: $1,000. Personal expenses: $900.

**2007-2008 Financial aid. Need-based:** 185 full-time freshmen applied for aid; 172 were judged to have need; 170 of these received aid. Average need met was 77%. Average scholarship/grant was $11,301; average loan $4,655. 58% of total undergraduate aid awarded as scholarships/grants, 42% as loans/jobs. **Non-need-based:** Awarded to 188 full-time undergraduates, including 45 freshmen. Scholarships awarded for academics, state residency.

**Application procedures. Admission:** Priority date 3/1; no deadline. $25 fee, may be waived for applicants with need. Application may be submitted online. Admission notification on a rolling basis beginning on or about 9/15. Must reply by May 1 or within 2 week(s) if notified thereafter. **Financial aid:** Priority date 3/15; no closing date. FAFSA, institutional form required. Applicants notified on a rolling basis starting 3/1; must reply within 2 week(s) of notification.

**Academics. Special study options:** Accelerated study, combined bachelor's/graduate degree, cooperative education, cross-registration, distance learning, double major, exchange student, honors, independent study, internships, study abroad, teacher certification program, Washington semester, weekend college. **Credit/placement by examination:** AP, CLEP, IB, institutional tests. **Support services:** Learning center, study skills assistance, tutoring, writing center.

**Majors. Biology:** General, biotechnology. **Business:** General, business admin, marketing. **Communications:** Organizational. **Education:** Early childhood, elementary. **Legal studies:** General, prelaw. **Liberal arts:** Arts/sciences. **Protective services:** Criminal justice. **Psychology:** General, child, forensic.

**Most popular majors.** Business/marketing 35%, education 9%, liberal arts 19%, psychology 20%.

**Computing on campus.** 200 workstations in dormitories, library, computer center, student center. Dormitories wired for high-speed internet access and linked to campus network. Commuter students can connect to campus network. Online library, helpline, wireless network available.

**Student life. Freshman orientation:** Mandatory. Preregistration for classes offered. **Policies:** No smoking or alcohol in dormitories. **Housing:** Guaranteed on-campus for all undergraduates. $100 nonrefundable deposit, deadline 5/1. **Activities:** Choral groups, dance, drama, international student organizations, music ensembles, Model UN, musical theater, student government, Interfaith Council, Habitat for Humanity, women in technology, Women of Culture, Alliance, Phi Beta Lambda.

**Athletics.** NCAA. **Intercollegiate:** Basketball W, cross-country W, soccer W, softball W, tennis W, volleyball W. **Team name:** Wildcats.

**Student services.** Adult student services, career counseling, student employment services, financial aid counseling, health services, minority student services, personal counseling, placement for graduates, women's services.

**Contact.** E-mail: admiss@baypath.edu
Phone: (413) 565-1000 ext. 331 Toll-free number: (800) 782-7284 ext. 331
Fax: (413) 565-1105
Julie Richardson, Dean of Enrollment Management, Traditional Programs, Bay Path College, 588 Longmeadow Street, Longmeadow, MA 01106

## Becker College
### Worcester, Massachusetts
CB member
**www.becker.edu**   CB code: 3079

- Private 4-year liberal arts college
- Residential campus in small city
- 1,694 degree-seeking undergraduates: 23% part-time, 66% women, 7% African American, 1% Asian American, 4% Hispanic American
- 78% of applicants admitted
- SAT or ACT (ACT writing optional) required

**General.** Founded in 1887. Regionally accredited. Campuses in Worcester and Leicester. Member of Colleges of the Worcester Consortium. **Degrees:** 125 bachelor's, 127 associate awarded. **ROTC:** Army, Naval, Air Force. **Location:** 49 miles from Boston, 39 miles from Providence, Rhode Island. **Calendar:** Semester, limited summer session. **Full-time faculty:** 49 total; 69% women. **Part-time faculty:** 82 total; 62% women. **Class size:** 68% < 20, 31% 20-39, less than 1% 40-49, less than 1% 50-99. **Special facilities:** Veterinary clinic, on-site preschool and day-care facility, 96-acre off-campus stable for equine programs.

**Freshman class profile.** 1,948 applied, 1,520 admitted, 425 enrolled.

| Mid 50% test scores | | | |
|---|---|---|---|
| SAT critical reading: | 450-540 | Rank in top tenth: | 8% |
| SAT math: | 370-420 | End year in good standing: | 84% |
| ACT composite: | 12-20 | Return as sophomores: | 69% |
| Rank in top quarter: | 40% | Out-of-state: | 34% |

**Basis for selection.** High school record, GPA, extracurricular activities important. Recommendations, interview considered. Additional prerequisites for nursing, veterinary technology, and veterinary science programs. Essay recommended. **Homeschooled:** Statement describing homeschool structure and mission, transcript of courses and grades, letter of recommendation (nonparent) required. Official transcript from high school with which student is affiliated.

**High school preparation.** Required and recommended units include English 4, mathematics 3, social studies 1, history 2 and science 2. 2 math including 1 algebra, 1 chemistry with lab, 1 biology with lab required for nursing, veterinary technician, veterinary science, pre-vet programs.

**2007-2008 Annual costs.** Tuition/fees: $23,600. Additional one-time charge of $285 for nursing program. Room/board: $9,300. Books/supplies: $1,000. Personal expenses: $1,170.

**2006-2007 Financial aid. Need-based:** 441 full-time freshmen applied for aid; 410 were judged to have need; 406 of these received aid. Average

need met was 47%. Average scholarship/grant was $8,575; average loan $2,304. 45% of total undergraduate aid awarded as scholarships/grants, 55% as loans/jobs. **Non-need-based:** Awarded to 254 full-time undergraduates, including 145 freshmen. Scholarships awarded for academics.

**Application procedures. Admission:** No deadline. $30 fee, may be waived for applicants with need. Application may be submitted online. Admission notification on a rolling basis. Must reply by May 1 or within 4 week(s) if notified thereafter. **Financial aid:** Priority date 3/1; no closing date. FAFSA required. Applicants notified on a rolling basis starting 2/1; must reply within 2 week(s) of notification.

**Academics. Special study options:** Accelerated study, cross-registration, distance learning, independent study, internships, liberal arts/career combination, teacher certification program. Member of 15-school Colleges of Worcester consortium. **Credit/placement by examination:** AP, CLEP, IB, institutional tests. 30 credit hours maximum toward associate degree, 60 toward bachelor's. **Support services:** Learning center, reduced course load, remedial instruction, study skills assistance, tutoring, writing center.

**Majors. Biology:** General. **Business:** Accounting, business admin, hospitality admin, human resources, marketing, tourism/travel. **Communications technology:** General. **Computer sciences:** Networking. **Education:** Early childhood, elementary. **Health:** Nursing (RN), preveterinary, veterinary technology/assistant. **Legal studies:** General, prelaw. **Liberal arts:** Arts/sciences. **Parks/recreation:** Health/fitness, sports admin. **Protective services:** Criminal justice. **Psychology:** General. **Public administration:** Human services. **Visual/performing arts:** Commercial/advertising art, interior design.

**Most popular majors.** Business/marketing 58%, health sciences 7%, psychology 6%, visual/performing arts 18%.

**Computing on campus.** 155 workstations in dormitories, library, computer center. Dormitories wired for high-speed internet access and linked to campus network. Commuter students can connect to campus network. Online library, helpline, wireless network available.

**Student life. Freshman orientation:** Mandatory. Preregistration for classes offered. **Housing:** Guaranteed on-campus for freshmen. Coed dorms, single-sex dorms, apartments, substance-free housing available. $300 deposit. Substance-free dormitory and over-21 housing available. **Activities:** Choral groups, dance, drama, student government, student newspaper, campus community service club, international club, animal health club, business club, commuter club, early childhood education club, outdoors club, travel club, nursing club.

**Athletics.** NCAA. **Intercollegiate:** Baseball M, basketball, cross-country, equestrian, field hockey W, football (tackle) M, golf M, ice hockey M, lacrosse, soccer, softball W, tennis, volleyball W. **Intramural:** Badminton, basketball, soccer, table tennis, volleyball. **Team name:** Hawks.

**Student services.** Adult student services, alcohol/substance abuse counseling, career counseling, student employment services, financial aid counseling, health services, on-campus daycare, personal counseling, placement for graduates. **Physically disabled:** Services for visually, speech, hearing impaired.

**Contact.** E-mail: admissions@beckercollege.edu
Phone: (508) 373-9400 Toll-free number: (877) 523-2537
Fax: (508) 890-1500
Karen Schedin, Director of Admissions, Becker College, 61 Sever Street, Worcester, MA 01609

---

## Bentley College
**Waltham, Massachusetts**
www.bentley.edu

**CB member**
**CB code: 3096**

- Private 4-year business college
- Residential campus in small city
- 4,148 degree-seeking undergraduates: 5% part-time, 40% women, 3% African American, 8% Asian American, 4% Hispanic American, 7% international
- 1,393 degree-seeking graduate students
- 38% of applicants admitted
- SAT or ACT with writing, application essay required
- 87% graduate within 6 years; 26% enter graduate study

**General.** Founded in 1917. Regionally accredited. **Degrees:** 1,092 bachelor's, 1 associate awarded; master's, doctoral offered. **ROTC:** Army, Air Force. **Location:** 10 miles from Boston. **Calendar:** Semester, extensive summer session. **Full-time faculty:** 267 total; 84% have terminal degrees,

12% minority, 39% women. **Part-time faculty:** 231 total; 36% have terminal degrees, 9% minority, 40% women. **Class size:** 30% < 20, 69% 20-39, less than 1% 40-49. **Special facilities:** Accounting center for electronic learning and business measurement, academic technology center, center for marketing technology, CyberLaw center, design and usability center, center for financial services: risk management program and trading room, women's leadership institute, service-learning center.

**Freshman class profile.** 6,689 applied, 2,531 admitted, 934 enrolled.

| Mid 50% test scores | | | |
|---|---|---|---|
| SAT critical reading: | 550-630 | Return as sophomores: | 92% |
| SAT math: | 600-680 | Out-of-state: | 56% |
| SAT writing: | 550-640 | Live on campus: | 97% |
| ACT composite: | 24-29 | International: | 8% |
| Rank in top quarter: | 81% | Fraternities: | 8% |
| Rank in top tenth: | 42% | Sororities: | 13% |

**Basis for selection.** Decisions based on the essential credentials needed to complete an applicant's file: application itself with the essay, secondary school transcript(s), college transcripts (if applicable), standardized test scores, recommendations. Any supplemental information submitted by the applicant will also be considered. Interviews recommended. **Homeschooled:** Statement describing homeschool structure and mission, transcript of courses and grades, letter of recommendation (nonparent) required. Interview strongly recommended.

**High school preparation.** 19 units recommended. Recommended units include English 4, mathematics 4, history 3, science 3 (laboratory 3) and foreign language 3. 2 additional units English, math, social or lab science, foreign language or speech recommended.

**2007-2008 Annual costs.** Tuition/fees: $32,896. Room/board: $10,940. Books/supplies: $1,000. Personal expenses: $1,300.

**2006-2007 Financial aid. Need-based:** 689 full-time freshmen applied for aid; 485 were judged to have need; 485 of these received aid. Average need met was 93%. Average scholarship/grant was $18,824; average loan $3,828. 71% of total undergraduate aid awarded as scholarships/grants, 29% as loans/jobs. **Non-need-based:** Awarded to 971 full-time undergraduates, including 362 freshmen. Scholarships awarded for academics, athletics, leadership, minority status. **Additional information:** Deadlines for receipt of CSS PROFILE: early decision 12/15, early action and regular decision 2/1.

**Application procedures. Admission:** Closing date 1/15 (postmark date). $50 fee, may be waived for applicants with need. Application may be submitted online. Admission notification 4/1. Must reply by 5/1. **Financial aid:** Closing date 2/1. FAFSA required. CSS profile required if student is applying for institutional grants. Applicants notified on a rolling basis starting 3/25.

**Academics. Special study options:** Accelerated study, combined bachelor's/graduate degree, cross-registration, double major, honors, independent study, internships, liberal arts/career combination, semester at sea, student-designed major, study abroad, Washington semester. 5-year bachelor's/master's programs in business administration, accountancy, finance, marketing analytics, information technology, real estate management, financial planning, taxation. **Credit/placement by examination:** AP, CLEP, IB, SAT, ACT, institutional tests. 30 credit hours maximum toward bachelor's degree. CLEP credit for French, German, Spanish not available to native speakers. Language exams require oral test with department. **Support services:** Learning center, reduced course load, study skills assistance, tutoring, writing center.

**Majors. Business:** General, accounting, business admin, communications, finance, managerial economics, marketing. **Computer sciences:** General. **English:** English lit. **History:** General. **Legal studies:** Paralegal. **Liberal arts:** Arts/sciences. **Math:** General. **Philosophy/religion:** Philosophy. **Public administration:** Policy analysis.

**Most popular majors.** Business/marketing 94%.

**Computing on campus.** PC or laptop required. 4,620 workstations in library, computer center. Dormitories wired for high-speed internet access and linked to campus network. Commuter students can connect to campus network. Online course registration, online library, helpline, repair service, student web hosting, wireless network available.

**Student life. Freshman orientation:** Available. Preregistration for classes offered. 3-day program, usually held in June; family members invited on the last day. **Policies:** Academic honesty system, minimum GPA for student leaders. **Housing:** Guaranteed on-campus for all undergraduates. Coed dorms, special housing for disabled, apartments, substance-free housing available. Health and wellness houses available. **Activities:** Bands, choral groups, dance, drama, Model UN, radio station, student government, student newspaper, College Democrats, College Republicans, People Respecting Individuality and Diversity through Education, Christian Fellowship, Habitat for Humanity, Muslim students association, Hillel, Newman Club, women's center.

**Athletics.** NCAA. **Intercollegiate:** Baseball M, basketball, cross-country, diving, field hockey W, football (tackle) M, golf M, ice hockey M, lacrosse, soccer, softball W, swimming, tennis, track and field, volleyball W. **Intramural:** Basketball, football (non-tackle) M, soccer, softball, volleyball. **Team name:** Falcons.

**Student services.** Adult student services, alcohol/substance abuse counseling, campus ministries, career counseling, student employment services, financial aid counseling, health services, minority student services, personal counseling, placement for graduates, veterans' counselor, women's services. **Physically disabled:** Services for visually, speech, hearing impaired. **Learning disabled:** Comprehensive services available.

**Contact.** E-mail: ugadmission@bentley.edu
Phone: (781) 891-2244 Toll-free number: (800) 523-2354
Fax: (781) 891-3414
Erika Vardaro, Director of Admissions, Bentley College, 175 Forest Street, Waltham, MA 02452-4705

---

## Berklee College of Music
**Boston, Massachusetts**
www.berklee.edu

**CB member**
**CB code: 3107**

- Private 4-year music college
- Commuter campus in very large city
- 4,090 full-time, degree-seeking undergraduates
- 34% of applicants admitted
- Application essay, interview required

**General.** Founded in 1945. Regionally accredited. Emphasis on contemporary musical idioms. **Degrees:** 883 bachelor's awarded. **Calendar:** Semester, extensive summer session. **Full-time faculty:** 189 total. **Part-time faculty:** 282 total. **Special facilities:** Concert performance center, synthesizer laboratories, recording studios, film scoring laboratories, media center, practice rooms, recital halls, technology labs.

**Freshman class profile.** 2,939 applied, 1,007 admitted, 694 enrolled.

**Basis for selection.** Musical training and experience, recommendations, academic record, test scores, extracurricular music activities, interview important. Auditions required. **Homeschooled:** Statement describing home-school structure and mission, state high school equivalency certificate required. **Learning Disabled:** Students with disabilities should contact Special Services Coordinator.

**High school preparation.** Recommended units include English 4, mathematics 1, history 1, science 1 (laboratory 1) and academic electives 6. Minimum 2 years recent formal musical study on principal instrument covering standard methods/materials and/or significant practical performance experience plus knowledge of written-music fundamentals normally required of all applicants.

**2008-2009 Annual costs.** Tuition/fees (projected): $31,298. Required fees include one-time charge for purchase of laptop, which all freshmen must purchase. Room/board: $14,360. Books/supplies: $464. Personal expenses: $2,354.

**2007-2008 Financial aid. Need-based:** Average need met was 24%. Average scholarship/grant was $6,882; average loan $3,726. 37% of total undergraduate aid awarded as scholarships/grants, 63% as loans/jobs. **Non-need-based:** Scholarships awarded for academics, music/drama.

**Application procedures. Admission:** Priority date 11/1; deadline 2/1 (postmark date). $150 fee, may be waived for applicants with need. Application must be submitted online. Admission notification 3/31. Applicants should submit completed application materials well in advance of deadline to ensure placement in desired entry class. **Financial aid:** Priority date 3/1; no closing date. FAFSA required. Applicants notified on a rolling basis starting 3/1; must reply within 3 week(s) of notification.

**Academics.** Bachelor's degree program includes 30 credits general education courses. Four-year professional diploma available (not including general education). **Special study options:** Accelerated study, cross-registration, distance learning, double major, ESL, internships, student-designed major, study abroad, teacher certification program. ProArts Consortium with Boston Architectural Center, Boston Conservatory, Emerson College, Massachusetts College of Art, School of the Museum of Fine Arts. **Credit/placement by examination:** CLEP, institutional tests. 60 credit hours maximum toward bachelor's degree. **Support services:** Learning center, pre-admission summer program, tutoring, writing center.

**Majors. Education:** Music. **Health:** Music therapy. **Visual/performing arts:** Jazz, music management, music performance, music theory/composition, piano/organ, voice/opera.

**Computing on campus.** PC or laptop required. 50 workstations in dormitories, library, computer center. Dormitories wired for high-speed internet access and linked to campus network. Online library, helpline, repair service, student web hosting, wireless network available.

**Student life. Freshman orientation:** Available. Series of events before and during registration week. **Housing:** Coed dorms available. $200 nonrefundable deposit. Residence space limited. **Activities:** Bands, choral groups, drama, music ensembles, musical theater, student government, student newspaper, black student union, Christian Fellowship, Berklee Cares, women musicians' network, Latinos association, GLBT Allies at Berklee, Korean student association, Amnesty International.

**Athletics. Intramural:** Basketball, football (non-tackle), ice hockey, soccer.

**Student services.** Career counseling, student employment services, personal counseling, veterans' counselor. **Physically disabled:** Services for visually impaired.

**Contact.** E-mail: admissions@berklee.edu
Phone: (617) 747-2222 Toll-free number: (800) 237-5533
Fax: (617) 747-2047
Damien Bracken, Director of Admissions/OSSE, Berklee College of Music, 1140 Boylston Street, Boston, MA 02215

---

## Boston Architectural College
**Boston, Massachusetts**
www.the-bac.edu

**CB code: 1168**

- Private 6-year architecture and design college
- Commuter campus in very large city
- 584 degree-seeking undergraduates: 3% African American, 4% Asian American, 6% Hispanic American
- 536 graduate students

**General.** Founded in 1889. Regionally accredited. Program offers practice-based learning with simultaneous employment in field and academic study. **Degrees:** 45 bachelor's awarded; master's, first professional offered. **Location:** Downtown. **Calendar:** Semester, limited summer session. **Full-time faculty:** 11 total; 27% women. **Part-time faculty:** 324 total; 37% women. **Class size:** 94% < 20, 4% 20-39, 1% 40-49. **Special facilities:** On-campus gallery featuring exhibits of architectural and interior design interest, CAD lab, photography studio.

**Freshman class profile.**

| | | | |
|---|---|---|---|
| GPA 3.50 or higher: | 17% | GPA 2.0-2.99: | 45% |
| GPA 3.0-3.49: | 31% | Return as sophomores: | 55% |

**Basis for selection.** Open admission. Portfolio required for transfer credits for design courses.

**2008-2009 Annual costs.** Tuition/fees (projected): $9,940. "Academic Only" program tuition is $13,272 plus $20 required fees. Books/supplies: $1,476. Personal expenses: $3,006.

**2007-2008 Financial aid. Need-based:** Average need met was 18%. Average scholarship/grant was $2,792; average loan $4,551. 21% of total undergraduate aid awarded as scholarships/grants, 79% as loans/jobs. **Non-need-based:** Scholarships awarded for academics, art, leadership.

**Application procedures. Admission:** Priority date 5/15; deadline 9/2 (receipt date). $50 fee, may be waived for applicants with need. Application may be submitted online. Admission notification on a rolling basis. Must reply by May 1 or within 2 week(s) if notified thereafter. **Financial aid:** Priority date 4/15; no closing date. FAFSA required. Applicants notified on a rolling basis starting 3/1; must reply within 2 week(s) of notification.

**Academics.** Bachelor of architecture or interior design awarded after 6-year program of concurrent work and academic curriculum. Students usually transfer into program during second or third years. **Special study options:** Cross-registration, distance learning, independent study, internships, liberal arts/career combination. Member Professional Arts Consortium. **Credit/placement by examination:** AP, CLEP, institutional tests. **Support services:** Learning center, tutoring, writing center.

**Majors. Architecture:** Architecture, environmental design, interior, landscape.

**Computing on campus.** 175 workstations in library, computer center. Online library, helpline, wireless network available.

**Student life. Freshman orientation:** Mandatory. Preregistration for classes offered. Several dates; includes writing test. **Policies:** Campus code of conduct. **Housing:** Dormitory space, when available, at ProArts Consortium schools. **Activities:** Student government.

**Student services.** Adult student services, career counseling, student employment services, financial aid counseling, minority student services, veterans' counselor. **Physically disabled:** Services for visually, speech, hearing impaired.

**Contact.** E-mail: admissions@the-bac.edu
Phone: (617) 585-0123 Toll-free number: (877) 585-0100
Fax: (617) 585-0121
Richard Moyer, Director of Admissions, Boston Architectural College, 320 Newbury Street, Boston, MA 02115-2795

## Boston College
**Chestnut Hill, Massachusetts**   **CB member**
www.bc.edu   **CB code: 3083**

- Private 4-year university affiliated with Roman Catholic Church
- Residential campus in small city
- 9,081 degree-seeking undergraduates: 52% women, 6% African American, 10% Asian American, 8% Hispanic American, 2% international
- 4,642 graduate students
- 27% of applicants admitted
- SAT and SAT Subject Tests or ACT with writing, application essay required
- 91% graduate within 6 years; 27% enter graduate study

**General.** Founded in 1863. Regionally accredited. **Degrees:** 2,350 bachelor's awarded; master's, doctoral, first professional offered. **ROTC:** Army, Naval, Air Force. **Location:** 6 miles from Boston. **Calendar:** Semester, extensive summer session. **Full-time faculty:** 675 total; 98% have terminal degrees, 12% minority, 39% women. **Part-time faculty:** 571 total. **Class size:** 39% < 20, 44% 20-39, 9% 40-49, 5% 50-99, 3% >100. **Special facilities:** Observatory, theatre arts center, chemistry center, recreation complex.

**Freshman class profile.** 28,850 applied, 7,869 admitted, 2,291 enrolled.

| Mid 50% test scores | | | |
|---|---|---|---|
| SAT critical reading: | 610-700 | Rank in top tenth: | 80% |
| SAT math: | 630-720 | Return as sophomores: | 96% |
| SAT writing: | 620-710 | Out-of-state: | 74% |
| ACT composite: | 28-32 | Live on campus: | 99% |
| Rank in top quarter: | 96% | International: | 2% |

**Basis for selection.** Evidence of academic ability, intellectual curiosity, strength of character, motivation, creativity, energy, and promise for personal growth and development very important. Recommendations by counselors and teachers, required personal statement and extracurricular activities important. 2 SAT Subject Tests of student's choice required if SAT is submitted. Portfolio recommended for studio art majors. **Learning Disabled:** May provide documentation of disability at option of applicant.

**High school preparation.** 20 units recommended. Recommended units include English 4, mathematics 4, social studies 4, science 4 (laboratory 4) and foreign language 4. 4 combined social studies and history recommended. 2 laboratory science (including 1 chemistry) required of nursing applicants.

**2007-2008 Annual costs.** Tuition/fees: $35,674. Room/board: $11,060. Books/supplies: $750. Personal expenses: $1,000.

**2006-2007 Financial aid. Need-based:** 1,219 full-time freshmen applied for aid; 960 were judged to have need; 960 of these received aid. Average need met was 100%. Average scholarship/grant was $21,777; average loan $3,617. 76% of total undergraduate aid awarded as scholarships/grants, 24% as loans/jobs. **Non-need-based:** Awarded to 511 full-time undergraduates, including 110 freshmen. Scholarships awarded for academics, athletics, leadership, ROTC.

**Application procedures. Admission:** Closing date 1/1 (postmark date). $70 fee, may be waived for applicants with need. Application may be submitted online. Admission notification 4/15. Must reply by 5/1. **Financial aid:** Priority date 2/1; no closing date. FAFSA, CSS PROFILE required. Applicants notified by 4/15; must reply by 5/1.

**Academics. Special study options:** Accelerated study, combined bachelor's/graduate degree, cross-registration, double major, ESL, exchange student, honors, independent study, internships, liberal arts/career combination, student-designed major, study abroad, teacher certification program, Washington semester. 3-2 program in engineering with Boston University; Tufts Medical School Early Acceptance Program. **Credit/placement by examination:** AP, CLEP, IB. 24 credit hours maximum toward bachelor's degree. **Support services:** Learning center, pre-admission summer program, reduced course load, study skills assistance, tutoring, writing center.

**Majors. Area/ethnic studies:** Hispanic-American/Latino/Chicano. **Biology:** General, biochemistry. **Business:** Accounting, business admin, finance, human resources, management information systems, managerial economics, operations. **Communications:** General. **Computer sciences:** General, computer science, information systems. **Education:** Early childhood, elementary, secondary. **English:** English lit. **Foreign languages:** Ancient Greek, classics, French, German, Italian, Latin, linguistics, Russian, Spanish. **Health:** Nursing (RN). **History:** General. **Math:** General. **Philosophy/religion:** Philosophy. **Physical sciences:** Chemistry, geology, geophysics, physics. **Psychology:** General. **Social sciences:** Economics, political science, sociology. **Visual/performing arts:** Art history/conservation, dramatic, film/cinema, studio arts.

**Most popular majors.** Biology 7%, business/marketing 24%, communications/journalism 11%, education 9%, English 9%, history 7%, social sciences 14%.

**Computing on campus.** 1,000 workstations in library, computer center, student center. Dormitories wired for high-speed internet access and linked to campus network. Commuter students can connect to campus network. Online course registration, online library, helpline, repair service, student web hosting, wireless network available.

**Student life. Freshman orientation:** Mandatory, $350 fee. Preregistration for classes offered. Three-day, 2-night program; 4-6 scheduled options are offered during the summer. **Policies:** Students under 21 are not allowed to be in possession of alcohol, and smoking is prohibited in all residence halls. Additionally prohibited in dorm rooms: halogen lights, space heaters, egg crate style foam mattress pads, and candles. **Housing:** Guaranteed on-campus for freshmen. Coed dorms, single-sex dorms, special housing for disabled, substance-free housing available. $250 partly refundable deposit, deadline 5/1. Honors house, multicultural floor, 24-hour quiet living floor, social justice floor available. Apartment-style housing and townhouse-style housing available for upperclassmen. **Activities:** Bands, campus ministries, choral groups, dance, drama, film society, international student organizations, literary magazine, music ensembles, musical theater, radio station, student government, student newspaper, symphony orchestra, TV station, 4Boston, Amnesty International, Appalachia Volunteers, Asian Caucus, Black Student Forum, Buddhist club, Hillel, Ignatian Society, Puerto Rican Association, Muslim students association.

**Athletics.** NCAA. **Intercollegiate:** Baseball M, basketball, cross-country, diving, fencing, field hockey W, football (tackle) M, golf, ice hockey, lacrosse W, rowing (crew) W, sailing, skiing, soccer, softball W, swimming, tennis, track and field, volleyball W. **Intramural:** Basketball, football (non-tackle), golf, ice hockey, racquetball, soccer, softball, squash, tennis, volleyball. **Team name:** Eagles.

**Student services.** Alcohol/substance abuse counseling, campus ministries, career counseling, services for economically disadvantaged, student employment services, financial aid counseling, health services, minority student services, on-campus daycare, personal counseling, placement for graduates, women's services. **Physically disabled:** Services for visually, speech, hearing impaired.

**Contact.** Phone: (617) 552-3100 Toll-free number: (800) 360-2522
Fax: (617) 552-0798
John Mahoney, Director of Undergraduate Admission, Boston College, 140 Commonwealth Avenue, Devlin Hall 208, Chestnut Hill, MA 02467-3809

## Boston Conservatory
**Boston, Massachusetts**   **CB member**
www.bostonconservatory.edu   **CB code: 3084**

- Private 4-year music and performing arts college
- Residential campus in very large city
- 459 degree-seeking undergraduates: 62% women
- 116 degree-seeking graduate students
- 34% of applicants admitted
- Application essay required
- 42% graduate within 6 years

**General.** Founded in 1867. Regionally accredited. **Degrees:** 66 bachelor's awarded; master's offered. **Location:** Downtown Boston. **Calendar:** Semester, limited summer session. **Full-time faculty:** 44 total. **Part-time faculty:** 128 total. **Class size:** 89% < 20, 9% 20-39, less than 1% 40-49, less than 1% 50-99. **Special facilities:** College operated theater.

**Freshman class profile.** 1,117 applied, 379 admitted, 154 enrolled.

| | | | |
|---|---|---|---|
| Return as sophomores: | 91% | Live on campus: | 98% |
| Out-of-state: | 75% | Sororities: | 5% |

**Basis for selection.** Audition carries most weight. Academic record and artistic background strongly considered. Test scores, recommendations, personal essay, school and community activities, interview important. Audition required. Interview required of music education, composition majors.

**High school preparation.** Required units include English 4, mathematics 3, social studies 2, history 2, science 2 and foreign language 2.

**2007-2008 Annual costs.** Tuition/fees: $30,110. Room/board: $15,230. Books/supplies: $750. Personal expenses: $1,705.

**2007-2008 Financial aid. Need-based:** 48% of total undergraduate aid awarded as scholarships/grants, 52% as loans/jobs. **Non-need-based:** Scholarships awarded for music/drama.

**Application procedures. Admission:** Priority date 12/1; deadline 2/1 (postmark date). $105 fee. Admission notification 4/1. Must reply by 5/1. **Financial aid:** Closing date 2/1. FAFSA, institutional form required. Applicants notified by 4/1; must reply by 5/1.

**Academics. Special study options:** Cross-registration, double major, ESL, independent study, teacher certification program. **Credit/placement by examination:** CLEP, institutional tests. 75 credit hours maximum toward bachelor's degree. **Support services:** Pre-admission summer program, study skills assistance, tutoring, writing center.

**Majors. Education:** Music. **Visual/performing arts:** Dance, music performance, music theory/composition, piano/organ, voice/opera.

**Computing on campus.** 20 workstations in dormitories, library, student center. Dormitories linked to campus network. Online library available.

**Student life. Freshman orientation:** Mandatory, $150 fee. Week prior to registration includes college life seminar, advising, parent luncheon, school tours, city-wide tours, placements, auditions. **Housing:** Coed dorms, single-sex dorms available. $250 deposit, deadline 5/1. **Activities:** International student organizations, literary magazine, student government, student newspaper, African American artists' association, community services association, Christian Fellowship, environmental awareness group, peer support aides, Taiwan Chinese student association, gay and lesbian artists' association, Organizacion De Artistas Hispanos, Korean Society.

**Student services.** Career counseling, health services, personal counseling.

**Contact.** E-mail: admissions@bostonconservatory.edu
Phone: (617) 912-9153 Fax: (617) 536-3176
Halley Shefler, Dean of Enrollment Services, Boston Conservatory, 8 The Fenway, Boston, MA 02215

## Boston University

| Boston, Massachusetts | CB member |
|---|---|
| www.bu.edu | CB code: 3087 |

- Private 4-year university
- Residential campus in very large city
- 16,673 degree-seeking undergraduates: 2% part-time, 60% women, 3% African American, 13% Asian American, 7% Hispanic American, 6% international
- 12,652 degree-seeking graduate students
- 59% of applicants admitted
- SAT or ACT with writing, SAT Subject Tests, application essay required
- 82% graduate within 6 years; 30% enter graduate study

**General.** Founded in 1839. Regionally accredited. **Degrees:** 3,883 bachelor's awarded; master's, doctoral, first professional offered. **ROTC:** Army, Naval, Air Force. **Location:** Downtown. **Calendar:** Semester, extensive summer session. **Full-time faculty:** 1,481 total; 76% have terminal degrees, 11% minority, 34% women. **Part-time faculty:** 1,008 total; 5% minority, 41% women. **Class size:** 52% < 20, 33% 20-39, 5% 40-49, 6% 50-99, 4%

>100. **Special facilities:** Biodiversity station in Ecuador, dedicated management library, planetarium, National Public Radio station, 20th century archives, professional theater/theater company, center for remote sensing, speech, language and hearing clinic, culinary center, communication multimedia lab.

**Freshman class profile.** 33,930 applied, 19,888 admitted, 4,163 enrolled.

| Mid 50% test scores | | Rank in top tenth: | 51% |
|---|---|---|---|
| SAT critical reading: | 580-680 | End year in good standing: | 93% |
| SAT math: | 590-690 | Return as sophomores: | 91% |
| SAT writing: | 590-670 | Out-of-state: | 79% |
| ACT composite: | 25-30 | Live on campus: | 99% |
| GPA 3.50 or higher: | 50% | International: | 7% |
| GPA 3.0-3.49: | 41% | Fraternities: | 1% |
| GPA 2.0-2.99: | 9% | Sororities: | 1% |
| Rank in top quarter: | 85% | | |

**Basis for selection.** Evidence of strong academic performance in challenging college-prep curriculum most important. TOEFL required for non-native English speakers. SAT Subject Tests in Chemistry and Math (level 2) required for accelerated medical and dental programs. Others required to submit 2 subject tests in subject areas of their choice. Interview required for accelerated medical/dental programs, all non-performance theater arts majors. Audition required for music, theater performance programs. Portfolio required of visual arts, stage management, theatrical design majors. Portfolio or audition required for College of Fine Arts.

**High school preparation.** 15 units required; 20 recommended. Required and recommended units include English 4, mathematics 3-4, social studies 3-4, science 3-4 (laboratory 3-4) and foreign language 2-4. Precalculus required. Social studies should include history.

**2007-2008 Annual costs.** Tuition/fees: $35,418. Room/board: $10,950. Books/supplies: $840. Personal expenses: $1,197.

**2007-2008 Financial aid. Need-based:** 2,410 full-time freshmen applied for aid; 1,933 were judged to have need; 1,928 of these received aid. Average need met was 88%. Average scholarship/grant was $19,069; average loan $4,736. 74% of total undergraduate aid awarded as scholarships/grants, 26% as loans/jobs. **Non-need-based:** Awarded to 3,814 full-time undergraduates, including 1,275 freshmen. Scholarships awarded for academics, alumni affiliation, art, athletics, leadership, music/drama, religious affiliation, ROTC, state residency. **Additional information:** Financial aid deadline for early decision applicants: 11/01; notification date: 2/15.

**Application procedures. Admission:** Closing date 1/1 (receipt date). $75 fee, may be waived for applicants with need. Application may be submitted online. Admission notification 4/15. Must reply by 5/1. Application deadline December 1 for accelerated medical and dental combined degree and trustee, Boston high school, Cardinal Medeiros Scholar programs. **Financial aid:** Closing date 2/15. FAFSA, CSS PROFILE required. Applicants notified on a rolling basis starting 3/15; must reply by 5/1 or within 2 week(s) of notification.

**Academics. Special study options:** Accelerated study, combined bachelor's/graduate degree, cooperative education, cross-registration, distance learning, double major, dual enrollment of high school students, ESL, honors, independent study, internships, liberal arts/career combination, semester at sea, student-designed major, study abroad, teacher certification program, Washington semester. Extensive opportunities for study abroad as well as internships available in South and Central America, Europe, Africa, China, Pacific Rim, Russia. Field study in marine science at Woods Hole Institute, in environmental/ecological science in Ecuador, and at Photonics Center, combined bachelor's/master's degrees, 6-year physical therapy (BS/DPT) program, 5-year occupational therapy (BS/MS) program; 7-year accelerated MD, DMD programs. **Credit/placement by examination:** AP, CLEP, IB, institutional tests. 32 credit hours maximum toward bachelor's degree. Credits assigned vary by school and college. Scores higher than minimums may result in additional credit depending on department. **Support services:** Learning center, study skills assistance, tutoring, writing center.

**Majors. Area/ethnic studies:** American, East Asian, Italian, Latin American, Russian/Slavic. **Biology:** General, biochemistry, ecology, marine, molecular. **Business:** Accounting, business admin, entrepreneurial studies, finance, hospitality admin, international, international finance, management information systems, market research, marketing, operations, organizational behavior. **Communications:** General, advertising, broadcast journalism, journalism, public relations. **Computer sciences:** General. **Conservation:** General, environmental science, environmental studies, management/policy. **Education:** General, art, bilingual, chemistry, Deaf/hearing impaired, drama/dance, early childhood, elementary, English, mathematics, music, physical, science, social studies, special. **Engineering:** General, aerospace, biomedical, computer, electrical, mechanical. **English:** English lit. **Foreign languages:** General, ancient Greek, classics, French, German, Italian, Latin, linguistics, modern Greek, Russian, Spanish. **Health:** Athletic training, communication disorders, dental lab technology. **History:** General. **Interdisciplinary:** Math/computer science, neuroscience, nutrition sciences. **Legal studies:** Legal secretary, paralegal. **Math:** General. **Parks/recreation:** Exercise sciences. **Philosophy/religion:** Philosophy, religion. **Physical sciences:** Astronomy, astrophysics, chemistry, geology, geophysics, physics, planetary. **Psychology:** General. **Social sciences:** Anthropology, archaeology, economics, geography, international relations, political science, sociology, urban studies. **Visual/performing arts:** General, acting, art history/conservation, cinematography, commercial/advertising art, directing/producing, drawing, music history, music performance, music theory/composition, painting, piano/organ, sculpture, theater design, theater history, voice/opera.

**Most popular majors.** Biology 6%, business/marketing 17%, communications/journalism 16%, engineering/engineering technologies 6%, health sciences 6%, psychology 8%, social sciences 17%.

**Computing on campus.** 750 workstations in dormitories, library, computer center, student center. Dormitories wired for high-speed internet access and linked to campus network. Commuter students can connect to campus network. Online course registration, online library, helpline, repair service, student web hosting, wireless network available.

**Student life. Freshman orientation:** Mandatory, $135 fee. Preregistration for classes offered. Summer program. **Policies:** Campus residents must abide by guest/visitor policy. **Housing:** Guaranteed on-campus for all undergraduates. Coed dorms, single-sex dorms, special housing for disabled, apartments, cooperative housing available. $650 nonrefundable deposit, deadline 5/1. Specialty residences or floors for students with common academic, cultural, or extracurricular interests available. **Activities:** Bands, choral groups, dance, drama, film society, literary magazine, opera, radio station, student government, student newspaper, symphony orchestra, over 400 student organizations.

**Athletics.** NCAA. **Intercollegiate:** Basketball, cross-country, diving, field hockey W, golf, ice hockey, lacrosse W, rowing (crew), soccer, softball W, swimming, tennis, track and field, wrestling M. **Intramural:** Basketball, football (non-tackle), ice hockey W, soccer, softball, swimming, tennis, volleyball, water polo. **Team name:** Terriers.

**Student services.** Adult student services, campus ministries, career counseling, student employment services, financial aid counseling, health services, minority student services, personal counseling, placement for graduates, veterans' counselor. **Physically disabled:** Services for visually, speech, hearing impaired. **Learning disabled:** Comprehensive services available.

**Contact.** E-mail: admissions@bu.edu
Phone: (617) 353-2300 Fax: (617) 353-9695
Kelly Walter, Director, Office of Undergraduate Admissions, Boston University, 121 Bay State Road, Boston, MA 02215

---

## Brandeis University
**Waltham, Massachusetts**
**www.brandeis.edu**

**CB member**
**CB code: 3092**

- Private 4-year university
- Residential campus in small city
- 3,203 degree-seeking undergraduates: 56% women, 3% African American, 9% Asian American, 4% Hispanic American, 7% international
- 1,596 degree-seeking graduate students
- 34% of applicants admitted
- SAT and SAT Subject Tests or ACT with writing, SAT Subject Tests, application essay required
- 88% graduate within 6 years

**General.** Founded in 1948. Regionally accredited. **Degrees:** 812 bachelor's awarded; master's, doctoral offered. **ROTC:** Army, Air Force. **Location:** 10 miles from Boston. **Calendar:** Semester, limited summer session. **Full-time faculty:** 351 total; 96% have terminal degrees, 12% minority, 39% women. **Part-time faculty:** 128 total; 70% have terminal degrees, 5% minority, 52% women. **Class size:** 66% < 20, 22% 20-39, 6% 40-49, 4% 50-99, 2% >100. **Special facilities:** Basic medical sciences research center, spatial orientation laboratory, center for complex systems, astronomical observatory.

---

**Freshman class profile.** 7,562 applied, 2,601 admitted, 704 enrolled.

| Mid 50% test scores | | | |
|---|---|---|---|
| SAT critical reading: | 630-720 | Rank in top quarter: | 96% |
| SAT math: | 650-740 | Rank in top tenth: | 71% |
| ACT composite: | 28-32 | Return as sophomores: | 94% |
| GPA 3.50 or higher: | 84% | Out-of-state: | 79% |
| GPA 3.0-3.49: | 14% | Live on campus: | 99% |
| GPA 2.0-2.99: | 2% | International: | 9% |

**Basis for selection.** Evidence of accomplishment and development most important. School and teacher statements, test scores also important. Students taking SAT must take 2 SAT Subject Tests from 2 subject areas. Interview recommended.

**High school preparation.** 16 units recommended. Recommended units include English 4, mathematics 3, history 1, science 1 (laboratory 1), foreign language 3 and academic electives 4.

**2007-2008 Annual costs.** Tuition/fees: $35,702. Room/board: $9,908. Books/supplies: $700. Personal expenses: $1,000.

**2007-2008 Financial aid. Need-based:** 523 full-time freshmen applied for aid; 387 were judged to have need; 375 of these received aid. Average need met was 83%. Average scholarship/grant was $23,806; average loan $4,540. 78% of total undergraduate aid awarded as scholarships/grants, 22% as loans/jobs. **Non-need-based:** Awarded to 857 full-time undergraduates, including 183 freshmen. Scholarships awarded for academics.

**Application procedures. Admission:** Closing date 1/15 (receipt date). $55 fee, may be waived for applicants with need. Application may be submitted online. Must reply by 5/1. **Financial aid:** Priority date 2/1; no closing date. FAFSA, CSS PROFILE required. Applicants notified on a rolling basis starting 4/1.

**Academics. Special study options:** Cross-registration, double major, independent study, internships, student-designed major, study abroad. BA/MA in physics, history; seminars at Boston Museum of Fine Arts and seminars available through Massachusetts Bay Marine Studies Consortium, early admission to Mt. Sinai Medical School (NY) and Tufts Medical School (MA). **Credit/placement by examination:** AP, CLEP, IB, institutional tests. **Support services:** Reduced course load, remedial instruction, study skills assistance, tutoring, writing center.

**Majors. Area/ethnic studies:** African-American, American, East Asian, European, Latin American, women's. **Biology:** General, biochemistry, biophysics. **Computer sciences:** Computer science. **Conservation:** Environmental studies. **English:** Creative writing, English lit. **Foreign languages:** Ancient Greek, classics, comparative lit, French, German, Hebrew, Latin, linguistics, Russian, Spanish. **Health:** Health care admin. **History:** General. **Interdisciplinary:** Global studies, neuroscience. **Math:** General. **Philosophy/religion:** Philosophy. **Physical sciences:** Chemistry, physics. **Psychology:** General. **Social sciences:** Anthropology, economics, sociology. **Visual/performing arts:** Art history/conservation, dramatic, studio arts.

**Most popular majors.** Area/ethnic studies 12%, biology 11%, English 6%, history 7%, interdisciplinary studies 8%, psychology 8%, social sciences 28%.

**Computing on campus.** 104 workstations in library, computer center, student center. Dormitories wired for high-speed internet access and linked to campus network. Commuter students can connect to campus network. Online course registration, helpline, repair service, student web hosting, wireless network available.

**Student life. Freshman orientation:** Mandatory, $183 fee. Preregistration for classes offered. 5-day program beginning weekend before Labor Day weekend. **Housing:** Guaranteed on-campus for freshmen. Coed dorms, single-sex dorms, special housing for disabled, apartments available. Thematic learning communities available. **Activities:** Bands, campus ministries, choral groups, dance, drama, film society, literary magazine, music ensembles, musical theater, radio station, student government, student newspaper, symphony orchestra, TV station, 246 recognized clubs and organizations.

**Athletics.** NCAA. **Intercollegiate:** Baseball M, basketball, cross-country, diving, fencing, golf M, sailing, soccer, softball W, swimming, tennis, track and field, volleyball W. **Intramural:** Basketball, equestrian, football (non-tackle) M, golf, ice hockey M, softball, squash, table tennis, tennis, volleyball, water polo, weight lifting. **Team name:** Judges.

**Student services.** Alcohol/substance abuse counseling, campus ministries, career counseling, student employment services, financial aid counseling, health services, minority student services, on-campus daycare, personal counseling, placement for graduates, veterans' counselor, women's services. **Physically disabled:** Services for visually, speech, hearing impaired.

**Contact.** E-mail: admissions@brandeis.edu
Phone: (781) 736-3500 Toll-free number: (800) 622-0622
Fax: (781) 736-3536
Gil Villanueva, Dean of Admissions, Brandeis University, Box 549110, Waltham, MA 02454-9110

## Bridgewater State College
**Bridgewater, Massachusetts**    **CB member**
**www.bridgew.edu**    **CB code: 3517**

- Public 4-year liberal arts and teachers college
- Commuter campus in large town
- 7,931 degree-seeking undergraduates: 15% part-time, 59% women, 6% African American, 2% Asian American, 2% Hispanic American, 1% international
- 1,215 degree-seeking graduate students
- 69% of applicants admitted
- SAT or ACT (ACT writing optional) required
- 48% graduate within 6 years

**General.** Founded in 1840. Regionally accredited. **Degrees:** 1,343 bachelor's awarded; master's offered. **ROTC:** Army, Air Force. **Location:** 30 miles from Boston, 35 miles from Providence, Rhode Island. **Calendar:** Semester, extensive summer session. **Full-time faculty:** 299 total; 89% have terminal degrees, 12% minority, 48% women. **Part-time faculty:** 288 total; 4% minority, 49% women. **Class size:** 45% < 20, 51% 20-39, 4% 40-49, less than 1% 50-99.

**Freshman class profile.** 6,498 applied, 4,507 admitted, 1,584 enrolled.

| Mid 50% test scores | | | |
|---|---|---|---|
| SAT critical reading: | 450-550 | Rank in top quarter: | 27% |
| SAT math: | 460-560 | Rank in top tenth: | 7% |
| ACT composite: | 19-23 | Return as sophomores: | 74% |
| GPA 3.50 or higher: | 15% | Out-of-state: | 7% |
| GPA 3.0-3.49: | 35% | Live on campus: | 65% |
| GPA 2.0-2.99: | 50% | International: | 1% |

**Basis for selection.** High school achievement most important, including weighted high school GPA and completion of 16 college preparatory courses. Test scores, essay, extracurricular activities also important. Class rank, recommendations considered. Essay recommended. **Learning Disabled:** Exemption from admissions standardized testing upon documentation of diagnostic test results. Must complete 16 required academic courses with minimum 3.0 GPA or present evidence of potential for academic success.

**High school preparation.** 16 units required. Required units include English 4, mathematics 3, social studies 1, history 1, science 3 (laboratory 2), foreign language 2 and academic electives 2.

**2007-2008 Annual costs.** Tuition/fees: $6,034; $12,174 out-of-state. Room/board: $7,670. Books/supplies: $1,000. Personal expenses: $1,800.

**2006-2007 Financial aid. Need-based:** 1,084 full-time freshmen applied for aid; 731 were judged to have need; 720 of these received aid. Average scholarship/grant was $1,844; average loan $1,265. 43% of total undergraduate aid awarded as scholarships/grants, 57% as loans/jobs. **Nonneed-based:** Awarded to 99 full-time undergraduates, including 24 freshmen. Scholarships awarded for academics, leadership, minority status, state residency.

**Application procedures. Admission:** Priority date 2/15; no deadline. $25 fee, may be waived for applicants with need. Application may be submitted online. Admission notification on a rolling basis beginning on or about 12/15. **Financial aid:** Priority date 3/1; no closing date. FAFSA required. Applicants notified on a rolling basis starting 4/1.

**Academics. Special study options:** Accelerated study, combined bachelor's/graduate degree, cross-registration, distance learning, double major, dual enrollment of high school students, ESL, exchange student, honors, independent study, internships, study abroad, teacher certification program, Washington semester. **Credit/placement by examination:** AP, CLEP, IB, institutional tests. **Support services:** Learning center, pre-admission summer program, reduced course load, remedial instruction, study skills assistance, tutoring, writing center.

**Majors. Architecture:** Urban/community planning. **Biology:** General, biochemistry, biomedical sciences, cellular/molecular, environmental. **Business:** Accounting, business admin, finance, international, management information systems, marketing, transportation. **Communications:** General. **Computer sciences:** Computer science. **Education:** Art, biology, drama/ dance, early childhood, elementary, English, health, health occupations, kindergarten/preschool, music, physical, special. **English:** Creative writing, English lit. **Foreign languages:** Spanish. **Health:** Athletic training, communication disorders, kinesiotherapy. **History:** General. **Legal studies:** General. **Math:** General. **Parks/recreation:** General, exercise sciences, sports admin. **Philosophy/religion:** Ethics, philosophy. **Physical sciences:** Chemistry, geochemistry, geology, physics. **Protective services:** Criminal justice. **Psychology:** General. **Public administration:** Social work. **Social sciences:** Anthropology, archaeology, economics, geography, international relations, political science, sociology, U.S. government, urban studies. **Transportation:** Airline/ commercial pilot, aviation management. **Visual/performing arts:** Art history/ conservation, crafts, dramatic, graphic design, photography, studio arts.

**Most popular majors.** Business/marketing 15%, communications/ journalism 7%, education 15%, psychology 13%, security/protective services 9%, social sciences 6%.

**Computing on campus.** PC or laptop required. 780 workstations in library, computer center, student center. Dormitories wired for high-speed internet access and linked to campus network. Commuter students can connect to campus network. Online course registration, online library, helpline, repair service, wireless network available.

**Student life. Freshman orientation:** Mandatory, $160 fee. Preregistration for classes offered. **Housing:** Coed dorms, single-sex dorms, apartments, substance-free housing available. $150 fully refundable deposit, deadline 5/1. Quiet floor, nonsmoking floor available in residence hall. Housing available over breaks for athletes, student teachers, international students. **Activities:** Bands, campus ministries, choral groups, dance, drama, literary magazine, music ensembles, musical theater, radio station, student government, student newspaper, Christian Fellowship, College Democrats, Afro-American Society, international club, La Sociedad Latina, Amnesty International, Big Brothers/Big Sisters, Habitat for Humanity.

**Athletics.** NCAA. **Intercollegiate:** Baseball M, basketball, cross-country, diving, field hockey W, football (tackle) M, lacrosse W, soccer, softball W, swimming, tennis, track and field, volleyball W, wrestling M. **Intramural:** Basketball, football (tackle) M, lacrosse M, soccer, softball, tennis, volleyball, water polo. **Team name:** Bears.

**Student services.** Adult student services, campus ministries, career counseling, student employment services, financial aid counseling, health services, minority student services, on-campus daycare, personal counseling, placement for graduates, veterans' counselor, women's services. **Physically disabled:** Services for visually, speech, hearing impaired.

**Contact.** E-mail: admission@bridgew.edu
Phone: (508) 531-1237 Fax: (508) 531-1746
Gregg Meyer, Director of Admissions, Bridgewater State College, Gates House, Bridgewater, MA 02325

## Cambridge College
**Cambridge, Massachusetts**
**www.cambridgecollege.edu**    **CB code: 3612**

- Private 4-year liberal arts and teachers college
- Commuter campus in very large city
- 1,199 degree-seeking undergraduates: 70% part-time, 67% women
- 3,388 degree-seeking graduate students

**General.** Regionally accredited. Cambridge College serves mostly working adults. **Degrees:** 180 bachelor's awarded; master's, doctoral offered. **Calendar:** Continuous, extensive summer session. **Full-time faculty:** 28 total; 68% have terminal degrees, 29% minority, 54% women. **Part-time faculty:** 1,065 total; 37% have terminal degrees, 30% minority, 60% women.

**Basis for selection.** Open admission. 3 years' work experience after high school recommended, including employment, volunteer work, training, community involvement. Placement testing may be used if applicant does not have high school degree or GED.

**2007-2008 Annual costs.** Tuition/fees: $10,350.

**2006-2007 Financial aid.** All financial aid based on need. 3 full-time freshmen applied for aid; 3 were judged to have need; 3 of these received aid. Average need met was 35%. Average loan was $1,312. 24% of total undergraduate aid awarded as scholarships/grants, 76% as loans/jobs.

**Application procedures. Admission:** No deadline. $30 fee. Admission notification on a rolling basis. **Financial aid:** No deadline. FAFSA, institutional form required. Applicants notified on a rolling basis starting 5/1.

**Academics. Special study options:** Accelerated study, cooperative education, distance learning, independent study, liberal arts/career combination, teacher certification program, weekend college. **Credit/placement by examination:** CLEP. **Support services:** Reduced course load, tutoring, writing center.

**Majors. Business:** Management science. **Psychology:** General, counseling, family. **Public administration:** Human services.

**Most popular majors.** Business/marketing 22%, liberal arts 48%, psychology 24%, public administration/social services 12%.

**Computing on campus.** Online course registration, online library, helpline, wireless network available.

**Student life. Freshman orientation:** Available.

**Student services.** Adult student services, services for economically disadvantaged, financial aid counseling. **Learning disabled:** Comprehensive services available.

**Contact.** E-mail: admit@cambridgecollege.edu
Phone: (888) 800-4723 Toll-free number: (800) 877-4723
Farah Ravanbakhsh, Senior Director, Admissions and Enrollment,
Cambridge College, 1000 Massachusetts Avenue, Cambridge, MA
02138-5304

---

## Clark University
### Worcester, Massachusetts
www.clarku.edu

CB member
CB code: 3279

- Private 4-year university and liberal arts college
- Residential campus in small city
- 2,217 degree-seeking undergraduates: 2% part-time, 61% women, 2% African American, 4% Asian American, 2% Hispanic American, 8% international
- 837 degree-seeking graduate students
- 56% of applicants admitted
- SAT or ACT (ACT writing optional), application essay required
- 76% graduate within 6 years; 30% enter graduate study

**General.** Founded in 1887. Regionally accredited. **Degrees:** 491 bachelor's awarded; master's, doctoral offered. **ROTC:** Army, Naval, Air Force. **Location:** 50 miles from Boston. **Calendar:** Semester, limited summer session. **Full-time faculty:** 173 total; 96% have terminal degrees, 17% minority, 41% women. **Part-time faculty:** 98 total. **Class size:** 58% < 20, 31% 20-39, 6% 40-49, 4% 50-99, less than 1% >100. **Special facilities:** Robert Goddard exhibition, map library, rare book room, NMR research facility, observatory, electronic music facility, arboretum, crafts studio, 2 theaters, environmental education laboratory, student-run recycling center, pulsed magnetic field laboratory, Holocaust studies center.

**Freshman class profile.** 5,201 applied, 2,918 admitted, 574 enrolled.

| Mid 50% test scores | | Rank in top quarter: | 74% |
|---|---|---|---|
| SAT critical reading: | 550-660 | Rank in top tenth: | 32% |
| SAT math: | 540-650 | Return as sophomores: | 88% |
| ACT composite: | 24-28 | Out-of-state: | 70% |
| GPA 3.50 or higher: | 52% | Live on campus: | 99% |
| GPA 3.0-3.49: | 35% | International: | 8% |
| GPA 2.0-2.99: | 13% | | |

**Basis for selection.** School achievement record and courses, recommendations, test scores most important. Special talents, accomplishments, motivation, and individual circumstances, including outside activities and jobs, also important. Interview recommended. Portfolio recommended for art majors.

**High school preparation.** 16 units recommended. Recommended units include English 4, mathematics 3, social studies 2, history 2, science 3 (laboratory 2) and foreign language 2.

**2007-2008 Annual costs.** Tuition/fees: $32,865. New student contingency fee: $50. Fifth-year tuition waived for eligible undergraduates admitted to accelerated bachelor's/master's programs. Room/board: $6,300. Books/supplies: $800. Personal expenses: $700.

**2007-2008 Financial aid. Need-based:** 401 full-time freshmen applied for aid; 310 were judged to have need; 301 of these received aid. Average need met was 94%. Average scholarship/grant was $18,954; average loan $4,531. **Non-need-based:** Awarded to 1,168 full-time undergraduates, including 308 freshmen. Scholarships awarded for academics, leadership.

**Application procedures. Admission:** Closing date 1/15 (postmark date). $55 fee, may be waived for applicants with need. Application may be submitted online. Admission notification 4/1. Must reply by 5/1. **Financial aid:** Closing date 2/1. FAFSA, CSS PROFILE required. Applicants notified by 3/31; must reply by 5/1 or within 2 week(s) of notification.

**Academics.** Interdisciplinary majors, special programs, and accelerated bachelor's/master's program with fifth-year tuition free available. **Special study options:** Combined bachelor's/graduate degree, cross-registration, double major, ESL, independent study, internships, liberal arts/career combination, student-designed major, study abroad, teacher certification program, Washington semester. Clark European Center in Luxembourg offers intensive May term including classes and field work. Courses also offered at Bermuda Biological Station. Students may also enroll in semester-long environmental science program at marine biological laboratory at Woods Hole Oceanographic Institute. 3-2 engineering programs with Columbia University, Worcester Polytechnic Institute, Washington University. **Credit/placement by examination:** AP, CLEP, IB, SAT, institutional tests. 16 credit hours maximum toward bachelor's degree. **Support services:** Reduced course load, study skills assistance, writing center.

**Majors. Area/ethnic studies:** Women's. **Biology:** General, biochemistry, bioinformatics, molecular. **Business:** General, business admin. **Communications:** General. **Computer sciences:** General, computer science. **Conservation:** Environmental science, environmental studies. **English:** English lit. **Foreign languages:** General, classics, comparative lit, French, Spanish. **History:** General. **Interdisciplinary:** Global studies, math/computer science, science/society. **Liberal arts:** Arts/sciences. **Math:** General. **Philosophy/religion:** Philosophy. **Physical sciences:** Chemistry, physics. **Psychology:** General. **Public administration:** General. **Social sciences:** Economics, geography, international relations, political science, sociology. **Visual/performing arts:** General, art, art history/conservation, dramatic, film/cinema, studio arts.

**Most popular majors.** Biology 7%, business/marketing 6%, communications/journalism 6%, English 7%, psychology 18%, social sciences 23%, visual/performing arts 13%.

**Computing on campus.** 58 workstations in dormitories, library, computer center, student center. Dormitories wired for high-speed internet access and linked to campus network. Commuter students can connect to campus network. Online course registration, online library, helpline, student web hosting, wireless network available.

**Student life. Freshman orientation:** Mandatory, $200 fee. Preregistration for classes offered. Program held during week prior to fall semester; includes course selection and registration. **Housing:** Guaranteed on-campus for freshmen. Coed dorms, single-sex dorms, special housing for disabled, apartments, substance-free housing available. $100 nonrefundable deposit, deadline 5/1. Some university-owned off-campus housing available. Year-round house, quiet house, other special interest houses available. All residence halls nonsmoking. **Activities:** Bands, campus ministries, choral groups, dance, drama, film society, international student organizations, literary magazine, music ensembles, Model UN, musical theater, radio station, student government, student newspaper, symphony orchestra, TV station, approximately 80 student clubs and organizations.

**Athletics.** NCAA. **Intercollegiate:** Baseball M, basketball, cross-country, diving, field hockey W, lacrosse M, rowing (crew), soccer, softball W, swimming, tennis, volleyball W. **Intramural:** Badminton, basketball, racquetball, soccer, softball, squash, volleyball, water polo. **Team name:** Cougars.

**Student services.** Adult student services, alcohol/substance abuse counseling, campus ministries, career counseling, services for economically disadvantaged, student employment services, financial aid counseling, health services, minority student services, personal counseling, placement for graduates, women's services. **Physically disabled:** Services for visually, speech, hearing impaired.

**Contact.** E-mail: admissions@clarku.edu
Phone: (508) 793-7431 Toll-free number: (800) 462-5275
Fax: (508) 793-8821
Harold Wingood, Dean of Admissions, Clark University, 950 Main Street, Worcester, MA 01610-1477

---

## College of the Holy Cross
### Worcester, Massachusetts
www.holycross.edu

CB member
CB code: 3282

- Private 4-year liberal arts college affiliated with Roman Catholic Church
- Residential campus in small city
- 2,817 degree-seeking undergraduates: 56% women, 4% African American, 5% Asian American, 5% Hispanic American, 1% international

- 33% of applicants admitted
- Application essay required
- 92% graduate within 6 years; 25% enter graduate study

**General.** Founded in 1843. Regionally accredited. **Degrees:** 644 bachelor's awarded. **ROTC:** Army, Naval, Air Force. **Location:** 45 miles from Boston. **Calendar:** Semester. **Full-time faculty:** 240 total; 94% have terminal degrees, 13% minority, 47% women. **Part-time faculty:** 48 total; 10% minority, 44% women. **Class size:** 55% < 20, 44% 20-39, less than 1% 40-49, less than 1% 50-99, less than 1% >100. **Special facilities:** Greenhouse, facilities for aquatic research, research-level scientific equipment.

**Freshman class profile.** 7,066 applied, 2,331 admitted, 719 enrolled.

| Mid 50% test scores | | | |
|---|---|---|---|
| SAT critical reading: | 590-690 | Return as sophomores: | 94% |
| SAT math: | 620-690 | Out-of-state: | 61% |
| Rank in top quarter: | 97% | Live on campus: | 100% |
| Rank in top tenth: | 65% | International: | 1% |

**Basis for selection.** Academic record, recommendations, interview, essay, extracurricular activities important. Evidence of superior achievement in analytical reading and writing of particular importance. Advanced placement and honors courses recommended. Standardized test scores are optional. Students have option to submit scores if they believe results present fuller picture of achievements and potential. Students who opt not to submit scores will not be at any disadvantage in admissions decisions. A personal interview is optional but highly recommended. **Homeschooled:** On-campus interview highly encouraged. Applicants should submit course work samples, personal statement, and college transcripts if applicable. If homeschooling associated with particular organization or program, submit description.

**High school preparation.** 20 units recommended. Recommended units include English 4, mathematics 4, social studies 2, history 2, science 4, foreign language 3 and academic electives 1.

**2008-2009 Annual costs.** Tuition/fees: $37,242. Room/board: $10,260. Books/supplies: $700. Personal expenses: $900.

**2007-2008 Financial aid. Need-based:** Average need met was 100%. Average scholarship/grant was $25,270; average loan $4,957. 79% of total undergraduate aid awarded as scholarships/grants, 21% as loans/jobs. **Non-need-based:** Scholarships awarded for academics, athletics, ROTC.

**Application procedures. Admission:** Closing date 1/15 (receipt date). $50 fee, may be waived for applicants with need. Application may be submitted online. Admission notification 4/1. Must reply by 5/1. **Financial aid:** Closing date 2/1. FAFSA required. CSS PROFILE required of all students applying for institutional aid. Applicants notified by 3/30; must reply by 5/1.

**Academics.** Students encouraged to participate in Oxford-style tutorials. 32 courses of 1 or more units required for graduation. 10 to 14 courses of 1 or more units required in major. **Special study options:** Accelerated study, cross-registration, double major, dual enrollment of high school students, honors, independent study, internships, liberal arts/career combination, semester at sea, student-designed major, study abroad, teacher certification program, Washington semester. First-year living and learning academic enrichment program. **Credit/placement by examination:** AP, CLEP, IB. **Support services:** Tutoring, writing center.

**Majors. Area/ethnic studies:** Asian, German, Russian/Slavic. **Biology:** General. **Business:** Accounting. **Computer sciences:** General. **Conservation:** Environmental studies. **English:** English lit. **Foreign languages:** Classics, comparative lit, French, German, Italian, Russian, Spanish. **History:** General. **Interdisciplinary:** Medieval/Renaissance. **Math:** General. **Philosophy/religion:** Philosophy, religion. **Physical sciences:** Chemistry, physics. **Psychology:** General. **Social sciences:** Anthropology, economics, political science, sociology. **Visual/performing arts:** Art history/conservation, dramatic, studio arts.

**Most popular majors.** Biology 6%, English 10%, foreign language 8%, history 11%, psychology 12%, social sciences 34%.

**Computing on campus.** 485 workstations in dormitories, library, computer center, student center. Dormitories wired for high-speed internet access and linked to campus network. Commuter students can connect to campus network. Online library, helpline, repair service, student web hosting, wireless network available.

**Student life. Freshman orientation:** Available, $210 fee. 2-day programs available in mid-June combined with a 3-day orientation prior to fall registration. **Policies:** Responsible drinking policy for students over 21. Initiation hazing prohibited. **Housing:** Guaranteed on-campus for all undergraduates. Coed dorms, special housing for disabled, apartments, substance-free housing available. $500 nonrefundable deposit, deadline 5/1. **Activities:**

Bands, choral groups, dance, drama, literary magazine, music ensembles, musical theater, radio station, student government, student newspaper, black student union, Purple Key Society, student program for urban development, women's forum, Latin American student organization, Asian student society, Muslim student association, Appalachia service project, Habitat for Humanity, association of bisexuals, gays and lesbians.

**Athletics.** NCAA. **Intercollegiate:** Baseball M, basketball, cross-country, diving, field hockey W, football (tackle) M, golf, ice hockey, lacrosse, rowing (crew), soccer, softball W, swimming, tennis, track and field, volleyball W. **Intramural:** Basketball, football (non-tackle), softball, tennis, volleyball. **Team name:** Crusaders.

**Student services.** Alcohol/substance abuse counseling, campus ministries, career counseling, student employment services, financial aid counseling, health services, minority student services, personal counseling, placement for graduates, women's services. **Physically disabled:** Services for visually, hearing impaired.

**Contact.** E-mail: admissions@holycross.edu
Phone: (508) 793-2443 Toll-free number: (800) 442-2421
Fax: (508) 793-3888
Ann McDermott, Director of Admissions, College of the Holy Cross, One College Street, Worcester, MA 01610-2395

---

## Curry College
**Milton, Massachusetts**
www.curry.edu

**CB member**
**CB code: 3285**

- Private 4-year nursing and liberal arts college
- Residential campus in large town
- 2,641 degree-seeking undergraduates: 22% part-time, 57% women, 7% African American, 1% Asian American, 2% Hispanic American
- 271 degree-seeking graduate students
- 66% of applicants admitted
- Application essay required
- 45% graduate within 6 years

**General.** Founded in 1879. Regionally accredited. **Degrees:** 599 bachelor's awarded; master's offered. **ROTC:** Army, Air Force. **Location:** 7 miles from downtown Boston. **Calendar:** Semester, limited summer session. **Full-time faculty:** 113 total; 60% have terminal degrees, 7% minority, 63% women. **Part-time faculty:** 325 total; 17% minority, 57% women. **Class size:** 64% < 20, 35% 20-39, less than 1% 40-49, less than 1% 50-99.

**Freshman class profile.** 3,739 applied, 2,472 admitted, 652 enrolled.

| Mid 50% test scores | | | |
|---|---|---|---|
| SAT critical reading: | 470-580 | Out-of-state: | 37% |
| SAT math: | 450-550 | Live on campus: | 90% |
| Return as sophomores: | 64% | International: | 1% |

**Basis for selection.** High school record, recommendations, extracurricular activities most important. Test scores also important. Interviews encouraged but not required. Interviews are strongly recommended. **Homeschooled:** Statement describing homeschool structure and mission, transcript of courses and grades, state high school equivalency certificate required. **Learning Disabled:** Wechsler Adult Intelligence Scale required of learning disabled applicants for admission. This replaces SAT requirement but SAT or ACT still recommended.

**High school preparation.** 16 units required. Required and recommended units include English 4, mathematics 3, social studies 2, science 2-3 (laboratory 2) and foreign language 2. 3 math through algebra II, 1 chemistry, and 1 biology required for nursing applicants.

**2007-2008 Annual costs.** Tuition/fees: $25,755. PAL (Program for Advancement of Learning) students pay additional program participation fee. Room/board: $10,290. Books/supplies: $700. Personal expenses: $1,000.

**2007-2008 Financial aid. Need-based:** 456 full-time freshmen applied for aid; 449 were judged to have need; 446 of these received aid. Average need met was 68.9%. Average scholarship/grant was $11,903; average loan $3,612. 69% of total undergraduate aid awarded as scholarships/grants, 31% as loans/jobs. **Non-need-based:** Awarded to 87 full-time undergraduates, including 30 freshmen. Scholarships awarded for academics, leadership.

**Application procedures. Admission:** Closing date 4/1 (postmark date). $40 fee, may be waived for applicants with need. Application may be submitted online. Admission notification on a rolling basis beginning on or about 1/1. Must reply by May 1 or within 2 week(s) if notified thereafter. **Financial aid:** Priority date 3/1; no closing date. FAFSA required. Applicants notified on a rolling basis starting 3/10; must reply by 5/1 or within 2 week(s) of notification.

**Academics. Special study options:** Accelerated study, double major, honors, independent study, internships, liberal arts/career combination, New York semester, semester at sea, student-designed major, study abroad, teacher certification program. **Credit/placement by examination:** AP, CLEP, SAT, institutional tests. 60 credit hours maximum toward bachelor's degree. **Support services:** Learning center, pre-admission summer program, reduced course load, remedial instruction, study skills assistance, tutoring, writing center.

**Majors. Biology:** General. **Business:** Business admin. **Communications:** General. **Computer sciences:** General. **Conservation:** Environmental science. **Education:** General, early childhood, elementary, special. **English:** English lit. **Health:** Health services, nursing (RN). **Liberal arts:** Arts/sciences. **Philosophy/religion:** Philosophy. **Protective services:** Criminal justice. **Psychology:** General. **Social sciences:** Sociology. **Visual/performing arts:** Graphic design, studio arts. **Other:** Politics and history.

**Most popular majors.** Business/marketing 14%, communications/journalism 13%, health sciences 24%, psychology 10%, security/protective services 22%.

**Computing on campus.** 100 workstations in dormitories, library, computer center. Dormitories wired for high-speed internet access and linked to campus network. Commuter students can connect to campus network. Helpline, student web hosting available.

**Student life. Freshman orientation:** Available, $150 fee. Preregistration for classes offered. 3 summer 2-day programs and a follow-up 2-day August program. **Housing:** Coed dorms, single-sex dorms, substance-free housing available. $200 nonrefundable deposit, deadline 5/1. Wellness, honors housing available. **Activities:** Campus ministries, choral groups, dance, drama, international student organizations, literary magazine, music ensembles, musical theater, radio station, student government, student newspaper, TV station, nursing association, student activities board, community service organization, Hillel, One Curry, Newman Club.

**Athletics.** NCAA. **Intercollegiate:** Baseball M, basketball, cross-country W, football (tackle) M, ice hockey M, lacrosse, soccer, softball W, tennis. **Intramural:** Basketball, cheerleading W, football (non-tackle), golf, rugby M, softball, tennis, volleyball. **Team name:** Colonels.

**Student services.** Adult student services, alcohol/substance abuse counseling, campus ministries, career counseling, student employment services, financial aid counseling, health services, minority student services, on-campus daycare, personal counseling, placement for graduates, veterans' counselor, women's services.

**Contact.** E-mail: curryadm@curry.edu
Phone: (617) 333-2210 Toll-free number: (800) 669-0686
Fax: (617) 333-2114
Jane Fidler, Dean of Admissions, Curry College, 1071 Blue Hill Avenue, Milton, MA 02186-9984

---

## Eastern Nazarene College

Quincy, Massachusetts
www.enc.edu

CB member
CB code: 3365

- Private 4-year liberal arts college affiliated with Church of the Nazarene
- Residential campus in small city
- 649 degree-seeking undergraduates
- 52% of applicants admitted
- SAT or ACT (ACT writing optional), application essay, interview required

**General.** Founded in 1900. Regionally accredited. **Degrees:** 197 bachelor's, 41 associate awarded; master's offered. **ROTC:** Army, Air Force. **Location:** 6 miles from Boston. **Calendar:** 4-1-4, limited summer session. **Full-time faculty:** 44 total. **Part-time faculty:** 22 total. **Class size:** 72% < 20, 22% 20-39, 2% 40-49, 3% 50-99. **Special facilities:** College-operated preschool.

### Freshman class profile.

| Mid 50% test scores | | | |
|---|---|---|---|
| SAT critical reading: | 440-580 | ACT composite: | 17-22 |
| SAT math: | 430-570 | Out-of-state: | 51% |
| SAT writing: | 440-580 | Live on campus: | 91% |

**Basis for selection.** Transcripts from high school(s), SAT/ACT scores, academic/character references, personal interview or essay most important. Audition required of music majors.

**High school preparation.** Required and recommended units include English 4, mathematics 2-4, social studies 1-2, history 1-2, science 2-4 and foreign language 2-4.

**2007-2008 Annual costs.** Tuition/fees: $20,574. Room/board: $7,395. Books/supplies: $1,000. Personal expenses: $2,000.

**Financial aid. Non-need-based:** Scholarships awarded for academics, alumni affiliation, leadership, music/drama, religious affiliation, state residency. **Additional information:** Participant in Massachusetts University pre-payment plan.

**Application procedures. Admission:** Priority date 3/15; no deadline. $25 fee, may be waived for applicants with need. Application may be submitted online. Admission notification on a rolling basis. Must reply by May 1 or within 3 week(s) if notified thereafter. **Financial aid:** Priority date 2/28; no closing date. FAFSA, institutional form required. Applicants notified on a rolling basis starting 3/15; must reply within 2 week(s) of notification.

**Academics.** Degree-completion program in business offered to professionals with equivalent of 2 years college work and professional experience. Associate degree also offered for those without prior college experience. **Special study options:** Accelerated study, cross-registration, double major, dual enrollment of high school students, exchange student, honors, independent study, internships, liberal arts/career combination, semester at sea, study abroad, teacher certification program, urban semester, Washington semester. **Credit/placement by examination:** AP, CLEP, IB, institutional tests. **Support services:** Learning center, reduced course load, remedial instruction, study skills assistance, tutoring, writing center.

**Majors. Biology:** General, biochemistry. **Business:** General, accounting/finance, business admin, entrepreneurial studies, marketing. **Communications:** General, advertising, journalism, public relations, radio/tv. **Computer sciences:** Computer science. **Education:** General, biology, chemistry, early childhood, elementary, English, history, mathematics, middle, music, physical, physics, science, social studies, special. **Engineering:** General, computer, electrical, physics. **English:** Composition, English lit. **Health:** Predental, premedicine, prepharmacy, preveterinary. **History:** General. **Interdisciplinary:** Biological/physical sciences. **Legal studies:** Prelaw. **Liberal arts:** Arts/sciences. **Math:** General. **Parks/recreation:** Health/fitness. **Philosophy/religion:** Religion. **Physical sciences:** Chemistry, physics. **Psychology:** General. **Public administration:** Social work. **Social sciences:** Sociology. **Theology:** Religious ed, sacred music, theology. **Visual/performing arts:** Dramatic, music performance, music theory/composition, piano/organ, theater arts management, voice/opera.

**Most popular majors.** Business/marketing 50%, education 9%, English 6%, liberal arts 6%, psychology 7%.

**Computing on campus.** 98 workstations in library, computer center. Dormitories wired for high-speed internet access and linked to campus network. Commuter students can connect to campus network. Online library, helpline, repair service available.

**Student life. Freshman orientation:** Mandatory. Preregistration for classes offered. **Policies:** No alcohol, drugs, or tobacco permitted. Religious observance required. **Housing:** Guaranteed on-campus for freshmen. Single-sex dorms, special housing for disabled, apartments available. $250 nonrefundable deposit, deadline 8/25. **Activities:** Bands, choral groups, drama, film society, music ensembles, musical theater, radio station, student government, student newspaper, TV station, MESA, Fellowship of Christian Athletes, inner-city ministry, Salvation Army student fellowships, nursing home ministry, children's ministry.

**Athletics.** NCAA. **Intercollegiate:** Baseball M, basketball, cross-country, soccer, softball W, tennis, volleyball W. **Intramural:** Basketball, football (non-tackle), lacrosse W, soccer, softball, volleyball. **Team name:** Crusaders.

**Student services.** Adult student services, alcohol/substance abuse counseling, campus ministries, career counseling, student employment services, financial aid counseling, health services, minority student services, on-campus daycare, personal counseling, placement for graduates. **Physically disabled:** Services for visually impaired.

**Contact.** E-mail: admissions@enc.edu
Phone: (617) 745-3711 Toll-free number: (800) 883-6288
Fax: (617) 745-3929
Rodney Neighbors, Director of Admissions, Eastern Nazarene College, 23 East Elm Avenue, Quincy, MA 02170-2999

---

## Elms College

Chicopee, Massachusetts
www.elms.edu

CB member
CB code: 3283

- Private 4-year liberal arts college affiliated with Roman Catholic Church
- Residential campus in small city

- 976 degree-seeking undergraduates
- 174 degree-seeking graduate students
- 84% of applicants admitted
- SAT or ACT with writing, application essay required

**General.** Founded in 1928. Regionally accredited. **Degrees:** 191 bachelor's, 6 associate awarded; master's offered. **ROTC:** Army, Air Force. **Location:** 2 miles from Springfield, 30 miles from Hartford, Connecticut. **Calendar:** Semester, extensive summer session. **Full-time faculty:** 50 total. **Part-time faculty:** 5 total. **Class size:** 79% < 20, 21% 20-39. **Special facilities:** Rare book collection, Federal Depository, Irish cultural center, Polish center for discovery and learning.

**Freshman class profile.** 550 applied, 464 admitted, 172 enrolled.

| Mid 50% test scores | | GPA 3.0-3.49: | 36% |
|---|---|---|---|
| SAT critical reading: | 420-530 | GPA 2.0-2.99: | 40% |
| SAT math: | 420-530 | Rank in top quarter: | 35% |
| SAT writing: | 440-540 | Rank in top tenth: | 10% |
| ACT composite: | 18-23 | Out-of-state: | 23% |
| GPA 3.50 or higher: | 23% | Live on campus: | 64% |

**Basis for selection.** Students should rank in top half of high school class. 2.5 GPA or better, minimum combined SAT score of 1000 (exclusive of Writing) recommended. Interview recommended. **Homeschooled:** Transcript of courses and grades, letter of recommendation (nonparent) required.

**High school preparation.** 12 units required; 20 recommended. Required and recommended units include English 4, mathematics 2-4, social studies 1-2, history 1-2, science 2-4 (laboratory 2) and foreign language 2-4. Biology, chemistry required for nursing applicants.

**2007-2008 Annual costs.** Tuition/fees: $23,755. Room/board: $8,820. Books/supplies: $525. Personal expenses: $900.

**Financial aid. Non-need-based:** Scholarships awarded for academics, alumni affiliation, leadership, religious affiliation, state residency.

**Application procedures. Admission:** No deadline. $30 fee, may be waived for applicants with need. Application may be submitted online. Admission notification on a rolling basis beginning on or about 12/15. Must reply by May 1 or within 2 week(s) if notified thereafter. **Financial aid:** Priority date 3/1; no closing date. FAFSA, institutional form required. Applicants notified on a rolling basis starting 3/10; must reply by 5/1 or within 2 week(s) of notification.

**Academics. Special study options:** Cross-registration, distance learning, double major, dual enrollment of high school students, ESL, exchange student, honors, independent study, internships, liberal arts/career combination, study abroad, teacher certification program, Washington semester, weekend college. **Credit/placement by examination:** AP, CLEP, IB, SAT, ACT, institutional tests. 6 credit hours maximum toward bachelor's degree. **Support services:** Learning center, reduced course load, study skills assistance, tutoring, writing center.

**Majors. Area/ethnic studies:** American, Spanish/Iberian. **Biology:** General. **Business:** Accounting, accounting/business management, business admin, international, marketing. **Communications:** General. **Computer sciences:** General. **Education:** General, bilingual, Deaf/hearing impaired, early childhood, elementary, English, ESL, secondary, special. **English:** English lit. **Foreign languages:** Spanish. **Health:** Audiology/hearing, audiology/speech pathology, communication disorders, facilities admin, health care admin, health services admin, nursing (RN), pediatric nursing, predental, premedicine, preop/surgical nursing, preveterinary, public health nursing, speech pathology, speech-language pathology assistant. **History:** General, American, European. **Interdisciplinary:** Biological/physical sciences. **Legal studies:** General, paralegal, prelaw. **Liberal arts:** Arts/sciences. **Math:** General. **Parks/recreation:** Sports admin. **Philosophy/religion:** Religion. **Physical sciences:** Chemistry. **Psychology:** General. **Public administration:** Social work. **Social sciences:** International relations, sociology. **Visual/performing arts:** Studio arts. **Other:** Natural Sciences.

**Computing on campus.** 70 workstations in dormitories, library, computer center, student center. Dormitories wired for high-speed internet access and linked to campus network. Commuter students can connect to campus network. Helpline, wireless network available.

**Student life. Freshman orientation:** Mandatory. Preregistration for classes offered. One-day programs held in June and August. **Housing:** Guaranteed on-campus for all undergraduates. Coed dorms available. **Activities:** Campus ministries, choral groups, dance, drama, international student organizations, literary magazine, music ensembles, radio station, student government, student newspaper, student government association, social work club, foreign language club, speech pathology and audiology club, Student Ambassadors organization, affirmative action committee, student nurse association.

**Athletics.** NCAA. **Intercollegiate:** Baseball M, basketball, cross-country, field hockey W, golf M, lacrosse W, soccer, softball W, swimming, volleyball. **Intramural:** Baseball M, basketball, cross-country, field hockey W, golf M, lacrosse W, soccer, softball W, swimming, volleyball. **Team name:** Blazers.

**Student services.** Adult student services, alcohol/substance abuse counseling, campus ministries, career counseling, student employment services, financial aid counseling, health services, minority student services, personal counseling, placement for graduates. **Physically disabled:** Services for visually, speech, hearing impaired.

**Contact.** E-mail: admissions@elms.edu
Phone: (413) 592-3189 Toll-free number: (800) 255-3567
Fax: (413) 594-2781
Joseph Wagner, Director of Admission, Elms College, 291 Springfield Street, Chicopee, MA 01013

---

## Emerson College
**Boston, Massachusetts**
www.emerson.edu

CB member
CB code: 3367

- Private 4-year college of communication and the arts
- Residential campus in very large city
- 3,293 degree-seeking undergraduates: 2% part-time, 55% women, 3% African American, 5% Asian American, 7% Hispanic American, 1% Native American, 2% international
- 904 degree-seeking graduate students
- 45% of applicants admitted
- SAT or ACT with writing, application essay required
- 72% graduate within 6 years; 12% enter graduate study

**General.** Founded in 1880. Regionally accredited. **Degrees:** 840 bachelor's awarded; master's, doctoral offered. **Calendar:** Semester, limited summer session. **Full-time faculty:** 159 total; 71% have terminal degrees, 14% minority, 45% women. **Part-time faculty:** 222 total; 35% have terminal degrees, 10% minority, 45% women. **Class size:** 62% < 20, 28% 20-39, 7% 40-49, 3% 50-99. **Special facilities:** 2 radio stations, 3 theaters, sound treated television studios, integrated digital newsroom, seven clinics/programs to observe speech and hearing therapy, media center, marketing research suite, film production facilities (with AVID nonlinear editing system), performance and production center.

**Freshman class profile.** 4,981 applied, 2,221 admitted, 843 enrolled.

| Mid 50% test scores | | GPA 2.0-2.99: | 3% |
|---|---|---|---|
| SAT critical reading: | 590-680 | Rank in top quarter: | 79% |
| SAT math: | 550-650 | Rank in top tenth: | 42% |
| SAT writing: | 580-670 | Return as sophomores: | 87% |
| ACT composite: | 25-29 | Out-of-state: | 80% |
| GPA 3.50 or higher: | 71% | Live on campus: | 98% |
| GPA 3.0-3.49: | 26% | International: | 2% |

**Basis for selection.** Secondary school record, recommendations, writing competency, and personal qualities as seen in extracurricular activities, community involvement, demonstrated leadership important. Applicants for programs in performing arts must submit resume of theater-related activities and either audition or interview, or submit a portfolio or an essay.

**High school preparation.** 16 units required; 20 recommended. Required and recommended units include English 4, mathematics 3, social studies 3, science 3, foreign language 3 and academic electives 4.

**2008-2009 Annual costs.** Tuition/fees (projected): $28,969. Room/board: $11,832. Books/supplies: $720. Personal expenses: $1,250.

**2007-2008 Financial aid. Need-based:** 627 full-time freshmen applied for aid; 454 were judged to have need; 454 of these received aid. Average need met was 75%. Average scholarship/grant was $12,900; average loan $3,698. 54% of total undergraduate aid awarded as scholarships/grants, 46% as loans/jobs. **Non-need-based:** Awarded to 651 full-time undergraduates, including 232 freshmen. Scholarships awarded for academics, music/drama. **Additional information:** Massachusetts Loan Plan available for parents of dependent undergraduates.

**Application procedures. Admission:** Closing date 1/5 (postmark date). $65 fee, may be waived for applicants with need. Application may be submitted online. Admission notification 4/1. Must reply by May 1 or within 2 week(s) if notified thereafter. **Financial aid:** Priority date 3/1; no closing date. FAFSA, CSS PROFILE required. Applicants notified by 4/1; must reply by 5/1 or within 3 week(s) of notification.

**Academics. Special study options:** Cross-registration, double major, honors, independent study, internships, liberal arts/career combination, student-designed major, study abroad, teacher certification program. Cross-registration available with Suffolk University and 6-member Boston ProArts Consortium (Berklee College of Music, Boston Architectural Center, Boston Conservatory, Massachusetts College of Art, and the School of the Museum of Fine Arts). **Credit/placement by examination:** AP, CLEP, IB, SAT, ACT, institutional tests. 32 credit hours maximum toward bachelor's degree. SAT or ACT math score may be used to waive semester course of math requirements. **Support services:** Learning center, reduced course load, study skills assistance, tutoring, writing center.

**Majors. Business:** Communications, marketing. **Communications:** General, advertising, broadcast journalism, journalism, media studies, political, public relations, publishing. **Education:** Autistic, Deaf/hearing impaired, drama/dance, speech, speech impaired. **English:** Creative writing, speech/rhetoric. **Health:** Audiology/hearing, audiology/speech pathology, communication disorders, speech pathology. **Visual/performing arts:** General, acting, cinematography, directing/producing, dramatic, film/cinema, play/screenwriting, theater arts management, theater design.

**Most popular majors.** Business/marketing 12%, communications/journalism 33%, English 18%, visual/performing arts 33%.

**Computing on campus.** 458 workstations in dormitories, library, computer center, student center. Dormitories wired for high-speed internet access and linked to campus network. Commuter students can connect to campus network. Online course registration, helpline, repair service, wireless network available.

**Student life. Freshman orientation:** Mandatory, $126 fee. Preregistration for classes offered. Four-day event preceding first day of classes. **Housing:** Coed dorms, substance-free housing available. $300 nonrefundable deposit, deadline 5/1. Living/learning communities available. **Activities:** Choral groups, dance, drama, film society, literary magazine, musical theater, radio station, student government, student newspaper, TV station, Hillel, Newman Club, Goodnews Fellowship, Islamic community, Alliance of Gays and Lesbians and Everyone, Latino student organization, international club, Earth Emerson, Asian Students for Intercultural Awareness, Amnesty International.

**Athletics.** NCAA. **Intercollegiate:** Baseball M, basketball, cross-country, golf, lacrosse, soccer, softball W, tennis, track and field, volleyball W. **Team name:** Lions.

**Student services.** Adult student services, campus ministries, career counseling, student employment services, financial aid counseling, health services, minority student services, personal counseling, placement for graduates. **Physically disabled:** Services for visually, speech, hearing impaired.

**Contact.** E-mail: admission@emerson.edu
Phone: (617) 824-8600 Fax: (617) 824-8609
Sara Ramirez, Director of Undergraduate Admission, Emerson College, 120 Boylston Street, Boston, MA 02116-4624

---

## Emmanuel College

**Boston, Massachusetts**
**www.emmanuel.edu**

CB member
CB code: 3368

- Private 4-year liberal arts college affiliated with Roman Catholic Church
- Residential campus in very large city
- 2,139 degree-seeking undergraduates: 23% part-time, 73% women, 6% African American, 2% Asian American, 4% Hispanic American, 1% international
- 179 degree-seeking graduate students
- 61% of applicants admitted
- SAT or ACT (ACT writing optional), application essay required
- 58% graduate within 6 years

**General.** Founded in 1919. Regionally accredited. Member of the Colleges of the Fenway consortium, which enables cross-registration with Massachusetts College of Pharmacy & Health Services, Wentworth Institute of Technology, Simmons College, Massachusetts College of Art, and Wheelock College. **Degrees:** 442 bachelor's awarded; master's offered. **ROTC:** Army. **Calendar:** Semester, limited summer session. **Full-time faculty:** 86 total; 79% have terminal degrees, 14% minority, 65% women. **Part-time faculty:** 132 total; 42% have terminal degrees, 4% minority, 64% women. **Class size:** 63% < 20, 37% 20-39.

**Freshman class profile.** 4,142 applied, 2,518 admitted, 582 enrolled.

| Mid 50% test scores | | | |
|---|---|---|---|
| SAT critical reading: | 480-580 | GPA 3.0-3.49: | 35% |
| SAT math: | 460-560 | GPA 2.0-2.99: | 25% |
| SAT writing: | 490-580 | Return as sophomores: | 80% |
| ACT composite: | 20-24 | Out-of-state: | 40% |
| GPA 3.50 or higher: | 40% | Live on campus: | 94% |
| | | International: | 2% |

**Basis for selection.** High school curriculum and record most important, followed by recommendations, test scores, essay, creativity, initiative. Interview recommended. **Homeschooled:** Portfolio, on-campus interview recommended.

**High school preparation.** 16 units recommended. Recommended units include English 4, mathematics 3, social studies 2, science 2 (laboratory 2) and foreign language 2.

**2007-2008 Annual costs.** Tuition/fees: $26,250. Room/board: $11,200. Books/supplies: $880. Personal expenses: $1,935.

**2007-2008 Financial aid. Need-based:** 516 full-time freshmen applied for aid; 475 were judged to have need; 475 of these received aid. Average need met was 76%. Average scholarship/grant was $15,007; average loan $4,055. 72% of total undergraduate aid awarded as scholarships/grants, 28% as loans/jobs. **Non-need-based:** Awarded to 656 full-time undergraduates, including 207 freshmen. Scholarships awarded for academics, alumni affiliation, leadership.

**Application procedures. Admission:** Priority date 12/1; deadline 3/1 (postmark date). $40 fee, may be waived for applicants with need. Application may be submitted online. Admission notification on a rolling basis beginning on or about 12/1. Must reply by May 1 or within 2 week(s) if notified thereafter. **Financial aid:** Priority date 4/1; no closing date. FAFSA, institutional form required. Applicants notified on a rolling basis starting 3/15.

**Academics.** Interdepartmental program allows students to concentrate in 2 departments. Internship offerings available in all areas of study. **Special study options:** Accelerated study, cross-registration, double major, exchange student, honors, independent study, internships, liberal arts/career combination, student-designed major, study abroad, teacher certification program, Washington semester. Degree completion opportunities at corporate sites for non-traditional students. **Credit/placement by examination:** AP, CLEP, IB, SAT, ACT, institutional tests. 32 credit hours maximum toward bachelor's degree. **Support services:** Learning center, pre-admission summer program, remedial instruction, study skills assistance, tutoring, writing center.

**Majors. Area/ethnic studies:** American. **Biology:** General, biochemistry, biostatistics. **Business:** Business admin. **Communications:** General. **Conservation:** Environmental studies. **Education:** Elementary, secondary. **English:** English lit. **Foreign languages:** Spanish. **Health:** Art therapy, nursing (RN). **History:** General. **Interdisciplinary:** Global studies, neuroscience. **Liberal arts:** Arts/sciences. **Math:** General. **Physical sciences:** Chemistry. **Psychology:** General, counseling, developmental. **Social sciences:** Political science, sociology. **Visual/performing arts:** Graphic design, studio arts.

**Most popular majors.** Business/marketing 28%, communications/journalism 9%, health sciences 10%, psychology 10%, social sciences 8%.

**Computing on campus.** 145 workstations in dormitories, library, computer center, student center. Dormitories wired for high-speed internet access and linked to campus network. Commuter students can connect to campus network. Online course registration, online library, helpline, student web hosting, wireless network available.

**Student life. Freshman orientation:** Mandatory, $100 fee. Preregistration for classes offered. Summer and fall program. **Policies:** No alcohol permitted on campus. **Housing:** Guaranteed on-campus for all undergraduates. Coed dorms, special housing for disabled, substance-free housing available. $200 nonrefundable deposit, deadline 5/1. **Activities:** Pep band, campus ministries, choral groups, dance, drama, international student organizations, literary magazine, musical theater, radio station, student government, student newspaper, symphony orchestra, Black student union, College Democrats, political forum, feminist coalition, Helping Unite Emmanuel Latinos to Lead & Achieve Success, peace and justice club, Republican club, social awareness club.

**Athletics.** NCAA. **Intercollegiate:** Basketball, cross-country, soccer, softball W, tennis W, track and field, volleyball. **Team name:** Saints.

**Student services.** Adult student services, alcohol/substance abuse counseling, campus ministries, career counseling, student employment services, financial aid counseling, health services, minority student services, personal counseling, placement for graduates. **Physically disabled:** Services for visually, speech, hearing impaired.

**Contact.** E-mail: enroll@emmanuel.edu
Phone: (617) 735-9715 Fax: (617) 735-9801
Sandra Robbins, Dean of Enrollment Management, Emmanuel College, 400 The Fenway, Boston, MA 02115

---

## Endicott College
### Beverly, Massachusetts
**CB member**
www.endicott.edu
**CB code: 3369**

- Private 4-year liberal arts college
- Residential campus in large town
- 2,128 degree-seeking undergraduates: 8% part-time, 57% women
- 344 degree-seeking graduate students
- 48% of applicants admitted
- SAT or ACT with writing, application essay required
- 64% graduate within 6 years

**General.** Founded in 1939. Regionally accredited. **Degrees:** 443 bachelor's, 6 associate awarded; master's offered. **ROTC:** Army, Air Force. **Location:** 24 miles from Boston. **Calendar:** 4-1-4, limited summer session. **Full-time faculty:** 74 total; 57% have terminal degrees, 5% minority, 51% women. **Part-time faculty:** 88 total; 30% have terminal degrees, 2% minority, 62% women. **Class size:** 52% < 20, 48% 20-39. **Special facilities:** Student-run restaurant/classroom, archives museum.

**Freshman class profile.** 3,549 applied, 1,709 admitted, 520 enrolled.

| Mid 50% test scores | | | |
|---|---|---|---|
| SAT critical reading: | 490-580 | Rank in top quarter: | 41% |
| SAT math: | 490-590 | Rank in top tenth: | 10% |
| SAT writing: | 490-570 | Return as sophomores: | 83% |
| ACT composite: | 21-24 | Out-of-state: | 58% |
| | | Live on campus: | 97% |

**Basis for selection.** School achievement record and SAT/ACT scores most important. Class rank, essay, volunteer work, extracurricular activities, leadership also important. Teacher, counselor recommendations considered. Interview recommended. **Homeschooled:** Verification that curriculum has been certified by local school system or state, or GED.

**High school preparation.** 16 units recommended. Recommended units include English 4, mathematics 3, social studies 2, history 1, science 2 and academic electives 4. One chemistry with laboratory and algebra required for nursing and athletic training programs.

**2007-2008 Annual costs.** Tuition/fees: $22,950. Room/board: $10,800. Books/supplies: $1,000. Personal expenses: $1,000.

**2007-2008 Financial aid. Need-based:** 334 full-time freshmen applied for aid; 276 were judged to have need; 275 of these received aid. Average need met was 57%. Average scholarship/grant was $7,267; average loan $3,710. 62% of total undergraduate aid awarded as scholarships/grants, 38% as loans/jobs. **Non-need-based:** Awarded to 620 full-time undergraduates, including 157 freshmen. Scholarships awarded for academics, alumni affiliation, art, leadership, ROTC, state residency.

**Application procedures. Admission:** Closing date 2/15. $40 fee, may be waived for applicants with need. Application may be submitted online. Admission notification on a rolling basis beginning on or about 11/1. Must reply by May 1 or within 1 week(s) if notified thereafter. **Financial aid:** Priority date 3/15; no closing date. FAFSA, institutional form required. Applicants notified on a rolling basis starting 3/15; must reply within 2 week(s) of notification.

**Academics. Special study options:** Accelerated study, combined bachelor's/graduate degree, cross-registration, distance learning, honors, independent study, internships, liberal arts/career combination, student-designed major, study abroad, teacher certification program. **Credit/placement by examination:** AP, CLEP, IB, SAT, institutional tests. 32 credit hours maximum toward bachelor's degree. **Support services:** Learning center, reduced course load, remedial instruction, study skills assistance, tutoring, writing center.

**Majors. Biology:** Biotechnology. **Business:** Accounting, business admin, hospitality admin. **Communications:** General. **Computer sciences:** Computer science. **Conservation:** Environmental studies. **Education:** Early childhood, elementary. **English:** English lit. **Foreign languages:** Spanish. **Health:** Art therapy, athletic training, nursing (RN). **History:** General. **Interdisciplinary:** Global studies. **Liberal arts:** Arts/sciences. **Parks/recreation:** Sports admin. **Protective services:** Criminal justice. **Psychology:** General. **Visual/performing arts:** Design, interior design.

**Most popular majors.** Business/marketing 27%, communications/journalism 7%, education 7%, health sciences 9%, liberal arts 7%, parks/recreation 11%, psychology 9%, security/protective services 7%, visual/performing arts 10%.

---

**Computing on campus.** 167 workstations in library, computer center. Dormitories wired for high-speed internet access and linked to campus network. Commuter students can connect to campus network. Online course registration, online library, helpline, repair service, wireless network available.

**Student life. Freshman orientation:** Available. Preregistration for classes offered. **Housing:** Guaranteed on-campus for freshmen. Coed dorms, single-sex dorms, apartments, substance-free housing available. $500 deposit, deadline 5/1. Single-parent housing, suite-type, modular housing available. **Activities:** Jazz band, campus ministries, choral groups, dance, drama, international student organizations, literary magazine, music ensembles, Model UN, musical theater, radio station, student government, student newspaper, TV station, intercultural club, Phi Theta Kappa, ALANA, Christian fellowship, political debate society, Rotaract Service Club.

**Athletics.** NCAA. **Intercollegiate:** Baseball M, basketball, cross-country, equestrian, field hockey W, football (tackle) M, golf M, lacrosse, soccer, softball W, tennis, volleyball. **Intramural:** Basketball, football (non-tackle), racquetball, soccer, softball, volleyball. **Team name:** Gulls.

**Student services.** Alcohol/substance abuse counseling, campus ministries, career counseling, financial aid counseling, health services, personal counseling.

**Contact.** E-mail: admissio@endicott.edu
Phone: (978) 921-1000 Toll-free number: (800) 325-1114
Fax: (978) 232-2520
Thomas Redman, Vice President for Admissions and Financial Aid, Endicott College, 376 Hale Street, Beverly, MA 01915-9985

---

## Fitchburg State College
### Fitchburg, Massachusetts
**CB member**
www.fsc.edu
**CB code: 3518**

- Public 4-year liberal arts and teachers college
- Residential campus in small city
- 3,605 degree-seeking undergraduates: 12% part-time, 55% women, 3% African American, 2% Asian American, 3% Hispanic American, 1% international
- 957 degree-seeking graduate students
- 66% of applicants admitted
- SAT or ACT (ACT writing optional), application essay required
- 47% graduate within 6 years

**General.** Founded in 1894. Regionally accredited. **Degrees:** 622 bachelor's awarded; master's offered. **ROTC:** Army. **Location:** 50 miles from Boston, 25 miles from Worcester. **Calendar:** Semester, limited summer session. **Full-time faculty:** 176 total; 90% have terminal degrees, 12% minority, 50% women. **Part-time faculty:** 78 total; 24% have terminal degrees, 3% minority, 53% women. **Class size:** 44% < 20, 55% 20-39, less than 1% 40-49. **Special facilities:** Teacher education laboratory school, 120-acre conservation area.

**Freshman class profile.** 3,391 applied, 2,230 admitted, 708 enrolled.

| Mid 50% test scores | | | |
|---|---|---|---|
| SAT critical reading: | 440-560 | GPA 2.0-2.99: | 54% |
| SAT math: | 460-560 | Return as sophomores: | 75% |
| SAT writing: | 450-540 | Out-of-state: | 9% |
| ACT composite: | 17-22 | Live on campus: | 69% |
| GPA 3.50 or higher: | 17% | Fraternities: | 1% |
| GPA 3.0-3.49: | 29% | Sororities: | 3% |

**Basis for selection.** Secondary school record, test scores, essay important. Recommendations considered. Interview recommended for nursing, undeclared major, computer science, business administration, communications/media majors. **Learning Disabled:** Students with professionally diagnosed learning disabilities exempt from standardized test requirements.

**High school preparation.** 16 units required. Required units include English 4, mathematics 3, social studies 1, history 1, science 3 (laboratory 2), foreign language 2 and academic electives 2. Additional units of math and science preferred for nursing, medical technology, computer science, business applicants.

**2007-2008 Annual costs.** Tuition/fees: $5,992; $12,072 out-of-state. Room/board: $6,632. Books/supplies: $600. Personal expenses: $1,500.

**Financial aid. Non-need-based:** Scholarships awarded for academics, alumni affiliation, leadership, state residency.

**Application procedures. Admission:** Priority date 1/1; no deadline. $10 fee ($40 out-of-state), may be waived for applicants with need. Application may be submitted online. Admission notification on a rolling basis beginning on or about 12/1. Must reply by May 1 or within 2 week(s) if notified thereafter. **Financial aid:** Priority date 2/1; no closing date. FAFSA required. Applicants notified on a rolling basis starting 3/15; must reply within 2 week(s) of notification.

**Academics.** Many major programs include internship, practicum, or clinical experience. All degree programs require completion of 60 credits in liberal arts and sciences. **Special study options:** Cross-registration, distance learning, double major, dual enrollment of high school students, honors, independent study, internships, liberal arts/career combination, student-designed major, study abroad, teacher certification program. **Credit/placement by examination:** AP, CLEP, institutional tests. 60 credit hours maximum toward bachelor's degree. **Support services:** Learning center, pre-admission summer program, reduced course load, remedial instruction, study skills assistance, tutoring, writing center.

**Honors college/program.** Selected freshmen students invited to join Leadership Academy based on high school preparation, test scores, and leadership potential. Students complete integrated sequence of courses over 4-year period. Students expected to demonstrate leadership through extracurricular activities, volunteer positions, and service learning placements. 25 new students accepted into program annually and 3.3 GPA required to continue.

**Majors. Architecture:** Technology. **Biology:** General, biotechnology, environmental, exercise physiology. **Business:** Accounting, business admin, finance, international, management science, marketing. **Communications:** General, digital media. **Computer sciences:** General, computer science. **Education:** General, biology, early childhood, elementary, English, geography, history, mathematics, middle, secondary, special, technology/industrial arts, trade/industrial. **Engineering technology:** Architectural, construction, electrical, energy systems, industrial, manufacturing. **English:** Creative writing, English lit, technical writing. **Health:** Nursing (RN). **History:** General. **Liberal arts:** Arts/sciences. **Math:** General. **Parks/recreation:** Exercise sciences, sports admin. **Protective services:** Criminal justice. **Psychology:** General, developmental, industrial. **Public administration:** Human services. **Social sciences:** Economics, geography, international economics, political science, sociology. **Visual/performing arts:** Cinematography, dramatic, graphic design, photography, theater design.

**Most popular majors.** Business/marketing 15%, education 14%, liberal arts 11%, security/protective services 7%, visual/performing arts 16%.

**Computing on campus.** PC or laptop required. 150 workstations in dormitories, library, computer center, student center. Dormitories wired for high-speed internet access and linked to campus network. Commuter students can connect to campus network. Online course registration, online library, helpline, wireless network available.

**Student life. Freshman orientation:** Mandatory. Preregistration for classes offered. Testing, academic advising, registration for classes key components of program. **Housing:** Coed dorms, special housing for disabled, apartments, substance-free housing available. $150 nonrefundable deposit, deadline 5/1. Quiet halls available. **Activities:** Bands, choral groups, dance, drama, literary magazine, radio station, student government, student newspaper, Christian Fellowship, black student union, Habitat for Humanity, Haitian American culture club, Latin American student organization, international student union, MASSPIRG, peer educators, rescue squad.

**Athletics.** NCAA. **Intercollegiate:** Baseball M, basketball, cross-country, field hockey W, football (tackle) M, ice hockey M, lacrosse W, soccer, softball W, track and field. **Intramural:** Basketball, bowling, football (nontackle), racquetball, soccer, softball, volleyball. **Team name:** Falcons.

**Student services.** Alcohol/substance abuse counseling, career counseling, services for economically disadvantaged, student employment services, financial aid counseling, health services, on-campus daycare, personal counseling. **Physically disabled:** Services for visually, speech, hearing impaired. **Learning disabled:** Comprehensive services available.

**Contact.** E-mail: admissions@fsc.edu
Phone: (978) 665-3144 Toll-free number: (800) 705-9692
Fax: (978) 665-4540
Pamela McCafferty, Dean of Enrollment Management, Fitchburg State College, 160 Pearl Street, Fitchburg, MA 01420-2697

---

## Framingham State College
**Framingham, Massachusetts**
www.framingham.edu

**CB member**
**CB code: 3519**

- Public 4-year liberal arts and teachers college
- Residential campus in small city

---

- 3,503 degree-seeking undergraduates: 12% part-time, 65% women, 4% African American, 2% Asian American, 4% Hispanic American, 1% international
- 778 degree-seeking graduate students
- 56% of applicants admitted
- SAT or ACT with writing required
- 43% graduate within 6 years

**General.** Founded in 1839. Regionally accredited. **Degrees:** 714 bachelor's awarded; master's offered. **ROTC:** Army. **Location:** 20 miles from Boston. **Calendar:** Semester, extensive summer session. **Full-time faculty:** 168 total; 81% have terminal degrees, 4% minority, 54% women. **Part-time faculty:** 65 total; 45% have terminal degrees, 8% minority, 55% women. **Class size:** 45% < 20, 54% 20-39, less than 1% 40-49, less than 1% 50-99. **Special facilities:** Greenhouse, early childhood demonstration lab, education curriculum library, learning center.

**Freshman class profile.** 3,940 applied, 2,208 admitted, 641 enrolled.

| Mid 50% test scores | | | |
|---|---|---|---|
| SAT critical reading: | 470-560 | Rank in top quarter: | 30% |
| SAT math: | 470-560 | Rank in top tenth: | 7% |
| GPA 3.50 or higher: | 19% | Return as sophomores: | 73% |
| GPA 3.0-3.49: | 32% | Out-of-state: | 5% |
| GPA 2.0-2.99: | 49% | Live on campus: | 76% |

**Basis for selection.** Strength of high school curriculum, weighted high school GPA, class rank, test scores most important. Some attention given to organized and volunteer activities, recommendations and special talents. Consideration given to students whose educational opportunities have been limited due to economic disadvantage. Admission standards policy of Massachusetts Board of Higher Education requires minimum of 16 college-preparatory courses with weighted GPA of 3.0. Students with lower GPA may qualify based on sliding scale combining SAT scores with GPA. Essay recommended. Portfolio required of studio art majors. **Homeschooled:** Students may be required to submit results of additional nationally normed tests, such as SAT Subject Tests. **Learning Disabled:** Students with diagnosed learning disability must submit individualized educational plan/504 plan along with all psychoeducational testing current within last 3 years.

**High school preparation.** 16 units required; 21 recommended. Required and recommended units include English 4, mathematics 3-4, social studies 1, history 1-2, science 3-4 (laboratory 2-3), foreign language 2-4 and academic electives 2. Math must include algebra I, algebra II, and geometry. Additional unit of math strongly recommended for computer science, math, pre-engineering, and science majors. Additional units of biology, chemistry, physics recommended for science majors. Foreign language must be 2 units of same language. All units must be college-preparatory level.

**2007-2008 Annual costs.** Tuition/fees: $5,799; $11,879 out-of-state. Fees include mandatory laptop purchase by new students. New England Regional tuition rate $1455. Room/board: $7,017. Books/supplies: $800. Personal expenses: $1,200.

**2006-2007 Financial aid. Need-based:** 579 full-time freshmen applied for aid; 369 were judged to have need; 369 of these received aid. Average need met was 79%. Average scholarship/grant was $4,238; average loan $3,401. 35% of total undergraduate aid awarded as scholarships/grants, 65% as loans/jobs. **Non-need-based:** Awarded to 129 full-time undergraduates, including 36 freshmen. Scholarships awarded for academics.

**Application procedures. Admission:** Priority date 2/15; deadline 5/15 (postmark date). $25 fee ($40 out-of-state), may be waived for applicants with need. Application may be submitted online. Admission notification on a rolling basis beginning on or about 1/15. Must reply by May 1 or within 2 week(s) if notified thereafter. Late applications may be considered. Some majors and on-campus housing may be filled by priority filing date of 2/15. Application fee waiver available to in-state students who submit College Board fee waiver. **Financial aid:** Priority date 3/1; no closing date. FAFSA required. Applicants notified on a rolling basis starting 4/15; must reply by 5/1 or within 2 week(s) of notification.

**Academics. Special study options:** Cross-registration, distance learning, double major, honors, independent study, internships, liberal arts/career combination, study abroad, teacher certification program, Washington semester. Pre-engineering program in conjunction with University of Massachusetts at Amherst, University of Massachusetts at Dartmouth, University of Massachusetts at Lowell. **Credit/placement by examination:** AP, CLEP, IB, institutional tests. 64 credit hours maximum toward bachelor's degree. **Support services:** Learning center, reduced course load, study skills assistance, tutoring, writing center.

**Majors. Agriculture:** Food science. **Biology:** General. **Business:** General, knowledge management. **Computer sciences:** General. **Education:** Early childhood, elementary. **English:** English lit. **Family/consumer sciences:** General, clothing/textiles, food/nutrition. **Foreign languages:** General. **Health:** Nursing (RN). **History:** General. **Liberal arts:** Arts/sciences. **Math:** General. **Physical sciences:** Chemistry. **Psychology:** General. **Social sciences:** Economics, geography, political science, sociology. **Visual/performing arts:** Art.

**Most popular majors.** Business/marketing 15%, communication technologies 9%, education 8%, English 7%, family/consumer sciences 11%, liberal arts 7%, psychology 10%, social sciences 11%.

**Computing on campus.** PC or laptop required. 232 workstations in dormitories, library, computer center, student center. Dormitories wired for high-speed internet access and linked to campus network. Commuter students can connect to campus network. Online course registration, online library, helpline, wireless network available.

**Student life. Freshman orientation:** Mandatory. Preregistration for classes offered. 1-day orientation offered in June, followed up by additional day in late August or early September. **Housing:** Coed dorms, single-sex dorms, substance-free housing available. $150 nonrefundable deposit, deadline 5/1. **Activities:** Choral groups, dance, drama, literary magazine, musical theater, radio station, student government, student newspaper, active sociologists, Hispanic student club, black student union, Christian Fellowship, Hillel, Newman Association, student union activities board, MASSPIRG, international student union.

**Athletics.** NCAA. **Intercollegiate:** Baseball M, basketball, cross-country, field hockey W, football (tackle) M, ice hockey M, lacrosse W, soccer, softball W, volleyball W. **Intramural:** Basketball, football (non-tackle), golf, lacrosse, soccer, softball, volleyball, weight lifting. **Team name:** Rams.

**Student services.** Adult student services, alcohol/substance abuse counseling, campus ministries, career counseling, services for economically disadvantaged, student employment services, financial aid counseling, health services, minority student services, personal counseling, placement for graduates, veterans' counselor, women's services. **Physically disabled:** Services for visually, hearing impaired.

**Contact.** E-mail: admiss@frc.mass.edu
Phone: (508) 626-4500 Fax: (508) 626-4017
Elizabeth Canella, Associate Dean of Admissions, Framingham State College, 100 State Street, Framingham, MA 01701-9101

## Franklin W. Olin College of Engineering
**Needham, Massachusetts**
**www.olin.edu**                    CB code: 2824

- Private 4-year engineering college
- Residential campus in large town
- 296 degree-seeking undergraduates: 43% women, 2% African American, 10% Asian American, 4% Hispanic American, 2% international
- 11% of applicants admitted
- SAT or ACT with writing, SAT Subject Tests, application essay required

**General.** Regionally accredited. **Degrees:** 71 bachelor's awarded. **Location:** 14 miles from Boston. **Calendar:** Semester. **Full-time faculty:** 31 total; 100% have terminal degrees, 16% minority, 39% women. **Part-time faculty:** 8 total; 88% have terminal degrees, 38% women. **Class size:** 52% < 20, 45% 20-39, 3% 40-49.

**Freshman class profile.** 1,054 applied, 111 admitted, 74 enrolled.

| Mid 50% test scores | | End year in good standing: | 99% |
|---|---|---|---|
| SAT critical reading: | 690-780 | Return as sophomores: | 95% |
| SAT math: | 740-800 | Out-of-state: | 85% |
| SAT writing: | 670-760 | Live on campus: | 100% |
| ACT composite: | 33-36 | International: | 5% |

**Basis for selection.** Secondary school achievement, course rigor, test scores, personal character most important; creativity and entrepreneurial spirit also very important. Cultural, economic, geographic diversity encouraged. After a review of all applications, a group of applicants chosen as candidates. Candidates required to attend 1 of 2 weekends on campus to participate in design project, individual interviews, and team exercises. Incoming class selected from this group. 2 SAT Subject Tests required: Math (Level 2 preferred, Level 1 accepted) and any science subject. **Homeschooled:** Statement describing homeschool structure and mission, transcript of courses and grades, letter of recommendation (nonparent) required.

**High school preparation.** Required units include English 4, mathematics 4, social studies 2, history 2, science 3 (laboratory 3) and foreign language 2. Require at least one year of calculus and one year of physics prior to high school graduation.

**2007-2008 Annual costs.** Every admitted student receives 4-year full-tuition scholarship; $11,400 room/board and $1,425 required fees for academic year. Books/supplies: $750.

**2007-2008 Financial aid. Need-based:** 34 full-time freshmen applied for aid; 8 were judged to have need; 8 of these received aid. Average need met was 100%. Average scholarship/grant was $8,583; average loan $1,458. 77% of total undergraduate aid awarded as scholarships/grants, 23% as loans/jobs. **Non-need-based:** Awarded to 299 full-time undergraduates, including 80 freshmen. Scholarships awarded for academics, leadership. **Additional information:** No financial aid forms necessary.

**Application procedures. Admission:** Closing date 12/1 (postmark date). $70 fee, may be waived for applicants with need. Application must be submitted online. Admission notification 3/21. Must reply by 5/1. **Financial aid:** Priority date 2/15; no closing date. FAFSA required. Applicants notified on a rolling basis starting 3/31; must reply by 5/1.

**Academics. Special study options:** Combined bachelor's/graduate degree, cross-registration, exchange student, independent study, internships, liberal arts/career combination, student-designed major, study abroad. **Credit/placement by examination:** AP, CLEP, institutional tests. **Support services:** Tutoring, writing center.

**Majors. Engineering:** General, electrical, mechanical.

**Computing on campus.** PC or laptop required. Dormitories wired for high-speed internet access and linked to campus network. Commuter students can connect to campus network. Online course registration, online library, helpline, repair service, student web hosting, wireless network available.

**Student life. Freshman orientation:** Available. **Policies:** All students sign honor code that addresses personal and academic integrity. **Housing:** Guaranteed on-campus for all undergraduates. Coed dorms available. **Activities:** Jazz band, choral groups, dance, drama, film society, music ensembles, musical theater, student government, symphony orchestra, Christian club, Support, Encourage and Recognize Volunteerism, international club, Korean club, political caucus, martial arts club.

**Athletics. Intramural:** Basketball, football (non-tackle), ice hockey, racquetball, soccer, softball, squash, tennis, volleyball.

**Student services.** Alcohol/substance abuse counseling, campus ministries, career counseling, financial aid counseling, health services, personal counseling, placement for graduates, women's services.

**Contact.** E-mail: info@olin.edu
Phone: (781) 292-2222 Fax: (781) 292-2210
Charles Nolan, Dean of Admission, Franklin W. Olin College of Engineering, Olin Way, Needham, MA 02492-1245

## Gordon College
**Wenham, Massachusetts**                    CB member
**www.gordon.edu**                           CB code: 3417

- Private 4-year liberal arts college affiliated with nondenominational tradition
- Residential campus in small town
- 1,521 degree-seeking undergraduates: 2% part-time, 63% women, 2% African American, 1% Asian American, 3% Hispanic American, 2% international
- 36 degree-seeking graduate students
- 71% of applicants admitted
- SAT or ACT with writing, application essay, interview required
- 71% graduate within 6 years

**General.** Founded in 1889. Regionally accredited. 100 acres of extensive woodlands and five ponds, full ropes course. **Degrees:** 374 bachelor's awarded; master's offered. **ROTC:** Army, Air Force. **Location:** 25 miles from Boston. **Calendar:** Semester, limited summer session. **Full-time faculty:** 90 total. **Part-time faculty:** 50 total. **Class size:** 65% < 20, 25% 20-39, 4% 40-49, 4% 50-99, 1% >100. **Special facilities:** Christian studies center, international office for Christians in the Visual Arts, electron microscope, gene sequencing machine, Shakespearean folios, center for balance and mobility.

**Freshman class profile.** 1,574 applied, 1,122 admitted, 458 enrolled.

| Mid 50% test scores | | | |
|---|---|---|---|
| SAT critical reading: | 530-650 | Rank in top tenth: | 32% |
| SAT math: | 520-630 | End year in good standing: | 94% |
| SAT writing: | 530-640 | Return as sophomores: | 85% |
| ACT composite: | 22-28 | Out-of-state: | 77% |
| Rank in top quarter: | 61% | Live on campus: | 99% |
| | | International: | 3% |

**Basis for selection.** High school course selection and grades, rank in class, essay of Christian commitment, test scores, references, interview important. School and community activities considered. SAT Subject Tests not required but may be used for placement. Audition required of music majors. Portfolio required of visual art majors. **Homeschooled:** Statement describing homeschool structure and mission, transcript of courses and grades, letter of recommendation (nonparent) required. Information regarding course of study, including description of curriculum and reading list, required. **Learning Disabled:** Students with diagnosed learning disability may submit documentation with application, as well as any learning plans used through high school.

**High school preparation.** 20 units required; 25 recommended. Required and recommended units include English 4, mathematics 2-3, social studies 2-3, science 2-3 (laboratory 1-3), foreign language 2-4 and academic electives 5. Academic profile should include AP, honors, or accelerated courses.

**2007-2008 Annual costs.** Tuition/fees: $25,748. Room/board: $6,906. Books/supplies: $800. Personal expenses: $1,000.

**2006-2007 Financial aid. Need-based:** 320 full-time freshmen applied for aid; 260 were judged to have need; 259 of these received aid. Average need met was 66%. Average scholarship/grant was $10,967; average loan $2,963, 58% of total undergraduate aid awarded as scholarships/grants, 42% as loans/jobs. **Non-need-based:** Awarded to 537 full-time undergraduates, including 291 freshmen. Scholarships awarded for academics, alumni affiliation, leadership, minority status, music/drama, religious affiliation.

**Application procedures. Admission:** Priority date 3/1; no deadline. $50 fee, may be waived for applicants with need. Application may be submitted online. Admission notification on a rolling basis beginning on or about 12/15. Must reply by May 1 or within 2 week(s) if notified thereafter. **Financial aid:** Closing date 3/1. FAFSA, CSS PROFILE required. Applicants notified on a rolling basis starting 4/15; must reply by 5/1 or within 2 week(s) of notification.

**Academics.** Study abroad in England, France, Israel, Italy, Egypt, Russia, China, Canada, Belize, Latin America, Uganda. Extensive domestic programs include marine biology, film studies in Hollywood. Great Books Honors Program in Jerusalem and Athens. Outdoor education immersion semester in urban Boston, South Africa. **Special study options:** Cooperative education, cross-registration, double major, honors, independent study, internships, liberal arts/career combination, student-designed major, study abroad, teacher certification program, urban semester, Washington semester. Gordon-in-Boston; Oregon Extension; co-op programs in arts, business, computer science, education, engineering, health professions, humanities, natural science, social/behavioral science. **Credit/placement by examination:** AP, CLEP, IB, SAT, institutional tests. **Support services:** Learning center, reduced course load, remedial instruction, study skills assistance, tutoring, writing center.

**Majors. Biology:** General, exercise physiology. **Business:** Accounting, business admin, finance. **Communications:** General. **Computer sciences:** Computer science. **Education:** Early childhood, elementary, middle, music, secondary, special. **English:** English lit. **Foreign languages:** General, French, German, Spanish. **History:** General. **Math:** General. **Parks/recreation:** General. **Philosophy/religion:** Christian, philosophy. **Physical sciences:** Chemistry, physics. **Psychology:** General. **Public administration:** Social work. **Social sciences:** Economics, international relations, political science, sociology. **Theology:** Youth ministry. **Visual/performing arts:** Art, dramatic, music performance.

**Most popular majors.** Biology 7%, business/marketing 8%, communications/journalism 7%, education 9%, English 9%, history 7%, philosophy/religious studies 9%, psychology 10%, visual/performing arts 8%.

**Computing on campus.** 125 workstations in dormitories, library, computer center, student center. Dormitories wired for high-speed internet access and linked to campus network. Commuter students can connect to campus network. Online library, helpline, repair service, wireless network available.

**Student life. Freshman orientation:** Mandatory. Preregistration for classes offered. 4-day program prior to fall semester. **Policies:** No alcohol or smoking allowed. Religious observance required. **Housing:** Guaranteed on-campus for freshmen. Coed dorms, single-sex dorms, special housing for disabled, apartments, substance-free housing available. $250 nonrefundable deposit. International hall, mentoring hall, theme houses. **Activities:** Bands, choral groups, drama, film society, literary magazine, music ensembles, musical theater, student government, student newspaper, symphony orchestra,

Society for New Politics, Advocates for Cultural Diversity, Christians for Social Action, fellowship group for children of missionaries, ministry to deaf persons, outreach service, short-term mission trips, Amnesty International, ALANA.

**Athletics.** NCAA. **Intercollegiate:** Baseball M, basketball, cross-country, field hockey W, golf, lacrosse, soccer, softball W, swimming, tennis, track and field, volleyball W. **Intramural:** Basketball, football (non-tackle), racquetball, soccer, softball, table tennis, volleyball. **Team name:** Fighting Scots.

**Student services.** Alcohol/substance abuse counseling, campus ministries, career counseling, student employment services, financial aid counseling, health services, minority student services, personal counseling, placement for graduates. **Physically disabled:** Services for visually, speech, hearing impaired.

**Contact.** E-mail: admissions@gordon.edu
Phone: (978) 867-4218 Toll-free number: (866) 464-6736
Fax: (978) 867-4682
Barbara Layne, Director of Admissions, Gordon College, 255 Grapevine Road, Wenham, MA 01984

---

## Hampshire College
**Amherst, Massachusetts**
www.hampshire.edu

CB member
CB code: 3447

- Private 4-year liberal arts college
- Residential campus in large town
- 1,412 degree-seeking undergraduates: 57% women, 4% African American, 4% Asian American, 5% Hispanic American, 1% Native American, 3% international
- 55% of applicants admitted
- Application essay required
- 71% graduate within 6 years; 10% enter graduate study

**General.** Founded in 1965. Regionally accredited. **Degrees:** 314 bachelor's awarded. **ROTC:** Army. **Location:** 90 miles from Boston, 20 miles from Springfield. **Calendar:** 4-1-4. **Full-time faculty:** 95 total; 84% have terminal degrees, 14% minority, 54% women. **Part-time faculty:** 54 total; 78% have terminal degrees, 18% minority, 46% women. **Class size:** 72% < 20, 28% 20-39, less than 1% 40-49. **Special facilities:** Bioshelter (integrated greenhouse/aquaculture facility), farm center, electronic music production studio, extensive film and photography facilities, fabrication center, national Yiddish book center, museum of picturebook art.

**Freshman class profile.** 2,571 applied, 1,421 admitted, 400 enrolled.

| Mid 50% test scores | | | |
|---|---|---|---|
| SAT critical reading: | 610-710 | GPA 2.0-2.99: | 19% |
| SAT math: | 540-660 | Rank in top quarter: | 58% |
| SAT writing: | 590-700 | Rank in top tenth: | 28% |
| ACT composite: | 25-30 | Return as sophomores: | 78% |
| GPA 3.50 or higher: | 47% | Out-of-state: | 85% |
| GPA 3.0-3.49: | 34% | Live on campus: | 99% |
| | | International: | 4% |

**Basis for selection.** Criteria include desire to do rigorous independent work, school record, academic writing samples, recommendations, school and community activities. Interview recommended.

**High school preparation.** 19 units required. Required units include English 4, mathematics 4, social studies 2, history 2, science 4 (laboratory 2) and foreign language 3.

**2008-2009 Annual costs.** Tuition/fees: $38,649. Room/board: $10,080. Books/supplies: $500. Personal expenses: $500.

**2007-2008 Financial aid. Need-based:** 255 full-time freshmen applied for aid; 227 were judged to have need; 226 of these received aid. Average need met was 97%. Average scholarship/grant was $23,880; average loan $3,000. 79% of total undergraduate aid awarded as scholarships/grants, 21% as loans/jobs. **Non-need-based:** Awarded to 646 full-time undergraduates, including 235 freshmen. Scholarships awarded for academics, leadership, minority status.

**Application procedures. Admission:** Priority date 11/15; deadline 1/15 (receipt date). $55 fee, may be waived for applicants with need. Application may be submitted online. Admission notification 4/1. Must reply by May 1 or within 2 week(s) if notified thereafter. **Financial aid:** Priority date 2/1; no closing date. FAFSA, CSS PROFILE required. Applicants notified by 4/1; Applicants notified on a rolling basis starting 4/1; must reply by 5/1 or within 2 week(s) of notification.

**Academics.** All students pursue individualized program of study. Requirements for graduation not based on credit, but on completion of division one courses in all 5 schools, an independent concentration consisting of combination of courses, independent project work, year-long thesis. **Special study options:** Exchange student, independent study, internships, student-designed major, study abroad, teacher certification program. Member 5-college consortium; may take classes at other member institutions. **Credit/placement by examination:** AP, CLEP, IB. **Support services:** Writing center.

**Majors. Agriculture:** Animal sciences. **Architecture:** Environmental design. **Area/ethnic studies:** African-American, American, Asian, Asian-American, Hispanic-American/Latino/Chicano, Latin American, women's. **Biology:** General. **Business:** General, international. **Communications:** General. **Computer sciences:** General, computer graphics, computer science. **Education:** General, early childhood, elementary, secondary. **English:** American lit, British lit, English lit. **Family/consumer sciences:** Family studies, food/nutrition. **Foreign languages:** Comparative lit, linguistics. **Health:** Predental, premedicine, preveterinary. **History:** General. **Interdisciplinary:** Behavioral sciences, biological/physical sciences, biopsychology, global studies, math/computer science, natural sciences, nutrition sciences, peace/conflict, science/society. **Legal studies:** General. **Liberal arts:** Arts/sciences. **Math:** General. **Philosophy/religion:** Judaic, philosophy, religion. **Physical sciences:** Chemistry, geology, physics. **Psychology:** General. **Social sciences:** General, anthropology, demography, economics, political science, sociology, urban studies. **Visual/performing arts:** General, art, art history/conservation, cinematography, dance, design, dramatic, drawing, film/cinema, multimedia, painting, photography, play/screenwriting, sculpture, studio arts.

**Most popular majors.** Area/ethnic studies 11%, biology 7%, English 12%, social sciences 17%, visual/performing arts 25%.

**Computing on campus.** 215 workstations in library, computer center, student center. Dormitories wired for high-speed internet access and linked to campus network. Commuter students can connect to campus network. Online course registration, helpline, student web hosting, wireless network available.

**Student life. Freshman orientation:** Mandatory, $140 fee. Preregistration for classes offered. Program held during week immediately before matriculation. **Policies:** Students design individual concentrations of study, test theory with off-campus study and community service, and complete original research and projects. **Housing:** Guaranteed on-campus for freshmen. Coed dorms, special housing for disabled, apartments available. $200 non-refundable deposit, deadline 5/1. **Activities:** Jazz band, choral groups, dance, drama, film society, music ensembles, student government, student newspaper, forum of international students, Excaliber, Jewish students, poetry club.

**Student services.** Career counseling, financial aid counseling, health services, minority student services, on-campus daycare, personal counseling, women's services. **Physically disabled:** Services for visually, hearing impaired.

**Contact.** E-mail: admissions@hampshire.edu
Phone: (413) 559-5471 Toll-free number: (877) 937-4267
Fax: (413) 559-5631
Karen Parker, Director of Admissions, Hampshire College, 893 West Street, Amherst, MA 01002-9988

---

## Harvard College
**Cambridge, Massachusetts**
www.college.harvard.edu

**CB member**
**CB code: 3434**

- Private 4-year university
- Residential campus in small city
- 6,648 degree-seeking undergraduates: 50% women, 8% African American, 16% Asian American, 7% Hispanic American, 1% Native American, 10% international
- 12,248 degree-seeking graduate students
- 9% of applicants admitted
- SAT or ACT with writing, SAT Subject Tests, application essay, interview required
- 97% graduate within 6 years

**General.** Founded in 1636. Regionally accredited. Harvard College is the undergraduate program within Harvard University, part of the faculty of arts and sciences, and offers programs in liberal arts. **Degrees:** 1,696 bachelor's awarded; master's, doctoral, first professional offered. **ROTC:** Army, Naval, Air Force. **Location:** 3 miles from Boston. **Calendar:** Semester, extensive summer session. **Full-time faculty:** 1,622 total; 99% have terminal degrees, 13% minority, 30% women. **Part-time faculty:** 450 total; 99% have terminal degrees, 16% minority, 35% women. **Special facilities:** Museum of Scandinavian and Germanic art, experimental forest in New York state, center for study of Italian Renaissance in Florence, Italy, center for

Byzantine studies in Washington, DC, Smithsonian astrophysical observatory.

**Freshman class profile.** 22,955 applied, 2,108 admitted, 1,659 enrolled.

| Mid 50% test scores | | | |
|---|---|---|---|
| SAT critical reading: | 700-800 | Rank in top quarter: | 100% |
| SAT math: | 700-790 | Rank in top tenth: | 95% |
| SAT writing: | 690-790 | Return as sophomores: | 96% |
| ACT composite: | 31-35 | Out-of-state: | 84% |
| | | International: | 10% |

**Basis for selection.** Secondary school record most important; character, creative ability in some discipline or activity, leadership, liveliness of mind, demonstrated stamina and ability to carry out demanding college program, and strong sense of social responsibility important. Any 3 SAT Subject Tests required. Interview with alumnus/alumna required of all applicants if possible; documentation of special talents encouraged.

**High school preparation.** Recommended units include English 4, mathematics 4, social studies 3, history 2, science 4 and foreign language 4. Applicants encouraged to take rigorous courses and make the most of any opportunities for enrichment.

**2007-2008 Annual costs.** Tuition/fees: $34,998. Room/board: $10,622.

**2007-2008 Financial aid.** All financial aid based on need. 1,072 full-time freshmen applied for aid; 906 were judged to have need; 906 of these received aid. Average need met was 100%. Average scholarship/grant was $34,806; average loan $3,631. 91% of total undergraduate aid awarded as scholarships/grants, 9% as loans/jobs. **Additional information:** Institution meets full need of all admitted students.

**Application procedures. Admission:** Priority date 12/1; deadline 1/1 (postmark date). $65 fee, may be waived for applicants with need. Application may be submitted online. Admission notification 4/1. Must reply by 5/1. **Financial aid:** Closing date 2/1. FAFSA required. CSS PROFILE required of all US citizens and US permanent residents plus all Canadians. Applicants notified by 4/1; must reply by 5/1 or within 2 week(s) of notification.

**Academics.** Require 12 one-term courses for completion of major and 32 one-term courses for graduation. **Special study options:** Accelerated study, cross-registration, double major, exchange student, honors, independent study, internships, student-designed major, study abroad, teacher certification program. **Credit/placement by examination:** AP, CLEP, IB, institutional tests. SAT Subject Test policy varies depending on subject matter and score. Sophomore standing available on basis of 4 AP exams with qualifying scores, or on basis of IB scores. Students with fewer than 4 AP qualifying scores eligible for placement in more challenging courses. **Support services:** Learning center, tutoring, writing center.

**Majors. Area/ethnic studies:** African-American, East Asian, Near/Middle Eastern, women's. **Biology:** General, biochemistry, evolutionary, neurobiology/physiology. **Computer sciences:** Computer science. **Conservation:** Environmental studies. **Engineering:** Science. **English:** English lit. **Foreign languages:** Ancient Greek, classics, comparative lit, German, Latin, linguistics, Romance, Sanskrit, Slavic. **History:** General, science/technology. **Interdisciplinary:** Classical/archaeology. **Liberal arts:** Arts/sciences. **Math:** General, applied, statistics. **Philosophy/religion:** Philosophy, religion. **Physical sciences:** Chemistry, geology, molecular physics, physics. **Psychology:** General. **Social sciences:** General, anthropology, economics, political science, sociology. **Visual/performing arts:** General, art history/conservation.

**Most popular majors.** Biology 12%, English 6%, history 9%, physical sciences 6%, psychology 8%, social sciences 38%.

**Computing on campus.** 605 workstations in dormitories, library, computer center. Dormitories wired for high-speed internet access and linked to campus network. Commuter students can connect to campus network. Online course registration, helpline, repair service available.

**Student life. Freshman orientation:** Mandatory. Week-long program in early September. **Housing:** Guaranteed on-campus for all undergraduates. Coed dorms, special housing for disabled, apartments available. All freshmen live together. Other students and some faculty members reside in 13 on-campus houses, self-contained communities offering seminars and tutorials. **Activities:** Bands, choral groups, dance, drama, film society, literary magazine, music ensembles, musical theater, opera, radio station, student government, student newspaper, symphony orchestra, TV station, over 320 official clubs available.

**Athletics.** NCAA. **Intercollegiate:** Baseball M, basketball, cross-country, diving, fencing, field hockey W, football (tackle) M, golf, ice hockey, lacrosse, rowing (crew), sailing, skiing, soccer, softball W, squash, swimming, tennis, track and field, volleyball, water polo, wrestling M. **Intramural:** Badminton, basketball, cross-country, equestrian, fencing, field hockey

W, football (tackle) M, gymnastics W, ice hockey, rowing (crew), rugby, sailing, skiing, soccer, softball, squash, swimming, table tennis, tennis, track and field, volleyball, wrestling M. **Team name:** Crimson.

**Student services.** Alcohol/substance abuse counseling, campus ministries, career counseling, services for economically disadvantaged, student employment services, financial aid counseling, health services, on-campus daycare, personal counseling, placement for graduates. **Physically disabled:** Services for visually, speech, hearing impaired.

**Contact.** E-mail: college@fas.harvard.edu
Phone: (617) 495-1551 Fax: (617) 495-8821
William Fitzsimmons, Dean of Admissions, Harvard College, 86 Brattle Street, Cambridge, MA 02138

## Hellenic College/Holy Cross
### Brookline, Massachusetts
www.hchc.edu

CB member
CB code: 3449

- Private 4-year liberal arts and seminary college affiliated with Eastern Orthodox Church
- Residential campus in large town
- 72 degree-seeking undergraduates: 32% women
- 115 degree-seeking graduate students
- 81% of applicants admitted
- SAT or ACT (ACT writing optional), application essay, interview required

**General.** Founded in 1937. Regionally accredited. **Degrees:** 22 bachelor's awarded; master's, first professional offered. **Location:** 5 miles from downtown Boston. **Calendar:** Semester, limited summer session. **Full-time faculty:** 14 total; 79% have terminal degrees, 50% women. **Part-time faculty:** 19 total; 47% have terminal degrees, 21% women. **Class size:** 49% < 20, 51% 20-39.

**Freshman class profile.** 36 applied, 29 admitted, 17 enrolled.

| Mid 50% test scores | | | |
|---|---|---|---|
| SAT critical reading: | 480-620 | GPA 3.0-3.49: | 60% |
| SAT math: | 460-520 | GPA 2.0-2.99: | 30% |
| SAT writing: | 430-610 | End year in good standing: | 85% |
| ACT composite: | 21-27 | Out-of-state: | 90% |
| GPA 3.50 or higher: | 10% | Live on campus: | 95% |

**Basis for selection.** High school achievement, GPA, 2 recommendations from instructors, test scores very important, school and community activities also important. For religious studies majors, 2 letters from clergy important if members of Orthodox Christian Church. **Homeschooled:** Transcript of courses and grades, state high school equivalency certificate required.

**High school preparation.** 15 units required. Required units include English 4, mathematics 2, social studies 2, history 2, science 3 and foreign language 2.

**2007-2008 Annual costs.** Tuition/fees: $17,325. Room/board: $10,890. Books/supplies: $1,000. Personal expenses: $1,500.

**Financial aid.** All financial aid based on need.

**Application procedures. Admission:** Priority date 5/1; deadline 8/15 (receipt date). $50 fee, may be waived for applicants with need. Application may be submitted online. Admission notification on a rolling basis. Students who apply by December 1 eligible to have application fee waived and receive priority consideration for scholarships; early applications encouraged. **Financial aid:** Closing date 4/1. FAFSA, institutional form required. Applicants notified on a rolling basis starting 10/1; must reply within 2 week(s) of notification.

**Academics. Special study options:** Cross-registration, exchange student, honors, independent study, internships, liberal arts/career combination, study abroad. **Credit/placement by examination:** AP, CLEP, IB, institutional tests. Credit granted varies by degree program. **Support services:** Tutoring.

**Majors. Education:** Elementary. **Family/consumer sciences:** Family studies. **Foreign languages:** Classics. **Liberal arts:** Arts/sciences. **Psychology:** General. **Theology:** Theology.

**Computing on campus.** Online library, wireless network available.

**Student life. Freshman orientation:** Available. **Policies:** Religious observance required for some students. **Housing:** Guaranteed on-campus for freshmen. Single-sex dorms, apartments available. $300 nonrefundable deposit.

**Activities:** Campus ministries, choral groups, dance, drama, music ensembles, student government, several Orthodox groups, prison ministry, missions group.

**Athletics. Intramural:** Basketball, soccer M, table tennis, tennis, volleyball.

**Student services.** Campus ministries, career counseling, student employment services, financial aid counseling, health services, personal counseling, placement for graduates.

**Contact.** E-mail: admissions@hchc.edu
Phone: (617) 850-1260 Toll-free number: (866) 424-2338
Fax: (617) 850-1460
Sonia Belcher, Director of Admissions and Records, Hellenic College/Holy Cross, 50 Goddard Avenue, Brookline, MA 02445

## Lasell College
### Newton, Massachusetts
www.lasell.edu

CB member
CB code: 3481

- Private 4-year business and liberal arts college
- Residential campus in small city
- 1,304 degree-seeking undergraduates: 2% part-time, 70% women, 6% African American, 3% Asian American, 5% Hispanic American, 2% international
- 82 degree-seeking graduate students
- 65% of applicants admitted
- SAT or ACT (ACT writing optional) required
- 51% graduate within 6 years

**General.** Founded in 1851. Regionally accredited. **Degrees:** 205 bachelor's awarded; master's offered. **Location:** 8 miles from Boston. **Calendar:** Semester. **Full-time faculty:** 57 total; 47% have terminal degrees, 9% minority, 67% women. **Part-time faculty:** 102 total; 11% have terminal degrees, 6% minority, 65% women. **Class size:** 66% < 20, 34% 20-39. **Special facilities:** Community based learning center, art and cultural center hosting an antique clothing collection, center for research on aging and intergenerational studies.

**Freshman class profile.** 2,775 applied, 1,816 admitted, 428 enrolled.

| Mid 50% test scores | | | |
|---|---|---|---|
| SAT critical reading: | 440-530 | Rank in top quarter: | 20% |
| SAT math: | 450-530 | Rank in top tenth: | 5% |
| GPA 3.50 or higher: | 10% | Return as sophomores: | 61% |
| GPA 3.0-3.49: | 23% | Out-of-state: | 53% |
| GPA 2.0-2.99: | 64% | Live on campus: | 93% |
| | | International: | 1% |

**Basis for selection.** Academic GPA, curriculum, class rank, interview, recommendations, extracurricular activities, and standardized test scores considered. Submission of an essay optional. Interview recommended.

**High school preparation.** 15 units required; 21 recommended. Required and recommended units include English 4, mathematics 3-4, social studies 2-3, history 2-3, science 2-3 (laboratory 2) and foreign language 2.

**2007-2008 Annual costs.** Tuition/fees: $21,850. Room/board: $9,550. Books/supplies: $1,000. Personal expenses: $2,000.

**2007-2008 Financial aid. Need-based:** Average need met was 69%. Average scholarship/grant was $12,006; average loan $3,400. 61% of total undergraduate aid awarded as scholarships/grants, 39% as loans/jobs. **Non-need-based:** Scholarships awarded for academics, alumni affiliation.

**Application procedures. Admission:** Priority date 3/15; no deadline. $40 fee, may be waived for applicants with need. Application may be submitted online. Admission notification on a rolling basis beginning on or about 12/15. Must reply by May 1 or within 2 week(s) if notified thereafter. **Financial aid:** Priority date 3/1; no closing date. FAFSA, institutional form required. Applicants notified on a rolling basis starting 2/15; must reply by 5/1 or within 2 week(s) of notification.

**Academics.** Free tutoring in writing, math, statistics, accounting, sciences, psychology, study skills, and other academic subjects. **Special study options:** Double major, honors, independent study, internships, liberal arts/career combination, semester at sea, student-designed major, study abroad, teacher certification program. Fifth-year master of science in management program. **Credit/placement by examination:** AP, CLEP, IB, SAT, ACT, institutional tests. **Support services:** Learning center, reduced course load, study skills assistance, tutoring.

**Majors. Business:** Accounting, accounting/business management, accounting/finance, business admin, entrepreneurial studies, fashion, finance, hospitality admin, hotel/motel admin, international, marketing, tourism/travel. **Communications:** General, advertising, digital media, journalism, media studies, public relations, radio/tv. **Conservation:** Environmental studies. **Education:** Early childhood, elementary, English, history, mathematics, secondary. **English:** Creative writing, English lit. **Family/consumer sciences:** Fashion consultant. **Health:** Athletic training. **History:** General. **Legal studies:** General, prelaw. **Liberal arts:** Humanities. **Parks/recreation:** Exercise sciences, sports admin. **Protective services:** Law enforcement admin. **Psychology:** General. **Public administration:** Human services. **Social sciences:** General, sociology. **Visual/performing arts:** Fashion design, graphic design. **Other:** Sport communication.

**Most popular majors.** Business/marketing 43%, liberal arts 7%, parks/recreation 7%, psychology 6%, social sciences 12%, visual/performing arts 13%.

**Computing on campus.** 175 workstations in dormitories, library, computer center, student center. Dormitories wired for high-speed internet access and linked to campus network. Commuter students can connect to campus network. Online course registration, online library, helpline, wireless network available.

**Student life. Freshman orientation:** Mandatory, $40 fee. Preregistration for classes offered. **Housing:** Guaranteed on-campus for all undergraduates. Coed dorms, single-sex dorms, substance-free housing available. $400 non-refundable deposit, deadline 5/1. Community service, wellness, and special interest housing available. **Activities:** Jazz band, campus ministries, choral groups, dance, drama, literary magazine, music ensembles, musical theater, radio station, student government, student newspaper.

**Athletics.** NCAA. **Intercollegiate:** Baseball M, basketball, cross-country, field hockey W, lacrosse, soccer, softball W, volleyball. **Intramural:** Basketball, football (non-tackle), soccer, softball, volleyball. **Team name:** Lasers.

**Student services.** Alcohol/substance abuse counseling, campus ministries, career counseling, student employment services, financial aid counseling, health services, personal counseling, placement for graduates.

**Contact.** E-mail: info@lasell.edu
Phone: (617) 243-2225 Toll-free number: (888) 527-3554
Fax: (617) 243-2380
James Tweed, Director of Undergraduate Admission, Lasell College, 1844 Commonwealth Avenue, Newton, MA 02466

## Lesley University
**Cambridge, Massachusetts**
www.lesley.edu/lc
**CB member**
**CB code: 3483**

- Private 4-year liberal arts and teachers college
- Residential campus in very large city
- 1,225 degree-seeking undergraduates: 6% part-time, 75% women, 5% African American, 4% Asian American, 5% Hispanic American, 2% international
- 4,662 degree-seeking graduate students
- 86% of applicants admitted
- SAT or ACT with writing, application essay, interview required
- 63% graduate within 6 years

**General.** Founded in 1909. Regionally accredited. Lesley University includes 2 undergraduate colleges, Lesley College and The Art Institute of Boston. Main campus in Cambridge. **Degrees:** 390 bachelor's awarded; master's, doctoral offered. **Calendar:** Semester, limited summer session. **Full-time faculty:** 72 total; 72% have terminal degrees, 14% minority, 60% women. **Part-time faculty:** 173 total; 25% have terminal degrees, 54% women. **Class size:** 76% < 20, 23% 20-39, less than 1% 40-49. **Special facilities:** Center for teaching resources, media production facility, fine arts studios.

**Freshman class profile.** 1,568 applied, 1,342 admitted, 343 enrolled.

| Mid 50% test scores | | | |
|---|---|---|---|
| SAT critical reading: | 450-600 | GPA 2.0-2.99: | 48% |
| SAT math: | 460-560 | Rank in top quarter: | 25% |
| SAT writing: | 480-580 | Rank in top tenth: | 15% |
| ACT composite: | 20-26 | Return as sophomores: | 70% |
| GPA 3.50 or higher: | 15% | Out-of-state: | 53% |
| GPA 3.0-3.49: | 36% | Live on campus: | 90% |
| | | International: | 2% |

**Basis for selection.** Primary focus given to academic record, both grades and challenging courses. Test scores, recommendations, interview, community service, leadership experience also considered.

**High school preparation.** 18 units required; 20 recommended. Required and recommended units include English 4, mathematics 3-4, social studies 1-2, history 1-2, science 3-4 (laboratory 2), foreign language 2 and academic electives 4.

**2008-2009 Annual costs.** Tuition/fees: $27,510. Room/board: $12,000. Books/supplies: $700. Personal expenses: $1,975.

**2007-2008 Financial aid. Need-based:** 327 full-time freshmen applied for aid; 258 were judged to have need; 250 of these received aid. Average need met was 70%. Average scholarship/grant was $12,625; average loan $4,029. 51% of total undergraduate aid awarded as scholarships/grants, 49% as loans/jobs. **Non-need-based:** Awarded to 420 full-time undergraduates, including 128 freshmen. Scholarships awarded for academics, art, leadership, minority status, state residency.

**Application procedures. Admission:** Priority date 2/15; no deadline. $40 fee, may be waived for applicants with need. Application may be submitted online. Admission notification on a rolling basis beginning on or about 1/15. Must reply by May 1 or within 2 week(s) if notified thereafter. **Financial aid:** Priority date 2/15; no closing date. FAFSA required. Applicants notified on a rolling basis starting 2/15.

**Academics.** Students complete between 450 and 650 hours of significant internship experience that begins freshman year. **Special study options:** Accelerated study, combined bachelor's/graduate degree, cross-registration, distance learning, double major, dual enrollment of high school students, exchange student, honors, independent study, internships, liberal arts/career combination, New York semester, student-designed major, study abroad, teacher certification program, Washington semester. **Credit/placement by examination:** AP, CLEP, IB, SAT, ACT, institutional tests. 16 credit hours maximum toward bachelor's degree. **Support services:** Learning center, pre-admission summer program, reduced course load, study skills assistance, tutoring, writing center.

**Majors. Area/ethnic studies:** American. **Biology:** General. **Business:** Business admin. **Communications technology:** General. **Conservation:** Environmental studies. **Education:** General, art, early childhood, early childhood special, elementary, English, kindergarten/preschool, mathematics, middle, science, secondary, social studies, special. **English:** English lit. **Family/consumer sciences:** Child development, family studies. **Health:** Art therapy, health services. **Interdisciplinary:** Global studies, natural sciences. **Liberal arts:** Arts/sciences. **Math:** General. **Social sciences:** General. **Visual/performing arts:** Art, studio arts.

**Most popular majors.** Business/marketing 7%, liberal arts 40%, psychology 14%, visual/performing arts 22%.

**Computing on campus.** 195 workstations in dormitories, library, computer center, student center. Dormitories wired for high-speed internet access and linked to campus network. Commuter students can connect to campus network. Online course registration, online library, helpline, wireless network available.

**Student life. Freshman orientation:** Mandatory. Begins 1 week prior to start of classes. **Housing:** Guaranteed on-campus for all undergraduates. Coed dorms, single-sex dorms, substance-free housing available. $300 deposit. Themed housing. **Activities:** Campus ministries, choral groups, dance, drama, film society, international student organizations, literary magazine, musical theater, student government, student newspaper, Women for Social Justice, Hillel, Third Wave Women's Group, Prism, Students For a Free Tibet, ALANA, Christian Fellowship.

**Athletics.** NCAA. **Intercollegiate:** Basketball, rowing (crew), soccer, softball W, volleyball. **Team name:** Lynx.

**Student services.** Adult student services, alcohol/substance abuse counseling, campus ministries, career counseling, student employment services, financial aid counseling, health services, minority student services, personal counseling, placement for graduates. **Physically disabled:** Services for visually, speech, hearing impaired. **Learning disabled:** Comprehensive services available.

**Contact.** E-mail: ugadm@lesley.edu
Phone: (617) 349-8800 Toll-free number: (800) 999-1959 ext. 8800
Fax: (617) 349-8810
Deb Kocar, Director of Admissions, Lesley University, 29 Everett Street, Cambridge, MA 02138-2790

## Massachusetts College of Art
**Boston, Massachusetts**
www.massart.edu
**CB member**
**CB code: 3516**

- Public 4-year visual arts college
- Residential campus in very large city

Four-Year Colleges

♦ 1,687 degree-seeking undergraduates: 11% part-time, 67% women, 3% African American, 6% Asian American, 6% Hispanic American, 1% Native American, 3% international
♦ 155 degree-seeking graduate students
♦ 56% of applicants admitted
♦ SAT or ACT with writing, application essay required
♦ 65% graduate within 6 years

**General.** Founded in 1873. Regionally accredited. **Degrees:** 277 bachelor's awarded; master's offered. **Calendar:** Semester, extensive summer session. **Full-time faculty:** 94 total. **Part-time faculty:** 197 total. **Class size:** 76% < 20, 24% 20-39, less than 1% 40-49. **Special facilities:** 7 art galleries, foundry, glass furnaces, ceramic kilns, video and film studios, performance and studio spaces, Polaroid 20X24 camera.

**Freshman class profile.** 1,315 applied, 735 admitted, 284 enrolled.

| Mid 50% test scores | | Rank in top quarter: | 45% |
|---|---|---|---|
| SAT critical reading: | 490-610 | Rank in top tenth: | 15% |
| SAT math: | 480-570 | Return as sophomores: | 82% |
| SAT writing: | 490-600 | Out-of-state: | 34% |
| GPA 3.50 or higher: | 31% | Live on campus: | 81% |
| GPA 3.0-3.49: | 44% | International: | 2% |
| GPA 2.0-2.99: | 25% | | |

**Basis for selection.** Emphasis on portfolio, academic record, essay, test scores, recommendations. Minimum GPA 3.0. For GPA between 2.0 and 2.9, SAT/ACT scores considered in combination with GPA on sliding scale. Applicants must meet Massachusetts public college admission standards. Portfolio of at least 15 pieces of artwork required, presented as 35 mm 2x2 slides. Work may also be submitted on VHS videotape or digital media. **Homeschooled:** General college preparatory program required for degree-seeking students. **Learning Disabled:** Testing may be waived for applicants with professionally certified learning disabilities.

**High school preparation.** 17 units required. Required units include English 4, mathematics 2, social studies 2, science 2 (laboratory 2), foreign language 2 and academic electives 2. At least 2 additional academic units of computer science, humanities, or visual and performing arts required. Additional math or science required. Social Studies requirement must include 1 U.S. history course. Foreign Language units must be in one language.

**2007-2008 Annual costs.** Tuition/fees: $7,450; $21,900 out-of-state. Tuition for New England resident students $13,000. Room/board: $10,360. Books/supplies: $2,000. Personal expenses: $1,250.

**2007-2008 Financial aid. Need-based:** 225 full-time freshmen applied for aid; 162 were judged to have need; 162 of these received aid. Average scholarship/grant was $6,572; average loan $3,611. 41% of total undergraduate aid awarded as scholarships/grants, 59% as loans/jobs. **Non-need-based:** Awarded to 205 full-time undergraduates, including 57 freshmen. Scholarships awarded for academics, art, leadership, state residency. **Additional information:** Tuition waiver available to Vietnam veterans.

**Application procedures. Admission:** Closing date 2/15. $30 fee ($65 out-of-state), may be waived for applicants with need. Application may be submitted online. Admission notification on a rolling basis. Must reply by May 1 or within 3 week(s) if notified thereafter. **Financial aid:** Priority date 3/1; no closing date. FAFSA required. Applicants notified on a rolling basis starting 3/15; must reply within 3 week(s) of notification.

**Academics.** Three-year certificates available. **Special study options:** Cross-registration, double major, exchange student, independent study, internships, liberal arts/career combination, student-designed major, study abroad. Member of American Independent Colleges of Art and Design (AICAD), College Academic Program Sharing (CAPS), Colleges of the Fenway, and Pro Arts Consortium. Exchange programs available in Holland, England, Germany, Ireland, Italy, France. Study abroad available in Spain, Greece, China, Mexico. **Credit/placement by examination:** CLEP, IB, institutional tests. **Support services:** Pre-admission summer program, reduced course load, remedial instruction, tutoring.

**Majors. Architecture:** Environmental design. **Education:** Art. **Visual/performing arts:** Art history/conservation, ceramics, cinematography, design, fashion design, fiber arts, film/cinema, graphic design, industrial design, metal/jewelry, multimedia, painting, photography, printmaking, sculpture, studio arts.

**Most popular majors.** Education 8%, visual/performing arts 92%.

**Computing on campus.** 250 workstations in library, computer center. Dormitories wired for high-speed internet access. Helpline, wireless network available.

**Student life. Freshman orientation:** Mandatory. **Housing:** Coed dorms available. $500 partly refundable deposit, deadline 5/1. Additional housing also available in Simmons College dorm. **Activities:** Dance, drama, film society, music ensembles, radio station, student government, student newspaper, TV station, minority student organization, gay/lesbian organization, student-run design firm, international student organization, nontraditional student organization.

**Athletics.** NCAA. **Intramural:** Basketball, cross-country, field hockey, football (non-tackle), ice hockey, soccer, softball W, table tennis, tennis, volleyball.

**Student services.** Adult student services, career counseling, student employment services, health services, personal counseling, placement for graduates, veterans' counselor. **Physically disabled:** Services for visually, hearing impaired.

**Contact.** E-mail: admissions@massart.edu
Phone: (617) 879-7222 Fax: (617) 879-7250
Lydia Polenco-Pena, Associate Director of Admissions, Massachusetts College of Art, 621 Huntington Avenue, Boston, MA 02115-5882

---

## Massachusetts College of Liberal Arts
**North Adams, Massachusetts**   CB member
**www.mcla.edu**   CB code: 3521

♦ Public 4-year liberal arts college
♦ Residential campus in large town
♦ 1,491 degree-seeking undergraduates: 11% part-time, 60% women, 4% African American, 1% Asian American, 4% Hispanic American
♦ 128 degree-seeking graduate students
♦ 71% of applicants admitted
♦ SAT or ACT (ACT writing optional), application essay required
♦ 48% graduate within 6 years

**General.** Founded in 1894. Regionally accredited. **Degrees:** 312 bachelor's awarded; master's offered. **Location:** 50 miles from Albany, New York, 120 miles from Boston. **Calendar:** Semester, limited summer session. **Full-time faculty:** 84 total; 76% have terminal degrees, 6% minority, 44% women. **Part-time faculty:** 96 total; 20% have terminal degrees, 48% women. **Class size:** 67% < 20, 33% 20-39, less than 1% 40-49.

**Freshman class profile.** 1,431 applied, 1,018 admitted, 354 enrolled.

| Mid 50% test scores | | GPA 2.0-2.99: | 54% |
|---|---|---|---|
| SAT critical reading: | 460-580 | End year in good standing: | 81% |
| SAT math: | 440-540 | Return as sophomores: | 71% |
| ACT composite: | 20-24 | Out-of-state: | 31% |
| GPA 3.50 or higher: | 15% | Live on campus: | 89% |
| GPA 3.0-3.49: | 31% | | |

**Basis for selection.** Secondary school record most important; test scores, essay also important; recommendations, extracurricular activities considered. Interview recommended. **Homeschooled:** State high school equivalency certificate required. **Learning Disabled:** Massachusetts law prohibits requiring standardized test scores from students with documented learning disabilities.

**High school preparation.** 16 units required. Required units include English 4, mathematics 3, science 3 (laboratory 2), foreign language 2 and academic electives 2.

**2007-2008 Annual costs.** Tuition/fees: $6,168; $17,474 out-of-state. Room/board: $7,309. Books/supplies: $700. Personal expenses: $1,300.

**2007-2008 Financial aid. Need-based:** 304 full-time freshmen applied for aid; 210 were judged to have need; 210 of these received aid. Average scholarship/grant was $5,426; average loan $2,060. 38% of total undergraduate aid awarded as scholarships/grants, 62% as loans/jobs. **Non-need-based:** Awarded to 241 full-time undergraduates, including 49 freshmen. Scholarships awarded for academics, alumni affiliation, art, leadership, minority status, music/drama.

**Application procedures. Admission:** Priority date 3/1; no deadline. $25 fee, may be waived for applicants with need. Application may be submitted online. Admission notification on a rolling basis beginning on or about 1/15. Must reply by May 1 or within 2 week(s) if notified thereafter. **Financial aid:** Priority date 3/1; no closing date. FAFSA, institutional form required. Applicants notified on a rolling basis starting 3/1; must reply by 5/1 or within 2 week(s) of notification.

**Academics. Special study options:** Cross-registration, distance learning, double major, dual enrollment of high school students, exchange student, honors, independent study, internships, liberal arts/career combination, student-designed major, study abroad, teacher certification program, Washington semester. **Credit/placement by examination:** AP, CLEP, IB, institutional tests. **Support services:** Learning center, pre-admission summer program, reduced course load, remedial instruction, tutoring, writing center.

**Majors. Biology:** General. **Business:** Business admin. **Computer sciences:** General. **Conservation:** Environmental studies. **Education:** General. **English:** English lit. **History:** General. **Math:** General. **Philosophy/religion:** Philosophy. **Physical sciences:** Physics. **Psychology:** General. **Social sciences:** Sociology. **Visual/performing arts:** General, arts management.

**Most popular majors.** Business/marketing 14%, English 28%, psychology 9%, social sciences 14%, visual/performing arts 11%.

**Computing on campus.** PC or laptop required. 125 workstations in dormitories, library, computer center. Dormitories linked to campus network. Helpline, wireless network available.

**Student life. Freshman orientation:** Mandatory, $75 fee. **Housing:** Guaranteed on-campus for all undergraduates. Coed dorms, special housing for disabled, apartments available. $100 nonrefundable deposit. **Activities:** Bands, choral groups, dance, drama, international student organizations, literary magazine, music ensembles, radio station, student government, student newspaper, TV station, interfaith association, Campus Christian Fellowship, Jewish student organization, Newman Club, Gay and Lesbian Allied student society, multicultural society.

**Athletics.** NCAA. **Intercollegiate:** Baseball M, basketball, cross-country, golf M, soccer, softball W, tennis W, volleyball W. **Intramural:** Basketball, bowling, equestrian, football (non-tackle), soccer, softball, swimming, tennis, volleyball, water polo M. **Team name:** Trailblazers.

**Student services.** Adult student services, career counseling, student employment services, health services, minority student services, personal counseling, placement for graduates, veterans' counselor, women's services. **Physically disabled:** Services for visually, hearing impaired.

**Contact.** E-mail: admissions@mcla.edu
Phone: (413) 662-5410 Toll-free number: (800) 292-6632
Fax: (413) 662-5179
Steve King, Assistant Dean of Enrollment Services; Director of Admission, Massachusetts College of Liberal Arts, 375 Church Street, North Adams, MA 01247

---

## Massachusetts College of Pharmacy and Health Sciences

**Boston, Massachusetts**
www.mcphs.edu

**CB member**
**CB code: 3512**

- Private 4-year health science and pharmacy college
- Commuter campus in very large city
- 2,411 degree-seeking undergraduates: 4% part-time, 68% women, 5% African American, 28% Asian American, 3% Hispanic American, 2% international
- 1,163 degree-seeking graduate students
- 65% of applicants admitted
- SAT or ACT (ACT writing optional), application essay required
- 69% graduate within 6 years

**General.** Founded in 1823. Regionally accredited. Member of Fenway College Consortium, 14-college library consortium, Worcester Consortium, and Manchester Area College Consortium. Students have access to Harvard Medical School library. Accelerated PharmD program available at Worcester campus and Manchester campus; physician assistant program offered at Boston and Manchester campuses. **Degrees:** 141 bachelor's awarded; master's, doctoral, first professional offered. **Calendar:** Semester, limited summer session. **Full-time faculty:** 188 total; 84% have terminal degrees, 60% women. **Part-time faculty:** 5 total; 80% have terminal degrees, 60% women. **Class size:** 13% < 20, 57% 20-39, 8% 40-49, 5% 50-99, 18% >100. **Special facilities:** Pharmacy practice lab, dental hygiene clinic, patient assessment lab, nursing skills and technology lab.

**Freshman class profile.** 2,517 applied, 1,638 admitted, 577 enrolled.

| Mid 50% test scores | | | |
|---|---|---|---|
| SAT critical reading: | 480-570 | Rank in top quarter: | 63% |
| SAT math: | 520-610 | Rank in top tenth: | 24% |
| SAT writing: | 490-580 | Return as sophomores: | 87% |
| ACT composite: | 21-25 | Out-of-state: | 50% |
| GPA 3.50 or higher: | 48% | Live on campus: | 77% |
| GPA 3.0-3.49: | 36% | International: | 2% |
| | | GPA 2.0-2.99: | 16% |

**Basis for selection.** School academic record most important, emphasis on math and science courses. Class rank, test scores, essays, counselor's

---

recommendation also very important. Student's interest, aptitude for pharmacy and allied health fields considered. **Homeschooled:** Require documentation of curriculum and program of study; equivalency exam. **Learning Disabled:** Must submit documents to Academic Support Services.

**High school preparation.** 18 units recommended. Recommended units include English 4, mathematics 3, social studies 1, history 1, science 2 (laboratory 2) and academic electives 5. Additional units of advanced math and science (especially chemistry) strongly recommended.

**2007-2008 Annual costs.** Tuition/fees: $22,700. Room/board: $11,720. Books/supplies: $800. Personal expenses: $2,040.

**2007-2008 Financial aid. Need-based:** 507 full-time freshmen applied for aid; 452 were judged to have need; 449 of these received aid. Average need met was 48%. Average scholarship/grant was $9,749; average loan $5,119. 25% of total undergraduate aid awarded as scholarships/grants, 75% as loans/jobs. **Non-need-based:** Awarded to 292 full-time undergraduates, including 113 freshmen. Scholarships awarded for academics.

**Application procedures. Admission:** Priority date 11/15; deadline 2/1 (postmark date). $70 fee, may be waived for applicants with need. Application may be submitted online. Admission notification on a rolling basis beginning on or about 1/10. Varies by program. **Financial aid:** Priority date 3/15; no closing date. FAFSA required. Applicants notified on a rolling basis.

**Academics.** Academic success seminars/workshops, peer mentors. **Special study options:** Accelerated study, combined bachelor's/graduate degree, cross-registration, distance learning, double major, dual enrollment of high school students, ESL, independent study, internships, liberal arts/career combination. **Credit/placement by examination:** AP, CLEP, IB, SAT, ACT, institutional tests. 6 credit hours maximum toward bachelor's degree. CLEP exams must be taken before student's first semester of enrollment in order for credit to be granted. **Support services:** Learning center, reduced course load, study skills assistance, tutoring, writing center.

**Majors. Health:** Dental hygiene, health services, medical radiologic technology/radiation therapy, nuclear medical technology, nursing (RN), premedicine, radiologic technology/medical imaging. **Physical sciences:** Chemistry. **Psychology:** Medical. **Other:** Pharmaceutical sciences/pharmaceutical marketing and management.

**Computing on campus.** 500 workstations in dormitories, library, computer center, student center. Dormitories wired for high-speed internet access and linked to campus network. Commuter students can connect to campus network. Online library, helpline, wireless network available.

**Student life. Freshman orientation:** Mandatory, $100 fee. Preregistration for classes offered. 2-day overnight program in summer; 1-day freshman parent orientation. **Policies:** ID's to be worn and displayed while on campus property. **Housing:** Guaranteed on-campus for freshmen. Coed dorms, substance-free housing available. $250 nonrefundable deposit, deadline 5/1. Women only floors available. **Activities:** Concert band, choral groups, dance, drama, international student organizations, music ensembles, musical theater, student government, student newspaper, symphony orchestra, Academy of Student Pharmacists, Kappa Psi fraternity, Vietnamese student association, student American dental hygienist association, black student union, physician assistant society, Academy of Students of Health Systems Pharmacy, campus activities board, student government association, Indian student organization.

**Athletics. Intramural:** Baseball, basketball, bowling, cross-country, field hockey W, football (non-tackle), golf, racquetball, soccer, softball, squash, table tennis, tennis, volleyball, water polo. **Team name:** Cardinals.

**Student services.** Adult student services, alcohol/substance abuse counseling, career counseling, student employment services, financial aid counseling, health services, minority student services, personal counseling, placement for graduates, veterans' counselor, women's services. **Physically disabled:** Services for visually, speech, hearing impaired.

**Contact.** E-mail: admissions@mcphs.edu
Phone: (617) 732-2850 Toll-free number: (800) 225-5506
Fax: (617) 732-2118
William Dunfey, Executive Director of Admissions, Massachusetts College of Pharmacy and Health Sciences, 179 Longwood Avenue, Boston, MA 02115-5896

---

## Massachusetts Institute of Technology

**Cambridge, Massachusetts**
web.mit.edu

**CB member**
**CB code: 3514**

- Private 4-year university
- Residential campus in small city

- 4,163 degree-seeking undergraduates: 1% part-time, 45% women, 7% African American, 26% Asian American, 12% Hispanic American, 1% Native American, 8% international
- 5,909 degree-seeking graduate students
- 12% of applicants admitted
- SAT Subject Tests, application essay required
- 93% graduate within 6 years; 48% enter graduate study

**General.** Founded in 1861. Regionally accredited. **Degrees:** 1,167 bachelor's awarded; master's, doctoral offered. **ROTC:** Army, Naval, Air Force. **Location:** One mile from Boston. **Calendar:** 4-1-4, limited summer session. **Full-time faculty:** 1,362 total; 91% have terminal degrees, 16% minority, 21% women. **Part-time faculty:** 443 total; 73% have terminal degrees, 8% minority, 24% women. **Class size:** 64% < 20, 19% 20-39, 4% 40-49, 9% 50-99, 3% >100. **Special facilities:** Museum, visual arts center, computer science and artificial intelligence laboratory, Institute for Soldier Nanotechnologies, Picower Institute for Learning and Memory.

**Freshman class profile.** 12,445 applied, 1,553 admitted, 1,067 enrolled.

| Mid 50% test scores | | End year in good standing: | 98% |
|---|---|---|---|
| SAT critical reading: | 660-760 | Return as sophomores: | 98% |
| SAT math: | 720-800 | Out-of-state: | 90% |
| SAT writing: | 660-750 | Live on campus: | 100% |
| ACT composite: | 31-34 | International: | 8% |
| Rank in top quarter: | 100% | Fraternities: | 51% |
| Rank in top tenth: | 97% | Sororities: | 28% |

**Basis for selection.** Holistic review of application. Important factors include character, creativity, grades, leadership, love of learning, personal accomplishments, quality of academic program, recommendations, resiliency, test scores. An applicant's context is considered. Non-native English speakers have the option of taking TOEFL in place of SAT Reasoning Test or ACT with Writing. Others must take SAT Reasoning Test or ACT with Writing. All students must take two SAT Subject Tests, one each in math and science. Interviews strongly recommended.

**High school preparation.** Recommended units include English 4, mathematics 4, social studies 2, science 4 and foreign language 2.

**2007-2008 Annual costs.** Tuition/fees: $34,986. Room/board: $10,400. Books/supplies: $1,114. Personal expenses: $1,700.

**2006-2007 Financial aid.** All financial aid based on need. 790 full-time freshmen applied for aid; 644 were judged to have need; 644 of these received aid. Average need met was 100%. Average scholarship/grant was $30,428; average loan $1,817. 86% of total undergraduate aid awarded as scholarships/grants, 14% as loans/jobs. **Additional information:** Filing deadline 2/15 for CSS PROFILE.

**Application procedures. Admission:** Closing date 1/1 (postmark date). $65 fee, may be waived for applicants with need. Application may be submitted online. Admission notification 3/20. Must reply by May 1 or within 2 week(s) if notified thereafter. **Financial aid:** Closing date 2/15. FAFSA, CSS PROFILE required. Applicants notified by 4/1; must reply by 5/1.

**Academics. Special study options:** Combined bachelor's/graduate degree, cooperative education, cross-registration, internships, semester at sea, study abroad, teacher certification program, Washington semester. Undergraduate research opportunities program; independent activities period; alternative freshman programs; cross-registration with Harvard University, Wellesley College, Massachusetts College of Art, School of the Museum of Fine Arts. **Credit/placement by examination:** AP, CLEP, IB, institutional tests. **Support services:** Learning center, pre-admission summer program, study skills assistance, tutoring, writing center.

**Majors. Architecture:** Architecture, urban/community planning. **Biology:** General. **Business:** General. **Communications:** Media studies. **Computer sciences:** Computer science. **Engineering:** Aerospace, biomedical, chemical, civil, electrical, environmental, materials, mechanical, nuclear, ocean. **English:** Creative writing, English lit. **Foreign languages:** General, linguistics. **History:** General. **Interdisciplinary:** Cognitive science, math/computer science, neuroscience, science/society. **Liberal arts:** Arts/sciences. **Math:** General. **Philosophy/religion:** Philosophy. **Physical sciences:** Chemistry, geology, physics. **Social sciences:** Anthropology, economics, political science.

**Most popular majors.** Biology 9%, business/marketing 8%, computer/information sciences 12%, engineering/engineering technologies 37%, mathematics 9%, physical sciences 11%.

**Computing on campus.** 1,100 workstations in dormitories, library, computer center, student center. Dormitories wired for high-speed internet access and linked to campus network. Commuter students can connect to campus network. Online course registration, online library, helpline, repair service, student web hosting, wireless network available.

**Student life. Freshman orientation:** Mandatory. Held last 2 weeks of August. Includes programs for parents. **Policies:** Many undergraduate buildings designated smoke-free. **Housing:** Guaranteed on-campus for freshmen. Coed dorms, single-sex dorms, special housing for disabled, apartments, cooperative housing, fraternity/sorority housing, substance-free housing available. Independent living group housing, housing for students with children, cultural theme housing, and living learning communities available. **Activities:** Bands, campus ministries, choral groups, dance, drama, film society, international student organizations, literary magazine, music ensembles, Model UN, musical theater, radio station, student government, student newspaper, symphony orchestra, TV station, numerous recognized organizations.

**Athletics.** NCAA. **Intercollegiate:** Baseball M, basketball, cross-country, diving, fencing, field hockey W, football (tackle) M, golf M, gymnastics, ice hockey W, lacrosse, rifle, rowing (crew), sailing, skiing, soccer, softball W, squash M, swimming, tennis, track and field, volleyball, water polo M, wrestling M. **Intramural:** Badminton, basketball, bowling, cross-country, football (non-tackle), ice hockey, rugby, soccer, softball, squash, table tennis, tennis, triathlon W, volleyball, water polo. **Team name:** Engineers.

**Student services.** Alcohol/substance abuse counseling, campus ministries, career counseling, student employment services, financial aid counseling, health services, on-campus daycare, personal counseling, placement for graduates. **Physically disabled:** Services for visually, speech, hearing impaired.

**Contact.** E-mail: admissions@mit.edu
Phone: (617) 253-3400 Fax: (617) 258-8304
Stuart Schmill, Director of Admissions, Massachusetts Institute of Technology, 77 Massachusetts Avenue, Rm 3-108, Cambridge, MA 02139-4307

---

## Massachusetts Maritime Academy
**Buzzards Bay, Massachusetts**
www.maritime.edu

CB member
CB code: 3515

- Public 4-year military and maritime college
- Residential campus in large town
- 1,062 degree-seeking undergraduates
- 40% of applicants admitted
- SAT or ACT (ACT writing optional), application essay required

**General.** Founded in 1891. Regionally accredited. **Degrees:** 198 bachelor's awarded; master's offered. **ROTC:** Army, Naval, Air Force. **Location:** 55 miles from Boston, 50 miles from Providence, Rhode Island. **Calendar:** 2 semesters and 8-week winter sea term. Limited summer session. **Full-time faculty:** 60 total. **Part-time faculty:** 20 total. **Class size:** 43% < 20, 57% 20-39, less than 1% 40-49. **Special facilities:** 540' training ship enterprise, slow-speed diesel simulator, video full-function bridge navigation simulator, commercial fishing simulator, spill management simulator, cargo handling simulator, hands-on aquaculture center, emergency management simulator.

**Freshman class profile.**

| Mid 50% test scores | | ACT composite: | 17-23 |
|---|---|---|---|
| SAT critical reading: | 440-560 | Live on campus: | 100% |
| SAT math: | 480-580 | | |

**Basis for selection.** School achievement record, test scores, extracurricular accomplishments most important. Character and personality emphasized, leadership potential desirable. Interview recommended.

**High school preparation.** 18 units required. Required units include English 4, mathematics 3, social studies 2, history 2, science 3 (laboratory 2) and foreign language 2. Math units must include 2 algebra, 1 plane geometry. Science units must include 1 chemistry, or two courses with a lab. Physics recommended.

**2007-2008 Annual costs.** Tuition/fees: $5,900; $15,114 out-of-state. Semester at Sea cost: $3,218. Room/board: $7,812. Books/supplies: $800. Personal expenses: $1,200.

**Financial aid. Non-need-based:** Scholarships awarded for academics, leadership, music/drama.

**Application procedures. Admission:** No deadline. $50 fee, may be waived for applicants with need. Application may be submitted online. Admission notification on a rolling basis beginning on or about 11/15. Must reply by May 1 or within 1 week(s) if notified thereafter. **Financial aid:** Priority date 4/30; no closing date. FAFSA, institutional form required. Applicants notified on a rolling basis starting 3/1.

**Academics.** Technical and practical training for third assistant engineer and third mate licenses. Graduates may apply for commissions in U.S. Navy, Coast Guard, Marine Reserve, Army, or Air Force. **Special study options:** Combined bachelor's/graduate degree, cooperative education, double major, internships, liberal arts/career combination, semester at sea. **Credit/placement by examination:** AP, CLEP, IB, institutional tests. 6 credit hours maximum toward bachelor's degree. **Support services:** Learning center, pre-admission summer program, reduced course load, study skills assistance, tutoring.

**Majors. Business:** Transportation. **Engineering:** General. **Engineering technology:** Industrial management. **Protective services:** Security management. **Transportation:** Maritime/Merchant Marine.

**Most popular majors.** Engineering/engineering technologies 50%, natural resources/environmental science 15%, security/protective services 15%, trade and industry 20%.

**Computing on campus.** PC or laptop required. 70 workstations in dormitories, library, computer center. Dormitories wired for high-speed internet access and linked to campus network. Commuter students can connect to campus network. Helpline, wireless network available.

**Student life. Freshman orientation:** Mandatory, $400 fee. Preregistration for classes offered. Held last 2 weeks of August, paramilitary style orientation. **Policies:** No mandatory military obligation. **Housing:** Guaranteed on-campus for all undergraduates. Coed dorms, substance-free housing available. All majors required to live on campus. **Activities:** Bands, drama, literary magazine, music ensembles, student government, student newspaper, Newman Club, marine careers group, Association of Industrial Plant Engineers.

**Athletics.** NCAA. **Intercollegiate:** Baseball M, cross-country, football (tackle) M, lacrosse M, rifle, rowing (crew), sailing, soccer M, softball W, track and field W, volleyball W. **Intramural:** Basketball, boxing M, football (tackle) M, ice hockey, racquetball, rifle, sailing, soccer, softball, swimming, table tennis, tennis, track and field W, volleyball, water polo, wrestling M. **Team name:** Buccaneers.

**Student services.** Adult student services, alcohol/substance abuse counseling, campus ministries, career counseling, student employment services, financial aid counseling, health services, personal counseling, placement for graduates, veterans' counselor, women's services. **Learning disabled:** Comprehensive services available.

**Contact.** E-mail: admissions@maritime.edu
Phone: (508) 830-5000 ext. 1102 Toll-free number: (800) 544-3411
Fax: (508) 830-5077
Roy Fulgueras, Director of Admissions, Massachusetts Maritime Academy, 101 Academy Drive, Buzzards Bay, MA 02532-1803

---

## Merrimack College

**North Andover, Massachusetts**     **CB member**
**www.merrimack.edu**     **CB code: 3525**

- Private 4-year business and liberal arts college affiliated with Roman Catholic Church
- Residential campus in large town
- 2,062 degree-seeking undergraduates: 11% part-time, 51% women
- 45 degree-seeking graduate students
- 71% of applicants admitted
- Application essay required
- 67% graduate within 6 years; 6% enter graduate study

**General.** Founded in 1947. Regionally accredited. Associated with Augustinian Friars. **Degrees:** 530 bachelor's, 3 associate awarded; master's offered. **ROTC:** Air Force. **Location:** 25 miles from Boston. **Calendar:** Semester, limited summer session. **Full-time faculty:** 139 total; 81% have terminal degrees, 10% minority, 40% women. **Part-time faculty:** 72 total; 49% have terminal degrees, 15% minority, 51% women. **Class size:** 53% < 20, 44% 20-39, less than 1% 40-49, 1% 50-99, less than 1% >100. **Special facilities:** Astronomy dome and telescope, arts center.

**Freshman class profile.** 3,657 applied, 2,600 admitted, 422 enrolled.

| Mid 50% test scores | | | |
|---|---|---|---|
| SAT critical reading: | 520-580 | Rank in top quarter: | 44% |
| SAT math: | 530-590 | Rank in top tenth: | 12% |
| ACT composite: | 21-26 | End year in good standing: | 81% |
| GPA 3.50 or higher: | 21% | Return as sophomores: | 81% |
| GPA 3.0-3.49: | 38% | Out-of-state: | 22% |
| GPA 2.0-2.99: | 41% | Live on campus: | 90% |

**Basis for selection.** School achievement record, course selection, class rank, essay, recommendations important. Interview recommended. **Home-schooled:** State certificate of completion, list of coursework, interview required.

**High school preparation.** 20 units required; 26 recommended. Required and recommended units include English 4, mathematics 3-4, social studies 1-2, history 1-2, science 3-4 (laboratory 3-4), foreign language 2-3 and academic electives 3. Math must include algebra I and II and plane geometry. 1 additional math and 3 science, including physics, required of math, science, engineering, and computer science applicants.

**2008-2009 Annual costs.** Tuition/fees: $29,810. Room/board: $10,190. Books/supplies: $800. Personal expenses: $2,750.

**2006-2007 Financial aid. Need-based:** 371 full-time freshmen applied for aid; 360 were judged to have need; 360 of these received aid. Average need met was 70%. Average scholarship/grant was $13,000; average loan $3,500. 80% of total undergraduate aid awarded as scholarships/grants, 20% as loans/jobs. **Non-need-based:** Awarded to 598 full-time undergraduates, including 65 freshmen. Scholarships awarded for academics, athletics, leadership, minority status, religious affiliation. **Additional information:** Accept the Challenge program provides tuition for students from Lawrence who meet program criteria.

**Application procedures. Admission:** Closing date 2/1 (postmark date). $60 fee, may be waived for applicants with need. Application may be submitted online. Admission notification 4/1. Admission notification on a rolling basis. Must reply by May 1 or within 2 week(s) if notified thereafter. **Financial aid:** Closing date 2/1. FAFSA required. Applicants notified by 3/15; must reply by 5/1 or within 2 week(s) of notification.

**Academics.** First-year seminars in civilization, inquiry, and conversation required. Associate degree and M.Ed programs offered through continuing education division only. **Special study options:** Accelerated study, cooperative education, cross-registration, double major, dual enrollment of high school students, ESL, independent study, internships, liberal arts/career combination, student-designed major, study abroad, teacher certification program, Washington semester. 5-year combined BA/BS program. **Credit/placement by examination:** AP, CLEP, IB, institutional tests. **Support services:** Learning center, reduced course load, remedial instruction, study skills assistance, tutoring, writing center.

**Majors. Biology:** General, biochemistry. **Business:** Business admin. **Communications:** General. **Computer sciences:** Computer science. **Conservation:** Environmental science. **Engineering:** General, civil, computer, electrical. **English:** English lit. **Foreign languages:** French, Romance, Spanish. **Health:** Athletic training, health services. **History:** General. **Liberal arts:** Arts/sciences. **Math:** General. **Philosophy/religion:** Philosophy, religion. **Physical sciences:** Chemistry, physics. **Psychology:** General. **Public administration:** Human services. **Social sciences:** Economics, political science, sociology. **Visual/performing arts:** Studio arts.

**Most popular majors.** Business/marketing 35%, communications/journalism 6%, English 6%, psychology 10%, social sciences 14%.

**Computing on campus.** 250 workstations in dormitories, library, computer center, student center. Dormitories wired for high-speed internet access and linked to campus network. Commuter students can connect to campus network. Online course registration, helpline, repair service, wireless network available.

**Student life. Freshman orientation:** Mandatory, $150 fee. Preregistration for classes offered. Two, 2-day June orientation sessions and a 3-day August pre-class orientation. **Policies:** All residence halls drug-free. **Housing:** Guaranteed on-campus for freshmen. Coed dorms, special housing for disabled, apartments, cooperative housing, substance-free housing available. $300 fully refundable deposit, deadline 5/1. Townhouses for upperclassmen. Applications accepted from groups of students for theme housing in townhouses. **Activities:** Bands, campus ministries, dance, drama, film society, international student organizations, music ensembles, Model UN, musical theater, student government, student newspaper, TV station, student tutoring group, community service organizations, College Democrats, College Republicans, Society Organized Against Racism, Latinos Organization.

**Athletics.** NCAA. **Intercollegiate:** Baseball M, basketball, cross-country, field hockey W, football (tackle) M, ice hockey M, lacrosse, soccer, softball W, tennis, volleyball W. **Intramural:** Basketball, ice hockey M, soccer, softball, volleyball. **Team name:** Warriors.

**Student services.** Adult student services, alcohol/substance abuse counseling, campus ministries, career counseling, student employment services, financial aid counseling, health services, minority student services, personal counseling, placement for graduates.

**Contact.** E-mail: admission@merrimack.edu
Phone: (978) 837-5100 Fax: (978) 837-5133
Jorge Hernandez, Director of Freshman Admission, Merrimack College, 315 Turnpike Street, North Andover, MA 01845

## Montserrat College of Art

| Beverly, Massachusetts | |
| --- | --- |
| www.montserrat.edu | CB member |
| | CB code: 9101 |

- Private 4-year visual arts college
- Residential campus in large town

**General.** Founded in 1970. Regionally accredited. **Location:** 18 miles from Boston. **Calendar:** Semester.

**Annual costs/financial aid.** Tuition/fees (2007-2008): $22,300. Room/board: $5,500. Books/supplies: $1,200. Personal expenses: $2,300. Need-based financial aid available to full-time and part-time students.

**Contact.** Phone: (978) 921-4242 ext. 1153
Dean of Admissions and Enrollment Management, 23 Essex Street, Beverly, MA 01915

## Mount Holyoke College

| South Hadley, Massachusetts | |
| --- | --- |
| www.mtholyoke.edu | CB member |
| | CB code: 3529 |

- Private 4-year liberal arts college for women
- Residential campus in large town
- 2,185 degree-seeking undergraduates: 2% part-time, 100% women, 5% African American, 12% Asian American, 5% Hispanic American, 1% Native American, 16% international
- 3 degree-seeking graduate students
- 52% of applicants admitted
- Application essay required
- 81% graduate within 6 years; 17% enter graduate study

**General.** Founded in 1837. Regionally accredited. Member of 5-college consortium with Amherst College, Hampshire College, Smith College, and University of Massachusetts at Amherst. **Degrees:** 518 bachelor's awarded; master's offered. **ROTC:** Army, Air Force. **Location:** 10 miles from Springfield, 90 miles from Boston. **Calendar:** Semester. **Full-time faculty:** 208 total; 94% have terminal degrees, 27% minority, 51% women. **Part-time faculty:** 28 total; 61% have terminal degrees, 32% minority, 64% women. **Class size:** 64% < 20, 29% 20-39, 3% 40-49, 4% 50-99, less than 1% >100. **Special facilities:** Nuclear accelerator, nuclear magnetic resonance equipment, electron microscope, bronze-casting foundry, solar greenhouse, Japanese meditation garden and tea house, equestrian center, language learning center with satellite communication and interactive video, child study center, environmental literacy center, greenhouse and botanical garden.

**Freshman class profile.** 3,194 applied, 1,671 admitted, 522 enrolled.

| Mid 50% test scores | | | |
| --- | --- | --- | --- |
| SAT critical reading: | 640-730 | GPA 2.0-2.99: | 5% |
| SAT math: | 590-690 | Rank in top quarter: | 86% |
| SAT writing: | 630-710 | Rank in top tenth: | 55% |
| ACT composite: | 26-30 | Return as sophomores: | 94% |
| GPA 3.50 or higher: | 70% | Out-of-state: | 80% |
| GPA 3.0-3.49: | 25% | Live on campus: | 99% |
| | | International: | 13% |

**Basis for selection.** School record most important, followed by special talents, particular goals, evidence of determination. Test scores optional. TOEFL exam required of non-native English speaking students. Personal interview on campus recommended if candidate lives within 200 miles of college, or with alumna admissions representative if applicant resides outside of area. **Homeschooled:** Detailed outline of study and 5 SAT Subject Tests recommended.

**High school preparation.** Recommended units include English 4, mathematics 3, history 3, science 3 (laboratory 3), foreign language 3 and academic electives 1. History requirement includes U.S. and world history. Either 4 units of one foreign language, or 2 units of one and 3 units of a second foreign language recommended.

**2008-2009 Annual costs.** Tuition/fees: $37,646. Room/board: $11,020. Books/supplies: $1,900.

**2007-2008 Financial aid.** **Need-based:** 362 full-time freshmen applied for aid; 307 were judged to have need; 307 of these received aid. Average need met was 100%. Average scholarship/grant was $27,269; average loan $3,713. 76% of total undergraduate aid awarded as scholarships/grants, 24% as loans/jobs. **Non-need-based:** Awarded to 142 full-time undergraduates, including 38 freshmen. Scholarships awarded for academics, leadership. **Additional information:** Parent loan plans include MASSPLAN, Achievers and PLUS. 10-month payment plan offered.

**Application procedures.** **Admission:** Closing date 1/15 (postmark date). $60 fee, may be waived for applicants with need. Application may be submitted online. Admission notification 4/1. Must reply by 5/1. **Financial aid:** Priority date 2/15, closing date 3/1. FAFSA, CSS PROFILE required. Applicants notified by 4/1; must reply by 5/1.

**Academics.** Honor system and self-scheduled examinations practiced. All students must complete minor. **Special study options:** Combined bachelor's/graduate degree, cooperative education, cross-registration, double major, exchange student, independent study, internships, liberal arts/career combination, semester at sea, student-designed major, study abroad, teacher certification program, Washington semester. Community-based learning courses. **Credit/placement by examination:** AP, CLEP, IB, institutional tests. 32 credit hours maximum toward bachelor's degree. **Support services:** Reduced course load, study skills assistance, tutoring, writing center.

**Majors.** **Architecture:** Architecture. **Area/ethnic studies:** African-American, American, Asian, European, German, Latin American, Russian/Slavic. **Biology:** General, biochemistry. **Computer sciences:** Computer science. **Conservation:** Environmental studies. **Education:** General. **English:** English lit. **Foreign languages:** Ancient Greek, classics, French, Italian, Latin, Romance, Spanish. **History:** General. **Interdisciplinary:** Ancient studies, medieval/Renaissance, neuroscience. **Math:** General, statistics. **Philosophy/religion:** Philosophy, religion. **Physical sciences:** Astronomy, chemistry, geology, physics. **Psychology:** General. **Social sciences:** Anthropology, economics, geography, international relations, political science, sociology. **Visual/performing arts:** Art history/conservation, dance, dramatic, film/cinema, studio arts. **Other:** Complex Organizations, Self-designed studies.

**Most popular majors.** Area/ethnic studies 7%, biology 8%, English 9%, foreign language 6%, psychology 8%, social sciences 29%, visual/performing arts 9%.

**Computing on campus.** 577 workstations in dormitories, library, computer center, student center. Dormitories wired for high-speed internet access and linked to campus network. Commuter students can connect to campus network. Online course registration, online library, helpline, repair service, student web hosting, wireless network available.

**Student life.** **Freshman orientation:** Available. Preregistration for classes offered. Program held week before start of classes. Specific orientation programs for international students, women of color. **Policies:** Smoke-free campus. **Housing:** Guaranteed on-campus for all undergraduates. Special housing for disabled, apartments available. $200 nonrefundable deposit, deadline 5/15. Kosher/halal kitchen available; special accommodations by need. **Activities:** Jazz band, campus ministries, choral groups, dance, drama, film society, international student organizations, literary magazine, music ensembles, Model UN, musical theater, radio station, student government, student newspaper, symphony orchestra.

**Athletics.** NCAA. **Intercollegiate:** Basketball W, cross-country W, diving W, equestrian W, field hockey W, golf W, lacrosse W, rowing (crew) W, soccer W, squash W, swimming W, tennis W, track and field W, volleyball W. **Intramural:** Badminton W, basketball W, soccer W. **Team name:** Lyons.

**Student services.** Adult student services, alcohol/substance abuse counseling, campus ministries, career counseling, student employment services, financial aid counseling, health services, minority student services, personal counseling, placement for graduates, women's services. **Physically disabled:** Services for visually, speech, hearing impaired.

**Contact.** E-mail: admission@mtholyoke.edu
Phone: (413) 538-2023 Fax: (413) 538-2409
Diane Anci, Dean of Admission, Mount Holyoke College, Newhall Center, South Hadley, MA 01075-1488

## Mount Ida College

| Newton, Massachusetts | |
| --- | --- |
| www.mountida.edu | CB member |
| | CB code: 3530 |

- Private 4-year business and liberal arts college
- Residential campus in small city
- 1,431 degree-seeking undergraduates
- 78% of applicants admitted
- SAT or ACT required

**General.** Founded in 1899. Regionally accredited. **Degrees:** 173 bachelor's, 41 associate awarded. **Location:** 8 miles from downtown Boston.

**Calendar:** Semester, limited summer session. **Full-time faculty:** 61 total. **Part-time faculty:** 107 total. **Class size:** 65% < 20, 34% 20-39, less than 1% 40-49, less than 1% 50-99. **Special facilities:** Darkroom, blueprint making facility, veterinary kennel and operating facility, dental laboratory, design labs.

## Freshman class profile.

| Mid 50% test scores | | | |
|---|---|---|---|
| SAT critical reading: | 390-480 | ACT composite: | 15-19 |
| SAT math: | 380-480 | Out-of-state: | 45% |
| SAT writing: | 390-480 | Live on campus: | 80% |

**Basis for selection.** Special requirements for science applicants and students interested in Learning Opportunities Program. Minimum 2.0 GPA required for admission to all bachelor's degree programs, except interior design, which requires 2.5 GPA. Veterinary science students must have some science background. Prefer art students to have art background. Portfolio recommended for art, interior design, fashion illustration majors. Interviews required for dental hygiene majors. Essay or personal statement strongly recommended. Interview and campus visit strongly recommended, may be required for certain programs.

**High school preparation.** 16 units recommended. Recommended units include English 4, mathematics 4, social studies 4 and science 4. 4 math, 2 physical science strongly recommended for science majors.

**2007-2008 Annual costs.** Tuition/fees: $21,330. Room/board: $10,635. Books/supplies: $800. Personal expenses: $525.

**Application procedures. Admission:** No deadline. $35 fee, may be waived for applicants with need. Application may be submitted online. Admission notification on a rolling basis beginning on or about 10/1. **Financial aid:** Priority date 5/1; no closing date. FAFSA, institutional form required. Applicants notified on a rolling basis starting 3/1; must reply within 3 week(s) of notification.

**Academics.** Professionally intensive courses of study coupled with liberal arts requirements. **Special study options:** ESL, honors, independent study, internships, student-designed major, study abroad, teacher certification program. Affiliation with Tufts Veterinary School and Tufts University School of Dental Medicine. **Credit/placement by examination:** CLEP, institutional tests. 12 credit hours maximum toward bachelor's degree. **Support services:** Learning center, reduced course load, remedial instruction, study skills assistance, tutoring.

**Majors. Agriculture:** Animal sciences, equestrian studies. **Biology:** General. **Business:** Business admin, fashion, hospitality admin, tourism/travel. **Education:** Early childhood. **Health:** Veterinary technology/assistant. **Legal studies:** General. **Liberal arts:** Arts/sciences. **Parks/recreation:** Sports admin. **Personal/culinary services:** Mortuary science. **Protective services:** Criminal justice. **Psychology:** General. **Public administration:** Human services. **Visual/performing arts:** Fashion design, interior design.

**Computing on campus.** 100 workstations in library, computer center. Dormitories wired for high-speed internet access and linked to campus network. Online library available.

**Student life. Freshman orientation:** Available. Preregistration for classes offered. Held in July. Students able to make housing selections. Orientation activities also held prior to first day of class in late August. **Housing:** Guaranteed on-campus for freshmen. Coed dorms, single-sex dorms, special housing for disabled, substance-free housing available. $350 deposit. **Activities:** Choral groups, dance, drama, literary magazine, musical theater, radio station, student government, student newspaper, TV station, black student achievement coalition, foundation for non-violent action, commuter council, career club, gay/lesbian/bisexual student group.

**Athletics.** NCAA. **Intercollegiate:** Basketball, cross-country, equestrian W, football (tackle) M, lacrosse M, soccer, softball W, volleyball. **Intramural:** Badminton, basketball, equestrian W, field hockey W, ice hockey, lacrosse M, rugby M, skiing M, soccer, softball, swimming M, tennis, volleyball. **Team name:** Mustangs.

**Student services.** Adult student services, alcohol/substance abuse counseling, career counseling, student employment services, financial aid counseling, health services, personal counseling, placement for graduates.

**Contact.** E-mail: admissions@mountida.edu
Phone: (617) 928-4553 Fax: (617) 928-4507
Jay Titus, Dean of Admissions, Mount Ida College, 777 Dedham Street, Newton, MA 02459

## New England Conservatory of Music
**Boston, Massachusetts** — CB member
www.newenglandconservatory.edu — CB code: 3659

- Private 4-year music college
- Commuter campus in very large city
- 384 degree-seeking undergraduates: 8% part-time, 43% women, 3% African American, 9% Asian American, 5% Hispanic American, 22% international
- 326 degree-seeking graduate students
- 29% of applicants admitted
- Application essay required
- 78% graduate within 6 years

**General.** Founded in 1867. Regionally accredited. In close proximity to Symphony Hall. Faculty includes members of Boston Symphony Orchestra. **Degrees:** 90 bachelor's awarded; master's, doctoral offered. **Location:** 2 miles from downtown. **Calendar:** Semester, limited summer session. **Full-time faculty:** 88 total; 26% have terminal degrees, 6% minority, 33% women. **Part-time faculty:** 126 total; 6% have terminal degrees, 11% minority, 27% women. **Class size:** 80% < 20, 20% 20-39. **Special facilities:** Listening library of 46,384 recordings.

**Freshman class profile.** 1,058 applied, 307 admitted, 95 enrolled.

| | | | |
|---|---|---|---|
| Return as sophomores: | 92% | Live on campus: | 100% |
| Out-of-state: | 90% | International: | 24% |

**Basis for selection.** Audition most important, followed by recommendations, essay, high school record. Accepted students permitted to postpone admission one-half year. SAT or ACT recommended. Live or taped auditions required. **Homeschooled:** Must provide curriculum overview.

**2007-2008 Annual costs.** Tuition/fees: $30,975. On-campus residents pay $335 health fee. Room/board: $11,300. Books/supplies: $700. Personal expenses: $2,386.

**2007-2008 Financial aid. Need-based:** 58 full-time freshmen applied for aid; 52 were judged to have need; 52 of these received aid. Average need met was 69%. Average scholarship/grant was $13,723; average loan $4,909. 68% of total undergraduate aid awarded as scholarships/grants, 32% as loans/jobs. **Non-need-based:** Awarded to 150 full-time undergraduates, including 36 freshmen. Scholarships awarded for academics, music/drama.

**Application procedures. Admission:** Priority date 12/1; no deadline. $100 fee. Application may be submitted online. Admission notification on a rolling basis beginning on or about 4/1. Must reply by May 1 or within 4 week(s) if notified thereafter. **Financial aid:** Closing date 12/1. FAFSA, institutional form required. Applicants notified by 4/1; must reply by 5/1 or within 2 week(s) of notification.

**Academics.** Undergraduate diploma available in lieu of bachelor's degree (performance-oriented, with fewer academic requirements). Artist's diploma (professional degree) available for particularly gifted performers. Graduate diploma also available. **Special study options:** Cross-registration, dual enrollment of high school students, ESL, independent study, internships, study abroad. 5-year double degree program with Tufts University; 5-year AB/MM program with Harvard University. **Credit/placement by examination:** CLEP, IB, institutional tests. 12 credit hours maximum toward bachelor's degree. **Support services:** Tutoring, writing center.

**Majors. Visual/performing arts:** Jazz, music history, music performance, music theory/composition, piano/organ, stringed instruments, voice/opera.

**Computing on campus.** 48 workstations in dormitories, library, computer center, student center. Online library, wireless network available.

**Student life. Freshman orientation:** Mandatory. Preregistration for classes offered. Held 5 days before start of classes. **Housing:** Guaranteed on-campus for freshmen. Coed dorms available. $500 fully refundable deposit, deadline 5/1. **Activities:** Bands, choral groups, music ensembles, opera, student government, student newspaper, symphony orchestra, Christian Fellowship, feminist and minority student organizations.

**Athletics. Team name:** Penguins.

**Student services.** Career counseling, student employment services, health services, personal counseling, placement for graduates. **Physically disabled:** Services for visually impaired.

**Contact.** E-mail: admissions@newenglandconservatory.edu
Phone: (617) 585-1101 Fax: (617) 585-1115
Christina Daly, Director of Admissions, New England Conservatory of Music, 290 Huntington Avenue, Boston, MA 02115

## New England Institute of Art
**Brookline, Massachusetts**
www.artinstitutes.edu/boston          CB code: 3636

- For-profit 4-year visual arts and technical college
- Commuter campus in very large city
- 1,684 degree-seeking undergraduates
- 44% of applicants admitted
- Application essay, interview required

**General.** Regionally accredited. **Degrees:** 253 bachelor's, 21 associate awarded. **Calendar:** Semester, extensive summer session. **Full-time faculty:** 30 total. **Part-time faculty:** 50 total. **Class size:** 79% < 20, 19% 20-39, 2% 40-49. **Special facilities:** Radio, TV, and audio production studios; drafting rooms.

**Freshman class profile.** 1,233 applied, 538 admitted, 538 enrolled.

**Basis for selection.** Essay and interview most important, followed by secondary school record. Class rank, recommendations, test scores considered. Second interview required for audio programs. Portfolio required for Media Arts and Animation program.

**2007-2008 Annual costs.** Tuition/fees: $20,900. Room/board: $11,300.

**Financial aid. Non-need-based:** Scholarships awarded for academics.

**Application procedures. Admission:** No deadline. $150 fee. Application may be submitted online. Admission notification on a rolling basis. **Financial aid:** Priority date 5/1; no closing date. FAFSA, institutional form required. Applicants notified on a rolling basis starting 3/1.

**Academics.** Bachelor's degrees offered in graphic design and multimedia/web design. Non-collegiate certificates offered in web site development and digital graphic design. **Special study options:** Internships. **Credit/placement by examination:** AP, CLEP, institutional tests. **Support services:** Learning center, remedial instruction, study skills assistance, tutoring.

**Majors. Communications:** Digital media. **Communications technology:** Graphics, photo/film/video, recording arts. **Computer sciences:** Web page design. **Visual/performing arts:** Commercial/advertising art, graphic design, illustration, multimedia.

**Computing on campus.** Dormitories wired for high-speed internet access. Student web hosting available.

**Student life. Freshman orientation:** Mandatory. Half-day program held prior to start of semester. **Policies:** Student code of conduct. **Housing:** Coed dorms, apartments available. $400 nonrefundable deposit. **Activities:** Drama, film society, literary magazine, radio station, student government.

**Student services.** Adult student services, alcohol/substance abuse counseling, career counseling, student employment services, financial aid counseling, personal counseling, placement for graduates.

**Contact.** E-mail: neiaadm@aii.edu
Phone: (617) 739-1700 Toll-free number: (800) 903-4425
Fax: (617) 582-4500
Ken Post, Vice President/Director of Admissions, New England Institute of Art, 10 Brookline Place West, Brookline, MA 02445-7295

## Newbury College
**Brookline, Massachusetts**
www.newbury.edu          CB member
          CB code: 3639

- Private 4-year business and liberal arts college
- Commuter campus in large city
- 1,200 degree-seeking undergraduates
- 84% of applicants admitted
- Application essay required

**General.** Founded in 1962. Regionally accredited. **Degrees:** 150 bachelor's, 60 associate awarded. **Location:** 3 miles from Boston. **Calendar:** Semester, limited summer session. **Full-time faculty:** 30 total. **Special facilities:** 7 culinary arts production kitchens, on-campus restaurant.

**Freshman class profile.** 1,850 applied, 1,550 admitted, 340 enrolled.

| Out-of-state: | 25% | Live on campus: | 35% |
|---|---|---|---|

**Basis for selection.** High school GPA and interviews important. 2 letters of recommendation and essay required. SAT or ACT recommended. SAT required for scholarship consideration but not for admissions. Interview recommended. **Learning Disabled:** Students reporting learning disability should submit copy of documents stating disability.

**High school preparation.** Recommended units include English 3, mathematics 3, social studies 3, history 3, science 2, foreign language 2 and computer science 1.

**2007-2008 Annual costs.** Tuition/fees: $20,000. Room/board: $10,100. Books/supplies: $630. Personal expenses: $1,000.

**Financial aid.** All financial aid based on need.

**Application procedures. Admission:** Priority date 3/1; no deadline. $50 fee, may be waived for applicants with need. Application may be submitted online. Admission notification on a rolling basis beginning on or about 1/1. Must reply by May 1 or within 4 week(s) if notified thereafter. **Financial aid:** Closing date 5/1. FAFSA required. Applicants notified on a rolling basis starting 3/1; must reply within 2 week(s) of notification.

**Academics.** Academic enrichment program available for students entering who demonstrate need for academic support. **Special study options:** Combined bachelor's/graduate degree, cross-registration, double major, honors, independent study, internships, liberal arts/career combination, study abroad, weekend college. **Credit/placement by examination:** CLEP, IB, institutional tests. 30 credit hours maximum toward associate degree, 60 toward bachelor's. **Support services:** Learning center, remedial instruction, study skills assistance, tutoring.

**Majors. Architecture:** Interior. **Business:** Accounting, business admin, finance, hospitality admin, hospitality/recreation, international, international marketing, marketing. **Communications:** General. **Computer sciences:** General, computer graphics, computer science. **Health:** Facilities admin, health care admin. **Legal studies:** General, paralegal, prelaw. **Personal/culinary services:** Chef training, culinary arts, restaurant/catering. **Protective services:** Law enforcement admin. **Psychology:** General. **Visual/performing arts:** Commercial/advertising art, graphic design, interior design.

**Most popular majors.** Business/marketing 66%, computer/information sciences 10%, legal studies 15%.

**Computing on campus.** 65 workstations in dormitories, library, computer center, student center. Dormitories wired for high-speed internet access and linked to campus network. Online library, helpline available.

**Student life. Freshman orientation:** Mandatory. Preregistration for classes offered. Information sessions and activities held a few days before each semester. **Housing:** Guaranteed on-campus for freshmen. Coed dorms, single-sex dorms available. $350 deposit, deadline 5/1. Summer housing available. **Activities:** Jazz band, dance, drama, radio station, student government, TV station, international student organization, black student union, Latino student association, Habitat for Humanity, innkeepers club, chef society, Alpha business club, radio club, programming board.

**Athletics.** NCAA. **Intercollegiate:** Basketball, cross-country, golf, soccer M, softball W, tennis, volleyball. **Intramural:** Basketball, softball W, volleyball, weight lifting. **Team name:** Nighthawks.

**Student services.** Alcohol/substance abuse counseling, campus ministries, career counseling, student employment services, financial aid counseling, personal counseling, placement for graduates.

**Contact.** E-mail: info@newbury.edu
Phone: (617) 730-7007 Toll-free number: (800) 639-2879
Fax: (617) 731-9618
Salvadore Liberto, Vice President for Enrollment & Dean of Admission, Newbury College, 129 Fisher Avenue, Brookline, MA 02445

## Nichols College
**Dudley, Massachusetts**
www.nichols.edu          CB member
          CB code: 3666

- Private 4-year business and liberal arts college
- Residential campus in small town
- 1,271 degree-seeking undergraduates
- 231 graduate students
- 77% of applicants admitted
- SAT or ACT (ACT writing recommended), application essay required
- 47% graduate within 6 years

**General.** Founded in 1815. Regionally accredited. **Degrees:** 188 bachelor's, 18 associate awarded; master's offered. **ROTC:** Army. **Location:** 20

miles from Worcester, 50 miles from Boston. **Calendar:** Semester, limited summer session. **Full-time faculty:** 34 total; 56% have terminal degrees, 3% minority, 29% women. **Part-time faculty:** 33 total; 21% have terminal degrees, 3% minority, 39% women. **Class size:** 35% < 20, 65% 20-39, less than 1% 40-49, less than 1% 50-99. **Special facilities:** Policy and cultural institute, observatory.

**Freshman class profile.** 1,894 applied, 1,456 admitted, 440 enrolled.

| Mid 50% test scores | | | |
|---|---|---|---|
| SAT critical reading: | 400-490 | GPA 2.0-2.99: | 66% |
| SAT math: | 420-520 | Return as sophomores: | 64% |
| SAT writing: | 420-470 | Out-of-state: | 41% |
| GPA 3.50 or higher: | 7% | Live on campus: | 93% |
| GPA 3.0-3.49: | 19% | International: | 1% |

**Basis for selection.** Secondary school record most important; test scores important, followed by recommendations, essay and interview. Interview recommended. **Homeschooled:** Statement describing homeschool structure and mission, interview, letter of recommendation (nonparent) required.

**High school preparation.** 16 units required. Required and recommended units include English 4, mathematics 3-4, social studies 2, science 2-3 (laboratory 2-3), foreign language 2 and academic electives 5. 2 foreign language recommended for liberal arts majors.

**2007-2008 Annual costs.** Tuition/fees: $25,700. Room/board: $8,960. Books/supplies: $1,050. Personal expenses: $1,200.

**2007-2008 Financial aid. Need-based:** 391 full-time freshmen applied for aid; 356 were judged to have need; 356 of these received aid. Average need met was 74%. Average scholarship/grant was $14,237; average loan $3,778. 57% of total undergraduate aid awarded as scholarships/grants, 43% as loans/jobs. **Non-need-based:** Awarded to 102 full-time undergraduates, including 44 freshmen. Scholarships awarded for academics, alumni affiliation, ROTC.

**Application procedures. Admission:** Priority date 3/1; no deadline. $25 fee, may be waived for applicants with need. Application may be submitted online. Admission notification on a rolling basis beginning on or about 10/1. Must reply by May 1 or within 2 week(s) if notified thereafter. **Financial aid:** Priority date 3/1, closing date 6/1. FAFSA required. Applicants notified on a rolling basis starting 2/26; must reply within 4 week(s) of notification.

**Academics. Special study options:** Combined bachelor's/graduate degree, cooperative education, distance learning, double major, honors, independent study, internships, liberal arts/career combination, study abroad, teacher certification program, Washington semester. **Credit/placement by examination:** AP, CLEP. 30 credit hours maximum toward bachelor's degree. **Support services:** Learning center, reduced course load, remedial instruction, study skills assistance, tutoring, writing center.

**Majors. Business:** Accounting, business admin, communications, finance, human resources, management information systems, managerial economics, marketing, training/development. **Education:** Secondary. **English:** English lit. **History:** General. **Math:** General. **Parks/recreation:** Sports admin. **Protective services:** Criminal justice. **Psychology:** General. **Social sciences:** Economics. **Other:** Arts and entertainment management.

**Most popular majors.** Business/marketing 91%.

**Computing on campus.** 69 workstations in library, computer center, student center. Dormitories wired for high-speed internet access and linked to campus network. Commuter students can connect to campus network. Online course registration, online library, helpline, repair service, wireless network available.

**Student life. Freshman orientation:** Mandatory. Preregistration for classes offered. Overnight pre-college summer programs for students and parents. **Housing:** Guaranteed on-campus for all undergraduates. Coed dorms, single-sex dorms, special housing for disabled, apartments, substance-free housing available. $250 deposit, deadline 5/1. **Activities:** Campus ministries, drama, literary magazine, radio station, student government, student newspaper, TV station, Institute for American Values, Republican club, Young Democrats, Umoja.

**Athletics.** NCAA. **Intercollegiate:** Baseball M, basketball, cheerleading, field hockey W, football (tackle) M, golf, ice hockey, lacrosse, soccer, softball W, tennis. **Intramural:** Basketball, football (non-tackle), football (tackle) M, racquetball, rugby, softball M, volleyball. **Team name:** Bison.

**Student services.** Alcohol/substance abuse counseling, campus ministries, career counseling, student employment services, financial aid counseling, health services, personal counseling, placement for graduates.

**Contact.** E-mail: admissions@nichols.edu
Phone: (508) 213-2203 Toll-free number: (800) 470-3379
Fax: (508) 943-9885
Diane Gillespie, Director of Admissions, Nichols College, PO Box 5000, Dudley, MA 01571-5000

## Northeastern University
**Boston, Massachusetts**     **CB member**
www.northeastern.edu     **CB code: 3667**

- Private 4-year university
- Residential campus in very large city
- 15,339 degree-seeking undergraduates: 51% women, 6% African American, 8% Asian American, 5% Hispanic American, 5% international
- 5,254 graduate students
- 39% of applicants admitted
- SAT or ACT with writing, application essay required
- 66% graduate within 6 years; 16% enter graduate study

**General.** Founded in 1898. Regionally accredited. 6 undergraduate colleges, 8 graduate and professional schools, 2 part-time undergraduate divisions, several suburban campuses. **Degrees:** 2,720 bachelor's awarded; master's, doctoral, first professional offered. **ROTC:** Army, Naval, Air Force. **Calendar:** Semester, extensive summer session. **Full-time faculty:** 911 total; 88% have terminal degrees, 37% women. **Part-time faculty:** 419 total. **Class size:** 49% < 20, 32% 20-39, 9% 40-49, 7% 50-99, 2% >100. **Special facilities:** African-American institute, science engineering research center, health sciences center, marine science center, center for subsurfacing and imaging systems, institute of chemical and biological analysis, research vessel.

**Freshman class profile.** 30,349 applied, 11,971 admitted, 2,871 enrolled.

| Mid 50% test scores | | | |
|---|---|---|---|
| SAT critical reading: | 570-660 | Rank in top tenth: | 42% |
| SAT math: | 600-680 | Return as sophomores: | 91% |
| ACT composite: | 25-29 | Out-of-state: | 65% |
| Rank in top quarter: | 77% | Live on campus: | 95% |
| | | International: | 6% |

**Basis for selection.** Academic achievement as measured by grades earned, quality of classes, test scores, class rank most important. Recommendations, personal statement, school and community activities also important. Portfolios/auditions required for art and design, music technology programs. **Homeschooled:** Transcript of courses and grades required. Students should submit comprehensive outline of academic curriculum, list of textbooks, special projects and activities.

**High school preparation.** 17 units required. Required and recommended units include English 4, mathematics 3-4, social studies 2, history 2, science 3-4 (laboratory 2-4) and foreign language 2-4. Each department and college of university may have more specific recommendations for additional preparation.

**2007-2008 Annual costs.** Tuition/fees: $31,899. Room/board: $11,420. Books/supplies: $900. Personal expenses: $900.

**2007-2008 Financial aid. Need-based:** 2,115 full-time freshmen applied for aid; 1,647 were judged to have need; 1,639 of these received aid. Average need met was 67%. Average scholarship/grant was $15,019; average loan $4,540. 57% of total undergraduate aid awarded as scholarships/grants, 43% as loans/jobs. **Non-need-based:** Awarded to 4,905 full-time undergraduates, including 1,194 freshmen. Scholarships awarded for academics, athletics, minority status.

**Application procedures. Admission:** Closing date 1/15 (postmark date). $75 fee, may be waived for applicants with need. Application may be submitted online. Admission notification 4/1. Must reply by May 1 or within 4 week(s) if notified thereafter. **Financial aid:** Closing date 2/15. FAFSA, CSS PROFILE required. Applicants notified on a rolling basis starting 2/15; must reply by 5/1.

**Academics. Special study options:** Accelerated study, combined bachelor's/graduate degree, cooperative education, cross-registration, distance learning, double major, ESL, exchange student, honors, independent study, internships, liberal arts/career combination, semester at sea, student-designed major, study abroad, teacher certification program, Washington semester. International cooperative experience. **Credit/placement by examination:** AP, CLEP, IB, institutional tests. **Support services:** Learning center, preadmission summer program, reduced course load, remedial instruction, study skills assistance, tutoring, writing center.

**Majors. Architecture:** Architecture. **Biology:** General, biochemistry, marine. **Business:** General, accounting, entrepreneurial studies, finance, human resources, international, logistics, management information systems, management science, marketing, operations. **Communications:** General, broadcast journalism, journalism, public relations. **Computer sciences:** General, computer science. **Conservation:** Environmental studies. **Education:** General, art, biology, chemistry, elementary, English, foreign languages, history, mathematics, music, social studies. **Engineering:** General, chemical, civil, computer, electrical, mechanical. **Engineering technology:** Computer, electrical, mechanical. **English:** British lit, English lit, speech/rhetoric. **Health:** Athletic training, audiology/speech pathology, clinical lab science, clinical lab technology, medical records admin, nursing (RN), recreational therapy, speech pathology. **History:** General. **Interdisciplinary:** Global studies, neuroscience. **Liberal arts:** Arts/sciences. **Math:** General. **Parks/recreation:** Health/fitness. **Philosophy/religion:** Philosophy. **Physical sciences:** Chemistry, geology, physics. **Protective services:** Criminal justice, police science, security services. **Psychology:** General. **Social sciences:** General, anthropology, economics, international relations, political science, sociology. **Visual/performing arts:** General, art, art history/conservation, commercial/advertising art, design, dramatic, music history, music management, music performance, studio arts.

**Most popular majors.** Business/marketing 25%, communications/journalism 7%, engineering/engineering technologies 14%, health sciences 9%, security/protective services 8%, social sciences 10%, visual/performing arts 7%.

**Computing on campus.** 1,993 workstations in dormitories, library, computer center, student center. Dormitories wired for high-speed internet access and linked to campus network. Commuter students can connect to campus network. Online course registration, online library, helpline, student web hosting, wireless network available.

**Student life. Freshman orientation:** Mandatory, $100 fee. Preregistration for classes offered. **Housing:** Guaranteed on-campus for freshmen. Coed dorms, special housing for disabled, apartments, fraternity/sorority housing, substance-free housing available. $400 deposit, deadline 5/1. Honors, wellness, quiet, living and learning, international, multicultural, leadership, college/program housing, and other academic themes available. **Activities:** Bands, choral groups, dance, drama, international student organizations, literary magazine, music ensembles, musical theater, radio station, student government, student newspaper, symphony orchestra, TV station, over 225 student organizations.

**Athletics.** NCAA. **Intercollegiate:** Baseball M, basketball, cross-country, diving W, field hockey W, football (tackle) M, ice hockey, rowing (crew), soccer, swimming W, track and field, volleyball W. **Intramural:** Basketball, ice hockey, racquetball, soccer, softball, squash, tennis, volleyball, water polo. **Team name:** Huskies.

**Student services.** Alcohol/substance abuse counseling, campus ministries, career counseling, services for economically disadvantaged, student employment services, financial aid counseling, health services, legal services, minority student services, personal counseling, placement for graduates, women's services. **Physically disabled:** Services for visually, speech, hearing impaired. **Learning disabled:** Comprehensive services available.

**Contact.** E-mail: admissions@neu.edu
Phone: (617) 373-2200 Fax: (617) 373-8780
Ronne Turner, Dean of Undergraduate Admissions, Northeastern University, 360 Huntington Avenue, 150 Richards Hall, Boston, MA 02115-9959

---

## Pine Manor College
**Chestnut Hill, Massachusetts**
www.pmc.edu

**CB member**
**CB code: 3689**

- Private 4-year liberal arts college for women
- Residential campus in very large city
- 491 degree-seeking undergraduates: 1% part-time, 100% women, 47% African American, 5% Asian American, 14% Hispanic American, 1% Native American, 6% international
- 10 degree-seeking graduate students
- 71% of applicants admitted
- SAT or ACT, application essay required
- 52% graduate within 6 years

**General.** Founded in 1911. Regionally accredited. **Degrees:** 74 bachelor's, 3 associate awarded; master's offered. **ROTC:** Army, Air Force. **Location:** 5 miles from Boston. **Calendar:** Semester, limited summer session. **Full-time faculty:** 32 total; 75% have terminal degrees, 12% minority, 75%

women. **Part-time faculty:** 44 total; 57% have terminal degrees, 14% minority, 75% women. **Class size:** 83% < 20, 17% 20-39. **Special facilities:** Center for inclusive leadership and social responsibility, child study center.

**Freshman class profile.** 589 applied, 416 admitted, 172 enrolled.

| | | | |
|---|---|---|---|
| Out-of-state: | 26% | **International:** | 5% |
| Live on campus: | 93% | | |

**Basis for selection.** School achievement record, test scores, GPA, and recommendations are important. Rolling deadline for SAT/ACT score submission. Interview recommended. **Learning Disabled:** Students may be required to submit learning disability documentation.

**High school preparation.** Required units include English 4, mathematics 3, social studies 2, science 3 and foreign language 2.

**2007-2008 Annual costs.** Tuition/fees: $17,750. Room/board: $10,570. Books/supplies: $800. Personal expenses: $1,000.

**2006-2007 Financial aid. Need-based:** 159 full-time freshmen applied for aid; 155 were judged to have need; 154 of these received aid. Average need met was 67%. Average scholarship/grant was $13,170; average loan $2,478. 64% of total undergraduate aid awarded as scholarships/grants, 36% as loans/jobs. **Non-need-based:** Awarded to 41 full-time undergraduates, including 19 freshmen. Scholarships awarded for academics, alumni affiliation, leadership.

**Application procedures. Admission:** No deadline. $25 fee, may be waived for applicants with need. Application may be submitted online. Admission notification on a rolling basis. Must reply by May 1 or within 2 week(s) if notified thereafter. **Financial aid:** Priority date 5/1; no closing date. FAFSA required. Applicants notified on a rolling basis starting 3/1; must reply by 5/1 or within 2 week(s) of notification.

**Academics.** All students required to participate in internship program. All students receive comprehensive advising. **Special study options:** Cross-registration, double major, honors, independent study, internships, liberal arts/career combination, semester at sea, student-designed major, study abroad, teacher certification program, Washington semester. Students with sophomore status or higher eligible to take courses offered by Marine Studies Consortium. **Credit/placement by examination:** AP, CLEP, IB, institutional tests. 24 credit hours maximum toward bachelor's degree. **Support services:** Learning center, reduced course load, study skills assistance, tutoring, writing center.

**Majors. Biology:** General. **Business:** Business admin. **Communications:** Media studies. **English:** English lit. **History:** General. **Liberal arts:** Arts/sciences. **Psychology:** General. **Social sciences:** Political science. **Visual/performing arts:** General.

**Most popular majors.** Biology 18%, business/marketing 19%, psychology 26%, visual/performing arts 11%.

**Computing on campus.** 108 workstations in dormitories, library, computer center, student center. Dormitories wired for high-speed internet access and linked to campus network. Commuter students can connect to campus network. Online course registration, helpline, repair service available.

**Student life. Freshman orientation:** Mandatory, $150 fee. Preregistration for classes offered. Held in June and September. **Housing:** Guaranteed on-campus for freshmen. Substance-free housing available. $250 nonrefundable deposit. Quiet residence halls available. **Activities:** Choral groups, dance, drama, literary magazine, radio station, student government, Ladies of Various Ebony Shades, African American, Latina, Asian, Native American and All club, Alianza Latina, Bisexuals, Gays, Lesbians and Allies in Diversity, Cape Verdean student alliance, dance ensemble, student government association, student health advisory board, Imani Christian club, Camerata singers.

**Athletics.** NCAA. **Intercollegiate:** Basketball W, cross-country W, lacrosse W, soccer W, softball W, tennis W, volleyball W. **Team name:** Gators.

**Student services.** Alcohol/substance abuse counseling, career counseling, services for economically disadvantaged, student employment services, financial aid counseling, health services, minority student services, personal counseling, placement for graduates, women's services.

**Contact.** E-mail: admission@pmc.edu
Phone: (617) 731-7104 Toll-free number: (800) 762-1357
Fax: (617) 731-7102
Robin Engel, Dean of Admissions and Financial Aid, Pine Manor College, 400 Heath Street, Chestnut Hill, MA 02467

## Regis College
**Weston, Massachusetts**
www.regiscollege.edu

CB member
CB code: 3723

- Private 4-year nursing and liberal arts college affiliated with Roman Catholic Church
- Residential campus in large town
- 934 degree-seeking undergraduates: 22% part-time, 91% women, 19% African American, 6% Asian American, 9% Hispanic American, 1% international
- 577 degree-seeking graduate students
- 77% of applicants admitted
- SAT or ACT (ACT writing optional), application essay required
- 54% graduate within 6 years; 29% enter graduate study

**General.** Founded in 1927. Regionally accredited. College founded by Sisters of St. Joseph. **Degrees:** 201 bachelor's, 124 associate awarded; master's, doctoral offered. **Location:** 12 miles from Boston. **Calendar:** Semester, limited summer session. **Full-time faculty:** 60 total; 77% have terminal degrees, 7% minority, 82% women. **Part-time faculty:** 64 total; 38% have terminal degrees, 6% minority, 77% women. **Class size:** 63% < 20, 35% 20-39, 2% 40-49, less than 1% 50-99. **Special facilities:** Philatelic museum, fine arts center, 2 digital imaging studios, music laboratory with electronic keyboards and computers.

**Freshman class profile.** 1,283 applied, 991 admitted, 263 enrolled.

| Mid 50% test scores | | | |
|---|---|---|---|
| SAT critical reading: | 400-500 | Rank in top tenth: | 3% |
| SAT math: | 400-500 | End year in good standing: | 81% |
| SAT writing: | 400-510 | Return as sophomores: | 70% |
| ACT composite: | 16-20 | Out-of-state: | 11% |
| Rank in top quarter: | 24% | Live on campus: | 75% |
| | | International: | 1% |

**Basis for selection.** All credentials within student's file reviewed. At times, interview or additional grades requested or guidance counselors spoken with. Interview highly recommended. Portfolio recommended for art majors. **Homeschooled:** Statement describing homeschool structure and mission, transcript of courses and grades, letter of recommendation (nonparent) required. **Learning Disabled:** Should apprise Director of Student Disabilities of disability status and document condition to receive appropriate accommodations.

**High school preparation.** 16 units required. Required units include English 4, mathematics 3, social studies 2, science 2 (laboratory 1), foreign language 2 and academic electives 3.

**2007-2008 Annual costs.** Tuition/fees: $25,990. Room/board: $11,600. Books/supplies: $900. Personal expenses: $1,520.

**2007-2008 Financial aid. Need-based:** 245 full-time freshmen applied for aid; 222 were judged to have need; 221 of these received aid. Average need met was 60%. Average scholarship/grant was $12,058; average loan $4,716. 60% of total undergraduate aid awarded as scholarships/grants, 40% as loans/jobs. **Non-need-based:** Awarded to 368 full-time undergraduates, including 125 freshmen. Scholarships awarded for academics, alumni affiliation, leadership, ROTC.

**Application procedures. Admission:** No deadline. $50 fee, may be waived for applicants with need. Application may be submitted online. Admission notification on a rolling basis beginning on or about 12/1. Must reply by May 1 or within 2 week(s) if notified thereafter. Students encouraged to apply by January 1. **Financial aid:** Priority date 2/15; no closing date. FAFSA, institutional form required. Applicants notified on a rolling basis starting 3/15.

**Academics.** First year seminar required. Internships required for some majors, encouraged for all; available semester, summer, school year; academic credit awarded. **Special study options:** Accelerated study, combined bachelor's/graduate degree, cross-registration, double major, ESL, exchange student, honors, independent study, internships, liberal arts/career combination, student-designed major, study abroad, teacher certification program, Washington semester. **Credit/placement by examination:** AP, CLEP, IB, SAT, institutional tests. 24 credit hours maximum toward bachelor's degree. **Support services:** Learning center, reduced course load, study skills assistance, tutoring, writing center.

**Majors. Biology:** General, biochemistry. **Business:** General. **Communications:** General, public relations. **Computer sciences:** General, computer science. **Education:** Mathematics. **English:** English lit. **Foreign languages:** Spanish. **Health:** Nursing (RN). **History:** General. **Interdisciplinary:** Museum. **Liberal arts:** Arts/sciences. **Psychology:** General. **Public**

**administration:** Social work. **Social sciences:** International relations, political science, sociology. **Visual/performing arts:** Dramatic, graphic design. **Other:** Human computer interaction, Law and government.

**Most popular majors.** Biology 7%, communications/journalism 8%, health sciences 53%, social sciences 9%.

**Computing on campus.** 196 workstations in library, computer center, student center. Dormitories wired for high-speed internet access and linked to campus network. Commuter students can connect to campus network. Online course registration, online library, helpline, wireless network available.

**Student life. Freshman orientation:** Mandatory, $195 fee. Preregistration for classes offered. Three 2-day programs in June, July, and August. 2-day program for entire class in September. **Policies:** Must complete series of effective decision-making courses in order to obtain guest privileges. **Housing:** Guaranteed on-campus for all undergraduates. Coed dorms, single-sex dorms, substance-free housing available. $450 nonrefundable deposit, deadline 5/1. All residences smoke-free. Quiet floors available. **Activities:** Campus ministries, choral groups, dance, drama, literary magazine, music ensembles, musical theater, radio station, student government, student newspaper, Asian American, African American, Hispanic, Asian, and Native American organizations, student organization for Latino culture, campus activities board, student government association, student athletic advisory committee.

**Athletics.** NCAA. **Intercollegiate:** Basketball, diving, field hockey W, lacrosse W, soccer W, softball W, swimming, tennis W, track and field W, volleyball W. **Intramural:** Basketball, soccer, softball. **Team name:** Regis Pride.

**Student services.** Adult student services, campus ministries, career counseling, student employment services, financial aid counseling, health services, minority student services, on-campus daycare, personal counseling, placement for graduates. **Physically disabled:** Services for visually, hearing impaired.

**Contact.** E-mail: admission@regiscollege.edu
Phone: (781) 768-7100 Toll-free number: (866) 438-7344
Fax: (781) 768-7071
Emily Keily, Director of Admission, Regis College, 235 Wellesley Street, Weston, MA 02493-1571

## Rhodec International
**Quincy, Massachusetts**
www.rhodec.edu/us

- For-profit 4-year virtual visual arts college
- Small city
- 160 degree-seeking undergraduates: 100% part-time, 92% women

**General.** Accredited by DETC. **Degrees:** 4 bachelor's, 24 associate awarded. **Calendar:** Continuous. **Part-time faculty:** 10 total.

**Basis for selection.** Open admission, but selective for some programs.

**2007-2008 Annual costs.** $224 to $447 per course, depending on number of credits.

**Application procedures. Admission:** No deadline. No application fee.

**Academics. Special study options:** Accelerated study, distance learning. **Credit/placement by examination:** CLEP.

**Majors. Visual/performing arts:** Interior design.

**Contact.** E-mail: uscontact@rhodec.edu
Phone: (617) 472-4942 Toll-free number: (877) 274-6332
Rhodec International, 59 Coddington Street, Suite 104, Quincy, MA 02169

## Salem State College
**Salem, Massachusetts**
www.salemstate.edu

CB member
CB code: 3522

- Public 4-year university
- Commuter campus in large town
- 7,014 degree-seeking undergraduates: 20% part-time, 63% women, 8% African American, 3% Asian American, 7% Hispanic American, 4% international
- 1,436 degree-seeking graduate students
- 60% of applicants admitted

- SAT or ACT (ACT writing optional) required
- 40% graduate within 6 years

**General.** Founded in 1854. Regionally accredited. **Degrees:** 1,059 bachelor's awarded; master's offered. **ROTC:** Army, Air Force. **Location:** 20 miles from Boston. **Calendar:** Semester, extensive summer session. **Full-time faculty:** 321 total; 9% minority, 50% women. **Part-time faculty:** 416 total; 4% minority, 58% women. **Class size:** 55% < 20, 43% 20-39, 1% 40-49, less than 1% 50-99. **Special facilities:** Media facility, center for creative and performing arts, observatories, glass blowing studio.

**Freshman class profile.** 6,890 applied, 4,118 admitted, 1,088 enrolled.

| Mid 50% test scores | | | |
|---|---|---|---|
| SAT critical reading: | 430-530 | Return as sophomores: | 73% |
| SAT math: | 430-540 | Out-of-state: | 5% |
| GPA 3.50 or higher: | 12% | Live on campus: | 55% |
| GPA 3.0-3.49: | 27% | International: | 2% |
| GPA 2.0-2.99: | 61% | | |

**Basis for selection.** Students with 3.0 GPA and college prep curriculum admitted. Students with less than 3.0 GPA admitted with balancing SAT/ACT scores. Special consideration possible. Some majors require higher GPA. Recommendations considered. Interview recommended. Portfolio required for art applicants. **Homeschooled:** Transcript of courses and grades, state high school equivalency certificate required.

**High school preparation.** 16 units required; 18 recommended. Required and recommended units include English 4, mathematics 3, social studies 2-3, history 1-2, science 3 (laboratory 2), foreign language 2, computer science 1 and visual/performing arts 1. Additional requirements for some programs.

**2007-2008 Annual costs.** Tuition/fees: $6,124; $12,264 out-of-state. Room/board: $8,561.

**Application procedures. Admission:** No deadline. $25 fee ($40 out-of-state), may be waived for applicants with need. Application may be submitted online. Admission notification on a rolling basis beginning on or about 1/3. Must reply within 30 days. **Financial aid:** Priority date 4/1; no closing date. FAFSA required. Applicants notified on a rolling basis starting 4/1; must reply within 2 week(s) of notification.

**Academics. Special study options:** Distance learning, double major, ESL, honors, independent study, internships, study abroad, teacher certification program. **Credit/placement by examination:** AP, CLEP, institutional tests. **Support services:** Learning center, pre-admission summer program, reduced course load, remedial instruction, tutoring, writing center.

**Majors. Biology:** General, biochemistry, ecology, marine. **Business:** Accounting, business admin, entrepreneurial studies, finance, human resources, international, management information systems, managerial economics, marketing. **Communications:** General, advertising, journalism, media studies, public relations. **Computer sciences:** General. **Education:** General, early childhood, elementary, middle, physical, secondary. **English:** Composition, English lit, technical writing. **Foreign languages:** Comparative lit, Spanish, translation. **Health:** Athletic training, clinical lab science, nuclear medical technology, nursing (RN). **History:** General, American, European, public archives. **Interdisciplinary:** Math/computer science. **Liberal arts:** Arts/sciences. **Math:** General. **Parks/recreation:** General, exercise sciences, health/fitness, sports admin. **Physical sciences:** Chemistry, geology. **Protective services:** Fire services admin, law enforcement admin. **Psychology:** General. **Public administration:** Social work. **Social sciences:** Cartography, economics, geography, political science, sociology. **Visual/performing arts:** Acting, art, art history/conservation, commercial/advertising art, dramatic, drawing, photography, printmaking, sculpture, theater design, theater history.

**Most popular majors.** Business/marketing 21%, communications/journalism 6%, education 12%, health sciences 12%, psychology 8%, security/protective services 8%, social sciences 8%.

**Computing on campus.** PC or laptop required. 84 workstations in library, computer center, student center. Dormitories wired for high-speed internet access and linked to campus network. Commuter students can connect to campus network. Online course registration, online library, helpline, repair service, student web hosting, wireless network available.

**Student life. Freshman orientation:** Mandatory, $85 fee. Preregistration for classes offered. Sessions held prior to start of semester. **Housing:** Coed dorms, substance-free housing available. $225 nonrefundable deposit, deadline 6/1. **Activities:** Bands, choral groups, dance, drama, literary magazine, music ensembles, musical theater, radio station, student government, student newspaper, Hillel, women's center, international student association, political science academy, Catholic student community, African American student association, Hispanic American society, student nurses association, criminal justice academy, MASSPIRG.

**Athletics.** NCAA. **Intercollegiate:** Baseball M, basketball, cross-country, field hockey W, golf M, ice hockey M, lacrosse, soccer, softball W, swimming W, tennis, track and field, volleyball W. **Intramural:** Archery, badminton, baseball M, basketball, field hockey W, football (non-tackle) M, golf, gymnastics, handball, ice hockey, racquetball, soccer, softball W, swimming, table tennis, tennis, volleyball. **Team name:** Vikings.

**Student services.** Adult student services, alcohol/substance abuse counseling, campus ministries, career counseling, services for economically disadvantaged, student employment services, financial aid counseling, health services, legal services, minority student services, on-campus daycare, personal counseling, placement for graduates, veterans' counselor, women's services. **Physically disabled:** Services for visually, speech, hearing impaired. **Learning disabled:** Comprehensive services available.

**Contact.** E-mail: admissions@salemstate.edu
Phone: (978) 542-6200 Fax: (978) 542-6893
Nate Bryant, Assistant Dean of Student Development, Salem State College, 352 Lafayette Street, Salem, MA 01970-5353

## School of the Museum of Fine Arts
**Boston, Massachusetts**
www.smfa.edu

CB code: 3794

- Private 4-year visual arts college
- Commuter campus in very large city
- 640 degree-seeking undergraduates: 6% part-time, 68% women, 2% African American, 4% Asian American, 5% Hispanic American, 1% Native American, 7% international
- 87 degree-seeking graduate students
- 82% of applicants admitted
- Application essay required
- 45% graduate within 6 years

**General.** Founded in 1876. All degree programs offered in affiliation with Tufts University, and all degree students may join sporting, musical, and other extracurricular activities offered at Tufts. Students may also cross-register at other schools in Boston's ProArts Consortium, including Emerson College, Berklee College of Music, Boston Conservatory, and Boston Architectural Center. **Degrees:** 142 bachelor's awarded; master's offered. **Location:** One mile from downtown. **Calendar:** Semester, limited summer session. **Full-time faculty:** 49 total; 71% have terminal degrees, 10% minority, 51% women. **Part-time faculty:** 34 total; 74% have terminal degrees, 3% minority, 56% women. **Class size:** 88% < 20, 11% 20-39, 1% 40-49. **Special facilities:** As a division of the Museum of Fine Arts, Boston (MFA), the Museum School is one of only three art schools in the nation that are affiliated with a museum. The MFA is one of the most comprehensive art museums in the world; the collection encompasses nearly 450,000 works of art, including a contemporary art collection. Recent acquisitions include works by Christian Boltanski, Chuck Close, Rineke Dijkstra, Robert Mangold, Takashi Murakami, Bridget Riley, Amy Sillman, Sarah Sze, and Kara Walker. Museum School students have free access to most Museum exhibits and are eligible for all Museum work-study positions. The Museum also hosts the School-s annual Traveling Scholars Exhibition.

**Freshman class profile.** 855 applied, 699 admitted, 135 enrolled.

| Mid 50% test scores | | | |
|---|---|---|---|
| SAT critical reading: | 520-640 | End year in good standing: | 86% |
| SAT math: | 480-590 | Return as sophomores: | 83% |
| SAT writing: | 490-600 | Out-of-state: | 62% |
| ACT composite: | 20-26 | Live on campus: | 44% |
| | | International: | 7% |

**Basis for selection.** Portfolio, previous schooling, and quality and content of essays important; grades and test scores important for BFA or BFA-E applicants, considered for diploma applicants. Combined Degree program applicants must apply to the Museum School and Tufts University simultaneously. Scores accepted on a rolling basis after February 1. Test scores not required for Diploma applicants. Portfolio required. Interview available by appointment. **Homeschooled:** Transcript of courses and grades required. Must have graduation date indicating successful completion of program; must be signed and dated by recognized record keeper, which may include outside testing agency, homeschool representative, or parent.

**2007-2008 Annual costs.** Tuition/fees: $27,970. Room only: $12,200. Books/supplies: $1,500. Personal expenses: $1,500.

**2007-2008 Financial aid. Need-based:** 91 full-time freshmen applied for aid; 77 were judged to have need; 77 of these received aid. Average need met was 36%. Average scholarship/grant was $15,002; average loan $3,416. 54% of total undergraduate aid awarded as scholarships/grants, 46% as loans/jobs. **Non-need-based:** Awarded to 122 full-time undergraduates, including 34 freshmen. Scholarships awarded for art.

**Application procedures. Admission:** Priority date 2/1; no deadline. $65 fee, may be waived for applicants with need. Application may be submitted online. Admission notification on a rolling basis beginning on or about 3/15. Must reply by May 1 or within 2 week(s) if notified thereafter. Students may apply early and request early notification of admission. **Financial aid:** Priority date 3/15; no closing date. FAFSA, institutional form required. Applicants notified on a rolling basis starting 4/15; must reply by 5/1 or within 2 week(s) of notification.

**Academics. Special study options:** Cross-registration, double major, ESL, exchange student, independent study, internships, liberal arts/career combination, New York semester, student-designed major, study abroad, teacher certification program. 5-year BFA/BA with Tufts University, studio art elective diploma program, optional fifth-year certificate program for Diploma recipients. **Credit/placement by examination:** AP, CLEP. **Support services:** Pre-admission summer program, study skills assistance, writing center.

**Majors. Communications technology:** Animation/special effects. **Education:** Art. **Visual/performing arts:** Art, ceramics, cinematography, drawing, illustration, metal/jewelry, multimedia, painting, photography, printmaking, sculpture, studio arts. **Other:** Video.

**Most popular majors.** Visual/performing arts 97%.

**Computing on campus.** 150 workstations in library, computer center, student center. Dormitories wired for high-speed internet access. Online course registration, wireless network available.

**Student life. Freshman orientation:** Mandatory, $125 fee. Preregistration for classes offered. Typically held during last week in August, right before beginning of semester. **Housing:** Coed dorms available. $450 nonrefundable deposit, deadline 5/1. **Activities:** Film society, student government, Outloud, chess club, infrasculpture, Amnesty International, photo club, vegan cooking collective, yoga club.

**Student services.** Adult student services, career counseling, student employment services, financial aid counseling, personal counseling, placement for graduates. **Physically disabled:** Services for hearing impaired.

**Contact.** E-mail: admissions@smfa.edu
Phone: (617) 369-3626 Toll-free number: (800) 643-6078
Fax: (617) 369-4264
Susan Clain, Dean of Admissions, School of the Museum of Fine Arts, 230 The Fenway, Boston, MA 02115

## Simmons College
**Boston, Massachusetts**
www.simmons.edu

**CB member**
**CB code: 3761**

- Private 4-year liberal arts college for women
- Residential campus in large city
- 2,064 degree-seeking undergraduates: 9% part-time, 100% women, 5% African American, 8% Asian American, 4% Hispanic American, 2% international
- 2,502 degree-seeking graduate students
- 57% of applicants admitted
- SAT or ACT (ACT writing optional), application essay required
- 77% graduate within 6 years

**General.** Founded in 1899. Regionally accredited. **Degrees:** 453 bachelor's awarded; master's, doctoral offered. **ROTC:** Army. **Location:** 2 miles from downtown. **Calendar:** Semester, extensive summer session. **Full-time faculty:** 245 total; 19% minority, 71% women. **Part-time faculty:** 342 total; 10% minority, 74% women. **Class size:** 61% < 20, 31% 20-39, 2% 40-49, 5% 50-99. **Special facilities:** Audiovisual media center, dream analysis lab, physical therapy lab.

**Freshman class profile.** 2,937 applied, 1,686 admitted, 479 enrolled.

| Mid 50% test scores | | | | |
|---|---|---|---|---|
| SAT critical reading: | 500-600 | Rank in top tenth: | | 18% |
| SAT math: | 480-590 | End year in good standing: | | 96% |
| SAT writing: | 510-610 | Return as sophomores: | | 83% |
| ACT composite: | 21-26 | Out-of-state: | | 47% |
| Rank in top quarter: | 58% | Live on campus: | | 90% |
| | | International: | | 3% |

**Basis for selection.** School achievement record most important. Test scores, 2 recommendations, essay, interview (if available), personal qualities also important. Interests, accomplishments considered.

**High school preparation.** 19 units required; 22 recommended. Required and recommended units include English 4, mathematics 3-4, social studies 3-4, history 3, science 3 and foreign language 3-4.

**2007-2008 Annual costs.** Tuition/fees: $28,302. Room/board: $11,138. Books/supplies: $800. Personal expenses: $1,250.

**2007-2008 Financial aid. Need-based:** Average need met was 69%. Average scholarship/grant was $13,088; average loan $3,615. 66% of total undergraduate aid awarded as scholarships/grants, 34% as loans/jobs. **Non-need-based:** Scholarships awarded for academics, alumni affiliation, leadership, minority status.

**Application procedures. Admission:** Priority date 2/1; deadline 4/1 (postmark date). $35 fee, may be waived for applicants with need. Application may be submitted online. Admission notification 4/15. Must reply by May 1 or within 2 week(s) if notified thereafter. **Financial aid:** Priority date 2/15, closing date 3/1. FAFSA required. Applicants notified on a rolling basis starting 3/15; must reply by 5/1 or within 4 week(s) of notification.

**Academics. Special study options:** Accelerated study, combined bachelor's/graduate degree, cross-registration, double major, dual enrollment of high school students, ESL, exchange student, honors, independent study, internships, liberal arts/career combination, semester at sea, student-designed major, study abroad, teacher certification program, Washington semester. Exchange programs with Mills College, Spelman College, Fisk University, American University, Colleges of the Fenway; double degree programs with Massachusetts College of Pharmacy and Health Sciences and Hebrew College. **Credit/placement by examination:** AP, CLEP, IB, institutional tests. 32 credit hours maximum toward bachelor's degree. **Support services:** Learning center, reduced course load, study skills assistance, tutoring, writing center.

**Majors. Area/ethnic studies:** African-American, East Asian, women's. **Biology:** General, biochemistry. **Business:** Business admin, finance, management information systems, sales/distribution. **Communications:** General, public relations. **Computer sciences:** General. **Conservation:** General, environmental science. **Education:** General, early childhood, elementary, ESL, middle, secondary, social studies, special. **English:** American lit, British lit, English lit. **Foreign languages:** Comparative lit, French, Spanish. **Health:** Nursing (RN), predental, premedicine, prepharmacy. **History:** General. **Interdisciplinary:** Biopsychology, nutrition sciences. **Math:** General. **Philosophy/religion:** Philosophy. **Physical sciences:** Chemistry, physics. **Psychology:** General. **Public administration:** Policy analysis. **Social sciences:** Economics, international relations, political science, sociology. **Visual/performing arts:** Art history/conservation, arts management, commercial/advertising art, graphic design, music history, music performance.

**Most popular majors.** Communications/journalism 11%, health sciences 30%, psychology 10%, public administration/social services 6%, social sciences 14%, visual/performing arts 7%.

**Computing on campus.** 250 workstations in dormitories, library, computer center, student center. Dormitories wired for high-speed internet access and linked to campus network. Commuter students can connect to campus network. Online course registration, online library, helpline, wireless network available.

**Student life. Freshman orientation:** Mandatory. Preregistration for classes offered. **Housing:** Special housing for disabled, substance-free housing available. $250 fully refundable deposit, deadline 5/1. Special interest housing available. **Activities:** Choral groups, dance, drama, film society, literary magazine, student government, student newspaper, Asian student association, black students organization, organizacion Latino Americana, international multicultural student association, Carribean culture association, Hillel, Amnesty International, feminist union, The Alliance, Students Take Action Now - Darfur (STAND).

**Athletics.** NCAA. **Intercollegiate:** Basketball W, diving W, field hockey W, rowing (crew) W, soccer W, softball W, swimming W, tennis W, track and field W, volleyball W. **Intramural:** Basketball W, diving W, softball W, tennis W, volleyball W. **Team name:** Sharks.

**Student services.** Adult student services, alcohol/substance abuse counseling, campus ministries, career counseling, student employment services, financial aid counseling, health services, personal counseling, placement for graduates, veterans' counselor, women's services. **Physically disabled:** Services for visually, speech, hearing impaired.

**Contact.** E-mail: ugadm@simmons.edu
Phone: (617) 521-2051 Toll-free number: (800) 345-8468
Fax: (617) 521-3190
Catherine Childs-Capolupo, Director of Undergraduate Admissions, Simmons College, 300 The Fenway, Boston, MA 02115-5898

## Smith College
**Northampton, Massachusetts**
www.smith.edu

**CB member**
**CB code: 3762**

- Private 4-year liberal arts college for women
- Residential campus in large town

- 2,569 degree-seeking undergraduates: 100% women, 7% African American, 12% Asian American, 6% Hispanic American, 1% Native American, 7% international
- 462 degree-seeking graduate students
- 52% of applicants admitted
- SAT or ACT (ACT writing optional), application essay required
- 86% graduate within 6 years

**General.** Founded in 1871. Regionally accredited. **Degrees:** 670 bachelor's awarded; master's, doctoral offered. **ROTC:** Army, Air Force. **Location:** 35 miles from Hartford, Connecticut, 90 miles from Boston. **Calendar:** Semester. **Full-time faculty:** 281 total; 98% have terminal degrees, 17% minority, 55% women. **Part-time faculty:** 28 total; 96% have terminal degrees, 4% minority, 50% women. **Class size:** 68% < 20, 26% 20-39, 3% 40-49, 4% 50-99, less than 1% >100. **Special facilities:** Physiology and horticultural laboratories, printmaking studio, darkroom and sculpture (including bronze casting studio) facilities, dance, theater and television studios, electronic music studio, recital hall, digital design studio, animal care facilities, electron microscopes, on-campus elementary school, multimedia language lab, greenhouses, astronomy observatories.

**Freshman class profile.** 3,329 applied, 1,726 admitted, 656 enrolled.

| Mid 50% test scores | | | |
|---|---|---|---|
| SAT critical reading: | 590-710 | Rank in top quarter: | 92% |
| SAT math: | 560-670 | Rank in top tenth: | 63% |
| SAT writing: | 590-700 | End year in good standing: | 92% |
| ACT composite: | 25-30 | Return as sophomores: | 90% |
| GPA 3.50 or higher: | 83% | Out-of-state: | 82% |
| GPA 3.0-3.49: | 16% | Live on campus: | 99% |
| GPA 2.0-2.99: | 1% | International: | 6% |

**Basis for selection.** Secondary school record, including GPA and difficulty of courses, recommendations most important. Class rank, essay, school and community activities and test scores also important. SAT Subject Tests recommended. 2 SAT Subject Tests recommended. Interview strongly recommended, may be conducted off-campus by alumna. **Homeschooled:** Statement describing homeschool structure and mission, transcript of courses and grades, interview, letter of recommendation (nonparent) required. Submit portfolio including transcript and evaluation of coursework and sample of short research or analytical paper with evaluator's remarks.

**High school preparation.** 16 units recommended. Recommended units include English 4, mathematics 4, history 2, science 3 (laboratory 3) and foreign language 3. 3 units of 1 foreign language or 2 each of 2 languages recommended.

**2007-2008 Annual costs.** Tuition/fees: $34,186. Room/board: $11,420. Books/supplies: $1,620. Personal expenses: $1,550.

**2007-2008 Financial aid. Need-based:** 496 full-time freshmen applied for aid; 396 were judged to have need; 396 of these received aid. Average need met was 100%. Average scholarship/grant was $26,530; average loan $3,538. 77% of total undergraduate aid awarded as scholarships/grants, 23% as loans/jobs. **Non-need-based:** Awarded to 170 full-time undergraduates, including 32 freshmen. Scholarships awarded for academics, state residency. **Additional information:** Financial aid policy guarantees to meet full financial need, as calculated by college, of all admitted students.

**Application procedures. Admission:** Closing date 1/15 (postmark date). $60 fee, may be waived for applicants with need. Application may be submitted online. Notification by early April. Must reply by May 1 or within 2 week(s) if notified thereafter. **Financial aid:** Closing date 2/15. FAFSA, CSS PROFILE required. Applicants notified by 4/1; must reply by 5/1.

**Academics.** Academic Honor Code; writing course required in freshman year. **Special study options:** Accelerated study, cross-registration, double major, exchange student, honors, independent study, internships, semester at sea, student-designed major, study abroad, teacher certification program, Washington semester. Member of Five College Consortium, program in engineering and technology, engineering science program within liberal arts curriculum leading to BS degree, post-baccalaureate certificate in American studies (available to international students). **Credit/placement by examination:** AP, CLEP, IB, institutional tests. 32 credit hours maximum toward bachelor's degree. **Support services:** Learning center, study skills assistance, tutoring, writing center.

**Majors. Area/ethnic studies:** African-American, American, Asian, Latin American, women's. **Biology:** General, biochemistry. **Computer sciences:** Computer science. **Education:** General. **Engineering:** General, biomedical, chemical, civil, computer, electrical, environmental, mechanical, mechanics, science. **English:** English lit. **Foreign languages:** Ancient Greek, classics, comparative lit, East Asian, French, German, Italian, Latin, Portuguese, Russian, Spanish. **History:** General. **Interdisciplinary:** Ancient studies, medieval/Renaissance, neuroscience. **Math:** General. **Philosophy/religion:** Philosophy, religion. **Physical sciences:** Astronomy, astrophysics, chemistry, geology, physics. **Psychology:** General. **Social sciences:** Anthropology, economics, political science, sociology. **Visual/performing arts:** Art, art history/conservation, dance, dramatic, film/cinema, studio arts.

**Most popular majors.** Area/ethnic studies 11%, English 7%, foreign language 11%, psychology 8%, social sciences 22%, visual/performing arts 10%.

**Computing on campus.** 600 workstations in dormitories, library, computer center, student center. Dormitories wired for high-speed internet access and linked to campus network. Commuter students can connect to campus network. Online course registration, online library, helpline, repair service, student web hosting, wireless network available.

**Student life. Freshman orientation:** Mandatory. Program 4-5 days prior to beginning of classes. Program includes Parent Day. **Policies:** Each residence self-governed within framework of college regulations. Residents determine house responsibilities. **Housing:** Guaranteed on-campus for all undergraduates. Cooperative housing available. $200 nonrefundable deposit, deadline 5/1. French-speaking house, senior house, nontraditional age house, apartment complexes for juniors and seniors available. **Activities:** Bands, campus ministries, choral groups, dance, drama, international student organizations, literary magazine, music ensembles, Model UN, musical theater, radio station, student government, student newspaper, TV station, service organizations, women's resource center, black student alliance, Asian student association, Hillel, Newman Club, Christian council, international relations club, Latina organization, Native American organization.

**Athletics.** NCAA. **Intercollegiate:** Basketball W, cross-country W, diving W, equestrian W, field hockey W, lacrosse W, rowing (crew) W, skiing W, soccer W, softball W, squash W, swimming W, tennis W, track and field W, volleyball W. **Intramural:** Basketball W, soccer W. **Team name:** Pioneers.

**Student services.** Adult student services, alcohol/substance abuse counseling, campus ministries, career counseling, services for economically disadvantaged, student employment services, financial aid counseling, health services, minority student services, on-campus daycare, personal counseling, placement for graduates, women's services. **Physically disabled:** Services for visually, speech, hearing impaired.

**Contact.** E-mail: admission@smith.edu
Phone: (413) 585-2500 Fax: (413) 585-2527
Debra Shaver, Director of Admission, Smith College, 7 College Lane, Northampton, MA 01063

## Springfield College
**Springfield, Massachusetts**
www.spfldcol.edu

CB member
CB code: 3763

- Private 4-year health science and liberal arts college
- Residential campus in small city
- 2,150 degree-seeking undergraduates
- 63% of applicants admitted
- SAT or ACT with writing, application essay required

**General.** Founded in 1885. Regionally accredited. Adult weekend programs at 10 sites across the country. **Degrees:** 930 bachelor's awarded; master's, doctoral offered. **ROTC:** Army, Air Force. **Location:** 90 miles from Boston, 26 miles from Hartford, Connecticut. **Calendar:** Semester, limited summer session. **Full-time faculty:** 176 total; 81% have terminal degrees, 10% minority, 44% women. **Part-time faculty:** 159 total; 9% minority, 50% women. **Class size:** 46% < 20, 52% 20-39, less than 1% 40-49, less than 1% 50-99, less than 1% >100. **Special facilities:** 81-acre campground and outdoor adventure area.

**Freshman class profile.** 2,321 applied, 1,456 admitted, 552 enrolled.

| Mid 50% test scores | | | |
|---|---|---|---|
| SAT critical reading: | 450-550 | Rank in top tenth: | 9% |
| SAT math: | 480-570 | Out-of-state: | 72% |
| Rank in top quarter: | 34% | Live on campus: | 98% |

**Basis for selection.** School achievement record, essay, extracurricular activities, personal references, and test scores important. Portfolio required of art majors. **Homeschooled:** Statement describing homeschool structure and mission, transcript of courses and grades, letter of recommendation (nonparent) required.

**High school preparation.** 16 units required. Required and recommended units include English 4, mathematics 3, social studies 2, history 1, science 3 (laboratory 2) and foreign language 3. Emphasis on science for majors in allied health fields.

**2007-2008 Annual costs.** Tuition/fees: $24,075. Room/board: $9,270. Books/supplies: $900. Personal expenses: $1,200.

**Financial aid. Additional information:** Co-operative education program available to students after freshman year.

**Application procedures. Admission:** Priority date 3/1; deadline 4/1 (postmark date). $50 fee, may be waived for applicants with need. Application may be submitted online. Admission notification on a rolling basis beginning on or about 12/1. Must reply by May 1 or within 2 week(s) if notified thereafter. Application closing date for athletic training, physical therapy majors 12/1; closing date for physician assistant and occupational therapy majors 2/1; SAT or ACT score reports must be received by February 1. **Financial aid:** Priority date 3/15; no closing date. FAFSA, institutional form, CSS PROFILE required. Applicants notified on a rolling basis starting 3/15; must reply by 5/1 or within 2 week(s) of notification.

**Academics.** Emphasis on practical fieldwork experiences to supplement classroom learning. **Special study options:** Combined bachelor's/graduate degree, cooperative education, cross-registration, double major, ESL, honors, independent study, internships, liberal arts/career combination, semester at sea, student-designed major, study abroad, teacher certification program. **Credit/placement by examination:** AP, CLEP, IB, SAT, ACT, institutional tests. 30 credit hours maximum toward bachelor's degree. **Support services:** Learning center, reduced course load, study skills assistance, tutoring, writing center.

**Majors. Biology:** General. **Business:** Business admin. **Computer sciences:** General, computer graphics, information systems. **Conservation:** General, environmental studies. **Education:** Art, early childhood, elementary, health, physical, secondary, special. **English:** English lit. **Health:** Art therapy, athletic training, clinical lab science, clinical lab technology, EMT paramedic, health care admin, medical records admin, physician assistant, predental, recreational therapy. **History:** General. **Interdisciplinary:** Biological/physical sciences. **Legal studies:** Prelaw. **Liberal arts:** Arts/sciences. **Math:** General. **Parks/recreation:** Exercise sciences, facilities management, health/fitness, sports admin. **Protective services:** Law enforcement admin. **Psychology:** General. **Public administration:** Community org/advocacy, human services. **Social sciences:** Political science, sociology. **Visual/performing arts:** Art, dance.

**Computing on campus.** 235 workstations in dormitories, library, computer center, student center. Dormitories wired for high-speed internet access and linked to campus network. Commuter students can connect to campus network. Helpline, wireless network available.

**Student life. Freshman orientation:** Mandatory, $100 fee. Orientation program immediately preceding fall semester. **Housing:** Guaranteed on-campus for all undergraduates. Coed dorms, single-sex dorms, special housing for disabled, apartments, substance-free housing available. **Activities:** Jazz band, choral groups, dance, drama, literary magazine, music ensembles, musical theater, radio station, student government, student newspaper, women's group, multicultural organization, Hot Line, community volunteer program, Alpha Phi Omega, service-oriented organizations, Newman Club, Association of Christian Athletes.

**Athletics.** NCAA. **Intercollegiate:** Baseball M, basketball, cross-country, diving, field hockey W, football (tackle) M, golf, gymnastics, lacrosse, soccer, softball W, swimming, tennis, track and field, volleyball, wrestling M. **Intramural:** Basketball, field hockey, football (non-tackle), handball, lacrosse, racquetball, soccer, softball, swimming, tennis, track and field, volleyball, wrestling M. **Team name:** Pride.

**Student services.** Adult student services, alcohol/substance abuse counseling, campus ministries, career counseling, student employment services, financial aid counseling, health services, minority student services, on-campus daycare, personal counseling, placement for graduates, veterans' counselor, women's services. **Physically disabled:** Services for visually, speech, hearing impaired.

**Contact.** E-mail: admissions@spfldcol.edu
Phone: (413) 748-3136 Toll-free number: (800) 343-1257
Fax: (413) 748-3694
Mary DeAngelo, Director of Admissions, Springfield College, 263 Alden Street, Springfield, MA 01109

---

## Stonehill College

**Easton, Massachusetts**
**www.stonehill.edu**

CB member
CB code: 3770

- Private 4-year business and liberal arts college affiliated with Roman Catholic Church
- Residential campus in large town
- 2,413 degree-seeking undergraduates: 3% part-time, 61% women, 2% African American, 2% Asian American, 4% Hispanic American

---

- 10 degree-seeking graduate students
- 52% of applicants admitted
- Application essay required
- 85% graduate within 6 years; 24% enter graduate study

**General.** Founded in 1948. Regionally accredited. **Degrees:** 632 bachelor's awarded; master's offered. **ROTC:** Army. **Location:** 22 miles from Boston. **Calendar:** Semester, limited summer session. **Full-time faculty:** 145 total; 81% have terminal degrees, 6% minority, 40% women. **Part-time faculty:** 113 total; 35% have terminal degrees, 7% minority, 40% women. **Class size:** 44% < 20, 55% 20-39, less than 1% 40-49, less than 1% 50-99. **Special facilities:** Observatory.

**Freshman class profile.** 5,704 applied, 2,960 admitted, 659 enrolled.

| Mid 50% test scores | | | |
|---|---|---|---|
| SAT critical reading: | 540-630 | GPA 2.0-2.99: | 8% |
| SAT math: | 550-640 | Rank in top quarter: | 89% |
| ACT composite: | 24-27 | Rank in top tenth: | 49% |
| GPA 3.50 or higher: | 62% | Return as sophomores: | 87% |
| GPA 3.0-3.49: | 30% | Out-of-state: | 52% |
| | | Live on campus: | 96% |

**Basis for selection.** School achievement record, class rank, test scores most important. Guidance counselor recommendation, activities, essay, campus visit also important. Other letters of recommendation also considered. **Homeschooled:** Statement describing homeschool structure and mission, transcript of courses and grades, state high school equivalency certificate required.

**High school preparation.** 17 units required; 20 recommended. Required and recommended units include English 4, mathematics 3-4, social studies 1, history 3, science 1-3 (laboratory 1-2), foreign language 2-3 and academic electives 2. Foreign language units should be in same language. 3 combined units in history, political science, social science required. Math units should consist of algegra I, algebra II, and geometry. Additional units in science and math recommended for science applicants. Additional math units recommended for business applicants.

**2007-2008 Annual costs.** Tuition/fees: $28,440. Room/board: $11,430.

**2007-2008 Financial aid. Need-based:** Average need met was 77%. Average scholarship/grant was $15,790; average loan $3,864. 67% of total undergraduate aid awarded as scholarships/grants, 33% as loans/jobs. **Non-need-based:** Scholarships awarded for academics, athletics, ROTC.

**Application procedures. Admission:** Closing date 1/15 (postmark date). $60 fee, may be waived for applicants with need. Application may be submitted online. Admission notification 4/1. Must reply by 5/1. **Financial aid:** Priority date 2/1; no closing date. FAFSA, CSS PROFILE required. Applicants notified by 4/1; must reply by 5/1.

**Academics.** Evening technology workshops and web-based electronic portfolios open to all students. **Special study options:** Combined bachelor's/graduate degree, cross-registration, double major, dual enrollment of high school students, honors, independent study, internships, liberal arts/career combination, New York semester, student-designed major, study abroad, teacher certification program, Washington semester. Full-time international internship sites in London, Brussels, Zaragoza, Dublin, Paris; Stonehill-Quebec exchange program; 3-2 computer engineering BA/BS program with University of Notre Dame, Indiana; Stonehill Undergraduate Research Experience (SURE) program. **Credit/placement by examination:** AP, CLEP, IB, institutional tests. 30 credit hours maximum toward bachelor's degree. **Support services:** Learning center, pre-admission summer program, reduced course load, study skills assistance, tutoring, writing center.

**Majors. Area/ethnic studies:** American. **Biology:** General, biochemistry. **Business:** Accounting, business admin, finance, international, marketing. **Communications:** General. **Computer sciences:** Computer science. **Education:** Early childhood, elementary. **Engineering:** Computer. **English:** English lit. **Foreign languages:** General. **Health:** Health care admin. **History:** General. **Interdisciplinary:** Gerontology, neuroscience. **Math:** General. **Philosophy/religion:** Philosophy, religion. **Physical sciences:** Chemistry. **Psychology:** General. **Public administration:** General. **Social sciences:** Criminology, economics, international relations, political science, sociology. **Visual/performing arts:** Studio arts. **Other:** Gender studies.

**Most popular majors.** Business/marketing 19%, communications/journalism 7%, education 7%, psychology 12%, social sciences 22%.

**Computing on campus.** 300 workstations in dormitories, library, computer center, student center. Dormitories wired for high-speed internet access and linked to campus network. Commuter students can connect to campus network. Online course registration, online library, helpline, student web hosting, wireless network available.

**Student life. Freshman orientation:** Available. Preregistration for classes offered. 2-day program in June. **Housing:** Guaranteed on-campus for all undergraduates. Coed dorms, single-sex dorms, special housing for disabled, substance-free housing available. $500 nonrefundable deposit, deadline 5/1. Special interest housing proposals considered for groups. **Activities:** Pep band, choral groups, dance, drama, film society, literary magazine, music ensembles, musical theater, radio station, student government, student newspaper, College Republicans, College Democrats, Amnesty International, BACCHUS, volunteer network, Habitat for Humanity, Circle K, politics society, environmental club, campus free thought alliance club.

**Athletics.** NCAA. **Intercollegiate:** Baseball M, basketball, cross-country, equestrian W, field hockey W, football (tackle) M, ice hockey M, lacrosse W, soccer, softball W, tennis, track and field, volleyball W. **Intramural:** Basketball, field hockey, football (non-tackle), handball, racquetball, soccer, softball, tennis, volleyball. **Team name:** Skyhawks.

**Student services.** Adult student services, alcohol/substance abuse counseling, campus ministries, career counseling, services for economically disadvantaged, student employment services, financial aid counseling, health services, minority student services, personal counseling, placement for graduates, women's services. **Physically disabled:** Services for visually, speech, hearing impaired.

**Contact.** E-mail: admissions@stonehill.edu
Phone: (508) 565-1373 Fax: (508) 565-1545
Brian Murphy, Dean of Admissions and Enrollment, Stonehill College, 320 Washington Street, Easton, MA 02357-0100

## Suffolk University

**Boston, Massachusetts**
www.suffolk.edu

**CB member**
**CB code: 3771**

- Private 4-year university
- Commuter campus in very large city
- 5,289 degree-seeking undergraduates: 9% part-time, 56% women, 3% African American, 6% Asian American, 5% Hispanic American, 9% international
- 3,460 degree-seeking graduate students
- 80% of applicants admitted
- SAT or ACT with writing required
- 52% graduate within 6 years; 26% enter graduate study

**General.** Founded in 1906. Regionally accredited. Campuses in Spain and Senegal. Branch campuses in Cape Cod, Merrimack, and Franklin. **Degrees:** 899 bachelor's awarded; master's, doctoral, first professional offered. **ROTC:** Army. **Location:** Downtown. **Calendar:** Semester, extensive summer session. **Full-time faculty:** 417 total; 92% have terminal degrees, 12% minority, 38% women. **Part-time faculty:** 494 total; 28% have terminal degrees, 16% minority, 41% women. **Class size:** 45% < 20, 54% 20-39, less than 1% 40-49, less than 1% 50-99. **Special facilities:** Marine biology station, poetry center, engergy research lab.

**Freshman class profile.** 8,044 applied, 6,403 admitted, 1,328 enrolled.

| Mid 50% test scores | | | |
|---|---|---|---|
| SAT critical reading: | 460-560 | Rank in top quarter: | 31% |
| SAT math: | 450-570 | Rank in top tenth: | 9% |
| SAT writing: | 460-560 | End year in good standing: | 84% |
| ACT composite: | 20-24 | Return as sophomores: | 72% |
| GPA 3.50 or higher: | 18% | Out-of-state: | 37% |
| GPA 3.0-3.49: | 35% | Live on campus: | 47% |
| GPA 2.0-2.99: | 46% | International: | 7% |

**Basis for selection.** High school record including courses taken, level of study, class rank, test scores, essay important. Counselor recommendation considered. Interview recommended. Portfolio required for BFA program applicants. **Homeschooled:** Transcript of courses and grades, state high school equivalency certificate, letter of recommendation (nonparent) required. Admission interview highly recommended. Transcript/Record of Courses and Grades OR written evaluation of work.

**High school preparation.** 17 units required; 21 recommended. Required and recommended units include English 4, mathematics 3-4, history 1-4, science 2-4 (laboratory 1), foreign language 2-3 and academic electives 4.

**2007-2008 Annual costs.** Tuition/fees: $24,250. Room/board: $13,360. Books/supplies: $1,000. Personal expenses: $2,473.

**2007-2008 Financial aid.** **Need-based:** 956 full-time freshmen applied for aid; 754 were judged to have need; 741 of these received aid. Average need met was 63%. Average scholarship/grant was $8,209; average loan $3,733. 54% of total undergraduate aid awarded as scholarships/grants, 46%

as loans/jobs. **Non-need-based:** Awarded to 1,187 full-time undergraduates, including 320 freshmen. Scholarships awarded for academics, alumni affiliation. **Additional information:** Foreign students may apply for institutional employment awards.

**Application procedures. Admission:** Closing date 3/1. $50 fee, may be waived for applicants with need. Application may be submitted online. Admission notification on a rolling basis beginning on or about 2/5. Must reply by May 1 or within 2 week(s) if notified thereafter. **Financial aid:** Closing date 3/1. FAFSA, institutional form required. Applicants notified on a rolling basis starting 3/1.

**Academics. Special study options:** Accelerated study, combined bachelor's/graduate degree, cooperative education, cross-registration, distance learning, double major, ESL, exchange student, honors, independent study, internships, liberal arts/career combination, study abroad, Washington semester. **Credit/placement by examination:** AP, CLEP, IB, SAT, ACT, institutional tests. 30 credit hours maximum toward associate degree, 30 toward bachelor's. **Support services:** Learning center, pre-admission summer program, reduced course load, remedial instruction, study skills assistance, tutoring, writing center.

**Honors college/program.** Prospective honors scholars must complete application available from the Office of Undergraduate Admission. Class rank, GPA, personal essay, interview, and the quality of the secondary school curriculum, including advanced placement, honors, and other types of accelerated courses, and any other relevant information considered. Applicants from the College of Arts and Sciences and Sawyer Business School will normally meet at least two of the following criteria: Academic GPA of 3.7/4.0; Class rank within upper 10 percent (if class rank is available); SAT scores of 1300; or ACT scores of 29; and TOEFL scores of 600, if applicable.

**Majors. Area/ethnic studies:** African-American, French, German, women's. **Biology:** General, biochemistry, biomedical sciences, biophysics, environmental, marine, radiobiology. **Business:** General, accounting, business admin, entrepreneurial studies, finance, international, management information systems, marketing, office technology. **Communications:** General, advertising, broadcast journalism, journalism, media studies, organizational, political, public relations. **Communications technology:** General, radio/tv. **Computer sciences:** General, computer science, information systems. **Conservation:** Environmental science. **Education:** General. **Engineering:** Computer, electrical, environmental. **Engineering technology:** Biomedical. **English:** Creative writing, English lit. **Foreign languages:** General, French, German, Spanish. **History:** General, American, European. **Legal studies:** Paralegal, prelaw. **Liberal arts:** Arts/sciences, humanities. **Math:** General. **Philosophy/religion:** Philosophy. **Physical sciences:** General, chemistry, physics. **Protective services:** Law enforcement admin. **Psychology:** General. **Public administration:** General, policy analysis. **Social sciences:** General, criminology, economics, international economics, international relations, political science, sociology, U.S. government. **Visual/performing arts:** General, acting, art, art history/conservation, arts management, commercial/advertising art, dramatic, film/cinema, interior design, studio arts, theater history.

**Most popular majors.** Business/marketing 42%, communications/journalism 17%, psychology 6%, social sciences 19%.

**Computing on campus.** 1,232 workstations in dormitories, library, computer center, student center. Dormitories wired for high-speed internet access and linked to campus network. Commuter students can connect to campus network. Online course registration, online library, helpline, wireless network available.

**Student life. Freshman orientation:** Available, $85 fee. Preregistration for classes offered. 3-day orientation held in June and August. **Housing:** Coed dorms, apartments, substance-free housing available. $600 fully refundable deposit, deadline 5/1. Strongly suggest housing deposit before March 15. Housing awarded on a first-come first-serve basis by date of the admission deposit. Housing deposit refundable in full until May 1. **Activities:** Jazz band, choral groups, dance, drama, literary magazine, music ensembles, musical theater, radio station, student government, student newspaper, TV station, Islamic cultural society, Newman Club, Jewish society, finance committee, student government association, student judiciary review board, Jumpstart Inc., S.O.U.L.S., Best Buddies, Up 'Til Dawn.

**Athletics.** NCAA. **Intercollegiate:** Baseball M, basketball, cross-country, golf M, ice hockey M, soccer M, softball W, tennis, volleyball W. **Intramural:** Basketball, football (non-tackle), soccer W, table tennis, volleyball. **Team name:** Rams.

**Student services.** Adult student services, alcohol/substance abuse counseling, campus ministries, career counseling, student employment services, financial aid counseling, health services, minority student services, personal counseling, placement for graduates, veterans' counselor, women's services. **Physically disabled:** Services for visually, speech, hearing impaired.

**Contact.** E-mail: admission@suffolk.edu
Phone: (617) 573-8460 Toll-free number: (800) 678-3365
Fax: (617) 742-4291
John Hamel, Director of Admissions, Suffolk University, 8 Ashburton Place, Boston, MA 02108

## Tufts University
### Medford, Massachusetts
**CB member**
**www.tufts.edu**
**CB code: 3901**

- Private 4-year university
- Residential campus in small city
- 5,015 degree-seeking undergraduates: 1% part-time, 51% women, 7% African American, 12% Asian American, 6% Hispanic American, 6% international
- 4,335 degree-seeking graduate students
- 28% of applicants admitted
- SAT and SAT Subject Tests or ACT with writing, application essay required
- 89% graduate within 6 years

**General.** Founded in 1852. Regionally accredited. **Degrees:** 1,361 bachelor's awarded; master's, doctoral, first professional offered. **ROTC:** Army, Naval, Air Force. **Location:** 5 miles from Boston. **Calendar:** Semester, limited summer session. **Full-time faculty:** 676 total; 42% women. **Part-time faculty:** 380 total; 46% women. **Class size:** 75% < 20, 19% 20-39, 2% 40-49, 2% 50-99, 2% >100. **Special facilities:** Computer-aided design laboratory, arts center, theater in the round, engineering project design center.

**Freshman class profile.** 15,365 applied, 4,229 admitted, 1,373 enrolled.

| Mid 50% test scores | | | |
|---|---|---|---|
| SAT critical reading: | 670-750 | Rank in top tenth: | 80% |
| SAT math: | 670-740 | Return as sophomores: | 96% |
| SAT writing: | 670-740 | Out-of-state: | 77% |
| ACT composite: | 29-32 | Live on campus: | 98% |
| Rank in top quarter: | 96% | International: | 5% |

**Basis for selection.** School achievement record most important. School recommendation, test scores, character, personality, extracurricular participation, special talents also important. Geographical distribution, alumni relationship, minority status, socioeconomic status all considered. For applicants who submit SAT scores: 2 SAT Subject Tests required of liberal arts applicants; Math 1 or 2 and either physics or chemistry required of engineering applicants. Interview optional but recommended. **Homeschooled:** Transcript of courses and grades required.

**High school preparation.** Recommended units include English 4, mathematics 3, history 2, science 2 and foreign language 3. 4 math, 2 laboratory science recommended for engineering, math, and science majors.

**2007-2008 Annual costs.** Tuition/fees: $36,700. Room/board: $10,160. Books/supplies: $800. Personal expenses: $1,200.

**2007-2008 Financial aid.** All financial aid based on need. 758 full-time freshmen applied for aid; 596 were judged to have need; 587 of these received aid. Average need met was 100%. 83% of total undergraduate aid awarded as scholarships/grants, 17% as loans/jobs.

**Application procedures. Admission:** Closing date 1/1 (postmark date). $70 fee, may be waived for applicants with need. Application may be submitted online. Admission notification 4/1. Must reply by 5/1. **Financial aid:** Closing date 2/15. FAFSA, CSS PROFILE required. Applicants notified by 4/1; must reply by 5/1.

**Academics. Special study options:** Combined bachelor's/graduate degree, cross-registration, double major, exchange student, independent study, internships, liberal arts/career combination, semester at sea, student-designed major, study abroad, teacher certification program, Washington semester. Experimental college, semester exchange with Lincoln University and Swarthmore College, 3-2 programs with New England Conservatory of Music (BA/BM), School of the Museum of Fine Arts (BA/BFA) European Center in Talloires, France. **Credit/placement by examination:** AP, CLEP, IB, institutional tests. Limit 1 year of credit by acceleration. **Support services:** Learning center, study skills assistance, tutoring.

**Majors. Area/ethnic studies:** African, African-American, American, Asian, Central/Eastern European, East Asian, European, Latin American, Near/Middle Eastern, Russian/Slavic, Western European, women's. **Biology:** General, ecology. **Computer sciences:** General, computer science, information systems, programming. **Education:** Early childhood. **Engineering:** General, architectural, biomedical, chemical, civil, computer, electrical, environmental, mechanical, physics, science. **English:** American lit, British lit, English lit. **Foreign languages:** General, ancient Greek, Chinese, classics, comparative lit, French, German, Italian, Japanese, Latin, Russian, Spanish. **History:** General. **Interdisciplinary:** Math/computer science, peace/conflict. **Liberal arts:** Arts/sciences. **Math:** General, applied. **Philosophy/religion:** Philosophy, religion. **Physical sciences:** Astronomy, chemistry, geology, physics. **Psychology:** General. **Social sciences:** Anthropology, archaeology, economics, international relations, political science, sociology. **Visual/performing arts:** Art history/conservation, music history, music theory/composition, musicology, studio arts, theater history.

**Most popular majors.** Engineering/engineering technologies 12%, psychology 8%, social sciences 34%, visual/performing arts 11%.

**Computing on campus.** 500 workstations in library, computer center. Dormitories wired for high-speed internet access and linked to campus network. Commuter students can connect to campus network. Online course registration, online library, helpline, repair service, wireless network available.

**Student life. Freshman orientation:** Available. Preregistration for classes offered. 3-day program prior to beginning of fall semester. **Housing:** Guaranteed on-campus for freshmen. Coed dorms, single-sex dorms, special housing for disabled, cooperative housing, fraternity/sorority housing, substance-free housing available. Culture, special interest, language houses available. **Activities:** Bands, campus ministries, choral groups, dance, drama, film society, international student organizations, literary magazine, music ensembles, musical theater, opera, radio station, student government, student newspaper, symphony orchestra, TV station, over 200 student organizations.

**Athletics.** NCAA. **Intercollegiate:** Baseball M, basketball, cross-country, diving, fencing W, field hockey W, football (tackle) M, golf M, ice hockey M, lacrosse, rowing (crew), rugby, sailing, soccer, softball W, squash, swimming, tennis, track and field, volleyball W. **Intramural:** Basketball, fencing M, handball, racquetball, softball, squash, tennis, volleyball. **Team name:** Jumbos.

**Student services.** Adult student services, alcohol/substance abuse counseling, campus ministries, career counseling, services for economically disadvantaged, student employment services, financial aid counseling, health services, legal services, minority student services, on-campus daycare, personal counseling, placement for graduates, women's services. **Physically disabled:** Services for visually, speech, hearing impaired.

**Contact.** E-mail: admissions.inquiry@ase.tufts.edu
Phone: (617) 627-3170 Fax: (617) 627-3860
Lee Coffin, Dean of Undergraduate Admissions and Enrollment Management, Tufts University, Bendetson Hall, Medford, MA 02155

## University of Massachusetts Amherst
### Amherst, Massachusetts
**CB member**
**www.umass.edu**
**CB code: 3917**

- Public 4-year university
- Residential campus in large town
- 19,621 degree-seeking undergraduates: 6% part-time, 50% women, 5% African American, 8% Asian American, 4% Hispanic American, 1% international
- 5,077 degree-seeking graduate students
- 66% of applicants admitted
- SAT or ACT (ACT writing recommended), application essay required
- 67% graduate within 6 years

**General.** Founded in 1863. Regionally accredited. **Degrees:** 4,235 bachelor's, 83 associate awarded; master's, doctoral offered. **ROTC:** Army, Air Force. **Location:** 90 miles from Boston, 30 miles from Springfield. **Calendar:** Semester, limited summer session. **Full-time faculty:** 1,175 total; 92% have terminal degrees, 18% minority, 36% women. **Part-time faculty:** 186 total; 55% have terminal degrees, 5% minority, 50% women. **Class size:** 40% < 20, 37% 20-39, 6% 40-49, 8% 50-99, 9% >100. **Special facilities:** Observatory, botanical gardens, sports arena with ice rink.

**Freshman class profile.** 27,138 applied, 17,815 admitted, 4,286 enrolled.

| Mid 50% test scores | | Rank in top tenth: | 22% |
|---|---|---|---|
| SAT critical reading: | 510-610 | Return as sophomores: | 84% |
| SAT math: | 520-630 | Out-of-state: | 23% |
| GPA 3.50 or higher: | 50% | Live on campus: | 96% |
| GPA 3.0-3.49: | 43% | International: | 1% |
| GPA 2.0-2.99: | 6% | Fraternities: | 5% |
| Rank in top quarter: | 58% | Sororities: | 5% |

**Basis for selection.** High school grades most important, followed by test scores, extra-curricular activities, essay and recommendations. Audition required of music majors and dance majors. Portfolio required of art and design majors. **Homeschooled:** Detailed transcript required. **Learning Disabled:** Applicants must submit diagnostic data and/or individualized educational plan. Massachusetts residents with documented learning disabilities are not required to submit standardized test scores for admissions consideration.

**High school preparation.** 16 units required. Required units include English 4, mathematics 3, social studies 2, science 3 (laboratory 2), foreign language 2 and academic electives 2.

**2007-2008 Annual costs.** Tuition/fees: $9,924; $20,499 out-of-state. Room/board: $8,052. Books/supplies: $1,000. Personal expenses: $1,000.

**2006-2007 Financial aid. Need-based:** 3,667 full-time freshmen applied for aid; 2,324 were judged to have need; 2,255 of these received aid. Average need met was 82%. Average scholarship/grant was $7,350; average loan $3,021. 49% of total undergraduate aid awarded as scholarships/grants, 51% as loans/jobs. **Non-need-based:** Awarded to 1,360 full-time undergraduates, including 521 freshmen. Scholarships awarded for academics, art, athletics, music/drama, ROTC, state residency.

**Application procedures. Admission:** Closing date 1/15 (postmark date). $40 fee ($50 out-of-state), may be waived for applicants with need. Application may be submitted online. Admission notification on a rolling basis beginning on or about 3/7. Must reply by 5/1. **Financial aid:** Priority date 3/1; no closing date. FAFSA required. Applicants notified on a rolling basis starting 4/1.

**Academics.** Students may take courses at Amherst, Hampshire, Mt. Holyoke and Smith Colleges at no extra charge. **Special study options:** Accelerated study, cooperative education, cross-registration, distance learning, double major, dual enrollment of high school students, ESL, exchange student, honors, independent study, internships, liberal arts/career combination, student-designed major, study abroad, teacher certification program, Washington semester. University Without Walls program offers individualized degrees to working adults; residential academic programs allow first-year students to live and take classes together. **Credit/placement by examination:** AP, CLEP, IB, institutional tests. 30 credit hours maximum toward bachelor's degree. Credit awarded for International Baccalaureate scores of 4-7. **Support services:** Learning center, study skills assistance, tutoring, writing center.

**Honors college/program.** First-year students admitted by invitation, approximately 500 freshmen admitted. Interdisciplinary seminars, enriched honors courses, colloquia, independent study, service learning offered; honors thesis, project, or activity required.

**Majors. Agriculture:** Animal sciences, economics, food science, plant sciences. **Architecture:** Environmental design, interior, landscape. **Area/ethnic studies:** African-American, Near/Middle Eastern, Russian/Slavic, women's. **Biology:** General, Biochemistry/biophysics and molecular biology, exercise physiology, microbiology. **Business:** Accounting, business admin, finance, hospitality admin, marketing. **Communications:** General, journalism. **Computer sciences:** Computer science. **Conservation:** Environmental science, forestry, management/policy, wildlife, wood science. **Education:** General. **Engineering:** Chemical, civil, computer, electrical, industrial, mechanical. **English:** English lit. **Family/consumer sciences:** Human nutrition. **Foreign languages:** Chinese, classics, comparative lit, French, Germanic, Italian, Japanese, linguistics, Portuguese, Spanish. **Health:** Communication disorders, nursing (RN), predental, premedicine, preveterinary. **History:** General. **Interdisciplinary:** Biological/physical sciences. **Legal studies:** General. **Liberal arts:** Humanities. **Math:** General. **Parks/recreation:** Sports admin. **Philosophy/religion:** Judaic, philosophy. **Physical sciences:** Astronomy, chemistry, geology, physics. **Psychology:** General. **Social sciences:** Anthropology, economics, geography, political science, sociology. **Visual/performing arts:** Art history/conservation, dance, dramatic, studio arts.

**Most popular majors.** Biology 7%, business/marketing 17%, communications/journalism 9%, health sciences 6%, psychology 8%, social sciences 13%.

**Computing on campus.** Dormitories wired for high-speed internet access and linked to campus network. Commuter students can connect to campus network. Online course registration, online library, helpline, repair service, student web hosting, wireless network available.

**Student life. Freshman orientation:** Mandatory. Preregistration for classes offered. Two-and-a-half-day sessions in June or July, with a make-up orientation at the end of August. **Policies:** Students required to live on campus through sophomore year unless living with relatives, married, or veteran of U.S. armed forces. **Housing:** Guaranteed on-campus for freshmen. Coed dorms, single-sex dorms, special housing for disabled, apartments, fraternity/sorority housing, substance-free housing available. Special interest housing; residential academic programs for first-year students. Gradual penalty for cancellation of housing up to $300. **Activities:** Bands, campus ministries, choral groups, dance, drama, film society, international student organizations, literary magazine, music ensembles, Model UN, musical theater, opera, radio station, student government, student newspaper, symphony orchestra, TV station, Over 280 student organizations.

**Athletics.** NCAA. **Intercollegiate:** Baseball M, basketball, cheerleading, cross-country, diving, field hockey W, football (tackle) M, ice hockey M, lacrosse, rowing (crew) W, skiing, soccer, softball W, swimming, tennis W, track and field. **Intramural:** Basketball, field hockey W, football (non-tackle), ice hockey, lacrosse W, soccer, softball, swimming, tennis, volleyball, wrestling. **Team name:** Minutemen/ Minutewomen.

**Student services.** Adult student services, alcohol/substance abuse counseling, campus ministries, career counseling, student employment services, financial aid counseling, health services, legal services, minority student services, on-campus daycare, personal counseling, placement for graduates, veterans' counselor, women's services. **Physically disabled:** Services for visually, speech, hearing impaired. **Learning disabled:** Comprehensive services available.

**Contact.** E-mail: mail@admissions.umass.edu
Phone: (413) 545-0222 Fax: (413) 545-4312
Kevin Kelly, Director of Admissions, University of Massachusetts Amherst, University Admissions Center, Amherst, MA 01003-9291

## University of Massachusetts Boston

| Boston, Massachusetts | CB member |
|---|---|
| www.umb.edu | CB code: 3924 |

- Public 4-year university
- Commuter campus in very large city
- 8,999 degree-seeking undergraduates: 29% part-time, 58% women, 16% African American, 13% Asian American, 8% Hispanic American, 3% international
- 2,827 degree-seeking graduate students
- 61% of applicants admitted
- SAT or ACT (ACT writing optional), application essay required
- 33% graduate within 6 years

**General.** Founded in 1964. Regionally accredited. **Degrees:** 1,418 bachelor's awarded; master's, doctoral offered. **Location:** 3 miles from downtown. **Calendar:** Semester, extensive summer session. **Full-time faculty:** 444 total; 95% have terminal degrees, 22% minority, 46% women. **Part-time faculty:** 418 total; 31% have terminal degrees, 11% minority, 58% women. **Class size:** 37% < 20, 56% 20-39, 2% 40-49, 4% 50-99, 1% >100. **Special facilities:** Tropical greenhouse, observatory, adaptive computer laboratory.

**Freshman class profile.** 4,213 applied, 2,581 admitted, 997 enrolled.

| Mid 50% test scores | | GPA 2.0-2.99: | 45% |
|---|---|---|---|
| SAT critical reading: | 460-570 | Return as sophomores: | 74% |
| SAT math: | 480-580 | Out-of-state: | 8% |
| GPA 3.50 or higher: | 22% | International: | 4% |
| GPA 3.0-3.49: | 33% | | |

**Basis for selection.** School achievement record, range of test scores, GPA most important. Recommendations, essay also important. Extracurricular activities considered. Grades for college preparatory background should be B- or better. Interview recommended for nontraditional students.

**High school preparation.** 16 units required. Required units include English 4, mathematics 3, social studies 1, history 1, science 3 (laboratory 2), foreign language 2 and academic electives 2.

**2007-2008 Annual costs.** Tuition/fees: $8,840; $20,658 out-of-state.

**2006-2007 Financial aid. Need-based:** 642 full-time freshmen applied for aid; 526 were judged to have need; 526 of these received aid. Average need met was 84%. Average scholarship/grant was $6,225; average loan $3,267. 49% of total undergraduate aid awarded as scholarships/grants, 51% as loans/jobs. **Non-need-based:** Awarded to 191 full-time undergraduates,

including 62 freshmen. Scholarships awarded for academics, leadership. **Additional information:** Some Massachusetts state employees and Massachusetts Vietnam veterans eligible for tuition waiver. Some waivers available based on talent and academic excellence.

**Application procedures. Admission:** Priority date 3/1; deadline 6/1. $40 fee ($60 out-of-state), may be waived for applicants with need. Application may be submitted online. Admission notification on a rolling basis. Must reply by May 1 or within 3 week(s) if notified thereafter. **Financial aid:** Priority date 3/1; no closing date. FAFSA required. Applicants notified on a rolling basis starting 3/21.

**Academics.** Certificates available in many areas, including communication studies, computer and information sciences, technical and business writing, international relations, accounting, hydrogeology, alcohol/substance abuse, Spanish translation, management information systems. **Special study options:** Accelerated study, combined bachelor's/graduate degree, cooperative education, cross-registration, distance learning, double major, dual enrollment of high school students, ESL, exchange student, honors, independent study, internships, liberal arts/career combination, student-designed major, study abroad, teacher certification program. 2-2 programs in engineering with area institutions. **Credit/placement by examination:** AP, CLEP, SAT, ACT, institutional tests. 90 credit hours maximum toward bachelor's degree. **Support services:** Learning center, pre-admission summer program, reduced course load, remedial instruction, study skills assistance, tutoring, writing center.

**Majors. Area/ethnic studies:** African-American, American, women's. **Biology:** General, biochemistry. **Business:** Business admin, labor relations. **Communications:** Media studies. **Computer sciences:** General. **Education:** Physical. **Engineering:** Physics. **English:** English lit. **Foreign languages:** Classics, French, German, Italian, Russian, Spanish. **Health:** Clinical lab science, nursing (RN). **History:** General. **Interdisciplinary:** Gerontology. **Legal studies:** General. **Math:** General. **Philosophy/religion:** Philosophy. **Physical sciences:** Chemistry, geology, physics. **Protective services:** Criminal justice. **Psychology:** General. **Public administration:** General, community org/advocacy, human services. **Social sciences:** General, anthropology, economics, geography, political science, sociology. **Visual/performing arts:** Art, dramatic.

**Most popular majors.** Business/marketing 22%, English 7%, health sciences 12%, psychology 12%, security/protective services 6%, social sciences 14%.

**Computing on campus.** 325 workstations in library, computer center, student center. Commuter students can connect to campus network. Online course registration, online library, helpline, repair service, wireless network available.

**Student life. Freshman orientation:** Mandatory, $25 fee. Preregistration for classes offered. **Housing:** Housing referral services available. **Activities:** Bands, campus ministries, choral groups, dance, drama, film society, international student organizations, literary magazine, music ensembles, radio station, student government, student newspaper, symphony orchestra, 70 organizations available.

**Athletics.** NCAA. **Intercollegiate:** Baseball M, basketball, cross-country, ice hockey M, lacrosse M, soccer, softball W, tennis, track and field, volleyball W. **Intramural:** Basketball, ice hockey M, racquetball, sailing, soccer, softball, squash, tennis, volleyball. **Team name:** Beacons.

**Student services.** Adult student services, alcohol/substance abuse counseling, campus ministries, career counseling, student employment services, health services, legal services, minority student services, on-campus daycare, personal counseling, placement for graduates, veterans' counselor, women's services. **Physically disabled:** Services for visually, speech, hearing impaired.

**Contact.** E-mail: undergrad@umb.edu
Phone: (617) 287-6100 Fax: (617) 287-5999
Liliana Mickle, Director of Admissions, University of Massachusetts Boston, 100 Morrissey Boulevard, Boston, MA 02125-3393

---

## University of Massachusetts Dartmouth

**North Dartmouth, Massachusetts**　　　**CB member**
**www.umassd.edu**　　　**CB code: 3786**

- Public 4-year university
- Commuter campus in large town
- 7,600 degree-seeking undergraduates: 10% part-time, 49% women, 7% African American, 3% Asian American, 2% Hispanic American, 1% Native American
- 952 degree-seeking graduate students

---

- 66% of applicants admitted
- SAT or ACT, application essay required

**General.** Founded in 1895. Regionally accredited. **Degrees:** 1,157 bachelor's awarded; master's, doctoral offered. **ROTC:** Army. **Location:** 60 miles from Boston, 30 miles from Providence, Rhode Island. **Calendar:** Semester, extensive summer session. **Full-time faculty:** 365 total; 82% have terminal degrees, 21% minority, 37% women. **Part-time faculty:** 341 total; 6% minority, 38% women. **Special facilities:** Observatory, marine research vessel, coastal marine laboratory, full art studios, Jewish culture and Portuguese studies centers, Robert F. Kennedy assassination archive.

**Freshman class profile.** 7,422 applied, 4,919 admitted, 1,700 enrolled.

| Mid 50% test scores | | | |
|---|---|---|---|
| SAT critical reading: | 470-570 | GPA 3.0-3.49: | 32% |
| SAT math: | 490-590 | GPA 2.0-2.99: | 49% |
| ACT composite: | 20-24 | Out-of-state: | 4% |
| GPA 3.50 or higher: | 19% | Live on campus: | 78% |

**Basis for selection.** High school record, test scores most important; class rank, essay, recommendations considered. Minimum high school GPA 2.0. Recommended high school GPA 3.0. Audition required for music majors; portfolio required for design majors. **Homeschooled:** State high school equivalency certificate required. Must get certification or equivalency from local high school. **Learning Disabled:** SAT scores may be waived for Massachusetts students with documented disability.

**High school preparation.** 16 units required. Required units include English 4, mathematics 3, social studies 1, history 1, science 3 (laboratory 2), foreign language 2 and academic electives 2. 1 U.S. history required. Programs in science, engineering and business require additional math. Science and engineering require physical science. 2 foreign language must be same language.

**2007-2008 Annual costs.** Tuition/fees: $8,595; $18,178 out-of-state. Room/board: $9,173. Books/supplies: $600. Personal expenses: $1,320.

**2007-2008 Financial aid. Need-based:** 1,560 full-time freshmen applied for aid; 1,155 were judged to have need; 1,155 of these received aid. Average need met was 93%. Average scholarship/grant was $6,433; average loan $4,841. 44% of total undergraduate aid awarded as scholarships/grants, 56% as loans/jobs. **Non-need-based:** Awarded to 495 full-time undergraduates, including 222 freshmen. Scholarships awarded for academics, minority status, ROTC, state residency.

**Application procedures. Admission:** No deadline. $40 fee ($60 out-of-state), may be waived for applicants with need. Application may be submitted online. Admission notification on a rolling basis beginning on or about 1/1. Must reply by May 1 or within 2 week(s) if notified thereafter. Competitive programs may be filled by March 1. Nursing closes by late January. Freshman applicants advised to apply before end of December and not later than March. **Financial aid:** Priority date 3/1; no closing date. FAFSA required. Applicants notified on a rolling basis starting 3/25; must reply within 3 week(s) of notification.

**Academics.** Alternative admissions program for academically disadvantaged Massachusetts residents; program offers special freshman curriculum and counseling support. **Special study options:** Combined bachelor's/graduate degree, cooperative education, cross-registration, distance learning, double major, dual enrollment of high school students, honors, independent study, internships, student-designed major, study abroad, teacher certification program, Washington semester. **Credit/placement by examination:** AP, CLEP, IB, SAT, ACT, institutional tests. 30 credit hours maximum toward bachelor's degree. **Support services:** Learning center, reduced course load, remedial instruction, study skills assistance, tutoring, writing center.

**Majors. Area/ethnic studies:** Women's. **Biology:** General. **Business:** Accounting, business admin, finance, management information systems, marketing. **Computer sciences:** General. **Education:** Art. **Engineering:** Civil, computer, electrical, mechanical, textile. **English:** English lit. **Foreign languages:** French, Portuguese, Spanish. **Health:** Clinical lab science, nursing (RN). **History:** General. **Liberal arts:** Arts/sciences. **Math:** General. **Philosophy/religion:** Philosophy. **Physical sciences:** Chemistry, physics. **Psychology:** General. **Social sciences:** Criminology, economics, political science, sociology. **Visual/performing arts:** General, art history/conservation, ceramics, commercial/advertising art, design, fiber arts, metal/jewelry, multimedia, painting, photography, sculpture, studio arts.

**Most popular majors.** Business/marketing 29%, engineering/engineering technologies 6%, English 6%, health sciences 9%, psychology 8%, social sciences 10%, visual/performing arts 12%.

**Computing on campus.** 650 workstations in dormitories, library, computer center, student center. Dormitories wired for high-speed internet access and linked to campus network. Commuter students can connect to campus network. Helpline, repair service, wireless network available.

**Student life. Freshman orientation:** Mandatory, $200 fee. Preregistration for classes offered. Three-day, 2-night program in June and July. **Housing:** Coed dorms, special housing for disabled, apartments, substance-free housing available. $200 nonrefundable deposit, deadline 5/1. Quiet substance-free, smoke-free housing, program-dedicated suites available. **Activities:** Bands, choral groups, dance, drama, literary magazine, music ensembles, musical theater, radio station, student government, student newspaper, symphony orchestra, women's center, Portuguese center, Unity House, Indian student organization, Arab student organization, Luso-American student organization, Taiwanese student organization, MASSPIRG.

**Athletics. NCAA. Intercollegiate:** Baseball M, basketball, cheerleading M, cross-country, diving, equestrian W, field hockey W, football (tackle) M, golf M, ice hockey M, lacrosse, soccer, softball W, swimming, tennis, track and field, volleyball W. **Intramural:** Badminton, basketball, cross-country, football (non-tackle), sailing, soccer, softball, swimming, table tennis, tennis, volleyball. **Team name:** Corsairs.

**Student services.** Adult student services, alcohol/substance abuse counseling, campus ministries, career counseling, student employment services, financial aid counseling, health services, minority student services, on-campus daycare, personal counseling, placement for graduates, veterans' counselor, women's services. **Physically disabled:** Services for visually, speech, hearing impaired.

**Contact.** E-mail: admissions@umassd.edu
Phone: (508) 999-8605 Fax: (508) 999-8755
Steven Briggs, Director of Admissions, University of Massachusetts Dartmouth, 285 Old Westport Road, North Dartmouth, MA 02747-2300

---

## University of Massachusetts Lowell
**Lowell, Massachusetts**  CB member
www.uml.edu  CB code: 3911

- Public 4-year university
- Commuter campus in small city
- 7,663 degree-seeking undergraduates: 22% part-time, 40% women, 5% African American, 8% Asian American, 5% Hispanic American, 1% international
- 2,756 degree-seeking graduate students
- 69% of applicants admitted
- SAT or ACT (ACT writing optional), application essay required
- 46% graduate within 6 years

**General.** Founded in 1894. Regionally accredited. **Degrees:** 1,381 bachelor's, 34 associate awarded; master's, doctoral offered. **ROTC:** Air Force. **Location:** 25 miles from Boston, 45 miles from Worcester. **Calendar:** Semester, extensive summer session. **Full-time faculty:** 406 total; 96% have terminal degrees, 20% minority, 34% women. **Part-time faculty:** 259 total; 4% minority. **Class size:** 49% < 20, 36% 20-39, 10% 40-49, 3% 50-99, 2% >100. **Special facilities:** Industrial history center, teaching and research laboratories in sound recording technology, digital imaging, wellness resource room.

**Freshman class profile.** 4,936 applied, 3,419 admitted, 1,243 enrolled.

| Mid 50% test scores | | | |
|---|---|---|---|
| SAT critical reading: | 480-570 | GPA 2.0-2.99: | 40% |
| SAT math: | 500-610 | Rank in top quarter: | 40% |
| GPA 3.50 or higher: | 25% | Rank in top tenth: | 15% |
| GPA 3.0-3.49: | 35% | Out-of-state: | 8% |
| | | Live on campus: | 54% |

**Basis for selection.** School record, test scores, recommendations most important. Interview recommended. Audition required of music majors. **Homeschooled:** Statement describing homeschool structure and mission, transcript of courses and grades, state high school equivalency certificate, letter of recommendation (nonparent) required.

**High school preparation.** 16 units required. Required units include English 4, mathematics 3, social studies 2, science 3 (laboratory 2), foreign language 2 and academic electives 2.

**2007-2008 Annual costs.** Tuition/fees: $8,732; $20,386 out-of-state. Room/board: $6,978. Books/supplies: $600. Personal expenses: $800.

**2007-2008 Financial aid. Need-based:** 989 full-time freshmen applied for aid; 644 were judged to have need; 644 of these received aid. Average need met was 94%. Average scholarship/grant was $5,939; average loan $3,845. 40% of total undergraduate aid awarded as scholarships/grants, 60% as loans/jobs. **Non-need-based:** Awarded to 693 full-time undergraduates, including 275 freshmen. Scholarships awarded for academics, art, athletics, ROTC.

**Application procedures. Admission:** Priority date 7/1; no deadline. $60 fee ($60 out-of-state), may be waived for applicants with need. Application may be submitted online. Admission notification on a rolling basis beginning on or about 4/1. Must reply by May 1 or within 2 week(s) if notified thereafter. **Financial aid:** Priority date 3/1; no closing date. FAFSA required. Applicants notified on a rolling basis starting 3/25.

**Academics.** Special focus on applied science and technology; coursework emphasizes context and implications of each discipline. Funded research initiatives available in nanotechnology, bioinformatics, advanced materials, photonics. **Special study options:** Accelerated study, combined bachelor's/graduate degree, cooperative education, cross-registration, distance learning, double major, dual enrollment of high school students, honors, internships, liberal arts/career combination, study abroad, teacher certification program. **Credit/placement by examination:** AP, CLEP, institutional tests. 30 credit hours maximum toward bachelor's degree. **Support services:** Learning center, pre-admission summer program, reduced course load, study skills assistance, tutoring, writing center.

**Majors. Area/ethnic studies:** American. **Biology:** General. **Business:** Business admin, entrepreneurial studies. **Computer sciences:** Computer science, information systems. **Conservation:** General, environmental science. **Education:** Health, music. **Engineering:** Chemical, civil, electrical, mechanical, polymer. **Engineering technology:** Civil, electrical, industrial. **English:** English lit. **Foreign languages:** General. **Health:** Clinical lab science, nursing (RN). **History:** General. **Liberal arts:** Arts/sciences. **Math:** General, applied. **Parks/recreation:** Exercise sciences. **Philosophy/religion:** Philosophy. **Physical sciences:** Chemistry, physics. **Protective services:** Law enforcement admin. **Psychology:** General. **Social sciences:** Economics, political science, sociology. **Visual/performing arts:** General, music performance, studio arts.

**Most popular majors.** Business/marketing 24%, computer/information sciences 8%, engineering/engineering technologies 15%, health sciences 8%, liberal arts 7%, psychology 6%, security/protective services 11%, visual/performing arts 6%.

**Computing on campus.** 4,000 workstations in dormitories, library, computer center, student center. Dormitories linked to campus network. Commuter students can connect to campus network. Online course registration, online library, helpline available.

**Student life. Freshman orientation:** Mandatory. Preregistration for classes offered. **Housing:** Coed dorms, single-sex dorms, special housing for disabled, apartments, cooperative housing available. $200 nonrefundable deposit. **Activities:** Bands, choral groups, dance, drama, film society, literary magazine, music ensembles, radio station, student government, student newspaper, symphony orchestra, Abundant Life Christian Fellowship, Chi Alpha, Latter-day Saints student association, association of students of African origin, Cambodian student association, Latin American student association, community service organization, College Democrats, College Republicans.

**Athletics. NCAA. Intercollegiate:** Baseball M, basketball, cross-country, field hockey W, football (tackle) M, golf M, ice hockey M, lacrosse M, rowing (crew), soccer, softball W, tennis, track and field, volleyball W. **Intramural:** Badminton, basketball, bowling, diving, equestrian W, ice hockey, racquetball, rowing (crew), soccer, softball, swimming, table tennis, tennis, volleyball. **Team name:** River Hawks.

**Student services.** Adult student services, alcohol/substance abuse counseling, campus ministries, career counseling, financial aid counseling, health services, personal counseling, placement for graduates, veterans' counselor. **Physically disabled:** Services for visually, speech, hearing impaired.

**Contact.** E-mail: admissions@uml.edu
Phone: (978) 934-3931 Toll-free number: (800) 410-4607
Fax: (978) 934-3086
Kerri Mead, Director Admissions, University of Massachusetts Lowell, 883 Broadway Street, Room 110, Lowell, MA 01854-5104

---

## Wellesley College
**Wellesley, Massachusetts**  CB member
www.wellesley.edu  CB code: 3957

- Private 4-year liberal arts college for women
- Residential campus in large town
- 2,247 degree-seeking undergraduates: 1% part-time, 100% women, 6% African American, 28% Asian American, 7% Hispanic American, 8% international
- 36% of applicants admitted
- SAT and SAT Subject Tests or ACT with writing, application essay required

**General.** Founded in 1870. Regionally accredited. **Degrees:** 568 bachelor's awarded. **ROTC:** Army, Air Force. **Location:** 12 miles from Boston. **Calendar:** Semester, limited summer session. **Full-time faculty:** 225 total; 98% have terminal degrees, 24% minority, 53% women. **Part-time faculty:** 89 total; 79% have terminal degrees, 20% minority, 72% women. **Class size:** 67% < 20, 31% 20-39, 1% 40-49, less than 1% 50-99. **Special facilities:** Science center with X-ray diffractometer, nuclear magnetic resonance, spectrometers (NMR and microMRI), electron microscopes, argon and dye lasers, observatory with three telescopes (6-, 12-, and 24-inch), cultural center, greenhouses, botanic gardens, arboretum, media and technology center with linear editing room for video, digital-based video editing suite, plotter, film recorder, slide scanner.

**Freshman class profile.** 4,017 applied, 1,434 admitted, 590 enrolled.

| Mid 50% test scores | | Rank in top quarter: | 98% |
|---|---|---|---|
| SAT critical reading: | 660-750 | Rank in top tenth: | 78% |
| SAT math: | 640-730 | Out-of-state: | 87% |
| SAT writing: | 660-730 | Live on campus: | 100% |
| ACT composite: | 29-32 | International: | 9% |

**Basis for selection.** Rigor of secondary school record, recommendations, test scores, essay, and character/personal qualities are very important. If SAT submitted, 2 SAT Subject Tests required. Interview recommended. **Homeschooled:** Statement describing homeschool structure and mission, transcript of courses and grades, letter of recommendation (nonparent) required. Applicants must meet home schooling requirements of their own state.

**High school preparation.** Recommended units include English 4, mathematics 4, social studies 4, history 4, science 3 (laboratory 2) and foreign language 4.

**2007-2008 Annual costs.** Tuition/fees: $34,994. Room/board: $10,826. Books/supplies: $800. Personal expenses: $1,200.

**2007-2008 Financial aid.** All financial aid based on need. 410 full-time freshmen applied for aid; 322 were judged to have need; 322 of these received aid. Average need met was 100%. Average scholarship/grant was $29,627; average loan $2,435. 88% of total undergraduate aid awarded as scholarships/grants, 12% as loans/jobs.

**Application procedures. Admission:** Closing date 1/15 (postmark date). $50 fee, may be waived for applicants with need. Application may be submitted online. Admission notification 4/1. Must reply by 5/1. Application fee waived for online applications and for students with financial need who apply by mail. **Financial aid:** Priority date 1/22, closing date 1/22. FAFSA, institutional form, CSS PROFILE required. Applicants notified by 4/1; must reply by 5/1.

**Academics. Special study options:** Cross-registration, double major, dual enrollment of high school students, exchange student, honors, independent study, internships, semester at sea, student-designed major, study abroad, teacher certification program, Washington semester. **Credit/placement by examination:** AP, CLEP, IB, institutional tests. **Support services:** Learning center, reduced course load, study skills assistance, tutoring, writing center.

**Majors. Architecture:** Architecture. **Area/ethnic studies:** African, African-American, American, Asian, Central/Eastern European, East Asian, European, Latin American, Russian/Slavic, women's. **Biology:** General, biochemistry. **Computer sciences:** General, computer science. **Conservation:** Environmental studies. **Engineering:** General. **English:** English lit. **Foreign languages:** General, ancient Greek, Chinese, classics, comparative lit, French, German, Italian, Japanese, Latin, linguistics, Russian, Spanish. **History:** General. **Interdisciplinary:** Biological/physical sciences, classical/archaeology, medieval/Renaissance, neuroscience, peace/conflict, science/society. **Math:** General. **Philosophy/religion:** Judaic, philosophy, religion. **Physical sciences:** Astronomy, chemistry, geology, physics. **Psychology:** General. **Social sciences:** Anthropology, archaeology, economics, international relations, political science, sociology. **Visual/performing arts:** Art history/conservation, dramatic, music history, studio arts.

**Most popular majors.** Area/ethnic studies 7%, biology 6%, English 6%, foreign language 12%, interdisciplinary studies 6%, psychology 9%, social sciences 30%, visual/performing arts 9%.

**Computing on campus.** 481 workstations in dormitories, library, computer center, student center. Dormitories wired for high-speed internet access and linked to campus network. Commuter students can connect to campus network. Online course registration, online library, helpline, repair service, student web hosting, wireless network available.

**Student life. Freshman orientation:** Mandatory. Preregistration for classes offered. Multiday program held in late August. **Housing:** Guaranteed on-campus for all undergraduates. Special housing for disabled, apartments, cooperative housing, substance-free housing available. $300 deposit, deadline 5/1. Pets allowed in dorm rooms. French and Spanish language houses available. **Activities:** Jazz band, campus ministries, choral groups, dance, drama, film society, international student organizations, literary magazine, music ensembles, Model UN, radio station, student government, student newspaper, symphony orchestra, black student club, Latina student club, Asian students union, Hillel, Al-Muslimat, Intervarsity Christian Fellowship, political and legislative action organization, Best Buddies, Habitat for Humanity.

**Athletics.** NCAA. **Intercollegiate:** Basketball W, cross-country W, diving W, fencing W, field hockey W, golf W, lacrosse W, rowing (crew) W, soccer W, softball W, swimming W, tennis W, track and field W, volleyball W. **Intramural:** Basketball W, ice hockey W, racquetball W, rowing (crew) W, rugby W, sailing W, soccer W, table tennis W. **Team name:** Wellesley Blue.

**Student services.** Adult student services, alcohol/substance abuse counseling, campus ministries, career counseling, services for economically disadvantaged, student employment services, financial aid counseling, health services, minority student services, on-campus daycare, personal counseling, placement for graduates, women's services. **Physically disabled:** Services for visually, hearing impaired.

**Contact.** E-mail: admission@wellesley.edu
Phone: (781) 283-2270 Fax: (781) 283-3678
Jennifer Desjarlais, Dean of Admission, Wellesley College, 106 Central Street, Wellesley, MA 02481-8203

## Wentworth Institute of Technology

**Boston, Massachusetts**     CB member
www.wit.edu     CB code: 3958

- Private 4-year engineering and technical college
- Residential campus in very large city
- 3,688 degree-seeking undergraduates: 10% part-time, 20% women, 3% African American, 5% Asian American, 3% Hispanic American, 3% international
- 80% of applicants admitted
- SAT or ACT (ACT writing optional), application essay required
- 49% graduate within 6 years

**General.** Founded in 1904. Regionally accredited. Cooperative education program. Member of Colleges of the Fenway. **Degrees:** 624 bachelor's, 70 associate awarded. **ROTC:** Army. **Location:** 2 miles from downtown. **Calendar:** Semester, limited summer session. **Full-time faculty:** 135 total; 50% have terminal degrees, 11% minority, 20% women. **Part-time faculty:** 142 total; 8% minority, 28% women. **Class size:** 38% < 20, 55% 20-39, 2% 40-49, 4% 50-99, less than 1% >100.

**Freshman class profile.** 2,329 applied, 1,867 admitted, 859 enrolled.

| Mid 50% test scores | | GPA 2.0-2.99: | 51% |
|---|---|---|---|
| SAT critical reading: | 450-550 | Return as sophomores: | 77% |
| SAT math: | 490-600 | Out-of-state: | 37% |
| ACT composite: | 19-25 | Live on campus: | 78% |
| GPA 3.50 or higher: | 13% | International: | 2% |
| GPA 3.0-3.49: | 33% | | |

**Basis for selection.** School achievement record most important, followed by test scores. **Homeschooled:** Transcript of courses and grades, letter of recommendation (nonparent) required. Course content description may be requested.

**High school preparation.** Required units include English 4, mathematics 4, social studies 1, science 2 (laboratory 1). 4 college-preparatory math, 1 physics recommended for many programs. Architecture program requires drafting.

**2007-2008 Annual costs.** Tuition/fees: $20,150. Tuition includes cost of laptop computer; students in architecture and design programs pay $2,000 in required fees for academic year. Room/board: $9,650. Books/supplies: $1,000. Personal expenses: $1,000.

**2006-2007 Financial aid. Need-based:** 976 full-time freshmen applied for aid; 584 were judged to have need; 584 of these received aid. Average need met was 40%. Average scholarship/grant was $1,484; average loan $2,533. 44% of total undergraduate aid awarded as scholarships/grants, 56% as loans/jobs. **Non-need-based:** Scholarships awarded for academics, leadership, state residency.

**Application procedures. Admission:** Priority date 5/1; no deadline. $30 fee, may be waived for applicants with need. Application may be submitted online. Admission notification on a rolling basis beginning on or about 10/30. Must reply by May 1 or within 2 week(s) if notified thereafter. Deposits are fully refundable if the student cancels enrollment on or before May 1st.

**Financial aid:** Priority date 3/1; no closing date. FAFSA required. Applicants notified on a rolling basis starting 3/15; must reply within 2 week(s) of notification.

**Academics.** Some bachelor's programs require 5 years. All bachelor's candidates required to complete 2 semesters full-time co-op. Architecture students enter 2-year core curriculum, must petition to enter junior year. **Special study options:** Cooperative education, cross-registration, distance learning, study abroad. Cross-registration with Simmons College, Emmanuel College, Wheelock College, Massachusetts College of Pharmacy and Health Sciences, Massachusetts College of Art (Colleges of the Fenway). **Credit/placement by examination:** AP, CLEP, IB, institutional tests. 32 credit hours maximum toward associate degree. Students may only receive maximum of one half of total credit requirement from credit by examination. **Support services:** Learning center, reduced course load, study skills assistance, tutoring.

**Majors. Architecture:** Architecture. **Business:** Construction management, operations. **Computer sciences:** General, computer science, information systems. **Conservation:** Environmental science. **Engineering:** Electrical, mechanical. **Engineering technology:** General, civil, computer, electrical, industrial management, mechanical. **Visual/performing arts:** Industrial design, interior design.

**Most popular majors.** Architecture 8%, business/marketing 22%, computer/information sciences 12%, engineering/engineering technologies 51%, visual/performing arts 7%.

**Computing on campus.** PC or laptop required. 370 workstations in dormitories, library, computer center. Dormitories wired for high-speed internet access and linked to campus network. Commuter students can connect to campus network. Online course registration, online library, helpline, repair service, wireless network available.

**Student life. Freshman orientation:** Mandatory. Preregistration for classes offered. Week-long session held week before classes begin. **Housing:** Coed dorms available. $500 fully refundable deposit, deadline 5/1. Apartments available for upperclassmen. **Activities:** Choral groups, drama, film society, international student organizations, music ensembles, musical theater, radio station, student government, student newspaper, honor society, society of women engineers, student association of interior design, solar-powered vehicle club, National Society of Black Engineers, Asian student association, architecture club.

**Athletics.** NCAA. **Intercollegiate:** Baseball M, basketball, golf M, ice hockey M, lacrosse M, rifle, soccer, softball W, tennis, volleyball. **Team name:** Leopards.

**Student services.** Alcohol/substance abuse counseling, career counseling, student employment services, financial aid counseling, health services, minority student services, personal counseling, placement for graduates, women's services.

**Contact.** E-mail: admissions@wit.edu
Phone: (617) 989-4000 Toll-free number: (800) 556-0610
Fax: (617) 989-4010
Maureen Dischino, Director of Admissions, Wentworth Institute of Technology, 550 Huntington Avenue, Boston, MA 02115

## Western New England College
**Springfield, Massachusetts**          **CB member**
www.wnec.edu                            **CB code: 3962**

- Private 4-year university
- Residential campus in small city
- 2,749 degree-seeking undergraduates: 11% part-time, 39% women, 3% African American, 2% Asian American, 3% Hispanic American
- 877 degree-seeking graduate students
- 73% of applicants admitted
- SAT or ACT (ACT writing optional) required
- 62% graduate within 6 years

**General.** Founded in 1919. Regionally accredited. **Degrees:** 601 bachelor's, 2 associate awarded; master's, first professional offered. **ROTC:** Army, Air Force. **Location:** 95 miles from Boston, 20 miles from Hartford. **Calendar:** Semester, limited summer session. **Full-time faculty:** 177 total; 89% have terminal degrees, 10% minority, 38% women. **Part-time faculty:** 137 total. **Class size:** 45% < 20, 55% 20-39, less than 1% 40-49.

**Freshman class profile.** 4,693 applied, 3,415 admitted, 722 enrolled.

| Mid 50% test scores | | | |
|---|---|---|---|
| SAT critical reading: | 470-560 | GPA 2.0-2.99: | 45% |
| SAT math: | 490-590 | Rank in top quarter: | 35% |
| ACT composite: | 20-24 | Rank in top tenth: | 13% |
| GPA 3.50 or higher: | 28% | Return as sophomores: | 75% |
| GPA 3.0-3.49: | 27% | Out-of-state: | 64% |
| | | Live on campus: | 93% |

**Basis for selection.** School achievement record, test scores, recommendation most important. Interview, class rank, extracurricular activities also considered. Interview and essay recommended.

**High school preparation.** 10 units required; 18 recommended. Required and recommended units include English 4, mathematics 2-4, social studies 1-2, history 1-2, science 1-2 (laboratory 1-2) and foreign language 2. One American history required. Additional science and math required for certain programs.

**2007-2008 Annual costs.** Tuition/fees: $25,942. Room/board: $9,998. Books/supplies: $1,000. Personal expenses: $1,270.

**Financial aid. Non-need-based:** Scholarships awarded for academics, music/drama, ROTC.

**Application procedures. Admission:** Priority date 3/1; no deadline. $50 fee, may be waived for applicants with need. Application may be submitted online. Admission notification on a rolling basis beginning on or about 12/1. Must reply by May 1 or within 2 week(s) if notified thereafter. **Financial aid:** Priority date 4/1; no closing date. FAFSA required. Applicants notified on a rolling basis starting 3/15; must reply by 5/1 or within 2 week(s) of notification.

**Academics. Special study options:** Accelerated study, combined bachelor's/graduate degree, cross-registration, distance learning, double major, dual enrollment of high school students, honors, independent study, internships, liberal arts/career combination, student-designed major, study abroad, teacher certification program, Washington semester. 3+3 law program. Accelerated part-time degree completion. 3+2 programs for completion of MBA or MSA for a variety of majors. **Credit/placement by examination:** AP, CLEP, IB, institutional tests. **Support services:** Pre-admission summer program, reduced course load, study skills assistance, tutoring, writing center.

**Majors. Biology:** General, molecular. **Business:** General, accounting, business admin, finance, management information systems, marketing. **Communications:** General, advertising, media studies. **Computer sciences:** Computer science, information systems. **Education:** Elementary, secondary. **Engineering:** Biomedical, electrical, industrial, mechanical. **English:** Creative writing, English lit. **History:** General. **Interdisciplinary:** Global studies. **Legal studies:** General. **Liberal arts:** Arts/sciences. **Math:** General. **Parks/recreation:** Sports admin. **Philosophy/religion:** Philosophy. **Physical sciences:** Chemistry. **Protective services:** Criminal justice. **Psychology:** General. **Public administration:** Social work. **Social sciences:** Economics, political science, sociology.

**Most popular majors.** Business/marketing 36%, engineering/engineering technologies 12%, parks/recreation 7%, psychology 12%, security/protective services 9%.

**Computing on campus.** 400 workstations in dormitories, library, computer center, student center. Dormitories wired for high-speed internet access and linked to campus network. Commuter students can connect to campus network. Online library, helpline, repair service, wireless network available.

**Student life. Freshman orientation:** Available. Preregistration for classes offered. Two-day program held over summer for students and parents. Parents assessed meals and materials fee. **Housing:** Guaranteed on-campus for freshmen. Coed dorms, special housing for disabled, apartments available. $300 nonrefundable deposit, deadline 5/1. **Activities:** Bands, campus ministries, choral groups, dance, drama, international student organizations, literary magazine, music ensembles, radio station, student government, student newspaper, United and Mutually Equal, Helping Hands Society.

**Athletics.** NCAA. **Intercollegiate:** Baseball M, basketball, bowling, cross-country, field hockey W, football (tackle) M, golf M, ice hockey M, lacrosse, soccer, softball W, swimming W, tennis, volleyball W, wrestling M. **Intramural:** Badminton, basketball, football (non-tackle), handball, soccer, softball, table tennis, volleyball, water polo. **Team name:** Golden Bears.

**Student services.** Adult student services, alcohol/substance abuse counseling, campus ministries, career counseling, student employment services, financial aid counseling, health services, minority student services, personal counseling, veterans' counselor. **Physically disabled:** Services for visually, hearing impaired.

**Contact.** E-mail: ugradmis@wnec.edu
Phone: (413) 782-1321 Toll-free number: (800) 325-1122 ext. 1321
Fax: (413) 782-1777
Charles Pollock, Vice President for Enrollment Management, Western New
England College, 1215 Wilbraham Road, Springfield, MA 01119-2684

## Westfield State College
**Westfield, Massachusetts**
www.wsc.ma.edu

**CB member**
**CB code: 3523**

- Public 4-year liberal arts and teachers college
- Residential campus in large town
- 4,540 degree-seeking undergraduates: 9% part-time, 54% women, 3% African American, 1% Asian American, 4% Hispanic American
- 426 degree-seeking graduate students
- 56% of applicants admitted
- SAT or ACT (ACT writing optional) required
- 56% graduate within 6 years

**General.** Founded in 1838. Regionally accredited. **Degrees:** 933 bachelor's awarded; master's offered. **ROTC:** Army, Air Force. **Location:** 10 miles from Springfield, 100 miles from Boston. **Calendar:** Semester, limited summer session. **Full-time faculty:** 180 total; 87% have terminal degrees, 11% minority, 49% women. **Part-time faculty:** 166 total; 44% women. **Class size:** 36% < 20, 59% 20-39, 5% 40-49, less than 1% 50-99, less than 1% >100. **Special facilities:** Electron microscope, natural history museum/collections.

**Freshman class profile.** 5,084 applied, 2,867 admitted, 952 enrolled.

| Mid 50% test scores | | | |
|---|---|---|---|
| | | GPA 3.0-3.49: | 37% |
| SAT critical reading: | 460-550 | GPA 2.0-2.99: | 46% |
| SAT math: | 460-560 | End year in good standing: | 84% |
| ACT composite: | 18-22 | Return as sophomores: | 76% |
| GPA 3.50 or higher: | 17% | Out-of-state: | 4% |

**Basis for selection.** School achievement record, test scores most important; school and community activities also important; recommendations considered. Essay recommended. Audition required of music majors. Portfolio required of art majors. **Homeschooled:** Requirements are based on AAC-ROA standards. **Learning Disabled:** SAT/ACT test score requirement waived for students with documented learning disability. Interview is required.

**High school preparation.** 16 units required. Required units include English 4, mathematics 3, social studies 1, history 1, science 3 (laboratory 2), foreign language 2 and academic electives 2.

**2007-2008 Annual costs.** Tuition/fees: $6,210; $12,290 out-of-state. New England Regional tuition and fees per year: $6695. Room/board: $6,458. Books/supplies: $950. Personal expenses: $1,750.

**Financial aid. Non-need-based:** Scholarships awarded for academics.

**Application procedures. Admission:** Closing date 3/1 (postmark date). $25 fee ($40 out-of-state), may be waived for applicants with need. Application may be submitted online. Admission notification 4/15. Admission notification on a rolling basis beginning on or about 1/1. Must reply by May 1 or within 2 week(s) if notified thereafter. **Financial aid:** Priority date 3/1; no closing date. FAFSA required. Applicants notified by 4/15.

**Academics. Special study options:** Cooperative education, cross-registration, distance learning, double major, dual enrollment of high school students, exchange student, honors, independent study, internships, student-designed major, study abroad, teacher certification program, Washington semester. **Credit/placement by examination:** AP, CLEP, institutional tests. 60 credit hours maximum toward bachelor's degree. Maximum of 3 credits awarded for AP tests in English. Students taking CLEP tests in English Composition with Essay or Freshman Composition must also submit writing portfolio; portfolio evaluated before credit can be awarded. Maximum of 3 credits awarded for composition. **Support services:** Learning center, pre-admission summer program, reduced course load, study skills assistance, tutoring, writing center.

**Majors. Architecture:** Urban/community planning. **Biology:** General. **Business:** General. **Communications:** General, broadcast journalism, journalism. **Computer sciences:** General, computer science, information systems. **Conservation:** Environmental science. **Education:** General, art, biology, business, elementary, English, history, kindergarten/preschool, mathematics, music, physical, science, special, technology/industrial arts. **English:** English lit. **Health:** Athletic training. **History:** General. **Liberal arts:** Arts/sciences. **Math:** General. **Parks/recreation:** General, health/fitness. **Physical sciences:** General. **Protective services:** Criminal justice. **Psychology:** General. **Public administration:** Social work. **Social sciences:** Economics, political science, sociology. **Visual/performing arts:** Art, dramatic.

**Most popular majors.** Business/marketing 15%, communications/journalism 9%, education 15%, liberal arts 6%, psychology 9%, security/protective services 19%.

**Computing on campus.** 275 workstations in dormitories, library, computer center, student center. Dormitories wired for high-speed internet access and linked to campus network. Commuter students can connect to campus network. Online course registration, online library, helpline, student web hosting, wireless network available.

**Student life. Freshman orientation:** Available. **Housing:** Guaranteed on-campus for freshmen. Coed dorms, special housing for disabled, apartments available. $100 deposit, deadline 6/1. Living/learning unit (academic intensive), quiet living section, all women section, designated smoking section (other housing smoke-free), movement science student section available. **Activities:** Bands, choral groups, drama, literary magazine, music ensembles, musical theater, radio station, student government, student newspaper, TV station, third world group, public interest research group, Campus Crusade, Circle K, Amnesty International, international relations club, Latino association for empowerment.

**Athletics.** NCAA. **Intercollegiate:** Baseball M, basketball, cheerleading, cross-country, diving W, field hockey W, football (tackle) M, lacrosse W, soccer, softball W, swimming W, track and field, volleyball W. **Intramural:** Badminton, basketball, bowling, football (tackle), racquetball, soccer, softball, table tennis, tennis, volleyball. **Team name:** Owls.

**Student services.** Adult student services, alcohol/substance abuse counseling, career counseling, services for economically disadvantaged, student employment services, health services, minority student services, personal counseling, placement for graduates, veterans' counselor. **Physically disabled:** Services for visually, speech, hearing impaired. **Learning disabled:** Comprehensive services available.

**Contact.** E-mail: admission@wsc.ma.edu
Phone: (413) 572-5218 Toll-free number: (800) 322-8401
Fax: (413) 572-0520
Michelle Mattie, Associate Dean, Enrollment Management, Westfield State College, 577 Western Avenue, Westfield, MA 01086-1630

## Wheaton College
**Norton, Massachusetts**
www.wheatoncollege.edu

**CB member**
**CB code: 3963**

- Private 4-year liberal arts college
- Residential campus in large town
- 1,551 degree-seeking undergraduates: 60% women, 5% African American, 3% Asian American, 3% Hispanic American, 3% international
- 37% of applicants admitted
- Application essay required
- 80% graduate within 6 years; 29% enter graduate study

**General.** Founded in 1834. Regionally accredited. **Degrees:** 424 bachelor's awarded. **ROTC:** Army. **Location:** 35 miles from Boston, 15 miles from Providence, Rhode Island. **Calendar:** Semester. **Full-time faculty:** 137 total; 88% have terminal degrees, 16% minority, 50% women. **Part-time faculty:** 48 total; 38% have terminal degrees, 10% minority, 58% women. **Class size:** 64% < 20, 30% 20-39, 4% 40-49, 2% 50-99. **Special facilities:** Observatory, language laboratory receiving international broadcasts via satellite.

**Freshman class profile.** 3,833 applied, 1,411 admitted, 418 enrolled.

| Mid 50% test scores | | | |
|---|---|---|---|
| | | Rank in top quarter: | 70% |
| SAT critical reading: | 580-670 | Rank in top tenth: | 44% |
| SAT math: | 560-650 | End year in good standing: | 95% |
| ACT composite: | 25-28 | Return as sophomores: | 88% |
| GPA 3.50 or higher: | 47% | Out-of-state: | 67% |
| GPA 3.0-3.49: | 33% | Live on campus: | 100% |
| GPA 2.0-2.99: | 20% | International: | 3% |

**Basis for selection.** School record, essay/writing sample, personal academic portfolio, extracurricular activities, recommendations, interview important. Standardized testing optional. Interviews strongly recommended. **Homeschooled:** Statement describing homeschool structure and mission, transcript of courses and grades required. **Learning Disabled:** Students who have diagnosed learning difference encouraged to submit supporting testing for review.

**High school preparation.** 20 units recommended. Recommended units include English 4, mathematics 4, social studies 3, history 2, science 3 (laboratory 2) and foreign language 4. English should emphasize composition skills.

**2007-2008 Annual costs.** Tuition/fees: $36,690. Freshmen pay one-time $50 general fee (non-refundable); all residents pay annual $120 technology fee. Room/board: $8,640. Books/supplies: $940. Personal expenses: $760.

**2007-2008 Financial aid. Need-based:** 285 full-time freshmen applied for aid; 226 were judged to have need; 226 of these received aid. Average need met was 97%. Average scholarship/grant was $22,563; average loan $4,224. 79% of total undergraduate aid awarded as scholarships/grants, 21% as loans/jobs. **Non-need-based:** Scholarships awarded for academics.

**Application procedures. Admission:** Closing date 1/15 (postmark date). $55 fee, may be waived for applicants with need. Application may be submitted online. Admission notification by 5/1. **Financial aid:** Closing date 2/1. FAFSA, CSS PROFILE required. Applicants notified by 4/1; must reply by 5/1.

**Academics. Special study options:** Accelerated study, combined bachelor's/graduate degree, cross-registration, double major, dual enrollment of high school students, exchange student, honors, independent study, internships, liberal arts/career combination, student-designed major, study abroad, teacher certification program, Washington semester. BS in engineering with George Washington University and Dartmouth College; MA in communications with Emerson College; MBA in management with Clark University and University of Rochester; BFA in studio art with School of the Museum of Fine Arts (Boston); MA in religion with Andover Newton Theological School; Doctor of Optometry with New England School of Optometry. **Credit/placement by examination:** AP, CLEP, IB, institutional tests. 8 credit hours maximum toward bachelor's degree. **Support services:** Learning center, reduced course load, study skills assistance, tutoring, writing center.

**Majors. Area/ethnic studies:** American, Asian, German, Italian, Russian/Slavic, women's. **Biology:** General, biochemistry, bioinformatics. **Computer sciences:** General, computer science. **Conservation:** General. **English:** Composition, English lit. **Foreign languages:** Classics, French, German, Italian, Latin, modern Greek, Russian, Spanish. **History:** General. **Interdisciplinary:** Biological/physical sciences, math/computer science. **Liberal arts:** Arts/sciences. **Math:** General. **Philosophy/religion:** Philosophy, religion. **Physical sciences:** Astronomy, chemistry, physics. **Psychology:** General. **Social sciences:** Anthropology, economics, international relations, political science, sociology. **Visual/performing arts:** Art history/conservation, studio arts. **Other:** African, American, Diaspora Studies, Mathematics and Economics, Religion and history, Theatre and English dramatic literature.

**Most popular majors.** Area/ethnic studies 8%, English 12%, history 9%, psychology 16%, social sciences 27%, visual/performing arts 13%.

**Computing on campus.** 348 workstations in library, computer center, student center. Dormitories wired for high-speed internet access and linked to campus network. Commuter students can connect to campus network. Online course registration, online library, helpline, repair service, student web hosting, wireless network available.

**Student life. Freshman orientation:** Mandatory. Preregistration for classes offered. Held 2-3 days prior to start of classes. **Housing:** Guaranteed on-campus for all undergraduates. Coed dorms, single-sex dorms, special housing for disabled, substance-free housing available. Special interest houses available: wellness, quiet, and theme. **Activities:** Bands, choral groups, dance, drama, film society, international student organizations, literary magazine, music ensembles, musical theater, radio station, student government, student newspaper, symphony orchestra, Amnesty International, student art league, Black students association, Latino students association, Asian and Southeast students association.

**Athletics.** NCAA. **Intercollegiate:** Baseball M, basketball, cross-country, diving, field hockey W, lacrosse, soccer, softball W, swimming, synchronized swimming W, tennis, track and field, volleyball W. **Intramural:** Badminton, basketball, soccer, softball, tennis, volleyball. **Team name:** Lyons.

**Student services.** Career counseling, student employment services, financial aid counseling, health services, minority student services, personal counseling, placement for graduates, women's services. **Physically disabled:** Services for visually, hearing impaired.

**Contact.** E-mail: admission@wheatoncollege.edu
Phone: (508) 286-8251 Toll-free number: (800) 394-6003
Fax: (508) 286-8271
Gail Berson, Vice President for Enrollment and Dean of Admission and Student Aid, Wheaton College, 26 East Main Street, Norton, MA 02766

---

## Wheelock College

**Boston, Massachusetts**
www.wheelock.edu

**CB member**
**CB code: 3964**

- Private 4-year liberal arts and teachers college
- Residential campus in very large city

---

- 787 degree-seeking undergraduates: 7% part-time, 93% women, 9% African American, 3% Asian American, 7% Hispanic American, 1% Native American, 1% international
- 269 degree-seeking graduate students
- 63% of applicants admitted
- SAT or ACT (ACT writing optional), application essay required

**General.** Founded in 1888. Regionally accredited. Member of the Colleges of the Fenway. **Degrees:** 169 bachelor's awarded; master's offered. **Location:** 2 miles from downtown. **Calendar:** Semester. **Full-time faculty:** 63 total; 87% have terminal degrees, 24% minority, 78% women. **Part-time faculty:** 80 total; 26% have terminal degrees, 25% minority, 78% women. **Class size:** 71% < 20, 29% 20-39, less than 1% 40-49.

**Freshman class profile.** 1,144 applied, 719 admitted, 224 enrolled.

| Mid 50% test scores | | | |
|---|---|---|---|
| SAT critical reading: | 440-530 | GPA 2.0-2.99: | 53% |
| SAT math: | 420-530 | Rank in top quarter: | 29% |
| SAT writing: | 440-530 | Rank in top tenth: | 9% |
| ACT composite: | 18-21 | Out-of-state: | 56% |
| GPA 3.50 or higher: | 16% | Live on campus: | 91% |
| GPA 3.0-3.49: | 30% | International: | 1% |

**Basis for selection.** School achievement record most important. Test scores, school and community activities considered. Interview recommended.

**High school preparation.** 16 units required. Required units include English 4, mathematics 3, social studies 2, science 2 (laboratory 1). Child development course recommended.

**2007-2008 Annual costs.** Tuition/fees: $26,080. Room/board: $10,400. Books/supplies: $880. Personal expenses: $1,000.

**2007-2008 Financial aid. Need-based:** Average need met was 69%. Average scholarship/grant was $11,699; average loan $3,124. 67% of total undergraduate aid awarded as scholarships/grants, 33% as loans/jobs. **Non-need-based:** Scholarships awarded for academics, job skills, leadership.

**Application procedures. Admission:** Priority date 3/1; no deadline. $35 fee, may be waived for applicants with need. Application must be submitted on paper. Admission notification on a rolling basis beginning on or about 1/1. Must reply by May 1 or within 2 week(s) if notified thereafter. **Financial aid:** Priority date 2/15; no closing date. FAFSA required. Applicants notified on a rolling basis starting 3/1; must reply by 5/1.

**Academics.** Fieldwork throughout all 4 years supplements classwork in day care, infant and toddler behavior, museum teaching, children in health care settings, elementary education, special education, social work programs. Students choose major and professional studies concentration in early childhood care and education, elementary school education, juvenile justice, social work, or child life. **Special study options:** Combined bachelor's/graduate degree, cross-registration, double major, independent study, internships, liberal arts/career combination, study abroad, teacher certification program. **Credit/placement by examination:** AP, CLEP, institutional tests. 32 credit hours maximum toward bachelor's degree. **Support services:** Learning center, pre-admission summer program, reduced course load, remedial instruction, study skills assistance, tutoring, writing center.

**Majors. Education:** Early childhood, elementary, special. **Family/consumer sciences:** Child care, child development. **Liberal arts:** Arts/sciences. **Public administration:** Social work. **Visual/performing arts:** General.

**Computing on campus.** 120 workstations in dormitories, library, computer center, student center. Dormitories wired for high-speed internet access and linked to campus network. Commuter students can connect to campus network. Online course registration, online library, helpline, repair service, wireless network available.

**Student life. Freshman orientation:** Mandatory, $200 fee. Preregistration for classes offered. Two-day program held in summer; students have choice of 2 sessions. **Housing:** Guaranteed on-campus for freshmen. Coed dorms, single-sex dorms, special housing for disabled, cooperative housing, substance-free housing available. $100 nonrefundable deposit, deadline 5/1. Smoke-free areas, wellness floor available. **Activities:** Choral groups, dance, drama, musical theater, student government, social work club, women's center, Boston Association for the Education of Young Children, child life council, sign language club, Bible study, juvenile justice and youth advocacy council.

**Athletics.** NCAA. **Intercollegiate:** Basketball, diving W, field hockey W, soccer W, softball W, swimming W, tennis M. **Intramural:** Basketball, racquetball, soccer, softball, squash, volleyball. **Team name:** Wildcats.

**Student services.** Alcohol/substance abuse counseling, career counseling, student employment services, financial aid counseling, health services, personal counseling, placement for graduates, women's services. **Physically disabled:** Services for visually, speech, hearing impaired.

**Contact.** E-mail: undergrad@wheelock.edu
Phone: (617) 879-2206 Toll-free number: (800) 734-5212
Fax: (617) 879-2449
Lisa Slavin, Dean of Enrollment and Financial Aid, Wheelock College, 200 The Riverway, Boston, MA 02215-4176

## Williams College
**Williamstown, Massachusetts**
www.williams.edu

**CB member**
**CB code: 3965**

- Private 4-year liberal arts college affiliated with United Church of Christ
- Residential campus in small town
- 1,962 degree-seeking undergraduates: 50% women, 10% African American, 11% Asian American, 9% Hispanic American, 7% international
- 49 degree-seeking graduate students
- 18% of applicants admitted
- SAT or ACT with writing, SAT Subject Tests, application essay required
- 95% graduate within 6 years

**General.** Founded in 1793. Regionally accredited. **Degrees:** 525 bachelor's awarded; master's offered. **ROTC:** Air Force. **Location:** 35 miles from Albany, New York, 150 miles from Boston. **Calendar:** 4-1-4. **Full-time faculty:** 268 total; 98% have terminal degrees, 18% minority, 39% women. **Part-time faculty:** 45 total; 82% have terminal degrees, 11% minority, 38% women. **Class size:** 73% < 20, 20% 20-39, 4% 40-49, 3% 50-99, less than 1% >100. **Special facilities:** Performing arts center, 2,000-acre experimental forest, environmental studies center, observatory, electron-scanning microscope, transmission microscopes, studio art center, nuclear magnetic resonance imager.

**Freshman class profile.** 6,478 applied, 1,194 admitted, 540 enrolled.

| Mid 50% test scores | | | |
|---|---|---|---|
| SAT critical reading: | 670-760 | Rank in top tenth: | 89% |
| SAT math: | 670-760 | Return as sophomores: | 97% |
| SAT writing: | 660-760 | Out-of-state: | 85% |
| ACT composite: | 29-33 | Live on campus: | 100% |
| Rank in top quarter: | 100% | International: | 9% |

**Basis for selection.** School achievement record, character and personal promise, test scores, essay important. College seeks diversity of social, economic, and geographic backgrounds. Leadership and accomplishment in extracurricular activities also considered.

**High school preparation.** College-preparatory program required. Recommended units include English 4, mathematics 4, social studies 3, science 3 (laboratory 3) and foreign language 4. Writing skills stressed. Course work should be at highest level available.

**2008-2009 Annual costs.** Tuition/fees: $37,640. Room/board: $9,890. Books/supplies: $800. Personal expenses: $1,200.

**2007-2008 Financial aid.** All financial aid based on need. 342 full-time freshmen applied for aid; 278 were judged to have need; 278 of these received aid. Average need met was 100%. Average scholarship/grant was $33,292; average loan $2,330. 90% of total undergraduate aid awarded as scholarships/grants, 10% as loans/jobs.

**Application procedures. Admission:** Closing date 1/1 (postmark date). $60 fee, may be waived for applicants with need. Application may be submitted online. Admission notification 4/1. Must reply by May 1 or within 2 week(s) if notified thereafter. **Financial aid:** Closing date 2/1. FAFSA, CSS PROFILE required. Applicants notified by 4/1; must reply by 5/1.

**Academics. Special study options:** Combined bachelor's/graduate degree, cross-registration, double major, exchange student, independent study, internships, New York semester, student-designed major, study abroad. Summer science research program, Williams in Oxford, Mystic maritime studies program, tutorials, 3-2 engineering program with Columbia University and Washington University. **Credit/placement by examination:** AP, CLEP, IB, institutional tests. **Support services:** Pre-admission summer program, study skills assistance, tutoring, writing center.

**Majors. Area/ethnic studies:** American, Asian. **Biology:** General. **Computer sciences:** Computer science. **English:** English lit. **Foreign languages:** Chinese, classics, comparative lit, French, German, Japanese, Russian, Spanish. **History:** General. **Math:** General. **Philosophy/religion:** Philosophy, religion. **Physical sciences:** Astronomy, astrophysics, chemistry, geology, physics. **Psychology:** General. **Social sciences:** Anthropology, economics, political science, sociology. **Visual/performing arts:** Art history/conservation, dramatic, studio arts.

**Most popular majors.** Biology 7%, English 11%, foreign language 7%, history 7%, mathematics 7%, physical sciences 7%, psychology 8%, social sciences 27%, visual/performing arts 10%.

**Computing on campus.** 247 workstations in library, computer center, student center. Dormitories wired for high-speed internet access and linked to campus network. Commuter students can connect to campus network. Online course registration, helpline, repair service, student web hosting, wireless network available.

**Student life. Freshman orientation:** Mandatory. **Housing:** Guaranteed on-campus for all undergraduates. Coed dorms, cooperative housing available. $200 nonrefundable deposit, deadline 5/1. **Activities:** Choral groups, dance, drama, literary magazine, music ensembles, radio station, student government, student newspaper, symphony orchestra, black student union, Purple Key, Asian Link, VISTA (Hispanic students), Korean club, minority coalition, nonviolent alternatives committee, women's club, Hillel.

**Athletics.** NCAA. **Intercollegiate:** Baseball M, basketball, cross-country, diving, field hockey W, football (tackle) M, golf, ice hockey, lacrosse, rowing (crew), skiing, soccer, softball W, squash, swimming, tennis, track and field, volleyball W, wrestling M. **Intramural:** Badminton, basketball, ice hockey M, skiing, soccer, softball, volleyball. **Team name:** Ephs.

**Student services.** Alcohol/substance abuse counseling, campus ministries, career counseling, services for economically disadvantaged, student employment services, financial aid counseling, health services, minority student services, personal counseling, placement for graduates. **Physically disabled:** Services for visually, hearing impaired.

**Contact.** E-mail: admission@williams.edu
Phone: (413) 597-2211 Fax: (413) 597-4052
Richard Nesbitt, Director of Admissions, Williams College, 33 Stetson Court, Williamstown, MA 01267

## Worcester Polytechnic Institute
**Worcester, Massachusetts**
www.wpi.edu

**CB member**
**CB code: 3969**

- Private 4-year university
- Residential campus in small city
- 3,009 degree-seeking undergraduates: 1% part-time, 26% women, 3% African American, 6% Asian American, 4% Hispanic American, 8% international
- 911 degree-seeking graduate students
- 66% of applicants admitted
- Application essay required
- 75% graduate within 6 years; 26% enter graduate study

**General.** Founded in 1865. Regionally accredited. Participation by most students in overseas or off-campus projects; over 20 project centers located throughout North America, Central America, Africa, Australia, Asia and Europe. **Degrees:** 571 bachelor's awarded; master's, doctoral offered. **ROTC:** Army, Naval, Air Force. **Location:** 35 miles from Boston. **Calendar:** Quarter, limited summer session. **Full-time faculty:** 232 total. **Part-time faculty:** 70 total. **Class size:** 70% < 20, 18% 20-39, 3% 40-49, 6% 50-99, 2% >100. **Special facilities:** Centers for life sciences and bioengineering, biomaterials, bioprocessing, comparative neuroimaging, molecular sensors, nanoscience and technology, untethered healthcare, water research, computer-controlled machining, holographic studies and laser technology, wireless information network studies, fuel cell, industrial mathematics and statistics; fire science laboratory, pavement research laboratory, atomic force microscopy laboratory.

**Freshman class profile.** 5,658 applied, 3,739 admitted, 805 enrolled.

| Mid 50% test scores | | | |
|---|---|---|---|
| SAT critical reading: | 560-670 | Rank in top tenth: | 48% |
| SAT math: | 630-710 | End year in good standing: | 94% |
| ACT composite: | 25-31 | Return as sophomores: | 94% |
| GPA 3.50 or higher: | 72% | Out-of-state: | 50% |
| GPA 3.0-3.49: | 24% | Live on campus: | 95% |
| GPA 2.0-2.99: | 4% | International: | 7% |
| Rank in top quarter: | 85% | Fraternities: | 34% |
| | | Sororities: | 47% |

**Basis for selection.** High school record including academic rigor most important. Extracurricular activities,recommendations, motivation, creativity, initiative important. In lieu of test scores, students may submit alternative documentation of potential for academic success. Students must submit SAT or ACT scores, or (in lieu of standardized test scores) they may choose WPI's Flex Path and submit alternative materials that they believe will better reflect their potential for success at WPI. Students who choose the Flex Path are encouraged to submit examples of academic work or extracurricular projects that reflect a high level of organization, motivation, creativity and problem-solving ability. Interviews offered, but not required. **Homeschooled:** Transcript of courses and grades, interview, letter of recommendation (nonparent) required. Please submit as much relevant support material as possible and outside recommendations. Detailed course descriptions are very helpful in the review process. Our general course requirements of 2 lab sciences and math through pre-calculus do apply to homeschooled applicants and it is important to be able to demonstrate competency in those areas.

**High school preparation.** 10 units required. Required and recommended units include English 4, mathematics 4, social studies 2, history 1, science 2-4 (laboratory 2) and foreign language 2. Math requirement should include trigonometry and pre-calculus analytic geometry. Science should include physics, chemistry, or biology.

**2007-2008 Annual costs.** Tuition/fees: $34,830. Room/board: $10,410. Books/supplies: $1,000. Personal expenses: $1,200.

**2006-2007 Financial aid. Need-based:** 690 full-time freshmen applied for aid; 596 were judged to have need; 592 of these received aid. Average need met was 67%. Average scholarship/grant was $16,660; average loan $4,928. 75% of total undergraduate aid awarded as scholarships/grants, 25% as loans/jobs. **Non-need-based:** Awarded to 948 full-time undergraduates, including 336 freshmen. Scholarships awarded for academics, leadership, minority status, ROTC.

**Application procedures. Admission:** Closing date 2/1 (postmark date). $60 fee, may be waived for applicants with need. Application may be submitted online. Admission notification 4/1. Must reply by May 1 or within 2 week(s) if notified thereafter. Second early action closing date January 1; notification date February 1. **Financial aid:** Closing date 2/1. FAFSA, CSS PROFILE required. Applicants notified by 4/1; must reply by 5/1.

**Academics.** Programs student-designed, stress projects and individualized study combining classroom and professional experience. **Special study options:** Accelerated study, combined bachelor's/graduate degree, cooperative education, cross-registration, double major, dual enrollment of high school students, ESL, honors, independent study, liberal arts/career combination, student-designed major, study abroad, teacher certification program, Washington semester. International scholars program, 3-2 BS/BA liberal arts programs with any Worcester Consortium college and selected other colleges. Accelerated 3-4 BS/DVM with Tufts University. 5-year BS/MS and BS/MBA programs. **Credit/placement by examination:** AP, CLEP, IB, institutional tests. 3 credit hours maximum toward bachelor's degree. **Support services:** Reduced course load, study skills assistance, tutoring, writing center.

**Majors. Biology:** General, biochemistry, biotechnology. **Business:** Business admin, management information systems, management science, operations. **Computer sciences:** Computer science, game design, web page design. **Engineering:** Aerospace, biomedical, chemical, civil, electrical, environmental, industrial, manufacturing, mechanical, physics, systems. **Engineering technology:** Industrial management. **English:** Technical writing. **Health:** Predental, premedicine, preveterinary. **Interdisciplinary:** Biological/physical sciences, global studies, science/society. **Legal studies:** Prelaw. **Liberal arts:** Humanities. **Math:** General, applied. **Physical sciences:** Chemistry, physics. **Social sciences:** General, economics.

**Most popular majors.** Biology 10%, business/marketing 7%, computer/information sciences 11%, engineering/engineering technologies 66%.

**Computing on campus.** 1,000 workstations in dormitories, library, computer center, student center. Dormitories wired for high-speed internet access and linked to campus network. Commuter students can connect to campus network. Online course registration, online library, helpline, repair service, student web hosting, wireless network available.

**Student life. Freshman orientation:** Available, $200 fee. Preregistration for classes offered. Program held in late August. **Housing:** Guaranteed on-campus for freshmen. Coed dorms, special housing for disabled, apartments, fraternity/sorority housing, substance-free housing available. **Activities:** Bands, choral groups, dance, drama, film society, literary magazine, music ensembles, musical theater, radio station, student government, student newspaper, symphony orchestra, African American cultural society, volunteer tutoring group, Big Brother/Big Sister, World House, European student association, Asian society, Hispanic student association, women's awareness group, students for social awareness, Amnesty International.

**Athletics.** NCAA. **Intercollegiate:** Baseball M, basketball, cross-country, field hockey W, football (tackle) M, rowing (crew), soccer, softball W, swimming, track and field, volleyball W, wrestling M. **Intramural:** Basketball, bowling, cross-country, fencing, football (non-tackle) M, racquetball, soccer, softball, swimming, table tennis, volleyball, water polo M, wrestling M. **Team name:** Engineers.

**Student services.** Adult student services, alcohol/substance abuse counseling, campus ministries, career counseling, student employment services, financial aid counseling, health services, minority student services, personal counseling, placement for graduates, veterans' counselor, women's services. **Physically disabled:** Services for visually, speech, hearing impaired. **Learning disabled:** Comprehensive services available.

**Contact.** E-mail: admissions@wpi.edu
Phone: (508) 831-5286 Fax: (508) 831-5875
Edward Connor, Director of Admission, Worcester Polytechnic Institute, 100 Institute Road, Worcester, MA 01609-2280

---

## Worcester State College
**Worcester, Massachusetts**
www.worcester.edu

**CB member**
**CB code: 3524**

- Public 4-year liberal arts and teachers college
- Commuter campus in small city
- 4,020 degree-seeking undergraduates: 17% part-time, 58% women, 4% African American, 3% Asian American, 5% Hispanic American, 2% international
- 478 degree-seeking graduate students
- SAT or ACT (ACT writing optional) required
- 40% graduate within 6 years

**General.** Founded in 1874. Regionally accredited. **Degrees:** 758 bachelor's awarded; master's offered. **ROTC:** Army, Naval, Air Force. **Location:** 45 miles from Boston, 65 miles from Hartford, Connecticut. **Calendar:** Semester, extensive summer session. **Full-time faculty:** 188 total; 74% have terminal degrees, 16% minority, 52% women. **Part-time faculty:** 231 total; 7% minority, 51% women. **Class size:** 50% < 20, 50% 20-39, less than 1% 40-49. **Special facilities:** Photographic labs; multimedia classrooms with satellite connectivity; speech, language and hearing clinic.

**Freshman class profile.** 3,810 applied, 2,030 admitted, 699 enrolled.

| Mid 50% test scores | | | |
|---|---|---|---|
| SAT critical reading: | 450-540 | GPA 2.0-2.99: | 51% |
| SAT math: | 460-560 | Return as sophomores: | 76% |
| ACT composite: | 20-24 | Out-of-state: | 4% |
| GPA 3.50 or higher: | 18% | Live on campus: | 52% |
| GPA 3.0-3.49: | 31% | International: | 1% |

**Basis for selection.** Open admission, but selective for some programs. Secondary school record most important; test scores important; extracurricular activities considered. Interview and personal essay recommended for academically weak. **Homeschooled:** Student must submit documentation that home school plan meets district curriculum standards. **Learning Disabled:** SAT waiver available for students with learning disabilties with IEP plan.

**High school preparation.** 16 units required. Required units include English 4, mathematics 3, social studies 1, history 1, science 3 (laboratory 2), foreign language 2 and academic electives 2. History unit must be US history.

**2007-2008 Annual costs.** Tuition/fees: $5,864; $11,944 out-of-state. Room/board: $7,958. Books/supplies: $984. Personal expenses: $1,200.

**2006-2007 Financial aid. Need-based:** 590 full-time freshmen applied for aid; 371 were judged to have need; 359 of these received aid. Average need met was 82%. Average scholarship/grant was $4,223; average loan $1,809. 58% of total undergraduate aid awarded as scholarships/grants, 42% as loans/jobs. **Non-need-based:** Awarded to 443 full-time undergraduates,

including 168 freshmen. **Additional information:** Veterans, Native Americans and those certified by Massachusetts Rehabilitation Commission and Massachusetts Commission for the Blind considered for tuition waivers while funds available. Tuition also waived for needy Massachusetts residents and in-state National Guard members.

**Application procedures. Admission:** Priority date 3/15; deadline 6/1 (receipt date). $20 fee, may be waived for applicants with need. Application may be submitted online. Admission notification on a rolling basis beginning on or about 12/1. Must reply by May 1 or within 4 week(s) if notified thereafter. **Financial aid:** Priority date 3/1; no closing date. FAFSA, institutional form required. Applicants notified on a rolling basis starting 3/1; must reply within 2 week(s) of notification.

**Academics. Special study options:** Combined bachelor's/graduate degree, cross-registration, distance learning, double major, ESL, exchange student, honors, independent study, internships, liberal arts/career combination, study abroad, teacher certification program, Washington semester. Foreign exchange student program. **Credit/placement by examination:** AP, CLEP, institutional tests. 30 credit hours maximum toward bachelor's degree. **Support services:** Learning center, pre-admission summer program, reduced course load, remedial instruction, study skills assistance, tutoring, writing center.

**Majors. Biology:** General, biotechnology. **Business:** Business admin. **Communications:** General, media studies. **Computer sciences:** General. **Education:** Elementary, kindergarten/preschool. **Foreign languages:** Spanish. **Health:** Adult health nursing, communication disorders, community health services, nursing (RN). **History:** General. **Interdisciplinary:** Biological/physical sciences. **Math:** General. **Physical sciences:** Chemistry. **Protective services:** Criminal justice. **Psychology:** General. **Social sciences:** Economics, geography, sociology, urban studies. **Other:** Health professions, related clinical sciences other.

**Most popular majors.** Biology 6%, business/marketing 22%, communications/journalism 9%, education 6%, health sciences 14%, psychology 15%, social sciences 8%.

**Computing on campus.** PC or laptop required. 102 workstations in dormitories, library, computer center, student center. Dormitories linked to campus network. Commuter students can connect to campus network. Online course registration, helpline, wireless network available.

**Student life. Freshman orientation:** Mandatory, $75 fee. Preregistration for classes offered. Four-hour parent orientation in Spring; 4.5-day session for students last week in August. **Housing:** Coed dorms, single-sex dorms, special housing for disabled, substance-free housing available. $150 nonrefundable deposit, deadline 2/15. **Activities:** Bands, campus ministries, choral groups, dance, drama, music ensembles, radio station, student government, student newspaper, TV station, student events committee, Third World Alliance, campus ambassadors, Gay-Straight Alliance, Surreal Games and Sci-Fi, Ski/Snow Board Club.

**Athletics.** NCAA. **Intercollegiate:** Baseball M, basketball, cheerleading, cross-country, field hockey W, football (tackle) M, golf M, ice hockey M, lacrosse W, soccer, softball W, tennis W, track and field, volleyball. **Intramural:** Baseball M, basketball, cheerleading, cross-country, field hockey W, football (tackle) M, golf M, ice hockey M, lacrosse W, rowing (crew), soccer, softball W, tennis W, track and field, volleyball. **Team name:** Lancers.

**Student services.** Alcohol/substance abuse counseling, campus ministries, career counseling, student employment services, financial aid counseling, health services, personal counseling, placement for graduates, veterans' counselor, women's services. **Physically disabled:** Services for visually, speech, hearing impaired.

**Contact.** E-mail: admissions@worcester.edu
Phone: (508) 929-8040 Toll-free number: (866) 972-2255
Fax: (508) 929-8183
Beth Axelson, Admissions Director, Worcester State College, 486 Chandler Street, Worcester, MA 01602-2597

# Michigan

## Adrian College
Adrian, Michigan
www.adrian.edu

CB member
CB code: 1001

- Private 4-year liberal arts college affiliated with United Methodist Church
- Residential campus in large town
- 1,269 degree-seeking undergraduates: 47% women, 4% African American, 1% Asian American, 2% Hispanic American, 4% international
- 64% of applicants admitted
- SAT or ACT (ACT writing optional) required
- 58% graduate within 6 years; 25% enter graduate study

**General.** Founded in 1859. Regionally accredited. **Degrees:** 157 bachelor's, 1 associate awarded. **Location:** 75 miles from Detroit, 30 miles from Toledo, Ohio. **Calendar:** Semester, limited summer session. **Full-time faculty:** 74 total; 95% have terminal degrees, 12% minority, 35% women. **Part-time faculty:** 58 total. **Class size:** 71% < 20, 27% 20-39, less than 1% 40-49, less than 1% 50-99. **Special facilities:** Observatory, planetarium, arboretum, solar greenhouse, human anatomy laboratory, writing laboratory, educational curriculum center.

**Freshman class profile.** 3,709 applied, 2,373 admitted, 492 enrolled.

| Mid 50% test scores | | | |
|---|---|---|---|
| SAT critical reading: | 430-520 | GPA 2.0-2.99: | 23% |
| SAT math: | 410-540 | Rank in top quarter: | 46% |
| ACT composite: | 20-25 | Rank in top tenth: | 17% |
| GPA 3.50 or higher: | 37% | End year in good standing: | 93% |
| GPA 3.0-3.49: | 39% | Return as sophomores: | 73% |
| | | International: | 7% |

**Basis for selection.** School achievement most important, followed by test scores. Applicants should rank in top half of high school class. School recommendations and extracurricular activities considered. ACT preferred. **Homeschooled:** Must have transcript approved by school district.

**High school preparation.** 16 units recommended. Recommended units include English 4, mathematics 3, social studies 1, history 1, science 2 (laboratory 1), foreign language 2 and academic electives 2.

**2007-2008 Annual costs.** Tuition/fees: $21,620. Room/board: $7,150. Books/supplies: $400. Personal expenses: $928.

**2007-2008 Financial aid. Need-based:** 418 full-time freshmen applied for aid; 376 were judged to have need; 376 of these received aid. Average need met was 100%. Average scholarship/grant was $9,211; average loan $4,485. 66% of total undergraduate aid awarded as scholarships/grants, 34% as loans/jobs. **Non-need-based:** Awarded to 936 full-time undergraduates, including 368 freshmen. Scholarships awarded for academics, alumni affiliation, art, leadership, music/drama, religious affiliation.

**Application procedures. Admission:** Closing date 3/15 (receipt date). No application fee. Application may be submitted online. Admission notification on a rolling basis. Must reply by May 1 or within 2 week(s) if notified thereafter. **Financial aid:** Closing date 3/1. FAFSA required. Applicants notified on a rolling basis starting 3/15; must reply by 5/1 or within 2 week(s) of notification.

**Academics. Special study options:** Combined bachelor's/graduate degree, cross-registration, double major, dual enrollment of high school students, ESL, exchange student, honors, independent study, internships, student-designed major, study abroad, teacher certification program, Washington semester. Philadelphia semester, bilingual multicultural program, exchange programs with Urban Life Center (Chicago), American College (London, England). **Credit/placement by examination:** AP, CLEP, IB, institutional tests. 15 credit hours maximum toward associate degree, 30 toward bachelor's. **Support services:** Learning center, pre-admission summer program, reduced course load, remedial instruction, study skills assistance, tutoring, writing center.

**Majors. Area/ethnic studies:** Japanese. **Biology:** General. **Business:** Accounting, business admin, international, international marketing, management science, marketing. **Communications:** General, journalism. **Conservation:** Environmental science, environmental studies. **Education:** General, art, elementary, health, multi-level teacher, music, physical, secondary, social science. **English:** English lit. **Foreign languages:** French, German, Spanish. **Health:** Predental, premedicine, prepharmacy, preveterinary. **History:** General. **Interdisciplinary:** Global studies. **Legal studies:** Prelaw. **Math:** General. **Parks/recreation:** Exercise sciences, health/fitness. **Philosophy/religion:** Philosophy, religion. **Physical sciences:** Chemistry, geology, physics, planetary. **Protective services:** Criminal justice. **Psychology:** General. **Public administration:** Social work. **Social sciences:** Economics, international relations, political science, sociology. **Theology:** Preministerial. **Visual/performing arts:** Art, arts management, dramatic, interior design, musical theater.

**Most popular majors.** Biology 8%, business/marketing 15%, communications/journalism 9%, health sciences 11%, history 6%, social sciences 8%, visual/performing arts 13%.

**Computing on campus.** 170 workstations in library, computer center, student center. Dormitories wired for high-speed internet access and linked to campus network. Commuter students can connect to campus network. Online course registration, online library, helpline, student web hosting, wireless network available.

**Student life. Freshman orientation:** Mandatory. Preregistration for classes offered. Week-long program in August. Students take placement exams and take a first-year trip. **Policies:** Freshmen, sophomores, and juniors required to live on campus unless living with family. **Housing:** Guaranteed on-campus for all undergraduates. Coed dorms, single-sex dorms, special housing for disabled, apartments, fraternity/sorority housing, substance-free housing available. $100 deposit, deadline 7/1. **Activities:** Bands, choral groups, dance, drama, international student organizations, literary magazine, music ensembles, musical theater, radio station, student government, student newspaper, symphony orchestra, Wesley Fellowship, Circle K, Religious Life Council, Habitat for Humanity, African-American Leaders Promoting Higher Achievement, Leaders in College Service, Catholic student organization.

**Athletics.** NCAA. **Intercollegiate:** Baseball M, basketball, cross-country, football (tackle) M, golf, ice hockey, lacrosse, soccer, softball W, tennis, track and field, volleyball W. **Intramural:** Basketball, bowling, football (non-tackle), lacrosse, racquetball, soccer, softball, tennis, volleyball. **Team name:** Bulldogs.

**Student services.** Adult student services, alcohol/substance abuse counseling, campus ministries, career counseling, student employment services, financial aid counseling, health services, minority student services, personal counseling, placement for graduates. **Physically disabled:** Services for visually, speech, hearing impaired.

**Contact.** E-mail: admissions@adrian.edu
Phone: (517) 265-5161 ext. 4326 Toll-free number: (800) 877-2246
Fax: (517) 264-3878
Carolyn Quinlan, Director of Admissions, Adrian College, 110 South Madison Street, Adrian, MI 49221-2575

## Albion College
Albion, Michigan
www.albion.edu

CB member
CB code: 1007

- Private 4-year liberal arts college affiliated with United Methodist Church
- Residential campus in small town
- 1,922 degree-seeking undergraduates: 55% women, 3% African American, 2% Asian American, 1% Hispanic American, 1% international
- 81% of applicants admitted
- SAT or ACT (ACT writing recommended), application essay required
- 72% graduate within 6 years

**General.** Founded in 1835. Regionally accredited. **Degrees:** 393 bachelor's awarded. **Location:** 55 miles from Lansing, 55 miles from Ann Arbor. **Calendar:** Semester, limited summer session. **Full-time faculty:** 136 total; 90% have terminal degrees, 10% minority, 42% women. **Part-time faculty:** 31 total; 23% have terminal degrees, 3% minority, 55% women. **Class size:** 61% < 20, 38% 20-39, 1% 40-49, less than 1% 50-99. **Special facilities:** Science complex, 144-acre nature center, observatory, equestrian center, institutes for public service, professional management, environmental studies, K-12 education, pre-medical and health care studies, honors studies, foundation for undergraduate research, scholarship, and creative activity.

**Freshman class profile.** 2,204 applied, 1,790 admitted, 503 enrolled.

| Mid 50% test scores | | | |
|---|---|---|---|
| SAT critical reading: | 520-660 | Rank in top quarter: | 64% |
| SAT math: | 530-650 | Rank in top tenth: | 30% |
| ACT composite: | 23-28 | Return as sophomores: | 84% |
| GPA 3.50 or higher: | 62% | Out-of-state: | 8% |
| GPA 3.0-3.49: | 28% | Live on campus: | 98% |
| GPA 2.0-2.99: | 10% | International: | 2% |

**Basis for selection.** Admission based on school achievement record, ACT/SAT test scores, recommendations from counselor or principal. SAT Subject Tests recommended. Interview recommended. Audition recommended for music and theater majors.

**High school preparation.** 15 units required; 17 recommended. Required and recommended units include English 4, mathematics 3, social studies 3, history 3, science 3 (laboratory 1), foreign language 3 and academic electives 3.

**2008-2009 Annual costs.** Tuition/fees: $28,880. Room/board: $8,190. Books/supplies: $650. Personal expenses: $350.

**2007-2008 Financial aid. Need-based:** 388 full-time freshmen applied for aid; 328 were judged to have need; 328 of these received aid. Average need met was 93%. Average scholarship/grant was $18,674; average loan $3,916. 79% of total undergraduate aid awarded as scholarships/grants, 21% as loans/jobs. **Non-need-based:** Awarded to 1,787 full-time undergraduates, including 474 freshmen. Scholarships awarded for academics, alumni affiliation, art, music/drama, state residency.

**Application procedures. Admission:** Priority date 12/1; deadline 3/1 (postmark date). $20 fee, may be waived for applicants with need. Application may be submitted online. Admission notification on a rolling basis beginning on or about 1/1. Must reply by May 1 or within 2 week(s) if notified thereafter. **Financial aid:** Priority date 3/1; no closing date. FAFSA required. Applicants notified on a rolling basis starting 3/15; must reply by 5/1 or within 2 week(s) of notification.

**Academics. Special study options:** Combined bachelor's/graduate degree, double major, dual enrollment of high school students, honors, independent study, internships, liberal arts/career combination, New York semester, semester at sea, student-designed major, study abroad, teacher certification program, urban semester, Washington semester. Environmental institute, public service institute, liberal arts program in professional management. **Credit/placement by examination:** AP, CLEP, IB, institutional tests. **Support services:** Learning center, reduced course load, study skills assistance, tutoring, writing center.

**Majors. Area/ethnic studies:** American. **Biology:** General, biochemistry. **Business:** Business admin. **Communications:** General. **Computer sciences:** General, computer science. **Conservation:** Environmental science, environmental studies. **Education:** Art, biology, chemistry, English, foreign languages, French, German, history, mathematics, music, physical, physics, science, social studies, Spanish. **English:** Creative writing, English lit. **Foreign languages:** French, German, Spanish. **History:** General. **Interdisciplinary:** Behavioral sciences, biological/physical sciences, math/computer science, natural sciences, neuroscience. **Math:** General. **Philosophy/religion:** Philosophy, religion. **Physical sciences:** Chemistry, geology, physics. **Psychology:** General. **Public administration:** Policy analysis. **Social sciences:** Anthropology, economics, international relations, political science, sociology. **Visual/performing arts:** General, art, art history/conservation, dramatic, music performance, studio arts.

**Most popular majors.** Biology 12%, business/marketing 16%, education 8%, English 8%, foreign language 6%, health sciences 6%, psychology 9%, social sciences 10%, visual/performing arts 8%.

**Computing on campus.** 435 workstations in dormitories, library, computer center, student center. Dormitories wired for high-speed internet access and linked to campus network. Commuter students can connect to campus network. Online course registration, online library, helpline, repair service, wireless network available.

**Student life. Freshman orientation:** Mandatory. Preregistration for classes offered. **Housing:** Guaranteed on-campus for all undergraduates. Coed dorms, single-sex dorms, special housing for disabled, apartments, cooperative housing, fraternity/sorority housing, substance-free housing available. Special interest annexes available. **Activities:** Bands, choral groups, dance, drama, international student organizations, literary magazine, music ensembles, musical theater, radio station, student government, student newspaper, symphony orchestra, 110 campus organizations.

**Athletics.** NCAA. **Intercollegiate:** Baseball M, basketball, cheerleading, cross-country, diving, equestrian, football (tackle) M, golf, soccer, softball W, swimming, tennis, track and field, volleyball W. **Intramural:** Badminton, basketball, diving, football (non-tackle), football (tackle) M, racquetball, rugby, soccer, softball, swimming, tennis, volleyball. **Team name:** Britons.

**Student services.** Alcohol/substance abuse counseling, campus ministries, career counseling, services for economically disadvantaged, student employment services, financial aid counseling, health services, minority student services, personal counseling, placement for graduates, women's services. **Physically disabled:** Services for visually, hearing impaired.

**Contact.** E-mail: admissions@albion.edu
Phone: (517) 629-0321 Toll-free number: (800) 858-6770
Fax: (517) 629-0569
Kevin Kropf, Director of Admission, Albion College, 611 East Porter Street, Albion, MI 49224-1831

---

## Alma College

**Alma, Michigan**
**www.alma.edu**

**CB member**
**CB code: 1010**

- Private 4-year liberal arts college affiliated with Presbyterian Church (USA)
- Residential campus in small town
- 1,304 degree-seeking undergraduates: 1% part-time, 56% women, 1% African American, 1% Asian American, 2% Hispanic American
- 78% of applicants admitted
- SAT or ACT (ACT writing optional) required
- 72% graduate within 6 years

**General.** Founded in 1886. Regionally accredited. Scottish heritage honored through marching band clad in kilts, Scottish dance troupe, student pipers, tartan, Alma Highland Festival and Games. **Degrees:** 241 bachelor's awarded. **ROTC:** Army. **Location:** 50 miles from Lansing, 45 miles from Saginaw. **Calendar:** 4-4-1 semester system. Limited summer session. **Full-time faculty:** 81 total; 88% have terminal degrees, 9% minority, 41% women. **Part-time faculty:** 38 total; 29% have terminal degrees, 8% minority, 53% women. **Class size:** 60% < 20, 36% 20-39, 1% 40-49, 3% 50-99. **Special facilities:** Planetarium, performing arts center, climbing wall, ecological station.

**Freshman class profile.** 2,044 applied, 1,598 admitted, 430 enrolled.

| Mid 50% test scores | | | |
|---|---|---|---|
| SAT critical reading: | 500-670 | Rank in top quarter: | 61% |
| SAT math: | 520-670 | Rank in top tenth: | 25% |
| SAT writing: | 500-620 | End year in good standing: | 93% |
| ACT composite: | 21-27 | Return as sophomores: | 83% |
| GPA 3.50 or higher: | 57% | Out-of-state: | 4% |
| GPA 3.0-3.49: | 29% | Live on campus: | 98% |
| GPA 2.0-2.99: | 14% | Fraternities: | 26% |
| | | Sororities: | 22% |

**Basis for selection.** Applicant should be in top half of class, have 3.0 high school GPA or 22 ACT or 1030 SAT (exclusive of Writing). Cocurricular activities considered. Portfolio recommended for art majors. Interview recommended for all, strongly recommended for academically weak and those whose grades and test scores show discrepancies.

**High school preparation.** 16 units required. Required and recommended units include English 4, mathematics 3, social studies 3, science 3 and foreign language 2.

**2007-2008 Annual costs.** Tuition/fees: $23,688. Room/board: $7,774. Books/supplies: $722. Personal expenses: $700.

**2007-2008 Financial aid. Need-based:** 419 full-time freshmen applied for aid; 336 were judged to have need; 336 of these received aid. Average need met was 88%. Average scholarship/grant was $17,631; average loan $4,936. 74% of total undergraduate aid awarded as scholarships/grants, 26% as loans/jobs. **Non-need-based:** Awarded to 410 full-time undergraduates, including 149 freshmen. Scholarships awarded for academics, alumni affiliation, art, music/drama. **Additional information:** Auditions required for music, drama, dance scholarship candidates. Portfolios required for art scholarship candidates.

**Application procedures. Admission:** Priority date 3/1; no deadline. $25 fee, may be waived for applicants with need. Application may be submitted online. Admission notification on a rolling basis beginning on or about 9/15. Must reply by May 1 or within 2 week(s) if notified thereafter. **Financial aid:** Priority date 3/1; no closing date. FAFSA required. Applicants notified on a rolling basis starting 3/1; must reply within 3 week(s) of notification.

**Academics.** One-month spring term provides special opportunities for study in United States or overseas. Students required to complete 2 spring terms. **Special study options:** Combined bachelor's/graduate degree, double major, dual enrollment of high school students, honors, independent study, internships, New York semester, student-designed major, study abroad, teacher certification program, urban semester, Washington semester. Pre-engineering 3-2 programs with University of Michigan, Michigan Technological University; pre-occupational therapy 3-2 program with Washington University (MO). **Credit/placement by examination:** AP, CLEP, IB, ACT, institutional tests. 32 credit hours maximum toward bachelor's degree. **Support services:** Pre-admission summer program, reduced course load, remedial instruction, study skills assistance, tutoring, writing center.

**Majors. Biology:** General, biochemistry. **Business:** Accounting, business admin, finance, international, marketing. **Communications:** Media studies. **Computer sciences:** Computer science. **Education:** General, elementary, secondary. **English:** English lit. **Foreign languages:** French, German, Spanish. **Health:** Medical illustrating, predental, premedicine, preveterinary. **History:** General. **Interdisciplinary:** Biological/physical sciences, gerontology. **Legal studies:** Prelaw. **Liberal arts:** Arts/sciences, humanities. **Math:** General. **Parks/recreation:** Exercise sciences. **Philosophy/religion:** Philosophy, religion. **Physical sciences:** Chemistry, physics. **Psychology:** General. **Social sciences:** Anthropology, economics, political science, sociology. **Theology:** Preministerial. **Visual/performing arts:** General, art, art history/conservation, dance, design, dramatic, graphic design, music performance, studio arts.

**Most popular majors.** Biology 10%, business/marketing 16%, communications/journalism 6%, English 8%, foreign language 6%, health sciences 8%, history 9%, psychology 7%, social sciences 10%, visual/performing arts 8%.

**Computing on campus.** 292 workstations in dormitories, library, computer center, student center. Dormitories wired for high-speed internet access and linked to campus network. Commuter students can connect to campus network. Online course registration, online library, helpline, student web hosting, wireless network available.

**Student life. Freshman orientation:** Mandatory, $315 fee. Preregistration for classes offered. One-week session begins last weekend of August and runs to Labor Day weekend. **Housing:** Guaranteed on-campus for all undergraduates. Coed dorms, single-sex dorms, fraternity/sorority housing, substance-free housing available. $100 nonrefundable deposit, deadline 5/1. Academic theme houses available. **Activities:** Bands, campus ministries, choral groups, dance, drama, international student organizations, literary magazine, music ensembles, Model UN, musical theater, opera, radio station, student government, student newspaper, symphony orchestra, College Republicans/College Democrats, Amnesty International, Big Brothers/Big Sisters, Catholic student organization, Habitat for Humanity, multicultural black student union, Students Offering Service.

**Athletics. NCAA. Intercollegiate:** Baseball M, basketball, cross-country, diving, football (tackle) M, golf, soccer, softball W, swimming, tennis, track and field, volleyball W. **Intramural:** Basketball, football (non-tackle), ice hockey, racquetball, soccer, softball, tennis, volleyball. **Team name:** Scots.

**Student services.** Alcohol/substance abuse counseling, campus ministries, career counseling, student employment services, financial aid counseling, health services, personal counseling. **Physically disabled:** Services for visually, hearing impaired.

**Contact.** E-mail: admissions@alma.edu
Phone: (989) 463-7139 Toll-free number: (800) 321-2562
Fax: (989) 463-7057
Evan Montague, Director of Admissions, Alma College, 614 West Superior Street, Alma, MI 48801-1599

---

## Andrews University
### Berrien Springs, Michigan
www.andrews.edu                                      CB code: 1030

- Private 4-year university affiliated with Seventh-day Adventists
- Residential campus in small town
- 1,622 degree-seeking undergraduates: 7% part-time, 56% women, 23% African American, 9% Asian American, 11% Hispanic American, 13% international
- 1,403 degree-seeking graduate students
- 57% of applicants admitted
- SAT or ACT (ACT writing optional), application essay required
- 54% graduate within 6 years

**General.** Founded in 1874. Regionally accredited. **Degrees:** 373 bachelor's, 4 associate awarded; master's, doctoral, first professional offered. **Location:** 10 miles from St. Joseph-Benton Harbor, 25 miles from South Bend, Indiana. **Calendar:** Semester, limited summer session. **Full-time faculty:** 203 total; 77% have terminal degrees, 28% minority, 32% women. **Part-time faculty:** 124 total; 18% have terminal degrees, 10% minority, 44% women. **Class size:** 62% < 20, 26% 20-39, 4% 40-49, 7% 50-99, 1% >100. **Special facilities:** Natural history museum, archaeology museum, performing arts center, arboretum.

**Freshman class profile.** 1,298 applied, 735 admitted, 337 enrolled.

| Mid 50% test scores | | | |
|---|---|---|---|
| SAT critical reading: | 470-610 | GPA 2.0-2.99: | 24% |
| SAT math: | 440-610 | Rank in top quarter: | 39% |
| SAT writing: | 420-540 | Rank in top tenth: | 16% |
| ACT composite: | 19-26 | Return as sophomores: | 77% |
| GPA 3.50 or higher: | 48% | Out-of-state: | 69% |
| GPA 3.0-3.49: | 27% | Live on campus: | 85% |
| | | International: | 12% |

**Basis for selection.** School achievement record, test scores, recommendations important. Interview recommended. Audition recommended for music majors. Portfolios recommended for architecture, art majors. **Homeschooled:** Portfolio required. **Learning Disabled:** Must advise student services of learning disability prior to admission interview and testing.

**High school preparation.** 13 units required; 15 recommended. Required and recommended units include English 3-4, mathematics 2-3, social studies 1, history 2, science 2 and academic electives 3. Additional 1 unit chemistry, 1 unit physics, 1 unit computer recommended.

**2008-2009 Annual costs.** Tuition/fees (projected): $20,541. Room/board: $6,330. Books/supplies: $1,000. Personal expenses: $600.

**Financial aid. Non-need-based:** Scholarships awarded for academics, alumni affiliation, leadership, music/drama, religious affiliation.

**Application procedures. Admission:** No deadline. $30 fee. Application must be submitted on paper. Admission notification on a rolling basis beginning on or about 1/1. **Financial aid:** Priority date 3/31; no closing date. FAFSA, institutional form required. Applicants notified on a rolling basis starting 3/15.

**Academics. Special study options:** Accelerated study, combined bachelor's/graduate degree, cooperative education, distance learning, double major, dual enrollment of high school students, ESL, honors, internships, student-designed major, study abroad, teacher certification program. **Credit/placement by examination:** AP, CLEP, IB, institutional tests. 32 credit hours maximum toward associate degree, 32 toward bachelor's. DANTES (for nontraditional students). **Support services:** Learning center, pre-admission summer program, reduced course load, remedial instruction, study skills assistance, tutoring, writing center.

**Majors. Agriculture:** Animal sciences, business, horticulture. **Architecture:** Architecture. **Biology:** General, biochemistry, biophysics, botany, molecular, zoology. **Business:** Accounting, business admin, entrepreneurial studies, finance, managerial economics, nonprofit/public, training/development. **Communications:** General, journalism, public relations. **Communications technology:** General. **Computer sciences:** General, information systems. **Conservation:** Environmental science. **Education:** Elementary, mathematics, secondary, social science, social studies. **Engineering:** General, electrical, industrial, mechanical. **Engineering technology:** Aerospace, electrical, mechanical. **English:** English lit. **Family/consumer sciences:** Family studies, food/nutrition. **Foreign languages:** French, Spanish. **Health:** Audiology/speech pathology, clinical lab science, dietetics, nursing (RN). **History:** General. **Interdisciplinary:** Biological/physical sciences, neuroscience. **Math:** General. **Mechanic/repair:** Aircraft. **Philosophy/religion:** Religion. **Physical sciences:** Chemistry, physics. **Psychology:** General. **Public administration:** Social work. **Social sciences:** General, anthropology, economics, international economic development, political science, sociology. **Theology:** Religious ed, sacred music, theology, youth ministry. **Transportation:** Aviation. **Visual/performing arts:** General, art, art history/conservation, ceramics, commercial/advertising art, design, graphic design, multimedia, music performance, painting, photography, printmaking, studio arts.

**Most popular majors.** Architecture 7%, biology 9%, business/marketing 10%, education 7%, health sciences 20%, visual/performing arts 6%.

**Computing on campus.** 130 workstations in dormitories, library, computer center. Dormitories wired for high-speed internet access and linked to campus network. Commuter students can connect to campus network. Online course registration, online library, helpline, repair service, student web hosting, wireless network available.

**Student life. Freshman orientation:** Mandatory. Preregistration for classes offered. Held week before fall registration. **Policies:** Students expected to abide by ethical and moral standards of the university, which are mission-driven as published in official documents. Resident students required to stay in dorm until age 22. Religious observance required. **Housing:** Guaranteed on-campus for all undergraduates. Single-sex dorms, apartments, substance-free housing available. $150 deposit. **Activities:** Concert band, choral groups, drama, music ensembles, musical theater, radio station, student government, student newspaper, symphony orchestra, Christian Youth Action.

**Athletics. Intramural:** Badminton, basketball, field hockey, football (non-tackle), soccer, softball, triathlon, volleyball.

**Student services.** Campus ministries, career counseling, student employment services, financial aid counseling, health services, on-campus daycare, personal counseling, placement for graduates, veterans' counselor. **Physically disabled:** Services for visually, speech, hearing impaired.

**Contact.** E-mail: enroll@andrews.edu
Phone: (800) 253-2874 Toll-free number: (800) 253-2874
Fax: (269) 471-3228
Stephen Payne, Vice President for Enrollment Management, Andrews University, 100 US Highway 31, Berrien Springs, MI 49104

---

## Aquinas College
**Grand Rapids, Michigan**
www.aquinas.edu                    **CB code: 1018**

- Private 4-year liberal arts college affiliated with Roman Catholic Church
- Residential campus in small city
- 1,779 degree-seeking undergraduates: 15% part-time, 64% women, 4% African American, 2% Asian American, 3% Hispanic American, 1% Native American
- 280 degree-seeking graduate students
- 81% of applicants admitted
- SAT or ACT (ACT writing optional) required
- 57% graduate within 6 years; 37% enter graduate study

**General.** Founded in 1886. Regionally accredited. **Degrees:** 329 bachelor's, 5 associate awarded; master's offered. **Location:** 140 miles from Detroit, 180 miles from Chicago. **Calendar:** Semester, extensive summer session. **Full-time faculty:** 91 total; 71% have terminal degrees, 7% minority, 50% women. **Part-time faculty:** 92 total; 29% have terminal degrees, 6% minority, 46% women. **Class size:** 58% < 20, 40% 20-39, 1% 40-49, less than 1% 50-99. **Special facilities:** Greenhouse, astronomy tower, nature trails, community theater.

**Freshman class profile.** 2,086 applied, 1,680 admitted, 412 enrolled.

| Mid 50% test scores | | Rank in top quarter: | 48% |
|---|---|---|---|
| ACT composite: | 20-25 | Rank in top tenth: | 17% |
| GPA 3.50 or higher: | 47% | Return as sophomores: | 74% |
| GPA 3.0-3.49: | 32% | Out-of-state: | 7% |
| GPA 2.0-2.99: | 21% | Live on campus: | 84% |

**Basis for selection.** GED not accepted. 2.5 high school GPA in academic subjects. Test scores important. Interview required for applicants with above average test scores but less than 2.5 high school GPA in academic subjects, recommended for others. Audition recommended for music majors. Portfolio recommended for art majors. **Homeschooled:** Transcript of courses and grades required. Greater emphasis placed upon results of ACT or SAT. Students may be required to complete Ability to Benefit test. **Learning Disabled:** Make appointment with Academic Achievement Center to express needed accommodations prior to enrollment.

**High school preparation.** 15 units required. Required units include English 4, mathematics 4, social studies 4 and science 3.

**2007-2008 Annual costs.** Tuition/fees: $20,048. Room/board: $6,422. Books/supplies: $737. Personal expenses: $727.

**2007-2008 Financial aid. Need-based:** 380 full-time freshmen applied for aid; 333 were judged to have need; 333 of these received aid. Average need met was 93%. Average scholarship/grant was $15,120; average loan $2,723. 75% of total undergraduate aid awarded as scholarships/grants, 25% as loans/jobs. **Non-need-based:** Scholarships awarded for academics, alumni affiliation, art, athletics, leadership, music/drama.

**Application procedures. Admission:** No deadline. No application fee. Application may be submitted online. Admission notification on a rolling basis beginning on or about 8/1. **Financial aid:** Priority date 3/1; no closing date. FAFSA required. Applicants notified on a rolling basis starting 2/15; must reply within 2 week(s) of notification.

**Academics. Special study options:** Accelerated study, cooperative education, cross-registration, distance learning, double major, dual enrollment of high school students, exchange student, honors, independent study, internships, liberal arts/career combination, student-designed major, study abroad,

teacher certification program. **Credit/placement by examination:** AP, CLEP, institutional tests. 30 credit hours maximum toward bachelor's degree. **Support services:** Learning center, remedial instruction, study skills assistance, tutoring, writing center,

**Majors. Biology:** General. **Business:** Accounting, business admin, communications, international, management information systems. **Communications:** General. **Computer sciences:** General. **Conservation:** Environmental science, environmental studies. **Education:** General, English, learning disabled, music, physical, science, social science, social studies, special. **English:** English lit. **Foreign languages:** French, German, Japanese, Spanish. **Health:** Athletic training. **History:** General. **Liberal arts:** Arts/sciences. **Math:** General. **Parks/recreation:** General, health/fitness, sports admin. **Philosophy/religion:** Philosophy, religion. **Physical sciences:** Chemistry. **Protective services:** Fire safety technology. **Psychology:** General. **Public administration:** Community org/advocacy. **Social sciences:** General, economics, geography, international relations, political science, sociology, urban studies. **Theology:** Sacred music. **Visual/performing arts:** Art, art history/conservation, arts management, theater arts management. **Other:** Sustainable business.

**Most popular majors.** Business/marketing 20%, communications/journalism 6%, education 19%, parks/recreation 6%, social sciences 9%.

**Computing on campus.** 155 workstations in dormitories, library, computer center, student center. Dormitories wired for high-speed internet access and linked to campus network. Commuter students can connect to campus network. Online library, helpline, wireless network available.

**Student life. Freshman orientation:** Mandatory, $100 fee. Preregistration for classes offered. 3 days during week before fall classes begin. Includes start of common freshman class. **Policies:** Students serve on administrative and faculty committees. **Housing:** Guaranteed on-campus for freshmen. Coed dorms, single-sex dorms, apartments, substance-free housing available. $100 deposit, deadline 8/15. Project/theme houses. **Activities:** Jazz band, campus ministries, choral groups, dance, drama, international student organizations, literary magazine, music ensembles, radio station, student government, student newspaper, community action volunteers, social action commission, community senate, Bible Study, College Democrats, College Republicans, Catholic studies club, Habitat for Humanity.

**Athletics. NAIA. Intercollegiate:** Baseball M, basketball, cross-country, golf, soccer, softball W, tennis, track and field, volleyball W. **Intramural:** Basketball, bowling, fencing M, golf, ice hockey M, lacrosse, skiing, soccer, softball, tennis, volleyball. **Team name:** Saints.

**Student services.** Adult student services, alcohol/substance abuse counseling, campus ministries, career counseling, student employment services, financial aid counseling, health services, minority student services, personal counseling, placement for graduates, veterans' counselor, women's services. **Physically disabled:** Services for visually, speech, hearing impaired.

**Contact.** E-mail: admissions@aquinas.edu
Phone: (616) 632-2900 Toll-free number: (800) 678-9593
Fax: (616) 732-4469
Thomas Mikowski, Dean of Admissions, Aquinas College, 1607 Robinson Road Southeast, Grand Rapids, MI 49506-1799

---

## Baker College of Allen Park
**Allen Park, Michigan**
www.baker.edu

- Private 4-year business and health science college
- Commuter campus in large city
- 2,204 degree-seeking undergraduates

**General.** Regionally accredited. **Location:** 10 miles from Detroit. **Calendar:** Quarter, limited summer session. **Full-time faculty:** 4 total. **Part-time faculty:** 100 total.

**Freshman class profile.** 900 applied, 900 admitted, 696 enrolled.

**Basis for selection.** Open admission, but selective for some programs. **Homeschooled:** Transcript of courses and grades required.

**2008-2009 Annual costs.** Tuition/fees (projected): $8,550.

**Application procedures. Admission:** No deadline. $20 fee, may be waived for applicants with need. Admission notification on a rolling basis.

**Academics. Special study options:** Combined bachelor's/graduate degree, cooperative education, distance learning, double major, dual enrollment of high school students, independent study, internships, teacher certification program. **Credit/placement by examination:** CLEP. **Support services:** Learning center, remedial instruction, study skills assistance, tutoring.

**Majors. Business:** Human resources. **Computer sciences:** Information technology. **Education:** Elementary, middle, secondary. **Health:** Health services. **Public administration:** Human services.

**Computing on campus.** 208 workstations in library, computer center, student center. Online library, helpline, wireless network available.

**Student life. Freshman orientation:** Mandatory.

**Contact.** Phone: (313) 425-3700
Steve Peterson, Vice President for Admissions, Baker College of Allen Park, 4500 Enterprise Drive, Allen Park, MI 48101

## Baker College of Auburn Hills
Auburn Hills, Michigan
www.baker.edu                                    CB code: 1457

▶ Private 4-year business and technical college
▶ Commuter campus in small city
▶ 3,701 degree-seeking undergraduates

**General.** Founded in 1990. Regionally accredited. Part of multicampus system specializing in career education. **Location:** 30 miles from Detroit. **Calendar:** Quarter, limited summer session. **Full-time faculty:** 11 total. **Part-time faculty:** 144 total. **Class size:** 45% < 20, 55% 20-39.

**Freshman class profile.** 1,484 applied, 1,484 admitted, 970 enrolled.

**Basis for selection.** Open admission. Specific entrance requirements for allied health programs and bachelor of business leadership degree program. Interview recommended.

**2008-2009 Annual costs.** Tuition/fees (projected): $8,550. Books/supplies: $1,000.

**Financial aid. Non-need-based:** Scholarships awarded for academics, alumni affiliation.

**Application procedures. Admission:** No deadline. $20 fee, may be waived for applicants with need. Application may be submitted online. Admission notification on a rolling basis. **Financial aid:** Priority date 2/21, closing date 9/1. FAFSA, institutional form required. Applicants notified on a rolling basis starting 4/1.

**Academics.** 2+2 system allows students to begin required courses in major while completing associate degree. **Special study options:** Accelerated study, combined bachelor's/graduate degree, distance learning, double major, dual enrollment of high school students, independent study, internships, liberal arts/career combination, teacher certification program. **Credit/placement by examination:** AP, CLEP, IB, institutional tests. 48 credit hours maximum toward associate degree, 96 toward bachelor's. **Support services:** Learning center, reduced course load, remedial instruction, study skills assistance, tutoring, writing center.

**Majors. Business:** General, accounting, business admin, management science. **Education:** General, elementary, middle, multi-level teacher, secondary.

**Computing on campus.** 131 workstations in library, computer center, student center. Commuter students can connect to campus network. Helpline available.

**Student life. Freshman orientation:** Mandatory. **Activities:** Accounting club, management club, interior design society, society of automotive engineers, marketing club.

**Student services.** Career counseling, student employment services, financial aid counseling, personal counseling, placement for graduates, veterans' counselor. **Physically disabled:** Services for visually, hearing impaired.

**Contact.** Phone: (248) 340-0600 Toll-free number: (888) 429-0410
Fax: (248) 340-0600
Jan Bohlen, Vice President for Admissions, Baker College of Auburn Hills, 1500 University Drive, Auburn Hills, MI 48326

## Baker College of Cadillac
Cadillac, Michigan
www.baker.edu                                    CB code: 1381

▶ Private 4-year business and health science college
▶ Commuter campus in large town
▶ 1,806 degree-seeking undergraduates

**General.** Founded in 1911. Regionally accredited. Part of multicampus system specializing in career education. **Location:** 90 miles from Grand Rapids, 45 miles from Traverse City. **Calendar:** Quarter, limited summer session. **Full-time faculty:** 4 total. **Part-time faculty:** 101 total. **Class size:** 68% < 20, 31% 20-39, 1% 40-49. **Special facilities:** Mock operating room, massage therapy room.

**Freshman class profile.** 595 applied, 595 admitted, 478 enrolled.

**Basis for selection.** Open admission. Some allied health programs require health appraisal. Interview recommended.

**2008-2009 Annual costs.** Tuition/fees (projected): $8,550. Books/supplies: $1,000.

**Financial aid. Non-need-based:** Scholarships awarded for academics.

**Application procedures. Admission:** No deadline. $20 fee, may be waived for applicants with need. Admission notification on a rolling basis beginning on or about 10/1. **Financial aid:** Priority date 2/21; no closing date. FAFSA, institutional form required. Applicants notified on a rolling basis starting 5/1.

**Academics. Special study options:** Accelerated study, combined bachelor's/graduate degree, cooperative education, distance learning, double major, dual enrollment of high school students, external degree, independent study, internships, liberal arts/career combination, weekend college. 2+2 bachelor's degree and bachelor of business leadership degree. **Credit/placement by examination:** AP, CLEP, IB, institutional tests. 48 credit hours maximum toward associate degree, 96 toward bachelor's. **Support services:** Learning center, reduced course load, remedial instruction, study skills assistance, tutoring, writing center.

**Majors. Business:** Accounting, business admin, human resources, office management. **Computer sciences:** Computer science. **Public administration:** Human services.

**Computing on campus.** 154 workstations in library, computer center. Commuter students can connect to campus network. Online library, helpline, repair service available.

**Student life. Freshman orientation:** Mandatory. Preregistration for classes offered. **Activities:** Student activities group, professional student organizations.

**Student services.** Career counseling, student employment services, financial aid counseling, personal counseling, placement for graduates, veterans' counselor. **Physically disabled:** Services for visually, hearing impaired.

**Contact.** E-mail: mike.tisdale@baker.edu
Phone: (231) 876-3100 Toll-free number: (888) 313-3463
Fax: (231) 775-8505
Mike Tisdale, Director of Admissions, Baker College of Cadillac, 9600 East 13th Street, Cadillac, MI 49601

## Baker College of Clinton Township
Clinton Township, Michigan
www.baker.edu                                    CB code: 1386

▶ Private 4-year business and technical college
▶ Commuter campus in very large city
▶ 5,608 degree-seeking undergraduates

**General.** Founded in 1911. Regionally accredited. Part of multicampus system specializing in career education. **Location:** 15 miles from Detroit. **Calendar:** Quarter, limited summer session. **Full-time faculty:** 17 total. **Part-time faculty:** 191 total. **Class size:** 25% < 20, 74% 20-39, less than 1% 40-49.

**Freshman class profile.** 2,709 applied, 2,709 admitted, 1,840 enrolled.

**Basis for selection.** Open admission, but selective for some programs. Physical exam may be required for some programs. Interview recommended. **Learning Disabled:** Students must complete special needs intake form signed by professional.

**High school preparation.** Recommended units include English 4, mathematics 4, social studies 2, science 3 and foreign language 4.

**2008-2009 Annual costs.** Tuition/fees (projected): $8,550. Books/supplies: $1,000. Personal expenses: $2,000.

**Financial aid. Non-need-based:** Scholarships awarded for academics, minority status.

**Application procedures. Admission:** Priority date 9/1; no deadline. $20 fee, may be waived for applicants with need. Application may be submitted online. Admission notification on a rolling basis. **Financial aid:** Priority date 2/21, closing date 9/1. FAFSA, institutional form required. Applicants notified on a rolling basis starting 4/1.

**Academics.** 2+2 system allows students to begin required courses in major while completing associate degree. **Special study options:** Accelerated study, combined bachelor's/graduate degree, cooperative education, distance learning, double major, dual enrollment of high school students, external degree, independent study, internships, teacher certification program. **Credit/placement by examination:** AP, CLEP, IB, institutional tests. 48 credit hours maximum toward associate degree, 96 toward bachelor's. **Support services:** Learning center, reduced course load, remedial instruction, study skills assistance, tutoring, writing center.

**Majors. Business:** Accounting, administrative services, business admin, human resources, management science, office management. **Computer sciences:** General, computer science. **Education:** Elementary, middle, multi-level teacher, secondary. **Health:** Health care admin, nursing (RN), office admin. **Public administration:** Human services.

**Computing on campus.** 120 workstations in library, computer center. Commuter students can connect to campus network. Helpline available.

**Student life. Freshman orientation:** Mandatory. Preregistration for classes offered.

**Student services.** Adult student services, career counseling, student employment services, financial aid counseling, personal counseling, placement for graduates, veterans' counselor. **Physically disabled:** Services for visually, hearing impaired.

**Contact.** E-mail: adm_mc@baker.edu
Phone: (586) 791-3000 Toll-free number: (888) 272-2842
Fax: (586) 791-6610
Annette Looser, Director of Admissions, Baker College of Clinton Township, 34401 Gratiot Avenue, Clinton Township, MI 48035

---

## Baker College of Flint
**Flint, Michigan**
www.baker.edu                                    CB code: 0806

- Private 4-year business and technical college
- Commuter campus in large city
- 5,808 degree-seeking undergraduates

**General.** Founded in 1911. Regionally accredited. Corporate services division offers degree-granting programs on campus and/or at work site, coordinated with corporate training and professional development programs. Part of multicampus system specializing in career education. **Location:** 10 miles from downtown, 60 miles from Detroit. **Calendar:** Quarter, limited summer session. **Full-time faculty:** 40 total. **Part-time faculty:** 304 total. **Special facilities:** Polysommnography sleep lab, orthotic/prosthetic lab.

**Freshman class profile.** 2,536 applied, 2,536 admitted, 1,806 enrolled.

| Out-of-state: | 2% | **Live on campus:** | 5% |
|---|---|---|---|

**Basis for selection.** Open admission, but selective for some programs. Health applicants must have health appraisal. Occupational therapy applicants must present minimum of 1 year biology, 1 year chemistry/physics, 2 years math including algebra or equivalent. All health programs require 2.0 GPA for entrance to professional classes. Class size may be limited. Trucking programs require drug screening prior to enrollment acceptance. Interview recommended.

**2008-2009 Annual costs.** Tuition/fees (projected): $8,550. Additional fees vary with program. Room only: $2,600. Books/supplies: $900.

**Financial aid. Non-need-based:** Scholarships awarded for academics, minority status.

**Application procedures. Admission:** Priority date 9/1; no deadline. $20 fee, may be waived for applicants with need. Admission notification on a rolling basis. **Financial aid:** Priority date 2/21, closing date 9/1. FAFSA, institutional form required. Applicants notified on a rolling basis starting 4/1.

**Academics.** 2+2 system allows students to begin required courses in major while completing associate degree. Calendar based on 10-week quarters. **Special study options:** Accelerated study, combined bachelor's/graduate degree, cooperative education, distance learning, double major, dual enrollment of high school students, external degree, independent study, internships. **Credit/placement by examination:** AP, CLEP, IB, institutional tests.

---

48 credit hours maximum toward associate degree, 96 toward bachelor's. **Support services:** Learning center, reduced course load, remedial instruction, study skills assistance, tutoring, writing center.

**Majors. Business:** Accounting, business admin, management information systems, office management, operations. **Computer sciences:** General. **Education:** Elementary, middle, multi-level teacher, secondary. **Engineering:** Mechanical. **Engineering technology:** Electrical. **Health:** Health care admin, medical records admin, nursing (RN). **Transportation:** Aviation management. **Visual/performing arts:** Commercial/advertising art, interior design.

**Most popular majors.** Business/marketing 65%, health sciences 25%.

**Computing on campus.** 300 workstations in library, computer center. Commuter students can connect to campus network. Helpline available.

**Student life. Freshman orientation:** Mandatory. Preregistration for classes offered. **Housing:** Guaranteed on-campus for freshmen. Coed dorms, substance-free housing available. $50 deposit, deadline 9/20. **Activities:** Literary magazine, National Association of Accountants, American Marketing Association, Interior Design Society, travel club, environmental club, physical therapy assistant club, medical assistants student organization, Health Information Management Association, graphic communications club, Society of Manufacturing Engineers student chapter.

**Athletics. Intramural:** Basketball, volleyball.

**Student services.** Career counseling, student employment services, on-campus daycare, personal counseling, placement for graduates, veterans' counselor. **Physically disabled:** Services for visually, hearing impaired.

**Contact.** E-mail: adm-fl@baker.edu
Phone: (810) 766-4000 Toll-free number: (800) 964-4299
Fax: (810) 766-4293
Jodi Cuneaz, Director of Admissions, Baker College of Flint, 1050 West Bristol Road, Flint, MI 48507

---

## Baker College of Jackson
**Jackson, Michigan**
www.baker.edu                                    CB code: 1887

- Private 4-year business and technical college
- Commuter campus in small city
- 1,813 degree-seeking undergraduates

**General.** Founded in 1994. Regionally accredited. Part of multicampus system specializing in career education. **Location:** 40 miles from Lansing, 40 miles from Ann Arbor. **Calendar:** Quarter, limited summer session. **Full-time faculty:** 5 total. **Part-time faculty:** 93 total.

**Freshman class profile.** 684 applied, 684 admitted, 607 enrolled.

**Basis for selection.** Open admission, but selective for some programs. Physical exam may be required for allied health programs. All health programs require specific GPA. Interview recommended.

**2008-2009 Annual costs.** Tuition/fees (projected): $8,550. Books/supplies: $975.

**Financial aid. Non-need-based:** Scholarships awarded for academics, minority status.

**Application procedures. Admission:** No deadline. $20 fee, may be waived for applicants with need. Application may be submitted online. Admission notification on a rolling basis. **Financial aid:** Priority date 2/21, closing date 9/1. FAFSA, institutional form required. Applicants notified on a rolling basis starting 4/1.

**Academics.** 2+2 system allows students to begin required courses in major while completing associate degree. **Special study options:** Accelerated study, combined bachelor's/graduate degree, cooperative education, distance learning, double major, dual enrollment of high school students, external degree, independent study, internships. **Credit/placement by examination:** AP, CLEP, IB, institutional tests. 48 credit hours maximum toward associate degree, 96 toward bachelor's. **Support services:** Learning center, reduced course load, remedial instruction, study skills assistance, tutoring, writing center.

**Majors. Business:** General, accounting. **Education:** Elementary, middle, multi-level teacher, secondary.

**Computing on campus.** 114 workstations in library, computer center. Commuter students can connect to campus network. Helpline available.

**Student life. Freshman orientation:** Mandatory. Preregistration for classes offered. **Activities:** Student government.

**Student services.** Career counseling, student employment services, personal counseling, placement for graduates, veterans' counselor. **Physically disabled:** Services for visually, hearing impaired.

**Contact.** E-mail: adm-jk@baker.edu
Phone: (517) 788-7800 Toll-free number: (888) 343-3683
Fax: (517) 789-7331
Kelli Stepka, Director of Admissions, Baker College of Jackson, 2800 Springport Road, Jackson, MI 49202

## Baker College of Muskegon
### Muskegon, Michigan
www.baker.edu                    CB code: 1527

▸ Private 4-year business and technical college
▸ Commuter campus in small city
▸ 5,010 degree-seeking undergraduates

**General.** Founded in 1888. Regionally accredited. Part of multicampus system specializing in career education. All associate degree programs include internship, co-op or clinical affiliation experience. **Location:** 40 miles from Grand Rapids. **Calendar:** Quarter, limited summer session. **Full-time faculty:** 17 total. **Part-time faculty:** 169 total. **Class size:** 38% < 20, 57% 20-39, 3% 40-49, 2% 50-99. **Special facilities:** Restaurant run by culinary and food and beverage management students.

**Freshman class profile.** 2,247 applied, 2,247 admitted, 1,708 enrolled.

**Basis for selection.** Open admission, but selective for some programs. 2.75 GPA required for admission to occupational therapy assisting, physical therapist assisting, veterinary technician, surgical technology, teacher preparation. Class size may be limited in some programs. Physical examination, background check required for some programs. Interview recommended. **Homeschooled:** Basic skills placement assessments in math, language arts, and reading part of orientation/registration process. **Learning Disabled:** Learning disability must be documented and presented to counseling staff before registering for classes.

**2008-2009 Annual costs.** Tuition/fees (projected): $8,550. Room only: $2,865. Books/supplies: $975. Personal expenses: $2,000.

**Financial aid. Non-need-based:** Scholarships awarded for academics, minority status.

**Application procedures. Admission:** Priority date 9/1; no deadline. $20 fee, may be waived for applicants with need. Application may be submitted online. Admission notification on a rolling basis. **Financial aid:** Priority date 2/21; no closing date. FAFSA, institutional form required. Applicants notified on a rolling basis starting 4/1.

**Academics.** 2-2 system allows students to begin required courses in major while completing associate degree. Maximum number of credits awarded for prior work and/or life experiences, 48 for associate and 144 for bachelor. **Special study options:** Accelerated study, combined bachelor's/graduate degree, cooperative education, distance learning, double major, dual enrollment of high school students, external degree, independent study, internships, liberal arts/career combination, teacher certification program. Accelerated bachelor of business administration offered in weekend delivery format. **Credit/placement by examination:** AP, CLEP, IB, institutional tests. 48 credit hours maximum toward associate degree, 144 toward bachelor's. **Support services:** Learning center, reduced course load, remedial instruction, study skills assistance, tutoring.

**Majors. Business:** Accounting, accounting/business management, administrative services, business admin, human resources, management science, marketing, office management, restaurant/food services. **Computer sciences:** General, computer science, information systems, systems analysis. **Education:** Elementary, kindergarten/preschool, middle, multi-level teacher, secondary. **Engineering technology:** Industrial management. **Health:** Health care admin. **Personal/culinary services:** General, culinary arts, restaurant/catering. **Public administration:** Human services. **Transportation:** Aviation management.

**Computing on campus.** 180 workstations in dormitories, library, computer center. Dormitories wired for high-speed internet access and linked to campus network. Commuter students can connect to campus network. Online course registration, online library, helpline, wireless network available.

**Student life. Freshman orientation:** Mandatory. Preregistration for classes offered. 3-4 hour session prior to start of quarter; includes COMPASS testing, registration, academic advising. **Policies:** No drug or alcohol use permitted anywhere on campus or in residence halls. **Housing:** Coed dorms,

special housing for disabled, apartments, substance-free housing available. $50 deposit, deadline 9/1. **Activities:** Student government, travel club, rehab club, residence hall association, culinary arts club, human resource management club.

**Athletics. Intramural:** Bowling.

**Student services.** Adult student services, career counseling, student employment services, financial aid counseling, personal counseling, placement for graduates, veterans' counselor. **Physically disabled:** Services for visually, hearing impaired.

**Contact.** E-mail: kathy.jacobson@baker.edu
Phone: (231) 777-5200 Toll-free number: (800) 937-0337
Fax: (231) 777-5201
Kathy Jacobson, Vice President and Director of Admissions, Baker College of Muskegon, 1903 Marquette Avenue, Muskegon, MI 49442

## Baker College of Owosso
### Owosso, Michigan
www.baker.edu                    CB code: 5270

▸ Private 4-year business and technical college
▸ Commuter campus in large town
▸ 2,911 degree-seeking undergraduates

**General.** Founded in 1911. Regionally accredited. Part of multicampus system, with affiliated graduate school, specializing in career education. Master's degree available at Flint campus. **Location:** 30 miles from Lansing, 300 miles from Flint. **Calendar:** Quarter, limited summer session. **Full-time faculty:** 8 total. **Part-time faculty:** 146 total. **Special facilities:** Diesel technology center.

**Freshman class profile.** 1,321 applied, 1,321 admitted, 1,111 enrolled.

| Out-of-state: | 3% | Live on campus: | 30% |
|---|---|---|---|

**Basis for selection.** Open admission. Limited enrollment for medical programs.

**2008-2009 Annual costs.** Tuition/fees (projected): $8,550. Room only: $2,700. Books/supplies: $1,000.

**Financial aid. Non-need-based:** Scholarships awarded for academics, minority status.

**Application procedures. Admission:** Priority date 9/1; no deadline. $20 fee, may be waived for applicants with need. Application may be submitted online. Admission notification on a rolling basis. **Financial aid:** Priority date 2/21, closing date 9/1. FAFSA, institutional form required. Applicants notified on a rolling basis starting 4/1.

**Academics.** 2+2 system allows students to begin required courses in major while completing associate degree. **Special study options:** Accelerated study, combined bachelor's/graduate degree, cooperative education, distance learning, double major, dual enrollment of high school students, external degree, independent study, internships. **Credit/placement by examination:** AP, CLEP, IB, institutional tests. 48 credit hours maximum toward associate degree, 96 toward bachelor's. **Support services:** Learning center, reduced course load, remedial instruction, study skills assistance, tutoring, writing center.

**Majors. Business:** Accounting, administrative services, business admin, human resources, management information systems, marketing, office management. **Communications technology:** Graphics. **Computer sciences:** General, computer graphics, computer science. **Education:** Elementary, middle, multi-level teacher, secondary. **Health:** Health care admin. **Public administration:** Human services.

**Computing on campus.** 226 workstations in dormitories, library, computer center. Dormitories wired for high-speed internet access. Commuter students can connect to campus network. Online library, helpline available.

**Student life. Freshman orientation:** Mandatory. Preregistration for classes offered. **Housing:** Guaranteed on-campus for freshmen. Coed dorms, substance-free housing available. $50 deposit. **Activities:** Student newspaper, accounting club, MLT club, interior design club, radiology club, graphics club.

**Athletics. Intramural:** Basketball, volleyball.

**Student services.** Adult student services, career counseling, services for economically disadvantaged, student employment services, financial aid counseling, on-campus daycare, personal counseling, placement for graduates, veterans' counselor. **Physically disabled:** Services for visually, speech, hearing impaired.

**Contact.** E-mail: michael.konopacke@baker.edu
Phone: (989) 729-3350 Toll-free number: (800) 879-3797
Fax: (989) 729-3359
Michael Konopacke, Vice President of Admissions, Baker College of Owosso, 1020 South Washington Street, Owosso, MI 48867

## Baker College of Port Huron
### Port Huron, Michigan
www.baker.edu                    CB code: 1413

- Private 4-year business and technical college
- Commuter campus in large town
- 1,642 degree-seeking undergraduates

**General.** Founded in 1911. Regionally accredited. Part of multicampus system specializing in career education. **Location:** 60 miles from Detroit. **Calendar:** Quarter, limited summer session. **Full-time faculty:** 12 total. **Part-time faculty:** 114 total. **Class size:** 58% < 20, 37% 20-39, 1% 40-49, 4% 50-99. **Special facilities:** Dental hygiene clinic.

**Freshman class profile.** 617 applied, 617 admitted, 553 enrolled.

**Basis for selection.** Open admission, but selective for some programs. Specific entrance requirements for health and human services programs. Waiting list for Dental Hygiene. Interview recommended.

**2008-2009 Annual costs.** Tuition/fees (projected): $8,550. Books/supplies: $1,000. Personal expenses: $2,000.

**Financial aid.** All financial aid based on need.

**Application procedures. Admission:** Priority date 9/1; no deadline. $20 fee, may be waived for applicants with need. Application may be submitted online. Admission notification on a rolling basis. **Financial aid:** Priority date 2/21; no closing date. FAFSA, institutional form required. Applicants notified on a rolling basis starting 4/1.

**Academics.** 2+2 system allows students to begin required courses in major while completing associate degree. Accelerated BBA available. **Special study options:** Accelerated study, combined bachelor's/graduate degree, cooperative education, distance learning, double major, dual enrollment of high school students, external degree, independent study, internships, liberal arts/career combination. **Credit/placement by examination:** AP, CLEP, IB, institutional tests. 48 credit hours maximum toward associate degree, 96 toward bachelor's. **Support services:** Learning center, reduced course load, remedial instruction, study skills assistance, tutoring, writing center.

**Majors. Business:** General, accounting, administrative services, business admin, human resources, international, management information systems, marketing, office management. **Computer sciences:** General, computer science, information systems. **Health:** Health care admin.

**Computing on campus.** 229 workstations in library, computer center. Commuter students can connect to campus network. Online course registration, helpline available.

**Student life. Freshman orientation:** Mandatory. Preregistration for classes offered. **Activities:** Dental hygiene society.

**Student services.** Adult student services, career counseling, student employment services, personal counseling, placement for graduates, veterans' counselor. **Physically disabled:** Services for visually, hearing impaired.

**Contact.** E-mail: daniel.kenny@baker.edu
Phone: (810) 985-7000 Toll-free number: (888) 262-2442
Fax: (810) 985-7066
Dan Kenny, Vice President of Admissions, Baker College of Port Huron, 3403 Lapeer Road, Port Huron, MI 48060-2597

## Calvin College
### Grand Rapids, Michigan                    CB member
www.calvin.edu                    CB code: 1095

- Private 4-year liberal arts college affiliated with Christian Reformed Church
- Residential campus in large city
- 4,078 degree-seeking undergraduates: 2% part-time, 54% women, 1% African American, 3% Asian American, 2% Hispanic American, 7% international
- 26 degree-seeking graduate students
- 95% of applicants admitted

- SAT or ACT (ACT writing optional), application essay required
- 75% graduate within 6 years; 35% enter graduate study

**General.** Founded in 1876. Regionally accredited. **Degrees:** 878 bachelor's awarded; master's offered. **ROTC:** Army. **Location:** 150 miles from Detroit and Chicago. **Calendar:** 4-1-4, limited summer session. **Full-time faculty:** 322 total; 83% have terminal degrees, 7% minority, 32% women. **Part-time faculty:** 85 total; 27% have terminal degrees, 9% minority, 48% women. **Class size:** 39% < 20, 58% 20-39, 2% 40-49, 1% 50-99. **Special facilities:** Ecosystem preserve and interpretive center, electron microscope, rhetoric center, observatory.

**Freshman class profile.** 2,277 applied, 2,169 admitted, 1,039 enrolled.

| Mid 50% test scores | | | |
|---|---|---|---|
| SAT critical reading: | 530-650 | Rank in top quarter: | 51% |
| SAT math: | 540-650 | Rank in top tenth: | 26% |
| ACT composite: | 23-28 | End year in good standing: | 95% |
| GPA 3.50 or higher: | 62% | Return as sophomores: | 89% |
| GPA 3.0-3.49: | 26% | Out-of-state: | 48% |
| GPA 2.0-2.99: | 12% | Live on campus: | 96% |
| | | International: | 8% |

**Basis for selection.** Genuine interest in Christian goals of college and 2.5 GPA required. Recommendation, personal statement important. Minimum 20 ACT or 470 SAT Verbal and 470 SAT Math recommended. GED accepted only for those age 19 years or over. SAT Subject Tests recommended. **Homeschooled:** Must provide some form of transcript with grades.

**High school preparation.** 12 units required; 17 recommended. Required and recommended units include English 3-4, mathematics 3, social studies 2-3, science 2 (laboratory 1), foreign language 2 and academic electives 3. Math must include algebra and geometry.

**2007-2008 Annual costs.** Tuition/fees: $21,685. Room/board: $7,460. Books/supplies: $680. Personal expenses: $875.

**2006-2007 Financial aid. Need-based:** 864 full-time freshmen applied for aid; 671 were judged to have need; 671 of these received aid. Average need met was 87%. Average scholarship/grant was $10,200; average loan $4,200. 60% of total undergraduate aid awarded as scholarships/grants, 40% as loans/jobs. **Non-need-based:** Awarded to 1,752 full-time undergraduates, including 527 freshmen. Scholarships awarded for academics, alumni affiliation, art, leadership, minority status, music/drama, religious affiliation, state residency.

**Application procedures. Admission:** Closing date 8/15 (postmark date). $35 fee, may be waived for applicants with need. Application may be submitted online. Admission notification on a rolling basis beginning on or about 11/1. Must reply by May 1 or within 4 week(s) if notified thereafter. **Financial aid:** Priority date 2/15; no closing date. FAFSA required. Applicants notified on a rolling basis starting 3/15.

**Academics.** Importance of faith perspective in all disciplines and co-curricular activities emphasized. **Special study options:** Accelerated study, combined bachelor's/graduate degree, double major, dual enrollment of high school students, honors, independent study, internships, student-designed major, study abroad, teacher certification program, urban semester, Washington semester. Overseas programs with Central College, January interim exchange with other colleges, academically-based service-learning. **Credit/placement by examination:** AP, CLEP, IB, institutional tests. **Support services:** Learning center, reduced course load, remedial instruction, study skills assistance, tutoring, writing center.

**Majors. Area/ethnic studies:** Asian. **Biology:** General, biochemistry, biotechnology. **Business:** General, accounting, business admin, communications, management information systems. **Communications:** General, digital media, media studies. **Computer sciences:** General, computer science, information systems, networking, programming. **Conservation:** Environmental science. **Education:** General, art, bilingual, biology, chemistry, Deaf/hearing impaired, early childhood, elementary, English, French, German, history, mathematics, mentally handicapped, middle, music, physical, physics, reading, secondary, social studies, Spanish, special, speech impaired. **Engineering:** General, chemical, civil, electrical, mechanical. **English:** English lit, speech/rhetoric. **Foreign languages:** Ancient Greek, Biblical, classics, Dutch/Flemish, French, German, Latin, modern Greek, Spanish. **Health:** Athletic training, audiology/speech pathology, communication disorders, predental, premedicine, preop/surgical nursing, prepharmacy, preveterinary, recreational therapy, speech pathology. **History:** General, American, European. **Interdisciplinary:** Biological/physical sciences, classical/archaeology, natural sciences. **Legal studies:** Prelaw. **Liberal arts:** Arts/sciences. **Math:** General. **Parks/recreation:** General, exercise sciences, health/fitness. **Philosophy/religion:** Philosophy, religion. **Physical sciences:** Chemistry, geology, physics. **Psychology:** General. **Public administration:** General, social work. **Social sciences:** General, economics, geography, international economic development, international relations, political science, sociology. **Theology:** Bible, sacred music. **Visual/performing arts:** General, art, art history/conservation, cinematography, conducting, dramatic, film/cinema, music history, music performance, music theory/composition, piano/organ, studio arts, voice/opera.

**Most popular majors.** Biology 7%, business/marketing 12%, education 6%, engineering/engineering technologies 7%, foreign language 6%, health sciences 8%, psychology 7%, social sciences 8%, visual/performing arts 7%.

**Computing on campus.** 900 workstations in dormitories, library, computer center. Dormitories wired for high-speed internet access and linked to campus network. Commuter students can connect to campus network. Online course registration, online library, helpline, student web hosting, wireless network available.

**Student life. Freshman orientation:** Mandatory, $75 fee. Two-day program held in summer. **Policies:** Strong emphasis on student leadership and service. Religious observance strongly expected and encouraged. First- and second-year students (under 21) not living at home required to live in residence halls. **Housing:** Guaranteed on-campus for freshmen. Single-sex dorms, apartments, substance-free housing available. $50 deposit, deadline 5/1. Project Neighborhood houses available. **Activities:** Bands, choral groups, dance, drama, film society, literary magazine, music ensembles, musical theater, radio station, student government, student newspaper, symphony orchestra, Amnesty International, Campus Crusade for Christ, Environmental Stewardship, Republicans club, InterVarsity Christian Fellowship, Liberals and Democrats, Young Life, Social Justice, Korean Christian Fellowship.

**Athletics.** NCAA. **Intercollegiate:** Baseball M, basketball, cross-country, diving, golf, soccer, softball W, swimming, tennis, track and field, volleyball W. **Intramural:** Badminton, basketball, football (non-tackle), golf, racquetball, soccer, softball, swimming, table tennis, tennis, track and field, volleyball, water polo. **Team name:** Knights.

**Student services.** Adult student services, alcohol/substance abuse counseling, campus ministries, career counseling, student employment services, financial aid counseling, health services, minority student services, personal counseling, placement for graduates. **Physically disabled:** Services for visually, speech, hearing impaired.

**Contact.** E-mail: admissions@calvin.edu
Phone: (616) 526-6106 Toll-free number: (800) 688-0122
Fax: (616) 526-6777
Dale Kuiper, Director of Admissions and Financial Aid, Calvin College, 3201 Burton Street Southeast, Grand Rapids, MI 49546

---

### Central Michigan University
**Mount Pleasant, Michigan**                     **CB member**
www.cmich.edu                                    **CB code: 1106**

- Public 4-year university
- Commuter campus in large town
- 19,632 degree-seeking undergraduates: 11% part-time, 56% women, 6% African American, 1% Asian American, 2% Hispanic American, 1% Native American, 1% international
- 6,142 degree-seeking graduate students
- 73% of applicants admitted
- ACT (writing optional) required
- 57% graduate within 6 years

**General.** Founded in 1892. Regionally accredited. 60 off-campus locations in the United States and surrounding countries. **Degrees:** 3,551 bachelor's awarded; master's, doctoral offered. **ROTC:** Army. **Location:** 70 miles from Lansing. **Calendar:** Semester, limited summer session. **Full-time faculty:** 737 total; 83% have terminal degrees, 18% minority, 38% women. **Part-time faculty:** 404 total; 26% have terminal degrees, 8% minority, 48% women. **Class size:** 32% < 20, 44% 20-39, 13% 40-49, 7% 50-99, 4% >100. **Special facilities:** Center for clinical care and education, English language institute, center for applied research and rural studies, Michigan services for children and young adults who are deaf-blind, psychological training and consultation center, language learning center, biological station, conservation genetics lab, water research center, museum of cultural and natural history, historical library, 255-acre natural woodland.

**Freshman class profile.** 15,220 applied, 11,165 admitted, 3,771 enrolled.

| Mid 50% test scores | | | |
|---|---|---|---|
| SAT critical reading: | 450-580 | Rank in top tenth: | 15% |
| SAT math: | 470-600 | End year in good standing: | 79% |
| ACT composite: | 20-24 | Return as sophomores: | 76% |
| GPA 3.50 or higher: | 39% | Out-of-state: | 3% |
| GPA 3.0-3.49: | 40% | Live on campus: | 94% |
| GPA 2.0-2.99: | 21% | International: | 2% |
| Rank in top quarter: | 39% | Fraternities: | 5% |
| | | Sororities: | 3% |

**Basis for selection.** School achievement record, test scores, recommendations important. Interview and essay recommended. Audition required for music majors. **Learning Disabled:** Students urged to register with Student Disability Services.

**High school preparation.** 19 units recommended. Recommended units include English 4, mathematics 4, social studies 2, history 2, science 3 (laboratory 2), foreign language 2, computer science 1 and visual/performing arts 1.

**2007-2008 Annual costs.** Tuition/fees: $9,120; $21,210 out-of-state. Four years guaranteed tuition plan. Room/board: $7,236. Books/supplies: $1,000. Personal expenses: $1,665.

**2006-2007 Financial aid. Need-based:** 2,992 full-time freshmen applied for aid; 2,000 were judged to have need; 1,950 of these received aid. Average need met was 84%. Average scholarship/grant was $5,020; average loan $3,909. 34% of total undergraduate aid awarded as scholarships/grants, 66% as loans/jobs. **Non-need-based:** Awarded to 2,593 full-time undergraduates, including 752 freshmen. Scholarships awarded for academics, alumni affiliation, art, athletics, leadership, minority status, music/drama, ROTC, state residency. **Additional information:** Tuition waiver for Native American students qualifying under state program criteria.

**Application procedures. Admission:** No deadline. $35 fee, may be waived for applicants with need. Application may be submitted online. Admission notification on a rolling basis. Must reply by May 1 or within 2 week(s) if notified thereafter. **Financial aid:** Priority date 3/1; no closing date. FAFSA required. Applicants notified on a rolling basis starting 4/1.

**Academics. Special study options:** Accelerated study, combined bachelor's/graduate degree, distance learning, double major, dual enrollment of high school students, ESL, honors, independent study, internships, semester at sea, student-designed major, study abroad, teacher certification program, Washington semester. Leadership Institute, Pre-professional studies. **Credit/placement by examination:** AP, CLEP, IB, SAT, ACT, institutional tests. Credit by examination may not be used to repeat any course previously taken. **Support services:** Learning center, pre-admission summer program, reduced course load, remedial instruction, study skills assistance, tutoring, writing center.

**Honors college/program.** Applicants must have 3.75 GPA or 3.6 GPA and 25 ACT.

**Majors. Architecture:** Interior. **Area/ethnic studies:** European, women's. **Biology:** General, biochemistry, biomedical sciences. **Business:** Accounting, actuarial science, business admin, entrepreneurial studies, fashion, finance, financial planning, hospitality admin, hotel/motel admin, human resources, international, logistics, management information systems, marketing, operations, purchasing, real estate, retailing. **Communications:** General, advertising, journalism, organizational, photojournalism, public relations. **Computer sciences:** Computer science, information technology. **Conservation:** General, environmental science, environmental studies. **Education:** Art, biology, business, chemistry, early childhood, elementary, emotionally handicapped, English, family/consumer sciences, French, geography, German, health, history, mathematics, mentally handicapped, music, physical, physics, science, Spanish, speech, technology/industrial arts. **Engineering:** Electrical, manufacturing, mechanical. **Engineering technology:** Automotive, computer systems, construction, electrical, manufacturing, mechanical. **English:** Creative writing, English lit. **Family/consumer sciences:** Child development, family systems, institutional food production. **Foreign languages:** French, German, Spanish. **Health:** Athletic training, clinical lab science, communication disorders, dietetics, health care admin, public health ed, recreational therapy. **History:** General. **Interdisciplinary:** Cognitive science, math/computer science, neuroscience. **Legal studies:** General. **Liberal arts:** Arts/sciences. **Math:** General, statistics. **Parks/recreation:** General, exercise sciences, facilities management, health/fitness, sports admin. **Philosophy/religion:** Philosophy, religion. **Physical sciences:** Astronomy, chemistry, geology, meteorology, oceanography, physics. **Psychology:** General. **Public administration:** Community org/advocacy, social work. **Social sciences:** General, anthropology, economics, geography, international relations, political science, sociology. **Visual/performing arts:** Acting, art, dramatic, graphic design, music theory/composition, studio arts, theater design.

**Most popular majors.** Business/marketing 26%, communications/journalism 8%, education 19%, parks/recreation 8%, social sciences 8%.

**Computing on campus.** 3,000 workstations in dormitories, library, computer center, student center. Dormitories wired for high-speed internet access and linked to campus network. Commuter students can connect to campus network. Online course registration, online library, helpline, repair service, student web hosting, wireless network available.

**Student life. Freshman orientation:** Mandatory, $175 fee. Preregistration for classes offered. One-day sessions; morning refreshments and lunch provided. **Housing:** Guaranteed on-campus for freshmen. Coed dorms, single-sex dorms, special housing for disabled, apartments, fraternity/sorority housing, substance-free housing available. $800 partly refundable deposit, deadline 5/1. Residential colleges for health professions, science and technology, language, school of music, school of business, honors, leadership, international students available. **Activities:** Bands, choral groups, dance, drama, film society, literary magazine, music ensembles, musical theater, radio station, student government, student newspaper, TV station, Asian cultural organization, Hispanic student organization, North American Indian student organization, organization for black unity, gay/lesbian/bisexual club, College Republicans, University Democrats, Baha'i club, Campus Crusade for Christ, Fellowship of Christian Athletes.

**Athletics.** NCAA. **Intercollegiate:** Baseball M, basketball, cross-country, field hockey W, football (tackle) M, gymnastics W, soccer W, softball W, track and field, volleyball W, wrestling M. **Intramural:** Basketball, football (non-tackle), golf, racquetball, soccer, softball, table tennis, tennis, volleyball, wrestling M. **Team name:** Chippewas.

**Student services.** Alcohol/substance abuse counseling, career counseling, student employment services, financial aid counseling, health services, minority student services, personal counseling, placement for graduates, veterans' counselor. **Physically disabled:** Services for visually, speech, hearing impaired.

**Contact.** E-mail: cmuadmit@cmich.edu
Phone: (989) 774-3076 Toll-free number: (888) 292-5366
Fax: (989) 774-7267
Betty Wagner, Director of Admissions, Central Michigan University, Admissions Office, Mount Pleasant, MI 48859

---

## Cleary University
### Howell, Michigan
### www.cleary.edu
**CB code: 1123**

- Private 4-year university and business college
- Commuter campus in small city
- 644 degree-seeking undergraduates: 40% part-time, 54% women, 8% African American, 1% Asian American, 2% Hispanic American
- 102 graduate students
- 90% of applicants admitted
- SAT or ACT (ACT writing optional) required

**General.** Founded in 1883. Regionally accredited. Campuses in Howell and Ann Arbor; extension sites throughout Southeastern Michigan. **Degrees:** 163 bachelor's, 57 associate awarded; master's offered. **Location:** 55 miles from Detroit, 27 miles from Ann Arbor. **Calendar:** Quarter, limited summer session. **Full-time faculty:** 8 total; 25% have terminal degrees, 12% minority, 62% women. **Part-time faculty:** 119 total; 12% have terminal degrees, 13% minority, 45% women. **Class size:** 89% < 20, 11% 20-39. **Special facilities:** Nature trails.

**Freshman class profile.** 72 applied, 65 admitted, 48 enrolled.

**Basis for selection.** 2.0 GPA, high school record or GED most important. 20 ACT or 1000 SAT (exclusive of Writing) recommended. Regular, special, guest, dual, provisional, transfer, and international admissions available. Applicants with below 2.0 GPA may be accepted if probable success in chosen program indicated.

**High school preparation.** 24 units recommended. Recommended units include English 4, mathematics 2, social studies 2, history 2, science 2 and academic electives 12.

**2008-2009 Annual costs.** Tuition/fees (projected): $14,880. Tuition prices guaranteed if student enrolled continuously. Tuition includes all books and fees.

**2006-2007 Financial aid. Need-based:** 46 full-time freshmen applied for aid; 46 were judged to have need; 46 of these received aid. Average need met was 35%. Average scholarship/grant was $915; average loan $1,103. 29% of total undergraduate aid awarded as scholarships/grants, 71% as loans/jobs. **Non-need-based:** Awarded to 63 full-time undergraduates, including 12 freshmen. Scholarships awarded for academics. **Additional information:** Filing electronically preferred; paper applications available. Tuition

---

guarantee based on continuous enrollment. Essay and recommendations required for scholarship consideration.

**Application procedures. Admission:** Closing date 8/15. $25 fee, may be waived for applicants with need. Application may be submitted online. Admission notification on a rolling basis. **Financial aid:** Priority date 3/15, closing date 8/15. FAFSA required. Applicants notified on a rolling basis; must reply within 2 week(s) of notification.

**Academics.** Compressed academic calendar reduces time to degree completion. First-time college students can complete bachelor's degree in 3.5 years and adults with previous college experience can complete degree in just over 1 year. **Special study options:** Accelerated study, combined bachelor's/graduate degree, cooperative education, distance learning, dual enrollment of high school students, independent study, internships. **Credit/placement by examination:** AP, CLEP, institutional tests. 36 credit hours maximum toward bachelor's degree. **Support services:** Pre-admission summer program, reduced course load, remedial instruction, study skills assistance, tutoring.

**Majors. Business:** Accounting, business admin, e-commerce, entrepreneurial studies, financial planning, human resources, management information systems, marketing, nonprofit/public, public finance. **Computer sciences:** Security.

**Computing on campus.** 60 workstations in computer center, student center. Commuter students can connect to campus network. Online library, helpline, wireless network available.

**Student life. Freshman orientation:** Mandatory. Preregistration for classes offered. **Activities:** Rotaract, automotive alley, Michigan quality council, quality improvement network, economic club.

**Student services.** Adult student services, career counseling, student employment services, financial aid counseling, placement for graduates, veterans' counselor.

**Contact.** E-mail: admissions@cleary.edu
Phone: (800) 686-1883 ext. 2249 Toll-free
number: (800) 686-1883 ext. 2249 Fax: (517) 552-7805
Carrie Bonofiglio, Director of Admissions, Cleary University, 3750 Cleary Drive, Howell, MI 48843

---

## College for Creative Studies
### Detroit, Michigan
**CB member**
### www.collegeforcreativestudies.edu
**CB code: 1035**

- Private 4-year visual arts college
- Commuter campus in very large city
- 1,307 degree-seeking undergraduates: 15% part-time, 42% women, 6% African American, 4% Asian American, 5% Hispanic American, 1% Native American, 4% international
- 39% of applicants admitted
- SAT or ACT (ACT writing optional) required
- 51% graduate within 6 years

**General.** Founded in 1926. Regionally accredited. **Degrees:** 259 bachelor's awarded. **Location:** 4 miles from downtown. **Calendar:** Semester, limited summer session. **Full-time faculty:** 51 total; 61% have terminal degrees, 14% minority, 31% women. **Part-time faculty:** 155 total; 29% minority, 43% women. **Special facilities:** Extensive studio space, art gallery for student exhibitions, foundry, computer studios, wood shop, metals shop, glassblowing studio, ceramic studio, fiber studio.

**Freshman class profile.** 1,260 applied, 488 admitted, 251 enrolled.

| Mid 50% test scores | | Return as sophomores: | 73% |
|---|---|---|---|
| ACT composite: | 18-23 | Out-of-state: | 22% |
| GPA 3.50 or higher: | 21% | Live on campus: | 70% |
| GPA 3.0-3.49: | 39% | International: | 3% |
| GPA 2.0-2.99: | 40% | | |

**Basis for selection.** Art portfolio, test scores, and high school record important. Minimum 2.5 high school GPA for applicants. ACT/SAT scores required. Portfolio required. **Homeschooled:** Transcript of courses and grades required.

**High school preparation.** 13 units recommended. Recommended units include English 4, mathematics 3, social studies 2, science 2 and foreign language 2. College-preparatory program recommended, art courses highly recommended.

**2008-2009 Annual costs.** Tuition/fees (projected): $28,275. College owned apartments available. Books/supplies: $2,500. Personal expenses: $1,500.

**2006-2007 Financial aid. Need-based:** 52% of total undergraduate aid awarded as scholarships/grants, 48% as loans/jobs. **Non-need-based:** Scholarships awarded for academics, art.

**Application procedures. Admission:** Priority date 3/1; deadline 8/1 (postmark date). $35 fee, may be waived for applicants with need. Application may be submitted online. Admission notification on a rolling basis beginning on or about 9/15. Must reply by May 1 or within 3 week(s) if notified thereafter. **Financial aid:** Priority date 7/1; no closing date. FAFSA required. Applicants notified on a rolling basis starting 3/15; must reply within 3 week(s) of notification.

**Academics. Special study options:** Cooperative education, cross-registration, double major, dual enrollment of high school students, exchange student, independent study, internships, New York semester, study abroad, teacher certification program. Advanced students may petition for 1 semester in New York studio space. **Credit/placement by examination:** AP, CLEP, IB, institutional tests. 6 credit hours maximum toward bachelor's degree. **Support services:** Learning center, pre-admission summer program, reduced course load, remedial instruction, study skills assistance, tutoring, writing center.

**Majors. Business:** Transportation. **Communications:** Digital media. **Communications technology:** Animation/special effects. **Production:** Furniture. **Visual/performing arts:** Ceramics, cinematography, commercial photography, commercial/advertising art, crafts, design, drawing, fiber arts, graphic design, illustration, industrial design, interior design, metal/jewelry, multimedia, painting, photography, printmaking, sculpture, studio arts.

**Computing on campus.** 400 workstations in dormitories, library, computer center. Dormitories wired for high-speed internet access and linked to campus network. Commuter students can connect to campus network. Online library, student web hosting, wireless network available.

**Student life. Freshman orientation:** Mandatory. Preregistration for classes offered. **Housing:** Apartments available. $200 fully refundable deposit, deadline 5/1. Furnished, college-owned apartments available. **Activities:** Student government, black student club, women artists club, industrial design students club.

**Student services.** Alcohol/substance abuse counseling, career counseling, student employment services, financial aid counseling, minority student services, personal counseling, placement for graduates. **Physically disabled:** Services for hearing impaired.

**Contact.** E-mail: admissions@collegeforcreativestudies.edu
Phone: (313) 664-7425 Toll-free number: (800) 952-2787
Fax: (313) 872-2739
Lori Watson, Director of Admissions, College for Creative Studies, 201 East Kirby, Detroit, MI 48202-4034

## Concordia University
### Ann Arbor, Michigan
www.cuaa.edu                                           CB code: 1094

- Private 4-year liberal arts and teachers college affiliated with Lutheran Church - Missouri Synod
- Residential campus in small city
- 493 degree-seeking undergraduates: 14% part-time, 54% women, 8% African American, 2% Asian American, 2% Hispanic American, 2% Native American, 1% international
- 553 degree-seeking graduate students
- 66% of applicants admitted
- SAT or ACT (ACT writing optional) required

**General.** Founded in 1962. Regionally accredited. **Degrees:** 112 bachelor's awarded; master's offered. **ROTC:** Army, Air Force. **Location:** 40 miles from Detroit. **Calendar:** Semester, limited summer session. **Full-time faculty:** 39 total; 5% minority, 33% women. **Part-time faculty:** 56 total; 12% minority, 55% women. **Class size:** 85% < 20, 14% 20-39, less than 1% 40-49. **Special facilities:** Earhart Manor (certified Michigan Historical Landmark).

**Freshman class profile.** 429 applied, 281 admitted, 94 enrolled.

| Mid 50% test scores | | | |
|---|---|---|---|
| SAT critical reading: | 460-690 | GPA 2.0-2.99: | 35% |
| SAT math: | 480-600 | End year in good standing: | 88% |
| SAT writing: | 430-680 | Return as sophomores: | 77% |
| ACT composite: | 19-26 | Out-of-state: | 22% |
| GPA 3.50 or higher: | 35% | Live on campus: | 95% |
| GPA 3.0-3.49: | 30% | International: | 2% |

**Basis for selection.** School achievement record most important. Test scores and rank in top half of class also important. Interview and essay recommended. Audition recommended for music majors. Portfolio recommended for art majors. **Homeschooled:** Letter of recommendation (nonparent) required. 300-500 word personal statement and resume or extracurricular activities sheet required. **Learning Disabled:** Require an explanation of the disability and written recommended accommodations from an appropriate professional.

**High school preparation.** 20 units recommended. Recommended units include English 4, mathematics 3, social studies 2, science 2 (laboratory 2), foreign language 2 and academic electives 5. Math should include two units of algebra and one unit of geometry.

**2007-2008 Annual costs.** Tuition/fees: $19,770. Additional one-time fees for all undergraduates include: $125 pre-enrollment deposit, $100 matriculation fee. Room/board: $7,350. Books/supplies: $600. Personal expenses: $1,200.

**2007-2008 Financial aid. Need-based:** Average need met was 35%. Average scholarship/grant was $11,796; average loan $5,633. 63% of total undergraduate aid awarded as scholarships/grants, 37% as loans/jobs. **Non-need-based:** Scholarships awarded for academics, alumni affiliation, art, athletics, leadership, music/drama, religious affiliation.

**Application procedures. Admission:** No deadline. $25 fee, may be waived for applicants with need. Application may be submitted online. Admission notification on a rolling basis. **Financial aid:** Closing date 3/1. FAFSA, institutional form required. Applicants notified on a rolling basis starting 3/1; must reply within 3 week(s) of notification.

**Academics. Special study options:** Accelerated study, cross-registration, double major, dual enrollment of high school students, exchange student, independent study, internships, liberal arts/career combination, student-designed major, study abroad, teacher certification program, weekend college. Accelerated degree program for mature students. **Credit/placement by examination:** AP, CLEP, IB, institutional tests. No limit on credit by examination. **Support services:** Reduced course load, remedial instruction, study skills assistance, tutoring, writing center.

**Majors. Biology:** General. **Business:** Business admin, hospitality admin. **Communications:** General, journalism. **Education:** Art, biology, chemistry, early childhood, elementary, English, health, history, mathematics, music, physical, psychology, science, secondary, social studies, Spanish, speech. **English:** English lit. **Family/consumer sciences:** Family studies. **Foreign languages:** Ancient Greek, Biblical, Spanish. **Health:** Premedicine. **History:** General. **Interdisciplinary:** Biological/physical sciences. **Legal studies:** Prelaw. **Math:** General. **Parks/recreation:** Health/fitness. **Philosophy/religion:** Philosophy, religion. **Physical sciences:** Chemistry, physics. **Protective services:** Law enforcement admin. **Psychology:** General. **Social sciences:** General, sociology. **Theology:** Preministerial, religious ed, sacred music. **Visual/performing arts:** Art, theater arts management. **Other:** Pre-engineering, Public safety.

**Most popular majors.** Business/marketing 18%, communications/journalism 9%, education 24%, security/protective services 7%, theological studies 9%.

**Computing on campus.** 80 workstations in library, computer center, student center. Dormitories wired for high-speed internet access and linked to campus network. Commuter students can connect to campus network. Online library, helpline, repair service, student web hosting, wireless network available.

**Student life. Freshman orientation:** Mandatory. Preregistration for classes offered. 3-day program includes academic, social, and orientation events. **Housing:** Guaranteed on-campus for all undergraduates. Single-sex dorms, apartments, substance-free housing available. $100 nonrefundable deposit, deadline 8/15. Students must live on campus (or with family member) until attaining junior status or 21 years of age. **Activities:** Bands, campus ministries, choral groups, dance, drama, music ensembles, musical theater, student government, student newspaper, several religious and community service groups.

**Athletics.** NAIA. **Intercollegiate:** Baseball M, basketball, cross-country, golf M, soccer, softball W, volleyball W. **Intramural:** Badminton, basketball, football (non-tackle), soccer, softball, table tennis, volleyball. **Team name:** Cardinals.

**Student services.** Adult student services, alcohol/substance abuse counseling, campus ministries, career counseling, student employment services, financial aid counseling, health services, personal counseling, placement for graduates, women's services. **Physically disabled:** Services for visually, speech, hearing impaired.

**Contact.** E-mail: admissions@cuaa.edu
Phone: (734) 995-7322 Toll-free number: (800) 253-0680
Fax: (734) 995-4610
Amy Becher, Executive Director of Enrollment Services, Concordia University, 4090 Geddes Road, Ann Arbor, MI 48105

## Cornerstone University
### Grand Rapids, Michigan
www.cornerstone.edu — CB code: 1253

- Private 4-year university and liberal arts college affiliated with Baptist faith
- Residential campus in small city
- 1,798 degree-seeking undergraduates: 20% part-time, 59% women, 12% African American, 1% Asian American, 3% Hispanic American, 1% international
- 625 degree-seeking graduate students
- 62% of applicants admitted
- SAT or ACT (ACT writing recommended), application essay required
- 46% graduate within 6 years; 10% enter graduate study

**General.** Founded in 1941. Regionally accredited. **Degrees:** 402 bachelor's, 61 associate awarded; master's, first professional offered. **Location:** 4 miles from downtown. **Calendar:** Semester, limited summer session. **Full-time faculty:** 66 total; 47% have terminal degrees, 4% minority, 33% women. **Part-time faculty:** 52 total; 6% have terminal degrees, 10% minority, 29% women. **Class size:** 59% < 20, 36% 20-39, 3% 40-49, 3% 50-99.

**Freshman class profile.** 981 applied, 611 admitted, 292 enrolled.

| Mid 50% test scores | | End year in good standing: | 90% |
|---|---|---|---|
| ACT composite: | 20-26 | Return as sophomores: | 70% |
| GPA 3.50 or higher: | 49% | Out-of-state: | 21% |
| GPA 3.0-3.49: | 32% | Live on campus: | 55% |
| GPA 2.0-2.99: | 18% | | |

**Basis for selection.** Statement of Christian commitment, pastoral reference, 2.5 high school GPA, and ACT score of 19. Students with lower scores and GPA may be admitted conditionally. Interview recommended. Audition required for music majors. **Homeschooled:** Statement describing homeschool structure and mission, transcript of courses and grades, letter of recommendation (nonparent) required.

**High school preparation.** Recommended units include English 4, mathematics 3, social studies 2, history 2, science 2 (laboratory 1), foreign language 2 and academic electives 4.

**2007-2008 Annual costs.** Tuition/fees: $18,360. Tuition includes laptop computer. Room/board: $6,300. Books/supplies: $1,000. Personal expenses: $1,234.

**2007-2008 Financial aid.** **Need-based:** 252 full-time freshmen applied for aid; 232 were judged to have need; 232 of these received aid. Average need met was 88%. Average scholarship/grant was $10,750; average loan $195. 53% of total undergraduate aid awarded as scholarships/grants, 47% as loans/jobs. **Non-need-based:** Scholarships awarded for academics, athletics, leadership, music/drama, state residency. **Additional information:** Audition required for music scholarship applicants.

**Application procedures.** **Admission:** No deadline. $25 fee, may be waived for applicants with need. Application may be submitted online. Admission notification on a rolling basis. **Financial aid:** Priority date 3/1; no closing date. FAFSA required. Applicants notified on a rolling basis starting 3/15; must reply within 2 week(s) of notification.

**Academics.** All students must complete internship in major field. Core curriculum. **Special study options:** Accelerated study, cross-registration, distance learning, double major, dual enrollment of high school students, ESL, honors, independent study, internships, liberal arts/career combination, study abroad, teacher certification program, urban semester, Washington semester, weekend college. **Credit/placement by examination:** AP, CLEP, IB, ACT, institutional tests. 15 credit hours maximum toward associate degree, 30 toward bachelor's. **Support services:** Learning center, reduced course load, remedial instruction, study skills assistance, tutoring, writing center.

**Honors college/program.** Requires 28 ACT; 12-15 admitted annually.

**Majors.** **Biology:** General, environmental. **Business:** Accounting, business admin, financial planning, international, management information systems, management science, marketing. **Communications:** General, digital media, media studies. **Computer sciences:** General. **Education:** Biology, early childhood, elementary, English, history, mathematics, music, physical, science, secondary, social science, social studies, voc/tech. **English:** American lit, creative writing, English lit, speech/rhetoric. **Family/consumer sciences:** Family systems, work/family studies. **Foreign languages:** Biblical. **Health:** Health services, predental, premedicine, preveterinary. **History:** General. **Math:** General. **Parks/recreation:** Exercise sciences, sports admin. **Philosophy/religion:** Philosophy. **Psychology:** General, family. **Public administration:** Social work. **Social sciences:** General. **Theology:** Bible, youth ministry. **Transportation:** Airline/commercial pilot. **Visual/performing arts:** Music performance, music theory/composition.

**Most popular majors.** Business/marketing 56%, education 19%.

**Computing on campus.** PC or laptop required. 117 workstations in dormitories, library, computer center, student center. Dormitories wired for high-speed internet access and linked to campus network. Commuter students can connect to campus network. Online course registration, online library, helpline, repair service, wireless network available.

**Student life.** **Freshman orientation:** Mandatory. Preregistration for classes offered. 4-day program held prior to start of Fall classes. **Policies:** Dry campus; chapel attendance required. Religious observance required. **Housing:** Guaranteed on-campus for all undergraduates. Single-sex dorms, apartments, substance-free housing available. $150 partly refundable deposit. Students under 21 with fewer than 63 credit hours must live on campus unless living with immediate family. **Activities:** Bands, campus ministries, choral groups, drama, literary magazine, music ensembles, musical theater, radio station, student government, student newspaper, symphony orchestra, student outreach committee, Young Republicans, cross-cultural ministries, social committee, fine arts committee, literature club, diversity club, right-to-life campus organization.

**Athletics.** NAIA. **Intercollegiate:** Basketball, cross-country, golf, soccer, softball W, track and field, volleyball W. **Intramural:** Basketball, football (non-tackle), ice hockey M, racquetball, soccer, softball, volleyball. **Team name:** Golden Eagles.

**Student services.** Adult student services, alcohol/substance abuse counseling, campus ministries, career counseling, student employment services, financial aid counseling, health services, personal counseling, placement for graduates, veterans' counselor. **Physically disabled:** Services for visually, hearing impaired.

**Contact.** E-mail: admissions@cornerstone.edu
Phone: (616) 222-1426 Toll-free number: (800) 787-9778
Fax: (616) 222-1418
Brent Rudin, Dean of Enrollment Management, Cornerstone University, 1001 East Beltline NE, Grand Rapids, MI 49525-5897

## Davenport University
### Grand Rapids, Michigan
www.davenport.edu — CB code: 1183

- Private 4-year university and business college
- Commuter campus in small city
- 10,579 degree-seeking undergraduates: 70% part-time, 73% women, 19% African American, 2% Asian American, 3% Hispanic American
- 765 degree-seeking graduate students
- 91% of applicants admitted

**General.** Founded in 1866. Regionally accredited. Locations in Alma, Bad Axe, Battle Creek, Bay City, Caro, Dearborn, Flint, Gaylord, Holland, Kalamazoo, Lansing, Lapeer, Midland, Romeo, Saginaw, South Bend/Mishawaka, Traverse City, Warren, Merrillville (Indiana), South Bend (Indiana). **Degrees:** 1,037 bachelor's, 683 associate awarded; master's offered. **Location:** 150 miles from Detroit, 175 miles from Chicago. **Calendar:** Semester, extensive summer session. **Full-time faculty:** 137 total; 19% have terminal degrees, 12% minority, 61% women. **Part-time faculty:** 1,008 total; 15% have terminal degrees, 19% minority, 54% women. **Class size:** 87% < 20, 13% 20-39, less than 1% 40-49.

**Freshman class profile.** 1,303 applied, 1,190 admitted, 893 enrolled.

| | | | |
|---|---|---|---|
| Out-of-state: | 3% | International: | 1% |
| Live on campus: | 1% | | |

**Basis for selection.** GPA and test scores important; prospective students without ACT or SAT scores may take standard COMPASS assessment as arranged by a Davenport representative. SAT or ACT recommended. Interview recommended.

**High school preparation.** Recommended units include English 6, mathematics 9 and social studies 9.

**2007-2008 Annual costs.** Tuition/fees: $12,445. Books/supplies: $1,600. Personal expenses: $1,170.

**2006-2007 Financial aid. Need-based:** 29% of total undergraduate aid awarded as scholarships/grants, 71% as loans/jobs. **Non-need-based:** Scholarships awarded for academics, alumni affiliation, athletics, leadership.

**Application procedures. Admission:** No deadline. $25 fee. Application may be submitted online. Admission notification on a rolling basis beginning on or about 9/1. **Financial aid:** Priority date 3/1; no closing date. FAFSA required. Applicants notified on a rolling basis starting 3/1; must reply within 2 week(s) of notification.

**Academics. Special study options:** Accelerated study, distance learning, dual enrollment of high school students, ESL, honors, independent study, internships, study abroad. **Credit/placement by examination:** AP, CLEP, IB, ACT, institutional tests. **Support services:** Learning center, remedial instruction, tutoring, writing center.

**Majors. Biology:** Bioinformatics. **Business:** General, accounting, business admin, finance, human resources, international, marketing. **Communications technology:** Animation/special effects. **Computer sciences:** General, networking, security. **Health:** Health care admin, management/clinical assistant, medical records admin, nursing (RN). **Legal studies:** Paralegal. **Parks/recreation:** Sports admin. **Protective services:** Security management. **Other:** Service management and marketing.

**Most popular majors.** Business/marketing 76%, computer/information sciences 14%, health sciences 6%.

**Computing on campus.** 3,224 workstations in library, computer center, student center. Dormitories wired for high-speed internet access and linked to campus network. Commuter students can connect to campus network. Online course registration, online library, wireless network available.

**Student life. Freshman orientation:** Mandatory. Preregistration for classes offered. **Housing:** Coed dorms, substance-free housing available. **Activities:** Minority student association.

**Athletics.** NAIA. **Intercollegiate:** Basketball, cross-country, golf, ice hockey M, lacrosse, soccer, track and field, volleyball. **Team name:** Panthers.

**Student services.** Career counseling, student employment services, financial aid counseling, placement for graduates.

**Contact.** E-mail: gradmiss@davenport.edu
Phone: (616) 698-7111 Toll-free number: (866) 925-3884
Cathryn Claerhout, Vice President for Admissions, Davenport University, 6191 Kraft Avenue SE, Grand Rapids, MI 49512-5926

## Eastern Michigan University
Ypsilanti, Michigan
www.emich.edu

CB member
CB code: 1201

- Public 4-year university
- Residential campus in small city
- 17,609 degree-seeking undergraduates: 30% part-time, 59% women, 18% African American, 2% Asian American, 3% Hispanic American, 1% Native American, 1% international
- 4,610 degree-seeking graduate students
- 75% of applicants admitted
- SAT or ACT (ACT writing optional) required
- 39% graduate within 6 years

**General.** Founded in 1849. Regionally accredited. **Degrees:** 2,945 bachelor's awarded; master's, doctoral offered. **ROTC:** Army, Naval, Air Force. **Location:** 7 miles from Ann Arbor, 35 miles from Detroit. **Calendar:** Semester, limited summer session. **Full-time faculty:** 756 total; 82% have terminal degrees, 17% minority, 48% women. **Part-time faculty:** 447 total; 13% minority, 60% women. **Class size:** 36% < 20, 51% 20-39, 7% 40-49, 5% 50-99, less than 1% >100. **Special facilities:** Corporate education center, observatory, laser laboratory, textiles research and training institute.

**Freshman class profile.** 9,736 applied, 7,290 admitted, 2,448 enrolled.

| Mid 50% test scores | | GPA 2.0-2.99: | 46% |
|---|---|---|---|
| SAT critical reading: | 450-570 | Rank in top quarter: | 33% |
| SAT math: | 450-580 | Rank in top tenth: | 10% |
| SAT writing: | 430-540 | End year in good standing: | 60% |
| ACT composite: | 18-24 | Return as sophomores: | 71% |
| GPA 3.50 or higher: | 20% | Out-of-state: | 13% |
| GPA 3.0-3.49: | 34% | Live on campus: | 68% |

**Basis for selection.** School achievement record and test scores important. Grades and test results combined to predict academic success. MELAB (Michigan English Language Assessment Battery) accepted in place of TOEFL

with minimum score 72 for unconditional acceptance. Essay recommended. Audition required of music majors. Portfolio required of art majors.

**High school preparation.** 21 units recommended. Recommended units include English 4, mathematics 4, social studies 2, history 1, science 4 (laboratory 1), foreign language 2 and academic electives 4. 2 units fine arts and 1 computer literacy also recommended.

**2007-2008 Annual costs.** Tuition/fees: $7,490; $19,925 out-of-state. Room/board: $6,942. Books/supplies: $900. Personal expenses: $1,150.

**2006-2007 Financial aid. Need-based:** 1,791 full-time freshmen applied for aid; 1,336 were judged to have need; 1,289 of these received aid. Average need met was 59%. Average scholarship/grant was $3,356; average loan $3,113. 32% of total undergraduate aid awarded as scholarships/grants, 68% as loans/jobs. **Non-need-based:** Awarded to 4,472 full-time undergraduates, including 1,575 freshmen. Scholarships awarded for academics, alumni affiliation, art, athletics, leadership, minority status, music/drama, ROTC, state residency.

**Application procedures. Admission:** Priority date 2/15; no deadline. $30 fee, may be waived for applicants with need. Application may be submitted online. Admission notification on a rolling basis beginning on or about 10/1. **Financial aid:** Priority date 3/15; no closing date. FAFSA required. Applicants notified on a rolling basis starting 3/1.

**Academics. Special study options:** Accelerated study, combined bachelor's/graduate degree, cooperative education, distance learning, double major, dual enrollment of high school students, ESL, external degree, honors, independent study, internships, student-designed major, study abroad, teacher certification program, Washington semester, weekend college. Dual enrollment program requires students to apply for admission to EMU. **Credit/placement by examination:** AP, CLEP, IB, SAT, ACT, institutional tests. 30 credit hours maximum toward bachelor's degree. **Support services:** Learning center, reduced course load, remedial instruction, tutoring, writing center.

**Honors college/program.** Admission based on high school GPA, test scores, letters of recommendation. Approximately 250 freshmen per year admitted; reduced class size emphasizing student-professor interaction.

**Majors. Architecture:** Architecture, urban/community planning. **Area/ethnic studies:** African-American, women's. **Biology:** General, biochemistry, toxicology. **Business:** General, accounting, actuarial science, business admin, construction management, entrepreneurial studies, fashion, finance, hospitality admin, international, labor studies, logistics, management information systems, managerial economics, marketing, office management. **Communications:** General, journalism, public relations. **Communications technology:** General, radio/tv. **Computer sciences:** General, computer science. **Education:** Art, biology, business, chemistry, computer, Deaf/hearing impaired, elementary, emotionally handicapped, English, foreign languages, French, German, history, mathematics, mentally handicapped, music, physical, physically handicapped, physics, reading, sales/marketing, science, secondary, social science, social studies, Spanish, special, speech impaired, technology/industrial arts, visually handicapped. **Engineering:** Physics. **Engineering technology:** CAD/CADD, computer, electrical, industrial, industrial management, manufacturing, mechanical, mechanical drafting, plastics. **English:** Composition, creative writing, English lit, speech/rhetoric, technical writing. **Family/consumer sciences:** Facilities/event planning. **Foreign languages:** French, German, Germanic, Japanese, linguistics, Spanish. **Health:** Athletic training, clinical lab science, dietetics, health care admin, music therapy, nursing (RN), predental, premedicine, prepharmacy, preveterinary, recreational therapy, speech pathology. **History:** General. **Interdisciplinary:** Biological/physical sciences, science/society. **Legal studies:** Paralegal, prelaw. **Math:** General, statistics. **Parks/recreation:** Facilities management, health/fitness. **Personal/culinary services:** Mortuary science. **Philosophy/religion:** Philosophy. **Physical sciences:** Chemistry, geology, geophysics, physics. **Psychology:** General. **Public administration:** General, social work. **Social sciences:** General, anthropology, criminology, economics, geography, political science, sociology. **Transportation:** Airline/commercial pilot, aviation management. **Visual/performing arts:** Art, art history/conservation, arts management, dance, dramatic, film/cinema, interior design, music performance.

**Most popular majors.** Business/marketing 21%, communications/journalism 6%, education 25%, health sciences 7%, social sciences 8%, visual/performing arts 8%.

**Computing on campus.** 1,500 workstations in dormitories, library, computer center, student center. Dormitories wired for high-speed internet access and linked to campus network. Commuter students can connect to campus network. Helpline, student web hosting, wireless network available.

**Student life. Freshman orientation:** Mandatory, $150 fee. Preregistration for classes offered. 4-day orientation held Saturday through Tuesday. **Housing:** Coed dorms, special housing for disabled, apartments, fraternity/sorority housing, substance-free housing available. $200 partly refundable deposit, deadline 5/1. Freshman housing, honors halls, in-hall academic services available. **Activities:** Bands, campus ministries, choral groups, dance, drama, film society, international student organizations, literary magazine, music ensembles, musical theater, radio station, student government, student newspaper, symphony orchestra, TV station, 10 honor societies, over 140 student organizations.

**Athletics.** NCAA. **Intercollegiate:** Baseball M, basketball, cross-country, diving, football (tackle) M, golf, gymnastics W, rowing (crew) W, soccer W, softball W, swimming, tennis W, track and field, volleyball W, wrestling M. **Intramural:** Badminton, basketball, bowling, cross-country, football (non-tackle), golf, racquetball, soccer, softball, swimming, table tennis, tennis, track and field, volleyball, weight lifting. **Team name:** Eagles.

**Student services.** Adult student services, alcohol/substance abuse counseling, campus ministries, career counseling, student employment services, health services, minority student services, on-campus daycare, personal counseling, placement for graduates, veterans' counselor, women's services. **Physically disabled:** Services for visually, speech, hearing impaired.

**Contact.** E-mail: admissions@emich.edu
Phone: (734) 487-3060 Toll-free number: (800) 468-6368
Fax: (734) 487-6559
Kathryn Orscheln, Director, Admissions, Eastern Michigan University, 400 Pierce Hall, Ypsilanti, MI 48197

---

## Ferris State University
**Big Rapids, Michigan**     CB member
www.ferris.edu     CB code: 1222

- Public 4-year university
- Residential campus in large town
- 11,421 degree-seeking undergraduates: 22% part-time, 47% women, 7% African American, 2% Asian American, 2% Hispanic American, 1% Native American, 1% international
- 1,214 degree-seeking graduate students
- SAT or ACT (ACT writing optional) required
- 41% graduate within 6 years

**General.** Founded in 1884. Regionally accredited. **Degrees:** 1,623 bachelor's, 863 associate awarded; master's, first professional offered. **ROTC:** Army. **Location:** 55 miles from Grand Rapids. **Calendar:** Semester, limited summer session. **Full-time faculty:** 532 total; 36% women. **Part-time faculty:** 316 total; 48% women. **Special facilities:** Observatory, wildlife museum, Jim Crow museum, art walk.

**Freshman class profile.** 2,340 enrolled.

| Mid 50% test scores | | | |
|---|---|---|---|
| | | GPA 2.0-2.99: | 39% |
| ACT composite: | 18-24 | Return as sophomores: | 73% |
| GPA 3.50 or higher: | 29% | Out-of-state: | 6% |
| GPA 3.0-3.49: | 32% | International: | 1% |

**Basis for selection.** School achievement record most important. General admission requirements: 2.5 GPA (509 GED) or 17 ACT/1210 SAT. Specific program requirements vary. ACT and SAT scores used for admissions purposes for marginal applicants. Interview recommended. Portfolio recommended of visual communication majors. **Learning Disabled:** Students with learning disabilities should submit documentation from professional psychologist or social worker to Disabilities Services Office in the Educational and Career Services Counseling Center.

**High school preparation.** 24 units recommended. Recommended units include English 4, mathematics 4, social studies 2, history 2, science 4 (laboratory 2), foreign language 3 and academic electives 3. 2 units in fine arts and 1 unit in computer literacy recommended.

**2007-2008 Annual costs.** Tuition/fees: $8,862; $16,062 out-of-state. Midwest Compact states of Illinois, Indiana, Kansas, Minnesota, Missouri, Nebraska, Ohio, and Wisconsin tuition is $13,050. Room/board: $7,646. Books/supplies: $1,246. Personal expenses: $860.

**2007-2008 Financial aid. Need-based:** 1,734 full-time freshmen applied for aid; 1,353 were judged to have need; 1,316 of these received aid. Average need met was 89%. Average scholarship/grant was $3,789; average loan $3,185. 31% of total undergraduate aid awarded as scholarships/grants, 69% as loans/jobs. **Non-need-based:** Awarded to 3,379 full-time undergraduates, including 1,216 freshmen. Scholarships awarded for academics, alumni affiliation, art, athletics, leadership, minority status, music/drama, religious affiliation, ROTC.

**Application procedures. Admission:** Closing date 8/1 (postmark date). $30 fee, may be waived for applicants with need. Application may be submitted online. Admission notification on a rolling basis beginning on or about 7/1. **Financial aid:** Priority date 3/1; no closing date. FAFSA required. Applicants notified on a rolling basis starting 3/1; must reply within 2 week(s) of notification.

**Academics. Special study options:** Accelerated study, combined bachelor's/graduate degree, cooperative education, cross-registration, distance learning, double major, dual enrollment of high school students, exchange student, external degree, honors, independent study, internships, liberal arts/career combination, study abroad, teacher certification program. **Credit/placement by examination:** AP, CLEP, SAT, ACT, institutional tests. **Support services:** Learning center, remedial instruction, study skills assistance, tutoring, writing center.

**Majors. Architecture:** Interior. **Biology:** General, biochemistry, biotechnology, environmental. **Business:** Accounting, accounting technology, accounting/finance, business admin, construction management, e-commerce, entrepreneurial studies, finance, golf management, hospitality admin, hospitality/recreation, hotel/motel admin, human resources, international, marketing, operations. **Communications:** General, advertising, public relations. **Communications technology:** Animation/special effects, graphic/printing, printing management, radio/tv. **Education:** Art, biology, business, chemistry, elementary, English, family/consumer sciences, health, history, mathematics, secondary, social science, social studies, voc/tech. **Engineering technology:** Automotive, electrical, energy systems, environmental, industrial, manufacturing, mechanical, plastics, quality control, surveying, telecommunications. **English:** British lit, composition, speech/rhetoric, technical writing. **Family/consumer sciences:** Child care. **Health:** Clinical lab science, health care admin, medical records admin, nuclear medical technology, nursing (RN). **History:** General. **Math:** General, applied, statistics. **Mechanic/repair:** Heavy equipment. **Parks/recreation:** Facilities management. **Physical sciences:** Chemistry. **Protective services:** Police science. **Psychology:** General. **Public administration:** General, social work. **Social sciences:** Sociology. **Visual/performing arts:** Art history/conservation, commercial/advertising art, design, graphic design, industrial design, interior design, metal/jewelry, music management, painting, photography, sculpture, studio arts. **Other:** Business Administration/Leadership-Organizational Development, Furniture design, Rubber technology.

**Most popular majors.** Business/marketing 26%, education 10%, engineering/engineering technologies 16%, health sciences 9%, security/protective services 11%, visual/performing arts 9%.

**Computing on campus.** 2,373 workstations in dormitories, library, computer center, student center. Dormitories wired for high-speed internet access and linked to campus network. Commuter students can connect to campus network. Online course registration, online library, helpline, repair service, wireless network available.

**Student life. Freshman orientation:** Mandatory, $75 fee. Preregistration for classes offered. **Policies:** All students sign ethics statement during orientation. **Housing:** Guaranteed on-campus for all undergraduates. Coed dorms, special housing for disabled, apartments, substance-free housing available. $200 nonrefundable deposit, deadline 6/1. Honors hall and substance free floors available. **Activities:** Bands, choral groups, dance, drama, music ensembles, radio station, student government, student newspaper, symphony orchestra, TV station, Alpha Omega Co-ed Christian Fraternity, Circle K, Diverse Sexuality and Gender Alliance, gospel choir, Habitat for Humanity, Indian students association, international student organization, Muslim student organization, National Organization for Women, Red Cross student chapter.

**Athletics.** NCAA. **Intercollegiate:** Basketball, cheerleading, cross-country, football (tackle) M, golf, ice hockey M, soccer W, softball W, tennis, track and field, volleyball W. **Intramural:** Badminton, basketball, football (non-tackle) M, golf, handball, ice hockey M, racquetball, softball, swimming, table tennis, tennis, volleyball, water polo M. **Team name:** Bulldogs.

**Student services.** Adult student services, alcohol/substance abuse counseling, campus ministries, career counseling, student employment services, financial aid counseling, health services, minority student services, on-campus daycare, personal counseling, placement for graduates, veterans' counselor. **Physically disabled:** Services for visually, speech, hearing impaired.

**Contact.** E-mail: admissions@ferris.edu
Phone: (231) 591-2100 Toll-free number: (800) 433-7747
Fax: (231) 591-3944
Kristen Salomonson, Dean of Enrollment Services, Ferris State University, 1201 South State Street, CSS 201, Big Rapids, MI 49307-2714

---

## Finlandia University
**Hancock, Michigan**
www.finlandia.edu     CB code: 1743

- Private 4-year university and liberal arts college affiliated with Evangelical Lutheran Church in America
- Commuter campus in small town

- 543 degree-seeking undergraduates: 14% part-time, 65% women, 1% African American, 3% Asian American, 1% Hispanic American, 2% Native American
- 72% of applicants admitted
- Application essay required

**General.** Founded in 1896. Regionally accredited. **Degrees:** 80 bachelor's, 32 associate awarded. **ROTC:** Army, Naval, Air Force. **Location:** 100 miles from Marquette, 220 miles from Green Bay, Wisconsin. **Calendar:** Semester, limited summer session. **Full-time faculty:** 42 total; 36% have terminal degrees, 5% minority, 76% women. **Part-time faculty:** 28 total; 21% have terminal degrees, 7% minority, 71% women. **Class size:** 72% < 20, 27% 20-39, 1% 40-49. **Special facilities:** Finnish-American historical archive.

**Freshman class profile.** 440 applied, 315 admitted, 82 enrolled.

| | | | |
|---|---|---|---|
| GPA 3.50 or higher: | 5% | Return as sophomores: | 61% |
| GPA 3.0-3.49: | 33% | Out-of-state: | 8% |
| GPA 2.0-2.99: | 58% | Live on campus: | 28% |

**Basis for selection.** One unit of algebra and chemistry with grade of 3.0 and 2.5 cumulative GPA required for nursing. 1 unit of algebra and biology with grade of 3.0 and 3.0 cumulative GPA required for physical therapist assistant. GPA of 2.0 required of all other programs. If GPA below 2.0, special consideration given in determining admission. Student may obtain admission into academic warning program based on placement test results. Nursing applicants should apply by March 15, physical therapy assistant applicants by April 15. SAT or ACT recommended. **Homeschooled:** Placement tests required. **Learning Disabled:** Must submit IEP and/or formal evaluation verifying diagnosed learning disability.

**High school preparation.** Recommended units include English 4, mathematics 2, science 2 (laboratory 2).

**2007-2008 Annual costs.** Tuition/fees: $17,514. Room/board: $5,800. Books/supplies: $1,300. Personal expenses: $100.

**2007-2008 Financial aid. Need-based:** 68 full-time freshmen applied for aid; 61 were judged to have need; 61 of these received aid. Average need met was 10%. Average scholarship/grant was $5,000; average loan $3,500. 40% of total undergraduate aid awarded as scholarships/grants, 60% as loans/jobs. **Non-need-based:** Awarded to 434 full-time undergraduates, including 65 freshmen. Scholarships awarded for academics, leadership, religious affiliation, state residency. **Additional information:** Work/study program; up to $2,800 per year.

**Application procedures. Admission:** Priority date 8/1; deadline 8/25 (postmark date). $30 fee, may be waived for applicants with need. Application may be submitted online. Admission notification on a rolling basis. **Financial aid:** Priority date 3/1, closing date 8/1. FAFSA, institutional form required. Applicants notified on a rolling basis starting 3/1; must reply within 2 week(s) of notification.

**Academics. Special study options:** Cooperative education, cross-registration, distance learning, double major, dual enrollment of high school students, ESL, exchange student, honors, independent study, internships, liberal arts/career combination, student-designed major, study abroad, teacher certification program. **Credit/placement by examination:** AP, CLEP, IB, SAT, ACT, institutional tests. 18 credit hours maximum toward associate degree, 30 toward bachelor's. **Support services:** Learning center, remedial instruction, study skills assistance, tutoring, writing center.

**Majors. Business:** General, accounting, business admin, fashion, international, international marketing, marketing. **Education:** Elementary. **Health:** Nursing (RN). **Liberal arts:** Arts/sciences. **Public administration:** Human services. **Visual/performing arts:** Art, ceramics, commercial/advertising art, design, drawing, fashion design, fiber arts, graphic design, illustration, interior design, painting, studio arts.

**Most popular majors.** Business/marketing 24%, education 6%, health sciences 22%, liberal arts 9%, psychology 17%, visual/performing arts 22%.

**Computing on campus.** 80 workstations in dormitories, library, computer center. Dormitories wired for high-speed internet access and linked to campus network. Online library, helpline available.

**Student life. Freshman orientation:** Mandatory. Preregistration for classes offered. Held the week before fall semester. **Housing:** Guaranteed on-campus for all undergraduates. Coed dorms, special housing for disabled, substance-free housing available. $100 nonrefundable deposit, deadline 8/25. **Activities:** Pep band, choral groups, drama, literary magazine, music ensembles, musical theater, student government, student newspaper, religious life committee, servant leadership program, local agency volunteer programs.

**Athletics.** NCAA. **Intercollegiate:** Baseball M, basketball, cross-country, ice hockey, skiing, soccer, softball W, volleyball W. **Intramural:** Bowling,

football (non-tackle), softball, swimming, table tennis, volleyball. **Team name:** Lions.

**Student services.** Adult student services, alcohol/substance abuse counseling, campus ministries, career counseling, services for economically disadvantaged, student employment services, financial aid counseling, personal counseling, placement for graduates. **Learning disabled:** Comprehensive services available.

**Contact.** E-mail: admissions@finlandia.edu
Phone: (906) 487-7274 Toll-free number: (877) 202-5491
Fax: (906) 487-7383
Martin Kinard, Director of Admissions, Finlandia University, 601 Quincy Street, Hancock, MI 49930-1882

## Grace Bible College
### Grand Rapids, Michigan
### www.gbcol.edu
**CB code: 0809**

- Private 4-year Bible and liberal arts college affiliated with Grace Gospel Fellowship
- Residential campus in small city
- 156 degree-seeking undergraduates: 4% part-time, 42% women, 2% African American, 2% Asian American, 2% Hispanic American, 1% international
- 68% of applicants admitted
- SAT or ACT (ACT writing optional) required
- 47% graduate within 6 years

**General.** Founded in 1945. Regionally accredited; also accredited by ABHE. **Degrees:** 23 bachelor's, 15 associate awarded. **ROTC:** Army. **Location:** 50 miles from Kalamazoo. **Calendar:** Semester. **Full-time faculty:** 7 total; 14% have terminal degrees, 29% women. **Part-time faculty:** 13 total; 31% have terminal degrees, 8% minority, 31% women. **Class size:** 73% < 20, 23% 20-39, 2% 40-49, 2% 50-99. **Special facilities:** College-operated recording studio.

**Freshman class profile.** 130 applied, 89 admitted, 42 enrolled.

| Mid 50% test scores | | | |
|---|---|---|---|
| SAT critical reading: | 480-530 | Rank in top quarter: | 38% |
| SAT math: | 490-520 | Rank in top tenth: | 7% |
| SAT writing: | 370-510 | End year in good standing: | 90% |
| ACT composite: | 19-25 | Return as sophomores: | 66% |
| GPA 3.50 or higher: | 36% | Out-of-state: | 21% |
| GPA 3.0-3.49: | 32% | Live on campus: | 75% |
| GPA 2.0-2.99: | 32% | International: | 2% |

**Basis for selection.** Evidence of personal salvation through Jesus Christ important. 2.5 GPA, 20 ACT, and rank in top half of class for regular admission. Probationary admission for those in third quarter of class. Interview may be recommended.

**High school preparation.** Recommended units include English 4, mathematics 3, social studies 3, science 3 and foreign language 1.

**2007-2008 Annual costs.** Tuition/fees: $12,140. Room/board: $6,400. Books/supplies: $511. Personal expenses: $911.

**2006-2007 Financial aid. Need-based:** 49 full-time freshmen applied for aid; 43 were judged to have need; 43 of these received aid. Average need met was 64%. Average scholarship/grant was $3,294; average loan $3,823. 40% of total undergraduate aid awarded as scholarships/grants, 60% as loans/jobs. **Non-need-based:** Awarded to 154 full-time undergraduates, including 92 freshmen. Scholarships awarded for academics, music/drama, religious affiliation.

**Application procedures. Admission:** Closing date 6/1 (receipt date). No application fee. Admission notification on a rolling basis. Must reply by May 1 or within 4 week(s) if notified thereafter. **Financial aid:** Priority date 3/1; no closing date. FAFSA required. Applicants notified on a rolling basis starting 5/15; must reply within 2 week(s) of notification.

**Academics.** All students major in Bible and theology in addition to degree major. **Special study options:** Combined bachelor's/graduate degree, cross-registration, double major, dual enrollment of high school students, independent study, internships, liberal arts/career combination. **Credit/placement by examination:** AP, CLEP, institutional tests. **Support services:** Reduced course load, remedial instruction, tutoring, writing center.

**Majors. Business:** General, accounting, business admin, international, management science, marketing. **Communications:** Digital media. **Communications technology:** Photo/film/video, recording arts. **Computer sciences:**

General, information technology, web page design. **Education:** Early childhood, elementary, music, secondary. **Liberal arts:** Arts/sciences. **Public administration:** Human services. **Theology:** Bible, missionary, pastoral counseling, religious ed, sacred music, theology, youth ministry.

**Most popular majors.** Communication technologies 17%, education 22%, interdisciplinary studies 9%, public administration/social services 9%, theological studies 35%.

**Computing on campus.** 25 workstations in library, computer center. Dormitories wired for high-speed internet access and linked to campus network. Helpline, wireless network available.

**Student life. Freshman orientation:** Mandatory. Preregistration for classes offered. Freshmen meet for 5 days prior to start of fall semester. **Policies:** Religious observance required. **Housing:** Guaranteed on-campus for freshmen. Single-sex dorms, apartments, substance-free housing available. $100 deposit, deadline 5/1. **Activities:** Jazz band, campus ministries, choral groups, drama, music ensembles, student government.

**Athletics.** NCCAA. **Intercollegiate:** Basketball, cross-country, soccer M, volleyball W. **Intramural:** Basketball M, bowling, golf, handball, racquetball, skiing, soccer, table tennis, tennis, volleyball. **Team name:** Tigers.

**Student services.** Campus ministries, career counseling, student employment services, financial aid counseling, health services, personal counseling, placement for graduates.

**Contact.** E-mail: gbc@gbcol.edu
Phone: (616) 538-2330 Toll-free number: (800) 968-1887
Fax: (616) 538-0599
Kevin Gilliam, Enrollment Director, Grace Bible College, 1011 Aldon Street SW, PO Box 910, Grand Rapids, MI 49509

---

# Grand Valley State University

**Allendale, Michigan**
www.gvsu.edu

**CB member**
**CB code: 1258**

- Public 4-year university
- Residential campus in small town
- 19,643 degree-seeking undergraduates: 12% part-time, 60% women, 5% African American, 3% Asian American, 3% Hispanic American, 1% Native American, 1% international
- 3,110 degree-seeking graduate students
- 69% of applicants admitted
- SAT or ACT (ACT writing recommended) required
- 51% graduate within 6 years

**General.** Founded in 1960. Regionally accredited. **Degrees:** 3,448 bachelor's awarded; master's offered. **Location:** 12 miles from Grand Rapids. **Calendar:** Semester, extensive summer session. **Full-time faculty:** 941 total; 67% have terminal degrees, 14% minority, 46% women. **Part-time faculty:** 511 total; 7% have terminal degrees, 6% minority, 52% women. **Class size:** 26% < 20, 57% 20-39, 9% 40-49, 6% 50-99, 1% >100. **Special facilities:** Cross-country fitness trail, recital hall, two Great Lakes research vessels, water resources research institute, center for presidential studies.

**Freshman class profile.** 13,435 applied, 9,335 admitted, 3,459 enrolled.

| Mid 50% test scores | | | |
|---|---|---|---|
| SAT critical reading: | 490-600 | GPA 2.0-2.99: | 3% |
| SAT math: | 500-610 | Rank in top quarter: | 60% |
| SAT writing: | 480-580 | Rank in top tenth: | 24% |
| ACT composite: | 22-26 | Return as sophomores: | 84% |
| GPA 3.50 or higher: | 60% | Out-of-state: | 4% |
| GPA 3.0-3.49: | 37% | Live on campus: | 84% |
| | | International: | 1% |

**Basis for selection.** Admission based on secondary school grades, courses, personal and academic data, ACT/SAT results. Audition required of music majors. Portfolio required of art majors. Interviews and essays required of some.

**High school preparation.** 20 units recommended. Required and recommended units include English 4, mathematics 3-4, social studies 3, science 3-4 (laboratory 1-2), foreign language 2 and academic electives 1. Math should include 2 algebra. English should include 1 composition. Also recommend 2 fine arts and computer literacy.

**2007-2008 Annual costs.** Tuition/fees: $7,240; $12,510 out-of-state. Per-credit-hour charge applies only to part-time students. Room/board: $7,048. Books/supplies: $900. Personal expenses: $1,000.

**2007-2008 Financial aid. Need-based:** 2,898 full-time freshmen applied for aid; 1,811 were judged to have need; 1,806 of these received aid. Average need met was 89%. Average scholarship/grant was $6,178; average loan $3,650. 49% of total undergraduate aid awarded as scholarships/grants, 51% as loans/jobs. **Non-need-based:** Awarded to 2,700 full-time undergraduates, including 950 freshmen. Scholarships awarded for academics, alumni affiliation, art, athletics, minority status, music/drama.

**Application procedures. Admission:** Priority date 2/1; deadline 5/1 (receipt date). $30 fee, may be waived for applicants with need. Application may be submitted online. Admission notification on a rolling basis beginning on or about 9/1. Must reply by 5/1. Application closing date February 1 for campus housing, scholarships. **Financial aid:** Priority date 3/1; no closing date. FAFSA required. Applicants notified on a rolling basis starting 4/1; must reply within 3 week(s) of notification.

**Academics. Special study options:** Combined bachelor's/graduate degree, distance learning, double major, dual enrollment of high school students, ESL, honors, independent study, internships, student-designed major, study abroad, teacher certification program, Washington semester. Undergraduates may take graduate level classes as seniors; co-op programs in education, engineering, health professions. **Credit/placement by examination:** AP, CLEP, IB, SAT, ACT, institutional tests. 32 credit hours maximum toward bachelor's degree. **Support services:** Learning center, preadmission summer program, remedial instruction, study skills assistance, tutoring, writing center.

**Honors college/program.** 3.5 GPA and 28 ACT required.

**Majors. Architecture:** Urban/community planning. **Area/ethnic studies:** Russian/Slavic. **Biology:** General, biochemistry, cellular/molecular. **Business:** Accounting, business admin, finance, human resources, international, management science, managerial economics, marketing, tourism promotion, tourism/travel. **Communications:** General, advertising, broadcast journalism, journalism, public relations. **Computer sciences:** General, computer science, information systems, programming. **Conservation:** Management/policy. **Education:** Music, physical, science, special. **Engineering:** Electrical, manufacturing, mechanical. **Engineering technology:** Occupational safety. **English:** Creative writing, English lit, technical writing. **Foreign languages:** Ancient Greek, classics, French, German, Latin, Spanish. **Health:** Athletic training, clinical lab science, medical radiologic technology/radiation therapy, nursing (RN), occupational health, predental, premedicine, prepharmacy, preveterinary. **History:** General. **Interdisciplinary:** Behavioral sciences, biological/physical sciences, biopsychology. **Legal studies:** General, paralegal. **Liberal arts:** Arts/sciences. **Math:** General, statistics. **Parks/recreation:** General, health/fitness. **Philosophy/religion:** Philosophy. **Physical sciences:** Chemistry, geochemistry, geology, physics. **Protective services:** Law enforcement admin, security services. **Psychology:** General, social. **Public administration:** General, social work. **Social sciences:** General, anthropology, economics, geography, international relations, political science, sociology. **Visual/performing arts:** Art, art history/conservation, ceramics, commercial/advertising art, dance, dramatic, film/cinema, metal/jewelry, painting, photography, printmaking, sculpture, studio arts.

**Most popular majors.** Business/marketing 19%, communications/journalism 7%, English 8%, health sciences 15%, psychology 6%, social sciences 8%.

**Computing on campus.** 1,700 workstations in dormitories, library, computer center, student center. Dormitories wired for high-speed internet access and linked to campus network. Commuter students can connect to campus network. Online course registration, helpline, repair service, student web hosting, wireless network available.

**Student life. Freshman orientation:** Mandatory, $75 fee. Preregistration for classes offered. One day long and held for small groups on 50 possible dates through May, June, July, and August. Students register for classes for full year. **Housing:** Guaranteed on-campus for freshmen. Coed dorms, apartments, fraternity/sorority housing, substance-free housing available. $150 deposit, deadline 2/1. Honors College, specialty, languages, engineering housing available. **Activities:** Bands, campus ministries, choral groups, dance, drama, international student organizations, literary magazine, music ensembles, musical theater, radio station, student government, student newspaper, symphony orchestra, TV station, 143 registered organizations.

**Athletics.** NCAA. **Intercollegiate:** Baseball M, basketball, cross-country, diving, football (tackle) M, golf, soccer W, softball W, swimming, tennis, track and field, volleyball W. **Intramural:** Archery, badminton, basketball, bowling, cross-country, diving, fencing, field hockey W, football (tackle) M, golf, gymnastics, racquetball, rowing (crew), skiing, skin diving, soccer, softball, squash, swimming, table tennis, tennis, volleyball, wrestling M. **Team name:** Lakers.

**Student services.** Adult student services, alcohol/substance abuse counseling, campus ministries, career counseling, services for economically disadvantaged, student employment services, financial aid counseling, health

services, minority student services, on-campus daycare, personal counseling, placement for graduates, women's services. **Physically disabled:** Services for visually, speech, hearing impaired.

**Contact.** E-mail: go2gvsu@gvsu.edu
Phone: (616) 331-2025 Toll-free number: (800) 748-0246
Fax: (616) 331-2000
Jodi Chycinski, Director of Admissions, Grand Valley State University, One Campus Drive, Allendale, MI 49401-9403

## Great Lakes Christian College
**Lansing, Michigan**
www.glcc.edu                    CB code: 7320

- Private 4-year Bible college affiliated with Church of Christ / Christian Church
- Residential campus in small city
- 260 degree-seeking undergraduates
- SAT or ACT (ACT writing optional) required

**General.** Founded in 1949. Accredited by ABHE. **Degrees:** 27 bachelor's, 6 associate awarded. **Location:** 90 miles from Detroit, 65 miles from Grand Rapids. **Calendar:** Semester, limited summer session. **Full-time faculty:** 10 total. **Part-time faculty:** 11 total.

**Freshman class profile.** 164 enrolled.

**Basis for selection.** Recommendations of character from applicant's minister and church leaders required. Students with GPA below 2.25 or ACT below 16 or SAT below 820 (exclusive of Writing) admitted on probation. **Homeschooled:** Transcript of courses and grades, letter of recommendation (nonparent) required.

**2007-2008 Annual costs.** Tuition/fees: $9,910. Room/board: $6,200. Books/supplies: $600. Personal expenses: $1,500.

**Financial aid. Non-need-based:** Scholarships awarded for academics, alumni affiliation, music/drama.

**Application procedures. Admission:** Priority date 8/1; no deadline. $30 fee, may be waived for applicants with need. Application may be submitted online. Admission notification on a rolling basis. **Financial aid:** Priority date 8/1; no closing date. FAFSA, institutional form required. Applicants notified on a rolling basis starting 5/1; must reply within 3 week(s) of notification.

**Academics. Special study options:** Double major, dual enrollment of high school students, internships. **Credit/placement by examination:** CLEP. **Support services:** Reduced course load, study skills assistance, tutoring.

**Majors. History:** General. **Theology:** Bible, religious ed, sacred music.

**Computing on campus.** 23 workstations in library, computer center, student center. Dormitories wired for high-speed internet access and linked to campus network. Commuter students can connect to campus network. Online library, wireless network available.

**Student life. Freshman orientation:** Mandatory. Preregistration for classes offered. **Policies:** Regular Christian service participation required of all full-time students. Religious observance required. **Housing:** Single-sex dorms, apartments, substance-free housing available. $200 deposit, deadline 6/1. **Activities:** Choral groups, drama, music ensembles, student government.

**Athletics.** NCCAA. **Intercollegiate:** Basketball M, soccer M, volleyball W. **Intramural:** Baseball M, volleyball M. **Team name:** Crusaders.

**Student services.** Campus ministries, financial aid counseling, personal counseling.

**Contact.** E-mail: admissions@glcc.edu
Phone: (517) 321-0242 ext. 221 Toll-free number: (800) 937-4522
Fax: (517) 321-5902
Lloyd Scharer, Director of Admissions & College Relations, Great Lakes Christian College, 6211 West Willow Highway, Lansing, MI 48917-1299

## Hillsdale College
**Hillsdale, Michigan**                 CB member
www.hillsdale.edu                       CB code: 1295

- Private 4-year liberal arts college
- Residential campus in large town

- 1,326 degree-seeking undergraduates: 3% part-time, 52% women, 2% international
- 64% of applicants admitted
- SAT or ACT (ACT writing optional), application essay required
- 72% graduate within 6 years; 51% enter graduate study

**General.** Founded in 1844. Regionally accredited. **Degrees:** 276 bachelor's awarded. **Location:** 120 miles from Detroit, 75 miles from Ann Arbor. **Calendar:** Semester, limited summer session. **Full-time faculty:** 110 total; 83% have terminal degrees, 27% women. **Part-time faculty:** 42 total; 38% have terminal degrees, 40% women. **Class size:** 77% < 20, 21% 20-39, less than 1% 40-49, less than 1% 50-99. **Special facilities:** Arboretum, preschool, K-12 private academy, economics library, special collections library for first editions, 685-acre lake biological station.

**Freshman class profile.** 1,401 applied, 897 admitted, 375 enrolled.

| Mid 50% test scores | | Rank in top tenth: | 47% |
|---|---|---|---|
| SAT critical reading: | 640-720 | End year in good standing: | 88% |
| SAT math: | 570-660 | Return as sophomores: | 88% |
| SAT writing: | 610-690 | Out-of-state: | 63% |
| ACT composite: | 25-30 | Live on campus: | 99% |
| GPA 3.50 or higher: | 82% | International: | 1% |
| GPA 3.0-3.49: | 15% | Fraternities: | 30% |
| GPA 2.0-2.99: | 3% | Sororities: | 40% |
| Rank in top quarter: | 75% | | |

**Basis for selection.** Minimum 3.3 GPA, class rank in top third preferred. Test scores, recommendations, interview, personal essay important. SAT Subject Tests recommended. Portfolio recommended for art majors. Audition required for music scholarship applicants. **Homeschooled:** Transcript of courses and grades required.

**High school preparation.** 16 units recommended. Recommended units include English 4, mathematics 4, social studies 1, history 2, science 3 (laboratory 1) and foreign language 2.

**2007-2008 Annual costs.** Tuition/fees: $19,090. Room/board: $7,340. Books/supplies: $800. Personal expenses: $500.

**2007-2008 Financial aid. Need-based:** 225 full-time freshmen applied for aid; 170 were judged to have need; 170 of these received aid. Average need met was 65%. Average scholarship/grant was $6,200; average loan $4,000. 84% of total undergraduate aid awarded as scholarships/grants, 16% as loans/jobs. **Non-need-based:** Awarded to 933 full-time undergraduates, including 284 freshmen. Scholarships awarded for academics, alumni affiliation, art, athletics, leadership, music/drama, state residency. **Additional information:** Campus employment available.

**Application procedures. Admission:** Priority date 11/15; deadline 2/15 (postmark date). $35 fee. Application may be submitted online. Admission notification on a rolling basis beginning on or about 12/1. Must reply by 5/1. **Financial aid:** Priority date 3/1, closing date 3/15. Institutional form required. CSS PROFILE required for returning students only. Applicants notified on a rolling basis starting 2/1; must reply by 5/1 or within 4 week(s) of notification.

**Academics.** Highly qualified students may study at Oxford University, England for semester or summer. Summer business program at Regents College, London, England as well as study abroad programs in France, Germany and Spain. **Special study options:** Accelerated study, double major, dual enrollment of high school students, honors, independent study, internships, study abroad, teacher certification program, Washington semester. **Credit/placement by examination:** AP, CLEP, IB, SAT, ACT, institutional tests. **Support services:** Reduced course load, study skills assistance, tutoring, writing center.

**Majors. Area/ethnic studies:** American, European. **Biology:** General. **Business:** General, accounting, business admin, finance, international marketing, marketing. **Communications:** General, journalism. **Computer sciences:** Computer science. **Education:** General, early childhood, elementary, multi-level teacher, physical, secondary. **English:** English lit, speech/rhetoric. **Foreign languages:** Classics, comparative lit, French, German, Spanish. **Health:** Predental, premedicine, prenursing, prepharmacy, preveterinary. **History:** General. **Interdisciplinary:** Math/computer science. **Legal studies:** Prelaw. **Liberal arts:** Arts/sciences. **Math:** General, computational. **Philosophy/religion:** Christian, philosophy, religion. **Physical sciences:** Chemistry, physics. **Psychology:** General. **Social sciences:** Economics, political science, sociology. **Theology:** Preministerial. **Visual/performing arts:** Art, dramatic.

**Most popular majors.** Biology 7%, business/marketing 15%, education 12%, English 11%, history 14%, social sciences 13%, visual/performing arts 7%.

**Computing on campus.** 200 workstations in library, computer center, student center. Dormitories wired for high-speed internet access and linked to campus network. Commuter students can connect to campus network. Online library, helpline, repair service, wireless network available.

**Student life. Freshman orientation:** Mandatory. Preregistration for classes offered. 3-day program in the fall. **Housing:** Guaranteed on-campus for all undergraduates. Single-sex dorms, apartments, fraternity/sorority housing, substance-free housing available. $200 nonrefundable deposit, deadline 5/1. **Activities:** Bands, choral groups, dance, drama, literary magazine, music ensembles, musical theater, student government, student newspaper, symphony orchestra, Catholic student council, Varsity H-Club, international relations club, student federation, enterprising leaders, Intervarsity Christian Fellowship, Fellowship of Christian Athletes, College Republicans, Young Life, Praxis, Charis.

**Athletics.** NCAA. **Intercollegiate:** Baseball M, basketball, cross-country, diving W, equestrian W, football (tackle) M, softball W, swimming W, track and field, volleyball W. **Intramural:** Basketball, football (non-tackle), handball, racquetball, soccer, softball, swimming, table tennis, tennis, track and field, volleyball. **Team name:** Chargers.

**Student services.** Campus ministries, career counseling, student employment services, financial aid counseling, health services, personal counseling, placement for graduates. **Physically disabled:** Services for visually impaired.

**Contact.** E-mail: admissions@hillsdale.edu
Phone: (517) 607-2327 Fax: (517) 607-2223
Jeffrey Lantis, Director of Admissions, Hillsdale College, 33 East College Street, Hillsdale, MI 49242

---

## Hope College
**Holland, Michigan**      **CB member**
**www.hope.edu**      **CB code: 1301**

- Private 4-year liberal arts college affiliated with Reformed Church in America
- Residential campus in small city
- 3,135 degree-seeking undergraduates: 2% part-time, 59% women, 2% African American, 2% Asian American, 3% Hispanic American, 1% international
- 83% of applicants admitted
- SAT or ACT (ACT writing optional), application essay required
- 78% graduate within 6 years; 28% enter graduate study

**General.** Founded in 1862. Regionally accredited. **Degrees:** 718 bachelor's awarded. **Location:** 30 miles from Grand Rapids, 160 miles from Chicago. **Calendar:** Semester, limited summer session. **Full-time faculty:** 219 total; 76% have terminal degrees, 12% minority, 43% women. **Part-time faculty:** 107 total; 32% have terminal degrees, 10% minority, 55% women. **Class size:** 51% < 20, 46% 20-39, 2% 40-49, 2% 50-99. **Special facilities:** Museum, Pelletron particle accelerator, biological field station, electron microscopes, laser research, cadaver lab.

**Freshman class profile.** 2,748 applied, 2,275 admitted, 819 enrolled.

| Mid 50% test scores | | Return as sophomores: | 88% |
|---|---|---|---|
| SAT critical reading: | 530-650 | Out-of-state: | 33% |
| SAT math: | 540-650 | Live on campus: | 99% |
| ACT composite: | 23-29 | International: | 1% |
| Rank in top quarter: | 66% | Fraternities: | 16% |
| Rank in top tenth: | 35% | Sororities: | 17% |
| End year in good standing: | 97% | | |

**Basis for selection.** Strength of curriculum, achievement, test scores, perceived ability to succeed important. Interviews recommended. **Home-schooled:** Paper of at least 3 pages from final 2 years of homeschooling, list of non-textbooks read in last 2 years of home schooling, letter of recommendation from adult outside of family required. **Learning Disabled:** Students should consult the director of the academic support program to ensure available resources and personnel to accommodate the disability.

**High school preparation.** 20 units required; 21 recommended. Required and recommended units include English 4, mathematics 3, social studies 2, science 3 (laboratory 1-2), foreign language 2 and academic electives 5.

**2008-2009 Annual costs.** Tuition/fees: $24,920. Room/board: $7,650.

**2007-2008 Financial aid. Need-based:** 691 full-time freshmen applied for aid; 526 were judged to have need; 525 of these received aid. Average need met was 86%. Average scholarship/grant was $15,276; average loan

$4,454. 70% of total undergraduate aid awarded as scholarships/grants, 30% as loans/jobs. **Non-need-based:** Awarded to 2,165 full-time undergraduates, including 689 freshmen. Scholarships awarded for academics, alumni affiliation, art, minority status, music/drama, religious affiliation.

**Application procedures. Admission:** Priority date 3/1; no deadline. $35 fee, may be waived for applicants with need. Application may be submitted online. Admission notification on a rolling basis beginning on or about 12/15. Must reply by May 1 or within 2 week(s) if notified thereafter. **Financial aid:** Priority date 3/1; no closing date. FAFSA, institutional form required. Applicants notified on a rolling basis starting 3/25.

**Academics.** Extensive undergraduate scientific research opportunities available. All fine arts divisions nationally accredited. **Special study options:** Distance learning, double major, ESL, independent study, internships, New York semester, student-designed major, study abroad, teacher certification program, urban semester, Washington semester. Internships in Chicago, New York City, Washington DC, Philadelphia. **Credit/placement by examination:** AP, CLEP, IB, institutional tests. 32 credit hours maximum toward bachelor's degree. **Support services:** Reduced course load, study skills assistance, tutoring, writing center.

**Majors. Area/ethnic studies:** Japanese, women's. **Biology:** General. **Business:** Accounting, business admin, managerial economics. **Communications:** General. **Computer sciences:** General. **Conservation:** Environmental science. **Education:** Art, biology, chemistry, drama/dance, emotionally handicapped, English, French, German, history, Latin, learning disabled, mathematics, music, physical, physics, science, social studies, Spanish. **Engineering:** General, physics. **English:** English lit. **Foreign languages:** Biblical, classics, French, German, Latin, Spanish. **Health:** Athletic training, nursing (RN). **History:** General. **Interdisciplinary:** Global studies. **Math:** General. **Parks/recreation:** Exercise sciences. **Philosophy/religion:** Philosophy, religion. **Physical sciences:** Chemistry, geochemistry, geology, geophysics, physics. **Psychology:** General. **Public administration:** Social work. **Social sciences:** Economics, political science, sociology. **Visual/performing arts:** Art history/conservation, dance, dramatic, jazz, music performance, piano/organ, stringed instruments, studio arts, voice/opera.

**Most popular majors.** Business/marketing 14%, communications/journalism 6%, education 17%, health sciences 6%, psychology 9%, social sciences 6%, visual/performing arts 6%.

**Computing on campus.** 350 workstations in dormitories, library, computer center, student center. Dormitories wired for high-speed internet access and linked to campus network. Commuter students can connect to campus network. Online library, helpline, repair service, student web hosting, wireless network available.

**Student life. Freshman orientation:** Mandatory. Preregistration for classes offered. 3-day orientation for students and parents begins Friday before school starts. **Policies:** Visitors of opposite gender not allowed after 12 a.m. on weekdays and 2 a.m. on weekends. No alcohol allowed on campus. **Housing:** Guaranteed on-campus for all undergraduates. Coed dorms, single-sex dorms, apartments, fraternity/sorority housing, substance-free housing available. $300 nonrefundable deposit, deadline 5/1. Cottages (houses on or near campus), theme housing available. **Activities:** Bands, campus ministries, choral groups, dance, drama, international student organizations, literary magazine, music ensembles, Model UN, musical theater, radio station, student government, student newspaper, symphony orchestra, Fellowship of Christian Athletes, Inter-Varsity Christian Fellowship, Fellowship of Christian Students, College Republicans and Democrats, international relations club, Higher Horizons, black student union, Hispanic students organization, Catholic student union.

**Athletics.** NCAA. **Intercollegiate:** Baseball M, basketball, cheerleading, cross-country, diving, football (tackle) M, golf, soccer, softball W, swimming, tennis, track and field, volleyball W. **Intramural:** Basketball, bowling, football (non-tackle), racquetball, soccer, softball, tennis, volleyball, water polo. **Team name:** Flying Dutchmen, Flying Dutch.

**Student services.** Adult student services, alcohol/substance abuse counseling, campus ministries, career counseling, student employment services, financial aid counseling, health services, minority student services, personal counseling, placement for graduates, women's services. **Physically disabled:** Services for visually, hearing impaired.

**Contact.** E-mail: admissions@hope.edu
Phone: (616) 395-7850 Toll-free number: (800) 968-7850
Fax: (616) 395-7130
Garrett Knoth, Admissions, Hope College, 69 East 10th Street, Holland, MI 49422-9000

## International Academy of Design and Technology: Detroit
**Troy, Michigan**
www.iadtdetroit.com/

- For-profit 4-year visual arts and technical college
- Small city
- 948 degree-seeking undergraduates

**General.** Accredited by ACICS. **Degrees:** 77 bachelor's, 40 associate awarded. **Calendar:** Semester. **Full-time faculty:** 20 total. **Part-time faculty:** 68 total.

**Freshman class profile.** 160 applied, 160 admitted, 157 enrolled.

**Basis for selection.** Open admission.

**2007-2008 Annual costs.** Tuition/fees: $16,620.

**2006-2007 Financial aid. Need-based:** 36% of total undergraduate aid awarded as scholarships/grants, 64% as loans/jobs.

**Application procedures. Admission:** No deadline. $50 fee. Admission notification on a rolling basis. **Financial aid:** No deadline.

**Academics. Credit/placement by examination:** CLEP.

**Majors. Communications technology:** Desktop publishing, graphics. **Computer sciences:** Game design. **Visual/performing arts:** Fashion design, graphic design, interior design.

**Contact.** Phone: (248) 457-2700
Jamie Morgan, Senior Director of Admissions, International Academy of Design and Technology: Detroit, 1850 Research Drive, Troy, MI 48083

## Kalamazoo College
**Kalamazoo, Michigan**
www.kzoo.edu
**CB member**
**CB code: 1365**

- Private 4-year liberal arts college
- Residential campus in small city
- 1,340 degree-seeking undergraduates: 58% women, 4% African American, 6% Asian American, 4% Hispanic American, 1% international
- 63% of applicants admitted
- SAT or ACT with writing, application essay required
- 78% graduate within 6 years

**General.** Founded in 1833. Regionally accredited. Study abroad centers in Kenya, Senegal, Ecuador, Spain, France, Germany, Mexico, and China. **Degrees:** 291 bachelor's awarded. **ROTC:** Army. **Location:** 140 miles from Detroit, 140 miles from Chicago. **Calendar:** Quarter. **Full-time faculty:** 101 total; 84% have terminal degrees, 16% minority, 46% women. **Part-time faculty:** 12 total; 50% have terminal degrees, 17% minority, 58% women. **Class size:** 64% < 20, 33% 20-39, 2% 40-49, 1% 50-99. **Special facilities:** 3 theaters, rare books collection, science center, 100 acre arboretum.

**Freshman class profile.** 2,092 applied, 1,310 admitted, 363 enrolled.

| Mid 50% test scores | | | |
|---|---|---|---|
| SAT critical reading: | 580-690 | Rank in top quarter: | 75% |
| SAT math: | 570-680 | Rank in top tenth: | 44% |
| ACT composite: | 26-30 | Return as sophomores: | 91% |
| GPA 3.50 or higher: | 69% | Out-of-state: | 28% |
| GPA 3.0-3.49: | 26% | Live on campus: | 100% |
| GPA 2.0-2.99: | 5% | International: | 1% |

**Basis for selection.** Curriculum, grades, essay, recommendations, and special accomplishments influence decision. Interview recommended. **Homeschooled:** Statement describing homeschool structure and mission, transcript of courses and grades, interview, letter of recommendation (nonparent) required.

**High school preparation.** 17 units required. Required and recommended units include English 4, mathematics 3-4, social studies 2, history 2, science 3-4 and foreign language 2-3.

**2007-2008 Annual costs.** Tuition/fees: $28,816. Room/board: $7,122. Books/supplies: $750. Personal expenses: $828.

**Financial aid. Non-need-based:** Scholarships awarded for academics, alumni affiliation. **Additional information:** Paid career development internship and senior project experiences available on campus.

**Application procedures. Admission:** Priority date 12/1; deadline 2/1 (postmark date). $35 fee, may be waived for applicants with need. Application must be submitted online. Admission notification 4/1. Must reply by 5/1. **Financial aid:** Priority date 2/15; no closing date. FAFSA, institutional form required. CSS PROFILE required for Early Decision applicants requesting need-based financial aid. Applicants notified on a rolling basis starting 3/21; must reply by 5/1.

**Academics.** Most students participate in career internships and study abroad. College subsidizes most study abroad expenses. Students complete a senior individualized project as part of graduation requirements. **Special study options:** Combined bachelor's/graduate degree, cross-registration, double major, dual enrollment of high school students, exchange student, independent study, internships, New York semester, study abroad, urban semester. **Credit/placement by examination:** AP, CLEP, IB, institutional tests. 18 credit hours maximum toward bachelor's degree. **Support services:** Learning center, reduced course load, study skills assistance, tutoring, writing center.

**Majors. Biology:** General. **Computer sciences:** General. **English:** Creative writing, English lit. **Family/consumer sciences:** Family studies. **Foreign languages:** Classics, French, German, Spanish. **Health:** Predental, premedicine, preveterinary. **History:** General. **Legal studies:** Prelaw. **Math:** General. **Philosophy/religion:** Philosophy, religion. **Physical sciences:** Chemistry, physics. **Psychology:** General. **Social sciences:** Anthropology, economics, political science, sociology. **Visual/performing arts:** Art, art history/conservation, dramatic.

**Most popular majors.** Biology 14%, English 12%, foreign language 6%, history 6%, psychology 9%, public administration/social services 27%.

**Computing on campus.** 130 workstations in library, computer center, student center. Dormitories wired for high-speed internet access and linked to campus network. Commuter students can connect to campus network. Online course registration, online library, helpline, student web hosting, wireless network available.

**Student life. Freshman orientation:** Mandatory. Preregistration for classes offered. Held the week before fall classes begin. **Housing:** Guaranteed on-campus for all undergraduates. Coed dorms available. Special-interest housing available. **Activities:** Bands, campus ministries, choral groups, dance, drama, international student organizations, literary magazine, music ensembles, musical theater, radio station, student government, student newspaper, symphony orchestra, African American student organization, women's equity coalition, volunteer bureau, environmental organization, film society, Habitat for Humanity, Amnesty International, coalition on racial diversity.

**Athletics.** NCAA. **Intercollegiate:** Baseball M, basketball, cross-country, diving, football (tackle) M, golf, soccer, softball W, swimming, tennis, volleyball W. **Intramural:** Basketball, cheerleading W, golf, gymnastics W, racquetball, rugby, skiing, soccer, softball, squash, table tennis, tennis, volleyball, water polo. **Team name:** Hornets.

**Student services.** Alcohol/substance abuse counseling, career counseling, student employment services, health services, personal counseling, placement for graduates, women's services.

**Contact.** E-mail: admission@kzoo.edu
Phone: (269) 337-7166 Toll-free number: (800) 253-3602
Fax: (269) 337-7390
Eric Staab, Dean of Admission, Kalamazoo College, Kalamazoo College Office of Admission, Kalamazoo, MI 49006-3295

## Kendall College of Art and Design of Ferris State University
**Grand Rapids, Michigan**
www.kcad.edu
**CB code: 1376**

- Public 4-year visual arts college
- Commuter campus in large city
- 1,043 degree-seeking undergraduates
- 39 graduate students
- 78% of applicants admitted
- ACT (writing optional), SAT Subject Tests, application essay required

**General.** Founded in 1928. Regionally accredited. **Degrees:** 140 bachelor's awarded; master's offered. **Location:** 175 miles from Detroit, 160 miles from Chicago. **Calendar:** Semester, limited summer session. **Full-time faculty:** 47 total; 6% have terminal degrees, 4% minority. **Part-time faculty:** 94 total; 3% have terminal degrees, 3% minority. **Special facilities:** 35,000-title slide collection.

**Freshman class profile.** 338 applied, 264 admitted, 239 enrolled.

**Basis for selection.** High school GPA, statement of purpose/essay, ACT or SAT test scores, and portfolio considered in admission process. Portfolio required. **Learning Disabled:** Highly recommended that students with learning disabilities meet college counselor to discuss education needs/assistance to help achieve learning success.

**2007-2008 Annual costs.** Tuition/fees: $13,094; $19,640 out-of-state. Studio art courses: $540 per credit hour in-state and $809 out-of-state. General education courses: $282 per credit hour in-state and $423 out-of-state. Books/supplies: $3,604. Personal expenses: $864.

**Financial aid.** All financial aid based on need.

**Application procedures. Admission:** Priority date 6/1; no deadline. $30 fee, may be waived for applicants with need. Application must be submitted on paper. Admission notification on a rolling basis. **Financial aid:** Closing date 2/15. FAFSA required. Applicants notified on a rolling basis starting 4/15; must reply within 4 week(s) of notification.

**Academics.** For bachelor's degree, 42-54 credits in major required, depending on specified major. **Special study options:** Combined bachelor's/graduate degree, double major, dual enrollment of high school students, independent study, internships, liberal arts/career combination, New York semester, study abroad, teacher certification program. **Credit/placement by examination:** AP, CLEP, institutional tests. 30 credit hours maximum toward bachelor's degree. **Support services:** Reduced course load, study skills assistance, tutoring, writing center.

**Majors. Education:** Art. **Production:** Furniture. **Visual/performing arts:** Art history/conservation, commercial/advertising art, design, digital art, drawing, graphic design, illustration, industrial design, interior design, metal/jewelry, multimedia, painting, photography, printmaking, sculpture, studio arts.

**Computing on campus.** 200 workstations in library, computer center. Commuter students can connect to campus network. Online course registration, online library available.

**Student life. Freshman orientation:** Available. Preregistration for classes offered. Held 2 weeks before classes begin. **Housing:** Apartments available. **Activities:** Student government, American Society of Interior Designers, Industrial Design Society of America, American Society of Illustrators, Grand Rapids Furniture Design Association.

**Student services.** Adult student services, career counseling, student employment services, financial aid counseling, personal counseling, placement for graduates, veterans' counselor. **Physically disabled:** Services for hearing impaired.

**Contact.** E-mail: brittons@ferris.edu
Phone: (616) 451-2787 Toll-free number: (800) 676-2787
Fax: (616) 831-9689
Sandy Britton, Director of Enrollment Management, Kendall College of Art and Design of Ferris State University, 17 Fountain Street NW, Grand Rapids, MI 49503-3002

## Kettering University

Flint, Michigan
www.kettering.edu

**CB member**
**CB code: 1246**

- Private 4-year university and engineering college
- Residential campus in small city
- 2,178 degree-seeking undergraduates: 15% women, 5% African American, 5% Asian American, 2% Hispanic American, 2% international
- 497 degree-seeking graduate students
- 72% of applicants admitted
- SAT or ACT (ACT writing optional) required
- 55% graduate within 6 years

**General.** Founded in 1919. Regionally accredited. Formerly GMI Engineering and Management Institute. **Degrees:** 395 bachelor's awarded; master's offered. **Location:** 70 miles from Detroit. **Calendar:** Semester, extensive summer session. **Full-time faculty:** 125 total; 82% have terminal degrees, 10% minority, 19% women. **Part-time faculty:** 13 total; 38% women. **Class**

size: 41% < 20, 49% 20-39, 7% 40-49, 3% 50-99. **Special facilities:** Computer-integrated manufacturing laboratory, GM-PACE e-design and e-manufacturing studio, acoustics laboratory, polymer optimization center, engine test center, SAE vehicle development laboratory, mechatronics laboratory, biomedical laboratories on campus and at nearby medical center, Ford design simulation studio, crash study lab, fuel cell research center.

**Freshman class profile.** 1,817 applied, 1,317 admitted, 385 enrolled.

| Mid 50% test scores | | | |
|---|---|---|---|
| SAT critical reading: | 500-620 | GPA 2.0-2.99: | 3% |
| SAT math: | 570-680 | Rank in top quarter: | 64% |
| ACT composite: | 24-29 | Rank in top tenth: | 32% |
| GPA 3.50 or higher: | 59% | Out-of-state: | 30% |
| GPA 3.0-3.49: | 38% | Live on campus: | 100% |
| | | International: | 2% |

**Basis for selection.** GED not accepted. Strength of preparation, performance in school, test scores, nonscholastic activities and achievements most important. Accepted students encouraged to confirm enrollment plans early so co-op employment search process can begin. SAT Subject Tests (especially math level II, chemistry, and physics), while not required, helpful when presented. Interview recommended. **Homeschooled:** Laboratory science experience very important and may need to be documented.

**High school preparation.** 10.5 units required; 21 recommended. Required and recommended units include English 3-4, mathematics 3.5-4, social studies 2, history 2, science 2-3 (laboratory 2-3), foreign language 2 and computer science 1. At least 1 unit of either chemistry or physics with laboratory required. Both chemistry and physics strongly recommended. Algebra I and II, geometry and trigonometry required. Drafting or CAD recommended, especially for those considering engineering.

**2007-2008 Annual costs.** Tuition/fees: $25,658. Room/board: $5,798. Books/supplies: $1,075. Personal expenses: $2,924.

**2006-2007 Financial aid. Need-based:** 365 full-time freshmen applied for aid; 333 were judged to have need; 333 of these received aid. Average need met was 71%. Average scholarship/grant was $12,579; average loan $2,513. 46% of total undergraduate aid awarded as scholarships/grants, 54% as loans/jobs. **Non-need-based:** Awarded to 1,641 full-time undergraduates, including 326 freshmen. Scholarships awarded for academics, leadership, state residency.

**Application procedures. Admission:** No deadline. $35 fee, may be waived for applicants with need. Application may be submitted online. Admission notification on a rolling basis beginning on or about 10/15. Must reply by May 1 or within 3 week(s) if notified thereafter. **Financial aid:** Priority date 2/14; no closing date. FAFSA required. Applicants notified on a rolling basis starting 2/1; must reply within 2 week(s) of notification.

**Academics.** All students required to participate in paid professional cooperative work experiences typically beginning freshman year. Students alternate 11-week terms of full-time study on campus with 12-week terms of full-time work experience with their co-op employer, generally located near home. **Special study options:** Accelerated study, combined bachelor's/graduate degree, cooperative education, distance learning, double major, dual enrollment of high school students, independent study, study abroad. Paid professional co-op experience in industry required of all undergraduates. Co-op typically begins in first year. Each 24-week semester divided into 11 weeks of classes and 12 weeks of co-op. **Credit/placement by examination:** AP, CLEP, IB, institutional tests. **Support services:** Learning center, study skills assistance, tutoring, writing center.

**Majors. Biology:** Biochemistry. **Business:** Business admin. **Computer sciences:** Computer science. **Engineering:** Computer, electrical, industrial, mechanical. **Math:** Applied. **Physical sciences:** Applied physics, chemistry. **Other:** Engineering physics.

**Most popular majors.** Engineering/engineering technologies 92%.

**Computing on campus.** 450 workstations in dormitories, library, computer center, student center. Dormitories wired for high-speed internet access and linked to campus network. Commuter students can connect to campus network. Online library, helpline, wireless network available.

**Student life. Freshman orientation:** Mandatory, $150 fee. Four-day program begins Thursday before start of classes. **Policies:** Grade requirement to be eligible to join or maintain active membership in Greek letter organizations. **Housing:** Guaranteed on-campus for freshmen. Coed dorms, apartments, fraternity/sorority housing, substance-free housing available. $100 fully refundable deposit, deadline 6/1. **Activities:** Jazz band, drama, music ensembles, radio station, student government, student newspaper, international club, Intervarsity Christian Fellowship, Christians in Action, Society of Automotive Engineers, Society of Women Engineers, National Society of Black Engineers, National Society of Hispanic Engineers, Habitat for Humanity, Asian American association.

**Athletics. Intramural:** Basketball, bowling, cross-country, football (non-tackle), golf, handball, ice hockey, lacrosse, racquetball, rifle, skin diving, soccer, softball, squash, table tennis, tennis, volleyball, water polo, weight lifting. **Team name:** Bulldogs.

**Student services.** Alcohol/substance abuse counseling, career counseling, student employment services, financial aid counseling, health services, minority student services, personal counseling, placement for graduates, women's services. **Physically disabled:** Services for visually, speech, hearing impaired.

**Contact.** E-mail: admissions@kettering.edu
Phone: (810) 762-7865 Toll-free number: (800) 955-4464 ext. 7865
Fax: (810) 762-9837
Barbara Sosin, Director of Admissions, Kettering University, 1700 West Third Avenue, Flint, MI 48504-4898

---

## Kuyper College
**Grand Rapids, Michigan**
www.kuyper.edu
CB code: 1672

- Private 4-year Bible college affiliated with Reformed Church
- Residential campus in large city
- 291 degree-seeking undergraduates: 14% part-time, 50% women, 3% African American, 2% Asian American, 4% Hispanic American, 9% international
- 2 degree-seeking graduate students
- 48% of applicants admitted
- SAT or ACT (ACT writing optional), application essay required
- 51% graduate within 6 years

**General.** Founded in 1939. Regionally accredited; also accredited by ABHE. **Degrees:** 61 bachelor's, 1 associate awarded. **Location:** 7 miles from downtown, 180 miles from Chicago. **Calendar:** Semester. **Full-time faculty:** 14 total; 43% have terminal degrees, 14% minority, 50% women. **Part-time faculty:** 16 total; 19% have terminal degrees, 12% minority, 44% women. **Class size:** 60% < 20, 35% 20-39, 5% 40-49.

**Freshman class profile.** 142 applied, 68 admitted, 68 enrolled.

| Mid 50% test scores | | | |
|---|---|---|---|
| SAT critical reading: | 450-540 | GPA 2.0-2.99: | 38% |
| SAT math: | 500-550 | Rank in top quarter: | 17% |
| SAT writing: | 520-580 | Rank in top tenth: | 3% |
| ACT composite: | 19-24 | Return as sophomores: | 68% |
| GPA 3.50 or higher: | 43% | Out-of-state: | 13% |
| GPA 3.0-3.49: | 17% | Live on campus: | 84% |
| | | International: | 7% |

**Basis for selection.** Secondary school record, test scores important. Applicants with 2.0-2.5 GPA evaluated individually and admitted on conditional acceptance. Interview required for borderline applicants. **Homeschooled:** Transcript of courses and grades required.

**2007-2008 Annual costs.** Tuition/fees: $12,685. Room/board: $6,100. Books/supplies: $649. Personal expenses: $815.

**2007-2008 Financial aid. Need-based:** 62 full-time freshmen applied for aid; 53 were judged to have need; 53 of these received aid. Average need met was 71%. Average scholarship/grant was $7,491; average loan $2,607. 63% of total undergraduate aid awarded as scholarships/grants, 37% as loans/jobs. **Non-need-based:** Awarded to 21 full-time undergraduates, including 4 freshmen. Scholarships awarded for academics, leadership, minority status.

**Application procedures. Admission:** Priority date 8/15; no deadline. $25 fee, may be waived for applicants with need. Application may be submitted online. Admission notification on a rolling basis. **Financial aid:** Priority date 3/1; no closing date. FAFSA, institutional form required. Applicants notified on a rolling basis starting 3/15; must reply within 2 week(s) of notification.

**Academics.** All students take 1 major in Bible/Theology, 1 major or concentration in professional ministry, and 1 or 2 minors in liberal arts. Faculty members are Calvinistic/Reformed, but present other theological perspectives. **Special study options:** Combined bachelor's/graduate degree, cooperative education, cross-registration, double major, dual enrollment of high school students, ESL, independent study, internships, study abroad, teacher certification program. **Credit/placement by examination:** AP, CLEP, SAT, ACT, institutional tests. **Support services:** Learning center, pre-admission summer program, reduced course load, remedial instruction, study skills assistance, tutoring, writing center.

**Majors. Business:** Accounting, business admin, international, office management. **Communications:** General, journalism, public relations. **Computer sciences:** General. **Education:** Elementary, secondary. **Family/consumer sciences:** Child development. **Health:** Prenursing. **Interdisciplinary:** Accounting/computer science. **Parks/recreation:** Exercise sciences. **Philosophy/religion:** Religion. **Public administration:** Social work. **Theology:** Bible, missionary, preministerial, theology, youth ministry. **Visual/performing arts:** Dramatic, film/cinema. **Other:** Music and worship.

**Most popular majors.** Education 8%, public administration/social services 21%, theological studies 67%.

**Computing on campus.** 54 workstations in dormitories, library, computer center. Dormitories linked to campus network. Commuter students can connect to campus network. Online library, helpline, student web hosting, wireless network available.

**Student life. Freshman orientation:** Available. Preregistration for classes offered. Held first week of fall semester. **Policies:** Smoke-free campus, alcohol and drug-free campus, standards of conduct and housing policies in accordance with school's moral values. **Housing:** Guaranteed on-campus for freshmen. Coed dorms, special housing for disabled, apartments, substance-free housing available. $100 nonrefundable deposit. **Activities:** Choral groups, drama, international student organizations, music ensembles, student government, Bible studies, student activities committee.

**Athletics. NCCAA. Intercollegiate:** Basketball. **Intramural:** Basketball, field hockey, football (non-tackle), soccer, softball, table tennis, volleyball. **Team name:** Cougars.

**Student services.** Alcohol/substance abuse counseling, campus ministries, career counseling, student employment services, financial aid counseling, health services, minority student services, personal counseling, placement for graduates, veterans' counselor. **Physically disabled:** Services for visually impaired. **Learning disabled:** Comprehensive services available.

**Contact.** E-mail: admissions@kuyper.edu
Phone: (616) 988-3621 Toll-free number: (800) 511-3749
Fax: (616) 988-3608
Larissa Lighthiser, Vice President for Enrollment, Kuyper College, 3333 East Beltline Avenue Northeast, Grand Rapids, MI 49525-9749

---

## Lake Superior State University
**Sault Ste. Marie, Michigan**
www.lssu.edu
CB member
CB code: 1421

- Public 4-year university
- Residential campus in small city
- 2,455 degree-seeking undergraduates: 16% part-time, 52% women, 2% African American, 1% Hispanic American, 7% Native American, 10% international
- 3 degree-seeking graduate students
- 91% of applicants admitted
- SAT or ACT (ACT writing recommended) required
- 44% graduate within 6 years

**General.** Founded in 1946. Regionally accredited. **Degrees:** 427 bachelor's, 108 associate awarded; master's offered. **Location:** 3 miles from Sault Sainte Marie, Canada. **Calendar:** Semester, limited summer session. **Full-time faculty:** 104 total; 10% minority, 41% women. **Part-time faculty:** 99 total; 17% minority. **Class size:** 40% < 20, 42% 20-39, 7% 40-49, 10% 50-99, less than 1% >100. **Special facilities:** Aquatic research laboratory with fish hatchery and toxicology lab, planetarium, natural science museum, 200-acre biology station, robotics laboratory, indoor rifle range, indoor ice arena.

**Freshman class profile.** 1,545 applied, 1,403 admitted, 483 enrolled.

| Mid 50% test scores | | | |
|---|---|---|---|
| ACT composite: | 18-24 | Return as sophomores: | 61% |
| Rank in top quarter: | 35% | Out-of-state: | 1% |
| Rank in top tenth: | 13% | Live on campus: | 63% |

**Basis for selection.** School achievement and test scores most important. Recommendations considered when applicant's academic record marginal. **Learning Disabled:** Students with learning disabilities referred to coordinator for Resource Center for Students with Disabilities.

**High school preparation.** 18 units recommended. Recommended units include English 4, mathematics 3, social studies 2, history 1, science 3 (laboratory 3) and foreign language 2. Specific academic units required vary by college program.

**2007-2008 Annual costs.** Tuition/fees: $7,386; $14,562 out-of-state. Residents of Ontario pay in-state tuition. Residents of Kansas, Minnesota, Missouri, Nebraska, and North Dakota eligible for Midwest Consortium agreement rate of $449 per credit. Room/board: $7,172. Books/supplies: $900. Personal expenses: $1,397.

**2006-2007 Financial aid. Need-based:** 439 full-time freshmen applied for aid; 428 were judged to have need; 428 of these received aid. Average need met was 70%. Average scholarship/grant was $4,298; average loan $3,111. 21% of total undergraduate aid awarded as scholarships/grants, 79% as loans/jobs. **Non-need-based:** Awarded to 1,102 full-time undergraduates, including 349 freshmen. Scholarships awarded for academics, alumni affiliation, athletics, state residency.

**Application procedures. Admission:** No deadline. $35 fee, may be waived for applicants with need. Application may be submitted online. Admission notification on a rolling basis beginning on or about 9/15. **Financial aid:** Priority date 2/21; no closing date. FAFSA required. Applicants notified on a rolling basis starting 11/1; must reply within 3 week(s) of notification.

**Academics. Special study options:** Combined bachelor's/graduate degree, cooperative education, cross-registration, distance learning, double major, dual enrollment of high school students, honors, independent study, internships, student-designed major, study abroad, teacher certification program, weekend college. **Credit/placement by examination:** AP, CLEP, IB, ACT, institutional tests. **Support services:** Learning center, tutoring, writing center.

**Majors. Biology:** General. **Business:** General, accounting, business admin, managerial economics. **Communications:** General. **Computer sciences:** General. **Conservation:** General, environmental science, fisheries, management/policy, wildlife. **Education:** Early childhood, elementary, multi-level teacher, secondary. **Engineering:** Computer, electrical, mechanical. **Engineering technology:** Electrical, industrial management, manufacturing. **English:** English lit. **Foreign languages:** French, Spanish. **Health:** Clinical lab science, nursing (RN), recreational therapy. **History:** General. **Interdisciplinary:** Math/computer science. **Legal studies:** Paralegal. **Liberal arts:** Arts/sciences. **Math:** General. **Parks/recreation:** Exercise sciences, facilities management. **Physical sciences:** Chemistry, geology. **Protective services:** Fire safety technology, law enforcement admin. **Psychology:** General. **Social sciences:** General, political science, sociology. **Visual/performing arts:** Studio arts. **Other:** Forensic chemistry.

**Most popular majors.** Business/marketing 19%, education 9%, engineering/engineering technologies 8%, health sciences 7%, security/protective services 21%, social sciences 8%.

**Computing on campus.** 450 workstations in library, computer center. Dormitories wired for high-speed internet access and linked to campus network. Commuter students can connect to campus network. Online course registration, online library, helpline, wireless network available.

**Student life. Freshman orientation:** Mandatory, $125 fee. Preregistration for classes offered. One-day program held during the summer; 4 dates available. **Housing:** Guaranteed on-campus for freshmen. Coed dorms, single-sex dorms, apartments, fraternity/sorority housing, substance-free housing available. $300 partly refundable deposit, deadline 6/15. **Activities:** Bands, choral groups, dance, drama, literary magazine, music ensembles, radio station, student government, student newspaper, symphony orchestra, Campus Crusade for Christ, Christian fellowship, Newman Center, Native American students' council, political science club, environmental awareness club, professional organizations.

**Athletics.** NCAA. **Intercollegiate:** Basketball, cross-country, ice hockey M, softball W, tennis, track and field, volleyball W. **Intramural:** Badminton, basketball, football (non-tackle) M, handball, ice hockey, racquetball, soccer, softball, tennis, track and field, volleyball, water polo, wrestling M. **Team name:** Lakers.

**Student services.** Adult student services, alcohol/substance abuse counseling, campus ministries, career counseling, services for economically disadvantaged, student employment services, financial aid counseling, health services, minority student services, on-campus daycare, personal counseling, placement for graduates, veterans' counselor. **Physically disabled:** Services for visually, speech, hearing impaired.

**Contact.** E-mail: admissions@lssu.edu
Phone: (906) 635-2231 Toll-free number: (888) 800-5778
Fax: (906) 635-6696
Susan Camp, Director of Admissions, Lake Superior State University, 650 West Easterday Avenue, Sault Ste. Marie, MI 49783-1699

---

## Lawrence Technological University
**Southfield, Michigan**   **CB member**
**www.ltu.edu**   **CB code: 1399**

- Private 4-year university
- Commuter campus in small city
- 2,361 degree-seeking undergraduates: 30% part-time, 22% women, 10% African American, 2% Asian American, 2% Hispanic American, 9% international
- 1,594 degree-seeking graduate students
- 60% of applicants admitted
- SAT or ACT (ACT writing optional), application essay required
- 45% graduate within 6 years

**General.** Founded in 1932. Regionally accredited. **Degrees:** 455 bachelor's, 19 associate awarded; master's, doctoral offered. **ROTC:** Army, Naval, Air Force. **Location:** 20 miles from Detroit. **Calendar:** Semester, extensive summer session. **Full-time faculty:** 114 total; 75% have terminal degrees, 11% minority, 23% women. **Part-time faculty:** 261 total; 41% have terminal degrees, 11% minority, 23% women. **Class size:** 74% < 20, 24% 20-39, less than 1% 40-49, less than 1% 50-99. **Special facilities:** Frank Lloyd Wright-designed residence for academic study.

**Freshman class profile.** 1,585 applied, 957 admitted, 337 enrolled.

| Mid 50% test scores | | | |
|---|---|---|---|
| SAT critical reading: | 450-600 | Rank in top tenth: | 16% |
| SAT math: | 540-630 | End year in good standing: | 74% |
| SAT writing: | 420-550 | Return as sophomores: | 67% |
| ACT composite: | 20-26 | Out-of-state: | 5% |
| GPA 3.50 or higher: | 36% | Live on campus: | 46% |
| GPA 3.0-3.49: | 31% | International: | 16% |
| GPA 2.0-2.99: | 32% | Fraternities: | 18% |
| Rank in top quarter: | 46% | Sororities: | 13% |

**Basis for selection.** Minimum 2.50 GPA required; Architecture/Transportation Design program requires 2.75. **Homeschooled:** Transcript of courses and grades, letter of recommendation (nonparent) required.

**High school preparation.** 12 units required. Required and recommended units include English 4, mathematics 3-4, social studies 3, history 2, science 2-4 (laboratory 2).

**2008-2009 Annual costs.** Tuition/fees: $21,979. Room/board: $8,071. Books/supplies: $1,235. Personal expenses: $1,945.

**2006-2007 Financial aid. Need-based:** 289 full-time freshmen applied for aid; 225 were judged to have need; 225 of these received aid. Average need met was 72%. Average scholarship/grant was $8,301; average loan $2,662. 49% of total undergraduate aid awarded as scholarships/grants, 51% as loans/jobs. **Non-need-based:** Awarded to 894 full-time undergraduates, including 222 freshmen. Scholarships awarded for academics, alumni affiliation, job skills, minority status, ROTC, state residency. **Additional information:** March 1 state deadline for Michigan Competitive Scholarship and Michigan Tuition Grant.

**Application procedures. Admission:** No deadline. $30 fee, may be waived for applicants with need. Application may be submitted online. Admission notification on a rolling basis. **Financial aid:** Priority date 4/1; no closing date. FAFSA required. Applicants notified on a rolling basis starting 3/1; must reply within 2 week(s) of notification.

**Academics. Special study options:** Cooperative education, cross-registration, distance learning, double major, dual enrollment of high school students, ESL, honors, independent study, internships, liberal arts/career combination, study abroad, weekend college. **Credit/placement by examination:** AP, CLEP, IB, institutional tests. **Support services:** Learning center, pre-admission summer program, reduced course load, remedial instruction, study skills assistance, tutoring, writing center.

**Majors. Architecture:** Architecture, environmental design, interior. **Biology:** Biochemistry, molecular. **Business:** Business admin, construction management. **Communications:** General. **Communications technology:** General. **Computer sciences:** Computer science, information technology. **Engineering:** Biomedical, civil, computer, electrical, mechanical. **Engineering technology:** General, industrial. **English:** English lit. **Interdisciplinary:** Math/computer science. **Liberal arts:** Humanities. **Math:** General. **Physical sciences:** Chemistry, physics. **Psychology:** General. **Visual/performing arts:** Design, illustration.

**Most popular majors.** Architecture 28%, computer/information sciences 9%, engineering/engineering technologies 53%.

**Computing on campus.** PC or laptop required. 100 workstations in dormitories, library, computer center, student center. Dormitories wired for high-speed internet access and linked to campus network. Commuter students can connect to campus network. Online course registration, online library, helpline, repair service, student web hosting, wireless network available.

**Student life. Freshman orientation:** Mandatory. Preregistration for classes offered. **Housing:** Special housing for disabled, apartments, substance-free housing available. $200 nonrefundable deposit, deadline 6/30. **Activities:** Literary magazine, music ensembles, student government, student newspaper, Campus Crusade for Christ, Alpha Kappa Alpha Sorority, Phi Beta Sigma Fraternity, National Society of Black Engineers, Young Republicans, Alpha Phi Omega.

**Athletics. Intramural:** Badminton, basketball, bowling, football (non-tackle) M, golf, racquetball, skiing, soccer, softball, table tennis, tennis, volleyball. **Team name:** Blue Devils.

**Student services.** Alcohol/substance abuse counseling, career counseling, services for economically disadvantaged, student employment services, financial aid counseling, minority student services, personal counseling, placement for graduates, veterans' counselor. **Physically disabled:** Services for visually, speech, hearing impaired.

**Contact.** E-mail: admissions@ltu.edu
Phone: (248) 204-3160 Toll-free number: (800) 225-5588
Fax: (248) 204-3188
Jane Rohrback, Director of Admissions, Lawrence Technological University, 21000 West Ten Mile Road, Southfield, MI 48075-1058

## Madonna University
**Livonia, Michigan**
**www.madonna.edu**                                    CB code: 1437

- Private 4-year university and liberal arts college affiliated with Roman Catholic Church
- Commuter campus in small city
- 2,779 degree-seeking undergraduates: 45% part-time, 76% women, 14% African American, 2% Asian American, 3% Hispanic American, 4% international
- 958 graduate students
- 77% of applicants admitted
- SAT or ACT (ACT writing optional), application essay required
- 42% graduate within 6 years

**General.** Founded in 1947. Regionally accredited. **Degrees:** 578 bachelor's, 22 associate awarded; master's offered. **Location:** 18 miles from Detroit, 20 miles from Ann Arbor. **Calendar:** Semester, limited summer session. **Full-time faculty:** 112 total; 97% have terminal degrees, 8% minority, 56% women. **Part-time faculty:** 222 total; 54% have terminal degrees, 14% minority, 51% women. **Class size:** 70% < 20, 27% 20-39, 1% 40-49, 1% 50-99.

**Freshman class profile.** 642 applied, 496 admitted, 189 enrolled.

| Mid 50% test scores | | End year in good standing: | 83% |
|---|---|---|---|
| ACT composite: | 21-25 | Return as sophomores: | 70% |
| GPA 3.50 or higher: | 51% | Out-of-state: | 1% |
| GPA 3.0-3.49: | 27% | Live on campus: | 19% |
| GPA 2.0-2.99: | 21% | International: | 3% |

**Basis for selection.** GPA and curriculum most important. Majors in sciences, allied health and nursing, and math require specific high school subjects. ACT test results important. Some majors require letters of recommendation. ACT preferred. Interview recommended.

**High school preparation.** College-preparatory program recommended. 19 units required. Required and recommended units include English 3-4, mathematics 2-4, social studies 3-4, history 4, science 3-4 (laboratory 1) and foreign language 2. 1 biology, 1 chemistry, 1 algebra required for nursing applicants; biology, 1 chemistry, 2 algebra required for medical and radiologic technology program applicants.

**2007-2008 Annual costs.** Tuition/fees: $11,680. Nursing students pay $437 per credit hour. Nonresident aliens pay $2,500 deposit. Room/board: $6,092. Books/supplies: $912. Personal expenses: $998.

**2006-2007 Financial aid. Need-based:** 123 full-time freshmen applied for aid; 89 were judged to have need; 89 of these received aid. Average need met was 60%. Average scholarship/grant was $5,283; average loan $1,980. 34% of total undergraduate aid awarded as scholarships/grants, 66% as loans/jobs. **Non-need-based:** Awarded to 403 full-time undergraduates,

including 81 freshmen. Scholarships awarded for academics, alumni affiliation, art, athletics, minority status, music/drama, religious affiliation, state residency.

**Application procedures. Admission:** Priority date 9/1; no deadline. $25 fee, may be waived for applicants with need. Application may be submitted online. Admission notification on a rolling basis. **Financial aid:** Priority date 2/21; no closing date. FAFSA required. Applicants notified on a rolling basis starting 4/1; must reply by 9/1 or within 2 week(s) of notification.

**Academics. Special study options:** Cooperative education, cross-registration, distance learning, double major, dual enrollment of high school students, ESL, independent study, internships, liberal arts/career combination, student-designed major, study abroad, teacher certification program, weekend college. **Credit/placement by examination:** AP, CLEP, IB, institutional tests. 30 credit hours maximum toward associate degree, 60 toward bachelor's. **Support services:** Learning center, pre-admission summer program, reduced course load, remedial instruction, study skills assistance, tutoring, writing center.

**Majors. Biology:** General, biochemistry. **Business:** Accounting, business admin, hospitality admin, human resources, international, management information systems, management science, marketing. **Communications:** General, journalism, public relations. **Computer sciences:** Computer science. **Conservation:** Environmental science. **Education:** Early childhood, elementary, learning disabled, mathematics, music, science, secondary, social studies. **Engineering technology:** Occupational safety. **English:** English lit, speech/rhetoric, technical writing. **Family/consumer sciences:** General, aging, child development, food/nutrition, merchandising. **Foreign languages:** American Sign Language, Spanish. **Health:** Clinical lab science, clinical lab technology, clinical nutrition, dietetics, health care admin, nursing (RN), predental, premedicine, prenursing. **History:** General. **Interdisciplinary:** Gerontology, natural sciences. **Legal studies:** Paralegal, prelaw. **Math:** General. **Philosophy/religion:** Philosophy, religion. **Physical sciences:** Chemistry, physics. **Protective services:** Criminal justice, firefighting, forensics. **Psychology:** General, industrial. **Public administration:** Social work. **Social sciences:** Sociology. **Theology:** Pastoral counseling, theology. **Visual/performing arts:** Graphic design, studio arts. **Other:** Applied science, Psychological trauma research, Television and video communications.

**Most popular majors.** Business/marketing 8%, education 8%, foreign language 6%, health sciences 24%, security/protective services 10%, social sciences 6%.

**Computing on campus.** 90 workstations in dormitories, library, computer center. Dormitories wired for high-speed internet access and linked to campus network. Commuter students can connect to campus network. Online course registration, online library, helpline, wireless network available.

**Student life. Freshman orientation:** Mandatory. Preregistration for classes offered. All day orientation in April, May, and June; evening orientation in January, May, July and August. **Policies:** Use of alcohol or drugs prohibited on campus; all buildings smoke-free; sexual assault, harassment policies in place. **Housing:** Single-sex dorms, substance-free housing available. $75 deposit, deadline 9/1. **Activities:** Campus ministries, choral groups, international student organizations, music ensembles, radio station, student government, student newspaper, TV station, social work student association, gerontology association, student-faculty academic clubs, athletic club, nursing student association, business professional association, student teacher association.

**Athletics.** NAIA. **Intercollegiate:** Baseball M, basketball, cross-country, golf, soccer, softball W, volleyball W. **Team name:** Crusaders.

**Student services.** Adult student services, alcohol/substance abuse counseling, campus ministries, career counseling, services for economically disadvantaged, student employment services, financial aid counseling, health services, minority student services, personal counseling, placement for graduates, women's services. **Physically disabled:** Services for visually, speech, hearing impaired.

**Contact.** E-mail: muinfo@madonna.edu
Phone: (734) 432-5339 Fax: (734) 432-5424
Michael Quattro, Director of Undergraduate Admission, Madonna University, 36600 Schoolcraft Road, Livonia, MI 48150-1176

## Marygrove College
**Detroit, Michigan**
**www.marygrove.edu**                                   CB code: 1452

- Private 4-year liberal arts college affiliated with Roman Catholic Church
- Commuter campus in very large city
- 700 degree-seeking undergraduates

- 2,175 graduate students
- ACT (writing recommended), application essay required

**General.** Founded in 1905. Regionally accredited. **Degrees:** 112 bachelor's, 4 associate awarded; master's offered. **Location:** 6 miles from downtown. **Calendar:** Semester, limited summer session. **Full-time faculty:** 56 total; 64% have terminal degrees, 41% minority, 59% women. **Part-time faculty:** 8 total; 25% have terminal degrees, 25% minority, 88% women. **Class size:** 84% < 20, 15% 20-39, less than 1% 40-49, less than 1% 50-99.

**Freshman class profile.**

| Mid 50% test scores | | Out-of-state: | 1% |
|---|---|---|---|
| ACT composite: | 14-19 | Live on campus: | 43% |

**Basis for selection.** School achievement record and test scores most important. Audition required of music, theater, dance majors. Portfolio required of art majors. Interview required of older applicants and academically weak applicants.

**High school preparation.** 16 units recommended. Recommended units include English 4, mathematics 2, social studies 2, science 2 and foreign language 2. One computer science recommended.

**2007-2008 Annual costs.** Tuition/fees: $14,690. Room/board: $6,600. Books/supplies: $1,040. Personal expenses: $2,200.

**Financial aid.** All financial aid based on need.

**Application procedures. Admission:** Priority date 12/1; deadline 3/15 (postmark date). $25 fee, may be waived for applicants with need. Application may be submitted online. Admission notification on a rolling basis. Must reply by 5/1. **Financial aid:** Priority date 3/15; no closing date. FAFSA, institutional form required. Applicants notified on a rolling basis starting 5/15; must reply within 2 week(s) of notification.

**Academics. Special study options:** Cooperative education, cross-registration, distance learning, double major, honors, independent study, internships, student-designed major, study abroad, teacher certification program. **Credit/placement by examination:** AP, CLEP, ACT, institutional tests. 16 credit hours maximum toward associate degree, 32 toward bachelor's. Credit awarded for score of 3 or higher on AP exam. Credit hours awarded determined by faculty. **Support services:** Learning center, preadmission summer program, reduced course load, remedial instruction, study skills assistance, tutoring, writing center.

**Majors. Biology:** General. **Business:** General, accounting, business admin, international. **Computer sciences:** General. **Conservation:** Environmental science. **Education:** General, early childhood, special. **English:** English lit. **Health:** Art therapy. **History:** General. **Interdisciplinary:** Natural sciences. **Math:** General. **Philosophy/religion:** Religion. **Physical sciences:** Chemistry. **Psychology:** General. **Public administration:** Social work. **Social sciences:** General, political science. **Visual/performing arts:** Art, dance, music performance, music theory/composition, studio arts.

**Computing on campus.** 50 workstations in library, computer center. Dormitories linked to campus network. Online course registration, helpline available.

**Student life. Freshman orientation:** Mandatory. Preregistration for classes offered. Two-day weekday program; students spend night in dorms. **Housing:** Coed dorms available. $250 deposit, deadline 8/1. **Activities:** Choral groups, dance, music ensembles, student government, business club, black social worker club, ensemble gospel choir, art club.

**Athletics.** USCAA. **Intercollegiate:** Basketball. **Team name:** Mustangs.

**Student services.** Campus ministries, career counseling, student employment services, financial aid counseling, health services, on-campus daycare, personal counseling, placement for graduates.

**Contact.** E-mail: info@marygrove.edu
Phone: (313) 927-1240 Toll-free number: (866) 313-1927
Fax: (313) 927-1345
John Ambrose, Director of Admissions, Marygrove College, 8425 West McNichols Road, Detroit, MI 48221

## Michigan Jewish Institute
**Oak Park, Michigan**
www.mji.edu
**CB code: 1505**

- Private 4-year business and liberal arts college affiliated with Jewish faith
- Commuter campus in very large city
- 75 degree-seeking undergraduates

**General.** Accredited by ACICS. **Degrees:** 3 bachelor's awarded. **Calendar:** Semester, limited summer session. **Full-time faculty:** 3 total. **Part-time faculty:** 15 total. **Special facilities:** Synagogue available on West Bloomfield campus.

**Basis for selection.** 2.0 GPA required; applicants with less than 2.0 GPA or with GED may be accepted under provisional status. **Homeschooled:** Statement describing homeschool structure and mission, transcript of courses and grades, interview, letter of recommendation (nonparent) required.

**High school preparation.** Recommended units include English 3, mathematics 3, social studies 1, history 2, science 3 (laboratory 1), foreign language 2 and computer science 1.

**2007-2008 Annual costs.** Tuition/fees: $10,800. Books/supplies: $1,215. Personal expenses: $1,060.

**Financial aid. Non-need-based:** Scholarships awarded for academics.

**Application procedures. Admission:** No deadline. $50 fee. Application may be submitted online. Admission notification on a rolling basis. HIgh school students may enroll in dual studies program to earn high school and college credits for the same courses. Students may also be admitted into the college for up to 6 months before high school graduation. Should an admitted student not complete high school within the 6 months, they will not be able to continue until proof of high school graduation or GED is provided.

**Academics. Special study options:** Accelerated study, cooperative education, distance learning, double major, dual enrollment of high school students, ESL, independent study, internships, liberal arts/career combination, study abroad, weekend college. **Credit/placement by examination:** AP, CLEP, IB, institutional tests. **Support services:** Learning center, reduced course load, remedial instruction, study skills assistance, tutoring.

**Majors. Business:** Business admin. **Computer sciences:** General. **Philosophy/religion:** Judaic. **Other:** Judaic education, Judaic organizational leadership.

**Most popular majors.** Area/ethnic studies 10%, business/marketing 30%, computer/information sciences 20%, education 10%, philosophy/religious studies 20%, theological studies 10%.

**Computing on campus.** PC or laptop required. 16 workstations in library, computer center, student center. Online library, helpline, wireless network available.

**Student life. Freshman orientation:** Available. Preregistration for classes offered. Scheduled onsite sessions and online tutorials available.

**Student services.** Adult student services, alcohol/substance abuse counseling, campus ministries, career counseling, student employment services, financial aid counseling, personal counseling.

**Contact.** E-mail: info@mji.edu
Phone: (248) 414-6900 ext. 102 Fax: (248) 414-6907
Fran Herman, Registrar, Michigan Jewish Institute, 25401 Coolidge Highway, Oak Park, MI 48237

## Michigan State University
**East Lansing, Michigan**
**CB member**
www.msu.edu
**CB code: 1465**

- Public 4-year university
- Residential campus in small city
- 35,772 degree-seeking undergraduates: 8% part-time, 53% women, 8% African American, 5% Asian American, 3% Hispanic American, 1% Native American, 4% international
- 8,596 degree-seeking graduate students
- 74% of applicants admitted
- SAT or ACT with writing, application essay required
- 74% graduate within 6 years; 20% enter graduate study

**General.** Founded in 1855. Regionally accredited. **Degrees:** 7,930 bachelor's awarded; master's, doctoral, first professional offered. **ROTC:** Army, Air Force. **Location:** 3 miles from Lansing, 80 miles from Detroit. **Calendar:** Semester, extensive summer session. **Full-time faculty:** 2,576 total; 93% have terminal degrees, 21% minority, 36% women. **Part-time faculty:** 378 total; 57% have terminal degrees, 13% minority, 54% women. **Class size:** 25% < 20, 46% 20-39, 7% 40-49, 10% 50-99, 12% >100. **Special**

**facilities:** Planetarium, botanical garden, center for environmental toxicology, superconducting cyclotron laboratory, pesticide research center, experimental farms, 2 museums, center for performing arts, 2 golf courses, agricultural and livestock pavilion, children's garden.

**Freshman class profile.** 24,436 applied, 18,040 admitted, 7,541 enrolled.

| Mid 50% test scores | | | |
|---|---|---|---|
| SAT critical reading: | 480-620 | GPA 2.0-2.99: | 6% |
| SAT math: | 520-650 | Rank in top quarter: | 69% |
| SAT writing: | 470-600 | Rank in top tenth: | 29% |
| ACT composite: | 23-27 | Return as sophomores: | 91% |
| GPA 3.50 or higher: | 65% | Out-of-state: | 11% |
| GPA 3.0-3.49: | 29% | Live on campus: | 91% |
| | | International: | 5% |

**Basis for selection.** Freshman admission based upon academic performance in high school, strength and quality of curriculum, recent trends in academic performance, class rank, test scores, leadership, talents, conduct and diversity of experience. Recommended that test scores be received no later than April. Audition required of music majors. **Homeschooled:** Submit grades, even if from parent. List or provide information on curriculum and be prepared to answer questions. Test scores have stronger emphasis; transcript required.

**High school preparation.** 14 units required. Required and recommended units include English 4, mathematics 3, social studies 2, history 1-2, science 2 (laboratory 2) and foreign language 2.

**2007-2008 Annual costs.** Tuition/fees: $9,640; $23,500 out-of-state. Room/board: $6,676. Books/supplies: $906. Personal expenses: $1,436.

**2007-2008 Financial aid.** All financial aid based on need. 5,151 full-time freshmen applied for aid; 3,296 were judged to have need; 3,282 of these received aid. Average need met was 79%. Average scholarship/grant was $7,339; average loan $3,385. 48% of total undergraduate aid awarded as scholarships/grants, 52% as loans/jobs.

**Application procedures. Admission:** No deadline. $35 fee, may be waived for applicants with need. Application may be submitted online. Admission notification on a rolling basis. Must reply by May 1 or within 2 week(s) if notified thereafter. Although Common Application accepted, use of internal application preferred. Early Action by invitation only. Test scores should be submitted by April. **Financial aid:** Priority date 3/15; no closing date. FAFSA required. Applicants notified on a rolling basis starting 3/15; must reply within 4 week(s) of notification.

**Academics. Special study options:** Accelerated study, cooperative education, distance learning, double major, dual enrollment of high school students, ESL, exchange student, honors, independent study, internships, liberal arts/career combination, student-designed major, study abroad, teacher certification program, weekend college. **Credit/placement by examination:** AP, CLEP, IB, SAT, ACT, institutional tests. 60 credit hours maximum toward bachelor's degree. **Support services:** Learning center, pre-admission summer program, reduced course load, remedial instruction, study skills assistance, tutoring, writing center.

**Honors college/program.** Selection criteria include test scores and class rank. Number admitted varies.

**Majors. Agriculture:** Animal sciences, business, communications, economics, food science, horticultural science, soil science. **Architecture:** Interior, landscape, urban/community planning. **Area/ethnic studies:** African-American, American, Asian, Central/Eastern European, Native American, Russian/Slavic, women's. **Biology:** General, biochemistry, Biochemistry/biophysics and molecular biology, botany, entomology, environmental, microbiology, molecular, molecular genetics, physiology, plant pathology, zoology. **Business:** Accounting, apparel, business admin, construction management, fashion, finance, hospitality admin, human resources, information resources management, logistics, management information systems, marketing, operations. **Communications:** General, advertising, journalism, public relations, radio/tv. **Computer sciences:** General, information systems. **Conservation:** Economics, environmental science, environmental studies, fisheries, forestry, wildlife. **Education:** General, art, biology, chemistry, computer, Deaf/hearing impaired, early childhood, elementary, family/consumer sciences, French, geography, German, health, history, kindergarten/preschool, learning disabled, mathematics, middle, music, physical, physics, reading, science, secondary, social science, social studies, Spanish, special. **Engineering:** General, agricultural, biomedical, chemical, civil, computer, electrical, materials, materials science, mechanical. **English:** English lit, technical writing. **Family/consumer sciences:** General, apparel marketing, child development, clothing/textiles, family/community services, textile manufacture, textile science. **Foreign languages:** Chinese, classics, East Asian, French, German, Japanese, linguistics, Russian, Spanish. **Health:** Audiology/speech pathology, clinical lab science, communication disorders, community health services, dietetics, marriage/family therapy, music therapy, nurse practitioner, nursing (RN), premedicine, veterinary technology/assistant. **History:**

General. **Interdisciplinary:** Biological/physical sciences, global studies, nutrition sciences, science/society. **Legal studies:** Prelaw. **Liberal arts:** Humanities. **Math:** General, computational, statistics. **Parks/recreation:** General, exercise sciences, facilities management. **Philosophy/religion:** Philosophy, religion. **Physical sciences:** General, astrophysics, chemical physics, chemistry, geology, geophysics, physics. **Protective services:** Criminal justice, law enforcement admin. **Psychology:** General. **Public administration:** General, policy analysis, social work. **Social sciences:** General, anthropology, economics, geography, international relations, political science, sociology. **Visual/performing arts:** Acting, art, art history/conservation, design, dramatic, fashion design, interior design, jazz, music pedagogy, music performance, music theory/composition, theater arts management. **Other:** Packaging.

**Most popular majors.** Biology 9%, business/marketing 19%, communications/journalism 12%, engineering/engineering technologies 6%, health sciences 6%, social sciences 10%.

**Computing on campus.** PC or laptop required. 2,000 workstations in dormitories, library, computer center, student center. Dormitories wired for high-speed internet access and linked to campus network. Commuter students can connect to campus network. Online course registration, helpline, repair service, student web hosting, wireless network available.

**Student life. Freshman orientation:** Mandatory, $175 fee. Preregistration for classes offered. Freshmen attend day-and-a-half session in summer; includes placement tests. **Housing:** Guaranteed on-campus for freshmen. Coed dorms, single-sex dorms, special housing for disabled, apartments, cooperative housing, fraternity/sorority housing, substance-free housing available. $250 fully refundable deposit, deadline 5/1. **Activities:** Bands, campus ministries, choral groups, dance, drama, film society, international student organizations, music ensembles, Model UN, musical theater, opera, radio station, student government, student newspaper, symphony orchestra, TV station, over 500 academic, athletic, social, religious, and political organizations.

**Athletics.** NCAA. **Intercollegiate:** Baseball M, basketball, cheerleading, cross-country, diving, field hockey W, football (tackle) M, golf, gymnastics W, ice hockey M, rowing (crew) W, soccer, softball W, swimming, tennis, track and field, volleyball W, wrestling M. **Intramural:** Archery, baseball M, basketball, cross-country, fencing, football (non-tackle) M, golf, gymnastics, ice hockey, lacrosse M, racquetball, rowing (crew) M, rugby, sailing, skiing, soccer, softball, squash, swimming, tennis, track and field, volleyball, water polo, wrestling M. **Team name:** Spartans.

**Student services.** Adult student services, alcohol/substance abuse counseling, career counseling, services for economically disadvantaged, student employment services, financial aid counseling, health services, legal services, minority student services, on-campus daycare, personal counseling, placement for graduates, veterans' counselor, women's services. **Physically disabled:** Services for visually, speech, hearing impaired. **Learning disabled:** Comprehensive services available.

**Contact.** E-mail: admis@msu.edu
Phone: (517) 355-8332 Fax: (517) 353-1647
James Cotter, Director of Admissions, Michigan State University, 250 Administration Building, East Lansing, MI 48824

## Michigan Technological University
Houghton, Michigan   · CB member
www.mtu.edu   CB code: 1464

- Public 4-year university
- Residential campus in small town
- 5,722 degree-seeking undergraduates: 8% part-time, 23% women, 2% African American, 1% Asian American, 1% Hispanic American, 1% Native American, 5% international
- 870 degree-seeking graduate students
- 84% of applicants admitted
- SAT or ACT (ACT writing optional) required
- 64% graduate within 6 years

**General.** Founded in 1885. Regionally accredited. **Degrees:** 966 bachelor's, 26 associate awarded; master's, doctoral offered. **ROTC:** Army, Air Force. **Location:** 210 miles from Green Bay, Wisconsin, 325 miles from Milwaukee. **Calendar:** Semester, limited summer session. **Full-time faculty:** 358 total; 85% have terminal degrees, 10% minority, 27% women. **Part-time faculty:** 64 total; 50% have terminal degrees, 6% minority, 48% women. **Class size:** 43% < 20, 36% 20-39, 8% 40-49, 10% 50-99, 3% >100. **Special facilities:** Mineral museum, performing arts center, forestry center and research forest, cosmic ray observatory, X-ray fluorescence spectrometer, process simulation and control center, remote sensing institute, computer-aided engineering lab, microfabrication lab, subsurface visualization lab.

**Freshman class profile.** 4,148 applied, 3,485 admitted, 1,223 enrolled.

| Mid 50% test scores | | | |
|---|---|---|---|
| SAT critical reading: | 530-650 | **GPA 2.0-2.99:** | 13% |
| SAT math: | 590-690 | **Rank in top quarter:** | 61% |
| SAT writing: | 500-620 | **Rank in top tenth:** | 30% |
| ACT composite: | 23-28 | **Return as sophomores:** | 83% |
| GPA 3.50 or higher: | 60% | **Out-of-state:** | 21% |
| GPA 3.0-3.49: | 27% | **Live on campus:** | 89% |
| | | **International:** | 5% |

**Basis for selection.** School record, class rank, test scores very important. Rank in top quarter of class preferred for engineering programs. Rank in top third to top half of class preferred for other bachelor's programs. Rank in top half of class preferred for associate degree programs. SAT or ACT scores must be received 30 days prior to start of term. Essay recommended. Interview recommended for borderline applicants. **Home-schooled:** ACT required.

**High school preparation.** 8 units required. Required and recommended units include English 3-4, mathematics 3-4, social studies 3, history 1, science 2-3, foreign language 2, computer science 1 and visual/performing arts 1. One computer literacy and 2 fine/performing arts recommended. Course requirements vary by program.

**2007-2008 Annual costs.** Tuition/fees: $9,829; $21,589 out-of-state. Room/board: $7,315. Books/supplies: $1,000. Personal expenses: $1,013.

**2007-2008 Financial aid. Need-based:** 986 full-time freshmen applied for aid; 714 were judged to have need; 714 of these received aid. Average need met was 84%. Average scholarship/grant was $7,523; average loan $4,146. 45% of total undergraduate aid awarded as scholarships/grants, 55% as loans/jobs. **Non-need-based:** Awarded to 3,359 full-time undergraduates, including 1,025 freshmen. Scholarships awarded for academics, alumni affiliation, art, athletics, job skills, leadership, ROTC, state residency.

**Application procedures. Admission:** Priority date 1/15; no deadline. No application fee. Application may be submitted online. Notification within 3 weeks of acceptance. Must reply by May 1 or within 2 week(s) if notified thereafter. **Financial aid:** Priority date 2/16; no closing date. FAFSA required. Applicants notified on a rolling basis starting 3/1; must reply within 4 week(s) of notification.

**Academics. Special study options:** Cooperative education, distance learning, double major, dual enrollment of high school students, ESL, exchange student, honors, independent study, internships, semester at sea, study abroad, teacher certification program. Dual enrollment programs with Northwestern Michigan College, Delta College, Oakland Community College, Adrian College, Albion College, Augsburg College, College of St. Scholastica, Mount Senario College, Lansing Community College, Olivet College, Northland College, University of Wisconsin-Superior. **Credit/placement by examination:** AP, CLEP, IB, SAT, ACT, institutional tests. **Support services:** Learning center, reduced course load, remedial instruction, study skills assistance, tutoring, writing center.

**Majors. Biology:** General, Biochemistry/biophysics and molecular biology, bioinformatics. **Business:** Business admin, construction management. **Communications:** General. **Communications technology:** Recording arts. **Computer sciences:** General, networking, system admin. **Conservation:** Environmental science, forestry, wildlife. **Engineering:** General, biomedical, chemical, civil, computer, electrical, environmental, geological, materials, mechanical, software, surveying. **Engineering technology:** Electrical, industrial, mechanical. **Health:** Clinical lab science. **History:** General. **Liberal arts:** Arts/sciences. **Math:** General. **Parks/recreation:** Exercise sciences. **Physical sciences:** Chemistry, geology, geophysics, physics. **Psychology:** General. **Social sciences:** General, anthropology, economics. **Visual/performing arts:** Theater design.

**Most popular majors.** Biology 6%, business/marketing 9%, computer/information sciences 6%, engineering/engineering technologies 65%.

**Computing on campus.** 1,300 workstations in dormitories, library, computer center, student center. Dormitories wired for high-speed internet access and linked to campus network. Commuter students can connect to campus network. Online course registration, online library, helpline, student web hosting, wireless network available.

**Student life. Freshman orientation:** Mandatory, $150 fee. Preregistration for classes offered. Week-long program before start of classes. **Policies:** Students must abide by rights and responsibilities policy on alcohol and illegal drugs; sexual assault policy; academic integrity policy. **Housing:** Guaranteed on-campus for freshmen. Coed dorms, special housing for disabled, apartments, fraternity/sorority housing, substance-free housing available. Alcohol-free, community governed, research scholar, honors, ROTC housing available. Computer science, first-year experience, healthy living, forest resources/environmental science learning communities available. **Activities:** Bands, campus ministries, choral groups, dance, drama, film society, international student organizations, literary magazine, music ensembles,

musical theater, opera, radio station, student government, student newspaper, symphony orchestra, numerous organizations.

**Athletics.** NCAA. **Intercollegiate:** Basketball, cross-country, football (tackle) M, ice hockey M, skiing, tennis, track and field, volleyball W. **Intramural:** Badminton, basketball, bowling, cross-country, football (non-tackle), golf, ice hockey, racquetball, rifle, soccer, softball, swimming, table tennis, tennis, volleyball, water polo, wrestling. **Team name:** Huskies.

**Student services.** Alcohol/substance abuse counseling, campus ministries, career counseling, student employment services, financial aid counseling, health services, minority student services, on-campus daycare, personal counseling, placement for graduates, veterans' counselor, women's services. **Physically disabled:** Services for visually, speech, hearing impaired.

**Contact.** E-mail: mtu4u@mtu.edu
Phone: (906) 487-2335 Toll-free number: (888) 688-1885
Fax: (906) 487-2125
Allison Carter, Director of Admissions, Michigan Technological University, 1400 Townsend Drive, Houghton, MI 49931-1295

## Michigan Theological Seminary
**Plymouth, Michigan**
**www.mts.edu**

- Private 4-year seminary college
- Small town
- 20 full-time, degree-seeking undergraduates
- 165 graduate students

**General. Degrees:** 3 bachelor's awarded; master's, first professional offered. **Calendar:** Semester. **Full-time faculty:** 5 total; 40% have terminal degrees, 60% minority.

**Basis for selection.** Transcripts, writing sample, and statement of faith most important.

**2008-2009 Annual costs.** Tuition/fees: $11,660.

**Application procedures. Admission:** No deadline. No application fee. Admission notification on a rolling basis.

**Academics. Special study options:** Independent study, internships, study abroad. **Credit/placement by examination:** CLEP.

**Majors. Theology:** Religious ed.

**Contact.** Phone: (734) 207-9581
Bethany Reedy, Registrar, Michigan Theological Seminary, 41550 East Ann Arbor Trail, Plymouth, MI 48170-1622

## Northern Michigan University
**Marquette, Michigan**      **CB member**
**www.nmu.edu**      **CB code: 1560**

- Public 4-year university
- Residential campus in large town
- 8,287 degree-seeking undergraduates: 7% part-time, 53% women, 1% African American, 1% Asian American, 1% Hispanic American, 2% Native American, 1% international
- 456 degree-seeking graduate students
- 78% of applicants admitted
- SAT or ACT (ACT writing optional) required
- 48% graduate within 6 years

**General.** Founded in 1899. Regionally accredited. Every full-time student receives a ThinkPad or MacBook notebook computer as part of tuition and fees, which are replaced every 2 years. **Degrees:** 1,221 bachelor's, 120 associate awarded; master's offered. **ROTC:** Army. **Location:** 300 miles from Milwaukee, 380 miles from Chicago. **Calendar:** Semester, limited summer session. **Full-time faculty:** 313 total; 78% have terminal degrees, 6% minority, 39% women. **Part-time faculty:** 130 total; 7% minority, 55% women. **Class size:** 29% < 20, 55% 20-39, 4% 40-49, 10% 50-99, 2% >100. **Special facilities:** Education center, center for teaching and learning science and math, art and design studios, observatory with 12.5 F:6 Newtonian telescope, 120-acre nature preserve.

**Freshman class profile.** 5,302 applied, 4,118 admitted, 1,394 enrolled.

| Mid 50% test scores | | | | |
|---|---|---|---|---|
| ACT composite: | 20-25 | GPA 2.0-2.99: | 40% | |
| GPA 3.50 or higher: | 29% | Return as sophomores: | 70% | |
| GPA 3.0-3.49: | 27% | Out-of-state: | 30% | |
| | | Live on campus: | 77% | |

**Basis for selection.** High school record, test scores most important. Recommendations considered. Students who do not fulfill normal requirements for admission may be conditionally admitted for freshman probation and college transition programs. Some certificate, diploma, and associate degree programs do not require test scores. Audition recommended for music, drama majors. Portfolio recommended for art majors. Interview, extracurricular activities, talent/ability considered for borderline students. **Homeschooled:** Transcript of courses and grades required.

**High school preparation.** 12 units required; 19 recommended. Required and recommended units include English 4, mathematics 4, social studies 4, science 4 and foreign language 3.

**2007-2008 Annual costs.** Tuition/fees: $6,709; $10,645 out-of-state. Excludes one-time $200 athletic fee for first time freshmen. All full-time students provided with laptop computer as part of tuition and fees. Room/board: $7,220. Books/supplies: $748. Personal expenses: $1,038.

**2006-2007 Financial aid. Need-based:** 1,605 full-time freshmen applied for aid; 1,074 were judged to have need; 1,044 of these received aid. Average need met was 67%. Average scholarship/grant was $3,665; average loan $3,025. 39% of total undergraduate aid awarded as scholarships/grants, 61% as loans/jobs. **Non-need-based:** Awarded to 2,156 full-time undergraduates, including 735 freshmen. Scholarships awarded for academics, alumni affiliation, art, athletics, leadership, minority status, music/drama, religious affiliation, ROTC, state residency. **Additional information:** Audition or portfolio required for music, drama, and art scholarship applicants. Alumni Dependent Tuition Program gives resident tuition rates to nonresident dependents of NMU alumni who received master's, baccalaureate, or associate degree; renewable.

**Application procedures. Admission:** No deadline. $30 fee, may be waived for applicants with need. Application may be submitted online. Admission notification on a rolling basis beginning on or about 9/15. **Financial aid:** Priority date 3/1; no closing date. FAFSA required. Applicants notified on a rolling basis starting 4/1; must reply within 2 week(s) of notification.

**Academics. Special study options:** Accelerated study, combined bachelor's/graduate degree, distance learning, double major, dual enrollment of high school students, ESL, exchange student, honors, independent study, internships, liberal arts/career combination, student-designed major, study abroad, teacher certification program, Washington semester, weekend college. **Credit/placement by examination:** AP, CLEP, IB, ACT, institutional tests. 11 credit hours maximum toward associate degree, 32 toward bachelor's. 8 credits may be counted toward certificate. **Support services:** Learning center, preadmission summer program, reduced course load, remedial instruction, study skills assistance, tutoring, writing center.

**Honors college/program.** Limited to 50 students; requires 3.5 GPA and 27 ACT or equivalent.

**Majors. Architecture:** Urban/community planning. **Biology:** General, biochemistry, botany, ecology, microbiology, physiology, zoology. **Business:** Accounting, accounting/finance, business admin, entrepreneurial studies, finance, financial planning, hospitality admin, management information systems, marketing, small business admin. **Communications:** General, digital media, media studies, public relations. **Computer sciences:** General, networking. **Conservation:** General, environmental science. **Education:** Art, biology, chemistry, elementary, English, French, geography, German, health, history, mathematics, mentally handicapped, music, physical, physics, science, secondary, social studies, Spanish, technology/industrial arts. **Engineering technology:** Construction, electrical, industrial, manufacturing, mechanical. **English:** Creative writing, English lit, technical writing. **Family/consumer sciences:** Child development, family studies. **Foreign languages:** French, Spanish. **Health:** Athletic training, clinical lab science, community health services, cytogenetics, cytotechnology, histologic technology, nursing (RN), predental, premedicine, prepharmacy, preveterinary, speech pathology. **History:** General. **Interdisciplinary:** Behavioral sciences. **Legal studies:** Prelaw. **Liberal arts:** Arts/sciences. **Math:** General. **Parks/recreation:** General, health/fitness, sports admin. **Philosophy/religion:** Philosophy. **Physical sciences:** Chemistry, geology, hydrology, physics. **Protective services:** Criminal justice, security services. **Psychology:** General, developmental, experimental. **Public administration:** General, social work. **Social sciences:** General, cartography, economics, geography, international relations, political science, sociology. **Visual/performing arts:** Art, ceramics, cinematography, design, digital art, dramatic, drawing, graphic design, illustration, industrial design, metal/jewelry, painting, photography, printmaking, sculpture. **Other:** Earth science teacher education, Entertainment/sports promotion, Forensic biochemistry, Human Centered Design, Pre-architecture, Pre-engineering, Pre-optometry.

**Most popular majors.** Biology 6%, business/marketing 13%, education 14%, health sciences 10%, social sciences 8%, visual/performing arts 8%.

**Computing on campus.** 9,900 workstations in library. Dormitories wired for high-speed internet access and linked to campus network. Commuter students can connect to campus network. Online course registration, online library, helpline, repair service, student web hosting, wireless network available.

**Student life. Freshman orientation:** Mandatory, $75 fee. Preregistration for classes offered. Three-day program held prior to start of classes. **Housing:** Guaranteed on-campus for all undergraduates. Coed dorms, special housing for disabled, apartments, substance-free housing available. $125 partly refundable deposit. **Activities:** Bands, campus ministries, choral groups, dance, drama, film society, international student organizations, literary magazine, music ensembles, musical theater, opera, radio station, student government, student newspaper, symphony orchestra, TV station, Campus Crusade for Christ, College Republicans, Circle K, Gonzo Media, Hong Meng: Asian culture, international volunteering student organization.

**Athletics.** NCAA. **Intercollegiate:** Basketball, cheerleading, cross-country W, diving W, football (tackle) M, golf M, ice hockey M, skiing, soccer W, swimming W, track and field W, volleyball W. **Intramural:** Basketball, field hockey W, football (non-tackle), ice hockey, lacrosse M, racquetball, soccer, softball, table tennis, volleyball. **Team name:** Wildcats.

**Student services.** Adult student services, campus ministries, career counseling, student employment services, financial aid counseling, health services, minority student services, personal counseling, placement for graduates, veterans' counselor. **Physically disabled:** Services for visually, hearing impaired.

**Contact.** E-mail: admiss@nmu.edu
Phone: (906) 227-2650 Toll-free number: (800) 682-9797
Fax: (906) 227-1747
Gerri Daniels, Director of Admissions, Northern Michigan University, 1401 Presque Isle Avenue, Marquette, MI 49855

## Northwood University: Michigan
**Midland, Michigan**
**www.northwood.edu**                                    **CB code: 1568**

- Private 4-year university and business college
- Residential campus in large town
- 1,979 degree-seeking undergraduates: 4% part-time, 35% women, 12% African American, 1% Asian American, 2% Hispanic American, 8% international
- 365 degree-seeking graduate students
- 80% of applicants admitted
- SAT or ACT (ACT writing optional), application essay required
- 51% graduate within 6 years

**General.** Founded in 1959. Regionally accredited. Specialty university offering only business degrees in professional management; 3 residential campuses in Michigan, Florida, and Texas; 48 program centers; library center in Maine. **Degrees:** 434 bachelor's, 279 associate awarded; master's offered. **Location:** 125 miles from Detroit, 25 miles from Saginaw. **Calendar:** Quarter, extensive summer session. **Full-time faculty:** 55 total; 26% have terminal degrees, 11% minority, 34% women. **Part-time faculty:** 39 total. **Class size:** 40% < 20, 49% 20-39, 9% 40-49, 1% 50-99. **Special facilities:** Creativity center, university-operated hotel.

**Freshman class profile.** 1,626 applied, 1,294 admitted, 457 enrolled.

| Mid 50% test scores | | | |
|---|---|---|---|
| SAT critical reading: | 410-540 | Rank in top tenth: | 9% |
| SAT math: | 430-550 | End year in good standing: | 72% |
| SAT writing: | 410-520 | Return as sophomores: | 74% |
| ACT composite: | 19-23 | Out-of-state: | 13% |
| GPA 3.50 or higher: | 24% | Live on campus: | 87% |
| GPA 3.0-3.49: | 33% | International: | 1% |
| GPA 2.0-2.99: | 40% | Fraternities: | 6% |
| Rank in top quarter: | 27% | Sororities: | 9% |

**Basis for selection.** Minimum 2.0 GPA and strong interest in business or related field important. Test scores considered. Students with lower GPA possibly admitted on probation. Interview recommended. **Homeschooled:** Transcript of courses and grades required.

**High school preparation.** 17 units recommended. Recommended units include English 4, mathematics 3, social studies 3, science 3 (laboratory 2), foreign language 1 and computer science 1.

**2007-2008 Annual costs.** Tuition/fees: $16,455. Room/board: $7,194. Books/supplies: $1,404. Personal expenses: $1,203.

**2007-2008 Financial aid. Need-based:** 367 full-time freshmen applied for aid; 320 were judged to have need; 319 of these received aid. Average need met was 54%. Average scholarship/grant was $6,272; average loan $3,194. 58% of total undergraduate aid awarded as scholarships/grants, 42% as loans/jobs. **Non-need-based:** Awarded to 923 full-time undergraduates, including 230 freshmen. Scholarships awarded for academics, alumni affiliation, athletics, leadership, minority status, ROTC.

**Application procedures. Admission:** No deadline. $25 fee, may be waived for applicants with need. Application may be submitted online. Admission notification on a rolling basis beginning on or about 9/1. **Financial aid:** No deadline. FAFSA required. Applicants notified on a rolling basis starting 3/1.

**Academics. Special study options:** Accelerated study, combined bachelor's/graduate degree, double major, dual enrollment of high school students, ESL, external degree, honors, independent study, internships, study abroad. **Credit/placement by examination:** AP, CLEP, IB, SAT, ACT, institutional tests. 12 credit hours maximum toward associate degree, 12 toward bachelor's. **Support services:** Learning center, reduced course load, remedial instruction, study skills assistance, tutoring, writing center.

**Majors. Business:** Accounting, banking/financial services, business admin, entrepreneurial studies, fashion, hotel/motel admin, international, management information systems, managerial economics, marketing, vehicle parts marketing. **Communications:** Advertising. **Computer sciences:** General. **Parks/recreation:** Sports admin.

**Most popular majors.** Business/marketing 92%, parks/recreation 6%.

**Computing on campus.** 215 workstations in dormitories, library, computer center. Dormitories wired for high-speed internet access and linked to campus network. Commuter students can connect to campus network. Online course registration, online library, helpline, student web hosting, wireless network available.

**Student life. Freshman orientation:** Mandatory. Preregistration for classes offered. Two-day programs held in early August and early September. **Housing:** Guaranteed on-campus for freshmen. Single-sex dorms, apartments, substance-free housing available. $100 fully refundable deposit. **Activities:** Jazz band, choral groups, dance, drama, student government, student newspaper, Business Professionals of America, American Marketing Association, ambassador club, Rotaract, law club, International Business Association, Minority Business Women, American Advertising Federation, The Church Reloaded, diversity club.

**Athletics.** NCAA. **Intercollegiate:** Baseball M, basketball, cheerleading, cross-country, football (tackle) M, golf, soccer, softball W, tennis, track and field, volleyball W. **Intramural:** Badminton, basketball, field hockey, football (non-tackle) M, soccer, tennis, volleyball. **Team name:** Timberwolves.

**Student services.** Adult student services, alcohol/substance abuse counseling, career counseling, student employment services, financial aid counseling, health services, minority student services, personal counseling, placement for graduates, veterans' counselor. **Physically disabled:** Services for visually, speech, hearing impaired.

**Contact.** E-mail: miadmit@northwood.edu
Phone: (989) 837-4273 Toll-free number: (800) 457-7878
Fax: (989) 837-4490
Daniel Toland, Dean of Admissions, Northwood University: Michigan, 4000 Whiting Drive, Midland, MI 48640

## Oakland University
**Rochester, Michigan**
www.oakland.edu
CB code: 1497

♦ Public 4-year university
♦ Commuter campus in small city
♦ 13,605 degree-seeking undergraduates: 26% part-time, 62% women, 8% African American, 4% Asian American, 2% Hispanic American, 1% international
♦ 3,791 degree-seeking graduate students
♦ 81% of applicants admitted
♦ 44% graduate within 6 years; 20% enter graduate study

**General.** Founded in 1957. Regionally accredited. **Degrees:** 2,112 bachelor's awarded; master's, doctoral offered. **ROTC:** Air Force. **Location:** 30 miles from Detroit. **Calendar:** Semester, limited summer session. **Full-time faculty:** 502 total; 88% have terminal degrees, 24% minority, 43% women. **Part-time faculty:** 424 total; 30% have terminal degrees, 12% minority, 58% women. **Class size:** 39% < 20, 41% 20-39, 6% 40-49, 11% 50-99, 2% >100. **Special facilities:** Music pavilion, engineering and science research laboratories, robotics laboratory, CAD-CAM laboratory, product development and manufacturing center.

**Freshman class profile.** 6,896 applied, 5,593 admitted, 2,340 enrolled.

| Mid 50% test scores | | | |
|---|---|---|---|
| ACT composite: | 19-24 | Return as sophomores: | 73% |
| GPA 3.50 or higher: | 32% | Out-of-state: | 1% |
| GPA 3.0-3.49: | 31% | Live on campus: | 34% |
| GPA 2.0-2.99: | 37% | International: | 1% |
| Rank in top quarter: | 38% | Fraternities: | 3% |
| End year in good standing: | 82% | Sororities: | 3% |

**Basis for selection.** Admission based on 2.5 GPA in academic subjects, school and community activities, recommendations. Applicants with minimum 2.0 GPA may be admitted to summer program. Engineering, business, education, nursing, and physical therapy programs require higher GPA. SAT or ACT recommended. Except for homeschooled students, ACT scores used only for placement and scholarship purposes. Audition required of music majors. **Homeschooled:** 25 ACT score.

**High school preparation.** Required and recommended units include English 4, mathematics 3, social studies 3, science 3 and foreign language 2. Recommend fine arts, computing.

**2007-2008 Annual costs.** Tuition/fees: $7,575; $17,625 out-of-state. Room/board: $6,670. Books/supplies: $1,178. Personal expenses: $1,534.

**2006-2007 Financial aid. Need-based:** 1,440 full-time freshmen applied for aid; 946 were judged to have need; 898 of these received aid. Average need met was 75%. Average scholarship/grant was $4,188; average loan $4,977. 40% of total undergraduate aid awarded as scholarships/grants, 60% as loans/jobs. **Non-need-based:** Awarded to 2,438 full-time undergraduates, including 1,149 freshmen. Scholarships awarded for academics, art, athletics, leadership, music/drama, state residency.

**Application procedures. Admission:** No deadline. $40 fee, may be waived for applicants with need. Application may be submitted online. Admission notification on a rolling basis. **Financial aid:** Priority date 2/15; no closing date. FAFSA required. Applicants notified on a rolling basis starting 3/15.

**Academics. Special study options:** Accelerated study, cooperative education, distance learning, double major, ESL, honors, independent study, internships, student-designed major, study abroad, teacher certification program. **Credit/placement by examination:** AP, CLEP, IB, ACT, institutional tests. 60 credit hours maximum toward bachelor's degree. **Support services:** Learning center, pre-admission summer program, reduced course load, remedial instruction, study skills assistance, tutoring, writing center.

**Majors. Area/ethnic studies:** African, East Asian, Latin American, Slavic, South Asian, women's. **Biology:** General, biochemistry, biophysics. **Business:** General, accounting, finance, human resources, management information systems, managerial economics, marketing, training/development. **Communications:** General, journalism. **Computer sciences:** General, information technology. **Education:** Elementary, music. **Engineering:** Computer, electrical, mechanical, physics. **English:** English lit. **Foreign languages:** General, French, German, linguistics, Spanish. **Health:** Clinical lab science, environmental health, nursing (RN), occupational health. **History:** General. **Liberal arts:** Arts/sciences. **Math:** General, statistics. **Philosophy/religion:** Philosophy. **Physical sciences:** Chemistry, physics. **Psychology:** General. **Public administration:** General. **Social sciences:** Anthropology, economics, political science, sociology. **Visual/performing arts:** Art history/conservation, drawing, music performance, music theory/composition, painting, photography, piano/organ, studio arts, theater design, voice/opera. **Other:** Engineering chemistry, engineering biology, Studio art: new media.

**Most popular majors.** Business/marketing 21%, communications/journalism 10%, education 14%, engineering/engineering technologies 7%, health sciences 12%, psychology 6%, social sciences 8%.

**Computing on campus.** 713 workstations in dormitories, library, computer center, student center. Dormitories linked to campus network. Commuter students can connect to campus network. Online course registration, online library, helpline, student web hosting, wireless network available.

**Student life. Freshman orientation:** Mandatory. Preregistration for classes offered. Held on weekdays from end of June through mid-July. 1.5-day program requires overnight stay in residence halls. Condensed 1-day orientation available. **Policies:** Freshmen must live on campus unless living with family. **Housing:** Guaranteed on-campus for freshmen. Coed dorms, special housing for disabled, apartments, fraternity/sorority housing, substance-free housing available. $100 nonrefundable deposit, deadline 9/1. Residence halls easily accessible to handicapped persons. Living/learning communities available. **Activities:** Bands, choral groups, dance, drama, film society, literary magazine, music ensembles, musical theater, radio station, student government, student newspaper, symphony orchestra, TV station, association of black students, Indian students association, Arab American association, College Democrats, College Republicans, Campus Crusade for Christ, Hillel, Muslim student association, Chinese friendship association, gay/straight alliance.

**Athletics.** NCAA. **Intercollegiate:** Baseball M, basketball, cross-country, diving, golf, soccer, softball W, swimming, tennis W, track and field, volleyball W. **Intramural:** Basketball, football (non-tackle), racquetball, soccer, table tennis, volleyball. **Team name:** Golden Grizzlies.

**Student services.** Alcohol/substance abuse counseling, campus ministries, career counseling, student employment services, financial aid counseling, health services, minority student services, on-campus daycare, personal counseling, placement for graduates. **Physically disabled:** Services for visually, speech, hearing impaired.

**Contact.** E-mail: ouinfo@oakland.edu
Phone: (248) 370-3360 Toll-free number: (800) 625-8648
Fax: (248) 370-4462
Eleanor Reynolds, Assistant Vice President Student Affairs, Oakland University, 101 North Foundation Hall, Rochester, MI 48309-4401

---

### Olivet College
**Olivet, Michigan**
www.olivetcollege.edu

CB member
CB code: 1595

- Private 4-year liberal arts college affiliated with Congregational Christian Churches and United Church of Christ
- Residential campus in rural community
- 920 degree-seeking undergraduates: 6% part-time, 40% women, 15% African American, 1% Asian American, 2% Hispanic American, 1% Native American, 2% international
- 45 graduate students
- 54% of applicants admitted
- ACT (writing recommended) required
- 37% graduate within 6 years

**General.** Founded in 1844. Regionally accredited. **Degrees:** 131 bachelor's awarded; master's offered. **Location:** 30 miles from Lansing, 120 miles from Detroit. **Calendar:** Semester, limited summer session. **Full-time faculty:** 37 total; 65% have terminal degrees, 8% minority, 43% women. **Part-time faculty:** 55 total; 14% have terminal degrees, 2% minority. **Class size:** 65% < 20, 33% 20-39, less than 1% 40-49, less than 1% 50-99, less than 1% >100. **Special facilities:** Observatory/planetarium, dynamic ecology laboratory, character education resource center, women's resource center, biological preserve.

**Freshman class profile.** 1,414 applied, 761 admitted, 210 enrolled.

| Mid 50% test scores | | Out-of-state: | 8% |
|---|---|---|---|
| ACT composite: | 17-21 | Live on campus: | 82% |
| Rank in top quarter: | 38% | Fraternities: | 10% |
| Rank in top tenth: | 25% | Sororities: | 10% |

**Basis for selection.** Minimum 2.6 GPA most important. Test scores, school achievement record, recommendations for those below 2.6 GPA important. Interview recommended. Portfolio recommended for art majors. **Homeschooled:** Transcript of courses and grades required.

**High school preparation.** 14 units required; 19 recommended. Required and recommended units include English 4, mathematics 3-4, social studies 2-3, science 3-4 (laboratory 1-2) and foreign language 2.

**2007-2008 Annual costs.** Tuition/fees: $19,302. Room/board: $6,346. Books/supplies: $900. Personal expenses: $1,000.

**Financial aid.** All financial aid based on need.

**Application procedures. Admission:** No deadline. $25 fee, may be waived for applicants with need. Application may be submitted online. Admission notification on a rolling basis beginning on or about 11/1. **Financial aid:** No deadline. FAFSA required. Applicants notified on a rolling basis starting 2/1; must reply within 3 week(s) of notification.

**Academics.** Olivet Plan degree program includes service learning experience, portfolio assessment measuring 6 essential competencies, senior experience, professional mentoring, and 3 1/2 week intensive learning term. **Special study options:** Cooperative education, double major, dual enrollment of high school students, honors, independent study, internships, liberal arts/career combination, student-designed major, teacher certification program. **Credit/placement by examination:** AP, CLEP, ACT, institutional tests. **Support services:** Learning center, pre-admission summer program, remedial instruction, tutoring, writing center.

**Majors. Biology:** General, biochemistry. **Business:** Business admin, financial planning, insurance, managerial economics, marketing. **Communications:** General, journalism, media studies. **Computer sciences:** Computer science. **Conservation:** Environmental science. **Education:** General, art, emotionally handicapped, music, speech. **English:** English lit. **Health:** Athletic training. **History:** General. **Interdisciplinary:** Biological/physical sciences. **Liberal arts:** Arts/sciences. **Math:** General. **Parks/recreation:** Health/fitness, sports admin. **Physical sciences:** Chemistry. **Protective services:** Criminal justice. **Psychology:** General. **Social sciences:** General, sociology. **Visual/performing arts:** Art, dramatic.

**Most popular majors.** Biology 12%, business/marketing 24%, English 7%, parks/recreation 14%, security/protective services 7%, social sciences 6%.

**Computing on campus.** 60 workstations in dormitories, library, computer center, student center. Dormitories wired for high-speed internet access and linked to campus network. Commuter students can connect to campus network. Online course registration, helpline, repair service, student web hosting, wireless network available.

**Student life. Freshman orientation:** Mandatory, $75 fee. Preregistration for classes offered. **Housing:** Guaranteed on-campus for all undergraduates. Coed dorms, single-sex dorms, apartments, fraternity/sorority housing, substance-free housing available. African American house, honors house, wellness floor available. **Activities:** Bands, choral groups, drama, literary magazine, music ensembles, musical theater, radio station, student government, student newspaper, symphony orchestra, Phi Kappa Delta, Psi Chi, international club, Earth Bound, black student union, N.O.W., campus media board, Students Organizing Community Service.

**Athletics.** NCAA. **Intercollegiate:** Baseball M, basketball, cross-country, diving, football (tackle) M, golf, soccer, softball W, swimming, tennis W, track and field, volleyball W, wrestling M. **Intramural:** Basketball, cheerleading, football (non-tackle) M, weight lifting M. **Team name:** Comets.

**Student services.** Adult student services, alcohol/substance abuse counseling, campus ministries, career counseling, services for economically disadvantaged, student employment services, financial aid counseling, health services, minority student services, personal counseling, placement for graduates, women's services. **Physically disabled:** Services for visually, speech, hearing impaired.

**Contact.** E-mail: admissions@olivetcollege.edu
Phone: (269) 749-7635 Toll-free number: (800) 456-7189
Fax: (269) 749-6617
Larry Vallar, Vice President for Enrollment Management, Olivet College, Admissions Office, Olivet, MI 49076

---

### Rochester College
**Rochester Hills, Michigan**
www.rc.edu

CB code: 1516

- Private 4-year liberal arts college affiliated with Church of Christ
- Residential campus in small city
- 957 degree-seeking undergraduates: 34% part-time, 62% women, 20% African American, 1% Asian American, 2% Hispanic American, 1% Native American, 2% international
- 10 degree-seeking graduate students
- 80% of applicants admitted
- ACT (writing optional), application essay required

**General.** Founded in 1959. Regionally accredited. **Degrees:** 273 bachelor's awarded; master's offered. **Location:** 25 miles from Detroit. **Calendar:** Semester, limited summer session. **Full-time faculty:** 46 total; 44% have terminal degrees, 39% women. **Part-time faculty:** 113 total; 15% have terminal degrees, 63% women. **Class size:** 86% < 20, 14% 20-39, less than 1% 40-49.

**Freshman class profile.** 210 applied, 167 admitted, 96 enrolled.

| Mid 50% test scores | | GPA 2.0-2.99: | 38% |
|---|---|---|---|
| ACT composite: | 18-25 | Rank in top quarter: | 28% |
| GPA 3.50 or higher: | 33% | Rank in top tenth: | 14% |
| GPA 3.0-3.49: | 26% | International: | 4% |

**Basis for selection.** ACT score and high school GPA most important. Recommendations and interview considered. **Homeschooled:** Transcript of courses and grades required.

**2007-2008 Annual costs.** Tuition/fees: $14,860. Room/board: $6,920. Books/supplies: $600. Personal expenses: $750.

**Financial aid. Non-need-based:** Scholarships awarded for academics, alumni affiliation, athletics, leadership, music/drama, state residency.

**Application procedures. Admission:** No deadline. $25 fee. Application may be submitted online. Admission notification on a rolling basis. **Financial aid:** Priority date 8/1; no closing date. FAFSA required. Applicants notified on a rolling basis starting 6/1; must reply within 2 week(s) of notification.

**Academics. Special study options:** Accelerated study, combined bachelor's/graduate degree, cross-registration, double major, dual enrollment of high school students, honors, independent study, internships, liberal arts/career combination, study abroad, teacher certification program, weekend college. **Credit/placement by examination:** AP, CLEP, IB, institutional tests. 32 credit hours maximum toward associate degree, 64 toward bachelor's. Credit awarded for successful completion of selected DANTES Subject Standardized Testing Program. **Support services:** Learning center, reduced course load, remedial instruction, study skills assistance, tutoring, writing center.

**Majors. Business:** Accounting, business admin, management information systems, marketing. **Communications:** General. **Computer sciences:** General. **Education:** General, early childhood, elementary, English, history, mathematics, middle, music, science, secondary. **English:** English lit. **History:** General. **Philosophy/religion:** Religion. **Psychology:** General. **Public administration:** Social work. **Theology:** Bible, theology. **Visual/performing arts:** Music performance.

**Most popular majors.** Business/marketing 35%, communications/journalism 6%, education 22%, psychology 20%.

**Computing on campus.** 34 workstations in dormitories, library, computer center. Dormitories wired for high-speed internet access and linked to campus network. Online library, helpline, student web hosting, wireless network available.

**Student life. Freshman orientation:** Mandatory, $100 fee. Preregistration for classes offered. **Housing:** Guaranteed on-campus for freshmen. Single-sex dorms, apartments available. $180 deposit, deadline 5/1. **Activities:** Bands, choral groups, drama, music ensembles, musical theater, opera, student government, student newspaper, service and mission organizations, student government, social clubs, departmental organizations, honor societies.

**Athletics.** NCCAA. **Intercollegiate:** Baseball M, basketball, soccer, softball W, volleyball W. **Intramural:** Basketball, football (non-tackle), softball, volleyball. **Team name:** Warriors.

**Student services.** Adult student services, alcohol/substance abuse counseling, campus ministries, career counseling, student employment services, financial aid counseling, minority student services, personal counseling, placement for graduates, veterans' counselor. **Physically disabled:** Services for visually, speech, hearing impaired.

**Contact.** E-mail: admissions@rc.edu
Phone: (248) 218-2031 Toll-free number: (800) 521-6010
Fax: (248) 218-2035
Larry Norman, Vice President for Enrollment Management, Rochester College, 800 West Avon Road, Rochester Hills, MI 48307

## Sacred Heart Major Seminary
**Detroit, Michigan**
www.shms.org                                    **CB code: 1686**

- Private 4-year seminary college affiliated with Roman Catholic Church
- Commuter campus in very large city
- 39 degree-seeking undergraduates: 5% part-time, 5% women
- 175 degree-seeking graduate students
- 100% of applicants admitted
- SAT or ACT (ACT writing optional), application essay required

**General.** Founded in 1919. Regionally accredited. Most B.A. students candidates for priesthood. 2-year programs leading to ordination as deacon or certification in pastoral-liturgical ministry offered. Pastoral ministry courses and degree programs open to men and women. Master level courses designed for laity who wish to minister in church. **Degrees:** 19 bachelor's, 5 associate awarded; master's, first professional offered. **Calendar:** Semester. **Full-time faculty:** 35 total; 71% have terminal degrees, 20% women. **Part-time faculty:** 24 total; 58% have terminal degrees, 21% women. **Class size:** 79% < 20, 21% 20-39.

**Freshman class profile.** 4 applied, 4 admitted, 4 enrolled.

| | | | |
|---|---|---|---|
| GPA 3.0-3.49: | 100% | Live on campus: | 100% |
| End year in good standing: | 75% | | |

**Basis for selection.** Recommendations of parish pastor, high school principal, and college counselor vital. School, community, and church-related activities viewed as important formative experiences. Religious commitment very important. Interview required for priesthood candidates.

**High school preparation.** Required and recommended units include English 4, mathematics 2, social studies 2, history 2, science 2 (laboratory 1), foreign language 2 and academic electives 1-2.

**2007-2008 Annual costs.** Tuition/fees: $12,530. Room/board: $7,000. Books/supplies: $1,310. Personal expenses: $3,150.

**2006-2007 Financial aid. Need-based:** Average need met was 75%. 88% of total undergraduate aid awarded as scholarships/grants, 12% as loans/jobs. **Non-need-based:** Scholarships awarded for academics, religious affiliation.

**Application procedures. Admission:** Closing date 8/1 (postmark date). $30 fee. Application must be submitted on paper. Admission notification on a rolling basis. **Financial aid:** No deadline. FAFSA, institutional form required. Applicants notified on a rolling basis.

**Academics.** 30 to 40% of undergraduate course work taken at other consortium colleges. **Special study options:** Cross-registration. **Credit/placement by examination:** AP, CLEP, institutional tests. 6 credit hours maximum toward associate degree, 12 toward bachelor's. Must accumulate 15 hours at SHMS before credit is recorded. **Support services:** Learning center, reduced course load, study skills assistance, tutoring.

**Majors. Liberal arts:** Arts/sciences. **Philosophy/religion:** Philosophy.

**Most popular majors.** Liberal arts 60%, philosophy/religious studies 40%.

**Computing on campus.** 12 workstations in library, computer center. Online library available.

**Student life. Freshman orientation:** Mandatory. 3 days for seminarians, 1 day for commuters at beginning of fall term. **Policies:** Religious observance required. **Housing:** Substance-free housing available. $110 fully refundable deposit, deadline 8/25. Guaranteed on-campus housing available to seminarians. **Activities:** Campus ministries, choral groups.

**Athletics. Intercollegiate:** Basketball M. **Intramural:** Handball M, racquetball M, soccer M, softball M, volleyball M.

**Student services.** Personal counseling.

**Contact.** Phone: (313) 883-8520 Toll-free number: (313) 883-8520
Fax: (313) 883-8530
John Lajiness, Director of Admissions and Enrollment Management, Sacred Heart Major Seminary, 2701 Chicago Boulevard, Detroit, MI 48206-1799

## Saginaw Valley State University
**University Center, Michigan**
www.svsu.edu                                    **CB code: 1766**

- Public 4-year university
- Commuter campus in small city
- 7,785 degree-seeking undergraduates: 19% part-time, 59% women, 8% African American, 1% Asian American, 2% Hispanic American, 3% international
- 1,678 degree-seeking graduate students
- 89% of applicants admitted
- ACT (writing optional) required

**General.** Founded in 1963. Regionally accredited. **Degrees:** 1,178 bachelor's awarded; master's offered. **Location:** 10 miles from Bay City and Saginaw. **Calendar:** Semester, limited summer session. **Full-time faculty:**

282 total; 79% have terminal degrees. **Part-time faculty:** 300 total. **Class size:** 30% < 20, 61% 20-39, 4% 40-49, 5% 50-99. **Special facilities:** Fine arts center, sculpture museum, observatory.

**Freshman class profile.** 4,821 applied, 4,279 admitted, 1,660 enrolled.

| Mid 50% test scores | | Rank in top tenth: | 18% |
|---|---|---|---|
| ACT composite: | 18-24 | End year in good standing: | 71% |
| GPA 3.50 or higher: | 37% | Return as sophomores: | 69% |
| GPA 3.0-3.49: | 30% | Out-of-state: | 1% |
| GPA 2.0-2.99: | 33% | Live on campus: | 66% |
| Rank in top quarter: | 41% | International: | 3% |

**Basis for selection.** Minimum high school GPA of 2.5 preferred. **Home-schooled:** Interview required.

**High school preparation.** Required and recommended units include English 4, mathematics 3-4, social studies 3-4, science 2-4 and foreign language 2. One unit of communications recommended.

**2007-2008 Annual costs.** Tuition/fees: $6,258; $14,283 out-of-state. Room/board: $6,630. Books/supplies: $900. Personal expenses: $941.

**2006-2007 Financial aid. Need-based:** 1,385 full-time freshmen applied for aid; 904 were judged to have need; 892 of these received aid. Average need met was 67%. Average scholarship/grant was $3,098; average loan $2,218. 38% of total undergraduate aid awarded as scholarships/grants, 62% as loans/jobs. **Non-need-based:** Awarded to 2,727 full-time undergraduates, including 1,139 freshmen. Scholarships awarded for academics, art, athletics, leadership, minority status, music/drama.

**Application procedures. Admission:** No deadline. $25 fee, may be waived for applicants with need. Application may be submitted online. Admission notification on a rolling basis. **Financial aid:** Priority date 2/14; no closing date. FAFSA required. Applicants notified on a rolling basis starting 3/20; must reply within 10 week(s) of notification.

**Academics. Special study options:** Accelerated study, combined bachelor's/graduate degree, cooperative education, distance learning, double major, dual enrollment of high school students, ESL, honors, independent study, internships, student-designed major, study abroad, teacher certification program. **Credit/placement by examination:** AP, CLEP, IB, ACT, institutional tests. 62 credit hours maximum toward bachelor's degree. **Support services:** Learning center, reduced course load, remedial instruction, study skills assistance, tutoring, writing center.

**Majors. Biology:** General, biochemistry. **Business:** General, accounting, business admin, finance, international, managerial economics, marketing, operations. **Communications:** General. **Computer sciences:** General, systems analysis. **Education:** Elementary, physical, special. **Engineering:** Electrical, mechanical. **Engineering technology:** General. **English:** English lit. **Foreign languages:** French, Spanish. **Health:** Athletic training, clinical lab science, health services, nursing (RN). **History:** General. **Interdisciplinary:** Global studies. **Math:** General, applied. **Parks/recreation:** Exercise sciences. **Physical sciences:** Chemical physics, chemistry, optics, physics. **Protective services:** Criminal justice. **Psychology:** General. **Public administration:** General, social work. **Social sciences:** Economics, political science, sociology. **Visual/performing arts:** Art, dramatic, graphic design, studio arts. **Other:** Applied studies, Business chemistry.

**Most popular majors.** Business/marketing 14%, education 30%, health sciences 10%, public administration/social services 6%, security/protective services 8%.

**Computing on campus.** 800 workstations in library, computer center, student center. Dormitories linked to campus network. Commuter students can connect to campus network. Online course registration, online library, helpline, student web hosting, wireless network available.

**Student life. Freshman orientation:** Mandatory, $55 fee. Preregistration for classes offered. Day-long sessions before each semester include university placement testing, advising, and registration. **Housing:** Coed dorms, special housing for disabled, apartments, substance-free housing available. $200 partly refundable deposit. **Activities:** Bands, choral groups, dance, drama, film society, literary magazine, music ensembles, musical theater, student government, student newspaper, over 75 campus organizations.

**Athletics.** NCAA. **Intercollegiate:** Baseball M, basketball, bowling M, cheerleading, cross-country, football (tackle) M, golf M, soccer, softball W, tennis W, track and field, volleyball W. **Intramural:** Badminton, basketball, football (non-tackle), golf, lacrosse, racquetball, soccer, softball, squash, table tennis, tennis, volleyball. **Team name:** Cardinals.

**Student services.** Adult student services, alcohol/substance abuse counseling, career counseling, services for economically disadvantaged, student employment services, financial aid counseling, health services, legal services, minority student services, personal counseling, placement for graduates, veterans' counselor, women's services. **Physically disabled:** Services for visually, hearing impaired.

**Contact.** E-mail: admissions@svsu.edu
Phone: (989) 964-4200 Toll-free number: (800) 968-9500
Fax: (989) 790-0180
James Dwyer, Director of Admissions, Saginaw Valley State University, 7400 Bay Road, University Center, MI 48710

---

## Siena Heights University
**Adrian, Michigan**
**www.sienahts.edu**

**CB member**
**CB code: 1719**

- Private 4-year university affiliated with Roman Catholic Church
- Residential campus in large town
- 855 full-time, degree-seeking undergraduates
- 275 graduate students
- SAT or ACT (ACT writing recommended) required

**General.** Founded in 1919. Regionally accredited. Branch campuses in Benton Harbor, Battle Creek, Kalamazoo, Lansing, Southfield, Monroe, and Jackson. Monroe County Community College, Lake Michigan College, and Southfield Community Center provide off-campus upper-division degree completion. **Degrees:** 642 bachelor's, 12 associate awarded; master's offered. **Location:** 30 miles from Toledo, Ohio; 60 miles from Detroit. **Calendar:** Semester, limited summer session. **Full-time faculty:** 66 total. **Part-time faculty:** 152 total. **Special facilities:** Montessori children's house on campus.

**Freshman class profile.**

| Mid 50% test scores | | Out-of-state: | 15% |
|---|---|---|---|
| ACT composite: | 17-21 | Live on campus: | 70% |

**Basis for selection.** School achievement record, test scores, self-motivation, and ability to benefit from available resources most important. SAT Subject Tests recommended. Interview required for art, theater, and music majors; audition required for music majors; portfolio required for art majors. Essay recommended for marginally qualified applicants. **Home-schooled:** Must complete GED for state or federal assistance.

**2007-2008 Annual costs.** Tuition/fees: $18,494. Room/board: $6,290. Books/supplies: $600. Personal expenses: $900.

**Financial aid. Non-need-based:** Scholarships awarded for academics, art, athletics, music/drama, religious affiliation.

**Application procedures. Admission:** No deadline. $25 fee, may be waived for applicants with need. Admission notification on a rolling basis. **Financial aid:** Priority date 3/15, closing date 8/15. FAFSA, institutional form, CSS PROFILE required. Applicants notified on a rolling basis starting 2/15.

**Academics. Special study options:** Combined bachelor's/graduate degree, cooperative education, double major, dual enrollment of high school students, exchange student, external degree, honors, independent study, internships, liberal arts/career combination, student-designed major, study abroad, teacher certification program, weekend college. 3-1 field experience/liberal arts in technical and nursing programs. **Credit/placement by examination:** AP, CLEP. 36 credit hours maximum toward bachelor's degree. **Support services:** Learning center, pre-admission summer program, reduced course load, remedial instruction, study skills assistance, tutoring, writing center.

**Majors. Area/ethnic studies:** American. **Biology:** General. **Business:** General, accounting, hospitality/recreation. **Communications:** General. **Computer sciences:** General. **Education:** Business, elementary, secondary. **English:** Creative writing, English lit. **Foreign languages:** Spanish. **Health:** Predental, premedicine, prepharmacy. **History:** General. **Interdisciplinary:** Natural sciences. **Legal studies:** Prelaw. **Liberal arts:** Arts/sciences. **Math:** General. **Parks/recreation:** Sports admin. **Philosophy/religion:** Philosophy, religion. **Physical sciences:** Chemistry. **Protective services:** Criminal justice. **Psychology:** General. **Public administration:** Social work. **Social sciences:** General. **Visual/performing arts:** Art, ceramics, commercial/advertising art, dramatic, drawing, metal/jewelry, painting, photography, sculpture, studio arts.

**Computing on campus.** 80 workstations in dormitories, library, computer center. Dormitories linked to campus network. Helpline available.

**Student life. Freshman orientation:** Available. Preregistration for classes offered. One-day program offered in April, May, June, July, and August. **Housing:** Guaranteed on-campus for all undergraduates. Coed dorms, single-sex dorms available. $50 deposit. **Activities:** Jazz band, choral groups, dance, drama, film society, literary magazine, music ensembles, musical theater, student government, student newspaper, Campus ministry, Siena Heights African American Knowledge Association, student programming association, Greek council, Students Against Violent Environments.

**Athletics.** NAIA. **Intercollegiate:** Baseball M, basketball, cross-country, golf M, soccer, softball W, track and field, volleyball W. **Intramural:** Basketball, softball, volleyball.

**Student services.** Adult student services, career counseling, student employment services, health services, personal counseling, placement for graduates.

**Contact.** E-mail: admissions@sienahts.edu
Phone: (517) 264-7180 Toll-free number: (800) 521-0009 ext. 7180
Fax: (517) 264-7745
Jeanine Novak, Dean of Admissions and Enrollment Services, Siena Heights University, 1247 East Siena Heights Drive, Adrian, MI 49221-1796

---

## Spring Arbor University
**Spring Arbor, Michigan**
**www.arbor.edu**                                    CB code: 1732

- Private 4-year university and liberal arts college affiliated with Free Methodist Church of North America
- Residential campus in rural community
- 2,611 degree-seeking undergraduates: 24% part-time, 68% women
- 1,191 degree-seeking graduate students
- 78% of applicants admitted
- SAT or ACT (ACT writing optional) required
- 59% graduate within 6 years; 25% enter graduate study

**General.** Founded in 1873. Regionally accredited. School of Adult Studies offers degree completion with courses and majors available at 14 regional sites. **Degrees:** 684 bachelor's, 4 associate awarded; master's offered. **ROTC:** Army, Air Force. **Location:** 8 miles from Jackson, 40 miles from Lansing. **Calendar:** Semester, limited summer session. **Full-time faculty:** 80 total; 60% have terminal degrees, 8% minority, 32% women. **Part-time faculty:** 48 total; 25% have terminal degrees, 8% minority, 52% women. **Class size:** 66% < 20, 28% 20-39, 5% 40-49, 1% 50-99. **Special facilities:** Trading center.

**Freshman class profile.** 1,485 applied, 1,154 admitted, 340 enrolled.

| Mid 50% test scores | | GPA 2.0-2.99: | 21% |
|---|---|---|---|
| SAT critical reading: | 470-600 | Rank in top quarter: | 47% |
| SAT math: | 460-600 | Rank in top tenth: | 21% |
| SAT writing: | 430-580 | Return as sophomores: | 72% |
| ACT composite: | 19-25 | Out-of-state: | 17% |
| GPA 3.50 or higher: | 48% | Live on campus: | 95% |
| GPA 3.0-3.49: | 29% | International: | 1% |

**Basis for selection.** 20 ACT/930 SAT and 2.6 GPA recommended. Applicants whose scores are below recommendations may be admitted conditionally. Interview recommended for borderline applicants. **Homeschooled:** Require letter of recommendation from parent/teacher and 2-3 page paper on homeschool experience.

**High school preparation.** 12 units required; 15 recommended. Required and recommended units include English 4, mathematics 3, history 2, science 2 (laboratory 2), foreign language 2 and computer science 1. Physical education or health-related course required.

**2007-2008 Annual costs.** Tuition/fees: $18,360. Per-credit-hour charges: $400 for 1-7 hours or 12 or more hours; $450 for 8-11 hours. Room/board: $6,370. Books/supplies: $660. Personal expenses: $804.

**2007-2008 Financial aid. Need-based:** 322 full-time freshmen applied for aid; 279 were judged to have need; 279 of these received aid. Average need met was 97%. Average scholarship/grant was $9,643; average loan $3,677. 56% of total undergraduate aid awarded as scholarships/grants, 44% as loans/jobs. **Non-need-based:** Scholarships awarded for academics, art, athletics, minority status, music/drama, religious affiliation.

**Application procedures. Admission:** Priority date 2/15; deadline 8/1 (receipt date). $30 fee, may be waived for applicants with need. Application may be submitted online. Admission notification on a rolling basis beginning on or about 9/1. **Financial aid:** Priority date 3/1; no closing date. FAFSA required. Applicants notified on a rolling basis starting 3/1; must reply within 2 week(s) of notification.

**Academics. Special study options:** Accelerated study, combined bachelor's/graduate degree, cross-registration, distance learning, double major, dual

---

enrollment of high school students, ESL, honors, independent study, internships, student-designed major, study abroad, teacher certification program, Washington semester, weekend college. Environmental study semester offered at AuSable Trails Institute in northern Michigan; cross-cultural program with several destinations. **Credit/placement by examination:** AP, CLEP, IB, SAT, ACT, institutional tests. 10 credit hours maximum toward associate degree, 60 toward bachelor's. No more than 1/3 of credits for major can be through credit by examination. **Support services:** Learning center, pre-admission summer program, reduced course load, remedial instruction, study skills assistance, tutoring.

**Majors. Biology:** General, biochemistry. **Business:** Accounting, actuarial science, business admin, finance, management information systems, managerial economics, operations. **Communications:** General, advertising, broadcast journalism, public relations. **Computer sciences:** Computer science. **Education:** Art, elementary, secondary, special. **Engineering technology:** General. **English:** Creative writing, English lit, speech/rhetoric. **Family/consumer sciences:** Family studies. **Foreign languages:** Spanish. **Health:** Health care admin, nursing (RN). **History:** General. **Interdisciplinary:** Global studies. **Math:** General. **Parks/recreation:** General, health/fitness. **Philosophy/religion:** Christian, philosophy, religion. **Physical sciences:** Chemistry, theoretical physics. **Psychology:** General. **Public administration:** Social work. **Social sciences:** General, political science, sociology, urban studies. **Theology:** Bible, missionary, pastoral counseling, sacred music, theology, youth ministry. **Visual/performing arts:** Art, design, film/cinema, graphic design. **Other:** Biology health careers.

**Most popular majors.** Business/marketing 35%, education 16%, family/consumer sciences 17%, health sciences 8%.

**Computing on campus.** 230 workstations in dormitories, library, computer center, student center. Dormitories wired for high-speed internet access and linked to campus network. Commuter students can connect to campus network. Online course registration, helpline, repair service, student web hosting, wireless network available.

**Student life. Freshman orientation:** Mandatory. Preregistration for classes offered. Three-day session held at the beginning of September; parents encouraged to attend first day. **Policies:** Emphasis placed on active commitment to Jesus Christ and his teachings. Chapel attendance required twice a week. Religious observance required. **Housing:** Guaranteed on-campus for freshmen. Single-sex dorms, special housing for disabled, apartments, substance-free housing available. $200 fully refundable deposit, deadline 5/1. **Activities:** Bands, campus ministries, choral groups, drama, film society, international student organizations, literary magazine, music ensembles, musical theater, radio station, student government, student newspaper, symphony orchestra, TV station, youth ministries, women in church ministry, prayer ministry, clown ministry, creative children's ministry, interfaith shelter, Action Jackson, Habitat for Humanity.

**Athletics.** NAIA, NCCAA. **Intercollegiate:** Baseball M, basketball, cross-country, golf M, soccer, softball W, tennis, track and field, volleyball W. **Intramural:** Basketball, field hockey M, football (non-tackle) M, golf M, soccer, softball, table tennis, tennis, volleyball. **Team name:** Cougars.

**Student services.** Adult student services, campus ministries, career counseling, student employment services, financial aid counseling, health services, minority student services, personal counseling, placement for graduates, veterans' counselor. **Physically disabled:** Services for visually, speech, hearing impaired.

**Contact.** E-mail: admissions@arbor.edu
Phone: (517) 750-6468 Toll-free number: (800) 968-0011
Fax: (517) 750-6620
Randy Comfort, Director of Admissions, Spring Arbor University, 106 East Main Street, Spring Arbor, MI 49283-9799

---

## University of Detroit Mercy
**Detroit, Michigan**                          CB member
**www.udmercy.edu**                            CB code: 1835

- Private 4-year university affiliated with Roman Catholic Church
- Commuter campus in very large city
- 2,989 degree-seeking undergraduates: 28% part-time, 67% women, 25% African American, 3% Asian American, 4% Hispanic American, 3% Native American, 4% international
- 2,436 degree-seeking graduate students
- 63% of applicants admitted
- SAT or ACT (ACT writing optional) required
- 51% graduate within 6 years

**General.** Founded in 1991. Regionally accredited. **Degrees:** 504 bachelor's awarded; master's, doctoral, first professional offered. **Calendar:** Semester, extensive summer session. **Full-time faculty:** 250 total; 88% have terminal degrees, 14% minority, 48% women. **Part-time faculty:** 321 total; 19% minority, 46% women. **Class size:** 61% < 20, 35% 20-39, 3% 40-49, 2% 50-99.

**Freshman class profile.** 2,686 applied, 1,690 admitted, 530 enrolled.

| Mid 50% test scores | | | |
|---|---|---|---|
| SAT critical reading: | 470-630 | Rank in top tenth: | 31% |
| SAT math: | 450-600 | Return as sophomores: | 78% |
| ACT composite: | 20-26 | Out-of-state: | 4% |
| Rank in top quarter: | 63% | Live on campus: | 45% |
| | | International: | 2% |

**Basis for selection.** High school GPA in college-preparatory work, test scores, counselor's recommendation considered. Interview required for University College applicants, recommended for all others.

**High school preparation.** 16 units required. Required and recommended units include English 4, mathematics 3-4, social studies 2, history 2, science 2-3 (laboratory 1) and academic electives 4. Units in speech, foreign language, music, art recommended.

**2008-2009 Annual costs.** Tuition/fees (projected): $27,319. Engineering and architecture students pay slightly higher tuition. Room/board: $8,250. Books/supplies: $1,420. Personal expenses: $2,567.

**Financial aid.** **Non-need-based:** Scholarships awarded for academics, alumni affiliation, athletics, leadership, minority status, music/drama, religious affiliation.

**Application procedures.** **Admission:** Closing date 7/1. $25 fee, may be waived for applicants with need. Application may be submitted online. Admission notification on a rolling basis beginning on or about 9/1. Must reply by May 1 or within 3 week(s) if notified thereafter. **Financial aid:** Priority date 3/1; no closing date. FAFSA required. Applicants notified on a rolling basis starting 3/1; must reply within 3 week(s) of notification.

**Academics.** **Special study options:** Combined bachelor's/graduate degree, cooperative education, distance learning, double major, dual enrollment of high school students, ESL, honors, independent study, internships, liberal arts/career combination, study abroad, teacher certification program, Washington semester, weekend college. Bachelor's degree completion program for registered nurses, 5-year program leading to master's degree in architecture. **Credit/placement by examination:** AP, CLEP, institutional tests. 30 credit hours maximum toward bachelor's degree. **Support services:** Learning center, reduced course load, remedial instruction, study skills assistance, tutoring, writing center.

**Majors.** **Architecture:** Architecture. **Biology:** General, biochemistry. **Business:** General, accounting, business admin, marketing. **Communications:** General, broadcast journalism, journalism, public relations. **Computer sciences:** General, computer science, systems analysis. **Education:** General, biology, chemistry, elementary, emotionally handicapped, history, mathematics, mentally handicapped, middle, reading, science, secondary, social science, social studies, special. **Engineering:** General, civil, computer, electrical, manufacturing, mechanical. **English:** Creative writing, English lit, speech/rhetoric, technical writing. **Health:** Dental hygiene, nursing (RN), predental, premedicine, substance abuse counseling. **History:** General. **Legal studies:** Paralegal, prelaw. **Liberal arts:** Arts/sciences. **Math:** General, applied. **Philosophy/religion:** Philosophy, religion. **Physical sciences:** Chemistry. **Protective services:** Criminal justice, law enforcement admin, police science. **Psychology:** General. **Public administration:** Social work. **Social sciences:** Economics, political science, sociology. **Visual/performing arts:** Dramatic.

**Most popular majors.** Biology 8%, business/marketing 12%, engineering/engineering technologies 13%, health sciences 36%.

**Computing on campus.** 250 workstations in dormitories, library, computer center, student center. Dormitories wired for high-speed internet access and linked to campus network. Commuter students can connect to campus network. Online library, helpline, repair service, student web hosting, wireless network available.

**Student life.** **Freshman orientation:** Available, $200 fee. Preregistration for classes offered. **Housing:** Coed dorms available. $100 deposit. International housing; intensive quiet floors; peace and justice floor; floor for women studying engineering, science, or architecture; honors floor available. **Activities:** Pep band, dance, drama, literary magazine, radio station, student government, student newspaper, American Institute of Architecture students, College Democrats, College Republicans, international student association, minority student association, NAACP, philosophy club, chemistry club, engineering societies, poet and writers forum, student environmental club.

**Athletics.** NCAA. **Intercollegiate:** Basketball, cheerleading, cross-country, fencing, golf, lacrosse, soccer, softball W, tennis W, track and field.

**Intramural:** Baseball M, basketball, racquetball, soccer M, softball, table tennis, tennis, volleyball. **Team name:** Detroit Titans.

**Student services.** Adult student services, alcohol/substance abuse counseling, campus ministries, career counseling, student employment services, financial aid counseling, health services, on-campus daycare, personal counseling, placement for graduates, veterans' counselor.

**Contact.** E-mail: admissions@udmercy.edu
Phone: (313) 993-1245 Toll-free number: (800) 635-5020
Fax: (313) 993-3326
Denise Williams, Director of Admissions, University of Detroit Mercy, 4001 West McNichols Road, Detroit, MI 48221-3038

## University of Michigan
**Ann Arbor, Michigan**
**www.umich.edu**

CB member
CB code: 1839

- Public 4-year university
- Residential campus in small city
- 25,916 degree-seeking undergraduates: 3% part-time, 50% women, 6% African American, 12% Asian American, 5% Hispanic American, 1% Native American, 5% international
- 13,261 degree-seeking graduate students
- 50% of applicants admitted
- SAT or ACT (ACT writing optional), application essay required
- 87% graduate within 6 years

**General.** Founded in 1817. Regionally accredited. Over 150 first-year seminars and several thousand undergraduate research opportunities. **Degrees:** 5,941 bachelor's awarded; master's, doctoral, first professional offered. **ROTC:** Army, Naval, Air Force. **Location:** 50 miles from Detroit. **Calendar:** Trimester, limited summer session. **Full-time faculty:** 2,367 total; 91% have terminal degrees, 23% minority, 37% women. **Part-time faculty:** 604 total; 75% have terminal degrees, 14% minority, 50% women. **Class size:** 45% < 20, 34% 20-39, 4% 40-49, 11% 50-99, 7% >100. **Special facilities:** Botanical garden, biological station in northern Michigan, arboretum, planetarium, laboratories, observatory, field station in the greater Yellowstone ecosystem, exhibit museum, art museum, herbarium, galleries.

**Freshman class profile.** 27,474 applied, 13,826 admitted, 5,992 enrolled.

| Mid 50% test scores | | | |
|---|---|---|---|
| SAT critical reading: | 590-690 | Return as sophomores: | 96% |
| SAT math: | 630-730 | Out-of-state: | 35% |
| ACT composite: | 27-31 | Live on campus: | 96% |
| Rank in top quarter: | 99% | International: | 4% |
| Rank in top tenth: | 92% | Fraternities: | 15% |
| | | Sororities: | 19% |

**Basis for selection.** Admissions based on school achievement record, including quality of school and courses elected, and test scores. Talents and extracurricular activities considered. Special consideration to educationally disadvantaged applicants. Audition required for music majors; portfolio required for art majors. **Homeschooled:** SAT Subject Test may be required.

**High school preparation.** 16 units required; 20 recommended. Required and recommended units include English 4, mathematics 3, social studies 3, history 3, science 3 (laboratory 1), foreign language 2-4, computer science 1, visual/performing arts 2 and academic electives 1.

**2007-2008 Annual costs.** Tuition/fees: $10,447; $31,301 out-of-state. Room/board: $8,190. Books/supplies: $1,020. Personal expenses: $2,000.

**2006-2007 Financial aid.** **Need-based:** 3,408 full-time freshmen applied for aid; 2,428 were judged to have need; 2,428 of these received aid. Average need met was 90%. Average scholarship/grant was $8,825; average loan $5,839. 50% of total undergraduate aid awarded as scholarships/grants, 50% as loans/jobs. **Non-need-based:** Awarded to 15,207 full-time undergraduates, including 4,585 freshmen. Scholarships awarded for academics, alumni affiliation, art, athletics, leadership, music/drama, religious affiliation, ROTC, state residency.

**Application procedures.** **Admission:** Closing date 2/1 (postmark date). $40 fee, may be waived for applicants with need. Application may be submitted online. Admission notification on a rolling basis beginning on or about 9/1. Must reply by 5/1. Students should apply early in the fall of senior year. Applications may be considered after 2/1 for School of Art and Design, School of Music, Theatre and Dance, School of Natural Resources and Environment, and School of Nursing programs on space availability basis. **Financial aid:** Priority date 2/15, closing date 4/30. FAFSA, CSS PROFILE required. Applicants notified on a rolling basis starting 3/15; must reply within 2 week(s) of notification.

**Academics.** Community health nursing program involves staying on-campus from Friday through Sunday for long weekend once a month for 47-credit master's degree. Small-scale, interdisciplinary instruction programs in residence halls; freshman and sophomore seminars, unique undergraduate research, and mentoring opportunities available. **Special study options:** Accelerated study, combined bachelor's/graduate degree, cooperative education, cross-registration, distance learning, double major, dual enrollment of high school students, ESL, exchange student, honors, independent study, internships, liberal arts/career combination, semester at sea, student-designed major, study abroad, teacher certification program, Washington semester, weekend college. Preferred admissions program to UM graduate/professional schools, graduate, business program available through branch campus, and weekend college for graduate students in public health, business administration and engineering. **Credit/placement by examination:** AP, CLEP, IB, institutional tests. 60 credit hours maximum toward bachelor's degree. Policies on credit by examination varies by exam. **Support services:** Learning center, reduced course load, study skills assistance, tutoring, writing center.

**Honors college/program.** 10% of each incoming freshman class admitted; grades, test scores, recommendations, and essay used in decision process.

**Majors. Architecture:** Architecture. **Area/ethnic studies:** African-American, American, Asian, Hispanic-American/Latino/Chicano, Latin American, Near/Middle Eastern, Russian/Slavic, women's. **Biology:** General, biochemistry, biophysics, cellular/molecular, ecology, microbiology. **Business:** Business admin, organizational behavior. **Communications:** General. **Computer sciences:** General. **Conservation:** Environmental studies. **Education:** Elementary, music, physical. **Engineering:** General, aerospace, biomedical, chemical, civil, computer, electrical, geological, industrial, marine, materials science, mechanical, nuclear, physics, science. **English:** British lit, creative writing. **Foreign languages:** Ancient Greek, classics, comparative lit, French, German, Hebrew, Italian, Latin, linguistics, modern Greek, Russian, Spanish. **Health:** Athletic training, dental hygiene, nursing (RN). **History:** General. **Interdisciplinary:** Ancient studies, classical/archaeology, medieval/Renaissance, neuroscience. **Liberal arts:** Humanities. **Math:** General, statistics. **Parks/recreation:** Exercise sciences, sports admin. **Philosophy/religion:** Judaic, philosophy, religion. **Physical sciences:** Astronomy, atmospheric science, chemistry, geology, oceanography, physics. **Psychology:** General. **Public administration:** Policy analysis. **Social sciences:** General, anthropology, economics, political science, sociology. **Visual/performing arts:** Art, art history/conservation, ceramics, dance, dramatic, drawing, fiber arts, film/cinema, graphic design, illustration, industrial design, jazz, metal/jewelry, music history, music performance, music theory/composition, printmaking, sculpture, theater design. **Other:** Pharmacy administration, policy and regulatory affairs.

**Most popular majors.** Biology 6%, business/marketing 6%, engineering/engineering technologies 15%, English 6%, psychology 11%, social sciences 18%, visual/performing arts 6%.

**Computing on campus.** 2,600 workstations in dormitories, library, computer center, student center. Dormitories wired for high-speed internet access and linked to campus network. Commuter students can connect to campus network. Online course registration, online library, helpline, repair service, student web hosting, wireless network available.

**Student life. Freshman orientation:** Mandatory, $232 fee. Preregistration for classes offered. Students must attend 1 of several 3-day summer programs. **Housing:** Guaranteed on-campus for freshmen. Coed dorms, single-sex dorms, special housing for disabled, apartments, cooperative housing, fraternity/sorority housing, substance-free housing available. Living-learning communities; substance-free dorms. **Activities:** Bands, campus ministries, choral groups, dance, drama, film society, international student organizations, literary magazine, music ensembles, Model UN, musical theater, opera, radio station, student government, student newspaper, symphony orchestra, TV station, over 1,000 student organizations.

**Athletics.** NCAA. **Intercollegiate:** Baseball M, basketball, cross-country, diving, field hockey W, football (tackle) M, golf, gymnastics, ice hockey M, rowing (crew) W, soccer, softball W, swimming, tennis, track and field, volleyball W, water polo W, wrestling M. **Intramural:** Badminton, basketball, cross-country, diving, football (non-tackle), golf, racquetball, soccer, softball, swimming, table tennis, tennis, track and field, volleyball, water polo, wrestling. **Team name:** Wolverines.

**Student services.** Adult student services, alcohol/substance abuse counseling, campus ministries, career counseling, student employment services, financial aid counseling, health services, legal services, minority student services, on-campus daycare, personal counseling, placement for graduates, women's services. **Physically disabled:** Services for visually, speech, hearing impaired.

**Contact.** E-mail: ugadmiss@umich.edu
Phone: (734) 764-7433 Fax: (734) 936-0740
Theodore Spencer, Associate Vice Provost and Executive Director, Undergraduate Admissions, University of Michigan, 1220 Student Activities Building, Ann Arbor, MI 48109-1316

## University of Michigan: Dearborn
**Dearborn, Michigan**     **CB member**
**www.umd.umich.edu**     **CB code: 1861**

- Public 4-year university
- Commuter campus in small city
- 6,212 degree-seeking undergraduates: 32% part-time, 52% women
- 1,829 degree-seeking graduate students
- 66% of applicants admitted
- SAT or ACT (ACT writing optional) required
- 50% graduate within 6 years

**General.** Founded in 1959. Regionally accredited. **Degrees:** 1,214 bachelor's awarded; master's offered. **ROTC:** Army, Naval, Air Force. **Location:** 10 miles from Detroit. **Calendar:** Semester, limited summer session. **Full-time faculty:** 292 total; 100% have terminal degrees, 30% minority, 35% women. **Part-time faculty:** 189 total; 100% have terminal degrees, 10% minority, 38% women. **Class size:** 31% < 20, 46% 20-39, 12% 40-49, 8% 50-99, less than 1% >100. **Special facilities:** Henry Ford's Fair Lane estate, environmental study area, extensive rotating art collection, engineering CAD-CAM robotics laboratory, Armenian research center.

**Freshman class profile.** 3,438 applied, 2,273 admitted, 903 enrolled.

| Mid 50% test scores | | | |
|---|---|---|---|
| ACT composite: | 21-26 | Rank in top tenth: | 25% |
| GPA 3.50 or higher: | 50% | Return as sophomores: | 81% |
| GPA 3.0-3.49: | 35% | Out-of-state: | 1% |
| GPA 2.0-2.99: | 15% | Fraternities: | 3% |
| Rank in top quarter: | 62% | Sororities: | 3% |

**Basis for selection.** Minimum 3.0 GPA with 500 SAT verbal and math or 22 ACT preferred; class rank considered. Interview recommended for applicants with less than 3.0 GPA or 20 ACT or 1000 SAT (exclusive of Writing). Essay recommended for all.

**High school preparation.** 15 units required; 20 recommended. Required and recommended units include English 4, mathematics 4, social studies 4, history 4, science 3 (laboratory 1) and foreign language 3. 1 unit information technology and 1 unit fine and performing arts recommended.

**2007-2008 Annual costs.** Tuition/fees: $8,009; $17,499 out-of-state. Books/supplies: $960. Personal expenses: $5,179.

**2006-2007 Financial aid. Need-based:** 570 full-time freshmen applied for aid; 336 were judged to have need; 336 of these received aid. Average need met was 47%. Average scholarship/grant was $3,817; average loan $2,732. 84% of total undergraduate aid awarded as scholarships/grants, 16% as loans/jobs. **Non-need-based:** Awarded to 2,590 full-time undergraduates, including 922 freshmen. Scholarships awarded for academics, alumni affiliation, athletics, job skills, leadership, minority status, ROTC.

**Application procedures. Admission:** Priority date 5/1; no deadline. $30 fee, may be waived for applicants with need. Application may be submitted online. Admission notification on a rolling basis beginning on or about 9/1. Must reply by May 1 or within 4 week(s) if notified thereafter. **Financial aid:** Priority date 2/15; no closing date. FAFSA required. Applicants notified on a rolling basis starting 3/1; must reply within 3 week(s) of notification.

**Academics. Special study options:** Accelerated study, cooperative education, cross-registration, distance learning, double major, dual enrollment of high school students, honors, independent study, internships, liberal arts/career combination, student-designed major, study abroad, teacher certification program, Washington semester. Professional development courses in education, engineering, liberal arts, and management. **Credit/placement by examination:** AP, CLEP, institutional tests. 30 credit hours maximum toward bachelor's degree. **Support services:** Learning center, pre-admission summer program, tutoring.

**Majors. Area/ethnic studies:** American. **Biology:** General, bacteriology, biochemistry, ecology. **Business:** Business admin, management science. **Communications:** General. **Computer sciences:** General, programming. **Conservation:** General, environmental studies. **Education:** General, art, business, chemistry, early childhood, foreign languages, mathematics, science, secondary, social studies. **Engineering:** General, computer, electrical, manufacturing, mechanical. **English:** English lit. **Foreign languages:** French,

Spanish. **Health:** Health care admin. **History:** General. **Interdisciplinary:** Behavioral sciences. **Liberal arts:** Arts/sciences. **Math:** General. **Philosophy/religion:** Philosophy. **Physical sciences:** Chemistry, physics. **Psychology:** General. **Public administration:** General. **Social sciences:** Anthropology, economics, political science, sociology. **Visual/performing arts:** Painting.

**Most popular majors.** Business/marketing 21%, education 24%, engineering/engineering technologies 18%.

**Computing on campus.** 140 workstations in library, computer center, student center. Commuter students can connect to campus network. Online course registration, helpline, wireless network available.

**Student life. Freshman orientation:** Mandatory, $50 fee. **Activities:** Choral groups, drama, film society, literary magazine, radio station, student government, student newspaper, TV station, Arab student union, African American association, campus engineers, Asian American association, student activities board, professional accounting society, Muslim student association.

**Athletics.** NAIA. **Intercollegiate:** Basketball, ice hockey M, volleyball W. **Intramural:** Basketball, ice hockey, softball, table tennis, tennis, volleyball. **Team name:** Wolves.

**Student services.** Adult student services, alcohol/substance abuse counseling, career counseling, student employment services, financial aid counseling, health services, on-campus daycare, personal counseling, placement for graduates, veterans' counselor, women's services. **Physically disabled:** Services for visually, speech, hearing impaired.

**Contact.** E-mail: admissions@umd.umich.edu
Phone: (313) 593-5100 Fax: (313) 436-9167
Christopher Tremblay, Director of Admissions, University of Michigan: Dearborn, 4901 Evergreen Road, 1145 UC, Dearborn, MI 48128-1491

## University of Michigan: Flint

Flint, Michigan
www.umflint.edu

CB member
CB code: 1853

- Public 4-year university and branch campus college
- Commuter campus in small city
- 5,655 degree-seeking undergraduates: 37% part-time, 62% women, 12% African American, 2% Asian American, 3% Hispanic American, 1% Native American, 1% international
- 1,022 degree-seeking graduate students
- 82% of applicants admitted
- SAT or ACT (ACT writing optional) required

**General.** Founded in 1956. Regionally accredited. Institution shares many resources of entire University of Michigan system. **Degrees:** 917 bachelor's awarded; master's, doctoral offered. **Location:** 60 miles from Detroit. **Calendar:** Semester, limited summer session. **Class size:** 44% < 20, 46% 20-39, 5% 40-49, 5% 50-99, less than 1% >100.

**Freshman class profile.** 1,901 applied, 1,554 admitted, 626 enrolled.

| Mid 50% test scores | | | |
|---|---|---|---|
| SAT critical reading: | 410-590 | Rank in top tenth: | 17% |
| SAT math: | 510-580 | End year in good standing: | 91% |
| ACT composite: | 19-24 | Return as sophomores: | 71% |
| GPA 3.50 or higher: | 33% | Out-of-state: | 1% |
| GPA 3.0-3.49: | 34% | International: | 2% |
| GPA 2.0-2.99: | 31% | Fraternities: | 1% |
| Rank in top quarter: | 42% | Sororities: | 1% |

**Basis for selection.** GPA of 2.7 or higher and test scores equaling national average automatically admitted. Essay and interview recommended. Audition required for art and music majors.

**High school preparation.** 12 units required; 21 recommended. Required and recommended units include English 4, mathematics 3-4, social studies 2, history 2, science 2-4 (laboratory 2) and foreign language 2. Fine arts and computer science courses recommended.

**2007-2008 Annual costs.** Tuition/fees: $7,343; $13,998 out-of-state. Books/supplies: $950. Personal expenses: $1,350.

**2006-2007 Financial aid. Need-based:** 377 full-time freshmen applied for aid; 266 were judged to have need; 254 of these received aid. Average need met was 63%. Average scholarship/grant was $4,119; average loan $3,034. 32% of total undergraduate aid awarded as scholarships/grants, 68% as loans/jobs. **Non-need-based:** Awarded to 1,212 full-time undergraduates, including 210 freshmen. Scholarships awarded for academics, art, leadership, music/drama. **Additional information:** SAT/ACT scores must be submitted for scholarship consideration.

**Application procedures. Admission:** No deadline. $30 fee, may be waived for applicants with need. Application may be submitted online. Admission notification on a rolling basis beginning on or about 12/1. Must reply by May 1 or within 2 week(s) if notified thereafter. **Financial aid:** Priority date 3/1; no closing date. FAFSA required. Applicants notified on a rolling basis starting 3/15.

**Academics. Special study options:** Combined bachelor's/graduate degree, cooperative education, distance learning, double major, dual enrollment of high school students, ESL, honors, independent study, internships, student-designed major, study abroad, teacher certification program. **Credit/placement by examination:** AP, CLEP, SAT, ACT, institutional tests. Maximum of 3 courses may be passed by examination in Arts & Sciences, School of Management and Nursing. **Support services:** Learning center, reduced course load, remedial instruction, study skills assistance, tutoring, writing center.

**Majors. Area/ethnic studies:** African-American. **Biology:** General, biomedical sciences, ecology, molecular, wildlife. **Business:** Accounting, actuarial science, business admin, finance, international, marketing, operations, organizational behavior. **Communications:** General, media studies, organizational. **Computer sciences:** General, computer science, information systems. **Conservation:** Environmental science. **Education:** General, art, biology, chemistry, elementary, English, foreign languages, French, history, mathematics, music, physics, science, secondary, social studies, Spanish. **Engineering:** Science. **English:** Composition, creative writing, English lit. **Foreign languages:** French, Spanish. **Health:** Clinical lab science, health care admin, health services, medical radiologic technology/radiation therapy, nursing (RN), public health ed. **History:** General. **Liberal arts:** Arts/sciences. **Math:** General. **Philosophy/religion:** Ethics, philosophy. **Physical sciences:** Chemistry, physics. **Protective services:** Law enforcement admin. **Psychology:** General, clinical. **Public administration:** General, social work. **Social sciences:** General, anthropology, economics, political science, sociology. **Visual/performing arts:** Acting, ceramics, dramatic, graphic design, music performance, painting, photography, printmaking, sculpture, studio arts, theater design, theater history.

**Most popular majors.** Business/marketing 15%, education 23%, health sciences 18%.

**Computing on campus.** 205 workstations in library, computer center, student center. Commuter students can connect to campus network. Online course registration, online library, helpline, repair service, student web hosting, wireless network available.

**Student life. Freshman orientation:** Mandatory, $60 fee. Preregistration for classes offered. One-day program for students and parents before start of fall semester. **Activities:** Bands, choral groups, dance, drama, literary magazine, music ensembles, musical theater, student government, student newspaper, TV station, College Democrats, College Republicans, Hillel student organization, Intervarsity Christian Fellowship, Muslim student association, Organization for University Tolerance, College Libertarians, Students Organizing Fun Activities Sober (SOFAS), poetry society, Voices for Women on Campus.

**Athletics. Intramural:** Basketball, football (non-tackle), racquetball, soccer, table tennis, volleyball.

**Student services.** Adult student services, alcohol/substance abuse counseling, career counseling, student employment services, financial aid counseling, health services, minority student services, on-campus daycare, personal counseling, women's services. **Physically disabled:** Services for visually, speech, hearing impaired.

**Contact.** E-mail: admissions@umflint.edu
Phone: (810) 762-3300 Fax: (810) 762-3272
Kimberley Buster-Williams, Director of Admissions, University of Michigan: Flint, 303 East Kearsley Street, Flint, MI 48502-1950

## Walsh College of Accountancy and Business Administration

Troy, Michigan
www.walshcollege.edu

CB code: 0372

- Private two-year upper-division business college
- Commuter campus in large city

**General.** Founded in 1922. Regionally accredited. **Degrees:** 374 bachelor's awarded; master's, doctoral offered. **Articulation:** Agreements with Henry Ford CC, Oakland CC, Macomb CC, Mott CC, Schoolcraft College, Washtenaw CC, St. Clair County CC, Wayne County CC, Kellogg CC, Jackson CC, Lansing CC, Lewis College of Business. **Location:** 17 miles from Detroit. **Calendar:** Semester, extensive summer session. **Full-time faculty:**

17 total. **Part-time faculty:** 150 total. **Class size:** 25% < 20, 70% 20-39, 5% 40-49.

**Student profile.** 1,047 degree-seeking undergraduates. 100% entered as juniors.

| | | | |
|---|---|---|---|
| Out-of-state: | 2% | 25 or older: | 64% |

**Basis for selection.** Open admission. College transcript required. 30 transferred credits must be in liberal arts, including course in English composition or written communication. Transfer accepted as juniors.

**2007-2008 Annual costs.** Tuition/fees: $8,280. Books/supplies: $2,016.

**Financial aid. Need-based:** 142 applied for aid; 121 were judged to have need; 121 of these received aid. Average need met was 47%. 23% of total undergraduate aid awarded as scholarships/grants, 77% as loans/jobs. **Non-need-based:** Awarded to 24 undergraduates. Scholarships awarded for academics.

**Application procedures. Admission:** Rolling admission. $25 fee, may be waived for applicants with need. Application may be submitted online. **Financial aid:** Priority date 3/1, no deadline. Applicants notified on a rolling basis. FAFSA required.

**Academics. Special study options:** Accelerated study, distance learning, double major, internships. Joint partnerships with area community colleges to offer 150-hour honors program in which students complete associate, bachelor and MBA degrees in 5 years. **Credit/placement by examination:** CLEP, IB. **Support services:** Reduced course load, study skills assistance, tutoring.

**Majors. Business:** General, accounting, business admin, finance. **Computer sciences:** General, information technology.

**Most popular majors.** Business/marketing 74%.

**Computing on campus.** 200 workstations in library, computer center. Commuter students can connect to campus network. Helpline available.

**Student life. Activities:** Student government, American Marketing Association, finance/economics club, National Association of Black Accountants, accounting club, Association of Information Technology Professionals, international club.

**Student services.** Career counseling, student employment services, financial aid counseling, placement for graduates. **Physically disabled:** Services for visually, hearing impaired.

**Contact.** E-mail: admissions@walshcollege.edu
Phone: (248) 823-1610 Toll-free number: (800) 925-7401
Fax: (248) 823-1662
Director of Admissions and Academic Advising, Walsh College of Accountancy and Business Administration, PO Box 7006, Troy, MI 48007-7006

---

## Wayne State University

**Detroit, Michigan**          **CB member**
www.wayne.edu               **CB code: 1898**

- Public 4-year university
- Commuter campus in very large city
- 19,964 degree-seeking undergraduates: 38% part-time, 58% women, 32% African American, 6% Asian American, 3% Hispanic American, 4% international
- 11,706 degree-seeking graduate students
- 83% of applicants admitted
- SAT or ACT (ACT writing optional) required

**General.** Founded in 1868. Regionally accredited. 5 off-campus locations and University Center at local community college. **Degrees:** 2,380 bachelor's awarded; master's, doctoral, first professional offered. **ROTC:** Air Force. **Location:** 3 miles from downtown. **Calendar:** Semester, extensive summer session. **Full-time faculty:** 978 total; 72% have terminal degrees, 25% minority, 40% women. **Part-time faculty:** 950 total; 17% have terminal degrees, 26% minority, 52% women. **Class size:** 54% < 20, 37% 20-39, 3% 40-49, 4% 50-99, 1% >100. **Special facilities:** 3 theaters.

**Freshman class profile.** 9,004 applied, 7,515 admitted, 3,188 enrolled.

| Mid 50% test scores | | | |
|---|---|---|---|
| ACT composite: | 17-24 | Out-of-state: | 1% |
| GPA 3.50 or higher: | 30% | Live on campus: | 23% |
| GPA 3.0-3.49: | 29% | International: | 4% |
| GPA 2.0-2.99: | 38% | Fraternities: | 1% |
| Return as sophomores: | 67% | Sororities: | 1% |

**Basis for selection.** High school record, test scores important. Minimum 2.75 GPA or 2.0 GPA combined with 21 ACT. Audition required of music applicants, recommended for dance and theater applicants; portfolio required for art applicants.

**High school preparation.** 17 units recommended. Recommended units include English 4, mathematics 3, social studies 3, science 3, foreign language 2 and visual/performing arts 2. Computer literacy.

**2007-2008 Annual costs.** Tuition/fees: $7,649; $16,400 out-of-state. Room/board: $6,702. Books/supplies: $885. Personal expenses: $2,105.

**2006-2007 Financial aid. Need-based:** 1,996 full-time freshmen applied for aid; 1,654 were judged to have need; 1,619 of these received aid. Average need met was 62%. Average scholarship/grant was $3,703; average loan $2,646. 28% of total undergraduate aid awarded as scholarships/grants, 72% as loans/jobs. **Non-need-based:** Awarded to 4,755 full-time undergraduates, including 1,402 freshmen. Scholarships awarded for academics, art, athletics, leadership, music/drama.

**Application procedures. Admission:** Closing date 8/1 (receipt date). $30 fee, may be waived for applicants with need. Application may be submitted online. Admission notification on a rolling basis beginning on or about 9/15. **Financial aid:** Priority date 3/1; no closing date. FAFSA required. Applicants notified on a rolling basis starting 4/15; must reply within 2 week(s) of notification.

**Academics. Special study options:** Accelerated study, combined bachelor's/graduate degree, cooperative education, cross-registration, distance learning, double major, dual enrollment of high school students, ESL, exchange student, honors, independent study, internships, liberal arts/career combination, study abroad, teacher certification program, weekend college. Off-campus courses for credit, city-wide adult education program. **Credit/placement by examination:** AP, CLEP, IB, institutional tests. 32 credit hours maximum toward bachelor's degree. **Support services:** Learning center, pre-admission summer program, remedial instruction, study skills assistance, tutoring, writing center.

**Majors. Area/ethnic studies:** African-American, American, Asian, East Asian, Hispanic-American/Latino/Chicano, women's. **Biology:** General. **Business:** Accounting, finance, labor studies, management information systems, marketing, organizational behavior. **Communications:** General, journalism, public relations, radio/tv. **Computer sciences:** General, information systems. **Conservation:** Environmental science. **Education:** Art, elementary, English, health, mathematics, physical, science, social studies, special, speech impaired, voc/tech. **Engineering:** Chemical, civil, electrical, industrial, mechanical. **Engineering technology:** Computer systems, electrical, electromechanical, industrial, mechanical. **English:** English lit. **Family/consumer sciences:** Apparel marketing, family studies, food/nutrition. **Foreign languages:** Classics, German, linguistics, Slavic. **Health:** Clinical lab science, communication disorders, medical radiologic technology/radiation therapy, nursing (RN), pathology assistant, speech pathology. **History:** General. **Math:** General. **Personal/culinary services:** Mortuary science. **Philosophy/religion:** Philosophy. **Physical sciences:** Chemistry, geology, physics. **Protective services:** Criminal justice. **Psychology:** General. **Public administration:** General, social work. **Social sciences:** Anthropology, economics, geography, political science, sociology, urban studies. **Visual/performing arts:** Art, art history/conservation, cinematography, dance, dramatic, film/cinema.

**Most popular majors.** Biology 6%, business/marketing 18%, education 14%, engineering/engineering technologies 8%, health sciences 9%, psychology 7%, visual/performing arts 8%.

**Computing on campus.** 1,000 workstations in library. Dormitories wired for high-speed internet access and linked to campus network. Commuter students can connect to campus network. Online course registration, helpline, repair service, wireless network available.

**Student life. Freshman orientation:** Mandatory, $75 fee. Preregistration for classes offered. **Housing:** Coed dorms, special housing for disabled, apartments, fraternity/sorority housing, substance-free housing available. $150 partly refundable deposit. **Activities:** Bands, choral groups, dance, drama, film society, literary magazine, music ensembles, musical theater, opera, student government, student newspaper, symphony orchestra, Indian student association, Golden Key honor society, Campus Crusade for Christ, friendship association of Chinese students.

**Athletics.** NCAA. **Intercollegiate:** Baseball M, basketball, cross-country, diving, fencing, football (tackle) M, golf M, ice hockey, softball W, swimming, tennis, volleyball W. **Intramural:** Badminton, basketball, bowling, football (non-tackle), football (tackle), racquetball, soccer, softball, tennis, volleyball. **Team name:** Warriors.

**Student services.** Adult student services, alcohol/substance abuse counseling, campus ministries, career counseling, services for economically disadvantaged, student employment services, financial aid counseling, health services, legal services, minority student services, on-campus daycare, personal counseling, placement for graduates, veterans' counselor, women's services. **Physically disabled:** Services for visually, speech, hearing impaired.

**Contact.**  E-mail: admissions@wayne.edu
Phone: (313) 577-3577 Toll-free number: (877) 978-4636
Fax: (313) 577-7536
Susan Zwieg, Director of University Admissions, Wayne State University, 42 West Warren, Detroit, MI 48202

## Western Michigan University
**Kalamazoo, Michigan**                          **CB member**
**www.wmich.edu**                                **CB code: 1902**

◆  Public 4-year university
◆  Residential campus in small city
◆  19,572 degree-seeking undergraduates: 12% part-time, 50% women, 6% African American, 2% Asian American, 2% Hispanic American, 1% Native American, 2% international
◆  1,168 degree-seeking graduate students
◆  86% of applicants admitted
◆  SAT or ACT (ACT writing optional) required

**General.** Founded in 1903. Regionally accredited. **Degrees:** 4,855 bachelor's awarded; master's, doctoral offered. **ROTC:** Army. **Location:** 140 miles from Detroit, 140 miles from Chicago. **Calendar:** Semester, extensive summer session. **Full-time faculty:** 913 total; 80% have terminal degrees, 14% minority, 39% women. **Part-time faculty:** 441 total; 55% women. **Class size:** 41% < 20, 39% 20-39, 10% 40-49, 7% 50-99, 4% >100. **Special facilities:** Van de Graaff particle accelerator, pilot plant for manufacturing and printing of paper and fiber recovery, aviation flight simulators, business technology park.

**Freshman class profile.** 11,791 applied, 10,179 admitted, 3,506 enrolled.

| Mid 50% test scores | | Rank in top tenth: | 10% |
|---|---|---|---|
| ACT composite: | 20-25 | Out-of-state: | 7% |
| GPA 3.50 or higher: | 29% | Live on campus: | 65% |
| GPA 3.0-3.49: | 39% | International: | 1% |
| GPA 2.0-2.99: | 32% | Fraternities: | 6% |
| Rank in top quarter: | 29% | Sororities: | 12% |

**Basis for selection.** School achievement record, test scores most important. Trend of grades and number of solid high school academic subjects completed considered; students not meeting college-preparatory program requirements may be admitted conditionally if they meet other admission requirements. Interview recommended. Audition required for dance, music, and theater applicants. Portfolio required for some art applicants. **Home-schooled:** State high school equivalency certificate, letter of recommendation (nonparent) required.

**High school preparation.** 15 units required; 18 recommended. Required and recommended units include English 4, mathematics 3, social studies 2-3, history 1, science 2 (laboratory 1), foreign language 2 and academic electives 2.

**2007-2008 Annual costs.** Tuition/fees: $7,260; $16,806 out-of-state. Room/board: $7,042. Books/supplies: $925. Personal expenses: $2,020.

**2007-2008 Financial aid. Need-based:** Average need met was 69%. Average scholarship/grant was $4,500; average loan $2,800. 34% of total undergraduate aid awarded as scholarships/grants, 66% as loans/jobs. **Non-need-based:** Scholarships awarded for academics, alumni affiliation, art, athletics, minority status, music/drama, ROTC, state residency.

**Application procedures. Admission:** No deadline. $35 fee, may be waived for applicants with need. Application may be submitted online. Admission notification on a rolling basis beginning on or about 9/15. **Financial aid:** Priority date 3/15; no closing date. FAFSA required. Applicants notified on a rolling basis starting 3/15.

**Academics. Special study options:** Accelerated study, combined bachelor's/graduate degree, cooperative education, cross-registration, distance learning, double major, dual enrollment of high school students, ESL, exchange student, honors, independent study, internships, student-designed major, study abroad, teacher certification program, weekend college. **Credit/placement by examination:** AP, CLEP, IB, SAT, ACT, institutional tests. Maximum semester hours of credit by examination which may be counted toward degree varies by department. Credit by examination may not be used to satisfy minimum residency requirement of 30 semester hours. **Support services:** Learning center, pre-admission summer program, reduced course load, remedial instruction, study skills assistance, tutoring, writing center.

**Honors college/program.** 3.6 GPA and 26 ACT or rank in top 10% of graduating class required. Academic essay, college cocurricular and community activities, and 2 recommendations from faculty also required. Academic program includes freshman/sophomore course clusters (3 courses in each group, at least 3 credits each), junior and senior seminars, honors thesis. 270 positions available each year.

**Majors. Area/ethnic studies:** African-American, women's. **Biology:** General, biochemistry, biomedical sciences. **Business:** General, accounting, e-commerce, finance, financial planning, information resources management, logistics, management science, managerial economics, travel services. **Communications:** General, advertising, journalism, organizational, public relations. **Computer sciences:** General, computer science. **Conservation:** Environmental studies. **Education:** Biology, business, chemistry, college student counseling, elementary, emotionally handicapped, English, family/consumer sciences, French, geography, German, health, history, Latin, mathematics, mentally handicapped, music, physical, physics, sales/marketing, science, social science, Spanish, technology/industrial arts. **Engineering:** Aerospace, chemical, civil, computer, electrical, industrial, manufacturing, mechanical, structural. **Engineering technology:** Industrial management. **English:** English lit. **Family/consumer sciences:** Clothing/textiles, family systems, institutional food production. **Foreign languages:** French, German, Latin, Spanish. **Health:** Athletic training, audiology/speech pathology, dietetics, music therapy, nursing (RN). **History:** General, public archives. **Interdisciplinary:** Global studies. **Math:** General, statistics. **Mechanic/repair:** Avionics. **Parks/recreation:** General, exercise sciences. **Philosophy/religion:** Philosophy, religion. **Physical sciences:** Chemistry, geochemistry, geology, geophysics, hydrology, physics. **Protective services:** Criminal justice. **Psychology:** General, social. **Public administration:** General, social work. **Social sciences:** Anthropology, economics, geography, political science, sociology. **Transportation:** Airline/commercial pilot, aviation management. **Visual/performing arts:** Acting, art, art history/conservation, cinematography, dance, dramatic, graphic design, industrial design, interior design, jazz, music performance, music theory/composition, musical theater, studio arts, theater design, theater history. **Other:** Business-oriented chemistry, Paper science and engineering, imaging, Student-planned major.

**Most popular majors.** Business/marketing 24%, communications/journalism 6%, education 19%, engineering/engineering technologies 6%, health sciences 6%, visual/performing arts 6%.

**Computing on campus.** 2,000 workstations in dormitories, library, computer center, student center. Dormitories wired for high-speed internet access and linked to campus network. Commuter students can connect to campus network. Online course registration, helpline, repair service, student web hosting, wireless network available.

**Student life. Freshman orientation:** Mandatory, $150 fee. Preregistration for classes offered. 2-day program in June; includes session for parents. **Policies:** Student code. **Housing:** Guaranteed on-campus for freshmen. Coed dorms, single-sex dorms, special housing for disabled, apartments, fraternity/sorority housing, substance-free housing available. $500 partly refundable deposit. Themed halls available. **Activities:** Bands, choral groups, dance, drama, film society, international student organizations, literary magazine, music ensembles, musical theater, opera, radio station, student government, student newspaper, symphony orchestra, Over 275 organizations available.

**Athletics.** NCAA. **Intercollegiate:** Baseball M, basketball, cross-country W, football (tackle) M, golf W, gymnastics W, ice hockey M, soccer, softball W, tennis, track and field W, volleyball W. **Intramural:** Badminton, basketball, bowling, equestrian, fencing, football (tackle), golf M, ice hockey, lacrosse, racquetball, rugby, sailing, skiing, soccer, softball, swimming, table tennis, tennis, volleyball. **Team name:** Broncos.

**Student services.** Adult student services, alcohol/substance abuse counseling, campus ministries, career counseling, student employment services, financial aid counseling, health services, minority student services, on-campus daycare, personal counseling, placement for graduates, veterans' counselor, women's services. **Physically disabled:** Services for visually, speech, hearing impaired.

**Contact.** E-mail: www.ask-wmu@wmich.edu
Phone: (269) 387-2000 Toll-free number: (800) 400-4968
Fax: (269) 387-2096
Penny Bundy, Director of Admissions, Western Michigan University, 1903
West Michigan Avenue, Kalamazoo, MI 49008-5211

## Yeshiva Beth Yehuda-Yeshiva Gedolah of Greater Detroit
### Oak Park, Michigan

CB code: 7010

▶ Private 5-year rabbinical college for men affiliated with Jewish faith
▶ Residential campus in large town

**General.** Accredited by AARTS. **Calendar:** Semester.

**Annual costs/financial aid.** Tuition/fees (2007-2008): $4,500. Room/board: $3,600. Books/supplies: $500. Personal expenses: $500.

**Contact.** Phone: (248) 968-3360
24600 Greenfield Road, Oak Park, MI 48237

# Minnesota

## Academy College
**Bloomington, Minnesota**
www.academycollege.edu
CB code: 3311

♦ For-profit 4-year junior and career college
♦ Large city
♦ 150 degree-seeking undergraduates: 6% part-time, 41% women, 21% African American, 6% Asian American, 3% Hispanic American, 1% Native American, 1% international
♦ Interview required

**General.** Accredited by ACICS. **Degrees:** 20 bachelor's, 30 associate awarded. **Calendar:** Quarter. **Full-time faculty:** 5 total. **Part-time faculty:** 50 total. **Class size:** 100% < 20.

**Freshman class profile.** 18 applied, 18 admitted, 18 enrolled.

**Basis for selection.** Open admission.

**2007-2008 Annual costs.** Tuition ranges from $305 to $400 per credit hour depending on program. Books/supplies: $700. Personal expenses: $2,200.

**2006-2007 Financial aid. Need-based:** 19 full-time freshmen applied for aid; 19 were judged to have need; 19 of these received aid. Average need met was 33%. Average scholarship/grant was $6,116; average loan $2,625. 22% of total undergraduate aid awarded as scholarships/grants, 78% as loans/jobs. **Non-need-based:** Awarded to 2 full-time undergraduates, including 2 freshmen.

**Application procedures. Admission:** No deadline. $30 fee. Application must be submitted on paper. Admission notification on a rolling basis. **Financial aid:** No deadline. FAFSA, institutional form required. Applicants notified on a rolling basis.

**Academics. Special study options:** Distance learning, internships. **Credit/placement by examination:** AP, CLEP. **Support services:** Learning center, reduced course load, study skills assistance, tutoring.

**Majors. Business:** Accounting, business admin. **Communications technology:** Graphics. **Computer sciences:** General, computer science.

**Computing on campus.** 100 workstations in library, computer center. Online library, wireless network available.

**Student life. Freshman orientation:** Mandatory.

**Student services.** Placement for graduates.

**Contact.** E-mail: admissions@academycollege.edu
Phone: (952) 851-0066 Toll-free number: (800) 292-9149
Fax: (952) 851-0094
Tracey Schantz, Campus Director, Academy College, 1101 East 78th Street, Bloomington, MN 55420

## Art Institutes International Minnesota
**Minneapolis, Minnesota**
www.artinstitutes.edu/minneapolis
CB code: 2332

♦ For-profit 4-year culinary school and visual arts college
♦ Commuter campus in large city
♦ 1,722 degree-seeking undergraduates
♦ Application essay, interview required

**General.** Accredited by ACICS. **Degrees:** 201 bachelor's, 69 associate awarded. **Calendar:** Quarter, extensive summer session. **Full-time faculty:** 56 total; 36% women. **Part-time faculty:** 63 total; 44% women. **Special facilities:** Student-run dining lab, art gallery, wireless internet, student lounge.

**Basis for selection.** Open admission. School tour required prior to admission. **Homeschooled:** Transcript of courses and grades, interview required. **Learning Disabled:** Notify Dean of Student Affairs.

**2007-2008 Annual costs.** Tuition/fees: $19,872. Typical full-time credit load 16 credits/quarter. Starter kits for most programs $550-850. Books/supplies: $1,649. Personal expenses: $2,880.

**Application procedures. Admission:** No deadline. $50 fee. Application may be submitted online. Admission notification on a rolling basis. **Financial aid:** FAFSA required.

**Academics. Special study options:** Cooperative education, distance learning, honors, independent study, internships, study abroad. **Credit/placement by examination:** AP, CLEP. **Support services:** Learning center, remedial instruction, study skills assistance, tutoring.

**Majors. Business:** Customer service, hospitality admin, hospitality/recreation, hotel/motel admin, marketing, merchandising, resort management, restaurant/food services, retailing, selling. **Communications:** Advertising, digital media, photojournalism. **Communications technology:** Animation/special effects, graphics. **Computer sciences:** Computer graphics, webmaster. **Personal/culinary services:** Restaurant/catering. **Visual/performing arts:** Commercial photography, commercial/advertising art, design, graphic design, interior design, multimedia, photography. **Other:** Hospitality management.

**Computing on campus.** 260 workstations in library, computer center, student center. Dormitories wired for high-speed internet access. Student web hosting, wireless network available.

**Student life. Freshman orientation:** Mandatory. Preregistration for classes offered. **Housing:** Apartments, substance-free housing available. $250 deposit. **Activities:** Campus ministries, film society, student government, student newspaper.

**Student services.** Alcohol/substance abuse counseling, campus ministries, career counseling, student employment services, financial aid counseling, personal counseling, placement for graduates. **Physically disabled:** Services for hearing impaired.

**Contact.** E-mail: aimadm@aii.edu
Phone: (612) 332-3361 Toll-free number: (800) 777-3643
Fax: (612) 332-3934
Mary Strand, Director of Admissions, Art Institutes International Minnesota, 15 South Ninth Street, Minneapolis, MN 55402

## Augsburg College
**Minneapolis, Minnesota**
www.augsburg.edu
CB member
CB code: 6014

♦ Private 4-year liberal arts college affiliated with Evangelical Lutheran Church in America
♦ Residential campus in large city
♦ 2,829 degree-seeking undergraduates: 17% part-time, 56% women, 6% African American, 4% Asian American, 2% Hispanic American, 1% Native American, 1% international
♦ 807 degree-seeking graduate students
♦ 61% of applicants admitted
♦ Application essay required
♦ 61% graduate within 6 years; 24% enter graduate study

**General.** Founded in 1869. Regionally accredited. **Degrees:** 539 bachelor's awarded; master's offered. **ROTC:** Army, Naval, Air Force. **Location:** 5 miles from downtown. **Calendar:** Differs by program, extensive summer session. **Full-time faculty:** 185 total; 97% have terminal degrees, 7% minority, 48% women. **Part-time faculty:** 244 total; 19% have terminal degrees, 2% minority, 62% women. **Class size:** 62% < 20, 36% 20-39, less than 1% 40-49, less than 1% 50-99. **Special facilities:** Center for atmospheric research.

**Freshman class profile.** 1,560 applied, 956 admitted, 411 enrolled.

| Mid 50% test scores | | | |
|---|---|---|---|
| SAT critical reading: | 510-640 | Rank in top quarter: | 34% |
| SAT math: | 500-640 | Rank in top tenth: | 16% |
| SAT writing: | 480-600 | End year in good standing: | 92% |
| ACT composite: | 19-25 | Return as sophomores: | 81% |
| GPA 3.50 or higher: | 32% | Out-of-state: | 13% |
| GPA 3.0-3.49: | 34% | Live on campus: | 86% |
| GPA 2.0-2.99: | 33% | International: | 1% |

**Basis for selection.** School achievement record, class rank in top half, test scores, essays and recommendations very important; extracurricular activities important. SAT or ACT recommended. Interview recommended.

**High school preparation.** 15 units required. Required and recommended units include English 4, mathematics 3, social studies 2-4, history 2, science 3 and foreign language 2.

**2007-2008 Annual costs.** Tuition/fees: $24,539. Room/board: $6,902. Books/supplies: $1,000. Personal expenses: $1,670.

**2006-2007 Financial aid. Need-based:** 37% of total undergraduate aid awarded as scholarships/grants, 63% as loans/jobs. **Non-need-based:** Scholarships awarded for academics, alumni affiliation, leadership, minority status, music/drama, religious affiliation.

**Application procedures. Admission:** Priority date 5/1; deadline 8/1 (receipt date). $25 fee, may be waived for applicants with need. Application may be submitted online. Admission notification on a rolling basis beginning on or about 11/1. Must reply by 5/1. **Financial aid:** Priority date 4/15, closing date 8/1. FAFSA required. Applicants notified on a rolling basis starting 3/1; must reply within 3 week(s) of notification.

**Academics. Special study options:** Combined bachelor's/graduate degree, cooperative education, cross-registration, double major, dual enrollment of high school students, ESL, honors, independent study, internships, liberal arts/career combination, student-designed major, study abroad, teacher certification program, urban semester, weekend college. Metro-urban studies internship program; global education program in Central America, Mexico, Namibia and Norway. **Credit/placement by examination:** AP, CLEP, IB, institutional tests. 1 credit hours maximum toward bachelor's degree. **Support services:** Learning center, reduced course load, remedial instruction, study skills assistance, tutoring.

**Majors. Area/ethnic studies:** Central/Eastern European, East Asian, Native American, Scandinavian, women's. **Biology:** General. **Business:** Accounting, accounting/business management, business admin, finance, international, management information systems, marketing. **Communications:** General, media studies, organizational. **Computer sciences:** Computer science. **Education:** General, biology, early childhood, elementary, emotionally handicapped, health, music, physical, secondary. **Engineering:** General. **English:** English lit. **Foreign languages:** French, German, Scandinavian, Spanish. **Health:** Clinical lab science, music therapy, nursing (RN), public health nursing. **History:** General. **Interdisciplinary:** Medieval/Renaissance. **Liberal arts:** Arts/sciences. **Math:** General. **Philosophy/religion:** Philosophy, religion. **Physical sciences:** Chemistry, physics. **Psychology:** General. **Public administration:** Social work. **Social sciences:** General, applied economics, economics, international relations, political science, sociology, urban studies. **Theology:** Youth ministry. **Visual/performing arts:** Art history/conservation, dramatic, film/cinema, music management, music performance, studio arts, theater history.

**Computing on campus.** 260 workstations in dormitories, library, computer center, student center. Dormitories wired for high-speed internet access and linked to campus network. Commuter students can connect to campus network. Online course registration, online library, helpline, student web hosting, wireless network available.

**Student life. Freshman orientation:** Available, $100 fee. Preregistration for classes offered. Students attend in June or July; lasts Friday through Saturday morning. **Housing:** Guaranteed on-campus for freshmen. Coed dorms, special housing for disabled, apartments, substance-free housing available. $350 partly refundable deposit, deadline 6/1. **Activities:** Bands, choral groups, drama, literary magazine, music ensembles, radio station, student government, student newspaper, symphony orchestra, Religious Life Commission, Fellowship of Christian Athletes, Black Student Union, Intertribal Student Union, Minnesota Public Interest Research Group, Global Awareness Community, International Association for Business Communication.

**Athletics.** NCAA. **Intercollegiate:** Baseball M, basketball, cross-country, football (tackle) M, golf, ice hockey, soccer, softball W, swimming W, tennis, track and field, volleyball W, wrestling M. **Intramural:** Basketball, softball, tennis, volleyball. **Team name:** Auggies.

**Student services.** Adult student services, alcohol/substance abuse counseling, campus ministries, career counseling, student employment services, financial aid counseling, health services, minority student services, personal counseling, placement for graduates. **Physically disabled:** Services for visually, speech, hearing impaired.

**Contact.** E-mail: admissions@augsburg.edu
Phone: (612) 330-1001 Toll-free number: (800) 788-5678
Fax: (612) 330-1590
Carrie Carroll, Director of Admissions, Augsburg College, 2211 Riverside Avenue, Minneapolis, MN 55454

## Bemidji State University
**Bemidji, Minnesota**
**www.bemidjistate.edu**                    CB code: 6676

◆ Public 4-year university
◆ Residential campus in large town

◆ 4,274 degree-seeking undergraduates: 23% part-time, 51% women
◆ 441 degree-seeking graduate students
◆ 86% of applicants admitted
◆ ACT (writing optional) required
◆ 45% graduate within 6 years

**General.** Founded in 1919. Regionally accredited. Arrowhead University Center located on Minnesota's Mesabi Iron Range offers several degree programs. **Degrees:** 821 bachelor's, 45 associate awarded; master's offered. **Location:** 150 miles from Duluth, 230 miles from Minneapolis-St. Paul. **Calendar:** Semester, extensive summer session. **Full-time faculty:** 224 total; 80% have terminal degrees, 5% minority, 42% women. **Part-time faculty:** 54 total; 52% women. **Class size:** 60% < 20, 33% 20-39, 3% 40-49, 2% 50-99, 1% >100. **Special facilities:** Freshwater aquatics laboratory, research center.

**Freshman class profile.** 1,955 applied, 1,674 admitted, 752 enrolled.

| Mid 50% test scores | | Return as sophomores: | 65% |
|---|---|---|---|
| ACT composite: | 20-24 | Out-of-state: | 2% |
| Rank in top quarter: | 50% | Live on campus: | 75% |
| Rank in top tenth: | 10% | | |

**Basis for selection.** Rank in top half of class or test scores above 50th percentile preferred. ACT scores considered for applicants in bottom half of class. Composite score of 21 or higher preferred. Interview recommended. Audition recommended for music applicants; portfolio recommended for art applicants. **Learning Disabled:** Students encouraged to identify themselves to Office of Disabilities to be apprised of services available.

**High school preparation.** 16 units required. Required and recommended units include English 4, mathematics 3, social studies 3, history 1, science 3 (laboratory 1), foreign language 2 and academic electives 1. 1 unit of art, music, world culture required.

**2007-2008 Annual costs.** Tuition/fees: $6,740; $6,740 out-of-state. Room/board: $5,874. Books/supplies: $800. Personal expenses: $1,245.

**2007-2008 Financial aid. Need-based:** 608 full-time freshmen applied for aid; 450 were judged to have need; 436 of these received aid. Average need met was 78%. Average scholarship/grant was $5,189; average loan $3,366. 48% of total undergraduate aid awarded as scholarships/grants, 52% as loans/jobs. **Non-need-based:** Awarded to 1,720 full-time undergraduates, including 433 freshmen. Scholarships awarded for academics, alumni affiliation, art, athletics, minority status, music/drama.

**Application procedures. Admission:** Priority date 8/15; no deadline. $20 fee. Application may be submitted online. Admission notification on a rolling basis. **Financial aid:** Priority date 5/15; no closing date. FAFSA, institutional form required. Applicants notified on a rolling basis starting 5/15.

**Academics. Special study options:** Accelerated study, combined bachelor's/graduate degree, cooperative education, distance learning, double major, dual enrollment of high school students, ESL, external degree, honors, independent study, internships, liberal arts/career combination, study abroad, teacher certification program. Exchange program with other Minnesota state universities, Euro-spring semester, Sino-summer semester. **Credit/placement by examination:** AP, CLEP, institutional tests. Department defined number of hours of credit by examination may be counted towards degree. **Support services:** Learning center, pre-admission summer program, reduced course load, remedial instruction, study skills assistance, tutoring, writing center.

**Majors. Area/ethnic studies:** Native American. **Biology:** General, marine. **Business:** Accounting, business admin. **Communications:** Journalism. **Computer sciences:** General, computer science. **Conservation:** General. **Education:** General, elementary, voc/tech. **Engineering:** Physics. **English:** English lit. **Foreign languages:** German, Spanish. **Health:** Clinical lab science, preop/surgical nursing. **History:** General. **Liberal arts:** Arts/sciences. **Math:** General. **Parks/recreation:** Health/fitness. **Philosophy/religion:** Philosophy. **Physical sciences:** Chemistry, geology, physics. **Protective services:** Criminal justice. **Psychology:** General. **Public administration:** Community org/advocacy, social work. **Social sciences:** General, economics, geography, political science, sociology. **Visual/performing arts:** Art, commercial/advertising art, dramatic.

**Most popular majors.** Business/marketing 12%, education 22%, engineering/engineering technologies 10%, health sciences 8%, psychology 10%, security/protective services 6%, visual/performing arts 6%.

**Computing on campus.** 1,600 workstations in dormitories, library, computer center, student center. Dormitories wired for high-speed internet access and linked to campus network. Commuter students can connect to campus network. Online course registration, online library, helpline, repair service, student web hosting, wireless network available.

**Student life. Freshman orientation:** Available, $25 fee. Preregistration for classes offered. One-day orientation for students and parents. **Policies:** Zero tolerance for discrimination, racism, sexual violence, illegal activities including drug use. **Housing:** Coed dorms, single-sex dorms, substance-free housing available. $100 partly refundable deposit. Single parents hall (includes child care facilities), quiet floors, hall/dorm for students older than average age. **Activities:** Bands, campus ministries, choral groups, dance, drama, film society, international student organizations, literary magazine, music ensembles, musical theater, opera, radio station, student government, student newspaper, symphony orchestra, TV station, Newman Center, Lutheran center, Young Republicans, Young Democrats, social service organization, veterans club, Council of Indian Students, Black Student Coalition.

**Athletics.** NCAA. **Intercollegiate:** Baseball M, basketball, cross-country, football (tackle) M, golf, ice hockey, soccer W, softball W, tennis W, track and field, volleyball W. **Intramural:** Badminton, baseball, basketball, field hockey, football (non-tackle), golf, ice hockey, racquetball, skiing, soccer, softball, table tennis, tennis, triathlon, volleyball, weight lifting M, wrestling M. **Team name:** Beavers.

**Student services.** Alcohol/substance abuse counseling, campus ministries, career counseling, services for economically disadvantaged, student employment services, financial aid counseling, health services, minority student services, on-campus daycare, personal counseling, placement for graduates, women's services. **Physically disabled:** Services for visually, speech, hearing impaired.

**Contact.** E-mail: admissions@bemidjistate.edu
Phone: (218) 755-2040 Toll-free number: (800) 475-2001
Fax: (218) 755-2074
Russ Kreager, Director of Admissions, Bemidji State University, 1500 Birchmont Drive NE, D-102, Bemidji, MN 56601

## Bethany Lutheran College

**Mankato, Minnesota**
**www.blc.edu**
**CB code: 6035**

- Private 4-year liberal arts college affiliated with Evangelical Lutheran Synod
- Residential campus in large town
- 586 degree-seeking undergraduates: 2% African American, 2% Asian American, 1% Hispanic American
- 83% of applicants admitted
- SAT or ACT (ACT writing recommended), application essay required
- 25% graduate within 6 years

**General.** Founded in 1927. Regionally accredited. **Degrees:** 106 bachelor's awarded. **ROTC:** Army. **Location:** 80 miles from Minneapolis-St. Paul. **Calendar:** Semester. **Full-time faculty:** 41 total; 78% have terminal degrees, 20% women. **Part-time faculty:** 24 total; 46% women. **Class size:** 70% < 20, 28% 20-39, less than 1% 40-49, less than 1% 50-99.

**Freshman class profile.** 404 applied, 336 admitted, 175 enrolled.

| Mid 50% test scores | | Rank in top quarter: | 39% |
|---|---|---|---|
| ACT composite: | 20-26 | Rank in top tenth: | 13% |
| GPA 3.50 or higher: | 49% | Return as sophomores: | 73% |
| GPA 3.0-3.49: | 33% | Out-of-state: | 26% |
| GPA 2.0-2.99: | 18% | Live on campus: | 87% |

**Basis for selection.** College-prep GPA, overall GPA, test scores most important. **Learning Disabled:** Students with learning disabilities must meet with head of tutorial program.

**High school preparation.** Recommended units include English 4, mathematics 3, social studies 3, history 3, science 3 (laboratory 1) and foreign language 2.

**2008-2009 Annual costs.** Tuition/fees: $18,710. Room/board: $5,800. Books/supplies: $800. Personal expenses: $1,200.

**2006-2007 Financial aid. Need-based:** 166 full-time freshmen applied for aid; 145 were judged to have need; 145 of these received aid. Average need met was 86%. Average scholarship/grant was $10,556; average loan $2,911. 69% of total undergraduate aid awarded as scholarships/grants, 31% as loans/jobs. **Non-need-based:** Awarded to 140 full-time undergraduates, including 45 freshmen. Scholarships awarded for academics, art, music/drama.

**Application procedures. Admission:** Closing date 7/1 (postmark date). No application fee. Application may be submitted online. Admission notification on a rolling basis beginning on or about 9/1. **Financial aid:** Priority date 4/15; no closing date. FAFSA, institutional form required. Applicants

notified on a rolling basis starting 3/1; must reply within 2 week(s) of notification.

**Academics. Special study options:** Cross-registration, double major, dual enrollment of high school students, independent study, internships, student-designed major, study abroad, teacher certification program. **Credit/placement by examination:** AP, CLEP, IB, SAT, ACT, institutional tests. 15 credit hours maximum toward associate degree, 15 toward bachelor's. **Support services:** Learning center, reduced course load, remedial instruction, tutoring.

**Majors. Biology:** Biomedical sciences. **Business:** Business admin. **Communications:** General. **Education:** Elementary. **English:** English lit. **History:** General. **Liberal arts:** Arts/sciences. **Physical sciences:** General, chemistry. **Psychology:** General. **Social sciences:** General, sociology. **Theology:** Sacred music. **Visual/performing arts:** Dramatic, studio arts.

**Most popular majors.** Business/marketing 7%, communications/journalism 26%, education 6%, English 7%, liberal arts 6%, psychology 6%, social sciences 8%, visual/performing arts 20%.

**Computing on campus.** 100 workstations in dormitories, library, computer center, student center. Dormitories wired for high-speed internet access and linked to campus network. Commuter students can connect to campus network. Helpline, repair service, student web hosting, wireless network available.

**Student life. Freshman orientation:** Mandatory. Preregistration for classes offered. **Policies:** Freshmen and sophomores not living with family required to live on campus. **Housing:** Guaranteed on-campus for all undergraduates. Single-sex dorms, apartments, substance-free housing available. **Activities:** Bands, choral groups, drama, literary magazine, music ensembles, musical theater, student government, student newspaper, TV station, spiritual life committee, Lutherans for Life, student senate, Lambda Pi Eta, scholastic leadership society.

**Athletics.** NCCAA. **Intercollegiate:** Baseball M, basketball, golf, soccer, softball W, tennis, volleyball W. **Intramural:** Baseball M, basketball, soccer, softball, tennis, volleyball. **Team name:** Vikings.

**Student services.** Campus ministries, career counseling, financial aid counseling, minority student services, personal counseling.

**Contact.** E-mail: admissions@blc.edu
Phone: (507) 344-7331 Toll-free number: (800) 944-3066
Fax: (507) 344-7376
Don Westphal, Dean of Admissions, Bethany Lutheran College, 700 Luther Drive, Mankato, MN 56001-4490

## Bethel University

**Saint Paul, Minnesota**
**www.bethel.edu**
**CB member**
**CB code: 6038**

- Private 4-year university and liberal arts college affiliated with Baptist General Conference
- Residential campus in large city
- 3,250 degree-seeking undergraduates: 18% part-time, 62% women, 3% African American, 3% Asian American, 2% Hispanic American
- 1,772 degree-seeking graduate students
- 88% of applicants admitted
- SAT or ACT (ACT writing optional), application essay required
- 76% graduate within 6 years; 38% enter graduate study

**General.** Founded in 1871. Regionally accredited. **Degrees:** 844 bachelor's, 5 associate awarded; master's, doctoral, first professional offered. **Location:** 10 miles from Minneapolis-St. Paul. **Calendar:** Differs by program, limited summer session. **Full-time faculty:** 171 total; 81% have terminal degrees, 12% minority, 40% women. **Part-time faculty:** 133 total; 27% have terminal degrees, 7% minority, 60% women. **Class size:** 51% < 20, 40% 20-39, 4% 40-49, 4% 50-99, 1% >100.

**Freshman class profile.** 1,643 applied, 1,447 admitted, 632 enrolled.

| Mid 50% test scores | | Rank in top quarter: | 58% |
|---|---|---|---|
| SAT critical reading: | 500-650 | Rank in top tenth: | 30% |
| SAT math: | 510-650 | Return as sophomores: | 85% |
| ACT composite: | 22-28 | Out-of-state: | 27% |
| GPA 3.50 or higher: | 59% | Live on campus: | 91% |
| GPA 3.0-3.49: | 27% | International: | 1% |
| GPA 2.0-2.99: | 13% | | |

**Basis for selection.** Rank in top half of class, 92 PSAT, 21 ACT, or 920 SAT (exclusive of Writing). Applicant must make personal statement regarding Christian commitment and agree to live in accordance with college's lifestyle. 2 recommendations required. Interview recommended for art, drama, and music applicants; audition recommended for music applicants; portfolio recommended for art applicants. **Homeschooled:** Transcript of courses and grades required.

**High school preparation.** 18 units recommended. Recommended units include English 4, mathematics 3, social studies 4, history 2, science 3 (laboratory 3), foreign language 2, computer science 1 and visual/performing arts 1.

**2008-2009 Annual costs.** Tuition/fees: $25,860. 2008-2009 housing for first-time students $4,540. Rate frozen as long as student continues to reside in campus housing. Room/board: $7,620. Books/supplies: $950. Personal expenses: $1,610.

**2006-2007 Financial aid. Need-based:** 522 full-time freshmen applied for aid; 437 were judged to have need; 437 of these received aid. Average need met was 78%. Average scholarship/grant was $11,590; average loan $3,662. 57% of total undergraduate aid awarded as scholarships/grants, 43% as loans/jobs. **Non-need-based:** Awarded to 842 full-time undergraduates, including 199 freshmen. Scholarships awarded for academics, alumni affiliation, art, job skills, leadership, music/drama, religious affiliation, state residency.

**Application procedures. Admission:** Priority date 3/1; no deadline. $25 fee, may be waived for applicants with need. Application may be submitted online. Admission notification on a rolling basis beginning on or about 2/1. **Financial aid:** Priority date 4/15; no closing date. FAFSA, institutional form required. Applicants notified on a rolling basis starting 3/1; must reply by 5/1 or within 3 week(s) of notification.

**Academics. Special study options:** Combined bachelor's/graduate degree, distance learning, double major, exchange student, honors, independent study, internships, liberal arts/career combination, New York semester, semester at sea, student-designed major, study abroad, teacher certification program, urban semester, Washington semester. Dual degree program for Engineering Science with the University of Minnesota and Washington University. South Africa term, Guatamala term, Spain term. **Credit/placement by examination:** AP, CLEP, IB, institutional tests. 32 credit hours maximum toward associate degree, 32 toward bachelor's. **Support services:** Learning center, reduced course load, study skills assistance, tutoring, writing center.

**Majors. Biology:** General. **Business:** Business admin, human resources, organizational behavior. **Communications:** General, journalism, media studies. **Computer sciences:** General. **Conservation:** Environmental science, environmental studies. **Education:** General, art, biology, business, chemistry, early childhood, elementary, English, ESL, French, health, mathematics, music, physical, science, social studies, Spanish. **Engineering:** Science. **English:** English lit. **Foreign languages:** French, Spanish. **Health:** Athletic training, community health services, nursing (RN). **History:** General. **Interdisciplinary:** Peace/conflict. **Math:** General. **Parks/recreation:** Exercise sciences, health/fitness. **Philosophy/religion:** Philosophy. **Physical sciences:** Chemistry, physics. **Psychology:** General. **Public administration:** Social work. **Social sciences:** Economics, international relations, political science. **Theology:** Bible, sacred music, youth ministry. **Visual/performing arts:** Art, dramatic, music performance. **Other:** Biochemistry and molecular biology, Christian ministries, Third World studies.

**Most popular majors.** Biology 6%, business/marketing 24%, communications/journalism 7%, education 12%, health sciences 17%, psychology 6%, theological studies 6%.

**Computing on campus.** 375 workstations in dormitories, library, computer center. Dormitories wired for high-speed internet access and linked to campus network. Commuter students can connect to campus network. Online course registration, online library, helpline, student web hosting, wireless network available.

**Student life. Freshman orientation:** Mandatory. Preregistration for classes offered. 2 days prior to the start of classes. **Policies:** High moral standards stressed. Use of tobacco and alcohol prohibited. **Housing:** Coed dorms, special housing for disabled, apartments, substance-free housing available. $150 fully refundable deposit. **Activities:** Bands, campus ministries, choral groups, dance, drama, literary magazine, music ensembles, musical theater, radio station, student government, student newspaper, symphony orchestra, United Cultures of Bethel, administrative fellowship groups, College Republicans, Habitat for Humanity, dormitory discipleship programs.

**Athletics.** NCAA. **Intercollegiate:** Baseball M, basketball, cross-country, football (tackle) M, golf M, ice hockey, soccer, softball W, tennis, track and field, volleyball W. **Intramural:** Badminton, basketball, football (non-tackle) M, softball, volleyball. **Team name:** Royals.

**Student services.** Adult student services, alcohol/substance abuse counseling, campus ministries, career counseling, student employment services, financial aid counseling, health services, minority student services, on-campus daycare, personal counseling, placement for graduates, women's services. **Physically disabled:** Services for visually, speech, hearing impaired.

**Contact.** E-mail: BUadmissions-cas@bethel.edu
Phone: (651) 638-6242 Toll-free number: (800) 255-8706 ext. 6242
Fax: (651) 635-1490
Jay Fedje, Director of Admissions, Bethel University, 3900 Bethel Drive, Saint Paul, MN 55112-6999

## Brown College
**Mendota Heights, Minnesota**
www.browncollege.edu                    **CB code: 1210**

- For-profit 4-year business and liberal arts college
- Commuter campus in small city
- 1,437 degree-seeking undergraduates
- Interview required

**General.** Founded in 1946. Accredited by ACCSCT. **Degrees:** 167 bachelor's, 303 associate awarded. **Location:** 14 miles from Minneapolis-St. Paul. **Calendar:** Quarter, extensive summer session. **Full-time faculty:** 156 total; 3% have terminal degrees, 10% minority, 38% women. **Part-time faculty:** 71 total; 4% have terminal degrees, 20% minority, 30% women.

**Basis for selection.** Open admission. ACCUPLACER Test required in lieu of other tests. **Learning Disabled:** IEP's and/or other requests for ADA-level accomodations accepted. Eligible students must complete brief Application for Auxiliary Aid and return with any supporting documentation available well in advance of enrollment.

**High school preparation.** Recommended units include English 4, mathematics 2 and science 1.

**2007-2008 Annual costs.** Tuition/fees: $16,340. Books/supplies: $2,000. Personal expenses: $1,600.

**Financial aid. Non-need-based:** Scholarships awarded for academics.

**Application procedures. Admission:** No deadline. $50 fee. Application may be submitted online. Admission notification on a rolling basis beginning on or about 1/1. **Financial aid:** Priority date 7/1; no closing date. FAFSA, institutional form required. Applicants notified on a rolling basis starting 1/1; must reply within 2 week(s) of notification.

**Academics. Special study options:** Cooperative education, internships, liberal arts/career combination. **Credit/placement by examination:** AP, CLEP, institutional tests. **Support services:** Learning center, reduced course load, remedial instruction, study skills assistance, tutoring, writing center.

**Majors. Business:** General. **Communications:** General. **Communications technology:** Graphics. **Computer sciences:** Information systems, information technology. **Protective services:** Criminal justice. **Visual/performing arts:** Design.

**Computing on campus.** PC or laptop required. 231 workstations in library, computer center. Commuter students can connect to campus network. Online course registration, online library, helpline, repair service, wireless network available.

**Student life. Freshman orientation:** Mandatory. **Housing:** Apartments available. **Activities:** Radio station, student government, student senate, Campus Crusade for Christ, minority students club.

**Athletics. Intramural:** Football (non-tackle) M.

**Student services.** Adult student services, career counseling, student employment services, financial aid counseling, placement for graduates.

**Contact.** E-mail: info@browncollege.edu
Phone: (651) 905-3240 Toll-free number: (800) 627-6966 ext. 240
Fax: (651) 905-3540
William Cowan, Admissions Director, Brown College, 1440 Northland Drive, Mendota Heights, MN 55120

## Capella University
**Minneapolis, Minnesota**
www.capella.edu                    **CB code: 3829**

- For-profit 4-year virtual college
- Very large city

**General.** Regionally accredited. **Calendar:** Quarter.

**Annual costs/financial aid.** Tuition/fees (2007-2008): $13,500. Need-based financial aid available to full-time and part-time students.

**Contact.** Phone: (888) 227-2736
225 South Sixth Street, 9th Floor, Minneapolis, MN 55402

## Carleton College
### Northfield, Minnesota
www.carleton.edu

**CB member**
**CB code: 6081**

- Private 4-year liberal arts college
- Residential campus in large town
- 1,986 degree-seeking undergraduates: 52% women, 5% African American, 10% Asian American, 5% Hispanic American, 1% Native American, 6% international
- 30% of applicants admitted
- SAT or ACT with writing, application essay required
- 93% graduate within 6 years; 23% enter graduate study

**General.** Founded in 1866. Regionally accredited. Interest in sustainability initiatives - green roofs, eco-building class, eco house built by students, 1.65 megawatt wind turbine. **Degrees:** 466 bachelor's awarded. **Location:** 35 miles from Minneapolis-St. Paul. **Calendar:** Trimester. **Full-time faculty:** 207 total; 92% have terminal degrees, 26% minority, 45% women. **Part-time faculty:** 20 total; 55% have terminal degrees, 15% minority, 45% women. **Class size:** 63% < 20, 34% 20-39, 2% 40-49, 1% 50-99. **Special facilities:** 955 acre arboretum, 35 acre virgin prairie, greenhouse, observatory, scanning and transmission electron microscope, refractor and reflector telescopes, nuclear magnet resonance spectrometer.

**Freshman class profile.** 4,840 applied, 1,444 admitted, 509 enrolled.

| Mid 50% test scores | | | |
|---|---|---|---|
| SAT critical reading: | 650-750 | Rank in top tenth: | 74% |
| SAT math: | 660-740 | End year in good standing: | 98% |
| SAT writing: | 650-730 | Return as sophomores: | 98% |
| ACT composite: | 29-33 | Out-of-state: | 77% |
| Rank in top quarter: | 92% | Live on campus: | 100% |
| | | International: | 7% |

**Basis for selection.** School achievement record and recommendations most important. Test scores, extracurricular school and community activities also important. SAT Subject Tests recommended. Interview recommended. **Learning Disabled:** Untimed standardized tests and GED accepted.

**High school preparation.** Recommended units include English 4, mathematics 3, social studies 3, science 3 (laboratory 1) and foreign language 3. 3 units distributed between history and social sciences recommended.

**2008-2009 Annual costs.** Tuition/fees (projected): $38,064. Room/board: $9,978. Books/supplies: $629. Personal expenses: $629.

**2006-2007 Financial aid. Need-based:** 373 full-time freshmen applied for aid; 252 were judged to have need; 252 of these received aid. Average need met was 100%. Average scholarship/grant was $25,686; average loan $3,978. 80% of total undergraduate aid awarded as scholarships/grants, 20% as loans/jobs. **Non-need-based:** Awarded to 354 full-time undergraduates, including 70 freshmen. Scholarships awarded for academics. **Additional information:** Full financial need of all admitted applicants met through combination of work, loans, grants.

**Application procedures. Admission:** Closing date 1/15 (postmark date). $30 fee, may be waived for applicants with need. Application may be submitted online. Admission notification 4/15. Must reply by May 1 or within 2 week(s) if notified thereafter. **Financial aid:** Priority date 2/15, closing date 2/15. FAFSA, CSS PROFILE required. Applicants notified by 4/1; must reply by 5/1 or within 2 week(s) of notification.

**Academics.** 15-20 freshman seminars offered, enrollment limited to 15 students each. **Special study options:** Accelerated study, cross-registration, double major, dual enrollment of high school students, independent study, internships, student-designed major, study abroad, teacher certification program, urban semester. **Credit/placement by examination:** AP, CLEP, IB, institutional tests. 36 credit hours maximum toward bachelor's degree. **Support services:** Learning center, tutoring, writing center.

**Majors. Area/ethnic studies:** African, African-American, American, Asian, Latin American, Russian/Slavic, women's. **Biology:** General. **Computer sciences:** Computer science. **English:** English lit. **Foreign languages:** Ancient Greek, classics, French, German, Hebrew, Latin, Romance, Russian, Spanish. **History:** General. **Interdisciplinary:** Math/computer science. **Math:**

**General. Philosophy/religion:** Philosophy, religion. **Physical sciences:** Chemistry, geology, physics. **Psychology:** General. **Social sciences:** Anthropology, economics, international relations, political science, sociology. **Visual/performing arts:** Art history/conservation, studio arts.

**Most popular majors.** Biology 10%, English 7%, history 7%, physical sciences 15%, social sciences 25%, visual/performing arts 8%.

**Computing on campus.** 300 workstations in library, computer center, student center. Dormitories wired for high-speed internet access and linked to campus network. Online course registration, online library, helpline, repair service, student web hosting, wireless network available.

**Student life. Freshman orientation:** Mandatory. Preregistration for classes offered. 4 days prior to start of fall classes. **Housing:** Guaranteed on-campus for all undergraduates. Coed dorms, special housing for disabled, apartments, substance-free housing available. 25 college-owned houses within 2 blocks of campus, some coeducational, with varying board options. Several for special interest groups. **Activities:** Bands, choral groups, dance, drama, film society, literary magazine, music ensembles, musical theater, radio station, student government, student newspaper, symphony orchestra, 132 registered student organizations.

**Athletics.** NCAA. **Intercollegiate:** Baseball M, basketball, cross-country, diving, football (tackle) M, golf, soccer, softball W, swimming, synchronized swimming W, tennis, track and field, volleyball W, wrestling M. **Intramural:** Basketball, ice hockey, racquetball, soccer, softball, table tennis, tennis, triathlon, volleyball. **Team name:** Knights.

**Student services.** Alcohol/substance abuse counseling, campus ministries, career counseling, student employment services, financial aid counseling, health services, minority student services, personal counseling, placement for graduates, women's services. **Physically disabled:** Services for visually, hearing impaired.

**Contact.** E-mail: admissions@carleton.edu
Phone: (507) 646-4190 Toll-free number: (800) 995-2275
Fax: (507) 646-4526
Paul Thiboutot, Dean of Admissions, Carleton College, 100 South College Street, Northfield, MN 55057

## College of St. Benedict
### St. Joseph, Minnesota
www.csbsju.edu

**CB member**
**CB code: 6104**

- Private 4-year liberal arts college for women affiliated with Roman Catholic Church
- Residential campus in small town
- 2,049 degree-seeking undergraduates: 100% women, 1% African American, 3% Asian American, 2% Hispanic American, 5% international
- 75% of applicants admitted
- SAT or ACT (ACT writing optional), application essay required
- 82% graduate within 6 years; 14% enter graduate study

**General.** Founded in 1887. Regionally accredited. Coeducational academic and campus life shared with St. John's University in nearby Collegeville. Access to all St. John's University facilities. **Degrees:** 440 bachelor's awarded. **ROTC:** Army. **Location:** 10 miles from St. Cloud, 70 miles from Minneapolis-St. Paul. **Calendar:** Semester, limited summer session. **Full-time faculty:** 155 total; 83% have terminal degrees, 8% minority, 57% women. **Part-time faculty:** 29 total; 24% have terminal degrees, 3% minority, 55% women. **Class size:** 46% < 20, 54% 20-39. **Special facilities:** Observatory, ecumenical center, museum and manuscript library, liturgical press, nature preserve, arboretum, natural history museum, pottery kiln.

**Freshman class profile.** 1,677 applied, 1,261 admitted, 537 enrolled.

| Mid 50% test scores | | | |
|---|---|---|---|
| SAT critical reading: | 500-630 | Rank in top quarter: | 77% |
| SAT math: | 540-660 | Rank in top tenth: | 43% |
| ACT composite: | 23-28 | End year in good standing: | 99% |
| GPA 3.50 or higher: | 84% | Return as sophomores: | 90% |
| GPA 3.0-3.49: | 15% | Out-of-state: | 15% |
| GPA 2.0-2.99: | 1% | Live on campus: | 100% |
| | | International: | 3% |

**Basis for selection.** Course selection, scholastic achievement, GPA, test scores and essay are most important. Extracurricular involvement, high school rank, and recommendation are also important. Students who have completed the application process by 11/15 will receive notification of their scholarship award on 12/20. Those that complete the application process by 12/15 will recieve notification of their scholarship award on 2/1. Interview recommended for conditionally accepted/academically weak applicants. **Homeschooled:** Applicants are not required to have a high school diploma but are required to provide appropriate documentation of college preparatory curriculum.

**High school preparation.** 15 units required. Required and recommended units include English 4, mathematics 3, social studies 2, science 2 (laboratory 2), foreign language 2 and academic electives 4.

**2007-2008 Annual costs.** Tuition/fees: $26,530. Room/board: $7,430. Books/supplies: $800. Personal expenses: $700.

**2007-2008 Financial aid. Need-based:** 443 full-time freshmen applied for aid; 361 were judged to have need; 361 of these received aid. Average need met was 92%. Average scholarship/grant was $16,350; average loan $3,718. 62% of total undergraduate aid awarded as scholarships/grants, 38% as loans/jobs. **Non-need-based:** Awarded to 1,909 full-time undergraduates, including 517 freshmen. Scholarships awarded for academics, art, leadership, music/drama, ROTC.

**Application procedures. Admission:** Priority date 11/15; no deadline. No application fee. Application may be submitted online. Admission notification on a rolling basis beginning on or about 10/1. A non-refundable enrollment deposit of $300 is due by May 1. **Financial aid:** Priority date 3/15; no closing date. FAFSA, institutional form required. Applicants notified on a rolling basis starting 3/15; must reply by 5/1.

**Academics. Special study options:** Combined bachelor's/graduate degree, cross-registration, double major, dual enrollment of high school students, ESL, exchange student, honors, independent study, internships, student-designed major, study abroad, teacher certification program, United Nations semester. 3-2 program in engineering with University of Minnesota, 3-1 program in dentistry with University of Minnesota, cross registration with St. Cloud State University. **Credit/placement by examination:** AP, CLEP, IB, institutional tests. **Support services:** Study skills assistance, tutoring, writing center.

**Majors. Area/ethnic studies:** Women's. **Biology:** General, biochemistry. **Business:** Accounting, business admin. **Computer sciences:** Computer science. **Conservation:** Environmental studies. **Education:** General, elementary. **English:** English lit, speech/rhetoric. **Foreign languages:** Classics, French, German, Spanish. **Health:** Dietetics, nursing (RN), predental, premedicine, prepharmacy, preveterinary. **History:** General. **Interdisciplinary:** Biological/physical sciences, math/computer science, natural sciences, nutrition sciences, peace/conflict. **Legal studies:** Prelaw. **Liberal arts:** Arts/sciences, humanities. **Math:** General. **Philosophy/religion:** Philosophy. **Physical sciences:** Chemistry, physics. **Psychology:** General. **Public administration:** Social work. **Social sciences:** General, economics, political science, sociology. **Theology:** Theology. **Visual/performing arts:** Art, dramatic.

**Most popular majors.** Biology 10%, business/marketing 8%, English 20%, health sciences 13%, psychology 13%, social sciences 9%.

**Computing on campus.** 643 workstations in dormitories, library, computer center, student center. Dormitories wired for high-speed internet access and linked to campus network. Commuter students can connect to campus network. Online course registration, helpline, repair service, student web hosting, wireless network available.

**Student life. Freshman orientation:** Mandatory. Preregistration for classes offered. Fall orientation begins the evening of move-in day and concludes with convocation the first day of classes. **Policies:** Freshmen and sophomores are required to live on campus. **Housing:** Guaranteed on-campus for freshmen. Special housing for disabled, apartments, substance-free housing available. Global initiative group house available. **Activities:** Bands, campus ministries, choral groups, dance, drama, international student organizations, literary magazine, music ensembles, Model UN, musical theater, opera, radio station, student government, student newspaper, symphony orchestra, Volunteers in Service to Others, College Republicans, College Democrats, Joints Events Council, Asia Club, Student Coalition for Global Solidarity, Students in Free Enterprise, Magis, Cultural Fusion Club, Outdoor Leadership Center.

**Athletics.** NCAA. **Intercollegiate:** Basketball W, cross-country W, diving W, golf W, ice hockey W, skiing W, soccer W, softball W, swimming W, tennis W, track and field W, volleyball W. **Intramural:** Badminton W, basketball W, racquetball W, soccer W, softball W, table tennis W, tennis W, volleyball W. **Team name:** Blazers.

**Student services.** Alcohol/substance abuse counseling, campus ministries, career counseling, student employment services, financial aid counseling, health services, minority student services, personal counseling, placement for graduates, women's services. **Physically disabled:** Services for hearing impaired.

**Contact.** E-mail: admissions@csbsju.edu
Phone: (320) 363-2196 Toll-free number: (800) 544-1489
Fax: (320) 363-2750
Michael Thorp, Dean of Admission, College of St. Benedict, PO Box 7155, Collegeville, MN 56321-7155

---

## College of St. Catherine
**St. Paul, Minnesota**
www.stkate.edu

**CB member**
**CB code: 6105**

- Private 4-year health science and liberal arts college for women affiliated with Roman Catholic Church
- Commuter campus in large city
- 3,731 degree-seeking undergraduates: 34% part-time, 97% women, 11% African American, 8% Asian American, 3% Hispanic American, 1% Native American, 2% international
- 1,424 degree-seeking graduate students
- 77% of applicants admitted
- SAT or ACT (ACT writing optional) required
- 59% graduate within 6 years

**General.** Founded in 1905. Regionally accredited. Men may attend classes through cross-registration. Traditional day, weekend and graduate programs offered on St. Paul campus. 2-year associate's program in various health professions at Minneapolis campus. **Degrees:** 511 bachelor's, 191 associate awarded; master's, doctoral offered. **ROTC:** Army, Air Force. **Location:** 6 miles from downtown. **Calendar:** 4-1-4, extensive summer session. **Full-time faculty:** 264 total; 8% minority, 80% women. **Special facilities:** Center for women's research, observatory.

**Freshman class profile.** 1,647 applied, 1,275 admitted, 350 enrolled.

| Mid 50% test scores | | Rank in top tenth: | 29% |
|---|---|---|---|
| ACT composite: | 22-26 | Return as sophomores: | 78% |
| GPA 3.50 or higher: | 68% | Out-of-state: | 13% |
| GPA 3.0-3.49: | 27% | Live on campus: | 80% |
| GPA 2.0-2.99: | 5% | International: | 2% |
| Rank in top quarter: | 65% | | |

**Basis for selection.** School achievement record with rank in top half of class and test scores important. Extracurricular and community involvement also considered. Recommendations important. Interview recommended for all applicants, required for marginal students. Audition recommended for music students; portfolio recommended for art students. Essay recommended for marginal students.

**High school preparation.** 15 units recommended. Recommended units include English 4, mathematics 3, social studies 2, science 2 and foreign language 4.

**2007-2008 Annual costs.** Tuition/fees: $24,423. Room/board: $6,788. Books/supplies: $625. Personal expenses: $400.

**2006-2007 Financial aid. Need-based:** 336 full-time freshmen applied for aid; 287 were judged to have need; 282 of these received aid. Average need met was 72%. Average scholarship/grant was $7,952; average loan $3,285. 52% of total undergraduate aid awarded as scholarships/grants, 48% as loans/jobs. **Non-need-based:** Awarded to 1,145 full-time undergraduates, including 285 freshmen. Scholarships awarded for academics, alumni affiliation, leadership. **Additional information:** Audition required for music scholarships.

**Application procedures. Admission:** No deadline. No application fee. Students must be accepted by 02/01 to be eligible to compete in merit scholarship competition. **Financial aid:** Priority date 4/15; no closing date. FAFSA, institutional form required. Applicants notified on a rolling basis starting 3/30; must reply within 2 week(s) of notification.

**Academics. Special study options:** Combined bachelor's/graduate degree, cross-registration, double major, exchange student, honors, independent study, internships, liberal arts/career combination, student-designed major, study abroad, teacher certification program, urban semester, Washington semester, weekend college. Cooperative program in fashion merchandising with Fashion Institute of Technology in New York City and Fashion Institute of Design in Los Angeles, academic year of study in New York City, exchange program with other Carondolet Colleges, internship program includes over 500 sites in Twin Cities area. **Credit/placement by examination:** AP, CLEP, IB, institutional tests. 32 credit hours maximum toward bachelor's degree. **Support services:** Learning center, reduced course load, study skills assistance, tutoring, writing center.

**Majors. Area/ethnic studies:** Women's. **Biology:** General, biochemistry. **Business:** Accounting, business admin, fashion, international, management information systems, sales/distribution. **Communications:** General. **Computer sciences:** General, information systems. **Education:** General, art, business, early childhood, elementary, English, family/consumer sciences, foreign languages, mathematics, middle, music, physical, secondary. **English:** English lit, speech/rhetoric. **Family/consumer sciences:** General, food/

nutrition. **Foreign languages:** American Sign Language, French, sign language interpretation, Spanish. **Health:** Dietetics, medical records admin, nursing (RN), predental, premedicine, prepharmacy, preveterinary, respiratory therapy technology. **History:** General. **Interdisciplinary:** Intercultural. **Legal studies:** Prelaw. **Math:** General. **Parks/recreation:** Exercise sciences. **Philosophy/religion:** Philosophy. **Physical sciences:** Chemistry, physics. **Psychology:** General. **Public administration:** Social work. **Social sciences:** General, economics, international relations, political science, sociology. **Theology:** Theology. **Visual/performing arts:** Art history/conservation, dramatic, fashion design, music performance, studio arts.

**Most popular majors.** Business/marketing 17%, English 9%, health sciences 26%.

**Computing on campus.** 350 workstations in dormitories, library, computer center, student center. Dormitories wired for high-speed internet access and linked to campus network. Commuter students can connect to campus network. Online course registration, online library, helpline available.

**Student life. Freshman orientation:** Mandatory. **Housing:** Guaranteed on-campus for freshmen. Apartments available. Apartments for student-parents available. **Activities:** Campus ministries, choral groups, dance, drama, international student organizations, literary magazine, music ensembles, musical theater, student government, student newspaper, Volunteers in Action, League of Women Voters, Minnesota Public Interest Research Group, Women of Color, clubs for majors, women's issues groups.

**Athletics. NCAA. Intercollegiate:** Basketball W, cross-country W, diving W, ice hockey W, soccer W, softball W, swimming W, tennis W, track and field W, volleyball W. **Intramural:** Basketball W, cheerleading W, football (non-tackle) W, golf W, lacrosse W, racquetball W, soccer W, softball W, tennis W, volleyball W. **Team name:** Wildcats.

**Student services.** Adult student services, campus ministries, career counseling, student employment services, financial aid counseling, health services, minority student services, on-campus daycare, personal counseling, placement for graduates, women's services. **Physically disabled:** Services for visually, speech, hearing impaired.

**Contact.** E-mail: admissions@stkate.edu
Phone: (651) 690-8850 Toll-free number: (800) 656-5283
Fax: (651) 690-8824
College of St. Catherine, 2004 Randolph Avenue #4-02, St. Paul, MN 55105

## College of St. Scholastica
**Duluth, Minnesota**                          **CB member**
**www.css.edu**                                **CB code: 6107**

▶ Private 4-year liberal arts college affiliated with Roman Catholic Church
▶ Residential campus in small city
▶ 1,986 degree-seeking undergraduates: 2% part-time, 69% women, 1% African American, 2% Asian American, 1% Hispanic American, 2% Native American, 4% international
▶ 707 degree-seeking graduate students
▶ 88% of applicants admitted
▶ SAT or ACT (ACT writing optional) required
▶ 64% graduate within 6 years; 26% enter graduate study

**General.** Founded in 1912. Regionally accredited. **Degrees:** 614 bachelor's awarded; master's, first professional offered. **ROTC:** Air Force. **Location:** 2 miles from downtown, 150 miles from Minneapolis-St. Paul. **Calendar:** Semester, limited summer session. **Full-time faculty:** 152 total; 59% have terminal degrees, 9% minority, 59% women. **Part-time faculty:** 109 total; 22% have terminal degrees, 6% minority, 62% women. **Class size:** 49% < 20, 45% 20-39, 2% 40-49, 2% 50-99, 1% >100. **Special facilities:** Wellness center with climbing wall.

**Freshman class profile.** 1,461 applied, 1,288 admitted, 487 enrolled.

| Mid 50% test scores | | | |
|---|---|---|---|
| SAT critical reading: | 530-650 | Rank in top quarter: | 52% |
| SAT math: | 530-660 | Rank in top tenth: | 23% |
| ACT composite: | 21-26 | End year in good standing: | 85% |
| GPA 3.50 or higher: | 56% | Return as sophomores: | 79% |
| GPA 3.0-3.49: | 30% | Out-of-state: | 14% |
| GPA 2.0-2.99: | 14% | Live on campus: | 84% |
| | | International: | 4% |

**Basis for selection.** School achievement record and test scores most important. Interview recommended.

**High school preparation.** Recommended units include English 4, mathematics 2, social studies 3, history 3, science 3 and foreign language 3.

**2007-2008 Annual costs.** Tuition/fees: $24,990. Room/board: $6,684. Books/supplies: $900. Personal expenses: $1,028.

**2007-2008 Financial aid. Need-based:** 436 full-time freshmen applied for aid; 394 were judged to have need; 393 of these received aid. Average need met was 83%. Average scholarship/grant was $6,641; average loan $3,938. 53% of total undergraduate aid awarded as scholarships/grants, 47% as loans/jobs. **Non-need-based:** Awarded to 1,571 full-time undergraduates, including 426 freshmen. Scholarships awarded for academics, alumni affiliation, religious affiliation, ROTC.

**Application procedures. Admission:** No deadline. $25 fee, may be waived for applicants with need. Application may be submitted online. Admission notification on a rolling basis beginning on or about 9/1. Must reply by May 1 or within 2 week(s) if notified thereafter. **Financial aid:** Priority date 3/15; no closing date. FAFSA, institutional form required. Applicants notified on a rolling basis starting 3/1; must reply by 5/1 or within 2 week(s) of notification.

**Academics. Special study options:** Accelerated study, combined bachelor's/graduate degree, cross-registration, distance learning, double major, dual enrollment of high school students, external degree, honors, independent study, internships, liberal arts/career combination, student-designed major, study abroad, teacher certification program, Washington semester. **Credit/placement by examination:** AP, CLEP, IB, institutional tests. 96 credit hours maximum toward bachelor's degree. All external credit meeting score expectations will be accepted; last 32 semester hours must be completed in residence. **Support services:** Pre-admission summer program, reduced course load, study skills assistance, tutoring, writing center.

**Honors college/program.** Should meet 2 of the following: top 15% of high school class, 26 ACT or 1100 (exclusive of Writing) SAT, GPA of 3.5; others may apply by contacting the honors director. Students must complete 20 honors credits, at least 8 of which are upper-level credits.

**Majors. Biology:** General, biochemistry, exercise physiology. **Business:** Accounting, business admin, marketing, organizational behavior. **Communications:** General, advertising, journalism. **Computer sciences:** General. **Education:** Elementary, multi-level teacher, school librarian, social science. **English:** English lit. **Health:** Health services, medical records admin, nursing (RN). **History:** General. **Interdisciplinary:** Global studies. **Liberal arts:** Humanities. **Math:** General. **Philosophy/religion:** Christian, religion. **Physical sciences:** Chemistry. **Psychology:** General. **Public administration:** Social work. **Social sciences:** General, applied economics. **Visual/performing arts:** Music performance.

**Most popular majors.** Biology 9%, business/marketing 29%, health sciences 33%.

**Computing on campus.** 205 workstations in dormitories, library, computer center, student center. Dormitories wired for high-speed internet access and linked to campus network. Commuter students can connect to campus network. Online course registration, online library, helpline, student web hosting, wireless network available.

**Student life. Freshman orientation:** Mandatory. Preregistration for classes offered. Combines academic advising with social activities. **Housing:** Guaranteed on-campus for freshmen. Coed dorms, special housing for disabled, apartments, substance-free housing available. $150 fully refundable deposit, deadline 5/1. Quiet or study wing; apartments for students with dependent children. **Activities:** Bands, campus ministries, choral groups, dance, drama, international student organizations, literary magazine, music ensembles, student government, student newspaper, TV station, Circle K, InterVarsity Christian Fellowship, American Indian student organization, Benedictine Friends, Volunteers Involved Through Action, Amnesty International, Kaleidoscope Multicultural Club, Habitat for Humanity, United for Africa.

**Athletics. NCAA. Intercollegiate:** Baseball M, basketball, cross-country, football (tackle) M, ice hockey M, skiing, soccer, softball W, tennis, track and field, volleyball W. **Intramural:** Badminton, basketball, bowling, football (non-tackle), tennis, volleyball. **Team name:** Saints.

**Student services.** Adult student services, alcohol/substance abuse counseling, campus ministries, career counseling, student employment services, financial aid counseling, health services, minority student services, personal counseling, placement for graduates, veterans' counselor, women's services. **Physically disabled:** Services for visually, hearing impaired.

**Contact.** E-mail: admissions@css.edu
Phone: (218) 723-6046 Toll-free number: (800) 249-6412
Fax: (218) 723-5991
Brian Dalton, Vice President for Enrollment Management, College of St. Scholastica, 1200 Kenwood Avenue, Duluth, MN 55811-4199

## College of Visual Arts
**Saint Paul, Minnesota**
www.cva.edu                                     CB code: 6147

- Private 4-year visual arts college
- Commuter campus in large city
- 170 degree-seeking undergraduates: 1% part-time, 58% women, 3% African American, 3% Asian American, 2% Hispanic American, 1% Native American, 1% international
- 98% of applicants admitted
- SAT or ACT (ACT writing optional), application essay required
- 26% graduate within 6 years

**General.** Founded in 1924. Regionally accredited. **Degrees:** 27 bachelor's awarded. **Calendar:** Semester, limited summer session. **Full-time faculty:** 7 total; 29% have terminal degrees, 71% women. **Part-time faculty:** 43 total; 12% have terminal degrees, 2% minority, 44% women. **Class size:** 99% < 20, 1% 20-39. **Special facilities:** Exhibition gallery, photography facilities, sculpture studio, printmaking studio, drawing studio, painting studio.

**Freshman class profile.** 115 applied, 113 admitted, 61 enrolled.

| Mid 50% test scores | | | |
|---|---|---|---|
| SAT critical reading: | 420-540 | End year in good standing: | 81% |
| SAT math: | 430-550 | Return as sophomores: | 69% |
| ACT composite: | 18-21 | Out-of-state: | 15% |
| | | International: | 2% |

**Basis for selection.** Statement of interest, test scores, transcript and portfolio very important. Students with 30+ college credits are not required to submit ACT/SAT scores. Review of portfolio required. **Homeschooled:** Transcript of courses and grades required. List of classes, textbooks used. **Learning Disabled:** Documentation of disabilities required.

**High school preparation.** Recommended units include English 4, mathematics 4, social studies 4, science 4 and foreign language 2. Progression of classes in art preferred.

**2007-2008 Annual costs.** Tuition/fees: $21,684. Books/supplies: $2,244.

**2007-2008 Financial aid. Need-based:** Average need met was 51%. Average scholarship/grant was $8,261; average loan $3,423. 36% of total undergraduate aid awarded as scholarships/grants, 64% as loans/jobs. **Non-need-based:** Scholarships awarded for academics, art.

**Application procedures. Admission:** Priority date 3/1; no deadline. $40 fee, may be waived for applicants with need. Application may be submitted online. Admission notification on a rolling basis beginning on or about 9/1. Must reply by May 1 or within 2 week(s) if notified thereafter. **Financial aid:** Priority date 3/1; no closing date. FAFSA, institutional form required. Applicants notified on a rolling basis starting 2/15; must reply within 2 week(s) of notification.

**Academics. Special study options:** Honors, independent study, internships, study abroad. **Credit/placement by examination:** AP, CLEP. **Support services:** Learning center, study skills assistance, tutoring, writing center.

**Majors. Visual/performing arts:** Commercial/advertising art, design, drawing, illustration, painting, photography, printmaking, sculpture, studio arts.

**Computing on campus.** 50 workstations in library, computer center. Online library, helpline available.

**Student life. Freshman orientation:** Mandatory. Preregistration for classes offered. **Housing:** Housing coordinator and roommate matching services. **Activities:** Film society, student government.

**Student services.** Alcohol/substance abuse counseling, career counseling, student employment services, financial aid counseling, personal counseling, placement for graduates.

**Contact.** E-mail: admissions@cva.edu
Phone: (651) 224-3416 Toll-free number: (800) 224-1536
Fax: (651) 224-8854
Jane Nordhorn, Director of Admissions, College of Visual Arts, 344 Summit Avenue, Saint Paul, MN 55102-2199

## Concordia College: Moorhead
**Moorhead, Minnesota**                          CB member
www.concordiacollege.edu                        CB code: 6113

- Private 4-year liberal arts college affiliated with Evangelical Lutheran Church in America
- Residential campus in small city

- 2,720 degree-seeking undergraduates: 1% part-time, 61% women, 1% African American, 2% Asian American, 1% Hispanic American, 4% international
- 10 degree-seeking graduate students
- 85% of applicants admitted
- SAT or ACT (ACT writing optional) required
- 69% graduate within 6 years

**General.** Founded in 1891. Regionally accredited. **Degrees:** 572 bachelor's awarded; master's offered. **ROTC:** Army, Air Force. **Location:** 234 miles from Minneapolis-St. Paul, 1 mile from Fargo, North Dakota. **Calendar:** Semester, limited summer session. **Full-time faculty:** 189 total; 75% have terminal degrees, 45% women. **Part-time faculty:** 74 total; 11% have terminal degrees, 51% women. **Class size:** 47% < 20, 48% 20-39, 3% 40-49, 2% 50-99. **Special facilities:** Observatory, microparticle accelerator, language villages, television production studio, biology research facility, nursing lab.

**Freshman class profile.** 2,517 applied, 2,152 admitted, 836 enrolled.

| Mid 50% test scores | | | |
|---|---|---|---|
| SAT critical reading: | 530-660 | GPA 2.0-2.99: | 7% |
| SAT math: | 530-670 | Rank in top quarter: | 50% |
| SAT writing: | 520-640 | Rank in top tenth: | 32% |
| ACT composite: | 22-27 | Return as sophomores: | 80% |
| GPA 3.50 or higher: | 69% | Out-of-state: | 29% |
| GPA 3.0-3.49: | 24% | Live on campus: | 98% |
| | | International: | 2% |

**Basis for selection.** Academic record (types of courses and grades) most important, followed by test scores and recommendations. Interview recommended.

**High school preparation.** Recommended units include English 4, mathematics 3, social studies 3, science 3 and foreign language 2. Computer science and exposure to fine arts recommended.

**2007-2008 Annual costs.** Tuition/fees: $22,350. Room/board: $5,700. Books/supplies: $740. Personal expenses: $1,170.

**2006-2007 Financial aid.** All financial aid based on need. 586 full-time freshmen applied for aid; 469 were judged to have need; 469 of these received aid. Average need met was 90%. Average scholarship/grant was $11,709; average loan $3,718. 61% of total undergraduate aid awarded as scholarships/grants, 39% as loans/jobs. **Additional information:** Students in ACCORD program (age 25 and older) may apply for tuition reductions for first 4 courses.

**Application procedures. Admission:** No deadline. $20 fee, may be waived for applicants with need. Application may be submitted online. Admission notification on a rolling basis beginning on or about 7/15. **Financial aid:** Priority date 4/15; no closing date. FAFSA, institutional form required. Applicants notified on a rolling basis starting 3/1.

**Academics. Special study options:** Cooperative education, cross-registration, distance learning, double major, exchange student, honors, independent study, internships, semester at sea, study abroad, teacher certification program, urban semester, Washington semester. Urban studies program in Chicago, Lutheran Consortium with Dar es Salaam University in Tanzania; master of science in nursing offered through consortium with Minnesota State University Moorhead and North Dakota State University. **Credit/placement by examination:** AP, CLEP, IB, SAT, ACT, institutional tests. 20 credit hours maximum toward bachelor's degree. **Support services:** Learning center, reduced course load, study skills assistance, tutoring, writing center.

**Majors. Area/ethnic studies:** French, German, Russian/Slavic, Scandinavian, Spanish/Iberian. **Biology:** General. **Business:** General, accounting, business admin, international, office management. **Communications:** General, advertising, broadcast journalism, journalism, media studies, public relations. **Computer sciences:** Computer science. **Conservation:** Environmental studies. **Education:** General, art, biology, business, chemistry, elementary, English, French, German, health, history, Latin, mathematics, music, physical, physics, science, secondary, social science, social studies, Spanish, speech. **English:** American lit, British lit, composition, creative writing, English lit. **Family/consumer sciences:** General, clothing/textiles, family studies, food/nutrition. **Foreign languages:** Classics, French, German, Latin, Russian, Scandinavian, Spanish. **Health:** Clinical lab science, facilities admin, health care admin, nursing (RN), predental, premedicine, prepharmacy, preveterinary. **History:** General. **Interdisciplinary:** Math/computer science. **Legal studies:** Prelaw. **Liberal arts:** Arts/sciences. **Math:** General, applied. **Parks/recreation:** Exercise sciences, health/fitness. **Philosophy/religion:** Philosophy, religion. **Physical sciences:** Chemistry, physics. **Psychology:** General. **Public administration:** Social work. **Social sciences:** Economics, international relations, political science, sociology. **Theology:** Theology. **Visual/performing arts:** Art, art history/conservation, conducting, dramatic, music performance, piano/organ, studio arts, voice/opera.

**Most popular majors.** Biology 8%, business/marketing 14%, communications/journalism 7%, education 16%, foreign language 6%, social sciences 9%, visual/performing arts 6%.

**Computing on campus.** 453 workstations in dormitories, library, computer center, student center. Dormitories wired for high-speed internet access and linked to campus network. Commuter students can connect to campus network. Online library, repair service, student web hosting, wireless network available.

**Student life. Freshman orientation:** Mandatory. Preregistration for classes offered. 4-day program one week prior to fall semester. **Housing:** Guaranteed on-campus for freshmen. Coed dorms, single-sex dorms, apartments, substance-free housing available. $200 fully refundable deposit, deadline 8/1. Students studying Spanish, French, or German have opportunity to live with native speakers in campus apartments. **Activities:** Bands, choral groups, dance, drama, literary magazine, music ensembles, musical theater, radio station, student government, student newspaper, TV station, Over 100 clubs and organizations.

**Athletics. NCAA. Intercollegiate:** Baseball M, basketball, cross-country, diving M, football (tackle) M, golf, ice hockey, soccer, softball W, swimming W, tennis, track and field, volleyball W, wrestling M. **Intramural:** Badminton, baseball M, basketball, bowling, cross-country, football (non-tackle), golf, ice hockey, racquetball, rugby, skiing, soccer, softball, swimming, table tennis, tennis, track and field, volleyball, weight lifting. **Team name:** Cobbers.

**Student services.** Adult student services, alcohol/substance abuse counseling, campus ministries, career counseling, student employment services, financial aid counseling, health services, minority student services, on-campus daycare, personal counseling, placement for graduates. **Physically disabled:** Services for visually, speech, hearing impaired.

**Contact.** E-mail: admissions@cord.edu
Phone: (218) 299-3004 Toll-free number: (800) 699-9897
Fax: (218) 299-4720
Scott Ellingson, Admissions Director, Concordia College: Moorhead, 901 Eighth Street South, Moorhead, MN 56562-9981

---

## Concordia University: St. Paul

**St. Paul, Minnesota**
www.csp.edu

**CB member**
**CB code: 6114**

- Private 4-year university affiliated with Lutheran Church - Missouri Synod
- Residential campus in large city
- 1,418 degree-seeking undergraduates: 8% part-time, 59% women, 9% African American, 6% Asian American, 1% Hispanic American, 1% international
- 631 degree-seeking graduate students
- 57% of applicants admitted
- SAT or ACT (ACT writing optional) required
- 45% graduate within 6 years

**General.** Founded in 1893. Regionally accredited. **Degrees:** 573 bachelor's, 16 associate awarded; master's offered. **ROTC:** Army, Naval, Air Force. **Calendar:** Semester, limited summer session. **Full-time faculty:** 89 total; 57% have terminal degrees, 3% minority, 48% women. **Part-time faculty:** 220 total; 7% minority, 46% women. **Class size:** 76% < 20, 23% 20-39, less than 1% 40-49, less than 1% 50-99.

**Freshman class profile.** 963 applied, 550 admitted, 201 enrolled.

| Mid 50% test scores | | | |
|---|---|---|---|
| ACT composite: | 18-24 | End year in good standing: | 78% |
| GPA 3.50 or higher: | 30% | Return as sophomores: | 71% |
| GPA 3.0-3.49: | 33% | Out-of-state: | 23% |
| GPA 2.0-2.99: | 36% | Live on campus: | 75% |
| Rank in top quarter: | 30% | | |
| Rank in top tenth: | 9% | | |

**Basis for selection.** School record, test scores, recommendations important. ACT preferred. Interview recommended.

**High school preparation.** 15 units required; 16 recommended. Required and recommended units include English 4, mathematics 2, social studies 1, history 1, science 2 (laboratory 2) and foreign language 1. 2 units of fine arts, 1 unit of health/physical education.

**2008-2009 Annual costs.** Tuition/fees: $24,900. Adult learners in degree completion programs have discounted tuition rates based on cost per credit. Rates vary by program. Room/board: $6,900. Books/supplies: $700. Personal expenses: $900.

---

**2007-2008 Financial aid. Need-based:** Average need met was 79%. Average scholarship/grant was $14,525; average loan $3,734. 48% of total undergraduate aid awarded as scholarships/grants, 52% as loans/jobs. **Non-need-based:** Scholarships awarded for academics, art, athletics, minority status, music/drama, religious affiliation. **Additional information:** Church districts and local congregations are major sources of aid for church-vocation students.

**Application procedures. Admission:** Priority date 5/1; deadline 8/1 (receipt date). $30 fee, may be waived for applicants with need. Application may be submitted online. Admission notification on a rolling basis. **Financial aid:** Priority date 5/1; no closing date. FAFSA, institutional form required. Applicants notified on a rolling basis starting 3/1; must reply within 3 week(s) of notification.

**Academics.** We have a variety of non-traditional undergraduate degree completion programs designed for working adults in both face-to-face and distance education formats. Approximately 40% of our undergraduates fall into this non-traditional category. **Special study options:** Accelerated study, cross-registration, distance learning, double major, dual enrollment of high school students, exchange student, honors, independent study, internships, study abroad, teacher certification program. **Credit/placement by examination:** AP, CLEP, IB, ACT, institutional tests. **Support services:** Learning center, reduced course load, study skills assistance, tutoring, writing center.

**Majors. Biology:** General. **Business:** Accounting, business admin, finance, management information systems, marketing. **Communications:** Media studies. **Education:** Art, bilingual, biology, chemistry, early childhood, elementary, English, ESL, health, history, kindergarten/preschool, mathematics, middle, music, physical, science, secondary, social studies. **English:** English lit. **Family/consumer sciences:** Child development, family studies. **History:** General. **Math:** General. **Parks/recreation:** Exercise sciences, health/fitness. **Protective services:** Criminal justice, law enforcement admin. **Psychology:** General. **Public administration:** Human services. **Social sciences:** Sociology. **Theology:** Missionary, religious ed, sacred music, theology. **Visual/performing arts:** Art, dramatic, studio arts.

**Most popular majors.** Business/marketing 54%, computer/information sciences 6%, education 7%, family/consumer sciences 11%.

**Computing on campus.** Dormitories wired for high-speed internet access and linked to campus network. Commuter students can connect to campus network. Helpline, repair service, wireless network available.

**Student life. Freshman orientation:** Mandatory. 3-day program prior to start of fall semester provides information about student life, support services, social programs, employment opportunities, and technology training. **Housing:** Guaranteed on-campus for freshmen. Coed dorms, single-sex dorms, special housing for disabled, apartments, substance-free housing available. $125 deposit. **Activities:** Bands, choral groups, dance, drama, music ensembles, musical theater, student government, student newspaper, TV station, Fellowship of Christian Athletes, Southeast Asian student association, United Minds of Joint Action, student senate, mission society.

**Athletics. NCAA. Intercollegiate:** Baseball M, basketball, cross-country, football (tackle) M, golf, soccer W, softball W, track and field, volleyball W. **Intramural:** Basketball, bowling, football (non-tackle), racquetball, skiing, soccer, softball, table tennis, volleyball. **Team name:** Golden Bears.

**Student services.** Adult student services, alcohol/substance abuse counseling, campus ministries, career counseling, services for economically disadvantaged, student employment services, financial aid counseling, health services, minority student services, on-campus daycare, personal counseling, placement for graduates. **Physically disabled:** Services for visually, speech, hearing impaired.

**Contact.** E-mail: admission@csp.edu
Phone: (651) 641-8230 Toll-free number: (800) 333-4705
Fax: (651) 603-6320
Kristin Schoon, Director of Undergraduate Admission, Concordia University: St. Paul, 275 Syndicate Street North, St. Paul, MN 55104-5494

---

## Crossroads College

**Rochester, Minnesota**
www.crossroadscollege.edu

**CB code: 6412**

- Private 4-year Bible college affiliated with Christian Church
- Residential campus in small city
- 184 degree-seeking undergraduates
- 62% of applicants admitted
- SAT or ACT (ACT writing recommended), application essay required

**General.** Founded in 1913. Accredited by ABHE. **Degrees:** 27 bachelor's, 5 associate awarded. **Location:** 85 miles from Minneapolis-St. Paul. **Calendar:** Semester, limited summer session. **Full-time faculty:** 7 total. **Part-time faculty:** 24 total. **Class size:** 79% < 20, 16% 20-39, 2% 40-49, 4% 50-99. **Special facilities:** 38-acre wooded area with nature trails, pond.

**Freshman class profile.** 69 applied, 43 admitted, 32 enrolled.

| Mid 50% test scores | | | |
|---|---|---|---|
| SAT critical reading: | 470-540 | Rank in top quarter: | 58% |
| SAT math: | 640-660 | Out-of-state: | 31% |
| ACT composite: | 17-23 | Live on campus: | 92% |

**Basis for selection.** High school rank, experience, aptitude for Christian ministry, character references, and personal statement of goals considered. High school GPA, rank and ACT/SAT scores determine number of credit hours a student may take during first semester if accepted. Interview recommended. **Learning Disabled:** Provide Vice President of Student Development with verification of learning disability.

**2008-2009 Annual costs.** Tuition/fees (projected): $13,210. Room only: $3,800. Books/supplies: $700. Personal expenses: $1,500.

**2007-2008 Financial aid. Need-based:** 48% of total undergraduate aid awarded as scholarships/grants, 52% as loans/jobs. **Non-need-based:** Scholarships awarded for academics, leadership, music/drama, religious affiliation.

**Application procedures. Admission:** Closing date 8/15 (receipt date). $30 fee. Admission notification on a rolling basis. **Financial aid:** Priority date 4/1; no closing date. FAFSA, institutional form required. Applicants notified on a rolling basis starting 2/1; must reply within 4 week(s) of notification.

**Academics.** Minors in religious music, counseling psychology, biblical and classical languages, missions, youth ministries. **Special study options:** Double major, independent study, internships, liberal arts/career combination, student-designed major. **Credit/placement by examination:** AP, CLEP, SAT, ACT, institutional tests. 30 credit hours maximum toward bachelor's degree. **Support services:** Reduced course load, remedial instruction, study skills assistance, tutoring, writing center.

**Majors. Psychology:** Counseling. **Theology:** Missionary, religious ed, sacred music, theology, youth ministry.

**Computing on campus.** 17 workstations in library, computer center. Dormitories wired for high-speed internet access. Wireless network available.

**Student life. Freshman orientation:** Mandatory. Preregistration for classes offered. 2-day session with some placement testing in August; one-day session in January. **Policies:** Attendance required at weekly Chapel and Spiritual Formation Group meetings; Field Service participation required. Religious observance required. **Housing:** Guaranteed on-campus for freshmen. Single-sex dorms, special housing for disabled, apartments, substance-free housing available. **Activities:** Choral groups, drama, music ensembles, student government, student newspaper, Christians outdoors, ambassadors group, international students fellowship.

**Athletics. Intercollegiate:** Baseball M, basketball, golf M, soccer M, softball W, tennis, volleyball W. **Intramural:** Bowling, golf, ice hockey, racquetball, skiing, soccer W, swimming, table tennis, tennis, volleyball. **Team name:** Knights.

**Student services.** Adult student services, campus ministries, career counseling, student employment services, financial aid counseling, personal counseling, placement for graduates, veterans' counselor.

**Contact.** E-mail: admissions@crossroads.edu
Phone: (507) 288-4563 ext. 313 Toll-free number: (800) 456-7651
Fax: (507) 288-9046
Scott Klaehn, Director of Admissions, Crossroads College, 920 Mayowood Road, SW, Rochester, MN 55902

---

## Crown College
### St. Bonifacius, Minnesota
**www.crown.edu**                                    CB code: 6639

- Private 4-year Bible and liberal arts college affiliated with Christian and Missionary Alliance
- Residential campus in small town
- 1,025 degree-seeking undergraduates: 36% part-time, 60% women
- 123 degree-seeking graduate students
- SAT or ACT (ACT writing optional); application essay required

---

**General.** Founded in 1916. Regionally accredited; also accredited by ABHE. **Degrees:** 164 bachelor's, 15 associate awarded; master's offered. **Location:** 25 miles from Minneapolis-St. Paul. **Calendar:** Semester, limited summer session. **Full-time faculty:** 37 total; 46% have terminal degrees, 3% minority, 27% women. **Part-time faculty:** 122 total; 23% have terminal degrees, less than 1% minority, 47% women. **Class size:** 66% < 20, 29% 20-39, 4% 40-49, 1% 50-99.

**Freshman class profile.**

| Mid 50% test scores | | | |
|---|---|---|---|
| SAT critical reading: | 490-650 | GPA 2.0-2.99: | 26% |
| SAT math: | 460-600 | Rank in top quarter: | 43% |
| ACT composite: | 19-24 | Rank in top tenth: | 12% |
| GPA 3.50 or higher: | 40% | Out-of-state: | 40% |
| GPA 3.0-3.49: | 32% | Live on campus: | 94% |

**Basis for selection.** Applicants must profess personal faith in Jesus Christ. Pastor's and general recommendations very important, academic records and test scores important. **Learning Disabled:** Applicant should meet with director of academic support.

**High school preparation.** Recommended units include English 4, mathematics 3, social studies 3, science 3 and foreign language 2.

**2008-2009 Annual costs.** Tuition/fees (projected): $19,198. Room/board: $6,986. Books/supplies: $1,500. Personal expenses: $2,272.

**2007-2008 Financial aid. Need-based:** 44% of total undergraduate aid awarded as scholarships/grants, 56% as loans/jobs. **Non-need-based:** Scholarships awarded for academics, alumni affiliation, leadership, minority status, music/drama, religious affiliation.

**Application procedures. Admission:** Closing date 8/18 (postmark date). $35 fee, may be waived for applicants with need. Application may be submitted online. Admission notification on a rolling basis. **Financial aid:** Priority date 4/1, closing date 8/1. FAFSA, institutional form required. Applicants notified on a rolling basis starting 4/1; must reply within 3 week(s) of notification.

**Academics. Special study options:** Accelerated study, distance learning, double major, dual enrollment of high school students, ESL, exchange student, honors, independent study, internships, liberal arts/career combination, study abroad, teacher certification program, urban semester, weekend college. 2-2 with nonaccredited Bible colleges. **Credit/placement by examination:** AP, CLEP, IB, ACT, institutional tests. 30 credit hours maximum toward associate degree, 30 toward bachelor's. **Support services:** Learning center, reduced course load, remedial instruction, study skills assistance, tutoring, writing center.

**Majors. Biology:** General. **Business:** General, business admin. **Communications:** General, digital media. **Computer sciences:** General, information systems, information technology. **Education:** Early childhood, elementary, English, history, music, secondary, social studies. **English:** English lit. **Foreign languages:** Linguistics. **Health:** Nursing (RN). **History:** General. **Liberal arts:** Arts/sciences. **Parks/recreation:** Sports admin. **Physical sciences:** General. **Psychology:** General. **Public administration:** Youth services. **Theology:** Bible, missionary, pastoral counseling, religious ed, theology, youth ministry. **Visual/performing arts:** Music performance.

**Computing on campus.** 60 workstations in library, computer center. Dormitories wired for high-speed internet access and linked to campus network. Commuter students can connect to campus network. Online library, helpline, wireless network available.

**Student life. Freshman orientation:** Available. Preregistration for classes offered. 2-day orientation program at the beginning of the spring semester, 4 days prior to fall semester. **Policies:** Religious observance required. **Housing:** Guaranteed on-campus for all undergraduates. Single-sex dorms, special housing for disabled, apartments, substance-free housing available. $50 deposit. **Activities:** Jazz band, choral groups, dance, drama, film society, literary magazine, music ensembles, musical theater, student government, student newspaper, Christian service groups, mission support groups, Student Missionary Society, ethnic clubs, activity planning group, student family association, Intercultural Experiences, College Conservatives, Missionary Cabinet.

**Athletics.** NCAA, NCCAA. **Intercollegiate:** Baseball M, basketball, cross-country, football (tackle) M, golf, soccer, softball W, volleyball W. **Intramural:** Basketball, football (non-tackle) M, soccer, volleyball. **Team name:** The Storm.

**Student services.** Adult student services, campus ministries, career counseling, student employment services, financial aid counseling, health services, personal counseling. **Physically disabled:** Services for visually, hearing impaired.

**Contact.** E-mail: info@crown.edu
Phone: (952) 446-4142 Toll-free number: (800) 682-7696
Fax: (952) 446-4149
Jill, Director of Admissions, Crown College, 8700 College View Drive, St. Bonifacius, MN 55375-9001

## DeVry University: Edina
### Edina, Minnesota
### www.devry.edu

- For-profit 4-year university
- Commuter campus in large town
- 161 degree-seeking undergraduates: 60% part-time, 39% women, 10% African American, 5% Asian American, 4% Hispanic American, 1% Native American
- 49 degree-seeking graduate students

**General. Degrees:** 17 bachelor's, 1 associate awarded; master's offered. **Calendar:** Semester. **Part-time faculty:** 1 total; 100% women.

**Freshman class profile.** 24 enrolled.

| Return as sophomores: | 33% | Out-of-state: | 13% |
|---|---|---|---|

**Basis for selection.** Interview and GPA important, test scores and class rank considered.

**2007-2008 Annual costs.** Tuition/fees: $13,020. Books/supplies: $1,300. Personal expenses: $5,082.

**Financial aid. Non-need-based:** Scholarships awarded for academics.

**Application procedures. Admission:** No deadline. $50 fee. Admission notification on a rolling basis. **Financial aid:** No deadline. FAFSA required. Applicants notified on a rolling basis.

**Academics. Special study options:** Accelerated study, distance learning. **Credit/placement by examination:** CLEP.

**Majors. Business:** Business admin. **Computer sciences:** Game design, networking, security.

**Most popular majors.** Business/marketing 94%, computer/information sciences 6%.

**Student life. Housing:** Private apartments, student-plan housing, private rooms available.

**Contact.** Phone: (877) 733-3879
DeVry University: Edina, 7700 France Avenue South, Suite 575, Edina, MN 55435

## Globe University
### Woodbury, Minnesota
### www.globeuniversity.edu          CB code: 2296

- For-profit 4-year business and health science college
- Commuter campus in small city
- 795 degree-seeking undergraduates
- Interview required

**General.** Accredited by ACICS. **Degrees:** 25 bachelor's, 152 associate awarded; master's offered. **Location:** 8 miles from Minneapolis-St. Paul. **Calendar:** Quarter, extensive summer session. **Full-time faculty:** 16 total. **Part-time faculty:** 42 total. **Class size:** 87% < 20, 13% 20-39.

**Basis for selection.** Open admission. **Learning Disabled:** Interview with Dean of Students.

**2007-2008 Annual costs.** Tuition/fees: $17,760. Books/supplies: $900.

**Application procedures. Admission:** No deadline. $50 fee. Application may be submitted online. Admission notification on a rolling basis. **Financial aid:** No deadline. FAFSA, institutional form required. Applicants notified on a rolling basis starting 5/1.

**Academics. Special study options:** Distance learning, independent study, internships, liberal arts/career combination. **Credit/placement by examination:** AP, CLEP, institutional tests. **Support services:** Learning center, reduced course load, study skills assistance, tutoring, writing center.

**Majors. Agriculture:** Animal sciences. **Business:** Accounting, business admin. **Computer sciences:** General, information technology, LAN/WAN management, security, system admin, web page design. **Engineering:** Software. **Engineering technology:** Computer, computer hardware, computer systems, software. **Health:** Office admin. **Legal studies:** Paralegal. **Parks/recreation:** Exercise sciences.

**Computing on campus.** 173 workstations in library, computer center. Commuter students can connect to campus network. Online library, helpline, repair service, wireless network available.

**Student life. Freshman orientation:** Mandatory. 4-hour orientation held prior to each quarter. **Activities:** Student government, student newspaper.

**Student services.** Career counseling, services for economically disadvantaged, student employment services, financial aid counseling, placement for graduates. **Physically disabled:** Services for hearing impaired.

**Contact.** E-mail: admissions@globeuniversity.edu
Phone: (651) 730-5100 Toll-free number: (800) 231-0660
Fax: (651) 730-5151
Christina Hilpipre, Director of Admissions, Globe University, 8089 Globe Drive, Woodbury, MN 55125

## Gustavus Adolphus College
### St. Peter, Minnesota          CB member
### www.gustavus.edu          CB code: 6253

- Private 4-year liberal arts college affiliated with Evangelical Lutheran Church in America
- Residential campus in small town
- 2,577 degree-seeking undergraduates: 57% women
- 80% of applicants admitted
- Application essay required
- 81% graduate within 6 years; 21% enter graduate study

**General.** Founded in 1862. Regionally accredited. **Degrees:** 595 bachelor's awarded. **ROTC:** Army. **Location:** 65 miles from Minneapolis-St. Paul. **Calendar:** 4-1-4, limited summer session. **Full-time faculty:** 180 total; 89% have terminal degrees, 10% minority, 43% women. **Part-time faculty:** 70 total; 26% have terminal degrees, 6% minority, 47% women. **Class size:** 54% < 20, 39% 20-39, 4% 40-49, 3% 50-99. **Special facilities:** Aboretum with walking and skiing paths, theme gardens, native woods and prairies, art museum, interpretive center.

**Freshman class profile.** 2,208 applied, 1,759 admitted, 690 enrolled.

| Mid 50% test scores | | Rank in top quarter: | 71% |
|---|---|---|---|
| SAT math: | 590-680 | Rank in top tenth: | 36% |
| ACT composite: | 24-29 | End year in good standing: | 90% |
| GPA 3.50 or higher: | 75% | Out-of-state: | 19% |
| GPA 3.0-3.49: | 20% | Live on campus: | 99% |
| GPA 2.0-2.99: | 5% | International: | 1% |

**Basis for selection.** School achievement record, test scores, recommendations, interview, essay or personal statement, school and community activities most important. Special consideration given to children of alumni and minority applicants. SAT or ACT recommended. **Homeschooled:** Statement describing homeschool structure and mission, interview, letter of recommendation (nonparent) required.

**High school preparation.** 17 units required; 22 recommended. Required and recommended units include English 4, mathematics 3-4, social studies 2, history 2, science 2-3 (laboratory 2-3), foreign language 2-3 and academic electives 2.

**2007-2008 Annual costs.** Tuition/fees: $28,535. Room/board: $6,775. Books/supplies: $900. Personal expenses: $630.

**2007-2008 Financial aid. Need-based:** 561 full-time freshmen applied for aid; 455 were judged to have need; 455 of these received aid. Average need met was 92%. Average scholarship/grant was $10,731; average loan $2,981. 77% of total undergraduate aid awarded as scholarships/grants, 23% as loans/jobs. **Non-need-based:** Awarded to 1,761 full-time undergraduates, including 480 freshmen. Scholarships awarded for academics, alumni affiliation, art, music/drama, religious affiliation, ROTC.

**Application procedures. Admission:** Closing date 4/1 (postmark date). No application fee. Application may be submitted online. Admission notification 4/15. Admission notification on a rolling basis beginning on or about 11/20. Must reply by May 1 or within 2 week(s) if notified thereafter. **Financial aid:** Priority date 2/15, closing date 4/15. FAFSA, institutional form required. CSS PROFILE required of students applying for need-based assistance. Applicants notified on a rolling basis starting 1/20; must reply by 5/1 or within 2 week(s) of notification.

**Academics. Special study options:** Cooperative education, cross-registration, double major, dual enrollment of high school students, exchange student, honors, independent study, internships, liberal arts/career combination, student-designed major, study abroad, teacher certification program, Washington semester. **Credit/placement by examination:** AP, CLEP, IB, institutional tests. **Support services:** Reduced course load, study skills assistance, tutoring, writing center.

**Majors. Area/ethnic studies:** Japanese, Russian/Slavic, Scandinavian, women's. **Biology:** General, biochemistry. **Business:** General, accounting, international. **Communications:** General. **Computer sciences:** General, computer science. **Conservation:** General, environmental studies. **Education:** General, elementary, secondary. **English:** English lit. **Foreign languages:** Classics, French, German, Japanese, Russian, Scandinavian, Spanish. **Health:** Athletic training, nursing (RN), predental, premedicine, preveterinary. **History:** General. **Legal studies:** Prelaw. **Math:** General. **Parks/recreation:** Health/fitness. **Philosophy/religion:** Philosophy, religion. **Physical sciences:** Chemistry, geology, physics. **Protective services:** Criminal justice. **Psychology:** General. **Social sciences:** Anthropology, economics, geography, political science, sociology. **Theology:** Sacred music. **Visual/performing arts:** Art, art history/conservation, dance, dramatic, music performance.

**Most popular majors.** Biology 8%, business/marketing 14%, communications/journalism 6%, education 8%, physical sciences 6%, psychology 7%, social sciences 18%.

**Computing on campus.** 440 workstations in dormitories, library, computer center, student center. Dormitories wired for high-speed internet access and linked to campus network. Commuter students can connect to campus network. Online course registration, online library, helpline, repair service, student web hosting, wireless network available.

**Student life. Freshman orientation:** Mandatory, $100 fee. Preregistration for classes offered. On-campus registration and pre-orientation sessions take place in June for students and families. Orientation program begins for first-year students four days prior to the beginning of classes. **Housing:** Guaranteed on-campus for all undergraduates. Coed dorms, special housing for disabled, apartments, substance-free housing available. $300 nonrefundable deposit, deadline 5/1. **Activities:** Bands, choral groups, dance, drama, literary magazine, music ensembles, musical theater, radio station, student government, student newspaper, symphony orchestra, TV station, over 100 religious, political, ethnic, and social service organizations.

**Athletics.** NCAA. **Intercollegiate:** Baseball M, basketball, cross-country, diving, football (tackle) M, golf, gymnastics W, ice hockey, skiing, soccer, softball W, swimming, tennis, track and field, volleyball W. **Intramural:** Badminton, basketball, football (non-tackle) M, golf, handball, ice hockey, lacrosse M, racquetball, rugby, skiing, soccer, softball, swimming, table tennis, tennis, volleyball. **Team name:** Gusties.

**Student services.** Alcohol/substance abuse counseling, campus ministries, career counseling, student employment services, financial aid counseling, health services, minority student services, personal counseling, placement for graduates, women's services. **Physically disabled:** Services for visually, hearing impaired.

**Contact.** E-mail: admission@gustavus.edu
Phone: (507) 933-7676 Toll-free number: (800) 487-8288
Fax: (507) 933-7474
Mark Anderson, Vice-President for Enrollment Management, Gustavus Adolphus College, 800 West College Avenue, St. Peter, MN 56082

---

## Hamline University

**St. Paul, Minnesota**
www.hamline.edu

**CB member**
**CB code: 6265**

- Private 4-year university and liberal arts college affiliated with United Methodist Church
- Residential campus in very large city
- 1,986 degree-seeking undergraduates: 3% part-time, 58% women, 5% African American, 6% Asian American, 2% Hispanic American, 1% Native American, 3% international
- 2,191 degree-seeking graduate students
- 78% of applicants admitted
- SAT or ACT (ACT writing optional), application essay required
- 69% graduate within 6 years; 27% enter graduate study

**General.** Founded in 1854. Regionally accredited. **Degrees:** 435 bachelor's awarded; master's, doctoral, first professional offered. **ROTC:** Air Force. **Location:** 5 miles from downtown. **Calendar:** 4-1-4, extensive summer session. **Full-time faculty:** 173 total; 87% have terminal degrees, 11% minority, 49% women. **Part-time faculty:** 307 total; 38% have terminal degrees, 6% minority, 54% women. **Class size:** 54% < 20, 36% 20-39, 6% 40-49, 4% 50-99. **Special facilities:** Music hall.

**Freshman class profile.** 2,018 applied, 1,570 admitted, 458 enrolled.

| Mid 50% test scores | | | |
|---|---|---|---|
| SAT critical reading: | 510-650 | Rank in top quarter: | 49% |
| SAT math: | 540-640 | Rank in top tenth: | 20% |
| SAT writing: | 510-620 | End year in good standing: | 88% |
| ACT composite: | 21-27 | Return as sophomores: | 82% |
| GPA 3.50 or higher: | 51% | Out-of-state: | 18% |
| GPA 3.0-3.49: | 29% | Live on campus: | 85% |
| GPA 2.0-2.99: | 20% | International: | 2% |
| | | Fraternities: | 3% |

**Basis for selection.** Class rank, high school GPA, and selection of college-preparatory courses of primary importance. Test scores, extracurricular activities, recommendations of teacher and guidance counselor also emphasized. ACT writing exam preferred but not required. Interview recommended.

**High school preparation.** 20 units recommended. Recommended units include English 4, mathematics 3, social studies 4, science 3 (laboratory 3), foreign language 2 and academic electives 4.

**2008-2009 Annual costs.** Tuition/fees: $28,143. Room/board: $7,784. Books/supplies: $1,200.

**2006-2007 Financial aid. Need-based:** 377 full-time freshmen applied for aid; 312 were judged to have need; 312 of these received aid. Average need met was 83%. Average scholarship/grant was $14,179; average loan $3,783. 70% of total undergraduate aid awarded as scholarships/grants, 30% as loans/jobs. **Non-need-based:** Awarded to 542 full-time undergraduates, including 128 freshmen. Scholarships awarded for academics, alumni affiliation, art, job skills, leadership, minority status, music/drama, religious affiliation, state residency.

**Application procedures. Admission:** Priority date 5/1; no deadline. No application fee. Application may be submitted online. Admission notification on a rolling basis beginning on or about 10/1. Must reply by May 1 or within 2 week(s) if notified thereafter. **Financial aid:** Priority date 3/1; no closing date. FAFSA required. Applicants notified on a rolling basis starting 3/1; must reply within 2 week(s) of notification.

**Academics.** Intensive fall semester course for conditionally-admitted students. **Special study options:** Combined bachelor's/graduate degree, cross-registration, double major, dual enrollment of high school students, ESL, exchange student, honors, independent study, internships, student-designed major, study abroad, teacher certification program, urban semester, Washington semester. **Credit/placement by examination:** AP, CLEP, IB. **Support services:** Learning center, study skills assistance, tutoring, writing center.

**Majors. Area/ethnic studies:** East Asian, Latin American, women's. **Biology:** General, biochemistry. **Business:** Business admin, international. **Communications:** General. **Conservation:** Environmental studies. **Education:** General, art, elementary, ESL, health, music, physical, science, secondary. **English:** English lit. **Foreign languages:** French, German, Spanish. **Health:** Athletic training, predental, premedicine, preveterinary. **History:** General. **Interdisciplinary:** Peace/conflict. **Legal studies:** General, paralegal. **Math:** General. **Parks/recreation:** Exercise sciences, health/fitness. **Philosophy/religion:** Philosophy, religion. **Physical sciences:** Chemistry, physics. **Protective services:** Criminal justice. **Psychology:** General. **Social sciences:** General, anthropology, criminology, economics, international relations, political science, sociology, urban studies. **Visual/performing arts:** Art history/conservation, dramatic, music performance, music theory/composition, studio arts.

**Most popular majors.** Business/marketing 10%, English 7%, legal studies 6%, psychology 11%, security/protective services 8%, social sciences 23%.

**Computing on campus.** 200 workstations in dormitories, library, computer center. Dormitories wired for high-speed internet access and linked to campus network. Commuter students can connect to campus network. Online course registration, online library, helpline, repair service, wireless network available.

**Student life. Freshman orientation:** Mandatory, $220 fee. 3 days immediately before classes begin. **Housing:** Guaranteed on-campus for all undergraduates. Coed dorms, special housing for disabled, apartments, fraternity/sorority housing, substance-free housing available. $50 deposit, deadline 5/1. Black Student Alliance House, Hmong Student Association House, Spanish Language House, residence halls organized around area of interest such as arts, weekends on campus, GLBT, social justice. **Activities:** Bands, choral groups, dance, drama, literary magazine, music ensembles, musical theater, radio station, student government, student newspaper, symphony orchestra, TV station, PRIDE Black Student Alliance, MPIRG, Intervarsity Christian Fellowship, Habitat for Humanity, Asian student association, Spectrum GLBT organization, Hand in Hand mentoring program, MA-MADADA Art League, Native American Student Association, Anthropological Society.

**Athletics.** NCAA. **Intercollegiate:** Baseball M, basketball, cross-country, diving, football (tackle) M, gymnastics W, ice hockey, soccer, softball W, swimming, tennis, track and field, volleyball W. **Intramural:** Basketball, bowling, football (non-tackle), volleyball. **Team name:** Pipers.

**Student services.** Alcohol/substance abuse counseling, campus ministries, career counseling, student employment services, financial aid counseling, health services, minority student services, personal counseling, placement for graduates, women's services. **Physically disabled:** Services for visually, speech, hearing impaired.

**Contact.** E-mail: cla-admis@hamline.edu
Phone: (651) 523-2207 Toll-free number: (800) 753-9753
Fax: (651) 523-2458
Steven Bjork, Associate Vice President for Admission and Career Services, Hamline University, 1536 Hewitt Avenue, St. Paul, MN 55104-1284

---

## Macalester College

**St. Paul, Minnesota**                    **CB member**
**www.macalester.edu**                     **CB code: 6390**

- Private 4-year liberal arts college affiliated with Presbyterian Church (USA)
- Residential campus in large city
- 1,912 degree-seeking undergraduates: 2% part-time, 58% women, 5% African American, 9% Asian American, 4% Hispanic American, 1% Native American, 12% international
- 41% of applicants admitted
- SAT or ACT (ACT writing optional), application essay required
- 86% graduate within 6 years; 28% enter graduate study

**General.** Founded in 1874. Regionally accredited. **Degrees:** 450 bachelor's awarded. **ROTC:** Naval, Air Force. **Location:** 5 miles from Minneapolis-St. Paul. **Calendar:** Semester. **Full-time faculty:** 157 total; 94% have terminal degrees, 20% minority, 47% women. **Part-time faculty:** 45 total; 58% have terminal degrees, 16% minority, 51% women. **Class size:** 68% < 20, 29% 20-39, 1% 40-49, 2% 50-99. **Special facilities:** Observatory with DT-M 16 inch F/8 cassegrain telescope, 250-acre nature preserve, nuclear accelerator, computer modeling facilities, laser spectroscopy laboratory, x-ray diffractometer and a nuclear magnetic spectrometer, fully equipped animal operant chamber, international research center, econometrics lab.

**Freshman class profile.** 4,967 applied, 2,015 admitted, 485 enrolled.

| Mid 50% test scores | | Rank in top tenth: | 68% |
|---|---|---|---|
| SAT critical reading: | 630-730 | End year in good standing: | 98% |
| SAT math: | 620-710 | Return as sophomores: | 94% |
| SAT writing: | 620-720 | Out-of-state: | 82% |
| ACT composite: | 28-32 | Live on campus: | 100% |
| Rank in top quarter: | 90% | International: | 13% |

**Basis for selection.** Test scores and curriculum most important. Leadership potential and extracurricular involvements also important, with special attention given to service to others. Students whose native language is not English must also submit the results of English as a Foreign Language (TOEFL) or the English Language Proficiency Test (ELPT). SAT Reading is not required of these students. Interview recommended. **Homeschooled:** Transcript of courses and grades, letter of recommendation (nonparent) required.

**High school preparation.** Recommended units include English 4, mathematics 3, social studies 3, science 3 (laboratory 3) and foreign language 3. Honors, AP, or IB level courses recommended.

**2008-2009 Annual costs.** Tuition/fees: $36,504. Room/board: $8,472. Books/supplies: $900. Personal expenses: $810.

**2007-2008 Financial aid.** Need-based: 366 full-time freshmen applied for aid; 320 were judged to have need; 320 of these received aid. Average need met was 100%. Average scholarship/grant was $24,674; average loan $2,811. 79% of total undergraduate aid awarded as scholarships/grants, 21% as loans/jobs. **Non-need-based:** Awarded to 115 full-time undergraduates, including 28 freshmen. Scholarships awarded for academics, minority status. **Additional information:** College meets full need for all admitted students. Minnesota Self Loan available to qualified students.

**Application procedures. Admission:** Closing date 1/15 (postmark date). $40 fee, may be waived for applicants with need. Application may be submitted online. Admission notification 3/30. Must reply by 5/1. **Financial aid:** Priority date 2/8, closing date 3/1. FAFSA, CSS PROFILE required. Applicants notified by 4/1; must reply by 5/1 or within 1 week(s) of notification.

**Academics.** Foreign language study and study abroad, as well as foreign student enrollment, are vital elements of the undergraduate experience at Macalester. **Special study options:** Cross-registration, double major, honors, independent study, internships, student-designed major, study abroad, teacher certification program, urban semester, Washington semester. BA/masters in architecture with Washington University of St. Louis, BA/BS in engineering with Washington University of St. Louis and with the University of Minnesota. **Credit/placement by examination:** AP, CLEP, IB, institutional tests. **Support services:** Learning center, remedial instruction, study skills assistance, tutoring.

**Majors. Area/ethnic studies:** Asian, Latin American, women's. **Biology:** General. **Computer sciences:** General. **Conservation:** Environmental studies. **English:** English lit. **Foreign languages:** Classics, French, German, Japanese, linguistics, Russian, Spanish. **History:** General. **Interdisciplinary:** Global studies, intercultural, neuroscience. **Liberal arts:** Humanities. **Math:** General. **Philosophy/religion:** Philosophy, religion. **Physical sciences:** Chemistry, geology, physics. **Psychology:** General. **Social sciences:** Anthropology, economics, geography, political science, sociology. **Visual/performing arts:** Art history/conservation, dramatic, studio arts.

**Most popular majors.** Biology 8%, foreign language 8%, interdisciplinary studies 8%, physical sciences 7%, psychology 6%, social sciences 30%, visual/performing arts 6%.

**Computing on campus.** 360 workstations in dormitories, library, computer center, student center. Dormitories wired for high-speed internet access and linked to campus network. Commuter students can connect to campus network. Online library, helpline, repair service, student web hosting, wireless network available.

**Student life. Freshman orientation:** Mandatory. Preregistration for classes offered. 5 days prior to classes in September. **Housing:** Guaranteed on-campus for freshmen. Coed dorms, apartments, substance-free housing available. $300 nonrefundable deposit, deadline 5/1. 6 language houses (French, German, Russian, Spanish, Japanese, Chinese), Jewish cultural house, vegetarian co-op housing available. 2-year residency requirement for first-year students, single-sex floors within coed dorms. **Activities:** Bands, campus ministries, choral groups, dance, drama, international student organizations, literary magazine, music ensembles, Model UN, radio station, student government, student newspaper, Voices of Tamani, production studio, theater club, Asian Student Alliance, GOP club, Habitat for Humanity, Model United Nations, Amnesty International, council for religious understanding, Young Dems.

**Athletics.** NCAA. **Intercollegiate:** Baseball M, basketball, cross-country, diving, football (tackle) M, golf, soccer, softball W, swimming, tennis, track and field, volleyball W, water polo W. **Intramural:** Badminton, basketball, bowling, football (non-tackle), racquetball, soccer, softball, table tennis, tennis, volleyball, water polo. **Team name:** Fighting Scots.

**Student services.** Alcohol/substance abuse counseling, campus ministries, career counseling, student employment services, financial aid counseling, health services, minority student services, personal counseling, placement for graduates. **Physically disabled:** Services for visually, speech, hearing impaired.

**Contact.** E-mail: admissions@macalester.edu
Phone: (651) 696-6357 Toll-free number: (800) 231-7974
Fax: (651) 696-6724
Lorne Robinson, Dean of Admissions and Financial Aid, Macalester College, 1600 Grand Avenue, St. Paul, MN 55105-1899

---

## Martin Luther College

**New Ulm, Minnesota**
**www.mlc-wels.edu**                       **CB code: 6435**

- Private 4-year college of theology and education affiliated with Wisconsin Evangelical Lutheran Synod
- Residential campus in large town
- 746 degree-seeking undergraduates: 7% part-time, 51% women, 1% Hispanic American, 1% international
- 46 degree-seeking graduate students
- 97% of applicants admitted
- ACT (writing optional) required
- 69% graduate within 6 years

**General.** Founded in 1995. Regionally accredited. Offers programs of study in early childhood education and staff ministry. **Degrees:** 186 bachelor's awarded; master's offered. **Location:** 90 miles from Minneapolis-St. Paul. **Calendar:** Semester, limited summer session. **Full-time faculty:** 53 total; 49% have terminal degrees, 13% women. **Part-time faculty:** 20 total; 30% have terminal degrees, 40% women. **Class size:** 43% < 20, 55% 20-39, 1% 40-49, less than 1% 50-99, less than 1% >100.

**Freshman class profile.** 234 applied, 226 admitted, 179 enrolled.

| Mid 50% test scores | | Rank in top tenth: | 16% |
|---|---|---|---|
| ACT composite: | 21-27 | Return as sophomores: | 89% |
| GPA 3.50 or higher: | 58% | Out-of-state: | 89% |
| GPA 3.0-3.49: | 26% | Live on campus: | 99% |
| GPA 2.0-2.99: | 16% | International: | 2% |
| Rank in top quarter: | 42% | | |

**Basis for selection.** Primarily pastor's letter of recommendation, high school transcript, and test scores required. Rating provided by student's high school considered.

**High school preparation.** 14 units required. Required units include English 4, mathematics 3, social studies 2, science 3 (laboratory 2), foreign language 2 and academic electives 2. 5 units in foreign language required for pastoral program.

**2008-2009 Annual costs.** Tuition/fees (projected): $10,350. Books/supplies: $800. Personal expenses: $1,525.

**2006-2007 Financial aid. Need-based:** 157 full-time freshmen applied for aid; 121 were judged to have need; 121 of these received aid. Average need met was 82%. Average scholarship/grant was $4,741; average loan $2,039. 58% of total undergraduate aid awarded as scholarships/grants, 42% as loans/jobs. **Non-need-based:** Awarded to 35 full-time undergraduates, including 56 freshmen. Scholarships awarded for academics, music/drama, religious affiliation.

**Application procedures. Admission:** Closing date 4/15 (postmark date). $25 fee, may be waived for applicants with need. Admission notification on a rolling basis beginning on or about 9/15. Must reply by May 1 or within 2 week(s) if notified thereafter. **Financial aid:** Priority date 4/15, closing date 9/30. FAFSA, institutional form required. Applicants notified by 3/1.

**Academics. Special study options:** Distance learning, double major, teacher certification program. **Credit/placement by examination:** AP, CLEP, ACT, institutional tests. **Support services:** Learning center, reduced course load, remedial instruction, study skills assistance, tutoring.

**Majors. Education:** Early childhood, elementary, multi-level teacher. **Theology:** Theology.

**Computing on campus.** 129 workstations in dormitories, library, computer center. Dormitories linked to campus network. Helpline, repair service available.

**Student life. Freshman orientation:** Mandatory, $20 fee. **Policies:** Religious observance required. **Housing:** Guaranteed on-campus for freshmen. Single-sex dorms available. $100 nonrefundable deposit, deadline 5/1. **Activities:** Bands, campus ministries, choral groups, dance, drama, literary magazine, music ensembles, musical theater, student government, symphony orchestra.

**Athletics.** NAIA, NCAA. **Intercollegiate:** Baseball M, basketball, cross-country, football (tackle) M, golf M, soccer, softball W, tennis, track and field, volleyball W. **Intramural:** Badminton, basketball, bowling, football (tackle) M, soccer, softball, tennis, volleyball. **Team name:** Knights.

**Student services.** Campus ministries, student employment services, financial aid counseling, health services, personal counseling.

**Contact.** E-mail: mlcadmit@mlc-wels.edu
Phone: (507) 354-8221 Fax: (507) 354-8225
Ronald Brutlag, Director of Admissions, Martin Luther College, 1995 Luther Court, New Ulm, MN 56073-3965

---

## Metropolitan State University
**St. Paul, Minnesota**
**www.metrostate.edu**                    **CB code: 1245**

▶ Public 4-year university
▶ Commuter campus in very large city
▶ 5,722 degree-seeking undergraduates: 63% part-time, 59% women
▶ 483 degree-seeking graduate students
▶ 53% of applicants admitted
▶ 24% graduate within 6 years

**General.** Founded in 1971. Regionally accredited. **Degrees:** 1,299 bachelor's awarded; master's, doctoral offered. **Calendar:** Semester, extensive summer session. **Full-time faculty:** 126 total; 82% have terminal degrees, 22% minority, 53% women. **Part-time faculty:** 391 total; 22% have terminal degrees, 14% minority, 46% women. **Class size:** 34% < 20, 64% 20-39, less than 1% 40-49, less than 1% 50-99.

**Freshman class profile.** 420 applied, 221 admitted, 77 enrolled.

| Mid 50% test scores | | Rank in top quarter: | 24% |
|---|---|---|---|
| ACT composite: | 16-24 | Rank in top tenth: | 8% |

**Basis for selection.** School achievement record and test scores most important. ACT or SAT at or above national median or high school rank in upper half of class. Interview and essays only used as part of the appeals process if admission was denied.

**High school preparation.** 16 units required. Required units include English 4, mathematics 3, social studies 3, science 3 (laboratory 1) and academic electives 3. 3 years of electives from language, world culture, or arts.

**2007-2008 Annual costs.** Tuition/fees: $5,293; $10,333 out-of-state. Books/supplies: $1,500. Personal expenses: $1,976.

**Financial aid. Non-need-based:** Scholarships awarded for academics, leadership, minority status, state residency.

**Application procedures. Admission:** Closing date 6/15. $20 fee, may be waived for applicants with need. Application may be submitted online. Admission notification on a rolling basis. **Financial aid:** Priority date 5/1; no closing date. FAFSA required. Applicants notified on a rolling basis starting 5/1; must reply within 2 week(s) of notification.

**Academics. Special study options:** Cross-registration, distance learning, double major, dual enrollment of high school students, external degree, independent study, internships, liberal arts/career combination, student-designed major, teacher certification program, weekend college. **Credit/placement by examination:** AP, CLEP, IB, institutional tests. 90 credit hours maximum toward bachelor's degree. **Support services:** Learning center, study skills assistance, tutoring, writing center.

**Majors. Area/ethnic studies:** Women's. **Biology:** General. **Business:** Accounting, business admin, finance, hospitality admin, human resources, information resources management, international, management information systems, marketing, operations, sales/distribution. **Communications:** General, advertising. **Computer sciences:** Computer science, information systems, security. **Education:** Biology, elementary, English, kindergarten/preschool, mathematics, social studies. **English:** Composition, English lit, technical writing. **Health:** Dental assistant, nursing (RN), substance abuse counseling. **History:** General. **Liberal arts:** Arts/sciences. **Math:** Applied. **Philosophy/religion:** Philosophy. **Protective services:** Criminal justice, police science. **Psychology:** General, developmental. **Public administration:** Human services, social work. **Social sciences:** General, economics. **Visual/performing arts:** Dramatic, play/screenwriting.

**Most popular majors.** Business/marketing 33%, health sciences 9%, liberal arts 16%, security/protective services 9%.

**Computing on campus.** 550 workstations in library, computer center. Commuter students can connect to campus network. Online course registration, helpline, wireless network available.

**Student life. Freshman orientation:** Mandatory, $10 fee. Preregistration for classes offered. Orientation sessions of 3-1/2 hours are held several times each semester. **Policies:** Annual registration required of all student organizations. **Activities:** Drama, international student organizations, literary magazine, student government, student newspaper, Asian student organization, Lavender Bridge, African-American student association, graduate student advisory committee, Voice of Indian Council for Educational Success, social work student association, psychology club, Muslim student association, Urban Teachers Student Program Organization.

**Student services.** Adult student services, career counseling, minority student services, personal counseling, women's services. **Physically disabled:** Services for visually, speech, hearing impaired.

**Contact.** E-mail: admission.metro@metrostate.edu
Phone: (651) 793-1300 Fax: (651) 793-1310
Monir Johnson, Admissions Director, Metropolitan State University, 700 East Seventh Street, St. Paul, MN 55106-5000

## Minneapolis College of Art and Design
**Minneapolis, Minnesota**  CB member
www.mcad.edu  CB code: 6411

- Private 4-year visual arts college
- Residential campus in very large city
- 731 degree-seeking undergraduates: 5% part-time, 53% women
- 41 degree-seeking graduate students
- 65% of applicants admitted
- SAT or ACT (ACT writing optional), application essay required
- 70% graduate within 6 years

**General.** Founded in 1886. Regionally accredited. **Degrees:** 152 bachelor's awarded; master's offered. **Calendar:** Semester, limited summer session. **Full-time faculty:** 36 total. **Part-time faculty:** 85 total. **Class size:** 80% < 20, 18% 20-39, 2% 40-49. **Special facilities:** Art and design galleries, personal on-campus studio space, 3-D animation, drawing, film, paper, painting, photo, print studios.

**Freshman class profile.** 489 applied, 318 admitted, 149 enrolled.

| Mid 50% test scores | | | |
|---|---|---|---|
| SAT critical reading: | 550-670 | GPA 3.0-3.49: | 38% |
| SAT math: | 490-650 | GPA 2.0-2.99: | 30% |
| SAT writing: | 500-720 | Return as sophomores: | 80% |
| ACT composite: | 20-28 | Out-of-state: | 60% |
| GPA 3.50 or higher: | 32% | Live on campus: | 81% |

**Basis for selection.** Bachelor of Fine Arts applicants required to submit a portfolio of creative work. For all students (BFA & BS), academic record and test scores reviewed. Level of interest and motivation determined through personal statement of interest, letter of recommendation and essay requirement. Tests not required for transfer applicants who have completed 12 or more satisfactory credits at the college level. Interview recommended; visual arts portfolio required.

**High school preparation.** Recommended units include English 4, social studies 4, history 4 and visual/performing arts 6.

**2007-2008 Annual costs.** Tuition/fees: $28,100. Housing costs vary; figure quoted is for double-occupancy (furnished) one-bedroom apartment. Required fees for 2007-2008 ($1,100) include cost of laptop computer that freshman must purchase ($900). Room only: $4,160. Books/supplies: $2,200. Personal expenses: $1,000.

**2007-2008 Financial aid. Need-based:** 132 full-time freshmen applied for aid; 112 were judged to have need; 111 of these received aid. Average need met was 57%. Average scholarship/grant was $10,506; average loan $3,866. 47% of total undergraduate aid awarded as scholarships/grants, 53% as loans/jobs. **Non-need-based:** Scholarships awarded for academics, alumni affiliation, art.

**Application procedures. Admission:** Priority date 2/15; deadline 5/1 (receipt date). $50 fee, may be waived for applicants with need. Application may be submitted online. Admission notification on a rolling basis. Must reply by 5/1. **Financial aid:** Priority date 3/15; no closing date. FAFSA required. Applicants notified on a rolling basis starting 4/1; must reply by 5/1 or within 2 week(s) of notification.

**Academics. Special study options:** Combined bachelor's/graduate degree, cooperative education, cross-registration, distance learning, exchange student, independent study, internships, New York semester, study abroad. **Credit/placement by examination:** AP, CLEP, IB. **Support services:** Learning center, reduced course load, study skills assistance, tutoring, writing center.

**Majors. Communications technology:** Animation/special effects. **Production:** Furniture. **Visual/performing arts:** General, cinematography, commercial/advertising art, design, drawing, illustration, multimedia, painting, photography, printmaking, sculpture, studio arts.

**Most popular majors.** Visual/performing arts 89%.

**Computing on campus.** PC or laptop required. 160 workstations in library, computer center, student center. Dormitories wired for high-speed internet access and linked to campus network. Commuter students can connect to campus network. Online library, helpline, repair service, student web hosting, wireless network available.

**Student life. Freshman orientation:** Mandatory. Preregistration for classes offered. 3 days in fall including 1 day for parents. **Housing:** Coed dorms, apartments available. $175 fully refundable deposit, deadline 5/1. **Activities:** Film society, radio station, student government.

**Student services.** Alcohol/substance abuse counseling, career counseling, student employment services, financial aid counseling, personal counseling.

**Contact.** E-mail: admissions@mcad.edu
Phone: (612) 874-3760 Toll-free number: (800) 874-6223
Fax: (612) 874-3701
William Mullen, Vice President, Enrollment Management, Minneapolis College of Art and Design, 2501 Stevens Avenue, Minneapolis, MN 55404

## Minnesota School of Business
**Minneapolis, Minnesota**
www.msbcollege.edu  CB code: 3313

- For-profit 4-year business and technical college
- Commuter campus in very large city

**General.** Accredited by ACICS. **Calendar:** Quarter.

**Annual costs/financial aid.** Tuition/fees (2007-2008): $17,810. Books/supplies: $1,500. Personal expenses: $2,178. Need-based financial aid available to full-time and part-time students.

**Contact.** Phone: (612) 861-2000
Director of Admissions, 1401 West 76 Street, Suite 500, Richfield, MN 55423

## Minnesota School of Business: Blaine
**Blaine, Minnesota**
www.msbcollege.edu

- For-profit 4-year branch campus and business college
- Very large city

**General.** Regionally accredited. **Calendar:** Quarter.

**Annual costs/financial aid.** Tuition/fees (2007-2008): $17,810.

**Contact.** 3680 Pheasant Ridge Dr. NE, Blaine, MN 55449

## Minnesota School of Business: Plymouth
**Plymouth, Minnesota**
www.msbcollege.edu

- For-profit 4-year business and technical college
- Small city
- 514 degree-seeking undergraduates

**General.** Accredited by ACICS. **Degrees:** 15 bachelor's, 140 associate awarded. **Calendar:** Quarter. **Full-time faculty:** 13 total. **Part-time faculty:** 74 total.

**Basis for selection.** Admissions based on results of Accuplacer entrance exam.

**2007-2008 Annual costs.** Tuition/fees: $17,810.

**Application procedures. Admission:** Closing date 10/1.

**Academics. Special study options:** Distance learning, independent study, internships, liberal arts/career combination. **Credit/placement by examination:** CLEP.

**Majors. Business:** Accounting, business admin. **Computer sciences:** Information technology. **Health:** Health care admin. **Other:** Health fitness specialist.

**Contact.** Phone: (866) 476-2121
Stacy Severson, Director of Admissions, Minnesota School of Business: Plymouth, 1455 County Road 101 North, Plymouth, MN 55447

## Minnesota School of Business: Rochester
**Rochester, Minnesota**
www.msbcollege.edu

- For-profit 4-year career college
- Small city
- 626 undergraduates

**General.** Accredited by ACICS. **Degrees:** 23 associate awarded. **Calendar:** Quarter. **Full-time faculty:** 8 total. **Part-time faculty:** 42 total.

**Basis for selection.** Admissions based on results of Accuplacer entrance exam.

**2007-2008 Annual costs.** Tuition/fees: $17,810.

**Application procedures. Admission:** Closing date 10/1. $50 fee. Application must be submitted online. Admission notification on a rolling basis.

**Academics. Special study options:** Distance learning. **Credit/placement by examination:** CLEP. **Support services:** Learning center, remedial instruction, study skills assistance, tutoring, writing center.

**Majors. Business:** Accounting, business admin.

**Computing on campus.** 14 workstations in library, student center. Online library, helpline, wireless network available.

**Contact.** Phone: (507) 536-9500
Shan Pollitt, Director of Admissions, Minnesota School of Business: Rochester, 2521 Pennington Drive NW, Rochester, MN 55901

## Minnesota School of Business: St. Cloud
### Waite Park, Minnesota
### www.msbcollege.edu

- For-profit 4-year virtual university, business, health science, technical and career college
- Small city
- 805 degree-seeking undergraduates

**General.** Accredited by ACICS. **Degrees:** 11 bachelor's, 119 associate awarded; master's offered. **Calendar:** Quarter, extensive summer session. **Full-time faculty:** 8 total. **Part-time faculty:** 48 total.

**Basis for selection.** Applicants to all diploma, associate, and bachelor degree programs must achieve minimum scores on the Accuplacer test administered at the college: 35 (reading comprehension), 35 (sentence skills), 21 (arithmetic). Alternatively, applicants to these programs must provide documentation of a bachelor's degree, minimum composite score of 21 on the ACT, or SAT score of 1485 (unless SAT was taken prior to March 2006, in which case composite score must be at least 990). Finally, if an applicant has already taken the CPAt exam through MSB/GC, entrance scores will be honored according to the requirements listed in the catalog at the time of past enrollment (though students may be required to take the Accuplacer exam for placement purposes). **Homeschooled:** State high school equivalency certificate required.

**2007-2008 Annual costs.** Tuition/fees: $17,810.

**Application procedures. Admission:** No deadline. $50 fee. Application must be submitted online. Admission notification on a rolling basis.

**Academics. Special study options:** Combined bachelor's/graduate degree, distance learning, internships. **Credit/placement by examination:** CLEP. **Support services:** Remedial instruction, study skills assistance, tutoring, writing center.

**Majors. Business:** Business admin.

**Computing on campus.** Online course registration, helpline, wireless network available.

**Contact.** E-mail: info@msbcollege.edu
Phone: (866) 403-3333
Candi Janssen, Director of Admissions, Minnesota School of Business: St. Cloud, 1201 Second Street South, Waite Park, MN 55387

## Minnesota School of Business: Shakopee
### Shakopee, Minnesota
### www.msbcollege.edu

- For-profit 4-year business and technical college
- Large town
- 445 degree-seeking undergraduates: 40% part-time, 81% women, 2% African American, 1% Asian American, 2% Hispanic American, 1% Native American
- 97% of applicants admitted

**General.** Accredited by ACICS. **Degrees:** 4 bachelor's, 65 associate awarded. **Calendar:** Quarter. **Full-time faculty:** 10 total. **Part-time faculty:** 29 total.

**Freshman class profile.** 136 applied, 132 admitted, 70 enrolled.

| | | | |
|---|---|---|---|
| **Return as sophomores:** | 64% | **International:** | 1% |

**Basis for selection.** SAT scores very important.

**2008-2009 Annual costs.** Tuition/fees (projected): $18,770.

**2007-2008 Financial aid. Need-based:** 41 full-time freshmen applied for aid; 40 were judged to have need; 40 of these received aid. Average need met was 45%. Average scholarship/grant was $4,500; average loan $3,500. 43% of total undergraduate aid awarded as scholarships/grants, 57% as loans/jobs. **Non-need-based:** Awarded to 39 full-time undergraduates, including 7 freshmen. Scholarships awarded for academics.

**Application procedures. Admission:** No deadline. $50 fee. Application may be submitted online. Admission notification on a rolling basis. **Financial aid:** No deadline. FAFSA, institutional form required. Applicants notified on a rolling basis.

**Academics. Special study options:** Combined bachelor's/graduate degree, distance learning, liberal arts/career combination. **Credit/placement by examination:** CLEP, SAT, ACT, institutional tests. 75 credit hours maximum toward associate degree, 75 toward bachelor's. **Support services:** Learning center, remedial instruction, study skills assistance, tutoring, writing center.

**Computing on campus.** 50 workstations in computer center. Online course registration, online library, helpline, wireless network available.

**Student life. Freshman orientation:** Available.

**Contact.** Phone: (866) 776-1200
Gretchen Seifert, Director of Admissions, Minnesota School of Business: Shakopee, 1200 Shakopee Town Square, Shakopee, MN 55379

## Minnesota State University: Mankato
### Mankato, Minnesota     CB member
### www.mnsu.edu     CB code: 6677

- Public 4-year university
- Commuter campus in large town
- 12,534 degree-seeking undergraduates
- 1,702 graduate students
- 89% of applicants admitted
- SAT or ACT (ACT writing optional) required
- 48% graduate within 6 years

**General.** Founded in 1867. Regionally accredited. **Degrees:** 2,078 bachelor's, 55 associate awarded; master's, doctoral offered. **ROTC:** Army. **Location:** 85 miles from Minneapolis-St. Paul. **Calendar:** Semester, extensive summer session. **Full-time faculty:** 492 total; 80% have terminal degrees, 7% minority, 41% women. **Part-time faculty:** 213 total; 8% have terminal degrees, 3% minority, 55% women. **Class size:** 38% < 20, 45% 20-39, 8% 40-49, 7% 50-99, 3% >100. **Special facilities:** 2 observatories, ropes course.

**Freshman class profile.** 5,653 applied, 5,016 admitted, 2,163 enrolled.

| Mid 50% test scores | | Return as sophomores: | 78% |
|---|---|---|---|
| ACT composite: | 20-24 | Out-of-state: | 14% |
| Rank in top quarter: | 27% | Live on campus: | 81% |
| Rank in top tenth: | 8% | | |

**Basis for selection.** Rank in top 50% of high school class or equivalent, most important. College preparatory courses also reviewed. ACT is used only when admission cannot be achieved using high school rank and college preparatory courses. Test scores due fifth class day of fall semester. Essays and/or recommendations used only for contract/admission review by faculty committees. **Homeschooled:** Must submit standardized test results in lieu of rank/record.

**High school preparation.** 16 units required. Required units include English 4, mathematics 3, social studies 2, history 1, science 3 (laboratory 3) and foreign language 2. One year world culture course or arts course.

**2007-2008 Annual costs.** Tuition/fees: $6,050; $12,854 out-of-state. Room/board: $5,354. Books/supplies: $820. Personal expenses: $2,600.

**2007-2008 Financial aid. Need-based:** Average need met was 75%. Average scholarship/grant was $4,138; average loan $3,025. 77% of total undergraduate aid awarded as scholarships/grants, 23% as loans/jobs. **Non-need-based:** Scholarships awarded for academics, alumni affiliation, art, athletics, leadership, minority status, music/drama.

**Application procedures. Admission:** $20 fee, may be waived for applicants with need. Application may be submitted online. Admission notification on a rolling basis. **Financial aid:** Priority date 3/15; no closing date. FAFSA required. Applicants notified on a rolling basis starting 3/30; must reply within 2 week(s) of notification.

**Academics. Special study options:** Combined bachelor's/graduate degree, cross-registration, distance learning, double major, dual enrollment of high school students, ESL, exchange student, external degree, honors, independent study, internships, semester at sea, student-designed major, study abroad, teacher certification program. **Credit/placement by examination:** AP, CLEP, IB, institutional tests. **Support services:** Learning center, reduced course load, remedial instruction, study skills assistance, tutoring, writing center.

**Majors. Agriculture:** Food science, plant sciences. **Architecture:** Urban/community planning. **Area/ethnic studies:** French, German, Scandinavian, women's. **Biology:** General, anatomy, bacteriology, biochemistry, biotechnology, botany, ecology, genetics, toxicology, zoology. **Business:** General, accounting, banking/financial services, business admin, finance, financial planning, human resources, insurance, international, investments/securities, management information systems, management science, operations. **Communications:** General, journalism, media studies, public relations. **Computer sciences:** General, computer science, information systems. **Conservation:** General, environmental studies. **Construction:** Maintenance. **Education:** General, art, biology, business, chemistry, computer, curriculum, drama/dance, elementary, English, family/consumer sciences, foreign languages, French, German, health, health occupations, history, mathematics, middle, music, physical, physics, school counseling, science, secondary, social science, social studies, Spanish, speech, speech impaired, technology/industrial arts, voc/tech. **Engineering:** General, civil, computer, electrical, mechanical. **Engineering technology:** Automotive, computer, electrical, manufacturing, mechanical. **English:** Creative writing, English lit, speech/rhetoric, technical writing. **Family/consumer sciences:** General, clothing/textiles, family studies, family/community services, food/nutrition, housing. **Foreign languages:** General, French, German, Spanish. **Health:** Athletic training, clinical lab assistant, clinical lab science, clinical lab technology, communication disorders, cytotechnology, dental hygiene, health care admin, licensed practical nurse, nursing (RN), predental, premedicine, preop/surgical nursing, prepharmacy, preveterinary, recreational therapy. **History:** General. **Interdisciplinary:** Biological/physical sciences. **Legal studies:** Prelaw. **Liberal arts:** Arts/sciences. **Math:** General. **Mechanic/repair:** Automotive. **Parks/recreation:** General, exercise sciences, facilities management, health/fitness, sports admin. **Philosophy/religion:** Philosophy. **Physical sciences:** Astronomy, chemistry, physics. **Protective services:** Corrections, law enforcement admin, police science. **Psychology:** General. **Public administration:** Human services, social work. **Social sciences:** Anthropology, criminology, economics, geography, international relations, political science, sociology, urban studies. **Transportation:** Aviation management. **Visual/performing arts:** General, art, art history/conservation, ceramics, commercial/advertising art, dramatic, drawing, fiber arts, interior design, music management, music performance, music theory/composition, painting, piano/organ, sculpture, studio arts, theater design, voice/opera.

**Most popular majors.** Business/marketing 20%, education 15%, engineering/engineering technologies 7%, health sciences 11%, security/protective services 7%.

**Computing on campus.** 900 workstations in dormitories, library, computer center, student center. Dormitories wired for high-speed internet access and linked to campus network. Commuter students can connect to campus network. Online course registration, online library, helpline, repair service, student web hosting, wireless network available.

**Student life. Freshman orientation:** Mandatory, $65 fee. Preregistration for classes offered. Includes overnight stay. **Housing:** Guaranteed on-campus for freshmen. Coed dorms, special housing for disabled available. $250 deposit. **Activities:** Bands, campus ministries, choral groups, dance, drama, literary magazine, music ensembles, musical theater, radio station, student government, student newspaper, symphony orchestra, Hmong student association, American Indian student association, Chicano LatinoAM student association, Fellowship of Christian Athletes, InterVarsity, MSU Pagan Organization.

**Athletics. NCAA. Intercollegiate:** Baseball M, basketball, bowling W, cheerleading, cross-country, diving, football (tackle) M, golf, ice hockey, soccer W, softball W, swimming, tennis, track and field, volleyball W, wrestling M. **Intramural:** Archery, basketball, bowling, fencing, football (non-tackle), golf, ice hockey, racquetball, rugby, skiing, soccer, softball, swimming, table tennis, tennis, track and field, triathlon, volleyball, wrestling M. **Team name:** Mavericks.

**Student services.** Adult student services, alcohol/substance abuse counseling, campus ministries, career counseling, services for economically disadvantaged, student employment services, financial aid counseling, health services, legal services, minority student services, on-campus daycare, personal counseling, placement for graduates, veterans' counselor, women's services. **Physically disabled:** Services for visually, speech, hearing impaired.

**Contact.** E-mail: admissions@mnsu.edu
Phone: (507) 389-1822 Toll-free number: (800) 722-0544
Fax: (507) 389-1511
Walt Wolff, Director of Admissions, Minnesota State University: Mankato, 122 Taylor Center, Mankato, MN 56001

## Minnesota State University: Moorhead
**Moorhead, Minnesota**
**www.mnstate.edu**      **CB code: 6678**

- Public 4-year university
- Residential campus in small city
- 6,638 degree-seeking undergraduates
- 82% of applicants admitted
- SAT or ACT (ACT writing recommended) required

**General.** Founded in 1885. Regionally accredited. **Degrees:** 1,400 bachelor's, 45 associate awarded; master's offered. **ROTC:** Army, Air Force. **Location:** 240 miles from Minneapolis-St. Paul. **Calendar:** Semester, limited summer session. **Full-time faculty:** 307 total. **Part-time faculty:** 185 total. **Special facilities:** Planetarium, biology museum.

**Freshman class profile.** 2,842 applied, 2,324 admitted, 1,224 enrolled.

| Mid 50% test scores | | | |
|---|---|---|---|
| | | **ACT composite:** | 19-24 |
| SAT critical reading: | 410-610 | **Rank in top quarter:** | 31% |
| SAT math: | 430-590 | **Rank in top tenth:** | 10% |

**Basis for selection.** Applicants must rank in top half of class or have minimum ACT composite score of 21 or equivalent scores on SAT or PSAT/NMSQT. Some applicants not meeting requirements will be admitted to transitional college program. Applicants must also fulfill minimum requirements of secondary course work. Students not meeting automatic admission standards may apply through alternative admissions program, New Center. **Learning Disabled:** Contact Office of Disability Services to make sure appropriate accommodations can be provided.

**High school preparation.** 16 units required. Required units include English 4, mathematics 3, social studies 3, science 3 (laboratory 1) and academic electives 3. One unit fine arts, .5 computer science recommended.

**2007-2008 Annual costs.** Tuition/fees: $5,948. Out-of-state students pay same rate as in-state. Room/board: $5,690. Books/supplies: $800. Personal expenses: $2,206.

**Financial aid. Non-need-based:** Scholarships awarded for academics, art, athletics, leadership, music/drama, state residency.

**Application procedures. Admission:** Closing date 8/1 (postmark date). $20 fee. Application may be submitted online. Admission notification on a rolling basis. **Financial aid:** Priority date 2/15; no closing date. FAFSA required. Applicants notified on a rolling basis starting 6/1; must reply within 2 week(s) of notification.

**Academics. Special study options:** Cross-registration, distance learning, double major, dual enrollment of high school students, exchange student, external degree, honors, independent study, internships, student-designed major, study abroad, teacher certification program. Reciprocal bachelor's degree programs with North Dakota State University. **Credit/placement by examination:** AP, CLEP, institutional tests. 12 credit hours maximum toward bachelor's degree. **Support services:** Pre-admission summer program, reduced course load, remedial instruction, study skills assistance, tutoring, writing center.

**Majors. Area/ethnic studies:** American, East Asian. **Biology:** General. **Business:** Accounting, business admin, finance, international, management information systems, marketing. **Communications:** Media studies. **Computer sciences:** General, computer science. **Education:** Art, biology, chemistry, elementary, English, health, kindergarten/preschool, mathematics, music, physical, physics, science, social studies, Spanish, special, speech. **Engineering technology:** Construction, industrial. **English:** English lit, speech/rhetoric. **Foreign languages:** Spanish. **Health:** Athletic training, audiology/speech pathology, clinical lab science, community health services, health care admin, nurse practitioner, predental, premedicine, prepharmacy, preveterinary. **History:** General. **Interdisciplinary:** Gerontology. **Legal studies:** General, paralegal. **Math:** General. **Parks/recreation:** Exercise sciences, health/fitness. **Philosophy/religion:** Philosophy. **Physical sciences:** Chemistry, physics. **Protective services:** Criminal justice. **Psychology:** General. **Public administration:** Social work. **Social sciences:** Anthropology, economics, political science, sociology. **Visual/performing arts:** Art, commercial/advertising art, dramatic, music management, music performance.

**Computing on campus.** 791 workstations in dormitories, library, computer center. Dormitories linked to campus network. Commuter students can connect to campus network. Online course registration, online library, helpline, repair service, student web hosting, wireless network available.

**Student life. Freshman orientation:** Available, $50 fee. Preregistration for classes offered. **Housing:** Coed dorms, single-sex dorms, special housing for disabled, apartments, fraternity/sorority housing available. $350 deposit. **Activities:** Bands, choral groups, dance, drama, literary magazine, music ensembles, musical theater, radio station, student government, student newspaper, symphony orchestra, TV station, 125 student clubs, including Spurs, Circle-K, Newman Club, United Campus Ministry, Spanish Club, Habitat for Humanity, Amnesty International, Model United Nations, Volunteer Visions.

**Athletics.** NCAA. **Intercollegiate:** Basketball, cross-country, diving W, football (tackle) M, golf W, soccer W, softball W, swimming W, tennis W, track and field, volleyball W, wrestling M. **Intramural:** Badminton, basketball, golf, ice hockey M, lacrosse M, racquetball, rugby, soccer, softball, swimming, tennis, track and field, volleyball, water polo, wrestling M. **Team name:** Dragons.

**Student services.** Adult student services, alcohol/substance abuse counseling, career counseling, student employment services, financial aid counseling, health services, minority student services, on-campus daycare, personal counseling, placement for graduates, veterans' counselor, women's services. **Physically disabled:** Services for visually, speech, hearing impaired.

**Contact.** E-mail: dragon@mnstate.edu
Phone: (218) 477-2161 Toll-free number: (800) 593-7246
Fax: (218) 477-4374
Gina Monson, Director of Admissions, Minnesota State University: Moorhead, Owens Hall, Moorhead, MN 56563

---

## National American University: Roseville
**Roseville, Minnesota**
www.national.edu

- For-profit 4-year university and branch campus college
- Very large city

**General.** Regionally accredited. **Calendar:** Quarter.

**Annual costs/financial aid.** Tuition/fees (2007-2008): $14,225.

**Contact.** 1550 West Highway 36, Roseville, MN 55431

---

## National American University: St. Paul
**Bloomington, Minnesota**
www.national.edu          CB code: 5358

- For-profit 4-year branch campus and business college
- Commuter campus in very large city

**General.** Founded in 1974. Regionally accredited. **Calendar:** Quarter.

**Annual costs/financial aid.** Tuition/fees (2007-2008): $14,225. Books/supplies: $1,000. Need-based financial aid available to full-time and part-time students.

**Contact.** Phone: (952) 883-0439
Director of Admissions, Mall of America West 112 West Market, Bloomington, MN 55425

---

## North Central University
**Minneapolis, Minnesota**
www.northcentral.edu        CB code: 0051

- Private 4-year university and Bible college affiliated with Assemblies of God
- Residential campus in large city
- 1,181 degree-seeking undergraduates: 9% part-time, 55% women
- 99% of applicants admitted

- SAT or ACT (ACT writing optional), application essay required
- 46% graduate within 6 years

**General.** Founded in 1930. Regionally accredited. **Degrees:** 167 bachelor's, 6 associate awarded. **ROTC:** Army, Air Force. **Location:** One mile from downtown. **Calendar:** Semester, limited summer session. **Full-time faculty:** 42 total; 55% have terminal degrees, 17% minority, 40% women. **Part-time faculty:** 75 total; 16% minority, 40% women. **Class size:** 49% < 20, 37% 20-39, 10% 40-49, 2% 50-99, 1% >100. **Special facilities:** Recording studio, youth and leadership center, word and worship center, children's literature library.

**Freshman class profile.** 402 applied, 398 admitted, 239 enrolled.

| Mid 50% test scores | | Rank in top quarter: | 31% |
|---|---|---|---|
| SAT critical reading: | 480-580 | Rank in top tenth: | 14% |
| SAT math: | 450-570 | End year in good standing: | 83% |
| ACT composite: | 18-24 | Return as sophomores: | 68% |
| GPA 3.50 or higher: | 31% | Out-of-state: | 60% |
| GPA 3.0-3.49: | 34% | Live on campus: | 94% |
| GPA 2.0-2.99: | 34% | | |

**Basis for selection.** School achievement record, essay and pastor's recommendation most important. Conditional admission available for students not in good standing at previous institution. Applicants with GPA below 2.2 or ACT scores below 18 may be admitted provisionally. The writing portions of the ACT and SAT are not required and not taken into consideration for scholarship. **Homeschooled:** Transcript of courses and grades required. Must meet their state's requirements for graduation.

**High school preparation.** 9 units recommended. Recommended units include English 3, mathematics 1, social studies 2, history 1, science 1 and foreign language 1.

**2007-2008 Annual costs.** Tuition/fees: $13,666. Room/board: $4,865. Books/supplies: $600.

**2006-2007 Financial aid. Need-based:** 41% of total undergraduate aid awarded as scholarships/grants, 59% as loans/jobs. **Non-need-based:** Scholarships awarded for academics, music/drama.

**Application procedures. Admission:** Closing date 6/1 (postmark date). $25 fee, may be waived for applicants with need. Application may be submitted online. Admission notification on a rolling basis. **Financial aid:** No deadline. FAFSA required. Applicants notified on a rolling basis starting 3/1; must reply within 2 week(s) of notification.

**Academics. Special study options:** Distance learning, double major, exchange student, independent study, internships, liberal arts/career combination, student-designed major, study abroad, teacher certification program, weekend college. **Credit/placement by examination:** AP, CLEP, SAT, ACT. **Support services:** Learning center, pre-admission summer program, reduced course load, remedial instruction, study skills assistance, tutoring, writing center.

**Majors. Business:** Business admin. **Communications:** Journalism, media studies. **Education:** Elementary, ESL, secondary. **English:** English lit. **Foreign languages:** American Sign Language, sign language interpretation. **Health:** Substance abuse counseling. **Parks/recreation:** Sports admin. **Philosophy/religion:** Christian, religion. **Psychology:** General. **Public administration:** Social work. **Social sciences:** Urban studies. **Theology:** Bible, missionary, pastoral counseling, religious ed, sacred music, theology, youth ministry. **Visual/performing arts:** Dramatic, music management, music performance. **Other:** Deaf Culture, Worship Arts, Youth Development Studies.

**Most popular majors.** Business/marketing 9%, education 9%, family/consumer sciences 6%, interdisciplinary studies 25%, psychology 10%, theological studies 23%, visual/performing arts 9%.

**Computing on campus.** 120 workstations in dormitories, library, computer center, student center. Dormitories wired for high-speed internet access and linked to campus network. Commuter students can connect to campus network. Online library, helpline, wireless network available.

**Student life. Freshman orientation:** Mandatory. Preregistration for classes offered. 4 optional dates in the summer months. **Policies:** North Central requires all members of the community to refrain from any form of sexual immorality. Students must refrain from the possession, use or distribution of non-medical drugs, alchoholic beverages and tobacco in any form. Religious observance required. **Housing:** Guaranteed on-campus for freshmen. Single-sex dorms, special housing for disabled, apartments, substance-free housing available. $150 partly refundable deposit, deadline 6/1. Honor dormitories available. **Activities:** Bands, campus ministries, choral groups, dance, drama, literary magazine, music ensembles, musical theater, student government, student newspaper, leadership development committee, student committee, The Northern Light, SIFE, Alpha Kai, Deaf Culture Fellowship, student senate, Student Missions Fellowship, student activities committee.

**Athletics.** NCAA, NCCAA. **Intercollegiate:** Baseball M, basketball, cross-country, golf M, soccer, softball W, track and field, volleyball W. **Intramural:** Football (non-tackle). **Team name:** Rams.

**Student services.** Campus ministries, career counseling, student employment services, financial aid counseling, health services, personal counseling, placement for graduates, women's services. **Physically disabled:** Services for visually, speech, hearing impaired.

**Contact.** E-mail: admissions@northcentral.edu
Phone: (612) 343-4460 Toll-free number: (800) 289-6222
Fax: (612) 343-4146
Troy Pearson, Director of Admissions, North Central University, 910 Elliot Avenue, Minneapolis, MN 55404

## Northwestern College
### Saint Paul, Minnesota
www.nwc.edu

CB code: 6489

- Private 4-year Bible and liberal arts college affiliated with nondenominational tradition
- Residential campus in very large city
- 1,845 degree-seeking undergraduates: 3% part-time, 59% women, 3% African American, 4% Asian American, 2% Hispanic American, 1% Native American
- 80 degree-seeking graduate students
- 93% of applicants admitted
- SAT or ACT (ACT writing optional), application essay required
- 60% graduate within 6 years; 12% enter graduate study

**General.** Founded in 1902. Regionally accredited. **Degrees:** 381 bachelor's, 8 associate awarded; master's offered. **ROTC:** Army, Air Force. **Location:** 9 miles from Minneapolis-St. Paul. **Calendar:** Semester, limited summer session. **Full-time faculty:** 96 total; 62% have terminal degrees, 7% minority, 38% women. **Part-time faculty:** 80 total; 28% have terminal degrees, 4% minority, 54% women. **Class size:** 50% < 20, 42% 20-39, 4% 40-49, 3% 50-99, 1% >100.

**Freshman class profile.** 1,109 applied, 1,029 admitted, 502 enrolled.

| Mid 50% test scores | | | |
|---|---|---|---|
| SAT critical reading: | 440-690 | Rank in top quarter: | 55% |
| SAT math: | 470-650 | Rank in top tenth: | 28% |
| ACT composite: | 22-27 | End year in good standing: | 91% |
| GPA 3.50 or higher: | 65% | Return as sophomores: | 83% |
| GPA 3.0-3.49: | 24% | Out-of-state: | 32% |
| GPA 2.0-2.99: | 11% | Live on campus: | 95% |

**Basis for selection.** Evidence that student will benefit from the education and contribute to the community important. School record, recommendations, test scores, essay, character, and religious affiliation very important. Audition required for music students. Portfolio recommended for art students. Interview recommended for borderline students.

**High school preparation.** 16 units recommended. Recommended units include English 4, mathematics 3, social studies 3, science 3, foreign language 2 and academic electives 1.

**2008-2009 Annual costs.** Tuition/fees: $22,250. Computer technology fee of $170. Room/board: $7,050. Books/supplies: $610. Personal expenses: $1,510.

**2006-2007 Financial aid. Need-based:** 477 full-time freshmen applied for aid; 388 were judged to have need; 387 of these received aid. Average need met was 70%. Average scholarship/grant was $12,098; average loan $3,020. 60% of total undergraduate aid awarded as scholarships/grants, 40% as loans/jobs. **Non-need-based:** Awarded to 1,450 full-time undergraduates, including 440 freshmen. Scholarships awarded for academics, alumni affiliation, leadership, music/drama. **Additional information:** Students enrolled at least half-time in the FOCUS or Distance Education degree programs may apply for financial aid from the same Federal and state sources as traditional undergraduates do. However, their expense budgets and aid are less due to lower tuition: FOCUS,,$315/credit; Center for Distance Education, $235/credit. Master's degree students with appropriate academic loads may apply for assistance from Federal student loan programs.

**Application procedures. Admission:** Priority date 5/1; deadline 8/1 (receipt date). $30 fee, may be waived for applicants with need. Application may be submitted online. Admission notification on a rolling basis beginning on or about 10/1. **Financial aid:** Priority date 3/1, closing date 6/1. FAFSA, institutional form required. Applicants notified on a rolling basis starting 3/1; must reply within 2 week(s) of notification.

**Academics.** Core curriulum built around a biblical worldview theme thoroughly integrates general education and biblical studies (64-68 credits). Transfer students meet core curriculum requirements on a proportional basis. **Special study options:** Combined bachelor's/graduate degree, distance learning, double major, exchange student, honors, independent study, internships, liberal arts/career combination, student-designed major, study abroad, teacher certification program, Washington semester. **Credit/placement by examination:** AP, CLEP, IB, SAT, ACT, institutional tests. 32 credit hours maximum toward associate degree, 32 toward bachelor's. **Support services:** Learning center, reduced course load, remedial instruction, study skills assistance, tutoring.

**Majors. Biology:** General. **Business:** Accounting, business admin, finance, international, management information systems, marketing. **Communications:** General, journalism, public relations, radio/tv. **Communications technology:** Animation/special effects. **Education:** Art, early childhood, elementary, English, ESL, mathematics, music, physical, social studies. **English:** Creative writing, English lit, technical writing. **History:** General. **Math:** General. **Parks/recreation:** Exercise sciences, health/fitness. **Protective services:** Criminal justice. **Psychology:** General. **Theology:** Bible, missionary, preministerial, youth ministry. **Visual/performing arts:** Dramatic, graphic design, music performance, music theory/composition, piano/organ, stringed instruments, studio arts, voice/opera. **Other:** Adult and family ministry.

**Most popular majors.** Biology 7%, business/marketing 11%, communications/journalism 13%, education 20%, psychology 8%, theological studies 17%, visual/performing arts 10%.

**Computing on campus.** PC or laptop required. 100 workstations in library, computer center, student center. Dormitories wired for high-speed internet access and linked to campus network. Commuter students can connect to campus network. Online course registration, online library, helpline, wireless network available.

**Student life. Freshman orientation:** Mandatory. Preregistration for classes offered. 6 one-day events during summer. General orientation: 4 days prior to start of classes. Multicultural orientation: 4 days prior to general orientation. **Policies:** Religious observance required. **Housing:** Guaranteed on-campus for freshmen. Single-sex dorms, special housing for disabled, apartments, substance-free housing available. **Activities:** Bands, choral groups, drama, literary magazine, music ensembles, musical theater, opera, radio station, student government, student newspaper, symphony orchestra, Student Missions Fellowship, The Gathering, transfer student organization, Guardian Angels, Mu Kappa, organization for students of color, Young Republicans.

**Athletics.** NCAA, NCCAA. **Intercollegiate:** Baseball M, basketball, cheerleading M, cross-country, football (tackle) M, golf M, soccer, softball W, tennis, track and field, volleyball W. **Intramural:** Basketball, football (non-tackle), softball, tennis, volleyball. **Team name:** Eagles.

**Student services.** Adult student services, campus ministries, career counseling, student employment services, financial aid counseling, health services, minority student services, personal counseling, placement for graduates.

**Contact.** E-mail: admissions@nwc.edu
Phone: (651) 631-5111 Toll-free number: (800) 827-6827
Fax: (651) 631-5680
Kenneth Faffler, Director of Admissions, Northwestern College, 3003 Snelling Avenue North, Saint Paul, MN 55113-1598

## Northwestern Health Sciences University
### Bloomington, Minnesota
www.nwhealth.edu

- Private two-year upper-division university and health science college
- Very large city

**General.** Regionally accredited. **Degrees:** 46 bachelor's awarded; master's, first professional offered. **Calendar:** Trimester, limited summer session. **Full-time faculty:** 65 total. **Part-time faculty:** 48 total.

**Student profile.** 82 degree-seeking undergraduates, 818 degree-seeking graduate students.

| | | | |
|---|---|---|---|
| Women: | 87% | Hispanic American: | 1% |
| African American: | 2% | Native American: | 1% |
| Asian American: | 1% | Part-time: | 28% |

**2007-2008 Annual costs.** Tuition/fees: $15,436. Reported costs are for upper-division Human Biology completion program (bachelor's), which is administered in conjunction with Doctor of Chiropractic degree program.

**Application procedures. Admission:** $50 fee. Application may be submitted online.

**Academics. Credit/placement by examination:** CLEP.

**Majors. Other:** Human biology.

**Computing on campus.** Wireless network available.

**Contact.** E-mail: admit@nwhealth.edu
Phone: (952) 888-4777 ext. 409
Bill Kuehl, Director of Admissions, Northwestern Health Sciences University, 2501 West 84th Street, Bloomington, MN 55431

## Oak Hills Christian College
**Bemidji, Minnesota**
www.oakhills.edu                     **CB code: 7247**

- Private 4-year Bible college affiliated with interdenominational tradition
- Residential campus in large town
- 163 degree-seeking undergraduates: 11% part-time, 45% women
- 95% of applicants admitted
- ACT (writing optional), application essay required
- 45% graduate within 6 years

**General.** Founded in 1946. Accredited by ABHE. **Degrees:** 26 bachelor's, 11 associate awarded. **Location:** 4 miles from Bemidji, 230 miles from Minneapolis-St. Paul. **Calendar:** Semester. **Full-time faculty:** 7 total; 71% have terminal degrees, 14% minority, 14% women. **Part-time faculty:** 13 total; 23% have terminal degrees, 38% women. **Class size:** 63% < 20, 31% 20-39, 6% 50-99. **Special facilities:** American Indian resource center.

**Freshman class profile.** 56 applied, 53 admitted, 31 enrolled.

| Mid 50% test scores | | Rank in top tenth: | 6% |
|---|---|---|---|
| ACT composite: | 17-23 | End year in good standing: | 49% |
| GPA 3.50 or higher: | 37% | Return as sophomores: | 47% |
| GPA 3.0-3.49: | 22% | Out-of-state: | 13% |
| GPA 2.0-2.99: | 37% | Live on campus: | 84% |
| Rank in top quarter: | 24% | | |

**Basis for selection.** Applicants must have high school GPA of 2.0 or above and/or ACT score of 18 or above to be eligible for consideration. Applicants not meeting minimum requirements considered on individual basis. SAT/ACT scores must be received at latest 4 weeks after first day of classes. Not required if student has 1 year of college credit or if 2 years out of high school. An essay or personal statement may generate an interview. **Homeschooled:** Transcript of courses and grades, letter of recommendation (nonparent) required. Proof of graduation from high school. **Learning Disabled:** All special education or diagnostic (IEP) records required. Interview may be requested.

**2008-2009 Annual costs.** Tuition/fees: $12,820. Room/board: $4,720. Books/supplies: $730. Personal expenses: $2,975.

**2006-2007 Financial aid. Need-based:** 21 full-time freshmen applied for aid; 18 were judged to have need; 18 of these received aid. Average need met was 56%. Average scholarship/grant was $5,786; average loan $1,873. 69% of total undergraduate aid awarded as scholarships/grants, 31% as loans/jobs. **Non-need-based:** Awarded to 14 full-time undergraduates, including 3 freshmen. Scholarships awarded for academics, alumni affiliation.

**Application procedures. Admission:** No deadline. $25 fee, may be waived for applicants with need. Application may be submitted online. Admission notification on a rolling basis. **Financial aid:** No deadline. FAFSA, institutional form required. Applicants notified on a rolling basis starting 3/1.

**Academics. Special study options:** Combined bachelor's/graduate degree, cooperative education, double major, honors, independent study, internships, study abroad. **Credit/placement by examination:** AP, CLEP, ACT, institutional tests. **Support services:** Reduced course load, remedial instruction, study skills assistance, tutoring.

**Majors. Psychology:** General. **Theology:** Bible, missionary, sacred music.

**Most popular majors.** Liberal arts 40%, theological studies 60%.

**Computing on campus.** 12 workstations in library. Dormitories wired for high-speed internet access and linked to campus network. Online library, wireless network available.

**Student life. Freshman orientation:** Mandatory. Preregistration for classes offered. Held first weekend prior to start of fall classes. **Policies:** Mandatory chapel, no alcohol, illegal drugs, gambling, or smoking on campus. Religious observance required. **Housing:** Guaranteed on-campus for freshmen. Single-sex dorms, special housing for disabled, apartments, substance-free housing available. $20 fully refundable deposit. Apartments for students with dependent children. **Activities:** Campus ministries, choral groups, drama, music ensembles, student government, married students group, students older than average group, women's group, engaged couples group, many outreach programs, single student cell groups.

**Athletics. Intercollegiate:** Basketball, volleyball W. **Intramural:** Basketball, football (non-tackle), golf, racquetball, soccer, softball, table tennis, volleyball. **Team name:** Wolfpack.

**Student services.** Adult student services, campus ministries, career counseling, student employment services, financial aid counseling, health services, minority student services, personal counseling, placement for graduates. **Physically disabled:** Services for visually, speech, hearing impaired. **Learning disabled:** Comprehensive services available.

**Contact.** E-mail: admissions@oakhills.edu
Phone: (218) 751-8671 ext. 1285 Toll-free
number: (888) 751-8670 ext. 1285 Fax: (218) 751-8825
Dan Hovestol, Admissions Director, Oak Hills Christian College, 1600 Oak Hills Road, SW, Bemidji, MN 56601-8826

## Pillsbury Baptist Bible College
**Owatonna, Minnesota**
www.pillsbury.edu                     **CB code: 0260**

- Private 4-year Bible college affiliated with Baptist faith
- Residential campus in large town
- 153 degree-seeking undergraduates: 7% part-time, 60% women
- ACT (writing optional), application essay required
- 41% graduate within 6 years

**General.** Accredited by ABHE. **Degrees:** 31 bachelor's, 5 associate awarded. **Location:** 50 miles from Minneapolis-St. Paul. **Calendar:** Semester, limited summer session. **Full-time faculty:** 19 total. **Part-time faculty:** 10 total.

**Freshman class profile.**

| Mid 50% test scores | | Return as sophomores: | 68% |
|---|---|---|---|
| ACT composite: | 18-24 | Out-of-state: | 43% |
| End year in good standing: | 80% | Live on campus: | 98% |

**Basis for selection.** Must demonstrate personal relationship with Jesus Christ and a Christian lifestyle; high school record, achievements and abilities important; ACT, statement, reference from pastor and teacher required. **Homeschooled:** GED may be required.

**High school preparation.** Recommended units include English 4, mathematics 3, social studies 3, science 3 and foreign language 2. Foreign language units should be in same language.

**2007-2008 Annual costs.** Tuition/fees: $8,970. Room/board: $4,436.

**2006-2007 Financial aid. Need-based:** 67% of total undergraduate aid awarded as scholarships/grants, 33% as loans/jobs.

**Application procedures. Admission:** No deadline. $25 fee. **Financial aid:** Priority date 4/15; no closing date.

**Academics. Special study options:** Double major, independent study, internships, study abroad. **Credit/placement by examination:** AP, CLEP, institutional tests. 10 credit hours maximum toward associate degree, 20 toward bachelor's. **Support services:** Remedial instruction, study skills assistance.

**Majors. Biology:** General. **Business:** Accounting, business admin. **Education:** Business, elementary, mathematics, music, physical, science, secondary, social studies. **Foreign languages:** Spanish. **Social sciences:** General. **Theology:** Bible, pastoral counseling, youth ministry. **Visual/performing arts:** Graphic design.

**Most popular majors.** Education 35%, theological studies 65%.

**Computing on campus.** 35 workstations in dormitories, library, computer center. Dormitories wired for high-speed internet access and linked to campus network. Helpline, wireless network available.

**Student life. Freshman orientation:** Mandatory. Preregistration for classes offered. **Policies:** Religious observance required. **Housing:** Guaranteed on-campus for all undergraduates. Single-sex dorms, substance-free housing available. **Activities:** Choral groups, drama, music ensembles, student government, student newspaper.

**Athletics.** NCCAA. **Intercollegiate:** Baseball M, basketball, golf, soccer M, softball W, volleyball W. **Team name:** Comets.

**Student services.** Career counseling, financial aid counseling, health services, personal counseling. **Physically disabled:** Services for hearing impaired.

**Contact.** E-mail: admissions@pillsbury.edu
Phone: (507) 451-2710 Toll-free number: (800) 747-4557
Jason Nicholson, Admissions Counselor, Pillsbury Baptist Bible College, 315 South Grove Avenue, Owatonna, MN 55060

---

## Rasmussen College: Brooklyn Park
**Brooklyn Park, Minnesota**
**www.rasmussen.edu**

- For-profit 4-year business college
- Small city

**General.** Regionally accredited. **Calendar:** Quarter.

**Annual costs/financial aid.** Regular courses: $345/credit; networking classes: $445/credit; child care classes: $255/credit.

**Contact.** 8301 93rd Avenue North, Brooklyn Park, MN 55445

---

## Rasmussen College: Eagan
**Eagan, Minnesota**
**www.rasmussen.edu**　　　　　**CB code: 2449**

- For-profit 4-year business and career college
- Small city
- 505 degree-seeking undergraduates: 70% part-time, 77% women

**General.** Regionally accredited. **Degrees:** 90 associate awarded. **Location:** 12 miles from Minneapolis-St. Paul. **Calendar:** Continuous, extensive summer session. **Full-time faculty:** 10 total. **Part-time faculty:** 11 total.

**Basis for selection.** Open admission. **Learning Disabled:** Student must submit documentation of learning disabilities if they wish to have special accomodations made.

**2007-2008 Annual costs.** Regular courses: $345/credit; networking classes: $445/credit; child care classes: $255/credit.

**Financial aid.** All financial aid based on need.

**Application procedures. Admission:** No deadline. $60 fee. Application must be submitted on paper. Admission notification on a rolling basis. **Financial aid:** No deadline. FAFSA, institutional form required. Applicants notified on a rolling basis.

**Academics. Special study options:** Distance learning, double major, honors. **Credit/placement by examination:** CLEP. **Support services:** Learning center, remedial instruction, study skills assistance, tutoring, writing center.

**Majors. Business:** Business admin.

**Computing on campus.** 90 workstations in library, computer center, student center. Online course registration, online library, helpline, wireless network available.

**Student life. Freshman orientation:** Mandatory.

**Contact.** Phone: (651) 687-9000 Toll-free number: (800) 852-6367
Fax: (651) 687-0507
Jon Peterson, Director of Admissions, Rasmussen College: Eagan, 3500 Federal Drive, Eagan, MN 55122

---

## Saint Cloud State University
**St. Cloud, Minnesota**
**www.stcloudstate.edu**　　　　　**CB code: 6679**

- Public 4-year university
- Commuter campus in small city
- 13,381 degree-seeking undergraduates: 12% part-time, 52% women, 3% African American, 2% Asian American, 1% Hispanic American, 1% Native American, 5% international
- 1,364 degree-seeking graduate students
- 76% of applicants admitted
- SAT or ACT (ACT writing optional) required
- 46% graduate within 6 years

**General.** Founded in 1869. Regionally accredited. **Degrees:** 2,487 bachelor's, 120 associate awarded; master's, doctoral offered. **ROTC:** Army. **Location:** 80 miles from Minneapolis-St. Paul. **Calendar:** Semester, limited summer session. **Full-time faculty:** 646 total; 80% have terminal degrees, 20% minority, 42% women. **Part-time faculty:** 217 total; 19% have terminal degrees, 10% minority, 54% women. **Class size:** 34% < 20, 54% 20-39, 6% 40-49, 3% 50-99, 3% >100. **Special facilities:** Planetarium, greenhouse, nature preserve, observatory, GIS cartographic center, aviation facilities, weather labs, National Hockey Center, AVID editing equipment.

**Freshman class profile.** 6,680 applied, 5,067 admitted, 2,381 enrolled.

| Mid 50% test scores | | Return as sophomores: | 71% |
|---|---|---|---|
| ACT composite: | 19-24 | Out-of-state: | 10% |
| Rank in top quarter: | 20% | Live on campus: | 80% |
| Rank in top tenth: | 6% | International: | 3% |

**Basis for selection.** Each application individually reviewed and evaluated using a combination of high school rank, GPA, curriculum, test scores, and other indicators of academic performance and potential.

**High school preparation.** 16 units required. Required units include English 4, mathematics 3, social studies 2, history 1, science 3 (laboratory 1), foreign language 2 and visual/performing arts 1.

**2007-2008 Annual costs.** Tuition/fees: $5,955; $12,097 out-of-state. Room/board: $5,592.

**Financial aid. Non-need-based:** Scholarships awarded for academics, art, athletics, leadership, music/drama.

**Application procedures. Admission:** Priority date 5/1; deadline 6/1 (receipt date). $20 fee, may be waived for applicants with need. Application may be submitted online. Admission notification on a rolling basis beginning on or about 9/15. Early application recommended for those who want to live on-campus. **Financial aid:** No deadline. FAFSA, institutional form required. Applicants notified on a rolling basis starting 6/15.

**Academics. Special study options:** Accelerated study, cooperative education, cross-registration, distance learning, double major, dual enrollment of high school students, ESL, honors, independent study, internships, student-designed major, study abroad, teacher certification program, weekend college. **Credit/placement by examination:** AP, CLEP, IB, institutional tests. 32 credit hours maximum toward bachelor's degree. **Support services:** Learning center, pre-admission summer program, remedial instruction, study skills assistance, tutoring, writing center.

**Majors. Area/ethnic studies:** Latin American, women's. **Biology:** General, aquatic, biochemistry, biotechnology, cellular/anatomical, ecology, marine. **Business:** General, accounting, business admin, entrepreneurial studies, finance, human resources, insurance, international, management information systems, marketing, real estate, tourism/travel. **Communications:** General, advertising, broadcast journalism, journalism, media studies, public relations, radio/tv. **Computer sciences:** General, computer science, networking, security. **Conservation:** Environmental science, environmental studies. **Education:** Art, biology, chemistry, drama/dance, driver/safety, early childhood, elementary, English, foreign languages, French, German, health, history, instructional media, kindergarten/preschool, mathematics, multi-level teacher, music, physical, physics, psychology, reading, science, secondary, social science, social studies, Spanish, special, speech, technology/industrial arts. **Engineering:** Computer, electrical, manufacturing, mechanical. **Engineering technology:** Surveying. **English:** American lit, composition, creative writing, English lit, speech/rhetoric. **Foreign languages:** French, German, linguistics, Spanish. **Health:** Audiology/speech pathology, clinical lab science, communication disorders, community health services, medical radiologic technology/radiation therapy, nuclear medical technology, nursing (RN), predental, premedicine, prepharmacy, preveterinary, public health ed, recreational therapy, substance abuse counseling. **History:** General. **Interdisciplinary:** Gerontology, natural sciences. **Legal studies:** Prelaw. **Liberal arts:** Arts/sciences, library science. **Math:** General, statistics. **Parks/**

recreation: General, health/fitness. **Philosophy/religion:** Philosophy. **Physical sciences:** General, atmospheric science, chemistry, geology, hydrology, meteorology, physics, planetary. **Protective services:** Criminal justice. **Psychology:** General, community. **Public administration:** General, social work. **Social sciences:** General, anthropology, economics, geography, international relations, political science, sociology, urban studies. **Transportation:** Air traffic control, airline/commercial pilot, aviation management, flight instructor. **Visual/performing arts:** Acting, art, art history/conservation, ceramics, dramatic, drawing, film/cinema, jazz, music history, music performance, painting, piano/organ, printmaking, sculpture, stringed instruments, studio arts, voice/opera. **Other:** Business economics, Communication studies, Earth science.

**Most popular majors.** Business/marketing 26%, communications/journalism 9%, education 13%, psychology 6%, social sciences 8%.

**Computing on campus.** 1,487 workstations in dormitories, library, computer center, student center. Dormitories wired for high-speed internet access and linked to campus network. Commuter students can connect to campus network. Online course registration, online library, helpline, repair service, student web hosting, wireless network available.

**Student life. Freshman orientation:** Mandatory. Preregistration for classes offered. Includes assistance with fall term registration. **Housing:** Coed dorms, single-sex dorms, special housing for disabled, apartments available. $100 fully refundable deposit, deadline 3/31. **Activities:** Bands, campus ministries, choral groups, dance, drama, film society, international student organizations, literary magazine, music ensembles, Model UN, musical theater, opera, radio station, student government, student newspaper, symphony orchestra, TV station, more than 240 clubs and departmental organizations.

**Athletics.** NCAA. **Intercollegiate:** Baseball M, basketball, cross-country, diving, football (tackle) M, golf, ice hockey, skiing W, soccer W, softball W, swimming, tennis, track and field, volleyball W, wrestling M. **Intramural:** Badminton, basketball, football (non-tackle), golf, ice hockey, racquetball, soccer, softball, tennis, volleyball, water polo. **Team name:** Huskies.

**Student services.** Adult student services, alcohol/substance abuse counseling, career counseling, student employment services, financial aid counseling, health services, minority student services, on-campus daycare, personal counseling, placement for graduates, veterans' counselor, women's services. **Physically disabled:** Services for visually, speech, hearing impaired.

**Contact.** E-mail: scsu4u@stcloudstate.edu
Phone: (320) 308-2244 Toll-free number: (877) 654-7278
Fax: (320) 308-2243
Jeff Rhodes, Director of Admissions, Saint Cloud State University, 720 Fourth Avenue South, St. Cloud, MN 56301

## St. John's University
**Collegeville, Minnesota**
www.csbsju.edu

**CB member**
**CB code: 6624**

- Private 4-year university and liberal arts college for men affiliated with Roman Catholic Church
- Residential campus in rural community
- 1,917 degree-seeking undergraduates
- 128 degree-seeking graduate students
- 74% of applicants admitted
- SAT or ACT (ACT writing optional), application essay required
- 80% graduate within 6 years; 14% enter graduate study

**General.** Founded in 1857. Regionally accredited. Coeducational academic and campus life shared with Saint Benedict in St. Joseph, MN. **Degrees:** 417 bachelor's awarded; master's, first professional offered. **ROTC:** Army. **Location:** 70 miles from Minneapolis-St. Paul, 15 miles from St. Cloud. **Calendar:** Semester, limited summer session. **Full-time faculty:** 153 total; 83% have terminal degrees, 9% minority, 35% women. **Part-time faculty:** 32 total; 28% have terminal degrees, 47% women. **Class size:** 46% < 20, 54% 20-39. **Special facilities:** Observatory, ecumenical center, museum and manuscript library, liturgical press, nature preserve, arboretum, natural history museum, pottery kiln.

**Freshman class profile.** 1,527 applied, 1,123 admitted, 515 enrolled.

| Mid 50% test scores | | | |
|---|---|---|---|
| SAT critical reading: | 490-630 | Rank in top quarter: | 53% |
| SAT math: | 500-650 | Rank in top tenth: | 23% |
| ACT composite: | 23-28 | End year in good standing: | 93% |
| GPA 3.50 or higher: | 63% | Return as sophomores: | 89% |
| GPA 3.0-3.49: | 32% | Out-of-state: | 15% |
| GPA 2.0-2.99: | 5% | Live on campus: | 100% |
| | | International: | 4% |

**Basis for selection.** Course selection, scholastic achievement, GPA, test scores and essay are most important. Extracurricular involvement, high school rank, and recommendation are also important. Students who have completed the application process by 11/15 will receive notification of their scholarship award on 12/20. Those that complete by 12/15 will receive notification of their scholarship award on 2/1. Interview recommended for academically weak/conditionally accepted students. **Homeschooled:** Applicants are not required to have a high school diploma, but are required to provide appropriate documentation of college preparatory curriculum.

**High school preparation.** 15 units required. Required and recommended units include English 4, mathematics 3, social studies 2, science 2 (laboratory 2), foreign language 2 and academic electives 4.

**2007-2008 Annual costs.** Tuition/fees: $26,530. Room/board: $6,870. Books/supplies: $800. Personal expenses: $700.

**2007-2008 Financial aid. Need-based:** 380 full-time freshmen applied for aid; 287 were judged to have need; 287 of these received aid. Average need met was 94%. Average scholarship/grant was $16,109; average loan $4,267. 63% of total undergraduate aid awarded as scholarships/grants, 37% as loans/jobs. **Non-need-based:** Awarded to 1,707 full-time undergraduates, including 481 freshmen. Scholarships awarded for academics, art, leadership, music/drama, ROTC.

**Application procedures. Admission:** Priority date 11/15; no deadline. No application fee. Application may be submitted online. Admission notification on a rolling basis. A non-refundable enrollment deposit of $300 is due by May 1. **Financial aid:** Priority date 3/15; no closing date. FAFSA, institutional form required. Applicants notified on a rolling basis starting 3/15; must reply by 5/1.

**Academics. Special study options:** Combined bachelor's/graduate degree, cross-registration, double major, dual enrollment of high school students, ESL, exchange student, honors, independent study, internships, student-designed major, study abroad, teacher certification program, United Nations semester. 3-2 program in engineering with University of Minnesota, 3-1 program in dentistry with University of Minnesota, cross registration with St. Cloud State University. **Credit/placement by examination:** AP, CLEP, IB, institutional tests. **Support services:** Study skills assistance, tutoring, writing center.

**Majors. Area/ethnic studies:** Women's. **Biology:** General, biochemistry. **Business:** Accounting, business admin. **Computer sciences:** Computer science. **Conservation:** Environmental science. **Education:** General, elementary. **English:** English lit, speech/rhetoric. **Foreign languages:** Classics, French, German, Spanish. **Health:** Dietetics, nursing (RN), predental, premedicine, prepharmacy, preveterinary. **History:** General. **Interdisciplinary:** Biological/physical sciences, math/computer science, natural sciences, nutrition sciences, peace/conflict. **Legal studies:** Prelaw. **Liberal arts:** Arts/sciences, humanities. **Math:** General. **Philosophy/religion:** Philosophy. **Physical sciences:** Chemistry, physics. **Psychology:** General. **Public administration:** Social work. **Social sciences:** General, economics, political science, sociology. **Theology:** Preministerial, theology. **Visual/performing arts:** Art, dramatic.

**Most popular majors.** Biology 10%, business/marketing 25%, English 13%, psychology 6%, social sciences 16%.

**Computing on campus.** 643 workstations in dormitories, library, computer center, student center. Dormitories wired for high-speed internet access and linked to campus network. Commuter students can connect to campus network. Online course registration, helpline, repair service, student web hosting, wireless network available.

**Student life. Freshman orientation:** Mandatory. Preregistration for classes offered. Fall orientation begins the evening of move-in day and concludes with convocation the first day of classes. **Policies:** Freshmen and sophomores are required to live on campus. **Housing:** Guaranteed on-campus for freshmen. Special housing for disabled, apartments, substance-free housing available. Earth-sheltered, solar-heated apartments available to upperclassmen; ROTC housing. **Activities:** Bands, campus ministries, choral groups, dance, drama, international student organizations, literary magazine, music ensembles, Model UN, musical theater, opera, radio station, student government, student newspaper, symphony orchestra, Volunteers in Service to Others, College Republicans, College Democrats, Joints Events Council, Asia club, Student Coalition for Global Solidarity, Students in Free Enterprise, Magis, Cultural Fusion Club, Outdoor Leadership center.

**Athletics.** NCAA. **Intercollegiate:** Baseball M, basketball M, cross-country M, diving M, football (tackle) M, golf M, ice hockey M, skiing M, soccer M, swimming M, tennis M, track and field M, wrestling M. **Intramural:** Basketball M, football (tackle) M, ice hockey M, racquetball M, soccer M, softball M, table tennis M, tennis M, volleyball M, water polo M. **Team name:** Johnnies.

**Student services.** Alcohol/substance abuse counseling, campus ministries, career counseling, student employment services, financial aid counseling, health services, minority student services, personal counseling, placement for graduates. **Physically disabled:** Services for hearing impaired.

**Contact.** E-mail: admissions@csbsju.edu
Phone: (320) 363-2196 Toll-free number: (800) 544-1489
Fax: (320) 363-2750
Michael Thorp, Dean of Admissions, St. John's University, PO Box 7155, Collegeville, MN 56321-7155

## St. Mary's University of Minnesota
**Winona, Minnesota**
www.smumn.edu

CB member
CB code: 6632

- Private 4-year university affiliated with Roman Catholic Church
- Residential campus in large town
- 1,979 degree-seeking undergraduates: 29% part-time, 53% women, 4% African American, 3% Asian American, 3% Hispanic American, 1% Native American, 1% international
- 3,690 degree-seeking graduate students
- 83% of applicants admitted
- SAT or ACT (ACT writing optional), application essay required
- 54% graduate within 6 years

**General.** Founded in 1912. Regionally accredited. **Degrees:** 401 bachelor's awarded; master's, doctoral offered. **ROTC:** Army. **Location:** 110 miles from Minneapolis-St. Paul, 45 miles from Rochester. **Calendar:** Semester, limited summer session. **Full-time faculty:** 105 total; 78% have terminal degrees, 3% minority, 37% women. **Part-time faculty:** 490 total; 32% have terminal degrees, 6% minority, 50% women. **Class size:** 57% < 20, 42% 20-39, less than 1% 40-49, less than 1% 50-99. **Special facilities:** Woodland and stream, nature preserve, observatory.

**Freshman class profile.** 1,410 applied, 1,169 admitted, 397 enrolled.

| Mid 50% test scores | | | |
|---|---|---|---|
| SAT critical reading: | 480-620 | Rank in top quarter: | 41% |
| SAT math: | 440-590 | Rank in top tenth: | 17% |
| ACT composite: | 19-25 | Return as sophomores: | 78% |
| GPA 3.50 or higher: | 32% | Out-of-state: | 37% |
| GPA 3.0-3.49: | 26% | Live on campus: | 97% |
| GPA 2.0-2.99: | 39% | International: | 1% |

**Basis for selection.** Minimum 2.5 GPA, upper half of class, 50th percentile on standardized tests, essay, college prep coursework required. Recommendations, interview, school and community activities considered. Interview recommended for academically marginal students.

**High school preparation.** 18 units required. Required and recommended units include English 4, mathematics 3, social studies 2, science 3 (laboratory 2), foreign language 2 and academic electives 6.

**2008-2009 Annual costs.** Tuition/fees: $24,150. Room/board: $6,380. Books/supplies: $1,220. Personal expenses: $850.

**2007-2008 Financial aid. Need-based:** 336 full-time freshmen applied for aid; 273 were judged to have need; 273 of these received aid. Average need met was 81%. Average scholarship/grant was $10,348; average loan $3,356. 63% of total undergraduate aid awarded as scholarships/grants, 37% as loans/jobs. **Non-need-based:** Awarded to 400 full-time undergraduates, including 124 freshmen. Scholarships awarded for academics, alumni affiliation, art, leadership, minority status, music/drama, religious affiliation.

**Application procedures. Admission:** Priority date 4/1; deadline 5/1 (postmark date). $25 fee, may be waived for applicants with need. Application may be submitted online. Admission notification 5/1. Admission notification on a rolling basis. Must reply by May 1 or within 2 week(s) if notified thereafter. **Financial aid:** Priority date 3/15; no closing date. FAFSA required. Applicants notified on a rolling basis starting 2/1; must reply within 3 week(s) of notification.

**Academics. Special study options:** Cooperative education, cross-registration, double major, dual enrollment of high school students, ESL, honors, independent study, internships, student-designed major, study abroad, teacher certification program, urban semester, Washington semester. **Credit/placement by examination:** AP, CLEP, IB, SAT, ACT, institutional tests. 8 credits per area allowed. **Support services:** Learning center, reduced course load, remedial instruction, study skills assistance, tutoring, writing center.

**Majors. Biology:** General, biophysics, environmental. **Business:** Accounting, business admin, human resources, international, management science, marketing. **Communications:** Journalism, public relations. **Communications technology:** General, desktop publishing. **Computer sciences:** Computer science, information systems. **Education:** Biology, chemistry, early childhood, English, foreign languages, French, mathematics, music, physics, science, social science, social studies, Spanish. **Engineering:** Physics. **Engineering technology:** Industrial. **English:** English lit, technical writing. **Foreign languages:** French, Spanish. **Health:** Clinical lab science, cytotechnology, health care admin, nuclear medical technology. **History:** General. **Interdisciplinary:** Math/computer science. **Math:** General. **Philosophy/religion:** Philosophy. **Physical sciences:** Chemistry, physics. **Protective services:** Criminal justice, law enforcement admin, police science. **Psychology:** General. **Public administration:** General, human services. **Social sciences:** General, political science, sociology. **Theology:** Pastoral counseling, preministerial, theology. **Visual/performing arts:** Commercial/advertising art, dramatic, music management, music performance, studio arts, voice/opera.

**Most popular majors.** Biology 6%, business/marketing 36%, education 7%, security/protective services 7%, visual/performing arts 7%.

**Computing on campus.** 365 workstations in dormitories, library, computer center, student center. Dormitories wired for high-speed internet access and linked to campus network. Commuter students can connect to campus network. Online course registration, online library, helpline, repair service, student web hosting available.

**Student life. Freshman orientation:** Mandatory. Preregistration for classes offered. Held during summer prior to fall enrollment. **Housing:** Guaranteed on-campus for all undergraduates. Coed dorms, single-sex dorms, special housing for disabled, apartments available. **Activities:** Bands, campus ministries, choral groups, dance, drama, international student organizations, literary magazine, music ensembles, musical theater, radio station, student government, student newspaper, Big and Little Pals, College Democrats, College Republicans, Collegians for Life, Community of Women, Inside-Out Christian Fellowship, international student association, LaSallian Collegians, liturgical ministers.

**Athletics.** NCAA. **Intercollegiate:** Baseball M, basketball, cross-country, diving, golf, ice hockey, soccer, softball W, swimming, tennis, track and field, volleyball W. **Intramural:** Basketball, golf, ice hockey M, racquetball, soccer, softball, tennis, volleyball. **Team name:** Cardinals.

**Student services.** Alcohol/substance abuse counseling, campus ministries, career counseling, student employment services, financial aid counseling, health services, personal counseling, placement for graduates. **Physically disabled:** Services for visually, hearing impaired.

**Contact.** E-mail: admissions@smumn.edu
Phone: (507) 457-1600 Toll-free number: (800) 635-5987
Fax: (507) 457-1722
Anthony Piscitiello, Vice President for Admissions, St. Mary's University of Minnesota, 700 Terrace Heights, #2, Winona, MN 55987-1399

## St. Olaf College
**Northfield, Minnesota**
www.stolaf.edu

CB member
CB code: 6638

- Private 4-year liberal arts college affiliated with Evangelical Lutheran Church in America
- Residential campus in large town
- 2,988 degree-seeking undergraduates: 55% women, 1% African American, 5% Asian American, 2% Hispanic American, 1% international
- 54% of applicants admitted
- SAT or ACT (ACT writing optional), application essay required
- 86% graduate within 6 years; 29% enter graduate study

**General.** Founded in 1874. Regionally accredited. **Degrees:** 670 bachelor's awarded. **Location:** 35 miles from Minneapolis-St. Paul. **Calendar:** 4-1-4, limited summer session. **Full-time faculty:** 197 total; 91% have terminal degrees, 7% minority, 41% women. **Part-time faculty:** 130 total; 62% have terminal degrees, 3% minority, 52% women. **Class size:** 60%

< 20, 33% 20-39, 2% 40-49, 4% 50-99, less than 1% >100. **Special facilities:** Norwegian-American Historical Society Archives; Kierkegaard Library, natural habitat includes 5 wetland areas, 45-acre native prairie grasses and bluebird trail of 70 houses.

**Freshman class profile.** 4,058 applied, 2,208 admitted, 751 enrolled.

| Mid 50% test scores | | | |
|---|---|---|---|
| SAT critical reading: | 600-720 | Rank in top quarter: | 82% |
| SAT math: | 600-700 | Rank in top tenth: | 54% |
| ACT composite: | 26-31 | End year in good standing: | 95% |
| GPA 3.50 or higher: | 71% | Return as sophomores: | 93% |
| GPA 3.0-3.49: | 22% | Out-of-state: | 48% |
| GPA 2.0-2.99: | 7% | Live on campus: | 100% |

**Basis for selection.** Academic achievement most important, with academic aptitude and personal qualifications, as well as leadership and significant involvement in school and community, strongly considered. Interview recommended. Audition required for music students. **Learning Disabled:** Personal interview recommended. Untimed standardized tests accepted.

**High school preparation.** 14 units required; 24 recommended. Required and recommended units include English 4, mathematics 2-4, social studies 1-2, history 1-2, science 2-4 (laboratory 1-2), foreign language 2-4 and academic electives 2-4.

**2008-2009 Annual costs.** Tuition/fees: $34,300. Room/board: $7,900. Books/supplies: $950. Personal expenses: $850.

**2007-2008 Financial aid. Need-based:** 596 full-time freshmen applied for aid; 466 were judged to have need; 466 of these received aid. Average need met was 100%. Average scholarship/grant was $15,483; average loan $4,053. 74% of total undergraduate aid awarded as scholarships/grants, 26% as loans/jobs. **Non-need-based:** Awarded to 1,398 full-time undergraduates, including 378 freshmen. Scholarships awarded for academics, leadership, music/drama. **Additional information:** Limited number of music lesson fee waivers available for music majors, awarded on audition basis only.

**Application procedures. Admission:** Priority date 1/15; no deadline. No application fee. Application may be submitted online. Admission notification on a rolling basis. Must reply by May 1 or within 2 week(s) if notified thereafter. **Financial aid:** Priority date 1/15, closing date 4/15. FAFSA, CSS PROFILE required. Applicants notified on a rolling basis starting 3/1; must reply by 5/1 or within 2 week(s) of notification.

**Academics.** Students may propose self-designed integrative majors. **Special study options:** Combined bachelor's/graduate degree, cross-registration, double major, dual enrollment of high school students, independent study, internships, student-designed major, study abroad, teacher certification program, urban semester, Washington semester. Great Conversation: 5-semester program emphasizing reading, writing, and outside-of-the-classroom discussion available to 70 incoming students each year; BA/BS in engineering with Washington University (MO), University of Minnesota, Minneapolis; center for experiential learning; center for integrative studies; joint law degree with Columbia University; undergraduate research in the sciences, Center for Integrative Studies study-travel programs in 38 different countries; includes Global semester, Term in Asia, Environmental Studies in Australia, ACM and HECUA program, 30-40 different interims, both domestic and abroad, all with a St. Olaf College faculty member as leader/instructor. **Credit/placement by examination:** AP, CLEP, IB, institutional tests. 5 credit hours maximum toward bachelor's degree. **Support services:** Learning center, pre-admission summer program, reduced course load, study skills assistance, tutoring, writing center.

**Majors. Area/ethnic studies:** American, Asian, Latin American, Russian/Slavic, women's. **Biology:** General. **Computer sciences:** Computer science. **Conservation:** Environmental studies. **Education:** Music, social studies. **English:** English lit. **Family/consumer sciences:** Family studies. **Foreign languages:** Ancient Greek, classics, French, German, Latin, Norwegian, Russian, Spanish. **Health:** Nursing (RN). **History:** General. **Interdisciplinary:** Ancient studies, medieval/Renaissance. **Liberal arts:** Arts/sciences. **Math:** General. **Parks/recreation:** Exercise sciences. **Philosophy/religion:** Philosophy, religion. **Physical sciences:** Chemistry, physics. **Psychology:** General. **Public administration:** Social work. **Social sciences:** Economics, political science, sociology. **Theology:** Sacred music. **Visual/performing arts:** Art, art history/conservation, dance, dramatic, music performance, music theory/composition. **Other:** American racial and multicultural studies.

**Most popular majors.** Area/ethnic studies 7%, biology 8%, English 8%, foreign language 7%, mathematics 7%, philosophy/religious studies 8%, physical sciences 6%, psychology 6%, social sciences 14%, visual/performing arts 12%.

**Computing on campus.** 969 workstations in dormitories, library, computer center, student center. Dormitories wired for high-speed internet access and linked to campus network. Commuter students can connect to campus network. Helpline, wireless network available.

**Student life. Freshman orientation:** Mandatory. Held 5 days before start of fall classes. **Policies:** Alcohol not permitted on campus. **Housing:** Guaranteed on-campus for all undergraduates. Coed dorms, special housing for disabled, substance-free housing available. $300 nonrefundable deposit, deadline 5/1. Honor houses, language houses, quiet halls, first-year only dorms. **Activities:** Bands, campus ministries, choral groups, dance, drama, film society, international student organizations, literary magazine, music ensembles, Model UN, musical theater, opera, radio station, student government, student newspaper, symphony orchestra, TV station, 137 registered student organizations.

**Athletics.** NCAA. **Intercollegiate:** Baseball M, basketball, cross-country, diving, football (tackle) M, golf, ice hockey, skiing, soccer, softball W, swimming, tennis, track and field, volleyball W, wrestling M. **Intramural:** Badminton, basketball, boxing, cross-country, diving, football (non-tackle), football (tackle), golf, ice hockey M, lacrosse, rowing (crew), rugby, skiing, soccer, softball, swimming, synchronized swimming, tennis, volleyball, water polo, wrestling. **Team name:** Oles.

**Student services.** Alcohol/substance abuse counseling, campus ministries, career counseling, services for economically disadvantaged, student employment services, financial aid counseling, health services, minority student services, personal counseling. **Physically disabled:** Services for visually, hearing impaired.

**Contact.** E-mail: admissions@stolaf.edu
Phone: (507) 786-3025 Toll-free number: (800) 800-3025
Fax: (507) 786-3832
Derek Gueldenzoph, Director of Admissions, St. Olaf College, 1520 St. Olaf Avenue, Northfield, MN 55057

## Southwest Minnesota State University
**Marshall, Minnesota**
**www.southwestmsu.edu** **CB code: 6703**

▸ Public 4-year liberal arts and technical college
▸ Residential campus in large town
▸ 2,600 degree-seeking undergraduates: 14% part-time, 55% women
▸ 354 degree-seeking graduate students
▸ SAT or ACT (ACT writing optional) required
▸ 40% graduate within 6 years; 8% enter graduate study

**General.** Founded in 1963. Regionally accredited. **Degrees:** 496 bachelor's, 4 associate awarded; master's offered. **Location:** 150 miles from Minneapolis-St. Paul. **Calendar:** Semester, limited summer session. **Full-time faculty:** 126 total; 75% have terminal degrees, 12% minority, 42% women. **Part-time faculty:** 76 total; 32% have terminal degrees, 7% minority, 42% women. **Class size:** 44% < 20, 49% 20-39, 5% 40-49, 2% 50-99, less than 1% >100. **Special facilities:** Natural history museum, anthropology museum, planetarium, wildlife area.

**Freshman class profile.**

| Mid 50% test scores | | | |
|---|---|---|---|
| ACT composite: | 19-23 | Rank in top tenth: | 6% |
| | | End year in good standing: | 85% |
| GPA 3.50 or higher: | 33% | Return as sophomores: | 67% |
| GPA 3.0-3.49: | 32% | Out-of-state: | 16% |
| GPA 2.0-2.99: | 33% | Live on campus: | 91% |
| Rank in top quarter: | 26% | International: | 1% |

**Basis for selection.** Class rank in top half of class or SAT combined score of 970 (exclusive of Writing) or ACT composite score of 21. Provisional admission may be granted to students who rank in top two-thirds of class or have ACT composite score of 19 or SAT combined score of 890. GED students must submit ACT. ACT recommended. PSAT/NMSQT may be submitted in place of SAT or ACT. Interview recommended for academically weak students; audition recommended for music students.

**High school preparation.** 15 units required. Required units include English 4, mathematics 3, social studies 3, history 1, science 3 and foreign language 2. Social studies units must include American history and geography.

**2007-2008 Annual costs.** Tuition/fees: $6,517. Room/board: $5,616. Books/supplies: $1,000. Personal expenses: $1,800.

**2007-2008 Financial aid. Need-based:** Average need met was 38%. Average scholarship/grant was $4,865; average loan $3,218. 45% of total undergraduate aid awarded as scholarships/grants, 55% as loans/jobs. **Non-need-based:** Scholarships awarded for academics, alumni affiliation, art, athletics, leadership, minority status, music/drama, state residency.

**Application procedures. Admission:** Priority date 8/15; deadline 9/1 (receipt date). $20 fee. Application may be submitted online. Admission notification on a rolling basis. **Financial aid:** Priority date 3/1; no closing date. FAFSA, institutional form required. Applicants notified on a rolling basis starting 5/15.

**Academics. Special study options:** Accelerated study, combined bachelor's/graduate degree, cooperative education, cross-registration, distance learning, double major, dual enrollment of high school students, ESL, exchange student, external degree, honors, independent study, internships, student-designed major, study abroad, teacher certification program. 2+2 bachelor's programs with Ridgewater College, St. Cloud Technical College, Minnesota West, South Central (Mankato) and Riverland College. **Credit/placement by examination:** AP, CLEP, ACT, institutional tests. 36 credit hours maximum toward associate degree, 36 toward bachelor's. **Support services:** Learning center, reduced course load, remedial instruction, study skills assistance, tutoring, writing center.

**Majors. Agriculture:** Agribusiness operations. **Biology:** General, cell/histology, ecology. **Business:** Accounting, business admin, finance, marketing. **Communications:** General, broadcast journalism, public relations. **Computer sciences:** General. **Education:** Art, biology, chemistry, drama/dance, early childhood, elementary, health, mathematics, music, physical, science, speech. **English:** Creative writing, English lit, speech/rhetoric. **Foreign languages:** Spanish. **History:** General. **Liberal arts:** Arts/sciences. **Math:** General. **Parks/recreation:** Health/fitness. **Philosophy/religion:** Philosophy. **Physical sciences:** Chemistry. **Protective services:** Fire services admin, law enforcement admin. **Psychology:** General. **Public administration:** General, social work. **Social sciences:** Political science, sociology. **Visual/performing arts:** Art, dramatic.

**Most popular majors.** Business/marketing 36%, education 16%, psychology 6%.

**Computing on campus.** 300 workstations in dormitories, library, computer center, student center. Dormitories wired for high-speed internet access and linked to campus network. Commuter students can connect to campus network. Online course registration, online library, helpline, repair service, student web hosting, wireless network available.

**Student life. Freshman orientation:** Available, $45 fee. Preregistration for classes offered. **Housing:** Coed dorms, single-sex dorms, special housing for disabled, apartments, substance-free housing available. $100 fully refundable deposit. **Activities:** Bands, choral groups, dance, drama, film society, international student organizations, literary magazine, music ensembles, musical theater, radio station, student government, student newspaper, symphony orchestra, TV station, Black Student Union, Inter-Varsity Christian Fellowship, Lutheran Student Commission, student activities committee, Republican Speakers Club, Young DFL, non-traditional students organization.

**Athletics.** NAIA. **Intercollegiate:** Baseball M, basketball, football (tackle) M, golf W, soccer W, softball W, tennis W, volleyball W, wrestling M. **Intramural:** Basketball, ice hockey M, racquetball, skiing, softball, tennis, track and field, volleyball, wrestling M. **Team name:** Mustangs.

**Student services.** Adult student services, alcohol/substance abuse counseling, campus ministries, career counseling, student employment services, financial aid counseling, health services, minority student services, on-campus daycare, personal counseling, placement for graduates, veterans' counselor, women's services. **Physically disabled:** Services for visually, speech, hearing impaired.

**Contact.** E-mail: shearerr@southwestmsu.edu
Phone: (507) 537-6286 Toll-free number: (800) 642-0684
Fax: (507) 537-7154
Richard Shearer, Enrollment Services Director, Southwest Minnesota State University, 1501 State Street, Marshall, MN 56258-1598

## University of Minnesota: Crookston
### Crookston, Minnesota
www.UMCrookston.edu          CB code: 6893

- Public 4-year branch campus college
- Commuter campus in small town
- 1,142 degree-seeking undergraduates: 15% part-time, 42% women, 5% African American, 2% Asian American, 2% Hispanic American, 1% Native American, 7% international
- 83% of applicants admitted
- SAT or ACT (ACT writing optional) required

**General.** Founded in 1965. Regionally accredited. Each student and faculty member issued laptop computer. **Degrees:** 222 bachelor's, 29 associate awarded. **ROTC:** Air Force. **Location:** 25 miles from Grand Forks, North Dakota, 170 miles from Winnipeg, Canada. **Calendar:** Semester, limited summer session. **Full-time faculty:** 52 total; 46% have terminal degrees,

10% minority, 31% women. **Part-time faculty:** 51 total; 22% have terminal degrees, 4% minority, 59% women. **Class size:** 47% < 20, 42% 20-39, 7% 40-49, 4% 50-99. **Special facilities:** 85-acre natural history area with prairie, marshes, and forests, teaching and outreach center.

**Freshman class profile.** 525 applied, 435 admitted, 241 enrolled.

| Mid 50% test scores | | End year in good standing: | 69% |
|---|---|---|---|
| SAT critical reading: | 390-490 | Out-of-state: | 34% |
| SAT math: | 410-560 | Live on campus: | 80% |
| ACT composite: | 18-23 | International: | 7% |
| Rank in top quarter: | 32% | Fraternities: | 3% |
| Rank in top tenth: | 13% | Sororities: | 1% |

**Basis for selection.** High school class rank and ACT test scores most important. ACT recommended. **Learning Disabled:** Students encouraged to contact Disability Services early in the admissions process to insure availability of appropriate services.

**High school preparation.** Recommended units include English 4, mathematics 3, social studies 2, science 3 and foreign language 2.

**2007-2008 Annual costs.** Tuition/fees: $8,821; $8,821 out-of-state. Room/board: $5,622. Books/supplies: $800. Personal expenses: $1,000.

**2007-2008 Financial aid. Need-based:** 46% of total undergraduate aid awarded as scholarships/grants, 54% as loans/jobs. **Non-need-based:** Scholarships awarded for academics, athletics, leadership, minority status, ROTC. **Additional information:** Tuition guarantee plan available to all students who apply for it.

**Application procedures. Admission:** Priority date 2/1; no deadline. $30 fee, may be waived for applicants with need. Application may be submitted online. Admission notification on a rolling basis beginning on or about 9/1. **Financial aid:** Priority date 2/15; no closing date. FAFSA required. Applicants notified on a rolling basis starting 3/15.

**Academics.** 10-week applied internship for all programs. **Special study options:** Cross-registration, distance learning, double major, dual enrollment of high school students, ESL, independent study, internships, student-designed major, study abroad, teacher certification program. **Credit/placement by examination:** AP, CLEP, IB, SAT, ACT. Proficiency examinations are administered by appropriate academic department, require no fee, and yield no credit or grade but may fulfill prerequisites for advanced courses or satisfy requirements. Special Examinations for Credit have fee of $50 per credit. Credits earned by examination do not count as residence credits. Exams given at discretion of appropriate academic department. **Support services:** Learning center, pre-admission summer program, reduced course load, remedial instruction, study skills assistance, tutoring, writing center.

**Majors. Agriculture:** Agribusiness operations, agronomy, animal sciences, business, equestrian studies, horticultural science, turf management. **Biology:** General. **Business:** Accounting, business admin, hospitality admin, management information systems. **Communications:** General. **Conservation:** General. **Education:** Agricultural, kindergarten/preschool. **Engineering:** Industrial. **Engineering technology:** Software. **Health:** Health care admin, health services. **Parks/recreation:** Sports admin. **Psychology:** Industrial. **Transportation:** Aviation.

**Most popular majors.** Agriculture 21%, business/marketing 29%, education 6%, engineering/engineering technologies 12%, interdisciplinary studies 6%, natural resources/environmental science 14%, parks/recreation 7%.

**Computing on campus.** PC or laptop required. 1,250 workstations in dormitories, library, computer center, student center. Dormitories wired for high-speed internet access and linked to campus network. Commuter students can connect to campus network. Online course registration, online library, helpline, repair service, student web hosting, wireless network available.

**Student life. Freshman orientation:** Mandatory, $75 fee. Preregistration for classes offered. The new student orientation program for the fall term begins three days before the first day of class. **Housing:** Coed dorms, apartments available. $100 nonrefundable deposit, deadline 9/1. **Activities:** Bands, campus ministries, choral groups, drama, international student organizations, musical theater, student government, campus ministry club, multicultural club, UMC Ambassadors, Students in Free Enterprise, Wildlife Society Chapter, Collegiate FFA, flying club, Habitat for Humanity, Rodeo Association, Student Athletic Advisory Committee.

**Athletics.** NCAA. **Intercollegiate:** Baseball M, basketball, cheerleading, equestrian W, football (tackle) M, golf, ice hockey M, soccer W, softball W, tennis W, volleyball W. **Intramural:** Basketball, bowling, racquetball, table tennis, tennis, volleyball. **Team name:** Golden Eagles.

**Student services.** Adult student services, alcohol/substance abuse counseling, campus ministries, career counseling, services for economically disadvantaged, student employment services, financial aid counseling, health services, minority student services, on-campus daycare, personal counseling, placement for graduates, women's services. **Physically disabled:** Services for visually, hearing impaired.

**Contact.** E-mail: info@umn.edu
Phone: (218) 281-8569 Toll-free number: (800) 862-6466
Fax: (218) 281-8575 ext. 369
Amber Evans-Dailey, Director of Admissions, University of Minnesota: Crookston, 2900 University Avenue, Crookston, MN 56716-5001

## University of Minnesota: Duluth
### Duluth, Minnesota
www.d.umn.edu                                    CB code: 6873

- Public 4-year university
- Residential campus in small city
- 9,184 degree-seeking undergraduates: 5% part-time, 47% women, 1% African American, 3% Asian American, 1% Hispanic American, 1% Native American, 1% international
- 1,091 degree-seeking graduate students
- 70% of applicants admitted
- SAT or ACT with writing required
- 51% graduate within 6 years; 16% enter graduate study

**General.** Founded in 1947. Regionally accredited. All buildings at UMD are connected by a unique skyway and concourse system. **Degrees:** 1,627 bachelor's awarded; master's, doctoral offered. **ROTC:** Air Force. **Location:** 130 miles from Minneapolis-St. Paul. **Calendar:** Semester, extensive summer session. **Full-time faculty:** 415 total; 94% have terminal degrees, 19% minority, 39% women. **Part-time faculty:** 149 total; 27% have terminal degrees, 8% minority, 48% women. **Class size:** 37% < 20, 48% 20-39, 6% 40-49, 5% 50-99, 5% >100. **Special facilities:** Planetarium, visual imaging laboratory, Tweed Museum of Art.

**Freshman class profile.** 7,653 applied, 5,393 admitted, 2,240 enrolled.

| Mid 50% test scores | | Rank in top tenth: | 15% |
|---|---|---|---|
| ACT composite: | 20-24 | Return as sophomores: | 79% |
| GPA 3.50 or higher: | 33% | Out-of-state: | 13% |
| GPA 3.0-3.49: | 42% | Live on campus: | 90% |
| GPA 2.0-2.99: | 25% | International: | 1% |
| Rank in top quarter: | 41% | | |

**Basis for selection.** 65th percentile of high school class or above typically admitted. Test scores are required. Students ranking between the 40th and 64th percentile are selectively admitted based on test scores and academic preparation. Essays or personal statements considered in an admissions decision appeals process. Audition required for music students. **Learning Disabled:** Students must meet our general admission policy.

**High school preparation.** 15 units required. Required units include English 4, mathematics 3, social studies 2, history 1, science 3 and foreign language 2. One year of physical and biological science required; mathematics sequence includes algebra, geometry, and higher algebra. Visual and performing arts courses and computer skills courses strongly recommended.

**2007-2008 Annual costs.** Tuition/fees: $9,600; $19,227 out-of-state. Room/board: $5,904. Books/supplies: $1,100. Personal expenses: $1,600.

**Financial aid. Non-need-based:** Scholarships awarded for academics, athletics, ROTC.

**Application procedures. Admission:** Priority date 2/1; deadline 8/1 (receipt date). $35 fee. Application may be submitted online. Admission notification on a rolling basis beginning on or about 9/15. Must reply by May 1 or within 4 week(s) if notified thereafter. Applications are accepted on a space available basis after 2/01. **Financial aid:** Priority date 3/31; no closing date. FAFSA required. Applicants notified on a rolling basis starting 3/1; must reply within 2 week(s) of notification.

**Academics. Special study options:** Cross-registration, distance learning, double major, dual enrollment of high school students, honors, independent study, internships, student-designed major, study abroad, teacher certification program. **Credit/placement by examination:** AP, CLEP, IB, ACT, institutional tests. **Support services:** Learning center, reduced course load, remedial instruction, study skills assistance, tutoring.

**Majors. Area/ethnic studies:** German, Native American, women's. **Biology:** General, biochemistry, cell/histology, molecular. **Business:** Accounting, actuarial science, business admin, finance, human resources, management information systems. **Communications:** General. **Computer sciences:** General, computer science, information systems. **Conservation:** Environmental science, environmental studies. **Education:** Art, biology, chemistry, early childhood, elementary, English, French, German, health, mathematics, middle, music, physical, physics, science, secondary, social studies, Spanish. **Engineering:** Chemical, civil, computer, electrical, mechanical. **English:** English lit. **Foreign languages:** French, German, Spanish. **Health:** Athletic training, communication disorders, health care admin, predental, premedicine, prepharmacy, preveterinary. **History:** General. **Legal studies:** Prelaw. **Math:** General, statistics. **Parks/recreation:** General, exercise sciences. **Philosophy/religion:** Philosophy. **Physical sciences:** Chemistry, geology, physics. **Psychology:** General. **Social sciences:** Anthropology, criminology, economics, geography, political science, sociology, urban studies. **Visual/performing arts:** Acting, art, art history/conservation, digital art, dramatic, graphic design, jazz, music pedagogy, music performance, musical theater, studio arts, theater design.

**Most popular majors.** Biology 7%, business/marketing 20%, education 14%, engineering/engineering technologies 7%, psychology 8%, social sciences 12%, visual/performing arts 6%.

**Computing on campus.** PC or laptop required. 465 workstations in library, computer center. Dormitories wired for high-speed internet access and linked to campus network. Commuter students can connect to campus network. Online course registration, online library, helpline, repair service, student web hosting, wireless network available.

**Student life. Freshman orientation:** Mandatory, $40 fee. Preregistration for classes offered. Academic advisement and registration (orientation) is held in March and April of student's senior year of high school. **Policies:** Smoke and alcohol free campus. **Housing:** Coed dorms, single-sex dorms, apartments, substance-free housing available. $200 partly refundable deposit, deadline 5/1. Housing facilities are fully accessible to persons with physical disabilities. All facilities are smoke free. **Activities:** Bands, campus ministries, choral groups, dance, drama, film society, international student organizations, literary magazine, music ensembles, musical theater, opera, radio station, student government, student newspaper, symphony orchestra, Intervarsity Christian Fellowship, Minnesota Public Interest Research Group, Anishinabe club, Black student association, Queer and Allied Students Union, Hispanic organization, Southeast Asian association, Students Engaged in Rewarding Volunteer Experiences.

**Athletics.** NCAA. **Intercollegiate:** Baseball M, basketball, cross-country, football (tackle) M, ice hockey, soccer W, softball W, tennis W, track and field, volleyball W. **Intramural:** Badminton, basketball, bowling, football (non-tackle), golf, ice hockey, sailing, skiing, soccer, softball, table tennis, tennis, track and field, volleyball, water polo. **Team name:** Bulldogs.

**Student services.** Campus ministries, career counseling, student employment services, financial aid counseling, health services, minority student services, on-campus daycare, personal counseling, placement for graduates, veterans' counselor, women's services. **Physically disabled:** Services for visually, speech, hearing impaired.

**Contact.** E-mail: umdadmis@d.umn.edu
Phone: (218) 726-7171 Toll-free number: (800) 232-1339
Fax: (218) 726-7040
Beth Esselstrom, Director of Admissions, University of Minnesota: Duluth, 25 Solon Campus Center, Duluth, MN 55812-3000

## University of Minnesota: Morris
### Morris, Minnesota
www.morris.umn.edu                                    CB code: 6890

- Public 4-year university and liberal arts college
- Residential campus in small town
- 1,686 degree-seeking undergraduates
- 76% of applicants admitted
- SAT or ACT with writing required
- 61% graduate within 6 years

**General.** Founded in 1959. Regionally accredited. **Degrees:** 317 bachelor's awarded. **Location:** 150 miles from Minneapolis-St. Paul; 100 miles from Fargo, North Dakota. **Calendar:** Semester, limited summer session. **Full-time faculty:** 119 total; 94% have terminal degrees, 15% minority, 43% women. **Part-time faculty:** 56 total; 20% have terminal degrees, 5% minority, 55% women. **Class size:** 69% < 20, 25% 20-39, 3% 40-49, 3% 50-99. **Special facilities:** Tropical conservatory, prairie gate press, historical center, experiment station, USDA soil laboratory, center for small towns, observatory.

**Freshman class profile.** 1,145 applied, 868 admitted, 363 enrolled.

| Mid 50% test scores | | | |
|---|---|---|---|
| SAT critical reading: | 520-700 | Rank in top quarter: | 60% |
| SAT math: | 560-680 | Rank in top tenth: | 32% |
| SAT writing: | 520-650 | Return as sophomores: | 84% |
| ACT composite: | 21-27 | Out-of-state: | 13% |
| | | Live on campus: | 98% |

**Basis for selection.** Admission based on four primary factors: high school performance, ACT/SAT scores, extra-curricular involvement/leadership experience/honors. Interview recommended. Audition required for music students receiving scholarships. **Homeschooled:** Submit porfolio of works studied.

**High school preparation.** 17 units recommended. Recommended units include English 4, mathematics 3, social studies 4, history 4, science 3 (laboratory 2) and foreign language 2. Science units must include 1 biological science and 1 physical science.

**2007-2008 Annual costs.** Tuition/fees: $9,331; $9,331 out-of-state. Tuition same for both In-state and out-of-state students except for Wisconsin residents, who pay lower rate due to reciprocity agreement. Room/board: $6,370. Books/supplies: $600. Personal expenses: $1,200.

**Financial aid. Non-need-based:** Scholarships awarded for academics, alumni affiliation, leadership, minority status, music/drama. **Additional information:** Land-grant program waiving tuition for Native Americans.

**Application procedures. Admission:** Priority date 12/15; deadline 3/15 (postmark date). $35 fee, may be waived for applicants with need. Application may be submitted online. Admission notification on a rolling basis beginning on or about 9/1. Must reply by May 1 or within 2 week(s) if notified thereafter. **Financial aid:** Priority date 3/1; no closing date. FAFSA required. Applicants notified on a rolling basis starting 3/1; must reply within 3 week(s) of notification.

**Academics.** Academic opportunities that allow students to assist faculty in research or teaching endeavors and receive a stipend or expense allowances include: The Undergraduate Research Opportunities Program, The Morris Academic Partnership, The Minority Mentorship Program, The Morris Administrative Internship, and The Student Internship Program. **Special study options:** Combined bachelor's/graduate degree, cooperative education, cross-registration, distance learning, double major, exchange student, honors, independent study, internships, liberal arts/career combination, New York semester, semester at sea, student-designed major, study abroad, teacher certification program, United Nations semester, urban semester, Washington semester. **Credit/placement by examination:** AP, CLEP, IB, ACT, institutional tests. No limit for credit by exam, but the credit awarded does not count as resident credit; must have 30 resident credits. **Support services:** Learning center, pre-admission summer program, reduced course load, study skills assistance, tutoring, writing center.

**Majors. Area/ethnic studies:** European, Latin American, Native American, women's. **Biology:** General. **Business:** Management science. **Communications:** General. **Computer sciences:** Computer science. **Conservation:** Environmental studies. **Education:** Elementary. **English:** English lit. **Foreign languages:** French, German, Spanish. **History:** General. **Liberal arts:** Humanities. **Math:** General, statistics. **Philosophy/religion:** Philosophy. **Physical sciences:** Chemistry, geology, physics. **Psychology:** General. **Public administration:** Social work. **Social sciences:** Anthropology, economics, political science, sociology. **Visual/performing arts:** Art history/conservation, dramatic, music performance, studio arts.

**Computing on campus.** 220 workstations in dormitories, library, computer center, student center. Dormitories wired for high-speed internet access and linked to campus network. Commuter students can connect to campus network. Online course registration, online library, helpline, repair service, wireless network available.

**Student life. Freshman orientation:** Mandatory. Preregistration for classes offered. Held 4 days prior to fall semester. **Housing:** Guaranteed on-campus for all undergraduates. Coed dorms, special housing for disabled, substance-free housing available. $200 deposit, deadline 8/1. **Activities:** Bands, choral groups, dance, drama, film society, literary magazine, music ensembles, musical theater, radio station, student government, student newspaper, symphony orchestra, TV station, Amnesty International, Big Friend/Little Friend, Campus Aglow Outreach, E-Quality, Habitat for Humanity, Intervarsity Christian Fellowship, Minnesota Public Interest Research Group (MPIRG), Morris Campus Student Association (MCSA), Positive Spirituality, Women of Color Association.

**Athletics.** NCAA. **Intercollegiate:** Baseball M, basketball, cross-country, diving W, football (tackle) M, golf, soccer, softball W, swimming W, tennis, track and field, volleyball W. **Intramural:** Baseball, basketball, bowling, field hockey, football (non-tackle), ice hockey, softball, triathlon, volleyball. **Team name:** Cougars.

**Student services.** Alcohol/substance abuse counseling, career counseling, student employment services, financial aid counseling, health services, minority student services, personal counseling, placement for graduates, veterans' counselor, women's services. **Physically disabled:** Services for visually, speech, hearing impaired. **Learning disabled:** Comprehensive services available.

**Contact.** E-mail: admissions@morris.umn.edu
Phone: (320) 589-6035 Toll-free number: (888) 866-3382
Fax: (320) 589-1673
Director of Admissions, University of Minnesota: Morris, 600 East 4th Street, Morris, MN 56267

---

## University of Minnesota: Twin Cities

Minneapolis, Minnesota  **CB member**
www.umn.edu/tc  **CB code: 6874**

- Public 4-year university
- Residential campus in very large city
- 28,703 degree-seeking undergraduates: 9% part-time, 53% women, 5% African American, 10% Asian American, 2% Hispanic American, 1% Native American, 2% international
- 17,810 degree-seeking graduate students
- 57% of applicants admitted
- SAT or ACT with writing required
- 61% graduate within 6 years

**General.** Founded in 1851. Regionally accredited. Campuses in Minneapolis and St. Paul. **Degrees:** 6,618 bachelor's awarded; master's, doctoral, first professional offered. **ROTC:** Army, Naval, Air Force. **Calendar:** Semester, extensive summer session. **Full-time faculty:** 1,760 total; 88% have terminal degrees, 14% minority, 33% women. **Part-time faculty:** 315 total; 70% have terminal degrees, 6% minority, 28% women. **Class size:** 43% < 20, 36% 20-39, 5% 40-49, 10% 50-99, 6% >100. **Special facilities:** West bank arts quarter, natural history museum, showboat, rehabilitation museum, arboretum, concert hall.

**Freshman class profile.** 26,097 applied, 14,823 admitted, 5,280 enrolled.

| Mid 50% test scores | | | |
|---|---|---|---|
| SAT critical reading: | 540-680 | Rank in top tenth: | 44% |
| SAT math: | 580-700 | Return as sophomores: | 88% |
| SAT writing: | 530-660 | Out-of-state: | 32% |
| ACT composite: | 24-29 | Live on campus: | 78% |
| Rank in top quarter: | 84% | International: | 3% |

**Basis for selection.** Successful completion of a college preparatory curriculum, high school rank percentile, grade point average, ACT or SAT scores, and strength of curriculum very important. Writing tests required. Results considered as secondary admission factor.

**High school preparation.** 16 units required. Required units include English 4, mathematics 3, social studies 3, history 1, science 3 and foreign language 2. 1 year of visual and/or performing arts also required. Management, biological sciences, and technology applicants require a fourth year of mathematics and 3 years of science including 1 year each of biological science, chemistry, and physics.

**2007-2008 Annual costs.** Tuition/fees: $9,885; $21,515 out-of-state. Reported costs represent College of Liberal Arts and include annual technology/collegiate fee of an average of $224. Mandatory technology/other fees may vary by program. Room/board: $7,062.

**2007-2008 Financial aid.** All financial aid based on need. 4,056 full-time freshmen applied for aid; 2,701 were judged to have need; 2,671 of these received aid. Average need met was 87%. Average scholarship/grant was $7,751; average loan $7,036. 43% of total undergraduate aid awarded as scholarships/grants, 57% as loans/jobs.

**Application procedures. Admission:** Priority date 12/15; no deadline. $45 fee, may be waived for applicants with need. Application may be submitted online. Admission notification on a rolling basis. Must reply by May 1 or within 2 week(s) if notified thereafter. **Financial aid:** Priority date 3/1; no closing date. FAFSA, institutional form required. Applicants notified on a rolling basis starting 2/15.

**Academics.** Four year graduation guarantee offered. **Special study options:** Accelerated study, combined bachelor's/graduate degree, cooperative education, cross-registration, distance learning, double major, dual enrollment of high school students, ESL, exchange student, external degree, honors, independent study, internships, liberal arts/career combination, student-designed major, study abroad, teacher certification program. Qualified undergraduates may take graduate-level classes. **Credit/placement by examination:** AP, CLEP, IB, SAT, ACT, institutional tests. **Support services:** Learning center, pre-admission summer program, reduced course load, remedial instruction, study skills assistance, tutoring, writing center.

**Majors. Agriculture:** Animal sciences, business, economics, food science. **Architecture:** Architecture, environmental design, landscape. **Area/ethnic studies:** African, African-American, American, East Asian, European, Hispanic-American/Latino/Chicano, Latin American, Native American, Near/Middle Eastern, Russian/Slavic, women's. **Biology:** General, bacteriology, biochemistry, biostatistics, cell/histology, ecology. **Business:** Accounting, actuarial science, business admin, human resources, insurance, international, labor relations, logistics, management information systems, marketing, sales/distribution. **Communications:** Journalism. **Computer sciences:** Computer science, networking. **Conservation:** General, fisheries, forest resources, forestry, wildlife. **Construction:** Maintenance. **Education:** Agricultural, art, business, early childhood, elementary, foundations, mathematics, music, physical, sales/marketing, technology/industrial arts. **Engineering:** Aerospace, agricultural, chemical, civil, computer, electrical, geological, materials, materials science, mechanical. **English:** English lit, speech/rhetoric. **Family/consumer sciences:** General, clothing/textiles, family studies, food/nutrition, housing. **Foreign languages:** General, ancient Greek, Chinese, classics, comparative lit, French, German, Hebrew, Italian, Japanese, Latin, linguistics, Portuguese, Russian, Scandinavian, Spanish. **Health:** Audiology/speech pathology, dental hygiene, music therapy, nurse anesthetist, nursing (RN), predental, premedicine, prepharmacy, preveterinary. **History:** General. **Interdisciplinary:** Biological/physical sciences, nutrition sciences. **Legal studies:** Prelaw. **Liberal arts:** Arts/sciences. **Math:** General, statistics. **Parks/recreation:** General. **Personal/culinary services:** Mortuary science. **Philosophy/religion:** Judaic, philosophy, religion. **Physical sciences:** Astronomy, astrophysics, chemistry, geology, geophysics, physics. **Psychology:** General. **Social sciences:** Anthropology, applied economics, criminology, econometrics, economics, geography, international relations, political science, sociology, urban studies. **Visual/performing arts:** Art history/conservation, commercial/advertising art, dance, design, dramatic, fashion design, film/cinema, interior design, music performance. **Other:** Bio-based products engineering.

**Most popular majors.** Biology 8%, business/marketing 9%, communications/journalism 6%, engineering/engineering technologies 10%, English 7%, psychology 7%, social sciences 12%, visual/performing arts 6%.

**Computing on campus.** Dormitories wired for high-speed internet access and linked to campus network. Commuter students can connect to campus network. Online course registration, online library, helpline, repair service, student web hosting, wireless network available.

**Student life. Freshman orientation:** Mandatory. **Housing:** Guaranteed on-campus for freshmen. Coed dorms, special housing for disabled, apartments, cooperative housing, fraternity/sorority housing, substance-free housing available. $100 fully refundable deposit, deadline 5/1. Honors housing available. 24 living and learning communities. **Activities:** Bands, choral groups, dance, drama, film society, international student organizations, literary magazine, music ensembles, musical theater, opera, radio station, student government, student newspaper, symphony orchestra, TV station, 600 student-run organizations.

**Athletics.** NCAA. **Intercollegiate:** Baseball, basketball, cheerleading, cross-country, diving, football (tackle), golf, gymnastics, ice hockey, rowing (crew) W, soccer W, softball W, swimming, tennis, track and field, volleyball W, wrestling M. **Intramural:** Badminton, baseball, basketball, bowling, fencing, football (tackle) M, golf, gymnastics, handball, ice hockey, judo, lacrosse, racquetball, rugby, sailing, skiing, soccer, softball, squash, swimming, synchronized swimming, tennis, volleyball, water polo, wrestling M. **Team name:** Gophers.

**Student services.** Adult student services, alcohol/substance abuse counseling, campus ministries, career counseling, services for economically disadvantaged, student employment services, financial aid counseling, health services, legal services, minority student services, on-campus daycare, personal counseling, placement for graduates, veterans' counselor, women's services. **Physically disabled:** Services for visually, speech, hearing impaired.

**Contact.** Phone: (612) 625-2008 Toll-free number: (800) 752-1000 Fax: (612) 626-1693
Wayne Sigler, Director of Admissions, University of Minnesota: Twin Cities, 240 Williamson Hall, 231 Pillsbury Drive SE, Minneapolis, MN 55455-0115

## University of St. Thomas
**Saint Paul, Minnesota**
www.stthomas.edu

CB member
CB code: 6110

- Private 4-year university and liberal arts college affiliated with Roman Catholic Church
- Commuter campus in very large city

- 5,939 degree-seeking undergraduates: 5% part-time, 49% women, 3% African American, 4% Asian American, 3% Hispanic American, 1% international
- 4,558 degree-seeking graduate students
- 80% of applicants admitted
- SAT or ACT (ACT writing optional), application essay required
- 71% graduate within 6 years

**General.** Founded in 1885. Regionally accredited. **Degrees:** 1,124 bachelor's awarded; master's, doctoral, first professional offered. **ROTC:** Army, Naval, Air Force. **Location:** 5 miles from downtown. **Calendar:** 4-1-4, limited summer session. **Class size:** 38% < 20, 59% 20-39, 1% 40-49, 2% 50-99, less than 1% >100.

**Freshman class profile.** 4,864 applied, 3,913 admitted, 1,315 enrolled.

| Mid 50% test scores | | Rank in top quarter: | 51% |
|---|---|---|---|
| SAT critical reading: | 520-640 | Rank in top tenth: | 21% |
| SAT math: | 520-640 | Return as sophomores: | 88% |
| ACT composite: | 23-27 | Out-of-state: | 21% |
| GPA 3.50 or higher: | 60% | Live on campus: | 92% |
| GPA 3.0-3.49: | 34% | International: | 1% |
| GPA 2.0-2.99: | 6% | | |

**Basis for selection.** Admissions decision by formula using a combination of high school rank and standardized test scores. Applicants who don't meet these conditions are given individual review. Interview recommended. **Homeschooled:** Submit course descriptions.

**High school preparation.** Required and recommended units include English 4, mathematics 3-4, social studies 2, science 2 and foreign language 4. Some departments may require 3 units social studies (includes 1 geography), 1 US history, 1 unit visual or performing arts.

**2008-2009 Annual costs.** Tuition/fees: $27,822. Room/board: $7,612.

**2007-2008 Financial aid. Need-based:** 960 full-time freshmen applied for aid; 477 were judged to have need; 477 of these received aid. Average need met was 82%. Average scholarship/grant was $13,690; average loan $3,766. 61% of total undergraduate aid awarded as scholarships/grants, 39% as loans/jobs. **Non-need-based:** Awarded to 1,173 full-time undergraduates, including 466 freshmen. Scholarships awarded for academics, music/drama, ROTC.

**Application procedures. Admission:** No deadline. No application fee. Application may be submitted online. Admission notification on a rolling basis. Applications accepted until class is full; reviewed starting 10/01. **Financial aid:** Priority date 4/1; no closing date. FAFSA required. Applicants notified on a rolling basis starting 3/1; must reply within 3 week(s) of notification.

**Academics. Special study options:** Cross-registration, double major, exchange student, honors, independent study, internships, semester at sea, student-designed major, study abroad, teacher certification program, urban semester, Washington semester. Renaissance Program in which students major in a liberal arts area, take career-oriented classes as a minor, and after graduation can take additional undergraduate business courses free of charge. **Credit/placement by examination:** AP, CLEP, IB, institutional tests. Typically credit by exam cap be used for only 1/8 of a student's courses. CLEP credit awarded if student scores at 50th percentile or above for those examinations that have been approved by the department in which the subject is usually taught. **Support services:** Learning center, reduced course load, study skills assistance, tutoring, writing center.

**Majors. Area/ethnic studies:** Women's. **Biology:** General, biochemistry. **Business:** Accounting, actuarial science, business admin, entrepreneurial studies, finance, human resources, international, marketing, operations, real estate. **Communications:** General, broadcast journalism, journalism, media studies. **Computer sciences:** General. **Conservation:** Environmental science, environmental studies. **Education:** Chemistry, drama/dance, elementary, English, foreign languages, French, German, health, mathematics, middle, music, physical, physics, science, secondary, social studies, Spanish. **Engineering:** General, electrical, mechanical. **English:** Creative writing, English lit. **Foreign languages:** Classics, comparative lit, French, German, Latin, Spanish. **Health:** Predental, preveterinary, public health ed. **History:** General. **Interdisciplinary:** Classical/archaeology, peace/conflict. **Legal studies:** Prelaw. **Liberal arts:** Arts/sciences. **Math:** General. **Philosophy/religion:** Philosophy, religion. **Physical sciences:** Chemistry, geology, physics. **Psychology:** General. **Public administration:** Social work. **Social sciences:** General, criminology, econometrics, economics, geography, international economics, international relations, political science, sociology. **Theology:** Theology. **Visual/performing arts:** Art history/conservation, dramatic, music performance. **Other:** Behavioral Neuroscience, Formation, Pre-Physical Therapy.

**Most popular majors.** Business/marketing 40%, communications/journalism 9%, education 7%, philosophy/religious studies 7%, social sciences 10%.

**Computing on campus.** Dormitories wired for high-speed internet access and linked to campus network. Commuter students can connect to campus network. Online course registration, online library, helpline, student web hosting, wireless network available.

**Student life. Freshman orientation:** Mandatory. Preregistration for classes offered. Held 2 days over summer; students and parents can stay overnight in the dorms. Separate programs for students and parents. **Housing:** Single-sex dorms, apartments available. $200 fully refundable deposit, deadline 5/1. Chemical-free lifestyle, women in science house, first year experience houses, Catholic women's and Catholic men's communities. **Activities:** Bands, choral groups, dance, drama, literary magazine, music ensembles, radio station, student government, student newspaper, Globally Minded Student Association, campus ministry, Volunteers in Action, HANA, Student Coalition for Social Justice, African Nations Students Association, Fellowship of Christian Athletes, St. Paul's Outreach student organization, theology club, Black Empowerment Student Alliance.

**Athletics.** NCAA. **Intercollegiate:** Baseball M, basketball, cross-country, football (tackle) M, golf, ice hockey, soccer, softball W, swimming, tennis, track and field, volleyball W. **Intramural:** Basketball, football (non-tackle), racquetball, soccer, softball, tennis, volleyball. **Team name:** Tommies.

**Student services.** Adult student services, alcohol/substance abuse counseling, campus ministries, career counseling, student employment services, financial aid counseling, health services, minority student services, on-campus daycare, personal counseling, veterans' counselor, women's services. **Physically disabled:** Services for visually, speech, hearing impaired. **Learning disabled:** Comprehensive services available.

**Contact.**  E-mail: admissions@stthomas.edu
Phone: (651) 962-6150 Toll-free number: (800) 328-6819 ext. 26150
Fax: (651) 962-6160
Marla Friederichs, Associate Vice President for Enrollment Management, University of St. Thomas, 2115 Summit Avenue, 32F, St. Paul, MN 55105-1096

## Walden University
**Minneapolis, Minnesota**
**www.waldenu.edu**

- For-profit two-year upper-division virtual university
- Large city
- 100% of applicants admitted

**General.** Walden University is a fully online institution offering programs in a variety of disciplines and degree levels, from undergraduate to doctorate. **Degrees:** 136 bachelor's awarded; master's, doctoral offered. **Calendar:** Differs by program, extensive summer session. **Full-time faculty:** 556 total. **Part-time faculty:** 327 total.

**Student profile.** 1,369 degree-seeking undergraduates, 27,838 degree-seeking graduate students. 708 applied as first time-transfer students, 708 admitted, 704 enrolled.

| | | | |
|---|---|---|---|
| Women: | 58% | Hispanic American: | 3% |
| African American: | 13% | International: | 36% |
| Asian American: | 1% | Part-time: | 94% |

**2008-2009 Annual costs.** Tuition/fees (projected): $11,520.

**Financial aid.** All financial aid based on need.

**Application procedures. Admission:** Rolling admission. $50 fee. Application may be submitted online. **Financial aid:** No deadline. Applicants notified on a rolling basis.

**Academics. Special study options:** Distance learning, dual enrollment of high school students, internships, student-designed major, teacher certification program. **Credit/placement by examination:** CLEP.

**Majors. Business:** Business admin, finance, human resources, international, knowledge management, management information systems, marketing.

**Computing on campus.** PC or laptop required. Commuter students can connect to campus network. Online library, helpline available.

**Student life. Activities:** Student newspaper.

**Student services.** Career counseling, financial aid counseling, veterans' counselor. **Physically disabled:** Services for visually, speech, hearing impaired. **Learning disabled:** Comprehensive services available.

**Contact.**  E-mail: admissions@waldenu.edu
Phone: (866) 492-5336 Toll-free number: (866) 492-5336
Dawn Wolff, Director of Admissions, Walden University, 650 South Exeter Street 8th Floor, Baltimore, MD 21202

## Winona State University
**Winona, Minnesota**
**www.winona.edu**                                  **CB code: 6680**

- Public 4-year university
- Residential campus in large town
- 7,443 degree-seeking undergraduates: 7% part-time, 62% women, 1% African American, 2% Asian American, 1% Hispanic American, 3% international
- 344 degree-seeking graduate students
- 82% of applicants admitted
- SAT and SAT Subject Tests or ACT (ACT writing optional) required
- 54% graduate within 6 years

**General.** Founded in 1858. Regionally accredited. **Degrees:** 1,548 bachelor's, 30 associate awarded; master's offered. **ROTC:** Army. **Location:** 90 miles from Minneapolis-St. Paul. **Calendar:** Semester, extensive summer session. **Full-time faculty:** 320 total. **Part-time faculty:** 130 total. **Class size:** 26% < 20, 60% 20-39, 5% 40-49, 6% 50-99, 2% >100.

**Freshman class profile.** 5,475 applied, 4,483 admitted, 1,735 enrolled.

| Mid 50% test scores | | | |
|---|---|---|---|
| SAT critical reading: | 460-580 | Return as sophomores: | 71.5% |
| SAT math: | 500-610 | Out-of-state: | 41% |
| ACT composite: | 21-24 | Live on campus: | 91% |
| Rank in top quarter: | 34% | International: | 1% |
| Rank in top tenth: | 10% | Fraternities: | 2% |
| | | Sororities: | 2% |

**Basis for selection.** 16 units of college prep high school courses and rank in top half of class or SAT combined score of 1000 (exclusive of Writing) or ACT composite score of 21 required for regular admission. Interview required for academically marginal students.

**High school preparation.** 16 units required. Required units include English 4, mathematics 3, social studies 2, history 1, science 3 (laboratory 3), foreign language 2 and academic electives 1. One English unit may be speech.

**2007-2008 Annual costs.** Tuition/fees: $6,336; $10,798 out-of-state. Fees include mandatory laptop lease for full-time students. Room/board: $6,110. Books/supplies: $500. Personal expenses: $600.

**2006-2007 Financial aid. Need-based:** 1,319 full-time freshmen applied for aid; 853 were judged to have need; 830 of these received aid. Average need met was 36%. Average scholarship/grant was $3,856; average loan $2,334. 37% of total undergraduate aid awarded as scholarships/grants, 63% as loans/jobs. **Non-need-based:** Awarded to 2,011 full-time undergraduates, including 797 freshmen. Scholarships awarded for academics, alumni affiliation, art, athletics, leadership, minority status, music/drama, ROTC, state residency.

**Application procedures. Admission:** Priority date 3/1; deadline 7/30 (postmark date). $20 fee. Application may be submitted online. Admission notification on a rolling basis beginning on or about 8/15. **Financial aid:** Priority date 3/1; no closing date. FAFSA required. Applicants notified on a rolling basis starting 5/1; must reply within 3 week(s) of notification.

**Academics. Special study options:** Accelerated study, cross-registration, distance learning, double major, dual enrollment of high school students, external degree, independent study, internships, student-designed major, study abroad, teacher certification program. **Credit/placement by examination:** AP, CLEP, IB, institutional tests. **Support services:** Learning center, reduced course load, study skills assistance, tutoring, writing center.

**Majors. Biology:** General, cell/histology, molecular. **Business:** General, accounting, administrative services, business admin, finance, human resources, management information systems, management science, managerial economics, market research, office/clerical, operations. **Communications:** General, advertising, broadcast journalism, journalism, media studies, photojournalism, public relations. **Communications technology:** General. **Computer sciences:** General, applications programming, computer science, information technology, programming. **Conservation:** General, environmental studies. **Education:** General, art, bilingual, biology, business, chemistry, curriculum, drama/dance, early childhood, elementary, emotionally handicapped, English, foreign languages, French, German, health, health occupations, history, learning disabled, mathematics, mentally handicapped, middle, multi-level teacher, multiple handicapped, music, physical, physically handicapped, physics, reading, science, secondary, social science, social studies, Spanish, special, speech. **Engineering:** Materials, materials science, polymer. **English:** Composition, English lit, speech/rhetoric. **Foreign languages:** General, French, German, Spanish. **Health:** Athletic training, clinical lab technology, cytotechnology, health care admin, nursing (RN), predental, premedicine, preop/surgical nursing, prepharmacy, preveterinary, public health ed, recreational therapy. **History:** General. **Interdisciplinary:** Biological/physical sciences. **Legal studies:** Paralegal, prelaw. **Liberal arts:** Arts/sciences. **Math:** General, applied, statistics. **Parks/recreation:** General, exercise sciences, facilities management, health/fitness, sports admin. **Physical sciences:** Chemistry, geology, physics, planetary, polymer chemistry. **Protective services:** Corrections, criminal justice, law enforcement admin, police science, security services. **Psychology:** General. **Public administration:** General, social work. **Social sciences:** General, economics, political science, sociology, urban studies. **Visual/performing arts:** General, art, commercial/advertising art, design, dramatic, music management, music performance, studio arts.

**Most popular majors.** Business/marketing 23%, education 18%, health sciences 11%.

**Computing on campus.** PC or laptop required. 1,600 workstations in dormitories, library, computer center, student center. Dormitories wired for high-speed internet access and linked to campus network. Commuter students can connect to campus network. Online course registration, helpline, repair service, student web hosting available.

**Student life. Freshman orientation:** Available, $25 fee. Preregistration for classes offered. **Housing:** Guaranteed on-campus for freshmen. Coed dorms, single-sex dorms, special housing for disabled, apartments available. $150 deposit, deadline 2/4. Residence hall with classrooms and faculty offices. **Activities:** Bands, choral groups, dance, drama, film society, literary magazine, music ensembles, musical theater, radio station, student government, student newspaper, symphony orchestra, TV station, over 130 organizations.

**Athletics.** NCAA. **Intercollegiate:** Baseball M, basketball, cross-country, football (tackle) M, golf, gymnastics W, soccer W, softball W, tennis, track and field W, volleyball W. **Intramural:** Archery, badminton, baseball M, basketball, bowling, cross-country, diving, equestrian, fencing, field hockey, golf, gymnastics W, handball, ice hockey, racquetball, rifle, rugby, skiing, soccer, softball, swimming, table tennis, tennis, track and field, volleyball, wrestling M. **Team name:** Warriors.

**Student services.** Adult student services, alcohol/substance abuse counseling, campus ministries, career counseling, services for economically disadvantaged, student employment services, financial aid counseling, health services, legal services, minority student services, on-campus daycare, personal counseling, placement for graduates, veterans' counselor, women's services. **Physically disabled:** Services for visually, speech, hearing impaired.

**Contact.** E-mail: admissions@winona.edu
Phone: (507) 457-5100 Toll-free number: (800) 342-5978
Fax: (507) 457-5620
Carl Stange, Director of Admissions, Winona State University, Office of Admissions, Winona, MN 55987

# Mississippi

## Alcorn State University

**Alcorn State, Mississippi**
www.alcorn.edu

**CB member**
**CB code: 1008**

- Public 4-year university and agricultural college
- Residential campus in rural community
- 3,004 degree-seeking undergraduates: 10% part-time, 65% women, 91% African American, 2% international
- 664 degree-seeking graduate students
- 59% of applicants admitted
- SAT or ACT (ACT writing optional), application essay, interview required
- 43% graduate within 6 years; 51% enter graduate study

**General.** Founded in 1871. Regionally accredited. School of Nursing is located in Natchez. **Degrees:** 399 bachelor's, 33 associate awarded; master's offered. **ROTC:** Army. **Location:** 40 miles from Natchez, 45 miles from Vicksburg. **Calendar:** Semester, limited summer session. **Full-time faculty:** 172 total; 62% have terminal degrees, 77% minority, 42% women. **Part-time faculty:** 47 total; 64% have terminal degrees, 66% minority, 70% women. **Class size:** 43% < 20, 43% 20-39, 7% 40-49, 6% 50-99. **Special facilities:** Nature trails, lakes.

**Freshman class profile.** 2,804 applied, 1,646 admitted, 514 enrolled.

| Mid 50% test scores | | | |
|---|---|---|---|
| SAT critical reading: | 390-460 | GPA 3.0-3.49: | 29% |
| SAT math: | 410-470 | GPA 2.0-2.99: | 49% |
| ACT composite: | 16-20 | Return as sophomores: | 63% |
| GPA 3.50 or higher: | 17% | Out-of-state: | 24% |
| | | Live on campus: | 81% |

**Basis for selection.** Test scores, school achievement record important; specific academic units considered. Test score requirements depend upon high school GPA. Audition required for music majors. **Homeschooled:** Transcript of courses and grades, state high school equivalency certificate required.

**High school preparation.** 15.5 units required. Required and recommended units include English 4, mathematics 3, social studies 3, science 3 (laboratory 2), foreign language 1 and academic electives 2. One advanced elective must be in foreign language or world geography. Half unit in computer application also required.

**2007-2008 Annual costs.** Tuition/fees: $4,320; $9,816 out-of-state. Room/board: $4,880. Books/supplies: $1,345. Personal expenses: $2,257.

**2007-2008 Financial aid. Need-based:** 505 full-time freshmen applied for aid; 484 were judged to have need; 484 of these received aid. Average need met was 86%. Average scholarship/grant was $3,768; average loan $2,640. 52% of total undergraduate aid awarded as scholarships/grants, 48% as loans/jobs. **Non-need-based:** Awarded to 992 full-time undergraduates, including 416 freshmen. Scholarships awarded for academics, athletics, ROTC.

**Application procedures. Admission:** No deadline. No application fee. Application must be submitted on paper. Admission notification on a rolling basis. **Financial aid:** Priority date 4/1; no closing date. FAFSA, institutional form required. Applicants notified on a rolling basis starting 4/1; must reply within 4 week(s) of notification.

**Academics. Special study options:** Accelerated study, cooperative education, distance learning, double major, honors, independent study, internships, liberal arts/career combination, teacher certification program. **Credit/placement by examination:** AP, CLEP, SAT, ACT, institutional tests. 15 credit hours maximum toward associate degree, 30 toward bachelor's. Student must earn 12 hours at Alcorn State University before credit by examination may be recorded on the student's transript. **Support services:** Learning center, pre-admission summer program, reduced course load, remedial instruction, tutoring.

**Majors. Agriculture:** General, business, economics. **Biology:** General. **Business:** Accounting, business admin. **Communications:** Media studies. **Computer sciences:** General, LAN/WAN management. **Education:** Elementary, special. **Engineering technology:** Robotics. **English:** English lit. **Family/consumer sciences:** Child development, food/nutrition. **Health:** Athletic training, nursing (RN). **History:** General. **Liberal arts:** Arts/sciences. **Math:**

General. **Parks/recreation:** General. **Physical sciences:** Chemistry. **Protective services:** Criminal justice. **Psychology:** General, educational. **Social sciences:** Economics, political science, sociology. **Visual/performing arts:** Music performance.

**Most popular majors.** Agriculture 7%, biology 12%, business/marketing 11%, education 6%, health sciences 13%, liberal arts 20%.

**Computing on campus.** 500 workstations in library, computer center, student center. Dormitories wired for high-speed internet access and linked to campus network. Commuter students can connect to campus network. Online course registration, helpline available.

**Student life. Freshman orientation:** Mandatory. Preregistration for classes offered. Entrance and placement exams given. **Housing:** Guaranteed on-campus for all undergraduates. Single-sex dorms available. $75 fully refundable deposit. **Activities:** Bands, choral groups, dance, drama, music ensembles, radio station, student government, student newspaper, TV station, Baptist Student Union, Wesley Foundation, NAACP, Black History Month Society, Young Women's Christian Association, Adventist Youth Society.

**Athletics.** NCAA. **Intercollegiate:** Baseball M, basketball, cross-country, football (tackle) M, golf, soccer W, softball W, tennis, track and field, volleyball W. **Intramural:** Basketball. **Team name:** Braves.

**Student services.** Career counseling, student employment services, health services, on-campus daycare, personal counseling, placement for graduates, veterans' counselor.

**Contact.** E-mail: ebarnes@alcorn.edu
Phone: (601) 877-6147 Toll-free number: (800) 222-6790
Fax: (601) 877-6347
Emanuel Barnes, Director of Admissions and Recruiting, Alcorn State University, 1000 ASU Drive #300, Alcorn State, MS 39096-7500

## Belhaven College

**Jackson, Mississippi**
www.belhaven.edu

**CB code: 1055**

- Private 4-year liberal arts college affiliated with Presbyterian Church (USA)
- Commuter campus in large city
- 2,071 degree-seeking undergraduates: 4% part-time, 66% women, 35% African American, 3% Hispanic American, 1% international
- 360 degree-seeking graduate students
- 64% of applicants admitted
- SAT or ACT (ACT writing optional), application essay required
- 39% graduate within 6 years

**General.** Founded in 1883. Regionally accredited. **Degrees:** 373 bachelor's, 42 associate awarded; master's offered. **ROTC:** Army, Air Force. **Location:** 188 miles from New Orleans, 200 miles from Memphis, Tennessee. **Calendar:** Semester, extensive summer session. **Full-time faculty:** 73 total; 78% have terminal degrees, 38% women. **Part-time faculty:** 161 total; 35% have terminal degrees, 40% women. **Class size:** 72% < 20, 23% 20-39, 4% 40-49, less than 1% 50-99, less than 1% >100.

**Freshman class profile.** 1,159 applied, 736 admitted, 253 enrolled.

| Mid 50% test scores | | | |
|---|---|---|---|
| SAT critical reading: | 490-640 | Return as sophomores: | 69% |
| SAT math: | 470-570 | Out-of-state: | 65% |
| ACT composite: | 20-26 | Live on campus: | 82% |
| | | International: | 1% |

**Basis for selection.** Test scores, school record, recommendations, and character important. ACT and SAT scores used for placement in math and English. Interview recommended for art, dance, music, and theater majors; portfolio recommended for art majors. Audition required for dance, music, and theater majors.

**High school preparation.** 16 units required. Required units include English 4, mathematics 2, social studies 1, science 1, computer science 1 and academic electives 8.

**2008-2009 Annual costs.** Tuition/fees: $16,360. Room/board: $6,120. Books/supplies: $1,400.

**2007-2008 Financial aid. Need-based:** Average need met was 60%. Average scholarship/grant was $8,602; average loan $3,714. 36% of total undergraduate aid awarded as scholarships/grants, 64% as loans/jobs. **Non-need-based:** Scholarships awarded for academics, alumni affiliation, art, athletics, music/drama.

**Application procedures. Admission:** No deadline. $25 fee, may be waived for applicants with need. Application may be submitted online. Admission notification on a rolling basis. Accepted applicants must reply within 30 days after acceptance. **Financial aid:** Priority date 3/1; no closing date. FAFSA required. Applicants notified on a rolling basis starting 2/1.

**Academics. Special study options:** Accelerated study, combined bachelor's/graduate degree, distance learning, double major, dual enrollment of high school students, ESL, honors, independent study, internships, student-designed major, study abroad, teacher certification program, weekend college. **Credit/placement by examination:** AP, CLEP, IB, SAT, ACT, institutional tests. 30 credit hours maximum toward bachelor's degree. **Support services:** Learning center, reduced course load, remedial instruction, study skills assistance, tutoring, writing center.

**Majors. Biology:** General. **Business:** Accounting, business admin. **Communications:** General. **Computer sciences:** General, computer science. **Education:** Elementary. **English:** Creative writing, English lit. **Health:** Health care admin. **History:** General. **Interdisciplinary:** Global studies. **Liberal arts:** Humanities. **Math:** General. **Parks/recreation:** Exercise sciences, sports admin. **Philosophy/religion:** Philosophy. **Physical sciences:** Chemistry. **Psychology:** General. **Social sciences:** General, political science. **Theology:** Bible. **Visual/performing arts:** Art, arts management, dance, dramatic. **Other:** Sports ministry.

**Computing on campus.** 40 workstations in library, computer center. Dormitories wired for high-speed internet access and linked to campus network. Commuter students can connect to campus network. Online course registration, online library available.

**Student life. Freshman orientation:** Mandatory. Preregistration for classes offered. Held 5 days before fall classes begin. **Housing:** Guaranteed on-campus for all undergraduates. Single-sex dorms, substance-free housing available. $100 fully refundable deposit, deadline 6/1. **Activities:** Bands, campus ministries, choral groups, dance, drama, international student organizations, literary magazine, music ensembles, student government, student newspaper, Black Student Association, Baptist Student Union, Fellowship of Christian Athletes, Reformed University Fellowship, Student Missions Fellowship, Highland Players.

**Athletics.** NAIA. **Intercollegiate:** Baseball M, basketball, cross-country, football (tackle) M, golf, soccer, softball W, tennis, volleyball W. **Intramural:** Basketball, football (non-tackle), soccer W, softball, volleyball, weight lifting W. **Team name:** Blazers.

**Student services.** Adult student services, campus ministries, career counseling, student employment services, financial aid counseling, health services, personal counseling.

**Contact.** E-mail: admission@belhaven.edu
Phone: (601) 968-5940 Toll-free number: (800) 960-5940
Fax: (601) 968-8946
Suzanne Sullivan, Director of Admission, Belhaven College, 1500 Peachtree Street, Jackson, MS 39202

---

## Blue Mountain College
**Blue Mountain, Mississippi**
**www.bmc.edu**                                      CB code: 1066

- Private 4-year liberal arts college affiliated with Southern Baptist Convention
- Commuter campus in rural community
- 406 degree-seeking undergraduates: 18% part-time, 64% women, 12% African American
- 26 degree-seeking graduate students
- 50% of applicants admitted
- SAT or ACT (ACT writing optional) required
- 50% graduate within 6 years

**General.** Founded in 1873. Regionally accredited. **Degrees:** 85 bachelor's awarded; master's offered. **Location:** 69 miles from Memphis, Tennessee. **Calendar:** Semester, limited summer session. **Full-time faculty:** 25 total; 68% have terminal degrees, 52% women. **Part-time faculty:** 17 total; 47% have terminal degrees, 6% minority, 59% women. **Class size:** 73% < 20, 24% 20-39, less than 1% 40-49, 3% 50-99.

**Freshman class profile.** 197 applied, 99 admitted, 59 enrolled.

| Mid 50% test scores | | Rank in top tenth: | 19% |
|---|---|---|---|
| ACT composite: | 18-23 | End year in good standing: | 92% |
| GPA 3.50 or higher: | 55% | Return as sophomores: | 72% |
| GPA 3.0-3.49: | 25% | Out-of-state: | 24% |
| GPA 2.0-2.99: | 15% | Live on campus: | 81% |
| Rank in top quarter: | 50% | | |

**Basis for selection.** High school record, test scores, and individual motivation considered.

**High school preparation.** 15 units recommended. Recommended units include English 4, mathematics 3, social studies 1, history 2, science 3 (laboratory 2) and foreign language 2.

**2007-2008 Annual costs.** Tuition/fees: $8,020. Room/board: $3,800. Books/supplies: $750. Personal expenses: $701.

**2007-2008 Financial aid. Need-based:** 47% of total undergraduate aid awarded as scholarships/grants, 53% as loans/jobs. **Non-need-based:** Scholarships awarded for academics, alumni affiliation, athletics, religious affiliation, state residency.

**Application procedures. Admission:** No deadline. $10 fee, may be waived for applicants with need. Application may be submitted online. Admission notification on a rolling basis beginning on or about 10/1. **Financial aid:** Priority date 6/1, closing date 8/1. FAFSA, institutional form required. Applicants notified on a rolling basis starting 5/1; must reply within 2 week(s) of notification.

**Academics.** Coordinated academic program for men and women preparing for church-related vocations. **Special study options:** Accelerated study, combined bachelor's/graduate degree, double major, honors, internships, teacher certification program. **Credit/placement by examination:** AP, CLEP, SAT, ACT, institutional tests. 30 credit hours maximum toward bachelor's degree. **Support services:** Learning center, reduced course load, remedial instruction.

**Majors. Biology:** General. **Business:** Business admin. **Education:** Biology, elementary, English, mathematics, music, physical, science, social science, Spanish. **English:** English lit. **Foreign languages:** Spanish. **Health:** Clinical lab technology. **History:** General. **Math:** General. **Parks/recreation:** Health/fitness. **Psychology:** General. **Social sciences:** General. **Theology:** Bible, sacred music, theology.

**Most popular majors.** Business/marketing 7%, education 62%, philosophy/religious studies 13%, psychology 10%.

**Computing on campus.** 69 workstations in dormitories, library, computer center. Dormitories wired for high-speed internet access. Online library, helpline, wireless network available.

**Student life. Freshman orientation:** Mandatory, $50 fee. Preregistration for classes offered. Held the week prior to the opening of the fall semester; designed to provide opportunities for learning methods that support college success. **Policies:** Smoking and alcoholic beverages forbidden. Chapel attendance is required of all full-time students. Unmarried, full-time students under the age of 21 are required to live on campus unless they are independent students, are living at home with their parents or immediate family members and commuting to school. **Housing:** Single-sex dorms, substance-free housing available. $50 fully refundable deposit. **Activities:** Choral groups, drama, literary magazine, music ensembles, musical theater, student government, Alpha Psi Omega, Baptist Student Union, Cap and Gown Honor Society, Mississippi Association of Educators student chapter, psychology club, Society of Mathematicians and Scientists, Vivace club, Ministerial Association, Koinonia.

**Athletics.** NAIA. **Intercollegiate:** Basketball, cross-country. **Intramural:** Basketball, cross-country, football (non-tackle) M, golf M, softball, swimming, table tennis, tennis W, volleyball W. **Team name:** Toppers.

**Student services.** Health services, personal counseling, placement for graduates. **Physically disabled:** Services for visually, hearing impaired.

**Contact.** E-mail: admissions@bmc.edu
Phone: (662) 685-4771 ext. 166 Toll-free number: (800) 235-0136
Fax: (662) 685-4776
Maria Teel, Director of Admissions, Blue Mountain College, PO Box 160, Blue Mountain, MS 38610-0160

---

## Delta State University
**Cleveland, Mississippi**                           CB member
**www.deltastate.edu**                               CB code: 1163

- Public 4-year university
- Commuter campus in large town

- 3,356 degree-seeking undergraduates
- 29% of applicants admitted
- SAT or ACT (ACT writing optional) required

**General.** Founded in 1924. Regionally accredited. **Degrees:** 603 bachelor's awarded; master's, doctoral offered. **Location:** 40 miles from Greenville, 110 miles from Memphis, Tennessee. **Calendar:** Semester, extensive summer session. **Full-time faculty:** 178 total. **Part-time faculty:** 77 total. **Special facilities:** Planetarium, airport.

**Freshman class profile.** 1,981 applied, 578 admitted, 477 enrolled.

| Mid 50% test scores | | GPA 2.0-2.99: | 35% |
|---|---|---|---|
| ACT composite: | 18-22 | Rank in top quarter: | 40% |
| GPA 3.50 or higher: | 27% | Out-of-state: | 15% |
| GPA 3.0-3.49: | 34% | Live on campus: | 100% |

**Basis for selection.** Combination of college preparatory curriculum, test scores, class rank. Mississippi residents must take ACT for admission. Interview required for art, music majors. Audition recommended for music majors; portfolio recommended for art majors.

**High school preparation.** 15 units required. Required units include English 4, mathematics 3, social studies 3, science 3 (laboratory 2), foreign language 1 and academic electives 1. Require .5 unit in computer applications.

**2007-2008 Annual costs.** Tuition/fees: $4,248; $10,258 out-of-state. Room/board: $4,896. Books/supplies: $700.

**2006-2007 Financial aid.** **Need-based:** 35% of total undergraduate aid awarded as scholarships/grants, 65% as loans/jobs. **Non-need-based:** Scholarships awarded for academics, alumni affiliation, art, athletics, leadership, music/drama, religious affiliation, ROTC, state residency.

**Application procedures.** **Admission:** Priority date 5/1; deadline 8/1 (receipt date). $15 fee. Application may be submitted online. Admission notification on a rolling basis beginning on or about 5/15. **Financial aid:** Priority date 3/1; no closing date. FAFSA, institutional form required. Applicants notified on a rolling basis starting 4/1; must reply within 2 week(s) of notification.

**Academics.** **Special study options:** Cooperative education, distance learning, double major, dual enrollment of high school students, honors, independent study, internships, teacher certification program, weekend college. **Credit/placement by examination:** AP, CLEP, SAT, ACT, institutional tests. 30 credit hours maximum toward bachelor's degree. **Support services:** Learning center, pre-admission summer program, remedial instruction, study skills assistance, tutoring, writing center.

**Majors. Biology:** General. **Business:** General, accounting, business admin, finance, hospitality admin, insurance, management information systems, marketing, office management. **Communications:** Journalism. **Education:** Elementary, English, mathematics, music, physical, social science, special. **English:** English lit. **Family/consumer sciences:** General. **Foreign languages:** General. **Health:** Athletic training, audiology/speech pathology, nursing (RN). **History:** General. **Math:** General. **Physical sciences:** Chemistry. **Protective services:** Criminal justice. **Psychology:** General. **Public administration:** Social work. **Social sciences:** General, political science. **Transportation:** Airline/commercial pilot, aviation. **Visual/performing arts:** General.

**Most popular majors.** Biology 7%, business/marketing 25%, education 23%, health sciences 10%.

**Computing on campus.** 293 workstations in library, computer center. Dormitories wired for high-speed internet access and linked to campus network. Commuter students can connect to campus network. Online course registration, student web hosting available.

**Student life. Freshman orientation:** Available, $35 fee. Preregistration for classes offered. Orientation provides opportunity for academic advisement and pre-registration. **Housing:** Guaranteed on-campus for all undergraduates. Single-sex dorms, apartments available. $50 deposit. **Activities:** Bands, choral groups, drama, literary magazine, music ensembles, musical theater, opera, student government, student newspaper, symphony orchestra, several religious, ethnic, social, political organizations available on campus.

**Athletics.** NCAA. **Intercollegiate:** Baseball M, basketball, cross-country W, diving, football (tackle) M, golf M, soccer, softball W, swimming, tennis. **Intramural:** Archery, badminton, basketball, bowling, cross-country, diving, football (non-tackle), golf, racquetball, rifle, soccer, softball, swimming, table tennis, tennis, triathlon, volleyball. **Team name:** Statesmen; Lady Statesmen.

**Student services.** Career counseling, student employment services, health services, on-campus daycare, personal counseling, placement for graduates. **Physically disabled:** Services for speech, hearing impaired.

**Contact.** E-mail: dheslep@deltastate.edu
Phone: (662) 846-4655 Fax: (662) 846-4684
Debbie Heslep, Dean of Enrollment Managaement, Delta State University, Kent Wyatt Hall Rm 117, Cleveland, MS 38733

---

### Jackson State University
**Jackson, Mississippi**
**www.jsums.edu**

CB member
CB code: 1341

- Public 4-year university
- Commuter campus in small city
- 6,823 degree-seeking undergraduates: 96% African American
- 1,875 graduate students
- 36% of applicants admitted
- SAT or ACT required
- 35% graduate within 6 years

**General.** Founded in 1877. Regionally accredited. **Degrees:** 834 bachelor's awarded; master's, doctoral offered. **ROTC:** Army. **Location:** 210 miles from Memphis, Tennessee, 190 miles from New Orleans. **Calendar:** Semester, extensive summer session. **Full-time faculty:** 384 total; 75% have terminal degrees, 38% minority, 42% women. **Part-time faculty:** 90 total; 46% have terminal degrees, 20% minority, 50% women. **Special facilities:** National research center, science observatory, academic research and computing center.

**Freshman class profile.** 6,499 applied, 2,341 admitted, 926 enrolled.

| Mid 50% test scores | | Rank in top quarter: | 34% |
|---|---|---|---|
| ACT composite: | 16-20 | End year in good standing: | 87% |
| GPA 3.50 or higher: | 17% | Return as sophomores: | 76% |
| GPA 3.0-3.49: | 27% | Out-of-state: | 37% |
| GPA 2.0-2.99: | 49% | Live on campus: | 75% |

**Basis for selection.** Test scores and high school transcript important. Audition recommended for music majors.

**High school preparation.** 15 units required. Required units include English 4, mathematics 3, social studies 3, science 3, foreign language 2 and academic electives 2.

**2007-2008 Annual costs.** Tuition/fees: $4,432; $9,976 out-of-state. Annual utility fee of $44 for residents and $96 for non-residents. Room/board: $5,534. Books/supplies: $800. Personal expenses: $2,250.

**2006-2007 Financial aid.** All financial aid based on need. 36% of total undergraduate aid awarded as scholarships/grants, 64% as loans/jobs.

**Application procedures.** **Admission:** Priority date 8/1; no deadline. No application fee. Application may be submitted online. Admission notification on a rolling basis beginning on or about 1/1. **Financial aid:** Priority date 4/1, closing date 5/1. FAFSA required. Applicants notified on a rolling basis starting 5/1.

**Academics.** **Special study options:** Distance learning, double major, dual enrollment of high school students, exchange student, honors, independent study, internships, study abroad, teacher certification program, weekend college. **Credit/placement by examination:** AP, CLEP, SAT, ACT. 30 credit hours maximum toward bachelor's degree. **Support services:** Learning center, pre-admission summer program, reduced course load, remedial instruction, study skills assistance, tutoring, writing center.

**Majors. Biology:** General. **Business:** Accounting, business admin, finance, marketing. **Communications:** Media studies. **Computer sciences:** General. **Education:** Business, elementary, instructional media, music, physical, social science, special. **Engineering:** Civil, computer, electrical. **Engineering technology:** Industrial. **English:** English lit, speech/rhetoric. **Foreign languages:** General. **Health:** Communication disorders, health care admin, predental. **History:** General. **Math:** General. **Physical sciences:** Atmospheric science, chemistry, physics. **Protective services:** Criminal justice. **Psychology:** General. **Public administration:** Social work. **Social sciences:** General, political science, sociology, urban studies. **Visual/performing arts:** General, music performance. **Other:** Childcare and family education, Professional interdiscplinary studies.

**Most popular majors.** Biology 8%, business/marketing 23%, education 20%, psychology 6%, security/protective services 9%.

**Computing on campus.** Dormitories wired for high-speed internet access and linked to campus network. Commuter students can connect to campus network. Online course registration, helpline, wireless network available.

**Student life. Freshman orientation:** Mandatory. Preregistration for classes offered. **Housing:** Single-sex dorms available. $50 nonrefundable deposit. **Activities:** Bands, choral groups, dance, drama, film society, literary magazine, music ensembles, opera, radio station, student government, student newspaper, symphony orchestra, TV station, Church of God in Christ (COGIC) club, NAACP, Alpha Phi Omega.

**Athletics.** NCAA. **Intercollegiate:** Baseball M, basketball, bowling, cross-country, football (tackle) M, golf, rifle, soccer W, softball W, tennis, track and field, volleyball W. **Intramural:** Basketball, rifle, swimming, tennis, volleyball. **Team name:** JSU Tigers.

**Student services.** Adult student services, career counseling, student employment services, financial aid counseling, health services, on-campus day-care, personal counseling, placement for graduates, veterans' counselor. **Physically disabled:** Services for visually, speech, hearing impaired.

**Contact.** E-mail: admappl@jsums.edu
Phone: (601) 979-2100 Toll-free number: (800) 848-6917
Fax: (601) 979-2237
Stephanie Chatman, Director of Admissions and Financial Aid, Jackson State University, 1400 JR Lynch Street, Jackson, MS 39217

## Magnolia Bible College
**Kosciusko, Mississippi**
www.magnolia.edu

**CB member**
**CB code: 0162**

- Private 4-year Bible college affiliated with Church of Christ
- Commuter campus in small town
- 35 degree-seeking undergraduates: 34% part-time, 23% women, 31% African American

**General.** Founded in 1976. Regionally accredited. **Degrees:** 6 bachelor's awarded. **Location:** 70 miles from Jackson. **Calendar:** Semester, limited summer session. **Full-time faculty:** 2 total; 50% have terminal degrees. **Part-time faculty:** 9 total; 33% have terminal degrees, 11% minority, 33% women. **Class size:** 100% < 20. **Special facilities:** Restoration artifacts collection, preaching laboratory.

**Freshman class profile.** 2 applied, 2 admitted, 2 enrolled.

| | | | |
|---|---|---|---|
| End year in good standing: | 100% | Live on campus: | 94% |
| Return as sophomores: | 100% | | |

**Basis for selection.** Open admission. Recommendations, religious commitment and personal character very important. Students encouraged to take ACT by end of first semester. Audition and portfolio recommended. **Home-schooled:** Complete junior year of high school with B average and score of 20 on ACT. Need transcript and letter of readiness from group leader or official.

**2008-2009 Annual costs.** Tuition/fees (projected): $6,540. Reduced tuition for Attala County residents: $1,950 full-time, $65 per credit hour, $90 required fees. Room only: $1,610. Books/supplies: $500. Personal expenses: $1,935.

**2007-2008 Financial aid. Need-based:** 92% of total undergraduate aid awarded as scholarships/grants, 8% as loans/jobs. **Non-need-based:** Scholarships awarded for academics, leadership, religious affiliation.

**Application procedures. Admission:** No deadline. No application fee. Application must be submitted on paper. Admission notification on a rolling basis. **Financial aid:** Priority date 8/1; no closing date. FAFSA, institutional form required. Applicants notified on a rolling basis starting 4/15; must reply within 4 week(s) of notification.

**Academics. Credit/placement by examination:** AP, CLEP, institutional tests. 30 credit hours maximum toward bachelor's degree. **Support services:** Remedial instruction, writing center.

**Majors. Theology:** Bible, missionary, pastoral counseling, religious ed, sacred music, theology.

**Computing on campus.** 3 workstations in dormitories, library, computer center. Dormitories wired for high-speed internet access. Online library, wireless network available.

**Student life. Freshman orientation:** Mandatory. **Policies:** Religious observance required. **Housing:** Single-sex dorms, apartments available. $100 deposit, deadline 8/1. Women students housed with families in area. **Activities:** Student government.

**Student services.** Personal counseling, placement for graduates.

**Contact.** E-mail: tbrown@magnolia.edu
Phone: (662) 289-2896 ext. 109 Toll-free number: (800) 748-8655
Fax: (662) 289-1850
Travis Brown, Director of Admissions, Magnolia Bible College, PO Box 1109, Kosciusko, MS 39090

## Millsaps College
**Jackson, Mississippi**
www.millsaps.edu

**CB code: 1471**

- Private 4-year business and liberal arts college affiliated with United Methodist Church
- Residential campus in large city
- 1,029 degree-seeking undergraduates: 1% part-time, 51% women, 11% African American, 4% Asian American, 1% Hispanic American, 1% international
- 108 degree-seeking graduate students
- 77% of applicants admitted
- SAT or ACT (ACT writing optional), application essay required
- 69% graduate within 6 years; 54% enter graduate study

**General.** Founded in 1890. Regionally accredited. 4,000-acre biocultural reserve and learning center available to students in the state of Yucatan, Mexico, where students excavate Mayan archaeological sites, conduct environmental jungle studies, research biology and geology of the area, and live in a sustainable solar-powered facility. **Degrees:** 199 bachelor's awarded; master's offered. **ROTC:** Army. **Location:** 190 miles from New Orleans, 210 miles from Memphis, Tennessee. **Calendar:** Semester, limited summer session. **Full-time faculty:** 91 total; 97% have terminal degrees, 7% minority, 43% women. **Part-time faculty:** 18 total; 33% have terminal degrees, 11% minority, 61% women. **Class size:** 68% < 20, 32% 20-39, less than 1% >100. **Special facilities:** Molecular biology/functional genomics research laboratory, fluorescence microscopy suite and imaging facility, GIS workstation with high-end GIS software, automated 24-hour food monitoring system for rats, animal microsurgical lab, hydro geologic monitoring stations, computational modeling lab, spectrometers, chromatographs, electrophoresis instruments, inert atmosphere reaction chamber, storm water and oil spill remediation research laboratory.

**Freshman class profile.** 1,253 applied, 968 admitted, 296 enrolled.

| Mid 50% test scores | | | |
|---|---|---|---|
| SAT critical reading: | 550-670 | Rank in top tenth: | 40% |
| SAT math: | 540-650 | End year in good standing: | 89% |
| ACT composite: | 23-29 | Return as sophomores: | 81% |
| GPA 3.50 or higher: | 55% | Out-of-state: | 57% |
| GPA 3.0-3.49: | 31% | Live on campus: | 96% |
| GPA 2.0-2.99: | 14% | International: | 1% |
| Rank in top quarter: | 66% | Fraternities: | 53% |
| | | Sororities: | 56% |

**Basis for selection.** Test scores, GPA in academic courses, recommendations, essays, and school and community activities are important. Advanced credit is awarded for A-Levels, International Baccalaureate, and some other systems. TOEFL is accepted for foreign language students. Auditions and portfolios are recommended. **Homeschooled:** Statement describing homeschool structure and mission, transcript of courses and grades, letter of recommendation (nonparent) required. **Learning Disabled:** If accomodations are needed, accepted students should contact Director of Services for Students with Disabilities to obtain forms to be completed by their healthcare providers.

**High school preparation.** 14 units required; 20 recommended. Required and recommended units include English 4, mathematics 3-4, social studies 2, history 2, science 3-4 (laboratory 1), foreign language 2 and computer science 2.

**2008-2009 Annual costs.** Tuition/fees: $24,754. Room/board: $8,800. Books/supplies: $1,000. Personal expenses: $1,000.

**2006-2007 Financial aid. Need-based:** 180 full-time freshmen applied for aid; 127 were judged to have need; 127 of these received aid. Average need met was 90%. Average scholarship/grant was $16,156; average loan $2,686. 77% of total undergraduate aid awarded as scholarships/grants, 23% as loans/jobs. **Non-need-based:** Awarded to 491 full-time undergraduates, including 136 freshmen. Scholarships awarded for academics, art, leadership, music/drama, religious affiliation.

**Application procedures. Admission:** No deadline. No application fee. Application may be submitted online. Admission notification on a rolling

basis beginning on or about 10/1. Must reply by May 1 or within 2 week(s) if notified thereafter. Early action priority deadline is 01/08, with notification 2 weeks after applying. **Financial aid:** Priority date 3/1; no closing date. FAFSA, institutional form required. Applicants notified on a rolling basis starting 3/15; must reply by 5/1 or within 2 week(s) of notification.

**Academics. Special study options:** Accelerated study, combined bachelor's/ graduate degree, double major, honors, independent study, internships, liberal arts/career combination, New York semester, semester at sea, student-designed major, study abroad, teacher certification program, United Nations semester, urban semester, Washington semester. Faith & Work Initiative; pre-professional programs include dentistry, engineering, law, medicine, ministry and social work. Interdisciplinary concentrations are available in American studies, Christian education, environmental studies, film studies, human services, international studies, and women's and gender studies, among others; undergraduate research, including field research opportunities in Alaska, Yellowstone, the Yucatan, and Europe; study abroad programs offered in Albania, Belgium, China, Costa Rica, England, France, Ghana, Germany, Greece, Italy, Ireland, Israel, Mexico (Yucatan), Japan, and Tanzania; direct exchange programs with Kansai Gaida University (Osaka, Japan) and with Queens University, the University of Ulster, and the Belfast Institute for Further and Higher Education (Belfast, Northern Ireland); dual degrees in engineering, applied science or nursing through agreements with Auburn University, Columbia University, Vanderbilt University, Washington University, and the University of Mississippi Medical Center; Ford Teaching Fellows program; Weiner Pre-Medical Fellows program for summer research. **Credit/placement by examination:** AP, CLEP, IB, institutional tests. 28 credit hours maximum toward bachelor's degree. Limited to two courses in any discipline and seven courses overall. **Support services:** Pre-admission summer program, reduced course load, study skills assistance, tutoring, writing center.

**Majors. Area/ethnic studies:** European. **Biology:** General, biochemistry. **Business:** Accounting, business admin. **Computer sciences:** Computer science. **Education:** Elementary. **English:** English lit. **Foreign languages:** Classics, French, Spanish. **History:** General. **Math:** General. **Philosophy/ religion:** Philosophy, religion. **Physical sciences:** Chemistry, geology, physics. **Psychology:** General. **Public administration:** General. **Social sciences:** Anthropology, economics, political science, sociology. **Visual/performing arts:** Art history/conservation, dramatic, studio arts.

**Most popular majors.** Biology 13%, business/marketing 20%, English 8%, history 7%, physical sciences 8%, psychology 13%, social sciences 10%.

**Computing on campus.** 150 workstations in dormitories, library, computer center, student center. Dormitories wired for high-speed internet access and linked to campus network. Commuter students can connect to campus network. Online course registration, online library, helpline, student web hosting, wireless network available.

**Student life. Freshman orientation:** Mandatory. Preregistration for classes offered. 3 days before classes start, emphasizes wellness education, interpersonal skills development, and the mission of the College and the community. Includes initial 8 days of educational and social activities and 8-week Foundations program held once weekly to explore student issues and involvement in campus activities. **Policies:** Students required to live on campus through sophomore year. Students with family in the area may be exempted from the policy. **Housing:** Guaranteed on-campus for freshmen. Coed dorms, single-sex dorms, fraternity/sorority housing, substance-free housing available. Community service dormitory and substance free dormitory wing available. **Activities:** Choral groups, dance, drama, film society, literary magazine, music ensembles, musical theater, student government, student newspaper, Circle K, Millsaps Christian Fellowship, Black student association, Habitat for Humanity, Catholic student association, Fellowship of Christian Athletes, College Republicans, Young Democrats, Multicultural Affairs Diversity Group, E.A.R.T.H. (environmental service club), Jewish cultural organization.

**Athletics.** NCAA. **Intercollegiate:** Baseball M, basketball, cheerleading, cross-country, football (tackle) M, golf, soccer, softball W, tennis, volleyball W. **Intramural:** Basketball, bowling, football (non-tackle), golf, racquetball, soccer, softball, table tennis, tennis, volleyball, weight lifting. **Team name:** Millsaps Majors, Lady Majors.

**Student services.** Adult student services, alcohol/substance abuse counseling, campus ministries, career counseling, student employment services, financial aid counseling, health services, minority student services, personal counseling, placement for graduates, women's services.

**Contact.** E-mail: admissions@millsaps.edu
Phone: (601) 974-1050 Toll-free number: (800) 352-1050
Fax: (601) 974-1059
Mathew Cox, Dean of Enrollment Management, Millsaps College, 1701 North State Street, Jackson, MS 39210-0001

## Mississippi College
**Clinton, Mississippi**
**www.mc.edu**                                      CB code: 1477

- Private 4-year university affiliated with Southern Baptist Convention
- Residential campus in large city
- 2,911 degree-seeking undergraduates: 14% part-time, 60% women, 24% African American, 1% Asian American, 1% Hispanic American, 4% international
- 1,497 degree-seeking graduate students
- 65% of applicants admitted
- SAT or ACT (ACT writing optional) required
- 61% graduate within 6 years; 5% enter graduate study

**General.** Founded in 1826. Regionally accredited. **Degrees:** 532 bachelor's awarded; master's, doctoral, first professional offered. **ROTC:** Army. **Location:** 10 miles from Jackson. **Calendar:** Semester, limited summer session. **Full-time faculty:** 165 total; 79% have terminal degrees, 4% minority, 46% women. **Part-time faculty:** 213 total; 46% have terminal degrees, 11% minority, 48% women. **Class size:** 49% < 20, 37% 20-39, 11% 40-49, 3% 50-99, less than 1% >100. **Special facilities:** Baptist healthplex, Choctaw trails.

**Freshman class profile.** 1,642 applied, 1,064 admitted, 541 enrolled.

| Mid 50% test scores | | | |
|---|---|---|---|
| SAT critical reading: | 460-580 | Rank in top quarter: | 57% |
| SAT math: | 450-580 | Rank in top tenth: | 25% |
| ACT composite: | 20-26 | Return as sophomores: | 77% |
| GPA 3.50 or higher: | 53% | Out-of-state: | 32% |
| GPA 3.0-3.49: | 23% | Live on campus: | 93% |
| GPA 2.0-2.99: | 22% | International: | 4% |

**Basis for selection.** ACT/SAT scores most important, followed by high school record. Recommendations considered in marginal cases. For placement purposes, provisional admission if ACT score is less than 18. Admission and advising affects course load and course selection. Audition recommended for music majors; portfolio recommended for art majors. **Homeschooled:** Transcript of courses and grades required.

**High school preparation.** 22 units recommended. Recommended units include English 4, mathematics 3, social studies 3, history 1, science 4 (laboratory 1), foreign language 1, computer science .5, academic electives 4.5. 2 units of advanced electives recommended.

**2008-2009 Annual costs.** Tuition/fees: $12,800. Room/board: $5,800. Books/supplies: $900. Personal expenses: $1,575.

**2007-2008 Financial aid. Need-based:** 527 full-time freshmen applied for aid; 296 were judged to have need; 294 of these received aid. Average need met was 81%. Average scholarship/grant was $11,184; average loan $4,069. 50% of total undergraduate aid awarded as scholarships/grants, 50% as loans/jobs. **Non-need-based:** Awarded to 1,238 full-time undergraduates, including 318 freshmen. Scholarships awarded for academics, alumni affiliation, art, leadership, music/drama, religious affiliation. **Additional information:** Student reply date for institutional scholarships: May 1.

**Application procedures. Admission:** No deadline. No application fee. Application may be submitted online. Admission notification on a rolling basis. Either SAT or ACT may be substituted for TOEFL scores for foreign students. **Financial aid:** Priority date 3/1; no closing date. FAFSA required. Applicants notified on a rolling basis starting 3/1; must reply by 5/1.

**Academics. Special study options:** Accelerated study, combined bachelor's/ graduate degree, distance learning, double major, dual enrollment of high school students, ESL, honors, independent study, internships, study abroad, teacher certification program. **Credit/placement by examination:** AP, CLEP, IB, institutional tests. 30 credit hours maximum toward bachelor's degree. **Support services:** Reduced course load, remedial instruction, study skills assistance, tutoring, writing center.

**Majors. Biology:** General, biochemistry. **Business:** Accounting, business admin, marketing. **Communications:** General, journalism, media studies, public relations. **Computer sciences:** General, computer science. **Education:** Art, biology, business, chemistry, elementary, English, French, mathematics, music, physical, secondary, social studies, Spanish, special. **Engineering:** Physics. **English:** English lit. **Foreign languages:** French, Spanish, translation. **Health:** Nursing (RN), premedicine. **History:** General. **Legal studies:** Paralegal, prelaw. **Math:** General. **Parks/recreation:** Exercise sciences, sports admin. **Philosophy/religion:** Christian. **Physical sciences:** Chemistry, physics. **Protective services:** Law enforcement admin. **Psychology:** General. **Public administration:** Social work. **Social sciences:** Political science, sociology. **Theology:** Sacred music. **Visual/performing arts:** Art, graphic design, interior design, music performance, music theory/composition, piano/organ, studio arts, voice/opera. **Other:** French and German.

**Most popular majors.** Biology 9%, business/marketing 21%, education 13%, health sciences 11%.

**Computing on campus.** 207 workstations in dormitories, library, computer center. Dormitories wired for high-speed internet access and linked to campus network. Commuter students can connect to campus network. Online course registration, helpline, student web hosting, wireless network available.

**Student life. Freshman orientation:** Available, $65 fee. Preregistration for classes offered. Held on a Thursday, Friday and Saturday in July. **Policies:** No alcohol allowed, no smoking in front of buildings. **Housing:** Single-sex dorms, special housing for disabled, apartments, substance-free housing available. $100 nonrefundable deposit, deadline 7/15. **Activities:** Bands, campus ministries, choral groups, drama, international student organizations, literary magazine, music ensembles, musical theater, opera, radio station, student government, student newspaper, Baptist student union, Civitan, Circle-K, Rotoract, Young Democrats, Young Republicans, Black Student Association, 5 women's social/service clubs, Reformed University Fellowship, Habitat for Humanity.

**Athletics.** NCAA. **Intercollegiate:** Baseball M, basketball, cheerleading, cross-country, equestrian W, football (tackle) M, golf, soccer, softball W, tennis, track and field, volleyball W. **Intramural:** Badminton, basketball, field hockey, football (non-tackle), soccer, softball, table tennis, tennis, volleyball. **Team name:** Choctaws.

**Student services.** Adult student services, campus ministries, career counseling, student employment services, financial aid counseling, health services, personal counseling, placement for graduates. **Physically disabled:** Services for visually, speech, hearing impaired.

**Contact.** E-mail: enrollment-services@mc.edu
Phone: (601) 925-3800 Toll-free number: (800) 738-1236
Fax: (601) 925-3950
Chad Phillips, Director of Admissions, Mississippi College, PO Box 4026, Clinton, MS 39058

---

## Mississippi State University
**Mississippi State, Mississippi**
www.msstate.edu

CB member
CB code: 1480

- Public 4-year university
- Commuter campus in large town
- 13,049 degree-seeking undergraduates: 10% part-time, 47% women
- 2,402 degree-seeking graduate students
- 70% of applicants admitted
- SAT or ACT (ACT writing optional) required
- 58% graduate within 6 years

**General.** Founded in 1878. Regionally accredited. Branches include Vicksburg Center for Graduate Studies in engineering, the Meridian Campus, and the Stennis Space Center on Gulf Coast. **Degrees:** 2,588 bachelor's awarded; master's, doctoral, first professional offered. **ROTC:** Army, Air Force. **Location:** 125 miles from Jackson. **Calendar:** Semester, extensive summer session. **Full-time faculty:** 851 total; 83% have terminal degrees, 16% minority, 34% women. **Part-time faculty:** 202 total; 39% have terminal degrees, 58% minority, 54% women. **Class size:** 37% < 20, 41% 20-39, 8% 40-49, 11% 50-99, 3% >100. **Special facilities:** Clock museum, antique tools and primitive machines museum, architecture, art, and design gallery, geological museum, costume and textiles collection, entomological museum.

**Freshman class profile.** 6,141 applied, 4,276 admitted, 2,281 enrolled.

| Mid 50% test scores | | Rank in top tenth: | 26% |
| --- | --- | --- | --- |
| SAT critical reading: | 490-630 | Return as sophomores: | 83% |
| SAT math: | 500-640 | Out-of-state: | 24% |
| ACT composite: | 20-27 | Live on campus: | 82% |
| GPA 3.50 or higher: | 38% | International: | 1% |
| GPA 3.0-3.49: | 29% | Fraternities: | 24% |
| GPA 2.0-2.99: | 32% | Sororities: | 26% |
| Rank in top quarter: | 26% | | |

**Basis for selection.** Admission based on standardized test scores, GPA, class rank. Students with academic deficiencies may be admitted after additional review. Requirements may vary by department; student should contact department to ensure that requirements are met. Successful completion of summer developmental program results in admission for fall term with mandatory participation in academic support program freshmen year. Audition, portfolio required. Interview recommended for architecture, professional golf management, and veterinary medicine students. **Homeschooled:** Transcript of courses and grades required.

**High school preparation.** 15.5 units required; 20.5 recommended. Required and recommended units include English 4, mathematics 3-4, social studies 1-2, history 2, science 3-4 (laboratory 2), foreign language 1, computer science .5. 1 unit World Geography.

**2007-2008 Annual costs.** Tuition/fees: $4,978; $11,469 out-of-state. Room/board: $6,951. Books/supplies: $1,000. Personal expenses: $1,828.

**2006-2007 Financial aid. Need-based:** 1,357 full-time freshmen applied for aid; 1,050 were judged to have need; 1,033 of these received aid. Average need met was 63%. Average scholarship/grant was $5,069; average loan $2,898. 38% of total undergraduate aid awarded as scholarships/grants, 62% as loans/jobs. **Non-need-based:** Awarded to 2,831 full-time undergraduates, including 858 freshmen. Scholarships awarded for academics, alumni affiliation, art, athletics, job skills, leadership, minority status, music/drama, ROTC, state residency. **Additional information:** No institutional closing date for FAFSA.

**Application procedures. Admission:** No deadline. $35 fee, may be waived for applicants with need. Application may be submitted online. Admission notification on a rolling basis beginning on or about 9/1. **Financial aid:** Priority date 4/1; no closing date. FAFSA required. Applicants notified on a rolling basis starting 12/1; must reply by 5/1.

**Academics. Special study options:** Cooperative education, distance learning, double major, dual enrollment of high school students, ESL, exchange student, honors, independent study, internships, liberal arts/career combination, student-designed major, study abroad, teacher certification program, weekend college. **Credit/placement by examination:** AP, CLEP, IB, SAT, ACT, institutional tests. Maximum of 25% of any curriculum may be earned by examination. **Support services:** Learning center, pre-admission summer program, reduced course load, remedial instruction, study skills assistance, tutoring, writing center.

**Honors college/program.** ACT composite score of 27 or above (SAT, 1230) AND a 3.75 high school core GPA.

**Majors. Agriculture:** General, agribusiness operations, agronomy, animal sciences, economics, food science, horticultural science, landscaping, plant protection, poultry. **Architecture:** Architecture, interior, landscape. **Biology:** General, bacteriology, biochemistry. **Business:** Accounting, business admin, construction management, finance, insurance, management information systems, managerial economics, marketing, real estate. **Communications:** General. **Computer sciences:** General. **Conservation:** Forestry, wildlife, wood science. **Education:** Agricultural, business, elementary, music, physical, secondary, special, voc/tech. **Engineering:** Aerospace, agricultural, biomedical, chemical, civil, computer, electrical, industrial, mechanical. **Engineering technology:** Industrial. **English:** English lit. **Family/consumer sciences:** General. **Foreign languages:** General. **Health:** Clinical lab science. **History:** General. **Interdisciplinary:** Biological/physical sciences. **Liberal arts:** Arts/sciences. **Math:** General. **Philosophy/religion:** Philosophy. **Physical sciences:** Chemistry, geology, physics. **Psychology:** General, educational. **Public administration:** Social work. **Social sciences:** Anthropology, economics, political science, sociology. **Visual/performing arts:** General.

**Most popular majors.** Agriculture 6%, business/marketing 24%, education 18%, engineering/engineering technologies 14%.

**Computing on campus.** 1,000 workstations in dormitories, library, computer center, student center. Dormitories wired for high-speed internet access and linked to campus network. Commuter students can connect to campus network. Online course registration, online library, helpline, student web hosting, wireless network available.

**Student life. Freshman orientation:** Available, $95 fee. Preregistration for classes offered. 2-day program for freshmen and a 1-day program for transfer students. Held three times during the summer and prior to the beginning of each semester. Orientation fees and parents' fees vary for freshman and transfer students. **Policies:** Residence halls are ADA accessible. **Housing:** Guaranteed on-campus for freshmen. Coed dorms, single-sex dorms, apartments, fraternity/sorority housing available. $50 nonrefundable deposit. **Activities:** Bands, campus ministries, choral groups, dance, drama, international student organizations, literary magazine, music ensembles, Model UN, musical theater, radio station, student government, student newspaper, symphony orchestra, TV station, more than 300 organizations on campus.

**Athletics.** NCAA. **Intercollegiate:** Baseball M, basketball, cross-country, football (tackle) M, golf, soccer W, softball W, tennis, track and field, volleyball W. **Intramural:** Badminton, basketball, bowling, football (non-tackle), golf, racquetball, soccer, softball, table tennis, tennis, volleyball, water polo, weight lifting. **Team name:** Bulldogs.

**Student services.** Adult student services, alcohol/substance abuse counseling, campus ministries, career counseling, services for economically disadvantaged, student employment services, financial aid counseling, health services, minority student services, on-campus daycare, personal counseling, placement for graduates, veterans' counselor. **Physically disabled:** Services for visually, speech, hearing impaired.

**Contact.** E-mail: admit@msstate.edu
Phone: (662) 325-2224 Fax: (662) 325-1678
Phil Bonfanti, Director of Admissions and Scholarships, Mississippi State University, Box 6334, Mississippi State, MS 39762

## Mississippi University for Women
Columbus, Mississippi
www.muw.edu

CB member
CB code: 1481

- Public 4-year university and liberal arts college
- Commuter campus in large town
- 2,003 degree-seeking undergraduates
- 46% of applicants admitted
- SAT or ACT (ACT writing recommended) required

**General.** Founded in 1884. Regionally accredited. **Degrees:** 363 bachelor's, 47 associate awarded; master's offered. **ROTC:** Army, Air Force. **Location:** 120 miles from Birmingham, Alabama, 160 miles from Memphis, Tennessee. **Calendar:** Semester, limited summer session. **Full-time faculty:** 136 total. **Part-time faculty:** 66 total. **Class size:** 60% < 20, 33% 20-39, 4% 40-49, 2% 50-99, 2% >100. **Special facilities:** Environmental education center.

**Freshman class profile.** 1,356 applied, 627 admitted, 241 enrolled.

| Mid 50% test scores | | | |
|---|---|---|---|
| SAT critical reading: | 380-560 | Out-of-state: | 10% |
| SAT math: | 480-570 | Live on campus: | 66% |
| ACT composite: | 18-24 | Fraternities: | 42% |
| Rank in top quarter: | 52% | Sororities: | 43% |

**Basis for selection.** Test scores, high school GPA, academic achievement considered in that order. Students with a 3.2 GPA or higher not required to provide test scores. Interview recommended.

**High school preparation.** 16 units required; 20 recommended. Required and recommended units include English 4, mathematics 3-4, social studies 3, science 3-4 (laboratory 2), foreign language 1 and academic electives 2. One elective of foreign language or world geography is required; other elective must be in foreign language, world geography, 4th year mathematics, or 4th year laboratory based science. Computer course of .5 units required.

**2007-2008 Annual costs.** Tuition/fees: $4,204; $10,723 out-of-state. Room/board: $4,740. Books/supplies: $800. Personal expenses: $2,671.

**2006-2007 Financial aid. Need-based:** 45% of total undergraduate aid awarded as scholarships/grants, 55% as loans/jobs. **Non-need-based:** Scholarships awarded for academics, alumni affiliation, leadership, minority status, music/drama, ROTC, state residency.

**Application procedures. Admission:** Priority date 5/1; no deadline. No application fee. Application may be submitted online. Admission notification on a rolling basis. **Financial aid:** Priority date 3/1; no closing date. FAFSA required. Applicants notified on a rolling basis starting 3/15; must reply within 2 week(s) of notification.

**Academics. Special study options:** Cross-registration, distance learning, double major, dual enrollment of high school students, honors, independent study, internships, study abroad, teacher certification program, weekend college. **Credit/placement by examination:** AP, CLEP, institutional tests. 60 credit hours maximum toward bachelor's degree. **Support services:** Learning center, pre-admission summer program, remedial instruction, tutoring.

**Majors. Biology:** General, microbiology. **Business:** Accounting, business admin. **Communications:** General, broadcast journalism, journalism. **Education:** Art, elementary, music, special. **English:** English lit. **Family/consumer sciences:** Clothing/textiles, family systems. **Foreign languages:** Spanish. **Health:** Nursing (RN), speech pathology. **History:** General. **Legal studies:** Paralegal. **Math:** General. **Parks/recreation:** Health/fitness. **Personal/culinary services:** Culinary arts. **Physical sciences:** General, chemistry. **Psychology:** General. **Social sciences:** General, political science. **Visual/performing arts:** General, graphic design, music theory/composition.

**Most popular majors.** Business/marketing 12%, education 17%, English 7%, family/consumer sciences 9%, health sciences 21%, psychology 6%, visual/performing arts 6%.

**Computing on campus.** 500 workstations in dormitories, library, computer center. Dormitories wired for high-speed internet access and linked to campus network. Commuter students can connect to campus network. Online course registration, online library, helpline, student web hosting available.

**Student life. Freshman orientation:** Available, $50 fee. Preregistration for classes offered. **Housing:** Guaranteed on-campus for all undergraduates. Single-sex dorms, apartments, substance-free housing available. $25 deposit, deadline 7/1. **Activities:** Jazz band, choral groups, drama, literary magazine, music ensembles, radio station, student government, student newspaper, TV station, Methodist, Presbyterian, Episcopal, Baptist, Catholic, Student Interfaith Association, Black student organizations, College Republicans, Young Democrats, International Student Association.

**Athletics. Intramural:** Badminton W, basketball, football (tackle) M, racquetball, softball, table tennis, tennis, volleyball.

**Student services.** Adult student services, alcohol/substance abuse counseling, career counseling, student employment services, financial aid counseling, health services, on-campus daycare, personal counseling, placement for graduates, veterans' counselor. **Physically disabled:** Services for visually, speech, hearing impaired.

**Contact.** E-mail: admissions@muw.edu
Phone: (662) 329-7106 Toll-free number: (877) 462-8439
Fax: (662) 241-7481
Cassie Derden, Director of Admissions, Mississippi University for Women, Box W-1613, Columbus, MS 39701

## Mississippi Valley State University
Itta Bena, Mississippi
www.mvsu.edu

CB member
CB code: 1482

- Public 4-year university and liberal arts college
- Commuter campus in small town
- 2,528 degree-seeking undergraduates
- 435 graduate students
- 25% of applicants admitted
- SAT or ACT (ACT writing optional) required

**General.** Founded in 1946. Regionally accredited. **Degrees:** 424 bachelor's awarded; master's offered. **ROTC:** Army. **Location:** 100 miles from Jackson, 130 miles from Memphis, Tennessee. **Calendar:** Semester, extensive summer session. **Full-time faculty:** 121 total; 63% have terminal degrees, 82% minority, 42% women. **Part-time faculty:** 47 total; 30% have terminal degrees, 92% minority, 62% women. **Class size:** 62% < 20, 32% 20-39, 2% 40-49, 3% 50-99, less than 1% >100.

**Freshman class profile.**

| Mid 50% test scores | | | |
|---|---|---|---|
| ACT composite: | 15-18 | GPA 3.0-3.49: | 22% |
| | | GPA 2.0-2.99: | 55% |
| GPA 3.50 or higher: | 10% | Rank in top quarter: | 27% |

**Basis for selection.** High school curriculum and test scores very important. Audition required for music education majors. Interview required of some students, but recommended for all students.

**High school preparation.** 16 units required; 18 recommended. Required and recommended units include English 4, mathematics 3, social studies 3, science 3 (laboratory 2), foreign language 1 and academic electives 2. Mathematics requirement includes algebra I and II and geometry. Social sciences must include US government and US history. Sciences must be chosen from introductory and advanced biology, physics, and chemistry. Advanced science or mathematics may be substituted for a foreign language.

**2007-2008 Annual costs.** Tuition/fees: $4,417; $10,198 out-of-state. Room/board: $4,542.

**Financial aid. Non-need-based:** Scholarships awarded for academics, athletics, minority status, ROTC.

**Application procedures. Admission:** Priority date 8/1; deadline 8/17 (receipt date). No application fee. Admission notification on a rolling basis. **Financial aid:** Priority date 3/1, closing date 5/1. FAFSA, institutional form required. Applicants notified on a rolling basis starting 4/1; must reply within 2 week(s) of notification.

**Academics. Special study options:** Cooperative education, double major, dual enrollment of high school students, honors, independent study, internships, teacher certification program. **Credit/placement by examination:** AP, CLEP, ACT. 30 credit hours maximum toward bachelor's degree.

**Support services:** Learning center, pre-admission summer program, reduced course load, remedial instruction, study skills assistance, tutoring, writing center.

**Majors. Biology:** General. **Business:** Accounting, business admin, office management. **Communications:** General. **Computer sciences:** General. **Education:** Biology, early childhood, elementary, English, mathematics, music, physical, social science. **Engineering technology:** Industrial. **English:** English lit, speech/rhetoric. **Health:** Environmental health. **History:** General. **Math:** General. **Physical sciences:** Chemistry. **Protective services:** Criminal justice. **Public administration:** General, social work. **Social sciences:** Political science, sociology. **Visual/performing arts:** Music management, studio arts.

**Most popular majors.** Business/marketing 12%, education 33%, English 6%, history 10%, public administration/social services 15%, security/protective services 6%.

**Computing on campus.** 600 workstations in dormitories, library, computer center. Dormitories wired for high-speed internet access and linked to campus network. Commuter students can connect to campus network. Online course registration, online library, wireless network available.

**Student life. Freshman orientation:** Mandatory, $75 fee. Preregistration for classes offered. **Housing:** Single-sex dorms, apartments available. $50 deposit, deadline 7/31. **Activities:** Bands, choral groups, dance, drama, music ensembles, radio station, student government, student newspaper, TV station, numerous honor societies, political, social, religious organizations, prelaw club.

**Athletics.** NCAA. **Intercollegiate:** Baseball M, basketball, bowling, cross-country, football (tackle) M, golf, soccer W, softball W, tennis, track and field, volleyball W. **Intramural:** Baseball M, basketball, bowling, cross-country, softball W, swimming, tennis, volleyball. **Team name:** Delta Devils (M), Devilettes (W).

**Student services.** Adult student services, career counseling, student employment services, financial aid counseling, health services, on-campus daycare, personal counseling, placement for graduates, veterans' counselor.

**Contact.** E-mail: nbtaylor@mvsu.edu
Phone: (662) 254-3347 Fax: (662) 254-3759
Nora Taylor, Director of Admissions and Recruitment, Mississippi Valley State University, 14000 Highway 82 West, Itta Bena, MS 38941-1400

---

## Rust College
### Holly Springs, Mississippi
### www.rustcollege.edu
**CB code: 1669**

- Private 4-year liberal arts college affiliated with United Methodist Church
- Residential campus in small town
- 967 degree-seeking undergraduates
- 40% of applicants admitted
- ACT (writing optional) required

**General.** Founded in 1866. Regionally accredited. **Degrees:** 130 bachelor's, 8 associate awarded. **Location:** 35 miles from Memphis, Tennessee. **Calendar:** Semester, limited summer session. **Full-time faculty:** 46 total. **Part-time faculty:** 4 total. **Class size:** 59% < 20, 19% 20-39, 4% 40-49, 12% 50-99, 5% >100. **Special facilities:** Histories, religious, poetry, speech writing books for ministers and ministerial students, Inuit and African art collections, international artifacts collection.

**Freshman class profile.** 5,129 applied, 2,073 admitted, 380 enrolled.

| Mid 50% test scores | | GPA 2.0-2.99: | 56% |
|---|---|---|---|
| ACT composite: | 14-17 | Return as sophomores: | 63% |
| GPA 3.50 or higher: | 12% | Out-of-state: | 54% |
| GPA 3.0-3.49: | 17% | | |

**Basis for selection.** School achievement record and recommendations most important. Test scores also important. **Homeschooled:** State high school equivalency certificate, letter of recommendation (nonparent) required.

**High school preparation.** 19 units required. Required units include English 4, mathematics 3, social studies 3, science 3 and academic electives 6.

**2007-2008 Annual costs.** Tuition/fees: $6,600. Room/board: $3,100. Books/supplies: $500. Personal expenses: $1,450.

**Financial aid. Non-need-based:** Scholarships awarded for academics, leadership, music/drama, religious affiliation, state residency.

---

**Application procedures. Admission:** Priority date 5/5; no deadline. $10 fee, may be waived for applicants with need. Admission notification on a rolling basis. Must reply by May 1 or within 2 week(s) if notified thereafter. **Financial aid:** Closing date 5/1. FAFSA, institutional form required. Applicants notified on a rolling basis starting 5/1; must reply within 2 week(s) of notification.

**Academics. Special study options:** Double major, honors, independent study, internships, liberal arts/career combination, study abroad, teacher certification program. Nursing and medical technology cooperative program with other institutions. **Credit/placement by examination:** CLEP, ACT, institutional tests. 12 credit hours maximum toward associate degree, 12 toward bachelor's. **Support services:** Learning center, pre-admission summer program, reduced course load, remedial instruction, study skills assistance, tutoring, writing center.

**Majors. Biology:** General. **Business:** Business admin. **Communications:** Broadcast journalism, journalism. **Computer sciences:** Computer science. **Education:** Biology, business, elementary, English, mathematics, social science. **English:** English lit. **Family/consumer sciences:** Child care. **Math:** General. **Physical sciences:** Chemistry. **Public administration:** Social work. **Social sciences:** General, political science, sociology.

**Most popular majors.** Biology 27%, business/marketing 14%, computer/information sciences 12%, English 7%, family/consumer sciences 12%, public administration/social services 8%, social sciences 9%.

**Computing on campus.** 220 workstations in dormitories, library, computer center. Dormitories wired for high-speed internet access and linked to campus network. Commuter students can connect to campus network. Online library, helpline, wireless network available.

**Student life. Freshman orientation:** Mandatory. Orientation and assessment program begins 1 week prior to registration. **Housing:** Guaranteed on-campus for all undergraduates. Single-sex dorms, apartments available. $50 deposit. **Activities:** Bands, choral groups, dance, drama, music ensembles, radio station, student government, student newspaper, TV station, Methodist Student Movement, Baptist Student Union, Catholic Student Association, pre-law club, NAACP, social work club, Sunday School Association, international student association, All Saints Student Movement.

**Athletics.** NCAA. **Intercollegiate:** Baseball M, basketball, cheerleading, cross-country, soccer M, softball W, tennis, track and field, volleyball. **Intramural:** Badminton, baseball, basketball, bowling, cheerleading, cross-country, football (non-tackle), soccer, softball, swimming, table tennis, tennis, track and field, volleyball, weight lifting. **Team name:** Bearcats.

**Student services.** Adult student services, career counseling, student employment services, health services, minority student services, on-campus daycare, personal counseling, placement for graduates, veterans' counselor.

**Contact.** E-mail: jbmcdonald@rustcollege.edu
Phone: (662) 252-8000 ext. 4059 Toll-free
number: (888) 886-8492 ext. 4059 Fax: (662) 252-8895
Johnny McDonald, Director of Enrollment Services, Rust College, 150 Rust Avenue, Holly Springs, MS 38635-2328

---

## Southeastern Baptist College
### Laurel, Mississippi
### www.southeasternbaptist.edu
**CB code: 1781**

- Private 4-year Bible college affiliated with Baptist faith
- Commuter campus in large town

**General.** Founded in 1949. Accredited by ABHE. **Location:** 90 miles from Jackson. **Calendar:** Semester.

**Annual costs/financial aid.** Tuition/fees (2007-2008): $4,600. Room: $1,050. Books/supplies: $300. Personal expenses: $350.

**Contact.** Phone: (601) 426-6346
Academic Dean, 4229 Highway 15 North, Laurel, MS 39440

---

## Tougaloo College
### Tougaloo, Mississippi
### www.tougaloo.edu
**CB member**
**CB code: 1807**

- Private 4-year liberal arts college affiliated with United Christian Mission Society and United Church of Christ
- Residential campus in large city
- 856 degree-seeking undergraduates: 5% part-time, 68% women, 99% African American

♦ 96% of applicants admitted

♦ SAT or ACT (ACT writing optional) required

**General.** Founded in 1869. Regionally accredited. Cooperative program with Brown University provides exchange of financial resources and students. Exchange opportunities available between New York and Boston universities in pre-med and other areas. **Degrees:** 128 bachelor's, 3 associate awarded. **ROTC:** Army, Naval. **Calendar:** Semester, limited summer session. **Full-time faculty:** 75 total. **Part-time faculty:** 25 total. **Class size:** 68% < 20, 30% 20-39, 2% 40-49, less than 1% 50-99. **Special facilities:** Large collection of civil rights documents, East and West African art and artifacts, collection of Mississippi Civil Rights original prints.

**Freshman class profile.** 1,058 applied, 1,012 admitted, 199 enrolled.

| Mid 50% test scores | | ACT composite: | 21-26 |
|---|---|---|---|
| SAT critical reading: | 450-530 | Out-of-state: | 24% |
| SAT math: | 380-470 | Live on campus: | 78% |

**Basis for selection.** Transcript, test scores important. Minimum 3.0 GPA and ACT composite score of 18 required of applicants in junior year of high school. Audition required for music majors. Portfolio recommended for art majors.

**High school preparation.** 16 units required. Required and recommended units include English 3, mathematics 2, social studies 2, science 2, foreign language 2 and academic electives 9.

**2007-2008 Annual costs.** Books/supplies: $500. Personal expenses: $500.

**Financial aid. Non-need-based:** Scholarships awarded for academics, athletics, ROTC.

**Application procedures. Admission:** Priority date 4/15; no deadline. $25 fee. Admission notification on a rolling basis. **Financial aid:** Priority date 4/15; no closing date. FAFSA, institutional form required. Applicants notified on a rolling basis starting 5/1; must reply within 2 week(s) of notification.

**Academics. Special study options:** Accelerated study, cooperative education, cross-registration, double major, exchange student, honors, independent study, internships, liberal arts/career combination, New York semester, student-designed major, study abroad, teacher certification program, Washington semester, weekend college. 3-2 program in pre-engineering and physical sciences with Brown University, Georgia Institute of Technology, University of Mississippi, University of Wisconsin Madison, Tuskegee Institute, Washington University St. Louis, Howard University, University of Memphis, Florida A&M. **Credit/placement by examination:** CLEP, IB, SAT, ACT, institutional tests. 12 credit hours maximum toward bachelor's degree. **Support services:** Learning center, pre-admission summer program, reduced course load, remedial instruction, study skills assistance, tutoring, writing center.

**Majors. Biology:** General. **Communications:** Media studies. **Education:** General, elementary, health, secondary. **English:** English lit. **History:** General. **Interdisciplinary:** Math/computer science. **Liberal arts:** Arts/sciences. **Math:** General. **Physical sciences:** Chemistry, physics. **Psychology:** General. **Social sciences:** Economics, political science, sociology. **Visual/performing arts:** Art.

**Computing on campus.** Dormitories linked to campus network. Commuter students can connect to campus network. Helpline, repair service available.

**Student life. Freshman orientation:** Mandatory. Preregistration for classes offered. **Housing:** Single-sex dorms, substance-free housing available. $50 deposit. **Activities:** Choral groups, dance, drama, music ensembles, radio station, student government, student newspaper, Baptist student union, biology club, Afro-American studies group, College Republicans, foreign students club, French club, pre-health club, prelaw club, honor societies, human services clubs.

**Athletics.** NAIA. **Intercollegiate:** Baseball M, basketball, cross-country, golf, tennis. **Intramural:** Badminton, baseball M, basketball, cheerleading, cross-country M, football (non-tackle) M, golf, soccer M, softball, tennis, track and field, volleyball. **Team name:** Bulldogs.

**Student services.** Adult student services, campus ministries, career counseling, student employment services, financial aid counseling, health services, personal counseling, placement for graduates, veterans' counselor.

**Contact.** E-mail: info@tougaloo.edu
Phone: (601) 977-7765 Toll-free number: (888) 424-2566
Junoesque Jacobs, Director of Admissions, Tougaloo College, 500 West County Line Road, Tougaloo, MS 39174

---

## University of Mississippi
**University, Mississippi**
www.olemiss.edu

CB member
CB code: 1840

♦ Public 4-year university

♦ Residential campus in large town

♦ 12,597 degree-seeking undergraduates: 9% part-time, 52% women, 13% African American, 1% Asian American, 1% Hispanic American, 1% international

♦ 2,200 degree-seeking graduate students

♦ 84% of applicants admitted

♦ 53% graduate within 6 years

**General.** Founded in 1844. Regionally accredited. **Degrees:** 2,376 bachelor's awarded; master's, doctoral, first professional offered. **ROTC:** Army, Naval, Air Force. **Location:** 75 miles from Memphis, Tennessee. **Calendar:** Semester, extensive summer session. **Full-time faculty:** 673 total; 18% minority, 37% women. **Part-time faculty:** 76 total; 5% minority, 55% women. **Special facilities:** Accredited teaching museum, William Faulkner home and grounds, Southern culture center, National Center for Physical Acoustics, 2 super computers, National Center for the Development of Natural Products, National School Food Service Management Institute, water and wetland resources center.

**Freshman class profile.** 7,898 applied, 6,639 admitted, 2,570 enrolled.

| Mid 50% test scores | | GPA 3.0-3.49: | 29% |
|---|---|---|---|
| SAT critical reading: | 460-600 | GPA 2.0-2.99: | 37% |
| SAT math: | 460-590 | Return as sophomores: | 81% |
| ACT composite: | 20-28 | International: | 1% |
| GPA 3.50 or higher: | 33% | | |

**Basis for selection.** School achievement record and test scores important. SAT or ACT may be required for students with core GPA of under 3.2. Essay required for Croff Institute for International Studies, honors college; audition required for music, theater majors. Portfolio recommended for art majors.

**High school preparation.** 15 units required. Required and recommended units include English 4, mathematics 3-4, social studies 1-2, history 2, science 3-4 (laboratory 2), foreign language 1-2, computer science .5 and academic electives 1. Mathematics units must include algebra and 2 higher courses. Social sciences units must include U.S. history and U.S. government. Academic electives must include 1 year world geography and fourth year math or science.

**2007-2008 Annual costs.** Tuition/fees: $4,932; $11,436 out-of-state. Room/board: $5,398.

**2006-2007 Financial aid. Need-based:** 1,524 full-time freshmen applied for aid; 933 were judged to have need; 911 of these received aid. Average need met was 50%. Average scholarship/grant was $5,491; average loan $3,195. 50% of total undergraduate aid awarded as scholarships/grants, 50% as loans/jobs. **Non-need-based:** Awarded to 6,454 full-time undergraduates, including 1,585 freshmen. Scholarships awarded for academics, alumni affiliation, art, athletics, leadership, minority status, music/drama, ROTC, state residency.

**Application procedures. Admission:** Priority date 4/1; deadline 7/20 (postmark date). $25 fee ($50 out-of-state), may be waived for applicants with need. Application may be submitted online. Admission notification on a rolling basis beginning on or about 9/15. **Financial aid:** Priority date 3/15; no closing date. FAFSA required. Applicants notified on a rolling basis starting 4/1; must reply within 3 week(s) of notification.

**Academics. Special study options:** Accelerated study, cooperative education, distance learning, double major, ESL, exchange student, honors, independent study, internships, study abroad, teacher certification program. **Credit/placement by examination:** AP, CLEP, IB, institutional tests. 63 credit hours maximum toward bachelor's degree. Student must earn 12 hours in residence before any credit-by-examination hours are recorded on transcript. **Support services:** Learning center, reduced course load, remedial instruction, study skills assistance, tutoring, writing center.

**Honors college/program.** Requires test scores, transcript, essays, and recommendations. 120 students admitted each fall. Unique courses which meet general education requirements taught by senior/master faculty. Senior thesis required.

**Majors. Area/ethnic studies:** African-American. **Biology:** General. **Business:** Accounting, business admin, finance, insurance, management information systems, managerial economics, marketing, real estate. **Communications:** Journalism. **Computer sciences:** General. **Education:** Elementary,

English, foreign languages, mathematics, science, social studies, special. **Engineering:** General, chemical, civil, electrical, geological, mechanical. **English:** English lit. **Family/consumer sciences:** General. **Foreign languages:** Classics, French, German, linguistics, Spanish. **Health:** Audiology/ speech pathology. **History:** General. **Legal studies:** Paralegal. **Liberal arts:** Arts/sciences. **Math:** General. **Parks/recreation:** Exercise sciences, facilities management. **Philosophy/religion:** Philosophy. **Physical sciences:** Chemistry, geology, physics. **Protective services:** Forensics, law enforcement admin. **Psychology:** General. **Public administration:** Policy analysis, social work. **Social sciences:** Anthropology, economics, international relations, political science, sociology. **Visual/performing arts:** General, art history/ conservation, dramatic. **Other:** Southern studies.

**Most popular majors.** Business/marketing 27%, education 11%, psychology 6%, social sciences 6%.

**Computing on campus.** 638 workstations in dormitories, library, computer center. Dormitories wired for high-speed internet access and linked to campus network. Commuter students can connect to campus network. Online course registration, online library, helpline, repair service, student web hosting, wireless network available.

**Student life. Freshman orientation:** Mandatory. Preregistration for classes offered. 2 days in June, additional session immediately before beginning of term. **Housing:** Guaranteed on-campus for freshmen. Single-sex dorms, apartments, fraternity/sorority housing, substance-free housing available. $150 nonrefundable deposit. Intensive study floors available to honors and other students. Special interest, graduate/older students, substance-free, environmental interest housing available. **Activities:** Bands, campus ministries, choral groups, dance, drama, international student organizations, music ensembles, musical theater, opera, radio station, student government, student newspaper, symphony orchestra, TV station, Wesley Foundation, Baptist student union, Black student union, Students for Environmental Awareness, Mortar Board, Habitat for Humanity, Students Envisioning Equality through Diversity.

**Athletics.** NCAA. **Intercollegiate:** Baseball M, basketball, cheerleading, cross-country, fencing, football (tackle) M, golf, lacrosse M, racquetball M, rifle W, rugby M, skiing M, soccer, softball W, tennis, track and field, volleyball W. **Intramural:** Badminton, basketball, bowling, football (tackle), golf, handball, rifle, soccer, softball, swimming, table tennis, tennis, track and field, volleyball, water polo. **Team name:** Rebels.

**Student services.** Adult student services, alcohol/substance abuse counseling, campus ministries, career counseling, student employment services, financial aid counseling, health services, legal services, minority student services, personal counseling, placement for graduates, veterans' counselor, women's services. **Physically disabled:** Services for visually, speech, hearing impaired.

**Contact.** E-mail: admissions@olemiss.edu
Phone: (662) 915-7226 Toll-free number: (800) 653-6477
Fax: (662) 915-5869
Charlotte Fant, Director of Admissions and Registrar, University of Mississippi, 145 Martindale, University, MS 38677-1848

## University of Mississippi Medical Center
### Jackson, Mississippi
www.umc.edu                                    CB code: 0358

- Public two-year upper-division health science college
- Commuter campus in large city
- 50% of applicants admitted

**General.** Founded in 1955. Regionally accredited. **Degrees:** 156 bachelor's awarded; master's, doctoral, first professional offered. **Location:** 200 miles from Memphis, Tennessee. **Calendar:** Quarter, limited summer session. **Full-time faculty:** 683 total; 80% have terminal degrees, 40% women. **Part-time faculty:** 161 total; 94% have terminal degrees, 44% women.

**Student profile.** 514 degree-seeking undergraduates, 1,145 degree-seeking graduate students. 1,534 applied as first time-transfer students, 761 admitted, 607 enrolled.

| | | | |
|---|---|---|---|
| Women: | 82% | Live on campus: | 3% |
| Part-time: | 20% | 25 or older: | 80% |
| Out-of-state: | 1% | | |

**Basis for selection.** College transcript required. Competitive admission to health science programs based on grades, recommendations, test scores, interviews. Transfer accepted as sophomores, juniors.

**2007-2008 Annual costs.** Tuition/fees: $5,104; $11,608 out-of-state. Tuition and fees quoted are for semester-based nursing program. Required fees vary by program. Books/supplies: $1,596.

**Financial aid.** All financial aid based on need.

**Application procedures. Admission:** Deadline 2/11. $10 fee. Admission notification 4/11. Must reply by 5/11. Application closing dates and reply dates vary by program. **Financial aid:** FAFSA, institutional form required.

**Academics.** Includes schools of medicine, nursing, health-related professions, and dentistry, graduate programs in medical and clinical health sciences, and 623-bed teaching hospital. Certificate programs in emergency medical technology and radiologic technology and clinical nuclear medicine offered. **Special study options:** Liberal arts/career combination. **Credit/ placement by examination:** CLEP. **Support services:** Pre-admission summer program, study skills assistance, tutoring.

**Majors. Health:** Clinical lab science, cytotechnology, dental hygiene, medical records admin.

**Computing on campus.** 75 workstations in library, computer center. Online library available.

**Student life. Housing:** Single-sex dorms, apartments available. $75 deposit. **Activities:** Student government, student newspaper, University Christian Fellowship, Catholic Student Organization.

**Athletics. Intramural:** Baseball, basketball, football (tackle) M, golf, soccer, softball, table tennis.

**Student services.** Alcohol/substance abuse counseling, campus ministries, career counseling, financial aid counseling, health services, minority student services, personal counseling. **Physically disabled:** Services for speech, hearing impaired.

**Contact.** Phone: (601) 984-1080
Barbara Westerfield, Registrar, University of Mississippi Medical Center, 2500 North State Street, Jackson, MS 39216

## University of Southern Mississippi
### Hattiesburg, Mississippi
www.usm.edu

CB member
CB code: 1479

- Public 4-year university
- Residential campus in small city
- 11,924 degree-seeking undergraduates: 14% part-time, 60% women, 29% African American, 1% Asian American, 1% Hispanic American, 1% international
- 2,668 degree-seeking graduate students
- 58% of applicants admitted
- 48% graduate within 6 years

**General.** Founded in 1910. Regionally accredited. Dual campus with main campus in Hattiesburg and nonresidential, nontraditional campus, in Long Beach, and other sites along Mississippi Gulf Coast. **Degrees:** 2,277 bachelor's awarded; master's, doctoral offered. **ROTC:** Army, Air Force. **Location:** 85 miles from Jackson, 110 miles from New Orleans. **Calendar:** Semester, extensive summer session. **Full-time faculty:** 720 total; 77% have terminal degrees, 11% minority, 43% women. **Part-time faculty:** 181 total; 34% have terminal degrees, 6% minority, 60% women. **Class size:** 55% < 20, 31% 20-39, 5% 40-49, 5% 50-99, 3% >100. **Special facilities:** Marine education center, aquarium.

**Freshman class profile.** 4,648 applied, 2,675 admitted, 860 enrolled.

| Mid 50% test scores | | Rank in top tenth: | 18% |
|---|---|---|---|
| SAT critical reading: | 440-590 | Return as sophomores: | 74% |
| SAT math: | 460-590 | Out-of-state: | 24% |
| ACT composite: | 19-24 | Live on campus: | 79% |
| GPA 3.50 or higher: | 24% | International: | 1% |
| GPA 3.0-3.49: | 26% | Fraternities: | 20% |
| GPA 2.0-2.99: | 49% | Sororities: | 17% |
| Rank in top quarter: | 44% | | |

**Basis for selection.** Test scores important; class rank considered. Applicants who do not meet stated criteria may be required to participate in screening process that will include diagnostic test. SAT or ACT recommended. Test not required of some students.

**High school preparation.** 16 units required; 18 recommended. Required and recommended units include English 4, mathematics 3, social studies 3, science 3, foreign language 2, computer science 1 and academic electives 2. Mathematics must include algebra I and II, geometry or higher mathematics. Social sciences must include US government, US history, world history, and economics or geography. Sciences must be chosen from introductory and advanced biology, physics, and chemistry. 2 units world geography, or additional science or mathematics may be substituted for 1 foreign language. 2 units of electives and .5 units of computer applications required.

**2007-2008 Annual costs.** Tuition/fees: $5,174; $11,952 out-of-state. Room/board: $5,218. Books/supplies: $1,000. Personal expenses: $2,634.

**2006-2007 Financial aid. Need-based:** 1,410 full-time freshmen applied for aid; 1,110 were judged to have need; 1,065 of these received aid. Average need met was 82%. Average scholarship/grant was $3,879; average loan $2,783. 45% of total undergraduate aid awarded as scholarships/grants, 55% as loans/jobs. **Non-need-based:** Awarded to 4,047 full-time undergraduates, including 939 freshmen.

**Application procedures. Admission:** No deadline. $25 fee, may be waived for applicants with need. Application may be submitted online. Admission notification on a rolling basis. **Financial aid:** Priority date 3/15; no closing date. FAFSA, institutional form required. Applicants notified on a rolling basis starting 4/1; must reply within 4 week(s) of notification.

**Academics. Special study options:** Accelerated study, combined bachelor's/graduate degree, cooperative education, distance learning, double major, dual enrollment of high school students, ESL, honors, internships, study abroad, teacher certification program. **Credit/placement by examination:** AP, CLEP, SAT, ACT, institutional tests. 30 credit hours maximum toward bachelor's degree. **Support services:** Learning center, pre-admission summer program, reduced course load, remedial instruction, study skills assistance, tutoring, writing center.

**Honors college/program.** Requires an ACT score of 24 or equivalent and essay.

**Majors. Architecture:** Interior, urban/community planning. **Area/ethnic studies:** American. **Biology:** General, marine. **Business:** Accounting, business admin, finance, human resources, management information systems, managerial economics, marketing. **Communications:** General, advertising, broadcast journalism, journalism. **Computer sciences:** General, data processing. **Education:** Business, Deaf/hearing impaired, elementary, music, physical, school counseling, special, technology/industrial arts. **Engineering technology:** Architectural, electrical, plastics. **English:** English lit. **Family/consumer sciences:** General, clothing/textiles, family studies, food/nutrition. **Foreign languages:** General. **Health:** Audiology/hearing, audiology/speech pathology, clinical lab science, nursing (RN). **History:** General. **Interdisciplinary:** Museum. **Legal studies:** Paralegal. **Liberal arts:** Library science. **Math:** General. **Parks/recreation:** General, health/fitness. **Personal/culinary services:** Mortuary science. **Philosophy/religion:** Philosophy. **Physical sciences:** Chemistry, geology, physics, polymer chemistry. **Protective services:** Criminal justice. **Psychology:** General. **Public administration:** Social work. **Social sciences:** Anthropology, geography, political science, sociology. **Visual/performing arts:** General, dance, dramatic.

**Most popular majors.** Business/marketing 20%, education 12%, health sciences 13%, psychology 7%.

**Computing on campus.** 484 workstations in dormitories, library, computer center, student center. Dormitories wired for high-speed internet access and linked to campus network. Commuter students can connect to campus network. Online course registration, online library, helpline, repair service, student web hosting, wireless network available.

**Student life. Freshman orientation:** Available. Preregistration for classes offered. **Housing:** Single-sex dorms, special housing for disabled, apartments, fraternity/sorority housing available. Freshmen who reside in area may live at home. All freshmen who request campus housing required to live in freshman dormitories. **Activities:** Bands, choral groups, dance, drama, film society, literary magazine, music ensembles, musical theater, opera, radio station, student government, student newspaper, symphony orchestra, honor societies, service and religious organizations, Young Republicans, Young Democrats.

**Athletics.** NCAA. **Intercollegiate:** Baseball M, basketball, cross-country, football (tackle) M, golf, rugby M, soccer W, softball W, tennis, track and field, volleyball W. **Intramural:** Badminton, basketball, bowling, golf, racquetball, soccer, softball, squash, swimming, table tennis, tennis, track and field, volleyball. **Team name:** Golden Eagles.

**Student services.** Adult student services, career counseling, student employment services, health services, minority student services, on-campus daycare, personal counseling, placement for graduates, veterans' counselor, women's services. **Physically disabled:** Services for visually, speech, hearing impaired. **Learning disabled:** Comprehensive services available.

**Contact.** E-mail: admissions@usm.edu
Phone: (601) 266-5000 Fax: (601) 266-5148
Kristi Motter, Director of Recruitment/Operations, University of Southern Mississippi, 118 College Drive #5166, Hattiesburg, MS 39406-0001

## Wesley College
### Florence, Mississippi
www.wesleycollege.edu                   CB code: 1923

- Private 4-year Bible college affiliated with Congregational Methodist Church
- Residential campus in small town
- 95 degree-seeking undergraduates
- 45% of applicants admitted
- SAT or ACT (ACT writing optional), application essay required

**General.** Founded in 1972. Accredited by ABHE. **Degrees:** 13 bachelor's awarded. **Location:** 12 miles from Jackson. **Calendar:** Semester, limited summer session. **Full-time faculty:** 5 total; 40% have terminal degrees, 20% women. **Part-time faculty:** 14 total; 21% have terminal degrees, 14% minority, 29% women. **Class size:** 82% < 20, 18% 20-39.

**Freshman class profile.**

| | | | |
|---|---|---|---|
| Rank in top quarter: | 12% | Out-of-state: | 46% |
| Rank in top tenth: | 2% | Live on campus: | 92% |

**Basis for selection.** Test scores, school achievement record, essay important. **Homeschooled:** Must have certified diploma, GED, or meet minimum ACT/SAT scores as specified in current college catalog. **Learning Disabled:** Copies of previous diagnostic records requested.

**High school preparation.** 15 units recommended. Recommended units include English 4, mathematics 2, social studies 4, science 3 and academic electives 2.

**2007-2008 Annual costs.** Tuition/fees: $8,270. Room/board: $3,900. Books/supplies: $700. Personal expenses: $650.

**Financial aid. Non-need-based:** Scholarships awarded for academics, alumni affiliation, leadership, religious affiliation.

**Application procedures. Admission:** Priority date 7/1; deadline 8/15 (receipt date). $25 fee. Application may be submitted online. Admission notification on a rolling basis. Must reply by May 1 or within 4 week(s) if notified thereafter. **Financial aid:** Closing date 5/14. FAFSA required. Applicants notified on a rolling basis starting 7/1; must reply within 2 week(s) of notification.

**Academics. Special study options:** Distance learning, double major, dual enrollment of high school students, independent study, internships. **Credit/placement by examination:** AP, CLEP, institutional tests. 15 credit hours maximum toward associate degree, 15 toward bachelor's. **Support services:** Learning center, reduced course load, remedial instruction, study skills assistance, tutoring.

**Majors. Philosophy/religion:** Religion. **Theology:** Bible, missionary, pastoral counseling, religious ed, theology, youth ministry.

**Most popular majors.** Theological studies 99%.

**Computing on campus.** 4 workstations in library, student center. Dormitories wired for high-speed internet access. Wireless network available.

**Student life. Freshman orientation:** Mandatory. Preregistration for classes offered. **Policies:** Religious observance required. **Housing:** Single-sex dorms, apartments, substance-free housing available. $50 deposit, deadline 8/15. **Activities:** Choral groups, drama, music ensembles, student government, missionary prayer band, ministerial partnership, Christian service program.

**Athletics.** NCCAA. **Intercollegiate:** Basketball M. **Intramural:** Basketball, table tennis, volleyball. **Team name:** Warriors.

**Student services.** Campus ministries, career counseling, student employment services, financial aid counseling, personal counseling.

**Contact.** E-mail: admissions@wesleycollege.edu
Phone: (601) 845-5747 Toll-free number: (800) 748-9972
Fax: (601) 845-2266
Nick Myers, Director of Enrollment, Wesley College, PO Box 1070, Florence, MS 39073-0070

# William Carey University
Hattiesburg, Mississippi
www.wmcarey.edu                    CB code: 1907

- Private 4-year university and liberal arts college affiliated with Baptist faith
- Commuter campus in small city
- 1,679 degree-seeking undergraduates: 13% part-time, 72% women, 29% African American, 1% Asian American, 1% Hispanic American, 1% Native American, 3% international
- 938 degree-seeking graduate students
- 96% of applicants admitted
- SAT or ACT (ACT writing optional) required
- 36% graduate within 6 years

**General.** Founded in 1906. Regionally accredited. **Degrees:** 497 bachelor's awarded; master's offered. **ROTC:** Army, Air Force. **Location:** 110 miles from New Orleans. **Calendar:** Trimester, extensive summer session. **Full-time faculty:** 93 total; 63% have terminal degrees, 3% minority, 53% women. **Part-time faculty:** 95 total; 43% have terminal degrees, 5% minority, 53% women. **Class size:** 57% < 20, 42% 20-39, less than 1% 40-49.

**Freshman class profile.** 426 applied, 411 admitted, 169 enrolled.

| Mid 50% test scores | | | |
|---|---|---|---|
| SAT critical reading: | 420-540 | Return as sophomores: | 75% |
| SAT math: | 430-580 | Out-of-state: | 8% |
| ACT composite: | 19-26 | Live on campus: | 82% |
| End year in good standing: | 87% | Fraternities: | 1% |
| | | Sororities: | 1% |

**Basis for selection.** ACT of 20 OR SAT of 950, exclusive of Writing, required. **Homeschooled:** Transcript of courses and grades required.

**High school preparation.** 16 units required. Required units include English 4, mathematics 3, social studies 2 and science 3.

**2007-2008 Annual costs.** Tuition/fees: $9,015. Room/board: $3,810. Books/supplies: $2,850. Personal expenses: $1,350.

**2007-2008 Financial aid.** Need-based: 17% of total undergraduate aid awarded as scholarships/grants, 83% as loans/jobs. **Non-need-based:** Scholarships awarded for academics, alumni affiliation, art, athletics, music/drama, religious affiliation.

**Application procedures. Admission:** Priority date 7/12; no deadline. $30 fee. Application may be submitted online. Admission notification on a rolling basis. Admissions application priority date: 30 days prior to beginning of term. **Financial aid:** Priority date 4/1, closing date 9/1. FAFSA required. Applicants notified on a rolling basis starting 6/1; must reply within 2 week(s) of notification.

**Academics. Special study options:** Accelerated study, cross-registration, distance learning, double major, dual enrollment of high school students, honors, independent study, internships, study abroad, teacher certification program. **Credit/placement by examination:** AP, CLEP, IB, ACT, institutional tests. 30 credit hours maximum toward bachelor's degree. **Support services:** Reduced course load, remedial instruction, study skills assistance, tutoring.

**Majors. Biology:** General. **Business:** Business admin. **Communications:** General, journalism. **Education:** Art, biology, drama/dance, elementary, English, mathematics, music, physical, social science, speech. **English:** English lit. **Health:** Health services, music therapy, nursing (RN). **History:** General. **Math:** General. **Parks/recreation:** Health/fitness. **Physical sciences:** Chemistry. **Psychology:** General. **Social sciences:** General. **Theology:** Bible, sacred music. **Visual/performing arts:** Art, dramatic, music performance, studio arts.

**Most popular majors.** Business/marketing 9%, education 15%, health sciences 28%, liberal arts 11%, psychology 13%.

**Computing on campus.** 50 workstations in library, computer center. Dormitories wired for high-speed internet access. Helpline available.

**Student life. Freshman orientation:** Mandatory. Preregistration for classes offered. Orientation for new students is held prior to the start of the fall term. **Policies:** Religious observance required. **Housing:** Guaranteed on-campus for freshmen. Single-sex dorms, apartments, substance-free housing available. $100 fully refundable deposit. **Activities:** Jazz band, choral groups, dance, drama, music ensembles, musical theater, student government, student newspaper, Baptist student union, Afro-American club, psychology club, Fellowship of Christian Athletes, honorary organizations, Church Related Vocations Fellowship, science society, student nurses association, student government association, music therapy association,.

**Athletics.** NAIA. **Intercollegiate:** Baseball M, basketball, golf, soccer, softball W. **Intramural:** Basketball, football (non-tackle) M, football (tackle), soccer, softball, tennis, volleyball. **Team name:** Crusaders.

**Student services.** Adult student services, alcohol/substance abuse counseling, campus ministries, career counseling, services for economically disadvantaged, student employment services, financial aid counseling, personal counseling, placement for graduates, veterans' counselor. **Physically disabled:** Services for visually impaired.

**Contact.** E-mail: admissions@wmcarey.edu
Phone: (601) 318-6103 Toll-free number: (800) 962-5991
Fax: (601) 318-6765
William Curry, Dean of Enrollment Management & Records, William Carey University, 498 Tuscan Avenue, Hattiesburg, MS 39401

# Missouri

## Avila University
### Kansas City, Missouri
www.avila.edu

CB code: 6109

- Private 4-year university and liberal arts college affiliated with Roman Catholic Church
- Commuter campus in very large city
- 1,065 degree-seeking undergraduates: 18% part-time, 68% women, 15% African American, 2% Asian American, 6% Hispanic American, 1% Native American, 3% international
- 509 degree-seeking graduate students
- 54% of applicants admitted
- SAT or ACT (ACT writing optional) required
- 38% graduate within 6 years; 29% enter graduate study

**General.** Founded in 1916. Regionally accredited. **Degrees:** 221 bachelor's awarded; master's offered. **ROTC:** Army. **Calendar:** Semester, extensive summer session. **Full-time faculty:** 68 total; 66% have terminal degrees, 7% minority, 66% women. **Part-time faculty:** 147 total; 24% have terminal degrees, 8% minority, 58% women. **Class size:** 74% < 20, 25% 20-39, less than 1% 40-49, less than 1% 50-99. **Special facilities:** Theater, radiological laboratory, 30 off-campus medical-clinical learning sites, campus media production facilities, nursing learning resource center, photography lab.

**Freshman class profile.** 707 applied, 381 admitted, 116 enrolled.

| Mid 50% test scores | | Rank in top quarter: | 43% |
|---|---|---|---|
| SAT critical reading: | 470-510 | Rank in top tenth: | 7% |
| SAT math: | 480-500 | End year in good standing: | 98% |
| ACT composite: | 20-24 | Return as sophomores: | 69% |
| GPA 3.50 or higher: | 46% | Out-of-state: | 26% |
| GPA 3.0-3.49: | 31% | Live on campus: | 74% |
| GPA 2.0-2.99: | 23% | | |

**Basis for selection.** Unconditional acceptance for applicants with minimum GPA of 2.5 and ACT composite of 20 or higher. Others may be considered. ACT/SAT not required if student has been out of high school 1 year or more. Use ACT subscores for placement in math and English. Audition recommended for drama, music students. **Homeschooled:** SAT or ACT and home school transcripts required. GED may be requested.

**High school preparation.** 17 units required. Required units include English 4, mathematics 3, social studies 3, science 3 (laboratory 1) and foreign language 3. One fine arts also recommended.

**2007-2008 Annual costs.** Tuition/fees: $18,850. Room/board: $5,800. Books/supplies: $800. Personal expenses: $2,200.

**2006-2007 Financial aid. Need-based:** 149 full-time freshmen applied for aid; 143 were judged to have need; 139 of these received aid. Average need met was 25.4%. Average scholarship/grant was $7,035; average loan $2,345. 54% of total undergraduate aid awarded as scholarships/grants, 46% as loans/jobs. **Non-need-based:** Awarded to 394 full-time undergraduates, including 103 freshmen. Scholarships awarded for academics, alumni affiliation, art, athletics, music/drama, religious affiliation. **Additional information:** Financial aid adjusted for increases in tuition based on need.

**Application procedures. Admission:** No deadline. $25 fee, may be waived for applicants with need. Application may be submitted online. Admission notification on a rolling basis. **Financial aid:** Priority date 3/1, closing date 4/1. FAFSA, institutional form required. Applicants notified on a rolling basis starting 2/1; must reply within 2 week(s) of notification.

**Academics.** Outcome-based core curriculum; interdisciplinary course work at junior level required; unique senior experience bridges transition from college to community. **Special study options:** Accelerated study, combined bachelor's/graduate degree, cooperative education, cross-registration, distance learning, double major, dual enrollment of high school students, ESL, exchange student, independent study, internships, liberal arts/career combination, study abroad, teacher certification program, Washington semester, weekend college. **Credit/placement by examination:** AP, CLEP, IB, SAT,

ACT, institutional tests. 32 credit hours maximum toward bachelor's degree. **Support services:** Learning center, reduced course load, remedial instruction, study skills assistance, tutoring, writing center.

**Majors. Biology:** General. **Business:** General, accounting, business admin, finance, international, marketing. **Communications:** General. **Computer sciences:** General. **Education:** Elementary, middle, secondary, special. **English:** English lit. **Health:** Facilities admin, nursing (RN). **History:** General. **Interdisciplinary:** Biological/physical sciences. **Legal studies:** Paralegal. **Philosophy/religion:** Religion. **Physical sciences:** Chemistry. **Psychology:** General. **Public administration:** Social work. **Social sciences:** Political science, sociology. **Visual/performing arts:** Dramatic, music performance, studio arts.

**Most popular majors.** Business/marketing 16%, education 8%, health sciences 33%, psychology 10%, visual/performing arts 9%.

**Computing on campus.** 150 workstations in dormitories, library, computer center, student center. Dormitories wired for high-speed internet access and linked to campus network. Commuter students can connect to campus network. Online course registration, online library, helpline, wireless network available.

**Student life. Freshman orientation:** Mandatory. Preregistration for classes offered. Held 3 days prior to first day of classes; programs available for freshmen-adult transfer students and friends/family of new students. **Policies:** First-time, first-year students not living at home with parents/guardians required to live on campus through sophomore year. **Housing:** Guaranteed on-campus for freshmen. Coed dorms, apartments, substance-free housing available. Single-sex floors available. Apartments available for single students are suite style allowing four students to occupy each suite with each student assigned a private bedroom. **Activities:** Campus ministries, choral groups, dance, drama, international student organizations, literary magazine, musical theater, student government, student newspaper, student nurses association, psychology club, Black Student Union, premedical club, English club, education club, association of radiological science, social work association, National Association of Masters in Psychology, Society of Life Scientists.

**Athletics.** NAIA. **Intercollegiate:** Baseball M, basketball, cheerleading M, football (tackle) M, golf W, soccer, softball W, volleyball W. **Intramural:** Basketball, table tennis, volleyball. **Team name:** Eagles.

**Student services.** Adult student services, alcohol/substance abuse counseling, campus ministries, career counseling, student employment services, financial aid counseling, health services, on-campus daycare, personal counseling, placement for graduates, veterans' counselor, women's services. **Physically disabled:** Services for visually, speech, hearing impaired.

**Contact.** E-mail: admission@avila.edu
Phone: (816) 501-2400 Toll-free number: (800) 462-8452
Fax: (816) 501-2453
Patricia Harper, Director of Admission, Avila University, 11901 Wornall Road, Kansas City, MO 64145-1007

## Baptist Bible College
### Springfield, Missouri
www.baptist.edu

CB code: 0991

- Private 4-year Bible and seminary college affiliated with Baptist faith
- Residential campus in small city
- 544 degree-seeking undergraduates: 18% part-time, 47% women, 1% African American, 1% Asian American, 3% Hispanic American, 1% Native American, 2% international

**General.** Founded in 1950. Candidate for regional accreditation; also accredited by ABHE. **Degrees:** 82 bachelor's, 7 associate awarded; master's offered. **Location:** 180 miles from Kansas City, 225 miles from St. Louis. **Calendar:** Semester, limited summer session. **Full-time faculty:** 39 total. **Part-time faculty:** 13 total.

**Freshman class profile.**

| Mid 50% test scores | | Out-of-state: | 71% |
|---|---|---|---|
| SAT math: | 430-540 | Live on campus: | 69% |
| ACT composite: | 18-23 | International: | 2% |

**Basis for selection.** Baptist pastor's recommendation required. **Homeschooled:** Ability To Benefit Test required by Financial Aid.

**2007-2008 Annual costs.** Tuition/fees: $13,610. Room/board: $5,400. Books/supplies: $800. Personal expenses: $2,164.

**Application procedures. Admission:** Priority date 8/1; no deadline. $40 fee. Application may be submitted online. Admission notification on a rolling basis. **Financial aid:** Closing date 5/1. FAFSA, institutional form required. Applicants notified on a rolling basis; must reply within 2 week(s) of notification.

**Academics. Special study options:** Distance learning. **Credit/placement by examination:** AP, CLEP, ACT. **Support services:** Learning center, reduced course load, remedial instruction, study skills assistance, tutoring.

**Majors. Business:** Administrative services. **Education:** Elementary, music. **Philosophy/religion:** Religion. **Theology:** Missionary, pastoral counseling, religious ed, sacred music, theology.

**Computing on campus.** 70 workstations in library, computer center, student center. Dormitories wired for high-speed internet access and linked to campus network. Online library, helpline, repair service available.

**Student life. Freshman orientation:** Mandatory. Preregistration for classes offered. **Policies:** Religious observance required. **Housing:** Guaranteed on-campus for freshmen. Single-sex dorms, apartments available. **Activities:** Concert band, choral groups, drama, music ensembles, radio station, student government, student newspaper.

**Athletics.** NCCAA. **Intercollegiate:** Basketball, soccer M, volleyball W. **Intramural:** Basketball. **Team name:** Patriots.

**Student services.** Campus ministries, career counseling, financial aid counseling, health services, on-campus daycare, personal counseling, veterans' counselor.

**Contact.** Phone: (417) 268-6013 Toll-free number: (800) 228-5754 Fax: (417) 268-6694
Terry Allcorn, Director of Admissions, Baptist Bible College, 628 East Kearney Street, Springfield, MO 65803

## Calvary Bible College and Theological Seminary
### Kansas City, Missouri
www.calvary.edu
CB code: 6331

- Private 4-year Bible and seminary college affiliated with nondenominational tradition
- Residential campus in large city
- 254 degree-seeking undergraduates: 25% part-time, 52% women, 5% African American, 3% Hispanic American, 3% Native American, 1% international
- 55 degree-seeking graduate students
- 44% graduate within 6 years

**General.** Founded in 1932. Regionally accredited; also accredited by ABHE. **Degrees:** 47 bachelor's, 5 associate awarded; master's, first professional offered. **ROTC:** Army. **Location:** 20 miles from Kansas City. **Calendar:** Semester, limited summer session. **Full-time faculty:** 13 total; 46% have terminal degrees, 23% women. **Part-time faculty:** 18 total; 39% have terminal degrees, 39% women.

**Freshman class profile.** 47 applied, 47 admitted, 30 enrolled.

| Mid 50% test scores | | | |
|---|---|---|---|
| SAT critical reading: | 530-620 | GPA 2.0-2.99: | 4% |
| SAT math: | 410-600 | Rank in top quarter: | 36% |
| ACT composite: | 20-25 | Rank in top tenth: | 9% |
| GPA 3.50 or higher: | 58% | Return as sophomores: | 75% |
| GPA 3.0-3.49: | 38% | Live on campus: | 84% |

**Basis for selection.** Open admission. Christian character stressed along with academic preparation. Pastor's and personal reference forms required. School achievement record and test scores considered. Applicants are required to submit a written Personal Testimony/Confirmation and Statement of Faith. Audition required for music students. **Homeschooled:** Transcripts are required in compliance with state's home school policies. **Learning Disabled:** Students should contact the Director of Admissions.

**2007-2008 Annual costs.** Tuition/fees: $8,500. Room/board: $4,000. Books/supplies: $500. Personal expenses: $1,000.

**2006-2007 Financial aid. Need-based:** 32 full-time freshmen applied for aid; 32 were judged to have need; 32 of these received aid. Average need met was 37%. Average scholarship/grant was $3,826. 44% of total undergraduate aid awarded as scholarships/grants, 56% as loans/jobs. **Non-need-based:** Awarded to 75 full-time undergraduates, including 21 freshmen. Scholarships awarded for academics, alumni affiliation, job skills, music/drama, religious affiliation, ROTC.

**Application procedures. Admission:** Closing date 7/15 (receipt date). $25 fee. Admission notification on a rolling basis. Must reply by 8/15. **Financial aid:** Priority date 3/1, closing date 4/1. FAFSA, institutional form required. Applicants notified on a rolling basis starting 5/1.

**Academics.** Each student carries major in Bible and theology and second major in a professional area. These majors prepare students for vocational and/or volunteer involvement in Christian ministry. **Special study options:** Cooperative education, double major, independent study, internships, student-designed major, teacher certification program. **Credit/placement by examination:** AP, CLEP, IB, institutional tests. **Support services:** Learning center, reduced course load, remedial instruction, study skills assistance, tutoring.

**Majors. Business:** Organizational behavior. **Communications:** Broadcast journalism, media studies. **Education:** Elementary, music, secondary. **Social sciences:** Urban studies. **Theology:** Bible, missionary, pastoral counseling, preministerial, religious ed, sacred music, theology, youth ministry. **Visual/performing arts:** Music performance, piano/organ, voice/opera. **Other:** Christian Broadcasting, Christian Education, Christian Ministry, Organizational Leadership.

**Most popular majors.** Education 27%, theological studies 66%.

**Computing on campus.** 23 workstations in library, student center. Dormitories wired for high-speed internet access. Online course registration, repair service, wireless network available.

**Student life. Freshman orientation:** Mandatory, $50 fee. **Policies:** Weekly Christian ministry, chapel and church attendance required. Single students required to live in college housing unless living with parents or at least 23 years of age. Religious observance required. **Housing:** Guaranteed on-campus for all undergraduates. Single-sex dorms, apartments available. $150 nonrefundable deposit, deadline 7/15. Duplexes available for married students. **Activities:** Pep band, campus ministries, choral groups, drama, music ensembles, musical theater, radio station, student government, Missionary Prayer Fellowship, short-term missions.

**Athletics.** NCCAA. **Intercollegiate:** Basketball, soccer M, volleyball W. **Team name:** Warriors.

**Student services.** Alcohol/substance abuse counseling, campus ministries, student employment services, financial aid counseling, health services, personal counseling, veterans' counselor, women's services.

**Contact.** E-mail: admissions@calvary.edu
Phone: (816) 326-3960 Toll-free number: (800) 326-3960
Fax: (816) 331-4474
Damon Horton, Director of Admissions and Financial Aid, Calvary Bible College and Theological Seminary, 15800 Calvary Road, Kansas City, MO 64147

## Central Bible College
### Springfield, Missouri
www.cbcag.edu
CB code: 6085

- Private 4-year Bible college affiliated with Assemblies of God
- Residential campus in small city
- 699 degree-seeking undergraduates: 11% part-time, 43% women
- 93% of applicants admitted
- Application essay required

**General.** Founded in 1922. Accredited by ABHE. **Degrees:** 113 bachelor's, 17 associate awarded. **ROTC:** Army, Air Force. **Location:** 210 miles from St. Louis, 174 miles from Kansas City. **Calendar:** Semester, extensive summer session. **Full-time faculty:** 37 total. **Part-time faculty:** 21 total.

**Freshman class profile.** 376 applied, 349 admitted, 182 enrolled.

| Mid 50% test scores | | | |
|---|---|---|---|
| SAT critical reading: | 400-620 | SAT writing: | 400-620 |
| SAT math: | 410-600 | ACT composite: | 18-24 |

**Basis for selection.** Special consideration given to members of Assemblies of God and all applicants who rank in top half of graduating class who meet entrance requirements. Interview recommended for all students; audition recommended for music students. **Homeschooled:** Transcript of courses and grades required.

**High school preparation.** Strong background in English, math, and science recommended. Computer literacy course recommended.

**2008-2009 Annual costs.** Tuition/fees: $10,630. Room/board: $5,032. Books/supplies: $550.

**Application procedures. Admission:** Priority date 8/15; no deadline. $25 fee, may be waived for applicants with need. Admission notification on a rolling basis. **Financial aid:** Priority date 5/1; no closing date. FAFSA required. Applicants notified on a rolling basis starting 5/15; must reply within 3 week(s) of notification.

**Academics. Special study options:** Accelerated study, cooperative education, cross-registration, double major, independent study, internships. **Credit/placement by examination:** CLEP, SAT, ACT, institutional tests. 24 credit hours maximum toward bachelor's degree. **Support services:** Reduced course load, remedial instruction, tutoring.

**Majors. Theology:** Bible, missionary, pastoral counseling, religious ed, sacred music, theology, youth ministry. **Other:** Ministry in arts.

**Computing on campus.** 20 workstations in library, computer center.

**Student life. Freshman orientation:** Mandatory, $175 fee. Preregistration for classes offered. **Policies:** Practices which are known to be morally wrong by Biblical teaching are not acceptable for members of the college community. Religious observance required. **Housing:** Guaranteed on-campus for freshmen. Single-sex dorms, apartments, substance-free housing available. **Activities:** Jazz band, choral groups, drama, music ensembles, radio station, student government, student newspaper, Campus Missions Fellowship, Delta Chi, FOCAL, student government association, student ministries, multicultural club.

**Athletics.** NCCAA. **Intercollegiate:** Basketball, soccer M, volleyball W. **Intramural:** Basketball, softball. **Team name:** Spartans.

**Student services.** Student employment services, financial aid counseling, health services, personal counseling, placement for graduates, veterans' counselor. **Physically disabled:** Services for hearing impaired.

**Contact.** E-mail: info@cbcag.edu
Phone: (417) 833-2551 ext. 1290 Toll-free number: (800) 831-4222
Fax: (417) 833-5141
Bill Davis, Registrar, Central Bible College, 3000 North Grant Avenue, Springfield, MO 65803-1069

---

## Central Christian College of the Bible
**Moberly, Missouri**
www.cccb.edu                    CB code: 6145

▶ Private 4-year Bible college affiliated with Christian Church
▶ Residential campus in large town

**General.** Founded in 1957. Accredited by ABHE. **Location:** 35 miles from Columbia. **Calendar:** Semester.

**Annual costs/financial aid.** Full-time students receive full scholarship for tuition only. Room and board $5,300 for two semesters. Required fees $575 per semester. Off-campus students pay a $625 facilities usage fee per semester. Books/supplies: $750. Personal expenses: $3,846. Need-based financial aid available to full-time and part-time students.

**Contact.** Phone: (888) 263-3900
Director of Admission, 911 East Urbandale Drive, Moberly, MO 65270-1997

---

## Central Methodist University
**Fayette, Missouri**
www.centralmethodist.edu            CB code: 6089

▶ Private 4-year university and liberal arts college affiliated with United Methodist Church
▶ Residential campus in small town
▶ 914 degree-seeking undergraduates: 3% part-time, 49% women, 8% African American, 1% Asian American, 2% Hispanic American, 1% Native American, 1% international
▶ 67% of applicants admitted
▶ SAT or ACT (ACT writing optional) required
▶ 42% graduate within 6 years

**General.** Founded in 1854. Regionally accredited. **Degrees:** 149 bachelor's, 2 associate awarded; master's offered. **ROTC:** Army, Air Force. **Location:** 25 miles from Columbia,150 miles from St. Louis. **Calendar:** Semester, limited summer session. **Full-time faculty:** 55 total; 60% have terminal degrees, 2% minority, 42% women. **Part-time faculty:** 34 total; 18% have terminal degrees, 47% women. **Class size:** 63% < 20, 29% 20-39, 5% 40-49, 3% 50-99. **Special facilities:** Observatory and laboratory, natural history museum, conservatory of music.

**Freshman class profile.** 1,127 applied, 758 admitted, 270 enrolled.

| Mid 50% test scores | | | |
|---|---|---|---|
| ACT composite: | 19-24 | Rank in top tenth: | 12% |
| GPA 3.50 or higher: | 36% | Return as sophomores: | 65% |
| GPA 3.0-3.49: | 33% | Out-of-state: | 11% |
| GPA 2.0-2.99: | 31% | Live on campus: | 96% |
| Rank in top quarter: | 33% | International: | 1% |

**Basis for selection.** Full acceptance requires 2.5 GPA and 20 ACT/940 SAT. Interview required for nursing applicants; audition recommended for drama, music students.

**High school preparation.** 24 units recommended. Recommended units include English 4, mathematics 3, social studies 3, science 3 and foreign language 2. 2 humanities recommended.

**2008-2009 Annual costs.** Tuition/fees: $17,980. Room/board: $6,000. Books/supplies: $900. Personal expenses: $2,250.

**2007-2008 Financial aid. Need-based:** 270 full-time freshmen applied for aid; 270 were judged to have need; 270 of these received aid. Average need met was 56%. Average scholarship/grant was $5,186; average loan $3,306. 66% of total undergraduate aid awarded as scholarships/grants, 34% as loans/jobs. **Non-need-based:** Awarded to 1,200 full-time undergraduates, including 478 freshmen. Scholarships awarded for academics, alumni affiliation, athletics, leadership, music/drama, religious affiliation, ROTC.

**Application procedures. Admission:** No deadline. $20 fee, may be waived for applicants with need. Application may be submitted online. Admission notification on a rolling basis beginning on or about 10/1. Must reply by May 1 or within 4 week(s) if notified thereafter. **Financial aid:** Priority date 3/15; no closing date. FAFSA required. Applicants notified on a rolling basis starting 1/30; must reply within 2 week(s) of notification.

**Academics.** Nursing students required to have notebook computer. **Special study options:** Accelerated study, combined bachelor's/graduate degree, distance learning, double major, dual enrollment of high school students, honors, independent study, internships, liberal arts/career combination, student-designed major, study abroad, teacher certification program. 3-year bachelor's degree, 2-week January travel program. **Credit/placement by examination:** AP, CLEP, IB, institutional tests. 32 credit hours maximum toward associate degree, 32 toward bachelor's. **Support services:** Learning center, pre-admission summer program, reduced course load, remedial instruction, study skills assistance, tutoring.

**Majors. Biology:** General, marine. **Business:** General, accounting, banking, financial services, business admin, entrepreneurial studies, international, management science. **Communications:** General. **Computer sciences:** Computer science. **Conservation:** Environmental science. **Education:** Biology, chemistry, early childhood, elementary, foreign languages, middle, music, physical, physics, science, secondary, social science, special. **English:** English lit. **Family/consumer sciences:** Child development. **Foreign languages:** Spanish. **Health:** Athletic training, nursing (RN). **History:** General. **Math:** General. **Parks/recreation:** Facilities management. **Philosophy/religion:** Philosophy, religion. **Physical sciences:** Chemistry, physics. **Protective services:** Law enforcement admin. **Psychology:** General. **Social sciences:** Political science, sociology. **Visual/performing arts:** Dramatic, music performance. **Other:** Marketing and Advertising.

**Most popular majors.** Business/marketing 28%, education 21%, health sciences 15%.

**Computing on campus.** 200 workstations in dormitories, library, student center. Dormitories wired for high-speed internet access and linked to campus network. Commuter students can connect to campus network. Online library, helpline, repair service, wireless network available.

**Student life. Freshman orientation:** Available, $100 fee. Preregistration for classes offered. **Housing:** Guaranteed on-campus for all undergraduates. Coed dorms, single-sex dorms, apartments, fraternity/sorority housing available. $100 fully refundable deposit. **Activities:** Bands, campus ministries, choral groups, drama, international student organizations, literary magazine, music ensembles, musical theater, radio station, student government, student newspaper, TV station, Alpha Phi Omega, prelaw club, religious, service, business, music organizations.

**Athletics.** NAIA. **Intercollegiate:** Baseball M, basketball, cross-country, football (tackle) M, soccer, softball W, track and field, volleyball W. **Intramural:** Basketball, football (tackle) M, golf, racquetball, soccer, softball, tennis, track and field, volleyball. **Team name:** Eagles.

**Student services.** Alcohol/substance abuse counseling, campus ministries, career counseling, student employment services, financial aid counseling, health services, personal counseling, placement for graduates.

**Contact.** E-mail: admissions@centralmethodist.edu
Phone: (660) 248-6251 Toll-free number: (877) 268-1854
Fax: (660) 248-1872
Lawrence Anderson, Director of Admissions, Central Methodist University, 411 Central Methodist Square, Fayette, MO 65248-1198

## Chamberlain College of Nursing
### St. Louis, Missouri
www.chamberlain.edu/collegeboard       CB code: 3139

- For-profit 4-year nursing college affiliated with United Church of Christ
- Commuter campus in very large city

**General.** Founded in 1889. Regionally accredited. **Calendar:** Semester.

**Annual costs/financial aid.** Above costs are for two of the required three semesters per year. Books/supplies: $1,100. Personal expenses: $550. Need-based financial aid available to full-time and part-time students.

**Contact.** Phone: (314) 768-7528
National Director of Admissions, 6150 Oakland Avenue, St. Louis, MO 63139

## College of the Ozarks
### Point Lookout, Missouri
www.cofo.edu       CB code: 6713

- Private 4-year liberal arts college affiliated with Presbyterian Church (USA)
- Residential campus in small town
- 1,336 degree-seeking undergraduates: 2% part-time, 56% women, 1% African American, 1% Asian American, 1% Hispanic American, 1% Native American, 1% international
- 12% of applicants admitted
- SAT or ACT (ACT writing optional), interview required
- 60% graduate within 6 years; 17% enter graduate study

**General.** Founded in 1906. Regionally accredited. No tuition; students work at a campus job rather than pay tuition. **Degrees:** 288 bachelor's awarded. **ROTC:** Army. **Location:** 2 miles from Branson, 45 miles from Springfield. **Calendar:** Semester. **Full-time faculty:** 88 total; 53% have terminal degrees, 1% minority, 30% women. **Part-time faculty:** 41 total; 12% have terminal degrees, 5% minority, 49% women. **Class size:** 58% < 20, 37% 20-39, 2% 40-49, 2% 50-99. **Special facilities:** Greenhouses, college-operated hotel, observatory, nature preserve.

**Freshman class profile.** 2,709 applied, 321 admitted, 283 enrolled.

| Mid 50% test scores | | Rank in top tenth: | 14% |
|---|---|---|---|
| ACT composite: | 21-26 | End year in good standing: | 75% |
| GPA 3.50 or higher: | 60% | Return as sophomores: | 84% |
| GPA 3.0-3.49: | 30% | Out-of-state: | 37% |
| GPA 2.0-2.99: | 10% | Live on campus: | 99% |
| Rank in top quarter: | 52% | International: | 1% |

**Basis for selection.** High school record, financial need, test scores, class rank, recommendations, activities and interview important. Academic interest and growth, development of intellectual skills considered. TOEFL for non-native English speakers. ACT preferred. Audition recommended for music students; portfolio recommended for art students. **Homeschooled:** We do not accept pass grades. Candidates must present a transcript with a letter or percentage grade.

**High school preparation.** College-preparatory program recommended. 24 units recommended. Recommended units include English 4, mathematics 3, social studies 3, science 2 (laboratory 1) and foreign language 2. Public speaking, visual and performing arts recommended.

**2008-2009 Annual costs.** Cost of full-time tuition met through combination of institutional work program and federal, state, and institutional funding. Required fees: $390. Full-time students participating in work program work 15 hours per week for 16 weeks and one 40-hour work week per semester. Part-time students (commuters only) pay $295 per credit hour for tuition and additional $390 per year as required fees. Room/board: $4,700. Books/supplies: $800. Personal expenses: $390.

**2007-2008 Financial aid. Need-based:** Average need met was 84%. Average scholarship/grant was $10,379. 85% of total undergraduate aid awarded as scholarships/grants, 15% as loans/jobs. **Non-need-based:** Scholarships awarded for academics, art, athletics, leadership, music/drama, ROTC, state residency.

**Application procedures. Admission:** Priority date 2/15; deadline 3/15 (receipt date). No application fee. Application may be submitted online. Admission notification on a rolling basis beginning on or about 2/1. Must reply by May 1 or within 2 week(s) if notified thereafter. **Financial aid:** Priority date 2/15; no closing date. FAFSA required. Applicants notified by 7/1.

**Academics.** Curriculum offers liberal arts foundation with intensive concentration in special areas. **Special study options:** Accelerated study, combined bachelor's/graduate degree, double major, dual enrollment of high school students, honors, independent study, internships, liberal arts/career combination, student-designed major, teacher certification program. 3-2 engineering program, interdisciplinary programs, paraprofessional counseling certificate, pre-professional programs, dietetics program. **Credit/placement by examination:** AP, CLEP, IB, ACT, institutional tests. **Support services:** Learning center, reduced course load, remedial instruction, study skills assistance, tutoring, writing center.

**Majors. Agriculture:** Agronomy, animal sciences, business, horticultural science, horticulture, mechanization. **Biology:** General. **Business:** Accounting, business admin, hospitality admin, international, managerial economics, marketing, restaurant/food services. **Communications:** General, broadcast journalism, journalism, public relations. **Computer sciences:** General, computer science. **Conservation:** Wildlife. **Education:** Agricultural, art, biology, business, chemistry, early childhood, elementary, English, family/consumer sciences, history, mathematics, music, physical, science, secondary, social studies, technology/industrial arts. **English:** English lit. **Family/consumer sciences:** General, child development, food/nutrition. **Foreign languages:** French, Spanish. **Health:** Dietetics, nursing (RN), prenursing. **History:** General. **Math:** General. **Parks/recreation:** Facilities management, health/fitness. **Philosophy/religion:** Philosophy, religion. **Physical sciences:** Chemistry. **Protective services:** Corrections, forensics, police science. **Psychology:** General. **Public administration:** Social work. **Social sciences:** Sociology. **Theology:** Sacred music. **Visual/performing arts:** Art, dramatic, studio arts, theater design.

**Most popular majors.** Agriculture 7%, business/marketing 17%, education 20%, psychology 7%, security/protective services 9%.

**Computing on campus.** 160 workstations in dormitories, library. Dormitories wired for high-speed internet access and linked to campus network. Commuter students can connect to campus network. Online course registration, online library, helpline, repair service, wireless network available.

**Student life. Freshman orientation:** Mandatory. Preregistration for classes offered. 10-day program held the week before classes begin. **Policies:** Convocations and chapel attendance required for some students. All full-time students must live in residence halls unless they meet one of the following criteria: 21 years of age or older, married, living with parents, or veteran of armed services. Religious observance required. **Housing:** Guaranteed on-campus for all undergraduates. Single-sex dorms, substance-free housing available. $100 fully refundable deposit. **Activities:** Bands, choral groups, drama, film society, literary magazine, music ensembles, musical theater, radio station, student government, student newspaper, Baptist Student Union, fire department, InterVarsity Christian Fellowship, wilderness activities club, Aggie club, Flying Falcons, business undergraduate society, Bonner Organization, College Republicans, College Democrats.

**Athletics.** NAIA. **Intercollegiate:** Baseball M, basketball, volleyball W. **Intramural:** Basketball, fencing, football (non-tackle) M, soccer, softball, swimming, tennis, volleyball. **Team name:** Bobcats.

**Student services.** Campus ministries, career counseling, student employment services, financial aid counseling, health services, on-campus daycare, personal counseling, placement for graduates, veterans' counselor.

**Contact.** E-mail: admiss4@cofo.edu
Phone: (417) 334-6411 ext. 4218 Toll-free number: (800) 222-0525
Fax: (417) 335-2618
Marci Linson, Dean of Admissions, College of the Ozarks, PO Box 17, Point Lookout, MO 65726-0017

## Columbia College
### Columbia, Missouri
### www.ccis.edu
**CB code: 6095**

▶ Private 4-year liberal arts college affiliated with Christian Church (Disciples of Christ)

▶ Commuter campus in small city

▶ 1,034 degree-seeking undergraduates: 18% part-time, 59% women, 6% African American, 1% Asian American, 2% Hispanic American, 1% Native American, 8% international

▶ 155 degree-seeking graduate students

▶ 57% of applicants admitted

▶ SAT or ACT (ACT writing optional) required

▶ 44% graduate within 6 years; 23% enter graduate study

**General.** Founded in 1851. Regionally accredited. Programs for adult students offered on campus and at 32 teaching locations in United States and Cuba. **Degrees:** 152 bachelor's, 4 associate awarded; master's offered. **ROTC:** Army, Naval, Air Force. **Location:** 120 miles from Kansas City, 120 miles from St. Louis. **Calendar:** Semester, limited summer session. **Full-time faculty:** 61 total; 88% have terminal degrees, 7% minority, 44% women. **Part-time faculty:** 24 total; 29% have terminal degrees, 12% minority, 46% women. **Class size:** 66% < 20, 34% 20-39.

**Freshman class profile.** 939 applied, 535 admitted, 208 enrolled.

| Mid 50% test scores | | | |
|---|---|---|---|
| SAT critical reading: | 460-600 | Rank in top quarter: | 35% |
| SAT math: | 600-660 | Rank in top tenth: | 16% |
| ACT composite: | 20-25 | Return as sophomores: | 56% |
| GPA 3.50 or higher: | 37% | Out-of-state: | 6% |
| GPA 3.0-3.49: | 30% | Live on campus: | 66% |
| GPA 2.0-2.99: | 28% | International: | 16% |

**Basis for selection.** School achievement, class rank, test scores most important. ACT preferred. Audition required for music students; portfolio required for art students. Interview recommended for academically weak students. **Homeschooled:** GED is required; ACT strongly recommended.

**High school preparation.** 12 units recommended. Recommended units include English 4, mathematics 3, social studies 2 and science 3.

**2007-2008 Annual costs.** Tuition/fees: $13,034. Room/board: $5,320. Books/supplies: $748. Personal expenses: $1,056.

**2006-2007 Financial aid. Need-based:** 170 full-time freshmen applied for aid; 107 were judged to have need; 103 of these received aid. Average need met was 72%. Average scholarship/grant was $6,255; average loan $2,988. 39% of total undergraduate aid awarded as scholarships/grants, 61% as loans/jobs. **Non-need-based:** Awarded to 534 full-time undergraduates, including 113 freshmen. Scholarships awarded for academics, alumni affiliation, art, athletics, leadership, music/drama, religious affiliation, ROTC, state residency.

**Application procedures. Admission:** No deadline. $25 fee, may be waived for applicants with need. Application may be submitted online. Admission notification on a rolling basis beginning on or about 3/15. **Financial aid:** Priority date 3/15; no closing date. FAFSA, institutional form required. Applicants notified on a rolling basis starting 3/1; must reply within 2 week(s) of notification.

**Academics.** Evening degree program available based on 8-week ongoing terms. **Special study options:** Accelerated study, cooperative education, cross-registration, distance learning, double major, dual enrollment of high school students, ESL, honors, independent study, internships, student-designed major, study abroad, teacher certification program. **Credit/placement by examination:** AP, CLEP, IB, SAT, ACT, institutional tests. 6 credit hours maximum toward associate degree, 12 toward bachelor's. **Support services:** Learning center, reduced course load, remedial instruction, study skills assistance, tutoring, writing center.

**Honors college/program.** High school GPA of 3.5 or greater, ACT in 78th percentile or higher required for admission.

**Majors. Area/ethnic studies:** American. **Biology:** General. **Business:** Accounting, business admin, finance, international, management science, marketing. **Communications:** General. **Computer sciences:** General, computer science. **Conservation:** Environmental studies. **English:** English lit. **History:** General. **Liberal arts:** Arts/sciences. **Math:** General. **Physical sciences:** Chemistry. **Protective services:** Forensics, law enforcement admin. **Psychology:** General. **Public administration:** Human services. **Social sciences:** Political science, sociology. **Visual/performing arts:** Art, ceramics, drawing, painting, photography, printmaking, studio arts. **Other:** Philosophy and Religious Studies.

**Most popular majors.** Biology 9%, business/marketing 32%, interdisciplinary studies 10%, security/protective services 12%, visual/performing arts 8%.

**Computing on campus.** 150 workstations in dormitories, library, computer center, student center. Dormitories wired for high-speed internet access and linked to campus network. Commuter students can connect to campus network. Online course registration, online library, helpline, student web hosting, wireless network available.

**Student life. Freshman orientation:** Mandatory, $25 fee. Preregistration for classes offered. Held weekend before classes start. **Policies:** Alcohol and illegal drugs forbidden on campus. **Housing:** Guaranteed on-campus for freshmen. Coed dorms, single-sex dorms, apartments, substance-free housing available. $100 fully refundable deposit. **Activities:** Choral groups, drama, international student organizations, literary magazine, student government, student newspaper, Black student association, Students in Free Enterprise, Student Leaders Advocating Teaching Excellence, Partners in Education, criminal justice association, Habitat for Humanity, Elysium Players, Fellowship of Christian Athletes.

**Athletics.** NAIA. **Intercollegiate:** Basketball, soccer M, softball W, volleyball W. **Intramural:** Basketball, soccer, softball, table tennis, tennis, volleyball. **Team name:** Cougars.

**Student services.** Adult student services, alcohol/substance abuse counseling, career counseling, services for economically disadvantaged, student employment services, financial aid counseling, health services, personal counseling, placement for graduates, veterans' counselor. **Physically disabled:** Services for hearing impaired.

**Contact.** E-mail: admissions@ccis.edu
Phone: (573) 875-7352 Toll-free number: (800) 231-2391 ext. 7352
Fax: (573) 875-7506
Regina Morin, Director of Admissions, Columbia College, 1001 Rogers Street, Columbia, MO 65216

## Conception Seminary College
### Conception, Missouri
### www.conception.edu
**CB code: 6112**

▶ Private 4-year seminary college for men affiliated with Roman Catholic Church

▶ Residential campus in rural community

▶ 95 degree-seeking undergraduates

▶ 95% of applicants admitted

▶ ACT, application essay required

**General.** Founded in 1883. Regionally accredited. Operated by Benedictine Monks of Conception Abbey, for both independent seminary students and candidates affiliated with sponsoring diocese. Women may enroll on part-time basis. **Degrees:** 16 bachelor's awarded. **Location:** 100 miles from Kansas City, 45 miles from St. Joseph. **Calendar:** Semester. **Full-time faculty:** 10 total. **Part-time faculty:** 18 total. **Class size:** 81% < 20, 19% 20-39. **Special facilities:** Basilica.

**Freshman class profile.** 20 applied, 19 admitted, 19 enrolled.

| | | | |
|---|---|---|---|
| Out-of-state: | 71% | Live on campus: | 100% |

**Basis for selection.** ACT composite scores tend to count more heavily than high school grades. Class rank considered. Applicants must be sponsored. Interview recommended.

**High school preparation.** 16 units required. Required units include English 4, social studies 4 and science 4.

**2008-2009 Annual costs.** Tuition/fees: $14,904. Room/board: $8,736. Books/supplies: $450. Personal expenses: $800.

**Financial aid. Non-need-based:** Scholarships awarded for academics.

**Application procedures. Admission:** Priority date 6/1; deadline 7/31 (receipt date). No application fee. Application may be submitted online. Admission notification on a rolling basis beginning on or about 2/1. Must reply by 8/10. Foreign applications require written certification of financial, ecclesiastical sponsorship. **Financial aid:** No deadline. FAFSA required. Applicants notified on a rolling basis starting 8/1; must reply by 8/20.

**Academics.** Curriculum combines liberal arts and pre-theology training to accommodate varying degrees of vocational commitment. **Special study options:** ESL, independent study. **Credit/placement by examination:** CLEP, institutional tests. 12 credit hours maximum toward bachelor's degree. **Support services:** Learning center, reduced course load, remedial instruction, tutoring.

**Majors. Philosophy/religion:** Philosophy.

**Computing on campus.** 15 workstations in dormitories, library, computer center. Dormitories wired for high-speed internet access and linked to campus network. Online library, helpline, repair service available.

**Student life. Freshman orientation:** Mandatory. Preregistration for classes offered. **Policies:** Religious observance required. **Housing:** Guaranteed on-campus for all undergraduates: Substance-free housing available. $50 deposit. **Activities:** Choral groups, drama, music ensembles, musical theater, student government, student newspaper, apostolic work, mission club, social concerns, community council, Inner-Life.

**Athletics. Intercollegiate:** Basketball M, soccer M, volleyball M. **Intramural:** Basketball M, football (non-tackle) M, racquetball M, soccer M, softball M, swimming M, table tennis M, tennis M, track and field M, volleyball M, weight lifting M. **Team name:** Blue Knights.

**Student services.** Adult student services, alcohol/substance abuse counseling, campus ministries, career counseling, financial aid counseling, health services, personal counseling.

**Contact.** E-mail: vocations@conception.edu
Phone: (660) 944-2886 Fax: (660) 944-2829
Br. Victor Schinstock, Director of Admissions, Conception Seminary College, Box 502, Conception, MO 64433-0502

---

## Culver-Stockton College

**Canton, Missouri**
**www.culver.edu**

**CB member**
**CB code: 6123**

- Private 4-year liberal arts college affiliated with Christian Church (Disciples of Christ)
- Residential campus in small town
- 807 degree-seeking undergraduates: 5% part-time, 59% women
- 76% of applicants admitted
- SAT or ACT (ACT writing optional) required
- 47% graduate within 6 years; 13% enter graduate study

**General.** Founded in 1853. Regionally accredited. **Degrees:** 165 bachelor's awarded. **Location:** 130 miles from St. Louis, 20 miles from Quincy, IL. **Calendar:** Semester, limited summer session. **Full-time faculty:** 51 total; 67% have terminal degrees, 8% minority, 28% women. **Part-time faculty:** 3 total; 33% have terminal degrees, 100% women. **Class size:** 67% < 20, 32% 20-39, less than 1% 40-49, less than 1% 50-99.

**Freshman class profile.** 1,233 applied, 932 admitted, 204 enrolled.

| Mid 50% test scores | | End year in good standing: | 87% |
|---|---|---|---|
| ACT composite: | 18-24 | Return as sophomores: | 70% |
| GPA 3.50 or higher: | 41% | Out-of-state: | 42% |
| GPA 3.0-3.49: | 24% | Live on campus: | 93% |
| GPA 2.0-2.99: | 34% | Fraternities: | 27% |
| Rank in top quarter: | 33% | Sororities: | 38% |
| Rank in top tenth: | 14% | | |

**Basis for selection.** Secondary school record, class rank, test scores most important; extracurricular activities, talent, personal qualities considered. **Learning Disabled:** Must request accommodations and submit appropriate documentation.

**High school preparation.** 15 units required. Required and recommended units include English 4, mathematics 2, social studies 3 and science 4.

**2007-2008 Annual costs.** Tuition/fees: $16,850. Room/board: $6,850. Books/supplies: $1,000. Personal expenses: $580.

**2007-2008 Financial aid. Need-based:** 199 full-time freshmen applied for aid; 182 were judged to have need; 182 of these received aid. Average need met was 76%. Average scholarship/grant was $11,565; average loan $3,436. 60% of total undergraduate aid awarded as scholarships/grants, 40% as loans/jobs. **Non-need-based:** Scholarships awarded for academics, alumni affiliation, art, athletics, job skills, leadership, music/drama, religious affiliation, state residency. **Additional information:** Interview required for scholarships, audition required for music students, portfolio required for art students.

**Application procedures. Admission:** Priority date 5/1; no deadline. No application fee. Application may be submitted online. Admission notification on a rolling basis. **Financial aid:** Priority date 3/1, closing date 6/1. FAFSA required. Applicants notified on a rolling basis starting 2/15; must reply within 2 week(s) of notification.

**Academics. Special study options:** Combined bachelor's/graduate degree, distance learning, double major, dual enrollment of high school students, honors, independent study, internships, liberal arts/career combination, semester at sea, student-designed major, study abroad, teacher certification program, Washington semester. **Credit/placement by examination:** AP, CLEP, IB, ACT, institutional tests. 94 credit hours maximum toward bachelor's degree. **Support services:** Learning center, reduced course load, remedial instruction, study skills assistance, tutoring, writing center.

**Majors. Biology:** General. **Business:** Accounting, business admin, finance, management information systems. **Education:** General, art, elementary, music, physical, speech. **English:** English lit. **Health:** Athletic training, nursing (RN). **History:** General. **Math:** General. **Parks/recreation:** Sports admin. **Philosophy/religion:** Religion. **Protective services:** Law enforcement admin. **Psychology:** General. **Visual/performing arts:** Art, arts management, dramatic.

**Most popular majors.** Business/marketing 23%, education 13%, health sciences 8%, psychology 15%, security/protective services 9%, visual/performing arts 13%.

**Computing on campus.** 110 workstations in dormitories, library, computer center, student center. Dormitories wired for high-speed internet access and linked to campus network. Commuter students can connect to campus network. Online library, helpline, repair service, student web hosting, wireless network available.

**Student life. Freshman orientation:** Mandatory, $100 fee. Preregistration for classes offered. Held for 3 days prior to the beginning of the fall semester. **Policies:** Students have voting representation on faculty committees. **Housing:** Guaranteed on-campus for all undergraduates. Coed dorms, single-sex dorms, fraternity/sorority housing, substance-free housing available. $100 deposit, deadline 8/15. All students under age 21 required to live on campus unless living with parents. **Activities:** Bands, campus ministries, choral groups, dance, drama, literary magazine, music ensembles, musical theater, radio station, student government, student newspaper, Disciples on Campus, Christian Fellowship Group, Fellowship of Christian Athletes, criminal justice club, psychology club, HOPE, student nurses organization.

**Athletics.** NAIA. **Intercollegiate:** Baseball M, basketball, cheerleading, cross-country, football (tackle) M, golf, soccer, softball W, track and field, volleyball W. **Intramural:** Basketball, football (non-tackle), racquetball, soccer, softball, table tennis, tennis, volleyball. **Team name:** Wildcats.

**Student services.** Adult student services, alcohol/substance abuse counseling, campus ministries, career counseling, student employment services, financial aid counseling, personal counseling, placement for graduates, veterans' counselor.

**Contact.** E-mail: enrollment@culver.edu
Phone: (800) 537-1883 Toll-free number: (800) 537-1883
Fax: (573) 288-6618
Jim Lynes, Director of Admissions, Culver-Stockton College, One College Hill, Canton, MO 63435-1299

---

## DeVry University: Kansas City

**Kansas City, Missouri**
**www.devry.edu**

**CB code: 6092**

- For-profit 4-year university
- Commuter campus in large city
- 950 degree-seeking undergraduates: 46% part-time, 29% women, 19% African American, 3% Asian American, 3% Hispanic American, 2% Native American
- 131 degree-seeking graduate students
- Interview required
- 36% graduate within 6 years

**General.** Founded in 1931. Regionally accredited. **Degrees:** 212 bachelor's, 28 associate awarded; master's offered. **Location:** 15 miles from downtown. **Calendar:** Semester, extensive summer session. **Full-time faculty:** 33 total; 9% minority, 27% women. **Part-time faculty:** 49 total; 14% minority, 41% women.

**Freshman class profile.**

| Return as sophomores: | 35% | Out-of-state: | 34% |
|---|---|---|---|

**Basis for selection.** Applicants must have high school diploma or equivalant degree from accredited postsecondary institution, and be at least 17 years of age on the first day of classes. New students may enter at beginning of any semester. CPT also accepted.

**High school preparation.** Required units include mathematics 1. Math unit must be algebra or higher.

**2007-2008 Annual costs.** Tuition/fees: $13,220. Books/supplies: $1,300. Personal expenses: $5,082.

**Financial aid.** All financial aid based on need.

**Application procedures. Admission:** No deadline. $50 fee, may be waived for applicants with need. Application may be submitted online. Admission notification on a rolling basis. **Financial aid:** No deadline. FAFSA required. Applicants notified on a rolling basis.

**Academics. Special study options:** Accelerated study, distance learning, weekend college. **Credit/placement by examination:** CLEP, institutional tests. **Support services:** Learning center, remedial instruction, tutoring.

**Majors. Biology:** Bioinformatics. **Business:** General, business admin. **Computer sciences:** General. **Engineering technology:** Computer. **Other:** Biomedical engineering technology, Technical management.

**Most popular majors.** Business/marketing 47%, computer/information sciences 29%, engineering/engineering technologies 21%.

**Computing on campus.** 1,300 workstations in library, computer center. Online course registration, online library, helpline available.

**Student life. Freshman orientation:** Mandatory. **Housing:** Private apartments, student-plan housing, private rooms available. **Activities:** Association of Information Technology Professionals, Campus Crusade for Christ, Institute for Electrical & Electronics Engineers, Phi Beta Lambda, Tau Alpha Pi, professional certification club, drama club, Gamma Beta Phi.

**Athletics. Intramural:** Volleyball.

**Student services.** Career counseling, student employment services, financial aid counseling, placement for graduates, veterans' counselor. **Physically disabled:** Services for visually, hearing impaired.

**Contact.** E-mail: ssmeed@kc.devry.edu
Phone: (816) 941-2810 Toll-free number: (800) 821-3766
Fax: (816) 941-0896
Shane Smeed, Director of Admissions, DeVry University: Kansas City, 11224 Holmes Street, Kansas City, MO 64131-3626

---

## Drury University
**Springfield, Missouri**
www.drury.edu

**CB member**
**CB code: 6169**

- Private 4-year university and liberal arts college affiliated with United Church of Christ and Christian Church (Disciples of Christ)
- Residential campus in large city
- 1,605 degree-seeking undergraduates: 2% part-time, 53% women
- 476 degree-seeking graduate students
- 76% of applicants admitted
- SAT or ACT (ACT writing optional) required
- 68% graduate within 6 years; 39% enter graduate study

**General.** Founded in 1873. Regionally accredited. **Degrees:** 340 bachelor's awarded; master's offered. **ROTC:** Army. **Location:** 220 miles from St. Louis, 170 miles from Kansas City. **Calendar:** Semester, limited summer session. **Full-time faculty:** 130 total; 88% have terminal degrees, 6% minority, 38% women. **Part-time faculty:** 47 total; 23% have terminal degrees, 4% minority, 49% women. **Class size:** 64% < 20, 33% 20-39, 2% 40-49, 1% 50-99. **Special facilities:** Science center, greenhouse, astronomical observation station, electronic music lab.

**Freshman class profile.** 1,193 applied, 903 admitted, 378 enrolled.

| Mid 50% test scores | | | |
|---|---|---|---|
| ACT composite: | 22-28 | Return as sophomores: | 82% |
| GPA 3.50 or higher: | 74% | Out-of-state: | 19% |
| GPA 3.0-3.49: | 19% | Live on campus: | 62% |
| GPA 2.0-2.99: | 7% | International: | 5% |
| Rank in top quarter: | 65% | Fraternities: | 37% |
| Rank in top tenth: | 33% | Sororities: | 33% |

**Basis for selection.** School achievement record, test scores, reference from high school counselor, essay important. Interview recommended for all students. Audition recommended for music, theater students; portfolio recommended for architecture, art students.

**High school preparation.** 12 units required. Required and recommended units include English 4, mathematics 3-4, social studies 3, science 3 and foreign language 2.

**2008-2009 Annual costs.** Tuition/fees: $18,409. Room/board: $6,384. Books/supplies: $1,500. Personal expenses: $1,500.

**2007-2008 Financial aid. Need-based:** 366 full-time freshmen applied for aid; 349 were judged to have need; 349 of these received aid. Average need met was 83%. Average scholarship/grant was $5,898; average loan $4,315. 31% of total undergraduate aid awarded as scholarships/grants, 69% as loans/jobs. **Non-need-based:** Awarded to 1,844 full-time undergraduates, including 439 freshmen. Scholarships awarded for academics, alumni affiliation, art, athletics, job skills, leadership, minority status, music/drama, religious affiliation.

**Application procedures. Admission:** Priority date 1/15; deadline 8/1 (postmark date). $25 fee, may be waived for applicants with need. Application may be submitted online. Admission notification on a rolling basis beginning on or about 10/1. Must reply by May 1 or within 3 week(s) if notified thereafter. Application fee waived if applicant visits campus. **Financial aid:** Closing date 3/15. FAFSA, institutional form required. Applicants notified on a rolling basis starting 3/30; must reply within 2 week(s) of notification.

**Academics.** General education curriculum leads to minor in global studies for each student. **Special study options:** Accelerated study, combined bachelor's/graduate degree, cooperative education, distance learning, double major, dual enrollment of high school students, ESL, honors, independent study, internships, liberal arts/career combination, student-designed major, study abroad, teacher certification program, Washington semester. Living-learning communities, leadership/community service communities, Drury Center in Volos, Greece. **Credit/placement by examination:** AP, CLEP, IB, institutional tests. **Support services:** Pre-admission summer program, reduced course load, remedial instruction, study skills assistance, tutoring, writing center.

**Majors. Architecture:** Architecture. **Biology:** General. **Business:** General, accounting, business admin, international, management information systems. **Communications:** General, advertising, public relations. **Computer sciences:** General, computer science, information systems. **Conservation:** Environmental science, environmental studies. **Education:** General, elementary, music, physical, secondary. **English:** Creative writing, English lit. **Foreign languages:** French, German, Spanish. **Health:** Predental, premedicine, preop/surgical nursing, preveterinary. **History:** General. **Liberal arts:** Arts/sciences. **Math:** General. **Parks/recreation:** Exercise sciences. **Philosophy/religion:** Philosophy. **Physical sciences:** Chemistry. **Psychology:** General. **Social sciences:** Criminology, economics, political science, sociology. **Visual/performing arts:** General, art, art history/conservation, arts management, commercial/advertising art, design, dramatic, jazz, music management, music performance, music theory/composition, piano/organ, studio arts, voice/opera.

**Most popular majors.** Architecture 9%, biology 9%, business/marketing 13%, communications/journalism 11%, English 6%, psychology 9%, social sciences 8%, visual/performing arts 12%.

**Computing on campus.** 338 workstations in dormitories, library, computer center, student center. Dormitories wired for high-speed internet access and linked to campus network. Commuter students can connect to campus network. Online course registration, online library, helpline, repair service, student web hosting, wireless network available.

**Student life. Freshman orientation:** Mandatory, $145 fee. Preregistration for classes offered. Four-day program; includes parent session. Registration for classes occurs separately in late June. **Housing:** Guaranteed on-campus for freshmen. Coed dorms, single-sex dorms, apartments, fraternity/sorority housing available. $200 fully refundable deposit, deadline 6/1. Living-learning communities, themed housing, leadership/service communities available. **Activities:** Bands, campus ministries, choral groups, dance, drama, film society, international student organizations, literary magazine, music ensembles, musical theater, opera, radio station, student government, student newspaper, symphony orchestra, TV station, Alliance of Minority Minds, Young Republicans, College Democrats, student government association, Student Union Board, Mortar Board, environmental club, Habitat for Humanity, Students in Free Enterprise.

**Athletics.** NCAA. **Intercollegiate:** Baseball M, basketball, cheerleading, cross-country, diving, golf, soccer, swimming, tennis, volleyball W. **Intramural:** Basketball, football (non-tackle) M, football (tackle), racquetball, soccer, softball, volleyball. **Team name:** Panthers.

**Student services.** Adult student services, alcohol/substance abuse counseling, campus ministries, career counseling, services for economically disadvantaged, student employment services, financial aid counseling, health

services, minority student services, personal counseling, placement for graduates, veterans' counselor, women's services. **Physically disabled:** Services for visually, speech, hearing impaired.

**Contact.** E-mail: druryad@drury.edu
Phone: (417) 873-7205 Toll-free number: (800) 922-2274
Fax: (417) 866-3873
Chip Parker, Director of Admission, Drury University, 900 North Benton Avenue, Springfield, MO 65802-3712

---

## Evangel University
### Springfield, Missouri
**www.evangel.edu**  **CB code: 6198**

- Private 4-year liberal arts college affiliated with Assemblies of God
- Residential campus in small city
- 1,534 degree-seeking undergraduates: 5% part-time, 60% women
- 123 degree-seeking graduate students
- 76% of applicants admitted
- SAT or ACT with writing required

**General.** Founded in 1955. Regionally accredited. **Degrees:** 388 bachelor's, 8 associate awarded; master's offered. **ROTC:** Army. **Location:** 170 miles from Kansas City, 212 miles from St. Louis. **Calendar:** Semester, limited summer session. **Full-time faculty:** 103 total. **Part-time faculty:** 54 total. **Class size:** 64% < 20, 29% 20-39, 4% 40-49, 3% 50-99.

**Freshman class profile.** 769 applied, 584 admitted, 344 enrolled.

| Mid 50% test scores | | | |
|---|---|---|---|
| ACT composite: | 18-25 | Out-of-state: | 57% |
| End year in good standing: | 94% | Live on campus: | 88% |

**Basis for selection.** Minimum 2.0 high school GPA, acceptance of college's moral and religious standards, acceptable ACT or SAT scores, rank in top half of graduating class. Statement of Christian faith required. Audition required for music, sport students. Essay and portfolio recommended. **Homeschooled:** Admissions based upon ACT/SAT scores and letters of recommendation.

**High school preparation.** Recommended units include English 3, mathematics 2, social studies 2 and science 1.

**2007-2008 Annual costs.** Tuition/fees: $14,340. Room/board: $5,120. Books/supplies: $1,000. Personal expenses: $1,750.

**2006-2007 Financial aid.** All financial aid based on need. 330 full-time freshmen applied for aid; 297 were judged to have need; 297 of these received aid. Average need met was 25%. Average scholarship/grant was $5,673; average loan $2,942. 32% of total undergraduate aid awarded as scholarships/grants, 68% as loans/jobs.

**Application procedures. Admission:** Closing date 8/1 (receipt date). $25 fee, may be waived for applicants with need. Application may be submitted online. Admission notification on a rolling basis. **Financial aid:** Priority date 4/1, closing date 6/1. FAFSA required. Applicants notified on a rolling basis starting 4/1; must reply within 3 week(s) of notification.

**Academics. Special study options:** Cross-registration, double major, dual enrollment of high school students, internships, liberal arts/career combination, study abroad, teacher certification program, Washington semester. **Credit/placement by examination:** AP, CLEP, IB, ACT, institutional tests. 30 credit hours maximum toward associate degree, 30 toward bachelor's. **Support services:** Learning center, reduced course load, remedial instruction, study skills assistance, tutoring, writing center.

**Majors. Biology:** General. **Business:** General, accounting, business admin, marketing. **Communications:** General, broadcast journalism, journalism. **Communications technology:** General. **Computer sciences:** General. **Education:** General, art, business, early childhood, elementary, English, foreign languages, mathematics, middle, music, physical, science, secondary, social studies, special. **English:** English lit, speech/rhetoric. **Foreign languages:** Spanish. **Health:** Clinical lab technology, predental, premedicine, preveterinary. **History:** General. **Interdisciplinary:** Math/computer science. **Legal studies:** Prelaw. **Math:** General. **Parks/recreation:** General. **Physical sciences:** Chemistry. **Protective services:** Criminal justice. **Psychology:** General. **Public administration:** Social work. **Social sciences:** General, criminology, political science, sociology. **Theology:** Bible, missionary, sacred music. **Visual/performing arts:** Dramatic, music performance, studio arts.

**Most popular majors.** Biology 6%, business/marketing 15%, communications/journalism 9%, education 14%, philosophy/religious studies 9%, psychology 7%, social sciences 7%.

**Computing on campus.** 312 workstations in dormitories, library, computer center, student center. Dormitories wired for high-speed internet access and linked to campus network. Online library, helpline, wireless network available.

**Student life. Freshman orientation:** Mandatory. Preregistration for classes offered. **Policies:** Religious observance required. **Housing:** Guaranteed on-campus for freshmen. Coed dorms, single-sex dorms, apartments, substance-free housing available. $200 deposit, deadline 8/1. **Activities:** Bands, choral groups, drama, literary magazine, music ensembles, radio station, student government, student newspaper, symphony orchestra, TV station, international students club, honor fraternities, student ministries.

**Athletics.** NAIA. **Intercollegiate:** Baseball M, basketball, cross-country, football (tackle) M, golf, softball W, tennis, track and field, volleyball W. **Intramural:** Basketball, football (non-tackle), soccer, softball, volleyball W. **Team name:** Crusaders.

**Student services.** Career counseling, student employment services, financial aid counseling, health services, on-campus daycare, personal counseling, placement for graduates, veterans' counselor. **Physically disabled:** Services for visually, hearing impaired.

**Contact.** E-mail: admission@evangel.edu
Phone: (417) 865-2811 Toll-free number: (800) 382-6435
Fax: (417) 865-9599
Cheri Meyer, Director of Admissions, Evangel University, 1111 North Glenstone, Springfield, MO 65802

---

## Fontbonne University
### St. Louis, Missouri
**www.fontbonne.edu**  **CB member**  **CB code: 6216**

- Private 4-year liberal arts college affiliated with Roman Catholic Church
- Commuter campus in large city
- 1,993 degree-seeking undergraduates: 23% part-time, 72% women, 34% African American, 1% Asian American, 1% Hispanic American, 1% international
- 859 degree-seeking graduate students
- 75% of applicants admitted
- SAT or ACT (ACT writing recommended) required
- 51% graduate within 6 years

**General.** Founded in 1923. Regionally accredited. **Degrees:** 466 bachelor's awarded; master's offered. **ROTC:** Army, Air Force. **Location:** 6 miles from downtown. **Calendar:** Semester, limited summer session. **Full-time faculty:** 69 total; 75% have terminal degrees, 12% minority, 68% women. **Part-time faculty:** 299 total. **Class size:** 81% < 20, 19% 20-39. **Special facilities:** Speech and hearing clinic.

**Freshman class profile.** 600 applied, 452 admitted, 191 enrolled.

| Mid 50% test scores | | | |
|---|---|---|---|
| SAT critical reading: | 500-630 | Rank in top quarter: | 28% |
| SAT math: | 470-630 | Rank in top tenth: | 7% |
| ACT composite: | 18-24 | End year in good standing: | 64% |
| GPA 3.50 or higher: | 28% | Return as sophomores: | 58% |
| GPA 3.0-3.49: | 24% | Out-of-state: | 18% |
| GPA 2.0-2.99: | 46% | Live on campus: | 64% |
| | | International: | 3% |

**Basis for selection.** High school GPA, class rank, test scores considered. Recommendations may be requested. Essay and interview recommended. Audition required for theater students; portfolio required for art students.

**High school preparation.** 16 units required. Required units include English 4, mathematics 3, social studies 3, science 3 (laboratory 1) and academic electives 3. Core electives 3 units. Must include foreign language and 1 unit visual or performing arts.

**2007-2008 Annual costs.** Tuition/fees: $18,320. Room/board: $6,971. Books/supplies: $650. Personal expenses: $1,300.

**2006-2007 Financial aid. Need-based:** 111 full-time freshmen applied for aid; 104 were judged to have need; 104 of these received aid. Average need met was 46%. Average scholarship/grant was $5,200; average loan $2,625. 34% of total undergraduate aid awarded as scholarships/grants, 66% as loans/jobs. **Non-need-based:** Awarded to 1,273 full-time undergraduates, including 153 freshmen. Scholarships awarded for academics, alumni affiliation, art, leadership, minority status, music/drama, religious affiliation, state residency.

**Application procedures. Admission:** Priority date 1/15; deadline 8/1. $25 fee, may be waived for applicants with need. Application may be submitted online. Admission notification on a rolling basis. Must reply by May 1 or within 3 week(s) if notified thereafter. **Financial aid:** Priority date 4/1; no closing date. FAFSA, institutional form required. Applicants notified on a rolling basis starting 2/1; must reply within 2 week(s) of notification.

**Academics. Special study options:** Accelerated study, cooperative education, cross-registration, distance learning, double major, dual enrollment of high school students, ESL, exchange student, honors, independent study, internships, liberal arts/career combination, student-designed major, study abroad, teacher certification program, weekend college. 3-2 program in social work or engineering with Washington University. **Credit/placement by examination:** AP, CLEP, institutional tests. **Support services:** Learning center, reduced course load, remedial instruction, study skills assistance, tutoring, writing center.

**Majors. Biology:** General, biotechnology. **Business:** Business admin, organizational behavior. **Communications:** General, advertising. **Computer sciences:** General. **Education:** Deaf/hearing impaired, early childhood, elementary, family/consumer sciences, middle, special. **English:** English lit. **Family/consumer sciences:** Clothing/textiles. **Health:** Dietetics, speech pathology. **History:** General. **Legal studies:** Prelaw. **Liberal arts:** Arts/sciences. **Math:** General. **Parks/recreation:** Sports admin. **Psychology:** General. **Public administration:** Human services. **Social sciences:** Sociology. **Visual/performing arts:** Art, dramatic, studio arts.

**Most popular majors.** Business/marketing 47%, education 18%, visual/performing arts 6%.

**Computing on campus.** 133 workstations in dormitories, library, computer center. Dormitories wired for high-speed internet access and linked to campus network. Commuter students can connect to campus network. Online course registration, online library, helpline, repair service, wireless network available.

**Student life. Freshman orientation:** Mandatory, $75 fee. Preregistration for classes offered. Held during week prior to classes, includes community service. **Housing:** Coed dorms, apartments, substance-free housing available. $150 deposit. Apartment style residence halls available. **Activities:** Choral groups, dance, drama, international student organizations, literary magazine, music ensembles, musical theater, radio station, student government, student newspaper, Fontbonne in Service and Humility, Go Deep (Spiritual Book Study), Pro-life Organization, Straights and Gays for Equality, Students for the Enhancement of Black Awareness.

**Athletics.** NCAA. **Intercollegiate:** Baseball M, basketball, bowling W, cross-country, golf, lacrosse, soccer, softball W, tennis, volleyball W. **Intramural:** Badminton, basketball, bowling M, football (non-tackle), soccer, softball, table tennis, tennis, volleyball. **Team name:** Griffins.

**Student services.** Adult student services, alcohol/substance abuse counseling, campus ministries, career counseling, student employment services, financial aid counseling, health services, minority student services, personal counseling, placement for graduates. **Physically disabled:** Services for speech, hearing impaired.

**Contact.** E-mail: fcadmission@fontbonne.edu
Phone: (314) 889-1400 Toll-free number: (800) 205-5862
Fax: (314) 889-1451
Peggy Musen, Associate Dean for Enrollment Management, Fontbonne University, 6800 Wydown Boulevard, St. Louis, MO 63105

## Global University
### Springfield, Missouri
### www.globaluniversity.edu
**CB code: 4916**

- Private 4-year Bible and seminary college affiliated with Assemblies of God
- Commuter campus in small city
- 4,858 degree-seeking undergraduates: 88% part-time, 35% women
- 272 degree-seeking graduate students

**General.** Founded in 1948. Accredited by DETC. Correspondence institution. All course work completed via distance education. **Degrees:** 5 bachelor's, 4 associate awarded; master's, first professional offered. **Location:** 200 miles to St. Louis, 170 miles to Kansas City. **Calendar:** Continuous, extensive summer session. **Full-time faculty:** 50 total. **Part-time faculty:** 400 total.

**Basis for selection.** Open admission.

**2007-2008 Annual costs.** Books/supplies: $600.

**Application procedures. Admission:** No deadline. $40 fee. Application may be submitted online. Admission notification on a rolling basis.

**Academics. Special study options:** Distance learning, external degree, independent study. **Credit/placement by examination:** CLEP. 16 credit hours maximum toward associate degree, 32 toward bachelor's. **Support services:** Study skills assistance.

**Majors. Theology:** Bible, missionary, religious ed, theology.

**Computing on campus.** Online library available.

**Contact.** E-mail: info@globaluniversity.edu
Phone: (417) 862-9533 Toll-free number: (800) 443-1083
Fax: (417) 862-0863
Lynne Kroh, Assistant Dean of Student Affairs, Global University, 1211 South Glenstone Avenue, Springfield, MO 65804

## Goldfarb School of Nursing at Barnes-Jewish College
### Saint Louis, Missouri
### www.barnesjewishcollege.edu
**CB code: 6329**

- Private 4-year nursing college
- Commuter campus in large city
- 488 degree-seeking undergraduates
- SAT or ACT (ACT writing recommended) required

**General.** Regionally accredited. Affiliated with Barnes-Jewish Hospital, and Washington University Medical Center. **Degrees:** 137 bachelor's, 225 associate awarded; master's offered. **Location:** Downtown. **Calendar:** Semester, extensive summer session. **Full-time faculty:** 49 total. **Part-time faculty:** 15 total. **Class size:** 20% < 20, 50% 20-39, 25% 40-49, 5% 50-99.

**Freshman class profile.**

| Out-of-state: | 1% | Live on campus: | 1% |
|---|---|---|---|

**Basis for selection.** High school or college level algebra, biology, chemistry are prerequisites. 2.75 GPA for undergraduate programs.

**High school preparation.** Recommended units include mathematics 4, science 4 (laboratory 4).

**2007-2008 Annual costs.** Tuition/fees: $12,560. Room only: $2,550.

**Application procedures. Admission:** No deadline. $50 fee. Application must be submitted on paper. Admission notification on a rolling basis.

**Academics. Special study options:** Combined bachelor's/graduate degree, liberal arts/career combination. **Credit/placement by examination:** AP, CLEP, IB, institutional tests. **Support services:** Tutoring, writing center.

**Majors. Health:** Nursing (RN).

**Computing on campus.** 60 workstations in dormitories, library, computer center, student center. Dormitories wired for high-speed internet access and linked to campus network. Commuter students can connect to campus network. Online library, helpline available.

**Student life. Housing:** Coed dorms, substance-free housing available. $150 deposit, deadline 5/1.

**Contact.** E-mail: bjcon-admissions@bjc.org
Phone: (314) 454-7057 Toll-free number: (800) 832-9009
Fax: (314) 454-5239
Elaine Dempsey, Director of Marketing and Enrollment, Goldfarb School of Nursing at Barnes-Jewish College, 306 South Kingshighway Boulevard, St. Louis, MO 63110-1091

## Grantham University
### Kansas City, Missouri
### www.grantham.edu
**CB code: 2244**

- For-profit 4-year virtual university
- Large city
- 8,500 full-time, degree-seeking undergraduates

**General.** Founded in 1951. Accredited by DETC. Degree programs are 100 percent online. **Degrees:** 167 bachelor's, 333 associate awarded; master's offered. **Calendar:** Continuous. **Part-time faculty:** 68 total.

**Basis for selection.** Open admission. High school diploma, GED, or equivalent required. Basic computer skills and use of computer with Windows, Internet access, e-mail account, printer also required.

**2007-2008 Annual costs.** Tuition/fees: $7,950. Tuition includes required textbooks, software and shipping (within U.S.).

**Financial aid. Additional information:** DANTES and some employer reimbursement programs available.

**Application procedures. Admission:** No deadline. No application fee. Application may be submitted online. Admission notification on a rolling basis. **Financial aid:** No deadline.

**Academics. Special study options:** Accelerated study, combined bachelor's/graduate degree, distance learning, independent study. **Credit/placement by examination:** CLEP, IB. 45 credit hours maximum toward associate degree, 90 toward bachelor's. **Support services:** Learning center, tutoring.

**Majors. Business:** Business admin, management information systems, office management. **Computer sciences:** General, applications programming, computer science, data processing, information systems, information technology, LAN/WAN management, systems analysis. **Engineering:** Computer, electrical. **Engineering technology:** Computer, electrical. **Protective services:** Law enforcement admin.

**Computing on campus.** PC or laptop required. Online library available.

**Student life. Freshman orientation:** Mandatory.

**Student services.** Adult student services, financial aid counseling, veterans' counselor.

**Contact.** E-mail: admissions@grantham.edu
Phone: (800) 955-2527 Toll-free number: (800) 955-2527
Fax: (816) 595-5757
DeAnn Wandler, Director of Admissions, Grantham University, 7200 Northwest 86th Street, Kansas City, MO 64153

## Hannibal-LaGrange College
**Hannibal, Missouri**
**www.hlg.edu**                                **CB code: 6266**

- Private 4-year liberal arts college affiliated with Southern Baptist Convention
- Commuter campus in large town
- 895 degree-seeking undergraduates: 3% African American, 1% Hispanic American, 1% Native American, 5% international
- 34 graduate students
- 97% of applicants admitted
- SAT or ACT (ACT writing optional), interview required
- 47% graduate within 6 years; 31% enter graduate study

**General.** Founded in 1858. Regionally accredited. Christian environment. **Degrees:** 191 bachelor's, 32 associate awarded; master's offered. **Location:** 100 miles from St. Louis. **Calendar:** Semester, limited summer session. **Full-time faculty:** 55 total; 34% have terminal degrees, 2% minority, 46% women. **Part-time faculty:** 85 total; 18% have terminal degrees, 4% minority, 52% women. **Class size:** 75% < 20, 24% 20-39, 1% 40-49. **Special facilities:** Nature trail, fine arts theater, mission center.

**Freshman class profile.** 362 applied, 350 admitted, 161 enrolled.

| Mid 50% test scores | | Return as sophomores: | 74% |
|---|---|---|---|
| ACT composite: | 18-26 | | |

**Basis for selection.** Most applicants admitted. Test scores important. 20 or above ACT composite required. Applicants with 16-19 ACT composite admitted provisionally. ACT administered on campus on registration day. Applications without English Composition 1 and college algebra must submit ACT scores and take mathematics placement exam. Interviews required for performance and honor students. **Homeschooled:** Transcript of courses and ACT score. **Learning Disabled:** Must provide appropriate documentation citing learning disability.

**High school preparation.** College-preparatory program recommended. Recommended units include English 2, mathematics 1, history 3, science 1 (laboratory 1).

**2007-2008 Annual costs.** Tuition/fees: $13,480. Room/board: $5,416. Books/supplies: $910. Personal expenses: $2,061.

**Financial aid. Non-need-based:** Scholarships awarded for academics, art, athletics, music/drama, religious affiliation. **Additional information:** Work-study opportunities vary according to on- and off-campus needs.

**Application procedures. Admission:** Closing date 8/26. $25 fee, may be waived for applicants with need. Application may be submitted online. Admission notification on a rolling basis beginning on or about 9/1. **Financial aid:** Closing date 7/1. FAFSA, institutional form required. Applicants notified on a rolling basis; must reply by 8/31.

**Academics. Special study options:** Accelerated study, cooperative education, distance learning, double major, dual enrollment of high school students, ESL, honors, independent study, internships, student-designed major, study abroad, teacher certification program, weekend college. Student-designed major in Liberal Studies. **Credit/placement by examination:** AP, CLEP, SAT, ACT, institutional tests. 16 credit hours maximum toward associate degree, 30 toward bachelor's. No more than 8 credit hours in one discipline. **Support services:** Reduced course load, remedial instruction, study skills assistance, tutoring.

**Honors college/program.** Minimum ACT-25, essay. Additional 21 hours plus research project, must maintain requirements for eligibility each semester.

**Majors. Biology:** General. **Business:** General, accounting, business admin, marketing, organizational behavior. **Communications:** General. **Computer sciences:** General. **Education:** General, art, business, early childhood, elementary, English, mathematics, music, physical, science, secondary, social studies. **English:** English lit. **Health:** Nursing (RN). **History:** General. **Liberal arts:** Arts/sciences. **Math:** General. **Parks/recreation:** Facilities management. **Philosophy/religion:** Christian. **Protective services:** Law enforcement admin. **Psychology:** General. **Public administration:** Human services. **Theology:** Bible, religious ed, sacred music. **Visual/performing arts:** Art, dramatic, music performance, piano/organ, studio arts, voice/opera. **Other:** Intercultural Missions.

**Most popular majors.** Business/marketing 33%, communications/journalism 6%, education 26%, public administration/social services 8%.

**Computing on campus.** 89 workstations in library, computer center. Dormitories linked to campus network. Commuter students can connect to campus network. Online library, repair service available.

**Student life. Freshman orientation:** Mandatory, $50 fee. Preregistration for classes offered. Conducted 4 days before classes begin. **Policies:** Students under 21 years of age at the beginning of the semester for which they enroll and who are not living with a parent or guardian are required to live residence housing unless they are living with an approved relative. Religious observance required. **Housing:** Single-sex dorms, special housing for disabled, apartments, substance-free housing available. $100 fully refundable deposit. **Activities:** Jazz band, campus ministries, choral groups, drama, music ensembles, student government, student newspaper, Christian Ministry Vocations Fellowship, Democratic club, Fellowship of Christian Athletes, Phi Beta Delta (men's service), Phi Beta Lambda, Gatekeepers (mentoring), Students for Life, Natures Investigation Circulus, Missouri State Teachers Association, Republican club, art club, science club.

**Athletics.** NAIA, NCCAA. **Intercollegiate:** Baseball M, basketball, golf M, soccer, softball W, swimming, track and field, volleyball, wrestling M. **Intramural:** Baseball M, basketball, racquetball, softball, table tennis, tennis, volleyball, weight lifting. **Team name:** Trojans.

**Student services.** Campus ministries, career counseling, student employment services, health services, personal counseling, placement for graduates. **Physically disabled:** Services for visually, hearing impaired.

**Contact.** E-mail: admissio@hlg.edu
Phone: (573) 629-3264 Toll-free number: (800) 454-1119
Fax: (573) 221-6594
Ray Carty, Vice President of Enrollment Management, Hannibal-LaGrange College, 2800 Palmyra Road, Hannibal, MO 63401

## Harris-Stowe State University
**St. Louis, Missouri**
**www.hssu.edu**                                **CB code: 6269**

- Public 4-year university
- Commuter campus in large city
- 1,800 degree-seeking undergraduates: 32% part-time, 69% women
- 76% of applicants admitted
- 15% graduate within 6 years

**General.** Founded in 1857. Regionally accredited. **Degrees:** 123 bachelor's awarded. **ROTC:** Army, Air Force. **Location:** Midtown. **Calendar:**

Semester, limited summer session. **Full-time faculty:** 57 total; 47% women. **Part-time faculty:** 124 total; 39% women. **Class size:** 70% < 20, 30% 20-39. **Special facilities:** Jazz institute.

**Freshman class profile.** 1,114 applied, 842 admitted, 448 enrolled.

| Mid 50% test scores | | | |
|---|---|---|---|
| ACT composite: | 14-18 | Rank in top tenth: | 3% |
| GPA 3.50 or higher: | 4% | Return as sophomores: | 39% |
| GPA 3.0-3.49: | 12% | Out-of-state: | 10% |
| GPA 2.0-2.99: | 59% | Live on campus: | 30% |
| Rank in top quarter: | 16% | Fraternities: | 1% |
| | | Sororities: | 1% |

**Basis for selection.** ACT composite score of 21, or combined ACT composite percentile rank and high school class percentile rank greater than or equal to 100. Full-time, first-year freshmen are encouraged to meet the Missouri High School Core Curriculum requirements. SAT or ACT recommended. Applicants with scores below 18 on any section of the ACT or below 440 on any section of the SAT must take Harris-Stowe State University's institutional placement test. **Learning Disabled:** Submit documentation of disability for review by Director of Academic Support Services.

**High school preparation.** Required and recommended units include English 4, mathematics 3, social studies 3, science 3 (laboratory 1), foreign language 2 and academic electives 7. 1 visual/performing arts required. Social studies must include American government. Electives must be from above list.

**2007-2008 Annual costs.** Tuition/fees: $5,090; $9,680 out-of-state. Books/supplies: $500. Personal expenses: $2,000.

**Financial aid. Non-need-based:** Scholarships awarded for academics, athletics, music/drama, state residency.

**Application procedures. Admission:** No deadline. $15 fee. Application must be submitted on paper. Admission notification on a rolling basis. **Financial aid:** Priority date 4/1; no closing date. FAFSA, institutional form required. Must reply within 3 week(s) of notification.

**Academics. Special study options:** Accelerated study, cooperative education, ESL, internships, student-designed major, teacher certification program. **Credit/placement by examination:** CLEP, SAT, ACT, institutional tests. **Support services:** Learning center, pre-admission summer program, reduced course load, remedial instruction, study skills assistance, tutoring, writing center.

**Majors. Business:** General, accounting, business admin, entrepreneurial studies, hospitality admin, marketing. **Computer sciences:** General, information systems, networking. **Education:** Early childhood, elementary, middle, multi-level teacher, secondary. **Health:** Health services admin. **Protective services:** Juvenile corrections, law enforcement admin. **Public administration:** General. **Social sciences:** Urban studies.

**Most popular majors.** Business/marketing 38%, computer/information sciences 6%, education 37%, security/protective services 9%.

**Computing on campus.** 205 workstations in dormitories, library, computer center. Dormitories wired for high-speed internet access. Commuter students can connect to campus network. Wireless network available.

**Student life. Freshman orientation:** Mandatory. Program directed by counseling staff during semester. **Housing:** Coed dorms available. $500 nonrefundable deposit. **Activities:** Choral groups, drama, literary magazine, music ensembles, student government, student newspaper, African American Studies Society, international student association, multicultural council, 100 Strong, Organization for Cultrual Progress, Student Ambassadors.

**Athletics.** NAIA. **Intercollegiate:** Baseball M, basketball, cheerleading, soccer, softball W, volleyball W. **Intramural:** Basketball, volleyball. **Team name:** Hornets.

**Student services.** Career counseling, student employment services, financial aid counseling, health services, personal counseling, placement for graduates, veterans' counselor.

**Contact.** E-mail: admissions@hssu.edu
Phone: (314) 340-3300 Fax: (314) 340-3555
Lashanda Boone, Executive Director of Enrollment Management, Harris-Stowe State University, 3026 Laclede Avenue, St. Louis, MO 63103-2199

## Hickey College
**St. Louis, Missouri**
www.hickeycollege.edu          CB code: 2308

- For-profit 4-year business and technical college
- Commuter campus in very large city

**General.** Founded in 1933. Accredited by ACICS. **Location:** 15 miles from downtown. **Calendar:** Semester.

**Annual costs/financial aid.** Tuition/fees (2007-2008): $12,240. Room/board: $5,520. Books/supplies: $1,000. Need-based financial aid available for full-time students.

**Contact.** Phone: (314) 434-2212
Admissions Manager, 940 West Port Plaza, St. Louis, MO 63146

## ITT Technical Institute: Arnold
**Arnold, Missouri**
www.itt-tech.edu          CB code: 2691

- For-profit 4-year technical college
- Commuter campus in large town

**General.** Accredited by ACICS. **Calendar:** Quarter.

**Annual costs/financial aid.** Tuition varies by program, $260-$368 per credit hour. Books/supplies: $3,100.

**Contact.** Phone: (636) 464-6600
Director of Recruitment, 1930 Meyer Drury Drive, Arnold, MO 63010

## ITT Technical Institute: Earth City
**Earth City, Missouri**
www.itt-tech.edu          CB code: 1216

- For-profit 4-year technical college
- Commuter campus in large city

**General.** Founded in 1936. Accredited by ACICS. **Location:** 15 miles from St. Louis. **Calendar:** Quarter.

**Annual costs/financial aid.** Tuition varies by program, $260-$368 per credit hour.

**Contact.** Phone: (314) 298-7800
Director of Recruitment, 13505 Lakefront Drive, Earth City, MO 63045

## Kansas City Art Institute
**Kansas City, Missouri**
www.kcai.edu          CB code: 6330

- Private 4-year visual arts college
- Commuter campus in large city
- 671 degree-seeking undergraduates: 55% women, 3% African American, 4% Asian American, 6% Hispanic American, 1% Native American, 1% international
- 63% of applicants admitted
- SAT or ACT with writing, application essay required
- 61% graduate within 6 years

**General.** Founded in 1885. Regionally accredited. **Degrees:** 122 bachelor's awarded. **Location:** 250 miles from St. Louis, 500 miles from Denver. **Calendar:** Semester, limited summer session. **Full-time faculty:** 51 total; 84% have terminal degrees, 2% minority, 37% women. **Part-time faculty:** 53 total; 77% have terminal degrees, 8% minority, 32% women. **Class size:** 82% < 20, 18% 20-39. **Special facilities:** Foundry, arboretum.

**Freshman class profile.** 538 applied, 339 admitted, 139 enrolled.

| Mid 50% test scores | | | |
|---|---|---|---|
| SAT critical reading: | 430-580 | GPA 2.0-2.99: | 27% |
| SAT math: | 430-590 | Rank in top quarter: | 39% |
| SAT writing: | 420-570 | Rank in top tenth: | 11% |
| ACT composite: | 20-25 | End year in good standing: | 85% |
| GPA 3.50 or higher: | 33% | Return as sophomores: | 76% |
| GPA 3.0-3.49: | 37% | Out-of-state: | 75% |
| | | Live on campus: | 90% |

**Basis for selection.** Portfolio, academic record, recommendations, test scores, personal interview important. Acceptable level of studio proficiency required prior to consideration of other credentials.

**High school preparation.** 20 units recommended. Recommended units include English 4, mathematics 3, social studies 3, science 3 and academic electives 3. 4 fine arts electives recommended.

**2007-2008 Annual costs.** Tuition/fees: $25,680. Room/board: $7,874. Books/supplies: $1,500. Personal expenses: $2,000.

**2007-2008 Financial aid. Need-based:** 152 full-time freshmen applied for aid; 108 were judged to have need; 108 of these received aid. Average need met was 73%. Average scholarship/grant was $15,724; average loan $5,657. 57% of total undergraduate aid awarded as scholarships/grants, 43% as loans/jobs. **Non-need-based:** Awarded to 173 full-time undergraduates, including 43 freshmen. Scholarships awarded for academics, art. **Additional information:** February 15 and March 15 priority application dates for merit scholarships; deadline July 1.

**Application procedures. Admission:** No deadline. $35 fee, may be waived for applicants with need. Application may be submitted online. Admission notification on a rolling basis beginning on or about 9/1. Must reply by May 1 or within 2 week(s) if notified thereafter. **Financial aid:** Priority date 3/15; no closing date. FAFSA required. Applicants notified on a rolling basis starting 4/1; must reply within 2 week(s) of notification.

**Academics. Special study options:** Double major, exchange student, independent study, internships, study abroad. **Credit/placement by examination:** AP, CLEP. 15 credit hours maximum toward bachelor's degree. **Support services:** Learning center, reduced course load, remedial instruction, study skills assistance, tutoring.

**Majors. English:** Creative writing. **Visual/performing arts:** Art history/conservation, ceramics, cinematography, fiber arts, graphic design, painting, photography, printmaking, sculpture.

**Most popular majors.** Visual/performing arts 50%.

**Computing on campus.** 50 workstations in library, computer center. Dormitories wired for high-speed internet access and linked to campus network. Commuter students can connect to campus network. Online course registration, online library, helpline, wireless network available.

**Student life. Freshman orientation:** Mandatory. Preregistration for classes offered. Three-day program held prior to start of academic year. **Housing:** Guaranteed on-campus for freshmen. Coed dorms, apartments, substance-free housing available. $125 deposit, deadline 5/1. **Activities:** Film society, student government.

**Student services.** Adult student services, career counseling, student employment services, financial aid counseling, minority student services, personal counseling, placement for graduates, veterans' counselor. **Physically disabled:** Services for visually, hearing impaired. **Learning disabled:** Comprehensive services available.

**Contact.** E-mail: admiss@kcai.edu
Phone: (816) 474-5224 Toll-free number: (800) 522-5224
Fax: (816) 802-3309
Larry Stone, Vice President for Enrollment Management, Kansas City Art Institute, 4415 Warwick Boulevard, Kansas City, MO 64111-1820

## Lester L. Cox College of Nursing and Health Sciences
**Springfield, Missouri**
www.coxcollege.edu                    CB code: 3932

▶ Private 4-year health science and nursing college
▶ Commuter campus in small city

**General.** Regionally accredited. **Calendar:** Semester.

**Annual costs/financial aid.** Tuition/fees (2007-2008): $9,720. Educational fee of $40 per credit hour. Room: $2,400. Books/supplies: $1,200.

**Contact.** Phone: (417) 269-3068
Director of Admission, 1423 North Jefferson Avenue, Springfield, MO 65802

## Lincoln University
**Jefferson City, Missouri**
www.lincolnu.edu                    CB code: 6366

▶ Public 4-year university and liberal arts college
▶ Commuter campus in large town
▶ 2,483 degree-seeking undergraduates: 20% part-time, 60% women, 45% African American, 1% Asian American, 1% Hispanic American, 4% international
▶ 168 degree-seeking graduate students

**General.** Founded in 1866. Regionally accredited. 1890 land-grant institution. **Degrees:** 297 bachelor's, 87 associate awarded; master's offered. **ROTC:** Army, Naval, Air Force. **Location:** 132 miles from St. Louis, 157 miles from Kansas City. **Calendar:** Semester, limited summer session. **Full-time faculty:** 125 total; 61% have terminal degrees, 33% minority, 49% women. **Part-time faculty:** 115 total; 27% minority, 49% women. **Class size:** 53% < 20, 41% 20-39, 4% 40-49, 1% 50-99. **Special facilities:** Ethnic studies center and archives, 3 research farms, agriculture and extension information center.

**Freshman class profile.** 1,549 applied, 1,477 admitted, 606 enrolled.

| Mid 50% test scores | | Rank in top quarter: | 16% |
|---|---|---|---|
| SAT critical reading: | 350-460 | Rank in top tenth: | 3% |
| SAT math: | 380-490 | Return as sophomores: | 53% |
| ACT composite: | 14-20 | Out-of-state: | 22% |
| GPA 3.50 or higher: | 10% | Live on campus: | 58% |
| GPA 3.0-3.49: | 19% | International: | 1% |
| GPA 2.0-2.99: | 55% | | |

**Basis for selection.** Open admission, but selective for some programs and for out-of-state students. Special requirements for Nursing and Education programs. ACT or SAT scores required but used for placement purposes only. Audition required for sacred music and music education students. **Homeschooled:** Must submit a transcript with the parent's notarized signature, demonstrating completion of the Missouri Minimum Core Curriculum or its equivalency, as determined by the University. **Learning Disabled:** Comprehensive documentation of disability by qualified professional must be on file to request accommodations.

**High school preparation.** 16 units recommended. Recommended units include English 4, mathematics 3, social studies 3, science 2 (laboratory 1), foreign language 2, visual/performing arts 1 and academic electives 1.

**2007-2008 Annual costs.** Tuition/fees: $5,995; $10,555 out-of-state. Students enrolled full-time must pay $241 per fall/spring semester or $81 per summer semester for insurance if they do not provide proof of other coverage. Enrollment in the student health insurance program is required for international students. Room/board: $4,590. Books/supplies: $950. Personal expenses: $166.

**2007-2008 Financial aid. Need-based:** 498 full-time freshmen applied for aid; 457 were judged to have need; 455 of these received aid. Average need met was 76%. Average scholarship/grant was $3,895; average loan $2,896. 56% of total undergraduate aid awarded as scholarships/grants, 44% as loans/jobs. **Non-need-based:** Awarded to 202 full-time undergraduates, including 49 freshmen. Scholarships awarded for academics, art, athletics, job skills, leadership, minority status, music/drama, ROTC, state residency.

**Application procedures. Admission:** Closing date 7/15 (postmark date). $20 fee. Application must be submitted on paper. Admission notification on a rolling basis. **Financial aid:** Priority date 3/1; no closing date. FAFSA, institutional form required. Applicants notified by 3/15; Applicants notified on a rolling basis starting 3/15; must reply within 2 week(s) of notification.

**Academics. Special study options:** Accelerated study, distance learning, double major, dual enrollment of high school students, exchange student, honors, independent study, internships, study abroad, teacher certification program. Senior citizen program, intersession courses. **Credit/placement by examination:** AP, CLEP, institutional tests. 15 credit hours maximum toward associate degree, 20 toward bachelor's. Total number of alternative credit hours cannot exceed 30. Students may receive credit only for courses numbered 100-299. Each examination may be taken only once. Students must be currently enrolled during the semester in which he/she elects to take the exam. **Support services:** Learning center, pre-admission summer program, reduced course load, remedial instruction, study skills assistance, tutoring, writing center.

**Majors. Agriculture:** General, business. **Biology:** General. **Business:** Accounting, administrative services, business admin, managerial economics, marketing. **Communications:** Journalism. **Computer sciences:** Information systems. **Conservation:** Environmental science. **Education:** Art, biology, business, chemistry, elementary, English, mathematics, middle, music, physical, physics, social science, special. **Engineering technology:** Civil, mechanical. **English:** English lit. **Family/consumer sciences:** Food/nutrition. **Foreign languages:** Spanish. **Health:** Clinical lab science, nursing (RN). **History:** General. **Liberal arts:** Arts/sciences. **Math:** General. **Physical sciences:** Chemistry, physics. **Protective services:** Law enforcement admin. **Psychology:** General. **Public administration:** General. **Social sciences:** Political science, sociology. **Theology:** Sacred music. **Visual/performing arts:** Studio arts. **Other:** Wellness.

**Most popular majors.** Business/marketing 22%, computer/information sciences 10%, education 14%, liberal arts 8%, security/protective services 10%.

**Computing on campus.** 250 workstations in dormitories, library, computer center, student center. Dormitories wired for high-speed internet access and linked to campus network. Commuter students can connect to campus network. Online library, helpline, repair service, wireless network available.

**Student life. Freshman orientation:** Mandatory. Preregistration for classes offered. Sessions offered throughout the year as needed. **Policies:** Unmarried freshmen and sophomores under 21 years of age, whose primary domicile is beyond a 60-mile radius of the university, are required to live in residence halls for four consecutive semesters. Armed Forces veterans and any student who has established a primary domicile one year prior to entering the University are exempted from this policy. **Housing:** Guaranteed on-campus for freshmen. Coed dorms, single-sex dorms, substance-free housing available. $125 fully refundable deposit, deadline 7/1. Honors housing. **Activities:** Bands, campus ministries, choral groups, dance, drama, international student organizations, literary magazine, music ensembles, radio station, student government, student newspaper, TV station, Baptist Student Center, College Republicans, College Democrats, Barrier Breakers, Wesley Foundation, Kathleen McGuire Newman Center.

**Athletics.** NCAA. **Intercollegiate:** Baseball M, basketball, cheerleading M, cross-country W, football (tackle) M, golf M, softball W, tennis W, track and field. **Intramural:** Basketball, bowling. **Team name:** Blue Tigers.

**Student services.** Career counseling, services for economically disadvantaged, financial aid counseling, health services, personal counseling, veterans' counselor. **Physically disabled:** Services for visually, speech, hearing impaired.

**Contact.** E-mail: enroll@lincolnu.edu
Phone: (573) 681-5599 Toll-free number: (800) 521-5052
Fax: (573) 681-5889
Mike Kosher, Director of Admissions, Lincoln University, 820 Chestnut Street/B-7 Young Hall, Jefferson City, MO 65102-0029

---

## Lindenwood University

**St. Charles, Missouri**
**www.lindenwood.edu**　　　　　　　　　**CB code: 6367**

- Private 4-year university and liberal arts college affiliated with Presbyterian Church (USA)
- Residential campus in very large city
- 5,872 degree-seeking undergraduates: 4% part-time, 57% women, 12% African American, 1% Asian American, 1% Hispanic American, 9% international
- 3,688 degree-seeking graduate students
- 58% of applicants admitted
- SAT or ACT (ACT writing recommended) required
- 40% graduate within 6 years

**General.** Founded in 1827. Regionally accredited. **Degrees:** 950 bachelor's awarded; master's, doctoral offered. **ROTC:** Army. **Location:** 20 miles from St. Louis. **Calendar:** 4-1-4, limited summer session. **Full-time faculty:** 201 total; 63% have terminal degrees, 4% minority, 52% women. **Part-time faculty:** 397 total; 53% have terminal degrees, 11% minority, 50% women. **Class size:** 44% < 20, 54% 20-39, 2% 40-49, less than 1% 50-99. **Special facilities:** Greenhouse, wetland program facility, success center.

**Freshman class profile.** 2,584 applied, 1,511 admitted, 903 enrolled.

| Mid 50% test scores | | | |
|---|---|---|---|
| SAT critical reading: | 420-530 | Rank in top quarter: | 12% |
| SAT math: | 460-590 | Rank in top tenth: | 2% |
| SAT writing: | 430-520 | Return as sophomores: | 62% |
| ACT composite: | 20-24 | Out-of-state: | 25% |
| GPA 3.50 or higher: | 31% | Live on campus: | 92% |
| GPA 3.0-3.49: | 32% | International: | 16% |
| GPA 2.0-2.99: | 36% | Fraternities: | 1% |
| | | Sororities: | 1% |

**Basis for selection.** Class rank, school record, high school GPA very important. **Homeschooled:** Transcript of courses and grades required.

**High school preparation.** 16 units recommended. Recommended units include English 4, mathematics 2, social studies 3, history 3, science 2 and foreign language 2.

**2008-2009 Annual costs.** Tuition/fees: $13,000. Room/board: $6,860. Books/supplies: $3,000. Personal expenses: $9,000.

**2007-2008 Financial aid. Need-based:** 55% of total undergraduate aid awarded as scholarships/grants, 45% as loans/jobs. **Non-need-based:** Scholarships awarded for academics, alumni affiliation, art, job skills, leadership, music/drama, ROTC.

**Application procedures. Admission:** No deadline. $30 fee, may be waived for applicants with need. Application may be submitted online. Admission notification on a rolling basis beginning on or about 9/1. Must reply by May 1 or within 4 week(s) if notified thereafter. **Financial aid:** Priority date 4/1; no closing date. FAFSA required. Applicants notified on a rolling basis.

**Academics. Special study options:** Accelerated study, combined bachelor's/graduate degree, cross-registration, distance learning, double major, dual enrollment of high school students, ESL, honors, independent study, internships, student-designed major, study abroad, teacher certification program. Bachelor of engineering with Washington University, 3-2 Lindenwood University/University of Missouri Columbia dual degree program in engineering and math or computer sciences, 2-2 program in engineering. **Credit/placement by examination:** AP, CLEP, IB, SAT, ACT, institutional tests. **Support services:** Learning center, reduced course load, study skills assistance, tutoring, writing center.

**Majors. Area/ethnic studies:** American. **Biology:** General, environmental. **Business:** General, accounting, business admin, communications, entrepreneurial studies, finance, hospitality admin, human resources, international, management information systems, marketing, nonprofit/public, retailing. **Communications:** General, advertising, digital media, journalism, media studies, organizational. **Computer sciences:** General, computer science, information technology. **Conservation:** Environmental science. **Education:** Art, biology, business, chemistry, early childhood, early childhood special, elementary, French, history, middle, physical, science, social science, social studies, Spanish, technology/industrial arts, trade/industrial. **English:** Creative writing, English lit. **Foreign languages:** French, Spanish. **Health:** Athletic training, health care admin. **History:** General. **Interdisciplinary:** Gerontology. **Math:** General. **Parks/recreation:** Exercise sciences, sports admin. **Personal/culinary services:** Funeral direction, mortuary science. **Philosophy/religion:** Christian, philosophy, religion. **Physical sciences:** Chemistry. **Protective services:** Criminal justice, fire services admin. **Psychology:** General. **Public administration:** General, human services, social work. **Social sciences:** Criminology, international relations, political science, sociology. **Theology:** Pastoral counseling, youth ministry. **Visual/performing arts:** General, acting, art, art history/conservation, arts management, dance, directing/producing, dramatic, fashion design, multimedia, music management, music performance, music theory/composition, musical theater, studio arts, theater arts management, theater design.

**Most popular majors.** Business/marketing 44%, communications/journalism 6%, education 13%, social sciences 8%, visual/performing arts 6%.

**Computing on campus.** 153 workstations in library, computer center, student center. Dormitories wired for high-speed internet access and linked to campus network. Commuter students can connect to campus network. Online library, helpline, wireless network available.

**Student life. Freshman orientation:** Mandatory. Preregistration for classes offered. **Policies:** Zero tolerance of illegal substances. **Housing:** Guaranteed on-campus for all undergraduates. Single-sex dorms, apartments, fraternity/sorority housing, substance-free housing available. $300 nonrefundable deposit. Housing for single parents with children available. **Activities:** Bands, campus ministries, choral groups, dance, drama, film society, international student organizations, literary magazine, music ensembles, musical theater, radio station, student government, student newspaper, TV station, Campus Crusade for Christ, intercultural club, American Humanics, Circle K, Reform Campus Fellowship, Lewis & Clark Historical Society, Eastern Debating Society, Christian Life Group, Fellowship of Christian Athletes, student government association.

**Athletics.** NAIA. **Intercollegiate:** Baseball M, basketball, bowling, cheerleading, cross-country, diving, field hockey W, football (tackle) M, golf, ice hockey, rifle, soccer, softball W, swimming, tennis, track and field, volleyball, water polo, wrestling M. **Intramural:** Basketball, bowling, football (non-tackle), soccer, softball, swimming, table tennis, tennis, volleyball, water polo. **Team name:** Lions.

**Student services.** Adult student services, campus ministries, career counseling, student employment services, financial aid counseling, placement for graduates, veterans' counselor. **Physically disabled:** Services for visually, hearing impaired.

**Contact.** E-mail: admissions@lindenwood.edu
Phone: (636) 949-4949 Fax: (636) 949-4989
Joe Parisi, Executive Director of Day Admissions, Lindenwood University, 209 South Kingshighway, St. Charles, MO 63301-1695

---

## Maryville University of Saint Louis

**St. Louis, Missouri**　　　　　　　　　**CB member**
**www.maryville.edu**　　　　　　　　　**CB code: 6399**

- Private 4-year university
- Commuter campus in very large city

- 2,674 degree-seeking undergraduates: 38% part-time, 78% women, 7% African American, 2% Asian American, 1% Hispanic American, 1% Native American
- 621 degree-seeking graduate students
- 68% of applicants admitted
- SAT or ACT (ACT writing optional) required
- 64% graduate within 6 years; 12% enter graduate study

**General.** Founded in 1872. Regionally accredited. **Degrees:** 609 bachelor's awarded; master's, doctoral offered. **ROTC:** Army. **Location:** 20 miles from downtown. **Calendar:** Semester, limited summer session. **Full-time faculty:** 108 total; 78% have terminal degrees, 10% minority, 58% women. **Part-time faculty:** 261 total; 24% have terminal degrees, 8% minority, 61% women. **Class size:** 67% < 20, 32% 20-39, less than 1% 40-49. **Special facilities:** Observatory, auditorium, outdoor walking trails, coffeehouse, teaching laboratory, clinical laboratories, communications laboratory, multimedia classrooms.

**Freshman class profile.** 1,243 applied, 843 admitted, 303 enrolled.

| Mid 50% test scores | | | |
|---|---|---|---|
| ACT composite: | 22-26 | Rank in top tenth: | 28% |
| GPA 3.50 or higher: | 60% | End year in good standing: | 96% |
| GPA 3.0-3.49: | 25% | Return as sophomores: | 82% |
| GPA 2.0-2.99: | 15% | Out-of-state: | 20% |
| Rank in top quarter: | 57% | Live on campus: | 62% |

**Basis for selection.** School record most important. Recommendations and extracurricular activities considered. ACT or SAT very important. Interview and 20 hours observation in clinical setting required for physical therapy students. Audition required for music therapy students; portfolio required for art education, graphic design, interior design, and studio art majors. **Homeschooled:** Increased weight placed on ACT or SAT scores.

**High school preparation.** 22 units required. Required and recommended units include English 4, mathematics 3, social studies 2, science 2, foreign language 3 and academic electives 8. Applicants for actuarial science, art, education, interior design, clinical laboratory science, nursing, occupational therapy, and physical therapy must meet other specific requirements.

**2008-2009 Annual costs.** Tuition/fees: $20,275. Room/board: $7,900. Books/supplies: $1,600. Personal expenses: $2,100.

**2007-2008 Financial aid. Need-based:** 255 full-time freshmen applied for aid; 212 were judged to have need; 212 of these received aid. Average need met was 72%. Average scholarship/grant was $10,481; average loan $5,576. 51% of total undergraduate aid awarded as scholarships/grants, 49% as loans/jobs. **Non-need-based:** Awarded to 392 full-time undergraduates, including 84 freshmen. Scholarships awarded for academics, art, leadership, minority status, religious affiliation, ROTC, state residency.

**Application procedures. Admission:** Closing date 8/15. $25 fee, may be waived for applicants with need. Application may be submitted online. Admission notification on a rolling basis. Must reply by May 1 or within 4 week(s) if notified thereafter. **Financial aid:** Priority date 3/1; no closing date. FAFSA required. Applicants notified on a rolling basis starting 2/1; must reply by 5/1 or within 2 week(s) of notification.

**Academics. Special study options:** Accelerated study, combined bachelor's/graduate degree, cooperative education, cross-registration, distance learning, double major, dual enrollment of high school students, honors, independent study, internships, liberal arts/career combination, semester at sea, student-designed major, study abroad, teacher certification program, Washington semester, weekend college. Prior learning assessment. **Credit/placement by examination:** AP, CLEP, IB, SAT, ACT, institutional tests. 30 credit hours maximum toward bachelor's degree. **Support services:** Learning center, reduced course load, study skills assistance, tutoring, writing center.

**Majors. Biology:** General, biomedical sciences. **Business:** General, accounting, accounting technology, actuarial science, business admin, e-commerce, management information systems, marketing. **Communications:** Media studies. **Computer sciences:** Computer science. **Conservation:** Environmental science, environmental studies. **Education:** Art, biology, chemistry, early childhood, elementary, English, history, mathematics, middle, secondary. **English:** English lit. **Health:** Clinical lab science, community health services, music therapy, nursing (RN), predental, premedicine, vocational rehab counseling. **History:** General. **Interdisciplinary:** Biological/physical sciences. **Legal studies:** Paralegal, prelaw. **Liberal arts:** Arts/sciences. **Math:** General, applied. **Physical sciences:** Chemistry. **Psychology:** General. **Social sciences:** Criminology, sociology. **Visual/performing arts:** Graphic design, interior design, studio arts.

**Most popular majors.** Business/marketing 31%, health sciences 29%, psychology 9%, visual/performing arts 8%.

**Computing on campus.** 434 workstations in dormitories, library, computer center, student center. Dormitories wired for high-speed internet access and linked to campus network. Commuter students can connect to campus network. Online course registration, online library, helpline, student web hosting, wireless network available.

**Student life. Freshman orientation:** Available. Preregistration for classes offered. Three-day program prior to start of classes. **Housing:** Guaranteed on-campus for all undergraduates. Coed dorms, apartments, substance-free housing available. $150 fully refundable deposit, deadline 5/1. **Activities:** Bands, campus ministries, choral groups, dance, drama, literary magazine, music ensembles, student government, student newspaper, student academic majors clubs, Baptist student union, Campus Crusade for Christ, Roman Catholic student community, Reformed Campus Fellowship, Association of Black Collegians, multicultural club, community service club, recycling initiative, leadership and values institute.

**Athletics.** NCAA. **Intercollegiate:** Baseball M, basketball, cross-country, golf, soccer, softball W, tennis, track and field, volleyball W. **Intramural:** Basketball, bowling, cheerleading, football (non-tackle), soccer, softball, table tennis, volleyball. **Team name:** Saints.

**Student services.** Adult student services, alcohol/substance abuse counseling, campus ministries, career counseling, student employment services, financial aid counseling, health services, minority student services, personal counseling, placement for graduates, veterans' counselor. **Physically disabled:** Services for visually, speech, hearing impaired.

**Contact.** E-mail: admissions@maryville.edu
Phone: (314) 529-9350 Toll-free number: (800) 627-9855 ext. 9350
Fax: (314) 529-9927
Shani Lenore, Director of Admissions, Maryville University of Saint Louis, 650 Maryville University Drive, St. Louis, MO 63141-7299

---

## Missouri Baptist University
**St. Louis, Missouri**
www.mobap.edu CB code: 2258

- Private 4-year university and liberal arts college affiliated with Baptist faith
- Commuter campus in very large city
- 1,414 degree-seeking undergraduates: 21% part-time, 58% women, 9% African American, 2% Hispanic American, 1% Native American, 4% international
- 1,192 graduate students
- 72% of applicants admitted
- 42% graduate within 6 years

**General.** Founded in 1963. Regionally accredited. **Degrees:** 280 bachelor's, 1 associate awarded; master's offered. **ROTC:** Army. **Location:** 10 miles from downtown. **Calendar:** Semester, limited summer session. **Full-time faculty:** 66 total; 50% have terminal degrees, 42% women. **Part-time faculty:** 137 total; 17% have terminal degrees, 43% women.

**Freshman class profile.** 432 applied, 313 admitted, 186 enrolled.

| Mid 50% test scores | | | |
|---|---|---|---|
| SAT critical reading: | 380-490 | Rank in top quarter: | 51% |
| SAT math: | 370-460 | Rank in top tenth: | 12% |
| ACT composite: | 19-24 | Return as sophomores: | 70% |

**Basis for selection.** Minimum 2.0 high school GPA. Minimum score of 20 is required for ACT and/or a minimum score of 950 (exclusive of Writing) on SAT. Final class rank must be in the upper 50 percent of the graduating class. Applicants with high school GPA below 2.0 may be admitted on a probational status. Interview and/or essay required for academically weak students; audition required for music majors. **Learning Disabled:** Students must self-identify to the Special Needs Access Office, provide current written documentation of a disability from a qualified professional or agency, and request accommodations from the university. Documentation must meet institutional documentation criteria, indicate a substantial limitation in the education environment, and be completed at least six weeks prior to the start of the semester or class.

**High school preparation.** 22 units required. Required and recommended units include English 4, mathematics 3, social studies 2, history 1, science 2 (laboratory 1), foreign language 2 and academic electives 3. One visual and performing arts required.

**2007-2008 Annual costs.** Tuition/fees: $15,850. Room/board: $6,350. Books/supplies: $2,200. Personal expenses: $2,047.

**Financial aid. Non-need-based:** Scholarships awarded for academics, alumni affiliation, athletics, leadership, music/drama, religious affiliation.

**Application procedures. Admission:** No deadline. $30 fee, may be waived for applicants with need. Application must be submitted on paper. Admission notification on a rolling basis. **Financial aid:** Priority date 4/1; no closing date. FAFSA, institutional form required. Applicants notified on a rolling basis starting 4/15; must reply within 2 week(s) of notification.

**Academics. Special study options:** Accelerated study, combined bachelor's/ graduate degree, cooperative education, cross-registration, distance learning, double major, dual enrollment of high school students, independent study, internships, liberal arts/career combination, student-designed major, study abroad, teacher certification program, urban semester, Washington semester. **Credit/placement by examination:** AP, CLEP, institutional tests. 45 credit hours maximum toward bachelor's degree. No single source may account for more than 30 of the 45 credit-hour maximum. **Support services:** Reduced course load, remedial instruction, study skills assistance, tutoring.

**Majors. Biology:** General, biotechnology. **Business:** Accounting, business admin, marketing, operations. **Communications:** General. **Computer sciences:** General. **Education:** Business, early childhood, elementary, health, middle, music, physical, science. **English:** English lit. **Family/consumer sciences:** Family studies. **Health:** Athletic training. **History:** General. **Math:** General. **Parks/recreation:** Sports admin. **Philosophy/religion:** Christian. **Physical sciences:** Chemistry. **Protective services:** Criminal justice. **Psychology:** General. **Public administration:** Human services. **Social sciences:** General. **Theology:** Religious ed, sacred music, theology. **Visual/performing arts:** Music performance. **Other:** Worship Arts.

**Most popular majors.** Business/marketing 32%, education 30%, psychology 6%, theological studies 7%.

**Computing on campus.** 55 workstations in dormitories, library, computer center. Dormitories wired for high-speed internet access and linked to campus network. Commuter students can connect to campus network. Online library, helpline, wireless network available.

**Student life. Freshman orientation:** Mandatory. **Policies:** Religious observance required. **Housing:** Single-sex dorms, apartments, substance-free housing available. $250 deposit, deadline 7/1. **Activities:** Bands, choral groups, drama, literary magazine, music ensembles, musical theater, opera, radio station, student government, student newspaper, Baptist Student Union, Fellowship of Christian Athletes, Student Mission, state teachers association, Ministerial Alliance, international club, science club, computer club, College Music Educators National Conference, Students in Free Enterprise.

**Athletics. NAIA. Intercollegiate:** Baseball M, basketball, bowling, cheerleading, cross-country, golf, lacrosse W, soccer, softball W, tennis W, track and field, volleyball, wrestling M. **Intramural:** Basketball, softball, volleyball. **Team name:** Spartans.

**Student services.** Adult student services, campus ministries, career counseling, student employment services, financial aid counseling, personal counseling, placement for graduates, veterans' counselor. **Physically disabled:** Services for visually, hearing impaired.

**Contact.** E-mail: admissions@mobap.edu
Phone: (314) 392-2290 Toll-free number: (877) 434-1115
Fax: (314) 392-2292
Terry Cruse, Director of Admissions, Missouri Baptist University, One College Park Drive, St. Louis, MO 63141-8698

## Missouri Southern State University
### Joplin, Missouri
www.mssu.edu                     CB code: 6322

- Public 4-year university and liberal arts college
- Commuter campus in large town
- 5,593 undergraduates
- 99% of applicants admitted

**General.** Founded in 1937. Regionally accredited. Extension courses offered in Lamar, Monett, Nevada (evening only), limited weekend courses. Television and online courses offered. **Degrees:** 609 bachelor's, 105 associate awarded; master's offered. **Location:** 138 miles from Kansas City, 126 miles from Tulsa, Oklahoma. **Calendar:** Semester, extensive summer session. **Full-time faculty:** 211 total. **Part-time faculty:** 84 total. **Class size:** 42% < 20, 53% 20-39, 3% 40-49, 1% 50-99, less than 1% >100. **Special facilities:** Biology pond, crime lab, child development center, small business development center, indoor "livefire" firearms range, performing arts center, greenhouse, law library, cyber coffee shop.

**Freshman class profile.** 1,425 applied, 1,404 admitted, 769 enrolled.

| | | | |
|---|---|---|---|
| Rank in top quarter: | 40% | Live on campus: | 30% |
| Rank in top tenth: | 17% | Fraternities: | 1% |
| Out-of-state: | 18% | Sororities: | 1% |

**Basis for selection.** Minimum 18 ACT or rank in upper 50% of class. Must score in 75th percentile on Michigan Test for English as foreign language. ACT recommended. **Learning Disabled:** Contact the Coordinator for Disability Services.

**High school preparation.** 16 units required. Required and recommended units include English 4, mathematics 3, social studies 3, science 2 (laboratory 1), foreign language 2 and academic electives 3. One unit from visual arts, music, dance or theater.

**2007-2008 Annual costs.** Tuition/fees: $4,276; $8,326 out-of-state. Room/ board: $4,720. Books/supplies: $600. Personal expenses: $1,500.

**Financial aid. Non-need-based:** Scholarships awarded for academics, alumni affiliation, art, athletics, job skills, leadership, minority status, music/drama, state residency.

**Application procedures. Admission:** Priority date 8/1; no deadline. $15 fee, may be waived for applicants with need. Application may be submitted online. Admission notification on a rolling basis beginning on or about 9/1. **Financial aid:** Priority date 2/15; no closing date. FAFSA required. Applicants notified on a rolling basis starting 2/15; must reply within 3 week(s) of notification.

**Academics. Special study options:** Accelerated study, cooperative education, distance learning, double major, dual enrollment of high school students, ESL, exchange student, honors, independent study, internships, liberal arts/career combination, study abroad, teacher certification program, weekend college. **Credit/placement by examination:** AP, CLEP, IB, SAT, ACT, institutional tests. **Support services:** Learning center, reduced course load, remedial instruction, study skills assistance, tutoring, writing center.

**Honors college/program.** Entrance by invitation. Approximately 50 students admitted each year. Application closing date March 1. Require 28 ACT or 3.5 GPA.

**Majors. Biology:** General, bacteriology, biochemistry, biotechnology, conservation, ecology, genetics, marine. **Business:** General, accounting, finance, financial planning, international, management science, marketing, operations. **Communications:** General, media studies. **Computer sciences:** General, computer science, information systems, programming. **Conservation:** General, management/policy. **Education:** General, art, biology, business, chemistry, early childhood, elementary, English, ESL, foreign languages, French, German, health, history, mathematics, middle, multi-level teacher, music, physical, physics, reading, science, secondary, social science, Spanish, special, speech, technology/industrial arts. **Engineering:** Industrial. **Engineering technology:** CAD/CADD, drafting. **English:** Creative writing, English lit, technical writing. **Foreign languages:** French, German, Spanish. **Health:** Environmental health, nursing (RN), predental, premedicine, prepharmacy, preveterinary. **History:** General. **Math:** General, computational. **Parks/recreation:** Health/fitness. **Physical sciences:** Chemistry, physics. **Protective services:** Forensics, law enforcement admin. **Psychology:** General. **Social sciences:** General, international relations, political science, sociology. **Visual/performing arts:** Dramatic, studio arts.

**Most popular majors.** Business/marketing 27%, education 19%, health sciences 8%, liberal arts 7%, security/protective services 9%.

**Computing on campus.** 522 workstations in library, computer center, student center. Dormitories wired for high-speed internet access and linked to campus network. Commuter students can connect to campus network. Online library, helpline, repair service, student web hosting, wireless network available.

**Student life. Freshman orientation:** Mandatory, $30 fee. Preregistration for classes offered. One-day introduction to campus and enrollment process during summer, plus 8-week course. **Housing:** Guaranteed on-campus for freshmen. Coed dorms, single-sex dorms, special housing for disabled, apartments, substance-free housing available. $150 deposit. Freshmen must live in residence halls if space is available, unless married, residing with relatives, or excused by the Coordinator of Student Housing. **Activities:** Bands, choral groups, dance, drama, film society, literary magazine, music ensembles, musical theater, radio station, student government, student newspaper, symphony orchestra, TV station, over 90 clubs and organizations available.

**Athletics. NCAA. Intercollegiate:** Baseball M, basketball, cheerleading, cross-country, football (tackle) M, golf M, soccer, softball W, tennis W, track and field, volleyball W. **Intramural:** Basketball, football (non-tackle), golf, racquetball, soccer, softball, table tennis, tennis, volleyball. **Team name:** Lions, Lady Lions.

**Student services.** Adult student services, career counseling, services for economically disadvantaged, student employment services, financial aid counseling, health services, on-campus daycare, personal counseling, placement for graduates, veterans' counselor. **Physically disabled:** Services for visually, hearing impaired. **Learning disabled:** Comprehensive services available.

**Contact.** E-mail: admissions@mssu.edu
Phone: (417) 625-9378 Toll-free number: (866) 818-6778
Fax: (417) 659-4429
Derek Skaggs, Director of Enrollment Services, Missouri Southern State University, 3950 East Newman Road, Joplin, MO 64801-1595

## Missouri State University
### Springfield, Missouri
www.missouristate.edu                    CB code: 6665

- Public 4-year university
- Commuter campus in small city
- 14,491 degree-seeking undergraduates: 12% part-time, 55% women, 3% African American, 2% Asian American, 2% Hispanic American, 1% Native American, 2% international
- 2,710 degree-seeking graduate students
- 75% of applicants admitted
- SAT or ACT (ACT writing optional) required
- 54% graduate within 6 years

**General.** Founded in 1906. Regionally accredited. **Degrees:** 2,807 bachelor's awarded; master's, doctoral offered. **ROTC:** Army. **Location:** 180 miles from Kansas City. **Calendar:** Semester, extensive summer session. **Full-time faculty:** 718 total; 8% have terminal degrees, 8% minority, 42% women. **Part-time faculty:** 329 total; 16% have terminal degrees, 3% minority, 52% women. **Class size:** 44% < 20, 40% 20-39, 8% 40-49, 6% 50-99, 2% >100. **Special facilities:** Observatory, 125-acre agriculture research and demonstration center, summer tent theater, archaeological research center, social research center, agriculture research center.

**Freshman class profile.** 7,677 applied, 5,755 admitted, 2,649 enrolled.

| Mid 50% test scores | | | |
|---|---|---|---|
| ACT composite: | 21-27 | Return as sophomores: | 74% |
| GPA 3.50 or higher: | 58% | Out-of-state: | 11% |
| GPA 3.0-3.49: | 30% | Live on campus: | 82% |
| GPA 2.0-2.99: | 12% | International: | 1% |
| Rank in top quarter: | 48% | Fraternities: | 6% |
| Rank in top tenth: | 21% | Sororities: | 10% |

**Basis for selection.** Applicant must have 108 or higher on selection index (sum of high school class rank percentile and test score percentile).

**High school preparation.** 16 units required. Required units include English 4, mathematics 3, social studies 3, science 2 (laboratory 1) and academic electives 3. 1 visual/performing arts required. Academic electives must include foreign language.

**2007-2008 Annual costs.** Tuition/fees: $5,988; $11,088 out-of-state. Room/board: $5,312. Books/supplies: $800. Personal expenses: $3,500.

**2007-2008 Financial aid. Need-based:** 2,060 full-time freshmen applied for aid; 1,410 were judged to have need; 1,393 of these received aid. Average need met was 69%. Average scholarship/grant was $5,406; average loan $3,003. 42% of total undergraduate aid awarded as scholarships/grants, 58% as loans/jobs. **Non-need-based:** Awarded to 4,676 full-time undergraduates, including 1,113 freshmen. Scholarships awarded for academics, alumni affiliation, art, athletics, job skills, leadership, minority status, music/drama, ROTC, state residency. **Additional information:** Extensive scholarship program offered to freshmen and transfer students. Out-of-state fee stipends available. Student employment service available to assist students in securing employment on campus and in community.

**Application procedures. Admission:** Priority date 3/1; deadline 7/20 (postmark date). $35 fee, may be waived for applicants with need. Application may be submitted online. Admission notification on a rolling basis beginning on or about 9/1. **Financial aid:** Priority date 3/31; no closing date. Institutional form required. Applicants notified on a rolling basis starting 4/1.

**Academics. Special study options:** Accelerated study, combined bachelor's/graduate degree, cooperative education, distance learning, double major, dual

enrollment of high school students, ESL, exchange student, honors, independent study, internships, student-designed major, study abroad, teacher certification program. London semester. **Credit/placement by examination:** AP, CLEP, IB, SAT, ACT, institutional tests. **Support services:** Learning center, pre-admission summer program, study skills assistance, tutoring, writing center.

**Honors college/program.** Minimum 27 ACT or 1220 (exclusive of Writing) SAT and rank in top 10th percentile of class required. Approximately 250 to 300 freshmen enroll each year. Program includes freshman honors seminar, honors general education courses, departmental honors courses, senior project, senior honors seminar.

**Majors. Agriculture:** General, agribusiness operations, agronomy, animal sciences, horticultural science. **Architecture:** Urban/community planning. **Biology:** General, cellular/molecular. **Business:** General, accounting, business admin, construction management, finance, hospitality admin, insurance, logistics, management information systems, marketing. **Communications:** General, journalism, media studies. **Computer sciences:** Computer science. **Conservation:** Wildlife. **Education:** Agricultural, art, biology, business, chemistry, early childhood, elementary, English, family/consumer sciences, French, German, history, Latin, mathematics, middle, music, physical, physics, science, Spanish, special, technology/industrial arts. **Engineering technology:** Industrial management. **English:** English lit, technical writing. **Family/consumer sciences:** Clothing/textiles, family studies, housing. **Foreign languages:** French, German, Latin, Spanish. **Health:** Athletic training, audiology/speech pathology, clinical lab science, dietetics, nursing (RN), preop/surgical nursing, radiologic technology/medical imaging, respiratory therapy technology. **History:** General. **Interdisciplinary:** Gerontology. **Liberal arts:** Humanities. **Math:** General. **Parks/recreation:** General, exercise sciences. **Philosophy/religion:** Philosophy, religion. **Physical sciences:** Chemistry, geology, physics. **Psychology:** General. **Public administration:** General, social work. **Social sciences:** Anthropology, cartography, criminology, economics, geography, political science, sociology. **Visual/performing arts:** General, art history/conservation, dance, design, dramatic, music performance, studio arts. **Other:** Electronic arts, Engineering physics, Entertainment mangement, Speech and theatre education.

**Most popular majors.** Business/marketing 32%, communications/journalism 6%, education 15%, psychology 6%, social sciences 6%.

**Computing on campus.** 1,800 workstations in dormitories, library, computer center, student center. Dormitories wired for high-speed internet access and linked to campus network. Commuter students can connect to campus network. Online library, helpline, student web hosting, wireless network available.

**Student life. Freshman orientation:** Mandatory, $40 fee. Preregistration for classes offered. Two-day program held during summer. **Housing:** Guaranteed on-campus for freshmen. Coed dorms, special housing for disabled, apartments, fraternity/sorority housing, substance-free housing available. $100 fully refundable deposit, deadline 7/1. Nontraditional, upper-class, honor, transfer student housing available. **Activities:** Bands, campus ministries, choral groups, dance, drama, film society, international student organizations, literary magazine, music ensembles, musical theater, radio station, student government, student newspaper, symphony orchestra, TV station, nearly 300 student organizations available.

**Athletics.** NCAA. **Intercollegiate:** Baseball M, basketball, cross-country, field hockey W, football (tackle) M, golf, soccer, softball W, swimming, track and field, volleyball W. **Intramural:** Basketball, bowling, football (non-tackle), golf, racquetball, soccer, softball, table tennis, tennis, track and field, volleyball, weight lifting, wrestling. **Team name:** Bears.

**Student services.** Adult student services, alcohol/substance abuse counseling, campus ministries, career counseling, services for economically disadvantaged, student employment services, financial aid counseling, health services, legal services, minority student services, on-campus daycare, personal counseling, placement for graduates, veterans' counselor. **Physically disabled:** Services for visually, speech, hearing impaired. **Learning disabled:** Comprehensive services available.

**Contact.** E-mail: info@missouristate.edu
Phone: (417) 836-5517 Toll-free number: (800) 492-7900
Fax: (417) 836-6334
Donald Simpson, Director of Admissions, Missouri State University, 901 South National Avenue, Springfield, MO 65897

## Missouri Technical School
### St. Louis, Missouri
www.motech.edu                    CB code: 2383

- For-profit 4-year engineering and technical college
- Commuter campus in very large city

**General.** Founded in 1932. Accredited by ACCSCT. **Location:** 20 miles from downtown. **Calendar:** Semester.

**Annual costs/financial aid.** Tuition is $500 per credit hour. Fees are $95 per 2-month term. Books/supplies: $800. Need-based financial aid available to full-time and part-time students.

**Contact.** Phone: (314) 569-3600
Director of Admissions, 1167 Corporate Lake Drive, St. Louis, MO 63132-1716

## Missouri University of Science and Technology
**Rolla, Missouri**
www.mst.edu

CB member
CB code: 6876

- Public 4-year university and engineering college
- Residential campus in large town
- 4,705 degree-seeking undergraduates: 7% part-time, 22% women, 5% African American, 2% Asian American, 2% Hispanic American, 1% Native American, 3% international
- 1,403 degree-seeking graduate students
- 67% of applicants admitted
- SAT or ACT (ACT writing optional) required
- 61% graduate within 6 years

**General.** Founded in 1870. Regionally accredited. **Degrees:** 834 bachelor's awarded; master's, doctoral offered. **ROTC:** Army, Naval, Air Force. **Location:** 100 miles from St. Louis, 100 miles from Springfield. **Calendar:** Semester, extensive summer session. **Full-time faculty:** 340 total; 86% have terminal degrees, 24% minority, 20% women. **Part-time faculty:** 63 total; 43% have terminal degrees, 13% minority, 25% women. **Class size:** 28% < 20, 51% 20-39, 10% 40-49, 7% 50-99, 5% >100. **Special facilities:** Computerized manufacturing system, nuclear reactor, observatory, experimental mine, museum of rocks, minerals, and gemstones, centers for environmental research, virtual reality laboratory, student design team center, wind tunnel.

**Freshman class profile.** 2,317 applied, 1,563 admitted, 977 enrolled.

| Mid 50% test scores | | | |
|---|---|---|---|
| SAT critical reading: | 530-670 | Rank in top tenth: | 38% |
| SAT math: | 590-690 | Return as sophomores: | 87% |
| ACT composite: | 25-30 | Out-of-state: | 21% |
| GPA 3.50 or higher: | 71% | Live on campus: | 95% |
| GPA 3.0-3.49: | 22% | International: | 1% |
| GPA 2.0-2.99: | 7% | Fraternities: | 30% |
| Rank in top quarter: | 69% | Sororities: | 27% |

**Basis for selection.** Admissions based on secondary school record, class rank, and standardized test scores. Recommendations considered. ACT or SAT score percentage, plus high school class rank percentile should equal 120 (minimum). Exceptions may be made on an individual basis. Campus visit and personal statement encouraged. **Homeschooled:** Transcript of courses and grades required. Must submit a standardized test score. **Learning Disabled:** Should submit voluntary declaration of disability to receive accommodation.

**High school preparation.** 17 units required. Required units include English 4, mathematics 4, social studies 3, science 3 (laboratory 1), foreign language 2 and academic electives 1. One fine arts required. Foreign language units must be in same language.

**2007-2008 Annual costs.** Tuition/fees: $8,172; $18,828 out-of-state. Room/board: $6,660. Books/supplies: $900. Personal expenses: $2,256.

**2006-2007 Financial aid. Need-based:** 756 full-time freshmen applied for aid; 583 were judged to have need; 583 of these received aid. Average need met was 46%. Average scholarship/grant was $4,978; average loan $3,708. 55% of total undergraduate aid awarded as scholarships/grants, 45% as loans/jobs. **Non-need-based:** Awarded to 1,346 full-time undergraduates, including 521 freshmen. Scholarships awarded for academics, alumni affiliation, athletics, job skills, leadership, minority status, music/drama, religious affiliation, ROTC, state residency.

**Application procedures. Admission:** Priority date 12/1; deadline 7/1 (postmark date). $35 fee, may be waived for applicants with need. Application may be submitted online. Admission notification on a rolling basis beginning on or about 10/1. Must reply by May 1 or within 3 week(s) if notified thereafter. **Financial aid:** Priority date 3/1; no closing date. FAFSA required. Applicants notified on a rolling basis; must reply within 3 week(s) of notification.

**Academics. Special study options:** Accelerated study, combined bachelor's/graduate degree, cooperative education, distance learning, double major, dual enrollment of high school students, ESL, honors, independent study, internships, liberal arts/career combination, student-designed major, study abroad, teacher certification program. **Credit/placement by examination:** AP, CLEP, IB, institutional tests. **Support services:** Learning center, pre-admission summer program, reduced course load, study skills assistance, tutoring, writing center.

**Majors. Biology:** General, biochemistry, biophysics. **Business:** General, business admin, management information systems. **Computer sciences:** General, computer science, information systems, information technology. **Engineering:** Aerospace, architectural, ceramic, chemical, civil, computer, electrical, environmental, geological, mechanical, mechanics, metallurgical, mining, nuclear, petroleum, polymer. **Engineering technology:** Industrial management. **English:** English lit, technical writing. **Health:** Predental, premedicine. **History:** General. **Legal studies:** Prelaw. **Math:** Applied. **Philosophy/religion:** Philosophy. **Physical sciences:** Chemistry, geochemistry, geology, geophysics, physics. **Psychology:** General. **Social sciences:** Economics.

**Most popular majors.** Computer/information sciences 9%, engineering/engineering technologies 71%.

**Computing on campus.** PC or laptop required. 812 workstations in dormitories, library, computer center. Dormitories wired for high-speed internet access and linked to campus network. Commuter students can connect to campus network. Online course registration, online library, helpline, repair service, student web hosting, wireless network available.

**Student life. Freshman orientation:** Mandatory, $135 fee. Preregistration for classes offered. Program includes meetings with advisers and placement testing. **Housing:** Guaranteed on-campus for freshmen. Coed dorms, special housing for disabled, apartments, cooperative housing, fraternity/sorority housing, substance-free housing available. $160 partly refundable deposit, deadline 6/1. Special accommodations for disabled students in co-ed dormitories. **Activities:** Bands, choral groups, dance, drama, literary magazine, music ensembles, musical theater, radio station, student government, student newspaper, symphony orchestra, Over 200 student groups avaliable.

**Athletics.** NCAA. **Intercollegiate:** Baseball M, basketball, cheerleading, cross-country, football (tackle) M, soccer, softball W, swimming M, track and field, volleyball W. **Intramural:** Badminton, basketball, bowling, cross-country, football (non-tackle), golf, racquetball, soccer, softball, swimming, table tennis, tennis, track and field, volleyball, weight lifting. **Team name:** Miners.

**Student services.** Adult student services, alcohol/substance abuse counseling, campus ministries, career counseling, student employment services, financial aid counseling, health services, legal services, minority student services, personal counseling, placement for graduates, women's services. **Physically disabled:** Services for visually, speech, hearing impaired. **Learning disabled:** Comprehensive services available.

**Contact.** E-mail: admissions@mst.edu
Phone: (573) 341-4164 Toll-free number: (800) 522-0938
Fax: (573) 341-4082
Lynn Stichnote, Director of Admissions, Missouri University of Science and Technology, 106 Parker Hall, Rolla, MO 65409

## Missouri Valley College
**Marshall, Missouri**
www.moval.edu

CB code: 6413

- Private 4-year liberal arts college affiliated with Presbyterian Church (USA)
- Residential campus in large town
- 1,419 degree-seeking undergraduates
- 57% of applicants admitted
- SAT or ACT (ACT writing optional) required

**General.** Founded in 1889. Regionally accredited. **Degrees:** 247 bachelor's, 4 associate awarded. **ROTC:** Army. **Location:** 75 miles from Kansas City. **Calendar:** Semester, limited summer session. **Full-time faculty:** 70 total. **Part-time faculty:** 50 total. **Class size:** 45% < 20, 54% 20-39, less than 1% 40-49, less than 1% 50-99.

**Freshman class profile.**

| | | | |
|---|---|---|---|
| Rank in top quarter: | 19% | International: | 8% |
| Rank in top tenth: | 6% | Fraternities: | 25% |
| Out-of-state: | 25% | Sororities: | 25% |
| Live on campus: | 90% | | |

**Basis for selection.** Interview, recommendations, high school record, test scores important; extracurricular activities, personal attributes also important; class rank considered. Essay recommended for academically weak students. Audition recommended for drama majors; portfolio recommended for art majors. **Homeschooled:** GED in addition to acceptable ACT/SAT score is sufficient.

**High school preparation.** Recommended units include English 4, mathematics 3, social studies 1, history 3, science 3 and foreign language 1.

**2008-2009 Annual costs.** Tuition/fees: $15,950. Room/board: $6,050. Books/supplies: $1,300. Personal expenses: $2,900.

**Financial aid. Non-need-based:** Scholarships awarded for academics, state residency.

**Application procedures. Admission:** Priority date 3/1; no deadline. $15 fee, may be waived for applicants with need. Application may be submitted online. Admission notification on a rolling basis. Must reply by May 1 or within 4 week(s) if notified thereafter. **Financial aid:** Priority date 3/1; no closing date. FAFSA required. Applicants notified on a rolling basis starting 2/1; must reply within 6 week(s) of notification.

**Academics. Special study options:** Combined bachelor's/graduate degree, double major, dual enrollment of high school students, ESL, external degree, independent study, internships, liberal arts/career combination, student-designed major, teacher certification program. **Credit/placement by examination:** AP, CLEP, SAT, ACT, institutional tests. 30 credit hours maximum toward bachelor's degree. **Support services:** Learning center, reduced course load, remedial instruction, study skills assistance, tutoring, writing center.

**Majors. Biology:** General. **Business:** Accounting, business admin. **Communications:** Media studies. **Computer sciences:** General. **Education:** Elementary, multiple handicapped, physical, secondary, social studies, special. **English:** English lit. **Health:** Athletic training, substance abuse counseling. **History:** General. **Interdisciplinary:** Biological/physical sciences. **Liberal arts:** Arts/sciences. **Math:** General. **Parks/recreation:** Exercise sciences, facilities management. **Protective services:** Law enforcement admin. **Psychology:** General. **Public administration:** General. **Social sciences:** Economics, political science, sociology. **Visual/performing arts:** Art, dramatic.

**Computing on campus.** 172 workstations in library, computer center, student center. Dormitories wired for high-speed internet access and linked to campus network. Commuter students can connect to campus network. Online library, helpline, repair service, wireless network available.

**Student life. Freshman orientation:** Available. Preregistration for classes offered. **Housing:** Guaranteed on-campus for all undergraduates. Single-sex dorms, apartments, fraternity/sorority housing available. **Activities:** Bands, choral groups, dance, drama, film society, literary magazine, music ensembles, musical theater, radio station, student government, student newspaper, symphony orchestra, TV station, international student organization, American Humanics, minority student union, Fellowship of Christian Athletes, student council for exceptional children.

**Athletics.** NAIA. **Intercollegiate:** Baseball M, basketball, cheerleading, cross-country, football (tackle) M, golf, rodeo, soccer, softball W, tennis, track and field, volleyball, wrestling. **Intramural:** Badminton, baseball M, basketball, bowling, cross-country, football (non-tackle), soccer, softball, table tennis, track and field, volleyball, weight lifting. **Team name:** Vikings.

**Student services.** Alcohol/substance abuse counseling, campus ministries, career counseling, student employment services, financial aid counseling, health services, placement for graduates, veterans' counselor.

**Contact.** E-mail: admissions@moval.edu
Phone: (660) 831-4114 Fax: (660) 831-4233
Tennille Langdon, Director of Admissions, Missouri Valley College, 500 East College Street, Marshall, MO 65340

---

## Missouri Western State University
### St. Joseph, Missouri
**www.missouriwestern.edu**     **CB code: 6625**

- ◆ Public 4-year business and liberal arts college
- ◆ Commuter campus in small city
- ◆ 5,301 degree-seeking undergraduates

**General.** Founded in 1915. Regionally accredited. **Degrees:** 659 bachelor's, 71 associate awarded. **ROTC:** Army. **Location:** 48 miles from Kansas City. **Calendar:** Semester, extensive summer session. **Full-time faculty:** 184 total. **Part-time faculty:** 127 total. **Class size:** 40% < 20, 53% 20-39, 3% 40-49, 4% 50-99, less than 1% >100. **Special facilities:** Biology nature study area, planetarium.

---

**Freshman class profile.**

| Mid 50% test scores | | | |
|---|---|---|---|
| ACT composite: | 16-22 | Out-of-state: | 6% |
| | | Live on campus: | 46% |

**Basis for selection.** Open admission, but selective for some programs. School record, test scores, interview, recommendations important for education, nursing, mathematics, computer science, social work applicants. Special talents important for music, art applicants. High school units mandated by state law may vary by program. Interview required for education, nursing, social work programs. Portfolio recommended for art majors, audition recommended for music majors.

**2007-2008 Annual costs.** Tuition/fees: $5,330; $9,290 out-of-state. Room/board: $5,784. Books/supplies: $800. Personal expenses: $1,500.

**2006-2007 Financial aid. Need-based:** 41% of total undergraduate aid awarded as scholarships/grants, 59% as loans/jobs. **Non-need-based:** Scholarships awarded for academics, alumni affiliation, art, athletics, job skills, leadership, minority status, music/drama, state residency.

**Application procedures. Admission:** Priority date 7/15; deadline 8/15. $15 fee, may be waived for applicants with need. Application may be submitted online. Admission notification on a rolling basis. **Financial aid:** Closing date 3/1. FAFSA, institutional form required. Applicants notified on a rolling basis starting 4/5; must reply within 3 week(s) of notification.

**Academics. Special study options:** Combined bachelor's/graduate degree, distance learning, double major, dual enrollment of high school students, honors, internships, liberal arts/career combination, teacher certification program, weekend college. **Credit/placement by examination:** AP, CLEP, institutional tests. 30 credit hours maximum toward associate degree, 30 toward bachelor's. **Support services:** Learning center, pre-admission summer program, reduced course load, remedial instruction, study skills assistance, tutoring, writing center.

**Majors. Biology:** General, biochemistry. **Business:** Accounting, business admin, finance, marketing. **Communications:** General. **Computer sciences:** General, information systems. **Education:** Art, elementary, English, French, middle, music, Spanish. **Engineering technology:** Computer, construction, electrical. **English:** English lit, speech/rhetoric. **Foreign languages:** French, Spanish. **Health:** Clinical lab technology, nursing (RN). **History:** General. **Interdisciplinary:** Natural sciences. **Liberal arts:** Arts/sciences. **Math:** General. **Parks/recreation:** Facilities management, health/fitness. **Physical sciences:** Chemistry. **Protective services:** Criminal justice. **Psychology:** General. **Public administration:** Social work. **Social sciences:** Economics, political science. **Visual/performing arts:** Art, graphic design.

**Computing on campus.** 300 workstations in dormitories, library, computer center, student center. Dormitories linked to campus network. Commuter students can connect to campus network. Online course registration available.

**Student life. Freshman orientation:** Available, $100 fee. Preregistration for classes offered. **Housing:** Coed dorms, apartments, fraternity/sorority housing available. $100 deposit. **Activities:** Bands, choral groups, dance, drama, music ensembles, musical theater, student government, student newspaper, symphony orchestra, over 70 organizations.

**Athletics.** NCAA. **Intercollegiate:** Baseball M, basketball, football (tackle) M, golf, soccer W, softball W, tennis W, volleyball W, wrestling M. **Intramural:** Archery, badminton, baseball M, basketball, bowling, golf, handball, racquetball, rugby M, soccer M, softball, table tennis, tennis, volleyball. **Team name:** Griffons.

**Student services.** Adult student services, alcohol/substance abuse counseling, career counseling, student employment services, financial aid counseling, health services, minority student services, on-campus daycare, personal counseling, placement for graduates, veterans' counselor.

**Contact.** E-mail: admissions@mwsc.edu
Phone: (816) 271-4200 Toll-free number: (800) 662-7041
Fax: (816) 271-5833
Howard McCauley, Director of Admissions, Missouri Western State University, 4525 Downs Drive, St. Joseph, MO 64507

---

## National American University: Kansas City
### Independence, Missouri
**www.national.edu**     **CB code: 5357**

- ◆ For-profit 4-year university
- ◆ Commuter campus in large city

**General.** Founded in 1941. Regionally accredited. **Location:** 8 miles from downtown. **Calendar:** Quarter.

**Annual costs/financial aid.** Need-based financial aid available to full-time and part-time students.

**Contact.** Phone: (866) 628-1288
Director of Admissions, 3620 Arrowhead Avenue, Independence, MO 64057

## Northwest Missouri State University
### Maryville, Missouri
www.nwmissouri.edu                    CB code: 6488

▶ Public 4-year university
▶ Residential campus in large town
▶ 5,607 degree-seeking undergraduates: 10% part-time, 56% women
▶ 850 degree-seeking graduate students
▶ 75% of applicants admitted
▶ SAT or ACT (ACT writing optional) required
▶ 55% graduate within 6 years; 99% enter graduate study

**General.** Founded in 1905. Regionally accredited. **Degrees:** 849 bachelor's, 36 associate awarded; master's offered. **ROTC:** Army. **Location:** 100 miles from Kansas City. **Calendar:** Trimester, extensive summer session. **Full-time faculty:** 250 total; 68% have terminal degrees, 8% minority, 44% women. **Part-time faculty:** 53 total; 19% have terminal degrees, 9% minority, 58% women. **Class size:** 42% < 20, 46% 20-39, 4% 40-49, 7% 50-99, less than 1% >100. **Special facilities:** Campus is state-recognized arboretum.

**Freshman class profile.** 4,433 applied, 3,306 admitted, 1,534 enrolled.

| Mid 50% test scores | | | |
|---|---|---|---|
| SAT critical reading: | 490-590 | Rank in top tenth: | 15% |
| SAT math: | 500-590 | End year in good standing: | 63% |
| ACT composite: | 19-24 | Return as sophomores: | 73% |
| GPA 3.50 or higher: | 42% | Out-of-state: | 24% |
| GPA 3.0-3.49: | 36% | Live on campus: | 93% |
| GPA 2.0-2.99: | 22% | International: | 2% |
| Rank in top quarter: | 41% | Fraternities: | 20% |
| | | Sororities: | 19% |

**Basis for selection.** School achievement record and test scores most important. Index based on class rank and national test. Audition recommended for dramatic arts and music students; portfolio recommended for art students. **Homeschooled:** Transcript of courses and grades, state high school equivalency certificate required.

**High school preparation.** 16 units required. Required and recommended units include English 4, mathematics 3-4, social studies 3, science 2-3 (laboratory 1), foreign language 2, visual/performing arts 1 and academic electives 3. One fine arts required. Foreign language and additional math and science highly recommended.

**2007-2008 Annual costs.** Tuition/fees: $6,438; $10,896 out-of-state. New student fee of $100. Primary textbooks included in tuition. Room/board: $6,276. Books/supplies: $500. Personal expenses: $1,400.

**Financial aid. Non-need-based:** Scholarships awarded for academics, alumni affiliation, art, athletics, job skills, leadership, minority status, music/drama, state residency.

**Application procedures. Admission:** No deadline. $25 fee, may be waived for applicants with need. Application may be submitted online. Admission notification on a rolling basis beginning on or about 9/1. **Financial aid:** Priority date 4/1; no closing date. FAFSA required. Applicants notified on a rolling basis starting 3/15; must reply within 2 week(s) of notification.

**Academics.** Laptop computers issued to every on-campus resident student. **Special study options:** Accelerated study, cross-registration, distance learning, double major, dual enrollment of high school students, ESL, exchange student, honors, independent study, internships, liberal arts/career combination, study abroad, teacher certification program, Washington semester. **Credit/placement by examination:** AP, CLEP, IB, SAT, ACT, institutional tests. **Support services:** Learning center, reduced course load, remedial instruction, study skills assistance, tutoring, writing center.

**Majors. Agriculture:** General, agribusiness operations, agronomy, animal sciences, economics, horticultural science. **Biology:** General, marine. **Business:** Accounting, administrative services, business admin, finance, international, management information systems, managerial economics, marketing. **Communications:** Advertising, journalism, organizational, public relations, radio/tv. **Computer sciences:** General, web page design. **Conservation:**

Wildlife. **Education:** Agricultural, art, biology, business, chemistry, curriculum, elementary, English, family/consumer sciences, mathematics, middle, multiple handicapped, music, physical, physics, science, social science, Spanish. **Engineering technology:** GIS. **English:** English lit, speech/rhetoric. **Family/consumer sciences:** Apparel marketing, family studies, institutional food production. **Foreign languages:** Spanish. **Health:** Clinical lab science, dietetics, preveterinary. **History:** General. **Interdisciplinary:** Biological/physical sciences, biopsychology. **Liberal arts:** Humanities. **Math:** General, statistics. **Parks/recreation:** General, facilities management. **Philosophy/religion:** Philosophy. **Physical sciences:** Chemistry, geology, physics. **Psychology:** General, industrial, psychobiology, social. **Public administration:** General. **Social sciences:** Economics, geography, political science, sociology. **Visual/performing arts:** Acting, dramatic, studio arts, theater design. **Other:** Alternative energy, Speech/theatre education.

**Most popular majors.** Agriculture 8%, business/marketing 22%, communications/journalism 11%, education 16%, psychology 12%.

**Computing on campus.** 5,000 workstations in dormitories, library, computer center, student center. Dormitories wired for high-speed internet access and linked to campus network. Commuter students can connect to campus network. Online course registration, online library, helpline, repair service, student web hosting, wireless network available.

**Student life. Freshman orientation:** Mandatory, $100 fee. Preregistration for classes offered. One-day program in June plus 4-day program held before classes begin in August. **Policies:** All campus locations are alcohol- and smoke-free. **Housing:** Guaranteed on-campus for freshmen. Coed dorms, special housing for disabled, apartments, fraternity/sorority housing available. $150 nonrefundable deposit. **Activities:** Bands, choral groups, dance, drama, film society, international student organizations, literary magazine, music ensembles, musical theater, radio station, student government, student newspaper, symphony orchestra, TV station, Wesley Center, Young Democrats, Pan-Hellenic council, Newman Center, College Republicans, peer education, volunteer center, Alliance of Black Collegians.

**Athletics.** NCAA. **Intercollegiate:** Baseball M, basketball, cross-country, football (tackle) M, soccer W, softball W, tennis, track and field, volleyball W. **Intramural:** Badminton, basketball, bowling, cross-country, football (nontackle), golf, racquetball, skiing, softball, swimming, table tennis, tennis, track and field, volleyball. **Team name:** Bearcats.

**Student services.** Alcohol/substance abuse counseling, campus ministries, career counseling, services for economically disadvantaged, student employment services, financial aid counseling, health services, minority student services, personal counseling, placement for graduates. **Physically disabled:** Services for visually, speech, hearing impaired.

**Contact.** E-mail: admissions@nwmissouri.edu
Phone: (660) 562-1562 Toll-free number: (800) 633-1175
Fax: (660) 562-1121
Beverly Schenkel, Dean of Enrollment Management, Northwest Missouri State University, 800 University Drive, Maryville, MO 64468-6001

## Ozark Christian College
### Joplin, Missouri
www.occ.edu                    CB code: 6542

▶ Private 4-year Bible college affiliated with nondenominational tradition
▶ Residential campus in large town
▶ 655 degree-seeking undergraduates: 16% part-time, 42% women, 1% African American, 1% Asian American, 2% Hispanic American, 1% Native American, 3% international
▶ 100% of applicants admitted
▶ SAT or ACT (ACT writing optional), application essay required
▶ 35% graduate within 6 years

**General.** Founded in 1942. Accredited by ABHE. **Degrees:** 121 bachelor's, 8 associate awarded. **Location:** 70 miles from Springfield, 100 miles from Tulsa, Oklahoma. **Calendar:** Semester, limited summer session. **Full-time faculty:** 33 total; 18% have terminal degrees, 9% women. **Part-time faculty:** 36 total; 11% have terminal degrees, 6% minority, 28% women. **Class size:** 66% < 20, 29% 20-39, 2% 40-49, 2% 50-99.

**Freshman class profile.** 276 applied, 276 admitted, 140 enrolled.

| | | | |
|---|---|---|---|
| Return as sophomores: | 65% | International: | 1% |
| Live on campus: | 90% | | |

**Basis for selection.** Secondary school record, test scores, essay important. 2 references required. Audition required for music ministry students. **Homeschooled:** Transcript of courses and grades required. Provide notarized transcript of grades signed by student and parents.

**High school preparation.** 15 units recommended. Recommended units include English 3, mathematics 2, history 1, science 2 and academic electives 7.

**2007-2008 Annual costs.** Tuition/fees: $7,830. Room/board: $4,050. Books/supplies: $600. Personal expenses: $1,500.

**2007-2008 Financial aid.** **Need-based:** 38% of total undergraduate aid awarded as scholarships/grants, 62% as loans/jobs. **Non-need-based:** Scholarships awarded for academics, leadership.

**Application procedures.** **Admission:** Closing date 8/5 (receipt date). $30 fee, may be waived for applicants with need. Application may be submitted online. Admission notification on a rolling basis. Applicant must submit high school transcript through first half of senior year. **Financial aid:** Priority date 4/1; no closing date. FAFSA required. Applicants notified on a rolling basis starting 6/1; must reply within 4 week(s) of notification.

**Academics.** **Special study options:** Combined bachelor's/graduate degree, distance learning, double major, independent study, internships. 5-year bachelor's degree program in theology, cooperative program with Missouri Southern State College for certification in elementary and secondary education as well as nursing. **Credit/placement by examination:** CLEP, ACT, institutional tests. **Support services:** Learning center, study skills assistance, tutoring.

**Majors.** **Theology:** Bible, missionary, religious ed, sacred music, theology.

**Computing on campus.** 23 workstations in library, computer center, student center. Dormitories wired for high-speed internet access and linked to campus network. Commuter students can connect to campus network. Online library, helpline, repair service, wireless network available.

**Student life.** **Freshman orientation:** Mandatory. **Housing:** Guaranteed on-campus for all undergraduates. Single-sex dorms, substance-free housing available. $90 deposit, deadline 8/5. **Activities:** Choral groups, drama, music ensembles, musical theater, radio station, student government.

**Athletics.** NCCAA. **Intercollegiate:** Basketball, soccer, volleyball W. **Intramural:** Basketball, racquetball, volleyball. **Team name:** Ambassadors.

**Student services.** Adult student services, career counseling, student employment services, financial aid counseling, health services, personal counseling, placement for graduates, veterans' counselor. **Physically disabled:** Services for hearing impaired.

**Contact.** E-mail: occadmin@occ.edu
Phone: (417) 624-2518 Fax: (417) 624-0090
Troy Nelson, Director of Admissions, Ozark Christian College, 1111 North Main Street, Joplin, MO 64801

## Park University
**Parkville, Missouri**
www.park.edu                                      **CB code: 6574**

- Private 4-year university
- Commuter campus in small town
- 11,824 degree-seeking undergraduates: 90% part-time, 50% women
- 578 degree-seeking graduate students
- 73% of applicants admitted

**General.** Founded in 1875. Regionally accredited. MetroPark School for adult education in Kansas City offers bachelor's degree. School for Extended Learning (SEL) offers degree programs in 21 states. **Degrees:** 2,584 bachelor's, 62 associate awarded; master's offered. **ROTC:** Army. **Location:** 12 miles from downtown Kansas City. **Calendar:** Semester, extensive summer session. **Full-time faculty:** 154 total; 64% have terminal degrees, 75% minority, 44% women. **Part-time faculty:** 818 total. **Special facilities:** 700 acres of woodland.

**Freshman class profile.** 523 applied, 383 admitted, 175 enrolled.

| Mid 50% test scores | | Rank in top tenth: | 8% |
|---|---|---|---|
| ACT composite: | 18-28 | Out-of-state: | 21% |
| Rank in top quarter: | 40% | Live on campus: | 35% |

**Basis for selection.** GPA (minimum 2.0), followed by test scores and rank in top half of class important. Exceptions considered on individual merit. Students with 3.0 GPA not required to submit SAT/ACT for admission; however, institutional placement test must be substituted. Entering freshmen with GPA of 2.0 to 3.0 must either be in top half of graduating class or submit satisfactory SAT/ACT scores. Interview recommended for academically weak students; audition recommended for music and theater students; portfolio recommended for art students.

**High school preparation.** 19 units recommended. Recommended units include English 3, mathematics 2, social studies 3, history 1, science 2 (laboratory 1), foreign language 2 and academic electives 6.

**2007-2008 Annual costs.** Tuition/fees: $7,800. Tuition varies by program and hours taken. Room/board: $5,460. Books/supplies: $1,200. Personal expenses: $2,745.

**2006-2007 Financial aid.** **Need-based:** 120 full-time freshmen applied for aid; 68 were judged to have need; 68 of these received aid. Average need met was 56%. Average scholarship/grant was $3,527; average loan $1,079. 28% of total undergraduate aid awarded as scholarships/grants, 72% as loans/jobs. **Non-need-based:** Awarded to 835 full-time undergraduates, including 72 freshmen. Scholarships awarded for academics, alumni affiliation, art, athletics, job skills, leadership, minority status, music/drama, religious affiliation, ROTC.

**Application procedures.** **Admission:** Priority date 4/15; deadline 8/1. $25 fee, may be waived for applicants with need. Application may be submitted online. Admission notification on a rolling basis. **Financial aid:** Priority date 4/1, closing date 8/1. FAFSA, institutional form required. Applicants notified on a rolling basis starting 4/1.

**Academics.** **Special study options:** Accelerated study, cross-registration, distance learning, double major, dual enrollment of high school students, ESL, honors, independent study, internships, student-designed major, study abroad, teacher certification program, Washington semester, weekend college. **Credit/placement by examination:** AP, CLEP, ACT, institutional tests. **Support services:** Learning center, reduced course load, remedial instruction, study skills assistance, tutoring, writing center.

**Majors.** **Biology:** General. **Business:** Accounting, accounting/business management, business admin, logistics, management information systems, managerial economics, marketing. **Communications:** General. **Computer sciences:** General, computer science. **Education:** Early childhood, elementary. **English:** English lit. **Family/consumer sciences:** Child development. **Foreign languages:** Spanish. **Health:** Athletic training. **History:** General. **Interdisciplinary:** Math/computer science, natural sciences. **Legal studies:** General. **Liberal arts:** Arts/sciences. **Math:** General. **Physical sciences:** Chemistry. **Protective services:** Fire services admin, law enforcement admin. **Psychology:** General. **Public administration:** General, social work. **Social sciences:** Economics, geography, political science, sociology. **Transportation:** Aviation management. **Visual/performing arts:** Dramatic, graphic design, interior design, studio arts.

**Most popular majors.** Business/marketing 66%, psychology 16%, security/protective services 9%.

**Computing on campus.** 570 workstations in dormitories, library, computer center, student center. Dormitories linked to campus network. Commuter students can connect to campus network. Online course registration available.

**Student life.** **Freshman orientation:** Mandatory. Preregistration for classes offered. **Housing:** Guaranteed on-campus for freshmen. Coed dorms, apartments available. $100 deposit. **Activities:** Choral groups, drama, literary magazine, radio station, student government, student newspaper, symphony orchestra, service organizations, Christian Fellowship, World Student Union, Brothers and Sisters United, accounting society, Latin American student organization, marketing club, honors club, non-traditional student organization.

**Athletics.** NAIA. **Intercollegiate:** Baseball M, basketball, cross-country, golf W, soccer, softball W, track and field, volleyball. **Intramural:** Basketball, soccer, softball, volleyball. **Team name:** Pirates.

**Student services.** Career counseling, student employment services, financial aid counseling, health services, on-campus daycare, personal counseling, placement for graduates, veterans' counselor. **Physically disabled:** Services for visually, speech, hearing impaired.

**Contact.** E-mail: admissions@park.edu
Phone: (816) 584-6214 Toll-free number: (800) 745-7275
Fax: (816) 741-4462
Cathy Colapietro, Director of Admissions and Student Financial Services, Park University, 8700 River Park Drive, Parkville, MO 64152

## Research College of Nursing
**Kansas City, Missouri**
www.researchcollege.edu                           **CB code: 6612**

- For-profit 4-year nursing college
- Residential campus in very large city
- 280 degree-seeking undergraduates: 1% part-time, 93% women

◗ 91 degree-seeking graduate students
◗ 68% of applicants admitted
◗ SAT or ACT (ACT writing optional) required

**General.** Founded in 1905. Regionally accredited. Natural science, social science and liberal arts courses taken at Rockhurst University. Students have access to facilities, organizations, sports and activities on both campuses. The undergraduate Bachelor of Science in Nursing is awarded jointly by Research College of Nursing and Rockhurst University. **Degrees:** 120 bachelor's awarded; master's offered. **ROTC:** Army. **Location:** 5 miles from downtown. **Calendar:** Semester, limited summer session. **Full-time faculty:** 30 total. **Part-time faculty:** 3 total. **Special facilities:** Medical library, 532-bed research medical center.

**Freshman class profile.** 244 applied, 165 admitted, 53 enrolled.

| Mid 50% test scores | | Out-of-state: | 25% |
|---|---|---|---|
| ACT composite: | 22-26 | Live on campus: | 77% |

**Basis for selection.** Academic record, high school GPA, rank in top half of class, counselor's recommendation, test scores very important. ACT score of 20 required. Interview, high school activities considered. Interview recommended for all; strongly recommended for applicants with ACT scores below 20.

**High school preparation.** 18 units recommended. Recommended units include English 4, mathematics 3, social studies 3, science 4 and foreign language 2. Visual or performing arts also recommended. Mathematics should include algebra II, science should include chemistry.

**2007-2008 Annual costs.** Tuition/fees: $22,720. Room/board: $6,600. Books/supplies: $720. Personal expenses: $915.

**Financial aid. Non-need-based:** Scholarships awarded for academics, alumni affiliation, leadership. **Additional information:** Financial aid handled by Rockhurst University for freshmen and sophomores.

**Application procedures. Admission:** Priority date 3/1; no deadline. $20 fee, may be waived for applicants with need. Admission notification on a rolling basis beginning on or about 10/1. Must reply by May 1 or within 4 week(s) if notified thereafter. **Financial aid:** Priority date 3/15; no closing date. FAFSA, institutional form required. Applicants notified on a rolling basis starting 3/15.

**Academics.** Students admitted into nursing program in freshman year guaranteed place in upper-division nursing courses if academic requirements maintained. **Special study options:** Accelerated study, cross-registration, double major, dual enrollment of high school students, exchange student, honors, independent study, study abroad. **Credit/placement by examination:** AP, CLEP, IB, ACT, institutional tests. 32 credit hours maximum toward bachelor's degree. **Support services:** Learning center, reduced course load, tutoring.

**Honors college/program.** Honors program for students who qualify.

**Majors. Health:** Nursing (RN).

**Computing on campus.** 300 workstations in dormitories, library, computer center. Commuter students can connect to campus network. Helpline available.

**Student life. Freshman orientation:** Mandatory, $50 fee. Preregistration for classes offered. **Housing:** Guaranteed on-campus for freshmen. Coed dorms, single-sex dorms, apartments, fraternity/sorority housing available. $200 fully refundable deposit. Freshman nursing students not living at home must live on Rockhurst College campus. All other undergraduates may choose to live on Research College campus or at Rockhurst College. **Activities:** Campus ministries, choral groups, drama, music ensembles, musical theater, radio station, student government, student newspaper, Alpha Phi Omega, Black Student Union, Young Republicans, Young Democrats, Missouri Student Nurses Association, National Student Nurses Association, Rockhurst Organization of Collegiate Women.

**Athletics.** NCAA. **Intercollegiate:** Baseball M, basketball, cross-country, golf, soccer, softball W, tennis, volleyball W. **Intramural:** Basketball, lacrosse, racquetball, rugby, table tennis, volleyball.

**Student services.** Campus ministries, career counseling, student employment services, financial aid counseling, health services, on-campus daycare, personal counseling, placement for graduates, veterans' counselor.

**Contact.**  Phone: (816) 995-2812 Toll-free number: (866) 855-0296
Fax: (816) 995-2813
Leslie Mendenhall, Director of Transfer and Graduate Recruitment, Research College of Nursing, 2525 East Meyer Boulevard, Kansas City, MO 64132-1199

## Rockhurst University
**Kansas City, Missouri**
**www.rockhurst.edu**

**CB member**
**CB code: 6611**

◗ Private 4-year business and liberal arts college affiliated with Roman Catholic Church
◗ Residential campus in very large city
◗ 1,598 degree-seeking undergraduates: 9% part-time, 60% women, 5% African American, 3% Asian American, 5% Hispanic American, 1% Native American, 1% international
◗ 791 degree-seeking graduate students
◗ 76% of applicants admitted
◗ SAT or ACT (ACT writing optional) required
◗ 65% graduate within 6 years

**General.** Founded in 1910. Regionally accredited. Students graduate with community service transcript in addition to academic transcript. **Degrees:** 389 bachelor's awarded; master's, doctoral offered. **ROTC:** Army. **Location:** 5 miles from downtown. **Calendar:** Semester, limited summer session. **Full-time faculty:** 119 total; 84% have terminal degrees, 5% minority, 47% women. **Part-time faculty:** 91 total; 37% have terminal degrees, 6% minority, 48% women. **Class size:** 28% < 20, 67% 20-39, 2% 40-49, 3% 50-99. **Special facilities:** Science center.

**Freshman class profile.** 1,833 applied, 1,388 admitted, 369 enrolled.

| Mid 50% test scores | | Rank in top quarter: | 55% |
|---|---|---|---|
| ACT composite: | 22-27 | Rank in top tenth: | 25% |
| GPA 3.50 or higher: | 63% | Out-of-state: | 39% |
| GPA 3.0-3.49: | 25% | Live on campus: | 90% |
| GPA 2.0-2.99: | 11% | International: | 1% |

**Basis for selection.** High school GPA, class rank, test scores, recommendations most important; school and community activities considered. ACT recommended. February ACT is deadline for scholarship increase. Interviews recommended for all students. Essay or personal statement may be required or requested. **Homeschooled:** Transcript of courses and grades, state high school equivalency certificate required. GED requested dependent on quality of grades presented on transcript.

**High school preparation.** 16 units recommended. Recommended units include English 4, mathematics 3, science 3 (laboratory 1) and academic electives 4. Recommend 3 units in foreign language and/or social studies.

**2007-2008 Annual costs.** Tuition/fees: $22,840. Room/board: $6,300. Books/supplies: $1,400. Personal expenses: $1,029.

**2007-2008 Financial aid. Need-based:** 366 full-time freshmen applied for aid; 334 were judged to have need; 334 of these received aid. Average need met was 100%. Average scholarship/grant was $4,855; average loan $3,581. 75% of total undergraduate aid awarded as scholarships/grants, 25% as loans/jobs. **Non-need-based:** Scholarships awarded for academics, alumni affiliation, athletics, leadership, music/drama, state residency. **Additional information:** Auditions, portfolios required for some scholarships.

**Application procedures. Admission:** No deadline. $25 fee, may be waived for applicants with need. Application may be submitted online. Admission notification on a rolling basis beginning on or about 9/1. Must reply by May 1 or within 2 week(s) if notified thereafter. **Financial aid:** Priority date 3/1, closing date 6/30. FAFSA required. Applicants notified on a rolling basis starting 1/30; must reply within 4 week(s) of notification.

**Academics.** Core curriculum based on 7 "modes of inquiry," different ways people approach reality to seek truth including artistic, literary, historical, scientific-causal, scientific-relational, philosophical, and theological. **Special study options:** Accelerated study, combined bachelor's/graduate degree, cooperative education, cross-registration, double major, dual enrollment of high school students, exchange student, honors, independent study, internships, New York semester, study abroad, teacher certification program, Washington semester. **Credit/placement by examination:** AP, CLEP, IB, SAT, ACT, institutional tests. 32 credit hours maximum toward bachelor's degree. **Support services:** Learning center, study skills assistance, tutoring, writing center.

**Majors. Biology:** General, biochemistry, bioinformatics. **Business:** Business admin, communications, nonprofit/public. **Communications:** General, organizational. **Computer sciences:** Computer science. **Education:** Elementary, secondary. **English:** English lit. **Foreign languages:** French, Spanish. **Health:** Clinical lab science, nursing (RN), speech pathology. **History:** General. **Interdisciplinary:** Global studies. **Math:** General. **Philosophy/religion:** Philosophy, religion. **Physical sciences:** Chemistry, physics. **Psychology:** General. **Public administration:** Community org/advocacy. **Social sciences:** General, economics, political science, sociology. **Visual/performing arts:** Dramatic.

**Most popular majors.** Biology 6%, business/marketing 22%, health sciences 33%, psychology 9%, social sciences 7%.

**Computing on campus.** 500 workstations in dormitories, library, computer center, student center. Dormitories wired for high-speed internet access and linked to campus network. Commuter students can connect to campus network. Online course registration, online library, helpline, student web hosting, wireless network available.

**Student life. Freshman orientation:** Mandatory, $70 fee. Preregistration for classes offered. Programs held 4 days before fall semester begins. Includes participation in first of many community service projects. **Policies:** Full-time unmarried freshmen and sophomores must live on campus if not living with family. **Housing:** Coed dorms, single-sex dorms, special housing for disabled, apartments, substance-free housing available. $200 nonrefundable deposit. Theme houses and student townhouse available. **Activities:** Campus ministries, choral groups, dance, drama, literary magazine, musical theater, student government, student newspaper, Alpha Phi Omega, Black Student Union, Multicultural Affairs Office, American Humanics, Appalachian Service Project, Peace of the World, Amnesty International, student alumni association.

**Athletics.** NCAA. **Intercollegiate:** Baseball M, basketball, golf, soccer, softball W, tennis, volleyball W. **Intramural:** Baseball M, basketball, cross-country, football (tackle) M, golf, handball M, racquetball, soccer, softball, table tennis, volleyball, wrestling M. **Team name:** Hawks.

**Student services.** Adult student services, alcohol/substance abuse counseling, campus ministries, career counseling, student employment services, financial aid counseling, health services, personal counseling, placement for graduates, veterans' counselor.

**Contact.** E-mail: admission@rockhurst.edu
Phone: (816) 501-4100 Toll-free number: (800) 842-6776
Fax: (816) 501-4241
Lane Ramey, Director of Freshman Admissions, Rockhurst University, 1100 Rockhurst Road, Kansas City, MO 64110-2561

---

## St. Louis Christian College
**Florissant, Missouri**
www.slcconline.edu                    CB code: 0334

▶ Private 4-year Bible college affiliated with Christian Church
▶ Residential campus in small city
▶ 318 degree-seeking undergraduates: 14% part-time, 39% women
▶ 39% of applicants admitted
▶ ACT (writing optional), application essay required

**General.** Founded in 1956. Candidate for regional accreditation; also accredited by ABHE. Christian Churches/Churches of Christ affiliation. Students highly involved in service and field education. **Degrees:** 25 bachelor's, 16 associate awarded. **Location:** 15 miles from downtown St. Louis. **Calendar:** Semester, limited summer session. **Full-time faculty:** 10 total. **Part-time faculty:** 15 total.

**Freshman class profile.** 97 applied, 38 admitted, 33 enrolled.

| Mid 50% test scores | | Out-of-state: | 54% |
|---|---|---|---|
| ACT composite: | 20-26 | Live on campus: | 73% |

**Basis for selection.** ACT score, high school class rank, and GPA very important. English and Math placement based on ACT subscores or ACCUPLACER tests. Interview recommended for all. Audition required for religious music students. **Homeschooled:** ACT required, GED recommended.

**High school preparation.** Recommended units include English 4, mathematics 3, social studies 3, science 3, foreign language 2 and academic electives 4.

**2007-2008 Annual costs.** Full-time residential students maintaining an acceptable GPA receive full scholarships for tuition; required fees are $990 annually. Full-time commuter students pay $130 per-credit-hour; required fees, $990. Room/board: $5,800. Books/supplies: $800. Personal expenses: $600.

**2007-2008 Financial aid. Need-based:** Average need met was 78%. Average scholarship/grant was $8,880; average loan $1,803. 62% of total undergraduate aid awarded as scholarships/grants, 38% as loans/jobs. **Non-need-based:** Scholarships awarded for academics, alumni affiliation, leadership, music/drama, religious affiliation.

**Application procedures. Admission:** Priority date 1/15; deadline 8/1 (receipt date). $15 fee, may be waived for applicants with need. Admission notification on a rolling basis beginning on or about 10/1. **Financial aid:**

---

Closing date 8/1. FAFSA, institutional form required. Applicants notified on a rolling basis starting 7/20; must reply within 2 week(s) of notification.

**Academics.** Preparation for ministries in preaching, education, youth work, mission fields, music, worship and pre-seminary education. **Special study options:** Cross-registration, internships. **Credit/placement by examination:** CLEP, ACT, institutional tests. 30 credit hours maximum toward associate degree, 30 toward bachelor's. **Support services:** Remedial instruction, tutoring, writing center.

**Majors. Education:** General. **Theology:** Bible, missionary, religious ed, sacred music, theology.

**Computing on campus.** 13 workstations in library, computer center. Dormitories linked to campus network.

**Student life. Freshman orientation:** Mandatory, $250 fee. Preregistration for classes offered. Held weekend before first day of class. **Policies:** Students involved in evangelistic activities of area churches. Religious observance required. **Housing:** Guaranteed on-campus for all undergraduates. Single-sex dorms, apartments available. $100 deposit, deadline 8/10. **Activities:** Choral groups, drama, music ensembles, student government, missions interest group, ministry teams.

**Athletics.** NCCAA. **Intercollegiate:** Baseball M, basketball M, volleyball W. **Intramural:** Baseball M, basketball, softball, tennis, volleyball. **Team name:** Soldiers.

**Student services.** Adult student services, campus ministries, career counseling, student employment services, personal counseling. **Physically disabled:** Services for visually, hearing impaired.

**Contact.** E-mail: admissions@slcconline.edu
Phone: (314) 837-6777 Toll-free number: (800) 877-7522
Fax: (314) 837-8291
Carrie Chapman, Director of Admissions, St. Louis Christian College, 1360 Grandview Drive, Florissant, MO 63033

---

## Saint Louis University
**St. Louis, Missouri**                    CB member
www.slu.edu                                CB code: 6629

▶ Private 4-year university affiliated with Roman Catholic Church
▶ Residential campus in very large city
▶ 7,365 degree-seeking undergraduates: 7% part-time, 58% women, 7% African American, 6% Asian American, 3% Hispanic American, 3% international
▶ 4,651 degree-seeking graduate students
▶ 80% of applicants admitted
▶ SAT or ACT (ACT writing optional) required
▶ 75% graduate within 6 years; 32% enter graduate study

**General.** Founded in 1818. Regionally accredited. Institution maintains campus with facilities in Madrid, Spain. **Degrees:** 1,562 bachelor's awarded; master's, doctoral, first professional offered. **ROTC:** Army, Air Force. **Location:** Midtown. **Calendar:** Semester, extensive summer session. **Full-time faculty:** 614 total; 90% have terminal degrees, 10% minority, 41% women. **Part-time faculty:** 338 total; 13% have terminal degrees, 9% minority, 54% women. **Class size:** 52% < 20, 38% 20-39, 4% 40-49, 4% 50-99, 2% >100. **Special facilities:** Vatican manuscripts microfilm library, art museums, biological station, entrepreneurial studies center, earthquake research center, supersonic wind tunnel, water tunnel, shock tube, flight simulators, airport, fabrication labs, sculpture/ceramics studio, performing arts center, physiology and gait research labs, practice clinics with actual clients in counseling and family therapy, child development, speech and hearing, psychology, dental, occupational and physical therapy, organic gardening and food service.

**Freshman class profile.** 9,169 applied, 7,340 admitted, 1,604 enrolled.

| Mid 50% test scores | | | |
|---|---|---|---|
| SAT critical reading: | 540-650 | Rank in top tenth: | 37% |
| SAT math: | 540-670 | End year in good standing: | 89% |
| ACT composite: | 24-29 | Return as sophomores: | 82% |
| GPA 3.50 or higher: | 66% | Out-of-state: | 65% |
| GPA 3.0-3.49: | 24% | Live on campus: | 87% |
| GPA 2.0-2.99: | 10% | International: | 2% |
| Rank in top quarter: | 68% | Fraternities: | 11% |
| | | Sororities: | 15% |

**Basis for selection.** Secondary school record, standardized test scores important; recommendations, essay, extracurricular activities, character/personal qualities, volunteer work considered. Academic performance is most important for international applicants. SAT or ACT writing component may be evaluated as a writing sample. Audition recommended for music majors;

portfolio recommended for art majors. **Homeschooled:** Appplicants are strongly recommended to present 5 academic courses each semester for all four years. These should include 4 years of English, 4 years of Mathematics (Algebra I and II, and Geometry), 3 years each of Natural Science, Social Science and Academic Electives, 2 years of foreign language. **Learning Disabled:** Students with learning disabilities are responsible for contacting Disabilities Services in order to learn about the accommodation process on campus and to receive academic accommodations within the classroom.

**High school preparation.** 20 units recommended. Recommended units include English 4, mathematics 4, social studies 3, science 3, foreign language 2 and academic electives 3.

**2008-2009 Annual costs.** Tuition/fees: $30,728. Room/board: $8,760. Books/supplies: $1,040. Personal expenses: $3,513.

**2006-2007 Financial aid. Need-based:** 1,196 full-time freshmen applied for aid; 939 were judged to have need; 939 of these received aid. Average need met was 62%. Average scholarship/grant was $14,006; average loan $3,017. 75% of total undergraduate aid awarded as scholarships/grants, 25% as loans/jobs. **Non-need-based:** Awarded to 2,422 full-time undergraduates, including 683 freshmen. Scholarships awarded for academics, art, athletics, leadership, music/drama, religious affiliation, ROTC. **Additional information:** Presidential scholarship applications are due by December 1. Martin Luther King Jr. scholarship applications have a priority date of February 1.

**Application procedures. Admission:** Closing date 12/1 (receipt date). $25 fee. Application may be submitted online. Admission notification 8/1. Admission notification on a rolling basis beginning on or about 9/15. Must reply by May 1 or within 2 week(s) if notified thereafter. **Financial aid:** Priority date 3/1; no closing date. FAFSA required. Applicants notified on a rolling basis starting 3/1; must reply by 5/1 or within 4 week(s) of notification.

**Academics. Special study options:** Accelerated study, combined bachelor's/graduate degree, cooperative education, cross-registration, distance learning, double major, dual enrollment of high school students, ESL, honors, independent study, internships, liberal arts/career combination, student-designed major, study abroad, teacher certification program. **Credit/placement by examination:** AP, CLEP, IB, SAT, ACT, institutional tests. 30 credit hours maximum toward bachelor's degree. **Support services:** Pre-admission summer program, reduced course load, study skills assistance, tutoring, writing center.

**Honors college/program.** Admission Requirements: 30 ACT/1360 SAT/3.8 GPA. There are approximately 125 freshman admitted each year. Academic offerings: Honors core classes, honors opportunities in major, senior honors thesis.

**Majors. Area/ethnic studies:** American, women's. **Biology:** General, biochemistry. **Business:** Business admin, human resources, management information systems, management science, marketing, organizational behavior, purchasing. **Communications:** General. **Computer sciences:** General. **Conservation:** Environmental science. **Education:** Multi-level teacher. **Engineering:** Aerospace, biomedical, computer, electrical, mechanical, physics. **Engineering technology:** Aerospace, electrical, industrial management. **English:** English lit. **Family/consumer sciences:** Food/nutrition. **Foreign languages:** General, classics, French, German, modern Greek, Russian, Spanish. **Health:** Athletic training, audiology/speech pathology, clinical lab science, cytotechnology, medical radiologic technology/radiation therapy, medical records admin, nuclear medical technology, nursing (RN). **History:** General. **Liberal arts:** Humanities. **Math:** General. **Parks/recreation:** Exercise sciences. **Philosophy/religion:** Philosophy. **Physical sciences:** Atmospheric science, chemistry, geology, geophysics, physics. **Protective services:** Corrections, law enforcement admin. **Psychology:** General. **Public administration:** Social work. **Social sciences:** Economics, international relations, political science, sociology, urban studies. **Theology:** Theology. **Transportation:** Airline/commercial pilot, aviation management. **Visual/performing arts:** Art history/conservation, dramatic, studio arts.

**Most popular majors.** Business/marketing 24%, engineering/engineering technologies 6%, health sciences 15%, psychology 7%, social sciences 6%.

**Computing on campus.** 750 workstations in dormitories, library, computer center, student center. Dormitories wired for high-speed internet access and linked to campus network. Commuter students can connect to campus network. Online course registration, online library, helpline, repair service, student web hosting, wireless network available.

**Student life. Freshman orientation:** Available. Preregistration for classes offered. Freshman orientation is a two-day program offered seven times during summer before fall enrollment. **Housing:** Coed dorms, single-sex dorms, special housing for disabled, apartments, fraternity/sorority housing, substance-free housing available. $200 fully refundable deposit, deadline

5/1. Foreign language housing available. **Activities:** Bands, campus ministries, choral groups, dance, drama, film society, international student organizations, literary magazine, music ensembles, Model UN, musical theater, radio station, student government, student newspaper, TV station, Black student alliance, College Democrats, College Republicans, student activities board, Muslim student association, Relay for Life, Amnesty International.

**Athletics.** NCAA. **Intercollegiate:** Baseball M, basketball, cross-country, diving, field hockey W, soccer, softball W, swimming, tennis, track and field, volleyball W. **Intramural:** Badminton, basketball, bowling, football (non-tackle), golf, handball, racquetball, soccer, softball, squash, swimming, table tennis, tennis, triathlon, volleyball. **Team name:** Billikens.

**Student services.** Adult student services, alcohol/substance abuse counseling, campus ministries, career counseling, services for economically disadvantaged, student employment services, financial aid counseling, health services, minority student services, personal counseling, veterans' counselor, women's services. **Physically disabled:** Services for visually, speech, hearing impaired.

**Contact.**  E-mail: admitme@slu.edu
Phone: (314) 977-2500 Toll-free number: (800) 758-3678
Fax: (314) 977-7136
Saint Louis University, 221 North Grand Boulevard, St. Louis, MO 63103-2097

## St. Luke's College
**Kansas City, Missouri**
**www.saintlukescollege.edu**                    CB code: 7127

- Private two-year upper-division nursing college affiliated with Episcopal Church
- Commuter campus in large city
- Application essay, interview required

**General.** Founded in 1903. Regionally accredited. **Degrees:** 50 bachelor's awarded. **Calendar:** Semester, limited summer session. **Full-time faculty:** 16 total. **Special facilities:** Simulated clinical settings for nursing students.

**Student profile.** 115 degree-seeking undergraduates. 100% entered as juniors.

**Basis for selection.** High school transcript, college transcript, application essay, interview required. Recommendations required. Health care-related work and community service considered. Transfer accepted as juniors.

**2008-2009 Annual costs.** Tuition/fees: $9,520. Books/supplies: $600.

**Application procedures. Admission:** Deadline 12/31. $35 fee. Admission notification 3/1. **Financial aid:** FAFSA, institutional form required.

**Academics. Special study options:** Combined bachelor's/graduate degree. **Credit/placement by examination:** AP, CLEP. **Support services:** Learning center, pre-admission summer program, study skills assistance, tutoring.

**Majors. Health:** Nursing (RN).

**Computing on campus.** 30 workstations in computer center. Helpline available.

**Student life. Activities:** Student government.

**Student services.** Career counseling, financial aid counseling, health services, personal counseling.

**Contact.**  E-mail: slc-admissions@saint-lukes.org
Phone: (816) 932-2367 Fax: (816) 932-9064
Marcia Shaw, Director of Admissions & Financial Aid, St. Luke's College, 8320 Ward Parkway, Suite 300, Kansas City, MO 64114

## Southeast Missouri State University
**Cape Girardeau, Missouri**                    CB member
**www.semo.edu**                                CB code: 6655

- Public 4-year university
- Residential campus in large town
- 8,485 degree-seeking undergraduates: 20% part-time, 60% women, 9% African American, 1% Asian American, 1% Hispanic American, 1% Native American, 1% international
- 819 degree-seeking graduate students
- 88% of applicants admitted

◆ SAT or ACT (ACT writing optional) required

◆ 51% graduate within 6 years

**General.** Founded in 1873. Regionally accredited. **Degrees:** 1,391 bachelor's, 17 associate awarded; master's offered. **ROTC:** Air Force. **Location:** 120 miles from St. Louis. **Calendar:** Semester, extensive summer session. **Full-time faculty:** 413 total; 78% have terminal degrees, 12% minority, 45% women. **Part-time faculty:** 201 total; 10% have terminal degrees, 4% minority, 60% women. **Class size:** 43% < 20, 54% 20-39, 2% 40-49, less than 1% 50-99, less than 1% >100. **Special facilities:** Demonstration farm, NASA Educator Resource Center, Southeast Explorer mobile teaching and learning center, Southeast Health on Wheels, the Holland School of Visual and Performing Arts at the River Campus, museum of archeology, history, and fine art.

**Freshman class profile.** 4,111 applied, 3,618 admitted, 1,805 enrolled.

| Mid 50% test scores | | | |
|---|---|---|---|
| SAT critical reading: | 460-610 | GPA 2.0-2.99: | 33% |
| SAT math: | 460-600 | Rank in top quarter: | 37% |
| SAT writing: | 490-640 | Rank in top tenth: | 14% |
| ACT composite: | 19-25 | End year in good standing: | 74% |
| GPA 3.50 or higher: | 37% | Return as sophomores: | 71% |
| GPA 3.0-3.49: | 28% | Out-of-state: | 14% |
| | | Live on campus: | 66% |

**Basis for selection.** Standard test scores, academic GPA, rigor of secondary school records very important. Nontraditional students may take the ASSET exam. ACT preferred. SAT accepted. Audition required for music and theater majors.

**High school preparation.** 17 units required. Required units include English 4, mathematics 3, social studies 2, history 1, science 3 (laboratory 1), visual/performing arts 1 and academic electives 3. Of social studies requirements, .5 units must be in U.S. government.

**2007-2008 Annual costs.** Tuition/fees: $5,925; $10,320 out-of-state. Room/board: $5,923. Books/supplies: $423. Personal expenses: $2,033.

**2007-2008 Financial aid. Need-based:** 1,315 full-time freshmen applied for aid; 903 were judged to have need; 880 of these received aid. Average need met was 60%. Average scholarship/grant was $4,448; average loan $3,163. 42% of total undergraduate aid awarded as scholarships/grants, 58% as loans/jobs. **Non-need-based:** Awarded to 1,331 full-time undergraduates, including 511 freshmen. Scholarships awarded for academics, alumni affiliation, art, athletics, job skills, leadership, minority status, music/drama, ROTC, state residency.

**Application procedures. Admission:** Priority date 12/15; deadline 5/1 (postmark date). $25 fee, may be waived for applicants with need. Application may be submitted online. Admission notification on a rolling basis beginning on or about 9/1. Must reply by 5/1. **Financial aid:** Priority date 3/1; no closing date. FAFSA required. Applicants notified on a rolling basis starting 4/1; must reply within 3 week(s) of notification.

**Academics. Special study options:** Accelerated study, distance learning, double major, dual enrollment of high school students, ESL, honors, independent study, internships, liberal arts/career combination, student-designed major, study abroad, teacher certification program. **Credit/placement by examination:** AP, CLEP, SAT, ACT, institutional tests. 30 credit hours maximum toward associate degree, 30 toward bachelor's. Departmental exams offered. **Support services:** Learning center, pre-admission summer program, reduced course load, remedial instruction, study skills assistance, tutoring, writing center.

**Majors. Agriculture:** General, agribusiness operations, animal sciences, horticultural science, plant sciences. **Biology:** General. **Business:** Accounting, administrative services, business admin, finance, marketing, office management. **Communications:** General. **Computer sciences:** General. **Conservation:** Environmental studies. **Education:** General, art, business, elementary, English, family/consumer sciences, foreign languages, kindergarten/preschool, mathematics, middle, music, physical, science, social studies, special, speech, technology/industrial arts. **Engineering:** Physics. **Engineering technology:** General, industrial. **English:** English lit, speech/rhetoric. **Family/consumer sciences:** General. **Foreign languages:** French, German, Spanish. **Health:** Clinical lab science, communication disorders, nursing (RN). **History:** General. **Liberal arts:** Humanities. **Math:** General. **Parks/recreation:** General, health/fitness, sports admin. **Philosophy/religion:** Philosophy. **Physical sciences:** Chemistry, physics. **Protective services:** Corrections. **Psychology:** General. **Public administration:** Social work. **Social sciences:** Anthropology, economics, political science. **Visual/performing arts:** General, art, dramatic. **Other:** Specialist in education.

**Most popular majors.** Business/marketing 14%, communications/journalism 6%, education 19%, liberal arts 13%.

**Computing on campus.** 1,311 workstations in dormitories, library, computer center, student center. Dormitories wired for high-speed internet access and linked to campus network. Online course registration, online library, helpline, student web hosting, wireless network available.

**Student life. Freshman orientation:** Mandatory, $50 fee. Preregistration for classes offered. One-day program offered many times throughout the semester. **Housing:** Coed dorms, fraternity/sorority housing, substance-free housing available. $150 partly refundable deposit. Apartments for students with dependents. **Activities:** Bands, campus ministries, choral groups, dance, drama, literary magazine, music ensembles, musical theater, opera, radio station, student government, student newspaper, symphony orchestra, Baptist Student Union, Lutheran Student Fellowship, Association of Black Collegians, Greek Life, College Republicans, College Democrats, Friends Without Borders, Indian Subcontinent Student Association.

**Athletics.** NCAA. **Intercollegiate:** Baseball M, basketball, cheerleading, cross-country, football (tackle) M, gymnastics W, soccer W, softball W, tennis W, track and field, volleyball W. **Intramural:** Badminton, basketball, bowling, football (non-tackle), golf, racquetball, soccer, softball, swimming, table tennis, tennis, volleyball, wrestling. **Team name:** Redhawks.

**Student services.** Adult student services, alcohol/substance abuse counseling, campus ministries, career counseling, services for economically disadvantaged, student employment services, financial aid counseling, health services, minority student services, on-campus daycare, personal counseling, placement for graduates, veterans' counselor. **Physically disabled:** Services for visually, speech, hearing impaired.

**Contact.** E-mail: admissions@semo.edu
Phone: (573) 651-2590 Fax: (573) 651-5936
Deborah Below, Director, Southeast Missouri State University, One University Plaza, Cape Girardeau, MO 63701

---

## Southwest Baptist University
**Bolivar, Missouri**
www.sbuniv.edu                          CB code: 6664

◆ Private 4-year university affiliated with Southern Baptist Convention

◆ Residential campus in small town

◆ 2,443 degree-seeking undergraduates: 26% part-time, 66% women, 4% African American, 1% Asian American, 1% Hispanic American, 1% Native American, 1% international

◆ 499 degree-seeking graduate students

◆ 65% of applicants admitted

◆ SAT or ACT (ACT writing optional) required

◆ 49% graduate within 6 years; 17% enter graduate study

**General.** Founded in 1878. Regionally accredited. **Degrees:** 337 bachelor's, 130 associate awarded; master's, doctoral offered. **ROTC:** Army. **Location:** 25 miles from Springfield, 120 miles from Kansas City. **Calendar:** Semester, extensive summer session. **Full-time faculty:** 110 total; 60% have terminal degrees, less than 1% minority, 37% women. **Part-time faculty:** 146 total; 24% have terminal degrees, less than 1% minority, 58% women. **Class size:** 64% < 20, 30% 20-39, 3% 40-49, 3% 50-99.

**Freshman class profile.** 1,674 applied, 1,081 admitted, 410 enrolled.

| Mid 50% test scores | | | |
|---|---|---|---|
| SAT critical reading: | 430-600 | Rank in top quarter: | 51% |
| SAT math: | 400-590 | Rank in top tenth: | 22% |
| ACT composite: | 20-26 | End year in good standing: | 88% |
| GPA 3.50 or higher: | 54% | Return as sophomores: | 72% |
| GPA 3.0-3.49: | 22% | Out-of-state: | 31% |
| GPA 2.0-2.99: | 23% | Live on campus: | 87% |
| | | International: | 1% |

**Basis for selection.** Must present proof of graduation from an accredited or approved high school or present an acceptable secondary certificate. Additionally, students must meet 2 of 3 qualifiers: 2.50 GPA, 21 ACT or 990 SAT score (exclusive of Writing), top 50% high school class rank. Interview required for conditionally admitted applicants, recommended for all. Audition recommended for music, speech, and theater students.

**High school preparation.** 13 units recommended. Recommended units include English 4, mathematics 3, social studies 2, science 2 and academic electives 2. 2 additional units of foreign language or computer science or 2 units of English, math, social studies or natural sciences recommended.

**2007-2008 Annual costs.** Tuition/fees: $14,950. Room/board: $4,550. Books/supplies: $1,000. Personal expenses: $1,000.

**2007-2008 Financial aid. Need-based:** 399 full-time freshmen applied for aid; 316 were judged to have need; 315 of these received aid. Average need met was 85%. Average scholarship/grant was $4,480; average loan $3,991. 44% of total undergraduate aid awarded as scholarships/grants, 56% as loans/jobs. **Non-need-based:** Awarded to 1,697 full-time undergraduates, including 457 freshmen. Scholarships awarded for academics, art, athletics, minority status, music/drama, state residency.

**Application procedures. Admission:** No deadline. $30 fee, may be waived for applicants with need. Application may be submitted online. Admission notification on a rolling basis beginning on or about 9/1. **Financial aid:** Priority date 3/15; no closing date. FAFSA, institutional form required. Applicants notified on a rolling basis starting 3/1; must reply within 2 week(s) of notification.

**Academics. Special study options:** Cooperative education, distance learning, double major, dual enrollment of high school students, honors, independent study, internships, student-designed major, study abroad, teacher certification program, Washington semester. **Credit/placement by examination:** AP, CLEP, IB, SAT, ACT, institutional tests. 16 credit hours maximum toward associate degree, 32 toward bachelor's. **Support services:** Learning center, reduced course load, remedial instruction, study skills assistance, tutoring, writing center.

**Majors. Biology:** General. **Business:** Accounting, business admin, customer service, finance, international, marketing, office management. **Communications:** General. **Computer sciences:** General, computer science. **Education:** Art, biology, chemistry, elementary, English, health, middle, music, physical, science, social studies. **English:** English lit. **Foreign languages:** Spanish. **Health:** Athletic training, clinical lab science, nursing (RN). **History:** General. **Math:** General. **Parks/recreation:** General, health/fitness, sports admin. **Philosophy/religion:** Religion. **Physical sciences:** Chemistry. **Protective services:** Law enforcement admin. **Psychology:** General. **Public administration:** Human services. **Social sciences:** Political science, sociology. **Theology:** Bible, missionary, religious ed, sacred music, theology. **Visual/performing arts:** Art, commercial/advertising art, dramatic. **Other:** Science and Christian faith.

**Most popular majors.** Business/marketing 15%, education 17%, health sciences 10%, psychology 14%, theological studies 12%.

**Computing on campus.** 261 workstations in dormitories, library, computer center, student center. Dormitories linked to campus network. Commuter students can connect to campus network. Online library, helpline, wireless network available.

**Student life. Freshman orientation:** Available. Preregistration for classes offered. 5 days prior to start of the fall semester. **Policies:** Religious observance required. **Housing:** Guaranteed on-campus for freshmen. Single-sex dorms, apartments, substance-free housing available. $100 deposit. **Activities:** Bands, campus ministries, choral groups, drama, international student organizations, music ensembles, opera, student government, student newspaper, symphony orchestra, University Missions, Student Government Association, Habitat for Humanity, Christian Service Organization, Theatrical Evangelism and Mission, Students in Free Enterprise, Discipleship-Now teams.

**Athletics.** NCAA. **Intercollegiate:** Baseball M, basketball, cheerleading, cross-country, football (tackle) M, golf M, soccer W, softball W, tennis, track and field, volleyball W. **Intramural:** Basketball, football (non-tackle), soccer, softball, table tennis, volleyball. **Team name:** Bearcats.

**Student services.** Campus ministries, career counseling, student employment services, financial aid counseling, health services, personal counseling, placement for graduates.

**Contact.** E-mail: dcrowder@sbuniv.edu
Phone: (417) 328-1810 Toll-free number: (800) 526-5859
Fax: (417) 328-1514
Darren Crowder, Director of Admissions, Southwest Baptist University, 1600 University Avenue, Bolivar, MO 65613-2597

---

## Stephens College

**Columbia, Missouri**
www.stephens.edu

**CB member**
**CB code:** 6683

- Private 4-year liberal arts college for women
- Residential campus in small city
- 861 degree-seeking undergraduates: 20% part-time, 97% women, 10% African American, 2% Asian American, 3% Hispanic American, 1% Native American
- 160 degree-seeking graduate students
- 71% of applicants admitted
- SAT or ACT (ACT writing optional), application essay required
- 57% graduate within 6 years; 21% enter graduate study

**General.** Founded in 1833. Regionally accredited. **Degrees:** 139 bachelor's, 1 associate awarded; master's offered. **ROTC:** Army, Naval, Air Force. **Location:** 125 miles from St. Louis and Kansas City. **Calendar:** Semester, limited summer session. **Full-time faculty:** 53 total; 42% have terminal degrees, 2% minority, 77% women. **Part-time faculty:** 60 total;

18% have terminal degrees, 12% minority, 70% women. **Class size:** 77% < 20, 22% 20-39, less than 1% 40-49, less than 1% 50-99. **Special facilities:** Professional-level theater, private elementary school and child study center, 60-horse stables, historical costume collection.

**Freshman class profile.** 735 applied, 522 admitted, 225 enrolled.

| Mid 50% test scores | | | |
|---|---|---|---|
| SAT critical reading: | 540-610 | Rank in top quarter: | 42% |
| SAT math: | 480-580 | Rank in top tenth: | 17% |
| ACT composite: | 21-26 | End year in good standing: | 78% |
| GPA 3.50 or higher: | 40% | Return as sophomores: | 68% |
| GPA 3.0-3.49: | 33% | Out-of-state: | 45% |
| GPA 2.0-2.99: | 26% | Live on campus: | 92% |
| | | Sororities: | 7% |

**Basis for selection.** School achievement record most important, followed by test scores. Interview recommended for all students; audition mandatory for dance, recommended for theater, musical theater students. **Homeschooled:** Statement describing homeschool structure and mission, letter of recommendation (nonparent) required. Statement should be short narrative written by the person primarily responsible for academic training. Statement should describe the nature of the secondary-level education.

**High school preparation.** 12 units recommended. Recommended units include English 4, mathematics 3, social studies 1, science 2 and foreign language 2.

**2008-2009 Annual costs.** Tuition/fees: $23,000. Room/board: $8,730. Books/supplies: $1,000. Personal expenses: $2,215.

**2007-2008 Financial aid. Need-based:** 202 full-time freshmen applied for aid; 181 were judged to have need; 181 of these received aid. Average need met was 79%. Average scholarship/grant was $6,576; average loan $4,009. 73% of total undergraduate aid awarded as scholarships/grants, 27% as loans/jobs. **Non-need-based:** Awarded to 657 full-time undergraduates, including 216 freshmen. Scholarships awarded for academics, alumni affiliation, athletics, leadership.

**Application procedures. Admission:** Priority date 4/1; no deadline. $25 fee, may be waived for applicants with need. Application may be submitted online. Admission notification on a rolling basis beginning on or about 9/15. **Financial aid:** Priority date 3/15; no closing date. FAFSA required. Applicants notified on a rolling basis starting 3/1.

**Academics. Special study options:** Combined bachelor's/graduate degree, cross-registration, distance learning, double major, dual enrollment of high school students, external degree, independent study, internships, liberal arts/career combination, semester at sea, student-designed major, study abroad, teacher certification program. **Credit/placement by examination:** AP, CLEP, IB, SAT, ACT. 10 credit hours maximum toward associate degree, 10 toward bachelor's. **Support services:** Learning center, pre-admission summer program, study skills assistance, tutoring, writing center.

**Majors. Agriculture:** Equine science. **Biology:** General. **Business:** Accounting, business admin, fashion, marketing. **Communications:** General, advertising, broadcast journalism, journalism, public relations. **Education:** General, early childhood, elementary. **English:** Creative writing, English lit. **Family/consumer sciences:** Clothing/textiles. **Health:** Medical records admin. **Legal studies:** Prelaw. **Liberal arts:** Arts/sciences. **Psychology:** General. **Visual/performing arts:** General, commercial/advertising art, dance, dramatic, fashion design.

**Most popular majors.** Business/marketing 19%, communications/journalism 6%, education 6%, English 7%, health sciences 9%, visual/performing arts 37%.

**Computing on campus.** 85 workstations in dormitories, library, computer center. Dormitories linked to campus network. Commuter students can connect to campus network. Online library, helpline, repair service, student web hosting, wireless network available.

**Student life. Freshman orientation:** Mandatory. Preregistration for classes offered. Typically held third week of August; one week prior to start of classes. Registration held mid-June on campus with academic advisor. **Housing:** Guaranteed on-campus for all undergraduates. Apartments available. $100 deposit. Pets allowed in dorm rooms. Freshman academic residence hall available. **Activities:** Choral groups, dance, drama, literary magazine, music ensembles, musical theater, radio station, student government, student newspaper, TV station, more than 45 clubs and organizations.

**Athletics.** NAIA. **Intercollegiate:** Basketball W, cross-country W, softball W, swimming W, tennis W, volleyball W. **Intramural:** Equestrian W. **Team name:** Stars.

**Student services.** Adult student services, career counseling, student employment services, financial aid counseling, health services, personal counseling, placement for graduates, women's services.

**Contact.** E-mail: apply@stephens.edu
Phone: (573) 876-7207 Toll-free number: (800) 876-7207
Fax: (573) 876-7237
David Adams, Dean of Enrollment Management, Stephens College, 1200
East Broadway, Columbia, MO 65215

## Truman State University
**Kirksville, Missouri**
**www.truman.edu**

**CB member**
**CB code: 6483**

- Public 4-year university and liberal arts college
- Residential campus in large town
- 5,496 degree-seeking undergraduates: 2% part-time, 57% women, 4% African American, 2% Asian American, 2% Hispanic American, 1% Native American, 4% international
- 258 degree-seeking graduate students
- 81% of applicants admitted
- SAT or ACT (ACT writing optional), application essay required
- 70% graduate within 6 years; 50% enter graduate study

**General.** Founded in 1867. Regionally accredited. **Degrees:** 1,149 bachelor's awarded; master's offered. **ROTC:** Army. **Location:** 195 miles from St. Louis, 170 miles from Kansas City. **Calendar:** Semester, extensive summer session. **Full-time faculty:** 336 total; 86% have terminal degrees, 10% minority, 40% women. **Part-time faculty:** 29 total; 31% have terminal degrees, 3% minority, 62% women. **Class size:** 37% < 20, 54% 20-39, 5% 40-49, 3% 50-99, less than 1% >100. **Special facilities:** Observatory, greenhouse, local history museum, farm, human performance laboratory, speech and hearing clinic, biofeedback laboratory, IR and NMR instrumentation, independent learning center for nursing.

**Freshman class profile.** 4,076 applied, 3,300 admitted, 1,405 enrolled.

| Mid 50% test scores | | Rank in top tenth: | 48% |
|---|---|---|---|
| SAT critical reading: | 570-690 | End year in good standing: | 88% |
| SAT math: | 560-670 | Return as sophomores: | 88% |
| ACT composite: | 25-30 | Out-of-state: | 19.5% |
| GPA 3.50 or higher: | 79% | Live on campus: | 90% |
| GPA 3.0-3.49: | 19% | International: | 5% |
| GPA 2.0-2.99: | 2% | Fraternities: | 22% |
| Rank in top quarter: | 80% | Sororities: | 18% |

**Basis for selection.** High school performance (class rank, GPA, college preparatory curriculum), test scores, essay most important; special ability, talent and achievement considered. Portfolio recommended for fine arts students. Audition required for music students. **Homeschooled:** Transcript of courses and grades required.

**High school preparation.** 16 units required; 17 recommended. Required and recommended units include English 4, mathematics 3-4, social studies 3, science 3 (laboratory 2) and foreign language 2. One fine arts required.

**2007-2008 Annual costs.** Tuition/fees: $6,432; $11,042 out-of-state. Room/board: $5,815. Books/supplies: $1,000. Personal expenses: $2,500.

**2006-2007 Financial aid.** **Need-based:** 1,063 full-time freshmen applied for aid; 537 were judged to have need; 537 of these received aid. Average need met was 83%. Average scholarship/grant was $2,857; average loan $2,074. 32% of total undergraduate aid awarded as scholarships/grants, 68% as loans/jobs. **Non-need-based:** Awarded to 4,392 full-time undergraduates, including 1,398 freshmen. Scholarships awarded for academics, alumni affiliation, art, athletics, leadership, minority status, music/drama, ROTC, state residency. **Additional information:** Out-of-state students whose parents work in Missouri may deduct $1 for every dollar paid in Missouri income taxes from out-of-state tuition.

**Application procedures.** **Admission:** Priority date 12/15; deadline 3/1 (postmark date). No application fee. Application may be submitted online. Admission notification on a rolling basis. Must reply by May 1 or within 3 week(s) if notified thereafter. **Financial aid:** Priority date 4/1; no closing date. FAFSA, institutional form required. Applicants notified on a rolling basis starting 3/1; must reply within 4 week(s) of notification.

**Academics.** **Special study options:** Combined bachelor's/graduate degree, double major, dual enrollment of high school students, exchange student, honors, independent study, internships, semester at sea, student-designed major, study abroad, teacher certification program, Washington semester. **Credit/placement by examination:** AP, CLEP, IB, institutional tests. **Support services:** Pre-admission summer program, study skills assistance, tutoring, writing center.

**Majors.** **Agriculture:** General, agronomy, animal sciences, business, equestrian studies. **Biology:** General, exercise physiology. **Business:** Accounting, business admin, finance, management information systems, marketing. **Communications:** General, journalism. **Computer sciences:** General. **Education:** Speech impaired. **English:** English lit, speech/rhetoric. **Foreign languages:** Classics, French, German, linguistics, Romance, Russian, Spanish. **Health:** Athletic training, communication disorders, health services, nursing (RN), predental, premedicine, prepharmacy, preveterinary. **History:** General. **Legal studies:** Prelaw. **Math:** General. **Parks/recreation:** Exercise sciences, health/fitness. **Philosophy/religion:** Philosophy, religion. **Physical sciences:** Chemistry, physics. **Protective services:** Criminal justice. **Psychology:** General. **Social sciences:** Economics, political science, sociology. **Visual/performing arts:** General, art, art history/conservation, commercial/advertising art, dramatic, music performance, studio arts.

**Most popular majors.** Biology 7%, business/marketing 19%, communications/journalism 7%, English 9%, health sciences 6%, parks/recreation 9%, psychology 9%, visual/performing arts 7%.

**Computing on campus.** 1,081 workstations in dormitories, library, computer center, student center. Dormitories wired for high-speed internet access and linked to campus network. Commuter students can connect to campus network. Online library, helpline, student web hosting, wireless network available.

**Student life.** **Freshman orientation:** Mandatory, $250 fee. Preregistration for classes offered. Sessions held during June and July; additional program begins week before beginning of fall semester. **Housing:** Coed dorms, single-sex dorms, special housing for disabled, apartments, fraternity/sorority housing, substance-free housing available. $150 partly refundable deposit, deadline 5/1. Smoke-free residence halls and apartments, international roommate options, quiet floors, faculty advisers in residence halls available. **Activities:** Bands, campus ministries, choral groups, dance, drama, international student organizations, literary magazine, music ensembles, Model UN, musical theater, radio station, student government, student newspaper, symphony orchestra, TV station, Alpha Phi Omega, Association of Black Collegians, College Republicans, Campus Christian Fellowship, Amnesty International, Blue Key, Cardinal Key, Circle-K, College Democrats, Baptist Student Union.

**Athletics.** NCAA. **Intercollegiate:** Baseball M, basketball, cross-country, football (tackle) M, golf, soccer, softball W, swimming, tennis, track and field, volleyball W, wrestling M. **Intramural:** Badminton, basketball, bowling, cross-country, football (non-tackle), golf, handball, racquetball, soccer, softball, swimming, table tennis, tennis, track and field, volleyball. **Team name:** Bulldogs.

**Student services.** Career counseling, services for economically disadvantaged, student employment services, financial aid counseling, health services, minority student services, personal counseling, placement for graduates, veterans' counselor, women's services. **Physically disabled:** Services for visually, speech, hearing impaired.

**Contact.** E-mail: admissions@truman.edu
Phone: (660) 785-4114 Toll-free number: (800) 892-7792
Fax: (660) 785-7456
Brad Chambers, Co-Director of Admissions, Truman State University, McClain Hall 205, Kirksville, MO 63501-9980

## University of Central Missouri
**Warrensburg, Missouri**
**www.ucmo.edu**

**CB code: 6090**

- Public 4-year university
- Commuter campus in large town
- 8,333 degree-seeking undergraduates: 16% part-time, 55% women, 6% African American, 1% Asian American, 2% Hispanic American, 1% Native American, 3% international
- 1,849 degree-seeking graduate students
- 81% of applicants admitted
- SAT or ACT (ACT writing optional) required
- 52% graduate within 6 years

**General.** Founded in 1871. Regionally accredited. **Degrees:** 1,654 bachelor's, 6 associate awarded; master's offered. **ROTC:** Army, Air Force. **Location:** 50 miles from Kansas City. **Calendar:** Semester, extensive summer session. **Full-time faculty:** 443 total; 68% have terminal degrees, 10% minority, 41% women. **Special facilities:** Airport, 260-acre farm, children's literature collection, musical instruments collection, child development lab, advanced technology library.

**Freshman class profile.** 3,887 applied, 3,132 admitted, 1,554 enrolled.

| Mid 50% test scores | | | |
|---|---|---|---|
| ACT composite: | 20-24 | Return as sophomores: | 70.7% |
| GPA 3.50 or higher: | 41% | Out-of-state: | 6% |
| GPA 3.0-3.49: | 31% | Live on campus: | 85% |
| GPA 2.0-2.99: | 27% | International: | 3% |
| Rank in top quarter: | 36% | Fraternities: | 9% |
| Rank in top tenth: | 12% | Sororities: | 6% |

**Basis for selection.** Applicant must be in top two-thirds of high school class, complete 16-unit core curriculum and have minimum ACT score of 20. TOEFL required for international students. Essay required for some programs; audition recommended for music students. **Homeschooled:** Recommend ACT, GED, or equivalent.

**High school preparation.** 16 units required. Required and recommended units include English 4, mathematics 3, social studies 3, science 2 (laboratory 1), foreign language 2 and academic electives 3. One fine/performing arts required.

**2007-2008 Annual costs.** Tuition/fees: $6,225; $11,845 out-of-state. Room/board: $5,846. Books/supplies: $500. Personal expenses: $1,400.

**Financial aid.** **Non-need-based:** Scholarships awarded for academics, alumni affiliation, art, athletics, leadership, minority status, music/drama, ROTC, state residency.

**Application procedures. Admission:** Priority date 6/1; no deadline. $30 fee, may be waived for applicants with need. Application may be submitted online. Admission notification on a rolling basis beginning on or about 8/18. **Financial aid:** Priority date 3/1; no closing date. FAFSA required. Applicants notified on a rolling basis starting 3/1; must reply within 2 week(s) of notification.

**Academics.** Online services and resources include library, technical support, writing center and bookstore. Extensive international exchange program. **Special study options:** Combined bachelor's/graduate degree, cooperative education, cross-registration, distance learning, double major, dual enrollment of high school students, ESL, honors, internships, liberal arts/career combination, student-designed major, study abroad, teacher certification program, weekend college. Engineering program with University of Missouri (Columbia, Rolla) and University of Indiana. **Credit/placement by examination:** AP, CLEP, IB, SAT, ACT, institutional tests. 15 credit hours maximum toward associate degree, 30 toward bachelor's. **Support services:** Learning center, remedial instruction, study skills assistance, tutoring, writing center.

**Honors college/program.** Minimum ACT score of 25; 319 freshmen admitted; requires 48 credit hours.

**Majors. Agriculture:** General, business, economics. **Biology:** General. **Business:** Accounting, actuarial science, business admin, finance, hotel/motel admin, human resources, management information systems, marketing, office management, tourism promotion. **Communications:** General, broadcast journalism, journalism, public relations. **Communications technology:** Graphic/printing. **Computer sciences:** General, data processing. **Education:** Agricultural, art, biology, business, chemistry, elementary, English, family/consumer sciences, foreign languages, French, German, mathematics, middle, music, physical, physics, science, secondary, social studies, Spanish, special, speech, technology/industrial arts. **Engineering technology:** Aerospace, architectural, construction, drafting, electrical, industrial. **English:** English lit, speech/rhetoric. **Family/consumer sciences:** General, child development, clothing/textiles, family studies. **Foreign languages:** French, German, Spanish. **Health:** Nursing (RN), speech pathology. **History:** General. **Math:** General. **Parks/recreation:** General, facilities management. **Physical sciences:** Chemistry, geology, physics, planetary. **Protective services:** Law enforcement admin. **Psychology:** General. **Public administration:** Social work. **Social sciences:** Economics, geography, political science, sociology. **Visual/performing arts:** Art, commercial/advertising art, dramatic, interior design, photography, studio arts.

**Most popular majors.** Business/marketing 19%, education 23%, engineering/engineering technologies 9%, health sciences 6%, security/protective services 8%, visual/performing arts 8%.

**Computing on campus.** 2,748 workstations in dormitories, library, computer center, student center. Dormitories wired for high-speed internet access and linked to campus network. Commuter students can connect to campus network. Online course registration, online library, helpline, student web hosting, wireless network available.

**Student life. Freshman orientation:** Mandatory. Preregistration for classes offered. 8 one-day sessions in early summer. **Housing:** Guaranteed on-campus for all undergraduates. Coed dorms, single-sex dorms, special housing for disabled, apartments, fraternity/sorority housing, substance-free housing available. $100 nonrefundable deposit, deadline 6/1. Honors hall, economy

suites. **Activities:** Bands, campus ministries, choral groups, dance, drama, film society, international student organizations, literary magazine, music ensembles, musical theater, opera, radio station, student government, student newspaper, symphony orchestra, TV station, Association of Black Collegiates, nontraditional student association, student ambassadors, College Republicans, College Democrats, United Students for Equal Access, Student Government Association.

**Athletics.** NCAA. **Intercollegiate:** Baseball M, basketball, bowling W, cross-country, football (tackle) M, golf M, soccer W, softball W, track and field, volleyball W, wrestling M. **Intramural:** Archery M, badminton M, basketball, bowling, cross-country, diving, football (tackle), golf, racquetball, rifle, rugby M, soccer, softball, swimming, table tennis, tennis, track and field, volleyball, water polo, weight lifting M, wrestling M. **Team name:** Mules (M), Jennies (W).

**Student services.** Adult student services, alcohol/substance abuse counseling, campus ministries, career counseling, student employment services, financial aid counseling, health services, minority student services, on-campus daycare, personal counseling, placement for graduates, veterans' counselor, women's services. **Physically disabled:** Services for visually, speech, hearing impaired.

**Contact.**  E-mail: admit@ucmovmb.ucmo.edu
Phone: (660) 543-4290 Toll-free number: (877) 729-8266
Fax: (660) 543-8517
Ann Nordyke, Chief Admissions Officer, University of Central Missouri, WDE 1400, Warrensburg, MO 64093

---

## University of Missouri: Columbia

| Columbia, Missouri | CB member |
|---|---|
| www.missouri.edu | CB code: 6875 |

- Public 4-year university
- Residential campus in small city
- 21,385 degree-seeking undergraduates: 5% part-time, 52% women, 6% African American, 3% Asian American, 2% Hispanic American, 1% Native American, 1% international
- 6,311 degree-seeking graduate students
- 86% of applicants admitted
- SAT or ACT (ACT writing optional) required
- 69% graduate within 6 years

**General.** Founded in 1839. Regionally accredited. Students with same academic interest housed in same residence hall and enrolled in 3 classes together. **Degrees:** 4,736 bachelor's awarded; master's, doctoral, first professional offered. **ROTC:** Army, Naval, Air Force. **Location:** 125 miles from Kansas City, 125 miles from St. Louis. **Calendar:** Semester, limited summer session. **Full-time faculty:** 1,074 total; 19% minority, 36% women. **Part-time faculty:** 68 total; 7% minority, 43% women. **Special facilities:** Observatory, research nuclear reactor, freedom of information center, Food for 21st Century program, engineering experiment station, center for research in social behavior, equine center, university research farms, child development laboratory, daily city newspaper production, nightly newscasts, black culture center.

**Freshman class profile.** 12,089 applied, 10,346 admitted, 4,981 enrolled.

| Mid 50% test scores | | | |
|---|---|---|---|
| SAT critical reading: | 530-650 | Out-of-state: | 19% |
| SAT math: | 540-650 | Live on campus: | 85% |
| ACT composite: | 23-28 | International: | 1% |
| Rank in top quarter: | 55% | Fraternities: | 31% |
| Rank in top tenth: | 27% | Sororities: | 36% |

**Basis for selection.** Admission based on required core courses and combination of high school rank and test scores. Individual programs may have additional requirements. Trial summer admission open to Missouri residents. Students must complete math and English with C or better to continue enrollment on probation in fall. ACT preferred.

**High school preparation.** 17 units required. Required units include English 4, mathematics 4, social studies 3, science 3 (laboratory 1) and foreign language 2. 1 fine arts required. Math must include algebra I and higher.

**2007-2008 Annual costs.** Tuition/fees: $8,099; $18,755 out-of-state. Room/board: $7,002. Books/supplies: $980. Personal expenses: $1,430.

**Financial aid.** **Non-need-based:** Scholarships awarded for academics, alumni affiliation, art, athletics, leadership, minority status, music/drama, ROTC, state residency. **Additional information:** Scholarship available for international students based on success during 1st semester.

**Application procedures. Admission:** Priority date 5/1; no deadline. $45 fee, may be waived for applicants with need. Application may be submitted online. Admission notification on a rolling basis. Must reply by May 1 or within 4 week(s) if notified thereafter. **Financial aid:** Priority date 3/1; no closing date. FAFSA required. Applicants notified on a rolling basis starting 4/1; must reply within 4 week(s) of notification.

**Academics.** Guaranteed admission to School of Law with 30 ACT, and maintenance of 3.3 GPA. Early admission to School of Medicine with 30 ACT, maintenance of 3.4 GPA, and required interview. Early admission to School of Nursing with 29 ACT and rank in top 10% of high school class. Project for Excellence in Teaching offered. **Special study options:** Accelerated study, combined bachelor's/graduate degree, cooperative education, cross-registration, distance learning, double major, dual enrollment of high school students, ESL, exchange student, external degree, honors, independent study, internships, New York semester, student-designed major, study abroad, teacher certification program, Washington semester. Evening college. **Credit/placement by examination:** AP, CLEP, IB, ACT, institutional tests. Credit by examination policy varies by school/college. **Support services:** Learning center, pre-admission summer program, reduced course load, study skills assistance, tutoring, writing center.

**Honors college/program.** 29 ACT or 1280 SAT and top 10% of high school graduating class required. If school does not rank, core GPA of 3.71 necessary. Core GPA includes all English courses, all math courses Algebra I and higher, and all science, social studies, and foreign language courses.

**Majors. Agriculture:** General, animal sciences, business; communications, economics, food science, plant sciences, soil science. **Area/ethnic studies:** African-American, East Asian, European, Latin American, South Asian, women's. **Biology:** General, biochemistry, conservation, microbiology. **Business:** General, accounting, banking/financial services, business admin, hotel/motel admin, international, marketing, real estate, restaurant/food services, travel services. **Communications:** General, advertising, broadcast journalism, journalism, photojournalism, radio/tv. **Computer sciences:** General, computer science, information technology. **Conservation:** Fisheries, forestry, wildlife. **Education:** General, agricultural, art, biology, business, chemistry, early childhood, elementary, English, foreign languages, mathematics, middle, multiple handicapped, music, physics, science, secondary, social studies, Spanish, voc/tech. **Engineering:** Agricultural, biomedical, chemical, civil, computer, electrical, industrial, mechanical. **English:** English lit. **Family/consumer sciences:** Clothing/textiles, family resources, family studies, food/nutrition, housing, human nutrition. **Foreign languages:** Classics, East Asian, French, German, linguistics, Russian, South Asian, Spanish. **Health:** Audiology/speech pathology, dietetics, health services admin, medical radiologic technology/radiation therapy, nuclear medical technology, nursing (RN), premedicine, prepharmacy, preveterinary, radiologic technology/medical imaging, respiratory therapy technology, sonography. **History:** General. **Interdisciplinary:** Behavioral sciences, nutrition sciences, peace/conflict. **Math:** General, statistics. **Military:** General. **Parks/recreation:** General, exercise sciences. **Philosophy/religion:** Philosophy, religion. **Physical sciences:** Atmospheric science, chemistry, geology, physics. **Psychology:** General. **Public administration:** Social work. **Social sciences:** Anthropology, archaeology, economics, geography, political science, sociology. **Visual/performing arts:** Art, dramatic.

**Most popular majors.** Biology 6%, business/marketing 19%, communications/journalism 12%, education 6%, engineering/engineering technologies 7%, health sciences 7%, psychology 6%, social sciences 7%.

**Computing on campus.** 1,179 workstations in dormitories, library, computer center, student center. Dormitories wired for high-speed internet access and linked to campus network. Commuter students can connect to campus network. Online course registration, online library, helpline, repair service, student web hosting, wireless network available.

**Student life. Freshman orientation:** Available. Preregistration for classes offered. Nineteen 2-day sessions during summer; parents invited. **Policies:** Alcohol-free and smoke-free campus buildings, residence halls, and Greek housing. **Housing:** Guaranteed on-campus for freshmen. Coed dorms, single-sex dorms, apartments, fraternity/sorority housing, substance-free housing available. $300 fully refundable deposit, deadline 4/1. Specialized living/learning communities and freshman interest groups in residence halls for fine arts, French, Spanish, women in engineering, men in engineering, wellness and service, journalism, service learning, first-time college students, international studies, nursing students. **Activities:** Bands, choral groups, dance, drama, film society, literary magazine, music ensembles, musical theater, opera, radio station, student government, student newspaper, symphony orchestra, TV station, Over 518 clubs available.

**Athletics.** NCAA. **Intercollegiate:** Baseball M, basketball, cross-country, diving, football (tackle) M, golf, gymnastics W, soccer W, softball W, swimming, tennis W, track and field, volleyball W, wrestling M. **Intramural:** Basketball, football (non-tackle), golf, soccer, softball, volleyball. **Team name:** Tigers.

**Student services.** Alcohol/substance abuse counseling, campus ministries, career counseling, services for economically disadvantaged, student employment services, financial aid counseling, health services, legal services, minority student services, on-campus daycare, personal counseling, placement for graduates, veterans' counselor, women's services. **Physically disabled:** Services for visually, speech, hearing impaired.

**Contact.** E-mail: mu4u@missouri.edu
Phone: (573) 882-7786 Toll-free number: (800) 225-6075
Fax: (573) 882-7887
Barbara Rupp, Director of Admissions, University of Missouri: Columbia, 230 Jesse Hall, Columbia, MO 65211

## University of Missouri: Kansas City

Kansas City, Missouri     **CB member**
www.umkc.edu     **CB code: 6872**

- Public 4-year university
- Commuter campus in large city
- 6,953 degree-seeking undergraduates: 21% part-time, 58% women, 14% African American, 6% Asian American, 4% Hispanic American, 1% Native American, 3% international
- 4,757 degree-seeking graduate students
- 60% of applicants admitted
- SAT or ACT (ACT writing optional) required
- 43% graduate within 6 years

**General.** Founded in 1929. Regionally accredited. **Degrees:** 1,428 bachelor's awarded; master's, doctoral, first professional offered. **ROTC:** Army. **Location:** 500 miles from Chicago, 250 miles from St. Louis. **Calendar:** Semester, extensive summer session. **Full-time faculty:** 684 total; 77% have terminal degrees, 22% minority, 42% women. **Part-time faculty:** 446 total; 36% have terminal degrees, 11% minority, 50% women. **Class size:** 54% < 20, 34% 20-39, 5% 40-49, 5% 50-99, 2% >100. **Special facilities:** Observatory, science and technology library, music conservatory, miniature toy museum.

**Freshman class profile.** 3,458 applied, 2,088 admitted, 959 enrolled.

| Mid 50% test scores | | | |
|---|---|---|---|
| SAT critical reading: | 560-660 | Rank in top tenth: | 34% |
| SAT math: | 560-690 | End year in good standing: | 71% |
| ACT composite: | 21-28 | Return as sophomores: | 71% |
| GPA 3.50 or higher: | 46% | Out-of-state: | 21% |
| GPA 3.0-3.49: | 28% | Live on campus: | 63% |
| GPA 2.0-2.99: | 26% | International: | 1% |
| Rank in top quarter: | 58% | Fraternities: | 12% |
| | | Sororities: | 20% |

**Basis for selection.** Admission based on class rank, test scores, and high school course requirements. Admission is very selective to combined arts and sciences/medical; highly selective to pharmacy program. Interview required for dentistry, medicine, and pharmacy applicants; audition required for dance and conservatory of music applicants. Portfolio recommended. **Homeschooled:** Applicants submit a transcript of course work as well as ACT or SAT score.

**High school preparation.** 17 units required. Required units include English 4, mathematics 4, social studies 3, science 3 (laboratory 1) and foreign language 2. 1 fine arts required.

**2007-2008 Annual costs.** Tuition/fees: $7,946; $18,642 out-of-state. Room/board: $7,046. Books/supplies: $990. Personal expenses: $4,170.

**2007-2008 Financial aid. Need-based:** 744 full-time freshmen applied for aid; 598 were judged to have need; 577 of these received aid. Average need met was 61%. Average scholarship/grant was $7,748; average loan $6,298. 36% of total undergraduate aid awarded as scholarships/grants, 64% as loans/jobs. **Non-need-based:** Awarded to 2,037 full-time undergraduates, including 359 freshmen. Scholarships awarded for academics, alumni affiliation, art, athletics, leadership, minority status, music/drama, state residency.

**Application procedures. Admission:** Priority date 4/1; no deadline. $35 fee, may be waived for applicants with need. Application may be submitted online. Admission notification on a rolling basis. Architecture, Medicine and Pharmacy programs have separate application deadlines and specific admissions requirements. **Financial aid:** Priority date 3/1; no closing date. FAFSA required. Applicants notified on a rolling basis starting 4/15; must reply within 2 week(s) of notification.

**Academics. Special study options:** Accelerated study, combined bachelor's/graduate degree, cooperative education, distance learning, double major, dual enrollment of high school students, ESL, honors, independent study, internships, liberal arts/career combination, student-designed major, study abroad, teacher certification program. **Credit/placement by examination:** AP, CLEP, IB, institutional tests. 30 credit hours maximum toward bachelor's degree.

**Support services:** Learning center, reduced course load, study skills assistance, tutoring, writing center.

**Majors. Architecture:** Urban/community planning. **Area/ethnic studies:** American. **Biology:** General. **Business:** General, accounting. **Computer sciences:** General, information systems. **Conservation:** Environmental science. **Education:** General, elementary, middle, music, secondary. **Engineering:** Civil, electrical, mechanical. **English:** English lit. **Foreign languages:** French, German, Spanish. **Health:** Clinical lab science, dental hygiene, nursing (RN). **History:** General. **Liberal arts:** Arts/sciences. **Math:** General. **Philosophy/religion:** Philosophy. **Physical sciences:** Chemistry, geology, physics. **Protective services:** Law enforcement admin. **Psychology:** General. **Social sciences:** Economics, geography, political science, sociology, urban studies. **Visual/performing arts:** Art, art history/conservation, dance, dramatic, music performance, music theory/composition, studio arts. **Other:** Communication studies, Electrical & computer engineering, History and Judaic studies, Mathematics & statistics.

**Most popular majors.** Business/marketing 13%, communications/journalism 6%, education 9%, health sciences 8%, liberal arts 15%, psychology 6%, social sciences 6%, visual/performing arts 6%.

**Computing on campus.** 680 workstations in dormitories, library, computer center, student center. Dormitories wired for high-speed internet access and linked to campus network. Commuter students can connect to campus network. Online course registration, online library, helpline, wireless network available.

**Student life. Freshman orientation:** Mandatory, $40 fee. Preregistration for classes offered. Several 2-day orientations during summer. **Housing:** Coed dorms, fraternity/sorority housing, substance-free housing available. $300 fully refundable deposit, deadline 7/1. University owned houses are available. **Activities:** Bands, choral groups, dance, drama, literary magazine, music ensembles, opera, radio station, student government, student newspaper, symphony orchestra, over 200 religious, political, ethnic, and social service organizations.

**Athletics.** NCAA. **Intercollegiate:** Basketball, cheerleading, cross-country, golf, soccer M, softball W, tennis, track and field, volleyball W. **Intramural:** Basketball, football (tackle), golf, racquetball, softball, table tennis, volleyball. **Team name:** Kangaroos.

**Student services.** Adult student services, alcohol/substance abuse counseling, campus ministries, career counseling, student employment services, financial aid counseling, health services, minority student services, on-campus daycare, personal counseling, placement for graduates, veterans' counselor, women's services. **Physically disabled:** Services for visually, speech, hearing impaired.

**Contact.** E-mail: admit@umkc.edu
Phone: (816) 235-1111 Toll-free number: (800) 775-8652
Fax: (816) 235-5544
Jennifer DeHaemers, Director of Admissions, University of Missouri: Kansas City, 5100 Rockhill Road, AC120, Kansas City, MO 64110-2499

---

## University of Missouri: St. Louis

| St. Louis, Missouri | **CB member** |
| --- | --- |
| www.umsl.edu | **CB code: 6889** |

- Public 4-year university
- Commuter campus in very large city
- 8,947 degree-seeking undergraduates: 35% part-time, 57% women, 18% African American, 3% Asian American, 2% Hispanic American, 2% international
- 2,972 degree-seeking graduate students
- 46% of applicants admitted
- SAT or ACT (ACT writing optional) required

**General.** Founded in 1963. Regionally accredited. **Degrees:** 2,039 bachelor's awarded; master's, doctoral, first professional offered. **ROTC:** Army, Air Force. **Location:** 7 miles from downtown. **Calendar:** Semester, extensive summer session. **Full-time faculty:** 447 total; 76% have terminal degrees, 21% minority, 48% women. **Part-time faculty:** 371 total; 27% have terminal degrees, 14% minority, 58% women. **Class size:** 45% < 20, 40% 20-39, 7% 40-49, 7% 50-99, 1% >100. **Special facilities:** Mercantile library, observatory, 3 art galleries, performing arts center.

**Freshman class profile.** 2,272 applied, 1,056 admitted, 498 enrolled.

| Mid 50% test scores | | | |
| --- | --- | --- | --- |
| SAT math: | 520-620 | End year in good standing: | 77% |
| ACT composite: | 21-26 | Return as sophomores: | 72% |
| Rank in top quarter: | 49% | Out-of-state: | 11% |
| Rank in top tenth: | 18% | International: | 4% |

**Basis for selection.** Class rank, test scores and high school course requirements most important. Audition required for music majors; not required for admission for the purpose of placement with instrument. **Home-schooled:** ACT scores are key factor in determining admission. Students should strive for score of 24 or higher.

**High school preparation.** 17 units required. Required units include English 4, mathematics 4, social studies 3, science 3 (laboratory 1) and foreign language 2. 1 fine art required.

**2007-2008 Annual costs.** Tuition/fees: $8,264; $18,920 out-of-state. Room/board: $7,394. Books/supplies: $900. Personal expenses: $4,130.

**2007-2008 Financial aid. Need-based:** 332 full-time freshmen applied for aid; 281 were judged to have need; 277 of these received aid. Average need met was 67%. Average scholarship/grant was $6,433; average loan $3,463. 31% of total undergraduate aid awarded as scholarships/grants, 69% as loans/jobs. **Non-need-based:** Awarded to 883 full-time undergraduates, including 131 freshmen. Scholarships awarded for academics, alumni affiliation, art, athletics, music/drama, ROTC, state residency.

**Application procedures. Admission:** Closing date 8/23. $35 fee, may be waived for applicants with need. Application may be submitted online. Admission notification on a rolling basis beginning on or about 10/1. **Financial aid:** Priority date 4/1; no closing date. FAFSA required. Applicants notified on a rolling basis starting 4/1; must reply within 2 week(s) of notification.

**Academics. Special study options:** Accelerated study, combined bachelor's/graduate degree, cooperative education, cross-registration, distance learning, double major, dual enrollment of high school students, ESL, exchange student, honors, independent study, internships, liberal arts/career combination, semester at sea, student-designed major, study abroad, teacher certification program. **Credit/placement by examination:** AP, CLEP, IB, SAT, ACT, institutional tests. 30 credit hours maximum toward bachelor's degree. **Support services:** Learning center, pre-admission summer program, study skills assistance, tutoring, writing center.

**Honors college/program.** Selection based on scores, class rank, extracurricular activities, test scores, 2 recommendations, essay, interview with Dean. Approximately 50 freshmen admitted each fall. Academic program includes honors classes.

**Majors. Biology:** General, biochemistry. **Business:** Accounting, business admin, finance, international, logistics, management information systems, marketing, operations, organizational behavior. **Communications:** General, media studies. **Computer sciences:** General. **Education:** General, early childhood, elementary, music, physical, secondary, special. **Engineering:** Civil, electrical, mechanical. **English:** English lit. **Foreign languages:** French, German, Spanish. **Health:** Health care admin, nursing (RN). **History:** General. **Liberal arts:** Arts/sciences. **Math:** General, applied. **Philosophy/religion:** Philosophy. **Physical sciences:** Chemistry, physics. **Psychology:** General. **Public administration:** General, social work. **Social sciences:** Anthropology, criminology, economics, political science, sociology. **Visual/performing arts:** Art, art history/conservation, dramatic.

**Most popular majors.** Business/marketing 28%, communications/journalism 7%, education 13%, health sciences 8%, psychology 7%, social sciences 11%.

**Computing on campus.** 1,300 workstations in dormitories, library, computer center, student center. Dormitories wired for high-speed internet access and linked to campus network. Commuter students can connect to campus network. Online course registration, online library, helpline, student web hosting, wireless network available.

**Student life. Freshman orientation:** Available. Preregistration for classes offered. One day program held several times throughout summer. Spring orientation session offered in January. **Housing:** Guaranteed on-campus for all undergraduates. Coed dorms, special housing for disabled, apartments, fraternity/sorority housing, substance-free housing available. $400 partly refundable deposit, deadline 7/1. Themed communities. **Activities:** Bands, choral groups, dance, drama, film society, international student organizations, literary magazine, music ensembles, Model UN, musical theater, opera, radio station, student government, student newspaper, Associated Black Collegians, Spanish club, Alpha Phi Omega, Amnesty International, Pan-Hellenic Council, College Republicans, Catholic Students at Newman Center, Campus Crusade for Christ, UMSL Life Group.

**Athletics.** NCAA. **Intercollegiate:** Baseball M, basketball, golf, ice hockey M, soccer, softball W, tennis, volleyball W. **Intramural:** Badminton, basketball, bowling, football (non-tackle), football (tackle), golf, racquetball, skiing, soccer, softball, swimming, table tennis, tennis, volleyball, weight lifting. **Team name:** Tritons.

**Student services.** Adult student services, alcohol/substance abuse counseling, campus ministries, career counseling, services for economically disadvantaged, student employment services, financial aid counseling, health services, minority student services, on-campus daycare, personal counseling, placement for graduates, veterans' counselor, women's services. **Physically disabled:** Services for visually, speech, hearing impaired.

**Contact.** E-mail: admissions@umsl.edu
Phone: (314) 516-5451 Toll-free number: (888) GO2-UMSL
Fax: (314) 516-5310
J McCalley, Associate Vice Provost, University of Missouri: St. Louis, One University Boulevard, St. Louis, MO 63121-4400

## Washington University in St. Louis
**St. Louis, Missouri**  CB member
www.wustl.edu  CB code: 6929

- Private 4-year university
- Residential campus in large city
- 6,467 degree-seeking undergraduates: 6% part-time, 50% women, 10% African American, 13% Asian American, 3% Hispanic American, 4% international
- 5,986 degree-seeking graduate students
- 17% of applicants admitted
- SAT or ACT (ACT writing optional), application essay required
- 92% graduate within 6 years

**General.** Founded in 1853. Regionally accredited. **Degrees:** 1,660 bachelor's awarded; master's, doctoral, first professional offered. **ROTC:** Army, Air Force. **Location:** 7 miles from downtown. **Calendar:** Semester, extensive summer session. **Full-time faculty:** 885 total; 98% have terminal degrees, 33% women. **Part-time faculty:** 181 total; 42% women. **Class size:** 73% < 20, 15% 20-39, 4% 40-49, 7% 50-99, 2% >100. **Special facilities:** Research center, 59-acre medical campus, observatory, plant growth facility, international writer's center, planetarium, business/economics experimental lab, lab science building, outdoor research center, theater.

**Freshman class profile.** 22,428 applied, 3,887 admitted, 1,338 enrolled.

| Mid 50% test scores | | Out-of-state: | 90% |
|---|---|---|---|
| SAT critical reading: | 680-750 | Live on campus: | 99% |
| SAT math: | 690-780 | International: | 5% |
| ACT composite: | 30-33 | Fraternities: | 25% |
| Return as sophomores: | 97% | Sororities: | 25% |

**Basis for selection.** Rigor of high school curriculum and academic performance, GPA, test scores, extracurricular activities, essay, and recommendations are very important. Counselor and teacher recommendations required of all applicants. Portfolio optional for students applying to the College of Art and the College of Architecture. Portfolio optional for students applying to the College of Art and the College of Architecture. **Homeschooled:** Letter of recommendation (nonparent) required. Recommendation from someone in the community who can give information on student's background.

**High school preparation.** 20 units recommended. Recommended units include English 4, mathematics 4, social studies 4, history 4, science 4 (laboratory 4) and foreign language 2.

**2008-2009 Annual costs.** Tuition/fees: $37,248. Room/board: $11,636. Books/supplies: $1,220. Personal expenses: $1,970.

**2007-2008 Financial aid.** **Need-based:** 939 full-time freshmen applied for aid; 525 were judged to have need; 515 of these received aid. Average need met was 100%. Average scholarship/grant was $25,706; average loan $4,868. 80% of total undergraduate aid awarded as scholarships/grants, 20% as loans/jobs. **Non-need-based:** Awarded to 1,063 full-time undergraduates, including 313 freshmen. Scholarships awarded for academics, ROTC.

**Application procedures.** **Admission:** Closing date 1/15. $55 fee, may be waived for applicants with need. Application may be submitted online. Admission notification 4/1. Must reply by 5/1. **Financial aid:** Closing date 2/15. FAFSA, CSS PROFILE required. Applicants notified by 4/1; must reply by 5/1.

**Academics.** **Special study options:** Accelerated study, combined bachelor's/graduate degree, cooperative education, cross-registration, double major, dual enrollment of high school students, ESL, exchange student, independent study, internships, liberal arts/career combination, student-designed major, study abroad, teacher certification program, Washington semester. University Scholars Program. **Credit/placement by examination:** AP, CLEP, IB, institutional tests. **Support services:** Learning center, pre-admission summer program, reduced course load, study skills assistance, tutoring, writing center.

**Majors.** **Architecture:** Architecture, technology. **Area/ethnic studies:** African-American, American, Asian, East Asian, European, German, Latin American, Near/Middle Eastern, women's. **Biology:** General, biochemistry, biophysics. **Business:** General, accounting, business admin, entrepreneurial studies, finance, human resources, international, international finance, managerial economics, marketing, operations. **Communications:** Advertising, journalism. **Computer sciences:** General, computer science, data processing, information systems. **Conservation:** Environmental studies. **Education:** General, art, biology, chemistry, drama/dance, elementary, English, French, German, history, mathematics, middle, physics, science, secondary, social science, social studies, Spanish. **Engineering:** Biomedical, chemical, civil, computer, electrical, mechanical, systems. **Engineering technology:** Architectural, biomedical, civil. **English:** American lit, British lit, English lit. **Foreign languages:** General, ancient Greek, Arabic, Chinese, classics, comparative lit, French, German, Germanic, Hebrew, Italian, Japanese, Latin, Spanish. **Health:** Predental, premedicine, prepharmacy, preveterinary. **History:** General. **Interdisciplinary:** Ancient studies, biological/physical sciences, biopsychology, math/computer science, neuroscience, science/society, systems science. **Legal studies:** Prelaw. **Liberal arts:** Arts/sciences, humanities. **Math:** General, applied, statistics. **Philosophy/religion:** Islamic, Judaic, philosophy, religion. **Physical sciences:** Chemistry, geology, physics, planetary. **Psychology:** General, industrial. **Social sciences:** General, anthropology, archaeology, economics, international relations, political science. **Visual/performing arts:** General, art, art history/conservation, ceramics, commercial/advertising art, dance, design, dramatic, drawing, fashion design, film/cinema, graphic design, illustration, music history, music theory/composition, painting, photography, printmaking, sculpture, studio arts, theater history, voice/opera.

**Most popular majors.** Biology 7%, business/marketing 14%, engineering/engineering technologies 13%, psychology 10%, social sciences 17%, visual/performing arts 10%.

**Computing on campus.** 2,500 workstations in dormitories, library, computer center, student center. Dormitories wired for high-speed internet access and linked to campus network. Commuter students can connect to campus network. Online course registration, online library, helpline, repair service, student web hosting, wireless network available.

**Student life.** **Freshman orientation:** Mandatory. Preregistration for classes offered. **Housing:** Guaranteed on-campus for freshmen. Coed dorms, apartments, cooperative housing, fraternity/sorority housing, substance-free housing available. $250 deposit, deadline 5/1. Special interest suites, upper-class housing, single-sex floors in coed buildings, on-campus transfer-specific housing, small-group housing available. **Activities:** Bands, campus ministries, choral groups, dance, drama, film society, international student organizations, literary magazine, music ensembles, Model UN, musical theater, opera, radio station, student government, student newspaper, symphony orchestra, TV station, Approximately 200 social clubs and organizations including religious, political, community service, ethnic, and many other organizations available.

**Athletics.** NCAA. **Intercollegiate:** Baseball M, basketball, cross-country, diving, football (tackle) M, soccer, softball W, swimming, tennis, track and field, volleyball W. **Intramural:** Badminton, basketball, bowling, cross-country, football (non-tackle), golf, racquetball, soccer, softball, swimming, table tennis, tennis, track and field, volleyball, water polo. **Team name:** Bears.

**Student services.** Adult student services, alcohol/substance abuse counseling, campus ministries, career counseling, student employment services, financial aid counseling, health services, minority student services, on-campus daycare, personal counseling, placement for graduates, veterans' counselor, women's services. **Physically disabled:** Services for visually, speech, hearing impaired.

**Contact.** E-mail: admissions@wustl.edu
Phone: (314) 935-6000 Toll-free number: (800) 638-0700
Fax: (314) 935-4290
Nanette Tarbouni, Director of Admissions, Washington University in St. Louis, Campus Box 1089, One Brookings Drive, St. Louis, MO 63130-4899

## Webster University
**St. Louis, Missouri**  CB member
www.webster.edu  CB code: 6933

- Private 4-year university
- Commuter campus in large city

- 3,523 degree-seeking undergraduates: 25% part-time, 58% women, 11% African American, 2% Asian American, 2% Hispanic American, 3% international
- 4,789 degree-seeking graduate students
- 56% of applicants admitted
- SAT or ACT (ACT writing recommended), application essay required
- 61% graduate within 6 years; 14% enter graduate study

**General.** Founded in 1915. Regionally accredited. Additional programs offered at five St. Louis area campuses. Undergraduate degrees offered at extended campus locations in California, South Carolina, Florida, as well as international campuses in Vienna, Austria; Leiden, The Netherlands; Geneva, Switzerland; Cha-am, Thailand; and London, United Kingdom. St. Louis Repertory Theatre, Opera Theatre of Saint Louis, Community Music School of Webster University. **Degrees:** 934 bachelor's awarded; master's, doctoral offered. **ROTC:** Army, Air Force. **Location:** 12 miles from St. Louis. **Calendar:** Semester, limited summer session. **Full-time faculty:** 171 total; 80% have terminal degrees, 47% women. **Part-time faculty:** 581 total. **Class size:** 86% < 20, 14% 20-39, less than 1% 40-49.

**Freshman class profile.** 1,677 applied, 934 admitted, 498 enrolled.

| Mid 50% test scores | | | |
|---|---|---|---|
| SAT critical reading: | 530-650 | Rank in top quarter: | 55% |
| SAT math: | 500-610 | Rank in top tenth: | 27% |
| ACT composite: | 21-28 | Return as sophomores: | 80% |
| GPA 3.50 or higher: | 52% | Out-of-state: | 33% |
| GPA 3.0-3.49: | 29% | Live on campus: | 55% |
| GPA 2.0-2.99: | 19% | International: | 2% |

**Basis for selection.** School achievement record, test scores important. Rank in top half of class recommended. Recommendation, essay, resume of activities considered. Interview recommended for all students. Audition required for dance, music, music theater, and theater students; portfolio required for art and film students. **Homeschooled:** Transcripts, ACT or SAT scores, recommendations from community leader or employer must be submitted.

**High school preparation.** 21 units recommended. Recommended units include English 4, mathematics 3, social studies 3, science 3 (laboratory 2), foreign language 2 and academic electives 3.

**2007-2008 Annual costs.** Tuition/fees: $19,330. Tuition $22,830 for theater conservatory students. Room/board: $8,220. Books/supplies: $800. Personal expenses: $1,500.

**2006-2007 Financial aid. Need-based:** 401 full-time freshmen applied for aid; 340 were judged to have need; 340 of these received aid. Average scholarship/grant was $5,585; average loan $2,632. 58% of total undergraduate aid awarded as scholarships/grants, 42% as loans/jobs. **Non-need-based:** Awarded to 1,554 full-time undergraduates, including 352 freshmen. Scholarships awarded for academics, art, music/drama.

**Application procedures. Admission:** Priority date 3/1; deadline 6/1. $35 fee, may be waived for applicants with need. Application may be submitted online. Admission notification on a rolling basis beginning on or about 9/1. Must reply by May 1 or within 4 week(s) if notified thereafter. **Financial aid:** Priority date 4/1; no closing date. FAFSA, institutional form required. Applicants notified on a rolling basis starting 2/9; must reply within 2 week(s) of notification.

**Academics.** Professional Actors Equity theater company in residence for theater program. Internships and practicums available in most areas. **Special study options:** Accelerated study, combined bachelor's/graduate degree, cooperative education, cross-registration, distance learning, double major, dual enrollment of high school students, ESL, exchange student, honors, independent study, internships, liberal arts/career combination, student-designed major, study abroad, teacher certification program. Certificate programs and combination bachelor's/master's degree in many subject areas, student leadership development program, individualized majors. **Credit/placement by examination:** AP, CLEP, IB. 64 credit hours maximum toward bachelor's degree. **Support services:** Learning center, reduced course load, remedial instruction, study skills assistance, tutoring, writing center.

**Majors. Area/ethnic studies:** American. **Biology:** General. **Business:** General, accounting, accounting/finance, business admin, finance, international, marketing. **Communications:** General, advertising, broadcast journalism, digital media, journalism, public relations. **Communications technology:** Recording arts. **Computer sciences:** Computer science. **Education:** General, music. **English:** English lit. **Foreign languages:** General, French, German, Spanish. **Health:** Nursing (RN). **History:** General. **Interdisciplinary:** Global studies. **Legal studies:** General, paralegal. **Liberal arts:** Arts/sciences, humanities. **Math:** General. **Philosophy/religion:** Ethics, philosophy, religion. **Psychology:** General. **Social sciences:** General, anthropology, economics, international relations, political science, sociology. **Visual/**

**performing arts:** Acting, art, cinematography, dance, directing/producing, dramatic, film/cinema, musical theater, photography, studio arts. **Other:** Media Literacy.

**Most popular majors.** Business/marketing 35%, communications/journalism 13%, computer/information sciences 6%, social sciences 7%, visual/performing arts 12%.

**Computing on campus.** 453 workstations in dormitories, library, computer center, student center. Dormitories wired for high-speed internet access and linked to campus network. Online course registration, online library, helpline, student web hosting, wireless network available.

**Student life. Freshman orientation:** Available. **Housing:** Guaranteed on-campus for freshmen. Coed dorms, apartments available. $150 fully refundable deposit, deadline 4/1. **Activities:** Jazz band, choral groups, dance, drama, film society, international student organizations, literary magazine, music ensembles, musical theater, opera, radio station, student government, student newspaper, symphony orchestra, TV station, Big Brothers & Sisters, Campus Crusade for Christ, Habitat for Humanity, international student association, Japanese student association, Latin American Student association, peer education zeitgeist, Vietnamese student association, Webster Lions Club, Webster LGBTQ Alliance.

**Athletics.** NCAA. **Intercollegiate:** Baseball M, basketball, cross-country W, golf M, soccer, softball W, tennis, volleyball W. **Intramural:** Bowling, soccer, table tennis, volleyball M. **Team name:** Gorloks.

**Student services.** Alcohol/substance abuse counseling, campus ministries, career counseling, student employment services, financial aid counseling, health services, minority student services, personal counseling, placement for graduates, women's services. **Physically disabled:** Services for visually, speech, hearing impaired.

**Contact.** E-mail: admit@webster.edu
Phone: (314) 968-6991 Toll-free number: (800) 753-6765
Fax: (314) 968-7115
Niel DeVasto, Director of Undergraduate Admissions, Webster University, 470 East Lockwood Avenue, St. Louis, MO 63119-3194

## Westminster College
**Fulton, Missouri**
www.westminster-mo.edu

**CB member**
**CB code: 6937**

- Private 4-year liberal arts college affiliated with Presbyterian Church (USA)
- Residential campus in large town
- 953 degree-seeking undergraduates: 1% part-time, 44% women, 4% African American, 2% Asian American, 2% Hispanic American, 1% Native American, 14% international
- 80% of applicants admitted
- SAT or ACT (ACT writing optional) required
- 59% graduate within 6 years; 28% enter graduate study

**General.** Founded in 1851. Regionally accredited. **Degrees:** 173 bachelor's awarded. **ROTC:** Army, Air Force. **Location:** 100 miles from St. Louis, 24 miles from Jefferson City. **Calendar:** Semester, limited summer session. **Full-time faculty:** 55 total; 69% have terminal degrees, 9% minority, 34% women. **Part-time faculty:** 36 total; 22% have terminal degrees, 58% women. **Class size:** 64% < 20, 36% 20-39. **Special facilities:** Winston Churchill Memorial and Library, 12th century church re-built on campus.

**Freshman class profile.** 931 applied, 744 admitted, 224 enrolled.

| Mid 50% test scores | | | |
|---|---|---|---|
| SAT critical reading: | 480-610 | Rank in top quarter: | 51% |
| SAT math: | 500-620 | Rank in top tenth: | 18% |
| SAT writing: | 470-610 | Return as sophomores: | 83% |
| ACT composite: | 23-28 | Out-of-state: | 19% |
| GPA 3.50 or higher: | 40% | Live on campus: | 97% |
| GPA 3.0-3.49: | 33% | International: | 12% |
| GPA 2.0-2.99: | 27% | Fraternities: | 60% |
| | | Sororities: | 40% |

**Basis for selection.** High school achievement (including class rank, involvement, ACT scores, curriculum, GPA) and recommendations most important. Interview recommended for borderline students, required for students with learning disabilities. **Learning Disabled:** Learning Disabilities Program applicants must have completed applications credentials and personal interview prior to April 1, including untimed SAT/ACT results.

**High school preparation.** 16 units required. Required and recommended units include English 4, mathematics 3, social studies 2, science 2 (laboratory 2), foreign language 2 and academic electives 2. Pre-med and pre-dental students should have at least 3 lab science, 1 advanced math.

**2008-2009 Annual costs.** Tuition/fees: $17,250. Room/board: $6,720. Books/supplies: $800. Personal expenses: $300.

**2007-2008 Financial aid. Need-based:** 193 full-time freshmen applied for aid; 149 were judged to have need; 149 of these received aid. Average need met was 94%. Average scholarship/grant was $11,498; average loan $2,556. 88% of total undergraduate aid awarded as scholarships/grants, 12% as loans/jobs. **Non-need-based:** Awarded to 411 full-time undergraduates, including 121 freshmen. Scholarships awarded for academics, alumni affiliation, leadership, minority status, music/drama, state residency.

**Application procedures. Admission:** Priority date 2/1; no deadline. No application fee. Application may be submitted online. Admission notification on a rolling basis beginning on or about 10/1. Must reply by May 1 or within 3 week(s) if notified thereafter. **Financial aid:** Priority date 2/15; no closing date. FAFSA required. Applicants notified on a rolling basis starting 3/1; must reply within 3 week(s) of notification.

**Academics.** First-year seminar fosters communication, critical thinking and study skills. **Special study options:** Combined bachelor's/graduate degree, cooperative education, cross-registration, double major, dual enrollment of high school students, exchange student, honors, independent study, internships, liberal arts/career combination, New York semester, student-designed major, study abroad, teacher certification program, urban semester, Washington semester. **Credit/placement by examination:** AP, CLEP, IB, institutional tests. 30 credit hours maximum toward bachelor's degree. **Support services:** Learning center, reduced course load, remedial instruction, study skills assistance, tutoring, writing center.

**Majors. Biology:** General, biochemistry. **Business:** Accounting, business admin, management information systems. **Communications:** Advertising, journalism, media studies. **Computer sciences:** General. **Conservation:** General, environmental science, environmental studies. **Education:** Elementary, middle, physical, secondary. **English:** English lit. **Foreign languages:** French, Spanish. **Health:** Athletic training. **History:** General. **Math:** General. **Philosophy/religion:** Philosophy, religion. **Physical sciences:** Chemistry, physics. **Psychology:** General. **Social sciences:** Anthropology, economics, international relations, political science, sociology.

**Most popular majors.** Biology 10%, business/marketing 30%, education 11%, liberal arts 11%, social sciences 10%.

**Computing on campus.** 200 workstations in library, computer center. Dormitories wired for high-speed internet access and linked to campus network. Commuter students can connect to campus network. Online course registration, online library, helpline, student web hosting, wireless network available.

**Student life. Freshman orientation:** Mandatory. Preregistration for classes offered. Held three days before classes start. **Housing:** Guaranteed on-campus for freshmen. Coed dorms, single-sex dorms, apartments, fraternity/sorority housing available. **Activities:** Bands, choral groups, dance, drama, literary magazine, music ensembles, Model UN, musical theater, student government, student newspaper, Young Democrats, Young Republicans, Big Brother-Big Sister program, Environmentally Concerned Students, Chapel Leadership Council, Habitat For Humanity, Fellowship of Christian Athletes.

**Athletics.** NCAA. **Intercollegiate:** Baseball M, basketball, cross-country W, football (tackle) M, golf, soccer, softball W, tennis, volleyball W. **Intramural:** Basketball, softball, volleyball. **Team name:** Blue Jays.

**Student services.** Alcohol/substance abuse counseling, campus ministries, career counseling, student employment services, financial aid counseling, health services, minority student services, personal counseling, placement for graduates, women's services. **Physically disabled:** Services for visually, speech, hearing impaired. **Learning disabled:** Comprehensive services available.

**Contact.** E-mail: admissions@westminster-mo.edu
Phone: (573) 592-5251 Toll-free number: (800) 475-3361
Fax: (573) 592-5255
George Wolf, Vice President and Dean of Enrollment Services, Westminster College, 501 Westminster Avenue, Fulton, MO 65251-1299

---

## William Jewell College

**Liberty, Missouri**
**www.jewell.edu**

**CB member**
**CB code: 6941**

- Private 4-year liberal arts college affiliated with Christian Church
- Residential campus in large town
- 1,329 degree-seeking undergraduates: 17% part-time, 60% women, 4% African American, 1% Asian American, 3% Hispanic American, 2% Native American

- 92% of applicants admitted
- SAT or ACT (ACT writing recommended), application essay required
- 65% graduate within 6 years; 24% enter graduate study

**General.** Founded in 1849. Regionally accredited. Campus in Harlaxton, England. **Degrees:** 330 bachelor's awarded. **Location:** 14 miles from downtown. **Calendar:** Semester, limited summer session. **Full-time faculty:** 78 total; 81% have terminal degrees, 5% minority, 51% women. **Part-time faculty:** 80 total; 15% have terminal degrees, 11% minority, 60% women. **Class size:** 73% < 20, 24% 20-39, 2% 40-49, less than 1% 50-99. **Special facilities:** Observatory, flow cytometer, high and low-ropes course, outdoor environmental learning lab, quimby pipe organ.

**Freshman class profile.** 990 applied, 911 admitted, 288 enrolled.

| Mid 50% test scores | | | |
|---|---|---|---|
| SAT critical reading: | 530-650 | Rank in top tenth: | 28% |
| SAT math: | 500-650 | End year in good standing: | 91% |
| ACT composite: | 22-28 | Return as sophomores: | 81% |
| GPA 3.50 or higher: | 69% | Out-of-state: | 35% |
| GPA 3.0-3.49: | 20% | Live on campus: | 91% |
| GPA 2.0-2.99: | 11% | Fraternities: | 27% |
| Rank in top quarter: | 62% | Sororities: | 42% |

**Basis for selection.** Admissions based on secondary school record. Class rank, standardized test scores, and essay also important. Audition or portfolio required for scholarship seeking music, theater, or art students.

**High school preparation.** 15 units required; 19 recommended. Required and recommended units include English 4, mathematics 3-4, social studies 3, science 3 (laboratory 1), foreign language 2-3 and academic electives 2.

**2008-2009 Annual costs.** Tuition/fees: $23,000. Base tuition now covers 12 to 18 credits per semester. Room/board: $6,130. Books/supplies: $1,000. Personal expenses: $1,800.

**2007-2008 Financial aid. Need-based:** 253 full-time freshmen applied for aid; 208 were judged to have need; 208 of these received aid. Average loan was $4,924. 71% of total undergraduate aid awarded as scholarships/grants, 29% as loans/jobs. **Non-need-based:** Awarded to 135 full-time undergraduates, including 33 freshmen. Scholarships awarded for academics, alumni affiliation, art, athletics, music/drama.

**Application procedures. Admission:** Priority date 12/1; deadline 8/15 (postmark date). $25 fee, may be waived for applicants with need. Application may be submitted online. Admission notification on a rolling basis beginning on or about 9/15. Must reply by May 1 or within 2 week(s) if notified thereafter. **Financial aid:** Priority date 3/1; no closing date. FAFSA required. Applicants notified on a rolling basis starting 2/15; must reply within 1.5 week(s) of notification.

**Academics.** Interdisciplinary core curriculum required. **Special study options:** Accelerated study, combined bachelor's/graduate degree, double major, dual enrollment of high school students, honors, independent study, internships, liberal arts/career combination, student-designed major, study abroad, teacher certification program, Washington semester. Pryor Leadership Studies. **Credit/placement by examination:** AP, CLEP, IB, SAT, ACT, institutional tests. No limit to credit by examination, but student must complete 30 hours in residence. **Support services:** Study skills assistance, tutoring, writing center.

**Honors college/program.** Oxbridge Honors Program allows students to study their major subject using tutorial mode of instruction used at Oxford University and Cambridge University (England). Minimum 3.8 GPA, ACT score of 28 required for admission.

**Majors. Biology:** General, biochemistry, molecular. **Business:** Accounting, business admin, international, managerial economics, nonprofit/public. **Communications:** General, organizational. **Computer sciences:** General, computer science, information systems. **Education:** Art, biology, chemistry, drama/dance, elementary, English, foreign languages, French, mathematics, music, physical, physics, secondary, social studies, Spanish, speech. **English:** English lit, speech/rhetoric. **Foreign languages:** French, Spanish. **Health:** Clinical lab science, nursing (RN). **History:** General. **Math:** General. **Parks/recreation:** General. **Philosophy/religion:** Philosophy, religion. **Physical sciences:** Chemistry, physics. **Psychology:** General. **Social sciences:** International relations, political science. **Theology:** Sacred music. **Visual/performing arts:** Art, dramatic, music performance, music theory/composition. **Other:** Bioethics.

**Most popular majors.** Business/marketing 19%, education 7%, health sciences 19%, psychology 10%.

**Computing on campus.** 232 workstations in library, computer center, student center. Dormitories wired for high-speed internet access and linked to campus network. Commuter students can connect to campus network. Online course registration, online library, helpline, student web hosting, wireless network available.

**Student life. Freshman orientation:** Mandatory. Preregistration for classes offered. 3-day program prior to the first day of classes. **Housing:** Guaranteed on-campus for freshmen. Coed dorms, single-sex dorms, special housing for disabled, fraternity/sorority housing, substance-free housing available. $300 nonrefundable deposit, deadline 5/1. Off-campus houses utilized as residence halls available. **Activities:** Bands, campus ministries, choral groups, dance, drama, music ensembles, musical theater, opera, radio station, student government, student newspaper, symphony orchestra, Young Democrats, College Republicans, Progressive Students for America, Amnesty International, Student Senate, UNITY, Rotaract, Fellowship of Christian Athletes, TPEXEIN.

**Athletics. NAIA. Intercollegiate:** Baseball M, basketball, cheerleading, cross-country, football (tackle) M, golf, soccer, softball W, tennis, track and field, volleyball W. **Intramural:** Basketball, football (non-tackle), golf, racquetball, soccer, softball, tennis, volleyball. **Team name:** Cardinals.

**Student services.** Adult student services, alcohol/substance abuse counseling, campus ministries, career counseling, student employment services, financial aid counseling, health services, minority student services, personal counseling, placement for graduates. **Physically disabled:** Services for hearing impaired.

**Contact.** E-mail: admission@william.jewell.edu
Phone: (816) 415-7511 Toll-free number: (888) 253-9355
Fax: (816) 415-5040
Bridget Gramling, Vice President for Enrollment, William Jewell College, 500 College Hill, Liberty, MO 64068

---

## William Woods University
**Fulton, Missouri**
www.williamwoods.edu

**CB member**
**CB code: 6944**

- Private 4-year university and liberal arts college affiliated with Christian Church (Disciples of Christ)
- Residential campus in large town
- 963 degree-seeking undergraduates: 18% part-time, 74% women, 3% African American, 1% Hispanic American, 1% Native American, 3% international
- 1,210 degree-seeking graduate students
- 85% of applicants admitted
- SAT or ACT (ACT writing optional) required
- 44% graduate within 6 years

**General.** Founded in 1870. Regionally accredited. Students may enroll in courses offered at 4 other mid-Missouri colleges and universities. **Degrees:** 237 bachelor's, 36 associate awarded; master's offered. **ROTC:** Army, Naval, Air Force. **Location:** 100 miles from St. Louis, 30 miles from Columbia. **Calendar:** Semester, limited summer session. **Full-time faculty:** 55 total; 62% have terminal degrees, 7% minority, 49% women. **Part-time faculty:** 194 total; 18% have terminal degrees, 7% minority, 36% women. **Class size:** 78% < 20, 22% 20-39. **Special facilities:** Equestrian studies facilities, observatory, broadcasting laboratory, computer laboratories, model courtroom, ASL interpreting laboratories.

**Freshman class profile.** 613 applied, 520 admitted, 186 enrolled.

| Mid 50% test scores | | Rank in top tenth: | 15% |
|---|---|---|---|
| SAT critical reading: | 460-600 | Return as sophomores: | 75% |
| SAT math: | 410-570 | Out-of-state: | 47% |
| ACT composite: | 19-25 | Live on campus: | 89% |
| GPA 3.50 or higher: | 37% | International: | 1% |
| GPA 3.0-3.49: | 35% | Fraternities: | 8% |
| GPA 2.0-2.99: | 27% | Sororities: | 39% |
| Rank in top quarter: | 39% | | |

**Basis for selection.** Secondary school record, class rank, test scores most important; extracurricular activities, 2 academic references also important; interview considered. Interview recommended for all students. Audition required for performing arts students; portfolio required for visual arts students. **Homeschooled:** Letter of recommendation (nonparent) required. GED required; ACT/SAT should be submitted.

**High school preparation.** 16 units required; 20 recommended. Required and recommended units include English 4, mathematics 3, social studies 2, history 3, science 3 (laboratory 3) and foreign language 2.

**2007-2008 Annual costs.** Tuition/fees: $16,080. Commuter students pay additional $50 fee per year. Room/board: $6,400. Books/supplies: $1,200. Personal expenses: $3,000.

**2007-2008 Financial aid. Need-based:** 145 full-time freshmen applied for aid; 141 were judged to have need; 139 of these received aid. Average need met was 82%. Average scholarship/grant was $11,738; average loan $4,026. 65% of total undergraduate aid awarded as scholarships/grants, 35% as loans/jobs. **Non-need-based:** Awarded to 387 full-time undergraduates, including 95 freshmen. Scholarships awarded for academics, alumni affiliation, art, athletics, leadership, music/drama, religious affiliation.

**Application procedures. Admission:** Priority date 3/1; no deadline. $25 fee, may be waived for applicants with need. Application may be submitted online. Admission notification on a rolling basis. Must reply by May 1 or within 3 week(s) if notified thereafter. **Financial aid:** Priority date 3/1; no closing date. FAFSA, institutional form required. Applicants notified on a rolling basis starting 3/15; must reply within 2 week(s) of notification.

**Academics.** ASL interpreting available. **Special study options:** Accelerated study, combined bachelor's/graduate degree, cross-registration, double major, dual enrollment of high school students, ESL, honors, independent study, internships, liberal arts/career combination, New York semester, student-designed major, study abroad, teacher certification program, Washington semester. Hollywood semester, qualified students may complete bachelor's degree in 3 years through Century Scholars program. **Credit/placement by examination:** AP, CLEP, IB, SAT, ACT, institutional tests. 30 credit hours maximum toward bachelor's degree. **Support services:** Reduced course load, study skills assistance, tutoring, writing center.

**Majors. Agriculture:** Equestrian studies. **Biology:** General. **Business:** Accounting, business admin, international, management information systems, managerial economics. **Communications:** General, advertising, broadcast journalism, journalism, public relations. **Computer sciences:** General. **Education:** General, art, elementary, English, mathematics, middle, physical, science, secondary, social science, special. **English:** Composition, English lit. **Foreign languages:** American Sign Language, Spanish. **Health:** Athletic training. **History:** General. **Legal studies:** General, paralegal. **Math:** General. **Parks/recreation:** Sports admin. **Physical sciences:** General. **Psychology:** General. **Public administration:** Social work. **Social sciences:** Political science. **Visual/performing arts:** Art, design, dramatic, graphic design, studio arts.

**Most popular majors.** Agriculture 16%, business/marketing 33%, communications/journalism 6%, foreign language 9%, legal studies 11%.

**Computing on campus.** 135 workstations in dormitories, library, computer center, student center. Dormitories wired for high-speed internet access and linked to campus network. Online course registration, online library, helpline, repair service, wireless network available.

**Student life. Freshman orientation:** Mandatory. Preregistration for classes offered. 7 days prior to start of fall term. **Policies:** All residence halls are no-smoking halls. Students under age 23 must reside on campus unless married or living with parent or guardian; lottery offered to students who wish to move off campus in spring for following fall semester. **Housing:** Guaranteed on-campus for all undergraduates. Coed dorms, single-sex dorms, special housing for disabled, apartments, fraternity/sorority housing, substance-free housing available. $250 partly refundable deposit, deadline 8/15. Senior housing, single rooms, independent housing, upper-class halls and apartments available. **Activities:** Campus ministries, choral groups, dance, drama, literary magazine, musical theater, radio station, student government, student newspaper, Big Brothers/Big Sisters, campus activities board, Association of Christian Ecumenical Students, community action network, international club, Jesters, Students for Social Work, departmental clubs.

**Athletics. NAIA. Intercollegiate:** Baseball M, basketball, cross-country, golf, soccer, softball W, track and field, volleyball. **Intramural:** Badminton, baseball M, basketball, equestrian, football (non-tackle), softball, table tennis, tennis, volleyball, weight lifting. **Team name:** Owls.

**Student services.** Adult student services, alcohol/substance abuse counseling, campus ministries, career counseling, financial aid counseling, health services, personal counseling. **Physically disabled:** Services for visually, speech, hearing impaired.

**Contact.** E-mail: admissions@williamwoods.edu
Phone: (573) 592-4221 Toll-free number: (800) 995-3159
Fax: (573) 592-1146
Jimmy Clay, Executive Director and Vice President of Enrollment Services, William Woods University, One University Avenue, Fulton, MO 65251-2388

# Montana

## Carroll College

**Helena, Montana**
**www.carroll.edu**

**CB member**
**CB code: 4041**

▶ Private 4-year liberal arts college affiliated with Roman Catholic Church
▶ Residential campus in large town
▶ 1,272 degree-seeking undergraduates: 6% part-time, 58% women, 1% Asian American, 2% Hispanic American, 1% Native American, 1% international
▶ SAT or ACT (ACT writing optional) required
▶ 61% graduate within 6 years

**General.** Founded in 1909. Regionally accredited. **Degrees:** 261 bachelor's, 1 associate awarded. **ROTC:** Army. **Location:** 90 miles from Great Falls, 240 miles from Billings. **Calendar:** Semester, limited summer session. **Full-time faculty:** 80 total. **Part-time faculty:** 54 total. **Special facilities:** Observatory, seismograph station, engineering lab, nursing lab including "SimMan" and "SimBaby".

**Freshman class profile.**

| Mid 50% test scores | | | |
|---|---|---|---|
| SAT critical reading: | 480-590 | GPA 2.0-2.99: | 20% |
| SAT math: | 480-590 | Rank in top quarter: | 53% |
| ACT composite: | 21-26 | Rank in top tenth: | 22% |
| GPA 3.50 or higher: | 54% | Return as sophomores: | 79% |
| GPA 3.0-3.49: | 26% | Out-of-state: | 48% |
| | | Live on campus: | 96% |

**Basis for selection.** School achievement record, test scores, recommendations most important. SAT Subject Tests required of home schooled and nonaccredited high school graduates. Personal statement required. Interview recommended for academically weak students. **Homeschooled:** SAT Subject Tests required.

**High school preparation.** 17 units recommended. Recommended units include English 4, mathematics 3, social studies 1, history 2, science 2 (laboratory 1), foreign language 2 and academic electives 2. 1 technology recommended, 1 theology recommended.

**2007-2008 Annual costs.** Tuition/fees: $19,620. Room/board: $6,608. Books/supplies: $800. Personal expenses: $1,600.

**Financial aid. Non-need-based:** Scholarships awarded for academics, athletics, leadership, music/drama, religious affiliation, ROTC.

**Application procedures. Admission:** Priority date 3/1; deadline 6/1 (receipt date). $35 fee. Application may be submitted online. Admission notification on a rolling basis beginning on or about 9/1. Must reply by May 1 or within 2 week(s) if notified thereafter. **Financial aid:** Priority date 3/1; no closing date. FAFSA required. Applicants notified on a rolling basis starting 3/1; must reply within 4 week(s) of notification.

**Academics. Special study options:** Accelerated study, cooperative education, double major, dual enrollment of high school students, ESL, exchange student, honors, independent study, internships, liberal arts/career combination, student-designed major, study abroad, teacher certification program. 3-2 engineering program with Notre Dame, Columbia University, USC, Gonzaga University, Montana State University-Bozeman, Montana Tech; complete Civil Engineering program ABATE. **Credit/placement by examination:** AP, CLEP, IB, SAT, ACT, institutional tests. 9 credit hours maximum toward associate degree, 18 toward bachelor's. **Support services:** Learning center, pre-admission summer program, reduced course load, study skills assistance, tutoring, writing center.

**Majors. Biology:** General. **Business:** Accounting, business admin, finance, managerial economics. **Communications:** General, public relations. **Conservation:** Environmental studies. **Education:** Elementary, ESL, physical, secondary. **Engineering:** Civil, software. **English:** Creative writing, English lit. **Foreign languages:** Biblical, French, Spanish. **Health:** Nursing (RN), predental, premedicine, prepharmacy, preveterinary. **History:** General. **Interdisciplinary:** Biological/physical sciences. **Math:** General. **Parks/recreation:** Health/fitness, sports admin. **Philosophy/religion:** Philosophy.

**Physical sciences:** Chemistry, physics. **Psychology:** General. **Public administration:** General. **Social sciences:** General, international relations, political science, sociology. **Theology:** Pastoral counseling. **Visual/performing arts:** Dramatic.

**Computing on campus.** 85 workstations in dormitories, library, computer center, student center. Dormitories wired for high-speed internet access and linked to campus network. Commuter students can connect to campus network. Online course registration, helpline, wireless network available.

**Student life. Freshman orientation:** Mandatory, $100 fee. Preregistration for classes offered. Four-day program. Fee includes cost of meals, entertainment, and various activities. **Policies:** Freshmen and sophomores required to live on campus. **Housing:** Guaranteed on-campus for freshmen. Coed dorms, single-sex dorms, apartments, substance-free housing available. $100 deposit, deadline 7/1. **Activities:** Pep band, choral groups, dance, drama, literary magazine, music ensembles, musical theater, radio station, student government, student newspaper, symphony orchestra, College Democrats, Circle K, cultural exchange club, Into the Streets service organization, peer mentors, social work club, sociology club, student community outreach experience, Young Republicans.

**Athletics.** NAIA. **Intercollegiate:** Basketball, cross-country, football (tackle) M, golf, soccer W, swimming, volleyball W. **Intramural:** Badminton, basketball, bowling, cross-country, golf, handball, racquetball, skiing, soccer, softball, swimming, table tennis, volleyball, water polo. **Team name:** Saints.

**Student services.** Adult student services, alcohol/substance abuse counseling, campus ministries, career counseling, student employment services, financial aid counseling, health services, personal counseling, placement for graduates, veterans' counselor.

**Contact.** E-mail: enroll@carroll.edu
Phone: (406) 447-4384 Toll-free number: (800) 992-3648
Fax: (406) 447-4533
Cynthia Thornquist, Director of Admissions and Enrollment, Carroll College, 1601 North Benton Avenue, Helena, MT 59625

## Montana State University: Billings

**Billings, Montana**
**www.msubillings.edu**

**CB member**
**CB code: 4298**

▶ Public 4-year university and technical college
▶ Commuter campus in small city
▶ 4,283 degree-seeking undergraduates: 24% part-time, 63% women, 1% African American, 1% Asian American, 4% Hispanic American, 6% Native American, 1% international
▶ 372 degree-seeking graduate students
▶ 100% of applicants admitted
▶ SAT or ACT (ACT writing recommended) required

**General.** Founded in 1927. Regionally accredited. College of Professional Studies and Lifelong Learning located in downtown Billings. **Degrees:** 513 bachelor's, 195 associate awarded; master's offered. **Location:** 224 miles from Helena, 560 miles from Denver. **Calendar:** Semester, limited summer session. **Full-time faculty:** 150 total; 90% have terminal degrees, 3% minority, 39% women. **Part-time faculty:** 118 total; 7% minority, 56% women. **Class size:** 47% < 20, 44% 20-39, 5% 40-49, 4% 50-99. **Special facilities:** Biological station, center for business enterprise, Montana Center for Disabilities, special education learning center, center for gerontological studies, small business institute, urban institute, public radio, center for applied economic research.

**Freshman class profile.** 1,415 applied, 1,410 admitted, 839 enrolled.

| Mid 50% test scores | | | |
|---|---|---|---|
| SAT critical reading: | 430-570 | Rank in top quarter: | 31% |
| SAT math: | 470-560 | Rank in top tenth: | 10% |
| ACT composite: | 19-24 | End year in good standing: | 60% |
| GPA 3.50 or higher: | 30% | Return as sophomores: | 65% |
| GPA 3.0-3.49: | 33% | Out-of-state: | 9% |
| GPA 2.0-2.99: | 35% | Live on campus: | 37% |

**Basis for selection.** Applicants must meet one of the following: 2.5 GPA, 22 ACT/1030 SAT (exclusive of Writing), or rank in upper half of graduating class. **Homeschooled:** Applicants may be admitted based on GED, ACT, or COMPASS scores.

**High school preparation.** 14 units required. Required units include English 4, mathematics 3, social studies 3, science 2 (laboratory 2). 2 years foreign language, computer science, visual and performing arts, or vocational education also recommended.

**2007-2008 Annual costs.** Tuition/fees: $5,132; $13,707 out-of-state. Room/board: $4,882. Books/supplies: $900. Personal expenses: $1,570.

**2006-2007 Financial aid. Need-based:** 555 full-time freshmen applied for aid; 419 were judged to have need; 409 of these received aid. Average need met was 50%. Average scholarship/grant was $3,780; average loan $2,255. 43% of total undergraduate aid awarded as scholarships/grants, 57% as loans/jobs. **Non-need-based:** Awarded to 886 full-time undergraduates, including 419 freshmen. Scholarships awarded for academics, alumni affiliation, art, athletics, job skills, leadership, minority status, music/drama, state residency. **Additional information:** Veterans and honors fee waivers offered.

**Application procedures. Admission:** Priority date 7/1; no deadline. $30 fee. Application must be submitted on paper. Admission notification on a rolling basis. **Financial aid:** Priority date 3/1; no closing date. FAFSA required. Applicants notified on a rolling basis starting 4/1; must reply within 3 week(s) of notification.

**Academics.** Full degree programs and many courses designed for working professionals. **Special study options:** Accelerated study, combined bachelor's/graduate degree, cooperative education, cross-registration, distance learning, double major, dual enrollment of high school students, ESL, external degree, honors, independent study, internships, liberal arts/career combination, study abroad, teacher certification program, weekend college. Evening College, with extensive online programs and courses. College of Technology offers training and retraining for employment by combining academics and vocational opportunities. **Credit/placement by examination:** AP, CLEP, SAT, ACT. **Support services:** Learning center, reduced course load, remedial instruction, study skills assistance, tutoring, writing center.

**Majors. Biology:** General. **Business:** General. **Communications:** General, media studies, public relations. **Conservation:** Environmental studies. **Education:** General, art, biology, chemistry, curriculum, elementary, English, foreign languages, health, history, mathematics, music, physical, physics, science, secondary, social science, social studies, Spanish, special. **English:** English lit. **Foreign languages:** Spanish. **Health:** Athletic training, health care admin, vocational rehab counseling. **History:** General. **Liberal arts:** Arts/sciences. **Math:** General. **Parks/recreation:** Health/fitness, sports admin. **Physical sciences:** Chemistry. **Protective services:** Criminal justice. **Psychology:** General. **Public administration:** Human services. **Social sciences:** Sociology. **Visual/performing arts:** Art, dramatic, music performance.

**Most popular majors.** Business/marketing 20%, communications/journalism 7%, education 31%, liberal arts 14%, psychology 10%.

**Computing on campus.** 1,050 workstations in dormitories, library, computer center, student center. Dormitories wired for high-speed internet access and linked to campus network. Commuter students can connect to campus network. Online course registration, online library, helpline, student web hosting, wireless network available.

**Student life. Freshman orientation:** Mandatory, $75 fee. Preregistration for classes offered. One-day orientations held throughout summer. **Housing:** Coed dorms, single-sex dorms, special housing for disabled, apartments, substance-free housing available. $75 fully refundable deposit. **Activities:** Bands, campus ministries, choral groups, drama, international student organizations, literary magazine, music ensembles, musical theater, radio station, student government, student newspaper, more than 50 student groups available.

**Athletics.** NCAA. **Intercollegiate:** Baseball M, basketball, cheerleading, cross-country, golf, soccer, softball W, tennis, volleyball W. **Intramural:** Archery, basketball, cross-country, golf, racquetball, skiing, softball, swimming, table tennis, tennis, volleyball. **Team name:** Yellowjackets.

**Student services.** Adult student services, alcohol/substance abuse counseling, campus ministries, career counseling, services for economically disadvantaged, student employment services, financial aid counseling, health services, legal services, minority student services, on-campus daycare, personal counseling, placement for graduates, veterans' counselor. **Physically disabled:** Services for visually, speech, hearing impaired.

**Contact.**  E-mail: cjohannes@msubillings.edu
Phone: (406) 657-2158 Toll-free number: (800) 656-6782
Fax: (406) 657-2051
Cheri Johannes, Director of Admissions, Montana State University: Billings, 1500 University Drive, Billings, MT 59101-0298

---

## Montana State University: Bozeman

**Bozeman, Montana**  **CB member**
**www.montana.edu**  **CB code: 4488**

- Public 4-year university
- Residential campus in large town

- 10,461 degree-seeking undergraduates: 15% part-time, 45% women, 1% Asian American, 1% Hispanic American, 2% Native American, 2% international
- 1,327 degree-seeking graduate students
- 64% of applicants admitted
- SAT or ACT with writing required
- 50% graduate within 6 years

**General.** Founded in 1893. Regionally accredited. **Degrees:** 1,837 bachelor's awarded; master's, doctoral offered. **ROTC:** Army, Air Force. **Location:** 139 miles from Billings. **Calendar:** Semester, limited summer session. **Full-time faculty:** 553 total; 80% have terminal degrees, 2% minority, 35% women. **Part-time faculty:** 249 total; 32% have terminal degrees, 1% minority, 57% women. **Class size:** 43% < 20, 36% 20-39, 8% 40-49, 8% 50-99, 5% >100. **Special facilities:** Museum of the Rockies, agricultural bioscience center, wind tunnel, electron microscope, center for biofilm engineering, planetarium, telecommunication center, geographic information and analysis center, thermal biology institute, rural dwellers center.

**Freshman class profile.** 5,768 applied, 3,696 admitted, 2,100 enrolled.

| Mid 50% test scores | | | |
|---|---|---|---|
| SAT critical reading: | 480-610 | Rank in top quarter: | 39% |
| SAT math: | 500-630 | Rank in top tenth: | 16% |
| ACT composite: | 21-26 | End year in good standing: | 90% |
| GPA 3.50 or higher: | 42% | Return as sophomores: | 71% |
| GPA 3.0-3.49: | 30% | Out-of-state: | 35% |
| GPA 2.0-2.99: | 27% | Live on campus: | 86% |
| | | International: | 2% |

**Basis for selection.** Minimum 2.5 GPA or 22 ACT/SAT equivalent, or rank in top half of graduating class. Completion of state college-preparatory requirements important. Students may use SAT/ACT math scores for placement or take departmental exam. Students with 27 ACT English or 640 SAT verbal can waive freshman composition. Varies by program. **Homeschooled:** GED required.

**High school preparation.** 14 units required. Required units include English 4, mathematics 3, social studies 3, science 2 (laboratory 2). 4 math recommended for science majors. Substitutions for foreign language requirement possible. 2 foreign language, preferably 2 computer science, visual and performing arts, or approved vocational education units.

**2007-2008 Annual costs.** Tuition/fees: $5,749; $16,274 out-of-state. Room/board: $6,926. Books/supplies: $1,050.

**2006-2007 Financial aid. Need-based:** 1,319 full-time freshmen applied for aid; 952 were judged to have need; 923 of these received aid. Average need met was 66%. Average scholarship/grant was $3,982; average loan $3,317. 34% of total undergraduate aid awarded as scholarships/grants, 66% as loans/jobs. **Non-need-based:** Awarded to 584 full-time undergraduates, including 161 freshmen. Scholarships awarded for academics, alumni affiliation, art, athletics, job skills, leadership, minority status, music/drama, ROTC, state residency.

**Application procedures. Admission:** No deadline. $30 fee. Application may be submitted online. Admission notification on a rolling basis. **Financial aid:** Priority date 3/1; no closing date. FAFSA required. Applicants notified on a rolling basis starting 4/1; must reply within 3 week(s) of notification.

**Academics. Special study options:** Combined bachelor's/graduate degree, cooperative education, cross-registration, distance learning, double major, ESL, exchange student, honors, independent study, internships, student-designed major, study abroad, teacher certification program. Combined bachelor's/master's programs in environmental design/architecture and construction engineering technology/construction engineering management. **Credit/placement by examination:** AP, CLEP, IB, SAT, ACT, institutional tests. No more than 30 semester credits earned by correspondence, extension, or continuing education counted toward bachelor's degree. **Support services:** Learning center, remedial instruction, study skills assistance, tutoring, writing center.

**Majors. Agriculture:** Business, horticultural science, plant sciences, range science. **Architecture:** Environmental design. **Biology:** General, bacteriology, biotechnology. **Business:** General. **Computer sciences:** Computer science. **Conservation:** General, management/policy. **Education:** Agricultural, elementary, music, secondary, technology/industrial arts. **Engineering:** Chemical, civil, computer, electrical, mechanical. **Engineering technology:** Construction. **English:** English lit. **Family/consumer sciences:** General. **Foreign languages:** General. **Health:** Nursing (RN). **History:** General. **Math:** General. **Parks/recreation:** Sports admin. **Philosophy/religion:** Philosophy. **Physical sciences:** Chemistry, physics, planetary. **Psychology:** General. **Social sciences:** Anthropology, economics, political science, sociology. **Visual/performing arts:** Art, cinematography.

**Most popular majors.** Biology 8%, business/marketing 11%, education 8%, engineering/engineering technologies 14%, family/consumer sciences 6%, health sciences 9%, social sciences 7%, visual/performing arts 8%.

**Computing on campus.** 850 workstations in dormitories, library, computer center. Dormitories wired for high-speed internet access and linked to campus network. Commuter students can connect to campus network. Online course registration, helpline, wireless network available.

**Student life. Freshman orientation:** Mandatory, $65 fee. Preregistration for classes offered. **Housing:** Guaranteed on-campus for freshmen. Coed dorms, single-sex dorms, apartments, fraternity/sorority housing, substance-free housing available. $200 nonrefundable deposit. Wellness, nonsmoking, older student floors available. **Activities:** Bands, campus ministries, choral groups, dance, drama, film society, international student organizations, literary magazine, music ensembles, musical theater, radio station, student government, student newspaper, TV station, campus service organizations, campus ministry, Circle-K, Native American club, international coordinating council, black student union, Campus Crusade for Christ, Intervarsity Christian Fellowship.

**Athletics.** NCAA. **Intercollegiate:** Basketball, cheerleading, cross-country, football (tackle) M, golf W, rodeo, skiing, tennis, track and field, volleyball W. **Intramural:** Archery, badminton, basketball, bowling, cross-country, golf, gymnastics, handball, racquetball, rodeo, skiing, soccer, softball, swimming, table tennis, tennis, track and field, volleyball, water polo, weight lifting, wrestling M. **Team name:** Bobcats.

**Student services.** Adult student services, alcohol/substance abuse counseling, campus ministries, career counseling, student employment services, financial aid counseling, health services, legal services, minority student services, on-campus daycare, personal counseling, placement for graduates, veterans' counselor, women's services. **Physically disabled:** Services for visually, speech, hearing impaired.

**Contact.** E-mail: admissions@montana.edu
Phone: (406) 994-2452 Toll-free number: (888) 678-2287
Fax: (406) 994-1923
Ronda Russell, Director, Admissions and Enrollment Services, Montana State University: Bozeman, PO Box 172190, Bozeman, MT 59717-2190

---

## Montana State University: Northern
**Havre, Montana**
**www.msun.edu**   CB code: 4538

- Public 4-year university and liberal arts college
- Commuter campus in large town
- 1,388 degree-seeking undergraduates
- SAT or ACT (ACT writing optional) required

**General.** Founded in 1929. Regionally accredited. Classes for military personnel available at resident center at Malmstrom Air Force Base, Great Falls. Extended campus in Great Falls. **Degrees:** 96 bachelor's, 27 associate awarded; master's offered. **Location:** 115 miles from Great Falls. **Calendar:** Semester, extensive summer session. **Full-time faculty:** 73 total. **Part-time faculty:** 30 total.

**Freshman class profile.**

| Mid 50% test scores | | | |
|---|---|---|---|
| | | ACT composite: | 16-21 |
| SAT critical reading: | 420-510 | Out-of-state: | 10% |
| SAT math: | 400-500 | Live on campus: | 31% |

**Basis for selection.** Test scores, 2.5 GPA or upper half of class, in conjunction with college preparatory program important.

**High school preparation.** 14 units required. Required units include English 4, mathematics 3, social studies 3, science 2 (laboratory 2) and academic electives 2.

**2007-2008 Annual costs.** Tuition/fees: $4,357; $14,493 out-of-state. Room/board: $5,627. Books/supplies: $800. Personal expenses: $558.

**Financial aid. Non-need-based:** Scholarships awarded for academics, athletics.

**Application procedures. Admission:** No deadline. $30 fee, may be waived for applicants with need. Application may be submitted online. Admission notification on a rolling basis. **Financial aid:** No deadline. FAFSA, institutional form required. Applicants notified on a rolling basis; must reply within 2 week(s) of notification.

**Academics. Special study options:** Accelerated study, combined bachelor's/graduate degree, cooperative education, distance learning, double major, dual enrollment of high school students, honors, independent study, internships,

---

liberal arts/career combination, teacher certification program. **Credit/placement by examination:** AP, CLEP, SAT, ACT, institutional tests. **Support services:** Learning center, pre-admission summer program, reduced course load, remedial instruction, study skills assistance, tutoring.

**Majors. Agriculture:** Business. **Area/ethnic studies:** Native American. **Biology:** General. **Business:** Business admin. **Communications:** General. **Computer sciences:** General. **Education:** General, elementary, mathematics, physical, science, secondary, social science, technology/industrial arts. **Engineering technology:** Civil, drafting, electrical. **English:** English lit. **Foreign languages:** French. **Health:** Nursing (RN). **Mechanic/repair:** Electronics/electrical. **Physical sciences:** Chemistry. **Visual/performing arts:** Studio arts.

**Computing on campus.** 250 workstations in dormitories, library, computer center, student center. Dormitories wired for high-speed internet access and linked to campus network. Commuter students can connect to campus network. Online course registration, online library, helpline, repair service available.

**Student life. Freshman orientation:** Mandatory. Preregistration for classes offered. **Housing:** Guaranteed on-campus for all undergraduates. Coed dorms, single-sex dorms, apartments available. $75 fully refundable deposit, deadline 9/1. Limited housing available for nontraditional students. **Activities:** Concert band, choral groups, dance, drama, music ensembles, musical theater, radio station, student government, student newspaper, North Star Ambassadors, Inter-Christian fellowship, Delta Alpha Theta, Sweetgrass Society, Northern Vets club.

**Athletics.** NAIA. **Intercollegiate:** Basketball, cheerleading, football (tackle) M, golf W, rodeo, volleyball W, wrestling M. **Intramural:** Badminton, basketball, bowling, football (non-tackle), racquetball, rodeo, skiing, soccer, softball, swimming, table tennis, tennis, volleyball, weight lifting. **Team name:** Lights, Skylights.

**Student services.** Adult student services, alcohol/substance abuse counseling, career counseling, services for economically disadvantaged, student employment services, financial aid counseling, health services, minority student services, on-campus daycare, personal counseling, placement for graduates, veterans' counselor. **Physically disabled:** Services for visually, speech, hearing impaired.

**Contact.** E-mail: admissions@msun.edu
Phone: (406) 265-3704 Toll-free number: (800) 662-6132
Fax: (406) 265-3792
Shauna Albrecht, Admissions Specialist, Director of Advising, Montana State University: Northern, Box 7751, Havre, MT 59501

---

## Montana Tech of the University of Montana
**Butte, Montana**
**www.mtech.edu**   CB code: 4487

- Public 4-year engineering and technical college
- Commuter campus in large town
- 2,137 degree-seeking undergraduates
- 174 graduate students
- 89% of applicants admitted
- 49% graduate within 6 years; 15% enter graduate study

**General.** Founded in 1893. Regionally accredited. **Degrees:** 262 bachelor's, 52 associate awarded; master's offered. **ROTC:** Army. **Location:** 82 miles from Bozeman, 65 miles from Helena. **Calendar:** Semester, extensive summer session. **Full-time faculty:** 124 total; 48% have terminal degrees, 36% women. **Part-time faculty:** 46 total; 11% have terminal degrees, 33% women. **Class size:** 65% < 20, 26% 20-39, 7% 40-49, 2% 50-99, less than 1% >100. **Special facilities:** Mineral museum, earthquake studies office.

**Freshman class profile.** 508 applied, 452 admitted, 443 enrolled.

| Mid 50% test scores | | | |
|---|---|---|---|
| | | GPA 2.0-2.99: | 28% |
| SAT critical reading: | 470-590 | Rank in top quarter: | 38% |
| SAT math: | 500-600 | Rank in top tenth: | 17% |
| SAT writing: | 430-560 | Return as sophomores: | 72% |
| ACT composite: | 19-25 | Out-of-state: | 10% |
| GPA 3.0-3.49: | 68% | Live on campus: | 80% |

**Basis for selection.** Rank in the top half of graduating class, or graduate with a minimum cumulative GPA of 2.5, or achieve a minimum composite score on the ACT of 22, or a minimum total score on the SAT of 1530. SAT or ACT recommended.

**High school preparation.** Required and recommended units include English 4, mathematics 3-4, social studies 3, history 3, science 2 (laboratory

2). Combined 3 years of foreign language, visual and performing arts, computer science, or vocational education required.

**2007-2008 Annual costs.** Tuition/fees: $5,635; $15,067 out-of-state. Room/board: $5,860. Books/supplies: $800. Personal expenses: $1,600.

**Financial aid.** All financial aid based on need.

**Application procedures. Admission:** Priority date 2/1; no deadline. $30 fee, may be waived for applicants with need. Application may be submitted online. Admission notification on a rolling basis. **Financial aid:** Priority date 3/1; no closing date. FAFSA, institutional form required. Applicants notified on a rolling basis starting 4/1; must reply within 2 week(s) of notification.

**Academics. Special study options:** Combined bachelor's/graduate degree, cooperative education, distance learning, double major, dual enrollment of high school students, honors, independent study, internships, liberal arts/career combination, student-designed major, teacher certification program. 3-2 liberal arts-engineering program with Carroll College, dual enrollment agreement with Flathead Valley Community College. **Credit/placement by examination:** AP, CLEP, IB, SAT, ACT, institutional tests. 10 credit hours maximum toward associate degree, 30 toward bachelor's. **Support services:** Learning center, pre-admission summer program, reduced course load, study skills assistance, tutoring.

**Majors. Biology:** General. **Business:** General, accounting, business admin, marketing. **Communications:** General. **Communications technology:** General. **Computer sciences:** General, applications programming, computer science, information systems, information technology, programming, systems analysis. **Engineering:** General, civil, computer, electrical, environmental, geological, materials, materials science, mechanical, metallurgical, mining, petroleum, science, software. **English:** Technical writing. **Health:** Medical informatics, nursing (RN), occupational health, predental, premedicine, prepharmacy, preveterinary. **Interdisciplinary:** Biological/physical sciences, science/society. **Legal studies:** Prelaw. **Liberal arts:** Arts/sciences. **Math:** General, applied, statistics. **Physical sciences:** Chemistry. **Production:** Welding.

**Most popular majors.** Business/marketing 9%, computer/information sciences 7%, engineering/engineering technologies 42%, health sciences 18%.

**Computing on campus.** 500 workstations in dormitories, library, computer center, student center. Dormitories wired for high-speed internet access and linked to campus network. Commuter students can connect to campus network. Online course registration, online library, helpline, repair service, student web hosting, wireless network available.

**Student life. Freshman orientation:** Mandatory. Preregistration for classes offered. Held several days before semester start. **Housing:** Guaranteed on-campus for freshmen. Coed dorms, special housing for disabled, apartments, substance-free housing available. $100 partly refundable deposit. **Activities:** Pep band, choral groups, music ensembles, radio station, student government, student newspaper, symphony orchestra, Baptist student union, international club, Circle-K, Baha'i club, Prospectors, American Indian Science and Engineering Society, Students in Engineering Programs, Abundant Campus Life Ministry, Newman Club.

**Athletics.** NAIA. **Intercollegiate:** Basketball, football (tackle) M, golf, volleyball W. **Intramural:** Basketball, football (non-tackle), handball, racquetball, softball, swimming, volleyball, weight lifting. **Team name:** Orediggers.

**Student services.** Adult student services, alcohol/substance abuse counseling, campus ministries, career counseling, student employment services, financial aid counseling, health services, minority student services, personal counseling, placement for graduates, veterans' counselor, women's services. **Physically disabled:** Services for visually, hearing impaired.

**Contact.** E-mail: admissions@mtech.edu
Phone: (406) 496-4178 Toll-free number: (800) 445-8324
Fax: (406) 496-4710
Tony Campeau, Director of Admissions, Montana Tech of the University of Montana, 1300 West Park Street, Butte, MT 59701-8997

---

## Rocky Mountain College
**Billings, Montana**
**www.rocky.edu**  CB code: 4660

- Private 4-year liberal arts college affiliated with United Church of Christ, United Methodist Church, United Presbyterian Church
- Commuter campus in small city
- 834 degree-seeking undergraduates: 6% part-time, 52% women
- 56 degree-seeking graduate students

---

- 69% of applicants admitted
- SAT or ACT with writing required

**General.** Founded in 1878. Regionally accredited. **Degrees:** 188 bachelor's, 1 associate awarded; master's offered. **Calendar:** Semester, limited summer session. **Full-time faculty:** 58 total. **Part-time faculty:** 75 total. **Class size:** 75% < 20, 23% 20-39, less than 1% 40-49, less than 1% 50-99. **Special facilities:** Outdoor recreation center, flight school, equestrian facilities, geology library, rock climbing wall.

**Freshman class profile.** 603 applied, 418 admitted, 171 enrolled.

| Mid 50% test scores | | | |
|---|---|---|---|
| SAT critical reading: | 460-590 | GPA 2.0-2.99: | 25% |
| SAT math: | 450-570 | Rank in top quarter: | 43% |
| ACT composite: | 19-24 | Rank in top tenth: | 21% |
| GPA 3.50 or higher: | 45% | Out-of-state: | 44% |
| GPA 3.0-3.49: | 30% | Live on campus: | 89% |
| | | International: | 7% |

**Basis for selection.** 2.5 GPA, ACT 21 or combined critical reading/math SAT of 1000 meets requirement for regular admission. Essay recommended for all students. Interview recommended for students not meeting regular admission requirements. Audition recommended for music, theater students. Portfolio recommended for art students. **Homeschooled:** Applicants must either have GED or pass ACT based on college entrance standards.

**High school preparation.** 13 units required. Required and recommended units include English 4, mathematics 2-3, social studies 2, history 2, science 2 (laboratory 1) and foreign language 1-2.

**2007-2008 Annual costs.** Tuition/fees: $17,679. Room/board: $5,700. Books/supplies: $900. Personal expenses: $1,000.

**Financial aid. Non-need-based:** Scholarships awarded for academics, alumni affiliation, art, athletics, leadership, minority status, music/drama, religious affiliation, state residency.

**Application procedures. Admission:** $35 fee, may be waived for applicants with need. Application may be submitted online. Admission notification on a rolling basis beginning on or about 9/1. Must reply by May 1 or within 4 week(s) if notified thereafter. Students who make their decision by Dec. 31 receive priority placement in housing and class selection. **Financial aid:** Priority date 3/1; no closing date. FAFSA, institutional form required. Applicants notified on a rolling basis starting 2/1; must reply within 4 week(s) of notification.

**Academics. Special study options:** Accelerated study, combined bachelor's/graduate degree, distance learning, double major, dual enrollment of high school students, ESL, honors, independent study, internships, student-designed major, study abroad, teacher certification program. 3-2 program in occupational therapy, degree completion program, master's in physician assistant studies. **Credit/placement by examination:** AP, CLEP, IB, SAT, ACT, institutional tests. 15 credit hours maximum toward associate degree, 31 toward bachelor's. **Support services:** Learning center, reduced course load, remedial instruction, study skills assistance, tutoring.

**Majors. Agriculture:** Business, equestrian studies. **Biology:** General. **Business:** Accounting, business admin, management science. **Communications:** General. **Computer sciences:** Computer science, information technology. **Conservation:** Environmental science, environmental studies. **Education:** General, art, biology, drama/dance, elementary, English, history, mathematics, middle, multi-level teacher, music, physical, secondary, social studies. **English:** English lit. **Health:** Athletic training. **History:** General. **Math:** General. **Parks/recreation:** Exercise sciences, health/fitness. **Physical sciences:** Chemistry, geology. **Psychology:** General. **Social sciences:** Economics, political science, sociology. **Transportation:** Airline/commercial pilot, aviation management. **Visual/performing arts:** Art, dramatic, music performance, theater design. **Other:** Philosophy and religious thought.

**Most popular majors.** Agriculture 6%, biology 6%, business/marketing 30%, education 11%, psychology 7%, visual/performing arts 8%.

**Computing on campus.** 104 workstations in dormitories, library, computer center, student center. Dormitories wired for high-speed internet access and linked to campus network. Commuter students can connect to campus network. Online course registration, online library, helpline, student web hosting, wireless network available.

**Student life. Freshman orientation:** Mandatory. Preregistration for classes offered. Held during the 4 days before classes start; includes mountain getaway trip. **Housing:** Guaranteed on-campus for freshmen. Coed dorms, apartments available. $150 nonrefundable deposit. Suites available. **Activities:** Bands, choral groups, drama, literary magazine, music ensembles, student government, student newspaper, Newman Club, intervarsity, American Indian science and engineering society, American Indian cultural association, health occupation groups, business club, precision flying team, ski club, equestrian club, Sojourner's club.

**Athletics.** NAIA. **Intercollegiate:** Basketball, cheerleading, equestrian, football (tackle) M, golf, skiing, soccer W, volleyball W. **Intramural:** Basketball, football (tackle) M, golf, handball, racquetball, skiing, soccer, softball, swimming, table tennis, tennis, volleyball. **Team name:** Battlin' Bears.

**Student services.** Adult student services, alcohol/substance abuse counseling, campus ministries, career counseling, student employment services, financial aid counseling, health services, on-campus daycare, personal counseling, placement for graduates. **Physically disabled:** Services for visually, speech, hearing impaired.

**Contact.** E-mail: admissions@rocky.edu
Phone: (406) 657-1021 Toll-free number: (800) 877-6259
Fax: (406) 657-1189
Laurie Rodriguez, Director of Admissions, Rocky Mountain College, 1511 Poly Drive, Billings, MT 59102-1796

## Salish Kootenai College
**Pablo, Montana**
www.skc.edu                                    CB code: 0898

- Private 4-year liberal arts college
- Commuter campus in rural community

**General.** Founded in 1977. Regionally accredited. **Location:** 55 miles from Missoula, 65 miles from Kalispell. **Calendar:** Quarter.

**Annual costs/financial aid.** Tuition for Native American students $74 per credit hour, $2,664 full-time. Tuition for students of Native American descent $91 per credit hour, $3,276 full-time. Required fees $897/year. Books/supplies: $750. Personal expenses: $1,800. Need-based financial aid available to full-time and part-time students.

**Contact.** Phone: (406) 275-4866
Admissions, Box 70, Pablo, MT 59855

## University of Great Falls
**Great Falls, Montana**
www.ugf.edu                                    CB code: 4058

- Private 4-year university and liberal arts college affiliated with Roman Catholic Church
- Residential campus in small city
- 612 degree-seeking undergraduates: 22% part-time, 63% women
- 78 degree-seeking graduate students
- 57% of applicants admitted
- Application essay required

**General.** Founded in 1932. Regionally accredited. **Degrees:** 117 bachelor's, 7 associate awarded; master's offered. **Location:** 600 miles from Seattle, 370 miles from Spokane, Washington. **Calendar:** Semester, limited summer session. **Full-time faculty:** 33 total. **Part-time faculty:** 69 total. **Class size:** 84% < 20, 16% 20-39. **Special facilities:** Herbarium.

**Freshman class profile.** 351 applied, 200 admitted, 148 enrolled.

| Mid 50% test scores | | | |
|---|---|---|---|
| SAT critical reading: | 330-430 | End year in good standing: | 80% |
| SAT math: | 360-490 | Return as sophomores: | 58% |
| ACT composite: | 18-24 | Out-of-state: | 27% |
| GPA 3.50 or higher: | 30% | Live on campus: | 76% |
| GPA 3.0-3.49: | 40% | | |
| GPA 2.0-2.99: | 28% | | |

**Basis for selection.** High school record and character most important. ACT/SAT scores may be considered when making scholarship decisions. SAT or ACT, SAT Subject Tests recommended. Interview recommended. **Homeschooled:** Transcript of courses and grades required. Applicants should submit SAT/ACT test scores, bibliography of school literature and essay describing and evaluating preparation for university-level work.

**High school preparation.** 20 units required; 22 recommended. Required and recommended units include English 4, mathematics 3, social studies 1-2, history 3, science 3 (laboratory 1) and academic electives 5.

**2007-2008 Annual costs.** Tuition/fees: $16,400. Room/board: $6,490. Books/supplies: $900. Personal expenses: $750.

**2007-2008 Financial aid.** **Need-based:** 34% of total undergraduate aid awarded as scholarships/grants, 66% as loans/jobs. **Non-need-based:** Scholarships awarded for academics, alumni affiliation, art, athletics, job skills, leadership, minority status, music/drama, religious affiliation, state residency.

**Application procedures.** **Admission:** Priority date 6/1; deadline 8/30 (postmark date). $35 fee, may be waived for applicants with need. Application may be submitted online. Admission notification on a rolling basis beginning on or about 10/1. Must reply by May 1 or within 2 week(s) if notified thereafter. Admission granted with 6th semester transcripts. **Financial aid:** Priority date 4/1; no closing date. FAFSA required. Applicants notified on a rolling basis starting 3/1; must reply within 2 week(s) of notification.

**Academics.** Trio Title IV Student Support Services program available to eligible students. **Special study options:** Combined bachelor's/graduate degree, cooperative education, cross-registration, distance learning, double major, dual enrollment of high school students, independent study, internships, liberal arts/career combination, teacher certification program. **Credit/placement by examination:** AP, CLEP, IB, SAT, ACT, institutional tests. 30 credit hours maximum toward associate degree, 30 toward bachelor's. **Support services:** Learning center, pre-admission summer program, reduced course load, remedial instruction, study skills assistance, tutoring, writing center.

**Majors.** **Biology:** General, botany. **Business:** Accounting, accounting/business management, business admin. **Computer sciences:** General, applications programming, computer graphics, computer science, data processing, LAN/WAN management, networking, programming, security, system admin, systems analysis. **Education:** Art, biology, chemistry, early childhood, elementary, English, gifted/talented, health, history, kindergarten/preschool, mathematics, middle, physical, psychology, reading, science, secondary, social science, social studies, special. **English:** English lit. **Health:** Preveterinary, substance abuse counseling. **History:** General. **Legal studies:** Paralegal. **Math:** General. **Parks/recreation:** Health/fitness. **Philosophy/religion:** Religion. **Physical sciences:** Chemistry. **Protective services:** Corrections, criminal justice, forensics, juvenile corrections, police science. **Psychology:** General. **Social sciences:** General, political science, sociology. **Visual/performing arts:** Art.

**Most popular majors.** Business/marketing 10%, education 37%, psychology 13%, security/protective services 13%.

**Computing on campus.** 120 workstations in dormitories, library, computer center, student center. Dormitories wired for high-speed internet access and linked to campus network. Commuter students can connect to campus network. Online course registration, online library, helpline, repair service, student web hosting, wireless network available.

**Student life.** **Freshman orientation:** Mandatory, $75 fee. Preregistration for classes offered. Programs held 3 days prior to fall and spring semesters; includes float trip down Missouri River. **Policies:** No drugs, alcohol, firearms or weapons allowed on campus. **Housing:** Guaranteed on-campus for freshmen. Coed dorms, special housing for disabled, apartments, substance-free housing available. $150 fully refundable deposit, deadline 8/25. **Activities:** Bands, choral groups, dance, drama, literary magazine, music ensembles, musical theater, student government, student newspaper, symphony orchestra, campus ministry, United Tribes Club, Americorps, drama club, art club, Students In Free Enterprise, international law and justice club, medical science club, student Montana education association, paralegal club.

**Athletics.** NAIA. **Intercollegiate:** Basketball, cross-country, golf, soccer W, softball W, volleyball W, wrestling M. **Intramural:** Baseball, basketball, bowling, cheerleading, football (non-tackle), softball, tennis, volleyball. **Team name:** Argonauts.

**Student services.** Adult student services, alcohol/substance abuse counseling, campus ministries, career counseling, services for economically disadvantaged, student employment services, financial aid counseling, health services, minority student services, on-campus daycare, personal counseling, placement for graduates, veterans' counselor, women's services. **Physically disabled:** Services for visually, hearing impaired.

**Contact.** E-mail: enroll@ugf.edu
Phone: (406) 791-5200 Toll-free number: (800) 856-9544
Fax: (406) 791-5209
April Clutter, Assistant Director of Admissions, University of Great Falls, 1301 20th Street South, Great Falls, MT 59405

## University of Montana: Missoula
**Missoula, Montana**                          CB member
www.umt.edu                                    CB code: 4489

- Public 4-year university and liberal arts college
- Residential campus in small city

- 11,586 degree-seeking undergraduates
- 95% of applicants admitted
- SAT or ACT (ACT writing recommended) required

**General.** Founded in 1893. Regionally accredited. Two-year technical college provides technical training, education and postsecondary academic preparation through general associate programs. **Degrees:** 1,692 bachelor's, 203 associate awarded; master's, doctoral, first professional offered. **ROTC:** Army. **Location:** 210 miles from Spokane, Washington. **Calendar:** Semester, extensive summer session. **Full-time faculty:** 548 total. **Part-time faculty:** 223 total. **Class size:** 45% < 20, 36% 20-39, 6% 40-49, 8% 50-99, 5% >100. **Special facilities:** Broadcast media center (public radio and TV) and performing arts building; 3 art galleries; wildlife biology museum; 29,000-acre experimental forest; biological research station; geology field camp; biological, biomedical, kinesiology, physiology, and forestry-related research centers and labs; environmental studies laboratory; primate colony; forensics lab; clinical psychology center; practical ethics center; Fort Missoula field research center.

**Freshman class profile.** 4,756 applied, 4,536 admitted, 2,111 enrolled.

| Mid 50% test scores | | | |
|---|---|---|---|
| SAT critical reading: | 460-600 | Out-of-state: | 27% |
| SAT math: | 470-600 | Live on campus: | 69% |
| SAT writing: | 460-580 | Fraternities: | 6% |
| ACT composite: | 20-25 | Sororities: | 5% |

**Basis for selection.** Must meet one of the following: 2.5 GPA, 22 ACT, 1540 SAT, or rank in top half of graduating class. TOEFL or Michigan Test and statement of intent and personal contribution required for international students. SAT/ACT not required for nontraditional students or international students.

**High school preparation.** Required and recommended units include English 4, mathematics 3, social studies 3, history 1-2, science 2 (laboratory 2), foreign language 2 and academic electives 2. Computer science, visual and performing arts, and/or vocational education.

**2007-2008 Annual costs.** Tuition/fees: $5,141; $15,504 out-of-state. Room/board: $6,026. Books/supplies: $800. Personal expenses: $3,248.

**Financial aid. Non-need-based:** Scholarships awarded for academics, art, athletics, leadership, music/drama, ROTC, state residency.

**Application procedures. Admission:** Priority date 3/1; no deadline. $30 fee. Admission notification on a rolling basis beginning on or about 9/15. **Financial aid:** Priority date 3/1; no closing date. FAFSA, institutional form, CSS PROFILE required. Applicants notified on a rolling basis starting 4/1; must reply by 8/1 or within 4 week(s) of notification.

**Academics. Special study options:** Combined bachelor's/graduate degree, cooperative education, cross-registration, distance learning, double major, ESL, exchange student, honors, independent study, internships, study abroad, teacher certification program. English language institute, combined programs with other institutions for bachelor in nursing and master in public administration with Montana State University - Bozeman. **Credit/placement by examination:** AP, CLEP, institutional tests. 10 credit hours maximum toward associate degree. Credit hours awarded determined by academic department. **Support services:** Learning center, pre-admission summer program, reduced course load, remedial instruction, study skills assistance, tutoring, writing center.

**Majors. Architecture:** Urban/community planning. **Area/ethnic studies:** Asian, Native American, women's. **Biology:** General, bacteriology, botany, cellular/molecular, zoology. **Business:** General, business admin, finance, international, management information systems, marketing. **Communications:** General, broadcast journalism, journalism. **Computer sciences:** Computer science. **Conservation:** General, forestry, wildlife. **Education:** General, art, biology, business, elementary, English, mathematics, music, physical, secondary. **English:** English lit, speech/rhetoric. **Foreign languages:** Classics, French, German, Japanese, Latin, Russian, Spanish. **Health:** Athletic training, clinical lab science. **History:** General. **Interdisciplinary:** Math/computer science. **Liberal arts:** Arts/sciences. **Math:** General. **Parks/recreation:** Exercise sciences, facilities management, health/fitness. **Philosophy/religion:** Philosophy. **Physical sciences:** Chemistry, geology, physics. **Psychology:** General. **Public administration:** Social work. **Social sciences:** Anthropology, cartography, criminology, economics, geography, international relations, political science, sociology. **Visual/performing arts:** General, art, art history/conservation, dance, dramatic, music performance, music theory/composition.

**Computing on campus.** 1,800 workstations in dormitories, library, computer center, student center. Dormitories wired for high-speed internet access and linked to campus network. Commuter students can connect to campus network. Online course registration, online library, helpline, repair service, wireless network available.

**Student life. Freshman orientation:** Mandatory, $45 fee. Preregistration for classes offered. Three-day summer session which includes parent track. **Housing:** Guaranteed on-campus for freshmen. Coed dorms, single-sex dorms, special housing for disabled, apartments, fraternity/sorority housing available. $120 deposit, deadline 3/1. Honors floors, international floors, quiet floors, activity dorms, personal development housing available. **Activities:** Bands, choral groups, dance, drama, literary magazine, music ensembles, musical theater, opera, radio station, student government, student newspaper, symphony orchestra, TV station, Associated Students of University of Montana, University of Montana Advocates, Mortar Board, Spurs, Circle-K, forestry student association, honors student association, Kyi-Yo (Native American organization), environmental action club, American Indian Business Leaders.

**Athletics.** NCAA. **Intercollegiate:** Basketball, cheerleading, cross-country, football (tackle) M, golf W, rodeo, soccer W, tennis, track and field, volleyball W. **Intramural:** Badminton, baseball M, basketball, football (tackle), golf, handball, racquetball, soccer, softball, swimming, table tennis, tennis, track and field, triathlon, volleyball. **Team name:** Grizzlies.

**Student services.** Adult student services, alcohol/substance abuse counseling, campus ministries, career counseling, services for economically disadvantaged, student employment services, financial aid counseling, health services, legal services, minority student services, on-campus daycare, personal counseling, placement for graduates, veterans' counselor, women's services. **Physically disabled:** Services for visually, speech, hearing impaired.

**Contact.** E-mail: admiss@umontana.edu
Phone: (406) 243-6266 Toll-free number: (800) 462-8636
Fax: (406) 243-5711
Jed Liston, Assistant Vice President for Enrollment Services, University of Montana: Missoula, Lommasson Center 103, Missoula, MT 59812

---

## University of Montana: Western
**Dillon, Montana**
www.umwestern.edu

**CB member**
**CB code: 4945**

- Public 4-year liberal arts and teachers college
- Residential campus in small town
- 1,148 degree-seeking undergraduates: 16% part-time, 54% women
- SAT or ACT with writing required

**General.** Founded in 1893. Regionally accredited. **Degrees:** 164 bachelor's, 35 associate awarded. **Location:** 65 miles from Butte, 145 miles from Idaho Falls. **Calendar:** Semester, extensive summer session. **Full-time faculty:** 50 total. **Part-time faculty:** 21 total. **Special facilities:** Outdoor education center, wildlife exhibit, office simulation center, public gallery, affiliation with La Cense, Mt Ranch.

**Freshman class profile.** 463 applied, 449 admitted, 252 enrolled.

| Mid 50% test scores | | | |
|---|---|---|---|
| SAT critical reading: | 370-500 | Rank in top quarter: | 20% |
| SAT math: | 380-510 | Rank in top tenth: | 4% |
| ACT composite: | 17-22 | Out-of-state: | 36% |
| | | Live on campus: | 99% |

**Basis for selection.** Open admission, but selective for some programs. School record, class rank, test scores most important. Writing scores required for admission. Open admission for Associate degree program. **Home-schooled:** State high school equivalency certificate required.

**High school preparation.** 16 units recommended. Recommended units include English 4, mathematics 3, social studies 3, science 3 (laboratory 3) and academic electives 2. Vocational education, computer education, foreign language, visual or performing arts recommended.

**2007-2008 Annual costs.** Tuition/fees: $3,659; $12,428 out-of-state. Room/board: $5,120. Books/supplies: $750. Personal expenses: $2,000.

**2006-2007 Financial aid. Need-based:** 55% of total undergraduate aid awarded as scholarships/grants, 45% as loans/jobs. **Non-need-based:** Scholarships awarded for academics, alumni affiliation, art, athletics, leadership, minority status, state residency. **Additional information:** Tuition and/or fee waiver for veterans and Native Americans.

**Application procedures. Admission:** Priority date 7/1; no deadline. $30 fee. Application may be submitted online. Admission notification on a rolling basis. **Financial aid:** Priority date 3/1; no closing date. FAFSA required. Applicants notified on a rolling basis starting 3/1; must reply within 2 week(s) of notification.

**Academics.** Offer classes in block scheduling system. All students take 1 course at a time in 3 week blocks. Blocks end with final exam and are followed by 4 day break prior to next block. 4 blocks per semester; most classes are 4 credits. **Special study options:** Cooperative education, distance learning, double major, dual enrollment of high school students, honors, independent study, internships, liberal arts/career combination, teacher certification program. **Credit/placement by examination:** AP, CLEP, institutional tests. 30 credit hours maximum toward associate degree, 30 toward bachelor's. **Support services:** Learning center, reduced course load, remedial instruction, study skills assistance, tutoring.

**Majors.** **Biology:** General. **Business:** General, business admin, communications, tourism/travel. **Conservation:** General, environmental studies, wildlife. **Education:** General, art, biology, business, chemistry, early childhood, elementary, English, health, history, mathematics, multi-level teacher, music, physical, school librarian, science, secondary, social studies, technology/industrial arts. **English:** English lit. **Liberal arts:** Arts/sciences. **Math:** Applied. **Physical sciences:** Chemistry, geology. **Social sciences:** General. **Visual/performing arts:** General, art, dramatic.

**Most popular majors.** Business/marketing 22%, education 54%, natural resources/environmental science 6%, social sciences 6%.

**Computing on campus.** 140 workstations in dormitories, library, computer center. Dormitories linked to campus network. Commuter students can connect to campus network. Online course registration, wireless network available.

**Student life.** **Freshman orientation:** Mandatory, $60 fee. Preregistration for classes offered. **Housing:** Guaranteed on-campus for freshmen. Coed dorms, single-sex dorms, special housing for disabled, apartments, substance-free housing available. $100 fully refundable deposit. Students with fewer than 30 credits not living with family required to live in dormitory. Transfer students under 21 with fewer than 30 credits not living with parents required to live on campus. **Activities:** Choral groups, drama, literary magazine, music ensembles, radio station, student government, student newspaper, admissions ambassadors, Chi Alpha-Christian fellowship, outdoor club, Polynesian club, rodeo club, IT club, Catholic campus ministry, academic clubs, community service.

**Athletics.** NAIA. **Intercollegiate:** Basketball, equestrian, football (tackle) M, golf, rodeo, volleyball W. **Intramural:** Basketball, golf, racquetball, skiing, soccer, softball, tennis, volleyball. **Team name:** Bulldogs, Lady Bulldogs.

**Student services.** Alcohol/substance abuse counseling, career counseling, student employment services, financial aid counseling, legal services, on-campus daycare, personal counseling, placement for graduates, veterans' counselor. **Physically disabled:** Services for visually, speech, hearing impaired.

**Contact.** E-mail: admissions@umwestern.edu
Phone: (406) 683-7331 Toll-free number: (877) 683-7331
Fax: (406) 683-7493
Catherine Redhead, Director of Admissions, University of Montana: Western, 710 South Atlantic Street, Dillon, MT 59725

# Nebraska

## Bellevue University
### Bellevue, Nebraska
### www.bellevue.edu
### CB code: 6053

- Private 4-year university and business college
- Commuter campus in large city
- 5,515 degree-seeking undergraduates: 32% part-time, 47% women
- 2,711 graduate students

**General.** Founded in 1965. Regionally accredited. Satellite operations throughout a five-state area in the Midwest. Focus on adult learners, non-traditional students and customized programs for organizations and corporations. **Degrees:** 1,782 bachelor's awarded; master's, doctoral offered. **ROTC:** Army, Air Force. **Calendar:** Differs by program, extensive summer session. **Full-time faculty:** 84 total; 44% have terminal degrees, 10% minority, 45% women. **Part-time faculty:** 226 total; 23% have terminal degrees, 4% minority. **Class size:** 72% < 20, 28% 20-39.

**Basis for selection.** Open admission, but selective for some programs. Students dismissed from another institution for academic or disciplinary reasons will be accepted for admission after 1 year has lapsed since dismissal from that institution. Admission to Professional Studies program requires roughly 60 transfer credit hours from accredited institution. Michigan English Language Assessment Battery used for placement after arrival. IELT also accepted. **Homeschooled:** Students should submit official verification of completion.

**High school preparation.** Recommended units include English 3, mathematics 3, social studies 3, history 3, science 3 (laboratory 1), foreign language 3 and academic electives 3.

**2008-2009 Annual costs.** Tuition/fees: $6,165. Prices vary depending on program. Books/supplies: $1,500. Personal expenses: $1,845.

**2006-2007 Financial aid. Need-based:** Average scholarship/grant was $2,706; average loan $2,176. 14% of total undergraduate aid awarded as scholarships/grants, 86% as loans/jobs. **Non-need-based:** Scholarships awarded for academics, athletics, leadership.

**Application procedures. Admission:** No deadline. $50 fee, may be waived for applicants with need. Application may be submitted online. Admission notification on a rolling basis. **Financial aid:** Priority date 4/15; no closing date. FAFSA, institutional form required. Applicants notified on a rolling basis starting 4/15; must reply within 2 week(s) of notification.

**Academics. Special study options:** Accelerated study, cross-registration, distance learning, double major, dual enrollment of high school students, ESL, independent study, internships, liberal arts/career combination, weekend college. **Credit/placement by examination:** AP, CLEP, IB, institutional tests. Offer 12 computer proficency exams, each worth 1 credit. Maximum of 12 credits allowed. **Support services:** Learning center, remedial instruction, study skills assistance, tutoring, writing center.

**Majors. Biology:** General. **Business:** General, accounting, business admin, e-commerce, human resources, management information systems, marketing. **Communications:** General. **Computer sciences:** General, information systems, information technology, web page design. **Conservation:** General, environmental science. **Education:** Physical. **English:** English lit. **Health:** Health care admin, premedicine, substance abuse counseling. **Legal studies:** Prelaw. **Liberal arts:** Arts/sciences. **Parks/recreation:** Sports admin. **Protective services:** Law enforcement admin. **Psychology:** General. **Public administration:** General, human services. **Social sciences:** General, sociology. **Visual/performing arts:** Art, art history/conservation, arts management, commercial/advertising art, studio arts.

**Most popular majors.** Business/marketing 45%, computer/information sciences 8%, health sciences 7%, security/protective services 10%.

**Computing on campus.** 600 workstations in library, computer center. Commuter students can connect to campus network. Online course registration, online library, helpline, wireless network available.

**Student life. Freshman orientation:** Available. Preregistration for classes offered. One day program typically held the beginning week of fall and winter terms. **Policies:** No alcohol at any student events. Any event must be coordinated through the Student Activities Office. **Housing:** Apartments available. **Activities:** Student government, Alpha Chi, Campus Crusade for Christ, computer graphic design club, Delta Epsilon Chi, economics club, institute of management accountants, international club, multicultural student organization, student advisory council, toastmasters.

**Athletics.** NAIA. **Intercollegiate:** Baseball M, basketball M, soccer, softball W, volleyball W. **Team name:** Bruins.

**Student services.** Career counseling, student employment services, financial aid counseling, personal counseling, placement for graduates, veterans' counselor. **Physically disabled:** Services for visually, speech, hearing impaired.

**Contact.** E-mail: info@bellevue.edu
Phone: (402) 293-2000 Toll-free number: (800) 756-7920
Fax: (402) 557-7230
Scott Kizzire, Director, Undergraduate Admissions, Bellevue University, 1000 Galvin Road South, Bellevue, NE 68005-3098

## Chadron State College
### Chadron, Nebraska
### www.csc.edu
### CB code: 6466

- Public 4-year business, liberal arts and teachers college
- Residential campus in small town
- 2,017 degree-seeking undergraduates

**General.** Founded in 1911. Regionally accredited. Limited distance education classes and programs offered online and at Scottsbluff, Alliance, Sidney, and throughout western Nebraska and eastern Wyoming. **Degrees:** 348 bachelor's awarded; master's offered. **ROTC:** Army. **Location:** 100 miles from Scottsbluff. **Calendar:** Semester, limited summer session. **Full-time faculty:** 97 total. **Part-time faculty:** 30 total. **Class size:** 65% < 20, 30% 20-39, 4% 40-49, less than 1% 50-99. **Special facilities:** Planetarium, herbarium, geological museum, high plains heritage center.

**Freshman class profile.** 1,270 applied, 1,270 admitted, 410 enrolled.

| Mid 50% test scores | | Rank in top quarter: | 26% |
|---|---|---|---|
| ACT composite: | 17-24 | Rank in top tenth: | 11% |
| GPA 3.50 or higher: | 31% | Out-of-state: | 29% |
| GPA 3.0-3.49: | 22% | Live on campus: | 90% |
| GPA 2.0-2.99: | 28% | | |

**Basis for selection.** Open admission, but selective for some programs. Test scores must be submitted for placement, but no minimum score required. Audition recommended for music program.

**High school preparation.** 12 units recommended. Recommended units include English 4, mathematics 3, social studies 3, science 2 (laboratory 2). Units in visual or performing arts, computer literacy, or foreign language recommended.

**2007-2008 Annual costs.** Tuition/fees: $4,212; $7,512 out-of-state. Room/board: $4,430. Books/supplies: $600. Personal expenses: $972.

**Financial aid. Non-need-based:** Scholarships awarded for academics, alumni affiliation, art, athletics, leadership, minority status, music/drama, state residency.

**Application procedures. Admission:** No deadline. $15 fee. Application may be submitted online. Admission notification on a rolling basis. **Financial aid:** Priority date 6/1; no closing date. FAFSA, institutional form required. Applicants notified on a rolling basis starting 4/1; must reply within 2 week(s) of notification.

**Academics. Special study options:** Accelerated study, combined bachelor's/graduate degree, cooperative education, distance learning, double major, dual enrollment of high school students, honors, independent study, internships, student-designed major, study abroad, teacher certification program. **Credit/placement by examination:** AP, CLEP, SAT, ACT, institutional tests. 65 credit hours maximum toward bachelor's degree. **Support services:** Learning center, pre-admission summer program, reduced course load, remedial instruction, study skills assistance, tutoring, writing center.

**Majors. Agriculture:** Range science. **Biology:** General. **Business:** Accounting, business admin, finance, management information systems, management science, office management. **Computer sciences:** Information systems. **Education:** Art, biology, business, chemistry, drama/dance, elementary, English, family/consumer sciences, history, mathematics, middle, music, physical, physics, science, secondary, social science, Spanish, technology/industrial arts, trade/industrial. **English:** English lit, speech/rhetoric. **Family/consumer sciences:** General. **Foreign languages:** Spanish. **History:** General.

**Legal studies:** General, prelaw. **Liberal arts:** Arts/sciences, library science. **Math:** General. **Parks/recreation:** General. **Physical sciences:** Chemistry. **Psychology:** General. **Public administration:** Social work. **Social sciences:** General, sociology. **Visual/performing arts:** Art, dramatic.

**Most popular majors.** Biology 11%, business/marketing 20%, education 27%.

**Computing on campus.** 120 workstations in dormitories, library, computer center, student center. Dormitories wired for high-speed internet access and linked to campus network. Commuter students can connect to campus network. Online course registration, online library, helpline, wireless network available.

**Student life. Freshman orientation:** Available, $50 fee. Preregistration for classes offered. Four or five 2-day weekend orientations held prior to start of fall term. **Housing:** Guaranteed on-campus for freshmen. Coed dorms, single-sex dorms, special housing for disabled, apartments, substance-free housing available. $100 deposit, deadline 6/1. **Activities:** Bands, choral groups, dance, drama, international student organizations, music ensembles, musical theater, student government, student newspaper, Circle K, student education association, multicultural club, Intervarsity Christian Fellowship, White Buffalo Club.

**Athletics.** NCAA. **Intercollegiate:** Basketball, football (tackle) M, golf W, track and field, volleyball W, wrestling M. **Intramural:** Archery, badminton, basketball, bowling, golf, racquetball, rugby M, softball, track and field, volleyball, wrestling M. **Team name:** Eagles.

**Student services.** Adult student services, alcohol/substance abuse counseling, career counseling, services for economically disadvantaged, student employment services, financial aid counseling, health services, on-campus daycare, personal counseling, placement for graduates, veterans' counselor. **Physically disabled:** Services for visually, speech, hearing impaired.

**Contact.** E-mail: inquire@csc.edu
Phone: (308) 432-6263 Toll-free number: (800) 242-3766
Fax: (308) 432-6229
Tena Cook, Director of Admissions, Chadron State College, 1000 Main Street, Chadron, NE 69337

## Clarkson College
**Omaha, Nebraska**
www.clarksoncollege.edu      **CB code: 2250**

- Private 4-year health science college affiliated with Episcopal Church
- Commuter campus in large city
- 697 degree-seeking undergraduates
- 135 graduate students
- Application essay required

**General.** Founded in 1888. Regionally accredited. **Degrees:** 116 bachelor's, 47 associate awarded; master's offered. **ROTC:** Army, Air Force. **Location:** 50 miles from Lincoln. **Calendar:** Semester, extensive summer session. **Full-time faculty:** 42 total; 52% have terminal degrees, 5% minority, 98% women. **Part-time faculty:** 53 total; 66% have terminal degrees, 4% minority, 72% women. **Class size:** 66% < 20, 30% 20-39, less than 1% 40-49, 3% 50-99. **Special facilities:** Health care clinical facilities for professional education (more than 180 clinical sites), fully energized radiologic technology lab.

**Freshman class profile.**

| Mid 50% test scores | | Out-of-state: | 79% |
|---|---|---|---|
| ACT composite: | 21-25 | | |

**Basis for selection.** Open admission, but selective for some programs. GPA, class rank, test scores, essay important. ACT recommended. **Homeschooled:** Must take GED and submit ACT scores. Essay required. Transcript or portfolio recommended.

**High school preparation.** 9 units required. Required and recommended units include English 3-4, mathematics 2-4, social studies 2-3, history 2, science 2-4 (laboratory 1-2) and foreign language 2.

**2007-2008 Annual costs.** Tuition/fees: $12,720. Distance learning fee: $40 per credit hour in 2007-08. Room only: $4,200. Books/supplies: $600. Personal expenses: $1,500.

**2006-2007 Financial aid. Need-based:** 21% of total undergraduate aid awarded as scholarships/grants, 79% as loans/jobs. **Non-need-based:** Scholarships awarded for academics, alumni affiliation, minority status, religious affiliation.

**Application procedures. Admission:** No deadline. $35 fee. Application must be submitted on paper. Admission notification on a rolling basis. Must reply by May 1 or within 4 week(s) if notified thereafter. Application deadlines may vary by program. Students should check with admissions office for program deadlines. **Financial aid:** Priority date 4/1; no closing date. FAFSA, institutional form required. Applicants notified on a rolling basis starting 4/13; must reply within 3 week(s) of notification.

**Academics. Special study options:** Accelerated study, combined bachelor's/graduate degree, cooperative education, cross-registration, distance learning, double major, dual enrollment of high school students, external degree, independent study, internships, study abroad. **Credit/placement by examination:** CLEP, institutional tests. 40 credit hours maximum toward associate degree, 88 toward bachelor's. Unlimited number of hours of credit by examination may be counted toward degree if residency requirement of 40 hours is met. **Support services:** Learning center, reduced course load, study skills assistance, tutoring, writing center.

**Majors. Business:** General, business admin. **Health:** Health care admin, medical radiologic technology/radiation therapy, nursing (RN), preop/surgical nursing, radiologic technology/medical imaging.

**Computing on campus.** 60 workstations in dormitories, library, computer center. Dormitories wired for high-speed internet access. Commuter students can connect to campus network. Online library, helpline, repair service available.

**Student life. Freshman orientation:** Mandatory. Preregistration for classes offered. One day program held on Friday before classes begin. **Housing:** Guaranteed on-campus for freshmen. Coed dorms, apartments available. $250 deposit, deadline 6/30. Board plan not available, kitchens located in each apartment. **Activities:** Student government, student newspaper, Christian Fellowship, Red Cross, National Student Nurses Association, Fellows club, Ambassador club, student leadership council.

**Athletics. Intercollegiate:** Skiing M.

**Student services.** Adult student services, alcohol/substance abuse counseling, career counseling, student employment services, financial aid counseling, health services, minority student services, on-campus daycare, personal counseling, placement for graduates. **Physically disabled:** Services for visually, hearing impaired.

**Contact.** E-mail: admiss@clarksoncollege.edu
Phone: (402) 552-3041 Toll-free number: (800) 647-5500
Fax: (402) 552-6057
Denise Work, Director of Admission, Clarkson College, 101 South 42nd Street, Omaha, NE 68131-2739

## College of Saint Mary
**Omaha, Nebraska**
www.csm.edu      **CB code: 6106**

- Private 4-year university, nursing, liberal arts and teachers college for women affiliated with Roman Catholic Church
- Commuter campus in large city
- 793 degree-seeking undergraduates: 22% part-time, 100% women, 10% African American, 1% Asian American, 7% Hispanic American, 1% Native American, 1% international
- 152 degree-seeking graduate students
- 42% of applicants admitted
- SAT or ACT (ACT writing optional) required
- 46% graduate within 6 years

**General.** Founded in 1923. Regionally accredited. Weekend accelerated master's program, integrated service learning. **Degrees:** 140 bachelor's, 67 associate awarded; master's, doctoral offered. **ROTC:** Army, Air Force. **Location:** 10 miles from downtown. **Calendar:** Semester, limited summer session. **Full-time faculty:** 59 total; 56% have terminal degrees, 10% minority, 80% women. **Part-time faculty:** 99 total; 20% have terminal degrees, 9% minority, 75% women. **Class size:** 77% < 20, 22% 20-39, less than 1% 40-49, 1% 50-99. **Special facilities:** Nursing labs, on-site child development center.

**Freshman class profile.** 650 applied, 275 admitted, 93 enrolled.

| Mid 50% test scores | | | |
|---|---|---|---|
| ACT composite: | 17-24 | Rank in top tenth: | 8% |
| GPA 3.50 or higher: | 41% | End year in good standing: | 70% |
| GPA 3.0-3.49: | 27% | Return as sophomores: | 61% |
| GPA 2.0-2.99: | 32% | Out-of-state: | 16% |
| Rank in top quarter: | 31% | Live on campus: | 82% |

**Basis for selection.** Test scores, secondary school record, class rank important. Recommendations considered. **Homeschooled:** Must take ACT exam and submit scores.

**High school preparation.** Required and recommended units include English 4, mathematics 2-3, social studies 2 and science 2-3. Chemistry and biology required of nursing, occupational therapy and preprofessional studies students.

**2007-2008 Annual costs.** Tuition/fees: $20,556. Room/board: $6,300.

**2007-2008 Financial aid. Need-based:** Average need met was 69%. Average scholarship/grant was $12,447; average loan $4,861. 46% of total undergraduate aid awarded as scholarships/grants, 54% as loans/jobs. **Non-need-based:** Scholarships awarded for academics, athletics, music/drama.

**Application procedures. Admission:** No deadline. $30 fee, may be waived for applicants with need. Application may be submitted online. Admission notification on a rolling basis. **Financial aid:** Priority date 3/1; no closing date. FAFSA required. Applicants notified on a rolling basis starting 3/1; must reply within 2 week(s) of notification.

**Academics. Special study options:** Accelerated study, combined bachelor's/graduate degree, cooperative education, distance learning, double major, exchange student, honors, independent study, internships, liberal arts/career combination, student-designed major, study abroad, teacher certification program, weekend college. **Credit/placement by examination:** AP, CLEP, IB, ACT, institutional tests. 15 credit hours maximum toward associate degree, 15 toward bachelor's. 30% of program may be earned through credit by examination. **Support services:** Learning center, reduced course load, remedial instruction, study skills assistance, tutoring, writing center.

**Majors. Biology:** General. **Business:** Business admin. **Computer sciences:** General. **Education:** Biology, chemistry, computer, early childhood, elementary, English, mathematics, middle, reading, science, secondary, social science, special. **English:** English lit. **Foreign languages:** Spanish. **Health:** Clinical lab technology, nursing (RN), predental, premedicine, prepharmacy, preveterinary. **Legal studies:** Paralegal. **Liberal arts:** Arts/sciences. **Math:** General. **Physical sciences:** General, chemistry. **Psychology:** General. **Theology:** Theology. **Visual/performing arts:** Studio arts.

**Most popular majors.** Business/marketing 27%, education 13%, health sciences 31%, legal studies 6%, liberal arts 13%.

**Computing on campus.** 90 workstations in dormitories, library, computer center, student center. Dormitories wired for high-speed internet access and linked to campus network. Commuter students can connect to campus network. Online course registration, online library, wireless network available.

**Student life. Freshman orientation:** Mandatory. Preregistration for classes offered. One-day program offered several times during late spring and summer. **Housing:** Guaranteed on-campus for freshmen. $125 nonrefundable deposit, deadline 8/1. Residence hall for single mothers with children available. **Activities:** Campus ministries, choral groups, student government, Do Unto Others board, residence hall council, Golden S, Student Nurse Association, campus activities board, Student Occupational Therapy Association, Student Education Association of Nebraska, business student association.

**Athletics.** NAIA. **Intercollegiate:** Basketball W, cheerleading M, cross-country W, soccer W, softball W, volleyball W. **Team name:** Flames.

**Student services.** Adult student services, alcohol/substance abuse counseling, campus ministries, career counseling, services for economically disadvantaged, student employment services, financial aid counseling, health services, minority student services, on-campus daycare, personal counseling, placement for graduates, veterans' counselor, women's services. **Physically disabled:** Services for visually, speech, hearing impaired.

**Contact.** E-mail: enroll@csm.edu
Phone: (402) 399-2355 Toll-free number: (800) 926-5534
Fax: (402) 399-2412
Diane Lee, Vice President of Enrollment Management, College of Saint Mary, 7000 Mercy Road, Omaha, NE 68106

## Concordia University
**Seward, Nebraska**
www.cune.edu                                    CB code: 6116

- Private 4-year university affiliated with Lutheran Church - Missouri Synod
- Residential campus in small town
- 1,066 degree-seeking undergraduates: 2% part-time, 55% women, 1% African American, 1% Hispanic American, 1% international
- 198 degree-seeking graduate students
- 77% of applicants admitted
- SAT or ACT (ACT writing optional) required
- 57% graduate within 6 years; 27% enter graduate study

**General.** Founded in 1894. Regionally accredited. Christ-centered and mission-minded environment. **Degrees:** 256 bachelor's awarded; master's offered. **ROTC:** Army, Air Force. **Location:** 25 miles from Lincoln, 75 miles from Omaha. **Calendar:** Semester, limited summer session. **Full-time faculty:** 56 total; 73% have terminal degrees, 2% minority, 30% women. **Part-time faculty:** 84 total; 34% have terminal degrees, 1% minority, 56% women. **Class size:** 48% < 20, 49% 20-39, 3% 40-49, less than 1% 50-99. **Special facilities:** Rock museum, observatory, arboretum.

**Freshman class profile.** 1,409 applied, 1,080 admitted, 264 enrolled.

| Mid 50% test scores | | | | |
|---|---|---|---|---|
| SAT critical reading: | 470-580 | Rank in top quarter: | 51% |
| SAT math: | 460-570 | Rank in top tenth: | 21% |
| ACT composite: | 21-27 | Return as sophomores: | 77% |
| GPA 3.50 or higher: | 61% | Out-of-state: | 64% |
| GPA 3.0-3.49: | 23% | Live on campus: | 99% |
| GPA 2.0-2.99: | 16% | | |

**Basis for selection.** High school GPA and SAT/ACT scores important in admissions decisions. Audition required for drama, music, and speech programs; portfolio required for art program. **Homeschooled:** Statement describing homeschool structure and mission, transcript of courses and grades, state high school equivalency certificate required.

**High school preparation.** 16 units recommended. Recommended units include English 4, mathematics 3, social studies 3, science 2 and foreign language 1. One unit each in music, art, and physical education recommended.

**2007-2008 Annual costs.** Tuition/fees: $19,790. Room/board: $5,070. Books/supplies: $700. Personal expenses: $1,200.

**Financial aid. Non-need-based:** Scholarships awarded for academics, alumni affiliation, art, athletics, leadership, music/drama, religious affiliation.

**Application procedures. Admission:** Priority date 7/1; deadline 8/1 (receipt date). No application fee. Application may be submitted online. Admission notification on a rolling basis beginning on or about 9/1. Must reply within 30 days of receipt of acceptance letter or request extension. **Financial aid:** Priority date 3/1; no closing date. FAFSA required. Applicants notified on a rolling basis starting 3/1; must reply within 4 week(s) of notification.

**Academics.** Curriculum for degree completion program for bachelor of arts in organizational management contains 16 modules taken sequentially one night a week for 18 months. Summer term offering hybrid online and face to face instruction. **Special study options:** Accelerated study, distance learning, double major, dual enrollment of high school students, ESL, exchange student, independent study, internships, study abroad, teacher certification program. Undergraduate students may take graduate level classes. **Credit/placement by examination:** AP, CLEP, IB, SAT, ACT. **Support services:** Learning center, reduced course load, study skills assistance, tutoring, writing center.

**Majors. Biology:** General. **Business:** General, accounting, business admin, communications, management information systems. **Communications:** General, journalism. **Computer sciences:** Computer science. **Education:** General, art, biology, business, chemistry, computer, elementary, English, ESL, family/consumer sciences, geography, health, history, mathematics, middle, multi-level teacher, music, physical, physics, science, secondary, social studies, Spanish, speech, technology/industrial arts. **English:** English lit, speech/rhetoric. **Foreign languages:** Spanish. **Health:** Predental, premedicine, prenursing, prepharmacy, preveterinary. **History:** General. **Interdisciplinary:** Behavioral sciences. **Legal studies:** Prelaw. **Math:** General. **Parks/recreation:** Exercise sciences, health/fitness, sports admin. **Physical sciences:** General, chemistry. **Psychology:** General. **Social sciences:** Geography. **Theology:** Preministerial, religious ed, sacred music, theology, youth ministry. **Visual/performing arts:** General, art, dramatic, graphic design, piano/organ, studio arts, voice/opera. **Other:** Health and Physical Education.

**Most popular majors.** Business/marketing 10%, education 29%, philosophy/religious studies 21%, psychology 6%, visual/performing arts 7%.

**Computing on campus.** 186 workstations in dormitories, library, computer center, student center. Dormitories wired for high-speed internet access and linked to campus network. Commuter students can connect to campus network. Online course registration, online library, helpline, student web hosting, wireless network available.

**Student life. Freshman orientation:** Mandatory. Preregistration for classes offered. 3 days before classes start. Includes community service events and community building. **Policies:** University responsibly maintains Christian standards of conduct among its students, faculty and staff. **Housing:** Guaranteed on-campus for all undergraduates. Single-sex dorms, special housing for disabled, apartments, substance-free housing available. $200 fully refundable deposit, deadline 8/24. **Activities:** Bands, campus ministries, choral groups, drama, literary magazine, music ensembles, musical theater, student government, student newspaper, symphony orchestra, Circle K, Ongoing Ambassadors for Christ, multicultural awareness club, Peers and Leaders Serving, Habitat for Humanity, Leaders in Physical Health Education, Mission Minded Students, Students in Free Enterprise, Students with Families Association.

**Athletics.** NAIA. **Intercollegiate:** Baseball M, basketball, cross-country, football (tackle) M, golf, soccer, softball W, tennis, track and field, volleyball W. **Intramural:** Basketball, bowling, football (non-tackle), racquetball, soccer, softball, table tennis, tennis, track and field, volleyball. **Team name:** Bulldogs.

**Student services.** Adult student services, alcohol/substance abuse counseling, campus ministries, career counseling, student employment services, financial aid counseling, health services, personal counseling, placement for graduates. **Physically disabled:** Services for visually, speech, hearing impaired.

**Contact.** E-mail: admiss@cune.edu
Phone: (800) 535-5494 Toll-free number: (800) 535-5494 ext. 7233
Fax: (402) 643-4073
Helen Schnell, Director of Undergraduate and Graduate Recruitment, Concordia University, 800 North Columbia Avenue, Seward, NE 68434-1556

## Creative Center
**Omaha, Nebraska**
**www.creativecenter.edu**

♦ For-profit 4-year visual arts and career college
♦ Commuter campus in large city
♦ 105 degree-seeking undergraduates: 4% part-time, 45% women
♦ Application essay, interview required

**General.** Accredited by ACCSCT. **Degrees:** 14 bachelor's, 31 associate awarded. **Calendar:** Semester, limited summer session. **Full-time faculty:** 3 total; 33% women. **Part-time faculty:** 12 total; 42% women. **Class size:** 62% 20-39, 38% 40-49.

**Basis for selection.** Students must provide a letter of recommendation, a letter of intent, a high school transcript and a portfolio to be reviewed and approved. Portfolio required.

**2008-2009 Annual costs.** Tuition/fees (projected): $18,800. Required fees vary by year and program.

**Financial aid.** **Non-need-based:** Scholarships awarded for academics, art.

**Application procedures.** **Admission:** No deadline. $100 fee. Application must be submitted on paper. Admission notification on a rolling basis. **Financial aid:** No deadline. FAFSA required. Applicants notified on a rolling basis starting 1/1.

**Academics.** **Credit/placement by examination:** CLEP. **Support services:** Reduced course load, study skills assistance, tutoring.

**Majors.** **Visual/performing arts:** Graphic design.

**Computing on campus.** PC or laptop required. 8 workstations in library. Online library, helpline, student web hosting, wireless network available.

**Student life.** **Freshman orientation:** Mandatory. Orientation held throughout first week of class.

**Student services.** Career counseling, financial aid counseling, placement for graduates.

**Contact.** E-mail: admissions@creativecenter.edu
Phone: (402) 898-1000 Toll-free number: (888) 898-1789
Fax: (402) 898-1301
Beth Connor, Admissions and Placement Coordinator, Creative Center, 10850 Emmet Street, Omaha, NE 68164

## Creighton University
**Omaha, Nebraska**          **CB member**
**www.creighton.edu**        **CB code: 6121**

♦ Private 4-year university affiliated with Roman Catholic Church
♦ Residential campus in large city
♦ 4,104 degree-seeking undergraduates: 7% part-time, 60% women, 3% African American, 8% Asian American, 4% Hispanic American, 1% Native American, 1% international
♦ 2,888 degree-seeking graduate students
♦ 81% of applicants admitted
♦ SAT or ACT (ACT writing optional), application essay required
♦ 75% graduate within 6 years; 40% enter graduate study

**General.** Founded in 1878. Regionally accredited. **Degrees:** 867 bachelor's, 3 associate awarded; master's, doctoral, first professional offered. **ROTC:** Army, Air Force. **Calendar:** Semester, extensive summer session. **Full-time faculty:** 501 total; 87% have terminal degrees, 12% minority, 41% women. **Part-time faculty:** 180 total; 51% have terminal degrees, 8% minority, 47% women. **Class size:** 46% < 20, 46% 20-39, 4% 40-49, 4% 50-99, less than 1% >100.

**Freshman class profile.** 4,274 applied, 3,476 admitted, 950 enrolled.

| Mid 50% test scores | | | |
|---|---|---|---|
| SAT critical reading: | 530-640 | Rank in top tenth: | 43% |
| SAT math: | 550-660 | End year in good standing: | 96% |
| SAT writing: | 520-640 | Return as sophomores: | 86% |
| ACT composite: | 24-30 | Out-of-state: | 69% |
| GPA 3.50 or higher: | 77% | Live on campus: | 96% |
| GPA 3.0-3.49: | 20% | International: | 1% |
| GPA 2.0-2.99: | 3% | Fraternities: | 27% |
| Rank in top quarter: | 74% | Sororities: | 28% |

**Basis for selection.** School record, type of school, test scores, letters of recommendation important, class rank considered. Applicants may elect to submit personal statement detailing qualifications not reflected in credentials. **Homeschooled:** GED required.

**High school preparation.** 16 units required; 21 recommended. Required and recommended units include English 4, mathematics 3-4, social studies 2-3, history 1, science 2-3, foreign language 2-3 and academic electives 3.

**2008-2009 Annual costs.** Tuition/fees: $28,542. Room/board: $8,516. Books/supplies: $1,000. Personal expenses: $1,400.

**2006-2007 Financial aid.** **Need-based:** 759 full-time freshmen applied for aid; 585 were judged to have need; 585 of these received aid. Average need met was 92%. Average scholarship/grant was $14,853; average loan $5,640. 61% of total undergraduate aid awarded as scholarships/grants, 39% as loans/jobs. **Non-need-based:** Awarded to 2,885 full-time undergraduates, including 817 freshmen. Scholarships awarded for academics, alumni affiliation, art, athletics, leadership, minority status, music/drama, ROTC.

**Application procedures.** **Admission:** Priority date 12/1; deadline 2/15 (postmark date). $40 fee, may be waived for applicants with need. Application may be submitted online. Admission notification on a rolling basis beginning on or about 12/1. Must reply by May 1 or within 2 week(s) if notified thereafter. Preferred reply date May 1 or as soon as possible if notified afterwards. March 1 is priority deadline for scholarship purposes for international students. **Financial aid:** Priority date 3/1; no closing date. FAFSA, institutional form required. Applicants notified on a rolling basis starting 3/15; must reply by 5/1 or within 4 week(s) of notification.

**Academics.** Sequences of courses offered in preengineering, predentistry, prelaw, premedicine, prepharmacy, prephysical therapy, preveterinary. Institution's students given admissions preference into all of university's professional schools. Core curriculum required (61 semester hours from 5 areas: cultures, ideas and civilizations; theology, philosophy and ethics; natural science; social and behavioral sciences; skills). **Special study options:** Accelerated study, combined bachelor's/graduate degree, cross-registration, distance learning, double major, dual enrollment of high school students, ESL, exchange student, honors, independent study, internships, liberal arts/career combination, study abroad, teacher certification program, Washington semester. 3-3 program in engineering with University of Detroit Mercy, 3-3 Law Program within Creighton University, study abroad opportunities at 110 partner institutions in 40 countries. **Credit/placement by examination:** AP, CLEP, IB, SAT, ACT, institutional tests. CLEP Subject Examinations must be taken with essay where applicable. **Support services:** Learning center, pre-admission summer program, reduced course load, remedial instruction, study skills assistance, tutoring, writing center.

**Majors. Area/ethnic studies:** American, Native American. **Biology:** General. **Business:** Accounting, communications, finance, international, management information systems, marketing. **Communications:** General, journalism, organizational. **Computer sciences:** Computer science, programming. **Conservation:** Environmental science. **Education:** Chemistry, elementary, Latin. **English:** American lit, British lit, composition, creative writing, English lit. **Foreign languages:** Ancient Greek, classics, French, German, Latin, Spanish. **Health:** EMT paramedic, health care admin, nursing (RN). **History:** General. **Interdisciplinary:** Math/computer science, peace/conflict. **Legal studies:** Prelaw. **Math:** General, applied. **Parks/recreation:** Exercise sciences. **Philosophy/religion:** Philosophy. **Physical sciences:** Atmospheric science, chemistry, physics. **Psychology:** General. **Public administration:** Social work. **Social sciences:** Anthropology, economics, international relations, political science, sociology. **Visual/performing arts:** Art, arts management, commercial/advertising art, dramatic.

**Most popular majors.** Biology 10%, business/marketing 22%, communications/journalism 8%, health sciences 20%, physical sciences 6%, psychology 7%.

**Computing on campus.** 520 workstations in dormitories, library, computer center, student center. Dormitories wired for high-speed internet access and linked to campus network. Commuter students can connect to campus network. Online course registration, online library, helpline, repair service, student web hosting, wireless network available.

**Student life. Freshman orientation:** Mandatory. Preregistration for classes offered. Welcome week first week of fall semester. **Housing:** Guaranteed on-campus for all undergraduates. Coed dorms, single-sex dorms, special housing for disabled, apartments, substance-free housing available. $100 deposit, deadline 5/1. **Activities:** Bands, campus ministries, choral groups, dance, drama, international student organizations, literary magazine, music ensembles, musical theater, student government, student newspaper, symphony orchestra, world hunger awareness group, Afro-American students association, international relations club, women's resource center, community service center, Christian life community, Young Democrats, Young Republican.

**Athletics.** NCAA. **Intercollegiate:** Baseball M, basketball, cross-country, golf, rowing (crew) W, soccer, softball W, tennis, volleyball W. **Intramural:** Badminton, basketball, bowling, football (non-tackle), golf, racquetball, soccer, softball, tennis, volleyball. **Team name:** Bluejays.

**Student services.** Adult student services, alcohol/substance abuse counseling, campus ministries, career counseling, services for economically disadvantaged, student employment services, financial aid counseling, health services, minority student services, on-campus daycare, personal counseling, placement for graduates, veterans' counselor, women's services. **Physically disabled:** Services for visually, speech, hearing impaired. **Learning disabled:** Comprehensive services available.

**Contact.** E-mail: admissions@creighton.edu
Phone: (402) 280-2703 Toll-free number: (800) 282-5835
Fax: (402) 280-2685
Mary Chase, Director of Admissions, Creighton University, 2500 California Plaza, Omaha, NE 68178-0001

---

## Dana College

**Blair, Nebraska**
**www.dana.edu**

**CB member**
**CB code: 6157**

◗ Private 4-year liberal arts college affiliated with Evangelical Lutheran Church in America

◗ Residential campus in small town

◗ 613 degree-seeking undergraduates: 1% part-time, 47% women, 3% African American, 1% Asian American, 4% Hispanic American

◗ 72% of applicants admitted

◗ SAT or ACT (ACT writing optional) required

◗ 50% graduate within 6 years

**General.** Founded in 1884. Regionally accredited. **Degrees:** 106 bachelor's awarded. **ROTC:** Army, Air Force. **Location:** 20 miles from Omaha. **Calendar:** 4-1-4, limited summer session. **Full-time faculty:** 35 total; 77% have terminal degrees, 3% minority, 60% women. **Part-time faculty:** 33 total; 21% have terminal degrees, 6% minority, 30% women. **Class size:** 72% < 20, 24% 20-39, 4% 40-49. **Special facilities:** Fine arts center, Danish heritage room, Danish immigrant archives.

**Freshman class profile.** 899 applied, 647 admitted, 185 enrolled.

| Mid 50% test scores | | GPA 2.0-2.99: | 33% |
|---|---|---|---|
| SAT critical reading: | 440-480 | Rank in top quarter: | 30% |
| SAT math: | 470-560 | Rank in top tenth: | 11% |
| ACT composite: | 20-25 | Return as sophomores: | 65% |
| GPA 3.50 or higher: | 41% | Out-of-state: | 40% |
| GPA 3.0-3.49: | 26% | Live on campus: | 95% |

**Basis for selection.** 2.0 cumulative GPA in college preparatory courses, standardized test scores important. Recommendations by school officials considered. **Homeschooled:** Transcript of courses and grades required. ACT composite of 18 or above or combined SAT score of 860 or above (exclusive of Writing), a signed parental transcript, plus one of the following: transcript from high school or college where courses were taken, GED score of 500 or above, portfolio of representative work.

**High school preparation.** 16 units recommended. Recommended units include English 4, mathematics 3, social studies 4, science 3 (laboratory 2) and foreign language 2.

**2007-2008 Annual costs.** Tuition/fees: $19,370. Room/board: $5,560. Books/supplies: $750. Personal expenses: $1,150.

**2007-2008 Financial aid. Need-based:** 183 full-time freshmen applied for aid; 159 were judged to have need; 159 of these received aid. Average need met was 96%. Average loan was $4,900. 46% of total undergraduate aid awarded as scholarships/grants, 54% as loans/jobs. **Non-need-based:** Awarded to 776 full-time undergraduates, including 284 freshmen. Scholarships awarded for academics, alumni affiliation, art, athletics, music/drama, religious affiliation, ROTC, state residency. **Additional information:** Auditions recommended for music and drama scholarship applicants. Portfolios recommended for art, graphic design, and cheerleading/dance scholarship applicants.

**Application procedures. Admission:** No deadline. No application fee. Application may be submitted online. Admission notification on a rolling basis. **Financial aid:** Priority date 4/7; no closing date. FAFSA, institutional form required. Applicants notified on a rolling basis starting 3/7; must reply within 3 week(s) of notification.

**Academics. Special study options:** Accelerated study, cross-registration, double major, dual enrollment of high school students, honors, independent study, internships, liberal arts/career combination, New York semester, semester at sea, student-designed major, study abroad, teacher certification program, United Nations semester, urban semester. **Credit/placement by examination:** AP, CLEP, IB, ACT, institutional tests. 30 credit hours maximum toward bachelor's degree. **Support services:** Learning center, reduced course load, remedial instruction, study skills assistance, tutoring.

**Majors. Biology:** General. **Business:** Accounting, business admin, management information systems. **Communications:** General, organizational. **Communications technology:** Animation/special effects. **Computer sciences:** Web page design. **Education:** General, art, biology, business, chemistry, drama/dance, elementary, English, foreign languages, German, history, mathematics, multi-level teacher, music, science, secondary, social science, social studies, Spanish, special, speech. **English:** English lit. **Foreign languages:** Spanish. **Health:** Clinical lab technology, predental, premedicine, prepharmacy, preveterinary. **History:** General. **Legal studies:** Prelaw. **Liberal arts:** Arts/sciences. **Math:** General. **Parks/recreation:** Health/fitness, sports admin. **Philosophy/religion:** Religion. **Physical sciences:** Chemistry. **Protective services:** Law enforcement admin. **Psychology:** General. **Public administration:** Social work. **Visual/performing arts:** Art, commercial/advertising art, musical theater. **Other:** Community journalism.

**Most popular majors.** Business/marketing 16%, education 29%, public administration/social services 8%, security/protective services 10%.

**Computing on campus.** 110 workstations in dormitories, library, computer center. Dormitories wired for high-speed internet access and linked to campus network. Commuter students can connect to campus network. Online library, student web hosting, wireless network available.

**Student life. Freshman orientation:** Mandatory. Preregistration for classes offered. **Housing:** Guaranteed on-campus for all undergraduates. Coed dorms, single-sex dorms, apartments, substance-free housing available. $100 fully refundable deposit. **Activities:** Bands, campus ministries, choral groups, dance, drama, literary magazine, music ensembles, musical theater, radio station, student government, student newspaper, TV station, Fellowship of Christian Athletes, social awareness organization, student activities board, German club, Help Our People Expand, communication club.

**Athletics.** NAIA. **Intercollegiate:** Baseball M, basketball, cross-country, football (tackle) M, golf W, soccer, softball W, track and field, volleyball W, wrestling M. **Intramural:** Basketball, bowling, handball, soccer, softball, swimming, table tennis, tennis, volleyball. **Team name:** Vikings.

**Student services.** Adult student services, alcohol/substance abuse counseling, campus ministries, career counseling, student employment services, financial aid counseling, health services, personal counseling, placement for graduates, veterans' counselor. **Physically disabled:** Services for visually, hearing impaired.

**Contact.** E-mail: admissions@acad2.dana.edu
Phone: (402) 426-7222 Toll-free number: (800) 444-3262
Fax: (402) 426-7386
Duane Heffelfinger, Dean of Enrollment, Dana College, 2848 College Drive, Blair, NE 68008-1099

---

## Doane College

Crete, Nebraska
www.doane.edu

CB member
CB code: 6165

- Private 4-year liberal arts college affiliated with United Church of Christ
- Residential campus in small town
- 921 degree-seeking undergraduates: 1% part-time, 53% women, 4% African American, 1% Asian American, 3% Hispanic American, 1% international
- 75% of applicants admitted
- SAT or ACT (ACT writing optional) required
- 63% graduate within 6 years

**General.** Founded in 1872. Regionally accredited. Campuses also in Lincoln and Grand Island. **Degrees:** 201 bachelor's awarded; master's offered. **ROTC:** Army, Air Force. **Location:** 25 miles from Lincoln, 75 miles from Omaha. **Calendar:** 4-1-4, limited summer session. **Full-time faculty:** 72 total; 72% have terminal degrees, 1% minority, 44% women. **Part-time faculty:** 60 total; 15% have terminal degrees, 45% women. **Class size:** 82% < 20, 18% 20-39. **Special facilities:** Arboretum, open-air theater, observatory, all-American rose test garden, ropes challenge course, fitness trail.

**Freshman class profile.** 1,027 applied, 773 admitted, 259 enrolled.

| Mid 50% test scores | | | |
|---|---|---|---|
| SAT critical reading: | 440-500 | GPA 2.0-2.99: | 29% |
| SAT math: | 460-520 | Rank in top quarter: | 39% |
| ACT composite: | 19-25 | Rank in top tenth: | 13% |
| GPA 3.50 or higher: | 47% | Return as sophomores: | 77% |
| GPA 3.0-3.49: | 24% | Out-of-state: | 30% |
| | | Live on campus: | 99% |

**Basis for selection.** Academic and personal record, recommendations, test scores important. Class rank considered. Interview required for academically marginal students; audition required for drama, music programs and forensics; portfolio required for art program.

**High school preparation.** 13 units recommended. Recommended units include English 4, mathematics 3, social studies 3 and science 3.

**2007-2008 Annual costs.** Tuition/fees: $19,150. Room/board: $5,410. Books/supplies: $800. Personal expenses: $1,030.

**2007-2008 Financial aid. Need-based:** 236 full-time freshmen applied for aid; 209 were judged to have need; 209 of these received aid. Average need met was 94%. Average scholarship/grant was $12,666; average loan $3,390. 47% of total undergraduate aid awarded as scholarships/grants, 53% as loans/jobs. **Non-need-based:** Scholarships awarded for academics, art, athletics, music/drama.

**Application procedures. Admission:** No deadline. No application fee. Application may be submitted online. Admission notification on a rolling basis beginning on or about 9/15. Must reply by May 1 or within 4 week(s) if notified thereafter. **Financial aid:** Priority date 3/1; no closing date. FAFSA required. Applicants notified on a rolling basis starting 3/1; must reply within 2 week(s) of notification.

**Academics.** Midwest Institute for International Students prepares students to meet English language requirement for admission to Doane and other American colleges. **Special study options:** Combined bachelor's/graduate degree, double major, ESL, honors, independent study, internships, student-designed major, study abroad, teacher certification program. 3-2 programs in engineering with Washington University, Columbia University, 3-2 program in environmental and forestry studies with Duke University. **Credit/placement by examination:** AP, CLEP, IB, SAT, ACT, institutional tests. 36 credit hours maximum toward bachelor's degree. International students who successfully complete Midwest Institute ESL program may be admitted without TOEFL scores. **Support services:** Learning center, reduced course load, remedial instruction, study skills assistance, tutoring, writing center.

**Majors. Biology:** General, biochemistry. **Business:** Accounting, business admin. **Communications:** General, journalism, media studies, organizational. **Computer sciences:** General, computer science, information systems. **Conservation:** Environmental studies. **Education:** Elementary, physical, special. **English:** English lit, speech/rhetoric. **Foreign languages:** French, German, Spanish. **History:** General. **Interdisciplinary:** Natural sciences. **Liberal arts:** Arts/sciences. **Math:** General. **Philosophy/religion:** Philosophy, religion. **Physical sciences:** Chemistry, physics. **Psychology:** General. **Public administration:** General. **Social sciences:** General, economics, international relations, political science, sociology. **Visual/performing arts:** Art, commercial/advertising art, dramatic.

**Most popular majors.** Biology 16%, business/marketing 17%, computer/information sciences 6%, education 23%, English 6%, social sciences 6%, visual/performing arts 7%.

**Computing on campus.** 400 workstations in dormitories, library, computer center, student center. Dormitories wired for high-speed internet access and linked to campus network. Commuter students can connect to campus network. Online course registration, online library, helpline, student web hosting, wireless network available.

**Student life. Freshman orientation:** Available. Preregistration for classes offered. **Housing:** Guaranteed on-campus for freshmen. Coed dorms, single-sex dorms available. $200 fully refundable deposit. Unmarried students under 22 not living with parents expected to live on campus. **Activities:** Bands, campus ministries, choral groups, dance, drama, film society, literary magazine, music ensembles, musical theater, radio station, student government, student newspaper, TV station, student education association, Doane speakers, Club Internationale, Fellowship of Christian Athletes, American Minority Student Alliance, College Republicans, Young Democrats.

**Athletics.** NAIA. **Intercollegiate:** Baseball M, basketball, bowling, cross-country, football (tackle) M, golf, soccer, softball W, tennis, track and field, volleyball W. **Intramural:** Basketball, football (tackle) M, golf, softball, swimming, tennis, volleyball. **Team name:** Tigers.

**Student services.** Adult student services, campus ministries, career counseling, student employment services, financial aid counseling, health services, personal counseling, placement for graduates, veterans' counselor.

**Contact.** E-mail: admissions@doane.edu
Phone: (402) 826-8222 Toll-free number: (800) 333-6263
Fax: (402) 826-8600
Cezar Mesquita, Dean of Admission, Doane College, 1014 Boswell Avenue, Crete, NE 68333

---

## Grace University

Omaha, Nebraska
www.graceuniversity.edu

CB code: 6248

- Private 4-year university and Bible college affiliated with interdenominational tradition
- Residential campus in very large city
- 358 degree-seeking undergraduates
- 68 graduate students
- ACT (writing optional), application essay required

**General.** Founded in 1943. Regionally accredited; also accredited by ABHE. **Degrees:** 77 bachelor's, 4 associate awarded; master's offered. **ROTC:** Army, Air Force. **Calendar:** Semester, limited summer session. **Full-time faculty:** 26 total. **Part-time faculty:** 44 total. **Class size:** 87% < 20, 8% 20-39, 1% 40-49, 3% 50-99, less than 1% >100.

**Basis for selection.** School achievement record, religious affiliation/commitment, test scores, recommendations, and student profile important. Conditional admission for students who have not taken SAT/ACT. Audition required for music programs. **Homeschooled:** ACT score of 20 or GED required.

**High school preparation.** Teacher education program requires 4 language arts, 2 mathematics, 2 sciences, 2 social sciences.

**2008-2009 Annual costs.** Tuition/fees (projected): $14,820. Room/board: $5,200. Books/supplies: $800.

**Financial aid. Non-need-based:** Scholarships awarded for academics, alumni affiliation, music/drama.

**Application procedures. Admission:** Priority date 2/1; no deadline. $35 fee, may be waived for applicants with need. Application may be submitted online. Admission notification on a rolling basis. **Financial aid:** Priority date 3/1; no closing date. FAFSA, institutional form required. Applicants

notified on a rolling basis starting 3/1; must reply within 2 week(s) of notification.

**Academics. Special study options:** Accelerated study, distance learning, double major, dual enrollment of high school students, ESL, independent study, internships, liberal arts/career combination, study abroad, teacher certification program. Adult degree completion program. **Credit/placement by examination:** AP, CLEP, ACT. 15 credit hours maximum toward bachelor's degree. Prior work/life experience limited to adult degree completion program. **Support services:** Learning center, reduced course load, study skills assistance, tutoring.

**Majors. Business:** Management science. **Communications:** Broadcast journalism, journalism. **Education:** Business, elementary, English, ESL, history, mathematics, middle, music, secondary, social science. **Health:** Nursing (RN). **Liberal arts:** Arts/sciences. **Psychology:** General. **Theology:** Bible, missionary, religious ed, sacred music, theology.

**Computing on campus.** 35 workstations in library, computer center. Dormitories wired for high-speed internet access and linked to campus network. Commuter students can connect to campus network. Online library, wireless network available.

**Student life. Freshman orientation:** Mandatory. Preregistration for classes offered. Held weekly throughout semester. **Policies:** Religious observance required. **Housing:** Guaranteed on-campus for freshmen. Single-sex dorms, apartments, substance-free housing available. $150 partly refundable deposit. **Activities:** Concert band, choral groups, drama, music ensembles, student government, student newspaper.

**Athletics.** NCCAA. **Intercollegiate:** Basketball, soccer M, volleyball W. **Intramural:** Basketball M, volleyball W. **Team name:** Royals.

**Student services.** Campus ministries, career counseling, student employment services, financial aid counseling, health services, personal counseling, placement for graduates.

**Contact.** E-mail: admissions@graceuniversity.edu
Phone: (402) 449-2831 Toll-free number: (800) 383-1422
Fax: (402) 449-2999
Angie Wayman, Director of Traditional Undergraduate Admissions, Grace University, 1311 South Ninth Street, Omaha, NE 68108-3629

---

## Hastings College

Hastings, Nebraska     **CB member**
www.hastings.edu     **CB code: 6270**

- Private 4-year liberal arts college affiliated with Presbyterian Church (USA)
- Residential campus in large town
- 1,067 degree-seeking undergraduates: 1% part-time, 46% women, 2% African American, 1% Asian American, 3% Hispanic American, 1% international
- 38 degree-seeking graduate students
- 78% of applicants admitted
- SAT or ACT (ACT writing optional) required
- 62% graduate within 6 years; 24% enter graduate study

**General.** Founded in 1882. Regionally accredited. Vocation and Values program asks the campus community to explore how faith intersects with vocation. **Degrees:** 258 bachelor's awarded; master's offered. **Location:** 90 miles from Lincoln, 150 miles from Omaha. **Calendar:** 4-1-4, limited summer session. **Full-time faculty:** 87 total; 71% have terminal degrees, 1% minority, 34% women. **Part-time faculty:** 36 total; 17% have terminal degrees, 3% minority, 56% women. **Special facilities:** Glass blowing studio, observatory, music studios, communications center.

**Freshman class profile.** 1,564 applied, 1,225 admitted, 311 enrolled.

| Mid 50% test scores | | | |
|---|---|---|---|
| SAT critical reading: | 500-600 | Rank in top quarter: | 40% |
| SAT math: | 490-600 | Rank in top tenth: | 16% |
| ACT composite: | 20-26 | Return as sophomores: | 81% |
| GPA 3.50 or higher: | 38% | Out-of-state: | 31% |
| GPA 3.0-3.49: | 38% | Live on campus: | 90% |
| GPA 2.0-2.99: | 24% | Fraternities: | 28% |
| | | Sororities: | 38% |

**Basis for selection.** Academic achievement record most important; counselor recommendations, test scores, class ranking also important. Placement interview strongly recommended for all applicants; interview required for allied health program; audition required for forensics, music, theater programs; portfolio required for art program. **Homeschooled:** ACT or SAT scores, satisfactory completion of high school graduation equivalency required. **Learning Disabled:** Interview recommended.

**High school preparation.** Required and recommended units include English 3-4, mathematics 3-4, social studies 4, history 4, science 3-4 (laboratory 3-4) and foreign language 2.

**2007-2008 Annual costs.** Tuition/fees: $19,604. Room/board: $5,432. Books/supplies: $730. Personal expenses: $1,650.

**Financial aid. Non-need-based:** Scholarships awarded for academics, alumni affiliation, art, athletics, leadership, music/drama.

**Application procedures. Admission:** No deadline. $20 fee, may be waived for applicants with need. Application may be submitted online. Admission notification on a rolling basis beginning on or about 10/15. **Financial aid:** No deadline. FAFSA, institutional form required. Applicants notified on a rolling basis starting 2/15; must reply within 2 week(s) of notification.

**Academics.** College offers 4-year liberal arts program of required courses in arts and humanities, math and science, communications, and other areas. **Special study options:** Combined bachelor's/graduate degree, double major, exchange student, independent study, internships, student-designed major, study abroad, teacher certification program, urban semester. 3-2 engineering programs with Columbia University, Georgia Institute of Technology, and Washington University, Missouri; International exchange program with colleges in England, Holland, Germany and Ireland; BA-BSN program with Creighton University. **Credit/placement by examination:** AP, CLEP, IB. 20 credit hours maximum toward bachelor's degree. All credit by examinations subject to approval of department. **Support services:** Learning center, reduced course load, study skills assistance, tutoring, writing center.

**Majors. Biology:** General. **Business:** Accounting, business admin, human resources, marketing. **Communications:** General, advertising, broadcast journalism, journalism, media studies, public relations, radio/tv. **Communications technology:** General. **Computer sciences:** General, computer science. **Education:** General, art, biology, business, chemistry, drama/dance, early childhood, elementary, English, foreign languages, history, mathematics, music, physical, physics, science, secondary, social science, social studies, special, speech. **English:** Creative writing, English lit, speech/rhetoric. **Foreign languages:** General, German, Spanish. **Health:** Health care admin, predental, premedicine, preveterinary. **History:** General. **Interdisciplinary:** Biopsychology. **Legal studies:** Prelaw. **Liberal arts:** Arts/sciences. **Math:** General. **Parks/recreation:** Exercise sciences, facilities management, health/fitness, sports admin. **Philosophy/religion:** Philosophy, religion. **Physical sciences:** Chemistry, physics. **Protective services:** Corrections. **Psychology:** General. **Public administration:** General, human services. **Social sciences:** Economics, international relations, political science, sociology. **Visual/performing arts:** Art, art history/conservation, dramatic, music history, music pedagogy, music performance, piano/organ, stringed instruments, voice/opera.

**Most popular majors.** Biology 6%, business/marketing 16%, communications/journalism 6%, education 15%, psychology 12%, social sciences 9%, visual/performing arts 15%.

**Computing on campus.** 181 workstations in library, computer center, student center. Dormitories wired for high-speed internet access and linked to campus network. Commuter students can connect to campus network. Online library, repair service, wireless network available.

**Student life. Freshman orientation:** Mandatory. Preregistration for classes offered. Weekend-long program, prior to the first day of class. Includes community service project. **Policies:** Alcohol not permitted on campus except in apartments for students of legal age; smoking forbidden in campus buildings. **Housing:** Guaranteed on-campus for all undergraduates. Coed dorms, single-sex dorms, apartments, substance-free housing available. $200 fully refundable deposit, deadline 8/1. Honors housing, campus houses, apartments available to upperclass students. **Activities:** Bands, choral groups, drama, literary magazine, music ensembles, musical theater, radio station, student government, student newspaper, symphony orchestra, TV station, Fellowship of Christian Athletes, student health advisory council, religious programs committee, Religion in Life Committee, Multicultural Student Union, Peer HIV Education Organization, College Democrats, College Republicans, Habitat for Humanity, gay/straight alliance.

**Athletics.** NAIA. **Intercollegiate:** Baseball M, basketball, cheerleading M, cross-country, football (tackle) M, golf, soccer, softball W, tennis, track and field, volleyball W, wrestling M. **Intramural:** Basketball, bowling, football (non-tackle), racquetball, softball, table tennis, volleyball. **Team name:** Broncos.

**Student services.** Adult student services, campus ministries, career counseling, student employment services, financial aid counseling, health services, minority student services, personal counseling, placement for graduates. **Physically disabled:** Services for hearing impaired.

**Contact.** E-mail: mmolliconi@hastings.edu
Phone: (402) 461-7403 Toll-free number: (800) 532-7642
Fax: (402) 461-7490
Mary Molliconi, Director of Admissions, Hastings College, 710 North
Turner Avenue, Hastings, NE 68901-7621

## ITT Technical Institute: Omaha
**Omaha, Nebraska**
www.itt-tech.edu                                  CB code: 2740

- For-profit 4-year technical college
- Commuter campus in large city

**General.** Accredited by ACICS. **Calendar:** Quarter.

**Contact.** Phone: (402) 331-2900
Director of Recruitment, 9814 M Street, Omaha, NE 68127

## Midland Lutheran College
**Fremont, Nebraska**
www.mlc.edu                                       CB code: 6406

- Private 4-year liberal arts college affiliated with Evangelical Lutheran
  Church in America
- Residential campus in large town
- 827 degree-seeking undergraduates
- 82% of applicants admitted
- ACT (writing optional) required

**General.** Founded in 1883. Regionally accredited. **Degrees:** 153 bachelor's awarded. **Location:** 35 miles from Omaha, 52 miles from Lincoln. **Calendar:** 4-1-4, limited summer session. **Full-time faculty:** 50 total. **Part-time faculty:** 28 total. **Class size:** 49% < 20, 47% 20-39, 3% 40-49, 2% 50-99. **Special facilities:** Planetarium/observatory, arboretum.

**Freshman class profile.** 815 applied, 670 admitted, 215 enrolled.

| Mid 50% test scores | | Rank in top tenth: | 9% |
|---|---|---|---|
| ACT composite: | 19-24 | Out-of-state: | 21% |
| Rank in top quarter: | 14% | Live on campus: | 80% |

**Basis for selection.** School achievement record, test scores, recommendation by school official, rank in top half of class reviewed. Applicants with lesser qualifications considered by review of test scores and personal educational objectives. Interview recommended for all students; audition recommended for drama, music programs.

**High school preparation.** 12 units recommended. Recommended units include English 4, mathematics 2, social studies 2, history 1, science 2 and foreign language 1.

**2007-2008 Annual costs.** Tuition/fees: $20,925. Room/board: $5,150. Books/supplies: $800. Personal expenses: $1,430.

**Financial aid. Non-need-based:** Scholarships awarded for academics, alumni affiliation, art, athletics, leadership, minority status, music/drama, religious affiliation.

**Application procedures. Admission:** No deadline. $30 fee, may be waived for applicants with need. Application may be submitted online. Admission notification on a rolling basis beginning on or about 10/1. **Financial aid:** Priority date 5/1; no closing date. FAFSA required. Applicants notified on a rolling basis starting 3/1; must reply within 4 week(s) of notification.

**Academics. Special study options:** Accelerated study, distance learning, double major, dual enrollment of high school students, independent study, internships, liberal arts/career combination, student-designed major, study abroad, teacher certification program. **Credit/placement by examination:** AP, CLEP, ACT, institutional tests. 32 credit hours maximum toward associate degree, 32 toward bachelor's. **Support services:** Learning center, reduced course load, study skills assistance, tutoring.

**Majors. Area/ethnic studies:** American. **Biology:** General. **Business:** General, accounting, business admin, management information systems, office management. **Communications:** General, journalism, public relations. **Computer sciences:** General, computer science, programming. **Conservation:** General. **Education:** General, art, biology, business, chemistry, early childhood, elementary, English, German, history, mathematics, middle, multilevel teacher, music, physical, science, secondary, social science, social studies, Spanish, speech. **English:** English lit. **Foreign languages:** Spanish. **Health:**

Athletic training, predental, premedicine, preop/surgical nursing, prepharmacy, preveterinary, respiratory therapy technology. **History:** General. **Legal studies:** Paralegal, prelaw. **Liberal arts:** Arts/sciences. **Math:** General. **Philosophy/religion:** Religion. **Physical sciences:** Chemistry. **Psychology:** General. **Public administration:** Human services. **Social sciences:** General, criminology, economics, sociology. **Visual/performing arts:** Art, commercial/advertising art, dramatic, studio arts.

**Most popular majors.** Business/marketing 32%, communications/journalism 8%, education 27%, health sciences 20%, social sciences 10%.

**Computing on campus.** 190 workstations in library, computer center, student center. Dormitories wired for high-speed internet access and linked to campus network. Online library, helpline, wireless network available.

**Student life. Freshman orientation:** Mandatory. Preregistration for classes offered. **Housing:** Guaranteed on-campus for freshmen. Coed dorms, single-sex dorms, special housing for disabled, substance-free housing available. $100 deposit, deadline 8/1. **Activities:** Bands, choral groups, dance, drama, literary magazine, music ensembles, musical theater, student government, student newspaper, Fellowship of Christian Athletes, Circle K, Religious Life Council.

**Athletics.** NAIA. **Intercollegiate:** Baseball M, basketball, cross-country, football (tackle) M, golf, soccer W, softball W, tennis, track and field, volleyball W. **Intramural:** Basketball, bowling, field hockey W, handball, racquetball, soccer M, softball, swimming, tennis, track and field, volleyball. **Team name:** Warriors.

**Student services.** Career counseling, student employment services, health services, personal counseling, placement for graduates.

**Contact.** E-mail: admissions@mlc.edu
Phone: (402) 941-6501 Toll-free number: (800) 642-8382
Fax: (402) 721-0250
Amy Poggendorf, Director of Admissions, Midland Lutheran College, 900 North Clarkson, Fremont, NE 68025

## Nebraska Christian College
**Papillion, Nebraska**
www.nechristian.edu                               CB code: 1332

- Private 4-year Bible college affiliated with Christian Church/Churches of Christ
- Residential campus in large town
- 149 degree-seeking undergraduates
- ACT with writing required

**General.** Founded in 1944. Accredited by ABHE. **Degrees:** 15 bachelor's, 6 associate awarded. **Location:** 110 miles from Omaha. **Calendar:** Semester. **Full-time faculty:** 11 total. **Part-time faculty:** 7 total.

**Freshman class profile.**

| Rank in top quarter: | 19% | Out-of-state: | 45% |
|---|---|---|---|
| Rank in top tenth: | 17% | | |

**Basis for selection.** Christian commitment and references very important; high school transcript or GED required. Transcript of any previous college work required.

**2008-2009 Annual costs.** Tuition/fees: $10,400. Room/board: $4,800. Books/supplies: $600. Personal expenses: $1,900.

**Financial aid. Non-need-based:** Scholarships awarded for academics, leadership.

**Application procedures. Admission:** Closing date 9/1. $25 fee. Application may be submitted online. Admission notification on a rolling basis. **Financial aid:** Priority date 6/1; no closing date. FAFSA, institutional form required. Applicants notified on a rolling basis starting 5/5.

**Academics. Special study options:** Double major, independent study, internships. **Credit/placement by examination:** CLEP.

**Majors. Theology:** Bible, missionary, religious ed, sacred music, theology.

**Computing on campus.** Dormitories wired for high-speed internet access.

**Student life. Freshman orientation:** Available. **Policies:** Religious observance required. **Housing:** Single-sex dorms, apartments available. $100 deposit. **Activities:** Choral groups, drama, music ensembles, student government.

**Athletics.** NCCAA. **Intercollegiate:** Basketball, soccer M, volleyball W. **Intramural:** Basketball M, football (non-tackle), soccer, volleyball. **Team name:** Parsons.

**Student services.** Adult student services, career counseling, student employment services, financial aid counseling, health services, personal counseling, placement for graduates.

**Contact.** E-mail: admissions@nechristian.edu
Phone: (402) 379-5000 Fax: (402) 379-5100
Tim Snyder, Director of Admissions, Nebraska Christian College, 12550 South 114th Street, Papillion, NE 68046

## Nebraska Methodist College of Nursing and Allied Health
**Omaha, Nebraska**
**www.methodistcollege.edu**                    **CB code: 6510**

- Private 4-year health science and nursing college affiliated with United Methodist Church
- Commuter campus in large city
- 504 degree-seeking undergraduates: 26% part-time, 92% women, 3% African American, 3% Asian American, 1% Hispanic American, 1% Native American
- 62 degree-seeking graduate students
- 76% of applicants admitted
- SAT or ACT (ACT writing recommended), application essay, interview required
- 76% graduate within 6 years

**General.** Founded in 1891. Regionally accredited. Health care classes offered at Josie Harper campus. **Degrees:** 101 bachelor's, 28 associate awarded; master's offered. **ROTC:** Army. **Location:** 120 miles from Des Moines, Iowa, 180 miles from Kansas City, Missouri. **Calendar:** Semester, limited summer session. **Full-time faculty:** 43 total; 28% have terminal degrees, 7% minority, 91% women. **Part-time faculty:** 62 total; 5% have terminal degrees, 3% minority, 86% women. **Class size:** 56% < 20, 36% 20-39, 5% 40-49, 4% 50-99. **Special facilities:** Human cadaver lab.

**Freshman class profile.** 96 applied, 73 admitted, 51 enrolled.

| Mid 50% test scores | | | |
|---|---|---|---|
| ACT composite: | 19-23 | Rank in top tenth: | 11% |
| GPA 3.50 or higher: | 36% | End year in good standing: | 96% |
| GPA 3.0-3.49: | 51% | Return as sophomores: | 81% |
| GPA 2.0-2.99: | 13% | Out-of-state: | 5% |
| Rank in top quarter: | 11% | Live on campus: | 80% |

**Basis for selection.** School achievement, test scores most important. Personal statement, interview important. Recommendations, school and community activities considered. **Homeschooled:** Transcript of courses and grades, state high school equivalency certificate required. Submit portfolio demonstrating range and depth of academic ability.

**High school preparation.** 10 units required. Required units include English 4, mathematics 2, social studies 2, science 2 (laboratory 2). Chemistry, biology, and algebra required. A background in physics is strongly recommended for applicants for radiologic technology, sonography, and physical therapist assistant.

**2008-2009 Annual costs.** Tuition/fees: $13,440. Room only: $6,150. Books/supplies: $1,500. Personal expenses: $1,300.

**2006-2007 Financial aid. Need-based:** 37 full-time freshmen applied for aid; 32 were judged to have need; 12 of these received aid. Average need met was 25%. Average scholarship/grant was $4,229; average loan $2,760. 34% of total undergraduate aid awarded as scholarships/grants, 66% as loans/jobs. **Non-need-based:** Awarded to 50 full-time undergraduates, including 10 freshmen. Scholarships awarded for academics, leadership, religious affiliation, ROTC.

**Application procedures. Admission:** Priority date 1/1; deadline 4/1 (receipt date). $25 fee. Application may be submitted online. Admission notification on a rolling basis beginning on or about 1/15. Must reply by 5/15. Application deadlines vary by program. **Financial aid:** Priority date 5/1; no closing date. FAFSA, institutional form required. Applicants notified on a rolling basis starting 3/1; must reply by 5/1 or within 4 week(s) of notification.

**Academics.** Peer tutoring available for most courses. **Special study options:** Accelerated study, distance learning, independent study, internships. **Credit/placement by examination:** AP, CLEP, institutional tests. 9 credit

hours maximum toward associate degree, 9 toward bachelor's. Credit by examination considered on an individual basis. **Support services:** Learning center, reduced course load, remedial instruction, study skills assistance, tutoring, writing center.

**Majors. Health:** Cardiovascular technology, nursing (RN), radiologic technology/medical imaging, respiratory therapy technology, sonography.

**Computing on campus.** 75 workstations in dormitories, library, computer center. Dormitories linked to campus network. Helpline available.

**Student life. Freshman orientation:** Mandatory. Preregistration for classes offered. One-day event for students and parents. **Housing:** Guaranteed on-campus for freshmen. Coed dorms, substance-free housing available. $50 deposit, deadline 6/1. **Activities:** Campus ministries, student government, student nurse association (state and national), allied health student association, College Ambassadors, minority student organization, Pathfinders, residence hall council.

**Student services.** Adult student services, alcohol/substance abuse counseling, campus ministries, career counseling, student employment services, financial aid counseling, health services, minority student services, personal counseling, placement for graduates, veterans' counselor.

**Contact.** E-mail: admissions@methodistcollege.edu
Phone: (402) 354-7200 Toll-free number: (800) 335-5510
Fax: (402) 354-7020
Deann Sterner, Director of Admissions, Nebraska Methodist College of Nursing and Allied Health, 720 North 87th Street, Omaha, NE 68114

## Nebraska Wesleyan University
**Lincoln, Nebraska**
**www.nebrwesleyan.edu**                    **CB code: 6470**

- Private 4-year liberal arts college affiliated with United Methodist Church
- Residential campus in small city
- 1,854 degree-seeking undergraduates: 11% part-time, 57% women, 2% African American, 1% Asian American, 1% Hispanic American
- 219 degree-seeking graduate students
- 80% of applicants admitted
- SAT or ACT (ACT writing optional) required
- 70% graduate within 6 years

**General.** Founded in 1887. Regionally accredited. Non-traditional programs on accelerated semesters. **Degrees:** 418 bachelor's awarded; master's offered. **ROTC:** Army, Air Force. **Location:** 55 miles from Omaha, 200 miles from Kansas City, Missouri. **Calendar:** Semester, limited summer session. **Full-time faculty:** 102 total; 82% have terminal degrees, 2% minority, 50% women. **Part-time faculty:** 71 total; 37% have terminal degrees, 4% minority, 62% women. **Class size:** 59% < 20, 38% 20-39, less than 1% 40-49, 2% 50-99. **Special facilities:** Planetarium, laboratory theatre, greenhouse, herbarium, nuclear magnetic resonance laboratory, sleep laboratory.

**Freshman class profile.** 1,632 applied, 1,300 admitted, 439 enrolled.

| Mid 50% test scores | | | |
|---|---|---|---|
| ACT composite: | 22-27 | Return as sophomores: | 82% |
| Rank in top quarter: | 64% | Out-of-state: | 8% |
| Rank in top tenth: | 27% | Live on campus: | 96% |
| End year in good standing: | 95% | Fraternities: | 14% |
| | | Sororities: | 22% |

**Basis for selection.** Students who rank in the top half of their graduating class or achieve an ACT composite score of 20 or an SAT combined score of 950 (exclusive of Writing) are invited to apply for admission. Campus visit recommended for all students; audition required for drama, music scholarships; portfolio required for art scholarships. **Homeschooled:** Transcript of courses and grades required. GED scores.

**High school preparation.** Recommended units include English 4, mathematics 3, social studies 3, science 3 and foreign language 2.

**2007-2008 Annual costs.** Tuition/fees: $20,252. Room/board: $5,340. Books/supplies: $800. Personal expenses: $1,800.

**2007-2008 Financial aid. Need-based:** 375 full-time freshmen applied for aid; 320 were judged to have need; 320 of these received aid. Average need met was 74%. Average scholarship/grant was $11,913; average loan $4,388. 67% of total undergraduate aid awarded as scholarships/grants, 33% as loans/jobs. **Non-need-based:** Awarded to 494 full-time undergraduates, including 132 freshmen. Scholarships awarded for academics, art, music/drama, religious affiliation.

**Application procedures. Admission:** Closing date 8/15 (postmark date). $20 fee, may be waived for applicants with need. Application may be submitted online. Admission notification on a rolling basis beginning on or about 1/15. Must reply by May 1 or within 4 week(s) if notified thereafter. **Financial aid:** No deadline. FAFSA required. Applicants notified on a rolling basis starting 3/1; must reply within 4 week(s) of notification.

**Academics. Special study options:** Combined bachelor's/graduate degree, double major, dual enrollment of high school students, exchange student, independent study, internships, liberal arts/career combination, semester at sea, study abroad, teacher certification program, United Nations semester, urban semester, Washington semester. 3-2 engineering with Washington University or Columbia University; Capitol Hill Internship Program; Chicago Center for Urban Life and Culture; summer research fellowships in the natural sciences; faculty led international study tours. **Credit/placement by examination:** AP, CLEP, IB, institutional tests. Unlimited number of hours of credit by examination may be counted toward degree. **Support services:** Reduced course load, study skills assistance, tutoring, writing center.

**Majors. Biology:** General, biochemistry, Biochemistry/biophysics and molecular biology. **Business:** Accounting, business admin, international. **Communications:** General, political. **Computer sciences:** Computer science, information technology. **Education:** Elementary, English, middle, music, physical, science, social science, special. **English:** English lit, speech/rhetoric. **Foreign languages:** French, German, Spanish. **Health:** Athletic training, nursing (RN). **History:** General. **Interdisciplinary:** Biopsychology, global studies. **Math:** General. **Parks/recreation:** Exercise sciences, health/fitness, sports admin. **Philosophy/religion:** Philosophy, religion. **Physical sciences:** Chemistry, physics. **Psychology:** General, industrial. **Public administration:** Social work. **Social sciences:** Economics, political science, sociology. **Visual/performing arts:** Art, dramatic, music performance, studio arts. **Other:** Business-sociology, Gender studies.

**Most popular majors.** Biology 7%, business/marketing 23%, education 9%, English 7%, health sciences 13%, parks/recreation 11%, psychology 7%, visual/performing arts 6%.

**Computing on campus.** 360 workstations in dormitories, library, computer center, student center. Dormitories wired for high-speed internet access and linked to campus network. Commuter students can connect to campus network. Online course registration, online library, helpline, repair service, student web hosting, wireless network available.

**Student life. Freshman orientation:** Mandatory. Preregistration for classes offered. Summer 1-day registration sessions in June; 4-day orientation program before fall classes begin. **Housing:** Guaranteed on-campus for all undergraduates. Coed dorms, single-sex dorms, apartments, fraternity/sorority housing, substance-free housing available. $100 nonrefundable deposit, deadline 7/1. Residence hall suites and townhomes. **Activities:** Bands, choral groups, drama, literary magazine, music ensembles, musical theater, opera, student government, student newspaper, student fellowship, Fellowship of Christian Athletes, Rainbow Club, College Republicans, Young Democrats, Nebraskans for Peace, international relations organization, Circle K, environmental action, global service learning.

**Athletics.** NAIA, NCAA. **Intercollegiate:** Baseball M, basketball, cross-country, football (tackle) M, golf, soccer, softball W, tennis, track and field, volleyball W. **Intramural:** Basketball, bowling, football (non-tackle), racquetball, soccer, softball, tennis, volleyball. **Team name:** Prairie Wolves.

**Student services.** Adult student services, campus ministries, career counseling, student employment services, financial aid counseling, health services, minority student services, personal counseling, placement for graduates, women's services. **Physically disabled:** Services for visually, speech, hearing impaired.

**Contact.** E-mail: admissions@nebrwesleyan.edu
Phone: (402) 465-2218 Toll-free number: (800) 541-3818
Fax: (402) 465-2177
Tara Sintek, Director of Admissions, Nebraska Wesleyan University, 5000 St. Paul Avenue, Lincoln, NE 68504

## Peru State College
**Peru, Nebraska**
**www.peru.edu**
CB code: 6468

♦ Public 4-year liberal arts and teachers college
♦ Residential campus in rural community
♦ 1,482 degree-seeking undergraduates

**General.** Founded in 1867. Regionally accredited. Elementary school teacher certification courses offered at Offutt Air Force Base. Online graduate degrees in education and organizational management offered. **Degrees:** 294 bachelor's awarded; master's offered. **Location:** 64 miles from Omaha, 67

miles from Lincoln. **Calendar:** Semester, limited summer session. **Full-time faculty:** 45 total; 78% have terminal degrees, 2% minority, 36% women. **Part-time faculty:** 60 total; 55% women.

**Freshman class profile.** 775 applied, 327 admitted, 219 enrolled.

**Out-of-state:** 7% **Live on campus:** 75%

**Basis for selection.** Open admission, but selective for out-of-state students. Out-of-state applicants must rank in top half of graduating class or have ACT score of 14 or SAT score of 560 (exclusive of Writing), and 2.0 GPA. SAT/ACT scores required of all, however scores are only used in admissions decisions for out-of-state applicants. **Homeschooled:** Transcript of courses and grades required.

**High school preparation.** 16 units recommended. Recommended units include English 4, mathematics 2, social studies 3, science 2 and foreign language 1.

**2007-2008 Annual costs.** Tuition/fees: $4,066; $7,366 out-of-state. Room/board: $4,816. Books/supplies: $600. Personal expenses: $1,000.

**2006-2007 Financial aid.** All financial aid based on need. 37% of total undergraduate aid awarded as scholarships/grants, 63% as loans/jobs.

**Application procedures. Admission:** Priority date 12/1; no deadline. No application fee. Application may be submitted online. Admission notification on a rolling basis beginning on or about 9/1. **Financial aid:** Priority date 3/1; no closing date. FAFSA, institutional form required. Applicants notified on a rolling basis starting 3/1; must reply within 2 week(s) of notification.

**Academics. Special study options:** Cooperative education, cross-registration, distance learning, double major, dual enrollment of high school students, honors, independent study, internships, liberal arts/career combination, study abroad, teacher certification program. **Credit/placement by examination:** CLEP, IB. 16 credit hours maximum toward bachelor's degree. **Support services:** Learning center, reduced course load, remedial instruction, study skills assistance, tutoring.

**Majors. Biology:** Plant physiology. **Business:** Business admin, office technology. **Computer sciences:** General, computer science, programming. **Education:** General, art, biology, computer, early childhood, elementary, English, history, mathematics, middle, music, physical, physics, science, secondary, social science, special, speech, voc/tech. **English:** English lit. **Interdisciplinary:** Natural sciences. **Math:** General. **Protective services:** Law enforcement admin. **Psychology:** General. **Social sciences:** General, sociology. **Visual/performing arts:** Art.

**Most popular majors.** Business/marketing 38%, education 47%, psychology 6%.

**Computing on campus.** 140 workstations in dormitories, library, computer center, student center. Dormitories linked to campus network.

**Student life. Freshman orientation:** Mandatory. Preregistration for classes offered. 5 different 1-day sessions in June, July, August. **Housing:** Guaranteed on-campus for freshmen. Coed dorms, single-sex dorms, apartments, substance-free housing available. $100 deposit. **Activities:** Bands, choral groups, drama, literary magazine, music ensembles, musical theater, student government, student newspaper, TV station, Fellowship of Christian Athletes, multicultural committee, Phi Beta Lambda, Peru Players, Women's Athletic Association, Ambassadors.

**Athletics.** NAIA. **Intercollegiate:** Baseball M, basketball, football (tackle) M, golf W, softball W, volleyball W. **Intramural:** Basketball, soccer, softball, swimming, table tennis, tennis, volleyball, water polo M. **Team name:** Bobcats.

**Student services.** Adult student services, alcohol/substance abuse counseling, campus ministries, career counseling, student employment services, financial aid counseling, health services, on-campus daycare, personal counseling, placement for graduates, veterans' counselor. **Physically disabled:** Services for visually, hearing impaired.

**Contact.** E-mail: admissions@oakmail.peru.edu
Phone: (402) 872-2221 Toll-free number: (800) 742-4412
Fax: (402) 872-2296
Micki Willis, Director of Recruitment and Admissions, Peru State College, Box 10, Peru, NE 68421-0010

## Union College
**Lincoln, Nebraska**
**www.ucollege.edu**
CB code: 6865

♦ Private 4-year liberal arts college affiliated with Seventh-day Adventists
♦ Residential campus in small city

- 867 degree-seeking undergraduates: 12% part-time, 56% women
- 71 graduate students
- 43% of applicants admitted
- SAT or ACT (ACT writing optional), application essay required
- 52% graduate within 6 years

**General.** Founded in 1889. Regionally accredited. **Degrees:** 139 bachelor's, 15 associate awarded; master's offered. **Location:** 50 miles from Omaha. **Calendar:** Semester, limited summer session. **Full-time faculty:** 59 total; 37% have terminal degrees, 14% minority, 37% women. **Part-time faculty:** 42 total; 17% have terminal degrees, 2% minority, 48% women. **Class size:** 69% < 20, 27% 20-39, 2% 40-49, 2% 50-99. **Special facilities:** Arboretum.

**Freshman class profile.** 903 applied, 386 admitted, 164 enrolled.

| Mid 50% test scores | | Rank in top quarter: | 22% |
|---|---|---|---|
| ACT composite: | 20-25 | Rank in top tenth: | 6% |
| GPA 3.50 or higher: | 47% | Return as sophomores: | 72% |
| GPA 3.0-3.49: | 29% | Out-of-state: | 87% |
| GPA 2.0-2.99: | 23% | Live on campus: | 98% |

**Basis for selection.** School achievement record and 3 references (including 1 from pastor) very important. Interview recommended for all students; audition recommended for music program; portfolio recommended for art program.

**High school preparation.** College-preparatory program recommended. 20 units required. Required and recommended units include English 3-4, mathematics 2-3, social studies 1, history 1, science 2-3 (laboratory 1), foreign language 1 and academic electives 3. 2 algebra, 1 geometry, trigonometry recommended for mathematics and science-related programs. Physics and chemistry recommended for nursing, biology, chemistry, physics, engineering, medical technology, premedicine, and predental programs.

**2007-2008 Annual costs.** Tuition/fees: $16,110. Room/board: $4,468. Books/supplies: $950. Personal expenses: $1,200.

**Financial aid.** **Non-need-based:** Scholarships awarded for academics. **Additional information:** Special institutional grants offered to all freshmen and sophomores demonstrating exceptional financial need.

**Application procedures.** **Admission:** No deadline. No application fee. Application may be submitted online. Admission notification on a rolling basis. **Financial aid:** Priority date 5/1; no closing date. FAFSA required. Applicants notified on a rolling basis starting 4/15; must reply by 5/1 or within 3 week(s) of notification.

**Academics.** **Special study options:** Cross-registration, double major, dual enrollment of high school students, ESL, honors, independent study, internships, student-designed major, study abroad, teacher certification program. **Credit/placement by examination:** AP, CLEP, IB, ACT, institutional tests. **Support services:** Learning center, reduced course load, remedial instruction, study skills assistance, tutoring, writing center.

**Majors.** **Biology:** General, biochemistry. **Business:** Accounting, business admin, finance, international finance, management science. **Communications:** Journalism, public relations. **Computer sciences:** Computer science, information systems, systems analysis. **Education:** General, elementary, secondary. **English:** Creative writing, English lit, speech/rhetoric. **Foreign languages:** French, German, Spanish. **History:** General. **Math:** General. **Parks/recreation:** Health/fitness, sports admin. **Philosophy/religion:** Religion. **Physical sciences:** Chemistry, physics. **Psychology:** General. **Public administration:** Social work. **Social sciences:** General. **Theology:** Pastoral counseling, religious ed, theology. **Visual/performing arts:** Commercial/advertising art, music performance, studio arts. **Other:** International Relief and Rescue.

**Most popular majors.** Biology 6%, business/marketing 18%, education 11%, health sciences 30%, visual/performing arts 7%.

**Computing on campus.** 80 workstations in dormitories, library, computer center, student center. Dormitories wired for high-speed internet access and linked to campus network. Commuter students can connect to campus network. Online library, helpline, student web hosting, wireless network available.

**Student life.** **Freshman orientation:** Mandatory. Preregistration for classes offered. **Policies:** Religious observance required. **Housing:** Guaranteed on-campus for all undergraduates. Single-sex dorms, apartments available. **Activities:** Concert band, choral groups, drama, literary magazine, music ensembles, student government, student newspaper, Collegiate Adventists for Better Living, Union for Christ, Union for Kids.

**Athletics.** **Intercollegiate:** Basketball, soccer. **Intramural:** Badminton, basketball, bowling, football (non-tackle), golf, gymnastics, racquetball, soccer, softball, tennis, volleyball. **Team name:** Warriors and Lady Warriors.

**Student services.** Campus ministries, career counseling, student employment services, financial aid counseling, health services, minority student services, personal counseling, placement for graduates. **Physically disabled:** Services for visually, speech, hearing impaired.

**Contact.** E-mail: ucenroll@ucollege.edu
Phone: (402) 486-2504 Toll-free number: (800) 228-4600
Fax: (402) 486-2895
Huda McClelland, Director of Admission, Union College, 3800 South 48th Street, Lincoln, NE 68506-4300

## University of Nebraska - Kearney
### Kearney, Nebraska
### www.unk.edu
CB code: 6467

- Public 4-year university
- Residential campus in large town
- 5,090 degree-seeking undergraduates: 9% part-time, 53% women, 1% African American, 1% Asian American, 4% Hispanic American, 8% international
- 1,295 degree-seeking graduate students
- 79% of applicants admitted
- SAT and SAT Subject Tests or ACT (ACT writing optional) required
- 58% graduate within 6 years

**General.** Founded in 1903. Regionally accredited. **Degrees:** 1,049 bachelor's awarded; master's offered. **Location:** 180 miles from Omaha. **Calendar:** Semester, extensive summer session. **Full-time faculty:** 306 total; 78% have terminal degrees, 7% minority, 45% women. **Part-time faculty:** 74 total; 27% have terminal degrees, 4% minority, 62% women. **Class size:** 37% < 20, 50% 20-39, 7% 40-49, 5% 50-99, less than 1% >100. **Special facilities:** Nebraska state art collection, state arboretum, planetarium.

**Freshman class profile.** 2,646 applied, 2,092 admitted, 996 enrolled.

| Mid 50% test scores | | Rank in top quarter: | 36% |
|---|---|---|---|
| SAT critical reading: | 410-600 | Rank in top tenth: | 15% |
| SAT math: | 410-520 | Return as sophomores: | 79% |
| SAT writing: | 440-540 | Out-of-state: | 9% |
| ACT composite: | 19-25 | Live on campus: | 83% |
| GPA 3.50 or higher: | 44% | International: | 9% |
| GPA 3.0-3.49: | 27% | Fraternities: | 11% |
| GPA 2.0-2.99: | 27% | Sororities: | 13% |

**Basis for selection.** Test scores, school achievement record most important. Applicants who show promise of academic success, but do not meet admission requirements, may be admitted on conditional basis.

**High school preparation.** 16 units required. Required units include English 4, mathematics 3, social studies 3, science 3 (laboratory 1), foreign language 2 and academic electives 1.

**2007-2008 Annual costs.** Tuition/fees: $5,021; $9,341 out-of-state. Room/board: $6,000. Books/supplies: $836. Personal expenses: $2,424.

**Financial aid.** **Non-need-based:** Scholarships awarded for academics, alumni affiliation, art, athletics, leadership, minority status, music/drama, state residency.

**Application procedures.** **Admission:** Priority date 8/1; no deadline. $45 fee. Application may be submitted online. Admission notification on a rolling basis beginning on or about 10/1. **Financial aid:** Priority date 4/1; no closing date. FAFSA, institutional form required. Applicants notified on a rolling basis starting 3/15; must reply within 2 week(s) of notification.

**Academics.** **Special study options:** Cooperative education, distance learning, double major, dual enrollment of high school students, ESL, exchange student, honors, independent study, internships, study abroad, teacher certification program. International student exchange program with Sapporo University and Kansai Gaidai, Japan; Nebraska semester abroad. **Credit/placement by examination:** CLEP, SAT, ACT, institutional tests. 45 credit hours maximum toward bachelor's degree. **Support services:** Learning center, study skills assistance, tutoring, writing center.

**Majors.** **Agriculture:** Business. **Biology:** General. **Business:** Business admin, office management, office/clerical, operations, tourism/travel. **Communications:** General, advertising, broadcast journalism, journalism. **Computer sciences:** General, information systems. **Education:** General, art, biology, business, chemistry, early childhood, elementary, English, ESL, family/consumer sciences, foreign languages, French, German, health, history, learning disabled, mathematics, mentally handicapped, middle, multiple handicapped, music, physical, physically handicapped, physics, science, secondary, social science, Spanish, special, speech, speech impaired, technology/industrial arts, trade/industrial. **English:** English lit, speech/rhetoric. **Family/**

consumer sciences: General, business, clothing/textiles, family studies, housing. **Foreign languages:** French, German, Spanish, translation. **Health:** Medical radiologic technology/radiation therapy, respiratory therapy technology, speech pathology. **History:** General. **Liberal arts:** Arts/sciences. **Math:** General. **Parks/recreation:** Facilities management, sports admin. **Philosophy/religion:** Philosophy. **Physical sciences:** Chemistry, physics. **Protective services:** Criminal justice, police science. **Psychology:** General. **Public administration:** Social work. **Social sciences:** General, economics, geography, international relations, political science, sociology. **Visual/performing arts:** General, art, art history/conservation, commercial/advertising art, dramatic, music performance, studio arts.

**Most popular majors.** Business/marketing 22%, education 18%, parks/recreation 6%, security/protective services 6%.

**Computing on campus.** 411 workstations in dormitories, library, computer center, student center. Dormitories wired for high-speed internet access and linked to campus network. Commuter students can connect to campus network. Online course registration, helpline, repair service, wireless network available.

**Student life. Freshman orientation:** Available. Preregistration for classes offered. **Housing:** Guaranteed on-campus for freshmen. Coed dorms, single-sex dorms, apartments, fraternity/sorority housing available. Honors residence hall available. **Activities:** Bands, choral groups, dance, drama, music ensembles, musical theater, radio station, student government, student newspaper, symphony orchestra, TV station, Young Republicans, Young Democrats, Alpha Phi Omega, Fellowship of Christian Athletes, international student association, People of Color.

**Athletics.** NCAA. **Intercollegiate:** Baseball M, basketball, cross-country, diving W, football (tackle) M, golf, softball W, swimming W, tennis, track and field, volleyball W, wrestling M. **Intramural:** Archery, badminton, basketball, bowling, cross-country, diving, football (non-tackle), golf, racquetball, soccer, softball, swimming, table tennis, tennis, track and field, volleyball, water polo, wrestling M. **Team name:** Lopers.

**Student services.** Alcohol/substance abuse counseling, career counseling, student employment services, financial aid counseling, health services, minority student services, on-campus daycare, personal counseling, placement for graduates, veterans' counselor, women's services. **Physically disabled:** Services for visually, hearing impaired.

**Contact.** E-mail: admissionsug@unk.edu
Phone: (308) 865-8526 Toll-free number: (800) 532-7639
Fax: (308) 865-8987
Dusty Newton, Director of Admissions, University of Nebraska - Kearney, 905 West 25th, Kearney, NE 68849

---

## University of Nebraska - Lincoln
### Lincoln, Nebraska
www.unl.edu

**CB member**
**CB code: 6877**

- Public 4-year university
- Residential campus in small city
- 18,053 degree-seeking undergraduates: 7% part-time, 46% women, 2% African American, 3% Asian American, 3% Hispanic American, 1% Native American, 3% international
- 4,144 degree-seeking graduate students
- 62% of applicants admitted
- SAT and SAT Subject Tests or ACT (ACT writing optional) required
- 63% graduate within 6 years

**General.** Founded in 1869. Regionally accredited. Nebraska's only land-grant university. Research opportunities impacting state's economic development available to students. **Degrees:** 3,217 bachelor's, 8 associate awarded; master's, doctoral, first professional offered. **ROTC:** Army, Naval, Air Force. **Location:** 50 miles from Omaha. **Calendar:** Semester, extensive summer session. **Full-time faculty:** 1,068 total; 96% have terminal degrees, 16% minority, 28% women. **Part-time faculty:** 14 total; 100% have terminal degrees, 7% minority, 29% women. **Class size:** 39% < 20, 42% 20-39, 6% 40-49, 7% 50-99, 7% >100. **Special facilities:** State museum, planetarium, center for performing arts, arboretum, center for Asian Culture, center for Great Plains studies, center for biomaterials and genetic research.

**Freshman class profile.** 9,598 applied, 5,978 admitted, 4,235 enrolled.

| Mid 50% test scores | | | |
|---|---|---|---|
| SAT critical reading: | 500-650 | Return as sophomores: | 83% |
| SAT math: | 530-670 | Out-of-state: | 21% |
| ACT composite: | 22-28 | Live on campus: | 90% |
| Rank in top quarter: | 53% | International: | 2% |
| Rank in top tenth: | 27% | Fraternities: | 22% |
| | | Sororities: | 24% |

**Basis for selection.** Students must meet minimum requirements of ACT composite score of 20 or higher, SAT combined score of 950 (exclusive of writing) or rank in top half of class. Audition required for music program. **Homeschooled:** Statement describing homeschool structure and mission, transcript of courses and grades required.

**High school preparation.** 16 units required. Required and recommended units include English 4, mathematics 4, social studies 3, history 1, science 3 (laboratory 1) and foreign language 2. Mathematics must include algebra I and II, geometry, and 1 higher level math. 2 units of foreign language must be in same language. At least 1 social studies should be U.S. and/or world history and 1 additional unit should be history, American government, and/or geography. College of Engineering & Technology requires 1 pre-calculus/trigonometry, 1 physics and 1 chemistry. Architecture requires 0.5 trigonometry or pre-calculus for pre-architecture.

**2007-2008 Annual costs.** Tuition/fees: $6,216; $16,236 out-of-state. Room/board: $6,523. Books/supplies: $950. Personal expenses: $2,009.

**2006-2007 Financial aid. Need-based:** 2,703 full-time freshmen applied for aid; 1,744 were judged to have need; 1,722 of these received aid. Average need met was 88%. Average scholarship/grant was $6,419; average loan $2,908. 49% of total undergraduate aid awarded as scholarships/grants, 51% as loans/jobs. **Non-need-based:** Awarded to 2,353 full-time undergraduates, including 922 freshmen. Scholarships awarded for academics, alumni affiliation, art, athletics, leadership, minority status, music/drama, state residency.

**Application procedures. Admission:** Priority date 1/15; deadline 5/1 (receipt date). $45 fee, may be waived for applicants with need. Application may be submitted online. Admission notification on a rolling basis beginning on or about 9/1. **Financial aid:** Priority date 4/15; no closing date. FAFSA required. Applicants notified on a rolling basis starting 4/1.

**Academics.** Comprehensive Education Program (CEP) is required of all entering students. Master of architecture professional degree available. **Special study options:** Accelerated study, combined bachelor's/graduate degree, cooperative education, cross-registration, distance learning, double major, dual enrollment of high school students, ESL, exchange student, external degree, honors, independent study, internships, liberal arts/career combination, student-designed major, study abroad, teacher certification program. **Credit/placement by examination:** AP, CLEP, IB, SAT, ACT, institutional tests. Individual colleges have different policies. **Support services:** Learning center, pre-admission summer program, reduced course load, remedial instruction, study skills assistance, tutoring, writing center.

**Honors college/program.** Formal application required. Acceptance based on evaluation of the student's potential by the faculty committee.

**Majors. Agriculture:** General, agronomy, animal sciences, business, communications, economics, food science, horticultural science, landscaping, mechanization, plant protection, products processing, range science, soil science. **Architecture:** Architecture, interior, landscape. **Area/ethnic studies:** Latin American, regional, Western European, women's. **Biology:** General, biochemistry, botany. **Business:** Accounting, actuarial science, business admin, finance, hospitality admin, international, management science, managerial economics, marketing. **Communications:** General, advertising, broadcast journalism, journalism. **Computer sciences:** General. **Conservation:** General, environmental studies, management/policy. **Education:** Agricultural, art, biology, business, chemistry, computer, Deaf/hearing impaired, elementary, English, ESL, foreign languages, French, German, health, history, mathematics, middle, multi-level teacher, music, physical, physics, reading, sales/marketing, science, social science, Spanish, technology/industrial arts, trade/industrial. **Engineering:** Agricultural, architectural, biomedical, chemical, civil, computer, electrical, industrial, mechanical. **Engineering technology:** Construction, electrical, industrial. **English:** English lit. **Family/consumer sciences:** General, clothing/textiles, food/nutrition, housing. **Foreign languages:** Ancient Greek, classics, French, German, Latin, Russian, Spanish. **Health:** Athletic training, community health services, predental, premedicine, prepharmacy, preveterinary, speech pathology, veterinary technology/assistant. **History:** General. **Interdisciplinary:** Ancient studies, medieval/Renaissance. **Liberal arts:** Arts/sciences, humanities. **Math:** General. **Parks/recreation:** Exercise sciences. **Philosophy/religion:** Philosophy. **Physical sciences:** Atmospheric science, chemistry, geology, hydrology, physics. **Protective services:** Forensics. **Psychology:** General. **Social sciences:** Anthropology, economics, geography, international relations, political science, sociology. **Visual/performing arts:** Art history/conservation, dance, dramatic, film/cinema, studio arts. **Other:** Child, youth and family studies, Ethnic studies, News & editorial, Technical education.

**Most popular majors.** Agriculture 8%, business/marketing 22%, education 14%, engineering/engineering technologies 12%.

**Computing on campus.** 650 workstations in dormitories, library, computer center, student center. Dormitories wired for high-speed internet access and linked to campus network. Commuter students can connect to campus network. Online course registration, online library, helpline, student web hosting available.

**Student life. Freshman orientation:** Available. Preregistration for classes offered. Day-long program conducted from mid-June to mid-July. **Policies:** No smoking allowed in University buildings. No alcohol or firearms on campus. **Housing:** Guaranteed on-campus for freshmen. Coed dorms, single-sex dorms, special housing for disabled, apartments, cooperative housing, fraternity/sorority housing, substance-free housing available. $400 partly refundable deposit, deadline 5/1. Pets allowed in dorm rooms. Special interest floors available. Freshmen required to live on campus if not living with parents or close relatives. **Activities:** Bands, choral groups, dance, drama, film society, literary magazine, music ensembles, musical theater, opera, radio station, student government, student newspaper, symphony orchestra, TV station, Afrikaan People's Union, University of Nebraska Inter-Tribal Exchange, Mexican-American student association, adult student network, Ecology Now, student foundation, student-alumni association, UNL Entrepreneurial Society.

**Athletics.** NCAA. **Intercollegiate:** Baseball M, basketball, bowling W, cross-country, diving W, football (tackle) M, golf, gymnastics, rifle W, rodeo, rowing (crew), soccer W, softball W, swimming W, tennis, track and field, volleyball W, wrestling M. **Intramural:** Football (non-tackle), soccer, softball, tennis, track and field, volleyball, water polo, wrestling M. **Team name:** Cornhuskers.

**Student services.** Adult student services, alcohol/substance abuse counseling, campus ministries, career counseling, services for economically disadvantaged, student employment services, financial aid counseling, health services, legal services, minority student services, on-campus daycare, personal counseling, placement for graduates, veterans' counselor, women's services. **Physically disabled:** Services for visually, speech, hearing impaired.

**Contact.** E-mail: admissions@unl.edu
Phone: (402) 472-2023 Toll-free number: (800) 742-8800
Fax: (402) 472-0670
Alan Cerveny, Dean of Admissions, University of Nebraska - Lincoln, 1410 Q Street, Lincoln, NE 68588-0417

---

## University of Nebraska - Omaha

Omaha, Nebraska        **CB member**
www.unomaha.edu        **CB code: 6420**

♦ Public 4-year university

♦ Commuter campus in large city

♦ 11,080 degree-seeking undergraduates: 22% part-time, 52% women, 6% African American, 3% Asian American, 4% Hispanic American, 1% Native American, 2% international

♦ 2,548 degree-seeking graduate students

♦ 86% of applicants admitted

♦ SAT or ACT (ACT writing optional) required

♦ 41% graduate within 6 years

**General.** Founded in 1908. Regionally accredited. Cooperative classes at Offutt Air Force Base. Cooperative programs with UNMC medical center. **Degrees:** 1,832 bachelor's awarded; master's, doctoral offered. **ROTC:** Army, Air Force. **Location:** 160 miles from Kansas City, Missouri. **Calendar:** Semester, extensive summer session. **Full-time faculty:** 487 total; 81% have terminal degrees, 17% minority, 42% women. **Part-time faculty:** 393 total; 23% have terminal degrees, 10% minority, 49% women. **Class size:** 31% < 20, 47% 20-39, 9% 40-49, 11% 50-99, 2% >100. **Special facilities:** Outdoor venture center, climbing wall, nature preserve, planetarium, Nebraska Book Arts Center.

**Freshman class profile.** 3,909 applied, 3,359 admitted, 1,680 enrolled.

| Mid 50% test scores | | | |
|---|---|---|---|
| SAT critical reading: | 390-520 | Rank in top tenth: | 11% |
| SAT math: | 380-440 | Return as sophomores: | 74% |
| ACT composite: | 19-25 | Out-of-state: | 6% |
| GPA 3.50 or higher: | 41% | Live on campus: | 30% |
| GPA 3.0-3.49: | 28% | International: | 2% |
| GPA 2.0-2.99: | 29% | Fraternities: | 5% |
| Rank in top quarter: | 34% | Sororities: | 4% |

**Basis for selection.** School achievement record, test scores important. Must have ACT score of 20, comparable SAT score or class rank in upper half of graduating class. Admitted for special talent consideration on case by case basis. Open admission for non-degree applicants and non-traditional adult freshman applicants. Audition required for music program. **Homeschooled:** Applicants must submit official GED scores verifying successful completion of the GED. An ACT composite score of 25+ may be substituted in lieu of the GED score.

**High school preparation.** 16 units required. Required units include English 4, mathematics 3, social studies 1, history 2, science 3 (laboratory 1), foreign language 2 and academic electives 1. Specific course requirements for programs in business administration, human resources and family services for College of Engineering and Technology.

**2007-2008 Annual costs.** Tuition/fees: $5,485; $14,522 out-of-state. Room/board: $4,840. Books/supplies: $800. Personal expenses: $2,050.

**2007-2008 Financial aid. Need-based:** 1,156 full-time freshmen applied for aid; 743 were judged to have need; 712 of these received aid. Average scholarship/grant was $1,673; average loan $2,040. 43% of total undergraduate aid awarded as scholarships/grants, 57% as loans/jobs. **Non-need-based:** Awarded to 1,682 full-time undergraduates, including 527 freshmen. Scholarships awarded for academics, alumni affiliation, art, athletics, leadership, minority status, music/drama, ROTC, state residency.

**Application procedures. Admission:** Closing date 8/1 (postmark date). $45 fee. Application may be submitted online. Admission notification on a rolling basis. **Financial aid:** Priority date 3/1; no closing date. FAFSA required. Applicants notified on a rolling basis starting 4/15; must reply within 2 week(s) of notification.

**Academics.** Associate degree program available on Omaha campus through University of Nebraska-Lincoln in construction, drafting and design technology, electronic technology, fire control and safety technology, fire protection, manufacturing technology. On-line courses in aviation studies also available. **Special study options:** Combined bachelor's/graduate degree, cooperative education, cross-registration, distance learning, double major, dual enrollment of high school students, ESL, exchange student, honors, independent study, internships, student-designed major, study abroad, teacher certification program. **Credit/placement by examination:** AP, CLEP, ACT, institutional tests. 30 credit hours maximum toward bachelor's degree. CLEP exams in American History and Western Civilization must be accompanied by essay. **Support services:** Reduced course load, study skills assistance, tutoring, writing center.

**Majors. Area/ethnic studies:** African-American, Latin American, women's. **Biology:** General, bioinformatics, biotechnology. **Business:** General, accounting, banking/financial services, finance, management information systems, managerial economics, market research, marketing, organizational behavior, real estate. **Communications:** General, broadcast journalism, journalism. **Computer sciences:** Computer science, security. **Conservation:** Environmental studies. **Education:** Elementary, music, physical, secondary, special, speech impaired. **Engineering:** Architectural, chemical, civil, computer, electrical, physics. **Engineering technology:** Construction, industrial, manufacturing. **English:** Creative writing, English lit, speech/rhetoric. **Family/consumer sciences:** General, communication, family resources. **Foreign languages:** French, German, Spanish. **Health:** Community health services, health care admin. **History:** General. **Interdisciplinary:** Gerontology, global studies, natural sciences. **Liberal arts:** Library science. **Math:** General. **Parks/recreation:** General. **Philosophy/religion:** Philosophy, religion. **Physical sciences:** Chemistry, geology, physics. **Protective services:** Criminal justice. **Psychology:** General. **Public administration:** General, social work. **Social sciences:** Geography, political science, sociology, urban studies. **Transportation:** Aviation, aviation management. **Visual/performing arts:** Art, art history/conservation, dramatic, music performance, music theory/composition, piano/organ, stringed instruments, studio arts, voice/opera.

**Most popular majors.** Biology 6%, business/marketing 28%, education 14%, security/protective services 10%.

**Computing on campus.** 2,300 workstations in dormitories, library, computer center, student center. Dormitories wired for high-speed internet access and linked to campus network. Commuter students can connect to campus network. Online course registration, online library, helpline, student web hosting, wireless network available.

**Student life. Freshman orientation:** Mandatory. Preregistration for classes offered. Held every week April 15 thru August 1st. **Housing:** Coed dorms, substance-free housing available. $250 partly refundable deposit. **Activities:** Bands, campus ministries, choral groups, dance, drama, film society, literary magazine, music ensembles, musical theater, opera, radio station, student government, student newspaper, symphony orchestra, TV station, American multi-cultural students, chapter summary Bible study, student government legislative & public relations, Campus Crusade for Christ, honor societies, Greek letter organizations.

**Athletics. NCAA. Intercollegiate:** Baseball M, basketball, cross-country W, football (tackle) M, golf W, ice hockey M, soccer W, softball W, swimming W, tennis W, track and field W, volleyball W, wrestling M. **Intramural:** Badminton, basketball, bowling, golf, gymnastics, handball, racquetball, soccer, softball, squash, swimming, tennis, volleyball, wrestling M. **Team name:** Mavericks.

**Student services.** Adult student services, alcohol/substance abuse counseling, campus ministries, career counseling, services for economically disadvantaged, student employment services, financial aid counseling, health services, minority student services, on-campus daycare, personal counseling, placement for graduates, veterans' counselor, women's services. **Physically disabled:** Services for visually, speech, hearing impaired.

**Contact.** E-mail: unoadm@mail.unomaha.edu
Phone: (402) 554-2393 Toll-free number: (800) 585-8648
Fax: (402) 554-3472
Jolene Adams, Director of Admissions, University of Nebraska - Omaha, 6001 Dodge Street, Omaha, NE 68182-0005

## University of Nebraska Medical Center
**Omaha, Nebraska**
www.unmc.edu                                            CB code: 6896

- Public two-year upper-division health science college
- Commuter campus in very large city
- 44% of applicants admitted

**General.** Founded in 1869. Regionally accredited. Students must have 30 plus transfer hours to be admitted to UNMC. **Degrees:** 402 bachelor's awarded; master's, doctoral, first professional offered. **ROTC:** Army, Air Force. **Calendar:** Semester, limited summer session. **Full-time faculty:** 804 total; 90% have terminal degrees, 18% minority, 40% women. **Part-time faculty:** 191 total; 80% have terminal degrees, 7% minority, 52% women.

**Student profile.** 812 degree-seeking undergraduates, 1,798 degree-seeking graduate students. 951 applied as first time-transfer students, 421 admitted, 366 enrolled. 16% entered as juniors, 12% entered as seniors. 5% transferred from two-year, 95% transferred from four-year institutions.

| | | | |
|---|---|---|---|
| Women: | 88% | International: | 1% |
| African American: | 1% | Part-time: | 7% |
| Asian American: | 2% | Out-of-state: | 10% |
| Hispanic American: | 3% | 25 or older: | 31% |

**Basis for selection.** College transcript required. Admissions requirements, application procedures, and closing dates vary by program. Health professions program applicants must have completed prerequisite courses at another institution. Transfer accepted as sophomores, juniors, seniors.

**2007-2008 Annual costs.** Tuition/fees: $5,450; $15,470 out-of-state. Tuition varies by program. Books/supplies: $900. Personal expenses: $1,500.

**Financial aid. Need-based:** 863 applied for aid; 729 were judged to have need; 719 of these received aid. Average need met was 55.86%. 34% of total undergraduate aid awarded as scholarships/grants, 66% as loans/jobs. **Non-need-based:** Awarded to 209 undergraduates. **Additional information:** Parental data collected from applicants for certain types of aid.

**Application procedures. Admission:** $45 fee, may be waived for applicants with need. **Financial aid:** Priority date 4/1, no deadline. Applicants notified on a rolling basis starting 5/1; must reply within 2 weeks of notification. FAFSA, institutional form required.

**Academics. Special study options:** Combined bachelor's/graduate degree, distance learning, honors. **Credit/placement by examination:** CLEP, IB, institutional tests. 24 credit hours maximum toward bachelor's degree.

**Majors. Health:** Clinical lab science, dental hygiene, medical radiologic technology/radiation therapy, nuclear medical technology, nursing (RN), radiologic technology/medical imaging, sonography.

**Computing on campus.** 108 workstations in library, computer center, student center. Commuter students can connect to campus network. Online library, helpline, repair service, wireless network available.

**Student life. Housing:** Apartments available. **Activities:** Student government, Committee on Minority Concerns, American Academy of Physician. Assistants, Religious Life Council, Christian Fellowship, Student Association for Rural Health, student services council, student professional organizations.

**Athletics. Intramural:** Basketball, softball, volleyball.

**Student services.** Alcohol/substance abuse counseling, career counseling, services for economically disadvantaged, financial aid counseling, health services, minority student services, on-campus daycare, personal counseling, veterans' counselor. **Physically disabled:** Services for hearing impaired.

**Contact.** E-mail: ttonjes@unmc.edu
Phone: (402) 559-6468 Toll-free number: (800) 626-8431 ext. 96468
Fax: (402) 559-6796
University of Nebraska Medical Center, 984230 Nebraska Medical Center, Omaha, NE 68198-4230

## Wayne State College
**Wayne, Nebraska**                                     CB member
www.wsc.edu                                             CB code: 6469

- Public 4-year liberal arts and teachers college
- Residential campus in small town
- 2,802 degree-seeking undergraduates: 8% part-time, 54% women, 3% African American, 1% Asian American, 2% Hispanic American, 1% Native American, 1% international
- 636 degree-seeking graduate students
- 52% graduate within 6 years

**General.** Founded in 1909. Regionally accredited. Campus is state arboretum. **Degrees:** 546 bachelor's awarded; master's offered. **ROTC:** Army. **Location:** 45 miles from Sioux City, Iowa. **Calendar:** Semester, extensive summer session. **Full-time faculty:** 132 total; 74% have terminal degrees, 4% minority, 46% women. **Part-time faculty:** 77 total; 16% have terminal degrees, 5% minority, 71% women. **Class size:** 43% < 20, 47% 20-39, 7% 40-49, 2% 50-99. **Special facilities:** Planetarium, outdoor amphitheater.

**Freshman class profile.** 1,356 applied, 1,356 admitted, 661 enrolled.

| Mid 50% test scores | | Rank in top tenth: | 11% |
|---|---|---|---|
| ACT composite: | 18-24 | Return as sophomores: | 75% |
| GPA 3.50 or higher: | 40% | Out-of-state: | 19% |
| GPA 3.0-3.49: | 26% | Live on campus: | 93% |
| GPA 2.0-2.99: | 30% | International: | 1% |
| Rank in top quarter: | 32% | | |

**Basis for selection.** Open admission.

**High school preparation.** 12 units recommended. Recommended units include English 4, mathematics 3, social studies 3 and science 2. Computer literacy, fine & performing arts and foreign language are also recommended.

**2007-2008 Annual costs.** Tuition/fees: $4,322; $7,622 out-of-state. Room/board: $4,800. Books/supplies: $900. Personal expenses: $930.

**2007-2008 Financial aid. Need-based:** 551 full-time freshmen applied for aid; 409 were judged to have need; 402 of these received aid. Average need met was 32%. Average scholarship/grant was $1,657; average loan $1,574. 40% of total undergraduate aid awarded as scholarships/grants, 60% as loans/jobs. **Non-need-based:** Awarded to 719 full-time undergraduates, including 225 freshmen. Scholarships awarded for academics, alumni affiliation, art, athletics, leadership, minority status, music/drama, religious affiliation, state residency.

**Application procedures. Admission:** Priority date 12/1; deadline 8/20. $30 fee. Application may be submitted online. Admission notification on a rolling basis beginning on or about 9/15. Maximum period of postponement: 1 semester. **Financial aid:** Priority date 4/1; no closing date. FAFSA required. Applicants notified on a rolling basis starting 3/1; must reply within 3 week(s) of notification.

**Academics. Special study options:** Cooperative education, distance learning, double major, dual enrollment of high school students, honors, independent study, internships, student-designed major, study abroad, teacher certification program. **Credit/placement by examination:** AP, CLEP, institutional tests. **Support services:** Learning center, reduced course load, study skills assistance, tutoring, writing center.

**Majors. Biology:** General. **Business:** Business admin. **Communications:** General, journalism, media studies. **Computer sciences:** General, information systems. **Education:** Art, biology, business, chemistry, drama/dance, early childhood, elementary, English, family/consumer sciences, foreign languages, geography, history, mathematics, middle, music, physical, psychology, social science, special, speech, technology/industrial arts. **Engineering technology:** General. **English:** English lit. **Family/consumer sciences:** General, food/nutrition. **Foreign languages:** General, Spanish. **Health:** Athletic training. **History:** General. **Math:** General. **Parks/recreation:** Exercise sciences, health/fitness, sports admin. **Physical sciences:** Chemistry. **Protective services:** Criminal justice. **Psychology:** General. **Social sciences:** General, geography, political science, sociology. **Visual/performing arts:** Art, dramatic, graphic design.

**Most popular majors.** Biology 6%, business/marketing 21%, communications/journalism 6%, education 24%, parks/recreation 7%, psychology 7%, security/protective services 7%.

**Computing on campus.** 365 workstations in library, computer center, student center. Dormitories wired for high-speed internet access and linked to campus network. Commuter students can connect to campus network. Online course registration, helpline, wireless network available.

**Student life. Freshman orientation:** Available, $75 fee. Preregistration for classes offered. **Housing:** Guaranteed on-campus for freshmen. Coed dorms, substance-free housing available. $100 fully refundable deposit. **Activities:** Bands, choral groups, dance, drama, literary magazine, music ensembles, musical theater, radio station, student government, student newspaper, TV station.

**Athletics.** NCAA. **Intercollegiate:** Baseball M, basketball, cross-country, football (tackle) M, golf, soccer W, softball W, track and field, volleyball W. **Intramural:** Archery, badminton, basketball, bowling, football (non-tackle), golf, handball, racquetball, softball, swimming, table tennis, tennis, track and field, volleyball, weight lifting M, wrestling M. **Team name:** Wildcats.

**Student services.** Alcohol/substance abuse counseling, campus ministries, career counseling, services for economically disadvantaged, student employment services, financial aid counseling, health services, minority student services, personal counseling, placement for graduates, veterans' counselor. **Physically disabled:** Services for visually, speech, hearing impaired.

**Contact.** E-mail: admit1@wsc.edu
Phone: (402) 375-7234 Toll-free number: (800) 228-9972
Fax: (402) 375-7204
Tammy Young, Director of Admissions, Wayne State College, 1111 Main Street, Wayne, NE 68787

## York College
**York, Nebraska**
**www.york.edu**                    CB code: 6984

- Private 4-year liberal arts and teachers college affiliated with Church of Christ
- Residential campus in small town
- 385 degree-seeking undergraduates: 6% part-time, 51% women, 5% African American, 2% Asian American, 4% Hispanic American, 1% international
- SAT or ACT (ACT writing optional) required
- 41% graduate within 6 years

**General.** Founded in 1956. Regionally accredited. **Degrees:** 64 bachelor's, 13 associate awarded. **ROTC:** Army, Naval, Air Force. **Location:** 50 miles from Lincoln. **Calendar:** Semester, limited summer session. **Full-time faculty:** 33 total; 36% have terminal degrees, 3% minority, 27% women. **Part-time faculty:** 24 total; 12% have terminal degrees, 42% women. **Class size:** 88% < 20, 10% 20-39, 2% 40-49. **Special facilities:** 35,000 sq. ft. indoor sports practice facility, historic prayer chapel.

**Freshman class profile.** 90 enrolled.

| Mid 50% test scores | | Rank in top tenth: | 13% |
|---|---|---|---|
| SAT critical reading: | 450-590 | End year in good standing: | 80% |
| SAT math: | 440-560 | Return as sophomores: | 55% |
| ACT composite: | 18-26 | Out-of-state: | 70% |
| GPA 3.50 or higher: | 30% | Live on campus: | 93% |
| GPA 3.0-3.49: | 34% | Fraternities: | 66% |
| GPA 2.0-2.99: | 34% | Sororities: | 76% |
| Rank in top quarter: | 25% | | |

**Basis for selection.** ACT/SAT test scores, high school GPA, class rank very important. Essay recommended but not required. **Homeschooled:** Transcript of courses and grades required.

**High school preparation.** 15 units required; 21 recommended. Required and recommended units include English 3-4, mathematics 2-4, social studies 1-4, history 1-4, science 2-4 and foreign language 3.

**2007-2008 Annual costs.** Tuition/fees: $14,000. Room/board: $4,500. Books/supplies: $1,500. Personal expenses: $2,400.

**2006-2007 Financial aid. Non-need-based:** Scholarships awarded for academics, alumni affiliation, athletics, job skills, leadership, music/drama.

**Application procedures. Admission:** Priority date 3/31; deadline 8/31. $20 fee, may be waived for applicants with need. Application may be submitted online. Admission notification on a rolling basis. Must reply by 9/1. **Financial aid:** Priority date 4/30; no closing date. FAFSA required. Applicants notified on a rolling basis starting 3/1; must reply within 4 week(s) of notification.

**Academics. Special study options:** Accelerated study, double major, dual enrollment of high school students, independent study, internships, student-designed major, teacher certification program. **Credit/placement by examination:** AP, CLEP, IB, SAT, ACT, institutional tests. 12 credit hours maximum toward associate degree, 32 toward bachelor's. **Support services:** Learning center, reduced course load, remedial instruction, study skills assistance, tutoring.

**Majors. Biology:** General. **Business:** Accounting, business admin, finance, human resources. **Communications:** General. **Education:** General, art, biology, business, drama/dance, elementary, English, history, mathematics, middle, multi-level teacher, music, physical, reading, secondary, social science, special, speech. **English:** English lit. **History:** General. **Math:** General. **Philosophy/religion:** Religion. **Physical sciences:** Chemistry. **Psychology:** General. **Theology:** Bible, religious ed. **Visual/performing arts:** Voice/opera.

**Most popular majors.** Biology 7%, business/marketing 26%, education 30%, liberal arts 11%, psychology 9%.

**Computing on campus.** 57 workstations in dormitories, library, computer center. Dormitories wired for high-speed internet access and linked to campus network. Online library, helpline, wireless network available.

**Student life. Freshman orientation:** Mandatory. Preregistration for classes offered. **Policies:** Students expected to conform to Christian norms. Alcohol and tobacco prohibited. Unmarried, full-time students under 21 required to live on campus or with relatives or staff off campus. **Housing:** Guaranteed on-campus for all undergraduates. Single-sex dorms, apartments, substance-free housing available. $75 fully refundable deposit, deadline 8/31. **Activities:** Campus ministries, choral groups, drama, music ensembles, musical theater, student government, student newspaper, service clubs, Chi Rho, spiritual life committee.

**Athletics.** NAIA. **Intercollegiate:** Baseball M, basketball, soccer, softball W, volleyball W, wrestling M. **Intramural:** Basketball, football (non-tackle), soccer, softball, table tennis, volleyball. **Team name:** Panthers.

**Student services.** Adult student services, campus ministries, career counseling, student employment services, financial aid counseling, health services, personal counseling, placement for graduates, veterans' counselor.

**Contact.** E-mail: enroll@york.edu
Phone: (402) 363-5627 Toll-free number: (800) 950-9675
Fax: (402) 363-5623
Christi Lones, Director of Admissions, York College, 1125 East 8th Street, York, NE 68467

# Nevada

## Art Institute of Las Vegas
Henderson, Nevada
www.ailv.artinstitutes.edu                    CB code: 3141

- For-profit 4-year culinary school and visual arts college
- Commuter campus in very large city
- 1,075 degree-seeking undergraduates
- Application essay required

**General.** Accredited by ACCSCT. **Degrees:** 123 bachelor's, 58 associate awarded. **Location:** 10 miles from Las Vegas. **Calendar:** Quarter, extensive summer session. **Full-time faculty:** 27 total; 4% have terminal degrees, 4% minority, 18% women. **Part-time faculty:** 54 total; 11% have terminal degrees, 22% minority, 43% women. **Class size:** 74% < 20, 23% 20-39, 2% 40-49, 1% 50-99. **Special facilities:** Student-run restaurant.

**Basis for selection.** Open admission, but selective for some programs. Competitive admissions to GAD and MAA programs. Applicants for GAD program must have 2.5 GPA . Applicants for both GAD and MAA must present acceptable portfolios. **Homeschooled:** Institution must be recognized by state or national department of education.

**2007-2008 Annual costs.** Tuition for full associate program: $48,272. Tuition for full bachelor's program: $82,752. Supply kit cost averages $11,000. Additional lab fees for culinary programs.

**2007-2008 Financial aid. Need-based:** 25% of total undergraduate aid awarded as scholarships/grants, 75% as loans/jobs. **Non-need-based:** Scholarships awarded for academics, state residency.

**Application procedures. Admission:** No deadline. $50 fee, may be waived for applicants with need. Application must be submitted on paper. Admission notification on a rolling basis. **Financial aid:** No deadline. Applicants notified on a rolling basis.

**Academics. Special study options:** Distance learning, independent study, internships, study abroad. **Credit/placement by examination:** AP, CLEP, IB, institutional tests. 28 credit hours maximum toward associate degree, 48 toward bachelor's. **Support services:** Learning center, pre-admission summer program, reduced course load, remedial instruction, study skills assistance, tutoring.

**Majors. Personal/culinary services:** Chef training. **Visual/performing arts:** General.

**Computing on campus.** 75 workstations in dormitories, library, computer center. Dormitories wired for high-speed internet access. Commuter students can connect to campus network. Online course registration, online library, student web hosting, wireless network available.

**Student life. Freshman orientation:** Mandatory. Preregistration for classes offered. One- or two-hour session held Thursday before start of classes. **Housing:** Apartments, substance-free housing available. **Activities:** Film society.

**Student services.** Adult student services, alcohol/substance abuse counseling, career counseling, services for economically disadvantaged, student employment services, financial aid counseling, personal counseling, placement for graduates. **Physically disabled:** Services for visually, speech, hearing impaired. **Learning disabled:** Comprehensive services available.

**Contact.** Phone: (702) 369-9944
Dewey McGuirk, Director of Admissions, Art Institute of Las Vegas, 2350 Corporate Circle, Henderson, NV 89074-7737

## DeVry University: Henderson
Henderson, Nevada
www.devry.edu

- For-profit 4-year university
- Commuter campus in large city

- 127 degree-seeking undergraduates: 55% part-time, 43% women, 20% African American, 14% Asian American, 22% Hispanic American, 1% international
- 49 degree-seeking graduate students

**General. Degrees:** 17 bachelor's, 7 associate awarded; master's offered. **Calendar:** Semester. **Full-time faculty:** 6 total. **Part-time faculty:** 6 total.

**Freshman class profile.**

| Return as sophomores: | 17% | International: | 4% |

**Basis for selection.** Academic record and interview most important.

**2007-2008 Annual costs.** Tuition/fees: $13,020. Books/supplies: $1,300. Personal expenses: $5,082.

**Financial aid. Non-need-based:** Scholarships awarded for academics.

**Application procedures. Admission:** No deadline. $50 fee. Admission notification on a rolling basis. **Financial aid:** No deadline. FAFSA required. Applicants notified on a rolling basis.

**Academics. Special study options:** Accelerated study, distance learning. **Credit/placement by examination:** CLEP.

**Majors. Business:** Business admin. **Other:** Technology management.

**Contact.** Phone: (702) 933-9700
DeVry University: Henderson, 2490 Paseo Verde Parkway, Suite 150, Henderson, NV 89074

## Great Basin College
Elko, Nevada
www.gbcnv.edu                    CB code: 4293

- Public 4-year community and teachers college
- Commuter campus in large town

**General.** Founded in 1967. Regionally accredited. **Location:** 280 miles from Reno, 220 miles from Salt Lake City. **Calendar:** Semester.

**Annual costs/financial aid.** Tuition/fees (2007-2008): $1,763; $7,148 out-of-state. Reduced tuition for nonresidents within 50 miles of Nevada border. Nonresident additional per-credit-hour charge: $60.25 for 1-6 credits, flat rate assessment of $5,385 for 7 credits and above. Room: $2,300. Books/supplies: $800. Need-based financial aid available to full-time and part-time students.

**Contact.** Phone: (775) 753-2311
Director of Enrollment Management, 1500 College Parkway, Elko, NV 89801

## International Academy of Design and Technology: Henderson
Henderson, Nevada
www.iadtvegas.com

- For-profit 3-year visual arts and technical college
- Very large city
- 418 degree-seeking undergraduates: 8% African American, 10% Asian American, 13% Hispanic American, 1% Native American

**General.** Accredited by ACICS. **Degrees:** 21 bachelor's, 30 associate awarded. **Location:** 10 miles from Las Vegas. **Calendar:** Quarter. **Full-time faculty:** 6 total. **Part-time faculty:** 23 total. **Class size:** 84% < 20, 16% 20-39.

**Basis for selection.** Open admission. **Homeschooled:** ACT or SAT scores.

**2007-2008 Annual costs.** Tuition/fees: $15,840. Costs of books and supplies vary from $4,200 to $9,600 for entire program depending on course of study. Additional fees may apply.

**Application procedures. Admission:** No deadline. $50 fee. Application may be submitted online.

**Academics. Special study options:** Distance learning, independent study, internships, study abroad. **Credit/placement by examination:** AP, CLEP. **Support services:** Tutoring.

**Majors. Computer sciences:** Game design. **Visual/performing arts:** Fashion design, graphic design, interior design.

**Computing on campus.** Online course registration, online library, wireless network available.

**Student life. Freshman orientation:** Mandatory.

**Contact.** E-mail: vegas_web@iadtvegas.com
Phone: (702) 990-0150 Toll-free number: (866) 400-4238
Maggie Balderas, Director of Admissions, International Academy of Design and Technology: Henderson, 2495 Village View Drive, Henderson, NV 89074

## ITT Technical Institute: Henderson
Henderson, Nevada
www.itt-tech.edu
CB code: 2710

- For-profit 4-year technical college
- Commuter campus in small city

**General.** Accredited by ACICS. **Calendar:** Quarter.

**Annual costs/financial aid.** Tuition varies by program, $260-$368 per credit hour.

**Contact.** Phone: (702) 558-5404
Director of Recruitment, 168 North Gibson Road, Henderson, NV 89014

## Morrison University
Reno, Nevada
www.morrison.neumont.edu
CB code: 2114

- For-profit 4-year university and business college
- Commuter campus in small city

**General.** Founded in 1902. Accredited by ACICS. **Location:** Half of mile from downtown. **Calendar:** Quarter.

**Annual costs/financial aid.** Tuition/fees (2007-2008): $9,000. Books/supplies: $825. Personal expenses: $1,800. Need-based financial aid available for full-time students.

**Contact.** Phone: (775) 850-0700 ext. 101
Director of Enrollment, 10315 Professional Circle, #201, Reno, NV 89521

## Nevada State College
Henderson, Nevada
www.nsc.nevada.edu

- Public 4-year nursing, liberal arts and teachers college
- Large city
- 1,545 degree-seeking undergraduates: 47% part-time, 74% women, 8% African American, 12% Asian American, 15% Hispanic American, 1% Native American

**General.** Regionally accredited. **Degrees:** 175 bachelor's awarded. **Calendar:** Semester, limited summer session. **Full-time faculty:** 68 total; 62% have terminal degrees, 25% minority, 63% women.

**Basis for selection.** 2.0 GPA required. **Homeschooled:** Transcript of courses and grades required. SAT/ACT required.

**High school preparation.** 12 units required. Required units include English 4, mathematics 3, social studies 3 and science 2.

**2007-2008 Annual costs.** Tuition/fees: $2,693; $10,790 out-of-state.

**Application procedures. Admission:** No deadline. $30 fee. Application may be submitted online. **Financial aid:** Closing date 5/1.

**Academics. Special study options:** Accelerated study, combined bachelor's/graduate degree, cooperative education, cross-registration, distance learning, double major, dual enrollment of high school students, ESL, independent study. **Credit/placement by examination:** AP, CLEP, institutional tests. **Support services:** Learning center, remedial instruction, tutoring.

**Majors. Biology:** General. **Business:** Accounting technology, business admin. **Communications:** General. **Computer sciences:** Computer science. **Conservation:** Environmental science. **Education:** Elementary, secondary, special. **English:** English lit. **Health:** Audiology/speech pathology, nursing (RN), speech pathology. **Interdisciplinary:** Systems science. **Protective services:** Corrections. **Psychology:** General. **Social sciences:** Economics.

**Most popular majors.** Education 25%, health sciences 57%, psychology 8%.

**Computing on campus.** 111 workstations in library, computer center, student center. Commuter students can connect to campus network. Online course registration, helpline, wireless network available.

**Student life. Freshman orientation:** Available. Preregistration for classes offered. **Activities:** Student newspaper.

**Contact.** E-mail: admissions@nsc.nevada.edu
Phone: (702) 992-2130
Patricia Ring, Admissions/Registrar, Nevada State College, 1125 Nevada State Drive, Henderson, NV 89002

## Sierra Nevada College
Incline Village, Nevada
www.sierranevada.edu
CB member
CB code: 4757

- Private 4-year liberal arts college
- Residential campus in small town
- 315 degree-seeking undergraduates
- 390 graduate students
- SAT or ACT with writing, application essay required

**General.** Founded in 1969. Regionally accredited. **Degrees:** 50 bachelor's awarded; master's offered. **ROTC:** Army. **Location:** 35 miles from Reno. **Calendar:** Semester, limited summer session. **Full-time faculty:** 15 total. **Part-time faculty:** 55 total. **Class size:** 84% < 20, 16% 20-39. **Special facilities:** Entertainment technology lab, center for environmental sciences.

**Freshman class profile.**

| Mid 50% test scores | | | |
|---|---|---|---|
| SAT critical reading: | 440-630 | Rank in top quarter: | 35% |
| SAT math: | 440-600 | Rank in top tenth: | 10% |
| ACT composite: | 18-26 | Out-of-state: | 71% |
| | | Live on campus: | 90% |

**Basis for selection.** Motivation as evidenced in personal interview and/or autobiographical statement very important. Applicants with GPA below 2.0 may be admitted provisionally, upon review by faculty admission committee. Interview recommended. **Homeschooled:** Submit any course plans or transcripts along with any home schooling plans that are available.

**High school preparation.** Recommended units include English 4, mathematics 3, social studies 2, history 2, science 2 and foreign language 2.

**2007-2008 Annual costs.** Tuition/fees: $22,305. Room/board: $8,410. Books/supplies: $750. Personal expenses: $2,035.

**Financial aid. Non-need-based:** Scholarships awarded for academics, art, athletics.

**Application procedures. Admission:** Priority date 2/15; no deadline. No application fee. Application may be submitted online. Admission notification on a rolling basis beginning on or about 11/1. Must reply by May 1 or within 3 week(s) if notified thereafter. **Financial aid:** Priority date 4/1; no closing date. FAFSA, institutional form required. Applicants notified on a rolling basis; must reply by 5/1 or within 4 week(s) of notification.

**Academics.** Interdisciplinary studies in business, environmental science, fine arts, and the humanities. **Special study options:** Combined bachelor's/graduate degree, double major, honors, independent study, internships, liberal arts/career combination, study abroad, teacher certification program. Tuition exchange. **Credit/placement by examination:** AP, CLEP, IB, SAT, ACT, institutional tests. 30 credit hours maximum toward bachelor's degree. **Support services:** Remedial instruction, study skills assistance, tutoring, writing center.

**Majors. Biology:** General, ecology. **Business:** Business admin, hospitality admin, resort management. **Computer sciences:** General, computer science. **Conservation:** Environmental science, management/policy. **English:** English lit. **Health:** Premedicine, prenursing, prepharmacy. **Interdisciplinary:** Global studies. **Liberal arts:** Arts/sciences. **Psychology:** General. **Visual/performing arts:** General, ceramics, drawing, painting, printmaking, sculpture, studio arts.

**Most popular majors.** Business/marketing 31%, English 9%, liberal arts 12%, psychology 7%, visual/performing arts 24%.

**Computing on campus.** PC or laptop required. 30 workstations in dormitories, library, computer center, student center. Dormitories wired for high-speed internet access and linked to campus network. Commuter students can connect to campus network. Online library, helpline, repair service, wireless network available.

**Student life. Freshman orientation:** Mandatory. Preregistration for classes offered. Week-long program held the week prior to first day of classes. **Housing:** Guaranteed on-campus for all undergraduates. Coed dorms, substance-free housing available. $200 nonrefundable deposit, deadline 5/1. **Activities:** Jazz band, choral groups, drama, literary magazine, music ensembles, musical theater, student government, student newspaper, recycling club, Christian club, Amnesty International.

**Athletics.** NCAA. **Intercollegiate:** Skiing. **Intramural:** Basketball, bowling, skiing, soccer, softball, volleyball. **Team name:** Eagles.

**Student services.** Alcohol/substance abuse counseling, career counseling, student employment services, financial aid counseling, health services, personal counseling, placement for graduates, veterans' counselor.

**Contact.** E-mail: admissions@sierranevada.edu
Phone: (775) 831-1314 Toll-free number: (866) 412-4636
Fax: (775) 831-6223
Julie McMillin, Dean of Admission and Financial Aid, Sierra Nevada College, 999 Tahoe Boulevard, Incline Village, NV 89451-4269

---

## University of Nevada: Las Vegas

| Las Vegas, Nevada | CB member |
| --- | --- |
| www.unlv.edu | CB code: 4861 |

- Public 4-year university
- Commuter campus in very large city
- 20,971 degree-seeking undergraduates: 26% part-time, 56% women, 9% African American, 17% Asian American, 13% Hispanic American, 1% Native American, 4% international
- 4,748 degree-seeking graduate students
- 68% of applicants admitted
- 39% graduate within 6 years

**General.** Founded in 1957. Regionally accredited. Credit courses available at Nellis Air Force Base. **Degrees:** 3,438 bachelor's awarded; master's, doctoral, first professional offered. **ROTC:** Army. **Location:** 268 miles from Los Angeles, 290 miles from Phoenix. **Calendar:** Semester, extensive summer session. **Full-time faculty:** 950 total; 88% have terminal degrees, 19% minority, 35% women. **Part-time faculty:** 727 total. **Class size:** 37% < 20, 41% 20-39, 9% 40-49, 10% 50-99, 2% >100. **Special facilities:** National supercomputing center for energy and environment, natural history museum, arboretum, 3 theaters, concert hall, international gaming institute, professional practice school for teachers.

**Freshman class profile.** 8,009 applied, 5,479 admitted, 2,967 enrolled.

| Mid 50% test scores | | Rank in top tenth: | 18% |
| --- | --- | --- | --- |
| SAT critical reading: | 450-560 | Return as sophomores: | 75% |
| SAT math: | 460-580 | Out-of-state: | 20% |
| ACT composite: | 19-24 | Live on campus: | 30% |
| GPA 3.50 or higher: | 31% | International: | 2% |
| GPA 3.0-3.49: | 47% | Fraternities: | 8% |
| GPA 2.0-2.99: | 21% | Sororities: | 6% |
| Rank in top quarter: | 50% | | |

**Basis for selection.** GED not accepted. High school record must show minimum 3.0 minimum GPA in core courses. ACT/SAT can waive GPA requirements, but all students must have the core. Recommendations, personal essay and test scores considered for students applying through Alternate Criteria program. ACT/SAT required for English and math course placement. SAT or ACT recommended. SAT/ACT required for students appealing admission through alternate criteria and for placement into English/math courses. Audition recommended for music, theater arts programs; portfolio recommended for art program. **Homeschooled:** Transcript of courses and grades, letter of recommendation (nonparent) required. Students must submit personal statement, 2 letters of recommendation, ACT/SAT test scores.

**High school preparation.** 13 units required. Required units include English 4, mathematics 3, social studies 3, science 3 (laboratory 2). Algebra or higher level math required.

**2007-2008 Annual costs.** Tuition/fees: $4,031; $14,842 out-of-state. Reduced tuition rate for out-of-state students who live within 50 miles of Nevada border and for those who reside in Western Undergraduate Exchange states. Room/board: $9,288. Books/supplies: $850. Personal expenses: $1,800.

**2006-2007 Financial aid.** **Need-based:** 1,700 full-time freshmen applied for aid; 1,014 were judged to have need; 980 of these received aid. Average need met was 56%. Average scholarship/grant was $3,791; average

loan $2,362. 44% of total undergraduate aid awarded as scholarships/grants, 56% as loans/jobs. **Non-need-based:** Awarded to 3,720 full-time undergraduates, including 1,076 freshmen. Scholarships awarded for academics, alumni affiliation, art, athletics, job skills, leadership, minority status, music/drama, ROTC, state residency. **Additional information:** Tuition reduction for state residents through consortium programs and for out-of-state students graduating from high schools in designated counties bordering Nevada, for military dependents residing in-state, and for dependents of children of alumni not residing in-state.

**Application procedures. Admission:** Priority date 2/1; deadline 7/20 (postmark date). $60 fee. Application may be submitted online. Admission notification on a rolling basis beginning on or about 7/1. **Financial aid:** Priority date 2/1; no closing date. FAFSA, institutional form required. Applicants notified on a rolling basis starting 3/20; must reply within 2 week(s) of notification.

**Academics. Special study options:** Accelerated study, combined bachelor's/graduate degree, cooperative education, cross-registration, distance learning, double major, dual enrollment of high school students, ESL, exchange student, honors, independent study, internships, student-designed major, study abroad, teacher certification program. 2+2 culinary arts program with College of Southern Nevada. **Credit/placement by examination:** AP, CLEP, IB, SAT, ACT, institutional tests. 30 credit hours maximum toward bachelor's degree. **Support services:** Learning center, pre-admission summer program, remedial instruction, study skills assistance, tutoring, writing center.

**Honors college/program.** Honors College applicants must complete the honors application, letters of recommendation, test scores, personal statements, and essay response.

**Majors. Architecture:** Architecture, interior, landscape, urban/community planning. **Area/ethnic studies:** Asian, Latin American, women's. **Biology:** General. **Business:** Accounting, finance, hospitality admin, human resources, international marketing, management information systems, managerial economics, marketing, real estate. **Communications:** General. **Computer sciences:** Computer science. **Conservation:** General, environmental studies, management/policy. **Education:** Adult/continuing, computer, early childhood, elementary, health, physical, secondary, special. **Engineering:** Civil, computer, electrical, mechanical, software. **Engineering technology:** Construction. **English:** English lit. **Foreign languages:** French, German, Spanish. **Health:** Athletic training, clinical lab science, health care admin, medical radiologic technology/radiation therapy, nuclear medical technology, nursing (RN), physics/radiologic health. **History:** General. **Interdisciplinary:** Nutrition sciences. **Liberal arts:** Arts/sciences. **Math:** General, applied. **Parks/recreation:** General, exercise sciences, health/fitness. **Personal/culinary services:** Culinary arts. **Philosophy/religion:** Philosophy. **Physical sciences:** Chemistry, geology, physics. **Psychology:** General. **Public administration:** Social work. **Social sciences:** Anthropology, political science, sociology. **Visual/performing arts:** Art, dance, dramatic, film/cinema, jazz, studio arts.

**Most popular majors.** Business/marketing 29%, communications/journalism 6%, education 9%, psychology 7%, social sciences 6%, visual/performing arts 6%.

**Computing on campus.** 250 workstations in dormitories, library, computer center, student center. Dormitories wired for high-speed internet access and linked to campus network. Commuter students can connect to campus network. Online course registration, online library, helpline, wireless network available.

**Student life. Freshman orientation:** Available, $90 fee. Two-day program. **Policies:** First-year residential, upper-class and Tonopah living/learning programs place students with others at similar levels and integrate classroom knowledge with life experience. **Housing:** Guaranteed on-campus for freshmen. Coed dorms, special housing for disabled, fraternity/sorority housing, substance-free housing available. $125 partly refundable deposit. All-female, study intensive floors available; handicapped accessible suites in all complexes. **Activities:** Bands, campus ministries, choral groups, dance, drama, film society, international student organizations, literary magazine, music ensembles, musical theater, opera, radio station, student government, student newspaper, symphony orchestra, TV station, Young Democrats/Republicans, Rebel Christian Fellowship, Hillel, ethnic student council, student organization of Latinos, black student association, Latter-day Saints student organization, Hawaii club.

**Athletics.** NCAA. **Intercollegiate:** Baseball M, basketball, cheerleading, cross-country W, diving, football (tackle) M, golf, soccer, softball W, swimming, tennis, track and field W, volleyball W. **Intramural:** Badminton, basketball, bowling, cross-country, diving W, football (tackle) M, golf, racquetball, soccer, softball, swimming, table tennis, tennis, track and field, volleyball. **Team name:** Rebels.

**Student services.** Adult student services, alcohol/substance abuse counseling, campus ministries, career counseling, services for economically disadvantaged, student employment services, financial aid counseling, health

services, minority student services, on-campus daycare, personal counseling, placement for graduates, veterans' counselor, women's services. **Physically disabled:** Services for visually, speech, hearing impaired. **Learning disabled:** Comprehensive services available.

**Contact.** E-mail: undergraduate.recruitment@unlv.edu
Phone: (702) 774-8658 Fax: (702) 774-8008
Cem Sunata, Registrar, University of Nevada: Las Vegas, 4505 Maryland Parkway Box 451021, Las Vegas, NV 89154-1021

## University of Nevada: Reno

| Reno, Nevada | CB member |
|---|---|
| www.unr.edu | CB code: 4844 |

- Public 4-year university
- Commuter campus in small city
- 12,659 degree-seeking undergraduates: 18% part-time, 53% women, 3% African American, 7% Asian American, 8% Hispanic American, 1% Native American, 2% international
- 2,628 degree-seeking graduate students
- 88% of applicants admitted
- 49% graduate within 6 years; 30% enter graduate study

**General.** Founded in 1874. Regionally accredited. **Degrees:** 1,962 bachelor's awarded; master's, doctoral, first professional offered. **ROTC:** Army. **Location:** 225 miles from San Francisco, 35 miles from Lake Tahoe. **Calendar:** Semester, extensive summer session. **Full-time faculty:** 592 total; 94% have terminal degrees, 14% minority, 36% women. **Part-time faculty:** 299 total; 29% have terminal degrees, 9% minority, 52% women. **Class size:** 32% < 20, 45% 20-39, 8% 40-49, 9% 50-99, 5% >100. **Special facilities:** Mineral museum, planetarium, arboretum, disability resource center, ethnic student resource center, internship center.

**Freshman class profile.** 4,683 applied, 4,111 admitted, 2,278 enrolled.

| Mid 50% test scores | | End year in good standing: | 78% |
|---|---|---|---|
| SAT critical reading: | 460-580 | Return as sophomores: | 77% |
| SAT math: | 460-590 | Out-of-state: | 16% |
| SAT writing: | 430-550 | Live on campus: | 53% |
| ACT composite: | 20-25 | International: | 2% |
| GPA 3.50 or higher: | 39% | Fraternities: | 11% |
| GPA 3.0-3.49: | 44% | Sororities: | 10% |
| GPA 2.0-2.99: | 17% | | |

**Basis for selection.** GED not accepted. Secondary school record most important, with 3.0 GPA in academic core of English, math, social sciences and natural sciences. If student does not meet GPA requirement, 1040 SAT or 22 ACT may be used in place of GPA requirement. All students applying for scholarships must submit test scores. Interview recommended for nursing program; audition recommended for music program; portfolio recommended for fine arts program.

**High school preparation.** 13 units required. Required units include English 4, mathematics 3, social studies 3, science 3 (laboratory 2).

**2007-2008 Annual costs.** Tuition/fees: $4,029; $14,839 out-of-state. Reduced tuition rate for out-of-state students who live within 50 miles of Nevada border. Nonresident additional per-credit-hour charge: $128.50 for 1-6 credits, flat rate assessment of $5405 for 7 credits and above. Room/board: $8,319.

**2006-2007 Financial aid. Need-based:** Average need met was 55%. Average scholarship/grant was $5,064; average loan $2,774. 52% of total undergraduate aid awarded as scholarships/grants, 48% as loans/jobs. **Non-need-based:** Awarded to 5,243 full-time undergraduates, including 1,360 freshmen. Scholarships awarded for academics, alumni affiliation, art, athletics, music/drama. **Additional information:** Reduced out-of-state tuition available for children of alumni and for non-residents from some neighboring counties in California and participants in WUE program.

**Application procedures. Admission:** Priority date 3/1; no deadline. $60 fee, may be waived for applicants with need. Application may be submitted online. Admission notification on a rolling basis. **Financial aid:** Priority date 2/15; no closing date. FAFSA required. Applicants notified on a rolling basis starting 4/1; must reply within 2 week(s) of notification.

**Academics. Special study options:** Distance learning, double major, dual enrollment of high school students, ESL, exchange student, honors, independent study, internships, study abroad, teacher certification program. **Credit/placement by examination:** AP, CLEP, IB, SAT, ACT, institutional tests. 60 credit hours maximum toward bachelor's degree. **Support services:** Learning center, remedial instruction, study skills assistance, tutoring, writing center.

**Majors. Agriculture:** Animal breeding, animal sciences, economics. **Area/ethnic studies:** Women's. **Biology:** General, biochemistry, biotechnology. **Business:** General, accounting, entrepreneurial studies, finance, hospitality admin, human resources, international, logistics, managerial economics, marketing. **Communications:** General, journalism. **Computer sciences:** General, computer science. **Conservation:** General, forestry, management/policy, wildlife. **Education:** Agricultural, art, business, elementary, English, family/consumer sciences, foreign languages, health, mathematics, music, physical, science, secondary, social science, social studies, special, speech, technology/industrial arts, trade/industrial. **Engineering:** Chemical, civil, computer, electrical, environmental, geological, mechanical, metallurgical, mining, physics, water resource. **Engineering technology:** Construction. **English:** Composition, creative writing, English lit. **Family/consumer sciences:** Child development, family studies, food/nutrition. **Foreign languages:** French, German, Spanish. **Health:** Nursing (RN), preveterinary, speech pathology. **History:** General. **Interdisciplinary:** Science/society. **Math:** General. **Philosophy/religion:** Philosophy. **Physical sciences:** Atmospheric science, chemistry, geology, geophysics, physics. **Psychology:** General, social. **Public administration:** Social work. **Social sciences:** Anthropology, criminology, geography, international relations, political science, sociology. **Visual/performing arts:** Art, art history/conservation, dramatic, interior design, music performance. **Other:** English language and linguistics, Health ecology.

**Most popular majors.** Biology 9%, business/marketing 14%, communications/journalism 6%, education 8%, engineering/engineering technologies 7%, health sciences 9%, liberal arts 6%, psychology 6%, social sciences 9%.

**Computing on campus.** 500 workstations in dormitories, library, computer center, student center. Dormitories wired for high-speed internet access and linked to campus network. Commuter students can connect to campus network. Online course registration, online library, helpline, repair service, student web hosting, wireless network available.

**Student life. Freshman orientation:** Mandatory, $99 fee. Preregistration for classes offered. Sessions held before each semester. Family members welcome. **Housing:** Coed dorms, single-sex dorms, special housing for disabled, apartments, substance-free housing available. $300 deposit. Special interest floors (fitness, arts and culture, stereo limitation, alcohol prohibition, honors) available. **Activities:** Bands, choral groups, dance, drama, international student organizations, literary magazine, music ensembles, Model UN, musical theater, opera, radio station, student government, student newspaper, Intervarsity Christian Fellowship, black student union, American Indian organization, Asian American Alliance, Chinese students association, Young Republicans, Young Democrats, Hillel, MEXA.

**Athletics.** NCAA. **Intercollegiate:** Baseball M, basketball, cross-country W, diving W, football (tackle) M, golf, rifle, skiing, soccer W, softball W, swimming W, tennis, track and field W, volleyball W. **Intramural:** Badminton, basketball, bowling, football (non-tackle), golf, racquetball, soccer, softball, swimming, table tennis, tennis, track and field, volleyball, water polo, weight lifting. **Team name:** Wolf Pack.

**Student services.** Adult student services, alcohol/substance abuse counseling, career counseling, services for economically disadvantaged, student employment services, financial aid counseling, health services, legal services, minority student services, on-campus daycare, personal counseling, placement for graduates, veterans' counselor, women's services. **Physically disabled:** Services for visually, speech, hearing impaired.

**Contact.** E-mail: asknevada@unr.edu
Phone: (775) 784-1110 Toll-free number: (866) 263-8232
Fax: (775) 784-4283
Melisa Choroszy, Associate Vice President, Enrollment Services, University of Nevada: Reno, Mail Stop 120, Reno, NV 89557

## University of Southern Nevada
Henderson, Nevada
www.usn.edu

- Private two-year upper-division university
- Commuter campus in very large city
- 26% of applicants admitted
- Application essay, interview required

**General.** Candidate for regional accreditation. **Calendar:** Differs by program. **Full-time faculty:** 54 total; 94% have terminal degrees, 33% minority, 54% women. **Part-time faculty:** 4 total; 75% have terminal degrees, 50% women. **Class size:** 50% 20-39, 50% 50-99.

**Student profile.** 139 degree-seeking undergraduates, 562 degree-seeking graduate students. 1,813 applied as first time-transfer students, 473 admitted, 338 enrolled. 62% transferred from two-year, 38% transferred from four-year institutions.

| | | | |
|---|---|---|---|
| **Women:** | 79% | **25 or older:** | 59% |
| **Out-of-state:** | 55% | | |

**Basis for selection.** College transcript, application essay, interview required. Must complete specified courses. Transfer accepted as juniors.

**2007-2008 Annual costs.** Tuition and fees vary by program from $25,000 to $34,975.

**Financial aid. Need-based:** 139 applied for aid; 139 were judged to have need; 139 of these received aid. Average need met was 91%. 5% of total undergraduate aid awarded as scholarships/grants, 95% as loans/jobs. **Non-need-based:** Scholarships awarded for academics.

**Application procedures. Admission:** Rolling admission. $100 fee. Application must be submitted on paper. **Financial aid:** Priority date 1/1, closing date 4/1. Applicants notified on a rolling basis starting 4/1; must reply within 2 weeks of notification.

**Academics. Special study options:** Accelerated study, combined bachelor's/graduate degree. **Credit/placement by examination:** CLEP.

**Majors. Health:** Nursing (RN).

**Computing on campus.** PC or laptop required. 15 workstations in library. Online library, helpline, repair service, wireless network available.

**Student services.** Financial aid counseling, placement for graduates.

**Contact.** E-mail: bsnadmission@usn.edu
Phone: (702) 968-2075 Fax: (702) 990-4435
University of Southern Nevada, 11 Sunset Way, Henderson, NV 89014

# New Hampshire

## Chester College of New England
**Chester, New Hampshire**          CB member
**www.chestercollege.edu**          CB code: 3977

- Private 4-year visual arts and liberal arts college
- Residential campus in rural community
- 222 degree-seeking undergraduates: 9% part-time, 64% women
- 13 graduate students
- 67% of applicants admitted
- Application essay, interview required

**General.** Founded in 1965. Regionally accredited. **Degrees:** 31 bachelor's awarded. **Location:** 10 miles from Manchester, 50 miles from Boston. **Calendar:** Semester, limited summer session. **Full-time faculty:** 14 total. **Part-time faculty:** 30 total. **Class size:** 88% < 20, 12% 20-39.

**Freshman class profile.** 154 applied, 103 admitted, 62 enrolled.

| Mid 50% test scores | | |
|---|---|---|
| SAT critical reading: | 440-610 | |
| SAT math: | 390-550 | |
| ACT composite: | 14-21 | |

| | |
|---|---|
| End year in good standing: | 92% |
| Return as sophomores: | 94% |
| Out-of-state: | 50% |
| Live on campus: | 60% |

**Basis for selection.** High school achievement record, recommendations important; SAT/ACT scores considered. Portfolio strongly recommended. **Homeschooled:** Statement describing homeschool structure and mission, interview, letter of recommendation (nonparent) required. Students may be required to complete an essay under examination conditions. SAT scores required.

**High school preparation.** Recommended units include English 4, mathematics 2, social studies 1, history 1 and science 2.

**2007-2008 Annual costs.** Tuition/fees: $15,930. Lab fees vary per student; average cost $600. Room/board: $7,850. Books/supplies: $1,100. Personal expenses: $1,000.

**Financial aid. Non-need-based:** Scholarships awarded for academics, art, state residency.

**Application procedures. Admission:** No deadline. $35 fee, may be waived for applicants with need. Application may be submitted online. Admission notification on a rolling basis beginning on or about 1/15. Must reply by May 1 or within 2 week(s) if notified thereafter. **Financial aid:** Priority date 3/15; no closing date. FAFSA required. Applicants notified on a rolling basis starting 12/1; must reply within 2 week(s) of notification.

**Academics. Special study options:** Cross-registration, double major, independent study, internships, liberal arts/career combination, student-designed major, study abroad. **Credit/placement by examination:** AP, CLEP, institutional tests. 60 credit hours maximum toward bachelor's degree. **Support services:** Reduced course load, remedial instruction, study skills assistance, tutoring.

**Majors. Computer sciences:** Web page design. **English:** Creative writing. **Liberal arts:** Arts/sciences. **Visual/performing arts:** Art, graphic design, photography, studio arts.

**Most popular majors.** Liberal arts 80%, visual/performing arts 20%.

**Computing on campus.** 42 workstations in library, computer center, student center. Dormitories wired for high-speed internet access. Online library available.

**Student life. Freshman orientation:** Mandatory. Preregistration for classes offered. Three-day orientation. **Housing:** Guaranteed on-campus for all undergraduates. Coed dorms, substance-free housing available. $300 nonrefundable deposit, deadline 8/15. **Activities:** Drama, literary magazine, student government.

**Athletics. Intramural:** Soccer, softball, table tennis, volleyball.

**Student services.** Career counseling, financial aid counseling, placement for graduates.

**Contact.** E-mail: admissions@chestercollege.edu
Phone: (603) 887-7401 Toll-free number: (800) 974-6372
Fax: (603) 887-1777
Lara Salazar, Admissions Counselor, Chester College of New England, 40 Chester Street, Chester, NH 03036

## Colby-Sawyer College
**New London, New Hampshire**          CB member
**www.colby-sawyer.edu**          CB code: 3281

- Private 4-year liberal arts college
- Residential campus in small town
- 942 degree-seeking undergraduates: 1% part-time, 65% women, 1% African American, 1% Asian American, 1% Hispanic American, 1% international
- 87% of applicants admitted
- SAT or ACT with writing, application essay required
- 60% graduate within 6 years; 8% enter graduate study

**General.** Founded in 1837. Regionally accredited. **Degrees:** 216 bachelor's, 2 associate awarded. **ROTC:** Army, Air Force. **Location:** 30 miles from Hanover, 35 miles from Concord. **Calendar:** Semester. **Full-time faculty:** 60 total; 73% have terminal degrees, 52% women. **Part-time faculty:** 67 total; 19% have terminal degrees, 63% women. **Class size:** 65% < 20, 35% 20-39, less than 1% 40-49. **Special facilities:** Fine arts center, laboratory school (preschool, K-3), library learning center, conservatory and greenhouse, science center, weather station.

**Freshman class profile.** 1,672 applied, 1,454 admitted, 352 enrolled.

| Mid 50% test scores | | |
|---|---|---|
| SAT critical reading: | 440-540 | |
| SAT math: | 440-530 | |
| ACT composite: | 18-22 | |
| GPA 3.50 or higher: | 17% | |
| GPA 3.0-3.49: | 40% | |

| | |
|---|---|
| GPA 2.0-2.99: | 42% |
| End year in good standing: | 84% |
| Return as sophomores: | 71% |
| Out-of-state: | 67% |
| Live on campus: | 98% |
| International: | 1% |

**Basis for selection.** High school transcript most important. Test scores, recommendations, school and community activities, essay also considered. Interviews highly recommended, but not required. Portfolio recommended for art program.

**High school preparation.** 15 units required. Required units include English 4, mathematics 3, social studies 3, science 3 (laboratory 3) and foreign language 2. Nursing applicants strongly encouraged to have 3 years of college-preparatory lab sciences, including biology and chemistry.

**2007-2008 Annual costs.** Tuition/fees: $28,010. Room/board: $9,900. Books/supplies: $750. Personal expenses: $1,000.

**2007-2008 Financial aid. Need-based:** 321 full-time freshmen applied for aid; 286 were judged to have need; 286 of these received aid. Average need met was 87%. Average scholarship/grant was $18,412; average loan $4,850. 70% of total undergraduate aid awarded as scholarships/grants, 30% as loans/jobs. **Non-need-based:** Awarded to 234 full-time undergraduates, including 90 freshmen. Scholarships awarded for academics, alumni affiliation, art, leadership, minority status, music/drama.

**Application procedures. Admission:** No deadline. $45 fee, may be waived for applicants with need. Application may be submitted online. Admission notification on a rolling basis beginning on or about 12/15. Must reply by May 1 or within 2 week(s) if notified thereafter. **Financial aid:** Priority date 2/15, closing date 3/1. FAFSA required. Applicants notified on a rolling basis starting 1/1; must reply by 5/1 or within 2 week(s) of notification.

**Academics.** Liberal arts and experiential education integrated. Internships or senior research projects required in all major programs. **Special study options:** Accelerated study, cross-registration, double major, dual enrollment of high school students, ESL, exchange student, honors, independent study, internships, semester at sea, student-designed major, study abroad, teacher certification program, Washington semester. **Credit/placement by examination:** AP, CLEP, IB, institutional tests. 30 credit hours maximum toward associate degree, 60 toward bachelor's. **Support services:** Learning center, reduced course load, study skills assistance, tutoring.

**Majors. Biology:** General. **Business:** Business admin. **Communications:** Media studies. **Conservation:** Environmental studies. **Education:** Art, early childhood, English, social studies. **English:** English lit. **Health:** Athletic training, nursing (RN). **Parks/recreation:** Exercise sciences, sports admin. **Psychology:** General, developmental. **Visual/performing arts:** Art, graphic design, studio arts.

**Most popular majors.** Business/marketing 12%, communications/journalism 7%, education 12%, health sciences 16%, parks/recreation 11%, psychology 17%, visual/performing arts 12%.

**Computing on campus.** 150 workstations in library, computer center, student center. Dormitories wired for high-speed internet access and linked to campus network. Commuter students can connect to campus network. Online library, helpline, wireless network available.

**Student life. Freshman orientation:** Mandatory. Preregistration for classes offered. Two days immediately preceding beginning of fall semester. **Housing:** Guaranteed on-campus for all undergraduates. Coed dorms, single-sex dorms, special housing for disabled, substance-free housing available. **Activities:** Choral groups, dance, drama, literary magazine, musical theater, radio station, student government, student newspaper, community service club, Safe Zones, cross cultural club, Christian Fellowship, Coalition for Peace and Justice, Student Democrats.

**Athletics.** NCAA. **Intercollegiate:** Baseball M, basketball, diving, equestrian, lacrosse W, skiing, soccer, swimming, tennis, track and field, volleyball W. **Intramural:** Basketball, football (non-tackle), golf, soccer, volleyball. **Team name:** Chargers.

**Student services.** Alcohol/substance abuse counseling, career counseling, student employment services, financial aid counseling, health services, personal counseling. **Physically disabled:** Services for visually, hearing impaired.

**Contact.** E-mail: admissions@colby-sawyer.edu
Phone: (603) 526-3700 Toll-free number: (800) 272-1015
Fax: (603) 526-3452
Tracey Perkins, Director of Admission Counseling, Colby-Sawyer College, 541 Main Street, New London, NH 03257-7835

## Daniel Webster College

**Nashua, New Hampshire**   **CB member**
**www.dwc.edu**   **CB code: 3648**

- Private 4-year college
- Residential campus in small city
- 703 degree-seeking undergraduates
- 117 degree-seeking graduate students
- 77% of applicants admitted
- SAT or ACT (ACT writing optional), application essay required
- 42% graduate within 6 years; 11% enter graduate study

**General.** Founded in 1965. Regionally accredited. **Degrees:** 196 bachelor's, 20 associate awarded; master's offered. **ROTC:** Army, Air Force. **Location:** 17 miles from Manchester, 35 miles from Boston. **Calendar:** Semester, limited summer session. **Full-time faculty:** 34 total; 71% have terminal degrees, 12% minority, 24% women. **Part-time faculty:** 44 total; 73% have terminal degrees, 7% minority, 23% women. **Class size:** 77% < 20, 23% 20-39. **Special facilities:** On-campus flight center, 35 aircraft including powered gliders, aerobatic planes, 3 flight simulators, air-traffic-control simulation system.

**Freshman class profile.** 1,136 applied, 871 admitted, 250 enrolled.

| Mid 50% test scores | | | |
|---|---|---|---|
| SAT critical reading: | 450-570 | GPA 2.0-2.99: | 38% |
| SAT math: | 470-600 | End year in good standing: | 89% |
| ACT composite: | 20-25 | Return as sophomores: | 76% |
| GPA 3.50 or higher: | 21% | Out-of-state: | 60% |
| GPA 3.0-3.49: | 40% | Live on campus: | 80% |

**Basis for selection.** High school transcript, recommendations, test scores and essay most important. Extracurricular activities considered. Interviews recommended. **Homeschooled:** Transcript of courses and grades, interview, letter of recommendation (nonparent) required.

**High school preparation.** 16 units required. Required and recommended units include English 4, mathematics 3-4, social studies 2, history 2, science 3 (laboratory 2) and foreign language 2. One computer science recommended.

**2008-2009 Annual costs.** Tuition/fees: $27,032. Room/board: $9,369. Books/supplies: $1,000. Personal expenses: $1,500.

**2006-2007 Financial aid. Need-based:** 56% of total undergraduate aid awarded as scholarships/grants, 44% as loans/jobs. **Non-need-based:** Scholarships awarded for academics, leadership.

**Application procedures. Admission:** No deadline. $35 fee, may be waived for applicants with need. Application may be submitted online. Admission notification on a rolling basis beginning on or about 12/1. Must reply by May 1 or within 2 week(s) if notified thereafter. **Financial aid:** Priority date 3/1; no closing date. FAFSA, institutional form required. Applicants notified on a rolling basis starting 3/15; must reply within 2 week(s) of notification.

**Academics.** Credit granted for pilot licenses. Flight students must have FAA Class II physical examination. Flight operations majors must pass FAA written examinations and flight tests to earn pilot ratings. **Special study options:** Accelerated study, cooperative education, cross-registration, distance learning, double major, dual enrollment of high school students, independent study, internships, liberal arts/career combination, study abroad, Washington semester. **Credit/placement by examination:** AP, CLEP, IB, institutional tests. 30 credit hours maximum toward associate degree, 30 toward bachelor's. **Support services:** Learning center, study skills assistance, tutoring, writing center.

**Majors. Business:** General, business admin, management information systems, marketing. **Computer sciences:** General, a.i./robotics, computer science, game design, information systems. **Engineering:** Aerospace, mechanical. **Parks/recreation:** Sports admin. **Protective services:** Emergency management/homeland security. **Psychology:** General. **Social sciences:** General. **Transportation:** Air traffic control, aviation, aviation management.

**Computing on campus.** 150 workstations in dormitories, library, computer center, student center. Dormitories wired for high-speed internet access and linked to campus network. Helpline, repair service, wireless network available.

**Student life. Freshman orientation:** Mandatory, $250 fee. 4-day program. **Housing:** Guaranteed on-campus for all undergraduates. Coed dorms, single-sex dorms, apartments, substance-free housing available. $400 non-refundable deposit, deadline 5/1. Townhouses attained by merit. Suites for 4 to 7 students available. **Activities:** Jazz band, choral groups, drama, film society, student government, student newspaper, Campus Crusade for Christ.

**Athletics.** NCAA. **Intercollegiate:** Baseball M, basketball, cross-country, golf, lacrosse M, soccer, softball W, volleyball W. **Intramural:** Basketball, skiing, soccer, volleyball. **Team name:** Eagles.

**Student services.** Adult student services, alcohol/substance abuse counseling, career counseling, student employment services, financial aid counseling, health services, personal counseling, placement for graduates, veterans' counselor.

**Contact.** E-mail: admissions@dwc.edu
Phone: (603) 577-6600 Toll-free number: (800) 325-6876
Fax: (603) 577-6001
Daniel Monahan, Dean of Admissions and Financial Assistance, Daniel Webster College, 20 University Drive, Nashua, NH 03063

## Dartmouth College

**Hanover, New Hampshire**   **CB member**
**www.dartmouth.edu**   **CB code: 3351**

- Private 4-year university and liberal arts college
- Residential campus in large town
- 4,085 degree-seeking undergraduates: 50% women, 7% African American, 14% Asian American, 6% Hispanic American, 4% Native American, 6% international
- 1,640 degree-seeking graduate students
- 15% of applicants admitted
- SAT and SAT Subject Tests or ACT with writing, application essay required
- 94% graduate within 6 years

**General.** Founded in 1769. Regionally accredited. **Degrees:** 1,021 bachelor's awarded; master's, doctoral, first professional offered. **ROTC:** Army. **Location:** 130 miles from Boston. **Calendar:** Quarter, extensive summer session. **Full-time faculty:** 492 total. **Part-time faculty:** 155 total. **Class size:** 64% < 20, 22% 20-39, 6% 40-49, 7% 50-99, 2% >100. **Special facilities:** Observatory, centers for humanities, social sciences, physical science, performing arts, ethics, life science, computation.

**Freshman class profile.** 14,176 applied, 2,166 admitted, 1,116 enrolled.

| Mid 50% test scores | | | |
|---|---|---|---|
| SAT critical reading: | 660-770 | GPA 3.0-3.49: | 16% |
| SAT math: | 670-780 | GPA 2.0-2.99: | 3% |
| SAT writing: | 660-770 | Return as sophomores: | 98% |
| ACT composite: | 29-34 | Out-of-state: | 96% |
| GPA 3.50 or higher: | 80% | Live on campus: | 100% |
| | | International: | 8% |

**Basis for selection.** Evidence of intellectual capability, motivation, and personal integrity of primary importance. Talent, accomplishment, and involvement in nonacademic areas also evaluated. 2 SAT Subject Tests of student's choice required. Interview optional.

**High school preparation.** Recommended units include English 4, mathematics 4, social studies 3, science 3 and foreign language 3. Strongest academic program available to applicant recommended.

**2008-2009 Annual costs.** Tuition/fees: $37,250. Room/board: $10,930. Books/supplies: $1,412. Personal expenses: $1,341.

**2006-2007 Financial aid.** All financial aid based on need. 669 full-time freshmen applied for aid; 512 were judged to have need; 512 of these received aid. Average need met was 100%. Average scholarship/grant was $30,269; average loan $3,212. 84% of total undergraduate aid awarded as scholarships/grants, 16% as loans/jobs.

**Application procedures. Admission:** Closing date 1/1 (postmark date). $70 fee, may be waived for applicants with need. Application may be submitted online. Admission notification 3/31. Must reply by 5/1. **Financial aid:** Closing date 2/1. FAFSA, CSS PROFILE required. Applicants notified by 3/31; must reply by 5/1.

**Academics.** Undergraduate research encouraged. **Special study options:** Combined bachelor's/graduate degree, double major, exchange student, honors, independent study, internships, semester at sea, student-designed major, study abroad, teacher certification program, Washington semester. Williams Mystic Seaport Maritime Studies program, study at Eugene O'Neill National Theater Institute, Twelve College Exchange, University of California-San Diego exchange program, McGill University exchange program, exchange programs with over 50 foreign universities, special academic programs in Washington, DC and Tucson, AZ. **Credit/placement by examination:** AP, CLEP, IB, SAT, ACT, institutional tests. **Support services:** Learning center, study skills assistance, tutoring, writing center.

**Majors. Area/ethnic studies:** African, African-American, Asian, Caribbean, German, Hispanic-American/Latino/Chicano, Latin American, Native American, Near/Middle Eastern, Russian/Slavic, Spanish/Iberian, women's. **Biology:** General, biochemistry, Biochemistry/biophysics and molecular biology, cell/histology, ecology, evolutionary, genetics, molecular. **Computer sciences:** Computer science. **Conservation:** General, environmental studies. **Engineering:** Biomedical, physics, science. **English:** English lit. **Foreign languages:** Arabic, Chinese, classics, comparative lit, French, German, Hebrew, Italian, Japanese, linguistics, Russian, South Asian, Spanish. **History:** General. **Interdisciplinary:** Ancient studies, classical/archaeology, neuroscience. **Math:** General. **Philosophy/religion:** Philosophy, religion. **Physical sciences:** Astronomy, chemistry, physics, planetary. **Psychology:** General. **Social sciences:** Anthropology, economics, geography, political science, sociology. **Visual/performing arts:** Art history/conservation, dramatic, film/cinema, studio arts.

**Most popular majors.** Area/ethnic studies 6%, English 7%, foreign language 6%, history 9%, psychology 10%, social sciences 31%.

**Computing on campus.** PC or laptop required. Dormitories wired for high-speed internet access and linked to campus network. Commuter students can connect to campus network. Online course registration, online library, helpline, repair service, student web hosting, wireless network available.

**Student life. Freshman orientation:** Mandatory. Held week before fall classes begin; freshmen trips led by Dartmouth outing club. **Housing:** Guaranteed on-campus for freshmen. Coed dorms, apartments, cooperative housing, fraternity/sorority housing, substance-free housing available. Academic affinity housing, faculty-in-residence programs, special interest housing available. **Activities:** Bands, campus ministries, choral groups, dance, drama, film society, international student organizations, literary magazine, music ensembles, Model UN, musical theater, opera, radio station, student government, student newspaper, symphony orchestra, TV station, community and service programs, religious groups, and political and ethnic organizations available.

**Athletics.** NCAA. **Intercollegiate:** Baseball M, basketball, cross-country, diving, equestrian, field hockey W, football (tackle) M, golf, ice hockey, lacrosse, rowing (crew), sailing, skiing, soccer, softball W, squash, swimming, tennis, track and field, volleyball W. **Intramural:** Baseball M, basketball, bowling, cross-country, football (non-tackle), golf, handball, ice hockey,

lacrosse, racquetball, skiing, soccer, softball, squash, swimming, table tennis, tennis, track and field, volleyball, water polo, wrestling M. **Team name:** Big Green.

**Student services.** Alcohol/substance abuse counseling, campus ministries, career counseling, student employment services, financial aid counseling, health services, minority student services, on-campus daycare, personal counseling, placement for graduates, women's services. **Physically disabled:** Services for visually, speech, hearing impaired.

**Contact.** E-mail: admissions.office@dartmouth.edu
Phone: (603) 646-2875 Fax: (603) 646-1216
Maria Laskaris, Dean of Admissions and Financial Aid, Dartmouth College, 6016 McNutt Hall, Hanover, NH 03755

## Franklin Pierce University
Rindge, New Hampshire — CB member
www.franklinpierce.edu — CB code: 3395

- Private 4-year liberal arts college
- Residential campus in small town
- 1,721 degree-seeking undergraduates: 1% part-time, 49% women
- 71% of applicants admitted
- SAT or ACT with writing, application essay required

**General.** Founded in 1962. Regionally accredited. 5 satellite campuses offer continuing education sequence of 8-week undergraduate and 12 week graduate sessions on-campus and on-line. Associate, bachelor's, MBA, DPT, MEd, DA offered through graduate and professional studies division campuses in Concord, Keene, Lebanon, Manchester and Portsmouth. **Degrees:** 278 bachelor's awarded; master's, doctoral offered. **ROTC:** Army, Air Force. **Location:** 20 miles from Keene, 60 miles from Boston. **Calendar:** Semester, limited summer session. **Full-time faculty:** 76 total; 82% have terminal degrees, 41% women. **Part-time faculty:** 90 total. **Class size:** 65% < 20, 33% 20-39, 1% 50-99, less than 1% >100. **Special facilities:** Graphics workshop, colonial archaeological dig site, glass blowing studio, ceramic kiln, black box theater.

**Freshman class profile.** 4,208 applied, 2,987 admitted, 531 enrolled.

| Mid 50% test scores | | | |
|---|---|---|---|
| SAT critical reading: | 440-550 | GPA 2.0-2.99: | 68% |
| SAT math: | 430-540 | Rank in top quarter: | 20% |
| SAT writing: | 420-520 | Rank in top tenth: | 7% |
| GPA 3.50 or higher: | 9% | Return as sophomores: | 68% |
| GPA 3.0-3.49: | 23% | Out-of-state: | 82% |
| | | Live on campus: | 97% |

**Basis for selection.** School achievement record, difficulty of course work, recommendations and school involvement primary considerations. Test scores also important. Interview recommended for all. **Homeschooled:** Letter of recommendation (nonparent) required.

**High school preparation.** 16 units required. Required units include English 4, mathematics 3, social studies 3, science 3 (laboratory 2) and academic electives 4.

**2007-2008 Annual costs.** Tuition/fees: $26,816. Room/board: $8,640. Books/supplies: $896. Personal expenses: $1,200.

**2007-2008 Financial aid. Need-based:** Average need met was 70%. Average scholarship/grant was $14,645; average loan $3,462. 59% of total undergraduate aid awarded as scholarships/grants, 41% as loans/jobs. **Non-need-based:** Scholarships awarded for academics, alumni affiliation, athletics, leadership, music/drama.

**Application procedures. Admission:** No deadline. No application fee. Application may be submitted online. Admission notification on a rolling basis beginning on or about 10/15. Must reply by May 1 or within 2 week(s) if notified thereafter. **Financial aid:** Closing date 3/1. FAFSA required. Applicants notified on a rolling basis starting 3/1; must reply within 2 week(s) of notification.

**Academics. Special study options:** Distance learning, double major, dual enrollment of high school students, ESL, exchange student, honors, independent study, internships, student-designed major, study abroad, teacher certification program, Washington semester. Walk Across Europe, Washington Internship, Arcadia Study Abroad, Vienna, Athens. **Credit/placement by examination:** AP, CLEP, IB, SAT, ACT, institutional tests. 30 credit hours maximum toward bachelor's degree. **Support services:** Learning center, reduced course load, remedial instruction, study skills assistance, tutoring, writing center.

**Majors. Area/ethnic studies:** American. **Biology:** General. **Business:** Accounting/finance, management information systems, management science, marketing. **Communications:** Media studies. **Computer sciences:** Information technology. **Conservation:** Environmental science. **Education:** General. **English:** English lit. **History:** General. **Liberal arts:** Arts/sciences. **Math:** General. **Parks/recreation:** Facilities management. **Protective services:** Criminal justice. **Psychology:** General. **Public administration:** Social work. **Social sciences:** Anthropology, political science. **Visual/performing arts:** Arts management, commercial/advertising art, dance, dramatic, music performance, studio arts.

**Most popular majors.** Business/marketing 15%, communications/journalism 12%, psychology 6%, security/protective services 12%, social sciences 10%, visual/performing arts 14%.

**Computing on campus.** 109 workstations in dormitories, library, computer center. Dormitories wired for high-speed internet access and linked to campus network. Commuter students can connect to campus network. Online library, helpline, repair service, wireless network available.

**Student life. Freshman orientation:** Mandatory. Preregistration for classes offered. Held immediately prior to start of semester. **Housing:** Guaranteed on-campus for all undergraduates. Coed dorms, special housing for disabled, apartments, substance-free housing available. $250 nonrefundable deposit, deadline 6/20. **Activities:** Jazz band, campus ministries, choral groups, dance, drama, international student organizations, literary magazine, music ensembles, musical theater, radio station, student government, student newspaper, TV station, student senate, law club, business club, black student alliance, Pierce Pals, community service, environmental awareness club, emergency medical services club, education club.

**Athletics.** NCAA. **Intercollegiate:** Baseball M, basketball, cross-country W, field hockey W, golf M, ice hockey M, lacrosse, rowing (crew), soccer, softball W, tennis, volleyball W. **Intramural:** Baseball M, basketball, cross-country, field hockey W, football (non-tackle), sailing, skiing, soccer, softball, table tennis, tennis, volleyball. **Team name:** Ravens.

**Student services.** Alcohol/substance abuse counseling, campus ministries, career counseling, student employment services, financial aid counseling, health services, personal counseling, placement for graduates, women's services. **Physically disabled:** Services for hearing impaired.

**Contact.** E-mail: admissions@franklinpierce.edu
Phone: (603) 899-4050 Toll-free number: (800) 437-0048
Fax: (603) 899-4394
Linda Quimby, Associate Director, Admissions, Franklin Pierce University, 40 University Drive, Rindge, NH 03461-0060

## Granite State College
### Concord, New Hampshire
www.granite.edu                    CB code: 0458

- Public 4-year liberal arts college
- Commuter campus in large town
- 1,065 degree-seeking undergraduates: 57% part-time, 75% women, 1% African American, 1% Hispanic American, 1% Native American
- 216 graduate students
- Application essay required
- 58% graduate within 6 years

**General.** Founded in 1972. Regionally accredited. **Degrees:** 218 bachelor's, 105 associate awarded. **ROTC:** Army. **Calendar:** Trimester, limited summer session. **Part-time faculty:** 142 total; 55% women. **Class size:** 89% < 20, 11% 20-39.

**Freshman class profile.** 80 applied, 80 admitted, 48 enrolled.

**Basis for selection.** Open admission. Accuplacer tests used for placement.

**2007-2008 Annual costs.** Tuition/fees: $6,920; $7,460 out-of-state. Books/supplies: $900. Personal expenses: $2,475.

**2006-2007 Financial aid. Need-based:** 33% of total undergraduate aid awarded as scholarships/grants, 67% as loans/jobs.

**Application procedures. Admission:** No deadline. $45 fee. Application may be submitted online. Admission notification on a rolling basis. **Financial aid:** No deadline. FAFSA, institutional form required. Applicants notified on a rolling basis starting 4/15.

**Academics. Special study options:** Accelerated study, cross-registration, distance learning, double major, independent study, internships, liberal arts/career combination, student-designed major. **Credit/placement by examination:** AP, CLEP, SAT, ACT, institutional tests. 32 credit hours maximum toward associate degree, 64 toward bachelor's. Exams must support degree

program. **Support services:** Learning center, remedial instruction, study skills assistance.

**Majors. Business:** Management science. **Education:** Early childhood. **Interdisciplinary:** Behavioral sciences. **Liberal arts:** Arts/sciences. **Protective services:** Criminal justice, law enforcement admin. **Other:** Applied technology.

**Most popular majors.** Business/marketing 26%, interdisciplinary studies 17%, liberal arts 48%.

**Computing on campus.** 128 workstations in computer center, student center. Online course registration, online library, helpline, wireless network available.

**Student life. Activities:** Alumni/learner association.

**Student services.** Adult student services, career counseling, financial aid counseling, veterans' counselor.

**Contact.** E-mail: ruth.nawn@granite.edu
Phone: (603) 228-3000 ext. 339 Toll-free number: (888) 228-3000 ext. 339
Fax: (603) 513-1387
Ruth Nawn, Associate Director of Admissions, Granite State College, 8 Old Suncook Road, Concord, NH 03301-7317

## Hesser College
### Manchester, New Hampshire
www.hesser.edu                    CB code: 3452

- For-profit 4-year business and junior college
- Residential campus in small city
- 3,800 undergraduates
- Application essay, interview required

**General.** Founded in 1900. Regionally accredited. Courses also available at centers in Nashua, Salem, Portsmouth, and Concord. **Degrees:** 161 bachelor's, 888 associate awarded. **Location:** 50 miles from Boston. **Calendar:** Semester, limited summer session. **Full-time faculty:** 50 total. **Part-time faculty:** 130 total.

**Freshman class profile.**

Out-of-state:          25%    Live on campus:          18%

**Basis for selection.** School achievement record most important. Admission granted to applicants in top 70% of graduating class with 2.0 high school GPA. Physical therapist and graphic design programs are selective. Portfolio recommended for fashion design, interior design and graphic design programs. **Learning Disabled:** Must meet with director of center for teaching, learning and assessment.

**2007-2008 Annual costs.** Books/supplies: $1,200. Personal expenses: $450.

**Financial aid.** All financial aid based on need. **Additional information:** Two private loans available to assist students in paying their balance; Tree Loan, SLM Loan.

**Application procedures. Admission:** No deadline. $20 fee, may be waived for applicants with need. Application may be submitted online. Admission notification on a rolling basis. **Financial aid:** Priority date 5/1; no closing date. FAFSA, institutional form required. Applicants notified on a rolling basis starting 3/1; must reply within 3 week(s) of notification.

**Academics. Special study options:** Accelerated study, independent study, internships. **Credit/placement by examination:** AP, CLEP, IB, institutional tests. Max of 50% of total program credits awarded via CLEP, DANTES and Advanced Placement exams. Max of 25% of total program credits awarded via institutional exams. **Support services:** Learning center, reduced course load, remedial instruction, tutoring, writing center.

**Majors. Business:** Accounting, business admin. **Protective services:** Law enforcement admin.

**Computing on campus.** 20 workstations in library, computer center. Dormitories wired for high-speed internet access. Helpline, repair service available.

**Student life. Freshman orientation:** Mandatory. Preregistration for classes offered. **Housing:** Guaranteed on-campus for freshmen. Single-sex dorms, substance-free housing available. $125 deposit. **Activities:** Choral groups, radio station, student government, TV station, special interest organizations relating to accounting, business, travel, and retailing, community service club.

**Athletics.** NJCAA. **Intercollegiate:** Baseball M, basketball, soccer, softball W, volleyball. **Intramural:** Basketball, cheerleading W, football (nontackle), soccer, volleyball. **Team name:** Blue Devils.

**Student services.** Alcohol/substance abuse counseling, career counseling, student employment services, financial aid counseling, health services, personal counseling, placement for graduates, veterans' counselor.

**Contact.** E-mail: admissions@hesser.edu
Phone: (603) 668-6660 ext. 2110 Toll-free
number: (800) 526-9231 ext. 2110 Fax: (603) 666-4722
Leann Gray, Director of Admissions, Hesser College, 3 Sundial Avenue, Manchester, NH 03103

## Keene State College
**Keene, New Hampshire**
www.keene.edu

**CB member**
**CB code: 3472**

- Public 4-year liberal arts and teachers college
- Residential campus in large town
- 4,658 degree-seeking undergraduates: 4% part-time, 58% women, 1% African American, 1% Hispanic American
- 98 degree-seeking graduate students
- 73% of applicants admitted
- SAT or ACT (ACT writing recommended), application essay required
- 58% graduate within 6 years

**General.** Founded in 1909. Regionally accredited. **Degrees:** 1,046 bachelor's, 41 associate awarded; master's offered. **ROTC:** Air Force. **Location:** 52 miles from Concord, 85 miles from Boston. **Calendar:** Semester, extensive summer session. **Full-time faculty:** 185 total; 94% have terminal degrees, 3% minority, 48% women. **Part-time faculty:** 246 total; less than 1% minority, 50% women. **Class size:** 53% < 20, 42% 20-39, 3% 40-49, 2% 50-99, less than 1% >100. **Special facilities:** Arboretum and gardens, center for Holocaust studies, child development center, community research center, curriculum materials library, small business institute, college-owned camp, 400-acre preserve, theater complex.

**Freshman class profile.** 4,676 applied, 3,425 admitted, 1,301 enrolled.

| Mid 50% test scores | | Rank in top quarter: | 20% |
|---|---|---|---|
| SAT critical reading: | 440-540 | Rank in top tenth: | 4% |
| SAT math: | 440-540 | End year in good standing: | 93% |
| SAT writing: | 440-540 | Return as sophomores: | 80% |
| GPA 3.50 or higher: | 15% | Out-of-state: | 53% |
| GPA 3.0-3.49: | 36% | Live on campus: | 95% |
| GPA 2.0-2.99: | 48% | | |

**Basis for selection.** High school record, including challenging courses, most important. SAT or ACT scores do not hold nearly as much weight as high school performance. Audition required for music education and music performance programs; portfolio required for art program. **Homeschooled:** Statement describing homeschool structure and mission required. **Learning Disabled:** Documented proof of disability required for some services.

**High school preparation.** 14 units required. Required units include English 4, mathematics 3, social studies 2, science 3 and academic electives 2.

**2007-2008 Annual costs.** Tuition/fees: $8,298; $15,848 out-of-state. New England Regional tuition is 150% of in-state public institution tuition. Room/board: $7,460. Books/supplies: $800. Personal expenses: $750.

**2006-2007 Financial aid. Need-based:** 947 full-time freshmen applied for aid; 661 were judged to have need; 652 of these received aid. Average need met was 67%. Average scholarship/grant was $5,061; average loan $3,155. 39% of total undergraduate aid awarded as scholarships/grants, 61% as loans/jobs. **Non-need-based:** Awarded to 814 full-time undergraduates, including 219 freshmen. Scholarships awarded for academics, alumni affiliation, art, music/drama.

**Application procedures. Admission:** Closing date 4/1 (receipt date). $35 fee, may be waived for applicants with need. Application may be submitted online. Admission notification on a rolling basis beginning on or about 12/1. Must reply by 5/1. **Financial aid:** Closing date 3/1. FAFSA required. Applicants notified on a rolling basis; must reply within 4 week(s) of notification.

**Academics. Special study options:** Cooperative education, double major, ESL, exchange student, honors, independent study, internships, liberal arts/career combination, student-designed major, study abroad, teacher certification program. **Credit/placement by examination:** AP, CLEP. 30 credit hours maximum toward associate degree, 60 toward bachelor's. **Support**

**services:** Learning center, pre-admission summer program, reduced course load, study skills assistance, tutoring, writing center.

**Majors. Architecture:** Architecture. **Area/ethnic studies:** American. **Biology:** General. **Business:** Business admin. **Communications:** General, journalism. **Computer sciences:** General. **Conservation:** Environmental studies. **Education:** Biology, chemistry, computer, early childhood, elementary, English, French, geography, health, history, mathematics, music, physical, science, secondary, social studies, Spanish, special, technology/industrial arts. **Engineering technology:** Architectural, occupational safety. **English:** English lit. **Foreign languages:** French, Spanish. **Health:** Athletic training, dietetics, substance abuse counseling. **History:** General, American, European. **Interdisciplinary:** Biological/physical sciences. **Math:** General. **Parks/recreation:** Health/fitness. **Physical sciences:** General, chemistry, geology. **Psychology:** General, clinical, developmental, experimental, social. **Social sciences:** General, economics, geography, sociology. **Visual/performing arts:** Acting, cinematography, commercial/advertising art, dance, directing/producing, film/cinema, graphic design, music history, music performance, music theory/composition, studio arts, theater design, theater history. **Other:** Chemistry physics, Computer mathematics, Individualized, Math physics, Music technology, Technology studies.

**Most popular majors.** Business/marketing 9%, communications/journalism 6%, education 19%, engineering/engineering technologies 11%, psychology 13%, social sciences 11%, visual/performing arts 10%.

**Computing on campus.** 500 workstations in dormitories, library, computer center, student center. Dormitories wired for high-speed internet access and linked to campus network. Commuter students can connect to campus network. Online course registration, online library, helpline, repair service, student web hosting, wireless network available.

**Student life. Freshman orientation:** Mandatory. Preregistration for classes offered. Two day session in June. Parents invited for additional fee. **Housing:** Coed dorms, single-sex dorms, apartments, fraternity/sorority housing, substance-free housing available. $100 nonrefundable deposit, deadline 5/1. Leadership, quiet, and music housing available. **Activities:** Bands, campus ministries, choral groups, dance, drama, film society, international student organizations, literary magazine, music ensembles, musical theater, radio station, student government, student newspaper, TV station, Habitat for Humanity, Amnesty International, student government, campus ecology, civil liberties union, student volunteer organization, environmental outing club, KSC Pride, Circle K.

**Athletics.** NCAA. **Intercollegiate:** Baseball M, basketball, cheerleading, cross-country, diving, field hockey W, lacrosse, soccer, softball W, swimming, track and field, volleyball W. **Intramural:** Badminton, basketball, cross-country, football (non-tackle), racquetball, soccer, softball, tennis, track and field, volleyball, water polo. **Team name:** Owls.

**Student services.** Adult student services, alcohol/substance abuse counseling, campus ministries, career counseling, student employment services, financial aid counseling, health services, minority student services, on-campus daycare, personal counseling, placement for graduates, veterans' counselor. **Physically disabled:** Services for visually, speech, hearing impaired.

**Contact.** E-mail: admissions@keene.edu
Phone: (603) 358-2276 Toll-free number: (800) 572-1909
Fax: (603) 358-2767
Margaret Richmond, Director of Admissions, Keene State College, 229 Main Street, Keene, NH 03435-2604

## Magdalen College
**Warner, New Hampshire**
www.magdalen.edu

**CB code: 3562**

- Private 4-year liberal arts college affiliated with Roman Catholic Church
- Residential campus in small town
- 69 degree-seeking undergraduates: 57% women, 1% African American, 6% Asian American, 3% Hispanic American, 3% international
- 76% of applicants admitted
- SAT or ACT (ACT writing recommended), application essay, interview required

**General.** Regionally accredited. **Degrees:** 11 bachelor's awarded. **Location:** 20 miles from Concord. **Calendar:** Semester. **Full-time faculty:** 7 total. **Part-time faculty:** 2 total. **Special facilities:** Observatory.

**Freshman class profile.** 41 applied, 31 admitted, 23 enrolled.

| Mid 50% test scores | | | |
|---|---|---|---|
| SAT critical reading: | 510-670 | Return as sophomores: | 72% |
| SAT math: | 390-570 | Out-of-state: | 78% |
| ACT composite: | 21-24 | Live on campus: | 100% |
| End year in good standing: | 95% | International: | 4% |

**Basis for selection.** Campus visit required (may be waived due to hardship). Academic GPA and high school transcript important.

**High school preparation.** 24 units recommended. Recommended units include English 4, mathematics 4, social studies 3, history 2, science 3, foreign language 2 and academic electives 6.

**2007-2008 Annual costs.** Tuition/fees: $11,470. Room/board: $6,500. Books/supplies: $350. Personal expenses: $200.

**Financial aid.** All financial aid based on need.

**Application procedures. Admission:** Closing date 5/1 (postmark date). $35 fee. Application must be submitted on paper. Admission notification on a rolling basis. Must reply by May 1 or within 4 week(s) if notified thereafter. **Financial aid:** Closing date 6/30. Institutional form required. Applicants notified by 7/1; must reply by 7/1 or within 4 week(s) of notification.

**Academics. Special study options:** Study abroad. **Credit/placement by examination:** CLEP. **Support services:** Learning center, pre-admission summer program, remedial instruction, study skills assistance, tutoring.

**Majors. Liberal arts:** Arts/sciences.

**Computing on campus.** 20 workstations in dormitories, library. Online library available.

**Student life. Freshman orientation:** Mandatory. 2-day program in early September. **Policies:** Dress code for class. Required attendance at meals. Curfews in dormitories. No-cut policy for class. Campus service required. Sunday mass required for Catholic students. Religious observance required. **Housing:** Guaranteed on-campus for all undergraduates. Single-sex dorms, substance-free housing available. $500 deposit, deadline 6/15. **Activities:** Choral groups, drama, music ensembles, musical theater, campus service organization, college choir.

**Athletics. Intramural:** Basketball, soccer, volleyball.

**Student services.** Campus ministries, career counseling, student employment services, financial aid counseling, personal counseling.

**Contact.** E-mail: admissions@magdalen.edu
Phone: (603) 456-2656 ext. 13 Toll-free number: (877) 498-1723
Fax: (603) 456-2660
Michael Rennie, Director of Admissions, Magdalen College, 511 Kearsarge Mountain Road, Warner, NH 03278

## New England College
### Henniker, New Hampshire
www.nec.edu                    CB code: 3657

- Private 4-year business, liberal arts and teachers college
- Residential campus in small town
- 1,052 degree-seeking undergraduates: 2% part-time, 47% women, 3% African American, 1% Asian American, 2% Hispanic American, 7% international
- 391 degree-seeking graduate students
- 70% of applicants admitted
- Application essay required
- 45% graduate within 6 years; 24% enter graduate study

**General.** Founded in 1946. Regionally accredited. Cross-registration with other 4-year institutions available through New Hampshire College and University Council. **Degrees:** 131 bachelor's awarded; master's offered. **ROTC:** Army, Air Force. **Location:** 18 miles from Concord. **Calendar:** Semester, limited summer session. **Full-time faculty:** 61 total; 75% have terminal degrees, 3% minority, 38% women. **Part-time faculty:** 88 total; 15% have terminal degrees, 1% minority, 49% women. **Class size:** 71% < 20, 27% 20-39, 2% 40-49. **Special facilities:** Educational innovation center.

**Freshman class profile.** 2,150 applied, 1,511 admitted, 306 enrolled.

| Mid 50% test scores | | | |
|---|---|---|---|
| SAT critical reading: | 380-500 | Rank in top tenth: | 6% |
| SAT math: | 380-500 | End year in good standing: | 74% |
| SAT writing: | 400-500 | Return as sophomores: | 63% |
| ACT composite: | 14-21 | Out-of-state: | 59% |
| GPA 3.50 or higher: | 11% | Live on campus: | 79% |
| GPA 3.0-3.49: | 22% | International: | 4% |
| GPA 2.0-2.99: | 58% | Fraternities: | 5% |
| Rank in top quarter: | 15% | Sororities: | 3% |

**Basis for selection.** School achievement record most important, followed by recommendations, essay or personal statement, evidence of leadership and extracurricular activities. Interview recommended for all; portfolio recommended for art program.

**High school preparation.** 12 units required. Required and recommended units include English 4, mathematics 3, social studies 3, science 3 (laboratory 1-2) and foreign language 2.

**2008-2009 Annual costs.** Tuition/fees: $26,472. Room/board: $9,288. Books/supplies: $640. Personal expenses: $1,250.

**2007-2008 Financial aid. Need-based:** 265 full-time freshmen applied for aid; 199 were judged to have need; 199 of these received aid. Average need met was 88%. Average scholarship/grant was $13,249; average loan $7,287. 56% of total undergraduate aid awarded as scholarships/grants, 44% as loans/jobs. **Non-need-based:** Awarded to 342 full-time undergraduates, including 101 freshmen. Scholarships awarded for academics, alumni affiliation, art, job skills, leadership, music/drama.

**Application procedures. Admission:** No deadline. $30 fee, may be waived for applicants with need. Application may be submitted online. Admission notification on a rolling basis beginning on or about 11/1. **Financial aid:** Priority date 4/1; no closing date. FAFSA, institutional form required. Applicants notified on a rolling basis starting 1/12; must reply within 2 week(s) of notification.

**Academics. Special study options:** Accelerated study, combined bachelor's/graduate degree, cross-registration, distance learning, double major, dual enrollment of high school students, ESL, exchange student, external degree, honors, independent study, internships, liberal arts/career combination, semester at sea, student-designed major, study abroad, teacher certification program, Washington semester. Exchange programs with Regent's College, London; American University of Paris; 18 colleges in Quebec, Canada; University of the Sunshine Coast, Australia. Students keep all financial aid when abroad. **Credit/placement by examination:** AP, CLEP, IB, institutional tests. 21 credit hours maximum toward associate degree, 21 toward bachelor's. **Support services:** Learning center, reduced course load, study skills assistance, tutoring, writing center.

**Majors. Biology:** General. **Business:** Accounting, business admin, entrepreneurial studies, finance, human resources, management information systems, marketing. **Communications:** General, advertising, public relations. **Computer sciences:** General. **Conservation:** Environmental science. **Education:** Art, biology, elementary, English, learning disabled, mathematics, physical, science, secondary, social science, social studies, special. **Engineering:** Civil. **English:** Creative writing, English lit. **Foreign languages:** Comparative lit. **Health:** Health care admin, premedicine. **History:** General. **Legal studies:** Prelaw. **Liberal arts:** Arts/sciences. **Math:** General. **Parks/recreation:** General, exercise sciences, facilities management, sports admin. **Philosophy/religion:** Philosophy. **Protective services:** Criminal justice. **Psychology:** General. **Social sciences:** Political science, sociology. **Visual/performing arts:** Art, art history/conservation, dramatic, photography.

**Most popular majors.** Business/marketing 14%, English 6%, health sciences 7%, parks/recreation 15%, psychology 9%, security/protective services 7%, social sciences 9%, visual/performing arts 10%.

**Computing on campus.** 176 workstations in library, computer center, student center. Dormitories wired for high-speed internet access and linked to campus network. Commuter students can connect to campus network. Online course registration, online library, helpline, wireless network available.

**Student life. Freshman orientation:** Available. Preregistration for classes offered. Held 3 days prior to first day of classes and 3 mid-summer options. **Housing:** Guaranteed on-campus for all undergrads. Coed dorms, apartments, fraternity/sorority housing, substance-free housing available. $100 nonrefundable deposit. Quiet study options, special interest housing available. **Activities:** Choral groups, dance, drama, international student organizations, literary magazine, radio station, student government, student newspaper, international student association, Hillel, Servcorps, environmental action committee, Womyn's Network, international diplomacy council, Adventure Bound, T.E.A.C.H.

**Athletics.** NCAA. **Intercollegiate:** Baseball M, basketball, cross-country, field hockey W, ice hockey, lacrosse, soccer, softball W. **Intramural:** Baseball M, basketball, ice hockey, soccer, softball, table tennis, tennis, volleyball. **Team name:** Pilgrims.

**Student services.** Adult student services, alcohol/substance abuse counseling, career counseling, student employment services, financial aid counseling, health services, personal counseling, placement for graduates, veterans' counselor.

**Contact.** E-mail: admission@nec.edu
Phone: (603) 428-2223 Toll-free number: (800) 521-7642
Fax: (603) 428-3155
Diane Raymond, Director of Admissions, New England College, 102 Bridge Street, Henniker, NH 03242

---

### Plymouth State University
**Plymouth, New Hampshire**     CB member
www.plymouth.edu     CB code: 3690

- Public 4-year university and teachers college
- Residential campus in small town
- 4,221 degree-seeking undergraduates: 50% women
- 863 graduate students
- 66% of applicants admitted
- SAT or ACT with writing, application essay required

**General.** Founded in 1871. Regionally accredited. **Degrees:** 616 bachelor's awarded; master's offered. **ROTC:** Army, Air Force. **Location:** 60 miles from Manchester, 115 miles from Boston. **Calendar:** Semester, limited summer session. **Full-time faculty:** 176 total. **Part-time faculty:** 171 total. **Class size:** 46% < 20, 48% 20-39, 4% 40-49, 2% 50-99, less than 1% >100. **Special facilities:** Planetarium, cultural arts center, child development and family center, geographic information systems lab, meteorology institute, center for the environment, climbing wall, ropes course.

**Freshman class profile.** 4,247 applied, 2,788 admitted, 1,012 enrolled.

| Mid 50% test scores | | | |
|---|---|---|---|
| SAT critical reading: | 420-520 | GPA 2.0-2.99: | 61% |
| SAT math: | 430-530 | Rank in top quarter: | 16% |
| ACT composite: | 17-22 | Rank in top tenth: | 4% |
| GPA 3.50 or higher: | 9% | Out-of-state: | 43% |
| GPA 3.0-3.49: | 27% | Live on campus: | 94% |

**Basis for selection.** Decision made by committee, based on school achievement record (most important) followed by test scores, recommendations, essay and extracurricular activites. SAT/ACT not required for resident or non-resident aliens. Audition required for music and theater programs. Portfolio required for art program. **Homeschooled:** Transcript of any work attempted in secondary school, SAT or ACT, GED or homeschool diploma, outline of homeschool curriculum required.

**High school preparation.** 13 units required; 18 recommended. Required and recommended units include English 4, mathematics 3, social studies 2-3, history 1-2, science 2-3 (laboratory 1) and foreign language 2.

**2007-2008 Annual costs.** Tuition/fees: $7,944; $15,494 out-of-state. New England Regional tuition: 150% of in-state public institution tuition. Room/board: $8,030. Books/supplies: $950. Personal expenses: $1,120.

**2006-2007 Financial aid. Need-based:** 858 full-time freshmen applied for aid; 601 were judged to have need; 592 of these received aid. Average need met was 59%. Average scholarship/grant was $5,062; average loan $2,602. 36% of total undergraduate aid awarded as scholarships/grants, 64% as loans/jobs. **Non-need-based:** Awarded to 1,020 full-time undergraduates, including 299 freshmen. Scholarships awarded for academics, minority status, music/drama.

**Application procedures. Admission:** Closing date 4/1 (postmark date). $35 fee, may be waived for applicants with need. Application may be submitted online. Admission notification on a rolling basis beginning on or about 11/1. Must reply by 5/1. **Financial aid:** Priority date 3/1; no closing date. FAFSA required. Applicants notified on a rolling basis starting 2/15; must reply by 5/1.

**Academics. Special study options:** Distance learning, double major, exchange student, honors, independent study, internships, student-designed major, study abroad, teacher certification program. **Credit/placement by examination:** AP, CLEP, institutional tests. 30 credit hours maximum toward bachelor's degree. **Support services:** Study skills assistance, tutoring, writing center.

**Majors. Architecture:** Urban/community planning. **Biology:** General, biotechnology, environmental. **Business:** General, accounting, business admin, marketing. **Communications:** General. **Computer sciences:** Computer science, information technology. **Conservation:** Environmental studies. **Education:** Art, early childhood, elementary, music. **English:** English lit. **Foreign languages:** French, Spanish. **Health:** Athletic training, public health ed. **History:** General. **Liberal arts:** Humanities. **Math:** General. **Parks/recreation:** Health/fitness. **Philosophy/religion:** Philosophy. **Physical sciences:** Atmospheric science, chemistry. **Protective services:** Criminal justice. **Psychology:** General. **Public administration:** General, social work. **Social sciences:** General, applied economics, geography, political science. **Visual/performing arts:** Art, commercial/advertising art, dramatic, studio arts. **Other:** Adventure education.

**Most popular majors.** Business/marketing 26%, education 17%, English 6%, parks/recreation 6%, visual/performing arts 7%.

**Computing on campus.** 500 workstations in dormitories, library, computer center, student center. Dormitories wired for high-speed internet access and linked to campus network. Commuter students can connect to campus network. Online course registration, online library, helpline, repair service, student web hosting, wireless network available.

**Student life. Freshman orientation:** Mandatory, $180 fee. Preregistration for classes offered. 5 sessions in June, one session in September. **Housing:** Guaranteed on-campus for freshmen. Coed dorms, apartments, fraternity/sorority housing, substance-free housing available. $90 deposit, deadline 5/1. Wellness housing, substance-free housing, music/theater/dance housing, honors housing, special interest housing, and community service housing available. **Activities:** Bands, choral groups, dance, drama, film society, international student organizations, literary magazine, music ensembles, musical theater, radio station, student government, student newspaper, Chi Alpha Christian Fellowship, multicultural student organization, Nicaragua club, volunteer club, social work club, health and wellness club, peer educators, Alternative Spring Break.

**Athletics.** NCAA. **Intercollegiate:** Baseball M, basketball, cheerleading M, diving W, field hockey W, football (tackle) M, ice hockey, lacrosse, skiing, soccer, softball W, swimming W, tennis W, volleyball W, wrestling M. **Intramural:** Basketball; bowling, cross-country, football (non-tackle), golf, racquetball, soccer, softball, table tennis, tennis, triathlon, volleyball. **Team name:** Panthers.

**Student services.** Alcohol/substance abuse counseling, campus ministries, career counseling, student employment services, financial aid counseling, health services, on-campus daycare, personal counseling, placement for graduates, veterans' counselor, women's services. **Physically disabled:** Services for visually, hearing impaired.

**Contact.** E-mail: plymouthadmit@plymouth.edu
Phone: (603) 535-2237 Toll-free number: (800) 842-6900
Fax: (603) 535-2714
Eugene Fahey, Senior Associate Director of Admission, Plymouth State University, 17 High Street MSC 52, Plymouth, NH 03264-1595

---

### Rivier College
**Nashua, New Hampshire**     CB member
www.rivier.edu     CB code: 3728

- Private 4-year liberal arts and teachers college affiliated with Roman Catholic Church
- Commuter campus in small city
- 1,432 degree-seeking undergraduates
- SAT or ACT with writing, application essay required

**General.** Founded in 1933. Regionally accredited. Founded in 1933 by the Sisters of the Presentation of Mary Convent. **Degrees:** 145 bachelor's, 116 associate awarded; master's offered. **ROTC:** Army, Naval, Air Force. **Location:** 19 miles from Manchester, 45 miles from Boston. **Calendar:** Semester, limited summer session. **Full-time faculty:** 71 total; 68% have terminal degrees, 62% women. **Part-time faculty:** 107 total; 19% have terminal degrees, 69% women. **Class size:** 62% < 20, 35% 20-39, 2% 40-49, less than 1% 50-99. **Special facilities:** Center for finance and economics, early childhood center/laboratory school, biology research lab.

**Freshman class profile.**

| | | | |
|---|---|---|---|
| Out-of-state: | 45% | Live on campus: | 68% |

**Basis for selection.** High school academic record (course selection, course level, grades), test scores, extracurricular activities, application essay, and letters of recommendation considered. Interview recommended for all; portfolio required for art programs.

**High school preparation.** 16 units recommended. Recommended units include English 4, mathematics 3, social studies 2, history 1, science 1 (laboratory 1), foreign language 2 and academic electives 3. Nursing program applicants must have completed chemistry and algebra.

**2008-2009 Annual costs.** Tuition/fees: $23,750. Room/board: $8,673. Books/supplies: $1,200. Personal expenses: $1,500.

**Financial aid. Non-need-based:** Scholarships awarded for academics, alumni affiliation, minority status.

**Application procedures. Admission:** Priority date 3/1; no deadline. $25 fee, may be waived for applicants with need. Application may be submitted online. Admission notification on a rolling basis beginning on or about 12/1. **Financial aid:** Priority date 2/1; no closing date. FAFSA required. Applicants notified on a rolling basis starting 3/1; must reply by 5/1 or within 2 week(s) of notification.

**Academics.** Formal programs for learning disabled students not offered, but college staffs Office of Special Needs Services with part-time learning disabilities specialist. **Special study options:** Combined bachelor's/graduate degree, cross-registration, double major, ESL, honors, independent study, internships, liberal arts/career combination, study abroad, teacher certification program. **Credit/placement by examination:** AP, CLEP, IB, institutional tests. 12 credit hours maximum toward associate degree, 12 toward bachelor's. **Support services:** Learning center, reduced course load, study skills assistance, tutoring, writing center.

**Honors college/program.** Honors program limited to 15 students per class. Special application and interview required. Scholarship available to all participants. SAT 1200 plus (exclusive of Writing), top 20% of high school class. Honors classes will fulfill some core requirements.

**Majors. Biology:** General. **Business:** Business admin, management information systems, management science. **Communications:** General, broadcast journalism, journalism, public relations. **Computer sciences:** Computer science. **Education:** General, biology, early childhood, elementary, English, foreign languages, history, mathematics, science, secondary, social science, social studies, Spanish. **Foreign languages:** Spanish. **Health:** Nursing (RN), predental, premedicine, preop/surgical nursing, preveterinary. **History:** General. **Interdisciplinary:** Math/computer science. **Legal studies:** Prelaw. **Liberal arts:** Arts/sciences. **Math:** General. **Psychology:** General. **Social sciences:** General, political science, sociology. **Visual/performing arts:** Commercial/advertising art, design, drawing, painting, photography, studio arts.

**Most popular majors.** Business/marketing 14%, education 24%, health sciences 22%, psychology 12%, social sciences 6%, visual/performing arts 7%.

**Computing on campus.** 150 workstations in dormitories, library, computer center, student center. Dormitories linked to campus network. Commuter students can connect to campus network. Online course registration, online library, helpline, repair service, wireless network available.

**Student life. Freshman orientation:** Mandatory, $100 fee. Preregistration for classes offered. 2-day on-campus program in June. Parallel program for parents. **Housing:** Guaranteed on-campus for all undergraduates. Coed dorms, special housing for disabled, substance-free housing available. $100 deposit, deadline 5/1. **Activities:** Campus ministries, choral groups, dance, drama, literary magazine, Model UN, student government, student newspaper, TV station, campus ministry, REACT (Rivier Environmental Activists), Amnesty International, international club, Chinese student association, America Reads, Americorps, Habitat for Humanity.

**Athletics.** NCAA. **Intercollegiate:** Baseball M, basketball, cross-country, soccer, softball W, track and field, volleyball. **Intramural:** Basketball, soccer, softball, table tennis, volleyball, weight lifting. **Team name:** Raiders.

**Student services.** Adult student services, alcohol/substance abuse counseling, campus ministries, career counseling, student employment services, financial aid counseling, health services, minority student services, on-campus daycare, personal counseling, placement for graduates.

**Contact.** E-mail: rivadmit@rivier.edu
Phone: (603) 897-8507 Toll-free number: (800) 447-4843
Fax: (603) 891-1799
David Boisvert, Director of Undergraduate Admissions, Rivier College, 420 Main Street, Nashua, NH 03060-5086

## St. Anselm College

**Manchester, New Hampshire**  **CB member**
www.anselm.edu  **CB code: 3748**

- Private 4-year nursing and liberal arts college affiliated with Roman Catholic Church
- Residential campus in small city

- 1,936 degree-seeking undergraduates: 1% part-time, 57% women, 1% African American, 1% Asian American, 1% Hispanic American, 1% Native American
- 69% of applicants admitted
- SAT or ACT (ACT writing optional), application essay required

**General.** Founded in 1889. Regionally accredited. Administered by Order of St. Benedict. **Degrees:** 472 bachelor's awarded. **ROTC:** Army, Air Force. **Location:** 50 miles from Boston. **Calendar:** Semester, limited summer session. **Full-time faculty:** 136 total; 94% have terminal degrees, 4% minority, 48% women. **Part-time faculty:** 70 total; 57% have terminal degrees, 4% minority, 47% women. **Class size:** 56% < 20, 40% 20-39, less than 1% 40-49, 2% 50-99, 1% >100. **Special facilities:** Observatory, politics institute, ice arena, humanities and performing arts center, art center.

**Freshman class profile.** 3,521 applied, 2,442 admitted, 571 enrolled.

| Mid 50% test scores | | GPA 2.0-2.99: | 38% |
|---|---|---|---|
| SAT critical reading: | 510-600 | Rank in top quarter: | 53% |
| SAT math: | 510-600 | Rank in top tenth: | 21% |
| ACT composite: | 22-26 | Out-of-state: | 83% |
| GPA 3.50 or higher: | 23% | Live on campus: | 96% |
| GPA 3.0-3.49: | 39% | | |

**Basis for selection.** School achievement record and character most important, followed by test scores, 2 recommendations, essay. Interview recommended. **Homeschooled:** Statement describing homeschool structure and mission, interview, letter of recommendation (nonparent) required.

**High school preparation.** 16 units required. Required and recommended units include English 4, mathematics 3-4, social studies 2, science 3-4 (laboratory 2) and foreign language 2-4.

**2007-2008 Annual costs.** Tuition/fees: $27,690. Room/board: $10,200. Books/supplies: $800.

**2007-2008 Financial aid. Need-based:** 488 full-time freshmen applied for aid; 387 were judged to have need; 384 of these received aid. Average need met was 82%. Average scholarship/grant was $14,350; average loan $4,683. 66% of total undergraduate aid awarded as scholarships/grants, 34% as loans/jobs. **Non-need-based:** Awarded to 1,164 full-time undergraduates, including 352 freshmen. Scholarships awarded for academics, athletics, state residency.

**Application procedures. Admission:** Priority date 3/1; no deadline. $55 fee, may be waived for applicants with need. Application may be submitted online. Admission notification on a rolling basis beginning on or about 1/1. Must reply by May 1 or within 2 week(s) if notified thereafter. **Financial aid:** Closing date 3/15. FAFSA, CSS PROFILE required. Applicants notified on a rolling basis starting 3/10; must reply by 5/1.

**Academics.** 4-semester humanities program required of all students. Special studies certificates in addition to major concentrations available in fine arts (visual arts, theater, music), international studies, communications, computational physical science, human relations and work, French, Spanish, German, Latin, Greek, Russian area studies, Latin American studies, Asian studies, Catholic studies, medieval studies, neuroscience, public policy studies, web design. **Special study options:** Cross-registration, honors, independent study, internships, liberal arts/career combination, New York semester, semester at sea, study abroad, teacher certification program, Washington semester. **Credit/placement by examination:** AP, CLEP, IB, institutional tests. 30 credit hours maximum toward bachelor's degree. **Support services:** Learning center, reduced course load, study skills assistance, tutoring, writing center.

**Majors. Biology:** General, biochemistry. **Business:** General, accounting, finance, managerial economics. **Computer sciences:** Computer science. **Conservation:** Environmental science. **Engineering:** General, physics. **English:** English lit. **Foreign languages:** Classics, French, Spanish. **Health:** Nursing (RN), predental, premedicine. **History:** General. **Interdisciplinary:** Biological/physical sciences, math/computer science. **Legal studies:** Prelaw. **Liberal arts:** Arts/sciences. **Math:** General. **Philosophy/religion:** Philosophy. **Physical sciences:** Chemistry, physics. **Protective services:** Criminal justice. **Psychology:** General. **Social sciences:** Economics, international relations, political science, sociology. **Theology:** Theology. **Visual/performing arts:** Art.

**Most popular majors.** Business/marketing 22%, health sciences 14%, history 6%, psychology 9%, social sciences 28%.

**Computing on campus.** 400 workstations in dormitories, library, computer center, student center. Dormitories wired for high-speed internet access and linked to campus network. Commuter students can connect to campus network. Online course registration, online library, helpline, repair service, wireless network available.

**Student life. Freshman orientation:** Available, $25 fee. Preregistration for classes offered. Held 3 days prior to fall semester. **Housing:** Guaranteed on-campus for all undergraduates. Coed dorms, single-sex dorms, special housing for disabled, apartments, substance-free housing available. $200 nonrefundable deposit, deadline 5/1. **Activities:** Bands, campus ministries, choral groups, dance, drama, film society, international student organizations, literary magazine, Model UN, musical theater, radio station, student government, student newspaper, TV station, Muslim student associations, black student alliance, Knights of Columbus, College Republicans, College Democrats, rugby club, Oxford Companions, volunteers center, music society, Radio Flyers.

**Athletics.** NCAA. **Intercollegiate:** Baseball M, basketball, cross-country, field hockey W, football (tackle) M, golf, ice hockey, lacrosse, skiing, soccer, softball W, tennis, volleyball W. **Intramural:** Basketball, football (non-tackle), handball, ice hockey, racquetball, skiing, soccer, softball, table tennis, tennis, volleyball. **Team name:** Hawks.

**Student services.** Alcohol/substance abuse counseling, campus ministries, career counseling, student employment services, financial aid counseling, health services, minority student services, personal counseling, placement for graduates, veterans' counselor.

**Contact.** E-mail: admission@anselm.edu
Phone: (603) 641-7500 Toll-free number: (888) 426-7356
Fax: (603) 641-7550
Nancy Griffin, Dean of Admission, St. Anselm College, 100 Saint Anselm Drive, Manchester, NH 03102-1310

---

## Southern New Hampshire University

**Manchester, New Hampshire**

www.snhu.edu

CB member
CB code: 3649

- Private 4-year university
- Residential campus in small city
- 1,953 degree-seeking undergraduates: 2% part-time, 55% women, 1% African American, 1% Asian American, 2% Hispanic American, 4% international
- 1,961 degree-seeking graduate students
- 65% of applicants admitted
- SAT or ACT with writing, application essay required
- 50% graduate within 6 years; 14% enter graduate study

**General.** Founded in 1932. Regionally accredited. Continuing Education Centers in Manchester, Nashua, Salem, Seacoast, Laconia (NH), Brunswick (ME) and online. Graduate programs in Manchester, Laconia, Nashua, Seacoast, Salem, Brunswick (ME), and online. **Degrees:** 1,104 bachelor's, 169 associate awarded; master's, doctoral offered. **ROTC:** Army, Air Force. **Location:** 55 miles from Boston. **Calendar:** Differs by program, extensive summer session. **Full-time faculty:** 130 total; 74% have terminal degrees, 10% minority, 40% women. **Part-time faculty:** 267 total; 40% women. **Class size:** 52% < 20, 48% 20-39. **Special facilities:** Culinary institute, financial studies center, advertising agency, audiovisual studio, psychology oberservation lab, career develpment center, iMAC graphics lab.

**Freshman class profile.** 3,565 applied, 2,306 admitted, 545 enrolled.

| Mid 50% test scores | | Rank in top quarter: | 19% |
|---|---|---|---|
| SAT critical reading: | 440-530 | Rank in top tenth: | 4% |
| SAT math: | 440-540 | End year in good standing: | 81% |
| SAT writing: | 440-530 | Return as sophomores: | 75% |
| GPA 3.50 or higher: | 11% | Out-of-state: | 62% |
| GPA 3.0-3.49: | 34% | Live on campus: | 87% |
| GPA 2.0-2.99: | 54% | International: | 4% |

**Basis for selection.** High school academic record weighed most heavily, including courses and course levels, grades, and class rank (if applicable). SAT/ACT scores, extracurricular activities, work experience, recommendations, and essay also considered. Interview required for 3-year bachelor's program. Creative writing majors must submit samples of their original writing. Culinary Arts and Baking and Pastry Arts applicants not required to submit SAT or ACT scores. Interview recommended.

**High school preparation.** Recommended units include English 4, mathematics 3, social studies 2, history 2, science 3 (laboratory 2) and foreign language 2.

**2008-2009 Annual costs.** Tuition/fees: $24,954. Room/board: $9,600. Books/supplies: $900. Personal expenses: $1,000.

**2007-2008 Financial aid. Need-based:** 464 full-time freshmen applied for aid; 411 were judged to have need; 411 of these received aid. Average need met was 69%. Average scholarship/grant was $12,160; average loan $4,555. 55% of total undergraduate aid awarded as scholarships/grants, 45%

as loans/jobs. **Non-need-based:** Awarded to 1,747 full-time undergraduates, including 445 freshmen. Scholarships awarded for academics, alumni affiliation, athletics, leadership, state residency.

**Application procedures. Admission:** Priority date 3/15; no deadline. $40 fee, may be waived for applicants with need. Application may be submitted online. Admission notification on a rolling basis. Must reply by May 1 or within 2 week(s) if notified thereafter. **Financial aid:** Priority date 3/15; no closing date. FAFSA required. Applicants notified on a rolling basis starting 3/1; must reply within 3 week(s) of notification.

**Academics.** All undergraduate day students required to have laptop computer. **Special study options:** Accelerated study, combined bachelor's/graduate degree, cooperative education, distance learning, double major, dual enrollment of high school students, ESL, honors, independent study, internships, semester at sea, student-designed major, study abroad, teacher certification program, United Nations semester, Washington semester, weekend college. Three-year honors program in business administration. **Credit/placement by examination:** AP, CLEP, IB. 15 credit hours maximum toward associate degree, 15 toward bachelor's. **Support services:** Learning center, reduced course load, remedial instruction, study skills assistance, tutoring.

**Majors. Business:** Accounting, business admin, hospitality admin, international, marketing, retailing, tourism/travel. **Communications:** General, advertising, digital media. **Computer sciences:** General. **Conservation:** Environmental studies. **Education:** General, business, early childhood, elementary, English, social studies. **English:** Creative writing, English lit. **Family/consumer sciences:** Child development. **History:** General. **Interdisciplinary:** Accounting/computer science. **Parks/recreation:** Sports admin. **Psychology:** General. **Public administration:** General. **Social sciences:** General, economics, political science. **Visual/performing arts:** Graphic design. **Other:** Justice Studies, Public Relations, Technical Management.

**Most popular majors.** Business/marketing 66%, psychology 6%.

**Computing on campus.** PC or laptop required. 674 workstations in library, computer center. Dormitories wired for high-speed internet access and linked to campus network. Commuter students can connect to campus network. Online course registration, online library, helpline, repair service, wireless network available.

**Student life. Freshman orientation:** Mandatory, $150 fee. Preregistration for classes offered. Five 1-day sessions held in June; 3-day program held at the opening of the fall term. **Housing:** Guaranteed on-campus for all undergraduates. Coed dorms, special housing for disabled, apartments, substance-free housing available. $10 fully refundable deposit, deadline 5/1. Women's floor and wellness housing. **Activities:** Campus ministries, choral groups, dance, drama, international student organizations, literary magazine, Model UN, musical theater, radio station, student government, student newspaper, TV station, over 50 clubs and organizations available.

**Athletics.** NCAA. **Intercollegiate:** Baseball M, basketball, cheerleading, cross-country, golf M, ice hockey M, lacrosse, soccer, softball W, tennis, volleyball W. **Intramural:** Basketball, football (tackle), racquetball, soccer, softball, table tennis, tennis, volleyball W. **Team name:** Penmen.

**Student services.** Adult student services, alcohol/substance abuse counseling, campus ministries, career counseling, student employment services, financial aid counseling, health services, personal counseling, placement for graduates, veterans' counselor. **Physically disabled:** Services for visually, speech, hearing impaired.

**Contact.** E-mail: admission@snhu.edu
Phone: (603) 645-9611 Toll-free number: (800) 642-4968
Fax: (603) 645-9693
Steve Soba, Director of Admission, Southern New Hampshire University, 2500 North River Road, Manchester, NH 03106-1045

---

## Thomas More College of Liberal Arts

**Merrimack, New Hampshire**

www.thomasmorecollege.edu

CB code: 3892

- Private 4-year liberal arts college affiliated with Roman Catholic Church
- Residential campus in large town
- 100 degree-seeking undergraduates
- 36% of applicants admitted
- SAT or ACT (ACT writing optional), application essay required

**General.** Founded in 1978. Regionally accredited. **Degrees:** 20 bachelor's awarded. **Location:** 45 miles from Boston. **Calendar:** Semester. **Full-time faculty:** 6 total. **Part-time faculty:** 3 total. **Class size:** 80% < 20, 10% 20-39, 10% 50-99.

**Freshman class profile.** 100 applied, 36 admitted, 26 enrolled.

| | | | |
|---|---|---|---|
| Out-of-state: | 96% | Live on campus: | 90% |

**Basis for selection.** Evidence of student's desire to learn important. Complete application includes essay, 2 academic letters of recommendation, high school transcript, and SAT or ACT scores. Interviews and/or visits are strongly recommended.

**High school preparation.** 17 units required. Required units include English 4, mathematics 3, social studies 2, history 2, science 2 (laboratory 2) and foreign language 2. Recommended languages: Latin, French, German. Recommended electives: music, art.

**2007-2008 Annual costs.** Tuition/fees: $12,250. Room/board: $8,300. Books/supplies: $600. Personal expenses: $100.

**Financial aid. Non-need-based:** Scholarships awarded for academics.

**Application procedures. Admission:** No deadline. No application fee. Application may be submitted online. Admission notification on a rolling basis beginning on or about 1/1. **Financial aid:** Priority date 5/1; no closing date. FAFSA required. Applicants notified on a rolling basis starting 5/15; must reply within 2 week(s) of notification.

**Academics.** Each student, regardless of major, takes 6-hour humanities course every semester throughout 4 years: philosophy, literature, politics, history, theology taught by faculty from various disciplines. **Special study options:** Independent study, study abroad. Sophomore semester in Rome. **Credit/placement by examination:** CLEP. **Support services:** Tutoring.

**Majors. Biology:** General. **English:** English lit. **Philosophy/religion:** Philosophy. **Social sciences:** Political science.

**Most popular majors.** English 43%, philosophy/religious studies 21%, social sciences 36%.

**Computing on campus.** 5 workstations in library.

**Student life. Freshman orientation:** Mandatory. **Policies:** Students are responsible, in main part, for care of campus. **Housing:** Guaranteed on-campus for all undergraduates. Single-sex dorms available. **Activities:** Choral groups.

**Student services.** Campus ministries, career counseling, financial aid counseling, personal counseling.

**Contact.** E-mail: admissions@thomasmorecollege.edu
Phone: (603) 880-8308 ext. 14 Toll-free number: (800) 880-8308 ext. 14
Fax: (603) 880-9280
Teddy Sifert, Director of Admissions, Thomas More College of Liberal Arts, Six Manchester Street, Merrimack, NH 03054-4818

---

## University of New Hampshire
**Durham, New Hampshire**          **CB member**
**www.unh.edu**                    **CB code: 3918**

- Public 4-year university
- Residential campus in small town
- 11,622 degree-seeking undergraduates: 2% part-time, 56% women, 1% African American, 2% Asian American, 2% Hispanic American, 1% international
- 2,449 degree-seeking graduate students
- 59% of applicants admitted
- SAT or ACT with writing, application essay required
- 73% graduate within 6 years

**General.** Founded in 1866. Regionally accredited. **Degrees:** 2,406 bachelor's, 145 associate awarded; master's, doctoral offered. **ROTC:** Army, Air Force. **Location:** 50 miles from Boston, 50 miles from Portland, Maine. **Calendar:** Semester, extensive summer session. **Full-time faculty:** 636 total; 84% have terminal degrees, 8% minority, 34% women. **Part-time faculty:** 297 total; 15% have terminal degrees, 2% minority, 65% women. **Class size:** 43% < 20, 34% 20-39, 7% 40-49, 9% 50-99, 6% >100. **Special facilities:** Journalism laboratory, optical observatory, marine research laboratory, experiential learning center, child development center, agricultural and equine facilities, electron microscope, sawmill.

**Freshman class profile.** 14,382 applied, 8,497 admitted, 2,646 enrolled.

| Mid 50% test scores | | Return as sophomores: | 87% |
|---|---|---|---|
| SAT critical reading: | 500-610 | Out-of-state: | 54% |
| SAT math: | 510-620 | Live on campus: | 97% |
| Rank in top quarter: | 66% | International: | 1% |
| Rank in top tenth: | 24% | Fraternities: | 4% |
| End year in good standing: | 94% | Sororities: | 2% |

**Basis for selection.** School achievement record most important, followed by course selection, class rank, recommendations, test scores. Cocurricular activities, character/leadership considered. SAT Subject Tests can satisfy a foreign language requirement for students in a BA program. Audition required for music programs. **Homeschooled:** Supporting documents include GED scores, transcripts, education plans, syllabi, SAT or ACT scores, homeschool association information.

**High school preparation.** 17 units required; 22 recommended. Required and recommended units include English 4, mathematics 3-4, social studies 3, science 3-4 (laboratory 2-3), foreign language 2-3 and academic electives 1. Additional requirements determined by intended major.

**2007-2008 Annual costs.** Tuition/fees: $11,070; $24,030 out-of-state. New England Regional Student Program tuition 175% of in-state public institution tuition. College of Earth and Physical Science charges an extra $705 per year. Whittemore School of Business charges an extra $691 per year. Room/board: $8,168. Books/supplies: $1,400. Personal expenses: $2,105.

**2006-2007 Financial aid. Need-based:** 2,409 full-time freshmen applied for aid; 1,740 were judged to have need; 1,722 of these received aid. Average need met was 83%. Average scholarship/grant was $3,097; average loan $2,210. 45% of total undergraduate aid awarded as scholarships/grants, 55% as loans/jobs. **Non-need-based:** Awarded to 3,056 full-time undergraduates, including 705 freshmen. Scholarships awarded for academics, art, athletics, leadership, music/drama, ROTC.

**Application procedures. Admission:** Closing date 2/1 (postmark date). $50 fee ($65 out-of-state), may be waived for applicants with need. Application may be submitted online. Admission notification 4/15. Admission notification on a rolling basis beginning on or about 11/15. Must reply by 5/1. **Financial aid:** Priority date 3/1; no closing date. FAFSA required. Applicants notified on a rolling basis starting 3/1.

**Academics.** General education requirement has 8 components. Students admitted as freshmen or as freshmen transfers must complete 4 writing intensive courses. **Special study options:** Combined bachelor's/graduate degree, cross-registration, double major, ESL, exchange student, honors, independent study, internships, semester at sea, student-designed major, study abroad, teacher certification program, Washington semester. Undergraduate research opportunities, International Undergraduate Opportunities Program. **Credit/placement by examination:** AP, CLEP, IB, institutional tests. 32 credit hours maximum toward associate degree, 64 toward bachelor's. **Support services:** Learning center, reduced course load, study skills assistance, tutoring, writing center.

**Majors. Agriculture:** Agronomy, animal sciences, business, dairy, dairy husbandry, equestrian studies, food science, horticultural science, plant sciences. **Architecture:** Urban/community planning. **Area/ethnic studies:** European, French, Western European, women's. **Biology:** General, bacteriology, biochemistry, microbiology, plant molecular, plant physiology, zoology. **Business:** General, accounting, business admin, entrepreneurial studies, finance, hospitality admin, hotel/motel admin, tourism/travel. **Communications:** General, digital media, journalism, media studies. **Computer sciences:** General, computer science. **Conservation:** General, economics, environmental science, environmental studies, forestry, wildlife. **Education:** Art, English, mathematics, music, science. **Engineering:** General, chemical, civil, computer, electrical, environmental, materials, materials science, mechanical, ocean. **English:** British lit, English lit. **Family/consumer sciences:** Child development, family studies, family/community services, food/nutrition, human nutrition. **Foreign languages:** Ancient Greek, classics, French, German, Latin, linguistics, modern Greek, Russian, Spanish. **Health:** Athletic training, clinical lab science, clinical lab technology, clinical nutrition, communication disorders, dietetics, health care admin, nursing (RN), recreational therapy, speech pathology. **History:** General. **Interdisciplinary:** Global studies, natural sciences. **Liberal arts:** Humanities. **Math:** General, applied. **Parks/recreation:** General, exercise sciences. **Personal/culinary services:** Restaurant/catering. **Philosophy/religion:** Philosophy. **Physical sciences:** Chemistry, geology, physics. **Psychology:** General. **Public administration:** Social work. **Social sciences:** Anthropology, criminology, economics, international relations, political science, sociology. **Visual/performing arts:** Music performance, music theory/composition, studio arts.

**Most popular majors.** Biology 7%, business/marketing 14%, engineering/engineering technologies 7%, English 7%, health sciences 9%, parks/recreation 6%, social sciences 20%.

**Computing on campus.** 345 workstations in library, computer center, student center. Dormitories wired for high-speed internet access and linked to campus network. Commuter students can connect to campus network. Online course registration, online library, helpline, repair service, student web hosting, wireless network available.

**Student life. Freshman orientation:** Available. Preregistration for classes offered. Course selection and registration held in June. Additional session in fall. Minority student orientation offered. **Housing:** Guaranteed on-campus for freshmen. Coed dorms, single-sex dorms, apartments, fraternity/sorority housing, substance-free housing available. $200 partly refundable deposit, deadline 5/1. 14 theme housing options available. **Activities:** Bands, choral groups, dance, drama, film society, literary magazine, music ensembles, musical theater, radio station, student government, student newspaper, symphony orchestra, TV station, Hillel, Diversity Support Coalition, honor societies, governance organizations, media and publications, hall councils, arts and entertainment groups, special interest groups, political and world affairs groups, religious groups.

**Athletics.** NCAA. **Intercollegiate:** Basketball, cross-country, diving W, field hockey W, football (tackle) M, gymnastics W, ice hockey, lacrosse W, skiing, soccer, swimming W, track and field, volleyball W. **Intramural:** Basketball, field hockey W, football (non-tackle), ice hockey, racquetball, soccer, softball, table tennis, tennis, volleyball. **Team name:** Wildcats.

**Student services.** Adult student services, alcohol/substance abuse counseling, campus ministries, career counseling, services for economically disadvantaged, student employment services, financial aid counseling, health services, legal services, minority student services, on-campus daycare, personal counseling, placement for graduates, veterans' counselor, women's services. **Physically disabled:** Services for visually, speech, hearing impaired.

**Contact.** E-mail: admissions@unh.edu
Phone: (603) 862-1360 Fax: (603) 862-0077
Robert McGann, Director of Admissions, University of New Hampshire, Grant House, Durham, NH 03824

---

## University of New Hampshire at Manchester
**Manchester, New Hampshire**    CB member
**www.unhm.unh.edu**    CB code: 2094

- Public 4-year university and liberal arts college
- Commuter campus in small city
- 773 degree-seeking undergraduates: 30% part-time, 54% women
- 67% of applicants admitted
- SAT or ACT (ACT writing optional), application essay required

**General.** Founded in 1985. Regionally accredited. **Degrees:** 107 bachelor's, 34 associate awarded; master's offered. **ROTC:** Army, Air Force. **Location:** 55 miles from Boston, 35 miles from Concord. **Calendar:** Semester, limited summer session. **Full-time faculty:** 36 total. **Part-time faculty:** 104 total.

**Freshman class profile.** 313 applied, 209 admitted, 116 enrolled.

| Mid 50% test scores | | ACT composite: | 18-23 |
|---|---|---|---|
| SAT critical reading: | 460-550 | Out-of-state: | 1% |
| SAT math: | 440-550 | | |

**Basis for selection.** Achievement in high school college preparatory program most important. SAT scores should be consistent with achievement. Recommendation, essay, interview very helpful for students of moderate achievement or in nontraditional cases. Non-native speakers of English must submit TOEFL scores. Interview recommended for college transition program. **Homeschooled:** Transcript of courses and grades, state high school equivalency certificate, letter of recommendation (nonparent) required. Encourage GED, SAT, syllabus of curriculum; diploma from homeschool association if available.

**High school preparation.** Required and recommended units include English 4, mathematics 3-4, social studies 2, science 3-4 (laboratory 3) and foreign language 2-3.

**2007-2008 Annual costs.** Tuition/fees: $8,515; $21,145 out-of-state. New England Regional Student tuition 150% of in-state public institution tuition. Books/supplies: $700. Personal expenses: $2,020.

**Financial aid. Non-need-based:** Scholarships awarded for academics, state residency.

**Application procedures. Admission:** Priority date 4/1; deadline 6/15 (postmark date). $45 fee ($60 out-of-state), may be waived for applicants with need. Admission notification on a rolling basis. Must reply by May 1

or within 3 week(s) if notified thereafter. **Financial aid:** Closing date 3/1. FAFSA required. Applicants notified on a rolling basis starting 4/1; must reply within 2 week(s) of notification.

**Academics. Special study options:** Combined bachelor's/graduate degree, cross-registration, double major, ESL, exchange student, external degree, independent study, internships, semester at sea, student-designed major, study abroad, teacher certification program, Washington semester. **Credit/placement by examination:** AP, CLEP, IB, institutional tests. 48 credit hours maximum toward associate degree, 64 toward bachelor's. ACT, PEP exams accepted to RN Baccalaureate program. **Support services:** Learning center, pre-admission summer program, reduced course load, remedial instruction, study skills assistance, tutoring.

**Majors. Biology:** General. **Business:** Business admin. **Communications:** General. **Computer sciences:** General. **Engineering technology:** Electrical. **English:** English lit. **Foreign languages:** Sign language interpretation. **Health:** Nursing (RN). **History:** General. **Liberal arts:** Arts/sciences, humanities. **Psychology:** General. **Social sciences:** Political science.

**Computing on campus.** 64 workstations in library, computer center. Commuter students can connect to campus network. Online library, helpline, wireless network available.

**Student life. Freshman orientation:** Mandatory, $30 fee. Preregistration for classes offered. 3-day (or evening) program held in June, August, and January. June attendees able to preregister for fall courses. **Housing:** Students may reside in dormitories at New Hampshire Technical Institute: Concord. **Activities:** Student government, student newspaper.

**Athletics. Team name:** Wildcats.

**Student services.** Career counseling. **Physically disabled:** Services for visually, speech, hearing impaired.

**Contact.** E-mail: unhm.admissions@unh.edu
Phone: (603) 641-4150 Fax: (603) 641-4342
Miho Bean, Associate Director of Admissions, University of New Hampshire at Manchester, 400 Commercial Street, Manchester, NH 03101-1113

# New Jersey

## Berkeley College

| | |
|---|---|
| West Paterson, New Jersey | **CB member** |
| www.berkeleycollege.edu | **CB code: 2061** |

- For-profit 4-year business college
- Commuter campus in large town
- 3,041 degree-seeking undergraduates: 14% part-time, 72% women, 23% African American, 5% Asian American, 35% Hispanic American, 1% Native American, 2% international

**General.** Founded in 1931. Regionally accredited. Branch campuses in Paramus, Newark, and Woodbridge, NJ. **Degrees:** 242 bachelor's, 227 associate awarded. **Location:** 20 miles from New York City. **Calendar:** Quarter, extensive summer session. **Full-time faculty:** 61 total. **Part-time faculty:** 130 total.

**Freshman class profile.**

| | | | |
|---|---|---|---|
| Return as sophomores: | 52% | Out-of-state: | 2% |

**Basis for selection.** Class rank, high school record, interview most important. Passing grade on school entrance/placement exam required. Interviews strongly recommended.

**2008-2009 Annual costs.** Tuition/fees: $19,050. Room/board: $9,000. Books/supplies: $1,300.

**Financial aid. Non-need-based:** Scholarships awarded for academics, alumni affiliation. **Additional information:** Alumni scholarship examination given in November and December. Full and partial scholarships awarded.

**Application procedures. Admission:** No deadline. $50 fee. Application may be submitted online. Admission notification on a rolling basis. Admitted applicants must reply within 2 weeks of notification. **Financial aid:** No deadline. FAFSA required. Applicants notified on a rolling basis starting 3/1; must reply within 6 week(s) of notification.

**Academics. Special study options:** Accelerated study, distance learning, internships, New York semester, study abroad. **Credit/placement by examination:** AP, CLEP, SAT, ACT, institutional tests. **Support services:** Learning center, remedial instruction, study skills assistance, tutoring, writing center.

**Majors. Business:** General, accounting, business admin, fashion, international, marketing, office management.

**Computing on campus.** 358 workstations in library, computer center, student center. Dormitories linked to campus network. Commuter students can connect to campus network. Online library, helpline, wireless network available.

**Student life. Freshman orientation:** Mandatory. **Housing:** Coed dorms available. $400 deposit. **Activities:** Choral groups, literary magazine, student government, Phi Beta Lambda, paralegal club, interior design club, athletic club, fashion and marketing club, Phi Theta Kappa.

**Athletics. Team name:** Bulldogs.

**Student services.** Adult student services, alcohol/substance abuse counseling, career counseling, student employment services, financial aid counseling, on-campus daycare, personal counseling, placement for graduates.

**Contact.** E-mail: admissions@berkeleycollege.edu
Phone: (973) 278-5400 ext. 1210 Toll-free number: (800) 446-5400
Fax: (973) 278-9141
Mary Claire Capp, Director for High School Admissions, Berkeley College, 44 Rifle Camp Road, West Paterson, NJ 07424-0440

## Beth Medrash Govoha

| | |
|---|---|
| Lakewood, New Jersey | |
| | **CB code: 2166** |

- Private 4-year rabbinical college for men affiliated with Jewish faith
- Residential campus in small city
- 2,318 degree-seeking undergraduates
- Interview required

**General.** Founded in 1943. Accredited by AARTS. **Degrees:** 447 bachelor's awarded; master's offered. **Calendar:** Semester. **Full-time faculty:** 130 total. **Part-time faculty:** 20 total.

**Basis for selection.** Interviews required.

**2007-2008 Annual costs.** Tuition/fees: $13,052. Room/board: $4,172. Books/supplies: $450.

**Application procedures. Admission:** Closing date 8/15. $125 fee, may be waived for applicants with need. **Financial aid:** No deadline.

**Academics. Credit/placement by examination:** CLEP.

**Majors. Theology:** Talmudic.

**Student life. Housing:** Apartments available.

**Student services.** Financial aid counseling, placement for graduates.

**Contact.** Phone: (732) 367-1060 Fax: (732) 367-7487
Rabbi Yaakov Pollak, Director of Admissions, Beth Medrash Govoha, 617 Sixth Street, Lakewood, NJ 08701

## Bloomfield College

| | |
|---|---|
| Bloomfield, New Jersey | **CB member** |
| www.bloomfield.edu | **CB code: 2044** |

- Private 4-year liberal arts and teachers college affiliated with Presbyterian Church (USA)
- Commuter campus in large town
- 2,033 degree-seeking undergraduates: 23% part-time, 66% women, 49% African American, 4% Asian American, 20% Hispanic American, 2% international
- 41% of applicants admitted
- SAT or ACT (ACT writing optional), application essay required
- 36% graduate within 6 years; 17% enter graduate study

**General.** Founded in 1868. Regionally accredited. **Degrees:** 253 bachelor's awarded. **ROTC:** Army. **Location:** 7 miles from Newark, 15 miles from New York City. **Calendar:** Semester, limited summer session. **Full-time faculty:** 70 total; 73% have terminal degrees, 23% minority, 61% women. **Part-time faculty:** 164 total; 12% have terminal degrees, 35% minority, 50% women. **Class size:** 72% < 20, 27% 20-39, less than 1% 50-99, less than 1% >100. **Special facilities:** Technology and multimedia center.

**Freshman class profile.** 2,750 applied, 1,133 admitted, 354 enrolled.

| Mid 50% test scores | | Rank in top quarter: | 7% |
|---|---|---|---|
| SAT critical reading: | 390-470 | End year in good standing: | 80% |
| SAT math: | 400-480 | Return as sophomores: | 70% |
| GPA 3.50 or higher: | 8% | Out-of-state: | 7% |
| GPA 3.0-3.49: | 23% | Live on campus: | 41% |
| GPA 2.0-2.99: | 68% | | |

**Basis for selection.** Acceptance for regular admission requires SAT combined score equal to 900 (exclusive of Writing) and minimum high school GPA of 2.70. Interviews not required but strongly recommended. Essays must be self-recommendations or reflections on previous educational experiences. Recent graded term paper can be substituted for essay. **Home-schooled:** Transcript of courses and grades, state high school equivalency certificate, interview, letter of recommendation (nonparent) required. Applicants must submit SAT scores and official transcript with information about organization that performed accreditation/conversion. **Learning Disabled:** Students must meet regular admission requirements, and should ask for special accommodations for SAT testing.

**High school preparation.** 14 units required.

**2007-2008 Annual costs.** Tuition/fees: $18,000. Room/board: $8,650. Books/supplies: $850. Personal expenses: $1,543.

**2007-2008 Financial aid. Need-based:** 330 full-time freshmen applied for aid; 292 were judged to have need; 290 of these received aid. Average need met was 66%. Average scholarship/grant was $13,449; average loan $4,860. 58% of total undergraduate aid awarded as scholarships/grants, 42% as loans/jobs. **Non-need-based:** Scholarships awarded for academics, alumni affiliation, athletics, religious affiliation.

**Application procedures. Admission:** Priority date 3/14; deadline 7/1 (receipt date). $40 fee, may be waived for applicants with need. Application may be submitted online. Admission notification on a rolling basis beginning on or about 10/1. **Financial aid:** Priority date 3/15, closing date 6/1. FAFSA required. Applicants notified on a rolling basis starting 3/1; must reply within 2 week(s) of notification.

**Academics.** Organized into 7 divisions: Business and Computer Information Systems, Creative Arts and Technology, Humanities, Natural Science and Mathematics, Nursing, and Social and Behavioral Sciences, and Education. **Special study options:** Accelerated study, cooperative education, distance learning, double major, dual enrollment of high school students, ESL, honors, independent study, internships, liberal arts/career combination, student-designed major, study abroad, teacher certification program, weekend college. Four-year clinical laboratory science program and allied health technologies major offered in conjunction with University of Medicine and Dentistry of New Jersey; joint BS/MS in computer information systems program offered with NJIT; special programs in advanced technology, allied health, computer classes; special programs for teachers. **Credit/placement by examination:** AP, CLEP. 16 credit hours maximum toward bachelor's degree. Maximum of 16 course units may be earned through CLEP examinations, portfolio assessment, and nursing assessment. **Support services:** Learning center, pre-admission summer program, reduced course load, remedial instruction, study skills assistance, tutoring, writing center.

**Majors. Biology:** General. **Business:** Accounting, business admin. **Computer sciences:** General, networking. **Education:** General, learning disabled. **English:** English lit. **Health:** Nursing (RN). **History:** General. **Math:** General, applied. **Philosophy/religion:** Philosophy, religion. **Physical sciences:** Chemistry. **Psychology:** General. **Social sciences:** Political science, sociology. **Visual/performing arts:** General. **Other:** Allied health technologies.

**Most popular majors.** Biology 6%, business/marketing 19%, education 8%, English 7%, health sciences 11%, psychology 14%, social sciences 20%, visual/performing arts 9%.

**Computing on campus.** 300 workstations in dormitories, library, computer center, student center. Dormitories wired for high-speed internet access and linked to campus network. Commuter students can connect to campus network. Online library, helpline, student web hosting, wireless network available.

**Student life. Freshman orientation:** Mandatory, $125 fee. Preregistration for classes offered. Conducted in August. **Policies:** Statement of Shared Values adopted, addressing student conduct and standards for behavior. **Housing:** Coed dorms, substance-free housing available. $150 fully refundable deposit, deadline 5/1. Honors house and creative arts an technology house available. Off-campus hotel also available. **Activities:** Choral groups, dance, drama, radio station, student government, student newspaper, African student association, Association of Latin American Students, Haitian student association, Team Infinite, Sisters in Support, Bible study, gospel choir, Muslim student association.

**Athletics.** NCAA. **Intercollegiate:** Baseball M, basketball, cross-country, soccer, softball W, tennis M, volleyball W. **Intramural:** Basketball. **Team name:** Deacons.

**Student services.** Adult student services, alcohol/substance abuse counseling, campus ministries, career counseling, student employment services, financial aid counseling, health services, personal counseling, placement for graduates. **Physically disabled:** Services for visually, speech, hearing impaired. **Learning disabled:** Comprehensive services available.

**Contact.** E-mail: admission@bloomfield.edu
Phone: (973) 748-9000 ext. 230 Toll-free number: (800) 848-4555
Fax: (973) 748-0916
Adam Castro, Director of Admissions, Bloomfield College, One Park Place, Bloomfield, NJ 07003

---

## Caldwell College

**Caldwell, New Jersey**               **CB member**
**www.caldwell.edu**                   **CB code: 2072**

- Private 4-year liberal arts college affiliated with Roman Catholic Church
- Commuter campus in large town
- 1,604 degree-seeking undergraduates: 28% part-time, 65% women, 17% African American, 2% Asian American, 13% Hispanic American, 6% international
- 404 degree-seeking graduate students
- 60% of applicants admitted
- SAT or ACT with writing, application essay required
- 51% graduate within 6 years

**General.** Founded in 1939. Regionally accredited. **Degrees:** 263 bachelor's awarded; master's offered. **ROTC:** Army. **Location:** 20 miles from New York City. **Calendar:** Semester, limited summer session. **Full-time faculty:** 79 total. **Part-time faculty:** 119 total. **Class size:** 79% < 20, 21% 20-39.

**Freshman class profile.** 1,850 applied, 1,106 admitted, 290 enrolled.

| Mid 50% test scores | | End year in good standing: | 92% |
|---|---|---|---|
| SAT critical reading: | 440-550 | Return as sophomores: | 71% |
| SAT math: | 430-570 | Out-of-state: | 7% |
| Rank in top quarter: | 23% | Live on campus: | 56% |
| Rank in top tenth: | 10% | International: | 13% |

**Basis for selection.** Class rank in top half, school achievement record, test scores, interview, extracurricular activities very important. Counselor's recommendation, volunteer work important. Essay, interview recommended for all, audition required for music programs, portfolio required for art programs.

**High school preparation.** 16 units required. Required units include English 4, mathematics 2, history 1, science 2 (laboratory 1), foreign language 2 and academic electives 5.

**2008-2009 Annual costs.** Tuition/fees: $23,600. Room/board: $9,650. Books/supplies: $1,200. Personal expenses: $1,000.

**2007-2008 Financial aid. Need-based:** 219 full-time freshmen applied for aid; 194 were judged to have need; 194 of these received aid. Average need met was 39%. Average scholarship/grant was $3,551; average loan $1,686. 52% of total undergraduate aid awarded as scholarships/grants, 48% as loans/jobs. **Non-need-based:** Awarded to 647 full-time undergraduates, including 196 freshmen. Scholarships awarded for academics, alumni affiliation, art, athletics, leadership, music/drama, religious affiliation.

**Application procedures. Admission:** Priority date 12/1; no deadline. $40 fee, may be waived for applicants with need. Application may be submitted online. Admission notification on a rolling basis beginning on or about 12/31. Must reply by May 1 or within 2 week(s) if notified thereafter. **Financial aid:** Priority date 4/1; no closing date. FAFSA, institutional form required. Applicants notified on a rolling basis starting 3/1; must reply within 4 week(s) of notification.

**Academics. Special study options:** Accelerated study, combined bachelor's/graduate degree, cooperative education, distance learning, double major, ESL, external degree, honors, independent study, internships, liberal arts/career combination, student-designed major, study abroad, teacher certification program, Washington semester, weekend college. Offers affiliation programs with institutions such as New York University, Columbia University, Temple University, UMDNJ and others where students earn bachelor's degree, typically in biology, and professional degree from the affiliated school. **Credit/placement by examination:** AP, CLEP, IB, institutional tests. 30 credit hours maximum toward bachelor's degree. Credit by exam only available during first year (30 credits) of matriculation. Credit toward major dependent on departmental approval. Prior Learning Assessment (PLA) for adult students who must attend PLA workshop. **Support services:** Learning center, pre-admission summer program, remedial instruction, study skills assistance, tutoring, writing center.

**Majors. Biology:** General. **Business:** Accounting, business admin, international, management science, marketing. **Communications:** General. **Computer sciences:** General, computer science. **Education:** Elementary. **English:** English lit. **Foreign languages:** French, Spanish. **Health:** Clinical lab technology. **History:** General. **Math:** General. **Physical sciences:** Chemistry. **Protective services:** Criminal justice. **Psychology:** General. **Social sciences:** General, political science, sociology. **Theology:** Theology. **Visual/performing arts:** Art, studio arts.

**Most popular majors.** Business/marketing 20%, communications/journalism 8%, education 12%, psychology 13%, security/protective services 9%.

**Computing on campus.** 210 workstations in dormitories, library, computer center, student center. Dormitories wired for high-speed internet access and linked to campus network. Commuter students can connect to campus network. Online course registration, online library, helpline, student web hosting, wireless network available.

**Student life. Freshman orientation:** Mandatory, $200 fee. Preregistration for classes offered. Held Sunday and Monday prior to beginning of classes in August. **Housing:** Guaranteed on-campus for all undergraduates. Coed dorms, substance-free housing available. $200 nonrefundable deposit, deadline 5/1. **Activities:** Jazz band, campus ministries, choral groups, drama, international student organizations, literary magazine, music ensembles, musical theater, student government, student newspaper, Circle K, black students cooperative union, Latin American student association, Portuguese club, Irish club.

**Athletics.** NCAA. **Intercollegiate:** Baseball M, basketball, cross-country W, golf M, soccer, softball W, tennis. **Intramural:** Basketball, football (non-tackle), soccer, softball, volleyball. **Team name:** Cougars.

**Student services.** Adult student services, alcohol/substance abuse counseling, campus ministries, career counseling, services for economically disadvantaged, student employment services, financial aid counseling, health services, minority student services, personal counseling, placement for graduates, women's services. **Physically disabled:** Services for visually, hearing impaired.

**Contact.** E-mail: admissions@caldwell.edu
Phone: (973) 618-3500 Toll-free number: (888) 864-9516
Fax: (973) 618-3600
Kathryn Reilly, Executive Director of Admissions and Financial Aid, Caldwell College, 9 Ryerson Avenue, Caldwell, NJ 07006-6195

## Centenary College
**Hackettstown, New Jersey**
www.centenarycollege.edu
**CB member**
**CB code: 2080**

▶ Private 4-year liberal arts college affiliated with United Methodist Church
▶ Residential campus in large town
▶ 2,238 degree-seeking undergraduates: 12% part-time, 66% women, 9% African American, 2% Asian American, 7% Hispanic American, 3% international
▶ 790 degree-seeking graduate students
▶ 70% of applicants admitted
▶ SAT or ACT, application essay required
▶ 51% graduate within 6 years

**General.** Founded in 1867. Regionally accredited. Laptop computers provided to all full-time students. **Degrees:** 409 bachelor's, 68 associate awarded; master's offered. **Location:** 55 miles from New York City. **Calendar:** Semester, limited summer session. **Full-time faculty:** 67 total; 57% have terminal degrees, 54% women. **Part-time faculty:** 261 total; 61% women. **Class size:** 60% < 20, 39% 20-39, 1% 40-49. **Special facilities:** Textile laboratory, equestrian center.

**Freshman class profile.** 1,244 applied, 874 admitted, 289 enrolled.

| Mid 50% test scores | | Rank in top quarter: | 22% |
|---|---|---|---|
| SAT critical reading: | 410-510 | Rank in top tenth: | 7% |
| SAT math: | 420-520 | Return as sophomores: | 72% |
| SAT writing: | 410-510 | Out-of-state: | 15% |
| ACT composite: | 20-21 | Live on campus: | 77% |
| GPA 3.50 or higher: | 6% | Fraternities: | 1% |
| GPA 3.0-3.49: | 21% | Sororities: | 1% |
| GPA 2.0-2.99: | 67% | | |

**Basis for selection.** School achievement record, standardized test scores most important. Interview, recommendations, community activities also strongly considered. Interviews required for academically marginal students with special needs; recommended for others. Portfolio required for art and design, graphic arts majors. **Homeschooled:** State high school equivalency certificate required. **Learning Disabled:** Interview with Director of Services, documentation of psycho-education evaluation and IEP required for supportive services programs.

**High school preparation.** 16 units required. Required and recommended units include English 4, mathematics 3-4, social studies 2, history 2, science 2-4 and foreign language 2. Major-related courses on high school level recommended.

**2007-2008 Annual costs.** Tuition/fees: $24,100. Additional fees required for equine majors and for comprehensive learning support program. Room/board: $8,900. Books/supplies: $1,200. Personal expenses: $850.

**2006-2007 Financial aid. Need-based:** 272 full-time freshmen applied for aid; 228 were judged to have need; 227 of these received aid. Average need met was 69%. Average scholarship/grant was $13,208; average loan $3,675. 59% of total undergraduate aid awarded as scholarships/grants, 41% as loans/jobs. **Non-need-based:** Awarded to 254 full-time undergraduates, including 68 freshmen. Scholarships awarded for academics, alumni affiliation, art, leadership, state residency.

**Application procedures. Admission:** Priority date 8/1; no deadline. $30 fee ($30 out-of-state), may be waived for applicants with need. Application may be submitted online. Admission notification on a rolling basis beginning on or about 9/15. Must reply by May 1 or within 4 week(s) if notified thereafter. **Financial aid:** Priority date 4/15; no closing date. FAFSA required. Applicants notified on a rolling basis starting 3/1.

**Academics.** Core curriculum required. Educational program balances career and liberal arts. **Special study options:** Accelerated study, cross-registration, distance learning, double major, honors, independent study, internships, liberal arts/career combination, student-designed major, study abroad, teacher certification program, weekend college. **Credit/placement by examination:** AP, CLEP, IB. 15 credit hours maximum toward associate degree, 30 toward bachelor's. **Support services:** Learning center, pre-admission summer program, reduced course load, remedial instruction, study skills assistance, tutoring, writing center.

**Majors. Agriculture:** Equestrian studies. **Biology:** General. **Business:** Accounting, business admin. **Communications:** General. **Computer sciences:** General. **English:** English lit. **History:** General. **Math:** General. **Protective services:** Criminal justice. **Psychology:** General. **Social sciences:** Political science, sociology. **Visual/performing arts:** Commercial/advertising art, dramatic, fashion design.

**Most popular majors.** Business/marketing 43%, English 6%, history 6%, psychology 8%, security/protective services 8%, social sciences 10%.

**Computing on campus.** PC or laptop required. Dormitories wired for high-speed internet access and linked to campus network. Commuter students can connect to campus network. Online course registration, online library, helpline, repair service, wireless network available.

**Student life. Freshman orientation:** Mandatory. Preregistration for classes offered. 3-day orientation prior to start of classes. **Housing:** Coed dorms, single-sex dorms, special housing for disabled, apartments available. $150 deposit, deadline 7/1. **Activities:** Campus ministries, choral groups, dance, drama, film society, international student organizations, literary magazine, Model UN, musical theater, radio station, student government, student newspaper, TV station, art guild, student activities committee, service groups, fashion group, academic clubs, professional and honor societies, special interest clubs, Students in Free Enterprise.

**Athletics.** NCAA. **Intercollegiate:** Baseball M, basketball, cross-country, equestrian, golf, lacrosse, soccer, softball W, volleyball W, wrestling M. **Intramural:** Basketball M, equestrian M. **Team name:** Cyclones.

**Student services.** Adult student services, alcohol/substance abuse counseling, campus ministries, career counseling, services for economically disadvantaged, student employment services, financial aid counseling, health services, minority student services, personal counseling, placement for graduates, women's services. **Learning disabled:** Comprehensive services available.

**Contact.** E-mail: admissions@centenarycollege.edu
Phone: (908) 852-1400 ext. 2217 Toll-free number: (800) 236-8679
Fax: (908) 852-3454
Diane Finnan, Vice President for Enrollment Management and Strategic Branding, Centenary College, 400 Jefferson Street, Hackettstown, NJ 07840-9989

## The College of New Jersey
**Ewing, New Jersey**
www.tcnj.edu
**CB code: 2519**

▶ Public 4-year liberal arts college
▶ Residential campus in large town
▶ 6,164 degree-seeking undergraduates: 2% part-time, 58% women, 6% African American, 8% Asian American, 8% Hispanic American
▶ 527 degree-seeking graduate students
▶ 47% of applicants admitted
▶ SAT or ACT (ACT writing optional), application essay required
▶ 83% graduate within 6 years; 25% enter graduate study

**General.** Founded in 1855. Regionally accredited. **Degrees:** 1,349 bachelor's awarded; master's offered. **ROTC:** Army, Air Force. **Location:** 35 miles from Philadelphia. **Calendar:** Semester, limited summer session. **Full-time faculty:** 335 total; 88% have terminal degrees, 24% minority, 46% women. **Part-time faculty:** 398 total; 21% have terminal degrees, 9% minority, 51% women. **Class size:** 42% < 20, 55% 20-39, 3% 40-49, less than 1% 50-99. **Special facilities:** Concert hall, electron microscopy lab, nuclear magnetic resonance lab, optical spectroscopy lab, observatory, planetarium, greenhouse.

**Freshman class profile.** 8,607 applied, 4,005 admitted, 1,297 enrolled.

| Mid 50% test scores | | Rank in top tenth: | 61% |
|---|---|---|---|
| SAT critical reading: | 560-650 | Return as sophomores: | 95% |
| SAT math: | 580-680 | Out-of-state: | 6% |
| SAT writing: | 560-660 | Live on campus: | 95% |
| Rank in top quarter: | 87% | | |

**Basis for selection.** Standardized test scores, high school rank and choice of curriculum very important. Extracurricular service, activities and community involvement are considered. Audition required for music; portfolio required for art. **Homeschooled:** Statement describing homeschool structure and mission, transcript of courses and grades, state high school equivalency certificate, letter of recommendation (nonparent) required.

**High school preparation.** 18 units required; 20 recommended. Required and recommended units include English 4, mathematics 3, social studies 2-3, science 3 (laboratory 2-3) and foreign language 2-3.

**2007-2008 Annual costs.** Tuition/fees: $11,307; $18,530 out-of-state. Room/board: $9,242. Books/supplies: $1,000. Personal expenses: $1,500.

**2007-2008 Financial aid.** **Need-based:** 1,069 full-time freshmen applied for aid; 619 were judged to have need; 573 of these received aid. Average need met was 54%. Average scholarship/grant was $13,878; average loan $3,676. 47% of total undergraduate aid awarded as scholarships/grants, 53% as loans/jobs. **Non-need-based:** Awarded to 2,047 full-time undergraduates, including 387 freshmen. Scholarships awarded for academics. **Additional information:** Merit scholarships available to New Jersey high school graduates based on academic distinction. Limited number of scholarships available to out-of-state students who demonstrate exceptional academic achievement in high school and on SAT.

**Application procedures.** **Admission:** Closing date 2/15 (postmark date). $60 fee, may be waived for applicants with need. Application may be submitted online. Admission notification on a rolling basis beginning on or about 1/15. Must reply by May 1 or within 3 week(s) if notified thereafter. **Financial aid:** Priority date 3/1, closing date 10/1. FAFSA required. Applicants notified on a rolling basis starting 6/1; must reply within 2 week(s) of notification.

**Academics.** **Special study options:** Combined bachelor's/graduate degree, cross-registration, double major, dual enrollment of high school students, exchange student, honors, independent study, internships, liberal arts/career combination, semester at sea, student-designed major, study abroad, teacher certification program, Washington semester. **Credit/placement by examination:** AP, CLEP, IB, SAT, institutional tests. 30 credit hours maximum toward bachelor's degree. **Support services:** Learning center, pre-admission summer program, reduced course load, remedial instruction, study skills assistance, tutoring, writing center.

**Majors.** **Area/ethnic studies:** Women's. **Biology:** General. **Business:** General, accounting, business admin, finance, international, marketing. **Communications:** General, journalism. **Computer sciences:** General. **Education:** Art, biology, chemistry, Deaf/hearing impaired, early childhood, elementary, English, foreign languages, health, history, mathematics, middle, physical, physics, social science, social studies, Spanish, special, speech, technology/industrial arts. **Engineering:** General, biomedical, civil, computer, electrical, mechanical, science. **English:** English lit, speech/rhetoric. **Foreign languages:** Spanish. **Health:** Nursing (RN), preop/surgical nursing. **History:** General. **Math:** General, statistics. **Philosophy/religion:** Philosophy. **Physical sciences:** Chemistry, physics. **Protective services:** Law enforcement admin. **Psychology:** General. **Social sciences:** Criminology, economics, international relations, political science, sociology. **Visual/performing arts:** General, art, commercial/advertising art, multimedia, studio arts.

**Most popular majors.** Biology 7%, business/marketing 13%, education 25%, English 11%, psychology 12%, visual/performing arts 6%.

**Computing on campus.** 581 workstations in dormitories, library, computer center, student center. Dormitories wired for high-speed internet access and linked to campus network. Commuter students can connect to campus network. Online course registration, online library, helpline, repair service, student web hosting, wireless network available.

**Student life.** **Freshman orientation:** Mandatory, $150 fee. Preregistration for classes offered. 4-part orientation program including June advisement week, summer readings, welcome week, college seminar. **Housing:** Guaranteed on-campus for freshmen. Coed dorms, single-sex dorms, special housing for disabled, apartments, substance-free housing available. $150 nonrefundable deposit, deadline 5/1. Pets allowed in dorm rooms. Housing for transfer students available. Faculty and students also have the opportunity to develop their own special interest learning communities on campus. **Activities:** Bands, campus ministries, choral groups, dance, drama, international student organizations, literary magazine, music ensembles, Model UN,

musical theater, opera, radio station, student government, student newspaper, symphony orchestra, TV station, Black Student Union, Amnesty International, Circle K, EOF Alliance, Friendship Day Committee, Islamic Society, Outreach Association, Students Acting for the Environment, Jewish Student Union.

**Athletics.** NCAA. **Intercollegiate:** Baseball M, basketball, cross-country, diving, field hockey W, football (tackle) M, golf M, lacrosse W, soccer, softball W, swimming, tennis, track and field, wrestling M. **Intramural:** Basketball, bowling, fencing, field hockey, football (non-tackle), golf M, ice hockey M, lacrosse M, racquetball, rugby, skiing, soccer, softball, swimming, tennis, volleyball, water polo. **Team name:** Lions.

**Student services.** Adult student services, alcohol/substance abuse counseling, campus ministries, career counseling, services for economically disadvantaged, student employment services, financial aid counseling, health services, minority student services, on-campus daycare, personal counseling, placement for graduates, veterans' counselor, women's services. **Physically disabled:** Services for visually, speech, hearing impaired.

**Contact.** E-mail: admiss@tcnj.edu
Phone: (609) 771-2131 Fax: (609) 637-5174
Lisa Angeloni, Dean of Admissions, The College of New Jersey, Box 7718, Ewing, NJ 08628

---

## College of St. Elizabeth
**Morristown, New Jersey**
**www.cse.edu**

CB member
CB code: 2090

- Private 4-year liberal arts college for women affiliated with Roman Catholic Church
- Residential campus in large town
- 1,112 degree-seeking undergraduates: 38% part-time, 93% women, 15% African American, 4% Asian American, 17% Hispanic American, 5% international
- 840 degree-seeking graduate students
- 82% of applicants admitted
- SAT or ACT (ACT writing optional), application essay required
- 67% graduate within 6 years

**General.** Founded in 1899. Regionally accredited. Men admitted to adult undergraduate programs and master's programs. **Degrees:** 281 bachelor's awarded; master's, doctoral offered. **Location:** 40 miles from New York City. **Calendar:** Semester, limited summer session. **Full-time faculty:** 68 total; 87% have terminal degrees, 4% minority, 60% women. **Part-time faculty:** 127 total; 31% have terminal degrees, 9% minority, 61% women. **Class size:** 86% < 20, 14% 20-39, less than 1% >100. **Special facilities:** Library of rare books and manuscripts, Greek theater, Shakespeare garden, Holocaust education resource center, center for Catholic women's history, center for theological and spiritual development.

**Freshman class profile.** 451 applied, 369 admitted, 160 enrolled.

| Mid 50% test scores | | End year in good standing: | 66% |
|---|---|---|---|
| SAT critical reading: | 390-500 | Return as sophomores: | 66% |
| SAT math: | 370-490 | Out-of-state: | 6% |
| SAT writing: | 390-510 | Live on campus: | 88% |
| Rank in top quarter: | 34% | International: | 3% |
| Rank in top tenth: | 14% | | |

**Basis for selection.** School achievement record and recommendations most important, followed by test scores, class rank; interview recommended. **Homeschooled:** Letter of recommendation (nonparent) required. Applicants processed on individual basis. Must provide approved curriculum guide.

**High school preparation.** 16 units required; 23 recommended. Required and recommended units include English 3-4, mathematics 2-3, history 1-3, science 1-2 (laboratory 1-2), foreign language 2 and academic electives 7.

**2007-2008 Annual costs.** Tuition/fees: $22,547. Room/board: $9,900. Books/supplies: $1,154. Personal expenses: $1,312.

**2007-2008 Financial aid.** **Need-based:** 72% of total undergraduate aid awarded as scholarships/grants, 28% as loans/jobs. **Non-need-based:** Scholarships awarded for academics, alumni affiliation, art, leadership, state residency.

**Application procedures.** **Admission:** Priority date 3/1; deadline 8/15 (receipt date). $35 fee, may be waived for applicants with need. Application may be submitted online. Admission notification on a rolling basis beginning on or about 11/15. Must reply by May 1 or within 2 week(s) if notified thereafter. **Financial aid:** Priority date 3/1; no closing date. FAFSA required. Applicants notified on a rolling basis starting 11/15; must reply by 5/1 or within 2 week(s) of notification.

**Academics.** Students with 60 undergraduate credits may take accelerated program in business or communication on Saturdays and complete bachelor's degree in 2 years. **Special study options:** Accelerated study, combined bachelor's/graduate degree, cross-registration, distance learning, double major, dual enrollment of high school students, ESL, exchange student, honors, independent study, internships, liberal arts/career combination, student-designed major, study abroad, teacher certification program, United Nations semester, weekend college. Accelerated co-ed baccalaureate program with majors in business, communication, nursing and psychology for adults over age 23 with classes evenings and on Saturdays. **Credit/placement by examination:** AP, CLEP, IB, institutional tests. 30 credit hours maximum toward bachelor's degree. Credit for prior work and/or life experience offered via portfolio. **Support services:** Learning center, pre-admission summer program, reduced course load, remedial instruction, study skills assistance, tutoring.

**Majors. Area/ethnic studies:** American. **Biology:** General, biochemistry. **Business:** Business admin. **Communications:** General. **Computer sciences:** Computer science. **Education:** Elementary, special. **English:** English lit. **Foreign languages:** Spanish. **Health:** Health care admin. **History:** General. **Interdisciplinary:** Global studies. **Math:** General. **Philosophy/religion:** Philosophy. **Physical sciences:** Chemistry. **Psychology:** General. **Social sciences:** Economics, sociology. **Theology:** Theology. **Visual/performing arts:** Art.

**Most popular majors.** Business/marketing 12%, communications/journalism 7%, education 12%, English 6%, health sciences 21%, interdisciplinary studies 7%, psychology 13%.

**Computing on campus.** 127 workstations in dormitories, library, computer center. Dormitories wired for high-speed internet access and linked to campus network. Commuter students can connect to campus network. Helpline, wireless network available.

**Student life. Freshman orientation:** Mandatory, $200 fee. Preregistration for classes offered. Comprehensive program held before start of classes for Women's College students. **Housing:** Guaranteed on-campus for all undergraduates. Substance-free housing available. $200 deposit. **Activities:** Campus ministries, choral groups, drama, literary magazine, music ensembles, student government, student newspaper, volunteer services center, international/intercultural club, Latin Roots, Students Take Action Committee, foreign language club, American Chemical Society Affiliates, psychology club, sociology club.

**Athletics.** NCAA. **Intercollegiate:** Basketball W, equestrian W, soccer W, softball W, swimming W, tennis W, volleyball W. **Intramural:** Volleyball W. **Team name:** Eagles.

**Student services.** Adult student services, alcohol/substance abuse counseling, campus ministries, career counseling, services for economically disadvantaged, student employment services, financial aid counseling, health services, minority student services, personal counseling, placement for graduates, women's services. **Physically disabled:** Services for visually, speech, hearing impaired.

**Contact.** E-mail: apply@cse.edu
Phone: (973) 290-4700 Toll-free number: (800) 210-7900
Fax: (973) 290-4710
Donna Tatarka, Dean of Admission, College of St. Elizabeth, 2 Convent Road, Morristown, NJ 07960-6989

## DeVry University: North Brunswick
**North Brunswick, New Jersey**
**www.devry.edu**                    CB code: 2113

- For-profit 4-year university
- Commuter campus in small city
- 1,370 degree-seeking undergraduates: 36% part-time, 26% women, 24% African American, 8% Asian American, 20% Hispanic American, 2% international
- Interview required

**General.** Founded in 1996. Regionally accredited. **Degrees:** 187 bachelor's, 196 associate awarded. **Location:** 30 miles from New York City. **Calendar:** Semester, extensive summer session. **Full-time faculty:** 41 total; 24% minority, 32% women. **Part-time faculty:** 103 total; 30% minority, 40% women.

## Freshman class profile.
**Out-of-state:**          8%     **International:**          1%

**Basis for selection.** Applicants must have high school diploma or equivalent, degree from an accredited postsecondary institution, or submit acceptable test scores and be at least 17 years of age on the first day of classes. New students may enter at beginning of any semester. SAT or ACT recommended. CPT also accepted.

**High school preparation.** Required units include mathematics 1. Math unit must be algebra or higher.

**2007-2008 Annual costs.** Tuition/fees: $13,220. Books/supplies: $1,300. Personal expenses: $3,152.

**Financial aid.** All financial aid based on need.

**Application procedures. Admission:** No deadline. $50 fee. Application may be submitted online. Admission notification on a rolling basis. **Financial aid:** No deadline. FAFSA required. Applicants notified on a rolling basis.

**Academics. Special study options:** Accelerated study, cooperative education, distance learning, weekend college. **Credit/placement by examination:** CLEP, institutional tests. **Support services:** Learning center, remedial instruction, tutoring.

**Majors. Business:** Business admin. **Computer sciences:** Networking, systems analysis. **Engineering technology:** Biomedical, electrical. **Other:** Technical management.

**Most popular majors.** Business/marketing 21%, computer/information sciences 58%, engineering/engineering technologies 21%.

**Computing on campus.** 575 workstations in library, computer center. Online course registration, online library, helpline available.

**Student life. Freshman orientation:** Mandatory. **Activities:** Student government, Phi Theta Kappa, Golden Key, Institution of Electrical and Electronics Engineers, cultural exchange club, chess club, art club, Crusade for Christ.

**Student services.** Career counseling, student employment services, financial aid counseling, on-campus daycare, placement for graduates, veterans' counselor. **Physically disabled:** Services for visually, hearing impaired.

**Contact.** E-mail: admissions@devry.edu
Phone: (732) 435-4850 Toll-free number: (800) 333-3879
Fax: (732) 435-4850
Gerald Wargo, Director of Admissions, DeVry University: North Brunswick, 630 US Highway One, North Brunswick, NJ 08902-3362

## Drew University
**Madison, New Jersey**                    CB member
**www.drew.edu**                           CB code: 2193

- Private 4-year university and liberal arts college affiliated with United Methodist Church
- Residential campus in large town
- 1,620 degree-seeking undergraduates: 2% part-time, 61% women, 6% African American, 5% Asian American, 8% Hispanic American, 2% international
- 921 degree-seeking graduate students
- 77% of applicants admitted
- 76% graduate within 6 years

**General.** Founded in 1867. Regionally accredited. **Degrees:** 357 bachelor's awarded; master's, doctoral, first professional offered. **Location:** 30 miles from New York City. **Calendar:** Semester, limited summer session. **Full-time faculty:** 157 total; 96% have terminal degrees, 18% minority, 47% women. **Part-time faculty:** 64 total. **Class size:** 68% < 20, 28% 20-39, 2% 40-49, 1% 50-99. **Special facilities:** 80-acre forest preserve, arboretum, photography gallery, observatory, research greenhouse, laser holography laboratory, center for the arts, music hall.

**Freshman class profile.** 3,816 applied, 2,940 admitted, 456 enrolled.

| Mid 50% test scores | | | |
|---|---|---|---|
| SAT critical reading: | 520-650 | GPA 2.0-2.99: | 18% |
| SAT math: | 510-630 | Rank in top quarter: | 64% |
| SAT writing: | 530-650 | Rank in top tenth: | 28% |
| ACT composite: | 20-27 | Return as sophomores: | 81% |
| GPA 3.50 or higher: | 41% | Out-of-state: | 44% |
| GPA 3.0-3.49: | 41% | Live on campus: | 91% |
| | | International: | 3% |

**Basis for selection.** School achievement record most important; test scores also important. Interview recommended. **Homeschooled:** Statement describing homeschool structure and mission, transcript of courses and grades required.

**High school preparation.** Recommended units include English 4, mathematics 3, social studies 2, history 2, science 2, foreign language 2 and academic electives 3.

**2007-2008 Annual costs.** Tuition/fees: $34,790. Room/board: $9,476. Books/supplies: $1,228. Personal expenses: $2,438.

**2006-2007 Financial aid. Need-based:** 81% of total undergraduate aid awarded as scholarships/grants, 19% as loans/jobs. **Non-need-based:** Scholarships awarded for academics, art, minority status, music/drama.

**Application procedures. Admission:** Closing date 2/15. $50 fee, may be waived for applicants with need. Application may be submitted online. Applicants notified by third week in March. Must reply by 5/1. **Financial aid:** Closing date 2/15. FAFSA, CSS PROFILE required. Applicants notified by 3/31; must reply by 5/1.

**Academics.** RISE program enables students to conduct scientific research with retired scientists. **Special study options:** Accelerated study, combined bachelor's/graduate degree, cross-registration, double major, exchange student, independent study, internships, New York semester, student-designed major, study abroad, teacher certification program, United Nations semester, Washington semester. Art, theater, Wall Street semesters in New York City, semesters in Brussels and London, summer semester in South Africa, 7-year dual degree (BA/MD) with UMDNJ-New Jersey Medical School, 5-year dual degree (BA/BS) with Columbia University and Washington University (St. Louis), month-long international seminars in January and May. **Credit/placement by examination:** AP, CLEP, IB, institutional tests. 32 credit hours maximum toward bachelor's degree. **Support services:** Learning center, pre-admission summer program, reduced course load, tutoring, writing center.

**Majors. Area/ethnic studies:** African, women's. **Biology:** General, biochemistry. **Computer sciences:** Computer science. **English:** English lit. **Foreign languages:** Chinese, classics, French, German, Spanish. **History:** General. **Interdisciplinary:** Behavioral sciences. **Math:** General. **Philosophy/religion:** Philosophy, religion. **Physical sciences:** Chemistry, physics. **Psychology:** General. **Social sciences:** Anthropology, economics, political science, sociology. **Visual/performing arts:** Art, art history/conservation, dramatic. **Other:** Biological Anthropology.

**Most popular majors.** English 8%, history 6%, interdisciplinary studies 10%, psychology 12%, social sciences 30%, visual/performing arts 10%.

**Computing on campus.** PC or laptop required. 2,500 workstations in library, computer center. Dormitories wired for high-speed internet access and linked to campus network. Commuter students can connect to campus network. Online course registration, online library, helpline, repair service, wireless network available.

**Student life. Freshman orientation:** Mandatory, $250 fee. Preregistration for classes offered. Week before start of fall semester. **Housing:** Guaranteed on-campus for all undergraduates. Coed dorms, special housing for disabled, substance-free housing available. Theme houses available. **Activities:** Campus ministries, choral groups, dance, drama, film society, literary magazine, music ensembles, radio station, student government, student newspaper, symphony orchestra, TV station, Amnesty International, Hispanic student organization, College Democrats, College Republicans, Pan-African student organization, Inter-Varsity Christian Fellowship, Jewish student organization/Hillel, Drew Environmental Action League, Students Against Violence Everywhere, The Alliance.

**Athletics.** NCAA. **Intercollegiate:** Baseball M, basketball, cross-country, equestrian, fencing, field hockey W, lacrosse, soccer, softball W, swimming, tennis. **Intramural:** Basketball, football (non-tackle), racquetball, soccer, softball, squash, table tennis, volleyball. **Team name:** Rangers.

**Student services.** Adult student services, alcohol/substance abuse counseling, campus ministries, career counseling, services for economically disadvantaged, student employment services, financial aid counseling, health services, minority student services, on-campus daycare, personal counseling, placement for graduates, women's services. **Physically disabled:** Services for visually, hearing impaired.

**Contact.** E-mail: cadm@drew.edu
Phone: (973) 408-3739 Fax: (973) 408-3068
Mary Beth Carey, Dean of College Admissions and Financial Assistance, Drew University, 36 Madison Avenue, Madison, NJ 07940-1493

---

## Fairleigh Dickinson University: College at Florham
**Madison, New Jersey**
**www.fdu.edu**                                    **CB code: 2262**

- Private 4-year university
- Residential campus in large town
- 2,470 degree-seeking undergraduates: 7% part-time, 53% women, 8% African American, 3% Asian American, 7% Hispanic American, 1% international
- 901 degree-seeking graduate students
- 63% of applicants admitted
- SAT or ACT (ACT writing optional) required
- 54% graduate within 6 years

**General.** Regionally accredited. Additional campus locations: Wroxton College, England and Vancouver, Canada. **Degrees:** 507 bachelor's awarded; master's offered. **ROTC:** Army, Air Force. **Location:** 27 miles from New York City. **Calendar:** Semester, extensive summer session. **Full-time faculty:** 120 total. **Part-time faculty:** 200 total. **Special facilities:** ITV multimedia classrooms, web-lab, center for students with learning disabilities.

**Freshman class profile.** 2,706 applied, 1,693 admitted, 489 enrolled.

| Mid 50% test scores | | | |
|---|---|---|---|
| SAT critical reading: | 460-560 | Rank in top tenth: | 11% |
| SAT math: | 460-570 | Return as sophomores: | 76% |
| SAT writing: | 470-560 | Out-of-state: | 21% |
| Rank in top quarter: | 32% | Live on campus: | 84% |

**Basis for selection.** GPA, test scores, difficulty of high school curriculum most important. **Homeschooled:** Applicant must take SAT or ACT. **Learning Disabled:** Separate application along with admissions application.

**High school preparation.** College-preparatory program required. 16 units required. Required and recommended units include English 4, mathematics 3, social studies 2, history 2, science 2-3 (laboratory 2-3), foreign language 2 and academic electives 3.

**2007-2008 Annual costs.** Tuition/fees: $28,228. Room/board: $9,582.

**Application procedures. Admission:** Priority date 3/15; no deadline. $40 fee, may be waived for applicants with need. Admission notification on a rolling basis beginning on or about 11/1. Must reply by May 1 or within 2 week(s) if notified thereafter.

**Academics. Special study options:** Accelerated study, combined bachelor's/graduate degree, cooperative education, cross-registration, distance learning, double major, external degree, honors, independent study, internships, liberal arts/career combination, study abroad, teacher certification program, Washington semester, weekend college. Nongovernmental organization status with United Nations affords students participatory opportunities. **Credit/placement by examination:** AP, CLEP, institutional tests. **Support services:** Learning center, remedial instruction, study skills assistance, tutoring, writing center.

**Majors. Biology:** General, marine. **Business:** Accounting, business admin, hospitality admin, managerial economics, marketing. **Communications:** General. **Computer sciences:** General. **English:** Creative writing, English lit. **Foreign languages:** French, Spanish. **Health:** Clinical lab science, health services, medical radiologic technology/radiation therapy, nursing (RN). **History:** General. **Liberal arts:** Humanities. **Math:** General. **Philosophy/religion:** Philosophy. **Physical sciences:** Chemistry. **Psychology:** General. **Social sciences:** Economics, political science, sociology. **Visual/performing arts:** General, cinematography, dramatic.

**Most popular majors.** Business/marketing 33%, communications/journalism 8%, liberal arts 8%, psychology 16%, social sciences 7%, visual/performing arts 12%.

**Computing on campus.** 170 workstations in dormitories, library, computer center. Dormitories wired for high-speed internet access and linked to campus network. Commuter students can connect to campus network. Online course registration, online library, helpline, student web hosting, wireless network available.

**Student life. Freshman orientation:** Mandatory. Preregistration for classes offered. **Housing:** Guaranteed on-campus for freshmen. Coed dorms, special housing for disabled, apartments available. $350 partly refundable deposit, deadline 5/1. **Activities:** Choral groups, dance, drama, film society, literary magazine, radio station, student government, student newspaper.

**Athletics.** NCAA. **Intercollegiate:** Baseball M, basketball, cross-country, field hockey W, football (tackle) M, golf M, lacrosse, soccer, softball W, swimming, tennis, volleyball W. **Intramural:** Basketball, bowling, football (tackle) M, ice hockey M, racquetball, soccer, softball. **Team name:** Devils.

**Student services.** Adult student services, alcohol/substance abuse counseling, campus ministries, career counseling, services for economically disadvantaged, student employment services, financial aid counseling, health services, minority student services, personal counseling, placement for graduates, women's services. **Learning disabled:** Comprehensive services available.

**Contact.** E-mail: globaleducation@fdu.edu
Phone: (800) 338-8803 Toll-free number: (800) 338-8803
Fax: (973) 443-8088
Bernetta Millonde, University Director of Admissions, Fairleigh Dickinson University: College at Florham, 285 Madison Avenue, Madison, NJ 07940

---

## Fairleigh Dickinson University: Metropolitan Campus
### Teaneck, New Jersey
**www.fdu.edu**  **CB code: 2263**

- Private 4-year university
- Commuter campus in large town
- 3,458 degree-seeking undergraduates: 36% part-time, 57% women, 16% African American, 6% Asian American, 18% Hispanic American, 7% international
- 2,534 degree-seeking graduate students
- 49% of applicants admitted
- SAT or ACT (ACT writing optional) required
- 38% graduate within 6 years

**General.** Founded in 1942. Regionally accredited. Additional campus at Wroxton College, England and Vancouver, Canada. **Degrees:** 589 bachelor's, 62 associate awarded; master's, doctoral offered. **ROTC:** Army, Air Force. **Location:** 13 miles from New York City. **Calendar:** Semester, extensive summer session. **Full-time faculty:** 185 total. **Part-time faculty:** 440 total. **Special facilities:** Computer labs, ITV multimedia classrooms, photonics lab, center for students with learning disabilities, center for psychological services, Web lab, marine biology lab, cyber crime lab.

**Freshman class profile.** 3,019 applied, 1,481 admitted, 453 enrolled.

| Mid 50% test scores | | | |
|---|---|---|---|
| SAT critical reading: | 440-530 | Rank in top tenth: | 14% |
| SAT math: | 450-560 | Return as sophomores: | 72% |
| SAT writing: | 430-530 | Out-of-state: | 9% |
| Rank in top quarter: | 42% | Live on campus: | 56% |
| | | International: | 11% |

**Basis for selection.** Rigor of secondary school record and GPA most important. Recommendations, standardized test scores, extracurricular activities important. **Learning Disabled:** Regional Center for College Students with Learning Disabilities requires separate application. Must also apply to university admissions.

**High school preparation.** 16 units required. Required and recommended units include English 4, mathematics 3, social studies 2, history 2, science 2-3 (laboratory 2-3), foreign language 2 and academic electives 3.

**2007-2008 Annual costs.** Tuition/fees: $26,232. Room/board: $10,422.

**Application procedures. Admission:** Priority date 3/15; no deadline. $40 fee, may be waived for applicants with need. Application may be submitted online. Admission notification on a rolling basis beginning on or about 11/15. Must reply by May 1 or within 2 week(s) if notified thereafter.

**Academics.** Core curriculum consists of 4 interdisciplinary courses. Marine biology majors spend 1 summer in Hilo, Hawaii, and 1 summer at Shoals Laboratory, Maine. FDU also offers University Honors Program and Global Scholars Program. **Special study options:** Accelerated study, combined bachelor's/graduate degree, cooperative education, distance learning, double major, ESL, honors, independent study, internships, liberal arts/career combination, student-designed major, study abroad, teacher certification program, Washington semester, weekend college. Nongovernmental organization status with United Nations affords students participatory opportunities. **Credit/placement by examination:** AP, CLEP, institutional

tests. **Support services:** Learning center, pre-admission summer program, reduced course load, remedial instruction, study skills assistance, tutoring, writing center.

**Majors. Biology:** General, biochemistry, marine. **Business:** Accounting, business admin, hospitality admin, managerial economics, marketing. **Communications:** General. **Computer sciences:** Computer science, information technology. **Conservation:** Environmental science. **Engineering:** Electrical. **Engineering technology:** Civil, construction, electrical, mechanical. **English:** English lit. **Foreign languages:** French, Spanish. **Health:** Clinical lab science, health services, medical radiologic technology/radiation therapy, nursing (RN). **History:** General. **Interdisciplinary:** Biological/physical sciences. **Liberal arts:** Humanities. **Math:** General. **Philosophy/religion:** Philosophy. **Physical sciences:** Chemistry. **Protective services:** Criminal justice. **Psychology:** General. **Social sciences:** Economics, international relations, political science, sociology. **Visual/performing arts:** General, dramatic.

**Most popular majors.** Business/marketing 12%, health sciences 8%, liberal arts 49%.

**Computing on campus.** 190 workstations in dormitories, library, computer center. Dormitories wired for high-speed internet access and linked to campus network. Commuter students can connect to campus network. Online course registration, online library, helpline, student web hosting, wireless network available.

**Student life. Freshman orientation:** Mandatory. Preregistration for classes offered. **Housing:** Guaranteed on-campus for freshmen. Coed dorms, single-sex dorms, apartments available. $350 partly refundable deposit, deadline 5/1. Honors and global scholar housing available. **Activities:** Pep band, campus ministries, dance, drama, international student organizations, literary magazine, radio station, student government, student newspaper, TV station, multicultural council, Indian Cultural Experience, Black Men's Alliance, Nubian Ladies, Hillel-Jewish Student Union.

**Athletics.** NCAA. **Intercollegiate:** Baseball M, basketball, bowling W, cross-country, fencing W, golf, soccer, softball W, tennis, track and field, volleyball W. **Intramural:** Badminton, baseball M, basketball, bowling, cheerleading, golf M, racquetball, skiing, soccer, table tennis, tennis, volleyball. **Team name:** Knights.

**Student services.** Adult student services, alcohol/substance abuse counseling, campus ministries, career counseling, services for economically disadvantaged, student employment services, financial aid counseling, health services, personal counseling, placement for graduates, women's services. **Learning disabled:** Comprehensive services available.

**Contact.** E-mail: globaleducation@fdu.edu
Phone: (201) 692-2553 Toll-free number: (800) 338-8803
Fax: (201) 692-7319
Bernetta Millonde, University Director of Admissions, Fairleigh Dickinson University: Metropolitan Campus, 1000 River Road, H-DH3-10, Teaneck, NJ 07666-1996

---

## Felician College
### Lodi, New Jersey
**www.felician.edu**  **CB code: 2321**

- Private 4-year liberal arts college affiliated with Roman Catholic Church
- Commuter campus in large city
- 1,615 degree-seeking undergraduates: 22% part-time, 78% women, 15% African American, 11% Asian American, 17% Hispanic American
- 94 degree-seeking graduate students
- 61% of applicants admitted
- SAT or ACT (ACT writing optional) required
- 36% graduate within 6 years

**General.** Founded in 1942. Regionally accredited. Additional campus in Rutherford. All programs spread through both campuses. **Degrees:** 115 bachelor's, 19 associate awarded; master's offered. **Location:** 12 miles from New York City. **Calendar:** Semester, limited summer session. **Full-time faculty:** 95 total; 59% women. **Part-time faculty:** 78 total. **Class size:** 76% < 20, 23% 20-39, less than 1% 40-49, less than 1% 50-99, less than 1% >100. **Special facilities:** Nursing skills laboratory, performance and theater facilities.

**Freshman class profile.** 1,561 applied, 948 admitted, 267 enrolled.

| Mid 50% test scores | | | |
|---|---|---|---|
| SAT critical reading: | 400-500 | Return as sophomores: | 60% |
| SAT math: | 390-490 | Out-of-state: | 5% |

**Basis for selection.** School achievement record, test scores most important. Interview, school and community activities, recommendations of high school counselor considered. Interview recommended for all; portfolio recommended for art programs.

**High school preparation.** 19 units recommended. Recommended units include English 4, mathematics 3, social studies 3, science 3 and academic electives 6. Biology, chemistry, algebra required for nursing and medical laboratory technology applicants.

**2007-2008 Annual costs.** Tuition/fees: $21,900. Room/board: $8,900. Books/supplies: $1,118. Personal expenses: $1,671.

**2006-2007 Financial aid. Need-based:** 252 full-time freshmen applied for aid; 226 were judged to have need; 226 of these received aid. Average need met was 85%. Average scholarship/grant was $7,000; average loan $3,500. 63% of total undergraduate aid awarded as scholarships/grants, 37% as loans/jobs. **Non-need-based:** Awarded to 705 full-time undergraduates, including 178 freshmen. Scholarships awarded for academics, alumni affiliation, athletics, religious affiliation.

**Application procedures. Admission:** No deadline. $30 fee, may be waived for applicants with need. Application may be submitted online. Admission notification on a rolling basis beginning on or about 3/15. Must reply by May 1 or within 2 week(s) if notified thereafter. **Financial aid:** Priority date 6/1; no closing date. FAFSA required. Applicants notified on a rolling basis starting 4/1; must reply within 2 week(s) of notification.

**Academics.** Post-baccalaureate certification available in elementary and secondary education. **Special study options:** Accelerated study, combined bachelor's/graduate degree, cooperative education, cross-registration, distance learning, double major, dual enrollment of high school students, ESL, honors, independent study, internships, liberal arts/career combination, student-designed major, study abroad, teacher certification program, weekend college. **Credit/placement by examination:** AP, CLEP, IB, SAT, institutional tests. 15 credit hours maximum toward associate degree, 30 toward bachelor's. **Support services:** Learning center, writing center.

**Majors. Biology:** General, toxicology. **Business:** Accounting, business admin, marketing. **Communications:** General, broadcast journalism, digital media, journalism. **Computer sciences:** General, computer science. **Education:** Early childhood, early childhood special, elementary, mathematics. **English:** English lit. **Health:** Cytotechnology, health services, nuclear medical technology, nursing (RN), nursing admin, respiratory therapy technology. **History:** General. **Interdisciplinary:** Natural sciences. **Liberal arts:** Humanities. **Math:** General. **Philosophy/religion:** Philosophy, religion. **Psychology:** General. **Social sciences:** Sociology. **Visual/performing arts:** Art, studio arts.

**Most popular majors.** Business/marketing 43%, education 30%, psychology 12%.

**Computing on campus.** 140 workstations in dormitories, library, computer center. Dormitories wired for high-speed internet access and linked to campus network. Commuter students can connect to campus network. Online library, repair service available.

**Student life. Freshman orientation:** Mandatory. 3 summer programs available. **Policies:** No drugs or alcohol on campus. **Housing:** Guaranteed on-campus for freshmen. Coed dorms, single-sex dorms, special housing for disabled available. $200 deposit. **Activities:** Choral groups, drama, international student organizations, literary magazine, student government, Angelicum Club, history club, RCIA, Kappa Sigma Xi, Aspiring Authors, Students in Free Enterprise, Kappa Gamma Pi.

**Athletics.** NAIA, NCAA. **Intercollegiate:** Baseball M, basketball, cross-country, golf M, soccer, softball W, track and field, volleyball W. **Intramural:** Basketball M, bowling. **Team name:** Golden Falcons.

**Student services.** Campus ministries, financial aid counseling, health services. **Learning disabled:** Comprehensive services available.

**Contact.** E-mail: admissions@inet.felician.edu
Phone: (201) 559-6131 Fax: (201) 559-6188
Cara Gibbons, Director of Undergraduate Admissions, Felician College, 262 South Main Street, Lodi, NJ 07644-2198

---

## Georgian Court University
**Lakewood, New Jersey**
www.georgian.edu

**CB member**
**CB code: 2274**

- Private 4-year university and liberal arts college for women affiliated with Roman Catholic Church
- Residential campus in large town

---

- 1,718 degree-seeking undergraduates: 19% part-time, 94% women, 8% African American, 2% Asian American, 8% Hispanic American, 1% international
- 835 degree-seeking graduate students
- 77% of applicants admitted
- 56% graduate within 6 years

**General.** Founded in 1908. Regionally accredited. Evening and graduate divisions coeducational. **Degrees:** 378 bachelor's awarded; master's offered. **Location:** 60 miles from New York City and Philadelphia. **Calendar:** Semester, limited summer session. **Full-time faculty:** 101 total; 82% have terminal degrees, 7% minority, 61% women. **Part-time faculty:** 206 total; 10% have terminal degrees, 3% minority, 55% women. **Class size:** 75% < 20, 25% 20-39. **Special facilities:** Arboretum, NASA Education Resource Center.

**Freshman class profile.** 563 applied, 433 admitted, 226 enrolled.

| | | | |
|---|---|---|---|
| GPA 3.50 or higher: | 21% | Rank in top tenth: | 6% |
| GPA 3.0-3.49: | 39% | Return as sophomores: | 72% |
| GPA 2.0-2.99: | 37% | Out-of-state: | 5% |
| Rank in top quarter: | 23% | Live on campus: | 71% |

**Basis for selection.** Completed high school program reviewed for rigor of courses and grades received. Students should be completing program of 16 academic units with grades of 2.5 or higher. Students not meeting criteria referred to faculty committee for review. SAT or ACT recommended. **Homeschooled:** Statement describing homeschool structure and mission required.

**High school preparation.** 16 units required. Required units include English 4, mathematics 2, history 1, (laboratory 1), foreign language 2 and academic electives 6.

**2007-2008 Annual costs.** Tuition/fees: $22,078. Room/board: $8,136. Books/supplies: $1,250. Personal expenses: $2,400.

**2007-2008 Financial aid. Need-based:** 218 full-time freshmen applied for aid; 196 were judged to have need; 196 of these received aid. Average need met was 83%. Average scholarship/grant was $17,663; average loan $3,388. 58% of total undergraduate aid awarded as scholarships/grants, 42% as loans/jobs. **Non-need-based:** Scholarships awarded for academics, alumni affiliation, art, athletics, leadership, minority status, music/drama, religious affiliation.

**Application procedures. Admission:** Closing date 8/1 (receipt date). $40 fee, may be waived for applicants with need. Application may be submitted online. Admission notification on a rolling basis beginning on or about 10/1. Must reply by May 1 or within 2 week(s) if notified thereafter. **Financial aid:** Priority date 3/1; no closing date. FAFSA, institutional form required. Applicants notified on a rolling basis starting 2/1; must reply within 2 week(s) of notification.

**Academics. Special study options:** Accelerated study, combined bachelor's/graduate degree, distance learning, double major, dual enrollment of high school students, ESL, honors, independent study, internships, liberal arts/career combination, study abroad, teacher certification program. **Credit/placement by examination:** AP, CLEP, institutional tests. 30 credit hours maximum toward bachelor's degree. **Support services:** Learning center, reduced course load, remedial instruction, study skills assistance, tutoring.

**Majors. Biology:** General, biochemistry. **Business:** Accounting, business admin. **Communications:** General. **Computer sciences:** General. **Education:** Elementary, special. **English:** English lit. **Foreign languages:** Spanish. **History:** General. **Interdisciplinary:** Natural sciences. **Liberal arts:** Arts/sciences, humanities. **Math:** General. **Philosophy/religion:** Religion. **Physical sciences:** Chemistry, physics. **Protective services:** Law enforcement admin. **Psychology:** General. **Public administration:** Social work. **Social sciences:** Sociology. **Visual/performing arts:** Art, art history/conservation, studio arts.

**Most popular majors.** Business/marketing 10%, education 35%, English 8%, history 6%, psychology 16%.

**Computing on campus.** 186 workstations in dormitories, library, computer center. Dormitories wired for high-speed internet access and linked to campus network. Commuter students can connect to campus network. Online course registration, online library, helpline, wireless network available.

**Student life. Freshman orientation:** Mandatory, $100 fee. Held during the week before classes begin. **Housing:** Guaranteed on-campus for all undergraduates. Substance-free housing available. $250 deposit, deadline 5/1. **Activities:** Bands, campus ministries, choral groups, international student organizations, literary magazine, music ensembles, student government, student newspaper, Council for Exceptional Children, Sisters United, Re-Entry

Women's Club, Alliance Francaise, Amnesty International, Black Student Union, LASO, Living/Learning Communities.

**Athletics.** NAIA, NCAA. **Intercollegiate:** Basketball W, cross-country W, lacrosse W, soccer W, softball W, tennis W, volleyball W. **Team name:** Lions.

**Student services.** Campus ministries, career counseling, financial aid counseling, health services, personal counseling. **Physically disabled:** Services for visually, speech, hearing impaired.

**Contact.** E-mail: admissions@georgian.edu
Phone: (732) 987-2200 ext. 2700 Toll-free number: (800) 458-8422
Fax: (732) 987-2000
Kathie Gallant, Director of Admissions, Georgian Court University, 900 Lakewood Avenue, Lakewood, NJ 08701-2697

---

## Kean University
**Union, New Jersey**      **CB member**
www.kean.edu      **CB code: 2517**

- Public 4-year university and liberal arts college
- Commuter campus in small city
- 10,137 degree-seeking undergraduates: 22% part-time, 63% women, 20% African American, 6% Asian American, 20% Hispanic American, 2% international
- 1,925 degree-seeking graduate students
- 67% of applicants admitted
- SAT or ACT (ACT writing optional), application essay required
- 42% graduate within 6 years

**General.** Founded in 1855. Regionally accredited. Institute for Foreign Service and Diplomacy. **Degrees:** 1,912 bachelor's awarded; master's offered. **ROTC:** Army, Air Force. **Location:** 12 miles from New York City. **Calendar:** Semester, limited summer session. **Full-time faculty:** 374 total; 89% have terminal degrees, 29% minority, 47% women. **Part-time faculty:** 915 total; 23% minority, 52% women. **Class size:** 43% < 20, 57% 20-39, less than 1% 40-49, less than 1% 50-99. **Special facilities:** Holocaust resource center, ethnic studies center.

**Freshman class profile.** 5,455 applied, 3,633 admitted, 1,478 enrolled.

| Mid 50% test scores | | Rank in top quarter: | 25% |
|---|---|---|---|
| SAT critical reading: | 400-500 | Rank in top tenth: | 6% |
| SAT math: | 410-520 | Return as sophomores: | 77% |
| GPA 3.50 or higher: | 14% | Out-of-state: | 3% |
| GPA 3.0-3.49: | 31% | Live on campus: | 38% |
| GPA 2.0-2.99: | 51% | International: | 2% |

**Basis for selection.** High school GPA at or above 2.50, test scores, counselor recommendations important. Consideration given to military service, work, personal life experiences. Non-U.S.-educated applicants evaluated based on academic record in home country. If needed, applicants advised of specific additional requirements.

**High school preparation.** 16 units required. Required and recommended units include English 4, mathematics 3, social studies 2, history 2, science 2 (laboratory 2), foreign language 2 and academic electives 5.

**2007-2008 Annual costs.** Tuition/fees: $8,505; $12,645 out-of-state. Room/board: $9,190.

**2007-2008 Financial aid. Need-based:** 1,238 full-time freshmen applied for aid; 935 were judged to have need; 912 of these received aid. Average need met was 55%. Average scholarship/grant was $6,925; average loan $3,466. 50% of total undergraduate aid awarded as scholarships/grants, 50% as loans/jobs. **Non-need-based:** Awarded to 674 full-time undergraduates, including 238 freshmen. Scholarships awarded for academics, alumni affiliation, art, leadership, music/drama.

**Application procedures. Admission:** Priority date 5/1; deadline 5/31 (postmark date). $50 fee, may be waived for applicants with need. Application may be submitted online. Admission notification on a rolling basis beginning on or about 11/1. Must reply by May 1 or within 2 week(s) if notified thereafter. **Financial aid:** Priority date 3/15; no closing date. FAFSA required. Applicants notified on a rolling basis starting 3/15; must reply by 5/1.

**Academics. Special study options:** Accelerated study, combined bachelor's/graduate degree, cooperative education, distance learning, double major, ESL, honors, independent study, internships, liberal arts/career combination, semester at sea, study abroad, teacher certification program, Washington semester, weekend college. 2-year bachelor's degree program for RNs, Foreign Transfer Programs, TraveLearn. **Credit/placement by examination:**

AP, CLEP, IB, SAT, institutional tests. 46 credit hours maximum toward bachelor's degree. **Support services:** Learning center, pre-admission summer program, reduced course load, remedial instruction, study skills assistance, tutoring, writing center.

**Majors. Biology:** General. **Business:** Accounting, business admin, finance, marketing. **Communications:** General. **Communications technology:** Printing management. **Computer sciences:** General, networking. **Education:** Elementary, kindergarten/preschool, music, physical, special, speech, technology/industrial arts. **Engineering technology:** Electrical, manufacturing. **English:** English lit. **Foreign languages:** Spanish. **Health:** Athletic training, clinical lab science, medical records admin. **History:** General. **Liberal arts:** Arts/sciences. **Math:** General. **Parks/recreation:** Facilities management. **Physical sciences:** Chemistry, geology. **Protective services:** Law enforcement admin. **Psychology:** General. **Public administration:** General, social work. **Social sciences:** Economics, political science, sociology. **Visual/performing arts:** Acting, art, art history/conservation, design, dramatic, film/cinema, industrial design, interior design, studio arts, theater design. **Other:** Philosophy and Religion, Psychology Rehabilitation, Science and Technology.

**Most popular majors.** Business/marketing 21%, education 20%, psychology 11%, visual/performing arts 7%.

**Computing on campus.** 1,650 workstations in dormitories, library, computer center, student center. Dormitories wired for high-speed internet access and linked to campus network. Commuter students can connect to campus network. Online course registration, student web hosting, wireless network available.

**Student life. Freshman orientation:** Mandatory, $50 fee. Preregistration for classes offered. **Housing:** Coed dorms, single-sex dorms, special housing for disabled, apartments, substance-free housing available. $100 nonrefundable deposit, deadline 5/1. Freshman housing, floor for women housing only. **Activities:** Bands, campus ministries, choral groups, dance, drama, film society, international student organizations, literary magazine, music ensembles, Model UN, musical theater, radio station, student government, student newspaper, TV station, Asian cultue club, association of Indian students, association of Latin American students, Intervarsity Christian fellowship, Haitian student association, Hamor's Head Club for Democrats, Jewish culture club, Muslim student association, Pan African student union.

**Athletics.** NCAA. **Intercollegiate:** Baseball M, basketball, cheerleading, cross-country, field hockey W, football (tackle) M, lacrosse, soccer, softball W, tennis W, track and field, volleyball W. **Intramural:** Basketball, football (non-tackle), soccer, softball, tennis, volleyball, weight lifting. **Team name:** Cougars.

**Student services.** Adult student services, alcohol/substance abuse counseling, campus ministries, career counseling, services for economically disadvantaged, student employment services, financial aid counseling, health services, minority student services, on-campus daycare, personal counseling, placement for graduates, veterans' counselor, women's services. **Physically disabled:** Services for visually, speech, hearing impaired. **Learning disabled:** Comprehensive services available.

**Contact.** E-mail: admitme@kean.edu
Phone: (908) 737-7100 Fax: (908) 737-7105
Audley Bridges, Director of Admissions, Kean University, 1000 Morris Avenue, Union, NJ 07083-0411

---

## Monmouth University
**West Long Branch, New Jersey**      **CB member**
www.monmouth.edu      **CB code: 2416**

- Private 4-year university
- Residential campus in small town
- 4,694 degree-seeking undergraduates: 8% part-time, 58% women, 4% African American, 2% Asian American, 5% Hispanic American
- 1,562 degree-seeking graduate students
- 57% of applicants admitted
- SAT or ACT with writing required
- 60% graduate within 6 years

**General.** Founded in 1933. Regionally accredited. **Degrees:** 962 bachelor's, 7 associate awarded; master's offered. **ROTC:** Air Force. **Location:** 50 miles from New York City, 75 miles from Philadelphia. **Calendar:** Semester, limited summer session. **Full-time faculty:** 251 total; 85% have terminal degrees, 16% minority, 49% women. **Part-time faculty:** 283 total; 20% have terminal degrees, 6% minority, 47% women. **Class size:** 44% < 20, 56% 20-39, less than 1% 40-49. **Special facilities:** Multimedia communications center with TV and radio station, sculpture garden, ice house-gallery.

**Freshman class profile.** 6,982 applied, 4,014 admitted, 946 enrolled.

| Mid 50% test scores | | | | |
|---|---|---|---|---|
| SAT critical reading: | 490-560 | GPA 2.0-2.99: | 34% |
| SAT math: | 500-580 | Rank in top quarter: | 39% |
| SAT writing: | 480-570 | Rank in top tenth: | 11% |
| ACT composite: | 21-24 | End year in good standing: | 97% |
| GPA 3.50 or higher: | 26% | Return as sophomores: | 80% |
| GPA 3.0-3.49: | 40% | Out-of-state: | 18% |
| | | Live on campus: | 82% |

**Basis for selection.** School record, GPA, test scores important followed by recommendations and essay. Resume of activities including community involvement and leadership positions required; audition recommended for music programs; portfolio recommended for art programs. Interview required for Music and Theatre Arts Department. **Homeschooled:** State high school equivalency certificate required. All students who submit portfolio of coursework in lieu of transcript must also complete institution's curriculum chart for homeschooled students.

**High school preparation.** 16 units required; 20 recommended. Required and recommended units include English 4, mathematics 3, social studies 2, history 2, science 2 (laboratory 1), foreign language 2 and academic electives 5.

**2007-2008 Annual costs.** Tuition/fees: $23,034. Room/board: $8,904. Books/supplies: $1,000. Personal expenses: $1,929.

**2007-2008 Financial aid. Need-based:** 782 full-time freshmen applied for aid; 599 were judged to have need; 598 of these received aid. Average need met was 71%. Average scholarship/grant was $11,468; average loan $4,197. 48% of total undergraduate aid awarded as scholarships/grants, 52% as loans/jobs. **Non-need-based:** Awarded to 3,886 full-time undergraduates, including 927 freshmen. Scholarships awarded for academics, alumni affiliation, art, athletics, leadership.

**Application procedures. Admission:** Priority date 12/1; deadline 3/1 (receipt date). $50 fee, may be waived for applicants with need. Application may be submitted online. Admission notification 4/1. Must reply by 5/1. All deposits non-refundable after May 1. **Financial aid:** No deadline. FAFSA required. Applicants notified on a rolling basis starting 2/15; must reply within 2 week(s) of notification.

**Academics. Special study options:** Accelerated study, combined bachelor's/graduate degree, cooperative education, cross-registration, double major, dual enrollment of high school students, honors, independent study, internships, liberal arts/career combination, student-designed major, study abroad, teacher certification program, Washington semester. **Credit/placement by examination:** AP, CLEP, IB, SAT, institutional tests. 30 credit hours maximum toward bachelor's degree. AP credit awarded only for institutional course equivalents. **Support services:** Learning center, reduced course load, remedial instruction, study skills assistance, tutoring, writing center.

**Honors college/program.** Students are admitted to the honors school with a minimum SAT score of 1200 (exclusive of Writing, with Critical Reading score no less than 510) and a GPA of at least 3.3.

**Majors. Biology:** General, environmental. **Business:** Business admin, international. **Communications:** General. **Computer sciences:** General. **Education:** General, special. **Engineering:** Software. **English:** English lit. **Foreign languages:** General. **Health:** Clinical lab science, health services, nursing (RN). **History:** General. **Math:** General. **Physical sciences:** Chemistry. **Protective services:** Criminal justice. **Psychology:** General. **Public administration:** Social work. **Social sciences:** General, anthropology, political science. **Visual/performing arts:** Art, dramatic, studio arts.

**Most popular majors.** Business/marketing 27%, communications/journalism 16%, education 16%, psychology 7%, security/protective services 6%, visual/performing arts 7%.

**Computing on campus.** 698 workstations in dormitories, library, computer center, student center. Dormitories wired for high-speed internet access and linked to campus network. Commuter students can connect to campus network. Online library, helpline, student web hosting, wireless network available.

**Student life. Freshman orientation:** Mandatory, $100 fee. Preregistration for classes offered. 2-day orientation held in July. **Policies:** No one who has not successfully completed at least 12 credit hours may associate with a fraternity or sorority. Students must have minimum 2.2 cumulative GPA and be registered full-time. Transfer students taking 12 or more credits may also associate. **Housing:** Coed dorms, apartments, substance-free housing available. $150 deposit. Honors, 24-hour quiet floors, leadership floors available. **Activities:** Bands, choral groups, dance, drama, international student organizations, literary magazine, music ensembles, musical theater, radio station, student government, student newspaper, TV station, Hillel, Christian Ambassadors, Catholic center, African-American student union, Latin American club, Circle K, Rotaract Club, alternative lifestyles clubs.

**Athletics.** NCAA. **Intercollegiate:** Baseball M, basketball, cross-country, field hockey W, football (tackle) M, golf, lacrosse W, sailing, soccer, softball W, tennis, track and field. **Intramural:** Badminton, basketball, football (non-tackle), soccer, softball, tennis, volleyball, water polo. **Team name:** Hawks.

**Student services.** Adult student services, alcohol/substance abuse counseling, campus ministries, career counseling, services for economically disadvantaged, student employment services, financial aid counseling, health services, legal services, personal counseling, placement for graduates, veterans' counselor, women's services. **Physically disabled:** Services for visually, speech, hearing impaired.

**Contact.** E-mail: admission@monmouth.edu
Phone: (732) 571-3456 Toll-free number: (800) 543-9671
Fax: (732) 263-5166
Lauren Cifelli, Director of Undergraduate Admission, Monmouth University, 400 Cedar Avenue, West Long Branch, NJ 07764-1898

---

## Montclair State University
**Upper Montclair, New Jersey**
**www.montclair.edu**

**CB member**
**CB code: 2520**

- Public 4-year university
- Residential campus in large town
- 12,559 degree-seeking undergraduates: 16% part-time, 61% women, 10% African American, 6% Asian American, 20% Hispanic American, 2% international
- 2,453 degree-seeking graduate students
- 57% of applicants admitted
- SAT required
- 61% graduate within 6 years; 23% enter graduate study

**General.** Founded in 1908. Regionally accredited. Includes Institute for the Humanities, Institute for the Advancement of Philosophy for Children, Institute for Critical Thinking, New Jersey School of Conservation in Stokes State Forest, Branchville, and Center for Continuing Education. **Degrees:** 2,482 bachelor's awarded; master's, doctoral offered. **ROTC:** Army, Naval, Air Force. **Location:** 14 miles from New York City. **Calendar:** Semester, limited summer session. **Full-time faculty:** 509 total; 92% have terminal degrees, 23% minority, 46% women. **Part-time faculty:** 766 total; 6% have terminal degrees, 8% minority, 58% women. **Class size:** 29% < 20, 67% 20-39, 2% 40-49, 2% 50-99, less than 1% >100.

**Freshman class profile.** 10,110 applied, 5,732 admitted, 2,098 enrolled.

| Mid 50% test scores | | | | |
|---|---|---|---|---|
| SAT critical reading: | 450-540 | Rank in top quarter: | 37% |
| SAT math: | 460-550 | Rank in top tenth: | 12% |
| SAT writing: | 450-540 | End year in good standing: | 88% |
| GPA 3.50 or higher: | 23% | Return as sophomores: | 82% |
| GPA 3.0-3.49: | 46% | Out-of-state: | 3% |
| GPA 2.0-2.99: | 30% | Live on campus: | 53% |
| | | International: | 1% |

**Basis for selection.** School achievement record most important. Extracurricular activities, test scores, community activities also important. Consideration given to disadvantaged applicants. Interview required for art, music, music therapy, speech, theater, and dance programs; audition required for dance, music, speech, theater programs; portfolio required for art programs. **Homeschooled:** Statement describing homeschool structure and mission, transcript of courses and grades required.

**High school preparation.** 16 units required. Required units include English 4, mathematics 3, social studies 2, science 2 (laboratory 2), foreign language 2 and academic electives 3. 4 mathematics (including trigonometry) required of computer science majors. Algebra II required for business administration majors. 3 additional units in English, social studies, science, mathematics, or foreign language required.

**2007-2008 Annual costs.** Tuition/fees: $8,895; $16,164 out-of-state. Room/board: $9,500. Books/supplies: $1,000. Personal expenses: $2,721.

**2007-2008 Financial aid. Need-based:** 1,371 full-time freshmen applied for aid; 1,035 were judged to have need; 980 of these received aid. Average need met was 64%. Average scholarship/grant was $6,904; average loan $3,531. 47% of total undergraduate aid awarded as scholarships/grants, 53% as loans/jobs. **Non-need-based:** Awarded to 956 full-time undergraduates, including 140 freshmen. Scholarships awarded for academics, alumni affiliation, art, leadership, minority status, music/drama, ROTC, state residency.

**Application procedures. Admission:** Closing date 3/1 (postmark date). $55 fee, may be waived for applicants with need. Application may be submitted online. Admission notification on a rolling basis beginning on or about 10/1. Must reply by 5/1. Immediate decision process available to seniors at some local high schools. **Financial aid:** Priority date 3/1; no closing date. FAFSA required. Applicants notified on a rolling basis starting 4/1; must reply within 2 week(s) of notification.

**Academics. Special study options:** Combined bachelor's/graduate degree, cooperative education, double major, ESL, honors, independent study, internships, study abroad, teacher certification program, Washington semester. Joint admission with UMDNJ. **Credit/placement by examination:** AP, CLEP, IB, institutional tests. 24 credit hours maximum toward bachelor's degree. **Support services:** Learning center, pre-admission summer program, reduced course load, remedial instruction, tutoring.

**Honors college/program.** Admission to Honors Program as freshman requires applicant to meet 2 of following criteria; rank in top 10 percent in high school class; score of at least 600 on either verbal or math SAT; combined SAT of at least 1200 (exclusive of Writing); unusual ability in creative arts or exceptional leadership or other extraordinary accomplishment.

**Majors. Area/ethnic studies:** Women's. **Biology:** General, biochemistry, molecular. **Business:** Business admin. **Communications:** Broadcast journalism, organizational, radio/tv. **Computer sciences:** General, computer science, information technology. **Education:** Business, drama/dance, health, physical, technology/industrial arts. **English:** English lit. **Family/consumer sciences:** General, food/nutrition. **Foreign languages:** Classics, French, Italian, Latin, linguistics, Spanish. **Health:** Athletic training, health services, music therapy. **History:** General. **Interdisciplinary:** Peace/conflict. **Liberal arts:** Arts/sciences, humanities. **Math:** General. **Philosophy/religion:** Philosophy, religion. **Physical sciences:** Chemistry, geology, physics. **Psychology:** General. **Social sciences:** Anthropology, economics, geography, political science, sociology. **Visual/performing arts:** Art, cinematography, dance, dramatic, fashion design, graphic design, illustration, music performance.

**Computing on campus.** 700 workstations in dormitories, library, computer center, student center. Dormitories wired for high-speed internet access and linked to campus network. Commuter students can connect to campus network. Online course registration, online library, helpline, repair service, wireless network available.

**Student life. Freshman orientation:** Mandatory. Preregistration for classes offered. 2-day program held in summer. **Housing:** Coed dorms, single-sex dorms, special housing for disabled, apartments available. $125 nonrefundable deposit, deadline 5/1. **Activities:** Bands, choral groups, dance, drama, international student organizations, literary magazine, music ensembles, musical theater, opera, radio station, student government, student newspaper, symphony orchestra, TV station, Newman Center, conservation club, college life union board, student intramural and leisure council.

**Athletics.** NCAA. **Intercollegiate:** Baseball M, basketball, diving, field hockey W, football (tackle) M, lacrosse, soccer, softball W, swimming, track and field, volleyball W. **Intramural:** Badminton, basketball, bowling, football (tackle) M, golf, racquetball, softball, tennis, volleyball, water polo. **Team name:** Red Hawks.

**Student services.** Adult student services, alcohol/substance abuse counseling, campus ministries, career counseling, services for economically disadvantaged, student employment services, financial aid counseling, health services, on-campus daycare, personal counseling, placement for graduates, veterans' counselor, women's services. **Physically disabled:** Services for visually impaired.

**Contact.** E-mail: undergraduate.admissions@mail.montclair.edu
Phone: (973) 655-4444 Toll-free number: (800) 331-9205
Fax: (973) 655-7700
Jason Langdon, Director of Admissions, Montclair State University, One Normal Avenue, Upper Montclair, NJ 07043-1624

---

## New Jersey City University
**Jersey City, New Jersey**
www.njcu.edu

**CB member**
**CB code: 2516**

- Public 4-year university
- Commuter campus in small city
- 6,242 degree-seeking undergraduates: 28% part-time, 62% women, 19% African American, 7% Asian American, 35% Hispanic American, 1% international
- 903 degree-seeking graduate students
- 49% of applicants admitted
- SAT or ACT, application essay required
- 32% graduate within 6 years

**General.** Founded in 1927. Regionally accredited. **Degrees:** 970 bachelor's awarded; master's offered. **Location:** 5 miles from New York City. **Calendar:** Semester, extensive summer session. **Full-time faculty:** 248 total; 84% have terminal degrees, 32% minority, 48% women. **Part-time faculty:** 426 total; 17% minority, 43% women. **Class size:** 59% < 20, 40% 20-39, less than 1% 40-49, less than 1% 50-99. **Special facilities:** Laboratory school for multihandicapped children, computer technology center, cooperative education, media studies center.

**Freshman class profile.** 2,901 applied, 1,421 admitted, 804 enrolled.

| Mid 50% test scores | | Live on campus: | 4% |
|---|---|---|---|
| SAT critical reading: | 400-500 | International: | 1% |
| SAT math: | 410-500 | Fraternities: | 2% |
| Return as sophomores: | 73% | Sororities: | 2% |
| Out-of-state: | 1% | | |

**Basis for selection.** High school courses, grades, class rank, and test scores most important, followed by essay or personal statement. Special program for educationally disadvantaged applicants available with above criteria. Interview recommended for all; audition required for music programs; portfolio recommended for art programs.

**High school preparation.** Required and recommended units include English 4, mathematics 4, social studies 4, science 4 (laboratory 2-3) and foreign language 2.

**2007-2008 Annual costs.** Tuition/fees: $8,155; $14,759 out-of-state. Room/board: $8,299. Books/supplies: $1,600. Personal expenses: $1,600.

**2006-2007 Financial aid. Need-based:** 552 full-time freshmen applied for aid; 507 were judged to have need; 482 of these received aid. Average need met was 60%. Average scholarship/grant was $7,143; average loan $2,733. 31% of total undergraduate aid awarded as scholarships/grants, 69% as loans/jobs. **Non-need-based:** Awarded to 310 full-time undergraduates, including 86 freshmen.

**Application procedures. Admission:** Closing date 4/1. $35 fee, may be waived for applicants with need. Admission notification on a rolling basis beginning on or about 1/1. Must reply by May 1 or within 3 week(s) if notified thereafter. **Financial aid:** Priority date 4/15; no closing date. FAFSA required. Applicants notified by 5/4.

**Academics.** Cooperative education placement offered in all majors. Professional diploma in school psychology offered. **Special study options:** Cooperative education, distance learning, double major, dual enrollment of high school students, ESL, honors, independent study, internships, liberal arts/career combination, study abroad, teacher certification program, Washington semester, weekend college. **Credit/placement by examination:** AP, CLEP, IB, institutional tests. 30 credit hours maximum toward bachelor's degree. **Support services:** Learning center, pre-admission summer program, reduced course load, remedial instruction, tutoring, writing center.

**Majors. Biology:** General. **Business:** Business admin. **Communications:** General. **Computer sciences:** General. **Education:** Early childhood, elementary, reading, special. **English:** English lit. **Foreign languages:** Spanish. **Health:** Clinical lab science, health services, nursing (RN). **History:** General. **Math:** General. **Philosophy/religion:** Philosophy. **Physical sciences:** Chemistry, geology, physics. **Protective services:** Firefighting, security services. **Psychology:** General. **Social sciences:** Economics, political science, sociology. **Visual/performing arts:** Art, studio arts.

**Most popular majors.** Business/marketing 29%, English 6%, psychology 10%, security/protective services 12%, social sciences 10%.

**Computing on campus.** 1,400 workstations in dormitories, library, computer center, student center. Dormitories wired for high-speed internet access and linked to campus network. Commuter students can connect to campus network. Online course registration, online library, helpline, wireless network available.

**Student life. Freshman orientation:** Mandatory. **Housing:** Coed dorms, substance-free housing available. $150 deposit, deadline 8/13. **Activities:** Bands, choral groups, dance, drama, film society, international student organizations, literary magazine, music ensembles, musical theater, opera, radio station, student government, student newspaper, Campus Christian fellowship, Black Freedom Society, Latin Power Association, Africana Journal.

**Athletics.** NCAA. **Intercollegiate:** Baseball M, basketball, bowling W, cross-country, soccer, softball W, track and field, volleyball. **Intramural:** Basketball, bowling, racquetball, soccer, softball, swimming, table tennis, volleyball, weight lifting. **Team name:** Gothic Knights.

**Student services.** Campus ministries, career counseling, student employment services, financial aid counseling, health services, on-campus daycare, personal counseling, placement for graduates, veterans' counselor, women's

services. **Physically disabled:** Services for visually, speech, hearing impaired.

**Contact.**   E-mail: admissions@njcu.edu
Phone: (201) 200-3234 Toll-free number: (888) 441-6528
Carmen Panlilio, Assistant Vice President for Admissions and Financial Aid, New Jersey City University, 2039 Kennedy Boulevard, Jersey City, NJ 07305-1597

## New Jersey Institute of Technology
**Newark, New Jersey**
**www.njit.edu**

**CB member**
**CB code: 2513**

- Public 4-year university
- Residential campus in very large city
- 4,967 degree-seeking undergraduates: 17% part-time, 19% women
- 2,735 degree-seeking graduate students
- 64% of applicants admitted
- SAT or ACT with writing required
- 52% graduate within 6 years

**General.** Founded in 1881. Regionally accredited. **Degrees:** 942 bachelor's awarded; master's, doctoral offered. **ROTC:** Army, Air Force. **Location:** 10 miles from New York City. **Calendar:** Semester, extensive summer session. **Full-time faculty:** 399 total; 100% have terminal degrees, 21% minority, 15% women. **Part-time faculty:** 247 total; 10% minority, 17% women. **Class size:** 43% < 20, 49% 20-39, 4% 40-49, 3% 50-99, less than 1% >100. **Special facilities:** Computer chip manufacturing laboratory, multi-lifecycle engineering center, numerous government and industry-sponsored research laboratories, hazardous waste management research center, factory floor manufacturing center, observatory.

**Freshman class profile.** 3,027 applied, 1,941 admitted, 784 enrolled.

| Mid 50% test scores | | | |
|---|---|---|---|
| SAT critical reading: | 470-570 | Out-of-state: | 4% |
| SAT math: | 540-640 | Live on campus: | 50% |
| Rank in top quarter: | 60% | International: | 5% |
| Rank in top tenth: | 12% | Fraternities: | 9% |
| Return as sophomores: | 80% | Sororities: | 4% |

**Basis for selection.** Class rank, test scores, secondary school record including grades and curriculum most important. Grades in mathematics and science very important, especially for engineering, engineering science and computer science applicants. Essay and interview required for honors college; interview and portfolio required for architecture programs. Interview required for conditional admission, educational opportunity program.

**High school preparation.** 16 units required. Required and recommended units include English 4, mathematics 4, social studies 1, history 1, science 2, foreign language 2 and academic electives 2. 3 mathematics required of management majors and science, technology and society majors. One laboratory science required for management majors.

**2008-2009 Annual costs.** Tuition/fees (projected): $11,350; $20,082 out-of-state. Room/board: $9,108. Books/supplies: $1,200. Personal expenses: $1,100.

**Financial aid. Non-need-based:** Scholarships awarded for academics, alumni affiliation, art, leadership, minority status, music/drama, ROTC, state residency. **Additional information:** Extensive co-op program for all majors.

**Application procedures. Admission:** Closing date 4/1. $50 fee, may be waived for applicants with need. Application may be submitted online. Admission notification on a rolling basis beginning on or about 11/15. Must reply by May 1 or within 2 week(s) if notified thereafter. **Financial aid:** Priority date 3/15, closing date 5/15. FAFSA required. Applicants notified on a rolling basis starting 3/1; must reply within 2 week(s) of notification.

**Academics.** All freshmen given personal computers for use at NJIT. Numerous research opportunities available. **Special study options:** Accelerated study, combined bachelor's/graduate degree, cooperative education, cross-registration, distance learning, double major, ESL, honors, independent study, internships, study abroad. Environmental Scholars Program, Career Advancement Plan, University Research Experience. **Credit/placement by examination:** AP, CLEP, SAT, institutional tests. **Support services:** Learning center, pre-admission summer program, reduced course load, remedial instruction, study skills assistance, tutoring.

**Majors. Architecture:** Architecture. **Biology:** General. **Business:** Business admin. **Computer sciences:** General, information systems, information technology. **Conservation:** Environmental science. **Engineering:** Biomedical, chemical, civil, computer, electrical, environmental, geological,

industrial, manufacturing, mechanical, science. **Engineering technology:** General. **English:** Technical writing. **History:** General. **Interdisciplinary:** Science/society. **Math:** Applied. **Physical sciences:** Chemistry, physics.

**Most popular majors.** Business/marketing 10%, computer/information sciences 17%, engineering/engineering technologies 64%.

**Computing on campus.** PC or laptop required. 1,500 workstations in dormitories, library, computer center, student center. Dormitories wired for high-speed internet access and linked to campus network. Commuter students can connect to campus network. Online course registration, online library, helpline, repair service, student web hosting, wireless network available.

**Student life. Freshman orientation:** Mandatory. **Housing:** Coed dorms available. $100 deposit, deadline 6/2. **Activities:** Dance, drama, literary magazine, radio station, student government, student newspaper, Arab student association, Black student engineers association, Caribbean student association, Chinese student association, Hispanic students in technology association, Intervarsity Christian Federation, Polish student association, Islamic student association, women engineers club.

**Athletics.** NCAA. **Intercollegiate:** Baseball M, basketball, cross-country, fencing, soccer, swimming, tennis, volleyball. **Intramural:** Badminton, basketball, bowling, cricket, fencing, racquetball, soccer, swimming, table tennis, tennis, track and field, volleyball, weight lifting. **Team name:** Highlanders.

**Student services.** Alcohol/substance abuse counseling, career counseling, student employment services, health services, on-campus daycare, personal counseling, placement for graduates, veterans' counselor, women's services. **Physically disabled:** Services for visually, speech, hearing impaired.

**Contact.**   E-mail: admissions@njit.edu
Phone: (973) 596-3300 Toll-free number: (800) 925-6548
Fax: (973) 596-3461
Kathy Kelly, Director of Admissions, New Jersey Institute of Technology, University Heights, Newark, NJ 07102

## Princeton University
**Princeton, New Jersey**
**www.princeton.edu**

**CB member**
**CB code: 2672**

- Private 4-year university
- Residential campus in large town
- 4,833 degree-seeking undergraduates: 47% women, 9% African American, 14% Asian American, 8% Hispanic American, 1% Native American, 9% international
- 2,356 degree-seeking graduate students
- 10% of applicants admitted
- SAT and SAT Subject Tests or ACT (ACT writing recommended), application essay required
- 95% graduate within 6 years

**General.** Founded in 1746. Regionally accredited. **Degrees:** 1,144 bachelor's awarded; master's, doctoral offered. **ROTC:** Army, Air Force. **Location:** 50 miles from New York City, 45 miles from Philadelphia. **Calendar:** Semester. **Full-time faculty:** 825 total; 93% have terminal degrees, 18% minority, 29% women. **Part-time faculty:** 190 total; 59% have terminal degrees, 17% minority, 43% women. **Class size:** 75% < 20, 14% 20-39, 2% 40-49, 5% 50-99, 4% >100. **Special facilities:** Institute for integrative genomics, center for theoretical physics, institute in neuroscience, center for creative and performing arts, center for human values, Princeton plasma physics laboratory, environmental institute, council of the humanities, institute for international and regional studies, observatory.

**Freshman class profile.** 18,942 applied, 1,838 admitted, 1,244 enrolled.

| Mid 50% test scores | | | |
|---|---|---|---|
| SAT critical reading: | 690-790 | Rank in top quarter: | 99% |
| SAT math: | 700-790 | Rank in top tenth: | 96% |
| SAT writing: | 690-780 | Return as sophomores: | 97% |
| ACT composite: | 30-34 | Out-of-state: | 81% |
| GPA 3.50 or higher: | 93% | Live on campus: | 100% |
| GPA 3.0-3.49: | 7% | International: | 11% |

**Basis for selection.** GED not accepted. School achievement record and recommendations of guidance counselor and 2 teachers very important. Test scores and essays also required of each applicant reviewed. Three SAT Subject Tests required. Interview recommended for all; audition recommended for music programs; portfolio recommended for creative writing, dance (video), visual arts programs. **Homeschooled:** Statement describing homeschool structure and mission required.

**High school preparation.** Recommended units include English 4, mathematics 4, social studies 2, history 2, science 4 (laboratory 2) and foreign language 4. One unit physics or chemistry (preferably both) and 4 mathematics urged for prospective engineering majors.

**2008-2009 Annual costs.** Tuition/fees: $34,290. Room/board: $11,405. Books/supplies: $1,200. Personal expenses: $2,295.

**2006-2007 Financial aid.** All financial aid based on need. 781 full-time freshmen applied for aid; 682 were judged to have need; 682 of these received aid. Average need met was 100%. Average scholarship/grant was $29,786. 97% of total undergraduate aid awarded as scholarships/grants, 3% as loans/jobs. **Additional information:** All aid need-based; all aid grant money (no loans); institution meets full demonstrated need.

**Application procedures. Admission:** Closing date 1/1 (postmark date). $65 fee, may be waived for applicants with need. Application may be submitted online. Admission notification 4/1. Must reply by 5/1. **Financial aid:** Priority date 2/1; no closing date. FAFSA, institutional form required. Applicants notified by 4/1; must reply by 5/1.

**Academics.** Independent project in junior year and senior thesis required for graduation. **Special study options:** Cross-registration, exchange student, independent study, student-designed major, study abroad, teacher certification program. **Credit/placement by examination:** AP, CLEP, IB, institutional tests. **Support services:** Learning center, pre-admission summer program, study skills assistance, tutoring, writing center.

**Majors. Architecture:** Architecture. **Area/ethnic studies:** East Asian, Near/Middle Eastern. **Biology:** Ecology, molecular. **Engineering:** Chemical, civil, computer, electrical, mechanical, operations research. **English:** English lit. **Foreign languages:** Classics, comparative lit, German, Italian, Slavic, Spanish. **History:** General. **Math:** General. **Philosophy/religion:** Philosophy, religion. **Physical sciences:** Astrophysics, chemistry, geology, physics. **Psychology:** General. **Public administration:** General. **Social sciences:** Anthropology, economics, political science, sociology. **Visual/performing arts:** Art history/conservation.

**Most popular majors.** Biology 8%, engineering/engineering technologies 15%, English 7%, history 9%, philosophy/religious studies 6%, physical sciences 6%, public administration/social services 7%, social sciences 25%.

**Computing on campus.** 500 workstations in dormitories, library, computer center, student center. Dormitories wired for high-speed internet access and linked to campus network. Commuter students can connect to campus network. Online course registration, online library, helpline, repair service, student web hosting, wireless network available.

**Student life. Freshman orientation:** Mandatory. 3-day orientation. Optional 1-week trip with Outdoor Action or Student Volunteer Council. **Housing:** Guaranteed on-campus for all undergraduates. Coed dorms, single-sex dorms, special housing for disabled available. Residential colleges for freshmen and sophomores. Kosher dining facilities available. **Activities:** Bands, campus ministries, choral groups, dance, drama, international student organizations, literary magazine, music ensembles, Model UN, musical theater, opera, radio station, student government, student newspaper, symphony orchestra, over 200 student organizations available.

**Athletics.** NCAA. **Intercollegiate:** Baseball M, basketball, cross-country, diving, fencing, field hockey W, football (tackle), golf, ice hockey, lacrosse, rowing (crew), soccer, softball W, squash, swimming, tennis, track and field, volleyball, water polo, wrestling M. **Intramural:** Badminton, basketball, bowling, football (non-tackle), golf, ice hockey, judo, racquetball, soccer, softball, tennis, water polo. **Team name:** Tigers.

**Student services.** Alcohol/substance abuse counseling, campus ministries, career counseling, student employment services, financial aid counseling, health services, minority student services, personal counseling, placement for graduates, women's services. **Physically disabled:** Services for visually, speech, hearing impaired.

**Contact.** E-mail: uaoffice@Princeton.edu
Phone: (609) 258-3060 Fax: (609) 258-6743
Janet Rapelye, Dean of Admission, Princeton University, Box 430, Princeton, NJ 08544-0430

## Rabbi Jacob Joseph School
Edison, New Jersey

▶ Private 4-year rabbinical college
▶ Large town

**General.** Accredited by AARTS. **Calendar:** Semester.

**Contact.** Phone: (732) 985-6533
One Plainfield Avenue, Edison, NJ 08817

## Rabbinical College of America
Morristown, New Jersey

CB code: 1546

▶ Private 4-year rabbinical college for men affiliated with Jewish faith
▶ Residential campus in large town

**General.** Founded in 1956. Accredited by AARTS. **Location:** One mile from downtown, 35 miles from New York City. **Calendar:** Semester.

**Annual costs/financial aid.** Tuition/fees (2007-2008): $9,700. Room/board: $6,800.

**Contact.** Phone: (973) 267-9404
Registrar, 226 Sussex Avenue, CN 1996, Morristown, NJ 07962-1996

## Ramapo College of New Jersey
Mahwah, New Jersey
www.ramapo.edu

CB member
CB code: 2884

▶ Public 4-year liberal arts college
▶ Residential campus in large town
▶ 5,131 degree-seeking undergraduates: 8% part-time, 47% women, 6% African American, 4% Asian American, 9% Hispanic American, 3% international
▶ 233 degree-seeking graduate students
▶ 49% of applicants admitted
▶ SAT, application essay required
▶ 65% graduate within 6 years

**General.** Founded in 1969. Regionally accredited. **Degrees:** 1,207 bachelor's awarded; master's offered. **ROTC:** Air Force. **Location:** 35 miles from New York City. **Calendar:** Semester, extensive summer session. **Full-time faculty:** 197 total; 95% have terminal degrees, 21% minority, 47% women. **Part-time faculty:** 237 total; 45% women. **Class size:** 30% < 20, 67% 20-39, 3% 40-49, less than 1% 50-99. **Special facilities:** International telecommunications center, electron microscope, Holocaust center, performing arts center, international and intercultural education office, environmental studies/sustainability education center, greenhouse center, astronomical observatory.

**Freshman class profile.** 4,983 applied, 2,421 admitted, 902 enrolled.

| Mid 50% test scores | | Rank in top tenth: | 35% |
|---|---|---|---|
| SAT critical reading: | 520-620 | Return as sophomores: | 90% |
| SAT math: | 540-630 | Out-of-state: | 2% |
| SAT writing: | 530-620 | Live on campus: | 85% |
| GPA 3.50 or higher: | 50% | International: | 3% |
| GPA 3.0-3.49: | 37% | Fraternities: | 16% |
| GPA 2.0-2.99: | 13% | Sororities: | 29% |
| Rank in top quarter: | 67% | | |

**Basis for selection.** School achievement record, test scores most important. Applicants should rank in top 25 percent of high school class. ESL or TOEFL assessment used to determine English language proficiency. Certain majors have additional entrance requirements.

**High school preparation.** 18 units required. Required and recommended units include English 4, mathematics 3, social studies 3, science 3 (laboratory 3), foreign language 2 and academic electives 3. Science units must include 3 lab. Math consists of algebra I, 1 geometry, and algebra II.

**2007-2008 Annual costs.** Tuition/fees: $9,965; $15,536 out-of-state. Room/board: $10,310. Books/supplies: $1,200. Personal expenses: $2,250.

**2006-2007 Financial aid. Need-based:** 638 full-time freshmen applied for aid; 436 were judged to have need; 419 of these received aid. Average need met was 79%. Average scholarship/grant was $19,348; average loan $2,622. 50% of total undergraduate aid awarded as scholarships/grants, 50% as loans/jobs. **Non-need-based:** Awarded to 1,184 full-time undergraduates, including 268 freshmen. Scholarships awarded for academics, job skills.

**Application procedures. Admission:** Closing date 3/1. $55 fee, may be waived for applicants with need. Application may be submitted online. Admission notification on a rolling basis beginning on or about 11/15. Must reply by 5/1. **Financial aid:** Priority date 3/1; no closing date. FAFSA required. Applicants notified on a rolling basis starting 4/1; must reply by 5/1 or within 2 week(s) of notification.

**Academics.** Thematic learning communities present curriculum of traditional majors and innovative programs in interdisciplinary fashion. **Special study options:** Accelerated study, combined bachelor's/graduate degree, cooperative education, distance learning, double major, dual enrollment of high school students, ESL, exchange student, external degree, honors, independent study, internships, liberal arts/career combination, student-designed major, study abroad, teacher certification program. **Credit/placement by examination:** AP, CLEP, IB, SAT. 65 credit hours maximum toward bachelor's degree. **Support services:** Learning center, pre-admission summer program, reduced course load, remedial instruction, study skills assistance, tutoring, writing center.

**Majors. Area/ethnic studies:** American. **Biology:** General, biochemistry, bioinformatics. **Business:** Accounting, business admin, international. **Communications:** General. **Computer sciences:** General, information systems. **Conservation:** Environmental science, environmental studies. **Foreign languages:** Comparative lit, Spanish. **Health:** Clinical lab science, health services. **History:** General. **Interdisciplinary:** Biological/physical sciences, global studies. **Legal studies:** General. **Liberal arts:** Arts/sciences, humanities. **Math:** General. **Physical sciences:** Chemistry, physics. **Psychology:** General. **Public administration:** Social work. **Social sciences:** Economics, political science, sociology. **Visual/performing arts:** Art, dramatic, multimedia.

**Most popular majors.** Biology 6%, business/marketing 21%, communications/journalism 12%, foreign language 6%, health sciences 7%, psychology 14%, visual/performing arts 8%.

**Computing on campus.** 1,058 workstations in dormitories, library, computer center, student center. Dormitories wired for high-speed internet access and linked to campus network. Commuter students can connect to campus network. Online course registration, online library, helpline, repair service, student web hosting, wireless network available.

**Student life. Freshman orientation:** Mandatory, $130 fee. Preregistration for classes offered. **Policies:** Smoking is prohibited in all physical buildings on campus. Smokers must stand 25 feet away from buildings. **Housing:** Guaranteed on-campus for freshmen. Coed dorms, special housing for disabled, apartments, cooperative housing, substance-free housing available. $200 partly refundable deposit, deadline 5/1. **Activities:** Campus ministries, choral groups, dance, drama, international student organizations, literary magazine, music ensembles, Model UN, musical theater, radio station, student government, student newspaper, TV station, United Asian Americans, College Democrats, College Republicans, Hillel, Intervarsity Christian Fellowship, Muslim student association, Community Builders Coalition, culture club.

**Athletics.** NCAA. **Intercollegiate:** Baseball M, basketball, cheerleading M, cross-country, field hockey W, lacrosse W, soccer, softball W, swimming, tennis, track and field, volleyball. **Intramural:** Basketball, bowling, football (non-tackle) M, soccer, softball, volleyball. **Team name:** Roadrunners.

**Student services.** Adult student services, alcohol/substance abuse counseling, campus ministries, career counseling, services for economically disadvantaged, student employment services, financial aid counseling, health services, minority student services, personal counseling, placement for graduates, veterans' counselor, women's services. **Physically disabled:** Services for visually, speech, hearing impaired. **Learning disabled:** Comprehensive services available.

**Contact.** E-mail: admissions@ramapo.edu
Phone: (201) 684-7300 Toll-free number: (800) 972-6276
Fax: (201) 684-7964
Peter Rice, Director of Admissions, Ramapo College of New Jersey, 505 Ramapo Valley Road, Mahwah, NJ 07430-1680

---

## Richard Stockton College of New Jersey

**Pomona, New Jersey**
www.stockton.edu

**CB member**
**CB code: 2889**

- Public 4-year liberal arts college
- Residential campus in large town
- 6,600 degree-seeking undergraduates: 11% part-time, 59% women, 8% African American, 5% Asian American, 6% Hispanic American
- 493 degree-seeking graduate students
- 54% of applicants admitted
- SAT or ACT (ACT writing optional), application essay required
- 67% graduate within 6 years; 20% enter graduate study

**General.** Founded in 1969. Regionally accredited. **Degrees:** 1,634 bachelor's awarded; master's, doctoral offered. **Location:** 12 miles from Atlantic City, 50 miles from Philadelphia. **Calendar:** Semester, extensive summer session. **Full-time faculty:** 259 total; 89% have terminal degrees, 22% minority, 51% women. **Part-time faculty:** 198 total; 7% minority, 41% women. **Class size:** 26% < 20, 67% 20-39, 4% 40-49, 1% 50-99, less than 1% >100. **Special facilities:** 400-acre outdoor research laboratory with arboretum, forestry nursery, ecologic succession plots and study preserve, child care center, interdisciplinary natural sciences laboratory, observatory, Holocaust center, geothermal plant, 7-acre marine science field station, ITV classroom, performing arts theater, hospital located on college grounds.

**Freshman class profile.** 3,962 applied, 2,158 admitted, 799 enrolled.

| Mid 50% test scores | | | |
|---|---|---|---|
| SAT critical reading: | 480-570 | GPA 2.0-2.99: | 23% |
| SAT math: | 500-580 | Rank in top quarter: | 48% |
| SAT writing: | 470-560 | Rank in top tenth: | 19% |
| ACT composite: | 18-21 | Return as sophomores: | 83% |
| GPA 3.50 or higher: | 46% | Out-of-state: | 2% |
| GPA 3.0-3.49: | 28% | Live on campus: | 86% |
| | | International: | 1% |

**Basis for selection.** Secondary school record, class rank, test scores most important; essay, recommendations, extracurricular activities also important; interview, work experience considered. **Homeschooled:** Statement describing homeschool structure and mission, transcript of courses and grades required.

**High school preparation.** 16 units required. Required and recommended units include English 4, mathematics 3, social studies 2, history 2, science 2 (laboratory 2), foreign language 2 and academic electives 5.

**2007-2008 Annual costs.** Tuition/fees: $9,091; $13,685 out-of-state. Room/board: $9,077. Books/supplies: $1,100. Personal expenses: $1,264.

**2007-2008 Financial aid. Need-based:** 659 full-time freshmen applied for aid; 507 were judged to have need; 482 of these received aid. Average need met was 74%. Average scholarship/grant was $8,148; average loan $3,557. 41% of total undergraduate aid awarded as scholarships/grants, 59% as loans/jobs. **Non-need-based:** Awarded to 931 full-time undergraduates, including 233 freshmen. Scholarships awarded for academics, art, leadership, minority status, music/drama, state residency.

**Application procedures. Admission:** Priority date 2/1; deadline 5/1 (postmark date). $50 fee, may be waived for applicants with need. Application may be submitted online. Admission notification on a rolling basis beginning on or about 11/1. Must reply by May 1 or within 2 week(s) if notified thereafter. **Financial aid:** Priority date 3/1; no closing date. FAFSA required. Applicants notified on a rolling basis starting 4/1; must reply within 2 week(s) of notification.

**Academics. Special study options:** Combined bachelor's/graduate degree, cross-registration, distance learning, double major, dual enrollment of high school students, honors, independent study, internships, liberal arts/career combination, semester at sea, student-designed major, study abroad, teacher certification program, Washington semester. Dual degree bachelor's program in engineering with Rutgers University and New Jersey Institute of Technology, preceptorial advising, opportunities for specialized research, extensive Washington internship available. **Credit/placement by examination:** AP, CLEP, IB, SAT, ACT, institutional tests. 32 credit hours maximum toward bachelor's degree. **Support services:** Learning center, pre-admission summer program, reduced course load, remedial instruction, study skills assistance, tutoring, writing center.

**Majors. Biology:** General, biochemistry, marine. **Business:** Hospitality admin. **Communications:** General. **Computer sciences:** Information systems. **Conservation:** Environmental studies. **Education:** Multi-level teacher. **English:** English lit. **Foreign languages:** General. **Health:** Audiology/speech pathology, nursing (RN). **History:** General. **Liberal arts:** Arts/sciences. **Math:** General. **Philosophy/religion:** Philosophy. **Physical sciences:** Chemistry, geology, physics. **Psychology:** General. **Public administration:** Social work. **Social sciences:** Criminology, economics, political science, sociology. **Visual/performing arts:** General.

**Most popular majors.** Biology 10%, business/marketing 19%, education 10%, psychology 11%, social sciences 15%.

**Computing on campus.** 3,375 workstations in dormitories, library, computer center, student center. Dormitories wired for high-speed internet access and linked to campus network. Commuter students can connect to campus network. Online course registration, online library, helpline, student web hosting, wireless network available.

**Student life. Freshman orientation:** Available, $50 fee. Preregistration for classes offered. Program includes parents' sessions. **Housing:** Guaranteed on-campus for freshmen. Coed dorms, special housing for disabled, substance-free housing available. $150 fully refundable deposit, deadline

5/1. Academic units available. **Activities:** Bands, choral groups, dance, drama, literary magazine, music ensembles, musical theater, radio station, student government, student newspaper, TV station, Books Without Borders, Unified Black Students Society, Christian Fellowship, Jewish student union, campus religious council, Circle K International, CHANGE, Amnesty International, coalition for women's rights, Certified Peer Educators.

**Athletics.** NCAA. **Intercollegiate:** Baseball M, basketball, cheerleading, cross-country, field hockey W, lacrosse M, rowing (crew) W, soccer, softball W, tennis W, track and field, volleyball W. **Intramural:** Basketball, football (non-tackle), soccer, softball, table tennis, volleyball. **Team name:** Ospreys.

**Student services.** Adult student services, alcohol/substance abuse counseling, campus ministries, career counseling, student employment services, health services, on-campus daycare, personal counseling, placement for graduates, veterans' counselor. **Physically disabled:** Services for visually, speech, hearing impaired. **Learning disabled:** Comprehensive services available.

**Contact.** E-mail: admissions@stockton.edu
Phone: (609) 652-4261 Toll-free number: (866) 772-2885
Fax: (609) 748-5541
John Iacovelli, Dean of Enrollment Management, Richard Stockton College of New Jersey, Jim Leeds Road, Pomona, NJ 08240-0195

## Rider University
**Lawrenceville, New Jersey**
www.rider.edu

**CB member**
**CB code: 2758**

- Private 4-year university
- Residential campus in large town
- 4,534 degree-seeking undergraduates: 14% part-time, 60% women, 9% African American, 3% Asian American, 5% Hispanic American, 3% international
- 1,029 degree-seeking graduate students
- 75% of applicants admitted
- SAT or ACT (ACT writing optional), application essay required
- 60% graduate within 6 years; 20% enter graduate study

**General.** Founded in 1865. Regionally accredited. Westminster College of the Arts, located in Lawrenceville and Princeton campuses. **Degrees:** 865 bachelor's, 10 associate awarded; master's offered. **ROTC:** Army. **Location:** 5 miles from Princeton, 3 miles from Trenton. **Calendar:** Semester, extensive summer session. **Full-time faculty:** 244 total; 96% have terminal degrees, 15% minority, 42% women. **Part-time faculty:** 301 total; 43% have terminal degrees, 8% minority, 51% women. **Class size:** 47% < 20, 47% 20-39, 5% 40-49, 1% 50-99, less than 1% >100. **Special facilities:** Holocaust/genocide center, teaching and learning center.

**Freshman class profile.** 6,213 applied, 4,672 admitted, 993 enrolled.

| Mid 50% test scores | | GPA 2.0-2.99: | 28% |
|---|---|---|---|
| SAT critical reading: | 470-570 | Rank in top quarter: | 38% |
| SAT math: | 480-590 | Rank in top tenth: | 12% |
| SAT writing: | 470-570 | Return as sophomores: | 83% |
| ACT composite: | 20-24 | Out-of-state: | 28% |
| GPA 3.50 or higher: | 36% | Live on campus: | 90% |
| GPA 3.0-3.49: | 36% | International: | 2% |

**Basis for selection.** High school curriculum most important, followed by GPA, test scores, essay, and recommendations. Extracurricular activities, interview considered. TOEFL required for international applicants. Interview recommended for all; audition required for music program with Westminster College of the Arts.

**High school preparation.** College-preparatory program required. 16 units required. Required and recommended units include English 4, mathematics 3-4, social studies 2, history 2, science 4 (laboratory 2) and foreign language 2. Algebra I and II and geometry required for business administration, science, mathematics majors.

**2007-2008 Annual costs.** Tuition/fees: $26,225. Room/board: $9,780. Books/supplies: $1,400. Personal expenses: $850.

**2007-2008 Financial aid. Need-based:** 823 full-time freshmen applied for aid; 672 were judged to have need; 672 of these received aid. Average need met was 72%. Average scholarship/grant was $14,041; average loan $3,735. 54% of total undergraduate aid awarded as scholarships/grants, 46% as loans/jobs. **Non-need-based:** Awarded to 1,314 full-time undergraduates, including 379 freshmen. Scholarships awarded for academics, alumni affiliation, art, athletics, leadership, minority status, music/drama, state residency.

**Application procedures. Admission:** No deadline. $50 fee, may be waived for applicants with need. Application may be submitted online. Admission notification on a rolling basis beginning on or about 12/15. Must reply by May 1 or within 4 week(s) if notified thereafter. Notification of admission decision sent within 3-4 weeks of receiving application. **Financial aid:** Priority date 3/1; no closing date. FAFSA required. Applicants notified on a rolling basis starting 3/15.

**Academics. Special study options:** Accelerated study, cross-registration, double major, ESL, honors, independent study, internships, liberal arts/career combination, study abroad, teacher certification program, weekend college. **Credit/placement by examination:** AP, CLEP, SAT, ACT, institutional tests. Policy varies by major. 30 hours of credit by general examination may be counted toward degree. No limit for subject examinations. Not acceptable for last 30 credits of degree program. 4-8 AP courses (24 credits) required for sophomore standing. **Support services:** Learning center, reduced course load, remedial instruction, study skills assistance, tutoring, writing center.

**Majors. Area/ethnic studies:** American. **Biology:** General, biochemistry. **Business:** Accounting, actuarial science, administrative services, business admin, entrepreneurial studies, finance, human resources, international, management science, managerial economics, marketing, office management, organizational behavior. **Communications:** Advertising, journalism. **Computer sciences:** General. **Conservation:** Environmental science. **Education:** Business, elementary, music, sales/marketing, science, secondary. **English:** English lit, speech/rhetoric. **Foreign languages:** French, German, Russian, Spanish. **History:** General. **Interdisciplinary:** Biopsychology. **Liberal arts:** Arts/sciences. **Math:** General. **Philosophy/religion:** Philosophy. **Physical sciences:** Chemistry, geology, oceanography, physics. **Psychology:** General. **Social sciences:** Economics, international relations, political science, sociology. **Theology:** Sacred music. **Visual/performing arts:** Art, arts management, music theory/composition, musical theater, piano/organ, studio arts, voice/opera.

**Computing on campus.** 300 workstations in dormitories, library, computer center, student center. Dormitories wired for high-speed internet access and linked to campus network. Commuter students can connect to campus network. Online course registration, online library, helpline, student web hosting, wireless network available.

**Student life. Freshman orientation:** Mandatory, $200 fee. Preregistration for classes offered. 2-day program for new students and their family members. **Housing:** Guaranteed on-campus for all undergraduates. Coed dorms, single-sex dorms, special housing for disabled, apartments, fraternity/sorority housing, substance-free housing available. $200 partly refundable deposit, deadline 5/1. Wellness, quiet, science, freshman experience, learning community, faculty-in-residence options, suites available. **Activities:** Bands, campus ministries, choral groups, dance, drama, film society, international student organizations, literary magazine, music ensembles, Model UN, musical theater, opera, radio station, student government, student newspaper, TV station, student entertainment council, residence hall association, finance board, Asian student organization, interfraternity council, hunger and homelessness awareness, College Republicans, Latin American student organization.

**Athletics.** NCAA. **Intercollegiate:** Baseball M, basketball, cheerleading, cross-country, diving, field hockey W, golf M, soccer, softball W, swimming, tennis, track and field, volleyball W, wrestling M. **Intramural:** Basketball, football (non-tackle), ice hockey M, lacrosse, soccer, softball, track and field, volleyball. **Team name:** Broncs.

**Student services.** Adult student services, alcohol/substance abuse counseling, campus ministries, career counseling, services for economically disadvantaged, student employment services, financial aid counseling, health services, minority student services, personal counseling, placement for graduates, veterans' counselor, women's services. **Physically disabled:** Services for visually, speech, hearing impaired.

**Contact.** E-mail: admissions@rider.edu
Phone: (609) 896-5042 Toll-free number: (800) 257-9026
Fax: (609) 895-6645
Sue Christian, Director of Undergraduate Admissions, Rider University, 2083 Lawrenceville Road, Lawrenceville, NJ 08648-3099

## Rowan University
**Glassboro, New Jersey**
www.rowan.edu

**CB member**
**CB code: 2515**

- Public 4-year university and liberal arts college
- Commuter campus in large town
- 8,499 degree-seeking undergraduates: 10% part-time, 52% women, 8% African American, 3% Asian American, 7% Hispanic American
- 786 degree-seeking graduate students

- 52% of applicants admitted
- SAT or ACT (ACT writing recommended), interview required
- 66% graduate within 6 years; 4% enter graduate study

**General.** Founded in 1923. Regionally accredited. **Degrees:** 1,828 bachelor's awarded; master's, doctoral offered. **ROTC:** Army. **Location:** 20 miles from Philadelphia. **Calendar:** Semester, extensive summer session. **Full-time faculty:** 405 total; 79% have terminal degrees, 21% minority, 42% women. **Part-time faculty:** 507 total; 9% minority, 44% women. **Class size:** 39% < 20, 60% 20-39, less than 1% 40-49, less than 1% 50-99, less than 1% >100. **Special facilities:** Observatory, glass-blowing museum, on-campus early childhood demonstration center, animal penthouse, greenhouse for biological studies, concert hall.

**Freshman class profile.** 8,088 applied, 4,178 admitted, 1,381 enrolled.

| Mid 50% test scores | | GPA 2.0-2.99: | 19% |
|---|---|---|---|
| SAT critical reading: | 490-590 | Rank in top quarter: | 47% |
| SAT math: | 510-620 | Rank in top tenth: | 17% |
| SAT writing: | 480-580 | Return as sophomores: | 86% |
| GPA 3.50 or higher: | 44% | Out-of-state: | 5% |
| GPA 3.0-3.49: | 36% | Live on campus: | 78% |

**Basis for selection.** School achievement record and test scores most important, followed by recommendations. Special admissions program for in-state disadvantaged and minority students. Audition required for music, theater programs; portfolio interview required for art program.

**High school preparation.** 16 units required. Required units include English 4, mathematics 3, social studies 2, science 2 (laboratory 2) and academic electives 5. Engineering applicants should have 3 units of laboratory science including physics and chemistry and 4 units of college preparatory math including precalculus. Calculus is strongly recommended.

**2007-2008 Annual costs.** Tuition/fees: $10,068; $17,376 out-of-state. Room/board: $9,242. Books/supplies: $900. Personal expenses: $1,000.

**2006-2007 Financial aid. Need-based:** 1,027 full-time freshmen applied for aid; 673 were judged to have need; 636 of these received aid. Average need met was 93%. Average scholarship/grant was $7,955; average loan $2,490. 31% of total undergraduate aid awarded as scholarships/grants, 69% as loans/jobs. **Non-need-based:** Awarded to 1,049 full-time undergraduates, including 262 freshmen. Scholarships awarded for academics, art, music/drama.

**Application procedures. Admission:** Closing date 3/1 (postmark date). $50 fee, may be waived for applicants with need. Application may be submitted online. Admission notification on a rolling basis beginning on or about 11/1. Must reply by 5/1. **Financial aid:** Closing date 3/15. FAFSA, institutional form required. Applicants notified on a rolling basis starting 5/1; must reply within 2 week(s) of notification.

**Academics.** Camden campus offers general education courses and major programs in elementary education, business administration, law/justice, and sociology. **Special study options:** Accelerated study, cooperative education, cross-registration, distance learning, double major, dual enrollment of high school students, ESL, external degree, honors, independent study, internships, liberal arts/career combination, student-designed major, study abroad, teacher certification program, weekend college. Cross-registration with Drexel University, Temple University, Rutgers-the State University of New Jersey, New Jersey Institute of Technology; combination programs with University of Medicine and Dentistry of New Jersey, Philadelphia College of Pharmacy and Science. **Credit/placement by examination:** AP, CLEP, IB, institutional tests, 30 credit hours maximum toward bachelor's degree. **Support services:** Pre-admission summer program, remedial instruction, study skills assistance, tutoring, writing center.

**Majors. Biology:** General, biochemistry. **Business:** Accounting, business admin, finance, human resources, management information systems, management science, marketing. **Communications:** Advertising, journalism, public relations. **Computer sciences:** Computer science. **Education:** General, art, early childhood, elementary, music, secondary, special. **Engineering:** General, chemical, civil, electrical, mechanical. **English:** Composition, English lit. **Foreign languages:** Spanish. **Health:** Athletic training. **History:** General. **Liberal arts:** Arts/sciences. **Math:** General. **Parks/recreation:** Health/fitness, sports admin. **Physical sciences:** Chemistry, physics. **Protective services:** Criminal justice. **Psychology:** General, developmental. **Social sciences:** Economics, geography, political science, sociology. **Visual/performing arts:** Art, dance, dramatic, film/cinema, jazz, music performance, music theory/composition, studio arts.

**Most popular majors.** Business/marketing 13%, communications/journalism 17%, education 18%, security/protective services 6%, social sciences 6%, visual/performing arts 6%.

**Computing on campus.** 1,200 workstations in library, computer center. Dormitories linked to campus network. Commuter students can connect to campus network. Online course registration, online library, helpline, repair service, student web hosting, wireless network available.

**Student life. Freshman orientation:** Available. Preregistration for classes offered. Overnight program for freshmen and their families during summer. **Housing:** Guaranteed on-campus for freshmen. Coed dorms, special housing for disabled, apartments available. $200 fully refundable deposit, deadline 5/1. Unmarried students under age 21 not living with parent/guardian required to live in college housing for freshman and sophomore years. **Activities:** Bands, choral groups, dance, drama, film society, literary magazine, music ensembles, musical theater, opera, radio station, student government, student newspaper, symphony orchestra, TV station, over 150 clubs and student organizations.

**Athletics.** NCAA. **Intercollegiate:** Baseball M, basketball, cross-country, diving, field hockey W, football (tackle) M, lacrosse W, soccer, softball W, swimming, track and field, volleyball W. **Intramural:** Basketball, bowling, golf, handball, racquetball, soccer, softball, table tennis, tennis, volleyball. **Team name:** Profs.

**Student services.** Adult student services, alcohol/substance abuse counseling, campus ministries, career counseling, student employment services, financial aid counseling, health services, legal services, minority student services, on-campus daycare, personal counseling, placement for graduates, veterans' counselor, women's services. **Physically disabled:** Services for visually, speech, hearing impaired.

**Contact.** E-mail: admissions@rowan.edu
Phone: (856) 256-4200 Toll-free number: (800) 447-1165
Fax: (856) 256-4430
Albert Betts, Director of Admissions, Rowan University, Savitz Hall, 201 Mullica Hill Road, Glassboro, NJ 08028

---

## Rutgers, The State University of New Jersey: Camden Regional Campus

**Camden, New Jersey** — CB member
www.rutgers.edu — CB code: 2742

- Public 4-year university
- Commuter campus in small city
- 3,657 degree-seeking undergraduates: 21% part-time, 56% women, 17% African American, 8% Asian American, 7% Hispanic American
- 1,418 degree-seeking graduate students
- 51% of applicants admitted
- SAT or ACT with writing required
- 52% graduate within 6 years

**General.** Founded in 1927. Regionally accredited. Undergraduate schools: Camden College of Arts and Sciences, University College-Camden, School of Business-Camden. Graduate degrees available at School of Business. Graduate schools: Graduate School-Camden, School of Law-Camden. **Degrees:** 873 bachelor's awarded; master's, first professional offered. **ROTC:** Army, Air Force. **Location:** One mile from Philadelphia. **Calendar:** Semester, extensive summer session. **Full-time faculty:** 230 total; 99% have terminal degrees, 16% minority, 40% women. **Part-time faculty:** 178 total; 99% have terminal degrees, 13% minority, 34% women. **Class size:** 39% < 20, 48% 20-39, 7% 40-49, 4% 50-99, 3% >100. **Special facilities:** Fine arts center.

**Freshman class profile.** 7,788 applied, 3,989 admitted, 380 enrolled.

| Mid 50% test scores | | Rank in top quarter: | 52% |
|---|---|---|---|
| SAT critical reading: | 490-590 | Rank in top tenth: | 23% |
| SAT math: | 500-620 | Out-of-state: | 4% |
| SAT writing: | 470-580 | Live on campus: | 46% |

**Basis for selection.** School achievement record (including grades, rank, strength of program, honors) and test scores most important. Extracurricular activities, talent, disadvantaged status considered. SAT Subject Tests required for applicants who will not have diploma from accredited high school by entrance date. May also be required of GED holders. SAT/ACT scores should be submitted by December of senior year. **Homeschooled:** SAT Subject Tests required for applicants who will not have diploma from accredited high school by entrance date.

**High school preparation.** 16 units required. Required and recommended units include English 4, mathematics 3-4, science 2, foreign language 2 and academic electives 5. Mathematics requirement includes algebra I and II and geometry. 4 mathematics, 1 chemistry, 1 physics required for engineering applicants.

**2007-2008 Annual costs.** Tuition/fees: $10,532; $19,700 out-of-state. Room/board: $9,024. Books/supplies: $733. Personal expenses: $1,453.

**Financial aid. Non-need-based:** Scholarships awarded for academics, alumni affiliation, art, athletics, leadership, minority status, music/drama, state residency.

**Application procedures. Admission:** Closing date 12/1. $60 fee, may be waived for applicants with need. Application must be submitted online. Admission notification on a rolling basis beginning on or about 2/28. Must reply by May 1 or within 2 week(s) if notified thereafter. May apply to up to 3 Rutgers colleges with 1 application. Students applying by December 1 notified by February 28. **Financial aid:** Priority date 3/15; no closing date. FAFSA required. Applicants notified on a rolling basis starting 2/1; must reply within 2 week(s) of notification.

**Academics. Special study options:** Accelerated study, combined bachelor's/graduate degree, cooperative education, cross-registration, distance learning, double major, dual enrollment of high school students, ESL, exchange student, honors, independent study, internships, liberal arts/career combination, student-designed major, study abroad, teacher certification program, weekend college. 8-year BA/MD with University of Medicine and Dentistry of New Jersey, 5-year BA or BS/MA in criminal justice with School of Criminal Justice-Newark, 2+2 BS and 2+3 dual bachelor's degree transfer programs with School of Engineering, BA in political science/MPA, BA in economics/MPA, BA/MS in biology, BA/MS in chemistry, BA/MA in English, BA/MA in history, BA/MA in liberal studies, BA/MS in mathematics, articulated bachelor's/dentistry program with University of Medicine and Dentistry of New Jersey. **Credit/placement by examination:** AP, CLEP, IB, institutional tests. No more than 8 credits given for elementary or intermediate levels of any foreign language. Graduating seniors may take no more than one examination in their final term. **Support services:** Learning center, pre-admission summer program, reduced course load, remedial instruction, study skills assistance, tutoring, writing center.

**Majors. Area/ethnic studies:** African-American. **Biology:** General, biomedical sciences. **Business:** Accounting, business admin, finance, hospitality admin, marketing. **Computer sciences:** Computer science. **Engineering:** Biomedical, ceramic, chemical, civil, electrical, mechanical, science. **English:** English lit. **Foreign languages:** French, German, Spanish. **Health:** Nursing (RN), predental, premedicine. **History:** General. **Interdisciplinary:** Biological/physical sciences. **Legal studies:** Prelaw. **Liberal arts:** Arts/sciences. **Math:** General. **Philosophy/religion:** Philosophy. **Physical sciences:** Chemistry, physics. **Protective services:** Criminal justice. **Psychology:** General. **Public administration:** Social work. **Social sciences:** Economics, political science, sociology, urban studies. **Visual/performing arts:** Art, dramatic.

**Most popular majors.** Business/marketing 24%, English 8%, psychology 15%, social sciences 13%.

**Computing on campus.** 187 workstations in dormitories, library, computer center, student center. Dormitories linked to campus network. Commuter students can connect to campus network. Helpline, repair service available.

**Student life. Freshman orientation:** Available. **Housing:** Coed dorms, special housing for disabled, apartments available. **Activities:** Drama, international student organizations, literary magazine, radio station, student government, student newspaper, accounting society, forensics society, political science association, Black student union, Latin American students organization, physics society, Jewish student union, marketing association, psychology club.

**Athletics.** NCAA. **Intercollegiate:** Baseball M, basketball, cross-country, golf M, rowing (crew) W, soccer, softball W, track and field, volleyball W. **Intramural:** Badminton, basketball, football (tackle) M, handball, racquetball, soccer, softball, squash, volleyball. **Team name:** Scarlet Raptors.

**Student services.** Career counseling, student employment services, health services, on-campus daycare, personal counseling, placement for graduates, veterans' counselor. **Physically disabled:** Services for visually, speech, hearing impaired.

**Contact.** Phone: (856) 225-6104 Fax: (856) 225-6498
Deborah Bowles, Director of Admissions, Rutgers, The State University of New Jersey: Camden Regional Campus, 406 Penn Street, Camden, NJ 08102

---

## Rutgers, The State University of New Jersey: New Brunswick/Piscataway Campus

Piscataway, New Jersey
www.rutgers.edu

CB member
CB code: 2765

- Public 4-year university
- Residential campus in large town

---

- 26,479 degree-seeking undergraduates: 6% part-time, 49% women, 9% African American, 24% Asian American, 8% Hispanic American, 2% international
- 6,901 degree-seeking graduate students
- 56% of applicants admitted
- SAT or ACT with writing required
- 73% graduate within 6 years

**General.** Founded in 1969. Regionally accredited. Undergraduate schools include Douglass College, Livingston College, Rutgers College, University College-New Brunswick, Cook College, School of Engineering, Mason Gross School of the Arts, Edward J. Bloustein School of Planning and Public Policy, College of Nursing, College of Pharmacy, School of Business-New Brunswick, School of Communication, Information and Library Studies. **Degrees:** 5,546 bachelor's awarded; master's, doctoral, first professional offered. **ROTC:** Army, Air Force. **Location:** 33 miles from New York City. **Calendar:** Semester, extensive summer session. **Full-time faculty:** 1,533 total; 99% have terminal degrees, 18% minority, 33% women. **Part-time faculty:** 833 total; 99% have terminal degrees, 17% minority, 52% women. **Class size:** 42% <20, 32% 20-39, 6% 40-49, 11% 50-99, 10% >100. **Special facilities:** Geology museum, ecological preserve, 2 theaters, center for urban policy research, institute for health, health care policy and aging research, journalism resources institute, laboratory for computer science research, center for mathematics, science and computer education.

**Freshman class profile.** 28,208 applied, 15,877 admitted, 5,519 enrolled.

| Mid 50% test scores | | | |
|---|---|---|---|
| SAT critical reading: | 530-630 | Rank in top quarter: | 81% |
| SAT math: | 560-670 | Rank in top tenth: | 41% |
| SAT writing: | 530-640 | Out-of-state: | 10% |
| | | Live on campus: | 86% |

**Basis for selection.** School achievement record (including grades, rank, strength of program, honors, AP) and test scores most important. Extracurricular activities, leadership talent, minority, disadvantaged status considered. State residents with educationally and economically disadvantaged backgrounds given consideration through state Educational Opportunity Fund program. SAT Subject Tests required of applicants who, by expected date of entrance, will not have diploma from accredited high school. May also be required of GED holders. Recommended that SAT/ACT be submitted by December of senior year. Interview, audition, portfolio review required for Mason Gross School of the Arts. **Homeschooled:** SAT Subject Tests required of applicants who, by expected date of entrance, will not have diploma from accredited high school.

**High school preparation.** 16 units required. Required and recommended units include English 4, mathematics 3-4, science 2, foreign language 2 and academic electives 5. Mathematics requirement includes algebra I and II and geometry. 4 mathematics, 1 chemistry, 1 physics required for engineering program. One biology, 1 chemistry required for nursing program. 5-9 academic electives required, depending on college.

**2007-2008 Annual costs.** Tuition/fees: $10,686; $19,854 out-of-state. Tuition and fees may vary by program. Room/board: $9,762. Books/supplies: $733. Personal expenses: $1,453.

**Financial aid. Non-need-based:** Scholarships awarded for academics, alumni affiliation, art, athletics, leadership, minority status, music/drama, state residency.

**Application procedures. Admission:** Closing date 12/1. $60 fee, may be waived for applicants with need. Application must be submitted online. Admission notification on a rolling basis. Must reply by May 1 or within 2 week(s) if notified thereafter. May apply to up to 3 Rutgers colleges with 1 application. Applications received by December 1 will be answered by February 28. **Financial aid:** Priority date 3/15; no closing date. FAFSA required. Applicants notified on a rolling basis starting 2/1; must reply within 2 week(s) of notification.

**Academics. Special study options:** Accelerated study, combined bachelor's/graduate degree, cooperative education, cross-registration, distance learning, double major, dual enrollment of high school students, ESL, exchange student, honors, independent study, internships, liberal arts/career combination, student-designed major, study abroad, teacher certification program, Washington semester, weekend college. Washington semester, 8-year BA or BS/MD with University of Medicine and Dentistry of New Jersey, 5-year BA/MBA, 5-year dual degrees in liberal arts and engineering, 5-year BA or BS/MPP with Edward J. Bloustein School of Planning and Public Policy, 5-year BA or BS/MA in criminal justice with School of Criminal Justice in Newark, 6-year BA in biology/MS in physician assistant, 5-year BA or BS/M.Ed. offered in conjunction with the Graduate School of Education, dual admission to Newark School of Law. **Credit/placement by examination:** AP, CLEP, IB, institutional tests. 30 credit hours maximum toward bachelor's degree. **Support services:** Learning center, pre-admission summer program, reduced course load, remedial instruction, study skills assistance, tutoring, writing center.

**Majors. Agriculture:** Animal sciences, food science, plant sciences. **Architecture:** Environmental design, urban/community planning. **Area/ethnic studies:** African, African-American, American, Caribbean, Central/Eastern European, East Asian, Hispanic-American/Latino/Chicano, Latin American, Near/Middle Eastern, Russian/Slavic, women's. **Biology:** General, bacteriology, biochemistry, biometrics, biotechnology, cell/histology, genetics, marine, molecular. **Business:** Accounting, business admin, finance, labor relations, management information systems, management science, marketing. **Communications:** General, journalism. **Computer sciences:** Computer science. **Conservation:** General, environmental studies, management/policy. **Engineering:** Biomedical, ceramic, chemical, civil, electrical, environmental, mechanical, science. **English:** English lit. **Foreign languages:** Chinese, classics, comparative lit, French, German, Italian, linguistics, Portuguese, Russian, Spanish. **Health:** Clinical lab technology, nursing (RN), physician assistant, predental, premedicine. **History:** General. **Interdisciplinary:** Medieval/Renaissance, nutrition sciences. **Legal studies:** Prelaw. **Math:** General, statistics. **Parks/recreation:** Exercise sciences. **Philosophy/religion:** Judaic, philosophy, religion. **Physical sciences:** Atmospheric science, chemistry, geology, physics. **Protective services:** Law enforcement admin. **Psychology:** General. **Public administration:** Social work. **Social sciences:** Anthropology, economics, geography, political science, sociology, urban studies. **Visual/performing arts:** Art, art history/conservation, dance, dramatic.

**Most popular majors.** Biology 10%, business/marketing 8%, communications/journalism 10%, engineering/engineering technologies 8%, psychology 10%, social sciences 16%.

**Computing on campus.** 1,450 workstations in dormitories, library, computer center, student center. Dormitories linked to campus network. Commuter students can connect to campus network. Helpline, repair service available.

**Student life. Freshman orientation:** Available. **Housing:** Guaranteed on-campus for freshmen. Coed dorms, single-sex dorms, special housing for disabled, apartments, cooperative housing, fraternity/sorority housing available. $100 deposit, deadline 6/15. Cooperative housing at Cook College only. Special interest housing, language and cultural houses, substance-free house, math/science/engineering house for women, first-year residence, transfer center, residence for single mothers and children available. **Activities:** Bands, campus ministries, choral groups, dance, drama, film society, international student organizations, literary magazine, music ensembles, musical theater, opera, radio station, student government, student newspaper, symphony orchestra, TV station, 400 organizations available.

**Athletics.** NCAA. **Intercollegiate:** Baseball M, basketball, cross-country, diving, fencing, field hockey W, football (tackle) M, golf, gymnastics W, lacrosse, rowing (crew), soccer, softball W, swimming, tennis, track and field, volleyball W, wrestling M. **Intramural:** Badminton, basketball, bowling, cross-country, golf, racquetball, soccer, softball, squash, swimming, table tennis, tennis, track and field, volleyball, water polo, wrestling M. **Team name:** Scarlet Knights.

**Student services.** Adult student services, career counseling, student employment services, health services, on-campus daycare, personal counseling, placement for graduates, veterans' counselor. **Physically disabled:** Services for visually, speech, hearing impaired.

**Contact.** Phone: (732) 932-4636 Fax: (732) 445-0237
Diane Harris, Associate Director of Undergraduate Admissions, Rutgers, The State University of New Jersey: New Brunswick/Piscataway Campus, 65 Davidson Road, Room 202, Piscataway, NJ 08854-8097

## Rutgers, The State University of New Jersey: Newark Regional Campus
**Newark, New Jersey**
www.rutgers.edu
CB code: 2753

- Public 4-year university
- Commuter campus in large city
- 6,115 degree-seeking undergraduates: 15% part-time, 56% women, 20% African American, 24% Asian American, 19% Hispanic American, 2% international
- 3,574 degree-seeking graduate students
- 49% of applicants admitted
- SAT or ACT with writing required
- 57% graduate within 6 years

**General.** Founded in 1930. Regionally accredited. Undergraduate schools: College of Nursing, Newark College of Arts and Sciences, University College-Newark, School of Management. **Degrees:** 1,295 bachelor's awarded; master's, doctoral, first professional offered. **ROTC:** Army, Air Force. **Location:** 10 miles from New York City. **Calendar:** Semester, extensive summer

session. **Full-time faculty:** 404 total; 99% have terminal degrees, 18% minority, 37% women. **Part-time faculty:** 221 total; 99% have terminal degrees, 4% minority, 44% women. **Class size:** 33% < 20, 38% 20-39, 13% 40-49, 13% 50-99, 3% >100. **Special facilities:** Biology learning center, jazz institute, animal behavior institute, center for molecular and behavioral neuroscience, center for negotiation and conflict resolution.

**Freshman class profile.** 13,085 applied, 6,442 admitted, 989 enrolled.

| Mid 50% test scores | | | |
|---|---|---|---|
| SAT critical reading: | 480-570 | Rank in top quarter: | 64% |
| SAT math: | 500-600 | Rank in top tenth: | 30% |
| SAT writing: | 490-580 | Out-of-state: | 5% |
| | | Live on campus: | 51% |

**Basis for selection.** School achievement record and test scores most important. Extracurricular activities, leadership talent, minority, disadvantaged status considered. State residents with educational and economically disadvantaged backgrounds given consideration through state Educational Opportunity Fund program. SAT Subject Tests required of applicants who, by expected date of entrance, will not have diploma from accredited high school. May also be required of GED holders. SAT/ACT scores should be submitted by December of senior year.

**High school preparation.** College-preparatory program required. 16 units required. Required and recommended units include English 4, mathematics 3-4, science 2, foreign language 2 and academic electives 5. Mathematics requirement includes algebra I, II and geometry. 4 mathematics, 1 chemistry, 1 physics required for engineering program. One biology, 1 chemistry required for nursing program. Foreign language recommended.

**2007-2008 Annual costs.** Tuition/fees: $10,267; $19,435 out-of-state. Tuition and fees may vary by program. Room/board: $10,034. Books/supplies: $733. Personal expenses: $1,453.

**Financial aid. Non-need-based:** Scholarships awarded for academics, alumni affiliation, art, athletics, leadership, minority status, music/drama, religious affiliation, state residency.

**Application procedures. Admission:** Priority date 12/1; no deadline. $60 fee, may be waived for applicants with need. Application must be submitted online. Admission notification on a rolling basis beginning on or about 2/28. Must reply by May 1 or within 2 week(s) if notified thereafter. May apply to up to 3 Rutgers colleges with 1 application. Applications completed by December 1 will be answered by February 28. **Financial aid:** Priority date 3/15; no closing date. FAFSA required. Applicants notified on a rolling basis starting 2/1; must reply within 2 week(s) of notification.

**Academics. Special study options:** Accelerated study, combined bachelor's/graduate degree, cooperative education, cross-registration, distance learning, double major, dual enrollment of high school students, ESL, exchange student, honors, independent study, internships, liberal arts/career combination, student-designed major, study abroad, teacher certification program, Washington semester, weekend college. 8-year BA/MD with University of Medicine and Dentistry of New Jersey, 5-year BA or BS/MA in criminal justice, 2-2 and 2-3 in engineering, dual admission to School of Law, 5-year BA/MBA, industrial engineering program with New Jersey Institute of Technology, bachelor's/dentistry program with Universtiy of Medicine and Dentistry of New Jersey. **Credit/placement by examination:** AP, CLEP, IB, institutional tests. 24 credit hours maximum toward bachelor's degree. **Support services:** Learning center, pre-admission summer program, reduced course load, remedial instruction, study skills assistance, tutoring, writing center.

**Honors college/program.** By invitation.

**Majors. Area/ethnic studies:** African, African-American, American, Caribbean, Hispanic-American/Latino/Chicano, women's. **Biology:** General, botany, zoology. **Business:** Accounting, business admin, finance, marketing. **Communications:** Journalism. **Computer sciences:** Computer science, information systems. **Conservation:** General. **Engineering:** Biomedical, ceramic, chemical, civil, electrical, mechanical. **English:** English lit. **Foreign languages:** French, Spanish. **Health:** Clinical lab science, clinical lab technology, nursing (RN), predental, premedicine. **History:** General. **Interdisciplinary:** Science/society. **Legal studies:** Prelaw. **Math:** General, applied. **Philosophy/religion:** Philosophy. **Physical sciences:** Chemistry, geology, physics. **Protective services:** Criminal justice. **Psychology:** General. **Public administration:** Social work. **Social sciences:** Anthropology, economics, political science, sociology. **Visual/performing arts:** Art, dramatic.

**Most popular majors.** Biology 8%, business/marketing 36%, health sciences 10%, psychology 7%, security/protective services 9%, social sciences 9%.

**Computing on campus.** 450 workstations in dormitories, library, computer center. Dormitories linked to campus network. Commuter students can connect to campus network. Helpline, repair service available.

**Student life. Freshman orientation:** Available. **Housing:** Coed dorms, special housing for disabled, apartments, fraternity/sorority housing available. $100 deposit. **Activities:** Choral groups, drama, international student organizations, radio station, student government, student newspaper, Black Organization of Students, Puerto Rican and Latin American student organizations, political, religious, and service organizations.

**Athletics.** NCAA. **Intercollegiate:** Baseball M, basketball, soccer, softball W, tennis, volleyball. **Intramural:** Basketball, racquetball, soccer, tennis, volleyball. **Team name:** Scarlet Raiders.

**Student services.** Career counseling, student employment services, health services, personal counseling, placement for graduates, veterans' counselor. **Physically disabled:** Services for visually, speech, hearing impaired.

**Contact.** Phone: (973) 353-5205 Fax: (973) 353-1440
Bruce Neimeyer, Director of Admissions at Newark, Rutgers, The State University of New Jersey: Newark Regional Campus, 249 University Avenue, Newark, NJ 07102-1896

---

## Saint Peter's College
**Jersey City, New Jersey**     **CB member**
**www.spc.edu**     **CB code: 2806**

- Private 4-year liberal arts college affiliated with Roman Catholic Church
- Commuter campus in small city
- 2,259 degree-seeking undergraduates: 13% part-time, 55% women, 22% African American, 9% Asian American, 27% Hispanic American, 4% international
- 641 degree-seeking graduate students
- 54% of applicants admitted
- SAT or ACT (ACT writing optional), application essay required
- 44% graduate within 6 years

**General.** Founded in 1872. Regionally accredited. Extensive evening program on main campus, at branch locations at Englewood Cliffs and South Amboy for adult learners, and other locations throughout metropolitan area. **Degrees:** 374 bachelor's, 38 associate awarded; master's offered. **ROTC:** Army, Air Force. **Location:** 3 miles from New York City. **Calendar:** Semester, extensive summer session. **Full-time faculty:** 108 total; 82% have terminal degrees, 11% minority, 44% women. **Part-time faculty:** 165 total; 17% minority, 34% women. **Class size:** 67% < 20, 33% 20-39.

**Freshman class profile.** 5,505 applied, 2,951 admitted, 544 enrolled.

| Mid 50% test scores | | End year in good standing: | 71% |
|---|---|---|---|
| SAT critical reading: | 420-510 | Return as sophomores: | 70% |
| SAT math: | 420-530 | Out-of-state: | 19% |
| GPA 3.50 or higher: | 35% | Live on campus: | 53% |
| GPA 3.0-3.49: | 30% | International: | 3% |
| GPA 2.0-2.99: | 35% | | |

**Basis for selection.** Admissions decision based on (in rank order) school achievement record, test scores, essay, letters of recommendation, class activities. Interview recommended.

**High school preparation.** 16 units required; 19 recommended. Required and recommended units include English 4, mathematics 3-4, history 2-3, science 2-3 (laboratory 1), foreign language 2 and academic electives 3.

**2007-2008 Annual costs.** Tuition/fees: $24,026. Room/board: $9,750. Books/supplies: $700. Personal expenses: $600.

**2006-2007 Financial aid. Need-based:** 536 full-time freshmen applied for aid; 448 were judged to have need; 446 of these received aid. Average need met was 75%. Average scholarship/grant was $16,336; average loan $2,416. 73% of total undergraduate aid awarded as scholarships/grants, 27% as loans/jobs. **Non-need-based:** Awarded to 446 full-time undergraduates, including 122 freshmen. Scholarships awarded for academics, athletics. **Additional information:** Cooperative education internships available in all majors, with average salaries exceeding $5,200.

**Application procedures. Admission:** Priority date 4/1; no deadline. No application fee. Application may be submitted online. Admission notification on a rolling basis beginning on or about 11/1. **Financial aid:** Priority date 3/15; no closing date. FAFSA required. Applicants notified on a rolling basis starting 2/15; must reply by 5/1 or within 2 week(s) of notification.

**Academics.** Joint Pre-Med/MD program with UMDNJ, joint Pre-Law/Law program with Seton Hall University. **Special study options:** Accelerated study, combined bachelor's/graduate degree, cooperative education, double major, dual enrollment of high school students, exchange student, honors, independent study, internships, liberal arts/career combination, student-designed major, study abroad, teacher certification program, Washington semester. Joint degree in clinical laboratory sciences with University of Medicine and Dentistry of New Jersey. **Credit/placement by examination:** AP, CLEP, IB, institutional tests. 30 credit hours maximum toward bachelor's degree. **Support services:** Learning center, pre-admission summer program, reduced course load, remedial instruction, study skills assistance, tutoring, writing center.

**Majors. Area/ethnic studies:** American. **Biology:** General, biochemistry, toxicology. **Business:** Accounting, actuarial science, banking/financial services, business admin, international, management information systems, managerial economics. **Communications:** General. **Computer sciences:** General, computer science, information systems, programming. **Education:** Elementary. **English:** English lit. **Foreign languages:** General, classics, Spanish. **Health:** Clinical lab science, cytotechnology, nursing (RN). **History:** General. **Interdisciplinary:** Biological/physical sciences. **Math:** General. **Philosophy/religion:** Philosophy, religion. **Physical sciences:** Chemistry, physics. **Psychology:** General. **Public administration:** Policy analysis. **Social sciences:** General, economics, political science, sociology, urban studies. **Visual/performing arts:** Studio arts.

**Computing on campus.** 225 workstations in dormitories, library, computer center, student center. Dormitories wired for high-speed internet access and linked to campus network. Commuter students can connect to campus network. Online library, helpline, student web hosting, wireless network available.

**Student life. Freshman orientation:** Mandatory, $200 fee. Preregistration for classes offered. 3-day sessions held throughout July. Program features academic advising, social activities, and introduction to community service. **Housing:** Guaranteed on-campus for all undergraduates. Coed dorms, special housing for disabled, apartments available. $200 partly refundable deposit, deadline 5/1. **Activities:** Choral groups, drama, international student organizations, literary magazine, radio station, student government, student newspaper, Alpha Phi Omega, Emmaus Spiritual Retreats, Circle K, Young Republicans, Hispanic culture club, Irish American club, Asian American student union, Black Action Committee, Indo-Pak culture club.

**Athletics.** NCAA. **Intercollegiate:** Baseball M, basketball, bowling, cheerleading, cross-country, diving, football (tackle) M, golf M, soccer, softball W, swimming, tennis, track and field, volleyball W. **Intramural:** Baseball M, basketball, bowling, racquetball, soccer, softball, swimming, table tennis, tennis, volleyball, water polo. **Team name:** Peacocks/Peahens.

**Student services.** Adult student services, alcohol/substance abuse counseling, campus ministries, career counseling, services for economically disadvantaged, student employment services, financial aid counseling, health services, minority student services, personal counseling, placement for graduates, veterans' counselor. **Physically disabled:** Services for visually, speech, hearing impaired.

**Contact.** E-mail: admissions@spc.edu
Phone: (201) 761-7100 Toll-free number: (888) 772-9933
Fax: (201) 761-7105
Joe Giglio, Director of Admission, Saint Peter's College, 2641 Kennedy Boulevard, Jersey City, NJ 07306

---

## Seton Hall University
**South Orange, New Jersey**     **CB member**
**www.shu.edu**     **CB code: 2811**

- Private 4-year university affiliated with Roman Catholic Church
- Residential campus in large town
- 4,896 degree-seeking undergraduates: 7% part-time, 56% women, 12% African American, 6% Asian American, 11% Hispanic American, 2% international
- 3,955 degree-seeking graduate students
- 72% of applicants admitted
- SAT or ACT with writing, application essay required
- 57% graduate within 6 years

**General.** Founded in 1856. Regionally accredited. Immaculate Conception Seminary and school of theology located on campus. Off-campus sites for nursing and education. **Degrees:** 1,098 bachelor's awarded; master's, doctoral, first professional offered. **ROTC:** Army. **Location:** 14 miles from New York City. **Calendar:** Semester, extensive summer session. **Full-time faculty:** 432 total; 88% have terminal degrees, 16% minority, 46% women. **Part-time faculty:** 526 total; 14% minority, 45% women. **Class size:** 50%

< 20, 48% 20-39, 1% 40-49, 1% 50-99, less than 1% >100. **Special facilities:** Computer graphics and communications laboratories, educational media center, nursing demonstration room, art center, music laboratories, special collections center.

**Freshman class profile.** 6,626 applied, 4,752 admitted, 1,260 enrolled.

| Mid 50% test scores | | | |
|---|---|---|---|
| SAT critical reading: | 470-580 | Return as sophomores: | 83% |
| SAT math: | 480-590 | Out-of-state: | 32% |
| Rank in top quarter: | 49% | Live on campus: | 74% |
| Rank in top tenth: | 21% | International: | 1% |

**Basis for selection.** School achievement record, test scores, recommendations, essay most important. Extracurricular activities, volunteer work, work experience important. Class rank, interview, talent/ability, character/personal qualities considered. Students who reside in Puerto Rico may submit SAT or TOEFL score along with PAA score; either ACT with Writing or SAT required, but not used in admission decisions. Interview strongly recommended. Audition required for music majors. **Homeschooled:** Statement describing homeschool structure and mission required. Must submit GED (total score of at least 225 with no individual score below 45), SAT/ACT scores, and a copy of their homeschool curriculum with a list of textbooks used for each of the major unit requirements.

**High school preparation.** 16 units required. Required units include English 4, mathematics 3, social studies 2, science 1 (laboratory 1), foreign language 2 and academic electives 4. Nursing majors must have additional 2 units in science (biology and chemistry).

**2007-2008 Annual costs.** Tuition/fees: $27,850. Required fees include lease of laptop computer. Room/board: $10,828. Books/supplies: $1,300. Personal expenses: $1,800.

**2006-2007 Financial aid. Need-based:** 989 full-time freshmen applied for aid; 851 were judged to have need; 837 of these received aid. Average need met was 69%. Average scholarship/grant was $6,000; average loan $2,674. 60% of total undergraduate aid awarded as scholarships/grants, 40% as loans/jobs. **Non-need-based:** Awarded to 2,712 full-time undergraduates, including 766 freshmen. Scholarships awarded for academics, alumni affiliation, athletics, leadership, minority status, ROTC, state residency.

**Application procedures. Admission:** Priority date 3/1; no deadline. $55 fee, may be waived for applicants with need. Application may be submitted online. Admission notification on a rolling basis beginning on or about 12/1. Must reply by May 1 or within 4 week(s) if notified thereafter. **Financial aid:** Priority date 2/15; no closing date. FAFSA required. Applicants notified on a rolling basis starting 3/1; must reply by 5/1 or within 4 week(s) of notification.

**Academics. Special study options:** Accelerated study, combined bachelor's/graduate degree, cooperative education, cross-registration, distance learning, double major, dual enrollment of high school students, ESL, honors, independent study, internships, liberal arts/career combination, study abroad, teacher certification program, Washington semester. **Credit/placement by examination:** AP, CLEP, IB, SAT, institutional tests. 30 credit hours maximum toward bachelor's degree. **Support services:** Pre-admission summer program, reduced course load, remedial instruction, study skills assistance, tutoring, writing center.

**Majors. Area/ethnic studies:** African-American, Asian. **Biology:** General, biochemistry. **Business:** Accounting, business admin, finance, labor relations, management information systems, managerial economics, marketing. **Communications:** General, journalism, public relations, radio/tv. **Computer sciences:** General. **Conservation:** Environmental studies. **Education:** Art, early childhood, elementary, health, secondary, special. **English:** English lit. **Foreign languages:** General, classics, French, Italian, Spanish. **Health:** Nursing (RN). **History:** General. **Liberal arts:** Arts/sciences, humanities. **Math:** General. **Parks/recreation:** Sports admin. **Philosophy/religion:** Christian, philosophy, religion. **Physical sciences:** Chemistry, physics. **Protective services:** Criminal justice. **Psychology:** General. **Public administration:** Social work. **Social sciences:** Anthropology, economics, international relations, political science, sociology. **Theology:** Religious ed, sacred music. **Visual/performing arts:** General, art history/conservation, commercial/advertising art, dramatic, music history, music performance, theater arts management.

**Most popular majors.** Biology 7%, business/marketing 19%, communications/journalism 11%, education 7%, health sciences 14%, security/protective services 6%, social sciences 12%.

**Computing on campus.** PC or laptop required. 350 workstations in dormitories, library, computer center, student center. Dormitories wired for high-speed internet access and linked to campus network. Online course registration, online library, helpline, repair service, student web hosting, wireless network available.

**Student life. Freshman orientation:** Mandatory, $225 fee. Preregistration for classes offered. 2-day program held at various times from June through July. **Policies:** 1.8 GPA housing requirement. **Housing:** Coed dorms, special housing for disabled, apartments, substance-free housing available. $250 deposit, deadline 5/1. **Activities:** Pep band, campus ministries, choral groups, drama, international student organizations, radio station, student government, student newspaper, TV station, Adelante, black students union, community service organizations, Puerto Rican Institute, Amnesty International, student ambassadors.

**Athletics.** NCAA. **Intercollegiate:** Baseball M, basketball, cross-country, golf M, soccer, softball W, swimming, tennis W, track and field, volleyball W. **Intramural:** Basketball, football (non-tackle), racquetball, soccer, softball, tennis, volleyball. **Team name:** Pirates.

**Student services.** Alcohol/substance abuse counseling, campus ministries, career counseling, services for economically disadvantaged, student employment services, financial aid counseling, health services, minority student services, personal counseling, placement for graduates. **Physically disabled:** Services for visually, speech, hearing impaired.

**Contact.** E-mail: thehall@shu.edu
Phone: (973) 761-9332 Toll-free number: (800) 843-4255
Fax: (973) 275-2040
Peter Nacy, Assistant Vice President for Admissions, Seton Hall University, 400 South Orange Avenue, South Orange, NJ 07079-2680

## Somerset Christian College
Zarephath, New Jersey
www.somerset.edu

CB code: 3933

- Private 4-year Bible college affiliated with Pillar of Fire International
- Commuter campus in small town
- 124 degree-seeking undergraduates
- SAT or ACT with writing, application essay required

**General.** Candidate for regional accreditation; also accredited by ABHE. **Degrees:** 16 associate awarded. **Location:** 45 miles from New York City and Philadelphia. **Calendar:** Semester, limited summer session. **Full-time faculty:** 5 total; 40% have terminal degrees, 20% minority, 20% women. **Part-time faculty:** 2 total; 100% have terminal degrees, 50% minority, 50% women. **Class size:** 48% < 20, 52% 20-39.

**Basis for selection.** Recommendations most important. High school record, standardized test scores, essay also important. **Homeschooled:** Interview, letter of recommendation (nonparent) required. Transcript of study including subjects, grades and cumulative GPA. Students must send proof of graduation date or GED scores. **Learning Disabled:** Students must have documented diagnosis and portfolio of prior school collaboration in accommodating students' learning disabilities.

**High school preparation.** 15 units required. Required units include English 4, mathematics 1, social studies 3, science 2, foreign language 2 and academic electives 3.

**2007-2008 Annual costs.** Tuition/fees: $6,940. Personal expenses: $1,120.

**Financial aid.** All financial aid based on need.

**Application procedures. Admission:** Closing date 8/30 (postmark date). $35 fee, may be waived for applicants with need. Application must be submitted online. Admission notification on a rolling basis. **Financial aid:** No deadline. FAFSA required. Applicants notified on a rolling basis starting 1/31.

**Academics. Special study options:** Distance learning, dual enrollment of high school students, independent study, internships. **Credit/placement by examination:** AP, CLEP, IB, institutional tests. **Support services:** Learning center, reduced course load, remedial instruction, study skills assistance, tutoring, writing center.

**Majors. Philosophy/religion:** Christian. **Theology:** Bible.

**Computing on campus.** 30 workstations in library, computer center. Online course registration, online library, wireless network available.

**Student life. Freshman orientation:** Mandatory. Preregistration for classes offered. **Policies:** Religious observance required. **Activities:** Student government, student newspaper.

**Student services.** Campus ministries, career counseling, financial aid counseling.

**Contact.** E-mail: info@somerset.edu
Phone: (732) 356-1595 Toll-free number: (800) 234-9305
Fax: (732) 356-4846
Linda Aarni, Director of Admissions, Somerset Christian College, 10
College Way, Zarephath, NJ 08890

## Stevens Institute of Technology

| Hoboken, New Jersey | CB member |
|---|---|
| www.stevens.edu | CB code: 2819 |

- Private 4-year university and engineering college
- Residential campus in small city
- 2,040 degree-seeking undergraduates: 26% women, 4% African American, 11% Asian American, 9% Hispanic American, 6% international
- 3,362 degree-seeking graduate students
- 51% of applicants admitted
- SAT or ACT (ACT writing optional), application essay, interview required
- 76% graduate within 6 years; 18% enter graduate study

**General.** Founded in 1870. Regionally accredited. **Degrees:** 299 bachelor's awarded; master's, doctoral offered. **ROTC:** Army, Air Force. **Location:** One mile from New York City. **Calendar:** Semester, extensive summer session. **Full-time faculty:** 243 total; 90% have terminal degrees, 13% minority, 15% women. **Part-time faculty:** 153 total. **Class size:** 43% < 20, 47% 20-39, 4% 40-49, 4% 50-99, 2% >100. **Special facilities:** Laboratory for coastal, ocean and naval engineering, environmental laboratory, design and manufacturing institute, advanced telecommunications institute, geoenvironmental laboratory, optical communications lab, quantum cascade laser, center for mass spectrometry, center for microchemical systems, computer visualization laboratory.

**Freshman class profile.** 2,783 applied, 1,413 admitted, 521 enrolled.

| Mid 50% test scores | | Rank in top quarter: | 80% |
|---|---|---|---|
| SAT critical reading: | 550-650 | Rank in top tenth: | 47% |
| SAT math: | 620-710 | Return as sophomores: | 89% |
| GPA 3.50 or higher: | 76% | Out-of-state: | 38% |
| GPA 3.0-3.49: | 20% | Live on campus: | 92% |
| GPA 2.0-2.99: | 4% | International: | 3% |

**Basis for selection.** GED not accepted. Admissions committee meets to review applicant's file once official transcript and standardized test scores received and interview requirement completed. Other information submitted considered as well. SAT Subject Tests required for accelerated premed, predentistry, or prelaw programs and recommended for all others. Students who live outside 250-mile radius and are unable to visit campus may schedule phone interview. Additional interview with departmental committee required of applicants to accelerated premed, predentistry, and prelaw programs. **Homeschooled:** Letter of recommendation (nonparent) required.

**High school preparation.** 16 units required. Required and recommended units include English 4, mathematics 4, social studies 2, history 2, science 3-4 (laboratory 3-4), foreign language 2 and academic electives 4. Business, engineering, computer science, and applied science programs require 2 algebra, 1 geometry, 1 pre-calculus or calculus, 1 chemistry, 1 physics, 1 biology.

**2007-2008 Annual costs.** Tuition/fees: $34,620. Room/board: $10,500. Books/supplies: $900. Personal expenses: $750.

**2007-2008 Financial aid. Need-based:** 441 full-time freshmen applied for aid; 380 were judged to have need; 378 of these received aid. Average need met was 81%. Average scholarship/grant was $14,888; average loan $3,684. 74% of total undergraduate aid awarded as scholarships/grants, 26% as loans/jobs. **Non-need-based:** Awarded to 1,264 full-time undergraduates, including 339 freshmen. Scholarships awarded for academics, leadership, music/drama, ROTC.

**Application procedures. Admission:** Priority date 11/15; deadline 2/1 (postmark date). $55 fee, may be waived for applicants with need. Application may be submitted online. Admission notification 4/1. Must reply by May 1 or within 2 week(s) if notified thereafter. **Financial aid:** Priority date 2/15; no closing date. FAFSA required. Applicants notified on a rolling basis starting 3/30; must reply by 5/1 or within 2 week(s) of notification.

**Academics. Special study options:** Accelerated study, combined bachelor's/graduate degree, cooperative education, cross-registration, distance learning, double major, dual enrollment of high school students, honors, independent study, internships, study abroad. 4-year bachelor's/master's programs in all engineering and science disciplines; dual enrollment program with New York University. **Credit/placement by examination:** AP, CLEP, IB.

**Support services:** Pre-admission summer program, reduced course load, remedial instruction, study skills assistance, tutoring, writing center.

**Majors. Biology:** Biochemistry, bioinformatics. **Business:** Business admin, management information systems. **Computer sciences:** General, networking, security. **Engineering:** General, biomedical, chemical, civil, computer, electrical, environmental, materials, materials science, mechanical, physics. **Engineering technology:** Industrial management. **English:** English lit. **History:** General. **Interdisciplinary:** Math/computer science. **Liberal arts:** Arts/sciences. **Math:** Applied. **Physical sciences:** Chemistry, physics.

**Most popular majors.** Biology 8%, business/marketing 13%, computer/information sciences 10%, engineering/engineering technologies 63%.

**Computing on campus.** PC or laptop required. 484 workstations in dormitories, library, computer center, student center. Dormitories wired for high-speed internet access and linked to campus network. Commuter students can connect to campus network. Online course registration, online library, helpline, repair service, student web hosting, wireless network available.

**Student life. Freshman orientation:** Mandatory, $400 fee. Preregistration for classes offered. 3-day freshman orientation, during which students travel into New York City for baseball games, museum trips, group activities and seminars on adjusting to college life. **Policies:** Honor system observed. **Housing:** Guaranteed on-campus for all undergraduates. Coed dorms, apartments, fraternity/sorority housing, substance-free housing available. $350 nonrefundable deposit, deadline 6/15. Freshmen not living at home must live on campus. **Activities:** Bands, choral groups, dance, drama, literary magazine, music ensembles, musical theater, radio station, student government, student newspaper, TV station, over 70 organizations.

**Athletics.** NCAA. **Intercollegiate:** Baseball M, basketball, cross-country, equestrian W, fencing, field hockey W, golf, lacrosse, soccer, swimming, tennis, track and field, volleyball, wrestling M. **Intramural:** Archery, badminton, basketball, cricket, football (non-tackle), lacrosse M, racquetball, soccer, softball, squash, tennis, volleyball. **Team name:** Ducks.

**Student services.** Alcohol/substance abuse counseling, campus ministries, career counseling, services for economically disadvantaged, student employment services, financial aid counseling, health services, minority student services, personal counseling, placement for graduates, veterans' counselor, women's services. **Physically disabled:** Services for visually, speech, hearing impaired.

**Contact.** E-mail: admissions@stevens.edu
Phone: (201) 216-5194 Toll-free number: (800) 458-5323
Fax: (201) 216-8348
Daniel Gallagher, Dean of University Admissions, Stevens Institute of Technology, 1 Castle Point on Hudson, Hoboken, NJ 07030

## Talmudical Academy of New Jersey

| Adelphia, New Jersey | |
|---|---|
| | CB code: 0686 |

- Private 4-year rabbinical college for men affiliated with Jewish faith
- Large town

**General.** Founded in 1967. Accredited by AARTS. **Calendar:** Semester.

**Annual costs/financial aid.** Tuition/fees (2007-2008): $9,200. Room/board: $2,500.

**Contact.** Phone: (732) 431-1600
Registrar and Admissions Director, Route 524, PO Box 7, Adelphia, NJ 07710

## Thomas Edison State College

| Trenton, New Jersey | CB member |
|---|---|
| www.tesc.edu | CB code: 0682 |

- Public 4-year liberal arts college
- Small city
- 15,963 degree-seeking undergraduates: 100% part-time, 38% women, 15% African American, 2% Asian American, 7% Hispanic American, 1% Native American, 2% international
- 460 degree-seeking graduate students

**General.** Founded in 1972. Regionally accredited. **Degrees:** 1,734 bachelor's, 398 associate awarded; master's offered. **Location:** 45 miles from Philadelphia, 76 miles from New York City. **Calendar:** Continuous.

**Basis for selection.** Open admission, but selective for some programs. Applicants should be at least 21 years old. Certain programs in health professions limited to persons holding appropriate certification. Admission to bachelor's degree nursing program limited to registered nurses (RNs) currently licensed in the USA. Admission to Master of Arts in Educational Leadership degree limited to person with valid Teacher's Certificate.

**2007-2008 Annual costs.** Tuition/fees: $4,300; $6,150 out-of-state. Two tuition plans available-either the Comprehensive Tuition Plan: $4,300 per year (state residents and military personnel), $6,150 (out-of-state), which covers up to 36 credits per year for all credit-earning options; or the Enrolled Options Plan: $1,275 per year (state residents and military personnel), $2,300 (out-of-state) and $3,140 (international) for annual enrollment tuition and a technology services fee ($97). Tests, portfolios, courses and other fees at additional cost.

**2006-2007 Financial aid.** Need-based: 16% of total undergraduate aid awarded as scholarships/grants, 84% as loans/jobs. **Additional information:** Financial aid applications should be received two months before each new term begins.

**Application procedures. Admission:** No deadline. $75 fee. Application may be submitted online. Admission notification on a rolling basis. **Financial aid:** No deadline. FAFSA, institutional form required. Applicants notified on a rolling basis.

**Academics.** Provides flexibility to complete degree, including credit by examination, assessment of experiential learning, guided study, online courses, e-pack courses and credit for corporate and military training. Contracts with subject matter experts to act as mentors to academic units of college. **Special study options:** Combined bachelor's/graduate degree, distance learning, dual enrollment of high school students, external degree, independent study. **Credit/placement by examination:** AP, CLEP. 60 credit hours maximum toward associate degree, 120 toward bachelor's.

**Majors. Agriculture:** Horticulture. **Biology:** General. **Business:** Accounting, business admin, entrepreneurial studies, finance, hospitality admin, human resources, international, labor relations, marketing, operations, real estate. **Communications:** General, journalism. **Computer sciences:** Computer science. **Conservation:** Environmental science, environmental studies, forestry. **Engineering technology:** Architectural drafting, biomedical, civil, computer systems, construction, electrical, manufacturing, mechanical, nuclear, surveying. **English:** English lit. **Family/consumer sciences:** Child care. **Foreign languages:** General. **Health:** Clinical lab science, cytotechnology, dental hygiene, facilities admin, health services, medical radiologic technology/radiation therapy, nuclear medical technology, nursing (RN), perfusion technology, public health ed, radiation protection, respiratory therapy technology, veterinary technology/assistant. **History:** General. **Interdisciplinary:** Gerontology, natural sciences. **Legal studies:** Paralegal. **Liberal arts:** Arts/sciences, humanities. **Math:** General. **Mechanic/repair:** Aircraft. **Parks/recreation:** General. **Philosophy/religion:** Philosophy, religion. **Protective services:** Criminal justice, emergency management/homeland security, fire safety technology, law enforcement admin. **Psychology:** General. **Public administration:** General, community org/advocacy, human services. **Social sciences:** General, anthropology, economics, political science, sociology. **Transportation:** Air traffic control. **Visual/performing arts:** Art, dramatic, photography. **Other:** Aviation flight technology, Engineering graphics, Health and Nutrition Counseling, Organization Leadership.

**Most popular majors.** Business/marketing 12%, engineering/engineering technologies 16%, health sciences 7%, liberal arts 28%, social sciences 9%.

**Computing on campus.** Commuter students can connect to campus network. Online library, wireless network available.

**Student services.** Adult student services, financial aid counseling, veterans' counselor. **Physically disabled:** Services for visually, hearing impaired.

**Contact.** E-mail: admissions@tesc.edu
Phone: (888) 442-8372 Toll-free number: (888) 442-8372
Fax: (609) 984-8447
David Hoftiezer, Admissions, Thomas Edison State College, 101 West State Street, Trenton, NJ 08608-1176

## University of Medicine and Dentistry of New Jersey: School of Health Related Professions
**Newark, New Jersey**
www.shrp.umdnj.edu
CB code: 0598

- Public two-year upper-division health science college
- Commuter campus in large city
- Application essay, interview required

**General.** Founded in 1976. Regionally accredited. Courses offered through videoconferencing in Newark, Scotch Plains, and Stratford. **Degrees:** 84 bachelor's, 75 associate awarded; master's, doctoral offered. **Location:** 15 miles from New York City. **Calendar:** Semester, limited summer session. **Full-time faculty:** 110 total. **Part-time faculty:** 20 total.

**Student profile.** 600 degree-seeking undergraduates.

| Out-of-state: | 3% | 25 or older: | 67% |
|---|---|---|---|

**Basis for selection.** Open admission. College transcript, application essay, interview required. Admission requirements vary per program; transfer applicants evaluated by faculty and associate dean. Minimum GPA and interview most important; health-related experience and letters of recommendation also important. Qualified minority, disabled and disadvantaged students encouraged to apply. Application procedures and closing dates vary per program. Transfer accepted as sophomores, juniors, seniors.

**2007-2008 Annual costs.** Tuition/fees: $8,160; $11,926 out-of-state. Books/supplies: $1,000.

**Application procedures. Admission:** Rolling admission. $50 fee. Application may be submitted online. **Financial aid:** Priority date 5/4. Notification of awards on rolling basis; students must reply within 3 weeks of notification. FAFSA, institutional form required.

**Academics. Special study options:** Accelerated study, combined bachelor's/graduate degree, cross-registration, distance learning, double major, dual enrollment of high school students, independent study, internships, liberal arts/career combination. **Credit/placement by examination:** CLEP, IB, institutional tests. Maximum of half of graduation requirement credits for professional component may be earned by examination.

**Majors. Biology:** Toxicology. **Health:** Clinical lab science, cytotechnology, dental hygiene, health services, medical radiologic technology/radiation therapy, nuclear medical technology, physician assistant, respiratory therapy technology, sonography.

**Computing on campus.** 50 workstations in library, computer center. Commuter students can connect to campus network. Online course registration, online library, helpline, repair service available.

**Student life. Activities:** Student professional organizations (by allied health specialty).

**Student services.** Adult student services, career counseling, student employment services, health services, on-campus daycare, personal counseling, placement for graduates, veterans' counselor.

**Contact.** E-mail: shrpadm@umdnj.edu
Phone: (973) 972-5454 Fax: (973) 972-7463
Brian Lewis, Assistant Dean for Enrollment Services, University of Medicine and Dentistry of New Jersey: School of Health Related Professions, 65 Bergen Street, Newark, NJ 07101-1709

## University of Medicine and Dentistry of New Jersey: School of Nursing
**Newark, New Jersey**
CB code: 0769

- Public 4-year nursing college
- Commuter campus in large city

**General.** Founded in 1992. Regionally accredited. **Location:** 10 miles from New York City. **Calendar:** Semester.

**Annual costs/financial aid.** Tuition/fees (2007-2008): $11,424; $15,872 out-of-state. Certain undergraduate degree programs are joint degree programs: associate degree with Middlesex County College, bachelor's degrees with Ramapo College and Rowan University. Tuition is determined for general education courses by joint degree partner. Tuition for nursing courses is determined by the School of Nursing. Books/supplies: $900. Need-based financial aid available to full-time and part-time students.

**Contact.** Phone: (973) 972-5336
Director of Admissions, 65 Bergen Street, Room 1126, Newark, NJ 07101

## Westminster Choir College of Rider University
**Princeton, New Jersey**
www.rider.edu/284.htm
CB code: 2974

- Private 4-year music college
- Residential campus in small town

**General.** Founded in 1926. Regionally accredited. **Location:** 50 miles from New York City and Philadelphia. **Calendar:** Semester.

**Annual costs/financial aid.** Books/supplies: $500. Personal expenses: $700. Need-based financial aid available for full-time students.

**Contact.** Phone: (609) 921-7144
Associate Director of Admissions, 101 Walnut Lane, Princeton, NJ 08540-3899

---

### William Paterson University of New Jersey

| Wayne, New Jersey | CB member |
|---|---|
| ww2.wpunj.edu | CB code: 2518 |

- Public 4-year university and liberal arts college
- Commuter campus in large town
- 8,760 degree-seeking undergraduates: 17% part-time, 56% women, 14% African American, 6% Asian American, 17% Hispanic American, 1% international
- 847 degree-seeking graduate students
- 70% of applicants admitted
- SAT or ACT (ACT writing optional) required
- 47% graduate within 6 years

**General.** Founded in 1855. Regionally accredited. **Degrees:** 1,684 bachelor's awarded; master's offered. **ROTC:** Air Force. **Location:** 20 miles from New York City. **Calendar:** Semester, limited summer session. **Full-time faculty:** 373 total; 89% have terminal degrees, 34% minority, 46% women. **Part-time faculty:** 601 total; 15% minority, 46% women. **Class size:** 47% < 20, 50% 20-39, 3% 40-49, less than 1% 50-99, less than 1% >100. **Special facilities:** 5 Silicon Graphics Iris workstations, satellite uplink and downlink capabilities, 2 theaters.

**Freshman class profile.** 5,992 applied, 4,206 admitted, 1,437 enrolled.

| Mid 50% test scores | | Rank in top tenth: | 9% |
|---|---|---|---|
| SAT critical reading: | 440-530 | Return as sophomores: | 76% |
| SAT math: | 440-540 | Out-of-state: | 3% |
| Rank in top quarter: | 25% | Live on campus: | 45% |

**Basis for selection.** School record and test score most important; recommendations also important; class rank and essay considered. Audition required for music programs; portfolio required for art programs. Essays recommended. **Homeschooled:** Transcript of courses and grades, state high school equivalency certificate required.

**High school preparation.** 16 units required. Required units include English 4, mathematics 3, social studies 2, science 2 (laboratory 2) and academic electives 5. Advanced math, literature, foreign language, social sciences required for academic electives.

**2007-2008 Annual costs.** Tuition/fees: $9,996; $16,242 out-of-state. Room/board: $10,250. Books/supplies: $800. Personal expenses: $1,500.

**2007-2008 Financial aid.** **Need-based:** 1,034 full-time freshmen applied for aid; 752 were judged to have need; 722 of these received aid. Average scholarship/grant was $7,740; average loan $3,397. 87% of total undergraduate aid awarded as scholarships/grants, 13% as loans/jobs. **Non-need-based:** Awarded to 977 full-time undergraduates, including 257 freshmen. Scholarships awarded for academics, alumni affiliation, minority status, music/drama.

**Application procedures. Admission:** Priority date 4/1; deadline 5/1 (postmark date). $50 fee, may be waived for applicants with need. Application may be submitted online. Admission notification on a rolling basis beginning on or about 10/1. Must reply by May 1 or within 2 week(s) if notified thereafter. **Financial aid:** Priority date 4/1; no closing date. FAFSA required. Applicants notified on a rolling basis starting 3/1; must reply within 2 week(s) of notification.

**Academics.** Honors programs available in biopsychology, humanities, cognitive science, life science and environmental ethics, music, nursing, performing and literary arts. **Special study options:** Accelerated study, combined bachelor's/graduate degree, cross-registration, distance learning, double major, dual enrollment of high school students, ESL, exchange student, honors, independent study, internships, study abroad, teacher certification program, Washington semester. Cluster courses (program that provides opportunities for students and faculty to study and learn together in courses grouped in interdisciplinary clusters of three), international exchange program. **Credit/placement by examination:** AP, CLEP, SAT, ACT, institutional tests. 90 credit hours maximum toward bachelor's degree. **Support services:** Learning center, pre-admission summer program, reduced course load, remedial instruction, study skills assistance, tutoring, writing center.

**Honors college/program.** Generally, accept students with 1200+ SAT scores (math and reading) and a solid B+ or above high school average. About 100 first-year students admitted to Honors College each year.

**Majors. Area/ethnic studies:** African, African-American, Caribbean, French, Latin American, women's. **Biology:** General, biotechnology. **Business:** Accounting, business admin, finance, international finance, managerial economics. **Communications:** General. **Computer sciences:** General, computer science. **Conservation:** General, environmental science. **Education:** Elementary, health, mathematics, music, physical, special. **English:** English lit. **Foreign languages:** French, Spanish. **Health:** Nursing (RN), public health nursing, speech pathology. **History:** General. **Math:** General. **Parks/recreation:** Exercise sciences. **Philosophy/religion:** Philosophy. **Physical sciences:** Chemistry. **Psychology:** General. **Social sciences:** Anthropology, economics, geography, political science, sociology. **Visual/performing arts:** Art, jazz, music management, music performance.

**Most popular majors.** Business/marketing 17%, communications/journalism 13%, education 8%, English 9%, health sciences 6%, psychology 10%, social sciences 15%, visual/performing arts 7%.

**Computing on campus.** 700 workstations in dormitories, library, computer center. Dormitories wired for high-speed internet access and linked to campus network. Commuter students can connect to campus network. Online course registration, online library, helpline, student web hosting, wireless network available.

**Student life. Freshman orientation:** Mandatory, $75 fee. 2-day program held twice in early summer. Freshmen and parents invited to stay overnight for nominal fee. **Housing:** Guaranteed on-campus for all undergraduates. Coed dorms, special housing for disabled, apartments, substance-free housing available. $150 nonrefundable deposit, deadline 4/1. Academic interest housing, 21-or-older dorm, apartment-style housing (for groups of students who are 21 or older, or who are 20 with 52 or more credits) available. Floor for women available in one residence hall. Intentional and learning communities offered. Special interest housing such as honors, nursing, quiet floors, theme floors available. **Activities:** Jazz band, campus ministries, dance, drama, film society, international student organizations, literary magazine, music ensembles, Model UN, radio station, student government, student newspaper, TV station, Black student association, Christian Fellowship Club, Jewish student association, Feminist Collective, Organization of Latin American Students, United Asian Americans, Coalition of Lesbians, Gays & Friends.

**Athletics.** NCAA. **Intercollegiate:** Baseball M, basketball, cross-country, field hockey W, football (tackle) M, soccer, softball W, swimming, track and field, volleyball W. **Intramural:** Basketball, field hockey W, soccer W, softball, volleyball. **Team name:** Pioneers.

**Student services.** Adult student services, alcohol/substance abuse counseling, campus ministries, career counseling, services for economically disadvantaged, student employment services, financial aid counseling, health services, legal services, minority student services, on-campus daycare, personal counseling, placement for graduates, veterans' counselor, women's services. **Physically disabled:** Services for visually, speech, hearing impaired.

**Contact.** E-mail: admissions@wpunj.edu
Phone: (973) 720-2125 Toll-free number: (877) 978-3923
Fax: (973) 720-2910
Colleen O'Connor, Director of Admissions, William Paterson University of New Jersey, 300 Pompton Road, Wayne, NJ 07470

# New Mexico

## Art Center Design College
**Albuquerque, New Mexico**
www.theartcenter.edu

CB code: 3039

▶ For-profit 4-year visual arts college
▶ Very large city
▶ 294 degree-seeking undergraduates
▶ SAT or ACT (ACT writing optional), application essay, interview required

**General.** Accredited by ACCSCT. **Degrees:** 25 bachelor's, 6 associate awarded. **Calendar:** Trimester, extensive summer session. **Full-time faculty:** 8 total. **Part-time faculty:** 25 total.

### Freshman class profile.

| Mid 50% test scores | | |
|---|---|---|
| SAT critical reading: | 450-520 | |
| SAT math: | | 370-450 |
| ACT composite: | | 17-23 |

**Basis for selection.** ACT test scores are required. **Homeschooled:** Transcript of courses and grades, state high school equivalency certificate, interview required.

**2007-2008 Annual costs.** Tuition/fees: $23,040. Books/supplies: $1,200.

**Application procedures. Admission:** No deadline. $25 fee. Application may be submitted online.

**Academics. Special study options:** Double major. **Credit/placement by examination:** CLEP, SAT, ACT. **Support services:** Learning center, tutoring.

**Majors. Biology:** Immunology. **Communications technology:** Animation/special effects. **Visual/performing arts:** Commercial/advertising art, interior design.

**Computing on campus.** 2 workstations in library, computer center. Online library, wireless network available.

**Student life. Freshman orientation:** Available. Preregistration for classes offered.

**Contact.** E-mail: inquire@theartcenter.edu
Phone: (505) 254-7575 Toll-free number: (800) 825-8753
Fax: (505) 254-4754
Colleen Gimbel-Froebe, Director of Admissions, Art Center Design College, 5000 Marble Avenue NE, Albuquerque, NM 87119

## College of Santa Fe
**Santa Fe, New Mexico**
www.csf.edu

CB member
CB code: 4676

▶ Private 4-year liberal arts college
▶ Residential campus in small city
▶ 657 degree-seeking undergraduates: 8% part-time, 49% women, 2% African American, 1% Asian American, 12% Hispanic American, 3% Native American
▶ 83% of applicants admitted
▶ SAT or ACT with writing, application essay, interview required
▶ 47% graduate within 6 years

**General.** Founded in 1947. Regionally accredited. **Degrees:** 119 bachelor's awarded. **Location:** 60 miles from Albuquerque. **Calendar:** Semester, limited summer session. **Full-time faculty:** 73 total; 77% have terminal degrees, 14% minority, 38% women. **Part-time faculty:** 105 total; 11% minority, 50% women. **Class size:** 89% < 20, 10% 20-39, less than 1% 40-49, less than 1% 50-99. **Special facilities:** Sound stages for film and video, visual arts center, theater center with two stages, digital arts laboratory, recording studios.

**Freshman class profile.** 624 applied, 516 admitted, 166 enrolled.

| Mid 50% test scores | | | | |
|---|---|---|---|---|
| SAT critical reading: | 540-640 | GPA 2.0-2.99: | 32% |
| SAT math: | 470-590 | Rank in top quarter: | 40% |
| SAT writing: | 510-620 | Rank in top tenth: | 12% |
| ACT composite: | 21-27 | Return as sophomores: | 68% |
| GPA 3.50 or higher: | 31% | Out-of-state: | 87% |
| GPA 3.0-3.49: | 36% | Live on campus: | 95% |

**Basis for selection.** Admissions based on secondary school record, interview, talent, ability, character, and personal qualities. Class rank, recommendations, standardized test scores, essay, and volunteer work also important. **Homeschooled:** Statement describing homeschool structure and mission, transcript of courses and grades, interview required.

**High school preparation.** 16 units required. Required and recommended units include English 4, mathematics 2-3, social studies 2, history 2, science 2-3 (laboratory 2-3), foreign language 2 and academic electives 6.

**2007-2008 Annual costs.** Tuition/fees: $26,072. Room/board: $8,458. Books/supplies: $1,180. Personal expenses: $1,380.

**Financial aid. Non-need-based:** Scholarships awarded for academics, alumni affiliation, art, athletics, leadership, minority status, music/drama.

**Application procedures. Admission:** Priority date 3/15; no deadline. $35 fee, may be waived for applicants with need. Application may be submitted online. Admission notification on a rolling basis beginning on or about 1/15. Must reply by May 1 or within 2 week(s) if notified thereafter. **Financial aid:** Priority date 3/15; no closing date. FAFSA required. Applicants notified on a rolling basis starting 3/1; must reply by 5/1 or within 2 week(s) of notification.

**Academics. Special study options:** Cooperative education, double major, dual enrollment of high school students, exchange student, independent study, internships, New York semester, semester at sea, student-designed major, study abroad. London semester, Lasallian Consortium for Study Abroad. **Credit/placement by examination:** AP, CLEP, institutional tests. 48 credit hours maximum toward bachelor's degree. **Support services:** Learning center, reduced course load, remedial instruction, study skills assistance, tutoring, writing center.

**Majors. Communications:** General. **English:** Creative writing, English lit. **Health:** Art therapy. **Interdisciplinary:** Global studies. **Psychology:** General. **Social sciences:** Political science. **Visual/performing arts:** Acting, art history/conservation, dramatic, film/cinema, graphic design, multimedia, music performance, music theory/composition, musical theater, musicology, painting, photography, sculpture, studio arts, theater arts management, theater design. **Other:** Environmental documentation.

**Most popular majors.** English 10%, psychology 6%, visual/performing arts 70%.

**Computing on campus.** 84 workstations in library, computer center. Dormitories wired for high-speed internet access and linked to campus network. Online course registration, online library, helpline, student web hosting, wireless network available.

**Student life. Freshman orientation:** Mandatory. Preregistration for classes offered. Four-day program involves meetings with faculty advisors, social activities, club sign-ups, off-campus trips to learn more about the community. **Housing:** Guaranteed on-campus for freshmen. Coed dorms, single-sex dorms, special housing for disabled, apartments, substance-free housing available. $200 fully refundable deposit. Separate quiet floors, substance-free floors. **Activities:** Choral groups, dance, drama, literary magazine, music ensembles, musical theater, student government, student newspaper, TV station.

**Athletics.** NAIA. **Intercollegiate:** Baseball M, golf, soccer, softball W, tennis. **Intramural:** Basketball, soccer, volleyball. **Team name:** Prairie Dogs.

**Student services.** Alcohol/substance abuse counseling, campus ministries, career counseling, financial aid counseling, health services, personal counseling. **Physically disabled:** Services for visually, speech, hearing impaired. **Learning disabled:** Comprehensive services available.

**Contact.** E-mail: admissions@csf.edu
Phone: (505) 473-6133 Toll-free number: (800) 456-2673
Fax: (505) 473-6129
J. Taylor Gantt, Associate Director, College of Santa Fe, 1600 Saint Michael's Drive, Santa Fe, NM 87505-7634

## College of the Southwest
**Hobbs, New Mexico**
www.csw.edu                                    **CB code: 4116**

- Private 4-year liberal arts and teachers college
- Commuter campus in large town
- 386 degree-seeking undergraduates: 15% part-time, 58% women
- 137 degree-seeking graduate students
- SAT or ACT (ACT writing optional) required

**General.** Founded in 1956. Regionally accredited. **Degrees:** 98 bachelor's awarded; master's offered. **Location:** 110 miles from Lubbock, Texas. **Calendar:** Semester, extensive summer session. **Full-time faculty:** 17 total; 100% have terminal degrees, 12% minority, 41% women. **Part-time faculty:** 31 total; 100% have terminal degrees, 6% minority, 48% women. **Class size:** 86% < 20, 13% 20-39, less than 1% 50-99.

**Freshman class profile.** 626 applied, 230 admitted, 123 enrolled.

| Mid 50% test scores | | | |
|---|---|---|---|
| SAT critical reading: | 350-480 | GPA 3.0-3.49: | 40% |
| SAT math: | 350-480 | GPA 2.0-2.99: | 32% |
| SAT writing: | 400-490 | Rank in top quarter: | 39% |
| ACT composite: | 15-21 | Rank in top tenth: | 10% |
| GPA 3.50 or higher: | 24% | Out-of-state: | 14% |

**Basis for selection.** Open admission, but selective for some programs. Applicants must meet 2 of 3 criteria: ACT 19 or SAT 910 (exclusive of Writing), 2.0 GPA; top half of graduating class. **Homeschooled:** Statement describing homeschool structure and mission, transcript of courses and grades, state high school equivalency certificate required. **Learning Disabled:** Students with special needs are required to submit diagnostic test results in which special need was evaluated during last 3 years, Individual Education Plan (IEP), and other supporting documentation.

**2007-2008 Annual costs.** Tuition/fees: $11,700. Room/board: $5,400. Books/supplies: $1,000. Personal expenses: $750.

**2007-2008 Financial aid. Need-based:** Average scholarship/grant was $8,266; average loan $1,750. 42% of total undergraduate aid awarded as scholarships/grants, 58% as loans/jobs. **Non-need-based:** Scholarships awarded for academics, alumni affiliation, athletics, leadership, music/drama, religious affiliation, state residency.

**Application procedures. Admission:** No deadline. $25 fee. Application may be submitted online. Admission notification on a rolling basis beginning on or about 7/1. **Financial aid:** Priority date 4/1, closing date 6/1. FAFSA, institutional form required. Applicants notified on a rolling basis starting 4/1; must reply within 2 week(s) of notification.

**Academics.** 6 hours religious studies, 3 hours economics required of all students. **Special study options:** Combined bachelor's/graduate degree, cooperative education, distance learning, double major, dual enrollment of high school students, internships, teacher certification program. Internet program for criminal justice degree only. **Credit/placement by examination:** AP, CLEP, IB, SAT, ACT. 45 credit hours maximum toward bachelor's degree. **Support services:** Reduced course load, remedial instruction, study skills assistance, tutoring.

**Majors. Biology:** General. **Business:** Accounting, business admin, management information systems, marketing. **Conservation:** General, environmental studies. **Education:** Bilingual, elementary, English, mathematics, physical, sales/marketing, science, secondary, social science, special. **English:** English lit. **History:** General. **Liberal arts:** Arts/sciences, humanities. **Math:** General. **Protective services:** Criminal justice. **Psychology:** General. **Social sciences:** General.

**Most popular majors.** Business/marketing 29%, education 40%, psychology 11%.

**Computing on campus.** 35 workstations in library, computer center. Dormitories wired for high-speed internet access. Online library, helpline, wireless network available.

**Student life. Freshman orientation:** Mandatory. Preregistration for classes offered. Held 1 week prior to beginning of classes. **Housing:** Single-sex dorms, apartments, substance-free housing available. $150 fully refundable deposit. **Activities:** Drama, literary magazine, music ensembles, student government, student newspaper, accounting, teaching, and game clubs, Students in Free Enterprise, Alpha Phi Omega, Southwest Cultural Pride Club, Sigma Tau Delta, CSW Alumni Association.

**Athletics.** NAIA. **Intercollegiate:** Baseball M, basketball M, cross-country, golf, soccer, softball W, track and field, volleyball W. **Intramural:** Badminton M, basketball, football (tackle) M, soccer W, table tennis, volleyball W. **Team name:** Mustangs.

**Student services.** Campus ministries, student employment services, financial aid counseling, personal counseling, placement for graduates, veterans' counselor.

**Contact.** E-mail: admissions@csw.edu
Phone: (505) 392-6563 Toll-free number: (800) 530-4400 ext. 1007
Fax: (505) 392-6006
Ashely Taylor, Admissions Coordinator, College of the Southwest, 6610 Lovington Highway #506, Hobbs, NM 88240

## Eastern New Mexico University
**Portales, New Mexico**
www.enmu.edu                                    **CB code: 4299**

- Public 4-year university
- Residential campus in large town
- 2,966 degree-seeking undergraduates: 20% part-time, 56% women, 6% African American, 1% Asian American, 31% Hispanic American, 3% Native American, 3% international
- 497 degree-seeking graduate students
- 70% of applicants admitted
- SAT or ACT (ACT writing optional) required

**General.** Founded in 1927. Regionally accredited. **Degrees:** 513 bachelor's, 15 associate awarded; master's offered. **Location:** 225 miles from Albuquerque, 120 miles from Lubbock, Texas. **Calendar:** Semester, extensive summer session. **Full-time faculty:** 154 total; 78% have terminal degrees, 20% minority, 45% women. **Part-time faculty:** 127 total; 15% have terminal degrees, 16% minority, 44% women. **Class size:** 58% < 20, 34% 20-39, 5% 40-49, 3% 50-99. **Special facilities:** Natural history museum, mineral museum, scanning and transmission electron microscopes.

**Freshman class profile.** 1,634 applied, 1,136 admitted, 543 enrolled.

| Mid 50% test scores | | | |
|---|---|---|---|
| SAT critical reading: | 440-530 | Rank in top quarter: | 33% |
| SAT math: | 440-540 | Rank in top tenth: | 11% |
| ACT composite: | 17-22 | End year in good standing: | 82% |
| GPA 3.50 or higher: | 34% | Return as sophomores: | 59% |
| GPA 3.0-3.49: | 35% | Out-of-state: | 21% |
| GPA 2.0-2.99: | 30% | Live on campus: | 73% |

**Basis for selection.** Test scores, school record, recommendations important. Students not meeting regular admission standards may be admitted on probation. **Homeschooled:** Transcript of courses and grades required.

**High school preparation.** 14 units recommended. Recommended units include English 4, mathematics 3, social studies 2, science 4 and foreign language 1.

**2007-2008 Annual costs.** Tuition/fees: $3,156; $8,700 out-of-state. Room/board: $4,888. Books/supplies: $1,100. Personal expenses: $3,214.

**2007-2008 Financial aid. Need-based:** 333 full-time freshmen applied for aid; 333 were judged to have need; 333 of these received aid. Average need met was 35%. Average scholarship/grant was $3,452; average loan $3,393. 42% of total undergraduate aid awarded as scholarships/grants, 58% as loans/jobs. **Non-need-based:** Awarded to 1,128 full-time undergraduates, including 399 freshmen. Scholarships awarded for academics, alumni affiliation, art, athletics, leadership, music/drama, state residency. **Additional information:** Not all merit scholarships are need-based.

**Application procedures. Admission:** Priority date 8/15; no deadline. No application fee. Application may be submitted online. Admission notification on a rolling basis. **Financial aid:** Priority date 3/1; no closing date. FAFSA required. Applicants notified by 4/1; must reply within 3 week(s) of notification.

**Academics. Special study options:** Accelerated study, cooperative education, distance learning, double major, dual enrollment of high school students, exchange student, honors, independent study, internships, student-designed major, study abroad, teacher certification program. **Credit/placement by examination:** AP, CLEP, ACT, institutional tests. 32 credit hours maximum toward associate degree, 50 toward bachelor's. **Support services:** Learning center, pre-admission summer program, remedial instruction, tutoring.

**Majors. Agriculture:** Agribusiness operations, dairy. **Biology:** General. **Business:** Accounting, business admin, finance, human resources, management information systems, managerial economics, marketing. **Communications:** General, broadcast journalism, journalism. **Computer sciences:** General, computer science. **Conservation:** Environmental science, wildlife. **Education:** Agricultural, business, early childhood, elementary, music, physical, sales/marketing, special. **Engineering technology:** General. **English:** English lit, speech/rhetoric. **Family/consumer sciences:** General. **Foreign languages:** Spanish. **Health:** Audiology/speech pathology, clinical lab science, nursing (RN). **History:** General. **Liberal arts:** Arts/sciences. **Math:** General. **Parks/recreation:** Health/fitness. **Philosophy/religion:** Religion. **Physical sciences:** Chemistry, geology, physics. **Protective services:** Criminal justice, forensics. **Psychology:** General. **Public administration:** Social work. **Social sciences:** General, anthropology, political science, sociology. **Transportation:** Aviation management. **Visual/performing arts:** Art, dramatic.

**Most popular majors.** Business/marketing 14%, education 19%, liberal arts 15%, psychology 6%.

**Computing on campus.** 493 workstations in dormitories, library, computer center. Dormitories linked to campus network. Commuter students can connect to campus network. Repair service available.

**Student life. Freshman orientation:** Mandatory, $60 fee. Preregistration for classes offered. **Housing:** Guaranteed on-campus for freshmen. Coed dorms, single-sex dorms, special housing for disabled, apartments, fraternity/sorority housing, substance-free housing available. $150 fully refundable deposit. **Activities:** Bands, choral groups, dance, drama, film society, literary magazine, music ensembles, musical theater, radio station, student government, student newspaper, symphony orchestra, TV station, several religious, political, honorary, and service organization.

**Athletics.** NCAA. **Intercollegiate:** Baseball M, basketball, cross-country, football (tackle) M, rodeo, soccer, softball W, tennis W, track and field, volleyball W. **Intramural:** Badminton, basketball, cross-country, football (tackle) M, golf, racquetball, soccer, softball, tennis, volleyball. **Team name:** Greyhounds.

**Student services.** Adult student services, career counseling, student employment services, financial aid counseling, health services, minority student services, on-campus daycare, personal counseling, placement for graduates, veterans' counselor. **Physically disabled:** Services for visually, speech, hearing impaired.

**Contact.** Phone: (575) 562-2178 Toll-free number: (800) 367-3668 Fax: (575) 562-2566
Donna Kittrell, Director of Enrollment Services, Eastern New Mexico University, Station Seven, Portales, NM 88130

---

## Institute of American Indian Arts
**Santa Fe, New Mexico**
**www.iaia.edu**
**CB code: 0180**

- Public 4-year visual arts college
- Residential campus in small city
- 184 degree-seeking undergraduates
- Application essay required

**General.** Founded in 1962. Regionally accredited. Dedicated to providing education in fine arts and cultural studies to American Indians and Alaska Natives. **Degrees:** 27 bachelor's, 12 associate awarded. **Location:** 60 miles from Albuquerque. **Calendar:** Semester. **Full-time faculty:** 19 total. **Part-time faculty:** 15 total. **Special facilities:** Contemporary Indian Art museum.

**Basis for selection.** Admissions decisions based on GPA, high school record, recommendations, SAT or ACT or Accuplacer test scores. SAT or ACT recommended. Personal statement of educational intention required.

**2007-2008 Annual costs.** Tuition/fees: $2,550. Room/board: $4,536. Books/supplies: $2,500. Personal expenses: $2,400.

**Financial aid. Non-need-based:** Scholarships awarded for academics, art. **Additional information:** For American Indian and Alaskan natives, financial aid available through Tribe or Native Corporation in which student is enrolled.

**Application procedures. Admission:** Closing date 8/4. $5 fee. Application may be submitted online. Admission notification on a rolling basis beginning on or about 5/1. Must reply by May 1 or within 1 week(s) if notified thereafter. **Financial aid:** Priority date 3/15; no closing date. FAFSA, institutional form required. Applicants notified on a rolling basis starting 5/1.

**Academics.** Most courses emphasize American Indian perspective. **Special study options:** Cross-registration, double major, exchange student, independent study, internships. **Credit/placement by examination:** AP, CLEP, SAT, ACT, institutional tests. **Support services:** Learning center, remedial instruction, study skills assistance, tutoring.

**Majors. English:** Creative writing. **Interdisciplinary:** Museum. **Visual/performing arts:** Studio arts. **Other:** Indigenous liberal studies, New media arts.

**Computing on campus.** 3 workstations in dormitories, library, computer center. Dormitories linked to campus network.

**Student life. Freshman orientation:** Mandatory. Preregistration for classes offered. Freshmen class orientation conducted each semester one week before registration. **Housing:** Guaranteed on-campus for freshmen. Coed dorms available. $150 deposit. **Activities:** Literary magazine, student government, student newspaper, TV station, student senate, Pow-Wow club, traditional dance club, museum club, photography club, theater club, campus cleanup club.

**Athletics. Intramural:** Badminton, basketball, bowling, skiing, softball, swimming, table tennis, tennis, volleyball.

**Student services.** Alcohol/substance abuse counseling, career counseling, student employment services, financial aid counseling, personal counseling, placement for graduates.

**Contact.** E-mail: admissions@iaia.edu
Phone: (505) 424-2332 Toll-free number: (800) 804-6422
Fax: (505) 424-4500
John Gritts, Director of Admissions, Records & Enrollment, Institute of American Indian Arts, 83 Avan Nu Po Road, Santa Fe, NM 87508-1300

---

## International Institute of the Americas: Albuquerque
**Albuquerque, New Mexico**
**www.iia.edu**

- For-profit 4-year branch campus college
- Commuter campus in large city
- 200 degree-seeking undergraduates
- Interview required

**General.** Accredited by ACICS. Additional campuses in Arizona: Phoenix, Mesa, and Tucson. **Degrees:** 1 bachelor's, 40 associate awarded. **Calendar:** Continuous, extensive summer session. **Full-time faculty:** 5 total; 20% have terminal degrees, 80% women. **Part-time faculty:** 11 total; 36% have terminal degrees, 54% women. **Special facilities:** Child activity center for students' children.

**Basis for selection.** Open admission.

**2008-2009 Annual costs.** Tuition/fees (projected): $11,400. Tuition and fees may vary by program.

**Financial aid.** All financial aid based on need.

**Application procedures. Admission:** No deadline. $200 fee. Application must be submitted on paper. Admission notification on a rolling basis. **Financial aid:** No deadline. FAFSA, institutional form required.

**Academics. Special study options:** Distance learning. **Credit/placement by examination:** CLEP. **Support services:** Learning center.

**Majors. Business:** Business admin.

**Computing on campus.** Commuter students can connect to campus network. Online library available.

**Student life. Freshman orientation:** Mandatory.

**Student services.** Career counseling, financial aid counseling, on-campus daycare, placement for graduates.

**Contact.** E-mail: jpalumbo@iia.edu
Phone: (505) 880-2877 Toll-free number: (888) 744-6340
Fax: (505) 352-0199
John Palumbo, VP of Admissions, International Institute of the Americas: Albuquerque, 4201 Central Avenue NW, Suite J, Albuquerque, NM 87105

## ITT Technical Institute: Albuquerque

**Albuquerque, New Mexico**
www.itt-tech.edu
**CB code: 2690**

- For-profit 4-year technical college
- Commuter campus in large city

**General.** Accredited by ACICS. **Calendar:** Quarter.

**Annual costs/financial aid.** Tuition varies by program, $260-$368 per credit hour.

**Contact.** Phone: (505) 828-1114
Director of Recruitment, 5100 Masthead Street Northeast, Albuquerque, NM 87109

## National American University: Rio Rancho

**Rio Rancho, New Mexico**
www.national.edu
**CB code: 5360**

- For-profit 4-year business college
- Large city
- 525 degree-seeking undergraduates

**General.** Founded in 1941. Regionally accredited. **Degrees:** 75 bachelor's, 15 associate awarded; master's offered. **ROTC:** Naval, Air Force. **Calendar:** Quarter, extensive summer session. **Part-time faculty:** 60 total.

**Basis for selection.** Open admission.

**2007-2008 Annual costs.** Tuition/fees: $11,930. Books/supplies: $675.

**Application procedures. Admission:** No deadline. $25 fee. Admission notification on a rolling basis. **Financial aid:** No deadline. Institutional form required. Applicants notified on a rolling basis.

**Academics. Special study options:** Combined bachelor's/graduate degree, distance learning, independent study. **Credit/placement by examination:** AP, CLEP. 45 credit hours maximum toward associate degree, 95 toward bachelor's. **Support services:** Tutoring.

**Majors. Business:** Accounting, business admin, management information systems.

**Most popular majors.** Business/marketing 82%, computer/information sciences 18%.

**Computing on campus.** 15 workstations in library, computer center.

**Student life. Activities:** Choral groups, literary magazine, music ensembles, TV station.

**Athletics. Team name:** Mavericks.

**Student services.** Adult student services, career counseling, student employment services, placement for graduates, veterans' counselor.

**Contact.** Phone: (505) 348-3750 Fax: (505) 348-3755
Nancy Pointer-Meason, Director of Admissions, National American University: Rio Rancho, 4775 Indian School Road Northeast, Suite 200, Albuquerque, NM 87110

## New Mexico Highlands University

**Las Vegas, New Mexico**
www.nmhu.edu
**CB member**
**CB code: 4532**

- Public 4-year university
- Commuter campus in large town
- 1,882 degree-seeking undergraduates: 24% part-time, 59% women
- 1,157 degree-seeking graduate students

**General.** Founded in 1893. Regionally accredited. **Degrees:** 366 bachelor's awarded; master's offered. **Location:** 68 miles from Santa Fe, 120 miles from Albuquerque. **Calendar:** Semester, limited summer session. **Full-time faculty:** 127 total; 82% have terminal degrees, 35% minority, 42% women.

**Freshman class profile.** 1,881 applied, 1,881 admitted, 360 enrolled.

| Mid 50% test scores | | | |
|---|---|---|---|
| SAT critical reading: | 390-480 | GPA 3.0-3.49: | 25% |
| SAT math: | 380-500 | GPA 2.0-2.99: | 52% |
| ACT composite: | 15-20 | Rank in top quarter: | 28% |
| GPA 3.50 or higher: | 18% | Rank in top tenth: | 10% |
| | | Return as sophomores: | 45% |

**Basis for selection.** Open admission. Minimum 2.0 GPA required. All tests used for placement purposes. COMPASS may be submitted in place of ACT. **Homeschooled:** Transcript of courses and grades, state high school equivalency certificate required.

**2007-2008 Annual costs.** Tuition/fees: $2,564; $3,656 out-of-state. Room/board: $4,476. Books/supplies: $756. Personal expenses: $1,494.

**Financial aid. Non-need-based:** Scholarships awarded for academics, athletics, leadership, minority status, music/drama, state residency. **Additional information:** Work study funds available on no-need basis to state residents.

**Application procedures. Admission:** No deadline. $15 fee, may be waived for applicants with need. Application may be submitted online. Admission notification on a rolling basis. **Financial aid:** Priority date 3/1, closing date 5/1. FAFSA, institutional form required. Applicants notified on a rolling basis starting 5/15; must reply within 2 week(s) of notification.

**Academics. Special study options:** Combined bachelor's/graduate degree, cooperative education, distance learning, double major, dual enrollment of high school students, ESL, honors, independent study, internships, liberal arts/career combination, teacher certification program. **Credit/placement by examination:** AP, CLEP, SAT, ACT, institutional tests. As approved by appropriate department. **Support services:** Learning center, tutoring, writing center.

**Majors. Biology:** General. **Business:** Accounting, business admin, finance, management information systems, marketing. **Communications:** Media studies. **Computer sciences:** Computer science. **Conservation:** Forest management. **Education:** Biology, computer, early childhood, elementary, mathematics, music, physical, science, special. **Engineering:** Computer. **English:** English lit. **Foreign languages:** Spanish. **History:** General. **Math:** General. **Parks/recreation:** Health/fitness. **Physical sciences:** Chemistry, forensic chemistry, geology. **Protective services:** Criminal justice, forensics. **Psychology:** General. **Public administration:** Social work. **Social sciences:** Anthropology, criminology, political science, sociology. **Visual/performing arts:** Art, music performance, studio arts.

**Computing on campus.** 250 workstations in dormitories, library, computer center, student center. Dormitories wired for high-speed internet access and linked to campus network. Commuter students can connect to campus network. Online library, repair service, wireless network available.

**Student life. Freshman orientation:** Mandatory. Preregistration for classes offered. **Housing:** Guaranteed on-campus for freshmen. Coed dorms, single-sex dorms, apartments available. $100 partly refundable deposit. **Activities:** Bands, choral groups, dance, drama, film society, music ensembles, musical theater, radio station, student government, student newspaper, TV station, social work club, international student club, several ethnic and religious groups.

**Athletics.** NAIA, NCAA. **Intercollegiate:** Baseball M, basketball, cheerleading M, cross-country, football (tackle) M, rodeo, soccer W, softball W, track and field W, volleyball W, wrestling M. **Intramural:** Baseball M, basketball, golf, handball, racquetball, rifle, rugby, skiing, softball, swimming, table tennis, tennis, track and field. **Team name:** Cowboys, Cowgirls.

**Student services.** Adult student services, career counseling, student employment services, financial aid counseling, health services, minority student services, on-campus daycare, personal counseling, placement for graduates, veterans' counselor. **Physically disabled:** Services for visually, speech, hearing impaired.

**Contact.** E-mail: admissions@nmhu.edu
Phone: (505) 454-3434 Toll-free number: (877) 850-9064
Fax: (505) 454-3552
John Coca, Director of Admissions, New Mexico Highlands University, Box 9000, Las Vegas, NM 87701

## New Mexico Institute of Mining and Technology

**Socorro, New Mexico**
www.nmt.edu
**CB member**
**CB code: 4533**

- Public 4-year engineering and liberal arts college
- Residential campus in small town

- 1,138 degree-seeking undergraduates: 4% part-time, 27% women, 1% African American, 3% Asian American, 24% Hispanic American, 3% Native American, 2% international
- 382 degree-seeking graduate students
- 55% of applicants admitted
- SAT or ACT (ACT writing optional) required
- 43% graduate within 6 years; 15% enter graduate study

**General.** Founded in 1889. Regionally accredited. Student employment opportunities in research facilities and in faculty research. **Degrees:** 225 bachelor's, 10 associate awarded; master's, doctoral offered. **Location:** 75 miles from Albuquerque. **Calendar:** Semester, limited summer session. **Full-time faculty:** 119 total; 97% have terminal degrees, 18% minority, 22% women. **Part-time faculty:** 26 total; 27% have terminal degrees, 15% minority, 23% women. **Class size:** 62% < 20, 31% 20-39, 3% 40-49, 4% 50-99, less than 1% >100. **Special facilities:** Experimental mine, mineral museum, laboratory for atmospheric physics and chemistry, energetic materials research, seismic research network, scanning electron microscope, scanning transmission electron microscope, transmission electron microscope, New Mexico Bureau of Geology, observatory.

**Freshman class profile.** 763 applied, 419 admitted, 249 enrolled.

| Mid 50% test scores | | | |
|---|---|---|---|
| SAT critical reading: | 530-660 | GPA 2.0-2.99: | 11% |
| SAT math: | 560-680 | Rank in top quarter: | 63% |
| ACT composite: | 23-29 | Rank in top tenth: | 31% |
| GPA 3.50 or higher: | 59% | Return as sophomores: | 73% |
| GPA 3.0-3.49: | 30% | Out-of-state: | 16% |

**Basis for selection.** Test scores and high school GPA most important. Minimum 2.5 GPA required. Minimum 21 ACT or 970 SAT (exclusive of Writing) required. Writing components accepted but not crucial to admission. Interview and recommendations considered if GPA and test scores are borderline or if other issues need to be addressed. **Homeschooled:** Must supply documentation of courses completed.

**High school preparation.** College-preparatory program recommended. 15 units required; 18 recommended. Required and recommended units include English 4, mathematics 3-4, social studies 2-3, history 1, science 2-4 (laboratory 2-3), foreign language 2 and academic electives 3.

**2007-2008 Annual costs.** Tuition/fees: $4,105; $11,761 out-of-state. Room/board: $5,300. Books/supplies: $902. Personal expenses: $1,635.

**Financial aid. Non-need-based:** Scholarships awarded for academics, alumni affiliation, minority status, state residency. **Additional information:** Campus research projects offer student employment based on merit.

**Application procedures. Admission:** Priority date 3/1; deadline 8/1. $15 fee, may be waived for applicants with need. Application may be submitted online. Admission notification on a rolling basis beginning on or about 3/1. Must reply by May 1 or within 2 week(s) if notified thereafter. **Financial aid:** Priority date 6/1; no closing date. FAFSA, institutional form required. Applicants notified on a rolling basis starting 4/1; must reply within 2 week(s) of notification.

**Academics. Special study options:** Accelerated study, cooperative education, distance learning, double major, dual enrollment of high school students, exchange student, independent study, internships, student-designed major, teacher certification program. **Credit/placement by examination:** AP, CLEP, institutional tests. No limit to number of credits. Must have permission of instructor. **Support services:** Pre-admission summer program, reduced course load, study skills assistance, tutoring, writing center.

**Majors. Biology:** General, biochemistry. **Business:** Business admin. **Computer sciences:** General, computer science, information technology. **Conservation:** General, environmental studies. **Engineering:** General, chemical, civil, electrical, environmental, materials, mechanical, metallurgical, mining, petroleum. **English:** Technical writing. **Math:** General, applied. **Physical sciences:** Astrophysics, atmospheric physics, chemistry, geology, geophysics, physics. **Psychology:** General.

**Most popular majors.** Biology 11%, computer/information sciences 12%, engineering/engineering technologies 44%, mathematics 8%, physical sciences 16%.

**Computing on campus.** 225 workstations in dormitories, library, computer center, student center. Dormitories wired for high-speed internet access and linked to campus network. Commuter students can connect to campus network. Helpline, student web hosting, wireless network available.

**Student life. Freshman orientation:** Available, $40 fee. Preregistration for classes offered. 2-day event held weekend before classes start. **Housing:**

Coed dorms, single-sex dorms, apartments, substance-free housing available. $100 partly refundable deposit, deadline 6/1. Students living on-campus must purchase meal plan. **Activities:** Bands, choral groups, dance, drama, film society, music ensembles, musical theater, radio station, student government, student newspaper, many organizations available.

**Athletics. Intramural:** Badminton, basketball, fencing, golf, racquetball, rifle, rugby, soccer, softball, table tennis, tennis, volleyball.

**Student services.** Adult student services, career counseling, student employment services, health services, on-campus daycare, personal counseling, placement for graduates. **Physically disabled:** Services for visually, hearing impaired.

**Contact.** E-mail: admission@admin.nmt.edu
Phone: (575) 835-5424 Toll-free number: (800) 428-8324
Fax: (575) 835-5989
Mike Kloeppel, Director of Admission, New Mexico Institute of Mining and Technology, 801 Leroy Place, Socorro, NM 87801

## New Mexico State University

**Las Cruces, New Mexico**
**www.nmsu.edu**

CB member
CB code: 4531

- Public 4-year university
- Commuter campus in small city
- 13,056 degree-seeking undergraduates: 13% part-time, 55% women, 3% African American, 1% Asian American, 43% Hispanic American, 3% Native American, 4% international
- 3,272 degree-seeking graduate students
- 85% of applicants admitted
- SAT or ACT with writing required
- 41% graduate within 6 years

**General.** Founded in 1888. Regionally accredited. **Degrees:** 2,120 bachelor's, 26 associate awarded; master's, doctoral offered. **ROTC:** Army, Air Force. **Location:** 42 miles from El Paso, Texas. **Calendar:** Semester, extensive summer session. **Full-time faculty:** 700 total; 77% have terminal degrees, 16% minority, 40% women. **Part-time faculty:** 261 total; 25% have terminal degrees, 15% minority, 56% women. **Class size:** 51% < 20, 33% 20-39, 7% 40-49, 7% 50-99, 2% >100. **Special facilities:** Observatory, horse farm, rodeo grounds, electron microscope, CRAY supercomputer, sports medicine training clinic.

**Freshman class profile.** 5,497 applied, 4,682 admitted, 2,223 enrolled.

| Mid 50% test scores | | | |
|---|---|---|---|
| SAT critical reading: | 420-550 | GPA 2.0-2.99: | 27% |
| SAT math: | 430-560 | Rank in top quarter: | 46% |
| SAT writing: | 420-550 | Rank in top tenth: | 18% |
| ACT composite: | 17-23 | Return as sophomores: | 75% |
| GPA 3.50 or higher: | 39% | Out-of-state: | 18% |
| GPA 3.0-3.49: | 34% | International: | 3% |

**Basis for selection.** School achievement record, test scores most important.

**High school preparation.** 10 units required. Required units include English 4, mathematics 3, science 2 (laboratory 2) and foreign language 1. English must include at least 2 composition, 1 of which must be at junior or senior level. Math must be algebra I, algebra II, geometry, trigonometry or advanced math. Will accept 1 foreign language or 1 fine arts.

**2007-2008 Annual costs.** Tuition/fees: $4,452; $14,180 out-of-state. Room/board: $5,766. Books/supplies: $918. Personal expenses: $3,578.

**2007-2008 Financial aid. Need-based:** 1,651 full-time freshmen applied for aid; 1,256 were judged to have need; 1,214 of these received aid. Average need met was 64%. Average scholarship/grant was $5,458; average loan $3,518. 51% of total undergraduate aid awarded as scholarships/grants, 49% as loans/jobs. **Non-need-based:** Awarded to 3,072 full-time undergraduates, including 848 freshmen. Scholarships awarded for academics, alumni affiliation, athletics, leadership, minority status, state residency.

**Application procedures. Admission:** No deadline. $20 fee. Application may be submitted online. Admission notification on a rolling basis. **Financial aid:** No deadline. FAFSA, institutional form required. Applicants notified on a rolling basis starting 3/1.

**Academics. Special study options:** Accelerated study, cooperative education, cross-registration, distance learning, double major, exchange student, honors, independent study, internships, student-designed major, study abroad, teacher certification program, weekend college. **Credit/placement**

by examination: AP, CLEP, institutional tests. **Support services:** Learning center, reduced course load, study skills assistance, tutoring, writing center.

**Majors. Agriculture:** General, agribusiness operations, agronomy, animal sciences, horticultural science, range science, soil science, turf management. **Architecture:** Urban/community planning. **Area/ethnic studies:** Women's. **Biology:** General, bacteriology, biochemistry, ecology, plant pathology. **Business:** General, accounting, business admin, finance, hospitality admin, international, marketing, real estate. **Communications:** Journalism. **Computer sciences:** General, information systems, information technology. **Conservation:** Environmental science, wildlife. **Education:** General, agricultural, early childhood, elementary, family/consumer sciences, music, physical, secondary. **Engineering:** Aerospace, agricultural, chemical, civil, electrical, industrial, mechanical, physics. **Engineering technology:** Surveying. **English:** English lit, speech/rhetoric. **Family/consumer sciences:** Clothing/textiles, family studies, food/nutrition. **Foreign languages:** General. **Health:** Athletic training, clinical lab science, environmental health, nursing (RN), public health ed. **History:** General. **Math:** General. **Parks/recreation:** Facilities management. **Philosophy/religion:** Philosophy. **Physical sciences:** Chemistry, geology, physics. **Protective services:** Criminal justice. **Psychology:** General. **Public administration:** Community org/advocacy, social work. **Social sciences:** Anthropology, economics, geography, political science, sociology. **Visual/performing arts:** General, cinematography, dance, dramatic, music performance, studio arts.

**Most popular majors.** Business/marketing 19%, education 13%, engineering/engineering technologies 11%, health sciences 7%.

**Computing on campus.** 743 workstations in dormitories, library, computer center, student center. Dormitories wired for high-speed internet access and linked to campus network. Commuter students can connect to campus network. Online course registration, online library, helpline, repair service, student web hosting, wireless network available.

**Student life. Freshman orientation:** Available. Preregistration for classes offered. **Housing:** Coed dorms, single-sex dorms, special housing for disabled, apartments, fraternity/sorority housing, substance-free housing available. $100 deposit, deadline 7/1. Upper division dorms available. **Activities:** Bands, campus ministries, choral groups, dance, drama, literary magazine, music ensembles, musical theater, opera, radio station, student government, student newspaper, symphony orchestra, TV station, Baptist student union, Catholic center, Young Democrats, College Republicans, black allied student association, Movimiento Estudiantil Chicano de Azatlan, Native American organization.

**Athletics.** NCAA. **Intercollegiate:** Baseball M, basketball, cross-country, equestrian, football (tackle) M, golf, softball W, swimming W, tennis, track and field W, volleyball W. **Intramural:** Archery, badminton, basketball, cheerleading, football (non-tackle), football (tackle), golf, racquetball, soccer, softball, tennis, volleyball, water polo, weight lifting, wrestling M. **Team name:** Aggies.

**Student services.** Adult student services, alcohol/substance abuse counseling, career counseling, student employment services, health services, personal counseling, placement for graduates, veterans' counselor. **Physically disabled:** Services for visually, speech, hearing impaired.

**Contact.** E-mail: admissions@nmsu.edu
Phone: (575) 646-3121 Toll-free number: (800) 662-6678
Fax: (575) 646-6330
Tyler Pruett, Director of Admissions, New Mexico State University, Box 30001, MSC 3A, Las Cruces, NM 88003-8001

---

## St. John's College

**Santa Fe, New Mexico**
**www.stjohnscollege.edu**

**CB member**
**CB code: 4737**

- Private 4-year liberal arts college
- Residential campus in small city
- 436 degree-seeking undergraduates: 40% women, 1% African American, 3% Asian American, 6% Hispanic American, 1% Native American, 2% international
- 98 degree-seeking graduate students
- 79% of applicants admitted
- Application essay required
- 56% graduate within 6 years

**General.** Founded in 1964. Regionally accredited. Second campus in Annapolis, MD, where students may transfer during their 4 years. **Degrees:** 104 bachelor's awarded; master's offered. **Location:** 60 miles from Albuquerque. **Calendar:** Semester, limited summer session. **Full-time faculty:** 73 total; 82% have terminal degrees, 4% minority, 26% women. **Part-time faculty:** 1 total; 100% have terminal degrees, 100% women. **Class size:**

97% < 20, 3% 20-39. **Special facilities:** Search and rescue center, Ptolemy stone, forest with hiking trails.

**Freshman class profile.** 344 applied, 271 admitted, 134 enrolled.

| Mid 50% test scores | | | |
|---|---|---|---|
| SAT critical reading: | 620-730 | Rank in top tenth: | 28% |
| SAT math: | 570-680 | Out-of-state: | 90% |
| ACT composite: | 25-30 | Live on campus: | 99% |
| Rank in top quarter: | 64% | International: | 4% |

**Basis for selection.** 3 essays describing educational and personal background and goals most important along with 2 letters of reference from teachers; secondary school reference from counselor or other school official also requested. High school achievement record considered. SAT or ACT required of early admission or home schooled applicants. Interview and 2-day campus visit strongly encouraged. **Homeschooled:** Statement describing homeschool structure and mission, transcript of courses and grades, letter of recommendation (nonparent) required. **Learning Disabled:** Campus visit required.

**High school preparation.** 5 units required; 22 recommended. Required and recommended units include English 4, mathematics 3, history 2, science 3 (laboratory 3) and foreign language 2-4. Math requirement includes 2 algebra, 1 geometry. Precalculus or trigonometry recommended.

**2008-2009 Annual costs.** Tuition/fees: $39,154. Room/board: $9,284. Books/supplies: $275. Personal expenses: $900.

**2006-2007 Financial aid. Need-based:** 73 full-time freshmen applied for aid; 66 were judged to have need; 66 of these received aid. Average need met was 93%. Average scholarship/grant was $18,888; average loan $3,225. 77% of total undergraduate aid awarded as scholarships/grants, 23% as loans/jobs. **Additional information:** 100% of need met for most of those qualified to receive aid. Families receive individual attention in determining need fairly. Independent students must submit parental data. Financial aid information also required of noncustodial parent in cases of separation or divorce. Aid awarded first-come, first-served until institutional money exhausted. Apply early by February 15; after April 1 aid difficult to obtain.

**Application procedures. Admission:** Priority date 3/1; no deadline. No application fee. Application may be submitted online. Admission notification on a rolling basis. Must reply by May 1 or within 2 week(s) if notified thereafter. Early application encouraged. **Financial aid:** Priority date 2/15; no closing date. FAFSA, CSS PROFILE required. Applicants notified on a rolling basis starting 12/1; must reply by 5/1.

**Academics. Special study options:** Accelerated study, internships. Great Books Program. **Credit/placement by examination:** CLEP. **Support services:** Tutoring, writing center.

**Majors. Liberal arts:** Arts/sciences.

**Computing on campus.** 20 workstations in library, computer center. Dormitories wired for high-speed internet access and linked to campus network. Commuter students can connect to campus network. Helpline, wireless network available.

**Student life. Freshman orientation:** Mandatory. Four-day program held twice a year. Includes on-campus service day, student activities fair, numerous community meals, and formal welcoming ceremony. **Housing:** Guaranteed on-campus for freshmen. Coed dorms, single-sex dorms, special housing for disabled, apartments, substance-free housing available. Single-sex suites, nonsmoking, nondrinking dorms available. **Activities:** Jazz band, choral groups, dance, drama, film society, literary magazine, music ensembles, musical theater, radio station, student government, student newspaper, Amnesty International, adult literacy, historic church restoration, Koran study group, women's literature group, peer counseling, community farm, soup kitchen, Beneficial Farm, Open Hands.

**Athletics. Intercollegiate:** Fencing. **Intramural:** Badminton, basketball, cross-country, fencing, racquetball, skiing, soccer, softball, squash, table tennis, tennis, volleyball.

**Student services.** Career counseling, student employment services, financial aid counseling, health services, personal counseling, placement for graduates.

**Contact.** E-mail: admissions@sjcsf.edu
Phone: (505) 984-6060 Toll-free number: (800) 331-5232
Fax: (505) 984-6162
Lawrence Clendenin, Director of Admissions, St. John's College, 1160 Camino Cruz Blanca, Santa Fe, NM 87505-4599

## University of New Mexico
### Albuquerque, New Mexico
www.unm.edu

CB member
CB code: 4845

- Public 4-year university
- Commuter campus in very large city
- 18,259 degree-seeking undergraduates
- 5,763 graduate students
- SAT or ACT (ACT writing recommended) required

**General.** Founded in 1889. Regionally accredited. Branch campuses in Valencia County, Los Alamos, Gallup, Taos. Graduate centers in Los Alamos and Santa Fe. **Degrees:** 2,996 bachelor's, 10 associate awarded; master's, doctoral, first professional offered. **ROTC:** Army, Naval, Air Force. **Location:** 2 miles from downtown. **Calendar:** Semester, limited summer session. **Full-time faculty:** 889 total. **Part-time faculty:** 526 total. **Special facilities:** 5 museums; observatory; meteoritics institute; arboretum; teaching hospital; major research facilities in ceramics, optoelectronics, space nuclear power, high power devices and systems; institute of lithography; Latin American institute; bureau of business and economic research.

### Freshman class profile.

| Mid 50% test scores | | |
|---|---|---|
| | ACT composite: | 19-25 |
| SAT critical reading: | 470-600 | |

**Basis for selection.** School achievement record (2.25 GPA required in college-preparatory units) most important. Test scores, class rank second. Essays, recommendations considered. Essay considered if student appeal denied. **Homeschooled:** Applicants must either pass GED, submit SAT Subject Test scores, or have 2.25 GPA and complete 13 college prep academic units. **Learning Disabled:** Student who is not admissable according to numerical admissions and self-discloses disability can be admitted after being approved by Special Admissions Committee.

**High school preparation.** 13 units required. Required units include English 4, mathematics 3, social studies 1, history 1, science 2 (laboratory 1) and foreign language 2. Foreign language requirements must be in same language. 1 science must be laboratory in biology, chemistry or physics. Math must be algebra I, geometry, algebra II, trigonometry or higher.

**2007-2008 Annual costs.** Tuition/fees: $4,571; $14,942 out-of-state. Room/board: $7,020.

**Financial aid. Non-need-based:** Scholarships awarded for academics, alumni affiliation, art, athletics, job skills, leadership, minority status, music/drama, religious affiliation, ROTC, state residency. **Additional information:** Regent scholarship program has priority date of 12/1. UNM scholars program has deadline of 2/1.

**Application procedures. Admission:** Closing date 6/15 (postmark date). $20 fee, may be waived for applicants with need. Application may be submitted online. Admission notification on a rolling basis. **Financial aid:** Priority date 3/1; no closing date. FAFSA required. Applicants notified on a rolling basis starting 4/15.

**Academics. Special study options:** Accelerated study, combined bachelor's/graduate degree, cooperative education, distance learning, double major, dual enrollment of high school students, ESL, exchange student, honors, independent study, internships, semester at sea, student-designed major, study abroad, teacher certification program, Washington semester, weekend college. **Credit/placement by examination:** AP, CLEP, IB, SAT, ACT, institutional tests. **Support services:** Learning center, reduced course load, remedial instruction, tutoring.

**Majors. Architecture:** Architecture, environmental design. **Area/ethnic studies:** African-American, American, Asian, European, Latin American, Native American, Russian/Slavic, women's. **Biology:** General, biochemistry. **Business:** Business admin. **Communications:** Journalism, media studies. **Computer sciences:** General. **Conservation:** Environmental science. **Education:** Art, early childhood, elementary, health, music, physical, secondary, special, technology/industrial arts. **Engineering:** Chemical, civil, computer, electrical, mechanical, nuclear, science. **English:** Speech/rhetoric. **Family/consumer sciences:** General, family studies, food/nutrition. **Foreign languages:** General, classics, comparative lit, French, German, linguistics, Portuguese, Russian, sign language interpretation, Spanish. **Health:** Audiology/speech pathology, clinical lab technology, dental hygiene, EMT paramedic, medical radiologic technology/radiation therapy, nursing (RN), physician assistant. **History:** General. **Liberal arts:** Arts/sciences, humanities. **Math:** General, statistics. **Parks/recreation:** General. **Philosophy/religion:** Philosophy, religion. **Physical sciences:** Astrophysics, chemistry, geology, physics. **Protective services:** Corrections. **Psychology:** General. **Public administration:** Community org/advocacy. **Social sciences:** Anthropology, economics, geography, political science, sociology.

**Visual/performing arts:** Art, art history/conservation, dance, dramatic, film/cinema, music performance, theater design.

**Computing on campus.** 479 workstations in dormitories, library, computer center, student center. Dormitories wired for high-speed internet access and linked to campus network. Commuter students can connect to campus network. Online course registration, online library, helpline, student web hosting, wireless network available.

**Student life. Freshman orientation:** Mandatory, $30 fee. Two-day sessions held June-August. **Housing:** Coed dorms, special housing for disabled, apartments, fraternity/sorority housing, substance-free housing available. $300 deposit. Special living options include senior housing, academic floors, scholar's wing, global learning center, freshman living learning community, outdoors/wellness, computer science, engineering units. **Activities:** Bands, choral groups, dance, drama, film society, literary magazine, music ensembles, musical theater, opera, radio station, student government, student newspaper, symphony orchestra, TV station, Panhellenic Council, RAZA En Accion, black student union, KIVA club, Del Otro Lado, NMPIRG, Hillel, Campus Crusade for Christ, progressive student alliance, international center.

**Athletics.** NCAA. **Intercollegiate:** Baseball M, basketball, cross-country, diving W, football (tackle) M, golf, skiing, soccer, softball W, swimming W, tennis, track and field, volleyball W. **Intramural:** Archery, badminton, basketball, bowling, cross-country, fencing, football (non-tackle), football (tackle) M, golf, racquetball, skiing, soccer, softball, swimming, table tennis, tennis, triathlon, volleyball, water polo. **Team name:** Lobos.

**Student services.** Adult student services, alcohol/substance abuse counseling, campus ministries, career counseling, services for economically disadvantaged, student employment services, financial aid counseling, health services, legal services, minority student services, on-campus daycare, personal counseling, placement for graduates, veterans' counselor, women's services. **Physically disabled:** Services for visually, speech, hearing impaired.

**Contact.** E-mail: apply@unm.edu
Phone: (505) 277-2446 Toll-free number: (800) 225-5866
Fax: (505) 277-6686
Tracy Hart, Director of Admissions and Recruiting Services, University of New Mexico, Office of Admissions, Albuquerque, NM 87196-4895

## Western New Mexico University
### Silver City, New Mexico
www.wnmu.edu

CB member
CB code: 4535

- Public 4-year university
- Commuter campus in large town
- 1,747 degree-seeking undergraduates: 22% part-time, 65% women, 4% African American, 1% Asian American, 47% Hispanic American, 2% Native American, 1% international
- 385 degree-seeking graduate students

**General.** Founded in 1893. Regionally accredited. **Degrees:** 148 bachelor's, 84 associate awarded; master's offered. **Location:** 155 miles from El Paso, Texas, 193 miles from Tucson, Arizona. **Calendar:** Semester, extensive summer session. **Full-time faculty:** 105 total; 88% have terminal degrees. **Part-time faculty:** 141 total. **Class size:** 78% < 20, 20% 20-39, less than 1% 40-49, less than 1% 50-99. **Special facilities:** Museum specializing in Native American cultures, fine arts center and gallery, amphitheater.

**Freshman class profile.** 785 applied, 785 admitted, 284 enrolled.

| Mid 50% test scores | | | | |
|---|---|---|---|---|
| SAT critical reading: | 410-580 | Return as sophomores: | 48% |
| SAT math: | 410-540 | Out-of-state: | 17% |
| ACT composite: | 16-21 | Live on campus: | 50% |
| | | International: | 1% |

**Basis for selection.** Open admission. COMPASS test used for placement. **Homeschooled:** State high school equivalency certificate required. If state high school equivalency certificate not received, student must take GED.

**High school preparation.** Recommended units include English 4, mathematics 3, social studies 2, history 1 and science 2.

**2007-2008 Annual costs.** Tuition/fees: $3,218; $11,887 out-of-state. Room/board: $5,145. Books/supplies: $810. Personal expenses: $2,060.

**2006-2007 Financial aid. Need-based:** 155 full-time freshmen applied for aid; 155 were judged to have need; 155 of these received aid. Average need met was 61%. Average scholarship/grant was $3,767; average loan $2,307. 45% of total undergraduate aid awarded as scholarships/grants, 55%

as loans/jobs. **Non-need-based:** Awarded to 347 full-time undergraduates, including 53 freshmen. Scholarships awarded for academics, athletics, state residency.

**Application procedures. Admission:** Priority date 8/1; no deadline. No application fee. Application may be submitted online. Admission notification on a rolling basis. **Financial aid:** Closing date 4/1. FAFSA, institutional form required. Applicants notified on a rolling basis starting 4/1; must reply within 2 week(s) of notification.

**Academics. Special study options:** Cooperative education, distance learning, double major, dual enrollment of high school students, honors, independent study, internships, liberal arts/career combination, teacher certification program. **Credit/placement by examination:** AP, CLEP, IB. 12 credit hours maximum toward associate degree, 32 toward bachelor's. **Support services:** Learning center, remedial instruction, study skills assistance, tutoring, writing center.

**Majors. Area/ethnic studies:** Hispanic-American/Latino/Chicano. **Biology:** General, botany, zoology. **Business:** General, accounting, business admin, managerial economics, marketing, operations. **Computer sciences:** General. **Conservation:** Wildlife. **Education:** General, art, biology, business, chemistry, elementary, ESL, health, mathematics, middle, music, physical, science, secondary, social science, social studies, Spanish, special, technology/industrial arts, voc/tech. **English:** English lit. **Foreign languages:** Spanish. **Health:** Clinical lab technology. **History:** General. **Liberal arts:** Arts/sciences. **Math:** General. **Physical sciences:** Chemistry. **Protective services:** Criminal justice, law enforcement admin. **Psychology:** General. **Public administration:** Social work. **Social sciences:** General, sociology. **Visual/performing arts:** Studio arts.

**Most popular majors.** Business/marketing 23%, education 22%, liberal arts 11%, public administration/social services 9%, security/protective services 7%.

**Computing on campus.** 150 workstations in dormitories, library, computer center. Dormitories linked to campus network. Commuter students can connect to campus network. Online course registration, online library, helpline available.

**Student life. Freshman orientation:** Available, $10 fee. Preregistration for classes offered. Two-day sessions held once a month from late May through mid-August. **Housing:** Guaranteed on-campus for all undergraduates. Coed dorms, single-sex dorms, special housing for disabled, apartments available. $75 deposit. **Activities:** Bands, campus ministries, choral groups, drama, music ensembles, musical theater, student government, student newspaper, symphony orchestra, Baptist student union, Society for the Advancement of Management, St. Francis Newman club, Chicano student organization, criminal justice, Native American club.

**Athletics.** NCAA. **Intercollegiate:** Basketball, cross-country, football (tackle) M, golf, softball W, tennis, volleyball W. **Intramural:** Basketball, racquetball, softball, swimming, tennis, volleyball. **Team name:** Mustangs.

**Student services.** Campus ministries, career counseling, student employment services, financial aid counseling, health services, minority student services, on-campus daycare, personal counseling, placement for graduates. **Physically disabled:** Services for visually, speech, hearing impaired.

**Contact.** E-mail: tresslerd@wnmu.edu
Phone: (505) 538-6106 Toll-free number: (800) 872-9668
Fax: (505) 538-6127
Dan Tressler, Director of Admissions, Western New Mexico University, Castorena 106, Silver City, NM 88062

# New York

## Adelphi University

**Garden City, New York**
www.adelphi.edu

**CB member**
**CB code: 2003**

- Private 4-year university
- Commuter campus in large town
- 4,973 degree-seeking undergraduates: 16% part-time, 72% women, 14% African American, 6% Asian American, 8% Hispanic American, 4% international
- 3,156 degree-seeking graduate students
- 69% of applicants admitted
- SAT or ACT with writing, application essay required
- 63% graduate within 6 years; 40% enter graduate study

**General.** Founded in 1896. Regionally accredited. **Degrees:** 1,134 bachelor's, 5 associate awarded; master's, doctoral offered. **ROTC:** Army, Air Force. **Location:** 20 miles from New York City. **Calendar:** Semester, limited summer session. **Full-time faculty:** 283 total; 89% have terminal degrees, 19% minority, 50% women. **Part-time faculty:** 657 total; 17% minority, 69% women. **Class size:** 42% < 20, 52% 20-39, 4% 40-49, 2% 50-99. **Special facilities:** Speech and hearing center, science library, observatory, day care facility, arboretum.

**Freshman class profile.** 6,165 applied, 4,245 admitted, 894 enrolled.

| Mid 50% test scores | | Rank in top quarter: | 48% |
|---|---|---|---|
| SAT critical reading: | 480-580 | Rank in top tenth: | 20% |
| SAT math: | 490-590 | End year in good standing: | 92% |
| SAT writing: | 480-580 | Return as sophomores: | 81% |
| ACT composite: | 20-24 | Out-of-state: | 14% |
| GPA 3.50 or higher: | 39% | Live on campus: | 45% |
| GPA 3.0-3.49: | 36% | International: | 3% |
| GPA 2.0-2.99: | 24% | | |

**Basis for selection.** 2.5 cumulative GPA and SAT combined score of 900 (exclusive of Writing) or higher very important. Rank in top third of class, school and community activities, references also important. SAT/ACT scores accepted on rolling basis. SAT recommended for General Studies entrants, not required for adult academic programs in University College. Applicants to dance, drama, music, or art require audition and portfolio review, education majors must have 2.75 minimum GPA. Interview required for honors college applicants. **Homeschooled:** State high school equivalency certificate required. GED required if not receiving diploma from accredited high school or academy. **Learning Disabled:** Fee-based learning disability program where students receive academic and counseling support, requires admission: interview required, SAT recommended, WAIS-III, WJ-III required. Accommodations for learning disabled students not in program without cost, including accommodative testing, scribes, academic assistance.

**High school preparation.** 16 units recommended. Recommended units include English 4, mathematics 3, science 3 and foreign language 2. 4 additional units recommended in either social studies, history, English, math, science or foreign language.

**2007-2008 Annual costs.** Tuition/fees: $23,000. Tuition, fees, and per-credit-hour charges for upper-division nursing, social work, and education programs are slightly higher. Room/board: $9,900. Books/supplies: $1,000. Personal expenses: $1,000.

**2006-2007 Financial aid. Need-based:** 713 full-time freshmen applied for aid; 579 were judged to have need; 567 of these received aid. Average need met was 33%. Average scholarship/grant was $4,965; average loan $3,449. 48% of total undergraduate aid awarded as scholarships/grants, 52% as loans/jobs. **Non-need-based:** Awarded to 2,224 full-time undergraduates, including 339 freshmen. Scholarships awarded for academics, alumni affiliation, art, athletics, job skills, leadership, minority status, music/drama, religious affiliation.

**Application procedures. Admission:** No deadline. $35 fee, may be waived for applicants with need. Application may be submitted online. Admission notification on a rolling basis beginning on or about 10/1. **Financial aid:** Priority date 3/15; no closing date. FAFSA required. Applicants notified on a rolling basis starting 2/15.

**Academics. Special study options:** Accelerated study, combined bachelor's/graduate degree, cross-registration, distance learning, double major, dual enrollment of high school students, ESL, honors, independent study, internships, liberal arts/career combination, student-designed major, study abroad, teacher certification program, Washington semester, weekend college. Learning disabled program combining matriculation with support services, ABLE for adults 21 and over, 1-year intensive general studies program for freshmen with HS records/SAT scores that do not meet school standards; students who successfully complete program invited to enroll in other school programs in their sophomore year. **Credit/placement by examination:** AP, CLEP, IB. 30 credit hours maximum toward bachelor's degree. **Support services:** Learning center, pre-admission summer program, reduced course load, study skills assistance, tutoring, writing center.

**Honors college/program.** SAT, 3.5 GPA, evidence of academic or creative writing and interview required. 60-80 freshmen admitted.

**Majors. Area/ethnic studies:** Latin American. **Biology:** General, biochemistry. **Business:** Accounting, business admin, finance. **Communications:** Journalism, media studies. **Computer sciences:** General, information systems. **Conservation:** Environmental studies. **Education:** Art, health, physical, secondary. **English:** English lit. **Foreign languages:** French, Spanish. **Health:** Audiology/speech pathology, nursing (RN). **History:** General. **Interdisciplinary:** Global studies. **Liberal arts:** Humanities. **Math:** General. **Parks/recreation:** Health/fitness. **Philosophy/religion:** Philosophy. **Physical sciences:** Chemistry, physics. **Protective services:** Law enforcement admin. **Psychology:** General. **Public administration:** Social work. **Social sciences:** General, anthropology, economics, political science, sociology. **Visual/performing arts:** Art history/conservation, dance, dramatic, studio arts.

**Most popular majors.** Business/marketing 16%, health sciences 24%, interdisciplinary studies 12%, psychology 8%, social sciences 11%.

**Computing on campus.** 664 workstations in dormitories, library, computer center, student center, student center. Dormitories wired for high-speed internet access and linked to campus network. Commuter students can connect to campus network. Online course registration, online library, helpline, repair service, student web hosting, wireless network available.

**Student life. Freshman orientation:** Mandatory, $255 fee. Preregistration for classes offered. 3-day orientation held on Garden City campus. **Housing:** Coed dorms, special housing for disabled, substance-free housing available. $300 nonrefundable deposit, deadline 5/4. Special housing available for students in honors college, performing arts, and Excel Program. **Activities:** Bands, choral groups, dance, drama, film society, literary magazine, music ensembles, musical theater, radio station, student government, student newspaper, symphony orchestra, nearly 80 clubs and organizations.

**Athletics.** NCAA. **Intercollegiate:** Baseball M, basketball, bowling W, cross-country, golf M, lacrosse, soccer, softball W, swimming, tennis, track and field, volleyball W. **Intramural:** Badminton, basketball, cheerleading W, football (non-tackle), soccer, volleyball, weight lifting M. **Team name:** Panthers.

**Student services.** Adult student services, alcohol/substance abuse counseling, campus ministries, career counseling, student employment services, financial aid counseling, health services, minority student services, on-campus daycare, personal counseling, placement for graduates, veterans' counselor. **Physically disabled:** Services for visually, speech, hearing impaired. **Learning disabled:** Comprehensive services available.

**Contact.** E-mail: admissions@adelphi.edu
Phone: (516) 877-3050 Toll-free number: (800) 233-5744
Fax: (516) 877-3039
Christine Murphy, Director of Admissions, Adelphi University, One South Avenue, Levermore 110, Garden City, NY 11530-0701

## Albany College of Pharmacy
**Albany, New York**
www.acp.edu

**CB code: 2013**

- Private 4-year health science and pharmacy college
- Residential campus in small city
- 1,015 degree-seeking undergraduates: 58% women, 2% African American, 13% Asian American, 1% Hispanic American, 8% international
- 407 graduate students
- 54% of applicants admitted
- SAT or ACT with writing, application essay required
- 57% graduate within 6 years

**General.** Founded in 1881. Regionally accredited. **Degrees:** 3 bachelor's awarded; first professional offered. **ROTC:** Army, Naval, Air Force. **Location:** 200 miles from New York City. **Calendar:** Semester, limited summer session. **Full-time faculty:** 82 total; 74% have terminal degrees, 12% minority, 49% women. **Part-time faculty:** 21 total; 14% minority, 81% women. **Class size:** 31% < 20, 44% 20-39, 4% 40-49, 2% 50-99, 20% >100. **Special facilities:** Turn-of-the-century antique pharmacy.

**Freshman class profile.** 1,050 applied, 567 admitted, 243 enrolled.

| Mid 50% test scores | | Rank in top quarter: | 86% |
|---|---|---|---|
| SAT critical reading: | 530-620 | Rank in top tenth: | 47% |
| SAT math: | 570-650 | End year in good standing: | 81% |
| SAT writing: | 510-600 | Return as sophomores: | 79% |
| ACT composite: | 23-28 | Out-of-state: | 11% |
| GPA 3.50 or higher: | 82% | Live on campus: | 96% |
| GPA 3.0-3.49: | 18% | International: | 8% |

**Basis for selection.** High school record, test scores, essay, letters of recommendation, New York State Regents Examinations considered. Special emphasis on science and mathematics grades.

**High school preparation.** 15 units required; 20 recommended. Required and recommended units include English 4, mathematics 4, social studies 4, science 3-4 (laboratory 3-4) and foreign language 4.

**2007-2008 Annual costs.** Tuition/fees: $22,950. Fees include mandatory laptop purchase. Room/board: $7,300.

**2007-2008 Financial aid. Need-based:** 232 full-time freshmen applied for aid; 190 were judged to have need; 189 of these received aid. Average need met was 51.25%. Average scholarship/grant was $7,982; average loan $3,345. 28% of total undergraduate aid awarded as scholarships/grants, 72% as loans/jobs. **Non-need-based:** Awarded to 178 full-time undergraduates, including 70 freshmen. Scholarships awarded for academics.

**Application procedures. Admission:** Priority date 2/1; deadline 3/1 (postmark date). $75 fee, may be waived for applicants with need. Application must be submitted online. Admission notification 3/15. Must reply by 5/1. **Financial aid:** Priority date 2/1, closing date 3/1. FAFSA required. Applicants notified on a rolling basis starting 3/25; must reply within 2 week(s) of notification.

**Academics. Special study options:** Accelerated study, combined bachelor's/graduate degree, cross-registration, internships. **Credit/placement by examination:** AP, CLEP. 30 credit hours maximum toward bachelor's degree. **Support services:** Study skills assistance, tutoring, writing center.

**Majors. Health:** Clinical lab science, cytotechnology, health services, pharmaceutical sciences.

**Computing on campus.** PC or laptop required. 30 workstations in library. Dormitories wired for high-speed internet access and linked to campus network. Commuter students can connect to campus network. Online library, helpline, repair service, wireless network available.

**Student life. Freshman orientation:** Mandatory, $250 fee. Usually held over first weekend prior to class start. **Policies:** College observes honor code. Residency required in first 2 years of study except for students living within 30-mile radius of campus. **Housing:** Guaranteed on-campus for freshmen. Coed dorms, substance-free housing available. $200 nonrefundable deposit, deadline 6/1. **Activities:** Concert band, choral groups, dance, literary magazine, student government, student newspaper, Academy of Student Pharmacists, student pharmaceutical society of state of NY, Phi Lambda Sigma.

**Athletics. Intercollegiate:** Basketball, soccer. **Intramural:** Basketball, football (non-tackle), tennis, volleyball. **Team name:** Panthers.

**Student services.** Alcohol/substance abuse counseling, campus ministries, career counseling, student employment services, financial aid counseling, health services, minority student services, personal counseling, placement for graduates.

**Contact.** E-mail: admissions@acp.edu
Phone: (518) 694-7221 Toll-free number: (888) 203-8010
Fax: (518) 694-7322
Carly Connors, Director of Admissions, Albany College of Pharmacy, 106 New Scotland Avenue, Albany, NY 12208-3492

---

**Alfred University**
**Alfred, New York**
www.alfred.edu

**CB member**
**CB code: 2005**

▶ Private 4-year university
▶ Residential campus in rural community

---

▶ 1,955 degree-seeking undergraduates
▶ 406 graduate students
▶ 74% of applicants admitted
▶ SAT or ACT (ACT writing optional), application essay required
▶ 64% graduate within 6 years; 31% enter graduate study

**General.** Founded in 1836. Regionally accredited. **Degrees:** 403 bachelor's awarded; master's, doctoral offered. **ROTC:** Army. **Location:** 75 miles from Rochester, 65 miles from Elmira. **Calendar:** Semester, limited summer session. **Full-time faculty:** 172 total; 44% women. **Part-time faculty:** 39 total; 31% women. **Class size:** 61% < 20, 33% 20-39, 2% 40-49, 4% 50-99, less than 1% >100. **Special facilities:** Observatory, carillon, 3 art galleries, library of ceramics, ceramics museum, equestrian center, Foster Lake.

**Freshman class profile.** 2,355 applied, 1,736 admitted, 518 enrolled.

| Mid 50% test scores | | Rank in top tenth: | 18% |
|---|---|---|---|
| SAT critical reading: | 490-610 | Return as sophomores: | 79% |
| SAT math: | 500-620 | Out-of-state: | 30% |
| ACT composite: | 22-27 | Live on campus: | 95% |
| Rank in top quarter: | 46% | | |

**Basis for selection.** Rigor of high school curriculum, grades, class rank, standardized ACT or SAT test results, extracurricular involvement, letters of recommendation, and character all factors. International students may submit TOEFL in lieu of SAT or ACT. Interview recommended. Portfolio required for students seeking admission to School of Art & Design. **Homeschooled:** Advise students to document courses taken and provide reading list. SAT or ACT mandatory and relied on heavily.

**High school preparation.** 16 units required. Required units include English 4, mathematics 2, social studies 2, science 2 (laboratory 2). 3-4 math for business college, 2-3 math for liberal arts and science college, 2 math for art and design college, 4 math for engineering school.

**2008-2009 Annual costs.** Tuition/fees: $24,278. Tuition info provided is for students enrolling in the College of Business or the College of Liberal Arts and Sciences. Costs for students enrolling in the School of Engineering vary by program and/or residency. Costs for students enrolling in the School of Art and Design vary by residency. Room/board: $10,796. Books/supplies: $900. Personal expenses: $500.

**2006-2007 Financial aid. Need-based:** 428 full-time freshmen applied for aid; 365 were judged to have need; 364 of these received aid. Average need met was 89%. Average scholarship/grant was $15,390; average loan $4,243. 73% of total undergraduate aid awarded as scholarships/grants, 27% as loans/jobs. **Non-need-based:** Awarded to 904 full-time undergraduates, including 254 freshmen. Scholarships awarded for academics, art, leadership, music/drama.

**Application procedures. Admission:** Priority date 2/1; no deadline. $40 fee, may be waived for applicants with need. Application may be submitted online. Admission notification on a rolling basis beginning on or about 11/15. Must reply by May 1 or within 2 week(s) if notified thereafter. **Financial aid:** Priority date 2/1, closing date 3/15. FAFSA, institutional form required. Applicants notified on a rolling basis starting 2/15; must reply by 5/1 or within 2 week(s) of notification.

**Academics.** Credit hours required for graduation vary from 120-138 depending on the major. There is a physical education requirement for all students. Additional graduation requirements vary by college. Preadmission summer program is required for students enrolling at AU through Opportunity Programs (EOP or HEOP). **Special study options:** Combined bachelor's/graduate degree, cooperative education, cross-registration, double major, ESL, exchange student, honors, independent study, internships, liberal arts/career combination, New York semester, semester at sea, student-designed major, study abroad, teacher certification program, United Nations semester, Washington semester. **Credit/placement by examination:** AP, CLEP, IB, SAT, ACT, institutional tests. **Support services:** Reduced course load, study skills assistance, tutoring, writing center.

**Majors. Biology:** General. **Business:** Accounting, business admin, finance, marketing. **Communications:** General. **Conservation:** Environmental studies. **Education:** Art, biology, business, chemistry, elementary, English, French, mathematics, middle, physics, social studies, Spanish. **Engineering:** Biomedical, ceramic, electrical, materials, materials science, mechanical. **English:** English lit. **Foreign languages:** French, German, Spanish. **Health:** Athletic training, clinical lab technology, predental, premedicine, preveterinary. **History:** General. **Interdisciplinary:** Biological/physical sciences, gerontology, intercultural. **Liberal arts:** Arts/sciences. **Math:** General. **Philosophy/religion:** Philosophy. **Physical sciences:** Chemistry, geology, physics. **Protective services:** Criminal justice. **Psychology:** General. **Social sciences:** Economics, political science, sociology. **Visual/performing arts:** Ceramics, dramatic, studio arts. **Other:** Glass Science Engineering.

**Most popular majors.** Business/marketing 11%, engineering/engineering technologies 15%, psychology 10%, visual/performing arts 32%.

**Computing on campus.** 450 workstations in dormitories, library, computer center, student center. Dormitories wired for high-speed internet access and linked to campus network. Commuter students can connect to campus network. Online course registration, online library, helpline, student web hosting, wireless network available.

**Student life. Freshman orientation:** Mandatory. Preregistration for classes offered. Starts the Wednesday before classes begin. Combination of academic and nonacademic activities to acclimate students to life on campus. **Policies:** Students must abide by Code of Honor. Policies against hazing and sexual harassment. All students required to live in residence halls 6 semesters. Students in poor academic standing required to live on campus. Exceptions granted for married students, students 23 and older, students living with parents/legal guardian and commuting from home, students with dependents, and veterans. **Housing:** Guaranteed on-campus for freshmen. Coed dorms, apartments, substance-free housing available. $300 nonrefundable deposit, deadline 5/1. Theme housing available (honors, language house, outdoor sports). **Activities:** Bands, choral groups, dance, drama, film society, literary magazine, music ensembles, musical theater, radio station, student government, student newspaper, symphony orchestra, TV station, Hillel, Brothers and Sisters in Christ, Spectrum, Student Volunteers for Community Action, Alpha Phi Omega, Habitat for Humanity, Christian fellowship, women's issues coalition.

**Athletics.** NCAA. **Intercollegiate:** Basketball, cross-country, diving, equestrian, football (tackle) M, lacrosse, skiing, soccer, softball W, swimming, tennis, track and field, volleyball W. **Intramural:** Basketball, football (non-tackle), lacrosse M, racquetball, skiing, soccer, softball, squash, tennis, volleyball. **Team name:** Saxons.

**Student services.** Alcohol/substance abuse counseling, campus ministries, career counseling, services for economically disadvantaged, student employment services, financial aid counseling, health services, minority student services, personal counseling, placement for graduates, women's services. **Physically disabled:** Services for visually, speech, hearing impaired.

**Contact.** E-mail: admissions@alfred.edu
Phone: (607) 871-2115 Toll-free number: (800) 541-9229
Fax: (607) 871-2198
Jeremy Spencer, Director of Admissions, Alfred University, Alumni Hall, Alfred, NY 14802-1205

---

## Bard College
**Annandale-on-Hudson, New York**  **CB member**
**www.bard.edu**  **CB code: 2037**

- Private 4-year liberal arts college affiliated with Episcopal Church
- Residential campus in small town
- 1,737 degree-seeking undergraduates: 3% part-time, 56% women, 2% African American, 3% Asian American, 3% Hispanic American, 1% Native American, 9% international
- 261 degree-seeking graduate students
- 27% of applicants admitted
- Application essay required
- 77% graduate within 6 years

**General.** Founded in 1860. Regionally accredited. **Degrees:** 334 bachelor's, 142 associate awarded; master's, doctoral offered. **Location:** 90 miles from New York City, 50 miles from Albany. **Calendar:** Semester. **Full-time faculty:** 140 total; 96% have terminal degrees, 16% minority, 44% women. **Part-time faculty:** 110 total; 89% have terminal degrees, 22% minority, 46% women. **Class size:** 72% < 20, 27% 20-39, less than 1% 40-49. **Special facilities:** Ecology field station contiguous to Hudson River Estuary Preserves; curatorial studies and art center; museum of late 20th-century art; archaeological field school; economics institute; center for studies in decorative arts, design and culture; Frank Gehry-designed performing arts center; Rafael Vinoly-designed science center.

**Freshman class profile.** 4,980 applied, 1,350 admitted, 491 enrolled.

| Mid 50% test scores | | Return as sophomores: | 88% |
|---|---|---|---|
| SAT critical reading: | 680-740 | Out-of-state: | 73% |
| SAT math: | 640-690 | Live on campus: | 99% |
| Rank in top quarter: | 85% | International: | 9% |
| Rank in top tenth: | 63% | | |

**Basis for selection.** School transcripts and achievement record, rigor of high school program, essays, academic recommendations, talents and dedication to activities, love of learning, and personal ambition important. Campus tour and information session recommended. Tape or CD, brief musical

autobiography, and audition required of conservatory applicants. **Home-schooled:** Statement describing homeschool structure and mission, transcript of courses and grades required.

**High school preparation.** 24 units recommended. Recommended units include English 4, mathematics 4, social studies 4, history 4, science 4 (laboratory 3) and foreign language 4.

**2008-2009 Annual costs.** Tuition/fees: $38,374. Fees for first-year students only: $230 security deposit and ID card; $650 for meals for Language and Thinking workshop. Room/board: $10,866. Books/supplies: $850. Personal expenses: $600.

**2007-2008 Financial aid. Need-based:** 322 full-time freshmen applied for aid; 290 were judged to have need; 290 of these received aid. Average need met was 89%. Average scholarship/grant was $25,971; average loan $3,721. 77% of total undergraduate aid awarded as scholarships/grants, 23% as loans/jobs. **Non-need-based:** Awarded to 56 full-time undergraduates, including 6 freshmen. Scholarships awarded for academics. **Additional information:** Excellence and Equal Cost Program for students who graduate in top 10 of public high school class lowers fees to levels equivalent to those at home state university or college.

**Application procedures. Admission:** Closing date 1/15 (receipt date). $50 fee, may be waived for applicants with need. Application must be submitted on paper. Admission notification 4/1. Must reply by May 1 or within 2 week(s) if notified thereafter. Applicants may be admitted through early action, regular procedure, or Immediate Decision Plan, which gives next-day decision after day-long program and individual interview. Sessions scheduled in early fall. **Financial aid:** Priority date 2/1, closing date 2/15. FAFSA, CSS PROFILE required. Applicants notified by 4/1; must reply by 5/1.

**Academics.** Strong tradition of independent study and tutorial work with faculty member. Writing-intensive, multidisciplinary programs. Extensive programs in languages, human rights and globalization and international affairs. Unique collaboration with The Rockefeller University. **Special study options:** Combined bachelor's/graduate degree, cross-registration, double major, dual enrollment of high school students, ESL, independent study, internships, New York semester, student-designed major, study abroad, Washington semester. Intensive language studies in Italy, Germany, France, Mexico, Russia, China, program in International Education (Central and Eastern Europe and Southern Africa). **Credit/placement by examination:** AP, CLEP, IB. **Support services:** Learning center, reduced course load, remedial instruction, study skills assistance, tutoring, writing center.

**Majors. Area/ethnic studies:** African, American, Asian, French, German, Italian, Latin American, Near/Middle Eastern, Russian/Slavic, Spanish/Iberian. **Biology:** General. **Computer sciences:** Computer science. **English:** American lit, British lit, creative writing, English lit. **Foreign languages:** General, ancient Greek, Arabic, Chinese, comparative lit, French, German, Hebrew, Italian, Japanese, Latin, Russian, Sanskrit, Spanish, translation. **Health:** Premedicine. **History:** General, American, Asian, European. **Interdisciplinary:** Global studies, medieval/Renaissance, neuroscience. **Legal studies:** Prelaw. **Liberal arts:** Arts/sciences. **Math:** General. **Philosophy/religion:** Judaic, philosophy, religion. **Physical sciences:** Chemistry, physics. **Psychology:** General. **Social sciences:** General, anthropology, archaeology, economics, political science, sociology. **Visual/performing arts:** General, acting, art history/conservation, cinematography, conducting, dance, directing/producing, dramatic, film/cinema, jazz, multimedia, music history, music performance, music theory/composition, photography, piano/organ, play/screenwriting, stringed instruments, studio arts, theater history, voice/opera. **Other:** Gender and Sexuality, Human Rights.

**Most popular majors.** English 14%, foreign language 8%, history 6%, psychology 6%, social sciences 19%, visual/performing arts 27%.

**Computing on campus.** 425 workstations in library, computer center, student center. Dormitories wired for high-speed internet access and linked to campus network. Commuter students can connect to campus network. Online course registration, online library, helpline, student web hosting, wireless network available.

**Student life. Freshman orientation:** Mandatory, $550 fee. 3-week writing-intensive Workshop in Language and Thinking held on campus in August immediately prior to fall semester; coincides with Bard Music Festival. **Policies:** All students members of the student government association, a democratic forum that allocates funds, takes action on campus issues, and provides student representation on administrative and faculty committees. **Housing:** Guaranteed on-campus for freshmen. Coed dorms, single-sex dorms, cooperative housing, substance-free housing available. Pets allowed in dorm rooms. **Activities:** Bands, campus ministries, choral groups, dance, drama, film society, international student organizations, literary magazine, music ensembles, Model UN, musical theater, opera, radio station, student government, student newspaper, symphony orchestra, over 120 organizations available.

**Athletics.** NCAA. **Intercollegiate:** Basketball, cross-country, soccer, squash M, tennis, track and field, volleyball. **Intramural:** Basketball, soccer, softball, squash. **Team name:** Raptors.

**Student services.** Adult student services, alcohol/substance abuse counseling, campus ministries, career counseling, services for economically disadvantaged, student employment services, financial aid counseling, health services, legal services, minority student services, personal counseling, placement for graduates, women's services. **Physically disabled:** Services for visually, hearing impaired.

**Contact.** E-mail: admissions@bard.edu
Phone: (845) 758-7472 Fax: (845) 758-5208
Mary Backlund, Director of Admission, Bard College, 30 Campus Road, Annandale-on-Hudson, NY 12504-5000

## Barnard College
**New York, New York**  **CB member**
**www.barnard.edu**  **CB code: 2038**

- Private 4-year liberal arts college for women
- Residential campus in very large city
- 2,346 degree-seeking undergraduates: 2% part-time, 100% women, 5% African American, 16% Asian American, 9% Hispanic American, 4% international
- 29% of applicants admitted
- SAT and SAT Subject Tests or ACT with writing, application essay required
- 89% graduate within 6 years

**General.** Founded in 1889. Regionally accredited. Cross-registration and shared facilities with Columbia University. Students receive Columbia University degrees. **Degrees:** 597 bachelor's awarded. **Calendar:** Semester. **Full-time faculty:** 198 total; 92% have terminal degrees, 17% minority, 61% women. **Part-time faculty:** 127 total; 86% have terminal degrees, 10% minority, 71% women. **Class size:** 71% < 20, 16% 20-39, 5% 40-49, 6% 50-99, 2% >100. **Special facilities:** Center for toddler development, center for research on women, theater, dance studios, access to 3600-acre nature preserve in upstate New York, greenhouse, access to geological observatory.

**Freshman class profile.** 4,574 applied, 1,315 admitted, 559 enrolled.

| Mid 50% test scores | | | |
|---|---|---|---|
| SAT critical reading: | 640-740 | Rank in top quarter: | 94% |
| SAT math: | 620-700 | Rank in top tenth: | 75% |
| SAT writing: | 650-730 | Return as sophomores: | 95% |
| ACT composite: | 28-31 | Out-of-state: | 70% |
| GPA 3.50 or higher: | 89% | Live on campus: | 99% |
| GPA 3.0-3.49: | 10% | International: | 4% |
| GPA 2.0-2.99: | 1% | | |

**Basis for selection.** High school record most important. Depth and difficulty of high school program considered. Test scores, recommendations, involvement in school and community activities, special talents, skills considered. Interview recommended.

**High school preparation.** 16 units recommended. Recommended units include English 4, mathematics 3, science 3 (laboratory 2) and foreign language 3. Additional units in social sciences, art, music also recommended.

**2007-2008 Annual costs.** Tuition/fees: $35,190. Room/board: $11,546.

**2007-2008 Financial aid.** All financial aid based on need. 312 full-time freshmen applied for aid; 248 were judged to have need; 248 of these received aid. Average need met was 100%. Average scholarship/grant was $29,509; average loan $3,052. 86% of total undergraduate aid awarded as scholarships/grants, 14% as loans/jobs.

**Application procedures. Admission:** Closing date 1/1 (postmark date). $55 fee, may be waived for applicants with need. Application must be submitted on paper. Admission notification 4/1. Must reply by May 1 or within 2 week(s) if notified thereafter. **Financial aid:** Closing date 2/1. FAFSA, institutional form, CSS PROFILE required. Applicants notified by 3/31; must reply by 5/1.

**Academics.** Interdisciplinary first year seminar mandatory. Coursework in global cultures, which may also fulfill other degree requirements, is mandatory. **Special study options:** Accelerated study, combined bachelor's/graduate degree, cross-registration, double major, dual enrollment of high school students, exchange student, honors, independent study, internships, liberal arts/career combination, student-designed major, study abroad, teacher certification program. Independent scholars program, BA/BS in engineering and applied science. **Credit/placement by examination:** AP, CLEP, IB, institutional tests. 30 credit hours maximum toward bachelor's degree. **Support services:** Pre-admission summer program, tutoring, writing center.

**Majors. Architecture:** Architecture, history/criticism. **Area/ethnic studies:** African, American, Asian, European, French, German, Latin American, Near/Middle Eastern, Russian/Slavic, Slavic, Spanish/Iberian, women's. **Biology:** General, biochemistry, biophysics, environmental. **Computer sciences:** General, computer science. **Conservation:** Environmental science, environmental studies. **Engineering:** Physics. **English:** English lit. **Foreign languages:** Ancient Greek, classics, comparative lit, French, German, Italian, Latin, linguistics, modern Greek, Russian, Spanish. **History:** General. **Interdisciplinary:** Ancient studies, biopsychology, medieval/Renaissance. **Math:** General, applied, statistics. **Philosophy/religion:** Philosophy, religion. **Physical sciences:** Astronomy, astrophysics, chemical physics, chemistry, geology, physics. **Psychology:** General. **Social sciences:** Anthropology, economics, geography, political science, sociology, urban studies. **Visual/performing arts:** General, art history/conservation, dance, dramatic, film/cinema, jazz.

**Most popular majors.** Area/ethnic studies 11%, English 11%, foreign language 6%, history 6%, psychology 15%, social sciences 25%, visual/performing arts 11%.

**Computing on campus.** 208 workstations in dormitories, library, computer center, student center. Dormitories wired for high-speed internet access and linked to campus network. Commuter students can connect to campus network. Online course registration, online library, helpline, repair service, wireless network available.

**Student life. Freshman orientation:** Mandatory, $275 fee. 8-day program. **Housing:** Guaranteed on-campus for all undergraduates. Special housing for disabled, apartments, substance-free housing available. $400 nonrefundable deposit, deadline 6/15. Coed dorms available through Columbia University. **Activities:** Bands, campus ministries, choral groups, dance, drama, film society, literary magazine, music ensembles, musical theater, opera, radio station, student government, student newspaper, symphony orchestra, TV station, more than 100 organizations.

**Athletics.** NCAA. **Intercollegiate:** Archery W, basketball W, cross-country W, diving W, fencing W, field hockey W, golf W, lacrosse W, rowing (crew) W, soccer W, softball W, swimming W, tennis W, track and field W, volleyball W. **Intramural:** Archery W, badminton W, basketball W, bowling W, cross-country W, fencing W, racquetball W, sailing W, soccer W, softball W, swimming W, tennis W, volleyball W. **Team name:** Lions.

**Student services.** Alcohol/substance abuse counseling, career counseling, student employment services, financial aid counseling, health services, personal counseling, placement for graduates, women's services. **Physically disabled:** Services for visually, speech, hearing impaired.

**Contact.** E-mail: admissions@barnard.edu
Phone: (212) 854-2014 Fax: (212) 854-6220
Jennifer Fondiller, Dean of Admissions, Barnard College, 3009 Broadway, New York, NY 10027-6598

## Beis Medrash Heichal Dovid
**Far Rockaway, New York**

- Private 4-year rabbinical college for men affiliated with Jewish faith
- Large city

**General.** Accredited by AARTS. **Calendar:** Semester.

**Contact.** Phone: (718) 868-2300 ext. 360
Registrar, 257 Beach 17th Street, Far Rockaway, NY 11691

## Berkeley College
**White Plains, New York**
**www.berkeleycollege.edu**  **CB code: 2064**

- For-profit 4-year business college
- Commuter campus in small city
- 704 degree-seeking undergraduates: 7% part-time, 68% women, 27% African American, 3% Asian American, 25% Hispanic American, 7% international

**General.** Founded in 1945. Regionally accredited. **Degrees:** 89 bachelor's, 30 associate awarded. **Location:** 28 miles from New York City. **Calendar:** Quarter, extensive summer session. **Full-time faculty:** 21 total. **Part-time faculty:** 14 total. **Special facilities:** Access to Manhattanville College facilities.

**Freshman class profile.**

| | | | |
|---|---|---|---|
| Return as sophomores: | 52% | International: | 4% |
| Out-of-state: | 18% | | |

**Basis for selection.** Class rank, high school record, interview most important. Passing grade on school entrance examination required. SAT/ACT considered if submitted. Interviews strongly recommended.

**2008-2009 Annual costs.** Tuition/fees: $19,050. Part-time students pay $75 administrative fee per quarter. Room/board: $9,000. Books/supplies: $1,300.

**Financial aid. Non-need-based:** Scholarships awarded for academics, alumni affiliation. **Additional information:** Alumni scholarship examination given in November and December. Full and partial scholarships awarded.

**Application procedures. Admission:** No deadline. $50 fee. Application may be submitted online. Admission notification on a rolling basis. Admitted applicants must reply within 2 weeks of notification. **Financial aid:** No deadline. FAFSA required. Applicants notified on a rolling basis starting 3/1; must reply within 6 week(s) of notification.

**Academics. Special study options:** Accelerated study, cooperative education, distance learning, ESL, internships, New York semester, study abroad. **Credit/placement by examination:** AP, CLEP, SAT, ACT, institutional tests. **Support services:** Learning center, remedial instruction, study skills assistance, tutoring.

**Majors. Business:** General, accounting, business admin, e-commerce, fashion, international, marketing, office management. **Health:** Health care admin.

**Computing on campus.** 150 workstations in library, computer center. Dormitories linked to campus network. Commuter students can connect to campus network. Online library, helpline, wireless network available.

**Student life. Freshman orientation:** Mandatory. **Housing:** Coed dorms available. $400 fully refundable deposit. **Activities:** Student government, student newspaper, accounting club, Berkeley club, Phi Beta Lambda, Phi Theta Kappa, international club, fashion club, paralegal club.

**Athletics. Intramural:** Basketball, softball, volleyball. **Team name:** Bulldogs.

**Student services.** Adult student services, career counseling, student employment services, financial aid counseling, personal counseling, placement for graduates.

**Contact.** E-mail: admissions@berkeleycollege.edu
Phone: (914) 694-1122 Toll-free number: (800) 446-5400
Fax: (914) 328-9469
Giselle Rivera, Director, High School Admissions, Berkeley College, 99 Church Street, White Plains, NY 10601

## Berkeley College of New York City
New York, New York
www.berkeleycollege.edu                    CB code: 0954

- For-profit 4-year business college
- Commuter campus in very large city
- 2,595 degree-seeking undergraduates: 10% part-time, 69% women, 23% African American, 4% Asian American, 24% Hispanic American, 1% Native American, 18% international
- 75% of applicants admitted

**General.** Founded in 1936. Regionally accredited. **Degrees:** 311 bachelor's, 170 associate awarded. **Location:** Midtown Manhattan. **Calendar:** Quarter, extensive summer session. **Full-time faculty:** 73 total. **Part-time faculty:** 103 total.

**Freshman class profile.** 2,412 applied, 1,799 admitted, 354 enrolled.

| Return as sophomores: | 52% | **International:** | 14% |
|---|---|---|---|
| **Out-of-state:** | 11% | | |

**Basis for selection.** High school record and interview most important. Institutional entrance tests required of all applicants. SAT or ACT accepted in lieu of institutional entrance exam.

**2008-2009 Annual costs.** Tuition/fees: $19,050. Part-time students pay $75 administrative fee per quarter. Books/supplies: $1,300.

**Financial aid. Non-need-based:** Scholarships awarded for academics, alumni affiliation. **Additional information:** Alumni scholarship examination given in November and December. Full and partial scholarships awarded.

**Application procedures. Admission:** No deadline. $50 fee. Application may be submitted online. Admission notification on a rolling basis.

Admitted applicants must reply within 2 weeks of notification. **Financial aid:** No deadline. FAFSA required. Applicants notified on a rolling basis starting 3/1; must reply within 6 week(s) of notification.

**Academics. Special study options:** Accelerated study, distance learning, ESL, internships, study abroad. **Credit/placement by examination:** AP, CLEP, SAT, ACT, institutional tests. **Support services:** Learning center, remedial instruction, study skills assistance, tutoring, writing center.

**Majors. Business:** General, accounting, business admin, fashion, international, marketing, office management. **Protective services:** Criminal justice.

**Computing on campus.** 200 workstations in library, computer center. Commuter students can connect to campus network. Online library, wireless network available.

**Student life. Freshman orientation:** Mandatory. **Housing:** $400 deposit. **Activities:** Student government, international club, multicultural club, fashion club, accounting club, paralegal club, student government.

**Athletics. Team name:** Bulldogs.

**Student services.** Adult student services, alcohol/substance abuse counseling, career counseling, student employment services, financial aid counseling, personal counseling, placement for graduates.

**Contact.** E-mail: admissions@berkeleycollege.edu
Phone: (212) 986-4343 Toll-free number: (800) 446-5400
Fax: (212) 818-1079
Linda Pinsky, Director of High School Admissions, Berkeley College of New York City, 3 East 43rd Street, New York, NY 10017

## Beth Hamedrash Shaarei Yosher Institute
Brooklyn, New York
CB code: 0731

- Private 5-year rabbinical college for men affiliated with Jewish faith
- Very large city

**General.** Founded in 1962. Accredited by AARTS. **Calendar:** Semester.

**Annual costs/financial aid.** Tuition/fees (2007-2008): $6,010. Room/board: $1,200. Personal expenses: $2,000.

**Contact.** Phone: (718) 854-2290
Director of Student Financial Aid, 4102-10 16th Avenue, Brooklyn, NY 11204

## Beth Hatalmud Rabbinical College
Brooklyn, New York
CB code: 7317

- Private 4-year rabbinical college for men affiliated with Jewish faith
- Very large city

**General.** Founded in 1950. Accredited by AARTS. **Calendar:** Semester.

**Contact.** Phone: (718) 259-2525
Director of Admissions, 2127 82nd Street, Brooklyn, NY 11214

## Boricua College
New York, New York
www.boricuacollege.edu                    CB code: 2901

- Private 4-year liberal arts college
- Commuter campus in very large city
- 1,004 degree-seeking undergraduates
- 54 graduate students
- 40% of applicants admitted
- Application essay, interview required
- 43% graduate within 6 years

**General.** Founded in 1974. Regionally accredited. Two centers in Brooklyn and one annex in the Bronx. **Degrees:** 190 bachelor's, 192 associate awarded; master's offered. **Calendar:** Semester, limited summer session. **Full-time faculty:** 58 total; 100% have terminal degrees, 36% women. **Part-time faculty:** 76 total; 100% have terminal degrees. **Class size:** 100% >100.

**Freshman class profile.** 924 applied, 369 admitted, 235 enrolled.

**Basis for selection.** Entrance examination, academic records, interview by the faculty, 2 letters of recommendation. Institutional tests required for admissions and placement. Final interview and approval by the faculty is required. **Learning Disabled:** Evaluation is done based on individual needs of the candidate.

**2007-2008 Annual costs.** Tuition/fees: $9,225. Books/supplies: $450. Personal expenses: $844.

**Application procedures. Admission:** No deadline. $25 fee, may be waived for applicants with need. Admission notification on a rolling basis. **Financial aid:** Priority date 4/30; no closing date. Applicants notified on a rolling basis; must reply within 3 week(s) of notification.

**Academics.** Academic load consists of 5 courses per semester: 3 applied studies courses (individualized instruction, colloquium, experiential), 1 theoretical, and 1 cultural class. Academic support services are available at different hours upon request. **Special study options:** Accelerated study, independent study, internships, liberal arts/career combination, teacher certification program. **Credit/placement by examination:** CLEP, IB, institutional tests. 30 credit hours maximum toward bachelor's degree. **Support services:** Reduced course load, tutoring.

**Majors. Area/ethnic studies:** Latin American. **Business:** Business admin. **Education:** Elementary. **Liberal arts:** Arts/sciences. **Public administration:** Human services.

**Computing on campus.** 120 workstations in library, computer center, student center. Online library, helpline, wireless network available.

**Student life. Freshman orientation:** Mandatory. Preregistration for classes offered. Based on appointments. **Policies:** Student regulations include a sexual harassment policy. **Activities:** Choral groups, dance, drama, opera, student government, student newspaper.

**Athletics. Intramural:** Basketball, volleyball.

**Student services.** Adult student services, career counseling, student employment services, personal counseling, placement for graduates.

**Contact.** E-mail: acruz@boricuacollege.edu
Phone: (212) 694-1000 ext. 650 Fax: (212) 694-1015
Abraham Cruz, Director of Admissions, Boricua College, 3755 Broadway, New York, NY 10032

---

## Briarcliffe College
**Bethpage, New York**
www.briarcliffe.edu                              **CB code: 3108**

- For-profit 4-year business and technical college
- Commuter campus in large town
- 1,990 degree-seeking undergraduates

**General.** Founded in 1966. Regionally accredited. **Degrees:** 350 bachelor's, 574 associate awarded. **Location:** 20 miles from New York City. **Calendar:** Semester, extensive summer session. **Full-time faculty:** 77 total. **Part-time faculty:** 147 total. **Class size:** 60% < 20, 39% 20-39, less than 1% 40-49.

**Basis for selection.** School achievement record important, recommendations suggested. Interviews recommended. **Homeschooled:** Not accepted.

**High school preparation.** Recommended units include English 4, mathematics 2, social studies 4 and science 1.

**2007-2008 Annual costs.** Tuition/fees: $15,979.

**Financial aid. Non-need-based:** Scholarships awarded for academics.

**Application procedures. Admission:** No deadline. $35 fee. Application may be submitted online. Admission notification on a rolling basis. **Financial aid:** No deadline. FAFSA, institutional form required. Applicants notified on a rolling basis.

**Academics. Special study options:** Independent study, internships, study abroad. 4-year BFA program with concentration in graphic design available. **Credit/placement by examination:** CLEP, institutional tests. 15 credit hours maximum toward associate degree, 15 toward bachelor's. **Support services:** Learning center, reduced course load, remedial instruction, study skills assistance, tutoring.

**Majors. Business:** Accounting, business admin, marketing. **Computer sciences:** Information technology, networking, programming. **Visual/performing arts:** General.

**Computing on campus.** 400 workstations in library, computer center. Commuter students can connect to campus network. Online library available.

**Student life. Freshman orientation:** Mandatory. Preregistration for classes offered. **Housing:** Single-sex dorms available. **Activities:** Student government, student newspaper.

**Athletics.** USCAA. **Intercollegiate:** Baseball M, basketball, bowling, lacrosse M; soccer M, softball W, volleyball W. **Team name:** Seahawks.

**Student services.** Financial aid counseling, placement for graduates.

**Contact.** E-mail: info@bcl.edu
Phone: (516) 918-3600 Fax: (516) 470-6020
Alan Shikowitz, Director of Admissions, Briarcliffe College, 1055 Stewart Avenue, Bethpage, NY 11714

---

## Canisius College
**Buffalo, New York**                              **CB member**
www.canisius.edu                              **CB code: 2073**

- Private 4-year liberal arts and teachers college affiliated with Roman Catholic Church
- Residential campus in large city
- 3,301 degree-seeking undergraduates: 3% part-time, 55% women, 6% African American, 1% Asian American, 2% Hispanic American, 3% international
- 1,491 degree-seeking graduate students
- 79% of applicants admitted
- SAT or ACT (ACT writing optional) required
- 65% graduate within 6 years

**General.** Founded in 1870. Regionally accredited. Campus connected by underground tunnel system, rapid transit stations near campus. **Degrees:** 926 bachelor's, 8 associate awarded; master's offered. **ROTC:** Army. **Calendar:** Semester, limited summer session. **Full-time faculty:** 213 total; 95% have terminal degrees, 7% minority, 39% women. **Part-time faculty:** 272 total; 19% have terminal degrees, 4% minority, 48% women. **Class size:** 42% < 20, 50% 20-39, 6% 40-49, less than 1% 50-99. **Special facilities:** Mini-planetarium, seismograph station, rare book room, digital media lab, human performance lab, animal care unit.

**Freshman class profile.** 3,695 applied, 2,914 admitted, 846 enrolled.

| Mid 50% test scores | | | |
|---|---|---|---|
| SAT critical reading: | 490-590 | Rank in top quarter: | 52% |
| SAT math: | 500-600 | Rank in top tenth: | 25% |
| ACT composite: | 22-27 | Return as sophomores: | 81% |
| GPA 3.50 or higher: | 47% | Out-of-state: | 8% |
| GPA 3.0-3.49: | 31% | Live on campus: | 75% |
| GPA 2.0-2.99: | 22% | International: | 2% |

**Basis for selection.** Primary emphasis placed on strength of academic record, achievement, class rank and SAT/ACT scores. Essays, recommendations important. Extracurricular activities, alumni affiliation factors. Interview and essay recommended.

**High school preparation.** 23 units recommended. Required and recommended units include English 4, mathematics 3, social studies 4, science 2-3 (laboratory 2), foreign language 2-3 and academic electives 4.

**2007-2008 Annual costs.** Tuition/fees: $26,427. Room/board: $9,770.

**2007-2008 Financial aid. Need-based:** 771 full-time freshmen applied for aid; 710 were judged to have need; 710 of these received aid. Average need met was 88.7%. Average scholarship/grant was $18,196; average loan $3,501. 72% of total undergraduate aid awarded as scholarships/grants, 28% as loans/jobs. **Non-need-based:** Awarded to 1,233 full-time undergraduates, including 299 freshmen. Scholarships awarded for academics, alumni affiliation, art, athletics, job skills, music/drama, religious affiliation, ROTC.

**Application procedures. Admission:** Priority date 3/1; deadline 5/1. $40 fee, may be waived for applicants with need. Application may be submitted online. Admission notification on a rolling basis beginning on or about 12/15. Must reply by 5/1. **Financial aid:** Priority date 2/15; no closing date. FAFSA required. Applicants notified on a rolling basis starting 3/1; must reply within 2 week(s) of notification.

**Academics.** Pre-professional programs include pre-engineering, prelaw, premedical, predentistry, preveterinary medicine, prepharmacy. **Special study options:** Combined bachelor's/graduate degree, cooperative education, cross-registration, distance learning, double major, dual enrollment of high school students, ESL, honors, independent study, internships, study abroad, teacher certification program. Early assurance for medical and dental school with SUNY Buffalo Medical and Dental Schools (New York state residents only), and the Upstate Medical School at Syracuse; 7-year joint degree programs with SUNY Buffalo Dental School, the Ohio College of Podiatric Medicine, the New York College of Podiatric Medicine and SUNY State College of Optometry in NYC; AS/BS with Fashion Institute of Technology. **Credit/placement by examination:** AP, CLEP, IB, SAT, ACT, institutional tests. 30 credit hours maximum toward bachelor's degree. **Support services:** Learning center, pre-admission summer program, reduced course load, remedial instruction, study skills assistance, tutoring, writing center.

**Majors. Area/ethnic studies:** European. **Biology:** General, biochemistry, bioinformatics. **Business:** Accounting, accounting technology, entrepreneurial studies, finance, international, management information systems, management science, marketing. **Communications:** General, digital media. **Computer sciences:** Computer science. **Conservation:** Environmental science. **Education:** Early childhood, early childhood special, elementary, physical, secondary. **English:** English lit. **Foreign languages:** French, Germanic, Spanish. **Health:** Athletic training, clinical lab science. **History:** General. **Liberal arts:** Arts/sciences, humanities. **Math:** General. **Philosophy/religion:** Philosophy, religion. **Physical sciences:** Chemistry, physics. **Protective services:** Criminal justice. **Psychology:** General. **Social sciences:** Anthropology, economics, international relations, political science, sociology, urban studies. **Visual/performing arts:** Art history/conservation.

**Most popular majors.** Biology 6%, business/marketing 22%, communications/journalism 11%, education 12%, mathematics 9%, psychology 10%, social sciences 9%.

**Computing on campus.** 500 workstations in dormitories, library, computer center, student center. Dormitories wired for high-speed internet access and linked to campus network. Commuter students can connect to campus network. Online course registration, online library, helpline, repair service, student web hosting, wireless network available.

**Student life. Freshman orientation:** Mandatory, $125 fee. Preregistration for classes offered. Program includes testing, advisement, registration, introduction to student services. **Policies:** Religious observance required. **Housing:** Coed dorms, special housing for disabled, apartments, substance-free housing available. $200 partly refundable deposit, deadline 5/1. Themed housing, science, honors, townhouses available. **Activities:** Bands, campus ministries, choral groups, dance, drama, film society, literary magazine, music ensembles, musical theater, radio station, student government, student newspaper, TV station, political science association, ethnic and social service organizations, international affairs society, social justice club, Circle K, Global Horizons, German club, Italian club, Little Theater.

**Athletics.** NCAA. **Intercollegiate:** Baseball M, basketball, cross-country, golf M, ice hockey M, lacrosse, soccer, softball W, swimming, synchronized swimming W, volleyball W. **Intramural:** Cheerleading, golf M, rowing (crew) W, rugby. **Team name:** Golden Griffins.

**Student services.** Adult student services, alcohol/substance abuse counseling, campus ministries, career counseling, services for economically disadvantaged, student employment services, financial aid counseling, health services, minority student services, personal counseling, placement for graduates, veterans' counselor. **Physically disabled:** Services for visually, speech, hearing impaired. **Learning disabled:** Comprehensive services available.

**Contact.** E-mail: admissions@canisius.edu
Phone: (716) 888-2200 Toll-free number: (800) 843-1517
Fax: (716) 888-3230
Ann Marie Moscovic, Director of Admissions, Canisius College, 2001 Main Street, Buffalo, NY 14208-1098

---

## Cazenovia College
**Cazenovia, New York**
**www.cazenovia.edu**                                    **CB code: 2078**

- Private 4-year liberal arts college
- Residential campus in small town
- 1,024 degree-seeking undergraduates: 8% part-time, 75% women, 4% African American, 1% Asian American, 2% Hispanic American, 1% Native American
- 78% of applicants admitted

**General.** Founded in 1824. Regionally accredited. **Degrees:** 158 bachelor's, 12 associate awarded. **ROTC:** Army, Air Force. **Location:** 20 miles from Syracuse. **Calendar:** Semester, limited summer session. **Full-time faculty:** 49 total; 59% women. **Part-time faculty:** 94 total; 58% women. **Class size:** 80% < 20, 19% 20-39, 2% 40-49. **Special facilities:** 160-acre farm and equine center, art and design facility and gallery.

**Freshman class profile.** 1,867 applied, 1,447 admitted, 330 enrolled.

| Mid 50% test scores | | | |
|---|---|---|---|
| ACT composite: | 18-24 | Rank in top quarter: | 34% |
| GPA 3.50 or higher: | 34% | Rank in top tenth: | 11% |
| GPA 3.0-3.49: | 32% | Out-of-state: | 24% |
| GPA 2.0-2.99: | 32% | Live on campus: | 95% |

**Basis for selection.** Rigor of secondary school record very important; interview, recommendations, school activities important. SAT or ACT recommended. Portfolio recommended for art, graphic and interior design, photography programs.

**High school preparation.** College-preparatory program recommended. 16 units recommended. Recommended units include English 4, mathematics 2, social studies 4 and science 2. Art courses recommended for art and design majors.

**2007-2008 Annual costs.** Tuition/fees: $21,490. Room/board: $8,940. Books/supplies: $1,000. Personal expenses: $200.

**2007-2008 Financial aid. Need-based:** 65% of total undergraduate aid awarded as scholarships/grants, 35% as loans/jobs. **Non-need-based:** Scholarships awarded for academics.

**Application procedures. Admission:** Priority date 3/1; no deadline. $30 fee, may be waived for applicants with need. Application may be submitted online. Admission notification on a rolling basis beginning on or about 11/1. Must reply by May 1 or within 2 week(s) if notified thereafter. **Financial aid:** Priority date 3/15; no closing date. FAFSA required. Applicants notified on a rolling basis starting 11/1; must reply by 5/1 or within 2 week(s) of notification.

**Academics. Special study options:** Combined bachelor's/graduate degree, double major, exchange student, honors, independent study, internships, student-designed major, study abroad, teacher certification program, Washington semester. **Credit/placement by examination:** AP, CLEP, IB, institutional tests. **Support services:** Learning center, pre-admission summer program, reduced course load, remedial instruction, study skills assistance, tutoring, writing center.

**Majors. Agriculture:** Equine science. **Business:** Accounting, business admin, fashion. **Communications:** General. **Conservation:** Environmental studies. **Education:** Early childhood, special. **English:** English lit. **Liberal arts:** Arts/sciences. **Parks/recreation:** Sports admin. **Protective services:** Criminal justice. **Psychology:** General. **Public administration:** Human services. **Social sciences:** General. **Visual/performing arts:** Design, fashion design, interior design, photography, studio arts.

**Most popular majors.** Business/marketing 22%, liberal arts 7%, public administration/social services 15%, visual/performing arts 32%.

**Computing on campus.** Dormitories wired for high-speed internet access and linked to campus network. Commuter students can connect to campus network. Helpline, wireless network available.

**Student life. Freshman orientation:** Mandatory. Preregistration for classes offered. **Housing:** Coed dorms, single-sex dorms available. $200 nonrefundable deposit, deadline 5/1. Single room suites available. **Activities:** Jazz band, campus ministries, choral groups, dance, drama, film society, musical theater, radio station, student government, student newspaper, human services club, overseas travel club, Young Democrats, Young Republicans, Cazventures outdoor club, Certified Peer Educators, You Are Not Alone-LGBT, Student Organization of Ethnic Diversity.

**Athletics.** NCAA. **Intercollegiate:** Baseball M, basketball, cheerleading, cross-country, equestrian, golf M, lacrosse, rowing (crew), soccer, softball W, volleyball W. **Intramural:** Basketball, bowling, equestrian, football (non-tackle), rowing (crew), skiing, soccer, softball, swimming, volleyball, weight lifting. **Team name:** Wildcats.

**Student services.** Alcohol/substance abuse counseling, campus ministries, career counseling, services for economically disadvantaged, student employment services, financial aid counseling, health services, personal counseling, placement for graduates. **Physically disabled:** Services for visually, speech, hearing impaired.

**Contact.** E-mail: admission@cazenovia.edu
Phone: (315) 655-7208 Toll-free number: (800) 654-3210
Fax: (315) 655-4860
Robert Croot, Vice President for Enrollment Management and Dean for Admissions and Financial Aid, Cazenovia College, 3 Sullivan Street, Cazenovia, NY 13035

## Central Yeshiva Tomchei Tmimim-Lubavitch
**Brooklyn, New York**
CB code: 0549

▶ Private 4-year rabbinical college for men affiliated with Jewish faith
▶ Very large city

**General.** Accredited by AARTS. **Calendar:** Continuous.

**Annual costs/financial aid.** Tuition/fees (2007-2008): $4,800. Room/board: $2,300.

**Contact.** Phone: (718) 859-7600
841-853 Ocean Parkway, Brooklyn, NY 11230

## City University of New York: Baruch College
**New York, New York** CB member
www.baruch.cuny.edu CB code: 2034

▶ Public 4-year business and liberal arts college
▶ Commuter campus in very large city
▶ 12,626 degree-seeking undergraduates: 24% part-time, 52% women, 11% African American, 30% Asian American, 17% Hispanic American, 13% international
▶ 3,217 degree-seeking graduate students
▶ 26% of applicants admitted
▶ SAT or ACT (ACT writing optional) required
▶ 57% graduate within 6 years

**General.** Founded in 1919. Regionally accredited. **Degrees:** 2,550 bachelor's awarded; master's offered. **ROTC:** Army. **Calendar:** Semester, extensive summer session. **Full-time faculty:** 501 total; 91% have terminal degrees, 31% minority, 38% women. **Part-time faculty:** 463 total; 23% have terminal degrees, 33% minority, 39% women. **Class size:** 27% < 20, 56% 20-39, 4% 40-49, 11% 50-99, 2% >100. **Special facilities:** Performing arts center (black box theater, gallery, various theaters and recital halls).

**Freshman class profile.** 17,114 applied, 4,414 admitted, 1,479 enrolled.

| Mid 50% test scores | | | |
|---|---|---|---|
| SAT critical reading: | 480-580 | Rank in top tenth: | 37% |
| SAT math: | 540-650 | End year in good standing: | 91% |
| GPA 3.50 or higher: | 30% | Return as sophomores: | 88% |
| GPA 3.0-3.49: | 63% | Out-of-state: | 5% |
| GPA 2.0-2.99: | 6% | International: | 6% |
| Rank in top quarter: | 67% | Fraternities: | 1% |
| | | Sororities: | 1% |

**Basis for selection.** Overall high school performance and 82 average or combined SAT score of 1200 required. **Homeschooled:** 1200 SAT required. **Learning Disabled:** No special requirements; recommended that students call Disability Service Office to discuss available services.

**High school preparation.** 16 units required. Required and recommended units include English 4, mathematics 3-4, social studies 4, science 2 (laboratory 2), foreign language 2-3 and academic electives 1.

**2007-2008 Annual costs.** Tuition/fees: $4,320; $11,120 out-of-state. Books/supplies: $1,016. Personal expenses: $2,706.

**2007-2008 Financial aid. Need-based:** 1,352 full-time freshmen applied for aid; 1,081 were judged to have need; 1,069 of these received aid. Average need met was 69%. Average scholarship/grant was $4,967; average loan $2,852. 71% of total undergraduate aid awarded as scholarships/grants, 29% as loans/jobs. **Non-need-based:** Awarded to 1,765 full-time undergraduates, including 1,043 freshmen. Scholarships awarded for academics, state residency.

**Application procedures. Admission:** Closing date 2/1 (postmark date). $65 fee. Application may be submitted online. Admission notification on a rolling basis beginning on or about 2/1. Must reply by May 1 or within 2 week(s) if notified thereafter. **Financial aid:** Priority date 3/15, closing date 4/30. FAFSA required. Applicants notified on a rolling basis starting 4/1; must reply by 6/1 or within 6 week(s) of notification.

**Academics.** 120 credit hours required for BA/BS degrees, 124 for BBA. Optional humanities seminar examining 2 or more disciplines in arts and sciences; joint business/liberal arts and science majors; programs in arts administration, management of musical enterprise, real estate, and metropolitan development. **Special study options:** Accelerated study, combined bachelor's/graduate degree, cross-registration, distance learning, double major, ESL, exchange student, honors, independent study, internships, liberal arts/career combination, student-designed major, study abroad. **Credit/placement by examination:** AP, CLEP, IB, institutional tests. 21 credit hours maximum toward bachelor's degree. No more than 21 credits through AP and/or college courses taken in high school. **Support services:** Learning center, pre-admission summer program, reduced course load, study skills assistance, tutoring, writing center.

**Honors college/program.** Applicants must have high standardized test scores (1300+ on the SAT, exclusive of Writing) and high school averages (90+). Leadership potential and community involvement sought. Applicants must supply teacher recommendations and essay.

**Majors. Architecture:** Urban/community planning. **Biology:** General. **Business:** General, accounting, actuarial science, business admin, communications, finance, human resources, labor relations, management information systems, managerial economics, operations, real estate, sales/distribution. **Communications:** General, advertising, journalism. **Computer sciences:** General, computer science, information systems. **Engineering:** Operations research. **English:** American lit, British lit, creative writing, English lit. **Foreign languages:** Comparative lit, Spanish. **History:** General. **Interdisciplinary:** Biological/physical sciences. **Liberal arts:** Arts/sciences. **Math:** General, statistics. **Philosophy/religion:** Philosophy. **Psychology:** General. **Public administration:** General. **Social sciences:** Economics, political science, sociology. **Visual/performing arts:** Arts management, design, music management.

**Most popular majors.** Business/marketing 76%, communications/journalism 6%.

**Computing on campus.** 1,300 workstations in library, computer center, student center. Online course registration, online library, helpline, wireless network available.

**Student life. Freshman orientation:** Mandatory. Half day-long, on-campus session offered on multiple days. **Activities:** Campus ministries, choral groups, dance, drama, film society, international student organizations, literary magazine, Model UN, musical theater, radio station, student government, student newspaper, Hillel, National Association of Black Accountants, Golden Key, International Honor Society, Asian student association, Muslim student association, United International Student Body, Model United Nations, Pre-Law Society, Caribbean student association.

**Athletics.** NCAA. **Intercollegiate:** Baseball M, basketball, cheerleading M, cross-country, soccer M, softball W, swimming, tennis, volleyball. **Intramural:** Badminton, basketball, cross-country, racquetball, table tennis, volleyball, weight lifting. **Team name:** Bearcats.

**Student services.** Adult student services, alcohol/substance abuse counseling, campus ministries, career counseling, student employment services, financial aid counseling, health services, legal services, personal counseling, placement for graduates, veterans' counselor. **Physically disabled:** Services for visually, speech, hearing impaired.

**Contact.** E-mail: admissions@baruch.cuny.edu
Phone: (646) 312-1400 Fax: (646) 312-1363
Marybeth Murphy, Vice President for Enrollment Management Services, City University of New York: Baruch College, One Bernard Baruch Way, Box H-0720, New York, NY 10010-5585

## City University of New York: Brooklyn College
**Brooklyn, New York** CB member
www.brooklyn.cuny.edu CB code: 2046

▶ Public 4-year liberal arts college
▶ Commuter campus in very large city
▶ 11,923 degree-seeking undergraduates: 25% part-time, 60% women, 27% African American, 14% Asian American, 12% Hispanic American, 6% international
▶ 2,956 degree-seeking graduate students
▶ 40% of applicants admitted
▶ SAT or ACT required
▶ 47% graduate within 6 years

**General.** Founded in 1930. Regionally accredited. **Degrees:** 1,994 bachelor's awarded; master's offered. **Location:** 10 miles from Manhattan. **Calendar:** Semester, extensive summer session. **Full-time faculty:** 530 total; 91% have terminal degrees, 28% minority, 43% women. **Part-time faculty:** 650 total; 27% minority, 48% women. **Class size:** 41% < 20, 50% 20-39, 5% 40-49, 3% 50-99, less than 1% >100. **Special facilities:** Astronomical observatory, greenhouse, applied sciences institute, institute for the humanities, infant study center, Brooklyn Center for the Performing Arts, particle accelerator.

**Freshman class profile.** 14,754 applied, 5,933 admitted, 1,322 enrolled.

| Mid 50% test scores | | Rank in top tenth: | 14% |
|---|---|---|---|
| SAT critical reading: | 450-560 | Return as sophomores: | 80% |
| SAT math: | 490-590 | Out-of-state: | 3% |
| GPA 3.50 or higher: | 22% | International: | 5% |
| GPA 3.0-3.49: | 57% | Fraternities: | 1% |
| GPA 2.0-2.99: | 21% | Sororities: | 1% |
| Rank in top quarter: | 48% | | |

**Basis for selection.** Students accepted based on SAT scores and academic average. Essay required for BA/MD, CHC and Scholars, interview recommended for scholars program. Audition required for music conservatory, theater programs; portfolio required for fine arts program.

**High school preparation.** Recommended units include English 4, mathematics 3, social studies 4, science 3, foreign language 3 and academic electives 4.

**2007-2008 Annual costs.** Tuition/fees: $4,377; $11,177 out-of-state. Books/supplies: $850. Personal expenses: $2,100.

**Financial aid. Non-need-based:** Scholarships awarded for academics, art, leadership, music/drama, state residency.

**Application procedures. Admission:** $65 fee. Admission notification on a rolling basis beginning on or about 1/15. **Financial aid:** Priority date 4/1; no closing date. FAFSA required. Applicants notified on a rolling basis starting 5/1.

**Academics. Special study options:** Accelerated study, combined bachelor's/graduate degree, distance learning, double major, dual enrollment of high school students, ESL, honors, independent study, internships, liberal arts/career combination, study abroad, teacher certification program, Washington semester, weekend college. **Credit/placement by examination:** AP, CLEP, IB, institutional tests. 35 credit hours maximum toward bachelor's degree. **Support services:** Learning center, pre-admission summer program, reduced course load, study skills assistance, tutoring, writing center.

**Majors. Area/ethnic studies:** African-American, American, Caribbean, Hispanic-American/Latino/Chicano, Latin American, women's. **Biology:** General. **Business:** Accounting, business admin. **Communications:** General, broadcast journalism, journalism, radio/tv. **Communications technology:** Radio/tv. **Computer sciences:** General. **Conservation:** Environmental studies. **Education:** General, bilingual, biology, chemistry, early childhood, elementary, English, French, kindergarten/preschool, mathematics, music, physical, physics, social studies, Spanish, special, speech, speech impaired. **English:** Creative writing, English lit, speech/rhetoric. **Family/consumer sciences:** Food/nutrition. **Foreign languages:** Classics, comparative lit, French, Italian, linguistics, Russian, Spanish. **Health:** Audiology/speech pathology, speech pathology. **History:** General. **Interdisciplinary:** Biological/physical sciences, math/computer science. **Math:** General, algebra, computational. **Parks/recreation:** Health/fitness. **Philosophy/religion:** Judaic, philosophy, religion. **Physical sciences:** Chemistry, geology, physics. **Psychology:** General. **Public administration:** Community org/advocacy. **Social sciences:** Anthropology, economics, political science, sociology. **Visual/performing arts:** Acting, art, art history/conservation, cinematography, dramatic, film/cinema, music performance, music theory/composition, play/screenwriting.

**Most popular majors.** Business/marketing 29%, computer/information sciences 6%, education 11%, health sciences 6%, psychology 13%, social sciences 9%.

**Computing on campus.** 2,000 workstations in library, computer center, student center. Online library, wireless network available.

**Student life. Freshman orientation:** Available. **Activities:** Concert band, choral groups, dance, drama, film society, literary magazine, music ensembles, radio station, student government, student newspaper, symphony orchestra, TV station, Hillel, Newman Club, student Christian association, Alpha Phi Omega, Christian fellowship, Islamic society, Caribbean student union, accounting society, lesbian/gay/bisexual/transgender alliance.

**Athletics.** NCAA. **Intercollegiate:** Basketball, cross-country, soccer M, softball W, tennis, track and field, volleyball. **Intramural:** Badminton W, basketball, racquetball, soccer M, softball W, tennis, track and field, volleyball. **Team name:** Bridges.

**Student services.** Adult student services, alcohol/substance abuse counseling, campus ministries, career counseling, services for economically disadvantaged, student employment services, financial aid counseling, health

services, on-campus daycare, personal counseling, placement for graduates, veterans' counselor, women's services. **Physically disabled:** Services for visually, speech, hearing impaired. **Learning disabled:** Comprehensive services available.

**Contact.** E-mail: adminqry@brooklyn.cuny.edu
Phone: (718) 951-5001 Fax: (718) 951-4506
City University of New York: Brooklyn College, 2900 Bedford Avenue, Brooklyn, NY 11210

## City University of New York: City College
New York, New York — CB member
www.ccny.cuny.edu — CB code: 2083

- Public 4-year university
- Commuter campus in very large city
- 10,683 degree-seeking undergraduates: 24% part-time, 50% women
- 2,878 degree-seeking graduate students
- 40% of applicants admitted
- SAT or ACT required
- 36% graduate within 6 years

**General.** Founded in 1847. Regionally accredited. **Degrees:** 1,278 bachelor's awarded; master's, doctoral offered. **Calendar:** Semester, extensive summer session. **Full-time faculty:** 519 total; 90% have terminal degrees, 32% minority, 38% women. **Part-time faculty:** 610 total; 33% have terminal degrees, 62% minority, 48% women. **Class size:** 43% < 20, 52% 20-39, 4% 40-49, less than 1% 50-99, less than 1% >100. **Special facilities:** Planetarium, weather station, ultra-fast laser spectroscopy laboratory, microwave laboratory, computer-aided design facilities, slide library, darkroom facilities, sonic music arts facility, structural biology center.

**Freshman class profile.** 17,816 applied, 7,204 admitted, 1,828 enrolled.

| Mid 50% test scores | | Rank in top quarter: | 33% |
|---|---|---|---|
| SAT critical reading: | 420-570 | Rank in top tenth: | 29% |
| SAT math: | 430-550 | End year in good standing: | 85% |
| GPA 3.50 or higher: | 20% | Return as sophomores: | 80% |
| GPA 3.0-3.49: | 26% | Out-of-state: | 2% |
| GPA 2.0-2.99: | 49% | International: | 10% |

**Basis for selection.** Academic average and number of academic units achieved in high school, SAT, or GED score of 325 or better important. Units recommended for admission must be acquired before graduation from any CUNY senior college. SAT section test scores of 450 or 20 ACT on math and verbal exempt student from taking placement exam. Interview required for biomedical education, audition required for music program; portfolio required for electronic design and multimedia. **Homeschooled:** Applicants must obtain GED or diploma through regionally accredited program.

**High school preparation.** 16 units recommended. Recommended units include English 4, mathematics 2, social studies 4, science 2 (laboratory 2) and foreign language 2. One unit of art or music recommended. For science and engineering students, 3 units of mathematics required.

**2007-2008 Annual costs.** Tuition/fees: $4,279; $11,079 out-of-state. Books/supplies: $938.

**2006-2007 Financial aid. Need-based:** 1,329 full-time freshmen applied for aid; 1,128 were judged to have need; 1,015 of these received aid. Average need met was 79%. Average scholarship/grant was $5,110; average loan $1,500. 67% of total undergraduate aid awarded as scholarships/grants, 33% as loans/jobs. **Non-need-based:** Awarded to 1,736 full-time undergraduates, including 782 freshmen. Scholarships awarded for academics, alumni affiliation, leadership.

**Application procedures. Admission:** Priority date 3/15; no deadline. $65 fee. Application may be submitted online. Admission notification on a rolling basis beginning on or about 1/15. **Financial aid:** Priority date 4/1; no closing date. FAFSA required. Applicants notified on a rolling basis starting 4/15.

**Academics. Special study options:** Accelerated study, combined bachelor's/graduate degree, cooperative education, cross-registration, dual enrollment of high school students, ESL, exchange student, honors, independent study, internships, liberal arts/career combination, study abroad, teacher certification program. Center for Worker Education, doctoral degrees through CUNY Graduate Center. **Credit/placement by examination:** AP, CLEP, IB, ACT, institutional tests. **Support services:** Learning center, pre-admission summer program, reduced course load, tutoring, writing center.

**Honors college/program.** Admits only new first-year students, who must apply by special application. The application deadline is November 1 for early admission and December 15 for regular admission. For the class admitted fall 2005 (Class of 2009), the average high school GPA was 93.9 (on a scale of 100) and the average SAT was 1376 (exclusive of Writing). Students are expected to achieve an overall 3.3 GPA by the end of their first year and a 3.5 GPA by the end of their second year, which must be maintained until graduation in four years. Detailed information about additional benefits, including full-tuition scholarships and study grants, and requirements of the CUNY Honors College can be accessed on the college's website.

**Majors. Architecture:** Architecture. **Area/ethnic studies:** African-American, Asian, Caribbean, Latin American. **Biology:** General, biochemistry. **Business:** General. **Communications:** General, advertising, journalism, public relations. **Computer sciences:** Computer science. **Education:** Art, bilingual, biology, chemistry, early childhood, elementary, English, foreign languages, French, history, mathematics, music, physics, science, secondary, social studies, Spanish. **Engineering:** Biomedical, chemical, civil, computer, electrical, mechanical. **English:** English lit. **Foreign languages:** General, comparative lit, French, Spanish. **Health:** Physician assistant, premedicine, prepharmacy, preveterinary. **History:** General. **Interdisciplinary:** Global studies. **Legal studies:** Prelaw. **Math:** General. **Philosophy/religion:** Judaic, philosophy. **Physical sciences:** Chemistry, geology, physics, planetary. **Psychology:** General. **Social sciences:** Anthropology, economics, international relations, political science, sociology. **Visual/performing arts:** General, art, art history/conservation, cinematography, commercial/advertising art, dramatic, film/cinema, graphic design, jazz, music performance, music theory/composition, studio arts.

**Most popular majors.** Architecture 6%, communications/journalism 6%, engineering/engineering technologies 16%, health sciences 7%, liberal arts 11%, psychology 10%, social sciences 10%, visual/performing arts 9%.

**Computing on campus.** 2,000 workstations in library, computer center, student center. Dormitories wired for high-speed internet access and linked to campus network. Commuter students can connect to campus network. Online course registration, online library, helpline, repair service, wireless network available.

**Student life. Freshman orientation:** Mandatory. Full-day program, including registration, held in spring and summer. **Housing:** Guaranteed on-campus for all undergraduates. Coed dorms, substance-free housing available. Housing office available. **Activities:** Jazz band, choral groups, dance, drama, film society, music ensembles, musical theater, radio station, student government, student newspaper, numerous religious, political, ethnic, and social service organizations.

**Athletics.** NCAA. **Intercollegiate:** Baseball M, basketball, cross-country, fencing, lacrosse M, soccer, tennis, track and field, volleyball. **Intramural:** Badminton M, basketball, fencing, soccer M, softball W, swimming, tennis, track and field, volleyball. **Team name:** Beavers.

**Student services.** Alcohol/substance abuse counseling, campus ministries, career counseling, services for economically disadvantaged, student employment services, financial aid counseling, health services, minority student services, on-campus daycare, personal counseling, placement for graduates, veterans' counselor, women's services. **Physically disabled:** Services for visually, speech, hearing impaired. **Learning disabled:** Comprehensive services available.

**Contact.** E-mail: admissions@ccny.cuny.edu
Phone: (212) 650-6977 Fax: (212) 650-6417
Joseph Fatozzi, Director of Admissions, City University of New York: City College, 160 Convent Avenue, New York, NY 10031

---

## City University of New York: College of Staten Island

**Staten Island, New York**                    **CB member**
**www.csi.cuny.edu**                            **CB code: 2778**

- Public 4-year liberal arts college
- Commuter campus in very large city
- 11,197 degree-seeking undergraduates: 28% part-time, 60% women, 9% African American, 8% Asian American, 11% Hispanic American, 3% international
- 866 degree-seeking graduate students
- 100% of applicants admitted
- Application essay, interview required
- 44% graduate within 6 years

**General.** Founded in 1955. Regionally accredited. **Degrees:** 1,019 bachelor's, 756 associate awarded; master's offered. **Location:** 10 miles from downtown Manhattan. **Calendar:** Semester, extensive summer session. **Full-time faculty:** 344 total; 84% have terminal degrees, 21% minority, 42% women. **Part-time faculty:** 537 total; 27% have terminal degrees, 14% minority, 50% women. **Class size:** 29% < 20, 53% 20-39, 15% 40-49, 3% 50-99, less than 1% >100. **Special facilities:** Astrophysical observatory, archives and special collections, artificial intelligence laboratory, center for developmental neuroscience and developmental disabilities, center for engineered polymeric materials, center for environmental science.

**Freshman class profile.** 7,399 applied, 7,399 admitted, 2,478 enrolled.

| Mid 50% test scores | | | |
|---|---|---|---|
| SAT critical reading: | 450-540 | GPA 2.0-2.99: | 51% |
| SAT math: | 460-550 | End year in good standing: | 71% |
| SAT writing: | 430-540 | Return as sophomores: | 82% |
| GPA 3.50 or higher: | 17% | Out-of-state: | 1% |
| GPA 3.0-3.49: | 29% | International: | 3% |

**Basis for selection.** High school record and GPA most important. Open admission for associate degree-seeking students. SAT or ACT recommended. Audition required for music programs; portfolio recommended for art programs.

**High school preparation.** 15 units required; 16 recommended. Required and recommended units include English 4, mathematics 2-3, social studies 4, science 2, foreign language 2 and academic electives 2.

**2007-2008 Annual costs.** Tuition/fees: $4,328; $11,128 out-of-state. Books/supplies: $938. Personal expenses: $1,697.

**2007-2008 Financial aid. Need-based:** 1,744 full-time freshmen applied for aid; 1,263 were judged to have need; 1,219 of these received aid. Average need met was 61%. Average scholarship/grant was $5,319; average loan $2,842. 76% of total undergraduate aid awarded as scholarships/grants, 24% as loans/jobs. **Non-need-based:** Awarded to 1,074 full-time undergraduates, including 613 freshmen. Scholarships awarded for academics, art, athletics, job skills, leadership, minority status, music/drama, state residency.

**Application procedures. Admission:** Priority date 3/15; no deadline. $65 fee, may be waived for applicants with need. Application must be submitted online. Admission notification on a rolling basis beginning on or about 12/15. **Financial aid:** Priority date 3/31; no closing date. FAFSA required. Applicants notified on a rolling basis starting 4/30.

**Academics. Special study options:** Accelerated study, cooperative education, cross-registration, distance learning, double major, dual enrollment of high school students, ESL, exchange student, external degree, honors, independent study, internships, liberal arts/career combination, student-designed major, study abroad, teacher certification program, weekend college. Cross-registration at any CUNY. **Credit/placement by examination:** AP, CLEP, IB, SAT, ACT, institutional tests. 30 credit hours maximum toward associate degree, 30 toward bachelor's. **Support services:** Learning center, pre-admission summer program, remedial instruction, study skills assistance, tutoring.

**Honors college/program.** Minimum 1250 SAT (exclusive of Writing) and 92 high school average required. 20 seats available.

**Majors. Area/ethnic studies:** African-American, American, women's. **Biology:** General, biochemistry. **Business:** General, accounting. **Communications:** General. **Computer sciences:** Computer science. **Education:** Biology, chemistry, English, history, mathematics, Spanish. **Engineering:** General. **English:** English lit. **Foreign languages:** Spanish. **Health:** Clinical lab science, nursing (RN). **History:** General. **Liberal arts:** Arts/sciences. **Math:** General. **Philosophy/religion:** Philosophy. **Physical sciences:** Chemistry, physics. **Psychology:** General. **Public administration:** Social work. **Social sciences:** Economics, international relations, political science. **Visual/performing arts:** Art, dramatic, film/cinema.

**Most popular majors.** Business/marketing 22%, liberal arts 17%, psychology 10%, social sciences 16%.

**Computing on campus.** 1,568 workstations in library, computer center, student center. Commuter students can connect to campus network. Online course registration, online library, helpline, student web hosting, wireless network available.

**Student life. Freshman orientation:** Mandatory. Scheduled at beginning of each semester, after or during time periods devoted to testing, advisement, and registration. Students with less than 6 credits are required to complete the orientation requirement during the first semester prior to completing 12 credits. **Activities:** Bands, choral groups, dance, drama, film society, literary magazine, music ensembles, musical theater, radio station, student government, student newspaper, Muslim student association, Israel club, Colleges Against Cancer, Chi Alpha Christian club, Hillel, armed forces club, international cultural dance club, Sri Lankan student association, South Asian student association, Middle Eastern club.

**Athletics.** NCAA. **Intercollegiate:** Baseball M, basketball, cross-country, diving, soccer, softball W, swimming, tennis, volleyball W. **Intramural:** Badminton, basketball, football (non-tackle), handball, racquetball, softball, table tennis, tennis. **Team name:** Dolphins.

**Student services.** Adult student services, alcohol/substance abuse counseling, campus ministries, career counseling, services for economically disadvantaged, student employment services, financial aid counseling, health services, minority student services, on-campus daycare, personal counseling, placement for graduates, veterans' counselor, women's services. **Physically disabled:** Services for visually, hearing impaired.

**Contact.** E-mail: admissions@mail.cuny.csi.edu
Phone: (718) 982-2010 Fax: (718) 982-2500
MaryBeth Reilly, Director of Recruitment and Admissions, City University of New York: College of Staten Island, 2800 Victory Boulevard 2A-104, Staten Island, NY 10314

## City University of New York: CUNY Online
**New York, New York**
**www.cuny.edu/online**

- Public 4-year virtual university
- Very large city
- 498 degree-seeking undergraduates: 66% part-time, 56% women
- Application essay required

**General.** Regionally accredited. CUNY Online offers a fully asynchronous online bachelor's degree program for students who have at least 30 earned credits. **Degrees:** 1 bachelor's awarded. **Calendar:** Semester, limited summer session. **Part-time faculty:** 36 total; 81% have terminal degrees, 25% minority, 50% women. **Class size:** 100% 20-39.

**Basis for selection.** Open admission, but selective for some programs. Accept only transfer applicants with at least 30 credits earned. SAT or ACT recommended. **Homeschooled:** State high school equivalency certificate required.

**2007-2008 Annual costs.** Tuition/fees: $4,330; $4,330 out-of-state.

**Application procedures. Admission:** Closing date 8/1 (receipt date). $70 fee, may be waived for applicants with need. Application must be submitted online. Admission notification on a rolling basis. **Financial aid:** Closing date 8/1.

**Academics. Special study options:** Distance learning. **Credit/placement by examination:** AP, CLEP, IB, SAT, ACT. **Support services:** Study skills assistance, tutoring.

**Majors. Business:** General. **Communications:** General.

**Computing on campus.** PC or laptop required. Helpline available.

**Contact.** E-mail: onlineba@mail.cuny.edu
Otilia Abraham, Coordinator of Admissions, City University of New York: CUNY Online, 101 West 31st Street, 7th Floor, New York, NY 10001

## City University of New York: Hunter College
**New York, New York** **CB member**
**www.hunter.cuny.edu** **CB code: 2301**

- Public 4-year liberal arts college
- Commuter campus in very large city
- 14,573 degree-seeking undergraduates: 27% part-time, 68% women, 12% African American, 18% Asian American, 19% Hispanic American, 10% international
- 4,108 degree-seeking graduate students
- 30% of applicants admitted
- SAT or ACT required
- 35% graduate within 6 years

**General.** Founded in 1870. Regionally accredited. **Degrees:** 2,116 bachelor's awarded; master's offered. **Calendar:** Semester, limited summer session. **Full-time faculty:** 664 total; 88% have terminal degrees, 27% minority, 50% women. **Part-time faculty:** 886 total; 38% have terminal degrees, 23% minority, 60% women. **Class size:** 41% < 20, 48% 20-39, 5% 40-49, 5% 50-99, less than 1% >100. **Special facilities:** Mathematics learning center, on-campus elementary and secondary schools.

**Freshman class profile.** 24,701 applied, 7,470 admitted, 1,906 enrolled.

| Mid 50% test scores | | | |
|---|---|---|---|
| SAT critical reading: | 480-550 | GPA 2.0-2.99: | 47% |
| SAT math: | 490-560 | Return as sophomores: | 80% |
| GPA 3.50 or higher: | 22% | Out-of-state: | 5% |
| GPA 3.0-3.49: | 26% | International: | 7% |

**Basis for selection.** Requirements vary by program. Indexing formula using weighted averages, high school academic units, and SAT scores for admission to some programs. SAT or ACT not required, but recommended, of first-time freshmen who graduated high school more than a year preceding admission.

**High school preparation.** 16 units recommended. Required and recommended units include English 2-4, mathematics 2-3, social studies 4, science 1-2 (laboratory 1), foreign language 2 and academic electives 1. 1 fine art or performing art recommended.

**2007-2008 Annual costs.** Tuition/fees: $4,349; $11,149 out-of-state. Dormitory availability very limited. Room only: $3,726. Books/supplies: $938. Personal expenses: $4,432.

**2006-2007 Financial aid. Need-based:** 1,489 full-time freshmen applied for aid; 1,129 were judged to have need; 1,107 of these received aid. Average need met was 76%. Average scholarship/grant was $5,443; average loan $2,952. 76% of total undergraduate aid awarded as scholarships/grants, 24% as loans/jobs. **Non-need-based:** Awarded to 2,558 full-time undergraduates, including 1,064 freshmen. Scholarships awarded for academics.

**Application procedures. Admission:** Closing date 3/15 (postmark date). $65 fee, may be waived for applicants with need. Admission notification on a rolling basis beginning on or about 1/15. **Financial aid:** Priority date 5/1; no closing date. FAFSA required. Applicants notified on a rolling basis starting 5/15.

**Academics. Special study options:** Accelerated study, combined bachelor's/graduate degree, cross-registration, distance learning, double major, dual enrollment of high school students, exchange student, honors, independent study, internships, liberal arts/career combination, student-designed major, study abroad, teacher certification program. BA/MA/MS programs in anthropology, biology/EOPS, economics, English, history, math, music, physics, social research (MS). **Credit/placement by examination:** AP, CLEP, IB, institutional tests. 30 credit hours maximum toward bachelor's degree. **Support services:** Learning center, reduced course load, remedial instruction, study skills assistance, tutoring, writing center.

**Majors. Area/ethnic studies:** African-American, Latin American, Near/Middle Eastern, women's. **Biology:** General, pharmacology. **Business:** Accounting. **Communications:** Media studies. **Computer sciences:** General. **Education:** General, art, biology, chemistry, drama/dance, early childhood, elementary, English, foreign languages, French, geography, German, health, history, Latin, mathematics, music, physical, physics, secondary, social studies, Spanish. **English:** British lit, creative writing, English lit. **Family/consumer sciences:** Food/nutrition. **Foreign languages:** General, ancient Greek, Chinese, classics, comparative lit, French, German, Hebrew, Italian, Latin, Romance, Russian, Spanish. **Health:** Adult health nursing, clinical lab science, clinical lab technology, maternal/child health nursing, nurse practitioner, nursing (RN), pediatric nursing, psychiatric nursing, public health nursing, speech pathology. **History:** General. **Liberal arts:** Humanities. **Math:** General, statistics. **Philosophy/religion:** Judaic, philosophy, religion. **Physical sciences:** Chemistry, physics. **Psychology:** General. **Social sciences:** Anthropology, archaeology, economics, geography, international relations, political science, sociology, urban studies. **Visual/performing arts:** Art history/conservation, cinematography, dance, dramatic, film/cinema, music performance, music theory/composition, studio arts.

**Most popular majors.** Business/marketing 8%, communications/journalism 7%, English 15%, health sciences 7%, psychology 14%, social sciences 22%, visual/performing arts 10%.

**Computing on campus.** 750 workstations in dormitories, library, computer center, student center. Commuter students can connect to campus network. Online course registration, online library, helpline, repair service, student web hosting, wireless network available.

**Student life. Freshman orientation:** Available. Preregistration for classes offered. **Housing:** Coed dorms, substance-free housing available. **Activities:** Bands, choral groups, dance, drama, film society, literary magazine, music ensembles, musical theater, radio station, student government, student newspaper, symphony orchestra, TV station, over 100 political, ethnic, social, and religious organizations.

**Athletics.** NCAA. **Intercollegiate:** Basketball, cross-country, fencing, football (non-tackle) W, soccer M, softball W, swimming W, tennis, track and field, volleyball, wrestling M. **Intramural:** Basketball, bowling, football (non-tackle), racquetball, swimming, table tennis, tennis, volleyball. **Team name:** Hawks.

**Student services.** Adult student services, alcohol/substance abuse counseling, campus ministries, career counseling, services for economically disadvantaged, student employment services, financial aid counseling, health services, legal services, minority student services, on-campus daycare, personal counseling, placement for graduates, veterans' counselor, women's services. **Physically disabled:** Services for visually, speech, hearing impaired.

**Contact.** E-mail: admissions@hunter.cuny.edu
Phone: (212) 772-4490
William Zlata, Director of Admissions, City University of New York: Hunter College, 695 Park Avenue, New York, NY 10021

## City University of New York: John Jay College of Criminal Justice
### New York, New York
www.jjay.cuny.edu/      CB code: 2115

- Public 4-year College of criminal justice and public safety
- Commuter campus in very large city
- 12,634 degree-seeking undergraduates: 24% part-time, 59% women, 23% African American, 7% Asian American, 40% Hispanic American, 4% international
- 1,755 degree-seeking graduate students
- 78% of applicants admitted
- SAT or ACT with writing required
- 42% graduate within 6 years; 30% enter graduate study

**General.** Founded in 1964. Regionally accredited. **Degrees:** 1,734 bachelor's, 173 associate awarded; master's offered. **Calendar:** Semester, limited summer session. **Full-time faculty:** 402 total; 81% have terminal degrees, 27% minority, 46% women. **Part-time faculty:** 629 total; 30% minority, 43% women. **Class size:** 23% < 20, 70% 20-39, 7% 40-49, less than 1% 50-99, less than 1% >100. **Special facilities:** Security laboratory, fire science laboratory, explosion-proof toxicology research laboratory.

**Freshman class profile.** 9,260 applied, 7,269 admitted, 2,813 enrolled.

| Mid 50% test scores | | | |
|---|---|---|---|
| SAT critical reading: | 420-520 | End year in good standing: | 70% |
| SAT math: | 420-510 | Return as sophomores: | 74% |
| SAT writing: | 370-420 | Out-of-state: | 7% |
| GPA 3.0-3.49: | 16% | International: | 3% |
| GPA 2.0-2.99: | 63% | | |

**Basis for selection.** Admission to associate degree programs requires minimum SAT score of 900 (exclusive of Writing), high school average of 72, or GED score of 300. Admission to baccalaureate degree program requires minimum SAT score from 960 to 1020 or minimum high school average of 80 and minimum of 12 academic units with a total of 4 units in English and mathematics with at least 1 unit in each discipline. **Homeschooled:** Applicants must have diploma issued by local registered high school, and minimum SAT of 1100.

**High school preparation.** 14 units required; 19 recommended. Required and recommended units include English 4, mathematics 3-4, social studies 2-4, (laboratory 2-3), foreign language 2-3 and visual/performing arts 1.

**2007-2008 Annual costs.** Tuition/fees: $4,279; $11,079 out-of-state. Books/supplies: $875. Personal expenses: $3,550.

**2006-2007 Financial aid.** **Need-based:** 2,488 full-time freshmen applied for aid; 2,140 were judged to have need; 1,982 of these received aid. Average need met was 85%. Average scholarship/grant was $3,125. 72% of total undergraduate aid awarded as scholarships/grants, 28% as loans/jobs. **Non-need-based:** Awarded to 835 full-time undergraduates, including 33 freshmen. Scholarships awarded for academics, state residency.

**Application procedures.** **Admission:** Priority date 12/1; deadline 5/1 (postmark date). $65 fee. Application may be submitted online. Admission notification on a rolling basis beginning on or about 1/15. Centralized application processing allows students to apply to 6 academic programs within CUNY system at same time. Admissions to John Jay on space-available basis. **Financial aid:** No deadline. FAFSA required. Applicants notified on a rolling basis starting 7/15; must reply within 2 week(s) of notification.

**Academics.** Degree requirements and curriculum combine professional education with the liberal arts. **Special study options:** Combined bachelor's/

graduate degree, cooperative education, cross-registration, distance learning, dual enrollment of high school students, ESL, exchange student, honors, independent study, internships, liberal arts/career combination, student-designed major, study abroad, weekend college. **Credit/placement by examination:** AP, CLEP, SAT, ACT, institutional tests. 32 credit hours maximum toward associate degree, 32 toward bachelor's. **Support services:** Learning center, pre-admission summer program, reduced course load, remedial instruction, tutoring, writing center.

**Majors. Computer sciences:** General. **Physical sciences:** General. **Protective services:** Law enforcement admin. **Psychology:** General. **Public administration:** General, community org/advocacy. **Social sciences:** Criminology, political science.

**Most popular majors.** Psychology 26%, security/protective services 55%, social sciences 16%.

**Computing on campus.** 1,700 workstations in library, computer center. Commuter students can connect to campus network. Online course registration, helpline available.

**Student life. Freshman orientation:** Available. Preregistration for classes offered. **Policies:** Students represented on college committees. **Activities:** Choral groups, dance, drama, musical theater, radio station, student government, student newspaper, Law Society, Irish club, Students against War and Racism, Haitian club, Christian Seekers Fellowship Club, Jewish Students Society, Newman Club, Betances Society, Black Student Society, ethnic organizations.

**Athletics.** NCAA. **Intercollegiate:** Baseball M, basketball, cross-country, diving W, rifle, soccer, softball W, swimming W, tennis, volleyball W. **Intramural:** Basketball, rifle, soccer M, swimming. **Team name:** Bloodhounds.

**Student services.** Adult student services, alcohol/substance abuse counseling, career counseling, services for economically disadvantaged, student employment services, financial aid counseling, health services, on-campus daycare, personal counseling, placement for graduates, veterans' counselor, women's services. **Physically disabled:** Services for visually, speech, hearing impaired.

**Contact.** E-mail: admiss@jjay.cuny.edu
Phone: (212) 237-8865 Fax: (212) 237-8777
Sandra Palleja, Dean of Admissions and Registration, City University of New York: John Jay College of Criminal Justice, 445 West 59th Street, New York, NY 10019

## City University of New York: Lehman College
### Bronx, New York
www.lehman.cuny.edu      CB member     CB code: 2312

- Public 4-year liberal arts college
- Commuter campus in very large city
- 8,236 degree-seeking undergraduates: 33% part-time, 71% women, 32% African American, 4% Asian American, 49% Hispanic American, 5% international
- 1,688 degree-seeking graduate students
- 32% of applicants admitted
- SAT or ACT (ACT writing optional) required
- 35% graduate within 6 years

**General.** Founded in 1931. Regionally accredited. **Degrees:** 1,292 bachelor's awarded; master's offered. **ROTC:** Army. **Location:** 8 miles from Manhattan. **Calendar:** Semester, limited summer session. **Full-time faculty:** 368 total; 75% have terminal degrees, 27% minority, 52% women. **Part-time faculty:** 458 total; 21% have terminal degrees, 37% minority, 55% women. **Class size:** 47% < 20, 52% 20-39, less than 1% 40-49, less than 1% 50-99. **Special facilities:** 2,500-seat performing arts center.

**Freshman class profile.** 14,155 applied, 4,474 admitted, 887 enrolled.

| Mid 50% test scores | | | |
|---|---|---|---|
| SAT critical reading: | 400-490 | End year in good standing: | 74% |
| SAT math: | 400-500 | Return as sophomores: | 75% |
| GPA 3.50 or higher: | 13% | Out-of-state: | 1% |
| GPA 3.0-3.49: | 63% | International: | 6% |
| GPA 2.0-2.99: | 24% | | |

**Basis for selection.** High school record, GPA, and college preparatory courses most important. Tests are used to exempt students from placement tests. **Homeschooled:** State high school equivalency certificate required.

**High school preparation.** 12 units required; 17 recommended. Required and recommended units include English 4, mathematics 2-3, social

studies 1-2, history 1-2, science 2-3 (laboratory 1), foreign language 2 and visual/performing arts 1.

**2007-2008 Annual costs.** Tuition/fees: $4,290; $11,090 out-of-state. Books/supplies: $938. Personal expenses: $2,717.

**2006-2007 Financial aid.** All financial aid based on need. 860 full-time freshmen applied for aid; 845 were judged to have need; 841 of these received aid. Average need met was 92%. Average scholarship/grant was $1,535; average loan $1,380. 72% of total undergraduate aid awarded as scholarships/grants, 28% as loans/jobs.

**Application procedures. Admission:** Priority date 1/15; deadline 8/15 (receipt date). $65 fee. Application may be submitted online. Admission notification on a rolling basis. **Financial aid:** No deadline. FAFSA required. Applicants notified on a rolling basis starting 3/1.

**Academics. Special study options:** Accelerated study, cooperative education, cross-registration, distance learning, double major, dual enrollment of high school students, ESL, exchange student, honors, independent study, internships, student-designed major, study abroad, teacher certification program, Washington semester, weekend college. Bilingual liberal arts (first 2 years may be taken in Spanish), professional writing concentration, 3-2 engineering program with City College. **Credit/placement by examination:** AP, CLEP, IB, institutional tests. 30 credit hours maximum toward bachelor's degree. **Support services:** Learning center, pre-admission summer program, reduced course load, remedial instruction, study skills assistance, tutoring, writing center.

**Honors college/program.** Criteria for selection include high school academic record, SAT/ACT scores, essay, 2 letters of recommendation and interview.

**Majors. Area/ethnic studies:** African-American, Latin American. **Biology:** General. **Business:** Accounting, business admin. **Communications:** General. **Computer sciences:** General, information systems. **Education:** Health, mathematics, physical. **English:** English lit, speech/rhetoric. **Family/consumer sciences:** Food/nutrition. **Foreign languages:** Comparative lit, French, Italian, linguistics, Spanish. **Health:** Audiology/speech pathology, facilities admin, nursing (RN). **History:** General. **Liberal arts:** Arts/sciences. **Math:** General. **Philosophy/religion:** Philosophy. **Physical sciences:** Chemistry, geology, physics. **Psychology:** General. **Public administration:** Social work. **Social sciences:** Anthropology, economics, geography, political science, sociology. **Visual/performing arts:** Art history/conservation, commercial/advertising art, music performance.

**Most popular majors.** Business/marketing 11%, education 28%, health sciences 16%, public administration/social services 9%, social sciences 16%.

**Computing on campus.** 88 workstations in library, computer center, student center. Commuter students can connect to campus network. Online library, helpline, repair service, student web hosting, wireless network available.

**Student life. Freshman orientation:** Mandatory. Preregistration for classes offered. **Activities:** Bands, choral groups, dance, drama, film society, literary magazine, music ensembles, musical theater, opera, radio station, student government, student newspaper, symphony orchestra, TV station, various religious, political, ethnic, and social service organizations.

**Athletics.** NCAA. **Intercollegiate:** Baseball M, basketball, cross-country, diving, softball W, swimming, tennis, track and field, volleyball. **Intramural:** Badminton, basketball, racquetball, soccer, softball, swimming, table tennis, tennis, volleyball. **Team name:** Lightning.

**Student services.** Adult student services, campus ministries, career counseling, services for economically disadvantaged, student employment services, financial aid counseling, health services, on-campus daycare, personal counseling, placement for graduates, veterans' counselor, women's services. **Physically disabled:** Services for visually, speech, hearing impaired.

**Contact.** E-mail: enroll@lehman.cuny.edu
Phone: (718) 960-8706 Fax: (718) 960-8712
Clarence Wilkes, Director of Admissions, City University of New York: Lehman College, 250 Bedford Park Boulevard West, Bronx, NY 10468

**General.** Founded in 1969. Regionally accredited. **Degrees:** 324 bachelor's, 345 associate awarded. **Calendar:** Semester, extensive summer session. **Full-time faculty:** 171 total; 60% have terminal degrees, 85% minority, 46% women. **Part-time faculty:** 273 total; 88% minority, 41% women. **Class size:** 34% < 20, 66% 20-39, less than 1% 40-49.

**Freshman class profile.** 4,267 applied, 4,267 admitted, 892 enrolled.

| Mid 50% test scores | | GPA 2.0-2.99: | 33% |
|---|---|---|---|
| SAT critical reading: | 380-460 | End year in good standing: | 82% |
| SAT math: | 380-480 | Return as sophomores: | 59% |
| GPA 3.50 or higher: | 2% | Out-of-state: | 1% |
| GPA 3.0-3.49: | 4% | International: | 2% |

**Basis for selection.** Open admission, but selective for some programs. Special requirements for nursing and baccalaureate programs with school record, class rank, and test scores considered. Discretionary policy admits 25 students each semester without high school diplomas. Must be 21 years old, legal residents of New York City.

**High school preparation.** 15 units recommended. Recommended units include English 4, mathematics 3, history 2, science 2 and academic electives 4.

**2007-2008 Annual costs.** Tuition/fees: $4,252; $11,052 out-of-state. Books/supplies: $798. Personal expenses: $1,653.

**Financial aid. Non-need-based:** Scholarships awarded for academics, leadership.

**Application procedures. Admission:** Priority date 7/8; no deadline. $65 fee, may be waived for applicants with need. Application may be submitted online. Admission notification on a rolling basis. **Financial aid:** Priority date 1/2, closing date 7/31. FAFSA required. Applicants notified on a rolling basis; must reply within 3 week(s) of notification.

**Academics. Special study options:** Combined bachelor's/graduate degree, cross-registration, distance learning, ESL, honors, independent study, internships, liberal arts/career combination, study abroad, teacher certification program. 2-year bachelor's program in nursing for RNs. **Credit/placement by examination:** AP, CLEP, IB, institutional tests. 15 credit hours maximum toward associate degree, 30 toward bachelor's. **Support services:** Learning center, pre-admission summer program, reduced course load, remedial instruction, tutoring.

**Majors. Biology:** General. **Business:** General, accounting. **Computer sciences:** Information systems. **Conservation:** Environmental science. **Education:** Early childhood, elementary, special. **English:** English lit. **Health:** Nursing (RN). **Liberal arts:** Arts/sciences. **Math:** General. **Psychology:** General. **Public administration:** General.

**Most popular majors.** Business/marketing 20%, psychology 6%.

**Computing on campus.** 450 workstations in library, computer center, student center. Wireless network available.

**Student life. Freshman orientation:** Available. Preregistration for classes offered. **Activities:** Jazz band, choral groups, dance, drama, literary magazine, radio station, student government, student newspaper, TV station, numerous religious, political, ethnic, and social service clubs.

**Athletics.** NCAA. **Intercollegiate:** Basketball, cross-country, soccer, softball W, track and field, volleyball. **Intramural:** Basketball, bowling, cheerleading W, soccer M, swimming, track and field W. **Team name:** Cougar.

**Student services.** Career counseling, student employment services, financial aid counseling, health services, on-campus daycare, personal counseling, placement for graduates, veterans' counselor, women's services. **Physically disabled:** Services for visually, speech, hearing impaired.

**Contact.** E-mail: enroll@mec.cuny.edu
Phone: (718) 270-6024 Fax: (718) 270-6411
Rose Banton, Director of Admissions, City University of New York: Medgar Evers College, 1665 Bedford Avenue, Brooklyn, NY 11225-2201

---

## City University of New York: Medgar Evers College

**Brooklyn, New York**              CB member
**www.mec.cuny.edu**              CB code: 2460

◗  Public 4-year business and liberal arts college
◗  Commuter campus in very large city
◗  5,245 degree-seeking undergraduates: 34% part-time, 75% women, 89% African American, 1% Asian American, 5% Hispanic American, 3% international

---

## City University of New York: New York City College of Technology

**Brooklyn, New York**              CB member
**www.citytech.cuny.edu**              CB code: 2550

◗  Public 4-year technical college
◗  Commuter campus in very large city
◗  12,630 degree-seeking undergraduates: 39% part-time, 49% women, 39% African American, 14% Asian American, 26% Hispanic American, 7% international

**General.** Founded in 1946. Regionally accredited. **Degrees:** 538 bachelor's, 867 associate awarded. **Calendar:** Semester, extensive summer session. **Full-time faculty:** 317 total; 84% have terminal degrees, 31% minority, 45% women. **Part-time faculty:** 653 total; 61% have terminal degrees, 37% minority, 41% women. **Class size:** 34% < 20, 58% 20-39, 8% 40-49, less than 1% 50-99. **Special facilities:** Ophthalmic dispensing and dental clinics, laboratory kitchens and dining room.

**Freshman class profile.** 11,618 applied, 10,186 admitted, 2,844 enrolled.

| Mid 50% test scores | | Return as sophomores: | 75% |
|---|---|---|---|
| SAT critical reading: | 350-450 | Out-of-state: | 1% |
| SAT math: | 370-470 | International: | 6% |
| SAT writing: | 340-430 | | |

**Basis for selection.** Open admission, but selective for some programs.

**High school preparation.** 14 units required; 17 recommended. Required and recommended units include English 4, mathematics 2-3, social studies 2-3, science 2-3 (laboratory 1-2), foreign language 1-2, visual/performing arts 1 and academic electives 1-2.

**2007-2008 Annual costs.** Tuition/fees: $4,289; $11,089 out-of-state. Books/supplies: $832. Personal expenses: $2,673.

**2007-2008 Financial aid.** Need-based: 2,210 full-time freshmen applied for aid; 1,942 were judged to have need; 1,884 of these received aid. Average need met was 58%. Average scholarship/grant was $913; average loan $2,211. 84% of total undergraduate aid awarded as scholarships/grants, 16% as loans/jobs. **Non-need-based:** Awarded to 397 full-time undergraduates, including 285 freshmen. Scholarships awarded for state residency. **Additional information:** Foreign students applying for aid must have resided in New York for at least 1 year.

**Application procedures. Admission:** Priority date 3/15; no deadline. $65 fee, may be waived for applicants with need. Application may be submitted online. Admission notification on a rolling basis. **Financial aid:** Priority date 5/15; no closing date. FAFSA required.

**Academics.** Students in health science programs work under supervision with patients in clinical settings. Industry standard facilities used in hospitality management program. **Special study options:** Distance learning, dual enrollment of high school students, ESL, honors, independent study, internships, study abroad, teacher certification program, weekend college. Bridge programs to higher education or careers in engineering technology, alternate format program for those out of high school 5 years with or without diploma. **Credit/placement by examination:** AP, CLEP, IB, institutional tests. 30 credit hours maximum toward associate degree. **Support services:** Learning center, pre-admission summer program, remedial instruction, study skills assistance, tutoring, writing center.

**Majors. Business:** Hospitality admin, tourism/travel. **Communications technology:** Graphic/printing. **Computer sciences:** General. **Construction:** Maintenance. **Education:** Technology/industrial arts. **Engineering technology:** Architectural, electromechanical, telecommunications. **Health:** Health services admin. **Legal studies:** Paralegal. **Math:** Applied. **Public administration:** Human services. **Visual/performing arts:** Commercial/advertising art, theater design.

**Most popular majors.** Architecture 7%, business/marketing 16%, computer/information sciences 30%, engineering/engineering technologies 7%, legal studies 7%, public administration/social services 9%, visual/performing arts 12%.

**Computing on campus.** Online course registration, online library, helpline, student web hosting, wireless network available.

**Student life. Freshman orientation:** Available. **Housing:** Some housing available at nearby university. **Activities:** Drama, musical theater, student government, student newspaper, full range of student clubs.

**Athletics.** NCAA. **Intercollegiate:** Basketball, cross-country, soccer M, softball W, tennis, volleyball. **Intramural:** Basketball, handball, soccer M, table tennis, track and field, volleyball. **Team name:** Yellow Jackets.

**Student services.** Adult student services, career counseling, services for economically disadvantaged, student employment services, financial aid counseling, health services, minority student services, on-campus daycare, personal counseling, placement for graduates. **Physically disabled:** Services for visually, speech, hearing impaired.

**Contact.** E-mail: admissions@citytech.cuny.edu
Phone: (718) 260-5500 Fax: (718) 260-5504
Alexis Chaconis, Director of Admissions, City University of New York: New York City College of Technology, 300 Jay Street Namm G17, Brooklyn, NY 11201

## City University of New York: Queens College

**Flushing, New York**
www.qc.cuny.edu

CB member
CB code: 2750

- Public 4-year liberal arts and teachers college
- Commuter campus in very large city
- 13,901 degree-seeking undergraduates: 26% part-time, 60% women, 9% African American, 20% Asian American, 18% Hispanic American, 7% international
- 3,633 degree-seeking graduate students
- 40% of applicants admitted
- SAT or ACT (ACT writing optional) required
- 52% graduate within 6 years; 20% enter graduate study

**General.** Founded in 1937. Regionally accredited. **Degrees:** 2,142 bachelor's awarded; master's offered. **ROTC:** Army, Naval. **Location:** 17 miles from Manhattan. **Calendar:** Semester, extensive summer session. **Full-time faculty:** 628 total; 86% have terminal degrees, 19% minority, 42% women. **Part-time faculty:** 693 total; 36% have terminal degrees, 19% minority, 50% women. **Class size:** 45% < 20, 45% 20-39, 4% 40-49, 5% 50-99, less than 1% >100. **Special facilities:** Louis Armstrong archives, Asian American/Asian research institute, center for biology of natural systems, Kupferberg center for the performing arts, speech, language, and learning center, environmental teaching and research center, Byzantine and modern Greek studies center, labor resource center, Italian American institute, center for Jewish studies, Michael Harrington center for democratic values and social change, worker education extension center, equity studies research center, center for improvement of education, neuroscience research center, Schutzman center for entrepreneurship.

**Freshman class profile.** 14,436 applied, 5,835 admitted, 1,778 enrolled.

| Mid 50% test scores | | End year in good standing: | 85% |
|---|---|---|---|
| SAT critical reading: | 450-550 | Return as sophomores: | 84% |
| SAT math: | 480-580 | Out-of-state: | 1% |
| SAT writing: | 490-550 | International: | 7% |
| GPA 3.50 or higher: | 26% | Fraternities: | 1% |
| GPA 3.0-3.49: | 71% | Sororities: | 1% |
| GPA 2.0-2.99: | 3% | | |

**Basis for selection.** Admission based on variety of factors including high school grades, strength of academic program, and test scores. Successful candidates will have chosen well-rounded program of study and attained at least B+ average. SAT Subject Tests recommended. SAT and SAT Subject Test required of scholarship and honors college applicants. Essay and interview recommended for scholarship, honors program; audition recommended for music, performance; portfolio recommended for bachelor of fine arts. Other criteria considered for appeals. **Homeschooled:** Transcript of courses and grades, state high school equivalency certificate required. Students must submit a letter from the superintendent of their school district confirming that all high school graduation requirements of the district have been met through home-schooling. If students cannot obtain the letter from the high school district, they must obtain a General Equivalency Development Diploma (GED). **Learning Disabled:** Untimed SAT/ACT accepted.

**High school preparation.** 16 units required; 17 recommended. Required and recommended units include English 4, mathematics 3, social studies 4, science 2-3 (laboratory 2-3) and foreign language 3.

**2007-2008 Annual costs.** Tuition/fees: $4,377; $11,177 out-of-state. Books/supplies: $879. Personal expenses: $3,526.

**2007-2008 Financial aid.** Need-based: 1,333 full-time freshmen applied for aid; 1,213 were judged to have need; 970 of these received aid. Average need met was 77%. Average scholarship/grant was $1,250; average loan $2,625. 63% of total undergraduate aid awarded as scholarships/grants, 37% as loans/jobs. **Non-need-based:** Awarded to 1,398 full-time undergraduates, including 553 freshmen. Scholarships awarded for academics, athletics, music/drama, state residency.

**Application procedures. Admission:** Priority date 1/1; no deadline. $65 fee, may be waived for applicants with need. Application must be submitted online. Admission notification on a rolling basis beginning on or about 1/15. Admitted applicants must reply by May 1 for some programs, within 4 weeks after notification for others. **Financial aid:** Priority date 2/1; no closing date. FAFSA, institutional form required. Applicants notified on a rolling basis starting 3/1; must reply within 3 week(s) of notification.

**Academics.** Required core liberal arts curriculum includes courses in the humanities, physical and biological sciences, scientific methodology and quantitative reasoning, social sciences, and pre-industrial/non-western civilization. **Special study options:** Accelerated study, combined bachelor's/graduate degree, cooperative education, cross-registration, distance learning, double major, dual enrollment of high school students, ESL, honors, independent study, internships, liberal arts/career combination, New York semester, student-designed major, study abroad, teacher certification program, weekend college. Albany semester, New York University internship, visiting student program at Fashion Institute of Technology. **Credit/placement by examination:** AP, CLEP, SAT, institutional tests. **Support services:** Learning center, pre-admission summer program, study skills assistance, tutoring, writing center.

**Honors college/program.** 40 students, average SAT of 1300 (exclusive of Writing) or higher, high school average 95 or higher, required to submit SAT Subject Test scores, interview required.

**Majors. Area/ethnic studies:** African, American, East Asian, Latin American, women's. **Biology:** General, biochemistry. **Business:** Accounting, actuarial science, finance, international, labor studies. **Communications:** Media studies. **Computer sciences:** Computer science. **Conservation:** Environmental science, environmental studies. **Education:** Art, early childhood, elementary, family/consumer sciences, music, physical. **English:** English lit. **Family/consumer sciences:** General. **Foreign languages:** Ancient Greek, comparative lit, French, German, Hebrew, Italian, Latin, linguistics, Russian, Spanish. **Health:** Communication disorders. **History:** General. **Interdisciplinary:** Nutrition sciences. **Math:** General. **Parks/recreation:** Exercise sciences. **Philosophy/religion:** Judaic, philosophy, religion. **Physical sciences:** Chemistry, geology, physics. **Psychology:** General. **Social sciences:** Anthropology, economics, political science, sociology, urban studies. **Visual/performing arts:** Art history/conservation, dance, dramatic, film/cinema, music performance, music theory/composition, studio arts. **Other:** Byzantine and Modern Greek Studies.

**Most popular majors.** Business/marketing 18%, communications/journalism 6%, education 11%, English 8%, psychology 14%, social sciences 20%.

**Computing on campus.** 2,300 workstations in library, computer center, student center. Commuter students can connect to campus network. Online course registration, online library, helpline, repair service, student web hosting, wireless network available.

**Student life. Freshman orientation:** Mandatory. Preregistration for classes offered. Held in June, July, August. **Policies:** Students found guilty of any form of academic dishonesty, such as plagiarism or cheating on an examination, are subject to discipline, including suspension or dismissal from the college. **Activities:** Bands, choral groups, dance, drama, film society, literary magazine, music ensembles, musical theater, radio station, student government, student newspaper, symphony orchestra, TV station, Catholic, Protestant, Hindu, Jewish, Greek Orthodox, Muslim, African American, Asian, Bangladeshi, Guyanese, Haitian, Hispanic, Italian, Irish, lesbian, and gay student organizations; honor societies; various clubs; political student associations.

**Athletics.** NCAA. **Intercollegiate:** Baseball M, basketball, cross-country, fencing W, soccer, softball W, swimming, tennis, track and field, volleyball W, water polo. **Intramural:** Basketball, cross-country, football (nontackle), ice hockey M, racquetball, soccer, softball, tennis, track and field, volleyball, water polo. **Team name:** Knights.

**Student services.** Adult student services, alcohol/substance abuse counseling, career counseling, student employment services, financial aid counseling, health services, minority student services, on-campus daycare, personal counseling, placement for graduates, veterans' counselor, women's services. **Physically disabled:** Services for visually, speech, hearing impaired.

**Contact.** E-mail: vincent.angrisani@qc.cuny.edu
Phone: (718) 997-5600 Fax: (718) 997-5617
Vincent Angrisani, Executive Director of Admissions, City University of New York: Queens College, 6530 Kissena Boulevard, Jefferson 117, Flushing, NY 11367-1597

---

## City University of New York: York College
**Jamaica, New York**     **CB member**
**www.york.cuny.edu**     **CB code: 2992**

- Public 4-year liberal arts college
- Commuter campus in very large city
- 5,868 degree-seeking undergraduates: 30% part-time, 67% women, 45% African American, 11% Asian American, 17% Hispanic American
- 45 degree-seeking graduate students

**General.** Founded in 1966. Regionally accredited. **Degrees:** 812 bachelor's awarded; master's offered. **Location:** 14 miles from midtown Manhattan. **Calendar:** Semester, limited summer session. **Full-time faculty:** 186 total; 50% minority, 48% women. **Part-time faculty:** 427 total; 56% minority, 46% women. **Class size:** 21% < 20, 40% 20-39, 4% 40-49, 17% 50-99, 17% >100. **Special facilities:** Theater, cardio-pneumo-simulator, flight simulator.

**Freshman class profile.**

| | | | |
|---|---|---|---|
| End year in good standing: | 78% | Out-of-state: | 1% |
| Return as sophomores: | 70% | | |

**Basis for selection.** 75 average with 12 high school academic units basic admission requirement; allowance made for higher average or test scores. Units recommended for admission must be acquired before graduation from any CUNY senior college. Admission requirements for CUNY senior colleges will be automatically satisfied with completion of our core requirement. Interview required for occupational therapy, nursing, physician assistant, and social work or for appeal.

**High school preparation.** 12 units required; 20 recommended. Required and recommended units include English 2-4, mathematics 2-4, social studies 4, science 3, foreign language 3, visual/performing arts 1 and academic electives 8-10.

**2007-2008 Annual costs.** Tuition/fees: $4,262; $11,062 out-of-state. Books/supplies: $938. Personal expenses: $1,628.

**2007-2008 Financial aid. Need-based:** 814 full-time freshmen applied for aid; 767 were judged to have need; 728 of these received aid. Average need met was 36%. Average scholarship/grant was $4,569; average loan $2,357. 87% of total undergraduate aid awarded as scholarships/grants, 13% as loans/jobs. **Non-need-based:** Awarded to 437 full-time undergraduates, including 292 freshmen. Scholarships awarded for academics.

**Application procedures. Admission:** Priority date 12/15; no deadline. $65 fee. Application may be submitted online. Admission notification on a rolling basis beginning on or about 1/1. Centralized application processing allows students to apply to 6 schools within CUNY system at same time. **Financial aid:** Priority date 5/1; no closing date. FAFSA required. Applicants notified on a rolling basis starting 3/1.

**Academics. Special study options:** Cooperative education, distance learning, double major, dual enrollment of high school students, ESL, honors, independent study, internships, liberal arts/career combination, study abroad, teacher certification program. Co-op programs in business, computer science, health professions. **Credit/placement by examination:** AP, CLEP, IB, institutional tests. 16 credit hours maximum toward bachelor's degree. Students with SAT/ACT scores exempt from CUNY skills assessment tests. **Support services:** Learning center, pre-admission summer program, remedial instruction, study skills assistance, tutoring, writing center.

**Majors. Area/ethnic studies:** African-American. **Biology:** General, biotechnology. **Business:** Accounting, business admin, management information systems, marketing. **Education:** Health, physical. **English:** English lit, speech/rhetoric. **Foreign languages:** French, Spanish. **Health:** Clinical lab technology, environmental health, nursing (RN). **History:** General. **Interdisciplinary:** Gerontology. **Liberal arts:** Arts/sciences. **Math:** General. **Philosophy/religion:** Philosophy. **Physical sciences:** Chemistry, geology, physics. **Psychology:** General. **Public administration:** Social work. **Social sciences:** Anthropology, economics, political science, sociology. **Visual/performing arts:** Art history/conservation, dramatic.

**Most popular majors.** Business/marketing 32%, education 9%, health sciences 9%, psychology 15%, public administration/social services 8%, social sciences 6%.

**Computing on campus.** 530 workstations in library, computer center, student center. Online library, wireless network available.

**Student life. Freshman orientation:** Available. Preregistration for classes offered. **Activities:** Jazz band, choral groups, drama, film society, literary magazine, musical theater, student government, student newspaper, TV station, 48 organizations.

**Athletics.** NCAA. **Intercollegiate:** Basketball, cheerleading, cross-country, soccer, softball W, swimming, tennis, track and field, volleyball, weight lifting. **Intramural:** Badminton, basketball, soccer M, softball W, swimming, table tennis, tennis, track and field, volleyball, weight lifting. **Team name:** Cardinals.

**Student services.** Adult student services, campus ministries, career counseling, student employment services, financial aid counseling, health services, on-campus daycare, personal counseling, placement for graduates, veterans' counselor. **Physically disabled:** Services for visually, speech, hearing impaired.

**Contact.** E-mail: admissions@york.cuny.edu
Phone: (718) 262-2165 Fax: (718) 262-2601
Diane Warmsley, Director of Admissions/Enrollment, City University of New York: York College, 94-20 Guy R. Brewer Boulevard, Jamaica, NY 11451-9989

---

## Clarkson University

**Potsdam, New York**                    **CB member**
**www.clarkson.edu**                     **CB code: 2084**

- Private 4-year university
- Residential campus in large town
- 2,521 degree-seeking undergraduates: 26% women, 3% African American, 3% Asian American, 2% Hispanic American, 2% international
- 406 degree-seeking graduate students
- 81% of applicants admitted
- SAT or ACT (ACT writing optional), application essay required
- 74% graduate within 6 years; 26% enter graduate study

**General.** Founded in 1896. Regionally accredited. **Degrees:** 591 bachelor's awarded; master's, doctoral, first professional offered. **ROTC:** Army, Air Force. **Location:** 140 miles from Syracuse, 70 miles from Watertown. **Calendar:** Semester, extensive summer session. **Full-time faculty:** 183 total; 86% have terminal degrees, 12% minority, 20% women. **Part-time faculty:** 28 total; 71% have terminal degrees, 29% women. **Class size:** 42% < 20, 31% 20-39, 7% 40-49, 16% 50-99, 3% >100. **Special facilities:** Center for advanced materials processing with multidisciplinary engineering labs, center for global competitiveness, center for leadership and entrepreneurship, center for excellence in communication, observatory, 200-acre nature preserve.

**Freshman class profile.** 2,983 applied, 2,408 admitted, 682 enrolled.

| Mid 50% test scores | | Rank in top quarter: | 73% |
|---|---|---|---|
| SAT critical reading: | 510-610 | Rank in top tenth: | 40% |
| SAT math: | 560-670 | End year in good standing: | 80% |
| SAT writing: | 500-630 | Return as sophomores: | 85% |
| ACT composite: | 23-29 | Out-of-state: | 30% |
| GPA 3.50 or higher: | 63% | Live on campus: | 93% |
| GPA 3.0-3.49: | 29% | International: | 3% |
| GPA 2.0-2.99: | 8% | | |

**Basis for selection.** School achievement record, test scores, recommendations, school and community involvement important. SAT Subject Tests recommended. Applicants whose TOEFL score falls below minimum required for admission can enter Clarkson Intensive English Program to study English as a Second Language in preparation for full-time study in a degree program. Interview recommended. **Homeschooled:** Transcript of courses and grades required. **Learning Disabled:** Documented information on disabilities necessary.

**High school preparation.** 16 units required. Required and recommended units include English 4, mathematics 3-4 and science 2-3.

**2008-2009 Annual costs.** Tuition/fees: $31,010. Room/board: $10,612. Books/supplies: $1,100. Personal expenses: $1,000.

**2007-2008 Financial aid. Need-based:** 574 full-time freshmen applied for aid; 499 were judged to have need; 499 of these received aid. Average need met was 86%. Average scholarship/grant was $14,270; average loan $5,100. 64% of total undergraduate aid awarded as scholarships/grants, 36% as loans/jobs. **Non-need-based:** Awarded to 448 full-time undergraduates, including 161 freshmen. Scholarships awarded for academics, alumni affiliation, leadership, minority status, ROTC.

**Application procedures. Admission:** Closing date 1/15 (postmark date). $50 fee, may be waived for applicants with need. Application may be submitted online. Admission notification on a rolling basis beginning on or about 2/1. Must reply by May 1 or within 2 week(s) if notified thereafter. Candidates encouraged to submit completed application between October 1 and March 1 of their final year in secondary school. **Financial aid:** Priority date 2/15; no closing date. FAFSA, institutional form required. Applicants notified on a rolling basis starting 3/19; must reply by 5/1 or within 2 week(s) of notification.

**Academics.** 3-year B.S. degree option. Students must be in top 10 percent of their high school class. Students apply Advanced Placement credits and/or work on special projects during the summer. **Special study options:** Accelerated study, combined bachelor's/graduate degree, cooperative education, cross-registration, double major, dual enrollment of high school students, ESL, honors, independent study, liberal arts/career combination, semester at sea, student-designed major, study abroad. 3-2 agreements with many area colleges. **Credit/placement by examination:** AP, CLEP, IB, institutional tests. 30 credit hours maximum toward bachelor's degree. **Support services:** Pre-admission summer program, study skills assistance, tutoring, writing center.

**Majors. Biology:** General, molecular. **Business:** Accounting/finance, e-commerce, entrepreneurial studies, logistics, management information systems. **Communications:** General, digital media. **Computer sciences:** General, computer science. **Conservation:** Environmental studies. **Engineering:** General, aerospace, chemical, civil, computer, electrical, environmental, mechanical, software. **Health:** Environmental health, occupational health, predental, premedicine, preveterinary. **History:** General. **Legal studies:** Prelaw. **Liberal arts:** Arts/sciences. **Math:** General, applied, statistics. **Physical sciences:** Chemistry, physics. **Psychology:** General. **Social sciences:** General, political science, sociology.

**Most popular majors.** Biology 7%, business/marketing 28%, engineering/engineering technologies 47%.

**Computing on campus.** 400 workstations in library, computer center. Dormitories wired for high-speed internet access and linked to campus network. Commuter students can connect to campus network. Online course registration, online library, helpline, repair service, student web hosting, wireless network available.

**Student life. Freshman orientation:** Available. Students meet housemates, classmates, advisers. Optional pre-orientation outing club trips; $125 charge for students who participate. **Housing:** Guaranteed on-campus for freshmen. Coed dorms, single-sex dorms, special housing for disabled, apartments, fraternity/sorority housing, substance-free housing available. Theme housing available. **Activities:** Bands, choral groups, drama, international student organizations, literary magazine, musical theater, radio station, student government, student newspaper, symphony orchestra, TV station, Inter-Varsity Christian Fellowship, American Indian science and engineering society, Black engineers society, Hispanic professional engineers society, women engineers society, special interest clubs.

**Athletics.** NCAA. **Intercollegiate:** Baseball M, basketball, cross-country, diving, golf M, ice hockey, lacrosse, skiing, soccer, swimming, volleyball W. **Intramural:** Basketball, football (tackle) M, ice hockey, racquetball, rowing (crew) M, soccer, softball, swimming, volleyball. **Team name:** Golden Knights.

**Student services.** Alcohol/substance abuse counseling, career counseling, services for economically disadvantaged, student employment services, financial aid counseling, health services, minority student services, personal counseling, placement for graduates, veterans' counselor, women's services. **Physically disabled:** Services for visually, speech, hearing impaired. **Learning disabled:** Comprehensive services available.

**Contact.** E-mail: admission@clarkson.edu
Phone: (315) 268-6480 Toll-free number: (800) 527-6577
Fax: (315) 268-7647
Brian Grant, Director of Admission, Clarkson University, Holcroft House, Potsdam, NY 13699-5605

---

## Colgate University

**Hamilton, New York**                   **CB member**
**www.colgate.edu**                      **CB code: 2086**

- Private 4-year liberal arts college
- Residential campus in small town
- 2,800 degree-seeking undergraduates: 52% women, 5% African American, 6% Asian American, 5% Hispanic American, 1% Native American, 5% international
- 6 degree-seeking graduate students
- 26% of applicants admitted
- SAT or ACT (ACT writing optional), application essay required
- 90% graduate within 6 years

**General.** Founded in 1819. Regionally accredited. **Degrees:** 674 bachelor's awarded; master's offered. **ROTC:** Army. **Location:** 38 miles from Syracuse, 25 miles from Utica. **Calendar:** Semester. **Full-time faculty:** 253 total; 97% have terminal degrees, 20% minority, 41% women. **Part-time faculty:** 55 total; 64% have terminal degrees, 13% minority, 54% women. **Class size:** 61% < 20, 37% 20-39, less than 1% 40-49, 1% 50-99, less than 1% >100. **Special facilities:** Anthropology museum, center for learning, teaching, and research, cable TV station, life sciences complex, geology/fossil collection, observatory, electron microscopes, laser lab, weather lab, geographic information system, center for outreach, volunteerism, and education.

**Freshman class profile.** 8,759 applied, 2,242 admitted, 746 enrolled.

| Mid 50% test scores | | | |
|---|---|---|---|
| SAT critical reading: | 620-720 | Rank in top quarter: | 83% |
| SAT math: | 630-710 | Rank in top tenth: | 64% |
| ACT composite: | 29-32 | Return as sophomores: | 94% |
| GPA 3.50 or higher: | 63% | Out-of-state: | 73% |
| GPA 3.0-3.49: | 31% | Live on campus: | 100% |
| GPA 2.0-2.99: | 6% | International: | 5% |

**Basis for selection.** School achievement record of primary importance. Teacher/counselor recommendations, test scores, and major talent or personal accomplishment considered. Disadvantaged, nontraditional, and minority applicants given special consideration. **Homeschooled:** Statement describing homeschool structure and mission, transcript of courses and grades, letter of recommendation (nonparent) required. **Learning Disabled:** Optional self-disclosure of disabilities in admissions process.

**High school preparation.** 16 units required; 20 recommended. Required and recommended units include English 4, mathematics 3-4, social studies 3-4, science 3-4 (laboratory 2-3) and foreign language 3-4. Foreign language units should be in 1 language.

**2008-2009 Annual costs.** Tuition/fees: $39,545. Room/board: $9,625. Books/supplies: $1,880.

**2007-2008 Financial aid. Need-based:** 276 full-time freshmen applied for aid; 219 were judged to have need; 219 of these received aid. Average need met was 100%. Average scholarship/grant was $30,297; average loan $1,877. 88% of total undergraduate aid awarded as scholarships/grants, 12% as loans/jobs. **Non-need-based:** Awarded to 167 full-time undergraduates, including 41 freshmen. Scholarships awarded for athletics.

**Application procedures. Admission:** Closing date 1/15 (postmark date). $55 fee, may be waived for applicants with need. Application may be submitted online. Admission notification 4/1. Must reply by 5/1. **Financial aid:** Closing date 1/15. FAFSA, CSS PROFILE required. Applicants notified by 4/1; must reply by 5/1 or within 2 week(s) of notification.

**Academics. Special study options:** Combined bachelor's/graduate degree, cross-registration, double major, honors, independent study, internships, semester at sea, student-designed major, study abroad, teacher certification program, urban semester, Washington semester. 3-4 architecture program with Washington University (MO), 3-2 program in engineering with Columbia University, Rensselaer Polytechnic Institute, and Washington University; Early Assurance Medical School program with American University; Extended study program during winter or summer breaks offer academic work in 13 locations around world including South Africa, Ireland, and China. **Credit/placement by examination:** AP, CLEP, IB, SAT, institutional tests. **Support services:** Learning center, pre-admission summer program, reduced course load, study skills assistance, tutoring, writing center.

**Majors. Area/ethnic studies:** African, African-American, Asian, Latin American, Native American, Russian/Slavic, women's. **Biology:** General, biochemistry, molecular. **Computer sciences:** General, computer science. **Conservation:** General, environmental studies. **Education:** General. **English:** English lit. **Foreign languages:** Classics, French, German, Japanese, Latin, modern Greek, Russian, Spanish. **Health:** Predental, premedicine, preveterinary. **History:** General. **Interdisciplinary:** Biological/physical sciences, math/computer science, natural sciences, neuroscience, peace/conflict. **Liberal arts:** Arts/sciences. **Math:** General. **Philosophy/religion:** Philosophy, religion. **Physical sciences:** Astronomy, astrophysics, chemistry, geology, physics. **Psychology:** General. **Social sciences:** General, anthropology, economics, geography, international economic development, international relations, political science, sociology. **Visual/performing arts:** Art, art history/conservation, dramatic, studio arts.

**Most popular majors.** Biology 7%, business/marketing 7%, English 10%, philosophy/religious studies 6%, social sciences 37%, visual/performing arts 6%.

**Computing on campus.** 848 workstations in dormitories, library, computer center, student center. Dormitories wired for high-speed internet access and linked to campus network. Commuter students can connect to campus network. Online course registration, helpline, repair service, student web hosting, wireless network available.

**Student life. Freshman orientation:** Mandatory. Preregistration for classes offered. 4-day program held 4 days before first day of classes. **Policies:** All students required to read, sign, and abide by Academic Honor Code. **Housing:** Guaranteed on-campus for all undergraduates. Coed dorms, special housing for disabled, apartments, cooperative housing, fraternity/sorority housing, substance-free housing available. $500 nonrefundable deposit, deadline 5/1. Theme housing (Peace Studies, La Casa Pan Latina, Harlem Renaissance Center, French-Italian House, etc.), accommodations for students

with special needs, townhouses for small groups of students available. **Activities:** Bands, choral groups, dance, drama, film society, literary magazine, music ensembles, musical theater, radio station, student government, student newspaper, symphony orchestra, TV station, over 125 campus organizations.

**Athletics.** NCAA. **Intercollegiate:** Basketball, cheerleading, cross-country, diving, field hockey W, football (tackle) M, golf M, ice hockey, lacrosse, rowing (crew), soccer, softball W, swimming, tennis, track and field, volleyball W. **Intramural:** Basketball, bowling, football (non-tackle), golf, ice hockey, racquetball, rifle, soccer, softball, squash, table tennis, tennis, volleyball. **Team name:** Raiders.

**Student services.** Alcohol/substance abuse counseling, campus ministries, career counseling, services for economically disadvantaged, student employment services, financial aid counseling, health services, minority student services, personal counseling, placement for graduates, women's services. **Physically disabled:** Services for visually, hearing impaired.

**Contact.** E-mail: admission@mail.colgate.edu
Phone: (315) 228-7401 Fax: (315) 228-7544
Gary Ross, Dean of Admission, Colgate University, 13 Oak Drive, Hamilton, NY 13346-1383

---

## College of Mount St. Vincent
**Riverdale, New York** — CB member
**www.mountsaintvincent.edu** — CB code: 2088

- Private 4-year liberal arts college affiliated with Roman Catholic Church
- Residential campus in very large city
- 1,417 degree-seeking undergraduates: 8% part-time, 73% women, 11% African American, 11% Asian American, 30% Hispanic American
- 111 degree-seeking graduate students
- 71% of applicants admitted
- SAT or ACT, application essay required
- 53% graduate within 6 years; 35% enter graduate study

**General.** Founded in 1847. Regionally accredited. Dual certification in elementary and special education and secondary and special education. 5-year program for master of science in education. **Degrees:** 267 bachelor's, 3 associate awarded; master's offered. **ROTC:** Air Force. **Location:** 12 miles from midtown Manhattan. **Calendar:** Semester, limited summer session. **Full-time faculty:** 73 total; 90% have terminal degrees, 6% minority, 58% women. **Part-time faculty:** 112 total; 36% minority, 56% women. **Class size:** 43% < 20, 56% 20-39, less than 1% 40-49. **Special facilities:** NMR spectrometer, computer graphics and animation center, computer classrooms, forensic science equipment.

**Freshman class profile.** 2,092 applied, 1,486 admitted, 394 enrolled.

| Mid 50% test scores | | | |
|---|---|---|---|
| SAT critical reading: | 450-540 | End year in good standing: | 84% |
| SAT math: | 430-530 | Return as sophomores: | 77% |
| GPA 3.50 or higher: | 13% | Out-of-state: | 16% |
| GPA 3.0-3.49: | 29% | Live on campus: | 64% |
| GPA 2.0-2.99: | 53% | International: | 1% |

**Basis for selection.** School achievement record (rank in top half of class, 3.0 high school GPA) most important, test scores and recommendations important, school and community activities considered. Interview recommended. **Learning Disabled:** Must submit IEP or other certification to receive service.

**High school preparation.** 16 units required; 20 recommended. Required and recommended units include English 4, mathematics 2-3, social studies 2-3, science 2-3 and foreign language 2-3. 3 math for nursing, science, and math majors; 3 science with lab for nursing and science majors.

**2007-2008 Annual costs.** Tuition/fees: $22,750. Room/board: $8,925. Books/supplies: $850. Personal expenses: $900.

**2006-2007 Financial aid. Need-based:** 360 full-time freshmen applied for aid; 304 were judged to have need; 304 of these received aid. Average need met was 78%. Average scholarship/grant was $9,000; average loan $2,200. 65% of total undergraduate aid awarded as scholarships/grants, 35% as loans/jobs. **Non-need-based:** Scholarships awarded for academics, alumni affiliation, leadership.

**Application procedures. Admission:** No deadline. $35 fee, may be waived for applicants with need. Application may be submitted online. Admission notification on a rolling basis beginning on or about 2/1. Must reply by May 1 or within 3 week(s) if notified thereafter. **Financial aid:** Priority date 3/1; no closing date. FAFSA required. Applicants notified on a rolling basis starting 3/1; must reply by 5/1 or within 3 week(s) of notification.

**Academics. Special study options:** Accelerated study, combined bachelor's/graduate degree, double major, honors, independent study, internships, liberal arts/career combination, study abroad, teacher certification program. 3-2 occupational therapy program with Columbia University, 3-2 physical therapy with New York Medical College. **Credit/placement by examination:** AP, CLEP, IB, institutional tests. 18 credit hours maximum toward bachelor's degree. **Support services:** Learning center, pre-admission summer program, reduced course load, remedial instruction, study skills assistance, tutoring, writing center.

**Majors. Biology:** General, biochemistry. **Business:** General, business admin. **Communications:** General. **English:** English lit. **Foreign languages:** General, French, Spanish. **Health:** Preop/surgical nursing. **History:** General. **Liberal arts:** Arts/sciences. **Math:** General. **Philosophy/religion:** Philosophy, religion. **Physical sciences:** Chemistry. **Psychology:** General. **Social sciences:** Economics, sociology.

**Most popular majors.** Business/marketing 15%, communications/journalism 12%, English 6%, health sciences 25%, liberal arts 17%, psychology 9%, social sciences 6%.

**Computing on campus.** 323 workstations in library, computer center. Dormitories wired for high-speed internet access and linked to campus network. Commuter students can connect to campus network. Online course registration, online library, helpline, repair service, wireless network available.

**Student life. Freshman orientation:** Mandatory, $125 fee. Preregistration for classes offered. 3 days with overnight for all freshmen; parent participation overnight optional. **Housing:** Guaranteed on-campus for all undergraduates. Coed dorms, single-sex dorms, special housing for disabled available. $200 fully refundable deposit, deadline 5/1. **Activities:** Campus ministries, choral groups, dance, drama, international student organizations, literary magazine, musical theater, radio station, student government, student newspaper, TV station, Culturally Aware Students of Today, Latino club, student nurses association, Circle-K, Student Action for Viable Earth, black student union, pep club, communications club.

**Athletics.** NCAA. **Intercollegiate:** Baseball M, basketball, cross-country, lacrosse, soccer, softball W, swimming, tennis, track and field W, volleyball. **Team name:** Dolphins.

**Student services.** Adult student services, campus ministries, career counseling, student employment services, financial aid counseling, health services, personal counseling, placement for graduates. **Physically disabled:** Services for visually, hearing impaired.

**Contact.** E-mail: admissions.office@mountsaintvincent.edu
Phone: (718) 405-3267 Toll-free number: (800) 665-2678
Fax: (718) 549-7945
Timothy Nash, VP & Dean of Admission and Financial Aid, College of Mount St. Vincent, 6301 Riverdale Avenue, Riverdale, NY 10471-1093

## College of New Rochelle

**New Rochelle, New York** — **CB member**
**www.cnr.edu** — **CB code: 2089**

- Private 4-year nursing and liberal arts college for women affiliated with Roman Catholic Church
- Residential campus in small city
- 933 degree-seeking undergraduates: 33% part-time, 95% women, 36% African American, 5% Asian American, 15% Hispanic American, 1% Native American, 1% international
- 862 degree-seeking graduate students
- 43% of applicants admitted
- SAT or ACT (ACT writing optional) required
- 52% graduate within 6 years

**General.** Founded in 1904. Regionally accredited. Independent institution in Roman Catholic tradition. Coeducational school of nursing and graduate school. **Degrees:** 241 bachelor's awarded; master's offered. **ROTC:** Army, Naval. **Location:** 14 miles from New York City. **Calendar:** Semester, limited summer session. **Full-time faculty:** 87 total; 87% have terminal degrees, 10% minority, 71% women. **Part-time faculty:** 145 total; 30% minority, 77% women. **Class size:** 73% < 20, 27% 20-39, less than 1% 50-99. **Special facilities:** 2 learning skills centers (including 1 for nursing), electron microscope, institute for entrepreneurial studies, computer graphics laboratory, model classroom, rare book collections of James Joyce, Thomas More, Ursuline Order.

**Freshman class profile.** 1,784 applied, 765 admitted, 128 enrolled.

| Mid 50% test scores | | | |
|---|---|---|---|
| SAT critical reading: | 450-530 | Rank in top tenth: | 28% |
| SAT math: | 460-530 | Return as sophomores: | 71% |
| ACT composite: | 18-23 | Out-of-state: | 16% |
| Rank in top quarter: | 51% | Live on campus: | 93% |

**Basis for selection.** Admissions based on secondary school record. Class rank and standardized test scores also important. Essay, interview recommended; portfolio required for art program.

**High school preparation.** 16 units required. Required and recommended units include English 4, mathematics 3, social studies 3, science 3 (laboratory 2) and foreign language 2. Biology, chemistry, 3 math required for nursing and physical therapy.

**2007-2008 Annual costs.** Tuition/fees: $23,700. All incoming freshmen given laptop at no additional cost. Room/board: $8,700. Books/supplies: $600. Personal expenses: $1,000.

**Financial aid. Non-need-based:** Scholarships awarded for academics, art, leadership.

**Application procedures. Admission:** No deadline. $20 fee, may be waived for applicants with need. Admission notification on a rolling basis beginning on or about 11/1. Must reply by May 1 or within 3 week(s) if notified thereafter. **Financial aid:** Priority date 3/1; no closing date. FAFSA, institutional form required. Applicants notified on a rolling basis starting 1/1; must reply within 2 week(s) of notification.

**Academics.** Laptop computers given to all undergraduate students. **Special study options:** Accelerated study, combined bachelor's/graduate degree, cooperative education, cross-registration, double major, exchange student, honors, independent study, internships, liberal arts/career combination, study abroad, teacher certification program, United Nations semester, Washington semester. Preprofessional programs in law, medicine, health. **Credit/placement by examination:** AP, CLEP, institutional tests. 15 credit hours maximum toward bachelor's degree. **Support services:** Learning center, reduced course load, remedial instruction, study skills assistance, tutoring, writing center.

**Majors. Area/ethnic studies:** American, women's. **Biology:** General. **Business:** General. **Communications:** Broadcast journalism, media studies. **Conservation:** Environmental studies. **Education:** General, art, elementary, special. **English:** English lit. **Foreign languages:** Classics, French, Latin, Spanish. **Health:** Art therapy, nursing (RN). **History:** General. **Interdisciplinary:** Biological/physical sciences, global studies. **Legal studies:** Prelaw. **Math:** General. **Philosophy/religion:** Philosophy, religion. **Physical sciences:** Chemistry. **Psychology:** General. **Public administration:** Social work. **Social sciences:** Economics, political science, sociology. **Visual/performing arts:** Art history/conservation, studio arts.

**Most popular majors.** Health sciences 67%, psychology 9%.

**Computing on campus.** 223 workstations in dormitories, library, computer center. Dormitories wired for high-speed internet access and linked to campus network. Commuter students can connect to campus network. Online course registration, online library, helpline, wireless network available.

**Student life. Freshman orientation:** Available. Preregistration for classes offered. **Housing:** Guaranteed on-campus for all undergraduates. Substance-free housing available. $100 deposit. **Activities:** Campus ministries, choral groups, dance, drama, film society, literary magazine, musical theater, student government, student newspaper, community services, Latin American Women Society, Black Student Union, CNR Drama, nurses gospel choir.

**Athletics.** NCAA. **Intercollegiate:** Basketball W, cross-country W, softball W, swimming W, tennis W, volleyball W. **Team name:** Blue Angels.

**Student services.** Adult student services, alcohol/substance abuse counseling, campus ministries, career counseling, services for economically disadvantaged, student employment services, financial aid counseling, health services, personal counseling, placement for graduates, women's services. **Physically disabled:** Services for visually, speech, hearing impaired.

**Contact.** E-mail: admission@cnr.edu
Phone: (914) 654-5452 Toll-free number: (800) 933-5923
Fax: (914) 654-5464
Stephanie Decker, Director of Admissions, College of New Rochelle, 29 Castle Place, New Rochelle, NY 10805-2339

## College of Saint Rose
**Albany, New York**
www.strose.edu

**CB member**
**CB code: 2091**

- Private 4-year liberal arts and teachers college affiliated with Roman Catholic Church
- Commuter campus in small city
- 3,116 degree-seeking undergraduates: 6% part-time, 72% women, 3% African American, 1% Asian American, 4% Hispanic American
- 1,774 degree-seeking graduate students
- 67% of applicants admitted
- SAT or ACT (ACT writing optional) required
- 68% graduate within 6 years

**General.** Founded in 1920. Regionally accredited. **Degrees:** 669 bachelor's awarded; master's offered. **ROTC:** Army, Naval, Air Force. **Location:** 140 miles from New York City. **Calendar:** Semester, limited summer session. **Full-time faculty:** 198 total; 82% have terminal degrees, 11% minority, 55% women. **Part-time faculty:** 283 total; 3% minority, 58% women. **Class size:** 55% < 20, 45% 20-39, less than 1% 40-49, less than 1% 50-99. **Special facilities:** Communications studio, speech and hearing clinic.

**Freshman class profile.** 3,842 applied, 2,558 admitted, 624 enrolled.

| Mid 50% test scores | | | |
|---|---|---|---|
| SAT critical reading: | 480-580 | GPA 2.0-2.99: | 27% |
| SAT math: | 480-580 | Rank in top quarter: | 48% |
| ACT composite: | 21-27 | Rank in top tenth: | 19% |
| GPA 3.50 or higher: | 44% | Return as sophomores: | 82% |
| GPA 3.0-3.49: | 29% | Out-of-state: | 11% |
| | | Live on campus: | 81% |

**Basis for selection.** School achievement record, test scores, recommendations most important. School and community involvement and interview also considered. Music applicants must read music, play at least 1 instrument, and pass audition using standard repertoire as guide. Art applicants must submit portfolio.

**High school preparation.** Required and recommended units include English 4, mathematics 4, social studies 4, history 4, science 4 (laboratory 2), foreign language 3-4 and academic electives 4.

**2007-2008 Annual costs.** Tuition/fees: $20,620. Room/board: $8,198. Books/supplies: $1,000. Personal expenses: $1,500.

**2006-2007 Financial aid. Need-based:** 602 full-time freshmen applied for aid; 520 were judged to have need; 519 of these received aid. Average need met was 49%. Average scholarship/grant was $3,190; average loan $1,805. 61% of total undergraduate aid awarded as scholarships/grants, 39% as loans/jobs. **Non-need-based:** Awarded to 319 full-time undergraduates, including 46 freshmen. Scholarships awarded for academics, alumni affiliation, art, athletics, minority status, music/drama.

**Application procedures. Admission:** Priority date 12/1; deadline 5/1 (receipt date). $35 fee, may be waived for applicants with need. Application may be submitted online. Admission notification on a rolling basis beginning on or about 12/1. Must reply by 5/1. **Financial aid:** Priority date 3/1; no closing date. FAFSA required. Applicants notified on a rolling basis starting 3/15; must reply by 5/1 or within 2 week(s) of notification.

**Academics. Special study options:** Accelerated study, combined bachelor's/graduate degree, cross-registration, double major, exchange student, independent study, internships, liberal arts/career combination, student-designed major, study abroad, teacher certification program. **Credit/placement by examination:** AP, CLEP, IB, institutional tests. 15 credit hours maximum toward bachelor's degree. **Support services:** Learning center, pre-admission summer program, reduced course load, remedial instruction, study skills assistance, tutoring, writing center.

**Majors. Area/ethnic studies:** American, women's. **Biology:** General, biochemistry, cell/histology. **Business:** Accounting, business admin. **Computer sciences:** General. **Conservation:** Environmental studies. **Education:** Art, biology, chemistry, elementary, English, mathematics, music, secondary, social studies, Spanish, trade/industrial. **English:** English lit. **Foreign languages:** Spanish. **Health:** Audiology/speech pathology, clinical lab science. **History:** General. **Liberal arts:** Arts/sciences. **Math:** General. **Philosophy/religion:** Religion. **Physical sciences:** Chemistry. **Protective services:** Law enforcement admin. **Psychology:** General. **Public administration:** Social work. **Social sciences:** Political science, sociology. **Visual/performing arts:** Commercial/advertising art, music performance.

**Most popular majors.** Business/marketing 9%, communication technologies 7%, education 45%, psychology 6%, visual/performing arts 8%.

**Computing on campus.** Dormitories wired for high-speed internet access and linked to campus network. Commuter students can connect to campus network. Helpline available.

**Student life. Freshman orientation:** Mandatory, $125 fee. Two-part orientation: 2-day overnight summer program and week-long program that begins 2 days prior to start of fall classes. **Housing:** Guaranteed on-campus for freshmen. Coed dorms, single-sex dorms, apartments available. $300 nonrefundable deposit, deadline 5/1. **Activities:** Bands, campus ministries, choral groups, dance, drama, international student organizations, literary magazine, music ensembles, musical theater, radio station, student government, student newspaper, symphony orchestra, TV station, many religious, ethnic, political, and social service organizations available.

**Athletics.** NCAA. **Intercollegiate:** Baseball M, basketball, cross-country, golf M, soccer, softball W, swimming, tennis W, volleyball W. **Intramural:** Basketball, soccer, volleyball. **Team name:** Golden Knights.

**Student services.** Adult student services, alcohol/substance abuse counseling, campus ministries, career counseling, services for economically disadvantaged, student employment services, financial aid counseling, health services, legal services, minority student services, personal counseling, placement for graduates. **Physically disabled:** Services for visually, speech, hearing impaired.

**Contact.** E-mail: admit@strose.edu
Phone: (518) 454-5111 Toll-free number: (800) 637-8556
Fax: (518) 454-2013
Mary Grondahl, Associate Vice President for Enrollment Planning and Undergraduate Admissions, College of Saint Rose, 432 Western Avenue, Albany, NY 12203

## Columbia University
**New York, New York**
www.columbia.edu

**CB member**
**CB code: 2116**

- Private 4-year university, engineering and liberal arts college
- Residential campus in very large city
- 5,602 degree-seeking undergraduates: 46% women, 9% African American, 18% Asian American, 10% Hispanic American, 1% Native American, 9% international
- 11% of applicants admitted
- SAT or ACT with writing, SAT Subject Tests, application essay required
- 93% graduate within 6 years

**General.** Founded in 1754. Regionally accredited. **Degrees:** 1,386 bachelor's awarded; master's, doctoral offered. **ROTC:** Army, Naval, Air Force. **Location:** 3 miles from midtown Manhattan. **Calendar:** Semester, extensive summer session. **Full-time faculty:** 790 total; 15% minority, 35% women. **Part-time faculty:** 267 total; 17% minority, 37% women. **Class size:** 52% < 20, 32% 20-39, 4% 40-49, 9% 50-99, 3% >100. **Special facilities:** Art and architecture galleries, cinemas, theaters, geological observatory, interactive graphics laboratory, telecommunications research center, plasma laboratory, materials laboratory, astronomical observatory.

**Freshman class profile.** 21,343 applied, 2,255 admitted, 1,333 enrolled.

| Mid 50% test scores | | | |
|---|---|---|---|
| SAT critical reading: | 660-760 | End year in good standing: | 97% |
| SAT math: | 670-780 | Return as sophomores: | 97% |
| SAT writing: | 650-760 | Out-of-state: | 75% |
| ACT composite: | 28-33 | Live on campus: | 99% |
| | | International: | 11% |

**Basis for selection.** School achievement record most important. Test scores, recommendations, essay, extracurricular activities also important. TOEFL required of all non-native speakers. Interview recommended for all; audition required for Juilliard program.

**High school preparation.** Recommended units include English 4, mathematics 4, history 4, science 4 (laboratory 4), foreign language 4 and academic electives 4.

**2007-2008 Annual costs.** Tuition/fees: $37,223. Room/board: $9,937. Books/supplies: $1,000. Personal expenses: $1,060.

**2007-2008 Financial aid.** All financial aid based on need. 852 full-time freshmen applied for aid; 691 were judged to have need; 691 of these received aid. Average need met was 100%. Average scholarship/grant was $32,035; average loan $3,346. 86% of total undergraduate aid awarded as scholarships/grants, 14% as loans/jobs.

**Application procedures. Admission:** Closing date 1/2 (receipt date). $70 fee, may be waived for applicants with need. Application may be submitted online. Admission notification 4/1. Must reply by 5/1. **Financial aid:** Closing date 3/1. FAFSA, CSS PROFILE required. Applicants notified by 4/1.

**Academics. Special study options:** Accelerated study, combined bachelor's/ graduate degree, cooperative education, cross-registration, double major, dual enrollment of high school students, ESL, independent study, internships, liberal arts/career combination, student-designed major, study abroad, teacher certification program. Combined 3-2 program with engineering; 3-2 programs with over 90 liberal arts colleges around the country. **Credit/ placement by examination:** AP, CLEP, IB, institutional tests. 16 credit hours maximum toward bachelor's degree. **Support services:** Tutoring.

**Majors. Architecture:** Architecture. **Area/ethnic studies:** African, African-American, American, Asian, Asian-American, Central/Eastern European, Chinese, East Asian, European, French, German, Hispanic-American/Latino/ Chicano, Italian, Japanese, Korean, Latin American, Near/Middle Eastern, Polish, regional, Russian/Slavic, Slavic, Spanish/Iberian, women's. **Biology:** General, biochemistry, biophysics, ecology, environmental, evolutionary. **Computer sciences:** Computer science. **Conservation:** General, environmental science. **Education:** General. **Engineering:** Biomedical, chemical, civil, computer, electrical, environmental, geological, materials, materials science, mechanical, mechanics, metallurgical, mining, operations research. **Engineering technology:** Industrial management. **English:** American lit, British lit, creative writing, English lit. **Foreign languages:** Ancient Greek, Biblical, Chinese, classics, comparative lit, East Asian, French, German, Germanic, Italian, Japanese, Korean, Latin, linguistics, modern Greek, Russian, Slavic, Spanish. **History:** General. **Interdisciplinary:** Ancient studies, classical/archaeology, intercultural, medieval/Renaissance, neuroscience. **Math:** General, applied, statistics. **Philosophy/religion:** Philosophy, religion. **Physical sciences:** Astronomy, astrophysics, chemical physics, chemistry, geochemistry, geology, geophysics, physics, planetary. **Psychology:** General. **Social sciences:** Anthropology, archaeology, economics, political science, sociology, urban studies. **Visual/performing arts:** General, art history/ conservation, dance, dramatic, film/cinema, jazz, studio arts, theater history.

**Most popular majors.** Engineering/engineering technologies 23%, English 8%, history 7%, social sciences 22%.

**Computing on campus.** 150 workstations in dormitories, library, computer center, student center. Dormitories wired for high-speed internet access and linked to campus network. Commuter students can connect to campus network. Online course registration, helpline, student web hosting, wireless network available.

**Student life. Freshman orientation:** Mandatory, $300 fee. Preregistration for classes offered. One week prgoram ending on Labor Day. **Housing:** Guaranteed on-campus for all undergraduates. Coed dorms, special housing for disabled, fraternity/sorority housing available. Special interest (group) housing available; single-sex first-year floor available. **Activities:** Bands, campus ministries, choral groups, dance, drama, film society, international student organizations, literary magazine, music ensembles, Model UN, musical theater, opera, radio station, student government, student newspaper, symphony orchestra, TV station, African-American, Hispanic, Asian-American, Gay/Lesbian student organizations, community service groups, religious groups of all denominations.

**Athletics.** NCAA. **Intercollegiate:** Archery W, baseball M, basketball, cross-country, diving, fencing, field hockey W, football (tackle) M, golf, lacrosse W, rowing (crew), soccer, softball W, swimming, tennis, track and field, volleyball W, wrestling M. **Intramural:** Basketball, football (non-tackle), racquetball, soccer, softball, squash, tennis, volleyball. **Team name:** Lions.

**Student services.** Alcohol/substance abuse counseling, campus ministries, career counseling, services for economically disadvantaged, student employment services, financial aid counseling, health services, minority student services, personal counseling, placement for graduates, women's services. **Physically disabled:** Services for visually, speech, hearing impaired.

**Contact.** Phone: (212) 854-2522 Fax: (212) 854-1209
Jessica Marinaccio, Dean of Undergraduate Admissions, Columbia University, 212 Hamilton Hall, MC 2807, New York, NY 10027

## Columbia University: School of General Studies
**New York, New York**
**www.gs.columbia.edu**                                   CB code: 2095

- Private 4-year university and liberal arts college
- Commuter campus in very large city

- 1,190 degree-seeking undergraduates: 41% part-time, 49% women, 6% African American, 12% Asian American, 8% Hispanic American, 1% Native American
- 36% of applicants admitted
- SAT or ACT (ACT writing optional), application essay required

**General.** Founded in 1947. Regionally accredited. Liberal arts division of university for nontraditional students whose undergraduate study has been interrupted or postponed for at least 1 year. Postbaccalaureate premedical program offered. **Degrees:** 251 bachelor's awarded. **ROTC:** Army, Air Force. **Calendar:** Semester, extensive summer session. **Full-time faculty:** 764 total; 100% have terminal degrees, 21% minority, 37% women. **Part-time faculty:** 239 total; 100% have terminal degrees, 37% minority, 37% women. **Special facilities:** Earth Institute, observatory.

**Freshman class profile.** 258 applied, 93 admitted, 47 enrolled.

**Basis for selection.** Maturity and varied backgrounds of students considered. Aptitude and motivation important together with academic performance and test scores. Interview requested when needed.

**2007-2008 Annual costs.** Tuition/fees: $36,013. Institutionally managed double-occupancy apartments available averaging $900/month rent. Books/supplies: $2,000.

**2007-2008 Financial aid.** All financial aid based on need. 54% of total undergraduate aid awarded as scholarships/grants, 46% as loans/jobs.

**Application procedures. Admission:** Priority date 3/1; deadline 6/1 (postmark date). $65 fee. Application may be submitted online. 4 to 6 weeks after receipt of application. Must reply by May 1 or within 2 week(s) if notified thereafter. **Financial aid:** Priority date 4/15, closing date 6/1. FAFSA, institutional form required. Applicants notified on a rolling basis; must reply within 3 week(s) of notification.

**Academics. Special study options:** Accelerated study, combined bachelor's/ graduate degree, cross-registration, double major, dual enrollment of high school students, ESL, exchange student, honors, independent study, internships, student-designed major, study abroad, teacher certification program. Dual degree program with Jewish Theological Seminary. **Credit/placement by examination:** AP, CLEP, SAT, ACT, institutional tests. 30 credit hours maximum toward bachelor's degree. **Support services:** Learning center, pre-admission summer program, reduced course load, remedial instruction, study skills assistance, tutoring, writing center.

**Majors. Architecture:** Architecture. **Area/ethnic studies:** African, African-American, American, Asian, East Asian, Hispanic-American/Latino/ Chicano, Latin American, Near/Middle Eastern, Russian/Slavic, women's. **Biology:** General, evolutionary. **Computer sciences:** General, computer science. **Conservation:** General, environmental studies. **Education:** Elementary, secondary. **English:** British lit, creative writing, English lit. **Foreign languages:** Classics, comparative lit, French, German, Italian, Portuguese, Russian, Spanish. **Health:** Premedicine. **History:** General. **Math:** General, applied, statistics. **Philosophy/religion:** Philosophy, religion. **Physical sciences:** Astronomy, astrophysics, chemistry, geochemistry, geology, geophysics, oceanography, physics. **Psychology:** General. **Public administration:** Human services. **Social sciences:** Economics, political science, sociology, urban studies. **Visual/performing arts:** General, art history/conservation, dance, dramatic, film/cinema, music performance, musicology, painting, sculpture, voice/opera.

**Most popular majors.** Foreign language 9%, history 7%, liberal arts 11%, mathematics 6%, social sciences 31%, visual/performing arts 6%.

**Computing on campus.** 347 workstations in dormitories, library, computer center, student center. Dormitories wired for high-speed internet access and linked to campus network. Commuter students can connect to campus network. Online course registration, online library, helpline, repair service, student web hosting, wireless network available.

**Student life. Freshman orientation:** Mandatory, $75 fee. Preregistration for classes offered. Generally held 1 week before classes start. Academic planning session (held prior to beginning of semester) required of all new students. **Housing:** Coed dorms, single-sex dorms, special housing for disabled, apartments, cooperative housing, fraternity/sorority housing available. $400 nonrefundable deposit. Limited on-campus housing available. Off-campus housing registry provides listings of Columbia-affiliated apartments. **Activities:** Bands, choral groups, dance, drama, film society, literary magazine, music ensembles, musical theater, opera, radio station, student government, student newspaper, symphony orchestra, TV station, many religious, political, and ethnic organizations.

**Athletics.** NCAA. **Intercollegiate:** Archery W, baseball M, basketball, cross-country, diving, fencing, field hockey W, football (tackle) M, golf, lacrosse W, rowing (crew), soccer, softball W, swimming, tennis, track and field, volleyball W, wrestling M. **Intramural:** Baseball M, basketball, boxing, cricket M, diving, fencing, lacrosse, racquetball, skiing, soccer, softball, squash, swimming, tennis, volleyball. **Team name:** Lions.

**Student services.** Adult student services, alcohol/substance abuse counseling, campus ministries, career counseling, services for economically disadvantaged, student employment services, financial aid counseling, health services, minority student services, personal counseling, placement for graduates, veterans' counselor, women's services. **Physically disabled:** Services for visually impaired. **Learning disabled:** Comprehensive services available.

**Contact.**  E-mail: gsdegree@columbia.edu
Phone: (212) 854-2772 Toll-free number: (800) 895-1169
Fax: (212) 854-6316
Curtis Rodgers, Dean of Admissions, Columbia University: School of General Studies, 408 Lewisohn Hall, Mail Code 4101, New York, NY 10027

---

## Concordia College
### Bronxville, New York
www.concordia-ny.edu

CB member
CB code: 2096

- Private 4-year liberal arts college affiliated with Lutheran Church - Missouri Synod
- Residential campus in small town
- 673 degree-seeking undergraduates: 5% part-time, 60% women, 11% African American, 8% Hispanic American, 10% international
- 67% of applicants admitted
- SAT or ACT with writing, application essay required
- 52% graduate within 6 years

**General.** Founded in 1881. Regionally accredited. Christian principles central to program of study. **Degrees:** 132 bachelor's, 2 associate awarded. **Location:** 14 miles from New York City. **Calendar:** Semester, limited summer session. **Full-time faculty:** 33 total; 67% have terminal degrees, 18% minority, 46% women. **Part-time faculty:** 44 total; 18% minority, 41% women. **Class size:** 62% < 20, 37% 20-39, 1% 40-49. **Special facilities:** Electric-piano laboratory, distance learning classroom, new media electronic and digital learning center.

**Freshman class profile.** 682 applied, 455 admitted, 128 enrolled.

| Mid 50% test scores | | | |
|---|---|---|---|
| SAT critical reading: | 410-490 | GPA 2.0-2.99: | 54% |
| SAT math: | 410-500 | Rank in top quarter: | 27% |
| ACT composite: | 16-20 | Rank in top tenth: | 13% |
| GPA 3.50 or higher: | 16% | Return as sophomores: | 73% |
| GPA 3.0-3.49: | 23% | Out-of-state: | 26% |
| | | International: | 14% |

**Basis for selection.** Test scores, school achievement record, interview important; community and church involvement considered. Interview required for some, recommended for others; audition required for music program. **Homeschooled:** Statement describing homeschool structure and mission, transcript of courses and grades, interview, letter of recommendation (nonparent) required. Show explanation of all course work studied and grades obtained. **Learning Disabled:** Students required to meet with learning specialist and submit most recent psychological assessment.

**High school preparation.** 15 units recommended. Recommended units include English 4, mathematics 3, social studies 2, science 2 (laboratory 2) and foreign language 2.

**2007-2008 Annual costs.** Tuition/fees: $21,950. Room/board: $8,520. Books/supplies: $900. Personal expenses: $1,500.

**Financial aid. Non-need-based:** Scholarships awarded for academics, athletics, leadership, music/drama.

**Application procedures. Admission:** Closing date 3/15 (postmark date). $50 fee, may be waived for applicants with need. Application may be submitted online. Admission notification on a rolling basis beginning on or about 12/1. Must reply by May 1 or within 4 week(s) if notified thereafter. **Financial aid:** Priority date 4/1; no closing date. FAFSA required. Applicants notified on a rolling basis starting 4/1; must reply by 5/1 or within 3 week(s) of notification.

**Academics. Special study options:** Combined bachelor's/graduate degree, cooperative education, cross-registration, distance learning, double major, ESL, exchange student, honors, independent study, internships, liberal arts/career combination, student-designed major, study abroad, teacher certification program. **Credit/placement by examination:** AP, CLEP, IB, institutional tests. 30 credit hours maximum toward associate degree, 30 toward bachelor's. **Support services:** Reduced course load, remedial instruction, study skills assistance, tutoring, writing center.

**Majors. Biology:** General, ecology. **Business:** General, accounting, business admin, finance, international. **Education:** General, elementary. **English:** English lit. **Health:** Premedicine. **History:** General. **Interdisciplinary:** Behavioral sciences. **Legal studies:** Prelaw. **Liberal arts:** Arts/sciences. **Math:** General. **Philosophy/religion:** Religion. **Physical sciences:** Geology. **Psychology:** General. **Public administration:** Social work. **Social sciences:** General. **Theology:** Religious ed, sacred music.

**Computing on campus.** 30 workstations in library, computer center. Dormitories wired for high-speed internet access and linked to campus network. Commuter students can connect to campus network. Online course registration, online library, helpline, repair service, wireless network available.

**Student life. Freshman orientation:** Mandatory. Preregistration for classes offered. Held at beginning of semester with adviser. **Housing:** Guaranteed on-campus for all undergraduates. Single-sex dorms available. $300 deposit, deadline 5/1. **Activities:** Jazz band, campus ministries, choral groups, drama, music ensembles, musical theater, student government, student newspaper, Christian service organizations, Afro-Latino American club, social work club, Prayer Partners, environmental club, In His Name, Lutheran Women League, Rotaract club.

**Athletics.** NCAA. **Intercollegiate:** Baseball M, basketball, cross-country, soccer, softball W, tennis, volleyball. **Intramural:** Basketball, football (nontackle), softball W, squash, tennis, volleyball. **Team name:** Clippers.

**Student services.** Adult student services, alcohol/substance abuse counseling, campus ministries, career counseling, student employment services, financial aid counseling, health services, minority student services, personal counseling, placement for graduates. **Learning disabled:** Comprehensive services available.

**Contact.**  E-mail: admission@concordia-ny.edu
Phone: (914) 337-9300 ext. 2155 Toll-free number: (800) 937-2655
Fax: (914) 395-4636
Donna Hoyt, Dean of Enrollment, Concordia College, 171 White Plains Road, Bronxville, NY 10708

---

## Cooper Union for the Advancement of Science and Art
### New York, New York
www.cooper.edu

CB member
CB code: 2097

- Private 4-year visual arts and engineering college
- Commuter campus in very large city
- 889 degree-seeking undergraduates: 37% women, 5% African American, 18% Asian American, 9% Hispanic American, 14% international
- 51 degree-seeking graduate students
- 11% of applicants admitted
- SAT or ACT (ACT writing recommended), application essay required
- 86% graduate within 6 years; 45% enter graduate study

**General.** Founded in 1859. Regionally accredited. Full-tuition scholarship school of architecture, art, and engineering. **Degrees:** 201 bachelor's awarded; master's offered. **Calendar:** Semester, limited summer session. **Full-time faculty:** 50 total; 90% have terminal degrees, 14% minority, 26% women. **Part-time faculty:** 165 total; 60% have terminal degrees, 30% minority, 32% women. **Class size:** 67% < 20, 32% 20-39, less than 1% 40-49, less than 1% >100.

**Freshman class profile.** 2,551 applied, 274 admitted, 203 enrolled.

| Mid 50% test scores | | | |
|---|---|---|---|
| SAT critical reading: | 610-700 | Rank in top quarter: | 98% |
| SAT math: | 640-770 | Rank in top tenth: | 93% |
| ACT composite: | 29-33 | End year in good standing: | 94% |
| GPA 3.50 or higher: | 55% | Return as sophomores: | 95% |
| GPA 3.0-3.49: | 37% | Out-of-state: | 40% |
| GPA 2.0-2.99: | 8% | Live on campus: | 80% |
| | | International: | 14% |

**Basis for selection.** Engineering applicants reviewed on high school record and program, essays, SAT, and required SAT Subject Test scores. Art and architecture applicants selected on basis of home test, high school record and program, SAT. All international students must apply from an address in United States. 2 SAT Subject Tests required for engineering applicants: 1

math and 1 chemistry or 1 math and 1 physics. Portfolios required for art applicants. All art and architecture applicants must complete a home test. **Homeschooled:** Statement describing homeschool structure and mission, transcript of courses and grades, letter of recommendation (nonparent) required. Must present proof of high school graduation certification (national) or equivalent.

**High school preparation.** 16 units required; 18 recommended. Required and recommended units include English 4, mathematics 1-4, social studies 1-4, history 1, science 1-4 (laboratory 3) and academic electives 8. 1 science required for architecture and art. 2 science and 4 math required for engineering including physics, chemistry, and precalculus; calculus preferred. 1 math required for art, 3 math for architecture including trigonometry or precalculus. 18 total units recommended for engineering.

**2007-2008 Annual costs.** Tuition/fees: $33,050. Every student admitted receives full-tuition scholarship (covering tuition only) for duration of enrollment. International students assessed annual filing fee of $1,700. Room only: $9,500. Books/supplies: $1,800. Personal expenses: $1,575.

**2006-2007 Financial aid. Need-based:** 120 full-time freshmen applied for aid; 76 were judged to have need; 76 of these received aid. Average need met was 92%. Average scholarship/grant was $3,156; average loan $2,639. 65% of total undergraduate aid awarded as scholarships/grants, 35% as loans/jobs. **Non-need-based:** Awarded to 900 full-time undergraduates, including 219 freshmen. Scholarships awarded for academics. **Additional information:** All students receive full-tuition scholarships valued at approximately $30,000 per year. Students able to document need receive financial aid package that may include combination of grants, loans, work-study, internships.

**Application procedures. Admission:** Priority date 12/1; deadline 1/1 (postmark date). $65 fee, may be waived for applicants with need. Application may be submitted online. Admission notification 4/1. Must reply by May 1 or within 4 week(s) if notified thereafter. Regular application closing date for architecture January 1, for fine arts January 10, for engineering February 1. **Financial aid:** Priority date 4/15, closing date 6/1. FAFSA, CSS PROFILE required. Applicants notified by 6/1; must reply by 6/30 or within 2 week(s) of notification.

**Academics.** Engineering tutorials and engineering mentor program available. All freshman engineering majors required to prove or acquire computer literacy. 128 credit hours required for graduation in art program, 135 in engineering, and 160 in architecture. Students may take classes in all 3 schools. Art students encouraged to take courses throughout 7 disciplines. Architecture students take 5 years of design culminating in thesis year. Engineering students encouraged to take coursework in other majors. **Special study options:** Combined bachelor's/graduate degree, cross-registration, exchange student, independent study, internships, student-designed major, study abroad. Research opportunities. Students may take up to 1 year off between studies to pursue related experiences. **Credit/placement by examination:** AP, CLEP, institutional tests. Varies depending upon school and department. **Support services:** Tutoring, writing center.

**Majors. Architecture:** Architecture. **Engineering:** General, chemical, civil, electrical, mechanical. **Visual/performing arts:** Graphic design, studio arts. **Other:** Interdisciplinary engineering.

**Most popular majors.** Architecture 9%, engineering/engineering technologies 57%, visual/performing arts 34%.

**Computing on campus.** 650 workstations in dormitories, library, computer center. Dormitories linked to campus network. Commuter students can connect to campus network. Online library, helpline, repair service, student web hosting, wireless network available.

**Student life. Freshman orientation:** Available, $100 fee. 2.5 days, of which 1.5 days usually spent away at camp. **Housing:** Coed dorms available. $500 fully refundable deposit, deadline 6/1. **Activities:** Bands, choral groups, dance, drama, film society, literary magazine, music ensembles, musical theater, student government, student newspaper, symphony orchestra, 90 registered clubs available.

**Athletics. Intercollegiate:** Basketball, cross-country, equestrian W, lacrosse M, soccer M, tennis, volleyball. **Intramural:** Badminton, baseball M, basketball, bowling, cross-country, fencing, golf, judo, soccer, softball, table tennis, tennis, volleyball. **Team name:** Pioneers.

**Student services.** Alcohol/substance abuse counseling, career counseling, student employment services, financial aid counseling, minority student services, personal counseling, placement for graduates, veterans' counselor. **Physically disabled:** Services for visually, hearing impaired.

**Contact.** E-mail: admissions@cooper.edu
Phone: (212) 353-4120 Fax: (212) 353-4342
Mitchell Lipton, Dean of Admissions and Records/Registrar, Cooper Union for the Advancement of Science and Art, 30 Cooper Square, Suite 300, New York, NY 10003-7183

## Cornell University
**Ithaca, New York**
www.cornell.edu

**CB member**
**CB code: 2098**

- Private 4-year university
- Residential campus in large town
- 13,455 degree-seeking undergraduates: 49% women, 5% African American, 16% Asian American, 6% Hispanic American, 1% Native American, 8% international
- 6,285 degree-seeking graduate students
- 21% of applicants admitted
- SAT or ACT with writing, application essay required
- 92% graduate within 6 years; 27% enter graduate study

**General.** Founded in 1865. Regionally accredited. 7 undergraduate colleges: agriculture and life sciences; architecture, art, and planning; arts and sciences; engineering; hotel administration; human ecology; industrial and labor relations. 6 graduate/professional colleges. **Degrees:** 3,467 bachelor's awarded; master's, doctoral, first professional offered. **ROTC:** Army, Naval, Air Force. **Location:** 60 miles from Syracuse. **Calendar:** Semester, extensive summer session. **Full-time faculty:** 1,728 total; 92% have terminal degrees, 16% minority, 30% women. **Part-time faculty:** 182 total; 68% have terminal degrees, 7% minority, 32% women. **Class size:** 60% < 20, 19% 20-39, 4% 40-49, 12% 50-99, 5% >100. **Special facilities:** Africana studies/research center, particle accelerator, biotechnology institute, supercomputer, national research centers, center for performing arts, observatory, marine laboratory, plantations, ornithology laboratory, life sciences institute.

**Freshman class profile.** 30,383 applied, 6,503 admitted, 3,055 enrolled.

| Mid 50% test scores | | | | |
|---|---|---|---|---|
| SAT critical reading: | 630-770 | End year in good standing: | 98% |
| SAT math: | 660-730 | Return as sophomores: | 96% |
| ACT composite: | 28-32 | Out-of-state: | 65% |
| Rank in top quarter: | 98% | Live on campus: | 100% |
| Rank in top tenth: | 87% | International: | 9% |

**Basis for selection.** School achievement record (difficulty of courses, grades earned), test scores, preparation and background for specific programs especially important. Essays, recommendations considered. Minority status considered. Some programs do not require Subject Tests. Please consult admissions office. Interview required for architecture, hotel administration programs; portfolio required for art, architecture programs. **Homeschooled:** Well-documented coursework required.

**High school preparation.** 16 units required. Required and recommended units include English 4, mathematics 3, social studies 3, history 3, science 3 (laboratory 3) and foreign language 3. Requirements vary by college.

**2007-2008 Annual costs.** Tuition/fees: $34,781. Tuition amounts listed are for Endowed/Private colleges only: Architecture, Art & Planning; Arts & Sciences; Engineering; Hotel Administration. Contract/State college amounts differ and vary by program. Room/board: $11,190. Books/supplies: $720. Personal expenses: $1,460.

**2007-2008 Financial aid.** All financial aid based on need. 1,407 full-time freshmen applied for aid; 1,310 were judged to have need; 1,310 of these received aid. Average need met was 100%. Average scholarship/grant was $21,824; average loan $5,180. 71% of total undergraduate aid awarded as scholarships/grants, 29% as loans/jobs.

**Application procedures. Admission:** Closing date 1/1 (receipt date). $65 fee, may be waived for applicants with need. Application may be submitted online. Notification on rolling basis, dates vary by program/college. Must reply by May 1 or within 2 week(s) if notified thereafter. Notification on rolling basis and dates vary by program/college. **Financial aid:** Closing date 2/11. FAFSA, institutional form, CSS PROFILE required. Applicants notified by 4/1; must reply by 5/1 or within 2 week(s) of notification.

**Academics.** Cornell/Hughes Scholars program for independent research in neurobiology, physiology, genetics and development, and biochemistry (molecular and cell biology), Cornell in Rome program for studies in architecture and fine arts, undergraduate research opportunities in traditional majors as well as in many interdisciplinary fields including American Indian studies, cognitive studies, agriculture, food and society, FALCON language programs. **Special study options:** Accelerated study, combined bachelor's/graduate degree, cooperative education, cross-registration, distance learning, double major, ESL, exchange student, honors, independent study, internships, liberal arts/career combination, New York semester, semester at sea, student-designed major, study abroad, teacher certification program, urban semester, Washington semester. **Credit/placement by examination:** AP, CLEP, IB, institutional tests. **Support services:** Learning center, pre-admission summer program, reduced course load, study skills assistance, tutoring, writing center.

**Majors. Agriculture:** General, agribusiness operations, agronomy, animal sciences, business, food science, horticultural science, international, ornamental horticulture, plant protection, plant sciences. **Architecture:** Architecture, landscape, urban/community planning. **Area/ethnic studies:** African-American, American, Asian, gay/lesbian, German, Near/Middle Eastern, Russian/Slavic, women's. **Biology:** General, animal genetics, animal physiology, bacteriology, biochemistry, biometrics, ecology, entomology, plant pathology. **Business:** Hotel/motel admin, labor relations, restaurant/food services. **Communications:** General. **Computer sciences:** Computer science, information technology. **Conservation:** General, economics. **Education:** General, agricultural, biology, chemistry, family/consumer sciences, mathematics, physics, science. **Engineering:** General, agricultural, chemical, civil, electrical, environmental, materials, mechanical, operations research, physics. **English:** English lit. **Family/consumer sciences:** General, consumer economics, family studies, food/nutrition. **Foreign languages:** Classics, comparative lit, French, German, Italian, linguistics, Russian, Spanish. **Health:** Premedicine. **History:** General. **Interdisciplinary:** Neuroscience, science/society. **Liberal arts:** Arts/sciences. **Math:** General. **Philosophy/religion:** Philosophy, religion. **Physical sciences:** Astronomy, atmospheric science, chemistry, geology, physics. **Psychology:** General. **Public administration:** General, community org/advocacy, policy analysis. **Social sciences:** General, anthropology, archaeology, economics, political science, sociology. **Visual/performing arts:** Art history/conservation, dance, dramatic, fiber arts, film/cinema, studio arts, theater design.

**Most popular majors.** Agriculture 13%, biology 12%, business/marketing 13%, engineering/engineering technologies 19%, social sciences 10%.

**Computing on campus.** 2,650 workstations in dormitories, library, computer center, student center. Dormitories wired for high-speed internet access and linked to campus network. Commuter students can connect to campus network. Online course registration, online library, helpline, repair service, student web hosting, wireless network available.

**Student life. Freshman orientation:** Available. Preregistration for classes offered. **Housing:** Guaranteed on-campus for freshmen. Coed dorms, single-sex dorms, special housing for disabled, apartments, cooperative housing, fraternity/sorority housing, substance-free housing available. $50 nonrefundable deposit, deadline 5/1. Ecology house, JAM (Just About Music), language house, international living center, Ujamaa residential college (Third World house), Risley residential college (theater and expressive arts), multicultural living learning unit, Akwe:Kon (Native American and Non-native American), Latino living center, transfer center. **Activities:** Bands, campus ministries, choral groups, dance, drama, film society, international student organizations, literary magazine, music ensembles, Model UN, musical theater, radio station, student government, student newspaper, symphony orchestra, TV station, Hillel, Campus Crusade for Christ, La Asociacion Latina, African, Native American, Caribbean, Vietnamese, international, and lesbian/gay/bisexual groups, debate.

**Athletics.** NCAA. **Intercollegiate:** Baseball M, basketball, cross-country, equestrian W, fencing W, field hockey W, football (tackle) M, golf M, gymnastics W, ice hockey, lacrosse, rowing (crew), soccer, softball W, squash, swimming, tennis, track and field, volleyball W, wrestling M. **Intramural:** Badminton, basketball, bowling, cross-country, fencing, football (non-tackle), golf, ice hockey, skiing, soccer, softball, squash, table tennis, tennis, track and field, volleyball, water polo, wrestling. **Team name:** Big Red.

**Student services.** Alcohol/substance abuse counseling, campus ministries, career counseling, student employment services, financial aid counseling, health services, minority student services, personal counseling, placement for graduates, veterans' counselor, women's services. **Physically disabled:** Services for visually, speech, hearing impaired.

**Contact.** E-mail: admissions@cornell.edu
Phone: (607) 255-5241 Fax: (607) 255-0659
Jason Locke, Director of Undergraduate Admissions, Cornell University, 410 Thurston Avenue, Ithaca, NY 14850-2488

---

## Culinary Institute of America
**Hyde Park, New York**
www.ciachef.edu
**CB member**
**CB code: 3301**

- Private 4-year culinary school
- Residential campus in large town
- 2,738 degree-seeking undergraduates: 41% women
- 75% of applicants admitted

- Application essay required
- 51% graduate within 6 years

**General.** Founded in 1946. Candidate for regional accreditation; also accredited by ACCSCT. **Degrees:** 304 bachelor's, 1,061 associate awarded. **Location:** 80 miles from New York City. **Calendar:** Semester. **Full-time faculty:** 128 total; 6% have terminal degrees, 23% women. **Part-time faculty:** 44 total; 54% women. **Special facilities:** 41 teaching kitchens and bakeshops, 5 restaurants, culinary library with over 70,000 volumes.

**Freshman class profile.** 1,115 applied, 832 admitted, 572 enrolled.

| | | | |
|---|---|---|---|
| GPA 3.50 or higher: | 23% | Rank in top tenth: | 6% |
| GPA 3.0-3.49: | 35% | End year in good standing: | 92% |
| GPA 2.0-2.99: | 39% | Return as sophomores: | 95% |
| Rank in top quarter: | 32% | Out-of-state: | 77% |

**Basis for selection.** School achievement record, 6 months work experience (particularly in hands-on food preparation), and interview important. SAT/ACT not used for admissions, but if tests taken recommended that students submit scores.

**High school preparation.** Recommended units include English 4, mathematics 3, social studies 2, history 2 and science 2.

**2007-2008 Annual costs.** Tuition/fees: $22,370. Room and board costs shown for typical undergraduate; costs may vary. Room/board: $6,890. Books/supplies: $975.

**Financial aid. Non-need-based:** Scholarships awarded for academics, alumni affiliation, job skills, leadership, minority status.

**Application procedures. Admission:** No deadline. $50 fee, may be waived for applicants with need. Application may be submitted online. Admission notification on a rolling basis. **Financial aid:** Priority date 12/15; no closing date. FAFSA required. Applicants notified by 4/1; must reply by 5/1 or within 4 week(s) of notification.

**Academics.** Curriculum devoted exclusively to culinary arts and baking and pastry arts education. Freshmen may enroll in one of 4 enrollment seasons throughout the year. All students complete 18-week paid externship program. Two-thirds of class time involves hands-on cooking, baking, table service, and dining room operations management in kitchens, bakeshops, and 5 student-staffed public restaurants. **Special study options:** Cross-registration, distance learning, internships. **Credit/placement by examination:** CLEP, institutional tests. **Support services:** Learning center, reduced course load, remedial instruction, study skills assistance, tutoring, writing center.

**Majors. Business:** Restaurant/food services. **Personal/culinary services:** Baking.

**Computing on campus.** 208 workstations in dormitories, library, computer center, student center. Dormitories wired for high-speed internet access and linked to campus network. Commuter students can connect to campus network. Online library, helpline, repair service, wireless network available.

**Student life. Freshman orientation:** Mandatory. **Housing:** Guaranteed on-campus for freshmen. Coed dorms, special housing for disabled, substance-free housing available. Hearing impaired student housing available. **Activities:** International student organizations, literary magazine, student government, student newspaper, Alliance, Eta Sigma Delta honor society, baking and pastry arts society, Black Culinarian Society, Chefs Supporting Agriculture, Culinary Christian Fellowship, ice carving society, global culinary society, garden society.

**Athletics. Intramural:** Basketball, football (tackle), ice hockey, racquetball, soccer, softball, tennis, volleyball. **Team name:** Flames.

**Student services.** Alcohol/substance abuse counseling, campus ministries, career counseling, student employment services, financial aid counseling, health services, personal counseling, placement for graduates, veterans' counselor. **Physically disabled:** Services for visually, speech, hearing impaired.

**Contact.** E-mail: admissions@culinary.edu
Phone: (845) 452-9430 Toll-free number: (800) 285-4627
Fax: (845) 451-1068
Rachel Birchwood, Director of Admissions, Culinary Institute of America, 1946 Campus Drive, Hyde Park, NY 12538-1499

---

## Daemen College
**Amherst, New York**
www.daemen.edu
**CB member**
**CB code: 2762**

- Private 4-year liberal arts college
- Residential campus in small city

- 1,571 degree-seeking undergraduates: 14% part-time, 74% women, 10% African American, 1% Asian American, 2% Hispanic American, 1% international
- 837 degree-seeking graduate students
- 68% of applicants admitted
- SAT or ACT (ACT writing optional) required
- 47% graduate within 6 years; 72% enter graduate study

**General.** Founded in 1947. Regionally accredited. **Degrees:** 279 bachelor's awarded; master's, first professional offered. **ROTC:** Army. **Location:** 9 miles from downtown Buffalo. **Calendar:** Semester, limited summer session. **Full-time faculty:** 88 total; 76% have terminal degrees, 8% minority, 53% women. **Part-time faculty:** 187 total; 14% have terminal degrees, 6% minority, 66% women. **Class size:** 69% < 20, 28% 20-39, 3% 40-49. **Special facilities:** Natural and health science research center, videoconference center, center for sustainable communities and civic engagement, Thomas J. Reynolds center for special education and after school programs.

**Freshman class profile.** 1,780 applied, 1,203 admitted, 363 enrolled.

| Mid 50% test scores | | | |
|---|---|---|---|
| SAT critical reading: | 450-550 | Rank in top tenth: | 17% |
| SAT math: | 460-570 | End year in good standing: | 87% |
| ACT composite: | 20-25 | Return as sophomores: | 70% |
| GPA 3.50 or higher: | 58% | Out-of-state: | 5% |
| GPA 3.0-3.49: | 40% | Live on campus: | 61% |
| GPA 2.0-2.99: | 2% | International: | 1% |
| Rank in top quarter: | 48% | Fraternities: | 1% |

**Basis for selection.** Emphasis on academic achievement and test scores with secondary consideration given to school activities and recommendations. Work experience also considered for entry into physician assistant program. 30 credit hour transfer limit on International Baccalaureate coursework. Applicants who have been out of high school for more than 2 years not required to submit SAT or ACT scores. Essay, interview required for physician assistant program; portfolio required for art program. **Home-schooled:** Applicants should provide evidence of equivalency of high school education by GED or attestation of equivalency by superintendent of schools in student's public school district of residence. This documentation needed for financial aid eligibility. **Learning Disabled:** Bring to the attention of Admission Office need for special accommodations and submit current medical evidence of disability and limitations that require accommodations. Feasibility determined considering nature and cost of accommodation, availability of funding, and whether accommodation will impact fundamental nature of course or program, among other factors.

**High school preparation.** 16 units recommended. Recommended units include English 4, mathematics 4, social studies 4, science 4 (laboratory 1). All science and allied health programs require 3 math and 3 science. Business program requires 3 math. Foreign language programs require 3 foreign language.

**2007-2008 Annual costs.** Tuition/fees: $18,750. Room/board: $8,610. Books/supplies: $800. Personal expenses: $800.

**2006-2007 Financial aid. Need-based:** 323 full-time freshmen applied for aid; 323 were judged to have need; 323 of these received aid. Average need met was 71.3%. Average scholarship/grant was $8,931; average loan $3,149. 61% of total undergraduate aid awarded as scholarships/grants, 39% as loans/jobs. **Non-need-based:** Awarded to 506 full-time undergraduates, including 47 freshmen. Scholarships awarded for academics, art, athletics, leadership.

**Application procedures. Admission:** No deadline. $25 fee, may be waived for applicants with need. Application may be submitted online. Admission notification on a rolling basis beginning on or about 10/15. Must reply by May 1 or within 2 week(s) if notified thereafter. **Financial aid:** Priority date 2/15; no closing date. FAFSA required. Applicants notified on a rolling basis starting 2/1; must reply within 2 week(s) of notification.

**Academics.** All professional programs require internships or field placements. There is a general service-learning requirement for graduation for all students. **Special study options:** Accelerated study, combined bachelor's/graduate degree, cross-registration, distance learning, double major, dual enrollment of high school students, exchange student, honors, independent study, internships, student-designed major, study abroad, teacher certification program, Washington semester, weekend college. Post-RN BS program in nursing. Weekend college for candidates of BS in business administration-general business and MS in childhood education or special education-childhood education, initial and professional certification. **Credit/placement by examination:** AP, CLEP, IB, institutional tests. No limit other than residency of 30 credit hours minimum required in courses completed at school (select programs may require a higher minimum). Veterans may

receive credit for military educational experiences. **Support services:** Learning center, pre-admission summer program, remedial instruction, study skills assistance, tutoring, writing center.

**Majors. Biology:** General, biochemistry. **Business:** Accounting, business admin. **Education:** Art, early childhood, elementary, special. **English:** English lit. **Foreign languages:** French, Spanish. **Health:** Community health, nursing (RN). **History:** General. **Interdisciplinary:** Natural sciences. **Math:** General. **Philosophy/religion:** Religion. **Psychology:** General. **Public administration:** Social work. **Social sciences:** Political science. **Visual/performing arts:** Art, graphic design, printmaking, studio arts.

**Most popular majors.** Biology 18%, business/marketing 11%, education 18%, health sciences 24%, psychology 8%, visual/performing arts 6%.

**Computing on campus.** 146 workstations in library, computer center, student center. Dormitories wired for high-speed internet access and linked to campus network. Commuter students can connect to campus network. Online library, repair service, wireless network available.

**Student life. Freshman orientation:** Mandatory, $105 fee. Preregistration for classes offered. Two sessions (2 days each) offered in July. **Housing:** Guaranteed on-campus for freshmen. Coed dorms, substance-free housing available. $100 fully refundable deposit, deadline 5/1. Coed apartment-style residence halls; some apartments are handicapped accessible. **Activities:** Choral groups, dance, drama, literary magazine, student government, student newspaper, student government association, multicultural association, Students without Borders, Black Student Union, Aiding Youth for Life, Amnesty International, environmental club, Voices of Zion.

**Athletics.** NAIA. **Intercollegiate:** Basketball, cross-country, golf M, soccer, volleyball W. **Intramural:** Basketball, football (non-tackle) M, softball. **Team name:** Wildcats.

**Student services.** Alcohol/substance abuse counseling, campus ministries, career counseling, student employment services, financial aid counseling, personal counseling, placement for graduates. **Physically disabled:** Services for hearing impaired.

**Contact.** E-mail: admissions@daemen.edu
Phone: (716) 839-8225 Toll-free number: (800) 462-7652
Fax: (716) 839-8229
Donna Shaffner, Dean of Admissions, Daemen College, 4380 Main Street, Amherst, NY 14226-3592

## Darkei Noam Rabbinical College
### Brooklyn, New York
CB code: 1270

- Private 5-year rabbinical college for men affiliated with Jewish faith
- Very large city

**General.** Founded in 1977. Accredited by AARTS. **Calendar:** Semester.

**Annual costs/financial aid.** Books/supplies: $300. Personal expenses: $3,000.

**Contact.** Phone: (718) 338-6464
Director of Admissions, 2822 Avenue J, Brooklyn, NY 11210

## Davis College
### Johnson City, New York
www.davisny.edu
CB code: 2233

- Private 4-year Bible college affiliated with nondenominational tradition
- Large town
- 219 degree-seeking undergraduates
- SAT or ACT (ACT writing optional) required

**General.** Regionally accredited; also accredited by ABHE. **Degrees:** 39 bachelor's, 10 associate awarded. **Location:** 2 miles from Binghamton. **Calendar:** Semester, limited summer session. **Full-time faculty:** 11 total. **Part-time faculty:** 13 total.

**Basis for selection.** Pastor recommendation, high school record most important. Applicants must give evidence of personal knowledge of the Lord Jesus Christ as Savior. Applicant lifestyle consistency with biblical principles important.

**2007-2008 Annual costs.** Tuition/fees: $10,650. Room/board: $5,800.

**Application procedures. Admission:** No deadline. $25 fee. Application may be submitted online. Admission notification on a rolling basis.

**Financial aid:** No deadline. FAFSA, institutional form required. Applicants notified on a rolling basis.

**Academics. Credit/placement by examination:** CLEP. **Support services:** Reduced course load, study skills assistance, tutoring.

**Majors. Theology:** Religious ed.

**Computing on campus.** Dormitories linked to campus network. Commuter students can connect to campus network. Wireless network available.

**Athletics. Intercollegiate:** Basketball, soccer, volleyball W. **Intramural:** Soccer, volleyball. **Team name:** Falcons.

**Contact.** E-mail: admissions@davisny.edu
Phone: (607) 729-1581 ext. 406 Toll-free number: (800) 331-4137 ext. 406
Fax: (607) 729-2962
Wes Ehret, Admissions Director, Davis College, 400 Riverside Drive, Johnson City, NY 13790

## DeVry Institute of Technology: New York

**Long Island City, New York**          **CB member**
**www.devry.edu**          **CB code: 4276**

- For-profit 4-year business and technical college
- Commuter campus in very large city
- 880 degree-seeking undergraduates: 29% part-time, 25% women, 34% African American, 10% Asian American, 29% Hispanic American, 1% Native American, 1% international
- 159 degree-seeking graduate students
- Interview required

**General.** Regionally accredited. **Degrees:** 152 bachelor's, 54 associate awarded; master's offered. **Calendar:** Semester, extensive summer session. **Full-time faculty:** 38 total; 42% minority, 13% women. **Part-time faculty:** 65 total; 29% minority, 29% women.

**Freshman class profile.**

| | | | |
|---|---|---|---|
| Return as sophomores: | 36% | International: | 1% |
| Out-of-state: | 4% | | |

**Basis for selection.** Applicants must have high school diploma or equivalent, or degree from an accredited postsecondary institution. Must demonstrate proficiency in basic college-level skills through test scores and/or institutionally administered placement examinations, and be at least 17 years of age on the first day of classes. New students may enter at beginning of any semester. SAT/ACT considered but not required for admission. If applicant chooses not to submit either, must take institution-administered admissions test.

**2007-2008 Annual costs.** Tuition/fees: $14,640. Books/supplies: $1,300. Personal expenses: $5,082.

**2006-2007 Financial aid.** All financial aid based on need.

**Application procedures. Admission:** No deadline. $50 fee. Application may be submitted online. Admission notification on a rolling basis. **Financial aid:** No deadline. FAFSA required. Applicants notified on a rolling basis.

**Academics. Special study options:** Accelerated study, distance learning. **Credit/placement by examination:** CLEP, institutional tests. **Support services:** Learning center, remedial instruction, tutoring.

**Majors. Business:** Business admin. **Computer sciences:** Networking, systems analysis. **Engineering technology:** Biomedical, computer, electrical. **Other:** Technical management.

**Most popular majors.** Business/marketing 49%, computer/information sciences 32%, engineering/engineering technologies 20%.

**Computing on campus.** 394 workstations in library, computer center. Online course registration, online library, helpline available.

**Student life. Freshman orientation:** Mandatory. **Housing:** Private apartments, student-plan housing, private rooms available. **Activities:** Muslim student association, martial arts club.

**Student services.** Career counseling, student employment services, financial aid counseling, placement for graduates, veterans' counselor. **Physically disabled:** Services for visually, hearing impaired.

**Contact.** Phone: (718) 472-2728
Newton Myvett, Director of Admissions, DeVry Institute of Technology: New York, 3020 Thomson Avenue, Long Island City, NY 11101-3051

## Dominican College of Blauvelt

**Orangeburg, New York**          **CB member**
**www.dc.edu**          **CB code: 2190**

- Private 4-year health science and liberal arts college
- Residential campus in small town
- 1,698 degree-seeking undergraduates: 26% part-time, 68% women, 19% African American, 8% Asian American, 18% Hispanic American, 1% international
- 188 degree-seeking graduate students
- 75% of applicants admitted
- SAT or ACT with writing required
- 40% graduate within 6 years

**General.** Founded in 1952. Regionally accredited. Private institution in Dominican tradition. **Degrees:** 272 bachelor's, 1 associate awarded; master's, doctoral offered. **Location:** 17 miles from New York City. **Calendar:** Differs by program, limited summer session. **Full-time faculty:** 67 total; 55% have terminal degrees, 6% minority, 75% women. **Part-time faculty:** 136 total; 7% have terminal degrees, 14% minority, 56% women. **Class size:** 73% < 20, 27% 20-39.

**Freshman class profile.** 1,474 applied, 1,107 admitted, 331 enrolled.

| Mid 50% test scores | | GPA 2.0-2.99: | 51% |
|---|---|---|---|
| SAT critical reading: | 370-470 | End year in good standing: | 65% |
| SAT math: | 390-480 | Return as sophomores: | 65% |
| SAT writing: | 400-480 | Out-of-state: | 28% |
| ACT composite: | 18-24 | Live on campus: | 78% |
| GPA 3.50 or higher: | 12% | International: | 1% |
| GPA 3.0-3.49: | 35% | | |

**Basis for selection.** Admissions based on secondary school records and standardized test scores. Interviews and written essays required in some cases. Meeting with admissions counselor not always required for admission but always desirable. Some applicants may be asked to meet with member of admissions staff. **Learning Disabled:** Students with current professional documentation of disabilities will be provided with reasonable accommodations to assure access to and full participation in mainstream of educational process.

**High school preparation.** 16 units required; 18 recommended. Required and recommended units include English 4, mathematics 3, social studies 3-4, science 3 (laboratory 1), foreign language 1-2 and academic electives 2.

**2007-2008 Annual costs.** Tuition/fees: $19,510. Room/board: $9,340. Books/supplies: $1,350. Personal expenses: $1,900.

**2007-2008 Financial aid. Need-based:** 320 full-time freshmen applied for aid; 302 were judged to have need; 302 of these received aid. Average need met was 62%. Average scholarship/grant was $11,745; average loan $3,466. 53% of total undergraduate aid awarded as scholarships/grants, 47% as loans/jobs. **Non-need-based:** Awarded to 340 full-time undergraduates, including 115 freshmen. Scholarships awarded for academics, athletics. **Additional information:** Individual financial aid counseling available.

**Application procedures. Admission:** No deadline. $35 fee, may be waived for applicants with need. Application may be submitted online. Admission notification on a rolling basis. **Financial aid:** Priority date 2/15; no closing date. FAFSA required. Applicants notified on a rolling basis starting 2/1.

**Academics. Special study options:** Accelerated study, combined bachelor's/graduate degree, cooperative education, distance learning, dual enrollment of high school students, honors, independent study, internships, teacher certification program, weekend college. Accelerated Bachelor of Science in Nursing for college graduates. **Credit/placement by examination:** AP, CLEP, IB, SAT, ACT, institutional tests. 30 credit hours maximum toward associate degree, 60 toward bachelor's. **Support services:** Learning center, remedial instruction, study skills assistance, tutoring, writing center.

**Majors. Biology:** General. **Business:** Accounting, business admin, finance, human resources, international, management information systems, marketing. **Computer sciences:** General. **Education:** General, biology, elementary, English, mathematics, multiple handicapped, secondary, social science, special. **English:** English lit. **Foreign languages:** Spanish. **Health:** Athletic training, health services, nursing (RN). **History:** General. **Legal studies:**

Prelaw. **Liberal arts:** Humanities. **Math:** General. **Psychology:** General. **Public administration:** Social work. **Social sciences:** General.

**Most popular majors.** Business/marketing 21%, education 11%, health sciences 29%, social sciences 12%.

**Computing on campus.** 140 workstations in dormitories, library, computer center. Dormitories wired for high-speed internet access and linked to campus network. Online library, wireless network available.

**Student life. Freshman orientation:** Mandatory. **Policies:** Alcohol-free campus. **Housing:** Guaranteed on-campus for all undergraduates. Coed dorms, substance-free housing available. $200 deposit. **Activities:** Campus ministries, choral groups, dance, drama, literary magazine, musical theater, student government, student newspaper, Dominicans Uniting Latinos for Cultural Education (DULCE), Helping Hands (community service).

**Athletics.** NAIA, NCAA. **Intercollegiate:** Baseball M, basketball, cross-country, golf M, lacrosse, soccer, softball W, volleyball W. **Intramural:** Basketball, softball, volleyball W. **Team name:** Chargers.

**Student services.** Alcohol/substance abuse counseling, campus ministries, career counseling, student employment services, financial aid counseling, health services, personal counseling, placement for graduates. **Physically disabled:** Services for visually, hearing impaired.

**Contact.** E-mail: admissions@dc.edu
Phone: (845) 848-7900 Toll-free number: (866) 432-4636
Fax: (845) 365-3150
Joyce Elbe, Director of Admissions, Dominican College of Blauvelt, 470 Western Highway, Orangeburg, NY 10962-1210

---

## Dowling College
**Oakdale, New York**
www.dowling.edu
**CB member**
**CB code: 2011**

- Private 4-year liberal arts college
- Commuter campus in large town
- 2,914 degree-seeking undergraduates: 26% part-time, 57% women, 11% African American, 2% Asian American, 11% Hispanic American, 6% international
- 2,405 degree-seeking graduate students
- 76% of applicants admitted
- SAT or ACT required
- 34% graduate within 6 years

**General.** Founded in 1955. Regionally accredited. School of Aviation situated at Brookhaven Airport. **Degrees:** 591 bachelor's awarded; master's, doctoral offered. **ROTC:** Air Force. **Location:** 50 miles from New York City. **Calendar:** Semester, extensive summer session. **Full-time faculty:** 121 total; 97% have terminal degrees, 3% minority, 36% women. **Part-time faculty:** 411 total; 16% have terminal degrees, 5% minority, 46% women. **Class size:** 65% < 20, 34% 20-39, less than 1% 40-49, less than 1% 50-99. **Special facilities:** College-owned fleet of aircraft, FRASCA flight simulators, virtual airport.

**Freshman class profile.** 2,607 applied, 1,987 admitted, 496 enrolled.

| Mid 50% test scores | | Rank in top quarter: | 20% |
|---|---|---|---|
| SAT critical reading: | 400-510 | Rank in top tenth: | 6% |
| SAT math: | 400-520 | Return as sophomores: | 64% |
| GPA 3.50 or higher: | 14% | Out-of-state: | 7% |
| GPA 3.0-3.49: | 44% | Live on campus: | 11% |
| GPA 2.0-2.99: | 38% | International: | 10% |

**Basis for selection.** Program of study, recent achievement, academic rank, school record, interview, standardized test scores, counselor's recommendation considered.

**High school preparation.** 16 units recommended. Recommended units include English 4, mathematics 3, social studies 3 and science 2. 4 additional units recommended.

**2007-2008 Annual costs.** Tuition/fees: $19,270. Room/board: $8,907. Books/supplies: $1,000. Personal expenses: $1,096.

**2007-2008 Financial aid. Need-based:** 308 full-time freshmen applied for aid; 297 were judged to have need; 266 of these received aid. Average need met was 28%. Average scholarship/grant was $2,572; average loan $3,589. 50% of total undergraduate aid awarded as scholarships/grants, 50% as loans/jobs. **Non-need-based:** Awarded to 1,571 full-time undergraduates, including 411 freshmen. Scholarships awarded for academics, alumni affiliation, athletics.

---

**Application procedures. Admission:** No deadline. $25 fee, may be waived for applicants with need. Application may be submitted online. Admission notification on a rolling basis. **Financial aid:** Priority date 4/30; no closing date. FAFSA required. Applicants notified on a rolling basis starting 3/1.

**Academics.** Optional winter term enables students to take 2 additional courses. **Special study options:** Accelerated study, combined bachelor's/graduate degree, cooperative education, double major, ESL, honors, independent study, internships, liberal arts/career combination, student-designed major, study abroad, teacher certification program, weekend college. Federal Aviation Administration cooperative program. **Credit/placement by examination:** AP, CLEP, IB, SAT, institutional tests. 30 credit hours maximum toward bachelor's degree. **Support services:** Learning center, preadmission summer program, reduced course load, remedial instruction, study skills assistance, tutoring.

**Majors. Biology:** General. **Business:** Accounting, business admin, finance, international, management information systems, marketing, tourism promotion, tourism/travel. **Computer sciences:** General, computer science. **Education:** General, art, biology, business, chemistry, elementary, English, foreign languages, mathematics, middle, multi-level teacher, music, science, secondary, social science, social studies, Spanish, special. **English:** English lit. **History:** General. **Liberal arts:** Arts/sciences. **Math:** General. **Psychology:** General. **Social sciences:** General, anthropology, economics, political science, sociology. **Transportation:** Aviation, aviation management. **Visual/performing arts:** General, art, dramatic, interior design.

**Most popular majors.** Area/ethnic studies 6%, business/marketing 23%, education 21%, liberal arts 11%, psychology 7%, social sciences 8%.

**Computing on campus.** 180 workstations in library, computer center. Dormitories wired for high-speed internet access and linked to campus network. Online course registration, online library, helpline available.

**Student life. Freshman orientation:** Available. Preregistration for classes offered. **Housing:** Coed dorms available. $200 deposit. **Activities:** Jazz band, choral groups, drama, literary magazine, music ensembles, musical theater, student government, student newspaper, symphony orchestra, 23 clubs and organizations related to academics, honor societies in business, education, economics, and psychology, Circle-K, computer science, scholarship society.

**Athletics.** NCAA. **Intercollegiate:** Baseball M, basketball, cheerleading, cross-country W, equestrian W, golf M, lacrosse M, rowing (crew), soccer, softball W, tennis, volleyball W. **Intramural:** Basketball, bowling, soccer, softball. **Team name:** Golden Lions.

**Student services.** Adult student services, alcohol/substance abuse counseling, campus ministries, career counseling, services for economically disadvantaged, student employment services, financial aid counseling, health services, personal counseling, placement for graduates. **Physically disabled:** Services for visually, speech, hearing impaired.

**Contact.** E-mail: admissions@dowling.edu
Phone: (631) 244-3030 Toll-free number: (800) 369-5464
Fax: (631) 563-3827
Frank Pizzardi, Director of Admissions Operations, Dowling College, 150 Idle Hour Boulevard, Oakdale, NY 11769-1999

---

## D'Youville College
**Buffalo, New York**
www.dyc.edu
**CB member**
**CB code: 2197**

- Private 4-year health science and liberal arts college
- Commuter campus in large city
- 1,532 degree-seeking undergraduates: 12% part-time, 76% women, 15% African American, 1% Asian American, 5% Hispanic American, 1% Native American, 11% international
- 1,356 degree-seeking graduate students
- 64% of applicants admitted
- SAT or ACT (ACT writing optional) required
- 52% graduate within 6 years

**General.** Founded in 1908. Regionally accredited. **Degrees:** 220 bachelor's awarded; master's, doctoral, first professional offered. **ROTC:** Army. **Location:** One mile from downtown. **Calendar:** Semester, extensive summer session. **Full-time faculty:** 147 total; 63% have terminal degrees, 9% minority. **Part-time faculty:** 127 total. **Class size:** 65% < 20, 31% 20-39, 3% 40-49, less than 1% 50-99. **Special facilities:** Equipment for blind and visually impaired including computer system with speech synthesizer, Braille printer, Versabraille, and print enhancer; physical therapy gait analysis lab; professional theater; gross anatomy lab.

**Freshman class profile.** 1,606 applied, 1,025 admitted, 216 enrolled.

| Mid 50% test scores | | Rank in top quarter: | 35% |
|---|---|---|---|
| SAT critical reading: | 450-540 | Rank in top tenth: | 13% |
| SAT math: | 450-560 | Return as sophomores: | 68% |
| ACT composite: | 20-25 | Out-of-state: | 10% |
| GPA 3.50 or higher: | 26% | Live on campus: | 49% |
| GPA 3.0-3.49: | 38% | International: | 2% |
| GPA 2.0-2.99: | 35% | | |

**Basis for selection.** High school GPA, class rank, test scores, type of high school program important. Interview, essay, letters of recommendation optional. 3 recommendations required for physician's assistant program. Interview required for physician's assistant and chiropractic programs.

**High school preparation.** 16 units recommended. Recommended units include English 4, mathematics 3, social studies 3, science 3 and foreign language 3. Biology and chemistry required for nursing, occupational therapy, physical therapy, dietetics, chiropractic and physician's assistant programs. 3 units of math required for accounting.

**2007-2008 Annual costs.** Tuition/fees: $17,800. Substantial tuition reduction depending on SAT scores. Room/board: $8,750. Books/supplies: $1,000. Personal expenses: $800.

**2006-2007 Financial aid. Need-based:** 175 full-time freshmen applied for aid; 159 were judged to have need; 157 of these received aid. Average need met was 77%. Average scholarship/grant was $9,335; average loan $4,482. 48% of total undergraduate aid awarded as scholarships/grants, 52% as loans/jobs. **Non-need-based:** Awarded to 308 full-time undergraduates, including 44 freshmen. Scholarships awarded for academics, leadership, religious affiliation, ROTC.

**Application procedures. Admission:** No deadline. $25 fee, may be waived for applicants with need. Application may be submitted online. Admission notification on a rolling basis. Must reply by May 1 or within 2 week(s) if notified thereafter. **Financial aid:** Priority date 3/1; no closing date. FAFSA required. Applicants notified on a rolling basis starting 4/1; must reply within 2 week(s) of notification.

**Academics. Special study options:** Accelerated study, combined bachelor's/ graduate degree, cross-registration, distance learning, double major, dual enrollment of high school students, exchange student, independent study, internships, liberal arts/career combination, study abroad, teacher certification program, weekend college. Career Discovery Program for undecided students; Teacher certification at the graduate level only. **Credit/placement by examination:** AP, CLEP, IB, institutional tests. 15 credit hours maximum toward bachelor's degree. Life experience may be granted credit through local Challenge Examinations. Prior to entering D'Youville, up to 15 credits may be earned via standardized examinations; additional 15 credits may be earned via standardized examinations after enrolling. **Support services:** Learning center, pre-admission summer program, reduced course load, remedial instruction, study skills assistance, tutoring, writing center.

**Majors. Biology:** General. **Business:** General, accounting, business admin, international. **Computer sciences:** Information technology. **English:** Creative writing, English lit, technical writing. **Health:** Health care admin, nursing (RN), physician assistant, predental, premedicine, preop/surgical nursing, prepharmacy, preveterinary. **History:** General. **Interdisciplinary:** Global studies. **Legal studies:** Prelaw. **Math:** General. **Philosophy/religion:** Philosophy. **Physical sciences:** Chemistry. **Psychology:** General. **Social sciences:** Sociology.

**Most popular majors.** Biology 10%, business/marketing 21%, health sciences 49%, interdisciplinary studies 10%.

**Computing on campus.** 100 workstations in dormitories, library, computer center, student center. Dormitories wired for high-speed internet access and linked to campus network. Commuter students can connect to campus network. Online library, helpline, repair service, student web hosting, wireless network available.

**Student life. Freshman orientation:** Mandatory, $25 fee. Preregistration for classes offered. Programs vary for traditional, transfer, and graduate students. **Housing:** Guaranteed on-campus for freshmen. Coed dorms, special housing for disabled, apartments, substance-free housing available. $100 deposit. Quiet floors for upper level students. **Activities:** Campus ministries, choral groups, drama, literary magazine, student government, student newspaper, Black Student Union, Latin American club, Lambda Sigma, writers club, Student Nurses Association, Asian Student Union.

**Athletics.** NCAA. **Intercollegiate:** Baseball M, basketball, cross-country W, golf, rowing (crew) W, soccer, softball W, volleyball. **Intramural:** Basketball, cheerleading W, cross-country, rowing (crew) W, skiing, table tennis, tennis. **Team name:** Spartans.

**Student services.** Adult student services, alcohol/substance abuse counseling, campus ministries, career counseling, services for economically disadvantaged, student employment services, financial aid counseling, health services, minority student services, personal counseling, placement for graduates, veterans' counselor. **Physically disabled:** Services for visually, speech, hearing impaired.

**Contact.** E-mail: admissions@dyc.edu
Phone: (716) 829-7600 Toll-free number: (800) 777-3921
Fax: (716) 829-7900
Ronald Dannecker, Director of Admissions, D'Youville College, 320 Porter Avenue, Buffalo, NY 14201-1084

---

## Eastman School of Music of the University of Rochester
### Rochester, New York
www.esm.rochester.edu          CB code: 2224

- Private 4-year music and performing arts college
- Residential campus in large city
- 504 degree-seeking undergraduates
- Application essay, interview required

**General.** Founded in 1921. Regionally accredited. Professional school within University of Rochester. Eastman students may take non-music classes, earn BA or BS degree, and attend social events at University of Rochester's River Campus. **Degrees:** 99 bachelor's awarded; master's, doctoral offered. **ROTC:** Naval. **Location:** 357 miles from New York City, 80 miles from Niagara Falls. **Calendar:** Semester, limited summer session. **Full-time faculty:** 95 total; 53% have terminal degrees, 10% minority, 26% women. **Part-time faculty:** 62 total; 5% minority, 48% women. **Class size:** 89% < 20, 9% 20-39, 1% 40-49, less than 1% 50-99. **Special facilities:** 4 performance halls including 3094-seat theater, computers for synthesis and analysis of music, complete analog and digital recording studios, music library containing over 700,000 items, over 135 practice rooms.

**Freshman class profile.**

| Out-of-state: | 75% | Fraternities: | 7% |
|---|---|---|---|
| Live on campus: | 99% | Sororities: | 11% |

**Basis for selection.** Proficiency in major area most important, in addition to academic record, test scores, interview, recommendations. Composition majors submit portfolio of scores. Some areas (jazz, composition, voice, piano) prescreened in advance of live audition. SAT and SAT Subject Tests or ACT recommended. Audition required for all; research/term paper required for theory majors; portfolio required for composition majors. Interview recommended for all, required for composition, music education, musical arts, theory majors. **Homeschooled:** Statement describing homeschool structure and mission, transcript of courses and grades, state high school equivalency certificate, interview, letter of recommendation (nonparent) required. SAT or ACT, at least 2 SAT Subject Tests required. Taking college credit classes also encouraged. **Learning Disabled:** To facilitate a smooth audition day experience, Admissions Office requests advance notice of any special considerations.

**High school preparation.** 16 units required. Required units include English 4.

**2007-2008 Annual costs.** Tuition/fees: $32,626. Room/board: $10,600. Books/supplies: $650. Personal expenses: $957.

**Financial aid. Non-need-based:** Scholarships awarded for academics, alumni affiliation, job skills, leadership, minority status, music/drama, state residency.

**Application procedures. Admission:** Closing date 12/1 (postmark date). $100 fee, may be waived for applicants with need. Application must be submitted online. Admission notification on a rolling basis beginning on or about 3/15. Must reply by May 1 or within 2 week(s) if notified thereafter. Admission review occurs following candidate's audition/interview. Regional auditions in Asia occur in fall, regional auditions in United States typically occur in January, auditions at Eastman School of Music occur in February and early March; typically, admission review and decisions following final audition date in Rochester. Separate (additional) application required for dual degree program. **Financial aid:** Closing date 2/28. FAFSA, institutional form required. Applicants notified on a rolling basis starting 3/15; must reply by 5/1 or within 2 week(s) of notification.

**Academics.** Arts leadership programs; orchestral studies and sacred music diploma programs. **Special study options:** Double major, ESL, independent study, internships, student-designed major, study abroad, teacher certification program. **Credit/placement by examination:** AP, CLEP, institutional tests. **Support services:** Pre-admission summer program, remedial instruction, study skills assistance, tutoring, writing center.

**Majors. Education:** Music. **Visual/performing arts:** Jazz, music performance, music theory/composition, piano/organ, voice/opera.

**Most popular majors.** Education 16%, visual/performing arts 84%.

**Computing on campus.** 50 workstations in dormitories, library, computer center, student center. Dormitories wired for high-speed internet access and linked to campus network. Commuter students can connect to campus network. Online course registration, online library, helpline, repair service, student web hosting, wireless network available.

**Student life. Freshman orientation:** Mandatory, $195 fee. Includes mandatory placement testing. **Policies:** Undergraduates required to live in college housing for first 3 years unless released by Assistant Dean of Residential Life. **Housing:** Guaranteed on-campus for freshmen. Coed dorms, single-sex dorms, special housing for disabled, fraternity/sorority housing, substance-free housing available. **Activities:** Bands, choral groups, literary magazine, music ensembles, opera, radio station, student government, student newspaper, symphony orchestra, international students association, Amnesty International, Intervarsity Christian Fellowship, Jewish students, Lambda, student association, graduate student association, musical organizations.

**Student services.** Adult student services, alcohol/substance abuse counseling, campus ministries, career counseling, student employment services, financial aid counseling, health services, personal counseling, placement for graduates. **Physically disabled:** Services for visually, speech impaired.

**Contact.** E-mail: admissions@esm.rochester.edu
Phone: (585) 274-1060 Toll-free number: (800) 388-9695
Fax: (585) 232-8601
Adrian Daly, Director of Admissions, Eastman School of Music of the University of Rochester, 26 Gibbs Street, Rochester, NY 14604-2599

## Elmira College
**Elmira, New York**
www.elmira.edu
**CB member**
**CB code: 2226**

- Private 4-year liberal arts college
- Residential campus in large town
- 1,176 degree-seeking undergraduates
- 76% of applicants admitted
- SAT or ACT (ACT writing optional), application essay required

**General.** Founded in 1855. Regionally accredited. **Degrees:** 337 bachelor's, 2 associate awarded; master's offered. **ROTC:** Army, Air Force. **Location:** 106 miles from Rochester, 90 miles from Syracuse. **Calendar:** 4-4-1. Limited summer session. **Full-time faculty:** 83 total. **Part-time faculty:** 119 total; 51% have terminal degrees, 3% minority, 63% women. **Class size:** 67% < 20, 33% 20-39, less than 1% 50-99. **Special facilities:** Center for Mark Twain Studies.

**Freshman class profile.** 1,798 applied, 1,368 admitted, 334 enrolled.

| Mid 50% test scores | | | |
|---|---|---|---|
| SAT critical reading: | 510-630 | **GPA 2.0-2.99:** | 38% |
| SAT math: | 500-620 | **Rank in top quarter:** | 65% |
| ACT composite: | 23-27 | **Rank in top tenth:** | 30% |
| **GPA 3.50 or higher:** | 38% | **Out-of-state:** | 59% |
| **GPA 3.0-3.49:** | 24% | **Live on campus:** | 98% |

**Basis for selection.** School academic record primary. Test scores, recommendations, essay, character and extracurricular activities important. Interview highly recommended.

**High school preparation.** 16 units required. Required and recommended units include English 4, mathematics 3, social studies 3, history 1, science 3 (laboratory 2), foreign language 2 and academic electives 2. 1 additional unit of foreign language recommended for foreign language and international business programs.

**2008-2009 Annual costs.** Tuition/fees: $33,200. Room/board: $10,100. Books/supplies: $450. Personal expenses: $550.

**2007-2008 Financial aid. Need-based:** Average need met was 83%. Average scholarship/grant was $21,674; average loan $4,738. 72% of total undergraduate aid awarded as scholarships/grants, 28% as loans/jobs. **Non-need-based:** Scholarships awarded for academics, leadership, ROTC. **Additional information:** Sibling Scholarship program provides 50% discounts on second family member's room and board, regardless of need.

**Application procedures. Admission:** Priority date 2/1; deadline 3/1 (postmark date). $50 fee, may be waived for applicants with need. Application may be submitted online. Admission notification on a rolling basis beginning on or about 10/15. Must reply by May 1 or within 2 week(s) if notified thereafter. **Financial aid:** Priority date 2/1, closing date 6/30. FAFSA required. Applicants notified on a rolling basis starting 2/1; must reply by 5/1 or within 2 week(s) of notification.

**Academics.** Mandatory writing program for all freshmen. 7.5-credit internship/community service, often done during 6-week spring term, required of all students. Off-campus study emphasized. **Special study options:** Accelerated study, combined bachelor's/graduate degree, double major, dual enrollment of high school students, ESL, exchange student, independent study, internships, liberal arts/career combination, student-designed major, study abroad, teacher certification program. Critical languages programs consortium member. **Credit/placement by examination:** AP, CLEP, IB, institutional tests. 30 credit hours maximum toward bachelor's degree. **Support services:** Reduced course load, study skills assistance, tutoring, writing center.

**Majors. Area/ethnic studies:** American. **Biology:** General, biochemistry. **Business:** Accounting, business admin, international, management information systems, managerial economics, marketing. **Conservation:** General, environmental studies. **Education:** Art, biology, chemistry, Deaf/hearing impaired, elementary, English, foreign languages, French, history, mathematics, middle, multi-level teacher, science, secondary, social science, social studies, Spanish, speech, speech impaired. **English:** British lit, English lit. **Foreign languages:** General, ancient Greek, classics, French, Latin, Spanish. **Health:** Audiology/speech pathology, clinical lab science, nursing (RN), predental, premedicine, preveterinary. **History:** General. **Legal studies:** Prelaw. **Math:** General. **Parks/recreation:** Sports admin. **Philosophy/religion:** Philosophy, religion. **Physical sciences:** Chemistry. **Protective services:** Criminal justice. **Psychology:** General. **Public administration:** Social work. **Social sciences:** General, anthropology, economics, international relations, political science, sociology. **Visual/performing arts:** Art, dramatic.

**Most popular majors.** Business/marketing 24%, education 21%, health sciences 10%, psychology 7%, social sciences 9%.

**Computing on campus.** 145 workstations in library, computer center. Dormitories wired for high-speed internet access and linked to campus network. Commuter students can connect to campus network. Wireless network available.

**Student life. Freshman orientation:** Mandatory, $350 fee. Preregistration for classes offered. 2-day summer registration program for testing, course registration, and get-acquainted activities. 4-day orientation program in the fall. **Housing:** Guaranteed on-campus for all undergraduates. Coed dorms, single-sex dorms, special housing for disabled, apartments, substance-free housing available. Quiet floors, tobacco- and alcohol-free floors available. All undergraduates required to live in college housing unless living with family or over the age of 25. **Activities:** Bands, choral groups, dance, drama, literary magazine, music ensembles, musical theater, radio station, student government, student newspaper, over 90 student interest groups.

**Athletics.** NCAA. **Intercollegiate:** Basketball, cheerleading, equestrian W, field hockey W, golf, ice hockey, lacrosse, soccer, softball W, tennis, volleyball W. **Intramural:** Badminton, basketball, bowling, football (non-tackle) M, football (tackle), handball, ice hockey, racquetball, skiing, skin diving, soccer, softball, squash, swimming, table tennis, tennis, volleyball. **Team name:** Soaring Eagles.

**Student services.** Alcohol/substance abuse counseling, campus ministries, career counseling, student employment services, financial aid counseling, health services, personal counseling, placement for graduates, veterans' counselor, women's services. **Physically disabled:** Services for visually, speech, hearing impaired.

**Contact.** E-mail: admissions@elmira.edu
Phone: (607) 735-1724 Toll-free number: (800) 935-6472
Fax: (607) 735-1718
Brett Moore, Director of Admissions, Elmira College, One Park Place, Elmira, NY 14901

## Eugene Lang College The New School for Liberal Arts
**New York, New York**
www.lang.edu
**CB code: 2521**

- Private 4-year liberal arts college
- Commuter campus in very large city
- 1,281 degree-seeking undergraduates: 4% part-time, 69% women, 4% African American, 5% Asian American, 7% Hispanic American, 1% Native American, 3% international

- 63% of applicants admitted
- SAT or ACT, application essay, interview required
- 53% graduate within 6 years

**General.** Founded in 1978. Regionally accredited. Students design own academic programs with advisers. Access to New York University and Cooper Union libraries, ability to select courses within The New School and Cooper Union. **Degrees:** 221 bachelor's awarded. **Location:** Located in Manhattan. **Calendar:** Semester, limited summer session. **Full-time faculty:** 53 total; 87% have terminal degrees, 26% minority, 53% women. **Part-time faculty:** 83 total; 17% minority, 49% women. **Class size:** 87% < 20, 12% 20-39, less than 1% 40-49, less than 1% 50-99, less than 1% >100. **Special facilities:** Photography laboratories, screening rooms, art galleries.

**Freshman class profile.** 1,670 applied, 1,056 admitted, 322 enrolled.

| Mid 50% test scores | | | |
|---|---|---|---|
| SAT critical reading: | 560-670 | GPA 2.0-2.99: | 28% |
| SAT math: | 490-610 | End year in good standing: | 91% |
| SAT writing: | 560-660 | Return as sophomores: | 73% |
| ACT composite: | 23-28 | Out-of-state: | 76% |
| GPA 3.50 or higher: | 22% | Live on campus: | 83% |
| GPA 3.0-3.49: | 49% | International: | 2% |

**Basis for selection.** Success in college preparatory studies most important supplemented by writing ability, intellectual curiosity, interview. Extracurricular/community activities, evidence of special talents, recommendations important. Telephone interviews available to students who cannot travel to New York. Essay required for BA/BFA; audition required for jazz, BA/BFA; portfolio required for art, BA/BFA.

**High school preparation.** 16 units required; 18 recommended. Required and recommended units include English 4, mathematics 3, social studies 3, history 2, science 3 and foreign language 2. Honors/AP courses recommended.

**2007-2008 Annual costs.** Tuition/fees: $31,310. Room/board: $11,750. Books/supplies: $2,050. Personal expenses: $1,550.

**2007-2008 Financial aid.** Need-based: 227 full-time freshmen applied for aid; 162 were judged to have need; 162 of these received aid. Average need met was 79%. Average scholarship/grant was $12,438; average loan $3,247. 80% of total undergraduate aid awarded as scholarships/grants, 20% as loans/jobs. **Non-need-based:** Awarded to 243 full-time undergraduates, including 91 freshmen. Scholarships awarded for academics, music/drama.

**Application procedures. Admission:** Closing date 2/1 (postmark date). $50 fee, may be waived for applicants with need. Application may be submitted online. Notification on a rolling basis beginning third week in March. Must reply by May 1 or within 3 week(s) if notified thereafter. **Financial aid:** Priority date 3/1; no closing date. FAFSA required. Applicants notified on a rolling basis starting 3/1; must reply within 4 week(s) of notification.

**Academics.** Students map out individual program of study within 5 broad areas of concentration. Seminars rather than lecture classes. **Special study options:** Accelerated study, combined bachelor's/graduate degree, cross-registration, distance learning, dual enrollment of high school students, ESL, exchange student, independent study, internships, student-designed major, study abroad, urban semester. **Credit/placement by examination:** CLEP, IB. **Support services:** Tutoring, writing center.

**Majors. Area/ethnic studies:** African-American, American, Caribbean, European, Latin American, Western European, women's. **Communications:** Journalism. **Education:** Foundations. **English:** American lit, British lit, creative writing, English lit. **Foreign languages:** Comparative lit. **History:** General. **Interdisciplinary:** Science/society. **Liberal arts:** Arts/sciences. **Philosophy/religion:** Philosophy, religion. **Psychology:** General. **Social sciences:** General, anthropology, economics, international relations, political science, sociology, urban studies. **Visual/performing arts:** General, art history/conservation, dance, music history, studio arts, theater history. **Other:** Culture and Media.

**Computing on campus.** 1,200 workstations in library, computer center, student center. Dormitories wired for high-speed internet access and linked to campus network. Commuter students can connect to campus network. Online course registration, online library, helpline, student web hosting, wireless network available.

**Student life. Freshman orientation:** Available. Preregistration for classes offered. One week before classes begin. **Housing:** Guaranteed on-campus for freshmen. Coed dorms, special housing for disabled, apartments, substance-free housing available. $250 nonrefundable deposit, deadline 7/1. **Activities:** Bands, choral groups, dance, drama, film society, international student organizations, literary magazine, opera, student government, student newspaper, symphony orchestra, Amnesty International, women's group, student union, Latino and African-American student organizations, gay/lesbian student organizations, volunteer groups, environmental group.

**Student services.** Career counseling, student employment services, financial aid counseling, health services, minority student services, personal counseling. **Learning disabled:** Comprehensive services available.

**Contact.**   E-mail: Lang@newschool.edu
Phone: (212) 229-5665 Toll-free number: (877) 528-3321
Fax: (212) 229-5355
Nicole Curvin, Director of Admissions, Eugene Lang College The New School for Liberal Arts, 65 West 11th Street (3rd floor), New York, NY 10011-8693

---

## Excelsior College
**Albany, New York**
**www.excelsior.edu**
CB member
CB code: 0759

- Private 4-year virtual liberal arts college
- Small city
- 33,422 degree-seeking undergraduates: 100% part-time, 60% women, 16% African American, 5% Asian American, 5% Hispanic American, 1% Native American, 1% international
- 884 degree-seeking graduate students

**General.** Founded in 1970. Regionally accredited. Provides Internet-based courses. No residency required. Professional academic advising provided. **Degrees:** 2,340 bachelor's, 2,628 associate awarded; master's offered. **Calendar:** Continuous, extensive summer session. **Full-time faculty:** 25 total; 60% women. **Part-time faculty:** 667 total; 60% women. **Class size:** 73% < 20, 27% 20-39. **Special facilities:** Comprehensive virtual library.

**Basis for selection.** Open admission, but selective for some programs. Admission to nursing program open to students with certain health care background.

**2007-2008 Annual costs.** Students charged $995 enrollment fee and $275 per credit hour. Because of nontraditional pricing, school does not charge set tuition based on 15 credit hours per semester.

**2006-2007 Financial aid.** All financial aid based on need. **Additional information:** Excelsior College is Title IV eligible for certain degree programs. College approved for all veterans educational benefit programs.

**Application procedures. Admission:** No deadline. $75 fee. Application may be submitted online. Admission notification on a rolling basis. Students may enroll at any time and are not divided into traditional classifications such as freshmen or sophomores. Applicants without high school diploma admitted as special students. **Financial aid:** Priority date 7/1; no closing date. FAFSA, institutional form required. Applicants notified on a rolling basis starting 8/1; must reply within 2 week(s) of notification.

**Academics.** Portfolio assessment option in subject areas where proficiency or performance examinations unavailable. Failing grades not placed in student records or figured into GPA. **Special study options:** Accelerated study, combined bachelor's/graduate degree, distance learning, external degree, honors, independent study. **Credit/placement by examination:** AP, CLEP. Some degrees can be earned entirely by examination. **Support services:** Reduced course load, study skills assistance, writing center.

**Majors. Biology:** General. **Business:** Accounting, business admin, finance, hospitality admin, human resources, insurance, international, management information systems, marketing, operations. **Communications:** General. **Computer sciences:** General, information systems, information technology. **Engineering technology:** General, computer systems, instrumentation, manufacturing, mechanical, nuclear. **English:** English lit. **Foreign languages:** General. **Health:** Health services, nursing (RN), optometric assistant. **History:** General. **Liberal arts:** Arts/sciences. **Math:** General. **Philosophy/religion:** Philosophy. **Physical sciences:** Chemistry, geology, optics, physics. **Protective services:** Criminal justice. **Psychology:** General. **Social sciences:** Economics, geography, political science, sociology. **Other:** Area studies, Electronic instrumentation technology.

**Most popular majors.** Business/marketing 8%, liberal arts 75%.

**Computing on campus.** Commuter students can connect to campus network. Online library, helpline available.

**Student life. Freshman orientation:** Available. Orientation conducted by mail. **Policies:** Students are kept informed of program developments through mailings, web, correspondence, and program newsletters.

**Student services.** Adult student services, career counseling, financial aid counseling, veterans' counselor.

**Contact.** E-mail: info@excelsior.edu
Phone: (518) 464-8500 Toll-free number: (888) 647-2388
Fax: (518) 464-8777
Annette Jeffes, Assistant VP for Enrollment Management, Admissions, Excelsior College, 7 Columbia Circle, Albany, NY 12203-5159

## Fashion Institute of Technology
New York, New York — CB member
www.fitnyc.edu — CB code: 2257

- Public 4-year visual arts and business college
- Commuter campus in very large city
- 7,535 degree-seeking undergraduates: 12% part-time, 86% women, 6% African American, 9% Asian American, 11% Hispanic American, 11% international
- 200 degree-seeking graduate students
- 43% of applicants admitted
- Application essay required
- 68% graduate within 6 years

**General.** Founded in 1944. Regionally accredited. SUNY institution. Specialized 2-year and 4-year programs provide professional preparation for fashion and design industries. **Degrees:** 1,081 bachelor's, 1,819 associate awarded; master's offered. **Calendar:** Semester, extensive summer session. **Full-time faculty:** 225 total; 12% minority, 55% women. **Part-time faculty:** 694 total; 15% minority, 50% women. **Class size:** 34% < 20, 66% 20-39. **Special facilities:** Textile and costume collection, fragrance laboratory, computer-aided design, textile, knitting, communications facility.

**Freshman class profile.** 3,873 applied, 1,656 admitted, 1,097 enrolled.

| | | | |
|---|---|---|---|
| GPA 3.50 or higher: | 28% | Return as sophomores: | 86% |
| GPA 3.0-3.49: | 42% | Out-of-state: | 39% |
| GPA 2.0-2.99: | 28% | Live on campus: | 65% |
| Rank in top quarter: | 40% | International: | 5% |
| Rank in top tenth: | 13% | | |

**Basis for selection.** Rank in class, portfolio, essay, community service, work experience, awards and honors considered. Portfolio required for art and design.

**High school preparation.** Required units include English 4, mathematics 2 and social studies 3. College preparatory program recommended.

**2007-2008 Annual costs.** Tuition/fees: $3,732; $10,316 out-of-state. Room/board: $10,095. Books/supplies: $1,600. Personal expenses: $1,500.

**Financial aid.** All financial aid based on need.

**Application procedures. Admission:** Priority date 1/1; deadline 2/1 (receipt date). $40 fee. Application may be submitted online. Admission notification 4/15. Admission notification on a rolling basis. Must reply by 5/1. No transfers can apply under early action. **Financial aid:** Priority date 2/1; no closing date. FAFSA, institutional form required. Applicants notified on a rolling basis starting 4/15; must reply within 2 week(s) of notification.

**Academics. Special study options:** Distance learning, exchange student, honors, internships, study abroad. One-year visiting student program with colleges and universities throughout United States. **Credit/placement by examination:** AP, CLEP, IB, SAT, ACT, institutional tests. See FIT's website for transfer credit policies. **Support services:** Learning center, reduced course load, remedial instruction, tutoring.

**Majors. Business:** Fashion, international marketing, market research, special products marketing. **Communications:** Advertising. **Communications technology:** Animation/special effects. **Education:** Technology/industrial arts. **Family/consumer sciences:** Clothing/textiles, textile manufacture. **Visual/performing arts:** Arts management, commercial photography, commercial/advertising art, fashion design, graphic design, illustration, industrial design, interior design, studio arts.

**Most popular majors.** Business/marketing 41%, communications/journalism 14%, visual/performing arts 40%.

**Computing on campus.** 1,500 workstations in dormitories, library, computer center, student center. Dormitories wired for high-speed internet access and linked to campus network. Commuter students can connect to campus network. Online course registration, helpline, repair service, student web hosting, wireless network available.

**Student life. Freshman orientation:** Mandatory. Preregistration for classes offered. **Housing:** Coed dorms, single-sex dorms, apartments, substance-free housing available. **Activities:** Choral groups, drama, literary magazine, radio station, student government, student newspaper, more than 60 groups and organizations available.

**Athletics.** NJCAA. **Intercollegiate:** Basketball, cross-country, tennis, volleyball W. **Intramural:** Bowling. **Team name:** Tigers.

**Student services.** Adult student services, career counseling, student employment services, health services, personal counseling, placement for graduates, veterans' counselor. **Physically disabled:** Services for visually, speech, hearing impaired.

**Contact.** E-mail: fitinfo@fitnyc.edu
Phone: (212) 217-3760
Dolores Lombardi, Director of Admissions, Fashion Institute of Technology, Seventh Avenue at 27th Street, New York, NY 10001-5992

## Five Towns College
Dix Hills, New York
www.fivetowns.edu — CB code: 3142

- For-profit 4-year music and liberal arts college
- Commuter campus in large town
- 1,093 degree-seeking undergraduates
- 58 graduate students
- 71% of applicants admitted
- SAT or ACT with writing, application essay, interview required

**General.** Founded in 1972. Regionally accredited. **Degrees:** 155 bachelor's, 15 associate awarded; master's, doctoral offered. **Location:** 40 miles from New York City. **Calendar:** Semester, limited summer session. **Full-time faculty:** 33 total. **Part-time faculty:** 96 total. **Class size:** 51% < 20, 43% 20-39, 6% 40-49, less than 1% 50-99. **Special facilities:** 24-, 48- and 72-track recording studios with ProTools and 5.1 surround sound, Korg MIDI technology studio, professional film/video arts studio and editing labs, theater technology lab.

**Freshman class profile.** 710 applied, 501 admitted, 231 enrolled.

| Mid 50% test scores | | | |
|---|---|---|---|
| | | ACT composite: | 17-19 |
| SAT critical reading: | 410-500 | Out-of-state: | 9% |
| SAT math: | 410-500 | Live on campus: | 20% |
| SAT writing: | 400-490 | | |

**Basis for selection.** Minimum 2.5 GPA required. Applicants for music and theater programs must pass audition and demonstrate competency in music, math, and English. **Learning Disabled:** Provide recent copy of individualized educational program and psychological report.

**High school preparation.** 18 units recommended. Recommended units include English 4, mathematics 3, social studies 3, science 2 and foreign language 2. Music harmony and other applied music classes recommended for music students.

**2008-2009 Annual costs.** Tuition/fees: $17,800. Room/board: $11,750. Books/supplies: $1,200. Personal expenses: $3,200.

**Financial aid. Non-need-based:** Scholarships awarded for academics, music/drama.

**Application procedures. Admission:** No deadline. $35 fee, may be waived for applicants with need. Admission notification on a rolling basis beginning on or about 11/1. **Financial aid:** Priority date 3/31; no closing date. FAFSA, institutional form required. Applicants notified on a rolling basis; must reply within 4 week(s) of notification.

**Academics.** Number of credit hours required for students in major field of study varies by program. **Special study options:** Combined bachelor's/graduate degree, distance learning, dual enrollment of high school students, independent study, internships, liberal arts/career combination, teacher certification program. **Credit/placement by examination:** AP, CLEP, institutional tests. **Support services:** Learning center, pre-admission summer program, reduced course load, remedial instruction, tutoring.

**Majors. Business:** Business admin. **Communications:** General, broadcast journalism, journalism, media studies, radio/tv. **Communications technology:** General, recording arts. **Education:** Elementary, music. **Visual/performing arts:** General, acting, cinematography, dramatic, film/cinema, jazz, music history, music management, music performance, music theory/composition, piano/organ, stringed instruments, theater design, voice/opera.

**Most popular majors.** Business/marketing 59%, education 8%, visual/performing arts 29%.

**Computing on campus.** 84 workstations in library, computer center, student center. Dormitories wired for high-speed internet access and linked to campus network. Helpline, repair service available.

**Student life. Freshman orientation:** Mandatory. **Housing:** Coed dorms, substance-free housing available. $250 deposit. **Activities:** Bands, choral groups, dance, drama, film society, music ensembles, musical theater, radio station, student government, student newspaper.

**Student services.** Alcohol/substance abuse counseling, career counseling, services for economically disadvantaged, student employment services, financial aid counseling, health services, personal counseling, placement for graduates. **Learning disabled:** Comprehensive services available.

**Contact.** E-mail: admissions@ftc.edu
Phone: (631) 656-2110 Fax: (631) 656-2172
Jerry Cohen, Dean of Enrollment Services, Five Towns College, 305 North Service Road, Dix Hills, NY 11746-6055

## Fordham University

Bronx, New York

www.fordham.edu

CB member

CB code: 2259

- Private 4-year university affiliated with Roman Catholic Church
- Residential campus in very large city
- 7,541 degree-seeking undergraduates: 6% part-time, 57% women, 6% African American, 6% Asian American, 12% Hispanic American, 2% international
- 6,306 degree-seeking graduate students
- 42% of applicants admitted
- SAT or ACT (ACT writing optional), application essay required
- 78% graduate within 6 years

**General.** Founded in 1841. Regionally accredited. Rose Hill campus in Bronx, Lincoln Center campus in Manhattan. **Degrees:** 1,670 bachelor's awarded; master's, doctoral, first professional offered. **ROTC:** Army, Naval, Air Force. **Calendar:** Semester, extensive summer session. **Full-time faculty:** 667 total; 96% have terminal degrees, 16% minority, 40% women. **Part-time faculty:** 736 total; 46% have terminal degrees, 13% minority, 47% women. **Class size:** 49% < 20, 48% 20-39, 1% 40-49, less than 1% 50-99, less than 1% >100. **Special facilities:** Environmental center in Armonk, seismic station, Fordham Hispanic Research, Third Age Center addressing issues of older population.

**Freshman class profile.** 22,035 applied, 9,281 admitted, 1,784 enrolled.

| Mid 50% test scores | | | |
|---|---|---|---|
| SAT critical reading: | 570-670 | GPA 2.0-2.99: | 5% |
| SAT math: | 560-660 | Rank in top quarter: | 78% |
| SAT writing: | 550-650 | Rank in top tenth: | 43% |
| ACT composite: | 25-29 | Return as sophomores: | 90% |
| GPA 3.50 or higher: | 72% | Out-of-state: | 50% |
| GPA 3.0-3.49: | 23% | Live on campus: | 73% |
| | | International: | 2% |

**Basis for selection.** School achievement record most important followed by test scores, class rank, extracurricular activities, recommendations, essay, personal characteristics. Special consideration given to children of alumni. SAT Subject Tests recommended. Audition required for dance and theater programs.

**High school preparation.** 22 units required; 25 recommended. Required and recommended units include English 4, mathematics 3-4, social studies 2, history 2, science 3-4, foreign language 2-3 and academic electives 6.

**2007-2008 Annual costs.** Tuition/fees: $32,720. Room/board: $12,300. Books/supplies: $820. Personal expenses: $1,500.

**2006-2007 Financial aid. Need-based:** 1,466 full-time freshmen applied for aid; 1,080 were judged to have need; 1,079 of these received aid. Average need met was 75%. Average scholarship/grant was $15,417; average loan $2,896. 69% of total undergraduate aid awarded as scholarships/grants, 31% as loans/jobs. **Non-need-based:** Awarded to 1,496 full-time undergraduates, including 546 freshmen. Scholarships awarded for academics, athletics, ROTC.

**Application procedures. Admission:** Closing date 1/15 (postmark date). $50 fee, may be waived for applicants with need. Application may be submitted online. Admission notification 4/1. Must reply by May 1 or within 2 week(s) if notified thereafter. **Financial aid:** Closing date 2/1. FAFSA, CSS PROFILE required. Applicants notified by 3/31; must reply by 5/1 or within 2 week(s) of notification.

**Academics. Special study options:** Combined bachelor's/graduate degree, distance learning, double major, ESL, exchange student, honors, independent study, internships, student-designed major, study abroad, teacher certification program, United Nations semester. Global Program in International Business. **Credit/placement by examination:** AP, CLEP, IB, institutional tests. 32 credit hours maximum toward bachelor's degree. Credit for CLEP examination only offered for liberal studies, adult continuing education school. **Support services:** Pre-admission summer program, tutoring, writing center.

**Majors. Area/ethnic studies:** African, African-American, American, Latin American, Near/Middle Eastern, Russian/Slavic, women's. **Biology:** General. **Business:** General, accounting, business admin, finance, international, management information systems, managerial economics, market research. **Communications:** General. **Computer sciences:** General. **English:** English lit. **Foreign languages:** Ancient Greek, classics, comparative lit, French, German, Italian, Latin, modern Greek, Russian, Spanish. **Health:** Predental, premedicine, prepharmacy, preveterinary. **History:** General. **Interdisciplinary:** Intercultural. **Legal studies:** Prelaw. **Math:** General. **Philosophy/religion:** Philosophy, religion. **Physical sciences:** Chemistry, physics. **Protective services:** Criminal justice. **Psychology:** General. **Public administration:** General, social work. **Social sciences:** Anthropology, economics, political science, sociology, urban studies. **Visual/performing arts:** Art, art history/conservation, dance, dramatic, film/cinema, photography, studio arts, theater design.

**Most popular majors.** Business/marketing 27%, communications/journalism 14%, English 6%, psychology 6%, social sciences 20%, visual/performing arts 6%.

**Computing on campus.** 900 workstations in dormitories, library, computer center. Dormitories wired for high-speed internet access and linked to campus network. Commuter students can connect to campus network. Online course registration, online library, helpline, repair service, wireless network available.

**Student life. Freshman orientation:** Mandatory, $110 fee. Comprehensive academic and social orientation 3 days prior to start of classes. **Housing:** Guaranteed on-campus for all undergraduates. Coed dorms, apartments, substance-free housing available. $200 partly refundable deposit, deadline 5/1. **Activities:** Bands, campus ministries, choral groups, dance, drama, film society, literary magazine, music ensembles, musical theater, radio station, student government, student newspaper, symphony orchestra, TV station, campus ministries, Rose Hill Ambassadors, international black student union, Progressive Students for Justice, Circle-K, commuter student association, Fordham University Emerging Leaders, Fordham University emergency medical services, weekend activities committee.

**Athletics.** NCAA. **Intercollegiate:** Baseball M, basketball, cross-country, diving, football (tackle) M, golf M, rowing (crew) W, soccer, softball W, squash M, swimming, tennis, track and field, volleyball W, water polo M. **Intramural:** Basketball, football (tackle), golf W, handball, racquetball, soccer, softball, swimming, tennis, triathlon, volleyball. **Team name:** Rams.

**Student services.** Adult student services, alcohol/substance abuse counseling, campus ministries, career counseling, student employment services, financial aid counseling, health services, personal counseling, placement for graduates. **Physically disabled:** Services for visually, hearing impaired.

**Contact.** E-mail: enroll@fordham.edu
Phone: (718) 817-4000 Toll-free number: (800) 367-3426
Fax: (718) 367-9404
Peter Farrell, Director of Admissions, Fordham University, East 441 Fordham Road, Bronx, NY 10458

## Globe Institute of Technology

New York, New York

www.globe.edu

CB code: 3333

- For-profit 4-year university and business college
- Commuter campus in very large city
- 2,305 degree-seeking undergraduates

**General.** Regionally accredited. **Degrees:** 200 bachelor's, 180 associate awarded. **ROTC:** Army, Naval, Air Force. **Calendar:** Semester, extensive summer session. **Full-time faculty:** 46 total. **Part-time faculty:** 170 total. **Class size:** 55% < 20, 40% 20-39, 5% 40-49.

**Freshman class profile.**

| Mid 50% test scores | | | |
|---|---|---|---|
| SAT critical reading: | 500-600 | SAT math: | 500-600 |
| | | SAT writing: | 500-600 |

**Basis for selection.** Open admission, but selective for some programs. Special requirements for video game development program. Interviews strongly recommended. **Learning Disabled:** Student should meet with school psychologist to discuss needs.

**2008-2009 Annual costs.** Tuition/fees: $11,040. Room/board: $5,000. Books/supplies: $800.

**Financial aid. Non-need-based:** Scholarships awarded for academics, athletics.

**Application procedures. Admission:** No deadline. $50 fee, may be waived for applicants with need. Application may be submitted online. Admission notification on a rolling basis. **Financial aid:** No deadline. FAFSA, institutional form required. Applicants notified on a rolling basis.

**Academics. Special study options:** Combined bachelor's/graduate degree, distance learning, ESL, honors, independent study, internships, liberal arts/career combination, weekend college. Video Game Development program admits only students in top 15% of graduating class and students with combined SAT score greater than 1950. **Credit/placement by examination:** AP, CLEP, institutional tests. 30 credit hours maximum toward associate degree, 60 toward bachelor's. **Support services:** Learning center, pre-admission summer program, reduced course load, remedial instruction, study skills assistance, tutoring, writing center.

**Majors. Business:** General, accounting, accounting technology, accounting/business management, accounting/finance, banking/financial services, business admin, customer service, finance, hospitality admin, hotel/motel admin, management information systems, nonprofit/public, office management, operations, resort management, restaurant/food services, small business admin, tourism/travel. **Computer sciences:** General, a.i./robotics, applications programming, computer graphics, computer science, database management, information technology, LAN/WAN management, networking, programming, security, system admin, systems analysis, vendor certification, web page design, webmaster. **Health:** Facilities admin, health care admin, office admin. **Legal studies:** Legal secretary, paralegal.

**Most popular majors.** Business/marketing 60%, computer/information sciences 20%, health sciences 10%, legal studies 10%.

**Computing on campus.** 200 workstations in library, computer center, student center. Dormitories wired for high-speed internet access. Commuter students can connect to campus network. Online course registration, online library, helpline, student web hosting, wireless network available.

**Student life. Freshman orientation:** Mandatory. Preregistration for classes offered. **Housing:** Guaranteed on-campus for all undergraduates. Coed dorms, apartments available. **Activities:** Dance, film society, literary magazine, student government, student newspaper, international club, Chinese club, Russian club, Latino club, Wall Street club, Carib club, film club, African club, dance club.

**Athletics.** NJCAA. **Intercollegiate:** Baseball M, basketball, bowling, cross-country, lacrosse M, soccer, softball W, track and field, volleyball W. **Team name:** Knights.

**Student services.** Adult student services, alcohol/substance abuse counseling, career counseling, services for economically disadvantaged, student employment services, financial aid counseling, minority student services, personal counseling, placement for graduates, women's services.

**Contact.** E-mail: admissions@globe.edu
Phone: (212) 349-4330 Toll-free number: (877) 394-5623
Fax: (212) 227-5920
Tatiana Garelik, Admission Director, Globe Institute of Technology, 291 Broadway, New York, NY 10007

## Hamilton College

**Clinton, New York**
**www.hamilton.edu**

**CB member**
**CB code: 2286**

- Private 4-year liberal arts college
- Residential campus in small town
- 1,810 degree-seeking undergraduates: 52% women, 4% African American, 7% Asian American, 5% Hispanic American, 1% Native American, 5% international
- 28% of applicants admitted
- SAT and SAT Subject Tests or ACT (ACT writing optional), application essay required
- 88% graduate within 6 years

**General.** Founded in 1812. Regionally accredited. **Degrees:** 455 bachelor's awarded. **ROTC:** Army, Air Force. **Location:** 10 miles from Utica, 50 miles from Syracuse. **Calendar:** Semester. **Full-time faculty:** 172 total; 96% have terminal degrees, 17% minority, 40% women. **Part-time faculty:** 45 total; 44% have terminal degrees, 16% minority, 58% women. **Class size:** 74% < 20, 24% 20-39, 2% 40-49, less than 1% 50-99, less than 1% >100. **Special facilities:** Observatory, nature preserve, electron microscope.

**Freshman class profile.** 4,962 applied, 1,376 admitted, 468 enrolled.

| Mid 50% test scores | | | |
|---|---|---|---|
| SAT critical reading: | 640-740 | Return as sophomores: | 93% |
| SAT math: | 640-720 | Out-of-state: | 69% |
| Rank in top quarter: | 90% | Live on campus: | 100% |
| Rank in top tenth: | 74% | International: | 5% |

**Basis for selection.** School achievement record, rank in high school class, school and community activities, application essay, graded example of expository writing, recommendations important. Test scores and interview also considered. Some preference given children of alumni. Special consideration given students from minority groups, disadvantaged backgrounds, and certain geographic regions. Students can fulfill test requirements with SAT or ACT or 3 SAT Subject Tests or 3 AP exams or any combination of these. Interview recommended for all; audition tape recommended for music applicants; portfolio recommended for studio art applicants.

**High school preparation.** 16 units recommended. Recommended units include English 4, mathematics 3, social studies 3, science 3 and foreign language 3.

**2007-2008 Annual costs.** Tuition/fees: $36,860. Room/board: $9,350.

**2007-2008 Financial aid. Need-based:** 256 full-time freshmen applied for aid; 191 were judged to have need; 191 of these received aid. Average need met was 100%. Average scholarship/grant was $27,356; average loan $3,157. 87% of total undergraduate aid awarded as scholarships/grants, 13% as loans/jobs. **Non-need-based:** Awarded to 125 full-time undergraduates, including 23 freshmen. Scholarships awarded for academics, leadership. **Additional information:** Will meet demonstrated need of all aided applicants.

**Application procedures. Admission:** Closing date 1/1 (postmark date). $50 fee, may be waived for applicants with need. Application may be submitted online. Admission notification 4/1. Must reply by 5/1. **Financial aid:** Closing date 2/8. FAFSA, institutional form, CSS PROFILE required. Applicants notified by 4/1; must reply by 5/1.

**Academics.** Sophomores may attain guaranteed early admission to one of 6 participating medical schools. Students must complete senior program or project in their concentration. May participate in Williams College Mystic Seaport Program. **Special study options:** Accelerated study, combined bachelor's/graduate degree, cross-registration, double major, ESL, independent study, internships, New York semester, student-designed major, study abroad, Washington semester. 3-2 program in engineering with Columbia University, Rensselaer Polytechnic Institute, Washington University (St. Louis); 3-3 program in law at Columbia University. **Credit/placement by examination:** AP, CLEP, IB, institutional tests. **Support services:** Learning center, pre-admission summer program, reduced course load, tutoring, writing center.

**Majors. Area/ethnic studies:** African-American, American, Asian, East Asian, Russian/Slavic, women's. **Biology:** General, biochemistry, molecular. **Communications:** General. **Computer sciences:** General. **English:** British lit, creative writing, English lit. **Foreign languages:** General, ancient Greek, Chinese, classics, comparative lit, French, German, Japanese, Latin, Russian, Spanish. **History:** General. **Interdisciplinary:** Biopsychology, neuroscience. **Liberal arts:** Arts/sciences. **Math:** General. **Philosophy/religion:** Philosophy, religion. **Physical sciences:** Chemistry, geology, physics. **Psychology:** General. **Public administration:** Policy analysis. **Social sciences:** Anthropology, archaeology, economics, international relations, political science, sociology. **Visual/performing arts:** Art history/conservation, dance, dramatic, studio arts.

**Most popular majors.** Biology 6%, English 6%, foreign language 10%, mathematics 6%, physical sciences 6%, psychology 6%, social sciences 33%, visual/performing arts 7%.

**Computing on campus.** 625 workstations in library, computer center, student center. Dormitories wired for high-speed internet access and linked to campus network. Commuter students can connect to campus network. Online course registration, online library, helpline, repair service, student web hosting, wireless network available.

**Student life. Freshman orientation:** Mandatory. One week prior to start of classes. **Policies:** Honor code covers all examinations, papers, research, and use of library. **Housing:** Guaranteed on-campus for all undergraduates. Coed dorms, special housing for disabled, apartments available. Special interest housing available including language houses and international house, quiet areas, substance-free areas. **Activities:** Bands, choral groups, dance, drama, film society, international student organizations, literary magazine, music ensembles, musical theater, radio station, student government, student newspaper, symphony orchestra, TV station, Newman Club, Jewish students organization, Black and Latin student union, women's center, La Vanguardia, Amnesty International, Muslim student organization, Asian cultural society.

**Athletics.** NCAA. **Intercollegiate:** Baseball M, basketball, cross-country, diving, field hockey W, football (tackle) M, golf M, ice hockey, lacrosse, rowing (crew), soccer, softball W, squash, swimming, tennis, track and field, volleyball W. **Intramural:** Basketball, cross-country, diving, fencing W, football (non-tackle), football (tackle) M, golf, handball, ice hockey, lacrosse, racquetball, soccer, softball, squash, swimming, tennis, volleyball. **Team name:** Continentals.

**Student services.** Adult student services, alcohol/substance abuse counseling, campus ministries, career counseling, student employment services, financial aid counseling, health services, minority student services, on-campus daycare, personal counseling, placement for graduates, women's services. **Physically disabled:** Services for visually, speech, hearing impaired.

**Contact.** E-mail: admission@hamilton.edu
Phone: (315) 859-4421 Toll-free number: (800) 843-2655
Fax: (315) 859-4457
Monica Inzer, Dean of Admissions and Financial Aid, Hamilton College, 198 College Hill Road, Clinton, NY 13323-1293

## Hartwick College
**Oneonta, New York**
**www.hartwick.edu**

CB member
CB code: 2288

- Private 4-year liberal arts college
- Residential campus in large town
- 1,513 degree-seeking undergraduates: 3% part-time, 56% women, 5% African American, 2% Asian American, 5% Hispanic American, 3% international
- 84% of applicants admitted
- Application essay required
- 60% graduate within 6 years; 19% enter graduate study

**General.** Founded in 1797. Regionally accredited. Additional campus for recreation, research, student residences. **Degrees:** 306 bachelor's awarded. **Location:** 68 miles from Binghamton, 75 miles from Albany. **Calendar:** 4-1-4, limited summer session. **Full-time faculty:** 108 total; 95% have terminal degrees, 7% minority, 44% women. **Part-time faculty:** 77 total; 46% women. **Class size:** 67% < 20, 31% 20-39, 1% 40-49, less than 1% 50-99. **Special facilities:** Environmental field station, museum, Native American artifact and library collections, tissue culture laboratory, electron microscope, 16-inch telescope, observatory, nuclear magnetic resonance spectrometer, fine and performing arts center.

**Freshman class profile.** 2,422 applied, 2,034 admitted, 455 enrolled.

| Mid 50% test scores | | Rank in top tenth: | 18% |
|---|---|---|---|
| SAT critical reading: | 490-610 | Return as sophomores: | 79% |
| SAT math: | 510-610 | Out-of-state: | 38% |
| ACT composite: | 21-27 | Live on campus: | 97% |
| GPA 3.50 or higher: | 31% | International: | 3% |
| GPA 3.0-3.49: | 28% | Fraternities: | 13% |
| GPA 2.0-2.99: | 39% | Sororities: | 7% |
| Rank in top quarter: | 45% | | |

**Basis for selection.** School achievement record, class rank, personal qualities, extracurricular activities, and recommendations considered. Test scores optional except for students applying to nursing program. SAT/ACT score submission not required for admission except for Nursing majors. Interview recommended for all; audition required for music program; portfolio recommended for art program. **Homeschooled:** Transcript of courses and grades, letter of recommendation (nonparent) required. Must meet all stated application requirements and submit SAT or ACT test score. At least 3 SAT Subject Tests strongly recommended. Transcripts should be submitted with course description and/or syllabi.

**High school preparation.** 19 units recommended. Recommended units include English 4, mathematics 3, social studies 2, history 2, science 3 (laboratory 2) and foreign language 3.

**2008-2009 Annual costs.** Tuition/fees: $31,900. New students (freshmen and transfers) must purchase laptop from college; cost of computer included in tuition. Room/board: $8,685. Books/supplies: $700. Personal expenses: $400.

**Financial aid. Non-need-based:** Scholarships awarded for academics, alumni affiliation, athletics, leadership, state residency.

**Application procedures. Admission:** Closing date 2/15 (postmark date). $35 fee, may be waived for applicants with need. Application may be submitted online. Admission notification 3/15. Must reply by 5/1. **Financial aid:** Priority date 2/15; no closing date. FAFSA, institutional form required. Applicants notified by 3/15; must reply within 2 week(s) of notification.

**Academics.** Curriculum XXI includes first-year seminar, core requirements and contemporary issues seminar. Senior thesis required. First-year students provided with notebook-sized personal computer. **Special study options:** Accelerated study, combined bachelor's/graduate degree, cross-registration, double major, exchange student, honors, independent study, internships, liberal arts/career combination, semester at sea, student-designed major, study abroad, teacher certification program, urban semester, Washington semester. Off-campus January term in Italy, Austria, France, Costa Rica, South Africa, Ireland, Spain; Philadelphia Urban Semester; Boston Semester; Outward Bound, NOLS programs; cooperative program in law with Albany Law School; 3-2 engineering with Clarkson University, Columbia University. **Credit/placement by examination:** AP, CLEP, IB, institutional tests. **Support services:** Reduced course load, study skills assistance, tutoring, writing center.

**Majors. Biology:** General, biochemistry. **Business:** Accounting, business admin. **Computer sciences:** General, information systems. **Education:** Music. **English:** English lit. **Foreign languages:** French, German, Spanish. **Health:** Clinical lab science, nursing (RN). **History:** General. **Liberal arts:** Arts/sciences. **Math:** General. **Philosophy/religion:** Philosophy, religion. **Physical sciences:** Chemistry, geology, physics. **Psychology:** General. **Social sciences:** Anthropology, economics, political science, sociology. **Visual/performing arts:** Art, art history/conservation, dramatic.

**Most popular majors.** Biology 7%, business/marketing 16%, English 11%, health sciences 10%, psychology 9%, social sciences 17%, visual/performing arts 7%.

**Computing on campus.** PC or laptop required. 56 workstations in library, computer center. Dormitories wired for high-speed internet access and linked to campus network. Commuter students can connect to campus network. Online library, helpline, repair service, student web hosting, wireless network available.

**Student life. Freshman orientation:** Mandatory, $300 fee. Preregistration for classes offered. Summer registration/parent orientation and 4-day pre-semester in residence program. **Housing:** Guaranteed on-campus for freshmen. Coed dorms, single-sex dorms, special housing for disabled, apartments, fraternity/sorority housing, substance-free housing available. Special interest housing, housing at environmental campus available. **Activities:** Bands, choral groups, dance, drama, literary magazine, music ensembles, musical theater, radio station, student government, student newspaper, TV station, over 60 academic and social organizations available.

**Athletics.** NCAA. **Intercollegiate:** Basketball, cheerleading M, cross-country, diving, equestrian W, field hockey W, football (tackle) M, lacrosse, soccer, swimming, tennis, volleyball W, water polo W. **Intramural:** Basketball, cross-country, equestrian, football (tackle), racquetball, soccer, squash, swimming, table tennis, tennis, volleyball, water polo. **Team name:** Hawks.

**Student services.** Alcohol/substance abuse counseling, campus ministries, career counseling, student employment services, financial aid counseling, health services, personal counseling, placement for graduates. **Physically disabled:** Services for visually, hearing impaired.

**Contact.** E-mail: admissions@hartwick.edu
Phone: (607) 431-4150 Toll-free number: (888) 427-8942
Fax: (607) 431-4154
Jacqueline Gregory, Director of Admissions, Hartwick College, Box 4022, Oneonta, NY 13820-4022

## Hilbert College
**Hamburg, New York**
**www.hilbert.edu**

CB code: 2334

- Private 4-year liberal arts college affiliated with Roman Catholic Church
- Commuter campus in large town
- 999 degree-seeking undergraduates: 20% part-time, 60% women, 6% African American, 2% Hispanic American, 2% Native American
- 90% of applicants admitted
- 55% graduate within 6 years; 10% enter graduate study

**General.** Founded in 1957. Regionally accredited. Affiliated with Franciscan Sisters of St. Joseph. Legal assistant program approved by American Bar Association. **Degrees:** 222 bachelor's, 28 associate awarded. **ROTC:** Army. **Location:** 10 miles from Buffalo. **Calendar:** Semester, limited summer session. **Full-time faculty:** 48 total; 44% have terminal degrees, 4%

minority, 48% women. **Part-time faculty:** 63 total; 21% have terminal degrees, 2% minority, 36% women. **Class size:** 64% < 20, 36% 20-39. **Special facilities:** Comprehensive law library.

**Freshman class profile.** 677 applied, 609 admitted, 214 enrolled.

| Mid 50% test scores | | Rank in top quarter: | 19% |
|---|---|---|---|
| SAT critical reading: | 380-490 | Rank in top tenth: | 4% |
| SAT math: | 400-500 | End year in good standing: | 79% |
| ACT composite: | 17-21 | Return as sophomores: | 71% |
| GPA 3.50 or higher: | 15% | Out-of-state: | 2% |
| GPA 3.0-3.49: | 27% | Live on campus: | 27% |
| GPA 2.0-2.99: | 54% | | |

**Basis for selection.** School achievement record and course selection important. Candidates must meet minimum academic criteria including high school GPA. SAT or ACT recommended. Essay, interview recommended. **Homeschooled:** Transcript of courses and grades, state high school equivalency certificate required. **Learning Disabled:** Separate statement directly to academic services required.

**High school preparation.** 16 units required; 21 recommended. Required and recommended units include English 4, mathematics 3-4, social studies 3-4, science 2-3 (laboratory 1-2) and foreign language 1-2.

**2008-2009 Annual costs.** Tuition/fees: $17,350. Room/board: $6,950. Books/supplies: $700. Personal expenses: $800.

**2007-2008 Financial aid. Need-based:** 206 full-time freshmen applied for aid; 189 were judged to have need; 189 of these received aid. Average need met was 67%. Average scholarship/grant was $8,380; average loan $3,953. 52% of total undergraduate aid awarded as scholarships/grants, 48% as loans/jobs. **Non-need-based:** Awarded to 133 full-time undergraduates, including 28 freshmen. Scholarships awarded for academics, job skills, leadership, minority status, state residency.

**Application procedures. Admission:** Priority date 6/30; deadline 9/1 (receipt date). $20 fee, may be waived for applicants with need. Application may be submitted online. Admission notification on a rolling basis beginning on or about 6/30. **Financial aid:** Priority date 3/1; no closing date. FAFSA required. Applicants notified on a rolling basis starting 3/15; must reply within 2 week(s) of notification.

**Academics. Special study options:** Combined bachelor's/graduate degree, cooperative education, cross-registration, distance learning, dual enrollment of high school students, honors, independent study, internships, study abroad, Washington semester. Member of Western New York consortium. **Credit/placement by examination:** AP, CLEP, IB, SAT, institutional tests. 18 credit hours maximum toward associate degree, 32 toward bachelor's. **Support services:** Learning center, reduced course load, tutoring, writing center.

**Majors. Business:** Accounting, business admin. **Communications:** Digital media. **Communications technology:** Photo/film/video. **English:** English lit. **Health:** Health services. **Legal studies:** Paralegal. **Liberal arts:** Arts/sciences. **Protective services:** Criminal justice, forensics, police science. **Psychology:** General. **Public administration:** Human services. **Social sciences:** Political science.

**Most popular majors.** Business/marketing 21%, psychology 9%, public administration/social services 7%, security/protective services 50%.

**Computing on campus.** 146 workstations in dormitories, library, computer center, student center. Dormitories wired for high-speed internet access. Online course registration, wireless network available.

**Student life. Freshman orientation:** Mandatory, $25 fee. 1-day programs held in June, July or August. **Housing:** Guaranteed on-campus for all undergraduates. Coed dorms, apartments available. $50 nonrefundable deposit, deadline 8/1. **Activities:** Campus ministries, choral groups, drama, literary magazine, student government, student newspaper, SADD, Human Service Association, Psychology Club, Great Expectations, Criminal Justice Club, Students in Free Enterprise, Common Grounds, Economic Crime Investigation Club.

**Athletics.** NCAA. **Intercollegiate:** Baseball M, basketball, cross-country, golf, soccer, softball W, volleyball. **Intramural:** Basketball, football (non-tackle), soccer, softball, table tennis, volleyball. **Team name:** Hawks.

**Student services.** Adult student services, alcohol/substance abuse counseling, campus ministries, career counseling, student employment services, financial aid counseling, minority student services, personal counseling, placement for graduates, veterans' counselor. **Physically disabled:** Services for visually, hearing impaired.

**Contact.** E-mail: admissions@hilbert.edu
Phone: (716) 649-7900 ext. 211 Toll-free number: (800) 649-8003
Fax: (716) 649-1152
Timothy Lee, Director of Admissions, Hilbert College, 5200 South Park Avenue, Hamburg, NY 14075-1597

## Hobart and William Smith Colleges
**Geneva, New York**
**www.hws.edu**
**CB member**
**CB code: 2294**

- Private 4-year liberal arts college
- Residential campus in large town
- 1,998 degree-seeking undergraduates: 54% women, 4% African American, 3% Asian American, 3% Hispanic American, 2% international
- 8 degree-seeking graduate students
- 55% of applicants admitted
- Application essay required
- 73% graduate within 6 years

**General.** Founded in 1822. Regionally accredited. Hobart and William Smith are coordinate colleges. All classes coeducational with one faculty, one President, one Board of Trustees, and one campus, but with separate deans, student governments, and athletic departments. **Degrees:** 433 bachelor's awarded; master's offered. **Location:** 50 miles from Syracuse, 40 miles from Rochester. **Calendar:** Semester. **Full-time faculty:** 183 total. **Part-time faculty:** 29 total. **Class size:** 68% < 20, 29% 20-39, 2% 40-49, 2% 50-99. **Special facilities:** 70-foot research vessel, 100-acre nature preserve, Finger Lakes Institute.

**Freshman class profile.** 4,165 applied, 2,270 admitted, 619 enrolled.

| Mid 50% test scores | | Rank in top quarter: | 68% |
|---|---|---|---|
| SAT critical reading: | 560-660 | Rank in top tenth: | 38% |
| SAT math: | 570-660 | End year in good standing: | 95% |
| ACT composite: | 25-28 | Return as sophomores: | 85% |
| GPA 3.50 or higher: | 34% | Out-of-state: | 61% |
| GPA 3.0-3.49: | 39% | Live on campus: | 100% |
| GPA 2.0-2.99: | 27% | International: | 2% |

**Basis for selection.** High school record, school and community activities, recommendations, and test scores important. Interview and talent considered. Economically and educationally disadvantaged NY state residents may apply through Higher Education Opportunity Program. Test scores are required for those students applying for the trustee and Blackwell scholarships. Interview recommended for all. Candidates for arts scholars program must submit portfolio or audition on campus. **Homeschooled:** Interview required. Students without a traditional, graded transcript must submit standardized test scores.

**High school preparation.** 20 units required. Required and recommended units include English 4, mathematics 3, social studies 2-3, history 2, science 3 (laboratory 2), foreign language 2-3 and academic electives 2-4. Mathematics must include algebra, geometry, and trigonometry sequence.

**2008-2009 Annual costs.** Tuition/fees: $38,860. Room/board: $9,686. Books/supplies: $1,000. Personal expenses: $600.

**2006-2007 Financial aid. Need-based:** 423 full-time freshmen applied for aid; 337 were judged to have need; 335 of these received aid. Average need met was 81%. Average scholarship/grant was $22,309; average loan $2,500. 78% of total undergraduate aid awarded as scholarships/grants, 22% as loans/jobs. **Non-need-based:** Awarded to 521 full-time undergraduates, including 178 freshmen. Scholarships awarded for academics, art, leadership, music/drama.

**Application procedures. Admission:** Closing date 2/1 (postmark date). $45 fee, may be waived for applicants with need. Application may be submitted online. Admission notification 4/1. Must reply by 5/1. **Financial aid:** Closing date 2/15. FAFSA, CSS PROFILE required. Applicants notified by 4/1; must reply by 5/1 or within 2 week(s) of notification.

**Academics.** All students must complete a major and a minor or a second major, 1 of which must be interdisciplinary. **Special study options:** Combined bachelor's/graduate degree, cross-registration, double major, ESL, exchange student, honors, independent study, internships, semester at sea, student-designed major, study abroad, teacher certification program, Washington semester. **Credit/placement by examination:** AP, CLEP, IB, institutional tests. Credit by examination counted toward degree limited to equivalent of 7 courses. **Support services:** Learning center, pre-admission summer program, reduced course load, study skills assistance, tutoring, writing center.

**Majors. Architecture:** Architecture. **Area/ethnic studies:** African, African-American, American, Asian, European, gay/lesbian, Hispanic-American/Latino/Chicano, Latin American, Russian/Slavic, women's. **Biology:** General, biochemistry. **Communications:** Media studies. **Computer sciences:** General, computer science. **Conservation:** Environmental studies. **English:** English lit. **Foreign languages:** Chinese, classics, comparative lit, French, Japanese, Latin, Russian, Spanish. **Health:** Predental, premedicine, preveterinary. **History:** General. **Interdisciplinary:** Math/computer science. **Math:** General. **Philosophy/religion:** Philosophy, religion. **Physical sciences:** Chemistry, geology, physics. **Psychology:** General. **Public administration:** Policy analysis. **Social sciences:** Anthropology, economics, international relations, political science, sociology, urban studies. **Visual/performing arts:** Art history/conservation, dance, dramatic, studio arts.

**Computing on campus.** 150 workstations in library, computer center. Dormitories wired for high-speed internet access and linked to campus network. Commuter students can connect to campus network. Online course registration, online library, helpline, repair service, student web hosting, wireless network available.

**Student life. Freshman orientation:** Mandatory. Preregistration for classes offered. 3-day program. **Housing:** Guaranteed on-campus for all undergraduates. Coed dorms, single-sex dorms, apartments, cooperative housing, fraternity/sorority housing, substance-free housing available. Theme residences, upperclassmen townhouses available. Extensive residential education program. **Activities:** Bands, choral groups, dance, drama, film society, literary magazine, music ensembles, musical theater, radio station, student government, student newspaper, symphony orchestra, service network, Literary Corps, international students club, denominational clubs, African-American student coalition, political educational network, Pan-African-Latin Organization, pride network, Big Brothers/Big Sisters, Latin American student organization.

**Athletics.** NCAA. **Intercollegiate:** Basketball, cross-country, diving W, field hockey W, football (tackle) M, golf, ice hockey M, lacrosse, rowing (crew), sailing, soccer, squash, swimming W, tennis. **Intramural:** Badminton, basketball, bowling, cross-country, diving M, equestrian, fencing, football (non-tackle), golf, ice hockey, lacrosse, racquetball, rugby, skiing, soccer, softball, squash, swimming, table tennis, tennis, track and field, volleyball, water polo. **Team name:** Statesmen (Hobart); Herons (William Smith).

**Student services.** Adult student services, alcohol/substance abuse counseling, campus ministries, career counseling, services for economically disadvantaged, student employment services, financial aid counseling, health services, legal services, minority student services, personal counseling, placement for graduates, women's services. **Physically disabled:** Services for visually, speech, hearing impaired.

**Contact.** E-mail: admissions@hws.edu
Phone: (315) 781-3622 Toll-free number: (800) 852-2256
Fax: (315) 781-3914
John Young, Director of Admissions, Hobart and William Smith Colleges, 629 South Main Street, Geneva, NY 14456

## Hofstra University
Hempstead, New York
www.hofstra.edu

CB member
CB code: 2295

- Private 4-year university
- Residential campus in large city
- 8,298 degree-seeking undergraduates: 8% part-time, 53% women, 9% African American, 5% Asian American, 8% Hispanic American, 1% Native American, 1% international
- 3,848 degree-seeking graduate students
- 54% of applicants admitted
- Application essay required
- 54% graduate within 6 years; 29% enter graduate study

**General.** Founded in 1935. Regionally accredited. **Degrees:** 1,808 bachelor's awarded; master's, doctoral, first professional offered. **ROTC:** Army. **Location:** 25 miles from New York City. **Calendar:** 4-1-4, extensive summer session. **Full-time faculty:** 544 total; 90% have terminal degrees, 16% minority, 42% women. **Part-time faculty:** 649 total; 39% have terminal degrees, 8% minority, 46% women. **Class size:** 47% < 20, 46% 20-39, 3% 40-49, 4% 50-99, less than 1% >100. **Special facilities:** Financial trading room, comprehensive media production facility, converged newsroom learning center, career center, writing center, linux beowolf cluster, digital language lab, technology, science and engineering labs, a rooftop observatory, 7 theaters, assessment centers for child observation and counseling, child care institute, cultural center, museum, arboretum, bird sanctuary.

**Freshman class profile.** 18,471 applied, 9,986 admitted, 1,735 enrolled.

| Mid 50% test scores | | | |
|---|---|---|---|
| SAT critical reading: | 540-630 | Rank in top quarter: | 56% |
| SAT math: | 550-630 | Rank in top tenth: | 26% |
| ACT composite: | 23-26 | End year in good standing: | 89% |
| GPA 3.50 or higher: | 41% | Return as sophomores: | 79% |
| GPA 3.0-3.49: | 34% | Out-of-state: | 49% |
| GPA 2.0-2.99: | 25% | Live on campus: | 79% |
| | | International: | 2% |

**Basis for selection.** Secondary school record, standardized test scores (SAT or ACT), personal essay and letters of recommendation most important. SAT Subject Tests recommended. No deadline (rolling) for SAT or ACT test scores. Standardized tests not required for admission to New Opportunities at Hofstra (NOAH), School of University Studies, Program for Academic Learning Skills (PALS) or International Applicants (TOEFL is required). Interview required of HEOP and academic learning skills applicants. Audition recommended for music, theater programs; portfolio recommended for fine arts program. **Homeschooled:** Statement describing homeschool structure and mission, transcript of courses and grades, state high school equivalency certificate required. Must provide at least 2 recommendations, including 1 from primary instructor or person who has primary responsibility for assessing applicant's academic performance. School required to certify completion of secondary school for all enrolled students prior to graduation. **Learning Disabled:** Students may apply to the Program for Academic Learning Skills. Application includes copy of psychological testing, WAISR or WISC.

**High school preparation.** 16 units required. Required and recommended units include English 4, mathematics 3-4, social studies 3-4, science 3-4 (laboratory 1-2) and foreign language 2-3. Social studies includes history; 4 math, 1 chemistry, and 1 physics required for engineering.

**2007-2008 Annual costs.** Tuition/fees: $26,730. Room/board: $10,300. Books/supplies: $1,000. Personal expenses: $1,150.

**2006-2007 Financial aid. Need-based:** 1,378 full-time freshmen applied for aid; 1,067 were judged to have need; 1,056 of these received aid. Average need met was 69%. Average scholarship/grant was $9,131; average loan $2,563. 43% of total undergraduate aid awarded as scholarships/grants, 57% as loans/jobs. **Non-need-based:** Awarded to 1,680 full-time undergraduates, including 472 freshmen. Scholarships awarded for academics, alumni affiliation, art, athletics, leadership, music/drama, ROTC, state residency. **Additional information:** Special financial aid funds may be available for applicants with special talents and those with superior academic ability.

**Application procedures. Admission:** No deadline. $50 fee, may be waived for applicants with need. Application may be submitted online. Admission notification on a rolling basis beginning on or about 2/1. Must reply by May 1 or within 2 week(s) if notified thereafter. **Financial aid:** Priority date 2/15; no closing date. FAFSA required. Applicants notified on a rolling basis starting 3/1.

**Academics. Special study options:** Accelerated study, combined bachelor's/graduate degree, cross-registration, distance learning, double major, dual enrollment of high school students, ESL, external degree, honors, independent study, internships, liberal arts/career combination, student-designed major, study abroad, teacher certification program, Washington semester, weekend college. **Credit/placement by examination:** AP, CLEP, IB, institutional tests. 30 credit hours maximum toward bachelor's degree. **Support services:** Learning center, pre-admission summer program, reduced course load, study skills assistance, tutoring, writing center.

**Honors college/program.** Applicants to Honors College are invited to participate based upon a careful review of academic achievement, writing ability, standardized test scores and extracurricular activities. Students invited to Honors College have a median SAT of 1300 (exclusive of Writing) and the vast majority graduated in the top 10% of the high school classes.

**Majors. Area/ethnic studies:** African, American, Asian, Caribbean, Hispanic-American/Latino/Chicano, Latin American, women's. **Biology:** General, biochemistry. **Business:** General, accounting, actuarial science, business admin, entrepreneurial studies, finance, international, labor studies, management information systems, managerial economics, marketing. **Communications:** General, broadcast journalism, journalism, media studies, public relations, radio/tv. **Computer sciences:** Computer science. **Conservation:** Environmental studies. **Education:** Art, biology, business, chemistry, early childhood, elementary, English, foreign languages, French, German, health, mathematics, multi-level teacher, music, physical, physics, science, secondary, social studies, Spanish. **Engineering:** Biomedical, civil, computer, electrical, environmental, industrial, manufacturing, mechanical, science. **English:** British lit, creative writing, English lit. **Foreign languages:** Chinese, classics, comparative lit, French, German, Hebrew, Italian, Latin, linguistics, Russian, Spanish. **Health:** Athletic training, audiology/speech pathology, community health, physician assistant, predental, premedicine, preveterinary. **History:** General. **Interdisciplinary:** Math/computer science, natural sciences. **Legal studies:** Prelaw. **Liberal arts:** Arts/sciences, humanities. **Math:** General, applied. **Philosophy/religion:** Judaic, philosophy, religion. **Physical sciences:** Chemistry, geology, physics. **Protective services:** Forensics. **Psychology:** General. **Social sciences:** General, anthropology, econometrics, economics, geography, political science, sociology. **Visual/performing arts:** Acting, art history/conservation, ceramics, dance, directing/producing, dramatic, jazz, metal/jewelry, music history, music management, music performance, music theory/composition, painting, photography, studio arts.

**Most popular majors.** Business/marketing 31%, communications/journalism 15%, education 9%, psychology 10%, social sciences 7%.

**Computing on campus.** 1,694 workstations in library, computer center. Dormitories wired for high-speed internet access and linked to campus network. Commuter students can connect to campus network. Online course registration, online library, helpline, repair service, student web hosting, wireless network available.

**Student life. Freshman orientation:** Available, $200 fee. Preregistration for classes offered. Several orientation programs for the undergraduate student population. Summer orientation is a 3-day/2-night program in which new students live on campus and begin preparation for the fall semester. **Housing:** Guaranteed on-campus for freshmen. Coed dorms, single-sex dorms, special housing for disabled, apartments, substance-free housing available. $300 nonrefundable deposit, deadline 5/1. Honors housing, living-learning center, and quiet floors available. **Activities:** Bands, campus ministries, choral groups, dance, drama, film society, international student organizations, literary magazine, music ensembles, musical theater, opera, radio station, student government, student newspaper, symphony orchestra, TV station, Hillel, Muslim student association, African people's organization, Organization of Latin Americans, College Republicans, Hofstra Democrats, Women of Action, progressive students union, Entertainment Unlimited.

**Athletics.** NCAA. **Intercollegiate:** Baseball M, basketball, cross-country, field hockey W, football (tackle) M, golf, lacrosse, soccer, softball W, tennis, volleyball W, wrestling M. **Intramural:** Badminton, basketball, football (non-tackle), soccer, softball, table tennis, tennis, volleyball. **Team name:** Pride.

**Student services.** Adult student services, alcohol/substance abuse counseling, campus ministries, career counseling, student employment services, financial aid counseling, health services, minority student services, on-campus daycare, personal counseling, placement for graduates. **Physically disabled:** Services for visually, speech, hearing impaired. **Learning disabled:** Comprehensive services available.

**Contact.** E-mail: admitme@hofstra.edu
Phone: (516) 463-6700 Toll-free number: (800) 463-7872
Fax: (516) 463-5100
Jessica Eads, Dean of Admissions and Financial Aid, Hofstra University, Admissions Center, 100 Hofstra University, Hempstead, NY 11549

---

## Holy Trinity Orthodox Seminary
**Jordanville, New York**
www.hts.edu
CB code: 2298

- Private 5-year seminary college for men affiliated with Russian Orthodox Church
- Residential campus in rural community
- 25 degree-seeking undergraduates
- Application essay required

**General.** Founded in 1948. Regionally accredited. **Degrees:** 4 bachelor's awarded. **Location:** 20 miles from Utica. **Calendar:** Semester, limited summer session. **Full-time faculty:** 6 total; 17% have terminal degrees, 17% women. **Part-time faculty:** 13 total; 8% have terminal degrees, 8% women. **Class size:** 100% < 20. **Special facilities:** Museum of Russian history, archives, icon painting studio.

**Freshman class profile.**

| Out-of-state: | 50% | Live on campus: | 100% |
|---|---|---|---|

**Basis for selection.** Orthodoxy/Orthodox baptism, knowledge of Russian, entrance exam required. Recommendation from spiritual father or parish priest important. **Homeschooled:** Letter of recommendation (nonparent) required.

**2007-2008 Annual costs.** Tuition/fees: $3,000. Room/board: $2,500. Books/supplies: $200.

**Financial aid. Additional information:** Work-study program can reasonably pay for room and board over the course of the academic year.

---

**Application procedures. Admission:** Closing date 5/1 (postmark date). No application fee.

**Academics. Special study options:** Distance learning. English as a Foreign Language. **Credit/placement by examination:** CLEP, institutional tests. **Support services:** Remedial instruction, tutoring.

**Majors. Theology:** Theology.

**Computing on campus.** 8 workstations in dormitories, library.

**Student life. Freshman orientation:** Mandatory. **Policies:** Closed campus. Religious observance required. **Housing:** Guaranteed on-campus for all undergraduates. Substance-free housing available. **Activities:** Choral groups, student newspaper.

**Contact.** E-mail: info@hts.edu
Phone: (315) 858-0945
Dc. Vladimir Tsurikov, Assistant Dean, Holy Trinity Orthodox Seminary, Box 36, Jordanville, NY 13361

---

## Houghton College
**Houghton, New York**
www.houghton.edu
CB member
CB code: 2299

- Private 4-year liberal arts college affiliated with Wesleyan Church
- Residential campus in rural community
- 1,324 degree-seeking undergraduates: 3% part-time, 64% women, 2% African American, 2% Asian American, 1% Hispanic American, 3% international
- 14 degree-seeking graduate students
- 84% of applicants admitted
- SAT or ACT (ACT writing optional), application essay required
- 72% graduate within 6 years; 33% enter graduate study

**General.** Founded in 1883. Regionally accredited. All students receive laptop computer as part of tuition. Extension campuses in suburban Buffalo and in the Adirondack State Park. Study abroad programs in London, Tanzania, and Australia. School of Music accredited by National Association of Schools of Music. **Degrees:** 336 bachelor's, 5 associate awarded; master's offered. **ROTC:** Army. **Location:** 60 miles from Buffalo, 70 miles from Rochester. **Calendar:** Semester, limited summer session. **Full-time faculty:** 94 total; 76% have terminal degrees, 6% minority, 32% women. **Part-time faculty:** 36 total; 28% have terminal degrees, 3% minority, 47% women. **Class size:** 66% < 20, 31% 20-39, less than 1% 40-49, 2% 50-99. **Special facilities:** Equestrian center with indoor riding ring, initiatives course, downhill and cross-country skiing facilities, ropes course, media arts computer lab, hiking and biking trails.

**Freshman class profile.** 1,005 applied, 843 admitted, 265 enrolled.

| Mid 50% test scores | | Rank in top quarter: | 64% |
|---|---|---|---|
| SAT critical reading: | 510-640 | Rank in top tenth: | 33% |
| SAT math: | 490-620 | End year in good standing: | 89% |
| SAT writing: | 510-630 | Return as sophomores: | 82% |
| ACT composite: | 21-28 | Out-of-state: | 38% |
| GPA 3.50 or higher: | 65% | Live on campus: | 97% |
| GPA 3.0-3.49: | 24% | International: | 4% |
| GPA 2.0-2.99: | 10% | | |

**Basis for selection.** Student's high school transcript and standardized test scores are of the utmost importance. Application essays, student's Christian character recommendation, and other intangibles are also considered. Interview recommended for all applicants. Audition and separate application required for entrance into the School of Music. Admission to the First-Year Honors Programs requires separate application, academic reference, writing sample, and interview. **Homeschooled:** Transcript of courses and grades required. Reading list recommended. **Learning Disabled:** Students must provide an IEP to receive services.

**High school preparation.** College-preparatory program recommended. 16 units recommended. Recommended units include English 4, mathematics 3, social studies 1, history 2, science 2 (laboratory 2) and foreign language 2.

**2008-2009 Annual costs.** Tuition/fees: $22,990. Tuition includes laptop computer, fees. Room/board: $6,930. Books/supplies: $900. Personal expenses: $750.

**2007-2008 Financial aid. Need-based:** 242 full-time freshmen applied for aid; 217 were judged to have need; 217 of these received aid. Average need met was 79%. Average scholarship/grant was $9,800; average loan $4,080. 59% of total undergraduate aid awarded as scholarships/grants, 41%

as loans/jobs. **Non-need-based:** Awarded to 458 full-time undergraduates, including 113 freshmen. Scholarships awarded for academics, alumni affiliation, art, athletics, music/drama, religious affiliation, ROTC, state residency.

**Application procedures. Admission:** No deadline. $40 fee, may be waived for applicants with need. Application may be submitted online. Admission notification on a rolling basis beginning on or about 1/1. Must reply by May 1 or within 4 week(s) if notified thereafter. **Financial aid:** Priority date 3/1; no closing date. FAFSA required. Applicants notified on a rolling basis starting 3/15; must reply by 5/1.

**Academics. Special study options:** Combined bachelor's/graduate degree, cross-registration, double major, exchange student, honors, independent study, internships, liberal arts/career combination, study abroad, teacher certification program, Washington semester. **Credit/placement by examination:** AP, CLEP, IB, SAT, ACT, institutional tests. 16 credit hours maximum toward associate degree, 32 toward bachelor's. **Support services:** Learning center, reduced course load, study skills assistance, tutoring, writing center.

**Majors. Agriculture:** Equestrian studies. **Biology:** General, biochemistry, environmental. **Business:** General, accounting, business admin. **Communications:** General, digital media, public relations. **Computer sciences:** Computer science, information technology. **Education:** General, biology, chemistry, elementary, English, ESL, foreign languages, French, history, mathematics, music, physical, physics, secondary, social studies, Spanish. **Engineering:** Physics. **English:** English lit. **Foreign languages:** French, Spanish. **Health:** Predental, premedicine, preveterinary, recreational therapy. **History:** General. **Interdisciplinary:** Intercultural. **Math:** General. **Parks/recreation:** General, health/fitness. **Philosophy/religion:** Philosophy, religion. **Physical sciences:** Chemistry, physics. **Psychology:** General. **Social sciences:** International relations, political science, sociology. **Theology:** Bible, missionary, preministerial, youth ministry. **Visual/performing arts:** Art, music performance, music theory/composition, piano/organ, stringed instruments, studio arts, voice/opera.

**Most popular majors.** Business/marketing 27%, education 14%, English 7%, philosophy/religious studies 10%, psychology 7%, theological studies 7%, visual/performing arts 6%.

**Computing on campus.** PC or laptop required. 8 workstations in dormitories, library, computer center, student center. Dormitories wired for high-speed internet access and linked to campus network. Commuter students can connect to campus network. Helpline, repair service, wireless network available.

**Student life. Freshman orientation:** Mandatory. Preregistration for classes offered. **Policies:** Drinking of alcoholic beverages and smoking on or off campus prohibited. Religious observance required. **Housing:** Guaranteed on-campus for freshmen. Single-sex dorms, special housing for disabled, apartments, substance-free housing available. $300 nonrefundable deposit, deadline 5/1. Townhouses and apartments available. **Activities:** Bands, campus ministries, choral groups, drama, international student organizations, literary magazine, music ensembles, musical theater, opera, student government, student newspaper, symphony orchestra, Allegany County Outreach, Global Christian Fellowship, Habitat for Humanity, Youth for Christ, Fellowship of Christian Athletes, intercultural student organization.

**Athletics.** NAIA. **Intercollegiate:** Basketball, cross-country, field hockey W, soccer, track and field, volleyball W. **Intramural:** Basketball, equestrian, football (non-tackle) M, racquetball, soccer, table tennis, volleyball, water polo. **Team name:** Highlanders.

**Student services.** Campus ministries, career counseling, student employment services, financial aid counseling, health services, personal counseling, placement for graduates.

**Contact.** E-mail: admission@houghton.edu
Phone: (585) 567-9353 Toll-free number: (800) 777-2556
Fax: (585) 567-9522
Wayne MacBeth, Vice President for Enrollment Management and Market Relations, Houghton College, 1 Willard Avenue/Box 128, Houghton, NY 14744-0128

## Iona College

**New Rochelle, New York**
www.iona.edu

**CB member**
**CB code: 2324**

- Private 4-year business and liberal arts college affiliated with Roman Catholic Church
- Residential campus in small city
- 3,480 degree-seeking undergraduates: 4% part-time, 54% women, 6% African American, 2% Asian American, 11% Hispanic American, 1% international

- 802 degree-seeking graduate students
- 59% of applicants admitted
- SAT or ACT (ACT writing optional), application essay required
- 60% graduate within 6 years; 76% enter graduate study

**General.** Founded in 1940. Regionally accredited. Independent institution in Roman Catholic, Christian Brothers tradition. **Degrees:** 713 bachelor's awarded; master's offered. **ROTC:** Army, Air Force. **Location:** 20 miles from New York City. **Calendar:** Semester, extensive summer session. **Full-time faculty:** 176 total; 92% have terminal degrees, 8% minority, 33% women. **Part-time faculty:** 227 total; 35% have terminal degrees, 10% minority, 40% women. **Class size:** 42% < 20, 52% 20-39, 6% 40-49. **Special facilities:** Extensive Irish and rare books collection.

**Freshman class profile.** 6,017 applied, 3,550 admitted, 908 enrolled.

| Mid 50% test scores | | | |
|---|---|---|---|
| SAT critical reading: | 530-640 | Rank in top quarter: | 54% |
| SAT math: | 550-660 | Rank in top tenth: | 31% |
| GPA 3.50 or higher: | 20% | Return as sophomores: | 86% |
| GPA 3.0-3.49: | 53% | Out-of-state: | 25% |
| GPA 2.0-2.99: | 27% | Live on campus: | 61% |
| | | International: | 1% |

**Basis for selection.** High school curriculum and GPA most important, followed by test scores, recommendations, interview, extracurricular activities, essays, grade trends. Interviews recommended. **Homeschooled:** Transcript of courses and grades, interview required.

**High school preparation.** 16 units required; 20 recommended. Required and recommended units include English 4, mathematics 3-4, social studies 1-2, history 1-2, science 2-3 (laboratory 2), foreign language 2 and academic electives 1-3.

**2007-2008 Annual costs.** Tuition/fees: $24,724. Room/board: $10,500. Books/supplies: $1,500. Personal expenses: $1,700.

**2007-2008 Financial aid. Need-based:** 898 full-time freshmen applied for aid; 688 were judged to have need; 684 of these received aid. Average need met was 25%. Average scholarship/grant was $3,841; average loan $2,081. 54% of total undergraduate aid awarded as scholarships/grants, 46% as loans/jobs. **Non-need-based:** Awarded to 3,279 full-time undergraduates, including 956 freshmen. Scholarships awarded for academics, alumni affiliation, athletics, ROTC.

**Application procedures. Admission:** Closing date 2/15 (postmark date). $50 fee, may be waived for applicants with need. Application may be submitted online. Admission notification 3/20. Must reply by 5/1. **Financial aid:** Closing date 4/15. FAFSA, institutional form required. Applicants notified on a rolling basis starting 12/20; must reply by 5/1 or within 2 week(s) of notification.

**Academics. Special study options:** Accelerated study, combined bachelor's/graduate degree, distance learning, double major, honors, independent study, internships, liberal arts/career combination, study abroad, teacher certification program, weekend college. **Credit/placement by examination:** AP, CLEP, SAT, ACT. 60 credit hours maximum toward bachelor's degree. **Support services:** Learning center, pre-admission summer program, reduced course load, tutoring, writing center.

**Majors. Biology:** General, biochemistry, environmental. **Business:** Accounting, business admin, finance, international, management information systems, marketing. **Communications:** General, advertising, journalism, media studies, public relations, radio/tv. **Computer sciences:** Computer science, networking, web page design. **Education:** Biology, early childhood, elementary, English, French, mathematics, secondary, social studies, Spanish. **English:** English lit. **Foreign languages:** French, Italian, Spanish. **Health:** Audiology/speech pathology, clinical lab science, health care admin. **History:** General. **Interdisciplinary:** Global studies. **Liberal arts:** Arts/sciences. **Math:** General, applied. **Philosophy/religion:** Philosophy, religion. **Physical sciences:** Chemistry, physics. **Protective services:** Law enforcement admin. **Psychology:** General. **Public administration:** Social work. **Social sciences:** Economics, political science, sociology. **Visual/performing arts:** Dramatic. **Other:** Italian teacher education.

**Most popular majors.** Business/marketing 36%, communications/journalism 15%, education 7%, psychology 11%, security/protective services 9%.

**Computing on campus.** 500 workstations in dormitories, library, computer center, student center. Dormitories wired for high-speed internet access and linked to campus network. Commuter students can connect to campus network. Online course registration, online library, helpline, repair service, wireless network available.

**Student life. Freshman orientation:** Mandatory. Preregistration for classes offered. Overnight summer program in June and July; 1-day welcome program. **Housing:** Coed dorms, special housing for disabled, apartments, substance-free housing available. $630 nonrefundable deposit, deadline 5/1. Honors program student housing available. **Activities:** Pep band, campus ministries, choral groups, dance, drama, film society, literary magazine, musical theater, radio station, student government, student newspaper, TV station, Gaelic Society, Council of Multicultural Leaders, Italian club, Students of Caribbean Ancestry, Hispanic Organization for Latin Awareness, Ancestry International, Democrats, Republicans, Students for American Awareness.

**Athletics.** NCAA. **Intercollegiate:** Baseball M, basketball, cross-country, diving, football (tackle) M, golf M, lacrosse W, rowing (crew), soccer, softball W, swimming, track and field, volleyball W, water polo. **Intramural:** Basketball, football (non-tackle), soccer, table tennis, volleyball. **Team name:** Gaels.

**Student services.** Adult student services, alcohol/substance abuse counseling, campus ministries, career counseling, student employment services, financial aid counseling, health services, minority student services, personal counseling, placement for graduates, veterans' counselor, women's services. **Physically disabled:** Services for speech impaired.

**Contact.** E-mail: icad@iona.edu
Phone: (914) 633-2502 Toll-free number: (800) 231-4662
Fax: (914) 633-2182
Kevin Cavanagh, Assistant VP for College Admissions, Iona College, 715 North Avenue, New Rochelle, NY 10801-1890

---

## Ithaca College
**Ithaca, New York**
www.ithaca.edu

**CB member**
**CB code: 2325**

- Private 4-year health science and liberal arts college
- Residential campus in large town
- 6,185 degree-seeking undergraduates: 1% part-time, 55% women, 3% African American, 4% Asian American, 4% Hispanic American, 2% international
- 393 degree-seeking graduate students
- 74% of applicants admitted
- SAT or ACT with writing, application essay required
- 77% graduate within 6 years; 30% enter graduate study

**General.** Founded in 1892. Regionally accredited. **Degrees:** 1,438 bachelor's awarded; master's, doctoral offered. **ROTC:** Army, Air Force. **Location:** 250 miles from New York City, 60 miles from Syracuse. **Calendar:** Semester, extensive summer session. **Full-time faculty:** 461 total; 92% have terminal degrees, 8% minority, 46% women. **Part-time faculty:** 212 total; 56% have terminal degrees, 5% minority, 50% women. **Class size:** 57% < 20, 37% 20-39, 3% 40-49, 3% 50-99, 1% >100. **Special facilities:** Digital audio/video labs, photography labs, cinematography postproduction studio, film animation lab, lighting studio, physical therapy and occupational therapy clinics, speech and hearing clinic, exercise science labs, greenhouse, tissue culture laboratory, simulated trading room, recording and electroacoustic music studio, observatory.

**Freshman class profile.** 11,235 applied, 8,326 admitted, 1,798 enrolled.

| Mid 50% test scores | | End year in good standing: | 93% |
|---|---|---|---|
| SAT critical reading: | 530-630 | Return as sophomores: | 87% |
| SAT math: | 540-630 | Out-of-state: | 56% |
| Rank in top quarter: | 66% | Live on campus: | 99% |
| Rank in top tenth: | 30% | International: | 2% |

**Basis for selection.** School achievement record, test scores most important. School and community activities, accomplishments, special talents, interview also important. Audition required for music, theater arts programs; portfolio recommended for BFA program. **Homeschooled:** Transcript of courses and grades, letter of recommendation (nonparent) required. Applicants encouraged to provide in-depth information regarding academic preparation.

**High school preparation.** 16 units required. Required units include English 4, mathematics 3, social studies 3, science 3, foreign language 2 and academic electives 1.

**2008-2009 Annual costs.** Tuition/fees: $30,606. Room/board: $11,126. Books/supplies: $1,130. Personal expenses: $1,470.

**Financial aid. Non-need-based:** Scholarships awarded for academics, alumni affiliation, leadership, minority status, music/drama, ROTC.

**Application procedures. Admission:** Closing date 2/1. $60 fee, may be waived for applicants with need. Application may be submitted online. Admission notification 4/15. Admission notification on a rolling basis beginning on or about 11/15. Must reply by May 1 or within 2 week(s) if notified

thereafter. **Financial aid:** Priority date 2/1; no closing date. FAFSA required. Applicants notified on a rolling basis starting 2/15.

**Academics.** Over 50 minors available. **Special study options:** Accelerated study, combined bachelor's/graduate degree, cross-registration, distance learning, double major, dual enrollment of high school students, honors, independent study, internships, liberal arts/career combination, student-designed major, study abroad, teacher certification program, Washington semester. London Center (England), Los Angeles program, study opportunities in over 50 countries. **Credit/placement by examination:** AP, CLEP, IB, institutional tests. 90 credit hours maximum toward bachelor's degree. **Support services:** Study skills assistance, tutoring, writing center.

**Majors. Biology:** General, biochemistry. **Business:** General, accounting, business admin, finance, international, managerial economics, market research, marketing. **Communications:** General, broadcast journalism, journalism, media studies, organizational, radio/tv. **Communications technology:** Recording arts. **Computer sciences:** General, computer science, information systems, information technology, programming. **Conservation:** General, environmental studies. **Education:** Art, biology, chemistry, Deaf/hearing impaired, English, foreign languages, French, German, health, history, mathematics, multi-level teacher, music, physical, physics, science, secondary, social studies, Spanish, speech impaired. **English:** Composition, creative writing, English lit, speech/rhetoric. **Foreign languages:** General, French, German, Italian, Spanish. **Health:** Athletic training, facilities admin, occupational therapy assistant, predental, premedicine, preveterinary, public health ed, recreational therapy, speech pathology. **History:** General. **Interdisciplinary:** Gerontology, intercultural, nutrition sciences. **Legal studies:** General, prelaw. **Liberal arts:** Arts/sciences. **Math:** General. **Parks/recreation:** Exercise sciences, health/fitness, sports admin. **Philosophy/religion:** Philosophy. **Physical sciences:** Chemistry, physics. **Psychology:** General, industrial. **Social sciences:** General, anthropology, applied economics, economics, political science, sociology. **Visual/performing arts:** General, acting, art, art history/conservation, arts management, cinematography, dance, dramatic, film/cinema, jazz, music performance, music theory/composition, photography, studio arts, theater arts management, theater design. **Other:** Sport Studies, Sports Information and Communication.

**Most popular majors.** Business/marketing 10%, communications/journalism 18%, English 7%, health sciences 11%, parks/recreation 7%, social sciences 8%, visual/performing arts 17%.

**Computing on campus.** 640 workstations in library, computer center. Dormitories wired for high-speed internet access and linked to campus network. Commuter students can connect to campus network. Online course registration, online library, helpline, repair service, student web hosting, wireless network available.

**Student life. Freshman orientation:** Available, $225 fee. Preregistration for classes offered. 2.5 days in summer and 4 days before school highlighted by placement tests and registration. Separate parent orientation program offered in summer. **Housing:** Guaranteed on-campus for all undergraduates. Coed dorms, single-sex dorms, special housing for disabled, apartments, fraternity/sorority housing, substance-free housing available. First-year students only, quiet study residence halls, music honor fraternity housing, smoke-free buildings and floors, co-ed by door buildings, honors floor, several freshmen seminar groups housed together, H.O.M.E. Program (Housing Offering a Multicultural Experience) available. **Activities:** Bands, campus ministries, choral groups, dance, drama, film society, literary magazine, music ensembles, musical theater, opera, radio station, student government, student newspaper, symphony orchestra, TV station, Jewish, Christian, Catholic, Muslim, and Christian Science organizations; African-Latino society; Amnesty International; BiGayla; community service network; Habitat for Humanity, Sex and Gender Education, Asia Society, Friends of Israel.

**Athletics.** NCAA. **Intercollegiate:** Baseball M, basketball, cross-country, diving, field hockey W, football (tackle) M, gymnastics W, lacrosse, rowing (crew), soccer, softball W, swimming, tennis, track and field, volleyball W, wrestling M. **Intramural:** Basketball, bowling, golf, ice hockey M, rowing (crew), rugby W, skiing, soccer, softball, tennis, volleyball. **Team name:** Bombers.

**Student services.** Adult student services, alcohol/substance abuse counseling, campus ministries, career counseling, student employment services, financial aid counseling, health services, minority student services, personal counseling, placement for graduates, veterans' counselor. **Physically disabled:** Services for visually, speech, hearing impaired.

**Contact.** E-mail: admission@ithaca.edu
Phone: (607) 274-3124 Toll-free number: (800) 429-4274
Fax: (607) 274-1900
Gerard Turbide, Director of Admission, Ithaca College, 100 Job Hall, Ithaca, NY 14850-7020

## Jewish Theological Seminary of America
**New York, New York**
www.jtsa.edu
CB code: 2339

- Private 4-year university and seminary college affiliated with Jewish faith
- Residential campus in very large city
- 180 degree-seeking undergraduates: 5% part-time, 61% women, 2% Hispanic American
- 374 degree-seeking graduate students
- 61% of applicants admitted
- SAT or ACT with writing, application essay required

**General.** Founded in 1886. Regionally accredited. **Degrees:** 47 bachelor's awarded; master's, doctoral, first professional offered. **ROTC:** Army, Naval, Air Force. **Calendar:** Semester, extensive summer session. **Full-time faculty:** 62 total; 95% have terminal degrees, 34% women. **Part-time faculty:** 69 total; 74% have terminal degrees, 48% women. **Class size:** 88% < 20, 11% 20-39, 2% 40-49. **Special facilities:** Jewish museum containing over 27,000 objects (paintings, sculptures, works on paper, artifacts, etc.), library containing largest collection of Hebraica and Judaica outside of Israel.

**Freshman class profile.** 102 applied, 62 admitted, 40 enrolled.

| Mid 50% test scores | | | |
|---|---|---|---|
| | | ACT composite: | 29-31 |
| SAT critical reading: | 650-730 | GPA 3.50 or higher: | 83% |
| SAT math: | 630-690 | GPA 3.0-3.49: | 17% |
| SAT writing: | 630-730 | Out-of-state: | 92% |

**Basis for selection.** GED not accepted. School achievement record, interest in Jewish studies, test scores, recommendations important; leadership potential considered. Interview recommended for residents in the New York area (within 100 mile radius).

**High school preparation.** Recommended units include English 4, mathematics 4, social studies 1, history 3, science 4, foreign language 4 and academic electives 4. Additional courses in Judaic studies, when available.

**2008-2009 Annual costs.** Tuition/fees: $15,000. Costs quoted paid to school only; separate costs assessed for dual-degree enrollment at Columbia University/Barnard College. Room/board: $9,200.

**2007-2008 Financial aid. Need-based:** 13 full-time freshmen applied for aid; 12 were judged to have need; 12 of these received aid. Average need met was 88%. Average scholarship/grant was $17,706; average loan $3,500. 87% of total undergraduate aid awarded as scholarships/grants, 13% as loans/jobs. **Non-need-based:** Awarded to 32 full-time undergraduates, including 17 freshmen. Scholarships awarded for academics, alumni affiliation, leadership.

**Application procedures. Admission:** Closing date 2/15. $65 fee, may be waived for applicants with need. Admission notification 4/1. Must reply by 5/1. Application deadline January 1 for double degree program with Barnard College, February 15 for joint program with Columbia University. **Financial aid:** Priority date 2/1, closing date 3/1. FAFSA, institutional form, CSS PROFILE required. Applicants notified on a rolling basis starting 4/1; must reply within 4 week(s) of notification.

**Academics. Special study options:** Cross-registration, distance learning, double major, exchange student, honors, independent study, liberal arts/career combination, student-designed major, study abroad, teacher certification program. BA/MA program with The Graduate School or William Davidson School of Jewish Education. **Credit/placement by examination:** AP, CLEP, institutional tests. 6 credit hours maximum toward bachelor's degree. **Support services:** Pre-admission summer program, remedial instruction, tutoring, writing center.

**Majors. Foreign languages:** General. **Philosophy/religion:** Judaic. **Theology:** Sacred music. **Visual/performing arts:** Music performance, music theory/composition.

**Computing on campus.** 50 workstations in dormitories, library, computer center. Dormitories wired for high-speed internet access and linked to campus network. Commuter students can connect to campus network.

**Student life. Freshman orientation:** Mandatory. **Policies:** Student life centers around supportive Jewish community. Undergraduates enrolled in joint degree programs with Barnard and Columbia participate in their extracurricular activities. **Housing:** Coed dorms, special housing for disabled available. **Activities:** Concert band, choral groups, dance, musical theater, student government, student newspaper, community service organization.

**Athletics. Intramural:** Basketball, bowling, field hockey W, lacrosse M, softball, volleyball.

**Student services.** Career counseling, student employment services, health services, personal counseling, placement for graduates.

**Contact.** E-mail: lcadmissions@jtsa.edu
Phone: (212) 678-8832 Fax: (212) 678-8947
Reina Cohen, Director of Admissions, Jewish Theological Seminary of America, 3080 Broadway, New York, NY 10027

## Juilliard School
**New York, New York**
www.juilliard.edu
CB code: 2340

- Private 4-year music and performing arts college
- Commuter campus in very large city
- 491 degree-seeking undergraduates: 45% women, 9% African American, 16% Asian American, 5% Hispanic American, 17% international
- 117 degree-seeking graduate students
- 6% of applicants admitted
- Application essay, interview required
- 74% graduate within 6 years

**General.** Founded in 1905. Regionally accredited. **Degrees:** 102 bachelor's awarded; master's, doctoral offered. **Calendar:** Semester. **Full-time faculty:** 113 total; 11% minority, 42% women. **Part-time faculty:** 152 total; 14% minority, 26% women. **Class size:** 95% < 20, 5% 20-39. **Special facilities:** Media center, over 100 practice rooms with over 200 pianos, scenery and costume shops, 15 2-story rehearsal studios, 5 theaters, 2 recital halls.

**Freshman class profile.** 2,311 applied, 149 admitted, 106 enrolled.

| | | | |
|---|---|---|---|
| Return as sophomores: | 95% | Live on campus: | 100% |
| Out-of-state: | 89% | International: | 15% |

**Basis for selection.** Quality of performance at audition most important. Foreign students given English proficiency examination at time of audition or may present TOEFL. Audition required. **Homeschooled:** Transcript of courses and grades, letter of recommendation (nonparent) required.

**High school preparation.** Extensive previous study in major field of dance, drama, or music required.

**2008-2009 Annual costs.** Tuition/fees: $28,640. Room/board: $11,250. Books/supplies: $4,100.

**2007-2008 Financial aid. Need-based:** 102 full-time freshmen applied for aid; 80 were judged to have need; 80 of these received aid. Average need met was 89%. Average scholarship/grant was $21,248; average loan $4,487. 74% of total undergraduate aid awarded as scholarships/grants, 26% as loans/jobs. **Non-need-based:** Awarded to 27 full-time undergraduates, including 8 freshmen. Scholarships awarded for music/drama.

**Application procedures. Admission:** Closing date 12/1. $100 fee, may be waived for applicants with need. Admission notification 4/1. Must reply by May 1 or within 2 week(s) if notified thereafter. Auditions held in March. Drama auditions in January and Febuary, application closing date December 1; notification by April 1, or 1 month after audition. **Financial aid:** Closing date 3/1. FAFSA, institutional form required. Applicants notified by 4/1; must reply by 5/1.

**Academics.** 3-year diploma program available in performing arts. **Special study options:** Accelerated study, cross-registration, double major, honors, liberal arts/career combination, study abroad. Eligible students can enroll in courses at Barnard College and Columbia College to fulfill liberal arts elective requirements. **Credit/placement by examination:** AP, CLEP, institutional tests. **Support services:** Tutoring.

**Majors. Visual/performing arts:** Dance, dramatic, jazz, music performance, music theory/composition, piano/organ, stringed instruments.

**Computing on campus.** 65 workstations in dormitories, library, computer center. Dormitories wired for high-speed internet access. Online library, wireless network available.

**Student life. Freshman orientation:** Mandatory, $200 fee. For all new students, begins 10 days before first day of classes. **Housing:** Guaranteed on-campus for freshmen. Coed dorms, substance-free housing available. $250 nonrefundable deposit, deadline 5/1. Single sex floor, quiet floor, graduate student only floor, substance-free floor available. **Activities:** Jazz band, choral groups, dance, drama, opera, student newspaper, symphony orchestra, ArtREACH, Korea Campus Crusade for Christ, Juilliard, Christian Fellowship, Amnesty Juilliard.

**Student services.** Alcohol/substance abuse counseling, career counseling, student employment services, financial aid counseling, health services, minority student services, personal counseling, placement for graduates.

**Contact.** E-mail: admissions@juilliard.edu
Phone: (212) 799-5000 ext. 223 Fax: (212) 769-6420
Lee Cioppa, Associate Dean for Admissions, Juilliard School, 60 Lincoln Center Plaza, New York, NY 10023-6588

## Kehilath Yakov Rabbinical Seminary
### Brooklyn, New York
**CB code: 0619**

- Private 4-year rabbinical college for men affiliated with Jewish faith
- Very large city

**General.** Accredited by AARTS. **Calendar:** Continuous.

**Contact.** Phone: (718) 963-3940
206 Wilson Street, Brooklyn, NY 11211

## Keuka College
### Keuka Park, New York
### www.keuka.edu
**CB member**
**CB code: 2350**

- Private 4-year liberal arts college affiliated with American Baptist Churches in the USA
- Residential campus in rural community
- 1,441 degree-seeking undergraduates: 22% part-time, 71% women
- 185 graduate students
- 75% of applicants admitted
- Application essay required
- 45% graduate within 6 years; 28% enter graduate study

**General.** Founded in 1890. Regionally accredited. **Degrees:** 286 bachelor's awarded; master's offered. **Location:** 50 miles from Rochester, 60 miles from Syracuse. **Calendar:** 4-1-4, limited summer session. **Full-time faculty:** 57 total; 91% have terminal degrees, 60% women. **Part-time faculty:** 44 total; 27% have terminal degrees, 61% women. **Class size:** 52% < 20, 46% 20-39, 1% 40-49, 1% 50-99. **Special facilities:** Lakefront for boating, sailing and science projects and research.

**Freshman class profile.** 889 applied, 666 admitted, 285 enrolled.

| Mid 50% test scores | | Rank in top tenth: | 5% |
|---|---|---|---|
| SAT critical reading: | 410-520 | End year in good standing: | 86% |
| SAT math: | 430-540 | Return as sophomores: | 65% |
| GPA 3.50 or higher: | 19% | Out-of-state: | 6% |
| GPA 3.0-3.49: | 38% | Live on campus: | 100% |
| GPA 2.0-2.99: | 41% | International: | 1% |
| Rank in top quarter: | 22% | | |

**Basis for selection.** Overall GPA, extracurricular activities, community service, leadership experience, letter of recommendation, quality of essay, SAT/ACT scores considered by committee. Interview recommended for all, required for some.

**High school preparation.** 18 units recommended. Recommended units include English 4, mathematics 3, social studies 3, history 2, science 3 (laboratory 2) and foreign language 3.

**2007-2008 Annual costs.** Tuition/fees: $20,550. Room/board: $8,530. Books/supplies: $950. Personal expenses: $1,000.

**2007-2008 Financial aid. Need-based:** 272 full-time freshmen applied for aid; 254 were judged to have need; 254 of these received aid. Average need met was 76%. Average scholarship/grant was $12,970; average loan $5,251. 55% of total undergraduate aid awarded as scholarships/grants, 45% as loans/jobs. **Non-need-based:** Awarded to 100 full-time undergraduates, including 46 freshmen. Scholarships awarded for academics, alumni affiliation, leadership, minority status, religious affiliation.

**Application procedures. Admission:** No deadline. $30 fee, may be waived for applicants with need. Application may be submitted online. Admission notification on a rolling basis beginning on or about 9/1. **Financial aid:** Priority date 3/15; no closing date. FAFSA required. Applicants notified on a rolling basis starting 3/1; must reply by 5/1 or within 2 week(s) of notification.

**Academics.** All students must complete 1 field period or internship each year, every 30 credit hours (experiential education). Field Period enables students to spend 4 weeks a year participating in an internship or international travel, or undertaking an independent project. **Special study options:** Accelerated study, combined bachelor's/graduate degree, cooperative education, cross-registration, double major, dual enrollment of high school students, independent study, internships, student-designed major, study abroad, teacher certification program. Albany semester; 3-1 in clinical science with New York Chiropractic College. **Credit/placement by examination:** AP, CLEP, institutional tests. 12 credit hours maximum toward bachelor's degree. **Support services:** Learning center, reduced course load, remedial instruction, study skills assistance, tutoring, writing center.

**Majors. Biology:** General, biochemistry. **Business:** Accounting, business admin, marketing. **Communications:** General. **Conservation:** Environmental science. **Education:** Biology, early childhood, English, mathematics, secondary, social studies, special. **English:** English lit. **Foreign languages:** American Sign Language, sign language interpretation. **Health:** Clinical lab science, nursing (RN). **Legal studies:** Prelaw. **Liberal arts:** Arts/sciences. **Math:** General. **Protective services:** Law enforcement admin. **Psychology:** General. **Public administration:** Social work. **Social sciences:** General, criminology, sociology.

**Most popular majors.** Business/marketing 20%, education 17%, health sciences 29%, security/protective services 14%.

**Computing on campus.** 140 workstations in dormitories, library, computer center. Dormitories wired for high-speed internet access and linked to campus network. Helpline, repair service, wireless network available.

**Student life. Freshman orientation:** Mandatory, $150 fee. Preregistration for classes offered. 2-session summer program. **Policies:** No smoking allowed in any campus building, including residence halls. **Housing:** Guaranteed on-campus for all undergraduates. Coed dorms, single-sex dorms, special housing for disabled, cooperative housing available. $150 deposit. Leadership, wellness, management, and theme housing. **Activities:** Bands, campus ministries, choral groups, dance, drama, film society, international student organizations, literary magazine, musical theater, radio station, student government, student newspaper, social work club, Keuka Leaders club, Keuka Circle (community service), Newman Club, minority support group, political action coalition, Student Nurse Association.

**Athletics.** NCAA. **Intercollegiate:** Baseball M, basketball, cross-country, golf, lacrosse, soccer, softball W, synchronized swimming W, tennis, volleyball W. **Intramural:** Basketball, football (non-tackle), soccer, softball, volleyball. **Team name:** Storm.

**Student services.** Adult student services, alcohol/substance abuse counseling, campus ministries, career counseling, student employment services, financial aid counseling, health services, minority student services, personal counseling, placement for graduates, women's services. **Physically disabled:** Services for visually, speech, hearing impaired.

**Contact.** E-mail: admissions@mail.keuka.edu
Phone: (315) 279-5254 Toll-free number: (800) 335-3852
Fax: (315) 279-5386
Carolanne Marquis, Executive Vice President, Keuka College, 141 Cental Avenue, Keuka Park, NY 14478-0098

## King's College
### New York, New York
### www.tkc.edu
**CB code: 2871**

- Private 4-year liberal arts college affiliated with nondenominational tradition
- Residential campus in very large city
- 215 degree-seeking undergraduates: 62% women, 2% African American, 2% Asian American, 3% Hispanic American, 6% international
- 75% of applicants admitted
- SAT or ACT (ACT writing optional), application essay required

**General.** Regionally accredited. **Degrees:** 26 bachelor's awarded. **Location:** The King's College campus is located in the Empire State Building in the center of midtown Manhattan, New York City. **Calendar:** Semester, limited summer session. **Full-time faculty:** 12 total; 100% have terminal degrees, 8% women. **Part-time faculty:** 13 total; 85% have terminal degrees, 31% women. **Class size:** 43% < 20, 57% 20-39.

**Freshman class profile.** 166 applied, 125 admitted, 44 enrolled.

| Mid 50% test scores | | Rank in top quarter: | 73% |
|---|---|---|---|
| SAT critical reading: | 590-690 | Rank in top tenth: | 41% |
| SAT math: | 530-610 | End year in good standing: | 95% |
| SAT writing: | 580-670 | Return as sophomores: | 64% |
| ACT composite: | 25-29 | Out-of-state: | 91% |
| GPA 3.50 or higher: | 87% | Live on campus: | 96% |
| GPA 3.0-3.49: | 11% | International: | 2% |
| GPA 2.0-2.99: | 2% | | |

**Basis for selection.** Admissions decisions based on combination of academic preparedness and leadership giftedness, primarily assessed through transcript, SAT or ACT scores, and essay. Short answer personal statements required in online application. **Homeschooled:** Transcript of courses and grades required. **Learning Disabled:** Documentation requested of any learning disabilities that will require special accommodation.

**High school preparation.** 16 units required. Required units include English 4, mathematics 3, social studies 2, science 3 and foreign language 2.

**2008-2009 Annual costs.** Tuition/fees: $22,850. Room only: $8,750. Books/supplies: $800. Personal expenses: $1,000.

**2006-2007 Financial aid. Need-based:** 38 full-time freshmen applied for aid; 32 were judged to have need; 32 of these received aid. Average need met was 95%. Average scholarship/grant was $11,563; average loan $4,583. 79% of total undergraduate aid awarded as scholarships/grants, 21% as loans/jobs. **Non-need-based:** Awarded to 68 full-time undergraduates, including 25 freshmen. Scholarships awarded for academics. **Additional information:** School does not participate in Title IV federal financial aid; students must file PROFILE and/or TAP application for institutional aid consideration.

**Application procedures. Admission:** Priority date 11/15; deadline 2/1 (postmark date). $30 fee, may be waived for applicants with need. Application may be submitted online. Admission notification 3/8. Must reply by May 1 or within 4 week(s) if notified thereafter. **Financial aid:** Priority date 3/1; no closing date. CSS PROFILE required. Applicants notified on a rolling basis starting 4/1; must reply by 7/31.

**Academics. Special study options:** Independent study, internships, study abroad. **Credit/placement by examination:** AP, CLEP, IB, institutional tests. **Support services:** Reduced course load, study skills assistance, tutoring.

**Majors. Business:** Business admin. **Other:** Politics, Philosophy, and Economics.

**Most popular majors.** Business/marketing 29%, education 32%, interdisciplinary studies 39%.

**Computing on campus.** PC or laptop required. Dormitories wired for high-speed internet access and linked to campus network. Commuter students can connect to campus network. Online course registration, online library, repair service, wireless network available.

**Student life. Freshman orientation:** Mandatory. Preregistration for classes offered. Held 1 week prior to classes. **Policies:** No alcoholic beverages/drug usage permitted on campus or in housing. **Housing:** Guaranteed on-campus for freshmen. Single-sex dorms, apartments available. $400 fully refundable deposit, deadline 6/15. **Activities:** Campus ministries, dance, drama, film society, music ensembles, student government, student newspaper.

**Athletics. Team name:** Pride.

**Student services.** Campus ministries, career counseling, student employment services, financial aid counseling.

**Contact.** E-mail: info@tkc.edu
Phone: (212) 659-7200 ext. 3610 Toll-free
number: (888) 969-7200 ext. 3610 Fax: (212) 659-3611
Brian Parker, Vice President of Admissions, King's College, 350 Fifth Avenue, Lower Lobby, New York, NY 10118

---

## Laboratory Institute of Merchandising
**New York, New York**                    CB member
**www.limcollege.edu**                     CB code: 2380

- For-profit 4-year College of Fashion Business
- Commuter campus in very large city
- 1,107 degree-seeking undergraduates: 4% part-time, 95% women, 9% African American, 6% Asian American, 16% Hispanic American, 1% international
- 63% of applicants admitted

---

- SAT or ACT (ACT writing optional), application essay, interview required
- 49% graduate within 6 years

**General.** Founded in 1939. Regionally accredited. **Degrees:** 188 bachelor's, 35 associate awarded. **Location:** Located in midtown Manhattan. **Calendar:** Semester, limited summer session. **Full-time faculty:** 26 total; 27% minority, 50% women. **Part-time faculty:** 118 total; 20% minority, 54% women. **Class size:** 69% < 20, 31% 20-39.

**Freshman class profile.** 837 applied, 525 admitted, 286 enrolled.

| Mid 50% test scores | | Rank in top quarter: | 17% |
|---|---|---|---|
| SAT critical reading: | 430-500 | Rank in top tenth: | 5% |
| SAT math: | 420-500 | End year in good standing: | 68% |
| ACT composite: | 17-23 | Return as sophomores: | 68% |
| GPA 3.50 or higher: | 9% | Out-of-state: | 61% |
| GPA 3.0-3.49: | 29% | Live on campus: | 74% |
| GPA 2.0-2.99: | 58% | International: | 1% |

**Basis for selection.** Interview, high school transcript, SAT/ACT score, letters of recommendation and college transcripts important. **Homeschooled:** Transcript of courses and grades, state high school equivalency certificate, interview, letter of recommendation (nonparent) required.

**2008-2009 Annual costs.** Tuition/fees: $19,825. Room/board: $18,700. Books/supplies: $1,100. Personal expenses: $2,000.

**2006-2007 Financial aid.** All financial aid based on need. 200 full-time freshmen applied for aid; 156 were judged to have need; 156 of these received aid. Average scholarship/grant was $5,428; average loan $2,363. 53% of total undergraduate aid awarded as scholarships/grants, 47% as loans/jobs.

**Application procedures. Admission:** No deadline. $40 fee, may be waived for applicants with need. Application may be submitted online. Admission notification on a rolling basis. **Financial aid:** Priority date 4/1; no closing date. FAFSA, institutional form required. Applicants notified on a rolling basis starting 2/15; must reply within 2 week(s) of notification.

**Academics.** Associate degree program distributed among liberal arts, business, and professional courses, including 2 work projects of 3 credits and 5 weeks each. Bachelor's degree programs distributed among liberal arts, business, and professional courses with a semester-long, 13-credit cooperative work project. Freshmen and sophomores participate in 3-credit, 5-week work project. Seniors participate in 16-week full-semester co-op. Curriculum also includes weekly field trips into fashion industry and guest lecturer series featuring fashion professionals. **Special study options:** Combined bachelor's/graduate degree, cooperative education, internships, study abroad. 3-credit class held winter/summer in France, England, Germany, Spain, Italy, or China. **Credit/placement by examination:** AP, CLEP, institutional tests. **Support services:** Learning center, pre-admission summer program, reduced course load, remedial instruction, study skills assistance, tutoring, writing center.

**Majors. Business:** Business admin, fashion, management science, marketing. **Family/consumer sciences:** Apparel marketing. **Other:** Visual merchandising.

**Most popular majors.** Business/marketing 40%, family/consumer sciences 51%, visual/performing arts 9%.

**Computing on campus.** 270 workstations in library, computer center, student center. Dormitories wired for high-speed internet access. Commuter students can connect to campus network. Online library, helpline available.

**Student life. Freshman orientation:** Mandatory. **Housing:** Coed dorms available. $1,100 partly refundable deposit. Affiliated with local YW-YMHA and Educational Housing Inc. in which traditional residence life experience available. **Activities:** Student government.

**Student services.** Alcohol/substance abuse counseling, career counseling, student employment services, financial aid counseling, personal counseling, placement for graduates.

**Contact.** E-mail: admissions@limcollege.edu
Phone: (212) 752-1530 ext. 289 Toll-free number: (800) 677-1323
Fax: (212) 750-3432
Kristina Gibson, Director of Admissions, Laboratory Institute of Merchandising, 12 East 53rd Street, New York, NY 10022

---

## Le Moyne College
**Syracuse, New York**                     CB member
**www.lemoyne.edu**                        CB code: 2366

- Private 4-year liberal arts college affiliated with Roman Catholic Church
- Residential campus in small city

- 2,490 degree-seeking undergraduates: 8% part-time, 61% women, 4% African American, 2% Asian American, 4% Hispanic American, 1% international
- 524 degree-seeking graduate students
- 69% of applicants admitted
- SAT or ACT (ACT writing optional), application essay required
- 68% graduate within 6 years; 37% enter graduate study

**General.** Founded in 1946. Regionally accredited. **Degrees:** 582 bachelor's awarded; master's offered. **ROTC:** Army, Air Force. **Location:** 2 miles from downtown. **Calendar:** Semester, extensive summer session. **Full-time faculty:** 158 total; 92% have terminal degrees, 17% minority, 42% women. **Part-time faculty:** 169 total; 30% have terminal degrees, 6% minority, 48% women. **Class size:** 39% < 20, 59% 20-39, 1% 40-49, less than 1% 50-99. **Special facilities:** Performing arts center.

**Freshman class profile.** 3,968 applied, 2,738 admitted, 578 enrolled.

| Mid 50% test scores | | Rank in top quarter: | 50% |
|---|---|---|---|
| SAT critical reading: | 490-600 | Rank in top tenth: | 22% |
| SAT math: | 500-610 | End year in good standing: | 92% |
| ACT composite: | 21-26 | Return as sophomores: | 84% |
| GPA 3.50 or higher: | 36% | Out-of-state: | 7% |
| GPA 3.0-3.49: | 36% | Live on campus: | 91% |
| GPA 2.0-2.99: | 28% | International: | 1% |

**Basis for selection.** High school courses and performance most important; class rank, test scores, recommendations, essay, interview, extracurricular activities also important. Students from underrepresented populations encouraged. February 1 priority date by which SAT scores must be received for fall term admission. Interview recommended. **Homeschooled:** Statement describing homeschool structure and mission, transcript of courses and grades, interview, letter of recommendation (nonparent) required. **Learning Disabled:** Interview strongly recommended.

**High school preparation.** 17 units required. Required and recommended units include English 4, mathematics 3-4, social studies 4, science 3-4 (laboratory 3) and foreign language 3. 4 math required for science and math majors.

**2008-2009 Annual costs.** Tuition/fees: $25,000. Room/board: $9,490. Books/supplies: $700. Personal expenses: $1,410.

**2006-2007 Financial aid. Need-based:** 502 full-time freshmen applied for aid; 444 were judged to have need; 441 of these received aid. Average need met was 82%. Average scholarship/grant was $15,998; average loan $3,291. 64% of total undergraduate aid awarded as scholarships/grants, 36% as loans/jobs. **Non-need-based:** Awarded to 1,369 full-time undergraduates, including 375 freshmen. Scholarships awarded for academics, alumni affiliation, athletics, leadership, minority status, ROTC. **Additional information:** Parent loan program at low interest, monthly payment plans and alternative loans for students.

**Application procedures. Admission:** Priority date 2/1; no deadline. $35 fee, may be waived for applicants with need. Application may be submitted online. Admission notification on a rolling basis beginning on or about 1/1. Must reply by May 1 or within 4 week(s) if notified thereafter. **Financial aid:** Priority date 2/1; no closing date. FAFSA, institutional form required. Applicants notified by 3/15; must reply by 5/1 or within 2 week(s) of notification.

**Academics.** Academic accommodations and services for students with documented disabilities. **Special study options:** Accelerated study, combined bachelor's/graduate degree, double major, dual enrollment of high school students, honors, independent study, internships, liberal arts/career combination, semester at sea, study abroad, teacher certification program, Washington semester. Certificate of Advanced Studies in Educational Leadership and Certificate of Advanced Studies in Nursing. **Credit/placement by examination:** AP, CLEP, IB. **Support services:** Learning center, remedial instruction, study skills assistance, tutoring, writing center.

**Majors. Biology:** General, biochemistry, ecology. **Business:** Accounting, business admin, finance, human resources, labor relations, management information systems, marketing, operations. **Communications:** General. **Computer sciences:** General. **English:** English lit. **Foreign languages:** French, Spanish. **Health:** Nursing (RN), predental, premedicine, prepharmacy, preveterinary. **History:** General. **Interdisciplinary:** Biological/physical sciences, peace/conflict. **Legal studies:** Prelaw. **Math:** General. **Philosophy/religion:** Philosophy, religion. **Physical sciences:** Chemistry, physics. **Psychology:** General. **Social sciences:** Criminology, economics, political science, sociology. **Visual/performing arts:** Dramatic.

**Most popular majors.** Biology 11%, business/marketing 33%, English 7%, psychology 17%, social sciences 15%.

**Computing on campus.** 325 workstations in dormitories, library, computer center, student center. Dormitories wired for high-speed internet access and linked to campus network. Commuter students can connect to campus network. Online course registration, online library, helpline, repair service, student web hosting, wireless network available.

**Student life. Freshman orientation:** Mandatory, $150 fee. Preregistration for classes offered. 4 summer orientation sessions of 2 days each and one fall orientation. **Housing:** Guaranteed on-campus for all undergraduates. Coed dorms, single-sex dorms, special housing for disabled, apartments, substance-free housing available. Living/Learning communities available. **Activities:** Bands, campus ministries, choral groups, dance, drama, film society, international student organizations, literary magazine, music ensembles, Model UN, musical theater, radio station, student government, student newspaper, TV station, international club, Amnesty International, Habitat for Humanity, Democrats Club, Republican Club, Gaelic Society, El Progreso, Pride in Our Work Ethnicity and Race, Muslim student association.

**Athletics.** NCAA. **Intercollegiate:** Baseball M, basketball, cross-country, diving, golf M, lacrosse, soccer, softball W, swimming, tennis, volleyball W. **Intramural:** Basketball, cross-country, football (non-tackle) M, racquetball, soccer, softball, volleyball. **Team name:** Dolphins.

**Student services.** Adult student services, alcohol/substance abuse counseling, campus ministries, career counseling, student employment services, financial aid counseling, health services, minority student services, personal counseling, placement for graduates. **Physically disabled:** Services for visually, speech, hearing impaired.

**Contact.** E-mail: admission@lemoyne.edu
Phone: (315) 445-4300 Toll-free number: (800) 333-4733
Fax: (315) 445-4711
Dennis Nicholson, Director of Admission, Le Moyne College, 1419 Salt Springs Road, Syracuse, NY 13214-1301

---

## Long Island University: Brooklyn Campus

**Brooklyn, New York**  **CB member**
**www.liu.edu**  **CB code: 2369**

- Private 4-year university and branch campus college
- Commuter campus in very large city
- 5,047 degree-seeking undergraduates: 15% part-time, 72% women, 35% African American, 16% Asian American, 12% Hispanic American, 1% international
- 3,023 degree-seeking graduate students
- 94% of applicants admitted

**General.** Founded in 1926. Regionally accredited. **Degrees:** 693 bachelor's, 35 associate awarded; master's, doctoral, first professional offered. **ROTC:** Army. **Location:** Short train ride to New York City. **Calendar:** Semester, extensive summer session. **Full-time faculty:** 310 total; 32% minority, 50% women. **Part-time faculty:** 482 total; 41% minority, 53% women.

**Freshman class profile.** 3,567 applied, 3,362 admitted, 1,100 enrolled.

| Mid 50% test scores | | GPA 2.0-2.99: | 45% |
|---|---|---|---|
| SAT critical reading: | 390-500 | Out-of-state: | 22% |
| SAT math: | 400-560 | Live on campus: | 25% |
| GPA 3.50 or higher: | 21% | International: | 1% |
| GPA 3.0-3.49: | 19% | | |

**Basis for selection.** Rigor of secondary school record, class rank, academic GPA, recommendations, test scores, essay considered. ACT or SAT required for admission to computer science, molecular biology, nursing, pharmacy, pre-athletic training, pre-occupational therapy, and pre-physician assistant majors. Interview, audition, and/or personal statement may be required for particular programs.

**High school preparation.** 16 units recommended. Recommended units include English 4, mathematics 2, social studies 3 and academic electives 4. Academic electives include any electives from fields of foreign languages, social studies, mathematics or natural science. Other electives include 3 credits of any studies except physical education and military science that lead to graduation from accredited high school.

**2007-2008 Annual costs.** Tuition/fees: $25,922. Room/board: $9,410.

**Application procedures. Admission:** Priority date 6/1; no deadline. $30 fee, may be waived for applicants with need. Application may be submitted online. Admission notification on a rolling basis. Some programs have February 1 application deadline. **Financial aid:** Priority date 3/15; no closing date. FAFSA required. Applicants notified on a rolling basis.

**Academics. Special study options:** Combined bachelor's/graduate degree, cooperative education, double major, ESL, honors, independent study, internships, student-designed major, study abroad, teacher certification program, United Nations semester, weekend college. **Credit/placement by examination:** AP, CLEP, IB, institutional tests. **Support services:** Learning center, pre-admission summer program, reduced course load, remedial instruction, study skills assistance, tutoring, writing center.

**Majors. Biology:** General, biochemistry. **Business:** Accounting, business admin, finance, sales/distribution. **Communications:** General, journalism. **Computer sciences:** General. **Education:** Art, biology, chemistry, elementary, English, mathematics, music, physical, Spanish, speech impaired. **English:** English lit, speech/rhetoric. **Foreign languages:** General. **Health:** Audiology/speech pathology, clinical lab science, community health, cytotechnology, nursing (RN), physician assistant. **History:** General. **Liberal arts:** Arts/sciences, humanities. **Math:** General. **Parks/recreation:** Exercise sciences. **Philosophy/religion:** Philosophy. **Physical sciences:** Chemistry. **Psychology:** General. **Public administration:** Social work. **Social sciences:** General, economics, political science, sociology. **Visual/performing arts:** General, commercial/advertising art, dance, music performance, studio arts.

**Most popular majors.** Biology 6%, business/marketing 12%, communications/journalism 7%, health sciences 31%, psychology 10%, social sciences 11%.

**Computing on campus.** 600 workstations in dormitories, library, computer center. Dormitories wired for high-speed internet access and linked to campus network. Online library, wireless network available.

**Student life. Freshman orientation:** Available, $35 fee. **Housing:** Coed dorms available. $150 deposit. **Activities:** Jazz band, choral groups, dance, drama, literary magazine, music ensembles, musical theater, radio station, student government, student newspaper, TV station.

**Athletics.** NCAA. **Intercollegiate:** Baseball M, basketball, cross-country, golf, lacrosse W, soccer, softball W, tennis W, track and field, volleyball W. **Team name:** Blackbirds.

**Student services.** Campus ministries, career counseling, student employment services, financial aid counseling, health services, personal counseling, placement for graduates. **Physically disabled:** Services for visually, speech, hearing impaired.

**Contact.** E-mail: admissions@brooklyn.liu.edu
Phone: (718) 488-1011 Toll-free number: (800) 548-7526
Fax: (718) 797-2399
Richard Sunday, Dean of Admissions, Long Island University: Brooklyn Campus, 1 University Plaza, Brooklyn, NY 11201

## Long Island University: C. W. Post Campus
**Brookville, New York**  CB member
**www.liu.edu**  CB code: 2070

- Private 4-year university, branch campus and liberal arts college
- Commuter campus in small town
- 5,139 degree-seeking undergraduates: 11% part-time, 63% women, 9% African American, 5% Asian American, 8% Hispanic American, 2% international
- 2,796 degree-seeking graduate students
- 85% of applicants admitted
- SAT or ACT (ACT writing optional), application essay required

**General.** Founded in 1954. Regionally accredited. **Degrees:** 899 bachelor's awarded; master's, doctoral offered. **ROTC:** Army. **Location:** 25 miles from New York City. **Calendar:** Semester, extensive summer session. **Full-time faculty:** 329 total; 16% minority, 44% women. **Part-time faculty:** 613 total; 12% minority, 52% women. **Special facilities:** Tilles center for the performing arts.

**Freshman class profile.** 5,204 applied, 4,432 admitted, 1,107 enrolled.

| Mid 50% test scores | | | |
|---|---|---|---|
| SAT critical reading: | 440-540 | GPA 2.0-2.99: | 49% |
| SAT math: | 430-550 | Out-of-state: | 12% |
| GPA 3.50 or higher: | 23% | Live on campus: | 57% |
| GPA 3.0-3.49: | 24% | International: | 4% |

**Basis for selection.** Rigor of secondary school record, class rank, GPA, recommendations, test scores, essay considered. Audition required for dance, music, and theater programs; interview recommended for communication arts, dance, and theater/film programs; portfolio required for art programs.

**High school preparation.** 16 units recommended. Recommended units include English 4, mathematics 3, social studies 4, science 3 (laboratory 3) and foreign language 2.

**2007-2008 Annual costs.** Tuition/fees: $25,950. Room/board: $9,600.

**Application procedures. Admission:** Priority date 3/1; no deadline. $30 fee, may be waived for applicants with need. Application may be submitted online. Admission notification on a rolling basis. **Financial aid:** Priority date 3/1; no closing date. FAFSA, CSS PROFILE required. Applicants notified on a rolling basis starting 3/1; must reply by 5/1.

**Academics. Special study options:** Accelerated study, combined bachelor's/graduate degree, cooperative education, cross-registration, double major, dual enrollment of high school students, ESL, honors, independent study, internships, student-designed major, study abroad, teacher certification program, United Nations semester, Washington semester, weekend college. **Credit/placement by examination:** AP, CLEP, IB, institutional tests. **Support services:** Learning center, pre-admission summer program, reduced course load, remedial instruction, study skills assistance, tutoring, writing center.

**Majors. Biology:** General, biomedical sciences, cell/histology. **Business:** Accounting, business admin. **Communications:** Advertising, journalism. **Communications technology:** Radio/tv. **Computer sciences:** Information systems, information technology. **Education:** Art, biology, chemistry, elementary, English, foreign languages, French, health, kindergarten/preschool, mathematics, music, physical, social studies, Spanish. **English:** English lit. **Foreign languages:** General, French, Italian, Spanish. **Health:** Art therapy, audiology/speech pathology, facilities admin, marriage/family therapy, medical radiologic technology/radiation therapy, medical records admin, nursing (RN). **History:** General. **Liberal arts:** Arts/sciences. **Math:** General, applied. **Philosophy/religion:** Philosophy. **Physical sciences:** Chemistry, geology, physics. **Protective services:** Forensics, law enforcement admin. **Psychology:** General. **Public administration:** General, social work. **Social sciences:** Economics, geography, international relations, political science, sociology. **Visual/performing arts:** Art history/conservation, arts management, cinematography, commercial/advertising art, dance, digital art, dramatic, music performance, photography, studio arts. **Other:** Earth science education.

**Most popular majors.** Business/marketing 18%, education 22%, health sciences 9%, psychology 7%, security/protective services 11%, social sciences 8%, visual/performing arts 9%.

**Computing on campus.** Dormitories wired for high-speed internet access and linked to campus network. Commuter students can connect to campus network. Repair service, wireless network available.

**Student life. Freshman orientation:** Available, $100 fee. Preregistration for classes offered. 2-day sessions for freshmen held in July and August prior to start of fall classes. **Housing:** Guaranteed on-campus for freshmen. Coed dorms, single-sex dorms available. $300 deposit, deadline 5/1. 24-hour intensified study housing available. **Activities:** Bands, choral groups, dance, drama, film society, literary magazine, music ensembles, musical theater, radio station, student government, student newspaper, TV station.

**Athletics.** NCAA. **Intercollegiate:** Baseball M, basketball, cross-country, field hockey W, football (tackle) M, lacrosse, soccer, softball W, swimming W, tennis W, volleyball W. **Team name:** Pioneers.

**Student services.** Adult student services, alcohol/substance abuse counseling, campus ministries, career counseling, student employment services, financial aid counseling, health services, personal counseling, placement for graduates, veterans' counselor. **Physically disabled:** Services for visually, speech, hearing impaired. **Learning disabled:** Comprehensive services available.

**Contact.** E-mail: enroll@cwpost.liu.edu
Phone: (516) 299-2900 Toll-free number: (800) 548-7526
Fax: (516) 299-2137
Joanne Graziano, Admissions Director, Long Island University: C. W. Post Campus, 720 Northern Boulevard, Brookville, NY 11548-1300

## Machzikei Hadath Rabbinical College
**Brooklyn, New York**
 CB code: 0726

- Private 5-year seminary college for men affiliated with Jewish faith
- Commuter campus in very large city

**General.** Founded in 1956. Accredited by AARTS. **Calendar:** Semester.

**Annual costs/financial aid.** Tuition/fees (2007-2008): $7,000.

**Contact.** Phone: (718) 854-8777 ext. 23
Director of Admissions, 5407 16th Avenue, Brooklyn, NY 11204

## Manhattan College
### Riverdale, New York
### www.manhattan.edu

**CB member**
**CB code: 2395**

- Private 4-year engineering and liberal arts college affiliated with Roman Catholic Church
- Residential campus in very large city
- 2,986 degree-seeking undergraduates: 49% women
- 402 graduate students
- 55% of applicants admitted
- SAT or ACT with writing, interview required

**General.** Founded in 1853. Regionally accredited. Independent institution in the Roman Catholic tradition sponsored by De La Salle Christian Brothers. **Degrees:** 687 bachelor's awarded; master's offered. **ROTC:** Army, Air Force. **Location:** 10 miles from midtown Manhattan. **Calendar:** Semester, extensive summer session. **Full-time faculty:** 182 total; 93% have terminal degrees, 14% minority, 34% women. **Part-time faculty:** 141 total; 33% have terminal degrees, 21% minority, 38% women. **Class size:** 52% < 20, 48% 20-39, less than 1% 40-49. **Special facilities:** Plant morphogenesis laboratory.

**Freshman class profile.** 5,166 applied, 2,823 admitted, 712 enrolled.

| Mid 50% test scores | | | |
|---|---|---|---|
| | | Out-of-state: | 31% |
| SAT critical reading: | 510-600 | Live on campus: | 80% |
| SAT math: | 510-620 | Fraternities: | 2% |
| ACT composite: | 23-26 | Sororities: | 3% |

**Basis for selection.** School achievement record and test scores most important. Essay, recommendations, and extracurricular activities also reviewed. Interview recommended.

**High school preparation.** 16 units required. Required and recommended units include English 4, mathematics 3-4, social studies 3, science 3 and foreign language 2-3. 4 mathematics, 4 science (including precalculus, chemistry, and physics) recommended of engineering majors and most science majors.

**2008-2009 Annual costs.** Tuition/fees (projected): $23,240. Program fees range from $1,000 to $1,900 depending on program. Room/board: $9,300. Books/supplies: $750. Personal expenses: $1,000.

**2007-2008 Financial aid.** All financial aid based on need. 58% of total undergraduate aid awarded as scholarships/grants, 42% as loans/jobs.

**Application procedures. Admission:** Closing date 3/1. $50 fee, may be waived for applicants with need. Application may be submitted online. Admission notification on a rolling basis beginning on or about 12/15. Must reply by 5/1. **Financial aid:** Priority date 2/15, closing date 4/15. FAFSA required. Applicants notified on a rolling basis starting 1/1; must reply by 5/1.

**Academics. Special study options:** Accelerated study, combined bachelor's/graduate degree, cooperative education, cross-registration, distance learning, double major, ESL, exchange student, honors, independent study, internships, study abroad, teacher certification program, Washington semester. **Credit/placement by examination:** AP, CLEP, institutional tests. 30 credit hours maximum toward bachelor's degree. **Support services:** Learning center, reduced course load, remedial instruction, study skills assistance, tutoring, writing center.

**Majors. Biology:** General, biochemistry. **Business:** General, accounting, finance, international, management information systems, managerial economics, statistics. **Communications:** General, broadcast journalism, journalism. **Computer sciences:** General, computer science, information systems. **Education:** General, biology, chemistry, computer, early childhood, elementary, English, foreign languages, French, health, history, mathematics, middle, physical, physics, science, secondary, social science, social studies, Spanish, special. **Engineering:** Chemical, civil, electrical, environmental, mechanical. **English:** Composition. **Foreign languages:** French, Spanish. **Health:** Nuclear medical technology, predental, premedicine, preveterinary. **History:** General. **Interdisciplinary:** Peace/conflict. **Legal studies:** Prelaw. **Math:** General. **Philosophy/religion:** Philosophy, religion. **Physical sciences:** Chemistry, physics. **Psychology:** General. **Social sciences:** Economics, sociology.

**Most popular majors.** Biology 6%, business/marketing 24%, communications/journalism 8%, education 15%, engineering/engineering technologies 21%, social sciences 6%.

**Computing on campus.** 320 workstations in library, computer center, student center. Dormitories wired for high-speed internet access and linked to campus network. Commuter students can connect to campus network. Online course registration, online library, helpline, repair service available.

**Student life. Freshman orientation:** Mandatory. **Housing:** Guaranteed on-campus for all undergraduates. Coed dorms available. $700 deposit, deadline 5/1. **Activities:** Bands, campus ministries, choral groups, dance, drama, literary magazine, music ensembles, musical theater, radio station, student government, student newspaper, TV station, African American club, Caribbean society, Chinese student association, Circle-K, Gaelic society, Young Conservatives, Democrats, Republicans, multicultural student union.

**Athletics.** NCAA. **Intercollegiate:** Baseball M, basketball, cheerleading, cross-country, golf M, lacrosse, soccer, softball W, swimming W, tennis, track and field, volleyball W. **Intramural:** Baseball M, basketball, cross-country, soccer, softball, track and field, volleyball. **Team name:** Jaspers.

**Student services.** Alcohol/substance abuse counseling, campus ministries, career counseling, student employment services, financial aid counseling, health services, personal counseling, placement for graduates, veterans' counselor. **Physically disabled:** Services for visually, hearing impaired.

**Contact.** E-mail: admit@manhattan.edu
Phone: (718) 862-7200 Toll-free number: (800) 622-9235
Fax: (718) 862-8019
William Bissett, Vice President for Enrollment Management, Manhattan College, 4513 Manhattan College Parkway, Riverdale, NY 10471

## Manhattan School of Music
### New York, New York
### www.msmnyc.edu

**CB code: 2396**

- Private 4-year music college
- Residential campus in very large city
- 415 degree-seeking undergraduates: 1% part-time, 50% women, 4% African American, 9% Asian American, 4% Hispanic American, 23% international
- 438 degree-seeking graduate students
- 37% of applicants admitted
- Application essay required
- 61% graduate within 6 years

**General.** Founded in 1917. Regionally accredited. **Degrees:** 85 bachelor's awarded; master's, doctoral offered. **Calendar:** Semester. **Full-time faculty:** 75 total; 28% have terminal degrees, 9% minority, 37% women. **Part-time faculty:** 314 total; 25% minority, 46% women. **Class size:** 85% < 20, 12% 20-39, 1% 50-99, 2% >100. **Special facilities:** 1,000-seat concert hall, 3 recital halls, 2 electronic music studios, recording studio, performance library, 2 addition performance spaces.

**Freshman class profile.** 945 applied, 346 admitted, 121 enrolled.

| | | | |
|---|---|---|---|
| GPA 3.50 or higher: | 65% | Out-of-state: | 87% |
| GPA 3.0-3.49: | 25% | Live on campus: | 99% |
| GPA 2.0-2.99: | 10% | International: | 23% |
| Return as sophomores: | 92% | | |

**Basis for selection.** Audition, availability of space in specific performance area, and academic record most important. SAT or ACT recommended. Audition required. **Homeschooled:** Statement describing homeschool structure and mission, transcript of courses and grades, letter of recommendation (nonparent) required. GED accepted, but if no GED, SAT or ACT required.

**High school preparation.** Recommended units include English 4, mathematics 3, social studies 4, history 4, science 3 and foreign language 4. Extensive music training required.

**2008-2009 Annual costs.** Tuition/fees: $30,475. Health fee of $2,250 required unless already insured. Room/board: $13,700. Books/supplies: $1,000. Personal expenses: $1,500.

**2007-2008 Financial aid. Need-based:** 69 full-time freshmen applied for aid; 58 were judged to have need; 55 of these received aid. Average need met was 42%. Average scholarship/grant was $15,229; average loan $3,833. 68% of total undergraduate aid awarded as scholarships/grants, 32% as loans/jobs. **Non-need-based:** Awarded to 41 full-time undergraduates, including 15 freshmen. Scholarships awarded for academics, alumni affiliation, leadership, music/drama.

**Application procedures. Admission:** Closing date 12/1 (receipt date). $100 fee, may be waived for applicants with need. Application must be submitted online. Admission notification 4/1. Must reply by May 1 or within 2 week(s) if notified thereafter. **Financial aid:** Closing date 3/1. FAFSA, institutional form, CSS PROFILE required. Applicants notified by 4/1; must reply by 5/1 or within 2 week(s) of notification.

**Academics. Special study options:** Cross-registration, ESL, independent study, study abroad. **Credit/placement by examination:** CLEP, institutional tests. 60 credit hours maximum toward bachelor's degree. **Support services:** Reduced course load, remedial instruction, tutoring.

**Majors. Visual/performing arts:** Music performance, music theory/composition.

**Computing on campus.** 14 workstations in computer center. Dormitories wired for high-speed internet access.

**Student life. Freshman orientation:** Mandatory. Preregistration for classes offered. Held 1-2 weeks before classes start. **Policies:** Undergraduate students required to live in residence hall for first 2 years. First-year transfer students required to live in residence hall for 1 year. Alcohol only allowed for those over 21 and only in designated areas. **Housing:** Guaranteed on-campus for freshmen. Coed dorms available. $500 nonrefundable deposit, deadline 6/15. **Activities:** Bands, choral groups, music ensembles, musical theater, opera, student government, symphony orchestra, Pan-African student union, international student association, Korean student association, resident community council, student council, politics discussion group, gay, lesbian and transgender club, Parallel Motion (a cappella choir), American music production.

**Student services.** Career counseling, student employment services, financial aid counseling. **Physically disabled:** Services for visually impaired.

**Contact.** E-mail: admission@msmnyc.edu
Phone: (917) 493-4501 Fax: (212) 749-3025
Amy Anderson, Assistant Dean for Admission and Financial Aid, Manhattan School of Music, 120 Claremont Avenue, New York, NY 10027-4698

## Manhattanville College
**Purchase, New York**
www.manhattanville.edu

**CB member**
**CB code: 2397**

- Private 4-year liberal arts and teachers college
- Residential campus in small town
- 1,752 degree-seeking undergraduates: 3% part-time, 67% women
- 1,177 graduate students
- 50% of applicants admitted
- SAT or ACT, application essay required
- 60% graduate within 6 years; 30% enter graduate study

**General.** Founded in 1841. Regionally accredited. Strong relationship with United Nations. **Degrees:** 356 bachelor's awarded; master's offered. **Location:** 25 miles from New York City. **Calendar:** Semester, extensive summer session. **Full-time faculty:** 97 total; 98% have terminal degrees, 12% minority, 52% women. **Part-time faculty:** 166 total; 98% have terminal degrees, 12% minority, 51% women. **Class size:** 73% < 20, 25% 20-39, 2% 40-49. **Special facilities:** Photography laboratory, observatory, environmental biology laboratory, TV production studio.

**Freshman class profile.** 3,927 applied, 1,951 admitted, 535 enrolled.

| Mid 50% test scores | | Rank in top quarter: | 47% |
|---|---|---|---|
| SAT critical reading: | 500-620 | Rank in top tenth: | 22% |
| SAT math: | 500-610 | End year in good standing: | 75% |
| ACT composite: | 20-25 | Return as sophomores: | 75% |
| GPA 3.50 or higher: | 21% | Out-of-state: | 45% |
| GPA 3.0-3.49: | 36% | Live on campus: | 85% |
| GPA 2.0-2.99: | 43% | International: | 10% |

**Basis for selection.** School achievement record, recommendations, test scores or samples of academic work most important. Essay, school and community activities. Interview strongly recommended. Portfolio required for fine arts program; audition recommended for dance, music and theater programs.

**High school preparation.** 16 units required. Required units include English 4, mathematics 3, social studies 2, science 2 and academic electives 5.

**2008-2009 Annual costs.** Tuition/fees: $31,620. Room/board: $13,040. Books/supplies: $800. Personal expenses: $1,550.

**Financial aid. Non-need-based:** Scholarships awarded for academics, alumni affiliation, art, leadership, music/drama. **Additional information:** Upper level

---

students may earn additional money and academic credit through internship program.

**Application procedures. Admission:** Closing date 3/1 (postmark date). $60 fee, may be waived for applicants with need. Application may be submitted online. Admission notification on a rolling basis beginning on or about 1/2. Must reply by May 1 or within 2 week(s) if notified thereafter. **Financial aid:** Closing date 3/1. FAFSA required. Applicants notified on a rolling basis starting 2/1; must reply by 5/1 or within 2 week(s) of notification.

**Academics.** Students must complete portfolio before graduation, which is individualized academic plan and profile. **Special study options:** Accelerated study, combined bachelor's/graduate degree, cooperative education, cross-registration, distance learning, double major, dual enrollment of high school students, ESL, exchange student, external degree, honors, independent study, internships, liberal arts/career combination, New York semester, student-designed major, study abroad, teacher certification program, Washington semester, weekend college. Study abroad programs in Oxford, Paris, Tokyo, Osaka, Madrid, Seville, Florence, Rome, Berlin, Galway and the world capitals program in Jerusalem, Santiago, Brussels, Buenos Aires, Prague, Moscow, and South Africa. **Credit/placement by examination:** AP, CLEP, IB, institutional tests. Up to 60 transfer credits allowed: up to 30 AP credits, up to 18 IB credits, no CLEP limit. **Support services:** Learning center, reduced course load, remedial instruction, study skills assistance, tutoring, writing center.

**Majors. Area/ethnic studies:** American, Asian, French. **Biology:** General, biochemistry. **Business:** Business admin, finance. **Communications:** General. **Computer sciences:** General. **Education:** General. **English:** English lit. **Foreign languages:** Romance. **History:** General. **Interdisciplinary:** Neuroscience. **Liberal arts:** Arts/sciences. **Math:** General. **Philosophy/religion:** Philosophy, religion. **Physical sciences:** Chemistry, physics. **Psychology:** General. **Social sciences:** Economics, political science, sociology. **Visual/performing arts:** Art history/conservation, dance, dramatic.

**Most popular majors.** Business/marketing 25%, education 9%, English 6%, history 8%, psychology 13%, social sciences 15%, visual/performing arts 11%.

**Computing on campus.** 270 workstations in dormitories, library, computer center, student center. Dormitories wired for high-speed internet access and linked to campus network. Commuter students can connect to campus network. Online course registration, online library, helpline, repair service, student web hosting, wireless network available.

**Student life. Freshman orientation:** Mandatory. Preregistration for classes offered. **Housing:** Coed dorms, substance-free housing available. $350 deposit, deadline 5/1. **Activities:** Bands, campus ministries, choral groups, dance, drama, film society, international student organizations, literary magazine, music ensembles, Model UN, musical theater, opera, radio station, student government, student newspaper, symphony orchestra, TV station, language and culture clubs, Students Organized Against Racism, women's resource center, gay/straight coalition, political science association, multicultural advisory board, Black student union.

**Athletics.** NCAA. **Intercollegiate:** Baseball M, basketball, cheerleading M, field hockey W, golf M, ice hockey, lacrosse, soccer, softball W, tennis. **Intramural:** Basketball. **Team name:** Valiants.

**Student services.** Adult student services, alcohol/substance abuse counseling, campus ministries, career counseling, services for economically disadvantaged, student employment services, financial aid counseling, health services, minority student services, personal counseling, placement for graduates, women's services. **Physically disabled:** Services for visually, speech, hearing impaired. **Learning disabled:** Comprehensive services available.

**Contact.** E-mail: admissions@mville.edu
Phone: (914) 323-5464 Toll-free number: (800) 328-4553
Fax: (914) 694-1732
Erica Padilla, Director of Admissions, Manhattanville College, 2900 Purchase Street, Purchase, NY 10577

## Mannes College The New School for Music
**New York, New York**
www.mannes.edu

**CB code: 2398**

- Private 4-year music college
- Commuter campus in very large city
- 189 degree-seeking undergraduates: 13% part-time, 57% women, 3% African American, 8% Asian American, 5% Hispanic American, 33% international
- 182 degree-seeking graduate students

- 34% of applicants admitted
- 66% graduate within 6 years

**General.** Founded in 1916. Regionally accredited. Division of The New School. **Degrees:** 25 bachelor's awarded; master's offered. **Location:** Located in Manhattan. **Calendar:** Semester, limited summer session. **Full-time faculty:** 5 total; 20% have terminal degrees, 20% women. **Part-time faculty:** 151 total; 11% minority, 40% women. **Class size:** 97% < 20, 2% 20-39, less than 1% 40-49, less than 1% 50-99, less than 1% >100. **Special facilities:** 2 concert halls.

**Freshman class profile.** 473 applied, 163 admitted, 59 enrolled.

| | | | |
|---|---|---|---|
| GPA 3.50 or higher: | 30% | Return as sophomores: | 91% |
| GPA 3.0-3.49: | 33% | Out-of-state: | 61% |
| GPA 2.0-2.99: | 33% | Live on campus: | 45% |
| End year in good standing: | 100% | International: | 44% |

**Basis for selection.** In order of importance: specific talent for major as evidenced by audition in major instrument or evaluation of previous accomplishment for composers and theory majors, general musicianship skills (ear, theory, etc.), academic record. Institutionally designed entrance examination, including major audition. Written examinations in music theory, dictation, ear training, and English usage. Audition required, essay recommended. Placement exams and interviews required for all Bachelor of Music, Bachelor of Science, Undergraduate Diploma, and Master of Music applicants. If applicant does not complete all sessions, application incomplete and will not be considered for acceptance. Tapes may be submitted for advisory opinion.

**High school preparation.** Required and recommended units include English 4, mathematics 4, social studies 2, science 4 (laboratory 2) and foreign language 2.

**2007-2008 Annual costs.** Tuition/fees: $30,410. Room/board: $11,750. Books/supplies: $2,050. Personal expenses: $1,550.

**2007-2008 Financial aid. Need-based:** 20 full-time freshmen applied for aid; 9 were judged to have need; 9 of these received aid. Average need met was 46%. Average scholarship/grant was $4,757; average loan $3,183. 14% of total undergraduate aid awarded as scholarships/grants, 86% as loans/jobs. **Non-need-based:** Awarded to 90 full-time undergraduates, including 13 freshmen. Scholarships awarded for academics, music/drama. **Additional information:** Closing date for scholarship applications 2 weeks prior to audition date.

**Application procedures. Admission:** Closing date 12/1 (postmark date). $100 fee. Application may be submitted online. Admission notification on a rolling basis beginning on or about 4/1. Must reply by May 1 or within 4 week(s) if notified thereafter. **Financial aid:** Priority date 3/1; no closing date. FAFSA required. Applicants notified on a rolling basis starting 3/1; must reply within 4 week(s) of notification.

**Academics. Special study options:** Cross-registration, double major, ESL, exchange student, independent study, internships. **Credit/placement by examination:** CLEP, institutional tests. **Support services:** Remedial instruction, tutoring, writing center.

**Majors. Visual/performing arts:** Conducting, music performance, music theory/composition, piano/organ, stringed instruments, studio arts, voice/opera.

**Computing on campus.** 15 workstations in library, computer center. Dormitories wired for high-speed internet access and linked to campus network. Commuter students can connect to campus network. Online course registration, helpline, student web hosting, wireless network available.

**Student life. Freshman orientation:** Available. **Housing:** Coed dorms, special housing for disabled available. $250 nonrefundable deposit, deadline 7/1. **Activities:** Jazz band, choral groups, dance, film society, international student organizations, literary magazine, music ensembles, opera, student government, student newspaper, symphony orchestra.

**Student services.** Career counseling, student employment services, financial aid counseling, health services, personal counseling. **Learning disabled:** Comprehensive services available.

**Contact.** E-mail: mannesadmissions@newschool.edu
Phone: (212) 580-0210 ext. 4862 Toll-free number: (800) 292-3040
Georgia Schmitt, Director of Admissions, Mannes College The New School for Music, 150 West 85th Street, New York, NY 10024

---

## Marist College

**Poughkeepsie, New York**

www.marist.edu

**CB member**

**CB code: 2400**

- Private 4-year liberal arts college
- Residential campus in small city

---

- 4,769 degree-seeking undergraduates: 6% part-time, 57% women, 3% African American, 2% Asian American, 5% Hispanic American
- 874 degree-seeking graduate students
- 42% of applicants admitted
- SAT or ACT with writing, application essay required
- 79% graduate within 6 years; 23% enter graduate study

**General.** Founded in 1929. Regionally accredited. Substantial internship opportunities for all majors. Students participate in community service program. **Degrees:** 1,152 bachelor's awarded; master's offered. **ROTC:** Army. **Location:** 75 miles from New York City, 75 miles from Albany. **Calendar:** Semester, limited summer session. **Full-time faculty:** 218 total; 78% have terminal degrees, 10% minority, 44% women. **Part-time faculty:** 375 total; 10% minority, 45% women. **Class size:** 55% < 20, 44% 20-39, less than 1% 40-49, less than 1% 50-99. **Special facilities:** Bureau of economic research, laboratory for environmental studies, management studies center, institute for public opinion, on-campus arboretum, online journalism laboratory.

**Freshman class profile.** 8,328 applied, 3,488 admitted, 1,019 enrolled.

| Mid 50% test scores | | | |
|---|---|---|---|
| SAT critical reading: | 520-620 | GPA 2.0-2.99: | 24% |
| SAT math: | 540-630 | Rank in top quarter: | 66% |
| SAT writing: | 530-630 | Rank in top tenth: | 29% |
| ACT composite: | 22-27 | Return as sophomores: | 91% |
| GPA 3.50 or higher: | 46% | Out-of-state: | 47% |
| GPA 3.0-3.49: | 30% | Live on campus: | 92% |

**Basis for selection.** Secondary school achievement record, rank in top third of class primary consideration. Test scores, recommendations, activities, personal and leadership qualities also important. Campus visits and information sessions with admission counselors strongly recommended. **Homeschooled:** Transcript of courses and grades, letter of recommendation (nonparent) required.

**High school preparation.** 17 units required. Required and recommended units include English 4, mathematics 3-4, social studies 2, history 1, science 3-4 (laboratory 2-3), foreign language 2-3 and academic electives 2. 1 U.S. history required. 4 math recommended for computer science and physical science majors, 2 social studies required, 2 social science recommended.

**2007-2008 Annual costs.** Tuition/fees: $24,040. Room/board: $10,250. Books/supplies: $1,230.

**2007-2008 Financial aid. Need-based:** 848 full-time freshmen applied for aid; 606 were judged to have need; 604 of these received aid. Average need met was 71%. Average scholarship/grant was $11,723; average loan $3,818. 65% of total undergraduate aid awarded as scholarships/grants, 35% as loans/jobs. **Non-need-based:** Awarded to 2,728 full-time undergraduates, including 836 freshmen. Scholarships awarded for academics, athletics, music/drama, ROTC, state residency.

**Application procedures. Admission:** Closing date 2/15 (postmark date). $50 fee, may be waived for applicants with need. Application may be submitted online. Admission notification 3/15. Must reply by 5/1. **Financial aid:** Priority date 2/15, closing date 5/1. FAFSA, institutional form required. Applicants notified on a rolling basis starting 3/15; must reply by 5/1 or within 2 week(s) of notification.

**Academics.** Paralegal certificates offered. **Special study options:** Accelerated study, combined bachelor's/graduate degree, cooperative education, cross-registration, distance learning, double major, dual enrollment of high school students, ESL, honors, independent study, internships, liberal arts/career combination, semester at sea, study abroad, teacher certification program, United Nations semester, Washington semester, weekend college. Undergraduates may take graduate classes. Cooperative education in arts, business, computer science, education, humanities, natural science, social/behavioral science, technologies. **Credit/placement by examination:** AP, CLEP, IB, SAT, ACT, institutional tests. ACT-PEP accepted on individual basis. **Support services:** Learning center, reduced course load, study skills assistance, tutoring, writing center.

**Majors. Area/ethnic studies:** American. **Biology:** General, biochemistry, biomedical sciences. **Business:** Accounting, business admin, fashion. **Communications:** Advertising, digital media, journalism, organizational, public relations, radio/tv. **Computer sciences:** Computer science, information systems, information technology, programming. **Conservation:** Environmental science. **Education:** Biology, chemistry, English, French, mathematics, social studies, Spanish, special. **English:** English lit. **Foreign languages:** French, Spanish. **Health:** Athletic training, clinical lab science. **History:** General. **Math:** General, applied, computational. **Philosophy/religion:** Philosophy.

**Physical sciences:** Chemistry. **Protective services:** Law enforcement admin. **Psychology:** General. **Public administration:** Social work. **Social sciences:** Economics, political science. **Visual/performing arts:** Art, art history/conservation, fashion design, studio arts.

**Most popular majors.** Business/marketing 26%, communications/journalism 22%, education 11%, liberal arts 6%, psychology 7%, security/protective services 6%.

**Computing on campus.** 646 workstations in dormitories, library, computer center, student center. Dormitories wired for high-speed internet access and linked to campus network. Commuter students can connect to campus network. Online course registration, online library, helpline, repair service, student web hosting, wireless network available.

**Student life. Freshman orientation:** Mandatory, $90 fee. 1-day orientation in June. **Housing:** Guaranteed on-campus for freshmen. Coed dorms, special housing for disabled, apartments, substance-free housing available. Garden apartments, townhouses, suites available. **Activities:** Bands, campus ministries, choral groups, dance, drama, film society, literary magazine, music ensembles, musical theater, radio station, student government, student newspaper, TV station, black student union, Asian Alliance, Circle K, ARCO, community service programs, Habitat for Humanity, political science club, council on theatre arts, social action clubs.

**Athletics.** NCAA. **Intercollegiate:** Baseball M, basketball, cross-country, diving, football (tackle) M, lacrosse, rowing (crew), soccer, softball W, swimming, tennis, track and field, volleyball W, water polo W. **Intramural:** Basketball, soccer, softball, volleyball. **Team name:** Red Foxes.

**Student services.** Adult student services, alcohol/substance abuse counseling, campus ministries, career counseling, student employment services, financial aid counseling, health services, personal counseling, placement for graduates, veterans' counselor. **Physically disabled:** Services for visually, hearing impaired. **Learning disabled:** Comprehensive services available.

**Contact.** E-mail: admission@marist.edu
Phone: (845) 575-3226 Toll-free number: (800) 436-5483
Fax: (845) 575-3215
Kent Rinehart, Dean of Undergraduate Admission, Marist College, 3399 North Road, Poughkeepsie, NY 12601-1387

## Marymount Manhattan College
**New York, New York**
**www.mmm.edu**
**CB member**
**CB code: 2405**

- Private 4-year liberal arts college
- Residential campus in very large city
- 1,813 degree-seeking undergraduates: 14% part-time, 76% women, 11% African American, 3% Asian American, 11% Hispanic American, 3% international
- 74% of applicants admitted
- SAT or ACT (ACT writing optional), application essay required
- 46% graduate within 6 years

**General.** Founded in 1936. Regionally accredited. **Degrees:** 347 bachelor's, 8 associate awarded. **Calendar:** Semester, limited summer session. **Full-time faculty:** 92 total; 86% have terminal degrees, 12% minority, 58% women. **Part-time faculty:** 193 total; 40% have terminal degrees, 17% minority, 58% women. **Class size:** 66% < 20, 33% 20-39, less than 1% 40-49. **Special facilities:** Communications and learning center, communication arts multimedia suite, center for science education.

**Freshman class profile.** 2,565 applied, 1,896 admitted, 490 enrolled.

| Mid 50% test scores | | | |
|---|---|---|---|
| SAT critical reading: | 490-600 | GPA 2.0-2.99: | 37% |
| SAT math: | 470-570 | Return as sophomores: | 58% |
| ACT composite: | 21-25 | Out-of-state: | 64% |
| GPA 3.50 or higher: | 20% | Live on campus: | 83% |
| GPA 3.0-3.49: | 43% | International: | 2% |

**Basis for selection.** High school GPA of 3.0 and SAT verbal and math scores of 450 each recommended. Letters of recommendation from teachers and administrators, extracurricular and community activities important. Rolling deadline for SAT/ACT score receipt. Interview recommended for all; audition required for acting, dance, and theater programs; portfolio recommended for art program. **Homeschooled:** Transcript of courses and grades required. Must submit official high school transcripts if high school attended before withdrawing. **Learning Disabled:** Interview and Wechsler Delta Adult Intelligence Scale test required.

**High school preparation.** 17 units required. Required and recommended units include English 4, mathematics 3, social studies 3, science 3 (laboratory 2), foreign language 2 and academic electives 4.

**2007-2008 Annual costs.** Tuition/fees: $20,570. Room/board: $12,250. Books/supplies: $1,000. Personal expenses: $1,500.

**2007-2008 Financial aid. Need-based:** 364 full-time freshmen applied for aid; 296 were judged to have need; 295 of these received aid. Average need met was 52%. Average scholarship/grant was $9,382; average loan $2,996. 66% of total undergraduate aid awarded as scholarships/grants, 34% as loans/jobs. **Non-need-based:** Awarded to 352 full-time undergraduates, including 94 freshmen. Scholarships awarded for academics, art, leadership, music/drama. **Additional information:** Limited international scholarships for top applicants.

**Application procedures. Admission:** Priority date 3/15; no deadline. $60 fee, may be waived for applicants with need. Application may be submitted online. Admission notification on a rolling basis beginning on or about 9/1. Must reply by May 1 or within 3 week(s) if notified thereafter. **Financial aid:** Priority date 3/15; no closing date. FAFSA required. Applicants notified on a rolling basis starting 3/15; must reply by 5/1 or within 3 week(s) of notification.

**Academics. Special study options:** Accelerated study, distance learning, double major, dual enrollment of high school students, exchange student, independent study, internships, liberal arts/career combination, study abroad, teacher certification program. 5-year bachelor's/master's program in computer science with Polytechnic University, programs with Laboratory Institute of Merchandising, New York School of Interior Design, Deutsches Haus at New York University, China Institute, New York Institute of Finance, American Institute of Banking, Hunter College of CUNY, Martha Graham School of Dance, HEOP. **Credit/placement by examination:** AP, CLEP, IB, SAT, ACT, institutional tests. 30 credit hours maximum toward bachelor's degree. Maximum of 12 credits for language proficiency. SAT Subject used for placement if submitted. **Support services:** Learning center, reduced course load, remedial instruction, study skills assistance, tutoring, writing center.

**Majors. Biology:** General. **Business:** Accounting, business admin. **Communications:** General. **English:** English lit. **Health:** Audiology/speech pathology. **History:** General. **Liberal arts:** Humanities. **Psychology:** General. **Social sciences:** International relations, political science, sociology. **Visual/performing arts:** Acting, art, art history/conservation, dance, dramatic, graphic design, studio arts. **Other:** Philosophy and Religious Studies.

**Most popular majors.** Business/marketing 8%, communications/journalism 26%, psychology 9%, social sciences 9%, visual/performing arts 37%.

**Computing on campus.** 215 workstations in library, computer center, student center. Dormitories wired for high-speed internet access and linked to campus network. Commuter students can connect to campus network. Wireless network available.

**Student life. Freshman orientation:** Mandatory. Preregistration for classes offered. 3 days of introductions, information, activities, and social engagements. **Housing:** Coed dorms available. $500 deposit, deadline 5/1. **Activities:** Choral groups, dance, drama, international student organizations, literary magazine, musical theater, radio station, student government, student newspaper, ethnic, religious, political, women's, environmental, and cultural groups, student professional organizations, and honor societies.

**Student services.** Adult student services, alcohol/substance abuse counseling, campus ministries, career counseling, student employment services, financial aid counseling, health services, personal counseling, placement for graduates. **Physically disabled:** Services for speech, hearing impaired. **Learning disabled:** Comprehensive services available.

**Contact.** E-mail: admissions@mmm.edu
Phone: (212) 517-0430 Toll-free number: (800) 627-9668
Fax: (212) 517-0448
Jim Rogers, Dean of Admissions, Marymount Manhattan College, 221 East 71st Street, New York, NY 10021-4597

## Medaille College
**Buffalo, New York**
**www.medaille.edu**
**CB code: 2422**

- Private 4-year liberal arts college
- Commuter campus in large city
- 1,640 degree-seeking undergraduates: 3% part-time, 64% women, 13% African American, 2% Hispanic American, 1% Native American
- 1,264 degree-seeking graduate students

- 79% of applicants admitted
- SAT or ACT with writing, application essay, interview required
- 34% graduate within 6 years; 27% enter graduate study

**General.** Founded in 1875. Regionally accredited. **Degrees:** 334 bachelor's, 90 associate awarded; master's offered. **ROTC:** Army. **Location:** 3 miles from downtown. **Calendar:** Semester, limited summer session. **Full-time faculty:** 97 total; 59% have terminal degrees, 13% minority, 40% women. **Part-time faculty:** 292 total; 9% have terminal degrees, 5% minority, 54% women. **Class size:** 70% < 20, 30% 20-39, less than 1% 40-49, less than 1% 50-99, less than 1% >100. **Special facilities:** New media institute.

**Freshman class profile.** 1,079 applied, 857 admitted, 420 enrolled.

| Mid 50% test scores | | GPA 2.0-2.99: | 47% |
|---|---|---|---|
| SAT critical reading: | 430-540 | End year in good standing: | 84% |
| SAT math: | 420-520 | Return as sophomores: | 64% |
| ACT composite: | 18-23 | Out-of-state: | 2% |
| GPA 3.50 or higher: | 20% | Live on campus: | 28% |
| GPA 3.0-3.49: | 27% | | |

**Basis for selection.** Motivation and maturity, as well as academic record and test scores, considered. SAT recommended.

**High school preparation.** 12 units required; 20 recommended. Required and recommended units include English 4, mathematics 2-3, social studies 4, history 2, science 2-3 (laboratory 2) and foreign language 2. 3 math, 3 science recommended for veterinary technology.

**2008-2009 Annual costs.** Tuition/fees: $18,230. Continuing students tuition is $17,420. Room/board: $8,846. Books/supplies: $1,100. Personal expenses: $1,100.

**2006-2007 Financial aid.** **Need-based:** 310 full-time freshmen applied for aid; 287 were judged to have need; 282 of these received aid. Average need met was 70%. Average scholarship/grant was $6,982; average loan $2,522. 36% of total undergraduate aid awarded as scholarships/grants, 64% as loans/jobs. **Non-need-based:** Awarded to 1,352 full-time undergraduates, including 535 freshmen. Scholarships awarded for academics, leadership.

**Application procedures.** **Admission:** Priority date 8/1; no deadline. $25 fee, may be waived for applicants with need. Application may be submitted online. Admission notification on a rolling basis beginning on or about 10/1. Must reply by May 1 or within 4 week(s) if notified thereafter. **Financial aid:** Priority date 3/1; no closing date. FAFSA required. Applicants notified on a rolling basis starting 3/1; must reply within 2 week(s) of notification.

**Academics.** All pre-professional programs require participation in at least 1 internship. Branch campuses in Amherst and Rochester. **Special study options:** Accelerated study, combined bachelor's/graduate degree, cross-registration, double major, honors, independent study, internships, liberal arts/career combination, student-designed major, teacher certification program, weekend college. Module system for full-time evening students and for full-time weekend students. **Credit/placement by examination:** AP, CLEP, IB, SAT. 30 credit hours maximum toward associate degree, 60 toward bachelor's. **Support services:** Learning center, reduced course load, remedial instruction, study skills assistance, tutoring.

**Majors. Biology:** General. **Business:** General, business admin. **Communications:** Media studies. **Computer sciences:** General. **Education:** General, biology, early childhood, elementary, English, middle, secondary, social studies. **English:** English lit. **Family/consumer sciences:** Child care. **Health:** Veterinary technology/assistant. **Interdisciplinary:** Biopsychology. **Liberal arts:** Arts/sciences. **Parks/recreation:** Sports admin. **Protective services:** Police science. **Psychology:** General. **Visual/performing arts:** General.

**Most popular majors.** Business/marketing 48%, education 12%.

**Computing on campus.** 120 workstations in dormitories, library, computer center, student center. Dormitories wired for high-speed internet access and linked to campus network. Wireless network available.

**Student life. Freshman orientation:** Mandatory. Preregistration for classes offered. **Housing:** Coed dorms, single-sex dorms, apartments, substance-free housing available. $100 deposit, deadline 9/1. **Activities:** Drama, film society, literary magazine, musical theater, radio station, student government, student newspaper, TV station, African American student union, child and youth services club, student volunteer center, multicultural association, SADD, international student society, resident student council.

**Athletics.** NCAA. **Intercollegiate:** Baseball M, basketball, bowling W, cross-country, golf, lacrosse, soccer, softball W, volleyball. **Team name:** Mavericks.

**Student services.** Adult student services, career counseling, student employment services, financial aid counseling, health services, personal counseling, placement for graduates, veterans' counselor. **Physically disabled:** Services for visually, speech, hearing impaired.

**Contact.** E-mail: admissionsug@medaille.edu
Phone: (716) 880-2200 Toll-free number: (800) 292-1582
Fax: (716) 880-2007
Greg Florczak, Director of Undergraduate Admissions, Medaille College, 18 Agassiz Circle, Buffalo, NY 14214

## Medaille College: Amherst
### Williamsville, New York

- Private 4-year liberal arts college
- Small town

**General. Calendar:** Semester.

**Annual costs/financial aid.** Tuition/fees (2007-2008): $16,590.

**Contact.** Phone: (716) 631-1061
400 Essjay Road, Suite 100, Williamsville, NY 14221

## Medaille College: Rochester
### Rochester, New York

- Private 4-year liberal arts college
- Small city

**General. Calendar:** Semester.

**Annual costs/financial aid.** Tuition/fees (2007-2008): $16,590.

**Contact.** Phone: (585) 272-0030
100 Corporate Woods, Suite 200, Rochester, NY 14623

## Mercy College
### Dobbs Ferry, New York
www.mercy.edu                                    CB code: 2409

- Private 4-year liberal arts college
- Commuter campus in large town
- 4,905 degree-seeking undergraduates: 31% part-time, 70% women, 25% African American, 3% Asian American, 27% Hispanic American, 1% international
- 3,366 degree-seeking graduate students
- 39% of applicants admitted
- Interview required

**General.** Founded in 1950. Regionally accredited. Campuses in Dobbs Ferry, White Plains, Yorktown Heights, Bronx, Manhattan. Mercy also has extensive online offerings. **Degrees:** 1,125 bachelor's, 134 associate awarded; master's, doctoral offered. **Location:** 20 miles from midtown Manhattan. **Calendar:** Semester, extensive summer session. **Full-time faculty:** 180 total; 78% have terminal degrees, 19% minority, 54% women. **Part-time faculty:** 600 total; 47% women.

**Freshman class profile.** 2,313 applied, 892 admitted, 608 enrolled.

| GPA 3.50 or higher: | 11% | Return as sophomores: | 62% |
|---|---|---|---|
| GPA 3.0-3.49: | 18% | Out-of-state: | 9% |
| GPA 2.0-2.99: | 44% | Live on campus: | 4% |

**Basis for selection.** Recommendations, essay, interview (if required), and activities most important. Most applicants must take placement examination to determine writing and mathematics skills; requirement may be waived under certain academic circumstances. Additional interview with program director required for nursing, occupational therapy, physical therapy, social work, veterinary technology, computer arts programs. **Home-schooled:** State high school equivalency certificate required.

**High school preparation.** 21 units required. Required units include English 4, mathematics 3, social studies 2, history 2, science 3 (laboratory 1), foreign language 3 and academic electives 3.

**2007-2008 Annual costs.** Tuition/fees: $14,170. Room/board: $9,444.

**2006-2007 Financial aid. Need-based:** 54% of total undergraduate aid awarded as scholarships/grants, 46% as loans/jobs. **Non-need-based:** Scholarships awarded for athletics.

**Application procedures. Admission:** No deadline. $37 fee, may be waived for applicants with need. Application may be submitted online. Admission notification on a rolling basis. **Financial aid:** Priority date 2/15; no closing date. FAFSA required. Applicants notified on a rolling basis starting 3/1; must reply within 4 week(s) of notification.

**Academics.** Some programs are on trimester and quarter schedule. Programs leading to provisional state certification offered in education. **Special study options:** Accelerated study, combined bachelor's/graduate degree, co-operative education, cross-registration, distance learning, double major, ESL, honors, independent study, internships, student-designed major, teacher certification program, weekend college. Program for college students with learning disabilities. **Credit/placement by examination:** AP, CLEP, institutional tests. 30 credit hours maximum toward associate degree, 30 toward bachelor's. **Support services:** Learning center, pre-admission summer program, reduced course load, remedial instruction, study skills assistance, tutoring, writing center.

**Majors. Agriculture:** Animal sciences. **Biology:** General. **Business:** Accounting, accounting/business management, business admin. **Computer sciences:** General, information systems. **Education:** Early childhood, elementary, English, ESL, mathematics, middle, social studies, Spanish, special. **English:** English lit. **Foreign languages:** Spanish. **Health:** Audiology/speech pathology, clinical lab science. **History:** General. **Liberal arts:** Arts/sciences. **Math:** General. **Protective services:** Law enforcement admin. **Psychology:** General. **Public administration:** Social work. **Social sciences:** General, political science, sociology. **Visual/performing arts:** Commercial/advertising art, music performance.

**Most popular majors.** Business/marketing 23%, health sciences 14%, psychology 13%, social sciences 27%.

**Computing on campus.** 588 workstations in dormitories, library, computer center, student center. Dormitories wired for high-speed internet access and linked to campus network. Commuter students can connect to campus network. Online course registration, online library, helpline, repair service, wireless network available.

**Student life. Freshman orientation:** Available. Preregistration for classes offered. **Policies:** Student services geared to commuter population with midday activities and programs. **Housing:** Coed dorms, substance-free housing available. $300 deposit, deadline 7/1. **Activities:** Campus ministries, dance, Model UN, student government, student newspaper, Reporter's Impact, green club, Dance Off Society Showstoppers, chess club, Latin American student association (LASA), student council, veterinary technology club, Italian club, accounting society.

**Athletics.** NCAA. **Intercollegiate:** Baseball M, basketball, cross-country, golf M, soccer, softball W, tennis M, track and field, volleyball W. **Intramural:** Badminton, baseball M, basketball, bowling. **Team name:** Mavericks.

**Student services.** Adult student services, alcohol/substance abuse counseling, career counseling, services for economically disadvantaged, student employment services, financial aid counseling, health services, minority student services, personal counseling, placement for graduates. **Physically disabled:** Services for visually, speech, hearing impaired.

**Contact.** E-mail: admissions@mercy.edu
Phone: (914) 674-7324 Toll-free number: (877) 637-2946
Fax: (914) 674-7382
Jeff Cutting, Executive Director of Admissions and Marketing, Mercy College, 555 Broadway, Dobbs Ferry, NY 10522

## Mesivta Torah Vodaath Seminary
**Brooklyn, New York**

**CB code: 0636**

- Private 5-year rabbinical college for men affiliated with Jewish faith
- Very large city

**General.** Founded in 1918. Accredited by AARTS. **Calendar:** Semester.

**Annual costs/financial aid.** Tuition/fees (2007-2008): $7,050. Room/board: $4,500.

**Contact.** Phone: (718) 941-8000
Director of Admissions, 425 East Ninth Street, Brooklyn, NY 11218

## Metropolitan College of New York
**New York, New York**
www.metropolitan.edu

**CB member**
**CB code: 4802**

- Private 4-year business and liberal arts college
- Commuter campus in very large city

- 651 degree-seeking undergraduates
- 336 graduate students
- 37% of applicants admitted
- Application essay, interview required

**General.** Founded in 1964. Regionally accredited. Students attend 3-semester full year with 1-month break. Off-site extensions for human services program in the Bronx, Staten Island and northeastern Queens. Students receive credit for applying studies to jobs or internship sites. **Degrees:** 227 bachelor's, 86 associate awarded; master's offered. **Location:** In downtown Manhattan. **Calendar:** Semester, extensive summer session. **Full-time faculty:** 32 total; 91% have terminal degrees, 41% minority, 31% women. **Part-time faculty:** 156 total; 33% minority, 49% women. **Class size:** 73% < 20, 27% 20-39.

**Freshman class profile.** 282 applied, 104 admitted, 92 enrolled.

**Basis for selection.** Academic record, test scores, previous volunteer experience, school and community activities, professional recommendations, motivation and communication skills as demonstrated in interviews considered. SAT or ACT recommended. Combined SAT score of 1050 (exclusive of Writing) or higher can be substituted for institution-administered Test of Adult Basic Education or ACCUPLACER required for admission.

**High school preparation.** 16 units required. Required units include English 4, mathematics 2, social studies 2, science 1 and foreign language 4.

**2007-2008 Annual costs.** Tuition/fees: $16,720. Tuition reported is undergraduate business program; other programs may vary in cost. Books/supplies: $1,500. Personal expenses: $726.

**2006-2007 Financial aid. Need-based:** 23% of total undergraduate aid awarded as scholarships/grants, 77% as loans/jobs. **Non-need-based:** Scholarships awarded for academics. **Additional information:** Limited merit scholarships.

**Application procedures. Admission:** Priority date 8/15; no deadline. $30 fee, may be waived for applicants with need. Application may be submitted online. Admission notification on a rolling basis beginning on or about 3/15. **Financial aid:** Priority date 8/15; no closing date. FAFSA required. Applicants notified on a rolling basis.

**Academics.** Class work integrated with field work. Class learning applied, documented and assessed in internship or employment setting. **Special study options:** Accelerated study, cooperative education, honors, internships, liberal arts/career combination, study abroad, teacher certification program, weekend college. **Credit/placement by examination:** CLEP, IB. 32 credit hours maximum toward bachelor's degree. **Support services:** Learning center, remedial instruction, tutoring.

**Majors. Area/ethnic studies:** African-American. **Business:** General, business admin, communications, managerial economics. **Communications:** General. **Education:** General. **Legal studies:** Prelaw. **Public administration:** Community org/advocacy, human services, social work. **Social sciences:** General, sociology, urban studies.

**Most popular majors.** Business/marketing 30%, public administration/social services 70%.

**Computing on campus.** 130 workstations in library, computer center.

**Student life. Freshman orientation:** Mandatory. **Activities:** Drama, student government, student newspaper, honor societies, networking club, dance committee.

**Student services.** Adult student services, career counseling, student employment services, financial aid counseling, personal counseling, placement for graduates, veterans' counselor. **Physically disabled:** Services for visually, hearing impaired.

**Contact.** Phone: (212) 343-1234 ext. 5001 Toll-free number: (800) 338-4465 Fax: (212) 343-8470
Steven Lenhart, Vice President of Enrollment Management, Metropolitan College of New York, 75 Varick Street, New York, NY 10013-1919

## Mirrer Yeshiva Central Institute
**Brooklyn, New York**

**CB code: 0661**

- Private 4-year rabbinical college for men affiliated with Jewish faith
- Very large city

**General.** Accredited by AARTS. **Calendar:** Continuous.

**Annual costs/financial aid.** Tuition/fees (2007-2008): $4,700. Room/board: $4,000.

**Contact.** Phone: (718) 645-0536
Admissions Director, 1795 Ocean Parkway, Brooklyn, NY 11223

## Molloy College

**Rockville Centre, New York**
www.molloy.edu

**CB member**
**CB code: 2415**

- Private 4-year liberal arts college affiliated with Roman Catholic Church
- Commuter campus in large town
- 2,848 degree-seeking undergraduates: 26% part-time, 79% women
- 869 graduate students
- 63% of applicants admitted
- SAT or ACT with writing, application essay required

**General.** Founded in 1955. Regionally accredited. Independent institution in Dominican tradition. **Degrees:** 518 bachelor's, 42 associate awarded; master's offered. **ROTC:** Army, Naval, Air Force. **Location:** 20 miles from New York City. **Calendar:** 4-1-4, limited summer session. **Full-time faculty:** 162 total; 64% have terminal degrees, 12% minority, 73% women. **Part-time faculty:** 330 total; 17% have terminal degrees, 9% minority, 65% women. **Class size:** 68% < 20, 31% 20-39, less than 1% 40-49, less than 1% 50-99. **Special facilities:** Weather station at Jones Beach, international business center.

**Freshman class profile.** 1,483 applied, 928 admitted, 372 enrolled.

| Mid 50% test scores | | | |
|---|---|---|---|
| SAT critical reading: | 460-570 | GPA 3.0-3.49: | 56% |
| SAT math: | 450-600 | GPA 2.0-2.99: | 17% |
| GPA 3.50 or higher: | 27% | Rank in top quarter: | 28% |
| | | Rank in top tenth: | 11% |

**Basis for selection.** Secondary school achievement with particular attention to grade 11 performance most important. Test scores also important. Recommendations, school and community activities, interview considered. Audition required for music program; portfolio required for art program. **Learning Disabled:** Applicants reviewed by separate committee.

**High school preparation.** 19 units required. Required units include English 4, mathematics 3, social studies 4, science 3 and foreign language 3. Science, math, and nursing majors must have 1 biology, 1 chemistry, and 3 math.

**2007-2008 Annual costs.** Tuition/fees: $18,570. Books/supplies: $900. Personal expenses: $2,040.

**2007-2008 Financial aid. Need-based:** 39% of total undergraduate aid awarded as scholarships/grants, 61% as loans/jobs. **Non-need-based:** Scholarships awarded for academics, art, athletics, leadership, music/drama.

**Application procedures. Admission:** No deadline. $30 fee, may be waived for applicants with need. Application may be submitted online. Admission notification on a rolling basis beginning on or about 12/1. **Financial aid:** Priority date 4/15, closing date 5/1. FAFSA required. Applicants notified on a rolling basis starting 3/1.

**Academics. Special study options:** Accelerated study, combined bachelor's/graduate degree, cooperative education, cross-registration, double major, ESL, honors, independent study, internships, liberal arts/career combination, student-designed major, study abroad, teacher certification program, weekend college. **Credit/placement by examination:** AP, CLEP, IB, SAT, ACT, institutional tests. 15 credit hours maximum toward associate degree, 30 toward bachelor's. **Support services:** Learning center, pre-admission summer program, reduced course load, remedial instruction, study skills assistance, tutoring, writing center.

**Majors. Biology:** General, ecology. **Business:** Accounting, business admin. **Communications:** General. **Computer sciences:** Computer science, information systems. **Education:** General, art, biology, elementary, English, history, mathematics, music, secondary, social studies, Spanish, special. **English:** English lit. **Foreign languages:** Spanish. **Health:** Audiology/speech pathology, health services admin, music therapy, nursing (RN). **History:** General. **Liberal arts:** Arts/sciences. **Math:** General. **Philosophy/religion:** Philosophy. **Protective services:** Law enforcement admin. **Psychology:** General. **Public administration:** Social work. **Social sciences:** Political science, sociology. **Visual/performing arts:** General, art, music performance.

**Most popular majors.** Business/marketing 9%, education 12%, health sciences 42%, security/protective services 7%.

**Computing on campus.** 420 workstations in library, computer center, student center. Commuter students can connect to campus network. Online course registration, online library, helpline, wireless network available.

**Student life. Freshman orientation:** Mandatory. **Activities:** Jazz band, choral groups, dance, drama, literary magazine, music ensembles, musical theater, student government, student newspaper, African American and Caribbean organization, Gaelic society, Out for Acceptance, social work club, Union Hispana de Molloy, Youth for Christ, HOPE Team.

**Athletics.** NCAA. **Intercollegiate:** Baseball M, basketball, cross-country, equestrian, lacrosse, soccer, softball W, tennis W, volleyball W. **Team name:** Lions.

**Student services.** Adult student services, alcohol/substance abuse counseling, campus ministries, career counseling, services for economically disadvantaged, student employment services, financial aid counseling, health services, personal counseling, veterans' counselor. **Physically disabled:** Services for visually, hearing impaired.

**Contact.** E-mail: admissions@molloy.edu
Phone: (516) 678-5000 ext. 6240 Toll-free number: (888) 466-5569
Fax: (516) 256-2247
Marguerite Lane, Director of Admissions, Molloy College, PO Box 5002, Rockville Centre, NY 11570

## Monroe College

**Bronx, New York**
www.monroecollege.edu

**CB code: 2463**

- For-profit 4-year business and health science college
- Commuter campus in very large city
- 6,232 degree-seeking undergraduates: 13% part-time, 71% women, 46% African American, 1% Asian American, 42% Hispanic American, 6% international
- 258 degree-seeking graduate students
- 58% of applicants admitted
- Application essay, interview required
- 53% graduate within 6 years; 15% enter graduate study

**General.** Founded in 1933. Regionally accredited. Branch campus in New Rochelle offers all programs, courses, and services available at main campus. **Degrees:** 925 bachelor's, 1,433 associate awarded; master's offered. **ROTC:** Army. **Calendar:** Semester, extensive summer session. **Full-time faculty:** 70 total; 40% have terminal degrees, 57% minority, 44% women. **Part-time faculty:** 160 total; 14% have terminal degrees, 71% minority, 60% women. **Class size:** 44% < 20, 55% 20-39, less than 1% 50-99.

**Freshman class profile.** 2,463 applied, 1,418 admitted, 1,254 enrolled.

| End year in good standing: | 92% | Live on campus: | 25% |
|---|---|---|---|
| Return as sophomores: | 81% | International: | 4% |
| Out-of-state: | 1% | | |

**Basis for selection.** Interview, school achievement record, test scores required. Modified open admissions for students who pass admissions test.

**2007-2008 Annual costs.** Tuition/fees: $10,684. Room/board: $10,738. Books/supplies: $900. Personal expenses: $4,772.

**Financial aid.** All financial aid based on need.

**Application procedures. Admission:** No deadline. $35 fee. Application may be submitted online. Admission notification on a rolling basis. **Financial aid:** Closing date 3/31. FAFSA required. Applicants notified on a rolling basis starting 7/1.

**Academics. Special study options:** Cooperative education, distance learning, dual enrollment of high school students, honors, internships, liberal arts/career combination, study abroad, weekend college. **Credit/placement by examination:** AP, CLEP, IB, institutional tests. 30 credit hours maximum toward associate degree, 30 toward bachelor's. **Support services:** Learning center, pre-admission summer program, remedial instruction, tutoring, writing center.

**Majors. Business:** Accounting, business admin. **Computer sciences:** General. **Health:** Health services admin. **Protective services:** Law enforcement admin.

**Most popular majors.** Business/marketing 60%, computer/information sciences 20%, security/protective services 17%.

**Computing on campus.** 800 workstations in dormitories, library, computer center. Dormitories wired for high-speed internet access and linked to

campus network. Commuter students can connect to campus network. Online course registration, online library, helpline, wireless network available.

**Student life. Freshman orientation:** Mandatory. Preregistration for classes offered. **Housing:** Coed dorms available. $100 deposit. Assistance for foreign students in securing local housing. Student apartments available near New Rochelle campus. On-campus housing at New Rochelle campus. **Activities:** Dance, student newspaper.

**Athletics.** NJCAA. **Intercollegiate:** Baseball M, basketball, soccer M, volleyball. **Intramural:** Basketball, softball M. **Team name:** Mustangs.

**Student services.** Adult student services, career counseling, student employment services, financial aid counseling, personal counseling, placement for graduates, veterans' counselor. **Physically disabled:** Services for visually, speech, hearing impaired.

**Contact.** E-mail: ejerome@monroecollege.edu
Phone: (718) 933-6700 Toll-free number: (800) 556-6676
Fax: (718) 364-3552
Evan Jerome, Director of Admissions, Monroe College, Monroe College Way, Bronx, NY 10468

---

## Mount St. Mary College
**Newburgh, New York**
www.msmc.edu

CB member
CB code: 2423

- Private 4-year liberal arts college
- Residential campus in large town
- 2,035 degree-seeking undergraduates: 17% part-time, 72% women, 10% African American, 3% Asian American, 9% Hispanic American
- 480 degree-seeking graduate students
- 77% of applicants admitted
- SAT or ACT with writing required
- 57% graduate within 6 years; 35% enter graduate study

**General.** Founded in 1954. Regionally accredited. Independent institution in Judeo-Christian tradition, founded by Dominican Sisters of Newburgh. **Degrees:** 422 bachelor's awarded; master's offered. **Location:** 58 miles from New York City. **Calendar:** Semester, limited summer session. **Full-time faculty:** 74 total; 90% have terminal degrees, 8% minority, 58% women. **Part-time faculty:** 145 total; 23% have terminal degrees, 6% minority, 54% women. **Class size:** 42% < 20, 55% 20-39, 2% 40-49, less than 1% 50-99. **Special facilities:** Elementary school on campus.

**Freshman class profile.** 1,600 applied, 1,231 admitted, 366 enrolled.

| Mid 50% test scores | | | |
|---|---|---|---|
| SAT critical reading: | 460-540 | GPA 2.0-2.99: | 33% |
| SAT math: | 450-550 | Rank in top quarter: | 30% |
| SAT writing: | 450-550 | Rank in top tenth: | 10% |
| ACT composite: | 19-23 | End year in good standing: | 82% |
| GPA 3.50 or higher: | 26% | Return as sophomores: | 72% |
| GPA 3.0-3.49: | 39% | Out-of-state: | 18% |
| | | Live on campus: | 74% |

**Basis for selection.** Admissions decisions based on total admission score which weighs high school average, class rank, and test scores as well as teacher/counselor recommendations. Interview recommended for all; essay required for special consideration, recommended for all others. **Home-schooled:** Transcript of courses and grades required. **Learning Disabled:** Must include IEP with application. Must meet with Director of Counseling and Coordinator of Services for Persons with Disabilities.

**High school preparation.** 20 units recommended. Recommended units include English 4, mathematics 3, social studies 4, science 3, foreign language 3, academic electives 3.5. Recommended math sequence is algebra, geometry, trigonometry. Biology and chemistry required for nursing majors.

**2007-2008 Annual costs.** Tuition/fees: $19,520. Room/board: $10,400. Books/supplies: $1,200. Personal expenses: $1,000.

**2007-2008 Financial aid. Need-based:** 337 full-time freshmen applied for aid; 272 were judged to have need; 271 of these received aid. Average need met was 61%. Average scholarship/grant was $8,102; average loan $4,833. 43% of total undergraduate aid awarded as scholarships/grants, 57% as loans/jobs. **Non-need-based:** Awarded to 301 full-time undergraduates, including 108 freshmen. Scholarships awarded for academics, ROTC.

**Application procedures. Admission:** Priority date 4/1; no deadline. $40 fee, may be waived for applicants with need. Application may be submitted online. Admission notification on a rolling basis beginning on or about 9/1. **Financial aid:** Closing date 2/15. FAFSA required. Applicants notified on a rolling basis starting 4/1; must reply within 2 week(s) of notification.

---

**Academics. Special study options:** Accelerated study, combined bachelor's/graduate degree, cooperative education, cross-registration, distance learning, double major, dual enrollment of high school students, exchange student, honors, independent study, internships, liberal arts/career combination, student-designed major, study abroad, teacher certification program. **Credit/placement by examination:** AP, CLEP, IB, SAT, ACT, institutional tests. 45 credit hours maximum toward bachelor's degree. **Support services:** Learning center, pre-admission summer program, reduced course load, remedial instruction, study skills assistance, tutoring, writing center.

**Majors. Biology:** General. **Business:** Accounting, business admin. **Computer sciences:** Information technology. **Education:** Early childhood, multilevel teacher, secondary. **English:** English lit. **Foreign languages:** Spanish. **Health:** Clinical lab science, nursing (RN). **History:** General. **Math:** General. **Physical sciences:** Chemistry. **Psychology:** General. **Public administration:** Human services. **Social sciences:** General, sociology.

**Most popular majors.** Business/marketing 21%, English 15%, health sciences 10%, history 12%, mathematics 6%, psychology 11%.

**Computing on campus.** 570 workstations in dormitories, library, computer center, student center. Dormitories wired for high-speed internet access and linked to campus network. Commuter students can connect to campus network. Online course registration, online library, helpline, student web hosting, wireless network available.

**Student life. Freshman orientation:** Mandatory, $200 fee. Preregistration for classes offered. Held the weekend before classes begin. **Housing:** Coed dorms, single-sex dorms, special housing for disabled available. $450 fully refundable deposit, deadline 5/1. **Activities:** Concert band, campus ministries, choral groups, dance, drama, film society, literary magazine, music ensembles, musical theater, radio station, student government, student newspaper, black student union, Habitat for Humanity, Big Brothers/Big Sisters, Christian fellowship, Latin student union.

**Athletics.** NCAA. **Intercollegiate:** Baseball M, basketball, cross-country, soccer, softball W, swimming, tennis, volleyball W. **Intramural:** Basketball, bowling, football (non-tackle) M, golf, soccer, softball, swimming, table tennis, volleyball. **Team name:** Blue Knights.

**Student services.** Adult student services, alcohol/substance abuse counseling, campus ministries, career counseling, services for economically disadvantaged, student employment services, financial aid counseling, health services, personal counseling, placement for graduates. **Physically disabled:** Services for visually impaired.

**Contact.** E-mail: admissions@msmc.edu
Phone: (845) 569-3248 Toll-free number: (888) 937-6762
Fax: (845) 562-6762
J. Randall Ognibene, Director of Admissions, Mount St. Mary College, 330 Powell Avenue, Newburgh, NY 12550

---

## Nazareth College of Rochester
**Rochester, New York**
www.naz.edu

CB member
CB code: 2511

- Private 4-year liberal arts college
- Residential campus in large city
- 2,120 degree-seeking undergraduates: 6% part-time, 75% women, 5% African American, 2% Asian American, 3% Hispanic American, 1% international
- 980 degree-seeking graduate students
- 74% of applicants admitted
- Application essay required
- 76% graduate within 6 years

**General.** Founded in 1924. Regionally accredited. **Degrees:** 468 bachelor's awarded; master's, doctoral offered. **ROTC:** Army, Air Force. **Location:** 7 miles from downtown. **Calendar:** Semester, extensive summer session. **Full-time faculty:** 152 total; 90% have terminal degrees, 14% minority, 57% women. **Part-time faculty:** 217 total; 23% have terminal degrees, 9% minority, 71% women. **Class size:** 57% < 20, 42% 20-39, less than 1% 40-49, less than 1% 50-99. **Special facilities:** Arts center, psychology research facility, speech clinic, center for service learning, physical therapy clinic.

**Freshman class profile.** 2,076 applied, 1,545 admitted, 458 enrolled.

| Mid 50% test scores | | | |
|---|---|---|---|
| SAT critical reading: | 530-630 | GPA 3.0-3.49: | 30% |
| SAT math: | 530-630 | GPA 2.0-2.99: | 31% |
| SAT writing: | 510-610 | Return as sophomores: | 83% |
| ACT composite: | 23-27 | Out-of-state: | 9% |
| GPA 3.50 or higher: | 37% | Live on campus: | 86% |
| | | International: | 1% |

**Basis for selection.** School achievement record, strength of high school academic program, class rank, recommendations most heavily considered. Standardized test optional institution. Interview recommended for all; audition required for music, music education, music theater, music therapy, and theater arts programs; portfolio required for art education, studio art programs.

**High school preparation.** 16 units required; 20 recommended. Required and recommended units include English 4, mathematics 3-4, social studies 3-4, science 3-4 (laboratory 2) and foreign language 3-4.

**2007-2008 Annual costs.** Tuition/fees: $22,844. Room/board: $9,420. Books/supplies: $900. Personal expenses: $1,100.

**2006-2007 Financial aid. Need-based:** 442 full-time freshmen applied for aid; 368 were judged to have need; 366 of these received aid. Average need met was 77%. Average scholarship/grant was $11,753; average loan $2,941. 59% of total undergraduate aid awarded as scholarships/grants, 41% as loans/jobs. **Non-need-based:** Awarded to 567 full-time undergraduates, including 174 freshmen. Scholarships awarded for academics, alumni affiliation, art, minority status, music/drama, ROTC, state residency.

**Application procedures. Admission:** Priority date 12/15; deadline 2/15 (postmark date). $40 fee, may be waived for applicants with need. Application may be submitted online. Admission notification on a rolling basis beginning on or about 3/1. Must reply by May 1 or within 4 week(s) if notified thereafter. **Financial aid:** Priority date 12/15, closing date 5/1. FAFSA required. CSS PROFILE required of early decision applicants only. Applicants notified on a rolling basis starting 2/20; must reply by 5/1 or within 2 week(s) of notification.

**Academics. Special study options:** Combined bachelor's/graduate degree, cross-registration, double major, exchange student, honors, independent study, internships, study abroad, teacher certification program, Washington semester. 2-2 bachelor's degree completion program for registered nurses and Monroe Community College graduates. **Credit/placement by examination:** AP, CLEP, IB, SAT, ACT. 30 credit hours maximum toward bachelor's degree. **Support services:** Reduced course load, remedial instruction, study skills assistance, tutoring, writing center.

**Majors. Area/ethnic studies:** American. **Biology:** General, biochemistry. **Business:** General, accounting. **Communications:** General. **Computer sciences:** Information systems. **Education:** Art, business, elementary, music, secondary, special. **English:** English lit. **Foreign languages:** French, German, Italian, Spanish. **Health:** Communication disorders, music therapy, speech pathology. **History:** General. **Interdisciplinary:** Peace/conflict. **Math:** General. **Philosophy/religion:** Philosophy, religion. **Physical sciences:** Chemistry. **Psychology:** General. **Public administration:** Social work. **Social sciences:** General, anthropology, economics, political science, sociology. **Visual/performing arts:** Art, art history/conservation, dramatic, music history, music performance, music theory/composition, studio arts.

**Most popular majors.** Business/marketing 12%, education 10%, English 8%, health sciences 19%, history 9%, psychology 9%, social sciences 10%, visual/performing arts 7%.

**Computing on campus.** 150 workstations in dormitories, library, computer center. Dormitories wired for high-speed internet access and linked to campus network. Commuter students can connect to campus network. Online library, helpline, wireless network available.

**Student life. Freshman orientation:** Mandatory, $100 fee. Preregistration for classes offered. Orientation charge included in first-year fees. 3-day weekend program includes community service. **Housing:** Coed dorms, single-sex dorms, special housing for disabled, apartments, substance-free housing available. $100 nonrefundable deposit, deadline 5/1. Foreign language houses, special interest and collective housing for students in various majors, quiet floor, honors floor available. **Activities:** Bands, choral groups, dance, drama, music ensembles, musical theater, radio station, student government, student newspaper, symphony orchestra, Amnesty International, Campus Ministry Council, Inter-Ethnic Coalition, Undergraduate Association, Club Cervantes, French club, Italian club, Rotaract, Women's Resource Network.

**Athletics.** NCAA. **Intercollegiate:** Basketball, cheerleading, cross-country, diving, equestrian, field hockey W, golf, lacrosse, soccer, softball W, swimming, tennis, track and field, volleyball W. **Intramural:** Basketball, racquetball, soccer, softball, swimming, tennis, volleyball. **Team name:** Golden Flyers.

**Student services.** Adult student services, alcohol/substance abuse counseling, campus ministries, career counseling, services for economically disadvantaged, student employment services, financial aid counseling, health services, minority student services, on-campus daycare, personal counseling, placement for graduates, women's services. **Physically disabled:** Services for visually, speech, hearing impaired.

**Contact.** E-mail: admissions@naz.edu
Phone: (585) 389-2860 Toll-free number: (800) 462-3944
Fax: (585) 389-2826
Thomas DaRin, Vice President for Enrollment Management, Nazareth College of Rochester, 4245 East Avenue, Rochester, NY 14618-3790

## New York Institute of Technology
**Old Westbury, New York**
**www.nyit.edu**                    CB code: 2561

- Private 4-year university and health science college
- Commuter campus in large town
- 6,267 degree-seeking undergraduates: 21% part-time, 37% women, 8% African American, 9% Asian American, 7% Hispanic American, 6% international
- 4,009 degree-seeking graduate students
- 69% of applicants admitted
- SAT or ACT (ACT writing recommended), application essay required
- 39% graduate within 6 years

**General.** Founded in 1955. Regionally accredited. 3-campus institution: Old Westbury in Nassau County, New York City, and Islip campus in Suffolk County. **Degrees:** 1,432 bachelor's, 41 associate awarded; master's, doctoral, first professional offered. **ROTC:** Army, Air Force. **Location:** 15 miles from New York City. **Calendar:** Semester, extensive summer session. **Full-time faculty:** 335 total; 58% have terminal degrees, 21% minority, 38% women. **Part-time faculty:** 613 total; 15% minority, 41% women. **Class size:** 65% < 20, 30% 20-39, 3% 40-49, 2% 50-99. **Special facilities:** Center for urban/suburban studies, center for neighborhood revitalization, Parkinson's disease treatment center, center for labor and industrial relations, center for energy, environment and economics, center for teaching and learning with technology, culinary arts center, center for entrepreneurial and small business services, center for business information technologies, motion graphics laboratory.

**Freshman class profile.** 4,073 applied, 2,797 admitted, 1,441 enrolled.

| Mid 50% test scores | | | |
|---|---|---|---|
| SAT critical reading: | 490-580 | Rank in top tenth: | 10% |
| SAT math: | 530-630 | Return as sophomores: | 72% |
| ACT composite: | 21-25 | Out-of-state: | 9% |
| GPA 3.50 or higher: | 43% | Live on campus: | 13% |
| GPA 3.0-3.49: | 47% | International: | 5% |
| GPA 2.0-2.99: | 10% | Fraternities: | 2% |
| Rank in top quarter: | 48% | Sororities: | 1% |

**Basis for selection.** 2 letters of recommendation required for 4-year nursing, occupational therapy, physical therapy, physician assistant and all education programs. Proof of 100 hours of volunteer or work experience required for physical therapy, physician assistant, occupational therapy programs. SAT important, minimum scores vary with program. Interview required for nursing, occupational therapy, physician assistant, physical therapy, BS/doctor of osteopathic medicine, and BS/Juris Doctor program applicants. Portfolio required for fine arts program.

**High school preparation.** 17 units required. Required and recommended units include English 4, mathematics 3, social studies 3-4, science 3 (laboratory 1) and academic electives 7. Freshmen in selected majors required to prove or acquire computer literacy.

**2007-2008 Annual costs.** Tuition/fees: $21,498. Room only charges apply to Manhattan campus; board charges vary on other campuses. Tuition/fee costs reported for nontechnology majors, vary for other programs. Room only: $12,254. Books/supplies: $1,400. Personal expenses: $2,550.

**2006-2007 Financial aid. Need-based:** 1,053 full-time freshmen applied for aid; 901 were judged to have need; 894 of these received aid. Average scholarship/grant was $3,484; average loan $3,058. 90% of total undergraduate aid awarded as scholarships/grants, 10% as loans/jobs. **Non-need-based:** Awarded to 3,019 full-time undergraduates, including 1,048 freshmen. Scholarships awarded for academics, athletics.

**Application procedures. Admission:** No deadline. $50 fee, may be waived for applicants with need. Application may be submitted online. Admission notification on a rolling basis beginning on or about 1/1. Must reply by May 1 or within 4 week(s) if notified thereafter. Application closing date for nursing, occupational therapy, physical therapy and physician assistant programs February 1. Notification to applicants to these programs sent March 1. Applicants to these programs must reply by May 1 or within 30 days if notified thereafter. No deferred admission to these programs. **Financial aid:** Priority date 3/1; no closing date. FAFSA required. Applicants notified on a rolling basis starting 3/15; must reply by 5/1 or within 2 week(s) of notification.

**Academics.** School focuses on career-oriented professional education, access to opportunity, applications-oriented research and service in public interest. **Special study options:** Accelerated study, combined bachelor's/graduate degree, cooperative education, cross-registration, distance learning, double major, dual enrollment of high school students, ESL, honors, independent study, internships, liberal arts/career combination, study abroad, teacher certification program, weekend college. Combined bachelor's/professional degree program in life sciences/osteopathic medicine, architectural technology/energy management, architectural technology/MBA, mechanical engineering/energy management, life sciences/physical therapy, life sciences/occupational therapy, behavioral sciences/law at Touro College Law Center. **Credit/placement by examination:** AP, CLEP, IB, institutional tests. 30 credit hours maximum toward associate degree, 60 toward bachelor's. **Support services:** Learning center, pre-admission summer program, reduced course load, remedial instruction, study skills assistance, tutoring, writing center.

**Majors. Architecture:** Architecture, technology. **Biology:** General. **Business:** Accounting, business admin, finance, hotel/motel admin, human resources, management information systems, marketing, restaurant/food services, tourism/travel. **Communications:** General, advertising, broadcast journalism, radio/tv. **Computer sciences:** General, computer graphics, computer science, networking. **Education:** Art, biology, business, chemistry, elementary, English, health occupations, mathematics, middle, physics, sales/marketing, science, social science, social studies, technology/industrial arts, trade/industrial, voc/tech. **Engineering:** Biomedical, computer, electrical, mechanical. **Engineering technology:** Aerospace, architectural, electrical, energy systems, environmental, manufacturing. **English:** English lit, technical writing. **Health:** Nursing (RN), physician assistant, premedicine. **Interdisciplinary:** Nutrition sciences. **Physical sciences:** Chemistry, physics. **Protective services:** Law enforcement admin. **Psychology:** General. **Social sciences:** General, economics, political science, sociology. **Visual/performing arts:** Commercial/advertising art, interior design, studio arts.

**Most popular majors.** Architecture 11%, business/marketing 27%, communications/journalism 10%, engineering/engineering technologies 7%, health sciences 12%, interdisciplinary studies 14%, visual/performing arts 10%.

**Computing on campus.** PC or laptop required. 1,210 workstations in dormitories, library, computer center, student center. Dormitories wired for high-speed internet access and linked to campus network. Commuter students can connect to campus network. Online library, helpline, student web hosting available.

**Student life. Freshman orientation:** Available. Preregistration for classes offered. One day at end of August. **Housing:** Guaranteed on-campus for all undergraduates. Coed dorms, special housing for disabled, apartments available. $275 nonrefundable deposit. Central Islip campus fully residential, special housing for graduate, architecture students. Off-campus housing available for Manhattan campus. **Activities:** Choral groups, dance, drama, film society, literary magazine, musical theater, radio station, student government, student newspaper, TV station, American Institute of Architecture Students, biomedical society, National Society of Black Engineers, Newman Club, Christian fellowship, Jewish student union, African people's organization, Community Connection, South Asian student association, Chinese student association.

**Athletics.** NCAA. **Intercollegiate:** Baseball M, basketball, boxing W, cross-country, lacrosse M, soccer, softball W, track and field, volleyball W. **Intramural:** Basketball, football (non-tackle), golf, soccer, softball, swimming, tennis, track and field, volleyball, weight lifting. **Team name:** Bears.

**Student services.** Adult student services, campus ministries, career counseling, student employment services, financial aid counseling, health services, personal counseling, placement for graduates, veterans' counselor. **Physically disabled:** Services for hearing impaired.

**Contact.**  E-mail: admissions@nyit.edu
Phone: (516) 686-7520 Toll-free number: (800) 345-6948
Fax: (516) 686-7613
Jacquelyn Nealon, Dean of Admissions, New York Institute of Technology, Box 8000, Old Westbury, NY 11568

---

## New York School of Interior Design
**New York, New York**
www.nysid.edu                              CB code: 0333

- Private 4-year visual arts college
- Commuter campus in very large city

- 685 degree-seeking undergraduates: 75% part-time, 92% women, 4% African American, 9% Asian American, 8% Hispanic American
- 18 degree-seeking graduate students
- 48% of applicants admitted
- Application essay required

**General.** Founded in 1916. The college is devoted exclusively to interior design education. **Degrees:** 32 bachelor's, 65 associate awarded; master's, first professional offered. **Location:** Located in Manhattan. **Calendar:** Semester, extensive summer session. **Full-time faculty:** 2 total; 50% women. **Part-time faculty:** 77 total; 34% have terminal degrees, 5% minority, 39% women. **Class size:** 91% < 20, 9% 50-99. **Special facilities:** Three galleries for architecture and interior design exhibits, lighting laboratory.

**Freshman class profile.** 122 applied, 58 admitted, 24 enrolled.

| | | | |
|---|---|---|---|
| GPA 3.50 or higher: | 25% | End year in good standing: | 80% |
| GPA 3.0-3.49: | 50% | Return as sophomores: | 20% |
| GPA 2.0-2.99: | 25% | Out-of-state: | 17% |

**Basis for selection.** High school transcripts, 2 letters of recommendation, essay, and portfolio in art/design. Portfolio required, interview recommended. **Homeschooled:** State high school equivalency certificate required.

**High school preparation.** 16 units recommended. Recommended units include English 4, mathematics 2, social studies 2, history 2, science 2 and foreign language 2. Studio art or drafting is recommended.

**2008-2009 Annual costs.** Tuition/fees: $19,790. Books/supplies: $1,000. Personal expenses: $900.

**2007-2008 Financial aid.** All financial aid based on need. 43% of total undergraduate aid awarded as scholarships/grants, 57% as loans/jobs.

**Application procedures. Admission:** Priority date 3/1; no deadline. $50 fee, may be waived for applicants with need. Application may be submitted online. Admission notification on a rolling basis beginning on or about 4/1. Must reply by May 1 or within 4 week(s) if notified thereafter. **Financial aid:** Priority date 5/1; no closing date. FAFSA, institutional form required. Applicants notified on a rolling basis starting 2/1; must reply within 2 week(s) of notification.

**Academics. Special study options:** Independent study, internships, study abroad. **Credit/placement by examination:** AP, CLEP, IB, institutional tests. 17 credit hours maximum toward associate degree, 41 toward bachelor's. **Support services:** Study skills assistance, tutoring, writing center.

**Majors. Visual/performing arts:** Interior design.

**Computing on campus.** 125 workstations in library, computer center. Commuter students can connect to campus network. Online course registration, helpline available.

**Student life. Freshman orientation:** Available. Preregistration for classes offered. General orientation is held the week before classes begin. **Activities:** Student chapter of American Society of Interior Designers.

**Student services.** Adult student services, career counseling, student employment services, financial aid counseling, personal counseling, placement for graduates.

**Contact.**  E-mail: admissions@nysid.edu
Phone: (212) 472-1500 ext. 204 Toll-free number: (800) 336-9743 ext. 204
Fax: (212) 472-1867
David Sprouls, Director of Admissions, New York School of Interior Design, 170 East 70th Street, New York, NY 10021-5110

---

## New York University
**New York, New York**                     CB member
www.nyu.edu                                CB code: 2562

- Private 4-year university
- Residential campus in very large city
- 20,899 degree-seeking undergraduates: 6% part-time, 62% women, 4% African American, 19% Asian American, 8% Hispanic American, 6% international
- 19,299 degree-seeking graduate students
- 37% of applicants admitted
- SAT or ACT with writing, SAT Subject Tests, application essay required
- 84% graduate within 6 years; 22% enter graduate study

**General.** Founded in 1831. Regionally accredited. School of Continuing and Professional Studies also available for adult degree and noncredit programs. **Degrees:** 5,713 bachelor's, 750 associate awarded; master's, doctoral, first professional offered. **ROTC:** Army, Naval. **Calendar:** Semester, extensive summer session. **Full-time faculty:** 2,132 total; 93% have terminal degrees, 40% women. **Part-time faculty:** 2,128 total; 79% have terminal degrees, 46% women. **Class size:** 58% < 20, 26% 20-39, 4% 40-49, 7% 50-99, 5% >100. **Special facilities:** Special academic facilities for arts, business, culture, education, international relations, language, law, media, music, public service, research, and social policy.

**Freshman class profile.** 34,389 applied, 12,615 admitted, 4,927 enrolled.

| Mid 50% test scores | | Rank in top quarter: | 93% |
|---|---|---|---|
| SAT critical reading: | 620-710 | Rank in top tenth: | 66% |
| SAT math: | 620-720 | Return as sophomores: | 92% |
| SAT writing: | 620-710 | Out-of-state: | 73% |
| ACT composite: | 28-31 | Live on campus: | 88% |
| GPA 3.50 or higher: | 70% | International: | 8% |
| GPA 3.0-3.49: | 28% | Fraternities: | 2% |
| GPA 2.0-2.99: | 2% | Sororities: | 1% |

**Basis for selection.** School achievement record most important. Standardized test scores, activities, essay, recommendations also important. Audition and/or submission of creative materials required for applicants to either Tisch School of the Arts or art and music programs within the School of Education. 2 SAT Subject Tests required of all students with exception of fine and performing arts students whose audition/portfolio is used in lieu of Subject Tests. Audition required for dance, drama, and music programs; portfolio required for art, theater design, photography, cinema studies, film, television, radio, and dramatic writing programs. Portfolios may include writing, photography, film or other creative work.

**High school preparation.** 16 units required. Required and recommended units include English 4, mathematics 3-4, history 4, science 3 (laboratory 2) and foreign language 2-3.

**2007-2008 Annual costs.** Tuition/fees: $35,290. Room/board: $12,200. Books/supplies: $700. Personal expenses: $1,000.

**2007-2008 Financial aid. Need-based:** 3,225 full-time freshmen applied for aid; 2,612 were judged to have need; 2,605 of these received aid. Average need met was 68%. Average scholarship/grant was $16,236; average loan $5,203. 57% of total undergraduate aid awarded as scholarships/grants, 43% as loans/jobs. **Non-need-based:** Awarded to 1,784 full-time undergraduates, including 327 freshmen. Scholarships awarded for academics. **Additional information:** Both need-based and merit scholarships available to first-time students. Range from $1,000 to $25,000.

**Application procedures. Admission:** Closing date 1/15 (postmark date). $65 fee, may be waived for applicants with need. Application may be submitted online. Admission notification 4/1. Must reply by May 1 or within 3 week(s) if notified thereafter. **Financial aid:** Closing date 2/15. FAFSA required. Applicants notified on a rolling basis starting 4/1; must reply by 5/1.

**Academics. Special study options:** Combined bachelor's/graduate degree, cross-registration, distance learning, double major, exchange student, honors, independent study, internships, liberal arts/career combination, student-designed major, study abroad, teacher certification program, Washington semester, weekend college. NYU offers an exchange program with several historically black colleges including Spelman, Bennett, Morehouse, and Tougaloo; 3-2 engineering program with Stevens Institute of Technology. **Credit/placement by examination:** AP, CLEP, IB. 32 credit hours maximum toward bachelor's degree. 8 to 32 hours of credit may be awarded for International Baccalaureate. **Support services:** Learning center, pre-admission summer program, reduced course load, study skills assistance, tutoring, writing center.

**Majors. Architecture:** Urban/community planning. **Area/ethnic studies:** African-American, East Asian, European, Latin American, Near/Middle Eastern. **Biology:** General, biochemistry. **Business:** General, accounting, finance, hotel/motel admin, international, labor relations, managerial economics, real estate, restaurant/food services. **Communications:** General, journalism, radio/tv. **Communications technology:** Radio/tv. **Computer sciences:** General, computer science. **Education:** Art, biology, chemistry, elementary, English, foreign languages, French, German, kindergarten/preschool, mathematics, physics, social studies, Spanish, special, speech impaired. **Engineering:** Operations research. **English:** American lit, British lit, English lit. **Family/consumer sciences:** Food/nutrition. **Foreign languages:** General, ancient Greek, classics, comparative lit, French, German, Hebrew, Italian, linguistics, modern Greek, Russian, Spanish. **Health:** Audiology/speech pathology, dental hygiene, nursing (RN). **History:** General. **Interdisciplinary:** Neuroscience. **Liberal arts:** Arts/sciences, humanities. **Math:** General. **Parks/recreation:** Facilities management. **Philosophy/religion:** Judaic, philosophy, religion. **Physical sciences:** Chemistry, physics. **Psychology:** General.

**Public administration:** General, community org/advocacy, social work. **Social sciences:** General, anthropology, economics, international relations, political science, sociology, urban studies. **Visual/performing arts:** Cinematography, commercial/advertising art, dance, dramatic, music management, music performance, music theory/composition, photography, studio arts. **Other:** Fundraising, Music technology.

**Most popular majors.** Business/marketing 14%, communications/journalism 9%, liberal arts 9%, social sciences 16%, visual/performing arts 20%.

**Computing on campus.** 2,600 workstations in dormitories, library, computer center, student center. Dormitories wired for high-speed internet access and linked to campus network. Commuter students can connect to campus network. Online course registration, online library, helpline, repair service, student web hosting, wireless network available.

**Student life. Freshman orientation:** Available. Preregistration for classes offered. Each undergraduate college handles own orientation. Charge and program determined and vary by school. **Housing:** Guaranteed on-campus for all undergraduates. Coed dorms, special housing for disabled, apartments, fraternity/sorority housing, substance-free housing available. $300 nonrefundable deposit, deadline 5/1. All freshmen who request housing on admissions application and meet all deadlines guaranteed 4 years of housing. First Year Residential Experience program available for new students. **Activities:** Bands, choral groups, dance, drama, film society, international student organizations, literary magazine, music ensembles, musical theater, opera, radio station, student government, student newspaper, symphony orchestra, TV station, over 350 clubs and organizations available.

**Athletics.** NCAA. **Intercollegiate:** Basketball, cheerleading, cross-country, diving, fencing, golf M, soccer, swimming, tennis, track and field, volleyball, wrestling M. **Intramural:** Basketball, bowling, football (non-tackle), soccer, softball, tennis, volleyball, weight lifting. **Team name:** Violets.

**Student services.** Adult student services, alcohol/substance abuse counseling, campus ministries, career counseling, services for economically disadvantaged, student employment services, financial aid counseling, health services, minority student services, personal counseling, placement for graduates, women's services. **Physically disabled:** Services for visually, speech, hearing impaired.

**Contact.** E-mail: admissions@nyu.edu
Phone: (212) 998-4500 Fax: (212) 995-4902
Barbara Hall, Associate Provost for Admissions and Financial Aid, New York University, 22 Washington Square North, New York, NY 10011-9108

---

## Niagara University

**Niagara University, New York**　　　　　**CB member**
**www.niagara.edu**　　　　　　　　　　　**CB code: 2558**

- ♦ Private 4-year university affiliated with Roman Catholic Church
- ♦ Residential campus in small city
- ♦ 3,219 degree-seeking undergraduates: 3% part-time, 62% women, 4% African American, 1% Asian American, 2% Hispanic American, 12% international
- ♦ 817 degree-seeking graduate students
- ♦ 77% of applicants admitted
- ♦ SAT or ACT (ACT writing optional) required
- ♦ 62% graduate within 6 years; 44% enter graduate study

**General.** Founded in 1856. Regionally accredited. Independent institution in the Vincentian tradition. **Degrees:** 644 bachelor's, 3 associate awarded; master's offered. **ROTC:** Army. **Location:** 20 miles from Buffalo, 90 miles from Toronto, Canada. **Calendar:** Semester, extensive summer session. **Full-time faculty:** 150 total; 90% have terminal degrees, 15% minority, 37% women. **Part-time faculty:** 227 total; 9% minority, 49% women. **Class size:** 43% < 20, 47% 20-39, 10% 40-49, less than 1% 50-99. **Special facilities:** Castellani Art Museum, Dwyer Ice Arena.

**Freshman class profile.** 3,078 applied, 2,358 admitted, 739 enrolled.

| Mid 50% test scores | | Rank in top quarter: | 42% |
|---|---|---|---|
| SAT critical reading: | 480-590 | Rank in top tenth: | 14% |
| SAT math: | 470-570 | End year in good standing: | 86% |
| ACT composite: | 19-25 | Return as sophomores: | 81% |
| GPA 3.50 or higher: | 43% | Out-of-state: | 9% |
| GPA 3.0-3.49: | 30% | Live on campus: | 77% |
| GPA 2.0-2.99: | 27% | International: | 2% |

**Basis for selection.** School achievement record, class rank, test scores most important. School recommendation also important. Character, personality, and extracurricular activities considered. Alumni relationship also considered. Interview, essay recommended for all; audition recommended for theater program. **Homeschooled:** Transcript of courses and grades required. Letter from district superintendent or local district official confirming that the student has received an education "substantially equivalent" to instruction given to students graduating from the public high school in that district.

**High school preparation.** 16 units required. Required units include English 4, mathematics 2, social studies 2, science 2, foreign language 2 and academic electives 4. 3 science (biology, chemistry mandatory, physics recommended) for math, science, nursing applicants. 2 foreign language required of all except business applicants. 3 math required for math, biology, business, biochemistry, chemistry, computer and information sciences, natural sciences, and nursing applicants. 3 social studies required for prospective social studies majors.

**2007-2008 Annual costs.** Tuition/fees: $22,425. Room/board: $9,300. Books/supplies: $900. Personal expenses: $750.

**2007-2008 Financial aid. Need-based:** 719 full-time freshmen applied for aid; 605 were judged to have need; 604 of these received aid. Average need met was 80%. Average scholarship/grant was $13,279; average loan $4,665. 63% of total undergraduate aid awarded as scholarships/grants, 37% as loans/jobs. **Non-need-based:** Awarded to 1,292 full-time undergraduates, including 392 freshmen. Scholarships awarded for academics, athletics, music/drama, ROTC. **Additional information:** Opportunity program available for academically and economically disadvantaged students.

**Application procedures. Admission:** Closing date 8/1 (receipt date). $30 fee, may be waived for applicants with need. Application may be submitted online. Admission notification on a rolling basis. Must reply by May 1 or within 4 week(s) if notified thereafter. **Financial aid:** Priority date 2/15; no closing date. FAFSA required. Applicants notified on a rolling basis starting 3/1; must reply within 3 week(s) of notification.

**Academics.** Academic exploration program for students undecided about their choice of major. **Special study options:** Accelerated study, combined bachelor's/graduate degree, cooperative education, cross-registration, double major, dual enrollment of high school students, ESL, exchange student, honors, independent study, internships, liberal arts/career combination, New York semester, study abroad, teacher certification program, Washington semester. **Credit/placement by examination:** AP, CLEP, institutional tests. 15 credit hours maximum toward associate degree, 15 toward bachelor's. **Support services:** Learning center, pre-admission summer program, reduced course load, remedial instruction, study skills assistance, tutoring, writing center.

**Majors. Biology:** General, biochemistry. **Business:** General, accounting, hospitality admin, hotel/motel admin, human resources, international, logistics, marketing, restaurant/food services, tourism/travel. **Communications:** General. **Computer sciences:** General, computer science, information systems. **Education:** General, biology, business, chemistry, early childhood, elementary, English, French, mathematics, secondary, social studies, Spanish, special. **English:** English lit. **Foreign languages:** French, Spanish. **Health:** Nursing (RN), predental, premedicine, preveterinary. **History:** General. **Legal studies:** Prelaw. **Liberal arts:** Arts/sciences. **Math:** General. **Philosophy/religion:** Philosophy, religion. **Physical sciences:** Chemistry. **Protective services:** Criminal justice. **Psychology:** General. **Public administration:** Social work. **Science technology:** Biological. **Social sciences:** General, criminology, political science, sociology. **Transportation:** General. **Visual/performing arts:** Dramatic.

**Most popular majors.** Business/marketing 35%, education 20%, security/protective services 8%, social sciences 6%.

**Computing on campus.** 150 workstations in dormitories, library, computer center, student center. Dormitories wired for high-speed internet access and linked to campus network. Online course registration, online library, helpline, repair service, wireless network available.

**Student life. Freshman orientation:** Available. Preregistration for classes offered. **Policies:** Freshmen not within reasonable commuting distance required to live on campus for 2 years. **Housing:** Guaranteed on-campus for all undergraduates. Coed dorms, apartments, substance-free housing available. $100 deposit, deadline 5/1. **Activities:** Pep band, campus ministries, choral groups, dance, drama, international student organizations, musical theater, radio station, student government, student newspaper, ethnic awareness society, Knights of Columbus, community action program, Muscular Dystrophy Association, foreign student council, St. Vincent DePaul Society, Black Student Union.

**Athletics.** NCAA. **Intercollegiate:** Baseball M, basketball, cross-country, diving, golf M, ice hockey, lacrosse, soccer, softball W, swimming, tennis, volleyball W. **Intramural:** Baseball M, basketball, bowling, golf, racquetball, skiing, softball, volleyball W, water polo. **Team name:** Purple Eagles.

**Student services.** Adult student services, alcohol/substance abuse counseling, campus ministries, career counseling, services for economically disadvantaged, student employment services, financial aid counseling, health services, minority student services, personal counseling, placement for graduates, veterans' counselor.

**Contact.** E-mail: admissions@niagara.edu
Phone: (716) 286-8700 Fax: (716) 286-8733
Harry Gong, Director of Admissions, Niagara University, Niagara University, NY 14109

## Nyack College
Nyack, New York
www.nyack.edu
CB code: 2560

- Private 4-year liberal arts college affiliated with Christian and Missionary Alliance
- Residential campus in large town
- 2,019 degree-seeking undergraduates
- Application essay required

**General.** Founded in 1882. Regionally accredited. Extension center in Manhattan. **Degrees:** 485 bachelor's, 16 associate awarded; master's, first professional offered. **Location:** 25 miles from New York City. **Calendar:** Differs by program, limited summer session. **Full-time faculty:** 167 total. **Part-time faculty:** 187 total.

**Freshman class profile.**

| Mid 50% test scores | | | |
|---|---|---|---|
| SAT critical reading: | 400-530 | GPA 3.0-3.49: | 23% |
| SAT math: | 380-530 | GPA 2.0-2.99: | 42% |
| ACT composite: | 18-25 | Rank in top quarter: | 29% |
| GPA 3.50 or higher: | 22% | Rank in top tenth: | 12% |
| | | Live on campus: | 85% |

**Basis for selection.** Applicants must have Christian commitment and sign agreement to abide by community life standards. Academic record, class rank, and test scores most important. Pastor's recommendation required for students applying to traditional undergraduate program. Interview recommended for those with unsatisfactory recommendations or academic concerns; audition required for music program. **Homeschooled:** Transcript of courses and grades required. **Learning Disabled:** Students should inform their admissions counselors.

**High school preparation.** 16 units required. Required and recommended units include English 4, foreign language 2 and academic electives 4. 3 in any combination of math and science and 3 in any combination of history and social science recommended.

**2008-2009 Annual costs.** Tuition/fees: $18,300. Room/board: $7,800. Books/supplies: $750. Personal expenses: $2,060.

**2007-2008 Financial aid. Need-based:** 54% of total undergraduate aid awarded as scholarships/grants, 46% as loans/jobs. **Non-need-based:** Scholarships awarded for academics, alumni affiliation, art, athletics, leadership, minority status, music/drama, religious affiliation, state residency.

**Application procedures. Admission:** No deadline. $25 fee, may be waived for applicants with need. Application may be submitted online. Admission notification on a rolling basis. **Financial aid:** Priority date 3/1; no closing date. FAFSA required. Applicants notified on a rolling basis starting 3/1; must reply by 4/1 or within 4 week(s) of notification.

**Academics.** Adult degree completion program offers accelerated study option for adult students, with classes held throughout the New York metropolitan and lower Hudson Valley regions, Washington, DC and Dayton, Ohio. **Special study options:** Accelerated study, distance learning, double major, ESL, honors, independent study, internships, liberal arts/career combination, study abroad, teacher certification program, Washington semester. Adult degree completion program. **Credit/placement by examination:** AP, CLEP, SAT, institutional tests. 30 credit hours maximum toward bachelor's degree. **Support services:** Learning center, pre-admission summer program, reduced course load, remedial instruction, study skills assistance, tutoring, writing center.

**Majors. Business:** Accounting, business admin. **Communications:** General. **Computer sciences:** General. **Education:** Elementary, ESL, music. **English:** English lit. **History:** General. **Liberal arts:** Arts/sciences. **Math:** General. **Philosophy/religion:** Philosophy, religion. **Psychology:** General. **Public administration:** Social work. **Social sciences:** General. **Theology:** Religious ed, sacred music, theology. **Visual/performing arts:** Music performance, music theory/composition.

**Computing on campus.** 180 workstations in dormitories, library, computer center, student center. Online library, wireless network available.

**Student life. Freshman orientation:** Mandatory, $100 fee. Preregistration for classes offered. Usually 4 days the week prior to classes starting. **Policies:** Alcohol, tobacco, and narcotic drug use and possession prohibited on and off campus. Religious observance required. **Housing:** Single-sex dorms, apartments, substance-free housing available. $150 deposit. **Activities:** Choral groups, drama, literary magazine, music ensembles, musical theater, radio station, student government, student newspaper, symphony orchestra, African American Association of Cultural Exchange, missions committee, drama ensemble, Association of Latin American Students, Asian student organization, mime and interpretive dance group, business club, WNYK Radio, Student Chapter of Music Educators National Conference.

**Athletics.** NCAA, NCCAA. **Intercollegiate:** Baseball M, basketball, cheerleading, cross-country, golf M, soccer, softball W, volleyball W. **Team name:** Warriors.

**Student services.** Adult student services, alcohol/substance abuse counseling, campus ministries, career counseling, services for economically disadvantaged, student employment services, financial aid counseling, health services, personal counseling, placement for graduates. **Physically disabled:** Services for visually, hearing impaired.

**Contact.** E-mail: admissions@nyack.edu
Phone: (845) 358-1710 ext. 350 Toll-free number: (800) 336-9225
Fax: (845) 358-3047
Heather Rosenberg, Director of Admissions, Nyack College, 1 South Boulevard, Nyack, NY 10960-3698

---

## Ohr Somayach Tanenbaum Education Center

**Monsey, New York**
**www.ohrsomayach.edu**                    **CB code: 3357**

---

▶ Private 4-year rabbinical college for men affiliated with Jewish faith

▶ Residential campus in large town

**General.** Founded in 1979. Accredited by AARTS. **Location:** Half a mile from Spring Valley, 33 miles from New York City. **Calendar:** Semester.

**Annual costs/financial aid.** Books/supplies: $300. Personal expenses: $725.

**Contact.** Phone: (845) 425-1370
Dean of Students, 244 Route 306, Monsey, NY 10952

---

## Pace University

**New York, New York**                    **CB member**
**www.pace.edu**                           **CB code: 2635**

---

▶ Private 4-year university

▶ Residential campus in very large city

▶ 7,178 degree-seeking undergraduates: 16% part-time, 60% women

▶ 3,802 degree-seeking graduate students

▶ 79% of applicants admitted

▶ SAT or ACT (ACT writing optional), application essay required

▶ 51% graduate within 6 years

**General.** Founded in 1906. Regionally accredited. Four schools and one college of the university are located on New York City and Pleasantville campuses: Dyson College of Arts and Sciences, Lienhard School of Nursing, School of Education, Lubin School of Business, and Seidenberg School of Computer Science and Information Systems. The School of Law and Lubin Graduate Center are located in White Plains. **Degrees:** 1,781 bachelor's, 72 associate awarded; master's, doctoral, first professional offered. **ROTC:** Army. **Calendar:** Semester, limited summer session. **Full-time faculty:** 438 total; 84% have terminal degrees, 16% minority, 42% women. **Part-time faculty:** 684 total; 24% have terminal degrees, 15% minority, 51% women. **Class size:** 53% < 20, 44% 20-39, 2% 40-49, 1% 50-99, less than 1% >100. **Special facilities:** Arts center, multimedia language laboratory, speech and hearing center, studio theater.

**Freshman class profile.** 7,338 applied, 5,769 admitted, 1,545 enrolled.

| Mid 50% test scores | | Rank in top tenth: | 12% |
|---|---|---|---|
| SAT critical reading: | 480-580 | End year in good standing: | 71% |
| SAT math: | 490-590 | Return as sophomores: | 75% |
| ACT composite: | 20-26 | Out-of-state: | 38% |
| GPA 3.50 or higher: | 26% | Live on campus: | 61% |
| GPA 3.0-3.49: | 32% | International: | 3% |
| GPA 2.0-2.99: | 41% | Fraternities: | 2% |
| Rank in top quarter: | 38% | Sororities: | 2% |

**Basis for selection.** 85 high school GPA, rank in top half of class, test scores, recommendations, personal statement important. Extracurricular activities also considered. Non-native speakers of English required to take TOEFL. Official scores must be sent directly to school. Notarized copies not acceptable. Interviews strongly recommended; audition required for dance, dramatic arts, theater; portfolio recommended for art programs. Applicants to Lienhard School of Nursing must be certified in CPR. **Learning Disabled:** Diagnostic tests recommended.

**High school preparation.** 16 units required; 20 recommended. Required and recommended units include English 4, mathematics 3-4, social studies 1-2, history 2-3, science 2 (laboratory 2), foreign language 2-3 and academic electives 2.

**2007-2008 Annual costs.** Tuition/fees: $30,158. As of Fall 2007, the Guaranteed Tuition Plan will be discontinued. Students admitted in Fall 2007 and after will have a traditional tuition program and be subject to possible annual tuition increases. Room/board: $10,320. Books/supplies: $800. Personal expenses: $1,350.

**2007-2008 Financial aid. Need-based:** 1,322 full-time freshmen applied for aid; 1,190 were judged to have need; 1,150 of these received aid. Average need met was 88%. Average scholarship/grant was $14,247; average loan $4,042. 65% of total undergraduate aid awarded as scholarships/grants, 35% as loans/jobs. **Non-need-based:** Awarded to 1,306 full-time undergraduates, including 324 freshmen. Scholarships awarded for academics, athletics.

**Application procedures. Admission:** Closing date 3/1 (postmark date). $45 fee, may be waived for applicants with need. Application may be submitted online. Admission notification on a rolling basis beginning on or about 12/15. Must reply by May 1 or within 2 week(s) if notified thereafter. **Financial aid:** Priority date 2/15; no closing date. FAFSA required. Applicants notified on a rolling basis starting 2/28; must reply by 5/1 or within 2 week(s) of notification.

**Academics.** Adult undergraduate degrees in liberal/general studies, business and computer science. **Special study options:** Accelerated study, combined bachelor's/graduate degree, cooperative education, cross-registration, distance learning, double major, dual enrollment of high school students, ESL, honors, independent study, internships, study abroad, teacher certification program. Evening and freshman studies programs, pre-freshman summer program, learning communities and service learning. **Credit/placement by examination:** AP, CLEP, IB, institutional tests. 30 credit hours maximum toward associate degree, 96 toward bachelor's. **Support services:** Learning center, reduced course load, remedial instruction, study skills assistance, tutoring, writing center.

**Honors college/program.** Honors Program requires entering freshmen have 90 or higher high school GPA, SAT verbal minimum of 550, SAT math minimum of 550. Honors program students may be enrolled in any of undergraduate schools at university.

**Majors. Area/ethnic studies:** Women's. **Biology:** General, biochemistry. **Business:** General, accounting, business admin, e-commerce, entrepreneurial studies, finance, hotel/motel admin, human resources, international, international marketing, management science, marketing. **Communications:** General, advertising, journalism. **Computer sciences:** General, computer science, information systems, systems analysis. **Conservation:** Environmental studies. **Education:** Biology, chemistry, early childhood, elementary, English, French, history, mathematics, physics, science, social studies, Spanish, speech impaired. **English:** English lit. **Foreign languages:** General, Spanish. **Health:** Clinical lab science, communication disorders, nursing (RN), speech pathology. **History:** General. **Liberal arts:** Arts/sciences. **Math:** General. **Philosophy/religion:** Philosophy, religion. **Physical sciences:** Chemistry, geology. **Protective services:** Forensics, law enforcement admin. **Psychology:** General. **Public administration:** Community org/advocacy. **Social sciences:** General, economics, political science. **Visual/performing arts:** Art history/conservation, commercial/advertising art, dramatic.

**Most popular majors.** Business/marketing 41%, communications/journalism 10%, computer/information sciences 9%, health sciences 11%, psychology 6%.

**Computing on campus.** 250 workstations in library, computer center. Dormitories linked to campus network. Commuter students can connect to campus network. Online library, helpline, wireless network available.

**Student life. Freshman orientation:** Available, $75 fee. Preregistration for classes offered. Held during summer for small groups (strongly recommended); held in fall before school starts for large groups. **Housing:** Coed dorms, apartments, substance-free housing available. $400 nonrefundable deposit, deadline 5/1. Apartment style housing for upperclassmen available. **Activities:** Choral groups, dance, drama, film society, international student organizations, literary magazine, Model UN, musical theater, radio station, student government, student newspaper, TV station, collegiate Italian American organization, Asian cultural society, international student organization, Jewish student association, Pace Christian Fellowship, Caribbean student association, Arab student association, African students association, Sabor Latino.

**Athletics.** NCAA. **Intercollegiate:** Baseball M, basketball, cross-country, equestrian W, football (tackle) M, golf, lacrosse M, soccer W, softball W, swimming, tennis, track and field, volleyball W. **Intramural:** Basketball, football (non-tackle) M, soccer, softball, volleyball. **Team name:** Setters.

**Student services.** Adult student services, career counseling, student employment services, health services, personal counseling, placement for graduates, veterans' counselor. **Physically disabled:** Services for visually, speech, hearing impaired.

**Contact.**  E-mail: infoctr@pace.edu
Phone: (212) 346-1323 Toll-free number: (800) 874-7223
Fax: (212) 346-1040
Joanna Broda, Executive Director of Admissions, Pace University, 1 Pace Plaza, New York, NY 10038

## Pace University: Pleasantville/Briarcliff
**Pleasantville, New York**
www.pace.edu                              CB code: 2685

- Private 4-year university
- Residential campus in small town

**General.** Regionally accredited. **Location:** 7 miles from White Plains, 30 miles from New York City. **Calendar:** Semester.

**Annual costs/financial aid.** Tuition/fees (2007-2008): $30,158. As of Fall 2007, the Guaranteed Tuition Plan will be discontinued. Students admitted in Fall 2007 and after will have a traditional tuition program and be subject to possible annual tuition increases. Room/board: $10,320. Books/supplies: $800. Personal expenses: $1,350. Need-based financial aid available to full-time and part-time students.

**Contact.**  Phone: (914) 773-3746
Director of Admission, 861 Bedford Road, Pleasantville, NY 10570

## Parsons The New School for Design
**New York, New York**
www.parsons.edu                           CB code: 2638

- Private 4-year visual arts college
- Commuter campus in very large city
- 3,537 degree-seeking undergraduates: 7% part-time, 79% women, 4% African American, 17% Asian American, 7% Hispanic American, 33% international
- 411 degree-seeking graduate students
- 50% of applicants admitted
- SAT or ACT required
- 69% graduate within 6 years

**General.** Founded in 1896. Regionally accredited. Division of The New School. **Degrees:** 455 bachelor's, 408 associate awarded; master's offered. **Location:** Located in Manhattan. **Calendar:** Semester, extensive summer session. **Full-time faculty:** 132 total; 61% have terminal degrees, 14% minority, 48% women. **Part-time faculty:** 860 total; 15% minority, 49% women. **Class size:** 88% < 20, 11% 20-39, less than 1% 40-49, less than 1% 50-99, less than 1% >100. **Special facilities:** Architecture studio, labs, galleries.

**Freshman class profile.** 2,559 applied, 1,284 admitted, 595 enrolled.

| Mid 50% test scores | | GPA 2.0-2.99: | 24% |
|---|---|---|---|
| SAT critical reading: | 480-600 | End year in good standing: | 94% |
| SAT math: | 490-610 | Return as sophomores: | 86% |
| SAT writing: | 480-590 | Out-of-state: | 74% |
| ACT composite: | 20-26 | Live on campus: | 77% |
| GPA 3.50 or higher: | 37% | International: | 24% |
| GPA 3.0-3.49: | 37% | | |

**Basis for selection.** Portfolio and home examination most important, followed by school achievement record and test scores. Activities, leadership, motivation considered. Applicants required to complete home examination of 4 specific art and design problems as supplement to portfolio. Portfolio required, essay recommended for all; interview recommended, required for those geographically close.

**High school preparation.** Required units include English 4, social studies 4, history 4 and visual/performing arts 4.

**2007-2008 Annual costs.** Tuition/fees: $32,640. Room/board: $11,750. Books/supplies: $2,050. Personal expenses: $1,550.

**2007-2008 Financial aid. Need-based:** 444 full-time freshmen applied for aid; 444 were judged to have need; 442 of these received aid. Average need met was 56%. Average scholarship/grant was $8,458; average loan $3,280. 66% of total undergraduate aid awarded as scholarships/grants, 34% as loans/jobs. **Non-need-based:** Awarded to 2,282 full-time undergraduates, including 428 freshmen. Scholarships awarded for academics, art.

**Application procedures. Admission:** $50 fee, may be waived for applicants with need. Application may be submitted online. Admission notification on a rolling basis. Must reply by May 1 or within 4 week(s) if notified thereafter. **Financial aid:** Priority date 3/1; no closing date. FAFSA required. Applicants notified on a rolling basis starting 3/1; must reply within 4 week(s) of notification.

**Academics. Special study options:** Accelerated study, cooperative education, cross-registration, distance learning, dual enrollment of high school students, ESL, exchange student, independent study, internships, liberal arts/career combination, student-designed major, study abroad, teacher certification program. Five-year combined BA/BFA, New York Studio Program. **Credit/placement by examination:** CLEP, IB, institutional tests. **Support services:** Pre-admission summer program, remedial instruction, tutoring, writing center.

**Majors. Architecture:** Architecture, environmental design, interior, landscape. **Business:** Fashion. **Visual/performing arts:** Art, ceramics, commercial photography, commercial/advertising art, design, drawing, fashion design, fiber arts, interior design, metal/jewelry, painting, photography, sculpture, studio arts.

**Most popular majors.** Visual/performing arts 97%.

**Computing on campus.** 1,200 workstations in library, computer center. Dormitories wired for high-speed internet access and linked to campus network. Commuter students can connect to campus network. Online course registration, helpline, student web hosting, wireless network available.

**Student life. Freshman orientation:** Mandatory. Orientation to school, programs, services, and New York City. **Housing:** Coed dorms, special housing for disabled, apartments, substance-free housing available. $250 deposit, deadline 7/1. **Activities:** Bands, dance, drama, film society, international student organizations, literary magazine, music ensembles, musical theater, opera, radio station, student government, student newspaper, symphony orchestra, women's group, student union, Latino and African-American student organizations, gay/lesbian student organizations, volunteer groups, environmental group.

**Student services.** Alcohol/substance abuse counseling, career counseling, services for economically disadvantaged, student employment services, financial aid counseling, health services, minority student services, personal counseling, placement for graduates.

**Contact.**  E-mail: parsadm@newschool.edu
Phone: (212) 229-8989 Toll-free number: (877) 528-3321
Fax: (212) 229-8975
Anthony Padilla, Director of Admission, Parsons The New School for Design, 65 Fifth Avenue, New York, NY 10011

## Paul Smith's College
**Paul Smiths, New York**
www.paulsmiths.edu                        CB code: 2640

- Private 4-year liberal arts college
- Residential campus in rural community
- 912 degree-seeking undergraduates
- 86% of applicants admitted

**General.** Founded in 1937. Regionally accredited. Hands-on experience in major, internship programs within college, and externships with leading companies. **Degrees:** 85 bachelor's, 111 associate awarded. **Location:** 150 miles from Albany, 20 miles from Lake Placid. **Calendar:** Semester, limited summer session. **Full-time faculty:** 57 total; 30% have terminal degrees, 33%

women. **Part-time faculty:** 26 total; 15% have terminal degrees, 50% women. **Class size:** 60% < 20, 31% 20-39, 5% 40-49, 4% 50-99. **Special facilities:** Sugar maple plantation, sawmill, on-campus restaurant, 14,200-acre forest, on-campus retail bakery.

## Freshman class profile.

| Out-of-state: | 35% | Live on campus: | 97% |
| --- | --- | --- | --- |

**Basis for selection.** High school background most important. Test scores, relevant experience, letters of recommendation and essay considered. Interview recommended. **Homeschooled:** Statement describing homeschool structure and mission, transcript of courses and grades, interview, letter of recommendation (nonparent) required.

**High school preparation.** 4 units required; 8 recommended. Required and recommended units include English 4, mathematics 2, science 2 (laboratory 2) and foreign language 2. High school subject requirements vary according to program.

**2008-2009 Annual costs.** Tuition/fees: $19,250. Program fees range from $580 to $1,880 depending on program. Room/board: $8,350. Books/supplies: $1,000. Personal expenses: $1,250.

**Financial aid. Non-need-based:** Scholarships awarded for academics. **Additional information:** Merit aid only for international students; no financial aid application required.

**Application procedures. Admission:** No deadline. $30 fee, may be waived for applicants with need. Application may be submitted online. Admission notification on a rolling basis beginning on or about 10/1. **Financial aid:** Priority date 3/31; no closing date. FAFSA required. Applicants notified on a rolling basis starting 3/5; must reply within 4 week(s) of notification.

**Academics. Special study options:** Combined bachelor's/graduate degree, double major, honors, independent study, internships, liberal arts/career combination, study abroad. **Credit/placement by examination:** AP, CLEP, IB, institutional tests. 15 credit hours maximum toward associate degree, 15 toward bachelor's. **Support services:** Learning center, reduced course load, remedial instruction, study skills assistance, tutoring, writing center.

**Majors. Biology:** General. **Business:** General, business admin, entrepreneurial studies, hospitality admin, hospitality/recreation, hotel/motel admin, resort management, restaurant/food services, tourism promotion, tourism/travel. **Conservation:** General, environmental science, fisheries, forest management, forest resources, forest sciences, forestry, management/policy, wildlife. **Health:** Predental, premedicine, preveterinary. **Interdisciplinary:** Biological/physical sciences. **Liberal arts:** Arts/sciences. **Parks/recreation:** General, facilities management. **Personal/culinary services:** Chef training, culinary arts, restaurant/catering.

**Most popular majors.** Business/marketing 17%, natural resources/environmental science 41%, parks/recreation 12%, personal/culinary services 27%.

**Computing on campus.** 140 workstations in library, computer center. Dormitories wired for high-speed internet access and linked to campus network. Commuter students can connect to campus network. Online library, helpline, student web hosting available.

**Student life. Freshman orientation:** Mandatory, $100 fee. **Housing:** Guaranteed on-campus for all undergraduates. Coed dorms, single-sex dorms, substance-free housing available. $100 nonrefundable deposit, deadline 5/1. **Activities:** Choral groups, literary magazine, radio station, student government, student newspaper, outing club, gaming and Anime club, conservation club, Junior American Culinary Federation, Christian Fellowship, fiber arts, fish and game club, ski and snowboard club, campus council.

**Athletics.** NAIA. **Intercollegiate:** Basketball, cross-country, rugby, soccer, volleyball W. **Intramural:** Basketball, ice hockey M, rugby, skiing, soccer, softball, volleyball, water polo. **Team name:** Bobcats.

**Student services.** Adult student services, alcohol/substance abuse counseling, campus ministries, career counseling, services for economically disadvantaged, student employment services, financial aid counseling, health services, personal counseling, placement for graduates. **Physically disabled:** Services for visually, hearing impaired.

**Contact.** E-mail: admiss@paulsmiths.edu
Phone: (518) 327-6227 Toll-free number: (800) 421-2605
Fax: (518) 327-6016
Bill Carter, Dean of Admissions, Paul Smith's College, PO Box 265, Routes 30 & 86, Paul Smiths, NY 12970-0265

---

## Polytechnic University

**Brooklyn, New York**
www.poly.edu

**CB member**
**CB code: 2668**

- Private 4-year university
- Commuter campus in very large city
- 1,467 degree-seeking undergraduates: 4% part-time, 19% women, 12% African American, 30% Asian American, 12% Hispanic American, 13% international
- 1,765 degree-seeking graduate students
- 73% of applicants admitted
- SAT or ACT, application essay required
- 47% graduate within 6 years; 22% enter graduate study

**General.** Founded in 1854. Regionally accredited. **Degrees:** 266 bachelor's awarded; master's, doctoral offered. **ROTC:** Army. **Location:** 2 miles from New York City. **Calendar:** Semester, extensive summer session. **Full-time faculty:** 140 total; 90% have terminal degrees, 24% minority, 19% women. **Part-time faculty:** 140 total; 63% have terminal degrees, 16% minority, 19% women. **Class size:** 55% < 20, 40% 20-39, 4% 40-49, 2% 50-99. **Special facilities:** Library of science and technology, center for advanced technology in telecommunications, institute of imaging sciences, center for construction management technology, transportation research institute, wireless research institute, urban infrastructure institute.

**Freshman class profile.** 1,482 applied, 1,075 admitted, 331 enrolled.

| Mid 50% test scores | | End year in good standing: | 78% |
| --- | --- | --- | --- |
| SAT critical reading: | 470-600 | Return as sophomores: | 84% |
| SAT math: | 560-680 | Out-of-state: | 8% |
| GPA 3.50 or higher: | 39% | Live on campus: | 29% |
| GPA 3.0-3.49: | 33% | International: | 13% |
| GPA 2.0-2.99: | 27% | Fraternities: | 6% |
| Rank in top quarter: | 61% | Sororities: | 3% |
| Rank in top tenth: | 31% | | |

**Basis for selection.** School achievement record, class rank, test scores, recommendations required. Special emphasis on mathematics and science areas. Interview recommended.

**High school preparation.** Required and recommended units include English 4, mathematics 4, social studies 3, science 4, foreign language 2 and academic electives 2. Requirements include 1 chemistry, pre-calculus, calculus.

**2007-2008 Annual costs.** Tuition/fees: $30,972. Room/board: $8,500. Books/supplies: $1,000. Personal expenses: $1,575.

**2006-2007 Financial aid. Need-based:** 379 full-time freshmen applied for aid; 297 were judged to have need; 297 of these received aid. Average need met was 93%. Average scholarship/grant was $8,413; average loan $2,917. 66% of total undergraduate aid awarded as scholarships/grants, 34% as loans/jobs. **Non-need-based:** Awarded to 1,105 full-time undergraduates, including 342 freshmen. Scholarships awarded for academics.

**Application procedures. Admission:** Priority date 2/1; no deadline. $50 fee, may be waived for applicants with need. Application may be submitted online. Admission notification on a rolling basis beginning on or about 2/1. Must reply by May 1 or within 4 week(s) if notified thereafter. **Financial aid:** Priority date 3/1; no closing date. FAFSA, institutional form, CSS PROFILE required. Applicants notified on a rolling basis starting 3/15; must reply within 2 week(s) of notification.

**Academics. Special study options:** Accelerated study, combined bachelor's/graduate degree, cooperative education, distance learning, double major, honors, internships, study abroad. Joint master's degree program in dental materials science with New York University. **Credit/placement by examination:** AP, CLEP, IB, institutional tests. 16 credit hours maximum toward bachelor's degree. Students with outstanding record or specialized competence may establish 16 credits maximum toward baccalaureate degree by passing comprehensive examinations. Each department determines courses in which examination available and examination format. **Support services:** Learning center, pre-admission summer program, remedial instruction, study skills assistance, tutoring, writing center.

**Honors college/program.** Students selected for Honors College must have superior high school academic records and interview with member of Honors College Faculty Governing Board.

**Majors. Biology:** Molecular biochemistry. **Business:** Construction management, management information systems. **Communications:** Journalism. **Computer sciences:** General, computer science. **Engineering:** Chemical, civil, computer, electrical, mechanical. **Liberal arts:** Arts/sciences. **Math:** General. **Physical sciences:** Chemistry, physics.

**Most popular majors.** Business/marketing 13%, computer/information sciences 15%, engineering/engineering technologies 65%.

**Computing on campus.** PC or laptop required. 104 workstations in dormitories, library, computer center, student center. Dormitories linked to campus network. Commuter students can connect to campus network. On-line library, helpline, repair service, student web hosting, wireless network available.

**Student life. Freshman orientation:** Available. **Housing:** Guaranteed on-campus for freshmen. Coed dorms, fraternity/sorority housing, substance-free housing available. $300 nonrefundable deposit. **Activities:** Film society, literary magazine, radio station, student government, student newspaper, Society of Women Engineers, Society of Black Engineers, Ambassador Society, ethnic and service organizations, Society of Hispanic Professional Engineers, Alpha Phi Omega service fraternity.

**Athletics.** NCAA. **Intercollegiate:** Baseball M, basketball, cross-country, judo, soccer, softball W, tennis, track and field, volleyball. **Intramural:** Basketball, bowling, football (non-tackle), golf, handball M, ice hockey M, racquetball, skiing, soccer, softball W, table tennis, track and field, volleyball, weight lifting. **Team name:** Blue Jays.

**Student services.** Career counseling, student employment services, placement for graduates.

**Contact.** E-mail: uadmit@poly.edu
Phone: (718) 260-3100 Toll-free number: (800) 765-9832
Fax: (718) 260-3446
Joy Colelli, Dean of Admissions and New Students, Polytechnic University, 6 Metrotech Center, Brooklyn, NY 11201-2999

---

## Pratt Institute
**Brooklyn, New York**
www.pratt.edu

**CB member**
**CB code: 2669**

▶ Private 4-year university and visual arts college
▶ Residential campus in very large city
▶ 3,040 degree-seeking undergraduates: 5% part-time, 60% women, 7% African American, 13% Asian American, 8% Hispanic American, 10% international
▶ 1,587 degree-seeking graduate students
▶ 43% of applicants admitted
▶ SAT or ACT with writing, application essay required

**General.** Founded in 1887. Regionally accredited. Additional campus located in Manhattan with associate degree programs, bachelor's degree in construction management program, and various graduate programs. **Degrees:** 566 bachelor's, 38 associate awarded; master's offered. **Location:** 2 miles from Manhattan. **Calendar:** Semester, extensive summer session. **Full-time faculty:** 119 total; 52% have terminal degrees, 8% minority, 36% women. **Part-time faculty:** 820 total; 16% minority, 43% women. **Class size:** 88% < 20, 12% 20-39, less than 1% 40-49, less than 1% 50-99. **Special facilities:** Wood and metal workshops, ceramics kiln studios and casting foundry, digital arts labs, printmaking workshop, fine arts center, center for community development.

**Freshman class profile.** 4,341 applied, 1,881 admitted, 586 enrolled.

| Mid 50% test scores | | | |
|---|---|---|---|
| SAT critical reading: | 510-640 | GPA 3.0-3.49: | 33% |
| SAT math: | 520-630 | GPA 2.0-2.99: | 13% |
| ACT composite: | 22-27 | Out-of-state: | 64% |
| GPA 3.50 or higher: | 53% | Live on campus: | 82% |
| | | International: | 10% |

**Basis for selection.** Admissions committee considers overall academic record which includes academic performance, portfolio, curriculum, test scores, recommendation, and essay. SAT Subject Tests recommended for applicants to architecture program. Interview not required. Letter of recommendation required for all applicants. Portfolio required for architecture, art and design programs.

**High school preparation.** 16 units recommended. Recommended units include English 4, mathematics 4, social studies 1, science 2 and academic electives 5. 4 math required for architecture and construction management applicants.

**2007-2008 Annual costs.** Tuition/fees: $31,080. All architecture students required to purchase laptop and software (discounted) during summer. All sophomore interior design majors required to purchase laptop computer. Laptop costs approximately $3,600. Room/board: $8,918. Books/supplies: $3,000. Personal expenses: $1,000.

**Financial aid. Non-need-based:** Scholarships awarded for academics, art.

**Application procedures. Admission:** Closing date 1/5 (postmark date). $50 fee, may be waived for applicants with need. Application may be submitted online. Admission notification 4/1. Must reply by May 1 or within 2 week(s) if notified thereafter. 2 regular admission deadlines: January 1 and February 1. January 1 applicants notified by March 1; February 1 applicants notified by beginning of April. AAS/AOS admissions on rolling basis. **Financial aid:** Closing date 2/1. FAFSA, institutional form required. Applicants notified on a rolling basis starting 3/11; must reply within 2 week(s) of notification.

**Academics. Special study options:** ESL, exchange student, independent study, internships, study abroad, teacher certification program. **Credit/placement by examination:** CLEP, institutional tests. **Support services:** Learning center, pre-admission summer program, reduced course load, study skills assistance, tutoring, writing center.

**Majors. Architecture:** Architecture. **Business:** Construction management. **Computer sciences:** Computer graphics. **Construction:** Site management. **Education:** Art. **English:** Creative writing. **Visual/performing arts:** Art history/conservation, cinematography, design, digital art, fashion design, industrial design, interior design, photography, studio arts. **Other:** Critical and visual studies.

**Most popular majors.** Architecture 17%, visual/performing arts 74%.

**Computing on campus.** 300 workstations in dormitories, library, computer center, student center. Dormitories wired for high-speed internet access and linked to campus network. Commuter students can connect to campus network. Online course registration, helpline, repair service, student web hosting, wireless network available.

**Student life. Freshman orientation:** Available. Preregistration for classes offered. **Housing:** Guaranteed on-campus for freshmen. Coed dorms, apartments, substance-free housing available. $300 fully refundable deposit, deadline 5/1. **Activities:** Film society, literary magazine, music ensembles, radio station, student government, student newspaper, TV station, Christian Fellowship, Jewish student union, Muslim student association, Asian student organization, The Agenda, Korean student association, environmental resource group, Gay/Lesbian at Pratt, New York Public Interest Research Group, Pratt Projects (socially conscious project design and creation).

**Athletics.** NCAA. **Intercollegiate:** Basketball M, cross-country, soccer, tennis, track and field, volleyball W. **Intramural:** Badminton, basketball, football (non-tackle) M, weight lifting. **Team name:** Canonneers.

**Student services.** Alcohol/substance abuse counseling, campus ministries, career counseling, student employment services, financial aid counseling, health services, minority student services, personal counseling, placement for graduates, veterans' counselor. **Physically disabled:** Services for visually, speech, hearing impaired.

**Contact.** E-mail: visit@pratt.edu
Phone: (718) 636-3514 Toll-free number: (800) 331-0834
Fax: (718) 636-3670
William Swan, Director of Admissions, Pratt Institute, 200 Willoughby Avenue, Brooklyn, NY 11205-3817

---

## Rabbinical Academy Mesivta Rabbi Chaim Berlin
**Brooklyn, New York**

**CB code: 0719**

▶ Private 4-year rabbinical college for men affiliated with Jewish faith
▶ Very large city

**General.** Accredited by AARTS. **Calendar:** Continuous.

**Annual costs/financial aid.** Tuition/fees (2007-2008): $8,000. Room/board: $3,000.

**Contact.** Phone: (718) 377-0777
Admissions Director, 1605 Coney Island Avenue, Brooklyn, NY 11230

---

## Rabbinical College Beth Shraga
**Monsey, New York**

▶ Private 4-year rabbinical college for men affiliated with Jewish faith
▶ Commuter campus in large town

**General. Calendar:** Continuous.

**Annual costs/financial aid.** Tuition/fees (2007-2008): $8,600. Room/board: $4,000.

**Contact.** Phone: (845) 356-1980
Admissions Director, PO Box 412, Monsey, NY 10952

## Rabbinical College Bobover Yeshiva B'nei Zion
### Brooklyn, New York
**CB code: 7011**

♦ Private 5-year rabbinical college for men affiliated with Jewish faith
♦ Very large city

**General.** Accredited by AARTS. **Calendar:** Continuous.

**Annual costs/financial aid.** Tuition/fees (2007-2008): $4,700. Room/board: $3,000. Books/supplies: $400. Personal expenses: $500.

**Contact.** Phone: (718) 438-2018
Director, 1577 48th Street, Brooklyn, NY 11219

## Rabbinical College Ch'san Sofer of New York
### Brooklyn, New York
**CB code: 0714**

♦ Private 4-year rabbinical college for men affiliated with Jewish faith
♦ Very large city

**General.** Founded in 1940. Accredited by AARTS. **Calendar:** Semester.

**Contact.** Phone: (718) 236-1171
Dean of the College, 1876 50th Street, Brooklyn, NY 11204

## Rabbinical College of Long Island
### Long Beach, New York
**CB code: 0675**

♦ Private 4-year rabbinical and teachers college for men affiliated with Jewish faith
♦ Large town

**General.** Founded in 1965. Accredited by AARTS. **Calendar:** Trimester.

**Contact.** Phone: (516) 431-7414
Director of Admissions, 205 West Beech Street, Long Beach, NY 11561

## Rabbinical College of Ohr Shimon Yisroel
### Brooklyn, New York

♦ Private 4-year rabbinical college for men
♦ Very large city

**General.** Accredited by AARTS. **Calendar:** Semester.

**Contact.** Phone: (718) 855-4092
215-217 Hewes Street, Brooklyn, NY 11211

## Rabbinical Seminary Adas Yereim
### Brooklyn, New York
**CB code: 0666**

♦ Private 4-year rabbinical college for men affiliated with Jewish faith
♦ Very large city

**General.** Founded in 1961. Accredited by AARTS. **Calendar:** Semester.

**Annual costs/financial aid.** Tuition/fees (2007-2008): $5,200.

**Contact.** Phone: (718) 388-1751
Director of Finances, 185 Wilson Street, Brooklyn, NY 11211

## Rabbinical Seminary of America
### Flushing, New York
**CB code: 2776**

♦ Private 5-year seminary college for men affiliated with Jewish faith
♦ Very large city

**General.** Founded in 1933. Accredited by AARTS. **Calendar:** Semester.

**Contact.** Phone: (718) 268-4700
Registrar, 76-01 147th Street, Flushing, NY 11367

## Rensselaer Polytechnic Institute
### Troy, New York
**CB member**
www.rpi.edu
**CB code: 2757**

♦ Private 4-year university
♦ Residential campus in small city
♦ 5,119 degree-seeking undergraduates: 27% women, 4% African American, 10% Asian American, 6% Hispanic American, 2% international
♦ 2,011 degree-seeking graduate students
♦ 49% of applicants admitted
♦ SAT or ACT with writing, application essay required
♦ 82% graduate within 6 years; 25% enter graduate study

**General.** Founded in 1824. Regionally accredited. **Degrees:** 1,244 bachelor's awarded; master's, doctoral offered. **ROTC:** Army, Naval, Air Force. **Location:** 10 miles from Albany, 150 miles from New York City. **Calendar:** Semester, extensive summer session. **Full-time faculty:** 400 total; 98% have terminal degrees, 17% minority, 21% women. **Part-time faculty:** 70 total; 9% minority, 23% women. **Class size:** 44% < 20, 41% 20-39, 6% 40-49, 9% 50-99, less than 1% >100. **Special facilities:** Center for Terahertz Research, Nanoscale Science and Engineering Center, linear accelerator laboratory, observatory, Incubator Center, Fresh Water Institute, Lighting Research Center, Social and Behavioral Research Laboratory, Center for Biotechnology and Interdisciplinary Studies, Computational Center for Nanotechnology Innovations, Geotechnical Centrifuge Research Center, Artificial Intelligence and Reasoning Lab, Human-Level Intelligence Laboratory.

**Freshman class profile.** 10,162 applied, 5,021 admitted, 1,288 enrolled.

| Mid 50% test scores | | Rank in top tenth: | 64% |
|---|---|---|---|
| SAT critical reading: | 600-690 | End year in good standing: | 94% |
| SAT math: | 650-730 | Return as sophomores: | 92% |
| SAT writing: | 580-670 | Out-of-state: | 63% |
| ACT composite: | 25-29 | Live on campus: | 98% |
| GPA 3.50 or higher: | 79% | International: | 2% |
| GPA 3.0-3.49: | 20% | Fraternities: | 26% |
| GPA 2.0-2.99: | 1% | Sororities: | 11% |
| Rank in top quarter: | 95% | | |

**Basis for selection.** School achievement record important, test scores and essay required, activities considered. SAT Subject Tests in a math and a science required of accelerated program applicants, or ACT (must include optional writing component) in lieu of SAT and SAT Subject Tests. TOEFL required of international applicants. Portfolio required for electronic arts, highly recommended for architecture.

**High school preparation.** 15 units required. Required and recommended units include English 4, mathematics 4, social studies 2-3 and science 3-4. Best suited applicants will have completed 4 math through precalculus, 3 science, and 2 social studies and/or history.

**2007-2008 Annual costs.** Tuition/fees: $35,878. Room/board: $10,420. Books/supplies: $1,802.

**2007-2008 Financial aid. Need-based:** 1,014 full-time freshmen applied for aid; 815 were judged to have need; 815 of these received aid. Average need met was 85%. Average scholarship/grant was $21,734; average loan $6,507. 74% of total undergraduate aid awarded as scholarships/grants, 26% as loans/jobs. **Non-need-based:** Awarded to 1,936 full-time undergraduates, including 595 freshmen. Scholarships awarded for academics, alumni affiliation, art, athletics, leadership, minority status, music/drama, ROTC.

**Application procedures. Admission:** Closing date 1/15 (postmark date). $70 fee, may be waived for applicants with need. Application may be submitted online. Admission notification 3/14. Must reply by 5/1. **Financial**

**aid:** Closing date 2/15. FAFSA, CSS PROFILE required. Applicants notified by 3/25.

**Academics.** Extensive accelerated program offerings available in virtually all Science departments including Computer Science, Physics, Applied Physics, Biology, Biology, Biochemistry and Biophysics, Geology and Hydrology, leading to the BS-PhD. **Special study options:** Accelerated study, combined bachelor's/graduate degree, cooperative education, cross-registration, distance learning, double major, dual enrollment of high school students, ESL, exchange student, honors, independent study, internships, liberal arts/career combination, student-designed major, study abroad. BS/MD with Albany Medical College; BS/JD with Columbia University and Albany Law School. **Credit/placement by examination:** AP, CLEP, IB. **Support services:** Learning center, pre-admission summer program, reduced course load, study skills assistance, tutoring, writing center.

**Majors. Architecture:** Architecture. **Biology:** General, biochemistry, biophysics. **Business:** Business admin. **Communications:** General, digital media. **Computer sciences:** General, computer science, information technology. **Conservation:** Environmental science. **Education:** Mathematics, science. **Engineering:** General, aerospace, biomedical, chemical, civil, computer, electrical, environmental, industrial, materials, mechanical, mechanics, nuclear, physics, science, systems. **Engineering technology:** Industrial management. **Foreign languages:** German. **Health:** Predental, premedicine. **Interdisciplinary:** Biological/physical sciences, science/society. **Legal studies:** Prelaw. **Liberal arts:** Arts/sciences. **Math:** General. **Philosophy/religion:** Philosophy. **Physical sciences:** Chemistry, geology, hydrology, physics. **Psychology:** General. **Social sciences:** Economics. **Visual/performing arts:** Studio arts. **Other:** Games and Simulation Arts and Sciences.

**Most popular majors.** Biology 6%, business/marketing 8%, computer/information sciences 13%, engineering/engineering technologies 55%.

**Computing on campus.** PC or laptop required. 3,115 workstations in dormitories, library, computer center, student center. Dormitories wired for high-speed internet access and linked to campus network. Commuter students can connect to campus network. Online course registration, online library, helpline, repair service, student web hosting, wireless network available.

**Student life. Freshman orientation:** Mandatory, $175 fee. Preregistration for classes offered. Held over 2-day period in July or August. **Policies:** College housing required of all freshmen unless student lives within 50-mile radius of campus with parent(s) or legal guardian(s). **Housing:** Guaranteed on-campus for freshmen. Coed dorms, special housing for disabled, apartments, fraternity/sorority housing, substance-free housing available. Living/learning program available. **Activities:** Bands, choral groups, dance, drama, film society, international student organizations, literary magazine, music ensembles, musical theater, radio station, student government, student newspaper, symphony orchestra, TV station, student-run union; 160 athletic, service, media, multicultural, performing arts, visual arts, religious clubs and organizations.

**Athletics.** NCAA. **Intercollegiate:** Baseball M, basketball, cross-country, diving, field hockey W, football (tackle) M, golf M, ice hockey, lacrosse, soccer, softball W, swimming, tennis, track and field. **Intramural:** Baseball, basketball, bowling, football (non-tackle), golf, ice hockey, racquetball, soccer, softball, swimming, table tennis, track and field, volleyball, water polo. **Team name:** Redhawks, Engineers.

**Student services.** Alcohol/substance abuse counseling, campus ministries, career counseling, services for economically disadvantaged, student employment services, financial aid counseling, health services, legal services, minority student services, personal counseling, placement for graduates, women's services. **Physically disabled:** Services for visually, speech, hearing impaired. **Learning disabled:** Comprehensive services available.

**Contact.** E-mail: admissions@rpi.edu
Phone: (518) 276-6216 Fax: (518) 276-4072
James Nondorf, Vice President for Enrollment, Rensselaer Polytechnic Institute, 110 Eighth Street, Troy, NY 12180-3590

---

## Roberts Wesleyan College
**Rochester, New York**
**www.roberts.edu**

CB member
CB code: 2759

- Private 4-year liberal arts college affiliated with Free Methodist Church of North America
- Residential campus in large city
- 1,312 degree-seeking undergraduates: 10% part-time, 69% women, 8% African American, 1% Asian American, 3% Hispanic American, 2% international
- 518 degree-seeking graduate students
- 63% of applicants admitted

- SAT or ACT (ACT writing recommended), application essay required
- 61% graduate within 6 years

**General.** Founded in 1866. Regionally accredited. **Degrees:** 378 bachelor's awarded; master's offered. **ROTC:** Army, Air Force. **Location:** 8 miles from downtown. **Calendar:** Semester, limited summer session. **Full-time faculty:** 112 total; 64% have terminal degrees, 10% minority, 46% women. **Part-time faculty:** 134 total; 20% have terminal degrees, 8% minority, 59% women. **Class size:** 66% < 20, 31% 20-39, 1% 40-49, 1% 50-99.

**Freshman class profile.** 1,531 applied, 957 admitted, 255 enrolled.

| Mid 50% test scores | | | |
|---|---|---|---|
| SAT critical reading: | 470-590 | GPA 2.0-2.99: | 22% |
| SAT math: | 450-590 | Rank in top quarter: | 44% |
| SAT writing: | 460-580 | Rank in top tenth: | 23% |
| ACT composite: | 20-25 | Return as sophomores: | 80% |
| GPA 3.50 or higher: | 45% | Out-of-state: | 13% |
| GPA 3.0-3.49: | 33% | Live on campus: | 76% |
| | | International: | 2% |

**Basis for selection.** Rank in top 30% of high school class, 2.9 GPA, recommendations, test scores, and interview important. Students expected to recognize Christian perspectives and values college upholds. Audition required for music program; portfolio required for art education, studio art. **Homeschooled:** Transcript of courses and grades, state high school equivalency certificate, letter of recommendation (nonparent) required. Strongly recommend applicants visit.

**High school preparation.** 12 units required. Required and recommended units include English 4, mathematics 2-4, social studies 2-3, history 3, science 4 (laboratory 3) and foreign language 3. Biology and chemistry required of nursing applicants.

**2007-2008 Annual costs.** Tuition/fees: $21,352. Room/board: $7,774. Books/supplies: $800. Personal expenses: $1,575.

**2006-2007 Financial aid. Need-based:** 194 full-time freshmen applied for aid; 180 were judged to have need; 180 of these received aid. Average need met was 81%. Average scholarship/grant was $12,647; average loan $5,037. 58% of total undergraduate aid awarded as scholarships/grants, 42% as loans/jobs. **Non-need-based:** Awarded to 221 full-time undergraduates, including 64 freshmen. Scholarships awarded for academics, alumni affiliation, art, athletics, music/drama, religious affiliation, ROTC, state residency. **Additional information:** Dollars for Scholars offer matching grants of up to $750.

**Application procedures. Admission:** Priority date 2/1; deadline 8/15 (postmark date). $35 fee, may be waived for applicants with need. Application may be submitted online. Admission notification on a rolling basis. Must reply by May 1 or within 2 week(s) if notified thereafter. **Financial aid:** Priority date 3/15; no closing date. FAFSA required. Applicants notified on a rolling basis starting 3/15; must reply by 5/1 or within 2 week(s) of notification.

**Academics. Special study options:** Cross-registration, distance learning, double major, dual enrollment of high school students, ESL, honors, independent study, internships, liberal arts/career combination, study abroad, teacher certification program, Washington semester. **Credit/placement by examination:** AP, CLEP, IB. 30 credit hours maximum toward bachelor's degree. **Support services:** Learning center, reduced course load, remedial instruction, study skills assistance, tutoring, writing center.

**Majors. Biology:** General, biochemistry. **Business:** General, accounting, business admin, human resources, marketing. **Communications:** General. **Computer sciences:** General, computer science. **Education:** Art, biology, chemistry, early childhood, elementary, English, history, kindergarten/preschool, mathematics, music, physics, science, social science, social studies, Spanish, special. **English:** English lit. **Foreign languages:** Spanish. **Health:** Nursing (RN), preop/surgical nursing. **History:** General. **Interdisciplinary:** Biological/physical sciences. **Liberal arts:** Arts/sciences, humanities. **Math:** General. **Philosophy/religion:** Religion. **Physical sciences:** Chemistry, physics. **Protective services:** Forensics, law enforcement admin. **Psychology:** General. **Public administration:** Social work. **Social sciences:** General, sociology. **Theology:** Bible, theology. **Visual/performing arts:** Commercial/advertising art, piano/organ, studio arts, voice/opera. **Other:** Economic Crime Investigation.

**Most popular majors.** Business/marketing 26%, education 20%, health sciences 19%, visual/performing arts 6%.

**Computing on campus.** 250 workstations in library, computer center. Dormitories wired for high-speed internet access and linked to campus network. Commuter students can connect to campus network. Online course registration, online library, helpline, wireless network available.

**Student life. Freshman orientation:** Mandatory. Preregistration for classes offered. **Policies:** Religious observance required. **Housing:** Guaranteed on-campus for freshmen. Single-sex dorms, special housing for disabled, apartments, substance-free housing available. $100 deposit, deadline 5/1. **Activities:** Bands, campus ministries, choral groups, dance, drama, international student organizations, music ensembles, musical theater, opera, radio station, student government, student newspaper, symphony orchestra.

**Athletics.** NAIA, NCCAA. **Intercollegiate:** Basketball, cross-country, golf, soccer, tennis, track and field, volleyball W. **Intramural:** Basketball, cross-country, football (non-tackle), racquetball, soccer, softball, table tennis, tennis, track and field, volleyball, water polo. **Team name:** Raiders.

**Student services.** Adult student services, alcohol/substance abuse counseling, campus ministries, career counseling, student employment services, financial aid counseling, health services, personal counseling, placement for graduates, veterans' counselor. **Physically disabled:** Services for visually, hearing impaired.

**Contact.** E-mail: admissions@roberts.edu
Phone: (585) 594-6400 Toll-free number: (800) 777-4792
Fax: (585) 594-6371
Linda Hoffman, Vice President for Admissions and Marketing, Roberts Wesleyan College, 2301 Westside Drive, Rochester, NY 14624-1997

---

## Rochester Institute of Technology

| **Rochester, New York** | **CB member** |
|---|---|
| **www.rit.edu** | **CB code: 2760** |

- Private 4-year university
- Residential campus in large city
- 12,779 degree-seeking undergraduates: 7% part-time, 32% women
- 2,513 graduate students
- 65% of applicants admitted
- SAT or ACT (ACT writing optional), application essay required
- 64% graduate within 6 years; 11% enter graduate study

**General.** Founded in 1829. Regionally accredited. University comprises 8 colleges, including National Technical Institute for the Deaf. **Degrees:** 2,432 bachelor's, 379 associate awarded; master's, doctoral offered. **ROTC:** Army, Naval, Air Force. **Location:** 5 miles from downtown, 70 miles from Buffalo. **Calendar:** Quarter, extensive summer session. **Full-time faculty:** 816 total; 70% have terminal degrees, 19% minority, 33% women. **Part-time faculty:** 417 total; 36% women. **Class size:** 40% < 20, 41% 20-39, 12% 40-49, 7% 50-99, less than 1% >100. **Special facilities:** Laser optics laboratory, observatory, animal care facility, color and black-and-white photography darkrooms, electronic prepress and publishing equipment, ceramic kilns, glass furnaces, blacksmithing area, student-operated restaurant, computer graphics and robotic labs, microelectronic, telecommunications, and computer engineering facilities, access to Internet 2 research network.

**Freshman class profile.** 11,012 applied, 7,112 admitted, 2,503 enrolled.

| Mid 50% test scores | | Return as sophomores: | 89% |
|---|---|---|---|
| SAT critical reading: | 530-630 | Out-of-state: | 51% |
| SAT math: | 560-670 | Live on campus: | 95% |
| ACT composite: | 24-29 | Fraternities: | 5% |
| Rank in top quarter: | 59% | Sororities: | 5% |
| Rank in top tenth: | 26% | | |

**Basis for selection.** Primary emphasis on high school grades in required courses, which vary by major. SAT or ACT given considerable weight. Class rank important. Candidates allowed to apply for up to 3 majors. ACT preferred for applicants to National Technical Institute for the Deaf. Interview recommended for all; portfolio required for art, crafts, and design programs. **Homeschooled:** Applicants should provide state certification of graduation if available.

**High school preparation.** 22 units required. Required and recommended units include English 4, mathematics 2-3, social studies 4, science 2-3 (laboratory 1-2), foreign language 2 and academic electives 10. Units required for social studies may be met with history courses. College of Engineering requires 4 math including precalculus.

**2008-2009 Annual costs.** Tuition/fees: $28,035. Room/board: $9,381. Books/supplies: $900. Personal expenses: $600.

**2006-2007 Financial aid. Need-based:** 2,071 full-time freshmen applied for aid; 1,736 were judged to have need; 1,733 of these received aid. Average need met was 88%. Average scholarship/grant was $12,700; average loan $5,000. 66% of total undergraduate aid awarded as scholarships/grants, 34% as loans/jobs. **Non-need-based:** Awarded to 3,218 full-time

undergraduates, including 776 freshmen. Scholarships awarded for academics, art, leadership, ROTC. **Additional information:** Most juniors and seniors participate in cooperative education program, earning an average $4,500-$6,500 per 3-month employment period through paid employment in jobs related to major.

**Application procedures. Admission:** Priority date 2/1; no deadline. $50 fee, may be waived for applicants with need. Application may be submitted online. Admission notification on a rolling basis beginning on or about 3/1. Must reply by May 1 or within 2 week(s) if notified thereafter. Applications received after March 15 will be processed if space available. **Financial aid:** Priority date 3/1; no closing date. FAFSA required. Applicants notified on a rolling basis starting 3/15; must reply by 5/1.

**Academics. Special study options:** Accelerated study, combined bachelor's/graduate degree, cooperative education, cross-registration, distance learning, double major, ESL, exchange student, honors, independent study, internships, liberal arts/career combination, student-designed major, study abroad, teacher certification program, weekend college. Accelerated bachelor's/master's degree programs, England semester, Japan semester, summer program in Croatia. **Credit/placement by examination:** AP, CLEP, IB, SAT, ACT, institutional tests. 45 credit hours maximum toward associate degree. **Support services:** Learning center, pre-admission summer program, reduced course load, study skills assistance, tutoring, writing center.

**Majors. Biology:** General, biochemistry, bioinformatics, biomedical sciences, biotechnology. **Business:** General, accounting, accounting/business management, business admin, finance, hospitality admin, hotel/motel admin, international, management information systems, market research, marketing, resort management, restaurant/food services, special products marketing, statistics, tourism promotion, tourism/travel, travel services. **Communications:** General, advertising, digital media, photojournalism, public relations. **Communications technology:** Animation/special effects, graphics, photo/film/video, printing management. **Computer sciences:** General, computer graphics, computer science, database management, game design, information technology, LAN/WAN management, networking, security, system admin, systems analysis, web page design, webmaster. **Engineering:** Aerospace, biomedical, computer, electrical, industrial, manufacturing, mechanical, polymer, software, systems. **Engineering technology:** Civil, computer, electrical, electromechanical, environmental, manufacturing, mechanical, occupational safety, telecommunications. **Family/consumer sciences:** Consumer economics, food/nutrition, human nutrition. **Foreign languages:** American Sign Language, sign language interpretation. **Health:** Medical illustrating, physician assistant, predental, premedicine, prepharmacy, preveterinary, sonography. **Interdisciplinary:** Math/computer science. **Legal studies:** Prelaw. **Math:** Applied, computational, probability, statistics. **Personal/culinary services:** Restaurant/catering. **Physical sciences:** Chemistry, physics, polymer chemistry. **Production:** Furniture, woodworking. **Protective services:** Law enforcement admin. **Psychology:** General. **Public administration:** Policy analysis. **Social sciences:** Economics, international relations. **Visual/performing arts:** Ceramics, cinematography, commercial photography, commercial/advertising art, crafts, design, graphic design, illustration, industrial design, interior design, metal/jewelry, multimedia, painting, photography, printmaking, sculpture, studio arts.

**Most popular majors.** Biology 6%, business/marketing 11%, computer/information sciences 16%, engineering/engineering technologies 27%, interdisciplinary studies 8%, visual/performing arts 16%.

**Computing on campus.** 2,500 workstations in dormitories, library, computer center. Dormitories wired for high-speed internet access and linked to campus network. Commuter students can connect to campus network. Online course registration, online library, helpline, repair service, student web hosting, wireless network available.

**Student life. Freshman orientation:** Mandatory, $165 fee. Preregistration for classes offered. Orientation in September prior to start of classes. **Policies:** Alcohol prohibited in campus residence halls. **Housing:** Guaranteed on-campus for freshmen. Coed dorms, special housing for disabled, apartments, fraternity/sorority housing, substance-free housing available. $300 nonrefundable deposit, deadline 5/1. Special interest houses for students in selected majors or groups, single-sex floors within coed dorms, special honors program floor available. **Activities:** Bands, campus ministries, choral groups, dance, drama, film society, international student organizations, literary magazine, music ensembles, musical theater, radio station, student government, student newspaper, Asian Culture Society, Electronic Gaming Society, Gospel Ensemble, Society of Women Engineers, Society of Hispanic Engineers, National Society of Black Engineers, Emerging Black Artists, Feminist Action, Catholic Newman Network, Outing club.

**Athletics.** NCAA. **Intercollegiate:** Baseball M, basketball, cheerleading, cross-country, diving, ice hockey, lacrosse, rowing (crew), soccer, softball W, swimming, tennis, track and field, volleyball W, wrestling M. **Intramural:** Badminton, basketball, football (non-tackle) M, golf, ice hockey, racquetball, soccer, softball, table tennis, tennis, volleyball. **Team name:** Tigers.

**Student services.** Adult student services, alcohol/substance abuse counseling, campus ministries, career counseling, services for economically disadvantaged, student employment services, financial aid counseling, health services, legal services, minority student services, on-campus daycare, personal counseling, placement for graduates, veterans' counselor, women's services. **Physically disabled:** Services for visually, speech, hearing impaired. **Learning disabled:** Comprehensive services available.

**Contact.** E-mail: admissions@rit.edu
Phone: (585) 475-6631 Fax: (585) 475-7424
Daniel Shelley, Assistant Vice President and Director of Undergraduate Admissions, Rochester Institute of Technology, 60 Lomb Memorial Drive, Rochester, NY 14623-5604

## Russell Sage College
**Troy, New York**
**www.sage.edu/rsc**
**CB member**
**CB code: 2764**

- Private 4-year liberal arts college for women
- Residential campus in small city
- 655 degree-seeking undergraduates: 4% part-time, 100% women, 5% African American, 4% Asian American, 3% Hispanic American, 1% Native American
- 76% of applicants admitted
- Application essay required
- 66% graduate within 6 years; 57% enter graduate study

**General.** Founded in 1916. Regionally accredited. Russell Sage College offers liberal arts and professional degree programs in business, nursing and health sciences, education, performing arts. RSC is a member of The Sage Colleges, including the coeducational Sage College of Albany and Sage Graduate School. **Degrees:** 223 bachelor's awarded. **ROTC:** Army, Naval, Air Force. **Location:** 10 miles from Albany, 150 miles from New York City. **Calendar:** Semester, extensive summer session. **Full-time faculty:** 55 total; 93% have terminal degrees, 7% minority, 62% women. **Part-time faculty:** 35 total; 43% have terminal degrees, 80% women. **Class size:** 64% < 20, 35% 20-39, less than 1% 50-99. **Special facilities:** Center for women's studies, New York State Theater Institute, INVEST nanotechnology business incubator.

**Freshman class profile.** 340 applied, 259 admitted, 82 enrolled.

| Mid 50% test scores | | | |
|---|---|---|---|
| SAT critical reading: | 530-600 | Rank in top quarter: | 63% |
| SAT math: | 520-580 | Rank in top tenth: | 28% |
| ACT composite: | 20-25 | End year in good standing: | 96% |
| GPA 3.50 or higher: | 46% | Return as sophomores: | 69% |
| GPA 3.0-3.49: | 42% | Out-of-state: | 11% |
| GPA 2.0-2.99: | 12% | Live on campus: | 78% |

**Basis for selection.** High school record, standardized test scores most important. Recommendations of school officials, intended major, school and community activities considered. Results from SAT or ACT examinations optional for applicants whose secondary school rank is in top 20% of graduating class. Interview recommended. **Homeschooled:** Statement describing homeschool structure and mission, transcript of courses and grades, interview, letter of recommendation (nonparent) required. **Learning Disabled:** The Sage Colleges promote self-advocacy for students with disabilities and facilitates a positive and adaptive learning environment for such students. Students seeking accommodations are required to present a recent evaluation of their disability conducted by a licensed professional. Upon admission, those requesting accommodations must contact the Coordinator of Disability Services in the Campus Life Office.

**High school preparation.** 16 units required. Required and recommended units include English 4, mathematics 3-4, social studies 4, science 3-4 (laboratory 2-3) and foreign language 2-3. Nursing program applicants must have 6 math/science combination including chemistry. Physical and occupational therapy students must have 4 math/science.

**2008-2009 Annual costs.** Tuition/fees: $26,740. Room/board: $9,200. Books/supplies: $1,000. Personal expenses: $1,260.

**2007-2008 Financial aid. Need-based:** 81 full-time freshmen applied for aid; 76 were judged to have need; 76 of these received aid. Average scholarship/grant was $6,200; average loan $2,750. 60% of total undergraduate aid awarded as scholarships/grants, 40% as loans/jobs. **Non-need-based:** Awarded to 477 full-time undergraduates, including 64 freshmen. Scholarships awarded for academics, alumni affiliation, leadership, music/drama.

**Application procedures. Admission:** Priority date 3/1; no deadline. $30 fee, may be waived for applicants with need. Application may be submitted online. Admission notification on a rolling basis beginning on or about 12/15. Must reply by May 1 or within 2 week(s) if notified thereafter. **Financial aid:** Priority date 3/1; no closing date. FAFSA required. Applicants notified on a rolling basis starting 3/1; must reply by 5/1 or within 2 week(s) of notification.

**Academics.** All students complete internship, field experience, or clinical experience. All students engage in service learning through 2 required courses: Women in the World (first year) and Women Changing the World (senior year). **Special study options:** Accelerated study, combined bachelor's/graduate degree, cross-registration, distance learning, double major, honors, independent study, internships, liberal arts/career combination, student-designed major, study abroad, teacher certification program. Early College for high school juniors, combined bachelor's/master's, bachelor's/doctoral programs with Sage Graduate School, 3+3 BA/JD with Albany Law School, 3+2 BS/BSE with Rensselaer Polytechnic Institute, BA/MS Accelerated Physician Assistant Program with Albany Medical College, BA/MS Early Assurance Program with Albany Medical College, BA/MD Early Assurance Program with Albany Medical College. **Credit/placement by examination:** AP, CLEP, IB, SAT, ACT, institutional tests. 30 credit hours maximum toward bachelor's degree. **Support services:** Learning center, pre-admission summer program, reduced course load, remedial instruction, study skills assistance, tutoring, writing center.

**Majors. Biology:** General, biochemistry. **Business:** Business admin. **Communications:** Media studies. **Education:** Elementary. **English:** English lit. **Foreign languages:** Spanish. **Health:** Art therapy, nursing (RN). **History:** General. **Interdisciplinary:** Biopsychology, global studies, nutrition sciences. **Math:** General. **Physical sciences:** Chemistry. **Protective services:** Criminal justice, forensics. **Psychology:** General. **Public administration:** Human services. **Social sciences:** Political science, sociology. **Visual/performing arts:** Dramatic, musical theater.

**Most popular majors.** Biology 8%, education 15%, health sciences 28%, psychology 12%, social sciences 9%, visual/performing arts 6%.

**Computing on campus.** 157 workstations in library, computer center, student center. Dormitories wired for high-speed internet access and linked to campus network. Commuter students can connect to campus network. Online course registration, online library, helpline, wireless network available.

**Student life. Freshman orientation:** Available, $200 fee. Preregistration for classes offered. 1-day welcome programs offered in June. 4-day orientation in September. **Policies:** Zero tolerance for drugs, harassment, or violence on campus. **Housing:** Guaranteed on-campus for all undergraduates. Substance-free housing available. $100 partly refundable deposit, deadline 5/1. Special houses available for honor students and students interested in language/international awareness activities. Over-21 residence hall available for seniors. 19th-century brownstone residences available. **Activities:** Campus ministries, choral groups, dance, drama, literary magazine, music ensembles, musical theater, student government, student newspaper, Black and Latina student alliance, gay and lesbian alliance, Fellowship of Christian Athletes, Hillel, Newman Community, Rotaract Club, Key Club, Sage Votes.

**Athletics.** NCAA. **Intercollegiate:** Basketball W, soccer W, softball W, tennis W, volleyball W. **Intramural:** Volleyball W. **Team name:** Gators.

**Student services.** Adult student services, alcohol/substance abuse counseling, campus ministries, career counseling, services for economically disadvantaged, student employment services, financial aid counseling, health services, minority student services, personal counseling, placement for graduates, women's services.

**Contact.** E-mail: rscadm@sage.edu
Phone: (518) 244-2217 Toll-free number: (888) 837-9724
Fax: (518) 244-6880
Kathy Rusch, Director of Admission, RSC, Russell Sage College, 45 Ferry Street, Troy, NY 12180-4115

## Sage College of Albany
**Albany, New York**
**www.sage.edu**
**CB code: 2343**

- Private 4-year business and liberal arts college
- Commuter campus in small city
- 883 degree-seeking undergraduates: 36% part-time, 72% women, 9% African American, 2% Asian American, 3% Hispanic American
- 67% of applicants admitted
- Application essay required

**General.** Founded in 1957. Regionally accredited. **Degrees:** 209 bachelor's, 49 associate awarded. **ROTC:** Army, Air Force. **Location:** 150 miles from New York City. **Calendar:** Semester, extensive summer session. **Full-time faculty:** 41 total; 66% have terminal degrees, 5% minority, 58% women. **Part-time faculty:** 47 total; 21% have terminal degrees, 43% women. **Class size:** 66% < 20, 34% 20-39, less than 1% 50-99. **Special facilities:** Fine arts studio, graphic design and interior design studios, award-winning Opalka Gallery.

**Freshman class profile.** 322 applied, 215 admitted, 80 enrolled.

| Mid 50% test scores | | GPA 2.0-2.99: | 45% |
|---|---|---|---|
| SAT critical reading: | 470-530 | Rank in top quarter: | 38% |
| SAT math: | 470-510 | Rank in top tenth: | 7% |
| ACT composite: | 19-22 | Return as sophomores: | 69% |
| GPA 3.50 or higher: | 24% | Out-of-state: | 16% |
| GPA 3.0-3.49: | 29% | Live on campus: | 78% |

**Basis for selection.** Recommendation of high school guidance counselor or teacher and academic record considered for all applicants. Applications reviewed on individual basis. SAT or ACT optional for applicants with secondary school rank in top 20% of graduating class. Interview recommended for all; portfolio required for art and design programs. **Home-schooled:** Statement describing homeschool structure and mission, transcript of courses and grades, interview, letter of recommendation (nonparent) required.

**High school preparation.** 16 units required. Required and recommended units include English 4, mathematics 2-3, social studies 4, science 2-3 and foreign language 2.

**2008-2009 Annual costs.** Tuition/fees: $19,490. Room/board: $9,350. Books/supplies: $1,000. Personal expenses: $1,260.

**2007-2008 Financial aid. Need-based:** 77 full-time freshmen applied for aid; 76 were judged to have need; 76 of these received aid. Average scholarship/grant was $6,200; average loan $2,600. 64% of total undergraduate aid awarded as scholarships/grants, 36% as loans/jobs. **Non-need-based:** Awarded to 275 full-time undergraduates, including 51 freshmen. Scholarships awarded for academics, art, leadership.

**Application procedures. Admission:** No deadline. $30 fee, may be waived for applicants with need. Application may be submitted online. Admission notification on a rolling basis beginning on or about 11/1. Must reply by May 1 or within 2 week(s) if notified thereafter. **Financial aid:** Priority date 3/1; no closing date. FAFSA required. Applicants notified on a rolling basis starting 3/1; must reply within 2 week(s) of notification.

**Academics.** College of Applied Studies offers specialties in art and design, business and communications, computer technologies, legal studies, creative studies. Four programs in fine arts (photography, graphic design, interior design, and fine arts) accredited by National Association of Schools of Art and Design. Transfer-friendly "two plus two" curriculum with professional study beginning in first 2 years; joint degrees in clinical biology and cytotechnology with Albany College of Pharmacy. Ease of transfer for community college graduates. **Special study options:** Cross-registration, distance learning, double major, honors, independent study, internships, liberal arts/career combination, student-designed major, study abroad. **Credit/placement by examination:** AP, CLEP, IB, SAT, ACT, institutional tests. 30 credit hours maximum toward associate degree, 30 toward bachelor's. **Support services:** Learning center, pre-admission summer program, reduced course load, remedial instruction, study skills assistance, tutoring, writing center.

**Majors. Biology:** General. **Business:** Accounting, business admin. **Communications:** Digital media. **Computer sciences:** General, networking, webmaster. **Education:** Physical. **Health:** Cytotechnology, nursing (RN). **Legal studies:** General, paralegal. **Liberal arts:** Arts/sciences. **Protective services:** Law enforcement admin. **Psychology:** General. **Social sciences:** General. **Visual/performing arts:** Graphic design, interior design, studio arts.

**Most popular majors.** Business/marketing 29%, education 10%, interdisciplinary studies 11%, legal studies 7%, visual/performing arts 23%.

**Computing on campus.** 183 workstations in library, computer center. Dormitories wired for high-speed internet access and linked to campus network. Commuter students can connect to campus network. Online course registration, online library, helpline, wireless network available.

**Student life. Freshman orientation:** Available, $125 fee. Preregistration for classes offered. New students may receive academic advising and register for classes (summer, fall, spring) beginning March 1st each year. One-day welcome programs offered in June. 4-day orientation in September. **Policies:** Zero tolerance for drugs, harassment or violence on campus. **Housing:** Guaranteed on-campus for freshmen. Coed dorms, apartments, substance-free housing available. $100 partly refundable deposit, deadline 5/1. Apartment-style suites available on adjacent campus. **Activities:** Literary magazine, student government, student newspaper, ALDANA (African American, Latino,

Desi's, Asian, Native American Alliance), Sage Votes, Association of Campus Events, Gay Straight Alliance.

**Athletics. Intramural:** Badminton, basketball, football (non-tackle), soccer, volleyball.

**Student services.** Adult student services, alcohol/substance abuse counseling, campus ministries, career counseling, services for economically disadvantaged, student employment services, financial aid counseling, health services, minority student services, personal counseling, placement for graduates, veterans' counselor.

**Contact.** E-mail: scaadm@sage.adm
Phone: (518) 292-1730 Toll-free number: (888) 837-9724
Fax: (518) 292-1912
Amy Sullivan, Director of Admission, Sage College of Albany, 140 New Scotland Avenue, Albany, NY 12208

## Saint Bonaventure University

**St. Bonaventure, New York**  **CB member**
**www.sbu.edu**  **CB code: 2793**

- Private 4-year university affiliated with Roman Catholic Church
- Residential campus in large town
- 1,905 degree-seeking undergraduates
- 459 graduate students
- 84% of applicants admitted

**General.** Founded in 1858. Regionally accredited. Catholic institution in Franciscan tradition. **Degrees:** 443 bachelor's awarded; master's offered. **ROTC:** Army. **Location:** 75 miles from Buffalo. **Calendar:** Semester, limited summer session. **Full-time faculty:** 145 total; 77% have terminal degrees, 6% minority, 30% women. **Part-time faculty:** 65 total; 3% minority, 52% women. **Class size:** 61% < 20, 39% 20-39. **Special facilities:** Observatory, digital media laboratory, permanent art collection, retreat facility, rare books collection.

**Freshman class profile.** 1,760 applied, 1,479 admitted, 527 enrolled.

| Mid 50% test scores | | GPA 2.0-2.99: | 39% |
|---|---|---|---|
| SAT critical reading: | 460-570 | Rank in top quarter: | 42% |
| SAT math: | 450-580 | Rank in top tenth: | 17% |
| SAT writing: | 460-560 | Out-of-state: | 26% |
| ACT composite: | 19-26 | Live on campus: | 95% |
| GPA 3.50 or higher: | 33% | International: | 1% |
| GPA 3.0-3.49: | 25% | | |

**Basis for selection.** Interview, high school GPA and curriculum most important. Recommendation, class rank, test scores, extracurricular activities also considered. Applicants to dual admission premed program with George Washington University must submit Biology SAT Subject Test scores. Essay recommended for all. **Homeschooled:** Statement describing homeschool structure and mission, transcript of courses and grades, letter of recommendation (nonparent) required. Course syllabus, book titles, and all course evaluations required to be considered for admission.

**High school preparation.** 19 units recommended. Recommended units include English 4, mathematics 3, social studies 4, science 3 and foreign language 2. Science majors must have 4 science, 4 math. Business majors need 4 math. Recommend 3 science lab.

**2007-2008 Annual costs.** Tuition/fees: $23,605. Room/board: $8,490. Books/supplies: $700. Personal expenses: $650.

**Financial aid. Non-need-based:** Scholarships awarded for academics, art, athletics, leadership, minority status, music/drama, religious affiliation, ROTC, state residency.

**Application procedures. Admission:** Priority date 2/1; deadline 4/30 (postmark date). $30 fee, may be waived for applicants with need. Application may be submitted online. Admission notification on a rolling basis beginning on or about 9/15. Must reply by May 1 or within 1 week(s) if notified thereafter. Applications considered until housing is closed. **Financial aid:** Priority date 2/1; no closing date. FAFSA, institutional form required. Applicants notified on a rolling basis starting 4/1; must reply by 5/1 or within 3 week(s) of notification.

**Academics. Special study options:** Accelerated study, combined bachelor's/graduate degree, cross-registration, distance learning, double major, dual enrollment of high school students, exchange student, honors, independent study, internships, liberal arts/career combination, student-designed major, study abroad, teacher certification program, Washington semester. **Credit/placement by examination:** AP, CLEP, IB, SAT, ACT, institutional tests.

30 credit hours maximum toward bachelor's degree. **Support services:** Learning center, pre-admission summer program, reduced course load, remedial instruction, study skills assistance, tutoring.

**Majors. Area/ethnic studies:** Women's. **Biology:** General, biochemistry, bioinformatics. **Business:** Accounting, finance, management information systems, management science. **Communications:** Journalism, media studies. **Computer sciences:** General, computer science. **Conservation:** General. **Education:** Elementary, physical, special. **English:** British lit, English lit. **Foreign languages:** Classics, French, Latin, Spanish. **History:** General. **Interdisciplinary:** Gerontology. **Math:** General. **Philosophy/religion:** Philosophy. **Physical sciences:** Chemistry, physics. **Psychology:** General. **Social sciences:** General, political science, sociology. **Theology:** Theology. **Visual/performing arts:** General, art history/conservation, dramatic.

**Most popular majors.** Business/marketing 31%, communications/journalism 17%, education 16%, psychology 6%, social sciences 11%.

**Computing on campus.** 321 workstations in dormitories, library, computer center, student center. Dormitories wired for high-speed internet access and linked to campus network. Commuter students can connect to campus network. Online course registration, helpline, repair service, student web hosting, wireless network available.

**Student life. Freshman orientation:** Mandatory, $150 fee. Preregistration for classes offered. 2-day session held in July. **Policies:** Students must live on campus until they are seniors or 21 years old unless they live within commuting distance. **Housing:** Guaranteed on-campus for all undergraduates. Single-sex dorms, special housing for disabled, apartments, substance-free housing available. $200 nonrefundable deposit, deadline 5/1. **Activities:** Bands, campus ministries, choral groups, dance, drama, international student organizations, literary magazine, music ensembles, Model UN, radio station, student government, student newspaper, TV station, Knights of Columbus, Irish society, black student union, Students In Free Enterprise, service learning organization.

**Athletics. NCAA. Intercollegiate:** Baseball M, basketball, cross-country, diving, golf M, lacrosse W, soccer, softball W, swimming, tennis. **Intramural:** Basketball, bowling, football (non-tackle) M, golf, racquetball, skiing, soccer, softball, swimming, table tennis, tennis, volleyball, water polo M. **Team name:** Bonnies.

**Student services.** Alcohol/substance abuse counseling, campus ministries, career counseling, services for economically disadvantaged, student employment services, financial aid counseling, health services, personal counseling, placement for graduates, veterans' counselor.

**Contact.** E-mail: admissions@sbu.edu
Phone: (716) 375-2400 Toll-free number: (800) 462-5050
Fax: (716) 375-4005
James DiRisio, Director of Admissions, Saint Bonaventure University, Route 417, St. Bonaventure, NY 14778-2284

---

## St. Francis College

**Brooklyn Heights, New York**  CB member
**www.stfranciscollege.edu**  CB code: 2796

- Private 4-year liberal arts college affiliated with Roman Catholic Church
- Commuter campus in very large city
- 2,224 degree-seeking undergraduates: 13% part-time, 54% women, 20% African American, 2% Asian American, 17% Hispanic American, 7% international
- 20 degree-seeking graduate students
- 88% of applicants admitted
- SAT, application essay required
- 60% graduate within 6 years

**General. Founded** in 1884. Regionally accredited. **Degrees:** 439 bachelor's, 18 associate awarded; master's offered. **ROTC:** Army, Air Force. **Location:** 5 minutes from Manhattan by subway. **Calendar:** Semester, limited summer session. **Full-time faculty:** 79 total; 82% have terminal degrees, 9% minority, 47% women. **Part-time faculty:** 134 total; 24% have terminal degrees, 20% minority, 34% women. **Class size:** 44% < 20, 55% 20-39, less than 1% 40-49, less than 1% 50-99. **Special facilities:** Television production and editing facility with 3 Ikegami cameras and 17 Mac G5 digital editing stations.

**Freshman class profile.** 1,643 applied, 1,453 admitted, 503 enrolled.

| Mid 50% test scores | | | |
|---|---|---|---|
| SAT critical reading: | 400-520 | GPA 2.0-2.99: | 50% |
| SAT math: | 390-520 | Return as sophomores: | 74% |
| GPA 3.50 or higher: | 18% | Out-of-state: | 2% |
| GPA 3.0-3.49: | 18% | International: | 7% |

**Basis for selection.** Academic achievement, test scores, counselor's recommendation, school and community activities, and admissions interview important. Degree-seeking students who do not meet criteria may be admitted after review and assessment of their educational background. SAT/ACT scores must be received by first day of class for fall-term admission. Interview required of academically weak applicants. **Homeschooled:** Statement describing homeschool structure and mission, state high school equivalency certificate required.

**High school preparation.** 18.5 units recommended. Recommended units include English 4, mathematics 2, social studies 4, science 2, visual/performing arts 1, academic electives 5.5. Applicants seeking BS should have completed 11th grade high school math or its equivalent.

**2007-2008 Annual costs.** Tuition/fees: $14,970. Books/supplies: $790. Personal expenses: $1,106.

**Financial aid. Non-need-based:** Scholarships awarded for academics, athletics.

**Application procedures. Admission:** No deadline. $35 fee, may be waived for applicants with need. Application may be submitted online. Admission notification on a rolling basis. Must reply by May 1 or within 2 week(s) if notified thereafter. **Financial aid:** Priority date 2/15; no closing date. FAFSA required. Applicants notified on a rolling basis starting 3/15; must reply within 2 week(s) of notification.

**Academics. Special study options:** Accelerated study, combined bachelor's/graduate degree, cooperative education, cross-registration, double major, dual enrollment of high school students, ESL, exchange student, honors, independent study, internships, student-designed major, study abroad, teacher certification program, Washington semester. Accelerated biomedical science program with New York College of Podiatric Medicine, medical technology program with St. Vincent's Catholic Medical Centers of New York and New York Methodist Hospital, joint affiliation program with St. Vincent's Catholic Medical Centers of New York in radiologic sciences, 7-year cooperative program with the New York University College of Dentistry, combined BA/MS in computer science with Polytechnic University. **Credit/placement by examination:** AP, CLEP, IB, SAT, ACT, institutional tests. 30 credit hours maximum toward associate degree, 96 toward bachelor's. **Support services:** Learning center, pre-admission summer program, remedial instruction, study skills assistance, tutoring, writing center.

**Majors. Biology:** General, biomedical sciences. **Business:** Accounting, business admin. **Communications:** General, digital media, public relations, radio/tv. **Computer sciences:** System admin. **Education:** Biology, chemistry, elementary, English, mathematics, physical, social studies, visually handicapped. **English:** English lit. **Foreign languages:** Spanish. **Health:** Clinical lab science, medical radiologic technology/radiation therapy, nursing (RN), physician assistant. **History:** General. **Liberal arts:** Arts/sciences. **Math:** General. **Philosophy/religion:** Philosophy, religion. **Physical sciences:** Chemistry. **Protective services:** Criminal justice. **Psychology:** General. **Social sciences:** Economics, political science, sociology. **Other:** Health Promotion and Science, International Cultural Studies.

**Most popular majors.** Business/marketing 21%, communications/journalism 10%, education 8%, health sciences 9%, liberal arts 14%, psychology 8%, social sciences 8%.

**Computing on campus.** 600 workstations in library, computer center, student center. Commuter students can connect to campus network. Helpline, wireless network available.

**Student life. Freshman orientation:** Mandatory. Preregistration for classes offered. **Housing:** Students may apply for housing at Polytechnic University, approximately 10-minute walk from college. **Activities:** Choral groups, dance, drama, literary magazine, student government, student newspaper, Latin American Society, Haitian Alliance, Caribbean student association, Christian club, Arab-American Society, French club, College Republicans, History and Political Science Society, Italian Historical Society, Model United Nations.

**Athletics. NCAA. Intercollegiate:** Basketball, cross-country, diving, soccer M, swimming, tennis, track and field, volleyball W, water polo. **Intramural:** Basketball, football (tackle) M, soccer M, volleyball. **Team name:** Terriers.

**Student services.** Adult student services, campus ministries, career counseling, services for economically disadvantaged, student employment services, financial aid counseling, health services, personal counseling, placement for graduates, veterans' counselor. **Physically disabled:** Services for visually, speech, hearing impaired.

**Contact.** E-mail: admissions@stfranciscollege.edu
Phone: (718) 489-3473 Fax: (718) 802-0453
Bro. George Larkin, Dean of Admissions, St. Francis College, 180 Remsen Street, Brooklyn Heights, NY 11201-9902

## St. John Fisher College
**Rochester, New York**
www.sjfc.edu

**CB member**
**CB code: 2798**

- Private 4-year liberal arts college affiliated with Roman Catholic Church
- Residential campus in large town
- 2,796 degree-seeking undergraduates: 6% part-time, 59% women, 5% African American, 2% Asian American, 3% Hispanic American
- 855 degree-seeking graduate students
- 61% of applicants admitted
- SAT or ACT (ACT writing optional) required
- 67% graduate within 6 years

**General.** Founded in 1948. Regionally accredited. **Degrees:** 646 bachelor's awarded; master's, doctoral, first professional offered. **ROTC:** Army, Air Force. **Location:** 6 miles from downtown. **Calendar:** Semester, extensive summer session. **Full-time faculty:** 182 total; 83% have terminal degrees, 13% minority, 44% women. **Part-time faculty:** 189 total; 6% minority, 59% women. **Class size:** 41% < 20, 55% 20-39, 2% 40-49, 2% 50-99. **Special facilities:** 2 electron microscopes, language laboratory, cyber cafe.

**Freshman class profile.** 3,209 applied, 1,944 admitted, 548 enrolled.

| Mid 50% test scores | | | |
|---|---|---|---|
| SAT critical reading: | 480-570 | GPA 3.0-3.49: | 36% |
| SAT math: | 500-600 | GPA 2.0-2.99: | 14% |
| SAT writing: | 470-560 | Rank in top quarter: | 54% |
| ACT composite: | 22-25 | Rank in top tenth: | 21% |
| GPA 3.50 or higher: | 50% | Return as sophomores: | 86% |

**Basis for selection.** Academic factors considered include high school GPA, strength of curriculum, class rank, and standardized test results. Extracurricular involvements, letters of recommendation, and personal interview also considered. Interview recommended for all. **Homeschooled:** Letter of recommendation (nonparent) required.

**High school preparation.** 16 units required. Required and recommended units include English 4, mathematics 3, social studies 4, science 3 and foreign language 3. 4 math required for programs needing college calculus.

**2007-2008 Annual costs.** Tuition/fees: $22,230. Room/board: $9,380. Books/supplies: $900. Personal expenses: $600.

**2006-2007 Financial aid. Need-based:** 543 full-time freshmen applied for aid; 450 were judged to have need; 450 of these received aid. Average need met was 85%. Average scholarship/grant was $12,846; average loan $4,483. 50% of total undergraduate aid awarded as scholarships/grants, 50% as loans/jobs. **Non-need-based:** Awarded to 1,941 full-time undergraduates, including 450 freshmen. Scholarships awarded for academics, leadership.

**Application procedures. Admission:** Priority date 12/1; no deadline. $30 fee, may be waived for applicants with need. Application may be submitted online. Admission notification on a rolling basis. Must reply by May 1 or within 3 week(s) if notified thereafter. **Financial aid:** Priority date 2/15; no closing date. FAFSA required. Applicants notified on a rolling basis starting 3/22; must reply by 5/1 or within 3 week(s) of notification.

**Academics.** All entering freshmen participate in one of the integrative learning communities as part of first-year experience. Experiential learning opportunities integrated into undergraduate programs. **Special study options:** Accelerated study, cross-registration, distance learning, double major, honors, independent study, internships, liberal arts/career combination, student-designed major, study abroad, teacher certification program, Washington semester, weekend college. 3-4 optometry program with Pennsylvania College of Optometry, 2-2 environmental science and forestry program with SUNY, 3-2 pre-engineering program with Clarkson University, SUNY Buffalo, Manhattan College, 2-2 pre-engineering program with University of Detroit Mercy, 4-2 pre-engineering program with Columbia University, University of Detroit. **Credit/placement by examination:** AP, CLEP, IB,

institutional tests. 66 credit hours maximum toward bachelor's degree. **Support services:** Reduced course load, remedial instruction, study skills assistance, tutoring, writing center.

**Majors. Area/ethnic studies:** American. **Biology:** General. **Business:** Accounting, business admin, finance, human resources, international, management information systems, management science, marketing. **Communications:** General, broadcast journalism, journalism. **Computer sciences:** General, computer science. **Education:** General, biology, chemistry, elementary, English, foreign languages, French, German, history, mathematics, physics, science, secondary, social science, social studies, Spanish, special. **English:** English lit. **Foreign languages:** French, Spanish. **Health:** Nursing (RN), preop/surgical nursing. **History:** General. **Liberal arts:** Arts/sciences. **Math:** General. **Parks/recreation:** Sports admin. **Philosophy/religion:** Philosophy, religion. **Physical sciences:** Chemistry, physics. **Psychology:** General. **Social sciences:** Anthropology, economics, political science, sociology.

**Most popular majors.** Business/marketing 22%, communications/journalism 8%, education 21%, health sciences 7%, history 6%, psychology 6%, social sciences 12%.

**Computing on campus.** 525 workstations in library, computer center. Dormitories wired for high-speed internet access and linked to campus network. Commuter students can connect to campus network. Online course registration, online library, helpline, student web hosting, wireless network available.

**Student life. Freshman orientation:** Mandatory. Preregistration for classes offered. Three-day program held weekend prior to start of classes. Day-long course registration in May, including full day of activities for parents. **Policies:** All housing smoke-free. **Housing:** Guaranteed on-campus for freshmen. Coed dorms, single-sex dorms, special housing for disabled available. $200 nonrefundable deposit. All residence halls accessible to students with disabilities. **Activities:** Pep band, campus ministries, choral groups, dance, drama, literary magazine, musical theater, student government, student newspaper, TV station, Circle K, Latino student union, black student union, Fisher Players, gospel choir, resident student association, commuter council, student activities board, Fisher Pride.

**Athletics.** NCAA. **Intercollegiate:** Baseball M, basketball, football (tackle) M, golf M, lacrosse, soccer, softball W, tennis, volleyball W. **Intramural:** Basketball, football (non-tackle) M, soccer, softball, volleyball. **Team name:** Cardinals.

**Student services.** Adult student services, campus ministries, career counseling, services for economically disadvantaged, student employment services, financial aid counseling, health services, on-campus daycare, personal counseling, placement for graduates, veterans' counselor. **Physically disabled:** Services for visually, hearing impaired.

**Contact.** E-mail: admissions@sjfc.edu
Phone: (585) 385-8064 Toll-free number: (800) 444-4640
Fax: (585) 385-8386
Stacy Ledermann, Director of Freshman Admissions, St. John Fisher College, 3690 East Avenue, Rochester, NY 14618-3597

## St. John's University
**Queens, New York**
www.stjohns.edu

**CB member**
**CB code: 2799**

- Private 4-year university affiliated with Roman Catholic Church
- Commuter campus in very large city
- 12,178 degree-seeking undergraduates: 4% part-time, 55% women, 16% African American, 16% Asian American, 14% Hispanic American, 4% international
- 4,904 degree-seeking graduate students
- 56% of applicants admitted
- SAT or ACT (ACT writing recommended) required
- 61% graduate within 6 years; 32% enter graduate study

**General.** Founded in 1870. Regionally accredited. Branch campuses in Staten Island, Manhattan, and Oakdale; graduate center in Rome, Italy. **Degrees:** 2,228 bachelor's, 62 associate awarded; master's, doctoral, first professional offered. **ROTC:** Army. **Location:** 10 miles from midtown Manhattan. **Calendar:** Semester, extensive summer session. **Full-time faculty:** 659 total; 87% have terminal degrees, 20% minority, 40% women. **Part-time faculty:** 820 total; 35% have terminal degrees, 17% minority, 41% women. **Class size:** 37% < 20, 50% 20-39, 7% 40-49, 4% 50-99, less than 1% >100. **Special facilities:** Speech and hearing clinic, instructional media center, health education resource center, writing institute, institute of Asian studies.

**Freshman class profile.** 27,754 applied, 15,410 admitted, 3,162 enrolled.

| Mid 50% test scores | | | |
|---|---|---|---|
| SAT critical reading: | 480-580 | Rank in top quarter: | 44% |
| SAT math: | 480-600 | Rank in top tenth: | 22% |
| GPA 3.50 or higher: | 32% | Return as sophomores: | 79% |
| GPA 3.0-3.49: | 33% | Out-of-state: | 23% |
| GPA 2.0-2.99: | 33% | Live on campus: | 49% |
| | | International: | 3% |

**Basis for selection.** School achievement record, standardized test scores, counselor/teacher recommendations, honor awards, extracurricular activities, personal essay used in admissions decisions. SAT not required if student has graduated or if time elapsed is more than 1 year prior to term of admission. Interview, personal statement, essay recommended for all; portfolio required for creative photography, fine art, graphic design, illustration programs. **Homeschooled:** Statement describing homeschool structure and mission, state high school equivalency certificate required.

**High school preparation.** 16 units required. Required and recommended units include English 4, mathematics 3, social studies 2, history 2, science 2 (laboratory 2), foreign language 2 and academic electives 1. Additional math/sciences classes highly recommended or required for certain majors.

**2007-2008 Annual costs.** Tuition/fees: $26,840. Tuition may vary by program and class year. Four-year fixed rate tuition plan available for incoming freshmen. Room/board: $12,070. Books/supplies: $1,000. Personal expenses: $2,700.

**2006-2007 Financial aid.** **Need-based:** 2,896 full-time freshmen applied for aid; 2,632 were judged to have need; 2,617 of these received aid. Average need met was 70%. Average scholarship/grant $9,701; average loan $3,603. 63% of total undergraduate aid awarded as scholarships/grants, 37% as loans/jobs. **Non-need-based:** Awarded to 8,609 full-time undergraduates, including 2,688 freshmen. Scholarships awarded for academics, alumni affiliation, art, athletics, leadership, music/drama, religious affiliation, ROTC.

**Application procedures. Admission:** No deadline. $50 fee, may be waived for applicants with need. Application may be submitted online. Admission notification on a rolling basis beginning on or about 12/1. Must reply by May 1 or within 2 week(s) if notified thereafter. Application closing date for pharmacy students February 1. **Financial aid:** Priority date 2/1; no closing date. FAFSA required. Applicants notified on a rolling basis starting 3/15; must reply within 2 week(s) of notification.

**Academics. Special study options:** Accelerated study, combined bachelor's/graduate degree, cross-registration, distance learning, double major, dual enrollment of high school students, ESL, honors, independent study, internships, liberal arts/career combination, study abroad, teacher certification program, weekend college. **Credit/placement by examination:** AP, CLEP, IB, SAT, ACT, institutional tests. Students must complete at least 50 percent of major courses and at least 30 credits on campus. **Support services:** Learning center, pre-admission summer program, reduced course load, study skills assistance, tutoring, writing center.

**Majors. Area/ethnic studies:** Asian. **Biology:** General, toxicology. **Business:** Accounting, actuarial science, business admin, finance, hospitality admin, insurance, management information systems, marketing. **Communications:** General, advertising, journalism, public relations. **Communications technology:** Photo/film/video. **Computer sciences:** General. **Conservation:** Environmental studies. **Education:** Biology, elementary, English, mathematics, physics, secondary, social studies, Spanish, special. **Engineering technology:** Telecommunications. **English:** English lit, speech/rhetoric. **Foreign languages:** French, Italian, Spanish. **Health:** Audiology/speech pathology, clinical lab science, health care admin, pathology assistant, physician assistant. **History:** General. **Legal studies:** General. **Liberal arts:** Arts/sciences. **Math:** General. **Parks/recreation:** Sports admin. **Personal/culinary services:** Mortuary science. **Philosophy/religion:** Philosophy. **Physical sciences:** General, chemistry, physics. **Protective services:** Law enforcement admin. **Psychology:** General. **Public administration:** General, human services. **Social sciences:** General, anthropology, economics, political science, sociology. **Theology:** Theology. **Visual/performing arts:** Graphic design, illustration, photography, studio arts.

**Most popular majors.** Business/marketing 23%, communications/journalism 10%, education 8%, health sciences 8%, legal studies 6%, psychology 7%, security/protective services 8%.

**Computing on campus.** PC or laptop required. 1,252 workstations in dormitories, library, computer center, student center. Dormitories wired for high-speed internet access and linked to campus network. Commuter students can connect to campus network. Online course registration, online library, helpline, repair service, student web hosting, wireless network available.

**Student life. Freshman orientation:** Mandatory, $175 fee. 3-day orientation program includes trip to Manhattan. **Housing:** Coed dorms available.

$500 nonrefundable deposit, deadline 5/1. Limited apartment housing available on Staten Island campus. **Activities:** Bands, campus ministries, choral groups, dance, drama, film society, literary magazine, musical theater, radio station, student government, student newspaper, TV station, over 180 organizations on all campuses.

**Athletics.** NCAA. **Intercollegiate:** Baseball M, basketball, cross-country W, fencing, golf, lacrosse M, soccer, softball W, tennis, track and field W, volleyball W. **Intramural:** Badminton, basketball, fencing, football (tackle), racquetball, soccer, softball, table tennis, tennis, volleyball, weight lifting. **Team name:** Red Storm.

**Student services.** Adult student services, alcohol/substance abuse counseling, campus ministries, career counseling, student employment services, financial aid counseling, health services, minority student services, personal counseling, placement for graduates, veterans' counselor. **Physically disabled:** Services for visually, speech, hearing impaired.

**Contact.** E-mail: admhelp@stjohns.edu
Phone: (718) 990-2000 Toll-free number: (888) 978-5646
Fax: (718) 990-2096
Beth Evans, Associate Vice President and Executive Director, Enrollment Management, St. John's University, 8000 Utopia Parkway, Queens, NY 11439

---

## St. Joseph's College
**Brooklyn, New York**
www.sjcny.edu

CB member
CB code: 2802

- Private 4-year liberal arts and teachers college
- Commuter campus in very large city
- 1,059 degree-seeking undergraduates: 31% part-time, 77% women, 37% African American, 7% Asian American, 12% Hispanic American, 1% international
- 231 degree-seeking graduate students
- 79% of applicants admitted
- SAT or ACT with writing required
- 71% graduate within 6 years

**General.** Founded in 1916. Regionally accredited. **Degrees:** 250 bachelor's awarded; master's offered. **Location:** 8 miles from Manhattan. **Calendar:** Semester, limited summer session. **Full-time faculty:** 47 total; 72% have terminal degrees, 28% minority, 60% women. **Part-time faculty:** 93 total; 39% minority, 52% women. **Class size:** 79% < 20, 21% 20-39. **Special facilities:** On-campus laboratory preschool for children 3-6 years old, model school for prospective teachers.

**Freshman class profile.** 874 applied, 688 admitted, 171 enrolled.

| Mid 50% test scores | | | |
|---|---|---|---|
| SAT critical reading: | 440-540 | GPA 3.0-3.49: | 42% |
| SAT math: | 430-550 | GPA 2.0-2.99: | 14% |
| GPA 3.50 or higher: | 44% | End year in good standing: | 73% |
| | | Return as sophomores: | 73% |

**Basis for selection.** High school achievement record, SAT/ACT scores, class rank, activities, recommendations important. Personal statements encouraged. Essay, interview recommended.

**High school preparation.** 18 units required. Required and recommended units include English 4, mathematics 3, social studies 4, science 2, foreign language 2-3 and academic electives 3. 3 units science recommended for science majors. No specific course requirements for general studies applicants.

**2008-2009 Annual costs.** Tuition/fees: $14,532. Books/supplies: $1,000. Personal expenses: $600.

**Financial aid. Non-need-based:** Scholarships awarded for academics, alumni affiliation, leadership.

**Application procedures. Admission:** No deadline. $25 fee, may be waived for applicants with need. Admission notification on a rolling basis. **Financial aid:** Priority date 2/25; no closing date. FAFSA, institutional form required. Applicants notified on a rolling basis starting 4/1; must reply by 5/1 or within 2 week(s) of notification.

**Academics. Special study options:** Accelerated study, honors, independent study, internships, teacher certification program, weekend college. Accelerated biomedical program with New York College of Podiatric Medicine. **Credit/placement by examination:** AP, CLEP, institutional tests. 30 credit hours maximum toward bachelor's degree. **Support services:** Reduced course load, tutoring, writing center.

**Majors. Biology:** General. **Business:** General, accounting, business admin, human resources. **Education:** General, early childhood, elementary, mathematics, middle, science, secondary, social studies, special. **English:** English lit, speech/rhetoric. **Foreign languages:** General. **Health:** Health care admin, prenursing. **History:** General. **Liberal arts:** Arts/sciences. **Math:** General. **Physical sciences:** Chemistry. **Psychology:** General. **Social sciences:** General, sociology.

**Most popular majors.** Business/marketing 22%, education 16%, health sciences 40%.

**Computing on campus.** 90 workstations in library, computer center. Dormitories wired for high-speed internet access. Commuter students can connect to campus network. Online course registration, online library available.

**Student life. Freshman orientation:** Mandatory. Preregistration for classes offered. **Activities:** Campus ministries, choral groups, dance, drama, literary magazine, musical theater, student government, student newspaper, Gaelic society, Hispanic awareness club, heritage gallery, Asian awareness, Japanese animation, political affairs, student ambassador club.

**Athletics.** USCAA. **Intercollegiate:** Basketball, cross-country, softball W, swimming W, tennis M, volleyball. **Intramural:** Basketball, table tennis, volleyball. **Team name:** Bears.

**Student services.** Adult student services, campus ministries, career counseling, student employment services, financial aid counseling, personal counseling, placement for graduates.

**Contact.** E-mail: asinfob@sjcny.edu
Phone: (718) 636-6868 Fax: (718) 636-8303
Theresa LaRocca-Meyer, Director of Admissions, St. Joseph's College, 245 Clinton Avenue, Brooklyn, NY 11205-3688

## St. Joseph's College: Suffolk Campus
**Patchogue, New York**
**www.sjcny.edu**                                   **CB code: 2841**

- Private 4-year branch campus and liberal arts college
- Commuter campus in large town
- 3,400 degree-seeking undergraduates: 20% part-time, 74% women
- 341 degree-seeking graduate students
- 79% of applicants admitted
- SAT or ACT (ACT writing recommended) required
- 66% graduate within 6 years

**General.** Founded in 1916. Regionally accredited. **Degrees:** 900 bachelor's awarded; master's offered. **ROTC:** Army, Air Force. **Location:** 60 miles from New York City. **Calendar:** 4-1-4, extensive summer session. **Full-time faculty:** 110 total; 64% have terminal degrees, 11% minority, 59% women. **Part-time faculty:** 270 total; 7% minority, 47% women. **Class size:** 55% < 20, 45% 20-39, less than 1% 40-49, less than 1% 50-99. **Special facilities:** Playhouse.

**Freshman class profile.** 1,393 applied, 1,100 admitted, 495 enrolled.

| Mid 50% test scores | | Rank in top tenth: | 19% |
|---|---|---|---|
| SAT critical reading: | 490-550 | End year in good standing: | 96% |
| SAT math: | 490-580 | Return as sophomores: | 81% |
| SAT writing: | 450-550 | Fraternities: | 1% |
| Rank in top quarter: | 55% | Sororities: | 2% |

**Basis for selection.** Grades in high school academic classes, GPA and rank in class most important. Performance on standardized tests important. Strongly factored in are letters of recommendation, personal statement and school/community activities. SAT Subject Tests recommended. Interview recommended. Essays required of scholarship candidates, strongly recommended for all others. **Homeschooled:** Transcript of courses and grades required. SAT or ACT required. Interview strongly recommended.

**High school preparation.** 18 units required. Required and recommended units include English 4, mathematics 3, social studies 4, science 3 (laboratory 3), foreign language 2 and academic electives 2. Social science unit must be American history.

**2007-2008 Annual costs.** Tuition/fees: $14,532. Books/supplies: $1,000. Personal expenses: $600.

**Financial aid. Non-need-based:** Scholarships awarded for academics.

**Application procedures. Admission:** Priority date 8/15; no deadline. $25 fee, may be waived for applicants with need. Application must be submitted on paper. Admission notification on a rolling basis beginning on or about 11/1. Must reply by May 1 or within 2 week(s) if notified thereafter. **Financial aid:** Priority date 2/25; no closing date. FAFSA, institutional form required. Applicants notified on a rolling basis starting 3/15; must reply within 2 week(s) of notification.

**Academics. Special study options:** Combined bachelor's/graduate degree, distance learning, double major, honors, independent study, internships, liberal arts/career combination, study abroad, teacher certification program, weekend college. 5-year program bachelor's/master's in computer science from Polytechnic University; 5-year BNS/MS in accounting. **Credit/placement by examination:** AP, CLEP, IB, institutional tests. 30 credit hours maximum toward bachelor's degree. **Support services:** Learning center, reduced course load, study skills assistance, tutoring, writing center.

**Majors. Biology:** General. **Business:** Accounting, business admin. **Communications:** General. **Computer sciences:** Computer science, information technology. **Education:** General, biology, early childhood, elementary, English, history, kindergarten/preschool, mathematics, middle, science, secondary, social studies, Spanish, special. **English:** English lit. **Foreign languages:** Spanish. **Health:** Facilities admin, predental, premedicine, preveterinary, recreational therapy. **History:** General. **Liberal arts:** Arts/sciences. **Math:** General. **Parks/recreation:** General. **Psychology:** General. **Social sciences:** General, criminology, economics, political science, sociology.

**Most popular majors.** Business/marketing 15%, education 47%, health sciences 8%, psychology 6%.

**Computing on campus.** 223 workstations in library, computer center. Commuter students can connect to campus network. Online course registration, online library, helpline, wireless network available.

**Student life. Freshman orientation:** Mandatory, $50 fee. Preregistration for classes offered. 1-day orientation in August just prior to start of classes. **Policies:** 2.7 average required to run for student government. **Activities:** Bands, choral groups, dance, drama, literary magazine, music ensembles, musical theater, student government, student newspaper, Amnesty International, student volunteer services, Circle K, Students Taking an Active Role in Society, Spanish club, Diversity Union, Habitat for Humanity, social sciences club, Lion's Club.

**Athletics.** NCAA. **Intercollegiate:** Baseball M, basketball, cross-country, equestrian, golf M, soccer, softball W, swimming, tennis, track and field, volleyball W. **Intramural:** Football (non-tackle). **Team name:** Golden Eagles.

**Student services.** Adult student services, alcohol/substance abuse counseling, campus ministries, career counseling, student employment services, financial aid counseling, minority student services, personal counseling, veterans' counselor. **Physically disabled:** Services for visually, hearing impaired.

**Contact.** E-mail: suffolkas@sjcny.edu
Phone: (631) 447-3219 Fax: (631) 447-3601
Gigi Lamens, Director of Admissions and Enrollment Planning, St. Joseph's College: Suffolk Campus, 155 West Roe Boulevard, Patchogue, NY 11772-2603

## St. Lawrence University
**Canton, New York**                                 **CB member**
**www.stlawu.edu**                                   **CB code: 2805**

- Private 4-year liberal arts college
- Residential campus in small town
- 2,160 degree-seeking undergraduates: 54% women, 3% African American, 2% Asian American, 3% Hispanic American, 1% Native American, 5% international
- 103 degree-seeking graduate students
- 44% of applicants admitted
- Application essay required
- 77% graduate within 6 years; 23% enter graduate study

**General.** Founded in 1856. Regionally accredited. **Degrees:** 500 bachelor's awarded; master's offered. **ROTC:** Army, Air Force. **Location:** 70 miles from Ottawa, Canada. **Calendar:** Semester, limited summer session. **Full-time faculty:** 171 total; 98% have terminal degrees, 16% minority, 47% women. **Part-time faculty:** 19 total; 32% have terminal degrees, 21% minority, 63% women. **Class size:** 67% < 20, 32% 20-39, less than 1% 40-49, less than 1% 50-99, less than 1% >100. **Special facilities:** 1,000 contiguous acres include woods and river habitat for conducting primary research; science facility; center for arts technology; golf course; crew boathouse; Adirondack Semester yurt village.

**Freshman class profile.** 4,645 applied, 2,030 admitted, 628 enrolled.

| Mid 50% test scores | | Rank in top quarter: | 74% |
|---|---|---|---|
| SAT critical reading: | 560-640 | Rank in top tenth: | 35% |
| SAT math: | 560-640 | End year in good standing: | 88% |
| SAT writing: | 560-640 | Return as sophomores: | 88% |
| ACT composite: | 25-29 | Out-of-state: | 59% |
| GPA 3.50 or higher: | 54% | Live on campus: | 100% |
| GPA 3.0-3.49: | 41% | International: | 5% |
| GPA 2.0-2.99: | 5% | | |

**Basis for selection.** Academic record most important; test scores, extracurricular activities, seriousness of purpose and intellectual promise important. Students for whom English is not the native language must submit official TOEFL results and are encouraged to submit SAT or ACT. Interview recommended.

**High school preparation.** 20 units recommended. Recommended units include English 4, mathematics 4, social studies 2, history 2, science 4 and foreign language 4.

**2008-2009 Annual costs.** Tuition/fees: $37,915. Room/board: $9,645. Books/supplies: $650.

**2007-2008 Financial aid. Need-based:** 454 full-time freshmen applied for aid; 389 were judged to have need; 389 of these received aid. Average need met was 94%. Average scholarship/grant was $24,660; average loan $3,303. 84% of total undergraduate aid awarded as scholarships/grants, 16% as loans/jobs. **Non-need-based:** Awarded to 535 full-time undergraduates, including 173 freshmen. Scholarships awarded for academics, alumni affiliation, athletics, minority status, ROTC.

**Application procedures. Admission:** Closing date 2/1 (postmark date). $60 fee, may be waived for applicants with need. Application may be submitted online. Admission notification 3/31. Must reply by May 1 or within 2 week(s) if notified thereafter. **Financial aid:** Closing date 2/1. FAFSA, institutional form required. Applicants notified by 3/31; must reply by 5/1 or within 2 week(s) of notification.

**Academics.** Quantitative Resource Center for math assistance. **Special study options:** Combined bachelor's/graduate degree, cross-registration, double major, exchange student, independent study, internships, student-designed major, study abroad, teacher certification program, Washington semester. Community-based learning; 3-2 program in engineering with Clarkson University, Columbia University, Rensselaer Polytechnic Institute, University of Rochester, University of Southern California, Washington University of St. Louis; early assurance programs in medicine with SUNY Health Science Center at Syracuse and in dentistry with SUNY at Buffalo; combined bachelor's/graduate degree program in business administration with Clarkson University, Union College and Rochester Institute of Technology; 14 study abroad programs in Australia, Europe, Kenya, Japan, Costa Rica, India, Canada, Trinidad and Tobago, China. **Credit/placement by examination:** AP, CLEP, IB, institutional tests. 60 credit hours maximum toward bachelor's degree. **Support services:** Pre-admission summer program, reduced course load, tutoring, writing center.

**Majors. Area/ethnic studies:** African, Asian, Canadian. **Biology:** General, biochemistry, biophysics, conservation, neurobiology/physiology. **Computer sciences:** Computer science. **Conservation:** Environmental studies. **English:** American lit, British lit, creative writing. **Foreign languages:** General, French, German, Spanish. **History:** General. **Interdisciplinary:** Global studies, math/computer science, neuroscience. **Math:** General. **Philosophy/religion:** Philosophy, religion. **Physical sciences:** Chemistry, geology, geophysics, physics. **Psychology:** General. **Social sciences:** Anthropology, economics, political science, sociology. **Visual/performing arts:** Dramatic, studio arts.

**Most popular majors.** Biology 6%, English 8%, foreign language 6%, history 8%, psychology 13%, social sciences 33%, visual/performing arts 10%.

**Computing on campus.** 330 workstations in dormitories, library, computer center, student center. Dormitories wired for high-speed internet access and linked to campus network. Online course registration, helpline, repair service, student web hosting, wireless network available.

**Student life. Freshman orientation:** Mandatory. Preregistration for classes offered. Orientation is three days preceding the start of fall classes. Programs are focused on academic introductions to the liberal arts, to the living-learning community concept, and St. Lawrence traditions. **Policies:** First-Year Program requires freshmen to reside in college with academic/administrative staff. **Housing:** Guaranteed on-campus for all undergraduates. Coed dorms, apartments, fraternity/sorority housing, substance-free housing available. Townhouse apartments for senior leaders, theme cottages/halls, some suites available. Students can petition to have quiet or single-sex halls within dormitory. **Activities:** Campus ministries, choral groups, dance, drama,

film society, literary magazine, music ensembles, Model UN, radio station, student government, student newspaper, TV station, Jewish Student organization, Black Student Union, environmental awareness organization, Habitat for Humanity, outing club, academic honorary societies, Circle K, Amnesty International.

**Athletics.** NCAA. **Intercollegiate:** Baseball M, basketball, cross-country, equestrian, field hockey W, football (tackle) M, golf, ice hockey, lacrosse, rowing (crew), skiing, soccer, softball W, squash, swimming, tennis, track and field, volleyball W. **Intramural:** Basketball, football (non-tackle) M, football (tackle) M, ice hockey, racquetball M, rugby, soccer, softball W, tennis, triathlon, volleyball. **Team name:** Saints.

**Student services.** Alcohol/substance abuse counseling, campus ministries, career counseling, services for economically disadvantaged, student employment services, financial aid counseling, health services, minority student services, personal counseling, placement for graduates. **Physically disabled:** Services for visually, hearing impaired.

**Contact.** E-mail: admissions@stlawu.edu
Phone: (315) 229-5261 Toll-free number: (800) 285-1856
Fax: (315) 229-5818
Teresa Cowdrey, Vice President and Dean of Admissions and Financial Aid, St. Lawrence University, Payson Hall, Canton, NY 13617

---

## St. Thomas Aquinas College
**Sparkill, New York**
**www.stac.edu**

**CB member**
**CB code: 2807**

- Private 4-year liberal arts college
- Commuter campus in large town
- 1,437 degree-seeking undergraduates: 7% part-time, 54% women, 6% African American, 3% Asian American, 15% Hispanic American, 1% international
- 216 degree-seeking graduate students
- 80% of applicants admitted
- SAT or ACT (ACT writing optional) required
- 52% graduate within 6 years

**General.** Founded in 1952. Regionally accredited. **Degrees:** 274 bachelor's, 17 associate awarded; master's offered. **ROTC:** Air Force. **Location:** 15 miles from New York City. **Calendar:** Semester, extensive summer session. **Full-time faculty:** 64 total; 89% have terminal degrees, 12% minority, 50% women. **Part-time faculty:** 87 total; 21% have terminal degrees, 6% minority, 38% women. **Class size:** 47% < 20, 52% 20-39, less than 1% 50-99. **Special facilities:** Arts, sciences and technology center, digital imaging laboratory.

**Freshman class profile.** 1,331 applied, 1,067 admitted, 326 enrolled.

| Mid 50% test scores | | GPA 2.0-2.99: | 61% |
|---|---|---|---|
| SAT critical reading: | 420-510 | Rank in top quarter: | 35% |
| SAT math: | 410-530 | Rank in top tenth: | 5% |
| SAT writing: | 420-520 | Return as sophomores: | 72% |
| ACT composite: | 17-22 | Out-of-state: | 30% |
| GPA 3.50 or higher: | 12% | Live on campus: | 58% |
| GPA 3.0-3.49: | 14% | International: | 1% |

**Basis for selection.** School achievement record, test scores, recommendation, and interview considered. Applicants should be in top half of class and have GPA above 3.0. Essay, interview recommended for all; portfolio recommended for art program. **Homeschooled:** Statement describing homeschool structure and mission, transcript of courses and grades, state high school equivalency certificate, letter of recommendation (nonparent) required.

**High school preparation.** 20 units required. Required units include English 4, mathematics 3, social studies 4, science 3 (laboratory 2) and foreign language 3.

**2008-2009 Annual costs.** Tuition/fees: $20,000. Room/board: $9,730. Books/supplies: $750. Personal expenses: $1,000.

**2006-2007 Financial aid. Need-based:** 294 full-time freshmen applied for aid; 216 were judged to have need; 211 of these received aid. Average need met was 56%. Average scholarship/grant was $9,225; average loan $3,278. 60% of total undergraduate aid awarded as scholarships/grants, 40% as loans/jobs. **Non-need-based:** Awarded to 296 full-time undergraduates, including 72 freshmen. Scholarships awarded for academics, athletics.

**Application procedures. Admission:** No deadline. $30 fee. Application may be submitted online. Admission notification on a rolling basis beginning on or about 10/1. **Financial aid:** Priority date 2/15; no closing date. FAFSA required. Applicants notified on a rolling basis starting 3/1; must reply by 5/1 or within 4 week(s) of notification.

**Academics. Special study options:** Accelerated study, combined bachelor's/ graduate degree, cooperative education, cross-registration, double major, dual enrollment of high school students, ESL, exchange student, honors, independent study, internships, liberal arts/career combination, study abroad, teacher certification program, Washington semester. **Credit/placement by examination:** AP, CLEP, IB, SAT, ACT, institutional tests. 15 credit hours maximum toward associate degree, 30 toward bachelor's. **Support services:** Learning center, pre-admission summer program, reduced course load, remedial instruction, study skills assistance, tutoring, writing center.

**Majors. Biology:** General. **Business:** General, accounting, business admin, finance, international marketing, marketing. **Communications:** General, broadcast journalism, journalism. **Computer sciences:** General. **Education:** General, art, biology, chemistry, elementary, English, foreign languages, history, mathematics, multi-level teacher, physics, science, secondary, social studies, Spanish, special. **Engineering:** General. **English:** English lit. **Foreign languages:** General, French, Spanish. **Health:** Art therapy, predental, premedicine, prenursing, prepharmacy, preveterinary. **History:** General. **Interdisciplinary:** Biological/physical sciences, math/computer science. **Legal studies:** Prelaw. **Liberal arts:** Arts/sciences. **Math:** General, applied. **Parks/ recreation:** Facilities management. **Philosophy/religion:** Philosophy, religion. **Physical sciences:** Chemistry, physics. **Protective services:** Law enforcement admin. **Psychology:** General. **Social sciences:** General. **Visual/ performing arts:** Art, commercial/advertising art, graphic design, studio arts.

**Most popular majors.** Business/marketing 23%, communications/ journalism 7%, education 12%, parks/recreation 6%, psychology 11%, security/ protective services 9%, social sciences 14%, visual/performing arts 6%.

**Computing on campus.** 200 workstations in dormitories, library, computer center, student center. Dormitories wired for high-speed internet access and linked to campus network. Commuter students can connect to campus network. Online library, helpline, wireless network available.

**Student life. Freshman orientation:** Mandatory, $75 fee. Preregistration for classes offered. **Housing:** Guaranteed on-campus for freshmen. Single-sex dorms, apartments, substance-free housing available. $250 nonrefundable deposit, deadline 5/1. **Activities:** Choral groups, dance, drama, literary magazine, music ensembles, musical theater, opera, radio station, student government, student newspaper, TV station, political union, business association, community service organization.

**Athletics.** NAIA, NCAA. **Intercollegiate:** Baseball M, basketball, cross-country, golf, lacrosse W, soccer, softball W, tennis, track and field. **Intramural:** Basketball, skiing, softball, tennis. **Team name:** Spartans.

**Student services.** Adult student services, alcohol/substance abuse counseling, campus ministries, career counseling, student employment services, financial aid counseling, health services, personal counseling, placement for graduates, veterans' counselor, women's services. **Physically disabled:** Services for visually, speech, hearing impaired. **Learning disabled:** Comprehensive services available.

**Contact.** E-mail: admissions@stac.edu
Phone: (845) 398-4100 Toll-free number: (800) 999-7822
Fax: (845) 398-4114
Danielle Mac Kay, Director of Admissions, St. Thomas Aquinas College, 125 Route 340, Sparkill, NY 10976

---

## Sarah Lawrence College

**Bronxville, New York**

**www.sarahlawrence.edu**

**CB member**

**CB code: 2810**

- ▸ Private 4-year liberal arts college
- ▸ Residential campus in small city
- ▸ 1,314 degree-seeking undergraduates: 4% part-time, 75% women, 4% African American, 5% Asian American, 5% Hispanic American, 1% Native American, 2% international
- ▸ 312 degree-seeking graduate students
- ▸ 44% of applicants admitted
- ▸ Application essay required
- ▸ 79% graduate within 6 years; 14% enter graduate study

**General.** Founded in 1926. Regionally accredited. **Degrees:** 282 bachelor's awarded; master's offered. **Location:** 15 miles from New York City. **Calendar:** Semester, limited summer session. **Full-time faculty:** 195 total; 23% minority, 52% women. **Part-time faculty:** 48 total; 21% minority,

58% women. **Class size:** 94% < 20, 3% 20-39, 2% 40-49, 2% 50-99. **Special facilities:** Visual arts center, student-run theater, early childhood center, greenhouse.

**Freshman class profile.** 2,801 applied, 1,236 admitted, 278 enrolled.

| | | | |
|---|---|---|---|
| GPA 3.50 or higher: | 64% | Rank in top tenth: | 37% |
| GPA 3.0-3.49: | 30% | Out-of-state: | 79% |
| GPA 2.0-2.99: | 6% | Live on campus: | 100% |
| Rank in top quarter: | 84% | International: | 4% |

**Basis for selection.** Student essays (one of which is a graded, analytical writing sample) and transcript most important. Letters of recommendation and extracurricular commitments also important. Interview considered. Students interested in visual art or music encouraged to submit slides, cassette tapes, or compositions. If on-campus interview not possible, applicant may arrange interview with an alumna/us or counselor.

**High school preparation.** College-preparatory program required. Required and recommended units include English 4, mathematics 2-4, social studies 4, history 2-4, science 2-4 and foreign language 2-4.

**2007-2008 Annual costs.** Tuition/fees: $38,090. Room/board: $13,316. Books/supplies: $600. Personal expenses: $800.

**2007-2008 Financial aid.** All financial aid based on need. 224 full-time freshmen applied for aid; 184 were judged to have need; 184 of these received aid. Average need met was 92%. Average scholarship/grant was $28,313; average loan $2,576. 76% of total undergraduate aid awarded as scholarships/ grants, 24% as loans/jobs.

**Application procedures. Admission:** Closing date 1/1 (postmark date). $60 fee, may be waived for applicants with need. Application may be submitted online. Admission notification 4/1. Must reply by 5/1. **Financial aid:** Closing date 2/1. FAFSA, CSS PROFILE required. Applicants notified by 4/1; must reply by 5/1.

**Academics.** 90% of classes are seminars with 11-12 students. Individual biweekly conferences with professors and self-designed independent study available. Students design own course of study with advisor. Although there are no formal majors, students may de facto create double major. Course work required in 3 of 4 divisions: humanities, social sciences, science and math, creative and performing arts. **Special study options:** Combined bachelor's/graduate degree, double major, exchange student, independent study, internships, student-designed major, study abroad, teacher certification program. Academic year in Oxford, Paris, Florence, Catania (Sicily), Cuba, guest year at Reed College (Oregon and its study abroad program) or guest year at Eugene Lang College of the New School (New York City); theater year in London. **Credit/placement by examination:** AP, CLEP, IB. **Support services:** Writing center.

**Majors. English:** English lit. **Liberal arts:** Arts/sciences. **Philosophy/ religion:** Judaic. **Social sciences:** Urban studies.

**Computing on campus.** 110 workstations in library, computer center. Dormitories wired for high-speed internet access and linked to campus network. Commuter students can connect to campus network. Online library, helpline, student web hosting available.

**Student life. Freshman orientation:** Mandatory. 9-day program held just before fall semester. **Housing:** Guaranteed on-campus for freshmen. Coed dorms, single-sex dorms, substance-free housing available. $500 nonrefundable deposit, deadline 5/1. Freshmen required to live on campus unless living at home. **Activities:** Jazz band, campus ministries, choral groups, dance, drama, film society, international student organizations, literary magazine, music ensembles, musical theater, radio station, student government, student newspaper, symphony orchestra, Amnesty International, Harambe (students of African descent), Hillel, Queer Variety Coalition, Beyond Compliance, Asian-Pacific Islander Coalition to Advance Diversity, Unidad (students of Latino descent), Our Time Musical Theater Troupe, The Experimental Music Club, SLC ACTS UP.

**Athletics. Intercollegiate:** Basketball M, equestrian, rowing (crew), softball W, swimming W, tennis, volleyball W. **Team name:** Gryphons.

**Student services.** Adult student services, alcohol/substance abuse counseling, career counseling, student employment services, financial aid counseling, health services, minority student services, personal counseling, placement for graduates. **Physically disabled:** Services for visually, speech, hearing impaired.

**Contact.** E-mail: slcadmit@sarahlawrence.edu
Phone: (914) 395-2510 Toll-free number: (800) 888-2858
Fax: (914) 395-2515
Stephen Schierloh, Dean of Admission, Sarah Lawrence College, One Mead Way, Bronxville, NY 10708-5999

## School of Visual Arts
**New York, New York**
www.sva.edu

**CB member**
**CB code: 2835**

- For-profit 4-year visual arts college
- Commuter campus in very large city
- 3,323 degree-seeking undergraduates: 3% part-time, 54% women, 4% African American, 13% Asian American, 10% Hispanic American, 13% international
- 424 degree-seeking graduate students
- 72% of applicants admitted
- SAT or ACT (ACT writing optional), application essay required
- 66% graduate within 6 years; 10% enter graduate study

**General.** Founded in 1947. Regionally accredited. Faculty composed entirely of working professionals. **Degrees:** 631 bachelor's awarded; master's offered. **Calendar:** Semester, limited summer session. **Full-time faculty:** 102 total; 55% have terminal degrees, 7% minority, 30% women. **Part-time faculty:** 728 total; 44% have terminal degrees, 7% minority, 37% women. **Class size:** 70% < 20, 28% 20-39, 2% 50-99, less than 1% >100. **Special facilities:** Visual arts museum, Milton Glaser design study center and archives, 8 student galleries including 9,000-square-foot gallery.

**Freshman class profile.** 2,565 applied, 1,851 admitted, 664 enrolled.

| Mid 50% test scores | | | |
|---|---|---|---|
| SAT critical reading: | 460-580 | GPA 3.0-3.49: | 35% |
| SAT math: | 440-560 | GPA 2.0-2.99: | 44% |
| SAT writing: | 460-570 | Return as sophomores: | 84% |
| ACT composite: | 20-25 | Out-of-state: | 56% |
| GPA 3.50 or higher: | 20% | Live on campus: | 70% |
| | | International: | 8% |

**Basis for selection.** Portfolio, academic record, interview important. Character and professional recommendations optional. Interview optional. Portfolio required for all programs. **Homeschooled:** Statement describing homeschool structure and mission, transcript of courses and grades, state high school equivalency certificate, interview, letter of recommendation (nonparent) required. GED.

**High school preparation.** Recommended units include English 4, social studies 4, history 4 and visual/performing arts 2.

**2008-2009 Annual costs.** Tuition/fees: $25,500. Additional fees vary by department. Room only: $11,350. Books/supplies: $2,100. Personal expenses: $1,600.

**2007-2008 Financial aid. Need-based:** 472 full-time freshmen applied for aid; 411 were judged to have need; 405 of these received aid. Average need met was 44%. Average scholarship/grant was $5,859; average loan $3,701. 29% of total undergraduate aid awarded as scholarships/grants, 71% as loans/jobs. **Non-need-based:** Awarded to 521 full-time undergraduates, including 116 freshmen. Scholarships awarded for art.

**Application procedures. Admission:** Priority date 2/1; no deadline. $50 fee, may be waived for applicants with need. Application may be submitted online. Admission notification on a rolling basis beginning on or about 2/1. Admitted applicants are encouraged to reply by April 15. **Financial aid:** Priority date 2/1; no closing date. FAFSA required. Applicants notified on a rolling basis starting 2/15; must reply within 4 week(s) of notification.

**Academics.** Curriculum designed to prepare students to graduate as working professionals in the arts. **Special study options:** ESL, exchange student, honors, internships, liberal arts/career combination, study abroad, teacher certification program. **Credit/placement by examination:** AP, CLEP, IB. **Support services:** Learning center, pre-admission summer program, reduced course load, remedial instruction, study skills assistance, tutoring, writing center.

**Honors college/program.** Additional application component.

**Majors. Visual/performing arts:** Art history/conservation, commercial/advertising art, interior design, photography, studio arts. **Other:** Film, video, animation.

**Computing on campus.** 728 workstations in library, computer center, student center. Dormitories wired for high-speed internet access and linked to campus network. Commuter students can connect to campus network. Online library, helpline, wireless network available.

**Student life. Freshman orientation:** Mandatory. Comprehensive 5-day program. **Housing:** Coed dorms, single-sex dorms, substance-free housing available. $800 nonrefundable deposit, deadline 5/1. **Activities:** Campus ministries, film society, international student organizations, literary magazine, radio station, student government, Korean Christian, animal rights, international film club, Campus Crusade for Christ, political, anime film club, fine art club, MFA Speakers, wrestling club.

**Athletics. Intramural:** Baseball, tennis.

**Student services.** Alcohol/substance abuse counseling, career counseling, student employment services, financial aid counseling, health services, personal counseling, placement for graduates, veterans' counselor, women's services. **Physically disabled:** Services for hearing impaired.

**Contact.** E-mail: admissions@sva.edu
Phone: (212) 592-2100 Toll-free number: (800) 436-4204
Fax: (212) 592-2116
Adam Rogers, Director of Admissions, School of Visual Arts, 209 East 23rd Street, New York, NY 10010-3994

## Shor Yoshuv Rabbinical College
**Lawrence, New York**
www.shoryoshuv.org

**CB code: 7129**

- Private 4-year rabbinical college for men affiliated with Jewish faith
- Very large city

**General.** Accredited by AARTS. **Calendar:** Continuous.

**Annual costs/financial aid.** Tuition/fees (2007-2008): $8,360. Room/board: $5,000.

**Contact.** Phone: (516) 239-9002
Admissions Director, One Cedar Lawn Avenue, Lawrence, NY 11559

## Siena College
**Loudonville, New York**
www.siena.edu

**CB member**
**CB code: 2814**

- Private 4-year liberal arts college affiliated with Roman Catholic Church
- Residential campus in large town
- 3,151 degree-seeking undergraduates: 4% part-time, 56% women, 2% African American, 4% Asian American, 4% Hispanic American
- 54% of applicants admitted
- SAT or ACT with writing, application essay required
- 79% graduate within 6 years

**General.** Founded in 1937. Regionally accredited. Affiliated with the Franciscan Friars. **Degrees:** 766 bachelor's awarded. **ROTC:** Army, Air Force. **Location:** 2 miles from Albany. **Calendar:** Semester, limited summer session. **Full-time faculty:** 187 total; 92% have terminal degrees, 9% minority, 37% women. **Part-time faculty:** 130 total; 46% have terminal degrees, 5% minority, 41% women. **Class size:** 32% < 20, 68% 20-39. **Special facilities:** Financial technology center featuring real-time capital market trading room, accounting lab, stock ticker, plasma data screens, 24 multimedia workstations.

**Freshman class profile.** 5,792 applied, 3,138 admitted, 780 enrolled.

| Mid 50% test scores | | | |
|---|---|---|---|
| SAT critical reading: | 500-590 | GPA 2.0-2.99: | 14% |
| SAT math: | 520-620 | Rank in top quarter: | 57% |
| SAT writing: | 490-590 | Rank in top tenth: | 21% |
| ACT composite: | 20-24 | Return as sophomores: | 87% |
| GPA 3.50 or higher: | 51% | Out-of-state: | 18% |
| GPA 3.0-3.49: | 35% | Live on campus: | 92% |

**Basis for selection.** School achievement record most important, priority given to students with challenging courses. Test scores, activities, recommendations also important. Interview required for Albany Medical School program finalists; recommended for all others. **Homeschooled:** Transcript of courses and grades required.

**High school preparation.** 13 units required; 19 recommended. Required and recommended units include English 4, mathematics 3-4, social studies 1, history 2-3, science 3-4 (laboratory 3-4) and foreign language 3.

**2007-2008 Annual costs.** Tuition/fees: $22,685. Room/board: $8,875. Books/supplies: $930. Personal expenses: $888.

**2006-2007 Financial aid. Need-based:** 629 full-time freshmen applied for aid; 488 were judged to have need; 487 of these received aid. Average need met was 76%. Average scholarship/grant was $11,995; average loan $2,943. 76% of total undergraduate aid awarded as scholarships/grants, 24%

as loans/jobs. **Non-need-based:** Awarded to 783 full-time undergraduates, including 229 freshmen. Scholarships awarded for academics, art, athletics, leadership, minority status, ROTC, state residency.

**Application procedures. Admission:** Closing date 3/1 (postmark date). $50 fee, may be waived for applicants with need. Application may be submitted online. Admission notification 3/15. Must reply by 5/1. **Financial aid:** Closing date 2/15. FAFSA required. Applicants notified by 4/1; must reply by 5/1.

**Academics.** Extensive internship program in capital district with state legislature, businesses, social agencies, libraries, and museums. **Special study options:** Accelerated study, combined bachelor's/graduate degree, cross-registration, double major, ESL, honors, independent study, internships, liberal arts/career combination, study abroad, teacher certification program, Washington semester. **Credit/placement by examination:** AP, CLEP, IB, institutional tests. 36 credit hours maximum toward bachelor's degree. 36 total credits permitted by proficiency examination, non-collegiate-sponsored instructional/experiential learning combined. **Support services:** Tutoring, writing center.

**Majors. Area/ethnic studies:** American. **Biology:** General, biochemistry, ecology. **Business:** Accounting, finance, marketing. **Computer sciences:** General. **English:** English lit. **Foreign languages:** Classics, French, Spanish. **History:** General. **Math:** General, applied, computational. **Philosophy/religion:** Philosophy, religion. **Physical sciences:** Chemistry, physics. **Psychology:** General. **Public administration:** Social work. **Social sciences:** Economics, political science, sociology. **Visual/performing arts:** General.

**Most popular majors.** Biology 11%, business/marketing 45%, English 7%, psychology 12%, social sciences 8%.

**Computing on campus.** 456 workstations in library, computer center. Dormitories wired for high-speed internet access and linked to campus network. Commuter students can connect to campus network. Online course registration, online library, helpline, wireless network available.

**Student life. Freshman orientation:** Mandatory, $180 fee. Preregistration for classes offered. 3-day summer program. **Housing:** Guaranteed on-campus for freshmen. Coed dorms, special housing for disabled, substance-free housing available. On-campus townhouses (men's and women's) available. **Activities:** Pep band, dance, drama, literary magazine, musical theater, radio station, student government, student newspaper, TV station, approximately 70 clubs and organizations.

**Athletics.** NCAA. **Intercollegiate:** Baseball M, basketball, cross-country, diving W, field hockey W, golf, lacrosse, soccer, softball W, swimming W, tennis, volleyball W, water polo W. **Intramural:** Basketball, football (non-tackle), golf, soccer, softball, volleyball. **Team name:** Saints.

**Student services.** Alcohol/substance abuse counseling, campus ministries, career counseling, services for economically disadvantaged, student employment services, financial aid counseling, health services, minority student services, personal counseling, placement for graduates, women's services. **Physically disabled:** Services for visually, speech, hearing impaired.

**Contact.** E-mail: admit@siena.edu
Phone: (518) 783-2423 Toll-free number: (888) 287-4362
Fax: (518) 783-2436
Heather Renault, Director for Admissions, Siena College, 515 Loudon Road, Loudonville, NY 12211-1462

---

## Skidmore College
**Saratoga Springs, New York**
www.skidmore.edu

**CB member**
**CB code: 2815**

- Private 4-year liberal arts college
- Residential campus in large town
- 2,771 degree-seeking undergraduates: 6% part-time, 60% women, 4% African American, 7% Asian American, 5% Hispanic American, 1% Native American, 3% international
- 54 degree-seeking graduate students
- 37% of applicants admitted
- SAT or ACT with writing, application essay required
- 81% graduate within 6 years; 19% enter graduate study

**General.** Founded in 1903. Regionally accredited. **Degrees:** 670 bachelor's awarded; master's offered. **ROTC:** Army, Air Force. **Location:** 30 miles from Albany. **Calendar:** Semester, limited summer session. **Full-time faculty:** 232 total; 84% have terminal degrees, 12% minority, 55% women. **Part-time faculty:** 112 total; 33% have terminal degrees, 12% minority, 58% women. **Class size:** 69% < 20, 28% 20-39, less than 1% 40-49, 1% 50-99, less than 1% >100. **Special facilities:** Fine and performing arts

facilities, equestrian center, 400 acres of woodlands and trails, teaching museum.

**Freshman class profile.** 6,768 applied, 2,479 admitted, 684 enrolled.

| Mid 50% test scores | | | |
|---|---|---|---|
| SAT critical reading: | 580-680 | Rank in top quarter: | 80% |
| SAT math: | 580-670 | Rank in top tenth: | 39% |
| SAT writing: | 590-690 | End year in good standing: | 95% |
| ACT composite: | 26-30 | Return as sophomores: | 94% |
| GPA 3.50 or higher: | 36% | Out-of-state: | 67% |
| GPA 3.0-3.49: | 45% | Live on campus: | 100% |
| GPA 2.0-2.99: | 19% | International: | 3% |

**Basis for selection.** Rigor of school record very important. Class rank, GPA, recommendations, and test scores also important. SAT Subject Tests recommended. 2 SAT Subject Tests recommended of all applicants. Interview recommended for all.

**High school preparation.** Recommended units include English 4, mathematics 4, social studies 4, science 4 (laboratory 3) and foreign language 4.

**2007-2008 Annual costs.** Tuition/fees: $36,860. Room/board: $9,836. Books/supplies: $1,054. Personal expenses: $1,000.

**2007-2008 Financial aid. Need-based:** 355 full-time freshmen applied for aid; 295 were judged to have need; 295 of these received aid. Average need met was 88%. Average scholarship/grant was $30,321; average loan $3,016. 85% of total undergraduate aid awarded as scholarships/grants, 15% as loans/jobs. **Non-need-based:** Awarded to 198 full-time undergraduates, including 113 freshmen. Scholarships awarded for music/drama.

**Application procedures. Admission:** Closing date 1/15 (postmark date). $60 fee, may be waived for applicants with need. Application may be submitted online. Admission notification 4/1. Must reply by 5/1. Enrollment deposit of $500 required on or before May 1. **Financial aid:** Closing date 1/15. FAFSA, CSS PROFILE required. Applicants notified by 4/1; must reply by 5/1.

**Academics. Special study options:** Accelerated study, combined bachelor's/graduate degree, cross-registration, distance learning, double major, dual enrollment of high school students, exchange student, external degree, honors, independent study, internships, liberal arts/career combination, student-designed major, study abroad, teacher certification program, Washington semester. 3+2 programs in engineering with Dartmouth College and Clarkson University, 4+1 MAT with Union College, 4+1 MBA with Clarkson University and the Graduate College at Union University. **Credit/placement by examination:** AP, CLEP, IB, SAT, ACT, institutional tests. Up to 60 hours may be counted toward degree. Maximum of 12 semester hours may be granted in credit through CLEP subject examinations. **Support services:** Pre-admission summer program, study skills assistance, tutoring, writing center.

**Majors. Area/ethnic studies:** American, Asian, French, women's. **Biology:** General. **Business:** General. **Computer sciences:** General. **Conservation:** Environmental studies. **Education:** Elementary. **English:** English lit. **Foreign languages:** Classics, French, German, Spanish. **History:** General. **Interdisciplinary:** Biopsychology, neuroscience. **Liberal arts:** Arts/sciences. **Math:** General. **Parks/recreation:** Exercise sciences. **Philosophy/religion:** Philosophy, religion. **Physical sciences:** Chemistry, geology, physics. **Psychology:** General. **Public administration:** Social work. **Social sciences:** Anthropology, economics, international relations, political science, sociology. **Visual/performing arts:** Art history/conservation, dance, dramatic, music history. **Other:** Biology/philosophy.

**Most popular majors.** Business/marketing 13%, English 8%, foreign language 8%, liberal arts 8%, psychology 8%, social sciences 18%, visual/performing arts 15%.

**Computing on campus.** Dormitories wired for high-speed internet access and linked to campus network. Commuter students can connect to campus network. Online course registration, online library, helpline, student web hosting, wireless network available.

**Student life. Freshman orientation:** Mandatory. Programs on and off campus. Fee for off-campus programs. **Housing:** Guaranteed on-campus for all undergraduates. Coed dorms, single-sex dorms, special housing for disabled, apartments available. $500 nonrefundable deposit, deadline 5/1. There is a gender neutral wing. Townhouse clusters available for upperclassmen. **Activities:** Bands, campus ministries, choral groups, dance, drama, film society, international student organizations, literary magazine, music ensembles, musical theater, opera, radio station, student government, student newspaper, symphony orchestra, TV station, 80 clubs and organizations.

**Athletics.** NCAA. **Intercollegiate:** Baseball M, basketball, diving, equestrian W, field hockey W, golf M, ice hockey M, lacrosse, rowing (crew), soccer, softball W, swimming, tennis, volleyball W. **Intramural:** Basketball, football (tackle) M, racquetball, soccer, softball, tennis, volleyball, water polo. **Team name:** Thoroughbreds.

**Student services.** Alcohol/substance abuse counseling, campus ministries, career counseling, services for economically disadvantaged, student employment services, financial aid counseling, health services, minority student services, on-campus daycare, personal counseling, placement for graduates, veterans' counselor. **Physically disabled:** Services for visually, speech, hearing impaired.

**Contact.** E-mail: admissions@skidmore.edu
Phone: (518) 580-5570 Toll-free number: (800) 867-6007
Fax: (518) 580-5584
Mary Lou Bates, Dean of Admissions and Financial Aid, Skidmore College, 815 North Broadway, Saratoga Springs, NY 12866

---

## State University of New York at Albany

**Albany, New York**      **CB member**
**www.albany.edu**      **CB code: 2532**

- Public 4-year university
- Residential campus in small city
- 12,449 degree-seeking undergraduates: 5% part-time, 49% women, 9% African American, 6% Asian American, 7% Hispanic American, 2% international
- 4,382 degree-seeking graduate students
- 52% of applicants admitted
- SAT or ACT with writing required
- 62% graduate within 6 years; 51% enter graduate study

**General.** Founded in 1844. Regionally accredited. Extensive internships in New York's Capital Region. International center for research and development in emerging field of nanotechnology. **Degrees:** 2,770 bachelor's awarded; master's, doctoral offered. **ROTC:** Army, Air Force. **Location:** 4 miles from downtown. **Calendar:** Semester, extensive summer session. **Full-time faculty:** 672 total; 93% have terminal degrees, 16% minority, 37% women. **Part-time faculty:** 640 total; 13% minority, 48% women. **Class size:** 26% < 20, 41% 20-39, 10% 40-49, 10% 50-99, 12% >100. **Special facilities:** Northeast Regional Forensic Institute; atmospheric science research center and Whiteface Mountain observation facility, microbeam analysis facility, large fine arts work areas, peptide synthesis facility, recombinant DNA sequencing laboratories, nanoscale science and engineering facilities.

**Freshman class profile.** 20,249 applied, 10,432 admitted, 2,519 enrolled.

| Mid 50% test scores | | | |
|---|---|---|---|
| SAT critical reading: | 500-590 | Rank in top quarter: | 49% |
| SAT math: | 510-610 | Rank in top tenth: | 15% |
| ACT composite: | 22-26 | Return as sophomores: | 84% |
| GPA 3.50 or higher: | 31% | Out-of-state: | 8% |
| GPA 3.0-3.49: | 49% | Live on campus: | 98% |
| GPA 2.0-2.99: | 20% | International: | 2% |

**Basis for selection.** Secondary school record, class rank, GPA, standardized test scores very important; essay, recommendations important.

**High school preparation.** 18 units required. Required and recommended units include English 4, mathematics 2-4, social studies 3, history 2, science 2-3 (laboratory 2-3), foreign language 1-3 and academic electives 4.

**2007-2008 Annual costs.** Tuition/fees: $6,018; $12,278 out-of-state. Room/board: $9,032. Books/supplies: $1,000. Personal expenses: $1,750.

**2006-2007 Financial aid. Need-based:** 2,035 full-time freshmen applied for aid; 1,354 were judged to have need; 1,337 of these received aid. Average need met was 70%. Average scholarship/grant was $5,510; average loan $3,324. 52% of total undergraduate aid awarded as scholarships/grants, 48% as loans/jobs. **Non-need-based:** Awarded to 972 full-time undergraduates, including 216 freshmen. Scholarships awarded for academics, athletics, state residency.

**Application procedures. Admission:** Priority date 1/15; deadline 3/1 (receipt date). $40 fee, may be waived for applicants with need. Application may be submitted online. Admission notification on a rolling basis beginning on or about 1/1. Must reply by May 1 or within 2 week(s) if notified thereafter. **Financial aid:** Priority date 3/15; no closing date. FAFSA required. Applicants notified on a rolling basis starting 3/15; must reply by 5/1 or within 2 week(s) of notification.

**Academics.** Project Renaissance year-long program for first-year students offers interdisciplinary course of study, close acquaintance with faculty in program, and community living. Participation open to all freshmen on first-come, first-served basis. **Special study options:** Accelerated study, combined bachelor's/graduate degree, cross-registration, distance learning, double major, dual enrollment of high school students, ESL, honors, independent study, internships, liberal arts/career combination, student-designed major, study abroad, Washington semester. Accelerated 5-year bachelor's/master's in 40 fields, internships with New York State Legislature, 3+3 program with Albany Law School, biology/dental program with Boston University Goldman School of Dental Medicine, bachelor's/doctor of optometry with SUNY State College, early assurance program with Albany Medical College and SUNY Upstate Medical University. **Credit/placement by examination:** AP, CLEP, IB. 60 credit hours maximum toward bachelor's degree. **Support services:** Pre-admission summer program, remedial instruction, study skills assistance, tutoring, writing center.

**Honors college/program.** Applicants admitted as Presidential or Douglass Scholars are invited to apply to the Honors College. The application consists of a short essay and is submitted for review by the Honors College Admission Committee. Approximately 125 freshmen will be admitted and enter the Honors College each fall. An additional 25 current University at Albany students will be admitted at the end of their first semester at the University.

**Majors. Area/ethnic studies:** African-American, Asian, Caribbean, Central/Eastern European, Chinese, East Asian, Japanese, Latin American, Russian/Slavic, women's. **Biology:** General, biochemistry, environmental, molecular. **Business:** Accounting, business admin. **Communications:** General. **Computer sciences:** General, information systems. **English:** English lit, speech/rhetoric. **Foreign languages:** Classics, French, Italian, linguistics, Russian, Spanish. **Health:** Predental, premedicine, prepharmacy, preveterinary. **History:** General. **Interdisciplinary:** Classical/archaeology, medieval/Renaissance. **Math:** General, applied. **Philosophy/religion:** Judaic, philosophy, religion. **Physical sciences:** Atmospheric science, chemistry, physics. **Protective services:** Criminal justice. **Psychology:** General. **Public administration:** Social work. **Social sciences:** Anthropology, economics, geography, political science, sociology, urban studies. **Visual/performing arts:** Art history/conservation, dramatic, music performance, music theory/composition, studio arts. **Other:** Globalization Studies.

**Most popular majors.** Biology 7%, business/marketing 14%, communications/journalism 8%, English 9%, history 6%, psychology 13%, social sciences 24%.

**Computing on campus.** 500 workstations in dormitories, library, computer center. Dormitories wired for high-speed internet access and linked to campus network. Commuter students can connect to campus network. Online course registration, online library, helpline, student web hosting, wireless network available.

**Student life. Freshman orientation:** Mandatory, $180 fee. Preregistration for classes offered. 2 days in summer with parental participation, 2 days in fall without parental participation. **Housing:** Guaranteed on-campus for freshmen. Coed dorms, apartments, substance-free housing available. $125 fully refundable deposit. Individualized services for disabled students available, including accessible housing information. **Activities:** Bands, campus ministries, choral groups, dance, drama, international student organizations, literary magazine, music ensembles, musical theater, radio station, student government, student newspaper, symphony orchestra, over 200 student groups.

**Athletics.** NCAA. **Intercollegiate:** Baseball M, basketball, cross-country, field hockey W, football (tackle) M, golf W, lacrosse, rugby, soccer, softball W, tennis W, track and field, volleyball W. **Intramural:** Basketball, football (non-tackle), racquetball, soccer, softball, tennis, track and field, volleyball. **Team name:** Great Danes.

**Student services.** Alcohol/substance abuse counseling, campus ministries, career counseling, services for economically disadvantaged, student employment services, financial aid counseling, health services, legal services, minority student services, on-campus daycare, personal counseling, placement for graduates, women's services. **Physically disabled:** Services for visually, speech, hearing impaired. **Learning disabled:** Comprehensive services available.

**Contact.** E-mail: ugadmissions@albany.edu
Phone: (518) 442-5435 Fax: (518) 442-5383
Robert Andrea, Director of Undergraduate Admission and Recruitment, State University of New York at Albany, Office of Undergraduate Admissions, University Hall 112, Albany, NY 12222

---

## State University of New York at Binghamton

**Binghamton, New York**      **CB member**
**www.binghamton.edu**      **CB code: 2535**

- Public 4-year university
- Residential campus in small city

- 11,435 degree-seeking undergraduates: 4% part-time, 48% women, 5% African American, 13% Asian American, 7% Hispanic American, 8% international
- 2,716 degree-seeking graduate students
- 39% of applicants admitted
- SAT or ACT with writing, application essay required
- 79% graduate within 6 years; 45% enter graduate study

**General.** Founded in 1946. Regionally accredited. Kosher kitchen, union hall, 4 libraries. **Degrees:** 2,875 bachelor's awarded; master's, doctoral offered. **ROTC:** Army, Air Force. **Location:** 50 miles from Ithaca, 70 miles from Syracuse. **Calendar:** Semester, extensive summer session. **Full-time faculty:** 575 total; 93% have terminal degrees, 24% minority, 38% women. **Part-time faculty:** 273 total; 10% minority, 53% women. **Class size:** 41% < 20, 38% 20-39, 7% 40-49, 8% 50-99, 6% >100. **Special facilities:** 190-acre nature preserve, 4-climate greenhouse, performing arts center (5 theaters), art/dance studios, sculpture foundry, research centers, electron microcopy laboratories, geographic information systems core facility, public archeology facility, integrated electronics engineering center, institute for child development, information commons, events center.

**Freshman class profile.** 25,242 applied, 9,799 admitted, 2,304 enrolled.

| Mid 50% test scores | | Rank in top quarter: | 85% |
|---|---|---|---|
| SAT critical reading: | 570-660 | Rank in top tenth: | 49% |
| SAT math: | 610-690 | End year in good standing: | 90% |
| ACT composite: | 25-29 | Return as sophomores: | 90% |
| GPA 3.50 or higher: | 71% | Out-of-state: | 10% |
| GPA 3.0-3.49: | 23% | Live on campus: | 94% |
| GPA 2.0-2.99: | 5% | International: | 10% |

**Basis for selection.** Admission based on academic strength as measured by quality of courses, grades and grade trend, and test scores. Evidence of intellectual curiosity, interest in others, and nonacademic pursuits sought through application. Geographic, socioeconomic, and ethnic diversity considered. SAT or ACT scores received on a rolling basis for fall-term admission. SAT Subject Test scores not applicable. Audition offered for music; portfolio review offered for art. **Homeschooled:** Students required to obtain documentation of equivalency from local school boards.

**High school preparation.** 16 units required. Required and recommended units include English 4, mathematics 3-4, social studies 2, history 3, science 2-3 and foreign language 3. 3 units of 1 foreign language or 2 each of 2 foreign languages required of liberal arts applicants.

**2007-2008 Annual costs.** Tuition/fees: $6,012; $12,272 out-of-state. Room/board: $9,188. Books/supplies: $800.

**2007-2008 Financial aid.** **Need-based:** 1,736 full-time freshmen applied for aid; 945 were judged to have need; 936 of these received aid. Average need met was 80%. Average scholarship/grant was $5,421; average loan $3,439. 36% of total undergraduate aid awarded as scholarships/grants, 64% as loans/jobs. **Non-need-based:** Awarded to 1,758 full-time undergraduates, including 564 freshmen. Scholarships awarded for academics, art, athletics, leadership, minority status, music/drama, state residency.

**Application procedures.** **Admission:** Priority date 12/1; no deadline. $40 fee, may be waived for applicants with need. Application may be submitted online. Admission notification on a rolling basis beginning on or about 4/1. Must reply by May 1 or within 4 week(s) if notified thereafter. **Financial aid:** Priority date 2/1; no closing date. FAFSA required. Applicants notified on a rolling basis starting 3/17; must reply within 2 week(s) of notification.

**Academics.** Learning community program is residentially based and targeted primarily for first-year students. **Special study options:** Accelerated study, combined bachelor's/graduate degree, cross-registration, distance learning, double major, dual enrollment of high school students, ESL, exchange student, honors, independent study, internships, liberal arts/career combination, student-designed major, study abroad, teacher certification program, Washington semester. Individualized major programs; early assurance (pre-med, special health care, dentistry and optometry); 3-2 and 4-1 combined BA or BS/MA or MS degree programs. **Credit/placement by examination:** AP, CLEP, IB, institutional tests. 32 credit hours maximum toward bachelor's degree. **Support services:** Learning center, pre-admission summer program, study skills assistance, tutoring, writing center.

**Majors.** **Area/ethnic studies:** African-American, Asian, Asian-American, Caribbean, Latin American. **Biology:** General, biochemistry, cellular/molecular, ecology, evolutionary. **Business:** Accounting, accounting/business management, business admin, entrepreneurial studies, finance, international, management information systems, management science, marketing. **Computer sciences:** General, computer science, information systems. **Conservation:** Environmental studies. **Engineering:** Biomedical, computer, electrical, industrial, mechanical, systems. **English:** Creative writing, English

lit, speech/rhetoric. **Family/consumer sciences:** Family studies. **Foreign languages:** Arabic, Biblical, classics, comparative lit, French, German, Hebrew, Italian, Latin, linguistics, Spanish. **Health:** Nursing (RN). **History:** General. **Interdisciplinary:** Global studies, medieval/Renaissance. **Math:** General. **Philosophy/religion:** Judaic, philosophy. **Physical sciences:** Applied physics, chemistry, geology, geophysics, physics. **Psychology:** General, psychobiology. **Social sciences:** Anthropology, economics, geography, international relations, political science, sociology. **Visual/performing arts:** Acting, art, art history/conservation, cinematography, dance, design, directing/producing, dramatic, drawing, film/cinema, music performance, painting, printmaking, sculpture, studio arts, theater design. **Other:** Consulting and leadership.

**Most popular majors.** Biology 7%, business/marketing 13%, engineering/engineering technologies 6%, English 9%, health sciences 7%, psychology 11%, social sciences 26%.

**Computing on campus.** 952 workstations in dormitories, library, computer center. Dormitories wired for high-speed internet access and linked to campus network. Commuter students can connect to campus network. Online course registration, online library, helpline, student web hosting, wireless network available.

**Student life.** **Freshman orientation:** Mandatory, $190 fee. Preregistration for classes offered. 2-day session held in summer. Parents invited to participate. **Housing:** Guaranteed on-campus for freshmen. Coed dorms, special housing for disabled, apartments, substance-free housing available. $250 nonrefundable deposit, deadline 5/1. Special interest housing and learning communities (residential community faculty masters) available. **Activities:** Bands, campus ministries, choral groups, dance, drama, film society, international student organizations, literary magazine, music ensembles, Model UN, musical theater, opera, radio station, student government, student newspaper, symphony orchestra, TV station, debate team, pre-law, pre-med/pre-health, pre-dental, pre-optometry, pre-vet clubs, student tour guides/ambassadors, honors programs/societies, scholars program, religious, ethnic, minority, women's, public interest, and voluntary service organizations.

**Athletics.** NCAA. **Intercollegiate:** Baseball M, basketball, cross-country, diving, golf M, lacrosse, soccer, softball W, swimming, tennis, track and field, volleyball W, wrestling M. **Intramural:** Basketball, bowling, football (non-tackle), racquetball, soccer, softball, table tennis, tennis, volleyball, water polo. **Team name:** Bearcats.

**Student services.** Adult student services, alcohol/substance abuse counseling, campus ministries, career counseling, services for economically disadvantaged, student employment services, financial aid counseling, health services, legal services, minority student services, on-campus daycare, personal counseling, placement for graduates, veterans' counselor, women's services. **Physically disabled:** Services for visually, speech, hearing impaired. **Learning disabled:** Comprehensive services available.

**Contact.** E-mail: admit@binghamton.edu
Phone: (607) 777-2171 Fax: (607) 777-4445
Cheryl Brown, Director of Admissions, State University of New York at Binghamton, Box 6001, Binghamton, NY 13902-6001

## State University of New York at Buffalo
**Buffalo, New York**    **CB member**
**www.buffalo.edu**    **CB code: 2925**

- Public 4-year university
- Commuter campus in large city
- 18,470 degree-seeking undergraduates: 6% part-time, 46% women, 7% African American, 9% Asian American, 3% Hispanic American, 10% international
- 8,968 degree-seeking graduate students
- 52% of applicants admitted
- SAT or ACT with writing required
- 63% graduate within 6 years; 35% enter graduate study

**General.** Founded in 1846. Regionally accredited. SUNY Buffalo is the largest and most comprehensive in the 64-campus State University of New York system. **Degrees:** 3,939 bachelor's awarded; master's, doctoral, first professional offered. **ROTC:** Army. **Location:** 10 miles from downtown. **Calendar:** Semester, extensive summer session. **Full-time faculty:** 1,193 total; 97% have terminal degrees, 24% minority, 34% women. **Part-time faculty:** 634 total; 97% have terminal degrees, 12% minority, 44% women. **Class size:** 35% < 20, 35% 20-39, 8% 40-49, 13% 50-99, 9% >100. **Special facilities:** Center for the arts, concert hall, anthropology research museum, multidisciplinary center for earthquake engineering research, New York State Center of Excellence in Bioinformatics & Life Sciences, center for computational research, poetry and rare books collection, New York State Center for Engineering Design and Industrial Innovation, pharmacy museum, virtual site museum, electronic poetry center, archeological survey center, numerous research centers.

### Freshman class profile.
19,831 applied, 10,245 admitted, 3,263 enrolled.

| Mid 50% test scores | | | |
|---|---|---|---|
| SAT critical reading: | 500-610 | Rank in top quarter: | 62% |
| SAT math: | 540-650 | Rank in top tenth: | 24% |
| ACT composite: | 23-27 | Return as sophomores: | 87% |
| GPA 3.50 or higher: | 27% | Out-of-state: | 7% |
| GPA 3.0-3.49: | 44% | Live on campus: | 74% |
| GPA 2.0-2.99: | 28% | International: | 9% |

**Basis for selection.** Freshmen evaluated based on secondary school performance, strength of curriculum, standardized test scores, and, in some cases, supplemental application. SAT Subject Test considered for placement for foreign language. Audition required for music. **Homeschooled:** Statement describing homeschool structure and mission, transcript of courses and grades, letter of recommendation (nonparent) required. Essay describing educational program, special projects, extracurricular activities, and special accomplishments required as well as 2 letters of recommendation: 1 from parent or other person providing education, 1 from person involved with other activities. If admitted, will need to submit letter from superintendent of local school district attesting to completion of program of home instruction meeting requirements of Section 100.10 of the Regulations of the Commissioner of Education, or passing score on GED. **Learning Disabled:** No separate admissions process: eligibility for services must be established by provision of disability documentation that meets institutional standards.

**High school preparation.** 17 units recommended. Recommended units include English 4, mathematics 3, social studies 4, science 3 and foreign language 3.

**2007-2008 Annual costs.** Tuition/fees: $6,218; $12,478 out-of-state. Room/board: $9,480.

**Financial aid. Non-need-based:** Scholarships awarded for academics, athletics, minority status, music/drama, state residency.

**Application procedures. Admission:** Priority date 11/1; no deadline. $40 fee, may be waived for applicants with need. Application may be submitted online. Admission notification on a rolling basis beginning on or about 2/1. Must reply by May 1 or within 2 week(s) if notified thereafter. **Financial aid:** Priority date 3/1; no closing date. FAFSA required. Applicants notified on a rolling basis starting 2/1; must reply by 5/1.

**Academics.** Over 300 baccalaureate, master's and doctoral degree programs within the College of Arts and Sciences plus 11 professional schools including Law, Medicine and Dentistry. **Special study options:** Accelerated study, combined bachelor's/graduate degree, cooperative education, cross-registration, distance learning, double major, dual enrollment of high school students, ESL, exchange student, honors, independent study, internships, liberal arts/career combination, student-designed major, study abroad, teacher certification program, Washington semester. Certificate programs, combined degree programs, early assurance program with School of Medicine and Dentistry, and Honors College. **Credit/placement by examination:** AP, CLEP, IB, SAT, ACT, institutional tests. Maximum of 30 credits from International Baccalaureate. **Support services:** Learning center, pre-admission summer program, reduced course load, remedial instruction, study skills assistance, tutoring, writing center.

**Majors. Architecture:** Architecture, environmental design. **Area/ethnic studies:** African-American, American, Asian, women's. **Biology:** General, biochemistry, bioinformatics, biomedical sciences, biophysics, biostatistics, biotechnology, pharmacology/toxicology. **Business:** Business admin. **Communications:** General, media studies. **Computer sciences:** Computer science, information systems. **Engineering:** General, aerospace, chemical, civil, computer, electrical, environmental, industrial, mechanical, physics, structural. **English:** English lit. **Foreign languages:** Classics, French, German, Italian, linguistics, Spanish. **Health:** Audiology/speech pathology, clinical lab science, nuclear medical technology, nursing (RN), pharmaceutical sciences. **History:** General. **Liberal arts:** Humanities. **Math:** General. **Parks/recreation:** Exercise sciences. **Philosophy/religion:** Philosophy. **Physical sciences:** Chemistry, geology, physics, theoretical physics. **Psychology:** General. **Social sciences:** Anthropology, economics, geography, political science, sociology. **Visual/performing arts:** Art, art history/conservation, dance, dramatic, film/cinema, music performance, studio arts. **Other:** Multi-interdisciplinary Studies.

**Most popular majors.** Biology 6%, business/marketing 18%, communications/journalism 9%, engineering/engineering technologies 11%, health sciences 6%, liberal arts 7%, psychology 10%, social sciences 9%.

**Computing on campus.** 2,435 workstations in dormitories, library, computer center. Dormitories wired for high-speed internet access and linked to campus network. Commuter students can connect to campus network. Online course registration, online library, helpline, repair service, student web hosting, wireless network available.

**Student life. Freshman orientation:** Available, $190 fee. Preregistration for classes offered. One-and-a-half-day programs include registration. **Policies:** University standards, administrative regulations and student conduct rules apply. **Housing:** Coed dorms, special housing for disabled, apartments, substance-free housing available. $200 fully refundable deposit, deadline 5/1. Shared interest, academic interest, freshmen, honors housing available. **Activities:** Bands, campus ministries, choral groups, dance, drama, film society, international student organizations, literary magazine, music ensembles, musical theater, radio station, student government, student newspaper, symphony orchestra, TV station, Over 300 registered organizations.

**Athletics.** NCAA. **Intercollegiate:** Baseball M, basketball, cross-country, diving, football (tackle) M, rowing (crew) W, soccer, softball W, swimming, tennis, track and field, volleyball W, wrestling M. **Intramural:** Badminton, basketball, bowling, cross-country, football (non-tackle), racquetball, soccer, softball, tennis, volleyball. **Team name:** Bulls.

**Student services.** Adult student services, alcohol/substance abuse counseling, campus ministries, career counseling, services for economically disadvantaged, student employment services, financial aid counseling, health services, legal services, minority student services, on-campus daycare, personal counseling, placement for graduates, veterans' counselor, women's services. **Physically disabled:** Services for visually, speech, hearing impaired.

**Contact.** E-mail: ub-admissions@buffalo.edu
Phone: (716) 645-6900 Toll-free number: (888) 822-3648
Fax: (716) 645-6411
Patricia Armstrong, Director of Admissions, State University of New York at Buffalo, 12 Capen Hall, Buffalo, NY 14260-1660

---

## State University of New York at Farmingdale
**Farmingdale, New York**
www.farmingdale.edu
CB member
CB code: 2526

- Public 4-year technical college
- Commuter campus in large town
- 5,569 degree-seeking undergraduates: 24% part-time, 43% women, 10% African American, 4% Asian American, 9% Hispanic American, 1% international
- 52% of applicants admitted

**General.** Founded in 1912. Regionally accredited. **Degrees:** 535 bachelor's, 580 associate awarded. **Location:** 30 miles from New York City. **Calendar:** Semester, extensive summer session. **Full-time faculty:** 182 total; 50% have terminal degrees, 20% minority, 43% women. **Part-time faculty:** 330 total; 14% have terminal degrees, 13% minority, 47% women. **Class size:** 27% < 20, 57% 20-39, 15% 40-49, 1% 50-99. **Special facilities:** CAD/CAM laboratory, fleet of single-engine and multi-engine aircraft, dental and health care laboratories, bioscience labs, Cold Springs Harbor Research lab on campus, manufacturing labs with plasmajet and advanced robotic technology, solar cell and hydrogen fuel cell research.

### Freshman class profile.
4,643 applied, 2,407 admitted, 1,023 enrolled.

| Mid 50% test scores | | | |
|---|---|---|---|
| SAT critical reading: | 430-510 | GPA 2.0-2.99: | 60% |
| SAT math: | 440-540 | Rank in top quarter: | 19% |
| SAT writing: | 420-500 | Rank in top tenth: | 4% |
| GPA 3.50 or higher: | 9% | Return as sophomores: | 74% |
| GPA 3.0-3.49: | 31% | Out-of-state: | 1% |

**Basis for selection.** School achievement record of primary importance. Applicants apply to and are accepted into a specific curriculum. Requirements vary according to program. SAT required for bachelor's degree students. Interview and portfolio required for advertising art and design, visual communications programs.

**High school preparation.** 20.5 units required. Required and recommended units include English 4, mathematics 2-4, social studies 4, science 2-4 and foreign language 2. Requirements vary by curriculum.

**2007-2008 Annual costs.** Tuition/fees: $5,340; $11,600 out-of-state. Room/board: $11,210. Books/supplies: $1,130. Personal expenses: $900.

**Financial aid. Non-need-based:** Scholarships awarded for academics.

**Application procedures. Admission:** No deadline. $40 fee, may be waived for applicants with need. Application may be submitted online. Admission notification on a rolling basis beginning on or about 11/1. Must reply by May 1 or within 4 week(s) if notified thereafter. Priority given to applications received by January 15 for dental hygiene program and nursing program. **Financial aid:** Priority date 4/1; no closing date. FAFSA, institutional form required. Applicants notified on a rolling basis starting 4/1.

**Academics. Special study options:** Distance learning, double major, honors, internships, study abroad. **Credit/placement by examination:** AP, CLEP, institutional tests. **Support services:** Learning center, remedial instruction, study skills assistance, tutoring, writing center.

**Majors. Agriculture:** Horticulture. **Biology:** General. **Business:** Business admin, operations. **Communications:** Media studies. **Computer sciences:** Programming. **Construction:** Maintenance. **Engineering technology:** Architectural, automotive, computer, computer systems, electrical, industrial, manufacturing, mechanical. **English:** Technical writing. **Health:** Dental hygiene, nursing (RN). **Interdisciplinary:** Science/society. **Math:** Applied. **Protective services:** Security management, security services. **Psychology:** Industrial. **Social sciences:** Applied economics. **Transportation:** Airline/commercial pilot, aviation management.

**Most popular majors.** Business/marketing 35%, communications/journalism 11%, computer/information sciences 13%, engineering/engineering technologies 17%, trade and industry 8%.

**Computing on campus.** 950 workstations in library, computer center, student center. Dormitories wired for high-speed internet access and linked to campus network. Commuter students can connect to campus network. Online course registration, online library, wireless network available.

**Student life. Freshman orientation:** Mandatory, $100 fee. Preregistration for classes offered. **Housing:** Coed dorms available. $100 deposit. **Activities:** Choral groups, drama, literary magazine, radio station, student government, student newspaper, African student association, Asian student alliance, Caribbean student organization, Christian fellowship.

**Athletics.** NCAA. **Intercollegiate:** Baseball M, basketball, cross-country, golf M, lacrosse, soccer, softball W, track and field, volleyball W. **Intramural:** Basketball, golf, racquetball, soccer, softball, squash, swimming, tennis, volleyball, weight lifting. **Team name:** Rams.

**Student services.** Alcohol/substance abuse counseling, campus ministries, career counseling, services for economically disadvantaged, student employment services, financial aid counseling, health services, on-campus daycare, personal counseling, placement for graduates, veterans' counselor. **Physically disabled:** Services for visually, speech, hearing impaired.

**Contact.** E-mail: admissions@farmingdale.edu
Phone: (631) 420-2200 Toll-free number: (800) 432-7646
Fax: (631) 420-2633
Jim Hall, Director of Admissions, State University of New York at Farmingdale, 2350 Broadhollow Road, Farmingdale, NY 11735-1021

---

## State University of New York at New Paltz

| New Paltz, New York | CB member |
|---|---|
| www.newpaltz.edu | CB code: 2541 |

- Public 4-year liberal arts college
- Residential campus in large town
- 5,803 degree-seeking undergraduates: 9% part-time, 68% women, 7% African American, 3% Asian American, 10% Hispanic American, 2% international
- 1,204 degree-seeking graduate students
- 36% of applicants admitted
- SAT or ACT (ACT writing optional) required
- 66% graduate within 6 years

**General.** Founded in 1828. Regionally accredited. More than 16 percent of undergraduates participate in international education each academic year. **Degrees:** 1,582 bachelor's awarded; master's offered. **Location:** 65 miles from Albany, 96 miles from New York City. **Calendar:** Semester, extensive summer session. **Full-time faculty:** 323 total; 66% have terminal degrees, 16% minority, 47% women. **Part-time faculty:** 389 total; 17% have terminal degrees, 12% minority, 61% women. **Class size:** 42% < 20, 50% 20-39, 4% 40-49, 3% 50-99, less than 1% >100. **Special facilities:** 3 theaters, recital hall, speech and hearing clinical center, music therapy training center, observatory, planetarium, theater collection, electronic classrooms.

**Freshman class profile.** 12,543 applied, 4,526 admitted, 943 enrolled.

| Mid 50% test scores | | | |
|---|---|---|---|
| SAT critical reading: | 520-600 | GPA 2.0-2.99: | 11% |
| SAT math: | 510-600 | Return as sophomores: | 86% |
| GPA 3.50 or higher: | 41% | Out-of-state: | 6% |
| GPA 3.0-3.49: | 48% | Live on campus: | 92% |
| | | International: | 3% |

**Basis for selection.** Secondary school curriculum and achievement, standardized test scores most important. Applicants, especially academically marginal, encouraged to send personal statements regarding academic work, recommendations from academic teachers, and any other pertinent information. Essay and recommendations encouraged for all; audition required for music, music therapy, theater arts programs; portfolio required for art education, scenography, studio art, and visual arts programs. **Homeschooled:** Must submit all data as required by NYS Commissioner of Education's regulations (Section 100.10).

**High school preparation.** Required and recommended units include English 4, mathematics 3-4, social studies 4, science 3-4 (laboratory 2-4) and foreign language 2-4.

**2007-2008 Annual costs.** Tuition/fees: $5,390; $11,650 out-of-state. Room/board: $8,070. Books/supplies: $1,250. Personal expenses: $1,100.

**2006-2007 Financial aid.** All financial aid based on need. 836 full-time freshmen applied for aid; 501 were judged to have need; 496 of these received aid. Average need met was 63%. Average scholarship/grant was $2,528; average loan $2,210. 50% of total undergraduate aid awarded as scholarships/grants, 50% as loans/jobs.

**Application procedures. Admission:** Closing date 4/1 (receipt date). $40 fee, may be waived for applicants with need. Application may be submitted online. Admission notification on a rolling basis beginning on or about 1/1. Must reply by May 1 or within 2 week(s) if notified thereafter. **Financial aid:** Priority date 3/15; no closing date. FAFSA required. Applicants notified on a rolling basis starting 4/1; must reply within 4 week(s) of notification.

**Academics.** Bachelor's degree completion program for registered nurses. **Special study options:** Combined bachelor's/graduate degree, cooperative education, cross-registration, distance learning, double major, ESL, exchange student, honors, independent study, internships, liberal arts/career combination, New York semester, student-designed major, study abroad, teacher certification program, United Nations semester. Student exchange programs in Australia, Brazil, Cuba, Czech Republic, Denmark, Ecuador, England, France, Greece, Ireland, Italy, Japan, The Netherlands, New Zealand, Spain, Uzbekistan, U.S. Virgin Islands and Zimbabwe. **Credit/placement by examination:** AP, CLEP, IB, SAT, institutional tests. 30 credit hours maximum toward bachelor's degree. **Support services:** Learning center, reduced course load, remedial instruction, study skills assistance, tutoring, writing center.

**Majors. Area/ethnic studies:** African-American, Asian, Latin American, women's. **Biology:** General, biotechnology. **Business:** General, accounting, business admin, finance, international, logistics. **Communications:** General, broadcast journalism, journalism, public relations. **Computer sciences:** General. **Education:** Art, biology, chemistry, early childhood special, elementary, English, foreign languages, French, German, history, learning disabled, mathematics, middle, physics, science, secondary, social science, social studies, Spanish, special, speech, speech impaired. **Engineering:** Computer, electrical. **English:** English lit, speech/rhetoric. **Foreign languages:** French, German, Spanish. **Health:** Communication disorders, music therapy, nursing (RN). **History:** General. **Interdisciplinary:** Biopsychology. **Legal studies:** Prelaw. **Liberal arts:** Arts/sciences. **Math:** General. **Philosophy/religion:** Philosophy. **Physical sciences:** Chemistry, geochemistry, geology, physics. **Psychology:** General. **Public administration:** Social work. **Social sciences:** General, anthropology, economics, geography, international relations, political science, sociology. **Visual/performing arts:** General, acting, art, art history/conservation, ceramics, commercial/advertising art, dramatic, metal/jewelry, painting, photography, piano/organ, printmaking, sculpture, studio arts, theater design, theater history, voice/opera.

**Most popular majors.** Business/marketing 14%, communications/journalism 8%, education 21%, English 11%, psychology 7%, social sciences 11%, visual/performing arts 10%.

**Computing on campus.** 600 workstations in dormitories, library, computer center, student center. Dormitories wired for high-speed internet access and linked to campus network. Commuter students can connect to campus network. Online course registration, online library, helpline, student web hosting available.

**Student life. Freshman orientation:** Available, $175 fee. Preregistration for classes offered. 3-day academic and transition program. **Housing:** Guaranteed on-campus for freshmen. Coed dorms, special housing for disabled, substance-free housing available. $100 partly refundable deposit, deadline

5/1. First-Year Initiative available. **Activities:** Bands, campus ministries, choral groups, dance, drama, literary magazine, music ensembles, radio station, student government, student newspaper, symphony orchestra, TV station, Jewish Action Movement, Black Student Union, Habitat for Humanity, Circle K International, equestrian club, NAACP, philosophy club, Korean culture union.

**Athletics.** NCAA. **Intercollegiate:** Baseball M, basketball, cross-country, field hockey W, lacrosse W, soccer, softball W, swimming, tennis, track and field, volleyball. **Intramural:** Basketball, cross-country, football (non-tackle), golf W, racquetball, softball, tennis, volleyball. **Team name:** Hawks.

**Student services.** Alcohol/substance abuse counseling, campus ministries, career counseling, services for economically disadvantaged, student employment services, financial aid counseling, health services, legal services, minority student services, on-campus daycare, personal counseling, placement for graduates, veterans' counselor, women's services. **Physically disabled:** Services for visually, speech, hearing impaired.

**Contact.** E-mail: admissions@newpaltz.edu
Phone: (845) 257-3200 Toll-free number: (888) 639-7589
Fax: (845) 257-3209
Kimberly Strano, Director of Freshmen and International Admission, State University of New York at New Paltz, 100 Hawk Drive, New Paltz, NY 12561-2499

## State University of New York at Oswego

Oswego, New York — CB member
www.oswego.edu — CB code: 2543

- Public 4-year university
- Residential campus in large town
- 6,962 degree-seeking undergraduates: 6% part-time, 54% women, 4% African American, 2% Asian American, 4% Hispanic American, 1% Native American, 1% international
- 737 degree-seeking graduate students
- 50% of applicants admitted
- SAT or ACT (ACT writing optional) required
- 59% graduate within 6 years; 26% enter graduate study

**General.** Founded in 1861. Regionally accredited. **Degrees:** 1,503 bachelor's awarded; master's offered. **ROTC:** Army. **Location:** 35 miles from Syracuse, 65 miles from Rochester. **Calendar:** Semester, limited summer session. **Full-time faculty:** 311 total; 78% have terminal degrees, 16% minority, 40% women. **Part-time faculty:** 198 total; 22% have terminal degrees, 8% minority, 44% women. **Class size:** 48% < 20, 36% 20-39, 8% 40-49, 4% 50-99, 3% >100. **Special facilities:** Weather facsimile machine, planetarium, cross-country ski facilities, advanced technology classrooms, biological field station.

**Freshman class profile.** 9,400 applied, 4,700 admitted, 1,389 enrolled.

| Mid 50% test scores | | | |
|---|---|---|---|
| SAT critical reading: | 510-590 | Rank in top tenth: | 13% |
| SAT math: | 520-580 | End year in good standing: | 89% |
| ACT composite: | 21-25 | Return as sophomores: | 78% |
| GPA 3.50 or higher: | 38% | Out-of-state: | 2% |
| GPA 3.0-3.49: | 38% | Live on campus: | 88% |
| GPA 2.0-2.99: | 24% | International: | 2% |
| Rank in top quarter: | 51% | Fraternities: | 6% |
| | | Sororities: | 5% |

**Basis for selection.** High school GPA and curriculum most important, followed by test scores, part II of application and letters of recommendation. Special talents considered. Applicants recommended to send both SAT and ACT; higher score accepted. Essay and interview recommended for all; audition recommended for music; portfolio required for graphic design and fine arts (BFA). **Homeschooled:** Proof of high school graduation or GED recognized by state of residency required. **Learning Disabled:** Advised to contact Office of Learning Services and/or Disability Services with copy of IEP if applicable.

**High school preparation.** 18 units required; 20 recommended. Required and recommended units include English 4, mathematics 3-4, social studies 4, science 3-4 (laboratory 2-3) and foreign language 2-4. Combined minimum of 6 math and science recommended.

**2007-2008 Annual costs.** Tuition/fees: $5,434; $11,694 out-of-state. Room/board: $9,470. Books/supplies: $800. Personal expenses: $850.

**2006-2007 Financial aid.** **Need-based:** 1,187 full-time freshmen applied for aid; 833 were judged to have need; 812 of these received aid. Average need met was 71%. Average scholarship/grant was $5,067; average loan $2,769. 41% of total undergraduate aid awarded as scholarships/grants,

59% as loans/jobs. **Non-need-based:** Awarded to 2,158 full-time undergraduates, including 633 freshmen. Scholarships awarded for academics, state residency.

**Application procedures.** **Admission:** Priority date 1/15; no deadline. $40 fee, may be waived for applicants with need. Application may be submitted online. Admission notification on a rolling basis beginning on or about 1/15. Must reply by May 1 or within 4 week(s) if notified thereafter. **Financial aid:** Priority date 3/1; no closing date. FAFSA required. Applicants notified on a rolling basis starting 3/1; must reply by 5/1 or within 3 week(s) of notification.

**Academics.** **Special study options:** Accelerated study, combined bachelor's/graduate degree, cross-registration, distance learning, double major, dual enrollment of high school students, ESL, exchange student, external degree, honors, independent study, internships, liberal arts/career combination, study abroad, teacher certification program, Washington semester. **Credit/placement by examination:** AP, CLEP, IB, SAT. 30 credit hours maximum toward bachelor's degree. **Support services:** Learning center, pre-admission summer program, reduced course load, remedial instruction, study skills assistance, tutoring, writing center.

**Honors college/program.** Approximately 80 freshmen enroll annually, distinct program of general education classes held in small class settings.

**Majors.** **Area/ethnic studies:** American, women's. **Biology:** General, zoology. **Business:** Accounting, business admin, finance, human resources, management science. **Communications:** General, broadcast journalism, journalism, public relations. **Computer sciences:** Computer science, information systems. **Education:** Agricultural, biology, business, chemistry, elementary, English, French, German, health occupations, history, mathematics, physics, science, secondary, social studies, Spanish, technology/industrial arts, trade/industrial, voc/tech. **English:** English lit. **Family/consumer sciences:** Child development. **Foreign languages:** French, German, linguistics, Spanish. **Health:** Medical radiologic technology/radiation therapy, perfusion technology, public health ed. **History:** General. **Interdisciplinary:** Cognitive science, global studies. **Legal studies:** Prelaw. **Math:** General, applied. **Philosophy/religion:** Philosophy. **Physical sciences:** Chemistry, geochemistry, geology, meteorology, physics. **Psychology:** General. **Social sciences:** Anthropology, econometrics, economics, political science, sociology. **Visual/performing arts:** Art, commercial/advertising art, dramatic.

**Most popular majors.** Business/marketing 17%, communications/journalism 9%, education 27%, psychology 10%, security/protective services 6%, visual/performing arts 6%.

**Computing on campus.** 750 workstations in dormitories, library, computer center, student center. Dormitories wired for high-speed internet access and linked to campus network. Commuter students can connect to campus network. Online course registration, online library, helpline, wireless network available.

**Student life.** **Freshman orientation:** Mandatory, $159 fee. Preregistration for classes offered. 2-day program for incoming students and families. **Housing:** Guaranteed on-campus for all undergraduates. Coed dorms, substance-free housing available. $100 fully refundable deposit, deadline 5/1. Pets allowed in dorm rooms. Global living and learning center, suites for upper-classmen, nontraditional student housing, first-year experience residence hall for incoming freshmen only, housing for 21 and over single suites available. **Activities:** Bands, choral groups, dance, drama, film society, literary magazine, music ensembles, musical theater, radio station, student government, student newspaper, symphony orchestra, TV station, Christian, Jewish, Catholic, and Baptist groups, black student union, Latin student union, Caribbean student association, international student association, Native American brotherhood, Students Educating Everyone About Disabilities.

**Athletics.** NCAA. **Intercollegiate:** Baseball M, basketball, cross-country, diving, field hockey W, golf M, ice hockey, lacrosse, soccer, softball W, swimming, tennis, track and field, volleyball W, wrestling M. **Intramural:** Basketball, football (non-tackle), golf, lacrosse, racquetball, skiing, soccer, softball, swimming, tennis, volleyball, weight lifting M, wrestling M. **Team name:** Lakers.

**Student services.** Adult student services, alcohol/substance abuse counseling, career counseling, services for economically disadvantaged, student employment services, financial aid counseling, health services, minority student services, on-campus daycare, personal counseling, placement for graduates, veterans' counselor, women's services. **Physically disabled:** Services for visually, speech, hearing impaired.

**Contact.** E-mail: admiss@oswego.edu
Phone: (315) 312-2250 Fax: (315) 312-3260
Joseph Grant, Vice President for Student Affairs and Enrollment, State University of New York at Oswego, 229 Sheldon Hall, Oswego, NY 13126-3599

## State University of New York at Purchase
**Purchase, New York**
**www.purchase.edu**                    **CB code: 2878**

- Public 4-year visual arts, business and liberal arts college
- Residential campus in large town
- 3,764 degree-seeking undergraduates: 6% part-time, 54% women, 8% African American, 3% Asian American, 10% Hispanic American, 2% international
- 159 degree-seeking graduate students
- 37% of applicants admitted
- SAT or ACT (ACT writing optional) required
- 51% graduate within 6 years

**General.** Founded in 1967. Regionally accredited. **Degrees:** 713 bachelor's awarded; master's offered. **Location:** 25 miles from New York City, 5 miles from White Plains. **Calendar:** Semester, extensive summer session. **Full-time faculty:** 144 total; 19% minority, 50% women. **Part-time faculty:** 228 total; 12% minority, 42% women. **Class size:** 73% < 20, 22% 20-39, 3% 40-49, 2% 50-99, less than 1% >100. **Special facilities:** Performing arts center, children's center, electron microscope.

**Freshman class profile.** 5,986 applied, 2,228 admitted, 785 enrolled.

| Mid 50% test scores | | | |
|---|---|---|---|
| SAT critical reading: | 500-610 | Rank in top quarter: | 34% |
| SAT math: | 480-590 | Rank in top tenth: | 2% |
| SAT writing: | 480-600 | Return as sophomores: | 82% |
| ACT composite: | 21-25 | Out-of-state: | 26% |
| GPA 3.50 or higher: | 27% | Live on campus: | 92% |
| GPA 3.0-3.49: | 34% | International: | 1% |
| | | GPA 2.0-2.99: | 38% |

**Basis for selection.** For liberal arts and sciences programs, high school achievement record or test scores important. For conservatory, performing arts and visual arts applicants, audition, interview, or portfolio most important. SAT recommended. Interview and essay required for film, theater design/technology programs; audition required for acting, dance, music programs; portfolio required for visual arts program.

**2007-2008 Annual costs.** Tuition/fees: $5,771; $12,031 out-of-state. Room/board: $9,444. Books/supplies: $1,500. Personal expenses: $700.

**2007-2008 Financial aid.** **Need-based:** Average need met was 76%. Average scholarship/grant was $4,712; average loan $4,399. 46% of total undergraduate aid awarded as scholarships/grants, 54% as loans/jobs. **Non-need-based:** Scholarships awarded for academics, art, minority status, music/drama. **Additional information:** All applicants automatically considered for scholarship upon review of applications, essays, auditions, and/or portfolio.

**Application procedures.** **Admission:** Priority date 3/1; deadline 7/15 (postmark date). $40 fee, may be waived for applicants with need. Application may be submitted online. Admission notification 5/1. Must reply by May 1 or within 2 week(s) if notified thereafter. Application deadlines vary by program. Priority date of 1/30 for students applying to acting, design/technology, and film programs. **Financial aid:** Priority date 2/1; no closing date. FAFSA required. Applicants notified on a rolling basis starting 3/1; must reply within 2 week(s) of notification.

**Academics.** **Special study options:** Cross-registration, distance learning, double major, ESL, independent study, internships, liberal arts/career combination, student-designed major, study abroad. Conservatory master-apprentice training in dance, music, acting, film, theater design technology, visual arts. **Credit/placement by examination:** AP, CLEP, institutional tests. 30 credit hours maximum toward bachelor's degree. **Support services:** Learning center, pre-admission summer program, remedial instruction, tutoring.

**Majors.** **Area/ethnic studies:** Women's. **Biology:** General, ecology. **Communications:** Journalism, media studies. **Conservation:** Environmental science, environmental studies. **English:** American lit, British lit, creative writing. **Foreign languages:** General. **History:** General. **Interdisciplinary:** Math/computer science. **Liberal arts:** Arts/sciences. **Math:** General. **Philosophy/religion:** Philosophy. **Physical sciences:** Chemistry. **Psychology:** General. **Social sciences:** Anthropology, economics, political science, sociology. **Visual/performing arts:** Art history/conservation, arts management, cinematography, commercial/advertising art, dance, dramatic, drawing, graphic design, music performance, music theory/composition, painting, photography, play/screenwriting, printmaking, sculpture, theater design, theater history.

**Most popular majors.** Communications/journalism 6%, English 7%, liberal arts 27%, social sciences 7%, visual/performing arts 38%.

**Computing on campus.** 350 workstations in dormitories, library, computer center. Dormitories linked to campus network. Commuter students can connect to campus network. Online course registration, online library, helpline, repair service, wireless network available.

**Student life.** **Freshman orientation:** Mandatory, $120 fee. **Housing:** Coed dorms, special housing for disabled, apartments, substance-free housing available. $100 fully refundable deposit. Freshman residence, wellness program, nonsmoking hall, nontraditional age hall, presidential scholars, learning community available. **Activities:** Jazz band, choral groups, dance, drama, film society, radio station, student government, student newspaper, TV station, philosophy club, chemistry society, literature club, dance club, ski club, Purchase Experimental Theatre, Organization of African People in America (OAPIA), Latinos Unidos, Gay/Lesbian/Bisexual and Transgendered Union.

**Athletics.** NCAA. **Intercollegiate:** Baseball M, basketball, cross-country, soccer, softball W, swimming W, tennis, volleyball. **Intramural:** Badminton, basketball, bowling, cross-country, fencing, golf, racquetball, skiing, soccer, softball, squash, swimming, table tennis, tennis, volleyball, water polo, weight lifting. **Team name:** Panthers.

**Student services.** Adult student services, career counseling, student employment services, health services, on-campus daycare, personal counseling, placement for graduates, veterans' counselor. **Physically disabled:** Services for visually, hearing impaired.

**Contact.** E-mail: admissn@purchase.edu
Phone: (914) 251-6300 Fax: (914) 251-6314
Stephanie McCaine, Stephanie McCaine, State University of New York at Purchase, 735 Anderson Hill Road, Purchase, NY 10577-1400

## State University of New York at Stony Brook
**Stony Brook, New York**                    **CB member**
**www.stonybrook.edu**                    **CB code: 2548**

- Public 4-year university
- Residential campus in large town
- 15,222 degree-seeking undergraduates: 7% part-time, 50% women, 9% African American, 22% Asian American, 8% Hispanic American, 6% international
- 6,707 degree-seeking graduate students
- 43% of applicants admitted
- SAT or ACT with writing required
- 59% graduate within 6 years

**General.** Founded in 1957. Regionally accredited. **Degrees:** 2,981 bachelor's awarded; master's, doctoral, first professional offered. **ROTC:** Army, Air Force. **Location:** 60 miles from New York City. **Calendar:** Semester, limited summer session. **Full-time faculty:** 919 total; 16% minority, 33% women. **Part-time faculty:** 586 total; 12% minority, 44% women. **Class size:** 36% < 20, 36% 20-39, 6% 40-49, 14% 50-99, 8% >100. **Special facilities:** Nuclear accelerator, natural science museum, 3-theater fine arts center, nature preserve, working arrangements with Cold Spring Harbor Laboratory and Brookhaven National Laboratory.

**Freshman class profile.** 24,060 applied, 10,382 admitted, 2,768 enrolled.

| Mid 50% test scores | | | |
|---|---|---|---|
| SAT critical reading: | 520-620 | Return as sophomores: | 89% |
| SAT math: | 560-660 | Out-of-state: | 8% |
| SAT writing: | 500-610 | Live on campus: | 78% |
| GPA 3.50 or higher: | 54% | International: | 6% |
| GPA 3.0-3.49: | 36% | | |
| | | GPA 2.0-2.99: | 10% |

**Basis for selection.** High school GPA, test scores and level of high school curriculum most important factors. Class rank, interview, letters of recommendation, extracurricular activities, essays considered. SAT Subject Tests recommended. Audition and musicianship examination required for major in music. Supplemental application with essay required for admission to Honors College, WISE (Women in Science & Engineering), Scholars for Medicine, Engineering Scholars for Medicine, Honors Program in Computer Science and for merit scholarship consideration. **Homeschooled:** State high school equivalency certificate required. Applicants required to take 5 Regents exams through their home school district or have their home district verify that they have fulfilled high school graduation requirements through home school curriculum. **Learning Disabled:** Applicants required to submit documentation of learning disability. Psychological and educational evaluation also required.

**High school preparation.** 16 units required; 19 recommended. Required and recommended units include English 4, mathematics 3-4, social studies 4, science 3-4 and foreign language 2-3. 4 math and 4 science recommended for applicants to science, engineering, and math programs.

**2007-2008 Annual costs.** Tuition/fees: $5,760; $12,020 out-of-state. Room/board: $8,734. Books/supplies: $900. Personal expenses: $1,292.

**2006-2007 Financial aid. Need-based:** 2,131 full-time freshmen applied for aid; 1,476 were judged to have need; 1,453 of these received aid. Average need met was 66%. Average scholarship/grant was $6,674; average loan $2,841. 56% of total undergraduate aid awarded as scholarships/grants, 44% as loans/jobs. **Non-need-based:** Awarded to 1,329 full-time undergraduates, including 457 freshmen. Scholarships awarded for academics, alumni affiliation, art, athletics, job skills, leadership, music/drama.

**Application procedures. Admission:** Priority date 12/1; no deadline. $40 fee, may be waived for applicants with need. Application may be submitted online. Admission notification on a rolling basis beginning on or about 2/1. Must reply by May 1 or within 2 week(s) if notified thereafter. **Financial aid:** Priority date 3/1; no closing date. FAFSA required. Applicants notified on a rolling basis starting 3/1; must reply by 5/1 or within 2 week(s) of notification.

**Academics. Special study options:** Combined bachelor's/graduate degree, cross-registration, distance learning, double major, dual enrollment of high school students, ESL, exchange student, honors, independent study, internships, New York semester, student-designed major, study abroad, teacher certification program, Washington semester. **Credit/placement by examination:** AP, CLEP, IB, institutional tests. 30 credit hours maximum toward bachelor's degree. **Support services:** Learning center, reduced course load, remedial instruction, tutoring, writing center.

**Honors college/program.** High grades in major subject areas, minimum cumulative unweighted high school average of 93, minimum combined SAT (exclusive of Writing) of 1300 or ACT score of 30, record of advanced or college-level course work, and evidence of writing ability required.

**Majors. Area/ethnic studies:** African-American, American, European, women's. **Biology:** General, biochemistry, marine, pharmacology. **Business:** Business admin. **Communications:** Journalism. **Computer sciences:** Computer science, information systems. **Conservation:** Environmental studies. **Engineering:** General, biomedical, computer hardware, electrical, mechanical. **English:** English lit. **Foreign languages:** Comparative lit, French, German, Italian, linguistics, Russian, Spanish. **Health:** Clinical lab science, cytotechnology, nursing (RN), respiratory therapy technology. **History:** General. **Liberal arts:** Humanities. **Math:** General, applied. **Philosophy/religion:** Philosophy, religion. **Physical sciences:** Astronomy, chemistry, geology, physics. **Psychology:** General. **Public administration:** Social work. **Social sciences:** Anthropology, economics, political science, sociology. **Visual/performing arts:** Art history/conservation, dramatic, studio arts.

**Most popular majors.** Biology 12%, business/marketing 7%, health sciences 19%, psychology 12%, social sciences 16%.

**Computing on campus.** 2,300 workstations in dormitories, library, computer center, student center. Dormitories wired for high-speed internet access and linked to campus network. Commuter students can connect to campus network. Online course registration, helpline, student web hosting available.

**Student life. Freshman orientation:** Mandatory, $180 fee. Preregistration for classes offered. 1-day session held in June or early August. **Housing:** Coed dorms, special housing for disabled, apartments, substance-free housing available. $200 fully refundable deposit, deadline 5/1. Single sex floors in coed dorms available. **Activities:** Bands, choral groups, dance, drama, film society, literary magazine, music ensembles, musical theater, opera, radio station, student government, student newspaper, symphony orchestra, Jewish, Protestant, Catholic, Islamic Society, Baha'i religious organizations, Inter-Varsity Christian Fellowship, international club, Chinese association, Indian student association, Pakistan club, African students association.

**Athletics.** NCAA. **Intercollegiate:** Baseball M, basketball, cross-country, diving, football (tackle) M, lacrosse, soccer, softball W, swimming, tennis, track and field, volleyball W. **Intramural:** Basketball, softball. **Team name:** Seawolves.

**Student services.** Adult student services, alcohol/substance abuse counseling, campus ministries, career counseling, services for economically disadvantaged, student employment services, financial aid counseling, health services, minority student services, on-campus daycare, personal counseling, placement for graduates, veterans' counselor, women's services. **Physically disabled:** Services for visually, speech, hearing impaired.

**Contact.** E-mail: enroll@stonybrook.edu
Phone: (631) 632-6868 Toll-free number: (800) 872-7869
Fax: (631) 632-9898
Judith Burke-Berhannan, Dean of Admissions, State University of New York at Stony Brook, 118 Administration Building, Stony Brook, NY 11794-1901

---

## State University of New York College at Brockport

**Brockport, New York**
**www.brockport.edu**

**CB member**
**CB code: 2537**

- Public 4-year liberal arts college
- Residential campus in small town
- 6,841 degree-seeking undergraduates: 9% part-time, 57% women, 6% African American, 1% Asian American, 3% Hispanic American, 1% international
- 1,198 degree-seeking graduate students
- 42% of applicants admitted
- SAT or ACT (ACT writing optional) required
- 59% graduate within 6 years; 27% enter graduate study

**General.** Founded in 1867. Regionally accredited. **Degrees:** 1,682 bachelor's awarded; master's offered. **ROTC:** Army, Naval, Air Force. **Location:** 16 miles from Rochester. **Calendar:** Semester, limited summer session. **Full-time faculty:** 315 total; 87% have terminal degrees, 16% minority, 46% women. **Part-time faculty:** 258 total; 27% have terminal degrees, 5% minority, 50% women. **Class size:** 42% < 20, 50% 20-39, 5% 40-49, 3% 50-99, less than 1% >100. **Special facilities:** Aquaculture ponds, unidata weather information system, weather radio receiver, nuclear laboratory, high resolution germanium detector, research vessel on Lake Ontario, electron microscope, two supercomputers, Doppler radar system, hydrotherapy room, parallel supercomputer, ultramodern dance facilities including green room.

**Freshman class profile.** 8,522 applied, 3,571 admitted, 1,038 enrolled.

| Mid 50% test scores | | | |
|---|---|---|---|
| SAT critical reading: | 500-600 | Rank in top quarter: | 52% |
| SAT math: | 480-580 | Rank in top tenth: | 14% |
| SAT writing: | 460-560 | End year in good standing: | 100% |
| ACT composite: | 21-25 | Return as sophomores: | 84% |
| GPA 3.50 or higher: | 51% | Out-of-state: | 8% |
| GPA 3.0-3.49: | 37% | Live on campus: | 93% |
| GPA 2.0-2.99: | 12% | International: | 1% |

**Basis for selection.** High school academic record including number of academic units, GPA, class rank, test scores important. Recommendations, essay, extracurricular activites considered. Recommend student take SAT or ACT for the first time in junior year of high school. Interview required in some cases; auditions required for dance and theater acting. **Home-schooled:** Statement describing homeschool structure and mission, transcript of courses and grades, state high school equivalency certificate, letter of recommendation (nonparent) required. Outline of courses completed at high school level, official test scores (SAT/ACT), personal essay, 2 letters of recommendation, and biography of books read during high school program required.

**High school preparation.** 18 units required. Required and recommended units include English 4, mathematics 3-4, social studies 4, science 3-4 (laboratory 1), foreign language 3, computer science 1, visual/performing arts 1 and academic electives 4.

**2007-2008 Annual costs.** Tuition/fees: $5,406; $11,666 out-of-state. Room/board: $8,830. Books/supplies: $1,000. Personal expenses: $1,974.

**2006-2007 Financial aid. Need-based:** 863 full-time freshmen applied for aid; 624 were judged to have need; 621 of these received aid. Average need met was 83%. Average scholarship/grant was $4,131; average loan $4,132. 43% of total undergraduate aid awarded as scholarships/grants, 57% as loans/jobs. **Non-need-based:** Awarded to 771 full-time undergraduates, including 257 freshmen. Scholarships awarded for academics, alumni affiliation, leadership, minority status, ROTC, state residency.

**Application procedures. Admission:** Priority date 2/1; no deadline. $40 fee, may be waived for applicants with need. Application may be submitted online. Admission notification on a rolling basis beginning on or about 11/15. Must reply by May 1 or within 3 week(s) if notified thereafter. **Financial aid:** Priority date 2/15; no closing date. FAFSA required. Applicants notified on a rolling basis starting 2/15; must reply within 4 week(s) of notification.

**Academics.** Time/credit-shortened B.S. degree, experiential learning, domestic and international internships through Delta College. 3-1-3 program allows 30 college credits to be earned during student's senior year of high school. **Special study options:** Accelerated study, combined bachelor's/graduate degree, cross-registration, distance learning, double major, dual enrollment of high school students, honors, independent study, internships, New York semester, semester at sea, student-designed major, study abroad, teacher certification program, Washington semester. **Credit/placement by examination:** AP, CLEP, IB, institutional tests. 90 credit hours maximum toward bachelor's degree. **Support services:** Learning center, pre-admission summer program, reduced course load, study skills assistance, tutoring, writing center.

**Honors college/program.** Freshman applicants should have high school average of at least a 91 and SAT of 1150 (exclusive of Writing) or ACT of 25. The average honors student has a 93 GPA and a 1220 SAT and/or 27 ACT.

**Majors. Area/ethnic studies:** African, African-American, women's. **Biology:** General, aquatic, biochemistry, biotechnology, cellular/molecular, environmental, exercise physiology. **Business:** Accounting, business admin, finance, international, international marketing. **Communications:** General, broadcast journalism, journalism, media studies. **Computer sciences:** General, computer science. **Conservation:** General, environmental science, environmental studies. **Education:** General, bilingual, biology, chemistry, developmentally delayed, elementary, English, health, history, mathematics, physical, physics, science, secondary, social studies, Spanish, special. **English:** Creative writing, English lit. **Foreign languages:** General, French, Spanish. **Health:** Athletic training, clinical lab technology, health care admin, nursing (RN), predental, premedicine, preveterinary. **History:** General. **Math:** General. **Parks/recreation:** General, facilities management, sports admin. **Philosophy/religion:** Philosophy. **Physical sciences:** Atmospheric science, chemistry, geology, hydrology, meteorology, physics, planetary. **Protective services:** Police science, security management. **Psychology:** General. **Public administration:** Social work. **Science technology:** Biological. **Social sciences:** Anthropology, international relations, political science, sociology. **Visual/performing arts:** General, art, dance, dramatic, studio arts.

**Most popular majors.** Business/marketing 15%, communications/journalism 7%, education 12%, English 6%, health sciences 12%, history 8%, psychology 7%, security/protective services 7%, social sciences 6%.

**Computing on campus.** 750 workstations in dormitories, library, computer center, student center. Dormitories wired for high-speed internet access and linked to campus network. Commuter students can connect to campus network. Online course registration, online library, helpline, wireless network available.

**Student life. Freshman orientation:** Available, $145 fee. Preregistration for classes offered. 24-hour program held in late June and early July. Students are given their course schedule and take a required Computer Skills Exam. A parent/family program runs parallel to the student orientation. **Housing:** Guaranteed on-campus for freshmen. Coed dorms, special housing for disabled, apartments, substance-free housing available. $100 nonrefundable deposit, deadline 5/1. Special living options available include freshman first-year experience program, transfer student program, health club, scholar floors, single-sex areas, adult, 24-hour quiet, academic excellence floors. **Activities:** Choral groups, dance, drama, international student organizations, music ensembles, musical theater, radio station, student government, student newspaper, TV station, Organization for Students of African Descent, Association of Latin American Students, Alpha Chi Honor Society, Caribbean club, women's center, Brockport Adult Student Organization, peer counseling, student alumni association, Native American student organization.

**Athletics.** NCAA. **Intercollegiate:** Baseball M, basketball, cross-country, diving, field hockey W, football (tackle) M, gymnastics W, ice hockey M, lacrosse, soccer, softball W, swimming, tennis W, track and field, volleyball W, wrestling M. **Intramural:** Badminton, basketball, bowling, football (non-tackle), racquetball, soccer, softball, table tennis, volleyball. **Team name:** Golden Eagles.

**Student services.** Alcohol/substance abuse counseling, campus ministries, career counseling, services for economically disadvantaged, student employment services, financial aid counseling, health services, legal services, minority student services, on-campus daycare, personal counseling, placement for graduates, veterans' counselor, women's services. **Physically disabled:** Services for visually, speech, hearing impaired.

**Contact.** E-mail: admit@brockport.edu
Phone: (585) 395-2751 Fax: (585) 395-5452
Bernard Valento, Director of Undergraduate Admissions, State University of New York College at Brockport, 350 New Campus Drive, Brockport, NY 14420-2915

## State University of New York College at Buffalo

**Buffalo, New York**
www.buffalostate.edu

CB member
CB code: 2533

- Public 4-year liberal arts and teachers college
- Commuter campus in large city
- 8,935 degree-seeking undergraduates: 10% part-time, 59% women, 14% African American, 2% Asian American, 5% Hispanic American, 1% Native American, 1% international
- 1,728 degree-seeking graduate students
- 47% of applicants admitted
- SAT or ACT (ACT writing optional), SAT Subject Tests required

**General.** Founded in 1867. Regionally accredited. **Degrees:** 1,791 bachelor's awarded; master's offered. **ROTC:** Army. **Location:** 450 miles from New York City, 250 miles from Cleveland. **Calendar:** Semester, limited summer session. **Full-time faculty:** 429 total; 77% have terminal degrees, 14% minority, 44% women. **Part-time faculty:** 358 total; 19% have terminal degrees, 7% minority, 53% women. **Special facilities:** Planetarium, performing arts center, center for environmental research and education, child care center, art center, Great Lakes research facility.

**Freshman class profile.** 9,762 applied, 4,631 admitted, 1,401 enrolled.

| Mid 50% test scores | | | |
|---|---|---|---|
| SAT critical reading: | 440-530 | Rank in top quarter: | 31% |
| SAT math: | 450-540 | Rank in top tenth: | 8% |
| GPA 3.50 or higher: | 23% | Out-of-state: | 1% |
| GPA 3.0-3.49: | 51% | Live on campus: | 54% |
| GPA 2.0-2.99: | 26% | Fraternities: | 1% |
| | | Sororities: | 1% |

**Basis for selection.** High school GPA, class rank, test scores important. Recommendations, essay, interview, volunteer work, work experience and extracurricular activities also considered. Portfolio required for fine arts program.

**High school preparation.** 17 units recommended. Required and recommended units include English 4, mathematics 2-3, science 2-3, foreign language 3 and academic electives 4.

**2007-2008 Annual costs.** Tuition/fees: $5,375; $11,635 out-of-state. Room/board: $8,514. Books/supplies: $900. Personal expenses: $1,000.

**2006-2007 Financial aid.** All financial aid based on need. 54% of total undergraduate aid awarded as scholarships/grants, 46% as loans/jobs.

**Application procedures. Admission:** No deadline. $40 fee, may be waived for applicants with need. Application may be submitted online. Admission notification on a rolling basis beginning on or about 12/15. Must reply by May 1 or within 4 week(s) if notified thereafter. **Financial aid:** Priority date 3/15, closing date 5/1. FAFSA required. Applicants notified on a rolling basis starting 5/1; must reply within 4 week(s) of notification.

**Academics. Special study options:** Cooperative education, cross-registration, distance learning, double major, dual enrollment of high school students, ESL, exchange student, honors, independent study, internships, liberal arts/career combination, New York semester, study abroad, teacher certification program, Washington semester. **Credit/placement by examination:** AP, CLEP, IB, institutional tests. 30 credit hours maximum toward bachelor's degree. **Support services:** Learning center, pre-admission summer program, reduced course load, remedial instruction, study skills assistance, tutoring.

**Honors college/program.** High school students must have GPA of 90 or higher (or rank within the top 10 percent of their graduating class) and SAT scores of 1100 (exclusive of Writing) or higher. Advanced Placement courses with grades of B or better, cocurricular activities, and community involvement also considered.

**Majors. Architecture:** Urban/community planning. **Biology:** General. **Business:** General, business admin, fashion, hospitality admin, hospitality/recreation, office management. **Communications:** General, broadcast journalism, journalism, media studies. **Computer sciences:** General, information systems, programming. **Education:** General, art, biology, business, chemistry, early childhood, elementary, emotionally handicapped, English, foreign languages, French, health occupations, mathematics, mentally handicapped, physically handicapped, physics, reading, sales/marketing, science, secondary, social studies, Spanish, technology/industrial arts, trade/industrial, voc/tech. **Engineering technology:** Electrical, electromechanical, industrial, mechanical. **English:** English lit. **Family/consumer sciences:** Clothing/textiles, food/nutrition. **Foreign languages:** French, Spanish. **Health:** Speech pathology. **History:** General. **Liberal arts:** Humanities. **Math:** General. **Parks/recreation:** Health/fitness. **Philosophy/religion:** Philosophy. **Physical sciences:** Chemistry, geology, physics, planetary. **Protective services:** Criminal justice, forensics. **Psychology:** General. **Public administration:** Social work. **Social sciences:** Anthropology, economics, geography, political science, sociology. **Visual/performing arts:** General, art history/conservation, commercial/advertising art, dramatic, fashion design, fiber arts, interior design, metal/jewelry, painting, photography, printmaking, sculpture, studio arts, theater arts management.

**Most popular majors.** Business/marketing 10%, communications/journalism 8%, education 28%, security/protective services 6%, social sciences 7%, visual/performing arts 7%.

**Computing on campus.** 900 workstations in dormitories, library, computer center, student center. Dormitories wired for high-speed internet access and linked to campus network. Commuter students can connect to campus network. Online course registration, online library, helpline, repair service, wireless network available.

**Student life. Freshman orientation:** Mandatory, $175 fee. Preregistration for classes offered. **Housing:** Coed dorms, apartments, substance-free housing available. $100 deposit, deadline 7/1. Apartments for students with dependent children available. **Activities:** Bands, campus ministries, choral groups, dance, drama, film society, international student organizations, literary magazine, music ensembles, radio station, student government, student newspaper, Newman Club, Amnesty International, public interest groups, African American student organization, Adelante Estudiantes, Native American student organization, Muslim student organization, Caribbean student organization.

**Athletics.** NCAA. **Intercollegiate:** Basketball, cross-country, diving, football (tackle) M, ice hockey M, lacrosse W, soccer, softball W, swimming, tennis W, track and field, volleyball W. **Intramural:** Basketball, football (tackle) M, racquetball, soccer, softball, volleyball. **Team name:** Bengals.

**Student services.** Adult student services, career counseling, student employment services, health services, minority student services, on-campus daycare, personal counseling, placement for graduates, veterans' counselor. **Physically disabled:** Services for visually, speech, hearing impaired.

**Contact.** E-mail: admissions@buffalostate.edu
Phone: (716) 878-4017 Fax: (716) 878-6100
Lesa Loritts, Director of Admissions, State University of New York College at Buffalo, 1300 Elmwood Avenue, Moot Hall, Buffalo, NY 14222-1095

## State University of New York College at Cortland

Cortland, New York
www.cortland.edu

CB member
CB code: 2538

- Public 4-year university, liberal arts and teachers college
- Residential campus in large town
- 5,904 degree-seeking undergraduates: 2% part-time, 57% women, 3% African American, 2% Asian American, 5% Hispanic American, 1% Native American
- 1,012 degree-seeking graduate students
- 44% of applicants admitted
- SAT or ACT (ACT writing recommended) required
- 56% graduate within 6 years

**General.** Founded in 1868. Regionally accredited. **Degrees:** 1,403 bachelor's awarded; master's offered. **ROTC:** Army, Air Force. **Location:** 35 miles from Syracuse, 18 miles from Ithaca. **Calendar:** Semester, limited summer session. **Full-time faculty:** 345 total; 55% have terminal degrees, 12% minority, 46% women. **Part-time faculty:** 256 total; 12% have terminal degrees, 5% minority, 54% women. **Class size:** 50% < 20, 41% 20-39, 3% 40-49, 5% 50-99, less than 1% >100. **Special facilities:** Outdoor education centers for field work, environmental center, geological field station, nature preserve for biological research.

**Freshman class profile.** 10,913 applied, 4,803 admitted, 1,196 enrolled.

| Mid 50% test scores | | Rank in top quarter: | 40% |
|---|---|---|---|
| SAT critical reading: | 480-560 | Rank in top tenth: | 8% |
| SAT math: | 500-590 | Return as sophomores: | 81% |
| GPA 3.50 or higher: | 33% | Out-of-state: | 2% |
| GPA 3.0-3.49: | 41% | Live on campus: | 98% |
| GPA 2.0-2.99: | 25% | | |

**Basis for selection.** Secondary school record, standardized test scores very important. Recommendations, personal statement, extracurricular activities, talent/ability, and class rank important. Additional consideration given for interview, alumni/ae relation, geographical residence, state residency, minority status, volunteer work, and work experience. Audition required for special talent: music program; portfolio recommended for special talent: art program.

**High school preparation.** Required and recommended units include English 4, mathematics 3-4, social studies 4, science 3-4 (laboratory 3) and foreign language 3-4. 2 units in math, science, or foreign language can be compensated for by 4+ units or advanced course work in another one of the three areas.

**2007-2008 Annual costs.** Tuition/fees: $5,439; $11,699 out-of-state. Room/board: $8,760. Books/supplies: $800. Personal expenses: $1,500.

**2007-2008 Financial aid. Need-based:** 1,069 full-time freshmen applied for aid; 673 were judged to have need; 659 of these received aid. Average need met was 73%. Average scholarship/grant was $1,589; average loan $1,950. 44% of total undergraduate aid awarded as scholarships/grants, 56% as loans/jobs. **Non-need-based:** Awarded to 1,371 full-time undergraduates, including 296 freshmen. Scholarships awarded for academics, leadership.

**Application procedures. Admission:** Priority date 3/1; no deadline. $40 fee, may be waived for applicants with need. Application may be submitted online. Admission notification on a rolling basis beginning on or about 1/2. Must reply by May 1 or within 4 week(s) if notified thereafter. **Financial aid:** Priority date 3/1, closing date 4/1. FAFSA required. Applicants notified on a rolling basis starting 3/1; must reply by 5/1 or within 4 week(s) of notification.

**Academics. Special study options:** Combined bachelor's/graduate degree, cooperative education, cross-registration, distance learning, double major, dual enrollment of high school students, exchange student, honors, independent study, internships, liberal arts/career combination, student-designed major, study abroad, teacher certification program, Washington semester. 13 study abroad programs in 11 countries. Students eligible to participate in more than 400 international study programs offered via SUNY. **Credit/placement by examination:** AP, CLEP, IB, institutional tests. 30 credit hours maximum toward bachelor's degree. **Support services:** Learning center, pre-admission summer program, reduced course load, study skills assistance, tutoring, writing center.

**Majors. Area/ethnic studies:** African-American. **Biology:** General. **Business:** General, management science. **Communications:** Broadcast journalism, health, journalism, organizational, public relations. **Education:** General, biology, chemistry, Deaf/hearing impaired, elementary, English, foreign languages, French, health, mathematics, middle, physical, physics, science, secondary, social studies, Spanish, special, speech. **English:** English lit. **Foreign languages:** French, Spanish. **Health:** Audiology/speech pathology. **History:** General. **Math:** General. **Parks/recreation:** General, exercise sciences, health/fitness. **Philosophy/religion:** Philosophy. **Physical sciences:** Chemistry, geochemistry, geology, physics, planetary. **Psychology:** General. **Social sciences:** Anthropology, criminology, economics, geography, international relations, political science, sociology. **Visual/performing arts:** Studio arts.

**Most popular majors.** Education 48%, parks/recreation 14%, social sciences 13%.

**Computing on campus.** 832 workstations in dormitories, library, computer center, student center. Dormitories linked to campus network. Commuter students can connect to campus network. Online course registration, online library, helpline, repair service available.

**Student life. Freshman orientation:** Available, $100 fee. **Housing:** Guaranteed on-campus for all undergraduates. Coed dorms, apartments, fraternity/sorority housing available. $150 deposit, deadline 5/1. **Activities:** Bands, choral groups, dance, drama, film society, literary magazine, music ensembles, musical theater, radio station, student government, student newspaper, symphony orchestra, TV station, Amnesty International, hunger homelessness coalition, New York Public Interest Research Group, Black, Latin, Jewish, & Asian student unions, community service council, Big Brothers/Big Sisters, Adopt-a-Grandparent program.

**Athletics.** NCAA. **Intercollegiate:** Baseball M, basketball, cross-country, diving, field hockey W, football (non-tackle) M, football (tackle) M, golf W, gymnastics W, ice hockey, lacrosse, racquetball, soccer, softball W, swimming, tennis W, track and field, volleyball W, wrestling M. **Intramural:** Archery, badminton, basketball, bowling, football (non-tackle), golf, racquetball, soccer, softball, table tennis, tennis, volleyball, water polo, weight lifting. **Team name:** Red Dragons.

**Student services.** Adult student services, campus ministries, career counseling, student employment services, financial aid counseling, health services, on-campus daycare, personal counseling, placement for graduates, veterans' counselor. **Physically disabled:** Services for visually, speech, hearing impaired.

**Contact.** E-mail: admissions@cortland.edu
Phone: (607) 753-4712 Fax: (607) 753-5998
Mark Yacavone, Director of Admissions, State University of New York College at Cortland, PO Box 2000, Cortland, NY 13045-0900

## State University of New York College at Fredonia

Fredonia, New York
www.fredonia.edu

CB member
CB code: 2539

- Public 4-year liberal arts college
- Residential campus in large town

- 5,067 degree-seeking undergraduates: 3% part-time, 56% women, 3% African American, 2% Asian American, 3% Hispanic American, 1% Native American
- 316 degree-seeking graduate students
- 56% of applicants admitted
- SAT or ACT (ACT writing optional) required
- 63% graduate within 6 years

**General.** Founded in 1826. Regionally accredited. **Degrees:** 1,060 bachelor's awarded; master's offered. **Location:** 45 miles from Buffalo, 50 miles from Erie, Pennsylvania. **Calendar:** Semester, limited summer session. **Full-time faculty:** 238 total; 80% have terminal degrees, 15% minority, 46% women. **Part-time faculty:** 208 total; 14% have terminal degrees, 5% minority, 47% women. **Class size:** 44% < 20, 43% 20-39, 6% 40-49, 5% 50-99, 2% >100. **Special facilities:** Arts center, communication lab, sounding recording studios, education and local history museums.

**Freshman class profile.** 5,893 applied, 3,322 admitted, 1,061 enrolled.

| Mid 50% test scores | | | |
|---|---|---|---|
| SAT critical reading: | 500-590 | Rank in top tenth: | 16% |
| SAT math: | 510-600 | End year in good standing: | 83% |
| ACT composite: | 21-26 | Return as sophomores: | 85% |
| GPA 3.50 or higher: | 35% | Out-of-state: | 2% |
| GPA 3.0-3.49: | 46% | Live on campus: | 90% |
| GPA 2.0-2.99: | 19% | Fraternities: | 3% |
| Rank in top quarter: | 45% | Sororities: | 3% |

**Basis for selection.** Academic achievement, test results, and subjects taken given priority. Counselor recommendations, resume with supporting materials important when priority credentials marginal. Audition required for acting, music, musical performance, musical theater, production design. Portfolio required for all Visual Arts and New Media program. **Home-schooled:** Submit all documentation of subject areas covered.

**High school preparation.** 20 units required; 23 recommended. Required and recommended units include English 4, mathematics 3-4, social studies 4, science 3-4 (laboratory 3), foreign language 3-4, computer science 1, visual/performing arts 1 and academic electives 1.

**2007-2008 Annual costs.** Tuition/fees: $5,544; $11,802 out-of-state. Room/board: $8,640. Books/supplies: $1,000. Personal expenses: $638.

**2006-2007 Financial aid. Need-based:** 902 full-time freshmen applied for aid; 627 were judged to have need; 614 of these received aid. Average need met was 78%. Average scholarship/grant was $3,063; average loan $2,944. 48% of total undergraduate aid awarded as scholarships/grants, 52% as loans/jobs. **Non-need-based:** Awarded to 785 full-time undergraduates, including 276 freshmen. Scholarships awarded for academics, alumni affiliation, art, athletics, leadership, minority status, music/drama.

**Application procedures. Admission:** No deadline. $40 fee, may be waived for applicants with need. Application may be submitted online. Admission notification on a rolling basis beginning on or about 12/1. Must reply by May 1 or within 4 week(s) if notified thereafter. **Financial aid:** Priority date 2/1, closing date 5/15. FAFSA required. Applicants notified on a rolling basis starting 3/10; must reply within 4 week(s) of notification.

**Academics.** Extensive interdisciplinary studies degree programs offered. **Special study options:** Accelerated study, combined bachelor's/graduate degree, distance learning, double major, honors, independent study, internships, student-designed major, study abroad, teacher certification program, Washington semester, Albany semester, over 90 exchange programs within SUNY system, 13 universities in engineering. **Credit/placement by examination:** AP, CLEP, IB. 30 credit hours maximum toward bachelor's degree. **Support services:** Learning center, study skills assistance, tutoring.

**Majors. Area/ethnic studies:** American. **Biology:** General, biochemistry, biotechnology, human/medical genetics. **Business:** Accounting, business admin, communications, finance, management information systems, management science. **Communications:** General, broadcast journalism, public relations. **Communications technology:** Recording arts. **Computer sciences:** General. **Conservation:** Environmental studies. **Education:** General, biology, chemistry, early childhood, elementary, English, foreign languages, French, mathematics, music, physics, secondary, social studies, Spanish, speech, speech impaired. **English:** English lit. **Foreign languages:** French, Spanish. **Health:** Audiology/speech pathology, clinical lab technology, communication disorders, music therapy. **History:** General. **Legal studies:** General, prelaw. **Math:** General. **Philosophy/religion:** Philosophy. **Physical sciences:** Chemistry, geochemistry, geology, geophysics, physics, planetary. **Protective services:** Criminal justice. **Psychology:** General. **Public administration:** Social work. **Social sciences:** Economics, political science, sociology. **Visual/performing arts:** Art, art history/conservation, ceramics, commercial/advertising art, dramatic, drawing, music history, music management, music

performance, music theory/composition, painting, piano/organ, printmaking, sculpture, studio arts, theater design, voice/opera.

**Most popular majors.** Business/marketing 14%, communications/journalism 8%, education 28%, psychology 8%, social sciences 8%, visual/performing arts 9%.

**Computing on campus.** 500 workstations in dormitories, library, computer center. Dormitories wired for high-speed internet access and linked to campus network. Commuter students can connect to campus network. Online course registration, online library, helpline, repair service, wireless network available.

**Student life. Freshman orientation:** Available, $105 fee. Preregistration for classes offered. 2-day program with students and parents in late June and early July; attendance strongly recommended. **Housing:** Guaranteed on-campus for all undergraduates. Coed dorms, single-sex dorms, apartments, substance-free housing available. $50 fully refundable deposit, deadline 5/1. **Activities:** Bands, campus ministries, choral groups, dance, drama, literary magazine, music ensembles, musical theater, opera, radio station, student government, student newspaper, symphony orchestra, TV station, Newman Club, Black student union, Young Republicans, service fraternities and sororities, Jewish student union, Young Democrats, Native American Student Association, Latinos Unidos, Intervarsity Christian Fellowship.

**Athletics.** NCAA. **Intercollegiate:** Baseball M, basketball, cross-country, ice hockey M, lacrosse W, soccer, softball W, swimming, tennis W, track and field, volleyball W. **Intramural:** Baseball M, basketball, field hockey W, handball, ice hockey, lacrosse M, racquetball, soccer, softball, volleyball, water polo. **Team name:** Blue Devils.

**Student services.** Alcohol/substance abuse counseling, campus ministries, career counseling, student employment services, financial aid counseling, health services, legal services, minority student services, on-campus daycare, personal counseling, placement for graduates, veterans' counselor. **Physically disabled:** Services for speech impaired.

**Contact.** E-mail: admissions.office@fredonia.edu
Phone: (716) 673-3251 Toll-free number: (800) 252-1212
Fax: (716) 673-3249
Christopher Dearth, Director of Admissions, State University of New York College at Fredonia, 178 Central Avenue, Fredonia, NY 14063-1136

---

## State University of New York College at Geneseo

Geneseo, New York   CB member
www.geneseo.edu   CB code: 2540

- Public 4-year liberal arts college
- Residential campus in small town
- 5,376 degree-seeking undergraduates: 2% part-time, 58% women, 2% African American, 6% Asian American, 3% Hispanic American, 2% international
- 153 degree-seeking graduate students
- 36% of applicants admitted
- SAT or ACT (ACT writing optional), application essay required
- 78% graduate within 6 years; 42% enter graduate study

**General.** Founded in 1871. Regionally accredited. **Degrees:** 1,142 bachelor's awarded; master's offered. **ROTC:** Army, Air Force. **Location:** 30 miles from Rochester. **Calendar:** Semester, limited summer session. **Full-time faculty:** 246 total; 82% have terminal degrees, 16% minority, 42% women. **Part-time faculty:** 84 total; 100% have terminal degrees, 14% minority, 52% women. **Class size:** 37% < 20, 50% 20-39, 6% 40-49, 6% 50-99, 2% >100. **Special facilities:** Nuclear accelerator, planetarium, 3 theaters, ice arena, arboretum.

**Freshman class profile.** 10,274 applied, 3,744 admitted, 1,035 enrolled.

| Mid 50% test scores | | | |
|---|---|---|---|
| SAT critical reading: | 620-700 | Rank in top quarter: | 88% |
| SAT math: | 630-690 | Rank in top tenth: | 57% |
| ACT composite: | 27-30 | End year in good standing: | 89% |
| GPA 3.50 or higher: | 85% | Return as sophomores: | 89% |
| GPA 3.0-3.49: | 13% | Out-of-state: | 1% |
| GPA 2.0-2.99: | 2% | Live on campus: | 100% |
| | | International: | 2% |

**Basis for selection.** Rigor of high school preparation, high school GPA, class rank, test scores, school and community activities, special talent, leadership, personal essay important. Special consideration given to minority applicants, children and grandchildren of alumni. Audition required for dramatic arts, music programs; portfolio required for art programs. **Home-schooled:** Statement describing homeschool structure and mission, transcript of courses and grades, state high school equivalency certificate required. Letter from high school offical or home school agency indicating the student is meeting production requirements.

**High school preparation.** College-preparatory program recommended. 20 units recommended. Recommended units include English 4, mathematics 4, social studies 4, science 4 and foreign language 4. Music, art also recommended. 4 math required for computer science and business majors.

**2007-2008 Annual costs.** Tuition/fees: $5,616; $11,876 out-of-state. Room/board: $8,550. Books/supplies: $800. Personal expenses: $750.

**2007-2008 Financial aid. Need-based:** 842 full-time freshmen applied for aid; 417 were judged to have need; 417 of these received aid. Average need met was 80%. Average scholarship/grant was $2,946; average loan $4,275. 44% of total undergraduate aid awarded as scholarships/grants, 56% as loans/jobs. **Non-need-based:** Awarded to 651 full-time undergraduates, including 283 freshmen. Scholarships awarded for academics, art, leadership, minority status, music/drama, religious affiliation, ROTC, state residency.

**Application procedures. Admission:** Closing date 1/1 (postmark date). $40 fee, may be waived for applicants with need. Application may be submitted online. Admission notification on a rolling basis beginning on or about 3/1. Must reply by 5/1. **Financial aid:** Closing date 2/15. FAFSA required. Applicants notified on a rolling basis starting 3/15; must reply by 5/1.

**Academics. Special study options:** Combined bachelor's/graduate degree, cross-registration, double major, honors, independent study, internships, study abroad, teacher certification program, Washington semester. Albany semester, 3-2 engineering, 3-3 engineering, 4-1 MBA, 3-4 dentistry, 3-4 optometry, 3-4 osteopathic medicine. **Credit/placement by examination:** AP, CLEP, IB, institutional tests. 30 credit hours maximum toward bachelor's degree. **Support services:** Learning center, pre-admission summer program, reduced course load, study skills assistance, tutoring, writing center.

**Majors. Area/ethnic studies:** African-American, American. **Biology:** General, biochemistry, biophysics. **Business:** General, accounting, business admin. **Communications:** General. **Computer sciences:** General. **Education:** Biology, chemistry, early childhood, elementary, English, French, history, mathematics, physics, science, social studies, Spanish, special. **English:** English lit. **Foreign languages:** Comparative lit, French, Spanish. **Health:** Communication disorders, speech pathology. **History:** General. **Interdisciplinary:** Natural sciences. **Math:** General. **Philosophy/religion:** Philosophy. **Physical sciences:** Chemistry, geochemistry, geology, geophysics, physics. **Psychology:** General. **Social sciences:** Anthropology, economics, geography, international relations, political science, sociology. **Visual/performing arts:** Art history/conservation, dramatic, music performance.

**Most popular majors.** Biology 11%, business/marketing 13%, education 19%, English 8%, psychology 10%, social sciences 18%.

**Computing on campus.** 900 workstations in dormitories, library, computer center, student center. Dormitories wired for high-speed internet access and linked to campus network. Commuter students can connect to campus network. Online course registration, helpline, student web hosting, wireless network available.

**Student life. Freshman orientation:** Available, $140 fee. Preregistration for classes offered. 5 sessions, 2 days each, during June and July. **Housing:** Guaranteed on-campus for freshmen. Coed dorms, substance-free housing available. $150 fully refundable deposit, deadline 5/1. Special interest housing available. Some fraternities/sororities have housing independent of college. **Activities:** Jazz band, choral groups, dance, drama, literary magazine, music ensembles, musical theater, radio station, student government, student newspaper, symphony orchestra, TV station, 168 organizations and clubs, interfaith center.

**Athletics.** NCAA. **Intercollegiate:** Basketball, cross-country, diving, equestrian W, field hockey W, ice hockey M, lacrosse, soccer, softball W, swimming, tennis W, track and field, volleyball W. **Intramural:** Badminton, basketball, football (non-tackle), golf, handball, ice hockey M, racquetball, rugby, skiing, soccer, softball, squash, swimming, table tennis, volleyball, water polo M. **Team name:** Blue Knights, Lady Knights.

**Student services.** Alcohol/substance abuse counseling, campus ministries, career counseling, services for economically disadvantaged, student employment services, health services, minority student services, personal counseling, placement for graduates, veterans' counselor, women's services. **Physically disabled:** Services for visually, speech, hearing impaired.

**Contact.** E-mail: admissions@geneseo.edu
Phone: (585) 245-5571 Toll-free number: (866) 245-5211
Fax: (585) 245-5550
Kris Shay, Director of Admissions, State University of New York College at Geneseo, 1 College Circle, Geneseo, NY 14454-1471

## State University of New York College at Old Westbury

**Old Westbury, New York**
**www.oldwestbury.edu**

**CB member**
**CB code: 2866**

- Public 4-year business and liberal arts college
- Commuter campus in small city
- 3,405 degree-seeking undergraduates: 15% part-time, 57% women, 30% African American, 6% Asian American, 19% Hispanic American, 1% international
- 53 degree-seeking graduate students
- 55% of applicants admitted
- SAT or ACT with writing required
- 36% graduate within 6 years; 79% enter graduate study

**General.** Founded in 1965. Regionally accredited. Curricular focus on interdisciplinary and multicultural academic programs. **Degrees:** 659 bachelor's awarded; master's offered. **ROTC:** Army, Air Force. **Location:** 25 miles from New York City. **Calendar:** Semester, limited summer session. **Full-time faculty:** 130 total; 77% have terminal degrees, 35% minority, 52% women. **Part-time faculty:** 140 total; 24% have terminal degrees, 23% minority, 49% women. **Class size:** 28% < 20, 71% 20-39, less than 1% 40-49, less than 1% 50-99. **Special facilities:** Language lab, performing arts theatre, recital hall, science laboratories, athletic center.

**Freshman class profile.** 3,976 applied, 2,185 admitted, 436 enrolled.

| Mid 50% test scores | | | |
|---|---|---|---|
| SAT critical reading: | 440-510 | Rank in top quarter: | 4% |
| SAT math: | 450-530 | Rank in top tenth: | 3% |
| SAT writing: | 420-500 | Return as sophomores: | 73% |
| ACT composite: | 18-22 | Out-of-state: | 3% |
| GPA 3.50 or higher: | 9% | Live on campus: | 65% |
| GPA 3.0-3.49: | 24% | International: | 1% |
| GPA 2.0-2.99: | 66% | Fraternities: | 1% |
| | | Sororities: | 1% |

**Basis for selection.** High school GPA, SAT scores, letters of recommendation, interview, personal essay important. SAT Subject Tests recommended. Essay and interview recommended for academically weak students. **Homeschooled:** Statement describing homeschool structure and mission required. Letter from superintendent of local school district verifying home schooling equivalent to high school curriculum required.

**High school preparation.** 18 units required; 19 recommended. Required and recommended units include English 4, mathematics 3, social studies 2, history 2, science 3 (laboratory 3), foreign language 2 and academic electives 2-3.

**2007-2008 Annual costs.** Tuition/fees: $5,177; $11,437 out-of-state. Room/board: $8,800. Books/supplies: $800. Personal expenses: $1,210.

**2006-2007 Financial aid. Need-based:** 351 full-time freshmen applied for aid; 349 were judged to have need; 315 of these received aid. Average need met was 47%. Average scholarship/grant was $5,893; average loan $1,595. 54% of total undergraduate aid awarded as scholarships/grants, 46% as loans/jobs. **Non-need-based:** Awarded to 72 full-time undergraduates, including 20 freshmen. Scholarships awarded for academics, alumni affiliation, state residency.

**Application procedures. Admission:** Priority date 12/1; no deadline. $40 fee, may be waived for applicants with need. Application may be submitted online. Admission notification on a rolling basis beginning on or about 1/7. Must reply by May 1 or within 2 week(s) if notified thereafter. **Financial aid:** Priority date 4/1; no closing date. FAFSA, institutional form required. Applicants notified on a rolling basis starting 4/15; must reply within 2 week(s) of notification.

**Academics.** All freshmen enroll in First-Year Experience program. **Special study options:** Combined bachelor's/graduate degree, cross-registration, distance learning, double major, ESL, exchange student, honors, independent study, internships, liberal arts/career combination, study abroad, teacher certification program, Washington semester. Minority access to research centers, Minority biomedical research. **Credit/placement by examination:** AP, CLEP, IB, SAT, institutional tests. 30 credit hours maximum toward bachelor's degree. Each department has own policy for accepting credit by examination in fulfillment of departmental requirements. 8 credits awarded for minimum of 2 years of active duty in any branch of military service. Veterans may also apply for credit based on specific formal courses of instruction given by military services. **Support services:** Learning center, pre-admission summer program, reduced course load, remedial instruction, study skills assistance, tutoring, writing center.

**Majors. Area/ethnic studies:** American. **Biology:** General, biochemistry. **Business:** Accounting, business admin, finance, labor relations, marketing. **Communications:** General. **Computer sciences:** General, information systems. **Education:** Bilingual, biology, chemistry, elementary, mathematics, middle, science, secondary, social studies, Spanish, special. **English:** English lit. **Foreign languages:** Comparative lit, Spanish. **Liberal arts:** Arts/sciences, humanities. **Math:** General. **Philosophy/religion:** Philosophy. **Physical sciences:** Chemistry. **Psychology:** General. **Social sciences:** General, criminology, sociology. **Visual/performing arts:** General.

**Most popular majors.** Business/marketing 28%, communications/journalism 7%, computer/information sciences 6%, education 17%, psychology 12%, social sciences 16%.

**Computing on campus.** 400 workstations in library, computer center, student center. Dormitories wired for high-speed internet access. Online course registration, online library, helpline, wireless network available.

**Student life. Freshman orientation:** Mandatory, $110 fee. Preregistration for classes offered. Held prior to fall term for 3 days; for new students and parents. A one-day orientation is held prior to the spring term for all new students. **Housing:** Guaranteed on-campus for all undergraduates. Coed dorms, substance-free housing available. $50 fully refundable deposit, deadline 5/1. **Activities:** Choral groups, dance, drama, film society, international student organizations, radio station, student government, student newspaper, women's center, Alianza Latina, African People's Organization, Big Brother/Big Sister club, Asian club, Access for All, Council for Unity, Shekinah Chorale.

**Athletics.** NCAA. **Intercollegiate:** Baseball M, basketball, cross-country, soccer M, softball W, swimming, volleyball W. **Intramural:** Badminton, cheerleading W, equestrian, football (tackle), racquetball, soccer, softball, swimming, tennis, volleyball, weight lifting. **Team name:** Panthers.

**Student services.** Alcohol/substance abuse counseling, campus ministries, career counseling, services for economically disadvantaged, student employment services, financial aid counseling, health services, on-campus daycare, personal counseling, women's services. **Physically disabled:** Services for visually, hearing impaired.

**Contact.** E-mail: enroll@oldwestbury.edu
Phone: (516) 876-3073 Fax: (516) 876-3307
Mary Marquez Bell, Vice President of Enrollment Services, State University of New York College at Old Westbury, Box 307, Old Westbury, NY 11568-0307

---

## State University of New York College at Oneonta

| Oneonta, New York | CB member |
|---|---|
| www.oneonta.edu | CB code: 2542 |

- Public 4-year liberal arts college
- Residential campus in large town
- 5,620 degree-seeking undergraduates: 2% part-time, 58% women, 3% African American, 2% Asian American, 5% Hispanic American, 2% international
- 129 degree-seeking graduate students
- 38% of applicants admitted
- SAT or ACT (ACT writing optional), application essay required
- 60% graduate within 6 years; 48% enter graduate study

**General.** Founded in 1887. Regionally accredited. **Degrees:** 1,297 bachelor's awarded; master's offered. **Location:** 75 miles from Albany, 175 miles from New York City. **Calendar:** Semester, extensive summer session. **Full-time faculty:** 263 total; 78% have terminal degrees, 18% minority, 46% women. **Part-time faculty:** 222 total; 18% have terminal degrees, 11% minority, 46% women. **Class size:** 42% <20, 42% 20-39, 12% 40-49, 3% 50-99, less than 1% >100. **Special facilities:** Observatory, biological field station in Cooperstown, volunteer center, science discovery center, college camp, children's center, music recording studio with tunable walls, computer art lab, DNA computing and genomics lab.

**Freshman class profile.** 12,540 applied, 4,767 admitted, 1,194 enrolled.

| Mid 50% test scores | | | |
|---|---|---|---|
| SAT critical reading: | 510-590 | Rank in top quarter: | 54% |
| SAT math: | 530-610 | Rank in top tenth: | 15% |
| ACT composite: | 22-25 | End year in good standing: | 93% |
| GPA 3.50 or higher: | 28% | Return as sophomores: | 81% |
| GPA 3.0-3.49: | 69% | Out-of-state: | 2% |
| GPA 2.0-2.99: | 3% | Live on campus: | 98% |
| | | International: | 4% |

**Basis for selection.** School achievement record, curriculum, test scores most important. Personal experiences, motivations, awards, honors and recommendations considered. Students scoring below 420 on SAT math or below 450 on SAT verbal must take placement tests. High school writing sample can be submitted in place of essay; interview recommended. **Homeschooled:** Statement describing homeschool structure and mission, transcript of courses and grades, state high school equivalency certificate, interview, letter of recommendation (nonparent) required.

**High school preparation.** 16 units required. Required and recommended units include English 4, mathematics 2-3, social studies 3, science 2-3 (laboratory 2) and foreign language 2-3. 15 specific units and 1 additional unit required in math, science, or foreign language.

**2007-2008 Annual costs.** Tuition/fees: $5,470; $11,730 out-of-state. Room/board: $7,966. Books/supplies: $900. Personal expenses: $1,070.

**2007-2008 Financial aid. Need-based:** 950 full-time freshmen applied for aid; 599 were judged to have need; 584 of these received aid. Average need met was 63%. Average scholarship/grant was $4,258; average loan $3,964. 51% of total undergraduate aid awarded as scholarships/grants, 49% as loans/jobs. **Non-need-based:** Awarded to 1,191 full-time undergraduates, including 285 freshmen. Scholarships awarded for academics.

**Application procedures. Admission:** Priority date 2/1; no deadline. $40 fee, may be waived for applicants with need. Application may be submitted online. Admission notification on a rolling basis beginning on or about 12/1. Must reply by May 1 or within 4 week(s) if notified thereafter. **Financial aid:** Priority date 3/15; no closing date. FAFSA required. Applicants notified on a rolling basis starting 3/1; must reply within 4 week(s) of notification.

**Academics. Special study options:** Combined bachelor's/graduate degree, cross-registration, distance learning, double major, honors, independent study, internships, liberal arts/career combination, New York semester, study abroad, teacher certification program, Washington semester. 3-1 program in fashion with Fashion Institute of Technology, 3-2 program in engineering with Alfred University, Clarkson University, Georgia Institute of Technology, Polytechnic Institute of New York, Rensselaer Polytechnic Institute, SUNY at Binghamton, SUNY Buffalo, and Syracuse University, 2-2 program in forestry with SUNY College of Environmental Science and Forestry, 2-2 programs in physical therapy, medical technology, respiratory care, and cytotechnology with SUNY Upstate Medical University, combined bachelor's/graduate degree programs in accounting and management with SUNY Binghamton, 4-1 MBA program with Rochester Institute of Technology, 2-3 option in physical therapy with SUNY Upstate Medical University, 3-1 option in fashion marketing and 2-2 option in fashion design with American Intercontinental University in London. **Credit/placement by examination:** AP, CLEP, IB. 36 credit hours maximum toward bachelor's degree. **Support services:** Learning center, pre-admission summer program, reduced course load, remedial instruction, study skills assistance, tutoring, writing center.

**Majors. Area/ethnic studies:** African-American, Hispanic-American/Latino/Chicano. **Biology:** General, biochemistry. **Business:** Accounting, fashion, managerial economics. **Communications:** General, media studies. **Communications technology:** Animation/special effects. **Computer sciences:** General, computer graphics, computer science. **Conservation:** Environmental science. **Education:** Biology, chemistry, early childhood, elementary, English, family/consumer sciences, foreign languages, French, history, mathematics, multi-level teacher, physics, science, social science, Spanish. **English:** English lit, speech/rhetoric. **Family/consumer sciences:** General, child development, clothing/textiles, family studies, food/nutrition. **Foreign languages:** French, Spanish. **History:** General. **Interdisciplinary:** Gerontology. **Math:** General, statistics. **Philosophy/religion:** Philosophy. **Physical sciences:** Atmospheric science, chemistry, geology, hydrology, physics. **Protective services:** Criminal justice. **Psychology:** General. **Social sciences:** Anthropology, economics, geography, political science, sociology. **Visual/performing arts:** Art history/conservation, dramatic, multimedia, music management, studio arts.

**Most popular majors.** Business/marketing 7%, education 20%, English 6%, family/consumer sciences 9%, psychology 7%, social sciences 8%, visual/performing arts 18%.

**Computing on campus.** 700 workstations in dormitories, library, computer center, student center. Dormitories wired for high-speed internet access and linked to campus network. Commuter students can connect to campus network. Online course registration, online library, helpline, student web hosting, wireless network available.

**Student life. Freshman orientation:** Available, $100 fee. Preregistration for classes offered. Meet adviser, select courses, register for classes. **Housing:** Guaranteed on-campus for freshmen. Coed dorms, substance-free housing available. $100 fully refundable deposit, deadline 5/1. Special interest housing options and apartment-style suites available within residence halls. **Activities:** Bands, campus ministries, choral groups, dance, drama, film society, international student organizations, literary magazine, music ensembles, Model UN, musical theater, opera, radio station, student government, student newspaper, symphony orchestra, TV station, service organizations, Newman Club, Asian Student Union, Hillel, HOLA Hispanic/Latino organization, Students of Color Coalition, Center for Social Responsibility and Community, Amnesty International, Students for a Free Tibet.

**Athletics. NCAA. Intercollegiate:** Baseball M, basketball, cross-country, field hockey W, lacrosse, soccer, softball W, swimming, tennis, track and field, volleyball W, wrestling M. **Intramural:** Basketball, football (non-tackle) W, soccer, softball, volleyball. **Team name:** Red Dragons.

**Student services.** Adult student services, alcohol/substance abuse counseling, campus ministries, career counseling, services for economically disadvantaged, student employment services, financial aid counseling, health services, minority student services, on-campus daycare, personal counseling, placement for graduates, veterans' counselor, women's services. **Physically disabled:** Services for visually, speech, hearing impaired.

**Contact.** E-mail: admissions@oneonta.edu
Phone: (607) 436-2524 Toll-free number: (800) 786-9123
Fax: (607) 436-3074
Karen Brown, Director of Admissions, State University of New York College at Oneonta, Admissions Office, 116 Alumni Hall, Oneonta, NY 13820-4016

## State University of New York College at Plattsburgh

| Plattsburgh, New York | CB member |
| www.plattsburgh.edu | CB code: 2544 |

- Public 4-year liberal arts and teachers college
- Residential campus in large town
- 5,516 degree-seeking undergraduates: 4% part-time, 57% women, 5% African American, 2% Asian American, 4% Hispanic American, 7% international
- 540 degree-seeking graduate students
- 46% of applicants admitted
- SAT or ACT (ACT writing optional) required
- 55% graduate within 6 years

**General.** Founded in 1889. Regionally accredited. Residential satellite campus for biotechnology and environmental science majors. **Degrees:** 1,238 bachelor's awarded; master's offered. **Location:** 60 miles from Montreal, Canada, 30 miles from Burlington, Vermont. **Calendar:** Semester, limited summer session. **Full-time faculty:** 268 total; 86% have terminal degrees, 12% minority, 41% women. **Part-time faculty:** 235 total; 21% have terminal degrees, 7% minority, 58% women. **Class size:** 47% < 20, 39% 20-39, 8% 40-49, 6% 50-99, less than 1% >100. **Special facilities:** Center for art, music, and theater, wilderness tract, planetarium, electron microscope, remote sensing laboratory, NMR spectrophotometer, computer operated infrared spectrophotometer, liquid scintillation counter, auditory research labs, speech and hearing clinic, Alzheimer's disease assistance center, virtual reality simulator lab, traumatic brain injury center.

**Freshman class profile.** 7,136 applied, 3,318 admitted, 975 enrolled.

| Mid 50% test scores | | Rank in top quarter: | 40% |
|---|---|---|---|
| SAT critical reading: | 490-580 | Rank in top tenth: | 13% |
| SAT math: | 500-590 | Return as sophomores: | 80% |
| ACT composite: | 20-25 | Out-of-state: | 6% |
| GPA 3.50 or higher: | 19% | Live on campus: | 91% |
| GPA 3.0-3.49: | 47% | International: | 6% |
| GPA 2.0-2.99: | 34% | | |

**Basis for selection.** Curriculum, high school GPA, class rank, test scores most important. Trend of grades, school and community activities, personal interview, and recommendations also considered. Equal opportunity program for academically and financially disadvantaged students. Essay and interview recommended for all; audition recommended for music, theater programs; portfolio recommended for art programs.

**High school preparation.** 14 units required; 21 recommended. Required and recommended units include English 4, mathematics 3-4, social studies 3, history 1, science 3-4, foreign language 3 and academic electives 2. Chemistry required for biochemistry, medical technology, nursing, food and nutrition programs.

**2007-2008 Annual costs.** Tuition/fees: $5,407; $11,667 out-of-state. Room/board: $7,970. Books/supplies: $950. Personal expenses: $2,287.

**2007-2008 Financial aid. Need-based:** 804 full-time freshmen applied for aid; 550 were judged to have need; 541 of these received aid. Average need met was 86%. Average scholarship/grant was $5,534; average loan $4,877. 42% of total undergraduate aid awarded as scholarships/grants, 58% as loans/jobs. **Non-need-based:** Awarded to 2,514 full-time undergraduates, including 609 freshmen. Scholarships awarded for academics, alumni affiliation, art, leadership, minority status, music/drama, ROTC, state residency.

**Application procedures. Admission:** Priority date 12/1; deadline 3/1 (receipt date). $40 fee, may be waived for applicants with need. Application may be submitted online. Admission notification on a rolling basis beginning on or about 1/15. Must reply by May 1 or within 4 week(s) if notified thereafter. **Financial aid:** Priority date 2/15; no closing date. FAFSA required. Applicants notified on a rolling basis starting 3/15; must reply within 6 week(s) of notification.

**Academics.** Credit for military experience, pass/fail option. **Special study options:** Combined bachelor's/graduate degree, cooperative education, cross-registration, distance learning, double major, dual enrollment of high school students, ESL, exchange student, honors, independent study, internships, liberal arts/career combination, student-designed major, study abroad, teacher certification program. Semester and academic year programs in Canada, study opportunities abroad in Argentina, Australia, Chile, Uruguay, England, 3-2 program in engineering with Clarkson University, SUNY Stony Brook and Binghamton, Syracuse University, McGill University and University of Vermont, 3-4 BA/OD with SUNY College of Optometry, 4-1 BS/MBA with Clarkson University. **Credit/placement by examination:** AP, CLEP, IB, SAT, ACT, institutional tests. 30 credit hours maximum toward bachelor's degree. **Support services:** Learning center, pre-admission summer program, reduced course load, remedial instruction, study skills assistance, tutoring, writing center.

**Majors. Area/ethnic studies:** Canadian, Latin American, women's. **Biology:** General, biochemistry, cell/histology, ecology. **Business:** General, accounting, business admin, entrepreneurial studies, finance, hotel/motel admin, international, marketing, restaurant/food services, tourism/travel. **Communications:** Journalism, media studies, organizational, radio/tv. **Computer sciences:** General. **Conservation:** General, environmental science. **Education:** Biology, chemistry, computer, early childhood, elementary, English, foreign languages, French, history, mathematics, multi-level teacher, physics, science, social science, social studies, Spanish, special. **English:** English lit, speech/rhetoric. **Family/consumer sciences:** Family studies, food/nutrition. **Foreign languages:** French, Spanish. **Health:** Audiology/speech pathology, clinical lab science, cytotechnology, nursing (RN). **History:** General. **Liberal arts:** Arts/sciences. **Math:** General. **Parks/recreation:** General. **Philosophy/religion:** Philosophy. **Physical sciences:** Chemistry, geology, physics. **Protective services:** Criminal justice. **Psychology:** General. **Public administration:** Social work. **Social sciences:** Anthropology, economics, geography, political science, sociology. **Visual/performing arts:** Art, dramatic.

**Most popular majors.** Business/marketing 21%, communications/journalism 7%, education 12%, health sciences 7%, psychology 8%, security/protective services 7%, social sciences 6%.

**Computing on campus.** 566 workstations in dormitories, library, computer center, student center. Dormitories wired for high-speed internet access and linked to campus network. Commuter students can connect to campus network. Online course registration, online library, helpline, repair service, student web hosting, wireless network available.

**Student life. Freshman orientation:** Available, $75 fee. Preregistration for classes offered. 2-night stay with meals included; simultaneous program for parents; includes course selection and registration. **Housing:** Guaranteed on-campus for all undergraduates. Coed dorms, special housing for disabled, substance-free housing available. $50 fully refundable deposit, deadline 7/1. Living/learning communities available. **Activities:** Bands, choral groups, dance, drama, film society, literary magazine, music ensembles, musical theater, radio station, student government, student newspaper, TV station, Akeba, El Pueblo, environmental action committee, Hillel, Inter-Varsity Christian Fellowship, Newman Association, Points of View, College Democrats, College Republicans.

**Athletics. NCAA. Intercollegiate:** Baseball M, basketball, cross-country, ice hockey, lacrosse M, soccer, softball W, tennis W, track and field, volleyball W. **Intramural:** Basketball, field hockey, football (non-tackle) M, racquetball, softball, tennis, volleyball. **Team name:** Cardinals.

**Student services.** Adult student services, alcohol/substance abuse counseling, campus ministries, career counseling, services for economically disadvantaged, student employment services, financial aid counseling, health services, legal services, minority student services, on-campus daycare, personal counseling, placement for graduates, veterans' counselor, women's

services. **Physically disabled:** Services for visually, speech, hearing impaired.

**Contact.** E-mail: admissions@plattsburgh.edu
Phone: (518) 564-2040 Toll-free number: (888) 673-0012
Fax: (518) 564-2045
Richard Higgins, Associate Vice President for Enrollment Management, State University of New York College at Plattsburgh, Kehoe Administration Building, Plattsburgh, NY 12901

## State University of New York College at Potsdam

**Potsdam, New York**  **CB member**
**www.potsdam.edu**  **CB code: 2545**

- Public 4-year liberal arts and teachers college
- Residential campus in large town
- 3,571 degree-seeking undergraduates: 3% part-time, 56% women, 2% African American, 1% Asian American, 3% Hispanic American, 1% Native American, 4% international
- 685 degree-seeking graduate students
- 66% of applicants admitted
- SAT or ACT (ACT writing optional) required
- 52% graduate within 6 years; 50% enter graduate study

**General.** Founded in 1816. Regionally accredited. First-year students may enroll in interdisciplinary program to study art, literature, science, and sociology of the Adirondacks. Extension offers undergraduate and graduate courses with emphasis on teacher education. **Degrees:** 716 bachelor's awarded; master's offered. **ROTC:** Army, Air Force. **Location:** 150 miles from Syracuse, 80 miles from Montreal, Canada. **Calendar:** Semester, limited summer session. **Full-time faculty:** 267 total; 86% have terminal degrees, 8% minority, 42% women. **Part-time faculty:** 110 total; 36% have terminal degrees, 3% minority, 62% women. **Class size:** 63% < 20, 32% 20-39, 2% 40-49, 2% 50-99, less than 1% >100. **Special facilities:** Electronic music and recording studios, planetarium, seismographic laboratory, 24-hour computer laboratory, concert hall, music theater, anthropology museum, biology museum, teaching resource center.

**Freshman class profile.** 4,112 applied, 2,734 admitted, 841 enrolled.

| Mid 50% test scores | | Rank in top quarter: | 32% |
|---|---|---|---|
| SAT critical reading: | 470-580 | Rank in top tenth: | 12% |
| SAT math: | 480-590 | End year in good standing: | 79% |
| ACT composite: | 20-24 | Return as sophomores: | 72% |
| GPA 3.50 or higher: | 33% | Out-of-state: | 4% |
| GPA 3.0-3.49: | 31% | Live on campus: | 92% |
| GPA 2.0-2.99: | 35% | International: | 3% |

**Basis for selection.** Admissions decisions based on secondary school record and standardized test scores. Class rank, talent, ability, activities and community service also important. Freshman applicants over the age of 22 are not required to submit SAT or ACT scores. Essays and interviews required for some, but not all applicants. Auditions required for music majors. Auditions encouraged for dance and theatre majors. Portfolios encouraged for art majors. **Homeschooled:** GED required. SAT or ACT required.

**High school preparation.** 13 units required; 21 recommended. Required and recommended units include English 4, mathematics 2-4, social studies 4, science 2-4 (laboratory 1-2), foreign language 4 and visual/performing arts 1.

**2007-2008 Annual costs.** Tuition/fees: $5,406; $11,666 out-of-state. Room/board: $8,420. Books/supplies: $1,000. Personal expenses: $1,300.

**2007-2008 Financial aid. Need-based:** 753 full-time freshmen applied for aid; 585 were judged to have need; 532 of these received aid. Average need met was 85%. Average scholarship/grant was $6,460; average loan $4,255. 54% of total undergraduate aid awarded as scholarships/grants, 46% as loans/jobs. **Non-need-based:** Awarded to 1,374 full-time undergraduates, including 461 freshmen. Scholarships awarded for academics, art, leadership, minority status, music/drama, ROTC. **Additional information:** Apply early to access limited, need-based awards.

**Application procedures. Admission:** No deadline. $40 fee, may be waived for applicants with need. Application may be submitted online. Admission notification on a rolling basis beginning on or about 10/1. Must reply by May 1 for guaranteed enrollment. **Financial aid:** Priority date 3/1; no closing date. FAFSA required. Applicants notified on a rolling basis starting 2/1; must reply within 4 week(s) of notification.

**Academics. Special study options:** Combined bachelor's/graduate degree, cross-registration, distance learning, double major, dual enrollment of high school students, exchange student, honors, independent study, internships, liberal arts/career combination, student-designed major, study abroad, teacher certification program. First-year students may enroll in interdisciplinary program to study art, literature, science, and sociology of the Adirondacks. Extension offers undergraduate and graduate courses with emphasis on teacher education. Combined degree options in engineering with Clarkson University and SUNY Binghamton; accounting, engineering or management with SUNY Utica/Rome. **Credit/placement by examination:** AP, CLEP, IB. Credit awarded for International Baccalaureate on course-by-course evaluation. **Support services:** Learning center, pre-admission summer program, reduced course load, study skills assistance, tutoring, writing center.

**Majors. Area/ethnic studies:** Women's. **Biology:** General, biochemistry. **Business:** Business admin, labor relations, managerial economics. **Computer sciences:** General. **Conservation:** Environmental studies. **Education:** Biology, chemistry, elementary, English, foreign languages, French, mathematics, music, physics, science, social studies, Spanish. **English:** English lit, speech/rhetoric. **Foreign languages:** French, Spanish. **History:** General. **Math:** General. **Philosophy/religion:** Philosophy. **Physical sciences:** Chemistry, geology, physics. **Protective services:** Criminal justice. **Psychology:** General. **Social sciences:** Anthropology, archaeology, economics, political science, sociology. **Visual/performing arts:** General, art, art history/conservation, dance, dramatic, music management, music performance, music theory/composition.

**Most popular majors.** Business/marketing 9%, education 29%, English 10%, history 6%, psychology 8%, social sciences 11%, visual/performing arts 12%.

**Computing on campus.** 690 workstations in dormitories, library, computer center, student center. Dormitories wired for high-speed internet access and linked to campus network. Commuter students can connect to campus network. Online course registration, online library, helpline, student web hosting, wireless network available.

**Student life. Freshman orientation:** Available, $165 fee. Preregistration for classes offered. Two-day program. **Policies:** Academic honor code outlines expectations for academic honesty and integrity; code of student rights, responsibilities, and conduct can be found in student handbook. **Housing:** Guaranteed on-campus for all undergraduates. Coed dorms, special housing for disabled, apartments, substance-free housing available. $50 fully refundable deposit, deadline 5/1. First year experience, study intensive, honors, and arts housing available. **Activities:** Bands, choral groups, dance, drama, international student organizations, literary magazine, music ensembles, musical theater, opera, radio station, student government, student newspaper, symphony orchestra, Intervarsity Christian Fellowship, SUNY Potsdam Campaign Against Hunger and Homelessness, Black Student Alliance, Potsdam Association of Native Americans, Caribbean Latin American Student Society, Politics Association, Circle K, Student Unitarian Universalists of Northern New York, Lesbian, Gay, Bisexual and Transgender Association.

**Athletics.** NCAA. **Intercollegiate:** Basketball, cheerleading, cross-country, equestrian, golf M, ice hockey, lacrosse, soccer, softball W, swimming, tennis W, volleyball W. **Intramural:** Basketball, football (non-tackle), racquetball, soccer, softball, tennis, volleyball, water polo, weight lifting. **Team name:** Bears.

**Student services.** Adult student services, alcohol/substance abuse counseling, campus ministries, career counseling, services for economically disadvantaged, student employment services, financial aid counseling, health services, legal services, minority student services, on-campus daycare, personal counseling, placement for graduates, veterans' counselor, women's services. **Physically disabled:** Services for visually, speech, hearing impaired.

**Contact.** E-mail: admissions@potsdam.edu
Phone: (315) 267-2180 Toll-free number: (877) 768-7326
Fax: (315) 267-2163
Thomas Nesbitt, Director of Admissions, State University of New York College at Potsdam, 44 Pierrepont Avenue, Potsdam, NY 13676

## State University of New York College of Environmental Science and Forestry

**Syracuse, New York**  **CB member**
**www.esf.edu**  **CB code: 2530**

- Public 4-year university and liberal arts college
- Residential campus in small city
- 1,455 degree-seeking undergraduates: 3% part-time, 37% women, 1% African American, 3% Asian American, 4% Hispanic American, 1% Native American, 1% international
- 485 degree-seeking graduate students
- 51% of applicants admitted

- SAT or ACT (ACT writing recommended), application essay required
- 67% graduate within 6 years; 31% enter graduate study

**General.** Founded in 1911. Regionally accredited. Doctoral granting; focused on the science, engineering, design and management of the environment and natural resources. **Degrees:** 280 bachelor's, 27 associate awarded; master's, doctoral offered. **ROTC:** Army, Air Force. **Location:** Downtown. **Calendar:** Semester, limited summer session. **Full-time faculty:** 143 total; 92% have terminal degrees, 12% minority, 24% women. **Part-time faculty:** 27 total; 74% have terminal degrees, 4% minority, 56% women. **Class size:** 77% < 20, 12% 20-39, 4% 40-49, 5% 50-99, 3% >100. **Special facilities:** 6 regional campuses and field stations used for field study and research, 25,000-acre multicampus forest system, ecological center, wildlife collection, semicommercial paper mill.

**Freshman class profile.** 1,349 applied, 685 admitted, 250 enrolled.

| Mid 50% test scores | | Rank in top tenth: | 24% |
|---|---|---|---|
| SAT critical reading: | 510-610 | End year in good standing: | 92% |
| SAT math: | 530-610 | Return as sophomores: | 84% |
| ACT composite: | 22-26 | Out-of-state: | 10% |
| Rank in top quarter: | 55% | Live on campus: | 90% |

**Basis for selection.** High school record most important, test scores, essay, and recommendations also important. Applicant should have strong college preparatory program with focus on mathematics and science for most programs and design background preferred for Landscape Architecture. Interview or participation in informational program recommended for all; portfolio required for some landscape architecture applicants. **Homeschooled:** Statement describing homeschool structure and mission required. If no superintendent's statement provided, student must have GED to enroll.

**High school preparation.** Required and recommended units include English 4, mathematics 3-4, social studies 3, history 1, science 3-4 (laboratory 3-4) and foreign language 3.

**2007-2008 Annual costs.** Tuition/fees: $5,100; $11,360 out-of-state. Room and board available through Syracuse University. Books/supplies: $1,200. Personal expenses: $450.

**2007-2008 Financial aid.** **Need-based:** 242 full-time freshmen applied for aid; 184 were judged to have need; 184 of these received aid. Average need met was 100%. Average scholarship/grant was $5,000; average loan $5,500. 10% of total undergraduate aid awarded as scholarships/grants, 90% as loans/jobs. **Non-need-based:** Awarded to 261 full-time undergraduates, including 126 freshmen. Scholarships awarded for academics, alumni affiliation, leadership, minority status, ROTC, state residency.

**Application procedures.** **Admission:** Priority date 12/1; no deadline. $40 fee, may be waived for applicants with need. Application may be submitted online. Admission notification on a rolling basis beginning on or about 2/1. Must reply by May 1 or within 4 week(s) if notified thereafter. **Financial aid:** Priority date 3/1; no closing date. FAFSA required. Applicants notified on a rolling basis starting 3/15; must reply within 2 week(s) of notification.

**Academics.** **Special study options:** Combined bachelor's/graduate degree, cooperative education, cross-registration, dual enrollment of high school students, ESL, honors, internships, study abroad, teacher certification program. Associate degree programs in forestry technology and land surveying technology offered through The Ranger School in Adirondack Mountains. **Credit/placement by examination:** AP, CLEP, IB. **Support services:** Learning center, pre-admission summer program, reduced course load, remedial instruction, study skills assistance, tutoring, writing center.

**Majors.** **Agriculture:** Animal sciences. **Architecture:** Landscape. **Biology:** Aquatic, biochemistry, biotechnology, conservation, environmental, wildlife. **Business:** Construction management. **Conservation:** General, environmental science, environmental studies, fisheries, forest management, forest resources, forest sciences, forestry, management/policy, wildlife, wood science. **Education:** Biology, chemistry, science. **Engineering:** General, environmental. **Physical sciences:** Chemistry. **Other:** Natural History and Interpretation, Paper Science and Engineering.

**Most popular majors.** Architecture 12%, biology 58%, engineering/engineering technologies 17%, natural resources/environmental science 11%.

**Computing on campus.** 150 workstations in dormitories, library, computer center. Dormitories wired for high-speed internet access and linked to campus network. Commuter students can connect to campus network. Online course registration, online library, helpline, wireless network available.

**Student life.** **Freshman orientation:** Mandatory, $50 fee. 4-day program prior to start of classes. **Housing:** Coed dorms, special housing for disabled, apartments, cooperative housing, fraternity/sorority housing, substance-free

housing available. $350 fully refundable deposit, deadline 5/1. All on-campus housing available through Syracuse University. School located adjacent to Syracuse University. **Activities:** Bands, campus ministries, choral groups, dance, drama, film society, literary magazine, music ensembles, musical theater, radio station, student government, student newspaper, symphony orchestra, TV station, undergraduate student association, Alpha Xi Sigma honor society, Wildlife Society, multicultural organization, environmental action coalition, woodsmen's team, creative minds club, green campus initiative, soccer club.

**Athletics.** **Intercollegiate:** Golf, soccer. **Intramural:** Basketball, football (non-tackle), racquetball, soccer, softball, tennis.

**Student services.** Alcohol/substance abuse counseling, campus ministries, career counseling, services for economically disadvantaged, student employment services, financial aid counseling, health services, legal services, minority student services, personal counseling, veterans' counselor, women's services. **Physically disabled:** Services for visually, speech, hearing impaired. **Learning disabled:** Comprehensive services available.

**Contact.** E-mail: esfinfo@esf.edu
Phone: (315) 470-6600 Toll-free number: (800) 777-7373
Fax: (315) 470-6933
Susan Sanford, Director of Admissions, State University of New York College of Environmental Science and Forestry, 106 Bray Hall, Syracuse, NY 13210

---

## State University of New York College of Technology at Canton
Canton, New York
www.canton.edu

CB code: 2523

- Public 4-year technical college
- Residential campus in small town
- 2,384 degree-seeking undergraduates: 8% part-time, 52% women, 9% African American, 1% Asian American, 4% Hispanic American, 2% Native American, 1% international
- 91% of applicants admitted
- 56% graduate within 6 years

**General.** Founded in 1906. Regionally accredited. **Degrees:** 86 bachelor's, 485 associate awarded. **ROTC:** Army, Air Force. **Location:** 135 miles from Syracuse, 120 miles from Montreal, Canada. **Calendar:** Semester, limited summer session. **Full-time faculty:** 107 total; 35% have terminal degrees, 8% minority, 42% women. **Part-time faculty:** 66 total; 4% have terminal degrees, 4% minority, 52% women. **Class size:** 36% < 20, 49% 20-39, 10% 40-49, 5% 50-99. **Special facilities:** Cross-country trails.

**Freshman class profile.** 2,125 applied, 1,931 admitted, 748 enrolled.

| Mid 50% test scores | | Rank in top tenth: | 1% |
|---|---|---|---|
| SAT critical reading: | 400-500 | Return as sophomores: | 75% |
| SAT math: | 410-520 | Out-of-state: | 4% |
| ACT composite: | 17-22 | Live on campus: | 74% |
| GPA 3.50 or higher: | 4% | International: | 1% |
| GPA 3.0-3.49: | 26% | Fraternities: | 2% |
| GPA 2.0-2.99: | 66% | Sororities: | 2% |
| Rank in top quarter: | 8% | | |

**Basis for selection.** High school record most important. Admission requirements vary according to program of study. COMPASS required for some. SAT or ACT required of bachelor's degree program applicants. SAT, ACT, SAT Subject Test scores received on rolling basis. Interview recommended. **Homeschooled:** Transcript of courses and grades required. Applicants must do 1 of following: present letter from superintendent from school district they reside in indicating completion of program equivalent to high school diploma; take GED exam; take 5 Regents Exams indicated in SUNY policy; complete 24 credit-hour program to earn GED. **Learning Disabled:** Students with documented needs should request accommodations through coordinator of Accommodative Services.

**High school preparation.** Required and recommended units include English 4, mathematics 3, social studies 4, history 3, science 3 (laboratory 1-2) and foreign language 1. Required high school courses vary with major. Engineering science technologies, health, and life sciences stress math and science; business technologies stress algebra.

**2007-2008 Annual costs.** Tuition/fees: $5,498; $8,358 out-of-state. Out-of-state tuition for bachelor's degree program: $10,610; $442 per credit hour. Room/board: $8,440. Books/supplies: $1,000. Personal expenses: $800.

**2006-2007 Financial aid.** **Need-based:** 66% of total undergraduate aid awarded as scholarships/grants, 34% as loans/jobs.

**Application procedures. Admission:** Priority date 3/1; no deadline. $40 fee, may be waived for applicants with need. Application may be submitted online. Admission notification on a rolling basis beginning on or about 11/1. Must reply by May 1 or within 4 week(s) if notified thereafter. Some enrolled freshmen must complete COMPASS placement test on campus before classes begin. Students notified of testing dates and whether they need COMPASS. **Financial aid:** Priority date 3/15; no closing date. FAFSA required. Applicants notified on a rolling basis starting 2/1; must reply within 4 week(s) of notification.

**Academics. Special study options:** Cross-registration, distance learning, dual enrollment of high school students, independent study, internships, liberal arts/career combination, student-designed major. Criminal justice students can complete Police Academy during spring semester of senior year. **Credit/placement by examination:** AP, CLEP, IB, institutional tests. 45 credit hours maximum toward associate degree. **Support services:** Learning center, reduced course load, remedial instruction, study skills assistance, tutoring, writing center.

**Majors. Business:** Finance, management information systems, operations. **Computer sciences:** Information technology. **Health:** Dental hygiene, facilities admin, health care admin, veterinary technology/assistant. **Legal studies:** General. **Protective services:** Criminalistics, emergency management/homeland security, law enforcement admin. **Other:** Alternative and renewable energy applications.

**Most popular majors.** Business/marketing 19%, computer/information sciences 8%, health sciences 20%, security/protective services 53%.

**Computing on campus.** 300 workstations in dormitories, library, computer center. Dormitories wired for high-speed internet access. Helpline, wireless network available.

**Student life. Freshman orientation:** Mandatory, $60 fee. Preregistration for classes offered. 2-day orientation for resident students and 1-day for commuters. **Policies:** All full-time students must live in college housing unless requirement waived by Residence Life office. **Housing:** Guaranteed on-campus for freshmen. Coed dorms, special housing for disabled, fraternity/sorority housing, substance-free housing available. $55 nonrefundable deposit, deadline 5/1. Pets allowed in dorm rooms. Some all-male or all-female floors and wings available. **Activities:** Concert band, campus ministries, choral groups, dance, film society, international student organizations, radio station, student government, student newspaper, Afro-Latin society, Native American organization, Habitat for Humanity, Big Brother/Big Sister, Peer Educators.

**Athletics.** NJCAA. **Intercollegiate:** Baseball M, basketball, ice hockey M, soccer, softball W, volleyball W. **Intramural:** Basketball, football (non-tackle), soccer, table tennis, tennis, volleyball. **Team name:** Kangaroos.

**Student services.** Adult student services, alcohol/substance abuse counseling, campus ministries, career counseling, services for economically disadvantaged, student employment services, financial aid counseling, health services, minority student services, personal counseling, placement for graduates, veterans' counselor. **Physically disabled:** Services for visually, speech, hearing impaired. **Learning disabled:** Comprehensive services available.

**Contact.** E-mail: admissions@canton.edu
Phone: (315) 386-7123 Toll-free number: (800) 388-7123
Fax: (315) 386-7929
Jonathan Kent, Director of Admissions, State University of New York College of Technology at Canton, 34 Cornell Drive, Canton, NY 13617-1098

## State University of New York Downstate Medical Center
**Brooklyn, New York**
www.downstate.edu          CB code: 2534

- Public two-year upper-division health science and nursing college
- Commuter campus in very large city
- Application essay, interview required

**General.** Founded in 1858. Regionally accredited. **Degrees:** 183 bachelor's awarded; master's, doctoral, first professional offered. **Articulation:** Agreements with St. Francis College, CUNY Medgar Evers College. **Location:** 4 miles from downtown Brooklyn, 6 miles from downtown Manhattan. **Calendar:** Semester, limited summer session. **Full-time faculty:** 720 total. **Part-time faculty:** 160 total.

**Student profile.** 309 degree-seeking undergraduates, 1,289 graduate students. 100% entered as juniors. 80% transferred from two-year, 20% transferred from four-year institutions.

| | | | |
|---|---|---|---|
| Women: | 83% | Out-of-state: | 4% |
| Part-time: | 37% | 25 or older: | 72% |

**Basis for selection.** College transcript, application essay, interview required. College of Medicine applicants apply through AMCAS: $65 application fee. Rolling admissions for College of Nursing and College of Health-Related Professions: $30 fee. Each program has different admission requirements. RN/BS program requires New York State Registered Nurse license. Prerequisite courses vary by program. Transfer accepted as juniors.

**2007-2008 Annual costs.** Tuition/fees: $4,745; $11,005 out-of-state. Reported room-only price is for double studio; other room-only prices vary by accommodation from $4,076 to $8,255. Room only: $4,525. Books/supplies: $1,358.

**Application procedures. Admission:** Deadline 4/1. $40 fee, may be waived for applicants with need. Application must be submitted on paper. Closing dates for applications differ, depending on program, and begin December 15. **Financial aid:** FAFSA required.

**Academics. Special study options:** Combined bachelor's/graduate degree, liberal arts/career combination. **Credit/placement by examination:** AP, CLEP. **Support services:** Learning center, reduced course load, tutoring.

**Majors. Health:** Nursing (RN), physician assistant, sonography.

**Student life. Housing:** Coed dorms available. **Activities:** Student government, student newspaper.

**Athletics. Intramural:** Basketball M.

**Student services.** Health services.

**Contact.** E-mail: admissions@downstate.edu
Phone: (718) 270-2446 Fax: (718) 270-7592
Shushawna DeOliveira, Director of Admissions & Enrollment, State University of New York Downstate Medical Center, 450 Clarkson Avenue, Box 60, Brooklyn, NY 11203-2098

## State University of New York Empire State College
**Saratoga Springs, New York**                    CB member
www.esc.edu                                        CB code: 2214

- Public 4-year liberal arts college
- Commuter campus in large town
- 10,731 degree-seeking undergraduates: 63% part-time, 60% women
- 657 degree-seeking graduate students
- 77% of applicants admitted
- Application essay required

**General.** Founded in 1971. Regionally accredited. No campus or classrooms; students meet with faculty and use facilities at regional centers and units throughout state. Centers in Genesee Valley (Rochester), Long Island (Old Westbury), Metropolitan New York, Hudson Valley (Hartsdale), and Buffalo. Coordinating center at Saratoga Springs. Units in Binghamton, Ithaca, Mid-Hudson (New Paltz), Mohawk Valley (Utica-Rome), North Country (Plattsburgh), Onondaga (Syracuse), Saratoga Springs, Watertown, and International Programs in Lebanon, Prague and several other locations. **Degrees:** 2,052 bachelor's, 735 associate awarded; master's offered. **Calendar:** Continuous, extensive summer session. **Full-time faculty:** 157 total; 99% have terminal degrees, 14% minority, 59% women. **Part-time faculty:** 1,113 total.

**Freshman class profile.** 1,749 applied, 1,344 admitted, 733 enrolled.

| | | | |
|---|---|---|---|
| Return as sophomores: | 49% | Out-of-state: | 2% |

**Basis for selection.** Requirements for undergraduate admission: completed application, possession of high school diploma or equivalent, ability to pursue college-level work, payment of nonrefundable orientation fee, and completion of the college's orientation process.

**2007-2008 Annual costs.** Tuition/fees: $4,575; $10,835 out-of-state. Books/supplies: $2,550. Personal expenses: $900.

**2006-2007 Financial aid.** All financial aid based on need. 28% of total undergraduate aid awarded as scholarships/grants, 72% as loans/jobs.

**Application procedures. Admission:** Priority date 6/1; no deadline. No application fee. Application may be submitted online. Admission notification on a rolling basis. **Financial aid:** Priority date 4/1; no closing date. FAFSA required. Applicants notified on a rolling basis; must reply within 3 week(s) of notification.

**Academics.** Learning contracts between faculty mentors and students lead to program completion and opportunities to obtain credit for prior college-level learning. **Special study options:** Accelerated study, combined bachelor's/graduate degree, cross-registration, distance learning, double major, external degree, independent study, internships, student-designed major, teacher certification program. Weekend residencies for some specialized programs. **Credit/placement by examination:** AP, CLEP, IB. 40 credit hours maximum toward associate degree, 96 toward bachelor's. **Support services:** Writing center.

**Majors. Business:** General, labor relations. **Education:** General. **History:** General. **Interdisciplinary:** Biological/physical sciences. **Liberal arts:** Arts/sciences. **Psychology:** General. **Public administration:** Community org/advocacy. **Social sciences:** General, economics. **Visual/performing arts:** Studio arts.

**Most popular majors.** Business/marketing 40%, English 7%, interdisciplinary studies 7%, physical sciences 7%, psychology 7%, public administration/social services 19%, visual/performing arts 6%.

**Computing on campus.** 100 workstations in computer center. Commuter students can connect to campus network. Online course registration, online library, helpline available.

**Student life. Freshman orientation:** Mandatory, $50 fee.

**Student services.** Adult student services, career counseling, student employment services, veterans' counselor.

**Contact.** E-mail: admissions@esc.edu
Phone: (518) 587-2100 Toll-free number: (800) 847-3000
Fax: (518) 587-9759
Jennifer Riley, Director of Admissions, State University of New York Empire State College, 111 West Avenue, Saratoga Springs, NY 12866-4391

---

## State University of New York Institute of Technology at Utica/Rome

**Utica, New York**
www.sunyit.edu

CB member
CB code: 0755

- Public 4-year business and nursing college
- Commuter campus in small city
- 1,913 degree-seeking undergraduates: 27% part-time, 44% women, 8% African American, 3% Asian American, 3% Hispanic American, 1% international
- 483 degree-seeking graduate students
- 39% of applicants admitted
- SAT or ACT (ACT writing optional) required

**General.** Founded in 1966. Regionally accredited. **Degrees:** 384 bachelor's awarded; master's offered. **ROTC:** Army. **Location:** 50 miles from Syracuse, 90 miles from Albany. **Calendar:** Semester, limited summer session. **Full-time faculty:** 88 total; 80% have terminal degrees, 20% minority, 34% women. **Part-time faculty:** 95 total; 24% have terminal degrees, 3% minority, 42% women. **Class size:** 55% < 20, 41% 20-39, 4% 40-49, less than 1% 50-99.

**Freshman class profile.** 1,610 applied, 628 admitted, 204 enrolled.

| Mid 50% test scores | | | |
|---|---|---|---|
| SAT critical reading: | 430-610 | GPA 2.0-2.99: | 43% |
| SAT math: | 460-640 | Rank in top quarter: | 49% |
| ACT composite: | 19-27 | Rank in top tenth: | 12% |
| GPA 3.50 or higher: | 19% | Return as sophomores: | 67% |
| GPA 3.0-3.49: | 38% | Out-of-state: | 3% |
| | | Live on campus: | 85% |

**Basis for selection.** Students must meet minimum SAT/ACT score ranges with competitive high school averages as well as minimum high school unit requirements. **Homeschooled:** Statement describing homeschool structure and mission, transcript of courses and grades, state high school equivalency certificate required. Statement from local public school superintendent that verifies home school curriculum matches NYS Regents Curriculum required.

**High school preparation.** 17 units required; 25 recommended. Required and recommended units include English 4, mathematics 3-4, social studies 2, history 2, science 3-4 (laboratory 3-4), foreign language 3 and academic electives 2.

**2007-2008 Annual costs.** Tuition/fees: $5,405; $11,665 out-of-state. Room/board: $7,950. Books/supplies: $900. Personal expenses: $1,315.

**2006-2007 Financial aid. Need-based:** 186 full-time freshmen applied for aid; 143 were judged to have need; 136 of these received aid. Average scholarship/grant was $2,462; average loan $1,234. 46% of total undergraduate aid awarded as scholarships/grants, 54% as loans/jobs. **Non-need-based:** Awarded to 249 full-time undergraduates, including 11 freshmen. Scholarships awarded for academics.

**Application procedures. Admission:** No deadline. $40 fee, may be waived for applicants with need. Application may be submitted online. Admission notification on a rolling basis beginning on or about 1/15. Must reply by May 1 or within 4 week(s) if notified thereafter. **Financial aid:** Priority date 3/15; no closing date. FAFSA required. Applicants notified on a rolling basis starting 3/17; must reply within 2 week(s) of notification.

**Academics. Special study options:** Accelerated study, combined bachelor's/graduate degree, cross-registration, distance learning, double major, dual enrollment of high school students, independent study, internships, liberal arts/career combination. **Credit/placement by examination:** AP, CLEP, IB, SAT, ACT, institutional tests. Credit awarded for International Baccalaureate varies by academic department. **Support services:** Learning center, remedial instruction, study skills assistance, tutoring, writing center.

**Majors. Business:** General, accounting, business admin, finance. **Computer sciences:** General, information systems. **Engineering:** Electrical. **Engineering technology:** Civil, computer, electrical, industrial, mechanical. **Health:** Health care admin, medical records admin, nursing (RN). **Math:** Applied. **Protective services:** Criminal justice. **Psychology:** General. **Social sciences:** Sociology.

**Most popular majors.** Business/marketing 22%, communications/journalism 8%, computer/information sciences 11%, engineering/engineering technologies 21%, health sciences 22%, psychology 7%, social sciences 7%.

**Computing on campus.** 244 workstations in dormitories, library, computer center, student center. Dormitories wired for high-speed internet access and linked to campus network. Commuter students can connect to campus network. Online course registration, online library, student web hosting, wireless network available.

**Student life. Freshman orientation:** Mandatory. Preregistration for classes offered. **Housing:** Guaranteed on-campus for freshmen. Coed dorms, special housing for disabled available. $150 fully refundable deposit, deadline 5/1. **Activities:** Jazz band, international student organizations, radio station, student government, student newspaper, TV station, black student union, Latino student association.

**Athletics.** NCAA. **Intercollegiate:** Baseball M, basketball, bowling, cross-country, golf, lacrosse M, soccer, softball W, volleyball W. **Intramural:** Badminton, basketball, bowling, golf, racquetball, soccer, softball, tennis, volleyball. **Team name:** Wildcats.

**Student services.** Alcohol/substance abuse counseling, campus ministries, career counseling, services for economically disadvantaged, student employment services, financial aid counseling, health services, legal services, minority student services, personal counseling, placement for graduates, veterans' counselor, women's services. **Physically disabled:** Services for visually, speech, hearing impaired.

**Contact.** E-mail: admissions@sunyit.edu
Phone: (315) 792-7500 Toll-free number: (866) 278-6948
Fax: (315) 792-7837
Jennifer Phelan-Ninh, Director of Admissions, State University of New York Institute of Technology at Utica/Rome, Box 3050, Utica, NY 13504-3050

---

## State University of New York Maritime College

**Throggs Neck, New York**
www.sunymaritime.edu

CB member
CB code: 2536

- Public 4-year maritime college
- Residential campus in very large city
- 1,327 degree-seeking undergraduates: 6% part-time, 10% women, 5% African American, 4% Asian American, 10% Hispanic American, 8% international
- 157 degree-seeking graduate students
- 70% of applicants admitted
- SAT or ACT (ACT writing optional) required
- 49% graduate within 6 years

**General.** Founded in 1874. Regionally accredited. Graduates eligible for commission as officers in Navy, Marine Corps, Coast Guard, Air Force, and commissioned Corps of the National Oceanic and Atmospheric Administration. 3 summer semesters at sea and regiment option required for students interested in obtaining U.S. Merchant Marine Officer's License. **Degrees:** 226 bachelor's, 4 associate awarded; master's offered. **ROTC:** Army, Naval. **Location:** 10 miles from New York City. **Calendar:** Semester, limited summer session. **Full-time faculty:** 67 total; 48% have terminal degrees, 3% minority, 18% women. **Part-time faculty:** 56 total; 18% have terminal degrees, 18% minority, 11% women. **Class size:** 33% < 20, 54% 20-39, 7% 40-49, 4% 50-99, 2% >100. **Special facilities:** 565-foot training ship, training tanker, Center for Simulated Marine Operations, bridge simulator, model basin and towing tank, CAD-CAM facilities, 2 diesel propulsion simulators, maritime museum, sailing center including several 1-ton ocean racers.

**Freshman class profile.** 1,158 applied, 807 admitted, 406 enrolled.

| Mid 50% test scores | | Rank in top quarter: | 29% |
|---|---|---|---|
| SAT critical reading: | 460-560 | Rank in top tenth: | 4% |
| SAT math: | 490-590 | Return as sophomores: | 85% |
| ACT composite: | 18-22 | Out-of-state: | 26% |
| GPA 3.50 or higher: | 19% | Live on campus: | 94% |
| GPA 3.0-3.49: | 30% | International: | 4% |
| GPA 2.0-2.99: | 49% | | |

**Basis for selection.** Quality and strength of preparation, school achievement record, including first semester senior grades, class rank, test scores, extracurricular activities considered. Interview and essay recommended. Interviews and essays are not required but highly recommended. **Home-schooled:** Transcript of courses and grades, state high school equivalency certificate required.

**High school preparation.** 18 units required. Required and recommended units include English 3, mathematics 3-4, social studies 3, history 3, science 3-4 (laboratory 1) and foreign language 3. Math requirement includes algebra, geometry, trigonometry; math beyond trigonometry recommended. Chemistry or physics required; both strongly recommended.

**2007-2008 Annual costs.** Tuition/fees: $6,364; $12,624 out-of-state. Additional required uniform charges. Room/board: $8,920. Books/supplies: $928. Personal expenses: $1,856.

**2006-2007 Financial aid. Need-based:** 211 full-time freshmen applied for aid; 127 were judged to have need; 125 of these received aid. Average need met was 50%. Average scholarship/grant was $4,689; average loan $3,171. 41% of total undergraduate aid awarded as scholarships/grants, 59% as loans/jobs. **Non-need-based:** Awarded to 72 full-time undergraduates, including 29 freshmen. Scholarships awarded for academics, leadership, ROTC, state residency. **Additional information:** All cadets who are United States citizens, physically qualified for Merchant Marine license, and not yet 25 at time of enrollment eligible to apply for Student Incentive Payment (SIP) of $3,000 per year from Maritime Administration of the Department of Transportation. Out-of-state students who elect to participate in SIP pay in-state tuition fees.

**Application procedures. Admission:** No deadline. $40 fee, may be waived for applicants with need. Application may be submitted online. Admission notification on a rolling basis. **Financial aid:** Priority date 3/1, closing date 7/15. FAFSA, institutional form required. Applicants notified on a rolling basis starting 3/15; must reply within 2 week(s) of notification.

**Academics.** Cadets acquire technical, professional, and leadership experience on training cruises to foreign and domestic ports during annual summer sea terms, while preparing for U.S. Merchant Marine Officer's License. **Special study options:** Cooperative education, distance learning, double major, dual enrollment of high school students, ESL, honors, independent study, internships, semester at sea. United States Coast Guard-issued deck and engine license program. **Credit/placement by examination:** AP, CLEP, IB, institutional tests. **Support services:** Learning center, pre-admission summer program, reduced course load, study skills assistance, tutoring, writing center.

**Majors. Business:** General, business admin, marketing, tourism/travel. **Engineering:** General, electrical, industrial, marine, mechanical. **Liberal arts:** Arts/sciences. **Physical sciences:** Atmospheric science.

**Most popular majors.** Business/marketing 53%, engineering/engineering technologies 38%, physical sciences 8%.

**Computing on campus.** 130 workstations in dormitories, library, computer center, student center. Dormitories wired for high-speed internet access and linked to campus network. Online course registration, online library, repair service, wireless network available.

**Student life. Freshman orientation:** Mandatory, $830 fee. Preregistration for classes offered. All incoming freshmen and transfers who pursue

U.S. Merchant Marine Officer's License required to participate in 2-week indoctrination period including 4-day orientation program and 10-day military-style physical training period. **Policies:** Maritime students organized as regiment of cadets to foster personal growth, development, leadership training, and experience. In system of increasing responsibility and privilege, first-class cadets (seniors) are regimental officers ashore. Cadet officers in charge of operation of training ship during summer sea terms. Participation in regiment optional for some programs. **Housing:** Guaranteed on-campus for all undergraduates. Coed dorms, special housing for disabled available. $100 fully refundable deposit, deadline 5/1. Most undergraduates required to live in on-campus housing. **Activities:** Bands, choral groups, music ensembles, student government, Newman Club, Eagle Scout Fraternity, cultural club, Afro-Caribbean club, Emerald Society, Pershing Rifles, honor guard.

**Athletics.** NCAA. **Intercollegiate:** Baseball M, basketball, cross-country, diving, lacrosse M, rifle, rowing (crew), sailing, soccer, softball W, swimming, tennis M, volleyball W, wrestling M. **Intramural:** Basketball, cross-country, football (tackle), racquetball, sailing, skiing, soccer, softball, squash, table tennis, tennis, volleyball, weight lifting. **Team name:** Privateers.

**Student services.** Alcohol/substance abuse counseling, campus ministries, career counseling, services for economically disadvantaged, financial aid counseling, health services, personal counseling, placement for graduates, veterans' counselor.

**Contact.** E-mail: admissions@sunymaritime.edu
Phone: (718) 409-7221 Toll-free number: (800) 654-1874
Fax: (718) 409-7465
Tara Fay, Senior Associate Director of Admissions, State University of New York Maritime College, 6 Pennyfield Avenue, Throggs Neck, NY 10465-4198

---

### State University of New York Upstate Medical University
**Syracuse, New York**
**www.upstate.edu**                                    CB code: 2547

- Public two-year upper-division health science and nursing college
- Residential campus in small city
- 36% of applicants admitted
- Application essay, interview required

**General.** Founded in 1834. Regionally accredited. Undergraduate level consists of upper-division programs. Affiliated with Crouse-Irving Memorial Hospital, Veteran's Administration Medical Center, Community General Hospital of Greater Syracuse, St. Joseph's Hospital Health Center, Hutchings Psychiatric Center. **Degrees:** 84 bachelor's awarded; master's, doctoral, first professional offered. **Articulation:** Agreements with SUNY Alfred, SUNY Canton, SUNY Cobleskill, SUNY Cortland, SUNY Delhi, SUNY Geneseo, SUNY Morrisville, SUNY Oswego, SUNY Oneonta, Cayuga CC, Columbia-Greene CC, Finger Lakes CC, Genesee CC, Jefferson CC, Mohawk Valley CC, Monroe CC, Niagara County CC, North Country CC, Onondaga CC, Sullivan CC, Tompkins Cortland CC. **Location:** 250 miles from New York City, 150 miles from Buffalo. **Calendar:** Semester, limited summer session. **Full-time faculty:** 27 total; 78% have terminal degrees, 59% women. **Part-time faculty:** 24 total; 75% have terminal degrees, 71% women. **Class size:** 92% < 20, 5% 20-39, less than 1% 40-49, 2% 50-99. **Special facilities:** Institutionally owned and operated 350-bed teaching hospital and Level 1 trauma center.

**Student profile.** 247 degree-seeking undergraduates, 979 degree-seeking graduate students. 445 applied as first time-transfer students, 159 admitted, 112 enrolled. 100% entered as juniors. 60% transferred from two-year, 40% transferred from four-year institutions.

| Women: | 72% | Part-time: | 34% |
|---|---|---|---|
| African American: | 6% | Out-of-state: | 4% |
| Asian American: | 4% | Live on campus: | 56% |
| Hispanic American: | 2% | 25 or older: | 61% |
| International: | 1% | | |

**Basis for selection.** High school transcript, college transcript, application essay, interview required. Evaluation of academic performance in courses required for admission. Personal interviews, recommendations, and essay also important. Applicants must complete admissions course requirements prior to admission. Final decision made at discretion of admissions committee, regardless of applicant's prior academic standing. Transfer accepted as juniors, seniors.

**2007-2008 Annual costs.** Tuition/fees: $4,876; $11,136 out-of-state. Room only: $5,600. Books/supplies: $900. Personal expenses: $1,360.

**Financial aid.** All financial aid based on need. 241 applied for aid; 241 were judged to have need; 241 of these received aid. Average need met was

98%. 32% of total undergraduate aid awarded as scholarships/grants, 68% as loans/jobs.

**Application procedures. Admission:** Rolling admission. $40 fee, may be waived for applicants with need. Application must be submitted on paper. Application deadline for physical therapy program March 15. Cardiovascular perfusion program completes admission process March 1, and Cytotechnology deadline March 1. Preference to New York residents. High school seniors may apply for admission 2 years prior to intended date of entry. Transfer students apply in fall 1 year prior to intended date of entry. High school seniors may apply for early admission. **Financial aid:** Applicants notified on a rolling basis; must reply within 2 weeks of notification. FAFSA required.

**Academics. Special study options:** Combined bachelor's/graduate degree, independent study. **Credit/placement by examination:** AP, CLEP, institutional tests. 36 credit hours maximum toward bachelor's degree. **Support services:** Reduced course load, tutoring.

**Majors. Health:** Clinical lab science, cytotechnology, nursing (RN), perfusion technology, respiratory therapy technology.

**Computing on campus.** 50 workstations in dormitories, library, computer center, student center. Dormitories wired for high-speed internet access and linked to campus network. Commuter students can connect to campus network. Helpline, student web hosting, wireless network available.

**Student life. Policies:** Students under 21 required to live on campus unless living at home. **Housing:** Guaranteed on-campus for all undergraduates. Coed dorms, apartments available. $150 deposit, deadline 8/1. **Activities:** Student government, campus activities governing board, Diversity in Allied Health.

**Athletics. Intramural:** Basketball, handball, racquetball, softball, table tennis, tennis, volleyball, water polo.

**Student services.** Alcohol/substance abuse counseling, career counseling, financial aid counseling, health services, minority student services, on-campus daycare, personal counseling, placement for graduates, veterans' counselor.

**Contact.** E-mail: admiss@upstate.edu
Phone: (315) 464-4570 Toll-free number: (800) 736-2171
Fax: (315) 464-8867
Jennifer Welch, Director of Admissions, State University of New York Upstate Medical University, 766 Irving Avenue, Syracuse, NY 13210

---

## Syracuse University
**Syracuse, New York**
www.syr.edu

CB member
CB code: 2823

- Private 4-year university
- Residential campus in small city
- 11,796 degree-seeking undergraduates: 1% part-time, 55% women, 7% African American, 9% Asian American, 6% Hispanic American, 1% Native American, 4% international
- 5,466 degree-seeking graduate students
- 51% of applicants admitted
- SAT or ACT with writing, application essay required
- 82% graduate within 6 years; 16% enter graduate study

**General.** Founded in 1870. Regionally accredited. **Degrees:** 2,819 bachelor's, 2 associate awarded; master's, doctoral, first professional offered. **ROTC:** Army, Air Force. **Location:** 150 miles from Albany, 250 miles from New York City. **Calendar:** Semester, extensive summer session. **Full-time faculty:** 906 total; 88% have terminal degrees, 18% minority, 35% women. **Part-time faculty:** 552 total; 6% minority, 48% women. **Class size:** 62% < 20, 26% 20-39, 5% 40-49, 5% 50-99, 3% >100. **Special facilities:** Newhouse Complex media laboratories, digital convergence center, Syracuse Center of Excellence in Environmental and Energy Systems, advanced flight simulator for aerospace engineering, Ballentine Investment Institute, community darkrooms, Syracuse Stage professional theater, Mary Ann Shaw Center for Public Service, Bernice M. Wright Child Development Laboratory School, Belfer Audio Laboratory and Archive, Gebbie Speech, Language, and Hearing Clinic.

**Freshman class profile.** 21,219 applied, 10,744 admitted, 3,098 enrolled.

| Mid 50% test scores | | Rank in top tenth: | 42% |
|---|---|---|---|
| SAT critical reading: | 540-650 | Return as sophomores: | 91% |
| SAT math: | 570-680 | Out-of-state: | 58% |
| ACT composite: | 24-29 | Live on campus: | 99% |
| GPA 3.50 or higher: | 59% | International: | 4% |
| GPA 3.0-3.49: | 32% | Fraternities: | 21% |
| GPA 2.0-2.99: | 9% | Sororities: | 24% |
| Rank in top quarter: | 70% | | |

**Basis for selection.** Most important: strong performance in challenging, college preparatory curriculum from accredited secondary school, strong qualitative factors, good citizenship. Other items of importance, but not strongest: secondary school counselor evaluation, 2 academic recommendations, standardized test scores. Personal characteristics, talents and interests considered. Applicants not admitted to their first-choice program will be considered for alternate programs on a space-available basis only if they checked this option on the admissions application. TOEFL exam is required of all applicants whose native language is not English. Interview and portfolio required for art, architecture programs; interview and audition required for drama and music programs. Interviews recommended for all other candidates, but not required. **Homeschooled:** Transcript of courses and grades, interview, letter of recommendation (nonparent) required. Submit detailed course descriptions/syllabus used. 2 recommendations from someone outside home required. For financial aid eligibility, letter from local school district must be submitted acknowledging that curriculum taught in home meets with school district approval, or GED.

**High school preparation.** 19 units required. Required units include English 4, mathematics 4, social studies 4, science 4 (laboratory 4) and foreign language 3.

**2008-2009 Annual costs.** Tuition/fees (projected): $33,426. Room/board: $11,656. Books/supplies: $1,230. Personal expenses: $866.

**2007-2008 Financial aid. Need-based:** 2,250 full-time freshmen applied for aid; 1,871 were judged to have need; 1,871 of these received aid. Average need met was 84%. Average scholarship/grant was $19,000; average loan $4,600. 71% of total undergraduate aid awarded as scholarships/grants, 29% as loans/jobs. **Non-need-based:** Awarded to 2,291 full-time undergraduates, including 560 freshmen. Scholarships awarded for academics, art, athletics, music/drama, ROTC.

**Application procedures. Admission:** Closing date 1/1 (postmark date). $70 fee, may be waived for applicants with need. Application may be submitted online. Admission notification on a rolling basis beginning on or about 3/15. Must reply by 5/1. **Financial aid:** Closing date 2/1. FAFSA, CSS PROFILE required. Applicants notified by 3/30; must reply by 5/1.

**Academics. Special study options:** Accelerated study, combined bachelor's/graduate degree, cooperative education, distance learning, double major, dual enrollment of high school students, ESL, honors, independent study, internships, liberal arts/career combination, student-designed major, study abroad, teacher certification program. Syracuse offers many undergraduate research opportunities, pre-professional programs, and minors. **Credit/placement by examination:** AP, CLEP, IB, institutional tests. 30 credit hours maximum toward bachelor's degree. Maximum of 30 semester hours of credit may be accepted from all forms of extra-institutional, experiential learning, and examination programs. **Support services:** Learning center, pre-admission summer program, study skills assistance, tutoring, writing center.

**Majors. Architecture:** Architecture, interior. **Area/ethnic studies:** African, African-American, American, Latin American, Russian/Slavic, women's. **Biology:** General, biochemistry, biophysics. **Business:** Accounting, business admin, entrepreneurial studies, finance, marketing, sales/distribution. **Communications:** General, advertising, journalism, public relations, radio/tv. **Computer sciences:** General, information systems. **Education:** Art, biology, chemistry, Deaf/hearing impaired, elementary, English, family/consumer sciences, mathematics, music, physical, physics, social studies, special. **Engineering:** Aerospace, biomedical, chemical, civil, computer, electrical, environmental, mechanical, operations research, physics. **English:** British lit, creative writing, speech/rhetoric. **Family/consumer sciences:** Clothing/textiles, consumer economics, family studies, food/nutrition, institutional food production. **Foreign languages:** General, classics, French, German, Italian, linguistics, Russian, Spanish. **Health:** Audiology/speech pathology, predental, premedicine, preveterinary. **History:** General. **Interdisciplinary:** Nutrition sciences. **Legal studies:** General. **Liberal arts:** Arts/sciences, library science. **Math:** General. **Philosophy/religion:** Philosophy, religion. **Physical sciences:** Chemistry, geology, physics. **Psychology:** General. **Public administration:** General, social work. **Social sciences:** General, anthropology, economics, geography, international relations, political science, sociology. **Visual/performing arts:** Art, art history/conservation, cinematography, commercial/advertising art, dramatic, music history, music performance, music theory/composition, painting, photography, sculpture, studio arts. **Other:** Classical civilization, Earth science teacher education, Graphic arts, Health & wellness, Recording & allied entertainment industries, Sports management, Supply chain management.

**Most popular majors.** Business/marketing 17%, communications/journalism 11%, engineering/engineering technologies 6%, psychology 6%, social sciences 13%, visual/performing arts 13%.

**Computing on campus.** 2,750 workstations in dormitories, library, computer center, student center. Dormitories wired for high-speed internet access and linked to campus network. Commuter students can connect to campus network. Online course registration, online library, helpline, repair service, student web hosting, wireless network available.

**Student life. Freshman orientation:** Mandatory. Preregistration for classes offered. Held for four days prior to the start of classes each fall. A variety of academic and social activities assist students in the transition from high school to college. **Policies:** Freshmen and sophomores required to live on campus. **Housing:** Guaranteed on-campus for freshmen. Coed dorms, special housing for disabled, apartments, fraternity/sorority housing, substance-free housing available. $350 partly refundable deposit, deadline 5/1. International living center, single-sex floors and wings of residence halls, numerous learning communities, and interest housing available. **Activities:** Bands, choral groups, dance, drama, film society, literary magazine, music ensembles, musical theater, opera, radio station, student government, student newspaper, symphony orchestra, TV station, student association, University Union Programming Board, African-American society, Asian Students in America, student environmental action coalition, AIDS task force, student volunteer groups.

**Athletics.** NCAA. **Intercollegiate:** Basketball, cross-country, diving, field hockey W, football (tackle) M, lacrosse, rowing (crew), soccer, softball W, swimming, tennis W, track and field, volleyball W. **Intramural:** Basketball, football (non-tackle), racquetball, soccer, softball, table tennis, tennis, volleyball. **Team name:** Orange.

**Student services.** Adult student services, alcohol/substance abuse counseling, campus ministries, career counseling, student employment services, financial aid counseling, health services, legal services, minority student services, on-campus daycare, personal counseling, placement for graduates, veterans' counselor, women's services. **Physically disabled:** Services for visually, speech, hearing impaired.

**Contact.** E-mail: orange@syr.edu
Phone: (315) 443-3611 Fax: (315) 443-4226
Susan Donovan, Dean of Admissions, Syracuse University, 100
Crouse-Hinds Hall, Syracuse, NY 13244-2130

---

## Talmudical Institute of Upstate New York
### Rochester, New York
**CB code: 1426**

- Private 5-year rabbinical and seminary college for men affiliated with Jewish faith
- Residential campus in large city

**General.** Founded in 1974. Accredited by AARTS. **Calendar:** Semester.

**Annual costs/financial aid.** Tuition/fees (2007-2008): $4,600. Room/board: $3,500.

**Contact.** Phone: (585) 473-2810
769 Park Avenue, Rochester, NY 14607

---

## Talmudical Seminary Oholei Torah
### Brooklyn, New York
**CB code: 0712**

- Private 4-year rabbinical and seminary college for men affiliated with Jewish faith
- Very large city

**General.** Founded in 1956. Accredited by AARTS. **Calendar:** Semester.

**Contact.** Phone: (718) 774-5215
667 Eastern Parkway, Brooklyn, NY 11213-3397

---

## Torah Teminah Talmudical Seminary
### Brooklyn, New York
**CB code: 7132**

- Private 4-year rabbinical and seminary college for men affiliated with Jewish faith
- Very large city

**General.** Accredited by AARTS. **Calendar:** Continuous.

**Annual costs/financial aid.** Tuition/fees (2007-2008): $8,350. Room/board: $3,000.

**Contact.** Phone: (718) 853-8500
555 Ocean Parkway, Brooklyn, NY 11218

---

## Touro College
### New York, New York
www.touro.edu
**CB code: 2902**

- Private 4-year liberal arts college
- Commuter campus in very large city
- 17,200 degree-seeking undergraduates

**General.** Founded in 1970. Regionally accredited. School of General Studies provides programs for part-time and adult students. **Degrees:** 2,189 bachelor's, 856 associate awarded; master's, doctoral, first professional offered. **Calendar:** Semester, limited summer session. **Full-time faculty:** 551 total. **Part-time faculty:** 988 total.

**Basis for selection.** For College of Liberal Arts and Sciences, 3.0 high school GPA, SAT verbal and math scores of 500 preferred. Recommendations from high school teachers and counselors and motivation important. High school experience less important for applicants to associate degree programs who take institutional admissions test. SAT or ACT recommended. SAT or ACT required for applicants to school of Health Sciences. Essay and interview recommended for College of Liberal Arts and Sciences.

**High school preparation.** 17 units recommended. Recommended units include English 4, mathematics 3, social studies 3, science 3 and foreign language 3. Requirements may vary by division.

**2007-2008 Annual costs.** Tuition/fees: $12,800. Room/board: $6,000. Books/supplies: $750. Personal expenses: $1,764.

**Application procedures. Admission:** No deadline. $50 fee, may be waived for applicants with need. Admission notification on a rolling basis. **Financial aid:** Priority date 5/15, closing date 6/1. FAFSA required. Applicants notified by 8/15.

**Academics. Special study options:** Accelerated study, combined bachelor's/graduate degree, distance learning, dual enrollment of high school students, ESL, honors, independent study, internships, liberal arts/career combination, student-designed major, study abroad, teacher certification program. **Credit/placement by examination:** AP, CLEP, institutional tests. **Support services:** Learning center, reduced course load, remedial instruction, tutoring.

**Majors. Biology:** General. **Business:** General, accounting, business admin, management information systems, managerial economics, marketing. **Communications:** General. **Computer sciences:** General. **Education:** Special. **English:** English lit, speech/rhetoric. **Foreign languages:** General, Hebrew. **Health:** Communication disorders, medical records technology, nursing (RN), physician assistant, predental, premedicine, prepharmacy, preveterinary. **History:** General. **Interdisciplinary:** Biological/physical sciences. **Liberal arts:** Arts/sciences. **Math:** General. **Philosophy/religion:** Judaic, philosophy. **Physical sciences:** Chemistry. **Psychology:** General. **Social sciences:** General, economics, political science, sociology.

**Computing on campus.** 400 workstations in library, computer center.

**Student life. Freshman orientation:** Available. **Housing:** Single-sex dorms available. $50 deposit. No board or meal plan available. Kitchen facilities in student housing. **Activities:** Literary magazine, student government, student newspaper, accounting and business society, biology club, debating society, Jewish Affairs Committee, foreign students association, Omicron Delta.

**Student services.** Adult student services, career counseling, student employment services, personal counseling, placement for graduates, veterans' counselor.

**Contact.** E-mail: lasadmit@adminm.touro.edu
Phone: (718) 252-7800 ext. 299 Fax: (718) 253-9455
Andre Baron, Director of Admissions, Touro College, 1602 Avenue J, Brooklyn, NY 11230

---

## U.T.A. Mesivta-Kiryas Jocl
### Monroe, New York

- Private 4-year rabbinical college for men affiliated with Jewish faith
- Large town

**General.** Accredited by AARTS. **Calendar:** Semester.

**Annual costs/financial aid.** Tuition/fees (2007-2008): $5,000. Room/board: $3,000.

**Contact.** Phone: (845) 783-9901
9 Nickelsburg Road, #312, Monroe, NY 10950-2169

## Union College

Schenectady, New York
www.union.edu

CB member
CB code: 2920

- Private 4-year engineering and liberal arts college
- Residential campus in small city
- 2,134 degree-seeking undergraduates: 48% women, 3% African American, 6% Asian American, 4% Hispanic American, 2% international
- 43% of applicants admitted
- Application essay required
- 86% graduate within 6 years; 36% enter graduate study

**General.** Founded in 1795. Regionally accredited. **Degrees:** 520 bachelor's awarded. **ROTC:** Army, Naval, Air Force. **Location:** 15 miles from Albany, 175 miles from New York City. **Calendar:** Trimester, limited summer session. **Full-time faculty:** 194 total; 95% have terminal degrees, 11% minority, 41% women. **Part-time faculty:** 42 total; 69% have terminal degrees, 17% minority, 52% women. **Class size:** 71% < 20, 26% 20-39, 3% 40-49. **Special facilities:** Horticultural garden, superconducting nuclear magnetic resonance spectrometer, electron scanning microscope, tandem pelletron positive ion accelerator, X-ray diffraction equipment, remote-controlled telescope.

**Freshman class profile.** 4,837 applied, 2,093 admitted, 560 enrolled.

| Mid 50% test scores | | | |
|---|---|---|---|
| SAT critical reading: | 560-660 | Rank in top quarter: | 87% |
| SAT math: | 590-680 | Rank in top tenth: | 64% |
| SAT writing: | 570-670 | End year in good standing: | 98% |
| ACT composite: | 25-29 | Return as sophomores: | 91% |
| GPA 3.50 or higher: | 52% | Out-of-state: | 62% |
| GPA 3.0-3.49: | 36% | Live on campus: | 99% |
| GPA 2.0-2.99: | 12% | International: | 3% |

**Basis for selection.** GED not accepted. Course selection and grades closely considered along with recommendations from high school and extracurricular record. Ethnic and geographic diversity sought in student body. Testing optional except for combined programs. Applicants for leadership in medicine and law and public policy programs required to submit the SAT and 2 SAT Subject Tests and must complete necessary tests no later than December of senior year. Portfolio recommended for art programs. **Homeschooled:** Interview required.

**High school preparation.** 16 units required; 24 recommended. Required and recommended units include English 4, mathematics 3-4, social studies 1-2, history 1-2, science 2-4 (laboratory 2-4) and foreign language 2-4.

**2008-2009 Annual costs.** Comprehensive fee: $48,552. Rebates offered to students living off-campus and/or not using a meal plan. Books/supplies: $450. Personal expenses: $808.

**2006-2007 Financial aid.** **Need-based:** 298 full-time freshmen applied for aid; 236 were judged to have need; 223 of these received aid. Average need met was 100%. Average scholarship/grant was $26,200; average loan $3,200. 81% of total undergraduate aid awarded as scholarships/grants, 19% as loans/jobs. **Non-need-based:** Awarded to 258 full-time undergraduates, including 57 freshmen. Scholarships awarded for academics, ROTC. **Additional information:** Cancellable loans given to eligible students who engage in public service work after graduation. Loans cancellable at rate of 20% for each year of service.

**Application procedures.** **Admission:** Closing date 1/15 (postmark date). $50 fee, may be waived for applicants with need. Application may be submitted online. Admission notification 4/1. Must reply by 5/1. Deposit for housing ($100) included in $500 Admission and Security deposit. If application filed online, supplemental graded, written essay from 11th or 12th grade required to complete application. **Financial aid:** Closing date 2/1. FAFSA, CSS PROFILE required. Applicants notified by 4/1; must reply by 5/1.

**Academics.** **Special study options:** Accelerated study, combined bachelor's/graduate degree, cross-registration, double major, dual enrollment of high school students, honors, independent study, internships, liberal arts/career

combination, student-designed major, study abroad, teacher certification program. **Credit/placement by examination:** AP, CLEP, IB, institutional tests. 4 credit hours maximum toward bachelor's degree. **Support services:** Study skills assistance, tutoring, writing center.

**Majors.** **Area/ethnic studies:** American. **Biology:** General, biochemistry. **Computer sciences:** General. **Engineering:** Electrical, mechanical. **English:** English lit. **Foreign languages:** General, classics. **History:** General. **Interdisciplinary:** Biological/physical sciences, neuroscience, science/society. **Liberal arts:** Arts/sciences, humanities. **Math:** General. **Philosophy/religion:** Philosophy. **Physical sciences:** Astronomy, chemistry, geology, physics. **Psychology:** General. **Social sciences:** General, anthropology, economics, political science, sociology. **Visual/performing arts:** General.

**Most popular majors.** Biology 11%, engineering/engineering technologies 10%, history 8%, liberal arts 8%, psychology 11%, social sciences 27%.

**Computing on campus.** 482 workstations in library, computer center, student center. Dormitories wired for high-speed internet access and linked to campus network. Commuter students can connect to campus network. Online course registration, online library, helpline, student web hosting, wireless network available.

**Student life.** **Freshman orientation:** Mandatory. Preregistration for classes offered. Begins Thursday and ends Sunday before classes begin. Orientation fee included in Admission and Security deposit. **Policies:** All students expected to live on campus during undergraduate years, provided housing available. **Housing:** Guaranteed on-campus for freshmen. Coed dorms, apartments, fraternity/sorority housing, substance-free housing available. $100 nonrefundable deposit, deadline 5/1. **Activities:** Bands, campus ministries, choral groups, dance, drama, film society, literary magazine, music ensembles, radio station, student government, student newspaper, symphony orchestra, TV station, African/Latino alliance of students, Asian student union, Big Brothers/Big Sisters, community action club, Newman Club, Jewish student union.

**Athletics.** NCAA. **Intercollegiate:** Baseball M, basketball, cross-country, diving, field hockey W, football (tackle) M, ice hockey, lacrosse, rowing (crew), soccer, softball W, swimming, tennis, track and field, volleyball W. **Intramural:** Basketball, football (non-tackle) M, ice hockey, lacrosse W, soccer, softball, volleyball. **Team name:** Dutchmen, Dutchwomen.

**Student services.** Campus ministries, career counseling, student employment services, financial aid counseling, health services, minority student services, personal counseling, placement for graduates. **Physically disabled:** Services for visually, hearing impaired.

**Contact.** E-mail: admissions@union.edu
Phone: (518) 388-6112 Toll-free number: (888) 843-6688
Fax: (518) 388-6986
Ann Brown, VP for Admissions and Financial Aid, Union College, Grant Hall, Schenectady, NY 12308-2311

## United States Merchant Marine Academy

Kings Point, New York
www.usmma.edu

CB member
CB code: 2923

- Public 4-year engineering, military and maritime college
- Residential campus in large town
- 995 degree-seeking undergraduates: 12% women
- 26% of applicants admitted
- SAT or ACT (ACT writing optional), application essay required

**General.** Founded in 1943. Regionally accredited. Accepted applicants appointed to academy as midshipmen, USNR. **Degrees:** 203 bachelor's awarded; master's offered. **Location:** 20 miles from New York City. **Calendar:** Trimester, limited summer session. **Full-time faculty:** 85 total; 41% have terminal degrees, 6% minority, 12% women. **Class size:** 45% < 20, 54% 20-39, less than 1% 40-49, less than 1% 50-99. **Special facilities:** US Merchant Marine Museum, computer-aided operational research facility, classes and instruction held on T/V Kings Pointer docked on campus, students given opportunity to study abroad for year at sea.

**Freshman class profile.** 1,754 applied, 462 admitted, 279 enrolled.

| Mid 50% test scores | | | |
|---|---|---|---|
| SAT critical reading: | 540-640 | Rank in top quarter: | 23% |
| SAT math: | 600-660 | Rank in top tenth: | 18% |
| ACT composite: | 25-29 | Out-of-state: | 86% |
| | | Live on campus: | 100% |

**Basis for selection.** Nomination by U.S. representatives or senators. Competitive standing determined by test scores, high school GPA, class rank, motivation, extracurricular activities, interest in academy, industry, citizenship, and recommendations from counselors, teachers, school principal. Must also meet medical requirements and pass physical fitness exercise regimen. Untimed test results not acceptable. Interview recommended. **Home-schooled:** Letter of recommendation (nonparent) required. Must have completed chemistry with lab or physics with lab through state-certified instructor.

**High school preparation.** 18 units required. Required and recommended units include English 4, mathematics 3-4, social studies 4, science 3-4 (laboratory 1-2), foreign language 2 and academic electives 8.

**2007-2008 Annual costs.** All midshipmen receive full tuition, room, board, and medical and dental expenses from the federal government. Total required freshmen fees include purchase of laptop computer, color printer, and PDA. International students pay required fees plus additional international student fee. Books/supplies: $692.

**2006-2007 Financial aid. Need-based:** 47% of total undergraduate aid awarded as scholarships/grants, 53% as loans/jobs. **Additional information:** Students paid by steamship companies while at sea.

**Application procedures. Admission:** Closing date 3/1 (postmark date). No application fee. Application may be submitted online. Admission notification on a rolling basis beginning on or about 11/1. Must reply by May 1 or within 2 week(s) if notified thereafter. **Financial aid:** Closing date 5/1. FAFSA, institutional form required. Applicants notified on a rolling basis starting 1/31.

**Academics. Special study options:** Honors, independent study, internships, semester at sea. Sea training on merchant vessels. **Credit/placement by examination:** CLEP, institutional tests. **Support services:** Learning center, remedial instruction, study skills assistance, tutoring.

**Majors. Engineering:** Marine, systems. **Engineering technology:** Industrial management. **Mechanic/repair:** Marine. **Transportation:** General, maritime/Merchant Marine.

**Most popular majors.** Engineering/engineering technologies 43%, trade and industry 57%.

**Computing on campus.** PC or laptop required. 1,200 workstations in dormitories, library. Dormitories wired for high-speed internet access and linked to campus network. Helpline, repair service, wireless network available.

**Student life. Freshman orientation:** Mandatory. 2-week orientation starting in early July. **Housing:** Guaranteed on-campus for all undergraduates. Coed dorms, substance-free housing available. Students required to live on campus. **Activities:** Bands, choral groups, drama, musical theater, student government, student newspaper, Christian Fellowship Community, Neumann Club.

**Athletics.** NCAA. **Intercollegiate:** Baseball M, basketball, cross-country, diving, football (tackle) M, golf, lacrosse M, rifle, rowing (crew), sailing, soccer M, softball W, swimming, tennis, track and field, volleyball W, wrestling M. **Intramural:** Badminton, baseball, basketball, bowling, boxing, cross-country, diving, football (tackle) M, golf, lacrosse M, racquetball, rifle, rowing (crew), rugby M, sailing, skiing, soccer, softball, swimming, tennis, track and field, volleyball, water polo, wrestling M. **Team name:** Mariners.

**Student services.** Alcohol/substance abuse counseling, campus ministries, career counseling, student employment services, financial aid counseling, health services, personal counseling, placement for graduates.

**Contact.** E-mail: admissions@usmma.edu
Phone: (516) 773-5391 Toll-free number: (866) 546-4778
Fax: (516) 773-5390
CAPT. Robert Johnson, Director of Admissions, United States Merchant Marine Academy, 300 Steamboat Road, Admissions Center, Kings Point, NY 11024-1699

---

## United States Military Academy

**West Point, New York**
**www.usma.edu**

CB member
CB code: 2924

- Public 4-year engineering and military college
- Residential campus in small town
- 4,487 degree-seeking undergraduates: 15% women
- 15% of applicants admitted
- SAT or ACT with writing, application essay required
- 81% graduate within 6 years; 2% enter graduate study

**General.** Founded in 1802. Regionally accredited. Cadets receive Bachelor of Science degree designed specifically to meet intellectual requirements of a commissioned officer in the Army. **Degrees:** 1,006 bachelor's awarded. **Location:** 50 miles from New York City. **Calendar:** Semester, limited summer session. **Full-time faculty:** 604 total; 63% have terminal degrees, 10% minority, 15% women. **Class size:** 96% < 20, 4% 20-39, less than 1% 40-49. **Special facilities:** West Point Museum, American Revolutionary-era Fort Putnam, 4,500-seat auditorium.

**Freshman class profile.** 10,838 applied, 1,627 admitted, 1,272 enrolled.

| Mid 50% test scores | | | |
|---|---|---|---|
| SAT critical reading: | 570-680 | Rank in top tenth: | 72% |
| SAT math: | 590-680 | End year in good standing: | 87% |
| ACT composite: | 26-29 | Return as sophomores: | 91% |
| Rank in top quarter: | 93% | Out-of-state: | 92% |
| | | Live on campus: | 100% |

**Basis for selection.** ACT/SAT, rigor of high school record, class rank, and faculty recommendations used to determine academic qualification. Demonstrated leadership potential, physical ability, medical exam and Candidate Fitness Assessment also important. Must be U.S. citizen, at least 17 but not yet 23 by July 1 of year admitted, unmarried, not pregnant, and without legal child support obligations. Naturalized citizens must provide documentation. Nomination by member of Congress required. Consideration also given to percentage of students from school who attend 4-year colleges after high school. Effective immediately, candidates for USMA Class of 2012 (entering USMA in 2008 and later) required to submit a writing score with their SAT and/or ACT exam. Interview recommended. **Learning Disabled:** No learning disabled at USMA.

**High school preparation.** 19 units recommended. Recommended units include English 4, mathematics 4, social studies 1, history 1, science 4 (laboratory 2), foreign language 2 and academic electives 3. English units should have strong emphasis on composition, grammar, literature and speech; math should include algebra, geometry, intermediate algebra, and trigonometry; U.S. history should include courses in geography, government and economics. Precalculus, calculus and basic computing course helpful.

**2007-2008 Annual costs.** All cadets active duty members of U.S. Army and receive annual salary of approximately $10,148. Tuition, room and board, medical, and dental care provided by Army. Deposit of $2,900 required for initial uniforms, books, supplies, equipment, and fees. If needed, loans for deposit available from $100 to $2,900.

**Financial aid. Additional information:** Cadets permitted to receive scholarships, but since there are no tuition, room, or board charges, scholarships stipulated for tuition, room or board only based on need rather than merit cannot be accepted. Scholarships may be used for textbooks, uniforms, and other expenses or used dollar for dollar to offset initial $2,900 deposit.

**Application procedures. Admission:** Closing date 2/28. No application fee. Application may be submitted online. Admission notification on a rolling basis beginning on or about 11/15. Must reply by 5/1. Candidates must notify admissions office in writing of intention to apply for early action by October 25. Nomination or medical exam results not necessary to apply, but required prior to admission.

**Academics.** Cadets must complete minimum basic requirement of 40 academic courses. 8 semesters of physical education and 4 military science courses required. Cumulative GPA of at least 2.0 required, while meeting appropriate physical fitness and proper conduct standards. **Special study options:** Double major, exchange student, honors, independent study, study abroad, Washington semester. **Credit/placement by examination:** CLEP. **Support services:** Learning center, reduced course load, remedial instruction, study skills assistance, tutoring.

**Majors. Area/ethnic studies:** East Asian, Latin American, Near/Middle Eastern, Russian/Slavic, Western European. **Business:** Business admin. **Computer sciences:** General, computer science, information systems. **Engineering:** Aerospace, chemical, civil, computer, electrical, mechanical, nuclear, operations research, physics, systems. **English:** American lit, British lit, English lit. **Foreign languages:** French, German, Portuguese, Russian, Spanish. **History:** General, American, European. **Interdisciplinary:** Behavioral sciences. **Legal studies:** General. **Math:** General. **Philosophy/religion:** Philosophy. **Physical sciences:** Chemistry, physics. **Psychology:** General. **Social sciences:** General, economics, geography, political science, sociology, U.S. government. **Other:** Military history.

**Computing on campus.** PC or laptop required. 1,000 workstations in dormitories, library, computer center. Dormitories wired for high-speed internet access and linked to campus network. Commuter students can connect to campus network. Online library, helpline, repair service, wireless network available.

**Student life. Freshman orientation:** Mandatory. **Policies:** Honor code. Cadets administer honor system with power to recommend dismissal. Military dress required. All cadets participate in intercollegiate, club or intramural level sport each semester. Seniors and juniors (after spring break) permitted to maintain cars. **Housing:** Guaranteed on-campus for all undergraduates.

Coed dorms, substance-free housing available. **Activities:** Pep band, choral groups, dance, drama, film society, literary magazine, music ensembles, musical theater, radio station, student government, student newspaper, TV station, more than 100 extracurricular activities.

**Athletics.** NCAA. **Intercollegiate:** Baseball M, basketball, cross-country, diving, football (tackle) M, golf M, gymnastics M, ice hockey M, lacrosse M, rifle, soccer, softball W, swimming, tennis, track and field, volleyball W, wrestling M. **Intramural:** Basketball, bowling, boxing M, cross-country, equestrian, football (tackle) M, golf, handball, lacrosse, racquetball, rowing (crew), rugby, skin diving, soccer, softball, swimming, tennis, track and field, volleyball M, wrestling M. **Team name:** Black Knights.

**Student services.** Career counseling, health services, legal services, personal counseling, placement for graduates, women's services.

**Contact.** E-mail: admissions@usma.edu
Phone: (845) 938-5760
Col. Deborah McDonald, Director of Admissions, United States Military Academy, 646 Swift Road, West Point, NY 10996-1905

## United Talmudical Seminary
**Brooklyn, New York**

CB code: 0696

▶ Private 5-year rabbinical college for men affiliated with Jewish faith
▶ Very large city

**General.** Founded in 1949. Accredited by AARTS. **Calendar:** Semester.

**Contact.** Phone: (718) 963-9260
Director of Admissions, 82 Lee Avenue, Brooklyn, NY 11211

## University of Rochester
**Rochester, New York**          **CB member**
**www.rochester.edu**            **CB code: 2928**

▶ Private 4-year university
▶ Residential campus in large city
▶ 4,964 degree-seeking undergraduates: 3% part-time, 50% women, 4% African American, 10% Asian American, 4% Hispanic American, 6% international
▶ 3,788 degree-seeking graduate students
▶ 41% of applicants admitted
▶ SAT or ACT (ACT writing optional), application essay required

**General.** Founded in 1850. Regionally accredited. **Degrees:** 1,324 bachelor's awarded; master's, doctoral, first professional offered. **ROTC:** Army, Naval, Air Force. **Location:** 2 miles from downtown. **Calendar:** Semester, extensive summer session. **Full-time faculty:** 515 total; 88% have terminal degrees, 12% minority, 27% women. **Part-time faculty:** 248 total; 4% minority, 55% women. **Class size:** 62% < 20, 22% 20-39, 6% 40-49, 7% 50-99, 3% >100. **Special facilities:** Eastman Theatre, art museum, music library, nuclear structure research laboratory, laser energetics laboratory, African and African-American Studies Institute, Susan B. Anthony Institute for Gender and Women's Studies, MK Gandhi Institute for Nonviolence, observatory, dental center, hospital, visual science center, optics institute, MRI scanner, cancer center, children's hospital, VR lab.

**Freshman class profile.** 11,676 applied, 4,815 admitted, 1,062 enrolled.

| Mid 50% test scores | | | |
|---|---|---|---|
| SAT critical reading: | 600-700 | Rank in top quarter: | 95% |
| SAT math: | 630-720 | Rank in top tenth: | 72% |
| ACT composite: | 27-31 | Out-of-state: | 54% |
| GPA 3.50 or higher: | 79% | Live on campus: | 100% |
| GPA 3.0-3.49: | 18% | International: | 8% |
| GPA 2.0-2.99: | 3% | Fraternities: | 15% |
| | | Sororities: | 16% |

**Basis for selection.** School achievement record and test scores most important. Recommendations, personal qualities, extracurricular activities important. Alumni relationship, minority status, special talents considered. SAT Subject Tests recommended. Audition required for music programs at Eastman School of Music. **Homeschooled:** Statement describing homeschool structure and mission required.

**High school preparation.** 32 units required.

**2008-2009 Annual costs.** Tuition/fees: $37,250. Room/board: $10,810. Books/supplies: $990. Personal expenses: $1,160.

**Financial aid. Non-need-based:** Scholarships awarded for academics, alumni affiliation, leadership, music/drama, ROTC, state residency. **Additional information:** Alternative loans and financing information available.

**Application procedures. Admission:** Closing date 1/1 (postmark date). $60 fee, may be waived for applicants with need. Application may be submitted online. Admission notification 4/1. Must reply by 5/1. **Financial aid:** Closing date 2/1. FAFSA, CSS PROFILE required. Applicants notified by 4/1; must reply by 5/1.

**Academics. Special study options:** Accelerated study, combined bachelor's/graduate degree, cross-registration, double major, dual enrollment of high school students, ESL, honors, independent study, internships, liberal arts/career combination, student-designed major, study abroad, teacher certification program, Washington semester. Senior Scholars Research Program allowing selected undergraduates to devote entire senior year to student-designed research project; Take Five, 5th year tuition-free to supplement regular requirements; Rochester Curriculum; Quest (1st-year course emphasizing how to learn). **Credit/placement by examination:** AP, CLEP, IB, institutional tests. **Support services:** Learning center, reduced course load, study skills assistance, tutoring, writing center.

**Majors. Area/ethnic studies:** African-American, Russian/Slavic, women's. **Biology:** General, bacteriology, biochemistry, cell/histology, ecology, embryology, molecular, molecular genetics. **Computer sciences:** General. **Conservation:** Environmental science, environmental studies. **Education:** Music. **Engineering:** General, biomedical, chemical, electrical, geological, mechanical, science. **English:** English lit. **Foreign languages:** General, classics, comparative lit, French, German, Japanese, linguistics, Russian, sign language interpretation, Spanish. **Health:** Nursing (RN). **History:** General. **Interdisciplinary:** Biological/physical sciences. **Liberal arts:** Arts/sciences. **Math:** General, applied, statistics. **Philosophy/religion:** Philosophy, religion. **Physical sciences:** Astronomy, chemistry, geology, optics, physics. **Psychology:** General, experimental. **Social sciences:** Anthropology, economics, political science. **Visual/performing arts:** Art history/conservation, film/cinema, jazz, music performance, music theory/composition, studio arts.

**Most popular majors.** Biology 11%, engineering/engineering technologies 8%, health sciences 7%, psychology 10%, social sciences 20%, visual/performing arts 12%.

**Computing on campus.** 450 workstations in dormitories, library, computer center, student center. Dormitories wired for high-speed internet access. Commuter students can connect to campus network. Online course registration, online library, helpline, repair service, wireless network available.

**Student life. Freshman orientation:** Mandatory, $200 fee. Preregistration for classes offered. Held 1 week prior to first day of classes. **Housing:** Guaranteed on-campus for freshmen. Coed dorms, single-sex dorms, special housing for disabled, apartments, fraternity/sorority housing, substance-free housing available. Special interest themes: drama, computers, film, health, international, music. Single-gender floors. **Activities:** Bands, choral groups, dance, drama, film society, international student organizations, literary magazine, music ensembles, Model UN, musical theater, opera, radio station, student government, student newspaper, symphony orchestra, TV station, over 220 student organizations.

**Athletics.** NCAA. **Intercollegiate:** Baseball M, basketball, cross-country, diving, field hockey W, football (tackle) M, golf M, lacrosse W, rowing (crew) W, soccer, softball W, squash, swimming, tennis, track and field, volleyball W. **Intramural:** Basketball, bowling, boxing, fencing, football (tackle) M, golf M, judo, racquetball, rugby, soccer, softball, squash, table tennis, tennis, volleyball, weight lifting. **Team name:** Yellowjackets.

**Student services.** Adult student services, alcohol/substance abuse counseling, campus ministries, career counseling, services for economically disadvantaged, student employment services, financial aid counseling, health services, minority student services, personal counseling, placement for graduates, women's services. **Physically disabled:** Services for visually, hearing impaired.

**Contact.** E-mail: admit@admissions.rochester.edu
Phone: (585) 275-3221 Toll-free number: (888) 822-2256
Fax: (585) 461-4595
Jonathan Burdick, Dean of Admissions and Financial Aid, University of Rochester, 300 Wilson Boulevard, Rochester, NY 14627-0251

## Utica College
**Utica, New York**              **CB member**
**www.utica.edu**                **CB code: 2932**

▶ Private 4-year college
▶ Residential campus in small city

- 2,336 degree-seeking undergraduates: 16% part-time, 60% women, 10% African American, 2% Asian American, 3% Hispanic American, 1% Native American, 2% international
- 559 degree-seeking graduate students
- 76% of applicants admitted
- Application essay required
- 49% graduate within 6 years; 39% enter graduate study

**General.** Founded in 1946. Regionally accredited. **Degrees:** 478 bachelor's awarded; master's, first professional offered. **ROTC:** Army, Air Force. **Location:** 50 miles from Syracuse. **Calendar:** Semester, limited summer session. **Full-time faculty:** 128 total; 83% have terminal degrees, 9% minority, 46% women. **Part-time faculty:** 195 total; 45% women. **Class size:** 73% < 20, 26% 20-39, 1% 40-49.

**Freshman class profile.** 2,541 applied, 1,936 admitted, 494 enrolled.

| Mid 50% test scores | | | |
|---|---|---|---|
| SAT critical reading: | 420-520 | Rank in top quarter: | 34% |
| SAT math: | 430-540 | Rank in top tenth: | 11% |
| SAT writing: | 410-510 | End year in good standing: | 86% |
| ACT composite: | 18-23 | Return as sophomores: | 67% |
| GPA 3.50 or higher: | 23% | Out-of-state: | 21% |
| GPA 3.0-3.49: | 41% | Live on campus: | 77% |
| GPA 2.0-2.99: | 34% | International: | 2% |

**Basis for selection.** Academic record, high school course of study, rank in class most important. Extracurricular activities, essay, interview, recommendations also important. SAT or ACT scores required only for freshmen applying to BS Health Studies/DPT Physical Therapy, BS Health Studies/MS Occupational Therapy, Nursing, or joint health professions programs, Higher Education Opportunity Program (HEOP), or for academic merit scholarships. Interview recommended. **Homeschooled:** Applicants must receive GED within first year of attendance. **Learning Disabled:** Written evaluation required, including discrepancy analysis completed by licensed psychologist or certified learning disability specialist indicating specific learning disability or disabilities.

**High school preparation.** 16 units required. Required units include English 4, mathematics 3, social studies 3, science 3, foreign language 2 and academic electives 1.

**2007-2008 Annual costs.** Tuition/fees: $24,584. Room/board: $10,030. Books/supplies: $850. Personal expenses: $706.

**2007-2008 Financial aid. Need-based:** 471 full-time freshmen applied for aid; 437 were judged to have need; 437 of these received aid. Average need met was 76%. Average scholarship/grant was $9,307; average loan $3,426. 71% of total undergraduate aid awarded as scholarships/grants, 29% as loans/jobs. **Non-need-based:** Awarded to 230 full-time undergraduates, including 58 freshmen. Scholarships awarded for academics.

**Application procedures. Admission:** No deadline. $40 fee, may be waived for applicants with need. Application may be submitted online. Admission notification on a rolling basis beginning on or about 9/1. January 15 application deadline for all joint medical programs, BS in Health Studies/MS in Occupational Therapy program, and BS in Health Studies/DPT in Physical Therapy program. February 15 application deadline for nursing program. **Financial aid:** Priority date 2/15; no closing date. FAFSA required. Applicants notified on a rolling basis starting 2/1; must reply by 5/1 or within 4 week(s) of notification.

**Academics. Special study options:** Accelerated study, combined bachelor's/graduate degree, cooperative education, cross-registration, distance learning, double major, dual enrollment of high school students, exchange student, honors, independent study, internships, liberal arts/career combination, study abroad, teacher certification program, United Nations semester, Washington semester, weekend college. BS Health Studies/MS Occupational Therapy weekend program; Economic Crime Investigation online program for transfer students. **Credit/placement by examination:** AP, CLEP, IB, SAT, institutional tests. 30 credit hours maximum toward bachelor's degree. **Support services:** Learning center, pre-admission summer program, reduced course load, remedial instruction, study skills assistance, tutoring, writing center.

**Majors. Biology:** General. **Business:** Accounting, business admin, managerial economics. **Communications:** General, journalism, public relations. **Computer sciences:** General. **Education:** Biology, business, chemistry, early childhood, elementary, English, ESL, mathematics, physics, secondary, social science, social studies, special. **English:** English lit. **Family/consumer sciences:** Child care. **Foreign languages:** General. **Health:** Facilities admin, health services, nursing (RN), recreational therapy. **History:** General. **Liberal arts:** Arts/sciences. **Math:** General. **Philosophy/religion:** Philosophy. **Physical sciences:** Chemistry, physics. **Protective services:** Criminal justice. **Psychology:** General. **Social sciences:** Economics, international relations, political science, sociology.

**Most popular majors.** Business/marketing 20%, communications/journalism 7%, health sciences 20%, psychology 9%, security/protective services 18%.

**Computing on campus.** 242 workstations in library, computer center, student center. Dormitories wired for high-speed internet access and linked to campus network. Helpline available.

**Student life. Freshman orientation:** Available, $50 fee. Preregistration for classes offered. Summer program for freshmen and parents held during the third week of July. **Policies:** All freshmen required to live in college residence for first 2 years, unless residing at home. **Housing:** Guaranteed on-campus for freshmen. Coed dorms, special housing for disabled, apartments, substance-free housing available. $200 deposit, deadline 5/1. Separate floors for men and women available in select residence halls. **Activities:** Concert band, choral groups, dance, drama, film society, literary magazine, radio station, student government, student newspaper, Latin American student union, Jewish student union, Young Democrats, College Republicans, women's resource center, Circle K, Students of African Descent Alliance, People Respecting Diversity Everywhere, gospel choir, Africa in Motion.

**Athletics.** NCAA. **Intercollegiate:** Baseball M, basketball, cross-country, diving, field hockey W, football (tackle) M, golf M, ice hockey, lacrosse, soccer, softball W, swimming, tennis, volleyball W, water polo W. **Intramural:** Basketball, bowling, football (non-tackle), racquetball, soccer, softball, tennis, volleyball, water polo. **Team name:** Pioneers.

**Student services.** Adult student services, alcohol/substance abuse counseling, campus ministries, career counseling, services for economically disadvantaged, student employment services, financial aid counseling, health services, minority student services, personal counseling, placement for graduates, veterans' counselor, women's services. **Physically disabled:** Services for visually, speech, hearing impaired.

**Contact.** E-mail: admiss@utica.edu
Phone: (315) 792-3006 Toll-free number: (800) 782-8884
Fax: (315) 792-3003
Patrick Quinn, Vice President for Enrollment Management, Utica College, 1600 Burrstone Road, Utica, NY 13502-4892

## Vassar College
**Poughkeepsie, New York**     CB member
www.vassar.edu     CB code: 2956

- Private 4-year liberal arts college
- Residential campus in small city
- 2,409 degree-seeking undergraduates: 1% part-time, 60% women, 5% African American, 10% Asian American, 7% Hispanic American, 6% international
- 1 degree-seeking graduate students
- 29% of applicants admitted
- SAT and SAT Subject Tests or ACT (ACT writing recommended), application essay required

**General.** Founded in 1861. Regionally accredited. **Degrees:** 604 bachelor's awarded; master's offered. **Location:** 75 miles from New York City. **Calendar:** Semester, limited summer session. **Full-time faculty:** 289 total; 89% have terminal degrees, 23% minority, 45% women. **Part-time faculty:** 57 total; 53% have terminal degrees, 14% minority, 56% women. **Class size:** 68% < 20, 31% 20-39, less than 1% 40-49, less than 1% 50-99, less than 1% >100. **Special facilities:** Environmental nature center, observatory, electron microscope, nursery school, experimental theater, art center and geology museum, intercultural center and outdoor amphitheater.

**Freshman class profile.** 6,393 applied, 1,830 admitted, 681 enrolled.

| Mid 50% test scores | | | |
|---|---|---|---|
| SAT critical reading: | 660-750 | Rank in top quarter: | 95% |
| SAT math: | 640-710 | Rank in top tenth: | 69% |
| SAT writing: | 650-740 | End year in good standing: | 98% |
| ACT composite: | 29-32 | Return as sophomores: | 91% |
| GPA 3.50 or higher: | 81% | Out-of-state: | 75% |
| GPA 3.0-3.49: | 19% | Live on campus: | 99% |
| | | International: | 7% |

**Basis for selection.** Academic credentials most important. Personal achievements, essay, and recommendations also considered carefully. Evidence that students have elected most demanding program available crucial. Disadvantaged status considered. 2 SAT Subject Tests of student's choice required. Optional interviews available with alumni.

**High school preparation.** 20 units recommended. Recommended units include English 4, mathematics 4, social studies 2, history 2, science 4 (laboratory 3) and foreign language 4. Advanced and accelerated courses recommended whenever possible. Minimum of 20 units recommended with additional unit in science, foreign language, and studies.

**2008-2009 Annual costs.** Tuition/fees: $40,210. Room/board: $9,040. Books/supplies: $860. Personal expenses: $1,200.

**2007-2008 Financial aid.** All financial aid based on need. 447 full-time freshmen applied for aid; 363 were judged to have need; 363 of these received aid. Average need met was 100%. Average scholarship/grant was $29,613; average loan $2,081. 84% of total undergraduate aid awarded as scholarships/grants, 16% as loans/jobs.

**Application procedures. Admission:** Closing date 1/1 (receipt date). $60 fee, may be waived for applicants with need. Application may be submitted online. Admission notification 4/1. Must reply by 5/1. **Financial aid:** Closing date 2/1. FAFSA, CSS PROFILE required. Applicants notified by 3/30; must reply by 5/1.

**Academics.** Introductory-level college course emphasizing written and oral communication required for freshmen. Majors declared through department, interdepartmental programs, multidisciplinary programs, and independent programs. Summer research with faculty. **Special study options:** Combined bachelor's/graduate degree, cooperative education, cross-registration, double major, exchange student, independent study, internships, liberal arts/career combination, student-designed major, study abroad, teacher certification program, urban semester, Washington semester. Independently designed junior year abroad programs; exchange programs with institutions in 12-college exchange as well as Fisk University, Hampton Institute, Howard University, Morehouse College, and Spelman College; 3-2 engineering program with Dartmouth College. **Credit/placement by examination:** AP, CLEP, IB, institutional tests. 4 credit hours maximum toward bachelor's degree. **Support services:** Learning center, reduced course load, study skills assistance, tutoring, writing center.

**Majors. Area/ethnic studies:** African, American, Asian, Latin American, women's. **Biology:** General, biochemistry. **Communications:** Media studies. **Computer sciences:** General. **Conservation:** Environmental studies. **English:** English lit. **Foreign languages:** Ancient Greek, Chinese, French, German, Italian, Japanese, Latin, Russian, Spanish. **History:** General. **Interdisciplinary:** Ancient studies, cognitive science, medieval/Renaissance, neuroscience, science/society. **Liberal arts:** Arts/sciences. **Math:** General. **Philosophy/religion:** Judaic, philosophy, religion. **Physical sciences:** Astronomy, chemistry, geology, physics. **Psychology:** General. **Social sciences:** Anthropology, economics, geography, international relations, political science, sociology, urban studies. **Visual/performing arts:** Art, dramatic, film/cinema.

**Most popular majors.** English 13%, history 6%, interdisciplinary studies 6%, psychology 9%, social sciences 29%, visual/performing arts 12%.

**Computing on campus.** 432 workstations in dormitories, library, computer center, student center. Dormitories wired for high-speed internet access and linked to campus network. Commuter students can connect to campus network. Online course registration, helpline, repair service, student web hosting, wireless network available.

**Student life. Freshman orientation:** Mandatory. Preregistration for classes offered. Held one week prior to start of classes. **Housing:** Guaranteed on-campus for all undergraduates. Coed dorms, single-sex dorms, special housing for disabled, apartments, cooperative housing, substance-free housing available. **Activities:** Bands, choral groups, dance, drama, film society, literary magazine, music ensembles, musical theater, opera, radio station, student government, student newspaper, symphony orchestra, TV station, Catholic community, Jewish union, Promoting Equality and Community Everywhere, Amnesty International, Young Socialists, Republican/Libertarian Coalition, AIDS education committee, Habitat for Humanity, Step Beyond (community service), African students union.

**Athletics.** NCAA. **Intercollegiate:** Baseball M, basketball, cross-country, diving, fencing, field hockey W, golf W, lacrosse, rowing (crew), soccer, squash, swimming, tennis, volleyball. **Intramural:** Badminton, basketball, bowling, golf, handball, soccer, softball, squash, tennis, volleyball, water polo. **Team name:** Brewers.

**Student services.** Alcohol/substance abuse counseling, campus ministries, career counseling, student employment services, financial aid counseling, health services, minority student services, on-campus daycare, personal counseling, placement for graduates, veterans' counselor, women's services. **Physically disabled:** Services for visually, hearing impaired.

**Contact.** E-mail: admissons@vassar.edu
Phone: (845) 437-7300 Toll-free number: (800) 827-7270
Fax: (845) 437-7063
David Borus, Dean of Admission and Financial Aid, Vassar College, Box 10, 124 Raymond Avenue, Poughkeepsie, NY 12604-0077

## Vaughn College of Aeronautics and Technology
Flushing, New York
www.vaughn.edu

CB member
CB code: 2001

- Private 4-year engineering and technical college
- Commuter campus in very large city
- 1,063 degree-seeking undergraduates: 26% part-time, 13% women, 20% African American, 11% Asian American, 36% Hispanic American, 1% Native American, 3% international
- 97% of applicants admitted
- SAT or ACT (ACT writing recommended), application essay required
- 34% graduate within 6 years; 1% enter graduate study

**General.** Founded in 1932. Regionally accredited. Engineering technology programs accredited by the Accreditation Board for Engineering and Technology. Management programs accredited by the International Assembly of Collegiate Business Education. **Degrees:** 103 bachelor's, 113 associate awarded; master's offered. **ROTC:** Army, Air Force. **Location:** 5 miles from Manhattan. **Calendar:** Semester, extensive summer session. **Full-time faculty:** 41 total; 27% have terminal degrees, 34% minority, 12% women. **Part-time faculty:** 73 total; 3% have terminal degrees, 29% minority, 16% women. **Class size:** 69% < 20, 30% 20-39, less than 1% 40-49. **Special facilities:** Fiber optic Unix-Novell computer system, 65-foot tower overlooking LaGuardia Airport, Frasca 142 flight simulator, nondestructive testing laboratory, composite materials laboratory and computerized engine test-cell.

**Freshman class profile.** 360 applied, 349 admitted, 197 enrolled.

| Mid 50% test scores | | | |
|---|---|---|---|
| SAT critical reading: | 470-560 | GPA 2.0-2.99: | 42% |
| SAT math: | 490-590 | End year in good standing: | 61% |
| GPA 3.50 or higher: | 16% | Return as sophomores: | 60% |
| GPA 3.0-3.49: | 42% | Out-of-state: | 6% |
| | | Live on campus: | 5% |

**Basis for selection.** High school transcripts or GED scores most important followed by SAT, ACT, or TOEFL. B.S. programs require strong performance in high school math and sciences courses. Open admissions to associate degree programs. SAT or ACT with Writing exam required for all first-time, first-year applicants to BS program. Interview recommended. **Homeschooled:** Statement describing homeschool structure and mission, transcript of courses and grades, state high school equivalency certificate required. **Learning Disabled:** Presentation of documental IEP necessary.

**High school preparation.** 14 units required; 18 recommended. Required and recommended units include English 4, mathematics 3-4, social studies 1-4 and science 2-4. Pre-calculus and physics required.

**2008-2009 Annual costs.** Tuition/fees (projected): $15,100. Room/board: $11,900. Books/supplies: $1,050. Personal expenses: $1,200.

**2007-2008 Financial aid. Need-based:** 125 full-time freshmen applied for aid; 125 were judged to have need; 125 of these received aid. Average need met was 85%. Average scholarship/grant was $2,200; average loan $3,500. 85% of total undergraduate aid awarded as scholarships/grants, 15% as loans/jobs. **Non-need-based:** Awarded to 429 full-time undergraduates, including 104 freshmen. Scholarships awarded for academics, alumni affiliation, job skills, ROTC.

**Application procedures. Admission:** Priority date 3/1; no deadline. $40 fee, may be waived for applicants with need. Application may be submitted online. Admission notification on a rolling basis beginning on or about 2/1. **Financial aid:** Priority date 1/15; no closing date. FAFSA required. Applicants notified by 4/15; must reply within 2 week(s) of notification.

**Academics. Special study options:** Accelerated study, distance learning, double major, independent study, internships, liberal arts/career combination. **Credit/placement by examination:** AP, CLEP, IB, SAT, ACT, institutional tests. 30 credit hours maximum toward associate degree, 60 toward bachelor's. **Support services:** Learning center, pre-admission summer program, reduced course load, remedial instruction, study skills assistance, tutoring, writing center.

**Majors. Business:** General. **Engineering technology:** CAD/CADD, electrical. **Mechanic/repair:** Aircraft, aircraft powerplant, avionics, communications systems. **Transportation:** Airline/commercial pilot, aviation, aviation management. **Other:** Mechatronic engineering.

**Most popular majors.** Business/marketing 6%, engineering/engineering technologies 19%, trade and industry 75%.

**Computing on campus.** 70 workstations in library, computer center, student center. Dormitories wired for high-speed internet access and linked to campus network. Commuter students can connect to campus network. Online library, helpline, repair service, wireless network available.

**Student life. Freshman orientation:** Mandatory. Preregistration for classes offered. One-day session held before classes begin. **Housing:** Guaranteed on-campus for all undergraduates. Coed dorms, substance-free housing available. $250 partly refundable deposit, deadline 6/15. **Activities:** Student government, student newspaper, American Institute of Aeronautics and Astronautics, Society of Automotive Engineers, Institute of Electrical and Electronics Engineers, flying club, Women in Aviation-International.

**Athletics. Intercollegiate:** Basketball M. **Intramural:** Basketball, soccer. **Team name:** Warriors.

**Student services.** Campus ministries, career counseling, services for economically disadvantaged, student employment services, financial aid counseling, health services, legal services, minority student services, personal counseling, placement for graduates, veterans' counselor.

**Contact.** E-mail: admitme@vaughn.edu
Phone: (718) 429-6600 ext. 118 Toll-free number: (800) 866-6828
Fax: (718) 779-2231
Vincent Papandrea, Director of Admissions, Vaughn College of Aeronautics and Technology, 86-01 23rd Avenue, Flushing, NY 11369

---

## Wagner College
**Staten Island, New York**
www.wagner.edu

CB member
CB code: 2966

- Private 4-year liberal arts college affiliated with Lutheran Church in America
- Residential campus in very large city
- 1,926 degree-seeking undergraduates: 2% part-time, 63% women, 5% African American, 2% Asian American, 5% Hispanic American, 1% international
- 359 degree-seeking graduate students
- 60% of applicants admitted
- SAT or ACT (ACT writing optional), application essay required
- 63% graduate within 6 years; 4% enter graduate study

**General.** Founded in 1883. Regionally accredited. **Degrees:** 432 bachelor's awarded; master's offered. **ROTC:** Army. **Location:** 10 miles from New York City. **Calendar:** Semester, limited summer session. **Full-time faculty:** 100 total; 84% have terminal degrees, 8% minority, 46% women. **Part-time faculty:** 149 total; 52% women. **Class size:** 63% < 20, 37% 20-39, less than 1% 40-49. **Special facilities:** Planetarium, electron microscopes.

**Freshman class profile.** 2,842 applied, 1,716 admitted, 524 enrolled.

| Mid 50% test scores | | GPA 2.0-2.99: | 10% |
|---|---|---|---|
| SAT critical reading: | 530-640 | Rank in top quarter: | 68% |
| SAT math: | 540-650 | Rank in top tenth: | 18% |
| SAT writing: | 530-640 | Return as sophomores: | 81% |
| ACT composite: | 24-28 | Out-of-state: | 57% |
| GPA 3.50 or higher: | 40% | Live on campus: | 82% |
| GPA 3.0-3.49: | 50% | International: | 1% |

**Basis for selection.** School achievement, test scores, recommendations, interview, special talents, essay all considered. Interview recommended for all; audition required for music, theater programs; portfolio recommended for art programs. Interview required for Physician Assistant program. **Homeschooled:** Transcript of courses and grades required.

**High school preparation.** 21 units required. Required units include English 4, mathematics 3, social studies 1, history 3, science 2 (laboratory 1), foreign language 2 and academic electives 6. 4 economics, arts, computers, or other elective areas of study required.

**2008-2009 Annual costs.** Tuition/fees: $31,000. Room/board: $9,250. Books/supplies: $725. Personal expenses: $1,260.

**2007-2008 Financial aid. Need-based:** 407 full-time freshmen applied for aid; 329 were judged to have need; 329 of these received aid. Average need met was 73%. Average scholarship/grant was $11,031; average loan $4,205. 51% of total undergraduate aid awarded as scholarships/grants, 49% as loans/jobs. **Non-need-based:** Awarded to 1,006 full-time undergraduates, including 240 freshmen. Scholarships awarded for academics, athletics, leadership, music/drama.

**Application procedures. Admission:** Closing date 2/15 (postmark date). $50 fee, may be waived for applicants with need. Application may be submitted online. Admission notification on a rolling basis beginning on or about 3/1. Must reply by May 1 or within 2 week(s) if notified thereafter.

**Financial aid:** Priority date 2/15; no closing date. FAFSA, institutional form required. Applicants notified on a rolling basis starting 3/1; must reply within 3 week(s) of notification.

**Academics. Special study options:** Combined bachelor's/graduate degree, double major, exchange student, honors, independent study, internships, study abroad, teacher certification program, United Nations semester, Washington semester. Learning community. **Credit/placement by examination:** AP, CLEP, IB, institutional tests. 9 credit hours maximum toward bachelor's degree. Up to 9 units may be awarded for credit by exam and prior experience. Each unit is equivalent to 3.3 credit hours. **Support services:** Reduced course load, tutoring, writing center.

**Majors. Biology:** General, bacteriology. **Business:** Accounting, business admin, finance, international, managerial economics, marketing. **Computer sciences:** Computer science. **Education:** General, early childhood, middle, secondary. **English:** English lit. **Foreign languages:** Spanish. **Health:** Nursing (RN), physician assistant, predental, premedicine. **History:** General. **Liberal arts:** Arts/sciences. **Math:** General. **Philosophy/religion:** Philosophy. **Physical sciences:** Chemistry, physics. **Psychology:** General. **Public administration:** Policy analysis. **Social sciences:** Anthropology, political science, sociology. **Visual/performing arts:** Arts management, dramatic, music performance, studio arts, theater design.

**Most popular majors.** Business/marketing 23%, education 8%, English 6%, health sciences 15%, psychology 8%, social sciences 8%, visual/performing arts 20%.

**Computing on campus.** 230 workstations in dormitories, library, computer center. Dormitories wired for high-speed internet access and linked to campus network. Commuter students can connect to campus network. Online library, helpline, wireless network available.

**Student life. Freshman orientation:** Mandatory. Freshmen move on-campus 3 days prior to start of fall semester. Orientation involves academic advisement and registration, social activities, and trip to Manhattan. **Housing:** Guaranteed on-campus for all undergraduates. Coed dorms, apartments, fraternity/sorority housing, substance-free housing available. $300 nonrefundable deposit, deadline 5/1. **Activities:** Bands, choral groups, dance, drama, literary magazine, music ensembles, musical theater, radio station, student government, student newspaper, Lutheran student club, Newman Society, Hillel, national honor societies, Amnesty International, Young Democrats, Young Republicans, Nubian Society, Muslim student association.

**Athletics. NCAA. Intercollegiate:** Baseball M, basketball, cross-country, football (tackle) M, golf, lacrosse, soccer W, softball W, swimming W, tennis, track and field, volleyball W, water polo W, wrestling M. **Intramural:** Basketball, bowling, cheerleading W, football (tackle) M, soccer, softball, table tennis, tennis, volleyball. **Team name:** Seahawks.

**Student services.** Alcohol/substance abuse counseling, campus ministries, career counseling, student employment services, financial aid counseling, health services, personal counseling, placement for graduates. **Physically disabled:** Services for visually, hearing impaired.

**Contact.** E-mail: adm@wagner.edu
Phone: (718) 390-3411 Toll-free number: (800) 221-1010
Fax: (718) 390-3105
Leigh-Ann Nowicki, Dean of Admissions, Wagner College, One Campus Road, Staten Island, NY 10301-4495

---

## Webb Institute
**Glen Cove, New York**
www.webb-institute.edu

CB member
CB code: 2970

- Private 4-year engineering and maritime college
- Residential campus in large town
- 91 degree-seeking undergraduates: 22% women, 2% Asian American, 2% Hispanic American
- 31% of applicants admitted
- SAT, SAT Subject Tests, interview required
- 62% graduate within 6 years; 30% enter graduate study

**General.** Founded in 1889. Regionally accredited. All students participate in 2-month paid winter work program in marine industry each year. **Degrees:** 21 bachelor's awarded. **Location:** 22 miles from New York City. **Calendar:** Semester. **Full-time faculty:** 11 total; 64% have terminal degrees, 9% women. **Part-time faculty:** 5 total; 60% have terminal degrees. **Class size:** 25% < 20, 75% 20-39. **Special facilities:** Adjoining nature preserve, model testing tank.

**Freshman class profile.** 95 applied, 29 admitted, 23 enrolled.

| Mid 50% test scores | | | |
|---|---|---|---|
| SAT critical reading: | 620-700 | Rank in top tenth: | 83% |
| SAT math: | 680-740 | End year in good standing: | 100% |
| SAT writing: | 600-710 | Return as sophomores: | 96% |
| GPA 3.50 or higher: | 100% | Out-of-state: | 78% |
| Rank in top quarter: | 100% | Live on campus: | 100% |

**Basis for selection.** GED not accepted. High school record, class rank, test scores, and interview with President of college most important. Character, motivation, and outside activities considered. **Homeschooled:** Statement describing homeschool structure and mission, transcript of courses and grades, letter of recommendation (nonparent) required.

**High school preparation.** 16 units required. Required units include English 4, mathematics 4, social studies 2, science 2 (laboratory 2) and academic electives 4.

**2008-2009 Annual costs.** All students receive 4-year, full-tuition scholarships. Room/board: $9,500. Books/supplies: $750. Personal expenses: $3,700.

**2006-2007 Financial aid.** All financial aid based on need. 6 full-time freshmen applied for aid; 6 were judged to have need; 6 of these received aid. Average need met was 80%. Average scholarship/grant was $3,000; average loan $2,625. 53% of total undergraduate aid awarded as scholarships/grants, 47% as loans/jobs.

**Application procedures. Admission:** Closing date 2/15 (postmark date). $25 fee, may be waived for applicants with need. Application must be submitted on paper. Admission notification on a rolling basis beginning on or about 3/15. Must reply by May 1 or within 2 week(s) if notified thereafter. **Financial aid:** Closing date 7/1. FAFSA required. Applicants notified by 8/1; must reply within 2 week(s) of notification.

**Academics.** Intensive single curriculum program demands high career motivation. **Special study options:** Double major, independent study, internships. **Credit/placement by examination:** CLEP. **Support services:** Study skills assistance.

**Majors. Engineering:** Marine.

**Computing on campus.** PC or laptop required. 100 workstations in dormitories, library, computer center, student center. Dormitories wired for high-speed internet access and linked to campus network. Repair service, wireless network available.

**Student life. Freshman orientation:** Mandatory. Held 1 week before classes start. **Housing:** Guaranteed on-campus for all undergraduates. Coed dorms, single-sex dorms, substance-free housing available. $150 deposit. **Activities:** Choral groups, drama, music ensembles, student government, free membership available to local YMCA, women engineers, society of American naval engineers, WebbWomen, society of naval architects and marine engineers.

**Athletics. Intercollegiate:** Basketball, cross-country, sailing, soccer, tennis, track and field, volleyball. **Intramural:** Basketball, cross-country, soccer, softball, triathlon, volleyball.

**Student services.** Alcohol/substance abuse counseling, career counseling, student employment services, financial aid counseling, health services, personal counseling, placement for graduates.

**Contact.** E-mail: admissions@webb-institute.edu
Phone: (516) 671-2213 Toll-free number: (866) 708-9322
Fax: (516) 674-9838
William Murray, Director of Enrollment Management, Webb Institute, 298 Crescent Beach Road, Glen Cove, NY 11542-1398

---

## Wells College
**Aurora, New York**
www.wells.edu

**CB member**
**CB code: 2971**

- Private 4-year liberal arts college
- Residential campus in rural community
- 544 degree-seeking undergraduates: 1% part-time, 77% women, 5% African American, 2% Asian American, 4% Hispanic American, 1% Native American, 2% international
- 64% of applicants admitted
- SAT or ACT (ACT writing recommended), application essay required
- 51% graduate within 6 years; 27% enter graduate study

**General.** Founded in 1868. Regionally accredited. **Degrees:** 82 bachelor's awarded. **ROTC:** Air Force. **Location:** 30 miles from Ithaca, 50 miles from Syracuse. **Calendar:** Semester. **Full-time faculty:** 48 total; 98% have terminal degrees, 19% minority, 58% women. **Part-time faculty:** 36 total; 33% have terminal degrees, 11% minority, 53% women. **Class size:** 80% < 20, 19% 20-39, 1% 40-49. **Special facilities:** Book arts center, lithography presses, digital imaging laboratory, boathouse with access to Cayuga Lake, indoor tennis courts, 9-hole golf course, science facility with growth chamber, NMR, and cold room.

**Freshman class profile.** 1,148 applied, 740 admitted, 174 enrolled.

| Mid 50% test scores | | | |
|---|---|---|---|
| SAT critical reading: | 510-640 | Rank in top quarter: | 60% |
| SAT math: | 490-590 | Rank in top tenth: | 25% |
| ACT composite: | 23-27 | End year in good standing: | 82% |
| GPA 3.50 or higher: | 54% | Return as sophomores: | 76% |
| GPA 3.0-3.49: | 30% | Out-of-state: | 40% |
| GPA 2.0-2.99: | 16% | Live on campus: | 99% |
| | | International: | 2% |

**Basis for selection.** Academic achievement record most important. Test scores, class rank, recommendations, essay, school and community extracurricular activities also important. Evidence of leadership ability through academic and cocurricular activities also considered. Interviews highly recommended. **Homeschooled:** Statement describing homeschool structure and mission, transcript of courses and grades, state high school equivalency certificate required. Please contact Admissions Office for additional information.

**High school preparation.** 17 units required; 23 recommended. Required and recommended units include English 4, mathematics 3-4, social studies 1, history 3, science 2-3 (laboratory 2-3), foreign language 2 and academic electives 2-3. Students encouraged to take 2 computer science, art, and/or music. AP and honors courses recommended.

**2008-2009 Annual costs.** Tuition/fees (projected): $19,480. Room/board: $8,420. Books/supplies: $800. Personal expenses: $800.

**2007-2008 Financial aid. Need-based:** 150 full-time freshmen applied for aid; 126 were judged to have need; 124 of these received aid. Average need met was 92%. Average scholarship/grant was $13,645; average loan $3,920. 69% of total undergraduate aid awarded as scholarships/grants, 31% as loans/jobs. **Non-need-based:** Awarded to 257 full-time undergraduates, including 98 freshmen. Scholarships awarded for academics, alumni affiliation, leadership.

**Application procedures. Admission:** Priority date 12/15; deadline 3/1 (postmark date). $40 fee, may be waived for applicants with need. Application may be submitted online. Admission notification 4/1. Must reply by 5/1. **Financial aid:** Priority date 2/15; no closing date. FAFSA required. CSS PROFILE required of early decision candidates only. Applicants notified on a rolling basis starting 3/1; must reply by 5/1.

**Academics.** Experiential learning integrated through internship and off-campus study programs, study abroad, research with professors, and community service. **Special study options:** Accelerated study, combined bachelor's/graduate degree, cross-registration, double major, independent study, internships, student-designed major, study abroad, teacher certification program, Washington semester. **Credit/placement by examination:** AP, CLEP, IB, SAT, ACT, institutional tests. 6 credit hours maximum toward bachelor's degree. **Support services:** Reduced course load, study skills assistance, tutoring, writing center.

**Majors. Area/ethnic studies:** African-American, American, women's. **Biology:** General, biochemistry, molecular. **Business:** General, managerial economics. **Computer sciences:** Computer science. **Conservation:** General, environmental science, environmental studies. **English:** English lit. **Foreign languages:** General, comparative lit, French, German, Spanish. **Health:** Predental, premedicine, preveterinary. **History:** General. **Interdisciplinary:** Global studies. **Legal studies:** Prelaw. **Liberal arts:** Humanities. **Math:** General. **Philosophy/religion:** Ethics, philosophy, religion. **Physical sciences:** Chemistry, physics. **Psychology:** General. **Public administration:** Policy analysis. **Social sciences:** Anthropology, economics, international relations, sociology, U.S. government. **Visual/performing arts:** General, art, art history/conservation, dance, dramatic, studio arts.

**Most popular majors.** Biology 7%, English 9%, psychology 17%, social sciences 24%, visual/performing arts 16%.

**Computing on campus.** 85 workstations in dormitories, library, computer center. Dormitories wired for high-speed internet access and linked to campus network. Commuter students can connect to campus network. Online library, repair service, wireless network available.

**Student life. Freshman orientation:** Mandatory. Preregistration for classes offered. General introduction held during 5-day orientation before classes begin. **Policies:** Honor code governs academic and co-curricular life. **Housing:** Guaranteed on-campus for all undergraduates. Coed dorms, single-sex dorms, substance-free housing available. $300 nonrefundable deposit, deadline 5/1. **Activities:** Choral groups, dance, drama, literary magazine, music ensembles, student government, student newspaper, Model United Nations, Amnesty International, American Red Cross Club, Wells College Democrats, College Republicans, Praising our Work, social and cultural organization, Women in Life-Long Learning.

**Athletics.** NCAA. **Intercollegiate:** Cross-country, field hockey W, lacrosse, soccer, softball W, swimming, tennis W. **Intramural:** Field hockey, golf, sailing, skiing, soccer, tennis, volleyball. **Team name:** Express.

**Student services.** Adult student services, campus ministries, career counseling, financial aid counseling, health services, minority student services, personal counseling, women's services.

**Contact.** E-mail: admissions@wells.edu
Phone: (315) 364-3264 Toll-free number: (800) 952-9355
Fax: (315) 364-3227
Susan Sloan, Director of Admissions, Wells College, 170 Main Street, Aurora, NY 13026

## Yeshiva and Kolel Bais Medrash Elyon
### Monsey, New York

- Private 4-year rabbinical college for men affiliated with Jewish faith
- Small city

**General.** Accredited by AARTS. **Calendar:** Semester.

**Annual costs/financial aid.** Tuition/fees (2007-2008): $7,800.

**Contact.** Phone: (845) 356-7064
Admissions Director, 73 Main Street, Monsey, NY 10952

## Yeshiva and Kollel Harbotzas Torah
### Brooklyn, New York

- Private 4-year rabbinical college for men affiliated with Jewish faith
- Very large city

**General.** Accredited by AARTS. **Calendar:** Semester.

**Annual costs/financial aid.** Tuition/fees (2007-2008): $4,600.

**Contact.** Phone: (718) 692-0208
1049 East 15th Street, Brooklyn, NY 11230

## Yeshiva Derech Chaim
### Brooklyn, New York
**CB code: 0552**

- Private 5-year rabbinical college for men affiliated with Jewish faith
- Very large city

**General.** Founded in 1975. Accredited by AARTS. **Calendar:** Semester.

**Annual costs/financial aid.** Tuition/fees (2007-2008): $8,300. Tuition includes board expenses. Room: $3,300. Books/supplies: $400.

**Contact.** Phone: (718) 438-3070
Admissions Director, 1573 39th Street, Brooklyn, NY 11218

## Yeshiva D'Monsey Rabbinical College
### Monsey, New York

- Private 4-year rabbinical college for men affiliated with Jewish faith
- Large town

**General.** Accredited by AARTS. **Calendar:** Semester.

**Annual costs/financial aid.** Tuition/fees (2007-2008): $3,000. Room/board: $3,000.

**Contact.** Phone: (845) 352-5852
2 Roman Boulevard, Monsey, NY 10952

## Yeshiva Gedolah Imrei Yosef D'Spinka
### Brooklyn, New York

- Private 4-year rabbinical college for men affiliated with Jewish faith
- Very large city

**General.** Accredited by AARTS. **Calendar:** Semester.

**Contact.** Phone: (718) 851-1600
Admissions Director, 1466 56th Street, Brooklyn, NY 11219

## Yeshiva Gedolah Zichron Moshe
### South Fallsburg, New York
**CB code: 0750**

- Private 4-year rabbinical college for men affiliated with Jewish faith
- Small town

**General.** Founded in 1969. Accredited by AARTS. **Calendar:** Semester.

**Annual costs/financial aid.** Books/supplies: $200. Personal expenses: $2,000.

**Contact.** Phone: (845) 434-5240
Dean of Admissions, Laurel Park Road, South Fallsburg, NY 12779

## Yeshiva Karlin Stolin
### Brooklyn, New York
**CB code: 1582**

- Private 4-year rabbinical college for men affiliated with Jewish faith
- Very large city

**General.** Accredited by AARTS. **Calendar:** Semester.

**Contact.** Phone: (718) 232-7800
1818 54th Street, Brooklyn, NY 11204-1545

## Yeshiva Mikdash Melech
### Brooklyn, New York
**CB code: 1432**

- Private 4-year rabbinical college for men affiliated with Jewish faith
- Residential campus in very large city
- 105 degree-seeking undergraduates: 1% international
- 13 graduate students
- Interview required

**General.** Accredited by AARTS. **Degrees:** 4 bachelor's awarded; master's, first professional offered. **Calendar:** Semester, extensive summer session. **Full-time faculty:** 6 total; 67% have terminal degrees. **Class size:** 100% < 20.

**Freshman class profile.**

| End year in good standing: | 98% | Live on campus: | 70% |
|---|---|---|---|

**Basis for selection.** Recommendations, school record, test scores, and class rank considered. **Homeschooled:** Statement describing homeschool structure and mission required.

**High school preparation.** Required units include English 3, mathematics 3, social studies 1, history 1, science 2 (laboratory 1), foreign language 1 and academic electives 1.

**2007-2008 Annual costs.** Tuition/fees: $6,500. Room/board: $3,800.

**Financial aid. Non-need-based:** Scholarships awarded for academics, leadership, religious affiliation.

**Application procedures. Admission:** No deadline. No application fee. Application must be submitted on paper. Admission notification on a rolling basis. **Financial aid:** No deadline. FAFSA required. Applicants notified on a rolling basis starting 5/1.

**Academics. Special study options:** Independent study, study abroad. **Credit/placement by examination:** CLEP. **Support services:** Remedial instruction, tutoring.

**Majors. Philosophy/religion:** Judaic. **Theology:** Talmudic.

**Student life. Freshman orientation:** Available. Preregistration for classes offered. **Policies:** Religious observance required. **Housing:** Guaranteed on-campus for freshmen. Substance-free housing available.

**Student services.** Adult student services, campus ministries, financial aid counseling.

**Contact.** E-mail: mikdashmelech@VERIZON.net
Phone: (718) 339-1090 Fax: (718) 998-9321
Rabbi Shmuel Beyda, Admissions Director, Yeshiva Mikdash Melech, 1326 Ocean Parkway, Brooklyn, NY 11230

## Yeshiva of Nitra
**Mount Kisco, New York**

CB code: 7131

- Private 4-year rabbinical college for men affiliated with Jewish faith
- Small city

**General.** Accredited by AARTS. **Calendar:** Continuous.

**Annual costs/financial aid.** Tuition/fees (2007-2008): $6,000. Room/board: $2,000.

**Contact.** Phone: (718) 387-0422
Pine Bridge Road, Mount Kisco, NY 10549

## Yeshiva of the Telshe Alumni
**Riverdale, New York**

- Private 4-year rabbinical college for men affiliated with Jewish faith
- Very large city

**General.** Accredited by AARTS. **Calendar:** Semester.

**Annual costs/financial aid.** Tuition/fees (2007-2008): $7,900. Room/board: $4,600.

**Contact.** Phone: (718) 601-3523
4904 Independence Avenue, Riverdale, NY 10471

## Yeshiva Shaar Hatorah
**Kew Gardens, New York**

CB code: 0743

- Private 4-year rabbinical college for men affiliated with Jewish faith
- Very large city

**General.** Founded in 1976. Accredited by AARTS. **Calendar:** Semester.

**Annual costs/financial aid.** Comprehensive fee (2007-2008): $12,750.

**Contact.** Phone: (718) 846-1940
Admissions Director, 117-06 84th Avenue, Kew Gardens, NY 11418

## Yeshiva Shaarei Torah of Rockland
**Suffern, New York**

- Private 4-year rabbinical college for men affiliated with Jewish faith
- Commuter campus in large town

**General.** Accredited by AARTS. **Calendar:** Semester.

**Annual costs/financial aid.** Tuition/fees (2007-2008): $7,000.

**Contact.** Phone: (845) 352-3431
Admissions Director, 91 West Carlton Road, Suffern, NY 10901

## Yeshiva University
**New York, New York**
www.yu.edu

CB member
CB code: 2990

- Private 4-year university, business and liberal arts college
- Residential campus in very large city
- 3,076 degree-seeking undergraduates

- 69% of applicants admitted
- SAT or ACT with writing, application essay, interview required
- 92% graduate within 6 years

**General.** Founded in 1886. Regionally accredited. Campus locations in Manhattan and the Bronx. **Degrees:** 589 bachelor's, 215 associate awarded; master's, doctoral, first professional offered. **Calendar:** Semester, limited summer session. **Full-time faculty:** 863 total. **Part-time faculty:** 389 total.

**Freshman class profile.** 2,169 applied, 1,506 admitted, 974 enrolled.

| Mid 50% test scores | | | |
|---|---|---|---|
| SAT critical reading: | 550-670 | SAT math: | 570-680 |
| | | Return as sophomores: | 88% |

**Basis for selection.** Equal weight given to high school GPA, test scores, ability and motivation as indicated in interview, school and community activities, recommendations of principal, guidance counselor, and/or employer. **Homeschooled:** Statement describing homeschool structure and mission, transcript of courses and grades, state high school equivalency certificate, interview required.

**2007-2008 Annual costs.** Tuition/fees: $30,560. Room/board: $9,410. Books/supplies: $1,166. Personal expenses: $3,101.

**Financial aid. Additional information:** Essays required of Distinguished Scholarship applicants.

**Application procedures. Admission:** Priority date 2/1; no deadline. $65 fee, may be waived for applicants with need. Application may be submitted online. Admission notification on a rolling basis beginning on or about 12/15. Must reply by May 1 or within 2 week(s) if notified thereafter. **Financial aid:** Priority date 4/15, closing date 5/1. FAFSA, institutional form required. Applicants notified on a rolling basis starting 4/1.

**Academics. Special study options:** Combined bachelor's/graduate degree, cross-registration, double major, dual enrollment of high school students, exchange student, honors, independent study, internships, student-designed major, study abroad, teacher certification program. **Credit/placement by examination:** CLEP, institutional tests. 44 credit hours maximum toward bachelor's degree. **Support services:** Reduced course load, tutoring, writing center.

**Honors college/program.** 1400 SAT (exclusive of Writing) or ACT equivalent, 2 nominations, interview required.

**Majors. Biology:** General. **Business:** Accounting, business admin. **Computer sciences:** General, computer science. **Education:** Elementary, foreign languages. **Engineering:** General. **English:** English lit, speech/rhetoric. **Foreign languages:** Classics, French, Hebrew. **Health:** Audiology/speech pathology, premedicine. **History:** General. **Math:** General. **Philosophy/religion:** Judaic, philosophy. **Physical sciences:** Chemistry, physics. **Psychology:** General. **Social sciences:** Economics, political science, sociology.

**Computing on campus.** 350 workstations in library, computer center, student center. Dormitories wired for high-speed internet access and linked to campus network. Online library, helpline, repair service, wireless network available.

**Student life. Freshman orientation:** Mandatory. Held the week before classes. **Policies:** Students participate in university governance through college senates. **Housing:** Guaranteed on-campus for all undergraduates. Single-sex dorms, apartments available. $250 nonrefundable deposit, deadline 6/1. **Activities:** Jazz band, choral groups, drama, literary magazine, music ensembles, musical theater, radio station, student government, student newspaper, neighborhood social service, preprofessional, special interest, and political clubs.

**Athletics.** NCAA. **Intercollegiate:** Baseball M, basketball, cross-country M, fencing M, golf M, soccer M, tennis M, volleyball M, wrestling M. **Intramural:** Basketball, tennis M, volleyball W. **Team name:** Macs.

**Student services.** Career counseling, student employment services, health services, personal counseling, placement for graduates.

**Contact.** E-mail: yuadmit@yu.edu
Phone: (212) 960-5277 Fax: (212) 960-0086
Michael Kranzler, Director of Undergraduate Admissions, Yeshiva University, 500 West 185th Street, New York, NY 10033

## Yeshivas Novominsk
**Brooklyn, New York**

- Private 4-year rabbinical college for men affiliated with Jewish faith
- Very large city

**General.** Accredited by AARTS. **Calendar:** Semester.

**Annual costs/financial aid.** Tuition/fees (2007-2008): $7,500. Room/board: $3,000.

**Contact.**   Phone: (718) 438-2727
1569 47th Street, Brooklyn, NY 11219

## Yeshivath Viznitz
### Monsey, New York

▶   Private 4-year rabbinical college for men
▶   Large town

**General.** Accredited by AARTS. **Calendar:** Semester.

**Contact.**   Phone: (914) 356-1010
25 Phyllis Terrace, Monsey, NY 10952

# North Carolina

## Appalachian State University

Boone, North Carolina

www.appstate.edu

CB member

CB code: 5010

- Public 4-year university
- Residential campus in large town
- 13,763 degree-seeking undergraduates: 5% part-time, 50% women, 4% African American, 1% Asian American, 2% Hispanic American
- 1,703 degree-seeking graduate students
- 65% of applicants admitted
- SAT or ACT with writing required

**General.** Founded in 1899. Regionally accredited. **Degrees:** 2,425 bachelor's awarded; master's, doctoral offered. **ROTC:** Army. **Location:** 87 miles from Winston-Salem. **Calendar:** Semester, extensive summer session. **Full-time faculty:** 737 total; 77% have terminal degrees, 8% minority, 44% women. **Part-time faculty:** 371 total; 24% have terminal degrees, 6% minority, 53% women. **Class size:** 42% < 20, 45% 20-39, 7% 40-49, 5% 50-99, 1% >100. **Special facilities:** Observatory, cultural museum, visual arts center, year round outdoor adventure camp.

**Freshman class profile.** 11,468 applied, 7,397 admitted, 2,737 enrolled.

| Mid 50% test scores | | GPA 2.0-2.99: | 4% |
|---|---|---|---|
| SAT critical reading: | 510-600 | Rank in top quarter: | 51% |
| SAT math: | 530-610 | Rank in top tenth: | 17% |
| SAT writing: | 490-590 | Return as sophomores: | 86% |
| ACT composite: | 21-26 | Out-of-state: | 10% |
| GPA 3.50 or higher: | 74% | Live on campus: | 97% |
| GPA 3.0-3.49: | 22% | Sororities: | 4% |

**Basis for selection.** GED not accepted. Satisfactory combination of grades and test scores or class rank and test scores required. SAT Math used for placement; CE clarification: no date, but on space basis. Audition required for music majors; portfolio required for art majors.

**High school preparation.** 13 units required. Required units include English 4, mathematics 4, social studies 1, history 1, science 3 (laboratory 1) and foreign language 2. Math units should include algebra I, algebra II, and geometry.

**2007-2008 Annual costs.** Tuition/fees: $4,241; $13,983 out-of-state. Room/board: $5,990. Books/supplies: $600. Personal expenses: $1,200.

**Financial aid. Non-need-based:** Scholarships awarded for academics, alumni affiliation, art, athletics, job skills, leadership, minority status, music/drama, religious affiliation, ROTC, state residency.

**Application procedures. Admission:** No deadline. $50 fee, may be waived for applicants with need. Application may be submitted online. Postponement allowed on individual basis for one term during academic year. **Financial aid:** Priority date 3/15; no closing date. FAFSA required. Applicants notified by 4/1; Applicants notified on a rolling basis starting 4/1; must reply within 3 week(s) of notification.

**Academics. Special study options:** Distance learning, double major, dual enrollment of high school students, ESL, exchange student, honors, independent study, internships, liberal arts/career combination, student-designed major, study abroad, teacher certification program. **Credit/placement by examination:** AP, CLEP, IB, SAT, ACT, institutional tests. **Support services:** Learning center, pre-admission summer program, remedial instruction, study skills assistance, tutoring, writing center.

**Majors. Architecture:** Urban/community planning. **Biology:** General, ecology. **Business:** Accounting, actuarial science, business admin, construction management, finance, hospitality admin, insurance, international, management information systems, marketing. **Communications:** General, advertising, journalism, public relations, radio/tv. **Computer sciences:** Computer science. **Education:** Art, biology, business, chemistry, drama/dance, elementary, English, family/consumer sciences, French, health, history, kindergarten/preschool, learning disabled, mathematics, middle, music, physical, physics, social studies, Spanish, technology/industrial arts. **Engineering technology:** Solar energy. **English:** English lit, speech/rhetoric. **Family/consumer sciences:** Child development, clothing/textiles, food/nutrition. **Foreign languages:** French, Spanish. **Health:** Athletic training, clinical lab science,

communication disorders, health care admin, music therapy, nursing (RN), public health ed. **History:** General. **Liberal arts:** Arts/sciences. **Math:** General, statistics. **Parks/recreation:** Exercise sciences, facilities management. **Philosophy/religion:** Philosophy, religion. **Physical sciences:** Chemistry, geology, physics. **Protective services:** Criminal justice. **Psychology:** General. **Public administration:** Social work. **Social sciences:** Anthropology, economics, geography, political science, sociology. **Visual/performing arts:** Art, arts management, dance, dramatic, graphic design, industrial design, interior design, music management, music performance, studio arts. **Other:** Geology, secondary education, Philosophy and Religion.

**Most popular majors.** Business/marketing 18%, communications/journalism 8%, education 19%, psychology 7%, social sciences 8%, visual/performing arts 7%.

**Computing on campus.** 2,500 workstations in dormitories, library, computer center, student center. Dormitories wired for high-speed internet access and linked to campus network. Commuter students can connect to campus network. Online course registration, online library, helpline, repair service, wireless network available.

**Student life. Freshman orientation:** Mandatory. Preregistration for classes offered. 2-day program throughout summer and at beginning of each semester and summer school session. **Housing:** Guaranteed on-campus for freshmen. Coed dorms, single-sex dorms, special housing for disabled, apartments, fraternity/sorority housing, substance-free housing available. $100 nonrefundable deposit, deadline 5/1. **Activities:** Bands, campus ministries, choral groups, dance, drama, film society, international student organizations, literary magazine, music ensembles, Model UN, musical theater, opera, radio station, student government, student newspaper, symphony orchestra, TV station, Campus Crusade for Christ, Habitat for Humanity, Order of the Black and Gold, ACLU, College Democrats/Republicans, Wesley Foundation, Westminster Canterbury Fellowship, Circle K.

**Athletics.** NCAA. **Intercollegiate:** Baseball M, basketball, cross-country, field hockey W, football (tackle) M, golf, soccer, softball W, tennis, track and field, volleyball W, wrestling M. **Intramural:** Archery, badminton, basketball, cheerleading, cross-country, fencing, field hockey W, football (non-tackle), football (tackle), golf, gymnastics, handball, racquetball, rugby M, soccer, softball, squash, swimming, table tennis, tennis, track and field, triathlon, volleyball, water polo, wrestling M. **Team name:** Mountaineers.

**Student services.** Adult student services, campus ministries, career counseling, student employment services, financial aid counseling, health services, on-campus daycare, personal counseling, placement for graduates, veterans' counselor, women's services. **Physically disabled:** Services for visually, speech, hearing impaired. **Learning disabled:** Comprehensive services available.

**Contact.** E-mail: admissions@appstate.edu
Phone: (828) 262-2000 Fax: (828) 262-3296
Paul Hiatt, Director of Admissions, Appalachian State University, ASU Box 32004, Boone, NC 28608

## Art Institute of Charlotte

Charlotte, North Carolina

www.artinstitutes.edu/charlotte

CB code: 3834

- For-profit 4-year visual arts college
- Commuter campus in very large city
- 880 degree-seeking undergraduates: 29% part-time, 69% women, 32% African American, 2% Asian American, 5% Hispanic American
- Application essay, interview required

**General.** Accredited by ACICS. **Degrees:** 19 bachelor's, 131 associate awarded. **Location:** 8 miles from Center City. **Calendar:** Quarter, extensive summer session. **Full-time faculty:** 37 total; 22% have terminal degrees, 32% minority, 46% women. **Part-time faculty:** 23 total; 17% have terminal degrees, 13% minority, 52% women. **Class size:** 54% < 20, 46% 20-39. **Special facilities:** Computer labs, interior design lighting laboratory, teaching restaurant open to the public.

**Basis for selection.** Interviews required. Applicant must provide a written essay and high school transcripts with minimum 2.0 GPA. SAT or ACT recommended. Students with a 2.0 average or lower required to take Accuplacer placement test. **Homeschooled:** Statement describing homeschool structure and mission, transcript of courses and grades, interview required.

**2007-2008 Annual costs.** Tuition/fees: $18,090. Annual tuition and fees vary by program. First-time students pay kit fee $670-$1220.

**Application procedures. Admission:** No deadline. $150 fee. Application may be submitted online. Admission notification on a rolling basis.

**Academics.** Students begin studies in the majors alongside general education classes from the first quarter. **Special study options:** Distance learning, internships, study abroad. **Credit/placement by examination:** AP, CLEP, SAT, ACT, institutional tests. **Support services:** Learning center, remedial instruction, study skills assistance, tutoring, writing center.

**Majors. Business:** Apparel. **Computer sciences:** Web page design. **Personal/culinary services:** Culinary arts. **Visual/performing arts:** Graphic design, interior design.

**Computing on campus.** 224 workstations in library, computer center, student center. Commuter students can connect to campus network. Online library, helpline, student web hosting, wireless network available.

**Student life. Freshman orientation:** Mandatory, Preregistration for classes offered. **Housing:** Apartments available. $450 fully refundable deposit. **Activities:** Student newspaper.

**Student services.** Alcohol/substance abuse counseling, career counseling, student employment services, financial aid counseling, personal counseling, placement for graduates, veterans' counselor.

**Contact.** E-mail: aichadm@aii.edu
Phone: (704) 357-8020 Toll-free number: (800) 872-4417
Fax: (704) 357-1133
Pamela Rogers, Senior Director of Admissions, Art Institute of Charlotte, Three LakePointe Plaza, Charlotte, NC 28217-4536

---

## Barton College
**Wilson, North Carolina**        CB member
www.barton.edu        CB code: 5016

- Private 4-year liberal arts college affiliated with Christian Church (Disciples of Christ)
- Residential campus in large town
- 1,103 degree-seeking undergraduates: 20% part-time, 71% women, 23% African American, 1% Asian American, 3% Hispanic American, 2% international
- 63% of applicants admitted
- SAT or ACT (ACT writing optional) required
- 37% graduate within 6 years

**General.** Founded in 1902. Regionally accredited. **Degrees:** 260 bachelor's awarded. **Location:** 45 miles from Raleigh. **Calendar:** 4-1-4, limited summer session. **Full-time faculty:** 73 total; 60% have terminal degrees, 7% minority, 52% women. **Part-time faculty:** 39 total; 13% have terminal degrees, 8% minority, 72% women. **Class size:** 67% < 20, 32% 20-39, less than 1% 40-49, less than 1% 50-99. **Special facilities:** Lula E. Rackley Gallery and the Virginia Thompson Graves Gallery of the Barton Museum, greenhouse, TV and music recording studios, photo developing labs and darkroom.

**Freshman class profile.** 1,409 applied, 882 admitted, 218 enrolled.

| Mid 50% test scores | | Rank in top quarter: | 31% |
|---|---|---|---|
| SAT critical reading: | 410-510 | Rank in top tenth: | 7% |
| SAT math: | 420-530 | End year in good standing: | 91% |
| ACT composite: | 17-21 | Return as sophomores: | 68% |
| GPA 3.50 or higher: | 22% | Out-of-state: | 26% |
| GPA 3.0-3.49: | 34% | Live on campus: | 81% |
| GPA 2.0-2.99: | 44% | International: | 1% |

**Basis for selection.** High school GPA, test scores, strong academic course study important. Interview recommended for marginal students; portfolio recommended for art students. **Homeschooled:** State high school equivalency certificate required.

**High school preparation.** 13 units required. Required and recommended units include English 4, mathematics 3, social studies 2, science 2 (laboratory 1), foreign language 2 and academic electives 1.

**2008-2009 Annual costs.** Tuition/fees: $19,938. Room/board: $6,782.

**2007-2008 Financial aid. Need-based:** 188 full-time freshmen applied for aid; 169 were judged to have need; 168 of these received aid. Average need met was 72%. Average scholarship/grant was $4,614; average loan $4,172. 40% of total undergraduate aid awarded as scholarships/grants, 60% as loans/jobs. **Non-need-based:** Awarded to 882 full-time undergraduates, including 211 freshmen. Scholarships awarded for academics, alumni affiliation, art, athletics, leadership, minority status, music/drama, religious affiliation, state residency.

---

**Application procedures. Admission:** No deadline. $25 fee, may be waived for applicants with need. Application may be submitted online. Admission notification on a rolling basis. Must reply by May 1 or within 2 week(s) if notified thereafter. **Financial aid:** Priority date 4/1; no closing date. FAFSA required. Applicants notified on a rolling basis starting 5/1; must reply within 2 week(s) of notification.

**Academics. Special study options:** Cooperative education, double major, ESL, honors, independent study, internships, liberal arts/career combination, study abroad, teacher certification program, Washington semester, weekend college. **Credit/placement by examination:** AP, CLEP, IB, SAT, ACT, institutional tests. 30 credit hours maximum toward bachelor's degree. **Support services:** Remedial instruction, study skills assistance, tutoring, writing center.

**Majors. Biology:** General. **Business:** Accounting, business admin, human resources. **Communications:** Media studies. **Computer sciences:** General. **Conservation:** Environmental science. **Education:** Art, Deaf/hearing impaired, elementary, learning disabled, middle, physical, social studies. **English:** English lit. **Foreign languages:** Spanish. **Health:** Athletic training, nursing (RN). **History:** General. **Interdisciplinary:** Gerontology. **Liberal arts:** Arts/sciences. **Math:** General. **Parks/recreation:** Health/fitness, sports admin. **Philosophy/religion:** Religion. **Physical sciences:** Chemistry. **Protective services:** Criminal justice. **Psychology:** General. **Public administration:** Social work. **Social sciences:** Political science. **Visual/performing arts:** Dramatic, studio arts.

**Most popular majors.** Business/marketing 22%, education 14%, health sciences 13%, public administration/social services 8%, security/protective services 7%.

**Computing on campus.** 176 workstations in dormitories, library, computer center, student center. Dormitories wired for high-speed internet access and linked to campus network. Commuter students can connect to campus network. Online library, helpline, wireless network available.

**Student life. Freshman orientation:** Mandatory, $75 fee. Preregistration for classes offered. Two-day sessions held during June. **Housing:** Guaranteed on-campus for freshmen. Coed dorms, single-sex dorms, special housing for disabled, fraternity/sorority housing, substance-free housing available. $150 nonrefundable deposit, deadline 5/1. Full-time freshmen and sophomores not living with parents required to live on campus. Special permission required for students under 23 to live off-campus. **Activities:** Pep band, campus ministries, choral groups, dance, drama, literary magazine, musical theater, student government, student newspaper, symphony orchestra, TV station, Disciples on Campus, Fellowship of Christian Athletes, Habitat for Humanity, Alpha Phi Omega, Campus Conservatives, College Democrats, diversity education team, political science club, Campus Crusade for Christ.

**Athletics.** NCAA. **Intercollegiate:** Baseball M, basketball, cross-country, golf M, soccer, softball W, tennis, volleyball W. **Intramural:** Badminton, basketball, football (non-tackle), soccer, softball, tennis, volleyball. **Team name:** Bulldogs.

**Student services.** Adult student services, campus ministries, career counseling, student employment services, financial aid counseling, health services, personal counseling, placement for graduates. **Physically disabled:** Services for visually, hearing impaired.

**Contact.** E-mail: enroll@barton.edu
Phone: (252) 399-6317 Toll-free number: (800) 345-4973
Fax: (252) 399-6572
Amanda Humphrey, Director of Admissions, Barton College, Box 5000, Wilson, NC 27893-7000

---

## Belmont Abbey College
**Belmont, North Carolina**        CB member
www.belmontabbeycollege.edu        CB code: 5055

- Private 4-year liberal arts college affiliated with Roman Catholic Church
- Residential campus in small town
- 1,300 degree-seeking undergraduates: 6% part-time, 61% women, 21% African American, 1% Asian American, 5% Hispanic American, 3% international
- 70% of applicants admitted
- SAT or ACT with writing, interview required
- 48% graduate within 6 years; 15% enter graduate study

**General.** Founded in 1876. Regionally accredited. **Degrees:** 130 bachelor's awarded. **ROTC:** Army, Naval, Air Force. **Location:** 10 miles from Charlotte. **Calendar:** Semester, limited summer session. **Full-time faculty:** 55 total; 73% have terminal degrees, 4% minority, 42% women. **Part-time**

**faculty:** 64 total; 16% have terminal degrees, 5% minority, 56% women. **Class size:** 59% < 20, 41% 20-39, less than 1% 40-49.

**Freshman class profile.** 1,034 applied, 721 admitted, 210 enrolled.

| Mid 50% test scores | | Rank in top tenth: | 10% |
|---|---|---|---|
| SAT critical reading: | 450-570 | End year in good standing: | 64% |
| SAT math: | 460-550 | Return as sophomores: | 64% |
| ACT composite: | 17-23 | Out-of-state: | 63% |
| GPA 3.50 or higher: | 25% | Live on campus: | 90% |
| GPA 3.0-3.49: | 22% | International: | 2% |
| GPA 2.0-2.99: | 52% | Fraternities: | 20% |
| Rank in top quarter: | 29% | Sororities: | 20% |

**Basis for selection.** GPA, class rank, high school curriculum, and test scores most important. Personal accomplishments, extracurricular activities, and letters of recommendation strongly considered.

**High school preparation.** 16 units required. Required and recommended units include English 4, mathematics 3-4, social studies 1, history 1, science 2, foreign language 2-3 and academic electives 3. For science majors 4 math, 1 chemistry, 1 physics, 1 additional science recommended.

**2007-2008 Annual costs.** Tuition/fees: $19,680. Room/board: $9,713. Books/supplies: $900. Personal expenses: $1,800.

**2007-2008 Financial aid. Need-based:** Average need met was 60%. Average scholarship/grant was $11,610; average loan $3,310. 66% of total undergraduate aid awarded as scholarships/grants, 34% as loans/jobs. **Non-need-based:** Scholarships awarded for academics, athletics, leadership, religious affiliation, state residency.

**Application procedures. Admission:** Closing date 8/1 (postmark date). $35 fee, may be waived for applicants with need. Application may be submitted online. Admission notification on a rolling basis beginning on or about 9/15. Must reply by May 1 or within 3 week(s) if notified thereafter. **Financial aid:** Priority date 4/1; no closing date. FAFSA required. Applicants notified on a rolling basis starting 3/1; must reply within 2 week(s) of notification.

**Academics. Special study options:** Accelerated study, double major, dual enrollment of high school students, honors, independent study, internships, liberal arts/career combination, study abroad, teacher certification program, weekend college. **Credit/placement by examination:** AP, CLEP, IB, institutional tests. 30 credit hours maximum toward bachelor's degree. **Support services:** Learning center, study skills assistance, tutoring, writing center.

**Majors. Biology:** General. **Business:** Accounting, business admin, international. **Computer sciences:** Programming. **Education:** General, elementary. **English:** English lit. **Health:** Predental, premedicine, prepharmacy, preveterinary. **History:** General. **Legal studies:** Prelaw. **Liberal arts:** Arts/sciences. **Philosophy/religion:** Philosophy, religion. **Protective services:** Criminal justice. **Psychology:** General. **Social sciences:** General, criminology, economics, political science, sociology. **Other:** Applied Psychology.

**Most popular majors.** Business/marketing 43%, education 28%, philosophy/religious studies 7%, social sciences 7%.

**Computing on campus.** 56 workstations in library, computer center, student center. Dormitories wired for high-speed internet access and linked to campus network. Commuter students can connect to campus network. Online course registration, online library, helpline, wireless network available.

**Student life. Freshman orientation:** Mandatory. Preregistration for classes offered. 4 days prior to class start. **Housing:** Coed dorms, single-sex dorms, special housing for disabled, apartments available. $400 deposit, deadline 8/24. 24-hour quiet (honors) dorm available. **Activities:** Campus ministries, choral groups, drama, international student organizations, literary magazine, musical theater, student government, student newspaper, black student union, Alpha Phi Omega.

**Athletics.** NCAA. **Intercollegiate:** Baseball M, basketball, cheerleading, cross-country, golf, lacrosse, soccer, softball W, volleyball W, wrestling M. **Intramural:** Basketball, bowling, cross-country, football (non-tackle) M, golf, softball, table tennis, volleyball. **Team name:** Crusaders.

**Student services.** Adult student services, alcohol/substance abuse counseling, campus ministries, career counseling, student employment services, financial aid counseling, health services, personal counseling, placement for graduates, veterans' counselor. **Physically disabled:** Services for visually, speech, hearing impaired.

**Contact.** E-mail: admissions@bac.edu
Phone: (704) 825-6665 Toll-free number: (888) 222-0110
Fax: (704) 825-6220
Roger Jones, Director of Admissions, Belmont Abbey College, 100 Belmont - Mt. Holly Road, Belmont, NC 28012-2795

---

## Bennett College
**Greensboro, North Carolina**
**www.bennett.edu**
**CB member**
**CB code: 5058**

- Private 4-year liberal arts college for women affiliated with United Methodist Church
- Residential campus in small city
- 662 degree-seeking undergraduates: 1% part-time, 100% women, 97% African American, 1% Hispanic American, 1% international
- 48% of applicants admitted
- Application essay required
- 35% graduate within 6 years

**General.** Founded in 1873. Regionally accredited. **Degrees:** 81 bachelor's awarded. **ROTC:** Army, Air Force. **Location:** 26 miles from Winston-Salem, 96 miles from Charlotte. **Calendar:** Semester, limited summer session. **Full-time faculty:** 52 total; 65% have terminal degrees, 75% minority, 60% women. **Part-time faculty:** 27 total; 22% have terminal degrees, 56% minority, 63% women. **Class size:** 72% < 20, 25% 20-39, 3% 40-49. **Special facilities:** Women's Leadership Institute, Carnegie Negro Library.

**Freshman class profile.** 1,293 applied, 618 admitted, 223 enrolled.

| Mid 50% test scores | | Rank in top quarter: | 16% |
|---|---|---|---|
| SAT critical reading: | 360-450 | Rank in top tenth: | 5% |
| SAT math: | 350-440 | End year in good standing: | 72% |
| ACT composite: | 15-18 | Return as sophomores: | 60% |
| GPA 3.50 or higher: | 10% | Out-of-state: | 75% |
| GPA 3.0-3.49: | 19% | Live on campus: | 98% |
| GPA 2.0-2.99: | 60% | | |

**Basis for selection.** School achievement record, test scores, recommendations of counselors, and applicant's personal statement important. SAT or ACT recommended. Interview recommended for borderline students. **Homeschooled:** Transcript of courses and grades, letter of recommendation (nonparent) required.

**High school preparation.** 18 units required. Required units include English 4, mathematics 3, social studies 2, science 2, foreign language 2 and academic electives 5.

**2007-2008 Annual costs.** Tuition/fees: $14,648. Room/board: $6,478. Books/supplies: $1,200. Personal expenses: $3,000.

**2007-2008 Financial aid. Need-based:** 220 full-time freshmen applied for aid; 211 were judged to have need; 208 of these received aid. Average need met was 43%. Average scholarship/grant was $7,834; average loan $3,252. 44% of total undergraduate aid awarded as scholarships/grants, 56% as loans/jobs. **Non-need-based:** Awarded to 51 full-time undergraduates, including 13 freshmen. Scholarships awarded for state residency.

**Application procedures. Admission:** No deadline. $30 fee, may be waived for applicants with need. Application may be submitted online. Admission notification on a rolling basis. **Financial aid:** Closing date 4/15. FAFSA, institutional form required. Applicants notified by 7/15.

**Academics.** Accepted students who do not meet required SAT or ACT score admitted to Academic Enrichment Program which provides tutoring, counseling and other support services. **Special study options:** Accelerated study, cooperative education, cross-registration, double major, exchange student, honors, independent study, internships, liberal arts/career combination, student-designed major, study abroad, teacher certification program, Washington semester. Dual degree programs in nursing and engineering with North Carolina Agricultural and Technical State University. **Credit/placement by examination:** AP, CLEP, SAT, ACT, institutional tests. **Support services:** Learning center, pre-admission summer program, reduced course load, remedial instruction, tutoring, writing center.

**Majors. Biology:** General. **Business:** Accounting, business admin. **Communications:** Media studies. **Computer sciences:** General. **Education:** Elementary, English, mathematics, mentally handicapped, middle, music. **English:** English lit. **Math:** General. **Physical sciences:** Chemistry. **Psychology:** General. **Public administration:** Social work. **Social sciences:** Political science, sociology. **Visual/performing arts:** General, arts management.

**Most popular majors.** Biology 16%, business/marketing 10%, communications/journalism 16%, education 9%, interdisciplinary studies 6%, psychology 14%, public administration/social services 9%, social sciences 14%.

**Computing on campus.** 130 workstations in dormitories, library, computer center. Dormitories wired for high-speed internet access. Commuter students can connect to campus network. Online library, wireless network available.

**Student life. Freshman orientation:** Mandatory, $100 fee. Preregistration for classes offered. **Housing:** Guaranteed on-campus for all undergraduates. Substance-free housing available. $100 deposit. Students with GPA of 3.0 may reside in honor residence hall. **Activities:** Choral groups, dance, drama, film society, literary magazine, music ensembles, radio station, student government, student newspaper, TV station, Student Christian Fellowship, NAACP, social work club, Women in Communications, student teachers association, psychology club, political science club.

**Athletics.** NCAA. **Intercollegiate:** Basketball W, cross-country W, softball W, tennis W, track and field W, volleyball W. **Intramural:** Basketball W, softball W, swimming W, tennis W, volleyball W. **Team name:** Belles.

**Student services.** Campus ministries, career counseling, student employment services, financial aid counseling, health services, on-campus daycare, personal counseling, placement for graduates.

**Contact.** E-mail: admiss@bennett.edu
Phone: (336) 370-8624 Toll-free number: (800) 413-5323
Fax: (336) 517-2166
Ulisa Bowles, Director of Admissions, Bennett College, 900 East Washington Street, Greensboro, NC 27401-3239

---

## Brevard College
**Brevard, North Carolina**                          **CB member**
**www.brevard.edu**                                 **CB code: 5067**

- Private 4-year liberal arts college affiliated with United Methodist Church
- Residential campus in small town
- 647 degree-seeking undergraduates: 3% part-time, 41% women, 7% African American, 1% Hispanic American, 1% Native American, 2% international
- 63% of applicants admitted
- SAT or ACT (ACT writing recommended), application essay required
- 32% graduate within 6 years

**General.** Founded in 1853. Regionally accredited. **Degrees:** 109 bachelor's awarded. **Location:** 33 miles from Asheville. **Calendar:** Semester. **Full-time faculty:** 57 total; 74% have terminal degrees, 46% women. **Part-time faculty:** 37 total; 30% have terminal degrees, 40% women. **Class size:** 77% < 20, 23% 20-39, less than 1% 50-99. **Special facilities:** Mountain climbing wall, ropes challenge course, Appalachian center for environmental solutions, fitness appraisal lab, transformational leadership, forest institute, performing arts center, policy center, academic enrichment center.

**Freshman class profile.** 1,050 applied, 663 admitted, 169 enrolled.

| Mid 50% test scores | | Rank in top quarter: | 17% |
|---|---|---|---|
| SAT critical reading: | 440-540 | Rank in top tenth: | 5% |
| SAT math: | 460-560 | End year in good standing: | 76% |
| ACT composite: | 18-25 | Return as sophomores: | 57% |
| GPA 3.50 or higher: | 28% | Out-of-state: | 53% |
| GPA 3.0-3.49: | 30% | Live on campus: | 93% |
| GPA 2.0-2.99: | 41% | International: | 2% |

**Basis for selection.** High school record, class rank, SAT/ACT scores, references, extracurricular activities, recommendations, essay, interview, talent/ability, character/personal qualities, volunteer work important. Essay, interview recommended for all students; portfolio required for art students; audition required for music students. **Homeschooled:** Statement describing homeschool structure and mission, transcript of courses and grades required. Legal documentation from homeschool agency, local school district, or State Department of Education and admissions interview required. **Learning Disabled:** Evaluation by licensed professional within past 3 years.

**High school preparation.** 22 units recommended. Recommended units include English 4, mathematics 3, social studies 4, history 1, science 3 (laboratory 1), foreign language 2 and academic electives 4. Math units should include 2 algebra and 1 geometry.

**2008-2009 Annual costs.** Tuition/fees: $20,050. Telecommunications fee $600 for on-campus residents. Room/board: $7,540. Books/supplies: $1,000. Personal expenses: $1,000.

**2007-2008 Financial aid. Need-based:** Average need met was 74%. Average scholarship/grant was $11,700; average loan $3,740. 76% of total undergraduate aid awarded as scholarships/grants, 24% as loans/jobs. **Non-need-based:** Scholarships awarded for academics, art, athletics, job skills, leadership, minority status, music/drama, religious affiliation, state residency.

**Application procedures. Admission:** No deadline. $30 fee, may be waived for applicants with need. Application may be submitted online. Admission notification on a rolling basis beginning on or about 7/1. **Financial aid:** Priority date 4/15; no closing date. FAFSA required. Applicants notified on a rolling basis starting 2/1; must reply within 4 week(s) of notification.

**Academics. Special study options:** Double major, dual enrollment of high school students, honors, independent study, internships, student-designed major, study abroad, teacher certification program. **Credit/placement by examination:** AP, CLEP, IB, SAT, ACT, institutional tests. 92 credit hours maximum toward bachelor's degree. **Support services:** Learning center, reduced course load, remedial instruction, study skills assistance, tutoring, writing center.

**Majors. Biology:** Ecology. **Business:** Business admin. **Conservation:** Environmental science, environmental studies. **Education:** General, art, drama/dance, elementary, English, mathematics, multi-level teacher, music, physical, science, secondary, social studies. **English:** English lit. **Health:** Health services, predental, premedicine, prenursing, preveterinary. **History:** General. **Interdisciplinary:** Biological/physical sciences. **Liberal arts:** Arts/sciences. **Math:** General. **Parks/recreation:** Exercise sciences, facilities management. **Philosophy/religion:** Religion. **Protective services:** Law enforcement admin. **Psychology:** General. **Visual/performing arts:** Art, dramatic, music performance.

**Most popular majors.** Business/marketing 17%, English 6%, interdisciplinary studies 14%, natural resources/environmental science 7%, parks/recreation 25%, visual/performing arts 15%.

**Computing on campus.** 100 workstations in dormitories, library, computer center, student center. Dormitories wired for high-speed internet access and linked to campus network. Online library, helpline, wireless network available.

**Student life. Freshman orientation:** Mandatory, $95 fee. Preregistration for classes offered. **Housing:** Guaranteed on-campus for all undergraduates. Coed dorms, single-sex dorms, substance-free housing available. All non-county or non-adjacent-county residents required to live on campus until age 21. **Activities:** Bands, choral groups, dance, drama, literary magazine, music ensembles, musical theater, opera, student government, student newspaper, recycling club, Fellowship of Christian Athletes, Omicron Delta Kappa, outing club, environmental educators, history club, Young Politicians of America, business club, debate society.

**Athletics.** NCAA. **Intercollegiate:** Baseball M, basketball, cheerleading, cross-country, football (tackle) M, golf M, soccer, softball W, tennis, track and field, volleyball W. **Intramural:** Archery, badminton, basketball, bowling, cross-country, equestrian, football (tackle) M, golf, skiing, soccer, softball, swimming, tennis, track and field, volleyball. **Team name:** Tornados.

**Student services.** Alcohol/substance abuse counseling, campus ministries, career counseling, student employment services, financial aid counseling, health services, personal counseling, placement for graduates, veterans' counselor. **Physically disabled:** Services for visually, speech, hearing impaired.

**Contact.** E-mail: admissions@brevard.edu
Phone: (828) 884-8300 Toll-free number: (800) 527-9090
Fax: (828) 884-3790
Ken Sigler, Director of Admissions, Brevard College, One Brevard College Drive, Brevard, NC 28712

---

## Cabarrus College of Health Sciences
**Concord, North Carolina**
**www.cabarruscollege.edu**                          **CB code: 5136**

- Private 4-year health science and nursing college
- Commuter campus in small city
- 353 degree-seeking undergraduates: 36% part-time, 88% women, 6% African American, 1% Asian American, 2% Hispanic American
- 62% of applicants admitted
- Application essay required
- 60% graduate within 6 years

**General.** Regionally accredited. **Degrees:** 15 bachelor's, 92 associate awarded. **Location:** 25 miles from Charlotte. **Calendar:** Semester, limited summer session. **Full-time faculty:** 26 total. **Part-time faculty:** 28 total. **Class size:** 67% < 20, 24% 20-39, 7% 40-49, 2% 50-99.

**Freshman class profile.** 66 applied, 41 admitted, 38 enrolled.

| Mid 50% test scores | | GPA 3.0-3.49: | 23% |
|---|---|---|---|
| SAT critical reading: | 460-540 | GPA 2.0-2.99: | 14% |
| SAT math: | 460-570 | Rank in top quarter: | 55% |
| ACT composite: | 19-28 | Rank in top tenth: | 6% |
| GPA 3.50 or higher: | 63% | | |

**Basis for selection.** School record, class rank, essay, test scores, and recommendations most important.

**High school preparation.** Required and recommended units include English 4, mathematics 2, science 2 (laboratory 2) and foreign language 2.

**2007-2008 Annual costs.** Tuition/fees: $8,750. Books/supplies: $1,300.

**Application procedures. Admission:** Priority date 3/1; no deadline. $35 fee. Application may be submitted online.

**Academics. Special study options:** Cross-registration, distance learning, liberal arts/career combination. **Credit/placement by examination:** AP, CLEP, institutional tests. 15 credit hours maximum toward associate degree, 15 toward bachelor's. **Support services:** Learning center, pre-admission summer program, study skills assistance.

**Majors. Health:** Health care admin, health services admin, nursing (RN).

**Computing on campus.** 24 workstations in library, computer center, student center. Commuter students can connect to campus network. Online library, wireless network available.

**Student life. Freshman orientation:** Mandatory. Preregistration for classes offered. 2-day orientation before start of first semester. **Activities:** Student government, student newspaper, Christian student union, association of nursing students, Rotaract.

**Student services.** Career counseling, financial aid counseling, on-campus daycare, personal counseling. **Physically disabled:** Services for hearing impaired.

**Contact.** E-mail: admissions@cabarruscollege.edu
Phone: (704) 783-1556 Fax: (704) 783-2077
Mark Ellison, Director of Admissions, Cabarrus College of Health Sciences, 401 Medical Park Drive, Concord, NC 28025-2405

## Campbell University
**Buies Creek, North Carolina**
www.campbell.edu

**CB member**
**CB code: 5100**

- Private 4-year university and liberal arts college affiliated with Baptist State Convention of North Carolina
- Residential campus in small town
- 2,806 degree-seeking undergraduates: 3% part-time, 52% women
- 1,809 degree-seeking graduate students
- 60% of applicants admitted
- SAT or ACT with writing required

**General.** Founded in 1887. Regionally accredited. **Degrees:** 932 bachelor's, 146 associate awarded; master's, doctoral, first professional offered. **ROTC:** Army. **Location:** 30 miles from Raleigh, 30 miles from Fayetteville. **Calendar:** Semester, extensive summer session. **Full-time faculty:** 196 total; 91% have terminal degrees, 33% women. **Part-time faculty:** 109 total; 47% have terminal degrees, 29% women. **Class size:** 54% < 20, 31% 20-39, 5% 40-49, 9% 50-99, less than 1% >100. **Special facilities:** Golf course, museum, geological collection, drug information center, nature trail.

**Freshman class profile.** 3,348 applied, 2,001 admitted, 899 enrolled.

| GPA 3.50 or higher: | 71% | Rank in top tenth: | 38% |
|---|---|---|---|
| GPA 3.0-3.49: | 21% | Out-of-state: | 22% |
| GPA 2.0-2.99: | 8% | Live on campus: | 80% |
| Rank in top quarter: | 80% | International: | 3% |

**Basis for selection.** 950 SAT (exclusive of Writing); GPA, course selection, class rank, and standardized test scores considered. Students with less than the acceptable threshold may be considered for probational admission. Candidates reviewed on an individual basis. Interview, essay recommended for all students; audition recommended for music programs.

**High school preparation.** 13 units recommended. Recommended units include English 4, mathematics 3, social studies 2, science 2 (laboratory 1) and foreign language 2. One social science should be U.S. History. Math units must include algebra I and II as well as geometry.

**2008-2009 Annual costs.** Tuition/fees (projected): $20,300. Room/board: $6,800. Books/supplies: $1,200. Personal expenses: $3,080.

**2007-2008 Financial aid. Need-based:** 716 full-time freshmen applied for aid; 597 were judged to have need; 597 of these received aid. Average need met was 100%. Average scholarship/grant was $5,459; average loan $2,918. 54% of total undergraduate aid awarded as scholarships/grants, 46% as loans/jobs. **Non-need-based:** Awarded to 2,892 full-time undergraduates, including 821 freshmen. Scholarships awarded for academics, athletics, music/drama, religious affiliation, ROTC, state residency.

**Application procedures. Admission:** No deadline. $35 fee, may be waived for applicants with need. Application may be submitted online. Admission notification on a rolling basis. **Financial aid:** Priority date 3/15; no closing date. FAFSA required. Applicants notified on a rolling basis starting 4/15; must reply within 2 week(s) of notification.

**Academics. Special study options:** Accelerated study, combined bachelor's/graduate degree, cooperative education, distance learning, double major, dual enrollment of high school students, exchange student, honors, independent study, internships, liberal arts/career combination, study abroad, teacher certification program, Washington semester. 3-2 engineering program with North Carolina State University. **Credit/placement by examination:** AP, CLEP, IB, SAT, institutional tests. 64 credit hours maximum toward bachelor's degree. **Support services:** Reduced course load, remedial instruction, study skills assistance, tutoring, writing center.

**Majors. Biology:** General, biochemistry. **Business:** General, accounting, business admin, communications, financial planning, international, management information systems. **Communications:** Advertising, broadcast journalism, journalism, public relations, radio/tv. **Computer sciences:** Computer graphics, computer science, information systems. **Education:** General, biology, elementary, English, family/consumer sciences, French, history, mathematics, middle, music, physical, social studies, Spanish. **English:** British lit, English lit. **Family/consumer sciences:** General, child development, family studies. **Foreign languages:** French, Spanish. **Health:** Athletic training, predental, premedicine, prepharmacy, preveterinary. **History:** General. **Legal studies:** Prelaw. **Math:** General. **Parks/recreation:** Exercise sciences, facilities management, health/fitness, sports admin. **Philosophy/religion:** Religion. **Physical sciences:** Chemistry. **Protective services:** Criminal justice. **Psychology:** General. **Public administration:** General, social work. **Social sciences:** Economics, international relations, political science. **Theology:** Sacred music. **Visual/performing arts:** Commercial/advertising art, dramatic, piano/organ, studio arts, voice/opera.

**Most popular majors.** Business/marketing 28%, health sciences 6%, liberal arts 12%, psychology 10%, social sciences 6%.

**Computing on campus.** 250 workstations in library, computer center, student center. Dormitories wired for high-speed internet access and linked to campus network. Commuter students can connect to campus network. Helpline, wireless network available.

**Student life. Freshman orientation:** Mandatory, $40 fee. Preregistration for classes offered. Two weekend sessions in summer available to incoming freshmen and their families for students entering in Fall. Short program before class start for students entering in Spring. **Policies:** Religious observance required. **Housing:** Guaranteed on-campus for all undergraduates. Single-sex dorms, special housing for disabled, apartments, substance-free housing available. $100 fully refundable deposit. **Activities:** Bands, choral groups, drama, international student organizations, literary magazine, music ensembles, musical theater, radio station, student government, student newspaper, Baptist Student Union, College Democrats/Republicans, Fellowship of Christian Athletes, North Carolina Student Legislators, Campus Crusade, Christians in Action, Campbell Catholic Community, Circle K.

**Athletics.** NCAA. **Intercollegiate:** Baseball M, basketball, cheerleading W, cross-country, golf, soccer, softball W, swimming W, tennis, track and field, volleyball W, wrestling M. **Intramural:** Basketball, cricket M, football (non-tackle), soccer, softball, swimming, table tennis, tennis, triathlon, volleyball, water polo. **Team name:** Fighting Camels.

**Student services.** Adult student services, alcohol/substance abuse counseling, campus ministries, career counseling, student employment services, financial aid counseling, health services, personal counseling, placement for graduates, veterans' counselor. **Physically disabled:** Services for visually, speech, hearing impaired.

**Contact.** E-mail: adm@mailcenter.campbell.edu
Phone: (910) 893-1200 ext. 1290 Toll-free
number: (800) 334-4111 ext. 1290 Fax: (910) 893-1288
Peggy Mason, Director of Admissions, Campbell University, PO Box 546, Buies Creek, NC 27506

## Carolina Christian College
**Winston-Salem, North Carolina**
**www.wsbc.edu**

- Private 4-year Bible college affiliated with Church of Christ
- Residential campus in small city
- 44 degree-seeking undergraduates

**General.** Accredited by ABHE. **Degrees:** 16 bachelor's, 2 associate awarded. **Calendar:** Semester. **Full-time faculty:** 2 total. **Part-time faculty:** 11 total.

**Basis for selection.** COMPASS test required.

**2007-2008 Annual costs.** Tuition/fees: $2,430.

**Application procedures. Admission:** No deadline. $50 fee. Admission notification on a rolling basis. **Financial aid:** No deadline.

**Academics. Credit/placement by examination:** CLEP.

**Majors. Theology:** Bible.

**Student life. Freshman orientation:** Available.

**Contact.** Phone: (336) 744-0900
Carolina Christian College, Box 777, Winston-Salem, NC 27105

## Catawba College
**Salisbury, North Carolina**          **CB member**
**www.catawba.edu**          **CB code: 5103**

- Private 4-year liberal arts college affiliated with United Church of Christ
- Residential campus in large town
- 1,291 degree-seeking undergraduates: 5% part-time, 50% women, 16% African American, 1% Asian American, 1% Hispanic American, 1% Native American, 1% international
- 32 degree-seeking graduate students
- 75% of applicants admitted
- SAT or ACT with writing, application essay required
- 38% graduate within 6 years; 13% enter graduate study

**General.** Founded in 1851. Regionally accredited. **Degrees:** 271 bachelor's awarded; master's offered. **ROTC:** Army. **Location:** 30 miles from Charlotte, 50 miles from Greensboro. **Calendar:** Semester, limited summer session. **Full-time faculty:** 70 total; 83% have terminal degrees, 3% minority, 40% women. **Part-time faculty:** 35 total; 40% have terminal degrees, 49% women. **Class size:** 59% < 20, 40% 20-39, 1% 40-49, less than 1% 50-99. **Special facilities:** Comprehensive three-manual Casavant pipe-organ, observatory, 45-acre outdoor biological laboratory, nature preserve.

**Freshman class profile.** 822 applied, 620 admitted, 266 enrolled.

| Mid 50% test scores | | Rank in top quarter: | 45% |
|---|---|---|---|
| SAT critical reading: | 450-570 | Rank in top tenth: | 13% |
| SAT math: | 470-580 | Return as sophomores: | 71% |
| ACT composite: | 18-25 | Out-of-state: | 45% |
| GPA 3.50 or higher: | 42% | Live on campus: | 93% |
| GPA 3.0-3.49: | 30% | International: | 2% |
| GPA 2.0-2.99: | 27% | | |

**Basis for selection.** School achievement record, class rank, standardized test scores, school recommendations important. SAT preferred, but ACT also accepted. Interview recommended for all students; audition recommended for drama, music programs.

**High school preparation.** 16 units required. Required and recommended units include English 4, mathematics 2-3, social studies 3, science 2-3 (laboratory 3), foreign language 2 and academic electives 1. Required credits must be academic subjects at college preparatory level.

**2008-2009 Annual costs.** Tuition/fees: $22,290. Room/board: $7,700. Books/supplies: $800. Personal expenses: $1,200.

**2007-2008 Financial aid. Need-based:** Average need met was 84%. Average scholarship/grant was $5,053; average loan $4,539. 45% of total undergraduate aid awarded as scholarships/grants, 55% as loans/jobs. **Non-need-based:** Awarded to 1,320 full-time undergraduates, including 115 freshmen. Scholarships awarded for academics, athletics, music/drama, state residency.

**Application procedures. Admission:** Priority date 3/15; no deadline. $30 fee, may be waived for applicants with need. Application may be submitted online. Admission notification on a rolling basis beginning on or about 10/1. **Financial aid:** Priority date 3/15; no closing date. FAFSA required. Applicants notified on a rolling basis starting 11/1; must reply within 2 week(s) of notification.

**Academics. Special study options:** Cross-registration, double major, dual enrollment of high school students, honors, independent study, internships, liberal arts/career combination, student-designed major, study abroad, teacher certification program. **Credit/placement by examination:** AP, CLEP, IB, institutional tests. 30 credit hours maximum toward bachelor's degree. **Support services:** Learning center, study skills assistance, tutoring, writing center.

**Majors. Biology:** General. **Business:** Accounting, business admin. **Communications:** General. **Computer sciences:** General. **Conservation:** Environmental science, environmental studies. **Education:** Elementary, gifted/talented, middle, music, physical. **English:** English lit. **Foreign languages:** French, Spanish. **Health:** Athletic training, recreational therapy. **History:** General. **Legal studies:** Prelaw. **Math:** General. **Parks/recreation:** General, health/fitness, sports admin. **Philosophy/religion:** Religion. **Physical sciences:** Chemistry. **Protective services:** Law enforcement admin. **Psychology:** General. **Public administration:** General. **Social sciences:** Political science, sociology. **Visual/performing arts:** Arts management, dramatic, music performance.

**Most popular majors.** Business/marketing 38%, education 8%, parks/recreation 6%, security/protective services 6%, visual/performing arts 13%.

**Computing on campus.** 100 workstations in dormitories, library, computer center. Dormitories wired for high-speed internet access and linked to campus network. Commuter students can connect to campus network. Helpline, repair service, wireless network available.

**Student life. Freshman orientation:** Mandatory. Orientation program week prior to start of fall classes. Optional summer orientation programs for students and parents at additional cost. **Housing:** Guaranteed on-campus for all undergraduates. Coed dorms, single-sex dorms, substance-free housing available. $200 deposit. **Activities:** Bands, choral groups, dance, drama, literary magazine, music ensembles, musical theater, student government, student newspaper, symphony orchestra, Alpha program, Athenian society, Helen Foil Beard Society, political science association, environmental service clubs, Fellowship of Christian Athletes, multi-cultural club, Philomathean club, volunteer club.

**Athletics.** NCAA. **Intercollegiate:** Baseball M, basketball, cross-country, field hockey W, football (tackle) M, golf, lacrosse M, soccer, softball W, swimming, tennis, volleyball W. **Intramural:** Basketball, cross-country, football (tackle) M, golf, handball, racquetball, soccer, softball, table tennis, tennis, volleyball. **Team name:** Catawba Indians.

**Student services.** Adult student services, alcohol/substance abuse counseling, campus ministries, career counseling, student employment services, financial aid counseling, health services, personal counseling, placement for graduates. **Physically disabled:** Services for hearing impaired.

**Contact.** E-mail: admission@catawba.edu
Phone: (704) 637-4402 Toll-free number: (800) 228-2922
Fax: (704) 637-4422
J Bitzer, Dean of Admissions, Catawba College, 2300 West Innes Street, Salisbury, NC 28144

## Chowan University
**Murfreesboro, North Carolina**          **CB member**
**www.chowan.edu**          **CB code: 5107**

- Private 4-year university and liberal arts college affiliated with Southern Baptist Convention
- Residential campus in rural community
- 893 degree-seeking undergraduates: 9% part-time, 52% women
- 56% of applicants admitted
- SAT or ACT (ACT writing optional) required
- 31% graduate within 6 years

**General.** Founded in 1848. Regionally accredited. **Degrees:** 89 bachelor's, 2 associate awarded. **Location:** 80 miles from Norfolk Virginia, 130 miles from Raleigh. **Calendar:** Semester, limited summer session. **Full-time faculty:** 50 total. **Part-time faculty:** 20 total. **Class size:** 64% < 20, 33% 20-39, 2% 40-49, less than 1% 50-99. **Special facilities:** Graphic communications center.

**Freshman class profile.** 2,942 applied, 1,660 admitted, 336 enrolled.

| Mid 50% test scores | | | |
|---|---|---|---|
| SAT critical reading: | 380-470 | Return as sophomores: | 43% |
| SAT math: | 380-480 | Out-of-state: | 55% |
| SAT writing: | 380-470 | Live on campus: | 84% |
| ACT composite: | 15-21 | Fraternities: | 11% |
| | | Sororities: | 20% |

**Basis for selection.** School achievement record most important. Essay, interview recommended for all students; audition required for music majors; portfolio required for graphic design and studio art majors. **Home-schooled:** State high school equivalency certificate required.

**High school preparation.** College-preparatory program recommended. Recommended units include English 4, mathematics 3, social studies 2, science 2 (laboratory 2) and academic electives 7.

**2007-2008 Annual costs.** Tuition/fees: $16,920. $90 Communications fee for residents only. Room/board: $7,000. Books/supplies: $864. Personal expenses: $1,000.

**Financial aid. Non-need-based:** Scholarships awarded for academics, athletics, leadership, music/drama, religious affiliation, state residency.

**Application procedures. Admission:** No deadline. $20 fee, may be waived for applicants with need. Application may be submitted online. Admission notification on a rolling basis. Must reply by May 1 or within 2 week(s) if notified thereafter. **Financial aid:** Priority date 3/1; no closing date. FAFSA required. Applicants notified on a rolling basis starting 3/1; must reply within 2 week(s) of notification.

**Academics. Special study options:** Distance learning, double major, dual enrollment of high school students, honors, independent study, internships, liberal arts/career combination, teacher certification program. **Credit/placement by examination:** AP, CLEP, IB, SAT. 15 credit hours maximum toward associate degree, 15 toward bachelor's. **Support services:** Learning center, reduced course load, remedial instruction, study skills assistance, tutoring.

**Majors. Biology:** General. **Business:** Accounting/business management, business admin, information resources management, marketing, small business admin. **Communications technology:** Graphics. **Education:** General, elementary, English, history, music, physical, secondary. **English:** English lit. **Health:** Athletic training, predental, premedicine, prenursing, prepharmacy, preveterinary. **History:** General. **Liberal arts:** Arts/sciences. **Parks/recreation:** Exercise sciences, health/fitness, sports admin. **Philosophy/religion:** Religion. **Physical sciences:** General. **Protective services:** Law enforcement admin. **Psychology:** General. **Visual/performing arts:** Graphic design, music performance, studio arts.

**Most popular majors.** Biology 12%, business/marketing 11%, communications/journalism 12%, education 17%, history 8%, parks/recreation 7%, psychology 7%, security/protective services 10%, visual/performing arts 10%.

**Computing on campus.** 219 workstations in dormitories, library, computer center. Dormitories wired for high-speed internet access and linked to campus network. Commuter students can connect to campus network. Online course registration, online library, helpline, repair service available.

**Student life. Freshman orientation:** Mandatory, $50 fee. Preregistration for classes offered. **Policies:** No alcohol on campus; restricted dorm visitation; academic honor code. **Housing:** Guaranteed on-campus for all undergraduates. Single-sex dorms, substance-free housing available. $200 partly refundable deposit, deadline 5/1. **Activities:** Bands, choral groups, drama, literary magazine, music ensembles, student government, Christian student union, Student National Education Association, Fellowship of Christian Athletes, Rotaract, international student association, Voices of Inspiration, College Democrats, College Republicans, history club, women's club.

**Athletics.** NCAA, NCCAA. **Intercollegiate:** Baseball M, basketball, cheerleading, cross-country W, football (tackle) M, golf, soccer, softball W, tennis, volleyball W. **Intramural:** Badminton, basketball, football (non-tackle) M, golf, handball, racquetball, softball, swimming, table tennis, tennis, volleyball W. **Team name:** Hawks.

**Student services.** Campus ministries, career counseling, student employment services, financial aid counseling, health services, personal counseling, placement for graduates, veterans' counselor.

**Contact.** E-mail: admissions@chowan.edu
Phone: (252) 398-1235 Toll-free number: (800) 488-4101
Fax: (252) 398-1190
Jonathan Wirt, Vice President for Enrollment Management, Chowan University, One University Place, Murfreesboro, NC 27855-9901

---

## Davidson College

Davidson, North Carolina
www.davidson.edu

CB member
CB code: 5150

- Private 4-year liberal arts college affiliated with Presbyterian Church (USA)
- Residential campus in small town
- 1,667 degree-seeking undergraduates: 50% women, 7% African American, 3% Asian American, 4% Hispanic American, 1% Native American, 3% international
- 28% of applicants admitted
- SAT or ACT (ACT writing optional), application essay required
- 92% graduate within 6 years

**General.** Founded in 1837. Regionally accredited. **Degrees:** 449 bachelor's awarded. **ROTC:** Army, Air Force. **Location:** 19 miles from Charlotte. **Calendar:** Semester. **Full-time faculty:** 167 total; 96% have terminal degrees, 16% minority, 36% women. **Part-time faculty:** 11 total; 82% have terminal degrees, 18% minority, 64% women. **Class size:** 71% < 20, 28% 20-39, 1% 40-49. **Special facilities:** Laser facility, electron microscope, campus arboretum.

**Freshman class profile.** 3,992 applied, 1,127 admitted, 467 enrolled.

| Mid 50% test scores | | | |
|---|---|---|---|
| SAT critical reading: | 630-730 | Rank in top tenth: | 83% |
| SAT math: | 640-710 | Return as sophomores: | 96% |
| ACT composite: | 28-32 | Out-of-state: | 80% |
| GPA 3.50 or higher: | 95% | Live on campus: | 100% |
| GPA 3.0-3.49: | 5% | International: | 4% |
| Rank in top quarter: | 98% | Fraternities: | 44% |

**Basis for selection.** GED not accepted. Course selection, rigor of program, grades, recommendations, essays, test scores, class rank considered. SAT and SAT Subject Tests or ACT recommended. Campus visit strongly recommended.

**High school preparation.** 16 units required. Required and recommended units include English 4, mathematics 3-4, science 2-4 and foreign language 2-4. Foreign language units should be in same language. 2 required, 4 recommended for social studies or history units.

**2008-2009 Annual costs.** Tuition/fees: $33,479. Room/board: $9,471. Books/supplies: $1,000. Personal expenses: $1,325.

**2006-2007 Financial aid. Need-based:** 231 full-time freshmen applied for aid; 152 were judged to have need; 148 of these received aid. Average need met was 100%. Average scholarship/grant was $19,364; average loan $2,974. 89% of total undergraduate aid awarded as scholarships/grants, 11% as loans/jobs. **Non-need-based:** Awarded to 724 full-time undergraduates, including 189 freshmen. Scholarships awarded for academics, art, athletics, leadership, minority status, music/drama, ROTC.

**Application procedures. Admission:** Closing date 1/2 (postmark date). $50 fee, may be waived for applicants with need. Admission notification 4/1. Must reply by 5/1. **Financial aid:** Closing date 2/15. FAFSA, CSS PROFILE required. Applicants notified by 4/1; must reply by 5/1.

**Academics.** 2-year interdisciplinary course in humanities available for freshmen and sophomores. Center for Special Studies supervises student-designed majors. **Special study options:** Cross-registration, double major, exchange student, honors, independent study, student-designed major, study abroad, teacher certification program, Washington semester. Visiting student program with Howard University and Morehouse College; Dean Rusk program in International Studies; Philadelphia Center Pro-School for Field Studies. **Credit/placement by examination:** AP, CLEP, IB, institutional tests. **Support services:** Tutoring, writing center.

**Majors. Biology:** General. **English:** English lit. **Foreign languages:** Classics, French, German, Spanish. **History:** General. **Math:** General. **Philosophy/religion:** Philosophy, religion. **Physical sciences:** Chemistry, physics. **Psychology:** General. **Social sciences:** Anthropology, economics, political science, sociology. **Visual/performing arts:** Art, dramatic.

**Most popular majors.** Biology 12%, English 14%, foreign language 9%, history 12%, psychology 6%, social sciences 29%.

**Computing on campus.** 142 workstations in dormitories, library, computer center, student center. Dormitories wired for high-speed internet access and linked to campus network. Commuter students can connect to campus network. Online course registration, helpline, repair service, wireless network available.

**Student life. Freshman orientation:** Mandatory, $100 fee. Preregistration for classes offered. **Housing:** Guaranteed on-campus for freshmen. Coed dorms, apartments, substance-free housing available. Substance-free, suite/apartment-style housing available. **Activities:** Bands, choral groups, dance, drama, literary magazine, music ensembles, musical theater, radio station, student government, student newspaper, symphony orchestra, black student coalition, Amnesty International, Young Democrats, College Republicans, Habitat for Humanity, Asia 3D, gender resource center.

**Athletics.** NCAA. **Intercollegiate:** Baseball M, basketball, cross-country, diving, field hockey W, football (tackle) M, golf M, lacrosse W, soccer, swimming, tennis, track and field, volleyball W, wrestling M. **Intramural:** Basketball, football (non-tackle), soccer, softball, volleyball. **Team name:** Wildcats.

**Student services.** Alcohol/substance abuse counseling, campus ministries, career counseling, financial aid counseling, health services, minority student services, personal counseling, placement for graduates. **Physically disabled:** Services for visually, hearing impaired.

**Contact.** E-mail: admission@davidson.edu
Phone: (704) 894-2230 Toll-free number: (800) 768-0380
Fax: (704) 894-2016
Christopher Gruber, Vice President and Dean of Admission and Financial Aid, Davidson College, Box 7156, Davidson, NC 28035-7156

---

## DeVry University: Charlotte
**Charlotte, North Carolina**
**www.devry.edu**

- For-profit 4-year university
- Commuter campus in very large city
- 107 degree-seeking undergraduates: 51% part-time, 54% women, 61% African American, 3% Asian American, 7% Hispanic American
- 113 degree-seeking graduate students
- Interview required

**General. Degrees:** 11 bachelor's awarded; master's offered. **Calendar:** Semester. **Full-time faculty:** 3 total. **Part-time faculty:** 9 total; 22% minority, 44% women.

**Freshman class profile.**

| | | | |
|---|---|---|---|
| Return as sophomores: | 44% | Out-of-state: | 19% |

**Basis for selection.** Academic record considered.

**2007-2008 Annual costs.** Tuition/fees: $13,020. Books/supplies: $1,300. Personal expenses: $5,082.

**Financial aid. Non-need-based:** Scholarships awarded for academics.

**Application procedures. Admission:** No deadline. $50 fee. Admission notification on a rolling basis. **Financial aid:** No deadline. FAFSA required. Applicants notified on a rolling basis.

**Academics. Special study options:** Accelerated study, distance learning. **Credit/placement by examination:** CLEP.

**Majors. Business:** Business admin. **Computer sciences:** General. **Other:** Technology management.

**Contact.** Phone: (704) 362-2345
DeVry University: Charlotte, 4521 Sharon Road, Charlotte, NC 28211

---

## Duke University
**Durham, North Carolina**
**www.duke.edu**

**CB member**
**CB code: 5156**

- Private 4-year university affiliated with United Methodist Church
- Residential campus in small city
- 6,260 degree-seeking undergraduates: 48% women, 10% African American, 19% Asian American, 6% Hispanic American, 6% international
- 7,027 degree-seeking graduate students
- 23% of applicants admitted
- SAT and SAT Subject Tests or ACT with writing, application essay required
- 94% graduate within 6 years; 23% enter graduate study

**General.** Founded in 1838. Regionally accredited. Duke University Marine Laboratory, located near Beaufort, offers semester and summer programs to qualified juniors, seniors, and graduate students from any college or university. **Degrees:** master's, doctoral, first professional offered. **ROTC:** Army, Naval, Air Force. **Location:** 30 miles from Raleigh, 170 miles from Richmond, Virginia. **Calendar:** Semester, extensive summer session. **Full-time faculty:** 990 total; 96% have terminal degrees, 18% minority, 27% women. **Class size:** 71% < 20, 21% 20-39, 3% 40-49, 4% 50-99, 2% >100. **Special facilities:** Phytotron, marine laboratory, primate center, free electron laser, nuclear magnetic resonance machine, nuclear laboratory, institute of the arts, science research center, institute of statistics and decision sciences, institute for public policy, institute for genomic sciences and policy, center for interdisciplinary and international studies, center for teaching, learning and writing, community service center, center for geometric computing, center for black culture, women's center, center for interdisciplinary engineering, medicine, and applied sciences.

**Freshman class profile.** 17,748 applied, 4,077 admitted, 1,700 enrolled.

| Mid 50% test scores | | Rank in top tenth: | 90% |
|---|---|---|---|
| SAT critical reading: | 660-750 | Return as sophomores: | 97% |
| SAT math: | 680-790 | Out-of-state: | 85% |
| SAT writing: | 680-780 | Live on campus: | 100% |
| ACT composite: | 29-34 | International: | 7% |
| Rank in top quarter: | 97% | | |

**Basis for selection.** GED not accepted. Courses, school achievement record, school and community activities, essays, recommendations, test scores considered. Special consideration to alumni children and minority applicants. Applicants requesting alumni interview must submit Part I of application by 10/1 for Early Decision or by 12/1 for regular decision. Students using ACT for admission need to submit SAT Subject Tests or AP scores for foreign language and mathematics placement. Applicants to Arts and Sciences submitting SAT must submit 2 SAT Subject Tests. Applicants to School of Engineering submitting SAT must take SAT Subject Test in mathematics and 1 other subject. Interview with alumnus/a in student's home area recommended, but not required; audition recommended for drama, music majors; portfolio recommended for art majors. **Homeschooled:** Transcript of courses and grades, letter of recommendation (nonparent) required.

**High school preparation.** Recommended units include English 4, mathematics 4, social studies 4, science 4 and foreign language 4. 4 math and 1 physics or chemistry required for engineering applicants, with calculus required before enrolling.

**2007-2008 Annual costs.** Tuition/fees: $35,512. Room/board: $9,940. Books/supplies: $940. Personal expenses: $1,640.

**Financial aid. Non-need-based:** Scholarships awarded for academics, alumni affiliation, art, athletics, leadership, minority status, religious affiliation, ROTC, state residency.

**Application procedures. Admission:** Closing date 1/2 (postmark date). $75 fee, may be waived for applicants with need. Application may be submitted online. Admission notification 4/1. Must reply by 5/1. **Financial aid:** Closing date 3/1. FAFSA, CSS PROFILE required. Applicants notified by 4/1; must reply by 5/1 or within 4 week(s) of notification.

**Academics.** International comparative studies with an emphasis in one or more areas. Special Focus Program for freshmen: engineering frontiers, evolution and humankind, forging social ideals, genome revolution, global health, memory and invention, visions of freedom. **Special study options:** Combined bachelor's/graduate degree, cross-registration, distance learning, double major, ESL, exchange student, honors, independent study, internships, New York semester, semester at sea, student-designed major, study abroad, teacher certification program, Washington semester. Art program/internship in New York City, marine biology semester in Beaufort. **Credit/placement by examination:** AP, CLEP, IB. **Support services:** Learning center, preadmission summer program, tutoring, writing center.

**Majors. Area/ethnic studies:** African-American, Asian, women's. **Biology:** General, anatomy. **Computer sciences:** General. **Conservation:** General. **Engineering:** Biomedical, civil, electrical, mechanical. **English:** British lit, English lit. **Foreign languages:** Ancient Greek, classics, French, German, Italian, Latin, Russian, Spanish. **History:** General. **Interdisciplinary:** Medieval/Renaissance, neuroscience. **Math:** General. **Philosophy/religion:** Philosophy, religion. **Physical sciences:** Chemistry, geology, physics. **Psychology:** General. **Public administration:** Policy analysis. **Social sciences:** Anthropology, economics, political science, sociology. **Visual/performing arts:** Art history/conservation, design, dramatic.

**Most popular majors.** Biology 9%, engineering/engineering technologies 12%, English 6%, psychology 10%, public administration/social services 9%, social sciences 30%.

**Computing on campus.** 450 workstations in dormitories, library, computer center, student center. Dormitories wired for high-speed internet access and linked to campus network. Commuter students can connect to campus network. Online course registration, online library, helpline, repair service, student web hosting, wireless network available.

**Student life. Freshman orientation:** Mandatory. Preregistration for classes offered. Held week prior to start of classes. **Housing:** Guaranteed on-campus for freshmen. Coed dorms, single-sex dorms, special housing for disabled, apartments, substance-free housing available. Special interest housing available for students in women's studies, the arts, languages, service (Alpha Phi Omega). All first-year students live together on East Campus. Most first-year residence halls have a faculty member in residence. All sophomores must live on West Campus. **Activities:** Bands, campus ministries, choral groups, dance, drama, film society, international student organizations, literary magazine, music ensembles, musical theater, opera, radio station, student government, student newspaper, symphony orchestra, TV station, Black Student Alliance, Hillel, Newman Club, Spanish American-Latin Student Association, Volunteers for Youth, Big Brother/Big Sister, Campus Crusade for Christ, Duke Democrats, College Republicans, Habitat for Humanity.

**Athletics.** NCAA. **Intercollegiate:** Baseball M, basketball, cross-country, diving, fencing, field hockey W, football (tackle) M, golf, lacrosse, rowing (crew) W, soccer, swimming, tennis, track and field, volleyball W, wrestling M. **Intramural:** Badminton, baseball, basketball, football (tackle) M, golf, racquetball, soccer M, softball, squash, swimming, table tennis, tennis, volleyball. **Team name:** Blue Devils.

**Student services.** Adult student services, alcohol/substance abuse counseling, campus ministries, career counseling, student employment services, financial aid counseling, health services, minority student services, on-campus daycare, personal counseling, placement for graduates, veterans' counselor, women's services. **Physically disabled:** Services for visually, speech, hearing impaired.

**Contact.** Phone: (919) 684-3214 Fax: (919) 681-8941
Christoph Guttentag, Dean of Undergraduate Admissions, Duke University, 2138 Campus Drive, Durham, NC 27708

---

## East Carolina University
**Greenville, North Carolina**
www.ecu.edu

**CB member**
**CB code: 5180**

- Public 4-year university
- Residential campus in small city
- 19,651 degree-seeking undergraduates: 12% part-time, 59% women, 16% African American, 2% Asian American, 2% Hispanic American, 1% Native American
- 6,039 degree-seeking graduate students
- 84% of applicants admitted
- SAT or ACT with writing required
- 54% graduate within 6 years

**General.** Founded in 1907. Regionally accredited. **Degrees:** 3,401 bachelor's awarded; master's, doctoral, first professional offered. **ROTC:** Army, Air Force. **Location:** 80 miles from Raleigh. **Calendar:** Semester, extensive summer session. **Full-time faculty:** 1,271 total; 87% have terminal degrees, 11% minority, 40% women. **Part-time faculty:** 158 total; 25% have terminal degrees, 4% minority, 58% women. **Class size:** 42% < 20, 34% 20-39, 5% 40-49, 8% 50-99, 2% >100. **Special facilities:** 2 accelerators, climbing wall, ropes course, global classroom, field station.

**Freshman class profile.** 14,653 applied, 12,328 admitted, 4,222 enrolled.

| Mid 50% test scores | | | |
|---|---|---|---|
| SAT critical reading: | 450-540 | GPA 2.0-2.99: | 19% |
| SAT math: | 470-560 | Rank in top quarter: | 40% |
| SAT writing: | 440-530 | Return as sophomores: | 77% |
| ACT composite: | 19-23 | Out-of-state: | 16% |
| GPA 3.50 or higher: | 45% | Live on campus: | 81% |
| GPA 3.0-3.49: | 36% | International: | 1% |

**Basis for selection.** Freshman admission decisions based on a formula that weighs class rank, high school GPA (unweighted), and standardized test scores. GED accepted for non-traditional freshmen. SAT preferred, ACT also accepted. Audition, statement of purpose and letter of recommendation required for music programs. **Homeschooled:** Transcript of courses and grades required.

**High school preparation.** 20 units required. Required units include English 4, mathematics 4, social studies 2, science 3 (laboratory 1), foreign

language 2 and academic electives 4. Recommended that during senior year student take the 4th math requirement, 1 foreign language, 1 natural science, 1 English. Social studies units must include 1 U.S. history, 1 fine art recommended.

**2007-2008 Annual costs.** Tuition/fees: $4,218; $14,732 out-of-state. Room/board: $7,450. Books/supplies: $800. Personal expenses: $1,600.

**Financial aid. Non-need-based:** Scholarships awarded for academics, alumni affiliation, art, athletics, minority status, ROTC.

**Application procedures. Admission:** Closing date 3/15 (postmark date). $60 fee, may be waived for applicants with need. Application may be submitted online. Admission notification on a rolling basis beginning on or about 10/1. Must reply by May 1 or within 2 week(s) if notified thereafter. Out-of-state freshman enrollment limited to 18% of incoming freshman class, and processed on space-available basis. Applications received prior to December 31 receive priority. **Financial aid:** Priority date 4/15; no closing date. FAFSA required. Applicants notified on a rolling basis starting 3/15; must reply within 3 week(s) of notification.

**Academics. Special study options:** Accelerated study, combined bachelor's/graduate degree, cooperative education, distance learning, double major, dual enrollment of high school students, exchange student, honors, independent study, internships, student-designed major, study abroad, teacher certification program, Washington semester. **Credit/placement by examination:** AP, CLEP, IB, SAT, institutional tests. **Support services:** Learning center, reduced course load, remedial instruction, study skills assistance, tutoring, writing center.

**Majors. Architecture:** Urban/community planning. **Area/ethnic studies:** African-American, women's. **Biology:** General, biochemistry, exercise physiology. **Business:** Accounting, accounting/business management, business admin, finance, hotel/motel admin, management information systems, marketing, office technology. **Communications:** General, broadcast journalism. **Computer sciences:** Computer science, information technology. **Education:** Art, business, drama/dance, elementary, English, family/consumer sciences, French, German, health, kindergarten/preschool, learning disabled, mathematics, middle, music, physical, sales/marketing, science, social studies, Spanish, special. **Engineering:** General. **Engineering technology:** Construction, drafting, industrial, manufacturing. **English:** English lit. **Family/consumer sciences:** Child development, clothing/textiles, family/community services. **Foreign languages:** French, German, Spanish. **Health:** Athletic training, audiology/speech pathology, clinical lab science, clinical nutrition, dietetics, environmental health, health services, marriage/family therapy, medical records admin, music therapy, nursing (RN), public health ed, recreational therapy, vocational rehab counseling. **History:** General, public archives. **Liberal arts:** Arts/sciences. **Math:** General. **Parks/recreation:** Exercise sciences, facilities management, sports admin. **Philosophy/religion:** Philosophy. **Physical sciences:** Chemistry, geology, physics. **Protective services:** Criminal justice. **Psychology:** General. **Public administration:** Social work. **Social sciences:** Anthropology, economics, geography, political science, sociology. **Visual/performing arts:** Acting, art, art history/conservation, ceramics, cinematography, dance, directing/producing, dramatic, drawing, fiber arts, graphic design, illustration, interior design, jazz, metal/jewelry, music performance, music theory/composition, painting, photography, piano/organ, printmaking, sculpture, stringed instruments, studio arts, voice/opera.

**Computing on campus.** 2,188 workstations in dormitories, library, computer center, student center. Dormitories wired for high-speed internet access and linked to campus network. Commuter students can connect to campus network. Online course registration, online library, helpline, repair service, student web hosting, wireless network available.

**Student life. Freshman orientation:** Mandatory, $100 fee. Preregistration for classes offered, 2-phase program: 1 summer session (overnight stay) and 1 session the day prior to start of classes. **Housing:** Guaranteed on-campus for freshmen. Coed dorms, single-sex dorms, fraternity/sorority housing, substance-free housing available. $200 partly refundable deposit, deadline 5/1. First-year student floor, leadership hall, extended quiet-hours floor, academic year residence halls available. **Activities:** Bands, campus ministries, choral groups, dance, drama, film society, international student organizations, literary magazine, music ensembles, Model UN, musical theater, opera, radio station, student government, student newspaper, symphony orchestra, TV station, 280 registered organizations.

**Athletics.** NCAA. **Intercollegiate:** Baseball M, basketball, cheerleading, cross-country, diving, football (tackle) M, golf, soccer W, softball W, swimming, tennis, track and field, volleyball. **Intramural:** Basketball, bowling, cross-country, football (non-tackle), golf, racquetball, softball, table tennis, tennis, volleyball. **Team name:** Pirates.

**Student services.** Adult student services, alcohol/substance abuse counseling, campus ministries, career counseling, student employment services, financial aid counseling, health services, minority student services, personal counseling, placement for graduates, veterans' counselor. **Physically disabled:** Services for visually, speech, hearing impaired.

**Contact.** E-mail: admis@ecu.edu
Phone: (252) 328-6640 Fax: (252) 328-6945
Donald Joyner, Director of Admissions, East Carolina University, Office of Undergraduate Admissions, Greenville, NC 27858-4353

---

## Elizabeth City State University

**Elizabeth City, North Carolina**    **CB member**
www.ecsu.edu    **CB code: 5629**

- Public 4-year liberal arts college
- Commuter campus in large town
- 2,658 degree-seeking undergraduates: 7% part-time, 62% women, 82% African American, 1% Hispanic American
- 136 degree-seeking graduate students
- 56% of applicants admitted
- SAT or ACT with writing required
- 49% graduate within 6 years

**General.** Founded in 1891. Regionally accredited. **Degrees:** 301 bachelor's awarded; master's offered. **ROTC:** Army. **Location:** 50 miles from Norfolk, Virginia. **Calendar:** Semester, extensive summer session. **Full-time faculty:** 135 total; 64% have terminal degrees, 52% minority, 38% women. **Part-time faculty:** 67 total; 8% have terminal degrees, 72% minority, 49% women. **Class size:** 61% < 20, 31% 20-39, 7% 40-49, less than 1% 50-99. **Special facilities:** Recording studio, boardwalk in nature preserves/wetlands, golf driving range.

**Freshman class profile.** 3,068 applied, 1,725 admitted, 588 enrolled.

| Mid 50% test scores | | | |
|---|---|---|---|
| SAT critical reading: | 380-460 | Rank in top tenth: | 8% |
| SAT math: | 380-460 | End year in good standing: | 79% |
| GPA 3.50 or higher: | 12% | Return as sophomores: | 79% |
| GPA 3.0-3.49: | 23% | Out-of-state: | 15% |
| GPA 2.0-2.99: | 60% | Live on campus: | 79% |
| Rank in top quarter: | 13% | Fraternities: | 3% |
| | | Sororities: | 6% |

**Basis for selection.** GPA and test scores considered. Special consideration given to residents from 21 neighboring counties. All applicants to any campus in the UNC system, except those exempted by current campus policies, must submit standardized test scores. SAT preferred, ACT accepted. **Homeschooled:** Statement describing homeschool structure and mission, transcript of courses and grades, letter of recommendation (nonparent) required. **Learning Disabled:** Important to ascertain in advance the extent of the learning disability in order to provide the available service(s).

**High school preparation.** 20 units required. Required units include English 4, mathematics 3, social studies 2, science 2 (laboratory 1) and foreign language 2. One additional laboratory science also required. Mathematics must include 1 algebra and 1 geometry. Social science must include 1 history.

**2007-2008 Annual costs.** Tuition/fees: $2,898; $11,779 out-of-state. Room/board: $5,147. Books/supplies: $670. Personal expenses: $1,200.

**Financial aid. Non-need-based:** Scholarships awarded for academics, athletics, minority status, ROTC, state residency.

**Application procedures. Admission:** Priority date 3/1; deadline 8/15. $30 fee, may be waived for applicants with need. Application may be submitted online. Admission notification on a rolling basis. **Financial aid:** Priority date 3/1, closing date 8/15. FAFSA required. Applicants notified on a rolling basis starting 6/1; must reply within 3 week(s) of notification.

**Academics. Special study options:** Combined bachelor's/graduate degree, cooperative education, distance learning, double major, honors, independent study, internships, liberal arts/career combination, teacher certification program, weekend college. **Credit/placement by examination:** AP, CLEP, IB, SAT. 48 credit hours maximum toward bachelor's degree. **Support services:** Learning center, pre-admission summer program, reduced course load, remedial instruction, study skills assistance, tutoring, writing center.

**Majors. Biology:** General. **Business:** Accounting, business admin. **Computer sciences:** Computer science. **Education:** Art, business, chemistry, elementary, English, history, learning disabled, mathematics, middle, physical, special, technology/industrial arts. **Engineering technology:** Industrial. **English:** English lit. **History:** General. **Math:** General. **Physical sciences:** Chemistry, geology, oceanography, physics. **Protective services:** Criminal justice. **Psychology:** General. **Public administration:** Social work. **Social**

sciences: General, political science, sociology. **Transportation:** Aviation. **Visual/performing arts:** Music management, studio arts.

**Computing on campus.** 350 workstations in dormitories, library, computer center, student center. Dormitories wired for high-speed internet access and linked to campus network. Commuter students can connect to campus network. Online course registration, online library, helpline, repair service, wireless network available.

**Student life. Freshman orientation:** Mandatory, $100 fee. Preregistration for classes offered. Three sessions held during summer months covering 2 1/2 days each. **Housing:** Guaranteed on-campus for freshmen. Coed dorms, single-sex dorms, apartments, substance-free housing available. $100 deposit, deadline 8/1. College-leased housing available. **Activities:** Bands, choral groups, dance, drama, literary magazine, music ensembles, radio station, student government, student newspaper, symphony orchestra, TV station, United Campus Religious Fellowship, honor and recognition societies in education, science, dramatics, journalism, student union program.

**Athletics.** NCAA. **Intercollegiate:** Baseball M, basketball, bowling W, boxing W, cheerleading, cross-country, football (tackle) M, golf, softball W, tennis, track and field, volleyball W, wrestling M. **Intramural:** Baseball M, basketball, boxing, football (non-tackle) M, softball, volleyball. **Team name:** Vikings.

**Student services.** Alcohol/substance abuse counseling, campus ministries, career counseling, student employment services, financial aid counseling, health services, personal counseling, placement for graduates, veterans' counselor. **Physically disabled:** Services for visually, speech, hearing impaired.

**Contact.** E-mail: gdeese@mail.ecsu.edu
Phone: (252) 335-3305 Toll-free number: (800) 347-3278
Fax: (252) 335-3537
Grady Deese, Director of Admissions, Elizabeth City State University, 1704 Weeksville Road, Campus Box 901, Elizabeth City, NC 27909

---

## Elon University

**Elon, North Carolina**    **CB member**
www.elon.edu    **CB code: 5183**

- Private 4-year university and liberal arts college affiliated with United Church of Christ
- Residential campus in large town
- 4,939 degree-seeking undergraduates: 2% part-time, 59% women, 6% African American, 1% Asian American, 2% Hispanic American, 2% international
- 517 degree-seeking graduate students
- 41% of applicants admitted
- SAT or ACT with writing, application essay required
- 73% graduate within 6 years; 16% enter graduate study

**General.** Founded in 1889. Regionally accredited. **Degrees:** 1,109 bachelor's awarded; master's, doctoral, first professional offered. **ROTC:** Army, Air Force. **Location:** 15 miles from Greensboro. **Calendar:** 4-1-4, extensive summer session. **Full-time faculty:** 311 total; 85% have terminal degrees, 9% minority, 46% women. **Part-time faculty:** 119 total; 49% have terminal degrees, 8% minority, 44% women. **Class size:** 50% < 20, 49% 20-39, less than 1% 40-49, less than 1% 50-99. **Special facilities:** Fine arts center, science center, academic pavilions.

**Freshman class profile.** 9,380 applied, 3,870 admitted, 1,286 enrolled.

| Mid 50% test scores | | | |
|---|---|---|---|
| SAT critical reading: | 560-650 | Rank in top quarter: | 66% |
| SAT math: | 570-660 | Rank in top tenth: | 29% |
| SAT writing: | 560-660 | End year in good standing: | 97% |
| ACT composite: | 24-28 | Return as sophomores: | 90% |
| GPA 3.50 or higher: | 76% | Out-of-state: | 77% |
| GPA 3.0-3.49: | 18% | Live on campus: | 100% |
| GPA 2.0-2.99: | 6% | International: | 2% |

**Basis for selection.** School achievement record most important, followed by test scores. Class rank, school and community activities, personal statement, recommendations also considered. Audition required for all performing arts programs. **Homeschooled:** Statement describing homeschool structure and mission, transcript of courses and grades, state high school equivalency certificate, letter of recommendation (nonparent) required.

**High school preparation.** Required and recommended units include English 4, mathematics 3-4, social studies 1, history 2-3, science 3 (laboratory 1) and foreign language 2-3. Algebra I, II and geometry required.

**2007-2008 Annual costs.** Tuition/fees: $22,166. Room/board: $7,296. Books/supplies: $900. Personal expenses: $1,500.

**2007-2008 Financial aid. Need-based:** 686 full-time freshmen applied for aid; 403 were judged to have need; 400 of these received aid. Average need met was 73%. Average scholarship/grant was $8,527; average loan $3,666. 62% of total undergraduate aid awarded as scholarships/grants, 38% as loans/jobs. **Non-need-based:** Awarded to 1,442 full-time undergraduates, including 426 freshmen. Scholarships awarded for academics, art, athletics, leadership, music/drama, ROTC, state residency.

**Application procedures. Admission:** Priority date 11/1; deadline 1/10 (postmark date). $50 fee, may be waived for applicants with need. Application may be submitted online. Admission notification 3/15. Must reply by May 1 or within 1 week(s) if notified thereafter. **Financial aid:** Priority date 2/15; no closing date. FAFSA, institutional form, CSS PROFILE required. Applicants notified on a rolling basis starting 3/30.

**Academics. Special study options:** Accelerated study, combined bachelor's/graduate degree, cross-registration, distance learning, double major, dual enrollment of high school students, ESL, exchange student, honors, independent study, internships, liberal arts/career combination, student-designed major, study abroad, teacher certification program, Washington semester. **Credit/placement by examination:** AP, CLEP, IB, SAT, ACT, institutional tests. **Support services:** Learning center, reduced course load, remedial instruction, study skills assistance, tutoring, writing center.

**Majors. Biology:** General. **Business:** Accounting, business admin, entrepreneurial studies, finance, international, management information systems, marketing. **Communications:** General, broadcast journalism, journalism. **Computer sciences:** General, computer science, information systems. **Conservation:** Environmental studies. **Education:** General, curriculum, elementary, middle, secondary, special. **Engineering:** General, chemical, computer, environmental, physics. **Engineering technology:** Environmental. **English:** British lit, creative writing, English lit. **Foreign languages:** General, French, Spanish. **Health:** Predental, premedicine, staff services technology. **History:** General. **Legal studies:** Prelaw. **Math:** General, applied. **Parks/recreation:** Exercise sciences, facilities management, sports admin. **Philosophy/religion:** Philosophy, religion. **Physical sciences:** Chemistry, physics. **Protective services:** Criminal justice. **Psychology:** General. **Public administration:** General, human services. **Social sciences:** Anthropology, economics, international relations, political science, sociology. **Visual/performing arts:** Art, art history/conservation, ceramics, dance, digital art, dramatic, music performance, musical theater, painting, photography, theater design. **Other:** Music technology, Professional writing and rhetoric.

**Most popular majors.** Business/marketing 23%, communications/journalism 18%, education 7%, parks/recreation 8%, psychology 6%, social sciences 9%, visual/performing arts 6%.

**Computing on campus.** 540 workstations in dormitories, library, computer center, student center. Dormitories wired for high-speed internet access and linked to campus network. Commuter students can connect to campus network. Online course registration, online library, helpline, repair service, student web hosting, wireless network available.

**Student life. Freshman orientation:** Mandatory. Preregistration for classes offered. Optional orientation during spring of high school senior year. Required orientation in August. **Policies:** Freshmen and sophomores are required to live on campus; housing is guaranteed. **Housing:** Guaranteed on-campus for freshmen. Coed dorms, single-sex dorms, apartments, fraternity/sorority housing, substance-free housing available. $500 fully refundable deposit, deadline 5/1. Theme suites based on academic interest available. **Activities:** Bands, campus ministries, choral groups, dance, drama, film society, literary magazine, music ensembles, Model UN, musical theater, radio station, student government, student newspaper, symphony orchestra, TV station, Intervarsity Christian Fellowship, Young Republicans, Black cultural society, Epsilon Sigma Alpha, liberal arts forum, Hillel, student media, Habitat for Humanity.

**Athletics.** NCAA. **Intercollegiate:** Baseball M, basketball, cheerleading, cross-country, football (tackle) M, golf, soccer, softball W, tennis, track and field W, volleyball W. **Intramural:** Basketball, bowling, football (non-tackle), golf, racquetball, soccer, table tennis, tennis, volleyball. **Team name:** Phoenix.

**Student services.** Adult student services, alcohol/substance abuse counseling, campus ministries, career counseling, student employment services, financial aid counseling, health services, minority student services, personal counseling, placement for graduates, veterans' counselor, women's services. **Physically disabled:** Services for visually, speech, hearing impaired.

**Contact.** E-mail: admissions@elon.edu
Phone: (336) 278-3566 Toll-free number: (800) 334-8448
Fax: (336) 278-7699
Susan Klopman, Dean of Admissions and Financial Planning, Elon University, 2700 Campus Box, Elon, NC 27244-2010

## Fayetteville State University
**Fayetteville, North Carolina**
www.uncfsu.edu

**CB member**
**CB code: 5212**

- Public 4-year university
- Commuter campus in small city
- 5,678 degree-seeking undergraduates: 22% part-time, 69% women
- 458 degree-seeking graduate students
- SAT or ACT with writing required

**General.** Founded in 1867. Regionally accredited. Courses leading to bachelor's degree also available at the Fort Bragg/Pope AFB Center, Seymour Johnson AFB, and online. **Degrees:** 685 bachelor's awarded; master's, doctoral offered. **ROTC:** Army, Air Force. **Location:** 60 miles from Raleigh. **Calendar:** Semester, limited summer session. **Full-time faculty:** 200 total. **Part-time faculty:** 40 total. **Special facilities:** Greenhouse, observatory, planetarium.

**Freshman class profile.**

| Mid 50% test scores | | Rank in top tenth: | 5% |
|---|---|---|---|
| SAT critical reading: | 380-460 | Out-of-state: | 16% |
| SAT math: | 370-470 | Live on campus: | 74% |
| Rank in top quarter: | 21% | | |

**Basis for selection.** 2.0 GPA, SAT scores, completion of 18 prescribed high school units required. All applicants, except those exempted by current campus policies, must submit a standardized test score. SAT preferred, ACT also accepted.

**High school preparation.** 19 units required. Required and recommended units include English 4, mathematics 3, social studies 2, history 1, science 3, foreign language 2 and academic electives 6. Foreign language units can be used as academic elective units.

**2007-2008 Annual costs.** Tuition/fees: $3,020; $13,202 out-of-state. Room/board: $4,870. Books/supplies: $350. Personal expenses: $750.

**Financial aid. Non-need-based:** Scholarships awarded for academics, alumni affiliation, athletics, music/drama, ROTC, state residency.

**Application procedures. Admission:** Closing date 7/1 (postmark date). $25 fee, may be waived for applicants with need. Application may be submitted online. Admission notification on a rolling basis beginning on or about 1/15. Must reply by 7/1. **Financial aid:** Priority date 3/1, closing date 4/1. FAFSA required. Applicants notified on a rolling basis starting 4/15; must reply within 2 week(s) of notification.

**Academics. Special study options:** Accelerated study, combined bachelor's/graduate degree, cooperative education, distance learning, double major, dual enrollment of high school students, honors, independent study, internships, study abroad, teacher certification program, weekend college. **Credit/placement by examination:** AP, CLEP, institutional tests. 30 credit hours maximum toward bachelor's degree. **Support services:** Learning center, pre-admission summer program, remedial instruction, tutoring.

**Majors. Biology:** General. **Business:** Accounting, business admin, office management. **Computer sciences:** General. **Education:** Business, English, health, mathematics, middle, music, physical, secondary, social science. **English:** British lit, English lit, speech/rhetoric. **History:** General. **Math:** General. **Physical sciences:** Chemistry. **Protective services:** Criminal justice. **Psychology:** General. **Public administration:** General. **Social sciences:** General, geography, political science, sociology. **Visual/performing arts:** General, dramatic.

**Most popular majors.** Business/marketing 22%, education 14%, psychology 11%, security/protective services 13%, social sciences 19%.

**Computing on campus.** 600 workstations in dormitories, library, computer center, student center. Dormitories wired for high-speed internet access and linked to campus network. Commuter students can connect to campus network. Online course registration, online library, helpline, wireless network available.

**Student life. Freshman orientation:** Mandatory, $45 fee. 3 Saturdays in July and August. **Housing:** Single-sex dorms available. $125 deposit, deadline 7/1. **Activities:** Bands, choral groups, drama, music ensembles, radio station, student government, student newspaper, TV station, Baptist student union, Federation of Young Democrats, NAACP, NCNW, Honda Campus All-Stars, art guild, Illusions modeling club.

**Athletics.** NCAA. **Intercollegiate:** Basketball, bowling W, cross-country, football (tackle) M, golf, softball W, tennis, track and field, volleyball W.

**Intramural:** Baseball M, basketball, bowling, football (tackle) M, golf, gymnastics, swimming, tennis M, volleyball. **Team name:** Broncos.

**Student services.** Alcohol/substance abuse counseling, career counseling, student employment services, financial aid counseling, health services, on-campus daycare, personal counseling, placement for graduates, veterans' counselor. **Physically disabled:** Services for visually impaired.

**Contact.** E-mail: rshabazz@uncfsu.edu
Phone: (910) 672-1371 Toll-free number: (800) 222-2594
Fax: (910) 672-1414
Charles Darlington, Director of Admissions, Fayetteville State University, 1200 Murchison Road, Fayetteville, NC 28301-4298

---

### Gardner-Webb University
**Boiling Springs, North Carolina**  **CB member**
www.gardner-webb.edu  **CB code: 5242**

- Private 4-year university and liberal arts college affiliated with Southern Baptist Convention
- Residential campus in small town
- 2,638 degree-seeking undergraduates: 15% part-time, 67% women, 18% African American, 1% Asian American, 2% Hispanic American
- 1,163 degree-seeking graduate students
- 70% of applicants admitted
- SAT or ACT (ACT writing optional) required
- 56% graduate within 6 years

**General.** Founded in 1905. Regionally accredited. **Degrees:** 585 bachelor's, 39 associate awarded; master's, doctoral offered. **ROTC:** Army, Air Force. **Location:** 45 miles from Charlotte, 60 miles from Greenville, SC. **Calendar:** Semester, extensive summer session. **Full-time faculty:** 135 total; 78% have terminal degrees, 49% women. **Part-time faculty:** 204 total. **Class size:** 100% 20-39. **Special facilities:** Observatory, adventure and ropes course, Lake Hollifield and Carillon.

**Freshman class profile.** 1,974 applied, 1,384 admitted, 419 enrolled.

| Mid 50% test scores | | | |
|---|---|---|---|
| SAT critical reading: | 440-580 | Return as sophomores: | 72% |
| SAT math: | 450-560 | Out-of-state: | 35% |
| Rank in top quarter: | 32% | Live on campus: | 98% |

**Basis for selection.** School achievement record most important, followed by test scores, recommendations, and school and community activities. Expected 2.5 GPA. Interview, portfolio, essay recommended for all students; audition required for music scholarships.

**High school preparation.** Recommended units include English 4, mathematics 3, social studies 2, science 2 and foreign language 2.

**2008-2009 Annual costs.** Tuition/fees: $20,465; $20,465 out-of-state. $170 communication fee, $30 residence hall activity fee for resident student, $200 student activities fee. Room/board: $6,500. Books/supplies: $1,000.

**Financial aid. Non-need-based:** Scholarships awarded for academics, athletics, leadership, music/drama, religious affiliation, ROTC, state residency.

**Application procedures. Admission:** No deadline. $40 fee, may be waived for applicants with need. Application may be submitted online. Admission notification on a rolling basis. **Financial aid:** No deadline. FAFSA required. Applicants notified on a rolling basis starting 3/1; must reply within 2 week(s) of notification.

**Academics. Special study options:** Combined bachelor's/graduate degree, double major, dual enrollment of high school students, honors, independent study, internships, liberal arts/career combination, New York semester, study abroad, teacher certification program, Washington semester. Spring Break in New York, Fall Break in Washington, Summer Costa Rica and Paris Trips. **Credit/placement by examination:** AP, CLEP, IB, SAT, ACT, institutional tests. 30 credit hours maximum toward bachelor's degree. **Support services:** Learning center, pre-admission summer program, reduced course load, remedial instruction, study skills assistance, tutoring, writing center.

**Honors college/program.** Students with 1170 SAT (exclusive of Writing) and 3.8 GPA average admitted.

**Majors. Biology:** General, environmental. **Business:** General, accounting, business admin, finance, international, management information systems. **Communications:** General, broadcast journalism, journalism, public relations. **Computer sciences:** General. **Education:** General, biology, chemistry, elementary, English, foreign languages, French, health, history, mathematics, middle, multi-level teacher, music, physical, science, secondary,

social science, Spanish. **English:** English lit. **Foreign languages:** General, American Sign Language, French, sign language interpretation, Spanish. **Health:** Athletic training, nursing (RN). **History:** General. **Legal studies:** Prelaw. **Math:** General. **Philosophy/religion:** Religion. **Physical sciences:** Chemistry. **Psychology:** General. **Social sciences:** General, political science, sociology. **Theology:** Religious ed, youth ministry. **Visual/performing arts:** Art, dramatic, music management, music performance, music theory/composition, photography, piano/organ, stringed instruments, studio arts, voice/opera.

**Most popular majors.** Business/marketing 32%, social sciences 31%.

**Computing on campus.** 150 workstations in library, computer center. Dormitories wired for high-speed internet access and linked to campus network. Commuter students can connect to campus network. Online course registration, online library, helpline, repair service, wireless network available.

**Student life. Freshman orientation:** Mandatory, $75 fee. Preregistration for classes offered. 3-day program typically held near the end of August, just before fall semester commences. **Policies:** Limited visitation hours: 12:00 noon to 12:00 midnight in dorm rooms. Lobbies open for visitation until 2:00 am. **Housing:** Guaranteed on-campus for all undergraduates. Single-sex dorms, apartments, substance-free housing available. $150 fully refundable deposit. Honors student residence hall available. **Activities:** Bands, campus ministries, choral groups, dance, drama, literary magazine, music ensembles, musical theater, opera, radio station, student government, student newspaper, symphony orchestra, Fellowship of Christian Athletes, student volunteer groups, student YMCA, gospel choir, bible studies, Young Republicans.

**Athletics.** NCAA, NCCAA. **Intercollegiate:** Baseball M, basketball, cheerleading, cross-country, football (tackle) M, golf, soccer, softball W, swimming, tennis, track and field, volleyball W, wrestling M. **Intramural:** Badminton, baseball M, basketball, football (non-tackle), racquetball, skiing, soccer, softball, swimming, table tennis, tennis, volleyball. **Team name:** Runnin' Bulldogs.

**Student services.** Campus ministries, career counseling, student employment services, financial aid counseling, personal counseling, placement for graduates, veterans' counselor. **Physically disabled:** Services for visually, speech, hearing impaired. **Learning disabled:** Comprehensive services available.

**Contact.** E-mail: admissions@gardner-webb.edu
Phone: (704) 406-4498 Toll-free number: (800) 253-6472
Fax: (704) 406-4488
Nathan Alexander, Assistant Vice President of Enrollment Management and Admissions, Gardner-Webb University, Box 817, Boiling Springs, NC 28017

---

### Greensboro College
**Greensboro, North Carolina**  **CB member**
www.gborocollege.edu  **CB code: 5260**

- Private 4-year liberal arts college affiliated with United Methodist Church
- Residential campus in large city
- 901 degree-seeking undergraduates: 6% part-time, 44% women
- 19 degree-seeking graduate students
- 64% of applicants admitted
- SAT or ACT with writing, application essay required
- 41% graduate within 6 years; 1% enter graduate study

**General.** Founded in 1838. Regionally accredited. **Degrees:** 187 bachelor's awarded; master's offered. **ROTC:** Army, Air Force. **Location:** 90 miles from Charlotte, 75 miles from Raleigh. **Calendar:** Semester, limited summer session. **Full-time faculty:** 68 total; 6% minority, 50% women. **Part-time faculty:** 71 total. **Class size:** 83% < 20, 17% 20-39. **Special facilities:** Historical museum, computer writing center, computerized music laboratories.

**Freshman class profile.** 1,027 applied, 657 admitted, 215 enrolled.

| Mid 50% test scores | | | |
|---|---|---|---|
| SAT critical reading: | 400-510 | Rank in top quarter: | 17% |
| SAT math: | 410-540 | Rank in top tenth: | 7% |
| ACT composite: | 17-23 | End year in good standing: | 53% |
| GPA 3.50 or higher: | 26% | Return as sophomores: | 35% |
| GPA 3.0-3.49: | 19% | Out-of-state: | 33% |
| GPA 2.0-2.99: | 52% | Live on campus: | 93% |

**Basis for selection.** High school curriculum most important, followed by grades, class rank, test scores, personal statement, school and community activities, high school caliber. Recommendations, interview considered. Interview recommended for all students. Audition required for music, theater majors; portfolio required for art majors. **Homeschooled:** Interview highly recommended and SAT/ACT required. **Learning Disabled:** Students wishing to receive accommodations facilitated by the Office of Disability Services are responsible for disclosure of physical, psychological, and learning disabilities. Accommodation of learning and psychological disabilities must be accompanied by appropriate documentation that includes professional evaluation, diagnosis, and recommendations.

**High school preparation.** Recommended units include English 4, mathematics 3, history 2, science 2 (laboratory 1) and foreign language 2. Remaining units must be selected from art, music, social science and physical education.

**2007-2008 Annual costs.** Tuition/fees: $20,810. Room/board: $7,930. Books/supplies: $800. Personal expenses: $900.

**Financial aid. Non-need-based:** Scholarships awarded for academics, alumni affiliation, art, leadership, music/drama, religious affiliation, state residency.

**Application procedures. Admission:** Priority date 12/15; no deadline. $35 fee, may be waived for applicants with need. Application may be submitted online. Admission notification on a rolling basis. Notification in 2 weeks of receiving complete application. Must reply by May 1 or within 4 week(s) if notified thereafter. **Financial aid:** Priority date 4/15; no closing date. FAFSA, institutional form required. Applicants notified on a rolling basis starting 2/1; must reply within 2 week(s) of notification.

**Academics. Special study options:** Accelerated study, cross-registration, double major, dual enrollment of high school students, ESL, honors, independent study, internships, liberal arts/career combination, student-designed major, study abroad, teacher certification program, weekend college. Academic success program, minor in ethics across the curriculum, minor in women's and gender studies, minor in computer science. **Credit/placement by examination:** AP, CLEP, IB, institutional tests. 45 credit hours maximum toward bachelor's degree. **Support services:** Learning center, reduced course load, study skills assistance, tutoring, writing center.

**Majors. Biology:** General. **Business:** Accounting, managerial economics. **Communications:** General. **Education:** General, art, biology, drama/dance, early childhood, elementary, emotionally handicapped, English, history, learning disabled, mathematics, mentally handicapped, middle, multiple handicapped, music, physical, social studies, Spanish, special. **English:** English lit. **Foreign languages:** French, Spanish. **Health:** Athletic training. **History:** General. **Liberal arts:** Arts/sciences. **Math:** General. **Parks/recreation:** Exercise sciences, health/fitness, sports admin. **Philosophy/religion:** Religion. **Physical sciences:** Chemistry. **Psychology:** General. **Social sciences:** Political science, sociology. **Visual/performing arts:** Dramatic, music performance, studio arts, theater design.

**Most popular majors.** Biology 7%, business/marketing 25%, education 15%, social sciences 12%, visual/performing arts 16%.

**Computing on campus.** 152 workstations in dormitories, library, computer center, student center. Dormitories wired for high-speed internet access and linked to campus network. Commuter students can connect to campus network. Online library, helpline, repair service, wireless network available.

**Student life. Freshman orientation:** Mandatory, $50 fee. Preregistration for classes offered. Three 2-day orientations held in May, June, and July. Additional program held in August, one week prior to start of class. **Housing:** Guaranteed on-campus for all undergraduates. Coed dorms, single-sex dorms, apartments, substance-free housing available. $200 partly refundable deposit. All students who have earned less than 58 credit hours required to live in college housing unless married, veterans, or residing with parents. All students encouraged to do so. Theme housing available, including community service housing. **Activities:** Bands, choral groups, dance, drama, international student organizations, literary magazine, music ensembles, Model UN, musical theater, opera, student government, student newspaper, Student Christian Fellowship, United African American Society, Student National Education Association, campus activity board, Fellowship of Christian Athletes, Los Amigos.

**Athletics.** NCAA. **Intercollegiate:** Baseball M, basketball, cheerleading, cross-country, football (tackle) M, golf M, lacrosse, soccer, softball W, swimming W, tennis, volleyball W. **Intramural:** Baseball M, basketball, football (non-tackle), skiing. **Team name:** Pride.

**Student services.** Adult student services, alcohol/substance abuse counseling, campus ministries, career counseling, student employment services, financial aid counseling, health services, personal counseling, placement for graduates. **Physically disabled:** Services for visually, speech, hearing impaired.

**Contact.** E-mail: admissions@gborocollege.edu
Phone: (336) 272-7102 ext. 211 Toll-free number: (800) 346-8226
Fax: (336) 378-0154
Tim Jackson, Director of Admissions, Greensboro College, 815 West Market Street, Greensboro, NC 27401-1875

## Guilford College
**Greensboro, North Carolina**
**www.guilford.edu**
CB member
CB code: 5261

- Private 4-year liberal arts college affiliated with Society of Friends (Quaker)
- Residential campus in small city
- 2,688 degree-seeking undergraduates: 16% part-time, 61% women, 22% African American, 2% Asian American, 2% Hispanic American, 1% Native American, 1% international
- 58% of applicants admitted
- Application essay required
- 58% graduate within 6 years; 17% enter graduate study

**General.** Founded in 1837. Regionally accredited. **Degrees:** 457 bachelor's awarded. **ROTC:** Army, Naval, Air Force. **Location:** 90 miles from Raleigh, 100 miles from Charlotte. **Calendar:** Semester, limited summer session. **Full-time faculty:** 135 total; 62% have terminal degrees, 16% minority, 47% women. **Part-time faculty:** 83 total; 42% have terminal degrees, 16% minority, 52% women. **Class size:** 66% < 20, 33% 20-39, less than 1% 40-49. **Special facilities:** Observatory, multimedia learning center for cultures and languages, telecommunications center, photography studio, outdoor sculpture studio, computer visualization laboratory.

**Freshman class profile.** 3,486 applied, 2,015 admitted, 491 enrolled.

| Mid 50% test scores | | | |
|---|---|---|---|
| SAT critical reading: | 490-630 | Rank in top quarter: | 45% |
| SAT math: | 500-610 | Rank in top tenth: | 20% |
| ACT composite: | 21-26 | End year in good standing: | 77% |
| GPA 3.50 or higher: | 30% | Return as sophomores: | 72% |
| GPA 3.0-3.49: | 30% | Out-of-state: | 61% |
| GPA 2.0-2.99: | 40% | Live on campus: | 98% |

**Basis for selection.** School achievement record and essay most important. Test scores, interview, recommendations, interests, leadership ability also important. Minimum SAT composite score of 1000 (exclusive of Writing) or ACT score of 22 recommended. SAT or ACT recommended. Applicant may choose to submit portfolio instead of standardized test scores. Portfolio should reflect student's academic, creative, and personal interests and accomplishments. It must include, but is not limited to, 3-5 writing samples (at least one should be a graded expository written work) and, if available, a junior/senior reading list. Auditions and portfolios recommended in music, theatre and art. **Homeschooled:** Interview required. Provide reason for homeschool.

**High school preparation.** 12 units recommended. Recommended units include English 4, mathematics 3, science 3 and foreign language 2.

**2008-2009 Annual costs.** Tuition/fees: $26,030. Parking fee $70, required athletic insurance $183. Room/board: $7,140. Books/supplies: $900. Personal expenses: $1,200.

**2006-2007 Financial aid. Need-based:** 331 full-time freshmen applied for aid; 306 were judged to have need; 303 of these received aid. Average need met was 76%. Average scholarship/grant was $17,188; average loan $5,300. 60% of total undergraduate aid awarded as scholarships/grants, 40% as loans/jobs. **Non-need-based:** Awarded to 454 full-time undergraduates, including 159 freshmen. Scholarships awarded for academics.

**Application procedures. Admission:** Priority date 1/15; deadline 2/15 (postmark date). $25 fee, may be waived for applicants with need. Application may be submitted online. Admission notification on a rolling basis beginning on or about 11/1. Must reply by May 1 or within 3 week(s) if notified thereafter. **Financial aid:** Priority date 3/1; no closing date. FAFSA required. Applicants notified on a rolling basis starting 2/15; must reply within 2 week(s) of notification.

**Academics.** Faculty tutoring for skills development and student tutoring for course-specific help available. Assistance available for non-remedial writing, organizational/time-management skills, and students with learning disabilities. Remedial assistance and reader service for the blind available. **Special study options:** Accelerated study, combined bachelor's/graduate degree, cooperative education, cross-registration, double major, ESL, exchange student, honors, independent study, internships, liberal arts/career combination, student-designed major, study abroad, teacher certification program, Washington semester, weekend college. 3-2 degree programs available in forestry and environmental studies with Duke University, and in physician assistant training with Bowman Gray School of Medicine at Wake Forest University. Many internships, work-study programs, accelerated degree programs in business management, computer information systems, psychology, and biology, dual majors, student-designed majors, study abroad in 9 countries, and cross-registration with members of the Greater Greensboro Consortium (8 colleges/universities). **Credit/placement by examination:** AP, CLEP, IB, SAT, ACT, institutional tests. 32 credit hours maximum toward bachelor's degree. **Support services:** Learning center, pre-admission summer program, reduced course load, remedial instruction, study skills assistance, tutoring, writing center.

**Majors. Area/ethnic studies:** African-American, women's. **Biology:** General, biomedical sciences. **Business:** Accounting, business admin. **Computer sciences:** General, information systems. **Conservation:** Environmental studies. **Education:** Elementary, physical, secondary. **English:** English lit. **Foreign languages:** French, German, Germanic, Spanish. **Health:** Athletic training. **History:** General. **Interdisciplinary:** Peace/conflict. **Math:** General. **Parks/recreation:** Exercise sciences, health/fitness, sports admin. **Philosophy/religion:** Philosophy, religion. **Physical sciences:** Chemistry, geology, physics. **Protective services:** Criminal justice, forensics. **Psychology:** General. **Social sciences:** Economics, international relations, political science, sociology. **Visual/performing arts:** Art, dramatic.

**Most popular majors.** Biology 11%, business/marketing 18%, computer/information sciences 8%, psychology 11%, security/protective services 11%, social sciences 8%, visual/performing arts 6%.

**Computing on campus.** 348 workstations in dormitories, library, computer center, student center. Dormitories wired for high-speed internet access and linked to campus network. Commuter students can connect to campus network. Helpline, repair service, wireless network available.

**Student life. Freshman orientation:** Mandatory, $75 fee. Preregistration for classes offered. One-day event in Spring; parents invited. **Policies:** Consistent with its Quaker heritage, college promotes and encourages student involvement in community service projects. **Housing:** Guaranteed on-campus for freshmen. Coed dorms, single-sex dorms, special housing for disabled, apartments, cooperative housing, substance-free housing available. $400 fully refundable deposit, deadline 5/1. Special interest housing available. Alternative houses with themes and community service project requirements. **Activities:** Bands, campus ministries, choral groups, dance, drama, film society, international student organizations, literary magazine, music ensembles, musical theater, radio station, student government, student newspaper, African American cultural society, Amnesty International, Project Community, community senate, Christian fellowship, Native American club, Hillel, Quaker Concerns, Guilford Action Network.

**Athletics.** NCAA. **Intercollegiate:** Baseball, basketball, cross-country, football (tackle) M, golf M, lacrosse, rugby, soccer, softball W, swimming W, tennis, volleyball W. **Intramural:** Baseball, basketball, cheerleading W, football (non-tackle), soccer, softball, table tennis, tennis, volleyball, water polo. **Team name:** Quakers.

**Student services.** Adult student services, alcohol/substance abuse counseling, campus ministries, career counseling, student employment services, financial aid counseling, health services, minority student services, personal counseling, placement for graduates, veterans' counselor, women's services. **Physically disabled:** Services for visually, speech, hearing impaired. **Learning disabled:** Comprehensive services available.

**Contact.** E-mail: admission@guilford.edu
Phone: (336) 316-2100 Toll-free number: (800) 992-7759
Fax: (336) 316-2954
B Doss, Vice President, Enrollment and Campus Life, Guilford College, Admissions, New Garden Hall, Greensboro, NC 27410-4108

---

## High Point University

| High Point, North Carolina | **CB member** |
| --- | --- |
| www.highpoint.edu | **CB code: 5293** |

- Private 4-year university affiliated with United Methodist Church
- Residential campus in small city
- 2,736 degree-seeking undergraduates: 9% part-time, 62% women
- 313 degree-seeking graduate students
- 73% of applicants admitted
- SAT or ACT (ACT writing optional) required
- 56% graduate within 6 years; 24% enter graduate study

**General.** Founded in 1924. Regionally accredited. **Degrees:** 581 bachelor's awarded; master's offered. **ROTC:** Army, Air Force. **Location:** 15 miles from Greensboro. **Calendar:** Semester, limited summer session. **Full-time faculty:** 129 total; 77% have terminal degrees, 8% minority, 40% women. **Part-time faculty:** 87 total. **Class size:** 67% < 20, 33% 20-39, less

than 1% 40-49, less than 1% >100. **Special facilities:** Athletic/convocation center, fine arts center.

**Freshman class profile.** 2,546 applied, 1,857 admitted, 749 enrolled.

| Mid 50% test scores | | Rank in top quarter: | 38% |
| --- | --- | --- | --- |
| SAT critical reading: | 460-570 | Rank in top tenth: | 17% |
| SAT math: | 460-570 | Return as sophomores: | 79% |
| SAT writing: | 460-560 | Out-of-state: | 72% |
| ACT composite: | 19-24 | Live on campus: | 97% |
| GPA 3.50 or higher: | 31% | Fraternities: | 10% |
| GPA 3.0-3.49: | 33% | Sororities: | 18% |
| GPA 2.0-2.99: | 36% | | |

**Basis for selection.** The most important factors are the academic transcript, including grades received and course selection, followed by standardized test scores (SAT or ACT). Other important factors are demonstrated leadership, extracurricular and community involvement, and special talent. Students who speak English as a second language must demonstrate proficiency in English. TOEFL preferred, other instruments considered. International students may submit TOEFL in lieu of SAT or ACT, unless they wish to play on intercollegiate athletic teams in which case either SAT or ACT required. Interview strongly encouraged. Applicants asked to provide short essay answers to specific questions, but personal essays invited and considered. **Learning Disabled:** Regardless of disability status, a person must meet the academic and technical standards required for admission.

**High school preparation.** 14 units required. Required and recommended units include English 4, mathematics 3, social studies 3, science 2 (laboratory 1), foreign language 2 and academic electives 2.

**2007-2008 Annual costs.** Tuition/fees: $19,850. Room/board: $7,960.

**2006-2007 Financial aid. Need-based:** 481 full-time freshmen applied for aid; 304 were judged to have need; 304 of these received aid. Average need met was 58%. Average scholarship/grant was $3,412; average loan $2,625. 53% of total undergraduate aid awarded as scholarships/grants, 47% as loans/jobs. **Non-need-based:** Awarded to 940 full-time undergraduates, including 265 freshmen. Scholarships awarded for academics, alumni affiliation, art, athletics, leadership, music/drama, religious affiliation, state residency.

**Application procedures. Admission:** Priority date 11/3; deadline 3/14 (postmark date). $40 fee, may be waived for applicants with need. Application may be submitted online. Admission notification on a rolling basis beginning on or about 1/1. Must reply by May 1 or within 4 week(s) if notified thereafter. **Financial aid:** Priority date 3/1; no closing date. FAFSA required. Applicants notified on a rolling basis starting 4/1; must reply within 3 week(s) of notification.

**Academics. Special study options:** Accelerated study, combined bachelor's/graduate degree, cooperative education, cross-registration, double major, dual enrollment of high school students, ESL, honors, independent study, internships, liberal arts/career combination, student-designed major, study abroad, teacher certification program. Dual degree programs with Duke University (forestry and environmental science) and Wake Forest University School of Medicine (medical technology). **Credit/placement by examination:** AP, CLEP, IB, SAT, ACT, institutional tests. 31 credit hours maximum toward bachelor's degree. **Support services:** Learning center, pre-admission summer program, reduced course load, study skills assistance, tutoring, writing center.

**Majors. Area/ethnic studies:** American. **Biology:** General. **Business:** Accounting, business admin, entrepreneurial studies, human resources, international, management information systems, marketing, organizational behavior. **Communications:** General. **Computer sciences:** General, computer science, security. **Conservation:** Forestry. **Education:** Art, early childhood, elementary, middle, physical, secondary, special. **English:** Composition, English lit. **Foreign languages:** General, French, Spanish. **Health:** Athletic training, clinical lab science. **History:** General. **Interdisciplinary:** Global studies. **Math:** General. **Parks/recreation:** Exercise sciences, facilities management, sports admin. **Philosophy/religion:** Philosophy, religion. **Physical sciences:** Chemistry. **Protective services:** Criminal justice. **Psychology:** General. **Social sciences:** Political science, sociology. **Visual/performing arts:** Art, dramatic, interior design, theater design. **Other:** Home furnishings marketing.

**Most popular majors.** Business/marketing 42%, computer/information sciences 8%, education 10%, psychology 6%, social sciences 7%.

**Computing on campus.** 950 workstations in library, computer center, student center. Dormitories wired for high-speed internet access and linked to campus network. Commuter students can connect to campus network. Online course registration, online library, helpline, repair service, student web hosting, wireless network available.

**Student life. Freshman orientation:** Mandatory. Preregistration for classes offered. **Housing:** Guaranteed on-campus for freshmen. Coed dorms, single-sex dorms, special housing for disabled, apartments, cooperative housing, fraternity/sorority housing, substance-free housing available. $200 fully refundable deposit, deadline 5/1. **Activities:** Bands, choral groups, dance, drama, literary magazine, music ensembles, musical theater, radio station, student government, student newspaper, TV station, Alpha Phi Omega, black cultural awareness, Board of Stewards, College Republicans, College Democrats, Fellowship of Christian Athletes, Model United Nations, Phi Theta Kappa Alumni Association, volunteer center.

**Athletics.** NCAA. **Intercollegiate:** Baseball M, basketball, cheerleading, cross-country, golf, soccer, tennis, track and field, volleyball W. **Intramural:** Badminton, basketball, bowling, golf, racquetball, soccer, softball, swimming, table tennis, tennis, track and field M, volleyball, water polo. **Team name:** Panthers.

**Student services.** Adult student services, alcohol/substance abuse counseling, campus ministries, career counseling, student employment services, financial aid counseling, health services, personal counseling, placement for graduates, veterans' counselor.

**Contact.**  E-mail: admiss@highpoint.edu
Phone: (336) 841-9216 Toll-free number: (800) 345-6993
Fax: (336) 888-6382
Andy Bills, Vice President of Enrollment, High Point University, 833 Montlieu Avenue, High Point, NC 27262-3598

## John Wesley College
**High Point, North Carolina**
www.johnwesley.edu                              **CB code: 5348**

- Private 4-year Bible college affiliated with interdenominational tradition
- Commuter campus in small city
- 107 degree-seeking undergraduates: 30% part-time, 33% women, 25% African American, 2% Asian American, 3% Hispanic American, 1% Native American
- 64% of applicants admitted
- Application essay, interview required
- 59% graduate within 6 years; 92% enter graduate study

**General.** Founded in 1932. Accredited by ABHE. **Degrees:** 38 bachelor's awarded. **Location:** 15 miles from Greensboro, 60 miles from Charlotte. **Calendar:** Semester, limited summer session. **Full-time faculty:** 3 total. **Part-time faculty:** 25 total. **Class size:** 98% < 20, 2% 20-39.

**Freshman class profile.** 14 applied, 9 admitted, 6 enrolled.

| | | | |
|---|---|---|---|
| End year in good standing: | 88% | Out-of-state: | 2% |
| Return as sophomores: | 35% | | |

**Basis for selection.** Future career in church-related vocations and motivation; religious commitment and personal statement very important. Positive personal testimony required. Finding and following God's will foremost. **Homeschooled:** Transcript of courses and grades required. Junior or higher standing, GPA 3.2 or higher, 16 or older, and recommendation from high school administrator or guidance counselor required.

**High school preparation.** 20 units recommended. Recommended units include English 4, mathematics 3, social studies 2, science 2 (laboratory 2).

**2007-2008 Annual costs.** Tuition/fees: $10,914. Room only: $2,344. Books/supplies: $1,000. Personal expenses: $2,600.

**Financial aid. Additional information:** Early Acceptance Scholarships, Academic Honor Scholarships, Married Student Credit and Minister/Missionary Dependent Scholarship available.

**Application procedures. Admission:** Closing date 8/8 (postmark date). $35 fee, may be waived for applicants with need. Application may be submitted online. Admission notification on a rolling basis. **Financial aid:** Priority date 3/15; no closing date. FAFSA required. Applicants notified on a rolling basis starting 6/1; must reply within 3 week(s) of notification.

**Academics.** All students major in Bible; second major optional. **Special study options:** Accelerated study, cooperative education, distance learning, double major, dual enrollment of high school students, independent study, internships, student-designed major. **Credit/placement by examination:** AP, CLEP, IB, institutional tests. 15 credit hours maximum toward associate degree, 30 toward bachelor's. **Support services:** Reduced course load.

**Majors. Business:** Business admin. **Education:** Elementary. **Theology:** Pastoral counseling, religious ed, theology.

**Most popular majors.** Business/marketing 45%, philosophy/religious studies 45%.

**Computing on campus.** 6 workstations in library, computer center. Dormitories wired for high-speed internet access. Online library available.

**Student life. Freshman orientation:** Mandatory. Preregistration for classes offered. Orientation activities held 2 business days before classes begin. **Policies:** Religious observance required. **Housing:** Apartments, substance-free housing available. $50 deposit, deadline 7/15. **Activities:** Campus ministries, drama, literary magazine, student government, evangelistic ministries, prison ministry, gospel music team, foreign missions involvement team.

**Athletics. Intramural:** Basketball, bowling, golf, table tennis, volleyball.

**Student services.** Campus ministries, student employment services, financial aid counseling, personal counseling, veterans' counselor.

**Contact.**  E-mail: aziemba@johnwesley.edu
Phone: (336) 889-2262 ext. 127 Fax: (336) 889-2261
Amanda Ziemba, Admissions Officer, John Wesley College, 2314 North Centennial, High Point, NC 27265-3197

## Johnson & Wales University: Charlotte
**Charlotte, North Carolina**
www.jwu.edu                              **CB code: 4360**

- Private 4-year university
- Commuter campus in very large city
- 2,569 degree-seeking undergraduates: 2% part-time, 55% women, 24% African American, 2% Asian American, 3% Hispanic American, 1% international
- 63% of applicants admitted

**General. Degrees:** 172 bachelor's, 586 associate awarded. **Calendar:** Quarter. **Full-time faculty:** 85 total. **Part-time faculty:** 16 total. **Class size:** 34% < 20, 60% 20-39, 5% 40-49, less than 1% 50-99.

**Freshman class profile.** 5,108 applied, 3,237 admitted, 721 enrolled.

| Mid 50% test scores | | | |
|---|---|---|---|
| SAT critical reading: | 410-530 | GPA 3.0-3.49: | 27% |
| SAT math: | 420-520 | GPA 2.0-2.99: | 50% |
| GPA 3.50 or higher: | 22% | Live on campus: | 63% |
| | | International: | 1% |

**Basis for selection.** Secondary school record, class rank, and interview important. SAT or ACT recommended of all; required for applicants to the honors programs.

**High school preparation.** 12 units recommended. Recommended units include English 4, mathematics 3, social studies 2 and science 3.

**2007-2008 Annual costs.** Tuition/fees: $21,717. Room/board: $8,550. Books/supplies: $900. Personal expenses: $594.

**2007-2008 Financial aid. Need-based:** 603 full-time freshmen applied for aid; 533 were judged to have need; 533 of these received aid. Average need met was 67%. Average scholarship/grant was $7,728; average loan $3,319. 44% of total undergraduate aid awarded as scholarships/grants, 56% as loans/jobs. **Non-need-based:** Awarded to 1,784 full-time undergraduates, including 571 freshmen. Scholarships awarded for academics, alumni affiliation, job skills, leadership.

**Application procedures. Admission:** No deadline. No application fee. Admission notification on a rolling basis beginning on or about 11/1. **Financial aid:** No deadline. FAFSA required. Applicants notified by 3/1.

**Academics.** Math center. **Special study options:** Accelerated study, cooperative education, dual enrollment of high school students, honors, independent study, internships, study abroad. **Credit/placement by examination:** CLEP, institutional tests. **Support services:** Learning center, pre-admission summer program, reduced course load, remedial instruction, study skills assistance, tutoring, writing center.

**Majors. Business:** Accounting, hotel/motel admin, management science, marketing, restaurant/food services, tourism/travel. **Other:** Sports/Entertainment/ Event Management.

**Most popular majors.** Business/marketing 7%, family/consumer sciences 92%.

**Computing on campus.** 160 workstations in library. Dormitories wired for high-speed internet access and linked to campus network. Commuter students can connect to campus network. Online library, helpline, wireless network available.

**Student life. Freshman orientation:** Available. **Housing:** Coed dorms, special housing for disabled available. $300 deposit. **Activities:** Choral groups, dance, literary magazine, music ensembles, student government, student newspaper.

**Athletics. Intramural:** Basketball, soccer, softball, volleyball. **Team name:** Wildcats.

**Student services.** Career counseling, student employment services, financial aid counseling, health services, personal counseling, veterans' counselor. **Physically disabled:** Services for visually, speech, hearing impaired.

**Contact.** E-mail: admissions.clt@jwu.edu
Phone: (980) 598-1100 Toll-free number: (866) 598-2427
Fax: (980) 598-1111
Brian Stanley, Director of Admissions, Johnson & Wales University: Charlotte, 801 West Trade Street, Charlotte, NC 28202

## Johnson C. Smith University
**Charlotte, North Carolina**
www.jcsu.edu

**CB member**
**CB code: 5333**

- Private 4-year university and liberal arts college
- Residential campus in very large city
- 1,463 degree-seeking undergraduates: 3% part-time, 58% women, 99% African American
- 46% of applicants admitted
- SAT or ACT (ACT writing optional) required
- 41% graduate within 6 years; 24% enter graduate study

**General.** Founded in 1867. Regionally accredited. **Degrees:** 228 bachelor's awarded. **ROTC:** Army, Air Force. **Location:** 244 miles from Atlanta. **Calendar:** Semester, limited summer session. **Full-time faculty:** 101 total; 73% have terminal degrees, 68% minority, 50% women. **Part-time faculty:** 19 total; 21% have terminal degrees, 68% minority, 47% women. **Class size:** 56% < 20, 44% 20-39, less than 1% 40-49. **Special facilities:** Technology center.

**Freshman class profile.** 5,299 applied, 2,436 admitted, 502 enrolled.

| Mid 50% test scores | | End year in good standing: | 91% |
|---|---|---|---|
| SAT critical reading: | 430-500 | Return as sophomores: | 64% |
| SAT math: | 440-510 | Out-of-state: | 79% |
| ACT composite: | 19-27 | Live on campus: | 95% |

**Basis for selection.** High school class rank, GPA, SAT or ACT scores important. Applicants encouraged to submit no more than 2 letters of recommendation from guidance counselors or teachers and personal essay to support application. Interviews are accepted but not required.

**High school preparation.** 16 units required. Required units include English 4, mathematics 2, social studies 2, science 1 and academic electives 7.

**2007-2008 Annual costs.** Tuition/fees: $15,754. Room/board: $6,132. Books/supplies: $1,750. Personal expenses: $2,400.

**2007-2008 Financial aid. Need-based:** 427 full-time freshmen applied for aid; 391 were judged to have need; 391 of these received aid. Average need met was 56%. Average scholarship/grant was $3,573; average loan $3,500. 32% of total undergraduate aid awarded as scholarships/grants, 68% as loans/jobs. **Non-need-based:** Awarded to 304 full-time undergraduates, including 182 freshmen. Scholarships awarded for academics, athletics, ROTC, state residency.

**Application procedures. Admission:** Priority date 8/1; no deadline. $25 fee, may be waived for applicants with need. Application may be submitted online. Admission notification on a rolling basis beginning on or about 10/1. **Financial aid:** Priority date 3/1; no closing date. FAFSA required. Applicants notified on a rolling basis starting 3/1; must reply within 2 week(s) of notification.

**Academics.** Requirements include 10 hours per year of community service, freshman and sophomore assessments in basic competencies, and exit exams in major field for seniors. Freshmen who have completed liberal studies program with honors may apply to enter Honors College as sophomores. **Special study options:** Accelerated study, cooperative education, cross-registration, double major, exchange student, honors, independent study, internships, liberal arts/career combination, study abroad, teacher certification program. **Credit/placement by examination:** AP, CLEP, institutional tests. **Support services:** Learning center, pre-admission summer program, reduced course load, study skills assistance, tutoring, writing center.

**Honors college/program.** Students receiving academic scholarships are expected to enroll in the Advanced Freshman Studies Program, which is preparatory for admission into the Honors College during the sophomore year. Students who complete the freshman year of the Liberal Studies Program with honors may be admitted into the Honors College in the sophomore year. Other students are invited to join the program based on their grades, high school preparation, and SAT scores as well as on references from both University and high school instructors.

**Majors. Biology:** General. **Business:** Business admin. **Communications:** Media studies. **Computer sciences:** General, information technology. **Education:** Elementary, health, mathematics, physical, social studies. **Engineering:** Computer. **English:** English lit. **Foreign languages:** French, Spanish. **History:** General. **Interdisciplinary:** Natural sciences. **Liberal arts:** Arts/sciences. **Math:** General. **Parks/recreation:** Sports admin. **Physical sciences:** Chemistry. **Psychology:** General. **Public administration:** Social work. **Social sciences:** General, criminology, economics, political science. **Visual/performing arts:** Music management. **Other:** Health and Physical Education/Fitness.

**Most popular majors.** Business/marketing 16%, communications/journalism 16%, computer/information sciences 8%, interdisciplinary studies 6%, parks/recreation 7%, psychology 6%, security/protective services 10%, social sciences 7%.

**Computing on campus.** PC or laptop required. 335 workstations in dormitories, library, computer center. Dormitories wired for high-speed internet access and linked to campus network. Commuter students can connect to campus network. Online course registration, online library, helpline, repair service, wireless network available.

**Student life. Freshman orientation:** Available, $100 fee. Three-day program in July for students and parents. **Housing:** Guaranteed on-campus for freshmen. Coed dorms, single-sex dorms, substance-free housing available. $150 nonrefundable deposit, deadline 7/15. Limited honors housing available. **Activities:** Bands, choral groups, dance, drama, literary magazine, music ensembles, student government, student newspaper, Student Christian association, Muslim student association, NAACP, National Association of Black Accountants, National Association of Black Engineers, Habitat for Humanity, College Democrats, Young Republicans.

**Athletics.** NCAA. **Intercollegiate:** Basketball, bowling W, cross-country, football (tackle) M, golf, softball W, tennis, track and field, volleyball W. **Intramural:** Basketball, football (non-tackle), table tennis. **Team name:** Golden Bulls.

**Student services.** Adult student services, alcohol/substance abuse counseling, campus ministries, career counseling, services for economically disadvantaged, student employment services, financial aid counseling, health services, minority student services, personal counseling, veterans' counselor. **Physically disabled:** Services for visually, speech, hearing impaired.

**Contact.** E-mail: admissions@jcsu.edu
Phone: (704) 378-1010 Toll-free number: (800) 782-7303
Fax: (704) 378-1242
Jocelyn Biggs, Director of Admissions, Johnson C. Smith University, 100 Beatties Ford Road, Charlotte, NC 28216-5398

## Lees-McRae College
**Banner Elk, North Carolina**
www.lmc.edu

**CB member**
**CB code: 5364**

- Private 4-year liberal arts college affiliated with Presbyterian Church (USA)
- Residential campus in rural community
- 871 degree-seeking undergraduates: 2% part-time, 60% women
- 74% of applicants admitted

**General.** Founded in 1900. Regionally accredited. **Degrees:** 204 bachelor's awarded. **Location:** 17 miles from Boone, 40 miles from Johnson City, Tennessee. **Calendar:** Semester, limited summer session. **Full-time faculty:** 43 total. **Part-time faculty:** 14 total. **Class size:** 71% < 20, 29% 20-39. **Special facilities:** Wireless campus, biology field station, Blue Ridge Wildlife Rehabilitation Institute.

**Freshman class profile.** 821 applied, 606 admitted, 203 enrolled.

| Mid 50% test scores | | ACT composite: | 19-24 |
|---|---|---|---|
| SAT critical reading: | 440-530 | Out-of-state: | 50% |
| SAT math: | 440-540 | Live on campus: | 96% |

**Basis for selection.** High school record and rank in top half of class preferred. Test scores optional. Recommendations considered. Interview recommended for all students; portfolio recommended for performing arts programs. Audition required for athletic, performing arts programs.

**High school preparation.** 18 units required. Required and recommended units include English 4, mathematics 3, social studies 2, history 1, science 2 (laboratory 1), foreign language 2 and academic electives 6.

**2007-2008 Annual costs.** Tuition/fees: $19,500. Room/board: $6,500. Books/supplies: $760. Personal expenses: $2,000.

**Financial aid. Non-need-based:** Scholarships awarded for academics, alumni affiliation, athletics, leadership, minority status, music/drama, religious affiliation, state residency.

**Application procedures. Admission:** Priority date 5/1; no deadline. No application fee. Application may be submitted online. Admission notification on a rolling basis beginning on or about 12/1. Accepting and notifying applicants of acceptance status begins after completion of 6 semesters in high school. **Financial aid:** Priority date 3/15; no closing date. FAFSA required. Applicants notified on a rolling basis starting 3/1; must reply within 2 week(s) of notification.

**Academics. Special study options:** Double major, ESL, honors, independent study, internships, liberal arts/career combination, student-designed major, study abroad, teacher certification program. 3-2 program Environmental Science/Forestry with Duke University. **Credit/placement by examination:** AP, CLEP, IB, ACT, institutional tests. 16 credit hours maximum toward bachelor's degree. **Support services:** Learning center, remedial instruction, study skills assistance, tutoring, writing center.

**Majors. Biology:** General. **Business:** Business admin. **Communications:** General. **Computer sciences:** Computer science, information systems. **Education:** Drama/dance, elementary, physical. **English:** English lit. **Health:** Predental, premedicine, preveterinary. **History:** General. **Liberal arts:** Arts/sciences. **Math:** General. **Philosophy/religion:** Religion. **Protective services:** Criminal justice. **Psychology:** General. **Social sciences:** International relations, sociology. **Visual/performing arts:** Dramatic.

**Most popular majors.** Biology 13%, business/marketing 17%, education 29%, psychology 10%, security/protective services 13%.

**Computing on campus.** 125 workstations in dormitories, library, computer center, student center. Dormitories wired for high-speed internet access and linked to campus network. Commuter students can connect to campus network. Online course registration, online library, helpline, wireless network available.

**Student life. Freshman orientation:** Mandatory. Preregistration for classes offered. 6 summer Freshmen Experience sessions (1 required) followed by August orientation. **Housing:** Guaranteed on-campus for freshmen. Coed dorms, single-sex dorms, substance-free housing available. **Activities:** Choral groups, dance, drama, international student organizations, music ensembles, musical theater, student government, Order of the Tower, student ambassadors, residence hall association, sports medicine club, Phi Beta Lambda, Circle K, campus after the class hours, EMS club.

**Athletics.** NCAA. **Intercollegiate:** Basketball, cheerleading, cross-country, golf M, lacrosse, soccer, softball W, tennis, track and field, volleyball. **Intramural:** Basketball, cross-country, football (non-tackle), golf, skiing, soccer, softball, table tennis, tennis, volleyball. **Team name:** Bobcats.

**Student services.** Alcohol/substance abuse counseling, campus ministries, career counseling, student employment services, financial aid counseling, health services, personal counseling, veterans' counselor.

**Contact.** E-mail: admissions@lmc.edu
Phone: (828) 898-8723 Toll-free number: (800) 280-4562
Fax: (828) 898-8707
Bill Sliwa, Vice President for Enrollment Management, Lees-McRae College, Box 128, Banner Elk, NC 28604

---

## Lenoir-Rhyne College

**Hickory, North Carolina**
www.lrc.edu

**CB member**
**CB code: 5365**

- Private 4-year liberal arts college affiliated with Evangelical Lutheran Church in America
- Residential campus in large town
- 1,366 degree-seeking undergraduates: 5% part-time, 64% women, 8% African American, 2% Asian American, 1% Hispanic American, 1% international
- 126 degree-seeking graduate students
- 84% of applicants admitted
- SAT or ACT with writing required
- 54% graduate within 6 years

**General.** Founded in 1891. Regionally accredited. **Degrees:** 316 bachelor's awarded; master's offered. **ROTC:** Army, Naval. **Location:** 50 miles from Charlotte. **Calendar:** Semester, limited summer session. **Full-time faculty:** 93 total; 81% have terminal degrees, 6% minority, 45% women. **Part-time faculty:** 70 total; 3% minority, 53% women. **Class size:** 72% < 20, 26% 20-39, 2% 40-49, less than 1% 50-99. **Special facilities:** Observatory, multimedia classrooms, outdoor classroom.

**Freshman class profile.** 1,770 applied, 1,478 admitted, 367 enrolled.

| Mid 50% test scores | | | |
|---|---|---|---|
| SAT critical reading: | 460-560 | GPA 2.0-2.99: | 13% |
| SAT math: | 470-580 | Rank in top quarter: | 58% |
| SAT writing: | 460-550 | Rank in top tenth: | 26% |
| ACT composite: | 19-24 | Return as sophomores: | 72% |
| GPA 3.50 or higher: | 67% | Out-of-state: | 21% |
| GPA 3.0-3.49: | 20% | Live on campus: | 83% |
| | | International: | 1% |

**Basis for selection.** School achievement record most important. Interview recommended for all students; audition required for music majors. **Homeschooled:** Transcript of courses and grades required.

**High school preparation.** 12 units required. Required units include English 4, mathematics 3, history 1, science 1 (laboratory 1) and foreign language 2. Chemistry required for nursing program. "History" refers to U.S. History; mathematics needs to include algebra I, algebra II, geometry.

**2008-2009 Annual costs.** Tuition/fees: $23,070. Room/board: $8,150. Books/supplies: $1,100. Personal expenses: $1,500.

**2006-2007 Financial aid. Need-based:** 340 full-time freshmen applied for aid; 310 were judged to have need; 310 of these received aid. Average need met was 33%. Average scholarship/grant was $12,337; average loan $2,513. 59% of total undergraduate aid awarded as scholarships/grants, 41% as loans/jobs. **Non-need-based:** Awarded to 551 full-time undergraduates, including 228 freshmen. Scholarships awarded for academics, athletics, job skills, leadership, minority status, music/drama, ROTC, state residency.

**Application procedures. Admission:** Priority date 12/1; deadline 8/15 (receipt date). $35 fee, may be waived for applicants with need. Application may be submitted online. Admission notification on a rolling basis beginning on or about 6/1. Must reply by May 1 or within 2 week(s) if notified thereafter. Students will not be put on the housing roster until the deposit is received. **Financial aid:** Priority date 3/1, closing date 8/1. FAFSA required. Applicants notified on a rolling basis starting 3/1; must reply within 2 week(s) of notification.

**Academics.** Special program for deaf, hearing-impaired and disabled students. **Special study options:** Accelerated study, combined bachelor's/graduate degree, cross-registration, distance learning, double major, dual enrollment of high school students, ESL, exchange student, external degree, honors, independent study, internships, liberal arts/career combination, student-designed major, study abroad, teacher certification program, Washington semester. **Credit/placement by examination:** AP, CLEP, IB, SAT, ACT, institutional tests. 16 credit hours maximum toward bachelor's degree. **Support services:** Learning center, pre-admission summer program, remedial instruction, study skills assistance, tutoring, writing center.

**Majors. Area/ethnic studies:** American. **Biology:** General. **Business:** Accounting, finance, international, management information systems, management science, marketing. **Communications:** General. **Computer sciences:** General, information systems. **Conservation:** Environmental studies, forestry. **Education:** Art, biology, chemistry, Deaf/hearing impaired, early childhood, elementary, English, ESL, history, mathematics, middle, music, physical, psychology, science, social science, social studies. **Engineering technology:** General. **English:** English lit. **Family/consumer sciences:** Child development. **Foreign languages:** French, German, Latin, Spanish. **Health:** Athletic training, clinical lab science, nursing (RN), premedicine. **History:** General. **Legal studies:** Prelaw. **Liberal arts:** Arts/sciences. **Math:** General. **Parks/recreation:** Sports admin. **Philosophy/religion:** Philosophy, religion. **Physical sciences:** Chemistry, physics. **Psychology:** General. **Public administration:** Human services. **Science technology:** Chemical. **Social sciences:** Economics, international relations, political science, sociology. **Theology:** Sacred music. **Visual/performing arts:** Arts management, dramatic, graphic design, music performance.

**Most popular majors.** Business/marketing 23%, education 10%, health sciences 16%, parks/recreation 7%, public administration/social services 6%, social sciences 9%.

**Computing on campus.** 112 workstations in library, computer center, student center. Dormitories wired for high-speed internet access and linked to campus network. Commuter students can connect to campus network. Online library, helpline, wireless network available.

**Student life. Freshman orientation:** Mandatory. Preregistration for classes offered. Held 2 days before start of classes. **Housing:** Guaranteed on-campus for all undergraduates. Coed dorms, special housing for disabled, fraternity/sorority housing available. $200 deposit. **Activities:** Bands, campus ministries, choral groups, dance, drama, film society, literary magazine, music ensembles, radio station, student government, student newspaper, Black student alliance, Campus Crusade for Christ, Fellowship of Christian Athletes, North Carolina Student Legislature, Intervarsity Christian Fellowship, College Democrats, Lutheran Student Movement, Circle K, Student Occupational Therapy Association, Gay Straight Alliance.

**Athletics.** NCAA. **Intercollegiate:** Baseball M, basketball, cheerleading, cross-country, football (tackle) M, golf, soccer, softball W, swimming W, tennis, track and field, volleyball W. **Intramural:** Basketball, football (non-tackle), lacrosse M, soccer, softball, volleyball. **Team name:** Bears.

**Student services.** Adult student services, campus ministries, career counseling, student employment services, financial aid counseling, health services, minority student services, personal counseling, veterans' counselor. **Physically disabled:** Services for hearing impaired.

**Contact.** E-mail: admission@lrc.edu
Phone: (828) 328-7300 Toll-free number: (800) 277-5721
Fax: (828) 328-7378
Karen Feezor, Director of Admissions, Lenoir-Rhyne College, PO Box 7227, Hickory, NC 28603

---

## Livingstone College

**Salisbury, North Carolina**
www.livingstone.edu

**CB member**
**CB code: 5367**

- Private 4-year liberal arts college affiliated with African Methodist Episcopal Zion Church
- Residential campus in large town
- 960 degree-seeking undergraduates
- 97% of applicants admitted
- SAT or ACT (ACT writing optional) required

**General.** Founded in 1879. Regionally accredited. **Degrees:** 122 bachelor's awarded. **ROTC:** Army. **Location:** 44 miles from Charlotte. **Calendar:** Semester. **Full-time faculty:** 51 total. **Part-time faculty:** 22 total. **Class size:** 64% < 20, 28% 20-39, 4% 40-49, 1% 50-99, 2% >100. **Special facilities:** Center for Negro and African life, literature and international studies.

**Freshman class profile.** 2,001 applied, 1,949 admitted, 331 enrolled.

| Mid 50% test scores | | | |
|---|---|---|---|
| | | ACT composite: | 13-16 |
| SAT critical reading: | 330-420 | Out-of-state: | 59% |
| SAT math: | 330-430 | Live on campus: | 85% |
| SAT writing: | 320-420 | | |

**Basis for selection.** School achievement record, test scores, recommendations important. College's placement test, instead of ELPT, used for advising and placement. Audition required for music majors; interview recommended for academically weak students.

**High school preparation.** 10 units required. Required and recommended units include English 4, mathematics 3, social studies 2, history 1, science 2 and foreign language 2.

**2007-2008 Annual costs.** Tuition/fees: $12,474. Room/board: $5,641. Books/supplies: $800. Personal expenses: $3,000.

**Financial aid. Non-need-based:** Scholarships awarded for academics, alumni affiliation, athletics, leadership, music/drama, religious affiliation, ROTC, state residency.

**Application procedures. Admission:** Priority date 5/15; no deadline. $25 fee, may be waived for applicants with need. Application may be submitted online. Admission notification on a rolling basis. Must reply by May 1 or within 4 week(s) if notified thereafter. **Financial aid:** Priority date 3/15, closing date 6/30. FAFSA required. Applicants notified by 5/1; must reply within 4 week(s) of notification.

**Academics. Special study options:** Accelerated study, cross-registration, double major, independent study, internships, teacher certification program. **Credit/placement by examination:** CLEP, institutional tests. **Support services:** Learning center, reduced course load, study skills assistance, tutoring.

**Majors. Biology:** General. **Business:** Accounting, business admin. **Computer sciences:** General. **Education:** Elementary. **Engineering:** General. **English:** English lit. **Health:** Predental, prepharmacy. **History:** General. **Legal studies:** General. **Math:** General. **Parks/recreation:** Sports admin. **Physical sciences:** Chemistry. **Protective services:** Criminal justice. **Psychology:** General. **Public administration:** Social work. **Social sciences:**

General, political science, sociology. **Theology:** Theology. **Visual/performing arts:** Dramatic.

**Most popular majors.** Business/marketing 24%, computer/information sciences 16%, psychology 6%, security/protective services 24%, social sciences 14%.

**Computing on campus.** 200 workstations in dormitories, library, computer center. Dormitories wired for high-speed internet access and linked to campus network.

**Student life. Freshman orientation:** Mandatory, $100 fee. Preregistration for classes offered. **Housing:** Single-sex dorms, special housing for disabled, apartments available. $100 deposit. **Activities:** Bands, choral groups, dance, drama, film society, music ensembles, musical theater, radio station, student government, pre-theological union, AME Zion Council.

**Athletics.** NCAA. **Intercollegiate:** Basketball, bowling, cross-country, football (tackle) M, softball W, tennis, track and field, volleyball W. **Intramural:** Basketball. **Team name:** Blue Bears.

**Student services.** Career counseling, student employment services, health services, personal counseling, placement for graduates, veterans' counselor.

**Contact.** Phone: (704) 216-6001 Toll-free number: (800) 835-3435
Fax: (704) 216-6215
Nicole Daniels, Director of Enrollment Management and Admission, Livingstone College, 701 West Monroe Street, Salisbury, NC 28144-5213

---

## Mars Hill College

**Mars Hill, North Carolina**
www.mhc.edu

**CB member**
**CB code: 5395**

- Private 4-year liberal arts college affiliated with Baptist faith
- Residential campus in small town
- 1,212 degree-seeking undergraduates
- 71% of applicants admitted
- SAT or ACT (ACT writing optional) required

**General.** Founded in 1856. Regionally accredited. **Degrees:** 242 bachelor's awarded. **Location:** 17 miles from Asheville. **Calendar:** Semester, extensive summer session. **Full-time faculty:** 71 total. **Part-time faculty:** 84 total. **Special facilities:** Satellite receiver for foreign language study, Appalachian archives and artifacts museum.

**Freshman class profile.** 1,305 applied, 921 admitted, 302 enrolled.

| Mid 50% test scores | | | |
|---|---|---|---|
| SAT critical reading: | 410-530 | Rank in top quarter: | 26% |
| SAT math: | 420-550 | Rank in top tenth: | 8% |
| ACT composite: | 16-22 | Out-of-state: | 44% |
| GPA 3.50 or higher: | 32% | Live on campus: | 84% |
| GPA 3.0-3.49: | 28% | Fraternities: | 8% |
| GPA 2.0-2.99: | 36% | Sororities: | 6% |

**Basis for selection.** School achievement record, test scores, school and community activities, recommendations from school officials all important. Students interested in early admission must apply as full-time students, achieve A average in courses, minimum SAT 1000 (exclusive of Writing) or ACT 22, and submit 2 recommendations from high school personnel. Audition required for music, theater programs. Essay, portfolio recommended; interview recommended for students who do not meet other admissions criteria. **Homeschooled:** Transcript of courses and grades required. **Learning Disabled:** Letter of documentation required.

**High school preparation.** 11 units required. Required and recommended units include English 4, mathematics 3, social studies 2, history 2, science 2, foreign language 2 and computer science 1.

**2007-2008 Annual costs.** Tuition/fees: $18,812. Room/board: $6,462. Books/supplies: $1,000. Personal expenses: $1,000.

**2007-2008 Financial aid. Need-based:** 70% of total undergraduate aid awarded as scholarships/grants, 30% as loans/jobs. **Non-need-based:** Scholarships awarded for academics, art, athletics, religious affiliation, state residency.

**Application procedures. Admission:** No deadline. $25 fee, may be waived for applicants with need. Application may be submitted online. Admission notification on a rolling basis. **Financial aid:** No deadline. FAFSA, institutional form required. Applicants notified on a rolling basis; must reply within 2 week(s) of notification.

**Academics. Special study options:** Accelerated study, cross-registration, distance learning, double major, dual enrollment of high school students, ESL, exchange student, independent study, internships, liberal arts/career combination, student-designed major, study abroad, teacher certification program. 3-2 physician assistant, 3-1 medical technology, 2-2 allied health programs. **Credit/placement by examination:** AP, CLEP, IB, SAT, ACT, institutional tests. 32 credit hours maximum toward bachelor's degree. **Support services:** Learning center, reduced course load, remedial instruction, study skills assistance, tutoring, writing center.

**Majors. Biology:** General, botany, zoology. **Business:** General, accounting, business admin, finance, international. **Communications:** General. **Computer sciences:** Computer science. **Education:** General, art, elementary, English, middle, music, physical, secondary. **English:** English lit. **Foreign languages:** Spanish. **Health:** Athletic training, clinical lab assistant, physician assistant, predental, premedicine, prepharmacy, preveterinary. **History:** General. **Interdisciplinary:** Biological/physical sciences. **Legal studies:** Prelaw. **Liberal arts:** Arts/sciences. **Math:** General. **Parks/recreation:** Facilities management, health/fitness. **Philosophy/religion:** Religion. **Physical sciences:** Chemistry. **Psychology:** General. **Public administration:** Social work. **Social sciences:** Political science, sociology. **Visual/performing arts:** Art, fashion design, music performance.

**Computing on campus.** 180 workstations in library, computer center, student center. Dormitories wired for high-speed internet access and linked to campus network. Commuter students can connect to campus network. Helpline, repair service, wireless network available.

**Student life. Freshman orientation:** Mandatory. Preregistration for classes offered. **Housing:** Guaranteed on-campus for all undergraduates. Single-sex dorms, special housing for disabled, apartments available. $250 deposit. College townhouses and apartments available to upperclassmen. **Activities:** Bands, campus ministries, choral groups, dance, drama, literary magazine, music ensembles, musical theater, student government, student newspaper, Christian Student Movement, Fellowship of Christian Athletes, The Refuge, Ladies of Distinction, Black Student Alliance, health care society, Green Students United, Bailey Mountain Cloggers.

**Athletics. NCAA. Intercollegiate:** Baseball M, basketball, cross-country, football (tackle) M, golf, lacrosse M, soccer, softball W, swimming, tennis, track and field, volleyball W. **Intramural:** Badminton, basketball, football (non-tackle), soccer, softball, tennis, volleyball, water polo M. **Team name:** Lions.

**Student services.** Adult student services, campus ministries, career counseling, services for economically disadvantaged, student employment services, financial aid counseling, health services, personal counseling, veterans' counselor.

**Contact.** E-mail: admissions@mhc.edu
Phone: (828) 689-1201 Toll-free number: (866) 642-4968
Fax: (828) 689-1473
Ed Hoffmeyer, Director of Admissions, Mars Hill College, Blackwell Hall, Box 370, Mars Hill, NC 28754

---

## Meredith College
### Raleigh, North Carolina
www.meredith.edu

CB member
CB code: 5410

- Private 4-year liberal arts college for women
- Residential campus in large city
- 1,937 degree-seeking undergraduates: 9% part-time, 100% women, 11% African American, 2% Asian American, 2% Hispanic American, 1% international
- 141 degree-seeking graduate students
- 88% of applicants admitted
- SAT or ACT (ACT writing optional) required
- 63% graduate within 6 years

**General.** Founded in 1891. Regionally accredited. **Degrees:** 372 bachelor's awarded; master's offered. **ROTC:** Army, Air Force. **Location:** 250 miles from Washington, DC, 375 miles from Atlanta. **Calendar:** Semester, limited summer session. **Full-time faculty:** 140 total; 90% have terminal degrees, 9% minority, 69% women. **Part-time faculty:** 152 total; 30% have terminal degrees, 5% minority, 72% women. **Class size:** 72% < 20, 26% 20-39, 1% 40-49, less than 1% 50-99, less than 1% >100. **Special facilities:** Amphitheatre, child care laboratory, experimental and clinical psychology laboratories, autism laboratory, astronomy observation deck, electron microscope suite, 15 student/faculty research laboratories, greenhouse.

**Freshman class profile.** 1,205 applied, 1,056 admitted, 464 enrolled.

| Mid 50% test scores | | | |
|---|---|---|---|
| SAT critical reading: | 460-580 | Rank in top quarter: | 50% |
| SAT math: | 460-570 | Rank in top tenth: | 21% |
| ACT composite: | 19-23 | Return as sophomores: | 74% |
| GPA 3.50 or higher: | 33% | Out-of-state: | 10% |
| GPA 3.0-3.49: | 38% | Live on campus: | 94% |
| GPA 2.0-2.99: | 29% | International: | 1% |

**Basis for selection.** GED not accepted. School record (courses taken, grades on academic subjects, and class rank), test scores, and recommendations important. Meredith seeks to enroll qualified students of varying backgrounds, interests and talents and has a need-blind admission policy. Essay and/or interview may be required of some; audition recommended for music majors; portfolio recommended for art majors. **Homeschooled:** SAT Reasoning and SAT Subject Tests (English, math, and foreign language or one of applicant's choice) required.

**High school preparation.** 16 units required. Required units include English 4, mathematics 3, science 3 and foreign language 2. 3 units required in social studies or history. At least 1 elective required, preferably from core academic subjects.

**2007-2008 Annual costs.** Tuition/fees: $22,400. Tuition includes laptop computer. Room/board: $6,300. Books/supplies: $750. Personal expenses: $1,250.

**2007-2008 Financial aid. Need-based:** 372 full-time freshmen applied for aid; 297 were judged to have need; 297 of these received aid. Average need met was 81%. Average scholarship/grant was $13,598; average loan $3,494. 63% of total undergraduate aid awarded as scholarships/grants, 37% as loans/jobs. **Non-need-based:** Awarded to 236 full-time undergraduates, including 112 freshmen. Scholarships awarded for academics, art, leadership, minority status, music/drama, religious affiliation, state residency.

**Application procedures. Admission:** Priority date 2/15; no deadline. $40 fee, may be waived for applicants with need. Application may be submitted online. Admission notification on a rolling basis beginning on or about 11/1. Must reply by May 1 or within 2 week(s) if notified thereafter. **Financial aid:** Priority date 2/15; no closing date. FAFSA required. Applicants notified on a rolling basis starting 3/15; must reply by 5/1 or within 2 week(s) of notification.

**Academics.** Undergraduate research program available to students in all disciplines. Post-baccalaureate dietetic internship program and post-baccalaureate certificate in paralegal studies available. **Special study options:** Accelerated study, combined bachelor's/graduate degree, cooperative education, cross-registration, double major, dual enrollment of high school students, honors, independent study, internships, liberal arts/career combination, New York semester, student-designed major, study abroad, teacher certification program, United Nations semester, Washington semester. Study Abroad includes summer programs, semester/year abroad opportunities, and individually-tailored semesters. 3-2 in engineering with N.C. State University. **Credit/placement by examination:** AP, CLEP, IB, institutional tests. **Support services:** Learning center, reduced course load, remedial instruction, study skills assistance, tutoring, writing center.

**Majors. Area/ethnic studies:** Women's. **Biology:** General, molecular. **Business:** Accounting, business admin, fashion. **Communications:** General, media studies. **Computer sciences:** General, computer science. **Conservation:** Environmental science, environmental studies. **Education:** Art, drama/dance, music, physical. **English:** English lit. **Family/consumer sciences:** General, child development. **Foreign languages:** French, Spanish. **Health:** Dietetics, health services. **History:** General, public archives. **Interdisciplinary:** Global studies. **Math:** General. **Parks/recreation:** Health/fitness. **Philosophy/religion:** Religion. **Physical sciences:** Chemistry. **Psychology:** General. **Public administration:** Social work. **Social sciences:** Economics, political science, sociology, U.S. government. **Visual/performing arts:** Dance, dramatic, fashion design, graphic design, interior design, music pedagogy, music performance, studio arts.

**Most popular majors.** Business/marketing 15%, communications/journalism 6%, family/consumer sciences 8%, health sciences 8%, psychology 12%, visual/performing arts 17%.

**Computing on campus.** PC or laptop required. 145 workstations in dormitories, library, computer center, student center. Dormitories wired for high-speed internet access and linked to campus network. Commuter students can connect to campus network. Online course registration, online library, helpline, repair service, wireless network available.

**Student life. Freshman orientation:** Mandatory. Preregistration for classes offered. 4-day program before start of classes with extra day for athletes, international students, and students with disabilities. **Policies:** Honor Code is a long-standing tradition that requires individual integrity and community responsibility of all students. Traditional-aged freshmen and sophomores must live on campus except if married or living with parents or other relatives by special permission. **Housing:** Guaranteed on-campus for freshmen. Substance-free housing available. $100 nonrefundable deposit, deadline 5/1. Pets allowed in dorm rooms. Campus housing available for all 4 years. All on-campus housing is "wellness housing.". **Activities:** Concert band, choral groups, dance, drama, international student organizations, literary magazine, music ensembles, Model UN, musical theater, student government, student newspaper, symphony orchestra, association for cultural awareness, unity council, service council, Habitat for Humanity, Angels for the Environment, College Democrats, College Republicans, Christian Association, Catholic Angels.

**Athletics.** NCAA. **Intercollegiate:** Basketball W, cross-country W, soccer W, softball W, tennis W, volleyball W. **Team name:** Avenging Angels.

**Student services.** Adult student services, alcohol/substance abuse counseling, campus ministries, career counseling, student employment services, financial aid counseling, health services, minority student services, personal counseling, placement for graduates. **Physically disabled:** Services for visually, speech, hearing impaired.

**Contact.** E-mail: admissions@meredith.edu
Phone: (919) 760-8581 Toll-free number: (800) 637-3348
Fax: (919) 760-2348
Heidi Fletcher, Director of Admissions, Meredith College, 3800 Hillsborough Street, Raleigh, NC 27607-5298

---

## Methodist University
### Fayetteville, North Carolina
**www.methodist.edu**  **CB code: 5426**

- Private 4-year liberal arts college affiliated with United Methodist Church
- Residential campus in small city
- 1,940 degree-seeking undergraduates: 13% part-time, 45% women
- 122 degree-seeking graduate students
- 54% of applicants admitted
- SAT or ACT (ACT writing optional) required
- 37% graduate within 6 years

**General.** Founded in 1956. Regionally accredited. **Degrees:** 290 bachelor's, 13 associate awarded; master's offered. **ROTC:** Army, Air Force. **Location:** 50 miles from Raleigh-Durham. **Calendar:** Semester, extensive summer session. **Full-time faculty:** 127 total; 77% have terminal degrees, 12% minority, 49% women. **Part-time faculty:** 86 total; 91% have terminal degrees, 17% minority, 43% women. **Class size:** 72% < 20, 27% 20-39, less than 1% 40-49, less than 1% 50-99. **Special facilities:** Computer-assisted English composition laboratory, psychology computer-experimental laboratory, nature trail, professional golf and tennis management center, 18-hole golf course and driving range, environmental simulation center (virtual reality laboratory).

**Freshman class profile.** 2,796 applied, 1,499 admitted, 437 enrolled.

| Mid 50% test scores | | Rank in top quarter: | 31% |
|---|---|---|---|
| SAT critical reading: | 440-530 | Rank in top tenth: | 12% |
| SAT math: | 450-570 | Return as sophomores: | 67% |
| SAT writing: | 410-520 | Out-of-state: | 51% |
| ACT composite: | 18-23 | Live on campus: | 89% |
| GPA 3.50 or higher: | 32% | International: | 4% |
| GPA 3.0-3.49: | 30% | Fraternities: | 1% |
| GPA 2.0-2.99: | 38% | Sororities: | 1% |

**Basis for selection.** High school record (GPA), curriculum, test scores carefully considered. All prospective student files reviewed on individual basis. Extracurricular achievements and teacher/counselor recommendations also considered. Students who transfer English 101 credits must take institutional English Placement Exam. SAT/ACT scores not required of transfer students with more than 31 semester hours of transferrable credit. Essay and interview recommended for all students; audition recommended for drama and music majors; portfolio recommended for art majors.

**High school preparation.** 16 units required; 20 recommended. Required and recommended units include English 4, mathematics 3-4, social studies 2, history 1-2, science 2-3 (laboratory 1-2), foreign language 2 and academic electives 4.

**2008-2009 Annual costs.** Tuition/fees: $21,944. Professional golf management, professional tennis management, and music students have additional fees. Room/board: $8,046. Books/supplies: $800. Personal expenses: $1,500.

**2006-2007 Financial aid. Need-based:** 449 full-time freshmen applied for aid; 350 were judged to have need; 350 of these received aid. Average need met was 71%. Average scholarship/grant was $8,746; average loan $2,330. 67% of total undergraduate aid awarded as scholarships/grants, 33% as loans/jobs. **Non-need-based:** Awarded to 1,124 full-time undergraduates, including 291 freshmen. Scholarships awarded for academics, alumni affiliation, leadership, music/drama, religious affiliation, ROTC, state residency.

**Application procedures. Admission:** No deadline. $25 fee, may be waived for applicants with need. Application may be submitted online. Admission notification on a rolling basis beginning on or about 9/1. Must reply by May 1 or within 2 week(s) if notified thereafter. **Financial aid:** Priority date 5/1, closing date 7/1. FAFSA required. Applicants notified on a rolling basis starting 3/1; must reply within 2 week(s) of notification.

**Academics. Special study options:** Accelerated study, double major, dual enrollment of high school students, ESL, exchange student, honors, independent study, internships, liberal arts/career combination, student-designed major, study abroad, teacher certification program, Washington semester, weekend college. **Credit/placement by examination:** AP, CLEP, IB, SAT, ACT, institutional tests. 45 credit hours maximum toward associate degree, 45 toward bachelor's. **Support services:** Learning center, reduced course load, remedial instruction, study skills assistance, tutoring, writing center.

**Majors. Biology:** General, botany, cellular/molecular, conservation, ecology, exercise physiology, microbiology, zoology. **Business:** Accounting, business admin, finance, golf management, hospitality admin, hospitality/recreation, management information systems, marketing, resort management, tourism/travel. **Communications:** General, journalism, media studies, organizational. **Computer sciences:** General, computer graphics, computer science, web page design. **Education:** General, art, biology, chemistry, elementary, English, foreign languages, mathematics, middle, music, physical, secondary, social studies, special. **Engineering technology:** Occupational safety. **English:** English lit, speech/rhetoric. **Foreign languages:** French, Spanish. **Health:** Athletic training, facilities admin, health care admin, physician assistant, predental, premedicine, prenursing, prepharmacy, preveterinary. **History:** General. **Legal studies:** Prelaw. **Liberal arts:** Arts/sciences. **Math:** General. **Parks/recreation:** Exercise sciences, facilities management, health/fitness, sports admin. **Philosophy/religion:** Philosophy, religion. **Physical sciences:** Chemistry, forensic chemistry. **Protective services:** Criminal justice. **Psychology:** General. **Public administration:** Social work. **Social sciences:** Political science, sociology. **Theology:** Religious ed. **Visual/performing arts:** General, art, ceramics, graphic design, music performance, painting, printmaking, sculpture, studio arts. **Other:** Professional tennis management.

**Most popular majors.** Biology 6%, business/marketing 47%, parks/recreation 8%, public administration/social services 6%, social sciences 6%.

**Computing on campus.** 220 workstations in library, computer center. Dormitories wired for high-speed internet access and linked to campus network. Commuter students can connect to campus network. Online course registration, online library, helpline, wireless network available.

**Student life. Freshman orientation:** Available, $50 fee. Preregistration for classes offered. Typically held the weekend (Friday and Saturday) after July 4th. **Housing:** Guaranteed on-campus for all undergraduates. Coed dorms, single-sex dorms, apartments, substance-free housing available. $100 nonrefundable deposit, deadline 5/1. Health/wellness hall, first-year experience hall available. Students must live on-campus through sophomore year unless living with parents/guardians. All residence halls are non-smoking facilities. **Activities:** Bands, campus ministries, choral groups, dance, drama, literary magazine, music ensembles, Model UN, musical theater, radio station, student government, student newspaper, symphony orchestra, Fellowship of Christian Athletes, Young Democrats/Republicans, African American culture society, student activities committee, commuting student organization.

**Athletics.** NCAA. **Intercollegiate:** Baseball M, basketball, cheerleading, cross-country, football (tackle) M, golf, lacrosse W, soccer, softball W, tennis, track and field, volleyball W. **Intramural:** Basketball, cheerleading W, football (non-tackle), golf, racquetball, soccer, softball, table tennis, tennis, volleyball. **Team name:** Monarchs.

**Student services.** Alcohol/substance abuse counseling, campus ministries, career counseling, student employment services, financial aid counseling, health services, personal counseling, placement for graduates, veterans' counselor, women's services. **Physically disabled:** Services for visually impaired.

**Contact.** E-mail: admissions@methodist.edu
Phone: (910) 630-7027 Toll-free number: (800) 488-7110
Fax: (910) 630-7285
Jamie Legg, Director of Admissions, Methodist University, 5400 Ramsey Street, Fayetteville, NC 28311-1498

## Miller-Motte Technical College
**Wilmington, North Carolina**
www.miller-motte.com

CB code: 3342

- For-profit 4-year technical college
- Commuter campus in small city
- 760 degree-seeking undergraduates
- Interview required

**General.** Accredited by ACICS. **Degrees:** 3 bachelor's, 173 associate awarded. **Location:** 145 miles from Raleigh. **Calendar:** Quarter, extensive summer session. **Full-time faculty:** 35 total. **Part-time faculty:** 30 total.

**Basis for selection.** Open admission, but selective for some programs. Minimum test score of 15 on Wonderlic test for admission, 18 for medical 19 surgical tech and 20 for MCSE.

**High school preparation.** 17 units recommended. Recommended units include English 4, mathematics 4, social studies 4, science 4 (laboratory 1).

**2007-2008 Annual costs.** Tuition/fees: $10,890. Books/supplies: $1,000. Personal expenses: $2,250.

**Financial aid.** All financial aid based on need.

**Application procedures. Admission:** No deadline. $35 fee. Application must be submitted on paper. Admission notification on a rolling basis. **Financial aid:** No deadline. FAFSA, institutional form required.

**Academics. Special study options:** Distance learning, double major, internships. **Credit/placement by examination:** CLEP, institutional tests. 46 credit hours maximum toward associate degree. **Support services:** Learning center, reduced course load, remedial instruction, study skills assistance, tutoring.

**Majors. Business:** Business admin. **Health:** Health services. **Protective services:** Law enforcement admin.

**Most popular majors.** Business/marketing 50%, health sciences 50%.

**Computing on campus.** 120 workstations in library, computer center. Commuter students can connect to campus network. Online library, repair service, student web hosting available.

**Student life. Freshman orientation:** Mandatory. Preregistration for classes offered. **Activities:** Student newspaper.

**Athletics. Team name:** Marlin.

**Student services.** Career counseling, financial aid counseling, placement for graduates.

**Contact.** Phone: (910) 392-4660 Toll-free number: (800) 784-2110 Fax: (910) 799-6224
Jennifer Rumbold, Director of Admissions, Miller-Motte Technical College, 5000 Market Street, Wilmington, NC 28405

## Montreat College
**Montreat, North Carolina**
www.montreat.edu

CB member
CB code: 5423

- Private 4-year liberal arts college affiliated with Presbyterian Church (USA)
- Residential campus in small town
- 984 degree-seeking undergraduates: 2% part-time, 61% women, 27% African American, 1% Asian American, 2% Hispanic American, 4% Native American, 2% international
- 161 degree-seeking graduate students
- 71% of applicants admitted
- SAT or ACT (ACT writing recommended), application essay required

**General.** Founded in 1916. Regionally accredited. **Degrees:** 190 bachelor's, 27 associate awarded; master's offered. **Location:** 16 miles from Asheville. **Calendar:** Semester, limited summer session. **Full-time faculty:** 46 total; 67% have terminal degrees, 13% minority, 35% women. **Class size:** 72% < 20, 26% 20-39, 2% 40-49. **Special facilities:** Scanning micron electroscope, ropes course, climbing wall, chapel of the prodigal, Black Mountain campus.

**Freshman class profile.** 427 applied, 304 admitted, 180 enrolled.

| Mid 50% test scores | | | |
|---|---|---|---|
| SAT critical reading: | 440-570 | Rank in top quarter: | 37% |
| SAT math: | 450-540 | Rank in top tenth: | 18% |
| GPA 3.50 or higher: | 37% | Out-of-state: | 31% |
| GPA 3.0-3.49: | 25% | Live on campus: | 100% |
| GPA 2.0-2.99: | 37% | International: | 1% |

**Basis for selection.** Decisions are criteria-based, using GPA and SAT/ACT scores as initial qualifiers. Essay, recommendation, and extracurricular activities also considered. Interview required for students who do not meet standard admission requirements. **Homeschooled:** Transcript of courses and grades, letter of recommendation (nonparent) required. **Learning Disabled:** Students with documented learning disabilities are referred to the Director of Student Success before an admissions decision is made.

**High school preparation.** 16 units required. Required units include English 4, mathematics 3, social studies 3, science 3, foreign language 1 and academic electives 2.

**2008-2009 Annual costs.** Tuition/fees (projected): $19,091. Room/board: $5,866. Books/supplies: $975. Personal expenses: $1,910.

**2006-2007 Financial aid. Need-based:** 64% of total undergraduate aid awarded as scholarships/grants, 36% as loans/jobs. **Non-need-based:** Scholarships awarded for academics, alumni affiliation, athletics, leadership, music/drama, religious affiliation, state residency.

**Application procedures. Admission:** Priority date 5/15; deadline 8/1 (postmark date). $30 fee, may be waived for applicants with need. Application may be submitted online. Admission notification on a rolling basis beginning on or about 9/15. **Financial aid:** Priority date 3/15; no closing date. FAFSA, institutional form required. Applicants notified on a rolling basis starting 1/15; must reply within 2 week(s) of notification.

**Academics. Special study options:** Accelerated study, double major, dual enrollment of high school students, independent study, internships, student-designed major, study abroad, teacher certification program, Washington semester. **Credit/placement by examination:** AP, CLEP, IB, institutional tests. 15 credit hours maximum toward associate degree, 30 toward bachelor's. **Support services:** Reduced course load, study skills assistance, tutoring, writing center.

**Majors. Area/ethnic studies:** American. **Biology:** General. **Business:** Accounting, business admin, international, marketing. **Communications:** Media studies. **Computer sciences:** General. **Conservation:** Environmental studies. **Education:** Elementary. **English:** English lit. **History:** General, American. **Parks/recreation:** General. **Philosophy/religion:** Christian. **Psychology:** General. **Public administration:** Human services. **Theology:** Bible, missionary, religious ed, youth ministry. **Visual/performing arts:** Music management, music performance.

**Most popular majors.** Business/marketing 72%.

**Computing on campus.** 60 workstations in library, computer center, student center. Dormitories wired for high-speed internet access and linked to campus network. Repair service, wireless network available.

**Student life. Freshman orientation:** Mandatory. Preregistration for classes offered. 5 days before classes start. There is also a pre-orientation program, Wilderness Journey, available at extra cost. **Policies:** No alcohol on campus. Religious observance required. **Housing:** Guaranteed on-campus for all undergraduates. Single-sex dorms, substance-free housing available. $100 fully refundable deposit, deadline 4/1. 351 spaces available for undergraduate students. **Activities:** Choral groups, dance, drama, music ensembles, musical theater, student government, student newspaper, missions club, Fellowship of Christian Athletes, Young Life.

**Athletics.** NAIA. **Intercollegiate:** Baseball M, basketball, cross-country, golf, soccer, softball W, track and field, volleyball W. **Intramural:** Basketball, football (non-tackle), soccer, softball, table tennis, tennis, volleyball. **Team name:** Cavaliers.

**Student services.** Adult student services, alcohol/substance abuse counseling, campus ministries, career counseling, student employment services, financial aid counseling, health services, personal counseling, placement for graduates, veterans' counselor. **Physically disabled:** Services for visually, speech, hearing impaired.

**Contact.** E-mail: admissions@montreat.edu
Phone: (828) 669-8012 ext. 3781 Toll-free number: (800) 622-6968
Fax: (828) 669-0120
Joey Higgins, Director of Admissions, Montreat College, Box 1267, Montreat, NC 28757-1267

## Mount Olive College

Mount Olive, North Carolina
www.mountolivecollege.edu

**CB member**
**CB code: 5435**

- Private 4-year liberal arts college affiliated with Free Will Baptists
- Residential campus in small town
- 3,116 degree-seeking undergraduates: 21% part-time, 67% women
- SAT or ACT (ACT writing optional) required

**General.** Founded in 1951. Regionally accredited. **Degrees:** 629 bachelor's, 140 associate awarded. **Location:** 13 miles from Goldsboro. **Calendar:** Differs by program, extensive summer session. **Full-time faculty:** 85 total; 79% have terminal degrees, 18% minority, 39% women. **Part-time faculty:** 218 total; 23% have terminal degrees, 6% minority, 43% women. **Class size:** 71% < 20, 29% 20-39, less than 1% >100.

**Freshman class profile.** 975 applied, 654 admitted, 404 enrolled.

| Mid 50% test scores | | | |
|---|---|---|---|
| SAT critical reading: | 420-510 | GPA 2.0-2.99: | 40% |
| SAT math: | 430-530 | Rank in top quarter: | 29% |
| ACT composite: | 15-21 | Rank in top tenth: | 7% |
| GPA 3.50 or higher: | 29% | Return as sophomores: | 64% |
| GPA 3.0-3.49: | 28% | Out-of-state: | 8% |
| | | Live on campus: | 49% |

**Basis for selection.** Open admission. School record, test scores, class rank important. Personal recommendations considered. Interview recommended for all students; portfolio recommended for art majors. Audition required for music majors.

**High school preparation.** 17 units required. Required units include English 4, mathematics 3, social studies 3, science 3 (laboratory 1) and academic electives 3.

**2008-2009 Annual costs.** Tuition/fees: $13,126. Room/board: $5,300. Books/supplies: $1,220.

**2006-2007 Financial aid. Need-based:** 375 full-time freshmen applied for aid; 317 were judged to have need; 313 of these received aid. Average need met was 65%. Average scholarship/grant was $7,351; average loan $2,030. 56% of total undergraduate aid awarded as scholarships/grants, 44% as loans/jobs. **Non-need-based:** Awarded to 536 full-time undergraduates, including 94 freshmen. Scholarships awarded for academics, art, athletics, leadership, music/drama, religious affiliation.

**Application procedures. Admission:** No deadline. $20 fee, may be waived for applicants with need. Application may be submitted online. Admission notification on a rolling basis beginning on or about 10/1. **Financial aid:** Priority date 3/1; no closing date. FAFSA required. Applicants notified on a rolling basis starting 2/14; must reply within 2 week(s) of notification.

**Academics. Special study options:** Accelerated study, cooperative education, distance learning, double major, dual enrollment of high school students, external degree, honors, independent study, internships, liberal arts/career combination, teacher certification program. Accelerated extension program at Seymour Johnson Air Force Base in Goldsboro; 55-week degree completion program in business offered in New Bern, Wilmington, and Raleigh-Research Triangle Park. **Credit/placement by examination:** AP, CLEP, institutional tests. 15 credit hours maximum toward associate degree, 30 toward bachelor's. **Support services:** Learning center, reduced course load, remedial instruction, study skills assistance, tutoring, writing center.

**Majors. Biology:** General. **Business:** Accounting, business admin, human resources, management information systems, organizational behavior. **Communications:** General. **Computer sciences:** General. **English:** English lit. **History:** General. **Liberal arts:** Arts/sciences. **Math:** General. **Parks/recreation:** General. **Philosophy/religion:** Religion. **Protective services:** Criminal justice. **Psychology:** General. **Visual/performing arts:** Design, studio arts.

**Most popular majors.** Business/marketing 52%, education 12%, security/protective services 15%.

**Computing on campus.** 50 workstations in library, computer center. Dormitories wired for high-speed internet access and linked to campus network. Commuter students can connect to campus network. Online library, repair service, wireless network available.

**Student life. Freshman orientation:** Available. **Policies:** Religious observance required. **Housing:** Guaranteed on-campus for freshmen. Single-sex dorms, apartments available. $50 nonrefundable deposit, deadline 3/15. **Activities:** Concert band, campus ministries, choral groups, international student organizations, music ensembles, musical theater, student government,

English society, political forum, recreation majors club, Fellowship of Christian Athletes, Phi Beta Lambda, minority students' organization, Fellowship of Christian Students, Free Spirit.

**Athletics.** NCAA. **Intercollegiate:** Baseball M, basketball, cross-country, golf, soccer, softball W, tennis, volleyball. **Intramural:** Badminton, baseball M, basketball, football (tackle) M, handball, racquetball, softball, table tennis, tennis, volleyball.

**Student services.** Adult student services, career counseling, student employment services, health services, personal counseling, placement for graduates, veterans' counselor.

**Contact.** E-mail: admissions@moc.edu
Phone: (919) 658-7164 Toll-free number: (800) 653-0854
Fax: (919) 658-7180
Tim Woodard, Director of Admissions, Mount Olive College, 634 Henderson Street, Mount Olive, NC 28365

## North Carolina Agricultural and Technical State University

Greensboro, North Carolina
www.ncat.edu

**CB member**
**CB code: 5003**

- Public 4-year Historically Black College/University (HBCU)
- Residential campus in small city
- 8,873 degree-seeking undergraduates: 9% part-time, 52% women, 92% African American, 1% Asian American, 1% Hispanic American
- 1,226 degree-seeking graduate students
- 56% of applicants admitted
- SAT or ACT with writing, SAT Subject Tests required

**General.** Founded in 1891. Regionally accredited. **Degrees:** 1,321 bachelor's awarded; master's, doctoral offered. **ROTC:** Army, Air Force. **Location:** 91 miles from Charlotte. **Calendar:** Semester, extensive summer session. **Full-time faculty:** 518 total. **Part-time faculty:** 323 total. **Special facilities:** African heritage center, microelectronics center, planetarium, herbarium, Olympic style track.

**Freshman class profile.** 5,598 applied, 3,147 admitted, 1,597 enrolled.

| Mid 50% test scores | | | |
|---|---|---|---|
| SAT critical reading: | 390-500 | GPA 3.0-3.49: | 25% |
| SAT math: | 400-510 | GPA 2.0-2.99: | 58% |
| ACT composite: | 15-20 | Rank in top quarter: | 10% |
| GPA 3.50 or higher: | 12% | Rank in top tenth: | 1% |
| | | International: | 1% |

**Basis for selection.** High school GPA, class rank, test scores, recommendations, course selection reviewed. SAT preferred, but ACT accepted. Audition recommended for music programs; portfolio recommended for art programs.

**High school preparation.** 19 units required. Required units include English 4, mathematics 4, social studies 1, history 1, science 3 (laboratory 1), foreign language 2 and academic electives 4.

**2007-2008 Annual costs.** Tuition/fees: $3,500; $12,942 out-of-state. Room/board: $5,379. Books/supplies: $800. Personal expenses: $1,700.

**2007-2008 Financial aid. Need-based:** Average need met was 52%. Average scholarship/grant was $4,803; average loan $3,182. 48% of total undergraduate aid awarded as scholarships/grants, 52% as loans/jobs. **Non-need-based:** Scholarships awarded for academics, athletics, music/drama, ROTC.

**Application procedures. Admission:** Priority date 6/1; no deadline. $45 fee. Admission notification on a rolling basis beginning on or about 9/15. Must reply by May 1 or within 2 week(s) if notified thereafter. **Financial aid:** Priority date 3/15; no closing date. FAFSA required. Applicants notified on a rolling basis starting 4/1; must reply within 2 week(s) of notification.

**Academics. Special study options:** Cooperative education, cross-registration, distance learning, double major, dual enrollment of high school students, honors, internships, study abroad, teacher certification program, weekend college. **Credit/placement by examination:** AP, CLEP, SAT, ACT, institutional tests. **Support services:** Learning center, reduced course load, remedial instruction, study skills assistance, tutoring, writing center.

**Majors. Agriculture:** Animal sciences, business, economics, plant sciences. **Architecture:** Landscape. **Biology:** General. **Business:** General, accounting, business admin, finance, managerial economics, marketing, transportation. **Communications:** General, broadcast journalism, journalism, public relations. **Computer sciences:** General. **Education:** General, agricultural, biology, business, chemistry, driver/safety, early childhood, elementary, English, family/consumer sciences, foreign languages, French, history, mathematics, music, physical, physics, social science, special, speech, technology/industrial arts, trade/industrial. **Engineering:** Agricultural, architectural, chemical, civil, electrical, materials, mechanical. **Engineering technology:** Industrial management, occupational safety. **English:** English lit, speech/rhetoric. **Family/consumer sciences:** General, clothing/textiles, family studies, family/community services, food/nutrition. **Foreign languages:** French. **Health:** Occupational health. **History:** General. **Math:** General. **Parks/recreation:** Facilities management, health/fitness. **Physical sciences:** Chemistry, physics. **Psychology:** General. **Public administration:** Social work. **Social sciences:** General, political science, sociology. **Visual/performing arts:** General, art, dramatic.

**Most popular majors.** Business/marketing 13%, communications/journalism 8%, engineering/engineering technologies 17%, psychology 11%, visual/performing arts 6%.

**Computing on campus.** 675 workstations in library, computer center. Dormitories wired for high-speed internet access and linked to campus network. Commuter students can connect to campus network. Online course registration, helpline available.

**Student life. Freshman orientation:** Mandatory, $10 fee. Preregistration for classes offered. **Housing:** Guaranteed on-campus for freshmen. Coed dorms, single-sex dorms, substance-free housing available. $150 deposit. **Activities:** Bands, choral groups, dance, drama, music ensembles, radio station, student government, student newspaper, symphony orchestra, TV station.

**Athletics.** NCAA. **Intercollegiate:** Baseball M, basketball, bowling W, cross-country, football (tackle) M, softball W, swimming W, tennis W, track and field, volleyball W, wrestling M. **Intramural:** Badminton, baseball M, basketball, bowling W, cross-country, football (tackle) M, golf, handball, racquetball, soccer, softball, swimming, table tennis, tennis, track and field, volleyball. **Team name:** Aggies.

**Student services.** Adult student services, alcohol/substance abuse counseling, career counseling, student employment services, health services, minority student services, personal counseling, placement for graduates, veterans' counselor. **Physically disabled:** Services for visually, speech, hearing impaired.

**Contact.** E-mail: uadmit@ncat.edu
Phone: (336) 334-7946 Toll-free number: (800) 443-8964
Fax: (336) 334-7478
Yvette Murph, Associate Vice Chancellor for Enrollment Management, North Carolina Agricultural and Technical State University, Webb Hall, Greensboro, NC 27411-0002

## North Carolina Central University

**Durham, North Carolina**                 **CB member**
**www.nccu.edu**                                   **CB code: 5495**

- Public 4-year university
- Commuter campus in small city
- 5,764 degree-seeking undergraduates
- 74% of applicants admitted
- SAT or ACT with writing required

**General.** Founded in 1910. Regionally accredited. Historically, the majority of students have been African American. **Degrees:** 810 bachelor's awarded; master's, first professional offered. **ROTC:** Army, Air Force. **Location:** 23 miles from Raleigh. **Calendar:** Semester, extensive summer session. **Full-time faculty:** 390 total. **Part-time faculty:** 259 total. **Class size:** 36% < 20, 47% 20-39, 11% 40-49, 6% 50-99, less than 1% >100. **Special facilities:** Collection of primary resources on black life and culture, art museum with works of Afro-American culture.

**Freshman class profile.** 3,513 applied, 2,585 admitted, 1,265 enrolled.

| Mid 50% test scores | | GPA 2.0-2.99: | 60% |
|---|---|---|---|
| SAT critical reading: | 380-470 | Rank in top quarter: | 16% |
| SAT math: | 370-460 | Rank in top tenth: | 5% |
| ACT composite: | 14-18 | Out-of-state: | 16% |
| GPA 3.50 or higher: | 12% | Live on campus: | 80% |
| GPA 3.0-3.49: | 20% | | |

**Basis for selection.** Academic achievement, class rank, test scores important. SAT preferred, ACT also accepted. Audition required for music programs. **Homeschooled:** Transcript of courses and grades, state high school equivalency certificate required.

**High school preparation.** 14 units required. Required units include English 4, mathematics 4, social studies 2, history 1, science 3 (laboratory 2) and foreign language 2. Social studies units must include 1 U.S. history. One foreign language, and 1 math recommended during 12th grade. Students who graduate high school in and after 2006 must have one additional math course from the following: pre-calculus, AP statistics, AP calculus, IB math level II, integrated math IV, discrete math, advanced models and functions.

**2007-2008 Annual costs.** Tuition/fees: $3,666; $13,411 out-of-state. Room/board: $5,226. Books/supplies: $1,500. Personal expenses: $1,575.

**Financial aid. Non-need-based:** Scholarships awarded for academics, alumni affiliation, athletics, minority status, music/drama, state residency. **Additional information:** Departmental grants based on need plus other available criteria.

**Application procedures. Admission:** Priority date 5/1; deadline 8/1. $30 fee. Application may be submitted online. Admission notification on a rolling basis. Early admission available with permission from high school principal and academic dean. **Financial aid:** Priority date 4/1; no closing date. FAFSA required. Applicants notified by 5/1; must reply within 2 week(s) of notification.

**Academics. Special study options:** Cooperative education, distance learning, double major, ESL, honors, independent study, internships, study abroad, teacher certification program. **Credit/placement by examination:** AP, CLEP, SAT, ACT, institutional tests. 30 credit hours maximum toward bachelor's degree. **Support services:** Learning center, remedial instruction, study skills assistance, tutoring, writing center.

**Majors. Biology:** General. **Business:** Accounting, business admin, hospitality admin. **Communications:** Media studies. **Computer sciences:** Computer science, information systems. **Conservation:** Environmental science. **Education:** Art, biology, chemistry, drama/dance, elementary, English, family/consumer sciences, French, health, history, kindergarten/preschool, mathematics, middle, music, physical, physics, Spanish. **English:** English lit. **Family/consumer sciences:** General. **Foreign languages:** French, Spanish. **Health:** Athletic training, nursing (RN), public health ed. **History:** General. **Math:** General. **Parks/recreation:** Facilities management, health/fitness. **Physical sciences:** Chemistry, physics. **Protective services:** Law enforcement admin. **Psychology:** General. **Public administration:** Social work. **Social sciences:** Geography, political science, sociology. **Visual/performing arts:** Art, dramatic, jazz.

**Most popular majors.** Business/marketing 18%, education 9%, family/consumer sciences 6%, health sciences 6%, psychology 7%, security/protective services 10%, social sciences 11%.

**Computing on campus.** 400 workstations in dormitories, library, computer center. Dormitories wired for high-speed internet access and linked to campus network. Commuter students can connect to campus network. Online course registration, online library, helpline, repair service, wireless network available.

**Student life. Freshman orientation:** Mandatory. Preregistration for classes offered. **Housing:** Coed dorms, single-sex dorms available. $100 deposit, deadline 6/1. Coed honors dormitory available. **Activities:** Bands, choral groups, dance, drama, literary magazine, radio station, student government, student newspaper.

**Athletics.** NAIA, NCAA. **Intercollegiate:** Basketball, bowling, cheerleading W, cross-country, football (tackle) M, golf, softball W, tennis, track and field, volleyball W. **Team name:** Eagles.

**Student services.** Career counseling, student employment services, health services, on-campus daycare, personal counseling, placement for graduates, veterans' counselor.

**Contact.** E-mail: admissions@nccu.edu
Phone: (919) 560-6298 Toll-free number: (877) 667-7533
Fax: (919) 530-7625
Jocelyn Foy, Director of Admissions, North Carolina Central University, PO Box 19717, Durham, NC 27707

## North Carolina School of the Arts

**Winston-Salem, North Carolina**          **CB member**
**www.ncarts.edu**                                **CB code: 5512**

- Public 4-year visual arts and performing arts college
- Residential campus in small city
- 743 degree-seeking undergraduates: 1% part-time, 40% women
- 121 graduate students

- 44% of applicants admitted
- 54% graduate within 6 years

**General.** Founded in 1963. Regionally accredited. State Conservatory with high school, undergraduate and graduate facilities. **Degrees:** 130 bachelor's awarded; master's offered. **Location:** 90 miles from Charlotte, 75 miles from Raleigh. **Calendar:** Trimester, limited summer session. **Full-time faculty:** 125 total; 31% have terminal degrees, 3% minority, 33% women. **Part-time faculty:** 35 total. **Class size:** 84% < 20, 14% 20-39, less than 1% 40-49, 1% 50-99. **Special facilities:** Stage production shop, film village with sound and recording stages.

**Freshman class profile.** 679 applied, 300 admitted, 185 enrolled.

| | | | |
|---|---|---|---|
| End year in good standing: | 77% | Live on campus: | 95% |
| Return as sophomores: | 74% | International: | 1% |
| Out-of-state: | 62% | | |

**Basis for selection.** Talent, achievement, career potential most important. Admission heavily dependent on audition. SAT combined score of 800 (exclusive of Writing) or ACT composite score of 19, school record, recommendations important. SAT or ACT recommended. Interview recommended for all students. Audition required for dance, drama, music programs; portfolio required for design, filmmaking, production programs.

**High school preparation.** 20 units required. Required and recommended units include English 4, mathematics 3, social studies 2, history 1, science 3 (laboratory 1), foreign language 2 and academic electives 4.

**2007-2008 Annual costs.** Tuition/fees: $5,061; $16,491 out-of-state. Required fees may vary by program. Room/board: $6,431. Books/supplies: $865. Personal expenses: $1,889.

**Financial aid. Non-need-based:** Scholarships awarded for academics, art, leadership, music/drama, state residency.

**Application procedures. Admission:** Priority date 3/1; no deadline. $60 fee, may be waived for applicants with need. Application may be submitted online. Admission notification on a rolling basis beginning on or about 4/1. Must reply by May 1 or within 3 week(s) if notified thereafter. Application closing date dependent upon audition. Applications must be submitted at least 2 weeks before audition date. Dance, drama and filmmaking interviews begin in January and end in early March. Music and technical theater auditions begin in November and end in early March. Decisions generally are made by April 1, or about 2 weeks after audition if later than April 1. **Financial aid:** Priority date 3/1; no closing date. FAFSA required. Applicants notified on a rolling basis starting 4/1; must reply within 2 week(s) of notification.

**Academics.** Professional training supplemented by strong general studies curriculum, small classes 7:1 student-teacher ratio. **Special study options:** Independent study, internships. **Credit/placement by examination:** AP, CLEP. **Support services:** Remedial instruction, study skills assistance, tutoring, writing center.

**Majors. Liberal arts:** Arts/sciences. **Visual/performing arts:** Cinematography, dance, dramatic, music performance, theater design.

**Computing on campus.** 28 workstations in dormitories, library, student center. Dormitories wired for high-speed internet access and linked to campus network. Online course registration available.

**Student life. Freshman orientation:** Mandatory, $75 fee. Includes academic assessment. **Housing:** Guaranteed on-campus for freshmen. Coed dorms, single-sex dorms, apartments available. $200 deposit, deadline 5/1. **Activities:** Jazz band, dance, drama, music ensembles, musical theater, opera, student government, student newspaper, symphony orchestra, spirituality committee, ADAPT-drug prevention team, C.A.R.E.-AIDS awareness and prevention team, Awareness for Gay and Lesbian Equality, Artists for Christ, Awareness of Black Arts, Minorities on the Move.

**Athletics. Team name:** Fighting Pickles.

**Student services.** Alcohol/substance abuse counseling, career counseling, student employment services, financial aid counseling, health services, personal counseling.

**Contact.** E-mail: admissions@ncarts.edu
Phone: (336) 770-3291 Fax: (336) 770-3370
Sheeler Lawson, Director of Admissions, North Carolina School of the Arts, 1533 South Main Street, Winston-Salem, NC 27127-2188

## North Carolina State University
**Raleigh, North Carolina**
www.ncsu.edu

CB member
CB code: 5496

- Public 4-year university
- Residential campus in large city
- 22,070 degree-seeking undergraduates: 7% part-time, 43% women, 9% African American, 5% Asian American, 3% Hispanic American, 1% Native American, 1% international
- 6,824 degree-seeking graduate students
- 60% of applicants admitted
- SAT or ACT with writing required
- 69% graduate within 6 years; 30% enter graduate study

**General.** Founded in 1887. Regionally accredited. **Degrees:** 4,601 bachelor's, 130 associate awarded; master's, doctoral, first professional offered. **ROTC:** Army, Naval, Air Force. **Location:** One mile from downtown. **Calendar:** Semester, extensive summer session. **Full-time faculty:** 1,723 total; 90% have terminal degrees, 18% minority, 30% women. **Part-time faculty:** 216 total; 65% have terminal degrees, 7% minority, 41% women. **Class size:** 32% < 20, 45% 20-39, 7% 40-49, 11% 50-99, 5% >100. **Special facilities:** 3 electron microscopes, phytotron, research farms, 2 campus theaters, craft center, stable isotope laboratory, teaching forest, wood products laboratory, coastal marine science laboratory, 80,000 acres of research forests and research farm lands, fiber, fabric, and garment manufacturing equipment.

**Freshman class profile.** 16,437 applied, 9,869 admitted, 4,791 enrolled.

| Mid 50% test scores | | Rank in top tenth: | 34% |
|---|---|---|---|
| SAT critical reading: | 520-610 | End year in good standing: | 87% |
| SAT math: | 550-660 | Return as sophomores: | 89% |
| SAT writing: | 510-610 | Out-of-state: | 8% |
| ACT composite: | 22-27 | Live on campus: | 77% |
| GPA 3.50 or higher: | 95% | International: | 1% |
| GPA 3.0-3.49: | 4% | Fraternities: | 6% |
| GPA 2.0-2.99: | 1% | Sororities: | 12% |
| Rank in top quarter: | 78% | | |

**Basis for selection.** GED not accepted. School academic record, standardized test scores important. Counselor evaluations, extracurricular activities also considered. Preference given to students with exceptionally strong high school record. Level and difficulty of courses considered. Weighted grades for advanced, honors, AP courses considered. All applicants to the UNC system, except those exempted by current campus policies, must submit standardized test scores. SAT preferred, ACT also accepted. Essay recommended for all students. Interview and portfolio required for College of Design applicants.

**High school preparation.** College-preparatory program required. 16 units required; 20 recommended. Required and recommended units include English 4, mathematics 4, social studies 1, history 1, science 3-4 (laboratory 1-2), foreign language 2 and academic electives 1-4. Science units should include 1 life or biological science, 1 physical science, and 1 laboratory science. Honors, advanced, AP and IB courses given extra weight.

**2007-2008 Annual costs.** Tuition/fees: $5,117; $17,315 out-of-state. Room/board: $7,370. Books/supplies: $930. Personal expenses: $1,230.

**2007-2008 Financial aid. Need-based:** 3,295 full-time freshmen applied for aid; 1,978 were judged to have need; 1,950 of these received aid. Average need met was 85%. Average scholarship/grant was $7,852; average loan $2,351. 71% of total undergraduate aid awarded as scholarships/grants, 29% as loans/jobs. **Non-need-based:** Awarded to 4,966 full-time undergraduates, including 1,386 freshmen. Scholarships awarded for academics, alumni affiliation, athletics, leadership, ROTC, state residency. **Additional information:** Freshman Merit Scholarships; students submitting complete admissions application by the November 1 Early Action deadline automatically considered, additional information may be required after initial review.

**Application procedures. Admission:** Priority date 11/1; deadline 2/1 (postmark date). $70 fee, may be waived for applicants with need. Application may be submitted online. Must reply by 5/1. Students applying under regular admission to College of Design must submit application by 12/1. Selected candidates will be invited to interview. **Financial aid:** Priority date 3/1; no closing date. FAFSA, institutional form required. CSS PROFILE recommended for early scholarship consideration. Applicants notified on a rolling basis starting 3/15.

**Academics. Special study options:** Accelerated study, combined bachelor's/graduate degree, cooperative education, cross-registration, distance learning, double major, dual enrollment of high school students, ESL, exchange student, external degree, honors, independent study, internships, liberal arts/career combination, student-designed major, study abroad, teacher certification program. 2+2 Engineering with University of North Carolina-Asheville and selected community colleges. **Credit/placement by examination:** AP, CLEP, IB, SAT, ACT, institutional tests. **Support services:** Learning center, pre-admission summer program, reduced course load, remedial instruction, study skills assistance, tutoring, writing center.

**Majors. Agriculture:** General, agribusiness operations, agronomy, animal sciences, education services, food science, horticultural science, mechanization, poultry, turf management. **Architecture:** Architecture, environmental design, landscape. **Area/ethnic studies:** African-American, German, women's. **Biology:** General, biochemistry, botany, microbiology, zoology. **Business:** Accounting, business admin, managerial economics. **Communications:** General. **Computer sciences:** Computer science. **Conservation:** General, environmental science, forest management, management/policy, wood science. **Education:** General, agricultural, elementary, English, French, health occupations, mathematics, middle, sales/marketing, science, social studies, Spanish, technology/industrial arts. **Engineering:** General, aerospace, agricultural, biomedical, chemical, civil, computer, construction, electrical, environmental, industrial, materials, mechanical, nuclear, textile. **Engineering technology:** Environmental. **English:** English lit. **Foreign languages:** French, Spanish. **History:** General. **Interdisciplinary:** Global studies, nutrition sciences, science/society. **Liberal arts:** Arts/sciences. **Math:** General, applied, statistics. **Parks/recreation:** Facilities management, sports admin. **Philosophy/religion:** Philosophy, religion. **Physical sciences:** Atmospheric science, chemistry, geology, oceanography, physics. **Psychology:** General. **Public administration:** Social work. **Social sciences:** Anthropology, criminology, political science, sociology. **Visual/performing arts:** Arts management, design, graphic design, industrial design. **Other:** Bioprocessing Science, Public Sector Leadership.

**Most popular majors.** Agriculture 7%, biology 10%, business/marketing 15%, communications/journalism 6%, engineering/engineering technologies 24%, social sciences 9%.

**Computing on campus.** 3,000 workstations in dormitories, library, computer center, student center. Dormitories wired for high-speed internet access and linked to campus network. Commuter students can connect to campus network. Online course registration, helpline, repair service, student web hosting, wireless network available.

**Student life. Freshman orientation:** Mandatory, $100 fee. Preregistration for classes offered. 2-day program. **Housing:** Guaranteed on-campus for freshmen. Coed dorms, single-sex dorms, special housing for disabled, apartments, fraternity/sorority housing, substance-free housing available. International student dormitory, Residential Scholars Program, residence hall for students interested in computers and visual and performing arts, first year college living and learning experience. **Activities:** Bands, choral groups, dance, drama, literary magazine, music ensembles, musical theater, radio station, student government, student newspaper, symphony orchestra, Alpha Phi Omega, Baptist Student Union, Campus Crusade for Christ, Circle-K, international student board, Young Democrats, Young Republicans, Society of Afro-American Culture, YMCA.

**Athletics.** NCAA. **Intercollegiate:** Baseball M, basketball, cheerleading, cross-country, diving, football (tackle) M, golf, gymnastics W, rifle, soccer, softball W, swimming, tennis, track and field, volleyball W, wrestling M. **Intramural:** Archery, badminton, baseball M, basketball, bowling, cross-country, fencing, field hockey W, football (non-tackle), golf, gymnastics, handball, ice hockey M, lacrosse M, racquetball, rugby M, sailing, skiing, skin diving, soccer, softball, squash, swimming, table tennis, tennis, track and field, volleyball, wrestling M. **Team name:** Wolfpack.

**Student services.** Adult student services, alcohol/substance abuse counseling, campus ministries, career counseling, student employment services, financial aid counseling, health services, legal services, minority student services, on-campus daycare, personal counseling, placement for graduates, veterans' counselor, women's services. **Physically disabled:** Services for visually, speech, hearing impaired.

**Contact.** E-mail: undergrad_admissions@ncsu.edu
Phone: (919) 515-2434 Fax: (919) 515-5039
Thomas Griffin, Director of Undergraduate Admissions, North Carolina State University, 203 Peele Hall, Box 7103, Raleigh, NC 27695-7103

## North Carolina Wesleyan College
**Rocky Mount, North Carolina**
www.ncwc.edu                                   CB code: 5501

- Private 4-year liberal arts college affiliated with United Methodist Church
- Residential campus in small city
- 1,510 degree-seeking undergraduates: 23% part-time, 58% women

- 63% of applicants admitted
- SAT or ACT (ACT writing optional) required

**General.** Founded in 1956. Regionally accredited. Adult students, 22 and older, can attend classes at sites in Raleigh, Goldsboro, and Rocky Mount. **Degrees:** 351 bachelor's awarded. **Location:** 57 miles from Raleigh. **Calendar:** Semester, extensive summer session. **Full-time faculty:** 52 total; 79% have terminal degrees, 4% minority, 48% women. **Part-time faculty:** 107 total; 48% have terminal degrees, 20% minority. **Class size:** 82% < 20, 18% 20-39. **Special facilities:** Black Mountain archival collection, center for the performing arts.

**Freshman class profile.** 1,245 applied, 781 admitted, 245 enrolled.

| Mid 50% test scores | | | |
|---|---|---|---|
| SAT critical reading: | 410-520 | Rank in top quarter: | 18% |
| SAT math: | 420-550 | Rank in top tenth: | 8% |
| SAT writing: | 400-510 | Out-of-state: | 42% |
| ACT composite: | 16-22 | Live on campus: | 85% |

**Basis for selection.** High school GPA most important, followed by SAT or ACT score, rigor of high school curriculum, and recommendations. Essay, school and community activities considered. SAT preferred. Essay, interview recommended for all students. **Homeschooled:** Statement describing homeschool structure and mission, interview required.

**High school preparation.** Recommended units include English 4, mathematics 3, social studies 2, science 2 (laboratory 2) and foreign language 2.

**2008-2009 Annual costs.** Tuition/fees (projected): $18,900. Room/board: $7,100. Books/supplies: $1,000. Personal expenses: $1,200.

**2006-2007 Financial aid.** All financial aid based on need. 78% of total undergraduate aid awarded as scholarships/grants, 22% as loans/jobs. **Additional information:** Scholarships based on GPA. Various scholarship and leadership awards available.

**Application procedures. Admission:** No deadline. $25 fee, may be waived for applicants with need. Application may be submitted online. Admission notification on a rolling basis. **Financial aid:** Priority date 3/1; no closing date. FAFSA required. Applicants notified on a rolling basis starting 1/1; must reply within 2 week(s) of notification.

**Academics. Special study options:** Accelerated study, cooperative education, cross-registration, distance learning, double major, dual enrollment of high school students, honors, independent study, internships, liberal arts/career combination, teacher certification program, weekend college. **Credit/placement by examination:** AP, CLEP, institutional tests. **Support services:** Learning center, pre-admission summer program, reduced course load, remedial instruction, study skills assistance, tutoring, writing center.

**Majors. Biology:** General. **Business:** Accounting, business admin. **Computer sciences:** Information systems. **Conservation:** General. **Education:** Elementary, middle, physical. **English:** English lit. **Health:** Premedicine. **History:** General. **Legal studies:** General. **Math:** General. **Philosophy/religion:** Religion. **Physical sciences:** Chemistry. **Protective services:** Criminal justice. **Psychology:** General. **Social sciences:** Anthropology, political science, sociology. **Visual/performing arts:** Dramatic.

**Most popular majors.** Business/marketing 38%, computer/information sciences 15%, legal studies 18%, psychology 8%.

**Computing on campus.** 223 workstations in dormitories, library, computer center, student center. Dormitories wired for high-speed internet access and linked to campus network. Commuter students can connect to campus network. Online course registration, helpline, repair service available.

**Student life. Freshman orientation:** Mandatory. Preregistration for classes offered. Takes place prior to start of fall classes. **Housing:** Guaranteed on-campus for freshmen. Coed dorms, single-sex dorms, special housing for disabled, fraternity/sorority housing, substance-free housing available. $100 deposit, deadline 7/15. **Activities:** Bands, choral groups, drama, literary magazine, music ensembles, student government, student newspaper, Black Student Association, Fellowship of Christian Athletes, College Republicans, Wesleyan Christian Fellowship.

**Athletics.** NCAA. **Intercollegiate:** Baseball M, basketball, cross-country W, football (tackle) M, golf M, lacrosse W, soccer, softball W, tennis, volleyball W. **Intramural:** Basketball, football (tackle) M, lacrosse W, soccer, softball, table tennis, tennis, volleyball. **Team name:** Bishops.

**Student services.** Adult student services, alcohol/substance abuse counseling, campus ministries, career counseling, student employment services, financial aid counseling, health services, personal counseling, placement for graduates, veterans' counselor. **Physically disabled:** Services for visually, hearing impaired.

**Contact.** E-mail: adm@ncwc.edu
Phone: (252) 985-5200 Toll-free number: (800) 488-6292
Fax: (252) 985-5295
Cecilia Summers, Director of Admissions, North Carolina Wesleyan
College, 3400 North Wesleyan Boulevard, Rocky Mount, NC 27804

## Peace College
### Raleigh, North Carolina
www.peace.edu

CB member
CB code: 5533

- Private 4-year liberal arts college for women affiliated with
  Presbyterian Church (USA)
- Residential campus in large city
- 658 degree-seeking undergraduates: 3% part-time, 100% women, 16%
  African American, 2% Asian American, 3% Hispanic American, 1%
  Native American
- 75% of applicants admitted
- SAT or ACT (ACT writing optional) required
- 37% graduate within 6 years; 11% enter graduate study

**General.** Founded in 1857. Regionally accredited. **Degrees:** 115 bachelor's awarded. **ROTC:** Army, Naval, Air Force. **Location:** Downtown. **Calendar:** Semester, limited summer session. **Full-time faculty:** 44 total; 86% have terminal degrees, 11% minority, 64% women. **Part-time faculty:** 47 total; 49% have terminal degrees, 13% minority, 55% women. **Class size:** 70% < 20, 27% 20-39, 2% 40-49, less than 1% 50-99.

**Freshman class profile.** 738 applied, 552 admitted, 188 enrolled.

| Mid 50% test scores | | | |
|---|---|---|---|
| SAT critical reading: | 430-520 | Rank in top quarter: | 25% |
| SAT math: | 420-510 | Rank in top tenth: | 10% |
| ACT composite: | 16-20 | End year in good standing: | 76% |
| GPA 3.50 or higher: | 37% | Return as sophomores: | 65% |
| GPA 3.0-3.49: | 25% | Out-of-state: | 12% |
| GPA 2.0-2.99: | 37% | Live on campus: | 60% |

**Basis for selection.** School achievement record, test scores, 2.0 GPA on college preparatory courses recommended. SAT combined score of 800 (exclusive of Writing) and above preferred or ACT of 17 minimum. Interview recommended for all students. Audition required for theatre, drama, and music majors; portfolio required for art programs.

**High school preparation.** 15 units required; 17 recommended. Required and recommended units include English 4, mathematics 3-4, social studies 2, history 2, science 2-3 and foreign language 2.

**2008-2009 Annual costs.** Tuition/fees: $22,993. Room/board: $7,820. Books/supplies: $1,300. Personal expenses: $2,200.

**2006-2007 Financial aid. Need-based:** 162 full-time freshmen applied for aid; 151 were judged to have need; 151 of these received aid. Average need met was 77%. Average scholarship/grant was $6,383; average loan $2,855. 66% of total undergraduate aid awarded as scholarships/grants, 34% as loans/jobs. **Non-need-based:** Awarded to 635 full-time undergraduates, including 161 freshmen. Scholarships awarded for academics.

**Application procedures. Admission:** Priority date 4/1; no deadline. $25 fee, may be waived for applicants with need. Application may be submitted online. Admission notification on a rolling basis beginning on or about 8/1. Must reply by May 1 or within 2 week(s) if notified thereafter. Prefer early admission candidates with SAT 1100 or above, 3.5 GPA in college preparatory courses, and rank in top 25% of class. On-campus interview required. **Financial aid:** Priority date 3/15; no closing date. FAFSA required. Applicants notified on a rolling basis starting 3/1; must reply by 5/1 or within 2 week(s) of notification.

**Academics. Special study options:** Cross-registration, double major, dual enrollment of high school students, honors, independent study, internships, liberal arts/career combination, study abroad. **Credit/placement by examination:** AP, CLEP, IB, SAT, ACT, institutional tests. 3 credit hours maximum toward bachelor's degree. CLEP credit is granted to students who have achieved the minimum score in designated subject tests. Students may petition program coordinators for additional or alternative credit, if warranted. **Support services:** Learning center, reduced course load, remedial instruction, study skills assistance, tutoring, writing center.

**Majors. Biology:** General. **Business:** Business admin, human resources. **Communications:** General. **English:** English lit. **Family/consumer sciences:** Child development. **Foreign languages:** Spanish. **History:** General. **Liberal arts:** Arts/sciences. **Psychology:** General. **Social sciences:** Anthropology, political science. **Visual/performing arts:** Design, music performance. **Other:** Leadership studies.

**Most popular majors.** Biology 11%, business/marketing 22%, communications/journalism 23%, liberal arts 6%, psychology 21%.

**Computing on campus.** 180 workstations in dormitories, library, computer center, student center. Dormitories wired for high-speed internet access and linked to campus network. Commuter students can connect to campus network. Online course registration, online library, helpline, repair service, student web hosting, wireless network available.

**Student life. Freshman orientation:** Mandatory, $75 fee. Preregistration for classes offered. 2-day program offered prior to start of classes. **Policies:** Honor code. Religious observance required. **Housing:** Guaranteed on-campus for freshmen. Special housing for disabled, substance-free housing available. $150 deposit, deadline 7/1. Freshmen and sophomores required to live on campus unless living with relatives in area. **Activities:** Choral groups, dance, drama, literary magazine, music ensembles, musical theater, opera, student government, student newspaper, Christian Association, honor societies, recreation association, Young Democrats/Republicans, Phi Theta Kappa, Student Environmental Action Coalition.

**Athletics.** NCAA. **Intercollegiate:** Basketball W, cross-country W, soccer W, softball W, tennis W, volleyball W. **Intramural:** Badminton W, basketball W, equestrian W, soccer W, softball W, swimming W, table tennis W, tennis W, volleyball W. **Team name:** Peace Pacers.

**Student services.** Adult student services, campus ministries, career counseling, student employment services, financial aid counseling, health services, personal counseling, placement for graduates.

**Contact.** E-mail: admissions@peace.edu
Phone: (919) 508-2000 Toll-free number: (800) 732-2347
Fax: (919) 508-2306
Matt Green, Dean of Enrollment, Peace College, 15 East Peace Street,
Raleigh, NC 27604-1194

## Pfeiffer University
### Misenheimer, North Carolina
www.pfeiffer.edu

CB member
CB code: 5536

- Private 4-year university and liberal arts college affiliated with United
  Methodist Church
- Residential campus in rural community
- 1,069 degree-seeking undergraduates: 10% part-time, 56% women,
  21% African American, 1% Asian American, 3% Hispanic American,
  4% international
- 971 degree-seeking graduate students
- 75% of applicants admitted
- SAT or ACT (ACT writing optional) required
- 50% graduate within 6 years

**General.** Founded in 1885. Regionally accredited. **Degrees:** 243 bachelor's awarded; master's offered. **ROTC:** Army. **Location:** 35 miles from Charlotte, 60 miles from Winston-Salem. **Calendar:** Semester, limited summer session. **Full-time faculty:** 77 total; 77% have terminal degrees, 13% minority, 39% women. **Part-time faculty:** 70 total. **Class size:** 77% < 20, 22% 20-39, less than 1% 40-49. **Special facilities:** Retreat center.

**Freshman class profile.** 745 applied, 559 admitted, 189 enrolled.

| Mid 50% test scores | | | |
|---|---|---|---|
| SAT critical reading: | 440-540 | Rank in top quarter: | 38% |
| SAT math: | 450-580 | Rank in top tenth: | 13% |
| ACT composite: | 18-24 | Return as sophomores: | 65% |
| GPA 3.50 or higher: | 28% | Out-of-state: | 31% |
| GPA 3.0-3.49: | 35% | Live on campus: | 74% |
| GPA 2.0-2.99: | 36% | International: | 3% |

**Basis for selection.** School achievement record, class rank, recommendations, and test scores reviewed. Interview recommended for all students; audition required for music programs.

**High school preparation.** 12 units required; 16 recommended. Required and recommended units include English 4, mathematics 3, social studies 2-4, history 2, science 2-3 (laboratory 1) and foreign language 2. Math should include algebra I and geometry.

**2008-2009 Annual costs.** Tuition/fees: $18,570; $18,570 out-of-state. Room/board: $7,360. Books/supplies: $750. Personal expenses: $600.

**Financial aid. Non-need-based:** Scholarships awarded for academics, alumni affiliation, athletics, leadership, music/drama, religious affiliation, state residency.

**Application procedures. Admission:** No deadline. $25 fee, may be waived for applicants with need. Application may be submitted online. Admission notification on a rolling basis beginning on or about 9/1. **Financial aid:** Priority date 5/1; no closing date. FAFSA required. Applicants notified on a rolling basis starting 3/1; must reply within 2 week(s) of notification.

**Academics. Special study options:** Accelerated study, combined bachelor's/graduate degree, cooperative education, distance learning, double major, dual enrollment of high school students, honors, independent study, internships, liberal arts/career combination, study abroad, teacher certification program, Washington semester, weekend college. **Credit/placement by examination:** AP, CLEP, IB, SAT, ACT, institutional tests. **Support services:** Learning center, reduced course load, remedial instruction, study skills assistance, tutoring.

**Majors. Biology:** General. **Business:** General, accounting, business admin. **Communications:** General. **Computer sciences:** General. **Conservation:** Environmental studies. **Education:** Elementary, music, physical, secondary, social science, special. **Engineering:** General. **English:** English lit. **Health:** Athletic training, health care admin, predental, premedicine, preveterinary. **History:** General. **Legal studies:** Prelaw. **Liberal arts:** Arts/sciences. **Math:** General. **Parks/recreation:** Facilities management, sports admin. **Philosophy/religion:** Religion. **Physical sciences:** Chemistry. **Protective services:** Criminal justice, police science. **Psychology:** General. **Social sciences:** Economics, sociology. **Theology:** Missionary, religious ed, sacred music, youth ministry. **Visual/performing arts:** Arts management, dramatic.

**Computing on campus.** 114 workstations in library, computer center. Dormitories linked to campus network. Commuter students can connect to campus network. Online library, repair service, wireless network available.

**Student life. Freshman orientation:** Available, $35 fee. **Housing:** Guaranteed on-campus for all undergraduates. Coed dorms, single-sex dorms, special housing for disabled, apartments, substance-free housing available. $150 deposit. Apartment-style housing with shared kitchen and bath available for older students not married. **Activities:** Bands, choral groups, dance, drama, literary magazine, music ensembles, musical theater, student government, student newspaper, religious organizations, political groups, service clubs, professional clubs.

**Athletics.** NCAA. **Intercollegiate:** Baseball M, basketball, cross-country, golf, lacrosse, soccer, softball W, swimming, tennis, volleyball W. **Intramural:** Basketball, lacrosse, soccer, softball, table tennis, tennis, volleyball. **Team name:** Falcons.

**Student services.** Alcohol/substance abuse counseling, campus ministries, career counseling, student employment services, financial aid counseling, health services, personal counseling, placement for graduates, veterans' counselor.

**Contact.** E-mail: admiss@pfeiffer.edu
Phone: (704) 463-1360 ext. 2060 Toll-free number: (800) 338-2060
Fax: (704) 463-1363
Steve Cumming, Director of Admissions, Pfeiffer University, Box 960, Misenheimer, NC 28109

## Piedmont Baptist College
**Winston-Salem, North Carolina**
**www.pbc.edu**                    CB code: 5555

- Private 4-year Bible and seminary college affiliated with Baptist faith
- Small city
- 258 degree-seeking undergraduates: 29% part-time, 41% women
- 111 degree-seeking graduate students
- 100% of applicants admitted
- ACT (writing optional), application essay required

**General.** Founded in 1945. Accredited by ABHE. **Degrees:** 33 bachelor's, 11 associate awarded; master's, doctoral offered. **Location:** 75 miles from Charlotte, 100 miles from Raleigh. **Calendar:** Semester, limited summer session. **Full-time faculty:** 20 total. **Part-time faculty:** 15 total. **Class size:** 77% < 20, 17% 20-39, 4% 40-49, 1% 50-99. **Special facilities:** Restored 18th Century Moravian community, Old Salem.

**Freshman class profile.** 62 applied, 62 admitted, 47 enrolled.

| | | | |
|---|---|---|---|
| Out-of-state: | 55% | Live on campus: | 44% |

**Basis for selection.** Student's life objectives and previous academic record important. Interview recommended for all students; audition required for music program.

**High school preparation.** Recommended units include English 4, mathematics 3, social studies 3, science 3 and foreign language 2.

**2008-2009 Annual costs.** Tuition/fees: $10,800. Room/board: $5,560. Books/supplies: $600. Personal expenses: $600.

**Application procedures. Admission:** Priority date 7/31; no deadline. $60 fee. Application may be submitted online. Admission notification on a rolling basis beginning on or about 12/1. Must reply by May 1 or within 2 week(s) if notified thereafter. **Financial aid:** No deadline. Institutional form required. Applicants notified on a rolling basis starting 3/1.

**Academics. Special study options:** Cooperative education, distance learning, double major, dual enrollment of high school students, independent study, internships, teacher certification program. **Credit/placement by examination:** AP, CLEP, institutional tests. **Support services:** Learning center, reduced course load, remedial instruction, study skills assistance, tutoring.

**Majors. Education:** Elementary, English, music, physical. **Theology:** Bible, missionary, youth ministry.

**Most popular majors.** Education 33%, philosophy/religious studies 60%.

**Computing on campus.** 26 workstations in library, computer center, student center. Dormitories linked to campus network. Commuter students can connect to campus network. Online course registration, online library, helpline, wireless network available.

**Student life. Freshman orientation:** Mandatory. Preregistration for classes offered. Held 2 days prior to registration, overviews basic rules and guidelines. **Policies:** Religious observance required. **Housing:** Guaranteed on-campus for freshmen. Single-sex dorms, apartments available. **Activities:** Choral groups, drama, music ensembles, student government, student newspaper, missions fellowship, preachers' fellowship, youth leaders' fellowship, educators' fellowship, music fellowship.

**Athletics.** NCCAA. **Intercollegiate:** Basketball, soccer M, volleyball W. **Team name:** Conquerors.

**Student services.** Campus ministries, career counseling, financial aid counseling, health services, personal counseling, placement for graduates, veterans' counselor.

**Contact.** E-mail: admissions@pbc.edu
Phone: (336) 725-8344 ext. 7900 Toll-free number: (800) 937-5097
Fax: (336) 725-5522
Kathy Holritz, Director of Admissions, Piedmont Baptist College, 420 South Boad Street, Winston-Salem, NC 27101-5133

## Queens University of Charlotte
**Charlotte, North Carolina**                    CB member
**www.queens.edu**                               CB code: 5560

- Private 4-year university affiliated with Presbyterian Church (USA)
- Residential campus in very large city
- 1,688 degree-seeking undergraduates: 35% part-time, 76% women, 18% African American, 2% Asian American, 4% Hispanic American, 1% Native American, 6% international
- 451 degree-seeking graduate students
- 79% of applicants admitted
- SAT or ACT with writing required
- 61% graduate within 6 years

**General.** Founded in 1857. Regionally accredited. **Degrees:** 274 bachelor's, 120 associate awarded; master's offered. **ROTC:** Army, Air Force. **Calendar:** Semester, limited summer session. **Full-time faculty:** 98 total; 68% have terminal degrees, 9% minority, 67% women. **Part-time faculty:** 94 total; 27% have terminal degrees, 15% minority, 61% women. **Class size:** 67% < 20, 31% 20-39, 3% 40-49, 2% 50-99. **Special facilities:** Rare books museum, recital hall.

**Freshman class profile.** 1,189 applied, 939 admitted, 292 enrolled.

| Mid 50% test scores | | | |
|---|---|---|---|
| SAT critical reading: | 470-570 | Rank in top quarter: | 45% |
| SAT math: | 460-570 | Rank in top tenth: | 21% |
| SAT writing: | 450-570 | Return as sophomores: | 67% |
| ACT composite: | 20-24 | Out-of-state: | 47% |
| GPA 3.50 or higher: | 41% | Live on campus: | 86% |
| GPA 3.0-3.49: | 34% | International: | 1% |
| GPA 2.0-2.99: | 25% | Fraternities: | 12% |
| | | Sororities: | 27% |

**Basis for selection.** High school courses taken, school achievement record, class rank, test scores important. Extracurricular activities, recommendations also considered. Official test scores must be received prior to admission. Interview recommended for all students. Audition required for drama, music, music therapy programs; portfolio recommended for art program. **Homeschooled:** Evidence of Home School registration in the home state (copy of Home School License) required.

**High school preparation.** Required units include English 4, mathematics 3, social studies 2, science 2 (laboratory 1) and foreign language 2. Chemistry recommended for nursing majors.

**2008-2009 Annual costs.** Tuition/fees: $22,068. Room/board: $7,882. Books/supplies: $800. Personal expenses: $1,150.

**2007-2008 Financial aid. Need-based:** 242 full-time freshmen applied for aid; 194 were judged to have need; 194 of these received aid. Average need met was 79%. Average scholarship/grant was $13,043; average loan $3,173. 63% of total undergraduate aid awarded as scholarships/grants, 37% as loans/jobs. **Non-need-based:** Awarded to 562 full-time undergraduates, including 143 freshmen. Scholarships awarded for academics, art, athletics, leadership, minority status, music/drama.

**Application procedures. Admission:** Priority date 12/1; no deadline. $40 fee, may be waived for applicants with need. Application may be submitted online. Admission notification on a rolling basis beginning on or about 10/15. Must reply by May 1 or within 3 week(s) if notified thereafter. **Financial aid:** Priority date 3/1; no closing date. FAFSA required. Applicants notified on a rolling basis starting 3/15; must reply by 5/1 or within 3 week(s) of notification.

**Academics.** 6 credit hours of internships required to enhance job placement and career opportunities. **Special study options:** Cross-registration, double major, dual enrollment of high school students, honors, independent study, internships, student-designed major, study abroad, teacher certification program, Washington semester, weekend college. John Belk International Program (3-week study tours in Europe and Asia), interdisciplinary core curriculum, professional golf management, Harvard Model UN, European internship program offered. **Credit/placement by examination:** AP, CLEP, IB, institutional tests. 43 credit hours maximum toward bachelor's degree. **Support services:** Reduced course load, tutoring, writing center.

**Majors. Area/ethnic studies:** American, European. **Biology:** General, biochemistry, environmental. **Business:** Business admin, management information systems, marketing. **Communications:** General, journalism, media studies, organizational. **Computer sciences:** Information systems. **Education:** General, elementary. **English:** British lit, creative writing, English lit. **Foreign languages:** General. **Health:** Music therapy, nursing (RN), predental, premedicine, preop/surgical nursing, prepharmacy, preveterinary. **History:** General. **Interdisciplinary:** Global studies. **Legal studies:** Prelaw. **Math:** General, statistics. **Philosophy/religion:** Religion. **Physical sciences:** Chemistry. **Psychology:** General. **Social sciences:** Political science, sociology. **Visual/performing arts:** Dramatic, music performance, studio arts.

**Most popular majors.** Business/marketing 25%, communications/journalism 13%, education 6%, health sciences 16%, psychology 9%.

**Computing on campus.** 109 workstations in dormitories, library, computer center. Dormitories wired for high-speed internet access and linked to campus network. Commuter students can connect to campus network. On-line library, helpline, wireless network available.

**Student life. Freshman orientation:** Mandatory. Preregistration for classes offered. 2-day program held at beginning of academic year. **Housing:** Guaranteed on-campus for freshmen. Coed dorms, special housing for disabled, substance-free housing available. $250 fully refundable deposit, deadline 5/1. **Activities:** Pep band, campus ministries, choral groups, dance, drama, international student organizations, literary magazine, music ensembles, Model UN, musical theater, student government, student newspaper, Students for Black Awareness, College Republicans, College Democrats, North Carolina Student Legislature, Justinian Society.

**Athletics.** NCAA. **Intercollegiate:** Basketball, cross-country, golf, lacrosse, soccer, softball W, tennis, track and field, volleyball W. **Intramural:** Basketball, football (non-tackle) M, soccer, softball, volleyball. **Team name:** Royals.

**Student services.** Adult student services, alcohol/substance abuse counseling, campus ministries, career counseling, student employment services, financial aid counseling, health services, minority student services, personal counseling, placement for graduates. **Physically disabled:** Services for visually impaired.

**Contact.** E-mail: admissions@queens.edu
Phone: (704) 337-2212 Toll-free number: (800) 849-0202
Fax: (704) 337-2403
William Lee, Director of Admissions, Queens University of Charlotte, 1900 Selwyn Ave, Charlotte, NC 28274

## Roanoke Bible College

**Elizabeth City, North Carolina**
www.roanokebible.edu  **CB code: 5597**

- Private 4-year Bible college affiliated with Church of Christ
- Residential campus in large town
- 141 degree-seeking undergraduates: 21% part-time, 45% women, 11% African American, 3% Hispanic American
- 55% of applicants admitted
- SAT or ACT (ACT writing optional), application essay required

**General.** Founded in 1948. Regionally accredited; also accredited by ABHE. **Degrees:** 36 bachelor's, 11 associate awarded. **Location:** 50 miles from Norfolk, Virginia. **Calendar:** Semester, limited summer session. **Full-time faculty:** 12 total; 33% have terminal degrees, 8% minority, 33% women. **Part-time faculty:** 15 total; 53% have terminal degrees, 7% minority, 20% women. **Class size:** 61% < 20, 21% 20-39.

**Freshman class profile.** 94 applied, 52 admitted, 30 enrolled.

| Mid 50% test scores | | | |
|---|---|---|---|
| SAT critical reading: | 400-530 | GPA 2.0-2.99: | 43% |
| SAT math: | 410-580 | Rank in top quarter: | 41% |
| ACT composite: | 19-24 | Rank in top tenth: | 14% |
| GPA 3.50 or higher: | 30% | Return as sophomores: | 38% |
| GPA 3.0-3.49: | 17% | Out-of-state: | 53% |
| | | Live on campus: | 90% |

**Basis for selection.** Evidence of Christian character, school achievement record, test scores, school and community activities, recommendations important. Interview recommended if questions arise from references or academic record. **Homeschooled:** Transcript of courses and grades, state high school equivalency certificate required.

**High school preparation.** 20 units required. Required and recommended units include English 4, mathematics 3, social studies 2, history 2, science 3 (laboratory 2), foreign language 2, computer science 1 and academic electives 4.

**2008-2009 Annual costs.** Tuition/fees: $9,150. Room/board: $5,890. Books/supplies: $900. Personal expenses: $2,500.

**2006-2007 Financial aid. Need-based:** 25 full-time freshmen applied for aid; 23 were judged to have need; 23 of these received aid. Average need met was 63%. Average scholarship/grant was $3,492; average loan $2,340. 43% of total undergraduate aid awarded as scholarships/grants, 57% as loans/jobs. **Non-need-based:** Awarded to 29 full-time undergraduates, including 5 freshmen. Scholarships awarded for academics, alumni affiliation, leadership, music/drama, religious affiliation.

**Application procedures. Admission:** No deadline. $50 fee, may be waived for applicants with need. Application may be submitted online. Admission notification on a rolling basis beginning on or about 9/1. Must reply by May 1 or within 2 week(s) if notified thereafter. **Financial aid:** Priority date 3/15; no closing date. FAFSA, institutional form required. Applicants notified on a rolling basis starting 4/1; must reply within 2 week(s) of notification.

**Academics. Special study options:** Distance learning, double major, dual enrollment of high school students, internships. Semester-long mission intern class overseas. **Credit/placement by examination:** AP, CLEP, institutional tests. 8 credit hours maximum toward associate degree, 16 toward bachelor's. **Support services:** Learning center, reduced course load, remedial instruction, study skills assistance, writing center.

**Majors. Business:** Nonprofit/public. **Foreign languages:** Linguistics. **Philosophy/religion:** Religion. **Theology:** Bible, missionary, pastoral counseling, religious ed, theology, youth ministry.

**Computing on campus.** 24 workstations in dormitories, library, computer center. Dormitories wired for high-speed internet access and linked to campus network.

**Student life. Freshman orientation:** Mandatory, $130 fee. Preregistration for classes offered. **Policies:** All students have opportunity to travel in choral group throughout country. Religious observance required. **Housing:** Guaranteed on-campus for all undergraduates. Single-sex dorms, special housing for disabled, apartments, substance-free housing available. $75 nonrefundable deposit, deadline 4/1. **Activities:** Campus ministries, choral groups, drama, music ensembles, musical theater, student government.

**Athletics. Intercollegiate:** Basketball, volleyball. **Intramural:** Basketball, football (non-tackle), golf, soccer, softball, table tennis, tennis, volleyball. **Team name:** Flames.

**Student services.** Career counseling, student employment services, financial aid counseling, personal counseling, placement for graduates. **Physically disabled:** Services for hearing impaired.

**Contact.** E-mail: admissions@roanokebible.edu
Phone: (252) 334-2028 Toll-free number: (800) 722-8980
Fax: (252) 334-2064
Garrett Lewis, Director of Enrollment Management, Roanoke Bible College, 715 North Poindexter Street, Elizabeth City, NC 27909

## St. Andrews Presbyterian College
Laurinburg, North Carolina — CB member
www.sapc.edu — CB code: 5214

- Private 4-year liberal arts college affiliated with Presbyterian Church (USA)
- Residential campus in large town
- 726 degree-seeking undergraduates: 4% part-time, 59% women
- 74% of applicants admitted
- SAT or ACT (ACT writing optional) required

**General.** Founded in 1958. Regionally accredited. **Degrees:** 164 bachelor's awarded. **Location:** 40 miles from Fayetteville, 20 miles from Pinehurst. **Calendar:** Semester, limited summer session. **Full-time faculty:** 42 total. **Part-time faculty:** 46 total. **Class size:** 81% < 20, 18% 20-39, less than 1% 40-49. **Special facilities:** Psychology laboratory complex, equestrian facilities, nature preserve, electronic fine arts center.

**Freshman class profile.** 1,065 applied, 788 admitted, 216 enrolled.

| Mid 50% test scores | | | |
|---|---|---|---|
| SAT critical reading: | 460-590 | Out-of-state: | 60% |
| SAT math: | 460-570 | Live on campus: | 96% |

**Basis for selection.** High school GPA, test scores, curriculum, type of high school very important. Recommendations important. Interview required for academically weak students, recommended for all other applicants. **Homeschooled:** Standardized test scores and interview required.

**High school preparation.** 16 units recommended. Required and recommended units include English 4, mathematics 3, social studies 3, history 1, science 3 and foreign language 2.

**2007-2008 Annual costs.** Tuition/fees: $18,192. Private living, lab fees, and equestrian fees additional. Room/board: $7,992.

**2007-2008 Financial aid. Need-based:** 187 full-time freshmen applied for aid; 149 were judged to have need; 149 of these received aid. Average need met was 80%. Average scholarship/grant was $11,066; average loan $3,347. 65% of total undergraduate aid awarded as scholarships/grants, 35% as loans/jobs. **Non-need-based:** Awarded to 415 full-time undergraduates, including 151 freshmen. Scholarships awarded for academics, alumni affiliation, athletics, leadership, music/drama, religious affiliation.

**Application procedures. Admission:** Priority date 5/1; no deadline. $30 fee. Application may be submitted online. Admission notification on a rolling basis beginning on or about 9/1. Housing deposit fully refundable until May 1st. **Financial aid:** Priority date 5/1; no closing date. FAFSA required. Applicants notified on a rolling basis starting 10/1; must reply within 2 week(s) of notification.

**Academics.** Academic programs include St. Andrew's General Education. **Special study options:** Cross-registration, double major, dual enrollment of high school students, exchange student, honors, independent study, internships, liberal arts/career combination, student-designed major, study abroad, teacher certification program, Washington semester. Courses offered abroad during winter or summer in Britain, Greece, India, Switzerland, Venezuela, China, Hawaii, former Soviet Union; exchange programs with Stirling University, Scotland and Kansai Gaidai University, Japan; study at Brunnenburg Castle, Italy, and Beijing Normal College of Foreign Languages. **Credit/placement by examination:** AP, CLEP, IB. 30 credit hours maximum toward bachelor's degree. **Support services:** Reduced course load, tutoring, writing center.

**Majors. Agriculture:** Equestrian studies. **Area/ethnic studies:** Asian. **Biology:** General. **Business:** General, business admin, international. **Communications:** Media studies. **Education:** Elementary, physical. **English:** Creative writing, English lit. **Health:** Athletic training, premedicine, prepharmacy, preveterinary. **History:** General, public archives. **Legal studies:** Prelaw. **Liberal arts:** Arts/sciences. **Math:** General. **Philosophy/religion:** Philosophy, religion. **Physical sciences:** Chemistry. **Psychology:** General. **Social sciences:** Political science. **Visual/performing arts:** General, art.

**Most popular majors.** Biology 12%, business/marketing 32%, education 12%, English 7%, parks/recreation 7%, psychology 7%.

**Computing on campus.** 100 workstations in library, computer center, student center. Dormitories wired for high-speed internet access and linked to campus network. Online library, repair service available.

**Student life. Freshman orientation:** Mandatory, $100 fee. 3 days prior to start of fall term. **Policies:** Honor code enforced. **Housing:** Guaranteed on-campus for all undergraduates. Coed dorms, single-sex dorms, special housing for disabled, substance-free housing available. $200 deposit, deadline 8/25. **Activities:** Choral groups, dance, drama, literary magazine, Model UN, musical theater, student government, student newspaper, Christian Student Fellowship, black student union, women's issues group, writer's forum, world culture club, Eco-Action, student activities union.

**Athletics.** NCAA. **Intercollegiate:** Baseball M, basketball, cross-country, equestrian, golf, lacrosse, soccer, softball W, tennis, track and field, volleyball W. **Intramural:** Basketball, bowling, racquetball, soccer, softball W, table tennis, volleyball. **Team name:** Knights.

**Student services.** Adult student services, alcohol/substance abuse counseling, career counseling, student employment services, financial aid counseling, health services, personal counseling, placement for graduates, women's services. **Physically disabled:** Services for visually, speech, hearing impaired.

**Contact.** E-mail: admissions@sapc.edu
Phone: (910) 277-5555 Toll-free number: (800) 763-0198
Fax: (910) 277-5087
Kirsten Simmons, Director of Admission, St. Andrews Presbyterian College, 1700 Dogwood Mile, Laurinburg, NC 28352

## St. Augustine's College
Raleigh, North Carolina — CB member
www.st-aug.edu — CB code: 5596

- Private 4-year liberal arts college affiliated with Episcopal Church
- Residential campus in large city
- 1,267 degree-seeking undergraduates
- Interview required

**General.** Founded in 1867. Regionally accredited. Home to historic St. Augustine's College Chapel and St. Agnes Hospital. **Degrees:** 187 bachelor's awarded. **ROTC:** Army, Air Force. **Location:** One mile from downtown. **Calendar:** Semester, limited summer session. **Full-time faculty:** 78 total. **Part-time faculty:** 42 total. **Class size:** 65% < 20, 33% 20-39, 2% 40-49, less than 1% 50-99. **Special facilities:** Archival collection tracing history of African-Americans in North Carolina and Delaney family.

**Freshman class profile.**

| Mid 50% test scores | | | |
|---|---|---|---|
| SAT critical reading: | 400-430 | Rank in top tenth: | 15% |
| SAT math: | 410-430 | Out-of-state: | 65% |
| ACT composite: | 15-17 | Live on campus: | 92% |
| Rank in top quarter: | 44% | Fraternities: | 6% |
| | | Sororities: | 12% |

**Basis for selection.** High school record (GPA and rank), standardized test scores and letters of recommendation reviewed. Alumni affiliation also considered. SAT or ACT recommended. Institutionally administered Accuplacer test is used for pre- and post-testing evaluation and placement purposes. Essay recommended. Auditions and interviews required of music majors. **Learning Disabled:** Students must self-identify. ADA Coordinator will assess level of disability and arrange for student to access the needed equipment or tutorials.

**High school preparation.** 20 units required. Required units include English 4, mathematics 3, social studies 2, science 2 and academic electives 9. One unit of algebra required, 2 units of laboratory recommended.

**2007-2008 Annual costs.** Tuition/fees: $13,206. Room/board: $6,590. Books/supplies: $900. Personal expenses: $1,530.

**Financial aid. Non-need-based:** Scholarships awarded for academics, art, athletics, leadership, minority status, music/drama, religious affiliation, ROTC, state residency.

**Application procedures. Admission:** Closing date 8/1 (postmark date). $25 fee, may be waived for applicants with need. Application may be submitted online. Admission notification on a rolling basis beginning on or about 1/1. **Financial aid:** Closing date 3/15. FAFSA, institutional form required. Applicants notified on a rolling basis starting 5/1; must reply within 2 week(s) of notification.

**Academics.** Required "Learning Community" program for all new freshmen and transfers. First year program includes skills enhancement and college survival tips. Community service requirement is part of course. **Special study options:** Accelerated study, cooperative education, cross-registration, double major, dual enrollment of high school students, honors, independent study, internships, liberal arts/career combination, study abroad, teacher certification program, weekend college. **Credit/placement by examination:** CLEP, IB, institutional tests. 15 credit hours maximum toward bachelor's degree. **Support services:** Learning center, pre-admission summer program, reduced course load, remedial instruction, study skills assistance, tutoring, writing center.

**Majors. Area/ethnic studies:** African-American. **Biology:** General, biomedical sciences. **Business:** Accounting, business admin, management science, real estate. **Communications:** General. **Computer sciences:** General, computer science. **Education:** Elementary. **Engineering:** General. **English:** English lit. **Health:** Occupational health, premedicine. **History:** General. **Legal studies:** Prelaw. **Math:** General. **Parks/recreation:** Health/fitness, sports admin. **Philosophy/religion:** Religion. **Physical sciences:** Chemistry. **Protective services:** Criminal justice, forensics. **Psychology:** General. **Social sciences:** Political science, sociology. **Visual/performing arts:** General, art, cinematography, music performance.

**Most popular majors.** Business/marketing 35%, communications/journalism 7%, computer/information sciences 12%, security/protective services 10%, social sciences 14%.

**Computing on campus.** 250 workstations in dormitories, library, computer center. Dormitories wired for high-speed internet access and linked to campus network. Commuter students can connect to campus network. Online course registration, online library, helpline, repair service available.

**Student life. Freshman orientation:** Mandatory, $60 fee. Preregistration for classes offered. 2-day orientations held in June, July, and August with students and parents. **Policies:** Alcohol and drug-free campus. No tolerance policy. No firearm policy. No smoking policy for all campus administrative buildings. Religious observance required. **Housing:** Guaranteed on-campus for freshmen. Single-sex dorms, substance-free housing available. $150 deposit. **Activities:** Bands, choral groups, dance, drama, film society, music ensembles, musical theater, radio station, student government, student newspaper, symphony orchestra, TV station, Christian Fellowship Organization, Young Democrats of America, Falcons for the Cause, NAACP, foreign language club, Falcon Battalion/Army ROTC, Student Service Corps, SAC Association for Black Journalists, International student association, Latin American students organization.

**Athletics.** NCAA. **Intercollegiate:** Baseball M; basketball, bowling W, cheerleading W, cross-country, football (tackle) M, golf, softball W, tennis, track and field, volleyball W. **Intramural:** Baseball M, basketball, softball W, volleyball. **Team name:** Falcons.

**Student services.** Adult student services, alcohol/substance abuse counseling, campus ministries, career counseling, services for economically disadvantaged, student employment services, financial aid counseling, health services, minority student services, personal counseling, placement for graduates, veterans' counselor. **Physically disabled:** Services for visually impaired.

**Contact.** E-mail: admissions@st-aug.edu
Phone: (919) 516-4012 Toll-free number: (800) 948-1126
Fax: (919) 516-5805
Jorge Sousa, Dean, Enrollment Management, St. Augustine's College, 1315 Oakwood Avenue, Raleigh, NC 27610-2298

---

## Salem College

**Winston-Salem, North Carolina**

**www.salem.edu**

**CB member**
**CB code: 5607**

- Private 4-year liberal arts college for women affiliated with Moravian Church in America
- Residential campus in small city
- 741 degree-seeking undergraduates: 16% part-time, 98% women, 19% African American, 1% Asian American, 4% Hispanic American, 13% international
- 218 degree-seeking graduate students
- 62% of applicants admitted
- SAT or ACT (ACT writing optional), application essay required
- 53% graduate within 6 years; 23% enter graduate study

**General.** Founded in 1772. Regionally accredited. Male students age 23 and over may enroll in adult program only and may not reside at the college. **Degrees:** 209 bachelor's awarded; master's offered. **Location:** 80 miles

from Charlotte, 25 miles from Greensboro. **Calendar:** 4-1-4, limited summer session. **Full-time faculty:** 57 total; 86% have terminal degrees, 9% minority, 61% women. **Part-time faculty:** 49 total; 37% have terminal degrees, 12% minority, 63% women. **Class size:** 84% < 20, 16% 20-39.

**Freshman class profile.** 420 applied, 260 admitted, 121 enrolled.

| Mid 50% test scores | | | |
|---|---|---|---|
| SAT critical reading: | 490-650 | Rank in top quarter: | 67% |
| SAT math: | 480-630 | Rank in top tenth: | 39% |
| ACT composite: | 21-31 | End year in good standing: | 92% |
| GPA 3.50 or higher: | 70% | Return as sophomores: | 77% |
| GPA 3.0-3.49: | 24% | Out-of-state: | 74% |
| GPA 2.0-2.99: | 6% | Live on campus: | 94% |
| | | International: | 25% |

**Basis for selection.** School achievement record, essay or personal statement, test scores important. Recommendations, interview, extracurricular and community activities, talent, minority status considered. Interview recommended for all students. Audition required for music program; portfolio recommended for art program.

**High school preparation.** College-preparatory program required. 16 units required. Required units include English 4, mathematics 3, social studies 2, science 3, foreign language 2 and academic electives 3. Math requirement includes 2 algebra and 1 geometry. On a case by case basis, a portion of this requirement may be waived for adult students.

**2007-2008 Annual costs.** Tuition/fees: $19,190. Room/board: $10,050. Books/supplies: $900. Personal expenses: $800.

**2006-2007 Financial aid. Need-based:** 86 full-time freshmen applied for aid; 81 were judged to have need; 81 of these received aid. Average need met was 100%. Average scholarship/grant was $9,828; average loan $2,359. 69% of total undergraduate aid awarded as scholarships/grants, 31% as loans/jobs. **Non-need-based:** Awarded to 494 full-time undergraduates, including 87 freshmen. Scholarships awarded for academics, alumni affiliation, leadership, minority status, music/drama, state residency.

**Application procedures. Admission:** Priority date 3/1; no deadline. $30 fee, may be waived for applicants with need. Application may be submitted online. Admission notification on a rolling basis beginning on or about 10/1. Must reply by May 1 or within 2 week(s) if notified thereafter. **Financial aid:** Priority date 3/1; no closing date. FAFSA required. Applicants notified on a rolling basis starting 3/1; must reply by 5/1 or within 2 week(s) of notification.

**Academics. Special study options:** Cross-registration, double major, dual enrollment of high school students, exchange student, honors, independent study, internships, liberal arts/career combination, student-designed major, study abroad, teacher certification program, United Nations semester, Washington semester. Cooperative engineering programs with Duke University and Vanderbilt University, 3-2 medical technology program with Wake Forest University's Bowman Gray School of Medicine; various study abroad options available through Brethren Colleges of America (BCA); St. Peters, Oxford; and St. Clare's, Oxford. **Credit/placement by examination:** AP, CLEP, IB, institutional tests. A maximum of 16 courses credit awarded through CLEP exam. **Support services:** Learning center, reduced course load, study skills assistance, tutoring, writing center.

**Majors. Area/ethnic studies:** American. **Biology:** General. **Business:** Accounting, business admin, international, nonprofit/public. **Communications:** General. **Education:** Music. **English:** Composition, creative writing, English lit. **Foreign languages:** French, German, Spanish. **Health:** Clinical lab technology. **History:** General. **Math:** General. **Philosophy/religion:** Philosophy, religion. **Physical sciences:** Chemistry. **Psychology:** General. **Social sciences:** Economics, international relations, sociology. **Visual/performing arts:** Art history/conservation, arts management, interior design, music performance, studio arts.

**Most popular majors.** Biology 8%, business/marketing 11%, communications/journalism 13%, English 10%, foreign language 6%, psychology 9%, social sciences 17%, visual/performing arts 11%.

**Computing on campus.** 54 workstations in library, computer center. Dormitories wired for high-speed internet access and linked to campus network. Commuter students can connect to campus network. Online library, helpline, wireless network available.

**Student life. Freshman orientation:** Mandatory. Preregistration for classes offered. 3 days before fall term begins. Separate orientation program for adult students. **Housing:** Guaranteed on-campus for freshmen. Apartments, substance-free housing available. $250 nonrefundable deposit, deadline 5/1. All full-time students under 23 years required to reside on-campus unless they reside with family within a 30 mile radius of the college. **Activities:** Marching band, choral groups, dance, drama, international student organizations, literary magazine, music ensembles, Model UN, musical theater, student government, student newspaper, College Republicans, College Democrats, Green Party, Catholic student association, campus activities council, Intervarsity Fellowship, Habitat for Humanity.

**Athletics.** NCAA. **Intercollegiate:** Basketball W, cross-country W, soccer W, swimming W, tennis W, volleyball W. **Team name:** Salem Spirit.

**Student services.** Adult student services, campus ministries, career counseling, financial aid counseling, health services, personal counseling, placement for graduates, women's services.

**Contact.** E-mail: admissions@salem.edu
Phone: (336) 721-2621 Toll-free number: (800) 327-2536
Fax: (336) 917-5572
Katherine Watts Knapp, Dean of Admissions and Financial Aid, Salem College, PO Box 10548, Winston-Salem, NC 27108

## Shaw University

**Raleigh, North Carolina**
www.shawuniversity.edu
**CB member**
**CB code: 5612**

- Private 4-year university and liberal arts college affiliated with Baptist faith
- Residential campus in large city
- 2,606 degree-seeking undergraduates: 10% part-time, 63% women, 85% African American, 1% international
- 210 degree-seeking graduate students
- 45% of applicants admitted
- SAT or ACT (ACT writing optional), application essay required
- 36% graduate within 6 years

**General.** Founded in 1865. Regionally accredited. **Degrees:** 371 bachelor's, 12 associate awarded; master's, first professional offered. **ROTC:** Army, Air Force. **Location:** 139 miles from Charlotte. **Calendar:** Semester, limited summer session. **Full-time faculty:** 116 total; 66% have terminal degrees, 82% minority, 33% women. **Part-time faculty:** 156 total; 38% have terminal degrees, 88% minority, 40% women. **Class size:** 70% < 20, 26% 20-39, 2% 40-49, 2% 50-99.

**Freshman class profile.** 5,632 applied, 2,535 admitted, 606 enrolled.

| Mid 50% test scores | | | |
|---|---|---|---|
| SAT critical reading: | 330-430 | GPA 2.0-2.99: | 74% |
| SAT math: | 320-420 | Rank in top quarter: | 12% |
| SAT writing: | 320-420 | Rank in top tenth: | 3% |
| ACT composite: | 11-16 | Return as sophomores: | 55% |
| GPA 3.50 or higher: | 4% | Out-of-state: | 52% |
| GPA 3.0-3.49: | 11% | Live on campus: | 72% |
| | | International: | 1% |

**Basis for selection.** 2.0 high school GPA desired. Interview, portfolio recommended for some. **Homeschooled:** Transcript of courses and grades, state high school equivalency certificate required.

**High school preparation.** 18 units required. Required units include English 3, mathematics 2, social studies 2, science 2 and academic electives 9. 9 electives in English, foreign language, mathematics, science.

**2007-2008 Annual costs.** Tuition/fees: $10,840. Room/board: $6,800. Books/supplies: $700. Personal expenses: $1,000.

**Financial aid. Non-need-based:** Scholarships awarded for academics, alumni affiliation, art, athletics, music/drama, religious affiliation.

**Application procedures. Admission:** Closing date 7/30. $25 fee, may be waived for applicants with need. Application may be submitted online. Admission notification on a rolling basis beginning on or about 8/1. **Financial aid:** Priority date 3/1; no closing date. FAFSA required. Applicants notified on a rolling basis starting 3/15; must reply within 2 week(s) of notification.

**Academics. Special study options:** Accelerated study, cross-registration, distance learning, double major, dual enrollment of high school students, external degree, honors, independent study, liberal arts/career combination, student-designed major, study abroad, teacher certification program, weekend college. **Credit/placement by examination:** CLEP, SAT, ACT, institutional tests. 30 credit hours maximum toward associate degree, 60 toward bachelor's. **Support services:** Learning center, reduced course load, study skills assistance, tutoring, writing center.

**Majors. Biology:** General. **Business:** Business admin, international. **Communications:** Media studies. **Computer sciences:** General, computer science. **Conservation:** General. **Education:** Elementary, English, mathematics. **English:** English lit. **Foreign languages:** Spanish. **Health:** Athletic training, audiology/speech pathology, recreational therapy. **Liberal arts:** Arts/

sciences. **Math:** General. **Parks/recreation:** General, exercise sciences. **Philosophy/religion:** Religion. **Physical sciences:** Chemistry, physics. **Protective services:** Criminal justice. **Psychology:** General. **Public administration:** General, social work. **Social sciences:** International relations, political science, sociology. **Visual/performing arts:** Dramatic.

**Most popular majors.** Business/marketing 29%, philosophy/religious studies 6%, psychology 9%, public administration/social services 6%, security/protective services 16%, social sciences 12%.

**Computing on campus.** 150 workstations in dormitories, library, computer center, student center. Dormitories wired for high-speed internet access and linked to campus network. Commuter students can connect to campus network. Online course registration, online library, helpline, repair service, student web hosting, wireless network available.

**Student life. Freshman orientation:** Available. **Housing:** Single-sex dorms, substance-free housing available. $100 deposit. **Activities:** Bands, campus ministries, choral groups, dance, drama, international student organizations, music ensembles, musical theater, radio station, student government, student newspaper, NAACP, business, sociology, criminal justice, accounting clubs, Christian Fellowship, northern exposure, Order of the Eastern Star.

**Athletics.** NCAA. **Intercollegiate:** Baseball M, basketball, bowling W, cross-country, football (tackle) M, softball W, tennis, track and field, volleyball W. **Intramural:** Basketball, tennis, volleyball. **Team name:** Bears.

**Student services.** Adult student services, alcohol/substance abuse counseling, campus ministries, career counseling, student employment services, financial aid counseling, health services, personal counseling, placement for graduates, veterans' counselor. **Physically disabled:** Services for visually, speech, hearing impaired.

**Contact.** E-mail: admissions@shawu.edu
Phone: (919) 546-8275 Toll-free number: (800) 214-6683
Fax: (919) 546-8271
Sandy Clifton, Interim Director of Admissions, Shaw University, 118 East South Street, Raleigh, NC 27601

## Southeastern Baptist Theological Seminary

**Wake Forest, North Carolina**
www.sebts.edu
**CB code: 7050**

- Private 4-year Bible and seminary college affiliated with Southern Baptist Convention
- Small town

**General.** Founded in 1950. Regionally accredited. **Location:** 20 miles from Raleigh, 30 miles from Durham. **Calendar:** Semester.

**Annual costs/financial aid.** Tuition/fees (2007-2008): $6,550. Non-Southern Baptist students per credit hour charge is $416.

**Contact.** Phone: (919) 761-2280
Dean of Students, PO Box 1889, Wake Forest, NC 27588

## University of North Carolina at Asheville

**Asheville, North Carolina**
www.unca.edu
**CB member**
**CB code: 5013**

- Public 4-year university and liberal arts college
- Residential campus in small city
- 3,251 degree-seeking undergraduates: 12% part-time, 58% women, 3% African American, 1% Asian American, 2% Hispanic American, 1% international
- 23 degree-seeking graduate students
- 76% of applicants admitted
- SAT or ACT with writing, application essay required
- 54% graduate within 6 years; 21% enter graduate study

**General.** Founded in 1927. Regionally accredited. **Degrees:** 578 bachelor's awarded; master's offered. **Location:** 130 miles from Charlotte, 200 miles from Atlanta. **Calendar:** Semester, limited summer session. **Full-time faculty:** 207 total; 85% have terminal degrees, 13% minority, 41% women. **Part-time faculty:** 117 total; 33% have terminal degrees, 51% women. **Class size:** 52% < 20, 46% 20-39, less than 1% 40-49, 1% 50-99. **Special facilities:** Botanical gardens, Jewish studies center, arboretum, environmental quality institute, distance learning facility, music recording studio, National Environmental Modeling and Analysis Center (NEMAC), astronomical research institute, National Climatic Data Center.

**Freshman class profile.** 2,653 applied, 2,014 admitted, 577 enrolled.

| Mid 50% test scores | | | |
|---|---|---|---|
| SAT critical reading: | 540-640 | Rank in top tenth: | 20% |
| SAT math: | 520-620 | End year in good standing: | 92% |
| SAT writing: | 510-620 | Return as sophomores: | 76% |
| ACT composite: | 22-26 | Out-of-state: | 17% |
| GPA 3.50 or higher: | 82% | Live on campus: | 90% |
| GPA 3.0-3.49: | 17% | International: | 1% |
| GPA 2.0-2.99: | 1% | Fraternities: | 1% |
| Rank in top quarter: | 56% | Sororities: | 3% |

**Basis for selection.** GED not accepted. High school curriculum, GPA, and class rank (top third), most important. Test scores important. Counselor recommendation and essay question required. Interview, extracurricular activities that support academic achievement considered. Students expected to have completed advanced coursework. Personal statements helpful. Interviews recommended. **Homeschooled:** Must provide a transcript documenting all courses taken, particularly UNC system minimum admissions requirements, units of credit received. Transcript must be signed by homeschool administrator. For North Carolina residents, a copy of the school's registration with the North Carolina Department of Non-Public Instruction is required. **Learning Disabled:** Untimed SAT accepted.

**High school preparation.** 15 units required. Required and recommended units include English 4, mathematics 4, social studies 1, history 1, science 3 (laboratory 1), foreign language 2 and academic electives 4. Science units should include biology and physical science such as chemistry or physics. One unit US history, 1 unit other social studies required. Math must include algebra I, II and geometry and 1 math course with algebra II as pre-requisite.

**2007-2008 Annual costs.** Tuition/fees: $4,164; $15,154 out-of-state. Room/board: $6,230. Books/supplies: $850. Personal expenses: $1,400.

**2006-2007 Financial aid. Need-based:** 392 full-time freshmen applied for aid; 202 were judged to have need; 200 of these received aid. Average need met was 81%. Average scholarship/grant was $4,608; average loan $2,440. 52% of total undergraduate aid awarded as scholarships/grants, 48% as loans/jobs. **Non-need-based:** Awarded to 426 full-time undergraduates, including 92 freshmen. Scholarships awarded for academics, alumni affiliation, art, athletics, job skills, leadership, minority status, music/drama, state residency.

**Application procedures. Admission:** Priority date 11/10; deadline 2/15 (postmark date). $50 fee, may be waived for applicants with need. Application may be submitted online. Admission notification 4/1. Must reply by 5/1. **Financial aid:** Priority date 3/1; no closing date. FAFSA required. Applicants notified on a rolling basis starting 3/15.

**Academics. Special study options:** Cross-registration, distance learning, double major, dual enrollment of high school students, exchange student, honors, independent study, internships, liberal arts/career combination, semester at sea, student-designed major, study abroad, teacher certification program, Washington semester. **Credit/placement by examination:** AP, CLEP, IB, institutional tests. 30 credit hours maximum toward bachelor's degree. AP and CLEP exam grades required for credit are subject to change. **Support services:** Learning center, reduced course load, remedial instruction, study skills assistance, tutoring, writing center.

**Majors. Area/ethnic studies:** Women's. **Biology:** General. **Business:** Accounting, business admin, operations. **Communications:** Media studies. **Computer sciences:** Computer science, web page design. **Conservation:** Environmental studies. **Engineering:** General. **English:** English lit. **Foreign languages:** Classics, French, German, Spanish. **Health:** Public health ed. **History:** General. **Liberal arts:** Arts/sciences. **Math:** General. **Philosophy/religion:** Philosophy, religion. **Physical sciences:** Atmospheric science, chemistry, physics. **Psychology:** General. **Social sciences:** Economics, political science, sociology. **Visual/performing arts:** Art, dramatic, studio arts.

**Most popular majors.** Business/marketing 12%, communications/journalism 6%, computer/information sciences 6%, English 8%, psychology 15%, social sciences 11%, visual/performing arts 10%.

**Computing on campus.** 390 workstations in dormitories, library, computer center, student center. Dormitories wired for high-speed internet access and linked to campus network. Commuter students can connect to campus network. Online course registration, online library, helpline, repair service, student web hosting, wireless network available.

**Student life. Freshman orientation:** Mandatory, $55 fee. Preregistration for classes offered. Two phase program held for one day in the summer and for two and one-half days before students begin classes. **Housing:** Guaranteed on-campus for freshmen. Coed dorms, single-sex dorms, special housing for disabled, substance-free housing available. $150 deposit, deadline 5/1. 24-hour quiet floors available. **Activities:** Bands, campus ministries,

choral groups, dance, drama, international student organizations, literary magazine, music ensembles, musical theater, radio station, student government, student newspaper, Baptist student union, international student association, InterVarsity Christian Fellowship, African American student association, Active Students for a Healthy Environment, University Ambassadors, Jewish student association, Asian Students in Asheville.

**Athletics.** NCAA. **Intercollegiate:** Baseball M, basketball, cheerleading, cross-country, soccer, tennis, track and field, volleyball W. **Intramural:** Badminton, basketball, football (non-tackle), golf, racquetball, soccer, softball, tennis, volleyball, water polo. **Team name:** Bulldogs.

**Student services.** Adult student services, alcohol/substance abuse counseling, campus ministries, career counseling, student employment services, financial aid counseling, health services, minority student services, personal counseling, placement for graduates, veterans' counselor, women's services. **Physically disabled:** Services for visually, hearing impaired.

**Contact.** E-mail: admissions@unca.edu
Phone: (828) 251-6481 Toll-free number: (800) 531-9842
Fax: (828) 251-6482
Pat McClellan, Dean of Academic Administration, University of North Carolina at Asheville, CPO#1320, UNCA, Asheville, NC 28804-8510

---

## University of North Carolina at Chapel Hill
**Chapel Hill, North Carolina**    **CB member**
www.unc.edu    **CB code: 5816**

- Public 4-year university
- Residential campus in large town
- 17,138 degree-seeking undergraduates: 2% part-time, 59% women, 11% African American, 7% Asian American, 4% Hispanic American, 1% Native American, 1% international
- 9,202 degree-seeking graduate students
- 35% of applicants admitted
- SAT or ACT with writing, application essay required

**General.** Founded in 1789. Regionally accredited. Entering freshmen required to own laptop meeting university specifications, as a part of the Carolina Computing Initiative; qualified students will receive special loans or grants. **Degrees:** 3,787 bachelor's awarded; master's, doctoral, first professional offered. **ROTC:** Army, Naval, Air Force. **Location:** 8 miles from Durham, 26 miles from Raleigh. **Calendar:** Semester, extensive summer session. **Full-time faculty:** 1,514 total; 89% have terminal degrees, 18% minority, 40% women. **Part-time faculty:** 107 total; 75% have terminal degrees, 10% minority, 45% women. **Class size:** 44% < 20, 38% 20-39, 6% 40-49, 6% 50-99, 6% >100. **Special facilities:** Planetarium, observatory, arboretum, botanical garden.

**Freshman class profile.** 20,090 applied, 6,999 admitted, 3,893 enrolled.

| Mid 50% test scores | | | |
|---|---|---|---|
| SAT critical reading: | 600-700 | Rank in top tenth: | 76% |
| SAT math: | 610-700 | End year in good standing: | 100% |
| SAT writing: | 590-690 | Return as sophomores: | 97% |
| ACT composite: | 26-31 | Out-of-state: | 17% |
| GPA 3.50 or higher: | 97% | Live on campus: | 83% |
| GPA 3.0-3.49: | 2% | International: | 1% |
| GPA 2.0-2.99: | 1% | Fraternities: | 13% |
| Rank in top quarter: | 95% | Sororities: | 17% |

**Basis for selection.** GED not accepted. High school record, including course selection and performance, very important. Test scores, essays, activities, and recommendations also receive strong consideration. Separate consideration given to out-of-state children of alumni. SAT preferred, ACT also accepted. Test score submission deadlines may vary. Audition required for drama and music programs; portfolio recommended for art program. **Homeschooled:** SAT Subject Tests recommended. Students should follow curriculum equivalent to that of high school students taking Advanced Placement and honors courses. **Learning Disabled:** Students may voluntarily supply documentation regarding disability and impact on educational experiences with application.

**High school preparation.** 18 units required; 20 recommended. Required and recommended units include English 4, mathematics 4, social studies 2-3, science 3-4 (laboratory 1), foreign language 2-4 and academic electives 2. One social studies must be U.S. history.

**2007-2008 Annual costs.** Tuition/fees: $5,340; $20,988 out-of-state. Fees may be higher for dental programs. Room/board: $7,960. Books/supplies: $1,000. Personal expenses: $1,200.

**2006-2007 Financial aid. Need-based:** 2,858 full-time freshmen applied for aid; 1,229 were judged to have need; 1,214 of these received aid. Average need met was 100%. Average scholarship/grant was $9,445; average loan $2,663. 70% of total undergraduate aid awarded as scholarships/grants, 30% as loans/jobs. **Non-need-based:** Awarded to 4,306 full-time undergraduates, including 1,427 freshmen. Scholarships awarded for academics, alumni affiliation, art, athletics, leadership, music/drama, religious affiliation, state residency. **Additional information:** Carolina meets 100% of all need documented for both resident and non-resident undergraduates who quality for need based aid, with a favorable mix of approximately 2/3 grants and scholarships and 1/3 loans and work study.

**Application procedures. Admission:** Closing date 1/15 (postmark date). $70 fee, may be waived for applicants with need. Application may be submitted online. On or around 01/15 for early notification; on or around 03/20 for regular notification. Must reply by 5/1. **Financial aid:** Priority date 3/1; no closing date. FAFSA, CSS PROFILE required. Applicants notified on a rolling basis starting 3/15; must reply by 5/1.

**Academics. Special study options:** Cross-registration, distance learning, double major, dual enrollment of high school students, honors, independent study, internships, student-designed major, study abroad, teacher certification program. **Credit/placement by examination:** AP, CLEP, IB, SAT, ACT, institutional tests. Credit by examination is non-transferable. **Support services:** Learning center, pre-admission summer program, reduced course load, study skills assistance, tutoring, writing center.

**Majors. Area/ethnic studies:** African-American, American, Asian, European, Latin American, Russian/Slavic, women's. **Biology:** General, biostatistics, pathology. **Business:** Business admin, human resources. **Communications:** General, media studies. **Computer sciences:** Computer science, information systems. **Conservation:** Environmental science, environmental studies. **Education:** Early childhood, elementary, middle. **English:** English lit. **Family/consumer sciences:** Food/nutrition. **Foreign languages:** Classics, comparative lit, German, linguistics. **Health:** Clinical lab science, dental hygiene, environmental health, health care admin, medical radiologic technology/radiation therapy, nursing (RN). **History:** General. **Interdisciplinary:** Peace/conflict. **Liberal arts:** Arts/sciences. **Math:** General, applied. **Parks/recreation:** Facilities management, health/fitness. **Philosophy/religion:** Philosophy, religion. **Physical sciences:** Chemistry, geology, physics. **Psychology:** General. **Public administration:** Policy analysis. **Social sciences:** Anthropology, archaeology, economics, geography, political science, sociology. **Visual/performing arts:** Art history/conservation, dramatic, music performance, studio arts. **Other:** Applied science, International studies, Romance languages French, Italian, Portuguese, Spanish.

**Most popular majors.** Biology 8%, business/marketing 8%, communications/journalism 13%, health sciences 7%, psychology 9%, social sciences 17%.

**Computing on campus.** PC or laptop required. 600 workstations in dormitories, library, computer center, student center. Dormitories wired for high-speed internet access and linked to campus network. Commuter students can connect to campus network. Online course registration, online library, helpline, repair service, student web hosting, wireless network available.

**Student life. Freshman orientation:** Mandatory, $155 fee. Preregistration for classes offered. 2-day summer orientation. **Policies:** Policies exist regarding: illegal drugs, honor code, student organizations, non-discrimination policy, no smoking policy, student possession and consumption of alcoholic beverages in facilities. **Housing:** Coed dorms, single-sex dorms, special housing for disabled, apartments, substance-free housing available. $200 nonrefundable deposit, deadline 5/15. Learning communities such as language houses (German, French, Spanish), connected learning, service and leadership, academic enhancement, substance free, health sciences, unitas, sustainability and women's experiences. **Activities:** Bands, campus ministries, choral groups, dance, drama, film society, international student organizations, literary magazine, music ensembles, Model UN, musical theater, opera, radio station, student government, student newspaper, symphony orchestra, TV station, Alpha Phi Omega co-ed service fraternity, Asian students association, Black Student Movement, Campus Crusade for Christ, Carolina Cancer Focus, Carolina Hispanic Association, College Republicans, Habitat for Humanity, Young Democrats.

**Athletics. NCAA. Intercollegiate:** Baseball M, basketball, cross-country, diving, fencing, field hockey W, football (tackle) M, golf, gymnastics W, lacrosse, rowing (crew) W, soccer, softball W, swimming, tennis, track and field, volleyball W, wrestling M. **Intramural:** Badminton, basketball, bowling, cross-country, football (non-tackle), golf, handball, racquetball, soccer, softball, swimming, table tennis, tennis, track and field, triathlon, volleyball, water polo. **Team name:** Tarheels.

**Student services.** Alcohol/substance abuse counseling, campus ministries, career counseling, student employment services, financial aid counseling, health services, legal services, minority student services, on-campus daycare, personal counseling, placement for graduates, veterans' counselor,

women's services. **Physically disabled:** Services for visually, speech, hearing impaired. **Learning disabled:** Comprehensive services available.

**Contact.** E-mail: unchelp@admissions.unc.edu
Phone: (919) 966-3621 Fax: (919) 962-3045
Stephen Farmer, Assistant Provost and Director of Undergraduate Admissions, University of North Carolina at Chapel Hill, Jackson Hall CB #2200, Chapel Hill, NC 27599-2200

## University of North Carolina at Charlotte
Charlotte, North Carolina — CB member
www.uncc.edu — CB code: 5105

- Public 4-year university
- Residential campus in very large city
- 17,481 degree-seeking undergraduates: 15% part-time, 52% women
- 3,543 degree-seeking graduate students
- 75% of applicants admitted
- SAT or ACT with writing required
- 45% graduate within 6 years

**General.** Founded in 1946. Regionally accredited. **Degrees:** 2,945 bachelor's awarded; master's, doctoral offered. **ROTC:** Army, Air Force. **Location:** 10 miles from downtown. **Calendar:** Semester, limited summer session. **Full-time faculty:** 945 total; 85% have terminal degrees, 21% minority, 41% women. **Part-time faculty:** 399 total; 25% have terminal degrees, 16% minority, 60% women. **Class size:** 33% < 20, 43% 20-39, 9% 40-49, 10% 50-99, 6% >100. **Special facilities:** Botanical and horticultural complex with controlled environment, 100-acre experimental ecological reserve, tropical rain forest conservatory, 46-acre wildlife refuge, 9,600-seat multipurpose student activity center.

**Freshman class profile.** 9,911 applied, 7,477 admitted, 2,955 enrolled.

| Mid 50% test scores | | | |
|---|---|---|---|
| SAT critical reading: | 470-560 | GPA 2.0-2.99: | 6% |
| SAT math: | 480-590 | Rank in top quarter: | 47% |
| SAT writing: | 460-550 | Rank in top tenth: | 15% |
| ACT composite: | 19-24 | Return as sophomores: | 77% |
| GPA 3.50 or higher: | 58% | Out-of-state: | 11% |
| GPA 3.0-3.49: | 36% | Live on campus: | 72% |
| | | International: | 1% |

**Basis for selection.** Overall performance in high school academic courses, senior year academic courses in progress, and SAT scores considered. SAT preferred, but ACT also accepted. Audition required for music; interview required for art, architecture, and music programs; portfolio required for art, architecture programs.

**High school preparation.** 16 units required. Required and recommended units include English 4, mathematics 4, social studies 2, history 1, science 3 (laboratory 1), foreign language 2 and academic electives 1. English should emphasize grammar, composition & literature; science should include at least 1 unit in a life or biological science and at least 1 unit in a physical science and 1 lab; foreign language units should be in same language. 1 social studies unit must be in U.S. history.

**2007-2008 Annual costs.** Tuition/fees: $4,153; $14,565 out-of-state. Room/board: $6,034. Books/supplies: $1,200. Personal expenses: $1,520.

**Financial aid. Non-need-based:** Scholarships awarded for academics, athletics, leadership, music/drama.

**Application procedures. Admission:** Closing date 7/1 (postmark date). $50 fee, may be waived for applicants with need. Application may be submitted online. Admission notification on a rolling basis beginning on or about 11/1. Must reply by May 1 or within 2 week(s) if notified thereafter. **Financial aid:** Priority date 4/1; no closing date. FAFSA required. Applicants notified on a rolling basis starting 4/1; must reply within 3 week(s) of notification.

**Academics. Special study options:** Accelerated study, cooperative education, cross-registration, distance learning, double major, dual enrollment of high school students, ESL, honors, independent study, internships, study abroad, teacher certification program, Washington semester, weekend college. Wilderness exploration program. **Credit/placement by examination:** AP, CLEP, IB, institutional tests. 30 credit hours maximum toward bachelor's degree. **Support services:** Learning center, pre-admission summer program, reduced course load, study skills assistance, tutoring, writing center.

**Honors college/program.** Minimum GPA 3.0 or high school rank and SAT scores predictive of 3.0 GPA. Must submit 2-3 page essay describing educational goals and objectives, as well as one letter of recommendation from a person who can address potential for success in Honors Program. Brief interview may be scheduled.

**Majors. Architecture:** Architecture. **Area/ethnic studies:** African-American. **Biology:** General. **Business:** Accounting, business admin, construction management, finance, international, management information systems, managerial economics, marketing, operations. **Communications:** General. **Computer sciences:** Computer science. **Education:** Art, chemistry, drama/dance, elementary, English, French, German, history, kindergarten/preschool, mathematics, mentally handicapped, middle, music, Spanish. **Engineering:** Civil, computer, electrical, mechanical. **Engineering technology:** Civil, electrical, mechanical. **English:** English lit. **Family/consumer sciences:** Family studies. **Foreign languages:** French, German, Spanish. **Health:** Athletic training, clinical lab science, nursing (RN). **History:** General. **Math:** General. **Parks/recreation:** Health/fitness. **Philosophy/religion:** Philosophy, religion. **Physical sciences:** Chemistry, geology, meteorology, physics. **Protective services:** Criminal justice, fire services admin. **Psychology:** General. **Public administration:** Social work. **Social sciences:** Anthropology, economics, geography, political science, sociology. **Visual/performing arts:** Art, art history/conservation, dance, dramatic, music performance, studio arts.

**Most popular majors.** Business/marketing 25%, communications/journalism 6%, education 7%, engineering/engineering technologies 9%, psychology 8%, social sciences 7%.

**Computing on campus.** 1,500 workstations in dormitories, library, computer center, student center. Dormitories wired for high-speed internet access and linked to campus network. Commuter students can connect to campus network. Online course registration, online library, helpline, student web hosting, wireless network available.

**Student life. Freshman orientation:** Available, $85 fee. Preregistration for classes offered. 2-day program for freshmen and parents. Parents fee $32. **Policies:** Students must follow code of student responsibility, code of student academic integrity, and university policy statements. **Housing:** Coed dorms, single-sex dorms, special housing for disabled, apartments, fraternity/sorority housing, substance-free housing available. $100 deposit. Housing for disabled students limited. Suite housing, honors housing, Greek village housing available. **Activities:** Bands, choral groups, dance, drama, literary magazine, music ensembles, musical theater, opera, student government, student newspaper, TV station, Campus Crusade for Christ, Hillel, College Democrats, College Republicans, feminist union, black student union, Latin American student organization, Muslim student association, Native American student organization, Asian student union.

**Athletics.** NCAA. **Intercollegiate:** Baseball M, basketball, cross-country, golf M, soccer, softball W, tennis, track and field, volleyball W. **Intramural:** Badminton, basketball, bowling, field hockey, football (non-tackle), golf, handball, lacrosse, racquetball, rugby, soccer, softball, swimming, table tennis, tennis, track and field, volleyball, water polo. **Team name:** Fortyniners.

**Student services.** Alcohol/substance abuse counseling, campus ministries, career counseling, student employment services, financial aid counseling, health services, minority student services, personal counseling, placement for graduates, veterans' counselor, women's services. **Physically disabled:** Services for visually, speech, hearing impaired.

**Contact.** E-mail: unccadm@uncc.edu
Phone: (704) 687-2213 Fax: (704) 687-6483
Tina McEntire, Director of Admissions, University of North Carolina at Charlotte, 9201 University City Boulevard, Charlotte, NC 28223-0001

---

## University of North Carolina at Greensboro

| Greensboro, North Carolina | CB member |
| --- | --- |
| www.uncg.edu | CB code: 5913 |

- Public 4-year university
- Residential campus in small city
- 13,245 degree-seeking undergraduates: 13% part-time, 68% women, 21% African American, 3% Asian American, 3% Hispanic American, 1% international
- 3,172 degree-seeking graduate students
- 60% of applicants admitted
- SAT or ACT with writing required
- 50% graduate within 6 years

**General.** Founded in 1891. Regionally accredited. **Degrees:** 2,195 bachelor's awarded; master's, doctoral offered. **ROTC:** Army, Air Force. **Location:** 90 miles from Raleigh. **Calendar:** Semester, extensive summer session. **Full-time faculty:** 810 total; 80% have terminal degrees, 14% minority, 51% women. **Part-time faculty:** 270 total; 46% have terminal degrees, 10% minority, 60% women. **Class size:** 45% < 20, 38% 20-39, 6% 40-49,

8% 50-99, 3% >100. **Special facilities:** Observatory, Silva cello music collection, Randall Jarrell collection, women's studies collection.

**Freshman class profile.** 6,411 applied, 3,840 admitted, 2,446 enrolled.

| Mid 50% test scores | | | |
| --- | --- | --- | --- |
| SAT critical reading: | 460-570 | Rank in top quarter: | 45% |
| SAT math: | 470-570 | Rank in top tenth: | 15% |
| SAT writing: | 450-560 | Return as sophomores: | 76% |
| GPA 3.50 or higher: | 60% | Out-of-state: | 9% |
| GPA 3.0-3.49: | 34% | Live on campus: | 81% |
| GPA 2.0-2.99: | 6% | International: | 1% |

**Basis for selection.** GED not accepted. Combined test scores and high school GPA based on academic courses most important. High school recommendations and activities considered. SAT preferred, but ACT accepted. Audition required for music program.

**High school preparation.** 15 units required. Required units include English 4, mathematics 4, social studies 2, science 3 (laboratory 1) and foreign language 2.

**2007-2008 Annual costs.** Tuition/fees: $4,029; $15,297 out-of-state. Room/board: $6,051. Books/supplies: $1,314. Personal expenses: $1,676.

**2007-2008 Financial aid. Need-based:** 1,901 full-time freshmen applied for aid; 1,681 were judged to have need; 1,649 of these received aid. Average need met was 57%. Average scholarship/grant was $5,831; average loan $3,247. 42% of total undergraduate aid awarded as scholarships/grants, 58% as loans/jobs. **Non-need-based:** Awarded to 5,733 full-time undergraduates, including 1,284 freshmen. Scholarships awarded for academics, alumni affiliation, art, athletics, leadership, music/drama, state residency.

**Application procedures. Admission:** Closing date 3/1. $45 fee, may be waived for applicants with need. Application must be submitted on paper. Admission notification on a rolling basis beginning on or about 3/1. Must reply by May 1 or within 4 week(s) if notified thereafter. **Financial aid:** Priority date 3/1; no closing date. FAFSA required. Applicants notified on a rolling basis starting 3/15; must reply within 3 week(s) of notification.

**Academics. Special study options:** Accelerated study, combined bachelor's/graduate degree, cross-registration, distance learning, double major, dual enrollment of high school students, honors, independent study, internships, study abroad, teacher certification program, Washington semester. Evening university. **Credit/placement by examination:** AP, CLEP, institutional tests. Up to 64 semester hours of any combination of transfer, correspondence, examination or other will be accepted. SAT Subject Test scores in some subjects may qualify for credit. **Support services:** Learning center, reduced course load, remedial instruction, study skills assistance, tutoring.

**Majors. Area/ethnic studies:** African-American, women's. **Biology:** General, biochemistry. **Business:** Accounting, business admin, finance, hospitality admin, international, managerial economics. **Communications:** Media studies. **Computer sciences:** Computer science, networking. **Education:** Art, biology, Deaf/hearing impaired, drama/dance, early childhood, elementary, English, French, German, health, mathematics, middle, music, physical, social science, social studies, Spanish, special, speech. **English:** English lit, speech/rhetoric. **Family/consumer sciences:** Child development, clothing/textiles, family studies, institutional food production. **Foreign languages:** Classics, French, German, Italian, Spanish. **Health:** Audiology/speech pathology, clinical lab science, nursing (RN), public health ed. **History:** General. **Interdisciplinary:** Nutrition sciences. **Liberal arts:** Arts/sciences. **Math:** General. **Parks/recreation:** General, exercise sciences. **Philosophy/religion:** Philosophy, religion. **Physical sciences:** Chemistry, physics. **Psychology:** General. **Public administration:** Social work. **Social sciences:** Anthropology, economics, geography, political science, sociology. **Visual/performing arts:** Art, dance, dramatic, interior design, jazz, music performance, music theory/composition, studio arts.

**Most popular majors.** Business/marketing 15%, education 13%, English 8%, family/consumer sciences 6%, health sciences 10%, social sciences 7%, visual/performing arts 10%.

**Computing on campus.** 600 workstations in dormitories, library, computer center, student center. Dormitories linked to campus network. Commuter students can connect to campus network. Online course registration, online library, helpline, wireless network available.

**Student life. Freshman orientation:** Available. **Housing:** Coed dorms, single-sex dorms, apartments available. $150 nonrefundable deposit, deadline 5/1. Residential college (academic/residential program), International House available. **Activities:** Bands, choral groups, dance, drama, film society, international student organizations, literary magazine, music ensembles, Model UN, musical theater, opera, radio station, student government, student newspaper, symphony orchestra, neo-black society, environmental awareness foundation, political awareness club, Habitat for Humanity, Rotaract Club, gay, lesbian and bisexual student association.

**Athletics.** NCAA. **Intercollegiate:** Baseball M, basketball, cross-country, golf, soccer, softball W, tennis, volleyball W, wrestling M. **Intramural:** Badminton, basketball, bowling, golf, racquetball, soccer, softball, swimming, table tennis, tennis, track and field, volleyball. **Team name:** Spartans.

**Student services.** Adult student services, campus ministries, career counseling, student employment services, financial aid counseling, health services, personal counseling, placement for graduates, veterans' counselor. **Physically disabled:** Services for visually, speech, hearing impaired.

**Contact.** E-mail: admissions@uncg.edu
Phone: (336) 334-5243 Fax: (336) 334-4180
Lise Keller, Director of Admissions, University of North Carolina at Greensboro, 1400 Spring Garden Street, Greensboro, NC 27402-6170

---

## University of North Carolina at Pembroke
**Pembroke, North Carolina**  CB member
**www.uncp.edu**  CB code: 5534

- Public 4-year university and liberal arts college
- Commuter campus in small town
- 5,002 degree-seeking undergraduates: 18% part-time, 62% women, 28% African American, 2% Asian American, 4% Hispanic American, 18% Native American, 1% international
- 601 degree-seeking graduate students
- 86% of applicants admitted
- SAT or ACT with writing required
- 38% graduate within 6 years

**General.** Founded in 1887. Regionally accredited. **Degrees:** 623 bachelor's awarded; master's offered. **ROTC:** Army, Air Force. **Location:** 35 miles from Fayetteville. **Calendar:** Semester, limited summer session. **Full-time faculty:** 277 total; 74% have terminal degrees, 18% minority, 43% women. **Part-time faculty:** 158 total; 28% have terminal degrees, 25% minority, 57% women. **Class size:** 47% < 20, 45% 20-39, 6% 40-49, 3% 50-99, less than 1% >100. **Special facilities:** Native American Resource Center, performing arts center.

**Freshman class profile.** 2,750 applied, 2,375 admitted, 1,119 enrolled.

| Mid 50% test scores | | | |
|---|---|---|---|
| SAT critical reading: | 420-510 | GPA 2.0-2.99: | 49% |
| SAT math: | 430-530 | Rank in top quarter: | 30% |
| SAT writing: | 400-490 | Rank in top tenth: | 9% |
| ACT composite: | 16-20 | Return as sophomores: | 72% |
| GPA 3.50 or higher: | 26% | Out-of-state: | 7% |
| GPA 3.0-3.49: | 24% | Live on campus: | 74% |
| | | International: | 1% |

**Basis for selection.** High school record, class standing, GPA, test scores, and college preparatory courses important. Tests not required for students over 21. Auditions and interviews may be required for acceptance to obtain programs.

**High school preparation.** 15 units required. Required units include English 4, mathematics 4, social studies 1, history 1, science 3 (laboratory 1) and foreign language 2.

**2008-2009 Annual costs.** Tuition/fees (projected): $3,635; $13,358 out-of-state. Room/board: $6,190. Books/supplies: $1,200. Personal expenses: $1,618.

**Financial aid. Non-need-based:** Scholarships awarded for alumni affiliation.

**Application procedures. Admission:** Priority date 7/15; no deadline. $40 fee, may be waived for applicants with need. Application may be submitted online. Admission notification on a rolling basis beginning on or about 9/15. **Financial aid:** Closing date 3/15. FAFSA required. Applicants notified on a rolling basis starting 4/15; must reply within 2 week(s) of notification.

**Academics.** Certification on secondary teaching level in English, biology, mathematics, social studies, and science education. **Special study options:** Accelerated study, cooperative education, cross-registration, distance learning, double major, dual enrollment of high school students, ESL, exchange student, external degree, honors, independent study, internships, study abroad, teacher certification program, Washington semester. **Credit/placement by examination:** AP, CLEP, institutional tests. 30 credit hours maximum toward bachelor's degree. **Support services:** Learning center, pre-admission summer program, reduced course load, remedial instruction, tutoring, writing center.

**Majors. Area/ethnic studies:** American, Native American. **Biology:** General. **Business:** Accounting, business admin. **Communications:** Media studies. **Computer sciences:** Computer science, information technology. **Conservation:** Environmental science. **Education:** Art, biology, elementary, English, kindergarten/preschool, mathematics, middle, music, physical, science, social studies, special. **English:** English lit. **Foreign languages:** Spanish. **Health:** Athletic training, nursing (RN), public health ed. **History:** General. **Math:** General. **Parks/recreation:** Facilities management, health/fitness. **Physical sciences:** Chemistry, physics. **Protective services:** Criminal justice. **Psychology:** General. **Public administration:** Social work. **Social sciences:** Political science, sociology. **Visual/performing arts:** Dramatic, music performance, studio arts. **Other:** Philosophy and religion.

**Most popular majors.** Biology 10%, business/marketing 12%, education 16%, health sciences 10%, parks/recreation 6%, public administration/social services 7%, social sciences 10%.

**Computing on campus.** 775 workstations in dormitories, library, computer center, student center. Dormitories wired for high-speed internet access and linked to campus network. Commuter students can connect to campus network. Online course registration, online library, helpline, wireless network available.

**Student life. Freshman orientation:** Mandatory, $50 fee. **Housing:** Coed dorms, single-sex dorms, apartments available. $175 deposit, deadline 7/15. Freshmen given preference for on-campus housing. Apartments available. **Activities:** Bands, choral groups, dance, drama, film society, literary magazine, music ensembles, musical theater, student government, student newspaper, TV station, Native American organization, African American student organization, Baptist student union, international student organization, Methodist campus ministry, Fellowship of Christian Athletes, campus association of social workers, American Medical Student Association, criminal justice club.

**Athletics.** NCAA. **Intercollegiate:** Baseball M, basketball, cheerleading, cross-country, football (tackle) M, golf M, soccer, softball W, tennis W, track and field, volleyball W, wrestling M. **Intramural:** Basketball, bowling, football (tackle) M, golf M, racquetball, soccer M, softball, volleyball, water polo M, wrestling M. **Team name:** Braves.

**Student services.** Campus ministries, career counseling, student employment services, financial aid counseling, health services, personal counseling, veterans' counselor. **Physically disabled:** Services for visually, hearing impaired.

**Contact.** E-mail: admissons@uncp.edu
Phone: (910) 521-6262 Toll-free number: (800) 949-8627
Fax: (910) 521-6497
Jackie Clark, Vice Chancellor for Enrollment Management, University of North Carolina at Pembroke, Box 1510, Pembroke, NC 28372

---

## University of North Carolina at Wilmington
**Wilmington, North Carolina**  CB member
**www.uncw.edu**  CB code: 5907

- Public 4-year university
- Commuter campus in small city
- 10,481 degree-seeking undergraduates: 7% part-time, 57% women, 5% African American, 2% Asian American, 3% Hispanic American, 1% Native American
- 984 degree-seeking graduate students
- 58% of applicants admitted
- SAT or ACT with writing, application essay required
- 65% graduate within 6 years; 20% enter graduate study

**General.** Founded in 1947. Regionally accredited. **Degrees:** 2,268 bachelor's awarded; master's, doctoral offered. **Location:** 125 miles from Raleigh. **Calendar:** Semester, extensive summer session. **Full-time faculty:** 544 total; 86% have terminal degrees, 14% minority, 40% women. **Part-time faculty:** 306 total; 33% have terminal degrees, 8% minority, 56% women. **Class size:** 27% < 20, 53% 20-39, 9% 40-49, 8% 50-99, 3% >100. **Special facilities:** Wildlife preserve, research vessel for marine biology laboratory.

**Freshman class profile.** 8,740 applied, 5,098 admitted, 1,920 enrolled.

| Mid 50% test scores | | | |
|---|---|---|---|
| SAT critical reading: | 530-610 | GPA 2.0-2.99: | 3% |
| SAT math: | 540-630 | Rank in top quarter: | 62% |
| SAT writing: | 510-600 | Rank in top tenth: | 25% |
| ACT composite: | 21-26 | End year in good standing: | 83% |
| GPA 3.50 or higher: | 81% | Return as sophomores: | 85% |
| GPA 3.0-3.49: | 16% | Out-of-state: | 18% |
| | | Live on campus: | 85% |

**Basis for selection.** High school record; rank in class, if provided; standardized test scores; and rigor of courses completed in high school are very important. SAT or ACT with writing preferred. Auditions for Music majors required. **Homeschooled:** Statement describing homeschool structure and mission, transcript of courses and grades, letter of recommendation (nonparent) required.

**High school preparation.** Required units include English 4, mathematics 4, social studies 2, history 1, science 3 (laboratory 1) and foreign language 2. Of the 2 social studies units, 1 unit must be U.S. history.

**2007-2008 Annual costs.** Tuition/fees: $4,398; $14,361 out-of-state. Room/board: $6,999. Books/supplies: $934. Personal expenses: $1,053.

**2006-2007 Financial aid. Need-based:** 1,012 full-time freshmen applied for aid; 545 were judged to have need; 545 of these received aid. Average need met was 88%. Average scholarship/grant was $3,763; average loan $2,792. 57% of total undergraduate aid awarded as scholarships/grants, 43% as loans/jobs. **Non-need-based:** Awarded to 386 full-time undergraduates, including 89 freshmen. Scholarships awarded for academics, athletics, leadership, minority status, music/drama, state residency.

**Application procedures. Admission:** Priority date 11/1; deadline 2/1 (postmark date). $45 fee, may be waived for applicants with need. Application may be submitted online. Admission notification 4/1. Must reply by May 1 or within 4 week(s) if notified thereafter. **Financial aid:** Priority date 3/15; no closing date. FAFSA, institutional form required. Applicants notified on a rolling basis starting 4/1; must reply within 3 week(s) of notification.

**Academics. Special study options:** Accelerated study, cooperative education, cross-registration, distance learning, double major, dual enrollment of high school students, ESL, exchange student, honors, independent study, internships, study abroad, teacher certification program. 2+2 engineering programs. **Credit/placement by examination:** AP, CLEP, IB, institutional tests. **Support services:** Learning center, reduced course load, remedial instruction, tutoring, writing center.

**Majors. Biology:** General, marine. **Business:** Accounting, business admin, finance, management information systems, managerial economics, marketing. **Communications:** General. **Computer sciences:** Computer science. **Conservation:** Environmental science, environmental studies. **Education:** Biology, chemistry, elementary, emotionally handicapped, English, French, history, kindergarten/preschool, learning disabled, mathematics, mentally handicapped, middle, multiple handicapped, music, physical, Spanish, special. **English:** Creative writing, English lit. **Foreign languages:** French, German, Spanish. **Health:** Athletic training, nursing (RN), recreational therapy. **History:** General. **Math:** General, statistics. **Parks/recreation:** Facilities management, health/fitness. **Philosophy/religion:** Philosophy, religion. **Physical sciences:** Chemistry, geology, physics. **Protective services:** Criminal justice. **Psychology:** General. **Public administration:** Social work. **Social sciences:** Anthropology, economics, geography, political science, sociology. **Visual/performing arts:** Art history/conservation, cinematography, dramatic, music performance, studio arts. **Other:** Health professions and related clinical sciences.

**Most popular majors.** Biology 7%, business/marketing 26%, communications/journalism 7%, education 11%, psychology 8%.

**Computing on campus.** 1,170 workstations in dormitories, library, computer center, student center. Dormitories wired for high-speed internet access and linked to campus network. Commuter students can connect to campus network. Online course registration, online library, helpline, repair service, student web hosting, wireless network available.

**Student life. Freshman orientation:** Mandatory, $80 fee. Preregistration for classes offered. **Housing:** Coed dorms, single-sex dorms, apartments, substance-free housing available. $100 nonrefundable deposit, deadline 5/1. Honors housing. **Activities:** Bands, campus ministries, choral groups, dance, drama, film society, international student organizations, literary magazine, music ensembles, musical theater, opera, radio station, student government, student newspaper, symphony orchestra, TV station, Baptist student union, black student alliance, College Republicans, Fellowship of Christian University Students, Global Serve, Alpha Phi Omega, Young Democrats, Newman Catholic Student Center, African American-Hispanic-Asian-Native American organizations.

**Athletics.** NCAA. **Intercollegiate:** Baseball M, basketball, cheerleading, cross-country, diving, golf, soccer, softball W, swimming, tennis, track and field, volleyball W. **Intramural:** Basketball, football (non-tackle), golf, soccer, softball, tennis, volleyball. **Team name:** Seahawks.

**Student services.** Adult student services, alcohol/substance abuse counseling, campus ministries, career counseling, student employment services, financial aid counseling, health services, minority student services, personal counseling, placement for graduates, veterans' counselor. **Physically disabled:** Services for visually, speech, hearing impaired.

**Contact.** E-mail: admissions@uncw.edu
Phone: (910) 962-3243 Toll-free number: (800) 228-5571
Fax: (910) 962-3038
Terrence Curran, Associate Provost, University of North Carolina at Wilmington, 601 South College Road, Wilmington, NC 28403-5904

---

## Wake Forest University
**Winston-Salem, North Carolina**
www.wfu.edu

**CB member**
**CB code: 5885**

- Private 4-year university
- Residential campus in small city
- 4,405 degree-seeking undergraduates: 1% part-time, 51% women, 7% African American, 5% Asian American, 2% Hispanic American, 1% Native American, 1% international
- 2,328 degree-seeking graduate students
- 42% of applicants admitted
- SAT or ACT with writing, application essay required
- 89% graduate within 6 years; 32% enter graduate study

**General.** Founded in 1834. Regionally accredited. All freshmen receive a personal computer and a color printer/scanner/copier. **Degrees:** 967 bachelor's awarded; master's, doctoral, first professional offered. **ROTC:** Army. **Location:** 4 miles from downtown. **Calendar:** Semester, limited summer session. **Full-time faculty:** 468 total; 90% have terminal degrees, 12% minority, 37% women. **Part-time faculty:** 198 total; 41% have terminal degrees, 6% minority, 50% women. **Class size:** 57% < 20, 36% 20-39, 5% 40-49, 2% 50-99, less than 1% >100. **Special facilities:** Museum of anthropology, center for nanotechnology and molecular materials, Reynolda house museum of American art, art gallery, archaeology laboratory, biomechanics laboratory, laser physics laboratory.

**Freshman class profile.** 7,177 applied, 3,041 admitted, 1,124 enrolled.

| Mid 50% test scores | | | |
|---|---|---|---|
| SAT critical reading: | 610-700 | Return as sophomores: | 94% |
| SAT math: | 630-710 | Out-of-state: | 77% |
| ACT composite: | 27-31 | Live on campus: | 99% |
| Rank in top quarter: | 91% | International: | 1% |
| Rank in top tenth: | 64% | Fraternities: | 35% |
| | | Sororities: | 48% |

**Basis for selection.** High school curriculum and achievement, test scores, school and community activities, essay, personal recommendations, special talents all important. Audition recommended for those competing for a Presidential Scholarship (for students with special talents in music, theater, art, dance, and debate).

**High school preparation.** 16 units required; 20 recommended. Required and recommended units include English 4, mathematics 3-4, social studies 2-4, science 1-4 and foreign language 2-4.

**2008-2009 Annual costs.** Tuition/fees: $36,975. Tuition covers cost of an IBM Thinkpad computer and inkjet printer for freshmen. Room/board: $9,945. Books/supplies: $850. Personal expenses: $1,350.

**2007-2008 Financial aid. Need-based:** 448 full-time freshmen applied for aid; 345 were judged to have need; 342 of these received aid. Average need met was 99%. Average scholarship/grant was $21,976; average loan $7,222. 62% of total undergraduate aid awarded as scholarships/grants, 38% as loans/jobs. **Non-need-based:** Awarded to 1,471 full-time undergraduates, including 341 freshmen. Scholarships awarded for academics, alumni affiliation, art, athletics, leadership, music/drama, religious affiliation, ROTC, state residency. **Additional information:** In fall 2008, freshmen with an annual family income of less than $40,000 will have their student loans capped at $4,000 per year during their college years. Other financial aid to the students will come from grant and scholarship increases and work-study opportunities.

**Application procedures. Admission:** Closing date 1/15. $50 fee, may be waived for applicants with need. Application may be submitted online. Admission notification 4/1. Must reply by 5/1. **Financial aid:** Priority date 2/1, closing date 3/1. FAFSA, CSS PROFILE required. Applicants notified by 4/1; must reply by 5/1 or within 4 week(s) of notification.

**Academics.** Language courses at all levels in Russian, Greek, Italian, Hebrew; elementary and intermediate courses in Chinese, Japanese and Arabic; elementary courses in Hindi, Portuguese. **Special study options:** Combined bachelor's/graduate degree, cross-registration, double major, dual enrollment of high school students, honors, independent study, internships, study abroad, teacher certification program, Washington semester. Semester in London, Venice, or Vienna and semester at universities in Dijon, Salamanca, Berlin, Moscow, Beijing, and Japan. **Credit/placement by examination:** AP, CLEP, IB, institutional tests. **Support services:** Learning center, reduced course load, study skills assistance, tutoring, writing center.

**Majors. Biology:** General, bacteriology. **Business:** General, accounting, finance, management science. **Communications:** General. **Computer sciences:** Computer science. **Education:** Elementary, social studies. **English:** English lit. **Foreign languages:** Ancient Greek, Chinese, classics, French, German, Japanese, Latin, Russian, Spanish. **Health:** Clinical lab science. **History:** General. **Math:** General. **Parks/recreation:** Exercise sciences. **Philosophy/religion:** Philosophy, religion. **Physical sciences:** Chemistry, physics. **Psychology:** General. **Social sciences:** Anthropology, econometrics, economics, political science, sociology. **Visual/performing arts:** Art history/conservation, dramatic, music history, music performance, studio arts.

**Most popular majors.** Biology 8%, business/marketing 18%, communications/journalism 8%, English 6%, foreign language 8%, history 7%, psychology 7%, social sciences 21%.

**Computing on campus.** PC or laptop required. 4,412 workstations in dormitories, library, computer center, student center. Dormitories wired for high-speed internet access and linked to campus network. Commuter students can connect to campus network. Online course registration, online library, helpline, repair service, student web hosting, wireless network available.

**Student life. Freshman orientation:** Mandatory. Preregistration for classes offered. Six days before Fall classes start. **Policies:** First- and second-year students with residential status required to live on campus. **Housing:** Guaranteed on-campus for all undergraduates. Coed dorms, apartments, fraternity/sorority housing, substance-free housing available. Theme housing. **Activities:** Bands, campus ministries, choral groups, dance, drama, film society, international student organizations, literary magazine, music ensembles, Model UN, radio station, student government, student newspaper, symphony orchestra, TV station, Black Student Alliance, College Democrats, College Republicans, Alpha Phi Omega, InterVarsity Christian Fellowship, Amnesty International, Habitat for Humanity, volunteer service corps.

**Athletics.** NCAA. **Intercollegiate:** Baseball M, basketball, cheerleading, cross-country, field hockey W, football (tackle) M, golf, soccer, tennis, track and field, volleyball W. **Intramural:** Basketball, bowling, cross-country, diving, equestrian W, football (non-tackle), golf, racquetball, soccer, softball, table tennis, tennis, volleyball, water polo, wrestling M. **Team name:** Demon Deacons.

**Student services.** Alcohol/substance abuse counseling, campus ministries, career counseling, student employment services, financial aid counseling, health services, minority student services, personal counseling, placement for graduates. **Physically disabled:** Services for visually, speech, hearing impaired.

**Contact.** E-mail: admissions@wfu.edu
Phone: (336) 758-5201 Fax: (336) 758-4324
Martha Allman, Director of Admissions, Wake Forest University, PO Box 7305, Winston-Salem, NC 27109-7305

---

## Warren Wilson College
**Asheville, North Carolina**
www.warren-wilson.edu

CB member
CB code: 5886

- Private 4-year liberal arts college affiliated with Presbyterian Church (USA)
- Residential campus in small city
- 869 degree-seeking undergraduates: 1% part-time, 61% women
- 73 degree-seeking graduate students
- 81% of applicants admitted
- SAT or ACT (ACT writing optional), application essay required
- 50% graduate within 6 years

**General.** Founded in 1894. Regionally accredited. **Degrees:** 152 bachelor's awarded; master's offered. **Location:** One mile from Asheville. **Calendar:** 4 consecutive 8-week terms. **Full-time faculty:** 62 total; 94% have terminal degrees, 11% minority, 48% women. **Part-time faculty:** 14 total; 71% have terminal degrees, 14% minority, 50% women. **Class size:** 81% < 20, 19% 20-39, less than 1% 40-49. **Special facilities:** 300-acre college farm, archaeological site, climbing wall, adventure challenge course, hiking trails.

**Freshman class profile.** 807 applied, 651 admitted, 235 enrolled.

| Mid 50% test scores | | | |
|---|---|---|---|
| SAT critical reading: | 540-670 | Rank in top tenth: | 21% |
| SAT math: | 500-610 | End year in good standing: | 84% |
| SAT writing: | 530-610 | Return as sophomores: | 73% |
| ACT composite: | 22-27 | Out-of-state: | 80% |
| Rank in top quarter: | 42% | Live on campus: | 98% |

**Basis for selection.** In order of importance: high school achievement, class rank, personal statement, recommendations, test scores, school and community activities. All records of examinations taken overseas plus TOEFL required of foreign applicants. Interview, portfolio recommended. **Home-schooled:** Submit transcript listing course titles and content, partial portfolio of sample work completed (graded papers), document that serves as diploma, copy of state rules under which school was formed or is recognized.

**High school preparation.** Required and recommended units include English 4, mathematics 3, history 3, science 2 (laboratory 2) and foreign language 2. Math requirement includes algebra I, II and geometry. Sciences must include 2 laboratories.

**2007-2008 Annual costs.** Tuition/fees: $21,384. All resident students required to work 15 hours per week in college's work program. $2,472 earnings credited toward tuition costs. Room/board: $6,700. Books/supplies: $870. Personal expenses: $775.

**Financial aid. Non-need-based:** Scholarships awarded for academics, art, job skills, leadership, religious affiliation, state residency.

**Application procedures. Admission:** Priority date 1/15; deadline 3/15 (receipt date). No application fee. Application may be submitted online. Admission notification on a rolling basis beginning on or about 2/1. Must reply by 5/1. **Financial aid:** Priority date 4/1; no closing date. FAFSA, institutional form required. Applicants notified on a rolling basis starting 3/1; must reply within 3 week(s) of notification.

**Academics. Special study options:** Cross-registration, double major, dual enrollment of high school students, ESL, exchange student, honors, independent study, internships, liberal arts/career combination, student-designed major, study abroad, teacher certification program, Washington semester. **Credit/placement by examination:** AP, CLEP, institutional tests. **Support services:** Reduced course load, study skills assistance, tutoring, writing center.

**Majors. Biology:** General. **Business:** Business admin. **Conservation:** General. **Education:** General, early childhood, elementary, middle, secondary. **English:** English lit. **Foreign languages:** General. **Health:** Premedicine, preveterinary. **History:** General. **Liberal arts:** Arts/sciences. **Math:** General. **Parks/recreation:** General. **Philosophy/religion:** Philosophy, religion. **Physical sciences:** Chemistry. **Psychology:** General. **Public administration:** Social work. **Social sciences:** Anthropology, economics, political science, sociology. **Visual/performing arts:** Art.

**Most popular majors.** Biology 7%, education 8%, history 8%, interdisciplinary studies 14%, natural resources/environmental science 16%, psychology 8%, social sciences 14%.

**Computing on campus.** 91 workstations in library, computer center, student center. Dormitories wired for high-speed internet access and linked to campus network. Commuter students can connect to campus network. Online course registration, online library, helpline, wireless network available.

**Student life. Freshman orientation:** Mandatory, $200 fee. 7-day orientation (late August) includes full day community service, dinner/discussion with faculty. **Policies:** Triad program requires students to work 15 hours/week at an on-campus job and do 100 hours community service by graduation, in addition to academics. **Housing:** Guaranteed on-campus for all undergraduates. Coed dorms, single-sex dorms, apartments, cooperative housing, substance-free housing available. **Activities:** Jazz band, choral groups, dance, drama, international student organizations, literary magazine, music ensembles, musical theater, student government, student newspaper, Amnesty International, Emmaus, Interfaith, Jewish student group, Buddhist experience, earth first, sustainable living.

**Athletics.** USCAA. **Intercollegiate:** Basketball, cross-country, soccer, swimming. **Intramural:** Basketball, football (non-tackle), soccer, table tennis, tennis, triathlon, volleyball. **Team name:** Owls.

**Student services.** Alcohol/substance abuse counseling, campus ministries, career counseling, student employment services, financial aid counseling, health services, minority student services, personal counseling, placement for graduates.

**Contact.** E-mail: admit@warren-wilson.edu
Phone: (828) 771-2073 Toll-free number: (800) 934-3536
Fax: (828) 298-1440
Richard Blomgren, Dean of Admission, Warren Wilson College, Office of
Admission, Asheville, NC 28815-9000

## Western Carolina University

| Cullowhee, North Carolina | CB member |
|---|---|
| www.wcu.edu | CB code: 5897 |

- Public 4-year university
- Residential campus in small town
- 7,006 degree-seeking undergraduates: 14% part-time, 53% women, 5% African American, 1% Asian American, 1% Hispanic American, 1% Native American, 1% international
- 1,543 degree-seeking graduate students
- 68% of applicants admitted
- SAT or ACT with writing required
- 47% graduate within 6 years

**General.** Founded in 1889. Regionally accredited. **Degrees:** 1,292 bachelor's awarded; master's, doctoral offered. **Location:** 55 miles from Asheville, 150 miles from Atlanta. **Calendar:** Semester, extensive summer session. **Full-time faculty:** 494 total; 71% have terminal degrees, 8% minority, 43% women. **Part-time faculty:** 204 total; 29% have terminal degrees, 7% minority, 49% women. **Class size:** 40% < 20, 53% 20-39, 6% 40-49, less than 1% 50-99. **Special facilities:** Center for applied technology, fine and performing arts center, collection of historical Native American artifacts and documents, center for the advancement of teaching, public policy institute, mountain heritage center.

**Freshman class profile.** 4,792 applied, 3,254 admitted, 1,259 enrolled.

| Mid 50% test scores | | | |
|---|---|---|---|
| SAT critical reading: | 450-550 | Rank in top quarter: | 33% |
| SAT math: | 470-560 | Rank in top tenth: | 11% |
| SAT writing: | 430-530 | End year in good standing: | 81% |
| ACT composite: | 18-23 | Return as sophomores: | 67% |
| GPA 3.50 or higher: | 42% | Out-of-state: | 8% |
| GPA 3.0-3.49: | 31% | Live on campus: | 95% |
| GPA 2.0-2.99: | 27% | International: | 1% |

**Basis for selection.** Secondary school record, test scores, class rank most important; recommendations, extracurricular activities, special talents and abilities, volunteer efforts, and paid work experiences considered. All applicants, except those exempted by current campus policies, must submit standardized test scores. SAT preferred, ACT also accepted. Essays not required but will be considered if submitted. Auditions required for music programs and portfolios recommended for art programs. **Homeschooled:** Must submit official transcript of all work completed and meet standards equivalent to those used for applicants from approved secondary schools.

**High school preparation.** 20 units required; 24 recommended. Required and recommended units include English 4, mathematics 4, social studies 2, history 1, science 3 (laboratory 3), foreign language 2 and academic electives 5-7.

**2007-2008 Annual costs.** Tuition/fees: $4,278; $13,861 out-of-state. Room/board: $5,305. Books/supplies: $605. Personal expenses: $1,287.

**2007-2008 Financial aid. Need-based:** 962 full-time freshmen applied for aid; 673 were judged to have need; 666 of these received aid. Average need met was 87%. Average scholarship/grant was $5,906; average loan $2,776. 55% of total undergraduate aid awarded as scholarships/grants, 45% as loans/jobs. **Non-need-based:** Awarded to 818 full-time undergraduates, including 194 freshmen. Scholarships awarded for academics, art, athletics, leadership, music/drama, state residency.

**Application procedures. Admission:** Priority date 3/1; deadline 6/1 (postmark date). $40 fee, may be waived for applicants with need. Application may be submitted online. Admission notification on a rolling basis beginning on or about 1/30. Must reply by 5/1. Housing deposit due upon receipt of student's acceptance. **Financial aid:** Priority date 3/31; no closing date. FAFSA, institutional form required. Applicants notified on a rolling basis starting 4/1.

**Academics. Special study options:** Combined bachelor's/graduate degree, cooperative education, distance learning, double major, dual enrollment of high school students, ESL, exchange student, honors, independent study, internships, student-designed major, study abroad, teacher certification program, Washington semester. **Credit/placement by examination:** AP, CLEP, IB, institutional tests. 45 credit hours maximum toward bachelor's

degree. **Support services:** Learning center, pre-admission summer program, reduced course load, study skills assistance, tutoring, writing center.

**Honors college/program.** First-year students who have at least one of the following are invited: 3.75 GPA in high school, top 10% of high school class, 1200 score on the SAT (exclusive of Writing), or 30 score on the ACT.

**Majors. Biology:** General. **Business:** Accounting, business admin, finance, hospitality admin, international, management information systems, marketing. **Communications:** General. **Computer sciences:** Computer science. **Conservation:** Environmental science, management/policy. **Education:** Art, elementary, English, German, kindergarten/preschool, mathematics, middle, music, physical, science, social studies, Spanish, special. **Engineering:** Electrical. **Engineering technology:** General, construction, electrical, industrial, manufacturing. **English:** English lit. **Foreign languages:** French, German, Spanish. **Health:** Athletic training, clinical lab science, communication disorders, dietetics, EMT paramedic, environmental health, health care admin, medical records admin, nursing (RN), recreational therapy. **History:** General. **Liberal arts:** Arts/sciences. **Math:** General. **Parks/recreation:** Facilities management, sports admin. **Philosophy/religion:** Philosophy. **Physical sciences:** Chemistry, geology. **Protective services:** Criminal justice, forensics. **Psychology:** General. **Public administration:** General, social work. **Social sciences:** General, anthropology, geography, political science, sociology. **Visual/performing arts:** Art, dramatic, interior design, music performance, studio arts. **Other:** Entrepreneurship, Motion picture and television production.

**Most popular majors.** Business/marketing 17%, communications/journalism 6%, education 16%, engineering/engineering technologies 7%, health sciences 12%, security/protective services 8%, visual/performing arts 6%.

**Computing on campus.** PC or laptop required. 226 workstations in dormitories, library, computer center, student center. Dormitories wired for high-speed internet access and linked to campus network. Commuter students can connect to campus network. Online course registration, online library, helpline, repair service, student web hosting, wireless network available.

**Student life. Freshman orientation:** Mandatory, $115 fee. Preregistration for classes offered. Six 2-day orientations held in June and July. **Housing:** Guaranteed on-campus for freshmen. Coed dorms, single-sex dorms, special housing for disabled, apartments, fraternity/sorority housing, substance-free housing available. $150 nonrefundable deposit, deadline 6/1. **Activities:** Bands, campus ministries, choral groups, dance, drama, film society, international student organizations, literary magazine, music ensembles, Model UN, musical theater, radio station, student government, student newspaper, TV station, black students association, forensics, College Democrats, College Republicans, Fellowship of Christian Athletes, Interfaith Council, black theatre ensemble, Project CARE.

**Athletics.** NCAA. **Intercollegiate:** Baseball M, basketball, cheerleading, cross-country, football (tackle) M, golf, soccer W, softball W, tennis W, track and field, volleyball W. **Intramural:** Badminton, basketball, bowling, football (non-tackle), football (tackle), racquetball, soccer, softball, swimming, table tennis, tennis, track and field, volleyball, water polo, weight lifting, wrestling M. **Team name:** Catamounts.

**Student services.** Alcohol/substance abuse counseling, campus ministries, career counseling, student employment services, financial aid counseling, health services, minority student services, on-campus daycare, personal counseling, placement for graduates, veterans' counselor, women's services. **Physically disabled:** Services for visually, speech, hearing impaired.

**Contact.** E-mail: admiss@wcu.edu
Phone: (828) 227-7317 Toll-free number: (877) 928-4968
Fax: (828) 227-7319
Alan Kines, Director of Admissions, Western Carolina University, 102
Camp Building, Cullowhee, NC 28723

## Wingate University

| Wingate, North Carolina | CB member |
|---|---|
| www.wingate.edu | CB code: 5908 |

- Private 4-year university and liberal arts college affiliated with Baptist faith
- Residential campus in small town
- 1,462 degree-seeking undergraduates: 4% part-time, 53% women, 14% African American, 2% Asian American, 2% Hispanic American, 1% Native American, 3% international
- 570 degree-seeking graduate students
- 61% of applicants admitted
- 46% graduate within 6 years; 20% enter graduate study

**General.** Founded in 1896. Regionally accredited. **Degrees:** 247 bachelor's awarded; master's, first professional offered. **ROTC:** Army, Air Force. **Location:** 25 miles from Charlotte. **Calendar:** Semester, limited summer session. **Full-time faculty:** 109 total; 94% have terminal degrees, 8% minority, 47% women. **Part-time faculty:** 62 total. **Class size:** 52% < 20, 47% 20-39, less than 1% 40-49, less than 1% 50-99. **Special facilities:** Outdoor recreation laboratory, 11-acre lake, performing arts center.

**Freshman class profile.** 3,119 applied, 1,899 admitted, 426 enrolled.

| Mid 50% test scores | | Rank in top quarter: | 43% |
|---|---|---|---|
| SAT critical reading: | 440-540 | Rank in top tenth: | 22% |
| SAT math: | 450-570 | End year in good standing: | 75% |
| ACT composite: | 18-24 | Return as sophomores: | 68% |
| GPA 3.50 or higher: | 50% | Out-of-state: | 27% |
| GPA 3.0-3.49: | 25% | Live on campus: | 89% |
| GPA 2.0-2.99: | 25% | | |

**Basis for selection.** Decisions based on secondary school record (GPA, class rank) and the rigor of secondary school record. Test scores are also considered. SAT or ACT recommended. 100% of applicants submitted test scores. SAT/ACT not required, but strongly recommended. Interview recommended for all students; portfolio recommended for art majors; audition required for music majors.

**High school preparation.** 13 units recommended. Recommended units include English 4, mathematics 3, social studies 2, science 2 (laboratory 1) and foreign language 2.

**2008-2009 Annual costs.** Tuition/fees: $19,350. Some music and art courses carry a fee. Room/board: $7,700. Books/supplies: $1,000. Personal expenses: $900.

**2007-2008 Financial aid. Need-based:** 380 full-time freshmen applied for aid; 300 were judged to have need; 300 of these received aid. Average need met was 82%. Average scholarship/grant was $6,282; average loan $2,049. 53% of total undergraduate aid awarded as scholarships/grants, 47% as loans/jobs. **Non-need-based:** Awarded to 1,690 full-time undergraduates, including 376 freshmen. Scholarships awarded for academics, alumni affiliation, art, athletics, music/drama, state residency. **Additional information:** Institutional aid may not be available after June 1.

**Application procedures. Admission:** Priority date 4/1; no deadline. $30 fee, may be waived for applicants with need. Application may be submitted online. Admission notification on a rolling basis beginning on or about 9/15. Must reply by May 1 or within 4 week(s) if notified thereafter. **Financial aid:** Priority date 5/1; no closing date. FAFSA required. Applicants notified on a rolling basis starting 3/1; must reply within 2 week(s) of notification.

**Academics.** Attendance to cultural events required as part of Lyceum program. Travel abroad available. Internships and undergraduate research under faculty supervision available. **Special study options:** Combined bachelor's/graduate degree, cross-registration, double major, dual enrollment of high school students, honors, independent study, internships, study abroad, teacher certification program. Adult Completion Program at the Wingate University School of Graduate Programs and Adult Education in downtown Mattews, NC. The program offers undergraduate courses in the evening for working adults. **Credit/placement by examination:** AP, CLEP, IB, SAT, ACT, institutional tests. 30 credit hours maximum toward bachelor's degree. **Support services:** Learning center, reduced course load, study skills assistance, tutoring, writing center.

**Majors. Area/ethnic studies:** American. **Biology:** General, environmental. **Business:** Accounting, business admin, finance, marketing. **Communications:** General, broadcast journalism, journalism, public relations. **Computer sciences:** Computer science. **Education:** Art, biology, elementary, English, mathematics, middle, music, physical, reading, social studies. **English:** English lit. **Foreign languages:** Spanish. **Health:** Athletic training, predental, premedicine, prepharmacy, preveterinary. **History:** General. **Interdisciplinary:** Math/computer science. **Legal studies:** Prelaw. **Liberal arts:** Arts/sciences. **Math:** General. **Parks/recreation:** Facilities management, sports admin. **Philosophy/religion:** Philosophy, religion. **Physical sciences:** Chemistry. **Psychology:** General. **Public administration:** Human services. **Social sciences:** Sociology. **Visual/performing arts:** Art, music management, music performance, piano/organ, studio arts, voice/opera. **Other:** Pre-Engineering Studies.

**Most popular majors.** Biology 6%, business/marketing 16%, communications/journalism 8%, education 12%, liberal arts 6%, psychology 6%, visual/performing arts 9%.

**Computing on campus.** 75 workstations in library, computer center, student center. Dormitories wired for high-speed internet access. Commuter students can connect to campus network. Wireless network available.

**Student life. Freshman orientation:** Mandatory. Preregistration for classes offered. Begins 4 days before classes. **Policies:** Honor Code. **Housing:** Guaranteed on-campus for all undergraduates. Single-sex dorms, special housing

for disabled, apartments, substance-free housing available. $300 deposit. **Activities:** Bands, campus ministries, choral groups, drama, international student organizations, literary magazine, music ensembles, student government, student newspaper, TV station, academic honors societies, greek life, Christian Student Union, minority student association, university and community assistance network, gospel choir, College Republicans, outdoor recreation and adventure club, running club.

**Athletics.** NCAA. **Intercollegiate:** Baseball M, basketball, cross-country, football (tackle) M, golf, lacrosse M, soccer, softball W, swimming, tennis, volleyball W. **Intramural:** Basketball, bowling, diving, football (tackle) M, golf, lacrosse W, racquetball, soccer, softball, swimming, table tennis, tennis, volleyball, water polo. **Team name:** Bulldogs.

**Student services.** Campus ministries, career counseling, student employment services, financial aid counseling, health services, minority student services, personal counseling, placement for graduates.

**Contact.** E-mail: admit@wingate.edu
Phone: (704) 233-8200 Toll-free number: (800) 755-5550
Fax: (704) 233-8110
Thomas Brown, Dean of Enrollment Management, Wingate University, Campus Box 3059, Wingate, NC 28174-0157

---

## Winston-Salem State University

**Winston-Salem, North Carolina**
**www.wssu.edu**

**CB member**
**CB code: 5909**

- Public 4-year university and health science college
- Commuter campus in small city
- 5,423 degree-seeking undergraduates: 11% part-time, 71% women, 82% African American, 1% Asian American, 1% Hispanic American, 1% international
- 398 degree-seeking graduate students
- 68% of applicants admitted
- SAT or ACT with writing required
- 44% graduate within 6 years

**General.** Founded in 1892. Regionally accredited. **Degrees:** 747 bachelor's awarded; master's offered. **ROTC:** Army. **Location:** 28 miles from Greensboro, 75 miles from Charlotte. **Calendar:** Semester, limited summer session. **Full-time faculty:** 325 total; 62% minority. **Part-time faculty:** 75 total; 40% minority. **Class size:** 42% < 20, 50% 20-39, 6% 40-49, 2% 50-99.

**Freshman class profile.** 3,345 applied, 2,270 admitted, 969 enrolled.

| Mid 50% test scores | | GPA 2.0-2.99: | 52% |
|---|---|---|---|
| SAT critical reading: | 400-480 | Rank in top quarter: | 3% |
| SAT math: | 400-490 | Rank in top tenth: | 1% |
| ACT composite: | 16-19 | Out-of-state: | 12% |
| GPA 3.50 or higher: | 13% | Live on campus: | 82% |
| GPA 3.0-3.49: | 33% | International: | 2% |

**Basis for selection.** Admissions based on secondary school record, class rank, and standardized tests scores. Extracurricular activities also important. SAT preferred. Interview recommended for all students; audition required for music program.

**High school preparation.** 15 units required. Required units include English 4, mathematics 4, social studies 1, history 1, science 3 and foreign language 2. Mathematics units must include or exceed algebra I, geometry and algebra II.

**2007-2008 Annual costs.** Tuition/fees: $3,299; $11,940 out-of-state. Room/board: $5,670. Personal expenses: $2,100.

**2006-2007 Financial aid. Need-based:** 958 full-time freshmen applied for aid; 931 were judged to have need; 786 of these received aid. Average need met was 51%. Average scholarship/grant was $2,049; average loan $2,164. 53% of total undergraduate aid awarded as scholarships/grants, 47% as loans/jobs. **Non-need-based:** Awarded to 583 full-time undergraduates, including 199 freshmen. Scholarships awarded for academics, athletics, ROTC, state residency.

**Application procedures. Admission:** Priority date 5/1; deadline 7/15. $40 fee, may be waived for applicants with need. Application may be submitted online. Admission notification on a rolling basis. **Financial aid:** Closing date 3/15. FAFSA required. Applicants notified by 5/15; must reply within 2 week(s) of notification.

**Academics. Special study options:** Accelerated study, cross-registration, distance learning, double major, ESL, honors, independent study, internships, liberal arts/career combination, study abroad, teacher certification program, Washington semester, weekend college. **Credit/placement by examination:** AP, CLEP, IB, institutional tests. 36 credit hours maximum toward bachelor's degree. **Support services:** Learning center, reduced course load, remedial instruction, study skills assistance, tutoring.

**Majors. Area/ethnic studies:** African-American. **Biology:** General, biotechnology, molecular. **Business:** Accounting, business admin, managerial economics. **Communications:** Media studies. **Computer sciences:** Computer science, information technology. **Education:** Art, early childhood, elementary, English, mathematics, middle, music, physical, social studies, Spanish, special. **English:** English lit. **Foreign languages:** Spanish. **Health:** Clinical lab science, nursing (RN), recreational therapy, vocational rehab counseling. **History:** General. **Interdisciplinary:** Gerontology. **Liberal arts:** Arts/sciences. **Math:** General. **Parks/recreation:** Exercise sciences, sports admin. **Physical sciences:** Chemistry. **Protective services:** Criminal justice. **Psychology:** General. **Public administration:** Social work. **Social sciences:** Political science, sociology. **Visual/performing arts:** Art, music management.

**Most popular majors.** Business/marketing 13%, health sciences 42%, parks/recreation 7%, social sciences 7%.

**Computing on campus.** PC or laptop required. 500 workstations in dormitories, library, computer center, student center. Dormitories wired for high-speed internet access and linked to campus network. Commuter students can connect to campus network. Online course registration, online library, wireless network available.

**Student life. Freshman orientation:** Available, $100 fee. Preregistration for classes offered. Held on a summer weekend. **Housing:** Coed dorms, single-sex dorms available. $75 nonrefundable deposit, deadline 5/14. **Activities:** Bands, dance, drama, radio station, student government, student newspaper, TV station, student religious council.

**Athletics.** NCAA. **Intercollegiate:** Basketball, bowling W, cheerleading M, cross-country, football (tackle) M, golf M, softball W, tennis, track and field, volleyball W. **Intramural:** Basketball M. **Team name:** Rams.

**Student services.** Adult student services, career counseling, student employment services, financial aid counseling, health services, personal counseling, veterans' counselor. **Physically disabled:** Services for visually impaired.

**Contact.** E-mail: admissions@wssu.edu
Phone: (336) 750-2070 Toll-free number: (800) 257-4052
Fax: (336) 750-2079
Tomikia LeGrande, Director of Admissions, Winston-Salem State University, 601 Martin Luther King Jr Drive, Winston-Salem, NC 27110

# North Dakota

## Dickinson State University
**Dickinson, North Dakota**
www.dsu.nodak.edu

CB code: 6477

- Public 4-year university
- Residential campus in large town
- 2,669 degree-seeking undergraduates: 33% part-time, 59% women, 1% African American, 1% Hispanic American, 2% Native American, 12% international

**General.** Founded in 1918. Regionally accredited. **Degrees:** 372 bachelor's, 68 associate awarded. **Location:** 100 miles from Bismarck, 300 miles from Billings, Montana. **Calendar:** Semester, limited summer session. **Full-time faculty:** 86 total; 45% have terminal degrees, 6% minority, 43% women. **Part-time faculty:** 102 total; 6% have terminal degrees, 4% minority, 63% women. **Class size:** 64% < 20, 29% 20-39, 4% 40-49, 3% 50-99. **Special facilities:** Nature preserve.

**Freshman class profile.** 554 applied, 509 admitted, 379 enrolled.

| Mid 50% test scores | | | |
|---|---|---|---|
| SAT critical reading: | 430-530 | Rank in top quarter: | 15% |
| SAT math: | 470-590 | Rank in top tenth: | 5% |
| ACT composite: | 18-23 | Out-of-state: | 34% |
| | | International: | 13% |

**Basis for selection.** Open admission, but selective for some programs. Minimum 20 ACT composite or minimum 2.0 GPA required for nursing program.

**High school preparation.** 13 units recommended. Recommended units include English 4, mathematics 3, social studies 3 and science 3. One algebra, 1 chemistry required for nursing program.

**2007-2008 Annual costs.** Tuition/fees: $4,749; $11,143 out-of-state. Tuition for Minnesota residents: $3,976. Tuition for South Dakota, Montana, Manitoba, Saskatchewan residents: $4,558. Room/board: $4,076. Books/supplies: $900. Personal expenses: $1,325.

**2006-2007 Financial aid. Need-based:** 38% of total undergraduate aid awarded as scholarships/grants, 62% as loans/jobs. **Non-need-based:** Scholarships awarded for academics, alumni affiliation, art, athletics, job skills, leadership, minority status, music/drama, religious affiliation, state residency. **Additional information:** Scholarships available to new students, priority deadline December 1.

**Application procedures. Admission:** No deadline. $35 fee. Application may be submitted online. Admission notification on a rolling basis. **Financial aid:** Priority date 3/15; no closing date. FAFSA required. Must reply within 2 week(s) of notification.

**Academics.** Limited evening classes available. **Special study options:** Accelerated study, combined bachelor's/graduate degree, cooperative education, distance learning, double major, dual enrollment of high school students, ESL, honors, independent study, internships, liberal arts/career combination, student-designed major, study abroad, teacher certification program. **Credit/placement by examination:** AP, CLEP, institutional tests. 8 credit hours maximum toward associate degree, 15 toward bachelor's. **Support services:** Learning center, remedial instruction, study skills assistance, tutoring, writing center.

**Majors. Agriculture:** Business. **Biology:** General. **Business:** General, accounting, administrative services, business admin, finance, management information systems, office management. **Communications:** General. **Computer sciences:** Computer science. **Education:** Art, biology, business, chemistry, computer, drama/dance, early childhood, elementary, English, foreign languages, health, history, mathematics, middle, music, physical, reading, science, secondary, social science, Spanish, speech. **English:** Creative writing, English lit. **Foreign languages:** Spanish. **Health:** Nursing (RN), predental, premedicine, preveterinary. **History:** General. **Interdisciplinary:** Behavioral sciences, natural sciences. **Legal studies:** Prelaw. **Liberal arts:** Arts/sciences. **Math:** General. **Parks/recreation:** Health/fitness. **Physical sciences:** Chemistry. **Psychology:** General. **Social sciences:** General, political science. **Visual/performing arts:** Art, dramatic, studio arts, theater design.

**Most popular majors.** Agriculture 11%, biology 7%, business/marketing 17%, education 11%, health sciences 10%, liberal arts 12%.

**Computing on campus.** 213 workstations in dormitories, library, computer center, student center. Dormitories wired for high-speed internet access and linked to campus network. Commuter students can connect to campus network. Online course registration, online library, helpline, repair service, wireless network available.

**Student life. Freshman orientation:** Mandatory, $25 fee. Preregistration for classes offered. **Housing:** Guaranteed on-campus for all undergraduates. Coed dorms, single-sex dorms, special housing for disabled, apartments, substance-free housing available. $50 fully refundable deposit. **Activities:** Bands, choral groups, dance, drama, film society, literary magazine, music ensembles, musical theater, student government, student newspaper.

**Athletics.** NAIA. **Intercollegiate:** Baseball M, basketball, cross-country, football (tackle) M, golf, rodeo, softball W, track and field, volleyball W, wrestling M. **Intramural:** Basketball, football (non-tackle), soccer, softball, volleyball. **Team name:** Blue Hawks.

**Student services.** Adult student services, career counseling, services for economically disadvantaged, student employment services, financial aid counseling, health services, minority student services, personal counseling, placement for graduates. **Physically disabled:** Services for visually, speech, hearing impaired. **Learning disabled:** Comprehensive services available.

**Contact.** E-mail: dsu.hawks@dickinsonstate.edu
Phone: (701) 483-2175 Toll-free number: (800) 279-4295
Fax: (701) 483-2409
Steve Glasser, Director of Enrollment Services, Dickinson State University, 291 Campus Drive, Dickinson, ND 58601-4896

## Jamestown College
**Jamestown, North Dakota**
www.jc.edu

CB code: 6318

- Private 4-year liberal arts college affiliated with Presbyterian Church (USA)
- Residential campus in large town
- 981 degree-seeking undergraduates: 4% part-time, 53% women, 1% African American, 1% Asian American, 1% Hispanic American, 1% Native American, 5% international
- 79% of applicants admitted
- 47% graduate within 6 years; 13% enter graduate study

**General.** Founded in 1883. Regionally accredited. **Degrees:** 191 bachelor's awarded. **Location:** 100 miles from Fargo and Bismarck. **Calendar:** Semester, limited summer session. **Full-time faculty:** 54 total; 52% have terminal degrees, 6% minority, 44% women. **Part-time faculty:** 27 total; 18% have terminal degrees, 63% women. **Class size:** 51% < 20, 40% 20-39, 6% 40-49, 2% 50-99, less than 1% >100.

**Freshman class profile.** 1,183 applied, 930 admitted, 270 enrolled.

| Mid 50% test scores | | | |
|---|---|---|---|
| SAT critical reading: | 410-570 | Rank in top quarter: | 29% |
| SAT math: | 450-590 | Rank in top tenth: | 18% |
| ACT composite: | 19-25 | Return as sophomores: | 67% |
| GPA 3.50 or higher: | 48% | Out-of-state: | 59% |
| GPA 3.0-3.49: | 32% | Live on campus: | 95% |
| GPA 2.0-2.99: | 20% | International: | 5% |

**Basis for selection.** Applicants with minimum 2.5 high school GPA or 18 ACT or 850 SAT (exclusive of writing) generally accepted. Applicants may be admitted on standard, conditional, or probationary basis. Interview recommended for all students. Audition required for music program; portfolio recommended for art program. **Homeschooled:** Letter of recommendation (nonparent) required.

**High school preparation.** College-preparatory program recommended. Recommended units include English 4, mathematics 3, social studies 3, science 4 and foreign language 2.

**2008-2009 Annual costs.** Tuition/fees: $15,035. Room/board: $4,850. Books/supplies: $1,000. Personal expenses: $1,300.

**2007-2008 Financial aid. Need-based:** 241 full-time freshmen applied for aid; 190 were judged to have need; 190 of these received aid. Average need met was 79%. Average scholarship/grant was $6,979; average loan $3,421. 50% of total undergraduate aid awarded as scholarships/grants, 50% as loans/jobs. **Non-need-based:** Awarded to 552 full-time undergraduates, including 171 freshmen. Scholarships awarded for academics, alumni affiliation, art, athletics, leadership, music/drama, religious affiliation. **Additional information:** FAFSA must be received by March 15th for North Dakota residents to be considered for North Dakota state grants.

**Application procedures. Admission:** Priority date 7/1; no deadline. $20 fee, may be waived for applicants with need. Application may be submitted online. Admission notification on a rolling basis. **Financial aid:** Priority date 3/1; no closing date. FAFSA required. Applicants notified on a rolling basis starting 2/1.

**Academics. Special study options:** Combined bachelor's/graduate degree, cooperative education, double major, dual enrollment of high school students, honors, independent study, internships, liberal arts/career combination, student-designed major, study abroad, teacher certification program. **Credit/placement by examination:** AP, CLEP, IB, SAT, ACT, institutional tests. Unlimited number of hours of credit by examination may be counted toward degree. **Support services:** Learning center, reduced course load, remedial instruction, study skills assistance, tutoring, writing center.

**Majors. Biology:** General, biochemistry. **Business:** Accounting, business admin, finance, financial planning, international, management information systems, managerial economics, marketing. **Communications:** General. **Computer sciences:** Computer science, information technology. **Education:** Biology, chemistry, early childhood, elementary, English, history, mathematics, music, physical, secondary, special. **English:** Composition, English lit. **Foreign languages:** French, German, Spanish. **Health:** Clinical lab science, nursing (RN), radiologic technology/medical imaging. **History:** General. **Math:** General, applied. **Parks/recreation:** Sports admin. **Philosophy/religion:** Religion. **Physical sciences:** Chemistry. **Protective services:** Criminal justice. **Psychology:** General. **Social sciences:** Political science. **Visual/performing arts:** Dramatic, music performance, studio arts.

**Most popular majors.** Biology 6%, business/marketing 21%, education 19%, health sciences 17%, social sciences 7%.

**Computing on campus.** 359 workstations in dormitories, library, computer center, student center. Dormitories wired for high-speed internet access and linked to campus network. Commuter students can connect to campus network. Online course registration, online library, helpline, repair service, student web hosting, wireless network available.

**Student life. Freshman orientation:** Mandatory. 3 days prior to classes. **Policies:** Weekly chapel service available on campus. Non-alcoholic nightclub available. **Housing:** Guaranteed on-campus for all undergraduates. Coed dorms, special housing for disabled, substance-free housing available. $100 fully refundable deposit. **Activities:** Bands, campus ministries, choral groups, dance, drama, music ensembles, musical theater, student government, student newspaper, honor societies, ministry teams, Students of Service, Fellowship of Christian Athletes, Jimmie Janes, Jimmie Ambassadors, Ignition.

**Athletics.** NAIA. **Intercollegiate:** Baseball M, basketball, cheerleading M, cross-country, football (tackle) M, golf, soccer, softball W, track and field, volleyball W, wrestling M. **Intramural:** Basketball, bowling, football (non-tackle), racquetball, soccer, softball, volleyball. **Team name:** Jimmies.

**Student services.** Alcohol/substance abuse counseling, campus ministries, career counseling, student employment services, financial aid counseling, on-campus daycare, personal counseling, placement for graduates.

**Contact.** E-mail: admissions@jc.edu
Phone: (701) 252-3467 ext. 2562 Toll-free number: (800) 336-2554
Fax: (701) 253-4318
Judy Erickson, Director of Admissions, Jamestown College, 6081 College Lane, Jamestown, ND 58405

---

## Mayville State University
**Mayville, North Dakota**
**www.mayvillestate.edu**                    **CB code: 6478**

- Public 4-year business and teachers college
- Residential campus in small town
- 769 degree-seeking undergraduates: 38% part-time, 58% women, 5% African American, 1% Asian American, 1% Hispanic American, 4% Native American, 4% international

**General.** Founded in 1889. Regionally accredited. Every student issued laptop computer. All students complete an Information Technology Certificate as part of their bachelor's degree. **Degrees:** 120 bachelor's, 8 associate awarded. **ROTC:** Army, Air Force. **Location:** 60 miles from Fargo, 40 miles from Grand Forks. **Calendar:** Semester, limited summer session. **Full-time faculty:** 35 total; 49% have terminal degrees, 3% minority, 40% women. **Part-time faculty:** 29 total; 24% have terminal degrees, 7% minority, 45% women. **Class size:** 68% < 20, 30% 20-39, 2% 40-49. **Special facilities:** Nature area, business incubation technology center, head start and child development center, undergraduate research labs.

**Freshman class profile.** 204 applied, 142 admitted, 90 enrolled.

| Mid 50% test scores | | |
|---|---|---|
| ACT composite: | 17-22 | Out-of-state: 45% |
| End year in good standing: | 78% | Live on campus: 95% |
| Return as sophomores: | 59% | International: 2% |

**Basis for selection.** Open admission, but selective for some programs. Admission to teacher education programs based on meeting GPA criteria, completion of PPST, and completion of specific prerequisites. ACT math scores used for placement. Interview recommended. **Homeschooled:** Transcript of courses and grades required. Must provide documentation equivalent to high school diploma.

**High school preparation.** College-preparatory program required. 17 units required; 18 recommended. Required and recommended units include English 4, mathematics 3, social studies 3, science 3 (laboratory 3) and foreign language 2. One unit of computer studies recommended.

**2007-2008 Annual costs.** Tuition/fees: $5,438; $7,335 out-of-state. Full-time tuition for South Dakota, Montana, Kansas, Michigan, Missouri, Nebraska, Manitoba, and Saskatchewan residents: $4,743. Full-time tuition for Minnesota residents: $4,082. All other states and Canadian provinces: $5,692. Room/board: $4,072. Books/supplies: $800. Personal expenses: $2,800.

**2006-2007 Financial aid. Need-based:** 128 full-time freshmen applied for aid; 99 were judged to have need; 98 of these received aid. Average need met was 40%. Average scholarship/grant was $2,726; average loan $2,718. 33% of total undergraduate aid awarded as scholarships/grants, 67% as loans/jobs. **Non-need-based:** Awarded to 294 full-time undergraduates, including 112 freshmen. Scholarships awarded for academics, athletics, leadership, minority status, music/drama, state residency.

**Application procedures. Admission:** No deadline. $35 fee. Application may be submitted online. Admission notification on a rolling basis beginning on or about 1/1. **Financial aid:** Priority date 2/15; no closing date. FAFSA required. Applicants notified on a rolling basis starting 5/1; must reply within 2 week(s) of notification.

**Academics. Special study options:** Accelerated study, cooperative education, distance learning, double major, dual enrollment of high school students, honors, internships, student-designed major, teacher certification program. 3-year business administration degree with cooperative education internship. **Credit/placement by examination:** AP, CLEP, institutional tests. 30 credit hours maximum toward bachelor's degree. **Support services:** Learning center, pre-admission summer program, remedial instruction, study skills assistance, tutoring.

**Majors. Biology:** General. **Business:** Business admin, office management. **Computer sciences:** General. **Education:** Biology, business, chemistry, elementary, English, geography, health, history, mathematics, physical, social science. **English:** English lit. **Family/consumer sciences:** Child care. **Health:** Athletic training, clinical lab science, predental, premedicine, prenursing, prepharmacy, preveterinary. **Legal studies:** Prelaw. **Math:** General. **Parks/recreation:** Health/fitness. **Physical sciences:** Chemistry. **Psychology:** General. **Social sciences:** General. **Other:** Health Education.

**Most popular majors.** Business/marketing 25%, education 53%, family/consumer sciences 8%, parks/recreation 8%.

**Computing on campus.** PC or laptop required. Dormitories wired for high-speed internet access and linked to campus network. Commuter students can connect to campus network. Online course registration, online library, helpline, repair service, wireless network available.

**Student life. Freshman orientation:** Mandatory, $35 fee. Preregistration for classes offered. Half-day events held in June and July. **Housing:** Guaranteed on-campus for all undergraduates. Single-sex dorms, apartments, substance-free housing available. $50 nonrefundable deposit. **Activities:** Bands, choral groups, drama, international student organizations, literary magazine, music ensembles, musical theater, radio station, student government, campus crusade, student education association, residence hall association, health and physical education club, student activities council, alumni ambassadors, minority/international student association.

**Athletics.** NAIA. **Intercollegiate:** Baseball M, basketball, football (tackle) M, softball W, volleyball W. **Intramural:** Badminton, basketball, bowling, football (non-tackle), golf, ice hockey M, racquetball, soccer, softball, table tennis, tennis, track and field, volleyball, weight lifting. **Team name:** Comets.

**Student services.** Adult student services, career counseling, student employment services, financial aid counseling, health services, on-campus daycare, personal counseling, placement for graduates, veterans' counselor. **Physically disabled:** Services for visually, hearing impaired.

**Contact.** E-mail: admit@mayvillestate.edu
Phone: (701) 788-4842 Toll-free number: (800) 437-4104
Fax: (701) 788-4748
Ray Gerszewski, Vice President for Student Affairs and Enrollment Management, Mayville State University, 330 Third Street, NE, Mayville, ND 58257-1299

## Medcenter One College of Nursing
**Bismarck, North Dakota**
www.medcenterone.com/collegeofnursing    CB code: 7051

- Private two-year upper-division nursing college
- Commuter campus in small city
- 63% of applicants admitted
- Application essay, interview required

**General.** Founded in 1988. Regionally accredited. Small college affiliated with a health system which provides a variety of clinical experiences. **Degrees:** 46 bachelor's awarded. **Articulation:** Agreement with Bismarck State College. **Location:** 190 miles from Fargo, 105 miles from Minot. **Calendar:** Semester, limited summer session. **Full-time faculty:** 10 total; 10% have terminal degrees, 10% minority, 100% women. **Part-time faculty:** 3 total; 100% women. **Class size:** 9% < 20, 18% 20-39, 73% 40-49.

**Student profile.** 89 degree-seeking undergraduates. 99 applied as first time-transfer students, 62 admitted, 47 enrolled. 100% entered as juniors. 88% transferred from two-year, 12% transferred from four-year institutions.

| Women: | 89% | Out-of-state: | 5% |
|--------|-----|---------------|-----|
| Part-time: | 2% | 25 or older: | 32% |

**Basis for selection.** High school transcript, college transcript, application essay, interview required. All students must transfer with minimum 64 credits of general education prerequisites, including 5 prerequisite science courses. Students not required to complete all prerequisites prior to applying but must have a minimum of 2 required sciences completed. Credits not completed at time of application must be completed prior to transfer. Overall college GPA, science GPA important. Transfer accepted as sophomores, juniors, seniors.

**2007-2008 Annual costs.** Tuition/fees: $10,017. Books/supplies: $1,069. Personal expenses: $1,000.

**Financial aid.** **Need-based:** 77 applied for aid; 66 were judged to have need; 66 of these received aid. Average need met was 97%. 44% of total undergraduate aid awarded as scholarships/grants, 56% as loans/jobs. **Non-need-based:** Awarded to 23 undergraduates.

**Application procedures.** **Admission:** Priority date 11/7. $40 fee. Application must be submitted on paper. **Financial aid:** Priority date 3/1, no deadline. Applicants notified on a rolling basis starting 6/1; must reply within 2 weeks of notification.

**Academics.** **Special study options:** Internships. **Credit/placement by examination:** CLEP, institutional tests. 30 credit hours maximum toward bachelor's degree.

**Majors.** **Health:** Nursing (RN).

**Computing on campus.** 17 workstations in library, computer center. Online library available.

**Student life.** **Activities:** Student government, student newspaper, Student Nurse Association, Student Organization.

**Student services.** Financial aid counseling, health services, personal counseling, placement for graduates.

**Contact.** E-mail: msmith@mohs.org
Phone: (701) 323-6833 Fax: (701) 323-6289
Mary Smith, Director of Student Services, Medcenter One College of Nursing, 512 North 7th Street, Bismarck, ND 58501-4425

## Minot State University
**Minot, North Dakota**
www.minotstateu.edu
CB code: 6479

- Public 4-year university and liberal arts college
- Commuter campus in large town
- 3,140 degree-seeking undergraduates: 29% part-time, 63% women, 3% African American, 1% Asian American, 2% Hispanic American, 4% Native American, 7% international

- 284 degree-seeking graduate students
- 80% of applicants admitted
- ACT required

**General.** Founded in 1913. Regionally accredited. **Degrees:** 449 bachelor's, 1 associate awarded; master's offered. **Location:** 105 miles from Bismarck, 225 miles from Grand Forks. **Calendar:** Semester, limited summer session. **Full-time faculty:** 179 total; 50% women. **Part-time faculty:** 78 total; 36% women. **Class size:** 70% < 20, 25% 20-39, 3% 40-49, 1% 50-99. **Special facilities:** Natural history museum, center for persons with disabilities, Native American collection, observatory, rural crime and justice center.

**Freshman class profile.** 642 applied, 516 admitted, 436 enrolled.

| Mid 50% test scores | | Live on campus: | 14% |
|---------------------|-----|----------------|-----|
| ACT composite: | 18-23 | International: | 8% |
| Out-of-state: | 11% | | |

**Basis for selection.** Secondary school record very important; ACT/SAT test scores, 16 ACT important.

**High school preparation.** 13 units required. Required and recommended units include English 4, mathematics 3, social studies 3, science 3 (laboratory 3). Science should include at least 3 units of biology, chemistry, physics, or physical science. Social science should not include consumer education, cooperative marketing, orientation to social science, or marriage/family. Math must be algebra I or above.

**2007-2008 Annual costs.** Tuition/fees: $4,773; $11,415 out-of-state. Room/board: $3,914.

**2007-2008 Financial aid.** **Need-based:** 403 full-time freshmen applied for aid; 259 were judged to have need; 257 of these received aid. Average need met was 86%. Average scholarship/grant was $3,545; average loan $3,629. 38% of total undergraduate aid awarded as scholarships/grants, 62% as loans/jobs. **Non-need-based:** Awarded to 520 full-time undergraduates, including 161 freshmen. Scholarships awarded for academics, alumni affiliation, art, athletics, minority status, music/drama, state residency. **Additional information:** Scholarship application deadline is 2/15.

**Application procedures.** **Admission:** Priority date 4/1; no deadline. $35 fee. Application may be submitted online. Admission notification on a rolling basis. **Financial aid:** Priority date 3/15; no closing date. FAFSA required. Applicants notified on a rolling basis starting 5/1; must reply within 2 week(s) of notification.

**Academics.** Wide variety of distance courses offered. **Special study options:** Accelerated study, cooperative education, distance learning, double major, dual enrollment of high school students, external degree, honors, independent study, internships, liberal arts/career combination, student-designed major, study abroad, teacher certification program. **Credit/placement by examination:** AP, CLEP, institutional tests. **Support services:** Learning center, reduced course load, remedial instruction, study skills assistance, tutoring, writing center.

**Majors.** **Biology:** General. **Business:** Accounting, business admin, finance, international, management information systems, marketing. **Communications:** Broadcast journalism, radio/tv. **Communications technology:** General. **Computer sciences:** General. **Education:** Art, biology, business, chemistry, Deaf/hearing impaired, elementary, English, foreign languages, French, German, history, mathematics, mentally handicapped, music, physical, physics, science, social science, Spanish, speech impaired. **English:** English lit, speech/rhetoric. **Foreign languages:** French, German, Spanish. **Health:** Clinical lab science, communication disorders, medical radiologic technology/radiation therapy, nursing (RN), substance abuse counseling. **History:** General. **Liberal arts:** Arts/sciences. **Math:** General. **Parks/recreation:** Health/fitness. **Physical sciences:** Chemistry, geology, physics, planetary. **Protective services:** Criminal justice. **Psychology:** General. **Public administration:** Social work. **Social sciences:** General, economics, geography, sociology. **Visual/performing arts:** Art, music performance.

**Most popular majors.** Business/marketing 29%, education 22%, health sciences 16%, security/protective services 8%.

**Computing on campus.** 300 workstations in dormitories, library, computer center, student center. Dormitories wired for high-speed internet access and linked to campus network. Commuter students can connect to campus network. Online course registration, online library, helpline, repair service, wireless network available.

**Student life.** **Freshman orientation:** Mandatory, $35 fee. Preregistration for classes offered. **Policies:** First-year students required to live in university housing (exceptions exist). **Housing:** Coed dorms, single-sex dorms, apartments, substance-free housing available. $100 deposit. **Activities:** Bands, choral groups, dance, drama, literary magazine, music ensembles, musical theater, opera, radio station, student government, student newspaper, symphony orchestra, TV station, disability awareness organization, Democratic Party, Republican Party, Intervarsity Christian Fellowship, Native American cultural awareness club, United Campus Ministries, Catholic student association, international awareness club, Student Education of Hard of Hearing/Deaf, National Student Speech/Hearing Association.

**Athletics.** NAIA. **Intercollegiate:** Baseball M, basketball, cheerleading W, cross-country, football (tackle) M, golf, softball W, track and field, volleyball W. **Intramural:** Basketball, bowling, racquetball, softball, track and field, volleyball. **Team name:** Beavers.

**Student services.** Adult student services, campus ministries, career counseling, services for economically disadvantaged, student employment services, financial aid counseling, health services, minority student services, personal counseling, placement for graduates, veterans' counselor, women's services. **Physically disabled:** Services for visually, speech, hearing impaired.

**Contact.**  E-mail: askmsu@minotstateu.edu
Phone: (701) 858-3350 Toll-free number: (800) 777-0750
Fax: (701) 839-6933
Tania Balas, Registrar, Minot State University, 500 University Avenue West, Minot, ND 58707-5002

---

## North Dakota State University

**Fargo, North Dakota**          CB member
**www.ndsu.edu**                 CB code: 6474

- Public 4-year university
- Residential campus in small city
- 10,403 degree-seeking undergraduates: 10% part-time, 45% women
- 2,124 degree-seeking graduate students
- 85% of applicants admitted
- SAT or ACT (ACT writing optional) required
- 50% graduate within 6 years

**General.** Founded in 1890. Regionally accredited. **Degrees:** 1,787 bachelor's awarded; master's, doctoral, first professional offered. **ROTC:** Army, Air Force. **Location:** 250 miles from Minneapolis-St. Paul. **Calendar:** Semester, limited summer session. **Full-time faculty:** 557 total; 82% have terminal degrees, 20% minority, 30% women. **Part-time faculty:** 98 total; 35% have terminal degrees, 3% minority, 45% women. **Class size:** 36% < 20, 42% 20-39, 8% 40-49, 10% 50-99, 5% >100. **Special facilities:** Fine arts center, regional studies institute, biotechnology institute, engineering computer center, center for writers, wellness center, technology park, downtown campus for art and architecture, equine center.

**Freshman class profile.** 4,381 applied, 3,719 admitted, 2,166 enrolled.

| Mid 50% test scores | | Rank in top tenth: | 15% |
|---|---|---|---|
| SAT critical reading: | 460-600 | Return as sophomores: | 82% |
| SAT math: | 490-640 | Out-of-state: | 57% |
| ACT composite: | 20-25 | Live on campus: | 86% |
| GPA 3.50 or higher: | 46% | International: | 2% |
| GPA 3.0-3.49: | 32% | Fraternities: | 3% |
| GPA 2.0-2.99: | 22% | Sororities: | 2% |
| Rank in top quarter: | 40% | | |

**Basis for selection.** All applicants must have completed college preparatory program in high school. Admission based on overall performance in high school, performance in college preparatory courses and standardized test scores. Admission to nursing, veterinary technology, architecture, pharmacy, electrical engineering, mechanical engineering programs based on academic record and test scores. Campus visit recommended for all students. Audition required for music programs. Secondary admission requirements for many programs. **Homeschooled:** Applicants advised to work with local school district for issuance of a Certificate of Graduation.

**High school preparation.** 13 units required. Required units include English 4, mathematics 3, social studies 3, science 3 (laboratory 3).

**2007-2008 Annual costs.** Tuition/fees: $5,975; $14,346 out-of-state. Tuition for South Dakota, Montana, Manitoba, Saskatchewan residents: $7,519. Room/board: $5,820. Books/supplies: $650. Personal expenses: $2,230.

**2006-2007 Financial aid.** **Need-based:** 1,934 full-time freshmen applied for aid; 1,345 were judged to have need; 1,317 of these received aid. Average need met was 36%. Average scholarship/grant was $3,275; average loan $3,370. 28% of total undergraduate aid awarded as scholarships/grants, 72% as loans/jobs. **Non-need-based:** Awarded to 3,148 full-time undergraduates, including 791 freshmen. Scholarships awarded for academics, alumni

affiliation, art, athletics, leadership, minority status, music/drama, ROTC, state residency.

**Application procedures.** **Admission:** Closing date 8/15 (receipt date). $35 fee. Application may be submitted online. Admission notification on a rolling basis. **Financial aid:** Closing date 3/15. FAFSA required. Applicants notified on a rolling basis starting 3/15.

**Academics.** **Special study options:** Combined bachelor's/graduate degree, cooperative education, cross-registration, distance learning, double major, dual enrollment of high school students, ESL, honors, independent study, internships, student-designed major, study abroad, teacher certification program. Tri-college, collaborative enrollment (ND University System). **Credit/placement by examination:** AP, CLEP, IB, ACT, institutional tests. **Support services:** Reduced course load, remedial instruction, study skills assistance, tutoring, writing center.

**Majors.** **Agriculture:** General, agribusiness operations, animal sciences, communications, crop production, economics, equestrian studies, food science, horticultural science, mechanization, plant protection, soil science, turf management. **Architecture:** Environmental design, landscape. **Area/ethnic studies:** Women's. **Biology:** General, Biochemistry/biophysics and molecular biology, biotechnology, botany, microbiology, zoology. **Business:** Accounting, actuarial science, business admin, hospitality admin, management information systems. **Communications:** Health, journalism, public relations. **Computer sciences:** Computer science. **Conservation:** Management/policy. **Education:** Agricultural, biology, chemistry, computer, elementary, English, family/consumer sciences, French, German, health, history, mathematics, music, physical, physics, science, social science, social studies, Spanish, speech. **Engineering:** Agricultural, civil, computer, construction, electrical, industrial, manufacturing, mechanical. **English:** English lit. **Family/consumer sciences:** Clothing/textiles, family studies. **Foreign languages:** Classics, French, Spanish. **Health:** Clinical lab science, dietetics, nursing (RN), pharmaceutical sciences, preveterinary, radiologic technology/medical imaging, respiratory therapy technology, veterinary technology/assistant. **History:** General. **Interdisciplinary:** Global studies. **Legal studies:** Prelaw. **Liberal arts:** Humanities. **Math:** General, statistics. **Parks/recreation:** General, sports admin. **Philosophy/religion:** Philosophy. **Physical sciences:** Chemistry, geology, physics. **Protective services:** Criminal justice. **Psychology:** General. **Social sciences:** General, anthropology, economics, political science, sociology. **Visual/performing arts:** Art, dramatic, interior design.

**Most popular majors.** Agriculture 8%, biology 6%, business/marketing 14%, engineering/engineering technologies 15%, family/consumer sciences 6%, health sciences 13%, history 7%.

**Computing on campus.** 500 workstations in dormitories, library, computer center, student center. Dormitories wired for high-speed internet access. Online course registration, online library, helpline, repair service, student web hosting, wireless network available.

**Student life.** **Freshman orientation:** Available, $10 fee. Offered in June, July or August and day before classes. **Policies:** No alcoholic beverages allowed on campus, code of student conduct. **Housing:** Guaranteed on-campus housing for freshmen. Coed dorms, single-sex dorms, apartments, fraternity/sorority housing, substance-free housing available. $50 partly refundable deposit. Housing is handicap accessible. Designated floors for engineering and architecture students; learning communities; wellness floors. **Activities:** Bands, choral groups, dance, drama, music ensembles, radio station, student government, student newspaper, Newman Center (Catholic), Lutheran Student Fellowship, United Campus Ministry, College Republicans, College Democrats, Circle-K, Mortar Board, international student association, Black Student Alliance, Native American student association.

**Athletics.** NCAA. **Intercollegiate:** Baseball M, basketball, cross-country, football (tackle) M, golf, soccer W, softball W, track and field, volleyball W, wrestling M. **Intramural:** Basketball, football (non-tackle), softball, volleyball. **Team name:** Bison.

**Student services.** Adult student services, alcohol/substance abuse counseling, campus ministries, career counseling, services for economically disadvantaged, student employment services, financial aid counseling, health services, minority student services, on-campus daycare, personal counseling, veterans' counselor. **Physically disabled:** Services for visually, speech, hearing impaired. **Learning disabled:** Comprehensive services available.

**Contact.**  E-mail: ndsu.admission@ndsu.edu
Phone: (701) 231-8643 Toll-free number: (800) 488-6378
Fax: (701) 231-8802
Jobey Lichtblau, Director of Admission, North Dakota State University, Ceres Hall 124, Fargo, ND 58105-5454

## Rasmussen College: Fargo
**Fargo, North Dakota**
www.rasmussen.edu                    CB code: 3343

- For-profit 4-year career college
- Commuter campus in small city
- 730 degree-seeking undergraduates: 49% part-time, 75% women, 1% Native American
- Interview required

**General.** Accredited by ACICS. **Degrees:** 173 associate awarded. **Calendar:** Quarter, extensive summer session. **Full-time faculty:** 9 total; 44% women. **Part-time faculty:** 15 total; 60% women.

**Basis for selection.** Open admission. Applicants must have high school diploma or GED and complete entrance assessments (STEP test).

**2007-2008 Annual costs.** Tuition/fees: $11,700. Per course tuition ranges from $845 to $1025 depending on course level. Personal expenses: $2,961.

**Financial aid.** All financial aid based on need. **Additional information:** Discount for members of the military and their families.

**Application procedures. Admission:** No deadline. $60 fee. Application may be submitted online. Admission notification on a rolling basis. **Financial aid:** No deadline. FAFSA, institutional form required. Applicants notified on a rolling basis starting 1/1.

**Academics. Special study options:** Distance learning, dual enrollment of high school students, liberal arts/career combination. **Credit/placement by examination:** AP, CLEP, institutional tests. 50% of program credits can be transfer or credit by examination credits. **Support services:** Reduced course load, remedial instruction, tutoring.

**Majors. Business:** Accounting, business admin. **Protective services:** Law enforcement admin.

**Computing on campus.** 110 workstations in library, computer center. Online library, helpline, wireless network available.

**Student life. Freshman orientation:** Mandatory. Preregistration for classes offered. 3-hour session held 1-2 weeks before classes begin. **Activities:** Student government.

**Student services.** Career counseling, student employment services, financial aid counseling, placement for graduates.

**Contact.** E-mail: fargoadmissions@rasmussen.edu
Phone: (701) 277-3889 Toll-free number: (800) 817-0009
Fax: (701) 277-5604
John Wilson, Director of Admissions, Rasmussen College: Fargo, 4012 19th Avenue SW, Fargo, ND 58103

## Trinity Bible College
**Ellendale, North Dakota**
www.trinitybiblecollege.edu              CB code: 0356

- Private 4-year Bible college affiliated with Assemblies of God
- Residential campus in rural community
- 283 degree-seeking undergraduates: 10% part-time, 48% women
- 100% of applicants admitted
- ACT (writing optional), application essay required
- 48% graduate within 6 years

**General.** Founded in 1948. Regionally accredited; also accredited by ABHE. **Degrees:** 41 bachelor's, 7 associate awarded. **Location:** 60 miles from Jamestown, 38 miles from Aberdeen. **Calendar:** Semester, limited summer session. **Full-time faculty:** 30 total. **Part-time faculty:** 10 total. **Special facilities:** Pentecostal heritage collection of rare and out-of-print works, teacher education laboratory.

**Freshman class profile.** 231 applied, 230 admitted, 60 enrolled.

| Return as sophomores: | 64% | Live on campus: | 85% |
|---|---|---|---|
| Out-of-state: | 77% | | |

**Basis for selection.** Applicants must have 14 ACT and 2.0 GPA to be admitted. References, school record, evidence of Christian testimony and lifestyle very important. Interview recommended. **Homeschooled:** Statement describing homeschool structure and mission, transcript of courses

and grades, letter of recommendation (nonparent) required. Minimum ACT scores of 14 English, 15 math required.

**2007-2008 Annual costs.** Tuition/fees: $11,970. Room/board: $4,660. Books/supplies: $700. Personal expenses: $1,636.

**Financial aid. Non-need-based:** Scholarships awarded for academics, alumni affiliation, art, leadership, music/drama, religious affiliation.

**Application procedures. Admission:** No deadline. $25 fee, may be waived for applicants with need. Admission notification on a rolling basis. **Financial aid:** Priority date 3/1, closing date 9/1. FAFSA required. Applicants notified on a rolling basis starting 3/1; must reply within 3 week(s) of notification.

**Academics.** All students major or minor in Biblical studies in conjunction with another major or minor of their choice. **Special study options:** Distance learning, double major, dual enrollment of high school students, independent study, internships, liberal arts/career combination, teacher certification program. **Credit/placement by examination:** AP, CLEP, IB, SAT, ACT, institutional tests. 30 credit hours maximum toward associate degree, 30 toward bachelor's. **Support services:** Learning center, reduced course load, remedial instruction, tutoring.

**Majors. Business:** General. **Education:** Elementary. **Philosophy/religion:** Religion. **Theology:** Bible, missionary, religious ed, theology. **Visual/performing arts:** Dramatic.

**Most popular majors.** Business/marketing 10%, education 20%, philosophy/religious studies 25%, theological studies 40%.

**Computing on campus.** 30 workstations in dormitories, library, computer center. Dormitories wired for high-speed internet access and linked to campus network. Online library, helpline, wireless network available.

**Student life. Freshman orientation:** Mandatory. Preregistration for classes offered. **Policies:** Religious observance required. **Housing:** Single-sex dorms, apartments, substance-free housing available. $150 deposit, deadline 8/31. **Activities:** Bands, choral groups, drama, music ensembles, radio station, student government, missions, photography, ministry clubs.

**Athletics.** NCCAA. **Intercollegiate:** Basketball, football (tackle) M. **Intramural:** Basketball, football (tackle) M, volleyball. **Team name:** Lions.

**Student services.** Campus ministries, career counseling, student employment services, financial aid counseling, personal counseling, placement for graduates, veterans' counselor.

**Contact.** E-mail: admissions@trinitybiblecollege.edu
Phone: (701) 349-3621 Toll-free number: (888) 822-2329
Fax: (701) 349-5786
Keyla Butts, Director of Enrollment Services, Trinity Bible College, 50 6th Avenue South, Ellendale, ND 58436-7150

## University of Mary
**Bismarck, North Dakota**
www.umary.edu                    CB code: 6428

- Private 4-year university affiliated with Roman Catholic Church
- Residential campus in small city
- 2,010 degree-seeking undergraduates: 20% part-time, 60% women, 3% African American, 1% Asian American, 2% Hispanic American, 5% Native American, 2% international
- 703 degree-seeking graduate students
- 85% of applicants admitted
- SAT or ACT (ACT writing optional) required
- 51% graduate within 6 years; 17% enter graduate study

**General.** Founded in 1959. Regionally accredited. Additional centers in Bismarck and Fargo. **Degrees:** 502 bachelor's, 1 associate awarded; master's, doctoral offered. **Location:** 6 miles from downtown. **Calendar:** Semester, limited summer session. **Full-time faculty:** 103 total; 40% have terminal degrees, 52% women. **Part-time faculty:** 185 total; 21% have terminal degrees, 2% minority, 48% women. **Class size:** 66% < 20, 24% 20-39, 2% 40-49, 7% 50-99, less than 1% >100. **Special facilities:** Climbing wall.

**Freshman class profile.** 1,008 applied, 855 admitted, 353 enrolled.

| Mid 50% test scores | | Rank in top tenth: | 17% |
|---|---|---|---|
| ACT composite: | 20-25 | End year in good standing: | 94% |
| GPA 3.50 or higher: | 50% | Return as sophomores: | 74% |
| GPA 3.0-3.49: | 32% | Out-of-state: | 44% |
| GPA 2.0-2.99: | 18% | Live on campus: | 92% |
| Rank in top quarter: | 47% | International: | 2% |

**Basis for selection.** Automatic acceptance for applicants in top half of class with 2.5 GPA and 19 ACT. Applicants not meeting these standards may be admitted with specific conditions for enrollment. Audition required for music program; interview recommended for academically weak students.

**High school preparation.** Recommended units include English 4, mathematics 3, social studies 4 and science 3.

**2008-2009 Annual costs.** Tuition/fees: $12,164. Room/board: $4,820. Books/supplies: $800. Personal expenses: $920.

**2006-2007 Financial aid. Need-based:** 50% of total undergraduate aid awarded as scholarships/grants, 50% as loans/jobs. **Non-need-based:** Scholarships awarded for academics, athletics, leadership, music/drama, state residency.

**Application procedures. Admission:** No deadline. $25 fee, may be waived for applicants with need. Application may be submitted online. Admission notification on a rolling basis. Must reply by May 1 or within 4 week(s) if notified thereafter. **Financial aid:** Priority date 3/15; no closing date. FAFSA required. Applicants notified on a rolling basis starting 4/1; must reply within 2 week(s) of notification.

**Academics. Special study options:** Accelerated study, combined bachelor's/graduate degree, cooperative education, distance learning, double major, dual enrollment of high school students, external degree, independent study, internships, liberal arts/career combination, semester at sea, study abroad, teacher certification program, weekend college. **Credit/placement by examination:** AP, CLEP, IB, institutional tests. 32 credit hours maximum toward associate degree, 96 toward bachelor's. **Support services:** Learning center, reduced course load, remedial instruction, study skills assistance, tutoring, writing center.

**Majors. Biology:** General. **Business:** Accounting, business admin, communications, finance, management science. **Communications:** General, public relations. **Computer sciences:** General, information systems. **Education:** Biology, business, early childhood, elementary, English, history, mathematics, mentally handicapped, music, physical, social science. **Engineering:** General. **English:** English lit. **Health:** Athletic training, clinical lab science, medical radiologic technology/radiation therapy, nursing (RN), respiratory therapy technology, substance abuse counseling. **Math:** General. **Parks/recreation:** Exercise sciences, health/fitness, sports admin. **Philosophy/religion:** Religion. **Protective services:** Criminal justice, law enforcement admin. **Psychology:** General. **Public administration:** Social work. **Social sciences:** General. **Theology:** Theology. **Visual/performing arts:** Music performance.

**Most popular majors.** Business/marketing 40%, education 10%, health sciences 19%, liberal arts 9%.

**Computing on campus.** 235 workstations in dormitories, library, computer center. Dormitories wired for high-speed internet access and linked to campus network. Commuter students can connect to campus network. Online course registration, online library, student web hosting, wireless network available.

**Student life. Freshman orientation:** Mandatory. Preregistration for classes offered. Two-day orientation for freshmen at beginning of fall term. **Housing:** Guaranteed on-campus for freshmen. Single-sex dorms, apartments, substance-free housing available. $100 fully refundable deposit. **Activities:** Bands, choral groups, dance, drama, literary magazine, music ensembles, musical theater, radio station, student government, student newspaper, campus ministry, Spurs, Circle-K, student nurses association, Young Democrats, College Republicans, student education association, social work club, music educators national conference.

**Athletics.** NCAA. **Intercollegiate:** Baseball M, basketball, cross-country, football (tackle) M, golf, soccer, softball W, tennis, track and field, volleyball W, wrestling M. **Intramural:** Badminton, basketball, bowling, football (non-tackle), golf, racquetball, soccer, softball, swimming, table tennis, tennis, volleyball, weight lifting. **Team name:** Marauders.

**Student services.** Adult student services, campus ministries, career counseling, services for economically disadvantaged, student employment services, financial aid counseling, health services, minority student services, personal counseling, placement for graduates, veterans' counselor. **Physically disabled:** Services for hearing impaired.

**Contact.** E-mail: marauder@umary.edu
Phone: (701) 355-8030 Toll-free number: (800) 288-6279
Fax: (701) 255-7687
Dave Heringer, Vice President for Enrollment Services, University of Mary, 7500 University Drive, Bismarck, ND 58504-9652

## University of North Dakota
**Grand Forks, North Dakota**
**www.und.edu**                                         **CB code: 6878**

- Public 4-year university
- Residential campus in small city
- 10,085 degree-seeking undergraduates: 13% part-time, 45% women, 1% African American, 1% Asian American, 1% Hispanic American, 3% Native American, 3% international
- 2,474 degree-seeking graduate students
- 70% of applicants admitted
- SAT or ACT (ACT writing optional) required
- 54% graduate within 6 years; 18% enter graduate study

**General.** Founded in 1883. Regionally accredited. **Degrees:** 1,963 bachelor's awarded; master's, doctoral, first professional offered. **ROTC:** Army, Air Force. **Location:** 320 miles from Minneapolis-St. Paul, 150 miles from Winnipeg, Canada. **Calendar:** Semester, extensive summer session. **Full-time faculty:** 565 total; 79% have terminal degrees, 11% minority, 39% women. **Part-time faculty:** 64 total; 34% have terminal degrees, 53% women. **Class size:** 41% < 20, 46% 20-39, 5% 40-49, 5% 50-99, 4% >100. **Special facilities:** Art museum, atmospherium, supercomputing center, native media center, American Indian center, biomedical research center, climate change and CO2 center, instructional and learning technologies center, peace studies center, renewable energy center, rural health center, children and family services training center, clinical education center, environmental training institute, ecological studies institute, hydrogen technology center, Native American aging resource center, behavioral research center, Indian law center, wellness center.

**Freshman class profile.** 3,783 applied, 2,649 admitted, 1,855 enrolled.

| Mid 50% test scores | | End year in good standing: | 82% |
|---|---|---|---|
| ACT composite: | 20-25 | Return as sophomores: | 74% |
| GPA 3.50 or higher: | 44% | Out-of-state: | 56% |
| GPA 3.0-3.49: | 33% | Live on campus: | 87% |
| GPA 2.0-2.99: | 23% | International: | 1% |
| Rank in top quarter: | 38% | Fraternities: | 8% |
| Rank in top tenth: | 15% | Sororities: | 11% |

**Basis for selection.** High school record and test scores most important. **Homeschooled:** Transcript of courses and grades required.

**High school preparation.** 13 units required. Required and recommended units include English 4, mathematics 3, social studies 3, science 3 (laboratory 3) and foreign language 1. Math must be algebra I and above.

**2007-2008 Annual costs.** Tuition/fees: $6,130; $14,523 out-of-state. Tuition for South Dakota, Montana, Saskatchewan, Manitoba residents: $7,538. Room/board: $5,451. Books/supplies: $800. Personal expenses: $2,070.

**2006-2007 Financial aid. Need-based:** 1,577 full-time freshmen applied for aid; 1,105 were judged to have need; 1,085 of these received aid. Average need met was 36%. Average scholarship/grant was $3,267; average loan $4,512. 24% of total undergraduate aid awarded as scholarships/grants, 76% as loans/jobs. **Non-need-based:** Awarded to 2,436 full-time undergraduates, including 721 freshmen. Scholarships awarded for academics, alumni affiliation, art, athletics, job skills, leadership, music/drama, religious affiliation, ROTC.

**Application procedures. Admission:** No deadline. $35 fee. Application may be submitted online. Admission notification on a rolling basis beginning on or about 9/1. **Financial aid:** Priority date 3/15; no closing date. FAFSA required. Applicants notified on a rolling basis starting 5/15; must reply within 4 week(s) of notification.

**Academics. Special study options:** Accelerated study, combined bachelor's/graduate degree, cooperative education, cross-registration, distance learning, double major, dual enrollment of high school students, ESL, exchange student, external degree, honors, independent study, internships, liberal arts/career combination, semester at sea, student-designed major, study abroad, teacher certification program, weekend college. **Credit/placement by examination:** AP, CLEP, IB, ACT, institutional tests. **Support services:** Learning center, pre-admission summer program, reduced course load, remedial instruction, study skills assistance, tutoring, writing center.

**Majors. Area/ethnic studies:** Native American. **Biology:** General, animal behavior, wildlife. **Business:** Accounting, accounting/finance, entrepreneurial studies, finance, management information systems, managerial economics, marketing. **Communications:** General. **Communications technology:** Graphics. **Computer sciences:** General, systems analysis. **Education:** Art, business, early childhood, elementary, mathematics, middle, music, physical, sales/marketing, science. **Engineering:** Chemical, civil, electrical, environmental, geological, mechanical. **Engineering technology:** Industrial, occupational safety. **English:** English lit. **Family/consumer sciences:** Food/nutrition. **Foreign languages:** General, classics, French, German, Scandinavian, Spanish. **Health:** Athletic training, audiology/speech pathology, clinical lab science, clinical nutrition, communication disorders, cytotechnology, dietetics, music therapy, nursing (RN), vocational rehab counseling. **History:** General. **Interdisciplinary:** Global studies. **Math:** General. **Parks/recreation:** Facilities management. **Philosophy/religion:** Philosophy, religion. **Physical sciences:** General, atmospheric science, chemistry, geology, physics. **Protective services:** Criminal justice, forensics. **Psychology:** General. **Public administration:** General, social work. **Social sciences:** General, anthropology, economics, geography, political science, sociology. **Transportation:** Air traffic control, airline/commercial pilot, aviation, aviation management, flight instructor. **Visual/performing arts:** General, art, dramatic, graphic design, music performance. **Other:** Fisheries and wildlife biology.

**Most popular majors.** Business/marketing 14%, education 9%, health sciences 11%, trade and industry 16%.

**Computing on campus.** 1,100 workstations in dormitories, library, computer center, student center. Dormitories wired for high-speed internet access and linked to campus network. Commuter students can connect to campus network. Online course registration, online library, helpline, student web hosting, wireless network available.

**Student life. Freshman orientation:** Available, $15 fee. Preregistration for classes offered. Held weekends before school opens in August. **Housing:** Guaranteed on-campus for freshmen. Coed dorms, single-sex dorms, special housing for disabled, apartments, fraternity/sorority housing available. $250 partly refundable deposit, deadline 5/1. **Activities:** Bands, campus ministries, choral groups, dance, drama, film society, international student organizations, literary magazine, music ensembles, musical theater, opera, radio station, student government, student newspaper, symphony orchestra, TV station, over 230 organizations available.

**Athletics.** NCAA. **Intercollegiate:** Baseball M, basketball, cross-country, diving, football (tackle) M, golf, ice hockey, soccer W, softball W, swimming, tennis W, track and field, volleyball W. **Intramural:** Badminton, basketball, cross-country, golf, ice hockey, racquetball, soccer W, softball W, swimming, tennis W, track and field, volleyball W. **Team name:** Fighting Sioux.

**Student services.** Adult student services, alcohol/substance abuse counseling, campus ministries, career counseling, services for economically disadvantaged, student employment services, financial aid counseling, health services, legal services, minority student services, on-campus daycare, personal counseling, placement for graduates, veterans' counselor, women's services. **Physically disabled:** Services for visually, speech, hearing impaired.

**Contact.** E-mail: enrollmentservices@mail.und.nodak.edu
Phone: (701) 777-3821 Toll-free number: (800) 225-5863
Fax: (701) 777-2721
Deborah Melby, Director, University of North Dakota, Twamley Hall Room 205 264 Centennial Drive Stop 8357, Grand Forks, ND 58202-8357

---

## Valley City State University
**Valley City, North Dakota**
**www.vcsu.edu**                         CB code: 6480

- Public 4-year liberal arts and teachers college
- Residential campus in small town
- 901 degree-seeking undergraduates: 25% part-time, 55% women, 4% African American, 1% Hispanic American, 2% Native American, 5% international
- 83 degree-seeking graduate students
- 92% of applicants admitted
- SAT or ACT (ACT writing optional) required
- 39% graduate within 6 years

**General.** Founded in 1889. Regionally accredited. All full-time undergraduate students are provided a laptop computer. **Degrees:** 192 bachelor's awarded; master's offered. **Location:** 60 miles from Fargo. **Calendar:** Semester, limited summer session. **Full-time faculty:** 54 total; 54% have terminal degrees, 4% minority, 52% women. **Part-time faculty:** 33 total; 18% have

terminal degrees, 52% women. **Special facilities:** Planetarium, medicine wheel, undergraduate research labs.

**Freshman class profile.** 271 applied, 248 admitted, 186 enrolled.

| Mid 50% test scores | | | |
|---|---|---|---|
| SAT critical reading: | 420-520 | Rank in top tenth: | 8% |
| SAT math: | 450-510 | End year in good standing: | 68% |
| ACT composite: | 18-23 | Out-of-state: | 35% |
| GPA 3.50 or higher: | 29% | Live on campus: | 85% |
| GPA 3.0-3.49: | 30% | International: | 4% |
| GPA 2.0-2.99: | 40% | Fraternities: | 3% |
| Rank in top quarter: | 25% | Sororities: | 3% |

**Basis for selection.** School achievement record and test scores important. **Homeschooled:** Transcript of courses and grades required.

**High school preparation.** 13 units required. Required and recommended units include English 4, mathematics 3, social studies 3, science 3 (laboratory 3) and foreign language 2.

**2007-2008 Annual costs.** Tuition/fees: $5,584; $12,165 out-of-state. Full-time tuition for South Dakota, Montana, Manitoba, Saskatchewan residents: $4,926. Full-time tuition for WUE students: $5,911. Room/board: $3,870. Books/supplies: $800. Personal expenses: $1,823.

**2006-2007 Financial aid. Need-based:** 191 full-time freshmen applied for aid; 130 were judged to have need; 128 of these received aid. Average need met was 70%. Average scholarship/grant was $4,644; average loan $3,052. 41% of total undergraduate aid awarded as scholarships/grants, 59% as loans/jobs. **Non-need-based:** Awarded to 255 full-time undergraduates, including 116 freshmen. Scholarships awarded for academics, alumni affiliation, athletics, leadership, minority status, music/drama.

**Application procedures. Admission:** No deadline. $35 fee. Application may be submitted online. Admission notification on a rolling basis beginning on or about 9/15. **Financial aid:** Priority date 3/15; no closing date. FAFSA required. Applicants notified on a rolling basis starting 2/1; must reply within 4 week(s) of notification.

**Academics. Special study options:** Combined bachelor's/graduate degree, cooperative education, distance learning, double major, dual enrollment of high school students, internships, liberal arts/career combination, student-designed major, teacher certification program. **Credit/placement by examination:** AP, CLEP, SAT, ACT, institutional tests. **Support services:** Reduced course load, study skills assistance, tutoring.

**Majors. Biology:** General. **Business:** Business admin, human resources, office management. **Computer sciences:** General. **Education:** Art, biology, business, chemistry, elementary, English, health, history, instructional media, mathematics, music, physical, science, secondary, social science, Spanish, technology/industrial arts, trade/industrial, voc/tech. **English:** English lit. **Foreign languages:** Spanish. **Health:** Predental, premedicine, prenursing, prepharmacy, preveterinary. **History:** General. **Legal studies:** Prelaw. **Liberal arts:** Arts/sciences. **Math:** General. **Parks/recreation:** Health/fitness. **Physical sciences:** Chemistry. **Psychology:** General. **Social sciences:** General. **Visual/performing arts:** Art.

**Most popular majors.** Business/marketing 22%, education 53%.

**Computing on campus.** PC or laptop required. 925 workstations in dormitories, library, computer center, student center. Dormitories wired for high-speed internet access and linked to campus network. Commuter students can connect to campus network. Online course registration, online library, helpline, repair service, student web hosting, wireless network available.

**Student life. Freshman orientation:** Available, $10 fee. Half-day sessions for students with concurrent sessions for parents; held on 2 separate days in June. **Policies:** Tobacco-free campus. **Housing:** Guaranteed on-campus for all undergraduates. Coed dorms, single-sex dorms, special housing for disabled, apartments, fraternity/sorority housing, substance-free housing available. $50 deposit. **Activities:** Bands, choral groups, drama, literary magazine, music ensembles, student government, student newspaper, inter-residence hall council, inter-fraternity/sorority council, inter-varsity Christian fellowship, Music Educators National Conference, Student National Education Association, Newman Club, Association of Information Technology Professionals, Faith Lutheran student club, international student club.

**Athletics.** NAIA. **Intercollegiate:** Baseball M, basketball, football (tackle) M, softball W, volleyball W. **Intramural:** Basketball, bowling, cross-country, football (non-tackle), golf, ice hockey, racquetball, softball, track and field, volleyball. **Team name:** Vikings.

**Student services.** Career counseling, student employment services, financial aid counseling, health services, on-campus daycare, personal counseling, placement for graduates, veterans' counselor.

**Contact.** E-mail: enrollment.services@vcsu.edu
Phone: (701) 845-7101 Toll-free number: (800) 532-8641 ext. 7101
Fax: (701) 845-7299
Dan Klein, Director of Enrollment Services, Valley City State University,
101 College Street SW, Valley City, ND 58072-4098

# Ohio

## Allegheny Wesleyan College
### Salem, Ohio
### www.awc.edu
### CB code: 4120

- Private 4-year Bible college affiliated with Allegheny Wesleyan Methodist Connection
- Residential campus in small town
- 44 degree-seeking undergraduates

**General.** Accredited by ABHE. Beautiful country setting on 45 acres. **Degrees:** 6 bachelor's awarded. **Calendar:** Semester. **Full-time faculty:** 5 total. **Part-time faculty:** 5 total.

**Freshman class profile.** 18 applied, 18 admitted, 17 enrolled.

**Basis for selection.** Open admission.

**2007-2008 Annual costs.** Tuition/fees: $4,700. Room/board: $3,200.

**Application procedures. Admission:** Priority date 4/25; deadline 8/26. $35 fee. Admission notification on a rolling basis. **Financial aid:** Priority date 8/26; no closing date.

**Academics. Credit/placement by examination:** AP, CLEP. **Support services:** Reduced course load, remedial instruction, tutoring.

**Majors. Theology:** Theology.

**Student life. Housing:** Coed dorms available. **Activities:** Student newspaper.

**Contact.** E-mail: college@awc.edu
Phone: (330) 337-6403 Toll-free number: (800) 292-3153 ext. 10
Fax: (330) 337-6255
Jeanne Zvaritch, Director of Admissions, Allegheny Wesleyan College, 2161 Woodside Road, Salem, OH 44460-9598

## Antioch University McGregor
### Yellow Springs, Ohio
### www.mcgregor.edu
### CB code: 4527

- Private 4-year branch campus and liberal arts college
- Commuter campus in small town
- 169 degree-seeking undergraduates

**General.** Founded in 1988. Regionally accredited. **Degrees:** 33 bachelor's awarded; master's offered. **Location:** 18 miles from Dayton. **Calendar:** Quarter, limited summer session. **Full-time faculty:** 60 total. **Part-time faculty:** 63 total. **Special facilities:** Nature reserve.

**Basis for selection.** Applicants must be over 21. Recommendations and motivation most important.

**2007-2008 Annual costs.** Tuition/fees: $13,185. Books/supplies: $1,800.

**Application procedures. Admission:** Priority date 6/1; deadline 11/1. $45 fee. Admission notification on a rolling basis. **Financial aid:** No deadline. Applicants notified on a rolling basis.

**Academics. Special study options:** Double major, independent study, student-designed major, weekend college. **Credit/placement by examination:** CLEP. 45 credit hours maximum toward bachelor's degree. **Support services:** Reduced course load, writing center.

**Majors. Business:** Business admin, human resources. **Liberal arts:** Arts/sciences, humanities. **Math:** General. **Public administration:** Human services.

**Most popular majors.** Business/marketing 29%, liberal arts 35%, psychology 20%, public administration/social services 12%.

**Computing on campus.** 35 workstations in library, computer center. Commuter students can connect to campus network. Online course registration, wireless network available.

**Student life. Freshman orientation:** Mandatory, $25 fee. **Activities:** Radio station.

**Student services.** Adult student services.

**Contact.** E-mail: sas@mcgregor.edu
Phone: (937) 769-1818 Fax: (937) 769-1804
Oscar Robinson, Executive Director of Operations and Registrar, Antioch University McGregor, 900 Dayton Street, Yellow Springs, OH 45387

## Art Academy of Cincinnati
### Cincinnati, Ohio
### www.artacademy.edu
### CB code: 1002

- Private 4-year visual arts college
- Commuter campus in large city
- 137 degree-seeking undergraduates: 7% part-time, 65% women, 6% African American, 3% Asian American, 3% Hispanic American, 1% Native American
- 3 degree-seeking graduate students
- 24% of applicants admitted
- SAT or ACT (ACT writing optional), application essay required

**General.** Founded in 1869. Regionally accredited. **Degrees:** 34 bachelor's awarded; master's offered. **Location:** One mile from downtown. **Calendar:** Semester, limited summer session. **Full-time faculty:** 15 total. **Part-time faculty:** 30 total. **Special facilities:** Glass-blowing facility and three art galleries.

**Freshman class profile.** 416 applied, 101 admitted, 32 enrolled.

| Mid 50% test scores | | ACT composite: | 18-23 |
|---|---|---|---|
| SAT critical reading: | 480-580 | Out-of-state: | 28% |
| SAT math: | 420-510 | Live on campus: | 47% |

**Basis for selection.** Academic background based upon GPA and ACT/SAT scores; portfolio review and interview very important; 1-page artist statement and 1 letter of recommendation. Portfolio required for all; interview required for those within 150 miles of campus. **Homeschooled:** Transcript of courses and grades, state high school equivalency certificate required.

**High school preparation.** 12 units recommended. Recommended units include English 4, mathematics 3, social studies 1 and science 2. 3-4 units art recommended.

**2008-2009 Annual costs.** Tuition/fees (projected): $21,300. Room/board: $6,800. Books/supplies: $1,200.

**Financial aid. Non-need-based:** Scholarships awarded for academics, art.

**Application procedures. Admission:** Priority date 3/1; deadline 6/30 (postmark date). No application fee. Application may be submitted online. Admission notification on a rolling basis. **Financial aid:** Priority date 4/1; no closing date. FAFSA required. Applicants notified on a rolling basis starting 3/1.

**Academics. Special study options:** Cross-registration, double major, exchange student, independent study, internships, New York semester, student-designed major, study abroad. **Credit/placement by examination:** AP, CLEP, institutional tests. **Support services:** Learning center, study skills assistance, tutoring, writing center.

**Majors. Visual/performing arts:** Art history/conservation, design, digital art, drawing, illustration, painting, photography, printmaking, sculpture, studio arts.

**Computing on campus.** 40 workstations in computer center. Dormitories wired for high-speed internet access.

**Student life. Freshman orientation:** Mandatory. Preregistration for classes offered. Held 5 days before school begins. **Housing:** Coed dorms available. $250 nonrefundable deposit, deadline 6/1. **Activities:** Film society, literary magazine, student government.

**Student services.** Career counseling, student employment services, financial aid counseling, personal counseling, placement for graduates, veterans' counselor. **Physically disabled:** Services for hearing impaired.

**Contact.** E-mail: admissions@artacademy.edu
Phone: (513) 562-8740 Toll-free number: (800) 323-5692
Fax: (513) 562-8778
John Wadell, Director of Admissions, Art Academy of Cincinnati, 1212 Jackson Street, Cincinnati, OH 45202

## Ashland University

| Ashland, Ohio | CB member |
|---|---|
| www.exploreashland.com | CB code: 1021 |

- Private 4-year university and liberal arts college affiliated with Brethren Church
- Residential campus in large town
- 2,712 degree-seeking undergraduates: 8% part-time, 54% women, 8% African American, 1% Asian American, 3% Hispanic American, 2% international
- 2,781 degree-seeking graduate students
- 83% of applicants admitted
- SAT or ACT (ACT writing optional), application essay required
- 58% graduate within 6 years

**General.** Founded in 1878. Regionally accredited. **Degrees:** 610 bachelor's, 9 associate awarded; master's, doctoral, first professional offered. **ROTC:** Air Force. **Location:** 60 miles from Cleveland, 80 miles from Columbus. **Calendar:** Semester, limited summer session. **Full-time faculty:** 234 total; 84% have terminal degrees, 6% minority, 42% women. **Part-time faculty:** 347 total; 33% have terminal degrees, 4% minority, 53% women. **Class size:** 58% < 20, 42% 20-39, less than 1% 40-49, less than 1% 50-99. **Special facilities:** Center for public affairs, business and economic research, convocation, numismatic, nonviolence, educational improvement, entrepreneurial studies; institute for middle level education.

**Freshman class profile.** 2,904 applied, 2,422 admitted, 646 enrolled.

| Mid 50% test scores | | Rank in top quarter: | 47% |
|---|---|---|---|
| SAT critical reading: | 450-560 | Rank in top tenth: | 16% |
| SAT math: | 480-580 | Return as sophomores: | 72% |
| SAT writing: | 450-460 | Out-of-state: | 6% |
| ACT composite: | 20-25 | Live on campus: | 87% |
| GPA 3.50 or higher: | 44% | International: | 1% |
| GPA 3.0-3.49: | 31% | Fraternities: | 2% |
| GPA 2.0-2.99: | 25% | Sororities: | 4% |

**Basis for selection.** School achievement record most important; test scores also important. Counselor's recommendation considered. Interview recommended for all; audition recommended for music, theater programs; portfolio recommended for art. **Homeschooled:** Transcript of courses and grades required. ACT or SAT test results.

**High school preparation.** Required and recommended units include English 3-4, mathematics 2-3, social studies 2-3, history 1, science 2-3, foreign language 2 and academic electives 1.

**2007-2008 Annual costs.** Tuition/fees: $22,898. Room/board: $8,374. Books/supplies: $800. Personal expenses: $1,461.

**2007-2008 Financial aid. Need-based:** 634 full-time freshmen applied for aid; 530 were judged to have need; 530 of these received aid. Average need met was 90%. Average scholarship/grant was $14,841; average loan $4,163. 55% of total undergraduate aid awarded as scholarships/grants, 45% as loans/jobs. **Non-need-based:** Awarded to 433 full-time undergraduates, including 99 freshmen. Scholarships awarded for academics, alumni affiliation, art, athletics, job skills, leadership, minority status, music/drama, religious affiliation.

**Application procedures. Admission:** No deadline. No application fee. Application may be submitted online. Admission notification on a rolling basis beginning on or about 9/15. Must reply by May 1 or within 4 week(s) if notified thereafter. **Financial aid:** Priority date 3/15; no closing date. FAFSA, institutional form required. Applicants notified on a rolling basis starting 3/15; must reply within 3 week(s) of notification.

**Academics. Special study options:** Double major, ESL, honors, independent study, internships, student-designed major, study abroad, teacher certification program, Washington semester, weekend college. Pre-MBA courses for graduated nonbusiness majors, bachelor's degree completion program for RNs. **Credit/placement by examination:** AP, CLEP, IB, SAT, ACT, institutional tests. 32 credit hours maximum toward associate degree, 32 toward bachelor's. **Support services:** Learning center, study skills assistance, tutoring, writing center.

**Majors. Area/ethnic studies:** American. **Biology:** General. **Business:** General, accounting, business admin, finance, franchise operations, management information systems, marketing, purchasing. **Communications:** General, journalism, radio/tv. **Computer sciences:** Computer science. **Conservation:** Environmental science. **Education:** Art, biology, business, chemistry, drama/dance, early childhood, English, family/consumer sciences, French, kindergarten/preschool, mathematics, middle, music, physical, science, social studies, Spanish, special. **English:** Creative writing, English lit. **Family/consumer sciences:** Family systems, food/nutrition. **Foreign languages:** French, Spanish. **Health:** Athletic training, nursing admin, recreational therapy. **History:** General. **Legal studies:** Prelaw. **Liberal arts:** Arts/sciences. **Math:** General. **Parks/recreation:** General, facilities management, sports admin. **Philosophy/religion:** Philosophy, religion. **Physical sciences:** Chemistry, geology, physics, planetary. **Protective services:** Law enforcement admin. **Psychology:** General. **Public administration:** Social work. **Social sciences:** Economics, political science, sociology. **Theology:** Bible, missionary, religious ed. **Visual/performing arts:** Commercial/advertising art, dramatic, music performance, music theory/composition, studio arts.

**Most popular majors.** Business/marketing 17%, education 37%, security/protective services 7%, social sciences 6%, visual/performing arts 7%.

**Computing on campus.** 191 workstations in dormitories, library, computer center, student center. Dormitories wired for high-speed internet access and linked to campus network. Commuter students can connect to campus network. Online library, helpline, repair service, wireless network available.

**Student life. Freshman orientation:** Available. Preregistration for classes offered. **Policies:** Dry campus. **Housing:** Guaranteed on-campus for all undergraduates. Coed dorms, single-sex dorms, apartments, fraternity/sorority housing, substance-free housing available. $200 fully refundable deposit, deadline 5/1. Scholar hall available. Apartments available to seniors. **Activities:** Bands, campus ministries, choral groups, dance, drama, international student organizations, literary magazine, music ensembles, musical theater, radio station, student government, student newspaper, symphony orchestra, TV station, Christian Fellowship, Newman Club, Fellowship of Christian Athletes, international club, Black Student Union, campus activities board, community care, adventure club, Republican/Democratic club.

**Athletics.** NCAA. **Intercollegiate:** Baseball M, basketball, cheerleading M, cross-country, diving, football (tackle) M, golf, soccer, softball W, swimming, tennis W, track and field, volleyball W, wrestling M. **Intramural:** Badminton, basketball, bowling, football (non-tackle), golf, racquetball, soccer, softball, swimming, table tennis, tennis, volleyball, wrestling M. **Team name:** Eagles.

**Student services.** Adult student services, alcohol/substance abuse counseling, campus ministries, career counseling, student employment services, financial aid counseling, health services, minority student services, personal counseling, veterans' counselor. **Physically disabled:** Services for visually, speech, hearing impaired.

**Contact.** E-mail: enrollme@ashland.edu
Phone: (419) 289-5052 Toll-free number: (800) 882-1548 ext. 5052
Fax: (419) 289-5999
Thomas Mansperger, Director of Admissions, Ashland University, 401 College Avenue, Ashland, OH 44805-9981

## Baldwin-Wallace College

| Berea, Ohio | CB member |
|---|---|
| www.bw.edu | CB code: 1050 |

- Private 4-year liberal arts college affiliated with United Methodist Church
- Residential campus in large town
- 3,491 degree-seeking undergraduates: 13% part-time, 57% women, 7% African American, 1% Asian American, 2% Hispanic American, 1% international
- 710 degree-seeking graduate students
- 66% of applicants admitted
- SAT or ACT (ACT writing optional), application essay required
- 68% graduate within 6 years

**General.** Founded in 1845. Regionally accredited. Campus in Beachwood, offering evening and Saturday classes for bachelor's and master's degrees in business, professional development and executive education. **Degrees:** 771 bachelor's awarded; master's offered. **ROTC:** Army, Air Force. **Location:** 15 miles from Cleveland. **Calendar:** Semester, limited summer session. **Full-time faculty:** 167 total; 81% have terminal degrees, 10% minority, 39% women. **Part-time faculty:** 223 total; 22% have terminal degrees, 9% minority, 44% women. **Class size:** 51% < 20, 48% 20-39, less than 1% 40-49, less than 1% 50-99. **Special facilities:** Observatory, 2 art galleries, 2 theaters, conservatory of music, 2 dance studios, cybercafe, arboretum, Lyceum Square (historical site).

**Freshman class profile.** 3,126 applied, 2,058 admitted, 740 enrolled.

| Mid 50% test scores | | Rank in top tenth: | 27% |
|---|---|---|---|
| SAT critical reading: | 500-610 | End year in good standing: | 97% |
| SAT math: | 490-600 | Return as sophomores: | 83% |
| SAT writing: | 470-590 | Out-of-state: | 16% |
| ACT composite: | 21-26 | Live on campus: | 86% |
| GPA 3.50 or higher: | 54% | International: | 1% |
| GPA 3.0-3.49: | 28% | Fraternities: | 14% |
| GPA 2.0-2.99: | 16% | Sororities: | 20% |
| Rank in top quarter: | 61% | | |

**Basis for selection.** Academic achievement (preferably 3.2 GPA) and class rank (preferably top 30%) most important. Test scores used to support data from high school record. 23 ACT, 550 SAT verbal, 550 SAT math recommended. Applicants must be graduates of accredited secondary school. Interview recommended for all; audition required for music, music education, music theater, and music therapy programs; portfolio recommended for art program. **Homeschooled:** Statement describing homeschool structure and mission, transcript of courses and grades, letter of recommendation (nonparent) required.

**High school preparation.** 17 units required; 24 recommended. Required and recommended units include English 4, mathematics 3-4, social studies 3-4, history 1, science 3-4 (laboratory 2), foreign language 1-2 and academic electives 3. Some flexibility in choice of subjects permitted.

**2007-2008 Annual costs.** Tuition/fees: $22,404. Conservatory tuition is higher. Room/board: $7,358. Books/supplies: $1,000. Personal expenses: $1,500.

**2007-2008 Financial aid. Need-based:** 708 full-time freshmen applied for aid; 610 were judged to have need; 610 of these received aid. Average need met was 92%. Average scholarship/grant was $13,273; average loan $3,905. 69% of total undergraduate aid awarded as scholarships/grants, 31% as loans/jobs. **Non-need-based:** Awarded to 1,047 full-time undergraduates, including 264 freshmen. Scholarships awarded for academics, alumni affiliation, leadership, minority status, music/drama, religious affiliation.

**Application procedures. Admission:** Priority date 3/1; no deadline. $25 fee, may be waived for applicants with need. Application may be submitted online. Admission notification on a rolling basis beginning on or about 10/1. Must reply by May 1 or within 3 week(s) if notified thereafter. **Financial aid:** Priority date 5/1, closing date 9/1. FAFSA required. Applicants notified on a rolling basis starting 2/14.

**Academics.** Weekend classes limited to nontraditional students. **Special study options:** Accelerated study, combined bachelor's/graduate degree, cross-registration, distance learning, double major, dual enrollment of high school students, ESL, exchange student, honors, independent study, internships, liberal arts/career combination, semester at sea, student-designed major, study abroad, teacher certification program, United Nations semester, Washington semester, weekend college. 3-2 in engineering with Case Western Reserve University, Columbia University (NY) and Washington University (MO); 3-2 in Social Work with Case Western Reserve University; 3/2 Accounting MBA, 3/2 Human Resources MBA and 3/2 Computer Science/Info. Systems MBA Programs. **Credit/placement by examination:** AP, CLEP, IB, SAT, ACT, institutional tests. **Support services:** Learning center, reduced course load, remedial instruction, study skills assistance, tutoring, writing center.

**Majors. Biology:** General, exercise physiology. **Business:** Accounting, business admin, finance, human resources, international, marketing, small business admin. **Communications:** General, media studies, public relations. **Computer sciences:** Computer science, networking, systems analysis, webmaster. **Education:** General, early childhood, learning disabled, middle, music. **English:** Creative writing, English lit. **Foreign languages:** French, German, Spanish. **Health:** Athletic training, communication disorders, music therapy. **History:** General. **Interdisciplinary:** Biological/physical sciences, global studies, neuroscience. **Math:** General. **Parks/recreation:** Health/fitness, sports admin. **Philosophy/religion:** Philosophy, religion. **Physical sciences:** Chemistry, physics. **Protective services:** Criminal justice. **Psychology:** General. **Social sciences:** Econometrics, economics, political science, sociology. **Visual/performing arts:** Art, art history/conservation, film/cinema, music history, music performance, music theory/composition, musical theater, piano/organ, studio arts, voice/opera. **Other:** Organizational leadership, Pre-Engineering, Theatre.

**Most popular majors.** Business/marketing 27%, education 14%, psychology 6%, visual/performing arts 7%.

**Computing on campus.** 543 workstations in dormitories, library, computer center, student center. Dormitories wired for high-speed internet access and linked to campus network. Commuter students can connect to campus network. Online course registration, online library, helpline, student web hosting, wireless network available.

**Student life. Freshman orientation:** Available, $75 fee. Preregistration for classes offered. 2-day program held in June, July, August. **Policies:** All full-time students required to live on campus first and second year. Residency exemptions made for commuting students living with families. **Housing:** Guaranteed on-campus for freshmen. Coed dorms, single-sex dorms, special housing for disabled, apartments, fraternity/sorority housing, substance-free housing available. Wellness halls, Sprout Houses (for single mothers and children), Carmel Living and Learning Center. **Activities:** Bands, campus ministries, choral groups, dance, drama, international student organizations, literary magazine, music ensembles, Model UN, musical theater, opera, radio station, student government, student newspaper, symphony orchestra, TV station, Campus Crusade for Christ, Hillel, Newman Student Organization, College Democrats, College Republicans, Black Student Alliance, Hispanic American Student Association, Middle Eastern Student Alliance, Certified Peer Educators, Habitat for Humanity.

**Athletics.** NCAA. **Intercollegiate:** Baseball M, basketball, cross-country, diving, football (tackle) M, golf, soccer, softball W, swimming, tennis, track and field, volleyball W, wrestling M. **Intramural:** Badminton, basketball, football (non-tackle), football (tackle) M, golf, racquetball, soccer, softball, tennis, volleyball, wrestling M. **Team name:** Yellow Jackets.

**Student services.** Adult student services, alcohol/substance abuse counseling, campus ministries, career counseling, student employment services, financial aid counseling, health services, minority student services, personal counseling. **Physically disabled:** Services for visually, speech, hearing impaired.

**Contact.** E-mail: admission@bw.edu
Phone: (440) 826-2222 Toll-free number: (877) 292-7759
Fax: (440) 826-3830
Susan Dileno, VP of Enrollment Management, Baldwin-Wallace College, 275 Eastland Road, Berea, OH 44017-2088

## Bluffton University
**Bluffton, Ohio**
www.bluffton.edu                           CB code: 1067

- Private 4-year liberal arts college affiliated with Mennonite Church
- Residential campus in small town
- 921 degree-seeking undergraduates: 2% part-time, 56% women, 4% African American, 1% Asian American, 2% Hispanic American, 2% international
- 116 degree-seeking graduate students
- 61% of applicants admitted
- SAT or ACT (ACT writing optional) required
- 56% graduate within 6 years

**General.** Founded in 1899. Regionally accredited. Christian faith, values, and service to others in the Anabaptist, peace church tradition. **Degrees:** 273 bachelor's awarded; master's offered. **Location:** 15 miles from Lima, 75 miles from Toledo. **Calendar:** Semester, limited summer session. **Full-time faculty:** 66 total; 65% have terminal degrees, 3% minority, 32% women. **Part-time faculty:** 50 total; 14% have terminal degrees, 8% minority, 48% women. **Class size:** 65% < 20, 29% 20-39, 5% 40-49, less than 1% 50-99, less than 1% >100. **Special facilities:** Nature preserve.

**Freshman class profile.** 1,343 applied, 817 admitted, 208 enrolled.

| Mid 50% test scores | | Rank in top quarter: | 44% |
|---|---|---|---|
| SAT critical reading: | 430-540 | Rank in top tenth: | 17% |
| SAT math: | 460-560 | Return as sophomores: | 68% |
| ACT composite: | 20-25 | Out-of-state: | 19% |
| GPA 3.50 or higher: | 43% | Live on campus: | 95% |
| GPA 3.0-3.49: | 39% | International: | 2% |
| GPA 2.0-2.99: | 18% | | |

**Basis for selection.** Class rank, school achievement record, and test scores very important. Campus visit and interview strongly recommended. Essay required for academically weak students; audition and portfolio required for scholarships in music and art. **Homeschooled:** Interview required.

**High school preparation.** College-preparatory program recommended. 16 units recommended. Recommended units include English 4, mathematics 3, social studies 3, science 3 and foreign language 3.

**2007-2008 Annual costs.** Tuition/fees: $21,780. Room/board: $7,294. Books/supplies: $1,100. Personal expenses: $1,330.

**2007-2008 Financial aid. Need-based:** 198 full-time freshmen applied for aid; 180 were judged to have need; 180 of these received aid. Average need met was 96%. Average scholarship/grant was $15,833; average loan

$4,620. 54% of total undergraduate aid awarded as scholarships/grants, 46% as loans/jobs. **Non-need-based:** Awarded to 163 full-time undergraduates, including 42 freshmen. Scholarships awarded for academics, art, job skills, leadership, minority status, music/drama, state residency.

**Application procedures. Admission:** Priority date 5/31; deadline 8/20 (receipt date). $20 fee, may be waived for applicants with need. Application may be submitted online. Admission notification on a rolling basis beginning on or about 6/1. **Financial aid:** Priority date 5/1, closing date 10/1. FAFSA required. Applicants notified on a rolling basis starting 3/1; must reply within 3 week(s) of notification.

**Academics. Special study options:** Accelerated study, combined bachelor's/ graduate degree, double major, dual enrollment of high school students, honors, independent study, internships, liberal arts/career combination, student-designed major, study abroad, teacher certification program, Washington semester. Degree-completion program for working adults 25 years and older. **Credit/placement by examination:** AP, CLEP, SAT, ACT, institutional tests. 20 credit hours maximum toward bachelor's degree. **Support services:** Learning center, remedial instruction, tutoring, writing center.

**Majors. Biology:** General. **Business:** Accounting, business admin, management information systems, organizational behavior. **Communications:** General. **Computer sciences:** Computer science, information systems, information technology. **Education:** Art, biology, business, chemistry, early childhood, elementary, English, family/consumer sciences, health, history, kindergarten/ preschool, mathematics, mentally handicapped, middle, music, physical, physics, science, secondary, social studies, special. **English:** English lit. **Family/ consumer sciences:** General, clothing/textiles, food/nutrition. **Foreign languages:** Spanish. **Health:** Premedicine. **History:** General. **Interdisciplinary:** Peace/conflict. **Math:** General. **Parks/recreation:** Facilities management, health/fitness, sports admin. **Philosophy/religion:** Religion. **Physical sciences:** Chemistry, physics. **Protective services:** Criminal justice. **Psychology:** General. **Public administration:** Social work. **Social sciences:** General, economics, sociology. **Theology:** Youth ministry. **Visual/ performing arts:** Art.

**Most popular majors.** Business/marketing 35%, education 22%, parks/ recreation 8%.

**Computing on campus.** 125 workstations in dormitories, library, computer center, student center. Dormitories wired for high-speed internet access and linked to campus network. Commuter students can connect to campus network. Online course registration, online library, helpline, repair service, student web hosting, wireless network available.

**Student life. Freshman orientation:** Mandatory. Preregistration for classes offered. Fall orientation begins Friday before classes and continues through first week of classes. Summer orientation 1-day event held over summer; students can choose 1 of 4 dates. **Policies:** No alcoholic beverages or tobacco allowed on campus. Honor system applies to all student activities. Students should feel comfortable with emphasis on faith and values. Voluntary chapel service once each week. **Housing:** Guaranteed on-campus for all undergraduates. Coed dorms, single-sex dorms, substance-free housing available. All traditional undergraduate students required to live on campus or commute from home. **Activities:** Bands, choral groups, dance, drama, international student organizations, literary magazine, music ensembles, musical theater, radio station, student government, student newspaper, departmental clubs, Brothers and Sisters in Christ, peace club, Habitat for Humanity, Fellowship of Christian Athletes, African American student organization, peer awareness leaders, College Republicans, Young Democrats.

**Athletics.** NCAA. **Intercollegiate:** Baseball M, basketball, cheerleading M, cross-country, football (tackle) M, soccer, softball W, tennis, track and field, volleyball W. **Intramural:** Basketball, bowling, football (non-tackle), softball, volleyball. **Team name:** Beavers.

**Student services.** Campus ministries, career counseling, student employment services, financial aid counseling, health services, minority student services, personal counseling, placement for graduates. **Physically disabled:** Services for visually, hearing impaired. **Learning disabled:** Comprehensive services available.

**Contact.** E-mail: admissions@bluffton.edu
Phone: (419) 358-3257 Toll-free number: (800) 488-3257
Fax: (419) 358-3081
Chris Jebsen, Director of Admissions, Bluffton University, 1 University Drive, Bluffton, OH 45817-2104

## Bowling Green State University

**Bowling Green, Ohio**
**www.bgsu.edu**

**CB member**
**CB code: 1069**

- Public 4-year university
- Residential campus in large town

- 15,391 degree-seeking undergraduates: 6% part-time, 54% women
- 2,430 degree-seeking graduate students
- 88% of applicants admitted
- SAT and SAT Subject Tests or ACT (ACT writing optional) required
- 57% graduate within 6 years

**General.** Founded in 1910. Regionally accredited. **Degrees:** 3,012 bachelor's awarded; master's, doctoral offered. **ROTC:** Army, Air Force. **Location:** 23 miles from Toledo. **Calendar:** Semester, limited summer session. **Full-time faculty:** 876 total; 76% have terminal degrees, 15% minority, 43% women. **Part-time faculty:** 236 total; 6% minority, 56% women. **Class size:** 36% < 20, 52% 20-39, 6% 40-49, 5% 50-99, 1% >100. **Special facilities:** Planetarium, film theater, sound recording archives, popular culture library, marine biology laboratory, educational memorabilia center.

**Freshman class profile.** 11,343 applied, 9,927 admitted, 3,241 enrolled.

| Mid 50% test scores | | | |
|---|---|---|---|
| SAT critical reading: | 470-590 | Rank in top quarter: | 33% |
| SAT math: | 450-580 | Rank in top tenth: | 12% |
| ACT composite: | 19-24 | End year in good standing: | 76% |
| GPA 3.50 or higher: | 31% | Return as sophomores: | 76% |
| GPA 3.0-3.49: | 32% | Out-of-state: | 13% |
| GPA 2.0-2.99: | 37% | Live on campus: | 89% |
| | | International: | 1% |

**Basis for selection.** Admissions decision based on high school sixth semester GPA and ACT or SAT test scores. Interview recommended for all; audition required for music; portfolio required for art programs. Essays required for honors program.

**High school preparation.** Recommended units include English 4, mathematics 3, social studies 3, science 3 (laboratory 2), foreign language 2 and visual/performing arts 1.

**2007-2008 Annual costs.** Tuition/fees: $9,060; $16,368 out-of-state. Room/ board: $6,878.

**2006-2007 Financial aid. Need-based:** 3,006 full-time freshmen applied for aid; 2,363 were judged to have need; 2,336 of these received aid. Average need met was 77%. Average scholarship/grant was $6,837; average loan $5,747. 36% of total undergraduate aid awarded as scholarships/grants, 64% as loans/jobs. **Non-need-based:** Awarded to 2,547 full-time undergraduates, including 716 freshmen. Scholarships awarded for academics, alumni affiliation, art, athletics, leadership, minority status, music/drama, ROTC, state residency.

**Application procedures. Admission:** Priority date 2/1; deadline 7/15 (postmark date). $40 fee, may be waived for applicants with need. Application may be submitted online. Admission notification on a rolling basis beginning on or about 10/1. Must reply by 5/1. **Financial aid:** No deadline. FAFSA required. Applicants notified on a rolling basis starting 4/15; must reply within 3 week(s) of notification.

**Academics.** Evening degree programs and career counseling offered for adults in the greater community. **Special study options:** Accelerated study, combined bachelor's/graduate degree, cooperative education, cross-registration, distance learning, double major, dual enrollment of high school students, exchange student, honors, independent study, internships, liberal arts/career combination, student-designed major, study abroad, teacher certification program, Washington semester. **Credit/placement by examination:** AP, CLEP, SAT, ACT, institutional tests. 30 hours toward bachelor's degree through portfolio program. **Support services:** Learning center, preadmission summer program, reduced course load, remedial instruction, study skills assistance, tutoring, writing center.

**Majors. Architecture:** Environmental design, interior. **Area/ethnic studies:** African, American, Asian, women's. **Biology:** General, bacteriology, ecology. **Business:** General, accounting, fashion, finance, hospitality admin, human resources, international, logistics, management information systems, managerial economics, operations, tourism promotion, tourism/travel. **Communications:** General, broadcast journalism, journalism, public relations. **Computer sciences:** General. **Conservation:** Management/policy. **Education:** General, art, biology, business, Deaf/hearing impaired, drama/dance, English, foreign languages, French, health, kindergarten/preschool, mathematics, middle, music, physical, sales/marketing, science, social studies, special, voc/tech. **Engineering technology:** Aerospace, construction, electrical, electromechanical, industrial, mechanical, quality control. **English:** Creative writing, English lit, speech/rhetoric, technical writing. **Family/ consumer sciences:** Aging, child development, family studies, food/ nutrition. **Foreign languages:** Classics, French, German, Latin, Russian, Spanish. **Health:** Athletic training, clinical lab science, communication disorders, dietetics, environmental health, health care admin, nursing (RN). **History:** General. **Interdisciplinary:** Gerontology, neuroscience. **Legal studies:** Prelaw. **Liberal arts:** Arts/sciences. **Math:** General, applied, statistics.

**Parks/recreation:** General, sports admin. **Philosophy/religion:** Philosophy. **Physical sciences:** Chemistry, geology, physics. **Protective services:** Criminal justice. **Psychology:** General. **Public administration:** General, social work. **Social sciences:** Economics, geography, international relations, political science, sociology. **Transportation:** Aviation management. **Visual/performing arts:** Acting, art, art history/conservation, cinematography, design, dramatic, film/cinema, music history, music performance, music theory/composition, piano/organ, studio arts, theater design, voice/opera. **Other:** Ethnic Studies, Popular Culture, Telecommunications.

**Most popular majors.** Business/marketing 14%, education 24%, English 7%, health sciences 7%, visual/performing arts 8%.

**Computing on campus.** 1,854 workstations in dormitories, library, computer center, student center. Dormitories wired for high-speed internet access and linked to campus network. Commuter students can connect to campus network. Online course registration, helpline, repair service available.

**Student life. Freshman orientation:** Available. Preregistration for classes offered. Normally held in summer. **Housing:** Guaranteed on-campus for freshmen. Coed dorms, fraternity/sorority housing, substance-free housing available. $200 deposit, deadline 5/1. No-alcohol wings, nonsmoking areas, residential housing communities available. **Activities:** Bands, choral groups, dance, drama, film society, international student organizations, literary magazine, music ensembles, musical theater, radio station, student government, student newspaper, symphony orchestra, TV station, Active Christians Today, African Peoples Association, Asian Communities, United Latino Student Union, World Student Association, Women's Group, College Democrats, College Republicans, Habitat for Humanity, Environmental Action Group.

**Athletics.** NCAA. **Intercollegiate:** Baseball M, basketball, cross-country, diving, football (tackle) M, golf, gymnastics W, ice hockey M, soccer, softball W, swimming, tennis, track and field, volleyball W. **Intramural:** Basketball, cross-country, football (non-tackle), golf, handball, ice hockey, racquetball, soccer, softball, swimming, tennis, track and field, volleyball. **Team name:** Falcons.

**Student services.** Adult student services, alcohol/substance abuse counseling, career counseling, services for economically disadvantaged, student employment services, financial aid counseling, health services, legal services, minority student services, personal counseling, placement for graduates, veterans' counselor, women's services. **Physically disabled:** Services for visually, speech, hearing impaired.

**Contact.** E-mail: admissions@bgnet.bgsu.edu
Phone: (419) 372-2478 Toll-free number: (866) Cho-osebgsu
Fax: (419) 372-6955
Gary Swegan, Assistant Vice Provost/Director of Admissions, Bowling Green State University, 110 McFall Center, Bowling Green, OH 43403-0085

## Bryant & Stratton College: Parma
**Parma, Ohio**
**www.bryantstratton.edu**                    **CB code: 0577**

◗ For-profit 4-year nursing and junior college
◗ Commuter campus in small city
◗ 696 degree-seeking undergraduates: 35% part-time, 84% women, 22% African American, 1% Asian American, 11% Hispanic American
◗ Interview required

**General.** Founded in 1854. Regionally accredited. On-line classes available. **Degrees:** 12 bachelor's, 56 associate awarded. **Location:** 10 miles from Cleveland. **Calendar:** Semester, extensive summer session. **Full-time faculty:** 16 total; 12% have terminal degrees, 62% women. **Part-time faculty:** 51 total; 2% have terminal degrees, 8% minority, 39% women. **Class size:** 81% < 20, 18% 20-39, less than 1% 40-49.

**Basis for selection.** Open admission, but selective for some programs. Interview and entrance test important; high school transcript preferred. Test of Adult Basic Education required for admission. Applicants with high school diploma or GED must take reading portion; others must take full test. Portfolio recommended. **Learning Disabled:** IEP plan required.

**2008-2009 Annual costs.** Tuition/fees (projected): $13,080. Books/supplies: $1,300. Personal expenses: $2,800.

**Financial aid.** All financial aid based on need. **Additional information:** Competitive and matching scholarships offered to high school seniors.

**Application procedures. Admission:** No deadline. $25 fee. Application must be submitted on paper. Admission notification on a rolling basis.

**Financial aid:** No deadline. FAFSA required. Applicants notified on a rolling basis starting 6/1.

**Academics. Special study options:** Combined bachelor's/graduate degree, distance learning, dual enrollment of high school students, internships. **Credit/placement by examination:** AP, CLEP, IB, institutional tests. 15 credit hours maximum toward associate degree, 15 toward bachelor's. **Support services:** Learning center, remedial instruction, study skills assistance, tutoring.

**Majors. Business:** Business admin. **Health:** Nursing (RN).

**Computing on campus.** 85 workstations in library, computer center. Online library, wireless network available.

**Student life. Freshman orientation:** Mandatory. Preregistration for classes offered. **Activities:** Student government, student newspaper.

**Student services.** Adult student services, career counseling, student employment services, financial aid counseling, personal counseling, placement for graduates.

**Contact.** E-mail: flnelly@bryantstratton.edu
Phone: (216) 265-315J ext. 229 Fax: (216) 265-0325
F. Nelly, Director of Admissions, Bryant & Stratton College: Parma, 12955 Snow Road, Parma, OH 44130-1013

## Bryant & Stratton College: Willoughby Hills
**Willoughby Hills, Ohio**
**www.bryantstratton.edu**                    **CB code: 3251**

◗ For-profit 4-year business college
◗ Commuter campus in small town
◗ 520 degree-seeking undergraduates
◗ Interview required

**General. Degrees:** 5 bachelor's, 55 associate awarded. **Location:** 15 miles from downtown Cleveland. **Calendar:** Continuous, limited summer session. **Full-time faculty:** 20 total. **Part-time faculty:** 35 total. **Class size:** 80% < 20, 20% 20-39.

**Basis for selection.** Open admission. Student's evaluation and diagnostic tests must show qualification for at least pre-college, preparatory math and English courses. Applicants must complete institutional entrance evaluation, math, writing and computer diagnostic tests for placement. **Learning Disabled:** Students with learning disability must provide instructional effectiveness plan from high school counselor.

**2007-2008 Annual costs.** Tuition/fees: $14,540. Books/supplies: $1,800. Personal expenses: $300.

**Financial aid. Non-need-based:** Scholarships awarded for academics.

**Application procedures. Admission:** Closing date 9/12 (receipt date). $25 fee. Application may be submitted online. Admission notification on a rolling basis. **Financial aid:** No deadline. FAFSA required. Applicants notified on a rolling basis.

**Academics.** ACTIVUM learning system facilitates students in developing technical and career-based skills through field trips, portfolio presentations, computer simulations and internship opportunities. **Special study options:** Accelerated study, distance learning, double major, dual enrollment of high school students, independent study, internships. Professional skills center offers medical coding courses and computer certification. **Credit/placement by examination:** AP, CLEP, institutional tests. 12 credit hours maximum toward associate degree, 12 toward bachelor's. **Support services:** Remedial instruction, study skills assistance, tutoring.

**Majors. Business:** Business admin.

**Computing on campus.** 120 workstations in library, computer center. Commuter students can connect to campus network. Online library, helpline, repair service, wireless network available.

**Student life. Freshman orientation:** Mandatory. Preregistration for classes offered. Various 4-hour sessions over 1-2 days prior to start of each term. **Activities:** Student government, student newspaper, student council, Institute of Management Accountants, PC users group, campus ambassador society.

**Athletics.** NJCAA. **Intercollegiate:** Soccer M. **Team name:** Bobcats.

**Student services.** Adult student services, student employment services, financial aid counseling, placement for graduates. **Physically disabled:** Services for visually, speech, hearing impaired.

**Contact.** E-mail: mejohnson@bryantstratton.edu
Phone: (440) 944-6800 Toll-free number: (800) 327-3151
Fax: (440) 944-9260
Melanie Johnson, Director of Admissions, Bryant & Stratton College:
Willoughby Hills, 27557 Chardon Road, Willoughby Hills, OH 44092

## Capital University
Columbus, Ohio — CB member
www.capital.edu — CB code: 1099

- Private 4-year university affiliated with Evangelical Lutheran Church in America
- Residential campus in very large city
- 2,634 degree-seeking undergraduates: 12% part-time, 62% women, 9% African American, 1% Asian American, 2% Hispanic American, 1% international
- 969 degree-seeking graduate students
- 75% of applicants admitted
- SAT or ACT (ACT writing optional) required
- 57% graduate within 6 years

**General.** Founded in 1830. Regionally accredited. **Degrees:** 651 bachelor's awarded; master's, first professional offered. **ROTC:** Army, Air Force. **Location:** 3 miles from downtown. **Calendar:** Semester, limited summer session. **Full-time faculty:** 217 total; 71% have terminal degrees, 12% minority, 45% women. **Part-time faculty:** 184 total; 15% have terminal degrees, 8% minority, 53% women. **Class size:** 67% < 20, 32% 20-39, less than 1% 40-49, less than 1% 50-99, less than 1% >100.

**Freshman class profile.** 3,394 applied, 2,539 admitted, 631 enrolled.

| Mid 50% test scores | | | |
|---|---|---|---|
| SAT critical reading: | 470-590 | GPA 2.0-2.99: | 24% |
| SAT math: | 470-590 | Rank in top quarter: | 46% |
| SAT writing: | 460-570 | Rank in top tenth: | 18% |
| ACT composite: | 21-26 | Return as sophomores: | 76% |
| GPA 3.50 or higher: | 41% | Out-of-state: | 4% |
| GPA 3.0-3.49: | 35% | Live on campus: | 79% |
| | | International: | 1% |

**Basis for selection.** Academic achievement in college-preparatory curriculum most important. Recommendations, test scores, and extracurricular activities considered. Interview recommended for all; audition required for music program; portfolio recommended for art, art therapy programs. **Homeschooled:** Statement describing homeschool structure and mission, transcript of courses and grades, letter of recommendation (nonparent) required.

**High school preparation.** 18 units required. Required units include English 4, mathematics 3, social studies 3, science 3 (laboratory 2), foreign language 2 and academic electives 1. Chemistry and algebra II for nursing applicants. One fine arts recommended.

**2008-2009 Annual costs.** Tuition/fees: $27,680. Room/board: $7,150. Books/supplies: $1,000. Personal expenses: $1,724.

**Financial aid. Non-need-based:** Scholarships awarded for academics, alumni affiliation, art, minority status, music/drama, religious affiliation, ROTC, state residency.

**Application procedures. Admission:** Priority date 4/15; no deadline. $25 fee, may be waived for applicants with need. Application may be submitted online. Admission notification on a rolling basis beginning on or about 9/15. Must reply by May 1 or within 2 week(s) if notified thereafter. **Financial aid:** Priority date 2/28; no closing date. FAFSA required. Applicants notified on a rolling basis starting 3/1; must reply by 5/1.

**Academics.** Teacher certification for learning disabilities and reading. Paralegal certification available from law school. **Special study options:** Combined bachelor's/graduate degree, cooperative education, cross-registration, double major, ESL, exchange student, honors, independent study, internships, liberal arts/career combination, student-designed major, study abroad, teacher certification program, Washington semester. Dual degree engineering program with Washington University, St. Louis, and Case Western Reserve; 3-2 occupational therapy program with Washington University, St. Louis. **Credit/placement by examination:** AP, CLEP, IB, SAT, ACT, institutional tests. 27 credit hours maximum toward bachelor's degree. **Support services:** Learning center, reduced course load, remedial instruction, study skills assistance, tutoring, writing center.

**Majors. Biology:** General, biochemistry. **Business:** General, accounting, business admin, finance, human resources, managerial economics, marketing. **Communications:** General, organizational, public relations, radio/tv. **Computer sciences:** Computer science. **Conservation:** Environmental studies. **Education:** General, early childhood, middle, music, physical, special.

**Engineering:** Computer. **English:** Creative writing, English lit. **Foreign languages:** French, Spanish. **Health:** Art therapy, athletic training, nursing (RN), nursing admin. **History:** General. **Legal studies:** Prelaw. **Math:** General. **Parks/recreation:** Exercise sciences, health/fitness. **Philosophy/religion:** Philosophy, religion. **Physical sciences:** Chemistry. **Psychology:** General. **Public administration:** General, social work. **Social sciences:** Criminology, economics, international relations, political science, sociology. **Visual/performing arts:** General, art, jazz, music management, music performance, music theory/composition, piano/organ, studio arts, voice/opera.

**Most popular majors.** Business/marketing 13%, education 18%, health sciences 16%, interdisciplinary studies 6%, psychology 6%, public administration/social services 13%, social sciences 9%.

**Computing on campus.** 105 workstations in dormitories, library, computer center, student center. Dormitories wired for high-speed internet access and linked to campus network. Commuter students can connect to campus network. Online course registration, online library, helpline, wireless network available.

**Student life. Freshman orientation:** Mandatory, $200 fee. One-day program in summer, 5-day program before start of classes. **Housing:** Guaranteed on-campus for freshmen. Coed dorms, special housing for disabled, apartments, substance-free housing available. $100 nonrefundable deposit, deadline 5/1. Honors housing, self-governing areas, and group cluster housing available. **Activities:** Bands, choral groups, dance, drama, literary magazine, music ensembles, musical theater, radio station, student government, student newspaper, symphony orchestra, TV station, Black student union, Young Republicans, Campus Democrats, Circle K, Ebony Brotherhood Association, international student association, Capateers (volunteers), Habitat for Humanity, university programming.

**Athletics.** NCAA. **Intercollegiate:** Baseball M, basketball, cross-country, football (tackle) M, golf, soccer, softball W, tennis, track and field, volleyball W. **Intramural:** Basketball, football (non-tackle), soccer, softball, tennis, volleyball. **Team name:** Crusaders.

**Student services.** Campus ministries, career counseling, student employment services, financial aid counseling, health services, minority student services, personal counseling, placement for graduates, veterans' counselor.

**Contact.** E-mail: admissions@capital.edu
Phone: (614) 236-6101 Toll-free number: (866) 544-6175
Fax: (614) 236-6926
Kimberly Ebbrecht, Director of Admission, Capital University, One College and Main, Columbus, OH 43209-2394

## Case Western Reserve University
Cleveland, Ohio — CB member
www.case.edu — CB code: 1105

- Private 4-year university
- Residential campus in very large city
- 4,120 degree-seeking undergraduates: 3% part-time, 42% women, 5% African American, 16% Asian American, 2% Hispanic American, 3% international
- 5,376 degree-seeking graduate students
- 75% of applicants admitted
- SAT or ACT with writing, application essay required
- 81% graduate within 6 years; 43% enter graduate study

**General.** Founded in 1826. Regionally accredited. **Degrees:** 903 bachelor's awarded; master's, doctoral, first professional offered. **ROTC:** Army, Air Force. **Location:** 4 miles from downtown. **Calendar:** Semester, extensive summer session. **Full-time faculty:** 727 total; 90% have terminal degrees, 16% minority, 41% women. **Part-time faculty:** 196 total; 66% have terminal degrees, 7% minority, 38% women. **Class size:** 62% < 20, 22% 20-39, 6% 40-49, 6% 50-99, 4% >100. **Special facilities:** Biology field station, observatory, interdisciplinary research centers, natural history museum, historical society, botanical garden.

**Freshman class profile.** 7,297 applied, 5,452 admitted, 1,133 enrolled.

| Mid 50% test scores | | | |
|---|---|---|---|
| SAT critical reading: | 580-690 | Return as sophomores: | 91% |
| SAT math: | 620-720 | Out-of-state: | 49% |
| SAT writing: | 580-680 | Live on campus: | 96% |
| ACT composite: | 26-31 | International: | 3% |
| Rank in top quarter: | 92% | Fraternities: | 33% |
| Rank in top tenth: | 66% | Sororities: | 26% |

**Basis for selection.** School achievement record and test scores most important. School and community activities, essays, recommendations, and interview also considered. Special consideration to applicants from culturally, educationally, or economically disadvantaged backgrounds. IELTS, AP International English test, or TOEFL required for all international students. Interview recommended for all; audition required for music, music education programs; portfolio required for art education program. Writing sample required. **Homeschooled:** Transcript of courses and grades, interview required. ACT/SAT scores required; at least 3 SAT Subject Tests highly recommended. Students are encouraged to submit at least two letters from outside instructors or employers.

**High school preparation.** 16 units required. Required and recommended units include English 4, mathematics 3-4, social studies 3-4, science 3 (laboratory 2-3) and foreign language 2-3. 3 laboratory science recommended. 4 mathematics, 1 chemistry and physics recommended for engineering. 3 laboratory science (1 chemistry) recommended for science, mathematics, and premedical.

**2007-2008 Annual costs.** Tuition/fees: $33,908. $400 technology fee for resident students only. Room/board: $9,938.

**2007-2008 Financial aid. Need-based:** 956 full-time freshmen applied for aid; 790 were judged to have need; 790 of these received aid. Average need met was 91%. Average scholarship/grant was $24,021; average loan $6,206. 72% of total undergraduate aid awarded as scholarships/grants, 28% as loans/jobs. **Non-need-based:** Awarded to 2,942 full-time undergraduates, including 890 freshmen. Scholarships awarded for academics, art, leadership, music/drama.

**Application procedures. Admission:** Closing date 1/15 (postmark date). No application fee. Application must be submitted online. Admission notification 4/1. Must reply by 5/1. **Financial aid:** Priority date 2/1; no closing date. FAFSA, institutional form required. Applicants notified on a rolling basis starting 2/15; must reply by 5/1 or within 2 week(s) of notification.

**Academics.** Preprofessional Scholars Program gives talented undergraduates conditional acceptances to graduate schools of medicine, dentistry, law, and social work. Most programs allow students to pursue combined bachelor's/master's. **Special study options:** Accelerated study, combined bachelor's/graduate degree, cooperative education, cross-registration, double major, dual enrollment of high school students, ESL, exchange student, honors, independent study, internships, liberal arts/career combination, student-designed major, study abroad, teacher certification program, Washington semester. Exchange program with Fisk University, 3-2 binary program in engineering, biochemistry, and astronomy. **Credit/placement by examination:** AP, CLEP, IB, institutional tests. **Support services:** Learning center, pre-admission summer program, reduced course load, study skills assistance, tutoring, writing center.

**Majors. Area/ethnic studies:** American, Asian, French, German, Japanese, women's. **Biology:** General, biochemistry, evolutionary. **Business:** Accounting, business admin. **Computer sciences:** General, computer science. **Conservation:** Environmental studies. **Education:** Art, music. **Engineering:** General, aerospace, biomedical, chemical, civil, computer, electrical, materials, materials science, mechanical, physics, polymer, systems. **English:** English lit. **Family/consumer sciences:** Human nutrition. **Foreign languages:** Classics, comparative lit, French, German, Spanish. **Health:** Communication disorders, dietetics, nursing (RN). **History:** General, science/technology. **Interdisciplinary:** Cognitive science, gerontology, natural sciences, nutrition sciences. **Math:** General, applied, statistics. **Philosophy/religion:** Philosophy, religion. **Physical sciences:** Astronomy, chemistry, geology, physics. **Psychology:** General. **Social sciences:** Anthropology, economics, international relations, political science, sociology. **Visual/performing arts:** Art history/conservation, dramatic. **Other:** Systems Biology.

**Most popular majors.** Biology 10%, business/marketing 9%, engineering/engineering technologies 28%, health sciences 8%, physical sciences 8%, psychology 8%, social sciences 10%.

**Computing on campus.** 415 workstations in dormitories, library, computer center, student center. Dormitories wired for high-speed internet access and linked to campus network. Commuter students can connect to campus network. Online course registration, online library, helpline, repair service, student web hosting, wireless network available.

**Student life. Freshman orientation:** Mandatory, $370 fee. Preregistration for classes offered. Four 3-day sessions beginning in July. **Housing:** Guaranteed on-campus for freshmen. Coed dorms, apartments, fraternity/sorority housing, substance-free housing available. Residential colleges for first-year students. Secured female-only floor available. Special-interest housing available. **Activities:** Bands, campus ministries, choral groups, dance, drama, film society, international student organizations, literary magazine, music ensembles, Model UN, musical theater, radio station, student government, student newspaper, symphony orchestra, University Christian Movement, Hillel Foundation, African-American Society, College Democrats, College Republicans, Habitat for Humanity.

**Athletics.** NCAA. **Intercollegiate:** Baseball M, basketball, cross-country, football (tackle) M, soccer, softball W, swimming, tennis, track and field, volleyball W, wrestling M. **Intramural:** Badminton, basketball, bowling, cross-country, football (non-tackle), football (tackle) M, golf, racquetball, soccer, softball, squash, swimming, table tennis, tennis, track and field, volleyball, water polo, weight lifting, wrestling M. **Team name:** Spartans.

**Student services.** Adult student services, alcohol/substance abuse counseling, campus ministries, career counseling, student employment services, financial aid counseling, health services, legal services, minority student services, personal counseling, placement for graduates, veterans' counselor, women's services. **Physically disabled:** Services for visually, speech, hearing impaired.

**Contact.** E-mail: admission@case.edu
Phone: (216) 368-4450 Fax: (216) 368-5111
Elizabeth Woyczynski, Director of Undergraduate Admission, Case Western Reserve University, Tomlinson Hall, Cleveland, OH 44106-7055

## Cedarville University
**Cedarville, Ohio**
**www.cedarville.edu**                    CB code: 1151

- Private 4-year university and liberal arts college affiliated with Baptist faith
- Residential campus in small town
- 2,951 degree-seeking undergraduates: 3% part-time, 55% women, 1% African American, 1% Asian American, 2% Hispanic American, 1% international
- 40 degree-seeking graduate students
- 76% of applicants admitted
- SAT or ACT (ACT writing recommended), application essay required
- 69% graduate within 6 years; 29% enter graduate study

**General.** Founded in 1887. Regionally accredited. **Degrees:** 702 bachelor's awarded; master's offered. **ROTC:** Army, Air Force. **Location:** 12 miles from Springfield, 20 miles from Dayton. **Calendar:** Semester, limited summer session. **Full-time faculty:** 212 total; 61% have terminal degrees, 6% minority, 27% women. **Part-time faculty:** 20 total; 5% minority, 60% women. **Class size:** 64% <20, 27% 20-39, 2% 40-49, 5% 50-99, 1% >100.

**Freshman class profile.** 2,654 applied, 2,014 admitted, 762 enrolled.

| Mid 50% test scores | | | |
|---|---|---|---|
| SAT critical reading: | 540-660 | Rank in top quarter: | 67% |
| SAT math: | 530-650 | Rank in top tenth: | 37% |
| SAT writing: | 520-640 | End year in good standing: | 92% |
| ACT composite: | 23-29 | Return as sophomores: | 85% |
| GPA 3.50 or higher: | 69% | Out-of-state: | 68% |
| GPA 3.0-3.49: | 24% | Live on campus: | 98% |
| GPA 2.0-2.99: | 7% | International: | 1% |

**Basis for selection.** Clear testimony of personal faith in Jesus Christ, evidence of consistent Christian lifestyle, above-average academic performance (academic records, class rank, test scores), personal references considered. Applications reviewed on a rolling basis. SAT and SAT Subject Tests or ACT recommended. Audition required for music majors; interview recommended for academically marginal students. **Learning Disabled:** Students encouraged to contact Coordinator of Disabilities Services.

**High school preparation.** Recommended units include English 4, mathematics 4, social studies 3, science 3 (laboratory 3) and foreign language 3. Additional mathematics and science recommended for nursing, science, engineering, and mathematics applicants.

**2007-2008 Annual costs.** Tuition/fees: $19,680. Room/board: $5,010. Books/supplies: $900. Personal expenses: $1,450.

**2006-2007 Financial aid. Need-based:** 654 full-time freshmen applied for aid; 499 were judged to have need; 498 of these received aid. Average need met was 34%. Average scholarship/grant was $2,905; average loan $2,687. 49% of total undergraduate aid awarded as scholarships/grants, 51% as loans/jobs. **Non-need-based:** Awarded to 2,190 full-time undergraduates, including 718 freshmen. Scholarships awarded for academics, alumni affiliation, athletics, leadership, minority status, music/drama, ROTC, state residency.

**Application procedures. Admission:** Priority date 3/1; no deadline. $30 fee, may be waived for applicants with need. Application may be submitted online. Admission notification on a rolling basis beginning on or about 8/1. Must reply by May 1 or within 2 week(s) if notified thereafter. **Financial aid:** Priority date 3/1; no closing date. FAFSA required. Applicants notified on a rolling basis starting 3/1; must reply within 4 week(s) of notification.

**Academics.** Special study options: Accelerated study, cooperative education, distance learning, double major, dual enrollment of high school students, honors, independent study, internships, liberal arts/career combination, student-designed major, study abroad, teacher certification program, Washington semester. **Credit/placement by examination:** AP, CLEP, IB, SAT, ACT, institutional tests. 40 credit hours maximum toward bachelor's degree. **Support services:** Reduced course load, remedial instruction, study skills assistance, tutoring, writing center.

**Majors.** **Area/ethnic studies:** American. **Biology:** General, cellular/molecular. **Business:** Accounting, business admin, finance, international, management information systems, marketing. **Communications:** General, radio/tv. **Communications technology:** General. **Computer sciences:** General, computer science. **Education:** Biology, early childhood, elementary, English, mathematics, middle, music, physical, physics, science, social studies, Spanish, special. **Engineering:** Computer, electrical, mechanical. **English:** English lit, technical writing. **Foreign languages:** Spanish. **Health:** Athletic training, clinical lab science, nursing (RN), predental, premedicine, preveterinary. **History:** General. **Interdisciplinary:** Global studies. **Legal studies:** Prelaw. **Math:** General. **Parks/recreation:** Exercise sciences, health/fitness, sports admin. **Philosophy/religion:** Philosophy. **Physical sciences:** Chemistry, physics. **Protective services:** Forensics, law enforcement admin. **Psychology:** General. **Public administration:** General, social work. **Social sciences:** General, political science, sociology. **Theology:** Missionary, pastoral counseling, religious ed, sacred music, theology, youth ministry. **Visual/performing arts:** Dramatic, graphic design, music pedagogy, music performance, music theory/composition, studio arts.

**Most popular majors.** Business/marketing 13%, communications/journalism 6%, education 17%, engineering/engineering technologies 6%, health sciences 10%, psychology 6%, theological studies 10%.

**Computing on campus.** 1,800 workstations in dormitories, library, student center. Dormitories linked to campus network. Commuter students can connect to campus network. Online course registration, helpline, repair service, wireless network available.

**Student life.** **Freshman orientation:** Mandatory, $105 fee. **Policies:** Alcohol, tobacco, and drugs prohibited. Religious observance required. **Housing:** Guaranteed on-campus for all undergraduates. Single-sex dorms, apartments available. $250 deposit, deadline 5/1. **Activities:** Bands, campus ministries, choral groups, drama, music ensembles, musical theater, radio station, student government, student newspaper, symphony orchestra, College Republicans, Emergency Medical Squad, Earth Stewardship Organization, Fellowship for World Missions, Students for Social Justice, Society for Technical Communicators, Society of Automotive Engineers International.

**Athletics.** NAIA, NCCAA. **Intercollegiate:** Baseball M, basketball, cheerleading, cross-country, golf M, soccer, softball W, tennis, track and field, volleyball W. **Intramural:** Badminton, basketball, bowling, cross-country, football (tackle) M, golf, racquetball, soccer, softball, table tennis, tennis, volleyball. **Team name:** Yellow Jackets.

**Student services.** Campus ministries, career counseling, student employment services, financial aid counseling, health services, personal counseling, placement for graduates, veterans' counselor. **Physically disabled:** Services for visually impaired.

**Contact.** E-mail: admissions@cedarville.edu
Phone: (937) 766-7700 Toll-free number: (800) 233-2784
Fax: (937) 766-7575
Roscoe Smith, Director of Admissions, Cedarville University, 251 North Main Street, Cedarville, OH 45314

---

## Central State University
**Wilberforce, Ohio**
www.centralstate.edu

**CB member**
**CB code: 1107**

- Public 4-year university and liberal arts college
- Residential campus in rural community
- 1,955 degree-seeking undergraduates: 7% part-time, 49% women, 92% African American, 1% Hispanic American
- 25 degree-seeking graduate students
- 38% of applicants admitted
- SAT or ACT (ACT writing optional) required

**General.** Founded in 1887. Regionally accredited. Ohio's only public historically black university. **Degrees:** 169 bachelor's awarded; master's offered. **ROTC:** Army, Air Force. **Location:** 18 miles from Dayton. **Calendar:** Semester, limited summer session. **Full-time faculty:** 106 total; 76% minority, 32% women. **Part-time faculty:** 76 total; 80% minority, 54% women. **Class size:** 60% < 20, 39% 20-39, less than 1% 40-49, less than

1% 50-99. **Special facilities:** Afro-American museum, hydraulics laboratory, computer numerically controlled equipment for machining and robotic welding, business incubator.

**Freshman class profile.** 5,717 applied, 2,159 admitted, 571 enrolled.

| Mid 50% test scores | | | |
|---|---|---|---|
| SAT critical reading: | 350-450 | GPA 2.0-2.99: | 64% |
| SAT math: | 340-450 | Rank in top quarter: | 16% |
| ACT composite: | 14-18 | Rank in top tenth: | 5% |
| GPA 3.50 or higher: | 4% | Return as sophomores: | 54% |
| GPA 3.0-3.49: | 12% | Out-of-state: | 46% |
| | | Live on campus: | 91% |

**Basis for selection.** Out-of-state residents must have 2.5 high school GPA and ACT score of 19 or SAT score of 910. Ohio residents must have 2.0 high school GPA and ACT score of 15 or SAT score of 720. Interview recommended. Personal essay required for admissions appeal process. **Homeschooled:** Transcript of courses and grades, state high school equivalency certificate, interview, letter of recommendation (nonparent) required. Ohio students need ONGP test results or OGT.

**High school preparation.** 16 units recommended. Recommended units include English 4, mathematics 3, social studies 3, science 3 and foreign language 2. 1 art recommended.

**2007-2008 Annual costs.** Tuition/fees: $5,294; $11,462 out-of-state. Room/board: $7,402. Books/supplies: $1,000. Personal expenses: $1,400.

**2007-2008 Financial aid.** **Need-based:** 561 full-time freshmen applied for aid; 522 were judged to have need; 521 of these received aid. 41% of total undergraduate aid awarded as scholarships/grants, 59% as loans/jobs. **Non-need-based:** Awarded to 521 full-time undergraduates, including 164 freshmen. Scholarships awarded for academics, alumni affiliation, art, athletics, leadership, music/drama, religious affiliation, ROTC.

**Application procedures.** **Admission:** No deadline. $20 fee, may be waived for applicants with need. Application may be submitted online. Admission notification on a rolling basis. **Financial aid:** Priority date 2/15; no closing date. FAFSA, institutional form required. Applicants notified on a rolling basis starting 5/1.

**Academics.** Special study options: Combined bachelor's/graduate degree, cooperative education, cross-registration, double major, honors, independent study, internships, study abroad, teacher certification program. **Credit/placement by examination:** AP, CLEP, SAT, ACT, institutional tests. 30 credit hours maximum toward bachelor's degree. **Support services:** Learning center, pre-admission summer program, reduced course load, tutoring, writing center.

**Majors.** **Biology:** General. **Business:** General, accounting. **Communications:** Broadcast journalism, radio/tv. **Computer sciences:** Computer science. **Education:** Early childhood, middle, multi-level teacher, secondary, special. **Engineering:** Environmental, manufacturing, water resource. **Engineering technology:** Industrial. **English:** English lit. **History:** General. **Math:** General. **Parks/recreation:** General. **Physical sciences:** Chemistry, geology. **Protective services:** Criminal justice. **Psychology:** General. **Public administration:** Social work. **Social sciences:** Economics, political science, sociology. **Visual/performing arts:** Art, jazz, music performance.

**Most popular majors.** Business/marketing 27%, communications/journalism 10%, education 15%, engineering/engineering technologies 7%, parks/recreation 7%, psychology 7%, social sciences 10%.

**Computing on campus.** 400 workstations in library, computer center, student center. Dormitories wired for high-speed internet access and linked to campus network. Online course registration, online library, helpline, wireless network available.

**Student life.** **Freshman orientation:** Mandatory, $125 fee. Preregistration for classes offered. **Housing:** Guaranteed on-campus for freshmen. Coed dorms, single-sex dorms available. $195 fully refundable deposit, deadline 8/1. **Activities:** Bands, campus ministries, choral groups, dance, drama, music ensembles, radio station, student government, student newspaper, TV station.

**Athletics.** NCAA. **Intercollegiate:** Basketball, cross-country, football (tackle) M, golf, tennis, track and field, volleyball. **Intramural:** Basketball, cross-country, football (non-tackle) M, racquetball, tennis. **Team name:** Marauders.

**Student services.** Alcohol/substance abuse counseling, campus ministries, career counseling, services for economically disadvantaged, student employment services, financial aid counseling, health services, on-campus daycare, personal counseling, placement for graduates.

**Contact.** E-mail: admissions@centralstate.edu
Phone: (937) 376-6348 Toll-free number: (800) 388-2781
Fax: (937) 376-6648
Robin Rucker, Associate Director of Admissions, Central State University,
PO Box 1004, Wilberforce, OH 45384-1004

## Cincinnati Christian University
Cincinnati, Ohio
www.ccuniversity.edu                          CB code: 1091

▶ Private 4-year university affiliated with Church of Christ/Christian
   Church
▶ Residential campus in very large city
▶ 775 degree-seeking undergraduates
▶ 202 graduate students
▶ SAT or ACT (ACT writing optional), application essay required

**General.** Founded in 1924. Regionally accredited; also accredited by ABHE.
Member of Greater Cincinnati Consortium of Colleges and Universities.
**Degrees:** 97 bachelor's, 6 associate awarded; master's, first professional
offered. **Location:** 10 miles from downtown. **Calendar:** Semester, limited
summer session. **Full-time faculty:** 34 total. **Part-time faculty:** 38 total.
**Class size:** 66% < 20, 25% 20-39, 3% 40-49, 5% 50-99.

### Freshman class profile.

| Mid 50% test scores | | | |
|---|---|---|---|
| SAT critical reading: | 450-580 | ACT composite: | 19-25 |
| SAT math: | 430-570 | Out-of-state: | 40% |
| SAT writing: | 430-560 | Live on campus: | 81% |

**Basis for selection.** High school academic record and standardized test
scores important. Minimum 2.5 GPA, 17 ACT composite/SAT 1215 for unconditional admission. Applicants age 25 or older can substitute English
proficiency test and essay for SAT/ACT requirement. Audition required for
music programs. **Learning Disabled:** GPA and standardized test scores must
meet minimum acceptance standards.

**2008-2009 Annual costs.** Tuition/fees (projected): $11,840. Room/
board: $6,260. Books/supplies: $800. Personal expenses: $1,950.

**2006-2007 Financial aid. Need-based:** 38% of total undergraduate aid
awarded as scholarships/grants, 62% as loans/jobs.

**Application procedures. Admission:** Closing date 7/1 (postmark date).
$40 fee, may be waived for applicants with need. Application may be sub-
mitted online. Admission notification on a rolling basis. **Financial aid:** Priority date 3/1; no closing date. FAFSA required. Applicants notified by 4/5;
must reply by 6/5 or within 2 week(s) of notification.

**Academics. Special study options:** Cross-registration, distance learning,
double major, independent study, internships, teacher certification program.
Adult degree completion program. **Credit/placement by examination:** AP,
CLEP, IB, institutional tests. 15 credit hours maximum toward associate
degree, 30 toward bachelor's. **Support services:** Learning center, reduced
course load, remedial instruction, study skills assistance, tutoring, writing
center.

**Majors. Computer sciences:** Data processing, information technology, LAN/
WAN management, programming. **Education:** Early childhood, elementary, middle, secondary, special. **Philosophy/religion:** Christian. **Psychology:** General. **Theology:** Bible, missionary, religious ed, sacred music.

**Most popular majors.** Education 11%, theological studies 70%.

**Computing on campus.** 57 workstations in dormitories, library, computer center, student center. Dormitories wired for high-speed internet access and linked to campus network. Online library, helpline, repair service,
wireless network available.

**Student life. Freshman orientation:** Mandatory. Preregistration for classes
offered. **Housing:** Guaranteed on-campus for all undergraduates. Single-sex
dorms, substance-free housing available. $75 nonrefundable deposit. **Activi-
ties:** Concert band, choral groups, drama, music ensembles, student government, student newspaper.

**Athletics.** NCCAA. **Intercollegiate:** Baseball M, basketball, soccer, volleyball W. **Intramural:** Basketball, cheerleading, football (tackle) M, soccer, track and field, volleyball. **Team name:** Eagles.

**Student services.** Career counseling, student employment services, financial aid counseling, health services, personal counseling. **Physically disabled:** Services for hearing impaired.

**Contact.** E-mail: cbcadmission@ccuniversity.edu
Phone: (513) 244-8141 Toll-free number: (800) 949-4228
Fax: (513) 244-8140
Jenny Baker, Admissions Director, Cincinnati Christian University, 2700
Glenway Avenue, Cincinnati, OH 45204-3200

## Cincinnati College of Mortuary Science
Cincinnati, Ohio
www.ccms.edu                                  CB code: 0945

▶ Private 4-year school of mortuary science
▶ Commuter campus in large city
▶ 125 degree-seeking undergraduates

**General.** Founded in 1882. Regionally accredited. **Degrees:** 32 bachelor's,
57 associate awarded. **Location:** 3 miles from downtown. **Calendar:** Quarter. **Full-time faculty:** 10 total. **Part-time faculty:** 4 total. **Class size:** 100%
50-99.

**Basis for selection.** Open admission.

**High school preparation.** 15 units recommended. Recommended units
include English 3, mathematics 1, social studies 2 and science 2.

**2007-2008 Annual costs.** Tuition/fees: $14,250. Books/supplies: $2,500.

**Financial aid.** All financial aid based on need.

**Application procedures. Admission:** No deadline. $25 fee. Applica-
tion may be submitted online. Admission notification on a rolling basis.
**Financial aid:** Priority date 7/1; no closing date. FAFSA required. Applicants notified on a rolling basis starting 3/1; must reply within 2 week(s) of
notification.

**Academics.** Program of study contingent on licensing requirements of
state in which student will practice. **Special study options:** Internships.
**Credit/placement by examination:** AP, CLEP, institutional tests. 41 credit
hours maximum toward associate degree, 56 toward bachelor's. **Support
services:** Reduced course load, tutoring.

**Majors. Personal/culinary services:** Mortuary science.

**Student life. Freshman orientation:** Mandatory. Preregistration for classes
offered. **Housing:** Some housing available in local funeral homes.

**Student services.** Career counseling, student employment services, personal counseling, veterans' counselor. **Physically disabled:** Services for hearing impaired.

**Contact.** Phone: (513) 761-2020 Fax: (513) 761-3333
Financial Aid/Admissions Officer, Cincinnati College of Mortuary Science,
645 West North Bend Road, Cincinnati, OH 45224-1428

## Cleveland Institute of Art
Cleveland, Ohio                               CB member
www.cia.edu                                   CB code: 1152

▶ Private 4-year visual arts college
▶ Commuter campus in very large city
▶ 478 degree-seeking undergraduates: 3% part-time, 53% women
▶ 3 degree-seeking graduate students
▶ 71% of applicants admitted
▶ SAT or ACT (ACT writing optional), application essay required
▶ 66% graduate within 6 years

**General.** Founded in 1882. Regionally accredited. **Degrees:** 109 bachelor's awarded; master's offered. **ROTC:** Army, Naval, Air Force. **Location:** 5 miles from downtown. **Calendar:** Semester, limited summer session. **Full-time faculty:** 43 total; 88% have terminal degrees, 9% minority,
46% women. **Part-time faculty:** 46 total; 59% have terminal degrees, 2%
minority, 46% women. **Class size:** 84% < 20, 15% 20-39, less than 1%
50-99. **Special facilities:** Individual studio spaces, woodshop, metalshop,
art galleries.

**Freshman class profile.** 407 applied, 291 admitted, 97 enrolled.

| Mid 50% test scores | | Rank in top quarter: | 31% |
|---|---|---|---|
| SAT critical reading: | 480-600 | Rank in top tenth: | 13% |
| SAT math: | 490-580 | End year in good standing: | 80% |
| ACT composite: | 19-23 | Return as sophomores: | 81% |
| GPA 3.50 or higher: | 24% | Out-of-state: | 41% |
| GPA 3.0-3.49: | 41% | Live on campus: | 70% |
| GPA 2.0-2.99: | 35% | International: | 5% |

**Basis for selection.** Portfolio of 12 to 20 pieces, high school transcripts, statement of purpose, test scores, and 2 letters of recommendation required. Interview strongly recommended. **Homeschooled:** Transcript of courses and grades, state high school equivalency certificate, letter of recommendation (nonparent) required. GED required.

**High school preparation.** 20 units recommended. Recommended units include English 4, mathematics 3, social studies 3, science 3 and academic electives 6. 2 years of art recommended.

**2007-2008 Annual costs.** Tuition/fees: $30,090. Room/board: $8,769. Books/supplies: $1,786. Personal expenses: $1,940.

**2007-2008 Financial aid. Need-based:** 83 full-time freshmen applied for aid; 78 were judged to have need; 78 of these received aid. Average need met was 63%. Average scholarship/grant was $15,597; average loan $4,607. 51% of total undergraduate aid awarded as scholarships/grants, 49% as loans/jobs. **Non-need-based:** Awarded to 99 full-time undergraduates, including 26 freshmen. Scholarships awarded for academics, art.

**Application procedures. Admission:** Priority date 7/1; no deadline. $30 fee, may be waived for applicants with need. Application may be submitted online. Admission notification on a rolling basis beginning on or about 10/1. Must reply by May 1 or within 2 week(s) if notified thereafter. **Financial aid:** Priority date 3/15; no closing date. FAFSA, institutional form required. Applicants notified on a rolling basis starting 3/16; must reply within 4 week(s) of notification.

**Academics. Special study options:** Combined bachelor's/graduate degree, cooperative education, cross-registration, exchange student, honors, independent study, internships, New York semester, study abroad. Study for up to 2 semesters at any Alliance of Independent Colleges of Art and Design. **Credit/placement by examination:** AP, CLEP, IB. 63 credit hours maximum toward bachelor's degree. **Support services:** Reduced course load, remedial instruction, study skills assistance, tutoring, writing center.

**Majors. Health:** Medical illustrating. **Visual/performing arts:** Ceramics, commercial/advertising art, digital art, drawing, fiber arts, illustration, industrial design, interior design, metal/jewelry, painting, photography, printmaking, sculpture.

**Computing on campus.** 303 workstations in dormitories, library, computer center. Dormitories wired for high-speed internet access and linked to campus network. Commuter students can connect to campus network. Online library, wireless network available.

**Student life. Freshman orientation:** Mandatory, $130 fee. Preregistration for classes offered. Orientation in two parts: summer program for students/parents and fall orientation for students only. **Housing:** Guaranteed on-campus for freshmen. Coed dorms, apartments, fraternity/sorority housing available. $150 nonrefundable deposit, deadline 6/15. **Activities:** Student government, student newspaper, student artist association, student leadership council, nature and hiking club, student activities program board, student independent exhibition committee, gay/lesbian association, Artists for Christ, ghost hunting club, survey student gallery.

**Student services.** Alcohol/substance abuse counseling, campus ministries, student employment services, financial aid counseling, health services, personal counseling.

**Contact.** E-mail: admiss@cia.edu
Phone: (216) 421-7418 Toll-free number: (800) 223-4700
Fax: (216) 754-3634
Sheila Wendeln, Director of Admissions, Cleveland Institute of Art, 11141 East Boulevard, Cleveland, OH 44106-1710

## Cleveland Institute of Music
**Cleveland, Ohio**
**www.cim.edu**                    **CB code: 1124**

- Private 4-year music college
- Residential campus in very large city
- 228 degree-seeking undergraduates
- 32% of applicants admitted
- SAT or ACT (ACT writing optional), application essay required

**General.** Founded in 1920. Regionally accredited. **Degrees:** 52 bachelor's awarded; master's, doctoral offered. **Location:** 2 miles from downtown. **Calendar:** Semester, limited summer session. **Full-time faculty:** 42 total. **Part-time faculty:** 69 total. **Special facilities:** Electronic music studios, audio recording facilities, large record, tape, CD library, technology learning center.

**Freshman class profile.** 524 applied, 169 admitted, 60 enrolled.

| Out-of-state: | 77% | Live on campus: | 100% |
|---|---|---|---|

**Basis for selection.** Audition most important. High school record, test scores, and letters of recommendation also reviewed. Incoming students must have scholastic and musical skills prerequisite to entering highly intensive, professionally oriented program. Institutional examinations including sight singing, ear training, and keyboard harmony required. Audition required. **Homeschooled:** Transcript of courses and grades required.

**High school preparation.** 16 units recommended. Recommended units include English 4, mathematics 3, social studies 3, science 3 and foreign language 3.

**2008-2009 Annual costs.** Tuition/fees (projected): $34,482. Room/board: $10,480. Books/supplies: $1,240. Personal expenses: $1,000.

**Financial aid. Non-need-based:** Scholarships awarded for academics, music/drama.

**Application procedures. Admission:** Closing date 12/1 (receipt date). $100 fee. Application must be submitted online. Admission notification 4/1. Admission notification on a rolling basis beginning on or about 3/1. Must reply by 5/1. Deferred admission from fall to spring semesters is dependent upon space availability. **Financial aid:** Priority date 2/15; no closing date. FAFSA, institutional form required. Applicants notified on a rolling basis starting 4/1; must reply by 5/1 or within 2 week(s) of notification.

**Academics. Special study options:** Cross-registration, double major, ESL, independent study, study abroad. **Credit/placement by examination:** AP, CLEP, IB, SAT, ACT, institutional tests. **Support services:** Learning center, reduced course load, remedial instruction, study skills assistance, tutoring, writing center.

**Majors. Communications technology:** Recording arts. **Visual/performing arts:** Music performance, music theory/composition, voice/opera.

**Computing on campus.** 36 workstations in dormitories, library, computer center, student center. Dormitories wired for high-speed internet access and linked to campus network. Helpline, repair service, wireless network available.

**Student life. Freshman orientation:** Mandatory. Held before the start of classes. **Policies:** Library privileges available through Case Western Reserve University. **Housing:** Coed dorms, substance-free housing available. **Activities:** Jazz band, choral groups, dance, drama, music ensembles, opera, student government, student newspaper, symphony orchestra, most student activities, athletics and student services available through Case Western Reserve University.

**Student services.** Alcohol/substance abuse counseling, career counseling, student employment services, financial aid counseling, health services, personal counseling, placement for graduates, veterans' counselor.

**Contact.** E-mail: cimadmission@po.cwru.edu
Phone: (216) 795-3107 Fax: (216) 795-3161
William Fay, Director of Admission, Cleveland Institute of Music, 11021 East Boulevard, Cleveland, OH 44106

## Cleveland State University
**Cleveland, Ohio**                    **CB member**
**www.csuohio.edu**                    **CB code: 1221**

- Public 4-year university
- Commuter campus in very large city
- 9,221 degree-seeking undergraduates: 24% part-time, 56% women, 23% African American, 3% Asian American, 3% Hispanic American, 2% international
- 4,777 degree-seeking graduate students

**General.** Founded in 1964. Regionally accredited. **Degrees:** 1,784 bachelor's awarded; master's, doctoral, first professional offered. **ROTC:** Army, Naval. **Calendar:** Semester, extensive summer session. **Full-time faculty:** 571 total; 92% have terminal degrees, 23% minority, 37% women. **Part-time faculty:** 453 total; 9% have terminal degrees, 18% minority, 52% women. **Class size:** 40% < 20, 44% 20-39, 6% 40-49, 8% 50-99, 2% >100.

**Freshman class profile.** 3,752 applied, 2,742 admitted, 1,196 enrolled.

| Mid 50% test scores | | | |
|---|---|---|---|
| SAT critical reading: | 400-530 | Rank in top quarter: | 28% |
| SAT math: | 400-550 | Rank in top tenth: | 11% |
| ACT composite: | 17-22 | Out-of-state: | 5% |
| GPA 3.50 or higher: | 18% | Live on campus: | 24% |
| GPA 3.0-3.49: | 26% | International: | 1% |
| GPA 2.0-2.99: | 51% | Fraternities: | 3% |
| | | Sororities: | 3% |

**Basis for selection.** Open admission, but selective for some programs and for out-of-state students. Special requirements for education and engineering programs. SAT/ACT must be submitted for counseling purposes, but scores not considered in admission decisions. Audition required for music majors.

**High school preparation.** 13 units required; 16 recommended. Required and recommended units include English 4, mathematics 4, social studies 1-3, science 2-3 (laboratory 1) and foreign language 2. 1 art recommended.

**2007-2008 Annual costs.** Tuition/fees: $7,920; $10,664 out-of-state. Room/board: $8,098. Books/supplies: $800. Personal expenses: $3,776.

**2007-2008 Financial aid. Need-based:** Average need met was 34%. Average scholarship/grant was $5,970; average loan $3,922. 36% of total undergraduate aid awarded as scholarships/grants, 64% as loans/jobs. **Non-need-based:** Scholarships awarded for academics, alumni affiliation, art, athletics, leadership, minority status, music/drama, religious affiliation, ROTC.

**Application procedures. Admission:** Priority date 7/15; deadline 8/15. $30 fee, may be waived for applicants with need. Application may be submitted online. Admission notification on a rolling basis beginning on or about 9/1. **Financial aid:** Priority date 2/15; no closing date. FAFSA required. Applicants notified on a rolling basis starting 3/15; must reply within 4 week(s) of notification.

**Academics. Special study options:** Accelerated study, cooperative education, cross-registration, distance learning, double major, dual enrollment of high school students, ESL, exchange student, honors, internships, student-designed major, study abroad, teacher certification program. **Credit/placement by examination:** AP, CLEP, IB, institutional tests. 90 credit hours maximum toward bachelor's degree. Unlimited AP exam credits accepted. **Support services:** Learning center, reduced course load, remedial instruction, study skills assistance, tutoring, writing center.

**Majors. Area/ethnic studies:** French, German, Italian, Spanish/Iberian, women's. **Business:** Accounting, finance, international, labor relations, management information systems, managerial economics, marketing, statistics. **Communications:** General. **Computer sciences:** General. **Conservation:** General, environmental studies. **Education:** Early childhood, elementary, physical, special. **Engineering:** Chemical, civil, electrical, mechanical. **Engineering technology:** Electrical. **English:** English lit. **Foreign languages:** French, German, linguistics, Spanish. **Health:** Audiology/hearing, nursing (RN). **History:** General. **Liberal arts:** Arts/sciences. **Math:** General. **Philosophy/religion:** Philosophy, religion. **Physical sciences:** Chemistry, geology, physics. **Psychology:** General. **Public administration:** Social work. **Social sciences:** General, anthropology, economics, political science, sociology, urban studies. **Visual/performing arts:** Art, dramatic.

**Most popular majors.** Business/marketing 19%, communications/journalism 9%, education 11%, engineering/engineering technologies 8%, health sciences 7%, psychology 7%, social sciences 14%.

**Computing on campus.** 711 workstations in dormitories, library, computer center, student center. Dormitories wired for high-speed internet access and linked to campus network. Online library, helpline available.

**Student life. Freshman orientation:** Available, $25 fee. Preregistration for classes offered. All-day program during summer. **Housing:** Coed dorms, fraternity/sorority housing available. $150 nonrefundable deposit, deadline 1/19. **Activities:** Bands, campus ministries, choral groups, dance, drama, film society, international student organizations, literary magazine, music ensembles, musical theater, opera, radio station, student government, student newspaper, symphony orchestra, Newman Center, Los Latinos Unidos, Hillel, University Christian Movement, Organization for Afro-American Unity, NAACP, environmental action group, College Democrats and Republicans.

**Athletics.** NCAA. **Intercollegiate:** Baseball M, basketball, cross-country W, diving, fencing, golf, soccer, softball W, swimming, tennis, track and field W, volleyball W, wrestling M. **Intramural:** Badminton, basketball, bowling, cross-country, fencing, field hockey W, golf, handball, racquetball, rowing (crew), sailing, soccer, squash, swimming, table tennis, tennis, track and field, volleyball, water polo, wrestling M. **Team name:** Vikings.

**Student services.** Adult student services, career counseling, student employment services, health services, personal counseling, placement for graduates, veterans' counselor. **Physically disabled:** Services for visually, speech, hearing impaired. **Learning disabled:** Comprehensive services available.

**Contact.** E-mail: admissions@csuohio.edu
Phone: (216) 687-2100 Toll-free number: (800) 278-6446
Fax: (216) 687-9210
Mark Nazario, Director, Undergraduate Admissions, Cleveland State University, 1806 East 22nd Street, Cleveland, OH 44115-2403

---

## College of Mount St. Joseph

Cincinnati, Ohio                                    CB member
www.msj.edu                                       CB code: 1129

- Private 4-year liberal arts college affiliated with Roman Catholic Church
- Commuter campus in very large city
- 1,916 degree-seeking undergraduates: 30% part-time, 68% women, 9% African American, 1% Asian American, 1% Hispanic American
- 308 degree-seeking graduate students
- 72% of applicants admitted
- SAT or ACT (ACT writing recommended) required
- 51% graduate within 6 years

**General.** Founded in 1920. Regionally accredited. **Degrees:** 366 bachelor's, 8 associate awarded; master's, doctoral offered. **ROTC:** Army, Air Force. **Location:** 7 miles from downtown Cincinnati. **Calendar:** Semester, extensive summer session. **Full-time faculty:** 117 total; 73% have terminal degrees, 5% minority, 61% women. **Part-time faculty:** 127 total; 26% have terminal degrees, 3% minority, 67% women. **Class size:** 57% < 20, 42% 20-39, 1% 40-49, less than 1% 50-99.

**Freshman class profile.** 1,153 applied, 835 admitted, 345 enrolled.

| Mid 50% test scores | | | |
|---|---|---|---|
| SAT critical reading: | 440-540 | GPA 2.0-2.99: | 31% |
| SAT math: | 440-550 | Rank in top quarter: | 33% |
| ACT composite: | 19-24 | Rank in top tenth: | 10% |
| GPA 3.50 or higher: | 28% | Return as sophomores: | 76% |
| GPA 3.0-3.49: | 40% | Out-of-state: | 16% |
| | | Live on campus: | 57% |

**Basis for selection.** Criteria for admission include college prep high school curriculum, strong grade point average, standardized test scores, evidence of leadership and extracurricular involvement, and personal background. Essays, recommendations and interviews may be required for some students. Audition required for music programs. Portfolio recommended for art programs. **Homeschooled:** Transcripts required along with any documentation from state or national home schooling accreditation agency. Also, a description of the courses completed is necessary. **Learning Disabled:** Students can apply for Project EXCEL, which helps students with learning disabilities.

**High school preparation.** 13 units required; 22 recommended. Required and recommended units include English 4, mathematics 2-4, social studies 1-2, history 1-2, science 2-4 (laboratory 1-2), foreign language 2, visual/performing arts 2 and academic electives 1-2. Mathematics must include a minimum of 1 year each of algebra and geometry. 1 fine arts required. May substitute 2 additional credits from other subjects in place of foreign language.

**2007-2008 Annual costs.** Tuition/fees: $21,200. Room/board: $6,500. Books/supplies: $800. Personal expenses: $600.

**2007-2008 Financial aid. Need-based:** 308 full-time freshmen applied for aid; 271 were judged to have need; 271 of these received aid. Average need met was 85%. Average scholarship/grant was $12,857; average loan $4,055. 54% of total undergraduate aid awarded as scholarships/grants, 46% as loans/jobs. **Non-need-based:** Awarded to 374 full-time undergraduates, including 87 freshmen. Scholarships awarded for academics, art, leadership, music/drama, ROTC, state residency. **Additional information:** College offers financial aid to full and part-time students. Unlimited, renewable merit-based scholarships offered.

**Application procedures. Admission:** Priority date 4/1; deadline 8/15 (postmark date). $25 fee, may be waived for applicants with need. Application may be submitted online. Admission notification on a rolling basis beginning on or about 10/1. Must reply by May 1 or within 4 week(s) if notified thereafter. **Financial aid:** Priority date 3/1; no closing date. FAFSA required. Applicants notified on a rolling basis starting 2/15; must reply by 5/1 or within 4 week(s) of notification.

**Academics.** Project EXCEL supports students with learning disabilities. **Special study options:** Accelerated study, cooperative education, cross-registration, distance learning, double major, honors, independent study, internships, liberal arts/career combination, study abroad, teacher certification program. **Credit/placement by examination:** AP, CLEP, IB, SAT, ACT, institutional tests. 32 credit hours maximum toward associate degree, 64 toward bachelor's. **Support services:** Learning center, reduced course load, remedial instruction, study skills assistance, tutoring, writing center.

**Majors. Biology:** General, biochemistry. **Business:** Accounting, business admin. **Communications:** General. **Computer sciences:** General. **Education:** Art, early childhood, middle, special. **English:** English lit. **Family/consumer sciences:** Aging. **Health:** Athletic training, nursing (RN). **History:** General. **Interdisciplinary:** Natural sciences. **Legal studies:** Paralegal. **Liberal arts:** Arts/sciences. **Math:** General. **Parks/recreation:** Sports admin. **Philosophy/religion:** Religion. **Physical sciences:** Chemistry. **Psychology:** General. **Public administration:** Social work. **Social sciences:** Criminology, sociology. **Theology:** Pastoral counseling, religious ed. **Visual/performing arts:** Art, graphic design, interior design, studio arts.

**Most popular majors.** Business/marketing 17%, education 9%, health sciences 29%, liberal arts 8%, visual/performing arts 10%.

**Computing on campus.** PC or laptop required. 278 workstations in library, computer center, student center. Commuter students can connect to campus network. Online course registration, online library, helpline, repair service, student web hosting, wireless network available.

**Student life. Freshman orientation:** Mandatory, $150 fee. Preregistration for classes offered. Orientation is two parts. A summer session, which includes a two-day, one night stay in the dorms and welcome weekend consisting of a service learning event, and a river cruise over the weekend before the start of classes. **Policies:** Smoke-free campus. All freshmen and sophomores under age 21 and unmarried who live outside 35-mile radius of college are required to live on campus and participate in a meal program. **Housing:** Guaranteed on-campus for freshmen. Coed dorms available. $100 fully refundable deposit, deadline 8/15. **Activities:** Bands, campus ministries, choral groups, dance, drama, literary magazine, music ensembles, musical theater, student government, student newspaper, Student Council for Exceptional Children, Circle K, Black Student Union, Alpha Phi Omega service organization, environmental awareness club, Young Democrats, Respect Life, student law club.

**Athletics. NCAA. Intercollegiate:** Baseball M, basketball, cheerleading M, cross-country, football (tackle) M, golf, lacrosse, soccer, softball W, tennis, track and field, volleyball W, wrestling M. **Intramural:** Basketball, football (non-tackle), racquetball, soccer, softball, tennis, volleyball. **Team name:** Lions.

**Student services.** Adult student services, alcohol/substance abuse counseling, campus ministries, career counseling, services for economically disadvantaged, student employment services, financial aid counseling, health services, minority student services, on-campus daycare, personal counseling, placement for graduates, veterans' counselor, women's services. **Physically disabled:** Services for visually, speech, hearing impaired. **Learning disabled:** Comprehensive services available.

**Contact.** E-mail: admissions@mail.msj.edu
Phone: (513) 244-4531 Toll-free number: (800) 654-9314
Fax: (513) 244-4629
Peggy Minnich, Director of Admission, College of Mount St. Joseph, 5701 Delhi Road, Cincinnati, OH 45233-1670

---

## College of Wooster
Wooster, Ohio
www.wooster.edu

**CB member**
**CB code: 1134**

- Private 4-year liberal arts college
- Residential campus in large town
- 1,754 degree-seeking undergraduates: 52% women, 4% African American, 3% Asian American, 2% Hispanic American, 5% international
- 74% of applicants admitted
- SAT or ACT with writing, application essay required
- 73% graduate within 6 years

**General.** Founded in 1866. Regionally accredited. **Degrees:** 433 bachelor's awarded. **Location:** 55 miles from Cleveland, 30 miles from Akron. **Calendar:** Semester, limited summer session. **Full-time faculty:** 167 total; 10% minority, 45% women. **Part-time faculty:** 23 total; 61% women. **Class size:** 58% <20, 37% 20-39, 4% 40-49, 1% 50-99, less than 1% >100.

**Freshman class profile.** 3,169 applied, 2,356 admitted, 545 enrolled.

| Mid 50% test scores | | | |
|---|---|---|---|
| SAT critical reading: | 540-670 | Rank in top tenth: | 27% |
| SAT math: | 560-650 | End year in good standing: | 97% |
| SAT writing: | 550-650 | Return as sophomores: | 86% |
| ACT composite: | 23-29 | Out-of-state: | 60% |
| GPA 3.50 or higher: | 54% | Live on campus: | 100% |
| GPA 3.0-3.49: | 34% | International: | 7% |
| GPA 2.0-2.99: | 12% | Fraternities: | 10% |
| Rank in top quarter: | 61% | Sororities: | 13% |

**Basis for selection.** Course pattern and academic performance most important. Recommendations, extracurricular activities, class rank, test scores, interview considered. Interview recommended for all; audition recommended for music; portfolio recommended for art programs.

**High school preparation.** Required and recommended units include English 4, mathematics 3-4, social studies 3-4, science 3-4, foreign language 2-3 and academic electives 2. Mathematics recommendation includes 2 algebra.

**2008-2009 Annual costs.** Tuition/fees: $33,770. Room/board: $8,650. Books/supplies: $900. Personal expenses: $600.

**2007-2008 Financial aid. Need-based:** 430 full-time freshmen applied for aid; 324 were judged to have need; 324 of these received aid. Average need met was 92%. Average scholarship/grant was $21,630; average loan $4,630. 77% of total undergraduate aid awarded as scholarships/grants, 23% as loans/jobs. **Non-need-based:** Awarded to 889 full-time undergraduates, including 267 freshmen. Scholarships awarded for academics, minority status, music/drama, religious affiliation, state residency.

**Application procedures. Admission:** Closing date 2/15. $40 fee, may be waived for applicants with need. Application may be submitted online. Admission notification 4/1. Must reply by May 1 or within 2 week(s) if notified thereafter. **Financial aid:** Priority date 2/15; no closing date. FAFSA, institutional form required. Either CSS PROFILE or institution application from prospectives. Applicants notified by 4/1; must reply by 5/1.

**Academics.** Centers in 6 cities for urban internships in social sciences. **Special study options:** Combined bachelor's/graduate degree, cooperative education, double major, exchange student, independent study, internships, New York semester, student-designed major, study abroad, teacher certification program, United Nations semester, urban semester, Washington semester. **Credit/placement by examination:** AP, CLEP, IB, institutional tests. 32 credit hours maximum toward bachelor's degree. **Support services:** Learning center, tutoring, writing center.

**Majors. Area/ethnic studies:** African, African-American, East Asian, Latin American, Near/Middle Eastern, Russian/Slavic, South Asian, Western European, women's. **Biology:** General, biochemistry, Biochemistry/biophysics and molecular biology, molecular. **Business:** Managerial economics. **Communications:** General. **Computer sciences:** General. **Education:** Music. **English:** American lit, British lit, English lit. **Foreign languages:** General, classics, comparative lit, French, German, Russian, Spanish. **Health:** Audiology/speech pathology, music therapy. **History:** General. **Math:** General. **Philosophy/religion:** Philosophy, religion. **Physical sciences:** Chemical physics, chemistry, geology, molecular physics, physics. **Psychology:** General. **Public administration:** Social work. **Social sciences:** Anthropology, archaeology, economics, international relations, political science, sociology, urban studies. **Visual/performing arts:** Art history/conservation, dance, dramatic, music history, music performance, music theory/composition, studio arts.

**Most popular majors.** Biology 9%, communications/journalism 7%, English 8%, history 11%, philosophy/religious studies 10%, physical sciences 8%, psychology 8%, social sciences 20%, visual/performing arts 9%.

**Computing on campus.** 275 workstations in dormitories, library, computer center, student center. Dormitories wired for high-speed internet access and linked to campus network. Commuter students can connect to campus network. Online library, helpline, repair service, student web hosting, wireless network available.

**Student life. Freshman orientation:** Mandatory. Held during 3 days prior to start of semester. **Housing:** Guaranteed on-campus for all undergraduates. Coed dorms, single-sex dorms, fraternity/sorority housing, substance-free housing available. Special housing for students participating in volunteer activities. **Activities:** Bands, campus ministries, choral groups, dance, drama, film society, international student organizations, literary magazine, music ensembles, Model UN, musical theater, radio station, student government, student newspaper, symphony orchestra, variety of religious, ethnic, and social service organizations available.

**Athletics. NCAA. Intercollegiate:** Baseball M, basketball, cross-country, diving, field hockey W, football (tackle) M, golf M, lacrosse, soccer, softball W, swimming, tennis, track and field, volleyball W. **Intramural:** Badminton, basketball, bowling, football (non-tackle), golf, racquetball, soccer, softball, swimming, tennis, volleyball, water polo M. **Team name:** Fighting Scots.

**Student services.** Alcohol/substance abuse counseling, campus ministries, career counseling, student employment services, financial aid counseling, health services, minority student services, personal counseling, placement for graduates. **Physically disabled:** Services for visually impaired.

**Contact.**  E-mail: admissions@wooster.edu
Phone: (330) 263-2322 Toll-free number: (800) 877-9905
Fax: (330) 263-2621
Mary Karen Vellines, Vice Pres. for Enrollment/Admissions, College of Wooster, 847 College Avenue, Wooster, OH 44691-2363

## Columbus College of Art and Design
### Columbus, Ohio
### www.ccad.edu
**CB code: 1085**

- Private 4-year visual arts college
- Residential campus in very large city
- 1,375 degree-seeking undergraduates: 5% part-time, 57% women, 8% African American, 2% Asian American, 3% Hispanic American, 1% Native American, 5% international
- 76% of applicants admitted
- SAT or ACT (ACT writing optional), application essay required
- 62% graduate within 6 years

**General.** Founded in 1879. Regionally accredited. Campus adjacent to Columbus Museum of Art. **Degrees:** 261 bachelor's awarded. **Location:** Downtown. **Calendar:** Semester, limited summer session. **Full-time faculty:** 80 total; 65% have terminal degrees, 9% minority, 34% women. **Part-time faculty:** 107 total; 23% have terminal degrees, 8% minority, 48% women. **Class size:** 67% < 20, 33% 20-39. **Special facilities:** Student exhibition hall.

**Freshman class profile.** 805 applied, 613 admitted, 286 enrolled.

| Mid 50% test scores | | Rank in top quarter: | 12% |
|---|---|---|---|
| SAT critical reading: | 460-570 | Rank in top tenth: | 4% |
| SAT math: | 430-530 | End year in good standing: | 75% |
| SAT writing: | 430-550 | Return as sophomores: | 77% |
| ACT composite: | 17-23 | Out-of-state: | 19% |
| GPA 3.50 or higher: | 11% | Live on campus: | 75% |
| GPA 3.0-3.49: | 25% | International: | 4% |
| GPA 2.0-2.99: | 64% | | |

**Basis for selection.** Portfolio and minimum high school GPA of 2.0 important. Portfolio required; interview recommended.

**High school preparation.** Recommended units include English 4, mathematics 2, science 2 and foreign language 2. 4 units art recommended.

**2007-2008 Annual costs.** Tuition/fees: $22,412. Room/board: $6,650. Books/supplies: $3,000. Personal expenses: $1,300.

**2007-2008 Financial aid. Need-based:** 302 full-time freshmen applied for aid; 270 were judged to have need; 269 of these received aid. Average need met was 66%. Average scholarship/grant was $12,623; average loan $5,286. 62% of total undergraduate aid awarded as scholarships/grants, 38% as loans/jobs. **Non-need-based:** Awarded to 309 full-time undergraduates, including 89 freshmen. Scholarships awarded for academics, art, ROTC, state residency.

**Application procedures. Admission:** No deadline. $25 fee, may be waived for applicants with need. Application may be submitted online. Admission notification on a rolling basis. **Financial aid:** Priority date 3/2, closing date 6/4. FAFSA required. Applicants notified on a rolling basis starting 3/15; must reply within 2 week(s) of notification.

**Academics. Special study options:** Accelerated study, cooperative education, cross-registration, double major, ESL, independent study, internships, New York semester, study abroad. **Credit/placement by examination:** AP, CLEP, SAT, ACT. **Support services:** Learning center, reduced course load, remedial instruction, study skills assistance, tutoring.

**Majors. Visual/performing arts:** Commercial/advertising art, fashion design, illustration, industrial design, interior design, photography, studio arts.

**Computing on campus.** 226 workstations in library, computer center, student center. Dormitories linked to campus network. Commuter students can connect to campus network. Online library, helpline, repair service available.

**Student life. Freshman orientation:** Mandatory. 3 days before first day of classes. **Housing:** Guaranteed on-campus for freshmen. Coed dorms, apartments, substance-free housing available. $200 fully refundable deposit, deadline 5/11. **Activities:** Literary magazine, student government, student newspaper, student Bible study, student spirituality group, gay/lesbian/bisexual group.

**Athletics. Intramural:** Basketball M, soccer M, volleyball.

**Student services.** Adult student services, career counseling, student employment services, financial aid counseling, personal counseling, placement for graduates.

**Contact.**  E-mail: admissions@ccad.edu
Phone: (614) 224-9101 ext. 3261 Toll-free number: (877) 997-2223
Fax: (614) 232-8344
Thomas Green, Director of Admissions, Columbus College of Art and Design, 107 North Ninth Street, Columbus, OH 43215-3875

## David N. Myers University
### Cleveland, Ohio
### www.myers.edu
**CB code: 1178**

- Private 4-year university
- Commuter campus in very large city
- 500 degree-seeking undergraduates
- SAT or ACT (ACT writing recommended) required

**General.** Founded in 1848. Regionally accredited. **Degrees:** 194 bachelor's, 28 associate awarded; master's offered. **Location:** Downtown. **Calendar:** Semester, extensive summer session. **Full-time faculty:** 19 total. **Part-time faculty:** 81 total.

**Basis for selection.** High school GPA, test scores very important. Students with GPA below 2.5 and ACT below 18 must take college placement exams. Interview recommended for all; essay required for external degree programs.

**High school preparation.** 21 units required. Required units include English 4, mathematics 3, social studies 3, history 2, science 3 (laboratory 1), foreign language 2 and academic electives 3.

**2007-2008 Annual costs.** Tuition/fees: $13,500. Room/board: $5,933. Books/supplies: $1,250.

**Financial aid. Non-need-based:** Scholarships awarded for academics, state residency.

**Application procedures. Admission:** No deadline. $25 fee. Admission notification on a rolling basis beginning on or about 4/1. **Financial aid:** Priority date 3/1; no closing date. FAFSA required. Applicants notified on a rolling basis starting 5/1; must reply within 4 week(s) of notification.

**Academics. Special study options:** Accelerated study, combined bachelor's/graduate degree, cooperative education, cross-registration, distance learning, double major, dual enrollment of high school students, external degree, independent study, internships, liberal arts/career combination, student-designed major, weekend college. **Credit/placement by examination:** CLEP, institutional tests. **Support services:** Learning center, pre-admission summer program, remedial instruction, tutoring.

**Majors. Business:** General, accounting, administrative services, business admin, finance, human resources, management information systems, management science, managerial economics, marketing, office management, office technology. **Computer sciences:** Information systems. **Engineering technology:** Industrial management. **Health:** Health care admin. **Legal studies:** Legal secretary, paralegal. **Liberal arts:** Arts/sciences. **Public administration:** General, human services.

**Computing on campus.** Commuter students can connect to campus network.

**Student life. Freshman orientation:** Available. **Activities:** Choral groups, student government, student newspaper, paralegal association, marketing club, administrative management society, Students in Free Enterprise.

**Athletics. Team name:** Mustangs.

**Student services.** Career counseling, student employment services, health services, personal counseling, placement for graduates, veterans' counselor.

**Contact.** E-mail: Admissions@myers.edu
Phone: (216) 432-8992 Toll-free number: (877) 366-9377
Fax: (216) 361-9274
Ron Brown, Vice President for Enrollment Management, David N. Myers University, 3921 Chester Avenue, Cleveland, OH 44114

---

## Defiance College

| | |
|---|---|
| **Defiance, Ohio** | **CB member** |
| **www.defiance.edu** | **CB code: 1162** |

- Private 4-year liberal arts college affiliated with United Church of Christ
- Residential campus in large town
- 869 degree-seeking undergraduates: 17% part-time, 53% women, 7% African American, 4% Hispanic American
- 80 degree-seeking graduate students
- 80% of applicants admitted
- SAT or ACT (ACT writing optional) required
- 51% graduate within 6 years

**General.** Founded in 1850. Regionally accredited. **Degrees:** 150 bachelor's, 5 associate awarded; master's offered. **Location:** 55 miles from Toledo, 45 miles from Fort Wayne, Indiana. **Calendar:** Semester, extensive summer session. **Full-time faculty:** 44 total; 57% have terminal degrees, 7% minority, 41% women. **Part-time faculty:** 53 total; 21% have terminal degrees, 8% minority, 43% women. **Class size:** 64% < 20, 34% 20-39, less than 1% 40-49, less than 1% 50-99. **Special facilities:** School for Advancing Humanity, wildlife sanctuary.

**Freshman class profile.** 919 applied, 738 admitted, 226 enrolled.

| Mid 50% test scores | | | |
|---|---|---|---|
| | | **ACT composite:** | 18-23 |
| **SAT critical reading:** | 410-530 | **Return as sophomores:** | 64% |
| **SAT math:** | 410-510 | **Out-of-state:** | 19% |
| **SAT writing:** | 400-520 | **Live on campus:** | 80% |

**Basis for selection.** School achievement record, test scores, college preparatory curriculum important. Minimum 2.25 high school GPA, 18 ACT composite or an SAT combined score of 850 (exclusive of Writing).

**High school preparation.** 15 units recommended. Recommended units include English 4, mathematics 3, social studies 2, science 3, foreign language 2 and visual/performing arts 1. One unit fine arts and 1 unit of computer proficiency recommended.

**2008-2009 Annual costs.** Tuition/fees: $21,830. Room/board: $7,150. Books/supplies: $1,350. Personal expenses: $1,200.

**Financial aid. Non-need-based:** Scholarships awarded for academics, leadership.

**Application procedures. Admission:** No deadline. $25 fee, may be waived for applicants with need. Application may be submitted online. Admission notification on a rolling basis beginning on or about 9/1. Must reply by May 1 or within 4 week(s) if notified thereafter. **Financial aid:** Priority date 3/1; no closing date. FAFSA required. Applicants notified on a rolling basis starting 3/15; must reply within 3 week(s) of notification.

**Academics.** Evening sessions available in many areas. Weekend college program for nontraditional students to pursue bachelor's or master's degree in several business majors. **Special study options:** Accelerated study, cooperative education, distance learning, double major, dual enrollment of high school students, honors, independent study, internships, student-designed major, study abroad, teacher certification program, weekend college. **Credit/placement by examination:** AP, CLEP, IB, institutional tests. 15 credit hours maximum toward associate degree, 30 toward bachelor's. **Support services:** Learning center, reduced course load, remedial instruction, study skills assistance, tutoring, writing center.

**Majors. Biology:** General. **Business:** General, accounting, business admin, management information systems. **Communications:** General, journalism, public relations. **Computer sciences:** General, computer science. **Conservation:** General, environmental studies. **Education:** General, art, biology, business, chemistry, early childhood, elementary, English, health, history, mathematics, middle, multi-level teacher, physical, science, secondary, social science, social studies, speech. **English:** English lit, speech/rhetoric. **Health:** Athletic training, clinical lab technology, health services, predental, premedicine, preveterinary. **History:** General. **Interdisciplinary:** Biological/physical sciences, math/computer science, natural sciences. **Legal studies:** Prelaw. **Liberal arts:** Arts/sciences. **Math:** General. **Parks/recreation:** Health/fitness, sports admin. **Philosophy/religion:** Religion. **Protective services:** Forensics. **Psychology:** General. **Public administration:** Social work. **Social sciences:** General, criminology. **Theology:** Religious ed. **Visual/**

**performing arts:** Art, commercial/advertising art, graphic design. **Other:** Computer forensics.

**Most popular majors.** Business/marketing 28%, education 16%, parks/recreation 9%, security/protective services 18%.

**Computing on campus.** 200 workstations in dormitories, library, computer center, student center. Dormitories wired for high-speed internet access and linked to campus network. Commuter students can connect to campus network. Online library, helpline, wireless network available.

**Student life. Freshman orientation:** Mandatory. Preregistration for classes offered. One-day sessions held in April, May, June, and August. **Policies:** Students must live and take meals on campus unless they are seniors, married, veterans, or living with parents or close relatives within approved commuting distance. **Housing:** Guaranteed on-campus for freshmen. Single-sex dorms, apartments, substance-free housing available. ADA-compliant rooms available in each hall. Service floors available. **Activities:** Concert band, choral groups, dance, drama, literary magazine, student government, student newspaper, American Marketing Association, Black Action Student Association, campus activities board, criminal justice society, Fellowship of Christian Athletes, student ecology club, Habitat for Humanity.

**Athletics.** NCAA. **Intercollegiate:** Baseball M, basketball, cross-country, football (tackle) M, golf, soccer, softball W, tennis, track and field, volleyball W. **Intramural:** Basketball, football (non-tackle), football (tackle) M, racquetball, volleyball. **Team name:** Yellow Jackets.

**Student services.** Adult student services, alcohol/substance abuse counseling, campus ministries, career counseling, student employment services, financial aid counseling, health services, minority student services, personal counseling, placement for graduates. **Physically disabled:** Services for hearing impaired.

**Contact.** E-mail: admissions@defiance.edu
Phone: (419) 783-2359 Toll-free number: (800) 520-4632
Fax: (419) 783-2468
Brad Harsha, Director of Admissions, Defiance College, 701 North Clinton Street, Defiance, OH 43512-1695

---

## Denison University

| | |
|---|---|
| **Granville, Ohio** | **CB member** |
| **www.denison.edu** | **CB code: 1164** |

- Private 4-year liberal arts college
- Residential campus in small town
- 2,212 degree-seeking undergraduates: 57% women, 5% African American, 3% Asian American, 2% Hispanic American, 4% international
- 39% of applicants admitted
- Application essay required
- 79% graduate within 6 years

**General.** Founded in 1831. Regionally accredited. **Degrees:** 550 bachelor's awarded. **ROTC:** Army. **Location:** 27 miles from Columbus. **Calendar:** Semester. **Full-time faculty:** 193 total; 98% have terminal degrees, 16% minority, 44% women. **Part-time faculty:** 19 total; 47% have terminal degrees, 26% minority, 47% women. **Class size:** 59% < 20, 41% 20-39, less than 1% 50-99. **Special facilities:** Field research station in 350-acre biological reserve, high resolution spectrometer lab, nuclear magnetic resonance spectrometer, planetarium, economics computer lab, harmonic systems lab, digital media lab, fine and performing arts MIX lab (intermedia experimental lab), geographic information systems lab.

**Freshman class profile.** 5,196 applied, 2,033 admitted, 586 enrolled.

| Mid 50% test scores | | | |
|---|---|---|---|
| **SAT critical reading:** | 580-690 | **Rank in top quarter:** | 82% |
| **SAT math:** | 580-670 | **Rank in top tenth:** | 53% |
| **ACT composite:** | 28-31 | **Return as sophomores:** | 93% |
| **GPA 3.50 or higher:** | 61% | **Out-of-state:** | 66% |
| **GPA 3.0-3.49:** | 34% | **Live on campus:** | 99% |
| **GPA 2.0-2.99:** | 5% | **International:** | 4% |

**Basis for selection.** Academic record, recommendations, talent and ability, character and personal qualities most important. School and community activities, essay and personal potential also important. Test scores considered. Interview recommended for all; audition required for visual and performing arts program; portfolio recommended for studio art programs.

**High school preparation.** 19 units required. Required units include English 4, mathematics 4, social studies 2, history 1, science 4, foreign language 3 and academic electives 1. 1 unit fine arts recommended.

**2007-2008 Annual costs.** Tuition/fees: $33,010. Room/board: $8,570.

**2007-2008 Financial aid. Need-based:** 358 full-time freshmen applied for aid; 271 were judged to have need; 271 of these received aid. Average need met was 99%. Average scholarship/grant was $21,848; average loan $3,931. 79% of total undergraduate aid awarded as scholarships/grants, 21% as loans/jobs. **Non-need-based:** Awarded to 1,981 full-time undergraduates, including 512 freshmen. Scholarships awarded for academics, art, leadership, music/drama, state residency.

**Application procedures. Admission:** Priority date 12/1; deadline 1/15 (postmark date). $40 fee, may be waived for applicants with need. Application may be submitted online. Admission notification 3/30. Must reply by May 1 or within 2 week(s) if notified thereafter. **Financial aid:** Priority date 2/15; no closing date. FAFSA required. Applicants notified by 3/30; must reply by 5/1 or within 2 week(s) of notification.

**Academics. Special study options:** Double major, honors, independent study, internships, New York semester, semester at sea, student-designed major, study abroad, teacher certification program, Washington semester. **Credit/placement by examination:** AP, CLEP, IB, institutional tests. **Support services:** Learning center, reduced course load, study skills assistance, tutoring, writing center.

**Majors. Area/ethnic studies:** African-American, East Asian, gay/lesbian, Latin American, Western European, women's. **Biology:** General, biochemistry. **Business:** Organizational behavior. **Communications:** General, digital media. **Computer sciences:** General. **Conservation:** General. **Education:** General, physical. **English:** British lit, English lit. **Foreign languages:** Classics, French, German, Spanish. **History:** General. **Math:** General. **Philosophy/religion:** Philosophy, religion. **Physical sciences:** Chemistry, geology, physics. **Psychology:** General. **Social sciences:** Anthropology, economics, political science, sociology. **Visual/performing arts:** Art history/conservation, dance, dramatic, film/cinema, studio arts.

**Most popular majors.** Biology 10%, communications/journalism 11%, education 6%, English 8%, psychology 8%, social sciences 24%, visual/performing arts 9%.

**Computing on campus.** Dormitories wired for high-speed internet access and linked to campus network. Commuter students can connect to campus network. Online library, helpline, student web hosting, wireless network available.

**Student life. Freshman orientation:** Mandatory. Preregistration for classes offered. Two summer orientation programs: A mandatory no-fee August orientation program or an optional but highly recommended June orientation program costing $175. **Housing:** Guaranteed on-campus for all undergraduates. Coed dorms, single-sex dorms, apartments, substance-free housing available. 3 student-constructed buildings using alternative energy resources accommodate 12 students. Apartment-style housing for high-GPA upper division students. **Activities:** Bands, campus ministries, choral groups, dance, drama, film society, international student organizations, literary magazine, music ensembles, musical theater, radio station, student government, student newspaper, symphony orchestra, TV station, over 130 organizations available.

**Athletics.** NCAA. **Intercollegiate:** Baseball M, basketball, cross-country, diving, field hockey W, football (tackle) M, golf M, lacrosse, soccer, softball W, swimming, tennis, track and field, volleyball W. **Intramural:** Basketball, equestrian, football (non-tackle), golf, ice hockey M, lacrosse M, racquetball, rifle, rugby, skiing, soccer, softball, squash, tennis, volleyball, water polo, wrestling M. **Team name:** Big Red.

**Student services.** Alcohol/substance abuse counseling, campus ministries, career counseling, student employment services, financial aid counseling, health services, minority student services, personal counseling, placement for graduates.

**Contact.** E-mail: admissions@denison.edu
Phone: (740) 587-6276 Toll-free number: (800) 336-4766
Fax: (740) 587-6306
Perry Robinson, VP and Director of Admissions, Denison University, Box H, Granville, OH 43023

---

## DeVry University: Columbus
**Columbus, Ohio**
www.devry.edu
**CB member**
**CB code: 1605**

▶  For-profit 4-year university
▶  Commuter campus in very large city
▶  2,379 degree-seeking undergraduates: 39% part-time, 37% women, 24% African American, 2% Asian American, 1% Hispanic American
▶  217 degree-seeking graduate students

▶  Interview required
▶  35% graduate within 6 years

**General.** Founded in 1952. Regionally accredited. **Degrees:** 458 bachelor's, 96 associate awarded; master's offered. **ROTC:** Army. **Location:** 5 miles from downtown. **Calendar:** Semester, extensive summer session. **Full-time faculty:** 50 total; 14% minority, 26% women. **Part-time faculty:** 50 total; 20% minority, 32% women.

**Freshman class profile.**

| Return as sophomores: | 52% | Out-of-state: | 2% |

**Basis for selection.** Applicants must have high school diploma or equivalent, demonstrate proficiency in basic college-level skills through SAT or ACT scores or institution-administered placement examinations, and be 17 years of age. New students may enter at beginning of any semester. SAT or ACT recommended. CPT also accepted.

**High school preparation.** Required units include mathematics 1. Math unit must be algebra or higher.

**2007-2008 Annual costs.** Tuition/fees: $13,220. Books/supplies: $1,300. Personal expenses: $5,082.

**Financial aid.** All financial aid based on need.

**Application procedures. Admission:** No deadline. $50 fee. Application may be submitted online. Admission notification on a rolling basis. **Financial aid:** No deadline. FAFSA required. Applicants notified on a rolling basis.

**Academics. Special study options:** Accelerated study, distance learning. **Credit/placement by examination:** CLEP, institutional tests. **Support services:** Learning center, tutoring.

**Majors. Business:** Business admin. **Computer sciences:** Networking, systems analysis. **Engineering technology:** Biomedical, computer, electrical. **Other:** Technical management.

**Most popular majors.** Business/marketing 49%, computer/information sciences 31%, engineering/engineering technologies 19%.

**Computing on campus.** 408 workstations in library, computer center, student center. Online course registration, online library, helpline available.

**Student life. Freshman orientation:** Mandatory. **Housing:** Private apartments, student-plan housing, private rooms available. **Activities:** DeVry student association, Tau Alpha Pi, DeVry Christian Alliance, Asian American student association, Future Accounting Society, Institute of Electrical and Electronics Engineers, Association of IT Professionals, minority student union.

**Athletics. Intramural:** Basketball, soccer, volleyball.

**Student services.** Career counseling, student employment services, financial aid counseling, placement for graduates, veterans' counselor. **Physically disabled:** Services for visually, hearing impaired.

**Contact.** E-mail: admissions@devry.edu
Phone: (614) 253-1525 Toll-free number: (800) 426-2206
Fax: (614) 253-0843
Bill Holtry, Dean of Admissions, DeVry University: Columbus, 1350 Alum Creek Drive, Columbus, OH 43209-2705

---

## Franciscan University of Steubenville
**Steubenville, Ohio**
www.franciscan.edu
**CB member**
**CB code: 1133**

▶  Private 4-year university affiliated with Roman Catholic Church
▶  Residential campus in large town
▶  1,976 degree-seeking undergraduates: 5% part-time, 60% women, 1% African American, 2% Asian American, 4% Hispanic American, 1% Native American, 1% international
▶  381 degree-seeking graduate students
▶  81% of applicants admitted
▶  SAT or ACT (ACT writing optional), application essay required
▶  67% graduate within 6 years

**General.** Founded in 1946. Regionally accredited. **Degrees:** 479 bachelor's, 39 associate awarded; master's offered. **ROTC:** Army. **Location:** 40 miles from Pittsburgh. **Calendar:** Semester, limited summer session. **Full-time faculty:** 115 total; 72% have terminal degrees, less than 1% minority, 24% women. **Part-time faculty:** 84 total; 12% have terminal degrees, 50% women. **Class size:** 48% < 20, 37% 20-39, 11% 40-49, 3% 50-99, less than

1% >100. **Special facilities:** Replica of Portiuncula (St. Mary of the Angels) Chapel as rebuilt by St. Francis of Assisi in 1207, Tomb of the Unborn Child.

**Freshman class profile.** 1,273 applied, 1,027 admitted, 442 enrolled.

| Mid 50% test scores | | Rank in top quarter: | 56% |
|---|---|---|---|
| SAT critical reading: | 540-660 | Rank in top tenth: | 33% |
| SAT math: | 520-640 | Return as sophomores: | 88% |
| ACT composite: | 22-28 | Out-of-state: | 80% |
| GPA 3.50 or higher: | 63% | Live on campus: | 88% |
| GPA 3.0-3.49: | 25% | International: | 2% |
| GPA 2.0-2.99: | 12% | Sororities: | 1% |

**Basis for selection.** Admission requirements include minimum 2.4 high school GPA, recommendations, interview when available, combined SAT score of 1000 (exclusive of Writing) or ACT composite of 21. Interview recommended. **Homeschooled:** Applicants should contact Admissions Office for requirements.

**High school preparation.** 15 units required. Required and recommended units include English 4, mathematics 3, social studies 2, history 2, science 3, foreign language 3 and academic electives 1. 10 units in 4 of the following fields: English, foreign language, social science, mathematics, natural sciences. Remaining 5 units may be in other subjects counted toward graduation. Majors in chemistry, engineering science, or mathematics should have 2 units algebra and 2 units geometry/trigonometry.

**2007-2008 Annual costs.** Tuition/fees: $18,180. Room/board: $6,300. Books/supplies: $800. Personal expenses: $1,200.

**Financial aid. Non-need-based:** Scholarships awarded for academics, leadership, religious affiliation.

**Application procedures. Admission:** Priority date 1/31; no deadline. $20 fee, may be waived for applicants with need. Application may be submitted online. Admission notification on a rolling basis beginning on or about 9/1. **Financial aid:** No deadline. FAFSA required. Applicants notified on a rolling basis starting 3/15; must reply within 3 week(s) of notification.

**Academics.** Students encouraged to spend 1 semester of sophomore year in study abroad program in Gaming, Austria. **Special study options:** Accelerated study, combined bachelor's/graduate degree, distance learning, double major, honors, independent study, internships, liberal arts/career combination, study abroad, teacher certification program. **Credit/placement by examination:** AP, CLEP, IB, institutional tests. 30 credit hours maximum toward associate degree, 30 toward bachelor's. **Support services:** Learning center, reduced course load, study skills assistance, tutoring, writing center.

**Honors college/program.** 1180 SAT (exclusive of Writing) and/or 26 ACT, 3.4 high school GPA, and a series of essays required. 40 freshmen admitted. Academic program consists of a great books seminar sequence.

**Majors. Biology:** General. **Business:** Accounting, business admin. **Communications:** General. **Computer sciences:** General, computer science. **Education:** Elementary. **English:** English lit. **Foreign languages:** Classics, French, German, Spanish. **Health:** Mental health services, nursing (RN). **History:** General. **Legal studies:** General. **Liberal arts:** Humanities. **Math:** General. **Philosophy/religion:** Philosophy. **Physical sciences:** Chemistry. **Psychology:** General. **Public administration:** Social work. **Social sciences:** Anthropology, economics, political science, sociology. **Theology:** Religious ed, sacred music, theology. **Visual/performing arts:** Dramatic.

**Most popular majors.** Business/marketing 11%, education 9%, health sciences 15%, theological studies 27%.

**Computing on campus.** 126 workstations in library, computer center. Commuter students can connect to campus network. Online library, helpline available.

**Student life. Freshman orientation:** Mandatory, $150 fee. Preregistration for classes offered. Held weekend before fall classes begin, from Friday morning to Sunday afternoon. **Housing:** Guaranteed on-campus for freshmen. Single-sex dorms available. $300 nonrefundable deposit. Household groups of 10-20 students in residence halls may develop distinctive environment for their group within the context of Christian and Franciscan perspective. **Activities:** Campus ministries, choral groups, drama, international student organizations, literary magazine, music ensembles, radio station, student government, student newspaper, campus ministry, International Student Organization, Human Life Concerns (pro-life), Works of Mercy Program, leadership development.

**Athletics. Intercollegiate:** Baseball M, basketball, cross-country, rugby M, soccer, tennis M, volleyball W. **Intramural:** Basketball, bowling, football (non-tackle), racquetball, soccer, softball, tennis, volleyball, weight lifting, wrestling M. **Team name:** Barons.

**Student services.** Adult student services, campus ministries, career counseling, student employment services, financial aid counseling, health services, personal counseling, veterans' counselor. **Physically disabled:** Services for visually, speech, hearing impaired.

**Contact.** E-mail: admissions@franciscan.edu
Phone: (740) 283-6226 Toll-free number: (800) 783-6220
Fax: (740) 284-5456
Margaret Weber, Director of Admissions, Franciscan University of Steubenville, 1235 University Boulevard, Steubenville, OH 43952-1763

## Franklin University
### Columbus, Ohio
www.franklin.edu · · · · · · · · · · · · · · · CB code: 1229

♦ Private 4-year university and business college
♦ Commuter campus in very large city

**General.** Founded in 1902. Regionally accredited. **Location:** Downtown Columbus. **Calendar:** Trimester.

**Annual costs/financial aid.** Tuition/fees (2007-2008): $7,650. Books/supplies: $750. Personal expenses: $2,150. Need-based financial aid available to full-time and part-time students.

**Contact.** Phone: (614) 797-4700
Chief Student Officer, 201 South Grant Avenue, Columbus, OH 43215-5399

## God's Bible School and College
### Cincinnati, Ohio
www.gbs.edu · · · · · · · · · · · · · · · CB code: 1238

♦ Private 4-year Bible college affiliated with interdenominational tradition
♦ Residential campus in large city

**General.** Founded in 1900. Accredited by ABHE. **Location:** One mile from downtown. **Calendar:** Semester.

**Annual costs/financial aid.** Tuition/fees (2007-2008): $4,980. Room/board: $3,300. Books/supplies: $550. Personal expenses: $2,400. Need-based financial aid available to full-time and part-time students.

**Contact.** Phone: (513) 721-7944 ext. 205
Director of Admissions, 1810 Young Street, Cincinnati, OH 45202-6838

## Heidelberg College
### Tiffin, Ohio
CB member
www.heidelberg.edu · · · · · · · · · · · · · · · CB code: 1292

♦ Private 4-year liberal arts college affiliated with United Church of Christ
♦ Residential campus in large town
♦ 1,255 degree-seeking undergraduates: 7% part-time, 48% women, 7% African American, 2% Hispanic American, 2% international
♦ 173 degree-seeking graduate students
♦ 73% of applicants admitted
♦ SAT or ACT (ACT writing optional) required
♦ 58% graduate within 6 years

**General.** Founded in 1850. Regionally accredited. **Degrees:** 240 bachelor's awarded; master's offered. **ROTC:** Army, Air Force. **Location:** 52 miles from Toledo, 80 miles from Cleveland. **Calendar:** Semester, limited summer session. **Full-time faculty:** 54 total; 82% have terminal degrees, 11% minority, 39% women. **Part-time faculty:** 94 total; 24% have terminal degrees, 7% minority, 49% women. **Class size:** 59% < 20, 39% 20-39, 1% 40-49, less than 1% 50-99. **Special facilities:** National center for water quality research, cadaver laboratory, four wooded lots for science research, archaeology laboratory, historic and military archaeology center.

## Freshman class profile. 1,860 applied, 1,366 admitted, 374 enrolled.

| Mid 50% test scores | | | |
|---|---|---|---|
| SAT critical reading: | 410-560 | Rank in top quarter: | 32% |
| SAT math: | 440-560 | Rank in top tenth: | 13% |
| SAT writing: | 410-560 | Return as sophomores: | 68% |
| ACT composite: | 19-24 | Out-of-state: | 9% |
| GPA 3.50 or higher: | 31% | Live on campus: | 91% |
| GPA 3.0-3.49: | 29% | International: | 3% |
| GPA 2.0-2.99: | 40% | Fraternities: | 11% |
| | | Sororities: | 18% |

**Basis for selection.** School achievement record is most important, followed by test scores. Special talents, community activities, and leadership qualities also considered. Audition required for music; interview recommended for academically weak students. **Learning Disabled:** Students with learning disabilites are strongly encouraged to self-report to the Academic Success Center after deciding to attend the College. Appointments to discuss possible services/accomodations are welcome.

**High school preparation.** 21 units recommended. Recommended units include English 4, mathematics 3, social studies 3, history 2, science 3 (laboratory 1), foreign language 2 and academic electives 3.

**2008-2009 Annual costs.** Tuition/fees (projected): $19,922. Room/board: $8,138. Books/supplies: $1,000. Personal expenses: $500.

**2007-2008 Financial aid. Need-based:** 356 full-time freshmen applied for aid; 299 were judged to have need; 299 of these received aid. Average need met was 88%. Average scholarship/grant was $11,519; average loan $4,514. 53% of total undergraduate aid awarded as scholarships/grants, 47% as loans/jobs. **Non-need-based:** Awarded to 234 full-time undergraduates, including 91 freshmen. Scholarships awarded for academics, music/drama, religious affiliation, state residency.

**Application procedures. Admission:** Priority date 1/1; deadline 8/1 (receipt date). $25 fee, may be waived for applicants with need. Application may be submitted online. Admission notification on a rolling basis beginning on or about 10/15. Must reply by May 1 or within 2 week(s) if notified thereafter. **Financial aid:** Priority date 3/1; no closing date. FAFSA required. Applicants notified on a rolling basis starting 3/15; must reply by 5/1 or within 2 week(s) of notification.

**Academics.** Freshman-level credit courses and graduate education course work offered at Sapporo, Japan campus. Program in Sport Management and Business Administration offered at Royal Racing Football Club, Montagnee in Belgium. **Special study options:** Accelerated study, combined bachelor's/graduate degree, cooperative education, cross-registration, double major, dual enrollment of high school students, exchange student, honors, independent study, internships, liberal arts/career combination, study abroad, teacher certification program, Washington semester. **Credit/placement by examination:** AP, CLEP, IB, SAT, ACT, institutional tests. 30 credit hours maximum toward bachelor's degree. **Support services:** Learning center, reduced course load, study skills assistance, tutoring, writing center.

**Majors. Biology:** General, environmental. **Business:** Accounting, business admin, management science. **Communications:** General, public relations. **Computer sciences:** General, computer science. **Conservation:** Management/policy. **Education:** Music, physical. **English:** English lit. **Foreign languages:** German, Spanish. **Health:** Athletic training, health care admin, predental, premedicine, prenursing, preveterinary. **History:** General. **Interdisciplinary:** Biological/physical sciences. **Legal studies:** Prelaw. **Math:** General. **Parks/recreation:** Sports admin. **Philosophy/religion:** Religion. **Physical sciences:** Chemistry, physics. **Protective services:** Law enforcement admin. **Psychology:** General. **Public administration:** General. **Social sciences:** General, anthropology, economics, political science. **Visual/performing arts:** Music management, music performance, music theory/composition, musical theater.

**Most popular majors.** Biology 8%, business/marketing 19%, communications/journalism 6%, education 16%, parks/recreation 11%, psychology 10%.

**Computing on campus.** 125 workstations in dormitories, library, computer center, student center. Dormitories wired for high-speed internet access and linked to campus network. Online course registration, helpline, repair service, wireless network available.

**Student life. Freshman orientation:** Mandatory. Preregistration for classes offered. 5 different 2-day summer sessions to choose from. **Housing:** Guaranteed on-campus for all undergraduates. Coed dorms, single-sex dorms, special housing for disabled, apartments, cooperative housing, substance-free housing available. $250 fully refundable deposit, deadline 8/1. Undergraduate specialty houses by major, interest, service groups available. **Activities:** Bands, campus ministries, choral groups, dance, drama, film society, international student organizations, literary magazine, music ensembles, Model

UN, musical theater, opera, radio station, student government, student newspaper, symphony orchestra, TV station, Black Student Union, Young Democrats, Young Republicans, Circle-K, religious organizations, World Student Union, Beta Beta Beta, political science organization.

**Athletics.** NCAA. **Intercollegiate:** Baseball M, basketball, cheerleading, cross-country, football (tackle) M, golf, soccer, softball W, tennis, track and field, volleyball W, wrestling M. **Intramural:** Archery, baseball M, basketball, bowling, golf, soccer, softball, table tennis, volleyball. **Team name:** Student Princes.

**Student services.** Adult student services, campus ministries, career counseling, student employment services, financial aid counseling, health services, minority student services, personal counseling, placement for graduates, women's services. **Physically disabled:** Services for visually, hearing impaired.

**Contact.** E-mail: adminfo@heidelberg.edu
Phone: (419) 448-2330 Toll-free number: (800) 434-3352
Fax: (419) 448-2334
Lindsay Sooy, Director of Admission, Heidelberg College, 310 East Market Street, Tiffin, OH 44883-2462

---

## Hiram College
**Hiram, Ohio**
**www.hiram.edu**

CB member
CB code: 1297

- Private 4-year liberal arts college affiliated with Christian Church (Disciples of Christ)
- Residential campus in rural community
- 1,256 degree-seeking undergraduates
- 77% of applicants admitted
- SAT or ACT (ACT writing optional), application essay required

**General.** Founded in 1850. Regionally accredited. Affiliated with John Cabot International University in Rome, Italy, Shoals Marine Laboratory in New Hampshire, Institute of European Studies, and Institute for Asian Studies. Exchange programs with Kansai University of Foreign Studies in Osaka, Japan, and Bosphorus University in Turkey. **Degrees:** 253 bachelor's awarded; master's offered. **Location:** 35 miles from Cleveland. **Calendar:** Semester, limited summer session. **Full-time faculty:** 68 total. **Part-time faculty:** 28 total. **Class size:** 88% < 20, 12% 20-39, less than 1% 40-49. **Special facilities:** 2 nature/science field research stations, observatory, center for literature and medicine.

**Freshman class profile.** 1,551 applied, 1,196 admitted, 334 enrolled.

| Mid 50% test scores | | | |
|---|---|---|---|
| SAT critical reading: | 480-610 | GPA 2.0-2.99: | 28% |
| SAT math: | 470-600 | Rank in top quarter: | 51% |
| ACT composite: | 20-26 | Rank in top tenth: | 23% |
| GPA 3.50 or higher: | 43% | Out-of-state: | 16% |
| GPA 3.0-3.49: | 29% | Live on campus: | 95% |

**Basis for selection.** School record, test scores, counselor and teacher recommendations emphasized. Extracurricular participation, alumni relationship considered. Interview required for scholarship candidates or academically marginal applicants; recommended for all others.

**High school preparation.** 20 units required; 21 recommended. Required and recommended units include English 4, mathematics 3, social studies 3, history 1, science 3 (laboratory 2), foreign language 2-3 and academic electives 2. One course in fine arts recommended.

**2007-2008 Annual costs.** Tuition/fees: $24,895. Room/board: $7,980. Books/supplies: $700. Personal expenses: $1,408.

**Financial aid. Non-need-based:** Scholarships awarded for academics, alumni affiliation, art, leadership, minority status, music/drama, religious affiliation, state residency.

**Application procedures. Admission:** Priority date 2/15; no deadline. $35 fee, may be waived for applicants with need. Application may be submitted online. Admission notification on a rolling basis beginning on or about 10/1. Must reply by May 1 or within 2 week(s) if notified thereafter. **Financial aid:** Priority date 2/15; no closing date. FAFSA required. Applicants notified on a rolling basis starting 2/15; must reply by 5/1 or within 2 week(s) of notification.

**Academics.** Prelaw, premed and preveterinary programs offered. **Special study options:** Accelerated study, combined bachelor's/graduate degree, cross-registration, double major, dual enrollment of high school students, ESL, exchange student, independent study, internships, student-designed major, study abroad, teacher certification program, Washington semester, weekend college. **Credit/placement by examination:** AP, CLEP, IB, institutional tests. 60 credit hours maximum toward bachelor's degree. **Support services:** Reduced course load, study skills assistance, tutoring, writing center.

**Majors. Biology:** General, biochemistry, biomedical sciences. **Business:** Accounting/finance, business admin. **Communications:** General. **Computer sciences:** General, computer science. **Conservation:** Environmental studies. **Education:** General, elementary. **English:** Creative writing, English lit. **Foreign languages:** Classics, French, German, Spanish. **History:** General. **Interdisciplinary:** Math/computer science. **Legal studies:** Prelaw. **Math:** General. **Philosophy/religion:** Philosophy, religion. **Physical sciences:** Chemistry, physics. **Psychology:** General. **Social sciences:** General, economics, political science, sociology. **Visual/performing arts:** Art history/conservation, dramatic, studio arts.

**Most popular majors.** Biology 13%, business/marketing 18%, communications/journalism 6%, education 7%, English 7%, social sciences 14%.

**Computing on campus.** 100 workstations in dormitories, library, computer center, student center. Dormitories wired for high-speed internet access and linked to campus network. Commuter students can connect to campus network. Online course registration, online library, helpline, student web hosting, wireless network available.

**Student life. Freshman orientation:** Mandatory, $240 fee. Preregistration for classes offered. Several orientation sessions held throughout late spring and summer. **Housing:** Guaranteed on-campus for all undergraduates. Coed dorms, single-sex dorms, substance-free housing available. $200 nonrefundable deposit, deadline 5/1. Dormitories include 24-hour and 12-hour quiet floors. **Activities:** Bands, choral groups, dance, drama, literary magazine, music ensembles, musical theater, radio station, student government, student newspaper, TV station, African-American Students United, environmental awareness club, Christian Fellowship, Network for Progressive Action, conservative student forum, Model United Nations, volunteer association, international organization, Intercultural Forum, Newman Club, Islamic Society.

**Athletics.** NCAA. **Intercollegiate:** Baseball M, basketball, cross-country, diving, football (tackle) M, golf, soccer, softball W, swimming, tennis, track and field, volleyball W. **Intramural:** Archery, basketball, football (nontackle), soccer, softball, tennis, volleyball, water polo. **Team name:** Terriers.

**Student services.** Campus ministries, career counseling, student employment services, health services, minority student services, personal counseling, placement for graduates, veterans' counselor.

**Contact.** E-mail: admission@hiram.edu
Phone: (330) 569-5169 Toll-free number: (800) 362-5280
Fax: (330) 569-5944
Sherman Dean, Director of Admission, Hiram College, Teachout Price Hall, Hiram, OH 44234

---

## John Carroll University

**University Heights, Ohio**
**www.jcu.edu**

**CB member**
**CB code: 1342**

- Private 4-year university and liberal arts college affiliated with Roman Catholic Church
- Residential campus in large town
- 3,022 degree-seeking undergraduates: 3% part-time, 54% women, 5% African American, 2% Asian American, 3% Hispanic American
- 691 graduate students
- 86% of applicants admitted
- SAT or ACT (ACT writing recommended), application essay required
- 74% graduate within 6 years; 83% enter graduate study

**General.** Founded in 1886. Regionally accredited. **Degrees:** 745 bachelor's awarded; master's offered. **ROTC:** Army. **Location:** 10 miles from Cleveland. **Calendar:** Semester, extensive summer session. **Full-time faculty:** 204 total; 92% have terminal degrees, 11% minority, 35% women. **Part-time faculty:** 189 total; 38% have terminal degrees, 50% women. **Class size:** 56% < 20, 44% 20-39, less than 1% 40-49. **Special facilities:** Science and technology center containing research facilities.

**Freshman class profile.** 3,309 applied, 2,830 admitted, 720 enrolled.

| Mid 50% test scores | | | |
|---|---|---|---|
| SAT critical reading: | 480-600 | Rank in top quarter: | 48% |
| SAT math: | 490-610 | Rank in top tenth: | 22% |
| SAT writing: | 480-590 | End year in good standing: | 93% |
| ACT composite: | 21-26 | Return as sophomores: | 84% |
| GPA 3.50 or higher: | 49% | Out-of-state: | 34% |
| GPA 3.0-3.49: | 34% | Live on campus: | 89% |
| GPA 2.0-2.99: | 17% | Fraternities: | 6% |
| | | Sororities: | 11% |

**Basis for selection.** Strength of high school curriculum, high school academic record, test scores, recommendations, extracurricular activities, essay most important. Interview highly recommended. **Homeschooled:** State high school equivalency certificate, interview, letter of recommendation (nonparent) required. Extra emphasis placed on standardized testing.

**High school preparation.** 16 units required; 21 recommended. Required and recommended units include English 4, mathematics 3-4, social studies 2-4, science 2-3 (laboratory 2-3), foreign language 2-3 and academic electives 3. Two units must be distributed between social studies and/or history; 4 recommended.

**2007-2008 Annual costs.** Tuition/fees: $26,434. Room/board: $7,790. Books/supplies: $1,200. Personal expenses: $1,000.

**Financial aid. Non-need-based:** Scholarships awarded for academics, minority status, ROTC, state residency. **Additional information:** Institutional form for need analysis required from upperclassmen and transfer students only.

**Application procedures. Admission:** Priority date 1/2; deadline 2/1 (postmark date). No application fee. Application may be submitted online. Admission notification on a rolling basis beginning on or about 12/15. Must reply by May 1 or within 4 week(s) if notified thereafter. **Financial aid:** Priority date 2/1; no closing date. FAFSA required. Applicants notified on a rolling basis starting 2/1; must reply by 5/1 or within 4 week(s) of notification.

**Academics.** Online course registration available for second semester freshmen. **Special study options:** Accelerated study, combined bachelor's/graduate degree, cooperative education, cross-registration, double major, dual enrollment of high school students, exchange student, honors, independent study, internships, liberal arts/career combination, student-designed major, study abroad, teacher certification program, Washington semester. **Credit/placement by examination:** AP, CLEP, IB, institutional tests. 30 credit hours maximum toward bachelor's degree. **Support services:** Learning center, reduced course load, study skills assistance, tutoring, writing center.

**Majors. Biology:** General. **Business:** Accounting, business admin, finance, logistics, managerial economics. **Communications:** General. **Computer sciences:** General, computer science. **Conservation:** Environmental studies. **Education:** Elementary, physical. **Engineering:** Physics. **English:** English lit. **Foreign languages:** Ancient Greek, comparative lit, French, German, Latin, Spanish. **Health:** Predental, premedicine, preveterinary. **History:** General. **Interdisciplinary:** Gerontology. **Legal studies:** Prelaw. **Liberal arts:** Arts/sciences. **Math:** General. **Philosophy/religion:** Philosophy, religion. **Physical sciences:** Chemistry, physics. **Psychology:** General. **Social sciences:** Economics, political science, sociology. **Visual/performing arts:** Art history/conservation.

**Most popular majors.** Biology 11%, business/marketing 29%, communications/journalism 11%, psychology 8%, social sciences 14%.

**Computing on campus.** 200 workstations in dormitories, library, computer center, student center. Dormitories wired for high-speed internet access and linked to campus network. Commuter students can connect to campus network. Online course registration, online library, helpline, repair service, student web hosting, wireless network available.

**Student life. Freshman orientation:** Mandatory, $325 fee. 2 day, one overnight for parents and students. Students take placement tests. **Policies:** Students must adhere to the Student Code of Conduct. All incoming freshman students required to live on campus freshman and sophomore years. **Housing:** Guaranteed on-campus for all undergraduates. Coed dorms, single-sex dorms, substance-free housing available. $300 fully refundable deposit, deadline 5/1. Suite-style housing available. **Activities:** Bands, campus ministries, choral groups, dance, drama, international student organizations, literary magazine, music ensembles, musical theater, radio station, student government, student newspaper, TV station, Christian Life Community, African American Alliance, EMS Association, Habitat for Humanity, Labre Project, Students in Free Enterprise, Public Relations Student Society of America.

**Athletics.** NCAA. **Intercollegiate:** Baseball M, basketball, cross-country, diving, football (tackle) M, golf, soccer, softball W, swimming, tennis, track and field, volleyball W, wrestling M. **Intramural:** Basketball, football (non-tackle), golf, racquetball, soccer, softball, table tennis, tennis, volleyball, water polo. **Team name:** Blue Streaks.

**Student services.** Adult student services, alcohol/substance abuse counseling, campus ministries, career counseling, student employment services, financial aid counseling, health services, minority student services, personal counseling, placement for graduates, veterans' counselor. **Physically disabled:** Services for visually, speech, hearing impaired.

**Contact.** E-mail: admission@jcu.edu
Phone: (216) 397-4294 Toll-free number: (888) 335-6800
Fax: (216) 397-4981
Thomas Fanning, Director of Admission and Retention, John Carroll University, 20700 North Park Boulevard, University Heights, OH 44118-4581

## Kent State University

Kent, Ohio

www.kent.edu

CB member

CB code: 1367

- Public 4-year university
- Residential campus in large town
- 17,674 degree-seeking undergraduates: 14% part-time, 59% women, 8% African American, 1% Asian American, 1% Hispanic American, 1% international
- 4,230 degree-seeking graduate students
- 80% of applicants admitted
- SAT or ACT (ACT writing optional) required
- 49% graduate within 6 years

**General.** Founded in 1910. Regionally accredited. **Degrees:** 3,744 bachelor's awarded; master's, doctoral offered. **ROTC:** Army, Air Force. **Location:** 50 miles from Cleveland, 11 miles from Akron. **Calendar:** Semester, extensive summer session. **Full-time faculty:** 881 total; 15% minority, 48% women. **Part-time faculty:** 595 total; 7% minority, 55% women. **Class size:** 51% < 20, 38% 20-39, 4% 40-49, 4% 50-99, 3% >100. **Special facilities:** 287-acre airport, liquid crystal institute, fashion museum, planetarium, ice arena, 18-hole golf course.

**Freshman class profile.** 12,364 applied, 9,854 admitted, 3,776 enrolled.

| Mid 50% test scores | | | |
|---|---|---|---|
| SAT critical reading: | 450-560 | Rank in top tenth: | 11% |
| SAT math: | 450-570 | End year in good standing: | 64% |
| ACT composite: | 19-24 | Return as sophomores: | 73% |
| GPA 3.50 or higher: | 27% | Out-of-state: | 13% |
| GPA 3.0-3.49: | 34% | Live on campus: | 82% |
| GPA 2.0-2.99: | 38% | International: | 1% |
| Rank in top quarter: | 32% | Fraternities: | 4% |
| | | Sororities: | 4% |

**Basis for selection.** Academic record, course work, test scores important. Varying criteria for nursing, education, flight, fashion design and merchandising, architecture, interior design, journalism and mass communication, 6-year medical program, music, dance, and honors college applicants. Interview required for 6-year medical program, recommended for all others. Audition required for dance, music, and musical theater students.

**High school preparation.** 16 units recommended. Recommended units include English 4, mathematics 3, social studies 3, science 3 (laboratory 2) and foreign language 3. One fine arts or third unit of foreign language recommended.

**2007-2008 Annual costs.** Tuition/fees: $8,430; $15,862 out-of-state. Room/board: $7,200. Books/supplies: $990.

**2007-2008 Financial aid. Need-based:** 2,972 full-time freshmen applied for aid; 2,421 were judged to have need; 2,421 of these received aid. Average need met was 63%. Average scholarship/grant was $5,762; average loan $4,234. 35% of total undergraduate aid awarded as scholarships/grants, 65% as loans/jobs. **Non-need-based:** Awarded to 2,508 full-time undergraduates, including 936 freshmen. Scholarships awarded for academics, alumni affiliation, art, athletics, leadership, minority status, music/drama, ROTC, state residency. **Additional information:** Participant in U.S. Department of Education's Quality Assurance Program and Experimental Sites Program.

**Application procedures. Admission:** Priority date 3/15; deadline 5/1 (postmark date). $30 fee, may be waived for applicants with need. Application may be submitted online. Admission notification on a rolling basis beginning on or about 10/1. **Financial aid:** Priority date 3/1; no closing date. FAFSA required. Applicants notified on a rolling basis starting 3/15; must reply within 2 week(s) of notification.

**Academics. Special study options:** Accelerated study, combined bachelor's/graduate degree, cooperative education, cross-registration, distance learning, double major, dual enrollment of high school students, ESL, exchange student, external degree, honors, independent study, internships, liberal arts/career combination, New York semester, student-designed major, study abroad, teacher certification program, Washington semester, weekend college. BS/MD. **Credit/placement by examination:** AP, CLEP, IB, institutional tests. 30 credit hours maximum toward bachelor's degree. **Support services:** Learning center, pre-admission summer program, reduced course load, remedial instruction, study skills assistance, tutoring, writing center.

**Honors college/program.** Approximately 250 incoming freshman admitted; high school class rank within top 10 percentile; 3.5 GPA or higher; 25 ACT composite (1140 SAT exclusive of Writing); small interactive classes (20 maximum); eight courses culminating with thesis project, portfolio, or course; two study abroad programs.

**Majors. Architecture:** Architecture. **Area/ethnic studies:** African-American, American, Latin American, Russian/Slavic. **Biology:** General, biotechnology, botany, zoology. **Business:** Accounting, business admin, fashion, finance, management information systems, management science, managerial economics, marketing. **Communications:** General, advertising, broadcast journalism, digital media, journalism, photojournalism, public relations, radio/tv. **Computer sciences:** Systems analysis. **Conservation:** General. **Education:** General, art, business, chemistry, early childhood, health, mathematics, middle, music, physical, science, social studies, special, technology/industrial arts, trade/industrial. **Engineering:** General, industrial. **English:** English lit, speech/rhetoric. **Family/consumer sciences:** Family studies, food/nutrition. **Foreign languages:** French, German, Latin, Russian, sign language interpretation, Spanish. **Health:** Athletic training, audiology/speech pathology, clinical lab science, nursing (RN), predental, premedicine, preveterinary. **History:** General. **Interdisciplinary:** Peace/conflict. **Legal studies:** Paralegal. **Liberal arts:** Arts/sciences, humanities. **Math:** General, applied. **Parks/recreation:** Facilities management. **Philosophy/religion:** Philosophy. **Physical sciences:** Chemistry, geology, physics. **Protective services:** Criminal justice. **Psychology:** General. **Social sciences:** Anthropology, geography, international relations, political science, sociology. **Transportation:** Aviation. **Visual/performing arts:** Art history/conservation, commercial/advertising art, crafts, dance, dramatic, fashion design, interior design, painting. **Other:** Ethnic Heritage.

**Most popular majors.** Business/marketing 23%, communications/journalism 7%, education 12%, health sciences 8%, psychology 6%, visual/performing arts 7%.

**Computing on campus.** 2,100 workstations in dormitories, library, computer center, student center. Dormitories wired for high-speed internet access and linked to campus network. Commuter students can connect to campus network. Online course registration, online library, helpline, repair service, student web hosting, wireless network available.

**Student life. Freshman orientation:** Mandatory, $100 fee. Preregistration for classes offered. **Housing:** Guaranteed on-campus for freshmen. Coed dorms, single-sex dorms, special housing for disabled, apartments, fraternity/sorority housing available. $200 nonrefundable deposit, deadline 6/4. Single undergraduate students must live in college housing first 4 semesters with some exemptions granted. Learning communities available. **Activities:** Bands, choral groups, dance, drama, film society, literary magazine, music ensembles, musical theater, opera, radio station, student government, student newspaper, TV station, social service, political and religious organizations available.

**Athletics.** NCAA. **Intercollegiate:** Baseball M, basketball, cross-country, field hockey W, football (tackle) M, golf, gymnastics W, soccer W, softball W, track and field, volleyball W, wrestling M. **Intramural:** Badminton, basketball, bowling, football (non-tackle), golf, racquetball, soccer, softball, table tennis, tennis, water polo, wrestling M. **Team name:** Golden Flashes.

**Student services.** Adult student services, alcohol/substance abuse counseling, campus ministries, career counseling, services for economically disadvantaged, student employment services, financial aid counseling, health services, legal services, minority student services, personal counseling, placement for graduates, veterans' counselor, women's services. **Physically disabled:** Services for visually, speech, hearing impaired.

**Contact.** E-mail: admissions@kent.edu
Phone: (330) 672-2444 Toll-free number: (800) 988-5368
Fax: (330) 672-2499
Nancy DellaVecchia, Director of Admissions, Kent State University, PO Box 5190, Kent, OH 44242-0001

## Kenyon College

Gambier, Ohio

www.kenyon.edu

CB member

CB code: 1370

- Private 4-year liberal arts college
- Residential campus in rural community

- 1,653 degree-seeking undergraduates: 52% women, 4% African American, 5% Asian American, 3% Hispanic American, 1% Native American, 3% international
- 29% of applicants admitted
- SAT or ACT (ACT writing optional), application essay required
- 84% graduate within 6 years; 18% enter graduate study

**General.** Founded in 1824. Regionally accredited. **Degrees:** 410 bachelor's awarded. **Location:** 50 miles from Columbus. **Calendar:** Semester. **Full-time faculty:** 152 total; 98% have terminal degrees, 10% minority, 42% women. **Part-time faculty:** 38 total; 60% have terminal degrees, 13% minority, 53% women. **Class size:** 22% < 20, 75% 20-39, 1% 40-49, less than 1% 50-99, less than 1% >100. **Special facilities:** Observatory, environmental center and nature preserve, science center.

**Freshman class profile.** 4,626 applied, 1,352 admitted, 458 enrolled.

| Mid 50% test scores | | | |
|---|---|---|---|
| SAT critical reading: | 630-730 | Rank in top quarter: | 94% |
| SAT math: | 610-690 | Rank in top tenth: | 73% |
| SAT writing: | 630-710 | End year in good standing: | 98% |
| ACT composite: | 28-32 | Return as sophomores: | 95% |
| GPA 3.50 or higher: | 79% | Out-of-state: | 85% |
| GPA 3.0-3.49: | 19% | Live on campus: | 100% |
| GPA 2.0-2.99: | 2% | International: | 4% |

**Basis for selection.** Secondary school record and personal character most important followed by test scores, class rank, recommendations, essay, talent, activities and interview. Alumni relationship, ethnicity, geographical residence and work experience considered. Non-native speakers of English required to submit TOEFL results. **Homeschooled:** Provide complete curriculum with texts and books used.

**High school preparation.** 21 units required; 24 recommended. Required and recommended units include English 4, mathematics 3-4, social studies 1, history 2-3, science 3-4 (laboratory 3), foreign language 3-4 and academic electives 3. 1 fine arts recommended.

**2008-2009 Annual costs.** Tuition/fees (projected): $40,240. Room/board: $6,590. Books/supplies: $1,300.

**2007-2008 Financial aid. Need-based:** 253 full-time freshmen applied for aid; 191 were judged to have need; 190 of these received aid. Average need met was 98%. Average scholarship/grant was $25,265; average loan $3,318. 84% of total undergraduate aid awarded as scholarships/grants, 16% as loans/jobs. **Non-need-based:** Awarded to 547 full-time undergraduates, including 158 freshmen. Scholarships awarded for academics, leadership, minority status.

**Application procedures. Admission:** Closing date 1/15 (postmark date). $50 fee, may be waived for applicants with need. Application may be submitted online. Admission notification 4/1. Must reply by 5/1. **Financial aid:** Closing date 2/15. FAFSA, CSS PROFILE required. Applicants notified by 4/1; must reply by 5/1.

**Academics. Special study options:** Accelerated study, combined bachelor's/graduate degree, double major, exchange student, honors, independent study, internships, liberal arts/career combination, New York semester, student-designed major, study abroad, urban semester, Washington semester. Cooperative 3-2 or 4-1 masters and teacher certification program with Bank Street College of Education; 3-2 engineering program with Case Western Reserve, Rensselaer Polytechnic Institute and Washington University; 3-2 environmental studies program with Duke University. **Credit/placement by examination:** AP, CLEP, IB, institutional tests. Credit determined for AP, IB or School Articulation Program (SCAP) counts toward 16 units required for graduation. No diversification requirements may be satisfied with AP credit. **Support services:** Study skills assistance, tutoring, writing center.

**Majors. Area/ethnic studies:** American, women's. **Biology:** General, biochemistry, molecular. **English:** English lit. **Foreign languages:** General, ancient Greek, Chinese, classics, French, German, Italian, Japanese, Latin, Russian, Spanish. **History:** General. **Interdisciplinary:** Neuroscience. **Math:** General. **Philosophy/religion:** Philosophy, religion. **Physical sciences:** Chemistry, physics. **Psychology:** General. **Social sciences:** Anthropology, economics, international relations, political science, sociology. **Visual/performing arts:** Art, art history/conservation, dance, dramatic, studio arts.

**Most popular majors.** Biology 6%, English 17%, foreign language 7%, history 7%, interdisciplinary studies 11%, psychology 7%, social sciences 20%, visual/performing arts 12%.

**Computing on campus.** 530 workstations in dormitories, library, computer center. Dormitories wired for high-speed internet access and linked to campus network. Commuter students can connect to campus network. Online library, helpline, student web hosting, wireless network available.

**Student life. Freshman orientation:** Mandatory. Held 4 days prior to start of classes. **Housing:** Guaranteed on-campus for all undergraduates. Coed dorms, single-sex dorms, special housing for disabled, apartments, fraternity/sorority housing, substance-free housing available. $350 nonrefundable deposit, deadline 5/1. Special accomodations can be made for married, international and disabled students. Fraternity and sorority housing available in room blocks only. Wellness and community service and social group halls on campus. **Activities:** Bands, campus ministries, choral groups, dance, drama, film society, international student organizations, literary magazine, music ensembles, Model UN, musical theater, opera, radio station, student government, student newspaper, symphony orchestra, Black Student Union, Christian Fellowship, Hillel, Asian Student Alliance, Associacion de Estudiantes Latino Americanos y de Naciones Tropicales Exoticas, Archon Society (community service organization), Allied Sexual Orientations, Amnesty International, Zen meditation group, political affairs club.

**Athletics.** NCAA. **Intercollegiate:** Baseball M, basketball, cross-country, diving, field hockey W, football (tackle) M, golf M, lacrosse, soccer, softball W, swimming, tennis, track and field, volleyball W. **Intramural:** Basketball, football (non-tackle), golf, racquetball, rugby, soccer, softball, tennis, volleyball, water polo. **Team name:** Lords/Ladies.

**Student services.** Alcohol/substance abuse counseling, campus ministries, career counseling, student employment services, financial aid counseling, health services, minority student services, personal counseling, placement for graduates, women's services. **Physically disabled:** Services for visually, hearing impaired.

**Contact.** E-mail: admissions@kenyon.edu
Phone: (740) 427-5776 Toll-free number: (800) 848-2468
Fax: (740) 427-5770
Jennifer Delahunty, Dean of Admissions, Kenyon College, Ransom Hall, Gambier, OH 43022

## Kettering College of Medical Arts
**Kettering, Ohio**
**www.kcma.edu**                                    **CB code: 0602**

- Private 4-year health science and nursing college affiliated with Seventh-day Adventists
- Commuter campus in large city
- 738 degree-seeking undergraduates: 45% part-time, 80% women, 8% African American, 2% Asian American, 2% Hispanic American
- 58 degree-seeking graduate students
- 50% of applicants admitted
- Application essay required

**General.** Founded in 1967. Regionally accredited. Institution is educational division of Kettering Health Network. **Degrees:** 54 bachelor's, 168 associate awarded; master's offered. **Location:** 5 miles from Dayton. **Calendar:** Semester, limited summer session. **Full-time faculty:** 53 total; 19% have terminal degrees, 9% minority, 66% women. **Part-time faculty:** 22 total; 9% have terminal degrees, 18% minority, 73% women. **Class size:** 65% < 20, 27% 20-39, 5% 40-49, 2% 50-99.

**Freshman class profile.** 204 applied, 101 admitted, 61 enrolled.

| Mid 50% test scores | | | |
|---|---|---|---|
| | | GPA 2.0-2.99: | 17% |
| SAT critical reading: | 490-560 | Rank in top quarter: | 53% |
| SAT math: | 490-580 | Rank in top tenth: | 22% |
| SAT writing: | 490-570 | End year in good standing: | 75% |
| ACT composite: | 20-24 | Return as sophomores: | 63% |
| GPA 3.50 or higher: | 52% | Out-of-state: | 3% |
| GPA 3.0-3.49: | 31% | Live on campus: | 3% |

**Basis for selection.** High school GPA, test scores, personal statements are important. Essay required for all applicants; interview required for physician assistant applicants.

**High school preparation.** 14 units recommended. Recommended units include English 4, mathematics 2 and science 3. Strong mathematics and science background recommended.

**2008-2009 Annual costs.** Tuition/fees (projected): $9,908. Tuition and fees may vary by program. Room only: $2,900. Books/supplies: $1,100. Personal expenses: $2,792.

**Financial aid. Non-need-based:** Scholarships awarded for academics.

**Application procedures. Admission:** No deadline. $25 fee, may be waived for applicants with need. Application may be submitted online. Admission notification on a rolling basis. **Financial aid:** Priority date 3/31; no closing date. FAFSA, institutional form required. Applicants notified on a rolling basis starting 5/15; must reply within 3 week(s) of notification.

**Academics.** **Special study options:** Accelerated study, cross-registration, distance learning, double major, dual enrollment of high school students, external degree, honors. **Credit/placement by examination:** AP, CLEP, SAT, ACT, institutional tests. **Support services:** Learning center, reduced course load, study skills assistance, tutoring, writing center.

**Majors.** **Health:** Nursing (RN), predental, premedicine, respiratory therapy technology, sonography.

**Computing on campus.** 32 workstations in library, computer center. Dormitories wired for high-speed internet access and linked to campus network. Online library, wireless network available.

**Student life.** **Freshman orientation:** Mandatory. Preregistration for classes offered. **Policies:** Religious observance required. **Housing:** Single-sex dorms, substance-free housing available. $75 nonrefundable deposit. **Activities:** Campus ministries, religious life organizations.

**Student services.** Campus ministries, career counseling, student employment services, financial aid counseling, health services, personal counseling, placement for graduates, veterans' counselor.

**Contact.** E-mail: studentadmissions@kcma.edu
Phone: (937) 395-8628 Toll-free number: (800) 433-5262
Fax: (937) 395-8338
Becky McDonald, Director of Enrollment Services, Kettering College of Medical Arts, 3737 Southern Boulevard, Kettering, OH 45429-1299

## Lake Erie College

Painesville, Ohio

www.lec.edu

**CB member**
**CB code: 1391**

- Private 4-year liberal arts college
- Residential campus in large town
- 795 degree-seeking undergraduates: 4% part-time, 57% women
- 153 degree-seeking graduate students
- 56% of applicants admitted
- SAT or ACT (ACT writing optional), application essay required

**General.** Founded in 1856. Regionally accredited. **Degrees:** 134 bachelor's awarded; master's offered. **Location:** 30 miles from Cleveland. **Calendar:** Semester, limited summer session. **Full-time faculty:** 34 total; 76% have terminal degrees, 6% minority, 50% women. **Part-time faculty:** 59 total; 22% have terminal degrees, 5% minority, 49% women. **Class size:** 82% < 20, 18% 20-39. **Special facilities:** Equestrian center.

**Freshman class profile.** 985 applied, 551 admitted, 397 enrolled.

| Mid 50% test scores | | | |
|---|---|---|---|
| SAT critical reading: | 410-550 | GPA 2.0-2.99: | 49% |
| SAT math: | 420-550 | Rank in top quarter: | 25% |
| SAT writing: | 410-530 | Rank in top tenth: | 11% |
| ACT composite: | 18-23 | Out-of-state: | 32% |
| GPA 3.50 or higher: | 22% | Live on campus: | 70% |
| GPA 3.0-3.49: | 28% | Sororities: | 8% |

**Basis for selection.** School achievement record, test scores, essay, reference letters and interview strongly considered. Special consideration of test scores for some applicants. Interview strongly recommended. **Homeschooled:** Statement describing homeschool structure and mission, transcript of courses and grades, interview, letter of recommendation (nonparent) required. **Learning Disabled:** Documentation of learning disability required.

**High school preparation.** Recommended units include English 4, mathematics 3, social studies 3, science 3 (laboratory 2) and foreign language 2. 1 fine arts and 1 physical education or health recommended.

**2008-2009 Annual costs.** Tuition/fees (projected): $25,070. Equestrian fee $880 per course. Room/board: $7,580. Books/supplies: $900. Personal expenses: $1,304.

**2006-2007 Financial aid.** **Need-based:** 72% of total undergraduate aid awarded as scholarships/grants, 28% as loans/jobs. **Non-need-based:** Scholarships awarded for academics, art, leadership, music/drama, state residency. **Additional information:** Twins' scholarship, sibling discount.

**Application procedures.** **Admission:** Priority date 3/1; deadline 8/1. $30 fee, may be waived for applicants with need. Application may be submitted online. Admission notification on a rolling basis beginning on or about 9/15. **Financial aid:** No deadline. FAFSA required. Applicants notified on a rolling basis; must reply within 2 week(s) of notification.

**Academics.** **Special study options:** Accelerated study, cross-registration, double major, dual enrollment of high school students, honors, independent study, internships, liberal arts/career combination, student-designed major, study abroad, teacher certification program, weekend college. **Credit/placement by examination:** AP, CLEP, IB, SAT, ACT, institutional tests. 32 credit hours maximum toward bachelor's degree. **Support services:** Learning center, reduced course load, study skills assistance, tutoring, writing center.

**Majors.** **Agriculture:** Animal breeding, equestrian studies, equine science, farm/ranch. **Biology:** General. **Business:** Accounting, business admin, international. **Communications:** General. **Conservation:** General, environmental studies. **Education:** General, curriculum, elementary, reading, secondary. **English:** English lit. **Foreign languages:** General, French, German, Italian, Spanish. **History:** General. **Legal studies:** Paralegal, prelaw. **Math:** General. **Physical sciences:** Chemistry. **Protective services:** Law enforcement admin. **Psychology:** General. **Social sciences:** General, sociology. **Visual/performing arts:** General, dance, studio arts, theater arts management.

**Most popular majors.** Agriculture 12%, biology 6%, business/marketing 24%, education 13%, interdisciplinary studies 8%, physical sciences 6%.

**Computing on campus.** 112 workstations in dormitories, library, computer center, student center. Dormitories wired for high-speed internet access and linked to campus network. Commuter students can connect to campus network. Online course registration, online library, helpline, repair service, wireless network available.

**Student life.** **Freshman orientation:** Mandatory, $200 fee. Preregistration for classes offered. One-day program during summer. **Housing:** Guaranteed on-campus for freshmen. Coed dorms, single-sex dorms, substance-free housing available. $150 nonrefundable deposit. Residence halls equipped with laundry and kitchen areas available. **Activities:** Choral groups, dance, drama, literary magazine, music ensembles, radio station, student government, student newspaper, honor, academic, and athletic associations, foreign language clubs, professional organizations, equestrian clubs, student activities council.

**Athletics.** NCAA. **Intercollegiate:** Baseball M, basketball, cross-country, equestrian, football (non-tackle) M, golf, lacrosse M, soccer, softball W, volleyball W. **Team name:** Storm.

**Student services.** Career counseling, student employment services, financial aid counseling, placement for graduates. **Physically disabled:** Services for visually impaired.

**Contact.** E-mail: admissions@lec.edu
Phone: (440) 375-7050 Toll-free number: (800) 916-0904
Fax: (440) 375-7005
Eric Felver, Director of Admissions, Lake Erie College, 391 West Washington Street, Painesville, OH 44077-3389

## Laura and Alvin Siegal College of Judaic Studies

Cleveland, Ohio

www.siegalcollege.edu

**CB code: 1190**

- Private 4-year liberal arts and teachers college affiliated with Jewish faith
- Commuter campus in large town
- 13 degree-seeking undergraduates: 100% part-time, 15% women
- 109 degree-seeking graduate students
- Application essay, interview required

**General.** Founded in 1963. Regionally accredited. **Degrees:** 1 bachelor's awarded; master's offered. **Location:** 10 miles from Cleveland. **Calendar:** Semester, extensive summer session. **Full-time faculty:** 8 total. **Part-time faculty:** 23 total.

**Basis for selection.** Interview and 2 recommendations most important. Essay important; high school record and community activities considered.

**High school preparation.** Graduation from Hebrew high school or good background in Hebrew language and Judaic subjects.

**2007-2008 Annual costs.** Tuition/fees: $15,775. Books/supplies: $500.

**2007-2008 Financial aid.** **Need-based:** 69% of total undergraduate aid awarded as scholarships/grants, 31% as loans/jobs.

**Application procedures.** **Admission:** No deadline. $50 fee. Admission notification on a rolling basis. **Financial aid:** No deadline. Institutional form required. Applicants notified on a rolling basis.

**Academics.** College specializes in Judaic and Hebrew studies and teacher education. **Special study options:** Cross-registration, distance learning, independent study, internships. **Credit/placement by examination:** AP, CLEP, IB. 45 credit hours maximum toward bachelor's degree. **Support services:** Reduced course load, study skills assistance.

**Majors. Foreign languages:** General, Hebrew. **Philosophy/religion:** Judaic. **Theology:** Bible, religious ed.

**Computing on campus.** 8 workstations in library. Online library, wireless network available.

**Student life. Freshman orientation:** Available. Preregistration for classes offered.

**Student services.** Adult student services, career counseling, financial aid counseling. **Physically disabled:** Services for hearing impaired.

**Contact.** E-mail: admissions@siegalcollege.edu
Phone: (216) 464-4050 Toll-free number: (888) 336-2257
Fax: (216) 464-5827
Ruth Kronick, Director of Student Services, Laura and Alvin Siegal College of Judaic Studies, 26500 Shaker Boulevard, Cleveland, OH 44122

## Lourdes College
**Sylvania, Ohio**
**www.lourdes.edu**

CB member
CB code: 1427

- Private 4-year liberal arts college affiliated with Roman Catholic Church
- Commuter campus in large town
- 1,700 degree-seeking undergraduates: 44% part-time, 83% women, 15% African American, 1% Asian American, 3% Hispanic American, 1% Native American
- 202 degree-seeking graduate students
- 80% of applicants admitted
- 32% graduate within 6 years

**General.** Founded in 1958. Regionally accredited. **Degrees:** 188 bachelor's, 30 associate awarded; master's offered. **ROTC:** Army, Air Force. **Location:** 10 miles from Toledo. **Calendar:** Semester, limited summer session. **Full-time faculty:** 77 total; 46% have terminal degrees, 4% minority, 71% women. **Part-time faculty:** 127 total; 16% have terminal degrees, 10% minority, 72% women. **Class size:** 61% < 20, 39% 20-39, less than 1% 40-49. **Special facilities:** Planetarium, life lab.

**Freshman class profile.** 405 applied, 326 admitted, 132 enrolled.

| Mid 50% test scores | | | |
|---|---|---|---|
| | | Rank in top quarter: | 19% |
| ACT composite: | 17-21 | Rank in top tenth: | 4% |
| GPA 3.50 or higher: | 13% | End year in good standing: | 80% |
| GPA 3.0-3.49: | 36% | Return as sophomores: | 70% |
| GPA 2.0-2.99: | 46% | Out-of-state: | 15% |

**Basis for selection.** Academic GPA very important, recommendations and interview considered. Conditional admission may be granted at the discretion of the Director of Admission to high school graduates with no prior college experience who have a high school G.P.A. below 2.0 on a 4.0 scale and transfer students who have attempted a minimum of 12 semester hours with a cumulative college G.P.A. below 2.0 on a 4.0 scale from a college accredited by the Higher Learning Commission. **Homeschooled:** Transcript of courses and grades required.

**High school preparation.** 18 units recommended. Recommended units include English 4, mathematics 3, social studies 3, science 3 (laboratory 2), foreign language 2 and visual/performing arts 1.

**2007-2008 Annual costs.** Tuition/fees: $14,040. Books/supplies: $656. Personal expenses: $3,440.

**2006-2007 Financial aid. Need-based:** 92 full-time freshmen applied for aid; 71 were judged to have need; 71 of these received aid. Average scholarship/grant was $6,677; average loan $2,557. 35% of total undergraduate aid awarded as scholarships/grants, 65% as loans/jobs. **Non-need-based:** Awarded to 656 full-time undergraduates, including 71 freshmen. Scholarships awarded for academics, art, minority status, state residency.

**Application procedures. Admission:** Priority date 8/25; no deadline. $25 fee, may be waived for applicants with need. Application may be submitted online. Admission notification on a rolling basis. **Financial aid:** Priority date 3/1; no closing date. FAFSA required. Applicants notified on a rolling basis starting 3/1; must reply within 4 week(s) of notification.

**Academics. Special study options:** Distance learning, double major, dual enrollment of high school students, independent study, internships, liberal arts/career combination, student-designed major, study abroad, teacher certification program, weekend college. **Credit/placement by examination:** AP, CLEP, institutional tests. **Support services:** Learning center, reduced course load, remedial instruction, study skills assistance, tutoring, writing center.

**Majors. Biology:** General. **Business:** Accounting/finance, business admin, human resources, management science, marketing. **Conservation:** Environmental science. **Education:** Early childhood, middle, secondary. **English:** English lit. **Health:** Health care admin, nursing (RN). **History:** General. **Philosophy/religion:** Religion. **Protective services:** Criminal justice. **Psychology:** General. **Public administration:** Social work. **Social sciences:** Sociology. **Visual/performing arts:** Art, art history/conservation.

**Most popular majors.** Business/marketing 25%, education 12%, health sciences 30%, interdisciplinary studies 10%.

**Computing on campus.** 161 workstations in library, computer center, student center. Helpline, wireless network available.

**Student life. Freshman orientation:** Mandatory. Preregistration for classes offered. **Activities:** Campus ministries, choral groups, film society, literary magazine, student government, student government association, Pi Alpha Theta (history), Sigma Theta Tau International (nursing), Kappa Gamma Pi (Catholic college graduate honor aociety), Phi Alpha (social work), Theta Alpha Kappa (theologians and students in religious studies), Sigma Phi Omega (gerontology), Zeta Delta Chi community service organization.

**Athletics. Team name:** Gray Wolves.

**Student services.** Adult student services, alcohol/substance abuse counseling, campus ministries, career counseling, services for economically disadvantaged, financial aid counseling, personal counseling. **Physically disabled:** Services for visually, speech, hearing impaired.

**Contact.** E-mail: lcadmits@lourdes.edu
Phone: (419) 885-5291 ext. 3680 Toll-free
number: (800) 878-3210 ext. 3680 Fax: (419) 882-3987
Amy Mergen, Director of Admissions, Lourdes College, 6832 Convent Boulevard, Sylvania, OH 43560-2898

## Malone College
**Canton, Ohio**
**www.malone.edu**

CB code: 1439

- Private 4-year liberal arts college affiliated with Evangelical Friends Church-Eastern Region
- Residential campus in small city
- 1,964 degree-seeking undergraduates: 10% part-time, 61% women, 6% African American, 1% Asian American, 1% Hispanic American, 1% international
- 332 degree-seeking graduate students
- 76% of applicants admitted
- SAT or ACT (ACT writing optional), application essay required
- 56% graduate within 6 years; 22% enter graduate study

**General.** Founded in 1892. Regionally accredited. Interdenominational Christian environment. **Degrees:** 492 bachelor's awarded; master's offered. **ROTC:** Army, Air Force. **Location:** 55 miles from Cleveland. **Calendar:** Semester, limited summer session. **Full-time faculty:** 108 total; 66% have terminal degrees, 5% minority, 45% women. **Part-time faculty:** 101 total; 23% have terminal degrees, 3% minority, 50% women. **Class size:** 53% < 20, 37% 20-39, 7% 40-49, 2% 50-99. **Special facilities:** Child development center.

**Freshman class profile.** 1,484 applied, 1,127 admitted, 392 enrolled.

| Mid 50% test scores | | | |
|---|---|---|---|
| SAT critical reading: | 480-580 | Rank in top quarter: | 49% |
| SAT math: | 470-570 | Rank in top tenth: | 23% |
| SAT writing: | 490-590 | End year in good standing: | 94% |
| ACT composite: | 20-25 | Return as sophomores: | 78% |
| GPA 3.50 or higher: | 48% | Out-of-state: | 17% |
| GPA 3.0-3.49: | 32% | Live on campus: | 86% |
| GPA 2.0-2.99: | 20% | International: | 1% |

**Basis for selection.** High school record, test scores and recommendations most important. Interview also considered and encouraged. Audition required for entrance into music programs; portfolio required during first semester for art programs. **Homeschooled:** Must have high school diploma, transcript, and ACT or SAT. **Learning Disabled:** Students disclosing learning disabilities must interview with Director of Disability Support Services.

**High school preparation.** 18 units required. Required units include English 4, mathematics 3, social studies 2, history 1, science 3 (laboratory 1), foreign language 2, visual/performing arts 1 and academic electives 2.

**2007-2008 Annual costs.** Tuition/fees: $18,870. Room/board: $6,600. Books/supplies: $930. Personal expenses: $1,200.

**2007-2008 Financial aid. Need-based:** 356 full-time freshmen applied for aid; 325 were judged to have need; 325 of these received aid. Average need met was 74%. Average scholarship/grant was $11,306; average loan $4,282. 51% of total undergraduate aid awarded as scholarships/grants, 49% as loans/jobs. **Non-need-based:** Awarded to 1,510 full-time undergraduates, including 381 freshmen. Scholarships awarded for academics, alumni affiliation, athletics, leadership, music/drama, religious affiliation. **Additional information:** Prepayment discounts and employer deferred payments available for students in adult degree-completion programs. Employer deferred payment plan is available for traditional undergraduate students.

**Application procedures. Admission:** Closing date 7/1 (postmark date). $20 fee, may be waived for applicants with need. Application may be submitted online. Admission notification on a rolling basis beginning on or about 9/1. **Financial aid:** Priority date 3/1, closing date 7/31. FAFSA required. Applicants notified on a rolling basis starting 3/1; must reply within 2 week(s) of notification.

**Academics.** 50-56 hours of general education courses organized under the 3 areas of 1) Foundations of Faith and Learning, 2) Foundational Skills, and 3) Engaging God's World. **Special study options:** Accelerated study, cross-registration, distance learning, double major, dual enrollment of high school students, exchange student, honors, independent study, internships, student-designed major, study abroad, teacher certification program, Washington semester, weekend college. 2 degree-completion programs for adult students in management, nursing; American Studies Program (Washington, D.C.), Australia Studies Centre (Sydney), China Studies Program (Shanghai), Latin American Studies Program (San Jose, Costa Rica), Middle East Studies Program (Cairo, Egypt), Russian Studies Program, Ugandan Studies Program, Los Angeles Film Studies Center, Contemporary Music Center (Martha's Vineyard), Washington Journalism Center, Daystar University in Kenya, Malone College Teacher Education semester in Guatemala. **Credit/placement by examination:** AP, CLEP, IB, SAT, ACT, institutional tests. 62 credit hours maximum toward bachelor's degree. External credit by exam limit is 20, excluding AP credit for which an additional 30 credits are available. Other credits available by in house exams. **Support services:** Reduced course load, remedial instruction, study skills assistance, tutoring, writing center.

**Majors. Biology:** General, zoology. **Business:** Accounting, business admin. **Communications:** General, journalism, public relations, radio/tv. **Communications technology:** Recording arts. **Computer sciences:** Computer science. **Education:** Art, early childhood, English, health, learning disabled, middle, music, physical, science, social studies, Spanish. **English:** English lit. **Foreign languages:** Spanish. **Health:** Clinical lab science, nursing (RN), public health ed. **History:** General. **Liberal arts:** Arts/sciences. **Math:** General. **Parks/recreation:** General, exercise sciences, health/fitness. **Philosophy/religion:** Philosophy. **Physical sciences:** Chemistry. **Psychology:** General. **Public administration:** Social work. **Social sciences:** Political science. **Theology:** Bible, pastoral counseling, sacred music, theology, youth ministry. **Visual/performing arts:** Dramatic, studio arts.

**Most popular majors.** Business/marketing 40%, education 17%, health sciences 15%, theological studies 6%.

**Computing on campus.** 205 workstations in dormitories, library, computer center, student center. Dormitories wired for high-speed internet access and linked to campus network. Online library, helpline, student web hosting, wireless network available.

**Student life. Freshman orientation:** Mandatory. Preregistration for classes offered. 5 days prior to start of semester, some on-campus events, community service, relationship-building activities. **Policies:** Christian institution with conservative campus lifestyle. Religious observance required. **Housing:** Single-sex dorms, substance-free housing available. $50 nonrefundable deposit. Full-time students required to live on campus unless 22 or older, holding senior status, married or commuting from home. Exceptions considered. **Activities:** Bands, choral groups, dance, drama, literary magazine, music ensembles, musical theater, radio station, student government, student newspaper, Campus Crusade for Christ, Habitat for Humanity, Helping Hands, multicultural student union, Nurses Christian Fellowship, Rotoract, spiritual life committee, Students in Action, Unity Under Christ, Fellowship of Christian Athletes.

**Athletics.** NAIA, NCCAA. **Intercollegiate:** Baseball M, basketball, cheerleading, cross-country, football (tackle) M, golf, soccer, softball W, tennis, track and field, volleyball W. **Intramural:** Basketball, bowling, football (non-tackle), football (tackle), skiing, soccer, softball, table tennis, volleyball, weight lifting. **Team name:** Pioneers.

**Student services.** Adult student services, campus ministries, career counseling, student employment services, financial aid counseling, health services, minority student services, personal counseling, placement for graduates. **Physically disabled:** Services for visually, speech, hearing impaired.

**Contact.** E-mail: admissions@malone.edu
Phone: (330) 471-8100 ext. 8145 Toll-free number: (800) 521-1146
Fax: (330) 471-8149
John Russell, Director of Admissions, Malone College, 515 25th Street Northwest, Canton, OH 44709-3897

---

## Marietta College
### Marietta, Ohio
### www.marietta.edu

**CB member**
**CB code: 1444**

- Private 4-year liberal arts college
- Residential campus in large town
- 1,466 degree-seeking undergraduates: 2% part-time, 51% women, 4% African American, 2% Asian American, 1% Hispanic American, 6% international
- 104 degree-seeking graduate students
- 75% of applicants admitted
- SAT or ACT (ACT writing optional) required
- 56% graduate within 6 years; 32% enter graduate study

**General.** Founded in 1835. Regionally accredited. **Degrees:** 255 bachelor's awarded; master's offered. **Location:** 120 miles from Columbus, 110 miles from Pittsburgh. **Calendar:** Semester, limited summer session. **Full-time faculty:** 96 total; 78% have terminal degrees, 5% minority, 35% women. **Part-time faculty:** 43 total; 40% have terminal degrees, 2% minority, 58% women. **Class size:** 68% < 20, 29% 20-39, 2% 40-49, less than 1% 50-99. **Special facilities:** Observatory, center for leadership development, greenhouse, cadaver lab, extensive fossil collection, many historically important documents from the beginning of the old Northwest Territory.

**Freshman class profile.** 2,320 applied, 1,751 admitted, 418 enrolled.

| Mid 50% test scores | | | |
|---|---|---|---|
| SAT critical reading: | 480-600 | Rank in top tenth: | 22% |
| SAT math: | 490-600 | End year in good standing: | 88% |
| ACT composite: | 20-26 | Return as sophomores: | 80% |
| GPA 3.50 or higher: | 49% | Out-of-state: | 42% |
| GPA 3.0-3.49: | 32% | Live on campus: | 93% |
| GPA 2.0-2.99: | 19% | International: | 7% |
| Rank in top quarter: | 53% | Fraternities: | 13% |
| | | Sororities: | 20% |

**Basis for selection.** High school curriculum, GPA, test scores most important. Recommendations and essay important. TOEFL used for admission and ESL placement. Interview recommended for all. Portfolio recommended for arts programs. **Homeschooled:** Statement describing home-school structure and mission, transcript of courses and grades, interview required. Chronicle of study and standardized test scores required.

**High school preparation.** 16 units required. Required units include English 4, mathematics 3, social studies 2, history 2, science 3 (laboratory 2), foreign language 2 and academic electives 1.

**2007-2008 Annual costs.** Tuition/fees: $24,822. Room/board: $7,390. Books/supplies: $680. Personal expenses: $615.

**2007-2008 Financial aid. Need-based:** 394 full-time freshmen applied for aid; 333 were judged to have need; 333 of these received aid. Average need met was 94%. Average scholarship/grant was $17,984; average loan $4,125. 71% of total undergraduate aid awarded as scholarships/grants, 29% as loans/jobs. **Non-need-based:** Awarded to 1,059 full-time undergraduates, including 300 freshmen. Scholarships awarded for academics, alumni affiliation, art, leadership, minority status, music/drama, state residency. **Additional information:** Auditions/portfolios for art, creative writing, music and theater required for competitive fine art scholarships.

**Application procedures. Admission:** Priority date 3/1; deadline 5/1 (postmark date). $25 fee, may be waived for applicants with need. Application may be submitted online. Admission notification on a rolling basis beginning on or about 9/1. Must reply by May 1 or within 2 week(s) if notified thereafter. **Financial aid:** Priority date 3/1, closing date 4/15. FAFSA, institutional form required. Applicants notified on a rolling basis starting 3/15; must reply by 5/1 or within 2 week(s) of notification.

**Academics.** Early Alert Program whereby professors can contact the Academic Resource Center to assist those students demonstrating need for additional academic support. **Special study options:** Combined bachelor's/graduate degree, double major, dual enrollment of high school students, ESL, exchange student, honors, independent study, internships, liberal arts/

career combination, student-designed major, study abroad, teacher certification program, Washington semester. Leadership program, investigative studies. **Credit/placement by examination:** AP, CLEP, IB, SAT, ACT, institutional tests. 36 credit hours maximum toward bachelor's degree. **Support services:** Reduced course load, remedial instruction, study skills assistance, tutoring, writing center.

**Majors. Biology:** General, biochemistry. **Business:** Accounting, communications, finance, human resources, international, management information systems, marketing. **Communications:** General, advertising, broadcast journalism, journalism, organizational, public relations, radio/tv. **Computer sciences:** General, computer science, information systems. **Conservation:** Environmental science, environmental studies. **Education:** General, early childhood, elementary, middle, multi-level teacher, secondary. **Engineering:** Petroleum. **English:** English lit. **Foreign languages:** Spanish. **Health:** Athletic training. **History:** General. **Math:** General. **Physical sciences:** Chemistry, geology, physics. **Psychology:** General. **Social sciences:** Economics, political science. **Visual/performing arts:** Commercial/advertising art, dramatic, studio arts.

**Most popular majors.** Business/marketing 22%, communications/journalism 14%, education 7%, health sciences 7%, social sciences 7%, visual/performing arts 10%.

**Computing on campus.** 350 workstations in dormitories, library, computer center, student center. Dormitories wired for high-speed internet access and linked to campus network. Commuter students can connect to campus network. Online library, helpline, repair service, wireless network available.

**Student life. Freshman orientation:** Mandatory, $250 fee. Preregistration for classes offered. Four-and-one-half day program. Culminating event either white-water rafting trip or dinner theater production. **Policies:** Student code of conduct, judicial system, no alcohol policy for students under age of 21. **Housing:** Guaranteed on-campus for freshmen. Coed dorms, single-sex dorms, special housing for disabled, apartments, fraternity/sorority housing, substance-free housing available. $200 deposit, deadline 5/1. Special interest theme housing (honors, arts and humanities house) available. **Activities:** Bands, choral groups, dance, drama, literary magazine, music ensembles, musical theater, radio station, student government, student newspaper, TV station, InterVarsity Christian Fellowship, Circle K, MC Democrats, MC Republicans, Habitat for Humanity, Feminist Majority Leadership, coalition for social change, American International Association, Charles Sumner Harrison organization, student global AIDS campaign.

**Athletics.** NCAA. **Intercollegiate:** Baseball M, basketball, cross-country, football (tackle) M, rowing (crew), soccer, softball W, tennis, track and field, volleyball W. **Intramural:** Basketball, football (non-tackle), handball, racquetball, soccer, softball, table tennis, volleyball. **Team name:** Pioneers.

**Student services.** Adult student services, alcohol/substance abuse counseling, career counseling, student employment services, financial aid counseling, health services, minority student services, personal counseling, placement for graduates. **Physically disabled:** Services for visually, speech, hearing impaired. **Learning disabled:** Comprehensive services available.

**Contact.** E-mail: admit@marietta.edu
Phone: (740) 376-4600 Toll-free number: (800) 331-7896
Fax: (740) 376-8888
Jason Turley, Director of Admission, Marietta College, 215 Fifth Street, Marietta, OH 45750-4005

---

## MedCentral College of Nursing
**Mansfield, Ohio**
**www.medcentral.edu**                **CB code: 3935**

- Private 4-year nursing college
- Commuter campus in small city
- 365 degree-seeking undergraduates
- 73% of applicants admitted
- SAT or ACT (ACT writing recommended) required

**General.** Regionally accredited. General electives taken at the Ohio State University-Mansfield. **Degrees:** 77 bachelor's awarded. **Location:** 60 miles from Cleveland, 60 miles from Columbus. **Calendar:** Quarter, extensive summer session. **Full-time faculty:** 20 total; 20% have terminal degrees, 80% women. **Part-time faculty:** 2 total.

**Freshman class profile.**

| Mid 50% test scores | | GPA 2.0-2.99: | 10% |
|---|---|---|---|
| ACT composite: | 18-28 | Rank in top quarter: | 80% |
| GPA 3.50 or higher: | 29% | Rank in top tenth: | 5% |
| GPA 3.0-3.49: | 61% | Live on campus: | 20% |

**Basis for selection.** Previous high school and college academic credentials very important. Co-curricular activities, work experience, students character also considered. **Homeschooled:** Transcript of courses and grades required. Require ACT/SAT.

**High school preparation.** 17 units required; 20 recommended. Required and recommended units include English 4, mathematics 3-4, social studies 2, history 1, science 3-4 (laboratory 2-3), foreign language 2, computer science 1 and academic electives 2.

**2007-2008 Annual costs.** Tuition/fees: $10,545. Room only: $4,890. Books/supplies: $2,000. Personal expenses: $3,000.

**Financial aid. Non-need-based:** Scholarships awarded for academics, leadership.

**Application procedures. Admission:** Priority date 5/1; deadline 7/1 (postmark date). $50 fee, may be waived for applicants with need. Application must be submitted on paper. Admission notification on a rolling basis beginning on or about 10/1. Must reply by 8/5. **Financial aid:** Priority date 4/2, closing date 9/15. FAFSA, institutional form required. Applicants notified on a rolling basis starting 4/1; must reply by 5/1 or within 2 week(s) of notification.

**Academics. Special study options:** Accelerated study, independent study. **Credit/placement by examination:** AP, CLEP, SAT, ACT, institutional tests. 48 credit hours maximum toward bachelor's degree. **Support services:** Learning center, remedial instruction, study skills assistance, tutoring, writing center.

**Majors. Health:** Nursing (RN).

**Computing on campus.** 150 workstations in library, computer center. Dormitories wired for high-speed internet access. Online library, wireless network available.

**Student life. Freshman orientation:** Mandatory. **Housing:** Guaranteed on-campus for freshmen. Apartments, substance-free housing available. $100 nonrefundable deposit, deadline 6/15. **Activities:** Student government, National Student Nurses Association.

**Student services.** Adult student services, alcohol/substance abuse counseling, campus ministries, career counseling, student employment services, financial aid counseling, personal counseling.

**Contact.** E-mail: admissions@medcentral.edu
Phone: (419) 520-2600 Toll-free number: (877) 645-4360
Fax: (419) 520-2662
Christopher Harris, Dean of Student Affairs, MedCentral College of Nursing, 335 Glessner Avenue, Mansfield, OH 44903-2265

---

## Mercy College of Northwest Ohio
**Toledo, Ohio**
**www.mercycollege.edu**                **CB code: 4685**

- Private 4-year health science and nursing college affiliated with Roman Catholic Church
- Commuter campus in large city
- 797 degree-seeking undergraduates: 49% part-time, 85% women, 6% African American, 4% Hispanic American
- 81% of applicants admitted
- SAT or ACT (ACT writing optional) required
- 33% graduate within 6 years

**General. Degrees:** 44 bachelor's, 136 associate awarded. **Calendar:** Semester, limited summer session. **Full-time faculty:** 60 total; 28% have terminal degrees, 3% minority, 88% women. **Part-time faculty:** 48 total; 12% have terminal degrees, 8% minority, 75% women. **Class size:** 56% < 20, 35% 20-39, 4% 40-49, 4% 50-99.

**Freshman class profile.** 208 applied, 168 admitted, 64 enrolled.

| Return as sophomores: | 77% | Live on campus: | 19% |
|---|---|---|---|
| Out-of-state: | 14% | | |

**Basis for selection.** Students reviewed by admission, progression and graduation committee. Must have minimum GPA of 2.3 to be admitted. Admission to programs of study may have higher GPA and specific course grade requirements.

**High school preparation.** 11 units required; 23 recommended. Required and recommended units include English 3-4, mathematics 2-4, social

**Four-Year Colleges**

studies 2-3, history 1, science 2-4 (laboratory 2-3), foreign language 2, computer science 1 and visual/performing arts 1.

**2007-2008 Annual costs.** Tuition/fees: $9,546. Actual cost is based on credit hours taken - 12 or more credits $278/ credit hour, less than 12 credit hours $310/credit hour. Books/supplies: $1,344. Personal expenses: $3,184.

**2006-2007 Financial aid. Need-based:** 46 full-time freshmen applied for aid; 43 were judged to have need; 43 of these received aid. Average need met was 45%. Average scholarship/grant was $6,485; average loan $2,920. 43% of total undergraduate aid awarded as scholarships/grants, 57% as loans/jobs. **Non-need-based:** Awarded to 177 full-time undergraduates, including 14 freshmen. Scholarships awarded for academics, alumni affiliation, religious affiliation, state residency.

**Application procedures. Admission:** Priority date 1/31; no deadline. $25 fee, may be waived for applicants with need. Application may be submitted online. Admission notification on a rolling basis. Must reply by May 1 or within 2 week(s) if notified thereafter. **Financial aid:** Priority date 4/1; no closing date. FAFSA required. Applicants notified on a rolling basis starting 3/1; must reply within 2 week(s) of notification.

**Academics. Special study options:** Combined bachelor's/graduate degree, distance learning, double major, independent study. **Credit/placement by examination:** AP, CLEP, institutional tests. **Support services:** Learning center, reduced course load, remedial instruction, study skills assistance, tutoring, writing center.

**Majors. Health:** Health care admin, nursing (RN).

**Computing on campus.** 24 workstations in library, computer center, student center. Online course registration, online library, wireless network available.

**Student life. Freshman orientation:** Mandatory. Preregistration for classes offered. **Housing:** Apartments available. $100 fully refundable deposit. **Activities:** Campus ministries, student government, student newspaper.

**Student services.** Adult student services, alcohol/substance abuse counseling, campus ministries, career counseling, services for economically disadvantaged, student employment services, financial aid counseling, personal counseling. **Physically disabled:** Services for visually, hearing impaired.

**Contact.** E-mail: admissions@mercycollege.edu
Phone: (419) 251-1313 Toll-free number: (888) 806-3729
Fax: (419) 251-1462
Shelly McCoy Grissom, Chief Admissions Officer, Mercy College of Northwest Ohio, 2221 Madison Avenue, Toledo, OH 43604

---

## Miami University: Oxford Campus
**Oxford, Ohio**
www.muohio.edu

**CB member**
**CB code: 1463**

- Public 4-year university
- Residential campus in small town
- 14,479 degree-seeking undergraduates: 2% part-time, 54% women, 3% African American, 3% Asian American, 2% Hispanic American, 1% Native American, 1% international
- 1,192 degree-seeking graduate students
- 75% of applicants admitted
- SAT or ACT with writing required
- 80% graduate within 6 years

**General.** Founded in 1809. Regionally accredited. Associate degree programs and certificates offered at branch campuses in Hamilton and Middletown with degrees conferred by main (Oxford) campus. **Degrees:** 4,086 bachelor's, 313 associate awarded; master's, doctoral offered. **ROTC:** Army, Naval, Air Force. **Location:** 35 miles from Cincinnati, 46 miles from Dayton. **Calendar:** Semester, extensive summer session. **Full-time faculty:** 813 total; 90% have terminal degrees, 14% minority, 39% women. **Part-time faculty:** 459 total; 33% have terminal degrees, 7% minority, 48% women. **Class size:** 34% < 20, 50% 20-39, 6% 40-49, 7% 50-99, 3% >100. **Special facilities:** Zoology museum.

**Freshman class profile.** 15,925 applied, 12,012 admitted, 3,488 enrolled.

| Mid 50% test scores | | | |
|---|---|---|---|
| SAT critical reading: | 540-640 | Rank in top quarter: | 72% |
| SAT math: | 570-660 | Rank in top tenth: | 35% |
| ACT composite: | 24-28 | Return as sophomores: | 89% |
| GPA 3.50 or higher: | 67% | Out-of-state: | 34% |
| GPA 3.0-3.49: | 30% | Live on campus: | 98% |
| GPA 2.0-2.99: | 3% | International: | 1% |

**Basis for selection.** Admission based upon academic performance, test scores, secondary school experience, community activities, and recommendations from the high school. Diversity of student body, applicant's special abilities, talents and achievements also considered. Essay recommended for all; audition required for music, theater programs; portfolio required for art, architecture programs. **Homeschooled:** Students who have not earned GED may present credentials that demonstrate levels of academic achievement, ability, and performance equivalent to that of high school graduates. Applicants may be requested to submit samples of work in various areas.

**High school preparation.** 16 units recommended. Recommended units include English 4, mathematics 3, social studies 3, science 3, foreign language 2 and visual/performing arts 1.

**2007-2008 Annual costs.** Tuition/fees: $11,925; $24,377 out-of-state. Tuition ranges from $7,161 to $9,911 depending on amount of built-in scholarship aid which varies by income. Room/board: $8,600. Books/supplies: $1,140. Personal expenses: $3,174.

**Financial aid. Non-need-based:** Scholarships awarded for academics, art, athletics, leadership, minority status, music/drama, ROTC, state residency.

**Application procedures. Admission:** Priority date 12/1; deadline 1/31 (postmark date). $45 fee, may be waived for applicants with need. Application may be submitted online. Admission notification 3/15. Must reply by May 1 or within 2 week(s) if notified thereafter. **Financial aid:** Priority date 2/15; no closing date. FAFSA required. Applicants notified on a rolling basis starting 3/20; must reply by 5/1 or within 3 week(s) of notification.

**Academics. Special study options:** Combined bachelor's/graduate degree, cooperative education, cross-registration, double major, exchange student, honors, independent study, internships, liberal arts/career combination, student-designed major, study abroad, teacher certification program, Washington semester. Undergraduate associates, undergraduate research program, science and engineering research semester, 3-1 medical technology with regional hospitals, 3-2 engineering with Case Western Reserve University and Columbia University, 3-2 forestry/environmental studies with Duke University, 3-1 arts/professional BA/MA awarded after completing junior year and first year of graduate school. **Credit/placement by examination:** AP, CLEP, IB, institutional tests. **Support services:** Learning center, pre-admission summer program, study skills assistance, tutoring.

**Majors. Architecture:** Interior, urban/community planning. **Area/ethnic studies:** African-American, American, Italian, women's. **Biology:** General, bacteriology, biochemistry, botany, zoology. **Business:** General, accounting, business admin, finance, human resources, management information systems, management science, managerial economics, marketing, operations, organizational behavior, purchasing, sales/distribution. **Communications:** General, journalism, media studies, public relations. **Computer sciences:** Computer science, systems analysis. **Conservation:** Environmental science, environmental studies, forestry, wood science. **Education:** Art, biology, chemistry, early childhood, elementary, English, French, German, health, kindergarten/preschool, Latin, mathematics, middle, music, physical, physics, science, social studies, Spanish, special, speech. **Engineering:** General, chemical, computer, electrical, manufacturing, mechanical, physics. **Engineering technology:** General, industrial management. **English:** American lit, British lit, creative writing, English lit, speech/rhetoric, technical writing. **Family/consumer sciences:** Family studies, food/nutrition, housing. **Foreign languages:** Ancient Greek, classics, comparative lit, French, German, Latin, linguistics, Russian, Spanish. **Health:** Athletic training, audiology/speech pathology, clinical lab science, dietetics, nursing (RN), predental, premedicine, speech pathology. **History:** General. **Legal studies:** Prelaw. **Math:** General, statistics. **Parks/recreation:** Exercise sciences, health/fitness, sports admin. **Philosophy/religion:** Philosophy, religion. **Physical sciences:** Chemistry, geology, physics. **Psychology:** General. **Public administration:** General, social work. **Social sciences:** Anthropology, economics, geography, international relations, political science, sociology. **Visual/performing arts:** Art, art history/conservation, commercial/advertising art, dramatic, music performance.

**Most popular majors.** Biology 6%, business/marketing 28%, education 10%, English 6%, social sciences 11%.

**Computing on campus.** 1,000 workstations in dormitories, library, computer center, student center. Dormitories wired for high-speed internet access and linked to campus network. Commuter students can connect to campus network. Online course registration, helpline, repair service, student web hosting available.

**Student life. Freshman orientation:** Available, $55 fee. Preregistration for classes offered. Held 2 days during June and July. **Housing:** Guaranteed on-campus for freshmen. Coed dorms, single-sex dorms, special housing for disabled, apartments, fraternity/sorority housing available. $400 nonrefundable deposit, deadline 5/1. All first-year students live in first-year student halls. Special arrangements include sorority suites in residence halls and an international hall. **Activities:** Bands, choral groups, dance, drama, film society, literary magazine, music ensembles, musical theater, opera, radio station, student government, student newspaper, symphony orchestra, TV station, Miami Service Network, minority affairs council, United Campus Ministries, Black student association, Miami student foundation, Association of International Students.

**Athletics.** NCAA. **Intercollegiate:** Baseball M, basketball, cross-country, diving, field hockey W, football (tackle) M, golf M, ice hockey M, soccer W, softball W, swimming, tennis W, track and field, volleyball W. **Intramural:** Archery, badminton, basketball, boxing M, cross-country, equestrian, field hockey W, football (tackle) M, golf, gymnastics, handball, ice hockey, lacrosse M, racquetball, rifle, rugby M, sailing, skiing, soccer, softball, squash, swimming, table tennis, tennis, track and field, volleyball, water polo, wrestling M. **Team name:** Red Hawks.

**Student services.** Alcohol/substance abuse counseling, campus ministries, career counseling, services for economically disadvantaged, student employment services, financial aid counseling, health services, legal services, minority student services, on-campus daycare, personal counseling, placement for graduates, veterans' counselor, women's services. **Physically disabled:** Services for visually, speech, hearing impaired.

**Contact.** E-mail: admission@muohio.edu
Phone: (513) 529-2531 Fax: (513) 529-1550
Laurie Koehler, Director of Admissions, Miami University: Oxford Campus, 301 South Campus Avenue, Oxford, OH 45056-3434

---

## Mount Carmel College of Nursing
**Columbus, Ohio**
www.mccn.edu

**CB member**
**CB code: 1502**

- Private 4-year nursing college affiliated with Roman Catholic
- Very large city
- 641 degree-seeking undergraduates
- 68% of applicants admitted

**General.** Regionally accredited. **Degrees:** 138 bachelor's awarded; master's offered. **Location:** Downtown. **Calendar:** Semester, limited summer session. **Full-time faculty:** 37 total. **Part-time faculty:** 22 total.

**Freshman class profile.** 147 applied, 100 admitted, 88 enrolled.

| Mid 50% test scores | ACT composite: | 19-22 |
|---|---|---|

**Basis for selection.** High school record and standardized test score most important.

**2007-2008 Annual costs.** Tuition/fees: $7,596.

**2007-2008 Financial aid. Need-based:** 52% of total undergraduate aid awarded as scholarships/grants, 48% as loans/jobs.

**Application procedures. Admission:** Priority date 2/1; no deadline. $30 fee. **Financial aid:** Priority date 3/1; no closing date. FAFSA, institutional form required. Applicants notified on a rolling basis.

**Academics. Credit/placement by examination:** CLEP.

**Majors. Health:** Nursing (RN).

**Contact.** E-mail: mccnadmissions@mchs.com
Phone: (614) 234-1085 Toll-free number: (800) 556-6942
Fax: (614) 234-2875
Kim Campbell, Director of Admissions, Mount Carmel College of Nursing, 127 South Davis Avenue, Columbus, OH 43222-1589

---

## Mount Union College
**Alliance, Ohio**
www.muc.edu

**CB member**
**CB code: 1492**

- Private 4-year liberal arts college affiliated with United Methodist Church
- Residential campus in large town
- 2,128 degree-seeking undergraduates: 3% part-time, 49% women, 4% African American, 1% Hispanic American, 2% international

- 78% of applicants admitted
- SAT or ACT (ACT writing optional), application essay required
- 65% graduate within 6 years; 26% enter graduate study

**General.** Founded in 1846. Regionally accredited. **Degrees:** 414 bachelor's awarded. **ROTC:** Army, Air Force. **Location:** 55 miles from Cleveland, 75 miles from Pittsburgh. **Calendar:** Semester, limited summer session. **Full-time faculty:** 125 total; 84% have terminal degrees, 11% minority, 34% women. **Part-time faculty:** 110 total; 6% have terminal degrees, 3% minority, 54% women. **Class size:** 56% < 20, 42% 20-39, 1% 40-49, less than 1% 50-99. **Special facilities:** 2 astronomical observatories, 141-acre nature center for ecological studies, bird observatory, scanning electron microscope facility.

**Freshman class profile.** 2,178 applied, 1,697 admitted, 593 enrolled.

| Mid 50% test scores | | Rank in top quarter: | 40% |
|---|---|---|---|
| SAT critical reading: | 450-580 | Rank in top tenth: | 13% |
| SAT math: | 460-570 | Return as sophomores: | 76% |
| ACT composite: | 19-25 | Out-of-state: | 11% |
| GPA 3.50 or higher: | 34% | Live on campus: | 93% |
| GPA 3.0-3.49: | 31% | International: | 1% |
| GPA 2.0-2.99: | 35% | | |

**Basis for selection.** Class rank, rigor of secondary school record, standardized test scores, academic GPA very important. Rolling deadline for SAT, ACT scores. Essay is required and interview recommended for all. Audition recommended for communications, music, and theater programs. Portfolio recommended for art and communications programs. **Home-schooled:** Statement describing homeschool structure and mission required.

**High school preparation.** 18 units recommended. Recommended units include English 4, mathematics 3, social studies 3, science 3 (laboratory 2), foreign language 2 and academic electives 1.

**2007-2008 Annual costs.** Tuition/fees: $22,050. Room/board: $6,700. Books/supplies: $750. Personal expenses: $590.

**2006-2007 Financial aid. Need-based:** 575 full-time freshmen applied for aid; 502 were judged to have need; 502 of these received aid. Average need met was 82%. Average scholarship/grant was $13,334; average loan $4,321. 67% of total undergraduate aid awarded as scholarships/grants, 33% as loans/jobs. **Non-need-based:** Awarded to 489 full-time undergraduates, including 152 freshmen. Scholarships awarded for academics, alumni affiliation, art, job skills, leadership, music/drama, religious affiliation, ROTC, state residency.

**Application procedures. Admission:** Priority date 3/1; no deadline. No application fee. Application may be submitted online. Admission notification on a rolling basis beginning on or about 10/1. Admission determined by space availability after May 1. **Financial aid:** Priority date 4/1; no closing date. FAFSA required. Applicants notified on a rolling basis starting 3/15; must reply within 4 week(s) of notification.

**Academics.** All freshmen must take Liberal Arts Experience course. **Special study options:** Accelerated study, cooperative education, double major, ESL, honors, independent study, internships, student-designed major, study abroad, teacher certification program. **Credit/placement by examination:** AP, CLEP, IB, institutional tests. 15 credit hours maximum toward bachelor's degree. **Support services:** Learning center, study skills assistance, tutoring, writing center.

**Majors. Area/ethnic studies:** American. **Biology:** General, biochemistry, environmental. **Business:** Accounting, business admin, international. **Communications:** General. **Computer sciences:** Programming, web page design. **Education:** Early childhood, health, middle, music, physical, special. **English:** Creative writing, English lit. **Foreign languages:** French, German, Japanese, Spanish. **Health:** Athletic training, clinical lab science. **History:** General. **Interdisciplinary:** Ancient studies, neuroscience. **Math:** General. **Parks/recreation:** Exercise sciences, sports admin. **Philosophy/religion:** Philosophy, religion. **Physical sciences:** Chemistry, geology, physics. **Psychology:** General. **Social sciences:** Economics, international relations, political science, sociology. **Visual/performing arts:** Dramatic, music performance, studio arts.

**Most popular majors.** Biology 7%, business/marketing 18%, education 21%, parks/recreation 11%, social sciences 9%.

**Computing on campus.** 220 workstations in dormitories, library, computer center, student center. Dormitories wired for high-speed internet access and linked to campus network. Commuter students can connect to campus network. Online course registration, online library, helpline, repair service, student web hosting, wireless network available.

**Student life. Freshman orientation:** Available. Preregistration for classes offered. 2-day summer orientation includes program for parents. Fall orientation held week before registration for students only. **Housing:** Guaranteed on-campus for all undergraduates. Coed dorms, single-sex dorms, special housing for disabled, fraternity/sorority housing, substance-free housing available. **Activities:** Bands, choral groups, dance, drama, literary magazine, music ensembles, musical theater, radio station, student government, student newspaper, academic clubs, academic honoraries, religious clubs, service organizations, Alpha Phi Omega, Black Student Union, Association of International Students, Association of Women Students, Religious Life Council, student activities council.

**Athletics.** NCAA. **Intercollegiate:** Baseball M, basketball, cheerleading, cross-country, diving, football (tackle) M, golf, soccer, softball W, swimming, tennis, track and field, volleyball W, wrestling M. **Intramural:** Badminton, basketball, bowling, diving, football (non-tackle), golf, gymnastics, racquetball, soccer, softball, swimming, tennis, volleyball, water polo, weight lifting. **Team name:** Purple Raiders.

**Student services.** Adult student services, alcohol/substance abuse counseling, campus ministries, career counseling, student employment services, financial aid counseling, health services, minority student services, personal counseling, placement for graduates. **Physically disabled:** Services for visually impaired.

**Contact.** E-mail: admission@muc.edu
Phone: (330) 823-2590 Toll-free number: (800) 334-6682
Fax: (330) 823-5097
Vince Heslop, Director of Enrollment Technology, Mount Union College, 1972 Clark Avenue, Alliance, OH 44601-3993

---

## Mount Vernon Nazarene University
**Mount Vernon, Ohio**
www.mvnu.edu                                    **CB code: 1531**

- Private 4-year university affiliated with Church of the Nazarene
- Residential campus in large town
- 2,033 degree-seeking undergraduates: 6% part-time, 59% women, 5% African American, 1% Asian American, 2% Hispanic American
- 348 degree-seeking graduate students
- 77% of applicants admitted
- SAT or ACT (ACT writing optional), application essay required
- 49% graduate within 6 years; 21% enter graduate study

**General.** Founded in 1964. Regionally accredited. **Degrees:** 457 bachelor's, 15 associate awarded; master's offered. **Location:** 45 miles from Columbus. **Calendar:** 4-1-4, limited summer session. **Full-time faculty:** 116 total; 60% have terminal degrees, 7% minority, 37% women. **Part-time faculty:** 139 total; 23% have terminal degrees, 1% minority, 38% women. **Class size:** 73% < 20, 22% 20-39, 2% 40-49, 3% 50-99. **Special facilities:** 70-acre biological research area and nature center, weather station.

**Freshman class profile.** 837 applied, 646 admitted, 351 enrolled.

| Mid 50% test scores | | Rank in top quarter: | 44% |
|---|---|---|---|
| SAT critical reading: | 460-560 | Rank in top tenth: | 18% |
| SAT math: | 460-570 | End year in good standing: | 86% |
| ACT composite: | 20-25 | Return as sophomores: | 71% |
| GPA 3.50 or higher: | 48% | Out-of-state: | 12% |
| GPA 3.0-3.49: | 27% | Live on campus: | 93% |
| GPA 2.0-2.99: | 24% | International: | 1% |

**Basis for selection.** High school record, ACT or SAT scores, recommendations important. Interview recommended. **Homeschooled:** Transcript of courses and grades, letter of recommendation (nonparent) required. Family members cannot complete either academic or character references. Employer can complete academic reference. Students who participate in accredited program must provide transcript from accrediting agency; otherwise, must provide a list of classes completed.

**High school preparation.** 21 units recommended. Required and recommended units include English 4, mathematics 3, social studies 3, science 3 (laboratory 3), foreign language 2-3, visual/performing arts 1 and academic electives 4. 1 health and physical education.

**2007-2008 Annual costs.** Tuition/fees: $18,064. Room/board: $5,286. Books/supplies: $1,000. Personal expenses: $1,746.

**2007-2008 Financial aid. Need-based:** 351 full-time freshmen applied for aid; 307 were judged to have need; 307 of these received aid. Average need met was 76%. Average scholarship/grant was $9,315; average loan $3,889. 55% of total undergraduate aid awarded as scholarships/grants, 45% as loans/jobs. **Non-need-based:** Awarded to 242 full-time undergraduates, including 77 freshmen. Scholarships awarded for academics, athletics, leadership, minority status, music/drama, religious affiliation, state residency.

**Application procedures. Admission:** Priority date 3/15; deadline 8/1 (receipt date). $25 fee, may be waived for applicants with need. Application may be submitted online. Admission notification on a rolling basis beginning on or about 9/1. **Financial aid:** Priority date 3/15; no closing date. FAFSA, institutional form required. Applicants notified on a rolling basis starting 2/15; must reply within 2 week(s) of notification.

**Academics.** Off-campus January term offers unique educational opportunities, including urban and international studies. **Special study options:** Combined bachelor's/graduate degree, cooperative education, cross-registration, distance learning, double major, dual enrollment of high school students, honors, independent study, internships, liberal arts/career combination, study abroad, teacher certification program, Washington semester. Cooperative pre-engineering program with Olivet Nazarene University, cooperative pre-occupational therapy/physical therapy/physician's assistant programs with Chatham College, and articulation agreements with Zane State College, Central Ohio Technical College, and North Central State College. Several opportunities for students to participate in service learning or mission trips. During the academic year, students may participate in one of the following trips: Germany, Hungary, Venezuela, Costa Rica, Nicaragua, Belize, Benin, Romania, or several out-of-state USA trips. **Credit/placement by examination:** AP, CLEP, IB, SAT, ACT, institutional tests. **Support services:** Reduced course load, study skills assistance.

**Majors. Biology:** General. **Business:** Accounting, business admin, finance, international, management information systems, marketing, office management. **Communications:** General, journalism. **Communications technology:** Graphics. **Computer sciences:** General, computer science. **Education:** General, art, biology, business, chemistry, early childhood, elementary, English, family/consumer sciences, health, history, mathematics, middle, music, physical, physics, science, secondary, social studies, Spanish, special. **English:** English lit. **Family/consumer sciences:** General. **Foreign languages:** Spanish. **Health:** Clinical lab science, nursing (RN), staff services technology. **History:** General. **Math:** General. **Parks/recreation:** Exercise sciences, health/fitness, sports admin. **Philosophy/religion:** Philosophy, religion. **Physical sciences:** Chemistry, physics. **Protective services:** Criminal justice. **Psychology:** General. **Public administration:** Social work. **Social sciences:** Sociology. **Theology:** Bible, pastoral counseling, religious ed, sacred music, youth ministry. **Visual/performing arts:** Art, design, dramatic, music performance. **Other:** Applied business technology, Intercultural studies, Video and radio broadcasting.

**Most popular majors.** Business/marketing 58%, education 8%.

**Computing on campus.** 292 workstations in dormitories, library, computer center, student center. Dormitories wired for high-speed internet access and linked to campus network. Commuter students can connect to campus network. Online course registration, online library, helpline, wireless network available.

**Student life. Freshman orientation:** Mandatory, $25 fee. Preregistration for classes offered. Sessions held in June, July, and August. **Policies:** Students expected to comply with university's published lifestyle guidelines. Religious observance required. **Housing:** Guaranteed on-campus for freshmen. Single-sex dorms, special housing for disabled, apartments, substance-free housing available. $100 fully refundable deposit, deadline 5/1. **Activities:** Bands, campus ministries, choral groups, drama, international student organizations, music ensembles, musical theater, opera, radio station, student government, student newspaper, Students in Free Enterprise, Fellowship of Christian Athletes, Young Republicans club, Association of Men, Association of Women, Association of Computing Machinery, American Sign Language club, Students with Concern.

**Athletics.** NAIA, NCCAA. **Intercollegiate:** Baseball M, basketball, cross-country, golf M, soccer, softball W, volleyball W. **Intramural:** Basketball, bowling, football (non-tackle), soccer, softball, volleyball. **Team name:** Cougars.

**Student services.** Adult student services, alcohol/substance abuse counseling, campus ministries, career counseling, student employment services, financial aid counseling, health services, minority student services, personal counseling, placement for graduates. **Physically disabled:** Services for visually, speech, hearing impaired.

**Contact.** E-mail: admissions@mvnu.edu
Phone: (740) 392-6868 ext. 4510 Toll-free number: (866) 462-6868
Fax: (740) 393-0511
Jay Mahan, Director of Admissions, Mount Vernon Nazarene University, 800 Martinsburg Road, Mount Vernon, OH 43050

---

## Muskingum College
**New Concord, Ohio**                          **CB member**
www.muskingum.edu                              **CB code: 1496**

- Private 4-year liberal arts college affiliated with Presbyterian Church (USA)
- Residential campus in small town

- 1,648 degree-seeking undergraduates: 6% part-time, 51% women, 4% African American, 1% Hispanic American, 2% international
- 322 degree-seeking graduate students
- 78% of applicants admitted
- SAT or ACT (ACT writing optional) required
- 60% graduate within 6 years; 16% enter graduate study

**General.** Founded in 1837. Regionally accredited. **Degrees:** 307 bachelor's awarded; master's offered. **Location:** 70 miles from Columbus, 125 miles from Pittsburgh. **Calendar:** Semester, limited summer session. **Full-time faculty:** 101 total; 85% have terminal degrees, 10% minority, 44% women. **Part-time faculty:** 36 total; 11% have terminal degrees, 6% minority, 58% women. **Class size:** 63% < 20, 35% 20-39, 2% 40-49. **Special facilities:** Biology field station, conservation facility.

**Freshman class profile.** 1,911 applied, 1,493 admitted, 430 enrolled.

| Mid 50% test scores | | | |
|---|---|---|---|
| SAT critical reading: | 420-570 | Rank in top tenth: | 25% |
| SAT math: | 460-560 | End year in good standing: | 65% |
| SAT writing: | 420-560 | Return as sophomores: | 71% |
| ACT composite: | 19-25 | Out-of-state: | 11% |
| GPA 3.50 or higher: | 36% | Live on campus: | 92% |
| GPA 3.0-3.49: | 32% | International: | 1% |
| GPA 2.0-2.99: | 31% | Fraternities: | 20% |
| Rank in top quarter: | 45% | Sororities: | 30% |

**Basis for selection.** School achievement record most important. Test scores, recommendations, extracurricular activities, interview considered. Special consideration to children of alumni. Essay and interview recommended for all; audition recommended for music programs; portfolio recommended for art programs. **Homeschooled:** Transcript of courses and grades, state high school equivalency certificate required. Portfolio of curriculum; statement of compliance with state truancy laws in cases where state certificate is not issued. **Learning Disabled:** Offer the PLUS Program for students with handicapping learning conditions, including learning disabilities. Students must indicate interest in this program when applying for admission, and must submit psychological evaluations to complete the application process.

**High school preparation.** 12 units required; 15 recommended. Required and recommended units include English 4, mathematics 2-3, social studies 2-3, science 2-3 and foreign language 2-3.

**2007-2008 Annual costs.** Tuition/fees: $18,170. Room/board: $7,000. Books/supplies: $1,000. Personal expenses: $900.

**2007-2008 Financial aid.** **Need-based:** 390 full-time freshmen applied for aid; 345 were judged to have need; 345 of these received aid. Average need met was 60%. Average scholarship/grant was $12,590; average loan $3,610. 68% of total undergraduate aid awarded as scholarships/grants, 32% as loans/jobs. **Non-need-based:** Awarded to 1,323 full-time undergraduates, including 364 freshmen. Scholarships awarded for academics, alumni affiliation, art, leadership, minority status, music/drama, religious affiliation, state residency. **Additional information:** Scholarship priority date February 1.

**Application procedures.** **Admission:** Closing date 8/1. No application fee. Application may be submitted online. Admission notification on a rolling basis beginning on or about 10/1. Must reply by May 1 or within 2 week(s) if notified thereafter. Application preferred filing date of March 1 for PLUS program. **Financial aid:** Priority date 3/15, closing date 8/1. FAFSA required. Applicants notified on a rolling basis starting 3/1; must reply by 5/1 or within 2 week(s) of notification.

**Academics.** **Special study options:** Accelerated study, distance learning, double major, dual enrollment of high school students, ESL, exchange student, independent study, internships, liberal arts/career combination, student-designed major, study abroad, teacher certification program, United Nations semester, Washington semester. **Credit/placement by examination:** AP, CLEP, IB, SAT, ACT, institutional tests. **Support services:** Learning center, pre-admission summer program, reduced course load, study skills assistance, tutoring, writing center.

**Majors. Biology:** General, conservation, molecular. **Business:** General, accounting, international marketing, managerial economics. **Communications:** General, digital media, journalism. **Computer sciences:** General, computer science. **Conservation:** Environmental science. **Education:** Early childhood, elementary, middle, secondary, special. **Engineering:** General, science. **English:** English lit. **Foreign languages:** French, German, Spanish. **Health:** Clinical lab technology, predental, premedicine, prenursing, prepharmacy, preveterinary, speech pathology. **History:** General. **Interdisciplinary:** Neuroscience. **Legal studies:** Prelaw. **Liberal arts:** Humanities. **Math:** General. **Philosophy/religion:** Philosophy, religion. **Physical sciences:** Chemistry, geology, physics, planetary. **Protective services:** Police

science. **Psychology:** General. **Social sciences:** Anthropology, economics, international relations, political science, sociology. **Theology:** Religious ed, theology. **Visual/performing arts:** Art, dramatic.

**Most popular majors.** Business/marketing 23%, communications/journalism 8%, education 24%, psychology 7%, social sciences 9%.

**Computing on campus.** 217 workstations in dormitories, library, computer center, student center. Dormitories wired for high-speed internet access and linked to campus network. Commuter students can connect to campus network. Online course registration, online library, helpline, repair service, student web hosting, wireless network available.

**Student life. Freshman orientation:** Available. Preregistration for classes offered. Six one-day sessions held on weekdays in May and June. **Housing:** Coed dorms, single-sex dorms, apartments, fraternity/sorority housing, substance-free housing available. $150 deposit, deadline 5/1. **Activities:** Bands, campus ministries, choral groups, dance, drama, international student organizations, literary magazine, music ensembles, Model UN, musical theater, radio station, student government, student newspaper, symphony orchestra, TV station, Christian Fellowship, Fellowship of Christian Athletes, political awareness program, SADD, Habitat for Humanity, Young Democrats, Young Republicans.

**Athletics.** NCAA. **Intercollegiate:** Baseball M, basketball, cheerleading, cross-country, football (tackle) M, golf, soccer, softball W, tennis, track and field, volleyball W, wrestling M. **Intramural:** Basketball, bowling, cross-country, football (non-tackle), golf, lacrosse, racquetball, rugby, soccer, softball, table tennis M, tennis, track and field, volleyball, wrestling M. **Team name:** Muskies.

**Student services.** Alcohol/substance abuse counseling, campus ministries, career counseling, student employment services, financial aid counseling, health services, on-campus daycare, personal counseling, placement for graduates. **Physically disabled:** Services for hearing impaired. **Learning disabled:** Comprehensive services available.

**Contact.** E-mail: adminfo@muskingum.edu
Phone: (740) 826-8137 Toll-free number: (800) 752-6082
Fax: (740) 826-8100
Beth DaLonzo, Senior Director of Admissions and Student Financial Services, Muskingum College, 163 Stormont Street, New Concord, OH 43762-1199

---

## Notre Dame College
**Cleveland, Ohio**
www.notredamecollege.edu

**CB member**
**CB code: 1566**

- Private 4-year liberal arts college affiliated with Roman Catholic Church
- Commuter campus in very large city
- 1,639 degree-seeking undergraduates
- 82 graduate students
- 56% of applicants admitted
- SAT or ACT, application essay required

**General.** Founded in 1922. Regionally accredited. Weekend college for adults who have graduated from high school 5 or more years prior to their first term of enrollment. **Degrees:** 121 bachelor's, 3 associate awarded; master's offered. **ROTC:** Army. **Location:** 10 miles from downtown Cleveland. **Calendar:** Semester, limited summer session. **Full-time faculty:** 38 total; 5% minority, 42% women. **Part-time faculty:** 80 total. **Special facilities:** Science research center.

**Freshman class profile.**

| Mid 50% test scores | | | |
|---|---|---|---|
| SAT critical reading: | 380-480 | Rank in top quarter: | 20% |
| SAT math: | 390-470 | Rank in top tenth: | 6% |
| ACT composite: | 17-21 | Out-of-state: | 17% |
| | | Live on campus: | 70% |

**Basis for selection.** School achievement record and test scores most important. Applicants should be in top half of class and have 2.5 high school GPA for unconditional admission. Extracurricular activities also considered. Interview recommended.

**High school preparation.** Recommended units include English 4, mathematics 3, social studies 2, history 1, science 3 (laboratory 3) and foreign language 3.

**2007-2008 Annual costs.** Tuition/fees: $21,090. Room/board: $7,156. Books/supplies: $1,428. Personal expenses: $1,470.

**Financial aid.** **Non-need-based:** Scholarships awarded for academics, state residency.

**Application procedures.** **Admission:** No deadline. $30 fee, may be waived for applicants with need. Application may be submitted online. Admission notification on a rolling basis. **Financial aid:** Closing date 5/1. FAFSA required. Applicants notified on a rolling basis starting 1/1; must reply within 2 week(s) of notification.

**Academics.** **Special study options:** Cooperative education, cross-registration, double major, exchange student, independent study, internships, student-designed major, study abroad, teacher certification program, weekend college. **Credit/placement by examination:** AP, CLEP, SAT, ACT, institutional tests. **Support services:** Learning center, reduced course load, remedial instruction, tutoring, writing center.

**Majors.** **Biology:** General, biochemistry. **Business:** Accounting, business admin, human resources, international, management information systems, managerial economics, marketing. **Communications:** General, digital media, public relations. **Education:** Early childhood, elementary, secondary. **English:** English lit. **Foreign languages:** Spanish. **Health:** Nursing (RN), predental, premedicine, prenursing. **History:** General. **Math:** General. **Physical sciences:** Chemistry. **Psychology:** General. **Social sciences:** Criminology, political science. **Theology:** Theology. **Visual/performing arts:** General, art history/conservation, arts management, studio arts.

**Most popular majors.** Business/marketing 41%, education 25%, psychology 14%.

**Computing on campus.** 67 workstations in dormitories, library, computer center.

**Student life.** **Freshman orientation:** Mandatory, $100 fee. Preregistration for classes offered. Three 2-day sessions held in June, July, and August. Evening orientation sessions held in August and January for adult students. **Housing:** Coed dorms, substance-free housing available. $150 deposit. **Activities:** Pep band, choral groups, drama, literary magazine, music ensembles, student government, student newspaper, campus ministry board, Black Scholars, multicultural student advisory board, St. Julie Scholars, psychology council, science and business clubs, Achievement in Research and Scholarship.

**Athletics.** NAIA. **Intercollegiate:** Baseball M, basketball, cross-country, diving W, field hockey W, golf, lacrosse W, soccer, softball W, swimming W, tennis M, track and field, volleyball W, wrestling M. **Intramural:** Soccer W, softball W, tennis, volleyball W. **Team name:** Falcons.

**Student services.** Adult student services, alcohol/substance abuse counseling, campus ministries, career counseling, student employment services, financial aid counseling, health services, personal counseling, placement for graduates. **Learning disabled:** Comprehensive services available.

**Contact.** E-mail: admissions@ndc.edu
Phone: (216) 381-1680 ext. 5355 Toll-free number: (877) 632-6446
Fax: (216) 381-3802
Dave Armstrong, Vice President for Enrollment, Notre Dame College, 4545 College Road, Cleveland, OH 44121-4293

---

## Oberlin College
**Oberlin, Ohio**
**www.oberlin.edu**

**CB member**
**CB code: 1587**

- Private 4-year music and liberal arts college
- Residential campus in small town
- 2,762 degree-seeking undergraduates: 2% part-time, 55% women, 6% African American, 8% Asian American, 5% Hispanic American, 1% Native American, 6% international
- 5 degree-seeking graduate students
- 31% of applicants admitted
- SAT or ACT with writing required
- 82% graduate within 6 years

**General.** Founded in 1833. Regionally accredited. **Degrees:** 706 bachelor's awarded; master's offered. **Location:** 34 miles from Cleveland. **Calendar:** 4-1-4. **Full-time faculty:** 266 total; 16% minority, 37% women. **Class size:** 68% < 20, 27% 20-39, 2% 40-49, 3% 50-99, less than 1% >100. **Special facilities:** Observatory, bog, environmental studies building, arboretum.

**Freshman class profile.** 7,014 applied, 2,193 admitted, 745 enrolled.

| Mid 50% test scores | | | |
|---|---|---|---|
| SAT critical reading: | 650-750 | Rank in top quarter: | 90% |
| SAT math: | 620-710 | Rank in top tenth: | 68% |
| ACT composite: | 27-31 | Return as sophomores: | 92% |
| GPA 3.50 or higher: | 63% | Out-of-state: | 91% |
| GPA 3.0-3.49: | 33% | Live on campus: | 100% |
| GPA 2.0-2.99: | 4% | International: | 7% |

**Basis for selection.** For college of arts and sciences: school achievement record, test scores, school and community leadership activities, recommendations, and interview important. Special consideration to applicants from minority and first generation college families and to foreign applicants. For conservatory: audition most important factor; admission selective. TOEFL required if English not first language. SAT Subject Tests recommended. Interview required for early admission candidates; recommended for all others. Audition required of applicants to conservatory; essay required of applicants to college of arts and sciences. **Homeschooled:** Interview, SAT Subject Tests, detailed portfolio required.

**High school preparation.** Required units include English 4, mathematics 4, social studies 3, science 3 and foreign language 3.

**2007-2008 Annual costs.** Tuition/fees: $36,500. Room/board: $9,280. Books/supplies: $830. Personal expenses: $978.

**2007-2008 Financial aid.** **Need-based:** 79% of total undergraduate aid awarded as scholarships/grants, 21% as loans/jobs. **Non-need-based:** Scholarships awarded for academics, leadership, music/drama, state residency.

**Application procedures.** **Admission:** Closing date 1/15 (postmark date). $35 fee, may be waived for applicants with need. Application may be submitted online. Admission notification 4/1. Must reply by May 1 or within 2 week(s) if notified thereafter. Application closing date for Conservatory of Music, February 15; application fee $100. **Financial aid:** Closing date 1/15. FAFSA, institutional form, CSS PROFILE required. Applicants notified by 4/1; must reply by 5/1 or within 2 week(s) of notification.

**Academics.** No core curriculum. Students required to take 9 credit hours in each academic division (Humanities, Social Sciences, and Math and Natural Science) and 9 hours related to cultural diversity. **Special study options:** Cross-registration, double major, dual enrollment of high school students, exchange student, honors, independent study, internships, liberal arts/career combination, New York semester, student-designed major, study abroad, teacher certification program, urban semester, Washington semester. 5-year dual degree program with music conservatory and liberal arts college, 3-2 engineering. **Credit/placement by examination:** AP, CLEP, IB, institutional tests. 30 credit hours maximum toward bachelor's degree. **Support services:** Learning center, remedial instruction, study skills assistance, tutoring, writing center.

**Majors.** **Area/ethnic studies:** African, African-American, American, East Asian, Latin American, Russian/Slavic, women's. **Biology:** General, biochemistry. **Computer sciences:** General. **Conservation:** Environmental studies. **Education:** Music. **English:** Creative writing, English lit. **Foreign languages:** Ancient Greek, classics, comparative lit, French, German, Latin, Russian, Spanish. **Health:** Predental, premedicine, preveterinary. **History:** General. **Interdisciplinary:** Neuroscience. **Legal studies:** Prelaw. **Math:** General. **Philosophy/religion:** Judaic, philosophy, religion. **Physical sciences:** Chemistry, geology, physics. **Psychology:** General. **Social sciences:** Anthropology, economics, political science, sociology. **Visual/performing arts:** Art history/conservation, conducting, dance, dramatic, film/cinema, jazz, music history, music theory/composition, piano/organ, stringed instruments, studio arts, voice/opera.

**Most popular majors.** Area/ethnic studies 8%, biology 10%, English 9%, history 7%, philosophy/religious studies 6%, social sciences 12%, visual/performing arts 26%.

**Computing on campus.** 340 workstations in dormitories, library, computer center. Dormitories wired for high-speed internet access and linked to campus network. Commuter students can connect to campus network. Online course registration, helpline, repair service, wireless network available.

**Student life.** **Freshman orientation:** Mandatory. Preregistration for classes offered. Held week prior to fall classes. Includes day of service. **Policies:** Students agree to follow honor code. **Housing:** Guaranteed on-campus for all undergraduates. Coed dorms, single-sex dorms, cooperative housing, substance-free housing available. **Activities:** Bands, choral groups, dance, drama, film society, literary magazine, music ensembles, musical theater, opera, radio station, student government, student newspaper, symphony orchestra, religious, political, inter-cultural, ethnic, social service, and gay/lesbian/bisexual organizations.

**Athletics.** NCAA. **Intercollegiate:** Baseball M, basketball, cross-country, diving, field hockey W, football (tackle) M, golf, lacrosse, soccer, softball

W, swimming, tennis, track and field, volleyball W. **Intramural:** Baseball M, basketball, bowling, football (non-tackle), handball, racquetball, rugby M, skin diving, soccer, softball, squash, table tennis, tennis, track and field, volleyball, weight lifting. **Team name:** Yeomen.

**Student services.** Alcohol/substance abuse counseling, campus ministries, career counseling, services for economically disadvantaged, student employment services, financial aid counseling, health services, minority student services, personal counseling, placement for graduates, women's services. **Physically disabled:** Services for visually, speech, hearing impaired.

**Contact.** E-mail: college.admissions@oberlin.edu
Phone: (440) 775-8411 Toll-free number: (800) 622-6243
Fax: (440) 775-6905
Debra Chermonte, Dean of Admissions and Financial Aid, Oberlin College, Carnegie Building, 101 North Professor Street, Oberlin, OH 44074

## Ohio Christian University
### Circleville, Ohio
**www.ohiochristian.edu**      **CB code: 1088**

- Private 4-year Bible college affiliated with Churches of Christ in Christian Union
- Residential campus in large town
- 616 degree-seeking undergraduates: 14% part-time, 55% women, 21% African American, 1% Hispanic American, 1% Native American, 1% international
- SAT or ACT (ACT writing optional), application essay required
- 47% graduate within 6 years

**General.** Founded in 1948. Candidate for regional accreditation; also accredited by ABHE. **Degrees:** 52 bachelor's, 2 associate awarded. **Location:** 25 miles from Columbus. **Calendar:** Semester, limited summer session. **Full-time faculty:** 14 total. **Part-time faculty:** 37 total. **Class size:** 74% < 20, 22% 20-39, 2% 40-49, 3% 50-99.

### Freshman class profile.

| Mid 50% test scores | | | |
|---|---|---|---|
| SAT critical reading: | 480-560 | Out-of-state: | 15% |
| SAT math: | 440-540 | Live on campus: | 37% |
| ACT composite: | 17-24 | International: | 1% |

**Basis for selection.** Open admission, but selective for some programs. Positive Christian testimony, potential for Christian service, sound academic performance, and personal character references important. Students without SAT or ACT may be admitted conditionally but must meet test requirement at earliest opportunity. Interview recommended for all; audition required for music majors.

**High school preparation.** 15 units recommended. Recommended units include English 4, mathematics 3, social studies 3, science 3 and foreign language 2.

**2008-2009 Annual costs.** Tuition/fees (projected): $13,635. Room/board: $5,990. Books/supplies: $500. Personal expenses: $1,506.

**2006-2007 Financial aid.** All financial aid based on need. Average scholarship/grant was $3,000; average loan $2,000. 53% of total undergraduate aid awarded as scholarships/grants, 47% as loans/jobs. **Additional information:** Religious affiliation tuition discount.

**Application procedures. Admission:** Priority date 4/1; no deadline. $25 fee, may be waived for applicants with need. Application may be submitted online. Admission notification on a rolling basis. Must reply by May 1 or within 2 week(s) if notified thereafter. **Financial aid:** Priority date 5/7; no closing date. FAFSA, institutional form, CSS PROFILE required. Applicants notified on a rolling basis starting 5/1; must reply within 2 week(s) of notification.

**Academics.** Every student is required to complete minimum of 30 hours in Bible and theology courses. **Special study options:** Accelerated study, combined bachelor's/graduate degree, distance learning, double major, dual enrollment of high school students, honors, independent study, internships, liberal arts/career combination, student-designed major, study abroad. **Credit/placement by examination:** AP, CLEP, ACT, institutional tests. **Support services:** Reduced course load, remedial instruction, study skills assistance, tutoring, writing center.

**Majors. Business:** General, accounting, accounting/business management, business admin. **Education:** General, early childhood, elementary, music, secondary. **Philosophy/religion:** Religion. **Psychology:** General. **Theology:** Missionary, pastoral counseling, religious ed, sacred music, theology, youth ministry.

**Most popular majors.** Education 8%, psychology 11%.

**Computing on campus.** 58 workstations in dormitories, library, computer center. Dormitories wired for high-speed internet access and linked to campus network. Online library, repair service, wireless network available.

**Student life. Freshman orientation:** Mandatory. Preregistration for classes offered. Held Sunday through Wednesday before classes start. **Policies:** Curfew of 11:30 pm (Monday-Thursday), 1:00 am (Friday), 12:00 am (Saturday-Sunday); dress code. Religious observance required. **Housing:** Guaranteed on-campus for freshmen. Single-sex dorms, apartments available. $50 deposit, deadline 8/1. **Activities:** Choral groups, drama, music ensembles, student government, Ministerial Association, Prison Ministries, S.H.I.N.E., World Gospel Mission Student Involvement, summer camp ministries.

**Athletics.** NCCAA. **Intercollegiate:** Baseball M, basketball, soccer M, softball W, volleyball W. **Intramural:** Basketball, golf, soccer, table tennis, volleyball. **Team name:** Trailblazers.

**Student services.** Adult student services, campus ministries, career counseling, student employment services, financial aid counseling, health services, minority student services, personal counseling, veterans' counselor. **Physically disabled:** Services for visually impaired.

**Contact.** E-mail: enroll@ohiochristian.edu
Phone: (740) 477-7701 Toll-free number: (800) 701-0222
Fax: (740) 477-7755
Mike Egenreider, Director of Admissions, Ohio Christian University, 1476 Lancaster Pike, Circleville, OH 43113

## Ohio Dominican University
### Columbus, Ohio
**www.ohiodominican.edu**      **CB member**    **CB code: 1131**

- Private 4-year university and liberal arts college affiliated with Roman Catholic Church
- Commuter campus in very large city
- 2,250 degree-seeking undergraduates: 24% part-time, 60% women, 23% African American, 1% Asian American, 2% Hispanic American, 1% international
- 522 degree-seeking graduate students
- 69% of applicants admitted
- SAT or ACT (ACT writing optional), application essay required
- 44% graduate within 6 years

**General.** Founded in 1911. Regionally accredited. **Degrees:** 397 bachelor's, 78 associate awarded; master's offered. **ROTC:** Army. **Location:** 4 miles from downtown. **Calendar:** Semester, limited summer session. **Full-time faculty:** 100 total; 65% have terminal degrees, 6% minority, 49% women. **Part-time faculty:** 100 total; 19% have terminal degrees, 15% minority, 48% women. **Class size:** 55% < 20, 45% 20-39, less than 1% 40-49.

**Freshman class profile.** 2,442 applied, 1,680 admitted, 399 enrolled.

| Mid 50% test scores | | | |
|---|---|---|---|
| ACT composite: | 19-23 | Rank in top tenth: | 9% |
| GPA 3.50 or higher: | 27% | Return as sophomores: | 59% |
| GPA 3.0-3.49: | 26% | Out-of-state: | 7% |
| GPA 2.0-2.99: | 46% | Live on campus: | 82% |
| Rank in top quarter: | 28% | International: | 1% |

**Basis for selection.** High school GPA, curriculum most important, followed by class rank, test scores, interview, recommendations, and activities. Interview required for in-state applicants; recommended for out-of-state. **Homeschooled:** Transcript of courses and grades, state high school equivalency certificate required.

**High school preparation.** College-preparatory program recommended. 16 units recommended. Recommended units include English 4, mathematics 3, social studies 3, science 3 and foreign language 3.

**2007-2008 Annual costs.** Tuition/fees: $21,794. Room/board: $7,200. Books/supplies: $950. Personal expenses: $1,500.

**Financial aid. Non-need-based:** Scholarships awarded for academics, athletics, state residency.

**Application procedures. Admission:** Priority date 4/1; no deadline. $25 fee. Application may be submitted online. Admission notification on a rolling basis beginning on or about 9/1. **Financial aid:** Priority date 4/1; no closing date. FAFSA required. Applicants notified on a rolling basis starting 3/1; must reply within 2 week(s) of notification.

**Academics. Special study options:** Cross-registration, distance learning, double major, dual enrollment of high school students, honors, independent study, internships, study abroad, teacher certification program, Washington semester. **Credit/placement by examination:** AP, CLEP, IB, ACT. No limit on credit hours by examination, but residency requirement must be met. **Support services:** Learning center, reduced course load, remedial instruction, study skills assistance, tutoring.

**Majors. Biology:** General. **Business:** Accounting, business admin, communications, international. **Communications:** General, public relations. **Computer sciences:** Information systems. **Education:** Art, biology, chemistry, elementary, English, instructional media, mathematics, middle, multiple handicapped, physics, science, secondary, social studies, special. **English:** English lit. **History:** General. **Liberal arts:** Arts/sciences. **Math:** General. **Philosophy/religion:** Philosophy. **Physical sciences:** Chemistry. **Protective services:** Criminal justice. **Psychology:** General. **Public administration:** Social work. **Social sciences:** Economics, political science, sociology. **Theology:** Theology. **Visual/performing arts:** Art, graphic design.

**Most popular majors.** Business/marketing 44%, education 21%, psychology 7%, social sciences 11%.

**Computing on campus.** 330 workstations in dormitories, library, computer center. Dormitories wired for high-speed internet access and linked to campus network. Commuter students can connect to campus network. Online course registration, online library, helpline, student web hosting available.

**Student life. Freshman orientation:** Mandatory, $125 fee. Preregistration for classes offered. **Housing:** Coed dorms, apartments available. $150 partly refundable deposit, deadline 8/15. **Activities:** Bands, choral groups, drama, literary magazine, radio station, student government, student newspaper, campus ministry, Black Student Union, American international membership club, resident student association, commuter student association, social work club, Pallete Club, psychology club.

**Athletics.** NAIA. **Intercollegiate:** Baseball M, basketball, cheerleading, cross-country, football (tackle) M, golf, soccer, softball W, tennis, volleyball W. **Intramural:** Badminton, basketball, golf, soccer, table tennis, tennis, volleyball. **Team name:** Panthers.

**Student services.** Adult student services, campus ministries, career counseling, student employment services, financial aid counseling, health services, personal counseling, placement for graduates, veterans' counselor.

**Contact.** E-mail: admissions@ohiodominican.edu
Phone: (614) 251-4500 Toll-free number: (800) 955-6446
Fax: (614) 251-4772
Nicole Evans, Director of Admissions, Ohio Dominican University, 1216 Sunbury Road, Columbus, OH 43219

---

## Ohio Northern University

Ada, Ohio
www.onu.edu
CB member
CB code: 1591

- Private 4-year university affiliated with United Methodist Church
- Residential campus in small town
- 2,534 degree-seeking undergraduates: 1% part-time, 46% women, 3% African American, 1% Asian American, 1% Hispanic American, 2% international
- 998 degree-seeking graduate students
- 88% of applicants admitted
- SAT or ACT (ACT writing optional) required
- 63% graduate within 6 years

**General.** Founded in 1871. Regionally accredited. **Degrees:** 440 bachelor's awarded; master's, first professional offered. **ROTC:** Army, Air Force. **Location:** 15 miles from Lima, 80 miles from Columbus. **Calendar:** Quarter, limited summer session. **Full-time faculty:** 229 total; 80% have terminal degrees, 9% minority, 37% women. **Part-time faculty:** 102 total; 24% have terminal degrees, 4% minority, 39% women. **Class size:** 57% < 20, 41% 20-39, less than 1% 40-49, 1% 50-99, less than 1% >100. **Special facilities:** Nature center, drug information center (College of Pharmacy), pharmacy museum.

**Freshman class profile.** 3,308 applied, 2,903 admitted, 722 enrolled.

| Mid 50% test scores | | | |
|---|---|---|---|
| SAT critical reading: | 510-630 | Rank in top quarter: | 65% |
| SAT math: | 550-660 | Rank in top tenth: | 38% |
| SAT writing: | 510-630 | Return as sophomores: | 81% |
| ACT composite: | 23-29 | Out-of-state: | 18% |
| GPA 3.50 or higher: | 66% | Live on campus: | 97% |
| GPA 3.0-3.49: | 22% | International: | 2% |
| GPA 2.0-2.99: | 12% | Fraternities: | 15% |
| | | Sororities: | 24% |

**Basis for selection.** Prefer ACT score of 20 or higher; secondary school record very important. Colleges of Pharmacy and Engineering have higher test score credentials for consideration. GPA, class rank, test scores, college prep curriculum, extracurricular activities are considered in admission decisions. College of Pharmacy has first review deadline of November 1. Admissions file including high school transcript, ACT/SAT scores, recommendations, essays, etc. must be complete by November 1 for College of Pharmacy applicants. Essay and interview recommended for all; audition recommended for music, performing arts programs; portfolio recommended for art program. **Homeschooled:** Statement describing homeschool structure and mission required.

**High school preparation.** 16 units required; 24 recommended. Required and recommended units include English 4, mathematics 2-4, social studies 2-3, history 2, science 2-3 (laboratory 2), foreign language 2, computer science 1, visual/performing arts 1 and academic electives 4. 4 units mathematics and science required for engineering and pharmacy applicants.

**2008-2009 Annual costs.** Tuition/fees (projected): $31,020. Room/board: $7,890. Books/supplies: $1,500. Personal expenses: $1,229.

**Financial aid. Non-need-based:** Scholarships awarded for academics, alumni affiliation, art, leadership, music/drama, ROTC, state residency.

**Application procedures. Admission:** Priority date 12/1; deadline 8/15 (receipt date). $30 fee, may be waived for applicants with need. Application may be submitted online. Admission notification on a rolling basis beginning on or about 7/15. Must reply by 5/1. Priority date for scholarship eligibility December 1. Pharmacy deadline is November 1 of senior year. **Financial aid:** Priority date 4/15, closing date 6/1. FAFSA, institutional form required. Applicants notified on a rolling basis starting 2/15; must reply within 2 week(s) of notification.

**Academics.** Pharmacy students are admitted directly to 6-year PharmD. program. **Special study options:** Combined bachelor's/graduate degree, cooperative education, distance learning, double major, dual enrollment of high school students, ESL, exchange student, honors, independent study, internships, liberal arts/career combination, study abroad, teacher certification program, Washington semester. **Credit/placement by examination:** AP, CLEP, IB, SAT, ACT, institutional tests. 45 credit hours maximum toward bachelor's degree. **Support services:** Pre-admission summer program, reduced course load, remedial instruction, study skills assistance, tutoring, writing center.

**Majors. Biology:** General, biochemistry, exercise physiology, molecular. **Business:** Accounting, business admin, finance, international, management science, marketing. **Communications:** General, broadcast journalism, journalism, organizational, public relations. **Computer sciences:** Computer graphics. **Conservation:** General, environmental studies. **Education:** General, art, biology, chemistry, early childhood, elementary, English, foreign languages, French, health, history, mathematics, middle, music, physical, physics, science, secondary, social studies, Spanish, technology/industrial arts. **Engineering:** General, civil, computer, electrical, mechanical. **Engineering technology:** Industrial. **English:** Composition, creative writing, English lit, technical writing. **Foreign languages:** French, German, Germanic, Spanish. **Health:** Athletic training, nursing (RN), physician assistant, predental, premedicine, preveterinary. **History:** General. **Liberal arts:** Arts/sciences. **Math:** General, statistics. **Parks/recreation:** Exercise sciences, health/fitness, sports admin. **Philosophy/religion:** Philosophy, religion. **Physical sciences:** Astronomy, chemistry, physics. **Protective services:** Criminal justice, forensics, law enforcement admin, police science. **Psychology:** General. **Social sciences:** General, international relations, political science, sociology. **Visual/performing arts:** Art, commercial/advertising art, dramatic, music management, music performance, music theory/composition, studio arts. **Other:** Pharmacy business.

**Most popular majors.** Biology 9%, business/marketing 19%, communications/journalism 6%, education 9%, engineering/engineering technologies 18%, health sciences 7%.

**Computing on campus.** 550 workstations in dormitories, library, computer center, student center. Dormitories wired for high-speed internet access and linked to campus network. Commuter students can connect to campus network. Online course registration, online library, helpline, repair service, wireless network available.

**Student life. Freshman orientation:** Mandatory. Preregistration for classes offered. 4 separate one-day orientations in June and July, on Monday or Friday. **Policies:** All students must reside on campus until 135 credit hours are reached. No smoking in residence halls. **Housing:** Guaranteed on-campus for freshmen. Coed dorms, single-sex dorms, special housing for disabled, apartments, fraternity/sorority housing, substance-free housing available. $200 fully refundable deposit, deadline 5/1. Honors residence halls available. **Activities:** Bands, campus ministries, choral groups, dance, drama, international student organizations, literary magazine, music ensembles, musical theater, opera, radio station, student government, student newspaper, symphony orchestra, TV station, Christian Legal Society, Fellowship of Christian Athletes, University Religious Association Council, Black Student Union, Amnesty International, College Republicans, Black Law Student Association, Habitat for Humanity, World Student Organization.

**Athletics.** NCAA. **Intercollegiate:** Baseball M, basketball, cross-country, diving, football (tackle) M, golf, soccer, softball W, swimming, tennis, track and field, volleyball W, wrestling M. **Intramural:** Badminton, basketball, bowling, football (non-tackle) M, racquetball, soccer, softball, swimming, table tennis M, tennis, track and field, volleyball, wrestling M. **Team name:** Polar Bears.

**Student services.** Alcohol/substance abuse counseling, campus ministries, career counseling, student employment services, financial aid counseling, health services, legal services, minority student services, personal counseling, placement for graduates. **Physically disabled:** Services for visually, speech, hearing impaired.

**Contact.** E-mail: admissions-ug@onu.edu
Phone: (419) 772-2260 Toll-free number: (888) 408-4668
Fax: (419) 772-2821
Deborah Miller, Director of Admissions, Ohio Northern University, 525 South Main Street, Ada, OH 45810

---

## Ohio State University: Columbus Campus
**Columbus, Ohio**          **CB member**
**www.osu.edu**          **CB code: 1592**

- Public 4-year university
- Residential campus in very large city
- 37,848 degree-seeking undergraduates: 6% part-time, 46% women, 7% African American, 5% Asian American, 3% Hispanic American, 2% international
- 13,359 degree-seeking graduate students
- 59% of applicants admitted
- SAT or ACT with writing, application essay required
- 71% graduate within 6 years

**General.** Founded in 1870. Regionally accredited. Additional campuses in Wooster, Marion, Lima, Newark, Mansfield. **Degrees:** 9,067 bachelor's, 358 associate awarded; master's, doctoral, first professional offered. **ROTC:** Army, Naval, Air Force. **Location:** 2 miles from downtown. **Calendar:** Quarter, extensive summer session. **Full-time faculty:** 3,118 total; 99% have terminal degrees, 19% minority, 31% women. **Part-time faculty:** 1,127 total; 14% minority, 49% women. **Class size:** 35% < 20, 39% 20-39, 8% 40-49, 12% 50-99, 7% >100. **Special facilities:** Radio telescope, dance notation bureau, extension center for educational research, biological science laboratory on Lake Erie, campus airport, environmental studies center, research vessel on Lake Erie, nuclear research reactor, supercomputer facility, arts center, cultural center, public service and public policy institute, polar research center, health policy studies center, mapping center, materials research center.

**Freshman class profile.** 21,508 applied, 12,697 admitted, 6,168 enrolled.

| Mid 50% test scores | | | |
|---|---|---|---|
| SAT critical reading: | 550-650 | Return as sophomores: | 92% |
| SAT math: | 580-680 | Out-of-state: | 15% |
| ACT composite: | 25-29 | Live on campus: | 92% |
| Rank in top quarter: | 89% | International: | 2% |
| Rank in top tenth: | 52% | Fraternities: | 8% |
| | | Sororities: | 14% |

**Basis for selection.** Secondary school record, class rank, test scores most important. Audition required for dance, music programs; portfolio required for art programs. **Homeschooled:** May be required to provide GED.

**High school preparation.** Required and recommended units include English 4, mathematics 3-4, social studies 2-3, science 2-3 (laboratory 2-3), foreign language 2-3, visual/performing arts 1 and academic electives 1.

**2007-2008 Annual costs.** Tuition/fees: $8,676; $21,285 out-of-state. Room/board: $7,365. Books/supplies: $1,317. Personal expenses: $3,966.

**2007-2008 Financial aid. Need-based:** 4,934 full-time freshmen applied for aid; 3,297 were judged to have need; 3,292 of these received aid. Average need met was 72%. Average scholarship/grant was $7,123; average loan $3,938. 42% of total undergraduate aid awarded as scholarships/grants, 58% as loans/jobs. **Non-need-based:** Awarded to 7,962 full-time undergraduates, including 2,437 freshmen. Scholarships awarded for academics, alumni affiliation, art, athletics, job skills, leadership, minority status, music/drama, ROTC, state residency.

**Application procedures. Admission:** Closing date 2/1 (postmark date). $40 fee, may be waived for applicants with need. Application may be submitted online. Admission notification on a rolling basis beginning on or about 12/1. Must reply by May 1 or within 4 week(s) if notified thereafter. **Financial aid:** Priority date 2/15; no closing date. FAFSA required. Applicants notified by 4/5; must reply by 5/1 or within 4 week(s) of notification.

**Academics. Special study options:** Accelerated study, combined bachelor's/graduate degree, cooperative education, cross-registration, distance learning, double major, dual enrollment of high school students, ESL, exchange student, honors, independent study, internships, liberal arts/career combination, semester at sea, student-designed major, study abroad, teacher certification program, Washington semester. **Credit/placement by examination:** AP, CLEP, IB, SAT, ACT, institutional tests. 45 credit hours maximum toward bachelor's degree. **Support services:** Learning center, pre-admission summer program, reduced course load, remedial instruction, study skills assistance, tutoring, writing center.

**Majors. Agriculture:** Agronomy, animal sciences, business, communications, economics, food processing, food science, landscaping, plant protection, plant sciences, turf management. **Architecture:** Architecture, environmental design, interior, landscape. **Area/ethnic studies:** African, African-American, Central/Eastern European, East Asian, Latin American, Near/Middle Eastern, Russian/Slavic, Western European, women's. **Biology:** General, biochemistry, botany, ecology, entomology, genetics, microbiology, molecular genetics, zoology. **Business:** General, accounting, actuarial science, fashion, finance, hospitality admin, hospitality/recreation, human resources, insurance, international, logistics, management information systems, managerial economics, marketing, operations, real estate, transportation. **Communications:** General, journalism, public relations. **Computer sciences:** General, computer science, information systems. **Conservation:** General, fisheries, forestry, management/policy, wildlife. **Education:** Agricultural, art, music, physical, special, technology/industrial arts, trade/industrial. **Engineering:** Aerospace, agricultural, ceramic, chemical, civil, computer, electrical, industrial, materials, materials science, mechanical, metallurgical, physics, systems. **Engineering technology:** Construction, surveying. **English:** Composition, English lit. **Family/consumer sciences:** General, clothing/textiles, family resources, family studies, family/community services, food/nutrition. **Foreign languages:** Arabic, Chinese, classics, comparative lit, French, German, Hebrew, Italian, Japanese, Latin, linguistics, modern Greek, Portuguese, Russian, Spanish. **Health:** Audiology/hearing, audiology/speech pathology, clinical lab science, dental hygiene, dietetics, medical radiologic technology/radiation therapy, medical records admin, perfusion technology, respiratory therapy technology. **History:** General. **Interdisciplinary:** Ancient studies, medieval/Renaissance, nutrition sciences, peace/conflict. **Liberal arts:** Arts/sciences. **Math:** General. **Parks/recreation:** Exercise sciences, facilities management, health/fitness, sports admin. **Philosophy/religion:** Islamic, Judaic, philosophy, religion. **Physical sciences:** Astronomy, chemistry, geology, geophysics, physics. **Production:** Welding. **Psychology:** General. **Public administration:** Social work. **Social sciences:** General, anthropology, criminology, economics, geography, international relations, political science, sociology, urban studies. **Transportation:** Aviation. **Visual/performing arts:** Art, art history/conservation, ceramics, dance, design, dramatic, drawing, industrial design, interior design, jazz, music history, music performance, music theory/composition, painting, photography, piano/organ, printmaking, sculpture, studio arts, voice/opera.

**Most popular majors.** Biology 6%, business/marketing 16%, communications/journalism 6%, engineering/engineering technologies 7%, family/consumer sciences 8%, health sciences 7%, psychology 6%, social sciences 15%.

**Computing on campus.** 800 workstations in dormitories, library, computer center, student center. Dormitories wired for high-speed internet access and linked to campus network. Commuter students can connect to campus network. Online course registration, online library, helpline, repair service, student web hosting, wireless network available.

**Student life. Freshman orientation:** Mandatory, $50 fee. Preregistration for classes offered. 27 2-day programs throughout summer (June-August) prior to enrollment. **Housing:** Guaranteed on-campus for freshmen. Coed dorms, special housing for disabled, apartments, cooperative housing, fraternity/sorority housing, substance-free housing available. $100 nonrefundable deposit. **Activities:** Bands, campus ministries, choral groups, dance, drama, film society, international student organizations, literary magazine, music ensembles, musical theater, opera, radio station, student government, student newspaper, symphony orchestra, TV station, over 800 organizations available.

**Athletics.** NCAA. **Intercollegiate:** Baseball M, basketball, cheerleading, cross-country, diving, fencing, field hockey W, football (tackle) M, golf, gymnastics, ice hockey, lacrosse, rifle, rowing (crew) W, soccer, softball W, swimming, synchronized swimming W, tennis, track and field, volleyball, wrestling M. **Intramural:** Archery, badminton, baseball M, basketball, bowling, cricket, diving, equestrian, fencing, football (non-tackle), golf, gymnastics, handball, ice hockey, lacrosse, racquetball, rifle, rowing (crew), rugby, sailing, skiing, soccer, softball, squash, swimming, table tennis, tennis, track and field, volleyball, water polo, wrestling. **Team name:** Buckeyes.

**Student services.** Adult student services, alcohol/substance abuse counseling, campus ministries, career counseling, services for economically disadvantaged, student employment services, financial aid counseling, health services, legal services, minority student services, on-campus daycare, personal counseling, placement for graduates, veterans' counselor, women's services. **Physically disabled:** Services for visually, speech, hearing impaired.

**Contact.** E-mail: askabuckeye@osu.edu
Phone: (614) 292-3980 Fax: (614) 292-4818
Mabel Freeman, Assistant Vice President for Undergraduate Admissions and First Year Experience, Ohio State University: Columbus Campus, 110 Enarson Hall, Columbus, OH 43210

---

## Ohio State University: Lima Campus
### Lima, Ohio
www.lima.ohio-state.edu                    CB code: 1541

- Public 4-year branch campus college
- Commuter campus in large town
- 1,194 degree-seeking undergraduates: 13% part-time, 49% women, 4% African American, 1% Asian American, 2% Hispanic American
- 65 degree-seeking graduate students
- Application essay required
- 35% graduate within 6 years

**General.** Founded in 1960. Regionally accredited. Branch campus of Ohio State University; all degrees awarded through main campus. **ROTC:** Army, Naval, Air Force. **Location:** 90 miles from Columbus. **Calendar:** Quarter, limited summer session. **Full-time faculty:** 40 total; 98% have terminal degrees, 12% minority, 32% women. **Part-time faculty:** 41 total; 12% minority, 54% women. **Class size:** 45% < 20, 40% 20-39, 7% 40-49, 8% 50-99. **Special facilities:** Greenhouse, nature trails, dinosaur museum.

**Freshman class profile.** 1,446 applied, 1,438 admitted, 500 enrolled.

| Mid 50% test scores | | | |
|---|---|---|---|
| SAT critical reading: | 440-560 | Rank in top quarter: | 28% |
| SAT math: | 420-580 | Rank in top tenth: | 9% |
| ACT composite: | 19-24 | Return as sophomores: | 65% |
| | | Out-of-state: | 1% |

**Basis for selection.** Open admission, but selective for out-of-state students. Out-of-state students evaluated on basis of GPA, class rank, principal/counselor recommendation, and SAT/ACT scores. SAT/ACT required for out-of-state students.

**High school preparation.** Required and recommended units include English 4, mathematics 3-4, social studies 2-3, science 2-3 (laboratory 2), foreign language 2-3, visual/performing arts 1 and academic electives 1.

**2007-2008 Annual costs.** Tuition/fees: $5,664; $17,559 out-of-state. Books/supplies: $1,317. Personal expenses: $3,426.

**2007-2008 Financial aid.** **Need-based:** Average need met was 63%. Average scholarship/grant was $3,477; average loan $3,814. 34% of total undergraduate aid awarded as scholarships/grants, 66% as loans/jobs. **Non-need-based:** Scholarships awarded for academics, alumni affiliation, art, athletics, job skills, leadership, minority status, music/drama, religious affiliation, ROTC, state residency.

**Application procedures. Admission:** Closing date 7/1 (postmark date). $40 fee, may be waived for applicants with need. Application may be submitted online. Admission notification on a rolling basis beginning on or about 12/1. Must reply by May 1 or within 4 week(s) if notified thereafter. **Financial aid:** Priority date 3/1; no closing date. FAFSA required. Applicants notified on a rolling basis starting 4/1; must reply within 4 week(s) of notification.

**Academics.** Students often leave campus after 1-3 years and complete bachelor's degree on Columbus campus. **Special study options:** Accelerated study, cooperative education, cross-registration, distance learning, double major, dual enrollment of high school students, ESL, exchange student, honors, independent study, internships, liberal arts/career combination, student-designed major, study abroad, teacher certification program, weekend college. **Credit/placement by examination:** AP, CLEP, SAT, ACT, institutional

---

tests. 45 credit hours maximum toward bachelor's degree. **Support services:** Learning center, remedial instruction, tutoring, writing center.

**Majors. Biology:** General. **Business:** General, financial planning, hospitality admin. **Education:** General. **English:** English lit. **Health:** Health services. **History:** General. **Math:** General. **Psychology:** General.

**Computing on campus.** 104 workstations in library, computer center. Commuter students can connect to campus network. Online course registration, online library, helpline available.

**Student life. Freshman orientation:** Mandatory. Preregistration for classes offered. Orientation services available throughout year, days and evenings. **Activities:** Campus ministries, choral groups, drama, international student organizations, music ensembles, musical theater, student government, Bible club, biology club, Buckeye Ag, Buckeye Scholars, Challengers club, English club, psychology club, gaming club.

**Athletics. Intramural:** Basketball, bowling, golf M, soccer, softball, volleyball. **Team name:** Barons.

**Student services.** Adult student services, campus ministries, career counseling, student employment services, financial aid counseling, on-campus daycare, personal counseling, placement for graduates. **Physically disabled:** Services for visually, speech, hearing impaired.

**Contact.** E-mail: admissions@lima.ohio-state.edu
Phone: (419) 995-8396 Fax: (419) 995-8483
Beth Keehn, Director of Admissions, Ohio State University: Lima Campus, 4240 Campus Drive, Lima, OH 45804-3596

---

## Ohio State University: Mansfield Campus
### Mansfield, Ohio
www.mansfield.ohio-state.edu                    CB code: 0744

- Public 4-year branch campus college
- Commuter campus in small city
- 1,180 degree-seeking undergraduates: 14% part-time, 55% women, 7% African American, 2% Asian American, 2% Hispanic American
- 70 degree-seeking graduate students
- Application essay required
- 30% graduate within 6 years

**General.** Founded in 1958. Regionally accredited. Branch campus of Ohio State University; all degrees awarded through main campus. **ROTC:** Army, Naval, Air Force. **Location:** 67 miles from Columbus. **Calendar:** Quarter, limited summer session. **Full-time faculty:** 45 total; 98% have terminal degrees, 11% minority, 33% women. **Part-time faculty:** 49 total; 4% minority, 55% women. **Class size:** 50% < 20, 38% 20-39, 5% 40-49, 6% 50-99, less than 1% >100. **Special facilities:** Archives and reading room, educational enrichment laboratory, language laboratory, elementary education suite.

**Freshman class profile.** 1,823 applied, 1,812 admitted, 527 enrolled.

| Mid 50% test scores | | | |
|---|---|---|---|
| SAT critical reading: | 460-550 | Rank in top tenth: | 4% |
| SAT math: | 450-550 | Return as sophomores: | 65% |
| ACT composite: | 19-24 | Out-of-state: | 1% |
| Rank in top quarter: | 25% | Live on campus: | 36% |

**Basis for selection.** Open admission, but selective for out-of-state students. Out-of-state applicants evaluated on basis of GPA, class rank, principal/counselor recommendations and test scores (either SAT or ACT). SAT/ACT required for out-of-state students.

**High school preparation.** Required and recommended units include English 4, mathematics 3-4, social studies 2-3, science 2-3 (laboratory 2-3), foreign language 2-3, visual/performing arts 1 and academic electives 1.

**2007-2008 Annual costs.** Tuition/fees: $5,664; $18,273 out-of-state. Room/board: $4,275. Books/supplies: $1,317. Personal expenses: $3,966.

**2007-2008 Financial aid. Need-based:** 391 full-time freshmen applied for aid; 312 were judged to have need; 308 of these received aid. Average need met was 64%. Average scholarship/grant was $4,720; average loan $4,028. 37% of total undergraduate aid awarded as scholarships/grants, 63% as loans/jobs. **Non-need-based:** Awarded to 87 full-time undergraduates, including 55 freshmen. Scholarships awarded for academics, alumni affiliation, art, athletics, job skills, leadership, minority status, music/drama, ROTC, state residency.

**Application procedures. Admission:** Closing date 7/1 (postmark date). $40 fee, may be waived for applicants with need. Application may be submitted online. Admission notification on a rolling basis beginning on or about 12/1. **Financial aid:** Priority date 3/1; no closing date. FAFSA required. Applicants notified on a rolling basis starting 4/5; must reply within 4 week(s) of notification.

**Academics.** Students often leave campus after 1-3 years and complete bachelor's degree on Columbus campus. **Special study options:** Accelerated study, cooperative education, cross-registration, distance learning, double major, dual enrollment of high school students, ESL, exchange student, honors, independent study, internships, liberal arts/career combination, student-designed major, study abroad, teacher certification program. **Credit/ placement by examination:** AP, CLEP, SAT, ACT, institutional tests. 45 credit hours maximum toward bachelor's degree. **Support services:** Learning center, remedial instruction, tutoring, writing center.

**Majors. Business:** Business admin. **Education:** Elementary. **English:** English lit. **History:** General. **Psychology:** General.

**Computing on campus.** 103 workstations in library, computer center, student center. Commuter students can connect to campus network. Online course registration, online library, helpline available.

**Student life. Freshman orientation:** Mandatory. Preregistration for classes offered. **Housing:** Coed dorms, substance-free housing available. $100 non-refundable deposit. **Activities:** Campus ministries, dance, drama, film society, student government, African American Student Union, campus acitivities board, College Crusade for Christ, College Democrats/Republicans, Diversity Alliance, economics and business club, Habitat for Humanity, Single Parent Network, Spanish club, Theta Alpha Pi.

**Athletics. Intercollegiate:** Basketball, cheerleading, soccer. **Intramural:** Basketball, bowling, football (non-tackle), golf, softball, table tennis, tennis, volleyball.

**Student services.** Adult student services, career counseling, student employment services, financial aid counseling, minority student services, personal counseling, placement for graduates. **Physically disabled:** Services for visually, speech, hearing impaired.

**Contact.** E-mail: admissions@mansfield.ohio-state.edu
Phone: (419) 755-4226 Fax: (419) 755-4241
Henry Thomas, Coordinator of Admissions and Financial Aid, Ohio State University: Mansfield Campus, 1680 University Drive, Mansfield, OH 44906

---

## Ohio State University: Marion Campus
**Marion, Ohio**
www.marion.ohio-state.edu          **CB code: 0752**

- Public 4-year branch campus college
- Commuter campus in large town
- 1,437 degree-seeking undergraduates: 14% part-time, 54% women, 6% African American, 4% Asian American, 2% Hispanic American
- 104 degree-seeking graduate students
- Application essay required
- 34% graduate within 6 years

**General.** Founded in 1958. Regionally accredited. Branch campus of Ohio State University; all degrees awarded through main campus. **ROTC:** Army, Naval, Air Force. **Location:** 44 miles from Columbus. **Calendar:** Quarter, limited summer session. **Full-time faculty:** 35 total; 97% have terminal degrees, 14% minority, 31% women. **Part-time faculty:** 71 total; 14% minority, 51% women. **Class size:** 40% < 20, 49% 20-39, 8% 40-49, 1% 50-99, 2% >100.

**Freshman class profile.** 1,075 applied, 1,069 admitted, 525 enrolled.

| Mid 50% test scores | | Rank in top quarter: | 32% |
|---|---|---|---|
| SAT critical reading: | 440-550 | Rank in top tenth: | 10% |
| SAT math: | 440-550 | Return as sophomores: | 72% |
| ACT composite: | 25-29 | | |

**Basis for selection.** Open admission, but selective for out-of-state students. Out-of-state students evaluated on basis of GPA class rank, principal/ counselor recommendation, and SAT/ACT scores. SAT/ACT required for all for placement and required for out-of-state students for admissions.

**High school preparation.** Required and recommended units include English 4, mathematics 3-4, social studies 2-3, science 2-3 (laboratory 2-3), foreign language 2-3, visual/performing arts 1 and academic electives 1.

---

**2007-2008 Annual costs.** Tuition/fees: $5,664; $18,273 out-of-state. Books/ supplies: $1,317. Personal expenses: $3,426.

**2007-2008 Financial aid. Need-based:** Average need met was 66%. Average scholarship/grant was $4,177; average loan $3,779. 36% of total undergraduate aid awarded as scholarships/grants, 64% as loans/jobs. **Non-need-based:** Scholarships awarded for academics, alumni affiliation, art, athletics, job skills, leadership, minority status, music/drama, ROTC, state residency.

**Application procedures. Admission:** Closing date 7/1 (postmark date). $40 fee, may be waived for applicants with need. Application may be submitted online. Admission notification on a rolling basis beginning on or about 12/1. Must reply by May 1 or within 4 week(s) if notified thereafter. **Financial aid:** Priority date 3/1; no closing date. FAFSA required. Applicants notified on a rolling basis starting 5/1; must reply within 4 week(s) of notification.

**Academics.** Students often leave campus after 1-3 years and complete bachelor's degree on Columbus campus. **Special study options:** Accelerated study, cooperative education, cross-registration, distance learning, double major, dual enrollment of high school students, ESL, exchange student, honors, independent study, internships, liberal arts/career combination, student-designed major, study abroad, teacher certification program. **Credit/ placement by examination:** AP, CLEP, SAT, ACT, institutional tests. 45 credit hours maximum toward bachelor's degree. **Support services:** Learning center, reduced course load, remedial instruction, tutoring, writing center.

**Majors. Business:** Business admin. **Education:** Elementary. **English:** English lit. **History:** General. **Psychology:** General.

**Computing on campus.** 174 workstations in library, computer center. Commuter students can connect to campus network. Online course registration, online library, helpline available.

**Student life. Freshman orientation:** Mandatory. Preregistration for classes offered. **Activities:** Campus ministries, choral groups, literary magazine, music ensembles, student government, Buckeye Ambassador, religious organizations (Christian and Pagan), political organizations (Democratic/ Republican), Education Society, honors organizations (Griffin Society), language organizations, theater and improv troupe, Student Government Impact (diversity student organization).

**Athletics. Intercollegiate:** Basketball, cheerleading, golf, soccer, volleyball W. **Intramural:** Basketball, softball, volleyball. **Team name:** Scarlet Wave.

**Student services.** Career counseling, student employment services, legal services, on-campus daycare, personal counseling, placement for graduates. **Physically disabled:** Services for visually, speech, hearing impaired.

**Contact.** E-mail: moreau.1@osu.edu
Phone: (740) 389-6786 ext. 6242 Fax: (740) 386-2439
Matt Moreau, Coordinator of Admissions, Ohio State University: Marion Campus, 1465 Mount Vernon Avenue, Marion, OH 43302

---

## Ohio State University: Newark Campus
**Newark, Ohio**
www.newark.osu.edu          **CB code: 0824**

- Public 4-year branch campus college
- Commuter campus in large town
- 2,325 degree-seeking undergraduates: 11% part-time, 52% women, 8% African American, 2% Asian American, 2% Hispanic American, 1% Native American
- 59 degree-seeking graduate students
- Application essay required
- 34% graduate within 6 years

**General.** Founded in 1957. Regionally accredited. Branch campus of Ohio State University; all degrees awarded through main campus. **Degrees:** 133 bachelor's, 105 associate awarded; master's offered. **ROTC:** Army, Naval, Air Force. **Location:** 28 miles from Columbus. **Calendar:** Quarter, limited summer session. **Full-time faculty:** 55 total; 98% have terminal degrees, 13% minority, 36% women. **Part-time faculty:** 90 total; 7% minority, 53% women. **Class size:** 34% < 20, 56% 20-39, 9% 40-49, 1% 50-99. **Special facilities:** Mathematics laboratory, writing laboratory.

**Freshman class profile.** 2,708 applied, 2,696 admitted, 1,172 enrolled.

| Mid 50% test scores | | | |
|---|---|---|---|
| SAT critical reading: | 440-560 | Rank in top quarter: | 25% |
| SAT math: | 440-560 | Rank in top tenth: | 5% |
| ACT composite: | 19-24 | Return as sophomores: | 62% |
| | | Live on campus: | 14% |

**Basis for selection.** Open admission, but selective for out-of-state students. Out-of-state applicants are evaluated based on GPA, class rank, recommendation by principal/counselor, and SAT/ACT score. SAT/ACT required for out-of-state students.

**High school preparation.** Required and recommended units include English 4, mathematics 3-4, social studies 2-3, science 2-3 (laboratory 2-3), foreign language 2-3, visual/performing arts 1 and academic electives 1.

**2007-2008 Annual costs.** Tuition/fees: $5,664; $18,273 out-of-state. Books/supplies: $1,317. Personal expenses: $3,426.

**2007-2008 Financial aid. Need-based:** Average need met was 62%. Average scholarship/grant was $4,739; average loan $3,850. 34% of total undergraduate aid awarded as scholarships/grants, 66% as loans/jobs. **Non-need-based:** Scholarships awarded for academics, alumni affiliation, art, athletics, job skills, leadership, minority status, music/drama, ROTC, state residency.

**Application procedures. Admission:** Closing date 7/1 (postmark date). $40 fee, may be waived for applicants with need. Application may be submitted online. Admission notification on a rolling basis beginning on or about 12/1. **Financial aid:** Priority date 3/1; no closing date. FAFSA required. Applicants notified on a rolling basis starting 5/1; must reply within 4 week(s) of notification.

**Academics.** Students often leave campus after 1-3 years and complete bachelor's degree on Columbus campus. **Special study options:** Accelerated study, cooperative education, cross-registration, distance learning, double major, dual enrollment of high school students, ESL, exchange student, honors, independent study, internships, liberal arts/career combination, student-designed major, study abroad, teacher certification program. **Credit/placement by examination:** AP, CLEP, SAT, ACT, institutional tests. 45 credit hours maximum toward bachelor's degree. **Support services:** Learning center, remedial instruction, tutoring, writing center.

**Majors. Business:** Business admin. **Education:** General. **English:** English lit. **Psychology:** General.

**Computing on campus.** 36 workstations in library, computer center, student center. Commuter students can connect to campus network. Online course registration, online library, helpline available.

**Student life. Freshman orientation:** Mandatory. Preregistration for classes offered. **Housing:** Coed dorms, substance-free housing available. $100 nonrefundable deposit. University-owned student apartments within 2-minute walk from campus. **Activities:** Campus ministries, choral groups, drama, international student organizations, literary magazine, Model UN, musical theater, student government, support groups, minority organization, international multicultural association, ski club, gay/straight alliance, academic and honors organizations.

**Athletics. Intercollegiate:** Baseball M, basketball, cross-country, golf M, softball W, volleyball. **Intramural:** Badminton, baseball M, basketball, football (non-tackle), soccer, softball, table tennis, tennis, volleyball. **Team name:** Titans.

**Student services.** Adult student services, campus ministries, career counseling, student employment services, financial aid counseling, minority student services, on-campus daycare, personal counseling, placement for graduates. **Physically disabled:** Services for visually, hearing impaired.

**Contact.** E-mail: barclay.3@osu.edu
Phone: (740) 366-3333 Fax: (740) 364-9645
Ann Donahue, Coordinator of Admissions, Ohio State University: Newark Campus, 1179 University Drive, Newark, OH 43055

---

## Ohio University

**Athens, Ohio**
www.ohio.edu

**CB member**
**CB code: 1593**

- Public 4-year university
- Residential campus in large town
- 16,920 degree-seeking undergraduates: 5% part-time, 51% women, 4% African American, 1% Asian American, 2% Hispanic American, 2% international
- 3,657 degree-seeking graduate students

---

- 82% of applicants admitted
- SAT or ACT (ACT writing optional) required
- 71% graduate within 6 years; 27% enter graduate study

**General.** Founded in 1804. Regionally accredited. **Degrees:** 3,970 bachelor's, 552 associate awarded; master's, doctoral, first professional offered. **ROTC:** Army, Air Force. **Location:** 75 miles from Columbus. **Calendar:** Quarter, extensive summer session. **Full-time faculty:** 873 total; 89% have terminal degrees, 18% minority, 36% women. **Part-time faculty:** 300 total; 59% have terminal degrees, 7% minority, 45% women. **Class size:** 44% < 20, 40% 20-39, 7% 40-49, 6% 50-99, 4% >100. **Special facilities:** University airport, nuclear accelerator, biotechnology research center, greenhouse, cartography center, meteorology center, contemporary history institute.

**Freshman class profile.** 13,020 applied, 10,679 admitted, 4,006 enrolled.

| Mid 50% test scores | | | |
|---|---|---|---|
| SAT critical reading: | 480-600 | Rank in top tenth: | 15% |
| SAT math: | 490-600 | End year in good standing: | 88% |
| SAT writing: | 480-580 | Return as sophomores: | 78% |
| ACT composite: | 21-26 | Out-of-state: | 10% |
| GPA 3.50 or higher: | 37% | Live on campus: | 97% |
| GPA 3.0-3.49: | 44% | International: | 2% |
| GPA 2.0-2.99: | 19% | Fraternities: | 13% |
| Rank in top quarter: | 41% | Sororities: | 17% |

**Basis for selection.** High school record as represented by rank in class, GPA, and curriculum completed most important. Secondary criteria test scores and recommendation. Rank in top third of class preferred. Audition required for dance and music programs.

**High school preparation.** 16 units required. Required units include English 4, mathematics 3, social studies 3, science 3 and foreign language 2. One unit visual or performing art recommended.

**2007-2008 Annual costs.** Tuition/fees: $8,907; $17,871 out-of-state. Room/board: $8,427. Books/supplies: $870. Personal expenses: $1,029.

**2007-2008 Financial aid. Need-based:** 3,520 full-time freshmen applied for aid; 2,293 were judged to have need; 2,255 of these received aid. Average need met was 60%. Average scholarship/grant was $5,597; average loan $3,434. 35% of total undergraduate aid awarded as scholarships/grants, 65% as loans/jobs. **Non-need-based:** Awarded to 5,313 full-time undergraduates, including 1,989 freshmen. Scholarships awarded for academics, art, athletics, minority status, music/drama, religious affiliation, ROTC.

**Application procedures. Admission:** Closing date 2/1 (receipt date). $45 fee, may be waived for applicants with need. Application may be submitted online. Admission notification on a rolling basis beginning on or about 10/1. Must reply by 5/1. **Financial aid:** Priority date 3/15, closing date 4/1. FAFSA required. Applicants notified on a rolling basis starting 4/1; must reply within 3 week(s) of notification.

**Academics.** Extensive learning community opportunities. **Special study options:** Accelerated study, combined bachelor's/graduate degree, cooperative education, cross-registration, distance learning, double major, dual enrollment of high school students, ESL, external degree, honors, independent study, internships, liberal arts/career combination, student-designed major, study abroad, teacher certification program. **Credit/placement by examination:** AP, CLEP, IB, institutional tests. Sophomore standing available by earning 45 quarter hours of credit based on AP scores. **Support services:** Learning center, pre-admission summer program, remedial instruction, study skills assistance, tutoring, writing center.

**Honors college/program.** Honors Tutorial College application deadline December 15, interview required.

**Majors. Area/ethnic studies:** African, African-American, Asian, European, Latin American, women's. **Biology:** General, botany, cellular/molecular, microbiology, wildlife, zoology. **Business:** Accounting, actuarial science, business admin, finance, human resources, international, management information systems, managerial economics, marketing. **Communications:** General, broadcast journalism, digital media, health, journalism, organizational, photojournalism, radio/tv. **Computer sciences:** Computer science, information technology. **Education:** Art, early childhood, elementary, English, family/consumer sciences, French, German, mathematics, middle, physical, science, secondary, social studies, Spanish, special. **Engineering:** Chemical, civil, electrical, industrial, mechanical. **Engineering technology:** Industrial. **English:** Creative writing, English lit, speech/rhetoric. **Family/consumer sciences:** Child development, clothing/textiles, family resources, family studies, food/nutrition, housing, institutional food production. **Foreign languages:** Ancient Greek, classics, French, German, Latin, linguistics, Russian, Spanish. **Health:** Athletic training, audiology/speech pathology, community health services, dietetics, environmental health, health care admin, nursing

(RN), occupational health. **History:** General. **Math:** General, applied. **Parks/recreation:** General, exercise sciences, health/fitness. **Philosophy/religion:** Philosophy, religion. **Physical sciences:** Astrophysics, atmospheric science, chemistry, geology, physics. **Psychology:** General. **Public administration:** Social work. **Social sciences:** Anthropology, cartography, criminology, economics, geography, political science, sociology, urban studies. **Transportation:** Aviation, aviation management. **Visual/performing arts:** Acting, art, art history/conservation, ceramics, cinematography, dance, dramatic, graphic design, music history, music performance, music theory/composition, painting, photography, piano/organ, play/screenwriting, printmaking, sculpture, theater arts management, voice/opera.

**Most popular majors.** Business/marketing 11%, communications/journalism 15%, education 12%, family/consumer sciences 7%, health sciences 7%, liberal arts 7%, parks/recreation 6%, social sciences 9%.

**Computing on campus.** 2,200 workstations in dormitories, library, computer center. Dormitories wired for high-speed internet access and linked to campus network. Commuter students can connect to campus network. Online course registration, helpline, repair service, student web hosting, wireless network available.

**Student life. Freshman orientation:** Mandatory. Preregistration for classes offered. Weekends in summer. **Housing:** Guaranteed on-campus for freshmen. Coed dorms, single-sex dorms, special housing for disabled, apartments, cooperative housing, fraternity/sorority housing, substance-free housing available. $200 nonrefundable deposit, deadline 5/1. International, intensive-study residence halls available. **Activities:** Bands, choral groups, dance, drama, film society, literary magazine, music ensembles, musical theater, opera, radio station, student government, student newspaper, symphony orchestra, TV station, over 300 professional, religious, ethnic, political, and social service organizations.

**Athletics.** NCAA. **Intercollegiate:** Baseball M, basketball, cross-country, diving, field hockey W, football (tackle) M, golf, soccer W, softball W, swimming W, track and field W, volleyball W, wrestling M. **Intramural:** Baseball M, basketball, bowling, cross-country, football (non-tackle), golf, racquetball, soccer, softball, swimming W, table tennis, tennis. **Team name:** Bobcats.

**Student services.** Adult student services, alcohol/substance abuse counseling, career counseling, services for economically disadvantaged, student employment services, financial aid counseling, health services, legal services, minority student services, personal counseling, placement for graduates, veterans' counselor. **Physically disabled:** Services for visually, hearing impaired.

**Contact.** E-mail: admissions@ohio.edu
Phone: (740) 593-4100 Fax: (740) 593-0560
T Garcia, Director of Undergraduate Admissions, Ohio University, 120 Chubb Hall, Athens, OH 45701-2979

---

## Ohio University: Chillicothe Campus
**Chillicothe, Ohio**
www.chillicothe.ohiou.edu                    CB code: 0775

▶ Public 4-year branch campus college
▶ Commuter campus in large town
▶ 1,695 degree-seeking undergraduates

**General.** Founded in 1946. Regionally accredited. **Degrees:** 178 associate awarded; master's offered. **Location:** 45 miles from Columbus. **Calendar:** Quarter, limited summer session. **Full-time faculty:** 45 total. **Part-time faculty:** 100 total.

**Basis for selection.** Open admission, but selective for some programs. Business, communications, education, and engineering colleges require high school GPA and ACT/SAT test scores. **Homeschooled:** State high school equivalency certificate required. Passing scores on Ohio graduation test or GED required.

**High school preparation.** Recommended units include English 4, mathematics 3, social studies 3, science 3 and foreign language 2. College-preparatory program strongly recommended including 1 visual or performing art.

**2007-2008 Annual costs.** Tuition/fees: $4,581; $8,904 out-of-state. Books/supplies: $848.

**Application procedures. Admission:** No deadline. $20 fee, may be waived for applicants with need. Application may be submitted online. Admission notification on a rolling basis. **Financial aid:** No deadline. FAFSA required. Applicants notified on a rolling basis.

---

**Academics.** Bachelor's programs in management, elementary education, criminal justice, nursing, technical and applied studies and self-designed major. Degree granted by Ohio University main campus. **Special study options:** Distance learning, double major, dual enrollment of high school students, external degree, independent study, internships, student-designed major, study abroad, teacher certification program. **Credit/placement by examination:** AP, CLEP, institutional tests. **Support services:** Learning center, pre-admission summer program, remedial instruction, study skills assistance, tutoring, writing center.

**Majors. Business:** Business admin. **Communications:** Organizational. **Education:** Early childhood, middle. **Engineering technology:** Environmental. **Health:** Nursing (RN). **Protective services:** Criminal justice. **Psychology:** General.

**Computing on campus.** 275 workstations in library, computer center, student center. Commuter students can connect to campus network. Online course registration, online library, helpline, student web hosting, wireless network available.

**Student life. Freshman orientation:** Available. Preregistration for classes offered. One-day session conducted prior to fall, winter and spring quarters. **Activities:** Drama, student government, student newspaper, National Communication Association, Ross County Association of Future Teachers, anime club, nursing student club, student programming club, human services association, law enforcement association, psychology club.

**Athletics. Team name:** Hilltoppers.

**Student services.** Adult student services, career counseling, services for economically disadvantaged, student employment services, financial aid counseling, personal counseling. **Physically disabled:** Services for visually, hearing impaired.

**Contact.** E-mail: lowej@ohio.edu
Phone: (740) 774-7240 Toll-free number: (877) 462-6824 ext. 240
Fax: (740) 774-7295
Jaime Lowe, Coordinator of Enrollment Services, Ohio University: Chillicothe Campus, 101 University Drive, Chillicothe, OH 45601

---

## Ohio University: Eastern Campus
**St. Clairsville, Ohio**
www.eastern.ohiou.edu                    CB code: 0828

▶ Public 4-year branch campus college
▶ Commuter campus in small town

**General.** Founded in 1957. Regionally accredited. **Location:** 7 miles from downtown, 14 miles from Wheeling, West Virginia. **Calendar:** Quarter.

**Annual costs/financial aid.** Tuition/fees (2007-2008): $4,521; $9,783 out-of-state. Need-based financial aid available to full-time and part-time students.

**Contact.** Phone: (740) 695-1720
Student Services Manager, 45425 National Road West, St. Clairsville, OH 43950-9724

---

## Ohio University: Lancaster Campus
**Lancaster, Ohio**
www.lancaster.ohiou.edu                    CB code: 0826

▶ Public 4-year branch campus college
▶ Large town
▶ 1,531 degree-seeking undergraduates

**General.** Founded in 1968. Regionally accredited. Some bachelor's and master's degrees available, awarded through Athens campus. **Degrees:** 70 associate awarded; master's offered. **ROTC:** Army, Naval, Air Force. **Location:** 30 miles from Columbus. **Calendar:** Quarter, extensive summer session. **Full-time faculty:** 30 total. **Part-time faculty:** 70 total.

**Basis for selection.** Open admission, but selective for some programs. Special requirements for business, education, engineering and communication programs. International students must take English fluency test through Ohio Program of Intensive English. ACT or SAT scores used in admission decisions to colleges of education, engineering.

**2007-2008 Annual costs.** Tuition/fees: $4,581; $8,904 out-of-state. Books/supplies: $500.

**Financial aid. Additional information:** Scholarship application deadline April 1.

**Application procedures. Admission:** No deadline. $20 fee, may be waived for applicants with need. Application may be submitted online. Admission notification on a rolling basis. **Financial aid:** Priority date 2/15; no closing date. FAFSA required. Applicants notified on a rolling basis; must reply within 2 week(s) of notification.

**Academics. Special study options:** Combined bachelor's/graduate degree, cross-registration, double major, independent study, internships, student-designed major. **Credit/placement by examination:** CLEP, institutional tests. **Support services:** Learning center, remedial instruction, tutoring.

**Computing on campus.** 98 workstations in library, computer center, student center. Online course registration, online library, helpline, student web hosting available.

**Student life. Freshman orientation:** Available. **Activities:** Choral groups, drama, student government, outdoor club, Young Democrats, Young Republicans, Christian Fellowship, adult support group.

**Athletics. Intercollegiate:** Baseball M, basketball, golf, softball W, tennis. **Intramural:** Skiing, table tennis, volleyball. **Team name:** Cougars.

**Student services.** Career counseling, student employment services, financial aid counseling, on-campus daycare, placement for graduates, veterans' counselor. **Physically disabled:** Services for visually, speech, hearing impaired.

**Contact.** Phone: (740) 654-6711 ext. 215 Toll-free number: (888) 446-4468 Fax: (740) 687-9497
Pat Fox, Enrollment Manager, Ohio University: Lancaster Campus, 1570 Granville Pike, Lancaster, OH 43130

---

## Ohio University: Southern Campus at Ironton
**Ironton, Ohio**
**www.southern.ohiou.edu**                    **CB code: 1912**

- Public 4-year branch campus college
- Commuter campus in large town
- 1,354 full-time, degree-seeking undergraduates

**General.** Founded in 1956. Regionally accredited. Student body reflects both traditional (65%) and non-traditional (45%) students who commute to all classes from 3-state area (OH, KY, WV). **Degrees:** 112 associate awarded; master's offered. **Location:** 20 miles from Huntington, West Virginia. **Calendar:** Quarter. **Full-time faculty:** 32 total. **Part-time faculty:** 122 total. **Special facilities:** Microwave link with main campus and other regional campuses, Ohio Horse Park, Nature Center.

**Basis for selection.** Open admission. Nursing applicants must have associate degree or diploma.

**2007-2008 Annual costs.** Tuition/fees: $4,395; $5,715 out-of-state. Books/supplies: $600.

**Financial aid. Non-need-based:** Scholarships awarded for academics, state residency.

**Application procedures. Admission:** No deadline. $20 fee, may be waived for applicants with need. Application may be submitted online. Admission notification on a rolling basis. **Financial aid:** Priority date 3/15; no closing date. FAFSA required. Applicants notified on a rolling basis.

**Academics. Special study options:** Dual enrollment of high school students, student-designed major, teacher certification program. **Credit/placement by examination:** CLEP, institutional tests. **Support services:** Learning center, study skills assistance, tutoring.

**Majors. Business:** Business admin. **Communications:** General, health, political. **Education:** Elementary. **Health:** Nursing (RN). **Protective services:** Criminal justice.

**Computing on campus.** Wireless network available.

**Student life. Freshman orientation:** Mandatory. Preregistration for classes offered. **Activities:** Drama, literary magazine, music ensembles, radio station, student government, student newspaper, TV station, Phi Alpha Xi service honor society, Los Amigos Internacionales club, diversity student council, student nurses association, ACTION (psychology club), art club.

**Athletics. Intercollegiate:** Equestrian.

**Student services.** Career counseling, financial aid counseling, personal counseling, placement for graduates, veterans' counselor.

**Contact.** E-mail: askousc@ohiou.edu
Phone: (740) 533-4600 Toll-free number: (800) 626-0513
Fax: (740) 533-4632
Robert Pleasant, Director of Enrollment Services, Ohio University: Southern Campus at Ironton, 1804 Liberty Avenue, Ironton, OH 45638

---

## Ohio University: Zanesville Campus
**Zanesville, Ohio**
**www.zanesville.ohiou.edu**                    **CB code: 0846**

- Public 4-year branch campus college
- Commuter campus in large town
- 1,681 degree-seeking undergraduates

**General.** Founded in 1946. Regionally accredited. **Degrees:** 126 associate awarded; master's offered. **Location:** 55 miles from Columbus. **Calendar:** Quarter, limited summer session. **Full-time faculty:** 35 total. **Part-time faculty:** 75 total.

**Freshman class profile.** 510 applied, 470 admitted, 323 enrolled.

**Basis for selection.** Open admission, but selective for some programs. Nursing admissions based on National League for Nursing test scores, high school GPA, and class rank. Admission to Colleges of Business, Engineering, and Communication based on high school rank and ACT scores. Essay, audition, and portfolio recommended for all; interview recommended for nursing program.

**High school preparation.** Recommended units include English 4, mathematics 3, social studies 3, science 3 and foreign language 2. One year of visual or performing arts recommended.

**2007-2008 Annual costs.** Tuition/fees: $4,581; $8,904 out-of-state. Books/supplies: $1,000. Personal expenses: $879.

**Application procedures. Admission:** No deadline. $20 fee, may be waived for applicants with need. Application may be submitted online. Admission notification on a rolling basis beginning on or about 1/1. **Financial aid:** Priority date 3/15; no closing date. FAFSA required. Applicants notified on a rolling basis starting 4/15; must reply within 2 week(s) of notification.

**Academics. Special study options:** Cross-registration, double major, dual enrollment of high school students, independent study, student-designed major, study abroad, teacher certification program. **Credit/placement by examination:** AP, CLEP, institutional tests. **Support services:** Learning center, reduced course load, remedial instruction, tutoring.

**Majors. Business:** General. **Communications:** Health, organizational. **Education:** Early childhood, middle. **Public administration:** Human services.

**Computing on campus.** 50 workstations in library, computer center. Commuter students can connect to campus network. Online course registration, online library, wireless network available.

**Student life. Freshman orientation:** Mandatory. Preregistration for classes offered. **Activities:** Literary magazine, radio station, student government, cultural events committee, student nursing association.

**Athletics. Intercollegiate:** Baseball M, basketball, golf, tennis, volleyball W. **Intramural:** Badminton, basketball, bowling, golf, skiing, table tennis, tennis, volleyball. **Team name:** Tracers.

**Student services.** Campus ministries, career counseling, student employment services, personal counseling, placement for graduates, veterans' counselor.

**Contact.** E-mail: ouzservices@ohio.edu
Phone: (740) 588-1439 Fax: (740) 588-1444
Monica Jones, Director of Student Services, Ohio University: Zanesville Campus, 1425 Newark Road, Zanesville, OH 43701

---

## Ohio Wesleyan University
**Delaware, Ohio**                    **CB member**
**www.owu.edu**                    **CB code: 1594**

- Private 4-year liberal arts college affiliated with United Methodist Church
- Residential campus in large town
- 1,960 degree-seeking undergraduates: 1% part-time, 52% women, 5% African American, 2% Asian American, 1% Hispanic American, 9% international

- 66% of applicants admitted
- SAT or ACT (ACT writing optional), application essay required
- 68% graduate within 6 years; 94% enter graduate study

**General.** Founded in 1842. Regionally accredited. **Degrees:** 371 bachelor's awarded. **ROTC:** Army, Air Force. **Location:** 25 miles from Columbus. **Calendar:** Semester, limited summer session. **Full-time faculty:** 136 total; 98% have terminal degrees, 7% minority, 35% women. **Part-time faculty:** 52 total; 48% have terminal degrees, 8% minority, 54% women. **Class size:** 56% < 20, 41% 20-39, 2% 40-49, less than 1% 50-99. **Special facilities:** 2 observatories, US Department of Agriculture laboratories, 2 nature field study preserves, science center; art museum.

**Freshman class profile.** 3,814 applied, 2,499 admitted, 576 enrolled.

| Mid 50% test scores | | Rank in top tenth: | 26% |
|---|---|---|---|
| SAT critical reading: | 530-650 | Return as sophomores: | 84% |
| SAT math: | 540-650 | Out-of-state: | 51% |
| ACT composite: | 24-29 | Live on campus: | 98% |
| GPA 3.50 or higher: | 36% | International: | 9% |
| GPA 3.0-3.49: | 31% | Fraternities: | 31% |
| GPA 2.0-2.99: | 33% | Sororities: | 24% |
| Rank in top quarter: | 49% | | |

**Basis for selection.** High school record (level of challenge and success) most important, followed by class rank, recommendations, test scores, essay, extracurricular activities, general aptitude, character, volunteerism, alumni affiliation. Special consideration given to music, fine art and theater talent. TOEFL required of non-native speakers of English. Interview recommended for all. Audition required for music programs. Portfolio recommended for art programs. Essay required of all applicants. **Homeschooled:** Statement describing homeschool structure and mission, state high school equivalency certificate, letter of recommendation (nonparent) required.

**High school preparation.** 16 units required. Required and recommended units include English 4, mathematics 3-4, social studies 3-4, science 3-4 and foreign language 2-3.

**2007-2008 Annual costs.** Tuition/fees: $31,930. Room/board: $8,030. Books/supplies: $2,050.

**2007-2008 Financial aid. Need-based:** 391 full-time freshmen applied for aid; 344 were judged to have need; 343 of these received aid. Average need met was 90%. Average scholarship/grant was $21,057; average loan $5,168. 77% of total undergraduate aid awarded as scholarships/grants, 23% as loans/jobs. **Non-need-based:** Awarded to 958 full-time undergraduates, including 282 freshmen. Scholarships awarded for academics, alumni affiliation, art, leadership, minority status, music/drama, religious affiliation, state residency.

**Application procedures. Admission:** Priority date 3/1; deadline 5/1 (postmark date). $35 fee, may be waived for applicants with need. Application may be submitted online. Admission notification on a rolling basis beginning on or about 10/1. Must reply by May 1 or within 2 week(s) if notified thereafter. **Financial aid:** Priority date 3/1, closing date 5/1. FAFSA, institutional form required. Applicants notified on a rolling basis starting 2/15; must reply by 5/1 or within 2 week(s) of notification.

**Academics.** Quantitative Skills Center provides individualized and alternative modes of instruction and tutoring to students who need assistance with math skills in any area of study. **Special study options:** Double major, dual enrollment of high school students, exchange student, honors, independent study, internships, New York semester, student-designed major, study abroad, teacher certification program, United Nations semester, urban semester, Washington semester. 3-2 engineering programs with Washington University (MO), Case Western Reserve University, California Institute of Technology (CA), Rensselaer Polytechnic Institute (NY), Alfred College of Ceramics (NY), and Polytechnic Institute of New York. **Credit/placement by examination:** AP, CLEP, IB, SAT, ACT, institutional tests. International Baccalaureate credit given for specific performance levels on higher exams. Students may receive exemption from certain requirements for test scores on SAT, SAT Subject Tests or ACT. **Support services:** Learning center, reduced course load, study skills assistance, tutoring, writing center.

**Majors. Area/ethnic studies:** African-American, East Asian, women's. **Biology:** General, bacteriology, biochemistry, botany, genetics, microbiology, zoology. **Business:** Accounting, international, managerial economics. **Communications:** Broadcast journalism, journalism. **Computer sciences:** General, computer science. **Conservation:** Environmental studies. **Education:** General, art, biology, chemistry, drama/dance, early childhood, elementary, foreign languages, French, German, health, kindergarten/preschool, Latin, mathematics, middle, multi-level teacher, music, physical, physics, science, secondary, social science, social studies, Spanish. **English:** American lit, British lit, composition, creative writing, English lit. **Foreign languages:** Biblical, classics, comparative lit, French, German, Latin, Spanish. **Health:** Predental, premedicine, preveterinary. **History:** General. **Interdisciplinary:**

Ancient studies, medieval/Renaissance, neuroscience. **Legal studies:** Prelaw. **Liberal arts:** Arts/sciences. **Math:** General, statistics. **Philosophy/religion:** Philosophy, religion. **Physical sciences:** Astronomy, chemistry, geology, physics. **Psychology:** General. **Social sciences:** Anthropology, economics, geography, international relations, political science, sociology, U.S. government, urban studies. **Theology:** Preministerial. **Visual/performing arts:** Art history/conservation, dance, dramatic, music performance, studio arts.

**Most popular majors.** Biology 11%, business/marketing 13%, education 7%, psychology 9%, social sciences 20%, visual/performing arts 6%.

**Computing on campus.** 300 workstations in dormitories, library, computer center, student center. Dormitories wired for high-speed internet access and linked to campus network. Commuter students can connect to campus network. Online library, helpline, repair service, student web hosting, wireless network available.

**Student life. Freshman orientation:** Mandatory. Preregistration for classes offered. 2 day session held in June and during the week before classes begin in August. **Housing:** Guaranteed on-campus for all undergraduates. Coed dorms, single-sex dorms, apartments, fraternity/sorority housing, substance-free housing available. $400 nonrefundable deposit, deadline 5/1. Pets allowed in dorm rooms. Small living units (SLUs) offer unique living opportunities to groups of 10-15 students. **Activities:** Bands, campus ministries, choral groups, dance, drama, international student organizations, literary magazine, music ensembles, Model UN, musical theater, opera, radio station, student government, student newspaper, symphony orchestra, B'nai B'rith Hillel Chapter, Christian Fellowship, Young Democrats, College Republicans, Student Union on Black Awareness, Sisters United, Tauheed, Gay, Lesbian, Bisexual and Transgender Center, women's resource center, Habitat for Humanity.

**Athletics.** NCAA. **Intercollegiate:** Baseball M, basketball, cross-country, diving, field hockey W, football (tackle) M, golf M, lacrosse, soccer, softball W, swimming, tennis, track and field, volleyball W. **Intramural:** Badminton, basketball, equestrian, football (non-tackle) M, golf, handball, lacrosse, racquetball, soccer, softball, squash, swimming, tennis, track and field, volleyball, water polo. **Team name:** Battling Bishops.

**Student services.** Alcohol/substance abuse counseling, campus ministries, career counseling, student employment services, financial aid counseling, health services, minority student services, on-campus daycare, personal counseling.

**Contact.** E-mail: owuadmit@owu.edu
Phone: (740) 368-3020 Toll-free number: (800) 922-8953
Fax: (740) 368-3314
Carol DelPropost, Assistant Vice President of Admission and Financial Aid, Ohio Wesleyan University, 75 South Sandusky Street, Delaware, OH 43015-2398

---

## Otterbein College
**Westerville, Ohio**
www.otterbein.edu

CB member
CB code: 1597

- Private 4-year liberal arts college affiliated with United Methodist Church
- Residential campus in large town
- 2,715 degree-seeking undergraduates: 16% part-time, 65% women, 6% African American, 1% Asian American, 2% Hispanic American
- 392 graduate students
- 81% of applicants admitted
- SAT or ACT (ACT writing optional) required

**General.** Founded in 1847. Regionally accredited. **Degrees:** 552 bachelor's awarded; master's offered. **ROTC:** Army, Air Force. **Location:** 12 miles from Columbus. **Calendar:** Quarter, limited summer session. **Full-time faculty:** 159 total; 91% have terminal degrees, 11% minority, 53% women. **Part-time faculty:** 116 total. **Special facilities:** Observatory, 3 performance stages, stables, 3 art galleries.

**Freshman class profile.** 3,360 applied, 2,729 admitted, 647 enrolled.

| | | | |
|---|---|---|---|
| GPA 3.50 or higher: | 51% | Rank in top quarter: | 55% |
| GPA 3.0-3.49: | 28% | Rank in top tenth: | 24% |
| GPA 2.0-2.99: | 21% | Live on campus: | 80% |

**Basis for selection.** School achievement record most important; test scores also important. Recommendations, essay, interview, and extracurricular activities considered. Students applying between May 1 and June 1 accepted on space-available basis. Visit recommended for all; audition required for music and theater programs; portfolio recommended for visual art program.

Essays required for scholarships. **Homeschooled:** Statement describing homeschool structure and mission, transcript of courses and grades required. Submit written documentation of successful completion of college preparatory high school equivalency. Transcripts from cooperating school district preferred. **Learning Disabled:** Students with diagnosed learning disabilities recommended to send documentation with admission application.

**High school preparation.** Recommended units include English 4, mathematics 3, social studies 3, science 3 and foreign language 2. One unit in fine arts recommended.

**2007-2008 Annual costs.** Tuition/fees: $25,065. Room/board: $7,149. Books/supplies: $700. Personal expenses: $1,017.

**Financial aid. Non-need-based:** Scholarships awarded for academics, alumni affiliation, art, leadership, minority status, music/drama, state residency.

**Application procedures. Admission:** Priority date 2/1; no deadline. $25 fee, may be waived for applicants with need. Application may be submitted online. Admission notification on a rolling basis beginning on or about 10/1. Must reply by May 1 or within 4 week(s) if notified thereafter. **Financial aid:** Priority date 4/1; no closing date. FAFSA required. Applicants notified on a rolling basis starting 2/15.

**Academics. Special study options:** Accelerated study, combined bachelor's/graduate degree, cross-registration, double major, dual enrollment of high school students, exchange student, honors, independent study, internships, liberal arts/career combination, student-designed major, study abroad, teacher certification program, Washington semester, weekend college. BA/BS in engineering with Washington University (MO) or Case Western Reserve University. **Credit/placement by examination:** AP, CLEP, IB, SAT, ACT, institutional tests. 60 credit hours maximum toward bachelor's degree. **Support services:** Learning center, reduced course load, remedial instruction, study skills assistance, tutoring, writing center.

**Honors college/program.** Presidential Scholars or must be in top 10% of high school class and have minimum composite ACT score of 25.

**Majors. Agriculture:** Equestrian studies. **Biology:** General, biochemistry, molecular. **Business:** General, accounting, actuarial science, business admin, finance, managerial economics. **Communications:** General, broadcast journalism, journalism, organizational, public relations. **Computer sciences:** Computer science. **Conservation:** General, environmental studies, management/policy. **Education:** General, art, biology, chemistry, early childhood, elementary, English, foreign languages, French, health, history, mathematics, middle, multi-level teacher, music, physical, physics, science, secondary, social studies, Spanish, special. **English:** Composition, creative writing, English lit. **Foreign languages:** French, Spanish. **Health:** Athletic training, nursing (RN), predental, premedicine, prepharmacy, preveterinary. **History:** General. **Legal studies:** Prelaw. **Math:** General. **Parks/recreation:** Health/fitness, sports admin. **Philosophy/religion:** Philosophy, religion. **Physical sciences:** Chemistry, physics. **Psychology:** General. **Social sciences:** Economics, international relations, political science, sociology. **Visual/performing arts:** General, acting, art, dramatic, music history, music performance, music theory/composition, theater design.

**Most popular majors.** Business/marketing 17%, communications/journalism 14%, education 15%, health sciences 10%, visual/performing arts 13%.

**Computing on campus.** 124 workstations in dormitories, library, computer center. Dormitories wired for high-speed internet access and linked to campus network. Commuter students can connect to campus network. Online course registration, helpline, wireless network available.

**Student life. Freshman orientation:** Mandatory. Preregistration for classes offered. One-day orientation held in July or August. **Housing:** Guaranteed on-campus for freshmen. Coed dorms, single-sex dorms, apartments, fraternity/sorority housing available. Theme housing available. **Activities:** Bands, choral groups, dance, drama, literary magazine, music ensembles, musical theater, opera, radio station, student government, student newspaper, symphony orchestra, TV station, Fellowship of Christian Athletes, Christian support group, Afro-American student union, Asian American student union, international students association, religious life council.

**Athletics.** NCAA. **Intercollegiate:** Baseball M, basketball, cross-country, equestrian, football (tackle) M, golf, soccer, softball W, tennis, track and field, volleyball W. **Intramural:** Basketball, bowling, football (non-tackle) M, handball, racquetball, soccer, softball, volleyball. **Team name:** Cardinals.

**Student services.** Adult student services, campus ministries, career counseling, student employment services, financial aid counseling, health services, minority student services, personal counseling, placement for graduates. **Physically disabled:** Services for visually, hearing impaired.

**Contact.** E-mail: uotterb@otterbein.edu
Phone: (614) 823-1500 Toll-free number: (800) 488-8144
Fax: (614) 823-1200
Cass Johnson, Director of Admission, Otterbein College, One Otterbein College, Westerville, OH 43081

## Pontifical College Josephinum
### Columbus, Ohio
### www.pcj.edu
CB code: 1348

- Private 4-year liberal arts and seminary college for men affiliated with Roman Catholic Church
- Residential campus in very large city
- 119 degree-seeking undergraduates: 2% Asian American, 9% Hispanic American, 6% international
- 52 degree-seeking graduate students
- 93% of applicants admitted
- SAT or ACT (ACT writing optional), application essay, interview required

**General.** Founded in 1892. Regionally accredited; also accredited by ATS. **Degrees:** 17 bachelor's awarded; master's, first professional offered. **Calendar:** Semester. **Full-time faculty:** 11 total; 54% have terminal degrees, 36% women. **Part-time faculty:** 20 total; 35% have terminal degrees, 40% women. **Class size:** 82% < 20, 18% 20-39.

**Freshman class profile.** 27 applied, 25 admitted, 22 enrolled.

| Mid 50% test scores | | End year in good standing: | 90% |
|---|---|---|---|
| SAT critical reading: | 510-670 | Return as sophomores: | 95% |
| SAT math: | 340-700 | Out-of-state: | 56% |
| SAT writing: | 450-560 | Live on campus: | 100% |
| ACT composite: | 17-31 | International: | 5% |

**Basis for selection.** School achievement record, recommendations from pastor and director of vocations required. **Homeschooled:** Transcript of courses and grades required.

**High school preparation.** 10 units required; 18 recommended. Required and recommended units include English 4, mathematics 2-4, social studies 2-4, science 1-4 and foreign language 1-2.

**2007-2008 Annual costs.** Tuition/fees: $15,677. Room/board: $7,494. Books/supplies: $350. Personal expenses: $2,500.

**2006-2007 Financial aid.** All financial aid based on need. 71% of total undergraduate aid awarded as scholarships/grants, 29% as loans/jobs.

**Application procedures. Admission:** Priority date 8/1; no deadline. $25 fee, may be waived for applicants with need. Application must be submitted on paper. Admission notification on a rolling basis beginning on or about 5/1. **Financial aid:** Priority date 9/2; no closing date. FAFSA, institutional form required. Applicants notified on a rolling basis starting 8/15; must reply within 2 week(s) of notification.

**Academics.** Students participate in supervised field experience and clinical pastoral education. **Special study options:** Double major, ESL, honors, independent study. **Credit/placement by examination:** AP, CLEP, institutional tests. 30 credit hours maximum toward bachelor's degree. **Support services:** Learning center, reduced course load, remedial instruction, tutoring, writing center.

**Majors. Area/ethnic studies:** Hispanic-American/Latino/Chicano, Latin American. **English:** English lit. **History:** General. **Liberal arts:** Humanities. **Philosophy/religion:** Philosophy, religion.

**Most popular majors.** English 15%, history 16%, philosophy/religious studies 68%.

**Computing on campus.** 16 workstations in library, computer center. Dormitories wired for high-speed internet access and linked to campus network. Online library available.

**Student life. Freshman orientation:** Mandatory. **Policies:** Daily chapel, evening prayer. Religious observance required. **Activities:** Choral groups, music ensembles, student government, Latin American Studies Organization.

**Athletics. Intramural:** Basketball M, soccer M, softball M.

**Student services.** Career counseling, health services, personal counseling.

**Contact.** Phone: (614) 985-2241 Toll-free number: (888) 252-5812
Fax: (614) 885-2307
Perry Cahall, Director of Admissions, Pontifical College Josephinum, 7625
North High Street, Columbus, OH 43235-1499

---

## Rabbinical College of Telshe
### Wickliffe, Ohio
**CB code: 1660**

- Private 4-year rabbinical and teachers college for men affiliated with Jewish faith
- Small city

**General.** Founded in 1941. Accredited by AARTS. **Calendar:** Semester.

**Annual costs/financial aid.** Tuition/fees (2007-2008): $7,500. Room/board: $3,600. Books/supplies: $300. Personal expenses: $1,000.

**Contact.** Phone: (440) 943-5300
Registrar, 28400 Euclid Avenue, Wickliffe, OH 44092-2584

---

## Shawnee State University
### Portsmouth, Ohio
### www.shawnee.edu
**CB code: 1790**

- Public 4-year university
- Commuter campus in large town
- 2,798 degree-seeking undergraduates: 18% part-time, 59% women, 3% African American, 1% Native American, 1% international
- 25 degree-seeking graduate students
- 26% graduate within 6 years; 26% enter graduate study

**General.** Founded in 1986. Regionally accredited. **Degrees:** 437 bachelor's, 242 associate awarded; master's offered. **Location:** 90 miles from Columbus, 90 miles from Cincinnati. **Calendar:** Semester, extensive summer session. **Full-time faculty:** 147 total; 56% have terminal degrees, 8% minority, 40% women. **Part-time faculty:** 142 total; 4% minority, 49% women. **Class size:** 61% < 20, 33% 20-39, 3% 40-49, 2% 50-99, less than 1% >100. **Special facilities:** Planetarium.

**Freshman class profile.** 2,939 applied, 2,939 admitted, 411 enrolled.

| Mid 50% test scores | | | |
|---|---|---|---|
| ACT composite: | 18-22 | Out-of-state: | 7% |
| Rank in top quarter: | 33% | Live on campus: | 38% |
| Rank in top tenth: | 13% | International: | 1% |
| End year in good standing: | 98% | Fraternities: | 6% |
| Return as sophomores: | 56% | Sororities: | 7% |

**Basis for selection.** Open admission, but selective for some programs. For admission to allied health programs: ACT required, interview recommended. **Homeschooled:** GED is required.

**High school preparation.** 16 units recommended. Recommended units include English 4, mathematics 3, social studies 3, science 3 and foreign language 2. Algebra, biology, chemistry required for allied health programs.

**2007-2008 Annual costs.** Tuition/fees: $5,832; $9,972 out-of-state. Room/board: $7,410. Books/supplies: $1,440. Personal expenses: $2,020.

**Financial aid. Non-need-based:** Scholarships awarded for academics. **Additional information:** ACT recommended for scholarship applicants.

**Application procedures. Admission:** No deadline. No application fee. Application may be submitted online. Admission notification on a rolling basis. Applicants to allied health programs advised to apply by February 1. **Financial aid:** Priority date 6/15; no closing date. FAFSA, institutional form required. Applicants notified on a rolling basis starting 5/1; must reply within 4 week(s) of notification.

**Academics. Special study options:** Cross-registration, distance learning, double major, dual enrollment of high school students, honors, independent study, internships, student-designed major, study abroad, teacher certification program, Washington semester. Distance learning is for the 4-year Nursing program only. **Credit/placement by examination:** AP, CLEP, institutional tests. SAT or ACT may be used in lieu of university-developed placement test. **Support services:** Learning center, pre-admission summer program, reduced course load, remedial instruction, study skills assistance, tutoring, writing center.

---

**Majors. Biology:** General. **Business:** Business admin, management information systems. **Education:** General, biology, chemistry, early childhood, history, kindergarten/preschool, mathematics, multi-level teacher, science, social science. **Engineering technology:** Computer, electrical, environmental, plastics. **English:** English lit. **Health:** Athletic training, nursing (RN), premedicine, prepharmacy, preveterinary. **History:** General. **Math:** General. **Parks/recreation:** Health/fitness, sports admin. **Physical sciences:** Atmospheric science, chemistry. **Psychology:** General. **Social sciences:** General, international relations, sociology. **Visual/performing arts:** General, ceramics, drawing, painting, photography, studio arts.

**Most popular majors.** Biology 8%, business/marketing 17%, education 14%, health sciences 6%, parks/recreation 7%, psychology 7%, social sciences 17%.

**Computing on campus.** 620 workstations in library, computer center, student center. Dormitories wired for high-speed internet access. Commuter students can connect to campus network. Online course registration, helpline, wireless network available.

**Student life. Freshman orientation:** Mandatory. Preregistration for classes offered. 1-day programs held throughout the summer. **Housing:** Coed dorms available. $35 nonrefundable deposit, deadline 6/30. **Activities:** Campus ministries, choral groups, drama, literary magazine, music ensembles, musical theater, student government, student newspaper, Health Executives and Administrators Learning Society, student programming board.

**Athletics.** NAIA. **Intercollegiate:** Baseball M, basketball, cross-country, golf M, soccer, softball W, tennis W, volleyball W. **Intramural:** Basketball, bowling, golf, racquetball, softball M, swimming, table tennis, tennis, volleyball. **Team name:** Bears.

**Student services.** Alcohol/substance abuse counseling, career counseling, services for economically disadvantaged, student employment services, financial aid counseling, health services, on-campus daycare, personal counseling, placement for graduates, veterans' counselor. **Physically disabled:** Services for visually, speech, hearing impaired.

**Contact.** E-mail: to_ssu@shawnee.edu
Phone: (740) 351-4778 Toll-free number: (800) 959-2778
Fax: (740) 351-3111
Bob Trusz, Director of Admissions, Shawnee State University, 940 Second Street, Portsmouth, OH 45662

---

## Tiffin University
### Tiffin, Ohio
### www.tiffin.edu
**CB member**
**CB code: 1817**

- Private 4-year university and business college
- Residential campus in large town
- 1,565 degree-seeking undergraduates: 6% part-time, 53% women
- 715 degree-seeking graduate students
- 71% of applicants admitted
- SAT or ACT (ACT writing optional) required
- 33% graduate within 6 years

**General.** Founded in 1888. Regionally accredited. Off-campus courses offered in Lima, Lorain, Columbus, Elyria and online. **Degrees:** 262 bachelor's, 5 associate awarded; master's offered. **ROTC:** Army. **Location:** 50 miles from Toledo, 90 miles from Columbus. **Calendar:** Semester, limited summer session. **Full-time faculty:** 48 total; 60% have terminal degrees, 8% minority, 48% women. **Part-time faculty:** 102 total. **Class size:** 69% < 20, 28% 20-39, 3% 40-49.

**Freshman class profile.** 1,852 applied, 1,324 admitted, 312 enrolled.

| | | | |
|---|---|---|---|
| GPA 3.50 or higher: | 18% | Live on campus: | 74% |
| GPA 3.0-3.49: | 31% | International: | 6% |
| GPA 2.0-2.99: | 50% | Fraternities: | 1% |
| Return as sophomores: | 63% | Sororities: | 1% |
| Out-of-state: | 20% | | |

**Basis for selection.** Test scores, GPA very important. Students below 2.0 GPA may be admitted conditionally into Learning Assistance Program. Interview required for academically weak applicants.

**High school preparation.** Required and recommended units include English 4, mathematics 3, social studies 3, science 3 and foreign language 2.

**2007-2008 Annual costs.** Tuition/fees: $16,800. Room/board: $7,080. Books/supplies: $1,200. Personal expenses: $2,300.

**2007-2008 Financial aid. Need-based:** 292 full-time freshmen applied for aid; 261 were judged to have need; 261 of these received aid. Average

need met was 18%. Average scholarship/grant was $6,555; average loan $3,281. 36% of total undergraduate aid awarded as scholarships/grants, 64% as loans/jobs. **Non-need-based:** Awarded to 1,274 full-time undergraduates, including 301 freshmen. Scholarships awarded for academics, alumni affiliation, athletics, leadership, music/drama, state residency.

**Application procedures. Admission:** No deadline. $20 fee, may be waived for applicants with need. Application may be submitted online. Admission notification on a rolling basis beginning on or about 9/15. **Financial aid:** No deadline. FAFSA required. Applicants notified by 1/15; Applicants notified on a rolling basis starting 1/15; must reply within 2 week(s) of notification.

**Academics. Special study options:** Accelerated study, combined bachelor's/ graduate degree, cross-registration, distance learning, double major, dual enrollment of high school students, honors, independent study, internships, study abroad, teacher certification program, Washington semester. **Credit/ placement by examination:** AP, CLEP, IB, SAT, ACT, institutional tests. 15 credit hours maximum toward associate degree, 30 toward bachelor's. **Support services:** Learning center, pre-admission summer program, reduced course load, remedial instruction, study skills assistance, tutoring.

**Majors. Business:** Accounting, business admin, finance, hospitality admin, human resources, international, logistics, marketing, nonprofit/public. **Communications:** General. **Computer sciences:** Information systems. **Education:** General. **English:** English lit. **Liberal arts:** Arts/sciences. **Parks/ recreation:** Sports admin. **Protective services:** Corrections, law enforcement admin. **Psychology:** General. **Social sciences:** International relations. **Visual/ performing arts:** Arts management.

**Most popular majors.** Business/marketing 52%, psychology 12%, security/ protective services 22%.

**Computing on campus.** 80 workstations in library, computer center, student center. Dormitories wired for high-speed internet access and linked to campus network. Commuter students can connect to campus network. Online course registration, online library, helpline, wireless network available.

**Student life. Freshman orientation:** Available, $25 fee. Preregistration for classes offered. Three-part program; first part occurs on a Saturday in April or May, or on a Friday in June; second part is a weekend in late July; third part occurs during first weekend of classes. **Policies:** Lower-division residential students required to be on meal plan. All undergraduates complete 26 hours of cb-curricular credit. **Housing:** Guaranteed on-campus for freshmen. Coed dorms, single-sex dorms, special housing for disabled, apartments, fraternity/sorority housing available. $49 partly refundable deposit. Theme housing, performing arts, leadership society, house units, junior/ senior house units. **Activities:** Bands, campus ministries, choral groups, dance, drama, international student organizations, literary magazine, music ensembles, musical theater, student government, student newspaper, Black United Students, Chamber of Fools, world student organization, Greek council, Campus Crusade for Christ, Delta Sigma Kappa, gospel choir, Habitat for Humanity.

**Athletics.** NAIA, NCAA. **Intercollegiate:** Baseball M, basketball, cross-country, football (tackle) M, golf, soccer, softball, squash W, tennis, track and field, volleyball W. **Team name:** Dragons.

**Student services.** Adult student services, career counseling, student employment services, financial aid counseling, personal counseling, placement for graduates, veterans' counselor.

**Contact.** E-mail: admissions@tiffin.edu
Phone: (419) 447-6443 Toll-free number: (800) 968-6446 ext. 3423
Fax: (419) 443-5006
Cam Cruickshank, Vice President for Admissions & Student Affairs, Tiffin University, 155 Miami Street, Tiffin, OH 44883

## Tri-State Bible College
**South Point, Ohio**
**www.tsbc.edu**

- Private 4-year Bible college
- Commuter campus in small town

**General.** Accredited by ABHE. **Calendar:** Semester.

**Annual costs/financial aid.** Tuition/fees (2007-2008): $4,960.

**Contact.** Phone: (740) 377-2520
506 Margaret Street, South Point, OH 45680

## Union Institute & University
**Cincinnati, Ohio**
**www.tui.edu**                                      **CB code: 0732**

- Private 4-year university and liberal arts college
- Commuter campus in very large city
- 929 degree-seeking undergraduates: 33% part-time, 63% women, 26% African American, 2% Asian American, 9% Hispanic American
- 776 graduate students
- Application essay, interview required
- 44% graduate within 6 years

**General.** Founded in 1964. Regionally accredited. Academic centers in Montpelie and Brattleboro, Vermont, North Miami Beach, Florida; Los Angeles and Sacramento, California. **Degrees:** 397 bachelor's awarded; master's, doctoral offered. **Location:** 2 miles from downtown. **Calendar:** Differs by program, extensive summer session. **Full-time faculty:** 58 total. **Part-time faculty:** 174 total.

**Basis for selection.** Maturity and evidence of ability to engage in self-directed learning is important. Programs designed for adult learners; majority are over age 25.

**2007-2008 Annual costs.** Tuition/fees: $13,224.

**Financial aid. Non-need-based:** Scholarships awarded for academics, state residency.

**Application procedures. Admission:** No deadline. $35 fee, may be waived for applicants with need. Application may be submitted online. Admission notification on a rolling basis. **Financial aid:** No deadline. FAFSA, institutional form required. Must reply within 4 week(s) of notification.

**Academics.** Individual tutorial-based courses. Many courses available through distance (internet-based) learning. Serves adult learners through individualized programs, carried out through faculty-mentored independent study and research. **Special study options:** Distance learning, double major, external degree, independent study, student-designed major, weekend college. **Credit/ placement by examination:** CLEP, institutional tests. 30 credit hours maximum toward bachelor's degree. **Support services:** Study skills assistance, tutoring.

**Majors. Biology:** General. **Business:** General, business admin, management information systems, organizational behavior, training/development. **Communications:** General. **Computer sciences:** General, information systems. **Education:** General, early childhood, elementary, ESL, special. **English:** English lit. **Health:** Health services, maternal/child health, substance abuse counseling. **History:** General. **Liberal arts:** Arts/sciences, humanities. **Protective services:** Criminal justice, law enforcement admin. **Psychology:** General. **Public administration:** General, social work. **Social sciences:** General, sociology. **Visual/performing arts:** General.

**Most popular majors.** Business/marketing 15%, education 18%, liberal arts 17%, psychology 8%, security/protective services 26%.

**Computing on campus.** 49 workstations in library, computer center. Commuter students can connect to campus network. Online course registration, online library, helpline available.

**Student life. Freshman orientation:** Available. Preregistration for classes offered. **Policies:** Programs for working adults.

**Student services.** Adult student services, financial aid counseling. **Physically disabled:** Services for visually, speech, hearing impaired.

**Contact.** E-mail: admissions@tui.edu
Phone: (802) 828-8568 Toll-free number: (800) 486-3116
Fax: (802) 828-8565
Rick Zand, Admissions Director, Union Institute & University, 440 East McMillan Street, Cincinnati, OH 45206

## University of Akron
**Akron, Ohio**
**www.uakron.edu**                          **CB member**
                                            **CB code: 1829**

- Public 4-year university
- Commuter campus in small city
- 17,988 degree-seeking undergraduates: 20% part-time, 49% women, 14% African American, 2% Asian American, 1% Hispanic American, 1% international

▶ 3,822 degree-seeking graduate students

▶ 37% graduate within 6 years

**General.** Founded in 1870. Regionally accredited. **Degrees:** 2,260 bachelor's, 363 associate awarded; master's, doctoral, first professional offered. **ROTC:** Army, Air Force. **Location:** 40 miles from Cleveland. **Calendar:** Semester, limited summer session. **Full-time faculty:** 737 total; 82% have terminal degrees, 16% minority, 41% women. **Part-time faculty:** 828 total; 30% have terminal degrees, 8% minority, 53% women. **Class size:** 41% < 20, 47% 20-39, 5% 40-49, 5% 50-99, 1% >100. **Special facilities:** Polymer training center, bath nature preserve field station, gas turbine testing facility, training center for fire and hazardous materials.

**Freshman class profile.** 11,410 applied, 9,314 admitted, 3,897 enrolled.

| Mid 50% test scores | | | |
|---|---|---|---|
| SAT critical reading: | 440-560 | GPA 2.0-2.99: | 39% |
| SAT math: | 440-580 | Rank in top quarter: | 30% |
| ACT composite: | 18-24 | Rank in top tenth: | 12% |
| GPA 3.50 or higher: | 26% | Return as sophomores: | 67% |
| GPA 3.0-3.49: | 27% | Out-of-state: | 4% |
| | | Live on campus: | 47% |

**Basis for selection.** Open admission, but selective for some programs. Open admissions to Summit College and Wayne College; all other colleges of the university select on basis of some or all of the following criteria: college prep curriculum, GPA, test scores, class rank, activities, leadership, recommendations, essays, portfolios, and auditions. Conditional admission possible for applicants with GPA less than 2.3 or test scores lower than 16 ACT/650 SAT (exclusive of Writing). Essay, interview required for honors program; audition required for dance, music programs. **Homeschooled:** Students required to obtain letter of exemption from school district.

**High school preparation.** 15 units recommended. Recommended units include English 4, mathematics 3, social studies 3, science 3 and foreign language 2.

**2007-2008 Annual costs.** Tuition/fees: $8,384; $17,632 out-of-state. Room/board: $8,003. Books/supplies: $900. Personal expenses: $1,520.

**2006-2007 Financial aid. Need-based:** 2,903 full-time freshmen applied for aid; 2,356 were judged to have need; 2,356 of these received aid. Average need met was 44%. Average scholarship/grant was $4,889; average loan $2,508. 39% of total undergraduate aid awarded as scholarships/grants, 61% as loans/jobs. **Non-need-based:** Awarded to 4,660 full-time undergraduates, including 1,443 freshmen. Scholarships awarded for academics, alumni affiliation, art, athletics, leadership, music/drama, ROTC, state residency.

**Application procedures. Admission:** Closing date 8/11 (receipt date). $30 fee. Application may be submitted online. Admission notification on a rolling basis beginning on or about 9/15. **Financial aid:** Priority date 2/1; no closing date. FAFSA, institutional form required. Applicants notified on a rolling basis starting 4/1; must reply within 2 week(s) of notification.

**Academics. Special study options:** Accelerated study, combined bachelor's/graduate degree, cooperative education, distance learning, double major, ESL, external degree, honors, independent study, internships, student-designed major, study abroad, teacher certification program, weekend college. Undergraduates may take graduate level classes. Dual enrollment offered for select graduate level programs. **Credit/placement by examination:** AP, CLEP, IB, institutional tests. 38 credit hours maximum toward associate degree, 38 toward bachelor's. **Support services:** Learning center, reduced course load, remedial instruction, study skills assistance, tutoring, writing center.

**Honors college/program.** Must have 2 out of 3 of following criteria: high school GPA 3.50; high school class rank in highest 10%; 27 ACT or 1200 SAT (exclusive of Writing). Some students with other unique qualifications may be admitted.

**Majors. Architecture:** Urban/community planning. **Biology:** General, animal physiology, biochemistry, botany, ecology, microbiology, zoology. **Business:** Accounting, business admin, e-commerce, financial planning, hotel/motel admin, human resources, international, management information systems, marketing, operations, sales/distribution. **Communications:** General, organizational, public relations, radio/tv. **Computer sciences:** Computer science, networking. **Education:** Art, drama/dance, early childhood, early childhood special, English, family/consumer sciences, French, mathematics, middle, music, physical, science, social studies, Spanish, special, voc/tech. **Engineering:** General, biomedical, chemical, civil, computer, electrical, mechanical, polymer. **Engineering technology:** Construction, electrical, manufacturing, mechanical, surveying. **English:** English lit. **Family/consumer sciences:** Child development, clothing/textiles, family systems, housing. **Foreign languages:** Classics, French, Spanish. **Health:** Athletic training, audiology/speech pathology, communication disorders, dietetics, licensed practical nurse, nursing (RN), recreational therapy, respiratory therapy technology. **History:** General. **Liberal arts:** Arts/sciences, humanities. **Math:** General, applied, statistics. **Parks/recreation:** Exercise sciences, sports admin. **Philosophy/**

**religion:** Philosophy. **Physical sciences:** Chemistry, geology, geophysics, physics, polymer chemistry. **Protective services:** Criminal justice, fire safety technology. **Psychology:** General. **Public administration:** Social work. **Social sciences:** General, cartography, criminology, economics, geography, international relations, sociology, U.S. government. **Visual/performing arts:** Art history/conservation, ceramics, dance, dramatic, graphic design, jazz, metal/jewelry, music history, music performance, music theory/composition, photography, piano/organ, printmaking, sculpture, stringed instruments, studio arts, voice/opera.

**Most popular majors.** Business/marketing 19%, communications/journalism 8%, education 17%, engineering/engineering technologies 11%, health sciences 13%.

**Computing on campus.** 3,100 workstations in dormitories, library, student center. Dormitories wired for high-speed internet access and linked to campus network. Commuter students can connect to campus network. Online course registration, online library, helpline, repair service, student web hosting, wireless network available.

**Student life. Freshman orientation:** Mandatory, $50 fee. Preregistration for classes offered. One-day program. **Policies:** All student organizations make own criteria for members, but some stipulated throughout university such as 2.0 GPA minimum requirement and good standing within university. **Housing:** Coed dorms, single-sex dorms, special housing for disabled, fraternity/sorority housing, substance-free housing available. $150 nonrefundable deposit, deadline 2/1. Honors housing available. **Activities:** Bands, campus ministries, choral groups, dance, drama, international student organizations, music ensembles, musical theater, radio station, student government, student newspaper, symphony orchestra, TV station, Chinese students and scholars association, Indian students association, Muslim students association, Black United Students, H.O.L.A., Hillel, College Republicans, College Democrats, Campus Focus, gospel choir.

**Athletics.** NCAA. **Intercollegiate:** Baseball M, basketball, cheerleading, cross-country, diving W, football (tackle) M, golf M, rifle, soccer, softball W, swimming W, tennis W, track and field, volleyball W. **Intramural:** Badminton, basketball, bowling, cross-country, golf, racquetball, skiing, soccer, softball, swimming, table tennis, track and field, volleyball W, wrestling M. **Team name:** Zips.

**Student services.** Adult student services, alcohol/substance abuse counseling, career counseling, student employment services, financial aid counseling, health services, minority student services, on-campus daycare, personal counseling, placement for graduates, veterans' counselor, women's services. **Physically disabled:** Services for visually, speech, hearing impaired.

**Contact.** E-mail: admissions@uakron.edu
Phone: (330) 972-7100 Toll-free number: (800) 655-4884
Fax: (330) 972-7022
Diane Raybuck, Director of Admissions; University of Akron, The University of Akron, Akron, OH 44325-2001

---

## University of Cincinnati
**Cincinnati, Ohio**
**www.uc.edu**

**CB member**
**CB code: 1833**

▶ Public 4-year university

▶ Commuter campus in large city

▶ 19,796 degree-seeking undergraduates: 15% part-time, 51% women, 11% African American, 3% Asian American, 2% Hispanic American, 1% international

▶ 8,099 degree-seeking graduate students

▶ 75% of applicants admitted

▶ SAT or ACT with writing, application essay required

▶ 52% graduate within 6 years

**General.** Founded in 1819. Regionally accredited. **Degrees:** 3,183 bachelor's, 161 associate awarded; master's, doctoral, first professional offered. **ROTC:** Army, Air Force. **Location:** 2 miles from downtown. **Calendar:** Quarter, extensive summer session. **Full-time faculty:** 1,209 total; 61% have terminal degrees, 18% minority, 39% women. **Part-time faculty:** 39 total; 18% have terminal degrees, 10% minority, 54% women. **Class size:** 47% < 20, 39% 20-39, 6% 40-49, 5% 50-99, 3% >100.

**Freshman class profile.** 11,876 applied, 8,902 admitted, 3,560 enrolled.

| Mid 50% test scores | | | |
|---|---|---|---|
| SAT critical reading: | 490-610 | GPA 2.0-2.99: | 20% |
| SAT math: | 500-630 | Rank in top quarter: | 46% |
| SAT writing: | 470-590 | Rank in top tenth: | 20% |
| ACT composite: | 21-27 | Return as sophomores: | 82% |
| GPA 3.50 or higher: | 46% | Out-of-state: | 9% |
| GPA 3.0-3.49: | 34% | Live on campus: | 71% |
| | | International: | 1% |

**Basis for selection.** Secondary school record, test scores most important; recommendations considered. Interview required for music programs; audition required for dance, music programs. **Homeschooled:** Transcript of courses and grades required. Release for home schooling from local Board of Education required.

**High school preparation.** 16 units required. Required and recommended units include English 4, mathematics 3-4, social studies 2, history 1, science 2-3, foreign language 2 and academic electives 2. Specific requirements may vary for each college.

**2007-2008 Annual costs.** Tuition/fees: $9,399; $23,922 out-of-state. Room/board: $8,799. Books/supplies: $1,185. Personal expenses: $3,474.

**2007-2008 Financial aid.** **Need-based:** 3,174 full-time freshmen applied for aid; 2,486 were judged to have need; 2,460 of these received aid. Average need met was 59%. Average scholarship/grant was $6,633; average loan $3,990. 42% of total undergraduate aid awarded as scholarships/grants, 58% as loans/jobs. **Non-need-based:** Awarded to 6,614 full-time undergraduates, including 1,944 freshmen. Scholarships awarded for academics, alumni affiliation, art, athletics, leadership, minority status, music/drama, ROTC, state residency.

**Application procedures.** **Admission:** Priority date 1/15; deadline 9/1 (postmark date). $40 fee, may be waived for applicants with need. Application may be submitted online. Admission notification on a rolling basis beginning on or about 10/1. **Financial aid:** No deadline. FAFSA required. Applicants notified on a rolling basis starting 3/10; must reply within 2 week(s) of notification.

**Academics.** Some engineering programs require students to acquire personal computers. **Special study options:** Accelerated study, combined bachelor's/graduate degree, cooperative education, distance learning, double major, ESL, honors, independent study, internships, liberal arts/career combination, study abroad, teacher certification program, Washington semester, weekend college. Learning at Large (students earn college credit without attending regularly scheduled classes). **Credit/placement by examination:** AP, CLEP, institutional tests. **Support services:** Pre-admission summer program, remedial instruction, study skills assistance, tutoring, writing center.

**Majors.** **Architecture:** Architecture, urban/community planning. **Area/ethnic studies:** African-American, Asian, French, German, Latin American, Spanish/Iberian. **Biology:** General. **Business:** Accounting, business admin, finance, management information systems, management science, operations, real estate. **Communications:** General, radio/tv. **Computer sciences:** General. **Education:** Art, early childhood, elementary, health, music, secondary. **Engineering:** General, aerospace, chemical, civil, computer, electrical, mechanical, mechanics, metallurgical, nuclear. **English:** British lit, English lit. **Family/consumer sciences:** Food/nutrition. **Foreign languages:** Classics, comparative lit, French, German, Latin, linguistics, Spanish. **Health:** Audiology/speech pathology, clinical lab science, health care admin, nuclear medical technology, nursing (RN), predental, premedicine, prepharmacy, preveterinary. **History:** General. **Liberal arts:** Arts/sciences. **Math:** General. **Philosophy/religion:** Judaic, philosophy. **Physical sciences:** Chemistry, geology, physics. **Protective services:** Criminal justice. **Psychology:** General. **Public administration:** Social work. **Social sciences:** Anthropology, economics, geography, international relations, political science, sociology, urban studies. **Visual/performing arts:** Art history/conservation, commercial/advertising art, conducting, dance, dramatic, fashion design, industrial design, interior design, jazz, music history, music performance, music theory/composition, piano/organ, studio arts, theater design, voice/opera. **Other:** Electronic media.

**Most popular majors.** Business/marketing 16%, education 6%, engineering/engineering technologies 12%, English 7%, health sciences 15%, security/protective services 6%, visual/performing arts 11%.

**Computing on campus.** 560 workstations in library, computer center. Dormitories linked to campus network. Commuter students can connect to campus network. Online course registration, helpline, repair service, wireless network available.

**Student life. Freshman orientation:** Available. Preregistration for classes offered. **Housing:** Guaranteed on-campus for freshmen. Coed dorms, single-sex dorms, apartments, fraternity/sorority housing available. **Activities:** Bands, choral groups, dance, drama, film society, music ensembles, musical theater, opera, radio station, student government, student newspaper, symphony orchestra, Women's Initiative Network, College Democrats, College Republicans.

**Athletics.** NCAA. **Intercollegiate:** Baseball M, basketball, cross-country, diving, football (tackle) M, golf, lacrosse W, soccer, swimming, tennis, track and field, volleyball W. **Intramural:** Archery W, badminton, baseball M, basketball, bowling, diving, golf, gymnastics W, handball, lacrosse, racquetball, soccer, softball, squash, swimming, table tennis, tennis, track and field, volleyball, wrestling M. **Team name:** Bearcats.

**Student services.** Adult student services, alcohol/substance abuse counseling, campus ministries, career counseling, services for economically disadvantaged, student employment services, financial aid counseling, health services, legal services, minority student services, on-campus daycare, personal counseling, placement for graduates, veterans' counselor, women's services. **Physically disabled:** Services for visually, speech, hearing impaired.

**Contact.** E-mail: admissions@uc.edu
Phone: (513) 556-1100 Toll-free number: (800) 827-8728
Fax: (513) 556-1105
Thomas Canepa, Assistant Vice President, Admissions, University of Cincinnati, PO Box 210091, Cincinnati, OH 45221-0091

## University of Dayton
Dayton, Ohio
www.udayton.edu
**CB member**
**CB code: 1834**

- Private 4-year university affiliated with Roman Catholic Church
- Residential campus in small city
- 7,154 degree-seeking undergraduates: 4% part-time, 49% women, 3% African American, 1% Asian American, 2% Hispanic American, 1% international
- 2,764 degree-seeking graduate students
- 82% of applicants admitted
- SAT or ACT (ACT writing optional), application essay required
- 76% graduate within 6 years

**General.** Founded in 1850. Regionally accredited. **Degrees:** 1,577 bachelor's awarded; master's, doctoral, first professional offered. **ROTC:** Army, Air Force. **Location:** 2 miles from downtown, 50 miles from Cincinnati. **Calendar:** Semester, extensive summer session. **Full-time faculty:** 457 total; 91% have terminal degrees, 13% minority, 34% women. **Part-time faculty:** 340 total; 7% minority, 43% women. **Class size:** 36% < 20, 54% 20-39, 6% 40-49, 4% 50-99, less than 1% >100. **Special facilities:** Research institute, portfolio management center, learning-teaching center, information sciences center, student-operated stores and coffee bars.

**Freshman class profile.** 8,742 applied, 7,156 admitted, 1,773 enrolled.

| Mid 50% test scores | | | |
|---|---|---|---|
| SAT critical reading: | 520-620 | Rank in top quarter: | 49% |
| SAT math: | 530-640 | Rank in top tenth: | 23% |
| ACT composite: | 23-28 | Return as sophomores: | 87% |
| GPA 3.50 or higher: | 51% | Out-of-state: | 39% |
| GPA 3.0-3.49: | 33% | Live on campus: | 92% |
| GPA 2.0-2.99: | 16% | International: | 1% |

**Basis for selection.** Considered factors include selection of courses in preparation for college, grade record and pattern in high school, class rank, results of SAT or ACT, character, and record of leadership and service. Will review PAA if presented. Interview recommended for all; audition required for all music programs. **Homeschooled:** Transcript of courses and grades required. Description of courses taken required, including bibliography of texts used for instruction. Examples of projects, homework or writing samples helpful. **Learning Disabled:** Prefer applicant provide documentation explaining disability for assessment.

**High school preparation.** 16 units recommended. Recommended units include English 4, mathematics 3, social studies 3, science 2 (laboratory 1) and academic electives 4. 2 units of foreign language required for admission to the College of Arts and Sciences.

**2008-2009 Annual costs.** Tuition/fees: $27,330. $1,299 additional cost to all new incoming students for purchase of computer from university. International students pay additional $75 per month for health and accident insurance. Engineering majors required to pay additional $750 per semester in fees. Room/board: $7,980. Books/supplies: $800. Personal expenses: $1,600.

**2006-2007 Financial aid.** **Need-based:** 1,339 full-time freshmen applied for aid; 972 were judged to have need; 969 of these received aid.

Average need met was 99%. Average scholarship/grant was $11,071; average loan $6,210. 57% of total undergraduate aid awarded as scholarships/grants, 43% as loans/jobs. **Non-need-based:** Awarded to 6,369 full-time undergraduates, including 1,544 freshmen. Scholarships awarded for academics, alumni affiliation, art, athletics, leadership, music/drama, ROTC, state residency.

**Application procedures. Admission:** Priority date 12/15; no deadline. $50 fee, may be waived for applicants with need. Application must be submitted online. Admission notification on a rolling basis beginning on or about 10/31. Must reply by May 1 or within 2 week(s) if notified thereafter. **Financial aid:** Priority date 3/31; no closing date. FAFSA required. Applicants notified on a rolling basis starting 2/20; must reply by 5/1 or within 3 week(s) of notification.

**Academics. Special study options:** Accelerated study, combined bachelor's/graduate degree, cooperative education, cross-registration, distance learning, double major, dual enrollment of high school students, ESL, exchange student, honors, independent study, internships, liberal arts/career combination, semester at sea, student-designed major, study abroad, teacher certification program, Washington semester. Domestic exchange program with other Marianist institutions; student-designed major in general studies only. **Credit/placement by examination:** AP, CLEP, IB, SAT, ACT, institutional tests. 24 credit hours maximum toward bachelor's degree. **Support services:** Learning center, pre-admission summer program, reduced course load, remedial instruction, study skills assistance, tutoring, writing center.

**Majors. Area/ethnic studies:** American. **Biology:** General, biochemistry, environmental. **Business:** General, accounting, business admin, entrepreneurial studies, finance, international, management information systems, managerial economics, marketing, operations. **Communications:** General, digital media, journalism, media studies, public relations. **Computer sciences:** General, computer science. **Conservation:** Environmental science. **Education:** Art, early childhood, foreign languages, French, German, middle, multi-level teacher, music, physical, secondary, Spanish, special. **Engineering:** Chemical, civil, computer, electrical, mechanical. **Engineering technology:** General, computer, electrical, industrial, manufacturing, mechanical. **English:** English lit. **Family/consumer sciences:** Food/nutrition. **Foreign languages:** French, German, Spanish. **Health:** Dietetics, music therapy, predental, premedicine. **History:** General. **Interdisciplinary:** Global studies. **Legal studies:** Prelaw. **Math:** General. **Parks/recreation:** Exercise sciences, facilities management, sports admin. **Philosophy/religion:** Philosophy, religion. **Physical sciences:** General, chemistry, geology, physics. **Protective services:** Criminal justice. **Psychology:** General. **Social sciences:** Econometrics, economics, political science, sociology. **Visual/performing arts:** Art history/conservation, design, dramatic, music performance, music theory/composition, photography, studio arts. **Other:** Human rights.

**Most popular majors.** Business/marketing 21%, communications/journalism 10%, computer/information sciences 9%, education 11%, engineering/engineering technologies 12%.

**Computing on campus.** PC or laptop required. Dormitories wired for high-speed internet access and linked to campus network. Commuter students can connect to campus network. Online course registration, online library, helpline, repair service, student web hosting, wireless network available.

**Student life. Freshman orientation:** Mandatory, $115 fee. Preregistration for classes offered. 2-3 days preceding the first day of classes. Virtual orientation also available online. **Housing:** Guaranteed on-campus for freshmen. Coed dorms, single-sex dorms, special housing for disabled, apartments, fraternity/sorority housing, substance-free housing available. $400 nonrefundable deposit, deadline 5/1. University-owned houses available. **Activities:** Bands, campus ministries, choral groups, dance, drama, international student organizations, literary magazine, music ensembles, Model UN, musical theater, opera, radio station, student government, student newspaper, symphony orchestra, TV station, Catholic Life, Campus Crusade for Christ, College Democrats, College Republicans, diversity discussion group, Indian student association, NAACP, Irish club, Italian club.

**Athletics.** NCAA. **Intercollegiate:** Baseball M, basketball, cheerleading, cross-country, football (tackle) M, golf, rowing (crew) W, soccer, softball W, tennis, track and field W, volleyball W. **Intramural:** Badminton, basketball, bowling, football (non-tackle), golf, racquetball, soccer, softball, tennis, volleyball, water polo, wrestling. **Team name:** Flyers.

**Student services.** Adult student services, alcohol/substance abuse counseling, campus ministries, career counseling, services for economically disadvantaged, student employment services, financial aid counseling, health services, minority student services, on-campus daycare, personal counseling, placement for graduates, women's services. **Physically disabled:** Services for visually, speech, hearing impaired. **Learning disabled:** Comprehensive services available.

**Contact.** E-mail: admission@udayton.edu
Phone: (937) 229-4411 Toll-free number: (800) 837-7433
Fax: (937) 229-4729
Robert Durkle, Director of Admission, University of Dayton, 300 College Park, Dayton, OH 45469-1300

## University of Findlay
**Findlay, Ohio**
www.findlay.edu                                    **CB code: 1223**

- Private 4-year university and health science college affiliated with Church of God
- Residential campus in large town
- 3,187 degree-seeking undergraduates: 11% part-time, 61% women, 3% African American, 1% Asian American, 1% Hispanic American, 7% international
- 1,384 degree-seeking graduate students
- 70% of applicants admitted
- SAT or ACT (ACT writing optional) required
- 51% graduate within 6 years

**General.** Founded in 1882. Regionally accredited. **Degrees:** 518 bachelor's, 78 associate awarded; master's, first professional offered. **ROTC:** Army, Air Force. **Location:** 45 miles from Toledo, 90 miles from Columbus. **Calendar:** Semester, limited summer session. **Full-time faculty:** 169 total; 52% have terminal degrees, 8% minority, 43% women. **Part-time faculty:** 130 total; 15% have terminal degrees, 4% minority, 55% women. **Class size:** 115% < 20, 75% 20-39, 8% 40-49, 6% 50-99. **Special facilities:** Two equestrian farms, cadaver lab, environmental resource training center, planetarium.

**Freshman class profile.** 2,948 applied, 2,052 admitted, 718 enrolled.

| Mid 50% test scores | | | |
|---|---|---|---|
| SAT critical reading: | 460-570 | Rank in top quarter: | 54% |
| SAT math: | 480-590 | Rank in top tenth: | 26% |
| SAT writing: | 480-580 | End year in good standing: | 88% |
| ACT composite: | 20-26 | Return as sophomores: | 77% |
| GPA 3.50 or higher: | 50% | Out-of-state: | 22% |
| GPA 3.0-3.49: | 29% | Live on campus: | 71% |
| GPA 2.0-2.99: | 20% | Fraternities: | 2% |
| | | Sororities: | 2% |

**Basis for selection.** Admissions based on school achievement record, curriculum, class rank, and recommendations. Essay required for special admissions program only; interview recommended for foundations program (special admissions program). **Homeschooled:** Statement describing homeschool structure and mission, state high school equivalency certificate, letter of recommendation (nonparent) required. Greater weight placed on standardized entrance exam scores for admission. Evaluation of GED if taken. **Learning Disabled:** Strongly encourage interview or campus visit.

**High school preparation.** College-preparatory program recommended. 16 units recommended. Recommended units include English 4, mathematics 2, social studies 2, history 1, science 4, foreign language 2 and academic electives 1. One fine arts unit recommended. Additional 1 math and 1 science for preveterinary and environmental programs.

**2007-2008 Annual costs.** Tuition/fees: $23,890. Pre-veterinary and equestrian students pay higher tuition in years one and two; pharmacy students pay higher tuition throughout the program. Room/board: $8,026. Books/supplies: $1,700.

**2006-2007 Financial aid. Need-based:** 637 full-time freshmen applied for aid; 488 were judged to have need; 488 of these received aid. Average need met was 71%. Average scholarship/grant was $11,972; average loan $3,029. 62% of total undergraduate aid awarded as scholarships/grants, 38% as loans/jobs. **Non-need-based:** Scholarships awarded for academics, alumni affiliation, athletics, music/drama, state residency.

**Application procedures. Admission:** Closing date 6/1 (receipt date). No application fee. Application may be submitted online. Admission notification on a rolling basis beginning on or about 9/1. Must reply by May 1 or within 4 week(s) if notified thereafter. Part-time applicants may be admitted year round to any of the six different program start dates. **Financial aid:** Priority date 8/1, closing date 9/1. FAFSA required. Applicants notified on a rolling basis starting 3/1; must reply within 2 week(s) of notification.

**Academics. Special study options:** Accelerated study, combined bachelor's/graduate degree, cooperative education, distance learning, double major, dual enrollment of high school students, ESL, external degree, honors, independent study, internships, liberal arts/career combination, semester at sea, student-designed major, study abroad, teacher certification program, Washington semester, weekend college. BS in nursing with Mount Carmel College of

Nursing and Lourdes College, 3-1 BA prgram with Art Institute Consortium. **Credit/placement by examination:** AP, CLEP, SAT, ACT, institutional tests. 15 credit hours maximum toward associate degree, 30 toward bachelor's. **Support services:** Learning center, reduced course load, remedial instruction, study skills assistance, tutoring, writing center.

**Majors. Agriculture:** Equestrian studies, farm/ranch. **Biology:** General. **Business:** General, accounting, business admin, entrepreneurial studies, finance, hospitality admin, hospitality/recreation, human resources, international, marketing. **Communications:** General, journalism, public relations. **Computer sciences:** General, computer science, systems analysis. **Education:** General, art, bilingual, biology, curriculum, developmentally delayed, drama/dance, driver/safety, early childhood, early childhood special, emotionally handicapped, English, ESL, evaluation, foreign languages, foundations, geography, health, history, kindergarten/preschool, learning disabled, mathematics, mentally handicapped, middle, multi-level teacher, multicultural, multiple handicapped, physical, psychology, reading, science, secondary, social science, social studies, Spanish, special, speech, testing/assessment. **Engineering technology:** Hazardous materials. **English:** Creative writing, English lit. **Foreign languages:** Japanese, Spanish. **Health:** Athletic training, environmental health, health care admin, nuclear medical technology, occupational health, physician assistant, premedicine, prenursing, preveterinary. **History:** General. **Legal studies:** Prelaw. **Math:** General. **Parks/recreation:** Exercise sciences, health/fitness, sports admin. **Philosophy/religion:** Philosophy, religion. **Protective services:** Law enforcement admin. **Psychology:** General. **Public administration:** Social work. **Social sciences:** General, economics, political science, sociology. **Theology:** Theology. **Visual/performing arts:** Art, commercial/advertising art, dramatic, theater design.

**Most popular majors.** Business/marketing 28%, education 17%, health sciences 20%.

**Computing on campus.** 400 workstations in dormitories, library, computer center, student center. Dormitories wired for high-speed internet access and linked to campus network. Commuter students can connect to campus network. Online course registration, online library, helpline, repair service, student web hosting, wireless network available.

**Student life. Freshman orientation:** Mandatory, $100 fee. Preregistration for classes offered. One-day registrations for students and orientation for parents during summer. 2-day orientation for students 2 days before classes begin. **Policies:** All freshmen, sophomores, and juniors under the age of 22 required to live on-campus. **Housing:** Guaranteed on-campus for freshmen. Coed dorms, single-sex dorms, special housing for disabled, apartments, fraternity/sorority housing, substance-free housing available. $150 nonrefundable deposit, deadline 7/1. Honors house and special interest houses. **Activities:** Bands, campus ministries, choral groups, dance, drama, literary magazine, music ensembles, musical theater, opera, radio station, student government, student newspaper, symphony orchestra, TV station, Circle-K, black student union, wilderness club, Campus Compact, College Democrats, College Republicans, Fellowship of Christian Athletes, Habitat for Humanity, international club, student government association.

**Athletics.** NCAA. **Intercollegiate:** Baseball M, basketball, cheerleading, cross-country, diving, equestrian, football (tackle) M, golf, soccer, softball W, swimming, tennis, track and field, volleyball W, wrestling M. **Intramural:** Basketball, bowling, football (non-tackle), golf, skiing, soccer, softball, table tennis, tennis, volleyball, water polo. **Team name:** Oilers.

**Student services.** Adult student services, alcohol/substance abuse counseling, campus ministries, career counseling, services for economically disadvantaged, student employment services, financial aid counseling, health services, minority student services, personal counseling, placement for graduates, veterans' counselor, women's services. **Physically disabled:** Services for visually, speech, hearing impaired.

**Contact.** E-mail: admissions@findlay.edu
Phone: (419) 434-4540 Toll-free number: (800) 548-0932
Fax: (419) 434-4898
Randall Langston, Director of Undergraduate Admissions, University of Findlay, 1000 North Main Street, Findlay, OH 45840-3653

## University of Rio Grande
Rio Grande, Ohio
www.rio.edu
CB code: 1663

- Private 4-year community and liberal arts college
- Commuter campus in rural community
- 1,861 degree-seeking undergraduates: 15% part-time, 61% women
- 222 degree-seeking graduate students
- 44% graduate within 6 years

**General.** Founded in 1876. Regionally accredited. Institution is both public and private. First 2 years are state subsidized, second 2 years are private, with higher tuition. Affiliated with Rio Grande Community College. **Degrees:** 192 bachelor's, 196 associate awarded; master's offered. **ROTC:** Army. **Location:** 12 miles from Gallipolis. **Calendar:** Semester, limited summer session. **Full-time faculty:** 92 total; 45% have terminal degrees, 8% minority, 40% women. **Part-time faculty:** 216 total; 1% have terminal degrees, less than 1% minority, 61% women. **Class size:** 70% < 20, 27% 20-39, 1% 40-49, 2% 50-99. **Special facilities:** Early childhood care center.

**Freshman class profile.** 2,628 applied, 1,963 admitted, 505 enrolled.

| | | | |
|---|---|---|---|
| GPA 3.50 or higher: | 28% | End year in good standing: | 67% |
| GPA 3.0-3.49: | 25% | Return as sophomores: | 57% |
| GPA 2.0-2.99: | 40% | Out-of-state: | 3% |
| Rank in top quarter: | 36% | Live on campus: | 27% |
| Rank in top tenth: | 18% | International: | 1% |

**Basis for selection.** Open admission, but selective for some programs. ACT required for nursing, medical laboratory technician, radiologic technology, diagnostic medical sonography, respiratory therapy, and education programs. Deferred admission for students demonstrating need for remedial work. Acceptance to Education department occurs at end of sophomore year. ACT scores not generally used in admission decisions but required with application. Scores used in decisions for nursing, medical laboratory technician, education, social work, honors programs. **Learning Disabled:** Students with any kind of special needs asked to meet with Director of Accessibility to determine education plan and for academic advising purposes.

**High school preparation.** 20 units required; 21 recommended. Required and recommended units include English 4, mathematics 3, social studies 3, history 2, science 3 (laboratory 1-2), foreign language 2 and academic electives 7-9. Chemistry, algebra, biology required for nursing applicants.

**2007-2008 Annual costs.** Tuition/fees: $16,600. Tuition reported is for private university sector of institution. Public community college in-state in-district tuition: $2,880 ($96 per credit hour); in-state out-of-district, $3,450 ($115 per credit hour). All public community college undergraduates pay $632 in required fees. Out-of-state community college students charged private tuition rate. Room/board: $6,840. Books/supplies: $1,000. Personal expenses: $1,571.

**2006-2007 Financial aid. Need-based:** 531 full-time freshmen applied for aid; 440 were judged to have need; 440 of these received aid. Average need met was 47%. Average scholarship/grant was $1,218. 65% of total undergraduate aid awarded as scholarships/grants, 35% as loans/jobs. **Non-need-based:** Awarded to 30 full-time undergraduates, including 19 freshmen. Scholarships awarded for academics, alumni affiliation, athletics, leadership, music/drama, state residency.

**Application procedures. Admission:** No deadline. $15 fee, may be waived for applicants with need. Application may be submitted online. Admission notification on a rolling basis. **Financial aid:** Priority date 3/15; no closing date. FAFSA, institutional form required. Applicants notified on a rolling basis starting 1/15; must reply within 3 week(s) of notification.

**Academics. Special study options:** Accelerated study, combined bachelor's/graduate degree, cooperative education, distance learning, double major, dual enrollment of high school students, ESL, honors, independent study, internships, liberal arts/career combination, student-designed major, study abroad, teacher certification program. **Credit/placement by examination:** AP, CLEP, institutional tests. **Support services:** Learning center, pre-admission summer program, reduced course load, remedial instruction, tutoring.

**Majors. Agriculture:** Business. **Area/ethnic studies:** American. **Biology:** General. **Business:** General, accounting, accounting technology, business admin, entrepreneurial studies, finance, human resources, international, managerial economics, marketing, office management, office technology, operations, real estate, restaurant/food services, retailing. **Communications:** General, journalism, media studies, public relations. **Computer sciences:** General, applications programming, computer science. **Conservation:** General, environmental studies, wildlife. **Education:** General, art, biology, business, chemistry, early childhood, elementary, English, health, history, mathematics, middle, multi-level teacher, music, physical, physics, reading, science, secondary, social science, special, speech. **Engineering technology:** Manufacturing. **English:** English lit. **Health:** Clinical lab science, health care admin, nursing (RN), premedicine. **History:** General. **Legal studies:** Prelaw. **Liberal arts:** Humanities. **Math:** General. **Parks/recreation:** Sports admin. **Physical sciences:** General, chemistry, physics. **Psychology:** General. **Public administration:** General, social work. **Social sciences:** General, archaeology, economics. **Theology:** Preministerial. **Visual/performing arts:** General, art, commercial/advertising art, dramatic, music management, studio arts.

**Most popular majors.** Business/marketing 18%, education 28%, health sciences 8%, natural resources/environmental science 10%, public administration/social services 12%.

**Computing on campus.** 300 workstations in library, computer center, student center. Dormitories wired for high-speed internet access and linked to campus network. Online course registration, online library, student web hosting, wireless network available.

**Student life. Freshman orientation:** Available, $40 fee. Preregistration for classes offered. Offered 4 times during the summer. **Housing:** Guaranteed on-campus for all undergraduates. Coed dorms, single-sex dorms, special housing for disabled, substance-free housing available. **Activities:** Bands, choral groups, dance, drama, literary magazine, music ensembles, musical theater, radio station, student government, student newspaper, TV station, international student organization, Valley Artist Services, Handicapped Coalition, Young Republicans, Rio Christian Fellowship, Student Ambassadors, Students in Free Enterprise.

**Athletics.** NAIA. **Intercollegiate:** Baseball M, basketball, cheerleading, cross-country, soccer, softball W, track and field, volleyball W. **Intramural:** Archery, badminton, basketball, equestrian, handball, racquetball, softball, swimming, tennis, water polo, wrestling M. **Team name:** Redmen.

**Student services.** Career counseling, student employment services, financial aid counseling, health services, on-campus daycare, personal counseling, placement for graduates, veterans' counselor. **Physically disabled:** Services for visually, speech, hearing impaired.

**Contact.** E-mail: jmabe@rio.edu
Phone: (740) 245-7206 Toll-free number: (800) 282-7201
Fax: (740) 245-7260
Mark Swann, Director of Admissions, University of Rio Grande, 218 North College Avenue, Rio Grande, OH 45674

---

## University of Toledo
Toledo, Ohio      **CB member**
www.utoledo.edu      **CB code: 1845**

- Public 4-year university
- Commuter campus in large city
- 15,476 degree-seeking undergraduates

**General.** Founded in 1872. Regionally accredited. **Degrees:** 2,707 bachelor's, 152 associate awarded; master's, doctoral, first professional offered. **ROTC:** Army, Air Force. **Location:** 6 miles from downtown. **Calendar:** Semester, extensive summer session. **Full-time faculty:** 1,107 total. **Part-time faculty:** 419 total. **Special facilities:** 2 observatories, ion accelerator, arboretum, planetarium, linear laser and nuclear physics laboratory, Lake Erie Research Center.

**Freshman class profile.**

| Mid 50% test scores | | | |
|---|---|---|---|
| SAT critical reading: | 450-570 | Rank in top tenth: | 16% |
| SAT math: | 450-590 | Out-of-state: | 3% |
| ACT composite: | 18-24 | Live on campus: | 47% |
| Rank in top quarter: | 36% | Fraternities: | 3% |
| | | Sororities: | 1% |

**Basis for selection.** Open admission, but selective for some programs and for out-of-state students. Out-of-state students need 2.0 GPA and 21 ACT or 980 SAT. Applicants to BS program in engineering need 3.0 GPA and 22 ACT or 1020 SAT. For admission to premedicine, predentistry, or preveterinary programs, 3.0 GPA and 25 ACT or 1130 SAT required. Applicants to computer science-engineering program need 3.0 GPA and 25 ACT or 1130 SAT, engineering technology 2.0 GPA and 21 ACT or 980 SAT, business college 2.25 GPA or 25 ACT or 1130 SAT. All SAT scores exclusive of Writing. Audition required for music program. **Homeschooled:** Official recognized transcript required. **Learning Disabled:** Registering with the Office of Accessibility recommended.

**High school preparation.** 16 units recommended. Recommended units include history 1, (laboratory 1) and foreign language 2. 4 math and chemistry required of engineering applicants.

**2007-2008 Annual costs.** Tuition/fees: $7,926; $16,738 out-of-state. Room/board: $8,374. Books/supplies: $690. Personal expenses: $2,204.

**Financial aid. Non-need-based:** Scholarships awarded for academics, art, athletics, leadership, minority status, music/drama, ROTC, state residency. **Additional information:** March priority date for federal aid. Students encouraged to apply as early as December for priority consideration for institutional aid.

**Application procedures. Admission:** No deadline. $40 fee, may be waived for applicants with need. Application may be submitted online. Admission notification on a rolling basis beginning on or about 10/1. Freshman applicants desiring on-campus housing encouraged to apply early. **Financial aid:** Priority date 4/1; no closing date. FAFSA required. Applicants

notified on a rolling basis starting 3/31; must reply within 4 week(s) of notification.

**Academics. Special study options:** Accelerated study, combined bachelor's/graduate degree, cooperative education, cross-registration, distance learning, double major, dual enrollment of high school students, ESL, exchange student, external degree, honors, independent study, internships, liberal arts/career combination, student-designed major, study abroad, teacher certification program, weekend college. **Credit/placement by examination:** AP, CLEP, institutional tests. 30 credit hours maximum toward associate degree, 30 toward bachelor's. **Support services:** Learning center, pre-admission summer program, reduced course load, remedial instruction, tutoring.

**Majors. Area/ethnic studies:** African-American, American, Asian, European, Latin American, Near/Middle Eastern, women's. **Biology:** General. **Business:** General, accounting, business admin, entrepreneurial studies, finance, human resources, international, logistics, management information systems, management science, market research, marketing, operations, organizational behavior. **Communications:** General. **Computer sciences:** Information systems. **Conservation:** Environmental studies. **Education:** General, art, business, English, French, German, health, kindergarten/preschool, mathematics, music, physical, science, secondary, social studies, Spanish, speech impaired, trade/industrial. **Engineering:** General, biomedical, chemical, civil, computer, electrical, industrial, mechanical. **Engineering technology:** Civil, electromechanical, mechanical. **English:** English lit. **Foreign languages:** French, German, linguistics, Spanish. **Health:** Facilities admin, medical records admin, nursing (RN), pharmaceutical sciences, predental, premedicine, preveterinary, public health ed, recreational therapy, respiratory therapy technology. **History:** General. **Interdisciplinary:** Medieval/Renaissance. **Legal studies:** Paralegal, prelaw. **Liberal arts:** Arts/sciences, humanities. **Math:** General. **Parks/recreation:** General, exercise sciences, health/fitness. **Philosophy/religion:** Philosophy, religion. **Physical sciences:** Astronomy, chemistry, geology, physics. **Protective services:** Criminal justice. **Psychology:** General. **Public administration:** Social work. **Social sciences:** Anthropology, economics, geography, international relations, political science, sociology, urban studies. **Visual/performing arts:** Art, art history/conservation, dramatic, film/cinema, studio arts.

**Computing on campus.** 2,800 workstations in dormitories, library, computer center, student center. Dormitories linked to campus network. Commuter students can connect to campus network. Online course registration, online library, helpline, repair service, wireless network available.

**Student life. Freshman orientation:** Available, $60 fee. **Housing:** Coed dorms, single-sex dorms, special housing for disabled, fraternity/sorority housing available. $200 deposit. **Activities:** Bands, choral groups, dance, drama, film society, music ensembles, musical theater, opera, radio station, student government, student newspaper, symphony orchestra, black student union, Campus Crusade for Christ, Hillel, Latino student union, University YMCA, gay and lesbian student union, international student association, Habitat for Humanity, Toledo Campus Ministry Fellowship.

**Athletics.** NCAA. **Intercollegiate:** Baseball M, basketball, cross-country, diving W, football (tackle) M, golf, soccer W, softball W, swimming W, tennis, track and field W, volleyball W. **Intramural:** Badminton, basketball, bowling M, diving W, fencing, golf, racquetball, soccer, softball, swimming W, table tennis, tennis, track and field W, volleyball, weight lifting. **Team name:** Rockets.

**Student services.** Adult student services, alcohol/substance abuse counseling, campus ministries, career counseling, services for economically disadvantaged, student employment services, financial aid counseling, health services, legal services, minority student services, on-campus daycare, personal counseling, placement for graduates, veterans' counselor, women's services. **Physically disabled:** Services for visually, speech, hearing impaired.

**Contact.** E-mail: enroll@utnet.utoledo.edu
Phone: (419) 530-8700 Toll-free number: (800) 586-5336
Fax: (419) 530-4504
William Pierce, Director of Admission, University of Toledo, 2801 West Bancroft Street, Toledo, OH 43606-3398

---

## Urbana University
Urbana, Ohio
www.urbana.edu      **CB code: 1847**

- Private 4-year liberal arts college
- Commuter campus in large town
- 1,500 full-time, degree-seeking undergraduates
- 200 graduate students
- SAT or ACT (ACT writing optional), application essay required

**General.** Founded in 1850. Regionally accredited. Branch sites in Bellefontaine, Piqua, Dayton, Springfield, London. **Degrees:** 197 bachelor's, 10 associate awarded; master's offered. **Location:** 42 miles from Columbus, 49 miles from Dayton. **Calendar:** Semester, limited summer session. **Full-time faculty:** 50 total. **Part-time faculty:** 70 total. **Special facilities:** Johnny Appleseed museum, rare books collection.

### Freshman class profile.

| Mid 50% test scores | | Out-of-state: | 1% |
|---|---|---|---|
| ACT composite: | 18-21 | Live on campus: | 50% |

**Basis for selection.** School achievement record, class rank, GPA, test scores, extra-curricular activities and honors important. Recommendations and interviews are required for some applicants. Special consideration given to children of alumni. For regular admission, composite score of 18 on ACT or equivalent on SAT required.

**High school preparation.** 15 units recommended. Required and recommended units include English 4, mathematics 2, social studies 2, science 2, foreign language 1 and academic electives 2.

**2007-2008 Annual costs.** Tuition/fees: $17,809. Room/board: $7,378. Books/supplies: $1,000. Personal expenses: $666.

**Financial aid. Non-need-based:** Scholarships awarded for academics, alumni affiliation, athletics, music/drama.

**Application procedures. Admission:** No deadline. $25 fee. Application may be submitted online. Admission notification on a rolling basis. **Financial aid:** Closing date 4/1. FAFSA required. Applicants notified on a rolling basis starting 3/1; must reply within 4 week(s) of notification.

**Academics. Special study options:** Accelerated study, cooperative education, cross-registration, double major, honors, independent study, internships, liberal arts/career combination, student-designed major, teacher certification program. Opportunity to study in Poland for one semester. **Credit/placement by examination:** AP, CLEP, institutional tests. 15 credit hours maximum toward associate degree, 15 toward bachelor's. **Support services:** Learning center, reduced course load, remedial instruction, tutoring, writing center.

**Majors. Business:** General, accounting, communications, human resources, marketing. **Communications:** General. **Computer sciences:** Information systems. **Education:** General, biology, elementary, English, mathematics, middle, science, secondary, social studies, special. **English:** English lit. **Health:** Athletic training, health services, predental, premedicine. **History:** General. **Interdisciplinary:** Biological/physical sciences. **Legal studies:** Prelaw. **Liberal arts:** Arts/sciences. **Math:** General. **Parks/recreation:** Sports admin. **Philosophy/religion:** Philosophy. **Protective services:** Criminal justice, law enforcement admin. **Psychology:** General. **Public administration:** Community org/advocacy. **Social sciences:** General, political science, sociology.

**Computing on campus.** 69 workstations in dormitories, library, computer center. Dormitories wired for high-speed internet access. Online library, repair service available.

**Student life. Freshman orientation:** Mandatory. Held the weekend before fall classes. **Housing:** Guaranteed on-campus for freshmen. Coed dorms, single-sex dorms available. $125 deposit, deadline 8/23. **Activities:** Bands, choral groups, drama, literary magazine, music ensembles, musical theater, student government, student newspaper, American Association of University Women, Association for Information Technology Professionals student chapter, business club, children's literature club, Gay/Straight Alliance, Habitat for Humanity, Johnny Appleseed club, science club, Sports Medicine Association, Student Ambassadors.

**Athletics.** NAIA. **Intercollegiate:** Baseball M, basketball, football (tackle) M, golf M, soccer, softball W, volleyball W. **Intramural:** Basketball, racquetball, swimming, synchronized swimming W, table tennis, volleyball, water polo. **Team name:** Blue Knights.

**Student services.** Adult student services, alcohol/substance abuse counseling, career counseling, student employment services, financial aid counseling, health services, personal counseling, placement for graduates, veterans' counselor.

**Contact.** E-mail: admiss@urbana.edu
Phone: (937) 484-1356 Toll-free number: (800) 787-2262 ext. 1356
Fax: (937) 484-1389
John Rangel, Director of Admissions, Urbana University, 579 College Way, Urbana, OH 43078

---

## Ursuline College
**Pepper Pike, Ohio**
www.ursuline.edu

**CB member**
**CB code: 1848**

- Private 4-year liberal arts college for women affiliated with Roman Catholic Church
- Residential campus in small town
- 1,158 degree-seeking undergraduates: 31% part-time, 93% women, 25% African American, 3% Asian American, 2% Hispanic American
- 377 degree-seeking graduate students
- 66% of applicants admitted
- SAT or ACT (ACT writing optional), application essay required
- 48% graduate within 6 years

**General.** Founded in 1871. Regionally accredited. Primarily women's college, but some men admitted. **Degrees:** 216 bachelor's awarded; master's offered. **ROTC:** Army. **Location:** 10 miles from Cleveland. **Calendar:** Semester, limited summer session. **Full-time faculty:** 70 total. **Part-time faculty:** 140 total. **Class size:** 79% < 20, 21% 20-39.

**Freshman class profile.** 436 applied, 287 admitted, 113 enrolled.

| Mid 50% test scores | | Rank in top quarter: | 37% |
|---|---|---|---|
| SAT critical reading: | 440-560 | Rank in top tenth: | 17% |
| SAT math: | 450-550 | End year in good standing: | 90% |
| ACT composite: | 18-23 | Return as sophomores: | 73% |
| GPA 3.50 or higher: | 36% | Out-of-state: | 3% |
| GPA 3.0-3.49: | 33% | Live on campus: | 66% |
| GPA 2.0-2.99: | 31% | | |

**Basis for selection.** Secondary school record, recommendations, standardized test scores and essay are very important. Community activities considered. Interview recommended for all. **Homeschooled:** Transcript of courses and grades, state high school equivalency certificate, letter of recommendation (nonparent) required. Official transcript from accrediting agency needed.

**High school preparation.** 17 units recommended. Recommended units include English 4, mathematics 3, social studies 3, science 3 (laboratory 2) and foreign language 2. One fine or performing arts recommended. Nursing students should have chemistry.

**2007-2008 Annual costs.** Tuition/fees: $21,110. Room/board: $7,036. Books/supplies: $1,000. Personal expenses: $700.

**2006-2007 Financial aid. Need-based:** 121 full-time freshmen applied for aid; 112 were judged to have need; 112 of these received aid. Average need met was 86%. Average scholarship/grant was $14,903; average loan $3,208. 48% of total undergraduate aid awarded as scholarships/grants, 52% as loans/jobs. **Non-need-based:** Awarded to 145 full-time undergraduates, including 24 freshmen. Scholarships awarded for academics, art, athletics, leadership, religious affiliation, ROTC.

**Application procedures. Admission:** No deadline. $25 fee, may be waived for applicants with need. Application may be submitted online. Applicants notified within 3 weeks of application. Must reply by May 1 or within 4 week(s) if notified thereafter. **Financial aid:** Priority date 3/15; no closing date. FAFSA, institutional form required. Applicants notified on a rolling basis starting 3/1; must reply within 2 week(s) of notification.

**Academics. Special study options:** Accelerated study, combined bachelor's/graduate degree, cooperative education, cross-registration, distance learning, double major, independent study, internships, liberal arts/career combination, New York semester, teacher certification program, weekend college. Optional junior year program in fashion merchandising or design at Fashion Institute of Technology in New York City for enrichment electives only. **Credit/placement by examination:** AP, CLEP, SAT, ACT, institutional tests. 43 credit hours maximum toward bachelor's degree. **Support services:** Learning center, reduced course load, remedial instruction, study skills assistance, tutoring, writing center.

**Majors. Area/ethnic studies:** American. **Biology:** General, biomedical sciences, biotechnology, environmental. **Business:** Accounting, business admin, fashion, human resources, management information systems, marketing. **Communications:** Public relations. **Education:** Art, early childhood, English, mathematics, middle, science, social studies, special. **English:** English lit. **Family/consumer sciences:** Work/family studies. **Health:** Facilities admin, health care admin, health services, nursing (RN), prenursing, preop/surgical nursing. **History:** General. **Interdisciplinary:** Historic preservation. **Legal studies:** Paralegal. **Liberal arts:** Humanities. **Math:** General. **Philosophy/religion:** Christian, philosophy. **Psychology:** General. **Public administration:** Social work. **Social sciences:** Sociology. **Visual/performing arts:** Art history/conservation, fashion design, graphic design, interior design, studio arts.

**Most popular majors.** Business/marketing 22%, education 10%, health sciences 37%, visual/performing arts 6%.

**Computing on campus.** 72 workstations in dormitories, library, computer center, student center. Dormitories wired for high-speed internet access and linked to campus network. Online library, wireless network available.

**Student life. Freshman orientation:** Available. Preregistration for classes offered. 3-day program offered prior to start of fall semester. **Housing:** $100 fully refundable deposit. **Activities:** Choral groups, drama, literary magazine, student government, student nurses, education association, campus service and spiritual life committees, ethnic groups, public relations society, peer mentors.

**Athletics.** NAIA. **Intercollegiate:** Basketball W, cross-country W, golf W, soccer W, softball W, tennis W, track and field W, volleyball W. **Team name:** Arrows.

**Student services.** Adult student services, campus ministries, career counseling, student employment services, financial aid counseling, minority student services, personal counseling. **Physically disabled:** Services for visually, speech, hearing impaired.

**Contact.** E-mail: admission@ursuline.edu
Phone: (440) 449-4203 Toll-free number: (888) 877-8546
Fax: (440) 684-6138
Director of Admissions, Ursuline College, 2550 Lander Road, Pepper Pike, OH 44124-4398

---

## Walsh University
**North Canton, Ohio**
**www.walsh.edu**
CB member
CB code: 1926

- Private 4-year university and liberal arts college affiliated with Roman Catholic Church
- Residential campus in small city
- 2,146 degree-seeking undergraduates: 20% part-time, 65% women
- 400 degree-seeking graduate students
- 79% of applicants admitted
- SAT or ACT (ACT writing optional) required
- 49% graduate within 6 years; 25% enter graduate study

**General.** Founded in 1958. Regionally accredited. **Degrees:** 363 bachelor's awarded; master's, doctoral offered. **Location:** 20 miles from Akron, 60 miles from Cleveland. **Calendar:** Semester, limited summer session. **Full-time faculty:** 98 total; 74% have terminal degrees, 13% minority, 53% women. **Part-time faculty:** 147 total; 11% have terminal degrees, 2% minority, 56% women. **Class size:** 55% < 20, 44% 20-39, less than 1% 40-49. **Special facilities:** Bioinformatics laboratory, prayer garden.

**Freshman class profile.** 1,313 applied, 1,035 admitted, 453 enrolled.

| Mid 50% test scores | | Rank in top quarter: | 41% |
|---|---|---|---|
| SAT critical reading: | 450-560 | Rank in top tenth: | 15% |
| SAT math: | 450-580 | End year in good standing: | 87% |
| ACT composite: | 19-25 | Return as sophomores: | 80% |
| GPA 3.50 or higher: | 41% | Out-of-state: | 4% |
| GPA 3.0-3.49: | 35% | Live on campus: | 74% |
| GPA 2.0-2.99: | 24% | | |

**Basis for selection.** Secondary school record and standardized test scores very important; class rank, recommendations, essay, and character important. Essay, interview recommended for all. **Homeschooled:** Transcript of courses and grades required.

**High school preparation.** 16 units recommended. Recommended units include English 4, mathematics 3, social studies 3, science 3, foreign language 2 and academic electives 1. Algebra, biology, and chemistry required for nursing applicants.

**2008-2009 Annual costs.** Tuition/fees (projected): $20,050. Room/board: $7,760. Books/supplies: $1,000. Personal expenses: $1,102.

**2007-2008 Financial aid. Need-based:** 427 full-time freshmen applied for aid; 371 were judged to have need; 371 of these received aid. Average need met was 72%. Average scholarship/grant was $3,854; average loan $2,420. 54% of total undergraduate aid awarded as scholarships/grants, 46% as loans/jobs. **Non-need-based:** Awarded to 1,640 full-time undergraduates, including 534 freshmen. Scholarships awarded for academics, alumni affiliation, athletics, music/drama, religious affiliation, state residency.

**Application procedures. Admission:** Closing date 8/15 (postmark date). $25 fee, may be waived for applicants with need. Application may be submitted online. Admission notification on a rolling basis beginning on or about 10/1. Must reply by 8/15. **Financial aid:** Priority date 3/15; no closing date. FAFSA, institutional form required. Applicants notified on a rolling basis starting 2/15.

**Academics.** Accelerated degree completion program for adults with evening and weekend classes, multiple locations. Structured first semester available for selected students. **Special study options:** Accelerated study, combined bachelor's/graduate degree, cross-registration, double major, dual enrollment of high school students, ESL, exchange student, external degree, honors, independent study, internships, liberal arts/career combination, study abroad, teacher certification program, Washington semester. CCSA Consortium for Study Abroad. **Credit/placement by examination:** AP, CLEP, institutional tests. 45 credit hours maximum toward bachelor's degree. **Support services:** Learning center, reduced course load, remedial instruction, study skills assistance, tutoring, writing center.

**Honors college/program.** 3.75 high school GPA, 27 ACT or 1200 SAT (exclusive of Writing), writing sample and interview required. Special English and history courses, upper-level seminar and thesis courses.

**Majors. Biology:** General. **Business:** General, accounting, business admin, finance, management information systems, marketing. **Communications:** General. **Computer sciences:** General. **Education:** Early childhood, elementary, emotionally handicapped, English, mathematics, mentally handicapped, middle, multiple handicapped, physical, reading, science, secondary, social science, social studies. **English:** English lit. **Foreign languages:** French, Spanish. **Health:** Clinical lab science, nursing (RN), predental, premedicine, preveterinary. **History:** General. **Interdisciplinary:** Biological/physical sciences, natural sciences. **Math:** General. **Philosophy/religion:** Philosophy, religion. **Physical sciences:** Chemistry. **Psychology:** General. **Social sciences:** Political science, sociology. **Theology:** Theology.

**Most popular majors.** Business/marketing 37%, communications/journalism 9%, education 21%, health sciences 11%, social sciences 6%.

**Computing on campus.** 346 workstations in dormitories, library, student center. Dormitories wired for high-speed internet access and linked to campus network. Commuter students can connect to campus network. Online course registration, online library, helpline, repair service, wireless network available.

**Student life. Freshman orientation:** Mandatory, $200 fee. Preregistration for classes offered. Occurs during student's choice of 1 of 5 weekends before classes begin in August. **Policies:** All full-time undergraduate students 23 and younger must live on campus (some exceptions permitted). **Housing:** Guaranteed on-campus for all undergraduates. Coed dorms, special housing for disabled, apartments, substance-free housing available. $200 deposit, deadline 8/15. Pets allowed in dorm rooms. Apartment-style residence hall with kitchens; quiet, themed floors for first-year students. **Activities:** Pep band, campus ministries, choral groups, dance, drama, international student organizations, literary magazine, music ensembles, radio station, student government, student newspaper, Circle-K, Black Student Union, Habitat for Humanity, Institute for Justice and Peace, commuter commission, major-related clubs.

**Athletics.** NAIA. **Intercollegiate:** Baseball M, basketball, cheerleading, cross-country, football (tackle) M, golf, soccer, softball W, tennis, track and field, volleyball W. **Intramural:** Basketball, bowling, football (non-tackle), golf, soccer, softball, swimming, table tennis, tennis, volleyball. **Team name:** Cavaliers.

**Student services.** Adult student services, alcohol/substance abuse counseling, campus ministries, career counseling, student employment services, financial aid counseling, health services, minority student services, personal counseling, placement for graduates, veterans' counselor. **Physically disabled:** Services for visually, speech impaired.

**Contact.** E-mail: admissions@walsh.edu
Phone: (330) 490-7172 Toll-free number: (800) 362-9846
Fax: (330) 490-7165
Brett Freshour, VP for Enrollment Management, Walsh University, 2020 East Maple Street, North Canton, OH 44720-3396

---

## Wilberforce University
**Wilberforce, Ohio**
**www.wilberforce.edu**
CB member
CB code: 1906

- Private 4-year liberal arts college affiliated with African Methodist Episcopal Church
- Residential campus in rural community
- 826 degree-seeking undergraduates
- 53% of applicants admitted

**General.** Founded in 1856. Regionally accredited. Cooperative education program required of all students. **Degrees:** 209 bachelor's awarded; master's offered. **ROTC:** Army, Air Force. **Location:** 18 miles from Dayton. **Calendar:** Semester, extensive summer session. **Full-time faculty:** 35 total. **Part-time faculty:** 49 total. **Special facilities:** African Methodist Episcopal Church archives.

**Freshman class profile.**

Out-of-state: 67%  Live on campus: 94%

**Basis for selection.** Class rank (top two-thirds), high school GPA, test scores most important. SAT or ACT recommended. Essay, interview recommended for all.

**High school preparation.** 15 units required. Required and recommended units include English 4, mathematics 2-3, social studies 2, science 2-3 and foreign language 2.

**2007-2008 Annual costs.** Tuition/fees: $11,560. Room/board: $5,320. Books/supplies: $1,000. Personal expenses: $1,500.

**Application procedures. Admission:** Priority date 1/1; deadline 4/1. $50 fee, may be waived for applicants with need. Admission notification on a rolling basis. **Financial aid:** Priority date 3/15, closing date 6/1. FAFSA, institutional form required. Applicants notified on a rolling basis starting 3/15; must reply within 2 week(s) of notification.

**Academics. Special study options:** Cooperative education, cross-registration, honors, internships, study abroad. **Credit/placement by examination:** AP, CLEP, institutional tests. 30 credit hours maximum toward bachelor's degree. **Support services:** Remedial instruction, tutoring.

**Majors. Biology:** General. **Business:** Accounting, business admin, finance, managerial economics. **Communications:** Journalism. **Computer sciences:** General, information systems. **Engineering:** Chemical, civil, electrical, mechanical. **English:** English lit. **Foreign languages:** Comparative lit. **Health:** Health care admin. **Interdisciplinary:** Biological/physical sciences. **Liberal arts:** Arts/sciences. **Math:** General. **Physical sciences:** Chemistry. **Psychology:** General. **Social sciences:** Economics, political science, sociology. **Visual/performing arts:** Studio arts.

**Computing on campus.** 49 workstations in library, computer center.

**Student life. Housing:** Guaranteed on-campus for freshmen. Single-sex dorms, apartments available. **Activities:** Choral groups, dance, drama, music ensembles, radio station, student government, student newspaper, Inter-Faith Fellowship, Interdenominational Ministerial Alliance, Alpha-Omega.

**Athletics.** NAIA. **Intercollegiate:** Basketball, cross-country, golf, track and field. **Intramural:** Baseball M, basketball, softball, table tennis, tennis, volleyball.

**Student services.** Career counseling, student employment services, health services, personal counseling, placement for graduates, veterans' counselor.

**Contact.** E-mail: admissions@wilberforce.edu
Phone: (937) 708-5721 Toll-free number: (800) 367-8568
Fax: (937) 376-4751
Lee Williams, Director of Admissions, Wilberforce University, 1055 North Bickett Road, Wilberforce, OH 45384-1001

## Wilmington College
**Wilmington, Ohio** — CB member
www.wilmington.edu — CB code: 1909

▶ Private 4-year liberal arts college affiliated with Society of Friends (Quaker)
▶ Residential campus in large town
▶ 1,428 degree-seeking undergraduates: 16% part-time, 57% women
▶ 43 graduate students
▶ 83% of applicants admitted
▶ SAT or ACT (ACT writing optional) required
▶ 56% graduate within 6 years

**General.** Founded in 1870. Regionally accredited. Affiliated with Wilmington Yearly Meeting of the Religious Society of Friends. Branch campuses in Cincinnati and other locations. BA in business offered at Cincinnati branch and Wilmington evening program. **Degrees:** 340 bachelor's awarded; master's offered. **Location:** 50 miles from Cincinnati, 60 miles from Columbus. **Calendar:** Semester, limited summer session. **Full-time faculty:** 72 total; 69% have terminal degrees, 1% minority, 43% women. **Part-time faculty:** 50 total; 52% women. **Class size:** 71% < 20, 27% 20-39, 2% 40-49, less

than 1% 50-99. **Special facilities:** Greenhouse, herbarium, observatory, electron microscope, live animal area, sports medicine center, Peace Resource Center containing Hiroshima/Nagasaki Memorial collection.

**Freshman class profile.** 1,922 applied, 1,603 admitted, 380 enrolled.

| Mid 50% test scores | | | |
|---|---|---|---|
| SAT critical reading: | 420-510 | Rank in top quarter: | 39% |
| SAT math: | 450-550 | Rank in top tenth: | 16% |
| ACT composite: | 18-23 | Return as sophomores: | 68% |
| GPA 3.50 or higher: | 33% | Out-of-state: | 3% |
| GPA 3.0-3.49: | 26% | Live on campus: | 88% |
| GPA 2.0-2.99: | 40% | International: | 1% |

**Basis for selection.** Previous academic record, test scores, counselor recommendation, and interview important. Essay, interview recommended for all.

**High school preparation.** 16 units required. Required and recommended units include English 4, mathematics 2, social studies 2, science 2 (laboratory 2), foreign language 2 and academic electives 4. 6 art units recommended.

**2007-2008 Annual costs.** Tuition/fees: $22,078. Room/board: $7,500. Books/supplies: $500. Personal expenses: $450.

**Financial aid. Non-need-based:** Scholarships awarded for academics, alumni affiliation, religious affiliation, state residency.

**Application procedures. Admission:** No deadline. $25 fee, may be waived for applicants with need. Application may be submitted online. Admission notification on a rolling basis. Online application does not require application fee. **Financial aid:** Priority date 3/31, closing date 6/1. FAFSA required. Applicants notified on a rolling basis starting 3/1; must reply by 5/1 or within 2 week(s) of notification.

**Academics. Special study options:** Accelerated study, cross-registration, double major, dual enrollment of high school students, honors, independent study, internships, liberal arts/career combination, student-designed major, study abroad, teacher certification program, Washington semester, weekend college. **Credit/placement by examination:** AP, CLEP, IB, SAT, ACT, institutional tests. 30 credit hours maximum toward bachelor's degree. **Support services:** Learning center, reduced course load, remedial instruction, study skills assistance, tutoring, writing center.

**Majors. Agriculture:** Agribusiness operations, agronomy, animal sciences, business, equine science, farm/ranch, production. **Biology:** General, bacteriology, biochemistry, environmental. **Business:** Accounting, business admin, management science, marketing, sales/distribution. **Communications:** General, journalism, media studies, public relations. **Computer sciences:** General, computer science. **Education:** General, agricultural, biology, chemistry, early childhood, elementary, English, health, history, mathematics, middle, multi-level teacher, physical, science, secondary, social science, social studies. **English:** English lit. **Foreign languages:** Spanish. **History:** General. **Legal studies:** Prelaw. **Liberal arts:** Arts/sciences. **Math:** General. **Parks/recreation:** Sports admin. **Physical sciences:** Astronomy, chemistry, geology, planetary. **Protective services:** Criminal justice. **Psychology:** General. **Public administration:** Social work. **Social sciences:** General, economics, political science, sociology. **Visual/performing arts:** Art, commercial/advertising art, dramatic.

**Most popular majors.** Agriculture 9%, business/marketing 24%, education 26%, psychology 10%.

**Computing on campus.** 156 workstations in library, computer center. Dormitories wired for high-speed internet access and linked to campus network. Commuter students can connect to campus network. Online course registration, helpline, student web hosting available.

**Student life. Freshman orientation:** Mandatory. Held 3 days prior to start of fall semester. **Housing:** Guaranteed on-campus for all undergraduates. Coed dorms, single-sex dorms, apartments, fraternity/sorority housing available. $100 nonrefundable deposit, deadline 8/15. Living/learning units available. **Activities:** Concert band, campus ministries, choral groups, drama, international student organizations, literary magazine, music ensembles, musical theater, student government, student newspaper, social service, international, education, and agriculture clubs, Christian Students, Young Friends (Quaker-Christian group), sports medicine association.

**Athletics.** NCAA. **Intercollegiate:** Baseball M, basketball, cheerleading, cross-country, football (tackle), golf, soccer, softball W, swimming, tennis, track and field, volleyball W, wrestling M. **Intramural:** Basketball, football (non-tackle), racquetball, soccer, softball, squash, table tennis, tennis, volleyball, weight lifting. **Team name:** Quakers.

**Student services.** Adult student services, alcohol/substance abuse counseling, campus ministries, career counseling, student employment services,

financial aid counseling, health services, minority student services, personal counseling, placement for graduates, veterans' counselor.

**Contact.** E-mail: admissions@wilmington.edu
Phone: (800) 341-9318 ext. 260 Fax: (937) 382-7077
Tina Garland, Director of Admission, Wilmington College, Box 1325 Pyle Center, Wilmington, OH 45177

---

## Wittenberg University

| Springfield, Ohio | CB member |
|---|---|
| www.wittenberg.edu | CB code: 1922 |

- Private 4-year liberal arts college affiliated with Evangelical Lutheran Church in America
- Residential campus in small city
- 1,897 degree-seeking undergraduates: 1% part-time, 54% women
- 5 degree-seeking graduate students
- 73% of applicants admitted
- Application essay required
- 61% graduate within 6 years

**General.** Founded in 1845. Regionally accredited. **Degrees:** 411 bachelor's awarded; master's offered. **ROTC:** Army, Air Force. **Location:** 25 miles from Dayton, 45 miles from Columbus. **Calendar:** Semester, limited summer session. **Full-time faculty:** 142 total; 92% have terminal degrees, 7% minority, 42% women. **Part-time faculty:** 53 total; 26% have terminal degrees, 4% minority, 58% women. **Class size:** 54% < 20, 44% 20-39, 1% 40-49, less than 1% 50-99, less than 1% >100. **Special facilities:** Observatory, East Asian art collection, Martin Luther library collection, humanities and technology center.

**Freshman class profile.** 2,887 applied, 2,096 admitted, 551 enrolled.

| Mid 50% test scores | | Rank in top quarter: | 50% |
|---|---|---|---|
| SAT critical reading: | 490-610 | Rank in top tenth: | 29% |
| SAT math: | 500-560 | Return as sophomores: | 80% |
| ACT composite: | 22-27 | Out-of-state: | 30% |
| GPA 3.50 or higher: | 45% | Live on campus: | 94% |
| GPA 3.0-3.49: | 31% | International: | 1% |
| GPA 2.0-2.99: | 23% | | |

**Basis for selection.** GED not accepted. In order of importance: school achievement record, courses taken, school attended, trend in work, test scores, counselor recommendation, extracurricular activities, and interview. Special consideration for children of alumni, minorities, Lutherans, residents of Clark County, and international students. Math and foreign language placement tests required. Interview recommended for all; portfolio required for art program; audition recommended for dance, music, theater programs. **Homeschooled:** On-campus interview.

**High school preparation.** Required and recommended units include English 4, mathematics 3-4, history 2-3, science 3-5 (laboratory 2) and foreign language 2-3.

**2007-2008 Annual costs.** Tuition/fees: $31,400. Room/board: $7,880. Books/supplies: $800. Personal expenses: $1,000.

**2006-2007 Financial aid.** All financial aid based on need. 493 full-time freshmen applied for aid; 427 were judged to have need; 427 of these received aid. Average need met was 90%. Average scholarship/grant was $20,408; average loan $3,035. 72% of total undergraduate aid awarded as scholarships/grants, 28% as loans/jobs. **Additional information:** Auditions required from applicants for music, theater, and dance scholarships. Portfolio required of applicants for art scholarships.

**Application procedures. Admission:** Closing date 3/15 (postmark date). $40 fee, may be waived for applicants with need. Application may be submitted online. Admission notification on a rolling basis. Must reply by May 1 or within 2 week(s) if notified thereafter. **Financial aid:** Priority date 3/15; no closing date. FAFSA required. Applicants notified on a rolling basis starting 3/1; must reply by 5/1 or within 2 week(s) of notification.

**Academics. Special study options:** Combined bachelor's/graduate degree, cross-registration, double major, dual enrollment of high school students, honors, independent study, internships, liberal arts/career combination, student-designed major, study abroad, teacher certification program, urban semester, Washington semester, weekend college. Semester programs with Duke University (marine biology), School of Visual Arts in New York, Camarillo Hospital in California, National Institutes of Health in Washington, D.C., Washington University (MO) (occupational therapy), Johns Hopkins Nursing Program; 3-2 engineering with Washington University (MO), Case Western Reserve University. **Credit/placement by examination:** AP,

---

CLEP, IB, institutional tests. **Support services:** Learning center, preadmission summer program, reduced course load, study skills assistance, tutoring, writing center.

**Majors. Area/ethnic studies:** American, East Asian, European, Russian/Slavic. **Biology:** General, biochemistry, molecular. **Business:** General, business admin, managerial economics, marketing. **Communications:** General. **Computer sciences:** Computer science. **Conservation:** Environmental studies. **Education:** General, elementary. **English:** English lit. **Foreign languages:** French, German, Spanish. **History:** General. **Interdisciplinary:** Biological/physical sciences, biopsychology, global studies, math/computer science. **Liberal arts:** Arts/sciences. **Math:** General. **Philosophy/religion:** Philosophy, religion. **Physical sciences:** General, chemistry, geology, physics. **Psychology:** General. **Social sciences:** General, economics, geography, political science, sociology, urban studies. **Visual/performing arts:** General, art.

**Most popular majors.** Biology 14%, business/marketing 12%, communications/journalism 7%, education 11%, English 7%, psychology 7%, social sciences 12%, visual/performing arts 6%.

**Computing on campus.** 900 workstations in dormitories, library, computer center, student center, student center. Dormitories wired for high-speed internet access and linked to campus network. Commuter students can connect to campus network. Online course registration, online library, helpline, student web hosting, wireless network available.

**Student life. Freshman orientation:** Mandatory. Preregistration for classes offered. Pre-orientation days offered 3 times during the summer. Full orientation held 3 days before the beginning of fall classes. **Housing:** Guaranteed on-campus for all undergraduates. Coed dorms, single-sex dorms, apartments, fraternity/sorority housing, substance-free housing available. $400 deposit, deadline 7/1. Substance-free residence hall, honors residence hall, special theme halls available. **Activities:** Bands, choral groups, dance, drama, international student organizations, literary magazine, music ensembles, musical theater, opera, radio station, student government, student newspaper, symphony orchestra, Newman Club, Concerned Black Students, Community Volunteer Service, Weaver Chapel Association, Project Woman, East Asian Studies Club, Hillel, Amnesty International, Habitat for Humanity.

**Athletics.** NCAA. **Intercollegiate:** Baseball M, basketball, cheerleading, cross-country, diving, field hockey W, football (tackle) M, golf, lacrosse, soccer, softball W, swimming, tennis, track and field, volleyball W. **Intramural:** Badminton, basketball, bowling, cricket M, diving, fencing, football (non-tackle), golf, gymnastics, handball M, ice hockey M, judo, racquetball, rugby, sailing, skiing, skin diving, soccer, softball, squash, swimming, table tennis, tennis, track and field, volleyball, water polo M, weight lifting. **Team name:** Tigers.

**Student services.** Adult student services, alcohol/substance abuse counseling, campus ministries, career counseling, student employment services, financial aid counseling, health services, minority student services, personal counseling, placement for graduates, veterans' counselor, women's services.

**Contact.** E-mail: admission@wittenberg.edu
Phone: (937) 327-6314 Toll-free number: (800) 677-7558 ext. 6314
Fax: (937) 327-6379
Michael Pochard, Assistant Director of Admission, Wittenberg University, Ward Street and North Wittenberg, Springfield, OH 45501-0720

---

## Wright State University

| Dayton, Ohio | CB member |
|---|---|
| www.wright.edu | CB code: 1179 |

- Public 4-year university
- Commuter campus in small city
- 11,912 degree-seeking undergraduates: 12% part-time, 55% women, 13% African American, 3% Asian American, 2% Hispanic American, 1% international
- 3,505 degree-seeking graduate students
- 43% graduate within 6 years

**General.** Founded in 1964. Regionally accredited. **Degrees:** 2,242 bachelor's, 69 associate awarded; master's, doctoral, first professional offered. **ROTC:** Army, Air Force. **Location:** 10 miles from downtown. **Calendar:** Quarter, extensive summer session. **Full-time faculty:** 652 total; 43% women. **Part-time faculty:** 3 total; 100% women. **Class size:** 55% < 20, 25% 20-39, 5% 40-49, 10% 50-99, 6% >100. **Special facilities:** Biological preserve, disabled-accessible garden of the senses.

## Freshman class profile. 5,866 applied, 4,898 admitted, 2,385 enrolled.

| Mid 50% test scores | | Rank in top tenth: | 14% |
|---|---|---|---|
| SAT critical reading: | 440-550 | Return as sophomores: | 67% |
| SAT math: | 430-570 | Out-of-state: | 3% |
| ACT composite: | 18-24 | Live on campus: | 58% |
| GPA 3.50 or higher: | 29% | International: | 1% |
| GPA 3.0-3.49: | 28% | Fraternities: | 5% |
| GPA 2.0-2.99: | 40% | Sororities: | 3% |
| Rank in top quarter: | 35% | | |

**Basis for selection.** Open admission, but selective for some programs. Liberal admission policy. College-preparatory curriculum, 2.0 minimum GPA required. Test scores important for selected programs. Audition required for acting, dance, directing/stage management, music programs; portfolio required for art, art education programs.

**High school preparation.** 15 units required. Required units include English 4, mathematics 3, social studies 3, science 3 (laboratory 3) and foreign language 2. Mathematics requirement includes 2 algebra. Art, music or theater recommended. Students not meeting course recommendations must make up deficiency prior to admission to program.

**2007-2008 Annual costs.** Tuition/fees: $7,278; $14,004 out-of-state. Room/board: $7,180.

**Financial aid.** **Non-need-based:** Scholarships awarded for academics, alumni affiliation, art, athletics, job skills, leadership, minority status, music/drama, ROTC. **Additional information:** Academic scholarship applications must be submitted by February 1.

**Application procedures.** **Admission:** No deadline. $30 fee. Application may be submitted online. Admission notification on a rolling basis beginning on or about 10/1. Application by January recommended for students desiring on-campus housing. **Financial aid:** Priority date 3/1; no closing date. FAFSA required. Applicants notified on a rolling basis starting 2/15; must reply within 2 week(s) of notification.

**Academics.** **Special study options:** Cooperative education, cross-registration, distance learning, double major, ESL, honors, independent study, internships, student-designed major, study abroad, teacher certification program. **Credit/placement by examination:** AP, CLEP, institutional tests. **Support services:** Learning center, pre-admission summer program, reduced course load, remedial instruction, tutoring, writing center.

**Majors.** **Area/ethnic studies:** African-American, women's. **Biology:** General, anatomy, biochemistry, pharmacology/toxicology. **Business:** Accounting, business admin, human resources, management information systems, management science, managerial economics, marketing, statistics. **Communications:** General, media studies, organizational. **Computer sciences:** General, computer science, information systems. **Education:** Art, business, early childhood, elementary, English, foreign languages, learning disabled, mathematics, mentally handicapped, multiple handicapped, music, physical, science, social studies. **Engineering:** General, biomedical, computer, electrical, materials, mechanical, physics, science, systems. **Engineering technology:** Biomedical, environmental. **English:** English lit. **Foreign languages:** General, classics, French, German, Latin, linguistics, modern Greek, Spanish. **Health:** Adult health nursing, clinical lab science, environmental health, nursing (RN), predental, premedicine, prepharmacy, preveterinary, vocational rehab counseling. **History:** General. **Interdisciplinary:** Systems science. **Legal studies:** Prelaw. **Liberal arts:** Arts/sciences. **Math:** General, applied, statistics. **Military:** General. **Philosophy/religion:** Philosophy, religion. **Physical sciences:** Chemistry, geology, physics. **Protective services:** Police science. **Psychology:** General. **Public administration:** General, social work. **Social sciences:** Anthropology, criminology, economics, geography, international relations, political science, sociology, urban studies. **Visual/performing arts:** Art, art history/conservation, arts management, dance, dramatic, drawing, film/cinema, music history, music performance, music theory/composition, photography, theater design.

**Most popular majors.** Business/marketing 18%, education 22%, engineering/engineering technologies 8%, health sciences 11%, psychology 6%, social sciences 9%.

**Computing on campus.** 600 workstations in dormitories, library, computer center, student center. Dormitories wired for high-speed internet access. Commuter students can connect to campus network. Online course registration, online library, helpline, student web hosting, wireless network available.

**Student life.** **Freshman orientation:** Available. Preregistration for classes offered. **Housing:** Coed dorms, special housing for disabled, apartments available. Honors dorm available. **Activities:** Bands, choral groups, dance, drama, literary magazine, music ensembles, musical theater, opera, radio station, student government, student newspaper, symphony orchestra, TV station, Black Student Union, Baptist Student Union, Student Association

for Escorts (SAFE), College Students for Special Wish, Fellowship of Christian Students, Circle-K, Model United Nations, Campus Crusade for Christ, Ohio College Democrats, Jewish Student Union.

**Athletics.** NCAA. **Intercollegiate:** Baseball M, basketball, cheerleading, cross-country, diving, golf M, soccer, softball W, swimming, tennis, track and field W, volleyball W. **Intramural:** Archery, baseball M, basketball, cricket M, cross-country, football (tackle), golf, handball, lacrosse M, soccer, softball, squash, tennis, volleyball W. **Team name:** Raiders.

**Student services.** Adult student services, campus ministries, career counseling, student employment services, financial aid counseling, health services, legal services, minority student services, personal counseling, placement for graduates, veterans' counselor, women's services. **Physically disabled:** Services for visually, speech, hearing impaired.

**Contact.** E-mail: admissions@wright.edu
Phone: (937) 775-5700 Toll-free number: (800) 247-1770
Fax: (937) 775-5795
Cathy Davis, Director of Admissions, Wright State University, 3640 Colonel Glenn Highway, Dayton, OH 45435

---

## Xavier University
**Cincinnati, Ohio**
www.xavier.edu

**CB member**
**CB code: 1965**

- Private 4-year university affiliated with Roman Catholic Church
- Residential campus in large city
- 3,814 degree-seeking undergraduates: 9% part-time, 56% women, 11% African American, 3% Asian American, 3% Hispanic American, 1% international
- 2,434 degree-seeking graduate students
- 73% of applicants admitted
- SAT or ACT (ACT writing optional), application essay required
- 76% graduate within 6 years; 21% enter graduate study

**General.** Founded in 1831. Regionally accredited. **Degrees:** 810 bachelor's, 25 associate awarded; master's, doctoral offered. **ROTC:** Army, Air Force. **Location:** 5 miles from downtown. **Calendar:** Semester, limited summer session. **Full-time faculty:** 309 total; 78% have terminal degrees, 16% minority, 47% women. **Part-time faculty:** 314 total; 21% have terminal degrees, 9% minority, 54% women. **Class size:** 51% < 20, 46% 20-39, 2% 40-49, less than 1% 50-99, less than 1% >100.

## Freshman class profile. 5,649 applied, 4,147 admitted, 858 enrolled.

| Mid 50% test scores | | Rank in top quarter: | 61% |
|---|---|---|---|
| SAT critical reading: | 520-640 | Rank in top tenth: | 29% |
| SAT math: | 530-640 | End year in good standing: | 94% |
| SAT writing: | 510-610 | Return as sophomores: | 88% |
| ACT composite: | 23-29 | Out-of-state: | 47% |
| GPA 3.50 or higher: | 59% | Live on campus: | 91% |
| GPA 3.0-3.49: | 27% | International: | 1% |
| GPA 2.0-2.99: | 14% | | |

**Basis for selection.** Previous academic performance, standardized test scores, rank in class, essay, and recommendations are all considered. Tests are required of all students. Interview recommended for all. **Homeschooled:** Statement describing homeschool structure and mission, transcript of courses and grades, interview required.

**High school preparation.** 21 units recommended. Recommended units include English 4, mathematics 3, social studies 3, science 3, foreign language 2 and academic electives 5. 1 health/physical education recommended.

**2008-2009 Annual costs.** Tuition/fees: $26,860. Room/board: $9,270. Books/supplies: $900. Personal expenses: $600.

**2007-2008 Financial aid.** **Need-based:** 675 full-time freshmen applied for aid; 500 were judged to have need; 499 of these received aid. Average need met was 78%. Average scholarship/grant was $10,815; average loan $4,616. 62% of total undergraduate aid awarded as scholarships/grants, 38% as loans/jobs. **Non-need-based:** Awarded to 1,521 full-time undergraduates, including 385 freshmen. Scholarships awarded for academics, alumni affiliation, art, athletics, job skills, music/drama, ROTC.

**Application procedures.** **Admission:** Closing date 2/1 (postmark date). $35 fee, may be waived for applicants with need. Application may be submitted online. Admission notification 1/15 and 3/15. Must reply by May 1 or within 2 week(s) if notified thereafter. **Financial aid:** Priority date 2/15; no closing date. FAFSA required. Applicants notified on a rolling basis starting 2/15; must reply by 5/1.

**Academics.** Strong emphasis on ethics and values in core curriculum. **Special study options:** Combined bachelor's/graduate degree, cooperative education, cross-registration, double major, dual enrollment of high school students, ESL, honors, independent study, internships, study abroad, teacher certification program, urban semester, Washington semester, weekend college. Cooperative science-engineering program (physics and chemistry) with University of Cincinnati, forestry program and environmental management programs with Duke University, Service Learning Semester. **Credit/placement by examination:** AP, CLEP, IB, institutional tests. 30 credit hours maximum toward associate degree, 60 toward bachelor's. **Support services:** Learning center, pre-admission summer program, reduced course load, remedial instruction, study skills assistance, tutoring, writing center.

**Majors. Biology:** General. **Business:** General, accounting, business admin, entrepreneurial studies, finance, human resources, international, management information systems, managerial economics, marketing. **Communications:** Advertising, organizational, public relations, radio/tv. **Computer sciences:** Computer science. **Conservation:** Management/policy. **Education:** General, biology, chemistry, early childhood, middle, Montessori teacher, music, physics, secondary, special. **English:** English lit. **Foreign languages:** Classics, French, German, Spanish. **Health:** Athletic training, clinical lab science, nursing (RN). **History:** General. **Interdisciplinary:** Natural sciences. **Liberal arts:** Arts/sciences. **Math:** General. **Parks/recreation:** Sports admin. **Philosophy/religion:** Philosophy. **Physical sciences:** Chemistry, physics. **Protective services:** Criminal justice. **Psychology:** General. **Public administration:** Social work. **Social sciences:** Economics, international relations, political science, sociology. **Theology:** Theology. **Visual/performing arts:** Studio arts.

**Most popular majors.** Business/marketing 24%, communications/journalism 7%, education 7%, liberal arts 14%, social sciences 7%.

**Computing on campus.** 250 workstations in dormitories, library, student center. Dormitories wired for high-speed internet access and linked to campus network. Commuter students can connect to campus network. Online course registration, online library, helpline, student web hosting, wireless network available.

**Student life. Freshman orientation:** Mandatory, $175 fee. Preregistration for classes offered. Held the Friday before the start of classes. **Policies:** Student handbook, responsible computer use, university alcohol policy, harassment code accountability procedures. **Housing:** Guaranteed on-campus for freshmen. Coed dorms, apartments, substance-free housing available. $200 fully refundable deposit, deadline 5/1. Special interest/theme housing available. **Activities:** Bands, campus ministries, choral groups, dance, drama, film society, international student organizations, literary magazine, music ensembles, musical theater, opera, radio station, student government, student newspaper, symphony orchestra, TV station, Black student association, center for peace and justice, Amnesty International, College Republicans, College Democrats, Earth Bread, Earthcare, Voices of Solidarity, Student Organization of Latinos.

**Athletics.** NCAA. **Intercollegiate:** Baseball M, basketball, cheerleading, cross-country, golf, soccer, swimming, tennis, track and field, volleyball W. **Intramural:** Basketball, bowling, football (non-tackle), golf, handball, racquetball, soccer, softball, tennis, volleyball. **Team name:** Musketeers.

**Student services.** Adult student services, alcohol/substance abuse counseling, campus ministries, career counseling, services for economically disadvantaged, student employment services, financial aid counseling, health services, minority student services, personal counseling, placement for graduates, veterans' counselor. **Physically disabled:** Services for visually, speech, hearing impaired. **Learning disabled:** Comprehensive services available.

**Contact.** E-mail: xuadmit@xavier.edu
Phone: (513) 745-3301 Toll-free number: (877) 982-3648
Fax: (513) 745-4319
Maureen Mathis, Co-Director for Admission, Xavier University, 3800 Victory Parkway, Cincinnati, OH 45207-5311

## Youngstown State University
**Youngstown, Ohio**
**www.ysu.edu**                      **CB code: 1975**

- Public 4-year university
- Commuter campus in small city
- 11,912 degree-seeking undergraduates: 19% part-time, 54% women, 14% African American, 1% Asian American, 2% Hispanic American, 1% international
- 1,042 degree-seeking graduate students
- 35% graduate within 6 years

**General.** Founded in 1908. Regionally accredited. **Degrees:** 1,449 bachelor's, 192 associate awarded; master's, doctoral offered. **ROTC:** Army,

Air Force. **Location:** 60 miles from Cleveland, 60 miles from Pittsburgh. **Calendar:** Semester, limited summer session. **Full-time faculty:** 429 total; 84% have terminal degrees, 18% minority, 40% women. **Part-time faculty:** 575 total; 6% minority, 54% women. **Class size:** 34% < 20, 53% 20-39, 7% 40-49, 5% 50-99, 2% >100. **Special facilities:** Planetarium, historic preservation center.

**Freshman class profile.** 4,582 applied, 3,731 admitted, 2,442 enrolled.

| Mid 50% test scores | | Rank in top tenth: | 10% |
|---|---|---|---|
| SAT critical reading: | 400-550 | End year in good standing: | 82% |
| SAT math: | 410-550 | Return as sophomores: | 73% |
| ACT composite: | 17-23 | Out-of-state: | 14% |
| GPA 3.50 or higher: | 19% | Live on campus: | 19% |
| GPA 3.0-3.49: | 26% | Fraternities: | 2% |
| GPA 2.0-2.99: | 43% | Sororities: | 3% |
| Rank in top quarter: | 23% | | |

**Basis for selection.** Open admission, but selective for some programs and for out-of-state students. Out-of-state applicants must be in top two-thirds of class, or have ACT composite score of 17 or combined SAT of 820. Open admission policy for Ohio residents and Mercer and Lawrence County, Pennsylvania residents. Selective admission to nursing, engineering and some other programs. Interview required for BS/MD program; audition required for music, BFA theater programs. **Homeschooled:** Students conditionally admitted if high school GPA below 2.00 and composite ACT score (or SAT equivalent) 17 or below. Official transcript showing documentation of grades 9-12 coursework completed and date of completion required. Copy of academic assessment (i.e., Iowa Basic Skills Test, California Achievement Test, etc.) reports submitted to appropriate superintendent of school pursuant to Section 3301-34-04 of Ohio Administrative Code also required. Curriculum outline, detailing course content, textbooks used, and any other relevant information regarding coursework must be submitted. Require proof of home school as required by legislation in each individual state.

**High school preparation.** 16 units recommended. Recommended units include English 4, mathematics 3, social studies 3, science 2 (laboratory 1) and foreign language 2. 1 fine and performing arts recommended. Recommended coursework should include English composition; algebra I and II, geometry; laboratory science; and US history and government.

**2007-2008 Annual costs.** Tuition/fees: $6,721; $12,394 out-of-state. Residents of any out-of-state area within 100 miles of campus are charged $9,414 yearly tuition. Per credit hour charge is $392. Room/board: $6,740. Books/supplies: $1,057. Personal expenses: $500.

**2006-2007 Financial aid.** **Need-based:** 33% of total undergraduate aid awarded as scholarships/grants, 67% as loans/jobs. **Non-need-based:** Scholarships awarded for academics, alumni affiliation, athletics, ROTC, state residency.

**Application procedures. Admission:** Priority date 2/15; deadline 8/15. $30 fee, may be waived for applicants with need. Application may be submitted online. Admission notification on a rolling basis. Students who apply by February 15 eligible for early registration and orientation. **Financial aid:** Priority date 2/15; no closing date. FAFSA, institutional form required. Applicants notified on a rolling basis starting 5/30; must reply within 2 week(s) of notification.

**Academics. Special study options:** Accelerated study, combined bachelor's/graduate degree, cooperative education, cross-registration, distance learning, double major, ESL, exchange student, honors, internships, student-designed major, study abroad, teacher certification program, urban semester, Washington semester, weekend college. Off-campus study with Lorain County Community College. **Credit/placement by examination:** AP, CLEP, IB, institutional tests. In select CLEP and AP tests, higher grade may make student eligible for more credits. **Support services:** Learning center, pre-admission summer program, reduced course load, remedial instruction, study skills assistance, tutoring, writing center.

**Majors. Area/ethnic studies:** African-American, American. **Biology:** General. **Business:** General, accounting, apparel, banking/financial services, business admin, fashion, finance, financial planning, hospitality admin, hospitality/recreation, human resources, management information systems, managerial economics, marketing, merchandising, office management, operations, public finance, purchasing, retailing, sales/distribution, selling, tourism promotion, tourism/travel. **Communications:** General, advertising, journalism, public relations, radio/tv. **Computer sciences:** General, computer science, information systems, information technology, programming. **Conservation:** Environmental science. **Education:** General, art, autistic, biology, business, chemistry, computer, drama/dance, early childhood, elementary, emotionally handicapped, English, family/consumer sciences, foreign languages, French, health, health occupations, history, kindergarten/preschool, learning disabled, mathematics, mentally handicapped, middle, multi-level teacher, multiple handicapped, music, physical, physics, science, secondary, social science, social studies, Spanish, special, speech. **Engineering:** General, chemical, civil, computer, electrical, industrial, materials, mechanical, structural. **Engineering technology:** General, civil, electrical, mechanical. **English:** English lit, speech/rhetoric, technical writing. **Family/consumer sciences:** General, clothing/textiles, family studies, family/community services, food/nutrition, work/family studies. **Foreign languages:** General, French, German, Italian, Spanish. **Health:** Athletic training, clinical lab science, community health, community health services, dietetics, facilities admin, nursing (RN), predental, premedicine, prepharmacy, preveterinary, public health ed, respiratory therapy technology. **History:** General. **Legal studies:** Prelaw. **Math:** General. **Parks/recreation:** Exercise sciences, health/fitness, sports admin. **Philosophy/religion:** Philosophy, religion. **Physical sciences:** General, astronomy, chemistry, geology, physics, planetary. **Protective services:** Corrections, criminal justice, forensics, law enforcement admin, security services. **Psychology:** General. **Public administration:** General, social work. **Social sciences:** General, anthropology, econometrics, economics, geography, international economics, political science, sociology. **Visual/performing arts:** General, acting, art, art history/conservation, commercial/advertising art, dramatic, jazz, music history, music performance, music theory/composition, painting, photography, piano/organ, printmaking, stringed instruments, studio arts, theater design, voice/opera.

**Most popular majors.** Business/marketing 16%, education 22%, engineering/engineering technologies 6%, health sciences 10%, security/protective services 7%.

**Computing on campus.** 1,619 workstations in dormitories, library, student center. Dormitories wired for high-speed internet access and linked to campus network. Commuter students can connect to campus network. Online course registration, online library, helpline, repair service, student web hosting, wireless network available.

**Student life. Freshman orientation:** Available, $50 fee. Orientation held in June, July, and August. **Housing:** Guaranteed on-campus for all undergraduates. Coed dorms, single-sex dorms, apartments, fraternity/sorority housing, substance-free housing available. $200 deposit. University scholars program honors facility available. **Activities:** Bands, choral groups, dance, drama, literary magazine, music ensembles, musical theater, opera, radio station, student government, student newspaper, symphony orchestra, College Republicans, Student Democrats, Pan-African student union, National Panhellenic Council, Hispanic-American organization, student athlete advisory council, interfraternity council, Golden Key, Omicron Delta Kappa, gospel choir, Panhellenic Council.

**Athletics.** NCAA. **Intercollegiate:** Baseball M, basketball, cross-country, football (tackle) M, golf, soccer W, softball W, swimming W, tennis, track and field, volleyball W. **Intramural:** Badminton, basketball, bowling, football (non-tackle), golf, handball, ice hockey, lacrosse, racquetball, soccer, softball, swimming, table tennis, tennis, volleyball, water polo. **Team name:** Penguins.

**Student services.** Adult student services, alcohol/substance abuse counseling, campus ministries, career counseling, student employment services, financial aid counseling, health services, minority student services, on-campus daycare, personal counseling, placement for graduates, veterans' counselor, women's services. **Physically disabled:** Services for visually, speech, hearing impaired.

**Contact.**  E-mail: enroll@ysu.edu
Phone: (330) 941-2000 Toll-free number: (877) 468-6978
Fax: (330) 941-3674
Sue Davis, Director of Undergraduate Admissions, Youngstown State University, One University Plaza, Youngstown, OH 44555-0001

# Oklahoma

## Bacone College
### Muskogee, Oklahoma
### www.bacone.edu
### CB code: 6030

▶ Private 4-year liberal arts college affiliated with American Baptist Churches in the USA
▶ Commuter campus in large town
▶ 880 degree-seeking undergraduates: 18% part-time, 51% women
▶ 64% of applicants admitted
▶ SAT or ACT required

**General.** Founded in 1880. Regionally accredited. Unique American Indian heritage and commitment to serving American Indians. Guided by Christian principles. **Degrees:** 84 bachelor's, 54 associate awarded. **Location:** 60 miles from Tulsa. **Calendar:** Semester, limited summer session. **Full-time faculty:** 26 total; 54% have terminal degrees, 35% minority, 73% women. **Part-time faculty:** 42 total; 17% have terminal degrees, 36% minority, 62% women. **Class size:** 70% < 20, 25% 20-39, 5% 40-49. **Special facilities:** Native American museum, Indian collection library.

**Freshman class profile.** 465 applied, 297 admitted, 278 enrolled.

| Mid 50% test scores | | | |
|---|---|---|---|
| SAT critical reading: | 340-430 | GPA 2.0-2.99: | 54% |
| SAT math: | 350-460 | Rank in top quarter: | 18% |
| ACT composite: | 14-20 | Rank in top tenth: | 6% |
| GPA 3.50 or higher: | 18% | Out-of-state: | 15% |
| GPA 3.0-3.49: | 24% | Live on campus: | 36% |

**Basis for selection.** 2.0 High School GPA and 18 ACT required. Additional standards for admission to nursing or radiography programs. ACT results used as basis for counseling. Interview recommended for nursing, radiologic technology programs. **Homeschooled:** Official transcript from an accredited homeschool organization or GED required; must have ACT score of 18.

**High school preparation.** Recommended units include English 4, mathematics 3, history 2, science 2 (laboratory 2).

**2007-2008 Annual costs.** Tuition/fees: $10,056. Room/board: $6,300. Books/supplies: $1,000. Personal expenses: $500.

**Financial aid.** All financial aid based on need.

**Application procedures. Admission:** No deadline. $25 fee, may be waived for applicants with need. Application may be submitted online. Admission notification on a rolling basis. **Financial aid:** Priority date 3/31; no closing date. FAFSA required. Applicants notified on a rolling basis starting 4/1; must reply within 2 week(s) of notification.

**Academics. Special study options:** Accelerated study, cross-registration, double major, dual enrollment of high school students, liberal arts/career combination. **Credit/placement by examination:** AP, CLEP, SAT, ACT, institutional tests. 15 credit hours maximum toward associate degree. **Support services:** Learning center, remedial instruction, tutoring.

**Majors. Business:** Business admin. **Education:** Early childhood, elementary, health, physical. **Health:** Nursing (RN). **Legal studies:** Prelaw.

**Most popular majors.** Business/marketing 12%, education 61%, parks/recreation 13%, social sciences 11%.

**Computing on campus.** 84 workstations in library, computer center. Commuter students can connect to campus network.

**Student life. Freshman orientation:** Mandatory. Preregistration for classes offered. **Housing:** Single-sex dorms available. $100 deposit. **Activities:** Choral groups, drama, student government, student newspaper, Christian Fellowship, Indian club, Black Student Union, cultural exchange student organization.

**Athletics.** NAIA. **Intercollegiate:** Baseball M, basketball, rodeo, soccer, softball W, wrestling. **Intramural:** Basketball, cross-country, football (tackle) M, golf, soccer, softball, table tennis, tennis, track and field, volleyball, wrestling. **Team name:** Warriors.

**Student services.** Career counseling, student employment services, health services, personal counseling, veterans' counselor. **Physically disabled:** Services for visually, speech, hearing impaired.

**Contact.** E-mail: admissionsoffice@bacone.edu
Phone: (918) 683-4581 ext. 7342 Toll-free
number: (888) 682-5514 ext. 7342 Fax: (918) 781-7416
Rev. Neil King, Director of Admissions, Bacone College, 2299 Old Bacone Road, Muskogee, OK 74403

## Cameron University
### Lawton, Oklahoma
### www.cameron.edu
### CB member
### CB code: 6080

▶ Public 4-year university and liberal arts college
▶ Commuter campus in small city
▶ 4,686 degree-seeking undergraduates: 31% part-time, 60% women
▶ 368 degree-seeking graduate students

**General.** Founded in 1909. Regionally accredited. **Degrees:** 552 bachelor's, 198 associate awarded; master's offered. **ROTC:** Army. **Location:** 100 miles from Oklahoma City. **Calendar:** Semester, limited summer session. **Full-time faculty:** 176 total; 70% have terminal degrees, 15% minority, 40% women. **Part-time faculty:** 97 total; 16% have terminal degrees, 10% minority, 54% women. **Class size:** 49% < 20, 44% 20-39, 5% 40-49, 2% 50-99.

**Freshman class profile.** 1,448 applied, 1,446 admitted, 864 enrolled.

| Mid 50% test scores | | | |
|---|---|---|---|
| ACT composite: | 16-21 | Rank in top tenth: | 9% |
| | | Return as sophomores: | 49% |
| GPA 3.50 or higher: | 30% | Out-of-state: | 3% |
| GPA 3.0-3.49: | 29% | Live on campus: | 7% |
| GPA 2.0-2.99: | 38% | Fraternities: | 2% |
| Rank in top quarter: | 26% | Sororities: | 2% |

**Basis for selection.** Open admission, but selective for some programs. 2.7 GPA and rank in top half of class, or ACT composite score of 20 required for bachelor's degree and associate of science or associate of arts programs. Open admissions for associate of applied science degree candidates only. Those who do not meet bachelor's criteria are admitted as associate degree candidates.

**High school preparation.** 15 units required. Required units include English 4, mathematics 3, history 3, science 2 (laboratory 2) and academic electives 3. One unit in government, geography, economics or non-Western culture.

**2007-2008 Annual costs.** Tuition/fees: $3,756; $9,105 out-of-state. Room/board: $3,492. Books/supplies: $1,050.

**2006-2007 Financial aid. Need-based:** 498 full-time freshmen applied for aid; 443 were judged to have need; 385 of these received aid. Average need met was 85%. Average scholarship/grant was $3,500; average loan $1,000. 58% of total undergraduate aid awarded as scholarships/grants, 42% as loans/jobs. **Non-need-based:** Awarded to 1,009 full-time undergraduates, including 453 freshmen. Scholarships awarded for academics, alumni affiliation, art, athletics, leadership, music/drama, ROTC.

**Application procedures. Admission:** Priority date 8/1; no deadline. $15 fee. Application may be submitted online. Admission notification on a rolling basis. **Financial aid:** Priority date 6/15; no closing date. FAFSA required. Applicants notified on a rolling basis starting 4/1; must reply within 2 week(s) of notification.

**Academics. Special study options:** Accelerated study, combined bachelor's/graduate degree, distance learning, double major, dual enrollment of high school students, honors, independent study, internships, liberal arts/career combination, study abroad, teacher certification program. **Credit/placement by examination:** AP, CLEP, IB, institutional tests. **Support services:** Learning center, pre-admission summer program, reduced course load, remedial instruction, study skills assistance, tutoring, writing center.

**Majors. Agriculture:** General, agronomy, animal sciences, horticultural science. **Biology:** General. **Business:** Accounting, business admin. **Communications:** General, broadcast journalism, journalism, public relations. **Computer sciences:** General, computer science, web page design. **Education:** General, art, biology, chemistry, early childhood, elementary, English, history, mathematics, music, physical, science, secondary, social studies. **Engineering technology:** Electrical, mechanical drafting. **English:** English lit. **Family/consumer sciences:** General. **Foreign languages:** General, linguistics. **Health:** Clinical lab technology. **History:** General. **Interdisciplinary:** Biological/physical sciences, natural sciences. **Math:** General. **Parks/**

recreation: Health/fitness. **Physical sciences:** Chemistry, physics. **Protective services:** Criminal justice. **Psychology:** General. **Social sciences:** Political science, sociology. **Visual/performing arts:** Art, dramatic, studio arts.

**Most popular majors.** Business/marketing 20%, education 9%, parks/recreation 8%, psychology 7%, security/protective services 12%.

**Computing on campus.** 450 workstations in dormitories, library, computer center. Dormitories wired for high-speed internet access and linked to campus network. Commuter students can connect to campus network. Online library, helpline, student web hosting, wireless network available.

**Student life. Freshman orientation:** Mandatory. 7 sessions annually, June through August. **Policies:** Student code of conduct; no alcohol on campus. **Housing:** Guaranteed on-campus for all undergraduates. Single-sex dorms, special housing for disabled, apartments, substance-free housing available. $200 fully refundable deposit, deadline 7/1. Quiet areas available. **Activities:** Bands, campus ministries, choral groups, drama, film society, international student organizations, literary magazine, music ensembles, musical theater, opera, radio station, student government, student newspaper, symphony orchestra, TV station, Ebony Society, Students of the Caribbean Alliance, American Indian student association, Latin alliance, Asian/Pacific Islander student association, Chi Alpha, Young Republicans.

**Athletics.** NCAA. **Intercollegiate:** Baseball M, basketball, cross-country M, golf, softball W, tennis, volleyball W. **Intramural:** Badminton, basketball, bowling, football (non-tackle), golf, racquetball, softball, tennis, volleyball. **Team name:** Aggies.

**Student services.** Campus ministries, career counseling, services for economically disadvantaged, student employment services, financial aid counseling, minority student services, veterans' counselor. **Physically disabled:** Services for visually, speech, hearing impaired.

**Contact.** E-mail: zoed@cameron.edu
Phone: (580) 581-2200 Toll-free number: (888) 454-7600
Fax: (580) 581-5514
Zoe DuRant, Director of Admissions, Cameron University, 2800 West Gore Boulevard, Lawton, OK 73505-6377

## DeVry University: Oklahoma City Center
**Oklahoma City, Oklahoma**
**www.devry.edu**

- For-profit 4-year college
- Very large city
- 44 degree-seeking undergraduates: 48% part-time, 27% women, 18% African American, 2% Hispanic American, 2% Native American
- 19 degree-seeking graduate students

**General.** Regionally accredited. **Degrees:** 2 bachelor's awarded; master's offered. **Calendar:** Semester. **Part-time faculty:** 1 total; 100% women.

**Freshman class profile.** 9 enrolled.

| | | | |
|---|---|---|---|
| Return as sophomores: | 33% | Out-of-state: | 22% |

**Basis for selection.** Applicants must have high school diploma or equivalent, or degree from accredited post-secondary institution, demonstrate proficiency in basic college-level skills through SAT or ACT scores or institution-administered placement examinations, and be at least 17 years of age. DeVry-administered admissions test required if SAT or ACT test scores are not submitted.

**2007-2008 Annual costs.** Books/supplies: $1,300. Personal expenses: $5,082.

**Financial aid. Non-need-based:** Scholarships awarded for academics.

**Application procedures. Admission:** No deadline. $50 fee. Admission notification on a rolling basis. **Financial aid:** No deadline. FAFSA required. Applicants notified on a rolling basis.

**Academics. Special study options:** Accelerated study, distance learning. **Credit/placement by examination:** CLEP.

**Contact.** DeVry University: Oklahoma City Center, Lakepointe Towers, 4013 NW Expressway Street, Oklahoma City, OK 73116

## East Central University
**Ada, Oklahoma**
**www.ecok.edu**                                    **CB code: 6186**

- Public 4-year university
- Commuter campus in large town

- 3,657 degree-seeking undergraduates: 19% part-time, 59% women, 4% African American, 1% Asian American, 3% Hispanic American, 21% Native American, 2% international
- 821 degree-seeking graduate students
- 96% of applicants admitted
- SAT or ACT (ACT writing optional) required
- 36% graduate within 6 years

**General.** Founded in 1909. Regionally accredited. **Degrees:** 621 bachelor's awarded; master's offered. **Location:** 86 miles from Oklahoma City. **Calendar:** Semester, extensive summer session. **Full-time faculty:** 161 total; 70% have terminal degrees, 9% minority, 43% women. **Part-time faculty:** 92 total; 18% have terminal degrees, 11% minority, 56% women.

**Freshman class profile.** 745 applied, 717 admitted, 558 enrolled.

| Mid 50% test scores | | End year in good standing: | 72% |
|---|---|---|---|
| ACT composite: | 18-23 | Return as sophomores: | 63% |
| GPA 3.50 or higher: | 42% | Out-of-state: | 2% |
| GPA 3.0-3.49: | 32% | Live on campus: | 40% |
| GPA 2.0-2.99: | 25% | International: | 1% |
| Rank in top quarter: | 42% | Fraternities: | 55% |
| Rank in top tenth: | 17% | Sororities: | 45% |

**Basis for selection.** Rank in top 50 percent of graduating class, 20 ACT score or SAT equivalent, 2.7 high school GPA and required course work.

**High school preparation.** 15 units required. Required and recommended units include English 4, mathematics 3, social studies 2, history 1, science 2 (laboratory 2) and academic electives 3. Additional courses from English, math, science, history, social sciences, foreign language, or computer science.

**2007-2008 Annual costs.** Tuition/fees: $3,841; $9,314 out-of-state. Room/board: $3,860. Books/supplies: $900.

**2007-2008 Financial aid. Need-based:** 46% of total undergraduate aid awarded as scholarships/grants, 54% as loans/jobs. **Non-need-based:** Scholarships awarded for academics, athletics.

**Application procedures. Admission:** No deadline. $20 fee. Application may be submitted online. Admission notification on a rolling basis. **Financial aid:** Closing date 3/1. FAFSA required. Applicants notified on a rolling basis starting 4/15; must reply within 2 week(s) of notification.

**Academics. Special study options:** Distance learning, double major, dual enrollment of high school students, exchange student, honors, independent study, internships, teacher certification program. **Credit/placement by examination:** AP, CLEP, ACT, institutional tests. 94 credit hours maximum toward bachelor's degree. Students do not receive CLEP or AP credit until 12 hours completed at ECU with GPA of 2.0 or higher. **Support services:** Learning center, pre-admission summer program, reduced course load, remedial instruction, study skills assistance, tutoring, writing center.

**Majors. Biology:** General. **Business:** General, accounting, administrative services, business admin, finance, managerial economics, marketing, office management, operations, sales/distribution. **Communications:** General, broadcast journalism, journalism. **Computer sciences:** General. **Education:** Agricultural, business, drama/dance, early childhood, elementary, English, family/consumer sciences, history, mathematics, mentally handicapped, music, physical, physically handicapped, science, social studies, special, speech, technology/industrial arts, trade/industrial. **English:** English lit, speech/rhetoric, technical writing. **Family/consumer sciences:** General, clothing/textiles. **Foreign languages:** Comparative lit. **Health:** Athletic training, environmental health, medical records technology, predental, premedicine, prepharmacy, preveterinary, vocational rehab counseling. **History:** General. **Legal studies:** Paralegal, prelaw. **Math:** General, applied. **Parks/recreation:** General, exercise sciences, health/fitness. **Physical sciences:** Chemistry, physics. **Protective services:** Criminal justice, police science. **Psychology:** General. **Public administration:** Community org/advocacy, human services, social work. **Social sciences:** General, cartography, criminology, political science, sociology. **Visual/performing arts:** Art, dramatic, piano/organ, studio arts, voice/opera.

**Most popular majors.** Business/marketing 11%, education 20%, health sciences 14%, public administration/social services 16%.

**Computing on campus.** 650 workstations in library, computer center. Online library, helpline, repair service, wireless network available.

**Student life. Freshman orientation:** Mandatory. Preregistration for classes offered. **Housing:** Coed dorms, single-sex dorms, special housing for disabled, apartments, fraternity/sorority housing available. **Activities:** Bands, choral groups, dance, drama, film society, literary magazine, music ensembles, musical theater, student government, student newspaper, Association of Black Students, Native American student association, Baptist Student Union, United Campus Ministry, Students with Disabilities, Church of Christ Bible Chair, Life House, Sigma Society, Panhellenic, Silent Friends Club.

**Athletics.** NCAA. **Intercollegiate:** Baseball M, basketball, cross-country, football (tackle) M, golf, soccer W, softball W, tennis, volleyball W. **Intramural:** Basketball, soccer, softball, volleyball. **Team name:** Tigers.

**Student services.** Adult student services, career counseling, student employment services, financial aid counseling, health services, minority student services, on-campus daycare, personal counseling, placement for graduates, veterans' counselor. **Physically disabled:** Services for visually, speech, hearing impaired.

**Contact.** E-mail: parmstro@ecok.edu
Phone: (580) 332-8000 Fax: (580) 559-5432
Pamla Armstrong, Registrar and Director of Admissions, East Central University, PMBJ8, 1100 East 14th Street, Ada, OK 74820

## Family of Faith College
### Shawnee, Oklahoma
### www.familyoffaithcollege.com

- Private 4-year Bible college
- Residential campus in rural community
- 23 degree-seeking undergraduates
- 100% of applicants admitted
- SAT or ACT (ACT writing optional), application essay required

**General.** Regionally accredited; also accredited by ABHE. **Degrees:** 2 bachelor's awarded. **Location:** Six from Shawnee, 30 miles from Oklahoma City. **Calendar:** Semester, limited summer session. **Full-time faculty:** 8 total. **Part-time faculty:** 4 total.

### Freshman class profile.

| Mid 50% test scores | | | |
|---|---|---|---|
| SAT critical reading: | 500-550 | SAT math: | 400-450 |
| | | ACT composite: | 20-24 |

**Basis for selection.** SAT/ACT not required for certificate programs. Academic and personal references required. ACT recommended. **Home-schooled:** Transcript of courses and grades, state high school equivalency certificate, letter of recommendation (nonparent) required.

**2007-2008 Annual costs.** Tuition/fees: $5,110. Room only: $1,600.

**Application procedures. Admission:** Closing date 6/1 (receipt date). $25 fee.

**Academics. Credit/placement by examination:** CLEP.

**Majors. Theology:** Bible, theology.

**Student life. Housing:** $50 fully refundable deposit.

**Contact.** E-mail: ffc@allegiance.tv
Phone: (405) 273-5331
Rhonda Gaines, Vice President of Student Affairs, Family of Faith College, PO Box 1805, Shawnee, OK 74802-1805

## ITT Technical Institute: Tulsa
### Tulsa, Oklahoma

- For-profit 4-year business and technical college
- Large city

**General.** Accredited by ACICS. **Calendar:** Quarter.

**Contact.** 4943 South 78th East Avenue, Tulsa, OK 74145

## Langston University
### Langston, Oklahoma
### www.lunet.edu
**CB member**
**CB code: 6361**

- Public 4-year university and liberal arts college
- Residential campus in rural community

- 2,461 degree-seeking undergraduates: 14% part-time, 60% women, 82% African American, 1% Hispanic American, 2% Native American, 2% international
- 245 degree-seeking graduate students
- SAT or ACT (ACT writing optional), application essay required

**General.** Founded in 1897. Regionally accredited. Branch campuses in Oklahoma City, Tulsa. **Degrees:** 335 bachelor's, 8 associate awarded; master's, doctoral offered. **ROTC:** Army, Air Force. **Location:** 40 miles from Oklahoma City, 90 miles from Tulsa. **Calendar:** Semester, limited summer session. **Full-time faculty:** 155 total. **Part-time faculty:** 7 total. **Special facilities:** International dairy goat research facility.

**Freshman class profile.** 2,756 applied, 1,157 admitted, 1,068 enrolled.

| | | | |
|---|---|---|---|
| **GPA 3.50 or higher:** | 3% | **GPA 2.0-2.99:** | 59% |
| **GPA 3.0-3.49:** | 14% | **International:** | 1% |

**Basis for selection.** Open admission, but selective for some programs. Minimum 2.7 GPA. Composite ACT of 20 or SAT equivalent required. March 1 priority date for SAT or ACT scores. Audition recommended for music program.

**High school preparation.** 15 units required. Required and recommended units include English 4, mathematics 3, social studies 2, history 1, science 2-8 (laboratory 2), foreign language 1-4 and academic electives 4. Remaining units must be additional work in these areas or in computer science, speech, economics, geography, government, psychology, or sociology. Required units must begin with algebra I. Required social sciences units must include 1 US history.

**2007-2008 Annual costs.** Tuition/fees: $3,596; $8,711 out-of-state. Room/board: $5,740. Books/supplies: $800. Personal expenses: $2,037.

**2006-2007 Financial aid.** All financial aid based on need. 559 full-time freshmen applied for aid; 477 were judged to have need; 472 of these received aid. Average need met was 61%. Average scholarship/grant was $854; average loan $2,499. 88% of total undergraduate aid awarded as scholarships/grants, 12% as loans/jobs.

**Application procedures. Admission:** Priority date 3/1; no deadline. $25 fee. Application may be submitted online. Admission notification on a rolling basis. **Financial aid:** Priority date 3/1, closing date 5/1. CSS PROFILE required. Applicants notified on a rolling basis starting 7/15; must reply within 2 week(s) of notification.

**Academics. Special study options:** Cooperative education, distance learning, double major, dual enrollment of high school students, honors, internships, liberal arts/career combination, study abroad, teacher certification program. **Credit/placement by examination:** AP, CLEP, SAT, ACT, institutional tests. 16 credit hours maximum toward associate degree, 30 toward bachelor's. **Support services:** Learning center, reduced course load, remedial instruction, tutoring.

**Majors. Agriculture:** Animal sciences, business, economics, farm/ranch. **Biology:** General, zoology. **Business:** Accounting, administrative services, business admin, human resources. **Communications:** General, broadcast journalism, journalism. **Communications technology:** General. **Computer sciences:** General. **Education:** General, business, elementary, family/consumer sciences, mathematics, music, physical, secondary, social studies, special, technology/industrial arts. **English:** English lit. **Family/consumer sciences:** General, clothing/textiles, family studies, food/nutrition. **Health:** Health care admin, preveterinary. **History:** General. **Legal studies:** Prelaw. **Math:** General. **Physical sciences:** Chemistry. **Protective services:** Corrections, police science. **Psychology:** General. **Social sciences:** General, economics, geography, sociology, urban studies. **Visual/performing arts:** Art, music performance.

**Most popular majors.** Business/marketing 22%, education 11%, health sciences 19%, liberal arts 8%, psychology 10%, security/protective services 7%, social sciences 6%.

**Computing on campus.** 300 workstations in library, computer center. Dormitories wired for high-speed internet access and linked to campus network.

**Student life. Freshman orientation:** Mandatory. Preregistration for classes offered. Begins 7 days prior to fall enrollment; includes social, cultural, and institutional activities along with registration and enrollment processes. **Policies:** All freshman and sophomore students are required to live on campus. Students must have a minimum 2.0 GPA to join student organizations. Students must have a minimum 2.5 GPA to be in SGA, campus royalty, or fraternities and sororities. **Housing:** Guaranteed on-campus for all undergraduates. Apartments available. $200 fully refundable deposit. **Activities:** Bands, choral groups, dance, drama, music ensembles, radio station, student government, student newspaper, TV station, Pan hellenic fraternities and sororities ,NAACP, NCNW.

**Athletics.** NAIA. **Intercollegiate:** Basketball, cheerleading, cross-country, football (tackle) M, softball W, track and field, volleyball W. **Intramural:** Basketball, football (non-tackle), track and field, volleyball. **Team name:** Lions.

**Student services.** Alcohol/substance abuse counseling, campus ministries, career counseling, services for economically disadvantaged, student employment services, financial aid counseling, health services, on-campus daycare, personal counseling, placement for graduates, veterans' counselor. **Physically disabled:** Services for visually, speech, hearing impaired.

**Contact.** E-mail: gtrobertson@lunet.edu
Phone: (405) 466-3428 Fax: (405) 466-3391
Gayle Robertson, Director of Enrollment Management, Langston University, Box 728, Langston, OK 73050

---

## Mid-America Christian University
### Oklahoma City, Oklahoma
### www.macu.edu
**CB code: 0918**

- Private 4-year university and liberal arts college affiliated with Church of God
- Residential campus in very large city
- 744 degree-seeking undergraduates: 12% African American, 1% Asian American, 4% Hispanic American, 7% Native American, 1% international
- 120 degree-seeking graduate students
- SAT or ACT (ACT writing optional) required
- 36% graduate within 6 years

**General.** Founded in 1953. Regionally accredited. **Degrees:** 166 bachelor's, 2 associate awarded; master's offered. **Location:** 10 miles from downtown. **Calendar:** Semester, limited summer session. **Full-time faculty:** 20 total; 35% have terminal degrees, 10% minority. **Part-time faculty:** 30 total; 20% minority. **Class size:** 67% < 20, 26% 20-39, 2% 40-49, 4% 50-99.

**Freshman class profile.**

| | | | |
|---|---|---|---|
| Out-of-state: | 64% | International: | 1% |
| Live on campus: | 82% | | |

**Basis for selection.** Applicants admitted who feel calling to full-time Christian vocations or seek God's will for their lives in a spiritual environment. 2 references required. Interview, audition recommended. **Homeschooled:** Applicants without a GED must have a minimum ACT score of 15 in English and 14 in math.

**High school preparation.** 16 units recommended. Recommended units include English 4, mathematics 2, social studies 2, science 2 and foreign language 2.

**2008-2009 Annual costs.** Tuition/fees: $12,800. Room/board: $5,176. Books/supplies: $800. Personal expenses: $660.

**Financial aid. Non-need-based:** Scholarships awarded for academics, leadership, minority status, music/drama.

**Application procedures. Admission:** Priority date 8/15; no deadline. $25 fee, may be waived for applicants with need. Application may be submitted online. Admission notification on a rolling basis beginning on or about 2/1. We allow students to provisionally enroll without graduation posted in senior year. **Financial aid:** Priority date 5/1; no closing date. FAFSA required. Applicants notified on a rolling basis starting 5/1.

**Academics.** Degree-completion program available for enrollees 25 years of age and above with approximately 2 years of college experience. Link program available for student lacking general education courses. **Special study options:** Combined bachelor's/graduate degree, distance learning, double major, dual enrollment of high school students, external degree, independent study, internships, liberal arts/career combination, teacher certification program, weekend college. **Credit/placement by examination:** AP, CLEP, SAT, ACT, institutional tests. 30 credit hours maximum toward associate degree, 30 toward bachelor's. Must be completed before accruing 30 credit hours. **Support services:** Remedial instruction, tutoring, writing center.

**Majors. Business:** Business admin, management information systems, management science, marketing. **Education:** Elementary, English, mathematics, music, secondary, social science, social studies. **English:** English lit. **Interdisciplinary:** Behavioral sciences. **Math:** General. **Philosophy/religion:** Religion. **Protective services:** Law enforcement admin. **Psychology:** Social. **Social sciences:** General. **Theology:** Bible, pastoral counseling, sacred music, theology. **Visual/performing arts:** Music performance.

**Most popular majors.** Computer/information sciences 7%, history 27%, philosophy/religious studies 15%, psychology 16%, theological studies 28%.

**Computing on campus.** 40 workstations in library, computer center, student center. Dormitories wired for high-speed internet access and linked to campus network. Online library, wireless network available.

**Student life. Freshman orientation:** Mandatory. Preregistration for classes offered. Held 1 day prior to start of classes. **Policies:** No smoking or drinking allowed on campus. Religious observance required. **Housing:** Guaranteed on-campus for freshmen. Single-sex dorms, substance-free housing available. $50 deposit. **Activities:** Concert band, choral groups, drama, music ensembles, musical theater, student government, Missions Club, Student Ministerial Fellowship, Ministry Refresher Institute.

**Athletics.** NCCAA. **Intercollegiate:** Baseball M, basketball, golf, soccer M, softball W, volleyball W. **Intramural:** Basketball, bowling, softball W, table tennis, volleyball. **Team name:** Evangels.

**Student services.** Campus ministries, career counseling, student employment services, financial aid counseling, health services, personal counseling, placement for graduates, veterans' counselor. **Physically disabled:** Services for speech impaired.

**Contact.** E-mail: info@macu.edu
Phone: (405) 692-3188 Toll-free number: (888) 436-3035
Fax: (405) 692-3165
Haley Hope, Director of Admissions, Mid-America Christian University, 3500 SW 119th Street, Oklahoma City, OK 73170

---

## Northeastern State University
### Tahlequah, Oklahoma
### www.nsuok.edu
**CB code: 6485**

- Public 4-year university
- Commuter campus in large town
- 8,181 degree-seeking undergraduates: 25% part-time, 62% women, 5% African American, 1% Asian American, 2% Hispanic American, 30% Native American, 3% international
- 1,070 degree-seeking graduate students
- 71% of applicants admitted
- ACT (writing optional) required
- 32% graduate within 6 years

**General.** Founded in 1851. Regionally accredited. **Degrees:** 1,473 bachelor's awarded; master's, first professional offered. **ROTC:** Army. **Location:** 60 miles from Tulsa, 30 miles from Muskogee. **Calendar:** Semester, extensive summer session. **Full-time faculty:** 304 total; 74% have terminal degrees, 14% minority, 45% women. **Part-time faculty:** 166 total; 31% have terminal degrees, 22% minority, 55% women. **Class size:** 42% < 20, 48% 20-39, 5% 40-49, 5% 50-99. **Special facilities:** Center for the Study of Literacy, Center for Tribal Studies, Oklahoma Institute for Learning Styles.

**Freshman class profile.** 2,273 applied, 1,609 admitted, 1,017 enrolled.

| Mid 50% test scores | | End year in good standing: | 71% |
|---|---|---|---|
| ACT composite: | 18-23 | Return as sophomores: | 63% |
| GPA 3.50 or higher: | 37% | Out-of-state: | 5% |
| GPA 3.0-3.49: | 39% | Live on campus: | 64% |
| GPA 2.0-2.99: | 23% | International: | 3% |
| Rank in top quarter: | 42% | Fraternities: | 13% |
| Rank in top tenth: | 17% | Sororities: | 10% |

**Basis for selection.** Admissions based on secondary school record, class rank, and standardized test scores. Audition required, interview recommended for music program. Interview recommended for drama program; portfolio recommended for graphic art program. Interview required for alternative admission. **Homeschooled:** Transcript of courses and grades required.

**High school preparation.** 15 units required. Required and recommended units include English 4, mathematics 3, social studies 2, history 1, science 2 (laboratory 2), foreign language 2 and academic electives 3.

**2007-2008 Annual costs.** Tuition/fees: $3,798; $9,318 out-of-state. Room/board: $5,592. Books/supplies: $990. Personal expenses: $1,080.

**2007-2008 Financial aid. Need-based:** 765 full-time freshmen applied for aid; 603 were judged to have need; 574 of these received aid. Average need met was 69%. Average scholarship/grant was $4,121; average loan $2,291. 64% of total undergraduate aid awarded as scholarships/grants, 36% as loans/jobs. **Non-need-based:** Awarded to 3,523 full-time undergraduates, including 696 freshmen. Scholarships awarded for academics, alumni affiliation, art, athletics, job skills, leadership, minority status, music/drama, religious affiliation, ROTC, state residency. **Additional information:** Participates in off-campus job location & development program to assist students with off-campus employers to earn money for college expenses.

**Application procedures. Admission:** Priority date 8/1; no deadline. No application fee. Application may be submitted online. Admission notification on a rolling basis. **Financial aid:** Priority date 4/1; no closing date. FAFSA, institutional form required. Applicants notified on a rolling basis starting 2/15.

**Academics.** NSU College of Optometry on campus. **Special study options:** Combined bachelor's/graduate degree, distance learning, double major, dual enrollment of high school students, honors, independent study, internships, student-designed major, teacher certification program, weekend college. **Credit/placement by examination:** AP, CLEP, IB, ACT, institutional tests. 30 credit hours maximum toward bachelor's degree. **Support services:** Learning center, pre-admission summer program, reduced course load, remedial instruction, study skills assistance, tutoring, writing center.

**Majors. Area/ethnic studies:** Native American. **Biology:** General, cell/histology, marine. **Business:** General, accounting, business admin, entrepreneurial studies, finance, human resources, international, logistics, management information systems, marketing, operations, tourism/travel. **Communications:** Advertising, journalism, public relations. **Computer sciences:** Computer science. **Conservation:** Environmental science. **Education:** Art, biology, chemistry, early childhood, elementary, English, learning disabled, mathematics, music, Native American, physical, physics, science, social studies, Spanish, speech. **Engineering:** Environmental. **Engineering technology:** General, industrial safety. **English:** English lit, speech/rhetoric. **Family/consumer sciences:** General, food/nutrition. **Foreign languages:** Spanish. **Health:** Audiology/speech pathology, clinical lab science, facilities admin, nursing (RN). **History:** General. **Math:** General. **Parks/recreation:** Exercise sciences. **Physical sciences:** Chemistry. **Protective services:** Law enforcement admin. **Psychology:** General, developmental. **Public administration:** Social work. **Social sciences:** Geography, political science, sociology. **Visual/performing arts:** Art, commercial/advertising art, design, dramatic, studio arts. **Other:** Organizationall leadership, Vision science.

**Most popular majors.** Business/marketing 21%, education 29%, psychology 8%, security/protective services 7%.

**Computing on campus.** 897 workstations in dormitories, library, computer center. Dormitories wired for high-speed internet access and linked to campus network. Commuter students can connect to campus network. Online library, helpline, student web hosting, wireless network available.

**Student life. Freshman orientation:** Mandatory. Preregistration for classes offered. Two-hour credit course meets two days prior to start of classes; seminars and one class meeting per week during the semester. **Housing:** Guaranteed on-campus for freshmen. Coed dorms, special housing for disabled, apartments, fraternity/sorority housing, substance-free housing available. $75 nonrefundable deposit. **Activities:** Bands, campus ministries, choral groups, dance, drama, international student organizations, literary magazine, music ensembles, Model UN, musical theater, student government, student newspaper, symphony orchestra, TV station, Native American student association, American Indian Science & Engineering Society, Association of Black Collegians, Indian University Scholar Society, Campus Christian Fellowship, Baptist campus ministries, Chi Alpha campus ministries, Fellowship of Christian Athletes, Sigma Theta Epsilon, RiverHawks for Christ.

**Athletics.** NCAA. **Intercollegiate:** Baseball M, basketball, football (tackle) M, golf, soccer, softball W, tennis W. **Intramural:** Basketball, football (non-tackle), golf, racquetball, soccer, softball, tennis, volleyball. **Team name:** RiverHawks.

**Student services.** Adult student services, alcohol/substance abuse counseling, campus ministries, career counseling, services for economically disadvantaged, student employment services, financial aid counseling, health services, personal counseling, placement for graduates, veterans' counselor. **Physically disabled:** Services for visually, speech, hearing impaired.

**Contact.** E-mail: nsuinfo@nsuok.edu
Phone: (918) 444-2200 Toll-free number: (800) 722-9614
Fax: (918) 458-2523
Dawn Cain, Director of Admissions, Northeastern State University, 600 North Grand Avenue, Tahlequah, OK 74464-2399

## Northwestern Oklahoma State University
**Alva, Oklahoma**
www.nwosu.edu                    CB code: 6493

▶ Public 4-year university and teachers college
▶ Commuter campus in small town

▶ 1,698 degree-seeking undergraduates: 22% part-time, 59% women, 5% African American, 1% Asian American, 4% Hispanic American, 5% Native American, 2% international
▶ 247 degree-seeking graduate students
▶ 100% of applicants admitted
▶ SAT or ACT (ACT writing optional) required
▶ 39% graduate within 6 years

**General.** Founded in 1897. Regionally accredited. **Degrees:** 381 bachelor's awarded; master's offered. **Location:** 160 miles from Oklahoma City, 70 miles from Enid. **Calendar:** Semester, limited summer session. **Full-time faculty:** 89 total; 49% have terminal degrees, 54% women. **Part-time faculty:** 65 total. **Class size:** 72% < 20, 25% 20-39, 1% 40-49, 1% 50-99. **Special facilities:** Farm.

**Freshman class profile.** 525 applied, 525 admitted, 352 enrolled.

| Mid 50% test scores | | | |
|---|---|---|---|
| SAT critical reading: | 420-510 | GPA 3.0-3.49: | 35% |
| SAT math: | 440-570 | GPA 2.0-2.99: | 29% |
| SAT writing: | 400-470 | Out-of-state: | 24% |
| ACT composite: | 18-23 | Live on campus: | 75% |
| GPA 3.50 or higher: | 34% | International: | 2% |

**Basis for selection.** Applicants with 2.7 GPA and in top 50 percent of class or with ACT composite score of 19 admitted unconditionally. Others admitted provisionally. Audition recommended for music program. **Home-schooled:** Transcript of courses and grades required.

**High school preparation.** 15 units required. Required and recommended units include English 4, mathematics 3, history 2, science 2 (laboratory 2), foreign language 2 and academic electives 3. 1 unit required from either government, economics, geography or non-Western culture.

**2007-2008 Annual costs.** Tuition/fees: $3,750; $9,300 out-of-state. Room/board: $3,400. Books/supplies: $900. Personal expenses: $1,200.

**2006-2007 Financial aid. Need-based:** 181 full-time freshmen applied for aid; 127 were judged to have need; 119 of these received aid. Average need met was 66%. Average scholarship/grant was $4,735; average loan $2,222. 56% of total undergraduate aid awarded as scholarships/grants, 44% as loans/jobs. **Non-need-based:** Awarded to 304 full-time undergraduates, including 95 freshmen. Scholarships awarded for academics, alumni affiliation, art, athletics, leadership, music/drama.

**Application procedures. Admission:** No deadline. $15 fee. Application may be submitted online. Admission notification on a rolling basis. **Financial aid:** No deadline. FAFSA required. Applicants notified on a rolling basis starting 5/1.

**Academics. Special study options:** Distance learning, double major, dual enrollment of high school students, honors, independent study, internships, study abroad, teacher certification program. 2-2 programs in many professional fields. **Credit/placement by examination:** AP, CLEP, SAT, ACT, institutional tests. **Support services:** Learning center, reduced course load, remedial instruction, tutoring, writing center.

**Majors. Agriculture:** General, business. **Biology:** General. **Business:** Accounting, business admin, e-commerce. **Communications:** Broadcast journalism, journalism, public relations. **Computer sciences:** General, information systems, programming. **Conservation:** Management/policy. **Education:** General, business, early childhood, elementary, English, health, learning disabled, mathematics, mentally handicapped, music, physical, science, social science, Spanish, special, technology/industrial arts. **English:** English lit, speech/rhetoric. **Health:** Nursing (RN). **History:** General. **Legal studies:** Prelaw. **Math:** General. **Parks/recreation:** Health/fitness. **Physical sciences:** Chemistry. **Protective services:** Police science. **Psychology:** General. **Public administration:** Social work. **Social sciences:** General, political science, sociology. **Visual/performing arts:** Dramatic, music performance, piano/organ, voice/opera.

**Most popular majors.** Agriculture 8%, business/marketing 23%, education 19%, health sciences 8%, parks/recreation 8%, psychology 9%.

**Computing on campus.** 93 workstations in library, computer center, student center. Commuter students can connect to campus network. Online library, wireless network available.

**Student life. Freshman orientation:** Mandatory. Preregistration for classes offered. First semester freshmen take Ranger Connection class for one semester, one hour per week. **Housing:** Guaranteed on-campus for all undergraduates. Single-sex dorms, special housing for disabled available. $75 fully refundable deposit. **Activities:** Bands, choral groups, dance, drama, music ensembles, musical theater, radio station, student government, student newspaper, TV station, Black student organization, Student Oklahoma

Education Association, Fellowship of Christian Athletes, College Republicans, Student Government Association, nontraditional students organization, Los Listos, University Democrats.

**Athletics.** NAIA. **Intercollegiate:** Baseball M, basketball, cross-country, football (tackle) M, golf, rodeo, soccer W, softball W. **Intramural:** Basketball, bowling, football (non-tackle), racquetball, softball, volleyball. **Team name:** Rangers.

**Student services.** Adult student services, career counseling, student employment services, financial aid counseling, health services, personal counseling, placement for graduates, veterans' counselor. **Physically disabled:** Services for visually, speech, hearing impaired.

**Contact.**  E-mail: recruit@nwosu.edu
Phone: (580) 327-8546 Fax: (580) 327-8413
Matt Adair, Director of Recruitment, Northwestern Oklahoma State University, 709 Oklahoma Boulevard, Alva, OK 73717-2799

## Oklahoma Baptist University
**Shawnee, Oklahoma**                     **CB member**
**www.okbu.edu**                          **CB code: 6541**

- Private 4-year university and liberal arts college affiliated with Southern Baptist Convention
- Residential campus in large town
- 1,424 degree-seeking undergraduates
- 75% of applicants admitted
- SAT or ACT (ACT writing optional) required

**General.** Founded in 1910. Regionally accredited. Each summer approximately 250 students, faculty and staff serve in projects around the world. About 300 students participate in local service projects during the year. **Degrees:** 313 bachelor's, 5 associate awarded; master's offered. **ROTC:** Air Force. **Location:** 35 miles from Oklahoma City, 90 miles from Tulsa. **Calendar:** Semester, limited summer session. **Full-time faculty:** 105 total. **Part-time faculty:** 55 total. **Class size:** 62% < 20, 31% 20-39, 3% 40-49, 3% 50-99. **Special facilities:** Planetarium (operated by students), greenhouse, music technology laboratory, biblical research library.

**Freshman class profile.** 1,082 applied, 812 admitted, 315 enrolled.

| Mid 50% test scores | | | |
|---|---|---|---|
| | | **ACT composite:** | 21-28 |
| SAT critical reading: | 520-610 | **Out-of-state:** | 38% |
| SAT math: | 490-570 | **Live on campus:** | 94% |

**Basis for selection.** Minimum 20 ACT or 950 SAT (exclusive of Writing), minimum 3.0 GPA or class rank in top half required. Interview recommended for borderline applicants; audition recommended for drama, music programs; portfolio recommended for art program.

**High school preparation.** 17 units recommended. Recommended units include English 4, mathematics 3, social studies 2, history 1, science 3 (laboratory 2), foreign language 2 and academic electives 2. Mathematics recommendation includes 2 algebra and 1 plane geometry.

**2007-2008 Annual costs.** Tuition/fees: $15,994. Room/board: $5,000. Books/supplies: $650. Personal expenses: $1,400.

**2006-2007 Financial aid. Need-based:** 274 full-time freshmen applied for aid; 221 were judged to have need; 221 of these received aid. Average need met was 67%. Average scholarship/grant was $3,980; average loan $2,508. 61% of total undergraduate aid awarded as scholarships/grants, 39% as loans/jobs. **Non-need-based:** Awarded to 1,568 full-time undergraduates, including 406 freshmen. Scholarships awarded for academics, alumni affiliation, art, athletics, job skills, leadership, music/drama, religious affiliation, ROTC, state residency.

**Application procedures. Admission:** Priority date 4/1; deadline 8/1 (postmark date). $25 fee, may be waived for applicants with need. Admission notification on a rolling basis. **Financial aid:** Priority date 3/1; no closing date. FAFSA, institutional form required. Applicants notified on a rolling basis starting 3/1; must reply by 5/1 or within 2 week(s) of notification.

**Academics.** Opportunities for January-term travel to Europe, Russia, South America; also opportunity to teach English in China and Hungary. **Special study options:** Accelerated study, combined bachelor's/graduate degree, cooperative education, double major, ESL, exchange student, honors, independent study, internships, liberal arts/career combination, student-designed major, study abroad, teacher certification program. Exchange program with Seinan Gakuin University, Japan, and Hong Kong Baptist College; opportunities for January-term travel to Europe, Russia, South America. **Credit/placement by examination:** AP, CLEP, IB, ACT, institutional tests. 32 credit

hours maximum toward bachelor's degree. Essay required for English, government, history exams; oral exam required for French, German and Spanish; lab exam required for information systems. **Support services:** Learning center, pre-admission summer program, reduced course load, remedial instruction, study skills assistance, tutoring.

**Majors. Biology:** General, biochemistry. **Business:** General, accounting, business admin, finance, international, international finance, management information systems, management science, marketing. **Communications:** General, broadcast journalism, journalism, public relations. **Computer sciences:** General, applications programming, computer science, information systems, systems analysis. **Education:** Art, biology, chemistry, early childhood, elementary, English, foreign languages, French, German, health, history, learning disabled, mathematics, mentally handicapped, music, physical, physics, science, secondary, social science, social studies, Spanish, special, speech. **English:** English lit, speech/rhetoric. **Foreign languages:** General, French, German, Spanish. **Health:** Athletic training, nursing (RN). **History:** General. **Interdisciplinary:** Math/computer science. **Liberal arts:** Arts/sciences. **Math:** General. **Parks/recreation:** Exercise sciences, facilities management, health/fitness, sports admin. **Philosophy/religion:** Philosophy, religion. **Physical sciences:** Chemistry, physics. **Psychology:** General. **Public administration:** Social work. **Social sciences:** General, anthropology, political science, sociology. **Theology:** Bible, missionary, religious ed, sacred music, theology. **Visual/performing arts:** Art, dramatic, music performance, music theory/composition, piano/organ, studio arts, voice/opera.

**Most popular majors.** Business/marketing 12%, education 16%, health sciences 12%, psychology 7%, theological studies 12%, visual/performing arts 8%.

**Computing on campus.** 200 workstations in dormitories, library, computer center. Dormitories wired for high-speed internet access and linked to campus network. Online course registration, online library available.

**Student life. Freshman orientation:** Mandatory. Preregistration for classes offered. Held during the 3 days immediately prior to start of fall semester. **Policies:** Campus is alcohol/drug/smoke free. **Housing:** Guaranteed on-campus for all undergraduates. Single-sex dorms, apartments, substance-free housing available. **Activities:** Bands, choral groups, drama, literary magazine, music ensembles, musical theater, opera, student government, student newspaper, symphony orchestra, TV station, Campus Crusade, FCA, Baptist Collegiate Ministries, Collegiate Republicans, Young Democrats, Black Student Fellowship, International Student Union, Native American Heritage Association, residence hall association.

**Athletics.** NAIA. **Intercollegiate:** Baseball M, basketball, cross-country, golf, soccer, softball W, tennis, track and field. **Intramural:** Badminton, basketball, bowling, racquetball, soccer, softball, swimming, table tennis, tennis, volleyball. **Team name:** Bison.

**Student services.** Campus ministries, career counseling, student employment services, financial aid counseling, health services, personal counseling, placement for graduates, veterans' counselor. **Physically disabled:** Services for visually, hearing impaired.

**Contact.**  E-mail: admissions@mail.okbu.edu
Phone: (405) 878-2033 Toll-free number: (800) 654-3285
Fax: (405) 878-2046
Bruce Perkins, Director of Admissions, Oklahoma Baptist University, 500 West University, Shawnee, OK 74804

## Oklahoma Christian University
**Oklahoma City, Oklahoma**
**www.oc.edu**                            **CB code: 6086**

- Private 4-year liberal arts college affiliated with Church of Christ
- Residential campus in very large city
- 1,998 degree-seeking undergraduates: 5% African American, 2% Asian American, 3% Hispanic American, 4% Native American
- 260 graduate students

**General.** Founded in 1950. Regionally accredited. **Degrees:** 234 bachelor's awarded; master's offered. **ROTC:** Army, Air Force. **Calendar:** Semester, extensive summer session. **Full-time faculty:** 103 total; 68% have terminal degrees, 7% minority, 29% women. **Part-time faculty:** 91 total; 25% have terminal degrees, 6% minority, 38% women. **Class size:** 53% < 20, 38% 20-39, 3% 40-49, 4% 50-99, less than 1% >100.

**Freshman class profile.** 1,899 applied, 1,618 admitted, 544 enrolled.

| Mid 50% test scores | | | |
|---|---|---|---|
| SAT critical reading: | 470-610 | GPA 3.0-3.49: | 32% |
| SAT math: | 470-640 | GPA 2.0-2.99: | 16% |
| ACT composite: | 19-26 | Rank in top quarter: | 47% |
| GPA 3.50 or higher: | 44% | Rank in top tenth: | 22% |
| | | Live on campus: | 96% |

**Basis for selection.** Open admission, but selective for some programs. Students are evaluated on both merit and character.

**High school preparation.** 15 units recommended. Recommended units include English 4, mathematics 4, social studies 3 and science 4.

**2008-2009 Annual costs.** Tuition/fees: $16,566. Room/board: $6,390. Books/supplies: $800. Personal expenses: $1,360.

**2006-2007 Financial aid. Need-based:** 435 full-time freshmen applied for aid; 375 were judged to have need; 375 of these received aid. Average need met was 40%. Average scholarship/grant was $1,280; average loan $2,521. 54% of total undergraduate aid awarded as scholarships/grants, 46% as loans/jobs. **Non-need-based:** Awarded to 1,940 full-time undergraduates, including 574 freshmen. Scholarships awarded for academics, art, athletics, leadership, music/drama, religious affiliation, ROTC.

**Application procedures. Admission:** Priority date 5/1; no deadline. $25 fee, may be waived for applicants with need. Application may be submitted online. Admission notification on a rolling basis. **Financial aid:** Priority date 3/15, closing date 8/31. FAFSA required. Applicants notified on a rolling basis starting 1/15; must reply within 4 week(s) of notification.

**Academics. Special study options:** Accelerated study, cross-registration, distance learning, double major, dual enrollment of high school students, ESL, exchange student, honors, independent study, internships, liberal arts/career combination, study abroad, teacher certification program. **Credit/placement by examination:** AP, CLEP, IB, institutional tests. 60 credit hours maximum toward bachelor's degree. **Support services:** Reduced course load, remedial instruction, study skills assistance, tutoring, writing center.

**Majors. Biology:** General, biochemistry. **Business:** General, accounting, business admin, management science, market research. **Communications:** General, advertising, broadcast journalism, journalism, public relations. **Computer sciences:** General, computer science, information systems. **Education:** Art, early childhood, elementary, English, ESL, mathematics, middle, music, physical, science, secondary, social studies, speech. **Engineering:** Computer, electrical, mechanical, physics. **Engineering technology:** Mechanical. **English:** Composition, creative writing, English lit, speech/rhetoric. **Family/consumer sciences:** Family studies, family/community services. **Foreign languages:** Spanish. **Health:** Clinical lab science, predental, premedicine, prenursing, prepharmacy, preveterinary. **History:** General. **Interdisciplinary:** Biological/physical sciences, math/computer science. **Legal studies:** Prelaw. **Liberal arts:** Arts/sciences. **Math:** General. **Parks/recreation:** Health/fitness. **Philosophy/religion:** Christian, religion. **Physical sciences:** Chemistry. **Psychology:** General. **Social sciences:** Political science. **Theology:** Bible, missionary, religious ed, theology, youth ministry. **Visual/performing arts:** Art, commercial/advertising art, design, dramatic, graphic design, interior design, music performance, piano/organ, studio arts, voice/opera.

**Computing on campus.** PC or laptop required. 1,850 workstations in dormitories, library, computer center, student center. Dormitories wired for high-speed internet access and linked to campus network. Commuter students can connect to campus network. Online course registration, online library, helpline, repair service, student web hosting, wireless network available.

**Student life. Freshman orientation:** Mandatory, $200 fee. Preregistration for classes offered. **Policies:** Single students must live on campus or with parents. Special arrangements considered. Religious observance required. **Housing:** Guaranteed on-campus for all undergraduates. Single-sex dorms, special housing for disabled, apartments, substance-free housing available. $100 partly refundable deposit. **Activities:** Bands, campus ministries, choral groups, drama, international student organizations, literary magazine, music ensembles, musical theater, opera, radio station, student government, student newspaper, symphony orchestra, TV station.

**Athletics.** NAIA. **Intercollegiate:** Baseball M, basketball, cheerleading W, cross-country, golf M, soccer, softball W, tennis, track and field. **Intramural:** Basketball, bowling, cross-country, football (non-tackle), golf M, soccer, softball, swimming, table tennis, tennis, track and field, volleyball. **Team name:** Eagles.

**Student services.** Alcohol/substance abuse counseling, campus ministries, career counseling, student employment services, financial aid counseling, health services, minority student services, personal counseling, placement for graduates, veterans' counselor. **Physically disabled:** Services for visually, speech, hearing impaired.

**Contact.** E-mail: info@oc.edu
Phone: (405) 425-5050 Toll-free number: (800) 877-5050
Fax: (405) 425-5069
Darci Thompson, Dean of Enrollment and Marketing, Oklahoma Christian University, Box 11000, Oklahoma City, OK 73136-1100

## Oklahoma City University
**Oklahoma City, Oklahoma**
www.okcu.edu

CB member
CB code: 6543

- Private 4-year university and liberal arts college affiliated with United Methodist Church
- Residential campus in very large city
- 2,129 degree-seeking undergraduates: 16% part-time, 62% women, 8% African American, 4% Asian American, 5% Hispanic American, 5% Native American, 17% international
- 1,719 degree-seeking graduate students
- 81% of applicants admitted
- SAT or ACT (ACT writing optional) required
- 47% graduate within 6 years

**General.** Founded in 1904. Regionally accredited. Institution embraces the United Methodist tradition of scholarship and service and welcomes all faiths. Service learning incorporated throughout the curriculum. **Degrees:** 498 bachelor's awarded; master's, first professional offered. **ROTC:** Army, Air Force. **Location:** 180 miles from Dallas, 350 miles from Kansas City. **Calendar:** Semester, limited summer session. **Full-time faculty:** 189 total; 78% have terminal degrees, 12% minority, 45% women. **Part-time faculty:** 151 total; 11% minority, 50% women. **Class size:** 71% < 20, 26% 20-39, 1% 40-49, 2% 50-99. **Special facilities:** Art center, entrepreneurship center, urban wilderness laboratory.

**Freshman class profile.** 998 applied, 808 admitted, 400 enrolled.

| Mid 50% test scores | | | |
|---|---|---|---|
| SAT critical reading: | 510-640 | Rank in top tenth: | 30% |
| SAT math: | 520-640 | End year in good standing: | 77% |
| ACT composite: | 22-27 | Return as sophomores: | 81% |
| GPA 3.50 or higher: | 58% | Out-of-state: | 50% |
| GPA 3.0-3.49: | 33% | Live on campus: | 94% |
| GPA 2.0-2.99: | 9% | International: | 11% |
| Rank in top quarter: | 60% | Fraternities: | 18% |
| | | Sororities: | 30% |

**Basis for selection.** School achievement record, which includes class rank, and test scores most important. Admissions interview and counselor recommendations also considered. Essay, interview recommended for all; audition required for dance, music programs; portfolio required for art, graphic design programs. **Homeschooled:** Present official transcript, including course work and grades, from home schooling experience. Demonstrate that individual is graduating no earlier than their class in the public school system. Submit official copy of ACT or SAT test scores.

**High school preparation.** 15 units required. Required units include English 4, mathematics 3, social studies 3, science 3 (laboratory 1) and foreign language 2. Mathematics requirement includes 2 algebra and 1 geometry, trigonometry, math analysis, or calculus. Social studies requirement includes 1 world history, 1 state history or civics, and 1 United States history.

**2007-2008 Annual costs.** Tuition/fees: $20,800. Room/board: $6,550. Books/supplies: $1,500. Personal expenses: $1,000.

**2006-2007 Financial aid. Need-based:** 83% of total undergraduate aid awarded as scholarships/grants, 17% as loans/jobs. **Non-need-based:** Scholarships awarded for academics, art, athletics, job skills, leadership, music/drama, religious affiliation.

**Application procedures. Admission:** Priority date 3/30; deadline 8/20 (postmark date). $30 fee, may be waived for applicants with need. Application may be submitted online. Admission notification on a rolling basis beginning on or about 10/15. Must reply by May 1 or within 2 week(s) if notified thereafter. **Financial aid:** Priority date 3/1, closing date 6/30. FAFSA, institutional form required. Applicants notified on a rolling basis starting 2/24; must reply within 2 week(s) of notification.

**Academics. Special study options:** Accelerated study, cooperative education, distance learning, double major, dual enrollment of high school students, ESL, exchange student, external degree, honors, independent study, internships, New York semester, student-designed major, study abroad, teacher certification program, Washington semester. **Credit/placement by examination:** AP, CLEP, IB, SAT, ACT, institutional tests. 30 credit hours maximum toward bachelor's degree. **Support services:** Learning center, reduced course load, study skills assistance, tutoring, writing center.

**Majors. Area/ethnic studies:** American. **Biology:** General, biochemistry, biophysics. **Business:** General, accounting, business admin, finance, international, management information systems, management science, managerial economics, marketing. **Communications:** Advertising, broadcast journalism, journalism, media studies, public relations, radio/tv. **Computer sciences:** General, computer science. **Education:** General, art, business, early childhood, elementary, English, foreign languages, French, German, health, history, mathematics, Montessori teacher, music, physical, science, secondary, social studies, Spanish, speech. **English:** English lit, speech/rhetoric. **Foreign languages:** French, German, Spanish. **Health:** Athletic training, nursing (RN), predental, premedicine, prepharmacy, preveterinary. **History:** General. **Interdisciplinary:** Biological/physical sciences. **Legal studies:** Prelaw. **Liberal arts:** Arts/sciences, humanities. **Math:** General. **Parks/recreation:** Health/fitness. **Philosophy/religion:** Philosophy, religion. **Physical sciences:** Chemistry, physics. **Protective services:** Corrections, law enforcement admin, police science. **Psychology:** General. **Public administration:** Social work. **Social sciences:** Economics, political science, sociology. **Theology:** Bible, religious ed, sacred music, youth ministry. **Visual/performing arts:** General, art, art history/conservation, arts management, cinematography, dance, dramatic, film/cinema, music management, music performance, music theory/composition, piano/organ, stringed instruments, studio arts, theater arts management, voice/opera. **Other:** Entertainment business.

**Most popular majors.** Business/marketing 7%, health sciences 13%, liberal arts 37%, visual/performing arts 20%.

**Computing on campus.** 218 workstations in dormitories, library, computer center, student center. Dormitories wired for high-speed internet access and linked to campus network. Commuter students can connect to campus network. Online course registration, online library, helpline, repair service, student web hosting, wireless network available.

**Student life. Freshman orientation:** Mandatory, $50 fee. Preregistration for classes offered. **Housing:** Guaranteed on-campus for all undergrads. Coed dorms, single-sex dorms, apartments, fraternity/sorority housing, substance-free housing available. $100 deposit. Learning communities available. **Activities:** Bands, choral groups, dance, drama, international student organizations, literary magazine, music ensembles, musical theater, opera, student government, student newspaper, symphony orchestra, TV station, Kappa Phi, Sigma Theta Epsilon, Association for People of Color, United Methodist Student Fellowship, Students of Arts Management, various, Alpha Phi Sorority, Gamma Phi Beta Sorority, Lambda Chi Alpha Fraternity, Kappa Sigma Fraternity.

**Athletics.** NAIA. **Intercollegiate:** Baseball M, basketball, cheerleading, golf, rowing (crew), soccer, softball W, volleyball W, wrestling. **Intramural:** Basketball, football (non-tackle) M, golf, softball, table tennis, volleyball. **Team name:** Stars.

**Student services.** Adult student services, campus ministries, career counseling, student employment services, financial aid counseling, health services, minority student services, personal counseling, placement for graduates, veterans' counselor. **Physically disabled:** Services for visually, hearing impaired.

**Contact.** E-mail: uadmissions@okcu.edu
Phone: (405) 208-5050 Toll-free number: (800) 633-7242
Fax: (405) 208-5916
Eduardo Prieto, Dean of Enrollment Services, Oklahoma City University, 2501 North Blackwelder Avenue, Oklahoma City, OK 73106

## Oklahoma Panhandle State University
**Goodwell, Oklahoma**
www.opsu.edu                     CB code: 6571

- Public 4-year agricultural and liberal arts college
- Residential campus in rural community
- 1,078 degree-seeking undergraduates: 12% part-time, 51% women, 7% African American, 1% Asian American, 13% Hispanic American, 3% Native American, 4% international
- 96% of applicants admitted
- 52% graduate within 6 years

**General.** Founded in 1909. Regionally accredited. **Degrees:** 196 bachelor's, 23 associate awarded. **Location:** 110 miles from Amarillo, Texas, 10 miles from Guymon. **Calendar:** Semester, limited summer session. **Full-time faculty:** 56 total; 38% have terminal degrees, 4% minority, 41% women. **Part-time faculty:** 35 total; 51% women. **Class size:** 78% < 20, 21% 20-39, less than 1% 40-49, less than 1% 50-99, less than 1% >100. **Special facilities:** Agronomy experiment station, historical museum, livestock facilities, farming area, rodeo arena, meat lab.

**Freshman class profile.** 313 applied, 301 admitted, 275 enrolled.

| Mid 50% test scores | | | |
|---|---|---|---|
| SAT critical reading: | 380-490 | GPA 3.0-3.49: | 36% |
| SAT math: | 410-570 | GPA 2.0-2.99: | 35% |
| ACT composite: | 16-21 | Out-of-state: | 54% |
| GPA 3.50 or higher: | 29% | Live on campus: | 90% |
| | | International: | 7% |

**Basis for selection.** Secondary school record, test scores and class rank most important. SAT or ACT recommended. Incoming students with no ACT scores, or a score of 19 or below, must take ACCUPLACER test. **Homeschooled:** Transcript of courses and grades required.

**High school preparation.** 15 units required. Required units include English 4, mathematics 3, social studies 2, history 1, science 2 (laboratory 2) and academic electives 3.

**2007-2008 Annual costs.** Tuition/fees: $3,249; $8,139 out-of-state. Room/board: $3,300. Books/supplies: $240.

**Financial aid.** All financial aid based on need.

**Application procedures. Admission:** No deadline. No application fee. Application may be submitted online. Admission notification on a rolling basis. **Financial aid:** Priority date 3/15; no closing date. FAFSA, institutional form required. Applicants notified by 5/1.

**Academics. Special study options:** Cooperative education, distance learning, double major, dual enrollment of high school students, ESL, independent study, internships, liberal arts/career combination, teacher certification program. **Credit/placement by examination:** AP, CLEP, SAT, ACT, institutional tests. 34 credit hours maximum toward associate degree, 60 toward bachelor's. **Support services:** Learning center, reduced course load, remedial instruction, study skills assistance, tutoring, writing center.

**Majors. Agriculture:** Agribusiness operations, agronomy, animal sciences, equine science. **Biology:** General. **Business:** Accounting, business admin. **Computer sciences:** General. **Education:** Agricultural, business, elementary. **Engineering technology:** Industrial. **English:** English lit. **Foreign languages:** Spanish. **Health:** Nursing (RN). **History:** General. **Interdisciplinary:** Biological/physical sciences. **Math:** General. **Parks/recreation:** Health/fitness. **Physical sciences:** Chemistry. **Psychology:** General. **Social sciences:** General. **Visual/performing arts:** Art.

**Most popular majors.** Agriculture 32%, biology 8%, business/marketing 8%, education 10%, health sciences 6%, parks/recreation 6%, psychology 9%.

**Computing on campus.** 75 workstations in library, computer center, student center. Dormitories wired for high-speed internet access. Online library, wireless network available.

**Student life. Freshman orientation:** Mandatory. Preregistration for classes offered. **Housing:** Guaranteed on-campus for all undergraduates. Single-sex dorms, apartments, substance-free housing available. **Activities:** Bands, choral groups, drama, music ensembles, musical theater, radio station, student government, student newspaper, Wesley Foundation, Baptist Student Union, Church of Christ Student Center, Circle-K, Newman Club, Methodist Student Center.

**Athletics.** NCAA. **Intercollegiate:** Baseball M, basketball, cheerleading, cross-country, football (tackle) M, golf, softball W, volleyball W. **Intramural:** Basketball, football (non-tackle), golf, soccer, softball, table tennis, volleyball. **Team name:** Aggies.

**Student services.** Adult student services, alcohol/substance abuse counseling, campus ministries, career counseling, student employment services, financial aid counseling, health services, minority student services, personal counseling, placement for graduates. **Physically disabled:** Services for visually, speech, hearing impaired.

**Contact.** E-mail: jolie@opsu.edu
Phone: (580) 349-1312 Toll-free number: (800) 664-6778
Fax: (580) 349-1371
Bobby Jenkins, Registrar and Director of Adminssion, Oklahoma Panhandle State University, OPSU Admissions, Goodwell, OK 73939-0430

## Oklahoma State University
**Stillwater, Oklahoma**                     CB member
http://osu.okstate.edu               CB code: 6546

- Public 4-year university
- Residential campus in small city
- 18,205 degree-seeking undergraduates: 12% part-time, 49% women, 4% African American, 2% Asian American, 2% Hispanic American, 10% Native American, 3% international

- 4,238 degree-seeking graduate students
- 88% of applicants admitted
- SAT or ACT (ACT writing optional) required
- 58% graduate within 6 years

**General.** Founded in 1890. Regionally accredited. Campuses in Oklahoma City, Okmulgee, Tulsa and Center for Health Sciences (includes College of Osteopathic Medicine) at Tulsa. Stillwater campus includes the Center for Veterinary Health Sciences. **Degrees:** 3,712 bachelor's awarded; master's, doctoral, first professional offered. **ROTC:** Army, Air Force. **Location:** 65 miles from Tulsa, 65 miles from Oklahoma City. **Calendar:** Semester, extensive summer session. **Full-time faculty:** 985 total; 91% have terminal degrees, 9% minority, 31% women. **Part-time faculty:** 231 total; 29% have terminal degrees, 8% minority, 52% women. **Class size:** 33% < 20, 41% 20-39, 11% 40-49, 10% 50-99, 4% >100. **Special facilities:** Laser research center with 8 laboratories and 30 laser systems, biotechnology and genetic engineering research center, telecommunication center.

**Freshman class profile.** 6,415 applied, 5,651 admitted, 3,209 enrolled.

| Mid 50% test scores | | | |
|---|---|---|---|
| SAT critical reading: | 490-610 | Rank in top tenth: | 27% |
| SAT math: | 510-630 | Return as sophomores: | 80% |
| ACT composite: | 22-27 | Out-of-state: | 21% |
| GPA 3.50 or higher: | 60% | Live on campus: | 88% |
| GPA 3.0-3.49: | 32% | International: | 1% |
| GPA 2.0-2.99: | 8% | Fraternities: | 23% |
| Rank in top quarter: | 59% | Sororities: | 27% |

**Basis for selection.** Applicants must earn a 3.0 high school GPA and rank in top 33% of their class, or have minimum 24 ACT or 1090 SAT (exclusive of Writing), or earn a 3.0 High School GPA in 15 required curricular units and have a 21 ACT or 980 SAT(exclusive of Writing). Early application encouraged. Test scores must be received no later than Friday before classes begin for fall-term admission. Interview recommended for academically borderline students. **Homeschooled:** Graduates of home school or unaccredited high schools must satisfy all the curricular requirements and meet the minimum ACT/SAT score requirements.

**High school preparation.** 15 units required. Required and recommended units include English 4, mathematics 3, social studies 2, history 1, science 2 (laboratory 2), foreign language 2, computer science 1 and academic electives 3.

**2007-2008 Annual costs.** Tuition/fees: $5,491; $14,916 out-of-state. Room/board: $6,267. Books/supplies: $940. Personal expenses: $2,350.

**2006-2007 Financial aid. Need-based:** 2,016 full-time freshmen applied for aid; 1,454 were judged to have need; 1,403 of these received aid. Average need met was 76%. Average scholarship/grant was $4,229; average loan $2,673. 52% of total undergraduate aid awarded as scholarships/grants, 48% as loans/jobs. **Non-need-based:** Awarded to 7,675 full-time undergraduates, including 1,968 freshmen. Scholarships awarded for academics, alumni affiliation, art, athletics, leadership, music/drama, ROTC, state residency.

**Application procedures. Admission:** No deadline. $40 fee, may be waived for applicants with need. Application may be submitted online. Admission notification on a rolling basis. Deferred admission allowed based on military deployments. **Financial aid:** No deadline. FAFSA required. Applicants notified on a rolling basis; must reply within 2 week(s) of notification.

**Academics. Special study options:** Accelerated study, combined bachelor's/graduate degree, cross-registration, distance learning, double major, dual enrollment of high school students, ESL, exchange student, honors, independent study, internships, semester at sea, student-designed major, study abroad, teacher certification program, Washington semester. **Credit/placement by examination:** AP, CLEP, IB, SAT, ACT. Maximum number of credit hours towards degree is subject to university "residence credit" policy. **Support services:** Learning center, pre-admission summer program, reduced course load, remedial instruction, study skills assistance, tutoring, writing center.

**Honors college/program.** ACT of 27 or SAT of 1210 (exclusive of Writing) and High School GPA of 3.75 required.

**Majors. Agriculture:** Animal sciences, business, communications, economics, food science, horticultural science, landscaping, soil science. **Architecture:** Architecture, landscape. **Area/ethnic studies:** American. **Biology:** General, biochemistry, botany, entomology, microbiology, physiology, zoology. **Business:** Accounting, business admin, finance, hospitality admin, international, management information systems, managerial economics, marketing. **Communications:** Journalism. **Computer sciences:** General. **Conservation:** Environmental science, forestry. **Education:** General, agricultural, elementary, music, physical, secondary, voc/tech. **Engineering:** Aerospace, agricultural, architectural, chemical, civil, electrical, industrial, mechanical.

**Engineering technology:** Construction, electrical, mechanical. **English:** English lit. **Family/consumer sciences:** Family studies, food/nutrition, housing. **Foreign languages:** French, German, Russian, Spanish. **Health:** Athletic training, public health ed, speech pathology. **History:** General. **Liberal arts:** Arts/sciences. **Math:** General, statistics. **Parks/recreation:** General. **Philosophy/religion:** Philosophy. **Physical sciences:** Chemistry, geology, physics. **Protective services:** Fire safety technology. **Psychology:** General. **Social sciences:** Economics, geography, political science, sociology. **Transportation:** Aviation. **Visual/performing arts:** Art, dramatic.

**Most popular majors.** Agriculture 8%, biology 6%, business/marketing 28%, education 8%, engineering/engineering technologies 11%, family/consumer sciences 7%.

**Computing on campus.** Dormitories wired for high-speed internet access and linked to campus network. Commuter students can connect to campus network. Online course registration, online library, helpline, repair service, wireless network available.

**Student life. Freshman orientation:** Mandatory. Preregistration for classes offered. One-day programs in June. Also ALPHA orientation program held the week before classes begin each fall semester. **Housing:** Guaranteed on-campus for freshmen. Coed dorms, single-sex dorms, special housing for disabled, apartments, fraternity/sorority housing, substance-free housing available. $150 fully refundable deposit. Learning communities, special interest housing available. **Activities:** Bands, campus ministries, choral groups, dance, drama, international student organizations, literary magazine, music ensembles, musical theater, opera, radio station, student government, student newspaper, symphony orchestra, TV station, Campus Crusade for Christ, Flying Aggies, Rodeo Club, Young Democrats, Young Republicans, Fire Protection Society, Alpha Pi Omega, National Organization for Women, African American student association, Hispanic student association.

**Athletics.** NCAA. **Intercollegiate:** Baseball M, basketball, cross-country, equestrian W, football (tackle) M, golf, soccer W, softball W, tennis, track and field, wrestling M. **Intramural:** Archery, badminton, basketball, bowling, cross-country, football (tackle), golf, racquetball, soccer, softball, squash, swimming, table tennis, tennis, track and field, volleyball, water polo, weight lifting, wrestling M. **Team name:** Cowboys, Cowgirls.

**Student services.** Adult student services, alcohol/substance abuse counseling, campus ministries, career counseling, student employment services, financial aid counseling, health services, legal services, minority student services, personal counseling, placement for graduates, veterans' counselor, women's services. **Physically disabled:** Services for visually, speech, hearing impaired.

**Contact.** E-mail: admissions@okstate.edu
Phone: (405) 744-5358 Toll-free number: (800) 233-5019 ext. 1
Fax: (405) 744-7092
Karen Lucas, Director of Undergraduate Admissions, Oklahoma State University, 219 Student Union, Stillwater, OK 74078-7042

---

## Oklahoma Wesleyan University
**Bartlesville, Oklahoma**     **CB member**
**www.okwu.edu**     **CB code: 6135**

- Private 4-year university and liberal arts college affiliated with Wesleyan Church
- Residential campus in large town
- 989 degree-seeking undergraduates
- 58 graduate students
- 48% of applicants admitted
- SAT or ACT required

**General.** Founded in 1909. Regionally accredited. **Degrees:** 213 bachelor's, 42 associate awarded; master's offered. **Location:** 40 miles from Tulsa. **Calendar:** Differs by program, limited summer session. **Full-time faculty:** 33 total; 48% have terminal degrees, 3% minority, 12% women. **Part-time faculty:** 2 total; 50% have terminal degrees, 50% women. **Class size:** 89% < 20, 10% 20-39, 1% 40-49, less than 1% 50-99. **Special facilities:** Historic mansion, fine arts center, city bike path.

**Freshman class profile.** 613 applied, 295 admitted, 110 enrolled.

| Mid 50% test scores | | | |
|---|---|---|---|
| SAT critical reading: | 430-520 | GPA 3.0-3.49: | 26% |
| SAT math: | 420-550 | GPA 2.0-2.99: | 12% |
| ACT composite: | 19-25 | Out-of-state: | 60% |
| GPA 3.50 or higher: | 62% | Live on campus: | 90% |

**Basis for selection.** In addition to required high school study, students must fulfill 2 out of 3 of the following: rank in top half of class, have 2.0

GPA, ACT score of 18. **Homeschooled:** Statement describing homeschool structure and mission, transcript of courses and grades required. Encouraged to apply.

**High school preparation.** 15 units required. Required units include English 4, mathematics 2, social studies 2, science 1 (laboratory 1).

**2008-2009 Annual costs.** Tuition/fees: $16,585. Room/board: $6,050. Books/supplies: $900. Personal expenses: $1,000.

**2007-2008 Financial aid. Need-based:** 25% of total undergraduate aid awarded as scholarships/grants, 75% as loans/jobs. **Non-need-based:** Scholarships awarded for academics, alumni affiliation, athletics, leadership, music/drama, religious affiliation, state residency.

**Application procedures. Admission:** No deadline. $25 fee, may be waived for applicants with need. Application may be submitted online. Admission notification on a rolling basis. Students must be accepted prior to beginning of classes. **Financial aid:** Priority date 4/1; no closing date. FAFSA, institutional form required. Applicants notified on a rolling basis starting 4/1; must reply by 5/1 or within 2 week(s) of notification.

**Academics. Special study options:** Distance learning, double major, dual enrollment of high school students, independent study, internships, student-designed major, study abroad, teacher certification program, Washington semester. **Credit/placement by examination:** AP, CLEP, institutional tests. 30 credit hours maximum toward associate degree, 36 toward bachelor's. **Support services:** Learning center, reduced course load, remedial instruction, study skills assistance, tutoring, writing center.

**Majors. Biology:** General. **Business:** General, business admin. **Communications:** General. **Computer sciences:** General, computer science. **Education:** Business, elementary, English, mathematics, music, physical, science, social studies. **English:** English lit. **History:** General. **Interdisciplinary:** Behavioral sciences. **Math:** General. **Parks/recreation:** Exercise sciences. **Philosophy/religion:** Christian. **Physical sciences:** Chemistry. **Psychology:** General. **Social sciences:** General, political science. **Theology:** Bible, missionary, sacred music, theology.

**Computing on campus.** 30 workstations in library, computer center, student center. Dormitories wired for high-speed internet access and linked to campus network. Online library, helpline, repair service, wireless network available.

**Student life. Freshman orientation:** Mandatory, $100 fee. Preregistration for classes offered. **Policies:** Religious observance required. **Housing:** Guaranteed on-campus for all undergraduates. Single-sex dorms, apartments, substance-free housing available. $200 fully refundable deposit. **Activities:** Bands, campus ministries, choral groups, music ensembles, student government, student newspaper, campus missionary fellowship, theology fellowship, Fellowship of Christian Athletes, Operation Saturation, Sudan fellowship, College Republicans.

**Athletics.** NAIA, NCCAA. **Intercollegiate:** Baseball M, basketball, cross-country, golf M, soccer, tennis, track and field, volleyball W. **Intramural:** Badminton, basketball, football (non-tackle), racquetball, softball, table tennis, volleyball. **Team name:** Eagles.

**Student services.** Adult student services, campus ministries, career counseling, student employment services, financial aid counseling, health services, placement for graduates, veterans' counselor.

**Contact.** E-mail: admissions@okwu.edu
Phone: (918) 335-6219 Toll-free number: (800) 468-6292
Fax: (918) 335-6229
Robert Myers, Executive Vice President, Oklahoma Wesleyan University, 2201 Silver Lake Road, Bartlesville, OK 74006

## Oral Roberts University

Tulsa, Oklahoma
www.oru.edu

**CB member**
**CB code: 6552**

- Private 4-year university and liberal arts college affiliated with nondenominational tradition
- Residential campus in large city
- 2,714 degree-seeking undergraduates: 9% part-time, 59% women
- 456 degree-seeking graduate students
- 75% of applicants admitted
- SAT or ACT (ACT writing optional), application essay required
- 54% graduate within 6 years

**General.** Founded in 1965. Regionally accredited. Integrated math and science academy sponsored by Oklahoma State Regents for Higher Education. **Degrees:** 551 bachelor's awarded; master's, doctoral, first professional

offered. **ROTC:** Air Force. **Location:** 7 miles from downtown. **Calendar:** Semester, limited summer session. **Full-time faculty:** 191 total; 62% have terminal degrees, 14% minority, 40% women. **Part-time faculty:** 101 total; 16% have terminal degrees, 16% minority, 52% women. **Class size:** 62% < 20, 32% 20-39, 2% 40-49, 3% 50-99, less than 1% >100. **Special facilities:** Prayer tower, mineralogical museum.

**Freshman class profile.** 1,201 applied, 904 admitted, 604 enrolled.

| Mid 50% test scores | | | |
|---|---|---|---|
| SAT critical reading: | 480-600 | GPA 2.0-2.99: | 19% |
| SAT math: | 440-580 | Rank in top quarter: | 45% |
| ACT composite: | 20-25 | Rank in top tenth: | 25% |
| GPA 3.50 or higher: | 49% | Return as sophomores: | 77% |
| GPA 3.0-3.49: | 31% | Out-of-state: | 73% |
| | | Live on campus: | 75% |

**Basis for selection.** Academic record, test scores, personal essay, minister's recommendation, other recommendations, extracurricular activities considered. Students must provide immunization records. Interview recommended for all; audition required for music program; portfolio recommended for art program. **Homeschooled:** Under special circumstances, applicants may be required to submit additional curricular information and/or proof of high school equivalency.

**High school preparation.** 16 units recommended. Recommended units include English 4, mathematics 2, social studies 2, science 1 (laboratory 1), foreign language 2 and academic electives 4. Students matriculating in a bachelor of science program may substitute additional mathematics for foreign language.

**2007-2008 Annual costs.** Tuition/fees: $17,400. Room/board: $7,350. Books/supplies: $1,500. Personal expenses: $1,500.

**2007-2008 Financial aid. Need-based:** 394 full-time freshmen applied for aid; 344 were judged to have need; 344 of these received aid. Average need met was 93%. Average scholarship/grant was $9,086; average loan $9,682. 19% of total undergraduate aid awarded as scholarships/grants, 81% as loans/jobs. **Non-need-based:** Awarded to 1,191 full-time undergraduates, including 208 freshmen. Scholarships awarded for academics, art, athletics, job skills, leadership, music/drama.

**Application procedures. Admission:** No deadline. $35 fee, may be waived for applicants with need. Application may be submitted online. Admission notification on a rolling basis. **Financial aid:** Priority date 3/15; no closing date. FAFSA required. Applicants notified on a rolling basis starting 2/15; must reply by 7/15.

**Academics.** An Academic Peer Advisor lives on each dorm wing and is available day and evening . **Special study options:** Accelerated study, combined bachelor's/graduate degree, distance learning, double major, dual enrollment of high school students, ESL, external degree, honors, independent study, internships, liberal arts/career combination, student-designed major, study abroad, teacher certification program, Washington semester, weekend college. **Credit/placement by examination:** AP, CLEP, institutional tests. 30 credit hours maximum toward associate degree, 30 toward bachelor's. **Support services:** Learning center, reduced course load, remedial instruction, study skills assistance, tutoring.

**Majors. Biology:** General, biochemistry. **Business:** Accounting, business admin, finance, international, international marketing, management information systems, management science, marketing, organizational behavior. **Communications:** General. **Computer sciences:** General, computer science. **Education:** Art, business, early childhood, elementary, English, foreign languages, health, mathematics, music, physical, science, social studies, Spanish, special. **Engineering:** General, biomedical, computer, electrical, mechanical, physics. **English:** Composition, English lit. **Foreign languages:** French, German, Spanish. **Health:** Clinical lab science, nursing (RN). **History:** General. **Liberal arts:** Arts/sciences. **Math:** General. **Parks/recreation:** Exercise sciences, facilities management, health/fitness. **Physical sciences:** Chemistry, physics. **Psychology:** General. **Public administration:** Social work. **Social sciences:** International relations, political science. **Theology:** Bible, missionary, pastoral counseling, religious ed, sacred music, theology. **Visual/performing arts:** Acting, art, commercial/advertising art, dance, design, dramatic, music performance, music theory/composition, piano/organ, studio arts, theater design, voice/opera.

**Most popular majors.** Business/marketing 26%, communications/journalism 11%, education 9%, health sciences 6%, psychology 6%, theological studies 12%, visual/performing arts 6%.

**Computing on campus.** 382 workstations in library, computer center. Dormitories linked to campus network. Commuter students can connect to campus network. Online course registration, online library, wireless network available.

**Student life. Freshman orientation:** Mandatory. Preregistration for classes offered. **Policies:** Single undergraduate students under 25 years of age must live in university housing or with parents. Religious observance required. **Housing:** Guaranteed on-campus for all undergraduates. Single-sex dorms, special housing for disabled, substance-free housing available. $125 nonrefundable deposit. **Activities:** Bands, campus ministries, choral groups, dance, drama, film society, international student organizations, literary magazine, music ensembles, musical theater, opera, radio station, student government, student newspaper, symphony orchestra, TV station, community outreach, international students association, missions club, Young Republicans, Young Democrats, student activist society, Model United Nations.

**Athletics.** NCAA. **Intercollegiate:** Baseball M, basketball, cross-country, golf, soccer, tennis, track and field, volleyball W. **Intramural:** Badminton, basketball, bowling, cross-country, football (non-tackle), golf, racquetball, softball, swimming, table tennis, tennis, volleyball, wrestling M. **Team name:** Golden Eagles.

**Student services.** Campus ministries, career counseling, student employment services, financial aid counseling, health services, personal counseling, placement for graduates, veterans' counselor. **Physically disabled:** Services for visually, speech, hearing impaired.

**Contact.** E-mail: admissions@oru.edu
Phone: (918) 496-6518 Toll-free number: (800) 678-8876
Fax: (918) 495-6222
Chris Belcher, Director of Admissions, Oral Roberts University, 7777 South Lewis Avenue, Tulsa, OK 74171

## Rogers State University
**Claremore, Oklahoma**
www.rsu.edu                      CB code: 6545

- ◆ Public 4-year university
- ◆ Commuter campus in large town
- ◆ 3,806 degree-seeking undergraduates: 42% part-time, 64% women, 3% African American, 1% Asian American, 3% Hispanic American, 28% Native American

**General.** Founded in 1909. Regionally accredited. **Degrees:** 155 bachelor's, 182 associate awarded. **ROTC:** Air Force. **Location:** 25 miles from Tulsa. **Calendar:** Semester, extensive summer session. **Full-time faculty:** 99 total. **Part-time faculty:** 113 total. **Class size:** 50% < 20, 46% 20-39, 4% 40-49, less than 1% 50-99. **Special facilities:** Conservation education reserve.

**Freshman class profile.**

| Mid 50% test scores | | Rank in top quarter: | 25% |
|---|---|---|---|
| ACT composite: | 17-22 | Rank in top tenth: | 8% |
| GPA 3.50 or higher: | 27% | Out-of-state: | 2% |
| GPA 3.0-3.49: | 30% | Live on campus: | 4% |
| GPA 2.0-2.99: | 39% | International: | 1% |

**Basis for selection.** Open admission, but selective for some programs. Bachelor degree programs require minimum ACT score of 20 and no curricular deficiencies. Open admission for associate degree programs. TOEFL required of students who are not native speakers of English. Essay required for returning suspension students only.

**High school preparation.** 15 units required; 17 recommended. Required and recommended units include English 4, mathematics 3, social studies 2, history 3, science 2 (laboratory 2) foreign language 2 and academic electives 3. Math should include algebra I and II; 1 computer science also recommended; history should include 1 unit of U.S. history and 1 of citizenship (government, geography, etc.).

**2007-2008 Annual costs.** Tuition/fees: $3,893; $8,858 out-of-state. Books/supplies: $700. Personal expenses: $1,200.

**Financial aid. Non-need-based:** Scholarships awarded for academics, athletics, leadership, music/drama.

**Application procedures. Admission:** No deadline. No application fee. Application may be submitted online. Admission notification on a rolling basis. **Financial aid:** Priority date 3/1; no closing date. FAFSA, institutional form required. Applicants notified on a rolling basis starting 4/1; must reply within 3 week(s) of notification.

**Academics. Special study options:** Cooperative education, distance learning, double major, dual enrollment of high school students, honors, independent study, internships, liberal arts/career combination. **Credit/placement by examination:** AP, CLEP, IB, institutional tests. 30 credit hours maximum toward associate degree, 45 toward bachelor's. **Support services:** Learning center, reduced course load, remedial instruction, study skills assistance, tutoring, writing center.

**Majors. Biology:** General. **Business:** Business admin. **Communications:** Broadcast journalism. **Computer sciences:** General. **Engineering technology:** Manufacturing. **History:** General. **Liberal arts:** Arts/sciences. **Protective services:** Law enforcement admin. **Psychology:** General. **Social sciences:** General.

**Most popular majors.** Biology 7%, business/marketing 39%, engineering/engineering technologies 16%, liberal arts 10%, social sciences 23%.

**Computing on campus.** 320 workstations in dormitories, library. Dormitories wired for high-speed internet access and linked to campus network. Online library, wireless network available.

**Student life. Freshman orientation:** Available. Preregistration for classes offered. **Housing:** Coed dorms, special housing for disabled, apartments, substance-free housing available. $200 fully refundable deposit. **Activities:** Drama, radio station, student government, TV station, Native American association, Baptist campus ministries, Defenders of Mother Earth, student art association, criminal justice association, student nursing association, Society for Computing and Business Machines, horse and agriculture club.

**Athletics.** NAIA. **Intercollegiate:** Baseball M, basketball, cheerleading, rodeo, soccer, softball W. **Intramural:** Basketball, bowling, football (non-tackle), soccer, softball, volleyball. **Team name:** Hillcats.

**Student services.** Adult student services, career counseling, services for economically disadvantaged, student employment services, financial aid counseling, health services, on-campus daycare, personal counseling, placement for graduates, veterans' counselor. **Physically disabled:** Services for visually, hearing impaired.

**Contact.** E-mail: admissions@rsu.edu
Phone: (918) 343-7546 Toll-free number: (800) 256-7511
Fax: (918) 343-7595
Lindsay Fields, Director of Enrollment Management, Rogers State University, 1701 West Will Rogers Boulevard, Claremore, OK 74017

## St. Gregory's University
**Shawnee, Oklahoma**
www.stgregorys.edu                      CB code: 6621

- ◆ Private 4-year university and liberal arts college affiliated with Roman Catholic Church
- ◆ Residential campus in large town
- ◆ 750 degree-seeking undergraduates: 47% part-time, 63% women, 7% African American, 7% Hispanic American, 8% Native American, 6% international
- ◆ 44 degree-seeking graduate students
- ◆ 72% of applicants admitted
- ◆ SAT or ACT (ACT writing optional), application essay required

**General.** Founded in 1875. Regionally accredited. A private institution in the Roman Catholic and Benedictine tradition. **Degrees:** 128 bachelor's, 43 associate awarded; master's offered. **ROTC:** Air Force. **Location:** 30 miles from Oklahoma City. **Calendar:** Semester, limited summer session. **Full-time faculty:** 39 total; 62% have terminal degrees, 5% minority, 46% women. **Part-time faculty:** 88 total; 23% have terminal degrees, 6% minority, 52% women. **Class size:** 93% < 20, 7% 20-39. **Special facilities:** Benedictine abbey, art museum.

**Freshman class profile.** 273 applied, 196 admitted, 84 enrolled.

| Mid 50% test scores | | Rank in top quarter: | 23% |
|---|---|---|---|
| SAT critical reading: | 430-560 | Rank in top tenth: | 13% |
| SAT math: | 440-500 | End year in good standing: | 91% |
| ACT composite: | 18-23 | Return as sophomores: | 58% |
| GPA 3.50 or higher: | 36% | Out-of-state: | 21% |
| GPA 3.0-3.49: | 36% | International: | 4% |
| GPA 2.0-2.99: | 28% | | |

**Basis for selection.** Core classes, GPA most important; test scores, class rank important. Interview required for students admitted on probation; audition required for dance, drama, and choral scholarships; portfolio required for art scholarships. **Homeschooled:** Interview required. **Learning Disabled:** Students with need beyond ADA standards may apply to Partners in Learning Program. Additional fee of approximately $7,000 required if admitted.

**High school preparation.** 17 units recommended. Recommended units include English 4, mathematics 3, social studies 2, history 2, science 2 (laboratory 2) and foreign language 2.

**2007-2008 Annual costs.** Tuition/fees: $14,710. Room/board: $6,150. Books/supplies: $900. Personal expenses: $2,000.

**2006-2007 Financial aid. Need-based:** 71 full-time freshmen applied for aid; 71 were judged to have need; 70 of these received aid. Average need met was 66%. Average scholarship/grant was $6,380; average loan $3,264. 37% of total undergraduate aid awarded as scholarships/grants, 63% as loans/jobs. **Non-need-based:** Awarded to 429 full-time undergraduates, including 113 freshmen. Scholarships awarded for academics, alumni affiliation, art, athletics, job skills, leadership, music/drama, religious affiliation.

**Application procedures. Admission:** Priority date 8/1; no deadline. $25 fee, may be waived for applicants with need. Application may be submitted online. Admission notification on a rolling basis. **Financial aid:** Priority date 4/1; no closing date. FAFSA, institutional form required. Applicants notified on a rolling basis starting 2/15; must reply within 3 week(s) of notification.

**Academics.** Tradition and Conversation seminars, a 4 semester, chronologically ordered sequence of discussion-based seminars on Western and Catholic intellectual traditions, required of all freshmen and sophomore students. Special accelerated programs for non-traditional students in Shawnee and Tulsa, Oklahoma. **Special study options:** Accelerated study, cooperative education, double major, ESL, honors, independent study, internships, student-designed major, study abroad, teacher certification program. **Credit/placement by examination:** AP, CLEP, IB, SAT, ACT, institutional tests. 12 credit hours maximum toward associate degree, 30 toward bachelor's. Course proficiency exams available in areas where no CLEP exams offered. **Support services:** Learning center, remedial instruction, study skills assistance, tutoring.

**Majors. Business:** Business admin. **Education:** General, elementary, secondary. **English:** English lit. **Interdisciplinary:** Natural sciences. **Liberal arts:** Arts/sciences, humanities. **Social sciences:** General. **Theology:** Theology.

**Most popular majors.** Business/marketing 43%, education 8%, liberal arts 9%, social sciences 15%.

**Computing on campus.** PC or laptop required. 60 workstations in dormitories, library, computer center, student center. Dormitories wired for high-speed internet access and linked to campus network. Commuter students can connect to campus network. Online library, helpline, repair service, student web hosting, wireless network available.

**Student life. Freshman orientation:** Mandatory. Preregistration for classes offered. Prior to start of fall term, 3 days plus evenings in first week of fall semester. **Policies:** Smoke-free; alcohol/drug-free; on-campus residency required under age 22. **Housing:** Guaranteed on-campus for freshmen. Single-sex dorms, substance-free housing available. $100 fully refundable deposit. **Activities:** Jazz band, choral groups, dance, drama, student government, student newspaper, Knights of Columbus, academic honor society, Fellowship of Christian Athletes, Buckley Retreat Team, history club, student alumni council, Students in Free Enterprise, Hispanic awareness student association.

**Athletics.** NAIA. **Intercollegiate:** Baseball M, basketball, cross-country, golf, soccer, softball W, volleyball W. **Intramural:** Basketball, football (non-tackle), racquetball, soccer, softball, table tennis, tennis, volleyball. **Team name:** Cavaliers.

**Student services.** Adult student services, alcohol/substance abuse counseling, campus ministries, career counseling, services for economically disadvantaged, student employment services, financial aid counseling, minority student services, personal counseling, placement for graduates, veterans' counselor. **Learning disabled:** Comprehensive services available.

**Contact.** E-mail: admissions@stgregorys.edu
Phone: (405) 878-5444 Toll-free number: (888) 784-7347
Fax: (405) 878-5198
Bill Halbach, Director of Admissions, St. Gregory's University, 1900 West MacArthur Drive, Shawnee, OK 74804

## Southeastern Oklahoma State University
**Durant, Oklahoma**
**www.sosu.edu**
**CB code: 6657**

- Public 4-year liberal arts and teachers college
- Commuter campus in large town
- 3,585 degree-seeking undergraduates: 21% part-time, 55% women
- 320 degree-seeking graduate students
- 72% of applicants admitted
- SAT or ACT (ACT writing optional) required
- 31% graduate within 6 years

**General.** Founded in 1909. Regionally accredited. Degree programs offered through satellite campus at Idabel and Higher Education Centers at Ardmore, McAlester, Tinker Air Force Base, Oklahoma City Community College, and Grayson County College. **Degrees:** 556 bachelor's awarded; master's offered. **Location:** 90 miles from Dallas, Texas. **Calendar:** Semester, extensive summer session. **Full-time faculty:** 142 total; 72% have terminal degrees, 20% minority, 38% women. **Part-time faculty:** 96 total; 23% have terminal degrees, 22% minority, 50% women. **Class size:** 47% < 20, 44% 20-39, 8% 40-49, 2% 50-99. **Special facilities:** Herbarium, equestrian facilities.

**Freshman class profile.** 1,130 applied, 810 admitted, 665 enrolled.

| Mid 50% test scores | | Rank in top quarter: | 43% |
|---|---|---|---|
| ACT composite: | 18-23 | Rank in top tenth: | 15% |
| GPA 3.50 or higher: | 40% | Out-of-state: | 23% |
| GPA 3.0-3.49: | 36% | Live on campus: | 51% |
| GPA 2.0-2.99: | 24% | International: | 1% |

**Basis for selection.** High school transcript and test scores important. Must have 2.7 GPA and rank in top half of class, 20 ACT or 940 SAT (exclusive of Writing), score in top half on ACT scores, or attain 2.7 GPA in 15 core units. Audition required for drama, music programs. Interview required for alternative admissions. **Homeschooled:** ACT score of 20 required.

**High school preparation.** 15 units required. Required and recommended units include English 4, mathematics 3, social studies 1, history 3, science 2 (laboratory 2), foreign language 1, computer science 1 and academic electives 3. One citizenship required.

**2007-2008 Annual costs.** Tuition/fees: $3,926; $9,720 out-of-state. Room/board: $4,530. Books/supplies: $800. Personal expenses: $1,447.

**2006-2007 Financial aid. Need-based:** 434 full-time freshmen applied for aid; 407 were judged to have need; 398 of these received aid. Average need met was 64%. Average scholarship/grant was $1,055; average loan $1,199. 58% of total undergraduate aid awarded as scholarships/grants, 42% as loans/jobs. **Non-need-based:** Awarded to 632 full-time undergraduates, including 232 freshmen. Scholarships awarded for academics, alumni affiliation, art, athletics, leadership, minority status, music/drama.

**Application procedures. Admission:** No deadline. $20 fee. Application may be submitted online. Admission notification on a rolling basis. **Financial aid:** Priority date 3/1; no closing date. FAFSA, institutional form required. Applicants notified on a rolling basis starting 4/15; must reply within 2 week(s) of notification.

**Academics.** Programs in aviation, ecology, energy, health-related sciences, and criminology. **Special study options:** Combined bachelor's/graduate degree, distance learning, double major, honors, independent study, internships, teacher certification program. **Credit/placement by examination:** AP, CLEP, IB, SAT, ACT, institutional tests. 60 credit hours maximum toward bachelor's degree. **Support services:** Learning center, pre-admission summer program, reduced course load, remedial instruction, study skills assistance, tutoring, writing center.

**Majors. Biology:** General, biotechnology. **Business:** Accounting, business admin, finance, management science, marketing. **Communications:** General. **Computer sciences:** General, information systems. **Conservation:** General, environmental science. **Education:** Art, elementary, English, mathematics, music, physical, science, secondary, social studies, Spanish, special. **Engineering:** Aerospace. **Engineering technology:** Occupational safety. **English:** English lit. **Foreign languages:** Spanish. **History:** General. **Math:** General. **Mechanic/repair:** Aircraft. **Parks/recreation:** General. **Physical sciences:** Chemistry. **Protective services:** Criminal justice. **Psychology:** General. **Social sciences:** Political science, sociology. **Transportation:** Airline/commercial pilot. **Visual/performing arts:** Art, dramatic, graphic design, music performance.

**Most popular majors.** Biology 6%, business/marketing 8%, education 25%, engineering/engineering technologies 10%, liberal arts 9%, parks/recreation 6%, psychology 7%.

**Computing on campus.** 2,138 workstations in dormitories, library, computer center, student center. Dormitories wired for high-speed internet access and linked to campus network. Commuter students can connect to campus network. Online course registration, online library, helpline, student web hosting, wireless network available.

**Student life. Freshman orientation:** Available, $20 fee. Preregistration for classes offered. **Policies:** No alcohol at university events on/off campus. **Housing:** Coed dorms, single-sex dorms, special housing for disabled available. $100 nonrefundable deposit. **Activities:** Bands, campus ministries, choral groups, dance, drama, international student organizations, literary magazine, music ensembles, musical theater, opera, radio station, student government, student newspaper, Black American Society, Wesley Center, student Bible center, Chi Alpha, Young Democrats, College Republicans, Muslim student association.

**Athletics.** NCAA. **Intercollegiate:** Baseball M, basketball, cross-country W, football (tackle) M, golf M, rodeo, softball W, tennis, volleyball W. **Intramural:** Basketball, bowling, football (non-tackle), football (tackle) M, rodeo, soccer, softball, volleyball W. **Team name:** Savage Storm.

**Student services.** Adult student services, alcohol/substance abuse counseling, campus ministries, career counseling, student employment services, financial aid counseling, health services, minority student services, personal counseling, placement for graduates, veterans' counselor. **Physically disabled:** Services for visually, speech, hearing impaired.

**Contact.** E-mail: admissions@sosu.edu
Phone: (580) 745-2060 Toll-free number: (800) 435-1327 ext. 2060
Fax: (580) 745-7502
Kristie Luke, Associate Dean of Admissions and Records/Registrar, Southeastern Oklahoma State University, 1405 North Fourth Avenue, PMB 4225, Durant, OK 74701-0607

---

## Southern Nazarene University
### Bethany, Oklahoma
**www.snu.edu**

CB member
CB code: 6036

- Private 4-year university and liberal arts college affiliated with Church of the Nazarene
- Residential campus in large town
- 1,665 degree-seeking undergraduates: 3% part-time, 49% women
- 425 degree-seeking graduate students

**General.** Founded in 1899. Regionally accredited. **Degrees:** 559 bachelor's, 2 associate awarded; master's offered. **ROTC:** Army, Air Force. **Location:** 10 miles from Oklahoma City. **Calendar:** Semester, limited summer session. **Full-time faculty:** 85 total. **Part-time faculty:** 60 total. **Special facilities:** Human cadaver laboratory, physics laser laboratory, laboratory school for children.

**Freshman class profile.** 320 enrolled.

**Basis for selection.** Open admission. Students admitted on probation if high school GPA below 2.5, composite ACT below 17, combined SAT below 700 (exclusive of Writing), or high school rank 40 percent or below. No test scores required for placement if student has 24 or more transfer credit hours or is over 25 years old. Interview recommended for all; audition recommended for music program. **Homeschooled:** Transcript of courses and grades required.

**High school preparation.** 13 units recommended. Recommended units include English 4, mathematics 3, social studies 2, science 2 and foreign language 2. One computer course recommended.

**2007-2008 Annual costs.** Tuition/fees: $15,924. Room/board: $5,620. Books/supplies: $600. Personal expenses: $1,200.

**Financial aid. Non-need-based:** Scholarships awarded for academics, athletics, ROTC, state residency.

**Application procedures. Admission:** Priority date 5/1; deadline 8/1. $25 fee, may be waived for applicants with need. Application may be submitted online. Admission notification on a rolling basis. **Financial aid:** Priority date 3/1; no closing date. FAFSA, institutional form required. Applicants notified on a rolling basis starting 5/1; must reply within 2 week(s) of notification.

**Academics. Special study options:** Combined bachelor's/graduate degree, distance learning, double major, dual enrollment of high school students, external degree, honors, independent study, internships, liberal arts/career combination, student-designed major, study abroad, teacher certification program, urban semester, Washington semester. **Credit/placement by examination:** AP, CLEP, IB, SAT, ACT, institutional tests. 30 credit hours maximum toward bachelor's degree. **Support services:** Remedial instruction, study skills assistance, tutoring, writing center.

**Majors. Area/ethnic studies:** American. **Biology:** General, biochemistry. **Business:** General, accounting, business admin, finance, marketing. **Communications:** General, journalism. **Communications technology:** General. **Computer sciences:** General, networking. **Conservation:** General. **Education:** General, early childhood, elementary, English, history, mathematics, music, physical, reading, science, secondary, Spanish, speech. **English:** English lit, speech/rhetoric. **Foreign languages:** Spanish. **Health:** Athletic training, clinical lab technology. **History:** General. **Interdisciplinary:** Behavioral sciences. **Legal studies:** Prelaw. **Liberal arts:** Arts/sciences. **Math:**

General. **Parks/recreation:** Exercise sciences. **Philosophy/religion:** Philosophy, religion. **Physical sciences:** Chemistry, physics. **Protective services:** Criminal justice. **Psychology:** General. **Social sciences:** General, political science, sociology. **Theology:** Missionary, religious ed, sacred music, theology. **Transportation:** Aviation management. **Visual/performing arts:** General, graphic design.

**Most popular majors.** Business/marketing 47%, health sciences 11%, psychology 12%.

**Computing on campus.** 120 workstations in library, computer center. Dormitories wired for high-speed internet access and linked to campus network. Helpline, repair service, wireless network available.

**Student life. Freshman orientation:** Mandatory. Preregistration for classes offered. **Policies:** Religious observance required. **Housing:** Guaranteed on-campus for freshmen. Single-sex dorms, apartments available. $50 deposit, deadline 8/1. Single students under 23 required to live on campus or with relatives. **Activities:** Bands, choral groups, drama, film society, music ensembles, student government, student newspaper, symphony orchestra, TV station, Gospel Team, Mission Crusaders, Circle-K, Spanish Club, Mortar Board.

**Athletics.** NAIA. **Intercollegiate:** Baseball M, basketball, cheerleading, cross-country, equestrian, football (tackle) M, golf, soccer, softball W, tennis, track and field, volleyball W. **Intramural:** Basketball, football (non-tackle), football (tackle) M, softball, tennis, track and field, volleyball. **Team name:** Crimson Storm.

**Student services.** Alcohol/substance abuse counseling, campus ministries, career counseling, services for economically disadvantaged, student employment services, financial aid counseling, health services, personal counseling, placement for graduates. **Physically disabled:** Services for visually, speech, hearing impaired.

**Contact.** E-mail: wrogers@snu.edu
Phone: (405) 491-6324 Toll-free number: (800) 648-9899
Fax: (405) 491-6320
Warren Rogers, Director of Admissions, Southern Nazarene University, 6729 NW 39th Expressway, Bethany, OK 73008

---

## Southwestern Christian University
### Bethany, Oklahoma
**www.swcu.edu**

CB code: 1433

- Private 4-year Bible college affiliated with Pentecostal Holiness Church
- Residential campus in large town
- 178 degree-seeking undergraduates: 6% part-time, 50% women
- 86 degree-seeking graduate students
- SAT or ACT with writing, application essay, interview required

**General.** Founded in 1946. Regionally accredited. **Degrees:** 28 bachelor's, 8 associate awarded; master's offered. **Location:** 10 miles from Oklahoma City. **Calendar:** Semester, limited summer session. **Full-time faculty:** 8 total; 25% have terminal degrees, 12% minority, 62% women. **Part-time faculty:** 26 total; 38% have terminal degrees, 15% minority, 42% women.

**Freshman class profile.**

| | | | |
|---|---|---|---|
| Out-of-state: | 13% | Live on campus: | 62% |

**Basis for selection.** Must have either 2.5 GPA or ACT score of 19. Written score of 6. Additonal materials and interview may be requested.

**High school preparation.** Required units include English 4, mathematics 2, social studies 2, history 2, science 2 (laboratory 2).

**2007-2008 Annual costs.** Tuition/fees: $9,020. Adult education program $320 per credit hour. Room/board: $4,400. Books/supplies: $750. Personal expenses: $1,100.

**Financial aid. Non-need-based:** Scholarships awarded for academics, alumni affiliation, leadership, music/drama, religious affiliation.

**Application procedures. Admission:** No deadline. No application fee. Application must be submitted on paper. Admission notification on a rolling basis. **Financial aid:** Priority date 8/1; no closing date. FAFSA required. Applicants notified on a rolling basis starting 5/1; must reply within 2 week(s) of notification.

**Academics.** Applied Biblical Leadership Education (ABLE), an adult studies completion program. **Special study options:** Accelerated study, cross-registration, double major, dual enrollment of high school students, honors, independent study, internships, liberal arts/career combination. **Credit/ placement by examination:** AP, CLEP, institutional tests. 30 credit hours maximum toward bachelor's degree. **Support services:** Learning center, reduced course load, remedial instruction, tutoring.

**Majors. Business:** Business admin. **Philosophy/religion:** Religion. **Theology:** Bible, missionary, pastoral counseling, religious ed, sacred music, theology, youth ministry. **Visual/performing arts:** Music performance.

**Computing on campus.** 9 workstations in library. Dormitories wired for high-speed internet access and linked to campus network. Online library, wireless network available.

**Student life. Freshman orientation:** Mandatory. Preregistration for classes offered. Held the week prior to classes; includes academic, financial aid and spiritual life orientation. **Policies:** Extracurricular Christian programs and activities emphasized. Mandatory dress code. Students sign lifestyle covenant agreeing to certain behaviors. Religious observance required. **Housing:** Single-sex dorms available. $100 nonrefundable deposit, deadline 8/15. **Activities:** Choral groups, drama, music ensembles, musical theater, student government, student newspaper, Southwestern Ministerial Association, Robert Hough Missionary Society, Christian Education Association.

**Athletics.** NCCAA. **Intercollegiate:** Basketball M, cross-country, golf M, soccer M, softball, volleyball W. **Intramural:** Baseball M, basketball, cheerleading, football (non-tackle) M, softball, table tennis, volleyball. **Team name:** Eagles.

**Student services.** Adult student services, campus ministries, career counseling, student employment services, financial aid counseling, personal counseling, placement for graduates, veterans' counselor.

**Contact.** E-mail: megan.miles@swcu.edu
Phone: (405) 789-7661 ext. 3442 Toll-free number: (888) 418-9272
Fax: (405) 495-0078
Director of Admissions, Southwestern Christian University, Box 340, Bethany, OK 73008

---

## Southwestern Oklahoma State University

**Weatherford, Oklahoma**   **CB member**
**www.swosu.edu**   **CB code: 6673**

- Public 4-year university
- Residential campus in large town
- 4,146 degree-seeking undergraduates: 12% part-time, 59% women, 5% African American, 1% Asian American, 5% Hispanic American, 7% Native American, 3% international
- 738 graduate students
- 90% of applicants admitted
- SAT or ACT (ACT writing optional) required
- 36% graduate within 6 years

**General.** Founded in 1901. Regionally accredited. Campus at Sayre offers lower division and remedial courses, as well as associate degrees. **Degrees:** 629 bachelor's, 124 associate awarded; master's, first professional offered. **Location:** 75 miles from Oklahoma City. **Calendar:** Semester, extensive summer session. **Full-time faculty:** 215 total; 58% have terminal degrees, 10% minority, 42% women. **Part-time faculty:** 15 total. **Class size:** 43% < 20, 42% 20-39, 8% 40-49, 6% 50-99.

**Freshman class profile.** 1,425 applied, 1,284 admitted, 917 enrolled.

| Mid 50% test scores | | Rank in top tenth: | 19% |
|---|---|---|---|
| ACT composite: | 18-24 | Return as sophomores: | 64% |
| GPA 3.50 or higher: | 48% | Out-of-state: | 9% |
| GPA 3.0-3.49: | 27% | Live on campus: | 55% |
| GPA 2.0-2.99: | 24% | International: | 1% |
| Rank in top quarter: | 38% | | |

**Basis for selection.** Bachelor degree programs require minimum ACT score of 19 and no curricular deficiencies. Open admission for certificate and associate degree programs. Last date to submit test scores is first day of classes. Essay required for returning suspension students only.

**High school preparation.** 15 units required; 17 recommended. Required and recommended units include English 4, mathematics 3, social studies 1, history 2, science 2 (laboratory 2), computer science 1 and academic electives 2-4. Social studies unit must be citizenship. Academic electives should be in fine arts. 3 units computer science or foreign language required.

**2007-2008 Annual costs.** Tuition/fees: $3,750; $8,550 out-of-state. Room/board: $4,700. Books/supplies: $1,230. Personal expenses: $996.

**2007-2008 Financial aid. Need-based:** 665 full-time freshmen applied for aid; 500 were judged to have need; 494 of these received aid. Average need met was 92%. Average scholarship/grant was $1,172; average loan $1,422. 46% of total undergraduate aid awarded as scholarships/grants, 54% as loans/jobs. **Non-need-based:** Scholarships awarded for academics, alumni affiliation, art, athletics, job skills, leadership, music/drama, state residency.

**Application procedures. Admission:** No deadline. $15 fee. Admission notification on a rolling basis. **Financial aid:** Priority date 3/1; no closing date. FAFSA, institutional form required. Applicants notified on a rolling basis starting 1/1.

**Academics. Special study options:** Accelerated study, combined bachelor's/graduate degree, distance learning, double major, independent study, internships, student-designed major, teacher certification program, weekend college. Weekend college for nursing only. **Credit/placement by examination:** AP, CLEP, IB, ACT, institutional tests. 62 credit hours maximum toward bachelor's degree. **Support services:** Pre-admission summer program, reduced course load, remedial instruction, study skills assistance, tutoring, writing center.

**Majors. Biology:** General, biophysics. **Business:** General, accounting, business admin, human resources, management information systems. **Communications:** General. **Computer sciences:** General, computer science, information systems. **Education:** Art, early childhood, elementary, English, health, history, learning disabled, mathematics, mentally handicapped, music, physical, science, social science, special, technology/industrial arts. **Engineering:** General, physics. **Engineering technology:** Manufacturing. **English:** English lit. **Health:** Athletic training, clinical lab technology, health care admin, medical records admin, music therapy, nursing (RN). **History:** General. **Math:** General. **Parks/recreation:** General, facilities management. **Physical sciences:** Chemistry, physics. **Protective services:** Criminal justice. **Psychology:** General. **Public administration:** Social work. **Social sciences:** Political science, sociology. **Theology:** Sacred music. **Visual/performing arts:** Commercial/advertising art, music management, music performance, music theory/composition, piano/organ, voice/opera.

**Most popular majors.** Business/marketing 20%, education 20%, health sciences 19%, parks/recreation 10%, visual/performing arts 7%.

**Computing on campus.** 200 workstations in library, computer center. Dormitories wired for high-speed internet access. Commuter students can connect to campus network. Online library, wireless network available.

**Student life. Freshman orientation:** Mandatory, $60 fee. Preregistration for classes offered. Class meets 1 hour per week for the first 8 weeks of the fall semester. **Housing:** Guaranteed on-campus for all undergraduates. Single-sex dorms, apartments available. $60 fully refundable deposit, deadline 8/1. **Activities:** Bands, campus ministries, choral groups, drama, international student organizations, literary magazine, music ensembles, Model UN, musical theater, student government, student newspaper, symphony orchestra, 7 religious organizations, 4 political organizations, and approximately 75 social and professional clubs.

**Athletics.** NCAA. **Intercollegiate:** Baseball M, basketball, cheerleading, cross-country W, football (tackle) M, golf, rodeo, soccer, softball W. **Intramural:** Basketball, bowling, football (non-tackle), golf, racquetball, soccer, softball, swimming, tennis, volleyball. **Team name:** Bulldogs.

**Student services.** Adult student services, alcohol/substance abuse counseling, career counseling, student employment services, financial aid counseling, health services, personal counseling, placement for graduates, veterans' counselor. **Physically disabled:** Services for visually, hearing impaired.

**Contact.** E-mail: admissions@swosu.edu
Phone: (580) 774-3009 Fax: (580) 774-3795
Todd Boyd, Director of Admissions, Southwestern Oklahoma State University, 100 Campus Drive, Weatherford, OK 73096

---

## Spartan College of Aeronautics and Technology

**Tulsa, Oklahoma**
**www.spartan.edu**   **CB code: 0336**

- For-profit 4-year technical college
- Commuter campus in large city
- 953 degree-seeking undergraduates
- Interview required

**General.** Founded in 1928. Accredited by ACCSCT. Multicampus institution with 2 technical campuses at Tulsa International Airport and Jones Airport in South Tulsa. **Location:** 100 miles from Oklahoma City. **Calendar:** Differs by program, extensive summer session. **Full-time faculty:** 63 total; 5% have terminal degrees, 10% women. **Part-time faculty:** 31 total; 10% women. **Class size:** 63% < 20, 37% 20-39.

### Freshman class profile.

| | | | |
|---|---|---|---|
| Out-of-state: | 83% | Live on campus: | 25% |

**Basis for selection.** Applicanst must demonstrate proficiency in college-level skills by submission of examination scores deemed appropriate by Spartan for the chosen program of study. Students wishing to attend flight training must obtain an FAA Class II flight certificate. SAT or ACT recommended. **Homeschooled:** Statement describing homeschool structure and mission, transcript of courses and grades, state high school equivalency certificate, interview required.

**2007-2008 Annual costs.** Tech program tuition $13,200 per academic year; flight program tuition approximately $17,000 per academic year; bachelor's program tuition $10,359 per academic year. Books/tools and supplies vary by program. Books/supplies: $1,148. Personal expenses: $1,610.

**Application procedures. Admission:** No deadline. $100 fee. Admission notification on a rolling basis. **Financial aid:** No deadline. FAFSA, institutional form required. Applicants notified on a rolling basis starting 2/1; must reply within 2 week(s) of notification.

**Academics. Special study options:** Independent study. **Credit/placement by examination:** CLEP, institutional tests. No more than half of credits required for degree may be earned through examination. **Support services:** Remedial instruction, tutoring.

**Majors. Mechanic/repair:** Avionics. **Transportation:** Aviation management. **Other:** Aviation maintenance technician.

**Computing on campus.** 40 workstations in library, student center. Online library, wireless network available.

**Student life. Freshman orientation:** Mandatory. Usually held on Friday immediately preceding Monday start date of classes. **Housing:** Apartments, substance-free housing available. **Activities:** Student government, student newspaper.

**Athletics. Intramural:** Basketball M, bowling, soccer M, softball M, table tennis M, volleyball M.

**Student services.** Career counseling, student employment services, financial aid counseling, personal counseling, placement for graduates, veterans' counselor.

**Contact.** E-mail: spartan@mail.spartan.edu
Phone: (918) 836-6886 Toll-free number: (800) 331-1204
Fax: (918) 831-5287
Damon Bowling, Vice President, Marketing, Spartan College of Aeronautics and Technology, Box 582833, Tulsa, OK 74158-2833

## University of Central Oklahoma
**Edmond, Oklahoma**  **CB member**
**www.ucok.edu**  **CB code: 6091**

- Public 4-year university
- Commuter campus in small city
- 14,181 degree-seeking undergraduates: 30% part-time, 58% women, 10% African American, 3% Asian American, 4% Hispanic American, 5% Native American, 6% international
- 1,364 degree-seeking graduate students
- 72% of applicants admitted
- SAT or ACT (ACT writing optional) required

**General.** Founded in 1890. Regionally accredited. **Degrees:** 2,111 bachelor's awarded; master's offered. **ROTC:** Army. **Location:** 12 miles from Oklahoma City. **Calendar:** Semester, extensive summer session. **Full-time faculty:** 434 total; 72% have terminal degrees, 15% minority, 48% women. **Part-time faculty:** 514 total; 14% minority, 65% women. **Class size:** 30% < 20, 53% 20-39, 13% 40-49, 4% 50-99, less than 1% >100. **Special facilities:** Jazz lab.

**Freshman class profile.** 4,450 applied, 3,219 admitted, 2,112 enrolled.

| Mid 50% test scores | | Rank in top tenth: | 14% |
|---|---|---|---|
| ACT composite: | 19-23 | Out-of-state: | 2% |
| GPA 3.50 or higher: | 37% | Live on campus: | 41% |
| GPA 3.0-3.49: | 37% | International: | 8% |
| GPA 2.0-2.99: | 25% | Fraternities: | 12% |
| Rank in top quarter: | 33% | Sororities: | 9% |

**Basis for selection.** Must have 2.7 GPA and rank in top 50% of class, or 2.7 GPA in 15 unit high school core, or minimum enhanced ACT composite score of 20.

**High school preparation.** 15 units required; 16 recommended. Required and recommended units include English 4, mathematics 3-4, social studies 1, history 2, science 2-3 (laboratory 2-3), foreign language 2 and academic electives 3.

**2007-2008 Annual costs.** Tuition/fees: $3,857; $9,729 out-of-state. Room/board: $6,915. Books/supplies: $1,000. Personal expenses: $2,000.

**2006-2007 Financial aid. Need-based:** 1,198 full-time freshmen applied for aid; 886 were judged to have need; 815 of these received aid. Average need met was 63%. Average scholarship/grant was $5,651; average loan $2,300. 37% of total undergraduate aid awarded as scholarships/grants, 63% as loans/jobs. **Non-need-based:** Awarded to 1,221 full-time undergraduates, including 222 freshmen. Scholarships awarded for academics, alumni affiliation, art, athletics, leadership, minority status, music/drama, ROTC, state residency.

**Application procedures. Admission:** No deadline. $25 fee. Application may be submitted online. Admission notification on a rolling basis beginning on or about 4/1. **Financial aid:** Priority date 5/31; no closing date. FAFSA, institutional form required. Applicants notified on a rolling basis starting 5/1; must reply by 6/30 or within 4 week(s) of notification.

**Academics. Special study options:** Accelerated study, distance learning, double major, dual enrollment of high school students, ESL, honors, independent study, internships, teacher certification program. **Credit/placement by examination:** AP, CLEP, ACT, institutional tests. 94 credit hours maximum toward bachelor's degree. **Support services:** Learning center, reduced course load, remedial instruction, tutoring, writing center.

**Majors. Biology:** General. **Business:** Accounting, actuarial science, apparel, business admin, finance, human resources, insurance, management information systems, managerial economics, marketing, nonprofit/public, operations. **Communications:** General, advertising, broadcast journalism, journalism, photojournalism, public relations. **Computer sciences:** General, information technology. **Education:** General, art, biology, business, chemistry, curriculum, drama/dance, early childhood, elementary, ESL, family/consumer sciences, French, German, health occupations, history, instructional media, mathematics, music, physical, physics, reading, science, social studies, Spanish, special, technology/industrial arts. **Engineering:** Biomedical, physics. **Engineering technology:** General, industrial safety. **English:** Composition, English lit. **Family/consumer sciences:** General, aging, child development, family systems, food/nutrition. **Foreign languages:** French, German, Spanish. **Health:** Audiology/speech pathology, clinical lab science, nursing (RN), public health ed, speech pathology. **History:** General. **Liberal arts:** Arts/sciences. **Math:** General, applied, statistics. **Parks/recreation:** General, exercise sciences. **Personal/culinary services:** Mortuary science. **Philosophy/religion:** Philosophy. **Physical sciences:** Chemistry, physics. **Protective services:** Corrections, criminal justice, forensics, juvenile corrections, police science. **Psychology:** General. **Social sciences:** Applied economics, economics, geography, political science, sociology, urban studies. **Visual/performing arts:** Art, art history/conservation, dance, dramatic, graphic design, interior design, music performance, piano/organ, stringed instruments, voice/opera.

**Most popular majors.** Business/marketing 27%, communications/journalism 9%, education 10%, liberal arts 13%.

**Computing on campus.** 450 workstations in dormitories, library, computer center, student center. Dormitories wired for high-speed internet access. Commuter students can connect to campus network. Helpline, wireless network available.

**Student life. Freshman orientation:** Mandatory, $35 fee. Preregistration for classes offered. 3-day orientation held the week before classes start in August. **Housing:** Coed dorms, single-sex dorms, apartments, fraternity/sorority housing, substance-free housing available. $150 fully refundable deposit. **Activities:** Bands, choral groups, dance, drama, music ensembles, musical theater, radio station, student government, student newspaper, symphony orchestra, TV station, Baptist Student Union, Fellowship of Christian Athletes, Young Democrats, Collegiate Republicans, Black student association, Malaysian student association, Association of Women Students, Webmasters.

**Athletics.** NCAA. **Intercollegiate:** Baseball M, basketball, cross-country, football (tackle) M, golf, soccer W, softball W, tennis, track and field, volleyball W, wrestling M. **Intramural:** Badminton, baseball M, basketball, bowling, football (non-tackle), golf, handball, soccer, softball, swimming, table tennis, tennis, track and field, volleyball, wrestling M. **Team name:** Bronchos.

**Student services.** Career counseling, student employment services, health services, personal counseling, placement for graduates, veterans' counselor. **Physically disabled:** Services for visually, speech, hearing impaired.

**Contact.** E-mail: admituco@ucok.edu
Phone: (405) 974-2338 Toll-free number: (800) 254-4215
Fax: (405) 341-4964
Linda Lofton, Director, Admissions & Records, University of Central
Oklahoma, 100 North University Drive, Edmond, OK 73034-0151

## University of Oklahoma
### Norman, Oklahoma
**CB member**
www.ou.edu
**CB code: 6879**

- Public 4-year university
- Residential campus in small city
- 20,400 degree-seeking undergraduates: 13% part-time, 51% women,
  6% African American, 6% Asian American, 4% Hispanic American,
  8% Native American, 2% international
- 9,214 graduate students
- 89% of applicants admitted
- SAT or ACT (ACT writing optional) required
- 63% graduate within 6 years

**General.** Founded in 1890. Regionally accredited. Faculty-in-residence program has faculty live in student dorms and mix with students. **Degrees:** 4,349 bachelor's awarded; master's, doctoral, first professional offered. **ROTC:** Army, Naval, Air Force. **Location:** 20 miles from Oklahoma City, 200 miles from Dallas. **Calendar:** Semester, extensive summer session. **Full-time faculty:** 1,412 total; 82% have terminal degrees, 17% minority, 41% women. **Part-time faculty:** 405 total; 52% have terminal degrees, 11% minority, 47% women. **Class size:** 48% < 20, 37% 20-39, 5% 40-49, 6% 50-99, 4% >100. **Special facilities:** Museum of science and history, biological station, history of science collection, western history collection, national severe storms laboratory, energy center, national weather center.

**Freshman class profile.** 8,768 applied, 7,788 admitted, 3,883 enrolled.

| Mid 50% test scores | | | |
|---|---|---|---|
| SAT critical reading: | 510-640 | GPA 2.0-2.99: | 5% |
| SAT math: | 540-660 | Rank in top quarter: | 67% |
| ACT composite: | 23-28 | Rank in top tenth: | 33% |
| GPA 3.50 or higher: | 65% | Return as sophomores: | 84% |
| GPA 3.0-3.49: | 30% | International: | 1% |

**Basis for selection.** Standardized test scores, class rank, and secondary school record very important. Prescribed set of requirements for residents and nonresidents that guarantee admission. Applicants who do not meet requirements for guaranteed admission, but do meet certain performance minimums, will be placed on wait list and admitted on space-available basis, with preference given to most academically qualified. High school GPA and class rank may be used in place of test scores for admission purposes. The latest date by which ACT or SAT scores must be received for admission purposes is the last day to enroll in classes for that fall term. Direct from high school applicants who are 21 years of age or older are not required to submit ACT or SAT scores. Audition required for dance, drama, music programs. **Homeschooled:** Must submit ACT or SAT score and submit a record or transcript of all courses completed at the high school level. **Learning Disabled:** Same admission criteria as all applicants, but students must self- identify after admission and provide documentation to receive special services.

**High school preparation.** 15 units required. Required and recommended units include English 4, mathematics 3, social studies 2, history 1, science 2 (laboratory 2), foreign language 2, computer science 1 and academic electives 3. Must have 1 U.S. history and 2 additional units from history, economics, geography, government, or non-western culture.

**2007-2008 Annual costs.** Tuition/fees: $6,507; $15,621 out-of-state. Computer course fees and other college level fees vary by college. Room/board: $7,058. Books/supplies: $953. Personal expenses: $3,425.

**2006-2007 Financial aid. Need-based:** 2,006 full-time freshmen applied for aid; 1,626 were judged to have need; 1,626 of these received aid. Average need met was 85%. Average scholarship/grant was $4,359; average loan $3,041. 33% of total undergraduate aid awarded as scholarships/grants, 67% as loans/jobs. **Non-need-based:** Scholarships awarded for academics, alumni affiliation, art, athletics, leadership, music/drama, religious affiliation, ROTC. **Additional information:** Institutional loans are available for early applicants who do not qualify for federal or state need-based aid.

**Application procedures. Admission:** Closing date 4/1 (receipt date). $40 fee, may be waived for applicants with need. Application may be submitted online. Admission notification on a rolling basis. April 1 application deadline for students applying for fall semesters, but freshman applicants are encouraged to apply as soon as junior year in high school is completed or by scholarship deadline of February 1. Online application fee may be waived, with appropriate documentation, for applicants with financial need. **Financial aid:** Priority date 3/1; no closing date. FAFSA required. Applicants notified on a rolling basis starting 3/15; must reply within 6 week(s) of notification.

**Academics.** College of Liberal Studies through distance learning provides non-traditional students with coherent interdisciplinary liberal arts programs. **Special study options:** Accelerated study, combined bachelor's/graduate degree, cooperative education, distance learning, double major, dual enrollment of high school students, ESL, external degree, honors, independent study, internships, liberal arts/career combination, semester at sea, student-designed major, study abroad, teacher certification program, Washington semester, weekend college. **Credit/placement by examination:** AP, CLEP, IB, SAT, ACT, institutional tests. Credit for prior work/life experience is awarded according to recommendations of the American Council on Education. Applicability of credits toward a degree vary depending on the college. Credit by examination may be counted toward a bachelor's degree, but total number of hours that may be applied vary depending on college. **Support services:** Learning center, pre-admission summer program, remedial instruction, study skills assistance, tutoring, writing center.

**Honors college/program.** Applicants should have a composite ACT of 29 or SAT of 1280 and be in top 10% of high school class or have grade point average of 3.75. Transfer students with fifteen or more college credit hours and cumulative GPA of 3.40 are eligible to apply. Offers an interdisciplinary curriculum and cum laude graduation to qualified undergraduate students from all majors.

**Majors. Architecture:** Architecture, environmental design. **Area/ethnic studies:** African-American, Native American, women's. **Biology:** Biochemistry, botany, microbiology, zoology. **Business:** Accounting, business admin, construction management, finance, management information systems, management science, managerial economics, marketing. **Communications:** General, advertising, broadcast journalism, journalism. **Computer sciences:** Computer science, information systems. **Conservation:** Environmental science. **Education:** Early childhood, elementary, English, foreign languages, mathematics, music, science, social studies, special. **Engineering:** General, aerospace, architectural, chemical, civil, computer, electrical, environmental, industrial, mechanical, petroleum, physics. **English:** English lit. **Foreign languages:** Chinese, classics, French, Germanic, linguistics, Russian, Spanish. **Health:** Clinical lab science, communication disorders, dental hygiene, medical radiologic technology/radiation therapy, nuclear medical technology, nursing (RN), sonography. **History:** General. **Interdisciplinary:** Global studies. **Liberal arts:** Arts/sciences, humanities. **Math:** General. **Parks/recreation:** Exercise sciences. **Philosophy/religion:** Philosophy, religion. **Physical sciences:** Astronomy, astrophysics, chemistry, geology, geophysics, meteorology, physics. **Psychology:** General. **Public administration:** General, social work. **Social sciences:** Anthropology, economics, geography, political science, sociology. **Transportation:** Aviation. **Visual/performing arts:** General, art history/conservation, dance, dramatic, film/cinema, interior design, music pedagogy, studio arts. **Other:** Human relations.

**Most popular majors.** Biology 6%, business/marketing 18%, communications/journalism 10%, engineering/engineering technologies 7%, health sciences 11%, social sciences 11%.

**Computing on campus.** 3,545 workstations in dormitories, library, computer center, student center. Dormitories wired for high-speed internet access and linked to campus network. Commuter students can connect to campus network. Online course registration, online library, helpline, repair service, student web hosting, wireless network available.

**Student life. Freshman orientation:** Available. Preregistration for classes offered. **Housing:** Guaranteed on-campus for freshmen. Coed dorms, single-sex dorms, special housing for disabled, apartments, fraternity/sorority housing, substance-free housing available. $175 fully refundable deposit. Honors, cultural, scholastic, National Merit housing available. **Activities:** Bands, campus ministries, choral groups, dance, drama, film society, international student organizations, literary magazine, music ensembles, Model UN, musical theater, opera, radio station, student government, student newspaper, symphony orchestra, TV station, American Indian, Black, Hispanic-American, Asian-American student associations, College Republicans, Young Democrats, Hillel Jewish student organization, Chi Alpha Christian Fellowship, Muslim student association, Alpha Phi Omega.

**Athletics.** NCAA. **Intercollegiate:** Baseball M, basketball, cross-country, football (tackle) M, golf, gymnastics, soccer W, softball W, tennis, track and field, volleyball W, wrestling M. **Intramural:** Badminton, basketball, cross-country, football (non-tackle), golf, handball, racquetball, soccer, softball, swimming, table tennis, tennis, volleyball. **Team name:** Sooners.

**Student services.** Adult student services, alcohol/substance abuse counseling, campus ministries, career counseling, services for economically disadvantaged, student employment services, financial aid counseling, health services, legal services, minority student services, on-campus daycare, personal counseling, placement for graduates, veterans' counselor, women's

services. **Physically disabled:** Services for visually, speech, hearing impaired.

**Contact.** E-mail: admrec@ou.edu
Phone: (405) 325-2252 Toll-free number: (800) 234-6868
Fax: (405) 325-7124
Patricia Lynch, Director of Admissions and Records, University of
Oklahoma, 1000 Asp Avenue, Norman, OK 73019-4076

## University of Science and Arts of Oklahoma
**Chickasha, Oklahoma**
www.usao.edu                                CB code: 6544

- Public 4-year university and liberal arts college
- Commuter campus in large town
- 1,096 degree-seeking undergraduates: 12% part-time, 62% women, 4% African American, 1% Asian American, 4% Hispanic American, 12% Native American, 4% international
- 94% of applicants admitted
- SAT or ACT (ACT writing optional) required
- 26% graduate within 6 years; 29% enter graduate study

**General.** Founded in 1908. Regionally accredited. Oklahoma's only public liberal arts college. Offers trimester system classes, allowing for three-year graduation. **Degrees:** 219 bachelor's awarded. **Location:** 48 miles from Oklahoma City. **Calendar:** Trimester, extensive summer session. **Full-time faculty:** 54 total; 91% have terminal degrees, 11% minority, 52% women. **Part-time faculty:** 37 total; 14% have terminal degrees, 5% minority, 49% women. **Class size:** 70% <20, 24% 20-39, 2% 40-49, 4% 50-99, less than 1% >100. **Special facilities:** Speech and hearing clinic, herbarium, child development center.

**Freshman class profile.** 348 applied, 326 admitted, 222 enrolled.

| Mid 50% test scores | | Rank in top tenth: | 19% |
|---|---|---|---|
| ACT composite: | 20-25 | End year in good standing: | 76% |
| GPA 3.50 or higher: | 49% | Return as sophomores: | 69% |
| GPA 3.0-3.49: | 31% | Out-of-state: | 2% |
| GPA 2.0-2.99: | 18% | Live on campus: | 64% |
| Rank in top quarter: | 48% | International: | 6% |

**Basis for selection.** One of the following is required for admission: minimum 23 ACT or 1050 SAT (exclusive of Writing), or minimum overall GPA of 3.0 and ranking in top 50% of high school graduating class, or GPA of 3.0 or higher in the 15-unit high school core curriculum and 20 ACT or 940 SAT. **Homeschooled:** Transcript of courses and grades required.

**High school preparation.** 15 units required; 21 recommended. Required and recommended units include English 4, mathematics 3-4, social studies 1, history 2, science 2-3 (laboratory 2-3), foreign language 2 and academic electives 3. 2 units of fine arts, drama and/or speech recommended.

**2007-2008 Annual costs.** Tuition/fees: $4,050; $9,630 out-of-state. Room/board: $4,690.

**2007-2008 Financial aid. Need-based:** 172 full-time freshmen applied for aid; 138 were judged to have need; 135 of these received aid. Average need met was 71%. Average scholarship/grant was $5,692; average loan $2,557. 59% of total undergraduate aid awarded as scholarships/grants, 41% as loans/jobs. **Non-need-based:** Awarded to 308 full-time undergraduates, including 72 freshmen. Scholarships awarded for academics, art, athletics, leadership, music/drama, state residency.

**Application procedures. Admission:** Closing date 8/31 (postmark date). $15 fee, may be waived for applicants with need. Application may be submitted online. Admission notification on a rolling basis beginning on or about 2/10. **Financial aid:** Priority date 3/15; no closing date. FAFSA, institutional form required. Applicants notified on a rolling basis starting 3/15; must reply within 4 week(s) of notification.

**Academics. Special study options:** Accelerated study, double major, dual enrollment of high school students, independent study, internships, liberal arts/career combination, student-designed major, teacher certification program. **Credit/placement by examination:** AP, CLEP, ACT, institutional tests. 62 credit hours maximum toward bachelor's degree. **Support services:** Learning center, reduced course load, remedial instruction, study skills assistance, tutoring, writing center.

**Majors. Area/ethnic studies:** Native American. **Biology:** General. **Business:** Business admin. **Communications:** General. **Computer sciences:** Computer science. **Education:** Deaf/hearing impaired, early childhood, elementary. **English:** English lit. **Health:** Speech pathology. **History:** General. **Interdisciplinary:** Natural sciences. **Math:** General. **Parks/recreation:** Health/

fitness. **Physical sciences:** Chemistry, physics. **Psychology:** General. **Social sciences:** Economics, political science, sociology. **Visual/performing arts:** Art, dramatic, studio arts.

**Most popular majors.** Business/marketing 21%, education 15%, English 7%, parks/recreation 8%, psychology 13%, visual/performing arts 11%.

**Computing on campus.** 175 workstations in library, computer center, student center. Dormitories wired for high-speed internet access and linked to campus network. Online library, helpline, repair service, student web hosting, wireless network available.

**Student life. Freshman orientation:** Mandatory. Preregistration for classes offered. **Housing:** Guaranteed on-campus for freshmen. Coed dorms, apartments available. $100 fully refundable deposit, deadline 4/1. **Activities:** Bands, campus ministries, choral groups, dance, drama, international student organizations, literary magazine, music ensembles, musical theater, student government, student newspaper, TV station, Ameslan Culture Club, Chi Alpha Christian Fellowship, College Democrats, College Republicans, African American student association, international student association, Inter-Tribal Heritage Club, student ambassadors, students with children club, feminist collective.

**Athletics.** NAIA. **Intercollegiate:** Baseball M, basketball, cheerleading, soccer, softball W. **Intramural:** Basketball, golf, softball M, volleyball. **Team name:** Drovers.

**Student services.** Alcohol/substance abuse counseling, career counseling, services for economically disadvantaged, student employment services, financial aid counseling, health services, minority student services, personal counseling, placement for graduates, veterans' counselor. **Physically disabled:** Services for visually, hearing impaired.

**Contact.** E-mail: usao-admissions@usao.edu
Phone: (405) 574-1357 Toll-free number: (800) 933-8726
Fax: (405) 574-1220
Joe Evans, Director of Admissions and Records, University of Science and Arts of Oklahoma, 1727 West Alabama, Chickasha, OK 73018-5322

## University of Tulsa
**Tulsa, Oklahoma**                          CB member
www.utulsa.edu                              CB code: 6883

- Private 4-year university affiliated with Presbyterian Church (USA)
- Residential campus in large city
- 2,920 degree-seeking undergraduates: 4% part-time, 48% women, 6% African American, 3% Asian American, 4% Hispanic American, 3% Native American, 11% international
- 1,165 degree-seeking graduate students
- 51% of applicants admitted
- SAT or ACT (ACT writing optional) required
- 64% graduate within 6 years; 42% enter graduate study

**General.** Founded in 1894. Regionally accredited. **Degrees:** 569 bachelor's awarded; master's, doctoral, first professional offered. **ROTC:** Air Force. **Location:** 100 miles from Oklahoma City. **Calendar:** Semester, limited summer session. **Full-time faculty:** 309 total; 96% have terminal degrees, 16% minority, 34% women. **Part-time faculty:** 71 total; 96% have terminal degrees, 6% minority, 46% women. **Class size:** 62% <20, 33% 20-39, 4% 40-49, 1% 50-99. **Special facilities:** Biotechnology institute, center for communicative disorders, communication lab, tall grass prairie preserve.

**Freshman class profile.** 3,804 applied, 1,944 admitted, 656 enrolled.

| Mid 50% test scores | | Rank in top tenth: | 64% |
|---|---|---|---|
| SAT critical reading: | 560-700 | End year in good standing: | 88% |
| SAT math: | 580-700 | Return as sophomores: | 88% |
| ACT composite: | 24-30 | Out-of-state: | 49% |
| GPA 3.50 or higher: | 70% | Live on campus: | 86% |
| GPA 3.0-3.49: | 20% | International: | 13% |
| GPA 2.0-2.99: | 10% | Fraternities: | 21% |
| Rank in top quarter: | 81% | Sororities: | 23% |

**Basis for selection.** Primary requirements are school achievement records and test scores. High school guidance counselor recommendation required. Extracurricular activities, community involvement, and talents are considered. Essays and interviews are recommended for all; audition required for music, theater programs; portfolio required for art program. **Homeschooled:** Statement describing homeschool structure and mission, transcript of courses and grades, letter of recommendation (nonparent) required.

**High school preparation.** College-preparatory program recommended. 16 units recommended. Recommended units include English 4, mathematics 3, social studies 1, history 2, science 3 (laboratory 2), foreign language 2 and academic electives 1. 4 mathematics and 4 physical science recommended for engineering and natural science students.

**2008-2009 Annual costs.** Tuition/fees: $23,940. A one-time $425 fee is charged first-time students for orientation, lifetime transcripts, course drop/add transactions, and graduation/commencement. Room/board: $7,776. Books/supplies: $1,200. Personal expenses: $2,628.

**2006-2007 Financial aid. Need-based:** 594 full-time freshmen applied for aid; 324 were judged to have need; 324 of these received aid. Average need met was 87%. Average scholarship/grant was $5,056; average loan $5,136. 30% of total undergraduate aid awarded as scholarships/grants, 70% as loans/jobs. **Non-need-based:** Awarded to 2,361 full-time undergraduates, including 599 freshmen. Scholarships awarded for academics, alumni affiliation, art, athletics, leadership, minority status, music/drama, religious affiliation.

**Application procedures. Admission:** Priority date 2/1; no deadline. $35 fee, may be waived for applicants with need. Application may be submitted online. Admission notification on a rolling basis beginning on or about 10/1. Must reply by May 1 or within 2 week(s) if notified thereafter. **Financial aid:** Priority date 4/1; no closing date. FAFSA, institutional form required. Applicants notified on a rolling basis starting 3/1; must reply by 5/1 or within 2 week(s) of notification.

**Academics. Special study options:** Accelerated study, combined bachelor's/graduate degree, double major, ESL, honors, independent study, internships, liberal arts/career combination, student-designed major, study abroad, teacher certification program, Washington semester. **Credit/placement by examination:** AP, CLEP, IB, SAT, ACT, institutional tests. 36 credit hours maximum toward bachelor's degree. **Support services:** Learning center, reduced course load, study skills assistance, tutoring, writing center.

**Majors. Area/ethnic studies:** Russian/Slavic. **Biology:** General, biochemistry. **Business:** Accounting, business admin, finance, international, management information systems, marketing, organizational behavior. **Communications:** General. **Computer sciences:** General, computer science, information technology. **Conservation:** Environmental studies. **Education:** Chemistry, Deaf/hearing impaired, early childhood, elementary, mathematics, music. **Engineering:** Chemical, electrical, mechanical, petroleum, physics. **Engineering technology:** Energy systems. **English:** English lit. **Foreign languages:** French, German, Spanish. **Health:** Athletic training, audiology/speech pathology, communication disorders, nursing (RN). **History:** General. **Interdisciplinary:** Global studies. **Legal studies:** General, prelaw. **Liberal arts:** Arts/sciences. **Math:** Applied. **Parks/recreation:** Exercise sciences. **Philosophy/religion:** Philosophy, religion. **Physical sciences:** Chemistry, geology, geophysics, physics. **Psychology:** General. **Social sciences:** Anthropology, economics, political science, sociology. **Visual/performing arts:** Art, art history/conservation, arts management, dramatic, film/cinema, music performance, music theory/composition, piano/organ, voice/opera.

**Most popular majors.** Biology 6%, business/marketing 22%, communications/journalism 6%, engineering/engineering technologies 13%, health sciences 7%, psychology 7%, visual/performing arts 10%.

**Computing on campus.** 900 workstations in dormitories, library, computer center, student center. Dormitories wired for high-speed internet access and linked to campus network. Commuter students can connect to campus network. Online course registration, online library, helpline, student web hosting, wireless network available.

**Student life. Freshman orientation:** Available. Preregistration for classes offered. Held the week prior to fall term, designed to help students form relationships with faculty, staff, and fellow students. **Housing:** Guaranteed on-campus for freshmen. Coed dorms, single-sex dorms, special housing for disabled, apartments, fraternity/sorority housing, substance-free housing available. $250 partly refundable deposit. Honors and language houses available. **Activities:** Bands, choral groups, dance, drama, literary magazine, music ensembles, musical theater, opera, radio station, student government, student newspaper, symphony orchestra, TV station, Baptist Student Union, Fellowship of Christian Athletes, Jewish student association, Young Democrats, Women's Law Caucus, Hispanic student association, College Republicans, International Fellowship House, Association of Black Collegians, volunteer income tax assistance project.

**Athletics.** NCAA. **Intercollegiate:** Basketball, cheerleading, cross-country, football (tackle) M, golf, rowing (crew) W, soccer, softball W, tennis, track and field, volleyball W. **Intramural:** Badminton, basketball, bowling, cross-country, diving, football (non-tackle), golf, racquetball, soccer, softball, squash, swimming, table tennis, tennis, track and field, volleyball, water polo, wrestling M. **Team name:** Golden Hurricane.

**Student services.** Adult student services, alcohol/substance abuse counseling, campus ministries, career counseling, student employment services, financial aid counseling, health services, legal services, minority student services, on-campus daycare, personal counseling, placement for graduates, veterans' counselor, women's services. **Physically disabled:** Services for visually, speech, hearing impaired.

**Contact.** E-mail: admission@utulsa.edu
Phone: (918) 631-2307 Toll-free number: (800) 331-3050
Fax: (918) 631-5003
John Corso, Associate Vice President of Enrollment and Student Services, University of Tulsa, 800 South Tucker Drive, Tulsa, OK 74104-3189

---

## Vatterott College
### Oklahoma City, Oklahoma
www.vatterott-college.com

CB code: 2899

- For-profit 4-year branch campus and career college
- Very large city
- 275 degree-seeking undergraduates

**General.** Accredited by ACCSCT. **Degrees:** 2 bachelor's, 76 associate awarded. **Calendar:** Continuous, 10-week sessions. **Full-time faculty:** 18 total. **Part-time faculty:** 4 total. **Class size:** 75% < 20, 25% 20-39.

**Basis for selection.** Open admission. Program-specific institutional entrance exams are administered.

**2007-2008 Annual costs.** Program cost ranges: $15,891 to $20,901 (certificate/diploma); $22,920 to $31,981 (associate degree); $57,458 (bachelor's degree).

**Financial aid.** All financial aid based on need.

**Application procedures. Admission:** No deadline. No application fee. **Financial aid:** No deadline. FAFSA required.

**Academics. Credit/placement by examination:** CLEP.

**Majors. Mechanic/repair:** Heating/ac/refrig.

**Student life. Freshman orientation:** Mandatory.

**Contact.** Phone: (405) 945-0088 Fax: (405) 945-0788
Mark Hybers, Director of Admissions, Vatterott College, 4621 NW 23rd Street, Oklahoma City, OK 73127

# Oregon

## Art Institute of Portland
**Portland, Oregon**
www.aipd.artinstitutes.edu

**CB member**
**CB code: 4231**

- For-profit 4-year visual arts and liberal arts college
- Commuter campus in large city
- 1,722 degree-seeking undergraduates: 42% part-time, 52% women, 1% African American, 6% Asian American, 6% Hispanic American, 2% Native American, 1% international
- 54% of applicants admitted
- Application essay, interview required

**General.** Founded in 1963. Regionally accredited. **Degrees:** 151 bachelor's, 24 associate awarded. **Calendar:** Quarter, extensive summer session. **Special facilities:** Specialized library, design laboratories, audio/visual laboratory.

**Freshman class profile.** 476 applied, 258 admitted, 255 enrolled.

| Return as sophomores: | 54% | Out-of-state: | 31% |
|---|---|---|---|

**Basis for selection.** Proof of graduation from secondary school/GED required. Interview, essay, college transcripts, and/or English/math placement exam considered.

**2007-2008 Annual costs.** Tuition/fees: $19,395. Room only: $8,250. Books/supplies: $2,457. Personal expenses: $2,700.

**Financial aid. Non-need-based:** Scholarships awarded for art. **Additional information:** Applicants encouraged to apply early for financial aid. Scholarship deadlines range from January 1 to March 1.

**Application procedures. Admission:** No deadline. $50 fee. Application may be submitted online. Admission notification on a rolling basis. **Financial aid:** Priority date 3/1; no closing date. FAFSA required. Applicants notified on a rolling basis starting 1/1; must reply within 5 week(s) of notification.

**Academics. Special study options:** Accelerated study, distance learning, honors, independent study, internships, liberal arts/career combination, study abroad. **Credit/placement by examination:** AP, CLEP, IB, SAT, ACT, institutional tests. Credit by examination only offered for courses in writing, computing, graphics, drawing, and math. **Support services:** Learning center, reduced course load, remedial instruction, study skills assistance, tutoring.

**Majors. Business:** Fashion. **Computer sciences:** Applications programming, computer graphics, web page design. **Visual/performing arts:** Art history/conservation, arts management, cinematography, commercial/advertising art, design, fashion design, graphic design, industrial design, interior design, multimedia.

**Most popular majors.** Computer/information sciences 24%, visual/performing arts 76%.

**Computing on campus.** 240 workstations in library, computer center. Dormitories wired for high-speed internet access. Commuter students can connect to campus network. Student web hosting, wireless network available.

**Student life. Freshman orientation:** Mandatory. Preregistration for classes offered. Held before each quarter-registration, advising and student and community services available. **Policies:** Student code of conduct published in catalog. No alcohol or drugs on campus or in housing. **Housing:** Special housing for disabled, apartments, substance-free housing available. $250 partly refundable deposit. Apartments for 2 or 4 students. **Activities:** Film society, student government, student newspaper.

**Student services.** Alcohol/substance abuse counseling, career counseling, student employment services, financial aid counseling, personal counseling, placement for graduates, veterans' counselor. **Physically disabled:** Services for visually, speech, hearing impaired.

**Contact.** E-mail: aipdadm@aii.edu
Phone: (503) 228-6528 Toll-free number: (888) 228-6528
Fax: (503) 227-1945
Alan Yanda, Director of Admissions, Art Institute of Portland, 1122 Northwest Davis Street, Portland, OR 97209-2911

## Cascade College
**Portland, Oregon**
www.cascade.edu

- Private 4-year branch campus and liberal arts college affiliated with Church of Christ
- Residential campus in very large city
- 262 degree-seeking undergraduates: 1% part-time, 59% women, 8% African American, 4% Asian American, 11% Hispanic American, 1% Native American, 2% international

**General.** Regionally accredited. **Degrees:** 48 bachelor's awarded. **Calendar:** Semester, limited summer session. **Full-time faculty:** 15 total. **Part-time faculty:** 22 total.

**Freshman class profile.**

| Return as sophomores: | 46% | International: | 2% |
|---|---|---|---|
| Live on campus: | 90% | | |

**Basis for selection.** Open admission.

**High school preparation.** Recommended units include English 4, mathematics 2, social studies 4, history 3, science 2 and foreign language 2.

**2008-2009 Annual costs.** Tuition/fees: $14,250. Room/board: $6,700.

**Financial aid. Non-need-based:** Scholarships awarded for academics, alumni affiliation, athletics, leadership, music/drama, religious affiliation.

**Application procedures. Admission:** No deadline. $25 fee, may be waived for applicants with need. Application may be submitted online. Admission notification on a rolling basis. **Financial aid:** No deadline. FAFSA required.

**Academics. Special study options:** Double major, independent study, internships, study abroad, teacher certification program. **Credit/placement by examination:** AP, CLEP, SAT, ACT. **Support services:** Tutoring.

**Majors. Biology:** General. **Business:** Business admin, marketing. **Communications:** General. **Education:** Early childhood, elementary. **English:** English lit. **Psychology:** General. **Theology:** Bible. **Other:** Interdisciplinary studies.

**Computing on campus.** 30 workstations in library, computer center, student center. Wireless network available.

**Student life. Freshman orientation:** Mandatory. Preregistration for classes offered. Occurs around third week of August. Includes on-campus orientation program, retreat at the Oregon coast, tour of Portland, placement testing and session for parents. **Policies:** Christian institution with specific expectations of behavior. Required daily chapel attendance. Curfew for freshmen. No alcohol on or off campus. Members of the opposite sex not permitted in rooms except during designated times. **Housing:** Single-sex dorms available. $75 partly refundable deposit. **Activities:** Bands, campus ministries, choral groups, drama, student government, Kappa Sigma Chi, Phi Phi Phi, Delta Sigma Rho, Lambda Chi Omega, Phi Alpha Sigma, drama/social club, nature society, diversity club.

**Athletics.** NAIA. **Intercollegiate:** Basketball, cross-country, soccer, track and field, volleyball W. **Intramural:** Basketball, football (tackle), table tennis. **Team name:** Thunderbirds.

**Student services.** Campus ministries, health services, personal counseling.

**Contact.** E-mail: admissions@cascade.edu
Phone: (503) 257-1202 Toll-free number: (800) 550-7678
Fax: (503) 257-1222
Ryan Fox, Director of Enrollment Management/Admissions, Cascade College, 9101 East Burnside Street, Portland, OR 97216

## Concordia University
**Portland, Oregon**
www.cu-portland.edu

**CB code: 4079**

- Private 4-year university and liberal arts college affiliated with Lutheran Church - Missouri Synod
- Commuter campus in very large city

- 1,036 degree-seeking undergraduates: 11% part-time, 67% women, 7% African American, 5% Asian American, 5% Hispanic American, 1% Native American, 2% international
- 470 degree-seeking graduate students
- 65% of applicants admitted
- SAT or ACT (ACT writing optional) required

**General.** Founded in 1905. Regionally accredited. **Degrees:** 203 bachelor's awarded; master's offered. **ROTC:** Air Force. **Location:** 5 miles from downtown. **Calendar:** Semester, limited summer session. **Full-time faculty:** 46 total; 63% have terminal degrees, 2% minority, 50% women. **Part-time faculty:** 115 total; 22% have terminal degrees, 3% minority, 56% women. **Class size:** 67% < 20, 32% 20-39, less than 1% 40-49, 1% 50-99. **Special facilities:** 2-way compressed video distance learning classroom.

**Freshman class profile.** 867 applied, 561 admitted, 183 enrolled.

| Mid 50% test scores | | | |
|---|---|---|---|
| SAT critical reading: | 430-560 | Rank in top quarter: | 55% |
| SAT math: | 430-560 | Rank in top tenth: | 25% |
| ACT composite: | 19-25 | Return as sophomores: | 71% |
| GPA 3.50 or higher: | 53% | Out-of-state: | 54% |
| GPA 3.0-3.49: | 24% | Live on campus: | 93% |
| GPA 2.0-2.99: | 23% | International: | 3% |

**Basis for selection.** 2.5 high school GPA, 480 SAT verbal, or 18 ACT required. **Homeschooled:** Statement describing homeschool structure and mission, state high school equivalency certificate, letter of recommendation (nonparent) required. Interview may be required.

**High school preparation.** 19 units recommended. Recommended units include English 4, mathematics 3, social studies 3, science 3, foreign language 2 and academic electives 3. One computer/keyboarding recommended.

**2008-2009 Annual costs.** Tuition/fees (projected): $22,100. Room/board: $6,400. Books/supplies: $800. Personal expenses: $1,600.

**Financial aid. Non-need-based:** Scholarships awarded for academics, athletics, leadership, music/drama, religious affiliation.

**Application procedures. Admission:** Priority date 3/1; deadline 7/1 (postmark date). $20 fee, may be waived for applicants with need. Application may be submitted online. Admission notification on a rolling basis beginning on or about 1/1. Must reply by May 1 or within 2 week(s) if notified thereafter. **Financial aid:** No deadline. FAFSA required. Applicants notified on a rolling basis starting 3/15; must reply by 5/1 or within 3 week(s) of notification.

**Academics. Special study options:** Accelerated study, cross-registration, distance learning, double major, dual enrollment of high school students, ESL, honors, independent study, internships, study abroad, teacher certification program. **Credit/placement by examination:** CLEP, institutional tests. **Support services:** Learning center, remedial instruction, tutoring, writing center.

**Majors. Biology:** General. **Business:** General, business admin, international. **Education:** General, biology, business, chemistry, early childhood, elementary, English, health, history, mathematics, middle, multi-level teacher, physical, science, secondary, social studies. **English:** English lit. **Health:** Athletic training, health care admin, nursing (RN), premedicine. **History:** General. **Liberal arts:** Arts/sciences. **Parks/recreation:** Health/fitness, sports admin. **Philosophy/religion:** Religion. **Physical sciences:** Chemistry. **Psychology:** General. **Public administration:** Social work. **Social sciences:** General. **Theology:** Religious ed, theology.

**Most popular majors.** Business/marketing 35%, education 24%, health sciences 8%, psychology 6%, public administration/social services 6%, theological studies 6%.

**Computing on campus.** PC or laptop required. 60 workstations in dormitories, library, computer center. Dormitories wired for high-speed internet access and linked to campus network. Commuter students can connect to campus network. Online course registration, online library, helpline, wireless network available.

**Student life. Freshman orientation:** Mandatory. Preregistration for classes offered. Usually day before classes begin. **Policies:** Optional attendance for chapel services. Lutheran format, mixture of traditional and contemporary services offered. **Housing:** Coed dorms, apartments, substance-free housing available. $50 deposit, deadline 5/1. School rents nearby houses to students with families and maintains referral file. Homestay option for international students. **Activities:** Campus ministries, choral groups, drama, international student organizations, literary magazine, music ensembles, radio station, student government, student newspaper, social service organization, Circle K, Spiritual Life, El Club Latino.

**Athletics.** NAIA. **Intercollegiate:** Baseball M, basketball, cross-country, golf, soccer, softball W, track and field, volleyball W. **Intramural:** Badminton, basketball, softball, tennis, volleyball. **Team name:** Cavaliers.

**Student services.** Adult student services, campus ministries, career counseling, financial aid counseling, health services, personal counseling, placement for graduates, veterans' counselor.

**Contact.** E-mail: admissions@cu-portland.edu
Phone: (503) 280-8501 Toll-free number: (800) 321-9371
Fax: (503) 280-8531
Bobi Swan, Dean of Admission, Concordia University, 2811 Northeast Holman Street, Portland, OR 97211-6099

---

## Corban College
Salem, Oregon
www.corban.edu
CB code: 4956

- Private 4-year liberal arts college affiliated with Baptist faith
- Residential campus in small city
- 861 degree-seeking undergraduates: 11% part-time, 60% women
- 55 graduate students
- 81% of applicants admitted
- SAT or ACT (ACT writing recommended), application essay required

**General.** Founded in 1935. Regionally accredited. **Degrees:** 171 bachelor's, 4 associate awarded; master's offered. **ROTC:** Army, Air Force. **Location:** 45 miles from Portland. **Calendar:** Semester, limited summer session. **Full-time faculty:** 36 total; 47% have terminal degrees, 8% minority, 22% women. **Part-time faculty:** 68 total; 13% have terminal degrees, 2% minority, 56% women. **Class size:** 66% < 20, 25% 20-39, 5% 40-49, 4% 50-99, less than 1% >100. **Special facilities:** Archaeological museum.

**Freshman class profile.**

| Mid 50% test scores | | | |
|---|---|---|---|
| SAT critical reading: | 490-600 | GPA 3.0-3.49: | 28% |
| SAT math: | 480-600 | GPA 2.0-2.99: | 13% |
| SAT writing: | 470-570 | Rank in top quarter: | 55% |
| ACT composite: | 20-25 | Rank in top tenth: | 27% |
| GPA 3.50 or higher: | 59% | Out-of-state: | 36% |
| | | Live on campus: | 94% |

**Basis for selection.** Commitment to Christianity, high school GPA, test scores, recommendations, essays, school and community activities considered. Audition required for music program.

**High school preparation.** 14 units recommended. Recommended units include English 4, mathematics 3, social studies 3, science 2 and foreign language 2.

**2008-2009 Annual costs.** Tuition/fees: $22,320. Room/board: $8,068. Books/supplies: $700. Personal expenses: $500.

**Financial aid. Non-need-based:** Scholarships awarded for academics, alumni affiliation, athletics, leadership, music/drama.

**Application procedures. Admission:** Priority date 3/1; deadline 8/1 (receipt date). $40 fee, may be waived for applicants with need. Application may be submitted online. Admission notification on a rolling basis beginning on or about 10/1. Must reply by May 1 or within 2 week(s) if notified thereafter. **Financial aid:** Priority date 2/15; no closing date. FAFSA required. Applicants notified by 3/1; must reply within 4 week(s) of notification.

**Academics. Special study options:** Accelerated study, combined bachelor's/graduate degree, cross-registration, distance learning, double major, honors, independent study, internships, liberal arts/career combination, study abroad, teacher certification program, Washington semester, weekend college. **Credit/placement by examination:** AP, CLEP, institutional tests. 20 credit hours maximum toward associate degree, 32 toward bachelor's. **Support services:** Learning center, reduced course load, tutoring.

**Majors. Business:** General, accounting, accounting/business management, accounting/finance, business admin, communications, finance, management information systems. **Communications:** General, journalism. **Computer sciences:** Computer science. **Education:** General, biology, business, elementary, English, history, mathematics, middle, multi-level teacher, music, physical, science, secondary, social science, social studies. **English:** English lit. **Health:** Predental, premedicine, prenursing, prepharmacy, preveterinary. **History:** General. **Legal studies:** Prelaw. **Liberal arts:** Arts/sciences, humanities. **Math:** General. **Parks/recreation:** Health/fitness, sports admin. **Philosophy/religion:** Religion. **Psychology:** General. **Public administration:**

Community org/advocacy. **Social sciences:** General. **Theology:** Bible, missionary, pastoral counseling, preministerial, religious ed, sacred music, theology, youth ministry. **Visual/performing arts:** Music performance, piano/organ, voice/opera.

**Most popular majors.** Business/marketing 29%, education 16%, liberal arts 12%, psychology 28%.

**Computing on campus.** 34 workstations in dormitories, library, computer center, student center. Dormitories wired for high-speed internet access and linked to campus network. Commuter students can connect to campus network. Online library, helpline, repair service, wireless network available.

**Student life. Freshman orientation:** Mandatory. Preregistration for classes offered. Students assigned to core group of 12-18 students, with adviser to answer questions and schedule classes for fall semester. Core group advisers often visit students in their homes. **Policies:** Religious observance required. **Housing:** Guaranteed on-campus for freshmen. Single-sex dorms, substance-free housing available. $100 deposit, deadline 8/1. **Activities:** Bands, choral groups, drama, literary magazine, music ensembles, musical theater, radio station, student government, student newspaper, symphony orchestra, Christian fellowships.

**Athletics.** NAIA, NCCAA. **Intercollegiate:** Baseball M, basketball, cross-country, golf M, soccer, softball W, volleyball W. **Intramural:** Basketball, football (non-tackle), soccer, softball, volleyball, weight lifting. **Team name:** Warriors.

**Student services.** Adult student services, campus ministries, career counseling, student employment services, financial aid counseling, health services, personal counseling, placement for graduates. **Physically disabled:** Services for visually, hearing impaired.

**Contact.** E-mail: admissions@corban.edu
Phone: (503) 375-7005 Toll-free number: (800) 845-3005
Fax: (503) 585-4316
Marty Ziesemer, Director of Admissions, Corban College, 5000 Deer Park Drive SE, Salem, OR 97317-9392

## DeVry University: Portland
**Portland, Oregon**
**www.devry.edu**

- For-profit 4-year university
- Commuter campus in very large city
- 66 degree-seeking undergraduates: 41% part-time, 45% women, 12% African American, 3% Asian American, 8% Hispanic American
- 51 degree-seeking graduate students

**General. Degrees:** 13 bachelor's awarded; master's offered. **Calendar:** Semester. **Part-time faculty:** 4 total; 25% women.

**Freshman class profile.** 12 enrolled.

| Return as sophomores: | 43% | Out-of-state: | 17% |
|---|---|---|---|

**Basis for selection.** Applicants must have high school diploma or equivalent, or a degree from accredited postsecondary institution, demonstrate proficiency in basic college-level skills through SAT or ACT scores or institution-administered placement exams, and be at least 17 years of age on the first day of classes. SAT/ACT tests considered but not required for admission. If applicant chooses not to submit either, must take DeVry-administered admissions test.

**2007-2008 Annual costs.** Tuition/fees: $13,020. Books/supplies: $1,300. Personal expenses: $5,082.

**Financial aid. Non-need-based:** Scholarships awarded for academics.

**Application procedures. Admission:** No deadline. $50 fee. Admission notification on a rolling basis. **Financial aid:** No deadline. FAFSA required. Applicants notified on a rolling basis.

**Academics. Special study options:** Accelerated study, distance learning. **Credit/placement by examination:** CLEP.

**Majors. Computer sciences:** Systems analysis. **Engineering technology:** Biomedical. **Other:** Technical management.

**Student life. Housing:** Private apartments, student-plan housing, private rooms available.

**Contact.** Phone: (866) 543-3879
DeVry University: Portland, Peterkort Center II, Portland, OR 97225

## Eastern Oregon University
**LaGrande, Oregon**
**www.eou.edu**                                              CB code: 4300

- Public 4-year university and liberal arts college
- Residential campus in large town
- 2,793 degree-seeking undergraduates: 36% part-time, 62% women, 1% African American, 2% Asian American, 4% Hispanic American, 3% Native American, 2% international
- 238 degree-seeking graduate students
- 52% of applicants admitted
- SAT or ACT (ACT writing optional) required

**General.** Founded in 1929. Regionally accredited. **Degrees:** 576 bachelor's awarded; master's offered. **ROTC:** Army. **Location:** 260 miles from Portland; 180 miles from Boise, Idaho. **Calendar:** Quarter, limited summer session. **Full-time faculty:** 104 total; 77% have terminal degrees, 6% minority, 42% women. **Part-time faculty:** 27 total; 41% have terminal degrees, 15% minority, 70% women. **Class size:** 55% < 20, 36% 20-39, 5% 40-49, 4% 50-99, less than 1% >100. **Special facilities:** Wildlife habitat laboratory, agriculture experiment station.

**Freshman class profile.** 725 applied, 378 admitted, 338 enrolled.

| Mid 50% test scores | | | |
|---|---|---|---|
| SAT critical reading: | 420-530 | GPA 2.0-2.99: | 31% |
| SAT math: | 410-530 | Rank in top quarter: | 37% |
| SAT writing: | 400-500 | Rank in top tenth: | 13% |
| ACT composite: | 18-23 | Return as sophomores: | 65% |
| GPA 3.50 or higher: | 36% | Out-of-state: | 33% |
| GPA 3.0-3.49: | 32% | Live on campus: | 59% |
| | | International: | 1% |

**Basis for selection.** Secondary school record most important; high school GPA of 3.0 in 14 subject areas required. Students not meeting these requirements must submit portfolio including essay and 2 letters of recommendation. Limited number of students not meeting requirements may be admitted. **Homeschooled:** State high school equivalency certificate, letter of recommendation (nonparent) required. Applicants must present certificate of completion and portfolio including essay, letters of recommendation, standardized test scores.

**High school preparation.** Required and recommended units include English 4, mathematics 3, science 2 (laboratory 1) and foreign language 2.

**2007-2008 Annual costs.** Tuition/fees: $6,072. Room/board: $8,100. Books/supplies: $1,152. Personal expenses: $1,353.

**2007-2008 Financial aid. Need-based:** 280 full-time freshmen applied for aid; 215 were judged to have need; 214 of these received aid. Average need met was 48%. Average scholarship/grant was $3,944; average loan $2,643. 38% of total undergraduate aid awarded as scholarships/grants, 62% as loans/jobs. **Non-need-based:** Awarded to 621 full-time undergraduates, including 174 freshmen. Scholarships awarded for academics, art, leadership, minority status, music/drama, state residency.

**Application procedures. Admission:** Priority date 12/1; deadline 9/15 (postmark date). $50 fee, may be waived for applicants with need. Application may be submitted online. Admission notification on a rolling basis beginning on or about 10/1. **Financial aid:** Priority date 3/1; no closing date. FAFSA required. Applicants notified on a rolling basis starting 4/1; must reply within 4 week(s) of notification.

**Academics.** Regional advisers for distance education students. **Special study options:** Combined bachelor's/graduate degree, cooperative education, cross-registration, distance learning, double major, dual enrollment of high school students, ESL, exchange student, external degree, honors, independent study, internships, liberal arts/career combination, semester at sea, student-designed major, study abroad, teacher certification program, weekend college. **Credit/placement by examination:** AP, CLEP, IB, institutional tests. 45 credit hours maximum toward bachelor's degree. **Support services:** Learning center, tutoring, writing center.

**Majors. Agriculture:** Agronomy, business, economics, range science, soil science. **Biology:** General. **Business:** General, accounting, business admin, managerial economics. **Computer sciences:** General, computer science, web page design. **Conservation:** General. **Education:** General, early childhood, elementary, ESL, German, middle, science, secondary, social science, social studies, Spanish. **English:** English lit. **Health:** Nursing (RN), ophthalmic lab technology, predental, premedicine, preop/surgical nursing, prepharmacy, preveterinary. **History:** General. **Legal studies:** Prelaw. **Liberal arts:** Arts/sciences. **Math:** General. **Parks/recreation:** Health/fitness. **Physical sciences:** Chemistry, physics. **Protective services:** Fire services admin. **Psychology:** General. **Social sciences:** Anthropology, political science, sociology. **Visual/performing arts:** Dramatic, studio arts.

**Most popular majors.** Business/marketing 28%, education 20%, liberal arts 23%.

**Computing on campus.** 150 workstations in dormitories, library, computer center, student center. Dormitories wired for high-speed internet access and linked to campus network. Commuter students can connect to campus network. Online course registration, online library, helpline, repair service, wireless network available.

**Student life. Freshman orientation:** Available. Preregistration for classes offered. **Housing:** Guaranteed on-campus for freshmen. Coed dorms, apartments available. **Activities:** Bands, choral groups, dance, drama, international student organizations, literary magazine, music ensembles, Model UN, musical theater, radio station, student government, student newspaper, symphony orchestra, international relations club, outdoor club, biology club, Fellowship of Christian Athletes, Latter-day Saints student association.

**Athletics.** NAIA. **Intercollegiate:** Baseball M, basketball, cheerleading, cross-country, football (tackle) M, rodeo, soccer W, softball W, track and field, volleyball W. **Intramural:** Badminton, baseball M, basketball, bowling, football (non-tackle), racquetball, softball, swimming, tennis, volleyball, water polo. **Team name:** Mountaineers.

**Student services.** Alcohol/substance abuse counseling, career counseling, student employment services, financial aid counseling, health services, minority student services, personal counseling, placement for graduates, veterans' counselor, women's services. **Physically disabled:** Services for visually, hearing impaired.

**Contact.** E-mail: admissions@eou.edu
Phone: (541) 962-3393 Toll-free number: (800) 452-8639
Fax: (541) 962-3418
Admissions Director, Eastern Oregon University, One University Boulevard, LaGrande, OR 97850

---

## Eugene Bible College
**Eugene, Oregon**
**www.ebc.edu**
**CB code: 4274**

- Private 4-year Bible college affiliated with Open Bible Standard Churches
- Residential campus in small city
- 137 degree-seeking undergraduates: 46% women
- 30% of applicants admitted
- Application essay required

**General.** Founded in 1925. Accredited by ABHE. **Degrees:** 35 bachelor's awarded. **Location:** 100 miles from Portland. **Calendar:** Quarter, extensive summer session. **Full-time faculty:** 10 total; 30% have terminal degrees, 20% minority, 40% women. **Part-time faculty:** 18 total; 28% have terminal degrees, 6% minority, 28% women. **Class size:** 54% < 20, 38% 20-39, 6% 40-49, 2% 50-99.

**Freshman class profile.** 122 applied, 37 admitted, 31 enrolled.

| Mid 50% test scores | | | |
|---|---|---|---|
| SAT critical reading: | 450-580 | GPA 2.0-2.99: | 32% |
| SAT math: | 430-610 | Rank in top quarter: | 29% |
| ACT composite: | 19-24 | Rank in top tenth: | 8% |
| GPA 3.50 or higher: | 27% | Out-of-state: | 48% |
| GPA 3.0-3.49: | 34% | Live on campus: | 70% |

**Basis for selection.** School achievement and activities, test scores, recommendations, personal essay most important. Religious affiliation or commitment important factor. SAT or ACT recommended. **Homeschooled:** CAT test, SAT Subject Test, or ITBS recommended.

**2007-2008 Annual costs.** Tuition/fees: $9,895. Room/board: $5,095. Books/supplies: $800. Personal expenses: $450.

**Financial aid. Non-need-based:** Scholarships awarded for academics, athletics, leadership, music/drama. **Additional information:** Some early acceptance awards possible for those admitted by May 15. Distance awards to those coming from over 1,000 miles away. Some awards for husbands and wives enrolled at same time.

**Application procedures. Admission:** Priority date 5/15; deadline 9/1 (receipt date). $30 fee. Application may be submitted online. Admission notification on a rolling basis. **Financial aid:** Priority date 5/1, closing date 9/1. FAFSA required. Applicants notified on a rolling basis starting 7/15; must reply within 4 week(s) of notification.

**Academics.** Transfer-track programs available in elementary education: first 2 years at college, final 2-3 years at other institutions. **Special study**

**options:** Cooperative education, distance learning, double major, dual enrollment of high school students, independent study, internships, liberal arts/career combination. **Credit/placement by examination:** AP, CLEP, institutional tests. **Support services:** Reduced course load, remedial instruction, study skills assistance, tutoring.

**Majors. Philosophy/religion:** Christian, religion. **Theology:** Bible, missionary, pastoral counseling, religious ed, sacred music, theology, youth ministry.

**Computing on campus.** 18 workstations in dormitories, library, computer center, student center. Dormitories wired for high-speed internet access. Repair service available.

**Student life. Freshman orientation:** Mandatory. Preregistration for classes offered. Week-long program ends with camping retreat to mountains with fellow students and faculty. **Policies:** Students required to sign Code of Conduct agreement. Student ministry/community service required. Religious observance required. **Housing:** Guaranteed on-campus for freshmen. Single-sex dorms, apartments, substance-free housing available. $75 deposit, deadline 9/1. **Activities:** Campus ministries, choral groups, drama, musical theater, student government.

**Athletics. Intramural:** Basketball, soccer, volleyball. **Team name:** Deacons.

**Student services.** Campus ministries, student employment services, financial aid counseling, personal counseling, placement for graduates, veterans' counselor.

**Contact.** E-mail: admissions@ebc.edu
Phone: (541) 485-1780 Toll-free number: (800) 322-2638
Fax: (541) 343-5801
Scott Thomas, Student Recruitment Coordinator, Eugene Bible College, 2155 Bailey Hill Road, Eugene, OR 97405

---

## George Fox University
**Newberg, Oregon**
**www.georgefox.edu**
**CB member**
**CB code: 4325**

- Private 4-year university and seminary college affiliated with Society of Friends (Quaker)
- Residential campus in large town
- 1,907 degree-seeking undergraduates: 12% part-time, 63% women, 1% African American, 5% Asian American, 4% Hispanic American, 2% Native American, 2% international
- 1,213 degree-seeking graduate students
- 83% of applicants admitted
- SAT or ACT (ACT writing optional), application essay required
- 65% graduate within 6 years; 26% enter graduate study

**General.** Founded in 1891. Regionally accredited. Volunteer service is encouraged through all-campus Serve Day and serve trips during school breaks. Freshman receive computer to keep upon graduating. **Degrees:** 510 bachelor's awarded; master's, doctoral, first professional offered. **ROTC:** Air Force. **Location:** 23 miles from Portland. **Calendar:** Semester, limited summer session. **Full-time faculty:** 167 total; 67% have terminal degrees, 7% minority, 38% women. **Part-time faculty:** 181 total; 22% have terminal degrees, 4% minority, 51% women. **Class size:** 60% < 20, 32% 20-39, 6% 40-49, 2% 50-99. **Special facilities:** Center for retreats and outdoor ministries, electron microscope, art galleries.

**Freshman class profile.** 1,264 applied, 1,049 admitted, 436 enrolled.

| Mid 50% test scores | | | |
|---|---|---|---|
| SAT critical reading: | 480-600 | Rank in top quarter: | 56% |
| SAT math: | 470-590 | Rank in top tenth: | 26% |
| SAT writing: | 460-580 | End year in good standing: | 89% |
| ACT composite: | 19-26 | Return as sophomores: | 80% |
| GPA 3.50 or higher: | 59% | Out-of-state: | 32% |
| GPA 3.0-3.49: | 30% | Live on campus: | 95% |
| GPA 2.0-2.99: | 11% | International: | 1% |

**Basis for selection.** Decision based on grade transcript, test scores, recommendations from teacher and counselor, church, school, and community activities. Interview recommended for all; audition recommended for drama, music programs. **Homeschooled:** Statement describing homeschool structure and mission, transcript of courses and grades, letter of recommendation (nonparent) required.

**High school preparation.** 16 units recommended. Recommended units include English 4, mathematics 3, social studies 2, history 2, science 2 (laboratory 2) and foreign language 2. 1 unit in health and physical education.

**2008-2009 Annual costs.** Tuition/fees: $25,190. Room/board: $8,000. Books/supplies: $700. Personal expenses: $1,380.

**2007-2008 Financial aid. Need-based:** 398 full-time freshmen applied for aid; 345 were judged to have need; 345 of these received aid. Average need met was 88%. Average scholarship/grant was $8,266; average loan $3,668. 69% of total undergraduate aid awarded as scholarships/grants, 31% as loans/jobs. **Non-need-based:** Awarded to 1,340 full-time undergraduates, including 357 freshmen. Scholarships awarded for academics, alumni affiliation, art, job skills, leadership, minority status, music/drama, religious affiliation. **Additional information:** Audition required for music and drama scholarships.

**Application procedures. Admission:** Priority date 2/1; no deadline. $40 fee, may be waived for applicants with need. Application may be submitted online. Admission notification on a rolling basis beginning on or about 10/1. Must reply by May 1 or within 2 week(s) if notified thereafter. **Financial aid:** Priority date 2/1; no closing date. FAFSA required. Applicants notified on a rolling basis starting 3/1; must reply within 6 week(s) of notification.

**Academics. Special study options:** Accelerated study, cross-registration, double major, dual enrollment of high school students, ESL, exchange student, honors, independent study, internships, student-designed major, study abroad, teacher certification program, Washington semester. **Credit/placement by examination:** AP, CLEP, IB, SAT, ACT, institutional tests. 32 credit hours maximum toward bachelor's degree. **Support services:** Learning center, reduced course load, remedial instruction, study skills assistance, tutoring, writing center.

**Majors. Biology:** General. **Business:** Accounting, business admin, management information systems. **Communications:** General, organizational. **Computer sciences:** General. **Education:** Elementary, health, music, physical. **Engineering:** General, electrical, mechanical. **English:** English lit. **Family/consumer sciences:** General. **Foreign languages:** Spanish. **Health:** Athletic training, nursing (RN). **History:** General. **Interdisciplinary:** Behavioral sciences, cognitive science, global studies. **Math:** General. **Parks/recreation:** Health/fitness. **Philosophy/religion:** Philosophy, religion. **Physical sciences:** Chemistry. **Psychology:** General. **Public administration:** Social work. **Social sciences:** Economics, political science, sociology. **Theology:** Bible. **Visual/performing arts:** Art, cinematography, dramatic. **Other:** Christian ministries, Interdisciplinary studies.

**Most popular majors.** Business/marketing 35%, interdisciplinary studies 14%, visual/performing arts 6%.

**Computing on campus.** 154 workstations in dormitories, library, computer center, student center. Dormitories wired for high-speed internet access and linked to campus network. Commuter students can connect to campus network. Online course registration, online library, helpline, repair service, wireless network available.

**Student life. Freshman orientation:** Mandatory. Preregistration for classes offered. One-day programs available during summer. New students attend 3-day program at the start of the semester. **Policies:** 3-year residency requirement for undergraduates. Required spiritual formation program and chapel program. Religious observance required. **Housing:** Guaranteed on-campus for all undergraduates. Single-sex dorms, special housing for disabled, apartments, substance-free housing available. Pets allowed in dorm rooms. Houses, theme floors, living learning communities. **Activities:** Bands, campus ministries, choral groups, drama, international student organizations, literary magazine, music ensembles, musical theater, radio station, student government, student newspaper, symphony orchestra, Christian services committee, Associated Student Community, multicultural club, Fellowship of Christian Athletes, Young Life, Residence Life, ADVANCE Leadership Development Program.

**Athletics.** NCAA. **Intercollegiate:** Baseball M, basketball, cross-country, golf, soccer, softball W, tennis, track and field, volleyball W. **Intramural:** Badminton, basketball, football (non-tackle), golf, racquetball, soccer, table tennis, tennis, volleyball. **Team name:** Bruins.

**Student services.** Alcohol/substance abuse counseling, campus ministries, career counseling, student employment services, financial aid counseling, health services, minority student services, personal counseling, veterans' counselor. **Physically disabled:** Services for visually, speech, hearing impaired.

**Contact.** E-mail: admissions@georgefox.edu
Phone: (503) 554-2240 Toll-free number: (800) 765-4369 ext. 2240
Fax: (503) 554-3110
Ryan Dougherty, Director of Undergraduate Admissions, George Fox University, 414 North Meridian Street, Newberg, OR 97132-2697

## ITT Technical Institute: Portland

**Portland, Oregon**
**www.itt-tech.edu**
**CB code: 0947**

- For-profit 4-year technical college
- Commuter campus in large city

**General.** Founded in 1979. Accredited by ACICS. **Location:** 10 miles from downtown. **Calendar:** Quarter.

**Annual costs/financial aid.** Tuition varies by program, $260-$368 per credit hour.

**Contact.** Phone: (503) 255-6500
Director of Recruitment, 6035 Northeast 78th Court, Portland, OR 97218

## Lewis & Clark College

**Portland, Oregon**
**www.lclark.edu**
**CB member**
**CB code: 4384**

- Private 4-year liberal arts college
- Residential campus in very large city
- 1,926 degree-seeking undergraduates: 61% women, 2% African American, 6% Asian American, 5% Hispanic American, 1% Native American, 5% international
- 1,598 degree-seeking graduate students
- 56% of applicants admitted
- Application essay required
- 71% graduate within 6 years; 10% enter graduate study

**General.** Founded in 1867. Regionally accredited. **Degrees:** 454 bachelor's awarded; master's, doctoral, first professional offered. **Calendar:** Semester, limited summer session. **Full-time faculty:** 221 total; 91% have terminal degrees, 10% minority, 45% women. **Part-time faculty:** 138 total; 33% have terminal degrees, 6% minority, 59% women. **Class size:** 61% < 20, 35% 20-39, 3% 40-49, 1% 50-99. **Special facilities:** Scanning electron microscope, 3 diode array UV/visible spectrometers, gas chromatography/mass spectrometer, X-ray fluorescence spectrometer, atomic absorption spectrometer, solar telescope with spectrograph, imaging laboratory with high resolution optical microscope, research astronomical observatory, holographic laboratory, electro-acoustic music studio, 85-rank Casavant organ, multi-media foreign language lab, greenhouse.

**Freshman class profile.** 5,351 applied, 2,998 admitted, 507 enrolled.

| Mid 50% test scores | | | |
|---|---|---|---|
| SAT critical reading: | 610-700 | Rank in top quarter: | 81% |
| SAT math: | 590-680 | Rank in top tenth: | 46% |
| SAT writing: | 590-680 | End year in good standing: | 93% |
| ACT composite: | 26-31 | Return as sophomores: | 88% |
| GPA 3.50 or higher: | 75% | Out-of-state: | 87% |
| GPA 3.0-3.49: | 22% | Live on campus: | 98% |
| GPA 2.0-2.99: | 3% | International: | 5% |

**Basis for selection.** School curriculum and achievement most important. Standardized tests, recommendations, extracurricular involvement, essay and interview also considered. Portfolio Path option offered for admission, requiring academic portfolio (including 5 graded writing samples) and 2 additional teacher recommendations; standardized test scores optional. Interviews optional, audition recommended for music scholarships, portfolio required for Portfolio Path applicants. **Homeschooled:** School's Portfolio Path for admissions recommended. GED required, interview recommended.

**High school preparation.** Recommended units include English 4, mathematics 4, social studies 4, science 3 (laboratory 2) and foreign language 3. One unit fine arts recommended.

**2007-2008 Annual costs.** Tuition/fees: $31,840. Room/board: $8,450. Books/supplies: $1,800. Personal expenses: $900.

**2007-2008 Financial aid. Need-based:** 373 full-time freshmen applied for aid; 275 were judged to have need; 275 of these received aid. Average need met was 86%. Average scholarship/grant was $22,425; average loan $4,205. 79% of total undergraduate aid awarded as scholarships/grants, 21% as loans/jobs. **Non-need-based:** Awarded to 304 full-time undergraduates, including 80 freshmen. Scholarships awarded for academics, leadership, music/drama.

**Application procedures. Admission:** Closing date 2/1 (receipt date). $50 fee, may be waived for applicants with need. Application may be submitted online. Admission notification 4/1. Must reply by May 1 or within 2 week(s) if notified thereafter. Non-refundable tuition deposit of $300 due 5/1 or 2 weeks after notification of admission. **Financial aid:** Priority date 3/1; no closing date. FAFSA, CSS PROFILE required. Applicants notified on a rolling basis starting 3/1.

**Academics. Special study options:** Accelerated study, combined bachelor's/ graduate degree, cross-registration, double major, dual enrollment of high school students, ESL, honors, independent study, internships, New York semester, student-designed major, study abroad, Washington semester. 3-2 engineering program with Columbia University, University of Southern California, Oregon Graduate Institute of Science and Engineering at OHSU, Washington University (St. Louis). **Credit/placement by examination:** AP, CLEP, IB, institutional tests. Up to 24 semester hours awarded for International Baccalaureate full diploma and a score of 36 or higher (16 hours for diploma with 32-35). Scores of 5 or higher on higher level exams get 4 credits. **Support services:** Learning center, reduced course load, study skills assistance, tutoring, writing center.

**Majors. Area/ethnic studies:** East Asian. **Biology:** General, biochemistry. **Communications:** General. **Computer sciences:** Computer science. **Conservation:** Environmental studies. **English:** English lit. **Foreign languages:** General, French, German, Spanish. **History:** General. **Interdisciplinary:** Math/computer science. **Liberal arts:** Arts/sciences. **Math:** General. **Philosophy/religion:** Philosophy, religion. **Physical sciences:** Chemistry, physics. **Psychology:** General. **Social sciences:** Anthropology, economics, international relations, political science, sociology. **Visual/performing arts:** Art, dramatic, music performance, studio arts.

**Most popular majors.** Biology 7%, English 8%, foreign language 8%, history 6%, psychology 12%, social sciences 26%, visual/performing arts 10%.

**Computing on campus.** 158 workstations in library, computer center, student center. Dormitories wired for high-speed internet access and linked to campus network. Commuter students can connect to campus network. Online library, helpline, repair service, student web hosting, wireless network available.

**Student life. Freshman orientation:** Mandatory. Preregistration for classes offered. Held the 4 days preceding class in late August. **Housing:** Guaranteed on-campus for freshmen. Coed dorms, single-sex dorms, substance-free housing available. Theme floors, apartment-style residence halls for upperclassmen available. **Activities:** Bands, campus ministries, choral groups, dance, drama, international student organizations, literary magazine, music ensembles, Model UN, musical theater, radio station, student government, student newspaper, symphony orchestra, TV station, Jewish student union, InterVarsity Christian Fellowship, Fellowship of Christian Athletes, Hawaii club, Amnesty International, black student union, Circle K, Forensics, Gringos y Latinos.

**Athletics.** NCAA. **Intercollegiate:** Baseball M, basketball, cross-country, football (tackle) M, golf, rowing (crew), soccer W, softball W, swimming, tennis, track and field, volleyball W. **Intramural:** Badminton, basketball, cross-country, softball, swimming, table tennis, tennis, volleyball, water polo. **Team name:** Pioneers, Pios.

**Student services.** Adult student services, alcohol/substance abuse counseling, campus ministries, career counseling, services for economically disadvantaged, student employment services, financial aid counseling, health services, legal services, minority student services, personal counseling, placement for graduates, veterans' counselor, women's services. **Physically disabled:** Services for visually, speech, hearing impaired.

**Contact.** E-mail: admissions@lclark.edu
Phone: (503) 768-7040 Toll-free number: (800) 444-4111
Fax: (503) 768-7055
Michael Sexton, Dean of Admissions, Lewis & Clark College, 0615 SW Palatine Hill Road, Portland, OR 97219-7899

---

## Linfield College

**McMinnville, Oregon**
**www.linfield.edu**

**CB member**
**CB code: 4387**

- Private 4-year business and liberal arts college affiliated with American Baptist Churches in the USA
- Residential campus in large town
- 1,646 degree-seeking undergraduates: 1% part-time, 54% women, 2% African American, 8% Asian American, 4% Hispanic American, 1% Native American, 2% international
- 80% of applicants admitted
- SAT or ACT (ACT writing optional), application essay required
- 69% graduate within 6 years; 15% enter graduate study

**General.** Founded in 1849. Regionally accredited. The McMinnville Campus serves students who are primarily in residence and pursuing a degree full-time. The Portland Campus serves primarily full-time transfer students completing a degree in nursing or health sciences. The Division of Continuing Education serves primarily part-time students who wish to complete a bachelor's degree online (some on site courses are available in Oregon as well). **Degrees:** 370 bachelor's awarded. **ROTC:** Air Force. **Location:** 38 miles from Portland. **Calendar:** 4-1-4, limited summer session. **Full-time faculty:** 110 total; 94% have terminal degrees, 7% minority, 44% women. **Part-time faculty:** 76 total; 36% have terminal degrees, 50% women. **Class size:** 62% < 20, 36% 20-39, 1% 40-49, 1% 50-99, less than 1% >100. **Special facilities:** Field station, anthropology museum, interactive writing laboratory.

**Freshman class profile.** 2,050 applied, 1,637 admitted, 476 enrolled.

| Mid 50% test scores | | | |
|---|---|---|---|
| SAT critical reading: | 490-610 | Rank in top tenth: | 33% |
| SAT math: | 500-610 | End year in good standing: | 95% |
| SAT writing: | 460-580 | Return as sophomores: | 81% |
| ACT composite: | 21-27 | Out-of-state: | 44% |
| GPA 3.50 or higher: | 62% | Live on campus: | 99% |
| GPA 3.0-3.49: | 31% | International: | 3% |
| GPA 2.0-2.99: | 7% | Fraternities: | 13% |
| Rank in top quarter: | 63% | Sororities: | 24% |

**Basis for selection.** High school grades, official transcripts, counselor's recommendation and/or teacher recommendation, test scores, and essay important. Interview recommended.

**High school preparation.** 17 units recommended. Recommended units include English 4, mathematics 4, social studies 3, science 3 and foreign language 2.

**2008-2009 Annual costs.** Tuition/fees: $27,414. Room/board: $7,860. Books/supplies: $650. Personal expenses: $1,100.

**2007-2008 Financial aid. Need-based:** 309 full-time freshmen applied for aid; 309 were judged to have need; 309 of these received aid. Average need met was 84%. Average scholarship/grant was $8,921; average loan $4,215. 61% of total undergraduate aid awarded as scholarships/grants, 39% as loans/jobs. **Non-need-based:** Awarded to 1,114 full-time undergraduates, including 268 freshmen. Scholarships awarded for academics, music/drama.

**Application procedures. Admission:** $40 fee, may be waived for applicants with need. Application may be submitted online. Admission notification 4/1. Must reply by May 1 or within 2 week(s) if notified thereafter. **Financial aid:** Priority date 2/1; no closing date. FAFSA required. Applicants notified by 4/1; must reply by 5/1.

**Academics. Special study options:** Cross-registration, distance learning, double major, ESL, external degree, independent study, internships, liberal arts/career combination, semester at sea, student-designed major, study abroad, teacher certification program, Washington semester. Broad participation in semester abroad programs at Linfield centers in Austria, China, Costa Rica, Ecuador, England, France, Ireland, Japan, Korea, Mexico and Norway, as well as shorter term study abroad opportunities through January term. **Credit/placement by examination:** AP, CLEP, IB, institutional tests. 30 credit hours maximum toward bachelor's degree. **Support services:** Learning center, reduced course load, study skills assistance, tutoring, writing center.

**Majors. Area/ethnic studies:** German. **Biology:** General. **Business:** General, accounting, finance, international. **Communications:** General, media studies. **Computer sciences:** Computer science. **Conservation:** Environmental studies. **Education:** Elementary, music. **English:** Creative writing, English lit. **Foreign languages:** French, German, Japanese, Spanish. **Health:** Athletic training, nursing (RN). **History:** General. **Math:** General. **Parks/recreation:** Exercise sciences, health/fitness. **Philosophy/religion:** Philosophy, religion. **Physical sciences:** General, applied physics, chemistry, physics. **Psychology:** General. **Social sciences:** Anthropology, economics, political science, sociology. **Visual/performing arts:** Art, design, dramatic, music performance, music theory/composition, studio arts.

**Most popular majors.** Biology 7%, business/marketing 24%, communications/journalism 6%, English 6%, parks/recreation 8%, social sciences 11%, visual/performing arts 6%.

**Computing on campus.** 250 workstations in dormitories, library, computer center, student center. Dormitories wired for high-speed internet access and linked to campus network. Commuter students can connect to campus network. Online course registration, online library, helpline, repair service, student web hosting, wireless network available.

**Student life. Freshman orientation:** Mandatory. 4-day program held at beginning of fall semester includes one-on-one advising, peer mentoring. **Housing:** Guaranteed on-campus for freshmen. Coed dorms, single-sex dorms, special housing for disabled, apartments, fraternity/sorority housing, substance-free housing available. **Activities:** Bands, choral groups, dance, drama, literary magazine, music ensembles, musical theater, opera, radio station, student government, student newspaper, symphony orchestra, multicultural student club, women's club, Hawaiian club, Fellowship of Christian Athletes, Progressive Student Union, Circle-K, Habitat for Humanity, Gay Straight Alliance, Linfield Republicans.

**Athletics.** NCAA. **Intercollegiate:** Baseball M, basketball, cross-country, football (tackle) M, golf, lacrosse W, soccer, softball, swimming, tennis, track and field, volleyball W. **Intramural:** Basketball, bowling, football (non-tackle), racquetball, soccer, softball, volleyball. **Team name:** Wildcats.

**Student services.** Adult student services, alcohol/substance abuse counseling, campus ministries, career counseling, student employment services, financial aid counseling, health services, minority student services, personal counseling, placement for graduates, veterans' counselor, women's services. **Physically disabled:** Services for visually, speech, hearing impaired.

**Contact.** E-mail: admission@linfield.edu
Phone: (503) 883-2213 Toll-free number: (800) 640-2287
Fax: (503) 883-2472
Lisa Knodle-Bragiel, Director of Admission, Linfield College, 900 SE
Baker Street, McMinnville, OR 97218-6894

## Marylhurst University
### Marylhurst, Oregon
www.marylhurst.edu **CB code: 0440**

- Private 4-year university and liberal arts college affiliated with Roman Catholic Church
- Commuter campus in large town
- 194 full-time, degree-seeking undergraduates
- 596 graduate students

**General.** Founded in 1893. Regionally accredited. **Degrees:** 168 bachelor's awarded; master's, first professional offered. **Location:** 10 miles from Portland. **Calendar:** Quarter, extensive summer session. **Full-time faculty:** 35 total. **Part-time faculty:** 340 total. **Class size:** 98% < 20, 2% 20-39.

**Basis for selection.** Open admission, but selective for some programs. High school GPA, record and recommendations considered.

**2007-2008 Annual costs.** Tuition/fees: $15,570. Books/supplies: $600. Personal expenses: $1,800.

**Financial aid. Non-need-based:** Scholarships awarded for academics.

**Application procedures. Admission:** No deadline. $20 fee. Application may be submitted online. Admission notification on a rolling basis. **Financial aid:** Priority date 6/1; no closing date. FAFSA, institutional form required. Applicants notified on a rolling basis starting 5/1.

**Academics. Special study options:** Distance learning, double major, ESL, honors, independent study, internships, student-designed major, weekend college. **Credit/placement by examination:** AP, CLEP, IB, institutional tests. 45 credit hours maximum toward bachelor's degree. **Support services:** Learning center, study skills assistance, tutoring, writing center.

**Majors. Business:** General, business admin, communications, real estate. **Communications:** General. **Conservation:** General, environmental studies. **Interdisciplinary:** Natural sciences. **Liberal arts:** Arts/sciences. **Philosophy/religion:** Philosophy, religion. **Psychology:** General. **Social sciences:** General. **Visual/performing arts:** Art, interior design, studio arts.

**Computing on campus.** 41 workstations in library. Online course registration available.

**Student life. Freshman orientation:** Available. **Activities:** Jazz band, choral groups, music ensembles, musical theater, symphony orchestra.

**Student services.** Adult student services, career counseling, financial aid counseling, personal counseling, veterans' counselor. **Physically disabled:** Services for visually, hearing impaired.

**Contact.** E-mail: admissions@marylhurst.edu
Phone: (503) 699-6268 Toll-free number: (800) 634-9982 ext. 6268
Fax: (503) 635-6585
Katie Abbot, Director of Admissions, Marylhurst University, PO Box 261, Marylhurst, OR 97036-0261

## Mount Angel Seminary
### St. Benedict, Oregon
www.mtangel.edu **CB code: 4491**

- Private 4-year seminary college for men affiliated with Roman Catholic Church
- Residential campus in small town
- 90 degree-seeking undergraduates
- 110 graduate students

**General.** Founded in 1887. Regionally accredited; also accredited by ATS. All undergraduates candidates for Roman Catholic priesthood. **Degrees:** 18 bachelor's awarded; master's, first professional offered. **Location:** 40 miles from Portland. **Calendar:** Semester. **Full-time faculty:** 25 total. **Part-time faculty:** 15 total.

**Freshman class profile.**

| | | | |
|---|---|---|---|
| Out-of-state: | 75% | Live on campus: | 100% |

**Basis for selection.** Primarily recommendations from sponsoring dioceses or clergymen, personal interview important. Test scores considered. SAT or ACT recommended. Interview recommended.

**2007-2008 Annual costs.** Tuition/fees: $13,681. Formation fee of $2,743 per year. Room/board: $8,934. Books/supplies: $800. Personal expenses: $1,000.

**Application procedures. Admission:** Closing date 6/15. $27 fee, may be waived for applicants with need. Admission notification on a rolling basis beginning on or about 9/1. **Financial aid:** No deadline. Institutional form required. Applicants notified on a rolling basis; must reply within 2 week(s) of notification.

**Academics. Special study options:** Cross-registration, double major, ESL. Interdivisional program, 3-week full-time pursuit of single approved course of study. **Credit/placement by examination:** CLEP, institutional tests.

**Majors. Liberal arts:** Arts/sciences. **Philosophy/religion:** Philosophy. **Theology:** Theology.

**Computing on campus.** 10 workstations in dormitories, library, computer center.

**Student life. Policies:** All full-time students working toward priesthood required to live on campus. Religious observance required. **Housing:** Guaranteed on-campus for all undergraduates. **Activities:** Student government.

**Athletics. Intramural:** Basketball M, racquetball M, soccer M, swimming M, volleyball M.

**Student services.** Health services, personal counseling.

**Contact.** Phone: (503) 845-3951 Fax: (503) 845-3126
Sr. Virginia Schroeder, Admissions Director, Mount Angel Seminary, One Abbey Drive, St. Benedict, OR 97373

## Multnomah Bible College
### Portland, Oregon
www.multnomah.edu **CB code: 4496**

- Private 4-year Bible and seminary college affiliated with interdenominational tradition
- Residential campus in large city
- 567 degree-seeking undergraduates: 8% part-time, 45% women, 1% African American, 4% Asian American, 3% Hispanic American, 1% Native American, 1% international
- 218 degree-seeking graduate students
- 81% of applicants admitted
- SAT or ACT (ACT writing recommended), application essay required
- 43% graduate within 6 years

**General.** Founded in 1936. Regionally accredited; also accredited by ABHE. Emphasis on preparation for Christian ministries. **Degrees:** 105 bachelor's awarded; master's, first professional offered. **Location:** 5 miles from downtown. **Calendar:** Semester, limited summer session. **Full-time faculty:** 31 total; 68% have terminal degrees, 6% minority, 16% women. **Part-time faculty:** 31 total; 19% have terminal degrees, 3% minority, 39% women. **Class size:** 53% < 20, 32% 20-39, 9% 40-49, 5% 50-99, less than 1% >100.

**Freshman class profile.** 143 applied, 116 admitted, 73 enrolled.

| Mid 50% test scores | | | |
|---|---|---|---|
| SAT critical reading: | 460-600 | GPA 3.0-3.49: | 23% |
| SAT math: | 470-580 | GPA 2.0-2.99: | 19% |
| SAT writing: | 460-590 | Rank in top quarter: | 38% |
| ACT composite: | 18-27 | Rank in top tenth: | 20% |
| GPA 3.50 or higher: | 58% | Return as sophomores: | 60% |
| | | International: | 1% |

**Basis for selection.** School achievement record, test scores, recommendations most important.

**High school preparation.** College-preparatory program recommended. Recommended units include English 4, mathematics 2, social studies 3, history 2, science 3 (laboratory 1) and foreign language 2.

**2007-2008 Annual costs.** Tuition/fees: $13,480. Room/board: $5,750. Books/supplies: $1,000. Personal expenses: $1,600.

**2006-2007 Financial aid. Need-based:** 212 full-time freshmen applied for aid; 176 were judged to have need; 124 of these received aid. Average need met was 20%. Average scholarship/grant was $3,496; average loan $2,257. 49% of total undergraduate aid awarded as scholarships/grants, 51% as loans/jobs. **Non-need-based:** Awarded to 115 full-time undergraduates, including 35 freshmen. Scholarships awarded for academics.

**Application procedures. Admission:** Priority date 3/1; deadline 7/15 (postmark date). $40 fee. Application must be submitted on paper. Admission notification on a rolling basis. Must reply by 8/15. **Financial aid:** Priority date 3/1, closing date 8/1. FAFSA, institutional form required. Applicants notified on a rolling basis starting 4/1; must reply within 3 week(s) of notification.

**Academics. Special study options:** Cooperative education, double major, internships, liberal arts/career combination, teacher certification program. **Credit/placement by examination:** AP, CLEP, IB, institutional tests. 20 credit hours maximum toward bachelor's degree. **Support services:** Reduced course load, study skills assistance.

**Majors. Communications:** General, journalism. **Education:** Elementary. **Foreign languages:** Ancient Greek, Hebrew. **History:** General. **Theology:** Bible, missionary, pastoral counseling, religious ed, sacred music, theology, youth ministry.

**Computing on campus.** 42 workstations in dormitories, library, computer center. Dormitories wired for high-speed internet access and linked to campus network. Commuter students can connect to campus network. Online library, helpline, wireless network available.

**Student life. Freshman orientation:** Mandatory. Orientation occurs three days before start of classes. **Policies:** No alcohol, smoking, gambling. Religious observance required. **Housing:** Guaranteed on-campus for freshmen. Single-sex dorms, apartments available. $125 fully refundable deposit, deadline 7/15. Houses for married students. **Activities:** Choral groups, drama, music ensembles, student government, student newspaper.

**Athletics. NCCAA. Intercollegiate:** Basketball, volleyball W. **Intramural:** Basketball, football (non-tackle), soccer, volleyball. **Team name:** Lions.

**Student services.** Campus ministries, career counseling, student employment services, financial aid counseling, health services, personal counseling, placement for graduates, veterans' counselor.

**Contact.** E-mail: admiss@multnomah.edu
Phone: (503) 255-0332 ext. 485 Toll-free number: (800) 275-4672
Fax: (503) 254-1268
Amy Stephens, Director of Admissions and Registrar, Multnomah Bible College, 8435 Northeast Glisan Street, Portland, OR 97220-5898

---

## Northwest Christian College

**Eugene, Oregon**
www.nwcc.edu

CB code: 4543

- Private 4-year liberal arts college affiliated with Christian Church (Disciples of Christ)
- Commuter campus in small city
- 395 degree-seeking undergraduates: 23% part-time, 59% women
- 89 degree-seeking graduate students
- 45% of applicants admitted
- SAT or ACT (ACT writing recommended), application essay required
- 51% graduate within 6 years

---

**General.** Founded in 1895. Regionally accredited. **Degrees:** 82 bachelor's, 7 associate awarded; master's offered. **ROTC:** Army. **Location:** 110 miles from Portland. **Calendar:** Semester, limited summer session. **Full-time faculty:** 27 total; 74% have terminal degrees, 4% minority, 52% women. **Part-time faculty:** 63 total; 21% have terminal degrees, 51% women. **Class size:** 90% <20, 10% 20-39.

**Freshman class profile.** 614 applied, 275 admitted, 52 enrolled.

| Mid 50% test scores | | | |
|---|---|---|---|
| SAT critical reading: | 440-580 | GPA 3.0-3.49: | 32% |
| SAT math: | 430-550 | GPA 2.0-2.99: | 31% |
| SAT writing: | 420-550 | Rank in top quarter: | 32% |
| ACT composite: | 18-23 | Rank in top tenth: | 5% |
| GPA 3.50 or higher: | 35% | Return as sophomores: | 53% |
| | | Out-of-state: | 23% |

**Basis for selection.** Admission based on evidence of ability to succeed academically and if applicant is appropriate match. Students failing to meet minimum admissions standards referred to admissions committee for final decision. Institution-developed math placement test used if student does not have ACT or SAT test scores. Interview recommended, personal statement required. **Homeschooled:** Greater reliance on standardized test scores to demonstrate admissibility. Flexible admission requirements enable student to demonstrate reasonable preparedness for college. **Learning Disabled:** Documented proof of disability.

**High school preparation.** 15 units required. Required units include English 4, mathematics 3, social studies 2, history 1, science 2 (laboratory 1) and foreign language 2. Computer literacy also recommended.

**2007-2008 Annual costs.** Tuition/fees: $21,481. Room/board: $6,770. Books/supplies: $825. Personal expenses: $900.

**2007-2008 Financial aid. Need-based:** Average need met was 75%. Average scholarship/grant was $13,411; average loan $1,919. 68% of total undergraduate aid awarded as scholarships/grants, 32% as loans/jobs. **Non-need-based:** Scholarships awarded for academics, athletics, leadership, music/drama, religious affiliation.

**Application procedures. Admission:** Priority date 7/1; no deadline. No application fee. Application may be submitted online. Admission notification on a rolling basis beginning on or about 10/15. **Financial aid:** Priority date 3/1; no closing date. FAFSA required. Applicants notified on a rolling basis starting 4/1.

**Academics. Special study options:** Accelerated study, distance learning, double major, ESL, independent study, internships, liberal arts/career combination, student-designed major, study abroad, teacher certification program. **Credit/placement by examination:** AP, CLEP, IB, institutional tests. 15 credit hours maximum toward associate degree, 30 toward bachelor's. **Support services:** Reduced course load, remedial instruction, tutoring, writing center.

**Majors. Biology:** Exercise physiology. **Business:** Accounting, business admin, management information systems. **Communications:** General. **Computer sciences:** General, programming. **Education:** Multi-level teacher. **English:** English lit. **Health:** Health services admin. **History:** General. **Interdisciplinary:** Intercultural. **Math:** General. **Psychology:** General. **Public administration:** Human services. **Social sciences:** General. **Theology:** Bible. **Visual/performing arts:** Music management.

**Most popular majors.** Business/marketing 63%, education 16%.

**Computing on campus.** 46 workstations in dormitories, library, computer center. Dormitories wired for high-speed internet access and linked to campus network. Commuter students can connect to campus network. Online library, wireless network available.

**Student life. Freshman orientation:** Mandatory, $156 fee. Preregistration for classes offered. 4 day program held immediately before fall term. **Policies:** Attendance at chapel is required of all students. Religious observance required. **Housing:** Guaranteed on-campus for freshmen. Coed dorms, apartments available. $100 fully refundable deposit, deadline 6/1. **Activities:** Concert band, campus ministries, choral groups, drama, literary magazine, music ensembles, student government, student newspaper, education club, TESOL club, psychology club, crochet club, dance club, golf club, running club, business club.

**Athletics. NAIA, USCAA. Intercollegiate:** Basketball, cross-country, soccer, softball W. **Intramural:** Basketball, volleyball W. **Team name:** Beacons.

**Student services.** Adult student services, alcohol/substance abuse counseling, campus ministries, career counseling, student employment services, financial aid counseling, health services, personal counseling, placement for graduates, veterans' counselor.

**Contact.** E-mail: admissions@nwcc.edu
Phone: (541) 684-7201 Toll-free number: (877) 463-6622
Fax: (541) 684-7317
Director of Admissions, Northwest Christian College, 828 East 11th
Avenue, Eugene, OR 97401-3745

## Oregon College of Art & Craft
### Portland, Oregon
### www.ocac.edu

- Private 4-year visual arts college
- Very large city

**General.** Candidate for regional accreditation. **Calendar:** Semester.

**Annual costs/financial aid.** Tuition/fees (2007-2008): $19,085. Fees
vary by area of concentration. Books/supplies: $1,700. Need-based finan-
cial aid available to full-time and part-time students.

**Contact.** Phone: (503) 297-5544 ext. 129
8245 SW Barnes Road, Portland, OR 97225-6349

## Oregon Health & Science University
### Portland, Oregon                     CB member
### www.ohsu.edu                         CB code: 4900

- Public 3-year university and health science college
- Commuter campus in very large city
- 591 degree-seeking undergraduates: 1% African American, 5% Asian
  American, 5% Hispanic American, 2% Native American, 1%
  international
- 1,864 graduate students

**General.** Founded in 1887. Regionally accredited. **Degrees:** 276 bachelor's awarded; master's, doctoral, first professional offered. **Calendar:** Quarter, limited summer session. **Full-time faculty:** 1,290 total. **Part-time faculty:** 510 total.

**Basis for selection.** Admission requirements vary by program.

**2007-2008 Annual costs.** Tuition/fees: $11,860; $20,176 out-of-state.
Tuition shown is for undergraduate nursing program; costs for other programs vary. Books/supplies: $461. Personal expenses: $2,285.

**2006-2007 Financial aid. Need-based:** 19% of total undergraduate aid
awarded as scholarships/grants, 81% as loans/jobs. **Non-need-based:** Scholarships awarded for academics, minority status, state residency.

**Application procedures. Admission:** Closing date 1/15 (postmark date).
$120 fee, may be waived for applicants with need. Application must be
submitted online. Admission notification on a rolling basis. Must reply by
5/1. **Financial aid:** Priority date 3/1; no closing date. FAFSA required. Applicants notified on a rolling basis starting 5/31.

**Academics.** Services offered in OHSU's Center for Diversity and Multicultural Affairs. **Special study options:** Accelerated study, combined bachelor's/
graduate degree, distance learning. **Credit/placement by examination:** CLEP,
IB. **Support services:** Pre-admission summer program, study skills assistance, tutoring.

**Majors. Health:** Clinical lab science, clinical lab technology, EMT paramedic, health services, medical radiologic technology/radiation therapy, nursing (RN).

**Computing on campus.** 60 workstations in library, computer center,
student center. Commuter students can connect to campus network. Online
library, helpline, wireless network available.

**Student life. Freshman orientation:** Available. Orientation varies by program. **Activities:** Student government, student newspaper.

**Athletics. Intramural:** Basketball, soccer, swimming, table tennis, tennis,
volleyball.

**Student services.** Career counseling, financial aid counseling, health services, personal counseling.

**Contact.** E-mail: proginfo@ohsu.edu
Phone: (503) 494-2998 Fax: (503) 494-3400
Jennifer Anderson, Director of Admissions, Oregon Health & Science
University, 3181 SW Sam Jackson Park Road, Portland, OR 97239

## Oregon Institute of Technology
### Klamath Falls, Oregon                CB member
### www.oit.edu                          CB code: 4587

- Public 4-year engineering, health science and technical college
- Commuter campus in small city
- 2,534 degree-seeking undergraduates: 1% African American, 6% Asian
  American, 4% Hispanic American, 2% Native American, 1%
  international
- 20 graduate students
- SAT or ACT with writing required

**General.** Founded in 1947. Regionally accredited. Portland MetroCenter
offers upper-division courses in electronics engineering technology, manufacturing engineering technology. Software engineering technology offered
at Capital Center in Portland-Metro area. **Degrees:** 451 bachelor's, 80 associate awarded; master's offered. **ROTC:** Army. **Location:** 280 miles from
Portland, 270 miles from Reno, Nevada. **Calendar:** Quarter, limited summer session. **Full-time faculty:** 133 total; 35% have terminal degrees, 5%
minority, 40% women. **Part-time faculty:** 90 total; 13% have terminal degrees, 6% minority, 37% women. **Class size:** 57% < 20, 37% 20-39, 4%
40-49, 2% 50-99. **Special facilities:** Center for research on geothermal energy, Oregon Renewable Energy Center.

**Freshman class profile.**

| Mid 50% test scores | | | |
|---|---|---|---|
| SAT critical reading: | 450-580 | GPA 2.0-2.99: | 8% |
| SAT math: | 480-610 | Rank in top quarter: | 56% |
| ACT composite: | 18-24 | Rank in top tenth: | 25% |
| GPA 3.50 or higher: | 53% | Out-of-state: | 8% |
| GPA 3.0-3.49: | 39% | Live on campus: | 54% |
| | | International: | 1% |

**Basis for selection.** Secondary school record and standardized test scores
very important. Class rank, recommendations, essay, interview, character/
personal qualities and work experience all considered. Applicants from nonstandard or unaccredited high schools must take 3 SAT Subject Tests: 1
English, 1 math, 1 other of student's choice. **Learning Disabled:** Tech opportunities available.

**High school preparation.** 14 units required. Required units include English 4, mathematics 3, social studies 3, science 2 (laboratory 1) and foreign
language 2.

**2007-2008 Annual costs.** Tuition/fees: $6,144; $16,179 out-of-state. Room/
board: $6,347. Books/supplies: $1,000. Personal expenses: $2,438.

**2006-2007 Financial aid. Need-based:** 186 full-time freshmen applied
for aid; 168 were judged to have need; 164 of these received aid. Average
need met was 20%. Average scholarship/grant was $3,943; average loan
$2,627. 35% of total undergraduate aid awarded as scholarships/grants, 65%
as loans/jobs. **Non-need-based:** Awarded to 84 full-time undergraduates,
including 26 freshmen. Scholarships awarded for academics, athletics, leadership, minority status.

**Application procedures. Admission:** Priority date 2/1; deadline 10/1.
$50 fee. Application may be submitted online. Admission notification on a
rolling basis beginning on or about 10/15. Must reply by May 1 or within 4
week(s) if notified thereafter. **Financial aid:** Priority date 3/1; no closing
date. FAFSA required. Applicants notified on a rolling basis starting 4/1;
must reply within 3 week(s) of notification.

**Academics. Special study options:** Combined bachelor's/graduate degree, cooperative education, cross-registration, distance learning, double major, dual enrollment of high school students, external degree, internships,
liberal arts/career combination, study abroad. **Credit/placement by examination:** AP, CLEP, SAT, ACT, institutional tests. No more than 25% of
credits submitted for graduation may be credit by examination. **Support
services:** Learning center, reduced course load, remedial instruction, study
skills assistance, tutoring.

**Majors. Business:** Accounting, business admin, entrepreneurial studies,
management information systems, marketing, operations, small business admin. **Communications:** General. **Computer sciences:** Information systems. **Conservation:** General. **Engineering technology:** Computer hardware, electrical, energy systems, manufacturing, mechanical, software,
surveying. **Health:** Clinical lab science, dental hygiene, health services, medical radiologic technology/radiation therapy, radiologic technology/medical
imaging, sonography. **Psychology:** General.

**Most popular majors.** Business/marketing 17%, engineering/
engineering technologies 33%, health sciences 31%, psychology 11%.

**Computing on campus.** 656 workstations in dormitories, library, computer center. Dormitories wired for high-speed internet access. Commuter

students can connect to campus network. Online course registration, online library, helpline, repair service, student web hosting, wireless network available.

**Student life. Freshman orientation:** Mandatory. Preregistration for classes offered. **Policies:** Student clubs are very community oriented and compete for community service awards. **Housing:** Coed dorms available. $150 partly refundable deposit, deadline 5/1. **Activities:** Choral groups, radio station, student government, student newspaper, symphony orchestra, TV station, Newman Club, Latter-day Saints, Christian Fellowship, Native American Club, international student club, Circle K, Latin American club, residence hall association, Phi Delta Theta, College Republicans.

**Athletics.** NAIA. **Intercollegiate:** Baseball M, basketball, cross-country, soccer W, softball W, track and field, volleyball W. **Intramural:** Basketball, cheerleading, cross-country, football (tackle) M, lacrosse M, soccer, softball, track and field, volleyball. **Team name:** Owls.

**Student services.** Adult student services, alcohol/substance abuse counseling, career counseling, student employment services, financial aid counseling, health services, personal counseling, placement for graduates, veterans' counselor. **Physically disabled:** Services for visually, hearing impaired.

**Contact.** E-mail: oit@oit.edu
Phone: (541) 885-1150 Toll-free number: (800) 422-2017
Fax: (541) 885-1115
John Duarte, Director of Admissions, Oregon Institute of Technology, 3201 Campus Drive, Klamath Falls, OR 97601

## Oregon State University
**Corvallis, Oregon**
www.oregonstate.edu

**CB member**
**CB code: 4586**

- Public 4-year university
- Residential campus in small city
- 15,515 degree-seeking undergraduates: 11% part-time, 47% women, 2% African American, 9% Asian American, 4% Hispanic American, 1% Native American, 2% international
- 3,080 degree-seeking graduate students
- 86% of applicants admitted
- SAT or ACT with writing, application essay required
- 61% graduate within 6 years

**General.** Founded in 1868. Regionally accredited. **Degrees:** 3,293 bachelor's awarded; master's, doctoral, first professional offered. **ROTC:** Army, Naval, Air Force. **Location:** 80 miles from Portland, 45 miles from Eugene. **Calendar:** Quarter, extensive summer session. **Full-time faculty:** 766 total; 75% have terminal degrees, 14% minority, 41% women. **Part-time faculty:** 400 total; 45% have terminal degrees, 8% minority, 54% women. **Class size:** 39% < 20, 32% 20-39, 9% 40-49, 12% 50-99, 7% >100. **Special facilities:** Arboretum, 13,429-acre forest, radiation center (with TRIGA Mark II Nuclear Reactor), wave research facility, marine science center museum and aquarium.

**Freshman class profile.** 8,149 applied, 6,971 admitted, 3,089 enrolled.

| Mid 50% test scores | | Rank in top tenth: | 19% |
|---|---|---|---|
| SAT critical reading: | 460-580 | Return as sophomores: | 81% |
| SAT math: | 490-610 | Out-of-state: | 13% |
| ACT composite: | 20-26 | Live on campus: | 78% |
| GPA 3.50 or higher: | 53% | International: | 2% |
| GPA 3.0-3.49: | 37% | Fraternities: | 16% |
| GPA 2.0-2.99: | 10% | Sororities: | 11% |
| Rank in top quarter: | 47% | | |

**Basis for selection.** GPA and essay most important. Students not meeting admission requirements may petition for exception. Students who do not meet subject requirements, who graduated from nonstandard or unaccredited high schools, or who graduated prior to 1987 must submit SAT Subject Test scores in addition to SAT or ACT. Applicants with GED not required to submit test scores. **Homeschooled:** Must submit SAT or ACT, and SAT Subject Tests.

**High school preparation.** 14 units required. Required and recommended units include English 4, mathematics 3, social studies 3, science 2 (laboratory 1-2) and foreign language 2.

**2007-2008 Annual costs.** Tuition/fees: $5,911; $18,187 out-of-state. Room/board: $7,251. Books/supplies: $1,350. Personal expenses: $2,181.

**Financial aid. Non-need-based:** Scholarships awarded for academics, athletics, job skills, leadership, minority status, ROTC, state residency.

**Application procedures. Admission:** Priority date 2/1; deadline 9/1. $50 fee. Application may be submitted online. Admission notification on a rolling basis beginning on or about 10/1. Must reply by May 1 or within 3 week(s) if notified thereafter. **Financial aid:** Priority date 2/1, closing date 5/1. FAFSA required. Applicants notified on a rolling basis starting 4/1; must reply within 4 week(s) of notification.

**Academics. Special study options:** Cooperative education, cross-registration, distance learning, double major, dual enrollment of high school students, ESL, exchange student, honors, independent study, internships, student-designed major, study abroad, teacher certification program, weekend college. **Credit/placement by examination:** AP, CLEP, IB, SAT, ACT, institutional tests. **Support services:** Learning center, remedial instruction, tutoring.

**Majors. Agriculture:** General, agronomy, animal sciences, business, economics, food science, horticultural science, plant sciences, range science. **Area/ethnic studies:** American. **Biology:** General, bacteriology, biochemistry, biophysics, biotechnology, botany, entomology, zoology. **Business:** Business admin. **Computer sciences:** General. **Conservation:** General, environmental science, fisheries, forest management, forest resources, management/policy, wildlife. **Education:** Technology/industrial arts. **Engineering:** Biomedical, chemical, civil, computer, construction, electrical, environmental, forest, industrial, manufacturing, mechanical, mining, nuclear, physics. **English:** English lit, speech/rhetoric. **Family/consumer sciences:** Clothing/textiles, family studies, food/nutrition, housing, merchandising. **Foreign languages:** French, German, Spanish. **Health:** Clinical lab technology, environmental health, health care admin, physics/radiologic health, public health ed. **History:** General. **Interdisciplinary:** Biological/physical sciences. **Liberal arts:** Arts/sciences. **Math:** General. **Parks/recreation:** General, health/fitness. **Philosophy/religion:** Philosophy. **Physical sciences:** Chemistry, geology, physics. **Psychology:** General. **Social sciences:** Anthropology, economics, geography, political science, sociology. **Visual/performing arts:** General, art, fashion design, interior design.

**Most popular majors.** Agriculture 6%, biology 7%, business/marketing 14%, engineering/engineering technologies 15%, family/consumer sciences 11%.

**Computing on campus.** 3,000 workstations in dormitories, library, computer center. Dormitories wired for high-speed internet access and linked to campus network. Commuter students can connect to campus network. Online course registration, helpline, repair service, student web hosting, wireless network available.

**Student life. Freshman orientation:** Available. Preregistration for classes offered. **Housing:** Coed dorms, special housing for disabled, apartments, cooperative housing, fraternity/sorority housing, substance-free housing available. $45 nonrefundable deposit. **Activities:** Bands, choral groups, dance, drama, film society, literary magazine, music ensembles, musical theater, opera, radio station, student government, student newspaper, symphony orchestra, TV station, 253 student organizations, 47 student honor and recognition societies.

**Athletics.** NCAA. **Intercollegiate:** Baseball M, basketball, cheerleading, cross-country W, football (tackle) M, golf, gymnastics W, rowing (crew), soccer, softball W, swimming W, volleyball W, wrestling M. **Intramural:** Badminton, basketball, bowling, cross-country, football (tackle) M, golf, racquetball, soccer, softball, swimming, tennis, track and field, volleyball, water polo, wrestling M. **Team name:** Beavers.

**Student services.** Adult student services, career counseling, student employment services, financial aid counseling, health services, legal services, minority student services, on-campus daycare, personal counseling, placement for graduates, veterans' counselor, women's services. **Physically disabled:** Services for visually, speech, hearing impaired.

**Contact.** E-mail: osuadmit@orst.edu
Phone: (541) 737-4411 Toll-free number: (800) 291-4192
Fax: (541) 737-2482
Michele Sandlin, Director of Admissions, Oregon State University, 104 Kerr Administration Building, Corvallis, OR 97331-2130

## Pacific Northwest College of Art
**Portland, Oregon**
www.pnca.edu

**CB code: 4504**

- Private 4-year visual arts college
- Commuter campus in large city
- 417 degree-seeking undergraduates: 10% part-time, 63% women, 1% African American, 4% Asian American, 5% Hispanic American, 1% Native American, 1% international
- 14 degree-seeking graduate students

♦ 59% of applicants admitted
♦ Application essay required

**General.** Founded in 1909. Regionally accredited. **Degrees:** 57 bachelor's awarded; master's offered. **Calendar:** Semester, limited summer session. **Full-time faculty:** 15 total. **Part-time faculty:** 40 total. **Class size:** 89% < 20, 11% 20-39. **Special facilities:** Student art galleries, printmaking center, individual studio spaces for seniors.

**Freshman class profile.** 297 applied, 175 admitted, 90 enrolled.

| | | | |
|---|---|---|---|
| GPA 3.50 or higher: | 30% | Out-of-state: | 54% |
| GPA 3.0-3.49: | 24% | Live on campus: | 48% |
| GPA 2.0-2.99: | 38% | International: | 1% |
| Return as sophomores: | 47% | | |

**Basis for selection.** Portfolio, essays important. 2.0 GPA recommended for academic courses. Greater emphasis on portfolio. Interview recommended. **Homeschooled:** Statement describing homeschool structure and mission, transcript of courses and grades, state high school equivalency certificate, letter of recommendation (nonparent) required. SAT/ACT exam recommended.

**High school preparation.** Recommended units include English 4, mathematics 3, social studies 3 and science 3. Visual arts classes recommended.

**2007-2008 Annual costs.** Tuition/fees: $19,359. Books/supplies: $985. Personal expenses: $615.

**Financial aid.** **Non-need-based:** Scholarships awarded for academics, art.

**Application procedures.** **Admission:** Priority date 3/1; no deadline. $35 fee, may be waived for applicants with need. Application may be submitted online. Admission notification on a rolling basis. Must reply by May 1 or within 2 week(s) if notified thereafter. **Financial aid:** Priority date 3/1, closing date 8/1. FAFSA required. Applicants notified on a rolling basis starting 4/1; must reply by 5/1 or within 4 week(s) of notification.

**Academics.** Thesis required part of fourth-year curriculum. **Special study options:** Cooperative education, cross-registration, dual enrollment of high school students, exchange student, independent study, internships, New York semester, student-designed major, study abroad. 5-year BA/BFA program with Reed College. **Credit/placement by examination:** AP, CLEP. **Support services:** Study skills assistance, tutoring, writing center.

**Majors.** **Visual/performing arts:** Graphic design, illustration, multimedia, painting, photography, printmaking, sculpture, studio arts.

**Computing on campus.** 130 workstations in library, computer center, student center. Commuter students can connect to campus network. Online library, wireless network available.

**Student life. Freshman orientation:** Available. Preregistration for classes offered. 1-2 days prior to the start of each semester. **Housing:** Coed dorms available. $450 deposit, deadline 6/15. Pets allowed in dorm rooms. Student housing available through partnership with College Housing Northwest. **Activities:** Film society, radio station, student government.

**Student services.** Career counseling, financial aid counseling, personal counseling.

**Contact.** E-mail: admissions@pnca.edu
Phone: (503) 821-8972 Fax: (503) 821-8978
Chris Sweet, Admissions, Pacific Northwest College of Art, 1241 NW Johnson Street, Portland, OR 97209

---

## Pacific University
### Forest Grove, Oregon
www.pacificu.edu                    CB code: 4601

♦ Private 4-year university affiliated with United Church of Christ
♦ Residential campus in large town
♦ 1,427 degree-seeking undergraduates: 3% part-time, 63% women, 1% African American, 24% Asian American, 4% Hispanic American, 1% Native American
♦ 1,502 degree-seeking graduate students
♦ 83% of applicants admitted
♦ SAT or ACT (ACT writing optional), application essay required
♦ 63% graduate within 6 years

**General.** Founded in 1849. Regionally accredited. Branch campuses in Portland and Eugene for selected professional programs. **Degrees:** 285 bachelor's awarded; master's, doctoral, first professional offered. **ROTC:** Army,

Air Force. **Location:** 25 miles from Portland. **Calendar:** 4-1-4, limited summer session. **Full-time faculty:** 92 total; 89% have terminal degrees, 9% minority, 42% women. **Part-time faculty:** 72 total; 6% minority, 56% women. **Class size:** 60% < 20, 35% 20-39, 2% 40-49, 3% 50-99, less than 1% >100. **Special facilities:** Wildlife refuge, Holocaust resource center, performing arts center, arboretum, internet studies center, ethics and social policy institute.

**Freshman class profile.** 1,258 applied, 1,050 admitted, 372 enrolled.

| Mid 50% test scores | | Rank in top quarter: | 74% |
|---|---|---|---|
| SAT critical reading: | 510-600 | Rank in top tenth: | 34% |
| SAT math: | 490-610 | Return as sophomores: | 80% |
| ACT composite: | 21-28 | Out-of-state: | 52% |
| GPA 3.50 or higher: | 68% | Live on campus: | 95% |
| GPA 3.0-3.49: | 25% | Fraternities: | 4% |
| GPA 2.0-2.99: | 7% | Sororities: | 4% |

**Basis for selection.** Strength of high school program, academic GPA, test scores, course selection, interview most important. 1000 SAT (exclusive of Writing) plus 3.0 GPA recommended. Recommendation, essay, extracurricular activities, leadership involvement also important. Audition required for music program; portfolio recommended for art program. **Homeschooled:** Statement describing homeschool structure and mission, transcript of courses and grades, state high school equivalency certificate, interview, letter of recommendation (nonparent) required.

**High school preparation.** 21 units recommended. Recommended units include English 4, mathematics 3, social studies 3, history 1, science 3 (laboratory 1), foreign language 2 and academic electives 4.

**2007-2008 Annual costs.** Tuition/fees: $26,470. Room/board: $7,170. Books/supplies: $900.

**2007-2008 Financial aid.** **Need-based:** 338 full-time freshmen applied for aid; 284 were judged to have need; 284 of these received aid. Average need met was 82%. Average scholarship/grant was $12,791; average loan $6,873. 63% of total undergraduate aid awarded as scholarships/grants, 37% as loans/jobs. **Non-need-based:** Awarded to 339 full-time undergraduates, including 109 freshmen. Scholarships awarded for academics, alumni affiliation, art, music/drama.

**Application procedures.** **Admission:** Priority date 2/15; deadline 8/15. $40 fee, may be waived for applicants with need. Application may be submitted online. Admission notification on a rolling basis beginning on or about 11/1. Must reply by May 1 or within 2 week(s) if notified thereafter. **Financial aid:** Priority date 3/1; no closing date. FAFSA required. Applicants notified on a rolling basis starting 3/1; must reply within 2 week(s) of notification.

**Academics. Special study options:** Combined bachelor's/graduate degree, cross-registration, double major, ESL, independent study, internships, liberal arts/career combination, study abroad, teacher certification program, Washington semester. 3-2 engineering programs with Oregon Graduate Institute and Washington University, 3-2 applied physics program, 4-1 computer science, 4-1 environmental science programs with Oregon Graduate Institute, exchange programs with University of Vienna, Beijing Normal University, University of Edinburgh, other institutions in Europe and Asia; cooperative arrangement with Northwest Film Center. **Credit/placement by examination:** AP, CLEP, IB, SAT, ACT, institutional tests. **Support services:** Learning center, reduced course load, tutoring, writing center.

**Majors. Biology:** General. **Business:** Business admin. **Communications:** General, journalism. **Computer sciences:** General. **Education:** General. **English:** Creative writing, English lit. **Foreign languages:** General, Chinese, French, German, Japanese, Spanish. **History:** General. **Liberal arts:** Arts/sciences. **Math:** General. **Parks/recreation:** Exercise sciences. **Philosophy/religion:** Philosophy. **Physical sciences:** Chemistry, physics. **Psychology:** General. **Public administration:** Social work. **Social sciences:** Economics, international relations, political science, sociology. **Visual/performing arts:** General, art, dramatic, multimedia, music performance.

**Most popular majors.** Biology 6%, business/marketing 11%, communications/journalism 7%, education 6%, English 6%, health sciences 9%, parks/recreation 12%, psychology 9%, social sciences 13%.

**Computing on campus.** 200 workstations in dormitories, library, computer center, student center. Dormitories wired for high-speed internet access and linked to campus network. Commuter students can connect to campus network. Online library, helpline, repair service, student web hosting, wireless network available.

**Student life. Freshman orientation:** Mandatory. Preregistration for classes offered. **Policies:** Unmarried freshman and sophomores under age 21 must live on campus unless living near campus with family. **Housing:** Guaranteed on-campus for freshmen. Coed dorms, single-sex dorms, special housing for disabled, apartments available. Limited number of houses available for married students. **Activities:** Bands, choral groups, dance, drama, film society, international student organizations, literary magazine, music ensembles, musical theater, radio station, student government, student newspaper, symphony orchestra, Hawaii club, Christian Fellowship, politics and law forum, Circle K, humanitarian center, gay and lesbian support group, ethnic diversity appreciation club, United Church of Christ student organization.

**Athletics.** NCAA. **Intercollegiate:** Baseball M, basketball, cheerleading, cross-country, golf, lacrosse W, soccer, softball W, swimming, tennis, track and field, volleyball W, wrestling. **Intramural:** Basketball, football (tackle), golf, handball, racquetball, soccer, softball, tennis, volleyball. **Team name:** Boxers.

**Student services.** Career counseling, student employment services, financial aid counseling, health services, personal counseling, placement for graduates, veterans' counselor.

**Contact.** E-mail: admissions@pacificu.edu
Phone: (503) 352-2218 Toll-free number: (800) 677-6712
Fax: (503) 352-2975
Karen Dunston, Director of Undergraduate Admission, Pacific University, 2043 College Way, Forest Grove, OR 97116-1797

## Pioneer Pacific College
### Wilsonville, Oregon
### www.pioneerpacific.edu
**CB code: 0492**

- For-profit 4-year technical college
- Commuter campus in large town
- 333 degree-seeking undergraduates: 22% part-time, 60% women
- Interview required

**General.** Accredited by ACICS. Five sites: Wilsonville - Main Campus, Wilsonville - Health Career Institute, Clackamas - Learning Site, Springfield - Branch Campus, and Portland - Oregon Culinary Institute. **Degrees:** 11 bachelor's, 204 associate awarded. **Location:** 20 miles from Portland. **Calendar:** Continuous, extensive summer session. **Full-time faculty:** 75 total. **Part-time faculty:** 90 total. **Class size:** 93% < 20, 7% 20-39.

**Basis for selection.** Open admission, but selective for some programs.

**2008-2009 Annual costs.** Tuition/fees (projected): $10,677. Costs vary by program from $7,250 to $22,053. Certain programs have additional lab fees. Personal expenses: $3,262.

**Financial aid.** All financial aid based on need.

**Application procedures. Admission:** No deadline. $50 fee. Application must be submitted on paper. Admission notification on a rolling basis. **Financial aid:** No deadline. FAFSA required. Applicants notified on a rolling basis starting 2/27.

**Academics. Special study options:** Accelerated study, honors, internships, liberal arts/career combination, weekend college. Externships. **Credit/placement by examination:** CLEP, institutional tests. **Support services:** Study skills assistance, tutoring.

**Majors. Business:** Business admin. **Computer sciences:** Information technology. **Health:** Health care admin. **Protective services:** Criminal justice.

**Most popular majors.** Business/marketing 36%, computer/information sciences 63%.

**Computing on campus.** 400 workstations in library, computer center. Online library, wireless network available.

**Student life. Freshman orientation:** Mandatory.

**Student services.** Career counseling, student employment services, financial aid counseling, placement for graduates.

**Contact.** E-mail: inquiries@pioneerpacific.edu
Phone: (503) 682-3903 Toll-free number: (866) 772-4636
Fax: (503) 682-1514
Todd Smith, Director of Admissions, Pioneer Pacific College, 27501 Southwest Parkway Avenue, Wilsonville, OR 97070

## Portland State University
### Portland, Oregon
### www.pdx.edu
**CB member**
**CB code: 4610**

- Public 4-year university
- Commuter campus in very large city

- 16,524 degree-seeking undergraduates: 31% part-time, 54% women, 4% African American, 10% Asian American, 5% Hispanic American, 1% Native American, 4% international
- 6,047 graduate students
- 91% of applicants admitted
- SAT or ACT with writing required

**General.** Founded in 1946. Regionally accredited. Courses offered at off-campus locations. **Degrees:** 3,143 bachelor's awarded; master's, doctoral offered. **ROTC:** Army, Air Force. **Location:** Downtown. **Calendar:** Quarter, extensive summer session. **Full-time faculty:** 751 total; 76% have terminal degrees, 14% minority, 45% women. **Part-time faculty:** 536 total; 24% have terminal degrees, 11% minority, 50% women. **Class size:** 30% < 20, 43% 20-39, 11% 40-49, 14% 50-99, 2% >100. **Special facilities:** Native American center.

**Freshman class profile.** 3,726 applied, 3,378 admitted, 1,671 enrolled.

| Mid 50% test scores | | | |
|---|---|---|---|
| SAT critical reading: | 460-590 | GPA 2.0-2.99: | 25% |
| SAT math: | 460-580 | Return as sophomores: | 68% |
| ACT composite: | 19-25 | Out-of-state: | 20% |
| GPA 3.50 or higher: | 33% | International: | 8% |
| GPA 3.0-3.49: | 42% | Fraternities: | 4% |
| | | Sororities: | 4% |

**Basis for selection.** 3.0 GPA or 1000 SAT (exclusive of Writing) or 21 ACT required for automatic admission. Various combinations of test scores and GPA also qualify for automatic admissions. Others may qualify under special action by admissions committee. Interview recommended for those who do not meet regular admission requirement.

**High school preparation.** 14 units required. Required and recommended units include English 4, mathematics 3, social studies 2, history 1, science 2 (laboratory 1) and foreign language 2. One unit laboratory science recommended.

**2007-2008 Annual costs.** Tuition/fees: $5,765; $17,831 out-of-state. Dormitory and meal service not managed by University available on campus. Books/supplies: $1,854. Personal expenses: $1,932.

**2007-2008 Financial aid. Need-based:** 1,002 full-time freshmen applied for aid; 752 were judged to have need; 740 of these received aid. Average need met was 57%. Average scholarship/grant was $5,275; average loan $3,375. 30% of total undergraduate aid awarded as scholarships/grants, 70% as loans/jobs. **Non-need-based:** Awarded to 928 full-time undergraduates, including 292 freshmen. Scholarships awarded for academics, art, athletics, music/drama, state residency.

**Application procedures. Admission:** Priority date 6/1; no deadline. $50 fee. Application must be submitted on paper. Admission notification on a rolling basis. **Financial aid:** Priority date 2/28; no closing date. FAFSA required. Applicants notified on a rolling basis; must reply within 4 week(s) of notification.

**Academics.** Community based service and research projects offered in Portland area. All students required to complete 45 credit hour multidisciplinary core curriculum, including community service learning experience. Teaching certification only offered at graduate level. **Special study options:** Accelerated study, combined bachelor's/graduate degree, cooperative education, distance learning, double major, ESL, exchange student, honors, independent study, internships, liberal arts/career combination, study abroad, teacher certification program, Washington semester. Haystack Summer Program in the arts and sciences. **Credit/placement by examination:** AP, CLEP, institutional tests. 45 credit hours maximum toward bachelor's degree. **Support services:** Pre-admission summer program, reduced course load, tutoring, writing center.

**Honors college/program.** Students with 1200 SAT (exclusive of Writing) and 3.5 GPA eligible to apply. Limited to 200 participants.

**Majors. Architecture:** Architecture, urban/community planning. **Area/ethnic studies:** African, Central/Eastern European, East Asian, European, Latin American, Near/Middle Eastern, women's. **Biology:** General, biochemistry. **Business:** General, accounting, business admin, finance, human resources, logistics, management information systems, marketing. **Computer sciences:** Computer science. **Conservation:** General. **Education:** Health. **Engineering:** Civil, computer, electrical, mechanical. **English:** English lit, speech/rhetoric. **Family/consumer sciences:** Family studies. **Foreign languages:** Chinese, French, German, Japanese, linguistics, Russian, Spanish. **Health:** Audiology/hearing, public health ed. **History:** General. **Interdisciplinary:** Biological/physical sciences. **Liberal arts:** Arts/sciences. **Math:** General. **Philosophy/religion:** Philosophy. **Physical sciences:** Chemistry, geology, physics. **Protective services:** Criminal justice, law enforcement admin. **Psychology:** General. **Social sciences:** General, anthropology, economics, geography, international relations, political science, sociology, urban studies. **Visual/performing arts:** Art, art history/conservation, commercial/

advertising art, design, dramatic, drawing, music performance, painting, printmaking, sculpture, studio arts.

**Most popular majors.** Business/marketing 26%, liberal arts 8%, psychology 7%, social sciences 16%.

**Computing on campus.** 725 workstations in dormitories, library, computer center, student center. Dormitories wired for high-speed internet access and linked to campus network. Commuter students can connect to campus network. Online course registration, online library, helpline, repair service, student web hosting, wireless network available.

**Student life. Freshman orientation:** Available. Preregistration for classes offered. **Housing:** Coed dorms, special housing for disabled, apartments, fraternity/sorority housing available. Pets allowed in dorm rooms. **Activities:** Bands, campus ministries, choral groups, dance, drama, film society, international student organizations, literary magazine, music ensembles, musical theater, opera, radio station, student government, student newspaper, symphony orchestra, student public interest research group, black cultural affairs board, United Indian Students in Higher Education, women's union, outdoor program, disabled student union, Hispanic student union.

**Athletics.** NCAA. **Intercollegiate:** Baseball M, basketball, cross-country, football (tackle) M, golf, soccer W, softball W, tennis, track and field, volleyball W, wrestling M. **Intramural:** Archery, basketball, football (tackle) M, golf, racquetball, soccer W, softball, volleyball. **Team name:** Vikings.

**Student services.** Adult student services, alcohol/substance abuse counseling, campus ministries, career counseling, student employment services, financial aid counseling, health services, minority student services, on-campus daycare, personal counseling, placement for graduates, veterans' counselor, women's services. **Physically disabled:** Services for visually, speech, hearing impaired.

**Contact.** E-mail: admissions@pdx.edu
Phone: (503) 725-3511 Toll-free number: (800) 547-8887 ext. 3511
Fax: (503) 725-5525
Agnes Hoffman, Vice Provost for Enrollment Management, Portland State University, PO Box 751-ADM, Portland, OR 97207-0751

## Reed College
**Portland, Oregon**
www.reed.edu

**CB member**
**CB code: 4654**

- Private 4-year liberal arts college
- Residential campus in very large city
- 1,426 degree-seeking undergraduates: 1% part-time, 55% women
- 28 degree-seeking graduate students
- 34% of applicants admitted
- SAT or ACT (ACT writing optional), application essay required
- 75% graduate within 6 years; 65% enter graduate study

**General.** Founded in 1909. Regionally accredited. **Degrees:** 279 bachelor's awarded; master's offered. **Location:** 5 miles from downtown. **Calendar:** Semester. **Full-time faculty:** 125 total; 91% have terminal degrees, 11% minority, 35% women. **Part-time faculty:** 10 total; 90% have terminal degrees, 10% minority, 30% women. **Class size:** 72% < 20, 24% 20-39, 2% 40-49, 3% 50-99, less than 1% >100. **Special facilities:** Nuclear research reactor, wildlife refuge, fish ladder.

**Freshman class profile.** 3,365 applied, 1,154 admitted, 347 enrolled.

| Mid 50% test scores | | GPA 2.0-2.99: | 1% |
|---|---|---|---|
| SAT critical reading: | 680-760 | Rank in top quarter: | 92% |
| SAT math: | 630-710 | Rank in top tenth: | 61% |
| SAT writing: | 650-730 | Return as sophomores: | 91% |
| ACT composite: | 28-32 | Out-of-state: | 93% |
| GPA 3.50 or higher: | 88% | Live on campus: | 96% |
| GPA 3.0-3.49: | 11% | International: | 5% |

**Basis for selection.** Academic achievement, essay, recommendations, test scores most important. Qualities of character, such as motivation, intellectual curiosity, individual responsibility, social consciousness are important. SAT Subject Tests recommended. Interview recommended. **Homeschooled:** Must document homeschool curriculum. High school diploma waived in some cases. Must be above age of compulsory education in home state. Require writing sample, essay, reference from evaluator or teacher not family member.

**High school preparation.** Recommended units include English 4, mathematics 4, social studies 1, history 3, science 3 and foreign language 3.

**2008-2009 Annual costs.** Tuition/fees: $38,190. Room/board: $9,920. Books/supplies: $950. Personal expenses: $900.

**2007-2008 Financial aid.** All financial aid based on need. Average need met was 100%. Average scholarship/grant was $29,915; average loan $2,322. 85% of total undergraduate aid awarded as scholarships/grants, 15% as loans/jobs. **Additional information:** College meets demonstrated need of continuing students who have attended Reed minimum of 2 semesters, who file financial aid applications on time, and who maintain satisfactory academic progress. Institutional aid consideration is for total of 8 semesters.

**Application procedures. Admission:** Closing date 1/15 (postmark date). $50 fee, may be waived for applicants with need. Application must be submitted on paper. Admission notification 4/1. Must reply by May 1 or within 2 week(s) if notified thereafter. **Financial aid:** Closing date 1/15. FAFSA, institutional form, CSS PROFILE required. Applicants notified by 4/1; must reply by 5/1 or within 2 week(s) of notification.

**Academics.** All students take 1-year course in humanities. After declaring major, students must pass qualifying exam prior to senior year. Seniors engage in 1-year research project in major field and prepare and defend thesis. **Special study options:** Combined bachelor's/graduate degree, cooperative education, cross-registration, double major, dual enrollment of high school students, exchange student, independent study, internships, liberal arts/career combination, study abroad. Computer science program with University of Washington, engineering arrangement with California Institute of Technology, Columbia University School of Engineering and Applied Sciences and Rensselaer Polytechnic Institute, forestry-environmental sciences degree arrangement with Nicholas School of the Environment of Duke University, art program in conjunction with Pacific Northwest College of Art. **Credit/placement by examination:** AP, CLEP, IB, institutional tests. 30 credit hours maximum toward bachelor's degree. **Support services:** Learning center, study skills assistance, tutoring, writing center.

**Majors. Area/ethnic studies:** American. **Biology:** General, biochemistry, molecular. **English:** Creative writing, English lit. **Foreign languages:** Chinese, classics, comparative lit, French, German, linguistics, Russian, Spanish. **History:** General. **Interdisciplinary:** Biological/physical sciences. **Math:** General. **Philosophy/religion:** Philosophy, religion. **Physical sciences:** Chemistry, physics. **Psychology:** General. **Social sciences:** Anthropology, economics, political science, sociology. **Visual/performing arts:** Art history/conservation, dramatic, studio arts.

**Most popular majors.** Biology 13%, English 8%, foreign language 7%, history 6%, philosophy/religious studies 14%, physical sciences 10%, psychology 8%, social sciences 19%, visual/performing arts 7%.

**Computing on campus.** 461 workstations in dormitories, library, computer center, student center. Dormitories wired for high-speed internet access and linked to campus network. Commuter students can connect to campus network. Online course registration, online library, helpline, repair service, student web hosting, wireless network available.

**Student life. Freshman orientation:** Mandatory. Preregistration for classes offered. Held 5 days before start of classes. **Policies:** Honor code in effect. First-year students required to live on campus. **Housing:** Guaranteed on-campus for freshmen. Coed dorms, single-sex dorms, special housing for disabled, apartments, cooperative housing, substance-free housing available. $100 partly refundable deposit, deadline 6/15. Chinese, French, German, Russian, and Spanish language houses available for upper division students. **Activities:** Choral groups, dance, drama, film society, literary magazine, music ensembles, radio station, student government, student newspaper, symphony orchestra, Christian Fellowship, Jewish Student Union, women's center, environmental coalition, politically active student groups, volunteer tutoring, language and outing clubs, poetry forum.

**Athletics. Intramural:** Archery, badminton, basketball M, diving, equestrian, fencing, golf, judo, rowing (crew), rugby, sailing, skiing, soccer, softball, squash, swimming, tennis, volleyball. **Team name:** Griffins.

**Student services.** Adult student services, alcohol/substance abuse counseling, career counseling, student employment services, financial aid counseling, health services, minority student services, personal counseling, placement for graduates. **Physically disabled:** Services for visually, speech, hearing impaired.

**Contact.** E-mail: admission@reed.edu
Phone: (503) 777-7511 Toll-free number: (800) 547-4750
Fax: (503) 777-7553
Paul Marthers, Dean of Admission, Reed College, 3203 SE Woodstock Boulevard, Portland, OR 97202-8199

## Southern Oregon University
**Ashland, Oregon**
www.sou.edu

**CB member**
**CB code: 4702**

- Public 4-year university and liberal arts college
- Residential campus in large town

♦ 4,058 degree-seeking undergraduates: 21% part-time, 58% women
♦ 399 degree-seeking graduate students
♦ 83% of applicants admitted
♦ SAT or ACT (ACT writing optional) required

**General.** Founded in 1926. Regionally accredited. Designated by National Aeronautical and Space Administration to cooperate in NASA-directed joint space research by undergraduates. **Degrees:** 769 bachelor's awarded; master's offered. **Location:** 180 miles from Eugene, 285 miles from Portland. **Calendar:** Quarter, extensive summer session. **Full-time faculty:** 207 total; 81% have terminal degrees. **Part-time faculty:** 104 total. **Class size:** 46% < 20, 42% 20-39, 6% 40-49, 5% 50-99, 1% >100. **Special facilities:** Herbarium, U.S. Fish and Wildlife forensics laboratory, public radio network studios, preschool and kindergarten, community television studio, center for visual arts, biotechnology center, institute for environmental economic and civic studies.

**Freshman class profile.** 1,887 applied, 1,565 admitted, 747 enrolled.

| Mid 50% test scores | | | |
|---|---|---|---|
| | | ACT composite: | 20-25 |
| SAT critical reading: | 450-580 | Out-of-state: | 24% |
| SAT math: | 460-570 | Live on campus: | 70% |

**Basis for selection.** 2.75 GPA from regionally accredited high school, 21 ACT, 1010 SAT (exclusive of Writing), and 14 required high school academic units. Requests for special admission for undergraduates reviewed individually. TOEFL required of non-native English speakers. SAT Subject Tests required of students graduating from nonstandard or unaccredited high schools. **Homeschooled:** Submit SAT and SAT Subject Tests.

**High school preparation.** 14 units required. Required units include English 4, mathematics 3, social studies 3, science 2 and foreign language 2.

**2007-2008 Annual costs.** Tuition/fees: $5,502; $17,580 out-of-state. Room/board: $7,482. Books/supplies: $1,155. Personal expenses: $2,475.

**Financial aid. Non-need-based:** Scholarships awarded for academics, alumni affiliation, art, athletics, leadership, minority status, music/drama, religious affiliation, state residency.

**Application procedures. Admission:** No deadline. $50 fee, may be waived for applicants with need. Application may be submitted online. Admission notification on a rolling basis. **Financial aid:** No deadline. FAFSA required. Applicants notified on a rolling basis starting 3/1; must reply within 2 week(s) of notification.

**Academics. Special study options:** Accelerated study, combined bachelor's/graduate degree, cooperative education, cross-registration, distance learning, double major, dual enrollment of high school students, ESL, exchange student, honors, independent study, internships, liberal arts/career combination, student-designed major, study abroad, teacher certification program. **Credit/placement by examination:** AP, CLEP, IB, institutional tests. 24 credit hours maximum toward bachelor's degree. **Support services:** Learning center, reduced course load, remedial instruction, study skills assistance, tutoring, writing center.

**Majors. Biology:** General. **Business:** General, accounting, business admin, hospitality admin, marketing. **Communications:** General, journalism, public relations. **Computer sciences:** General, computer science, programming, security. **Conservation:** Environmental studies. **Education:** General. **English:** English lit, speech/rhetoric. **Foreign languages:** General, Spanish. **Health:** Athletic training, nursing (RN), predental, premedicine, preop/surgical nursing, prepharmacy, preveterinary. **History:** General. **Interdisciplinary:** Biological/physical sciences, math/computer science. **Legal studies:** Prelaw. **Math:** General. **Parks/recreation:** Health/fitness, sports admin. **Physical sciences:** Chemistry, geology, physics. **Protective services:** Criminal justice, law enforcement admin, police science. **Psychology:** General. **Social sciences:** General, anthropology, criminology, economics, geography, political science, sociology. **Visual/performing arts:** Art, dramatic, music management.

**Computing on campus.** 750 workstations in dormitories, library, computer center, student center. Dormitories wired for high-speed internet access and linked to campus network. Commuter students can connect to campus network. Online course registration, online library, helpline, student web hosting, wireless network available.

**Student life. Freshman orientation:** Mandatory. Preregistration for classes offered. Early registration in July, orientation few days before start of classes. **Housing:** Guaranteed on-campus for freshmen. Coed dorms, special housing for disabled, apartments, substance-free housing available. $50 deposit. Special quiet, nonsmoking, older student or freshmen residence halls available. **Activities:** Bands, choral groups, dance, drama, literary magazine, music ensembles, musical theater, opera, radio station, student government, student newspaper, symphony orchestra, TV station, 100 clubs.

**Athletics.** NAIA. **Intercollegiate:** Basketball, cross-country, football (tackle) M, soccer W, softball W, tennis W, track and field, volleyball W, wrestling M. **Intramural:** Badminton, baseball M, basketball, bowling, golf, racquetball, rugby, sailing, skiing, soccer, softball, swimming, table tennis, tennis, track and field, volleyball, water polo. **Team name:** Raiders.

**Student services.** Adult student services, alcohol/substance abuse counseling, career counseling, services for economically disadvantaged, student employment services, financial aid counseling, health services, legal services, minority student services, on-campus daycare, personal counseling, placement for graduates, veterans' counselor, women's services. **Physically disabled:** Services for visually, speech, hearing impaired. **Learning disabled:** Comprehensive services available.

**Contact.** E-mail: admissions@sou.edu
Phone: (541) 552-6411 Toll-free number: (800) 482-7672
Fax: (541) 552-6614
Mark Bottorff, Assistant Vice President of Enrollment Services and Director of Admissions, Southern Oregon University, 1250 Siskiyou Boulevard, Ashland, OR 97520-5032

## University of Oregon
Eugene, Oregon
www.uoregon.edu

CB member
CB code: 4846

♦ Public 4-year university
♦ Residential campus in small city
♦ 16,422 degree-seeking undergraduates: 8% part-time, 52% women, 2% African American, 6% Asian American, 4% Hispanic American, 1% Native American, 5% international
♦ 3,267 degree-seeking graduate students
♦ 87% of applicants admitted
♦ SAT or ACT with writing required
♦ 67% graduate within 6 years; 28% enter graduate study

**General.** Founded in 1876. Regionally accredited. **Degrees:** 4,093 bachelor's awarded; master's, doctoral, first professional offered. **ROTC:** Army. **Location:** 110 miles from Portland. **Calendar:** Quarter, extensive summer session. **Full-time faculty:** 815 total; 98% have terminal degrees, 21% minority, 40% women. **Part-time faculty:** 352 total; 88% have terminal degrees, 16% minority, 49% women. **Class size:** 39% < 20, 41% 20-39, 4% 40-49, 9% 50-99, 7% >100. **Special facilities:** Art museum, natural and cultural history museum, sports marketing center, entrepreneurship center, chemistry laboratory, instrumentation center, computer music center, mountain observatory, marine biology institute.

**Freshman class profile.** 11,287 applied, 9,813 admitted, 3,587 enrolled.

| Mid 50% test scores | | End year in good standing: | 88% |
|---|---|---|---|
| SAT critical reading: | 490-610 | Return as sophomores: | 84% |
| SAT math: | 500-610 | Out-of-state: | 32% |
| GPA 3.50 or higher: | 50% | Live on campus: | 83% |
| GPA 3.0-3.49: | 40% | International: | 5% |
| GPA 2.0-2.99: | 10% | Fraternities: | 11% |
| Rank in top quarter: | 57% | Sororities: | 11% |
| Rank in top tenth: | 23% | | |

**Basis for selection.** Students with minimum 3.25 GPA and 16 college preparatory units guaranteed admission. For all others, secondary school record and test scores most important. Audition required for dance and music programs. Portfolio required for arts, architecture, and interior architecture programs. Essay required for all students with fewer than 16 college preparatory units or GPA below 3.25. **Homeschooled:** 1540 SAT/22 ACT and average score of 470 (940 total) for SAT Subject Tests in Math I or II and a second test of your choice required. Second language test strongly recommended to meet the second language proficiency requirements. **Learning Disabled:** If student does not meet admission requirements and has self-identified a documented disability, then a secondary review will take place by the disability review committee.

**High school preparation.** 14 units required; 16 recommended. Required and recommended units include English 4, mathematics 3, social studies 3, science 2 (laboratory 1) and foreign language 2.

**2007-2008 Annual costs.** Tuition/fees: $6,168; $19,332 out-of-state. Additional program-specific fees may apply. Room/board: $8,166. Books/supplies: $1,050. Personal expenses: $2,496.

**2007-2008 Financial aid. Need-based:** 2,097 full-time freshmen applied for aid; 1,251 were judged to have need; 1,165 of these received aid. Average need met was 60%. Average scholarship/grant was $4,776; average loan $4,351. 36% of total undergraduate aid awarded as scholarships/grants,

64% as loans/jobs. **Non-need-based:** Awarded to 2,726 full-time undergraduates, including 950 freshmen. Scholarships awarded for academics, athletics, leadership, minority status, music/drama, ROTC, state residency.

**Application procedures. Admission:** Priority date 11/1; deadline 1/15 (postmark date). $50 fee, may be waived for applicants with need. Application may be submitted online. Admission notification on a rolling basis beginning on or about 9/15. Must reply by May 1 or within 4 week(s) if notified thereafter. Additional application deadlines: Clark Honors College, 11/1 early notification, 1/15 standard notification; Architecture, 1/15; Interior Architecture, 1/15; Digital Arts, 2/1; Landscape Architecture, 2/15; Art, 3/1; School of Music and Dance, 1/15. **Financial aid:** Priority date 3/1, closing date 6/30. FAFSA required. Applicants notified on a rolling basis starting 4/15; must reply within 4 week(s) of notification.

**Academics. Special study options:** Cross-registration, distance learning, double major, ESL, exchange student, honors, independent study, internships, liberal arts/career combination, semester at sea, student-designed major, study abroad, teacher certification program. **Credit/placement by examination:** AP, CLEP, IB, SAT, ACT, institutional tests. **Support services:** Learning center, remedial instruction, study skills assistance, tutoring.

**Honors college/program.** SAT/ACT scores, unweighted GPA, rigor and breadth of coursework, diversity, 2 teacher recommendations and personal essay considered. Approximately 150 spaces available per year.

**Majors. Architecture:** Architecture, interior, landscape. **Area/ethnic studies:** Asian, Russian/Slavic, women's. **Biology:** General, biochemistry, marine, physiology. **Business:** General, accounting. **Communications:** Advertising, digital media, journalism, media studies, public relations. **Computer sciences:** General. **Conservation:** Environmental science, environmental studies. **Education:** General, early childhood, elementary, middle, music. **English:** English lit. **Foreign languages:** Ancient Greek, Chinese, classics, comparative lit, French, German, Italian, Japanese, Latin, linguistics, Romance, Russian, Spanish. **Health:** Communication disorders. **History:** General. **Interdisciplinary:** Ancient studies, biological/physical sciences, global studies, math/computer science, medieval/Renaissance. **Liberal arts:** Humanities. **Math:** General. **Philosophy/religion:** Judaic, philosophy, religion. **Physical sciences:** Chemistry, geology, physics. **Psychology:** General. **Public administration:** General, human services. **Social sciences:** General, anthropology, economics, geography, political science, sociology. **Visual/performing arts:** Art, art history/conservation, ceramics, dance, design, dramatic, fiber arts, jazz, metal/jewelry, multimedia, music performance, music theory/composition, painting, photography, printmaking, sculpture, studio arts. **Other:** Ethnic studies.

**Most popular majors.** Biology 6%, business/marketing 14%, communications/journalism 9%, foreign language 7%, psychology 8%, social sciences 18%, visual/performing arts 7%.

**Computing on campus.** 1,700 workstations in dormitories, library, computer center, student center. Dormitories wired for high-speed internet access and linked to campus network. Commuter students can connect to campus network. Online course registration, online library, helpline, repair service, student web hosting, wireless network available.

**Student life. Freshman orientation:** Mandatory. Preregistration for classes offered. Two-day session for students and family held during the summer. **Housing:** Coed dorms, special housing for disabled, apartments, fraternity/sorority housing, substance-free housing available. $250 partly refundable deposit, deadline 3/31. Single-sex halls, residential academic programs, special interest or theme halls, graduate student and family housing available. **Activities:** Bands, choral groups, dance, drama, literary magazine, music ensembles, musical theater, opera, radio station, student government, student newspaper, symphony orchestra.

**Athletics.** NCAA. **Intercollegiate:** Baseball M, basketball, cheerleading M, cross-country, football (tackle) M, golf, lacrosse W, soccer W, softball W, tennis, track and field, volleyball W, wrestling M. **Intramural:** Badminton, basketball, cross-country, football (non-tackle), golf, racquetball, soccer, softball, swimming, table tennis, tennis, track and field, volleyball, wrestling M. **Team name:** Ducks.

**Student services.** Adult student services, alcohol/substance abuse counseling, career counseling, services for economically disadvantaged, student employment services, financial aid counseling, health services, legal services, minority student services, on-campus daycare, personal counseling, placement for graduates, veterans' counselor, women's services. **Physically disabled:** Services for visually, speech, hearing impaired. **Learning disabled:** Comprehensive services available.

**Contact.** E-mail: uoadmit@uoregon.edu
Phone: (541) 346-3201 Toll-free number: (800) 232-3825
Fax: (541) 346-5815
Brian Henley, Director of Admissions, University of Oregon, 1217
University of Oregon, Eugene, OR 97403-1217

---

## University of Portland
Portland, Oregon     **CB member**
www.up.edu     **CB code: 4847**

- Private 4-year university affiliated with Roman Catholic Church
- Residential campus in large city
- 2,967 degree-seeking undergraduates: 1% part-time, 63% women, 1% African American, 10% Asian American, 4% Hispanic American, 1% Native American, 2% international
- 575 degree-seeking graduate students
- 59% of applicants admitted
- SAT or ACT (ACT writing optional), application essay required

**General.** Founded in 1901. Regionally accredited. **Degrees:** 672 bachelor's awarded; master's offered. **ROTC:** Army, Air Force. **Calendar:** Semester, limited summer session. **Full-time faculty:** 199 total; 91% have terminal degrees, 4% minority, 43% women. **Part-time faculty:** 100 total; 6% have terminal degrees, 3% minority, 46% women. **Class size:** 35% < 20, 56% 20-39, 7% 40-49, 2% 50-99, less than 1% >100.

**Freshman class profile.** 7,139 applied, 4,195 admitted, 805 enrolled.

| Mid 50% test scores | | | |
|---|---|---|---|
| SAT critical reading: | 530-640 | Rank in top tenth: | 50% |
| SAT math: | 540-640 | End year in good standing: | 94% |
| GPA 3.50 or higher: | 73% | Return as sophomores: | 85% |
| GPA 3.0-3.49: | 24% | Out-of-state: | 66% |
| GPA 2.0-2.99: | 3% | Live on campus: | 94% |
| Rank in top quarter: | 81% | International: | 1% |

**Basis for selection.** School achievement record, test scores, counselor recommendation, essay important. **Homeschooled:** Applicants need record of courses, SAT or ACT scores, letter of recommendation. Interview strongly encouraged.

**High school preparation.** Required and recommended units include English 3-4, mathematics 2-3, social studies 2, history 2, science 2 and academic electives 7. Engineering, math, and some science majors require additional math and science courses.

**2007-2008 Annual costs.** Tuition/fees: $27,890. Room/board: $8,300. Books/supplies: $1,000. Personal expenses: $800.

**2006-2007 Financial aid. Need-based:** 597 full-time freshmen applied for aid; 388 were judged to have need; 387 of these received aid. Average need met was 89%. Average scholarship/grant was $13,838; average loan $2,912. 72% of total undergraduate aid awarded as scholarships/grants, 28% as loans/jobs. **Non-need-based:** Awarded to 1,969 full-time undergraduates, including 562 freshmen. Scholarships awarded for academics, music/drama, ROTC.

**Application procedures. Admission:** Priority date 2/1; deadline 6/1 (postmark date). $50 fee, may be waived for applicants with need. Application may be submitted online. Admission notification on a rolling basis beginning on or about 10/1. Must reply by May 1 or within 2 week(s) if notified thereafter. **Financial aid:** Priority date 3/1; no closing date. FAFSA, institutional form required. Applicants notified on a rolling basis starting 3/15; must reply within 3 week(s) of notification.

**Academics. Special study options:** Cross-registration, double major, honors, independent study, internships, liberal arts/career combination, study abroad, teacher certification program, Washington semester. **Credit/placement by examination:** AP, CLEP, IB, institutional tests. 45 credit hours maximum toward bachelor's degree. **Support services:** Learning center, study skills assistance, tutoring, writing center.

**Majors. Biology:** General. **Business:** Accounting, business admin, finance, international, marketing. **Communications:** Media studies, organizational. **Computer sciences:** Computer science. **Conservation:** Environmental science, environmental studies. **Education:** Elementary, music, secondary. **Engineering:** Civil, computer, electrical, environmental, mechanical. **English:** English lit. **Foreign languages:** French, German, Spanish. **Health:** Nursing (RN). **History:** General. **Math:** General. **Philosophy/religion:** Philosophy. **Physical sciences:** Chemistry, physics. **Psychology:** General. **Public administration:** Social work. **Social sciences:** Political science, sociology. **Theology:** Theology. **Visual/performing arts:** Dramatic, theater arts management.

**Most popular majors.** Biology 9%, business/marketing 15%, education 6%, engineering/engineering technologies 9%, foreign language 7%, health sciences 19%, social sciences 8%.

**Computing on campus.** 400 workstations in dormitories, library, computer center, student center. Dormitories wired for high-speed internet access and linked to campus network. Commuter students can connect to campus network. Online course registration, online library, helpline, student web hosting, wireless network available.

**Student life. Freshman orientation:** Available. Preregistration for classes offered. Held 3 days before classes begin. **Housing:** Guaranteed on-campus for freshmen. Coed dorms, single-sex dorms available. $100 nonrefundable deposit, deadline 5/1. Rental houses available. **Activities:** Bands, campus ministries, choral groups, dance, drama, film society, international student organizations, literary magazine, music ensembles, musical theater, radio station, student government, student newspaper, symphony orchestra, campus ministry, volunteer services, black student union, international club, Hawaiian club, Society of Women Engineeers, feminist discussion group, Bible study group.

**Athletics.** NCAA. **Intercollegiate:** Baseball M, basketball, cross-country, golf, soccer, tennis, track and field, volleyball W. **Intramural:** Basketball, bowling, football (non-tackle), golf, skiing, soccer, softball, swimming, table tennis, tennis, volleyball, water polo, weight lifting. **Team name:** Pilots.

**Student services.** Adult student services, alcohol/substance abuse counseling, campus ministries, career counseling, student employment services, financial aid counseling, health services, personal counseling, placement for graduates, veterans' counselor. **Physically disabled:** Services for visually, speech, hearing impaired.

**Contact.** E-mail: admissio@up.edu
Phone: (503) 943-7147 Toll-free number: (888) 627-5601
Fax: (503) 943-7315
Jason McDonald, Dean of Admissions, University of Portland, 5000 North Willamette Boulevard, Portland, OR 97203-5798

## Warner Pacific College
**Portland, Oregon**
www.warnerpacific.edu                                    **CB code: 4595**

- Private 4-year liberal arts college affiliated with Church of God
- Residential campus in very large city
- 722 degree-seeking undergraduates: 63% women, 5% African American, 3% Asian American, 5% Hispanic American, 1% international
- 61 degree-seeking graduate students
- SAT or ACT, application essay required
- 49% graduate within 6 years; 20% enter graduate study

**General.** Founded in 1937. Regionally accredited. **Degrees:** 177 bachelor's, 10 associate awarded; master's offered. **ROTC:** Army, Naval, Air Force. **Location:** 44 miles from Salem, 10 miles from Vancouver, Washington. **Calendar:** Semester, limited summer session. **Full-time faculty:** 29 total; 97% have terminal degrees, 28% minority. **Part-time faculty:** 30 total; 97% have terminal degrees. **Class size:** 79% <20, 19% 20-39, 2% 40-49. **Special facilities:** Field station for wildlife observation and study.

**Freshman class profile.** 755 applied, 337 admitted, 98 enrolled.

| Mid 50% test scores | | | |
|---|---|---|---|
| SAT critical reading: | 450-580 | GPA 3.0-3.49: | 37% |
| SAT math: | 490-580 | GPA 2.0-2.99: | 35% |
| SAT writing: | 430-550 | End year in good standing: | 80% |
| ACT composite: | 17-25 | Return as sophomores: | 51% |
| GPA 3.50 or higher: | 28% | Out-of-state: | 32% |
| | | Live on campus: | 69% |

**Basis for selection.** Open admission, but selective for some programs. High school GPA important; test scores, essay and signed lifestyle agreement required. **Homeschooled:** Statement describing homeschool structure and mission, transcript of courses and grades, state high school equivalency certificate, interview, letter of recommendation (nonparent) required.

**High school preparation.** 11 units recommended. Recommended units include English 4, mathematics 2, social studies 3 and science 2.

**2007-2008 Annual costs.** Tuition/fees: $21,500. Room/board: $6,028. Books/supplies: $600. Personal expenses: $2,350.

**2006-2007 Financial aid.** **Need-based:** 78 full-time freshmen applied for aid; 72 were judged to have need; 72 of these received aid. Average need met was 75%. Average scholarship/grant was $6,472; average loan $4,182. 56% of total undergraduate aid awarded as scholarships/grants, 44% as loans/jobs. **Non-need-based:** Awarded to 391 full-time undergraduates, including 102 freshmen. Scholarships awarded for academics, alumni affiliation, athletics, leadership, minority status, music/drama, religious affiliation.

**Application procedures. Admission:** No deadline. $50 fee ($50 out-of-state), may be waived for applicants with need. Application may be submitted online. Admission notification on a rolling basis. **Financial aid:** Priority date 3/1, closing date 8/30. FAFSA required. Applicants notified on a rolling basis starting 3/1; must reply within 4 week(s) of notification.

**Academics. Special study options:** Accelerated study, cooperative education, cross-registration, double major, independent study, internships, liberal arts/career combination, student-designed major, study abroad, teacher certification program, Washington semester. 2-2 nursing program with Walla Walla School of Nursing. **Credit/placement by examination:** AP, CLEP, institutional tests. 30 credit hours maximum toward associate degree, 30 toward bachelor's. No more than 45 total alternative credits (maximum 30 of any one type). **Support services:** Learning center, reduced course load, remedial instruction, study skills assistance, tutoring.

**Majors. Area/ethnic studies:** American. **Biology:** General. **Business:** Business admin, international. **Education:** Elementary, music, physical, secondary. **English:** English lit. **Family/consumer sciences:** Family studies. **History:** General. **Liberal arts:** Arts/sciences. **Philosophy/religion:** Religion. **Physical sciences:** General. **Psychology:** General. **Public administration:** Social work. **Social sciences:** General. **Theology:** Preministerial.

**Most popular majors.** Business/marketing 40%, family/consumer sciences 40%.

**Computing on campus.** Dormitories wired for high-speed internet access and linked to campus network.

**Student life. Freshman orientation:** Available. Preregistration for classes offered. **Policies:** Religious observance required. **Housing:** Guaranteed on-campus for freshmen. Single-sex dorms, special housing for disabled, apartments available. $100 deposit. **Activities:** Bands, choral groups, drama, music ensembles, student government.

**Athletics.** NAIA, NCCAA. **Intercollegiate:** Basketball, cross-country, soccer, track and field, volleyball W. **Intramural:** Badminton, basketball, football (non-tackle), volleyball. **Team name:** Knights.

**Student services.** Adult student services, campus ministries, career counseling, student employment services, financial aid counseling, health services, minority student services, personal counseling, placement for graduates.

**Contact.** E-mail: admissions@warnerpacific.edu
Phone: (503) 517-1020 Toll-free number: (800) 804-1510
Fax: (503) 517-1352
Shannon Mackey, Executive Director of Enrollment Management, Warner Pacific College, 2219 SE 68th Avenue, Portland, OR 97215-4026

## Western Oregon University
**Monmouth, Oregon**                                    **CB member**
www.wou.edu                                              **CB code: 4585**

- Public 4-year liberal arts and teachers college
- Residential campus in small town
- 4,390 degree-seeking undergraduates: 12% part-time, 58% women
- 564 degree-seeking graduate students
- 86% of applicants admitted
- SAT or ACT with writing required

**General.** Founded in 1856. Regionally accredited. **Degrees:** 724 bachelor's, 5 associate awarded; master's offered. **ROTC:** Army, Naval, Air Force. **Location:** 15 miles from Salem, 60 miles from Portland. **Calendar:** Quarter, limited summer session. **Full-time faculty:** 174 total; 84% have terminal degrees, 10% minority, 47% women. **Part-time faculty:** 138 total; 11% have terminal degrees, 17% minority, 54% women. **Class size:** 50% <20, 39% 20-39, 6% 40-49, 4% 50-99, less than 1% >100. **Special facilities:** Arctic museum, teaching research institute, early childhood and training development center.

**Freshman class profile.** 3,193 applied, 2,732 admitted, 970 enrolled.

| Mid 50% test scores | | | |
|---|---|---|---|
| SAT critical reading: | 420-530 | GPA 3.0-3.49: | 38% |
| SAT math: | 430-530 | GPA 2.0-2.99: | 27% |
| SAT writing: | 400-510 | Rank in top quarter: | 36% |
| ACT composite: | 17-23 | Rank in top tenth: | 13% |
| GPA 3.50 or higher: | 35% | Out-of-state: | 13% |
| | | Live on campus: | 84% |

**Basis for selection.** 2.75 GPA required. 1000 SAT (exclusive of Writing) strongly recommended, but only used in admissions decision if applicant does not meet GPA or college preparation requirements. If applicant does not meet academic requirements, other evidence of potential in the form of interviews, portfolios, auditions, and essays considered. **Home-schooled:** 1000 SAT (exclusive of writing) or 21 ACT or minimum 1410 SAT Subject Tests combined score in 3 subjects; must take 1 SAT Reasoning Test, 1 SAT Subject Test in math, and second exam in foreign language.

**High school preparation.** 14 units required. Required and recommended units include English 4, mathematics 3, social studies 2, history 1, science 2 (laboratory 1) and foreign language 2.

**2007-2008 Annual costs.** Tuition/fees: $5,982; $16,332 out-of-state. Room/board: $7,055. Books/supplies: $1,125. Personal expenses: $2,475.

**2006-2007 Financial aid. Need-based:** 38% of total undergraduate aid awarded as scholarships/grants, 62% as loans/jobs. **Non-need-based:** Scholarships awarded for academics, art, athletics, leadership, minority status, music/drama, ROTC, state residency.

**Application procedures. Admission:** No deadline. $50 fee. Application may be submitted online. Admission notification on a rolling basis. **Financial aid:** Priority date 3/1; no closing date. FAFSA required. Applicants notified on a rolling basis starting 3/20; must reply within 2 week(s) of notification.

**Academics. Special study options:** Distance learning, double major, dual enrollment of high school students, honors, independent study, internships, student-designed major, study abroad, teacher certification program. Preprofessional studies, interdisciplinary studies, nondegree licensure programs, service learning and career development. **Credit/placement by examination:** AP, CLEP, IB, SAT, ACT, institutional tests. 48 credit hours maximum toward bachelor's degree. **Support services:** Learning center, remedial instruction, study skills assistance, tutoring, writing center.

**Majors. Biology:** General. **Business:** General. **Communications:** General. **Computer sciences:** General. **Education:** General, biology, chemistry, elementary, health, instructional media, middle, multi-level teacher, physical, reading, science, secondary, social studies, Spanish. **English:** English lit, speech/rhetoric. **Foreign languages:** Sign language interpretation, Spanish. **History:** General. **Interdisciplinary:** Biological/physical sciences, math/computer science, natural sciences. **Liberal arts:** Arts/sciences. **Math:** General. **Philosophy/religion:** Philosophy. **Physical sciences:** Chemistry, geology, planetary. **Protective services:** Corrections, fire services admin, law enforcement admin. **Psychology:** General. **Public administration:** General. **Social sciences:** General, anthropology, economics, geography, political science, sociology. **Visual/performing arts:** General, art, dance, dramatic, studio arts, theater arts management.

**Most popular majors.** Business/marketing 12%, education 43%, interdisciplinary studies 6%, psychology 7%, security/protective services 6%, social sciences 8%.

**Computing on campus.** 411 workstations in dormitories, library, computer center, student center. Dormitories wired for high-speed internet access and linked to campus network. Commuter students can connect to campus network. Online course registration, online library, helpline, repair service, wireless network available.

**Student life. Freshman orientation:** Available. Held last weekend in June and 2nd and 3rd weekends in July on Friday and/or Saturday. **Policies:** No alcohol permitted in residence halls. **Housing:** Guaranteed on-campus for freshmen. Coed dorms, special housing for disabled, apartments, substance-free housing available. $35 nonrefundable deposit, deadline 10/1. Family housing, housing by learning communities, community living options available. **Activities:** Bands, choral groups, dance, drama, international student organizations, literary magazine, music ensembles, Model UN, musical theater, student government, student newspaper, symphony orchestra, TV station, Baptist student union, Big Brother/Big Sister, multicultural student union, Campus Crusade for Christ, Circle K, environmental action committee.

**Athletics.** NCAA. **Intercollegiate:** Baseball M, basketball, cheerleading, cross-country, football (tackle) M, soccer W, softball W, track and field, volleyball W. **Intramural:** Basketball, bowling, cross-country, football (non-tackle), football (tackle) M, golf, racquetball, rifle, skiing, soccer, softball, swimming, table tennis, tennis, track and field, triathlon, volleyball, water polo, weight lifting, wrestling. **Team name:** Wolves.

**Student services.** Adult student services, alcohol/substance abuse counseling, campus ministries, career counseling, services for economically disadvantaged, student employment services, financial aid counseling, health services, minority student services, on-campus daycare, personal counseling, placement for graduates, veterans' counselor, women's services. **Physically disabled:** Services for visually, speech, hearing impaired.

**Contact.** E-mail: wolfgram@wou.edu
Phone: (503) 838-8211 Toll-free number: (877) 877-1593
Fax: (503) 838-8067
David McDonald, Dean of Admissions, Enrollment Management, and Retention, Western Oregon University, 345 North Monmouth Avenue, Monmouth, OR 97361

## Willamette University
**Salem, Oregon**
www.willamette.edu

**CB member**
**CB code: 4954**

- Private 4-year university and liberal arts college affiliated with United Methodist Church
- Residential campus in small city
- 1,821 degree-seeking undergraduates: 1% part-time, 55% women, 1% African American, 6% Asian American, 4% Hispanic American, 1% international
- 720 degree-seeking graduate students
- 77% of applicants admitted
- SAT or ACT with writing, application essay required
- 80% graduate within 6 years

**General.** Founded in 1842. Regionally accredited. Tokyo International University of America sister school. **Degrees:** 475 bachelor's awarded; master's, first professional offered. **Location:** 45 miles from Portland. **Calendar:** Semester. **Full-time faculty:** 200 total; 12% minority, 40% women. **Part-time faculty:** 110 total; 6% minority, 38% women. **Class size:** 67% < 20, 33% 20-39, less than 1% 40-49, less than 1% 50-99. **Special facilities:** Art museum, American headquarters for International Debate Education Association, papers and memorabilia of Senator Mark O. Hatfield, botanical gardens, Japanese gardens, rose gardens, rural retreat center, indoor climbing wall, wildlife refuge field station, digital art and music studios, 2 electron microscopes (scanning and transmission).

**Freshman class profile.** 2,983 applied, 2,301 admitted, 435 enrolled.

| Mid 50% test scores | | | | |
|---|---|---|---|---|
| SAT critical reading: | 570-690 | GPA 2.0-2.99: | 6% |
| SAT math: | 550-660 | Rank in top quarter: | 76% |
| SAT writing: | 550-660 | Rank in top tenth: | 47% |
| ACT composite: | 25-29 | Return as sophomores: | 87% |
| GPA 3.50 or higher: | 75% | Out-of-state: | 68% |
| GPA 3.0-3.49: | 19% | Live on campus: | 97% |

**Basis for selection.** School record most important, followed by test scores, essay, recommendations, school and community activities, interview. Audition recommended for music, theater programs; portfolio recommended for art program. **Homeschooled:** Recommend submission of accredited transcript from governing agency, if available.

**High school preparation.** 20 units recommended. Recommended units include English 4, mathematics 4, social studies 1, history 2, science 3 (laboratory 3) and foreign language 3.

**2007-2008 Annual costs.** Tuition/fees: $31,968. Optional health insurance: $405. Room/board: $7,570. Books/supplies: $1,800.

**2007-2008 Financial aid. Need-based:** 347 full-time freshmen applied for aid; 275 were judged to have need; 275 of these received aid. Average need met was 92%. Average scholarship/grant was $19,469; average loan $4,199. 74% of total undergraduate aid awarded as scholarships/grants, 26% as loans/jobs. **Non-need-based:** Awarded to 819 full-time undergraduates, including 241 freshmen. Scholarships awarded for academics, music/drama.

**Application procedures. Admission:** Closing date 2/1 (postmark date). $50 fee, may be waived for applicants with need. Application may be submitted online. Admission notification 4/1. Must reply by May 1 or within 2 week(s) if notified thereafter. **Financial aid:** Closing date 2/1. FAFSA required. CSS PROFILE recommended of early action applicants. Applicants notified by 4/1; must reply by 5/1 or within 2 week(s) of notification.

**Academics. Special study options:** Accelerated study, combined bachelor's/graduate degree, cooperative education, double major, exchange student, independent study, internships, student-designed major, study abroad, urban semester, Washington semester. Interdisciplinary freshman study program, undergraduate research grants, field studies program in ecology in Hawaii, Ecuador, American Southwest, Oregon; 3-2 program, master's degree in management; 3-2 program, bachelor's degree in computer science with Oregon Graduate Institute, University of Oregon; 3-2 program, master's degree in forestry with Duke University. **Credit/placement by examination:** AP, CLEP, IB, institutional tests. 28 credit hours maximum toward bachelor's degree. **Support services:** Reduced course load, study skills assistance, tutoring, writing center.

**Majors.** **Area/ethnic studies:** American, Asian, Japanese, Latin American, women's. **Biology:** General. **Computer sciences:** General. **Conservation:** Environmental science. **Education:** Music. **English:** English lit, speech/rhetoric. **Foreign languages:** Classics, comparative lit, French, German, Spanish. **History:** General. **Interdisciplinary:** Global studies. **Liberal arts:** Humanities. **Math:** General. **Parks/recreation:** Exercise sciences. **Philosophy/religion:** Philosophy, religion. **Physical sciences:** Chemistry, physics. **Psychology:** General. **Social sciences:** Anthropology, economics, political science, sociology. **Visual/performing arts:** Art history/conservation, dramatic, film/cinema, music performance, music theory/composition, piano/organ, stringed instruments, studio arts, voice/opera. **Other:** Science studies.

**Most popular majors.** Biology 7%, business/marketing 10%, English 11%, foreign language 8%, physical sciences 6%, psychology 8%, social sciences 18%, visual/performing arts 7%.

**Computing on campus.** 400 workstations in dormitories, library, computer center, student center. Dormitories wired for high-speed internet access and linked to campus network. Commuter students can connect to campus network. Online course registration, online library, helpline, repair service, student web hosting, wireless network available.

**Student life.** **Freshman orientation:** Mandatory. 5-day program before start of semester. **Housing:** Guaranteed on-campus for freshmen. Coed dorms, apartments, fraternity/sorority housing, substance-free housing available. International studies house, nonsmoking residence hall, quiet study residence hall, substance-free hall available. **Activities:** Bands, campus ministries, choral groups, dance, drama, film society, international student organizations, literary magazine, music ensembles, Model UN, musical theater, opera, student government, student newspaper, symphony orchestra, More than 100 student organizations available.

**Athletics.** NCAA. **Intercollegiate:** Baseball M, basketball, cross-country, football (tackle) M, golf, rowing (crew), soccer, softball W, swimming, tennis, track and field, volleyball W. **Intramural:** Badminton, basketball, bowling, football (non-tackle), racquetball, soccer, softball, table tennis, tennis, volleyball, water polo, weight lifting. **Team name:** Bearcats.

**Student services.** Alcohol/substance abuse counseling, campus ministries, career counseling, student employment services, financial aid counseling, health services, minority student services, personal counseling, veterans' counselor, women's services. **Physically disabled:** Services for visually, speech, hearing impaired.

**Contact.** E-mail: libarts@willamette.edu
Phone: (503) 370-6303 Toll-free number: (877) 542-2787
Fax: (503) 375-5363
Madeleine Rhyneer, Vice President for Admissions and Financial Aid,
Willamette University, 900 State Street, Salem, OR 97301-3922

# Pennsylvania

---

## Albright College

Reading, Pennsylvania
www.albright.edu

**CB member**
**CB code: 2004**

- Private 4-year liberal arts college affiliated with United Methodist Church
- Residential campus in small city
- 2,153 degree-seeking undergraduates: 1% part-time, 59% women, 8% African American, 2% Asian American, 5% Hispanic American, 4% international
- 16 degree-seeking graduate students
- 77% of applicants admitted
- SAT or ACT (ACT writing optional), application essay required
- 60% graduate within 6 years

**General.** Founded in 1856. Regionally accredited. **Degrees:** 492 bachelor's awarded; master's offered. **Location:** 50 miles from Philadelphia. **Calendar:** 4-1-4, limited summer session. **Full-time faculty:** 108 total; 77% have terminal degrees, 15% minority, 48% women. **Part-time faculty:** 55 total; 31% have terminal degrees, 4% minority, 60% women. **Class size:** 59% < 20, 39% 20-39, 1% 40-49, less than 1% >100. **Special facilities:** Satellite dish for foreign language program, transmission and scanning electron microscopes, Holocaust resource center, center for local government, center for cultural ecology, center for Latin American studies.

**Freshman class profile.** 3,353 applied, 2,595 admitted, 512 enrolled.

| Mid 50% test scores | | Rank in top tenth: | 23% |
|---|---|---|---|
| SAT critical reading: | 450-560 | End year in good standing: | 90% |
| SAT math: | 450-570 | Return as sophomores: | 74% |
| ACT composite: | 18-22 | Out-of-state: | 35% |
| GPA 3.50 or higher: | 40% | Live on campus: | 78% |
| GPA 3.0-3.49: | 29% | International: | 5% |
| GPA 2.0-2.99: | 30% | Fraternities: | 3% |
| Rank in top quarter: | 46% | Sororities: | 4% |

**Basis for selection.** High school performance (with emphasis on difficulty of curriculum pursued), personal statement, and recommendations most important. Community service, extracurricular activity and test scores considered. Interview recommended.

**High school preparation.** 16 units required; 20 recommended. Required and recommended units include English 4, mathematics 2-3, social studies 2, history 1-2, science 3-4 (laboratory 1-2), foreign language 2-3 and academic electives 2. Bachelor of science applicants should have 1 additional unit in science and 1 in math. 2 units of laboratory science recommended.

**2008-2009 Annual costs.** Tuition/fees: $30,570. $3,721 per course (worth 4 credits). Room/board: $8,670. Books/supplies: $800. Personal expenses: $1,000.

**2007-2008 Financial aid. Need-based:** 467 full-time freshmen applied for aid; 437 were judged to have need; 430 of these received aid. Average need met was 79%. Average scholarship/grant was $16,975; average loan $4,698. 67% of total undergraduate aid awarded as scholarships/grants, 33% as loans/jobs. **Non-need-based:** Awarded to 442 full-time undergraduates, including 104 freshmen. Scholarships awarded for academics, alumni affiliation, art, leadership, minority status, music/drama, religious affiliation.

**Application procedures. Admission:** Priority date 3/1; no deadline. $25 fee, may be waived for applicants with need. Application may be submitted online. Admission notification on a rolling basis beginning on or about 10/1. Must reply by May 1 or within 2 week(s) if notified thereafter. **Financial aid:** Priority date 3/1; no closing date. FAFSA required. Applicants notified on a rolling basis starting 2/15; must reply by 5/1 or within 2 week(s) of notification.

**Academics.** Flexible curriculum combines liberal arts education with hands-on experiences. Institution emphasizes faculty-student collaboration and has an active undergraduate research program, which also funds summer projects with faculty. **Special study options:** Accelerated study, combined bachelor's/graduate degree, cross-registration, double major, dual enrollment of high school students, ESL, exchange student, honors, independent study, internships, liberal arts/career combination, semester at sea, student-designed major, study abroad, teacher certification program, urban semester, Washington semester. Interdisciplinary studies, student research. **Credit/placement by examination:** AP, CLEP, IB, SAT, ACT. 28 credit hours maximum toward bachelor's degree. **Support services:** Learning center, pre-admission summer program, reduced course load, study skills assistance, tutoring, writing center.

**Majors. Area/ethnic studies:** American, Latin American, women's. **Biology:** General, biochemistry. **Business:** Accounting, business admin, finance, international, marketing. **Communications:** General. **Computer sciences:** General, information systems. **Conservation:** General, environmental science, environmental studies. **Education:** Art, early childhood, elementary, secondary, special. **English:** English lit. **Family/consumer sciences:** Clothing/textiles. **Foreign languages:** French, Spanish. **Health:** Predental, premedicine, preveterinary. **History:** General. **Math:** General. **Philosophy/religion:** Philosophy, religion. **Physical sciences:** Chemistry, optics, physics. **Psychology:** General. **Social sciences:** Anthropology, criminology, economics, political science, sociology. **Visual/performing arts:** Dramatic, studio arts.

**Most popular majors.** Business/marketing 27%, psychology 13%, social sciences 15%, visual/performing arts 8%.

**Computing on campus.** 271 workstations in dormitories, library, computer center, student center, student center. Dormitories wired for high-speed internet access and linked to campus network. Online library, helpline, wireless network available.

**Student life. Freshman orientation:** Mandatory. Preregistration for classes offered. Held the 4 days prior to start of fall classes. **Housing:** Guaranteed on-campus for all undergraduates. Coed dorms, substance-free housing available. $100 nonrefundable deposit, deadline 6/1. Honors housing, break housing suite, all freshmen housing, all-female floors, all-male floors, single rooms, single-sex suites/apartments/wings. **Activities:** Bands, choral groups, dance, drama, international student organizations, literary magazine, music ensembles, musical theater, radio station, student government, student newspaper, TV station, Newman Association, Hillel, Christian Fellowship, African American society, Asian American society, environmental action group, American Association of University Women, human services organization.

**Athletics.** NCAA. **Intercollegiate:** Baseball M, basketball, cheerleading, cross-country, field hockey W, football (tackle) M, golf M, soccer, softball W, swimming, tennis, track and field, volleyball W. **Intramural:** Basketball, bowling, football (non-tackle), softball, volleyball. **Team name:** Lions.

**Student services.** Adult student services, campus ministries, career counseling, student employment services, financial aid counseling, health services, minority student services, personal counseling, women's services. **Physically disabled:** Services for visually, hearing impaired.

**Contact.** E-mail: admission@albright.edu
Phone: (610) 921-7512 Toll-free number: (800) 252-1856
Fax: (610) 921-7294
Gregory Eichhorn, Vice-President for Enrollment Management and Dean of Admissions, Albright College, 13th & Bern Streets, Reading, PA 19612-5234

---

## Allegheny College

Meadville, Pennsylvania
www.allegheny.edu

**CB member**
**CB code: 2006**

- Private 4-year liberal arts college affiliated with United Methodist Church
- Residential campus in large town
- 2,163 degree-seeking undergraduates: 1% part-time, 56% women, 2% African American, 3% Asian American, 2% Hispanic American, 1% international
- 57% of applicants admitted
- SAT or ACT (ACT writing recommended), application essay required
- 71% graduate within 6 years; 39% enter graduate study

**General.** Founded in 1815. Regionally accredited. **Degrees:** 363 bachelor's awarded. **Location:** 90 miles from Pittsburgh and Cleveland. **Calendar:** Semester, limited summer session. **Full-time faculty:** 145 total; 91% have terminal degrees, 12% minority, 41% women. **Part-time faculty:** 24 total; 29% have terminal degrees, 4% minority, 58% women. **Class size:** 58% < 20, 37% 20-39, 4% 40-49, less than 1% 50-99. **Special facilities:** Science complex, video conference facilities, planetarium, observatory, GIS lab, smart classrooms, solid-volume glass sculpture grouping, environmental research reserve, 80-acre protected forest, Center for Political Participation, Center for Experiential Learning, Center for Economic and Environment Development, language learning center, seismometer station, art studios, dance studio and performance area, art galleries.

**Freshman class profile.** 4,354 applied, 2,487 admitted, 584 enrolled.

| Mid 50% test scores | | Rank in top tenth: | 46% |
|---|---|---|---|
| SAT critical reading: | 560-660 | End year in good standing: | 99% |
| SAT math: | 560-650 | Return as sophomores: | 87% |
| ACT composite: | 24-28 | Out-of-state: | 43% |
| GPA 3.50 or higher: | 79% | Live on campus: | 98% |
| GPA 3.0-3.49: | 18% | International: | 1% |
| GPA 2.0-2.99: | 3% | Fraternities: | 14% |
| Rank in top quarter: | 77% | Sororities: | 13% |

**Basis for selection.** Rigor of high school program most important, followed by high school achievement. Test scores important. Essay, minority status, alumni ties, geography considered. One recommendation from guidance counselor and 1 from teacher required. Interview recommended. **Homeschooled:** Campus visit and individual interview with admissions counselor to discuss portfolios recommended. Recommendation from a nonfamily member, description of the level of instruction. **Learning Disabled:** Recommended interview with Director of Student Support Services.

**High school preparation.** 16 units required. Required units include English 4, mathematics 3, social studies 3, science 3, foreign language 2 and academic electives 1.

**2008-2009 Annual costs.** Tuition/fees: $32,000. Room/board: $8,000. Books/supplies: $900. Personal expenses: $800.

**2007-2008 Financial aid. Need-based:** 491 full-time freshmen applied for aid; 403 were judged to have need; 403 of these received aid. Average need met was 95%. Average scholarship/grant was $18,078; average loan $5,420. 74% of total undergraduate aid awarded as scholarships/grants, 26% as loans/jobs. **Non-need-based:** Awarded to 846 full-time undergraduates, including 229 freshmen. Scholarships awarded for academics, leadership, minority status, state residency.

**Application procedures. Admission:** Closing date 2/15 (postmark date). $35 fee, may be waived for applicants with need. Application may be submitted online. Admission notification 4/1. Must reply by 5/1. **Financial aid:** Priority date 2/15; no closing date. FAFSA required. Applicants notified on a rolling basis starting 3/1; must reply by 5/1 or within 4 week(s) of notification.

**Academics.** Experiential learning term; teacher partnerships with Columbia University Teachers College, Xavier School of Education and University of Pittsburgh; business school partnership with Simon Graduate School of Business Administration at University of Rochester; medical school partnerships with Jefferson Medical College and Drexel College of Medicine; accelerated master's degree program with Carnegie Mellon University for public policy and management, arts management, health policy and management, information systems management, and information technology; marine biology study programs. **Special study options:** Combined bachelor's/graduate degree, double major, dual enrollment of high school students, ESL, exchange student, independent study, internships, student-designed major, study abroad, Washington semester. Graduate school partnerships, marine biology study program, combined degree programs (3-2, 3-4), summer study program, double minor. **Credit/placement by examination:** AP, CLEP, IB, institutional tests. 20 credit hours maximum toward bachelor's degree. Math and science department exams available for placement. **Support services:** Learning center, reduced course load, study skills assistance, tutoring, writing center.

**Majors. Area/ethnic studies:** Women's. **Biology:** General, biochemistry. **Business:** Managerial economics. **Communications:** General, journalism, media studies. **Computer sciences:** Computer science. **Conservation:** Environmental science, environmental studies. **Education:** General. **Engineering:** Software. **English:** Creative writing, English lit, technical writing. **Foreign languages:** French, German, Spanish. **Health:** Predental, premedicine, prenursing, prepharmacy, preveterinary. **History:** General. **Interdisciplinary:** Neuroscience. **Legal studies:** Prelaw. **Math:** General. **Philosophy/religion:** Philosophy, religion. **Physical sciences:** Chemistry, geology, physics. **Psychology:** General. **Social sciences:** Applied economics, economics, international relations, political science. **Visual/performing arts:** Art, art history/conservation, dramatic, music performance, studio arts. **Other:** Art and technology, Environmental geology, Health/medical preparatory.

**Most popular majors.** Biology 12%, English 9%, interdisciplinary studies 7%, physical sciences 6%, psychology 14%, social sciences 24%.

**Computing on campus.** 311 workstations in dormitories, library, computer center, student center. Dormitories wired for high-speed internet access and linked to campus network. Commuter students can connect to campus network. Online library, helpline, repair service, student web hosting, wireless network available.

**Student life. Freshman orientation:** Mandatory. 4-day session held 4 days before fall classes begin. **Policies:** Honor code. **Housing:** Guaranteed on-campus for all undergraduates. Coed dorms, single-sex dorms, special housing for disabled, apartments, fraternity/sorority housing, substance-free housing available. Special interest housing, theme-based student apartments available, townhouses, wellness floors. **Activities:** Bands, choral groups, dance, drama, literary magazine, music ensembles, musical theater, radio station, student government, student newspaper, symphony orchestra, TV station, Association for Asian and Asian-American Awareness, Advancement of Black Culture, Union Latina, Habitat for Humanity, Newman Association, Hillel, Christian Outreach, Students for Environmental Action, Alpha Phi Omega, Americorps Bonner Leaders.

**Athletics.** NCAA. **Intercollegiate:** Baseball M, basketball, cross-country, diving, football (tackle) M, golf, lacrosse W, soccer, softball W, swimming, tennis, track and field, volleyball W. **Intramural:** Basketball, bowling, football (non-tackle), golf, racquetball, soccer, softball, tennis, volleyball. **Team name:** Gators.

**Student services.** Adult student services, alcohol/substance abuse counseling, campus ministries, career counseling, student employment services, financial aid counseling, health services, minority student services, personal counseling, placement for graduates. **Physically disabled:** Services for visually, hearing impaired.

**Contact.** E-mail: admissions@allegheny.edu
Phone: (814) 332-4351 Toll-free number: (800) 521-5293
Fax: (814) 337-0431
Jennifer Winge, Director of Admissions, Allegheny College, 520 North Main Street, Meadville, PA 16335

## Alvernia College
Reading, Pennsylvania
www.alvernia.edu
CB member
CB code: 2431

- Private 4-year liberal arts college affiliated with Roman Catholic Church
- Residential campus in small city
- 1,922 degree-seeking undergraduates: 19% part-time, 69% women, 11% African American, 1% Asian American, 6% Hispanic American, 1% Native American, 1% international
- 564 degree-seeking graduate students
- 76% of applicants admitted
- SAT or ACT (ACT writing optional) required
- 59% graduate within 6 years

**General.** Founded in 1958. Regionally accredited. Affiliated with Bernardine Sisters, Third Order of St. Francis. **Degrees:** 423 bachelor's, 7 associate awarded; master's, doctoral offered. **ROTC:** Army. **Location:** 60 miles from Philadelphia. **Calendar:** Semester, limited summer session. **Full-time faculty:** 81 total; 62% have terminal degrees, 9% minority, 58% women. **Part-time faculty:** 211 total; 21% have terminal degrees, 7% minority, 45% women. **Class size:** 64% < 20, 36% 20-39.

**Freshman class profile.** 1,290 applied, 985 admitted, 303 enrolled.

| Mid 50% test scores | | GPA 2.0-2.99: | 50% |
|---|---|---|---|
| SAT critical reading: | 420-520 | Rank in top quarter: | 18% |
| SAT math: | 420-530 | Rank in top tenth: | 4% |
| SAT writing: | 410-500 | End year in good standing: | 89% |
| ACT composite: | 17-21 | Return as sophomores: | 71% |
| GPA 3.50 or higher: | 18% | Out-of-state: | 20% |
| GPA 3.0-3.49: | 31% | Live on campus: | 77% |

**Basis for selection.** Important factors include academic performance, standardized test scores, class rank, extracurricular activities, and community involvement. Essay, interview recommended for all. Interview required of nursing, occupational therapy and physical therapist assistant applicants.

**High school preparation.** Recommended units include English 4, mathematics 4, social studies 3, science 2 and foreign language 2.

**2007-2008 Annual costs.** Tuition/fees: $21,614. Room/board: $8,250. Books/supplies: $1,400. Personal expenses: $1,196.

**2006-2007 Financial aid. Need-based:** 296 full-time freshmen applied for aid; 269 were judged to have need; 269 of these received aid. Average need met was 66%. Average scholarship/grant was $10,369; average loan $3,876. 56% of total undergraduate aid awarded as scholarships/grants, 44% as loans/jobs. **Non-need-based:** Awarded to 189 full-time undergraduates, including 48 freshmen. Scholarships awarded for academics, alumni affiliation, ROTC.

**Application procedures. Admission:** No deadline. $25 fee, may be waived for applicants with need. Admission notification on a rolling basis. Must reply by May 1 or within 2 week(s) if notified thereafter. **Financial aid:** No deadline. FAFSA required. Applicants notified on a rolling basis starting 2/1; must reply within 2 week(s) of notification.

**Academics. Special study options:** Accelerated study, combined bachelor's/ graduate degree, cross-registration, double major, dual enrollment of high school students, ESL, honors, independent study, internships, student-designed major, study abroad, teacher certification program, Washington semester. **Credit/placement by examination:** AP, CLEP, IB, institutional tests. 30 credit hours maximum toward associate degree, 30 toward bachelor's. Total of 30 credits allowed for all experiential credit, CLEP, life experience, challenge exam. **Support services:** Learning center, pre-admission summer program, reduced course load, remedial instruction, study skills assistance, tutoring, writing center.

**Majors. Biology:** General. **Business:** General, accounting, human resources, marketing. **Communications:** General. **Computer sciences:** General. **Education:** General, biology, chemistry, early childhood, elementary, English, mathematics, science, social studies, special. **English:** English lit. **Health:** Athletic training, nursing (RN), substance abuse counseling. **History:** General. **Interdisciplinary:** Biological/physical sciences. **Liberal arts:** Arts/sciences. **Parks/recreation:** Sports admin. **Philosophy/religion:** Religion. **Physical sciences:** Chemistry. **Protective services:** Forensics, law enforcement admin. **Psychology:** General. **Public administration:** Social work. **Social sciences:** General, political science. **Theology:** Theology.

**Most popular majors.** Business/marketing 17%, education 17%, health sciences 25%, security/protective services 20%.

**Computing on campus.** 273 workstations in dormitories, library, computer center, student center. Dormitories wired for high-speed internet access and linked to campus network. Commuter students can connect to campus network. Online course registration, online library, helpline, wireless network available.

**Student life. Freshman orientation:** Mandatory. Preregistration for classes offered. Held weekend before classes start. **Housing:** Coed dorms, single-sex dorms, special housing for disabled available. Single-sex townhouses available. Single-sex floors in dorms. **Activities:** Choral groups, dance, drama, literary magazine, music ensembles, student government, student newspaper.

**Athletics.** NCAA. **Intercollegiate:** Baseball M, basketball, cross-country, field hockey W, golf M, ice hockey M, lacrosse, soccer, softball W, tennis, volleyball W. **Intramural:** Basketball, cheerleading W, lacrosse M, volleyball M. **Team name:** Crusaders.

**Student services.** Adult student services, campus ministries, career counseling, services for economically disadvantaged, student employment services, financial aid counseling, health services, personal counseling, placement for graduates, veterans' counselor. **Physically disabled:** Services for visually impaired.

**Contact.** E-mail: admissions@alvernia.edu
Phone: (610) 796-8220 Toll-free number: (888) 258-3764
Fax: (610) 796-8336
Jeff Dittman, Dean of Undergraduate Admission, Alvernia College, 400 St. Bernardine Street, Reading, PA 19607-1799

---

## Arcadia University

**Glenside, Pennsylvania**
www.arcadia.edu

**CB member**
**CB code: 2039**

- Private 4-year university affiliated with Presbyterian Church (USA)
- Residential campus in large town
- 1,889 full-time, degree-seeking undergraduates
- 1,528 graduate students
- 75% of applicants admitted
- SAT or ACT with writing, application essay required

**General.** Founded in 1853. Regionally accredited. **Degrees:** 398 bachelor's awarded; master's, doctoral offered. **ROTC:** Army. **Location:** 10 miles from Philadelphia. **Calendar:** Semester, limited summer session. **Full-time faculty:** 102 total; 16% minority, 48% women. **Part-time faculty:** 294 total; 10% minority, 57% women. **Class size:** 66% < 20, 32% 20-39, 1% 40-49, less than 1% 50-99, less than 1% >100. **Special facilities:** Observatory housing 14-inch Schmidt-Cassegrain telescope with extensive astrophotography capabilities, Grey Towers Castle (national historic landmark) used as residence hall.

**Freshman class profile.** 3,767 applied, 2,836 admitted, 498 enrolled.

| Mid 50% test scores | | | |
|---|---|---|---|
| SAT critical reading: | 500-610 | GPA 2.0-2.99: | 14% |
| SAT math: | 480-590 | Rank in top quarter: | 58% |
| SAT writing: | 500-600 | Rank in top tenth: | 29% |
| ACT composite: | 20-26 | End year in good standing: | 78% |
| GPA 3.50 or higher: | 56% | Out-of-state: | 51% |
| GPA 3.0-3.49: | 30% | Live on campus: | 86% |

**Basis for selection.** Emphasis placed on academic records, including type of program followed, courses taken, grades earned, class rank. Standardized test scores, counselor/ teacher recommendations, participation in school and community activities important. Character references also considered. Supplementary materials demonstrating student's talents and potential recommended. Portfolio review required for fine arts department. Auditions required for BFA in acting. **Homeschooled:** Portfolio representing academic record/work and level of achievement for grades 9-12 required.

**High school preparation.** 19 units recommended. Recommended units include English 4, mathematics 3, social studies 2, history 2, science 3 (laboratory 3) and foreign language 2. Additional units in foreign language, math, and/or laboratory science recommended. Math includes algebra II and geometry.

**2008-2009 Annual costs.** Tuition/fees (projected): $29,700. Room/ board: $10,280. Books/supplies: $1,000.

**2007-2008 Financial aid. Need-based:** Average need met was 80%. Average scholarship/grant was $14,470; average loan $5,065. **Non-need-based:** Scholarships awarded for academics, alumni affiliation, art, leadership, music/drama.

**Application procedures. Admission:** Priority date 1/15; deadline 3/1. $30 fee, may be waived for applicants with need. Application may be submitted online. Admission notification on a rolling basis beginning on or about 9/1. Must reply by May 1 or within 2 week(s) if notified thereafter. **Financial aid:** Priority date 3/1; no closing date. FAFSA, institutional form required. Applicants notified on a rolling basis starting 2/15; must reply by 5/1.

**Academics. Special study options:** Accelerated study, combined bachelor's/ graduate degree, cooperative education, cross-registration, distance learning, double major, dual enrollment of high school students, exchange student, honors, independent study, internships, liberal arts/career combination, student-designed major, study abroad, teacher certification program, Washington semester. Combined programs leading to graduate degrees in physical therapy, physician assistant studies (option to combine with public health), forensic science, international peace and conflict resolution. Combined with other universities for degrees in engineering, nursing, optometry. **Credit/ placement by examination:** AP, CLEP, IB, institutional tests. 64 credit hours maximum toward bachelor's degree. **Support services:** Learning center, pre-admission summer program, reduced course load, remedial instruction, study skills assistance, tutoring, writing center.

**Majors. Biology:** General. **Business:** General, accounting, business admin, finance, human resources, international, management information systems, marketing. **Communications:** General, media studies, radio/tv. **Computer sciences:** General, computer science, programming. **Conservation:** Environmental studies. **Education:** General, art, biology, chemistry, early childhood, elementary, English, mathematics, multi-level teacher, science, secondary, social science, social studies, special. **Engineering:** General. **English:** English lit. **Foreign languages:** Spanish. **Health:** Art therapy, health care admin, health services admin, medical illustrating. **History:** General. **Interdisciplinary:** Biological/physical sciences. **Legal studies:** General. **Liberal arts:** Arts/sciences. **Math:** General. **Philosophy/religion:** Philosophy. **Physical sciences:** Chemistry. **Psychology:** General. **Social sciences:** International relations, political science, sociology. **Visual/performing arts:** General, acting, art history/conservation, ceramics, commercial/advertising art, dramatic, graphic design, interior design, metal/jewelry, painting, photography, printmaking, studio arts, theater history. **Other:** Global legal studies, Sound and music, Sport Psychology.

**Most popular majors.** Biology 7%, business/marketing 15%, communications/journalism 7%, education 15%, psychology 10%, social sciences 9%, visual/performing arts 15%.

**Computing on campus.** 150 workstations in library, computer center. Dormitories wired for high-speed internet access and linked to campus network. Commuter students can connect to campus network. Online course registration, helpline, repair service, wireless network available.

**Student life. Freshman orientation:** Mandatory. Preregistration for classes offered. **Housing:** Guaranteed on-campus for all undergraduates. Coed dorms, single-sex dorms, special housing for disabled, apartments, substance-free housing available. $300 nonrefundable deposit, deadline 5/1. Living and learning community available. **Activities:** Choral groups, dance, drama, literary magazine, music ensembles, musical theater, radio station, student government, student newspaper, TV station, approximately 45 clubs and organizations.

**Athletics.** NCAA. **Intercollegiate:** Baseball M, basketball, equestrian, field hockey W, golf, lacrosse W, soccer, softball W, swimming, tennis, volleyball W. **Intramural:** Basketball, field hockey W, football (non-tackle), skiing, soccer, softball, swimming M, tennis, volleyball, weight lifting. **Team name:** Scarlet Knights.

**Student services.** Adult student services, alcohol/substance abuse counseling, career counseling, services for economically disadvantaged, student employment services, financial aid counseling, health services, minority student services, personal counseling, placement for graduates.

**Contact.** E-mail: admiss@arcadia.edu
Phone: (215) 572-2910 Toll-free number: (887) 272-2342
Fax: (215) 881-8767
Mark Laureziosa, Assistant Vice President of Enrollment Management, Arcadia University, 450 South Easton Road, Glenside, PA 19038-3295

## Art Institute of Philadelphia
### Philadelphia, Pennsylvania
### www.artinstitutes.edu/Philadelphia          CB code: 2033

- For-profit 4-year visual arts college
- Commuter campus in very large city
- 2,515 full-time, degree-seeking undergraduates
- Application essay, interview required

**General.** Founded in 1966. Accredited by ACICS. **Degrees:** 300 bachelor's, 290 associate awarded. **Calendar:** Quarter, extensive summer session. **Full-time faculty:** 100 total. **Part-time faculty:** 120 total. **Special facilities:** Recording studio utilizing Pro-tools software, digital photography laboratory, nonlinear digital editing suites, and full-service chef instructor/student-run restaurant.

**Basis for selection.** Open admission. Portfolio recommended.

**High school preparation.** Background or strong interest in chosen major preferred.

**2007-2008 Annual costs.** Costs vary by program and course of study. Diploma program, $14, 436; associate degree program, $31,383 - $48,120; bachelor's degree program, $72, 180. Additional fees may apply.

**Financial aid. Additional information:** Institute-sponsored scholarships available.

**Application procedures. Admission:** No deadline. $50 fee. Application may be submitted online. Admission notification on a rolling basis. **Financial aid:** Closing date 5/1. FAFSA, institutional form required. Applicants notified on a rolling basis starting 3/1; must reply within 2 week(s) of notification.

**Academics.** Academic program designed to simulate working environment, focusing course work on job-related skills. **Special study options:** Independent study, internships. **Credit/placement by examination:** CLEP, IB, SAT, ACT, institutional tests. **Support services:** Learning center, reduced course load, remedial instruction, study skills assistance, tutoring.

**Majors. Communications technology:** Animation/special effects. **Computer sciences:** Web page design. **Visual/performing arts:** Cinematography, commercial/advertising art, design, industrial design, interior design.

**Computing on campus.** 507 workstations in dormitories, library, computer center. Dormitories wired for high-speed internet access. Online library, student web hosting available.

**Student life. Freshman orientation:** Available. **Housing:** Coed dorms, apartments available. **Activities:** Student government.

**Student services.** Career counseling, student employment services, financial aid counseling, personal counseling, placement for graduates.

**Contact.** E-mail: aiphadm@aii.edu
Phone: (215) 567-7080 Toll-free number: (800) 275-2474
Fax: (215) 405-6399
Larry McHugh, Director of Admissions, Art Institute of Philadelphia, 1622 Chestnut Street, Philadelphia, PA 19103-5198

## Art Institute of Pittsburgh
### Pittsburgh, Pennsylvania
### www.artinstitutes.edu/pittsburgh          CB code: 2029

- For-profit 4-year visual arts and technical college
- Commuter campus in large city
- 7,900 degree-seeking undergraduates
- Application essay, interview required

**General.** Founded in 1921. Regionally accredited; also accredited by ACICS. **Degrees:** 430 bachelor's, 210 associate awarded. **Calendar:** Continuous, extensive summer session. **Full-time faculty:** 207 total. **Part-time faculty:** 692 total. **Special facilities:** Photography laboratory, art gallery for students and faculty, traveling exhibits, 24-track recording studio, restaurant.

**Freshman class profile.**

| | | | |
|---|---|---|---|
| Out-of-state: | 50% | Live on campus: | 50% |

**Basis for selection.** High school transcript most important. Essay required. Interview required. Limited portfolio required for some programs. **Homeschooled:** Statement describing homeschool structure and mission, transcript of courses and grades, state high school equivalency certificate, letter of recommendation (nonparent) required.

**High school preparation.** Prefer students with demonstrated interest in chosen major.

**2008-2009 Annual costs.** Tuition/fees (projected): $20,556. Tuition and fees may vary. Culinary lab fee for food courses, $250; $100 lab fee per online course. Room only: $5,978. Books/supplies: $1,445.

**Application procedures. Admission:** No deadline. $50 fee. Application may be submitted online. Admission notification on a rolling basis. **Financial aid:** No deadline. FAFSA, institutional form required. Applicants notified on a rolling basis starting 4/15.

**Academics. Special study options:** Cross-registration, distance learning, internships, study abroad. **Credit/placement by examination:** AP, CLEP. **Support services:** Learning center, remedial instruction, tutoring, writing center.

**Majors. Business:** Fashion. **Communications technology:** Animation/special effects. **Computer sciences:** Web page design. **Personal/culinary services:** Chef training, restaurant/catering. **Visual/performing arts:** Cinematography, commercial/advertising art, design, industrial design, interior design, photography.

**Computing on campus.** 225 workstations in dormitories, library, computer center. Dormitories wired for high-speed internet access and linked to campus network. Commuter students can connect to campus network. Online course registration, online library, helpline, student web hosting, wireless network available.

**Student life. Freshman orientation:** Mandatory. Preregistration for classes offered. One-day program held before start of classes. **Housing:** Coed dorms, apartments, substance-free housing available. $100 deposit. **Activities:** Drama, film society, international student organizations, student government, student newspaper, community relations activities, student success task force, student council.

**Athletics. Intramural:** Basketball M.

**Student services.** Career counseling, student employment services, financial aid counseling, personal counseling, placement for graduates, veterans' counselor. **Physically disabled:** Services for visually, speech, hearing impaired.

**Contact.** E-mail: aipadm@aii.edu
Phone: (412) 263-6600 Toll-free number: (800) 275-2470
Fax: (412) 263-6667
Jeffrey Bucklew, Director of Admissions, Art Institute of Pittsburgh, 420 Boulevard of the Allies, Pittsburgh, PA 15219-1328

## Art Institute Online
### Pittsburgh, Pennsylvania
### www.aionline.edu          CB code: 3835

- For-profit 4-year virtual college
- Large city
- 9,000 undergraduates

**General.** Accredited by ACICS. A division of The Art Institute of Pittsburgh. **Degrees:** 160 bachelor's, 86 associate awarded. **Calendar:** Quarter. **Full-time faculty:** 285 total. **Part-time faculty:** 285 total.

**Basis for selection.** 2.0 high school GPA required. Applicants must submit completed enrollment agreement and $100 enrollment fee within 10 days of application. Applicants not accepted for admission will receive full refund of all fees paid.

**2007-2008 Annual costs.** Tuition/fees: $13,024.

**Application procedures. Admission:** No deadline. $50 fee. Application may be submitted online. Admission notification on a rolling basis.

**Academics. Credit/placement by examination:** CLEP.

**Majors. Business:** Hotel/motel admin. **Communications:** Advertising. **Computer sciences:** Web page design. **Family/consumer sciences:** Merchandising. **Personal/culinary services:** Restaurant/catering. **Visual/performing arts:** Graphic design, interior design. **Other:** Game art and design.

**Student life. Freshman orientation:** Mandatory. Online student orientation teaches use of online software program and acquaints students with overall classroom environment. Conducted prior to beginning of classes.

**Contact.** E-mail: aioadm@aii.edu
Phone: (877) 872-8869 Toll-free number: (877) 872-8869
Fax: (412) 995-4320
Donald Fisher, Admissions Director, Art Institute Online, 1400 Penn Avenue, Pittsburgh, PA 15222

---

## Baptist Bible College of Pennsylvania
### Clarks Summit, Pennsylvania
www.bbc.edu
CB code: 2036

- Private 4-year Bible and seminary college affiliated with Baptist faith
- Residential campus in small city
- 668 degree-seeking undergraduates: 5% part-time, 59% women, 1% African American, 1% Asian American, 2% Hispanic American, 2% international
- 206 degree-seeking graduate students
- 76% of applicants admitted
- SAT or ACT (ACT writing optional), application essay required
- 49% graduate within 6 years

**General.** Founded in 1932. Regionally accredited; also accredited by ABHE. Part of each student's curriculum includes ministry/service experiences in churches or social agencies. **Degrees:** 157 bachelor's, 25 associate awarded; master's, doctoral, first professional offered. **Location:** 7 miles from Scranton, 20 miles from Wilkes-Barre. **Calendar:** Semester, limited summer session. **Full-time faculty:** 35 total; 57% have terminal degrees, 3% minority, 29% women. **Part-time faculty:** 16 total; 19% have terminal degrees, 6% minority, 50% women. **Class size:** 70% < 20, 20% 20-39, 4% 40-49, 6% 50-99, 1% >100.

**Freshman class profile.** 450 applied, 344 admitted, 164 enrolled.

| Mid 50% test scores | | | |
|---|---|---|---|
| SAT critical reading: | 460-570 | GPA 2.0-2.99: | 22% |
| SAT math: | 430-560 | End year in good standing: | 92% |
| ACT composite: | 20-24 | Return as sophomores: | 69% |
| GPA 3.50 or higher: | 48% | Out-of-state: | 70% |
| GPA 3.0-3.49: | 25% | Live on campus: | 96% |

**Basis for selection.** Academic record, test scores, references/recommendations most important. Audition required, interview recommended for all; portfolio required for music programs.

**2007-2008 Annual costs.** Tuition/fees: $15,060. Room/board: $5,600. Books/supplies: $600. Personal expenses: $1,144.

**2006-2007 Financial aid. Non-need-based:** Scholarships awarded for academics, leadership, music/drama, religious affiliation.

**Application procedures. Admission:** Priority date 5/1; deadline 8/15 (postmark date). $30 fee. Application may be submitted online. Admission notification on a rolling basis. Must reply by May 1 or within 4 week(s) if notified thereafter. **Financial aid:** Closing date 5/1. FAFSA, institutional form required. Applicants notified on a rolling basis starting 4/1.

---

**Academics. Special study options:** Combined bachelor's/graduate degree, distance learning, double major, dual enrollment of high school students, independent study, internships, study abroad, teacher certification program. **Credit/placement by examination:** AP, CLEP, IB, SAT, ACT, institutional tests. **Support services:** Reduced course load, remedial instruction, study skills assistance, tutoring, writing center.

**Majors. Business:** Administrative services. **Communications:** General. **Education:** Early childhood, elementary, health, mathematics, multi-level teacher, music, physical, science, secondary, social studies. **Parks/recreation:** Health/fitness. **Theology:** Missionary, preministerial, sacred music, youth ministry.

**Most popular majors.** Communications/journalism 9%, education 27%, psychology 11%, theological studies 52%.

**Computing on campus.** 30 workstations in library, computer center. Dormitories wired for high-speed internet access and linked to campus network. Online course registration, online library, wireless network available.

**Student life. Freshman orientation:** Mandatory. Preregistration for classes offered. Parent and student orientation weekend includes sessions on academics, student life, finances, and interaction with faculty. **Policies:** Religious observance required. **Housing:** Guaranteed on-campus for all undergraduates. Single-sex dorms, special housing for disabled, substance-free housing available. $250 deposit, deadline 5/1. **Activities:** Choral groups, drama, music ensembles, student government, student newspaper, several religious and service groups.

**Athletics.** NCAA, NCCAA. **Intercollegiate:** Baseball M, basketball, cheerleading W, cross-country, golf M, soccer, softball W, tennis W, track and field, volleyball, wrestling M. **Intramural:** Basketball, soccer, softball M, volleyball. **Team name:** Defenders.

**Student services.** Adult student services, alcohol/substance abuse counseling, career counseling, student employment services, financial aid counseling, health services, personal counseling, placement for graduates.

**Contact.** E-mail: admissions@bbc.edu
Phone: (570) 586-2400 ext. 9271 Toll-free number: (800) 585-9271
Fax: (570) 585-9299
Glenn Amos, Vice President for Enrollment Management, Baptist Bible College of Pennsylvania, 538 Venard Road, Clarks Summit, PA 18411-1297

---

## Bloomsburg University of Pennsylvania
### Bloomsburg, Pennsylvania
CB member
www.bloomu.edu
CB code: 2646

- Public 4-year university and liberal arts college
- Residential campus in large town
- 7,667 degree-seeking undergraduates: 5% part-time, 58% women, 7% African American, 1% Asian American, 2% Hispanic American, 1% international
- 780 degree-seeking graduate students
- 61% of applicants admitted
- SAT or ACT (ACT writing optional) required
- 61% graduate within 6 years; 19% enter graduate study

**General.** Founded in 1839. Regionally accredited. **Degrees:** 1,516 bachelor's awarded; master's, doctoral offered. **ROTC:** Army, Air Force. **Location:** 40 miles from Wilkes-Barre, 80 miles from Harrisburg. **Calendar:** Semester, extensive summer session. **Full-time faculty:** 379 total; 84% have terminal degrees, 14% minority, 41% women. **Part-time faculty:** 46 total; 17% have terminal degrees, 4% minority, 54% women. **Class size:** 24% < 20, 64% 20-39, 6% 40-49, 4% 50-99, 3% >100.

**Freshman class profile.** 9,868 applied, 6,009 admitted, 1,685 enrolled.

| Mid 50% test scores | | | |
|---|---|---|---|
| SAT critical reading: | 460-540 | GPA 2.0-2.99: | 21% |
| SAT math: | 470-570 | Rank in top quarter: | 36% |
| SAT writing: | 440-530 | Rank in top tenth: | 9% |
| GPA 3.50 or higher: | 40% | Return as sophomores: | 81% |
| GPA 3.0-3.49: | 38% | Out-of-state: | 12% |
| | | Live on campus: | 89% |

**Basis for selection.** School achievement record and class rank most important. School's recommendation considered in borderline cases.

**High school preparation.** 16 units required; 19 recommended. Required and recommended units include English 4, mathematics 3-4, social studies 2, history 2, science 3-4, foreign language 2, computer science 1 and academic electives 2.

**2007-2008 Annual costs.** Tuition/fees: $6,623; $14,390 out-of-state. Room/board: $6,030. Books/supplies: $900. Personal expenses: $2,400.

**2007-2008 Financial aid. Need-based:** 1,493 full-time freshmen applied for aid; 1,418 were judged to have need; 1,297 of these received aid. Average need met was 69%. Average scholarship/grant was $5,489; average loan $3,223. 46% of total undergraduate aid awarded as scholarships/grants, 54% as loans/jobs. **Non-need-based:** Awarded to 1,460 full-time undergraduates, including 441 freshmen. Scholarships awarded for academics, art, athletics, job skills, leadership, minority status, music/drama, ROTC, state residency.

**Application procedures. Admission:** Priority date 12/1; no deadline. $30 fee, may be waived for applicants with need. Application may be submitted online. Admission notification on a rolling basis beginning on or about 9/18. Must reply by May 1 or within 2 week(s) if notified thereafter. **Financial aid:** Priority date 3/15; no closing date. FAFSA required. Applicants notified on a rolling basis starting 4/1.

**Academics. Special study options:** Combined bachelor's/graduate degree, cooperative education, distance learning, double major, dual enrollment of high school students, honors, independent study, internships, study abroad, teacher certification program. **Credit/placement by examination:** AP, CLEP, SAT, institutional tests. 64 credit hours maximum toward bachelor's degree. **Support services:** Learning center, pre-admission summer program, reduced course load, remedial instruction, study skills assistance, tutoring, writing center.

**Majors. Biology:** General. **Business:** Accounting, business admin, managerial economics. **Communications:** General, media studies. **Computer sciences:** General, computer science. **Education:** Business, early childhood, elementary, science, social studies, special. **Engineering:** Electrical. **English:** English lit, speech/rhetoric. **Foreign languages:** French, German, sign language interpretation, Spanish. **Health:** Audiology/speech pathology, clinical lab science, medical radiologic technology/radiation therapy, nursing (RN), physics/radiologic health. **History:** General. **Math:** General. **Parks/recreation:** Exercise sciences. **Philosophy/religion:** Philosophy. **Physical sciences:** Chemistry, geology, physics. **Protective services:** Criminal justice. **Psychology:** General. **Public administration:** Social work. **Social sciences:** Anthropology, economics, geography, political science, sociology. **Visual/performing arts:** Art history/conservation, dramatic, studio arts. **Other:** Computer forensics.

**Most popular majors.** Business/marketing 22%, education 16%, English 9%, health sciences 9%, social sciences 9%.

**Computing on campus.** 1,250 workstations in dormitories, library, computer center, student center. Dormitories wired for high-speed internet access and linked to campus network. Online course registration, helpline, wireless network available.

**Student life. Freshman orientation:** Mandatory, $77 fee. One-day program in July and 3-day program prior to start of classes. **Housing:** Guaranteed on-campus for freshmen. Coed dorms, apartments, cooperative housing, substance-free housing available. $100 nonrefundable deposit, deadline 5/1. **Activities:** Bands, campus ministries, choral groups, dance, drama, international student organizations, literary magazine, music ensembles, Model UN, radio station, student government, student newspaper, symphony orchestra, TV station, Bloomsburg Christian Fellowship, Hillel, University Democrats, College Republicans, community government association, Black Cultural Society, Student Organization of Latinos, Habitat for Humanity.

**Athletics.** NCAA. **Intercollegiate:** Baseball M, basketball, cross-country, field hockey W, football (tackle) M, lacrosse W, soccer, softball W, swimming, tennis, track and field, wrestling M. **Intramural:** Basketball, field hockey W, football (non-tackle) M, racquetball, soccer, softball, tennis, volleyball, wrestling M. **Team name:** Huskies.

**Student services.** Adult student services, alcohol/substance abuse counseling, campus ministries, career counseling, services for economically disadvantaged, student employment services, financial aid counseling, health services, legal services, minority student services, on-campus daycare, personal counseling, placement for graduates, veterans' counselor, women's services. **Physically disabled:** Services for visually, speech, hearing impaired.

**Contact.** E-mail: buadmiss@bloomu.edu
Phone: (570) 389-4316 Fax: (570) 389-4741
Christopher Keller, Director of Admissions and Records, Bloomsburg University of Pennsylvania, 104 Student Service Center, Bloomsburg, PA 17815

---

## Bryn Athyn College of the New Church
**Bryn Athyn, Pennsylvania**
www.brynathyn.edu                                    **CB code: 2002**

- Private 4-year liberal arts college affiliated with General Church of the New Jerusalem (Swedenborgian)
- Residential campus in small town

- 118 degree-seeking undergraduates: 3% part-time, 54% women
- 18 degree-seeking graduate students
- 97% of applicants admitted
- SAT or ACT with writing, application essay required

**General.** Founded in 1876. Regionally accredited. **Degrees:** 22 bachelor's, 23 associate awarded; master's, first professional offered. **Location:** 15 miles from Philadelphia. **Calendar:** Trimester. **Full-time faculty:** 20 total; 70% have terminal degrees, 50% women. **Part-time faculty:** 19 total; 26% have terminal degrees, 42% women. **Class size:** 95% < 20, 5% 20-39. **Special facilities:** Performing arts center, archives, ecological restoration trust.

**Freshman class profile.** 59 applied, 57 admitted, 47 enrolled.

| Mid 50% test scores | | | |
|---|---|---|---|
| SAT critical reading: | 430-570 | GPA 3.50 or higher: | 33% |
| SAT math: | 500-580 | GPA 3.0-3.49: | 35% |
| SAT writing: | 410-550 | GPA 2.0-2.99: | 32% |
| | | Out-of-state: | 24% |

**Basis for selection.** Applicants expected to have interest in the New Church. School achievement record important; test scores considered. TOEFL required of non-native English speakers. SAT may be required of some Canadian applicants. Interview recommended; may be required. **Home-schooled:** SAT Subject Tests in literature and math recommended.

**High school preparation.** 15 units recommended. Recommended units include English 4, mathematics 3, history 3, science 3 and foreign language 2. 3 units social studies and/or history required.

**2007-2008 Annual costs.** Tuition/fees: $10,114. Room/board: $5,574. Books/supplies: $950. Personal expenses: $700.

**2007-2008 Financial aid. Need-based:** 84% of total undergraduate aid awarded as scholarships/grants, 16% as loans/jobs. **Non-need-based:** Scholarships awarded for academics, leadership, religious affiliation.

**Application procedures. Admission:** Priority date 2/1; deadline 7/1 (receipt date). $30 fee, may be waived for applicants with need. Application may be submitted online. Admission notification on a rolling basis beginning on or about 2/1. Must reply by 8/1. **Financial aid:** Closing date 6/1. FAFSA, institutional form required. Applicants notified on a rolling basis starting 4/30; must reply by 9/30.

**Academics. Special study options:** Accelerated study, cooperative education, cross-registration, distance learning, ESL, independent study, internships, student-designed major, study abroad, teacher certification program. **Credit/placement by examination:** AP, CLEP, IB, SAT, ACT, institutional tests. **Support services:** Remedial instruction, study skills assistance, tutoring, writing center.

**Majors. Biology:** General. **Education:** General, biology, English, history. **English:** English lit. **Foreign languages:** Classics. **History:** General. **Interdisciplinary:** Biological/physical sciences, math/computer science. **Philosophy/religion:** Philosophy, religion. **Physical sciences:** General. **Psychology:** General.

**Most popular majors.** Education 14%, English 14%, history 14%, interdisciplinary studies 41%, philosophy/religious studies 14%.

**Computing on campus.** 55 workstations in dormitories, library, computer center, student center. Dormitories wired for high-speed internet access and linked to campus network. Online library, helpline, repair service, wireless network available.

**Student life. Freshman orientation:** Mandatory. **Policies:** No alcohol on campus, restricted dorm visiting, required chapel attendance. Religious observance required. **Housing:** Guaranteed on-campus for all undergraduates. Single-sex dorms available. $150 fully refundable deposit, deadline 7/15. Satellite housing available. **Activities:** Choral groups, drama, international student organizations, student government, student newspaper, CARE.

**Athletics. Intercollegiate:** Badminton, ice hockey M, lacrosse, soccer, volleyball W. **Team name:** Blaze.

**Student services.** Campus ministries, career counseling, student employment services, financial aid counseling, health services, personal counseling.

**Contact.** E-mail: admissions@brynathyn.edu
Phone: (267) 502-2511 Fax: (267) 502-2658
Sean Lawing, Director of Admissions, Bryn Athyn College of the New Church, PO Box 717, Bryn Athyn, PA 19009-0717

## Bryn Mawr College

**Bryn Mawr, Pennsylvania**
www.brynmawr.edu

**CB member**
**CB code: 2049**

- Private 4-year liberal arts college for women
- Residential campus in very large city
- 1,275 degree-seeking undergraduates: 1% part-time, 100% women, 6% African American, 12% Asian American, 3% Hispanic American, 7% international
- 488 degree-seeking graduate students
- 45% of applicants admitted
- SAT and SAT Subject Tests or ACT (ACT writing optional), application essay required
- 84% graduate within 6 years; 21% enter graduate study

**General.** Founded in 1885. Regionally accredited. Academic exchange with Haverford College, Swarthmore College, and University of Pennsylvania. Extracurricular and social coordination with Haverford. **Degrees:** 301 bachelor's awarded; master's, doctoral offered. **ROTC:** Air Force. **Location:** 11 miles from Philadelphia. **Calendar:** Semester, limited summer session. **Full-time faculty:** 153 total; 97% have terminal degrees, 17% minority, 49% women. **Part-time faculty:** 23 total; 65% have terminal degrees, 17% minority, 61% women. **Class size:** 71% < 20, 24% 20-39, 3% 40-49, 2% 50-99, less than 1% >100. **Special facilities:** Collections of minerals, archaeological and anthropological artifacts.

**Freshman class profile.** 2,106 applied, 958 admitted, 352 enrolled.

| Mid 50% test scores | | | |
|---|---|---|---|
| SAT critical reading: | 620-730 | Rank in top tenth: | 62% |
| SAT math: | 580-690 | Return as sophomores: | 94% |
| SAT writing: | 620-720 | Out-of-state: | 87% |
| ACT composite: | 26-30 | Live on campus: | 100% |
| Rank in top quarter: | 91% | International: | 6% |

**Basis for selection.** School achievement record, recommendations, essay most important. Test scores, school and community activities, extracurricular achievements important. For those submitting SAT, 2 SAT Subject Tests required. Interview recommended. **Homeschooled:** Statement describing homeschool structure and mission, transcript of courses and grades, state high school equivalency certificate, interview, letter of recommendation (nonparent) required. Interview required, but may be completed with admissions officer or alumna.

**High school preparation.** 16 units recommended. Required and recommended units include English 4, mathematics 3, social studies 2, history 2, science 2 (laboratory 1), foreign language 3 and academic electives 2.

**2007-2008 Annual costs.** Tuition/fees: $34,650. Room/board: $11,024. Books/supplies: $1,000. Personal expenses: $1,000.

**2007-2008 Financial aid.** All financial aid based on need. 240 full-time freshmen applied for aid; 177 were judged to have need; 177 of these received aid. Average need met was 100%. Average scholarship/grant was $26,061; average loan $3,397. 82% of total undergraduate aid awarded as scholarships/grants, 18% as loans/jobs.

**Application procedures. Admission:** Closing date 1/15 (postmark date). $50 fee, may be waived for applicants with need. Application may be submitted online. Admission notification 4/1. Must reply by 5/1. **Financial aid:** Priority date 2/5, closing date 3/1. FAFSA, CSS PROFILE required. Applicants notified by 3/23; must reply by 5/1.

**Academics.** Most examinations self-scheduled. **Special study options:** Accelerated study, combined bachelor's/graduate degree, cross-registration, double major, dual enrollment of high school students, exchange student, independent study, internships, liberal arts/career combination, student-designed major, study abroad, teacher certification program. 3-2 Program in City and Regional Planning with the University of Pennsylvania. A.B./B.S. 3-2 engineering programs with University of Pennsylvania. **Credit/placement by examination:** AP, CLEP, IB, institutional tests. 32 credit hours maximum toward bachelor's degree. **Support services:** Preadmission summer program, reduced course load, study skills assistance, tutoring, writing center.

**Majors. Architecture:** Urban/community planning. **Area/ethnic studies:** East Asian. **Biology:** General. **Computer sciences:** Computer science. **English:** English lit. **Foreign languages:** Ancient Greek, classics, comparative lit, French, German, Italian, Latin, Russian, Spanish. **History:** General. **Interdisciplinary:** Classical/archaeology. **Math:** General. **Philosophy/religion:** Philosophy, religion. **Physical sciences:** Astronomy, chemistry, geology, physics. **Psychology:** General. **Social sciences:** Anthropology, archaeology, economics, political science, sociology, urban studies. **Visual/performing arts:** Art history/conservation, studio arts.

**Most popular majors.** Biology 6%, English 11%, foreign language 12%, history 9%, mathematics 9%, physical sciences 6%, psychology 8%, social sciences 31%.

**Computing on campus.** 200 workstations in dormitories, library, computer center, student center. Dormitories linked to campus network. Commuter students can connect to campus network. Online course registration, online library, helpline, repair service, student web hosting, wireless network available.

**Student life. Freshman orientation:** Mandatory. Week-long program; students divided into groups of 10-20 students based on residence hall assignments. **Policies:** Self-governing student body, academic and social honor code, Customs and Traditions programs. **Housing:** Guaranteed on-campus for all undergraduates. Coed dorms, apartments, cooperative housing, substance-free housing available. $200 deposit, deadline 6/1. Students may live at Haverford. Foreign language houses available (Chinese, French, German, Hebrew, Italian, Russian, Spanish). Special housing available for non-traditional-aged students. **Activities:** Bands, campus ministries, choral groups, dance, drama, film society, international student organizations, literary magazine, music ensembles, Model UN, musical theater, radio station, student government, student newspaper, Mujeres, Rainbow Alliance, investment group, Jewish student union.

**Athletics.** NCAA. **Intercollegiate:** Badminton W, basketball W, cross-country W, field hockey W, lacrosse W, rowing (crew) W, soccer W, swimming W, tennis W, track and field W, volleyball W. **Intramural:** Tennis W, volleyball W. **Team name:** Owls.

**Student services.** Adult student services, alcohol/substance abuse counseling, campus ministries, career counseling, services for economically disadvantaged, student employment services, financial aid counseling, health services, minority student services, personal counseling, placement for graduates, women's services. **Physically disabled:** Services for visually, speech, hearing impaired.

**Contact.** E-mail: admissions@brynmawr.edu
Phone: (610) 526-5152 Toll-free number: (800) 262-1885
Fax: (610) 526-7471
Jennifer Rickard, Dean of Admissions and Financial Aid, Bryn Mawr College, 101 North Merion Avenue, Bryn Mawr, PA 19010-2899

## Bucknell University

**Lewisburg, Pennsylvania**
www.bucknell.edu

**CB member**
**CB code: 2050**

- Private 4-year university
- Residential campus in small town
- 3,495 degree-seeking undergraduates: 51% women, 3% African American, 7% Asian American, 3% Hispanic American, 3% international
- 101 degree-seeking graduate students
- 30% of applicants admitted
- SAT or ACT with writing, application essay required
- 90% graduate within 6 years; 26% enter graduate study

**General.** Founded in 1846. Regionally accredited. **Degrees:** 862 bachelor's awarded; master's offered. **ROTC:** Army. **Location:** 75 miles from Harrisburg, 195 miles from Philadelphia. **Calendar:** Semester, limited summer session. **Full-time faculty:** 317 total; 96% have terminal degrees, 10% minority, 38% women. **Part-time faculty:** 23 total; 48% have terminal degrees, 4% minority, 35% women. **Class size:** 57% < 20, 39% 20-39, 1% 40-49, 2% 50-99, less than 1% >100. **Special facilities:** Observatory, 63-acre nature preserve, center for performing arts, poetry center, greenhouse, outdoor naturalistic primate facility, engineering structural test lab, gas chromatograph/mass spectrometer, nuclear magnetic resonance spectrometer, herbarium, 18-hole golf course, small business development center.

**Freshman class profile.** 8,943 applied, 2,673 admitted, 887 enrolled.

| Mid 50% test scores | | | |
|---|---|---|---|
| SAT critical reading: | 600-690 | Rank in top tenth: | 72% |
| SAT math: | 630-710 | End year in good standing: | 97% |
| SAT writing: | 600-690 | Return as sophomores: | 94% |
| ACT composite: | 27-31 | Out-of-state: | 77% |
| Rank in top quarter: | 93% | Live on campus: | 99% |
| | | International: | 2% |

**Basis for selection.** Emphasis on school achievement. Test scores, recommendations, special talents and abilities, evidence of volunteer work, personal qualities important. If English is not student's first language and student submits SAT scores with Critical Reading score below 550, TOEFL required. SAT Subject Test in foreign language required for any student planning to enroll in foreign language study. Interview recommended for all; audition required for music program; portfolio recommended for art program. **Homeschooled:** Statement describing homeschool structure and mission, interview required. Interview, SAT, graded English paper, writing sample (not from English class), program description or certification from homeschooler's accrediting agency or school district, name/address/phone number of homeschool supervisor required.

**High school preparation.** 16 units required; 20 recommended. Required and recommended units include English 4, mathematics 3-4, social studies 2, history 2, science 2-3, foreign language 2-4 and academic electives 1.

**2008-2009 Annual costs.** Tuition/fees: $39,652. Room/board: $8,728. Books/supplies: $750. Personal expenses: $1,000.

**2007-2008 Financial aid. Need-based:** 535 full-time freshmen applied for aid; 422 were judged to have need; 422 of these received aid. Average need met was 100%. Average scholarship/grant was $21,300; average loan $4,500. 73% of total undergraduate aid awarded as scholarships/grants, 27% as loans/jobs. **Non-need-based:** Awarded to 205 full-time undergraduates, including 88 freshmen. Scholarships awarded for academics, art, athletics, leadership, music/drama, ROTC.

**Application procedures. Admission:** Closing date 1/15 (postmark date). $60 fee, may be waived for applicants with need. Application may be submitted online. Admission notification 4/1. Must reply by 5/1. **Financial aid:** Closing date 1/1. FAFSA, CSS PROFILE required. Applicants notified by 4/1; must reply by 5/1.

**Academics. Special study options:** Combined bachelor's/graduate degree, double major, dual enrollment of high school students, honors, independent study, internships, liberal arts/career combination, student-designed major, study abroad, teacher certification program, Washington semester. **Credit/placement by examination:** AP, CLEP, IB, institutional tests. No policy limit on number of credits; only a few courses offer this option. **Support services:** Learning center, study skills assistance, tutoring, writing center.

**Majors. Area/ethnic studies:** East Asian, Latin American, women's. **Biology:** General, animal behavior, biochemistry, cellular/molecular. **Business:** Accounting, business admin. **Computer sciences:** General. **Conservation:** Environmental studies. **Education:** General, early childhood, elementary, music, secondary. **Engineering:** Biomedical, chemical, civil, computer, electrical, mechanical. **English:** Creative writing, English lit. **Foreign languages:** Classics, French, German, Russian, Spanish. **History:** General. **Interdisciplinary:** Neuroscience. **Liberal arts:** Humanities. **Math:** General. **Philosophy/religion:** Philosophy, religion. **Physical sciences:** Chemistry, geology, physics. **Psychology:** General. **Social sciences:** Anthropology, econometrics, economics, geography, international relations, political science, sociology. **Visual/performing arts:** General, art history/conservation, dramatic, music history, music performance, music theory/composition, studio arts.

**Most popular majors.** Biology 10%, business/marketing 12%, engineering/engineering technologies 13%, English 7%, foreign language 6%, psychology 6%, social sciences 22%.

**Computing on campus.** 608 workstations in dormitories, library, computer center, student center. Dormitories wired for high-speed internet access and linked to campus network. Commuter students can connect to campus network. Online course registration, online library, helpline, repair service, wireless network available.

**Student life. Freshman orientation:** Mandatory, $50 fee. Preregistration for classes offered. Held 5 days prior to start of classes. **Policies:** All first-year students must sign statement of student responsibility. **Housing:** Guaranteed on-campus for all undergraduates. Coed dorms, single-sex dorms, special housing for disabled, apartments, fraternity/sorority housing, substance-free housing available. Special interest houses, substance-free floors, quiet floors available. Six residential colleges with themes: arts, humanities, global, environment, social justice, technology and society. **Activities:** Bands, campus ministries, choral groups, dance, drama, film society, international student organizations, literary magazine, music ensembles, Model UN, musical theater, opera, radio station, student government, student newspaper, symphony orchestra, Hillel, Fellowship of Christians, Students for Asian Awareness, Chinese culture association, Brothers and Sisters Empowered, Japan Society, Muslim student association, O.H.L.A.S. (formerly Le Cumbre Hispanic).

**Athletics.** NCAA. **Intercollegiate:** Baseball M, basketball, cross-country, diving, field hockey W, football (tackle) M, golf, lacrosse, rowing (crew) W, soccer, softball W, swimming, tennis, track and field, volleyball W, water

polo, wrestling M. **Intramural:** Basketball, bowling, cross-country, football (non-tackle), golf, racquetball, soccer, softball, squash, table tennis, tennis, volleyball, weight lifting M. **Team name:** Bison.

**Student services.** Alcohol/substance abuse counseling, campus ministries, career counseling, financial aid counseling, health services, minority student services, personal counseling, placement for graduates, women's services. **Physically disabled:** Services for visually, hearing impaired.

**Contact.** E-mail: admissions@bucknell.edu
Phone: (570) 577-1101 Fax: (570) 577-3538
Kurt Thiede, Vice President for Enrollment Management and Dean of Admissions, Bucknell University, Freas Hall, Lewisburg, PA 17837-9988

| Cabrini College | |
|---|---|
| Radnor, Pennsylvania | **CB member** |
| www.cabrini.edu | **CB code: 2071** |

- Private 4-year liberal arts college affiliated with Roman Catholic Church
- Residential campus in large town
- 1,820 degree-seeking undergraduates: 7% part-time, 66% women, 6% African American, 2% Asian American, 3% Hispanic American, 1% international
- 1,197 degree-seeking graduate students
- 75% of applicants admitted
- SAT or ACT (ACT writing optional) required
- 59% graduate within 6 years

**General.** Founded in 1957. Regionally accredited. College sponsored by Missionary Sisters of the Sacred Heart (international religious order serving six continents). **Degrees:** 336 bachelor's awarded; master's offered. **ROTC:** Army, Air Force. **Location:** 18 miles from Philadelphia, 5 miles from King of Prussia. **Calendar:** Semester, extensive summer session. **Full-time faculty:** 64 total; 80% have terminal degrees, 5% minority, 55% women. **Part-time faculty:** 203 total; 21% have terminal degrees, 10% minority, 51% women. **Class size:** 51% < 20, 47% 20-39, 2% 40-49, less than 1% 50-99. **Special facilities:** College-operated preschool (off-campus), human performance lab, video studio, graphic design lab.

**Freshman class profile.** 4,015 applied, 3,021 admitted, 514 enrolled.

| Mid 50% test scores | | | |
|---|---|---|---|
| SAT critical reading: | 440-530 | Rank in top quarter: | 20% |
| SAT math: | 440-520 | Rank in top tenth: | 6% |
| GPA 3.50 or higher: | 26% | End year in good standing: | 88% |
| GPA 3.0-3.49: | 33% | Return as sophomores: | 66% |
| GPA 2.0-2.99: | 41% | Out-of-state: | 41% |
| | | Live on campus: | 87% |

**Basis for selection.** School achievement record, test scores, academic potential, and personal qualities most important. Special consideration for children of alumni and students with special backgrounds, skills or abilities. Community action required. Non-English-speaking international students may take TOEFL instead of SAT/ACT. Interview recommended for all; portfolio recommended for studio art program. **Homeschooled:** Transcript of courses and grades, state high school equivalency certificate required. Provide as much external testing data as possible. Standardized test scores given more weight for homeschooled students.

**High school preparation.** 18 units required; 21 recommended. Required and recommended units include English 4, mathematics 3-4, social studies 3, science 3, foreign language 2 and academic electives 2. Two arts and humanities also recommended. Additional math and science units recommended for science students.

**2007-2008 Annual costs.** Tuition/fees: $28,030. Room/board: $10,290. Books/supplies: $960. Personal expenses: $360.

**2007-2008 Financial aid. Need-based:** 457 full-time freshmen applied for aid; 395 were judged to have need; 395 of these received aid. Average need met was 69%. Average scholarship/grant was $7,022; average loan $3,811. 67% of total undergraduate aid awarded as scholarships/grants, 33% as loans/jobs. **Non-need-based:** Awarded to 1,525 full-time undergraduates, including 493 freshmen. Scholarships awarded for academics, alumni affiliation.

**Application procedures. Admission:** Priority date 5/1; no deadline. $35 fee, may be waived for applicants with need. Application may be submitted online. Admission notification on a rolling basis beginning on or about 10/1. **Financial aid:** Closing date 4/1. FAFSA required. Applicants notified on a rolling basis starting 3/1.

**Academics.** Education fieldwork opportunities provided to education majors from sophomore to senior years. Students participate in community service. Internship or co-op programs offered in all majors. **Special study options:** Accelerated study, combined bachelor's/graduate degree, cooperative education, cross-registration, distance learning, double major, exchange student, honors, independent study, internships, liberal arts/career combination, student-designed major, study abroad, teacher certification program, Washington semester. Exchange programs with Eastern University, Rosemont College, Valley Forge Military College; cross-registration with Southeastern Pennsylvania Consortium for Higher Education (8-member consortium of private colleges/universities). **Credit/placement by examination:** AP, CLEP, IB, SAT, institutional tests. 30 credit hours maximum toward bachelor's degree. DANTES. **Support services:** Learning center, reduced course load, remedial instruction, study skills assistance, tutoring, writing center.

**Majors. Area/ethnic studies:** American. **Biology:** General. **Business:** Accounting, business admin, finance, human resources, management information systems, marketing. **Communications:** General. **Computer sciences:** General, information technology. **Education:** General, early childhood, elementary, kindergarten/preschool, special. **English:** English lit. **Foreign languages:** French, Spanish. **Health:** Clinical lab science, premedicine. **History:** General. **Liberal arts:** Arts/sciences. **Math:** General. **Parks/recreation:** Exercise sciences. **Philosophy/religion:** Philosophy, religion. **Physical sciences:** Chemistry. **Psychology:** General. **Public administration:** Social work. **Social sciences:** Criminology, political science, sociology. **Visual/performing arts:** Graphic design.

**Most popular majors.** Business/marketing 30%, communications/journalism 14%, education 17%, social sciences 8%.

**Computing on campus.** 426 workstations in dormitories, library, computer center. Dormitories wired for high-speed internet access and linked to campus network. Commuter students can connect to campus network. Online course registration, online library, helpline, student web hosting, wireless network available.

**Student life. Freshman orientation:** Mandatory, $210 fee. Preregistration for classes offered. 3-day program prior to the beginning of the fall semester. **Housing:** Coed dorms, single-sex dorms, special housing for disabled, apartments available. $350 fully refundable deposit, deadline 5/1. Special interest housing options designated for intensified study, honors, Hispanic culture and community service. **Activities:** Campus ministries, choral groups, dance, drama, international student organizations, literary magazine, music ensembles, musical theater, radio station, student government, student newspaper, TV station, Ethnic Student Alliance, Outreach to the Homeless, Cavaliers for Life, Amnesty International, Latinos Unidos, Student Ambassadors, Cavalier Pride.

**Athletics.** NCAA. **Intercollegiate:** Basketball, cross-country, field hockey W, golf M, lacrosse, soccer, softball W, swimming W, tennis, track and field, volleyball W. **Intramural:** Badminton, basketball, cricket, football (non-tackle), lacrosse, racquetball, rugby, soccer, softball, squash, swimming, tennis, volleyball, water polo. **Team name:** Cavaliers.

**Student services.** Adult student services, alcohol/substance abuse counseling, campus ministries, career counseling, student employment services, financial aid counseling, health services, minority student services, personal counseling, placement for graduates. **Physically disabled:** Services for visually, hearing impaired.

**Contact.** E-mail: admit@cabrini.edu
Phone: (610) 902-8552 Toll-free number: (800) 848-1003
Fax: (610) 902-8508
Mark Osborn, Vice President for Enrollment Management, Cabrini College, 610 King of Prussia Road, Radnor, PA 19087-3698

---

## California University of Pennsylvania

| California, Pennsylvania | CB member |
| --- | --- |
| www.cup.edu | CB code: 2647 |

- Public 4-year university
- Commuter campus in small town
- 6,606 degree-seeking undergraduates: 10% part-time, 52% women, 6% African American, 1% Asian American, 1% Hispanic American, 1% international
- 1,376 degree-seeking graduate students
- 64% of applicants admitted
- SAT required
- 53% graduate within 6 years; 32% enter graduate study

**General.** Founded in 1852. Regionally accredited. Green-oriented; utilizes geothermal technologies to reduce energy consumption. **Degrees:** 1,087 bachelor's, 29 associate awarded; master's offered. **ROTC:** Army, Air Force. **Location:** 38 miles from Pittsburgh. **Calendar:** Semester, limited summer

session. **Full-time faculty:** 268 total; 72% have terminal degrees, 13% minority. **Part-time faculty:** 104 total; 12% have terminal degrees, 8% minority. **Class size:** 28% < 20, 50% 20-39, 11% 40-49, 10% 50-99, less than 1% >100. **Special facilities:** Fine arts gallery, international corporate art collection, 98-acre farm with recreational facilities.

**Freshman class profile.** 4,028 applied, 2,587 admitted, 1,260 enrolled.

| Mid 50% test scores | | Rank in top quarter: | 28% |
| --- | --- | --- | --- |
| SAT critical reading: | 460-530 | Rank in top tenth: | 7% |
| SAT math: | 470-540 | End year in good standing: | 89% |
| SAT writing: | 450-540 | Return as sophomores: | 79% |
| ACT composite: | 19-21 | Out-of-state: | 7% |
| GPA 3.50 or higher: | 24% | Live on campus: | 75% |
| GPA 3.0-3.49: | 36% | International: | 1% |
| GPA 2.0-2.99: | 39% | | |

**Basis for selection.** School achievement record, test scores, activities, recommendations, interview considered. Essay recommended. **Homeschooled:** Transcript of courses and grades required.

**High school preparation.** 19 units required; 21 recommended. Required and recommended units include English 4, mathematics 3, social studies 2, history 2, science 1 (laboratory 1), foreign language 2 and academic electives 6.

**2007-2008 Annual costs.** Tuition/fees: $6,851; $10,046 out-of-state. Room/board: $8,548. Books/supplies: $800. Personal expenses: $1,552.

**2006-2007 Financial aid. Need-based:** 1,066 full-time freshmen applied for aid; 841 were judged to have need; 836 of these received aid. Average need met was 89%. Average scholarship/grant was $4,642; average loan $2,792. 48% of total undergraduate aid awarded as scholarships/grants, 52% as loans/jobs. **Non-need-based:** Awarded to 1,611 full-time undergraduates, including 568 freshmen. Scholarships awarded for academics, alumni affiliation, art, athletics, leadership, minority status, music/drama, religious affiliation, ROTC, state residency.

**Application procedures. Admission:** Priority date 5/1; no deadline. $25 fee, may be waived for applicants with need. Application may be submitted online. Admission notification on a rolling basis. **Financial aid:** Priority date 5/1; no closing date. FAFSA required. Applicants notified on a rolling basis starting 4/1; must reply within 3 week(s) of notification.

**Academics. Special study options:** Accelerated study, combined bachelor's/graduate degree, cooperative education, cross-registration, distance learning, double major, dual enrollment of high school students, exchange student, external degree, honors, independent study, internships, liberal arts/career combination, student-designed major, study abroad, teacher certification program, urban semester, Washington semester, weekend college. **Credit/placement by examination:** AP, CLEP, IB, SAT, institutional tests. **Support services:** Learning center, pre-admission summer program, reduced course load, remedial instruction, study skills assistance, tutoring, writing center.

**Honors college/program.** Minimum 1100 SAT (exclusive of Writing), 3.0 GPA, letter of recommendation required. Admitted students work with adviser and dean to design course of study.

**Majors. Biology:** General. **Business:** Accounting, business admin. **Communications:** General. **Computer sciences:** General. **Conservation:** Environmental science. **Education:** General, elementary, kindergarten/preschool, special. **Engineering technology:** General, computer, electrical. **English:** English lit. **Foreign languages:** General, French, German, Russian, Spanish. **Health:** Athletic training, clinical lab technology, communication disorders, nursing (RN). **History:** General. **Interdisciplinary:** Gerontology. **Liberal arts:** Arts/sciences. **Math:** General. **Parks/recreation:** Facilities management, sports admin. **Philosophy/religion:** Philosophy. **Physical sciences:** General, chemistry, geology, physics. **Protective services:** Criminal justice. **Psychology:** General. **Public administration:** Social work. **Social sciences:** General, geography, political science. **Visual/performing arts:** Art, commercial/advertising art, dramatic, graphic design.

**Most popular majors.** Business/marketing 12%, education 21%, engineering/engineering technologies 8%, health sciences 8%, parks/recreation 6%, psychology 6%, security/protective services 8%.

**Computing on campus.** 1,220 workstations in dormitories, library, computer center, student center. Dormitories wired for high-speed internet access and linked to campus network. Commuter students can connect to campus network. Online course registration, online library, helpline available.

**Student life. Freshman orientation:** Mandatory. Preregistration for classes offered. One-day session held in July or August. **Policies:** Freshman students under 21 and not commuting from parental home required to live in dormitory. **Housing:** Coed dorms, special housing for disabled, fraternity/

sorority housing, substance-free housing available. $235 deposit. **Activities:** Bands, campus ministries, choral groups, dance, drama, film society, international student organizations, literary magazine, music ensembles, musical theater, opera, radio station, student government, student newspaper, symphony orchestra, TV station.

**Athletics.** NCAA. **Intercollegiate:** Baseball M, basketball, cheerleading, cross-country, football (tackle) M, golf, rugby, soccer, softball, swimming W, tennis W, track and field, volleyball. **Intramural:** Archery, badminton, baseball M, basketball, bowling, cheerleading, cross-country, fencing, football (non-tackle), football (tackle), golf, gymnastics, handball, ice hockey, judo, lacrosse, racquetball, rugby, skiing, skin diving M, soccer, softball W, swimming W, table tennis, tennis W, track and field, triathlon, volleyball, weight lifting, wrestling M. **Team name:** Vulcans.

**Student services.** Adult student services, alcohol/substance abuse counseling, campus ministries, career counseling, services for economically disadvantaged, student employment services, financial aid counseling, health services, legal services, minority student services, personal counseling, placement for graduates, veterans' counselor, women's services. **Physically disabled:** Services for visually, speech, hearing impaired. **Learning disabled:** Comprehensive services available.

**Contact.** E-mail: inquiry@cup.edu
Phone: (724) 938-4404 Fax: (724) 938-4564
William Edmonds, Dean of Admissions, California University of Pennsylvania, 250 University Avenue, California, PA 15419-1394

## Carlow University
### Pittsburgh, Pennsylvania
**www.carlow.edu**                                    **CB code: 2421**

- Private 4-year university and liberal arts college for women affiliated with Roman Catholic Church
- Commuter campus in large city
- 1,555 degree-seeking undergraduates: 25% part-time, 94% women, 16% African American, 1% Asian American, 1% Hispanic American, 1% Native American
- 609 degree-seeking graduate students
- 60% of applicants admitted
- SAT or ACT with writing required
- 48% graduate within 6 years; 98% enter graduate study

**General.** Founded in 1929. Regionally accredited. Founded by the Sisters of Mercy in 1929 and member of the Conference for Mercy Higher Education. **Degrees:** 332 bachelor's awarded; master's, doctoral offered. **ROTC:** Army, Naval, Air Force. **Location:** 3 miles from downtown. **Calendar:** Semester, limited summer session. **Full-time faculty:** 84 total; 67% have terminal degrees, 6% minority, 74% women. **Part-time faculty:** 149 total; 9% minority, 70% women. **Class size:** 83% < 20, 16% 20-39, 1% 50-99. **Special facilities:** Early learning center and school, science and technology research labs, greenhouse, darkroom, biochamber, children's science lab, International Poetry Forum archives, Women of Spirit Institute.

**Freshman class profile.** 1,101 applied, 661 admitted, 218 enrolled.

| Mid 50% test scores | | | |
|---|---|---|---|
| SAT critical reading: | 450-560 | Rank in top quarter: | 46% |
| SAT math: | 430-530 | Rank in top tenth: | 13% |
| ACT composite: | 18-24 | End year in good standing: | 72% |
| GPA 3.50 or higher: | 42% | Return as sophomores: | 75% |
| GPA 3.0-3.49: | 35% | Out-of-state: | 3% |
| GPA 2.0-2.99: | 23% | Live on campus: | 66% |

**Basis for selection.** Secondary school GPA, rank, record, and course work most important. SAT or ACT also considered. 3.0 GPA and class ranking in upper two-fifths of graduating class strengthen the application. International students must take TOEFL and ACT or SAT exams. Essay, interview recommended for all and in some cases required. Portfolio recommended for all art programs. **Homeschooled:** Personal interview and portfolio from most recent year highly recommended.

**High school preparation.** 18 units required. Required and recommended units include English 4, mathematics 3-4, social studies 2, history 2, science 3-4 (laboratory 2) and academic electives 4. Applicants to professional nursing programs must have 4 units English, 3 units social sciences, 2 units math (1 must be algebra), and 2 units laboratory science, including chemistry.

**2007-2008 Annual costs.** Tuition/fees: $19,514. Nursing supplemental tuition is $150 per credit; student teaching fee is $222 for 3 to 6 credits. Room/board: $7,684. Books/supplies: $700. Personal expenses: $1,000.

**2006-2007 Financial aid. Need-based:** Average need met was 70%. 60% of total undergraduate aid awarded as scholarships/grants, 40% as loans/jobs. **Non-need-based:** Scholarships awarded for academics, athletics, leadership.

**Application procedures. Admission:** Priority date 2/15; deadline 7/1. $20 fee, may be waived for applicants with need. Application may be submitted online. Admission notification on a rolling basis beginning on or about 7/1. Must reply by May 1 or within 2 week(s) if notified thereafter. **Financial aid:** Priority date 4/1; no closing date. FAFSA required. Applicants notified on a rolling basis starting 2/15; must reply within 4 week(s) of notification.

**Academics. Special study options:** Accelerated study, combined bachelor's/graduate degree, cross-registration, distance learning, double major, ESL, honors, independent study, internships, liberal arts/career combination, semester at sea, student-designed major, study abroad, teacher certification program, weekend college. 3+2 programs: biology/environmental engineering, chemistry/chemical engineering, math/engineering with Carnegie Mellon University, biology/environmental science and management with Duquesne University. 3+3 JD Law Program. First Year Experience for freshmen, graduate certificates and minors in nursing, social sciences, education, and accounting. **Credit/placement by examination:** AP, CLEP, IB, institutional tests. 30 credit hours maximum toward bachelor's degree. **Support services:** Learning center, reduced course load, remedial instruction, study skills assistance, tutoring.

**Majors. Biology:** General. **Business:** General, accounting, auditing, communications, human resources. **Communications:** General, media studies. **Computer sciences:** Information systems. **Conservation:** Environmental science. **Education:** Art, early childhood, elementary, social studies, special. **Engineering:** Environmental. **English:** Creative writing, English lit, technical writing. **Foreign languages:** Spanish. **Health:** Art therapy, health services admin, nursing (RN). **History:** General. **Liberal arts:** Arts/sciences. **Math:** General. **Philosophy/religion:** Philosophy. **Physical sciences:** Chemistry. **Psychology:** General. **Public administration:** Policy analysis, social work. **Social sciences:** Political science, sociology. **Theology:** Theology. **Visual/performing arts:** Art, art history/conservation, commercial/advertising art, multimedia, photography. **Other:** Chemistry/chemical engineering, Mathematics/engineering, Scientific/medical marketing.

**Most popular majors.** Business/marketing 14%, education 24%, health sciences 20%, psychology 7%.

**Computing on campus.** 134 workstations in dormitories, library, computer center, student center. Dormitories wired for high-speed internet access and linked to campus network. Commuter students can connect to campus network. Online course registration, online library, helpline, repair service, student web hosting, wireless network available.

**Student life. Freshman orientation:** Mandatory. Preregistration for classes offered. Held 2 days prior to semester, includes seminars, team-building activities, social events. **Housing:** $100 deposit. **Activities:** Campus ministries, choral groups, drama, international student organizations, literary magazine, student government, student newspaper, community outreach, Alpha Phi Omega, eco club, social work association, united Black students, Alternative Spring Break, FEMME, PRIDE, Chi Eta Phi.

**Athletics.** NAIA. **Intercollegiate:** Basketball W, soccer W, softball W, tennis W, volleyball W. **Team name:** The Celtics.

**Student services.** Adult student services, alcohol/substance abuse counseling, campus ministries, career counseling, student employment services, financial aid counseling, health services, minority student services, on-campus daycare, personal counseling, placement for graduates, women's services. **Physically disabled:** Services for visually, speech, hearing impaired.

**Contact.** E-mail: admissions@carlow.edu
Phone: (412) 578-6059 Toll-free number: (800) 333-2275
Fax: (412) 578-6668
Susan Winstel, Associate Director of Admissions, Carlow University, 3333 Fifth Avenue, Pittsburgh, PA 15213-3165

## Carnegie Mellon University
### Pittsburgh, Pennsylvania                          **CB member**
**www.cmu.edu**                                       **CB code: 2074**

- Private 4-year university
- Residential campus in large city
- 5,758 degree-seeking undergraduates: 2% part-time, 39% women, 5% African American, 24% Asian American, 5% Hispanic American, 14% international
- 4,644 degree-seeking graduate students

- 28% of applicants admitted
- SAT or ACT with writing, application essay required
- 87% graduate within 6 years

**General.** Founded in 1900. Regionally accredited. **Degrees:** 1,215 bachelor's awarded; master's, doctoral offered. **ROTC:** Army, Naval, Air Force. **Location:** 5 miles from downtown. **Calendar:** Semester, limited summer session. **Full-time faculty:** 830 total; 98% have terminal degrees, 16% minority, 26% women. **Part-time faculty:** 182 total; 98% have terminal degrees, 10% minority, 41% women. **Class size:** 65% < 20, 23% 20-39, 3% 40-49, 7% 50-99, 2% >100. **Special facilities:** Botanical institute, rare books collection, recording studios, design studios, photo shoot studio, music halls.

**Freshman class profile.** 22,356 applied, 6,259 admitted, 1,416 enrolled.

| Mid 50% test scores | | | |
|---|---|---|---|
| SAT critical reading: | 620-720 | Rank in top quarter: | 93% |
| SAT math: | 690-790 | Rank in top tenth: | 73% |
| SAT writing: | 620-710 | Return as sophomores: | 95% |
| ACT composite: | 29-33 | Out-of-state: | 81% |
| GPA 3.50 or higher: | 71% | Live on campus: | 99% |
| GPA 3.0-3.49: | 27% | International: | 13% |
| | | GPA 2.0-2.99: | 2% |

**Basis for selection.** Academic and artistic potential, standardized tests, activities, jobs, interests, and other personalized information important. Deadline for fine arts applicants is 12/1. SAT Subject Test required for drama, design, art, or music school applicants. All other applicants must take appropriate tests, preferably by December, but no later than January. Interview recommended for all; audition required for drama, music programs; portfolio required for art, design programs. **Homeschooled:** Transcript of courses and grades, letter of recommendation (nonparent) required. Submit syllabus/course descriptions of work done; transcript of grades/evaluations; recommendation from counselor, representative of state board of education, homeschool association, or other person of authority.

**High school preparation.** Required and recommended units include English 4, mathematics 4, science 3 (laboratory 3), foreign language 2 and academic electives 3-4. Requirements vary by program.

**2007-2008 Annual costs.** Tuition/fees: $37,354. Room/board: $9,660. Books/supplies: $966. Personal expenses: $1,335.

**2007-2008 Financial aid. Need-based:** 942 full-time freshmen applied for aid; 730 were judged to have need; 727 of these received aid. Average need met was 82%. Average scholarship/grant was $20,072; average loan $4,442. 71% of total undergraduate aid awarded as scholarships/grants, 29% as loans/jobs. **Non-need-based:** Awarded to 1,433 full-time undergraduates, including 374 freshmen. Scholarships awarded for academics, art, leadership, minority status, music/drama, state residency. **Additional information:** Early need analysis offered; merit awards available. Students notified within week to 10 days of receipt of financial aid application.

**Application procedures. Admission:** Closing date 1/1 (postmark date). $70 fee, may be waived for applicants with need. Application may be submitted online. Admission notification 4/15. Must reply by 5/1. **Financial aid:** Priority date 2/15, closing date 5/1. FAFSA, institutional form required.

**Academics. Special study options:** Combined bachelor's/graduate degree, cooperative education, cross-registration, distance learning, double major, dual enrollment of high school students, exchange student, independent study, internships, liberal arts/career combination, student-designed major, study abroad, teacher certification program, Washington semester. **Credit/placement by examination:** AP, CLEP, IB, institutional tests. **Support services:** Learning center, pre-admission summer program, study skills assistance, tutoring, writing center.

**Majors. Architecture:** Architecture, history/criticism, technology. **Area/ethnic studies:** European, Latin American, Russian/Slavic. **Biology:** General, biophysics. **Business:** Business admin, managerial economics. **Communications:** General. **Computer sciences:** Computer science, information systems. **Conservation:** Management/policy. **Engineering:** General, biomedical, chemical, civil, computer, electrical, environmental, materials, materials science, mechanical, metallurgical, operations research. **English:** Creative writing, English lit, technical writing. **Foreign languages:** General, Chinese, French, German, Japanese, Spanish. **History:** General, European. **Interdisciplinary:** Behavioral sciences, biopsychology, cognitive science, systems science. **Liberal arts:** Arts/sciences. **Math:** General, applied, computational, probability, statistics. **Philosophy/religion:** Ethics, logic, philosophy. **Physical sciences:** Astrophysics, chemical physics, chemistry, physics. **Psychology:** General, cognitive, psychobiology. **Public administration:** Policy analysis. **Social sciences:** General, economics, international relations, political science. **Visual/performing arts:** Art, design, dramatic, industrial design, jazz, music performance, music theory/composition, piano/organ, stringed instruments, voice/opera.

**Most popular majors.** Business/marketing 10%, computer/information sciences 9%, engineering/engineering technologies 30%, interdisciplinary studies 8%, physical sciences 6%, visual/performing arts 10%.

**Computing on campus.** 388 workstations in dormitories, library. Dormitories wired for high-speed internet access and linked to campus network. Commuter students can connect to campus network. Online course registration, online library, helpline, repair service, student web hosting, wireless network available.

**Student life. Freshman orientation:** Mandatory, $190 fee. Week-long program held one week before start of classes. **Policies:** Freshmen required to live on campus. **Housing:** Guaranteed on-campus for freshmen. Coed dorms, single-sex dorms, special housing for disabled, apartments, fraternity/sorority housing, substance-free housing available. $600 nonrefundable deposit, deadline 5/1. Special interest group housing available. **Activities:** Bands, campus ministries, choral groups, dance, drama, film society, international student organizations, literary magazine, music ensembles, Model UN, musical theater, radio station, student government, student newspaper, symphony orchestra, TV station, Alpha Phi Omega, Hillel, minority women's club, service clubs, National Society of Black Engineers, Society of Women Engineers, Phi Beta Kappa, fraternities and sororities.

**Athletics.** NCAA. **Intercollegiate:** Basketball, cheerleading, cross-country, diving, football (tackle) M, golf M, soccer, swimming, tennis, track and field, volleyball W. **Intramural:** Badminton, basketball, bowling, cross-country, fencing, football (non-tackle), golf, racquetball, soccer, softball, squash, swimming, table tennis, tennis, track and field, volleyball, water polo. **Team name:** Tartans.

**Student services.** Alcohol/substance abuse counseling, campus ministries, career counseling, student employment services, financial aid counseling, health services, on-campus daycare, personal counseling, placement for graduates, women's services. **Physically disabled:** Services for visually, speech, hearing impaired. **Learning disabled:** Comprehensive services available.

**Contact.** E-mail: undergraduate-admissions@andrew.cmu.edu
Phone: (412) 268-2082 Fax: (412) 268-7838
Michael Steidel, Director of Admissions, Carnegie Mellon University, 5000 Forbes Avenue, Pittsburgh, PA 15213-3890

---

## Cedar Crest College
**Allentown, Pennsylvania**
www.cedarcrest.edu

CB member
CB code: 2079

- Private 4-year liberal arts college for women
- Residential campus in small city
- 1,709 degree-seeking undergraduates: 43% part-time, 96% women, 6% African American, 2% Asian American, 7% Hispanic American, 1% Native American
- 102 degree-seeking graduate students
- 62% of applicants admitted
- SAT or ACT (ACT writing optional) required
- 63% graduate within 6 years; 28% enter graduate study

**General.** Founded in 1867. Regionally accredited. Men admitted to evening and weekend classes and daytime programs in nursing and nuclear medicine. **Degrees:** 333 bachelor's awarded; master's offered. **ROTC:** Army. **Location:** 55 miles from Philadelphia, 100 miles from New York City. **Calendar:** Semester, extensive summer session. **Full-time faculty:** 92 total; 73% have terminal degrees, 3% minority, 55% women. **Part-time faculty:** 83 total; 20% have terminal degrees, 1% minority, 75% women. **Class size:** 67% < 20, 27% 20-39, 3% 40-49, 3% 50-99, less than 1% >100. **Special facilities:** Wildlife sanctuary, outdoor Greek theater, arboretum, sculpture garden, aquatic center, college-operated museums.

**Freshman class profile.** 1,543 applied, 952 admitted, 221 enrolled.

| Mid 50% test scores | | | |
|---|---|---|---|
| SAT critical reading: | 490-580 | Rank in top quarter: | 60% |
| SAT math: | 480-580 | Rank in top tenth: | 25% |
| SAT writing: | 470-570 | End year in good standing: | 90% |
| ACT composite: | 20-27 | Return as sophomores: | 80% |
| GPA 3.50 or higher: | 29% | Out-of-state: | 44% |
| GPA 3.0-3.49: | 34% | Live on campus: | 82% |
| | | GPA 2.0-2.99: | 37% |

**Basis for selection.** Secondary school curriculum and grades most important. Test scores important. Special talents, potential for academic and personal growth considered. Interview and essay recommended for all.

**High school preparation.** 16 units required. Required and recommended units include English 4, mathematics 3, social studies 3, science 2 (laboratory 2), foreign language 2 and academic electives 3. Special natural science requirements for nuclear medicine and nursing.

**2008-2009 Annual costs.** Tuition/fees (projected): $26,542. Average per-credit-hour cost is $568. Room/board: $9,008. Books/supplies: $1,000. Personal expenses: $300.

**2007-2008 Financial aid. Need-based:** 216 full-time freshmen applied for aid; 190 were judged to have need; 190 of these received aid. Average need met was 80%. Average scholarship/grant was $15,001; average loan $3,816. 60% of total undergraduate aid awarded as scholarships/grants, 40% as loans/jobs. **Non-need-based:** Awarded to 203 full-time undergraduates, including 62 freshmen. Scholarships awarded for academics, alumni affiliation, art, leadership, music/drama.

**Application procedures. Admission:** No deadline. $30 fee, may be waived for applicants with need. Application may be submitted online. Admission notification on a rolling basis beginning on or about 8/2. Must reply by May 1 or within 2 week(s) if notified thereafter. **Financial aid:** No deadline. FAFSA, institutional form required. Applicants notified on a rolling basis starting 11/1; must reply by 5/1 or within 3 week(s) of notification.

**Academics. Special study options:** Accelerated study, combined bachelor's/graduate degree, cross-registration, distance learning, double major, dual enrollment of high school students, ESL, honors, independent study, internships, liberal arts/career combination, student-designed major, study abroad, teacher certification program, Washington semester. **Credit/placement by examination:** AP, CLEP, IB, SAT, ACT, institutional tests. 18 credit hours maximum toward bachelor's degree. **Support services:** Reduced course load, remedial instruction, study skills assistance, tutoring, writing center.

**Majors. Biology:** General, biochemistry, environmental, genetics. **Business:** Accounting, business admin, marketing. **Communications:** General. **Computer sciences:** General. **Education:** Elementary, secondary. **English:** English lit. **Family/consumer sciences:** Food/nutrition. **Foreign languages:** Spanish. **Health:** Nuclear medical technology. **History:** General. **Interdisciplinary:** Neuroscience. **Math:** General. **Physical sciences:** Chemistry. **Psychology:** General. **Public administration:** Social work. **Social sciences:** Criminology, political science. **Visual/performing arts:** General, art, dance, dramatic, studio arts.

**Most popular majors.** Biology 9%, business/marketing 12%, education 6%, health sciences 29%, psychology 13%.

**Computing on campus.** 195 workstations in dormitories, library, computer center, student center. Dormitories wired for high-speed internet access and linked to campus network. Commuter students can connect to campus network. Online course registration, online library, helpline, repair service, student web hosting, wireless network available.

**Student life. Freshman orientation:** Available. Preregistration for classes offered. 5-day academic and social program in August mandatory. 2-day academic testing and advising program in June suggested. **Policies:** Drinking under age 21 prohibited; honor philosophy exists. **Housing:** Special housing for disabled available. **Activities:** Concert band, choral groups, dance, drama, international student organizations, literary magazine, music ensembles, musical theater, radio station, student government, student newspaper, TV station, Sister Inc., Hillel, Crest Christian Fellowship, political society, SADD, Alpha Phi Omega, Islamic Awareness, Amnesty International.

**Athletics.** NCAA. **Intercollegiate:** Basketball W, cross-country W, field hockey W, lacrosse W, soccer W, softball W, tennis W, volleyball W. **Intramural:** Basketball W, soccer W, softball W, triathlon W, volleyball W. **Team name:** Falcons.

**Student services.** Adult student services, alcohol/substance abuse counseling, campus ministries, career counseling, student employment services, financial aid counseling, health services, personal counseling, placement for graduates. **Physically disabled:** Services for visually, speech, hearing impaired.

**Contact.** E-mail: cccadmis@cedarcrest.edu
Phone: (610) 740-3780 Toll-free number: (800) 360-1222
Fax: (610) 606-4647
Judith Neyhart, Executive Vice President for Enrollment, Cedar Crest College, 100 College Drive, Allentown, PA 18104-6196

## Central Pennsylvania College
**Summerdale, Pennsylvania**
www.centralpenn.edu                    CB code: 1061

- For-profit 4-year business and technical college
- Commuter campus in rural community

- 1,102 degree-seeking undergraduates: 34% part-time, 67% women, 20% African American, 1% Asian American, 5% Hispanic American, 1% Native American
- Application essay, interview required
- 61% graduate within 6 years

**General.** Founded in 1881. Regionally accredited. **Degrees:** 165 bachelor's, 104 associate awarded. **Location:** 5 miles from Harrisburg. **Calendar:** Trimester, extensive summer session. **Full-time faculty:** 26 total; 23% have terminal degrees, 58% women. **Part-time faculty:** 84 total. **Special facilities:** Student-staffed restaurant, travel agency, online campus store, mock courtroom, optometric room, multimedia lab, child-care facility, advanced technology education center, conference facility, crime lab.

**Freshman class profile.**

| Out-of-state: | 11% | Live on campus: | 56% |
|---|---|---|---|

**Basis for selection.** Open admission, but selective for some programs. High school achievement record very important for admission to physical therapist assistant and paralegal programs. Minimum SAT score of 900 (exclusive of Writing) required for admission into physical therapy assistant program. **Homeschooled:** Provide transcript of courses completed with grades and include parent/teacher/academy signatures. **Learning Disabled:** Students meet with academic dean to discuss provisions needed for individual learning experience.

**2007-2008 Annual costs.** Tuition/fees: $12,648. Room/board: $6,360. Books/supplies: $1,200. Personal expenses: $1,000.

**Financial aid. Non-need-based:** Scholarships awarded for academics, alumni affiliation, job skills, leadership, minority status, state residency.

**Application procedures. Admission:** Priority date 5/1; no deadline. No application fee. Application may be submitted online. Admission notification on a rolling basis. **Financial aid:** Priority date 3/15; no closing date. FAFSA, institutional form required. Applicants notified on a rolling basis starting 2/1; must reply within 2 week(s) of notification.

**Academics. Special study options:** Distance learning, double major, honors, internships, study abroad. **Credit/placement by examination:** AP, CLEP, IB, institutional tests. 15 credit hours maximum toward associate degree, 15 toward bachelor's. **Support services:** Reduced course load, remedial instruction, study skills assistance, tutoring, writing center.

**Majors. Business:** Accounting, business admin. **Communications:** General. **Computer sciences:** Computer science, web page design. **Legal studies:** General. **Protective services:** Criminal justice, emergency management/homeland security.

**Most popular majors.** Business/marketing 42%, communications/journalism 9%, computer/information sciences 16%, security/protective services 33%.

**Computing on campus.** 150 workstations in library, computer center. Dormitories wired for high-speed internet access and linked to campus network. Commuter students can connect to campus network. Online course registration, online library, helpline, wireless network available.

**Student life. Freshman orientation:** Mandatory. Preregistration for classes offered. **Policies:** Dress code, mandatory attendance, ethics policies, no alcohol or drugs. **Housing:** Guaranteed on-campus for freshmen. Apartments available. $250 deposit. All resident housing is either single-gender townhouses or apartments. **Activities:** Choral groups, literary magazine, student government, student newspaper, Debit Debit Credit, Gamma Beta Phi, Delta Epsilon Chi, technology club, Club MED, Toastmasters, Young Republicans.

**Athletics.** NJCAA. **Intercollegiate:** Basketball, bowling, golf. **Intramural:** Basketball, football (non-tackle), softball, tennis, volleyball. **Team name:** Silver Knights.

**Student services.** Adult student services, alcohol/substance abuse counseling, career counseling, student employment services, financial aid counseling, on-campus daycare, personal counseling, placement for graduates.

**Contact.** E-mail: admissions@centralpenn.edu
Phone: (717) 728-2201 Toll-free number: (800) 759-2727
Fax: (717) 732-5254
Katie Borrelli, Director of Admissions, Central Pennsylvania College, College Hill & Valley Roads, Summerdale, PA 17093-0309

## Chatham University
**Pittsburgh, Pennsylvania**
www.chatham.edu

CB member
CB code: 2081

▶ Private 4-year university and liberal arts college for women

▶ Residential campus in large city

▶ 651 degree-seeking undergraduates: 10% part-time, 99% women, 10% African American, 2% Asian American, 2% Hispanic American, 6% international

▶ 968 degree-seeking graduate students

▶ 76% of applicants admitted

▶ Application essay required

▶ 48% graduate within 6 years

**General.** Founded in 1869. Regionally accredited. **Degrees:** 108 bachelor's awarded; master's, doctoral offered. **ROTC:** Army, Naval, Air Force. **Location:** 5 miles from downtown. **Calendar:** Semester, limited summer session. **Full-time faculty:** 85 total; 91% have terminal degrees, 5% minority, 69% women. **Part-time faculty:** 174 total; 11% minority, 68% women. **Class size:** 71% < 20, 26% 20-39, less than 1% 40-49, 2% 50-99. **Special facilities:** Broadcast studio, science complex and greenhouse, proscenium theatre, arboretum.

**Freshman class profile.** 600 applied, 453 admitted, 175 enrolled.

| Mid 50% test scores | | | |
|---|---|---|---|
| SAT critical reading: | 480-580 | Rank in top quarter: | 41% |
| SAT math: | 440-560 | Rank in top tenth: | 18% |
| ACT composite: | 21-26 | Return as sophomores: | 69% |
| GPA 3.50 or higher: | 45% | Out-of-state: | 28% |
| GPA 3.0-3.49: | 31% | Live on campus: | 97% |
| GPA 2.0-2.99: | 23% | International: | 8% |

**Basis for selection.** School achievement record, essays, and test scores most important, though test scores are not required. Students who do not submit SAT/ACT scores required to submit a graded writing sample and resume/list of activities. Portfolios may also be submitted. Activities, talents, volunteer work, paid work, alumnae relationship, class rank, and recommendations considered. TOEFL or IELTS required for international students. Applicants who choose not to submit the SAT/ACT required to submit a graded writing sample or list of curricular and co-curricular activities. Applicants also have the option to submit a portfolio or special project/activity. Campus visit or interviews recommended for all.

**High school preparation.** 11 units required; 15 recommended. Required and recommended units include English 4, mathematics 2-3, science 2-3 and foreign language 2. Require 3 units of social science.

**2007-2008 Annual costs.** Tuition/fees: $25,816. Room/board: $7,892. Books/supplies: $860. Personal expenses: $2,862.

**2007-2008 Financial aid. Need-based:** 145 full-time freshmen applied for aid; 135 were judged to have need; 135 of these received aid. Average need met was 88%. Average scholarship/grant was $4,937; average loan $5,546. 56% of total undergraduate aid awarded as scholarships/grants, 44% as loans/jobs. **Non-need-based:** Awarded to 448 full-time undergraduates, including 119 freshmen. Scholarships awarded for academics, alumni affiliation, leadership, music/drama, state residency.

**Application procedures. Admission:** Priority date 3/15; deadline 8/1. $35 fee, may be waived for applicants with need. Application may be submitted online. Admission notification on a rolling basis beginning on or about 10/15. Must reply by May 1 or within 2 week(s) if notified thereafter. **Financial aid:** Priority date 5/1; no closing date. FAFSA required. Applicants notified on a rolling basis starting 2/15; must reply by 5/1 or within 2 week(s) of notification.

**Academics.** All students eligible through PACE Center to receive free tutoring in every course offered. Specialized courses offered for students having academic difficulties, as well as career preparation courses to help students choose a career path. **Special study options:** Accelerated study, combined bachelor's/graduate degree, cooperative education, cross-registration, distance learning, double major, dual enrollment of high school students, ESL, exchange student, honors, independent study, internships, liberal arts/career combination, semester at sea, student-designed major, study abroad, teacher certification program, Washington semester. Five-year bachelors/masters programs on campus and with other institutions. **Credit/placement by examination:** AP, CLEP, IB. 12 credit hours maximum toward bachelor's degree. **Support services:** Learning center, reduced course load, remedial instruction, study skills assistance, tutoring, writing center.

**Majors. Architecture:** Interior. **Area/ethnic studies:** Women's. **Biology:** General, biochemistry. **Business:** Accounting, business admin, international, managerial economics, marketing. **Communications:** General, broadcast journalism, journalism, public relations. **Conservation:** Environmental

science, environmental studies. **Education:** Early childhood, elementary. **Engineering:** General. **English:** Creative writing, English lit. **Foreign languages:** French, Spanish. **Health:** Nursing (RN). **History:** General. **Interdisciplinary:** Intercultural. **Legal studies:** Prelaw. **Math:** General. **Parks/recreation:** Exercise sciences. **Physical sciences:** Chemistry, physics. **Protective services:** Forensics. **Psychology:** General. **Public administration:** Policy analysis, social work. **Social sciences:** Economics, international relations, political science. **Visual/performing arts:** Art history/conservation, arts management, dramatic, photography, studio arts. **Other:** Film & Digitial Technology.

**Most popular majors.** Biology 11%, business/marketing 7%, English 8%, health sciences 8%, psychology 17%, public administration/social services 7%, social sciences 7%, visual/performing arts 12%.

**Computing on campus.** PC or laptop required. 300 workstations in dormitories, library, computer center. Dormitories wired for high-speed internet access and linked to campus network. Commuter students can connect to campus network. Online course registration, online library, helpline, repair service, student web hosting, wireless network available.

**Student life. Freshman orientation:** Mandatory. Preregistration for classes offered. Held immediately before classes begin in late August. Mini-orientations held during late spring and summer when students can register for courses. **Policies:** Honor code. **Housing:** Guaranteed on-campus for all undergraduates. Apartments, substance-free housing available. $150 nonrefundable deposit, deadline 5/1. Intercultural residence hall, community service floor and environmental floor within larger residence hall available. **Activities:** Choral groups, dance, drama, international student organizations, literary magazine, music ensembles, musical theater, student government, student newspaper, black student union, Christian Fellowship, Jewish organization, feminist collective, Gateway student association, Green Horizons, Mortar Board, Students Against Sexual Oppression.

**Athletics.** NCAA. **Intercollegiate:** Basketball W, cross-country W, ice hockey W, soccer W, softball W, swimming W, tennis W, volleyball W, water polo W. **Team name:** Cougars.

**Student services.** Adult student services, campus ministries, career counseling, services for economically disadvantaged, student employment services, financial aid counseling, health services, personal counseling, placement for graduates, women's services. **Physically disabled:** Services for visually, speech, hearing impaired.

**Contact.** E-mail: admissions@chatham.edu
Phone: (412) 365-1825 Toll-free number: (800) 837-1290
Fax: (412) 365-1609
Michael Poll, Vice President of Admissions, Chatham University, Woodland Road, Pittsburgh, PA 15232

## Chestnut Hill College
**Philadelphia, Pennsylvania**
www.chc.edu

CB member
CB code: 2082

▶ Private 4-year liberal arts college affiliated with Roman Catholic Church

▶ Residential campus in very large city

▶ 1,248 degree-seeking undergraduates: 21% part-time, 68% women, 37% African American, 2% Asian American, 6% Hispanic American, 1% international

▶ 740 degree-seeking graduate students

▶ 74% of applicants admitted

▶ SAT or ACT (ACT writing optional), application essay required

▶ 55% graduate within 6 years; 30% enter graduate study

**General.** Founded in 1924. Regionally accredited. Additional campus at Sugar Loaf Hill. **Degrees:** 207 bachelor's, 1 associate awarded; master's, doctoral offered. **Location:** 17 miles from center city. **Calendar:** Semester, limited summer session. **Full-time faculty:** 71 total; 82% have terminal degrees, 7% minority, 72% women. **Part-time faculty:** 200 total; 28% have terminal degrees, 10% minority, 53% women. **Class size:** 84% < 20, 16% 20-39. **Special facilities:** Observatory, planetarium, Irish literature collection, multimedia center, smart classrooms.

**Freshman class profile.** 1,614 applied, 1,195 admitted, 232 enrolled.

| Mid 50% test scores | | | |
|---|---|---|---|
| SAT critical reading: | 440-550 | GPA 2.0-2.99: | 49% |
| SAT math: | 420-530 | End year in good standing: | 84% |
| SAT writing: | 440-540 | Return as sophomores: | 68% |
| ACT composite: | 17-21 | Out-of-state: | 33% |
| GPA 3.50 or higher: | 19% | Live on campus: | 70% |
| GPA 3.0-3.49: | 32% | International: | 2% |

**Basis for selection.** Secondary school record, essay very important. Standardized test scores, recommendations, character, interview, extracurricular activities important. Alumni connection, talent, volunteer activity, work experience considered. Open admissions to accelerated program in the School of Continuing and Professional Studies. Students placed in writing, math, and language courses on basis of placement tests administered by the college. **Homeschooled:** Must subscribe to a homeschool agency.

**High school preparation.** 16 units recommended. Recommended units include English 4, mathematics 3, social studies 4, science 3 and foreign language 2.

**2008-2009 Annual costs.** Tuition/fees (projected): $26,000. Room/board: $8,550. Books/supplies: $1,000. Personal expenses: $1,400.

**2007-2008 Financial aid. Need-based:** Average need met was 79%. Average scholarship/grant was $14,403; average loan $5,827. 39% of total undergraduate aid awarded as scholarships/grants, 61% as loans/jobs. **Non-need-based:** Scholarships awarded for academics, alumni affiliation, leadership, religious affiliation. **Additional information:** Application priority date 1/15 for merit-based scholarships.

**Application procedures. Admission:** Priority date 1/20; no deadline. $35 fee, may be waived for applicants with need. Application may be submitted online. Admission notification on a rolling basis. Must reply by May 1 or within 3 week(s) if notified thereafter. **Financial aid:** Closing date 4/15. FAFSA required. Applicants notified on a rolling basis starting 1/31; must reply by 5/1 or within 3 week(s) of notification.

**Academics.** Montessori certification available with elementary and preelementary education. Secondary education certification available in major field of study. Interdisciplinary bachelor's degree in international business, language, and culture. **Special study options:** Combined bachelor's/graduate degree, cooperative education, cross-registration, double major, dual enrollment of high school students, ESL, exchange student, honors, independent study, internships, student-designed major, study abroad, teacher certification program. 2-2 double bachelor's program in biology or chemistry and medical technology with Thomas Jefferson University School of Allied Health Sciences, 3-2 BA/MS psychology, 3-2 BS/MS applied technology, 5-year BS/MEd elementary education with emphasis in special education. **Credit/placement by examination:** AP, CLEP, IB, institutional tests. 12 credit hours maximum toward bachelor's degree. **Support services:** Learning center, pre-admission summer program, reduced course load, remedial instruction, study skills assistance, tutoring, writing center.

**Majors. Biology:** General, biochemistry, molecular. **Business:** Accounting, accounting/business management, business admin, communications, human resources, international, marketing. **Communications technology:** General. **Computer sciences:** General, information technology. **Conservation:** Environmental science. **Education:** Early childhood, elementary, multilevel teacher, music. **English:** English lit. **Family/consumer sciences:** Child care. **Foreign languages:** French, Spanish. **Health:** Health care admin. **History:** General. **Interdisciplinary:** Math/computer science. **Liberal arts:** Arts/sciences. **Math:** General. **Physical sciences:** Chemistry. **Protective services:** Forensics, law enforcement admin. **Psychology:** General. **Public administration:** Human services. **Social sciences:** Political science, sociology.

**Most popular majors.** Business/marketing 27%, education 10%, psychology 12%, public administration/social services 18%, security/protective services 13%.

**Computing on campus.** PC or laptop required. 40 workstations in library, computer center. Commuter students can connect to campus network. Helpline, wireless network available.

**Student life. Freshman orientation:** Available. Preregistration for classes offered. Held 2 or 3 times during the summer. Additional program held the few days before classes begin. **Housing:** Coed dorms, substance-free housing available. $200 nonrefundable deposit, deadline 5/1. **Activities:** Jazz band, campus ministries, choral groups, dance, drama, literary magazine, music ensembles, musical theater, radio station, student government, student newspaper, symphony orchestra, TV station, African-American awareness society, ecology club, gay/straight alliance, hospitality club, Hispanics in Action, Mosaic of Cultures club, Students for Peace and Justice, College Democrats, College Republicans.

**Athletics.** NCAA. **Intercollegiate:** Baseball M, basketball, cross-country, golf, lacrosse W, soccer, softball W, tennis, volleyball W. **Team name:** Griffins.

**Student services.** Adult student services, alcohol/substance abuse counseling, campus ministries, career counseling, services for economically disadvantaged, student employment services, financial aid counseling, health services, personal counseling, placement for graduates.

**Contact.** E-mail: chcapply@chc.edu
Phone: (215) 248-7001 Toll-free number: (800) 248-0052
Fax: (215) 248-7082
William Fritz, Director of Admissions, School of Undergraduate Studies, Chestnut Hill College, 9601 Germantown Avenue, Philadelphia, PA 19118-2693

---

## Cheyney University of Pennsylvania
**Cheyney, Pennsylvania**     CB member
**www.cheyney.edu**     CB code: 2648

- Public 4-year university
- Residential campus in small town
- 1,318 degree-seeking undergraduates
- 47% of applicants admitted
- SAT or ACT, application essay required

**General.** Founded in 1837. Regionally accredited. Courses offered at Philadelphia Urban Center. **Degrees:** 149 bachelor's awarded; master's offered. **ROTC:** Army. **Location:** 25 miles from Philadelphia. **Calendar:** Semester, limited summer session. **Full-time faculty:** 89 total. **Part-time faculty:** 24 total. **Class size:** 40% < 20, 58% 20-39, 2% 50-99. **Special facilities:** Planetarium, weather station, theater arts center.

**Freshman class profile.** 3,283 applied, 1,552 admitted, 281 enrolled.

| | | | |
|---|---|---|---|
| Out-of-state: | 17% | Live on campus: | 88% |

**Basis for selection.** Test scores, class rank, GPA, counselor recommendation, extracurricular activities important. 830 SAT (exclusive of writing) or 17 ACT required. SAT Subject Tests recommended. Interview recommended.

**High school preparation.** 13 units required. Required units include English 4, mathematics 3, history 2, science 2 and foreign language 2.

**2007-2008 Annual costs.** Tuition/fees: $6,412; $14,179 out-of-state. Tuition for MD, NY, NJ and DE is $10,354. Room/board: $6,856. Books/supplies: $1,200.

**Financial aid. Non-need-based:** Scholarships awarded for academics, athletics.

**Application procedures. Admission:** Priority date 6/15; deadline 3/31. $20 fee, may be waived for applicants with need. Application may be submitted online. Admission notification on a rolling basis. **Financial aid:** Priority date 3/15; no closing date. FAFSA required. Applicants notified on a rolling basis starting 4/1; must reply within 2 week(s) of notification.

**Academics.** Health and physical education courses required of most students. **Special study options:** Cooperative education, cross-registration, distance learning, double major, independent study, internships, teacher certification program. **Credit/placement by examination:** AP, CLEP, institutional tests. 23 credit hours maximum toward bachelor's degree. **Support services:** Learning center, pre-admission summer program, reduced course load, remedial instruction, tutoring.

**Majors. Biology:** General. **Business:** Accounting, business admin. **Communications:** General. **Communications technology:** General. **Computer sciences:** General. **Education:** Early childhood, elementary, special. **English:** English lit. **Family/consumer sciences:** Clothing/textiles. **Foreign languages:** French, Spanish. **Health:** Clinical lab science. **Interdisciplinary:** Biological/physical sciences. **Math:** General. **Parks/recreation:** Facilities management. **Physical sciences:** Chemistry. **Psychology:** General. **Social sciences:** General, economics, geography, political science, sociology. **Visual/performing arts:** Art, dramatic.

**Most popular majors.** Business/marketing 28%, communications/journalism 6%, parks/recreation 6%, psychology 12%, social sciences 35%.

**Computing on campus.** 296 workstations in dormitories, library, computer center, student center. Dormitories wired for high-speed internet access and linked to campus network. Online course registration, helpline, repair service available.

**Student life. Freshman orientation:** Mandatory. **Policies:** Ecumenical services held on campus. **Housing:** Guaranteed on-campus for freshmen. Coed dorms, single-sex dorms available. $100 deposit, deadline 5/11. Freshmen-only dormitory available. **Activities:** Bands, choral groups, dance, drama, film society, music ensembles, radio station, student government, student newspaper, TV station, Shades of Unity, Toastmasters, business club, education club, NAACP, Latino Students in Action, LaOriginale, Commuter Students Association.

**Athletics.** NCAA. **Intercollegiate:** Basketball, bowling W, cross-country, football (tackle) M, tennis W, track and field, volleyball W. **Intramural:** Basketball, football (tackle) M. **Team name:** Wolves.

**Student services.** Career counseling, student employment services, health services, personal counseling, placement for graduates, veterans' counselor.

**Contact.** E-mail: gstemley@cheyney.edu
Phone: (610) 399-2275 Toll-free number: (800) 243-9639
Fax: (610) 399-2099
Gemma Stemley, Director of Admissions, Cheyney University of Pennsylvania, 1837 University Circle, Cheyney, PA 19319-0019

---

## Clarion University of Pennsylvania
**Clarion, Pennsylvania**        **CB member**
**www.clarion.edu**        **CB code: 2649**

- Public 4-year business and teachers college
- Residential campus in small town
- 5,691 degree-seeking undergraduates: 10% part-time, 60% women, 5% African American, 1% Asian American, 1% Hispanic American, 1% international
- 773 degree-seeking graduate students
- 69% of applicants admitted
- SAT or ACT (ACT writing optional) required
- 50% graduate within 6 years

**General.** Founded in 1867. Regionally accredited. **Degrees:** 946 bachelor's, 144 associate awarded; master's offered. **ROTC:** Army. **Location:** 85 miles from Pittsburgh, 75 miles from Erie. **Calendar:** Semester, limited summer session. **Full-time faculty:** 246 total; 11% minority, 45% women. **Part-time faculty:** 83 total; 5% minority, 59% women. **Class size:** 22% < 20, 58% 20-39, 9% 40-49, 7% 50-99, 3% >100. **Special facilities:** Planetarium.

**Freshman class profile.** 4,297 applied, 2,951 admitted, 1,439 enrolled.

| Mid 50% test scores | | Rank in top tenth: | 9% |
|---|---|---|---|
| SAT critical reading: | 430-530 | Return as sophomores: | 72% |
| SAT math: | 420-530 | Out-of-state: | 5% |
| GPA 3.50 or higher: | 33% | Live on campus: | 89% |
| GPA 3.0-3.49: | 33% | Fraternities: | 1% |
| GPA 2.0-2.99: | 30% | Sororities: | 6% |
| Rank in top quarter: | 25% | | |

**Basis for selection.** School achievement record, class rank, GPA, test scores considered. Audition required of music program applicants; Nursing students must complete NLN entrance exam. **Homeschooled:** Transcript of courses and grades required.

**High school preparation.** 13 units required; 19 recommended. Required and recommended units include English 4, mathematics 3-4, social studies 3-4, science 3-4 (laboratory 1) and foreign language 2.

**2007-2008 Annual costs.** Tuition/fees: $6,867; $12,044 out-of-state. Tuition for incoming out of state residents with SAT of 1100 or higher and at least a 3.5 GPA or the top 20% of their graduating class is $7,766. Room/board: $5,808. Books/supplies: $850. Personal expenses: $2,235.

**2006-2007 Financial aid. Need-based:** 1,192 full-time freshmen applied for aid; 968 were judged to have need; 929 of these received aid. Average need met was 61%. Average scholarship/grant was $5,316; average loan $2,505. 57% of total undergraduate aid awarded as scholarships/grants, 43% as loans/jobs. **Non-need-based:** Awarded to 1,382 full-time undergraduates, including 408 freshmen. Scholarships awarded for academics, art, athletics, leadership, minority status, music/drama, state residency.

**Application procedures. Admission:** No deadline. $30 fee, may be waived for applicants with need. Application may be submitted online. Admission notification on a rolling basis beginning on or about 9/1. **Financial aid:** Closing date 4/15. FAFSA required. Applicants notified on a rolling basis starting 3/1.

---

**Academics. Special study options:** Accelerated study, combined bachelor's/graduate degree, cooperative education, distance learning, double major, dual enrollment of high school students, honors, independent study, internships, liberal arts/career combination, study abroad, teacher certification program. Co-op program in engineering with two participating schools; co-op in speech pathology and audiology with Gallaudet University. Joint and collaborative programs in MSLS/JD, pharmacy, osteopathic medicine, nanotechnology, master of nursing, language, radiologic science, respiratory care and industrial technology. **Credit/placement by examination:** AP, CLEP, IB, institutional tests. 38 credit hours maximum toward bachelor's degree. **Support services:** Learning center, pre-admission summer program, remedial instruction, study skills assistance, tutoring, writing center.

**Majors. Biology:** General, molecular. **Business:** Accounting, business admin, finance, international, labor relations, managerial economics, marketing, real estate. **Communications:** General. **Computer sciences:** General, information systems. **Conservation:** Environmental science. **Education:** Early childhood, elementary, special. **English:** English lit, speech/rhetoric. **Foreign languages:** French, Spanish. **Health:** Audiology/speech pathology, clinical lab technology, medical radiologic technology/radiation therapy, nursing (RN). **History:** General. **Interdisciplinary:** Biological/physical sciences. **Liberal arts:** Arts/sciences, library science. **Math:** General, applied. **Philosophy/religion:** Philosophy. **Physical sciences:** Chemistry, geology, physics. **Psychology:** General, social. **Social sciences:** Anthropology, economics, political science, sociology. **Visual/performing arts:** Art, dramatic, music management.

**Most popular majors.** Business/marketing 20%, communications/journalism 10%, education 20%, health sciences 9%, liberal arts 7%, social sciences 8%.

**Computing on campus.** 1,143 workstations in dormitories, library, computer center, student center. Dormitories wired for high-speed internet access and linked to campus network. Commuter students can connect to campus network. Online course registration, online library, helpline, student web hosting, wireless network available.

**Student life. Freshman orientation:** Mandatory, $150 fee. Preregistration for classes offered. One-day session held in January, spring and summer. **Policies:** Students who live on campus are guaranteed a room on campus the following year. **Housing:** Coed dorms, single-sex dorms, apartments, fraternity/sorority housing, substance-free housing available. $100 nonrefundable deposit. **Activities:** Bands, choral groups, dance, drama, literary magazine, music ensembles, musical theater, radio station, student government, student newspaper, TV station, Koinonia Christian Fellowship, African American Caucus, Newman Association, Hip Hop Dance Team, NAACP, Young Democrats, Eagle Ambassadors, People Reaching Out and Understanding Disabilities, Students Together Against Rape, University Activities Board.

**Athletics.** NCAA. **Intercollegiate:** Baseball M, basketball, cross-country W, diving, football (tackle) M, golf M, soccer W, softball W, swimming, tennis W, track and field W, volleyball W, wrestling M. **Intramural:** Badminton, basketball, bowling, golf, racquetball, soccer, softball, swimming, table tennis, tennis, track and field, volleyball, water polo, wrestling. **Team name:** Golden Eagles.

**Student services.** Adult student services, alcohol/substance abuse counseling, campus ministries, career counseling, services for economically disadvantaged, student employment services, financial aid counseling, health services, minority student services, on-campus daycare, personal counseling, placement for graduates, veterans' counselor, women's services. **Physically disabled:** Services for visually, speech, hearing impaired.

**Contact.** E-mail: admissions@clarion.edu
Phone: (814) 393-2306 Toll-free number: (800) 672-7171
Fax: (814) 393-2030
William Bailey, Dean of Enrollment Management, Clarion University of Pennsylvania, 840 Wood Street, Clarion, PA 16214

---

## Curtis Institute of Music
**Philadelphia, Pennsylvania**
**www.curtis.edu**        **CB code: 2100**

- Private 4-year music college
- Commuter campus in very large city
- 137 degree-seeking undergraduates: 46% women, 5% African American, 9% Asian American, 1% Hispanic American, 41% international
- 23 degree-seeking graduate students
- 11% of applicants admitted
- SAT required

**General.** Founded in 1924. Regionally accredited. **Degrees:** 29 bachelor's awarded; master's offered. **Calendar:** Semester. **Full-time faculty:** 1 total; 100% women. **Part-time faculty:** 87 total; 9% have terminal degrees, 13% minority, 33% women. **Special facilities:** More than 82,000 titles in audio-visual materials, sheet music, and books.

**Freshman class profile.** 224 applied, 24 admitted, 14 enrolled.

| | | | |
|---|---|---|---|
| Out-of-state: | 81% | **International:** | 14% |

**Basis for selection.** Admission based on audition. Preference given to applicants demonstrating potential rather than proficiency. Test scores considered for applicants to bachelor's degree program. **Homeschooled:** Transcript of courses and grades, state high school equivalency certificate required.

**High school preparation.** Major emphasis on applied music activities.

**2008-2009 Annual costs.** Required fees $2,115; for bachelor of music students $2,215; additional expenses per year $15,850 (includes books, supplies, living expenses and miscellaneous).

**2007-2008 Financial aid.** All financial aid based on need. Average need met was 80%. Average scholarship/grant was $6,559; average loan $3,857. 46% of total undergraduate aid awarded as scholarships/grants, 54% as loans/jobs.

**Application procedures. Admission:** Closing date 12/11 (postmark date). $135 fee, may be waived for applicants with need. Application may be submitted online. Admission notification 4/1. Must reply by 5/1. **Financial aid:** Closing date 3/1. FAFSA, institutional form required. Applicants notified by 4/1; must reply by 5/1.

**Academics. Special study options:** Double major, ESL. **Credit/placement by examination:** AP, CLEP, institutional tests. 47 credit hours maximum toward bachelor's degree. **Support services:** Remedial instruction, study skills assistance.

**Majors. Visual/performing arts:** Music performance, music theory/composition.

**Computing on campus.** 16 workstations in library, computer center, student center. Online library, repair service available.

**Student life. Freshman orientation:** Mandatory. Preregistration for classes offered. **Activities:** Music ensembles, opera, student government, symphony orchestra.

**Student services.** Alcohol/substance abuse counseling, career counseling, financial aid counseling, health services, personal counseling.

**Contact.** E-mail: admissions@curtis.edu
Phone: (215) 893-5262 Fax: (215) 893-7900
Christopher Hodges, Admissions Officer, Curtis Institute of Music, 1726 Locust Street, Philadelphia, PA 19103-6187

---

### Delaware Valley College
**Doylestown, Pennsylvania**        CB member
www.delval.edu        CB code: 2510

- Private 4-year agricultural and liberal arts college
- Residential campus in large town
- 1,851 degree-seeking undergraduates: 11% part-time, 58% women, 3% African American, 1% Asian American, 2% Hispanic American
- 86 degree-seeking graduate students
- 66% of applicants admitted
- SAT or ACT (ACT writing recommended), application essay required
- 54% graduate within 6 years

**General.** Founded in 1896. Regionally accredited. **Degrees:** 325 bachelor's, 12 associate awarded; master's offered. **Location:** 20 miles from Philadelphia, 70 miles from New York City. **Calendar:** Semester, extensive summer session. **Full-time faculty:** 83 total; 59% have terminal degrees, 7% minority, 37% women. **Part-time faculty:** 94 total; 15% have terminal degrees, 5% minority, 38% women. **Class size:** 54% < 20, 38% 20-39, 3% 40-49, 4% 50-99, less than 1% >100. **Special facilities:** Equine facility with indoor and outdoor arena, animal farms, dairy, farm market, arboretum greenhouses, tissue culture laboratories.

**Freshman class profile.** 1,932 applied, 1,273 admitted, 476 enrolled.

| Mid 50% test scores | | | |
|---|---|---|---|
| SAT critical reading: | 460-560 | Rank in top quarter: | 38% |
| SAT math: | 460-560 | Rank in top tenth: | 14% |
| SAT writing: | 450-550 | End year in good standing: | 76% |
| ACT composite: | 20-25 | Return as sophomores: | 76% |
| GPA 3.50 or higher: | 52% | Out-of-state: | 45% |
| GPA 3.0-3.49: | 32% | Live on campus: | 88% |
| GPA 2.0-2.99: | 16% | Fraternities: | 4% |
| | | Sororities: | 5% |

**Basis for selection.** Academic achievement, class rank, test scores, letters of recommendation from math or science teacher and guidance counselor, grades in math and science considered. Interview, essay recommended. **Homeschooled:** State high school equivalency certificate required.

**High school preparation.** 15 units required. Required units include English 3, mathematics 2, social studies 2, science 2 (laboratory 1) and academic electives 6. For business administration 1 unit science only. Agriculture, biology, and chemistry majors need 6 additional units, business majors 7.

**2007-2008 Annual costs.** Tuition/fees: $24,710. Required fees for commuters $1,100; freshman commuters pay an additional $450. Room/board: $8,964. Books/supplies: $1,000. Personal expenses: $1,100.

**2006-2007 Financial aid. Need-based:** 433 full-time freshmen applied for aid; 373 were judged to have need; 373 of these received aid. Average need met was 75%. Average scholarship/grant was $14,370; average loan $3,233. 80% of total undergraduate aid awarded as scholarships/grants, 20% as loans/jobs. **Non-need-based:** Awarded to 714 full-time undergraduates, including 188 freshmen. Scholarships awarded for academics, alumni affiliation, music/drama.

**Application procedures. Admission:** Priority date 5/1; no deadline. $35 fee, may be waived for applicants with need. Application may be submitted online. Admission notification on a rolling basis beginning on or about 10/31. Must reply by May 1 or within 4 week(s) if notified thereafter. **Financial aid:** Priority date 4/1; no closing date. FAFSA required. Applicants notified on a rolling basis starting 2/1; must reply by 5/1.

**Academics.** Students complete 500 hour employment program related to major. **Special study options:** Accelerated study, combined bachelor's/graduate degree, cooperative education, cross-registration, distance learning, double major, honors, independent study, internships, liberal arts/career combination, study abroad, teacher certification program, weekend college. **Credit/placement by examination:** AP, CLEP, institutional tests. Credit for 5 courses may be granted through examination. **Support services:** Learning center, pre-admission summer program, reduced course load, remedial instruction, study skills assistance, tutoring, writing center.

**Majors. Agriculture:** Agribusiness operations, agronomy, animal sciences, crop production, dairy, food science, horticultural science, ornamental horticulture, turf management. **Biology:** General, zoology. **Business:** Accounting, business admin, management information systems, marketing. **Communications:** Digital media. **Conservation:** Wildlife. **Education:** Secondary. **English:** English lit. **Math:** General. **Physical sciences:** Chemistry. **Protective services:** Law enforcement admin.

**Most popular majors.** Agriculture 50%, biology 9%, business/marketing 20%, security/protective services 8%.

**Computing on campus.** 150 workstations in dormitories, library, computer center, student center. Dormitories wired for high-speed internet access and linked to campus network. Online library, helpline, repair service, wireless network available.

**Student life. Freshman orientation:** Mandatory. **Housing:** Guaranteed on-campus for freshmen. Coed dorms, single-sex dorms available. $200 deposit, deadline 5/1. **Activities:** Concert band, choral groups, drama, literary magazine, music ensembles, radio station, student government, student newspaper, Christian Fellowship, Hillel, Future Farmers of America, Minority Leadership Coalition, environmental awareness club, Alpha Phi Omega, DVC Volunteer Corps, Newman Club, equine club, business club.

**Athletics.** NCAA. **Intercollegiate:** Baseball M, basketball M, cheerleading M, cross-country, field hockey W, football (tackle) M, golf M, soccer, softball W, track and field, volleyball W, wrestling M. **Intramural:** Basketball, bowling, cross-country, equestrian, football (tackle) M, golf M, lacrosse M, soccer M, softball, tennis, volleyball. **Team name:** Aggies.

**Student services.** Adult student services, career counseling, student employment services, health services, personal counseling, placement for graduates. **Physically disabled:** Services for visually, speech, hearing impaired.

**Contact.** E-mail: admitme@deval.edu
Phone: (215) 489-2211 Toll-free number: (800) 233-5825
Fax: (215) 230-2968
Stephen Zenko, Director of Admissions, Delaware Valley College, 700 East
Butler Avenue, Doylestown, PA 18901-2697

---

## DeSales University
**Center Valley, Pennsylvania**          **CB member**
**www.desales.edu**                      **CB code: 2021**

- Private 4-year university affiliated with Roman Catholic Church
- Residential campus in small town
- 2,207 degree-seeking undergraduates: 25% part-time, 58% women
- 759 degree-seeking graduate students
- 77% of applicants admitted
- SAT or ACT required
- 67% graduate within 6 years; 29% enter graduate study

**General.** Founded in 1964. Regionally accredited. **Degrees:** 443 bachelor's awarded; master's offered. **ROTC:** Army. **Location:** 7 miles from Allentown, 50 miles from Philadelphia. **Calendar:** Semester, limited summer session. **Full-time faculty:** 103 total; 71% have terminal degrees, 47% women. **Part-time faculty:** 78 total; 56% women.

**Freshman class profile.** 1,797 applied, 1,387 admitted, 391 enrolled.

| Mid 50% test scores | | Rank in top tenth: | 23% |
|---|---|---|---|
| SAT critical reading: | 480-590 | End year in good standing: | 96% |
| SAT math: | 490-600 | Return as sophomores: | 79% |
| ACT composite: | 19-22 | Out-of-state: | 24% |
| Rank in top quarter: | 45% | Live on campus: | 89% |

**Basis for selection.** High school achievement most important. Test scores and recommendations also considered. Essay, interview recommended for all; audition required for dance, theater programs. Interview required for physician assistant program.

**High school preparation.** 16 units required; 18 recommended. Required and recommended units include English 4, mathematics 3-4, social studies 3-4, science 2 (laboratory) and foreign language 2. Biology, chemistry, 3 math recommended for biology major. 3 math, including 2 algebra, recommended for business major. Chemistry, physics, 3 math recommended for chemistry major. Biology, chemistry, physics, 2 math recommended for nursing major. 2 biology, chemistry, or physics, and 3 math recommended for pre-med major. 4 math recommended for math major.

**2007-2008 Annual costs.** Tuition/fees: $23,900. Room/board: $8,750. Books/supplies: $800. Personal expenses: $1,800.

**2007-2008 Financial aid. Need-based:** 335 full-time freshmen applied for aid; 276 were judged to have need; 276 of these received aid. Average need met was 74%. Average scholarship/grant was $7,108; average loan $3,275. 57% of total undergraduate aid awarded as scholarships/grants, 43% as loans/jobs. **Non-need-based:** Awarded to 1,091 full-time undergraduates, including 291 freshmen. Scholarships awarded for academics, leadership, music/drama.

**Application procedures. Admission:** Priority date 3/1; deadline 8/1. $30 fee, may be waived for applicants with need. Application may be submitted online. Admission notification on a rolling basis. Must reply by May 1 or within 2 week(s) if notified thereafter. **Financial aid:** Priority date 2/1, closing date 5/1. FAFSA required. Applicants notified on a rolling basis starting 2/15; must reply by 5/1 or within 2 week(s) of notification.

**Academics. Special study options:** Accelerated study, cross-registration, distance learning, double major, dual enrollment of high school students, ESL, honors, independent study, internships, liberal arts/career combination, semester at sea, study abroad, teacher certification program, weekend college. BS in medical studies, MS in physician assistant studies; cross-registration at consortium schools: Cedar Crest, Moravian, Muhlenberg, Lafayette, Lehigh. **Credit/placement by examination:** AP, CLEP, institutional tests. 24 credit hours maximum toward bachelor's degree. For AP credit for Physics B must complete lab component. Must submit research paper for CLEP English Composition with Essay to obtain 6 credits. **Support services:** Learning center, pre-admission summer program, reduced course load, study skills assistance, tutoring.

**Majors. Biology:** General, biochemistry. **Business:** General, accounting, business admin, e-commerce, finance, human resources, management information systems, management science, marketing. **Communications:** General. **Computer sciences:** General, computer science. **Conservation:** Environmental science. **Education:** Elementary, special. **English:** English lit. **Foreign languages:** Spanish. **Health:** Clinical lab science, nursing (RN), physician assistant. **History:** General. **Legal studies:** General. **Liberal arts:**

Arts/sciences. **Math:** General. **Parks/recreation:** Exercise sciences, sports admin. **Philosophy/religion:** Philosophy. **Physical sciences:** Chemistry. **Protective services:** Criminal justice. **Psychology:** General. **Social sciences:** Political science. **Theology:** Theology. **Visual/performing arts:** Dance, dramatic, film/cinema.

**Most popular majors.** Business/marketing 24%, education 8%, health sciences 16%, psychology 6%, security/protective services 9%, visual/performing arts 14%.

**Computing on campus.** 150 workstations in library, computer center, student center. Dormitories wired for high-speed internet access and linked to campus network. Commuter students can connect to campus network. Online course registration, online library, helpline, student web hosting, wireless network available.

**Student life. Freshman orientation:** Mandatory, $100 fee. Preregistration for classes offered. One-day academic orientation in June; 3-day social and academic orientation in August. **Policies:** Students under 21 cannot possess or be in presence of alcohol. Access to dorm rooms of opposite sex restricted during certain hours. **Housing:** Guaranteed on-campus for all undergraduates. Single-sex dorms, substance-free housing available. Pets allowed in dorm rooms. Town houses for upperclassmen, common-interest housing available. **Activities:** Pep band, campus ministries, choral groups, dance, drama, film society, international student organizations, literary magazine, music ensembles, musical theater, radio station, student government, student newspaper, TV station, pro-life club, accounting and finance club, Habitat For Humanity, Spanish Alliance, Best Buddies, Esto Vir, Lion's Club, natural science club.

**Athletics.** NCAA. **Intercollegiate:** Baseball M, basketball, cross-country, field hockey W, golf M, lacrosse M, soccer, softball W, tennis, track and field, volleyball W. **Intramural:** Basketball, football (non-tackle), soccer, softball, volleyball. **Team name:** Bulldogs.

**Student services.** Adult student services, alcohol/substance abuse counseling, campus ministries, career counseling, services for economically disadvantaged, student employment services, financial aid counseling, health services, minority student services, personal counseling, placement for graduates, veterans' counselor.

**Contact.** E-mail: admiss@desales.edu
Phone: (610) 282-4443 Toll-free number: (877) 433-7253
Fax: (610) 282-0131
Mary Birkhead, Director of Admissions, DeSales University, 2755 Station Avenue, Center Valley, PA 18034-9568

---

## DeVry University: Fort Washington
**Fort Washington, Pennsylvania**
**www.devry.edu**                        **CB code: 3866**

- For-profit 4-year university
- Commuter campus in large town
- 812 degree-seeking undergraduates: 45% part-time, 33% women, 35% African American, 4% Asian American, 6% Hispanic American, 1% international
- 116 degree-seeking graduate students
- Interview required

**General. Degrees:** 107 bachelor's, 21 associate awarded; master's offered. **Location:** 35 miles from Philadelphia. **Calendar:** Semester, extensive summer session. **Full-time faculty:** 29 total; 28% minority, 34% women. **Part-time faculty:** 90 total; 12% minority, 38% women.

**Freshman class profile.** 182 enrolled.

| Return as sophomores: | 52% | International: | 1% |
|---|---|---|---|
| Out-of-state: | 16% | | |

**Basis for selection.** Applicants must have high school diploma or equivalent, or a degree from accredited postsecondary institution, demonstrate proficiency in basic college-level skills through SAT or ACT scores or institution-administered placement exams, and be at least 17 years of age on the first day of classes. New students may enter at beginning of any semester. CPT also accepted.

**High school preparation.** Math unit must be algebra or higher.

**2007-2008 Annual costs.** Tuition/fees: $14,640. Books/supplies: $1,300. Personal expenses: $5,082.

**Financial aid.** All financial aid based on need.

**Application procedures. Admission:** No deadline. $50 fee. Application may be submitted online. Admission notification on a rolling basis. **Financial aid:** No deadline. FAFSA required. Applicants notified on a rolling basis.

**Academics. Special study options:** Accelerated study, distance learning. **Credit/placement by examination:** CLEP. **Support services:** Learning center, remedial instruction, tutoring.

**Majors. Business:** Business admin. **Computer sciences:** Networking, systems analysis. **Engineering technology:** Biomedical, computer, electrical. **Other:** Technical management.

**Most popular majors.** Business/marketing 51%, computer/information sciences 30%, engineering/engineering technologies 18%.

**Computing on campus.** 407 workstations in library, computer center. Online course registration, online library, helpline available.

**Student life. Freshman orientation:** Mandatory. **Activities:** Campus Crusade for Christ, electronic gamers club, creative arts club.

**Athletics. Intramural:** Volleyball.

**Student services.** Career counseling, student employment services, financial aid counseling, placement for graduates, veterans' counselor. **Physically disabled:** Services for visually, hearing impaired.

**Contact.** E-mail: admissions@phi.devry.edu
Phone: (215) 591-5701 Toll-free number: (866) 303-3879
Fax: (215) 591-5745
Steve Cohen, Director of Admission, DeVry University: Fort Washington, 1140 Virginia Drive, Fort Washington, PA 19034-3204

## Dickinson College
Carlisle, Pennsylvania
www.dickinson.edu
CB member
CB code: 2186

- Private 4-year liberal arts college
- Residential campus in large town
- 2,349 degree-seeking undergraduates: 55% women, 4% African American, 5% Asian American, 5% Hispanic American, 6% international
- 42% of applicants admitted
- Application essay required
- 83% graduate within 6 years; 29% enter graduate study

**General.** Founded in 1783. Regionally accredited. **Degrees:** 562 bachelor's awarded. **ROTC:** Army. **Location:** 100 miles from Philadelphia, 90 miles from Washington, DC. **Calendar:** Semester, limited summer session. **Full-time faculty:** 188 total; 96% have terminal degrees, 10% minority, 42% women. **Part-time faculty:** 39 total; 49% have terminal degrees, 49% women. **Class size:** 70% < 20, 29% 20-39, 1% 40-49. **Special facilities:** Arts center, planetarium and multiple telescope observatory, intercontinental satellite communications for study-abroad programs, study of contemporary issues center.

**Freshman class profile.** 5,844 applied, 2,442 admitted, 621 enrolled.

| Mid 50% test scores | | End year in good standing: | 98% |
|---|---|---|---|
| SAT critical reading: | 600-690 | Return as sophomores: | 91% |
| SAT math: | 590-680 | Out-of-state: | 78% |
| ACT composite: | 27-30 | Live on campus: | 100% |
| Rank in top quarter: | 79% | International: | 5% |
| Rank in top tenth: | 48% | | |

**Basis for selection.** Academic potential as shown by school achievement record most important. Extracurricular activities very important. Counselor recommendation required. Motivation, personal character considered. Special consideration given to applicants of color. Preference given to academically qualified children of alumni if they satisfy above criteria. All standardized tests optional. SAT or ACT recommended. Interview recommended.

**High school preparation.** 16 units required. Required and recommended units include English 4, mathematics 3, social studies 2, science 3 (laboratory 2), foreign language 2-3 and academic electives 2.

**2008-2009 Annual costs.** Tuition/fees: $38,259. Room/board: $9,600. Books/supplies: $1,000. Personal expenses: $1,200.

**2007-2008 Financial aid. Need-based:** 386 full-time freshmen applied for aid; 300 were judged to have need; 297 of these received aid. Average

need met was 96%. Average scholarship/grant was $24,542; average loan $4,175. 79% of total undergraduate aid awarded as scholarships/grants, 21% as loans/jobs. **Non-need-based:** Awarded to 321 full-time undergraduates, including 68 freshmen. Scholarships awarded for academics, alumni affiliation, leadership, ROTC.

**Application procedures. Admission:** Closing date 2/1 (postmark date). $65 fee, may be waived for applicants with need. Application may be submitted online. Admission notification 3/31. Must reply by May 1 or within 2 week(s) if notified thereafter. **Financial aid:** Closing date 2/1. FAFSA, CSS PROFILE required. Applicants notified by 3/31; must reply by 5/1 or within 2 week(s) of notification.

**Academics.** Certificates in interdepartmental programs offered in Latin American studies in conjunction with bachelor's degree. Prebusiness, prelaw and premedical preparation available in conjunction with majors listed. **Special study options:** Accelerated study, combined bachelor's/graduate degree, cross-registration, double major, ESL, exchange student, independent study, internships, liberal arts/career combination, student-designed major, study abroad, teacher certification program, Washington semester. 3-2 engineering programs with University of Pennsylvania, Case Western Reserve University, Rensselaer Polytechnic Institute; 3-3 law degree with Dickinson School of Law of Penn State University. **Credit/placement by examination:** AP, CLEP, IB, institutional tests. **Support services:** Tutoring, writing center.

**Majors. Area/ethnic studies:** American, East Asian, Italian, Russian/ Slavic, women's. **Biology:** General, biochemistry. **Business:** International. **Computer sciences:** General. **Conservation:** Environmental science, environmental studies. **English:** English lit. **Foreign languages:** Classics, French, German, Italian, Russian, Spanish. **History:** General. **Interdisciplinary:** Medieval/Renaissance, neuroscience. **Legal studies:** General, prelaw. **Math:** General. **Philosophy/religion:** Judaic, philosophy, religion. **Physical sciences:** Chemistry, geology, physics. **Psychology:** General. **Public administration:** Policy analysis. **Social sciences:** Anthropology, archaeology, economics, international relations, political science, sociology. **Visual/ performing arts:** Dramatic, studio arts. **Other:** Dance and music.

**Most popular majors.** Biology 8%, business/marketing 8%, English 9%, foreign language 10%, history 8%, psychology 7%, social sciences 22%.

**Computing on campus.** 600 workstations in dormitories, library, computer center, student center. Dormitories wired for high-speed internet access and linked to campus network. Commuter students can connect to campus network. Online course registration, online library, helpline, repair service, wireless network available.

**Student life. Freshman orientation:** Mandatory. Preregistration for classes offered. **Housing:** Guaranteed on-campus for all undergraduates. Coed dorms, special housing for disabled, apartments, fraternity/sorority housing, substance-free housing available. Theme, foreign language, arts, environmental, multicultural housing available. **Activities:** Bands, choral groups, dance, drama, film society, international student organizations, literary magazine, music ensembles, Model UN, musical theater, radio station, student government, student newspaper, symphony orchestra, public affairs, social service, religious, multicultural, foreign student organizations, College Democrats, Young Republicans, debate club.

**Athletics.** NCAA. **Intercollegiate:** Baseball M, basketball, cross-country, field hockey W, football (tackle) M, golf, lacrosse, soccer, softball W, swimming, tennis, track and field, volleyball W. **Intramural:** Badminton, basketball M, bowling M, field hockey W, football (non-tackle) M, football (tackle) M, golf, racquetball, soccer, softball, squash, table tennis, tennis, volleyball M. **Team name:** Red Devils.

**Student services.** Adult student services, alcohol/substance abuse counseling, career counseling, student employment services, financial aid counseling, health services, minority student services, on-campus daycare, personal counseling, placement for graduates. **Physically disabled:** Services for visually, speech, hearing impaired.

**Contact.** E-mail: admit@dickinson.edu
Phone: (717) 245-1231 Toll-free number: (800) 644-1773
Fax: (717) 245-1442
Catherine Davenport, Dean of Admissions, Dickinson College, PO Box 1773, Carlisle, PA 17013-2896

## Drexel University
Philadelphia, Pennsylvania
www.drexel.edu
CB member
CB code: 2194

- Private 5-year university
- Commuter campus in very large city

- 12,722 degree-seeking undergraduates: 17% part-time, 44% women, 8% African American, 12% Asian American, 3% Hispanic American, 7% international
- 7,215 degree-seeking graduate students
- 72% of applicants admitted
- SAT or ACT (ACT writing optional) required

**General.** Founded in 1891. Regionally accredited. Most undergraduate programs require up to 18 months work experience within 5-year program of study. **Degrees:** 2,366 bachelor's, 27 associate awarded; master's, doctoral, first professional offered. **ROTC:** Army, Naval, Air Force. **Calendar:** Quarter, extensive summer session. **Class size:** 51% < 20, 40% 20-39, 3% 40-49, 5% 50-99, 2% >100. **Special facilities:** Art collection, observatory, rifle range.

**Freshman class profile.** 16,867 applied, 12,097 admitted, 2,396 enrolled.

| Mid 50% test scores | | | |
|---|---|---|---|
| SAT critical reading: | 530-630 | Out-of-state: | 54% |
| SAT math: | 560-670 | Live on campus: | 87% |
| ACT composite: | 23-28 | International: | 8% |

**Basis for selection.** Academic average, counselor's recommendation and test scores most important, followed by class rank, school, community and church activities. Employment also considered. Essay required for most majors for media arts and design programs. Portfolio required for graphic design, music industry, photography and fashion design. Audition required for dance.

**High school preparation.** Required and recommended units include mathematics 3, science 1 (laboratory 1) and foreign language 1. Engineering applicants required to have 4 units math (including algebra I and II, geometry, trigonometry, and pre-calculus) and 2 units lab science (including chemistry and physics). Science applicants required to have 4 units math (including algebra I and II, geometry, and trigonometry) and 2 units lab science (including biology, chemistry, or physics). Most other applicants must have algebra I and II and geometry as required math units and one lab science.

**2008-2009 Annual costs.** Tuition/fees: $30,440. Tuition listed is for 5-year program with co-op quarter terms. Room/board: $12,135. Books/supplies: $1,800. Personal expenses: $2,925.

**Financial aid. Non-need-based:** Scholarships awarded for academics, alumni affiliation, art, athletics, leadership, music/drama, ROTC.

**Application procedures. Admission:** Closing date 3/1 (postmark date). $75 fee, may be waived for applicants with need. Application may be submitted online. Admission notification on a rolling basis. Must reply by May 1 or within 2 week(s) if notified thereafter. **Financial aid:** Closing date 3/1. FAFSA required. Applicants notified on a rolling basis starting 3/15.

**Academics. Special study options:** Accelerated study, combined bachelor's/graduate degree, cooperative education, distance learning, double major, ESL, honors, independent study, internships, semester at sea, study abroad, teacher certification program, weekend college. 3-3 programs in engineering with Lincoln University, Indiana University of Pennsylvania and Eastern Mennonite College. **Credit/placement by examination:** AP, CLEP, IB, institutional tests. 30 credit hours maximum toward bachelor's degree. **Support services:** Learning center, pre-admission summer program, reduced course load, remedial instruction, study skills assistance, tutoring, writing center.

**Majors. Architecture:** Architecture. **Biology:** General. **Business:** General, hotel/motel admin, managerial economics. **Computer sciences:** Computer science, information systems, security, web page design. **Conservation:** Environmental science, environmental studies. **Engineering:** Architectural, biomedical, chemical, civil, computer, construction, electrical, environmental, industrial, materials, mechanical, software. **Engineering technology:** General. **English:** English lit, technical writing. **Health:** Clinical lab assistant, health care admin, nursing (RN), physician assistant, substance abuse counseling. **History:** General. **Interdisciplinary:** Biological/physical sciences, nutrition sciences. **Liberal arts:** Humanities. **Math:** General. **Parks/recreation:** Sports admin. **Personal/culinary services:** Chef training, restaurant/catering. **Physical sciences:** Chemistry, physics. **Protective services:** Law enforcement admin. **Psychology:** General. **Social sciences:** Anthropology, international relations, political science, sociology. **Visual/performing arts:** Cinematography, dance, design, fashion design, graphic design, interior design, photography, play/screenwriting, theater arts management. **Other:** Communications and applied technology, Design and merchandising.

**Most popular majors.** Business/marketing 24%, computer/information sciences 11%, engineering/engineering technologies 22%, health sciences 16%, visual/performing arts 11%.

**Computing on campus.** PC or laptop required. 610 workstations in dormitories, library, computer center, student center. Dormitories wired for high-speed internet access and linked to campus network. Commuter students can connect to campus network. Online course registration, online library, helpline, repair service, student web hosting, wireless network available.

**Student life. Freshman orientation:** Available. Preregistration for classes offered. 2-day overnight sessions held in July; 3-day program prior to start of classes. **Policies:** Freshmen required to live on campus unless living with parents. **Housing:** Guaranteed on-campus for freshmen. Coed dorms, special housing for disabled, apartments, fraternity/sorority housing available. $200 nonrefundable deposit, deadline 7/1. **Activities:** Bands, campus ministries, choral groups, dance, drama, film society, literary magazine, music ensembles, musical theater, radio station, student government, student newspaper, TV station, Newman Center, Hillel, Alpha Phi Omega, NAACP, Eye Openers, Disciples in Deed, Drexel Christian Fellowship, Jewish Heritage Program.

**Athletics.** NCAA. **Intercollegiate:** Basketball, diving, field hockey W, golf M, lacrosse, rowing (crew), soccer, softball W, swimming, tennis, wrestling M. **Intramural:** Badminton, basketball, football (non-tackle), soccer, softball, squash, table tennis, tennis, volleyball. **Team name:** Dragons.

**Student services.** Adult student services, career counseling, student employment services, financial aid counseling, health services, minority student services, personal counseling, placement for graduates. **Physically disabled:** Services for visually, speech, hearing impaired.

**Contact.** E-mail: enroll@drexel.edu
Phone: (215) 895-2400 Toll-free number: (800) 237-3935
Fax: (215) 895-5939
Joan McDonald, Admissions Director, Drexel University, 3141 Chestnut Street, Philadelphia, PA 19104-2875

---

## Duquesne University
**Pittsburgh, Pennsylvania**
www.duq.edu

CB member
CB code: 2196

- Private 4-year university affiliated with Roman Catholic Church
- Residential campus in large city
- 5,562 degree-seeking undergraduates: 6% part-time, 58% women, 3% African American, 2% Asian American, 1% Hispanic American, 2% international
- 4,459 graduate students
- 74% of applicants admitted
- SAT or ACT with writing, application essay required
- 70% graduate within 6 years; 33% enter graduate study

**General.** Founded in 1878. Regionally accredited. **Degrees:** 1,321 bachelor's awarded; master's, doctoral, first professional offered. **ROTC:** Army, Naval, Air Force. **Calendar:** Semester, extensive summer session. **Full-time faculty:** 442 total; 86% have terminal degrees, 6% minority, 40% women. **Part-time faculty:** 438 total; 6% minority, 50% women. **Class size:** 50% < 20, 39% 20-39, 4% 40-49, 5% 50-99, 3% >100. **Special facilities:** Recording complex, recital hall, electronic studio, keyboard lab, music technology center, academic research center for pharmaceutical information, pharmaceutical technology center, pharmacy manufacturing lab, phenomenology center, health sciences cadaver lab, computational sciences liberal arts center, international nursing center, nurse managed wellness center.

**Freshman class profile.** 5,374 applied, 3,993 admitted, 1,361 enrolled.

| Mid 50% test scores | | | |
|---|---|---|---|
| SAT critical reading: | 510-600 | Rank in top quarter: | 56% |
| SAT math: | 510-610 | Rank in top tenth: | 26% |
| SAT writing: | 510-600 | End year in good standing: | 96% |
| ACT composite: | 22-26 | Return as sophomores: | 88% |
| GPA 3.50 or higher: | 57% | Out-of-state: | 21% |
| GPA 3.0-3.49: | 31% | Live on campus: | 89% |
| GPA 2.0-2.99: | 12% | International: | 1% |

**Basis for selection.** School achievement record, standardized test scores, recommendations, essay very important. Decisions based on overall GPA, standardized test scores, curriculum, volunteer activities, etc. Interview recommended for all; audition required for music program. **Homeschooled:** Transcript of courses and grades required. **Learning Disabled:** Documentation of learning disabilities may be required.

**High school preparation.** 16 units required. Required units include English 4, mathematics 2, social studies 2, science 2, foreign language 2 and academic electives 4. 8 units in any combination from areas of social studies, language, math, and science required.

**2007-2008 Annual costs.** Tuition/fees: $23,950. Room/board: $8,546. Books/supplies: $600. Personal expenses: $600.

**2006-2007 Financial aid. Need-based:** 1,154 full-time freshmen applied for aid; 924 were judged to have need; 924 of these received aid. Average need met was 90%. Average scholarship/grant was $11,279; average loan $3,355. 49% of total undergraduate aid awarded as scholarships/grants, 51% as loans/jobs. **Non-need-based:** Awarded to 4,902 full-time undergraduates, including 1,523 freshmen. Scholarships awarded for academics, athletics, music/drama, ROTC.

**Application procedures. Admission:** Priority date 11/1; deadline 7/1 (receipt date). $50 fee, may be waived for applicants with need. Application may be submitted online. Admission notification on a rolling basis beginning on or about 9/15. Must reply by May 1 or within 2 week(s) if notified thereafter. **Financial aid:** Closing date 5/1. FAFSA, institutional form required. Applicants notified on a rolling basis starting 3/1; must reply by 5/1 or within 3 week(s) of notification.

**Academics. Special study options:** Accelerated study, combined bachelor's/graduate degree, cross-registration, distance learning, double major, dual enrollment of high school students, ESL, exchange student, external degree, honors, independent study, internships, liberal arts/career combination, semester at sea, student-designed major, study abroad, teacher certification program, Washington semester, weekend college. **Credit/placement by examination:** AP, CLEP, IB, institutional tests. 90 credit hours maximum toward bachelor's degree. **Support services:** Learning center, pre-admission summer program, reduced course load, remedial instruction, study skills assistance, tutoring, writing center.

**Honors college/program.** 1300 SAT or ACT equivalent, 3.5 GPA and ranking in the top 10% of graduating class (if high school ranks seniors). Other well qualified students may apply. Approximately 100 incoming freshmen admitted each year.

**Majors. Biology:** General, biochemistry. **Business:** General, accounting, communications, entrepreneurial studies, finance, international, investments/securities, logistics, management information systems, management science, managerial economics, marketing, nonprofit/public. **Communications:** General, journalism, public relations. **Computer sciences:** Computer science, web page design, webmaster. **Conservation:** Environmental science. **Education:** General, early childhood, elementary, English, Latin, mathematics, multi-level teacher, music, secondary, social studies, Spanish. **English:** English lit, speech/rhetoric. **Foreign languages:** General, ancient Greek, classics, Latin, Spanish. **Health:** Athletic training, health care admin, music therapy, nursing (RN), premedicine. **History:** General. **Math:** General. **Philosophy/religion:** Philosophy. **Physical sciences:** Chemistry, physics. **Psychology:** General. **Social sciences:** Economics, international relations, political science, sociology. **Theology:** Theology. **Visual/performing arts:** Art history/conservation, dramatic, music performance, studio arts. **Other:** Computer software, applications, Public relations, advertising, and applied communications.

**Most popular majors.** Biology 10%, business/marketing 24%, communications/journalism 7%, education 11%, health sciences 20%, liberal arts 6%.

**Computing on campus.** 917 workstations in dormitories, library, computer center, student center. Dormitories wired for high-speed internet access and linked to campus network. Commuter students can connect to campus network. Online course registration, online library, helpline, repair service, student web hosting, wireless network available.

**Student life. Freshman orientation:** Mandatory, $135 fee. Preregistration for classes offered. 5-day program in August; includes volunteer opportunities. **Policies:** All recognized student organizations must have faculty or staff adviser, have purpose consistent with university mission, and abide by Code of Rights, Responsibilities and Conduct. **Housing:** Guaranteed on-campus for all undergraduates. Coed dorms, special housing for disabled, apartments, fraternity/sorority housing, substance-free housing available. $300 nonrefundable deposit, deadline 5/1. Single-sex, sorority and fraternity, international, and club wings available. **Activities:** Bands, choral groups, dance, drama, film society, international student organizations, literary magazine, music ensembles, musical theater, opera, radio station, student government, student newspaper, symphony orchestra, TV station, black student union, university volunteers, Latin American student association, Evergreen, Indian student association, St. Vincent de Paul Society, College Republicans, Asian student association, Young Democrats.

**Athletics.** NCAA. **Intercollegiate:** Baseball M, basketball, cross-country, football (tackle) M, golf M, lacrosse W, rowing (crew) W, soccer, swimming, tennis, track and field, volleyball W, wrestling M. **Intramural:** Badminton, basketball, football (non-tackle), skiing, soccer, softball, swimming, table tennis, tennis, volleyball, water polo, weight lifting. **Team name:** Dukes.

**Student services.** Adult student services, alcohol/substance abuse counseling, campus ministries, career counseling, services for economically disadvantaged, student employment services, financial aid counseling, health services, minority student services, on-campus daycare, personal counseling, placement for graduates, women's services. **Physically disabled:** Services for visually, speech, hearing impaired.

**Contact.** E-mail: admissions@duq.edu
Phone: (412) 396-6222 Toll-free number: (800) 456-0590
Fax: (412) 396-6223
Paul - James Cukanna, Associate Vice President, Enrollment Management, Duquesne University, 600 Forbes Avenue, Administration Building, Pittsburgh, PA 15282-0201

---

## East Stroudsburg University of Pennsylvania

**East Stroudsburg, Pennsylvania**
**www4.esu.edu**

**CB member**
**CB code: 2650**

- Public 4-year university
- Residential campus in large town
- 5,841 degree-seeking undergraduates: 7% part-time, 56% women, 5% African American, 1% Asian American, 5% Hispanic American
- 822 degree-seeking graduate students
- 66% of applicants admitted
- SAT or ACT (ACT writing optional) required
- 52% graduate within 6 years

**General.** Founded in 1893. Regionally accredited. **Degrees:** 1,137 bachelor's awarded; master's offered. **ROTC:** Army, Air Force. **Location:** 40 miles from Allentown and Scranton. **Calendar:** Semester, extensive summer session. **Full-time faculty:** 272 total; 79% have terminal degrees, 13% minority, 43% women. **Part-time faculty:** 74 total; 24% have terminal degrees, 7% minority, 64% women. **Class size:** 28% < 20, 50% 20-39, 19% 40-49, 3% 50-99, less than 1% >100. **Special facilities:** 30-acre ecological studies area, business accelerator program.

**Freshman class profile.** 5,799 applied, 3,820 admitted, 1,190 enrolled.

| Mid 50% test scores | | Rank in top quarter: | 36% |
|---|---|---|---|
| SAT critical reading: | 440-520 | Rank in top tenth: | 5% |
| SAT math: | 450-540 | End year in good standing: | 84% |
| SAT writing: | 430-520 | Return as sophomores: | 82% |
| GPA 3.50 or higher: | 31% | Out-of-state: | 34% |
| GPA 3.0-3.49: | 38% | Live on campus: | 85% |
| GPA 2.0-2.99: | 31% | | |

**Basis for selection.** Academic achievement primary factor in selection process. Whole-person assessment also used, taking into account school and community activities, achievements and aspirations.

**High school preparation.** Recommended units include English 4, mathematics 4, social studies 3, history 3, science 3 (laboratory 2) and foreign language 2.

**2007-2008 Annual costs.** Tuition/fees: $6,809; $14,575 out-of-state. Tuition for incoming out of state residents who are high achieving science and technology majors (biology, chemistry, computer science, mathematics, and physics) is $7,766. Room/board: $5,686. Books/supplies: $1,000. Personal expenses: $2,168.

**2006-2007 Financial aid. Need-based:** 1,040 full-time freshmen applied for aid; 695 were judged to have need; 654 of these received aid. Average need met was 75%. Average scholarship/grant was $4,170; average loan $2,519. 45% of total undergraduate aid awarded as scholarships/grants, 55% as loans/jobs. **Non-need-based:** Awarded to 1,386 full-time undergraduates, including 355 freshmen. Scholarships awarded for academics, alumni affiliation, art, athletics, job skills, leadership, minority status, music/drama, religious affiliation, state residency.

**Application procedures. Admission:** Closing date 4/1 (postmark date). $35 fee, may be waived for applicants with need. Application may be submitted online. Admission notification on a rolling basis beginning on or about 11/15. Must reply by May 1 or within 3 week(s) if notified thereafter. **Financial aid:** Closing date 3/1. FAFSA required. Applicants notified by 4/1; must reply by 5/1.

**Academics. Special study options:** Accelerated study, combined bachelor's/graduate degree, cross-registration, distance learning, double major, dual enrollment of high school students, exchange student, honors, independent study, internships, student-designed major, study abroad, teacher certification program, urban semester. **Credit/placement by examination:** AP, CLEP, SAT, institutional tests. 24 credit hours maximum toward bachelor's degree.

**Support services:** Learning center, pre-admission summer program, reduced course load, remedial instruction, study skills assistance, tutoring, writing center.

**Majors. Biology:** General, biochemistry, biotechnology, ecology, marine. **Business:** Business admin, hospitality admin. **Communications:** General. **Communications technology:** General. **Computer sciences:** General, security. **Education:** Early childhood, elementary, health, physical, special. **English:** English lit. **Foreign languages:** French, Spanish. **Health:** Athletic training, audiology/speech pathology, clinical lab science, health services admin, nursing (RN). **History:** General. **Interdisciplinary:** Biological/physical sciences. **Liberal arts:** Arts/sciences, humanities. **Math:** General. **Parks/recreation:** Exercise sciences, facilities management. **Philosophy/religion:** Philosophy. **Physical sciences:** General, chemistry, geology, physics. **Psychology:** General. **Social sciences:** General, economics, geography, political science, sociology. **Visual/performing arts:** General, dramatic, graphic design.

**Most popular majors.** Biology 6%, business/marketing 12%, education 23%, health sciences 9%, parks/recreation 11%, psychology 8%, social sciences 10%.

**Computing on campus.** 223 workstations in dormitories, library, computer center, student center. Dormitories linked to campus network. Online course registration, helpline, wireless network available.

**Student life. Freshman orientation:** Available, $65 fee. Preregistration for classes offered. 2-day event during summer with joint and separate sessions for parents. **Housing:** Guaranteed on-campus for freshmen. Coed dorms, single-sex dorms, special housing for disabled, apartments, substance-free housing available. $150 nonrefundable deposit, deadline 5/1. **Activities:** Bands, campus ministries, choral groups, dance, drama, literary magazine, music ensembles, musical theater, radio station, student government, student newspaper, symphony orchestra, Latin American Students Association, Campus Democrats, Young Republicans, African American Student Alliance, Fellowship of Christian Athletes, Newman Club, Women for Awareness.

**Athletics.** NCAA. **Intercollegiate:** Baseball M, basketball, cross-country, field hockey W, football (tackle) M, lacrosse W, soccer, softball W, swimming W, tennis, track and field, volleyball, wrestling M. **Intramural:** Badminton, basketball, football (non-tackle), racquetball, soccer, softball, tennis, volleyball, water polo. **Team name:** Warriors.

**Student services.** Adult student services, campus ministries, career counseling, student employment services, financial aid counseling, health services, minority student services, on-campus daycare, personal counseling, placement for graduates, veterans' counselor, women's services. **Physically disabled:** Services for visually, speech, hearing impaired.

**Contact.** E-mail: undergrads@po-box.esu.edu
Phone: (570) 422-3542 Toll-free number: (877) 230-5547
Fax: (570) 422-3933
Henry Gardner, Associate Provost for Enrollment Management, East Stroudsburg University of Pennsylvania, 200 Prospect Street, East Stroudsburg, PA 18301-2999

---

## Eastern University
**St. Davids, Pennsylvania**
www.eastern.edu                    CB code: 2220

- Private 4-year university affiliated with American Baptist Churches in the USA
- Residential campus in small town
- 2,449 degree-seeking undergraduates
- 68% of applicants admitted
- SAT or ACT (ACT writing recommended), application essay required

**General.** Founded in 1952. Regionally accredited. **Degrees:** 572 bachelor's, 29 associate awarded; master's, doctoral, first professional offered. **ROTC:** Army, Air Force. **Location:** 10 miles from Philadelphia. **Calendar:** Semester, limited summer session. **Full-time faculty:** 115 total; 86% have terminal degrees, 22% minority, 42% women. **Part-time faculty:** 275 total; 28% have terminal degrees, 21% minority, 48% women. **Class size:** 70% < 20, 29% 20-39, less than 1% 40-49, less than 1% 50-99, less than 1% >100. **Special facilities:** Planetarium, observatory.

**Freshman class profile.** 1,549 applied, 1,058 admitted, 421 enrolled.

| Mid 50% test scores | | | |
|---|---|---|---|
| SAT critical reading: | 460-590 | GPA 2.0-2.99: | 25% |
| SAT math: | 450-570 | Rank in top quarter: | 43% |
| SAT writing: | 460-590 | Rank in top tenth: | 14% |
| ACT composite: | 15-24 | Out-of-state: | 51% |
| GPA 3.50 or higher: | 43% | Live on campus: | 94% |
| GPA 3.0-3.49: | 31% | International: | 1% |

**Basis for selection.** SAT, GPA, and class rank most important. Interest in school mission, slope of grades, attendance, interviews also evaluated. Interview recommended.

**High school preparation.** Recommended units include English 4, mathematics 3, social studies 2, science 3 and foreign language 3.

**2007-2008 Annual costs.** Tuition/fees: $21,395. Room/board: $8,350. Books/supplies: $1,000. Personal expenses: $1,800.

**Application procedures. Admission:** No deadline. $25 fee, may be waived for applicants with need. Application may be submitted online. Admission notification on a rolling basis. **Financial aid:** No deadline. FAFSA, institutional form required. Applicants notified on a rolling basis starting 4/1.

**Academics. Special study options:** Accelerated study, cross-registration, double major, honors, independent study, student-designed major, study abroad, teacher certification program, Washington semester. **Credit/placement by examination:** AP, CLEP, IB, SAT, ACT. 30 credit hours maximum toward associate degree, 60 toward bachelor's. **Support services:** Pre-admission summer program, remedial instruction, study skills assistance, tutoring, writing center.

**Honors college/program.** Students must be in top 9% of class and have 1300 SAT (exclusive of Writing) or 30 ACT, or extraordinary leadership abilities with significant academic achievements.

**Majors. Biology:** General, biochemistry. **Business:** Accounting/finance, business admin, management information systems, marketing, nonprofit/public. **Communications:** General. **Conservation:** General. **Education:** Elementary. **Foreign languages:** French, Spanish. **Health:** Nursing (RN). **History:** General. **Math:** General. **Parks/recreation:** Health/fitness. **Physical sciences:** Astronomy, chemistry. **Psychology:** General. **Public administration:** Social work. **Social sciences:** Economics, political science, sociology. **Theology:** Bible, missionary, theology, youth ministry. **Visual/performing arts:** Art history/conservation, dance.

**Most popular majors.** Business/marketing 39%, education 9%, health sciences 10%, psychology 6%, theological studies 9%.

**Computing on campus.** 131 workstations in dormitories, library, computer center, student center. Dormitories wired for high-speed internet access and linked to campus network. Commuter students can connect to campus network. Repair service available.

**Student life. Freshman orientation:** Mandatory. Preregistration for classes offered. Held 3 days before fall semester. **Policies:** Smoke-free campus. **Housing:** Coed dorms, apartments, substance-free housing available. $150 nonrefundable deposit, deadline 8/1. Students required to live on campus unless they receive permission from Dean of Students Office. **Activities:** Bands, choral groups, dance, drama, literary magazine, music ensembles, musical theater, student government, student newspaper, black student league, Penn State Education Association, yacht club, gospel outreach, Fellowship of Christian Athletes, Habitat for Humanity, Evangelicals for Social Action, students organized against racism, prison ministry, Latinos Unidos.

**Athletics.** NCAA. **Intercollegiate:** Baseball M, basketball, cross-country M, field hockey W, golf M, lacrosse, soccer, softball W, tennis, volleyball W. **Intramural:** Basketball, cheerleading, soccer, volleyball. **Team name:** Eagles.

**Student services.** Adult student services, alcohol/substance abuse counseling, campus ministries, career counseling, financial aid counseling, health services, legal services, minority student services, personal counseling, veterans' counselor, women's services. **Physically disabled:** Services for visually, speech, hearing impaired.

**Contact.** E-mail: ugadm@eastern.edu
Phone: (610) 341-5967 Toll-free number: (800) 452-0996
Fax: (610) 341-1723
David Urban, Executive Director for Enrollment, Eastern University, 1300 Eagle Road, St. Davids, PA 19087-3696

## Edinboro University of Pennsylvania

**Edinboro, Pennsylvania**      **CB member**
www.edinboro.edu      **CB code: 2651**

- Public 4-year liberal arts and teachers college
- Commuter campus in small town
- 6,127 degree-seeking undergraduates: 10% part-time, 56% women, 10% African American, 1% Asian American, 1% Hispanic American, 1% international
- 1,028 degree-seeking graduate students
- 82% of applicants admitted
- 48% graduate within 6 years

**General.** Founded in 1857. Regionally accredited. Extensive programs and services for physically and learning disabled students available. Credit courses, continuing education, workshops, and seminars offered at Porreco Extension Center in Erie. **Degrees:** 1,097 bachelor's, 82 associate awarded; master's offered. **ROTC:** Army. **Location:** 18 miles from Erie. **Calendar:** Semester, extensive summer session. **Full-time faculty:** 323 total; 9% minority, 46% women. **Part-time faculty:** 34 total; 9% minority, 35% women. **Class size:** 26% < 20, 55% 20-39, 12% 40-49, 8% 50-99, less than 1% >100. **Special facilities:** Observatory, planetarium, natural wildlife museum, robotics laboratory, center for performing arts, speech and hearing clinic.

**Freshman class profile.** 3,612 applied, 2,944 admitted, 1,296 enrolled.

| Mid 50% test scores | | | |
|---|---|---|---|
| SAT critical reading: | 410-520 | GPA 2.0-2.99: | 33% |
| SAT math: | 400-510 | Rank in top quarter: | 20% |
| ACT composite: | 15-20 | Rank in top tenth: | 5% |
| GPA 3.50 or higher: | 26% | Return as sophomores: | 69% |
| GPA 3.0-3.49: | 27% | Out-of-state: | 14% |
| | | Live on campus: | 77% |

**Basis for selection.** High school curriculum, test scores, GPA, and class rank most important. Recommendations and activities record also reviewed. Interview and essay recommended for all; audition required for music program; portfolio recommended for art program. **Homeschooled:** Transcript of courses and grades, interview, letter of recommendation (nonparent) required.

**High school preparation.** 15 units recommended. Recommended units include English 4, mathematics 3, social studies 4, science 3, foreign language 2, computer science 1 and academic electives 3.

**2007-2008 Annual costs.** Tuition/fees: $6,767; $9,356 out-of-state. Room/board: $5,976. Books/supplies: $900. Personal expenses: $1,300.

**2006-2007 Financial aid. Need-based:** 1,210 full-time freshmen applied for aid; 1,025 were judged to have need; 987 of these received aid. Average need met was 57%. Average scholarship/grant was $2,194; average loan $2,107. 52% of total undergraduate aid awarded as scholarships/grants, 48% as loans/jobs. **Non-need-based:** Awarded to 5,082 full-time undergraduates, including 995 freshmen. Scholarships awarded for academics, alumni affiliation, art, athletics, job skills, leadership, minority status, music/drama, religious affiliation, ROTC, state residency.

**Application procedures. Admission:** Priority date 4/1; no deadline. $30 fee, may be waived for applicants with need. Application may be submitted online. Admission notification on a rolling basis beginning on or about 7/1. Must reply by May 1 or within 4 week(s) if notified thereafter. **Financial aid:** Priority date 3/15, closing date 5/1. FAFSA required. Applicants notified on a rolling basis starting 3/20; must reply within 2 week(s) of notification.

**Academics.** 60 credits of general education electives required for bachelor's degree. Associate degree counseling, peer tutoring, peer mentors, academic advising center, and trial admissions program offered. **Special study options:** Combined bachelor's/graduate degree, cooperative education, cross-registration, distance learning, double major, dual enrollment of high school students, honors, independent study, internships, liberal arts/career combination, student-designed major, study abroad, teacher certification program. **Credit/placement by examination:** AP, CLEP, SAT, ACT, institutional tests. 30 credit hours maximum toward associate degree, 30 toward bachelor's. **Support services:** Learning center, pre-admission summer program, reduced course load, remedial instruction, study skills assistance, tutoring, writing center.

**Majors. Area/ethnic studies:** Latin American, women's. **Biology:** General. **Business:** Accounting, business admin, marketing, operations. **Communications:** General, broadcast journalism, journalism. **Computer sciences:** General. **Conservation:** Environmental science. **Education:** Elementary, special. **English:** English lit. **Foreign languages:** German, Spanish. **Health:** Clinical lab technology, communication disorders, nursing (RN), predental, premedicine, preveterinary. **History:** General. **Interdisciplinary:** Biological/

physical sciences. **Liberal arts:** Arts/sciences, humanities. **Math:** General. **Parks/recreation:** Health/fitness, sports admin. **Philosophy/religion:** Philosophy. **Physical sciences:** Chemistry, geology, physics, planetary. **Protective services:** Criminal justice. **Psychology:** General. **Public administration:** Social work. **Social sciences:** General, anthropology, economics, geography, political science, sociology. **Visual/performing arts:** Art, art history/conservation, ceramics, dramatic, drawing, fiber arts, graphic design, painting, photography, printmaking, sculpture.

**Most popular majors.** Business/marketing 8%, communications/journalism 7%, education 10%, health sciences 9%, liberal arts 8%, psychology 6%, security/protective services 10%, social sciences 7%, visual/performing arts 16%.

**Computing on campus.** 717 workstations in dormitories, library, computer center, student center. Dormitories wired for high-speed internet access and linked to campus network. Commuter students can connect to campus network. Online course registration, online library, helpline, repair service, wireless network available.

**Student life. Freshman orientation:** Available. Preregistration for classes offered. Summer program. **Policies:** Zero tolerance policy for alcohol and drugs on campus. **Housing:** Guaranteed on-campus for freshmen. Coed dorms, single-sex dorms, special housing for disabled, substance-free housing available. $75 partly refundable deposit, deadline 5/1. Living/learning communities available. **Activities:** Bands, choral groups, dance, drama, film society, literary magazine, radio station, student government, student newspaper, TV station, 89 organizations on campus.

**Athletics.** NCAA. **Intercollegiate:** Basketball, cross-country, football (tackle) M, soccer W, softball W, swimming, track and field, volleyball W, wrestling M. **Intramural:** Basketball, football (non-tackle), racquetball, soccer, softball, volleyball, wrestling M. **Team name:** The Fighting Scots.

**Student services.** Adult student services, alcohol/substance abuse counseling, campus ministries, career counseling, student employment services, financial aid counseling, health services, minority student services, personal counseling, placement for graduates, veterans' counselor. **Physically disabled:** Services for visually, speech, hearing impaired. **Learning disabled:** Comprehensive services available.

**Contact.** E-mail: eup_admissions@edinboro.edu
Phone: (814) 732-2761 Toll-free number: (800) 626-2203
Fax: (814) 732-2420
James Cooney, Director of Undergraduate Admissions, Edinboro University of Pennsylvania, 200 East Normal Street, Edinboro, PA 16444

## Elizabethtown College

**Elizabethtown, Pennsylvania**      **CB member**
www.etown.edu      **CB code: 2225**

- Private 4-year liberal arts college affiliated with Church of the Brethren
- Residential campus in large town
- 2,233 degree-seeking undergraduates: 15% part-time, 65% women
- 32 degree-seeking graduate students
- 58% of applicants admitted
- SAT or ACT (ACT writing optional), application essay required
- 70% graduate within 6 years; 22% enter graduate study

**General.** Founded in 1899. Regionally accredited. **Degrees:** 482 bachelor's, 11 associate awarded; master's offered. **Location:** 20 miles from Harrisburg, 90 miles from Philadelphia. **Calendar:** Semester, limited summer session. **Full-time faculty:** 129 total; 83% have terminal degrees, 9% minority, 42% women. **Part-time faculty:** 171 total; 18% have terminal degrees, 6% minority, 52% women. **Class size:** 68% < 20, 30% 20-39, 1% 40-49, less than 1% 50-99, less than 1% >100. **Special facilities:** Anabaptist and Pietist groups center, global citizenship center, Brethren Colleges Abroad headquarters.

**Freshman class profile.** 3,370 applied, 1,968 admitted, 503 enrolled.

| Mid 50% test scores | | | |
|---|---|---|---|
| SAT critical reading: | 510-610 | Rank in top tenth: | 34% |
| SAT math: | 520-620 | Return as sophomores: | 86% |
| ACT composite: | 21-26 | Out-of-state: | 31% |
| Rank in top quarter: | 67% | Live on campus: | 97% |
| | | International: | 1% |

**Basis for selection.** School achievement record most important. College preparatory program strongly recommended. Co-curricular activities also considered, particularly service-oriented activities. Applicants should be in top quarter of class. Students may waive SAT/ACT score from admissions and merit-based scholarship decisions if they are ranked in top 10% of class or have 3.5 GPA if school does not rank. Interview required for occupational therapy and honors program. For international business applicants, essay must demonstrate interest in that subject area. Audition required for music, music education, music therapy programs; portfolio required for art program. **Homeschooled:** Letter of recommendation (nonparent) required.

**High school preparation.** 15 units required; 20 recommended. Required and recommended units include English 3-4, mathematics 3-4, social studies 2, history 2, science 2-4 (laboratory 2-3), foreign language 2 and academic electives 2.

**2008-2009 Annual costs.** Tuition/fees: $30,650. Room/board: $7,950. Books/supplies: $800. Personal expenses: $700.

**2007-2008 Financial aid. Need-based:** 421 full-time freshmen applied for aid; 362 were judged to have need; 362 of these received aid. Average need met was 84%. Average scholarship/grant was $16,581; average loan $3,638. 71% of total undergraduate aid awarded as scholarships/grants, 29% as loans/jobs. **Non-need-based:** Awarded to 648 full-time undergraduates, including 181 freshmen. Scholarships awarded for academics, art, music/drama, religious affiliation.

**Application procedures. Admission:** Priority date 3/1; no deadline. $30 fee, may be waived for applicants with need. Application may be submitted online. Admission notification on a rolling basis beginning on or about 12/1. Must reply by May 1 or within 2 week(s) if notified thereafter. December 15 closing date for occupational therapy program. March 1 closing date for international business. January 15 closing date for honors program. **Financial aid:** Priority date 3/15; no closing date. FAFSA, institutional form required. Applicants notified on a rolling basis starting 3/1; must reply by 5/1 or within 2 week(s) of notification.

**Academics. Special study options:** Combined bachelor's/graduate degree, double major, dual enrollment of high school students, ESL, exchange student, external degree, honors, independent study, internships, liberal arts/career combination, study abroad, teacher certification program, Washington semester. 2-2 program with Thomas Jefferson University in nursing, laboratory sciences, diagnostic imaging; 3-3 program in physical therapy (DPT) with Thomas Jefferson University; 3-2 in engineering with Penn State; 3-2 with Duke University in forestry and environmental management; 3-3 in physical therapy with Widener University and University of Maryland, Baltimore; 3+4 in dentistry with Temple University; agreements for MBA programs at Lehigh University, Rutgers University, Loyola College (MD), Penn State University, Harrisburg. **Credit/placement by examination:** AP, CLEP, IB, institutional tests. Credit by examination unlimited provided student is able to fulfill residency requirement. Credit for International Baccalaureate awarded only for subject exams and only for earned scores from 4-7. **Support services:** Learning center, reduced course load, study skills assistance, tutoring, writing center.

**Majors. Biology:** General, biochemistry, biotechnology. **Business:** Accounting, actuarial science, business admin, international, management information systems, managerial economics. **Communications:** Advertising, media studies, public relations. **Computer sciences:** General, information systems. **Conservation:** Environmental science, forest management, forest sciences. **Education:** Biology, chemistry, early childhood, elementary, English, history, mathematics, multi-level teacher, music, science, social science, social studies. **Engineering:** General, computer, electrical, industrial, mechanics, physics. **English:** English lit, technical writing. **Foreign languages:** French, German, Japanese, Spanish. **Health:** Clinical lab science, music therapy, predental, premedicine, preveterinary. **History:** General. **Math:** General, applied. **Philosophy/religion:** Christian, ethics, philosophy, religion. **Physical sciences:** Chemistry, physics. **Psychology:** General. **Public administration:** Social work. **Social sciences:** Anthropology, criminology, economics, political science, sociology. **Visual/performing arts:** Art, theater arts management.

**Most popular majors.** Business/marketing 30%, communications/journalism 8%, education 12%, English 6%, social sciences 9%.

**Computing on campus.** 200 workstations in dormitories, library, computer center, student center. Dormitories wired for high-speed internet access and linked to campus network. Commuter students can connect to campus network. Online course registration, online library, helpline, student web hosting, wireless network available.

**Student life. Freshman orientation:** Mandatory. One-day summer program in June and multi-day program at beginning of fall semester. **Policies:** All residence halls are smoke-free. **Housing:** Guaranteed on-campus for all undergraduates. Coed dorms, single-sex dorms, special housing for disabled, apartments, substance-free housing available. Special housing available for students involved in service learning and community service. **Activities:** Bands, choral groups, dance, drama, international student organizations, literary magazine, music ensembles, musical theater, radio station, student government, student newspaper, symphony orchestra, TV station, Newman club, Intervarsity Christian Fellowship, Hillel, Circle-K, Habitat for Humanity, Amnesty International, Colors United, College Democrats, Republican club.

**Athletics.** NCAA. **Intercollegiate:** Baseball M, basketball, cross-country, diving, field hockey W, golf M, lacrosse, soccer, softball W, swimming, tennis, track and field, volleyball W, wrestling M. **Intramural:** Basketball, racquetball, soccer, softball, tennis, volleyball. **Team name:** Blue Jays.

**Student services.** Adult student services, alcohol/substance abuse counseling, campus ministries, career counseling, student employment services, financial aid counseling, health services, minority student services, personal counseling, placement for graduates, veterans' counselor, women's services. **Physically disabled:** Services for visually, hearing impaired. **Learning disabled:** Comprehensive services available.

**Contact.** E-mail: admissions@etown.edu
Phone: (717) 361-1400 Fax: (717) 361-1365
Debra Murray, Director of Admissions, Elizabethtown College, One Alpha Drive, Elizabethtown, PA 17022-2298

---

## Franklin & Marshall College
Lancaster, Pennsylvania
www.fandm.edu

CB member
CB code: 2261

- Private 4-year liberal arts college
- Residential campus in small city
- 2,063 degree-seeking undergraduates: 49% women, 4% African American, 4% Asian American, 4% Hispanic American, 8% international
- 37% of applicants admitted
- Application essay required
- 84% graduate within 6 years; 25% enter graduate study

**General.** Founded in 1787. Regionally accredited. **Degrees:** 466 bachelor's awarded. **Location:** 60 miles from Philadelphia, 120 miles from Washington, DC. **Calendar:** Semester, limited summer session. **Full-time faculty:** 184 total; 97% have terminal degrees, 10% minority, 35% women. **Part-time faculty:** 54 total; 63% have terminal degrees, 7% minority, 46% women. **Class size:** 52% < 20, 46% 20-39, 1% 40-49, less than 1% 50-99. **Special facilities:** Observatory, science library, retail sales complex, bronze casting foundry, field house, planetarium, natural history museum, concert hall, performing arts center, Writers House.

**Freshman class profile.** 5,018 applied, 1,873 admitted, 570 enrolled.

| Mid 50% test scores | | | |
|---|---|---|---|
| SAT critical reading: | 600-690 | Rank in top quarter: | 87% |
| SAT math: | 610-690 | Rank in top tenth: | 57% |
| GPA 3.50 or higher: | 63% | Return as sophomores: | 91% |
| GPA 3.0-3.49: | 30% | Out-of-state: | 68% |
| GPA 2.0-2.99: | 7% | Live on campus: | 99% |
| | | International: | 10% |

**Basis for selection.** School achievement record, test scores or graded writing samples, extracurricular activities, recommendations, essay considered. SAT or ACT recommended. Submission of standardized test scores optional for all students. If students choose to omit scores, two recent graded writing samples must then be submitted. Interview required for early decision applicants, strongly recommended for others. Auditions and portfolios recommended for all students who wish to demonstrate particular talent. **Homeschooled:** Interview required. Interview, accrediting and evaluative documenation from home state, and SAT or ACT required. 3 SAT Subject Tests highly recommended.

**High school preparation.** Required and recommended units include English 4, mathematics 3-4, social studies 1-3, history 2-3, science 2-3 (laboratory 2-3), foreign language 2-4 and visual/performing arts 1.

**2008-2009 Annual costs.** Tuition/fees: $38,630. Room/board: $9,870. Books/supplies: $650. Personal expenses: $950.

**2007-2008 Financial aid. Need-based:** Average need met was 100%. Average scholarship/grant was $23,468; average loan $4,012. 80% of total undergraduate aid awarded as scholarships/grants, 20% as loans/jobs. **Non-need-based:** Scholarships awarded for academics, art, leadership, music/drama.

**Application procedures. Admission:** Closing date 2/1 (postmark date). $50 fee, may be waived for applicants with need. Application may be submitted online. Admission notification 4/1. Must reply by May 1 or within 2 week(s) if notified thereafter. **Financial aid:** Priority date 2/1, closing date 3/1. FAFSA, institutional form, CSS PROFILE required. Applicants notified by 3/15; must reply by 5/1.

**Academics.** Interdisciplinary minors offered. **Special study options:** Accelerated study, combined bachelor's/graduate degree, cross-registration, double major, dual enrollment of high school students, exchange student, honors, independent study, internships, liberal arts/career combination, New York semester, semester at sea, student-designed major, study abroad, teacher certification program, Washington semester. 3-2 programs in forestry, engineering, environmental studies; Columbia University's New York/Paris program. **Credit/placement by examination:** AP, CLEP, IB, institutional tests. 64 credit hours maximum toward bachelor's degree. **Support services:** Preadmission summer program, reduced course load, tutoring, writing center.

**Majors.** **Area/ethnic studies:** African, African-American, American. **Biology:** General, biochemistry. **Business:** Business admin. **Conservation:** Environmental science, environmental studies. **English:** Creative writing, English lit. **Foreign languages:** Ancient Greek, classics, French, German, Latin, Spanish. **History:** General. **Interdisciplinary:** Behavioral sciences, biopsychology, neuroscience. **Math:** General. **Philosophy/religion:** Philosophy, religion. **Physical sciences:** Astronomy, astrophysics, chemistry, geology, physics. **Psychology:** General. **Social sciences:** Anthropology, economics, political science, sociology. **Visual/performing arts:** Art history/conservation, dance, dramatic, studio arts.

**Most popular majors.** Biology 10%, business/marketing 14%, English 9%, foreign language 6%, interdisciplinary studies 9%, social sciences 25%, visual/performing arts 6%.

**Computing on campus.** 125 workstations in library, computer center. Dormitories wired for high-speed internet access and linked to campus network. Commuter students can connect to campus network. Online course registration, online library, helpline, repair service, student web hosting, wireless network available.

**Student life.** **Freshman orientation:** Mandatory, $200 fee. Preregistration for classes offered. 5 days prior to start of classes, includes noncredit pre-semester academic experience. **Policies:** Freshmen and sophomores required to live in college housing. **Housing:** Guaranteed on-campus for freshmen. Coed dorms, special housing for disabled, apartments, substance-free housing available. French house, arts house, international house available to upperclassmen, community outreach house, men's and women's floors. **Activities:** Bands, choral groups, dance, drama, literary magazine, music ensembles, musical theater, opera, radio station, student government, student newspaper, symphony orchestra, TV station, East Asian society, Catholic Campus Community, Hillel, Christian Fellowship, Habitat for Humanity, Voices for Women, Coalition for Choice, Environmental Action Alliance, Black student union, Mi Gente Latina.

**Athletics.** NCAA. **Intercollegiate:** Baseball M, basketball, cross-country, field hockey W, football (tackle) M, golf, lacrosse, rowing (crew) W, soccer, softball W, squash, swimming, tennis, track and field, volleyball W, wrestling M. **Intramural:** Archery, badminton, basketball, bowling, cross-country, football (non-tackle) M, soccer, softball, squash, table tennis, tennis, volleyball. **Team name:** Diplomats.

**Student services.** Alcohol/substance abuse counseling, campus ministries, career counseling, student employment services, financial aid counseling, health services, minority student services, on-campus daycare, personal counseling, placement for graduates, women's services.

**Contact.** E-mail: admission@fandm.edu
Phone: (717) 291-3953 Fax: (717) 291-4389
Eric Maguire, Director of Admission, Franklin & Marshall College, PO Box 3003, Lancaster, PA 17604-3003

## Gannon University

Erie, Pennsylvania
www.gannon.edu

CB member
CB code: 2270

- Private 4-year university affiliated with Roman Catholic Church
- Residential campus in small city
- 2,460 degree-seeking undergraduates: 7% part-time, 60% women, 5% African American, 1% Asian American, 2% Hispanic American, 1% international
- 1,375 degree-seeking graduate students
- 83% of applicants admitted
- SAT or ACT (ACT writing optional) required
- 64% graduate within 6 years

**General.** Founded in 1925. Regionally accredited. **Degrees:** 436 bachelor's, 39 associate awarded; master's, doctoral offered. **ROTC:** Army. **Location:** 120 miles from Pittsburgh, 90 miles from Cleveland. **Calendar:** Semester, extensive summer session. **Full-time faculty:** 190 total; 69% have terminal degrees, 11% minority, 42% women. **Part-time faculty:** 144 total; 22% have terminal degrees, 3% minority, 47% women. **Class size:** 57% < 20, 42% 20-39, less than 1% 40-49, less than 1% 50-99. **Special facilities:** Environmental studies center, computer integrated enterprise manufacturing center, floating laboratory providing hands-on environmental study on Lake Erie.

**Freshman class profile.** 2,909 applied, 2,423 admitted, 617 enrolled.

| Mid 50% test scores | | | |
|---|---|---|---|
| SAT critical reading: | 460-570 | Rank in top quarter: | 53% |
| SAT math: | 470-590 | Rank in top tenth: | 25% |
| ACT composite: | 19-25 | End year in good standing: | 86% |
| GPA 3.50 or higher: | 52% | Return as sophomores: | 81% |
| GPA 3.0-3.49: | 27% | Out-of-state: | 28% |
| GPA 2.0-2.99: | 20% | Live on campus: | 78% |

**Basis for selection.** High school record important, including course selection, GPA, class rank, standardized test scores, recommendations, personal statement. Admission requirements vary by program. Limited number of students who do not meet all admissions requirements may be accepted into General Studies program. **Homeschooled:** Interview required. **Learning Disabled:** Applicants screened through director must be interviewed.

**High school preparation.** 16 units required. Required units include English 4. Remaining 12 required academic units based on planned major.

**2007-2008 Annual costs.** Tuition/fees: $21,346. Room/board: $8,300. Books/supplies: $1,000. Personal expenses: $1,324.

**2007-2008 Financial aid.** **Need-based:** 598 full-time freshmen applied for aid; 542 were judged to have need; 541 of these received aid. Average need met was 83%. Average scholarship/grant was $14,749; average loan $3,384. 73% of total undergraduate aid awarded as scholarships/grants, 27% as loans/jobs. **Non-need-based:** Awarded to 728 full-time undergraduates, including 195 freshmen. Scholarships awarded for academics, athletics, leadership, music/drama, religious affiliation, ROTC.

**Application procedures.** **Admission:** No deadline. $25 fee, may be waived for applicants with need. Application may be submitted online. Admission notification on a rolling basis beginning on or about 9/1. Early application especially recommended for health science programs since space is limited. Closing date for occupational therapy, physican's assistant, radiological science programs January 15. Closing date for medical program December 15. **Financial aid:** Priority date 3/15; no closing date. FAFSA, institutional form required. Applicants notified on a rolling basis starting 11/1; must reply by 5/1 or within 4 week(s) of notification.

**Academics.** Preferred admission to doctorate physical therapy program granted to students with bachelor's degree from Gannon in physical therapy. Occupational therapy and physician assistant programs are 5-year master's degree programs. **Special study options:** Accelerated study, combined bachelor's/graduate degree, distance learning, double major, dual enrollment of high school students, external degree, honors, independent study, internships, liberal arts/career combination, study abroad, teacher certification program, Washington semester. **Credit/placement by examination:** AP, CLEP, IB, institutional tests. 36 credit hours maximum toward bachelor's degree. **Support services:** Learning center, reduced course load, remedial instruction, study skills assistance, tutoring, writing center.

**Honors college/program.** Minimum 1150 SAT score (exclusive of Writing), 3.0 GPA, rank in top tenth of high school class, college preparatory curriculum, extracurricular activities, community service. Recommendation, interview and essay required. Approximately 50 freshmen admitted per year.

**Majors.** **Biology:** General, bioinformatics. **Business:** Accounting, business admin, finance, insurance, international, management information systems, marketing. **Communications:** Advertising, journalism. **Communications technology:** Radio/tv. **Computer sciences:** General, programming. **Conservation:** Environmental science. **Education:** Business, early childhood, elementary, foreign languages, multi-level teacher, secondary, social studies, special. **Engineering:** Chemical, electrical, environmental, industrial, mechanical. **English:** British lit, English lit. **Foreign languages:** General. **Health:** Clinical lab science, dietetics, nursing (RN), physician assistant, premedicine, respiratory therapy technology. **History:** General. **Legal studies:** Paralegal, prelaw. **Liberal arts:** Arts/sciences. **Math:** General. **Parks/recreation:** Sports admin. **Personal/culinary services:** Mortuary science. **Philosophy/religion:** Philosophy. **Physical sciences:** Chemistry. **Protective services:** Criminal justice. **Psychology:** General. **Public administration:** Social work. **Science technology:** Biological. **Social sciences:** General, political science. **Theology:** Theology. **Visual/performing arts:** General, dramatic.

**Most popular majors.** Biology 7%, business/marketing 16%, education 6%, health sciences 24%, security/protective services 9%.

**Computing on campus.** 350 workstations in dormitories, library, computer center, student center. Dormitories wired for high-speed internet access and linked to campus network. Commuter students can connect to campus network. Online library, helpline, wireless network available.

**Student life.** **Freshman orientation:** Mandatory, $60 fee. Preregistration for classes offered. 4 separate sessions during summer. Open to parents and students. **Housing:** Guaranteed on-campus for freshmen. Coed dorms, special housing for disabled, apartments, substance-free housing available. $100 fully refundable deposit. **Activities:** Pep band, campus ministries, choral groups, dance, drama, international student organizations, literary magazine, music ensembles, musical theater, radio station, student government, student newspaper, Social Concerns, minority student union, College Democrats, College Republicans, activities programming board, debate, Vitality Through Exercise, residence union.

**Athletics.** NCAA. **Intercollegiate:** Baseball M, basketball, cross-country, diving, football (tackle) M, golf, lacrosse W, soccer, softball W, swimming, volleyball W, water polo, wrestling M. **Intramural:** Basketball, football (non-tackle), handball, racquetball, soccer, volleyball, wrestling M. **Team name:** Golden Knights.

**Student services.** Adult student services, alcohol/substance abuse counseling, campus ministries, career counseling, services for economically disadvantaged, student employment services, financial aid counseling, health services, minority student services, personal counseling, placement for graduates, veterans' counselor. **Learning disabled:** Comprehensive services available.

**Contact.** E-mail: admissions@gannon.edu
Phone: (814) 871-7240 Toll-free number: (800) 426-6668
Fax: (814) 871-5803
Terrance Kizina, Director of Admission, Gannon University, 109 University Square, Erie, PA 16541-0001

## Geneva College
**Beaver Falls, Pennsylvania**  **CB member**
www.geneva.edu  **CB code: 2273**

- Private 4-year liberal arts college affiliated with Reformed Presbyterian Church of North America
- Residential campus in large town
- 1,639 degree-seeking undergraduates: 8% part-time, 55% women, 12% African American, 1% Asian American, 1% Hispanic American, 1% international
- 241 graduate students
- 84% of applicants admitted
- SAT or ACT (ACT writing optional), application essay required
- 54% graduate within 6 years

**General.** Founded in 1848. Regionally accredited. **Degrees:** 439 bachelor's, 19 associate awarded; master's offered. **ROTC:** Army. **Location:** 35 miles from Pittsburgh. **Calendar:** Semester, extensive summer session. **Full-time faculty:** 85 total. **Part-time faculty:** 130 total. **Special facilities:** Collection of artifacts and records of Pittsburgh steel industry, technology development center, observatory, high adventure ropes course.

**Freshman class profile.** 1,093 applied, 916 admitted, 352 enrolled.

| Mid 50% test scores | | | |
|---|---|---|---|
| SAT critical reading: | 470-600 | Rank in top tenth: | 19% |
| SAT math: | 470-610 | Return as sophomores: | 76% |
| ACT composite: | 20-25 | Out-of-state: | 31% |
| Rank in top quarter: | 27% | Live on campus: | 87% |

**Basis for selection.** Academic performance and test scores most important. Recommendations and extracurricular activities considered. Interview recommended for all; audition required for music program. **Homeschooled:** Transcript of courses and grades required. Help in preparing homeschooler's transcript available if necessary.

**High school preparation.** 16 units required. Required units include English 4, mathematics 2, social studies 3, science 1, foreign language 2 and academic electives 4. Engineering students should have 1 unit of chemistry and physics, 4 units of college-preparatory mathematics including trigonometry or precalculus.

**2007-2008 Annual costs.** Tuition/fees: $19,430. Room/board: $7,200. Books/supplies: $800. Personal expenses: $1,150.

**2007-2008 Financial aid. Need-based:** 324 full-time freshmen applied for aid; 278 were judged to have need; 278 of these received aid. Average need met was 85%. Average scholarship/grant was $13,139; average loan $3,704. 69% of total undergraduate aid awarded as scholarships/grants, 31% as loans/jobs. **Non-need-based:** Scholarships awarded for academics, music/drama, religious affiliation.

**Application procedures. Admission:** No deadline. $40 fee, may be waived for applicants with need. Application may be submitted online. Admission notification on a rolling basis beginning on or about 9/1. Must reply by May 1 or within 3 week(s) if notified thereafter. **Financial aid:** Priority date 3/15; no closing date. FAFSA required. Applicants notified on a rolling basis starting 3/1; must reply by 5/1 or within 4 week(s) of notification.

**Academics. Special study options:** Accelerated study, combined bachelor's/graduate degree, cooperative education, cross-registration, double major, dual enrollment of high school students, honors, independent study, internships, liberal arts/career combination, student-designed major, study abroad, teacher certification program, Washington semester. **Credit/placement by examination:** AP, CLEP, IB, SAT, ACT, institutional tests. 30 credit hours maximum toward bachelor's degree. **Support services:** Pre-admission summer program, reduced course load, remedial instruction, study skills assistance, tutoring, writing center.

**Majors. Biology:** General. **Business:** Accounting, business admin, human resources. **Communications:** General. **Computer sciences:** General. **Education:** General, biology, chemistry, elementary, English, history, mathematics, music, physics, social studies, special. **Engineering:** General, chemical. **English:** Composition, English lit, speech/rhetoric. **Health:** Speech pathology. **History:** General. **Liberal arts:** Arts/sciences. **Math:** Applied. **Philosophy/religion:** Philosophy. **Physical sciences:** Chemistry, physics. **Psychology:** General. **Public administration:** Social work. **Social sciences:** Political science, sociology. **Theology:** Bible, youth ministry. **Visual/performing arts:** Music management, music performance.

**Computing on campus.** 50 workstations in dormitories, library, computer center, student center. Dormitories wired for high-speed internet access and linked to campus network. Commuter students can connect to campus network. Online library, helpline, repair service, wireless network available.

**Student life. Freshman orientation:** Mandatory. Held 5 days prior to start of classes. **Policies:** Smoking, drinking, social or ballroom dancing not permitted on campus. Students must live on campus unless married, commuting, or over age 24. Religious observance required. **Housing:** Guaranteed on-campus for all undergraduates. Single-sex dorms, apartments, substance-free housing available. $150 fully refundable deposit. Special interest, theme houses available. **Activities:** Bands, campus ministries, choral groups, dance, drama, international student organizations, literary magazine, music ensembles, radio station, student government, student newspaper, community service club, Young Republicans, black student organization.

**Athletics.** NCAA, NCCAA. **Intercollegiate:** Baseball M, basketball, cross-country, football (tackle) M, soccer, softball W, tennis W, track and field, volleyball W. **Intramural:** Basketball, football (tackle) M, racquetball, soccer, softball, volleyball. **Team name:** Golden Tornadoes.

**Student services.** Campus ministries, career counseling, student employment services, financial aid counseling, health services, minority student services, personal counseling, placement for graduates. **Physically disabled:** Services for visually, hearing impaired.

**Contact.** E-mail: admissions@geneva.edu
Phone: (724) 847-6500 Toll-free number: (800) 847-8255
Fax: (724) 847-6776
David Layton, Dean of Undergraduate Enrollment, Geneva College, 3200 College Avenue, Beaver Falls, PA 15010

## Gettysburg College
**Gettysburg, Pennsylvania**  **CB member**
www.gettysburg.edu  **CB code: 2275**

- Private 4-year liberal arts college
- Residential campus in large town
- 2,485 degree-seeking undergraduates: 1% part-time, 53% women
- 36% of applicants admitted
- SAT or ACT (ACT writing optional), application essay required
- 81% graduate within 6 years

**General.** Founded in 1832. Regionally accredited. **Degrees:** 648 bachelor's awarded. **ROTC:** Army. **Location:** 36 miles from Harrisburg, 80 miles from Washington, DC. **Calendar:** Semester. **Full-time faculty:** 199 total; 84% have terminal degrees, 13% minority, 45% women. **Part-time faculty:** 86 total; 7% have terminal degrees, 10% minority, 42% women. **Class size:** 509% < 20, 29% 20-39, 19% 40-49, less than 1% 50-99. **Special facilities:** Observatory, planetarium, intercultural resource center, women's resource center, child study center, public service center, optics and plasma physics laboratories, infrared and NMR spectrometers, proton accelerator, science center, outdoor climbing wall, music conservatory.

**Freshman class profile.** 6,126 applied, 2,180 admitted, 695 enrolled.

| Mid 50% test scores | | End year in good standing: | 91% |
|---|---|---|---|
| SAT critical reading: | 610-690 | Return as sophomores: | 91% |
| SAT math: | 610-670 | Out-of-state: | 77% |
| Rank in top quarter: | 89% | Live on campus: | 100% |
| Rank in top tenth: | 66% | International: | 2% |

**Basis for selection.** Academic record, recommendations, and activities most important. Audition required for music program; portfolio recommended for art program. Interview strongly recommended. **Homeschooled:** Statement describing homeschool structure and mission, transcript of courses and grades, interview, letter of recommendation (nonparent) required.

**High school preparation.** Required and recommended units include English 4, mathematics 3-4, history 3-4, science 3-4 (laboratory 3-4) and foreign language 3-4. History requirement can be fulfilled with social studies units, depending on available high school courses.

**2007-2008 Annual costs.** Tuition/fees: $35,990. Room/board: $8,630. Books/supplies: $500.

**2007-2008 Financial aid. Need-based:** 460 full-time freshmen applied for aid; 362 were judged to have need; 362 of these received aid. Average need met was 100%. Average scholarship/grant was $24,157; average loan $3,848. 83% of total undergraduate aid awarded as scholarships/grants, 17% as loans/jobs. **Non-need-based:** Scholarships awarded for academics, music/drama.

**Application procedures. Admission:** Closing date 2/1 (postmark date). $55 fee, may be waived for applicants with need. Application may be submitted online. Admission notification 4/1. Must reply by May 1 or within 2 week(s) if notified thereafter. **Financial aid:** Closing date 2/15. FAFSA, CSS PROFILE required. Applicants notified by 3/26; must reply by 5/1.

**Academics. Special study options:** Combined bachelor's/graduate degree, double major, independent study, internships, semester at sea, student-designed major, study abroad, teacher certification program, United Nations semester, Washington semester. 3-2 programs in engineering with Columbia University, Rensselaer Polytechnic Institute, and Washington University in St. Louis; 3-2 program in nursing with Johns Hopkins University; pre-law and health professions advising available. **Credit/placement by examination:** AP, CLEP, IB, SAT, institutional tests. **Support services:** Study skills assistance, tutoring, writing center.

**Majors. Area/ethnic studies:** African-American, American, Asian, Asian-American, East Asian, Japanese, Latin American, women's. **Biology:** General, biochemistry, conservation, molecular. **Business:** Business admin, finance, international, management science, marketing, nonprofit/public. **Communications:** General, journalism. **Computer sciences:** General, computer science. **Conservation:** General, environmental science, environmental studies, forestry, management/policy, water/wetlands/marine. **Education:** Music. **Engineering:** General, biomedical, chemical, civil, computer, electrical, environmental, mechanical, mechanics, physics, science. **English:** American lit, British lit, creative writing, English lit. **Foreign languages:** Classics, comparative lit, French, German, Japanese, Latin, Spanish. **Health:** Health services, nursing (RN), predental, premedicine, prepharmacy, preveterinary. **History:** General, American, Asian, European. **Interdisciplinary:** Behavioral sciences, biological/physical sciences, global studies, math/computer science, medieval/Renaissance, natural sciences, neuroscience, peace/conflict. **Legal studies:** Prelaw. **Liberal arts:** Arts/sciences. **Math:** General. **Parks/recreation:** Exercise sciences, health/fitness, sports admin. **Philosophy/religion:** Philosophy, religion. **Physical sciences:** Astronomy, chemistry, physics. **Psychology:** General. **Social sciences:** Anthropology, economics, international relations, political science, sociology, U.S. government. **Theology:** Preministerial. **Visual/performing arts:** General, art, art history/conservation, dramatic, film/cinema, music performance, music theory/composition, piano/organ, studio arts, theater arts management, voice/opera.

**Most popular majors.** Biology 10%, business/marketing 17%, English 7%, history 8%, psychology 9%, social sciences 22%.

**Computing on campus.** 620 workstations in library, computer center, student center. Dormitories wired for high-speed internet access and linked to campus network. Commuter students can connect to campus network. Online course registration, online library, helpline, repair service, student web hosting, wireless network available.

**Student life. Freshman orientation:** Mandatory. Preregistration for classes offered. Begins 5 days prior to the start of fall semester classes. **Housing:** Guaranteed on-campus for all undergraduates. Coed dorms, single-sex dorms, apartments, fraternity/sorority housing, substance-free housing available. $500 nonrefundable deposit, deadline 5/1. Special interest and theme housing available. **Activities:** Bands, choral groups, dance, drama, film society, literary magazine, music ensembles, musical theater, radio station, student government, student newspaper, symphony orchestra, TV station, over 100 clubs available.

**Athletics.** NCAA. **Intercollegiate:** Baseball M, basketball, cheerleading, cross-country, field hockey W, football (tackle) M, golf, lacrosse, soccer, softball W, swimming, tennis, track and field, volleyball W, wrestling M. **Intramural:** Badminton, basketball, field hockey, football (non-tackle), golf, lacrosse W, skiing, soccer, softball, volleyball, weight lifting. **Team name:** Bullets.

**Student services.** Campus ministries, career counseling, student employment services, financial aid counseling, health services, minority student services, personal counseling, placement for graduates, women's services.

**Contact.** E-mail: admiss@gettysburg.edu
Phone: (717) 337-6100 Toll-free number: (800) 431-0803
Fax: (717) 337-6145
Gail Sweezey, Director of Admissions, Gettysburg College, 300 North Washington Street, Gettysburg, PA 17325-1484

---

## Gratz College
**Melrose Park, Pennsylvania**
**www.gratz.edu**
CB code: 2280

- Private 4-year College of Jewish Studies affiliated with Jewish faith
- Commuter campus in very large city
- 10 degree-seeking undergraduates
- 200 graduate students
- Application essay required

**General.** Founded in 1895. Regionally accredited. **Degrees:** 1 bachelor's awarded; master's, doctoral offered. **Location:** 6 miles from Philadelphia. **Calendar:** Semester, limited summer session. **Full-time faculty:** 10 total. **Part-time faculty:** 125 total. **Special facilities:** Jewish music library and rare book collection, oral history Holocaust archives, Holocaust Awareness Museum.

**Basis for selection.** Application, personal statement, transcripts, and two recommendations important. Interview recommended. **Learning Disabled:** Students asked to submit written documentation concerning learning disability to Dean of Students.

**2007-2008 Annual costs.** Tuition/fees: $11,340. Books/supplies: $550. Personal expenses: $500.

**Application procedures. Admission:** No deadline. $50 fee, may be waived for applicants with need. Admission notification on a rolling basis. **Financial aid:** Priority date 6/1; no closing date. FAFSA, institutional form required. Applicants notified on a rolling basis starting 11/1.

**Academics.** All education programs relate specifically to Jewish Studies. For bachelor's in Jewish Studies, 42 liberal arts credits from another accredited college or university required. **Special study options:** Cross-registration, distance learning, double major, independent study, internships, study abroad, teacher certification program. **Credit/placement by examination:** CLEP, institutional tests. **Support services:** Reduced course load, remedial instruction, tutoring.

**Majors. Philosophy/religion:** Judaic, religion.

**Computing on campus.** 4 workstations in library, student center. Wireless network available.

**Student life. Freshman orientation:** Available. Preregistration for classes offered. **Activities:** Choral groups, student government.

**Student services.** Adult student services, career counseling, financial aid counseling, personal counseling, placement for graduates.

**Contact.** E-mail: admissions@gratz.edu
Phone: (215) 635-7300 ext. 140 Toll-free number: (800) 475-4635 ext. 140
Fax: (215) 635-7399
Ruthann Crosby, Director of Student Life, Gratz College, 7605 Old York Road, Melrose Park, PA 19027

---

## Grove City College
**Grove City, Pennsylvania**
**www.gcc.edu**
CB member
CB code: 2277

- Private 4-year liberal arts college affiliated with Presbyterian Church (USA)
- Residential campus in small town
- 2,490 degree-seeking undergraduates: 1% part-time, 49% women, 1% African American, 2% Asian American, 1% Hispanic American, 1% international

- 55% of applicants admitted
- SAT or ACT (ACT writing optional), application essay, interview required
- 82% graduate within 6 years; 22% enter graduate study

**General.** Founded in 1876. Regionally accredited. **Degrees:** 537 bachelor's awarded. **Location:** 60 miles from Pittsburgh. **Calendar:** Semester, extensive summer session. **Full-time faculty:** 140 total; 81% have terminal degrees, less than 1% minority, 24% women. **Part-time faculty:** 71 total; 20% have terminal degrees, 1% minority, 46% women. **Class size:** 40% < 20, 46% 20-39, 8% 40-49, 5% 50-99, 1% >100.

**Freshman class profile.** 1,916 applied, 1,057 admitted, 655 enrolled.

| Mid 50% test scores | | | |
|---|---|---|---|
| SAT critical reading: | 570-700 | Rank in top quarter: | 83% |
| SAT math: | 570-690 | Rank in top tenth: | 52% |
| ACT composite: | 25-30 | Return as sophomores: | 90% |
| GPA 3.50 or higher: | 83% | Out-of-state: | 50% |
| GPA 3.0-3.49: | 15% | Live on campus: | 91% |
| GPA 2.0-2.99: | 2% | International: | 1% |

**Basis for selection.** High school record, GPA or class rank, test scores, recommendations, interview, character, and extracurricular activities very important. Audition required for music program. **Homeschooled:** Transcript of courses and grades, interview, letter of recommendation (nonparent) required. Outside activities important.

**High school preparation.** 17 units recommended. Recommended units include English 4, mathematics 3, social studies 2, history 2, science 3 (laboratory 2) and foreign language 3. Engineering, science, and math applicants must have 4 math and 4 science.

**2007-2008 Annual costs.** Tuition/fees: $11,500. Tuition includes cost of tablet PC and printer. Room/board: $6,134. Books/supplies: $900. Personal expenses: $350.

**2007-2008 Financial aid. Need-based:** 421 full-time freshmen applied for aid; 280 were judged to have need; 267 of these received aid. Average need met was 62%. Average scholarship/grant was $6,284. 70% of total undergraduate aid awarded as scholarships/grants, 30% as loans/jobs. **Non-need-based:** Awarded to 878 full-time undergraduates, including 233 freshmen. Scholarships awarded for academics, leadership, minority status. **Additional information:** Institutional aid applications required for institutional scholarships, loans, and student employment.

**Application procedures. Admission:** Closing date 2/1 (postmark date). $50 fee, may be waived for applicants with need. Application may be submitted online. Decision letters mailed 3/15. Must reply by 5/1. **Financial aid:** Closing date 4/15. Institutional form required. Applicants notified on a rolling basis starting 3/15; must reply by 5/1.

**Academics.** All students required to complete 3-year interdisciplinary humanities sequence, which includes religion, philosophy, history, philosophy of science, science/faith/technology, literature, art, and music. **Special study options:** Accelerated study, double major, independent study, internships, study abroad, teacher certification program, Washington semester. **Credit/placement by examination:** AP, CLEP, IB. **Support services:** Reduced course load, tutoring.

**Majors. Biology:** General, biochemistry, molecular. **Business:** Accounting, business admin, communications, entrepreneurial studies, international, managerial economics, marketing. **Communications:** General. **Computer sciences:** General, applications programming, systems analysis. **Education:** Biology, chemistry, early childhood, elementary, English, French, history, mathematics, music, physics, science, secondary, social studies, Spanish. **Engineering:** Electrical, mechanical. **Engineering technology:** Industrial management. **English:** English lit. **Foreign languages:** French, Spanish. **Health:** Predental, premedicine, preveterinary. **History:** General. **Interdisciplinary:** Math/computer science. **Legal studies:** Prelaw. **Math:** General. **Philosophy/religion:** Philosophy, religion. **Physical sciences:** Chemistry, physics. **Psychology:** General. **Social sciences:** Economics, political science, sociology. **Visual/performing arts:** Music management, music performance.

**Most popular majors.** Biology 11%, business/marketing 19%, education 12%, engineering/engineering technologies 9%, English 6%, history 7%, philosophy/religious studies 6%, social sciences 9%.

**Computing on campus.** PC or laptop required. 50 workstations in library, computer center. Dormitories wired for high-speed internet access and linked to campus network. Commuter students can connect to campus network. Online course registration, online library, helpline, repair service, student web hosting, wireless network available.

**Student life. Freshman orientation:** Available. Preregistration for classes offered. One-day programs in June. **Policies:** Alcohol not permitted on campus. Chapel program consists of lectures, vespers, and seminars. Students must attend 16 chapels per semester. Religious observance required. **Housing:** Guaranteed on-campus for all undergraduates. Single-sex dorms, apartments, substance-free housing available. **Activities:** Bands, campus ministries, choral groups, dance, drama, international student organizations, literary magazine, music ensembles, musical theater, opera, radio station, student government, student newspaper, symphony orchestra, TV station, Fellowship of Christian Athletes, Salt Company, Warriors for Christ, Young Life, Neuman club, College Republicans, College Democrats, outing club, orientation board, Life Advocates.

**Athletics.** NCAA. **Intercollegiate:** Baseball M, basketball, cheerleading M, cross-country, diving, football (tackle) M, golf, soccer, softball W, swimming, tennis, track and field, volleyball W, water polo W. **Intramural:** Badminton, basketball, bowling, football (non-tackle), golf M, handball M, racquetball, soccer W, softball, swimming W, tennis, volleyball. **Team name:** Wolverines.

**Student services.** Campus ministries, career counseling, student employment services, financial aid counseling, health services, minority student services, personal counseling, placement for graduates.

**Contact.** E-mail: admissions@gcc.edu
Phone: (724) 458-2100 Fax: (724) 458-3395
Jeffrey Mincey, Director of Admissions, Grove City College, 100 Campus Drive, Grove City, PA 16127-2104

## Gwynedd-Mercy College
**Gwynedd Valley, Pennsylvania**     **CB member**
www.gmc.edu     **CB code: 2278**

- Private 4-year health science and liberal arts college affiliated with Roman Catholic Church
- Residential campus in large town
- 1,933 degree-seeking undergraduates: 31% part-time, 75% women, 16% African American, 2% Asian American, 1% Hispanic American, 1% international
- 580 degree-seeking graduate students
- 42% of applicants admitted
- SAT or ACT (ACT writing optional) required
- 75% graduate within 6 years

**General.** Founded in 1948. Regionally accredited. Affiliated with the Religious Sisters of Mercy. 8-week evening sessions running 12 months for business and accounting majors. Accelerated degree program begins every 6 weeks. **Degrees:** 395 bachelor's, 224 associate awarded; master's offered. **Location:** 20 miles from Philadelphia. **Calendar:** Semester, limited summer session. **Full-time faculty:** 82 total; 62% have terminal degrees, 1% minority, 67% women. **Part-time faculty:** 223 total; 22% have terminal degrees, 7% minority, 57% women. **Class size:** 69% < 20, 27% 20-39, 1% 40-49, 2% 50-99, less than 1% >100. **Special facilities:** Lincoln-era collection, nursery laboratory school for early childhood education.

**Freshman class profile.** 3,311 applied, 1,400 admitted, 291 enrolled.

| Mid 50% test scores | | | |
|---|---|---|---|
| SAT critical reading: | 440-540 | Rank in top tenth: | 4% |
| SAT math: | 440-540 | Return as sophomores: | 75% |
| Rank in top quarter: | 26% | Out-of-state: | 11% |
| | | Live on campus: | 74% |

**Basis for selection.** School achievement record most important, followed by test scores and recommendations. Extracurricular activities considered. Nursing program very competitive.

**High school preparation.** 16 units required. Required units include English 4, mathematics 3, history 1, science 3 and academic electives 3. Chemistry required for applicants to nursing, cardiovascular, biology, medical technology programs. Biology required for cardiovascular, health information technology programs. Physics required for radiation therapy, medical technology, biology programs. Chemistry or physics required for respiratory therapy.

**2008-2009 Annual costs.** Tuition/fees (projected): $22,790. Tuition and fees for nursing and allied health programs $23,840 for full-time, and $570 per credit hour for part-time. Room/board: $8,990. Books/supplies: $650. Personal expenses: $1,000.

**2006-2007 Financial aid. Need-based:** 261 full-time freshmen applied for aid; 222 were judged to have need; 220 of these received aid. Average need met was 74%. Average scholarship/grant was $11,613; average loan $2,339. 66% of total undergraduate aid awarded as scholarships/grants, 34%

as loans/jobs. **Non-need-based:** Scholarships awarded for academics, leadership.

**Application procedures. Admission:** Closing date 8/20 (receipt date). $25 fee, may be waived for applicants with need. Application may be submitted online. Admission notification on a rolling basis beginning on or about 9/20. Must reply by May 1 or within 3 week(s) if notified thereafter. Nursing program usually filled by May 1. **Financial aid:** Priority date 3/1, closing date 7/15. FAFSA, institutional form required. Applicants notified on a rolling basis starting 3/1; must reply by 5/1 or within 2 week(s) of notification.

**Academics. Special study options:** Accelerated study, cooperative education, cross-registration, double major, dual enrollment of high school students, ESL, honors, independent study, internships, liberal arts/career combination, teacher certification program, weekend college. **Credit/placement by examination:** AP, CLEP, institutional tests. Credit by examination cannot be applied to open electives. **Support services:** Learning center, reduced course load, remedial instruction, study skills assistance, tutoring, writing center.

**Majors. Biology:** General. **Business:** Accounting, business admin. **Computer sciences:** General. **Education:** Biology, business, elementary, mathematics, special. **English:** English lit. **Family/consumer sciences:** Aging. **Health:** Cardiovascular technology, clinical lab science, medical radiologic technology/radiation therapy, medical records admin, nursing (RN), premedicine, preveterinary, respiratory therapy technology. **History:** General. **Math:** General. **Protective services:** Law enforcement admin. **Psychology:** General. **Social sciences:** Sociology.

**Most popular majors.** Business/marketing 41%, education 20%, health sciences 23%.

**Computing on campus.** 217 workstations in library, computer center, student center. Dormitories wired for high-speed internet access and linked to campus network. Commuter students can connect to campus network. Online course registration, online library, helpline, wireless network available.

**Student life. Freshman orientation:** Available. Preregistration for classes offered. Multiple full-day sessions offered during the summer. **Housing:** Coed dorms, special housing for disabled available. $250 deposit, deadline 5/1. **Activities:** Campus ministries, choral groups, drama, literary magazine, musical theater, student government, student newspaper, business society, honor societies, Mercy Corps, resident council, commuter club, education club, peer counseling, psychology/sociology club.

**Athletics. NCAA. Intercollegiate:** Baseball M, basketball, cross-country, field hockey W, golf M, lacrosse W, soccer, softball W, tennis, track and field, volleyball W. **Intramural:** Volleyball. **Team name:** Griffins.

**Student services.** Adult student services, campus ministries, career counseling, student employment services, financial aid counseling, health services, minority student services, on-campus daycare, personal counseling, placement for graduates.

**Contact.** E-mail: admissions@gmc.edu
Phone: (215) 646-7300 ext. 530 Toll-free number: (800) 342-5462
Fax: (215) 641-5556
James Abbuhl, Vice President for Enrollment Management,
Gwynedd-Mercy College, 1325 Sumneytown Pike, Gwynedd Valley, PA 19437-0901

## Harrisburg University of Science and Technology
**Harrisburg, Pennsylvania**
**www.harrisburgu.net**

- Private 4-year university
- Small city
- 141 degree-seeking undergraduates
- 86% of applicants admitted

**General.** Regionally accredited. **Degrees:** 8 bachelor's awarded; master's offered. **Calendar:** Trimester. **Full-time faculty:** 9 total. **Part-time faculty:** 17 total.

**Basis for selection.** Admissions based on high school record. SAT or ACT recommended. Interview and essay or personal statement recommended.

**Application procedures. Admission:** $30 fee. Admission notification on a rolling basis.

**Academics. Credit/placement by examination:** CLEP.

**Majors. Biology:** Biotechnology. **Business:** E-commerce. **Computer sciences:** General, information technology. **Conservation:** Environmental science. **Science technology:** Biological. **Social sciences:** Geography.

**Contact.** E-mail: admissions@harrisburgu.net
Phone: (717) 901-5160
Harrisburg University of Science and Technology, 304 Market Street, Harrisburg, PA 17101

## Haverford College
**Haverford, Pennsylvania**
**www.haverford.edu**
CB member
CB code: 2289

- Private 4-year liberal arts college
- Residential campus in large town
- 1,169 degree-seeking undergraduates: 54% women, 8% African American, 11% Asian American, 8% Hispanic American, 1% Native American, 4% international
- 25% of applicants admitted
- SAT or ACT with writing, SAT Subject Tests, application essay required
- 91% graduate within 6 years; 22% enter graduate study

**General.** Founded in 1833. Regionally accredited. Founded by the Society of Friends (Quakers), but now independent. **Degrees:** 289 bachelor's awarded. **Location:** 10 miles from Philadelphia. **Calendar:** Semester. **Full-time faculty:** 113 total; 95% have terminal degrees, 26% minority, 47% women. **Part-time faculty:** 16 total; 62% have terminal degrees, 19% minority, 62% women. **Class size:** 76% < 20, 19% 20-39, 3% 40-49, less than 1% 50-99. **Special facilities:** Observatory, arboretum, fine arts foundry.

**Freshman class profile.** 3,492 applied, 877 admitted, 315 enrolled.

| Mid 50% test scores | | Rank in top tenth: | 89% |
|---|---|---|---|
| SAT critical reading: | 650-750 | Return as sophomores: | 96% |
| SAT math: | 640-740 | Out-of-state: | 88% |
| SAT writing: | 650-740 | Live on campus: | 100% |
| Rank in top quarter: | 99% | International: | 2% |

**Basis for selection.** School record, test scores, extracurricular achievements, and recommendations important. College seeks diversity of social, economic, and geographic backgrounds. Some preference given to children of alumni. First-year applicants must take SAT or ACT plus 2 SAT Subject Tests before deadline for decision plan chosen. Interview required of applicants living within 150 miles of college, recommended for others. **Homeschooled:** Statement describing homeschool structure and mission, transcript of courses and grades, interview, letter of recommendation (nonparent) required.

**High school preparation.** 13 units required. Required and recommended units include English 4, mathematics 3-4, social studies 2, science 1-2 (laboratory 1) and foreign language 3.

**2007-2008 Annual costs.** Tuition/fees: $35,390. Room/board: $10,880. Books/supplies: $1,194. Personal expenses: $1,468.

**2007-2008 Financial aid.** All financial aid based on need. 182 full-time freshmen applied for aid; 142 were judged to have need; 142 of these received aid. Average need met was 100%. Average scholarship/grant was $29,084; average loan $2,905. 89% of total undergraduate aid awarded as scholarships/grants, 11% as loans/jobs.

**Application procedures. Admission:** Closing date 1/15. $60 fee, may be waived for applicants with need. Application may be submitted online. Admission notification 4/15. Must reply by May 1 or within 2 week(s) if notified thereafter. **Financial aid:** Closing date 1/31. FAFSA, CSS PROFILE required. Applicants notified by 4/8; must reply by 5/1.

**Academics.** Academic Flexibility Program allows for advanced independent work and interdepartmental majors. Ample opportunity for student-faculty research. Senior seminars, comprehensive examination and/or senior thesis required for completion of all major programs. **Special study options:** Cross-registration, double major, exchange student, independent study, internships, liberal arts/career combination, student-designed major, study abroad, teacher certification program. Exchange programs with Spelman College (GA), Claremont McKenna College and Pitzer College (CA), Fisk University (TN); cross-registration with Bryn Mawr College, Swarthmore College, noncredit internships also available; 3-2 engineering program with California Institute of Technology. **Credit/placement by examination:** AP, CLEP, IB, SAT, ACT, institutional tests. **Support services:** Learning center, study skills assistance, tutoring, writing center.

**Majors. Architecture:** Urban/community planning. **Area/ethnic studies:** East Asian. **Biology:** General. **Computer sciences:** General. **English:** English lit. **Foreign languages:** Ancient Greek, classics, comparative lit, French, German, Italian, Latin, Russian, Spanish. **History:** General. **Liberal arts:** Arts/sciences. **Math:** General. **Philosophy/religion:** Philosophy, religion. **Physical sciences:** Astronomy, chemistry, geology, physics. **Psychology:** General. **Social sciences:** Anthropology, archaeology, economics, political science, sociology, urban studies. **Visual/performing arts:** Art history/conservation, studio arts.

**Most popular majors.** Biology 15%, history 9%, liberal arts 7%, philosophy/religious studies 6%, physical sciences 11%, psychology 7%, social sciences 29%.

**Computing on campus.** 300 workstations in dormitories, library, computer center, student center. Dormitories wired for high-speed internet access and linked to campus network. Commuter students can connect to campus network. Online course registration, online library, helpline, student web hosting, wireless network available.

**Student life. Freshman orientation:** Mandatory, $180 fee. Preregistration for classes offered. Directly precedes the start of the fall semester. **Policies:** Student conduct regulated by academic and social honor code, which allows for unsupervised examinations. Students serve on campus governance and policy-making committees. **Housing:** Guaranteed on-campus for all undergraduates. Coed dorms, single-sex dorms, apartments, substance-free housing available. Students may live at Bryn Mawr College through dormitory exchange program. Students at both colleges may eat meals on either campus. **Activities:** Campus ministries, choral groups, dance, drama, international student organizations, literary magazine, music ensembles, musical theater, radio station, student government, student newspaper, Quaker activities committee, Hillel, Christian Fellowship, environmental action committee, black students league, Puerto Rican students association, Asian students association, Bisexual/Gay/Lesbian alliance, Eighth Dimension Volunteer Service Program.

**Athletics. NCAA. Intercollegiate:** Baseball M, basketball, cricket M, cross-country, fencing, field hockey W, lacrosse, soccer, softball W, squash, tennis, track and field, volleyball W. **Intramural:** Basketball, soccer, tennis.

**Student services.** Alcohol/substance abuse counseling, campus ministries, career counseling, student employment services, financial aid counseling, health services, minority student services, personal counseling, placement for graduates, women's services. **Physically disabled:** Services for visually, speech, hearing impaired.

**Contact.** E-mail: admission@haverford.edu
Phone: (610) 896-1350 Fax: (610) 896-1338
Jess Lord, Dean of Admission and Financial Aid, Haverford College, 370 Lancaster Avenue, Haverford, PA 19041-1392

---

## Holy Family University
### Philadelphia, Pennsylvania
**www.holyfamily.edu**

CB member
CB code: 2297

- Private 4-year university and liberal arts college affiliated with Roman Catholic Church
- Commuter campus in very large city
- 2,122 degree-seeking undergraduates: 32% part-time, 76% women
- 1,167 degree-seeking graduate students
- 57% of applicants admitted
- SAT or ACT (ACT writing optional) required
- 69% graduate within 6 years; 3% enter graduate study

**General.** Founded in 1954. Regionally accredited. Additional campuses in Newtown, Bensalem, and South Philadelphia. **Degrees:** 342 bachelor's, 23 associate awarded; master's offered. **Location:** 12 miles from downtown. **Calendar:** Semester, extensive summer session. **Full-time faculty:** 99 total; 70% have terminal degrees, 11% minority, 65% women. **Part-time faculty:** 275 total; 12% have terminal degrees, 12% minority, 55% women. **Class size:** 79% < 20, 21% 20-39. **Special facilities:** Early childhood center with nursery school and kindergarten.

**Freshman class profile.** 1,097 applied, 626 admitted, 322 enrolled.

| Mid 50% test scores | | | |
|---|---|---|---|
| SAT critical reading: | 430-510 | GPA 2.0-2.99: | 23% |
| SAT math: | 420-510 | End year in good standing: | 85% |
| SAT writing: | 410-490 | Return as sophomores: | 85% |
| ACT composite: | 19-20 | Out-of-state: | 15% |
| GPA 3.50 or higher: | 13% | Live on campus: | 25% |
| GPA 3.0-3.49: | 64% | International: | 1% |

**Basis for selection.** High school record most important, followed by recommendations, interview and test scores. Motivation, schoolwork and community activities considered. Essay, interview recommended. **Home-schooled:** State-issued equivalency diploma required. **Learning Disabled:** Students must meet with Counseling Center to be evaluated. Results and formal report shared with Admission department and acceptance decision is made. Results discussed with student.

**High school preparation.** 14 units required; 16 recommended. Required and recommended units include English 4, mathematics 3, history 2, science 2, foreign language 2 and academic electives 3. All students must have algebra I, algebra II, and geometry. Math majors need trigonometry. Nursing requires biology, chemistry, and science electives. Science requires biology, chemistry, and trigonometry.

**2008-2009 Annual costs.** Tuition/fees: $21,590. Room/board: $9,400. Books/supplies: $948. Personal expenses: $600.

**2006-2007 Financial aid. Need-based:** Average need met was 89%. 49% of total undergraduate aid awarded as scholarships/grants, 51% as loans/jobs. **Non-need-based:** Scholarships awarded for academics, alumni affiliation, athletics.

**Application procedures. Admission:** No deadline. $25 fee, may be waived for applicants with need. Application may be submitted online. Admission notification on a rolling basis. Must reply by May 1 or within 2 week(s) if notified thereafter. **Financial aid:** Priority date 3/1; no closing date. FAFSA, institutional form required. Applicants notified on a rolling basis starting 3/15; must reply within 2 week(s) of notification.

**Academics. Special study options:** Accelerated study, combined bachelor's/graduate degree, cooperative education, double major, dual enrollment of high school students, independent study, internships, study abroad, teacher certification program. **Credit/placement by examination:** AP, CLEP, IB, institutional tests. 30 credit hours maximum toward bachelor's degree. **Support services:** Pre-admission summer program, remedial instruction, study skills assistance, tutoring, writing center.

**Majors. Biology:** General, biochemistry. **Business:** Accounting, business admin, finance, human resources, international, management information systems. **Communications:** Media studies. **Education:** Art, biology, chemistry, early childhood, elementary, English, French, history, mathematics, social science, social studies, Spanish, special. **English:** American lit, English lit. **Foreign languages:** French, Spanish. **Health:** Clinical lab science, nursing (RN), radiologic technology/medical imaging. **History:** General. **Liberal arts:** Humanities. **Math:** General. **Parks/recreation:** Sports admin. **Philosophy/religion:** Religion. **Physical sciences:** Chemistry. **Protective services:** Criminal justice, fire services admin. **Psychology:** General, industrial. **Public administration:** Social work. **Social sciences:** Economics, sociology. **Visual/performing arts:** Studio arts.

**Most popular majors.** Business/marketing 24%, education 26%, health sciences 27%.

**Computing on campus.** 300 workstations in dormitories, library, computer center. Dormitories wired for high-speed internet access and linked to campus network. Commuter students can connect to campus network. Online course registration, online library, helpline, repair service, wireless network available.

**Student life. Freshman orientation:** Mandatory. **Policies:** Mature and intelligent student conduct expected in accordance with college's interests, standards, and ideals. **Housing:** Guaranteed on-campus for freshmen. Coed dorms, apartments, substance-free housing available. $200 nonrefundable deposit, deadline 3/15. On-campus housing available for some athletes. **Activities:** Campus ministries, choral groups, drama, literary magazine, music ensembles, musical theater, radio station, student government, student newspaper, TV station, community health and welfare organizations, social and departmental clubs, honor societiesministry team.

**Athletics. NCAA. Intercollegiate:** Basketball, cross-country, golf M, lacrosse W, soccer, softball W, tennis W, track and field, volleyball W. **Intramural:** Basketball, bowling, cheerleading W, football (non-tackle), racquetball, table tennis, volleyball. **Team name:** Tigers.

**Student services.** Adult student services, alcohol/substance abuse counseling, campus ministries, career counseling, student employment services, financial aid counseling, health services, minority student services, personal counseling, placement for graduates. **Physically disabled:** Services for visually, speech, hearing impaired. **Learning disabled:** Comprehensive services available.

**Contact.** E-mail: undergra@holyfamily.edu
Phone: (215) 637-3050 Toll-free number: (800) 637-1191
Fax: (215) 281-1022
Lauren Campbell, Director of Admissions, Holy Family University, 9801 Frankford Avenue, Philadelphia, PA 19114-2009

## Immaculata University
### Immaculata, Pennsylvania
www.immaculata.edu

CB member
CB code: 2320

- Private 4-year university and liberal arts college affiliated with Roman Catholic Church
- Residential campus in large town
- 2,647 degree-seeking undergraduates: 61% part-time, 77% women, 10% African American, 2% Asian American, 2% Hispanic American, 1% international
- 933 degree-seeking graduate students
- 80% of applicants admitted
- SAT or ACT (ACT writing recommended) required
- 55% graduate within 6 years

**General.** Founded in 1920. Regionally accredited. **Degrees:** 437 bachelor's, 31 associate awarded; master's, doctoral offered. **Location:** 20 miles from Philadelphia. **Calendar:** Semester, limited summer session. **Full-time faculty:** 100 total; 74% have terminal degrees, 6% minority, 71% women. **Part-time faculty:** 321 total; 26% have terminal degrees, 57% women. **Class size:** 77% < 20, 23% 20-39, less than 1% 40-49.

**Freshman class profile.** 1,335 applied, 1,071 admitted, 286 enrolled.

| Mid 50% test scores | | | |
|---|---|---|---|
| SAT critical reading: | 440-540 | GPA 2.0-2.99: | 38% |
| SAT math: | 410-530 | Return as sophomores: | 70% |
| GPA 3.50 or higher: | 28% | Out-of-state: | 38% |
| GPA 3.0-3.49: | 32% | Live on campus: | 84% |

**Basis for selection.** Class rank, academic program, test scores, counselor recommendation important. Minimum 2.3 GPA preferred. Interviews, essay recommended. Audition required for music program. **Homeschooled:** Transcript of courses and grades required. **Learning Disabled:** Proof of psychological or educational testing date must be supplied.

**High school preparation.** 16 units required; 20 recommended. Required and recommended units include English 4, mathematics 2-3, social studies 2-3, science 2-4 (laboratory 1), foreign language 2-3 and academic electives 4. Music required for music majors.

**2007-2008 Annual costs.** Tuition/fees: $22,650. Tuition and fees for entering freshmen guaranteed to not increase for the 4 years they are enrolled. Room/board: $9,800.

**2007-2008 Financial aid. Need-based:** 254 full-time freshmen applied for aid; 225 were judged to have need; 225 of these received aid. Average need met was 26%. Average scholarship/grant was $5,907; average loan $3,507. 41% of total undergraduate aid awarded as scholarships/grants, 59% as loans/jobs. **Non-need-based:** Awarded to 822 full-time undergraduates, including 267 freshmen. Scholarships awarded for academics, alumni affiliation, art, job skills, leadership, minority status, music/drama, religious affiliation, state residency.

**Application procedures. Admission:** Priority date 3/1; no deadline. $35 fee, may be waived for applicants with need. Application may be submitted online. Admission notification on a rolling basis beginning on or about 9/15. Must reply by May 1 or within 2 week(s) if notified thereafter. **Financial aid:** Priority date 2/15, closing date 4/15. FAFSA required. Applicants notified on a rolling basis starting 2/1; must reply within 2 week(s) of notification.

**Academics. Special study options:** Accelerated study, combined bachelor's/graduate degree, cross-registration, distance learning, double major, dual enrollment of high school students, honors, independent study, internships, liberal arts/career combination, semester at sea, study abroad, teacher certification program, Washington semester. **Credit/placement by examination:** AP, CLEP, IB, SAT, ACT, institutional tests. 30 credit hours maximum toward associate degree, 63 toward bachelor's. **Support services:** Learning center, reduced course load, remedial instruction, study skills assistance, tutoring, writing center.

**Majors. Biology:** General. **Business:** Accounting, business admin, fashion, finance, human resources. **Computer sciences:** Information systems. **Conservation:** Environmental studies. **Education:** Business, elementary, family/consumer sciences, music. **English:** English lit. **Foreign languages:** French, German, Spanish. **Health:** Dietetics, health care admin, music therapy, nursing (RN), premedicine. **History:** General. **Interdisciplinary:** Biological/physical sciences, biopsychology, math/computer science. **Math:** General. **Parks/recreation:** Exercise sciences. **Physical sciences:** Chemistry. **Protective services:** Criminal justice. **Psychology:** General. **Public administration:** Policy analysis. **Social sciences:** Economics, international relations, political science, sociology. **Theology:** Theology. **Visual/performing arts:** Music performance.

**Most popular majors.** Business/marketing 38%, health sciences 43%.

**Computing on campus.** 326 workstations in dormitories, library, computer center, student center. Dormitories wired for high-speed internet access and linked to campus network. Commuter students can connect to campus network. Online course registration, online library, helpline, wireless network available.

**Student life. Freshman orientation:** Mandatory. Preregistration for classes offered. 2-day session held in summer. **Housing:** Coed dorms, single-sex dorms, special housing for disabled, apartments available. $250 partly refundable deposit. **Activities:** Bands, campus ministries, choral groups, dance, drama, international student organizations, literary magazine, music ensembles, musical theater, student government, student newspaper, symphony orchestra, African American cultural society, American Music Therapy Association, Modern Foreign Language Association.

**Athletics.** NCAA. **Intercollegiate:** Basketball, cross-country W, field hockey W, golf, lacrosse, soccer, softball W, tennis, volleyball W. **Intramural:** Basketball, cross-country W, field hockey W, lacrosse W, soccer W, softball W, swimming W, tennis W, volleyball W. **Team name:** Mighty Macs.

**Student services.** Adult student services, alcohol/substance abuse counseling, campus ministries, career counseling, student employment services, financial aid counseling, health services, minority student services, personal counseling, placement for graduates. **Physically disabled:** Services for visually, hearing impaired.

**Contact.** E-mail: admiss@immaculata.edu
Phone: (610) 647-4400 ext. 3060 Toll-free number: (877) 428-6329
Fax: (610) 640-0836
Rebecca Bowlby, Director of Admission, Immaculata University, PO Box 642, Immaculata, PA 19345-0642

## Indiana University of Pennsylvania
### Indiana, Pennsylvania
www.iup.edu

CB member
CB code: 2652

- Public 4-year university
- Residential campus in large town
- 11,338 degree-seeking undergraduates: 6% part-time, 55% women, 11% African American, 1% Asian American, 2% Hispanic American, 1% international
- 2,162 degree-seeking graduate students
- 65% of applicants admitted
- SAT or ACT (ACT writing optional) required
- 51% graduate within 6 years

**General.** Founded in 1875. Regionally accredited. Branch campuses located in Punxsutawney and Armstrong County. **Degrees:** 2,314 bachelor's, 8 associate awarded; master's, doctoral offered. **ROTC:** Army. **Location:** 50 miles from Pittsburgh. **Calendar:** Semester, extensive summer session. **Full-time faculty:** 645 total; 13% minority, 47% women. **Part-time faculty:** 75 total; 3% minority, 64% women. **Special facilities:** Museums, ski slopes, nature preserve, lodge, and sailing base.

**Freshman class profile.** 9,322 applied, 6,013 admitted, 2,550 enrolled.

| Mid 50% test scores | | | |
|---|---|---|---|
| SAT critical reading: | 430-530 | Rank in top tenth: | 9% |
| SAT math: | 430-540 | Return as sophomores: | 73% |
| SAT writing: | 420-520 | Out-of-state: | 5% |
| Rank in top quarter: | 28% | International: | 1% |

**Basis for selection.** School achievement record, recommendations and extracurricular activities considered, test scores, and high school rank important. Audition required for music program; portfolio required for art program. **Homeschooled:** Transcript of courses and grades required.

**High school preparation.** 4 units recommended. Recommended units include English 3, mathematics 3, social studies 3, science 3 and foreign language 2. Additional .5 unit computer science recommended.

**2007-2008 Annual costs.** Tuition/fees: $6,695; $14,461 out-of-state. Required fees for out-of-state students: $1,606. Tuition for OH, VA, WV, IN and MI residents; branch campus students from any state; out of state students with a high school GPA of at least 3.0, or any transfer student with GPA of at least 3.0 is $7,766. Room/board: $5,442. Books/supplies: $1,000. Personal expenses: $2,633.

**2006-2007 Financial aid. Need-based:** 2,221 full-time freshmen applied for aid; 1,706 were judged to have need; 1,695 of these received aid. Average need met was 78%. Average scholarship/grant was $5,512; average loan $2,973. 47% of total undergraduate aid awarded as scholarships/grants, 53% as loans/jobs. **Non-need-based:** Awarded to 2,053 full-time undergraduates, including 738 freshmen. Scholarships awarded for academics, alumni affiliation, art, athletics, job skills, leadership, music/drama, ROTC, state residency.

**Application procedures. Admission:** Priority date 12/31; no deadline. $35 fee, may be waived for applicants with need. Application may be submitted online. Admission notification on a rolling basis beginning on or about 9/1. Must reply by May 1 or within 2 week(s) if notified thereafter. **Financial aid:** Priority date 4/15; no closing date. FAFSA required. Applicants notified on a rolling basis starting 3/15.

**Academics. Special study options:** Accelerated study, combined bachelor's/graduate degree, cooperative education, cross-registration, distance learning, double major, dual enrollment of high school students, ESL, exchange student, external degree, honors, independent study, internships, liberal arts/career combination, student-designed major, study abroad, teacher certification program, urban semester, Washington semester, weekend college. **Credit/placement by examination:** AP, CLEP, IB, SAT, ACT, institutional tests. Unlimited number of hours of credit by examination may be counted toward degree. **Support services:** Learning center, pre-admission summer program, remedial instruction, study skills assistance, tutoring, writing center.

**Majors. Architecture:** Urban/community planning. **Biology:** General, biochemistry. **Business:** General, accounting, business admin, fashion, finance, hospitality admin, human resources, international, management information systems, marketing, office management. **Communications:** General, journalism. **Computer sciences:** General. **Education:** Deaf/hearing impaired, early childhood, elementary, physically handicapped, social science, special, speech impaired, trade/industrial. **Engineering technology:** Occupational safety. **English:** English lit. **Family/consumer sciences:** General, consumer economics, family studies, food/nutrition. **Foreign languages:** French, German, Spanish. **Health:** Clinical lab science, environmental health, nuclear medical technology, nursing (RN), respiratory therapy technology. **History:** General. **Interdisciplinary:** Biological/physical sciences. **Math:** General, applied. **Parks/recreation:** Health/fitness. **Philosophy/religion:** Philosophy, religion. **Physical sciences:** General, applied physics, chemistry, geology, physics. **Psychology:** General. **Social sciences:** Anthropology, criminology, economics, geography, international relations, political science, sociology. **Visual/performing arts:** Art, dramatic, multimedia, music performance, studio arts. **Other:** Disability services, Economics and mathematics, French for international trade.

**Most popular majors.** Business/marketing 23%, communications/journalism 8%, education 8%, family/consumer sciences 6%, health sciences 7%, social sciences 16%, visual/performing arts 9%.

**Computing on campus.** 3,500 workstations in dormitories, library, computer center. Dormitories wired for high-speed internet access and linked to campus network. Commuter students can connect to campus network. Online course registration, helpline, repair service, student web hosting, wireless network available.

**Student life. Freshman orientation:** Mandatory, $140 fee. Preregistration for classes offered. **Housing:** Guaranteed on-campus for freshmen. Coed dorms, special housing for disabled, apartments, substance-free housing available. $80 nonrefundable deposit, deadline 5/15. Honors college dormitory, substance-free housing, academic specialty floors available. **Activities:** Bands, campus ministries, choral groups, dance, drama, international student organizations, music ensembles, musical theater, radio station, student government, student newspaper, symphony orchestra, TV station, Alpha Phi Omega National Service Fraternity (coeducational), Gamma Sigma Sigma Service Sorority, African American Cultural Center, Campus Crusade for Christ, Coalition for Christian Outreach, Newman Center, Panhellenic Association, NAACP.

**Athletics.** NCAA. **Intercollegiate:** Baseball M, basketball, cross-country, diving, field hockey W, football (tackle) M, golf M, lacrosse W, soccer W, softball W, swimming, tennis W, track and field, volleyball W. **Intramural:** Archery, badminton, basketball, bowling, cross-country, fencing, football (non-tackle), golf, racquetball, soccer, softball, table tennis, tennis, track and field, volleyball, water polo, weight lifting, wrestling M. **Team name:** Crimson Hawks.

**Student services.** Adult student services, alcohol/substance abuse counseling, campus ministries, career counseling, services for economically disadvantaged, student employment services, financial aid counseling, health services, legal services, minority student services, on-campus daycare, personal counseling, placement for graduates, veterans' counselor, women's services. **Physically disabled:** Services for visually, speech, hearing impaired.

**Contact.** E-mail: admissions_inquiry@iup.edu
Phone: (724) 357-2230 Toll-free number: (800) 442-6830
Fax: (724) 357-6281
Rhonda Luckey, Vice President for Student Affairs, Indiana University of Pennsylvania, 117 John Sutton Hall, 1011 South Drive, Indiana, PA 15705-1088

## Juniata College

**Huntingdon, Pennsylvania**
www.juniata.edu

**CB member**
**CB code: 2341**

- Private 4-year liberal arts college
- Residential campus in small town
- 1,410 degree-seeking undergraduates: 1% part-time, 55% women
- 67% of applicants admitted
- Application essay required
- 77% graduate within 6 years; 31% enter graduate study

**General.** Founded in 1876. Regionally accredited. **Degrees:** 350 bachelor's awarded. **Location:** 30 miles from Altoona and State College. **Calendar:** Semester, limited summer session. **Full-time faculty:** 97 total; 92% have terminal degrees, 6% minority, 37% women. **Part-time faculty:** 36 total; 28% have terminal degrees, 3% minority, 56% women. **Class size:** 70% < 20, 26% 20-39, 4% 40-49, less than 1% 50-99. **Special facilities:** Nature preserve, environmental studies field station, observatory, early childhood education center.

**Freshman class profile.** 1,958 applied, 1,318 admitted, 377 enrolled.

| Mid 50% test scores | | Rank in top tenth: | 36% |
|---|---|---|---|
| SAT critical reading: | 530-630 | End year in good standing: | 98% |
| SAT math: | 540-630 | Return as sophomores: | 84% |
| GPA 3.50 or higher: | 69% | Out-of-state: | 39% |
| GPA 3.0-3.49: | 25% | Live on campus: | 97% |
| GPA 2.0-2.99: | 6% | International: | 4% |
| Rank in top quarter: | 77% | | |

**Basis for selection.** School achievement record most important. Standardized test scores, school and community activities, recommendations and essay also important. SAT or ACT recommended. Students may submit SAT or ACT scores either directly from the testing agency or from the guidance counselor. If a student chooses not to submit standardized test scores, then must submit two graded papers. Interview recommended. **Homeschooled:** Interview required.

**High school preparation.** 16 units required; 18 recommended. Required and recommended units include English 4, mathematics 3-4, social studies 1, history 3, science 3-4 (laboratory 2) and foreign language 2.

**2008-2009 Annual costs.** Tuition/fees (projected): $30,280. Room/board: $8,420. Books/supplies: $600. Personal expenses: $1,000.

**2007-2008 Financial aid. Need-based:** 315 full-time freshmen applied for aid; 271 were judged to have need; 271 of these received aid. Average need met was 85%. Average scholarship/grant was $17,666; average loan $4,315. 75% of total undergraduate aid awarded as scholarships/grants, 25% as loans/jobs. **Non-need-based:** Awarded to 535 full-time undergraduates, including 160 freshmen. Scholarships awarded for academics, art.

**Application procedures. Admission:** Priority date 12/1; deadline 3/15 (postmark date). $30 fee, may be waived for applicants with need. Application may be submitted online. Admission notification on a rolling basis beginning on or about 2/28. Must reply by May 1 or within 2 week(s) if notified thereafter. **Financial aid:** Closing date 3/1. FAFSA required. Applicants notified on a rolling basis starting 2/21; must reply by 5/1.

**Academics.** Majors replaced by Programs of Emphasis. Over 50% of students design individualized POE. **Special study options:** Combined bachelor's/graduate degree, distance learning, double major, dual enrollment of high school students, ESL, exchange student, honors, independent study, internships, student-designed major, study abroad, teacher certification program, urban semester, Washington semester. Marine biology with Oregon Marine Program; 3-3 law with Duquesne University; 3-2 engineering with Columbia University, Pennsylvania State University, Clarkson University, Washington University; 3-4 dentistry with Temple University; 3-4 medicine with Tulane University School of Medicine, Lake Erie College of Osteopathic Medicine; 3-4 optometry with Pennsylvania College of Optometry; 3-4 podiatry with Temple University School of Podiatric Medicine and Ohio College of Podiatric Medicine; nursing with Jefferson College of Health Professions, Johns Hopkins University, Case Western Reserve University; biotechnology, cytogenetics/cytotechnology, diagnostic imaging/cardiovascular technology, occupational therapy with Jefferson College of

Health Professions; physical therapy with Widener University, Drexel University; medical technology with Jefferson College of Health Professions, Altoona Regional Health Systems, Lancaster General College of Nursing & Health Sciences. **Credit/placement by examination:** AP, CLEP, IB, institutional tests. Unlimited number of hours of credit by examination may be counted toward degree. **Support services:** Reduced course load, study skills assistance, tutoring, writing center.

**Majors. Biology:** General, biochemistry, botany, cell/histology, ecology, marine, microbiology, molecular, zoology. **Business:** General, accounting, business admin, entrepreneurial studies, finance, human resources, information resources management, international, marketing. **Communications:** General, digital media, health. **Computer sciences:** General, information technology. **Conservation:** Environmental science, environmental studies, wildlife. **Education:** General, biology, chemistry, early childhood, early childhood special, elementary, English, French, German, mathematics, multi-level teacher, physics, science, secondary, social studies, Spanish, special. **Engineering:** General, physics. **English:** English lit. **Foreign languages:** General, French, German, Russian, Spanish. **Health:** Predental, premedicine, prenursing, prepharmacy, preveterinary. **History:** General. **Interdisciplinary:** Global studies, museum, natural sciences, peace/conflict. **Legal studies:** Prelaw. **Liberal arts:** Arts/sciences, humanities. **Math:** General. **Philosophy/religion:** Philosophy, religion. **Physical sciences:** General, chemistry, geology, physics. **Psychology:** General. **Public administration:** General, social work. **Social sciences:** General, anthropology, criminology, international relations, political science, sociology. **Visual/performing arts:** Art history/conservation, dramatic, studio arts, theater arts management.

**Most popular majors.** Biology 17%, business/marketing 13%, education 8%, interdisciplinary studies 9%, physical sciences 9%, psychology 6%, social sciences 10%.

**Computing on campus.** 360 workstations in library, computer center, student center. Dormitories wired for high-speed internet access and linked to campus network. Commuter students can connect to campus network. Online course registration, online library, helpline, repair service, wireless network available.

**Student life. Freshman orientation:** Available. Preregistration for classes offered. 2 days in summer, parallel programs for new students and their parents. **Housing:** Guaranteed on-campus for all undergraduates. Coed dorms, single-sex dorms, apartments, substance-free housing available. $400 nonrefundable deposit, deadline 5/1. Special interest housing available. **Activities:** Bands, campus ministries, choral groups, dance, drama, film society, international student organizations, literary magazine, music ensembles, Model UN, musical theater, radio station, student government, student newspaper, symphony orchestra, Catholic Council, Fellowship of Christian Athletes, emergency services club, Habitat for Humanity, outreach club, responsible justice coalition.

**Athletics.** NCAA. **Intercollegiate:** Baseball M, basketball, cross-country, field hockey W, football (tackle) M, soccer, softball W, swimming W, tennis, track and field, volleyball. **Intramural:** Basketball, bowling, soccer, volleyball. **Team name:** Eagles.

**Student services.** Adult student services, alcohol/substance abuse counseling, campus ministries, career counseling, student employment services, financial aid counseling, health services, personal counseling, placement for graduates. **Physically disabled:** Services for visually, hearing impaired.

**Contact.** E-mail: admissions@juniata.edu
Phone: (814) 641-3420 Toll-free number: (877) 586-4282
Fax: (814) 641-3100
Michelle Bartol, Dean of Enrollment, Juniata College, 1800 Moore Street, Huntingdon, PA 16652-2196

---

## Keystone College
La Plume, Pennsylvania
www.keystone.edu

CB member
CB code: 2351

- Private 4-year junior and liberal arts college
- Residential campus in small town
- 1,757 degree-seeking undergraduates: 24% part-time, 62% women, 2% African American, 1% Hispanic American, 1% international
- 95% of applicants admitted
- SAT or ACT (ACT writing optional), application essay required

**General.** Founded in 1868. Regionally accredited. Students may enroll in up to 12 credits as nonmatriculating prior to making formal application to college. Trimester system for Adult Weekender Program. **Degrees:** 224 bachelor's, 89 associate awarded. **ROTC:** Army, Air Force. **Location:** 15 miles from Scranton. **Calendar:** Semester, limited summer session. **Full-time faculty:** 59 total; 37% have terminal degrees, 3% minority, 64% women. **Part-time faculty:** 189 total; 8% have terminal degrees, 3% minority, 53% women.

**Class size:** 79% < 20, 21% 20-39, less than 1% 40-49. **Special facilities:** Observatory, children's center, Microsoft-certified systems engineer training site, water discovery center, urban forestry center, restaurant (operated by culinary students), delayed harvest trout stream, Cisco training site, countryside conservancy, PRAXIS testing location.

**Freshman class profile.** 932 applied, 884 admitted, 376 enrolled.

| Mid 50% test scores | | | |
|---|---|---|---|
| SAT critical reading: | 380-490 | GPA 2.0-2.99: | 62% |
| SAT math: | 390-490 | Rank in top quarter: | 12% |
| SAT writing: | 390-490 | Rank in top tenth: | 2% |
| ACT composite: | 16-20 | Return as sophomores: | 70% |
| GPA 3.50 or higher: | 6% | Out-of-state: | 17% |
| GPA 3.0-3.49: | 24% | Live on campus: | 48% |
| | | International: | 1% |

**Basis for selection.** School achievement record, extracurricular activities, test scores, recommendations, class rank, preparation in proposed major area of study considered. Portfolio and interviews required for all art and art education applications. **Homeschooled:** Statement describing homeschool structure and mission, interview required. Portfolio of high school level work also required. **Learning Disabled:** Current psychological report and Individualized Educational Program or 504 plan should be submitted at time of application. On-campus interview generally required to ensure that the college provides a level of support needed for the student to be academically sucessful.

**High school preparation.** 15 units required. Required and recommended units include English 4, mathematics 3-4, social studies 2, history 2, science 2-3 (laboratory 1), foreign language 2 and academic electives 2. Foreign language recommended for art, communications, and liberal arts curricula. 4 math and 3 science (including 2 lab) recommended for allied health, environmental science, pre-medical tracks, and forensic biology.

**2007-2008 Annual costs.** Tuition/fees: $17,265. Room/board: $8,400. Books/supplies: $1,400. Personal expenses: $2,040.

**2006-2007 Financial aid. Need-based:** Average need met was 70%. Average scholarship/grant was $12,312; average loan $2,625. 56% of total undergraduate aid awarded as scholarships/grants, 44% as loans/jobs. **Non-need-based:** Awarded to 59 full-time undergraduates, including 13 freshmen. Scholarships awarded for academics, art, job skills, leadership, ROTC.

**Application procedures. Admission:** Priority date 5/1; deadline 7/1 (receipt date). $30 fee, may be waived for applicants with need. Application may be submitted online. Admission notification on a rolling basis. Must reply by May 1 or within 3 week(s) if notified thereafter. **Financial aid:** Priority date 5/1; no closing date. FAFSA required. Applicants notified on a rolling basis starting 2/2; must reply by 5/1 or within 2 week(s) of notification.

**Academics.** Students in good academic and financial standing who have not received at least 1 job offer or acceptance into transfer or graduate program within 6 months after graduating and fulfilling requirements of Career Development Center will be provided with additional courses and career counseling at no extra charge. **Special study options:** Combined bachelor's/graduate degree, cooperative education, cross-registration, distance learning, double major, dual enrollment of high school students, ESL, honors, independent study, internships, study abroad, teacher certification program, weekend college. 2-2, 2-3, 3+3, 4-3 programs with various 4-year institutions for students studying allied health, health sciences, and environmental sciences. **Credit/placement by examination:** AP, CLEP, IB, SAT, ACT, institutional tests. 12 credit hours maximum toward associate degree, 18 toward bachelor's. Maximum of 32 credits for associate degree-seekers and 64 credits for bachelor's degree-seekers awarded for prior work and/or life experience. **Support services:** Learning center, pre-admission summer program, reduced course load, remedial instruction, study skills assistance, tutoring, writing center.

**Honors college/program.** Admissions requirements 1100 SAT (exclusive of Writing), 24 ACT, top 10% of class or 3.0 GPA. Students who do not meet criteria considered on case-by-case basis.

**Majors. Biology:** General, biochemistry, biomedical sciences, environmental. **Business:** General, accounting, accounting/business management, business admin, management information systems. **Communications:** General, journalism. **Computer sciences:** General, information systems, information technology, LAN/WAN management, networking, systems analysis. **Conservation:** General, management/policy, water/wetlands/marine. **Education:** General, art, early childhood, elementary, mathematics, multi-level teacher, social studies. **Family/consumer sciences:** General, child care, child development, family systems. **Health:** Predental, premedicine, prepharmacy, preveterinary. **Interdisciplinary:** Biological/physical sciences, natural sciences. **Legal studies:** Prelaw. **Parks/recreation:** General, facilities management, sports admin. **Protective services:** Criminal justice, criminalistics, law enforcement admin. **Social sciences:** General. **Visual/**

**performing arts:** Art, ceramics, drawing, illustration, painting, printmaking, sculpture, studio arts.

**Computing on campus.** 120 workstations in dormitories, library, computer center, student center. Dormitories wired for high-speed internet access and linked to campus network. Commuter students can connect to campus network. Online course registration, helpline, wireless network available.

**Student life. Freshman orientation:** Mandatory, $125 fee. Preregistration for classes offered. One-day program during summer for placement testing. Multi-day overnight program prior to start of classes; includes canoeing, hiking, camping, volunteer service, theatre, creative writing, and music. **Housing:** Guaranteed on-campus for all undergraduates. Coed dorms, single-sex dorms, special housing for disabled, substance-free housing available. $100 nonrefundable deposit, deadline 5/1. Smoke-free housing. **Activities:** Campus ministries, choral groups, drama, international student organizations, literary magazine, musical theater, radio station, student government, student newspaper, art society, Phi Theta Kappa, Circle K, equestrian club, FADE (Facing Alcohol and Drugs Through Education), service learning, multi-ethnic cultural association.

**Athletics.** NCAA. **Intercollegiate:** Baseball M, basketball, cross-country, golf M, soccer, softball W, tennis, track and field, volleyball W. **Intramural:** Basketball, football (non-tackle), lacrosse, soccer, softball, table tennis, tennis, volleyball, weight lifting. **Team name:** Giants.

**Student services.** Adult student services, alcohol/substance abuse counseling, campus ministries, career counseling, services for economically disadvantaged, student employment services, financial aid counseling, health services, minority student services, on-campus daycare, personal counseling, placement for graduates, veterans' counselor, women's services.

**Contact.** E-mail: admissions@keystone.edu
Phone: (570) 945-8111 Toll-free number: (877) 426-5534
Fax: (570) 945-7916
Sarah Keating, Director of Admissions, Keystone College, One College Green, La Plume, PA 18440-1099

---

## King's College
### Wilkes-Barre, Pennsylvania
www.kings.edu

CB member
CB code: 2353

- Private 4-year business and liberal arts college affiliated with Roman Catholic Church
- Residential campus in small city
- 2,031 degree-seeking undergraduates: 5% part-time, 48% women, 2% African American, 1% Asian American, 3% Hispanic American
- 209 degree-seeking graduate students
- 78% of applicants admitted
- 72% graduate within 6 years; 27% enter graduate study

**General.** Founded in 1946. Regionally accredited. **Degrees:** 436 bachelor's, 2 associate awarded; master's offered. **ROTC:** Army, Air Force. **Location:** 110 miles from Philadelphia, 140 miles from New York City. **Calendar:** Semester, extensive summer session. **Full-time faculty:** 125 total; 81% have terminal degrees, 3% minority, 40% women. **Part-time faculty:** 83 total; 23% have terminal degrees, 1% minority, 47% women. **Class size:** 55% < 20, 44% 20-39, 1% 40-49. **Special facilities:** Rooftop greenhouse, molecular biology laboratory.

**Freshman class profile.** 2,107 applied, 1,651 admitted, 557 enrolled.

| Mid 50% test scores | | | |
|---|---|---|---|
| SAT critical reading: | 460-560 | Rank in top quarter: | 33% |
| SAT math: | 460-550 | Rank in top tenth: | 12% |
| GPA 3.50 or higher: | 37% | Return as sophomores: | 82% |
| GPA 3.0-3.49: | 34% | Out-of-state: | 33% |
| GPA 2.0-2.99: | 29% | Live on campus: | 71% |

**Basis for selection.** Class rank and academic GPA very important. Standardized test scores important. SAT or ACT recommended. Students may choose a standardized test option/essay choice in which an official graded writing sample from either junior or senior year is submitted and notarized by the high school guidance office. Students choosing this option are required to notify the Office of Admission on the application. A student's decision is non-reversible and must be made prior to application review. Interview recommended. **Homeschooled:** Transcript of courses and grades, state high school equivalency certificate required. **Learning Disabled:** Learning-disabled students applying for the first-year academic studies program must submit supplemental application with appropriate documentation. Contact Director of Academic Skills Center during admission process.

**High school preparation.** 16 units required; 22 recommended. Required and recommended units include English 4, mathematics 3-4, social studies 3-4, history 3-4, science 3-4 and foreign language 2-3.

**2007-2008 Annual costs.** Tuition/fees: $23,450. Room/board: $8,930.

**2007-2008 Financial aid. Need-based:** 523 full-time freshmen applied for aid; 459 were judged to have need; 459 of these received aid. Average need met was 78%. Average scholarship/grant was $12,479; average loan $4,140. 70% of total undergraduate aid awarded as scholarships/grants, 30% as loans/jobs. **Non-need-based:** Awarded to 521 full-time undergraduates, including 142 freshmen. Scholarships awarded for academics, leadership, ROTC. **Additional information:** Most minority students receive some aid in the form of a diversity scholarship.

**Application procedures. Admission:** No deadline. $30 fee, may be waived for applicants with need. Application may be submitted online. Admission notification on a rolling basis beginning on or about 10/1. Must reply by May 1 or within 2 week(s) if notified thereafter. **Financial aid:** Priority date 2/15; no closing date. FAFSA, institutional form required. Applicants notified on a rolling basis starting 3/1; must reply within 2 week(s) of notification.

**Academics. Special study options:** Accelerated study, cross-registration, distance learning, double major, dual enrollment of high school students, ESL, honors, independent study, internships, student-designed major, study abroad, teacher certification program, Washington semester, weekend college. Preprofessional programs in dentistry, medicine, pharmacy, veterinary science. **Credit/placement by examination:** AP, CLEP, IB, institutional tests. 15 credit hours maximum toward associate degree, 30 toward bachelor's. **Support services:** Learning center, pre-admission summer program, reduced course load, study skills assistance, tutoring, writing center.

**Majors. Biology:** General. **Business:** Accounting, business admin, finance, human resources, international, marketing. **Communications:** Media studies. **Computer sciences:** General, computer science. **Conservation:** Environmental science, environmental studies. **Education:** Early childhood, elementary, special. **English:** English lit. **Foreign languages:** French, Spanish. **Health:** Athletic training, clinical lab science, health services. **History:** General. **Interdisciplinary:** Biological/physical sciences, neuroscience. **Math:** General. **Philosophy/religion:** Philosophy. **Physical sciences:** Chemistry. **Protective services:** Criminal justice. **Psychology:** General. **Social sciences:** Economics, political science, sociology. **Theology:** Theology. **Visual/performing arts:** Dramatic.

**Most popular majors.** Business/marketing 28%, communications/journalism 8%, education 10%, psychology 7%, security/protective services 9%, social sciences 6%.

**Computing on campus.** 350 workstations in dormitories, library, computer center, student center. Dormitories wired for high-speed internet access and linked to campus network. Commuter students can connect to campus network. Online course registration, helpline, repair service, student web hosting, wireless network available.

**Student life. Freshman orientation:** Mandatory, $150 fee. Preregistration for classes offered. Held the 4 days prior to start of fall classes. **Housing:** Guaranteed on-campus for all undergraduates. Coed dorms, single-sex dorms, apartments available. $200 partly refundable deposit, deadline 8/8. **Activities:** Campus ministries, choral groups, dance, drama, literary magazine, music ensembles, radio station, student government, student newspaper, association of campus events, organizations of various majors, Campion Society, Blood Council, Circle K, politics society, environmental awareness and outdoors club, residence hall council, service fraternity and sorority.

**Athletics.** NCAA. **Intercollegiate:** Baseball M, basketball, cheerleading, cross-country, field hockey W, football (tackle) M, golf M, lacrosse, soccer, softball W, swimming, tennis, volleyball W, wrestling M. **Intramural:** Basketball, soccer. **Team name:** Monarchs.

**Student services.** Adult student services, campus ministries, career counseling, student employment services, financial aid counseling, health services, personal counseling, placement for graduates.

**Contact.** E-mail: admissions@kings.edu
Phone: (570) 208-5858 Toll-free number: (888) 546-4772
Fax: (570) 208-5971
Michelle Lawrence-Schmude, Director of Admissions, King's College, 133 North River Street, Wilkes-Barre, PA 18711

---

## Kutztown University of Pennsylvania
### Kutztown, Pennsylvania
www.kutztown.edu

CB member
CB code: 2653

- Public 4-year university
- Residential campus in small town

- 8,768 degree-seeking undergraduates: 6% part-time, 58% women, 7% African American, 1% Asian American, 4% Hispanic American, 1% international
- 719 degree-seeking graduate students
- 65% of applicants admitted
- SAT or ACT (ACT writing optional) required
- 55% graduate within 6 years

**General.** Founded in 1866. Regionally accredited. **Degrees:** 1,589 bachelor's awarded; master's offered. **ROTC:** Army. **Location:** 20 miles from Allentown and Reading. **Calendar:** Semester, extensive summer session. **Full-time faculty:** 437 total; 63% have terminal degrees, 13% minority, 45% women. **Part-time faculty:** 55 total; 7% minority, 53% women. **Class size:** 30% < 20, 54% 20-39, 4% 40-49, 7% 50-99, 5% >100. **Special facilities:** Observatory, on-campus preschool, Pennsylvania German heritage cultural center, planetarium.

**Freshman class profile.** 9,002 applied, 5,888 admitted, 1,902 enrolled.

| Mid 50% test scores | | | |
|---|---|---|---|
| SAT critical reading: | 440-530 | Rank in top tenth: | 6% |
| SAT math: | 440-540 | End year in good standing: | 78% |
| SAT writing: | 430-520 | Return as sophomores: | 78% |
| ACT composite: | 17-21 | Out-of-state: | 13% |
| GPA 3.50 or higher: | 18% | Live on campus: | 88% |
| GPA 3.0-3.49: | 33% | International: | 1% |
| GPA 2.0-2.99: | 49% | Fraternities: | 2% |
| Rank in top quarter: | 28% | Sororities: | 3% |

**Basis for selection.** School records and academic aptitude tests most important. Recommendations, essays, extracurricular activities considered. SAT Subject Tests (biology and chemistry) required for medical technology program. Audition required for music program; portfolio and/or art test required for art education, communication design, crafts, and fine arts programs. **Homeschooled:** Applicants must submit supporting data from Pennsylvania Home Schooling Association.

**High school preparation.** 16 units recommended. Recommended units include English 4, mathematics 3, social studies 4, science 3 and foreign language 2. Course recommendations vary for specific programs.

**2007-2008 Annual costs.** Tuition/fees: $6,873; $14,640 out-of-state. Room/board: $6,960. Books/supplies: $1,100. Personal expenses: $2,600.

**2006-2007 Financial aid. Need-based:** 1,739 full-time freshmen applied for aid; 1,212 were judged to have need; 1,212 of these received aid. Average need met was 52%. Average scholarship/grant was $4,917; average loan $2,496. 43% of total undergraduate aid awarded as scholarships/grants, 57% as loans/jobs. **Non-need-based:** Awarded to 618 full-time undergraduates, including 148 freshmen. Scholarships awarded for academics, art, athletics, leadership, minority status, music/drama, state residency.

**Application procedures. Admission:** Priority date 1/1; no deadline. $35 fee, may be waived for applicants with need. Application may be submitted online. Admission notification on a rolling basis beginning on or about 4/15. Must reply by May 1 or within 4 week(s) if notified thereafter. **Financial aid:** Priority date 2/15; no closing date. FAFSA required. Applicants notified on a rolling basis starting 3/30; must reply by 5/1 or within 4 week(s) of notification.

**Academics. Special study options:** Combined bachelor's/graduate degree, cross-registration, distance learning, double major, dual enrollment of high school students, honors, independent study, internships, liberal arts/career combination, student-designed major, study abroad, teacher certification program. **Credit/placement by examination:** AP, CLEP, IB, SAT, ACT, institutional tests. **Support services:** Learning center, pre-admission summer program, remedial instruction, study skills assistance, tutoring, writing center.

**Majors. Biology:** General. **Business:** Accounting, business admin, finance, human resources, international, management science, marketing. **Communications:** General, digital media. **Computer sciences:** Information technology. **Conservation:** Environmental science. **Education:** General, early childhood, elementary, kindergarten/preschool, reading, secondary, special, speech impaired, visually handicapped. **English:** English lit, speech/rhetoric, technical writing. **Foreign languages:** French, German, Russian, Spanish. **Health:** Clinical lab science, nursing (RN). **History:** General. **Interdisciplinary:** Biological/physical sciences. **Liberal arts:** Arts/sciences, library science. **Math:** General. **Philosophy/religion:** Philosophy. **Physical sciences:** Chemistry, geology, oceanography, physics. **Protective services:** Criminal justice. **Psychology:** General. **Public administration:** General, social work. **Social sciences:** General, anthropology, geography, political science, sociology. **Visual/performing arts:** General, art, commercial/advertising art, crafts, dramatic, studio arts.

**Most popular majors.** Business/marketing 15%, education 17%, English 8%, psychology 9%, security/protective services 6%, social sciences 8%, visual/performing arts 14%.

**Computing on campus.** 673 workstations in dormitories, library, computer center, student center. Dormitories wired for high-speed internet access and linked to campus network. Commuter students can connect to campus network. Online course registration, online library, helpline, student web hosting, wireless network available.

**Student life. Freshman orientation:** Mandatory, $80 fee. Preregistration for classes offered. 2-day, one overnight session in June, plus 2-day informational program preceding fall semester. **Policies:** No alcohol or drugs. **Housing:** Guaranteed on-campus for freshmen. Coed dorms, single-sex dorms, apartments, cooperative housing, substance-free housing available. $125 nonrefundable deposit, deadline 5/1. **Activities:** Bands, choral groups, dance, drama, film society, international student organizations, literary magazine, music ensembles, musical theater, radio station, student government, student newspaper, symphony orchestra, TV station, Student Alliance for Learning, Success and Achievement, black student union, Minority Achievement Coalition, Brothers and Sisters Seeking Excellence, Feminist Majority Leadership Alliance, Circle K, volunteer center, social work club.

**Athletics.** NCAA. **Intercollegiate:** Baseball M, basketball, cheerleading W, cross-country, field hockey W, football (tackle) M, golf W, soccer, softball W, swimming, tennis, track and field, volleyball W, wrestling M. **Intramural:** Badminton, basketball, cross-country, football (non-tackle), golf, soccer, softball, swimming, tennis, volleyball, weight lifting. **Team name:** Golden Bears.

**Student services.** Adult student services, alcohol/substance abuse counseling, career counseling, services for economically disadvantaged, student employment services, financial aid counseling, health services, minority student services, on-campus daycare, personal counseling, veterans' counselor, women's services. **Physically disabled:** Services for visually, speech, hearing impaired.

**Contact.** E-mail: admission@kutztown.edu
Phone: (610) 683-4060 Toll-free number: (877) 628-1915
Fax: (610) 683-1375
William Stahler, Director of Admissions, Kutztown University of Pennsylvania, Admissions Office, Kutztown, PA 19530-0730

---

## La Roche College
**Pittsburgh, Pennsylvania**
www.laroche.edu

CB member
CB code: 2379

- Private 4-year liberal arts college affiliated with Roman Catholic Church
- Commuter campus in large city
- 1,306 degree-seeking undergraduates: 13% part-time, 66% women, 5% African American, 1% Asian American, 1% Hispanic American, 1% Native American, 12% international
- 140 degree-seeking graduate students
- 73% of applicants admitted
- SAT or ACT required

**General.** Founded in 1963. Regionally accredited. Founded and sponsored by Sisters of Divine Providence. **Degrees:** 311 bachelor's, 23 associate awarded; master's offered. **ROTC:** Army, Air Force. **Calendar:** Semester, limited summer session. **Full-time faculty:** 64 total; 88% have terminal degrees, 8% minority, 50% women. **Part-time faculty:** 123 total; 17% have terminal degrees, 55% women. **Class size:** 74% < 20, 25% 20-39, less than 1% 40-49.

**Freshman class profile.** 944 applied, 685 admitted, 295 enrolled.

| Mid 50% test scores | | | |
|---|---|---|---|
| SAT critical reading: | 410-510 | GPA 2.0-2.99: | 36% |
| SAT math: | 410-510 | Rank in top quarter: | 24% |
| SAT writing: | 430-510 | Rank in top tenth: | 8% |
| ACT composite: | 15-19 | Out-of-state: | 8% |
| GPA 3.50 or higher: | 23% | Live on campus: | 76% |
| GPA 3.0-3.49: | 37% | International: | 17% |

**Basis for selection.** Depth and rigor of curriculum considered. Standardized test scores considered in relation to other factors. Recommendation from guidance counselor important. Extracurricular involvement considered. Essay, interview recommended.

**High school preparation.** 16 units required; 18 recommended. Required and recommended units include English 4, mathematics 3, social studies 3, history 3, science 3 (laboratory 2) and foreign language 2.

**2007-2008 Annual costs.** Tuition/fees: $19,270. Room/board: $7,942. Books/supplies: $800. Personal expenses: $900.

**2007-2008 Financial aid. Need-based:** 283 full-time freshmen applied for aid; 283 were judged to have need; 281 of these received aid. Average need met was 90%. Average scholarship/grant was $3,090; average loan $2,304. 55% of total undergraduate aid awarded as scholarships/grants, 45% as loans/jobs. **Non-need-based:** Awarded to 23 full-time undergraduates, including 12 freshmen. Scholarships awarded for academics.

**Application procedures. Admission:** No deadline. $50 fee, may be waived for applicants with need. Application may be submitted online. Admission notification on a rolling basis beginning on or about 9/15. **Financial aid:** Priority date 2/15, closing date 5/1. FAFSA required. Applicants notified on a rolling basis starting 2/15; must reply within 2 week(s) of notification.

**Academics. Special study options:** Accelerated study, combined bachelor's/ graduate degree, cross-registration, distance learning, double major, ESL, independent study, internships, student-designed major, study abroad, teacher certification program, Washington semester. **Credit/placement by examination:** AP, CLEP, institutional tests. 60 credit hours maximum toward bachelor's degree. **Support services:** Learning center, reduced course load, remedial instruction, study skills assistance, tutoring, writing center.

**Majors. Architecture:** Interior. **Biology:** General. **Business:** Accounting, finance, international, management science, marketing, real estate. **Computer sciences:** General, computer science, information technology. **Education:** Elementary, English. **English:** Composition, English lit. **Foreign languages:** Spanish. **Health:** Medical radiologic technology/radiation therapy, nursing (RN), respiratory therapy technology. **History:** General. **Liberal arts:** Arts/sciences. **Math:** General. **Philosophy/religion:** Religion. **Physical sciences:** Chemistry. **Protective services:** Criminal justice. **Psychology:** General. **Public administration:** Human services. **Social sciences:** International relations, sociology. **Theology:** Religious ed. **Visual/performing arts:** Dance, design. **Other:** National security studies.

**Most popular majors.** Architecture 9%, business/marketing 24%, education 12%, health sciences 10%, psychology 9%, security/protective services 7%, visual/performing arts 10%.

**Computing on campus.** 200 workstations in dormitories, library, computer center. Dormitories wired for high-speed internet access and linked to campus network. Commuter students can connect to campus network. Online course registration, online library, helpline, wireless network available.

**Student life. Freshman orientation:** Mandatory. Preregistration for classes offered. **Housing:** Coed dorms available. $100 nonrefundable deposit, deadline 5/1. **Activities:** Campus ministries, choral groups, dance, drama, international student organizations, literary magazine, radio station, student government, student newspaper, campus ministry, professional organizations, multicultural student organization, Project Achievement, environment club, black student coalition, African Student Forum, GLOBE (international students), Rotaract Club, community service.

**Athletics.** NCAA. **Intercollegiate:** Baseball M, basketball, cross-country, golf M, soccer, softball W, volleyball W. **Intramural:** Basketball, racquetball, soccer, softball, table tennis, tennis, volleyball. **Team name:** Redhawks.

**Student services.** Adult student services, alcohol/substance abuse counseling, campus ministries, career counseling, services for economically disadvantaged, student employment services, financial aid counseling, health services, minority student services, personal counseling, placement for graduates, veterans' counselor. **Physically disabled:** Services for visually impaired. **Learning disabled:** Comprehensive services available.

**Contact.** E-mail: admissions@laroche.edu
Phone: (412) 536-1271 Toll-free number: (800) 838-4572
Fax: (412) 536-1048
Thomas Hassett, Director of Admissions, La Roche College, 9000 Babcock Boulevard, Pittsburgh, PA 15237

---

## La Salle University

**Philadelphia, Pennsylvania**
**www.lasalle.edu**

**CB member**
**CB code: 2363**

- Private 4-year university and liberal arts college affiliated with Roman Catholic Church
- Residential campus in very large city
- 4,024 degree-seeking undergraduates: 22% part-time, 61% women, 16% African American, 4% Asian American, 8% Hispanic American, 1% international
- 1,785 degree-seeking graduate students
- 63% of applicants admitted

---

- SAT or ACT (ACT writing optional), application essay required
- 74% graduate within 6 years

**General.** Founded in 1863. Regionally accredited. **Degrees:** 927 bachelor's, 17 associate offered; master's, doctoral offered. **ROTC:** Army, Air Force. **Location:** 6 miles from downtown. **Calendar:** Semester, extensive summer session. **Full-time faculty:** 232 total; 80% have terminal degrees, 9% minority, 47% women. **Part-time faculty:** 145 total; 8% minority, 48% women. **Class size:** 48% < 20, 51% 20-39, 1% 40-49. **Special facilities:** Art museum, cable-access television station, restored home and gardens of 18th-century American portrait painter Charles Wilson Peale.

**Freshman class profile.** 5,401 applied, 3,376 admitted, 825 enrolled.

| Mid 50% test scores | | | |
|---|---|---|---|
| SAT critical reading: | 480-570 | Out-of-state: | 51% |
| SAT math: | 470-570 | Live on campus: | 89% |
| Rank in top quarter: | 50% | International: | 1% |
| Rank in top tenth: | 20% | Fraternities: | 7% |
| Return as sophomores: | 84% | Sororities: | 18% |

**Basis for selection.** High school GPA, class rank, test scores most important. Activities, recommendations considered. Admission through Academic Discovery Program, provides counseling and tutorial support for students who need academic assistance and meet certain criteria of financial need. Interview recommended.

**High school preparation.** 16 units required. Required units include English 4, mathematics 3, history 1, science 1 (laboratory 1), foreign language 2 and academic electives 5.

**2007-2008 Annual costs.** Tuition/fees: $29,510. Room/board: $10,660. Books/supplies: $500. Personal expenses: $1,119.

**2007-2008 Financial aid. Need-based:** 690 full-time freshmen applied for aid; 598 were judged to have need; 598 of these received aid. Average need met was 73%. Average scholarship/grant was $15,998; average loan $3,762. 67% of total undergraduate aid awarded as scholarships/grants, 33% as loans/jobs. **Non-need-based:** Awarded to 944 full-time undergraduates, including 240 freshmen. Scholarships awarded for academics, athletics, ROTC.

**Application procedures. Admission:** No deadline. $35 fee, may be waived for applicants with need. Application may be submitted online. Admission notification on a rolling basis beginning on or about 12/15. Must reply by May 1 or within 2 week(s) if notified thereafter. **Financial aid:** Priority date 2/15; no closing date. FAFSA required. Applicants notified on a rolling basis starting 3/15; must reply by 5/1 or within 2 week(s) of notification.

**Academics. Special study options:** Accelerated study, combined bachelor's/ graduate degree, cooperative education, double major, dual enrollment of high school students, ESL, honors, independent study, internships, study abroad, teacher certification program. 3-2 with Thomas Jefferson University. **Credit/placement by examination:** AP, CLEP, SAT, institutional tests. 70 credit hours maximum toward bachelor's degree. **Support services:** Learning center, pre-admission summer program, reduced course load, remedial instruction, tutoring, writing center.

**Majors. Area/ethnic studies:** Central/Eastern European, regional, Russian/ Slavic. **Biology:** General, biochemistry. **Business:** General, accounting, banking/ financial services, business admin, communications, finance, human resources, insurance, international, international marketing, labor relations, management science, managerial economics, market research, marketing, nonprofit/public, operations, organizational behavior, statistics. **Communications:** General, broadcast journalism, digital media, journalism, media studies, public relations, radio/tv. **Communications technology:** Desktop publishing, radio/tv. **Computer sciences:** General, applications programming, computer graphics, computer science, database management, information systems, information technology, programming, web page design. **Conservation:** General, environmental science. **Education:** General, bilingual, biology, chemistry, developmentally delayed, early childhood, early childhood special, elementary, emotionally handicapped, English, foreign languages, French, German, history, mathematics, mentally handicapped, middle, multi-level teacher, physically handicapped, science, secondary, social science, social studies, Spanish, special. **English:** American lit, British lit, composition, English lit, speech/rhetoric, technical writing. **Foreign languages:** General, Biblical, classics, comparative lit, French, German, Italian, Latin, Spanish. **Health:** Audiology/hearing, audiology/speech pathology, nursing (RN), predental, premedicine, preveterinary, speech pathology. **History:** General, American. **Interdisciplinary:** Biological/physical sciences, math/computer science, nutrition sciences, peace/conflict, systems science. **Legal studies:** Prelaw. **Liberal arts:** Arts/sciences. **Math:** General, applied, statistics. **Philosophy/religion:** Philosophy, religion. **Physical sciences:** Chemistry, geology, planetary. **Protective services:** Criminal justice. **Psychology:** General. **Public administration:** General, social work. **Social sciences:**

General, criminology, economics, international economics, international relations, political science, sociology, U.S. government. **Theology:** Religious ed. **Visual/performing arts:** Art history/conservation, cinematography, film/cinema, music history, studio arts.

**Most popular majors.** Business/marketing 21%, communications/journalism 10%, education 7%, health sciences 26%, public administration/social services 9%.

**Computing on campus.** 181 workstations in library, computer center. Dormitories wired for high-speed internet access and linked to campus network. Commuter students can connect to campus network. Online course registration, online library, helpline, repair service, student web hosting, wireless network available.

**Student life. Freshman orientation:** Mandatory, $100 fee. Preregistration for classes offered. **Policies:** Nonalcoholic nightclub and eatery available 7 days a week. **Housing:** Guaranteed on-campus for all undergraduates. Coed dorms, special housing for disabled, apartments, substance-free housing available. $200 deposit, deadline 5/1. Campus owned and operated townhouses available. **Activities:** Jazz band, campus ministries, choral groups, dance, drama, film society, international student organizations, literary magazine, musical theater, radio station, student government, student newspaper, TV station, black student union, Hillel, women's center, social work association, veterans club, Young Socialist Alliance, student council for exceptional children, urban center.

**Athletics.** NCAA. **Intercollegiate:** Baseball M, basketball, cheerleading, cross-country, diving, field hockey W, football (tackle) M, golf, lacrosse W, rowing (crew), soccer, softball W, swimming, tennis, track and field, volleyball W. **Intramural:** Basketball, football (non-tackle), rugby M, softball, volleyball. **Team name:** Explorers.

**Student services.** Adult student services, alcohol/substance abuse counseling, campus ministries, career counseling, services for economically disadvantaged, student employment services, health services, minority student services, on-campus daycare, personal counseling, placement for graduates, veterans' counselor.

**Contact.** E-mail: admiss@lasalle.edu
Phone: (215) 951-1500 Toll-free number: (800) 328-1910
Fax: (215) 951-1656
Robert Voss, Dean of Admissions and Financial Aid, La Salle University, 1900 West Olney Avenue, Philadelphia, PA 19141-1199

---

## Lafayette College

| | |
|---|---|
| Easton, Pennsylvania | **CB member** |
| www.lafayette.edu | **CB code: 2361** |

- Private 4-year engineering and liberal arts college affiliated with Presbyterian Church (USA)
- Residential campus in large town
- 2,366 degree-seeking undergraduates: 1% part-time, 48% women, 5% African American, 3% Asian American, 5% Hispanic American, 6% international
- 35% of applicants admitted
- SAT or ACT with writing, application essay required
- 89% graduate within 6 years

**General.** Founded in 1826. Regionally accredited. **Degrees:** 556 bachelor's awarded. **ROTC:** Army. **Location:** 80 miles from New York City, 60 miles from Philadelphia. **Calendar:** Semester, limited summer session. **Full-time faculty:** 199 total; 100% have terminal degrees, 10% minority, 32% women. **Part-time faculty:** 35 total; 46% have terminal degrees, 9% minority, 57% women. **Class size:** 59% < 20, 35% 20-39, 3% 40-49, 3% 50-99, less than 1% >100. **Special facilities:** Advanced computer-aided design laboratory, satellite downlink capability.

**Freshman class profile.** 6,364 applied, 2,224 admitted, 594 enrolled.

| Mid 50% test scores | | | |
|---|---|---|---|
| SAT critical reading: | 570-680 | GPA 2.0-2.99: | 11% |
| SAT math: | 610-710 | Rank in top quarter: | 92% |
| SAT writing: | 570-680 | Rank in top tenth: | 66% |
| ACT composite: | 25-30 | Return as sophomores: | 95% |
| GPA 3.50 or higher: | 49% | Out-of-state: | 73% |
| GPA 3.0-3.49: | 40% | Live on campus: | 99% |
| | | International: | 7% |

**Basis for selection.** Academic performance, class rank, quality of courses taken, personal qualities, extracurricular record, recommendations, and standardized test results important. Special consideration to applicants who will contribute diversity to student body. SAT Subject Tests recommended. SAT Subject Tests, if submitted, may be considered for placement in math and

foreign languages. Interview recommended for all; portfolio recommended for art program.

**High school preparation.** 16 units recommended. Recommended units include English 4, mathematics 3, science 2 (laboratory 2), foreign language 2 and academic electives 5. 4 math, chemistry, physics required of bachelor of science degree candidates.

**2008-2009 Annual costs.** Tuition/fees (projected): $36,090. Room/board: $11,248. Books/supplies: $850. Personal expenses: $900.

**2006-2007 Financial aid. Need-based:** 442 full-time freshmen applied for aid; 368 were judged to have need; 348 of these received aid. Average need met was 100%. Average scholarship/grant was $24,355; average loan $3,606. 89% of total undergraduate aid awarded as scholarships/grants, 11% as loans/jobs. **Non-need-based:** Awarded to 300 full-time undergraduates, including 116 freshmen. Scholarships awarded for academics, leadership, ROTC. **Additional information:** Parent loans, up to $7,500 annually, available with college absorbing interest while student is enrolled. Family has 8 years after graduation to repay. Not limited to those demonstrating need.

**Application procedures. Admission:** Closing date 1/1. $60 fee, may be waived for applicants with need. Application may be submitted online. Admission notification 4/1. Must reply by 5/1. **Financial aid:** Closing date 2/15. FAFSA, CSS PROFILE required. Applicants notified on a rolling basis starting 3/15; must reply by 5/1.

**Academics.** Self-designed majors include psychobiology, pre-architecture, area studies. Interdisciplinary minors also offered. **Special study options:** Accelerated study, cross-registration, distance learning, double major, exchange student, honors, independent study, internships, liberal arts/career combination, New York semester, semester at sea, student-designed major, study abroad, urban semester, Washington semester. Interim sessions here and abroad. **Credit/placement by examination:** AP, CLEP, institutional tests. **Support services:** Reduced course load, tutoring.

**Majors. Area/ethnic studies:** American. **Biology:** General, biochemistry. **Computer sciences:** General. **Engineering:** General, chemical, civil, electrical, mechanical. **English:** English lit. **Foreign languages:** French, German, Russian, Spanish. **History:** General. **Math:** General. **Philosophy/religion:** Philosophy, religion. **Physical sciences:** Chemistry, geology, physics. **Psychology:** General. **Social sciences:** Anthropology, economics, international relations, political science, sociology. **Visual/performing arts:** Music history, studio arts.

**Most popular majors.** Biology 6%, engineering/engineering technologies 18%, English 7%, history 6%, psychology 7%, social sciences 31%.

**Computing on campus.** 600 workstations in library, computer center. Dormitories wired for high-speed internet access and linked to campus network. Commuter students can connect to campus network. Online course registration, online library, helpline, repair service, student web hosting, wireless network available.

**Student life. Freshman orientation:** Mandatory. **Housing:** Guaranteed on-campus for freshmen. Coed dorms, single-sex dorms, special housing for disabled, apartments, fraternity/sorority housing, substance-free housing available. $500 deposit, deadline 5/1. Scholars house, black cultural center, Hillel House, arts house, special interest group floors in residence halls available. **Activities:** Bands, choral groups, dance, drama, film society, international student organizations, literary magazine, music ensembles, musical theater, radio station, student government, student newspaper, Hillel, Black collegians association, women's association, apartheid awareness association, environmental awareness and protection group, community outreach center.

**Athletics.** NCAA. **Intercollegiate:** Baseball M, basketball, cross-country, diving, fencing, field hockey W, football (tackle) M, golf, lacrosse, rowing (crew), rugby M, soccer, softball W, swimming, tennis, track and field, volleyball W. **Intramural:** Badminton, basketball, bowling, cheerleading, cross-country, equestrian, racquetball, soccer, softball, squash, swimming, table tennis, tennis, track and field, volleyball, water polo, wrestling M. **Team name:** Leopards.

**Student services.** Adult student services, career counseling, student employment services, health services, on-campus daycare, personal counseling, placement for graduates.

**Contact.** E-mail: admissions@lafayette.edu
Phone: (610) 330-5100 Fax: (610) 330-5355
Carol Rowlands, Director of Admissions, Lafayette College, 118 Markle Hall, Easton, PA 18042-1770

## Lancaster Bible College

**Lancaster, Pennsylvania**
www.lbc.edu                     CB code: 2388

- Private 4-year Bible college affiliated with nondenominational tradition
- Residential campus in small city
- 655 degree-seeking undergraduates: 14% part-time, 50% women
- 137 degree-seeking graduate students
- SAT or ACT (ACT writing recommended), application essay required

**General.** Founded in 1933. Regionally accredited; also accredited by ABHE. **Degrees:** 121 bachelor's, 24 associate awarded; master's offered. **Location:** 64 miles from Philadelphia. **Calendar:** Semester, limited summer session. **Full-time faculty:** 48 total; 52% have terminal degrees, 25% women. **Part-time faculty:** 43 total; 37% have terminal degrees, 42% women. **Class size:** 57% < 20, 33% 20-39, 4% 40-49, 6% 50-99.

**Freshman class profile.**

| Mid 50% test scores | | | |
|---|---|---|---|
| SAT critical reading: | 480-580 | Rank in top quarter: | 34% |
| SAT math: | 460-570 | Rank in top tenth: | 16% |
| ACT composite: | 17-23 | Out-of-state: | 33% |
| | | Live on campus: | 92% |

**Basis for selection.** Application must include personal spiritual testimony, academic transcripts, SAT or ACT scores, and 3 references. Interview recommended for all; audition required for religious music program. **Homeschooled:** Yearly evaluations should be included with application.

**2007-2008 Annual costs.** Tuition/fees: $14,520. Room/board: $6,170. Books/supplies: $700. Personal expenses: $1,750.

**Financial aid. Non-need-based:** Scholarships awarded for academics, alumni affiliation, leadership, music/drama, state residency.

**Application procedures. Admission:** Priority date 8/1; no deadline. $25 fee, may be waived for applicants with need. Admission notification on a rolling basis. **Financial aid:** Priority date 5/1; no closing date. FAFSA required. Applicants notified on a rolling basis starting 3/15; must reply within 3 week(s) of notification.

**Academics. Special study options:** Accelerated study, double major, independent study, internships, study abroad, teacher certification program. **Credit/placement by examination:** AP, CLEP, SAT, ACT, institutional tests. 15 credit hours maximum toward associate degree, 30 toward bachelor's. **Support services:** Learning center, reduced course load, remedial instruction, study skills assistance, tutoring.

**Majors. Education:** Elementary, physical. **Theology:** Bible.

**Most popular majors.** Education 9%, theological studies 91%.

**Computing on campus.** 35 workstations in library, student center. Dormitories wired for high-speed internet access and linked to campus network. Commuter students can connect to campus network. Online library, helpline available.

**Student life. Freshman orientation:** Mandatory, $40 fee. Preregistration for classes offered. 2 days prior to start of classes. **Policies:** Religious observance required. **Housing:** Guaranteed on-campus for freshmen. Single-sex dorms available. **Activities:** Concert band, choral groups, drama, international student organizations, music ensembles, student government, student newspaper, Christian Counseling Fellowship, married couples fellowship, Helpers in Service teams, student missionary fellowship, resident affairs council, commuter affairs council.

**Athletics.** NCCAA. **Intercollegiate:** Baseball M, basketball, cheerleading, cross-country, lacrosse W, soccer, volleyball. **Intramural:** Basketball, football (non-tackle) M, soccer, softball, table tennis, tennis, volleyball. **Team name:** Chargers.

**Student services.** Campus ministries, career counseling, student employment services, financial aid counseling, health services, personal counseling, placement for graduates. **Learning disabled:** Comprehensive services available.

**Contact.** E-mail: admissions@lbc.edu
Phone: (717) 560-8271 Toll-free number: (866) 522-4968
Fax: (717) 560-8213
Joanne Roper, Associate Vice President for Admissions, Lancaster Bible College, 901 Eden Road, Lancaster, PA 17608-3403

## Lebanon Valley College

**Annville, Pennsylvania**                     CB member
www.lvc.edu                     CB code: 2364

- Private 4-year liberal arts college affiliated with United Methodist Church
- Residential campus in small town
- 1,705 degree-seeking undergraduates: 5% part-time, 55% women, 1% African American, 2% Asian American, 3% Hispanic American
- 128 degree-seeking graduate students
- 71% of applicants admitted
- 70% graduate within 6 years; 18% enter graduate study

**General.** Founded in 1866. Regionally accredited. **Degrees:** 411 bachelor's, 5 associate awarded; master's, doctoral offered. **Location:** 7 miles from Hershey, 25 miles from Harrisburg. **Calendar:** Semester, limited summer session. **Full-time faculty:** 100 total; 89% have terminal degrees, 7% minority, 37% women. **Part-time faculty:** 91 total; 25% have terminal degrees, 4% minority, 33% women. **Class size:** 52% < 20, 47% 20-39, less than 1% 40-49, less than 1% 50-99. **Special facilities:** Electronic pianos, sound recording studio, transmission electron microscope, scanning electron microscope, Fourier transform infrared spectrometer, atomic absorption spectrometer, nuclear magnetic resonance spectrometer, molecular modeling lab, campus wetlands area for research, arboretum, physical therapy wellness pool.

**Freshman class profile.** 2,131 applied, 1,514 admitted, 451 enrolled.

| Mid 50% test scores | | | |
|---|---|---|---|
| SAT critical reading: | 480-600 | Rank in top tenth: | 36% |
| SAT math: | 490-620 | End year in good standing: | 90% |
| SAT writing: | 480-600 | Return as sophomores: | 83% |
| ACT composite: | 20-26 | Out-of-state: | 23% |
| Rank in top quarter: | 71% | Live on campus: | 88% |

**Basis for selection.** Record of high school achievement in challenging college prep courses is most important. Recommendations, test scores (optional), school and community activities evaluated. Submission of standardized test scores is optional for all applicants. Essay and interview recommended for all; interview required for physical therapy program; audition required for music program.

**High school preparation.** College-preparatory program required. 16 units required. Required and recommended units include English 4, mathematics 3, social studies 1, history 2, science 2-3 (laboratory 2) and foreign language 2-3.

**2007-2008 Annual costs.** Tuition/fees: $27,800. Room/board: $7,430. Books/supplies: $900. Personal expenses: $1,000.

**2007-2008 Financial aid. Need-based:** 426 full-time freshmen applied for aid; 375 were judged to have need; 374 of these received aid. Average need met was 88%. Average scholarship/grant was $17,087; average loan $4,427. 74% of total undergraduate aid awarded as scholarships/grants, 26% as loans/jobs. **Non-need-based:** Awarded to 446 full-time undergraduates, including 119 freshmen. Scholarships awarded for academics, alumni affiliation, music/drama.

**Application procedures. Admission:** No deadline. $30 fee, may be waived for applicants with need. Application may be submitted online. Admission notification on a rolling basis beginning on or about 10/15. Must reply by May 1 or within 2 week(s) if notified thereafter. Regular applications procedures apply. Permission from school district necessary. **Financial aid:** Priority date 3/1; no closing date. FAFSA, institutional form required. Applicants notified on a rolling basis starting 3/1; must reply by 5/1 or within 2 week(s) of notification.

**Academics. Special study options:** Combined bachelor's/graduate degree, double major, dual enrollment of high school students, independent study, internships, liberal arts/career combination, student-designed major, study abroad, teacher certification program, urban semester, Washington semester. **Credit/placement by examination:** AP, CLEP, IB, institutional tests. 15 credit hours maximum toward associate degree, 30 toward bachelor's. **Support services:** Reduced course load, study skills assistance, tutoring, writing center.

**Majors. Area/ethnic studies:** American. **Biology:** General, Biochemistry/biophysics and molecular biology. **Business:** Accounting, actuarial science, business admin. **Communications:** Digital media. **Communications technology:** Recording arts. **Computer sciences:** Computer science. **Education:** Elementary, music. **English:** English lit. **Foreign languages:** French, German, Spanish. **Health:** Health care admin, health services. **History:** General. **Interdisciplinary:** Intercultural. **Math:** General. **Philosophy/religion:**

Philosophy, religion. **Physical sciences:** Chemistry, physics. **Psychology:** General, psychobiology. **Social sciences:** Criminology, economics, political science, sociology. **Visual/performing arts:** Music management, music performance, studio arts.

**Most popular majors.** Biology 7%, business/marketing 15%, education 18%, English 6%, health sciences 9%, psychology 11%, social sciences 10%, visual/performing arts 7%.

**Computing on campus.** 138 workstations in library, computer center, student center. Dormitories wired for high-speed internet access and linked to campus network. Commuter students can connect to campus network. Online course registration, online library, helpline, student web hosting, wireless network available.

**Student life. Freshman orientation:** Mandatory. Preregistration for classes offered. One-day programs in May and July; 3-day program in August. **Housing:** Guaranteed on-campus for all undergraduates. Coed dorms, single-sex dorms, special housing for disabled, apartments, substance-free housing available. Community service, suites, theme housing available. **Activities:** Bands, choral groups, drama, literary magazine, music ensembles, musical theater, radio station, student government, student newspaper, symphony orchestra, College Republicans, Circle K, College Democrats, Cornerstone, Down to Earth, Best Buddies, L.E.A.D., Student Action for Earth, Students Acting for Global Awareness.

**Athletics.** NCAA. **Intercollegiate:** Baseball M, basketball, cross-country, field hockey W, football (tackle) M, golf M, ice hockey M, soccer, softball W, swimming, tennis, track and field, volleyball W. **Intramural:** Basketball, football (non-tackle), racquetball, softball. **Team name:** Flying Dutchmen.

**Student services.** Alcohol/substance abuse counseling, campus ministries, career counseling, student employment services, financial aid counseling, health services, minority student services, personal counseling, placement for graduates. **Physically disabled:** Services for visually, speech impaired. **Learning disabled:** Comprehensive services available.

**Contact.** E-mail: admission@lvc.edu
Phone: (717) 867-6181 Toll-free number: (866) 582-4236
Fax: (717) 867-6026
Susan Sarisky, Director of Admission, Lebanon Valley College, 101 North College Avenue, Annville, PA 17003-1400

---

## Lehigh University
**Bethlehem, Pennsylvania**
www.lehigh.edu

CB member
CB code: 2365

- Private 4-year university
- Residential campus in small city
- 4,732 degree-seeking undergraduates: 2% part-time, 41% women, 3% African American, 6% Asian American, 4% Hispanic American, 2% international
- 1,895 degree-seeking graduate students
- 32% of applicants admitted
- SAT or ACT with writing, application essay required
- 83% graduate within 6 years

**General.** Founded in 1865. Regionally accredited. **Degrees:** 1,170 bachelor's awarded; master's, doctoral offered. **ROTC:** Army. **Location:** 50 miles from Philadelphia, 75 miles from New York City. **Calendar:** Semester, limited summer session. **Full-time faculty:** 440 total; 99% have terminal degrees, 18% minority, 27% women. **Part-time faculty:** 189 total; 16% minority, 46% women. **Special facilities:** Two aberration-corrected electron microscopes, financial service laboratory, broadband seismic station, multidirectional experimental laboratory, electron optical labs, particle accelerator, rock climbing wall.

**Freshman class profile.** 12,155 applied, 3,882 admitted, 1,166 enrolled.

| Mid 50% test scores | | | |
|---|---|---|---|
| SAT critical reading: | 600-680 | Return as sophomores: | 93% |
| SAT math: | 640-710 | Out-of-state: | 75% |
| Rank in top quarter: | 99% | Live on campus: | 99% |
| Rank in top tenth: | 90% | International: | 3% |

**Basis for selection.** All submitted material considered. Campus visit recommended.

**High school preparation.** 16 units required. Required units include English 4, mathematics 3, social studies 2, (laboratory 2), foreign language 2 and academic electives 3. Chemistry required, physics recommended for

engineering and science candidates. Waivers in math granted by some departments to well-qualified candidates.

**2007-2008 Annual costs.** Tuition/fees: $35,610. Room/board: $9,340. Books/supplies: $1,000. Personal expenses: $1,210.

**2007-2008 Financial aid. Need-based:** 709 full-time freshmen applied for aid; 474 were judged to have need; 474 of these received aid. Average need met was 97%. Average scholarship/grant was $24,722; average loan $3,375. 80% of total undergraduate aid awarded as scholarships/grants, 20% as loans/jobs. **Non-need-based:** Awarded to 681 full-time undergraduates, including 156 freshmen. Scholarships awarded for academics, art, athletics, leadership, music/drama, ROTC.

**Application procedures. Admission:** Closing date 1/1 (postmark date). $65 fee, may be waived for applicants with need. Application may be submitted online. Admission notification 4/1. Must reply by 5/1. **Financial aid:** Closing date 2/1. FAFSA, CSS PROFILE required. Applicants notified by 3/30; must reply by 5/1 or within 3 week(s) of notification.

**Academics. Special study options:** Accelerated study, combined bachelor's/graduate degree, cooperative education, cross-registration, distance learning, double major, ESL, exchange student, external degree, honors, independent study, internships, liberal arts/career combination, study abroad, teacher certification program, urban semester, Washington semester. **Credit/placement by examination:** AP, CLEP, IB, institutional tests. **Support services:** Learning center, study skills assistance, tutoring, writing center.

**Majors. Architecture:** Architecture. **Area/ethnic studies:** African-American, American, Asian, Russian/Slavic, women's. **Biology:** General, biochemistry, molecular. **Business:** Accounting, finance, logistics, management science, managerial economics, marketing. **Communications:** Journalism. **Computer sciences:** Computer science, information systems. **Conservation:** Environmental science. **Engineering:** Biomedical, chemical, civil, computer, electrical, environmental, industrial, materials, mechanical, mechanics, physics, structural. **English:** English lit. **Foreign languages:** Classics, French, German, Spanish. **Health:** Predental, premedicine. **History:** General. **Interdisciplinary:** Biological/physical sciences, biopsychology, cognitive science, global studies, science/society. **Math:** General, statistics. **Philosophy/religion:** Philosophy, religion. **Physical sciences:** Astronomy, astrophysics, chemistry, physics. **Psychology:** General. **Social sciences:** General, anthropology, international relations, political science, sociology, urban studies. **Visual/performing arts:** Art, art history/conservation, design, dramatic, music history. **Other:** Applied science, Classical civilization, Computer science & business, Journalism/science writing.

**Most popular majors.** Business/marketing 30%, engineering/engineering technologies 28%, psychology 7%, social sciences 8%.

**Computing on campus.** 580 workstations in library, computer center. Dormitories wired for high-speed internet access and linked to campus network. Commuter students can connect to campus network. Online course registration, online library, helpline, repair service, student web hosting, wireless network available.

**Student life. Freshman orientation:** Mandatory, $191 fee. Preregistration for classes offered. Four-day program held prior to the first day of classes. **Policies:** Project Impact program strives to alter drinking culture and bring about enduring changes in pattern of student life. **Housing:** Guaranteed on-campus for freshmen. Coed dorms, apartments, fraternity/sorority housing, substance-free housing available. $500 nonrefundable deposit, deadline 5/1. Special interest housing (theme housing); residential college (Taylor College) available. **Activities:** Bands, campus ministries, choral groups, dance, drama, film society, international student organizations, literary magazine, music ensembles, Model UN, musical theater, radio station, student government, student newspaper, symphony orchestra, Global Union, Asian cultural society, Fellowship of Christian Athletes, Omicron Delta Kappa, Chinese culture club, Black student union, Muslim students association, Alpha Phi Omega Service Fraternity, Best Buddies.

**Athletics.** NCAA. **Intercollegiate:** Baseball M, basketball, cross-country, diving, field hockey W, football (tackle) M, golf, lacrosse, rowing (crew) W, soccer, softball W, swimming, tennis, track and field, volleyball W, wrestling M. **Intramural:** Basketball, football (non-tackle), soccer, softball, volleyball. **Team name:** Mountain Hawks.

**Student services.** Alcohol/substance abuse counseling, campus ministries, career counseling, student employment services, financial aid counseling, health services, minority student services, on-campus daycare, personal counseling, placement for graduates, veterans' counselor, women's services.

**Contact.** E-mail: admissions@lehigh.edu
Phone: (610) 758-3100 Fax: (610) 758-4361
Bruce Gardiner, Director of Admissions, Lehigh University, 27 Memorial Drive West, Bethlehem, PA 18015-3094

## Lincoln University

**Lincoln University, Pennsylvania**
**www.lincoln.edu**

**CB member**
**CB code: 2367**

- Public 4-year university and liberal arts college
- Residential campus in rural community
- 1,898 degree-seeking undergraduates: 2% part-time, 60% women, 96% African American, 1% Hispanic American, 3% international
- 545 degree-seeking graduate students
- 38% of applicants admitted
- SAT or ACT (ACT writing optional), application essay required
- 40% graduate within 6 years

**General.** Founded in 1854. Regionally accredited. **Degrees:** 229 bachelor's awarded; master's offered. **ROTC:** Army. **Location:** 45 miles from Philadelphia. **Calendar:** Semester, limited summer session. **Full-time faculty:** 99 total; 71% have terminal degrees, 71% minority, 64% women. **Part-time faculty:** 95 total; 28% have terminal degrees, 68% minority, 56% women. **Class size:** 38% < 20, 60% 20-39, 2% 40-49, 1% 50-99.

**Freshman class profile.** 5,488 applied, 2,068 admitted, 633 enrolled.

| Mid 50% test scores | | | |
|---|---|---|---|
| SAT critical reading: | 370-450 | Rank in top quarter: | 17% |
| SAT math: | 360-450 | Rank in top tenth: | 5% |
| ACT composite: | 14-18 | Return as sophomores: | 66% |
| GPA 3.50 or higher: | 7% | Out-of-state: | 61% |
| GPA 3.0-3.49: | 33% | Live on campus: | 99% |
| GPA 2.0-2.99: | 52% | International: | 2% |

**Basis for selection.** Admissions based on secondary school record and class rank; recommendations, standardized test scores, talent, and ability also important.

**High school preparation.** 21 units required. Required units include English 4, mathematics 3, social studies 3, science 3 and academic electives 5. 2 arts or humanities required.

**2007-2008 Annual costs.** Tuition/fees: $7,762; $11,602 out-of-state. Out-of-state students pay additional $588 in fees. Room/board: $7,278.

**2007-2008 Financial aid. Need-based:** 609 full-time freshmen applied for aid; 564 were judged to have need; 556 of these received aid. Average need met was 46%. Average scholarship/grant was $5,863; average loan $3,707. 36% of total undergraduate aid awarded as scholarships/grants, 64% as loans/jobs. **Non-need-based:** Awarded to 756 full-time undergraduates, including 258 freshmen. Scholarships awarded for academics, alumni affiliation, leadership, music/drama.

**Application procedures. Admission:** Priority date 4/1; no deadline. $20 fee, may be waived for applicants with need. Application may be submitted online. Admission notification on a rolling basis beginning on or about 2/15. **Financial aid:** Closing date 5/1. FAFSA required. Applicants notified on a rolling basis starting 4/1; must reply within 3 week(s) of notification.

**Academics. Special study options:** Exchange student, honors, independent study, internships, study abroad, teacher certification program. 3-2 in advanced science/engineering with Drexel University; Penn State University; Howard University; University of Delaware, Temple University, Widener University, and New Jersey Institute of Technology. **Credit/placement by examination:** AP, CLEP, IB, SAT, institutional tests. **Support services:** Learning center, reduced course load, remedial instruction, study skills assistance, tutoring, writing center.

**Majors. Biology:** General. **Business:** Accounting, actuarial science, business admin, finance, human resources. **Communications:** General, journalism. **Computer sciences:** General. **Conservation:** Environmental science. **Education:** Early childhood, elementary, English, mathematics, music, secondary, special. **Engineering:** General. **English:** English lit. **Foreign languages:** French, Japanese, Spanish. **Health:** Recreational therapy. **History:** General. **Math:** General. **Parks/recreation:** Health/fitness. **Philosophy/religion:** Philosophy, religion. **Physical sciences:** General, chemistry, physics. **Protective services:** Criminal justice. **Psychology:** General. **Public administration:** General, human services. **Social sciences:** Anthropology, economics, international relations, political science, sociology. **Visual/performing arts:** Studio arts.

**Most popular majors.** Biology 7%, business/marketing 12%, communications/journalism 9%, education 15%, parks/recreation 11%, psychology 6%, security/protective services 10%, social sciences 15%.

**Computing on campus.** 167 workstations in dormitories, library, computer center. Dormitories wired for high-speed internet access and linked to campus network. Commuter students can connect to campus network. Online library, repair service, wireless network available.

**Student life. Freshman orientation:** Mandatory, $158 fee. Preregistration for classes offered. **Housing:** Guaranteed on-campus for freshmen. Coed dorms, single-sex dorms, apartments available. $275 deposit. **Activities:** Jazz band, choral groups, dance, drama, music ensembles, radio station, student government, student newspaper, TV station, Music Educator National Conference, Mu Phi Alpha, Tolson Society, law society, Phi Kappa Epsilon honor society, fashion club, religious organizations, and social clubs.

**Athletics.** NCAA. **Intercollegiate:** Baseball M, basketball, cross-country, soccer, tennis, track and field, volleyball W. **Intramural:** Baseball M, basketball, bowling, boxing W, cheerleading W, cross-country, diving, football (tackle) M, softball, swimming, tennis, track and field, volleyball. **Team name:** Lions.

**Student services.** Alcohol/substance abuse counseling, campus ministries, career counseling, student employment services, financial aid counseling, health services, personal counseling, women's services.

**Contact.** E-mail: admiss@lincoln.edu
Phone: (484) 365-7206 Toll-free number: (800) 790-0191
Fax: (484) 365-8109
Michael Taylor, Director of Admissions, Lincoln University, PO Box 179, Lincoln University, PA 19352-0999

## Lock Haven University of Pennsylvania

**Lock Haven, Pennsylvania**
**www.lhup.edu**

**CB member**
**CB code: 2654**

- Public 4-year university and liberal arts college
- Residential campus in small town
- 4,779 degree-seeking undergraduates: 6% part-time, 56% women, 7% African American, 1% Asian American, 2% Hispanic American, 1% international
- 241 degree-seeking graduate students
- 74% of applicants admitted
- SAT or ACT (ACT writing optional) required
- 51% graduate within 6 years

**General.** Founded in 1870. Regionally accredited. Branch campus in Clearfield. **Degrees:** 761 bachelor's, 66 associate awarded; master's offered. **ROTC:** Army. **Location:** 26 miles from Williamsport, 35 miles from State College. **Calendar:** Semester, limited summer session. **Full-time faculty:** 238 total; 71% have terminal degrees, 13% minority, 44% women. **Part-time faculty:** 17 total; 6% minority, 47% women. **Class size:** 27% < 20, 53% 20-39, 14% 40-49, 5% 50-99, less than 1% >100. **Special facilities:** Rural retreat conference center, cadaver dissection laboratory, electron microscope, primate laboratory.

**Freshman class profile.** 4,776 applied, 3,524 admitted, 1,233 enrolled.

| Mid 50% test scores | | | |
|---|---|---|---|
| SAT critical reading: | 420-510 | GPA 2.0-2.99: | 37% |
| SAT math: | 420-520 | Rank in top quarter: | 25% |
| SAT writing: | 410-500 | Rank in top tenth: | 6% |
| ACT composite: | 16-22 | Return as sophomores: | 70% |
| GPA 3.50 or higher: | 29% | Out-of-state: | 10% |
| GPA 3.0-3.49: | 33% | Live on campus: | 80% |
| | | International: | 1% |

**Basis for selection.** Course selection, grades received, and test scores most important. Preferred test score report date February 1. Interview required for nursing program; audition required for music programs. **Home-schooled:** Provide as much documentation as possible. Interview required.

**High school preparation.** 16 units required; 21 recommended. Required and recommended units include English 4, mathematics 3-4, social studies 2, history 2, science 3-4 (laboratory 2-3) and foreign language 2. 4 units math required for math, computer science, biology, physics, and chemistry majors. 1 unit each biology, chemistry, physics required for health science majors. 1 unit each biology, anatomy and physiology, chemistry recommended for health and physical education majors.

**2007-2008 Annual costs.** Tuition/fees: $6,679; $12,445 out-of-state. Beginning Fall 2007, all freshmen are required to have a laptop computer for use in the classroom. Computers can be purchased through the university; cost of computer is not included in mandatory fees. The university has a small number of laptops available to students who cannot afford to make such a purchase. Room/board: $6,188. Books/supplies: $900. Personal expenses: $1,090.

**2007-2008 Financial aid. Need-based:** 1,195 full-time freshmen applied for aid; 932 were judged to have need; 932 of these received aid.

Average need met was 73%. Average scholarship/grant was $5,182; average loan $3,500. 47% of total undergraduate aid awarded as scholarships/grants, 53% as loans/jobs. **Non-need-based:** Awarded to 797 full-time undergraduates, including 192 freshmen. Scholarships awarded for academics, art, athletics, leadership, minority status, music/drama, ROTC, state residency.

**Application procedures. Admission:** Priority date 3/1; no deadline. $25 fee, may be waived for applicants with need. Application may be submitted online. Admission notification on a rolling basis beginning on or about 10/1. Must reply by May 1 or within 2 week(s) if notified thereafter. **Financial aid:** Closing date 3/15. FAFSA required. Applicants notified on a rolling basis starting 4/1; must reply within 2 week(s) of notification.

**Academics. Special study options:** Combined bachelor's/graduate degree, cross-registration, distance learning, double major, dual enrollment of high school students, honors, independent study, internships, student-designed major, study abroad, teacher certification program. Exchange program with institutions in Taiwan, Russia, Australia, France, England, Poland, Germany, Scotland, Costa Rica, China, Japan, Croatia, Italy, Kenya, Mexico. 2-2 program in music education with Clarion University of Pennsylvania and Millersville University of Pennsylvania. **Credit/placement by examination:** AP, CLEP, IB, SAT, institutional tests. 30 credit hours maximum toward bachelor's degree. **Support services:** Learning center, preadmission summer program, reduced course load, remedial instruction, study skills assistance, tutoring, writing center.

**Majors. Biology:** General. **Business:** Accounting, business admin. **Communications:** Journalism. **Computer sciences:** General, computer science. **Education:** Elementary, kindergarten/preschool, special. **English:** English lit, speech/rhetoric. **Foreign languages:** French, German, Spanish. **History:** General. **Interdisciplinary:** Biological/physical sciences. **Legal studies:** Paralegal. **Liberal arts:** Arts/sciences. **Math:** General. **Parks/recreation:** Facilities management, sports admin. **Philosophy/religion:** Philosophy. **Physical sciences:** Chemistry, geology, physics. **Protective services:** Law enforcement admin. **Psychology:** General. **Public administration:** Social work. **Social sciences:** General, economics, geography, international relations, political science, sociology. **Visual/performing arts:** Art, dramatic, studio arts. **Other:** Health and Physical Education, Health Sciences.

**Most popular majors.** Business/marketing 10%, education 16%, health sciences 10%, parks/recreation 18%, security/protective services 9%.

**Computing on campus.** PC or laptop required. 290 workstations in dormitories, library, computer center, student center. Dormitories wired for high-speed internet access and linked to campus network. Commuter students can connect to campus network. Online course registration, online library, helpline, repair service, student web hosting, wireless network available.

**Student life. Freshman orientation:** Available, $75 fee. Overnight new student and parent programs, run concurrently, held during June. **Housing:** Guaranteed on-campus for freshmen. Coed dorms, apartments, substance-free housing available. $100 deposit, deadline 5/1. **Activities:** Bands, choral groups, dance, drama, literary magazine, music ensembles, musical theater, radio station, student government, student newspaper, symphony orchestra, TV station, Newman Club, Black Cultural Society, Campus Crusade, Commonwealth Association of Students, Fellowship of Christian Athletes, social service society, Full Gospel Fellowship, New Life Student Fellowship.

**Athletics.** NCAA. **Intercollegiate:** Baseball M, basketball, boxing, cheerleading, cross-country, field hockey W, football (tackle) M, lacrosse W, soccer, softball W, swimming W, track and field, volleyball W, wrestling M. **Intramural:** Badminton, basketball, cross-country, field hockey W, golf, racquetball, skiing, soccer, softball, tennis, volleyball, water polo, wrestling M. **Team name:** Bald Eagles, Lady Eagles.

**Student services.** Adult student services, alcohol/substance abuse counseling, campus ministries, career counseling, student employment services, financial aid counseling, health services, minority student services, personal counseling, placement for graduates, veterans' counselor, women's services. **Physically disabled:** Services for visually, speech impaired.

**Contact.** E-mail: admissions@lhup.edu
Phone: (570) 484-2027 Toll-free number: (800) 332-8900
Fax: (570) 484-2201
Stephen Lee, Director of Admissions, Lock Haven University of Pennsylvania, Akeley Hall, Lock Haven, PA 17745

## Lycoming College
**Williamsport, Pennsylvania**
www.lycoming.edu
**CB member**
**CB code: 2372**

- Private 4-year liberal arts college affiliated with United Methodist Church
- Residential campus in small city

- 1,402 degree-seeking undergraduates: 1% part-time, 55% women
- 78% of applicants admitted
- SAT or ACT (ACT writing optional), application essay required
- 70% graduate within 6 years; 20% enter graduate study

**General.** Founded in 1812. Regionally accredited. **Degrees:** 319 bachelor's awarded. **ROTC:** Army. **Location:** 90 miles from Harrisburg, 170 miles from Philadelphia. **Calendar:** Semester, limited summer session. **Full-time faculty:** 84 total; 92% have terminal degrees, 8% minority, 37% women. **Part-time faculty:** 39 total; 13% have terminal degrees, 41% women. **Class size:** 62% < 20, 34% 20-39, 3% 40-49, 1% 50-99, less than 1% >100. **Special facilities:** Planetarium, Clean Water Institute, graphics computer lab, Polling Institute.

**Freshman class profile.** 1,585 applied, 1,236 admitted, 399 enrolled.

| Mid 50% test scores | | | |
|---|---|---|---|
| SAT critical reading: | 460-570 | Rank in top tenth: | 19% |
| SAT math: | 470-580 | Return as sophomores: | 79% |
| SAT writing: | 450-560 | Out-of-state: | 39% |
| ACT composite: | 20-25 | Live on campus: | 95% |
| Rank in top quarter: | 43% | International: | 1% |

**Basis for selection.** Academic achievement as reflected in school record, class rank, and test scores most important. Curriculum, counselor and teacher recommendations also considered. Interview recommended for all; portfolio recommended for art program and creative writing program; audition recommended for music and theater programs.

**High school preparation.** 16 units required. Required and recommended units include English 4, mathematics 3-4, social studies 3-4, science 2-3 (laboratory 2-3), foreign language 2-3 and academic electives 2.

**2007-2008 Annual costs.** Tuition/fees: $27,129. Room/board: $7,238. Books/supplies: $800. Personal expenses: $800.

**2007-2008 Financial aid. Need-based:** 366 full-time freshmen applied for aid; 318 were judged to have need; 318 of these received aid. Average need met was 83%. Average scholarship/grant was $16,572; average loan $4,399. 73% of total undergraduate aid awarded as scholarships/grants, 27% as loans/jobs. **Non-need-based:** Awarded to 322 full-time undergraduates, including 116 freshmen. Scholarships awarded for academics, art, leadership, minority status, music/drama.

**Application procedures. Admission:** Priority date 4/1; deadline 7/1 (receipt date). $35 fee, may be waived for applicants with need. Application may be submitted online. Admission notification on a rolling basis beginning on or about 12/15. Must reply by May 1 or within 4 week(s) if notified thereafter. **Financial aid:** Priority date 3/1; no closing date. FAFSA, institutional form required. Applicants notified on a rolling basis starting 3/1; must reply by 5/1.

**Academics.** Teacher certification offered on elementary and secondary levels; special education certification as part of bachelor of arts program. **Special study options:** Accelerated study, combined bachelor's/graduate degree, cross-registration, double major, honors, independent study, internships, student-designed major, study abroad, teacher certification program, United Nations semester, urban semester, Washington semester. **Credit/placement by examination:** AP, CLEP, IB, institutional tests. 64 credit hours maximum toward bachelor's degree. **Support services:** Learning center, study skills assistance, tutoring, writing center.

**Majors. Area/ethnic studies:** American. **Biology:** General. **Business:** Accounting, actuarial science, business admin. **Communications:** General. **Computer sciences:** General. **English:** English lit. **Foreign languages:** French, German, Spanish. **History:** General. **Math:** General. **Philosophy/religion:** Philosophy, religion. **Physical sciences:** Astronomy, chemistry, physics. **Protective services:** Criminal justice. **Psychology:** General. **Social sciences:** Anthropology, archaeology, economics, political science, sociology. **Visual/performing arts:** Art, art history/conservation, dramatic.

**Most popular majors.** Biology 12%, business/marketing 17%, communications/journalism 8%, psychology 14%, social sciences 16%, visual/performing arts 11%.

**Computing on campus.** 125 workstations in library, computer center, student center. Dormitories wired for high-speed internet access and linked to campus network. Commuter students can connect to campus network. Online course registration, online library, helpline, repair service, student web hosting, wireless network available.

**Student life. Freshman orientation:** Mandatory, $200 fee. Preregistration for classes offered. 2-day, 1-night event for students and parents. Choose 1 of 3 dates. **Policies:** Students must live in college-owned residence halls or apartments. **Housing:** Guaranteed on-campus for all undergraduates. Coed dorms, single-sex dorms, apartments, fraternity/sorority housing, substance-free housing available. $100 nonrefundable deposit, deadline 5/1. Substance-free housing, study-intensive housing, Creative Arts Society housing available. **Activities:** Bands, campus ministries, choral groups, dance, drama, film society, literary magazine, music ensembles, musical theater, radio station, student government, student newspaper, symphony orchestra, TV station, Circle K, Habitat for Humanity, College Democrats, College Republicans, environmental awareness foundation, Black Student Union, Big Brothers/Big Sisters, Colleges Against Cancer, Religious Experiences at Lycoming.

**Athletics.** NCAA. **Intercollegiate:** Basketball, cross-country, football (tackle) M, golf M, lacrosse, soccer, softball W, swimming, tennis, volleyball W, wrestling M. **Intramural:** Basketball, football (non-tackle), soccer, softball, volleyball. **Team name:** Warriors.

**Student services.** Alcohol/substance abuse counseling, campus ministries, career counseling, student employment services, financial aid counseling, health services, personal counseling, placement for graduates, women's services.

**Contact.** E-mail: admissions@lycoming.edu
Phone: (570) 321-4026 Toll-free number: (800) 345-3920 ext. 4026
Fax: (570) 321-4317
James Spencer, Vice President for Admissions and Financial Aid, Lycoming College, 700 College Place, Williamsport, PA 17701

## Mansfield University of Pennsylvania
Mansfield, Pennsylvania
www.mansfield.edu      CB code: 2655

- Public 4-year university and liberal arts college
- Residential campus in small town
- 2,849 degree-seeking undergraduates: 7% part-time, 62% women, 5% African American, 1% Asian American, 2% Hispanic American, 1% Native American, 1% international
- 387 degree-seeking graduate students
- 70% of applicants admitted
- SAT or ACT (ACT writing optional) required
- 48% graduate within 6 years; 16% enter graduate study

**General.** Founded in 1857. Regionally accredited. **Degrees:** 566 bachelor's, 36 associate awarded; master's offered. **Location:** 50 miles from Williamsport, 30 miles from Corning, New York. **Calendar:** Semester, limited summer session. **Full-time faculty:** 138 total; 92% have terminal degrees, 17% minority, 44% women. **Part-time faculty:** 64 total; 86% have terminal degrees, 11% minority, 64% women. **Class size:** 43% < 20, 45% 20-39, 5% 40-49, 5% 50-99, less than 1% >100. **Special facilities:** Planetarium, solar collector, science museum, animal collection, fisheries research boat, leadership institute.

**Freshman class profile.** 3,367 applied, 2,349 admitted, 670 enrolled.

| Mid 50% test scores | | | |
|---|---|---|---|
| SAT critical reading: | 430-530 | Rank in top quarter: | 32% |
| SAT math: | 430-540 | Rank in top tenth: | 12% |
| SAT writing: | 420-510 | Return as sophomores: | 73% |
| ACT composite: | 17-22 | Out-of-state: | 20% |
| GPA 3.50 or higher: | 45% | Live on campus: | 80% |
| GPA 3.0-3.49: | 26% | Fraternities: | 3% |
| GPA 2.0-2.99: | 28% | Sororities: | 1% |

**Basis for selection.** Class rank, high school curriculum, test scores important; counselor's recommendation, extracurricular activities considered. Special consideration given to applicants eligible for Equal Education Opportunity Program. Entry competitive in X-ray technology, respiratory therapy, fisheries, music, art programs, premed, nursing, biology, chemistry. Essay recommended for all; interview required for radiology program; audition required for music program; portfolio required for art program. **Homeschooled:** Statement describing homeschool structure and mission, transcript of courses and grades required.

**High school preparation.** 21 units required; 25 recommended. Required and recommended units include English 4, mathematics 3-4, history 4, science 2-3 (laboratory 2-3), foreign language 2-4 and academic electives 6.

**2007-2008 Annual costs.** Tuition/fees: $6,979; $14,746 out-of-state. Tuition for NY residents is $8,544. Room/board: $6,236. Books/supplies: $1,200. Personal expenses: $800.

**2006-2007 Financial aid. Need-based:** Average need met was 68%. Average scholarship/grant was $4,065; average loan $2,733. 46% of total undergraduate aid awarded as scholarships/grants, 54% as loans/jobs. **Non-need-based:** Awarded to 211 full-time undergraduates, including 65 freshmen. Scholarships awarded for academics, art, athletics, leadership, music/drama, state residency.

**Application procedures. Admission:** No deadline. $25 fee, may be waived for applicants with need. Application may be submitted online. Admission notification on a rolling basis beginning on or about 7/1. Must reply by May 1 or within 2 week(s) if notified thereafter. Applicants to competitive programs should apply by January 15. **Financial aid:** Priority date 3/15; no closing date. FAFSA, institutional form required. Applicants notified on a rolling basis starting 3/15; must reply within 2 week(s) of notification.

**Academics. Special study options:** Cooperative education, cross-registration, distance learning, double major, dual enrollment of high school students, ESL, exchange student, external degree, honors, independent study, internships, liberal arts/career combination, student-designed major, study abroad, teacher certification program, Washington semester. Online programs. **Credit/placement by examination:** AP, CLEP, IB, SAT, institutional tests. **Support services:** Learning center, pre-admission summer program, reduced course load, remedial instruction, study skills assistance, tutoring, writing center.

**Majors. Architecture:** Urban/community planning. **Biology:** General, biochemistry, cell/histology, marine, molecular. **Business:** Accounting, actuarial science, business admin, human resources, international, marketing, tourism promotion, tourism/travel. **Communications:** General, broadcast journalism, journalism, public relations. **Computer sciences:** General, computer science, information systems. **Conservation:** General, environmental studies, fisheries. **Education:** Art, biology, chemistry, early childhood, elementary, English, foreign languages, French, German, history, mathematics, middle, multi-level teacher, music, physics, secondary, social studies, Spanish, special. **English:** English lit, speech/rhetoric. **Foreign languages:** French, German, Spanish. **Health:** Clinical lab science, clinical lab technology, music therapy, predental, premedicine, preop/surgical nursing, prepharmacy, preveterinary. **History:** General. **Legal studies:** Prelaw. **Liberal arts:** Arts/sciences. **Math:** General. **Philosophy/religion:** Philosophy. **Physical sciences:** Chemistry, geology, physics. **Protective services:** Law enforcement admin. **Psychology:** General. **Public administration:** Social work. **Social sciences:** General, anthropology, economics, geography, political science, sociology. **Visual/performing arts:** Art, art history/conservation, dramatic, music management, music performance, piano/organ, studio arts, voice/opera.

**Most popular majors.** Business/marketing 10%, communications/journalism 7%, education 12%, English 7%, health sciences 8%, public administration/social services 9%, security/protective services 14%, visual/performing arts 8%.

**Computing on campus.** 715 workstations in dormitories, library, computer center, student center. Dormitories wired for high-speed internet access and linked to campus network. Commuter students can connect to campus network. Online course registration, online library, helpline, wireless network available.

**Student life. Freshman orientation:** Mandatory, $65 fee. Preregistration for classes offered. 2-day program for students and parents. **Housing:** Guaranteed on-campus for all undergraduates. Coed dorms, fraternity/sorority housing available. **Activities:** Bands, choral groups, dance, drama, literary magazine, music ensembles, musical theater, radio station, student government, student newspaper, symphony orchestra, TV station, Black Awareness Association, Inter-Varsity Christian Fellowship, Commonwealth Association of Students.

**Athletics.** NCAA. **Intercollegiate:** Baseball M, basketball, cross-country, diving W, field hockey W, soccer W, softball W, swimming W, track and field. **Intramural:** Basketball, football (non-tackle) M, soccer, softball, tennis, volleyball, water polo. **Team name:** Mounties.

**Student services.** Adult student services, alcohol/substance abuse counseling, campus ministries, career counseling, services for economically disadvantaged, student employment services, financial aid counseling, health services, minority student services, on-campus daycare, personal counseling, placement for graduates, veterans' counselor, women's services. **Physically disabled:** Services for visually, speech, hearing impaired.

**Contact.** E-mail: admissions@mansfield.edu
Phone: (570) 662-4243 Toll-free number: (800) 577-6826
Fax: (570) 662-4121
Brian Barden, Executive Director of Enrollment Services, Mansfield University of Pennsylvania, Alumni Hall, Mansfield, PA 16933

## Marywood University

**Scranton, Pennsylvania**
www.marywood.edu

CB member
CB code: 2407

- Private 4-year university affiliated with Roman Catholic Church
- Residential campus in small city
- 1,950 degree-seeking undergraduates: 6% part-time, 71% women, 1% African American, 2% Asian American, 3% Hispanic American, 1% international
- 1,149 degree-seeking graduate students
- 73% of applicants admitted
- SAT or ACT (ACT writing optional) required
- 60% graduate within 6 years

**General.** Founded in 1915. Regionally accredited. Off-campus and distance education degree program available. **Degrees:** 376 bachelor's awarded; master's, doctoral offered. **ROTC:** Army, Air Force. **Location:** 110 miles from Philadelphia, 120 miles from New York City. **Calendar:** Semester, extensive summer session. **Full-time faculty:** 133 total; 84% have terminal degrees, 53% women. **Part-time faculty:** 174 total; 57% women. **Class size:** 54% < 20, 44% 20-39, less than 1% 40-49, 1% 50-99. **Special facilities:** Arboretum, assistive technology lab, science multimedia laboratory, interactive voice laboratory, music computer laboratory, nursing laboratory, video conferencing facility, speech and hearing clinic, healthy family center, early childhood center, center for athletics and wellness.

**Freshman class profile.** 1,756 applied, 1,289 admitted, 478 enrolled.

| Mid 50% test scores | | | |
|---|---|---|---|
| SAT critical reading: | 470-560 | GPA 2.0-2.99: | 41% |
| SAT math: | 470-560 | Rank in top quarter: | 43% |
| SAT writing: | 460-560 | Rank in top tenth: | 16% |
| ACT composite: | 19-23 | Return as sophomores: | 80% |
| GPA 3.50 or higher: | 25% | Out-of-state: | 38% |
| GPA 3.0-3.49: | 32% | Live on campus: | 75% |

**Basis for selection.** Class rank and high school achievement weighed alongside performance on SAT/ACT. Course selection, achievement outside classroom, involvement in activities in and out of school, and letters or recommendations also considered. TOEFL used for admission of non-native English speakers. Essay recommended for all. Interview required for physician's assistant program; recommended for all others. Audition required for music program; portfolio recommended for art program. **Learning Disabled:** Students may request accommodation by submitting documentation to admissions office or coordinator of services for students with disabilities.

**High school preparation.** 16 units required. Required units include English 4, mathematics 2, social studies 3, science 1 (laboratory 1) and academic electives 6. Biological science must be laboratory science.

**2007-2008 Annual costs.** Tuition/fees: $24,090. Room/board: $10,410. Books/supplies: $900. Personal expenses: $800.

**2007-2008 Financial aid. Need-based:** 381 full-time freshmen applied for aid; 330 were judged to have need; 329 of these received aid. Average need met was 84%. Average scholarship/grant was $14,835; average loan $3,657. 65% of total undergraduate aid awarded as scholarships/grants, 35% as loans/jobs. **Non-need-based:** Awarded to 446 full-time undergraduates, including 122 freshmen. Scholarships awarded for academics, alumni affiliation, art, leadership, minority status, music/drama.

**Application procedures. Admission:** No deadline. $35 fee, may be waived for applicants with need. Application may be submitted online. Admission notification on a rolling basis beginning on or about 10/1. Must reply by May 1 or within 3 week(s) if notified thereafter. **Financial aid:** Priority date 2/15; no closing date. FAFSA required. Applicants notified on a rolling basis starting 2/15; must reply by 5/1 or within 3 week(s) of notification.

**Academics.** Healthy Family Center provides opportunities for study and research in nutrition, dietetics, and athletic performance; Robert J. Mellow Center for Athletics and Wellness provides full support for athletic training program. **Special study options:** Combined bachelor's/graduate degree, cross-registration, distance learning, double major, dual enrollment of high school students, ESL, honors, independent study, internships, semester at sea, student-designed major, study abroad, teacher certification program. Study abroad programs in China, India, Ghana, Australia; agreements also with Ireland, Italy, Spain, England, Costa Rica. **Credit/placement by examination:** AP, CLEP, IB, institutional tests. 30 credit hours maximum toward associate degree, 66 toward bachelor's. **Support services:** Learning center, pre-admission summer program, reduced course load, remedial instruction, study skills assistance, tutoring, writing center.

**Majors. Biology:** General, biotechnology. **Business:** Accounting, business admin, financial planning, hospitality admin, international, marketing. **Communications:** Advertising, digital media, public relations. **Computer sciences:** General. **Conservation:** Environmental science. **Education:** Art, biology, elementary, emotionally handicapped, ESL, family/consumer sciences, French, mathematics, music, science, secondary, social science, Spanish, special. **English:** English lit. **Foreign languages:** French, Spanish. **Health:** Art therapy, athletic training, audiology/speech pathology, clinical lab science, dietetics, health care admin, music therapy, nursing (RN), physician assistant. **History:** General. **Math:** General. **Parks/recreation:** Health/fitness. **Philosophy/religion:** Religion. **Protective services:** Law enforcement admin. **Psychology:** General, industrial. **Public administration:** Social work. **Social sciences:** General. **Theology:** Sacred music. **Transportation:** Aviation management. **Visual/performing arts:** Arts management, ceramics, dramatic, graphic design, illustration, interior design, music performance, musical theater, painting, photography, sculpture.

**Most popular majors.** Business/marketing 7%, education 16%, English 7%, health sciences 21%, psychology 7%, visual/performing arts 16%.

**Computing on campus.** 382 workstations in dormitories, library, computer center, student center. Dormitories wired for high-speed internet access and linked to campus network. Commuter students can connect to campus network. Online course registration, online library, helpline, repair service, student web hosting available.

**Student life. Freshman orientation:** Mandatory, $175 fee. Preregistration for classes offered. Includes program for families, held in midsummer for 2 days. Additional 2-day program prior to start of classes. **Policies:** First and second-year students under 21 not living at home with families in area required to live on campus. **Housing:** Guaranteed on-campus for freshmen. Coed dorms, single-sex dorms, special housing for disabled, apartments available. Volunteer services residential community and international students residential community available. **Activities:** Jazz band, campus ministries, dance, drama, international student organizations, music ensembles, musical theater, radio station, student government, student newspaper, TV station, Amnesty International, Collegiate Volunteers, environmental club, Volunteers in Action, Psi Chi, Peer Mediators, Gay-Straight Alliance, Americorps.

**Athletics.** NCAA. **Intercollegiate:** Baseball M, basketball, cross-country, field hockey W, lacrosse, soccer, softball W, tennis, volleyball W. **Intramural:** Badminton, basketball, football (non-tackle), football (tackle) M, ice hockey, racquetball, softball W, table tennis, volleyball W, water polo. **Team name:** Pacers.

**Student services.** Adult student services, alcohol/substance abuse counseling, campus ministries, career counseling, services for economically disadvantaged, student employment services, financial aid counseling, health services, minority student services, on-campus daycare, personal counseling, placement for graduates, women's services. **Physically disabled:** Services for visually, speech, hearing impaired. **Learning disabled:** Comprehensive services available.

**Contact.** E-mail: yourfuture@marywood.edu
Phone: (570) 348-6234 Toll-free number: (866) 279-9663
Fax: (570) 961-4763
Robert Reese, Director of University Admissions, Marywood University, 2300 Adams Avenue, Scranton, PA 18509-1598

## Mercyhurst College

**Erie, Pennsylvania**
www.mercyhurst.edu

CB code: 2410

- Private 4-year liberal arts college affiliated with Roman Catholic Church
- Residential campus in small city
- 3,921 degree-seeking undergraduates: 10% part-time, 58% women
- 283 graduate students
- 66% of applicants admitted
- SAT or ACT (ACT writing recommended) required
- 65% graduate within 6 years; 24% enter graduate study

**General.** Founded in 1926. Regionally accredited. **Degrees:** 579 bachelor's, 216 associate awarded; master's offered. **ROTC:** Army. **Location:** 100 miles from Pittsburgh, 90 miles from Buffalo, New York. **Calendar:** Trimester, limited summer session. **Full-time faculty:** 168 total; 47% have terminal degrees, 5% minority, 48% women. **Part-time faculty:** 133 total; 5% have terminal degrees, 5% minority, 41% women. **Class size:** 49% < 20, 38% 20-39, less than 1% 40-49, less than 1% 50-99. **Special facilities:** Observatory, archeological materials preservation laboratory.

**Freshman class profile.** 3,583 applied, 2,354 admitted, 671 enrolled.

| Mid 50% test scores | | | |
|---|---|---|---|
| SAT critical reading: | 480-580 | Rank in top quarter: | 43% |
| SAT math: | 480-580 | Rank in top tenth: | 18% |
| ACT composite: | 20-24 | End year in good standing: | 86% |
| GPA 3.50 or higher: | 46% | Return as sophomores: | 81% |
| GPA 3.0-3.49: | 32% | Out-of-state: | 60% |
| GPA 2.0-2.99: | 22% | Live on campus: | 93% |

**Basis for selection.** Admissions based on secondary school record. Class rank, standardized test scores, talent, ability, character, and personal qualities also important. Essay, interview recommended for all; audition required for dance, music programs; portfolio required for art program. **Homeschooled:** SAT/ACT and transcript preferred.

**High school preparation.** 16 units required. Required and recommended units include English 4, mathematics 3, social studies 4, history 1, science 2 (laboratory 1) and foreign language 2.

**2007-2008 Annual costs.** Tuition/fees: $21,876. Room/board: $7,800. Books/supplies: $1,000. Personal expenses: $2,000.

**Financial aid. Non-need-based:** Scholarships awarded for academics, alumni affiliation, art, athletics, leadership, minority status, music/drama, religious affiliation, ROTC.

**Application procedures. Admission:** Priority date 3/15; no deadline. $30 fee, may be waived for applicants with need. Application may be submitted online. Admission notification on a rolling basis beginning on or about 11/15. Must reply by May 1 or within 2 week(s) if notified thereafter. **Financial aid:** Priority date 3/1; no closing date. FAFSA required. Applicants notified on a rolling basis starting 2/15; must reply by 5/1 or within 2 week(s) of notification.

**Academics.** Education department offers graduate student-taught special education programs for learning disabled students. **Special study options:** Accelerated study, combined bachelor's/graduate degree, cooperative education, cross-registration, double major, dual enrollment of high school students, honors, independent study, internships, liberal arts/career combination, New York semester, semester at sea, student-designed major, study abroad, teacher certification program, Washington semester, weekend college. **Credit/placement by examination:** AP, CLEP, IB, SAT, ACT, institutional tests. 30 credit hours maximum toward bachelor's degree. **Support services:** Learning center, pre-admission summer program, reduced course load, remedial instruction, study skills assistance, tutoring, writing center.

**Majors. Biology:** General, biochemistry. **Business:** Accounting, business admin, finance, hospitality admin, international. **Communications:** General. **Computer sciences:** General. **Education:** Art, biology, business, chemistry, early childhood, elementary, English, family/consumer sciences, foreign languages, mathematics, music, science, secondary, social science, special. **English:** English lit. **Family/consumer sciences:** General. **Foreign languages:** General. **Health:** Art therapy, health services, medical records technology. **History:** General. **Interdisciplinary:** Global studies. **Math:** General. **Philosophy/religion:** Philosophy, religion. **Physical sciences:** Chemistry, geology. **Protective services:** Criminal justice, forensics. **Psychology:** General. **Public administration:** Social work. **Social sciences:** Anthropology, political science, sociology. **Theology:** Religious ed. **Visual/performing arts:** Dance, music performance, studio arts.

**Most popular majors.** Business/marketing 29%, education 16%, interdisciplinary studies 7%, security/protective services 8%.

**Computing on campus.** 350 workstations in dormitories, library, computer center, student center. Dormitories wired for high-speed internet access and linked to campus network. Commuter students can connect to campus network. Online course registration, online library, helpline, repair service, student web hosting, wireless network available.

**Student life. Freshman orientation:** Mandatory, $150 fee. Preregistration for classes offered. 3 days prior to start of classes. **Housing:** Guaranteed on-campus for all undergraduates. Single-sex dorms, apartments, substance-free housing available. $350 fully refundable deposit. **Activities:** Bands, choral groups, dance, drama, film society, literary magazine, music ensembles, musical theater, opera, radio station, student government, student newspaper, symphony orchestra, campus ministry, Association of Black Collegians, Habitat for Humanity, Amnesty International, ambassadors club.

**Athletics.** NCAA. **Intercollegiate:** Baseball M, basketball, cheerleading, cross-country, field hockey W, football (tackle) M, golf, ice hockey, lacrosse, rowing (crew), soccer, softball W, swimming M, tennis, volleyball, water polo, wrestling M. **Intramural:** Basketball, bowling, football (nontackle) M, ice hockey, skiing, soccer, softball, table tennis. **Team name:** Lakers.

**Student services.** Adult student services, alcohol/substance abuse counseling, campus ministries, career counseling, services for economically disadvantaged, student employment services, financial aid counseling, health services, personal counseling, placement for graduates, veterans' counselor. **Physically disabled:** Services for hearing impaired. **Learning disabled:** Comprehensive services available.

**Contact.** E-mail: admissions@mercyhurst.edu
Phone: (814) 824-2202 Toll-free number: (800) 825-1926
Fax: (814) 824-2071
Emily Crawford, Director of Admissions, Mercyhurst College, 501 East 38th Street, Erie, PA 16546-0001

---

## Messiah College
**Grantham, Pennsylvania**
www.messiah.edu

**CB member**
**CB code: 2411**

- Private 4-year liberal arts college affiliated with interdenominational tradition
- Residential campus in small town
- 2,798 degree-seeking undergraduates: 1% part-time, 63% women, 2% African American, 2% Asian American, 1% Hispanic American, 2% international
- 79% of applicants admitted
- Application essay required
- 74% graduate within 6 years; 17% enter graduate study

**General.** Founded in 1909. Regionally accredited. Students able to take coursework at Temple University. **Degrees:** 668 bachelor's awarded. **Location:** 10 miles from Harrisburg, 20 miles from Gettysburg. **Calendar:** Semester, limited summer session. **Full-time faculty:** 172 total; 81% have terminal degrees, 4% minority, 37% women. **Part-time faculty:** 116 total; 4% minority. **Class size:** 49% < 20, 49% 20-39, 1% 40-49, less than 1% 50-99, less than 1% >100. **Special facilities:** Historical library and archives, natural history museum, service and learning center, Anabaptist, Pietist, Wesleyan studies institute.

**Freshman class profile.** 2,496 applied, 1,961 admitted, 725 enrolled.

| Mid 50% test scores | | | |
|---|---|---|---|
| SAT critical reading: | 520-640 | GPA 2.0-2.99: | 6% |
| SAT math: | 520-640 | Rank in top quarter: | 67% |
| SAT writing: | 510-630 | Rank in top tenth: | 34% |
| ACT composite: | 22-27 | Return as sophomores: | 86% |
| GPA 3.50 or higher: | 76% | Out-of-state: | 47% |
| GPA 3.0-3.49: | 18% | Live on campus: | 98% |
| | | International: | 1% |

**Basis for selection.** Admitted students normally in top third of class and have B average or better. Statement of Christian commitment required. SAT or ACT recommended. Tests required of standard choice applicants. Students in the top 20% of high school class may apply without test scores, but must submit graded writing sample and have on-campus interview. Interview required for students who apply by the "Write Choice" application method, strongly recommended for all others. **Homeschooled:** Comprehensive transcript of senior year academic program as well as courses and course evaluations of 9th through 11th grades required. Include independent evaluation by qualified educator if available. **Learning Disabled:** Autobiographical statement required. Psychoeducational report (done within last 4 years) and interview required only after admissions decision. High school IEP recommended.

**High school preparation.** 16 units required; 20 recommended. Required and recommended units include English 4, mathematics 2-3, social studies 2, history 2, science 2-3 (laboratory 2-3), foreign language 2 and academic electives 4.

**2007-2008 Annual costs.** Tuition/fees: $24,420. Room/board: $7,340. Books/supplies: $900. Personal expenses: $1,200.

**2007-2008 Financial aid. Need-based:** 606 full-time freshmen applied for aid; 516 were judged to have need; 516 of these received aid. Average need met was 75%. Average scholarship/grant was $12,374; average loan $3,758. 61% of total undergraduate aid awarded as scholarships/grants, 39% as loans/jobs. **Non-need-based:** Awarded to 935 full-time undergraduates, including 270 freshmen. Scholarships awarded for academics, art, leadership, music/drama, religious affiliation.

**Application procedures. Admission:** Priority date 5/1; no deadline. $30 fee, may be waived for applicants with need. Application may be submitted online. Admission notification on a rolling basis beginning on or about 7/1. Must reply by May 1 or within 4 week(s) if notified thereafter. **Financial aid:** Priority date 4/1; no closing date. FAFSA required. Applicants notified on a rolling basis starting 3/15; must reply by 5/1 or within 4 week(s) of notification.

**Academics.** Supplemental instructional support available. **Special study options:** Accelerated study, double major, dual enrollment of high school students, ESL, exchange student, honors, independent study, internships, student-designed major, study abroad, teacher certification program, urban semester, Washington semester. Pass/Fail option. **Credit/placement by examination:** AP, CLEP, IB, institutional tests. 32 credit hours maximum toward bachelor's degree. **Support services:** Learning center, pre-admission summer program, reduced course load, remedial instruction, study skills assistance, tutoring, writing center.

**Majors. Biology:** General, biochemistry. **Business:** Accounting, business admin, e-commerce, entrepreneurial studies, human resources, international, managerial economics, marketing. **Communications:** General, journalism, radio/tv. **Computer sciences:** Computer science, information systems. **Conservation:** Environmental science, environmental studies. **Education:** Art, biology, chemistry, early childhood, elementary, English, family/consumer sciences, French, German, mathematics, music, physical, social studies, Spanish. **Engineering:** General. **English:** English lit. **Family/consumer sciences:** Family/community services. **Foreign languages:** French, German, Spanish. **Health:** Athletic training, clinical nutrition, nursing (RN), recreational therapy. **History:** General. **Interdisciplinary:** Biopsychology. **Liberal arts:** Humanities. **Math:** General. **Parks/recreation:** General, exercise sciences, sports admin. **Philosophy/religion:** Philosophy, religion. **Physical sciences:** Chemistry, physics. **Protective services:** Criminal justice. **Psychology:** General. **Public administration:** Social work. **Social sciences:** Economics, political science, sociology. **Theology:** Bible, religious ed. **Visual/performing arts:** Art history/conservation, arts management, dramatic, studio arts.

**Most popular majors.** Business/marketing 13%, communications/journalism 6%, education 12%, English 7%, health sciences 9%, parks/recreation 6%.

**Computing on campus.** 571 workstations in dormitories, library, computer center, student center. Dormitories wired for high-speed internet access and linked to campus network. Commuter students can connect to campus network. Online course registration, online library, helpline, student web hosting, wireless network available.

**Student life. Freshman orientation:** Mandatory. Preregistration for classes offered. 4-day orientation for students and parents during fall welcome weekend; includes placement exams and service day. **Policies:** Students generally required to live on campus unless married or living with relatives. Religious observance required. **Housing:** Guaranteed on-campus for all undergraduates. Coed dorms, single-sex dorms, special housing for disabled, apartments, substance-free housing available. $200 nonrefundable deposit, deadline 5/1. **Activities:** Bands, campus ministries, choral groups, dance, drama, film society, literary magazine, music ensembles, musical theater, radio station, student government, student newspaper, symphony orchestra, outreach teams, World Christian Fellowship, Nurses Christian Fellowship, Newman Club, Powerhouse band, Acclamation dance, Alliance of Confessing Theologies, service trips.

**Athletics.** NCAA. **Intercollegiate:** Baseball M, basketball, cross-country, field hockey W, golf M, lacrosse, soccer, softball W, tennis, track and field, volleyball W, wrestling M. **Intramural:** Basketball, football (non-tackle), racquetball, soccer, softball, volleyball. **Team name:** Falcons.

**Student services.** Campus ministries, career counseling, student employment services, financial aid counseling, health services, minority student services, on-campus daycare, personal counseling, placement for graduates. **Physically disabled:** Services for visually, speech, hearing impaired.

**Contact.** E-mail: admiss@messiah.edu
Phone: (717) 691-6000 Toll-free number: (800) 233-4220
Fax: (717) 796-5374
Chopka John, Dean for Enrollment Management, Messiah College, PO Box 3005, Grantham, PA 17027-0800

---

## Millersville University of Pennsylvania
Millersville, Pennsylvania    CB member
www.millersville.edu    CB code: 2656

- Public 4-year university and liberal arts college
- Residential campus in small town
- 7,164 degree-seeking undergraduates: 8% part-time, 56% women, 7% African American, 2% Asian American, 4% Hispanic American
- 630 degree-seeking graduate students
- 57% of applicants admitted
- SAT or ACT (ACT writing recommended) required
- 67% graduate within 6 years

**General.** Founded in 1855. Regionally accredited. **Degrees:** 1,397 bachelor's, 1 associate awarded; master's offered. **ROTC:** Army. **Location:** 5

miles from Lancaster, 35 miles from Harrisburg. **Calendar:** 4-1-4, limited summer session. **Full-time faculty:** 308 total; 96% have terminal degrees, 18% minority, 46% women. **Part-time faculty:** 126 total; 35% have terminal degrees, 7% minority, 52% women. **Class size:** 24% < 20, 67% 20-39, 5% 40-49, 3% 50-99, 1% >100. **Special facilities:** Early childhood center, teleconferencing center, weather station, foreign language lab, 2 art galleries.

**Freshman class profile.** 6,723 applied, 3,820 admitted, 1,345 enrolled.

| Mid 50% test scores | | | |
|---|---|---|---|
| SAT critical reading: | 470-570 | Rank in top tenth: | 14% |
| SAT math: | 480-580 | Return as sophomores: | 83% |
| SAT writing: | 460-560 | Out-of-state: | 4% |
| Rank in top quarter: | 44% | Live on campus: | 84% |

**Basis for selection.** High school record most important, followed by class rank, test scores and recommendations. Special consideration to students with special talents. Educationally and economically disadvantaged students may be admitted to Aim for Success enrichment program if they demonstrate potential for college success. Applicants without SAT scores may enroll as non-degree students and be admitted to degree-seeking status after completing 12 credits with 2.0 GPA. Interview required for applicants to disadvantaged program; recommended for all others. Audition required for music applicants; portfolio recommended for art applicants. RN required for nursing program.

**High school preparation.** 15 units required; 21 recommended. Required and recommended units include English 4, mathematics 3, social studies 3, history 2, science 3 (laboratory 1), foreign language 2 and academic electives 4.

**2007-2008 Annual costs.** Tuition/fees: $6,624; $14,391 out-of-state. Room/board: $6,876. Books/supplies: $900. Personal expenses: $1,714.

**2006-2007 Financial aid. Need-based:** 1,158 full-time freshmen applied for aid; 758 were judged to have need; 734 of these received aid. Average need met was 69%. Average scholarship/grant was $4,868; average loan $2,505. 48% of total undergraduate aid awarded as scholarships/grants, 52% as loans/jobs. **Non-need-based:** Awarded to 749 full-time undergraduates, including 213 freshmen. Scholarships awarded for academics, athletics, minority status.

**Application procedures. Admission:** Priority date 1/1; no deadline. $50 fee, may be waived for applicants with need. Application may be submitted online. Admission notification on a rolling basis beginning on or about 9/15. Extensions of reply date for accepted applicants granted upon request until May 1. **Financial aid:** Closing date 3/15. FAFSA required. Applicants notified on a rolling basis starting 3/19; must reply within 2 week(s) of notification.

**Academics. Special study options:** Accelerated study, combined bachelor's/graduate degree, cooperative education, cross-registration, distance learning, double major, dual enrollment of high school students, honors, independent study, internships, study abroad, teacher certification program. Adult and Continuing Education (ACE) program, off-campus study, learning disabilities services. **Credit/placement by examination:** AP, CLEP, institutional tests. **Support services:** Learning center, pre-admission summer program, reduced course load, remedial instruction, study skills assistance, tutoring, writing center.

**Majors. Biology:** General. **Business:** Business admin. **Communications:** General. **Computer sciences:** General. **Education:** Art, elementary, English, foreign languages, mathematics, music, science, secondary, social studies, special, technology/industrial arts. **Engineering technology:** Industrial, occupational safety. **English:** English lit. **Foreign languages:** French, German, Spanish. **Health:** Nursing (RN). **History:** General. **Math:** General. **Philosophy/religion:** Philosophy. **Physical sciences:** Atmospheric science, chemistry, geology, oceanography, physics. **Psychology:** General. **Public administration:** Social work. **Social sciences:** General, anthropology, economics, geography, international relations, political science, sociology. **Visual/performing arts:** Art.

**Most popular majors.** Biology 6%, business/marketing 12%, communications/journalism 8%, education 17%, engineering/engineering technologies 6%, English 7%, psychology 8%, social sciences 11%, visual/performing arts 6%.

**Computing on campus.** 580 workstations in dormitories, library, computer center, student center. Dormitories wired for high-speed internet access and linked to campus network. Commuter students can connect to campus network. Online course registration, online library, helpline, repair service, wireless network available.

**Student life. Freshman orientation:** Mandatory, $290 fee. Six-day program in August includes parents. **Housing:** Guaranteed on-campus for freshmen. Coed dorms, apartments, substance-free housing available. $125 partly refundable deposit, deadline 4/1. Academic interest housing available for several subject areas. University-affiliated apartments and dormitory for single students adjacent to campus. **Activities:** Bands, campus ministries, choral groups, dance, drama, literary magazine, music ensembles, musical theater, radio station, student government, student newspaper, symphony orchestra, TV station, University Christian Fellowship, black student union, College Republicans, Circle K, InterVarsity Christian Fellowship, Hillel, Habitat For Humanity.

**Athletics.** NCAA. **Intercollegiate:** Baseball M, basketball, cheerleading M, cross-country, field hockey W, football (tackle) M, golf M, lacrosse W, soccer, softball W, swimming W, tennis, track and field, volleyball W, wrestling M. **Intramural:** Badminton, basketball, golf, racquetball, soccer, softball, tennis, volleyball. **Team name:** Marauders.

**Student services.** Adult student services, alcohol/substance abuse counseling, campus ministries, career counseling, services for economically disadvantaged, student employment services, financial aid counseling, health services, minority student services, on-campus daycare, personal counseling, placement for graduates, veterans' counselor, women's services. **Physically disabled:** Services for visually, speech, hearing impaired.

**Contact.** E-mail: admissions@millersville.edu
Phone: (717) 872-3371 Toll-free number: (800) 682-3648
Fax: (717) 871-2147
Douglas Zander, Director of Admissions, Millersville University of Pennsylvania, PO Box 1002, Millersville, PA 17551-0302

## Misericordia University
Dallas, Pennsylvania
www.misericordia.edu

**CB member**
**CB code: 2087**

- Private 4-year health science and liberal arts college affiliated with Roman Catholic Church
- Residential campus in large town
- 2,003 degree-seeking undergraduates: 26% part-time, 74% women, 1% African American, 1% Asian American, 1% Hispanic American, 1% Native American
- 280 degree-seeking graduate students
- 74% of applicants admitted
- SAT or ACT (ACT writing optional) required
- 67% graduate within 6 years; 25% enter graduate study

**General.** Founded in 1924. Regionally accredited. Guaranteed Placement Program (within six months of graduation); Women with Children program for single women. **Degrees:** 473 bachelor's awarded; master's, doctoral offered. **ROTC:** Army, Air Force. **Location:** 9 miles from Wilkes-Barre, 20 miles from Scranton. **Calendar:** Semester, limited summer session. **Full-time faculty:** 94 total; 80% have terminal degrees, 5% minority, 52% women. **Part-time faculty:** 159 total; 9% have terminal degrees, less than 1% minority, 54% women. **Class size:** 60% < 20, 38% 20-39, 1% 40-49, less than 1% 50-99.

**Freshman class profile.** 1,289 applied, 949 admitted, 372 enrolled.

| Mid 50% test scores | | Rank in top quarter: | 53% |
|---|---|---|---|
| SAT critical reading: | 460-550 | Rank in top tenth: | 16% |
| SAT math: | 460-560 | End year in good standing: | 88% |
| ACT composite: | 19-24 | Return as sophomores: | 81% |
| GPA 3.50 or higher: | 34% | Out-of-state: | 25% |
| GPA 3.0-3.49: | 36% | Live on campus: | 83% |
| GPA 2.0-2.99: | 30% | | |

**Basis for selection.** In order of importance: high school achievement, test scores, character, recommendations from school teachers or counselors. Test scores weighed more heavily for health science programs. Essay, interview recommended. Essay required for occupational therapy applicants. **Homeschooled:** If applicant not affiliated with specific organization, college will accept transcript from home schooling parent that shows course work completed and grades achieved. GED not required. **Learning Disabled:** Essay, 3 letters of recommendation, documentation of disability, test results (i.e., WAIS) required. SAT/ACT not required.

**High school preparation.** 16 units required. Required units include English 4, mathematics 4, social studies 4 and science 4. 2 units science and algebra required for allied health applicants. Strong math background required for computer science, physical therapy, chemistry and biology applicants.

**2007-2008 Annual costs.** Tuition/fees: $21,950. Room/board: $9,100. Books/supplies: $850. Personal expenses: $500.

**2007-2008 Financial aid. Need-based:** 352 full-time freshmen applied for aid; 308 were judged to have need; 308 of these received aid. Average need met was 73%. Average scholarship/grant was $11,435; average loan $4,753. 61% of total undergraduate aid awarded as scholarships/grants, 39% as loans/jobs. **Non-need-based:** Awarded to 319 full-time undergraduates, including 85 freshmen. Scholarships awarded for academics, alumni affiliation, leadership, minority status, state residency.

**Application procedures. Admission:** No deadline. $25 fee, may be waived for applicants with need. Application may be submitted online. Admission notification on a rolling basis beginning on or about 9/1. Must reply by May 1 or within 4 week(s) if notified thereafter. Essay required for applicants to 5-year occupational therapy bachelor's/master's program. Closing date for applications to 5-year physical therapy bachelor's/master's program is February 1. **Financial aid:** Priority date 3/1, closing date 5/1. FAFSA, institutional form required. Applicants notified on a rolling basis starting 3/15; must reply by 5/1.

**Academics. Special study options:** Accelerated study, combined bachelor's/graduate degree, cross-registration, distance learning, double major, dual enrollment of high school students, honors, independent study, internships, student-designed major, study abroad, teacher certification program, weekend college. **Credit/placement by examination:** AP, CLEP, IB, SAT, ACT, institutional tests. 40 credit hours maximum toward bachelor's degree. **Support services:** Learning center, pre-admission summer program, study skills assistance, tutoring, writing center.

**Majors. Biology:** General, biochemistry. **Business:** Accounting, business admin, management science, marketing. **Communications:** General. **Computer sciences:** General, information technology. **Education:** Elementary, special. **English:** English lit. **Health:** Clinical lab science, medical radiologic technology/radiation therapy, nursing (RN). **History:** General. **Liberal arts:** Arts/sciences. **Math:** General. **Parks/recreation:** Sports admin. **Philosophy/religion:** Philosophy. **Physical sciences:** Chemistry. **Psychology:** General. **Public administration:** Social work.

**Most popular majors.** Business/marketing 17%, education 18%, health sciences 39%, psychology 6%.

**Computing on campus.** 100 workstations in dormitories, library, computer center, student center. Dormitories wired for high-speed internet access and linked to campus network. Commuter students can connect to campus network. Online course registration, online library, helpline, repair service, wireless network available.

**Student life. Freshman orientation:** Mandatory, $200 fee. Preregistration for classes offered. One-day testing for math and English placement. **Housing:** Coed dorms, substance-free housing available. $100 nonrefundable deposit, deadline 5/1. Leadership house, service house, apartment building for women with children located adjacent to campus. **Activities:** Jazz band, campus ministries, choral groups, dance, drama, literary magazine, music ensembles, radio station, student government, student newspaper, TV station, student nurses association, Council for Exceptional Children, Circle-K, Peer Associates, Diversity Institute.

**Athletics.** NCAA. **Intercollegiate:** Baseball M, basketball, cheerleading M, cross-country, field hockey W, golf M, lacrosse, soccer, softball W, swimming, tennis W, track and field, volleyball W. **Intramural:** Basketball, cross-country, football (non-tackle), racquetball, soccer, softball, tennis, volleyball. **Team name:** Cougars.

**Student services.** Adult student services, alcohol/substance abuse counseling, campus ministries, career counseling, services for economically disadvantaged, student employment services, financial aid counseling, health services, minority student services, personal counseling, placement for graduates, women's services. **Physically disabled:** Services for visually, speech, hearing impaired. **Learning disabled:** Comprehensive services available.

**Contact.** E-mail: admiss@misericordia.edu
Phone: (570) 674-6264 Toll-free number: (866) 262-6363
Fax: (570) 675-2441
Glenn Bozinski, Director of Admissions, Misericordia University, 301 Lake Street, Dallas, PA 18612-1098

## Moore College of Art and Design
Philadelphia, Pennsylvania
www.moore.edu

**CB code: 2417**

- Private 4-year visual arts college for women
- Residential campus in very large city
- 557 degree-seeking undergraduates
- 62% of applicants admitted
- Interview required

**General.** Founded in 1848. Regionally accredited. **Degrees:** 107 bachelor's awarded. **Location:** 90 miles from New York City. **Calendar:** Semester, limited summer session. **Full-time faculty:** 32 total. **Part-time faculty:** 112 total. **Class size:** 80% < 20, 20% 20-39. **Special facilities:** Professional galleries.

**Freshman class profile.** 491 applied, 302 admitted, 117 enrolled.

| Mid 50% test scores | | | |
|---|---|---|---|
| SAT critical reading: | 460-560 | GPA 3.0-3.49: | 50% |
| SAT math: | 420-520 | GPA 2.0-2.99: | 36% |
| ACT composite: | 16-22 | Out-of-state: | 44% |
| GPA 3.50 or higher: | 14% | Live on campus: | 65% |

**Basis for selection.** High school record, interview, portfolio, and test scores important. 850 SAT (exclusive of writing) or 18 ACT and 2.5 GPA required. Students must complete writing placement essay. Portfolio required; essay recommended for all. **Learning Disabled:** Students who request accommodations must provide qualifying documentation on professional letterhead and contain dates of assessment, signatures, titles, and license/certification numbers of diagnosing professionals. Documentation should be no more than 3 years old.

**High school preparation.** 14 units recommended. Recommended units include English 4, mathematics 2, social studies 4, science 2 and foreign language 2. 3 art recommended.

**2008-2009 Annual costs.** Tuition/fees (projected): $27,724. Room/board: $10,500. Books/supplies: $2,000. Personal expenses: $2,000.

**Financial aid. Non-need-based:** Scholarships awarded for academics, art, leadership.

**Application procedures. Admission:** Closing date 3/1 (postmark date). $40 fee, may be waived for applicants with need. Application may be submitted online. Admission notification on a rolling basis beginning on or about 11/15. Must reply by May 1 or within 3 week(s) if notified thereafter. **Financial aid:** Priority date 3/1, closing date 5/1. FAFSA required. Applicants notified on a rolling basis starting 2/15; must reply within 2 week(s) of notification.

**Academics. Special study options:** Double major, exchange student, independent study, internships, teacher certification program. **Credit/placement by examination:** AP, CLEP, institutional tests. 6 credit hours maximum toward bachelor's degree. **Support services:** Pre-admission summer program, reduced course load, study skills assistance, tutoring.

**Majors. Education:** Art. **Interdisciplinary:** Museum. **Visual/performing arts:** Art history/conservation, fashion design, fiber arts, graphic design, illustration, interior design, photography, studio arts.

**Most popular majors.** Visual/performing arts 95%.

**Computing on campus.** PC or laptop required. 125 workstations in dormitories, library, computer center. Dormitories wired for high-speed internet access. Online course registration, wireless network available.

**Student life. Freshman orientation:** Mandatory, $55 fee. Held 4 days prior to beginning of semester. **Housing:** Guaranteed on-campus for freshmen. Apartments, substance-free housing available. $250 partly refundable deposit, deadline 7/15. **Activities:** Student government, student newspaper, environmental committee, Emerging Leaders in the Arts, judicial board, residence life mentors.

**Student services.** Adult student services, career counseling, student employment services, financial aid counseling, health services, personal counseling, placement for graduates.

**Contact.** E-mail: admiss@moore.edu
Phone: (215) 965-4014 Toll-free number: (800) 523-2025
Fax: (215) 568-3547
Heeseung Lee, Director of Admissions, Moore College of Art and Design, The Parkway at 20th Street, Philadelphia, PA 19103-1179

## Moravian College
**Bethlehem, Pennsylvania**
www.moravian.edu

**CB member**
**CB code: 2418**

- Private 4-year liberal arts college affiliated with Moravian Church in America
- Residential campus in small city
- 1,661 degree-seeking undergraduates: 5% part-time, 58% women, 2% African American, 2% Asian American, 3% Hispanic American, 1% international
- 133 graduate students
- 64% of applicants admitted
- SAT or ACT with writing, application essay required
- 75% graduate within 6 years; 21% enter graduate study

**General.** Founded in 1742. Regionally accredited. Member of Lehigh Valley Association of Independent Colleges Consortium. Sixth oldest college in country. **Degrees:** 378 bachelor's awarded; master's offered. **ROTC:** Army. **Location:** 60 miles from Philadelphia, 90 miles from New York City. **Calendar:** Semester, extensive summer session. **Full-time faculty:** 118 total; 92% have terminal degrees, 5% minority, 49% women. **Part-time faculty:** 83 total; 37% have terminal degrees, 2% minority, 57% women. **Class size:** 63% < 20, 36% 20-39, 1% 40-49, less than 1% 50-99.

**Freshman class profile.** 2,189 applied, 1,401 admitted, 401 enrolled.

| Mid 50% test scores | | | |
|---|---|---|---|
| SAT critical reading: | 500-600 | Return as sophomores: | 86% |
| SAT math: | 500-610 | Out-of-state: | 38% |
| SAT writing: | 490-590 | Live on campus: | 88% |
| Rank in top quarter: | 54% | International: | 2% |
| Rank in top tenth: | 29% | Fraternities: | 10% |
| | | Sororities: | 22% |

**Basis for selection.** High school record and standardized test scores important. Academic credentials, character, extracurricular involvement, volunteer work and potential for contribution considered. Interviews strongly recommended; audition required for music applicants; portfolio required for art applicants. **Homeschooled:** Letter of recommendation (nonparent) required. Interview strongly encouraged in order to share educational background in detail.

**High school preparation.** 16 units required; 18 recommended. Required and recommended units include English 4, mathematics 3-4, social studies 4, science 3 (laboratory 2) and foreign language 2-3. 4 math units recommended for business, science, or math students.

**2007-2008 Annual costs.** Tuition/fees: $28,388. Room/board: $7,993. Books/supplies: $850. Personal expenses: $1,336.

**2007-2008 Financial aid. Need-based:** 351 full-time freshmen applied for aid; 303 were judged to have need; 303 of these received aid. Average need met was 83%. Average scholarship/grant was $16,505; average loan $4,271. 63% of total undergraduate aid awarded as scholarships/grants, 37% as loans/jobs. **Non-need-based:** Awarded to 396 full-time undergraduates, including 103 freshmen. Scholarships awarded for academics, alumni affiliation, leadership, music/drama, religious affiliation, ROTC.

**Application procedures. Admission:** Priority date 3/1; deadline 3/1 (postmark date). $40 fee, may be waived for applicants with need. Application may be submitted online. Admission notification 3/15. Must reply by 5/1. **Financial aid:** Priority date 2/14, closing date 3/15. FAFSA, CSS PROFILE required. Applicants notified on a rolling basis starting 4/1; must reply by 5/1 or within 2 week(s) of notification.

**Academics.** Learning Center offers partial but responsive program for learning disabled students. **Special study options:** Combined bachelor's/graduate degree, cross-registration, double major, honors, independent study, internships, student-designed major, study abroad, teacher certification program, Washington semester. Allied health program with Thomas Jefferson University, forestry program cooperative with Duke University, engineering programs cooperative with Lehigh University and Washington University (MO), dental program cooperative with Temple University. **Credit/placement by examination:** AP, CLEP, IB, SAT, ACT, institutional tests. Some courses not included in credit-by-examination option. **Support services:** Learning center, study skills assistance, tutoring, writing center.

**Majors. Area/ethnic studies:** German. **Biology:** General, biochemistry. **Business:** Accounting, business admin, international. **Computer sciences:** Computer science. **Conservation:** Environmental science, environmental studies. **Education:** Music, science, social science. **English:** Creative writing, English lit. **Foreign languages:** Classics, French, German, Spanish. **Health:** Clinical lab science, nursing (RN). **History:** General. **Interdisciplinary:** Neuroscience. **Math:** General. **Philosophy/religion:** Philosophy, religion. **Physical sciences:** Chemistry, geology, physics. **Protective services:** Criminal justice. **Psychology:** General. **Social sciences:** Economics, political science, sociology. **Theology:** Sacred music. **Visual/performing arts:** Art, art history/conservation, dramatic, graphic design, music performance, music theory/composition, studio arts. **Other:** Neuroscience.

**Most popular majors.** Biology 6%, business/marketing 20%, English 7%, health sciences 8%, history 6%, psychology 13%, social sciences 17%, visual/performing arts 11%.

**Computing on campus.** 263 workstations in library, computer center. Dormitories wired for high-speed internet access and linked to campus network. Commuter students can connect to campus network. Online library, helpline, repair service, wireless network available.

**Student life. Freshman orientation:** Mandatory, $100 fee. Preregistration for classes offered. Three-day program held immediately prior to fall semester. **Housing:** Guaranteed on-campus for all undergraduates. Coed dorms, single-sex dorms, apartments, fraternity/sorority housing, substance-free housing available. $400 nonrefundable deposit, deadline 5/1. Special interest housing and substance free housing available. Townhouses and suites available. **Activities:** Bands, campus ministries, choral groups, dance, drama, international student organizations, literary magazine, music ensembles, musical theater, radio station, student government, student newspaper, symphony orchestra, Hillel Society, Newman Association, international club, Moravian College Christian Fellowship, Spectrum, Catacombs, Campus Community Connection, The Forum, multicultural club, The Learning Connection.

**Athletics.** NCAA. **Intercollegiate:** Baseball M, basketball, cross-country, field hockey W, football (tackle) M, golf M, lacrosse, soccer, softball W, tennis, track and field, volleyball W. **Intramural:** Basketball, football (non-tackle), soccer, softball, table tennis, tennis, volleyball. **Team name:** Greyhounds.

**Student services.** Adult student services, alcohol/substance abuse counseling, campus ministries, career counseling, student employment services, financial aid counseling, health services, minority student services, personal counseling, placement for graduates. **Physically disabled:** Services for visually, speech, hearing impaired.

**Contact.** E-mail: admissions@moravian.edu
Phone: (610) 861-1320 Toll-free number: (800) 441-3191
Fax: (610) 625-7930
James Mackin, Director of Admission, Moravian College, 1200 Main Street, Bethlehem, PA 18018

---

## Mount Aloysius College
Cresson, Pennsylvania
www.mtaloy.edu                    CB code: 2420

- Private 4-year liberal arts college affiliated with Roman Catholic Church
- Commuter campus in small town
- 1,483 degree-seeking undergraduates: 22% part-time, 72% women, 2% African American, 1% Hispanic American, 1% international
- 51 degree-seeking graduate students
- 87% of applicants admitted
- SAT or ACT (ACT writing optional), application essay required
- 41% graduate within 6 years

**General.** Founded in 1939. Regionally accredited. **Degrees:** 148 bachelor's, 237 associate awarded; master's offered. **Location:** 12 miles from Altoona, 90 miles from Pittsburgh. **Calendar:** Semester, limited summer session. **Full-time faculty:** 58 total; 38% have terminal degrees, 71% women. **Part-time faculty:** 112 total; less than 1% minority, 49% women. **Class size:** 67% < 20, 32% 20-39, less than 1% 40-49. **Special facilities:** Health and science center with mock operating room, telehealth/telenursing, ecumenical library.

**Freshman class profile.** 951 applied, 830 admitted, 307 enrolled.

| Mid 50% test scores | | | |
|---|---|---|---|
| SAT critical reading: | 410-500 | GPA 3.0-3.49: | 40% |
| SAT math: | 410-510 | GPA 2.0-2.99: | 31% |
| SAT writing: | 400-490 | Return as sophomores: | 66% |
| ACT composite: | 16-19 | Out-of-state: | 8% |
| GPA 3.50 or higher: | 26% | Live on campus: | 50% |
| | | International: | 1% |

**Basis for selection.** School record, test scores, activities, talent, and character most important. Nursing entrance test not required for students with SAT of 900 (exclusive of Writing) or higher. Placement test waived if student scores 500 or higher in either section. Interview required for students with lower SAT scores and GPA. Interviews and essays required for physical therapist assistant majors. **Learning Disabled:** Admission interview required.

**High school preparation.** 16 units required; 21 recommended. Required and recommended units include English 4, mathematics 3, social studies 3, history 3, science 3, foreign language 2 and academic electives 3. Algebra and 2 lab sciences required for nursing. Algebra, chemistry required for physical therapist assistant, radiography and medical imaging applicants. Biology required for occupational therapy assistant applicants.

**2007-2008 Annual costs.** Tuition/fees: $15,990. Room/board: $7,700. Books/supplies: $1,400. Personal expenses: $2,750.

**2006-2007 Financial aid. Need-based:** 309 full-time freshmen applied for aid; 274 were judged to have need; 274 of these received aid. Average

need met was 23%. Average scholarship/grant was $2,120; average loan $2,394. 57% of total undergraduate aid awarded as scholarships/grants, 43% as loans/jobs. **Non-need-based:** Awarded to 72 full-time undergraduates, including 70 freshmen. Scholarships awarded for academics, art, leadership, music/drama, religious affiliation.

**Application procedures. Admission:** No deadline. $30 fee, may be waived for applicants with need. Application may be submitted online. Admission notification on a rolling basis beginning on or about 8/1. **Financial aid:** Priority date 2/15; no closing date. FAFSA required. Applicants notified on a rolling basis starting 3/15; must reply within 4 week(s) of notification.

**Academics. Special study options:** Accelerated study, combined bachelor's/graduate degree, distance learning, honors, independent study, internships, student-designed major, teacher certification program. **Credit/placement by examination:** AP, CLEP, institutional tests. 15 credit hours maximum toward associate degree, 30 toward bachelor's. **Support services:** Learning center, pre-admission summer program, reduced course load, remedial instruction, study skills assistance, tutoring, writing center.

**Majors. Business:** Accounting, accounting/business management, business admin. **Computer sciences:** General, information technology. **Education:** Early childhood, elementary. **English:** English lit. **Foreign languages:** Sign language interpretation. **Health:** Health services, nursing (RN), physician assistant, radiologic technology/medical imaging. **History:** General. **Interdisciplinary:** Behavioral sciences, math/computer science. **Legal studies:** Prelaw. **Liberal arts:** Arts/sciences, humanities. **Protective services:** Criminal justice. **Psychology:** General. **Social sciences:** General, criminology, political science.

**Most popular majors.** Business/marketing 20%, education 7%, health sciences 29%, liberal arts 20%, security/protective services 8%.

**Computing on campus.** 175 workstations in dormitories, library, computer center, student center. Dormitories linked to campus network. Helpline, repair service available.

**Student life. Freshman orientation:** Mandatory. **Housing:** Guaranteed on-campus for all undergraduates. Coed dorms available. **Activities:** Choral groups, drama, student government, student newspaper, campus ministry, nursing, occupational therapy assistant, business, Phi Theta Kappa, student programming council.

**Athletics.** NCAA. **Intercollegiate:** Baseball M, basketball, cross-country, golf, soccer, softball W, volleyball W. **Intramural:** Baseball M, basketball, football (tackle), golf, skiing, soccer, softball W, table tennis, tennis, volleyball. **Team name:** Mounties.

**Student services.** Alcohol/substance abuse counseling, campus ministries, career counseling, student employment services, financial aid counseling, health services, on-campus daycare, personal counseling, placement for graduates, veterans' counselor. **Physically disabled:** Services for hearing impaired.

**Contact.** E-mail: admissions@mtaloy.edu
Phone: (814) 886-6383 Toll-free number: (888) 823-2220
Fax: (814) 886-6441
Frank Crouse, Vice President for Enrollment Management/Dean of Admissions, Mount Aloysius College, 7373 Admiral Peary Highway, Cresson, PA 16630

---

## Muhlenberg College
Allentown, Pennsylvania              CB member
www.muhlenberg.edu              CB code: 2424

- Private 4-year liberal arts college affiliated with Evangelical Lutheran Church in America
- Residential campus in small city
- 2,324 degree-seeking undergraduates: 4% part-time, 58% women, 2% African American, 2% Asian American, 4% Hispanic American
- 37% of applicants admitted
- Application essay required
- 83% graduate within 6 years; 35% enter graduate study

**General.** Founded in 1848. Regionally accredited. **Degrees:** 542 bachelor's, 5 associate awarded. **ROTC:** Army. **Location:** 55 miles from Philadelphia, 90 miles from New York City. **Calendar:** Semester, limited summer session. **Full-time faculty:** 161 total; 89% have terminal degrees, 6% minority, 48% women. **Part-time faculty:** 114 total; 10% have terminal degrees, 10% minority, 39% women. **Class size:** 65% < 20, 34% 20-39, less than 1% 40-49, less than 1% 50-99, less than 1% >100. **Special facilities:** 3-theater complex, electronic music studio, natural history museum, 38-acre environmental field station, greenhouse, two electron microscopes, isolation laboratories, DNA sequencer, 20-foot boat for marine studies, 60-acre arboretum.

**Freshman class profile.** 4,703 applied, 1,750 admitted, 551 enrolled.

| Mid 50% test scores | | | |
|---|---|---|---|
| SAT critical reading: | 550-650 | GPA 2.0-2.99: | 20% |
| SAT math: | 560-660 | Rank in top quarter: | 80% |
| SAT writing: | 560-660 | Rank in top tenth: | 47% |
| ACT composite: | 24-29 | End year in good standing: | 98% |
| GPA 3.50 or higher: | 40% | Return as sophomores: | 92% |
| GPA 3.0-3.49: | 40% | Out-of-state: | 91% |
| | | Live on campus: | 99% |

**Basis for selection.** High school courses, grades, class rank, test scores, personal qualities, essay, recommendations, special talents and activities important. Interview strongly recommended. Test scores optional; SAT/ACT required for consideration for Assured Admission Medical and Dental Programs, Merit Scholarships, honors programs. Audition recommended for dance, drama, music programs; portfolio recommended for art program. **Homeschooled:** Statement describing homeschool structure and mission, transcript of courses and grades, state high school equivalency certificate, letter of recommendation (nonparent) required. Interview strongly recommended.

**High school preparation.** 16 units required; 20 recommended. Required and recommended units include English 4, mathematics 3-4, social studies 1, history 2-3, science 2-4 (laboratory 2), foreign language 2-3 and academic electives 2. Advanced placement and accelerated courses encouraged.

**2007-2008 Annual costs.** Tuition/fees: $33,090. Room/board: $7,940.

**2007-2008 Financial aid. Need-based:** 339 full-time freshmen applied for aid; 234 were judged to have need; 234 of these received aid. Average need met was 91%. Average scholarship/grant was $19,116; average loan $3,398. 82% of total undergraduate aid awarded as scholarships/grants, 18% as loans/jobs. **Non-need-based:** Awarded to 907 full-time undergraduates, including 231 freshmen. Scholarships awarded for academics, art, leadership, music/drama.

**Application procedures. Admission:** Closing date 2/15 (postmark date). $50 fee, may be waived for applicants with need. Application may be submitted online. Admission notification 3/15. Must reply by 5/1. **Financial aid:** Closing date 2/15. FAFSA, institutional form, CSS PROFILE required. Applicants notified by 4/1; must reply by 5/1.

**Academics. Special study options:** Accelerated study, combined bachelor's/graduate degree, cross-registration, double major, exchange student, honors, independent study, internships, student-designed major, study abroad, teacher certification program, Washington semester. Study abroad with Lehigh Valley Association of Independent Colleges; over 60 agreements with foreign universities for study abroad; 3-2 or 4-2 combined Degree Program in Engineering with Columbia University or Washington University. MC/Penn Dental Program-University of Pennsylvania. Combined program with Drexel University College of Medicine. 7-year Optometry Program-State University of New York 3-2 or 4-2. Combined Degree Program in Environmental Science or Forestry. **Credit/placement by examination:** AP, CLEP, IB, SAT, ACT, institutional tests. 68 credit hours maximum toward bachelor's degree. 68 credit hours equivalent to 17 course units. **Support services:** Learning center, reduced course load, study skills assistance, tutoring, writing center.

**Majors. Area/ethnic studies:** American, German, Russian/Slavic. **Biology:** General, biochemistry. **Business:** Accounting, business admin, finance, human resources, management information systems. **Communications:** General. **Computer sciences:** General. **Conservation:** Environmental science. **English:** English lit. **Foreign languages:** General, French, German, Spanish. **History:** General. **Interdisciplinary:** Natural sciences, neuroscience. **Math:** General. **Philosophy/religion:** Philosophy, religion. **Physical sciences:** General, chemistry, physics. **Psychology:** General. **Social sciences:** Anthropology, economics, international relations, political science, sociology. **Visual/performing arts:** Art, dance, dramatic, film/cinema.

**Most popular majors.** Biology 8%, business/marketing 24%, communications/journalism 9%, English 7%, psychology 10%, social sciences 12%, visual/performing arts 14%.

**Computing on campus.** 490 workstations in dormitories, library, computer center. Dormitories wired for high-speed internet access and linked to campus network. Commuter students can connect to campus network. Helpline, repair service, wireless network available.

**Student life. Freshman orientation:** Mandatory, $120 fee. Preregistration for classes offered. 3-day program prior to start of classes in August. **Policies:** Students share responsibility for maintaining high standards and must pledge to abide by Academic Behavior Code. **Housing:** Guaranteed on-campus for all undergraduates. Coed dorms, single-sex dorms, special

housing for disabled, apartments, fraternity/sorority housing, substance-free housing available. $400 deposit, deadline 5/1. College-owned houses in neighborhood surrounding campus. **Activities:** Bands, campus ministries, choral groups, dance, drama, international student organizations, literary magazine, music ensembles, musical theater, radio station, student government, student newspaper, TV station, over 100 clubs and organizations.

**Athletics.** NCAA. **Intercollegiate:** Baseball M, basketball, cheerleading, cross-country, field hockey W, football (tackle) M, golf, lacrosse, soccer, softball W, tennis, track and field, volleyball W, wrestling M. **Intramural:** Basketball, cross-country, football (non-tackle) M, racquetball, soccer, softball, tennis, volleyball. **Team name:** Mules.

**Student services.** Adult student services, alcohol/substance abuse counseling, campus ministries, career counseling, student employment services, financial aid counseling, health services, minority student services, personal counseling, placement for graduates, women's services. **Physically disabled:** Services for visually, speech, hearing impaired.

**Contact.** E-mail: admissions@muhlenberg.edu
Phone: (484) 664-3200 Fax: (484) 664-3234
Christopher Hooker-Haring, Dean of Admission and Financial Aid, Muhlenberg College, 2400 Chew Street, Allentown, PA 18104

---

## Neumann College
### Aston, Pennsylvania
### www.neumann.edu
**CB member**
**CB code: 2628**

- Private 4-year liberal arts college affiliated with Roman Catholic Church
- Residential campus in large town
- 2,499 degree-seeking undergraduates: 21% part-time, 65% women, 13% African American, 1% Asian American, 2% Hispanic American, 2% international
- 585 degree-seeking graduate students
- 95% of applicants admitted
- SAT or ACT required
- 56% graduate within 6 years; 20% enter graduate study

**General.** Founded in 1965. Regionally accredited. Provides Catholic education in Franciscan tradition. **Degrees:** 392 bachelor's, 23 associate awarded; master's, doctoral offered. **ROTC:** Army. **Location:** 19 miles from Philadelphia. **Calendar:** Semester, limited summer session. **Full-time faculty:** 89 total; 53% have terminal degrees, 4% minority. **Part-time faculty:** 200 total; 15% have terminal degrees, 5% minority. **Class size:** 46% < 20, 51% 20-39, 2% 40-49, 2% 50-99. **Special facilities:** Franciscan studies institute, Betty Neumann archives.

**Freshman class profile.** 2,490 applied, 2,359 admitted, 540 enrolled.

| Mid 50% test scores | | | |
|---|---|---|---|
| SAT critical reading: | 400-490 | Rank in top tenth: | 30% |
| SAT math: | 400-490 | End year in good standing: | 90% |
| GPA 3.50 or higher: | 5% | Return as sophomores: | 74% |
| GPA 3.0-3.49: | 45% | Out-of-state: | 32% |
| GPA 2.0-2.99: | 50% | Live on campus: | 72% |
| Rank in top quarter: | 50% | International: | 3% |

**Basis for selection.** Acceptance depends on major applied for, SAT scores and high school GPA. Interview recommended. **Homeschooled:** State high school equivalency certificate required.

**High school preparation.** 16 units required; 17 recommended. Required and recommended units include English 4, mathematics 2, social studies 2, science 2-3, foreign language 2 and academic electives 4.

**2007-2008 Annual costs.** Tuition/fees: $19,486. Room/board: $8,838. Books/supplies: $1,500. Personal expenses: $1,000.

**2006-2007 Financial aid.** All financial aid based on need. 490 full-time freshmen applied for aid; 490 were judged to have need; 490 of these received aid. Average scholarship/grant was $17,000; average loan $3,000. 50% of total undergraduate aid awarded as scholarships/grants, 50% as loans/jobs.

**Application procedures. Admission:** No deadline. $35 fee, may be waived for applicants with need. Admission notification on a rolling basis. Must reply by May 1 or within 2 week(s) if notified thereafter. **Financial aid:** No deadline. FAFSA required. Applicants notified on a rolling basis; must reply within 2 week(s) of notification.

**Academics. Special study options:** Accelerated study, combined bachelor's/graduate degree, cooperative education, distance learning, double major, honors, independent study, internships, liberal arts/career combination, student-designed major, study abroad, teacher certification program, weekend college. **Credit/placement by examination:** AP, CLEP, institutional tests. 15 credit hours maximum toward associate degree, 30 toward bachelor's. **Support services:** Learning center, reduced course load, remedial instruction, study skills assistance, tutoring, writing center.

**Majors. Biology:** General. **Business:** Accounting, business admin, international, marketing. **Communications:** General. **Computer sciences:** General. **Conservation:** Environmental studies. **Education:** Early childhood, elementary. **English:** English lit. **Health:** Clinical lab technology, nursing (RN). **Liberal arts:** Arts/sciences. **Parks/recreation:** Health/fitness, sports admin. **Philosophy/religion:** Religion. **Protective services:** Criminal justice. **Psychology:** General. **Social sciences:** Political science.

**Most popular majors.** Business/marketing 11%, education 13%, health sciences 14%, legal studies 8%, liberal arts 30%, parks/recreation 7%, psychology 7%.

**Computing on campus.** 300 workstations in dormitories, library, computer center. Dormitories wired for high-speed internet access and linked to campus network. Commuter students can connect to campus network. Online library, helpline, wireless network available.

**Student life. Freshman orientation:** Mandatory. Preregistration for classes offered. Held the last weekend before classes begin. **Policies:** Alcohol-free campus. **Housing:** Guaranteed on-campus for all undergraduates. Coed dorms, apartments available. $200 deposit, deadline 8/1. **Activities:** Jazz band, choral groups, dance, drama, international student organizations, literary magazine, music ensembles, musical theater, student government, student newspaper, TV station, Black student union, environmental club, bio/sci club, business association, professional education society, student nurses association, psychology club.

**Athletics.** NCAA. **Intercollegiate:** Baseball M, basketball, field hockey W, golf M, ice hockey, lacrosse, soccer, softball W, tennis, volleyball W. **Intramural:** Basketball, lacrosse M, softball W, table tennis, tennis, volleyball. **Team name:** Knights.

**Student services.** Adult student services, campus ministries, career counseling, services for economically disadvantaged, student employment services, financial aid counseling, health services, on-campus daycare, personal counseling, placement for graduates.

**Contact.** E-mail: neumann@neumann.edu
Phone: (610) 558-5616 Toll-free number: (800) 963-8626
Fax: (610) 558-5652
Dennis Murphy, Vice President for Enrollment Managament, Neumann College, One Neumann Drive, Aston, PA 19014-1298

---

### Peirce College
**Philadelphia, Pennsylvania**
www.peirce.edu
**CB member**
**CB code: 2674**

- Private 4-year business and technical college
- Commuter campus in very large city
- 2,172 degree-seeking undergraduates: 59% part-time, 73% women, 55% African American, 1% Asian American, 6% Hispanic American, 2% international
- 75% graduate within 6 years

**General.** Founded in 1865. Regionally accredited. **Degrees:** 239 bachelor's, 251 associate awarded. **Calendar:** Semester, limited summer session. **Full-time faculty:** 30 total; 60% have terminal degrees, 30% minority, 53% women. **Part-time faculty:** 137 total; 18% have terminal degrees, 26% minority. **Class size:** 91% < 20, 9% 20-39.

**Freshman class profile.** 63 enrolled.

| | | | |
|---|---|---|---|
| End year in good standing: | 77% | Out-of-state: | 15% |
| Return as sophomores: | 60% | International: | 1% |

**Basis for selection.** Open admission.

**2007-2008 Annual costs.** Tuition/fees: $13,750. Books/supplies: $1,000. Personal expenses: $2,000.

**2006-2007 Financial aid. Need-based:** 18 full-time freshmen applied for aid; 18 were judged to have need; 18 of these received aid. Average need met was 90%. Average scholarship/grant was $5,252; average loan $2,236. 38% of total undergraduate aid awarded as scholarships/grants, 62% as loans/jobs. **Non-need-based:** Awarded to 344 full-time undergraduates,

---

including 8 freshmen. Scholarships awarded for academics, leadership. **Additional information:** Tuition discounts available for US students serving in US military and in protect-and-serve fields.

**Application procedures. Admission:** No deadline. $50 fee, may be waived for applicants with need. Application may be submitted online. Admission notification on a rolling basis. **Financial aid:** Priority date 6/1; no closing date. FAFSA required. Applicants notified on a rolling basis; must reply within 3 week(s) of notification.

**Academics. Special study options:** Accelerated study, cooperative education, distance learning, independent study, weekend college. **Credit/placement by examination:** AP, CLEP, IB, institutional tests. 30 credit hours maximum toward associate degree, 90 toward bachelor's. **Support services:** Learning center, reduced course load, study skills assistance, tutoring.

**Majors. Business:** Business admin. **Computer sciences:** Information systems. **Legal studies:** Paralegal.

**Most popular majors.** Business/marketing 55%, computer/information sciences 25%, legal studies 20%.

**Computing on campus.** PC or laptop required. 36 workstations in library, computer center, student center. Online course registration, online library, helpline, wireless network available.

**Student life. Freshman orientation:** Mandatory, $483 fee. Preregistration for classes offered. **Activities:** Chi Alpha Epsilon Honor Society, Delta Mu Delta Honor Society, paralegal student association, information technology student association.

**Student services.** Adult student services, career counseling, services for economically disadvantaged, student employment services, financial aid counseling, health services. **Physically disabled:** Services for visually, hearing impaired.

**Contact.** E-mail: info@peirce.edu
Phone: (215) 670-9214 Toll-free number: (888) 467-3472 ext. 9214
Fax: (215) 670-9366
Nadine Maher, Dean of Enrollment Management, Peirce College, 1420 Pine Street, Philadelphia, PA 19102-4699

---

### Penn State Abington
**Abington, Pennsylvania**
www.abington.psu.edu
**CB code: 2660**

- Public 4-year branch campus college
- Commuter campus in small city
- 2,902 degree-seeking undergraduates: 13% part-time, 49% women, 13% African American, 15% Asian American, 6% Hispanic American, 1% international
- 80% of applicants admitted
- SAT or ACT with writing required
- 48% graduate within 6 years; 22% enter graduate study

**General.** Founded in 1950. Regionally accredited. **Degrees:** 375 bachelor's, 45 associate awarded. **ROTC:** Army, Air Force. **Location:** 15 miles from Philadelphia. **Calendar:** Semester, limited summer session. **Full-time faculty:** 105 total; 59% have terminal degrees, 11% minority, 46% women. **Part-time faculty:** 105 total; 30% have terminal degrees, 8% minority, 49% women. **Class size:** 35% < 20, 56% 20-39, 3% 40-49, 4% 50-99, 2% >100.

**Freshman class profile.** 3,604 applied, 2,870 admitted, 870 enrolled.

| Mid 50% test scores | | Rank in top quarter: | 29% |
|---|---|---|---|
| SAT critical reading: | 400-520 | Rank in top tenth: | 10% |
| SAT math: | 420-540 | Return as sophomores: | 73% |
| GPA 3.50 or higher: | 19% | Out-of-state: | 9% |
| GPA 3.0-3.49: | 31% | International: | 1% |
| GPA 2.0-2.99: | 49% | | |

**Basis for selection.** Admission decisions based upon high school GPA, standardized test scores, class rank, personal statements, activities. Essay considered if submitted; portfolios required for select majors. **Home-schooled:** Provide complete documentation showing courses studied and all evaluations presented from homeschool evaluator or supervisor assigned to student in cooperation with local school district or evaluator approved through program.

**High school preparation.** Required units include English 4, mathematics 3, social studies 3, science 3 and foreign language 2.

**2007-2008 Annual costs.** Tuition/fees: $11,006; $16,506 out-of-state. Books/supplies: $1,168. Personal expenses: $1,854.

**2006-2007 Financial aid. Need-based:** 725 full-time freshmen applied for aid; 559 were judged to have need; 548 of these received aid. Average need met was 68%. Average scholarship/grant was $6,317; average loan $2,557. 54% of total undergraduate aid awarded as scholarships/grants, 46% as loans/jobs. **Non-need-based:** Awarded to 485 full-time undergraduates, including 328 freshmen. Scholarships awarded for academics, alumni affiliation, athletics, ROTC.

**Application procedures. Admission:** Priority date 11/30; no deadline. $50 fee, may be waived for applicants with need. Application may be submitted online. Admission notification on a rolling basis beginning on or about 11/1. All freshmen applications processed at University Park Campus. **Financial aid:** Priority date 2/15; no closing date. FAFSA required. Applicants notified on a rolling basis starting 3/1.

**Academics. Special study options:** Accelerated study, combined bachelor's/ graduate degree, cooperative education, distance learning, double major, dual enrollment of high school students, ESL, exchange student, external degree, honors, independent study, internships, liberal arts/career combination, student-designed major, study abroad, teacher certification program. **Credit/ placement by examination:** AP, CLEP, IB, SAT. 60 credit hours maximum toward bachelor's degree. **Support services:** Learning center, pre-admission summer program, remedial instruction, study skills assistance, tutoring, writing center.

**Majors. Agriculture:** General, agribusiness operations, agronomy, animal sciences, education services, food science, horticultural science, landscaping, mechanization, soil science, turf management. **Area/ethnic studies:** African-American, American, East Asian, Latin American, women's. **Biology:** General, bacteriology, biochemistry, biomedical sciences. **Business:** General, accounting, actuarial science, communications, finance, hospitality admin, labor relations, management information systems, managerial economics, marketing, organizational behavior. **Communications:** General, advertising, journalism. **Computer sciences:** General, information systems. **Conservation:** General, forest sciences, forest technology. **Education:** Adult/ continuing, art, elementary, foreign languages, secondary, special. **Engineering:** Aerospace, agricultural, architectural, biomedical, chemical, civil, computer, electrical, environmental, industrial, materials science, mechanical, mining, nuclear, petroleum, science. **English:** English lit. **Family/ consumer sciences:** Family studies, human nutrition. **Foreign languages:** Classics, comparative lit, French, German, Italian, Japanese, Russian, Spanish. **Health:** Communication disorders, health care admin, nursing (RN), premedicine. **History:** General. **Interdisciplinary:** Biological/physical sciences, medieval/Renaissance. **Liberal arts:** Arts/sciences. **Math:** General, statistics. **Parks/recreation:** General, exercise sciences. **Philosophy/ religion:** Judaic, philosophy, religion. **Physical sciences:** Astronomy, atmospheric science, chemistry, geology, physics. **Protective services:** Criminal justice, law enforcement admin. **Psychology:** General, social. **Science technology:** Biological. **Social sciences:** Anthropology, applied economics, archaeology, economics, geography, international relations, political science, sociology. **Visual/performing arts:** General, acting, art, art history/ conservation, film/cinema, graphic design, theater design. **Other:** Rehabilitation and therapeutic studies.

**Most popular majors.** Business/marketing 38%, computer/information sciences 7%, psychology 17%, security/protective services 16%.

**Computing on campus.** 150 workstations in library, computer center. Commuter students can connect to campus network. Online course registration, online library, helpline, repair service, student web hosting, wireless network available.

**Student life. Freshman orientation:** Mandatory, $30 fee. Preregistration for classes offered. Three-part process before classes start: 1-day orientation, advising appointment, and new student day. **Policies:** Acts of intolerance and high-risk drinking discouraged at all locations. All facilities designated smoke-free. Students expected to abide by The Penn State Principles. **Activities:** Campus ministries, dance, drama, film society, literary magazine, student government, student newspaper, Christian Fellowship, Asian club, black student union, Hillel, lesbian and gay alliance, Latino student association, Italian American organization, Muslim student association, Praise and Worship gospel association.

**Athletics. Intercollegiate:** Baseball M, basketball, golf, lacrosse, soccer, softball, tennis, volleyball W. **Intramural:** Basketball, cross-country, football (non-tackle) M, handball, soccer, softball, tennis, volleyball. **Team name:** Nittany Lions.

**Student services.** Adult student services, alcohol/substance abuse counseling, career counseling, services for economically disadvantaged, student employment services, financial aid counseling, health services, minority student services, personal counseling, placement for graduates, veterans' counselor. **Physically disabled:** Services for visually, speech, hearing impaired.

**Contact.** E-mail: admissions@psu.edu
Phone: (814) 865-5471 Fax: (814) 863-7590
Anne Rohrbach, Executive Director for Undergraduate Admissions, Penn State Abington, 201 Shields Building, University Park, PA 16802-1294

## Penn State Altoona
**Altoona, Pennsylvania**
**www.aa.psu.edu**                                    CB code: 2660

- Public 4-year branch campus college
- Residential campus in small city
- 3,854 degree-seeking undergraduates: 5% part-time, 49% women, 6% African American, 2% Asian American, 2% Hispanic American, 1% international
- 70% of applicants admitted
- SAT or ACT with writing required
- 65% graduate within 6 years; 22% enter graduate study

**General.** Founded in 1929. Regionally accredited. **Degrees:** 316 bachelor's, 95 associate awarded. **ROTC:** Army, Air Force. **Location:** 2 miles from downtown. **Calendar:** Semester, limited summer session. **Full-time faculty:** 150 total; 72% have terminal degrees, 9% minority, 42% women. **Part-time faculty:** 150 total; 23% have terminal degrees, 3% minority, 47% women. **Class size:** 39% < 20, 45% 20-39, 5% 40-49, 10% 50-99, less than 1% >100. **Special facilities:** MAC lab, CAD lab, robotics lab, manufacturing lab, automation lab, environmental studies lab, comprehensive art studio space.

**Freshman class profile.** 5,930 applied, 4,122 admitted, 1,494 enrolled.

| Mid 50% test scores | | Rank in top tenth: | 8% |
|---|---|---|---|
| SAT critical reading: | 450-550 | Return as sophomores: | 84% |
| SAT math: | 460-570 | Out-of-state: | 16% |
| GPA 3.50 or higher: | 11% | International: | 1% |
| GPA 3.0-3.49: | 45% | Fraternities: | 4% |
| GPA 2.0-2.99: | 44% | Sororities: | 2% |
| Rank in top quarter: | 32% | | |

**Basis for selection.** Admission decisions based upon high school GPA, test scores, class rank, personal statements, and activities. Essay considered if submitted; portfolios required for select majors. **Homeschooled:** Provide complete documentation showing courses studied and all evaluations presented from homeschool evaluator or supervisor assigned to student in cooperation with local school district or evaluator approved through program.

**High school preparation.** Required units include English 4, mathematics 3, social studies 3, science 3 and foreign language 2.

**2007-2008 Annual costs.** Tuition/fees: $11,464; $17,246 out-of-state. Room/board: $7,750. Books/supplies: $1,168. Personal expenses: $2,916.

**2006-2007 Financial aid. Need-based:** 1,203 full-time freshmen applied for aid; 924 were judged to have need; 886 of these received aid. Average need met was 63%. Average scholarship/grant was $5,387; average loan $2,751. 41% of total undergraduate aid awarded as scholarships/grants, 59% as loans/jobs. **Non-need-based:** Awarded to 809 full-time undergraduates, including 293 freshmen. Scholarships awarded for academics, alumni affiliation, athletics, ROTC.

**Application procedures. Admission:** Priority date 11/30; no deadline. $50 fee, may be waived for applicants with need. Application may be submitted online. Admission notification on a rolling basis beginning on or about 11/1. All freshmen applications processed at University Park Campus. **Financial aid:** Priority date 2/15; no closing date. FAFSA required. Applicants notified on a rolling basis starting 3/1.

**Academics. Special study options:** Cooperative education, cross-registration, distance learning, double major, dual enrollment of high school students, ESL, honors, independent study, internships, liberal arts/career combination, student-designed major, study abroad, teacher certification program. **Credit/placement by examination:** AP, CLEP, IB, SAT. 60 credit hours maximum toward bachelor's degree. **Support services:** Learning center, remedial instruction, study skills assistance, tutoring, writing center.

**Majors. Agriculture:** General, agribusiness operations, agronomy, animal sciences, education services, food science, horticultural science, landscaping, mechanization, soil science, turf management. **Area/ethnic studies:** African-American, American, East Asian, Latin American, women's. **Biology:** General, bacteriology, biochemistry, biomedical sciences. **Business:** General, accounting, actuarial science, finance, hospitality admin, labor relations, management information systems, managerial economics, marketing, organizational behavior. **Communications:** General, advertising, journalism. **Computer sciences:** General, information systems. **Conservation:**

General, environmental studies, forest sciences, forest technology. **Education:** Adult/continuing, art, elementary, foreign languages, secondary, special. **Engineering:** Aerospace, agricultural, architectural, biomedical, chemical, civil, computer, electrical, environmental, industrial, materials science, mechanical, mining, nuclear, petroleum, science. **English:** English lit. **Family/consumer sciences:** Family studies, human nutrition. **Foreign languages:** Classics, comparative lit, French, German, Italian, Japanese, Russian, Spanish. **Health:** Communication disorders, health care admin, nursing (RN), premedicine. **History:** General. **Interdisciplinary:** Biological/physical sciences, medieval/Renaissance. **Liberal arts:** Arts/sciences. **Math:** General, statistics. **Parks/recreation:** Exercise sciences, facilities management. **Philosophy/religion:** Judaic, philosophy, religion. **Physical sciences:** Astronomy, atmospheric science, chemistry, geology, physics. **Protective services:** Criminal justice, law enforcement admin. **Psychology:** General. **Science technology:** Biological. **Social sciences:** Anthropology, applied economics, archaeology, economics, geography, international relations, political science, sociology. **Visual/performing arts:** General, acting, art, art history/conservation, film/cinema, graphic design, theater design. **Other:** Rehabilitation and therapeutic studies.

**Most popular majors.** Business/marketing 17%, education 15%, engineering/engineering technologies 8%, family/consumer sciences 7%, psychology 11%, security/protective services 17%.

**Computing on campus.** 450 workstations in dormitories, library, computer center. Dormitories wired for high-speed internet access and linked to campus network. Commuter students can connect to campus network. Online course registration, online library, helpline, student web hosting, wireless network available.

**Student life. Freshman orientation:** Mandatory. Preregistration for classes offered. Begins Saturday prior to start of classes and runs 2 weeks. **Policies:** Acts of intolerance and high-risk drinking discouraged at all locations. All facilities designated as smoke-free. **Housing:** Coed dorms, special housing for disabled, substance-free housing available. $100 partly refundable deposit, deadline 5/1. Suites, special interest housing available. **Activities:** Bands, campus ministries, choral groups, dance, drama, film society, international student organizations, literary magazine, music ensembles, student government, student newspaper, black student union, Circle K, Latin American student association, Catholic campus community, Students About Living Truth, Jewish student association, Asian student association, German club, Eco-Action, Being United for Social Transformation.

**Athletics.** NAIA. **Intercollegiate:** Baseball M, basketball, cross-country, diving, golf, soccer, softball W, swimming, tennis, volleyball W. **Intramural:** Badminton, basketball, football (non-tackle), football (tackle), racquetball, soccer, softball, table tennis, track and field, triathlon, volleyball, weight lifting. **Team name:** Nittany Lions.

**Student services.** Adult student services, alcohol/substance abuse counseling, campus ministries, career counseling, services for economically disadvantaged, student employment services, financial aid counseling, health services, minority student services, personal counseling, placement for graduates, veterans' counselor, women's services. **Physically disabled:** Services for visually, speech, hearing impaired.

**Contact.** E-mail: admissions@psu.edu
Phone: (814) 865-5471 Fax: (814) 863-7590
Anne Rohrbach, Executive Director for Undergraduate Admissions, Penn State Altoona, 201 Shields Building, University Park, PA 16802-1294

---

### Penn State Beaver
**Monaca, Pennsylvania**
**www.br.psu.edu**                    CB code: 2660

▸ Public 4-year branch campus college

▸ Residential campus in small town

▸ 697 degree-seeking undergraduates: 6% part-time, 37% women, 8% African American, 3% Asian American, 2% Hispanic American

▸ 92% of applicants admitted

▸ SAT or ACT with writing required

▸ 47% graduate within 6 years; 22% enter graduate study

**General.** Founded in 1964. Regionally accredited. **Degrees:** 57 bachelor's, 2 associate awarded. **Location:** 30 miles from Pittsburgh. **Calendar:** Semester, limited summer session. **Full-time faculty:** 30 total; 70% have terminal degrees, 20% minority, 50% women. **Part-time faculty:** 24 total; 29% have terminal degrees, 46% women. **Class size:** 39% < 20, 53% 20-39, 5% 40-49, 3% 50-99.

**Freshman class profile.** 891 applied, 822 admitted, 301 enrolled.

| Mid 50% test scores | | | |
|---|---|---|---|
| SAT critical reading: | 420-530 | Rank in top quarter: | 28% |
| SAT math: | 430-560 | Rank in top tenth: | 7% |
| GPA 3.50 or higher: | 11% | Return as sophomores: | 73% |
| GPA 3.0-3.49: | 33% | Out-of-state: | 15% |
| GPA 2.0-2.99: | 52% | International: | 1% |

**Basis for selection.** Admission decisions based upon high school GPA as well as other factors, including standardized verbal and math test scores, class rank, personal statements, activities lists. Essay considered if submitted; portfolios required for select majors. **Homeschooled:** Helpful if applicants provide complete documentation showing courses studied and all evaluations from home school evaluator or supervisor assigned to student in cooperation with local school district or evaluator approved through program.

**High school preparation.** Required units include English 4, mathematics 3, social studies 3, science 3 and foreign language 2.

**2007-2008 Annual costs.** Tuition/fees: $11,006; $16,506 out-of-state. Room/board: $7,750. Books/supplies: $1,168. Personal expenses: $2,916.

**2006-2007 Financial aid. Need-based:** 218 full-time freshmen applied for aid; 174 were judged to have need; 172 of these received aid. Average need met was 71%. Average scholarship/grant was $5,555; average loan $2,669. 46% of total undergraduate aid awarded as scholarships/grants, 54% as loans/jobs. **Non-need-based:** Awarded to 186 full-time undergraduates, including 123 freshmen. Scholarships awarded for academics, alumni affiliation, athletics, ROTC.

**Application procedures. Admission:** Priority date 11/30; no deadline. $50 fee, may be waived for applicants with need. Application may be submitted online. Admission notification on a rolling basis beginning on or about 11/1. All freshmen applications processed at University Park Campus. **Financial aid:** Priority date 2/15; no closing date. FAFSA required. Applicants notified on a rolling basis starting 3/1.

**Academics. Special study options:** Accelerated study, cross-registration, distance learning, double major, dual enrollment of high school students, ESL, honors, independent study, internships, semester at sea, study abroad. **Credit/placement by examination:** AP, CLEP, IB, SAT. 60 credit hours maximum toward bachelor's degree. **Support services:** Learning center, pre-admission summer program, reduced course load, remedial instruction, study skills assistance, tutoring, writing center.

**Majors. Agriculture:** General, agribusiness operations, agronomy, animal sciences, education services, food science, horticultural science, landscaping, mechanization, soil science, turf management. **Area/ethnic studies:** African-American, American, East Asian, Latin American, women's. **Biology:** General, bacteriology, biochemistry, biomedical sciences. **Business:** Accounting, actuarial science, business admin, finance, hospitality admin, labor relations, management information systems, managerial economics, marketing, organizational behavior. **Communications:** General, advertising, journalism. **Computer sciences:** General, information systems. **Conservation:** General, forest sciences, forest technology. **Education:** Adult/continuing, art, elementary, foreign languages, secondary, special. **Engineering:** Aerospace, agricultural, architectural, biomedical, chemical, civil, computer, electrical, environmental, industrial, materials science, mechanical, mining, nuclear, petroleum, science. **English:** English lit. **Family/consumer sciences:** Family studies, human nutrition. **Foreign languages:** Classics, comparative lit, French, German, Italian, Japanese, Russian, Spanish. **Health:** Communication disorders, health care admin, nursing (RN), premedicine. **History:** General. **Interdisciplinary:** Biological/physical sciences, medieval/Renaissance. **Liberal arts:** Arts/sciences. **Math:** General, statistics. **Parks/recreation:** Exercise sciences, facilities management. **Philosophy/religion:** Judaic, philosophy, religion. **Physical sciences:** Astronomy, atmospheric science, chemistry, geology, physics. **Protective services:** Criminal justice, law enforcement admin. **Psychology:** General. **Science technology:** Biological. **Social sciences:** Anthropology, applied economics, archaeology, economics, geography, international relations, political science, sociology. **Visual/performing arts:** General, acting, art, art history/conservation, film/cinema, graphic design, theater design. **Other:** Rehabilitation and therapeutic studies.

**Most popular majors.** Business/marketing 40%, communications/journalism 12%, computer/information sciences 23%, psychology 25%.

**Computing on campus.** 127 workstations in library, computer center, student center. Dormitories wired for high-speed internet access and linked to campus network. Commuter students can connect to campus network. Online course registration, online library, helpline, repair service, student web hosting, wireless network available.

**Student life. Freshman orientation:** Mandatory, $30 fee. Preregistration for classes offered. One-day orientation session just before classes begin.

**Policies:** Acts of intolerance and high-risk drinking discouraged at all locations. All facilities designated as smoke-free. **Housing:** Coed dorms available. $100 partly refundable deposit, deadline 5/1. Townhouses available. **Activities:** Campus ministries, drama, film society, literary magazine, radio station, student government, student newspaper, Common Ground Christian club, Big Brothers/Big Sisters mentoring program.

**Athletics.** NJCAA. **Intercollegiate:** Baseball M, basketball, soccer M, softball W, volleyball W. **Intramural:** Basketball, bowling, football (non-tackle), table tennis, volleyball. **Team name:** Nittany Lions.

**Student services.** Adult student services, alcohol/substance abuse counseling, campus ministries, career counseling, services for economically disadvantaged, student employment services, financial aid counseling, health services, personal counseling, placement for graduates, veterans' counselor. **Physically disabled:** Services for visually, speech, hearing impaired.

**Contact.** E-mail: admissions@psu.edu
Phone: (814) 865-5471 Fax: (814) 863-7590
Anne Rohrbach, Executive Director for Undergraduate Admissions, Penn State Beaver, 201 Shields Building, University Park, PA 16802-1294

---

## Penn State Berks
### Reading, Pennsylvania
### www.bk.psu.edu
**CB code: 2660**

- Public 4-year branch campus college
- Residential campus in small city
- 2,557 degree-seeking undergraduates: 8% part-time, 42% women, 8% African American, 4% Asian American, 4% Hispanic American, 1% international
- 75% of applicants admitted
- SAT or ACT with writing required
- 61% graduate within 6 years; 22% enter graduate study

**General.** Founded in 1924. Regionally accredited. **Degrees:** 225 bachelor's, 58 associate awarded. **ROTC:** Army. **Location:** 5 miles from downtown. **Calendar:** Semester, limited summer session. **Full-time faculty:** 109 total; 68% have terminal degrees, 11% minority, 42% women. **Part-time faculty:** 81 total; 15% have terminal degrees, 5% minority, 47% women. **Class size:** 37% < 20, 42% 20-39, 12% 40-49, 10% 50-99.

**Freshman class profile.** 3,354 applied, 2,532 admitted, 929 enrolled.

| Mid 50% test scores | | | |
|---|---|---|---|
| SAT critical reading: | 420-540 | Rank in top quarter: | 24% |
| SAT math: | 430-560 | Rank in top tenth: | 5% |
| GPA 3.50 or higher: | 7% | Return as sophomores: | 80% |
| GPA 3.0-3.49: | 28% | Out-of-state: | 9% |
| GPA 2.0-2.99: | 64% | International: | 1% |

**Basis for selection.** Admission decisions based upon high school GPA, test scores, class rank, personal statements, and activities. Essay considered if submitted; portfolios required for select majors. **Homeschooled:** Complete documentation showing courses studied and all evaluations presented from home school evaluator or supervisor assigned to student in cooperation with local school district or evaluator approved through program required.

**High school preparation.** Required units include English 4, mathematics 3, social studies 3, science 3 and foreign language 2.

**2007-2008 Annual costs.** Tuition/fees: $11,464; $17,246 out-of-state. Room/board: $8,420. Books/supplies: $1,168. Personal expenses: $2,916.

**2006-2007 Financial aid. Need-based:** 776 full-time freshmen applied for aid; 544 were judged to have need; 530 of these received aid. Average need met was 61%. Average scholarship/grant was $5,447; average loan $2,668. 42% of total undergraduate aid awarded as scholarships/grants, 58% as loans/jobs. **Non-need-based:** Awarded to 326 full-time undergraduates, including 138 freshmen. Scholarships awarded for academics, alumni affiliation, athletics, ROTC.

**Application procedures. Admission:** Priority date 11/30; no deadline. $50 fee, may be waived for applicants with need. Application may be submitted online. Admission notification on a rolling basis beginning on or about 11/1. All freshmen applications processed at University Park Campus. **Financial aid:** Priority date 2/15; no closing date. FAFSA required. Applicants notified on a rolling basis starting 3/1.

**Academics. Special study options:** Accelerated study, cooperative education, cross-registration, distance learning, dual enrollment of high school students, honors, independent study, internships, study abroad. **Credit/**

**placement by examination:** AP, CLEP, IB, SAT. 60 credit hours maximum toward bachelor's degree. **Support services:** Learning center, preadmission summer program, remedial instruction, study skills assistance, tutoring, writing center.

**Majors. Agriculture:** General, agribusiness operations, agronomy, animal sciences, education services, food science, horticultural science, landscaping, mechanization, soil science, turf management. **Area/ethnic studies:** African-American, American, East Asian, Latin American, women's. **Biology:** General, bacteriology, biochemistry, biomedical sciences. **Business:** General, accounting, actuarial science, finance, hospitality admin, labor relations, management information systems, managerial economics, marketing, organizational behavior. **Communications:** General, advertising, journalism. **Computer sciences:** General, information systems. **Conservation:** General, forest sciences, forest technology. **Education:** Adult/continuing, art, elementary, foreign languages, secondary, special. **Engineering:** Aerospace, agricultural, architectural, biomedical, chemical, civil, computer, electrical, environmental, industrial, materials science, mechanical, mining, nuclear, petroleum, science. **English:** English lit, technical writing. **Family/consumer sciences:** Family studies, human nutrition. **Foreign languages:** General, classics, comparative lit, French, German, Italian, Japanese, Russian, Spanish. **Health:** Communication disorders, health care admin, nursing (RN), premedicine. **History:** General. **Interdisciplinary:** Biological/physical sciences, medieval/Renaissance. **Liberal arts:** Arts/sciences. **Math:** General, statistics. **Parks/recreation:** Exercise sciences, facilities management. **Philosophy/religion:** Judaic, philosophy, religion. **Physical sciences:** Astronomy, atmospheric science, chemistry, geology, physics. **Protective services:** Criminal justice, law enforcement admin. **Psychology:** General. **Science technology:** Biological. **Social sciences:** Anthropology, applied economics, archaeology, economics, geography, international relations, political science, sociology. **Visual/performing arts:** General, acting, art, art history/conservation, film/cinema, graphic design, theater design. **Other:** Rehabilitation and therapeutic studies.

**Most popular majors.** Business/marketing 37%, computer/information sciences 14%, engineering/engineering technologies 7%, English 7%, interdisciplinary studies 10%, parks/recreation 8%, psychology 7%.

**Computing on campus.** 311 workstations in dormitories, library, computer center, student center. Dormitories wired for high-speed internet access and linked to campus network. Commuter students can connect to campus network. Online course registration, online library, helpline, repair service, student web hosting, wireless network available.

**Student life. Freshman orientation:** Mandatory. Preregistration for classes offered. Week prior to the start of classes. **Policies:** All facilities smoke-free. **Housing:** Coed dorms, special housing for disabled, substance-free housing available. $100 partly refundable deposit, deadline 5/1. Honor students, suites, special interest houses available. **Activities:** Pep band, campus ministries, choral groups, dance, drama, film society, international student organizations, radio station, student government, student newspaper, Christian Fellowship, Dimensions-the Ethnic Society, multicultural dance group, substance free, Rainbow Alliance, political science club, spiritual praise choir, yoga and meditation society.

**Athletics.** NCAA. **Intercollegiate:** Baseball M, basketball, cross-country, golf M, soccer, softball W, tennis, volleyball W. **Intramural:** Badminton, basketball, football (non-tackle), golf, table tennis, volleyball. **Team name:** NIttany Lions.

**Student services.** Adult student services, alcohol/substance abuse counseling, career counseling, services for economically disadvantaged, student employment services, financial aid counseling, health services, minority student services, personal counseling, placement for graduates, veterans' counselor. **Physically disabled:** Services for visually, speech, hearing impaired. **Learning disabled:** Comprehensive services available.

**Contact.** E-mail: admissions@psu.edu
Phone: (814) 865-5471 Fax: (814) 863-7590
Anne Rohrbach, Executive Director for Undergraduate Admissions, Penn State Berks, 201 Shields Building, University Park, PA 16802-1294

---

## Penn State Brandywine
### Media, Pennsylvania
### www.de.psu.edu
**CB code: 2660**

- Public 4-year branch campus college
- Commuter campus in small town
- 1,455 degree-seeking undergraduates: 10% part-time, 43% women, 15% African American, 9% Asian American, 3% Hispanic American
- 80% of applicants admitted
- SAT or ACT with writing required
- 39% graduate within 6 years; 22% enter graduate study

**General.** Founded in 1966. Regionally accredited. **Degrees:** 179 bachelor's, 3 associate awarded. **ROTC:** Army, Air Force. **Location:** 20 miles from Philadelphia. **Calendar:** Semester, limited summer session. **Full-time faculty:** 61 total; 57% have terminal degrees, 15% minority, 51% women. **Part-time faculty:** 54 total; 17% have terminal degrees, 7% minority, 50% women. **Class size:** 36% < 20, 54% 20-39, 6% 40-49, 3% 50-99, less than 1% >100.

**Freshman class profile.** 1,745 applied, 1,401 admitted, 434 enrolled.

| Mid 50% test scores | | GPA 2.0-2.99: | 58% |
|---|---|---|---|
| SAT critical reading: | 410-520 | Rank in top quarter: | 23% |
| SAT math: | 420-540 | Rank in top tenth: | 6% |
| GPA 3.50 or higher: | 12% | Return as sophomores: | 69% |
| GPA 3.0-3.49: | 29% | Out-of-state: | 4% |

**Basis for selection.** Admission decisions based on high school GPA, as well as other factors, which may include standardized verbal and math test scores, class rank, personal statements, and list of activities. Essay considered if submitted; portfolios required for select majors. **Homeschooled:** Applicants should provide complete documentation showing courses studied and all evaluations presented from evaluator or supervisor assigned to student in cooperation with local school district or evaluator approved through program.

**High school preparation.** Required units include English 4, mathematics 3, social studies 3, science 3 and foreign language 2.

**2007-2008 Annual costs.** Tuition/fees: $11,006; $16,506 out-of-state. Books/supplies: $1,168. Personal expenses: $1,854.

**2006-2007 Financial aid. Need-based:** 386 full-time freshmen applied for aid; 272 were judged to have need; 263 of these received aid. Average need met was 69%. Average scholarship/grant was $5,922; average loan $2,351. 53% of total undergraduate aid awarded as scholarships/grants, 47% as loans/jobs. **Non-need-based:** Awarded to 276 full-time undergraduates, including 171 freshmen. Scholarships awarded for academics, alumni affiliation, athletics, ROTC.

**Application procedures. Admission:** Priority date 11/30; no deadline. $50 fee, may be waived for applicants with need. Application may be submitted online. Admission notification on a rolling basis beginning on or about 11/1. All freshmen applications processed at University Park Campus. **Financial aid:** Priority date 2/15; no closing date. FAFSA required. Applicants notified on a rolling basis starting 3/1.

**Academics. Special study options:** Combined bachelor's/graduate degree, distance learning, double major, dual enrollment of high school students, ESL, honors, independent study, internships, study abroad, teacher certification program. **Credit/placement by examination:** AP, CLEP, IB, SAT. 60 credit hours maximum toward bachelor's degree. **Support services:** Learning center, pre-admission summer program, reduced course load, remedial instruction, study skills assistance, tutoring, writing center.

**Majors. Agriculture:** General, agribusiness operations, agronomy, animal sciences, education services, food science, horticultural science, landscaping, mechanization, soil science, turf management. **Area/ethnic studies:** African-American, American, East Asian, Latin American, women's. **Biology:** General, bacteriology, biochemistry, biomedical sciences. **Business:** Accounting, actuarial science, business admin, finance, hospitality admin, labor relations, management information systems, managerial economics, marketing, organizational behavior. **Communications:** General, advertising, journalism. **Computer sciences:** General, information systems. **Conservation:** General, forest sciences, forest technology. **Education:** Adult/continuing, art, elementary, foreign languages, secondary, special. **Engineering:** Aerospace, agricultural, architectural, biomedical, chemical, civil, computer, electrical, environmental, industrial, materials science, mechanical, mining, nuclear, petroleum, science. **English:** English lit. **Family/consumer sciences:** Family studies, human nutrition. **Foreign languages:** Classics, comparative lit, French, German, Italian, Japanese, Russian, Spanish. **Health:** Communication disorders, health care admin, nursing (RN), premedicine. **History:** General. **Interdisciplinary:** Biological/physical sciences, medieval/Renaissance. **Liberal arts:** Arts/sciences. **Math:** General, statistics. **Parks/recreation:** Exercise sciences, facilities management. **Philosophy/religion:** Judaic, philosophy, religion. **Physical sciences:** Astronomy, atmospheric science, chemistry, geology, physics. **Protective services:** Criminal justice, law enforcement admin. **Psychology:** General. **Science technology:** Biological. **Social sciences:** Anthropology, applied economics, archaeology, economics, geography, international relations, political science, sociology. **Visual/performing arts:** General, acting, art, art history/conservation, film/cinema, graphic design, theater design. **Other:** Rehabilitation and therapeutic studies.

**Most popular majors.** Business/marketing 39%, communications/journalism 12%, computer/information sciences 13%, education 6%, English 6%, family/consumer sciences 13%, liberal arts 9%.

**Computing on campus.** 142 workstations in library, computer center, student center. Commuter students can connect to campus network. Online course registration, online library, helpline, repair service, student web hosting, wireless network available.

**Student life. Freshman orientation:** Available. Preregistration for classes offered. Held in summer, prior to fall semester. **Policies:** Acts of intolerance and high-risk drinking discouraged at all locations. All facilities designated smoke-free. **Activities:** Choral groups, dance, drama, film society, international student organizations, literary magazine, student government, student newspaper, black student league, Nittany Christian Fellowship, gay-straight alliance, gospel ensemble, Jewish student league.

**Athletics. Intercollegiate:** Baseball M, basketball, soccer, tennis, volleyball W. **Intramural:** Basketball, soccer. **Team name:** Nittany Lions.

**Student services.** Adult student services, alcohol/substance abuse counseling, career counseling, services for economically disadvantaged, student employment services, financial aid counseling, health services, minority student services, personal counseling, placement for graduates, veterans' counselor, women's services. **Physically disabled:** Services for visually, speech, hearing impaired.

**Contact.** E-mail: admissions@psu.edu
Phone: (814) 865-5471 Fax: (814) 863-7590
Anne Rohrbach, Executive Director for Undergraduate Admissions, Penn State Brandywine, 201 Shields Building, University Park, PA 16802-1294

---

### Penn State Dubois
**DuBois, Pennsylvania**
**www.ds.psu.edu**                   CB code: 2660

- Public 4-year branch campus college
- Commuter campus in small town
- 724 degree-seeking undergraduates: 15% part-time, 51% women, 1% African American
- 88% of applicants admitted
- SAT or ACT with writing required
- 46% graduate within 6 years; 22% enter graduate study

**General.** Founded in 1935. Regionally accredited. **Degrees:** 52 bachelor's, 87 associate awarded. **Location:** 120 miles from Pittsburgh. **Calendar:** Semester, limited summer session. **Full-time faculty:** 43 total; 65% have terminal degrees, 14% minority, 44% women. **Part-time faculty:** 46 total; 20% have terminal degrees, 50% women. **Class size:** 67% < 20, 29% 20-39, less than 1% 40-49, 2% 50-99, less than 1% >100.

**Freshman class profile.** 539 applied, 472 admitted, 228 enrolled.

| Mid 50% test scores | | GPA 2.0-2.99: | 53% |
|---|---|---|---|
| SAT critical reading: | 410-500 | Rank in top quarter: | 21% |
| SAT math: | 420-550 | Rank in top tenth: | 5% |
| GPA 3.50 or higher: | 11% | Return as sophomores: | 82% |
| GPA 3.0-3.49: | 35% | Out-of-state: | 2% |

**Basis for selection.** Admission decisions based upon high school GPA, as well as other factors, which may include standardized verbal and math test scores, class rank, personal statements, and list of activities. Essay considered if submitted; portfolios required for select majors. **Homeschooled:** Applicants should provide complete documentation showing the courses studied and all evaluations presented from evaluator or supervisor assigned to student in cooperation with local school district or evaluator who is approved through the program.

**High school preparation.** Required units include English 4, mathematics 3, social studies 3, science 3 and foreign language 2.

**2007-2008 Annual costs.** Tuition/fees: $10,996; $16,496 out-of-state. Books/supplies: $1,168. Personal expenses: $1,854.

**2006-2007 Financial aid. Need-based:** 176 full-time freshmen applied for aid; 151 were judged to have need; 148 of these received aid. Average need met was 65%. Average scholarship/grant was $5,363; average loan $2,555. 52% of total undergraduate aid awarded as scholarships/grants, 48% as loans/jobs. **Non-need-based:** Awarded to 163 full-time undergraduates, including 69 freshmen. Scholarships awarded for academics, alumni affiliation, athletics, ROTC.

**Application procedures. Admission:** Priority date 11/30; no deadline. $50 fee, may be waived for applicants with need. Application may be submitted online. Admission notification on a rolling basis beginning on or about 11/1. All freshmen applications processed at University Park Campus. **Financial aid:** Priority date 2/15; no closing date. FAFSA required. Applicants notified on a rolling basis starting 3/1.

**Academics.** **Special study options:** Accelerated study, cross-registration, distance learning, double major, dual enrollment of high school students, honors, independent study, internships, student-designed major, study abroad. **Credit/placement by examination:** AP, CLEP, IB, SAT. 60 credit hours maximum toward bachelor's degree. **Support services:** Learning center, reduced course load, remedial instruction, study skills assistance, tutoring, writing center.

**Majors.** **Agriculture:** General, agribusiness operations, agronomy, animal sciences, education services, food science, horticultural science, landscaping, mechanization, soil science, turf management. **Area/ethnic studies:** African-American, American, East Asian, Latin American, women's. **Biology:** General, bacteriology, biochemistry, biomedical sciences. **Business:** Accounting, actuarial science, business admin, finance, hospitality admin, labor relations, management information systems, managerial economics, marketing, organizational behavior. **Communications:** General, advertising, journalism. **Computer sciences:** General, information systems. **Conservation:** General, forest sciences, forest technology. **Education:** Adult/continuing, art, elementary, foreign languages, secondary, special. **Engineering:** Aerospace, agricultural, architectural, biomedical, chemical, civil, computer, electrical, environmental, industrial, materials science, mechanical, mining, nuclear, petroleum, science. **English:** English lit. **Family/consumer sciences:** Family studies, human nutrition. **Foreign languages:** Classics, comparative lit, French, German, Italian, Japanese, Russian, Spanish. **Health:** Communication disorders, health care admin, nursing (RN), premedicine. **History:** General. **Interdisciplinary:** Biological/physical sciences, medieval/Renaissance. **Liberal arts:** Arts/sciences. **Math:** General, statistics. **Parks/recreation:** Exercise sciences, facilities management. **Philosophy/religion:** Judaic, philosophy, religion. **Physical sciences:** Astronomy, atmospheric science, chemistry, geology, physics. **Protective services:** Criminal justice, law enforcement admin. **Psychology:** General. **Science technology:** Biological. **Social sciences:** Anthropology, applied economics, archaeology, economics, geography, international relations, political science, sociology. **Visual/performing arts:** General, acting, art, art history/conservation, film/cinema, graphic design, theater design. **Other:** Rehabilitation and therapeutic studies.

**Most popular majors.** Business/marketing 56%, family/consumer sciences 25%, liberal arts 19%.

**Computing on campus.** 212 workstations in computer center, student center. Commuter students can connect to campus network. Online course registration, online library, helpline, repair service, student web hosting available.

**Student life.** **Freshman orientation:** Available. Preregistration for classes offered. Both fall and spring orientations available. **Policies:** Acts of intolerance and high risk drinking discouraged at all locations. All facilities designated smoke free. Students expected to abide by The Penn State Principles. **Activities:** Choral groups, drama, film society, literary magazine, student government, student newspaper, diversity club, women's liaison committee, veterans club, adult learner student organization, environmental conservation and outing club, Campus Crusade for Christ, world cultures club.

**Athletics.** **Intercollegiate:** Basketball M, cross-country, volleyball W. **Intramural:** Basketball, table tennis, volleyball. **Team name:** Nittany Lions.

**Student services.** Adult student services, alcohol/substance abuse counseling, career counseling, services for economically disadvantaged, student employment services, financial aid counseling, health services, personal counseling, placement for graduates, veterans' counselor, women's services. **Physically disabled:** Services for visually, speech, hearing impaired.

**Contact.** E-mail: admissions@psu.edu
Phone: (814) 865-5471 Fax: (814) 863-7590
Anne Rohrbach, Executive Director for Undergraduate Admissions, Penn State Dubois, 201 Shields Building, University Park, PA 16802-1294

## Penn State Erie, The Behrend College
### Erie, Pennsylvania
www.pserie.psu.edu                        CB code: 2660

- Public 4-year branch campus college
- Residential campus in small city
- 3,843 degree-seeking undergraduates: 5% part-time, 35% women, 3% African American, 2% Asian American, 2% Hispanic American, 1% international
- 138 degree-seeking graduate students
- 79% of applicants admitted
- SAT or ACT with writing required
- 63% graduate within 6 years; 22% enter graduate study

**General.** Founded in 1926. Regionally accredited. **Degrees:** 649 bachelor's, 29 associate awarded; master's offered. **ROTC:** Army. **Calendar:** Semester, limited summer session. **Full-time faculty:** 208 total; 59% have terminal degrees, 11% minority, 32% women. **Part-time faculty:** 72 total; 15% have terminal degrees, 3% minority, 43% women. **Class size:** 32% < 20, 43% 20-39, 18% 40-49, 4% 50-99, 2% >100. **Special facilities:** Observatory, natural area for science field trips and experimentation, hiking trails, cross-country skiing.

**Freshman class profile.** 3,689 applied, 2,908 admitted, 1,162 enrolled.

| Mid 50% test scores | | | |
|---|---|---|---|
| SAT critical reading: | 460-560 | Rank in top quarter: | 39% |
| SAT math: | 480-590 | Rank in top tenth: | 12% |
| GPA 3.50 or higher: | 19% | Return as sophomores: | 83% |
| GPA 3.0-3.49: | 49% | Out-of-state: | 9% |
| GPA 2.0-2.99: | 32% | International: | 1% |

**Basis for selection.** Admission decisions based on high school GPA, standardized test scores, class rank, personal statements, and activities. Essay considered if submitted; portfolios required for select majors. **Homeschooled:** Complete documentation helpful, showing courses studied and all evaluations presented from homeschool evaluator, supervisor assigned to student in cooperation with local school district, or evaluator approved through program.

**High school preparation.** Required units include English 4, mathematics 3, social studies 3, science 3 and foreign language 2.

**2007-2008 Annual costs.** Tuition/fees: $11,464; $17,246 out-of-state. Room/board: $7,750. Books/supplies: $1,168. Personal expenses: $2,916.

**2006-2007 Financial aid.** **Need-based:** 892 full-time freshmen applied for aid; 684 were judged to have need; 656 of these received aid. Average need met was 67%. Average scholarship/grant was $5,352; average loan $2,897. 41% of total undergraduate aid awarded as scholarships/grants, 59% as loans/jobs. **Non-need-based:** Awarded to 801 full-time undergraduates, including 228 freshmen. Scholarships awarded for academics, alumni affiliation, athletics, ROTC.

**Application procedures.** **Admission:** Priority date 11/30; no deadline. $50 fee, may be waived for applicants with need. Application may be submitted online. Admission notification on a rolling basis beginning on or about 11/1. All freshmen applications processed at University Park Campus. **Financial aid:** Priority date 2/15; no closing date. FAFSA required. Applicants notified on a rolling basis starting 3/1.

**Academics.** **Special study options:** Accelerated study, combined bachelor's/graduate degree, cooperative education, distance learning, double major, dual enrollment of high school students, honors, independent study, internships, liberal arts/career combination, semester at sea, study abroad, teacher certification program. **Credit/placement by examination:** AP, CLEP, IB, SAT, institutional tests. 60 credit hours maximum toward bachelor's degree. **Support services:** Learning center, pre-admission summer program, remedial instruction, study skills assistance, tutoring, writing center.

**Majors.** **Agriculture:** General, agribusiness operations, agronomy, animal sciences, education services, food science, horticultural science, landscaping, mechanization, soil science, turf management. **Area/ethnic studies:** African-American, American, East Asian, Latin American, women's. **Biology:** General, bacteriology, biochemistry, biomedical sciences. **Business:** Accounting, actuarial science, business admin, finance, hospitality admin, international, labor relations, management information systems, managerial economics, marketing, organizational behavior. **Communications:** General, advertising, journalism, media studies. **Computer sciences:** General, computer science, information systems. **Conservation:** General, forest sciences, forest technology. **Education:** Adult/continuing, art, elementary, foreign languages, secondary, special. **Engineering:** Aerospace, agricultural, architectural, biomedical, chemical, civil, computer, electrical, environmental, industrial, materials science, mechanical, mining, nuclear, petroleum, polymer, science, software. **Engineering technology:** Mechanical. **English:** Creative writing, English lit. **Family/consumer sciences:** Family studies, human nutrition. **Foreign languages:** Classics, comparative lit, French, German, Italian, Japanese, Russian, Spanish. **Health:** Communication disorders, health care admin, nursing (RN), premedicine. **History:** General. **Interdisciplinary:** Biological/physical sciences, medieval/Renaissance. **Liberal arts:** Arts/sciences. **Math:** General, statistics. **Parks/recreation:** Exercise sciences, facilities management. **Philosophy/religion:** Judaic, philosophy, religion. **Physical sciences:** General, astronomy, atmospheric science, chemistry, geology, physics. **Protective services:** Criminal justice, law enforcement admin. **Psychology:** General. **Science technology:** Biological. **Social sciences:** Anthropology, applied economics, archaeology, economics, geography, international relations, political science, sociology. **Visual/performing arts:** General, acting, art, art history/conservation, film/cinema, graphic design, theater design. **Other:** Rehabilitation and therapeutic studies.

**Most popular majors.** Business/marketing 39%, engineering/ engineering technologies 30%.

**Computing on campus.** 778 workstations in dormitories, library, computer center, student center. Dormitories wired for high-speed internet access and linked to campus network. Commuter students can connect to campus network. Online course registration, online library, helpline, repair service, student web hosting, wireless network available.

**Student life. Freshman orientation:** Mandatory. Preregistration for classes offered. Held during the 3 days before start of classes. **Policies:** Acts of intolerance and high-risk drinking discouraged at all locations. All facilities designated as smoke-free. **Housing:** Coed dorms, single-sex dorms, special housing for disabled, apartments, substance-free housing available. $100 partly refundable deposit, deadline 5/1. Suites, special interest housing available. **Activities:** Bands, campus ministries, choral groups, dance, drama, film society, international student organizations, literary magazine, music ensembles, radio station, student government, student newspaper, Asian student organization, Association of Black Collegians, National Society of Black Engineers, human relations programming council, multicultural council, Irish American society, Women Today, College Republicans, InterVarsity Christian Fellowship, gospel choir.

**Athletics.** NCAA. **Intercollegiate:** Baseball M, basketball, cross-country, golf, soccer, softball W, swimming, tennis, track and field, volleyball W, water polo. **Intramural:** Badminton, basketball, bowling, football (non-tackle), golf, soccer, softball, swimming, table tennis, track and field, triathlon, volleyball. **Team name:** Behrend Lions.

**Student services.** Adult student services, alcohol/substance abuse counseling, campus ministries, career counseling, services for economically disadvantaged, student employment services, financial aid counseling, health services, minority student services, on-campus daycare, personal counseling, placement for graduates, veterans' counselor, women's services. **Physically disabled:** Services for visually, speech, hearing impaired.

**Contact.** E-mail: admissions@psu.edu
Phone: (814) 865-5471 Fax: (814) 863-7590
Anne Rohrbach, Executive Director for Undergraduate Admissions, Penn State Erie, The Behrend College, 201 Shields Building, University Park, PA 16801-1294

## Penn State Fayette, The Eberly Campus
**Uniontown, Pennsylvania**
www.fe.psu.edu                    CB code: 2660

▶ Public 4-year branch campus college
▶ Commuter campus in large town
▶ 942 degree-seeking undergraduates: 21% part-time, 58% women, 7% African American, 1% Hispanic American
▶ 90% of applicants admitted
▶ SAT or ACT with writing required
▶ 44% graduate within 6 years; 22% enter graduate study

**General.** Founded in 1934. Regionally accredited. **Degrees:** 63 bachelor's, 101 associate awarded. **Location:** 40 miles from Pittsburgh. **Calendar:** Semester, limited summer session. **Full-time faculty:** 55 total; 51% have terminal degrees, 7% minority, 36% women. **Part-time faculty:** 33 total; 24% have terminal degrees, 3% minority, 52% women. **Class size:** 53% < 20, 41% 20-39, 5% 40-49, 2% 50-99.

**Freshman class profile.** 605 applied, 542 admitted, 246 enrolled.

| Mid 50% test scores | | | |
|---|---|---|---|
| SAT critical reading: | 400-510 | GPA 2.0-2.99: | 46% |
| SAT math: | 400-520 | Rank in top quarter: | 37% |
| GPA 3.50 or higher: | 16% | Rank in top tenth: | 8% |
| GPA 3.0-3.49: | 36% | Return as sophomores: | 78% |
| | | Out-of-state: | 2% |

**Basis for selection.** Admission decisions based on high school GPA, as well as other factors, which may include standardized verbal and math test scores, class rank, personal statements, and activities lists. Essay considered if submitted; portfolios required for select majors. **Homeschooled:** Complete documentation helpful, showing courses studied and all evaluations presented from home school evaluator, supervisor assigned to student in cooperation with local school district, or evaluator approved through program. **Learning Disabled:** Prospective students with disabilities are encouraged to contact or visit the Office for Disability Services in their junior or senior years in high school in order to find out more about disability services at the college level.

**High school preparation.** Required units include English 4, mathematics 3, social studies 3, science 3 and foreign language 2.

**2007-2008 Annual costs.** Tuition/fees: $10,996; $16,496 out-of-state. Books/supplies: $1,168. Personal expenses: $1,854.

**2006-2007 Financial aid. Need-based:** 187 full-time freshmen applied for aid; 160 were judged to have need; 159 of these received aid. Average need met was 72%. Average scholarship/grant was $5,551; average loan $2,538. 47% of total undergraduate aid awarded as scholarships/grants, 53% as loans/jobs. **Non-need-based:** Awarded to 215 full-time undergraduates, including 76 freshmen. Scholarships awarded for academics, alumni affiliation, athletics, ROTC.

**Application procedures. Admission:** Priority date 11/30; no deadline. $50 fee, may be waived for applicants with need. Application may be submitted online. Admission notification on a rolling basis beginning on or about 11/1. All freshmen applications processed at University Park Campus. **Financial aid:** Priority date 2/15; no closing date. FAFSA required. Applicants notified on a rolling basis starting 3/1.

**Academics. Special study options:** Accelerated study, cross-registration, distance learning, double major, dual enrollment of high school students, honors, independent study, internships, student-designed major, study abroad, weekend college. **Credit/placement by examination:** AP, CLEP, IB, SAT. 60 credit hours maximum toward bachelor's degree. **Support services:** Learning center, remedial instruction, study skills assistance, tutoring, writing center.

**Majors. Agriculture:** General, agribusiness operations, agronomy, animal sciences, education services, food science, horticultural science, landscaping, mechanization, soil science, turf management. **Area/ethnic studies:** African-American, American, East Asian, Latin American, women's. **Biology:** General, bacteriology, biochemistry, biomedical sciences. **Business:** Accounting, actuarial science, business admin, finance, hospitality admin, labor relations, management information systems, managerial economics, marketing, organizational behavior. **Communications:** General, advertising, journalism. **Computer sciences:** General, information systems. **Conservation:** General, forest sciences, forest technology. **Education:** Adult/ continuing, art, elementary, foreign languages, secondary, special. **Engineering:** Aerospace, agricultural, architectural, biomedical, chemical, civil, computer, electrical, environmental, industrial, materials science, mechanical, mining, nuclear, petroleum, science. **English:** English lit. **Family/ consumer sciences:** Family studies, human nutrition. **Foreign languages:** Classics, comparative lit, French, German, Italian, Japanese, Russian, Spanish. **Health:** Communication disorders, health care admin, nursing (RN), premedicine. **History:** General. **Interdisciplinary:** Biological/physical sciences, medieval/Renaissance. **Liberal arts:** Arts/sciences. **Math:** General, statistics. **Parks/recreation:** Exercise sciences, facilities management. **Philosophy/religion:** Judaic, philosophy, religion. **Physical sciences:** Astronomy, atmospheric science, chemistry, geology, physics. **Protective services:** Criminal justice, law enforcement admin. **Psychology:** General. **Science technology:** Biological. **Social sciences:** Anthropology, applied economics, archaeology, economics, geography, international relations, political science, sociology. **Visual/performing arts:** General, acting, art, art history/ conservation, film/cinema, graphic design, theater design. **Other:** Rehabilitation and therapeutic studies.

**Most popular majors.** Business/marketing 29%, family/consumer sciences 25%, liberal arts 6%, security/protective services 38%.

**Computing on campus.** 196 workstations in library, computer center, student center. Commuter students can connect to campus network. Online course registration, online library, helpline, repair service, student web hosting available.

**Student life. Freshman orientation:** Available. Preregistration for classes offered. **Policies:** Acts of intolerance and high-risk drinking discouraged at all locations. All facilities designated smoke-free. **Activities:** Drama, musical theater, student government, student newspaper, adult student organization, humanities society, Christian club, minority students association, Women in Science Engineering & Technology, Students Against Destructive Decisions.

**Athletics. Intercollegiate:** Baseball M, basketball, golf M, softball W, volleyball W. **Intramural:** Basketball, football (non-tackle), racquetball, softball, tennis. **Team name:** Nittany Lions.

**Student services.** Adult student services, alcohol/substance abuse counseling, career counseling, services for economically disadvantaged, student employment services, financial aid counseling, health services, on-campus daycare, personal counseling, placement for graduates, veterans' counselor. **Physically disabled:** Services for visually, speech, hearing impaired.

**Contact.** E-mail: admissions@psu.edu
Phone: (814) 865-5471 Fax: (814) 863-7590
Anne Rohrbach, Executive Director for Undergraduate Admissions, Penn State Fayette, The Eberly Campus, 201 Shields Building, University Park, PA 16802-1294

## Penn State Greater Allegheny
### McKeesport, Pennsylvania
### www.mk.psu.edu

- Public 4-year branch campus college
- Residential campus in large town
- 681 degree-seeking undergraduates: 6% part-time, 43% women, 20% African American, 3% Asian American, 4% Hispanic American, 1% international
- 86% of applicants admitted
- SAT or ACT with writing required
- 49% graduate within 6 years; 22% enter graduate study

**General.** Founded in 1947. Regionally accredited. **Degrees:** 84 bachelor's, 5 associate awarded. **Location:** 15 miles from Pittsburgh. **Calendar:** Semester, limited summer session. **Full-time faculty:** 36 total; 72% have terminal degrees, 22% minority, 47% women. **Part-time faculty:** 35 total; 14% have terminal degrees, 9% minority, 49% women. **Class size:** 57% < 20, 39% 20-39, 2% 40-49, 2% 50-99. **Special facilities:** Computer-based lab science equipment, special computer labs for systems integration and networking.

**Freshman class profile.** 712 applied, 612 admitted, 270 enrolled.

| Mid 50% test scores | | | |
|---|---|---|---|
| SAT critical reading: | 400-520 | Rank in top quarter: | 28% |
| SAT math: | 400-540 | Rank in top tenth: | 10% |
| GPA 3.50 or higher: | 9% | Return as sophomores: | 81% |
| GPA 3.0-3.49: | 33% | Out-of-state: | 22% |
| GPA 2.0-2.99: | 55% | Live on campus: | 43% |

**Basis for selection.** Admission decisions based upon high school GPA, as well as other factors, which may include standardized verbal and math test scores, class rank, personal statements, and list of activities. Essay considered if submitted; portfolios required for select majors. **Homeschooled:** Applicants should provide complete documentation showing the courses studied and all evaluations presented from evaluator or supervisor assigned to student in cooperation with local school district or evaluator who is approved through the program.

**High school preparation.** Required units include English 4, mathematics 3, social studies 3, science 3 and foreign language 2.

**2007-2008 Annual costs.** Tuition/fees: $11,006; $16,506 out-of-state. Room/board: $7,750. Books/supplies: $1,168. Personal expenses: $2,916.

**2006-2007 Financial aid. Need-based:** 205 full-time freshmen applied for aid; 179 were judged to have need; 178 of these received aid. Average need met was 73%. Average scholarship/grant was $6,430; average loan $2,555. 54% of total undergraduate aid awarded as scholarships/grants, 46% as loans/jobs. **Non-need-based:** Awarded to 226 full-time undergraduates, including 134 freshmen. Scholarships awarded for academics, alumni affiliation, athletics, ROTC.

**Application procedures. Admission:** Priority date 11/30; no deadline. $50 fee, may be waived for applicants with need. Application may be submitted online. Admission notification on a rolling basis beginning on or about 11/1. **Financial aid:** Priority date 2/15; no closing date. FAFSA required. Applicants notified on a rolling basis starting 3/1.

**Academics. Special study options:** Accelerated study, cross-registration, distance learning, double major, dual enrollment of high school students, honors, independent study, internships, study abroad. **Credit/placement by examination:** AP, CLEP, IB, SAT. 60 credit hours maximum toward bachelor's degree. **Support services:** Learning center, pre-admission summer program, remedial instruction, study skills assistance, tutoring, writing center.

**Majors. Agriculture:** General, agribusiness operations, agronomy, animal sciences, education services, food science, horticultural science, landscaping, mechanization, soil science, turf management. **Area/ethnic studies:** African-American, American, East Asian, Latin American, women's. **Biology:** General, bacteriology, biochemistry, biomedical sciences. **Business:** Accounting, actuarial science, business admin, finance, hospitality admin, labor relations, management information systems, managerial economics, marketing, organizational behavior. **Communications:** General, advertising, journalism. **Computer sciences:** General, information systems. **Conservation:** General, forest sciences, forest technology. **Education:** Adult/continuing, art, elementary, foreign languages, secondary, special. **Engineering:** Aerospace, agricultural, architectural, biomedical, chemical, civil, computer, electrical, environmental, industrial, materials science, mechanical, mining, nuclear, petroleum, science. **English:** English lit. **Family/consumer sciences:** Family studies, human nutrition. **Foreign languages:** Classics, comparative lit, French, German, Italian, Japanese, Russian, Spanish. **Health:** Communication disorders, health care admin, nursing (RN),

premedicine. **History:** General. **Interdisciplinary:** Biological/physical sciences, medieval/Renaissance. **Liberal arts:** Arts/sciences. **Math:** General, statistics. **Parks/recreation:** General, exercise sciences. **Philosophy/religion:** Judaic, philosophy, religion. **Physical sciences:** Astronomy, atmospheric science, chemistry, geology, physics. **Protective services:** Criminal justice, law enforcement admin. **Psychology:** General. **Science technology:** Biological. **Social sciences:** Anthropology, applied economics, archaeology, economics, geography, international relations, political science, sociology. **Visual/performing arts:** General, acting, art, art history/conservation, film/cinema, graphic design, theater design. **Other:** Rehabilitation and therapeutic studies.

**Most popular majors.** Business/marketing 41%, communications/journalism 11%, computer/information sciences 29%, psychology 20%.

**Computing on campus.** 203 workstations in dormitories, library, computer center, student center. Dormitories wired for high-speed internet access and linked to campus network. Commuter students can connect to campus network. Online course registration, online library, helpline, student web hosting, wireless network available.

**Student life. Freshman orientation:** Mandatory. Preregistration for classes offered. Orientation held prior to start of semester. **Policies:** Acts of intolerance and high-risk drinking discouraged at all locations. All facilities designated as smoke-free. Students expected to abide by The Penn State Principles. **Housing:** Coed dorms, substance-free housing available. $100 partly refundable deposit, deadline 5/1. **Activities:** Dance, drama, literary magazine, radio station, student government, student newspaper, black student union, Christian Fellowship, gospel choir, Spanish club, multicultural organization.

**Athletics. Intercollegiate:** Baseball M, basketball, golf, soccer M, softball W, volleyball W. **Intramural:** Basketball, football (non-tackle), soccer, softball, volleyball.

**Student services.** Adult student services, alcohol/substance abuse counseling, campus ministries, career counseling, services for economically disadvantaged, student employment services, financial aid counseling, health services, minority student services, personal counseling, placement for graduates, veterans' counselor, women's services. **Physically disabled:** Services for visually, speech, hearing impaired.

**Contact.** E-mail: admissions@psu.edu
Phone: (814) 865-5471 Fax: (814) 863-7590
Anne Rohrbach, Executive Director for Undergraduate Admissions, Penn State Greater Allegheny, 201 Shields Building, University Park, PA 16802-1294

## Penn State Harrisburg
### Middletown, Pennsylvania
### www.hbg.psu.edu
**CB code: 2660**

- Public 4-year branch campus college
- Residential campus in small town
- 2,294 degree-seeking undergraduates: 16% part-time, 46% women, 9% African American, 7% Asian American, 4% Hispanic American, 2% international
- 1,357 degree-seeking graduate students
- 70% of applicants admitted
- SAT or ACT with writing required

**General.** Founded in 1966. Regionally accredited. **Degrees:** 548 bachelor's, 9 associate awarded; master's, doctoral offered. **ROTC:** Army. **Location:** 8 miles from Harrisburg. **Calendar:** Semester, limited summer session. **Full-time faculty:** 195 total; 85% have terminal degrees, 28% minority, 39% women. **Part-time faculty:** 101 total; 39% have terminal degrees, 6% minority, 48% women. **Class size:** 44% < 20, 51% 20-39, 4% 40-49, less than 1% 50-99. **Special facilities:** Black cultural arts center, humanities gallery, American studies archives.

**Freshman class profile.** 2,689 applied, 1,882 admitted, 422 enrolled.

| Mid 50% test scores | | | |
|---|---|---|---|
| SAT critical reading: | 460-570 | Rank in top quarter: | 35% |
| SAT math: | 480-580 | Rank in top tenth: | 9% |
| GPA 3.50 or higher: | 12% | Return as sophomores: | 82% |
| GPA 3.0-3.49: | 49% | Out-of-state: | 24% |
| GPA 2.0-2.99: | 39% | International: | 2% |

**Basis for selection.** Admissions based on secondary school record and standardized test scores.

**High school preparation.** Required units include English 4, mathematics 3, social studies 3, science 3 and foreign language 2.

**2007-2008 Annual costs.** Tuition/fees: $11,454; $17,236 out-of-state. Room/board: $8,610. Books/supplies: $1,168. Personal expenses: $2,916.

**2006-2007 Financial aid. Need-based:** 301 full-time freshmen applied for aid; 226 were judged to have need; 217 of these received aid. Average need met was 62%. Average scholarship/grant was $5,857; average loan $2,855. 38% of total undergraduate aid awarded as scholarships/grants, 62% as loans/jobs. **Non-need-based:** Awarded to 312 full-time undergraduates, including 78 freshmen. Scholarships awarded for academics, alumni affiliation, athletics, ROTC.

**Application procedures. Admission:** Priority date 11/30; no deadline. $50 fee, may be waived for applicants with need. Application may be submitted online. Admission notification on a rolling basis beginning on or about 11/1. All freshmen applications processed at University Park Campus. **Financial aid:** Priority date 2/15; no closing date. FAFSA required. Applicants notified on a rolling basis starting 3/1.

**Academics. Special study options:** Accelerated study, cooperative education, cross-registration, distance learning, double major, dual enrollment of high school students, honors, independent study, internships, student-designed major, study abroad, teacher certification program, weekend college. **Credit/placement by examination:** AP, CLEP, IB, SAT. 60 credit hours maximum toward bachelor's degree. **Support services:** Learning center, study skills assistance, tutoring, writing center.

**Majors. Area/ethnic studies:** American. **Business:** Business admin, finance, international, management information systems, marketing, organizational behavior. **Communications:** General. **Computer sciences:** General, information systems. **Education:** Elementary, social studies. **Engineering:** Electrical, environmental, mechanical, structural. **English:** English lit. **Health:** Health care admin, nursing (RN). **Liberal arts:** Humanities. **Math:** Applied. **Protective services:** Criminal justice. **Psychology:** General. **Public administration:** Policy analysis. **Social sciences:** Sociology.

**Most popular majors.** Business/marketing 28%, communications/journalism 6%, computer/information sciences 8%, education 12%, engineering/engineering technologies 19%, psychology 8%, security/protective services 6%.

**Computing on campus.** 520 workstations in library, computer center. Dormitories wired for high-speed internet access and linked to campus network. Commuter students can connect to campus network. Online course registration, online library, helpline, repair service, student web hosting, wireless network available.

**Student life. Freshman orientation:** Available. Preregistration for classes offered. Held 2 days prior to the start of classes. **Policies:** Acts of intolerance and high-risk drinking discouraged at all locations. All facilities designated smoke-free. **Housing:** Special housing for disabled, apartments, substance-free housing available. $100 partly refundable deposit, deadline 5/1. Special interest housing. **Activities:** Choral groups, dance, drama, international student organizations, literary magazine, music ensembles, radio station, student government, student newspaper, black student union, Christian Fellowship, resident community council.

**Athletics. Intercollegiate:** Baseball M, basketball, cross-country, golf, soccer, softball W, tennis, volleyball W. **Intramural:** Badminton, basketball, racquetball, tennis. **Team name:** Nittany Lions.

**Student services.** Adult student services, alcohol/substance abuse counseling, career counseling, services for economically disadvantaged, student employment services, financial aid counseling, health services, minority student services, on-campus daycare, personal counseling, placement for graduates, veterans' counselor, women's services. **Physically disabled:** Services for visually, speech, hearing impaired.

**Contact.** E-mail: admissions@psu.edu
Phone: (814) 865-5471 Fax: (814) 863-7590
Anne Rohrbach, Executive Director for Undergraduate Admissions, Penn State Harrisburg, 201 Shields Building, University Park, PA 16802-1294

---

## Penn State Hazleton
**Hazleton, Pennsylvania**
**www.hn.psu.edu**                                    **CB code: 2660**

- Public 4-year branch campus college
- Residential campus in large town
- 1,192 degree-seeking undergraduates: 3% part-time, 40% women, 8% African American, 4% Asian American, 7% Hispanic American
- 89% of applicants admitted

- SAT or ACT (ACT writing optional) required
- 57% graduate within 6 years; 22% enter graduate study

**General.** Founded in 1934. Regionally accredited. **Degrees:** 39 bachelor's, 42 associate awarded. **ROTC:** Army, Air Force. **Location:** 4 miles from Hazleton. **Calendar:** Semester, limited summer session. **Full-time faculty:** 51 total; 65% have terminal degrees, 16% minority, 41% women. **Part-time faculty:** 33 total; 24% have terminal degrees, 9% minority, 33% women. **Class size:** 43% < 20, 45% 20-39, 5% 40-49, 6% 50-99. **Special facilities:** Weather station.

**Freshman class profile.** 1,613 applied, 1,441 admitted, 571 enrolled.

| Mid 50% test scores | | | |
|---|---|---|---|
| SAT critical reading: | 420-530 | Rank in top quarter: | 24% |
| SAT math: | 420-540 | Rank in top tenth: | 6% |
| GPA 3.50 or higher: | 9% | Return as sophomores: | 80% |
| GPA 3.0-3.49: | 35% | Out-of-state: | 25% |

with **GPA 2.0-2.99:** 54% at top.

**Basis for selection.** Admission decisions based on high school GPA, as well as other factors, which may include standardized verbal and math test scores, class rank, personal statements, and activities lists. Essay considered if submitted; portfolios required for select majors. **Homeschooled:** Complete documentation helpful, showing courses studied and all evaluations presented from homeschool evaluator, supervisor assigned to student in cooperation with local school district, or evaluator approved through program.

**High school preparation.** Required units include English 4, mathematics 3, social studies 3, science 3 and foreign language 2.

**2007-2008 Annual costs.** Tuition/fees: $11,006; $16,506 out-of-state. Room/board: $7,750. Books/supplies: $1,168. Personal expenses: $2,916.

**2006-2007 Financial aid. Need-based:** 477 full-time freshmen applied for aid; 374 were judged to have need; 363 of these received aid. Average need met was 63%. Average scholarship/grant was $5,391; average loan $2,673. 45% of total undergraduate aid awarded as scholarships/grants, 55% as loans/jobs. **Non-need-based:** Awarded to 257 full-time undergraduates, including 156 freshmen. Scholarships awarded for academics, alumni affiliation, athletics, ROTC.

**Application procedures. Admission:** Priority date 11/30; no deadline. $50 fee, may be waived for applicants with need. Application may be submitted online. Admission notification on a rolling basis beginning on or about 11/1. All freshman applications processed at University Park Campus. **Financial aid:** Priority date 2/15; no closing date. FAFSA required. Applicants notified on a rolling basis starting 3/1.

**Academics. Special study options:** Accelerated study, cross-registration, distance learning, double major, dual enrollment of high school students, ESL, honors, independent study, internships, student-designed major, study abroad. **Credit/placement by examination:** AP, CLEP, IB, SAT. 60 credit hours maximum toward bachelor's degree. **Support services:** Learning center, remedial instruction, study skills assistance, tutoring, writing center.

**Honors college/program.** 300 admitted university-wide each year.

**Majors. Agriculture:** General, agribusiness operations, agronomy, animal sciences, education services, food science, horticultural science, landscaping, mechanization, soil science, turf management. **Area/ethnic studies:** African-American, American, East Asian, Latin American, women's. **Biology:** General, bacteriology, biochemistry, biomedical sciences. **Business:** Accounting, actuarial science, business admin, finance, hospitality admin, labor relations, management information systems, managerial economics, marketing, organizational behavior. **Communications:** General, advertising, journalism. **Computer sciences:** General, information systems. **Conservation:** General, forest sciences, forest technology. **Education:** Adult/continuing, art, elementary, foreign languages, secondary, special. **Engineering:** Aerospace, agricultural, architectural, biomedical, chemical, civil, computer, electrical, environmental, industrial, materials science, mechanical, mining, nuclear, petroleum, science. **English:** English lit. **Family/consumer sciences:** Family studies, human nutrition. **Foreign languages:** Classics, comparative lit, French, German, Italian, Japanese, Russian, Spanish. **Health:** Communication disorders, health care admin, nursing (RN), premedicine. **History:** General. **Interdisciplinary:** Biological/physical sciences, medieval/Renaissance. **Liberal arts:** Arts/sciences. **Math:** General, statistics. **Parks/recreation:** Exercise sciences, facilities management. **Philosophy/religion:** Judaic, philosophy, religion. **Physical sciences:** Astronomy, atmospheric science, chemistry, geology, physics. **Protective services:** Criminal justice, law enforcement admin. **Psychology:** General. **Science technology:** Biological. **Social sciences:** Anthropology, applied economics, archaeology, economics, geography, international relations, political science, sociology. **Visual/performing arts:** General, acting, art, art history/conservation, film/cinema, graphic design, theater design. **Other:** Rehabilitation and therapeutic studies.

**Most popular majors.** Business/marketing 41%, computer/information sciences 23%, liberal arts 36%.

**Computing on campus.** 166 workstations in library, student center. Dormitories wired for high-speed internet access and linked to campus network. Commuter students can connect to campus network. Online course registration, online library, helpline, repair service, student web hosting, wireless network available.

**Student life. Freshman orientation:** Available. Preregistration for classes offered. Testing and academic advising in June; formal orientation in August and September. **Policies:** Acts of intolerance and high-risk drinking discouraged at all locations. All facilities designated as smoke-free. Students expected to abide by The Penn State Principles. **Housing:** Coed dorms, substance-free housing available. $100 partly refundable deposit, deadline 5/1. Townhouses, suites available. **Activities:** Campus ministries, choral groups, dance, drama, literary magazine, radio station, student government, student newspaper, multicultural club, Circle K, Allies, Fellowship of Christian Athletes, Helping Hands.

**Athletics. Intercollegiate:** Baseball M, basketball, cheerleading, golf, soccer M, softball W, tennis, volleyball W. **Intramural:** Rifle, softball, table tennis, tennis, volleyball. **Team name:** Nittany Lions.

**Student services.** Adult student services, alcohol/substance abuse counseling, campus ministries, career counseling, services for economically disadvantaged, student employment services, financial aid counseling, health services, legal services, minority student services, personal counseling, placement for graduates, veterans' counselor, women's services. **Physically disabled:** Services for visually, speech, hearing impaired.

**Contact.** E-mail: admissions@psu.edu
Phone: (814) 865-5471 Fax: (814) 863-7590
Anne Rohrbach, Executive Director for Undergraduate Admissions, Penn State Hazleton, 201 Shields Building, University Park, PA 16802-1294

---

## Penn State Lehigh Valley
**Fogelsville, Pennsylvania**
www.lv.psu.edu                    CB code: 2660

- Public 4-year branch campus college
- Commuter campus in rural community
- 685 degree-seeking undergraduates: 15% part-time, 40% women, 3% African American, 6% Asian American, 10% Hispanic American, 1% international
- 80% of applicants admitted
- SAT or ACT with writing required
- 49% graduate within 6 years; 22% enter graduate study

**General.** Regionally accredited. **Degrees:** 65 bachelor's, 8 associate awarded. **ROTC:** Army. **Location:** 15 miles from Allentown, 30 miles from Easton. **Calendar:** Semester, limited summer session. **Full-time faculty:** 27 total; 78% have terminal degrees, 15% minority, 52% women. **Part-time faculty:** 58 total; 21% have terminal degrees, 7% minority, 38% women. **Class size:** 68% < 20, 26% 20-39, 4% 40-49, 2% 50-99.

**Freshman class profile.** 908 applied, 722 admitted, 243 enrolled.

| Mid 50% test scores | | Rank in top quarter: | 35% |
|---|---|---|---|
| SAT critical reading: | 420-530 | Rank in top tenth: | 8% |
| SAT math: | 450-570 | Return as sophomores: | 72% |
| GPA 3.50 or higher: | 11% | Out-of-state: | 7% |
| GPA 3.0-3.49: | 34% | International: | 1% |
| GPA 2.0-2.99: | 53% | | |

**Basis for selection.** Admission decisions based on high school GPA, standardized test scores, class rank, personal statements, and activities. Essay considered if submitted; portfolios required for select majors. **Homeschooled:** Applicants should provide complete documentation showing courses studied and all evaluations presented from evaluator or supervisor assigned to student in cooperation with local school district or evaluator approved through program.

**High school preparation.** Required units include English 4, mathematics 3, social studies 3, science 3 and foreign language 2.

**2007-2008 Annual costs.** Tuition/fees: $11,006; $16,506 out-of-state. Books/supplies: $1,168. Personal expenses: $1,854.

**2006-2007 Financial aid. Need-based:** 167 full-time freshmen applied for aid; 115 were judged to have need; 113 of these received aid. Average need met was 65%. Average scholarship/grant was $5,623; average loan $2,865. 45% of total undergraduate aid awarded as scholarships/grants, 55%

as loans/jobs. **Non-need-based:** Awarded to 82 full-time undergraduates, including 55 freshmen. Scholarships awarded for academics, alumni affiliation, athletics, ROTC.

**Application procedures. Admission:** Priority date 11/30; no deadline. $50 fee, may be waived for applicants with need. Application may be submitted online. Admission notification on a rolling basis beginning on or about 11/1. All freshmen applications processed at University Park Campus. **Financial aid:** Priority date 2/15; no closing date. FAFSA required. Applicants notified on a rolling basis starting 3/1.

**Academics. Special study options:** Accelerated study, cooperative education, cross-registration, distance learning, dual enrollment of high school students, honors, independent study, internships, study abroad. **Credit/ placement by examination:** AP, CLEP, IB, SAT. 60 credit hours maximum toward bachelor's degree. **Support services:** Learning center, reduced course load, study skills assistance, tutoring, writing center.

**Majors. Agriculture:** General, agribusiness operations, agronomy, animal sciences, education services, food science, horticultural science, landscaping, mechanization, soil science, turf management. **Area/ethnic studies:** African-American, American, East Asian, Latin American, women's. **Biology:** General, bacteriology, biochemistry, biomedical sciences. **Business:** General, accounting, actuarial science, finance, hospitality admin, labor relations, management information systems, managerial economics, marketing, organizational behavior. **Communications:** General, advertising, journalism. **Computer sciences:** General, information systems. **Conservation:** General, forest sciences, forest technology. **Education:** Adult/continuing, art, elementary, foreign languages, secondary, special. **Engineering:** Aerospace, agricultural, architectural, biomedical, chemical, civil, computer, electrical, environmental, industrial, materials science, mechanical, mining, nuclear, petroleum, science. **English:** English lit, technical writing. **Family/ consumer sciences:** Family studies, human nutrition. **Foreign languages:** General, classics, comparative lit, French, German, Italian, Japanese, Russian, Spanish. **Health:** Communication disorders, health care admin, nursing (RN), premedicine. **History:** General. **Interdisciplinary:** Biological/ physical sciences, medieval/Renaissance. **Liberal arts:** Arts/sciences. **Math:** General, statistics. **Parks/recreation:** Exercise sciences, facilities management. **Philosophy/religion:** Judaic, philosophy, religion. **Physical sciences:** Astronomy, atmospheric science, chemistry, geology, physics. **Protective services:** Criminal justice, law enforcement admin. **Psychology:** General. **Science technology:** Biological. **Social sciences:** Anthropology, applied economics, archaeology, economics, geography, international relations, political science, sociology. **Visual/performing arts:** General, acting, art, art history/ conservation, film/cinema, graphic design, theater design. **Other:** Rehabilitation and therapeutic studies.

**Most popular majors.** Business/marketing 51%, computer/information sciences 23%, psychology 23%.

**Computing on campus.** 155 workstations in dormitories, library, computer center, student center. Commuter students can connect to campus network. Online course registration, online library, helpline, repair service, student web hosting, wireless network available.

**Student life. Freshman orientation:** Mandatory. Preregistration for classes offered. One-day program held prior to start of classes. **Policies:** Acts of intolerance and high risk drinking discouraged at all locations. All facilities designated as smoke-free. Students expected to abide by The Penn State Principles. **Activities:** Drama, student government, student newspaper, Asian club, Christian Fellowship, Habitat for Humanity.

**Athletics. Intercollegiate:** Golf, tennis. **Intramural:** Basketball, football (non-tackle), soccer. **Team name:** Nittany Lions.

**Student services.** Adult student services, alcohol/substance abuse counseling, career counseling, services for economically disadvantaged, student employment services, financial aid counseling, health services, minority student services, personal counseling, placement for graduates, veterans' counselor. **Physically disabled:** Services for visually, speech, hearing impaired. **Learning disabled:** Comprehensive services available.

**Contact.** E-mail: admission@psu.edu
Phone: (814) 865-5471 Fax: (814) 863-7590
Anne Rohrbach, Executive Director for Undergraduate Admissions, Penn State Lehigh Valley, 201 Shields Building, University Park, PA 16802-1294

---

## Penn State Mont Alto
**Mont Alto, Pennsylvania**
www.ma.psu.edu                    CB code: 2660

- Public 4-year branch campus college
- Residential campus in rural community
- 1,025 degree-seeking undergraduates: 19% part-time, 59% women, 12% African American, 3% Asian American, 3% Hispanic American

- 89% of applicants admitted
- SAT or ACT with writing required
- 51% graduate within 6 years; 22% enter graduate study

**General.** Founded in 1929. Regionally accredited. **Degrees:** 30 bachelor's, 104 associate awarded. **ROTC:** Army. **Location:** 12 miles from Chambersburg. **Calendar:** Semester, limited summer session. **Full-time faculty:** 52 total; 50% have terminal degrees, 8% minority, 54% women. **Part-time faculty:** 51 total; 12% have terminal degrees, 2% minority, 55% women. **Class size:** 52% < 20, 39% 20-39, 6% 40-49, 3% 50-99.

**Freshman class profile.** 927 applied, 826 admitted, 365 enrolled.

| Mid 50% test scores | | | |
|---|---|---|---|
| SAT critical reading: | 440-550 | Rank in top quarter: | 34% |
| SAT math: | 430-560 | Rank in top tenth: | 13% |
| GPA 3.50 or higher: | 15% | Return as sophomores: | 74% |
| GPA 3.0-3.49: | 33% | Out-of-state: | 30% |
| GPA 2.0-2.99: | 51% | International: | 1% |

**Basis for selection.** Admission decisions based upon high school GPA, as well as other factors, which may include standardized verbal and math test scores, class rank, personal statements, and list of activities. Essay considered if submitted; portfolios required for select majors. **Homeschooled:** Applicants should provide complete documentation showing the courses studied and all evaluations presented from evaluator or supervisor assigned to student in cooperation with local school district or evaluator who is approved through the program.

**High school preparation.** Required units include English 4, mathematics 3, social studies 3, science 3 and foreign language 2.

**2007-2008 Annual costs.** Tuition/fees: $11,006; $16,506 out-of-state. Room/board: $7,750. Books/supplies: $1,168. Personal expenses: $2,916.

**2006-2007 Financial aid. Need-based:** 341 full-time freshmen applied for aid; 281 were judged to have need; 275 of these received aid. Average need met was 70%. Average scholarship/grant was $5,881; average loan $2,828. 46% of total undergraduate aid awarded as scholarships/grants, 54% as loans/jobs. **Non-need-based:** Awarded to 249 full-time undergraduates, including 172 freshmen. Scholarships awarded for academics, alumni affiliation, athletics, ROTC.

**Application procedures. Admission:** Priority date 11/30; no deadline. $50 fee, may be waived for applicants with need. Application may be submitted online. Admission notification on a rolling basis beginning on or about 11/1. All freshmen applications processed at University Park Campus. **Financial aid:** Priority date 2/15; no closing date. FAFSA required. Applicants notified on a rolling basis starting 3/1.

**Academics. Special study options:** Accelerated study, cross-registration, distance learning, double major, dual enrollment of high school students, honors, independent study, internships, study abroad. **Credit/placement by examination:** AP, CLEP, IB, SAT. 60 credit hours maximum toward bachelor's degree. **Support services:** Learning center, remedial instruction, study skills assistance, tutoring, writing center.

**Majors. Agriculture:** General, agribusiness operations, agronomy, animal sciences, education services, food science, horticultural science, landscaping, mechanization, soil science, turf management. **Area/ethnic studies:** African-American, American, East Asian, Latin American, women's. **Biology:** General, bacteriology, biochemistry, biomedical sciences. **Business:** Accounting, actuarial science, business admin, finance, hospitality admin, labor relations, management information systems, managerial economics, marketing, organizational behavior. **Communications:** General, advertising, journalism. **Computer sciences:** General, information systems. **Conservation:** General, forest sciences, forest technology. **Education:** Adult/continuing, art, elementary, foreign languages, secondary, special. **Engineering:** Aerospace, agricultural, architectural, biomedical, chemical, civil, computer, electrical, environmental, industrial, materials science, mechanical, mining, nuclear, petroleum, science. **English:** English lit. **Family/consumer sciences:** Family studies, human nutrition. **Foreign languages:** Classics, comparative lit, French, German, Italian, Japanese, Russian, Spanish. **Health:** Communication disorders, health care admin, nursing (RN), premedicine. **History:** General. **Interdisciplinary:** Biological/physical sciences, medieval/Renaissance. **Liberal arts:** Arts/sciences. **Math:** General, statistics. **Parks/recreation:** General, exercise sciences. **Philosophy/religion:** Judaic, philosophy, religion. **Physical sciences:** Astronomy, atmospheric science, chemistry, geology, physics. **Protective services:** Criminal justice, law enforcement admin. **Psychology:** General. **Science technology:** Biological. **Social sciences:** Anthropology, applied economics, archaeology, economics, geography, international relations, political science, sociology. **Visual/performing arts:** General, acting, art, art history/conservation, film/cinema, graphic design, theater design. **Other:** Rehabilitation and therapeutic studies.

**Most popular majors.** Business/marketing 27%, English 17%, family/consumer sciences 40%, health sciences 17%.

**Computing on campus.** 164 workstations in computer center, student center. Dormitories wired for high-speed internet access and linked to campus network. Commuter students can connect to campus network. Online course registration, online library, helpline, repair service, student web hosting, wireless network available.

**Student life. Freshman orientation:** Available. Preregistration for classes offered. **Policies:** Acts of intolerance and high-risk drinking discouraged at all locations. All facilities designated as smoke-free. **Housing:** Coed dorms, special housing for disabled, substance-free housing available. Suites, special interest housing, townhouses available. **Activities:** Jazz band, campus ministries, dance, drama, student government, student newspaper, Christian Fellowship, language club, multicultural club, volunteer club, black student union, Asian student association.

**Athletics. Intercollegiate:** Basketball, cheerleading, cross-country, golf, soccer, softball W, tennis, volleyball W. **Intramural:** Badminton, basketball, racquetball, soccer, softball, volleyball. **Team name:** Nittany Lions.

**Student services.** Adult student services, alcohol/substance abuse counseling, campus ministries, career counseling, services for economically disadvantaged, student employment services, financial aid counseling, health services, minority student services, placement for graduates, veterans' counselor, women's services. **Physically disabled:** Services for visually, speech, hearing impaired.

**Contact.** E-mail: admissions@psu.edu
Phone: (814) 865-5471 Fax: (814) 863-7590
Anne Rohrbach, Executive Director for Undergraduate Admissions, Penn State Mont Alto, 201 Shields Building, University Park, PA 16802-1294

---

## Penn State New Kensington
**New Kensington, Pennsylvania**
**www.nk.psu.edu**      CB code: 2660

- Public 4-year branch campus college
- Commuter campus in large town
- 734 degree-seeking undergraduates: 19% part-time, 44% women, 3% African American, 1% Asian American, 1% Hispanic American
- 86% of applicants admitted
- SAT or ACT with writing required
- 42% graduate within 6 years; 22% enter graduate study

**General.** Founded in 1958. Regionally accredited. **Degrees:** 75 bachelor's, 38 associate awarded. **Location:** 22 miles from Pittsburgh. **Calendar:** Semester, limited summer session. **Full-time faculty:** 38 total; 60% have terminal degrees, 16% minority, 45% women. **Part-time faculty:** 48 total; 27% have terminal degrees, 8% minority, 42% women. **Class size:** 63% < 20, 32% 20-39, 3% 40-49, 3% 50-99.

**Freshman class profile.** 561 applied, 482 admitted, 211 enrolled.

| Mid 50% test scores | | | |
|---|---|---|---|
| | | GPA 2.0-2.99: | 48% |
| SAT critical reading: | 430-540 | Rank in top quarter: | 29% |
| SAT math: | 440-570 | Rank in top tenth: | 9% |
| GPA 3.50 or higher: | 16% | Return as sophomores: | 69% |
| GPA 3.0-3.49: | 35% | Out-of-state: | 4% |

**Basis for selection.** Admission decisions based upon high school GPA, as well as other factors, which may include standardized verbal and math test scores, class rank, personal statements, and list of activities. Essay considered if submitted; portfolios required for select majors. **Homeschooled:** Applicants should provide complete documentation showing the courses studied and all evaluations presented from evaluator or supervisor assigned to student in cooperation with local school district or evaluator who is approved through the program.

**High school preparation.** Required units include English 4, mathematics 3, social studies 3, science 3 and foreign language 2.

**2007-2008 Annual costs.** Tuition/fees: $11,006; $16,506 out-of-state. Books/supplies: $1,168. Personal expenses: $1,854.

**2006-2007 Financial aid. Need-based:** 180 full-time freshmen applied for aid; 139 were judged to have need; 136 of these received aid. Average need met was 71%. Average scholarship/grant was $4,768; average loan $2,501. 48% of total undergraduate aid awarded as scholarships/grants, 52% as loans/jobs. **Non-need-based:** Awarded to 155 full-time undergraduates, including 99 freshmen. Scholarships awarded for academics, alumni affiliation, athletics, ROTC.

**Application procedures. Admission:** Priority date 11/30; no deadline. $50 fee, may be waived for applicants with need. Application may be submitted online. Admission notification on a rolling basis beginning on or about 11/1. All freshmen applications processed at University Park Campus. **Financial aid:** Priority date 2/15; no closing date. FAFSA required. Applicants notified on a rolling basis starting 3/1.

**Academics. Special study options:** Cross-registration, distance learning, double major, dual enrollment of high school students, external degree, honors, independent study, internships, study abroad. **Credit/placement by examination:** AP, CLEP, IB, SAT. 60 credit hours maximum toward bachelor's degree. **Support services:** Learning center, remedial instruction, study skills assistance, tutoring, writing center.

**Majors. Agriculture:** General, agribusiness operations, agronomy, animal sciences, education services, food science, horticultural science, landscaping, mechanization, soil science, turf management. **Area/ethnic studies:** African-American, American, East Asian, Latin American, women's. **Biology:** General, bacteriology, biochemistry, biomedical sciences. **Business:** Accounting, actuarial science, business admin, finance, hospitality admin, labor relations, management information systems, managerial economics, marketing, organizational behavior. **Communications:** General, advertising, journalism. **Computer sciences:** General, information systems. **Conservation:** General, forest sciences, forest technology. **Education:** Adult/continuing, art, elementary, foreign languages, secondary, special. **Engineering:** Aerospace, agricultural, architectural, biomedical, chemical, civil, computer, electrical, environmental, industrial, materials science, mechanical, mining, nuclear, petroleum, science. **English:** English lit. **Family/consumer sciences:** Family studies, human nutrition. **Foreign languages:** Classics, comparative lit, French, German, Italian, Japanese, Russian, Spanish. **Health:** Communication disorders, health care admin, nursing (RN), premedicine. **History:** General. **Interdisciplinary:** Biological/physical sciences, medieval/Renaissance. **Liberal arts:** Arts/sciences. **Math:** General, statistics. **Parks/recreation:** Exercise sciences, facilities management. **Philosophy/religion:** Judaic, philosophy, religion. **Physical sciences:** Astronomy, atmospheric science, chemistry, geology, physics. **Protective services:** Criminal justice, law enforcement admin. **Psychology:** General. **Science technology:** Biological. **Social sciences:** Anthropology, applied economics, archaeology, economics, geography, international relations, political science, sociology. **Visual/performing arts:** General, acting, art, art history/conservation, film/cinema, graphic design, theater design. **Other:** Rehabilitation and therapeutic studies.

**Most popular majors.** Business/marketing 48%, communications/journalism 11%, computer/information sciences 25%, engineering/engineering technologies 9%, psychology 7%.

**Computing on campus.** 265 workstations in computer center. Commuter students can connect to campus network. Online course registration, online library, helpline, repair service, student web hosting, wireless network available.

**Student life. Freshman orientation:** Mandatory, $25 fee. Preregistration for classes offered. 2-day program held prior to beginning of classes. **Policies:** Acts of intolerance and high-risk drinking discouraged at all locations. All facilities designated as smoke-free. Students expected to abide by The Penn State Principles. **Activities:** Jazz band, choral groups, dance, drama, literary magazine, musical theater, student government, student newspaper, multicultural club, Society of Women Engineers, Spanish culture club.

**Athletics. Intercollegiate:** Basketball, cheerleading, golf, volleyball W. **Intramural:** Basketball, football (non-tackle), racquetball, soccer, softball, table tennis, volleyball. **Team name:** Nittany Lions.

**Student services.** Adult student services, alcohol/substance abuse counseling, campus ministries, career counseling, services for economically disadvantaged, student employment services, financial aid counseling, health services, minority student services, placement for graduates, veterans' counselor, women's services. **Physically disabled:** Services for visually, speech, hearing impaired.

**Contact.** E-mail: admissions@psu.edu
Phone: (814) 865-5471 Fax: (814) 863-7590
Anne Rohrbach, Executive Director for Undergraduate Admissions, Penn State New Kensington, 201 Shields Building, University Park, PA 16802-1294

## Penn State Schuylkill
**Schuylkill Haven, Pennsylvania**
www.sl.psu.edu                    CB code: 2660

- Public 4-year branch campus college
- Residential campus in small town
- 827 degree-seeking undergraduates: 10% part-time, 54% women, 29% African American, 2% Asian American, 3% Hispanic American

- 81% of applicants admitted
- SAT or ACT with writing required
- 53% graduate within 6 years; 22% enter graduate study

**General.** Founded in 1934. Regionally accredited. **Degrees:** 50 bachelor's, 33 associate awarded. **Location:** 4 miles from Pottsville. **Calendar:** Semester, limited summer session. **Full-time faculty:** 38 total; 74% have terminal degrees, 5% minority, 34% women. **Part-time faculty:** 21 total; 24% have terminal degrees, 10% minority, 38% women. **Class size:** 41% < 20, 52% 20-39, 6% 40-49, 1% 50-99, less than 1% >100.

**Freshman class profile.** 993 applied, 806 admitted, 337 enrolled.

| Mid 50% test scores | | | |
|---|---|---|---|
| SAT critical reading: | 380-500 | GPA 2.0-2.99: | 67% |
| SAT math: | 380-520 | Rank in top quarter: | 28% |
| GPA 3.50 or higher: | 5% | Rank in top tenth: | 10% |
| GPA 3.0-3.49: | 27% | Return as sophomores: | 80% |
| | | Out-of-state: | 35% |

**Basis for selection.** Admission decisions based upon high school GPA, standardized test scores, class rank, personal statements, and activities. Essay considered if submitted; portfolios required for select majors. **Homeschooled:** Applicants should provide complete documentation showing courses studied and all evaluations presented from evaluator or supervisor assigned to student in cooperation with local school district or evaluator approved through program.

**High school preparation.** Required units include English 4, mathematics 3, social studies 3, science 3 and foreign language 2.

**2007-2008 Annual costs.** Tuition/fees: $10,996; $16,496 out-of-state. Books/supplies: $1,168. Personal expenses: $1,854.

**2006-2007 Financial aid. Need-based:** 287 full-time freshmen applied for aid; 256 were judged to have need; 252 of these received aid. Average need met was 70%. Average scholarship/grant was $6,296; average loan $2,687. 51% of total undergraduate aid awarded as scholarships/grants, 49% as loans/jobs. **Non-need-based:** Awarded to 233 full-time undergraduates, including 156 freshmen. Scholarships awarded for academics, alumni affiliation, athletics, ROTC.

**Application procedures. Admission:** Priority date 11/30; no deadline. $50 fee, may be waived for applicants with need. Application may be submitted online. Admission notification on a rolling basis beginning on or about 11/1. All freshmen applications processed at University Park Campus. **Financial aid:** Priority date 2/15; no closing date. FAFSA required. Applicants notified on a rolling basis starting 3/1.

**Academics. Special study options:** Accelerated study, cooperative education, distance learning, double major, dual enrollment of high school students, honors, independent study, internships, student-designed major, study abroad. **Credit/placement by examination:** AP, CLEP, IB, SAT. 60 credit hours maximum toward bachelor's degree. **Support services:** Learning center, study skills assistance, tutoring, writing center.

**Majors. Agriculture:** General, agribusiness operations, agronomy, animal sciences, education services, food science, horticultural science, landscaping, mechanization, soil science, turf management. **Area/ethnic studies:** African-American, American, East Asian, Latin American, women's. **Biology:** General, bacteriology, biochemistry, biomedical sciences, toxicology. **Business:** General, accounting, actuarial science, finance, hospitality admin, labor relations, management information systems, managerial economics, marketing, organizational behavior. **Communications:** General, advertising, journalism. **Computer sciences:** General, information systems. **Conservation:** General, forest sciences, forest technology. **Education:** Adult/continuing, art, elementary, foreign languages, secondary, special. **Engineering:** Aerospace, agricultural, architectural, biomedical, chemical, civil, computer, electrical, environmental, industrial, materials science, mechanical, mining, nuclear, petroleum, science. **English:** English lit. **Family/consumer sciences:** Family studies, human nutrition. **Foreign languages:** Classics, comparative lit, French, German, Italian, Japanese, Russian, Spanish. **Health:** Communication disorders, health care admin, nursing (RN), premedicine. **History:** General. **Interdisciplinary:** Biological/physical sciences, medieval/Renaissance. **Liberal arts:** Arts/sciences, humanities. **Math:** General, statistics. **Parks/recreation:** Exercise sciences, facilities management. **Philosophy/religion:** Judaic, philosophy, religion. **Physical sciences:** Astronomy, atmospheric science, chemistry, geology, physics. **Protective services:** Criminal justice, law enforcement admin. **Psychology:** General. **Science technology:** Biological. **Social sciences:** Anthropology, applied economics, archaeology, economics, geography, international relations, political science, sociology. **Visual/performing arts:** General, acting, art, art history/conservation, film/cinema, graphic design, theater design. **Other:** Rehabilitation and therapeutic studies.

**Most popular majors.** Business/marketing 16%, computer/information sciences 8%, psychology 40%, security/protective services 36%.

**Computing on campus.** 165 workstations in computer center, student center. Dormitories wired for high-speed internet access and linked to campus network. Commuter students can connect to campus network. Online course registration, online library, helpline, repair service, student web hosting, wireless network available.

**Student life. Freshman orientation:** Available. Preregistration for classes offered. 3-day program held prior to start of classes. **Policies:** Acts of intolerance and high-risk drinking discouraged at all locations. All facilities designated as smoke-free. Students expected to abide by The Penn State Principles. **Housing:** Special housing for disabled, apartments, substance-free housing available. $100 partly refundable deposit, deadline 5/1. **Activities:** Campus ministries, choral groups, dance, drama, international student organizations, musical theater, student government, student newspaper, Campus Crusade for Christ, criminal justice club, religious and philosophical forum, united minority leaders, Keystone honor society.

**Athletics. Intercollegiate:** Basketball, cross-country, golf M, soccer M, softball W, volleyball W. **Intramural:** Basketball, football (non-tackle) M, soccer, softball, table tennis, volleyball. **Team name:** Nittany Lions.

**Student services.** Adult student services, career counseling, services for economically disadvantaged, student employment services, financial aid counseling, health services, minority student services, personal counseling, placement for graduates, veterans' counselor. **Physically disabled:** Services for visually impaired.

**Contact.** E-mail: admissions@psu.edu
Phone: (814) 865-5471 Fax: (814) 863-7590
Anne Rohrbach, Executive Director for Undergraduate Admissions, Penn State Schuylkill, 201 Shields Building, University Park, PA 16802-1294

---

## Penn State Shenango
### Sharon, Pennsylvania
**www.shenango.psu.edu** — CB code: 2660

- Public two-year upper-division branch campus college
- Commuter campus in large town
- 79% of applicants admitted

**General.** Founded in 1965. Regionally accredited. **Degrees:** 46 bachelor's, 56 associate awarded. **Articulation:** Agreement with Youngstown State University. **Location:** 17 miles from Youngstown, Ohio. **Calendar:** Semester, limited summer session. **Full-time faculty:** 29 total; 55% have terminal degrees, 10% minority, 45% women. **Part-time faculty:** 46 total; 20% have terminal degrees, 48% women. **Class size:** 64% < 20, 31% 20-39, 4% 40-49, 1% 50-99. **Special facilities:** Scanning electron microscope.

**Student profile.** 677 degree-seeking undergraduates. 62 applied as first time-transfer students, 49 admitted, 35 enrolled. 20% entered as juniors, 14% entered as seniors. 30% transferred from two-year, 70% transferred from four-year institutions.

| | | | |
|---|---|---|---|
| Women: | 65% | Part-time: | 30% |
| African American: | 8% | Out-of-state: | 13% |
| Asian American: | 1% | 25 or older: | 46% |
| Hispanic American: | 1% | | |

**Basis for selection.** High school transcript, college transcript required. Transfer accepted as sophomores, juniors, seniors.

**2007-2008 Annual costs.** Tuition/fees: $11,006; $16,506 out-of-state. Books/supplies: $1,168. Personal expenses: $1,854.

**Financial aid. Need-based:** 409 applied for aid; 379 were judged to have need; 377 of these received aid. Average need met was 71%. 46% of total undergraduate aid awarded as scholarships/grants, 54% as loans/jobs. **Non-need-based:** Awarded to 161 undergraduates. Scholarships awarded for academics, alumni affiliation, athletics, ROTC.

**Application procedures. Admission:** Rolling admission. $50 fee, may be waived for applicants with need. Application may be submitted online. All freshmen applications processed at University Park Campus. **Financial aid:** Closing date 5/1. Schools required to obtain student aid information through National Student Loan Data System (NSLDS). FAFSA required.

**Academics. Special study options:** Accelerated study, cross-registration, distance learning, double major, dual enrollment of high school students, honors, independent study, internships, student-designed major, study abroad. **Credit/placement by examination:** AP, CLEP, IB, SAT. 60 credit hours maximum toward bachelor's degree. **Support services:** Learning center, remedial instruction, study skills assistance, tutoring, writing center.

**Majors. Agriculture:** General, agribusiness operations, agronomy, animal sciences, education services, food science, horticultural science, landscaping, mechanization, soil science, turf management. **Area/ethnic studies:** African-American, American, East Asian, Latin American, women's. **Biology:** General, bacteriology, biochemistry, biomedical sciences. **Business:** Accounting, actuarial science, business admin, finance, hospitality admin, labor relations, management information systems, managerial economics, marketing, organizational behavior. **Communications:** General, advertising, journalism. **Computer sciences:** General, information systems. **Conservation:** General, forest sciences, forest technology. **Education:** Adult/continuing, art, elementary, foreign languages, secondary, special. **Engineering:** Aerospace, agricultural, architectural, biomedical, chemical, civil, computer, electrical, environmental, industrial, materials science, mechanical, mining, nuclear, petroleum, science. **English:** English lit. **Family/consumer sciences:** Family studies, human nutrition. **Foreign languages:** Classics, comparative lit, French, German, Italian, Japanese, Russian, Spanish. **Health:** Communication disorders, health care admin, nursing (RN), premedicine. **History:** General. **Interdisciplinary:** Biological/physical sciences, medieval/Renaissance. **Liberal arts:** Arts/sciences. **Math:** General, statistics. **Parks/recreation:** Exercise sciences, facilities management. **Philosophy/religion:** Judaic, philosophy, religion. **Physical sciences:** Astronomy, atmospheric science, chemistry, geology, physics. **Protective services:** Criminal justice, law enforcement admin. **Psychology:** General. **Science technology:** Biological. **Social sciences:** Anthropology, applied economics, archaeology, economics, geography, international relations, political science, sociology. **Visual/performing arts:** General, acting, art, art history/conservation, film/cinema, graphic design, theater design. **Other:** Rehabilitation and therapeutic studies.

**Most popular majors.** Business/marketing 50%, family/consumer sciences 44%, liberal arts 7%.

**Computing on campus.** 132 workstations in library, computer center, student center. Commuter students can connect to campus network. Online course registration, online library, helpline, repair service, student web hosting, wireless network available.

**Student life. Policies:** Acts of intolerance and high risk drinking discouraged at all locations. All facilities designated as smoke-free. Students expected to abide by The Penn State Principles. **Activities:** Literary magazine, student government, environmental club, Students for Cultural Diversity, Women in Transition, Word of God Bible study club, Adults Seeking Knowledge.

**Athletics. Intramural:** Basketball, golf, softball, volleyball. **Team name:** Nittany Lions.

**Student services.** Adult student services, alcohol/substance abuse counseling, career counseling, student employment services, financial aid counseling, health services, minority student services, placement for graduates, veterans' counselor, women's services. **Physically disabled:** Services for visually, speech, hearing impaired.

**Contact.** E-mail: admissions@psu.edu
Phone: (814) 865-5471 Fax: (814) 863-7590
Anne Rohrbach, Executive Director for Undergraduate Admissions, Penn State Shenango, 201 Shields Building, University Park, PA 16802-1294

---

## Penn State University Park
### University Park, Pennsylvania
**www.psu.edu** — CB member, CB code: 2660

- Public 4-year university
- Residential campus in large town
- 35,876 degree-seeking undergraduates: 2% part-time, 45% women, 4% African American, 5% Asian American, 4% Hispanic American, 2% international
- 6,156 degree-seeking graduate students
- 51% of applicants admitted
- SAT or ACT with writing required
- 85% graduate within 6 years; 22% enter graduate study

**General.** Founded in 1855. Regionally accredited. **Degrees:** 9,604 bachelor's, 71 associate awarded; master's, doctoral, first professional offered. **ROTC:** Army, Naval, Air Force. **Location:** 90 miles from Harrisburg. **Calendar:** Semester, extensive summer session. **Full-time faculty:** 2,344 total; 77% have terminal degrees, 18% minority, 37% women. **Part-time faculty:** 307 total; 29% have terminal degrees, 8% minority, 50% women. **Class size:** 33% < 20, 42% 20-39, 9% 40-49, 10% 50-99, 8% >100. **Special facilities:** Art museum, earth and mineral science museum and art gallery, anthropology museum, entomological museum, sports museum, land-grant frescoes, agricultural museum, Pennsylvania space grant consortium.

**Freshman class profile.** 39,551 applied, 20,156 admitted, 6,495 enrolled.

| Mid 50% test scores | | | |
|---|---|---|---|
| SAT critical reading: | 530-630 | Rank in top quarter: | 81% |
| SAT math: | 560-670 | Rank in top tenth: | 45% |
| GPA 3.50 or higher: | 65% | Return as sophomores: | 94% |
| GPA 3.0-3.49: | 31% | Out-of-state: | 32% |
| GPA 2.0-2.99: | 4% | International: | 4% |

**Basis for selection.** Admission decisions based upon high school GPA, standardized test scores, class rank, personal statements, and activities. Essay considered if submitted; portfolios required for select majors. **Home-schooled:** Applicants should provide complete documentation showing courses studied and all evaluations presented from evaluator or supervisor assigned to student in cooperation with local school district or evaluator approved through program.

**High school preparation.** Required units include English 4, mathematics 3, social studies 3, science 3 and foreign language 2. 3 units required in arts and humanities. Additional requirements for some programs.

**2007-2008 Annual costs.** Tuition/fees: $12,844; $23,712 out-of-state. Room/board: $7,750. Books/supplies: $1,168. Personal expenses: $2,916.

**2006-2007 Financial aid. Need-based:** 6,038 full-time freshmen applied for aid; 3,915 were judged to have need; 3,672 of these received aid. Average need met was 65%. Average scholarship/grant was $5,815; average loan $2,737. 40% of total undergraduate aid awarded as scholarships/grants, 60% as loans/jobs. **Non-need-based:** Awarded to 9,094 full-time undergraduates, including 2,188 freshmen. Scholarships awarded for academics, alumni affiliation, athletics, ROTC.

**Application procedures. Admission:** Priority date 11/30; no deadline. $50 fee, may be waived for applicants with need. Application may be submitted online. Admission notification on a rolling basis beginning on or about 11/1. **Financial aid:** Priority date 2/15; no closing date. FAFSA required. Applicants notified on a rolling basis starting 3/1.

**Academics. Special study options:** Accelerated study, combined bachelor's/graduate degree, cooperative education, cross-registration, distance learning, double major, dual enrollment of high school students, ESL, exchange student, external degree, honors, independent study, internships, liberal arts/career combination, student-designed major, study abroad, teacher certification program, Washington semester, weekend college. **Credit/placement by examination:** AP, CLEP, IB, SAT, institutional tests. 60 credit hours maximum toward bachelor's degree. **Support services:** Learning center, pre-admission summer program, study skills assistance, tutoring, writing center.

**Honors college/program.** 300 students admitted each year. Generally, students with excellent high school records (near top of class in grades and schedule strength) and 1350 SAT (exclusive of Writing) are competitive applicants.

**Majors. Agriculture:** General, agribusiness operations, agronomy, animal sciences, education services, food science, horticultural science, landscaping, mechanization, soil science, turf management. **Architecture:** Architecture, landscape. **Area/ethnic studies:** African-American, American, East Asian, Latin American, women's. **Biology:** General, bacteriology, biochemistry, biomedical sciences. **Business:** Accounting, actuarial science, finance, hospitality admin, labor relations, management information systems, managerial economics, marketing, organizational behavior. **Communications:** General, advertising, journalism. **Computer sciences:** General, information systems. **Conservation:** General, forest sciences, forest technology. **Education:** Adult/continuing, art, elementary, foreign languages, music, secondary, special. **Engineering:** Aerospace, agricultural, architectural, biomedical, chemical, civil, computer, electrical, environmental, industrial, materials science, mechanical, mining, nuclear, petroleum, science. **English:** English lit. **Family/consumer sciences:** Family studies, human nutrition. **Foreign languages:** Classics, comparative lit, French, German, Italian, Japanese, Russian, Spanish. **Health:** Communication disorders, health care admin, nursing (RN), premedicine. **History:** General. **Interdisciplinary:** Biological/physical sciences, medieval/Renaissance. **Liberal arts:** Arts/sciences. **Math:** General, statistics. **Parks/recreation:** Exercise sciences, facilities management. **Philosophy/religion:** Judaic, philosophy, religion. **Physical sciences:** Astronomy, atmospheric science, chemistry, geology, physics. **Protective services:** Law enforcement admin. **Psychology:** General. **Science technology:** Biological. **Social sciences:** Anthropology, applied economics, archaeology, economics, geography, international relations, political science, sociology. **Visual/performing arts:** General, acting, art, art history/conservation, film/cinema, graphic design, music performance, theater design.

**Most popular majors.** Business/marketing 16%, communications/journalism 9%, education 6%, engineering/engineering technologies 13%, social sciences 6%.

**Computing on campus.** 3,900 workstations in dormitories, library, computer center, student center, student center. Dormitories wired for high-speed internet access and linked to campus network. Commuter students can connect to campus network. Online course registration, online library, helpline, repair service, student web hosting, wireless network available.

**Student life. Freshman orientation:** Mandatory. Preregistration for classes offered. Held the 2 days prior to start of classes. **Policies:** Acts of intolerance and high-risk drinking discouraged at all locations. All facilites designated as smoke-free. **Housing:** Coed dorms, single-sex dorms, special housing for disabled, apartments, fraternity/sorority housing, substance-free housing available. $100 partly refundable deposit, deadline 5/1. Suites, special interest housing available. **Activities:** Bands, campus ministries, choral groups, dance, drama, film society, international student organizations, literary magazine, music ensembles, Model UN, musical theater, opera, radio station, student government, student newspaper, symphony orchestra, TV station, adult learners, eco-action, Habitat for Humanity, minorities in agriculture and natural resources, National Society of Black Engineers, College Democrats, College Libertarians, Womyn's Concerns, Black Caucus, Alliance Christian Fellowship.

**Athletics.** NCAA. **Intercollegiate:** Baseball M, basketball, cheerleading, cross-country, diving, fencing, field hockey W, football (tackle) M, golf, gymnastics, lacrosse, soccer, softball W, swimming, tennis, track and field, volleyball, wrestling M. **Intramural:** Badminton, basketball, bowling, cross-country, diving, football (non-tackle), football (tackle), golf, gymnastics, racquetball, soccer, softball, squash, swimming, tennis, track and field, volleyball, wrestling. **Team name:** Nittany Lions.

**Student services.** Adult student services, alcohol/substance abuse counseling, campus ministries, career counseling, services for economically disadvantaged, student employment services, financial aid counseling, health services, legal services, minority student services, on-campus daycare, personal counseling, placement for graduates, veterans' counselor, women's services. **Physically disabled:** Services for visually, speech, hearing impaired.

**Contact.** E-mail: admissions@psu.edu
Phone: (814) 865-5471 Fax: (814) 863-7590
Anne Rohrbach, Executive Director for Undergraduate Admissions, Penn State University Park, 201 Shields Building, University Park, PA 16802-1294

---

## Penn State Wilkes-Barre
### Lehman, Pennsylvania
www.wb.psu.edu

CB code: 2660

- Public 4-year branch campus college
- Commuter campus in small city
- 563 degree-seeking undergraduates: 9% part-time, 29% women, 3% African American, 2% Asian American, 2% Hispanic American
- 84% of applicants admitted
- SAT or ACT with writing required
- 49% graduate within 6 years; 22% enter graduate study

**General.** Founded in 1916. Regionally accredited. **Degrees:** 64 bachelor's, 18 associate awarded. **ROTC:** Army, Air Force. **Location:** 10 miles from Wilkes-Barre. **Calendar:** Semester, limited summer session. **Full-time faculty:** 37 total; 54% have terminal degrees, 16% minority, 16% women. **Part-time faculty:** 22 total; 23% have terminal degrees, 54% women. **Class size:** 62% < 20, 36% 20-39, 2% 40-49, less than 1% 50-99.

**Freshman class profile.** 630 applied, 531 admitted, 173 enrolled.

| Mid 50% test scores | | | |
|---|---|---|---|
| SAT critical reading: | 430-530 | Rank in top quarter: | 35% |
| SAT math: | 440-560 | Rank in top tenth: | 9% |
| GPA 3.50 or higher: | 15% | Return as sophomores: | 75% |
| GPA 3.0-3.49: | 37% | Out-of-state: | 6% |
| GPA 2.0-2.99: | 47% | International: | 1% |

**Basis for selection.** Admission decisions based upon high school GPA, standardized test scores, class rank, personal statements, and activities. Essay considered if submitted; portfolios required for select majors. **Home-schooled:** Applicants should provide complete documentation showing courses studied and all evaluations presented from evaluator or supervisor assigned to student in cooperation with local school district or evaluator approved through program. **Learning Disabled:** Prospective students with disabilities encouraged to contact or visit the Office for Disability Services in their junior or senior years in high school in order to find out more about disability services at the college level.

**High school preparation.** Required units include English 4, mathematics 3, social studies 3, science 3 and foreign language 2.

**2007-2008 Annual costs.** Tuition/fees: $11,006; $16,506 out-of-state. Books/supplies: $1,168. Personal expenses: $1,854.

**2006-2007 Financial aid. Need-based:** 165 full-time freshmen applied for aid; 131 were judged to have need; 130 of these received aid. Average need met was 65%. Average scholarship/grant was $5,475; average loan $2,454. 47% of total undergraduate aid awarded as scholarships/grants, 53% as loans/jobs. **Non-need-based:** Awarded to 180 full-time undergraduates, including 92 freshmen. Scholarships awarded for academics, alumni affiliation, athletics, ROTC.

**Application procedures. Admission:** Priority date 11/30; no deadline. $50 fee, may be waived for applicants with need. Application may be submitted online. Admission notification on a rolling basis beginning on or about 11/30. All freshmen applications processed at University Park Campus. **Financial aid:** Priority date 2/15; no closing date. FAFSA required. Applicants notified on a rolling basis starting 3/1.

**Academics. Special study options:** Accelerated study, cross-registration, distance learning, double major, dual enrollment of high school students, honors, independent study, internships, student-designed major, study abroad. **Credit/placement by examination:** AP, CLEP, IB, SAT. 60 credit hours maximum toward bachelor's degree. **Support services:** Learning center, study skills assistance, tutoring, writing center.

**Majors. Agriculture:** General, agribusiness operations, agronomy, animal sciences, education services, food science, horticultural science, landscaping, mechanization, soil science, turf management. **Area/ethnic studies:** African-American, American, East Asian, Latin American, women's. **Biology:** General, bacteriology, biochemistry, biomedical sciences. **Business:** Accounting, actuarial science, business admin, finance, hospitality admin, labor relations, management information systems, managerial economics, marketing, organizational behavior. **Communications:** General, advertising, journalism. **Computer sciences:** General, information systems. **Conservation:** General, forest sciences, forest technology. **Education:** Adult/continuing, art, elementary, foreign languages, secondary, special. **Engineering:** Aerospace, agricultural, architectural, biomedical, chemical, civil, computer, electrical, environmental, industrial, materials science, mechanical, mining, nuclear, petroleum, science. **English:** English lit. **Family/consumer sciences:** Family studies, human nutrition. **Foreign languages:** Classics, comparative lit, French, German, Italian, Japanese, Russian, Spanish. **Health:** Communication disorders, health care admin, nursing (RN), premedicine. **History:** General. **Interdisciplinary:** Biological/physical sciences, medieval/Renaissance. **Liberal arts:** Arts/sciences. **Math:** General, statistics. **Parks/recreation:** General, exercise sciences. **Philosophy/religion:** Judaic, philosophy, religion. **Physical sciences:** Astronomy, atmospheric science, chemistry, geology, physics. **Protective services:** Criminal justice, law enforcement admin. **Psychology:** General. **Science technology:** Biological. **Social sciences:** Anthropology, applied economics, archaeology, economics, geography, international relations, political science, sociology. **Visual/performing arts:** General, acting, art, art history/conservation, film/cinema, graphic design, theater design. **Other:** Rehabilitation and therapeutic studies.

**Most popular majors.** Business/marketing 38%, computer/information sciences 20%, security/protective services 36%.

**Computing on campus.** 196 workstations in library, computer center, student center. Commuter students can connect to campus network. Online course registration, online library, helpline, repair service, student web hosting, wireless network available.

**Student life. Freshman orientation:** Mandatory. Preregistration for classes offered. One-day session held prior to start of classes. **Policies:** Acts of intolerance and high-risk drinking discouraged at all locations. All facilities designated smoke-free. Students expected to abide by The Penn State Principles. **Activities:** Radio station, student government, student newspaper, Model United Nations, students for justice club.

**Athletics. Intercollegiate:** Baseball M, basketball M, cross-country, golf, soccer, volleyball W. **Intramural:** Basketball, football (tackle), racquetball, softball, volleyball. **Team name:** Nittany Lions.

**Student services.** Adult student services, alcohol/substance abuse counseling, campus ministries, career counseling, services for economically disadvantaged, student employment services, financial aid counseling, health services, minority student services, personal counseling, placement for graduates. **Physically disabled:** Services for visually, hearing impaired.

**Contact.** E-mail: admissions@psu.edu
Phone: (814) 865-5471 Fax: (814) 863-7590
Anne Rohrbach, Executive Director for Undergraduate Admissions, Penn State Wilkes-Barre, 201 Shields Building, University Park, PA 16802-1294

## Penn State Worthington Scranton
### Dunmore, Pennsylvania
www.sn.psu.edu                    CB code: 2660

- Public 4-year branch campus college
- Commuter campus in large town
- 1,185 degree-seeking undergraduates: 17% part-time, 50% women, 2% African American, 1% Asian American, 3% Hispanic American
- 86% of applicants admitted
- SAT or ACT with writing required
- 43% graduate within 6 years; 22% enter graduate study

**General.** Founded in 1923. Regionally accredited. **Degrees:** 111 bachelor's, 78 associate awarded. **ROTC:** Army, Air Force. **Location:** One mile from Scranton. **Calendar:** Semester, limited summer session. **Full-time faculty:** 55 total; 62% have terminal degrees, 13% minority, 51% women. **Part-time faculty:** 54 total; 11% have terminal degrees, 4% minority, 59% women. **Class size:** 40% < 20, 54% 20-39, 3% 40-49, 2% 50-99.

**Freshman class profile.** 903 applied, 773 admitted, 306 enrolled.

| Mid 50% test scores | | | |
|---|---|---|---|
| SAT critical reading: | 420-530 | Rank in top quarter: | 19% |
| SAT math: | 410-520 | Rank in top tenth: | 5% |
| GPA 3.50 or higher: | 6% | Return as sophomores: | 76% |
| GPA 3.0-3.49: | 32% | Out-of-state: | 2% |

| | | | |
|---|---|---|---|
| GPA 2.0-2.99: | | | 61% |

**Basis for selection.** Admission decisions based upon high school GPA, as well as other factors, which may include standardized verbal and math test scores, class rank, personal statements, and list of activities. Essay considered if submitted; portfolios required for select majors. **Homeschooled:** Provide complete documentation showing courses studied and all evaluations presented from evaluator or supervisor assigned to student in cooperation with local school district or evaluator who is approved through the program.

**High school preparation.** Required units include English 4, mathematics 3, social studies 3, science 3 and foreign language 2.

**2007-2008 Annual costs.** Tuition/fees: $10,986; $16,486 out-of-state. Books/supplies: $1,168. Personal expenses: $1,854.

**2006-2007 Financial aid. Need-based:** 269 full-time freshmen applied for aid; 220 were judged to have need; 217 of these received aid. Average need met was 60%. Average scholarship/grant was $5,195; average loan $2,613. 45% of total undergraduate aid awarded as scholarships/grants, 55% as loans/jobs. **Non-need-based:** Awarded to 172 full-time undergraduates, including 73 freshmen. Scholarships awarded for academics, alumni affiliation, athletics, ROTC.

**Application procedures. Admission:** Priority date 11/30; no deadline. $50 fee, may be waived for applicants with need. Application may be submitted online. Admission notification on a rolling basis beginning on or about 11/1. All freshmen applications processed at University Park Campus. **Financial aid:** Priority date 2/15; no closing date. FAFSA required. Applicants notified on a rolling basis starting 3/1.

**Academics. Special study options:** Accelerated study, cooperative education, cross-registration, distance learning, double major, dual enrollment of high school students, honors, independent study, internships, study abroad. **Credit/placement by examination:** AP, CLEP, IB, SAT. 60 credit hours maximum toward bachelor's degree. **Support services:** Learning center, remedial instruction, study skills assistance, tutoring, writing center.

**Majors. Agriculture:** General, agribusiness operations, agronomy, animal sciences, business, education services, food science, horticultural science, landscaping, mechanization, soil science, turf management. **Area/ethnic studies:** African-American, American, East Asian, Latin American, women's. **Biology:** General, bacteriology, biochemistry, biomedical sciences. **Business:** Accounting, actuarial science, business admin, finance, hospitality admin, labor relations, management information systems, managerial economics, marketing, organizational behavior. **Communications:** General, advertising, journalism. **Computer sciences:** General, information systems. **Conservation:** General, forest sciences, forest technology. **Education:** Adult/continuing, art, elementary, foreign languages, secondary, special. **Engineering:** Aerospace, agricultural, architectural, biomedical, chemical, civil, computer, electrical, environmental, industrial, materials science, mechanical, mining, nuclear, petroleum, science. **English:** English lit. **Family/consumer sciences:** Family studies, human nutrition. **Foreign languages:** Classics, comparative lit, French, German, Italian, Japanese, Russian, Spanish. **Health:** Communication disorders, health care admin, nursing (RN), premedicine. **History:** General. **Interdisciplinary:** Biological/physical sciences, medieval/Renaissance. **Liberal arts:** Arts/sciences. **Math:** General, statistics. **Parks/recreation:** Exercise sciences, facilities management. **Philosophy/religion:**

Judaic, philosophy, religion. **Physical sciences:** Astronomy, atmospheric science, chemistry, geology, physics. **Protective services:** Criminal justice, law enforcement admin. **Psychology:** General. **Science technology:** Biological. **Social sciences:** Anthropology, applied economics, archaeology, economics, geography, international relations, political science, sociology. **Visual/performing arts:** General, acting, art, art history/conservation, film/cinema, graphic design, theater design. **Other:** Rehabilitation and therapeutic studies.

**Most popular majors.** Business/marketing 52%, computer/information sciences 17%, family/consumer sciences 24%.

**Computing on campus.** 180 workstations in library, computer center, student center. Commuter students can connect to campus network. Online course registration, online library, helpline, repair service, student web hosting, wireless network available.

**Student life. Freshman orientation:** Available. Preregistration for classes offered. **Policies:** Acts of intolerance and high-risk drinking discouraged at all locations. All facilities designated as smoke-free. Students expected to abide by The Penn State Principles. **Activities:** Jazz band, choral groups, drama, literary magazine, music ensembles, student government, student newspaper, community human service organization, Faith and Values, German club, Lighthouse club, multicultural club, veterans club, public affairs club.

**Athletics. Intercollegiate:** Baseball M, basketball, cross-country, soccer M, softball W. **Intramural:** Basketball, soccer, softball, volleyball, weight lifting. **Team name:** Nittany Lions.

**Student services.** Adult student services, alcohol/substance abuse counseling, career counseling, services for economically disadvantaged, student employment services, financial aid counseling, health services, personal counseling, placement for graduates, veterans' counselor, women's services. **Physically disabled:** Services for visually, speech, hearing impaired.

**Contact.** E-mail: admissions@psu.edu
Phone: (814) 865-5471 Fax: (814) 863-7590
Anne Rohrbach, Executive Director for Undergraduate Admissions, Penn State Worthington Scranton, 201 Shields Building, University Park, PA 16802-1294

---

## Penn State York
### York, Pennsylvania
**www.yk.psu.edu**

**CB code: 2660**

- Public 4-year branch campus college
- Commuter campus in large town
- 1,070 degree-seeking undergraduates: 24% part-time, 44% women, 5% African American, 6% Asian American, 5% Hispanic American
- 84% of applicants admitted
- SAT or ACT with writing required
- 45% graduate within 6 years; 22% enter graduate study

**General.** Founded in 1926. Regionally accredited. **Degrees:** 100 bachelor's, 82 associate awarded. **Calendar:** Semester, extensive summer session. **Full-time faculty:** 59 total; 61% have terminal degrees, 17% minority, 36% women. **Part-time faculty:** 55 total; 18% have terminal degrees, 2% minority, 47% women. **Class size:** 59% < 20, 37% 20-39, 2% 40-49, 2% 50-99.

**Freshman class profile.** 1,328 applied, 1,118 admitted, 333 enrolled.

| Mid 50% test scores | | | |
|---|---|---|---|
| SAT critical reading: | 410-530 | GPA 2.0-2.99: | 62% |
| SAT math: | 440-550 | Rank in top quarter: | 24% |
| GPA 3.50 or higher: | 9% | Rank in top tenth: | 6% |
| GPA 3.0-3.49: | 27% | Return as sophomores: | 71% |
| | | Out-of-state: | 11% |

**Basis for selection.** Admission decisions based upon high school GPA and other factors, which may include standardized verbal and math test scores, class rank, personal statements, activities lists. Essay considered if submitted; portfolios required for select majors. **Homeschooled:** Complete documentation showing courses studied and all evaluations from home school evaluator or supervisor assigned to student in cooperation with local school district or evaluator approved through program.

**High school preparation.** Required units include English 4, mathematics 3, social studies 3, science 3 and foreign language 2.

**2007-2008 Annual costs.** Tuition/fees: $10,986; $16,486 out-of-state. Books/supplies: $1,168. Personal expenses: $1,854.

**2006-2007 Financial aid. Need-based:** 241 full-time freshmen applied for aid; 185 were judged to have need; 182 of these received aid. Average need met was 66%. Average scholarship/grant was $4,869; average loan $2,506. 48% of total undergraduate aid awarded as scholarships/grants, 52% as loans/jobs. **Non-need-based:** Awarded to 212 full-time undergraduates, including 99 freshmen. Scholarships awarded for academics, alumni affiliation, athletics, ROTC.

**Application procedures. Admission:** Priority date 11/30; no deadline. $50 fee, may be waived for applicants with need. Application may be submitted online. Admission notification on a rolling basis beginning on or about 11/1. All freshmen applications processed at University Park Campus. **Financial aid:** Priority date 2/15; no closing date. FAFSA required. Applicants notified on a rolling basis starting 3/1.

**Academics. Special study options:** Accelerated study, cross-registration, distance learning, double major, ESL, honors, independent study, internships, student-designed major, study abroad. **Credit/placement by examination:** AP, CLEP, IB, SAT. 60 credit hours maximum toward bachelor's degree. **Support services:** Learning center, pre-admission summer program, reduced course load, remedial instruction, study skills assistance, tutoring, writing center.

**Majors. Agriculture:** General, agribusiness operations, agronomy, animal sciences, education services, food science, horticultural science, landscaping, mechanization, soil science, turf management. **Area/ethnic studies:** African-American, American, East Asian, Latin American, women's. **Biology:** General, bacteriology, biochemistry, biomedical sciences. **Business:** Accounting, actuarial science, business admin, finance, hospitality admin, labor relations, management information systems, managerial economics, marketing, organizational behavior. **Communications:** General, advertising, journalism. **Computer sciences:** General, information systems. **Conservation:** General, forest sciences, forest technology. **Education:** Adult/continuing, art, elementary, foreign languages, secondary, special. **Engineering:** Aerospace, agricultural, architectural, biomedical, chemical, civil, computer, electrical, environmental, industrial, materials science, mechanical, mining, nuclear, petroleum, science. **English:** English lit. **Family/consumer sciences:** Family studies, human nutrition. **Foreign languages:** Classics, comparative lit, French, German, Italian, Japanese, Russian, Spanish. **Health:** Communication disorders, health care admin, nursing (RN), premedicine. **History:** General. **Interdisciplinary:** Biological/physical sciences, medieval/Renaissance. **Liberal arts:** Arts/sciences. **Math:** General, statistics. **Parks/recreation:** Exercise sciences, facilities management. **Philosophy/religion:** Judaic, philosophy, religion. **Physical sciences:** Astronomy, atmospheric science, chemistry, geology, physics. **Protective services:** Criminal justice, law enforcement admin. **Psychology:** General. **Science technology:** Biological. **Social sciences:** Anthropology, applied economics, archaeology, economics, geography, international relations, political science, sociology. **Visual/performing arts:** General, acting, art, art history/conservation, film/cinema, graphic design, theater design. **Other:** Rehabilitation and therapeutic studies.

**Most popular majors.** Business/marketing 44%, communications/journalism 7%, computer/information sciences 24%, interdisciplinary studies 11%.

**Computing on campus.** 169 workstations in computer center. Commuter students can connect to campus network. Online course registration, online library, helpline, repair service, student web hosting, wireless network available.

**Student life. Freshman orientation:** Mandatory. Preregistration for classes offered. Full-day event in August. **Policies:** Acts of intolerance and high-risk drinking discouraged at all locations. All facilities designated as smoke-free. Students expected to abide by The Penn State Principles. **Activities:** Campus ministries, dance, drama, literary magazine, Model UN, student government, student newspaper, black student union, Christian Fellowship, Hispanic students association, Rainbow Alliance, veterans club, Asian culture club, foreign policy club, debate club.

**Athletics. Intercollegiate:** Baseball M, basketball, soccer, tennis, volleyball. **Intramural:** Badminton, basketball, football (non-tackle) M, handball, soccer, softball, table tennis, tennis, volleyball. **Team name:** Nittany Lions.

**Student services.** Adult student services, alcohol/substance abuse counseling, campus ministries, career counseling, services for economically disadvantaged, student employment services, financial aid counseling, health services, minority student services, personal counseling, placement for graduates, veterans' counselor, women's services. **Physically disabled:** Services for visually, speech, hearing impaired. **Learning disabled:** Comprehensive services available.

**Contact.** E-mail: admissions@psu.edu
Phone: (814) 865-5471 Fax: (814) 863-7590
Anne Rohrbach, Executive Director for Undergraduate Admissions, Penn State York, 201 Shields Building, University Park, PA 16802-1294

## Pennsylvania College of Art and Design
**Lancaster, Pennsylvania**
www.pcad.edu — CB code: 2681

- Private 4-year visual arts college
- Commuter campus in small city
- 252 degree-seeking undergraduates: 7% part-time, 60% women, 4% African American, 3% Asian American, 3% Hispanic American, 1% Native American
- 57% of applicants admitted
- Application essay, interview required
- 59% graduate within 6 years; 5% enter graduate study

**General.** Regionally accredited. **Degrees:** 37 bachelor's awarded. **Location:** 75 miles from Philadelphia, 75 miles from Baltimore. **Calendar:** Semester, limited summer session. **Full-time faculty:** 12 total; 92% have terminal degrees, 17% women. **Part-time faculty:** 34 total; 44% have terminal degrees, 44% women. **Special facilities:** Visual arts gallery.

**Freshman class profile.** 190 applied, 108 admitted, 87 enrolled.

| | | | |
|---|---|---|---|
| End year in good standing: | 80% | Out-of-state: | 20% |
| Return as sophomores: | 76% | | |

**Basis for selection.** Portfolio review, interview, personal statement, and high school transcripts required. Students with a GPA below 2.5 are required to submit two letters of recommendation. **Homeschooled:** Transcript of courses and grades, state high school equivalency certificate, interview required.

**2007-2008 Annual costs.** Tuition/fees: $15,205. Books/supplies: $1,265. Personal expenses: $1,111.

**Application procedures. Admission:** No deadline. $40 fee, may be waived for applicants with need. Application must be submitted on paper. Admission notification on a rolling basis. Must reply by May 1 or within 2 week(s) if notified thereafter.

**Academics. Special study options:** Dual enrollment of high school students, internships. **Credit/placement by examination:** AP, CLEP, institutional tests.

**Majors. Visual/performing arts:** Graphic design, illustration, photography, studio arts.

**Computing on campus.** Online library, wireless network available.

**Student life. Freshman orientation:** Mandatory. **Housing:** Housing referral service available. **Activities:** Literary magazine, student government.

**Student services.** Career counseling, student employment services.

**Contact.** E-mail: admissions@pcad.edu
Phone: (717) 396-7833 Fax: (717) 396-1339
Director of Admission, Pennsylvania College of Art and Design, PO Box 59, Lancaster, PA 17608-0059

## Pennsylvania College of Technology
**Williamsport, Pennsylvania** — CB member
www.pct.edu — CB code: 2989

- Public 4-year technical college
- Commuter campus in small city
- 6,565 degree-seeking undergraduates: 13% part-time, 34% women, 3% African American, 1% Asian American, 1% Hispanic American, 1% Native American
- 49% graduate within 6 years

**General.** Founded in 1965. Regionally accredited. **Degrees:** 484 bachelor's, 1,193 associate awarded. **ROTC:** Army. **Location:** 85 miles from Harrisburg, 70 miles from Wilkes-Barre. **Calendar:** Semester, limited summer session. **Full-time faculty:** 293 total; 28% women. **Part-time faculty:** 200 total; 51% women. **Special facilities:** Automotive technology center, aviation center, plastics manufacturing center, community arts center, earth science center.

**Freshman class profile.** 3,066 applied, 2,911 admitted, 1,631 enrolled.

**Basis for selection.** Open admission, but selective for some programs. Competitive admissions to health science programs, using GPA, SAT scores, high school rank, selected course grades, completed developmental course work. Some programs have more specific requirements. SAT recommended for all bachelor's programs, dental hygiene, radiography, occupational therapy assistant, nursing applicants; college placement exams required for all applicants. Portfolio required for graphic design program. **Homeschooled:** Transcript of courses and grades, state high school equivalency certificate required. Must provide proof of graduation from an organization governed by the State Board of Education, such as Pennsylvania Homeschoolers Accreditation Agency. Otherwise must present GED.

**2007-2008 Annual costs.** Tuition/fees: $11,250; $14,130 out-of-state. Room/board: $7,770. Books/supplies: $1,000. Personal expenses: $2,450.

**Financial aid. Non-need-based:** Scholarships awarded for academics, alumni affiliation.

**Application procedures. Admission:** Closing date 7/1 (postmark date). $50 fee, may be waived for applicants with need. Application may be submitted online. Admission notification on a rolling basis. **Financial aid:** Priority date 4/1; no closing date. FAFSA, institutional form required. Applicants notified on a rolling basis starting 6/1; must reply by 7/1 or within 4 week(s) of notification.

**Academics. Special study options:** Accelerated study, cooperative education, cross-registration, distance learning, dual enrollment of high school students, exchange student, honors, independent study, internships, student-designed major, study abroad, weekend college. **Credit/placement by examination:** AP, CLEP, institutional tests. 30 credit hours maximum toward associate degree, 30 toward bachelor's. **Support services:** Learning center, pre-admission summer program, remedial instruction, study skills assistance, tutoring.

**Majors. Business:** Accounting, business admin, management information systems. **Communications technology:** Graphic/printing. **Computer sciences:** Networking, security, systems analysis, web page design. **Construction:** Masonry. **Engineering technology:** Architectural, automotive, civil, construction, environmental, heat/ac/refrig, manufacturing, mechanical, plastics. **Health:** Adult health nursing, cardiovascular technology, dental hygiene, EMT paramedic, surgical technology. **Mechanic/repair:** Avionics, electronics/electrical, heating/ac/refrig, industrial electronics. **Parks/recreation:** Exercise sciences. **Personal/culinary services:** Chef training. **Visual/performing arts:** Commercial/advertising art.

**Most popular majors.** Business/marketing 16%, computer/information sciences 16%, engineering/engineering technologies 40%, health sciences 15%.

**Computing on campus.** 1,820 workstations in dormitories, library, computer center, student center. Dormitories wired for high-speed internet access and linked to campus network. Commuter students can connect to campus network. Online course registration, online library, helpline, wireless network available.

**Student life. Freshman orientation:** Available. Preregistration for classes offered. 2-day sessions offered throughout summer. **Policies:** No illegal drugs and no alcohol on campus. Smoke-free buildings and housing environments. **Housing:** Coed dorms, substance-free housing available. $300 deposit. Coed apartments available. **Activities:** Campus ministries, dance, radio station, student government, Alpha Omega Fellowship, Campus Crusade for Christ, Earth Smart, human services club, multicultural society, occupational therapy assistant club, physicians assistant club, Skills USA, student nurses association.

**Athletics. Intercollegiate:** Archery, baseball M, basketball, bowling, cross-country, golf, soccer, softball W, tennis, volleyball. **Intramural:** Archery, badminton, basketball, bowling, football (non-tackle), golf, lacrosse, racquetball, soccer, softball, table tennis, tennis, volleyball, weight lifting, wrestling M. **Team name:** Wildcats.

**Student services.** Adult student services, alcohol/substance abuse counseling, career counseling, student employment services, financial aid counseling, health services, on-campus daycare, personal counseling, placement for graduates, veterans' counselor, women's services. **Physically disabled:** Services for visually, speech, hearing impaired.

**Contact.** E-mail: admissions@pct.edu
Phone: (570) 327-4761 Toll-free number: (800) 367-9222
Fax: (570) 321-5551
Chester Schuman, Director of Admissions, Pennsylvania College of Technology, One College Avenue, Williamsport, PA 17701

## Philadelphia Biblical University
**Langhorne, Pennsylvania**
www.pbu.edu — CB code: 2661

- Private 4-year university and Bible college affiliated with Protestant Evangelical tradition
- Residential campus in small town

- 1,060 degree-seeking undergraduates: 6% part-time, 54% women, 12% African American, 3% Asian American, 2% Hispanic American, 2% international
- 296 degree-seeking graduate students
- 98% of applicants admitted
- SAT or ACT (ACT writing optional), application essay required
- 60% graduate within 6 years; 35% enter graduate study

**General.** Founded in 1913. Regionally accredited; also accredited by ABHE. **Degrees:** 252 bachelor's awarded; master's, first professional offered. **ROTC:** Air Force. **Location:** 17 miles from Philadelphia; 5 miles from Trenton, New Jersey. **Calendar:** Semester, limited summer session. **Full-time faculty:** 53 total; 58% have terminal degrees, 9% minority, 32% women. **Part-time faculty:** 78 total; 20% have terminal degrees, 8% minority, 35% women. **Class size:** 57% < 20, 39% 20-39, 1% 40-49, 2% 50-99. **Special facilities:** Wooded walking trail.

**Freshman class profile.** 366 applied, 357 admitted, 213 enrolled.

| Mid 50% test scores | | | |
|---|---|---|---|
| SAT critical reading: | 470-580 | Rank in top quarter: | 36% |
| SAT math: | 450-560 | Rank in top tenth: | 8% |
| ACT composite: | 20-24 | End year in good standing: | 99% |
| GPA 3.50 or higher: | 50% | Return as sophomores: | 82% |
| GPA 3.0-3.49: | 26% | Out-of-state: | 56% |
| GPA 2.0-2.99: | 21% | Live on campus: | 90% |
| | | International: | 2% |

**Basis for selection.** High school GPA, pastor's references, autobiography, SAT or ACT scores required for some. Some applicants not meeting academic admissions requirements may be admitted and placed in remedial program. Interview recommended for all; audition required for music program. **Homeschooled:** Letter of recommendation (nonparent) required.

**High school preparation.** 15 units recommended. Recommended units include English 4, mathematics 1, social studies 3, science 2 and foreign language 2.

**2008-2009 Annual costs.** Tuition/fees (projected): $17,785. Room/board: $7,150. Books/supplies: $900. Personal expenses: $1,200.

**2007-2008 Financial aid. Need-based:** 168 full-time freshmen applied for aid; 147 were judged to have need; 147 of these received aid. Average need met was 77%. Average scholarship/grant was $10,569; average loan $4,416. 63% of total undergraduate aid awarded as scholarships/grants, 37% as loans/jobs. **Non-need-based:** Awarded to 265 full-time undergraduates, including 62 freshmen. Scholarships awarded for academics, leadership, minority status.

**Application procedures. Admission:** No deadline. $25 fee, may be waived for applicants with need. Application may be submitted online. Admission notification on a rolling basis beginning on or about 9/1. Must reply by May 1 or within 4 week(s) if notified thereafter. **Financial aid:** Priority date 5/1; no closing date. FAFSA required. Applicants notified on a rolling basis starting 3/15.

**Academics.** Students may participate in semester studies in Israel. **Special study options:** Accelerated study, combined bachelor's/graduate degree, double major, dual enrollment of high school students, honors, internships, study abroad, teacher certification program. Cooperative agreement with Bucks County Community College. **Credit/placement by examination:** AP, CLEP, IB, SAT, ACT, institutional tests. 12 credit hours maximum toward bachelor's degree. **Support services:** Learning center, reduced course load, remedial instruction, study skills assistance, tutoring, writing center.

**Majors. Business:** Business admin. **Education:** Early childhood, elementary, English, mathematics, music, physical, social studies. **Parks/recreation:** Health/fitness. **Public administration:** Social work. **Theology:** Bible, missionary, pastoral counseling, religious ed, sacred music, theology. **Visual/performing arts:** Music performance, music theory/composition.

**Most popular majors.** Education 12%, philosophy/religious studies 75%.

**Computing on campus.** 71 workstations in dormitories, library, student center. Dormitories wired for high-speed internet access and linked to campus network. Commuter students can connect to campus network. Online course registration, online library, helpline, wireless network available.

**Student life. Freshman orientation:** Mandatory. Preregistration for classes offered. **Policies:** Religious observance required. **Housing:** Guaranteed on-campus for freshmen. Single-sex dorms, special housing for disabled, apartments, substance-free housing available. $100 fully refundable deposit, deadline 7/15. **Activities:** Concert band, campus ministries, choral groups, drama, international student organizations, music ensembles, musical theater, opera, student government, student newspaper, symphony orchestra, student

missionary fellowship, commuter council, resident council, student theological society, cultural awareness association, student business club, social committee.

**Athletics.** NCAA, NCCAA. **Intercollegiate:** Baseball M, basketball, field hockey W, golf M, soccer, softball W, tennis, volleyball. **Intramural:** Basketball, football (non-tackle), soccer, table tennis, tennis, volleyball. **Team name:** Eagles.

**Student services.** Alcohol/substance abuse counseling, campus ministries, career counseling, student employment services, financial aid counseling, health services, personal counseling, placement for graduates. **Physically disabled:** Services for visually, hearing impaired.

**Contact.** E-mail: admissions@pbu.edu
Phone: (215) 702-4235 Toll-free number: (800) 366-0049
Fax: (215) 702-4248
Lisa Yoder, Director of Admissions, Philadelphia Biblical University, 200 Manor Avenue, Langhorne, PA 19047-2990

## Philadelphia University
**Philadelphia, Pennsylvania**
www.philau.edu

CB member
CB code: 2666

- Private 4-year university
- Residential campus in very large city
- 2,796 degree-seeking undergraduates: 8% part-time, 69% women, 10% African American, 4% Asian American, 3% Hispanic American, 2% international
- 522 degree-seeking graduate students
- 64% of applicants admitted
- SAT or ACT (ACT writing optional) required
- 50% graduate within 6 years

**General.** Founded in 1884. Regionally accredited. **Degrees:** 527 bachelor's, 4 associate awarded; master's, doctoral offered. **Location:** 7 miles from Center City. **Calendar:** Semester, limited summer session. **Full-time faculty:** 111 total; 73% have terminal degrees, 9% minority, 39% women. **Part-time faculty:** 335 total; 11% minority, 38% women. **Class size:** 65% < 20, 34% 20-39, less than 1% 40-49, less than 1% 50-99. **Special facilities:** Computer-aided design laboratories in architecture, graphic design and fashion design; CAD facilities, university design center, rapid prototyping.

**Freshman class profile.** 4,015 applied, 2,574 admitted, 737 enrolled.

| Mid 50% test scores | | | |
|---|---|---|---|
| SAT critical reading: | 480-560 | Rank in top tenth: | 11% |
| SAT math: | 490-590 | Return as sophomores: | 77% |
| SAT writing: | 470-560 | Out-of-state: | 55% |
| GPA 3.50 or higher: | 50% | Live on campus: | 90% |
| GPA 3.0-3.49: | 31% | International: | 2% |
| GPA 2.0-2.99: | 19% | Fraternities: | 1% |
| Rank in top quarter: | 38% | Sororities: | 1% |

**Basis for selection.** Academic record, GPA, and test scores most important. Extracurricular activities, counselor's recommendation and interview considered. Interview, essay recommended.

**High school preparation.** 15 units required; 19 recommended. Required and recommended units include English 4, mathematics 3-4, social studies 2-3, history 1-2, science 3-4 (laboratory 2), foreign language 2 and academic electives 2.

**2007-2008 Annual costs.** Tuition/fees: $25,456. Room/board: $8,358. Books/supplies: $1,400. Personal expenses: $1,789.

**2007-2008 Financial aid. Need-based:** 632 full-time freshmen applied for aid; 523 were judged to have need; 523 of these received aid. Average need met was 72%. Average scholarship/grant was $13,651; average loan $3,373. 56% of total undergraduate aid awarded as scholarships/grants, 44% as loans/jobs. **Non-need-based:** Awarded to 849 full-time undergraduates, including 255 freshmen. Scholarships awarded for academics, athletics.

**Application procedures. Admission:** No deadline. $35 fee, may be waived for applicants with need. Application may be submitted online. Admission notification on a rolling basis. Must reply by May 1 or within 3 week(s) if notified thereafter. **Financial aid:** Closing date 4/15. FAFSA required. Applicants notified on a rolling basis starting 2/10; must reply by 5/1.

**Academics. Special study options:** Accelerated study, combined bachelor's/graduate degree, distance learning, double major, honors, independent study, internships, liberal arts/career combination, study abroad, weekend college.

**Credit/placement by examination:** AP, CLEP, SAT, institutional tests. 60 credit hours maximum toward bachelor's degree. **Support services:** Learning center, reduced course load, remedial instruction, study skills assistance, tutoring, writing center.

**Majors. Architecture:** Architecture, interior, landscape. **Biology:** General, biochemistry, environmental. **Business:** Accounting, apparel, business admin, fashion, finance, international, management information systems, marketing. **Communications:** Digital media. **Communications technology:** Animation/special effects, graphics. **Conservation:** Environmental studies. **Engineering:** General, architectural, industrial, mechanical, textile. **Family/consumer sciences:** Apparel marketing, clothing/textiles, textile science. **Health:** Health care admin, premedicine. **Interdisciplinary:** Biopsychology. **Legal studies:** Prelaw. **Physical sciences:** Chemistry. **Psychology:** General. **Visual/performing arts:** Fashion design, fiber arts, graphic design, industrial design, interior design. **Other:** Professional communications.

**Most popular majors.** Architecture 19%, business/marketing 39%, visual/performing arts 27%.

**Computing on campus.** 400 workstations in library, computer center, student center. Dormitories wired for high-speed internet access and linked to campus network. Commuter students can connect to campus network. Online course registration, online library, helpline, student web hosting, wireless network available.

**Student life. Freshman orientation:** Mandatory, $100 fee. Preregistration for classes offered. Three-day residential program in summer. **Housing:** Guaranteed on-campus for freshmen. Coed dorms, single-sex dorms, apartments, substance-free housing available. $300 deposit, deadline 5/1. Townhouses available. **Activities:** Choral groups, dance, drama, international student organizations, student government, student newspaper, professional (major-related) organizations, Black awareness society, Hillel, Christian fellowship, community service corps, Minaret, Gemini Theatre, Phila Capella, Gay Lesbian Bisexual Allies Coalition.

**Athletics.** NCAA. **Intercollegiate:** Baseball M, basketball, cross-country, field hockey W, golf M, lacrosse W, rowing (crew), soccer, softball W, tennis, volleyball W. **Intramural:** Basketball, cross-country, football (tackle) M, skiing, soccer, softball, swimming, tennis, volleyball W. **Team name:** Rams.

**Student services.** Adult student services, alcohol/substance abuse counseling, career counseling, student employment services, financial aid counseling, health services, personal counseling, placement for graduates. **Physically disabled:** Services for visually, hearing impaired. **Learning disabled:** Comprehensive services available.

**Contact.** E-mail: admissions@philau.edu
Phone: (215) 951-2800 Toll-free number: (800) 951-7287
Fax: (215) 951-2907
Christine Greb, Director of Admissions, Philadelphia University, School House Lane and Henry Avenue, Philadelphia, PA 19144-5497

---

## Point Park University

**Pittsburgh, Pennsylvania**
www.pointpark.edu

**CB member**
**CB code: 2676**

- Private 4-year university
- Commuter campus in large city
- 3,089 degree-seeking undergraduates: 21% part-time, 59% women, 19% African American, 1% Asian American, 2% Hispanic American, 1% international
- 476 degree-seeking graduate students
- 75% of applicants admitted
- Application essay, interview required
- 46% graduate within 6 years

**General.** Founded in 1960. Regionally accredited. **Degrees:** 637 bachelor's, 10 associate awarded; master's offered. **ROTC:** Army, Air Force. **Location:** Downtown. **Calendar:** Semester, extensive summer session. **Full-time faculty:** 109 total; 58% have terminal degrees, 14% minority, 40% women. **Part-time faculty:** 212 total. **Class size:** 77% < 20, 22% 20-39, less than 1% 40-49, less than 1% 50-99. **Special facilities:** Children's school, Pittsburgh Playhouse, 3-theater performing arts center.

**Freshman class profile.** 2,681 applied, 2,021 admitted, 460 enrolled.

| Mid 50% test scores | | | |
|---|---|---|---|
| SAT critical reading: | 460-570 | GPA 2.0-2.99: | 35% |
| SAT math: | 430-540 | Rank in top quarter: | 33% |
| SAT writing: | 440-560 | Rank in top tenth: | 13% |
| ACT composite: | 19-24 | Return as sophomores: | 73% |
| GPA 3.50 or higher: | 30% | Out-of-state: | 31% |
| GPA 3.0-3.49: | 35% | Live on campus: | 71% |
| | | International: | 2% |

**Basis for selection.** High school record, class rank, test scores most important. Recommendations, extracurricular activities, talent, character also important. Audition required for some majors, portfolio recommended for multimedia, technical theater, stage management programs.

**High school preparation.** Recommended units include English 4, mathematics 4, social studies 4, history 4, science 4, foreign language 2, visual/performing arts 2 and academic electives 2.

**2007-2008 Annual costs.** Tuition/fees: $18,990. Cost of tuition in bachelor of arts and bachelor of fine arts programs within conservatory of performing arts: $21,420 or $608 per credit hour. Room/board: $8,440. Books/supplies: $1,000. Personal expenses: $1,851.

**2007-2008 Financial aid. Need-based:** Average need met was 73%. Average scholarship/grant was $9,121; average loan $5,491. 47% of total undergraduate aid awarded as scholarships/grants, 53% as loans/jobs. **Non-need-based:** Scholarships awarded for academics, alumni affiliation, art, athletics, job skills, leadership, music/drama.

**Application procedures. Admission:** No deadline. $40 fee, may be waived for applicants with need. Application may be submitted online. Admission notification on a rolling basis beginning on or about 10/1. Must reply by May 1 or within 2 week(s) if notified thereafter. **Financial aid:** Priority date 5/1; no closing date. FAFSA required. Applicants notified on a rolling basis starting 2/15; must reply within 2 week(s) of notification.

**Academics. Special study options:** Accelerated study, cooperative education, cross-registration, double major, ESL, honors, independent study, internships, student-designed major, study abroad, teacher certification program, weekend college. Numerous off-campus programs for college credits. Several accelerated programs available. Offers professionally oriented programs in arts, business, communications, and technology. **Credit/placement by examination:** AP, CLEP, IB, institutional tests. 30 credit hours maximum toward associate degree, 60 toward bachelor's. **Support services:** Learning center, pre-admission summer program, reduced course load, remedial instruction, study skills assistance, tutoring.

**Majors. Biology:** General, biotechnology. **Business:** Accounting, business admin, human resources. **Communications:** Advertising, broadcast journalism, journalism, media studies, photojournalism. **Computer sciences:** Information technology. **Conservation:** Environmental science. **Education:** Biology, drama/dance, early childhood, elementary, English, mathematics. **Engineering technology:** Civil, mechanical. **English:** English lit. **History:** General. **Interdisciplinary:** Behavioral sciences. **Legal studies:** General. **Personal/culinary services:** Mortuary science. **Protective services:** Criminal justice, law enforcement admin. **Psychology:** General. **Public administration:** General. **Social sciences:** General, international relations, political science. **Visual/performing arts:** Cinematography, dance, dramatic, photography.

**Most popular majors.** Business/marketing 19%, communications/journalism 11%, education 7%, engineering/engineering technologies 6%, security/protective services 13%, visual/performing arts 25%.

**Computing on campus.** 183 workstations in library, computer center, student center. Dormitories wired for high-speed internet access and linked to campus network. Commuter students can connect to campus network. Online library, helpline, student web hosting, wireless network available.

**Student life. Freshman orientation:** Mandatory. Preregistration for classes offered. Held in summer months, includes placement testing if needed for major. **Policies:** Policies regarding student conduct, plagiarism and resident life. **Housing:** Guaranteed on-campus for all undergraduates. Coed dorms, single-sex dorms, special housing for disabled available. $350 fully refundable deposit, deadline 7/15. Quiet floors, single-gender floors available. **Activities:** Choral groups, dance, drama, film society, international student organizations, literary magazine, musical theater, radio station, student government, student newspaper, TV station, black student union, Amnesty International.

**Athletics.** NAIA. **Intercollegiate:** Baseball M, basketball, cross-country, soccer, softball W, volleyball W. **Intramural:** Basketball M, tennis, volleyball, weight lifting M. **Team name:** Pioneers.

**Student services.** Adult student services, alcohol/substance abuse counseling, career counseling, student employment services, financial aid counseling, health services, on-campus daycare, personal counseling, placement for graduates, veterans' counselor. **Physically disabled:** Services for visually, speech, hearing impaired.

**Contact.** E-mail: enroll@pointpark.edu
Phone: (412) 392-3430 Toll-free number: (800) 321-0129
Fax: (412) 392-3902
Joell Minford, Director of Admissions, Point Park University, 201 Wood Street, Pittsburgh, PA 15222-1984

## Restaurant School
**Philadelphia, Pennsylvania**
www.walnuthillcollege.edu                    **CB code: 4883**

- For-profit 4-year culinary school and business college
- Commuter campus in very large city

**General.** Accredited by ACCSCT. **Calendar:** Semester.

**Annual costs/financial aid.** Tuition/fees (2007-2008): $17,880. Room: $5,000.

**Contact.** Phone: (215) 222-4200 ext. 3011
Director of Admissions, 4207 Walnut Street, Philadelphia, PA 19104

## Robert Morris University
**Moon Township, Pennsylvania**          **CB member**
www.rmu.edu                               **CB code: 2769**

- Private 4-year university
- Commuter campus in large town
- 3,878 degree-seeking undergraduates: 17% part-time, 46% women, 8% African American, 1% Asian American, 1% Hispanic American, 2% international
- 1,002 degree-seeking graduate students
- 76% of applicants admitted
- SAT or ACT (ACT writing optional) required
- 51% graduate within 6 years; 5% enter graduate study

**General.** Founded in 1921. Regionally accredited. **Degrees:** 773 bachelor's awarded; master's, doctoral offered. **ROTC:** Army, Air Force. **Location:** 17 miles from Pittsburgh. **Calendar:** Semester, limited summer session. **Full-time faculty:** 174 total; 83% have terminal degrees, 14% minority, 39% women. **Part-time faculty:** 180 total; 30% have terminal degrees, 6% minority, 48% women. **Class size:** 46% < 20, 47% 20-39, 7% 40-49, less than 1% 50-99.

**Freshman class profile.** 2,938 applied, 2,223 admitted, 666 enrolled.

| Mid 50% test scores | | Rank in top tenth: | 12% |
|---|---|---|---|
| SAT critical reading: | 440-530 | Return as sophomores: | 74% |
| SAT math: | 470-570 | Out-of-state: | 19% |
| ACT composite: | 19-24 | Live on campus: | 76% |
| GPA 3.50 or higher: | 37% | International: | 3% |
| GPA 3.0-3.49: | 35% | Fraternities: | 4% |
| GPA 2.0-2.99: | 27% | Sororities: | 5% |
| Rank in top quarter: | 32% | | |

**Basis for selection.** Academic potential, high school GPA, class rank, test scores, and evidence of motivation important. Interview required of restricted-status applicants, recommended for all others.

**High school preparation.** 16 units required; 18 recommended. Required and recommended units include English 4, mathematics 3, social studies 4, science 2, foreign language 2 and academic electives 3.

**2007-2008 Annual costs.** Tuition/fees: $17,900. Room/board: $8,520. Books/supplies: $1,100. Personal expenses: $1,800.

**2007-2008 Financial aid. Need-based:** 588 full-time freshmen applied for aid; 500 were judged to have need; 500 of these received aid. Average need met was 78%. Average scholarship/grant was $10,151; average loan $5,420. 39% of total undergraduate aid awarded as scholarships/grants, 61% as loans/jobs. **Non-need-based:** Awarded to 853 full-time undergraduates, including 225 freshmen. Scholarships awarded for academics, athletics.

**Application procedures. Admission:** Priority date 12/1; deadline 7/1 (postmark date). $30 fee, may be waived for applicants with need. Application may be submitted online. Admission notification on a rolling basis beginning on or about 8/1. Must reply by May 1 or within 3 week(s) if notified thereafter. **Financial aid:** No deadline. FAFSA required. Applicants notified on a rolling basis starting 3/15.

**Academics. Special study options:** Combined bachelor's/graduate degree, cooperative education, cross-registration, distance learning, double major, honors, independent study, internships, study abroad, teacher certification program, weekend college. **Credit/placement by examination:** AP, CLEP, SAT, ACT, institutional tests. 30 credit hours maximum toward bachelor's degree. **Support services:** Pre-admission summer program, reduced course load, remedial instruction, study skills assistance, tutoring.

**Majors. Business:** Accounting, actuarial science, business admin, finance, hospitality admin, management information systems, marketing, operations, organizational behavior. **Communications:** General. **Computer sciences:** Information systems. **Conservation:** Environmental science. **Education:** Business, elementary. **Engineering:** Manufacturing, software. **English:** English lit. **Health:** Health care admin, health services admin, medical radiologic technology/radiation therapy, nursing (RN). **Math:** Applied. **Parks/recreation:** Sports admin. **Psychology:** General. **Social sciences:** General, economics. **Transportation:** Aviation management. **Visual/performing arts:** Design.

**Most popular majors.** Business/marketing 61%, communications/journalism 7%.

**Computing on campus.** 300 workstations in library, computer center, student center. Dormitories wired for high-speed internet access and linked to campus network. Commuter students can connect to campus network. Online course registration, online library, helpline, wireless network available.

**Student life. Freshman orientation:** Mandatory. Preregistration for classes offered. 3-day program. **Housing:** Coed dorms, single-sex dorms, special housing for disabled, apartments, substance-free housing available. $150 nonrefundable deposit, deadline 5/1. **Activities:** Bands, campus ministries, drama, international student organizations, literary magazine, musical theater, student government, student newspaper, TV station, minority student organization, campus activities board, inter-residence hall council, interfraternity council/Panhellenic council, honor societies.

**Athletics.** NCAA. **Intercollegiate:** Basketball, cross-country, field hockey W, football (tackle) M, golf, ice hockey, lacrosse, rowing (crew) W, soccer, softball W, tennis, track and field, volleyball W. **Intramural:** Basketball, football (non-tackle) M, softball, volleyball W. **Team name:** Colonials.

**Student services.** Adult student services, alcohol/substance abuse counseling, campus ministries, career counseling, student employment services, financial aid counseling, health services, minority student services, personal counseling, placement for graduates, veterans' counselor. **Physically disabled:** Services for visually, speech, hearing impaired.

**Contact.** E-mail: admissions@rmu.edu
Phone: (412) 397-5200 Toll-free number: (800) 762-0097
Fax: (412) 397-2425
Robert Morris University, 6001 University Boulevard, Moon Township, PA 15108-1189

## Rosemont College
**Rosemont, Pennsylvania**                **CB member**
www.rosemont.edu                          **CB code: 2763**

- Private 4-year liberal arts college for women affiliated with Roman Catholic Church
- Residential campus in small town
- 551 degree-seeking undergraduates: 28% part-time, 95% women, 36% African American, 6% Asian American, 8% Hispanic American, 1% international
- 389 degree-seeking graduate students
- 60% of applicants admitted
- SAT or ACT, application essay required
- 59% graduate within 6 years; 17% enter graduate study

**General.** Founded in 1921. Regionally accredited. **Degrees:** 107 bachelor's awarded; master's offered. **ROTC:** Army, Air Force. **Location:** 11 miles from Philadelphia. **Calendar:** Semester, limited summer session. **Full-time faculty:** 32 total; 91% have terminal degrees, 3% minority, 59% women. **Part-time faculty:** 134 total; 81% have terminal degrees, 7% minority, 53% women. **Class size:** 89% < 20, 11% 20-39.

**Freshman class profile.** 367 applied, 221 admitted, 68 enrolled.

| Mid 50% test scores | | Rank in top quarter: | 46% |
|---|---|---|---|
| SAT critical reading: | 410-500 | Rank in top tenth: | 24% |
| SAT math: | 420-500 | End year in good standing: | 95% |
| SAT writing: | 410-510 | Return as sophomores: | 76% |
| GPA 3.50 or higher: | 35% | Out-of-state: | 30% |
| GPA 3.0-3.49: | 47% | Live on campus: | 90% |
| GPA 2.0-2.99: | 18% | | |

**Basis for selection.** School achievement record and curriculum, recommendations, test scores, extracurricular activities strongly considered. Interview recommended. **Homeschooled:** Statement describing homeschool structure and mission, transcript of courses and grades, letter of recommendation (nonparent) required.

**High school preparation.** 18 units required. Required units include English 4, mathematics 2, social studies 2, history 2, science 2 (laboratory 2), foreign language 2 and academic electives 2.

**2007-2008 Annual costs.** Tuition/fees: $22,835. Room/board: $9,200. Books/supplies: $800. Personal expenses: $1,000.

**2007-2008 Financial aid. Need-based:** 64 full-time freshmen applied for aid; 58 were judged to have need; 58 of these received aid. Average need met was 80%. Average scholarship/grant was $18,109; average loan $3,504. 71% of total undergraduate aid awarded as scholarships/grants, 29% as loans/jobs. **Non-need-based:** Scholarships awarded for academics, alumni affiliation, art, job skills, religious affiliation.

**Application procedures. Admission:** No deadline. $35 fee, may be waived for applicants with need. Application may be submitted online. Admission notification on a rolling basis. Must reply by May 1 or within 2 week(s) if notified thereafter. $300 deposit required of all students intending to enroll. Refundable only if college notified by May 1 of decision not to attend. **Financial aid:** Priority date 2/15; no closing date. FAFSA required. Applicants notified on a rolling basis starting 2/15; must reply by 5/1 or within 4 week(s) of notification.

**Academics. Special study options:** Accelerated study, combined bachelor's/graduate degree, cross-registration, distance learning, double major, ESL, exchange student, honors, independent study, internships, liberal arts/career combination, student-designed major, study abroad, teacher certification program, Washington semester. **Credit/placement by examination:** AP, CLEP, IB, SAT, institutional tests. 30 credit hours maximum toward bachelor's degree. Students may be exempted if they demonstrate mastery of subject as determined by particular department. **Support services:** Learning center, reduced course load, remedial instruction, study skills assistance, tutoring, writing center.

**Majors. Area/ethnic studies:** Asian, women's. **Biology:** General, biochemistry. **Business:** General, accounting, business admin, communications, hospitality admin, human resources, management science, managerial economics, organizational behavior. **Communications:** General. **Conservation:** Environmental science. **English:** English lit. **Foreign languages:** General, French, German, Italian, Spanish. **History:** General. **Liberal arts:** Arts/sciences, humanities. **Math:** General. **Philosophy/religion:** Philosophy, religion. **Physical sciences:** Chemistry. **Protective services:** Criminal justice. **Psychology:** General. **Social sciences:** General, economics, political science, sociology. **Visual/performing arts:** Art history/conservation.

**Most popular majors.** Business/marketing 17%, English 14%, psychology 13%, social sciences 6%, visual/performing arts 17%.

**Computing on campus.** 100 workstations in dormitories, library, computer center, student center. Dormitories wired for high-speed internet access and linked to campus network. Commuter students can connect to campus network. Online course registration, online library, helpline, student web hosting, wireless network available.

**Student life. Freshman orientation:** Mandatory, $280 fee. Preregistration for classes offered. Orientation approximately 3 days; includes academics component. **Housing:** Guaranteed on-campus for all undergraduates. Substance-free housing available. **Activities:** Bands, campus ministries, choral groups, dance, drama, international student organizations, literary magazine, music ensembles, Model UN, musical theater, opera, radio station, student government, student newspaper, premed club, politics club, Rosemont Alcohol and Drug Awareness Resource, multicultural society, Best Buddies, Triad, art society.

**Athletics.** NCAA. **Intercollegiate:** Basketball W, field hockey W, lacrosse W, softball W, tennis W, volleyball W. **Team name:** Ramblers.

**Student services.** Adult student services, alcohol/substance abuse counseling, campus ministries, career counseling, student employment services, financial aid counseling, health services, legal services, minority student services, on-campus daycare, personal counseling, placement for graduates, veterans' counselor, women's services. **Physically disabled:** Services for visually, speech, hearing impaired.

**Contact.** E-mail: admissions@rosemont.edu
Phone: (610) 526-2966 Toll-free number: (800) 331-0708
Fax: (610) 520-4399
Rennie Andrews, Dean of Undergraduate Women's College Admissions, Rosemont College, 1400 Montgomery Avenue, Rosemont, PA 19010-1699

## St. Charles Borromeo Seminary - Overbrook

**Wynnewood, Pennsylvania**
www.scs.edu                                    CB code: 2794

- Private 4-year seminary college for men affiliated with Roman Catholic Church
- Residential campus in large town
- 54 degree-seeking undergraduates: 2% African American, 6% Hispanic American, 4% international
- 116 degree-seeking graduate students
- 100% of applicants admitted
- Application essay, interview required
- 50% graduate within 6 years

**General.** Founded in 1832. Regionally accredited; also accredited by ATS. College and theology divisions enroll full-time seminary students. Religious studies division enrolls part-time undergraduate and graduate students who wish to pursue theological studies. Part-time programs open to men and women. **Degrees:** 12 bachelor's awarded; master's, first professional offered. **Location:** 4 miles from central Philadelphia. **Calendar:** Semester, limited summer session. **Full-time faculty:** 18 total; 67% have terminal degrees, 17% women. **Part-time faculty:** 7 total; 43% have terminal degrees, 43% women. **Class size:** 97% < 20, 3% 20-39. **Special facilities:** Rare book and special collections.

**Freshman class profile.** 7 applied, 7 admitted, 7 enrolled.

| End year in good standing: | 100% | Out-of-state: | 57% |
|---|---|---|---|
| Return as sophomores: | 100% | Live on campus: | 100% |

**Basis for selection.** Sponsorship by diocese or religious community required for admission to college and theology divisions. Seminary applicants holding bachelor's degree from accredited institution may enter special pre-theology program. SAT or ACT recommended. **Homeschooled:** Transcript of courses and grades, letter of recommendation (nonparent) required.

**High school preparation.** 20 units recommended. Recommended units include English 4, mathematics 3, social studies 3, science 3 and foreign language 3. 3 to 4 units of religious education recommended. GED accepted on individual basis.

**2007-2008 Annual costs.** Tuition/fees: $12,321. Room/board: $8,269. Books/supplies: $800. Personal expenses: $500.

**Application procedures. Admission:** Priority date 3/1; deadline 7/15. No application fee. Admission notification on a rolling basis beginning on or about 4/1. Level of admission dependent on academic background in philosophy, theology, and classical languages.

**Academics.** Strong emphasis on philosophy, theology, classical languages, and liberal arts. **Special study options:** Accelerated study, ESL, independent study. **Credit/placement by examination:** AP, CLEP, institutional tests. 30 credit hours maximum toward bachelor's degree. **Support services:** Reduced course load, tutoring.

**Majors. Philosophy/religion:** Philosophy.

**Computing on campus.** 60 workstations in library, computer center. Online library, wireless network available.

**Student life. Freshman orientation:** Mandatory. **Policies:** Religious observance required. **Housing:** Guaranteed on-campus for all undergraduates. Substance-free housing available. On-campus housing available for seminarians in college and theology divisions. On-campus housing available to students in religious studies division during summer session. **Activities:** Choral groups, drama, music ensembles, student government, student newspaper, Seminarians for Life.

**Athletics. Intramural:** Basketball M, football (tackle) M, soccer M, volleyball M.

**Student services.** Campus ministries, financial aid counseling, health services, personal counseling.

**Contact.** E-mail: frdd@adphila.org
Phone: (610) 785-6271 Fax: (610) 617-9267
Rev. David Diamond, Vice Rector, St. Charles Borromeo Seminary -
Overbrook, 100 East Wynnewood Road, Wynnewood, PA 19096

## St. Francis University
### Loretto, Pennsylvania
www.francis.edu

CB member
CB code: 2797

- Private 4-year university and liberal arts college affiliated with Roman Catholic Church
- Residential campus in rural community
- 1,513 degree-seeking undergraduates: 7% part-time, 63% women
- 516 degree-seeking graduate students
- 85% of applicants admitted
- SAT or ACT (ACT writing optional), application essay required
- 61% graduate within 6 years

**General.** Founded in 1847. Regionally accredited. **Degrees:** 290 bachelor's, 1 associate awarded; master's, doctoral offered. **ROTC:** Army. **Location:** 90 miles from Pittsburgh, 20 miles from Altoona. **Calendar:** Semester, limited summer session. **Full-time faculty:** 99 total; 73% have terminal degrees, 3% minority, 48% women. **Part-time faculty:** 79 total; 24% have terminal degrees, 2% minority, 34% women. **Class size:** 52% < 20, 43% 20-39, 1% 40-49, 3% 50-99. **Special facilities:** Rural health and wellness institute, small business development center, global competitiveness center, Southern Alleghenies art museum, center for remote and medically under served areas, nature trail.

**Freshman class profile.** 1,342 applied, 1,146 admitted, 412 enrolled.

| Mid 50% test scores | | | |
|---|---|---|---|
| SAT critical reading: | 460-550 | Rank in top quarter: | 28% |
| SAT math: | 460-580 | Rank in top tenth: | 22% |
| ACT composite: | 19-26 | Return as sophomores: | 82% |
| GPA 3.50 or higher: | 52% | Out-of-state: | 25% |
| GPA 3.0-3.49: | 32% | Live on campus: | 85% |
| GPA 2.0-2.99: | 16% | Fraternities: | 10% |
| | | Sororities: | 10% |

**Basis for selection.** High school record most important, followed by test scores, counselor's recommendations, major area of interest, activities, honors. Relationship to alumni also considered. Campus visit highly recommended. Admission to professional track programs places more weight on test scores. Interview highly recommended. **Learning Disabled:** Send documentation to the Academic Center for Enrichment.

**High school preparation.** Required and recommended units include English 4, mathematics 2-4, social studies 2, science 1, foreign language 2 and academic electives 7. One natural science for nonscience majors, 2 for science majors also required. One science unit must include laboratory. Remaining units in academic electives. 4 math and 2 science required for physician assistant and occupational therapy. 4 math and 4 science required for physical therapy.

**2007-2008 Annual costs.** Tuition/fees: $23,494. Room/board: $7,984. Books/supplies: $800. Personal expenses: $1,250.

**2006-2007 Financial aid. Need-based:** 379 full-time freshmen applied for aid; 350 were judged to have need; 349 of these received aid. Average need met was 73%. Average scholarship/grant was $13,688; average loan $2,785. 66% of total undergraduate aid awarded as scholarships/grants, 34% as loans/jobs. **Non-need-based:** Awarded to 492 full-time undergraduates, including 162 freshmen. Scholarships awarded for academics, alumni affiliation, athletics, music/drama, religious affiliation.

**Application procedures. Admission:** Priority date 3/1; deadline 7/30 (receipt date). $30 fee, may be waived for applicants with need. Application may be submitted online. Admission notification on a rolling basis beginning on or about 10/1. Must reply by May 1 or within 2 week(s) if notified thereafter. Application closing date for physical therapy, occupational therapy and physican assistant January 15. Notification by February 1. **Financial aid:** Priority date 5/1; no closing date. FAFSA required. Applicants notified on a rolling basis starting 3/1.

**Academics. Special study options:** Combined bachelor's/graduate degree, cooperative education, distance learning, double major, honors, independent study, internships, liberal arts/career combination, semester at sea, student-designed major, study abroad, teacher certification program, Washington semester. **Credit/placement by examination:** AP, CLEP, IB, SAT, ACT, institutional tests. 15 credit hours maximum toward associate degree, 30 toward bachelor's. **Support services:** Learning center, pre-admission summer program, reduced course load, remedial instruction, study skills assistance, tutoring, writing center.

**Honors college/program.** 3.25 GPA, 1150 SAT (580 CR, exclusive of Writing), and position in top 1/5 of high school class required. About 40 applicants admitted.

**Majors. Area/ethnic studies:** American, French. **Biology:** General, marine. **Business:** Accounting, business admin, finance, management information systems, marketing. **Communications:** General, public relations. **Computer sciences:** General, computer science, information systems, programming. **Conservation:** Environmental science, environmental studies, forest management, forestry. **Education:** General, biology, chemistry, elementary, English, foreign languages, French, history, mathematics, multi-level teacher, psychology, secondary, social science, social studies, Spanish, special, speech. **Engineering:** General, environmental. **English:** English lit. **Foreign languages:** General, French, Spanish. **Health:** Clinical lab technology, nursing (RN), physician assistant. **History:** General. **Interdisciplinary:** Biological/physical sciences, math/computer science. **Math:** General. **Philosophy/religion:** Philosophy, religion. **Physical sciences:** Chemistry. **Psychology:** General. **Public administration:** General, social work. **Social sciences:** Economics, political science, sociology. **Other:** Exercise physiology.

**Most popular majors.** Biology 7%, business/marketing 32%, education 11%, health sciences 23%, social sciences 8%.

**Computing on campus.** PC or laptop required. 40 workstations in dormitories, library, computer center, student center. Dormitories wired for high-speed internet access and linked to campus network. Commuter students can connect to campus network. Online library, helpline, repair service, wireless network available.

**Student life. Freshman orientation:** Mandatory. Preregistration for classes offered. Held at various times during spring and summer. **Policies:** All students required to live on campus until 21st birthday unless commuter status or a senior by September 1 of academic year. **Housing:** Guaranteed on-campus for freshmen. Coed dorms, single-sex dorms, special housing for disabled, apartments, fraternity/sorority housing, substance-free housing available. $100 deposit, deadline 5/1. **Activities:** Bands, choral groups, drama, music ensembles, musical theater, radio station, student government, student newspaper, TV station, Secular Franciscan Order, student activities organization, multicultural awareness club, Historians' Round Table, Knights of Columbus, Peace and Justice Center, current affairs club, pro-life club, prelaw club.

**Athletics.** NCAA. **Intercollegiate:** Basketball, cross-country, diving W, field hockey W, football (tackle) M, golf, lacrosse W, soccer, softball W, swimming W, tennis, track and field, volleyball. **Intramural:** Basketball, cross-country, football (non-tackle), golf, skiing, soccer, softball, swimming, table tennis, tennis, track and field, volleyball. **Team name:** Red Flash.

**Student services.** Adult student services, alcohol/substance abuse counseling, campus ministries, career counseling, student employment services, financial aid counseling, health services, minority student services, personal counseling, placement for graduates, veterans' counselor.

**Contact.** E-mail: admissions@francis.edu
Phone: (814) 472-3100 Toll-free number: (800) 342-5732
Fax: (814) 472-3335
Erin McCloskey, Dean for Enrollment Management, St. Francis University, Box 600, Loretto, PA 15940

## Saint Joseph's University
### Philadelphia, Pennsylvania
www.sju.edu

CB member
CB code: 2801

- Private 4-year university affiliated with Roman Catholic Church
- Residential campus in very large city
- 4,825 degree-seeking undergraduates: 14% part-time, 52% women, 8% African American, 3% Asian American, 3% Hispanic American, 2% international
- 2,097 degree-seeking graduate students
- 62% of applicants admitted
- SAT or ACT (ACT writing optional), application essay required
- 75% graduate within 6 years; 20% enter graduate study

**General.** Founded in 1851. Regionally accredited. Founded by the Society of Jesus. **Degrees:** 1,025 bachelor's, 6 associate awarded; master's, doctoral offered. **ROTC:** Army, Naval, Air Force. **Location:** 8 miles from downtown. **Calendar:** Semester, extensive summer session. **Full-time faculty:** 277 total; 89% have terminal degrees, 13% minority, 40% women. **Part-time faculty:** 337 total; 9% minority, 39% women. **Class size:** 42% < 20, 53% 20-39, 4% 40-49, less than 1% 50-99.

**Freshman class profile.** 8,779 applied, 5,407 admitted, 1,090 enrolled.

| Mid 50% test scores | | | |
|---|---|---|---|
| SAT critical reading: | 530-620 | **GPA 2.0-2.99:** | 22% |
| SAT math: | 540-630 | **Return as sophomores:** | 88% |
| ACT composite: | 23-28 | **Out-of-state:** | 57% |
| GPA 3.50 or higher: | 36% | **Live on campus:** | 97% |
| GPA 3.0-3.49: | 42% | **International:** | 1% |

**Basis for selection.** GED not accepted. Careful consideration given to applicant's high school curriculum, extracurricular activities, recalculated academic GPA, and standardized test scores. Preference is given to those applicants who have taken more demanding curriculum.

**High school preparation.** 12 units required. Required units include English 4, mathematics 3, history 1, science 2 (laboratory 1) and foreign language 2.

**2007-2008 Annual costs.** Tuition/fees: $30,985. Room/board: $10,550.

**2007-2008 Financial aid. Need-based:** 769 full-time freshmen applied for aid; 566 were judged to have need; 566 of these received aid. Average need met was 85%. Average scholarship/grant was $14,383; average loan $3,047. 48% of total undergraduate aid awarded as scholarships/grants, 52% as loans/jobs. **Non-need-based:** Awarded to 3,605 full-time undergraduates, including 1,023 freshmen. Scholarships awarded for academics, art, athletics, minority status, music/drama, ROTC.

**Application procedures. Admission:** Closing date 2/1 (postmark date). $60 fee, may be waived for applicants with need. Application may be submitted online. Admission notification 3/1. Must reply by May 1 or within 2 week(s) if notified thereafter. **Financial aid:** Priority date 2/15, closing date 5/1. FAFSA required. Applicants notified on a rolling basis starting 3/15.

**Academics. Special study options:** Accelerated study, combined bachelor's/graduate degree, cooperative education, distance learning, double major, dual enrollment of high school students, ESL, honors, independent study, internships, student-designed major, study abroad, teacher certification program, Washington semester, weekend college. Jesuit student exchange. **Credit/placement by examination:** AP, CLEP, IB, institutional tests. **Support services:** Learning center, pre-admission summer program, reduced course load, study skills assistance, tutoring, writing center.

**Majors. Area/ethnic studies:** European, French. **Biology:** General, biochemistry. **Business:** Accounting, actuarial science, business admin, finance, international, international marketing, management information systems, marketing, purchasing, special products marketing. **Communications:** General. **Computer sciences:** General, information systems. **Conservation:** Environmental studies. **Education:** Elementary, English, foreign languages, mathematics, science, secondary, social studies, special. **English:** English lit. **Foreign languages:** French, German, Italian, Latin, Spanish. **Health:** Facilities admin, health services. **History:** General. **Legal studies:** General. **Liberal arts:** Humanities. **Math:** General. **Philosophy/religion:** Philosophy, religion. **Physical sciences:** Chemistry, physics. **Psychology:** General. **Public administration:** General. **Social sciences:** General, criminology, economics, international relations, political science, sociology. **Visual/performing arts:** General.

**Most popular majors.** Business/marketing 46%, education 11%, English 6%, psychology 7%, social sciences 12%.

**Computing on campus.** 675 workstations in dormitories, library, computer center, student center. Dormitories wired for high-speed internet access and linked to campus network. Commuter students can connect to campus network. Online course registration, online library, helpline, repair service, student web hosting, wireless network available.

**Student life. Freshman orientation:** Available, $210 fee. **Housing:** Guaranteed on-campus for freshmen. Coed dorms, single-sex dorms, apartments, substance-free housing available. $400 partly refundable deposit, deadline 5/1. Special accommodations may be arranged for disabled students based upon need. **Activities:** Bands, campus ministries, choral groups, dance, drama, film society, international student organizations, literary magazine, music ensembles, musical theater, radio station, student government, student newspaper, black student union, Hand-in-Hand, College Democrats, College Republicans, Up-Til-Dawn, Project Mexico, Habitat for Humanity, Students for Life.

**Athletics.** NCAA. **Intercollegiate:** Baseball M, basketball, cheerleading, cross-country, field hockey W, golf M, lacrosse, rowing (crew), soccer, softball W, tennis, track and field. **Intramural:** Basketball, football (nontackle), golf M, rugby, soccer, softball, tennis, volleyball. **Team name:** Hawks.

**Student services.** Adult student services, alcohol/substance abuse counseling, campus ministries, career counseling, services for economically disadvantaged, student employment services, financial aid counseling, health

services, minority student services, personal counseling, women's services. **Physically disabled:** Services for visually, speech, hearing impaired. **Learning disabled:** Comprehensive services available.

**Contact.** E-mail: admit@sju.edu
Phone: (610) 660-1300 Toll-free number: (888) 232-4295
Fax: (610) 660-1314
Director of Admissions, Saint Joseph's University, 5600 City Avenue, Philadelphia, PA 19131

## St. Vincent College
**Latrobe, Pennsylvania** — CB member
www.stvincent.edu — CB code: 2808

- Private 4-year liberal arts college affiliated with Roman Catholic Church
- Residential campus in large town
- 1,617 degree-seeking undergraduates: 2% part-time, 50% women, 3% African American, 1% Asian American, 2% Hispanic American, 1% international
- 208 degree-seeking graduate students
- 62% of applicants admitted
- SAT or ACT (ACT writing optional), application essay required
- 71% graduate within 6 years

**General.** Founded in 1846. Regionally accredited. Affiliated with Order of Saint Benedict. **Degrees:** 331 bachelor's awarded; master's offered. **ROTC:** Air Force. **Location:** 35 miles from Pittsburgh. **Calendar:** Semester, extensive summer session. **Full-time faculty:** 91 total; 84% have terminal degrees, 2% minority, 24% women. **Part-time faculty:** 112 total; 29% have terminal degrees, less than 1% minority, 38% women. **Class size:** 42% < 20, 58% 20-39, less than 1% 40-49. **Special facilities:** Planetarium, observatory, radio telescope, wetlands program, rare book collection, spectrophotometer, spectrometer, physiograph workstations, nature reserve.

**Freshman class profile.** 1,855 applied, 1,146 admitted, 424 enrolled.

| Mid 50% test scores | | | |
|---|---|---|---|
| SAT critical reading: | 480-590 | **GPA 2.0-2.99:** | 11% |
| SAT math: | -600 | **Rank in top quarter:** | 54% |
| SAT writing: | 470-570 | **Rank in top tenth:** | 24% |
| ACT composite: | 20-26 | **Return as sophomores:** | 84% |
| GPA 3.50 or higher: | 62% | **Out-of-state:** | 16% |
| GPA 3.0-3.49: | 27% | **Live on campus:** | 89% |

**Basis for selection.** High school curriculum and grades most important; class rank, test scores, and essay important. Recommendations from school counselor considered. Interview recommended for all; audition required for music, theater programs; portfolio required for art, art therapy programs. **Learning Disabled:** All prior test results related to learning disability should be submitted.

**High school preparation.** 16 units required; 20 recommended. Required and recommended units include English 4, mathematics 3, social studies 3, science 1-3 (laboratory 1), foreign language 2 and academic electives 5. One plane geometry, 1 intermediate algebra, .5 trigonometry, and 1 physics required for 3-2 engineering program applicants.

**2007-2008 Annual costs.** Tuition/fees: $24,106. Room/board: $7,380. Books/supplies: $1,300. Personal expenses: $1,280.

**2007-2008 Financial aid. Need-based:** 419 full-time freshmen applied for aid; 333 were judged to have need; 333 of these received aid. Average need met was 91%. Average scholarship/grant was $15,854; average loan $3,580. 77% of total undergraduate aid awarded as scholarships/grants, 23% as loans/jobs. **Non-need-based:** Awarded to 1,524 full-time undergraduates, including 227 freshmen. Scholarships awarded for academics, alumni affiliation, leadership, minority status, music/drama, religious affiliation.

**Application procedures. Admission:** Priority date 2/1; deadline 5/1 (postmark date). $25 fee, may be waived for applicants with need. Application may be submitted online. Admission notification on a rolling basis beginning on or about 10/1. Must reply by May 1 or within 3 week(s) if notified thereafter. **Financial aid:** Priority date 3/1, closing date 5/1. FAFSA required. Applicants notified on a rolling basis starting 3/1; must reply within 2 week(s) of notification.

**Academics.** College attempts to place career orientation in context of broader human and religious values with emphasis on liberal arts core curriculum. **Special study options:** Accelerated study, combined bachelor's/graduate degree, cooperative education, cross-registration, distance learning, double major, dual enrollment of high school students, external degree, honors, independent study, internships, liberal arts/career combination, study abroad, teacher certification program. 3-2 engineering BA/BS program with University of Pittsburgh, Catholic University of America, Pennsylvania State; 4-1 BS/MBA, 3-3 BA/JD, 3-2 occupational therapy, physical therapy, and physician's assistant, 2-4 pharmacy programs with Duquesne University; 3-4 podiatry with Ohio College of Pediatric Medicine and Pennsylvania College of Pediatric Medicine. **Credit/placement by examination:** AP, CLEP, IB, institutional tests. 62 credit hours maximum toward bachelor's degree. **Support services:** Learning center, pre-admission summer program, reduced course load, remedial instruction, study skills assistance, tutoring, writing center.

**Majors. Biology:** General, biochemistry, bioinformatics. **Business:** Accounting, business admin, finance, international, marketing. **Communications:** General. **Communications technology:** General. **Computer sciences:** General. **Conservation:** General, environmental science, environmental studies, management/policy. **Education:** Art, business, elementary, physics, psychology. **Engineering:** General. **English:** English lit. **Foreign languages:** French, Spanish. **Health:** Office assistant, predental, premedicine, prepharmacy, preveterinary. **History:** General. **Legal studies:** Prelaw. **Liberal arts:** Arts/sciences. **Math:** General. **Philosophy/religion:** Philosophy. **Physical sciences:** Chemistry, physics. **Psychology:** General. **Public administration:** Policy analysis. **Social sciences:** Anthropology, economics, political science, sociology. **Theology:** Religious ed, theology. **Visual/performing arts:** Art history/conservation, arts management, graphic design, music performance, studio arts.

**Most popular majors.** Biology 7%, business/marketing 24%, communications/journalism 7%, history 10%, psychology 15%, social sciences 9%.

**Computing on campus.** 286 workstations in dormitories, library, computer center, student center. Dormitories wired for high-speed internet access and linked to campus network. Commuter students can connect to campus network. Online course registration, helpline, wireless network available.

**Student life. Freshman orientation:** Mandatory, $125 fee. Preregistration for classes offered. 6 weeks of activities to acclimate students to college on academic and social levels. **Housing:** Guaranteed on-campus for all undergraduates. Coed dorms, apartments available. $100 nonrefundable deposit, deadline 5/1. **Activities:** Pep band, campus ministries, choral groups, dance, drama, international student organizations, literary magazine, music ensembles, radio station, student government, student newspaper, TV station, pro-life club, Student Democrats, College Republicans, academic/social action/special interest groups, prelaw club, student educational association.

**Athletics.** NCAA. **Intercollegiate:** Baseball M, basketball, cross-country, field hockey W, football (tackle) M, golf, lacrosse, soccer, softball W, swimming, tennis, track and field M, volleyball W. **Intramural:** Basketball, football (non-tackle), soccer, softball, table tennis, volleyball. **Team name:** Bearcats.

**Student services.** Adult student services, alcohol/substance abuse counseling, campus ministries, career counseling, student employment services, financial aid counseling, health services, on-campus daycare, personal counseling, placement for graduates. **Physically disabled:** Services for visually, speech, hearing impaired. **Learning disabled:** Comprehensive services available.

**Contact.** E-mail: admission@stvincent.edu
Phone: (724) 537-4540 Toll-free number: (800) 782-5549
Fax: (724) 532-5069
David Collins, Assistant Vice President of Admission and Financial Aid, St. Vincent College, 300 Fraser Purchase Road, Latrobe, PA 15650-2690

---

## Seton Hill University

**Greensburg, Pennsylvania**
www.setonhill.edu

**CB member**
**CB code: 2812**

- Private 4-year university and liberal arts college affiliated with Roman Catholic Church
- Residential campus in large town
- 1,535 degree-seeking undergraduates: 18% part-time, 62% women
- 327 degree-seeking graduate students
- 63% of applicants admitted
- Application essay required
- 53% graduate within 6 years; 34% enter graduate study

**General.** Founded in 1918. Regionally accredited. **Degrees:** 274 bachelor's awarded; master's offered. **ROTC:** Army, Air Force. **Location:** 35 miles from Pittsburgh. **Calendar:** Semester, limited summer session. **Full-time faculty:** 69 total; 88% have terminal degrees, 7% minority, 56% women. **Part-time faculty:** 136 total; 39% have terminal degrees, 6% minority, 62% women. **Class size:** 62% < 20, 36% 20-39, 2% 40-49. **Special facilities:**

Child development center, kindergarten, women in business center, Catholic Holocaust education center.

**Freshman class profile.** 1,701 applied, 1,079 admitted, 322 enrolled.

| Mid 50% test scores | | | |
|---|---|---|---|
| SAT critical reading: | 450-550 | Rank in top tenth: | 23% |
| SAT math: | 450-570 | End year in good standing: | 94% |
| GPA 3.50 or higher: | 46% | Return as sophomores: | 73% |
| GPA 3.0-3.49: | 25% | Out-of-state: | 22% |
| GPA 2.0-2.99: | 29% | Live on campus: | 87% |
| Rank in top quarter: | 49% | International: | 3% |

**Basis for selection.** School achievement record most important, followed by test scores and recommendations. Applicants from minorities or low-income families encouraged, accepted on basis of motivation and potential. SAT or ACT recommended. Students who have not taken SAT or ACT may submit 2 graded writing samples for consideration. Interview recommended for all; audition required for music, theater programs; portfolio required for art program. Additional application required for physician assistant program. **Homeschooled:** Must provide SAT/ACT scores and official transcript issued by a school district or agency approving the curriculum, or GED.

**High school preparation.** 15 units required. Required and recommended units include English 4, mathematics 2, social studies 2, science 1 (laboratory 1), foreign language 2 and academic electives 4. 4 math units recommended for science majors.

**2007-2008 Annual costs.** Tuition/fees: $25,006. Room/board: $7,740. Books/supplies: $1,000. Personal expenses: $2,500.

**2007-2008 Financial aid. Need-based:** 293 full-time freshmen applied for aid; 274 were judged to have need; 272 of these received aid. Average need met was 81%. Average scholarship/grant was $17,293; average loan $4,815. 69% of total undergraduate aid awarded as scholarships/grants, 31% as loans/jobs. **Non-need-based:** Awarded to 284 full-time undergraduates, including 112 freshmen. Scholarships awarded for academics, alumni affiliation, art, athletics, job skills, music/drama.

**Application procedures. Admission:** Priority date 5/1; deadline 8/15 (receipt date). $35 fee, may be waived for applicants with need. Application may be submitted online. Admission notification on a rolling basis beginning on or about 9/1. **Financial aid:** Priority date 5/1; no closing date. FAFSA, institutional form required. Applicants notified on a rolling basis starting 11/15; must reply by 5/1 or within 2 week(s) of notification.

**Academics. Special study options:** Accelerated study, combined bachelor's/graduate degree, cross-registration, distance learning, double major, ESL, exchange student, honors, independent study, internships, liberal arts/career combination, New York semester, semester at sea, student-designed major, study abroad, teacher certification program, United Nations semester, Washington semester, weekend college. **Credit/placement by examination:** AP, CLEP, IB, SAT, ACT. 30 credit hours maximum toward bachelor's degree. **Support services:** Learning center, pre-admission summer program, reduced course load, remedial instruction, study skills assistance, tutoring, writing center.

**Majors. Biology:** General, biochemistry. **Business:** Accounting, actuarial science, business admin, entrepreneurial studies, finance, hospitality admin, human resources, international, management information systems, marketing, sales/distribution. **Communications:** General, journalism. **Computer sciences:** Computer science. **Education:** Art, biology, chemistry, English, family/consumer sciences, foreign languages, mathematics, music, Spanish. **Engineering:** General. **English:** Creative writing, English lit. **Family/consumer sciences:** General, child care, child development. **Foreign languages:** Spanish. **Health:** Art therapy, clinical lab science, dietetics, music therapy, nursing (RN), physician assistant. **History:** General. **Legal studies:** Prelaw. **Math:** General. **Philosophy/religion:** Religion. **Physical sciences:** Chemistry. **Protective services:** Criminal justice, forensics. **Psychology:** General. **Public administration:** Human services, social work. **Social sciences:** Economics, international relations, political science, sociology. **Theology:** Sacred music. **Visual/performing arts:** Acting, art history/conservation, arts management, ceramics, commercial/advertising art, dramatic, drawing, metal/jewelry, music performance, painting, printmaking, sculpture, studio arts, theater arts management, theater design. **Other:** Actuary science.

**Most popular majors.** Business/marketing 46%, health sciences 6%, psychology 7%, public administration/social services 7%, visual/performing arts 8%.

**Computing on campus.** 326 workstations in dormitories, library, computer center, student center. Dormitories wired for high-speed internet access and linked to campus network. Commuter students can connect to campus network. Online course registration, helpline, repair service, student web hosting, wireless network available.

**Student life. Freshman orientation:** Mandatory, $25 fee. Preregistration for classes offered. One-day, on-campus family orientation in summer. Four-day orientation during weekend and weekdays prior to start of classes. **Policies:** Residence hall students involved in setting community standards. **Housing:** Guaranteed on-campus for all undergraduates. Coed dorms, single-sex dorms, substance-free housing available. **Activities:** Bands, campus ministries, choral groups, dance, drama, international student organizations, literary magazine, music ensembles, musical theater, student government, student newspaper, symphony orchestra, social work club, liturgical groups, Respect Life, Operation Christmas Basket, Association of Black Collegians, National Coalition Building Institute, Helping Hands, Habitat for Humanity.

**Athletics. NCAA. Intercollegiate:** Baseball M, basketball, cross-country, equestrian W, field hockey W, football (tackle) M, golf, lacrosse, soccer, softball W, tennis, track and field, volleyball W, wrestling M. **Intramural:** Basketball W, equestrian W, soccer W, softball W, volleyball W. **Team name:** Griffins.

**Student services.** Adult student services, alcohol/substance abuse counseling, campus ministries, career counseling, services for economically disadvantaged, student employment services, financial aid counseling, health services, minority student services, on-campus daycare, personal counseling, placement for graduates, veterans' counselor. **Physically disabled:** Services for visually, speech, hearing impaired.

**Contact.**  E-mail: admit@setonhill.edu
Phone: (724) 838-4255 Toll-free number: (800) 826-6234
Fax: (724) 830-1294
Sherri Bett, Director of Admissions, Seton Hill University, 1 Seton Hill Drive, Greensburg, PA 15601

---

## Shippensburg University of Pennsylvania
**Shippensburg, Pennsylvania**               CB member
**www.ship.edu**                            CB code: 2657

- Public 4-year university
- Residential campus in small town
- 6,560 degree-seeking undergraduates: 4% part-time, 53% women, 6% African American, 1% Asian American, 2% Hispanic American
- 1,011 degree-seeking graduate students
- 75% of applicants admitted
- SAT or ACT (ACT writing optional) required
- 65% graduate within 6 years

**General.** Founded in 1871. Regionally accredited. **Degrees:** 1,323 bachelor's awarded; master's offered. **ROTC:** Army. **Location:** 40 miles from Harrisburg. **Calendar:** Semester, extensive summer session. **Full-time faculty:** 328 total; 89% have terminal degrees, 14% minority, 41% women. **Part-time faculty:** 54 total; 30% have terminal degrees, 4% minority, 50% women. **Class size:** 27% < 20, 60% 20-39, 12% 40-49, less than 1% 50-99. **Special facilities:** On-campus elementary school for student teachers, planetarium, vertebrate museum, greenhouse, herbarium, electron microscope, NMR spectrometer, fashion archives, interfaith spiritual center, women's center, performing arts center.

**Freshman class profile.** 6,164 applied, 4,648 admitted, 1,727 enrolled.

| Mid 50% test scores | | Rank in top quarter: | 25% |
|---|---|---|---|
| SAT critical reading: | 450-540 | Rank in top tenth: | 7% |
| SAT math: | 440-550 | End year in good standing: | 77% |
| GPA 3.50 or higher: | 27% | Return as sophomores: | 74% |
| GPA 3.0-3.49: | 35% | Out-of-state: | 6% |
| GPA 2.0-2.99: | 37% | Live on campus: | 88% |

**Basis for selection.** Secondary school record and test scores important. Summer Bridge Program provides access and academic support to students who do not meet regular admission criteria but have demonstrated potential, desire, and motivation to succeed in college. Rolling date for test scores, but application cannot be considered for admission until test scores are received. Interviews advisable in some situations. **Homeschooled:** Transcript of courses and grades, state high school equivalency certificate required. Those working with accredited agency must submit copy of both annual evaluation and homeschool diploma. All others encouraged to schedule interview and present portfolio, and must provide GED results. Grade transcripts required (if available). **Learning Disabled:** Students must register with Office of Disability Services and provide documentation from qualified professional that verifies disability. Documentation must be less than 3 years old. Reasonable support services provided.

**High school preparation.** 15 units recommended. Recommended units include English 4, mathematics 3, social studies 3, science 3 (laboratory 3) and foreign language 2.

**2007-2008 Annual costs.** Tuition/fees: $6,849; $14,615 out-of-state. Tuition for transfer students from five neighboring MD community colleges with dual admission agreements is $7,766. Room/board: $6,272. Books/supplies: $1,080. Personal expenses: $1,187.

**2007-2008 Financial aid. Need-based:** 1,378 full-time freshmen applied for aid; 885 were judged to have need; 875 of these received aid. Average need met was 69%. Average scholarship/grant was $4,916; average loan $3,294. 43% of total undergraduate aid awarded as scholarships/grants, 57% as loans/jobs. **Non-need-based:** Awarded to 929 full-time undergraduates, including 258 freshmen. Scholarships awarded for academics, athletics.

**Application procedures. Admission:** No deadline. $30 fee, may be waived for applicants with need. Application may be submitted online. Admission notification on a rolling basis. Must reply by April 1 or request a May 1 extension in writing. **Financial aid:** Priority date 3/15; no closing date. FAFSA required. Applicants notified on a rolling basis; must reply within 2 week(s) of notification.

**Academics.** Web-based online courses and programs also available. **Special study options:** Accelerated study, combined bachelor's/graduate degree, cooperative education, distance learning, double major, dual enrollment of high school students, honors, independent study, internships, study abroad, teacher certification program, Washington semester. **Credit/placement by examination:** AP, CLEP, IB, SAT, ACT, institutional tests. 30 credit hours maximum toward bachelor's degree. **Support services:** Learning center, pre-admission summer program, reduced course load, remedial instruction, study skills assistance, tutoring, writing center.

**Majors. Biology:** General. **Business:** Accounting, business admin, finance, logistics, management science, marketing. **Communications:** Journalism. **Computer sciences:** General, systems analysis. **Conservation:** Environmental studies. **Education:** Elementary. **English:** English lit, speech/rhetoric. **Foreign languages:** French, Spanish. **Health:** Health care admin. **History:** General. **Math:** General. **Parks/recreation:** Exercise sciences. **Physical sciences:** Chemistry, geology, physics. **Protective services:** Criminal justice. **Psychology:** General. **Public administration:** General, social work. **Social sciences:** Economics, geography, political science, sociology. **Visual/performing arts:** Art.

**Most popular majors.** Business/marketing 21%, communications/journalism 6%, education 15%, English 8%, psychology 7%, security/protective services 9%, social sciences 7%.

**Computing on campus.** 800 workstations in dormitories, library, computer center, student center. Dormitories wired for high-speed internet access and linked to campus network. Commuter students can connect to campus network. Online course registration, online library, helpline, wireless network available.

**Student life. Freshman orientation:** Mandatory, $50 fee. Orientation held in summer and prior to fall and spring semesters. **Policies:** University student code of conduct in effect. **Housing:** Guaranteed on-campus for freshmen. Coed dorms, single-sex dorms, special housing for disabled, apartments, substance-free housing available. $100 partly refundable deposit, deadline 4/1. **Activities:** Bands, campus ministries, choral groups, dance, drama, international student organizations, literary magazine, music ensembles, musical theater, radio station, student government, student newspaper, symphony orchestra, TV station, African American student organization, Fellowship of Christian Athletes, Christian Fellowship, Jewish student organization, Big Brother-Big Sister, nontraditional student organization, Latino student organization, Asian student organization.

**Athletics. NCAA. Intercollegiate:** Baseball M, basketball, cross-country, field hockey W, football (tackle) M, lacrosse W, soccer, softball W, swimming, tennis W, track and field, volleyball W, wrestling M. **Intramural:** Basketball, racquetball, soccer, softball, tennis, volleyball. **Team name:** Raiders.

**Student services.** Adult student services, campus ministries, career counseling, student employment services, financial aid counseling, health services, minority student services, on-campus daycare, personal counseling, placement for graduates, veterans' counselor, women's services. **Physically disabled:** Services for visually, hearing impaired.

**Contact.**  E-mail: admiss@ship.edu
Phone: (717) 477-1231 Toll-free number: (800) 822-8028
Fax: (717) 477-4016
Thomas Speakman, Dean of Enrollment Services, Shippensburg University of Pennsylvania, 1871 Old Main Drive, Shippensburg, PA 17257-2299

---

## Slippery Rock University of Pennsylvania
**Slippery Rock, Pennsylvania**              CB member
**www.sru.edu**                             CB code: 2658

- Public 4-year university
- Residential campus in rural community

- 7,521 degree-seeking undergraduates: 7% part-time, 56% women, 5% African American, 1% Asian American, 1% Hispanic American, 1% international
- 740 degree-seeking graduate students
- 70% of applicants admitted
- SAT or ACT (ACT writing optional) required
- 53% graduate within 6 years

**General.** Founded in 1889. Regionally accredited. **Degrees:** 1,532 bachelor's awarded; master's, doctoral offered. **ROTC:** Army. **Location:** 50 miles from Pittsburgh. **Calendar:** Semester, extensive summer session. **Full-time faculty:** 331 total; 87% have terminal degrees, 18% minority, 46% women. **Part-time faculty:** 35 total; 11% have terminal degrees, 20% minority, 40% women. **Class size:** 17% < 20, 60% 20-39, 15% 40-49, 6% 50-99, 2% >100. **Special facilities:** Environmental education centers.

**Freshman class profile.** 4,736 applied, 3,324 admitted, 1,508 enrolled.

| Mid 50% test scores | | | |
|---|---|---|---|
| SAT critical reading: | 450-530 | Rank in top tenth: | 10% |
| SAT math: | 460-550 | Return as sophomores: | 78% |
| ACT composite: | 19-23 | Out-of-state: | 11% |
| GPA 3.50 or higher: | 35% | Live on campus: | 96% |
| GPA 3.0-3.49: | 35% | International: | 1% |
| GPA 2.0-2.99: | 30% | Fraternities: | 8% |
| Rank in top quarter: | 35% | Sororities: | 9% |

**Basis for selection.** Recommended minimum 2.5 GPA, or 76 percent or higher average. Minimum score of 900 SAT (exclusive of Writing) or 20 ACT recommended. Interview recommended for all; audition required for dance, music, music education, and music therapy programs. **Homeschooled:** Documentation of homeschool diploma or certification information regarding how homeschool material covered required.

**High school preparation.** 16 units recommended. Recommended units include English 4, mathematics 3, social studies 3, history 3, science 3 (laboratory 1) and foreign language 2.

**2007-2008 Annual costs.** Tuition/fees: $6,671; $9,260 out-of-state. Tuition for out-of-state residents with at least 3.0 GPA is $7,766. Room/board: $7,862. Books/supplies: $1,278. Personal expenses: $1,689.

**2007-2008 Financial aid.** **Need-based:** 1,394 full-time freshmen applied for aid; 1,036 were judged to have need; 1,018 of these received aid. Average need met was 68%. Average scholarship/grant was $3,524; average loan $3,379. 44% of total undergraduate aid awarded as scholarships/grants, 56% as loans/jobs. **Non-need-based:** Awarded to 2,632 full-time undergraduates, including 775 freshmen. Scholarships awarded for academics, alumni affiliation, art, athletics, job skills, leadership, minority status, music/drama, ROTC, state residency. **Additional information:** May 1 closing date for Pennsylvania state grants.

**Application procedures.** **Admission:** No deadline. $30 fee, may be waived for applicants with need. Application may be submitted online. Admission notification on a rolling basis beginning on or about 9/15. Must reply by May 1 or within 2 week(s) if notified thereafter. **Financial aid:** Priority date 5/1; no closing date. FAFSA required. Applicants notified on a rolling basis starting 3/15; must reply within 4 week(s) of notification.

**Academics.** **Special study options:** Combined bachelor's/graduate degree, distance learning, double major, exchange student, honors, independent study, internships, liberal arts/career combination, study abroad, teacher certification program. **Credit/placement by examination:** AP, CLEP, IB, SAT, ACT, institutional tests. 45 credit hours maximum toward bachelor's degree. **Support services:** Learning center, pre-admission summer program, reduced course load, remedial instruction, study skills assistance, tutoring, writing center.

**Majors. Biology:** General. **Business:** Business admin. **Communications:** General. **Computer sciences:** General, information technology. **Conservation:** General. **Education:** Elementary, school counseling, special. **Engineering technology:** Occupational safety. **English:** English lit. **Foreign languages:** French, Spanish. **Health:** Athletic training, clinical lab technology, clinical/medical social work, cytotechnology, music therapy, nursing (RN). **History:** General. **Interdisciplinary:** Science/society. **Math:** General. **Parks/recreation:** Facilities management, health/fitness. **Philosophy/religion:** Philosophy. **Physical sciences:** Chemistry, geology, physics. **Psychology:** General. **Public administration:** Social work. **Social sciences:** Anthropology, criminology, economics, geography, political science, sociology. **Visual/performing arts:** Art, dance, dramatic, music performance.

**Most popular majors.** Business/marketing 15%, education 21%, health sciences 13%, parks/recreation 11%, visual/performing arts 6%.

**Computing on campus.** 1,253 workstations in dormitories, library, computer center, student center. Dormitories wired for high-speed internet access and linked to campus network. Commuter students can connect to campus network. Online course registration, online library, helpline, repair service available.

**Student life. Freshman orientation:** Mandatory, $90 fee. Preregistration for classes offered. Several sessions held during summer months. **Housing:** Guaranteed on-campus for freshmen. Coed dorms, single-sex dorms, special housing for disabled, apartments, substance-free housing available. $175 nonrefundable deposit. Special interest residence hall floors in education, humanities and fine arts, honors, wellness, technology, math/science, intensive study, ROTC, nontraditional/grad available. **Activities:** Bands, campus ministries, choral groups, dance, drama, international student organizations, literary magazine, music ensembles, musical theater, radio station, student government, student newspaper, symphony orchestra, TV station, Amnesty International, Black Action Society, Campus Crusade for Christ, environmental science society, Latino student organization.

**Athletics.** NCAA. **Intercollegiate:** Baseball M, basketball, cheerleading, cross-country, diving, field hockey W, football (tackle) M, golf, soccer, softball W, swimming, tennis, track and field, volleyball W, water polo, wrestling M. **Intramural:** Badminton, basketball, cross-country, diving, football (non-tackle), golf, racquetball, soccer, softball, swimming, tennis, track and field, triathlon, volleyball, water polo, weight lifting, wrestling. **Team name:** Pride.

**Student services.** Adult student services, alcohol/substance abuse counseling, campus ministries, career counseling, services for economically disadvantaged, student employment services, financial aid counseling, health services, legal services, minority student services, on-campus daycare, personal counseling, placement for graduates, veterans' counselor, women's services. **Physically disabled:** Services for visually, speech, hearing impaired.

**Contact.** E-mail: asktherock@sru.edu
Phone: (800) 929-4778 Toll-free number: (800) 778-9111
Fax: (724) 738-2913
Mimi Conner, Associate Director of Admissions, Slippery Rock University of Pennsylvania, 1 Morrow Way, Slippery Rock, PA 16057-1383

## Susquehanna University
**Selinsgrove, Pennsylvania**
www.susqu.edu

**CB member**
**CB code: 2820**

- Private 4-year university and liberal arts college affiliated with Evangelical Lutheran Church in America
- Residential campus in small town
- 1,976 degree-seeking undergraduates: 1% part-time, 54% women, 3% African American, 2% Asian American, 2% Hispanic American, 1% international
- 86% of applicants admitted
- Application essay required
- 82% graduate within 6 years; 24% enter graduate study

**General.** Founded in 1858. Regionally accredited. Associate degrees available in evening and only to residents of the greater Selinsgrove area. **Degrees:** 441 bachelor's, 7 associate awarded. **ROTC:** Army. **Location:** 50 miles from Harrisburg. **Calendar:** Semester, limited summer session. **Full-time faculty:** 121 total; 93% have terminal degrees, 16% minority, 40% women. **Part-time faculty:** 68 total; 50% women. **Class size:** 53% < 20, 46% 20-39, 1% 40-49, less than 1% 50-99. **Special facilities:** Ecology field station, film library, music library, rare book room, 24-hour study center, arboretum, observatory, 450-seat teaching theater, child development center, satellite dishes, distribution system for foreign language broadcasts, video conferencing facility, high technology center for business and communications.

**Freshman class profile.** 2,373 applied, 2,042 admitted, 593 enrolled.

| Mid 50% test scores | | | |
|---|---|---|---|
| SAT critical reading: | 520-610 | End year in good standing: | 89% |
| SAT math: | 530-610 | Return as sophomores: | 84% |
| ACT composite: | 22-27 | Out-of-state: | 45% |
| Rank in top quarter: | 61% | Live on campus: | 99% |
| Rank in top tenth: | 34% | International: | 1% |

**Basis for selection.** School record and class rank most important, test scores secondary. Application essay, interview, teacher and counselor evaluations, activities, and interest in the university considered. Students have option of submitting 2 graded writing samples in place of SAT or ACT scores. Interview highly recommended for all. Audition required for music majors. Portfolio required for writing and graphic design majors. **Home-schooled:** Student should have detailed description of course work taken.

**High school preparation.** 18 units required; 25 recommended. Required and recommended units include English 4, mathematics 3-4, social studies 1-3, history 1, science 3-4 (laboratory 2-3), foreign language 2-3 and academic electives 2-3.

**2008-2009 Annual costs.** Tuition/fees: $31,080. Room/board: $8,800. Books/supplies: $750. Personal expenses: $750.

**2007-2008 Financial aid. Need-based:** 476 full-time freshmen applied for aid; 386 were judged to have need; 386 of these received aid. Average need met was 84%. Average scholarship/grant was $18,973; average loan $3,745. 75% of total undergraduate aid awarded as scholarships/grants, 25% as loans/jobs. **Non-need-based:** Awarded to 777 full-time undergraduates, including 237 freshmen. Scholarships awarded for academics, alumni affiliation, leadership, minority status, music/drama, ROTC. **Additional information:** Graduated pay scale for federal work-study program.

**Application procedures. Admission:** Closing date 3/1 (postmark date). $35 fee, may be waived for applicants with need. Application may be submitted online. Admission notification 5/1. Admission notification on a rolling basis beginning on or about 1/15. Must reply by 5/1. **Financial aid:** Priority date 3/1, closing date 5/1. FAFSA, CSS PROFILE required. Applicants notified on a rolling basis starting 2/15; must reply by 5/1.

**Academics. Special study options:** Accelerated study, combined bachelor's/graduate degree, cross-registration, distance learning, double major, dual enrollment of high school students, exchange student, honors, independent study, internships, liberal arts/career combination, semester at sea, student-designed major, study abroad, teacher certification program, United Nations semester, urban semester, Washington semester. Internships abroad, 3-2 forestry or environmental management with Duke University, semester in London for junior business majors, 150-hour option in accounting to meet American Institute of CPA requirements, dentistry with Temple University, 2-2 allied health with Thomas Jefferson University. **Credit/placement by examination:** AP, CLEP, IB, SAT, ACT, institutional tests. 30 credit hours maximum toward associate degree, 65 toward bachelor's. **Support services:** Reduced course load, study skills assistance, tutoring, writing center.

**Majors. Biology:** General, biochemistry, ecology. **Business:** Accounting, business admin. **Communications:** General. **Computer sciences:** Computer science, information systems. **Conservation:** Environmental science. **Education:** Early childhood, elementary, music. **English:** Creative writing, English lit. **Foreign languages:** French, German, Spanish. **History:** General. **Interdisciplinary:** Global studies. **Math:** General. **Philosophy/religion:** Philosophy, religion. **Physical sciences:** Chemistry, physics. **Psychology:** General. **Social sciences:** Economics, political science, sociology. **Visual/performing arts:** Art, art history/conservation, dramatic, graphic design, music performance.

**Most popular majors.** Business/marketing 25%, communications/journalism 14%, education 12%, English 7%, social sciences 7%, visual/performing arts 6%.

**Computing on campus.** 305 workstations in dormitories, library, computer center, student center. Dormitories wired for high-speed internet access and linked to campus network. Commuter students can connect to campus network. Online course registration, online library, helpline, student web hosting, wireless network available.

**Student life. Freshman orientation:** Mandatory. Preregistration for classes offered. Four-day program; includes community service projects. **Housing:** Guaranteed on-campus for all undergraduates. Coed dorms, apartments, fraternity/sorority housing, substance-free housing available. $400 nonrefundable deposit, deadline 5/1. Volunteer services living groups, scholars' house, international student house, townhouses available. **Activities:** Bands, choral groups, dance, drama, film society, international student organizations, literary magazine, music ensembles, musical theater, opera, radio station, student government, student newspaper, symphony orchestra, volunteer services program, investment club, Habitat for Humanity, Student Environmental Action Coalition, Hispanic and Latino student organization, black student organization, Asian student organization, Big Brothers/Big Sisters, Hillel.

**Athletics.** NCAA. **Intercollegiate:** Baseball M, basketball, cheerleading, cross-country, field hockey W, football (tackle) M, golf, lacrosse, rowing (crew), soccer, softball W, swimming, tennis, track and field, volleyball W. **Intramural:** Baseball M, basketball, football (non-tackle), ice hockey M, racquetball, soccer, softball, tennis, volleyball. **Team name:** Crusaders.

**Student services.** Adult student services, alcohol/substance abuse counseling, campus ministries, career counseling, student employment services, financial aid counseling, health services, minority student services, on-campus daycare, personal counseling, placement for graduates, veterans' counselor, women's services. **Physically disabled:** Services for visually impaired.

**Contact.** E-mail: suadmiss@susqu.edu
Phone: (570) 372-4260 Toll-free number: (800) 326-9672
Fax: (570) 372-2722
Chris Markle, Director of Admissions, Susquehanna University, 514 University Avenue, Selinsgrove, PA 17870-1164

## Swarthmore College
Swarthmore, Pennsylvania
www.swarthmore.edu

CB member
CB code: 2821

- ♦ Private 4-year liberal arts college
- ♦ Residential campus in small town
- ♦ 1,480 degree-seeking undergraduates: 52% women, 8% African American, 17% Asian American, 10% Hispanic American, 1% Native American, 7% international
- ♦ 18% of applicants admitted
- ♦ SAT and SAT Subject Tests or ACT with writing, application essay required
- ♦ 94% graduate within 6 years; 21% enter graduate study

**General.** Founded in 1864. Regionally accredited. Quaker tradition. **Degrees:** 353 bachelor's awarded. **ROTC:** Army, Naval, Air Force. **Location:** 11 miles from Philadelphia. **Calendar:** Semester. **Full-time faculty:** 167 total; 100% have terminal degrees, 14% minority, 40% women. **Part-time faculty:** 36 total; 69% have terminal degrees, 17% minority, 64% women. **Class size:** 74% < 20, 23% 20-39, 2% 40-49, 1% 50-99, less than 1% >100. **Special facilities:** 330-acre arboretum, observatory, performing arts center, solar energy laboratory, Friends historical library, peace collection, LEED certified science center, civic and social responsibility center.

**Freshman class profile.** 5,242 applied, 930 admitted, 365 enrolled.

| Mid 50% test scores | | | |
|---|---|---|---|
| SAT critical reading: | 680-780 | Rank in top tenth: | 91% |
| SAT math: | 680-760 | Return as sophomores: | 97% |
| SAT writing: | 680-760 | Out-of-state: | 85% |
| ACT composite: | 27-33 | Live on campus: | 100% |
| Rank in top quarter: | 96% | International: | 8% |

**Basis for selection.** High school record, recommendations, class rank, test scores, essay, reading and experience in school and out, intellectual capacity and character important. Social responsibility considered. Students interested in engineering strongly encouraged to take Math Level 2 SAT Subject Tests. TOEFL or IELTS strongly encouraged for non-U.S. citizens whose first language is not English. Interview strongly recommended. Portfolios recommended if intended major is in the arts or music. **Home-schooled:** Include supplementary materials giving evidence of intellectual passion, personal commitments, special talents and interests. Additional essay on reasons for decision to homeschool and its consequences would be helpful. **Learning Disabled:** Proper documentation required.

**High school preparation.** Recommended units include English 4, mathematics 3 and science 3. 3 history/social studies, study of 1 or 2 foreign languages, and coursework in art and music recommended.

**2008-2009 Annual costs.** Tuition/fees: $36,490. Room/board: $11,314. Books/supplies: $1,080. Personal expenses: $1,052.

**2007-2008 Financial aid. Need-based:** 239 full-time freshmen applied for aid; 176 were judged to have need; 176 of these received aid. Average need met was 100%. Average scholarship/grant was $30,073; average loan $2,163. 87% of total undergraduate aid awarded as scholarships/grants, 13% as loans/jobs. **Non-need-based:** Awarded to 11 full-time undergraduates, including 1 freshmen. Scholarships awarded for academics, leadership, state residency. **Additional information:** 100% of demonstrated financial need met for all admitted students.

**Application procedures. Admission:** Closing date 1/2 (postmark date). $60 fee, may be waived for applicants with need. Application may be submitted online. Admission notification 4/1. Must reply by 5/1. **Financial aid:** Closing date 2/15. FAFSA, institutional form, CSS PROFILE required. Applicants notified by 4/1; must reply by 5/1.

**Academics. Special study options:** Accelerated study, cross-registration, double major, exchange student, honors, independent study, internships, student-designed major, study abroad, teacher certification program. Cooperative exchange programs with Rice and Tufts universities and Harvey Mudd, Pomona, Mills, and Middlebury colleges. **Credit/placement by examination:** AP, CLEP, IB, institutional tests. One course generally equals one credit. **Support services:** Study skills assistance, tutoring, writing center.

**Majors. Area/ethnic studies:** Asian, German. **Biology:** General, biochemistry. **Computer sciences:** General. **Education:** General. **Engineering:** General. **English:** English lit. **Foreign languages:** Ancient Greek, Chinese, classics, comparative lit, French, German, Japanese, Latin, linguistics, Russian, Spanish. **History:** General. **Interdisciplinary:** Medieval/Renaissance. **Math:** General. **Philosophy/religion:** Philosophy, religion. **Physical sciences:** Astronomy, astrophysics, chemical physics, chemistry, physics. **Psychology:** General, psychobiology. **Social sciences:** Economics, political science, sociology. **Visual/performing arts:** Art history/conservation, dance, dramatic, film/cinema, studio arts.

**Most popular majors.** Biology 10%, foreign language 9%, mathematics 6%, philosophy/religious studies 6%, physical sciences 6%, psychology 9%, social sciences 28%.

**Computing on campus.** 180 workstations in dormitories, library, computer center, student center. Dormitories wired for high-speed internet access and linked to campus network. Commuter students can connect to campus network. Online course registration, online library, helpline, repair service, student web hosting, wireless network available.

**Student life. Freshman orientation:** Mandatory. Four-day program held before beginning of classes. 3 multi-day optional preorientation programs. **Policies:** New students required to live on campus. **Housing:** Guaranteed on-campus for all undergraduates. Coed dorms, single-sex dorms, substance-free housing available. Gender-neutral housing (sharing rooms and/or bathrooms). **Activities:** Jazz band, campus ministries, choral groups, dance, drama, film society, international student organizations, literary magazine, music ensembles, opera, radio station, student government, student newspaper, symphony orchestra, more than 100 clubs and organizations.

**Athletics.** NCAA. **Intercollegiate:** Badminton W, baseball M, basketball, cross-country, field hockey W, golf M, lacrosse, soccer, softball W, swimming, tennis, track and field, volleyball W. **Intramural:** Basketball, football (non-tackle), soccer, softball, table tennis, tennis, volleyball. **Team name:** Garnet Tide, Garnet.

**Student services.** Alcohol/substance abuse counseling, campus ministries, career counseling, services for economically disadvantaged, student employment services, financial aid counseling, health services, minority student services, personal counseling, placement for graduates, women's services. **Physically disabled:** Services for visually, hearing impaired.

**Contact.** E-mail: admissions@swarthmore.edu
Phone: (610) 328-8300 Toll-free number: (800) 667-3110
Fax: (610) 328-8580
James Bock, Dean of Admissions and Financial Aid, Swarthmore College, 500 College Avenue, Swarthmore, PA 19081

---

## Talmudical Yeshiva of Philadelphia
### Philadelphia, Pennsylvania
**CB code: 1037**

- Private 4-year rabbinical college for men affiliated with Jewish faith
- Residential campus in very large city
- 112 degree-seeking undergraduates: 7% international
- 92% of applicants admitted
- Interview required

**General.** Founded in 1953. Accredited by AARTS. First Talmudic degree and ordination available. **Degrees:** 13 bachelor's awarded; first professional offered. **Calendar:** Trimester, extensive summer session. **Full-time faculty:** 5 total. **Part-time faculty:** 1 total.

**Freshman class profile.** 40 applied, 37 admitted, 34 enrolled.

| | | | |
|---|---|---|---|
| End year in good standing: | 97% | Live on campus: | 100% |
| Return as sophomores: | 75% | International: | 3% |
| Out-of-state: | 93% | | |

**Basis for selection.** Institutional examinations required.

**High school preparation.** 20 units required. Required and recommended units include English 4, social studies 3, science 3 and foreign language 2.

**2007-2008 Annual costs.** Tuition/fees: $7,300. Room/board: $6,000. Books/supplies: $900.

**2006-2007 Financial aid.** All financial aid based on need. 27 full-time freshmen applied for aid; 25 were judged to have need; 25 of these received aid. 98% of total undergraduate aid awarded as scholarships/grants, 2% as loans/jobs.

**Application procedures. Admission:** Priority date 1/15; no deadline. No application fee. Admission notification on a rolling basis beginning on or about 7/15. **Financial aid:** Priority date 8/1, closing date 5/1. FAFSA, institutional form required. Applicants notified on a rolling basis starting 3/15; must reply within 2 week(s) of notification.

**Academics. Credit/placement by examination:** CLEP, IB, institutional tests. **Support services:** Tutoring.

**Majors. Theology:** Talmudic.

**Student life. Policies:** Religious observance required. **Housing:** Guaranteed on-campus for all undergraduates.

**Student services.** Career counseling, health services, personal counseling, placement for graduates.

**Contact.** Phone: (215) 473-1212 Fax: (215) 477-5065
Rabbi Uri Mandelbaum, Admissions Director, Talmudical Yeshiva of Philadelphia, 6063 Drexel Road, Philadelphia, PA 19131

---

## Temple University
### Philadelphia, Pennsylvania
### www.temple.edu
**CB member**
**CB code: 2906**

- Public 4-year university
- Commuter campus in very large city
- 24,861 degree-seeking undergraduates: 11% part-time, 55% women, 17% African American, 10% Asian American, 3% Hispanic American, 3% international
- 7,851 degree-seeking graduate students
- 63% of applicants admitted
- SAT or ACT with writing, application essay required
- 59% graduate within 6 years

**General.** Founded in 1884. Regionally accredited. Campuses in Ambler, Fort Washington, downtown Philadelphia, Harrisburg, Japan and other international locations. **Degrees:** 4,808 bachelor's, 7 associate awarded; master's, doctoral, first professional offered. **ROTC:** Army, Naval, Air Force. **Location:** 2 miles from downtown. **Calendar:** Semester, extensive summer session. **Full-time faculty:** 1,306 total; 70% have terminal degrees, 16% minority, 37% women. **Part-time faculty:** 1,447 total; 14% minority, 43% women. **Class size:** 42% < 20, 44% 20-39, 9% 40-49, 4% 50-99, 2% >100. **Special facilities:** Observatory, planetarium, arboretum, technology center.

**Freshman class profile.** 16,659 applied, 10,559 admitted, 4,089 enrolled.

| Mid 50% test scores | | | |
|---|---|---|---|
| SAT critical reading: | 490-590 | Rank in top quarter: | 52% |
| SAT math: | 490-590 | Rank in top tenth: | 19% |
| ACT composite: | 20-25 | Return as sophomores: | 85% |
| GPA 3.50 or higher: | 41% | Out-of-state: | 28% |
| GPA 3.0-3.49: | 40% | Live on campus: | 79% |
| GPA 2.0-2.99: | 19% | International: | 1% |

**Basis for selection.** Admissions process holistic; every aspect of student's academic history considered. Interview and essay required for health professions applicants. Audition required for dance, music programs; portfolio required for art. **Homeschooled:** Statement describing homeschool structure and mission, transcript of courses and grades, letter of recommendation (nonparent) required.

**High school preparation.** 16 units required; 22 recommended. Required and recommended units include English 4, mathematics 3-4, social studies 2, history 1-2, science 2-3 (laboratory 1-2), foreign language 2 and academic electives 1-3.

**2007-2008 Annual costs.** Tuition/fees: $10,802; $19,320 out-of-state. Room/board: $8,518. Books/supplies: $1,000. Personal expenses: $3,900.

**2006-2007 Financial aid. Need-based:** 3,639 full-time freshmen applied for aid; 2,660 were judged to have need; 2,608 of these received aid. Average need met was 86%. Average scholarship/grant was $5,511; average loan $2,618. 56% of total undergraduate aid awarded as scholarships/grants, 44% as loans/jobs. **Non-need-based:** Awarded to 11,643 full-time undergraduates, including 2,585 freshmen. Scholarships awarded for academics, art, athletics, music/drama, ROTC.

**Application procedures. Admission:** Closing date 3/1 (postmark date). $50 fee, may be waived for applicants with need. Application may be submitted online. Admission notification on a rolling basis beginning on or about 10/15. Must reply by May 1 or within 2 week(s) if notified thereafter.

**Financial aid:** Closing date 3/1. FAFSA required. Applicants notified on a rolling basis starting 2/15; must reply by 5/1 or within 3 week(s) of notification.

**Academics. Special study options:** Combined bachelor's/graduate degree, cooperative education, cross-registration, distance learning, double major, dual enrollment of high school students, ESL, exchange student, honors, independent study, internships, liberal arts/career combination, student-designed major, study abroad, teacher certification program. Programs in Japan, Italy, Costa Rica, France, Germany, Ghana, India, Spain, Turkey, United Kingdom and Brazil. **Credit/placement by examination:** AP, CLEP, IB, institutional tests. **Support services:** Learning center, pre-admission summer program, reduced course load, remedial instruction, study skills assistance, tutoring, writing center.

**Majors. Agriculture:** Horticultural science. **Architecture:** Architecture, landscape, urban/community planning. **Area/ethnic studies:** African-American, American, Asian, Latin American, women's. **Biology:** General, biochemistry, biophysics. **Business:** General, accounting, actuarial science, business admin, entrepreneurial studies, finance, hospitality admin, insurance, international, labor relations, management information systems, marketing, real estate. **Communications:** Advertising, journalism, organizational, public relations. **Computer sciences:** General, information technology. **Conservation:** Environmental studies. **Education:** Art, business, elementary, English, foreign languages, mathematics, music, physical, science, social studies, trade/industrial. **Engineering:** Civil, electrical, mechanical. **Engineering technology:** General, civil, environmental. **English:** English lit, speech/rhetoric. **Foreign languages:** Classics, French, German, Hebrew, Italian, linguistics, Russian, Spanish. **Health:** Audiology/speech pathology, medical records admin, music therapy, nursing (RN), public health ed, recreational therapy. **History:** General. **Liberal arts:** Arts/sciences. **Math:** General. **Parks/recreation:** General. **Philosophy/religion:** Judaic, philosophy, religion. **Physical sciences:** Chemistry, geology, physics. **Protective services:** Criminal justice. **Psychology:** General. **Public administration:** Social work. **Social sciences:** Anthropology, economics, political science, sociology. **Visual/performing arts:** Acting, art, art history/conservation, ceramics, dance, dramatic, fiber arts, film/cinema, graphic design, jazz, metal/jewelry, music history, music pedagogy, music performance, music theory/composition, painting, photography, printmaking, sculpture, voice/opera.

**Most popular majors.** Business/marketing 21%, communications/journalism 11%, education 11%, social sciences 7%, visual/performing arts 12%.

**Computing on campus.** 3,565 workstations in dormitories, library, computer center, student center. Dormitories wired for high-speed internet access and linked to campus network. Commuter students can connect to campus network. Online course registration, online library, helpline, repair service, student web hosting, wireless network available.

**Student life. Freshman orientation:** Mandatory. Preregistration for classes offered. Includes placement testing. **Housing:** Guaranteed on-campus for freshmen. Coed dorms, special housing for disabled, apartments available. $250 fully refundable deposit, deadline 5/1. Living/learning centers available. **Activities:** Bands, campus ministries, choral groups, dance, drama, film society, international student organizations, literary magazine, music ensembles, musical theater, opera, radio station, student government, student newspaper, symphony orchestra, Newman Club, Hillel, Young Democrats, Young Republicans, professional organizations, public service organization, cultural organization.

**Athletics.** NCAA. **Intercollegiate:** Baseball M, basketball, cheerleading, cross-country, fencing W, field hockey W, football (tackle) M, golf M, gymnastics, lacrosse W, rowing (crew), soccer, softball W, tennis, track and field, volleyball W. **Intramural:** Basketball, football (non-tackle) M, racquetball, soccer M, softball, table tennis, tennis, volleyball, water polo. **Team name:** Owls.

**Student services.** Adult student services, alcohol/substance abuse counseling, campus ministries, career counseling, services for economically disadvantaged, student employment services, financial aid counseling, health services, legal services, personal counseling, placement for graduates, veterans' counselor. **Physically disabled:** Services for visually, speech, hearing impaired. **Learning disabled:** Comprehensive services available.

**Contact.** E-mail: tuadm@temple.edu
Phone: (215) 204-7200 Toll-free number: (888) 340-2222
Fax: (215) 204-5694
Timm Rinehart, Associate Vice President, Enrollment Management, Temple University, 103 Conwell Hall, Philadelphia, PA 19122-6096

---

## Thiel College
**Greenville, Pennsylvania**
**www.thiel.edu**

**CB member**
**CB code: 2910**

- Private 4-year liberal arts college affiliated with Evangelical Lutheran Church in America
- Residential campus in small town

---

- 1,179 degree-seeking undergraduates: 4% part-time, 46% women, 6% African American, 1% Asian American, 1% Hispanic American, 4% international
- 75% of applicants admitted
- SAT or ACT with writing, interview required
- 38% graduate within 6 years

**General.** Founded in 1866. Regionally accredited. **Degrees:** 180 bachelor's, 2 associate awarded. **Location:** 75 miles from Pittsburgh, 75 miles from Cleveland. **Calendar:** Semester, limited summer session. **Full-time faculty:** 68 total; 68% have terminal degrees, 9% minority, 37% women. **Part-time faculty:** 49 total; 16% have terminal degrees, 2% minority, 47% women. **Class size:** 55% < 20, 43% 20-39, 2% 40-49, less than 1% 50-99, less than 1% >100. **Special facilities:** Wildlife sanctuary, black box theater, neuro-science program.

**Freshman class profile.** 1,328 applied, 999 admitted, 371 enrolled.

| Mid 50% test scores | | | |
|---|---|---|---|
| SAT critical reading: | 410-530 | Rank in top quarter: | 28% |
| SAT math: | 420-530 | Rank in top tenth: | 14% |
| ACT composite: | 17-23 | End year in good standing: | 57% |
| GPA 3.50 or higher: | 23% | Return as sophomores: | 57% |
| GPA 3.0-3.49: | 21% | Out-of-state: | 28% |
| GPA 2.0-2.99: | 51% | Live on campus: | 91% |
| | | International: | 3% |

**Basis for selection.** High school GPA, class rank, curriculum, and recommendation important. Essay required. **Learning Disabled:** Students with disabilities must submit evidence of disability to Office of Special Needs.

**High school preparation.** 16 units recommended. Recommended units include English 4, mathematics 2, social studies 3, science 2 (laboratory 2), foreign language 2 and academic electives 1. Engineering, math, and science majors should complete 3 years of college preparatory math and science.

**2007-2008 Annual costs.** Tuition/fees: $20,214. Room/board: $7,840. Books/supplies: $800. Personal expenses: $1,600.

**2007-2008 Financial aid. Need-based:** 321 full-time freshmen applied for aid; 298 were judged to have need; 298 of these received aid. Average need met was 74%. Average scholarship/grant was $13,794; average loan $4,466. 67% of total undergraduate aid awarded as scholarships/grants, 33% as loans/jobs. **Non-need-based:** Scholarships awarded for academics, alumni affiliation, leadership, music/drama, religious affiliation, state residency.

**Application procedures. Admission:** Priority date 4/1; deadline 6/30 (receipt date). $35 fee, may be waived for applicants with need. Application may be submitted online. Admission notification on a rolling basis beginning on or about 9/15. Must reply by May 1 or within 2 week(s) if notified thereafter. **Financial aid:** Priority date 3/15; no closing date. FAFSA required. Applicants notified on a rolling basis starting 2/15; must reply within 2 week(s) of notification.

**Academics. Special study options:** Combined bachelor's/graduate degree, cooperative education, distance learning, double major, dual enrollment of high school students, honors, independent study, internships, liberal arts/career combination, semester at sea, study abroad, teacher certification program, United Nations semester, Washington semester. 3-2 engineering with Case Western Reserve University and University of Pittsburgh, 3-2 engineering technologies with Point Park College, Pittsburgh, cooperative program with Art Institute of Pittsburgh, cooperative engineering with Youngstown State University, exchange with Duke University in forestry. **Credit/placement by examination:** AP, CLEP, IB, SAT, ACT, institutional tests. 30 credit hours maximum toward bachelor's degree. **Support services:** Learning center, reduced course load, remedial instruction, study skills assistance, tutoring, writing center.

**Majors. Biology:** General. **Business:** Accounting, actuarial science, business admin, communications, international, management information systems. **Communications:** General. **Communications technology:** Radio/tv. **Computer sciences:** General, information systems. **Conservation:** General, environmental studies. **Education:** Biology, chemistry, elementary, English, history, mathematics, physics, science, social studies. **English:** English lit. **Health:** Audiology/speech pathology, clinical lab technology, cytotechnology. **History:** General. **Interdisciplinary:** Neuroscience. **Math:** General. **Personal/culinary services:** General, mortuary science. **Philosophy/religion:** Philosophy, religion. **Physical sciences:** Chemistry, physics. **Protective services:** Criminal justice. **Psychology:** General. **Social sciences:** Political science, sociology. **Theology:** Religious ed. **Visual/performing arts:** General, art, commercial/advertising art. **Other:** Binary engineering, Neuroscience.

**Most popular majors.** Business/marketing 34%, computer/information sciences 6%, education 10%, English 6%, psychology 11%, social sciences 6%.

**Computing on campus.** PC or laptop required. 300 workstations in dormitories, library, computer center, student center. Dormitories wired for high-speed internet access and linked to campus network. Commuter students can connect to campus network. Online course registration, helpline, wireless network available.

**Student life. Freshman orientation:** Mandatory, $275 fee. Preregistration for classes offered. Weekend before classes start. **Housing:** Guaranteed on-campus for all undergraduates. Coed dorms, apartments, fraternity/ sorority housing, substance-free housing available. $150 partly refundable deposit, deadline 6/30. Special interest housing, learning/living environment available. **Activities:** Bands, campus ministries, choral groups, dance, drama, international student organizations, literary magazine, music ensembles, musical theater, radio station, student government, student newspaper, symphony orchestra, TV station, Organization of Black Collegiates, Lutheran student movement, Circle K.

**Athletics.** NCAA. **Intercollegiate:** Baseball M, basketball, cheerleading, cross-country, football (tackle) M, soccer, softball W, track and field, volleyball W, wrestling M. **Intramural:** Badminton, basketball, softball, table tennis, volleyball. **Team name:** Tomcats.

**Student services.** Alcohol/substance abuse counseling, campus ministries, career counseling, student employment services, financial aid counseling, health services, minority student services, personal counseling, placement for graduates. **Physically disabled:** Services for visually, hearing impaired.

**Contact.** E-mail: admission@thiel.edu
Phone: (724) 589-2345 Toll-free number: (800) 248-4435
Fax: (724) 589-2013
Sonya Lapikas, Director of Admissions, Thiel College, 75 College Avenue, Greenville, PA 16125-2181

## Thomas Jefferson University: College of Health Professions
**Philadelphia, Pennsylvania**
www.jefferson.edu/jchp

CB code: 2903

- Private two-year upper-division health science and nursing college
- Residential campus in very large city
- 40% of applicants admitted
- Application essay required

**General.** Founded in 1824. Regionally accredited. Associate degree programs available in evening division. **Degrees:** 370 bachelor's, 80 associate awarded; master's, doctoral, first professional offered. **Articulation:** Agreements with Bloomsburg U of Pennsylvania, Bucks County CC, Cabrini College, CC of Philadelphia, Delaware County CC, Elizabethtown College, Juniata College, Keystone JC, La Salle U, Lebanon Valley College of Pennsylvania, Manor JC, Moravian College, Penn State: Delaware County Campus, St. Joseph's U, Shippensburg U of Pennsylvania, Susquehanna U, Villanova U, Gordon College, Burlington County College, Camden County College, Gloucester County College, Penn State: Abington Campus, Rider U, Muhlenberg College, Middlesex County College, Cumberland County College, Arcadia U. **ROTC:** Naval, Air Force. **Calendar:** Semester, limited summer session. **Full-time faculty:** 150 total. **Part-time faculty:** 55 total. **Special facilities:** Rare book collection, simulation labs, human performance lab (gait research), simulation building.

**Student profile.** 827 degree-seeking undergraduates, 1,802 degree-seeking graduate students. 1,462 applied as first time-transfer students, 585 admitted, 451 enrolled. 80% entered as juniors, 20% entered as seniors. 55% transferred from two-year, 45% transferred from four-year institutions.

| | | | |
|---|---|---|---|
| Women: | 83% | International: | 1% |
| African American: | 9% | Part-time: | 18% |
| Asian American: | 8% | Out-of-state: | 27% |
| Hispanic American: | 3% | Live on campus: | 30% |

**Basis for selection.** College transcript, application essay required. Decisions based on review of college transcripts, recommendations, written personal statement, and interview. Specific prerequisite credit requirements for each program. Volunteer experiences strongly recommended; 2 site visits required for OT applicants. Transfer accepted as sophomores, juniors, seniors.

**2007-2008 Annual costs.** Tuition/fees: $23,685. Books/supplies: $1,495. Personal expenses: $855.

**Financial aid. Need-based:** 40% of total undergraduate aid awarded as scholarships/grants, 60% as loans/jobs. **Non-need-based:** Scholarships awarded for academics, leadership, state residency.

**Application procedures. Admission:** Priority date 3/1. $50 fee, may be waived for applicants with need. Application may be submitted online. **Financial aid:** Applicants notified on a rolling basis starting 11/15; must reply within 2 weeks of notification. FAFSA, institutional form required.

**Academics.** Plan College Education Program allows qualified high school seniors to reserve a place for future enrollment after completion of required college program. **Special study options:** Accelerated study, combined bachelor's/graduate degree, distance learning, independent study, internships, study abroad. **Credit/placement by examination:** AP, CLEP, institutional tests. 30 credit hours maximum toward bachelor's degree. **Support services:** Pre-admission summer program, study skills assistance, tutoring, writing center.

**Majors. Biology:** Biotechnology. **Health:** Cardiovascular technology, clinical lab science, cytotechnology, nursing (RN), preop/surgical nursing, sonography. **Science technology:** Biological.

**Computing on campus.** 100 workstations in library, computer center, student center. Dormitories wired for high-speed internet access. Commuter students can connect to campus network. Online course registration, online library, helpline, wireless network available.

**Student life. Housing:** Guaranteed on-campus for all undergraduates. Coed dorms, special housing for disabled, apartments available. **Activities:** Choral groups, international student organizations, student government, student newspaper, African American student society, Chinese students and scholars society, Hands of Hope, Jewish student association, Medical Professionals for Choice, Asian professional society, Latino health organization, occupational therapy association, physical therapy association, Student Nurses Association of Pennsylvania.

**Athletics. Intramural:** Basketball, football (non-tackle) M, golf, racquetball, rugby, softball, squash, swimming, table tennis, tennis, volleyball, water polo.

**Student services.** Adult student services, alcohol/substance abuse counseling, career counseling, student employment services, financial aid counseling, health services, minority student services, on-campus daycare, personal counseling, placement for graduates, veterans' counselor. **Physically disabled:** Services for visually, speech, hearing impaired.

**Contact.** E-mail: jchp@jefferson.edu
Phone: (215) 503-8890 Toll-free number: (877) 533-3247
Fax: (215) 503-7241
Karen Astle, Assistant Dean for Admission, Thomas Jefferson University: College of Health Professions, 130 South Ninth Street, Edison Building, Suite 100, Philadelphia, PA 19107

## University of Pennsylvania
**Philadelphia, Pennsylvania**
www.upenn.edu

CB member
CB code: 2926

- Private 4-year university
- Residential campus in very large city
- 9,687 degree-seeking undergraduates: 3% part-time, 49% women, 8% African American, 17% Asian American, 6% Hispanic American, 10% international
- 9,229 degree-seeking graduate students
- 16% of applicants admitted
- SAT and SAT Subject Tests or ACT with writing, application essay required
- 94% graduate within 6 years; 20% enter graduate study

**General.** Founded in 1740. Regionally accredited. **Degrees:** 2,823 bachelor's, 2 associate awarded; master's, doctoral, first professional offered. **ROTC:** Army, Naval, Air Force. **Location:** One mile from downtown. **Calendar:** Semester, limited summer session. **Full-time faculty:** 1,395 total; 100% have terminal degrees, 17% minority. **Part-time faculty:** 693 total; 100% have terminal degrees, 14% minority, 46% women. **Class size:** 74% < 20, 15% 20-39, 3% 40-49, 6% 50-99, 1% >100. **Special facilities:** Arthropology museum, contemporary art institute, arboretum, astronomical observatory, large animal research center, women's center, undergraduate research center, wind tunnel.

**Freshman class profile.** 22,645 applied, 3,628 admitted, 2,385 enrolled.

| Mid 50% test scores | | | |
|---|---|---|---|
| SAT critical reading: | 650-750 | Rank in top tenth: | 96% |
| SAT math: | 680-770 | End year in good standing: | 97% |
| SAT writing: | 660-750 | Return as sophomores: | 98% |
| ACT composite: | 29-33 | Out-of-state: | 81% |
| GPA 3.50 or higher: | 81% | Live on campus: | 99% |
| GPA 3.0-3.49: | 16% | International: | 11% |
| GPA 2.0-2.99: | 3% | Fraternities: | 29% |
| Rank in top quarter: | 99% | Sororities: | 25% |

**Basis for selection.** Transcript indicating rigor of course work and achievement/evaluation most important criteria. Co-curricular involvements and testing strongly considered, as are counselor and faculty recommendations. Personal commentary (essays) and interview considered as well. Interested in diverse geographic, economic, racial, ethnic student body. Portfolio suggested for Architecture and Fine Arts programs. **Homeschooled:** Statement describing homeschool structure and mission, transcript of courses and grades, letter of recommendation (nonparent) required. Commentary from primary instructor most important, and at least 1 other academic reference highly recommended. SAT Subject Tests in major academic areas highly recommended.

**High school preparation.** 20 units recommended. Recommended units include English 4, mathematics 4, social studies 2, history 2, science 4 and foreign language 4.

**2007-2008 Annual costs.** Tuition/fees: $35,916. Room/board: $10,208. Books/supplies: $1,042. Personal expenses: $2,067.

**2006-2007 Financial aid.** All financial aid based on need. 1,254 full-time freshmen applied for aid; 951 were judged to have need; 951 of these received aid. Average need met was 100%. Average scholarship/grant was $26,102; average loan $2,381. 81% of total undergraduate aid awarded as scholarships/grants, 19% as loans/jobs.

**Application procedures. Admission:** Closing date 1/1 (postmark date). $75 fee, may be waived for applicants with need. Application may be submitted online. Admission notification 4/1. Must reply by 5/1. Rolling admission notification for nursing school applicants; notification begins on or about February 15. **Financial aid:** Priority date 2/15; no closing date. FAFSA, institutional form, CSS PROFILE required. Applicants notified by 4/1; must reply by 5/1.

**Academics. Special study options:** Accelerated study, combined bachelor's/graduate degree, cross-registration, double major, ESL, exchange student, honors, independent study, internships, liberal arts/career combination, student-designed major, study abroad, teacher certification program, Washington semester. **Credit/placement by examination:** AP, CLEP, IB, institutional tests. No maximum number of semester hours of credit by examination counted toward degree. **Support services:** Learning center, pre-admission summer program, remedial instruction, study skills assistance, tutoring, writing center.

**Majors. Architecture:** Architecture, environmental design. **Area/ethnic studies:** African, African-American, American, East Asian, South Asian, women's. **Biology:** General, biochemistry, bioinformatics, biomedical sciences, biophysics. **Business:** Accounting, actuarial science, business admin, e-commerce, finance, human resources, insurance, international, management information systems, marketing, operations, real estate, sales/distribution, transportation. **Communications:** General. **Computer sciences:** General, computer graphics, networking. **Conservation:** Environmental studies. **Education:** General, elementary. **Engineering:** Biomedical, chemical, computer, electrical, environmental, materials, materials science, mechanical, systems. **English:** English lit. **Foreign languages:** Classics, comparative lit, East Asian, French, German, Italian, linguistics, Russian, Semitic, Spanish. **Health:** Community health services, health care admin, nursing (RN). **History:** General, science/technology. **Interdisciplinary:** Cognitive science, global studies, natural sciences, neuroscience. **Legal studies:** General. **Liberal arts:** Arts/sciences, humanities. **Math:** General, statistics. **Philosophy/religion:** Judaic, logic, philosophy, religion. **Physical sciences:** Chemistry, geology, physics. **Psychology:** General. **Public administration:** Policy analysis. **Social sciences:** General, anthropology, economics, international relations, political science, sociology, urban studies. **Visual/performing arts:** General, art history/conservation, dramatic, film/cinema, studio arts.

**Most popular majors.** Biology 6%, business/marketing 21%, engineering/engineering technologies 9%, health sciences 7%, interdisciplinary studies 6%, social sciences 18%.

**Computing on campus.** 1,295 workstations in dormitories, library, computer center, student center. Dormitories wired for high-speed internet access and linked to campus network. Commuter students can connect to campus network. Online course registration, online library, helpline, repair service, student web hosting, wireless network available.

**Student life. Freshman orientation:** Mandatory. Preregistration for classes offered. **Housing:** Guaranteed on-campus for freshmen. Coed dorms, special housing for disabled, apartments, fraternity/sorority housing, substance-free housing available. $200 nonrefundable deposit, deadline 5/1. Private off-campus housing available. **Activities:** Bands, choral groups, dance, drama, film society, literary magazine, music ensembles, musical theater, opera, radio station, student government, student newspaper, symphony orchestra, TV station, various religious, political, ethnic, social service, performing arts, cultural, and sports organizations.

**Athletics.** NCAA. **Intercollegiate:** Baseball M, basketball, cross-country, diving, fencing, field hockey W, football (tackle) M, golf, gymnastics W, lacrosse, rowing (crew), soccer, softball W, squash, swimming, tennis, track and field, volleyball W, wrestling M. **Intramural:** Basketball, cross-country, football (non-tackle), golf, soccer, softball, table tennis, tennis, track and field, volleyball. **Team name:** Quakers.

**Student services.** Adult student services, alcohol/substance abuse counseling, campus ministries, career counseling, services for economically disadvantaged, student employment services, financial aid counseling, health services, minority student services, on-campus daycare, personal counseling, placement for graduates, veterans' counselor, women's services. **Physically disabled:** Services for visually, speech, hearing impaired.

**Contact.** E-mail: info@admissions.ugao.upenn.edu
Phone: (215) 898-7507 Fax: (215) 898-9670
Eric Furda, Dean of Admissions, University of Pennsylvania, 1 College Hall, Philadelphia, PA 19104

---

## University of Pittsburgh
**Pittsburgh, Pennsylvania**
www.pitt.edu

**CB member**
**CB code: 2927**

- Public 4-year university
- Residential campus in large city
- 16,798 degree-seeking undergraduates: 7% part-time, 51% women, 8% African American, 5% Asian American, 1% Hispanic American, 1% international
- 9,466 degree-seeking graduate students
- 56% of applicants admitted
- SAT or ACT (ACT writing optional) required
- 75% graduate within 6 years; 38% enter graduate study

**General.** Founded in 1787. Regionally accredited. Regional campuses in Johnstown, Bradford, Titusville, and Greensburg. **Degrees:** 3,713 bachelor's awarded; master's, doctoral, first professional offered. **ROTC:** Army, Naval, Air Force. **Location:** 3 miles from downtown. **Calendar:** Semester, extensive summer session. **Full-time faculty:** 1,550 total. **Part-time faculty:** 535 total. **Class size:** 43% < 20, 35% 20-39, 6% 40-49, 10% 50-99, 6% >100. **Special facilities:** Observatory, nationality rooms, performance hall, American music center, ecology laboratory.

**Freshman class profile.** 19,056 applied, 10,591 admitted, 3,419 enrolled.

| Mid 50% test scores | | | |
|---|---|---|---|
| SAT critical reading: | 570-670 | Return as sophomores: | 90% |
| SAT math: | 580-670 | Out-of-state: | 25% |
| ACT composite: | 24-30 | Live on campus: | 95% |
| Rank in top quarter: | 81% | International: | 1% |
| Rank in top tenth: | 48% | Fraternities: | 7% |
| | | Sororities: | 8% |

**Basis for selection.** GED not accepted. High school record, class rank, test scores, and activities considered. College of General Studies applicants must apply directly to that college, not through Admissions and Financial Aid. Students admitted as freshmen into School of Arts and Sciences, School of Engineering, School of Nursing, and College of Business Administration. Students may be conditionally accepted into the School of Pharmacy, PharmD program with the provision that they successfully complete 4 terms (2 years) of preprofessional study in School of Arts and Sciences. Interview and essay recommended for all; audition required for music program; portfolio recommended for studio art program; essay required for pharmacy applicants. **Homeschooled:** Statement describing homeschool structure and mission, transcript of courses and grades required. In some cases, committee will request end-of-year reviews by state-approved educator, if transcript from an approved homeschooling association not provided, and/or course descriptions. In all cases, high school diploma or equivalent required showing date of graduation at end of senior year.

**High school preparation.** 15 units required. Required and recommended units include English 4, mathematics 3, social studies 1-3, history 1, science 3 (laboratory 3), foreign language 3, computer science 1 and academic electives 3. 4 electives required with 3 in single foreign language recommended. Total units required varies by academic college.

**2007-2008 Annual costs.** Tuition/fees: $12,876; $22,386 out-of-state. Room/board: $8,300. Books/supplies: $700. Personal expenses: $1,500.

**2007-2008 Financial aid. Need-based:** 2,707 full-time freshmen applied for aid; 1,903 were judged to have need; 1,861 of these received aid. Average need met was 78%. Average scholarship/grant was $8,577; average loan $4,674. 52% of total undergraduate aid awarded as scholarships/grants, 48% as loans/jobs. **Non-need-based:** Awarded to 4,017 full-time undergraduates, including 1,238 freshmen. Scholarships awarded for academics, athletics.

**Application procedures. Admission:** Priority date 3/1; no deadline. $45 fee, may be waived for applicants with need. Application may be submitted online. Admission notification on a rolling basis beginning on or about 10/5. Must reply by May 1 or within 3 week(s) if notified thereafter. **Financial aid:** Priority date 3/1; no closing date. FAFSA, institutional form required. Applicants notified on a rolling basis starting 3/15; must reply by 5/1 or within 3 week(s) of notification.

**Academics.** Accelerated high school program enables students to take courses in School of Arts and Sciences while in high school. **Special study options:** Accelerated study, combined bachelor's/graduate degree, cooperative education, cross-registration, distance learning, double major, dual enrollment of high school students, ESL, exchange student, external degree, honors, independent study, internships, liberal arts/career combination, student-designed major, study abroad, teacher certification program, Washington semester. Freshman seminars, early admission to some graduate programs for exceptional students. **Credit/placement by examination:** AP, CLEP, IB, SAT, ACT, institutional tests. 60 credit hours maximum toward bachelor's degree. College of Arts and Sciences does not accept CLEP. **Support services:** Learning center, pre-admission summer program, reduced course load, remedial instruction, study skills assistance, tutoring, writing center.

**Majors. Area/ethnic studies:** African-American. **Biology:** General, ecology, microbiology, molecular. **Business:** Accounting, business admin, finance, marketing. **Communications:** Media studies. **Computer sciences:** Computer science, information systems. **Education:** Physical. **Engineering:** Biomedical, chemical, civil, computer, electrical, materials, mechanical, physics. **English:** British lit, creative writing, speech/rhetoric. **Foreign languages:** Chinese, classics, French, German, Italian, Japanese, linguistics, Polish, Russian, Slavic, Spanish. **Health:** Audiology/speech pathology, dental hygiene, dietetics, medical records admin, nursing (RN), orthotics/prosthetics. **History:** General, science/technology. **Interdisciplinary:** Biological/physical sciences. **Liberal arts:** Arts/sciences, humanities. **Math:** General, applied, statistics. **Philosophy/religion:** Philosophy, religion. **Physical sciences:** General, chemistry, geology, physics. **Protective services:** Corrections. **Psychology:** General, educational. **Public administration:** General, social work. **Social sciences:** General, anthropology, economics, political science, sociology, urban studies. **Visual/performing arts:** Art history/conservation, dramatic, film/cinema, studio arts.

**Most popular majors.** Business/marketing 15%, engineering/engineering technologies 11%, English 11%, health sciences 10%, psychology 9%, social sciences 12%.

**Computing on campus.** 600 workstations in dormitories, library, computer center, student center. Dormitories wired for high-speed internet access and linked to campus network. Commuter students can connect to campus network. Online library, helpline, repair service, wireless network available.

**Student life. Freshman orientation:** Available. Preregistration for classes offered. **Housing:** Guaranteed on-campus for freshmen. Coed dorms, single-sex dorms, fraternity/sorority housing, substance-free housing available. $325 fully refundable deposit. Rooms can be adapted to meet disabled students' particular needs. **Activities:** Bands, campus ministries, choral groups, dance, drama, film society, international student organizations, literary magazine, music ensembles, Model UN, radio station, student government, student newspaper, TV station, approximately 450 student organizations.

**Athletics.** NCAA. **Intercollegiate:** Baseball M, basketball, cross-country, diving, football (tackle) M, gymnastics W, soccer, softball W, swimming, tennis W, track and field, volleyball W, wrestling M. **Intramural:** Badminton, basketball, football (tackle) M, racquetball, soccer, squash, swimming, volleyball, wrestling M. **Team name:** Panthers.

**Student services.** Adult student services, alcohol/substance abuse counseling, campus ministries, career counseling, student employment services, financial aid counseling, health services, personal counseling, placement for graduates, veterans' counselor. **Physically disabled:** Services for visually, speech, hearing impaired.

**Contact.** E-mail: oafa@pitt.edu
Phone: (412) 624-7488 Fax: (412) 648-8815
Betsy Porter, Director, Office of Admissions and Financial Aid, University of Pittsburgh, 4227 Fifth Avenue, 1st Floor, Alumni Hall, Pittsburgh, PA 15260

## University of Pittsburgh at Bradford
**Bradford, Pennsylvania**    CB member
**www.upb.pitt.edu**    CB code: 2935

- Public 4-year university
- Residential campus in large town
- 1,354 degree-seeking undergraduates: 12% part-time, 58% women, 4% African American, 2% Asian American, 1% Hispanic American
- 84% of applicants admitted
- SAT or ACT (ACT writing optional) required
- 43% graduate within 6 years; 21% enter graduate study

**General.** Founded in 1963. Regionally accredited. **Degrees:** 184 bachelor's, 35 associate awarded. **ROTC:** Army. **Location:** 160 miles from Pittsburgh, 79 miles from Buffalo, New York. **Calendar:** Semester, extensive summer session. **Full-time faculty:** 69 total; 62% have terminal degrees, 14% minority, 41% women. **Part-time faculty:** 66 total; 17% have terminal degrees, 3% minority, 61% women. **Class size:** 56% < 20, 39% 20-39, 3% 40-49, 2% 50-99. **Special facilities:** Located in the Allegheny National Forest.

**Freshman class profile.** 737 applied, 620 admitted, 323 enrolled.

| Mid 50% test scores | | | |
|---|---|---|---|
| SAT critical reading: | 420-530 | GPA 2.0-2.99: | 35% |
| SAT math: | 440-560 | Rank in top quarter: | 30% |
| SAT writing: | 430-510 | Rank in top tenth: | 6% |
| ACT composite: | 17-22 | End year in good standing: | 70% |
| GPA 3.50 or higher: | 31% | Return as sophomores: | 72% |
| GPA 3.0-3.49: | 31% | Out-of-state: | 16% |
| | | Live on campus: | 81% |

**Basis for selection.** School achievement record, test scores, interview most important. Essay and recommendations considered. **Homeschooled:** Required: Complete listing of courses taken/completed/in progress, syllabus for each course, textbook used, 1 recommendation from educator, 1 outside recommendation, personal essay, personal interview, state requirement satisfaction.

**High school preparation.** 15 units required. Required and recommended units include English 4, mathematics 2-2.5, history 1, science 1-2 (laboratory 1-2), foreign language 2 and academic electives 5. Engineering and math students must have trigonometry and physics with a lab. Nursing majors must have 3 social science and 1 each of chemistry and biology with labs in both.

**2007-2008 Annual costs.** Tuition/fees: $11,300; $20,880 out-of-state. Room/board: $6,850. Books/supplies: $1,000. Personal expenses: $1,500.

**2007-2008 Financial aid. Need-based:** Average need met was 78%. Average scholarship/grant was $5,277; average loan $3,407. 44% of total undergraduate aid awarded as scholarships/grants, 56% as loans/jobs. **Non-need-based:** Awarded to 130 full-time undergraduates, including 54 freshmen. Scholarships awarded for academics, alumni affiliation, ROTC, state residency.

**Application procedures. Admission:** Priority date 5/1; no deadline. $45 fee, may be waived for applicants with need. Application may be submitted online. Admission notification on a rolling basis beginning on or about 11/15. Must reply by May 1 or within 2 week(s) if notified thereafter. **Financial aid:** Priority date 3/1; no closing date. FAFSA required. Applicants notified on a rolling basis starting 4/1; must reply within 2 week(s) of notification.

**Academics.** Student services include: on-going individual academic, personal and career counseling; strategies for maintaining and improving GPA; assistance with study skills and life management issues; cultural enrichment activities; computer learning lab services; graduate school assistance. **Special study options:** Combined bachelor's/graduate degree, cross-registration, distance learning, double major, dual enrollment of high school students, external degree, independent study, internships, semester at sea, study abroad, teacher certification program. 3-4 pre-optometry program with Pennsylvania College of Optometry, 1-4 pharmacy program with Oakland campus. **Credit/placement by examination:** AP, CLEP, IB, SAT, ACT, institutional tests. 30 credit hours maximum toward associate degree, 90 toward bachelor's. **Support services:** Learning center, reduced course load, remedial instruction, study skills assistance, tutoring.

**Majors. Biology:** General. **Business:** General, accounting, business admin, entrepreneurial studies, hospitality admin. **Communications:** Public relations, radio/tv. **Computer sciences:** Applications programming, computer science. **Conservation:** Environmental studies. **Education:** General, elementary, physical, secondary, social science. **Engineering:** General, chemical, civil, electrical, industrial, mechanical, science. **Engineering technology:** Petroleum. **English:** Creative writing, English lit, speech/rhetoric. **Health:**

Athletic training, nursing (RN), radiologic technology/medical imaging. **Interdisciplinary:** Biological/physical sciences. **Liberal arts:** Humanities. **Math:** Applied. **Parks/recreation:** Sports admin. **Physical sciences:** General, chemistry. **Protective services:** Corrections, law enforcement admin. **Psychology:** General. **Social sciences:** General, demography, economics, political science, sociology. **Visual/performing arts:** General.

**Most popular majors.** Biology 6%, business/marketing 19%, communications/journalism 6%, education 7%, health sciences 13%, parks/recreation 6%, security/protective services 9%, social sciences 19%.

**Computing on campus.** 118 workstations in library, computer center, student center. Dormitories wired for high-speed internet access and linked to campus network. Commuter students can connect to campus network. Online library, helpline, repair service, student web hosting, wireless network available.

**Student life. Freshman orientation:** Mandatory, $90 fee. Preregistration for classes offered. 2-day program for students and parents in July; additional 3-day program immediately prior to start of classes. **Housing:** Guaranteed on-campus for freshmen. Coed dorms, special housing for disabled, apartments, substance-free housing available. $125 nonrefundable deposit, deadline 5/1. Townhouse/apartment style housing available. **Activities:** Campus ministries, choral groups, dance, drama, literary magazine, radio station, student government, student newspaper, black action committee, Christ in Action, Collegiate Liberals of America, Conservative Union, Habitat for Humanity, ideology expression club.

**Athletics.** NCAA. **Intercollegiate:** Baseball M, basketball, cross-country, golf, soccer, softball W, swimming, volleyball W. **Intramural:** Basketball, football (non-tackle), golf, ice hockey, soccer, softball, swimming, table tennis, tennis, volleyball, water polo. **Team name:** Panthers.

**Student services.** Adult student services, alcohol/substance abuse counseling, campus ministries, career counseling, student employment services, financial aid counseling, health services, personal counseling, placement for graduates, veterans' counselor.

**Contact.** E-mail: admissions@upb.pitt.edu
Phone: (814) 362-7555 Toll-free number: (800) 872-1787
Fax: (814) 362-5150
Alexander Nazemetz, Director of Admissions, University of Pittsburgh at Bradford, 300 Campus Drive, Bradford, PA 16701

## University of Pittsburgh at Greensburg
**Greensburg, Pennsylvania**
www.upg.pitt.edu                           CB code: 2936

- Public 4-year branch campus and liberal arts college
- Commuter campus in large town
- 1,771 degree-seeking undergraduates: 7% part-time, 50% women, 5% African American, 2% Asian American, 1% Hispanic American
- 85% of applicants admitted
- SAT or ACT with writing required
- 57% graduate within 6 years

**General.** Founded in 1963. Regionally accredited. **Degrees:** 261 bachelor's awarded. **ROTC:** Army, Air Force. **Location:** 35 miles from Pittsburgh. **Calendar:** Semester, limited summer session. **Full-time faculty:** 74 total. **Part-time faculty:** 59 total. **Class size:** 40% < 20, 49% 20-39, 4% 40-49, 7% 50-99. **Special facilities:** Wildlife sanctuary and nature trail, humanities village, behavioral science village, natural sciences and new technologies village, international village.

**Freshman class profile.** 1,425 applied, 1,217 admitted, 490 enrolled.

| Mid 50% test scores | | GPA 2.0-2.99: | 31% |
|---|---|---|---|
| SAT critical reading: | 490-560 | Rank in top quarter: | 27% |
| SAT math: | 480-600 | Rank in top tenth: | 5% |
| SAT writing: | 450-510 | Return as sophomores: | 73% |
| ACT composite: | 20-23 | Out-of-state: | 3% |
| GPA 3.50 or higher: | 29% | Live on campus: | 72% |
| GPA 3.0-3.49: | 40% | | |

**Basis for selection.** High school curriculum and grades most important, followed by class rank and SAT/ACT scores. Interviews, essays and letters of recommendation all optional. **Homeschooled:** Transcript of courses and grades required.

**High school preparation.** 15 units required; 20 recommended. Required and recommended units include English 4, mathematics 2-4, social studies 2, history 2, science 1-2 (laboratory 1), foreign language 3, computer science 1 and academic electives 1-3. If student is missing foreign

language unit, must have enough academic elective units to meet the minimum total units required (15).

**2007-2008 Annual costs.** Tuition/fees: $11,320; $20,900 out-of-state. Room/board: $7,000. Books/supplies: $1,000. Personal expenses: $1,500.

**2007-2008 Financial aid. Need-based:** 407 full-time freshmen applied for aid; 324 were judged to have need; 317 of these received aid. Average need met was 66%. Average scholarship/grant was $5,651; average loan $4,270. 44% of total undergraduate aid awarded as scholarships/grants, 56% as loans/jobs. **Non-need-based:** Awarded to 339 full-time undergraduates, including 167 freshmen. Scholarships awarded for academics, leadership, minority status.

**Application procedures. Admission:** No deadline. $45 fee, may be waived for applicants with need. Application may be submitted online. Admission notification on a rolling basis beginning on or about 9/1. Must reply by May 1 or within 3 week(s) if notified thereafter. **Financial aid:** Priority date 2/15; no closing date. FAFSA required. Applicants notified on a rolling basis starting 3/15; must reply within 3 week(s) of notification.

**Academics. Special study options:** Combined bachelor's/graduate degree, cross-registration, double major, dual enrollment of high school students, exchange student, independent study, internships, liberal arts/career combination, student-designed major, study abroad. **Credit/placement by examination:** AP, CLEP, SAT, ACT, institutional tests. 30 credit hours maximum toward bachelor's degree. **Support services:** Learning center, reduced course load, remedial instruction, study skills assistance, tutoring, writing center.

**Majors. Area/ethnic studies:** American. **Biology:** General. **Business:** Accounting, business admin, management information systems. **Communications:** General, journalism, public relations. **Computer sciences:** Information systems. **Conservation:** General. **English:** Composition, English lit. **Health:** Predental, premedicine, prepharmacy, preveterinary. **History:** General. **Liberal arts:** Arts/sciences. **Math:** Applied. **Protective services:** Law enforcement admin. **Psychology:** General. **Social sciences:** General, anthropology, criminology, political science.

**Most popular majors.** Business/marketing 33%, English 13%, psychology 26%, security/protective services 10%.

**Computing on campus.** 400 workstations in dormitories, library, computer center. Dormitories wired for high-speed internet access and linked to campus network. Commuter students can connect to campus network. Online library, helpline, repair service, student web hosting, wireless network available.

**Student life. Freshman orientation:** Mandatory, $55 fee. **Housing:** Coed dorms, substance-free housing available. $150 deposit, deadline 5/1. **Activities:** Choral groups, dance, drama, international student organizations, literary magazine, musical theater, radio station, student government, student newspaper, student activities board, honor societies, academic societies, Alpha Phi Omega, Circle K, Amnesty International, Christian fellowship club, College Republicans, college democrats.

**Athletics.** NCAA. **Intercollegiate:** Baseball M, basketball, cross-country, golf, soccer, softball W, tennis, volleyball W. **Intramural:** Baseball M, basketball, golf, racquetball, skiing, soccer, softball, table tennis, tennis, volleyball. **Team name:** Bobcats.

**Student services.** Adult student services, alcohol/substance abuse counseling, career counseling, student employment services, financial aid counseling, health services, personal counseling, placement for graduates. **Physically disabled:** Services for visually, hearing impaired.

**Contact.** E-mail: upgadmit@pitt.edu
Phone: (724) 836-9880 Fax: (724) 836-7160
Heather Kabala, Director of Admissions, University of Pittsburgh at Greensburg, 150 Finoli Drive, Greensburg, PA 15601

## University of Pittsburgh at Johnstown
**Johnstown, Pennsylvania**                 CB member
www.upj.pitt.edu                            CB code: 2934

- Public 4-year engineering and liberal arts college
- Residential campus in small city
- 3,116 degree-seeking undergraduates: 6% part-time, 47% women, 2% African American, 1% Asian American, 1% Hispanic American
- 88% of applicants admitted
- SAT or ACT (ACT writing recommended), application essay required
- 59% graduate within 6 years

**General.** Founded in 1927. Regionally accredited. **Degrees:** 577 bachelor's, 16 associate awarded. **Location:** 70 miles from Pittsburgh. **Calendar:** Semester, limited summer session. **Full-time faculty:** 143 total; 68% have terminal degrees, 8% minority, 37% women. **Part-time faculty:** 51 total; 37% have terminal degrees, 2% minority, 37% women. **Class size:** 31% < 20, 57% 20-39, 8% 40-49, 3% 50-99, less than 1% >100. **Special facilities:** 40-acre nature preserve maintained by biology department, performing arts center.

**Freshman class profile.** 1,749 applied, 1,542 admitted, 852 enrolled.

| Mid 50% test scores | | | |
|---|---|---|---|
| SAT critical reading: | 450-540 | GPA 2.0-2.99: | 24% |
| SAT math: | 470-560 | Rank in top quarter: | 35% |
| SAT writing: | 460-540 | Rank in top tenth: | 11% |
| ACT composite: | 18-22 | Return as sophomores: | 73% |
| GPA 3.50 or higher: | 42% | Out-of-state: | 1% |
| GPA 3.0-3.49: | 33% | Live on campus: | 76% |

**Basis for selection.** College preparatory curriculum, high school achievement, test scores, and class rank very important. Recommendations and essay considered. Interview recommended.

**High school preparation.** 15 units required. Required and recommended units include English 4, mathematics 2-3, social studies 4, science 2 (laboratory 1-2) and foreign language 2. One each of trigonometry, physics, and chemistry required for engineering technology program.

**2007-2008 Annual costs.** Tuition/fees: $11,332; $20,912 out-of-state. Room/board: $6,400. Books/supplies: $1,000. Personal expenses: $1,500.

**2007-2008 Financial aid. Need-based:** 769 full-time freshmen applied for aid; 648 were judged to have need; 632 of these received aid. Average need met was 52%. Average scholarship/grant was $5,357; average loan $3,801. 51% of total undergraduate aid awarded as scholarships/grants, 49% as loans/jobs. **Non-need-based:** Awarded to 814 full-time undergraduates, including 295 freshmen. Scholarships awarded for academics, athletics, leadership, minority status, state residency.

**Application procedures. Admission:** No deadline. $45 fee, may be waived for applicants with need. Application may be submitted online. Admission notification on a rolling basis beginning on or about 9/1. Must reply by May 1 or within 2 week(s) if notified thereafter. **Financial aid:** Priority date 4/1; no closing date. FAFSA required. Applicants notified on a rolling basis starting 3/15; must reply within 2 week(s) of notification.

**Academics. Special study options:** Accelerated study, combined bachelor's/graduate degree, cooperative education, cross-registration, distance learning, double major, dual enrollment of high school students, independent study, internships, liberal arts/career combination, student-designed major, study abroad, teacher certification program. **Credit/placement by examination:** AP, CLEP, IB, SAT, ACT, institutional tests. 90 credit hours maximum toward bachelor's degree. **Support services:** Learning center, reduced course load, study skills assistance, tutoring, writing center.

**Majors. Area/ethnic studies:** American. **Biology:** General. **Business:** General, accounting, finance, managerial economics, marketing. **Communications:** General, journalism. **Computer sciences:** General. **Conservation:** Environmental studies. **Education:** Biology, chemistry, elementary, english, mathematics, science, secondary, social science, social studies. **Engineering technology:** Civil, electrical, mechanical. **English:** American lit, British lit, creative writing. **Health:** Predental, premedicine, preveterinary. **History:** General. **Legal studies:** Prelaw. **Liberal arts:** Arts/sciences. **Math:** General. **Physical sciences:** Chemistry, geology. **Psychology:** General. **Social sciences:** General, economics, geography, political science, sociology. **Visual/performing arts:** Dramatic.

**Most popular majors.** Biology 6%, business/marketing 21%, communications/journalism 10%, education 16%, engineering/engineering technologies 11%, psychology 6%, social sciences 11%.

**Computing on campus.** 150 workstations in library, computer center. Dormitories wired for high-speed internet access and linked to campus network. Commuter students can connect to campus network. Online library, helpline, student web hosting, wireless network available.

**Student life. Freshman orientation:** Mandatory, $55 fee. Preregistration for classes offered. One-day program. **Policies:** To be eligible to hold office within group or organization, student must be full-time and have minimum 2.0 GPA. **Housing:** Guaranteed on-campus for all undergraduates. Coed dorms, apartments, substance-free housing available. $350 fully refundable deposit, deadline 7/1. Townhouses, lodges, and single-sex residences available. **Activities:** Concert band, campus ministries, choral groups, dance, drama, literary magazine, music ensembles, Model UN, musical theater, radio station, student government, student newspaper, TV station, Newman Students Association, Black Action Society, Student Outreach Through Service, Time Out Christian Fellowship, Student Council on World Affairs,

political science club, honor societies, academic clubs, Habitat for Humanity.

**Athletics.** NCAA. **Intercollegiate:** Baseball M, basketball, cross-country W, golf, soccer, track and field W, volleyball W, wrestling M. **Intramural:** Basketball, football (non-tackle), softball, volleyball. **Team name:** Mountain Cats.

**Student services.** Adult student services, alcohol/substance abuse counseling, campus ministries, career counseling, student employment services, financial aid counseling, health services, personal counseling, placement for graduates, veterans' counselor. **Physically disabled:** Services for visually, speech, hearing impaired.

**Contact.** E-mail: upjadmit@pitt.edu
Phone: (814) 269-7050 Toll-free number: (800) 765-4875
Fax: (814) 269-7044
James Gyure, Director of Admissions, University of Pittsburgh at Johnstown, 450 Schoolhouse Road, 157 Blackington Hall, Johnstown, PA 15904-1200

## University of Scranton
### Scranton, Pennsylvania
**CB member**
www.scranton.edu
**CB code: 2929**

- Private 4-year university and liberal arts college affiliated with Roman Catholic Church
- Residential campus in small city
- 3,994 degree-seeking undergraduates: 4% part-time, 57% women, 1% African American, 2% Asian American, 5% Hispanic American
- 1,495 degree-seeking graduate students
- 66% of applicants admitted
- SAT or ACT (ACT writing optional), application essay required
- 77% graduate within 6 years

**General.** Founded in 1888. Regionally accredited. **Degrees:** 894 bachelor's, 1 associate awarded; master's, doctoral offered. **ROTC:** Army, Air Force. **Location:** 125 miles from Philadelphia, 125 miles from New York City. **Calendar:** Semester, limited summer session. **Full-time faculty:** 258 total; 84% have terminal degrees, 9% minority, 37% women. **Part-time faculty:** 254 total; 12% have terminal degrees, 2% minority, 52% women. **Class size:** 38% < 20, 42% 20-39, 19% 40-49, less than 1% 50-99. **Special facilities:** 2 cyber-cafes, conference and retreat center at Chapman Lake, performing arts center with seating for 700.

**Freshman class profile.** 7,609 applied, 5,033 admitted, 1,030 enrolled.

| Mid 50% test scores | | | |
|---|---|---|---|
| SAT critical reading: | 510-600 | Rank in top quarter: | 63% |
| SAT math: | 520-620 | Rank in top tenth: | 27% |
| GPA 3.50 or higher: | 40% | Return as sophomores: | 90% |
| GPA 3.0-3.49: | 42% | Out-of-state: | 59% |
| GPA 2.0-2.99: | 18% | Live on campus: | 86% |

**Basis for selection.** Program taken, GPA, SAT scores, class rank most important. Essay, extracurricular/leadership activities, recommendations important. **Homeschooled:** State high school equivalency certificate required.

**High school preparation.** 16 units required. Required and recommended units include English 4, mathematics 3-4, social studies 2-3, history 2-3, science 3 (laboratory 1) and foreign language 2. Science and business students should have 4 math; science students should have 4 science.

**2007-2008 Annual costs.** Tuition/fees: $28,758. Room/board: $10,610. Books/supplies: $900. Personal expenses: $1,100.

**2007-2008 Financial aid. Need-based:** 853 full-time freshmen applied for aid; 717 were judged to have need; 710 of these received aid. Average need met was 75%. Average scholarship/grant was $14,767; average loan $3,345. 72% of total undergraduate aid awarded as scholarships/grants, 28% as loans/jobs. **Non-need-based:** Awarded to 729 full-time undergraduates, including 218 freshmen. Scholarships awarded for academics, minority status, ROTC.

**Application procedures. Admission:** Closing date 3/1 (postmark date). $40 fee, may be waived for applicants with need. Application may be submitted online. Admission notification on a rolling basis beginning on or about 1/15. Must reply by May 1 or within 2 week(s) if notified thereafter. **Financial aid:** Priority date 2/15; no closing date. FAFSA required. Applicants notified on a rolling basis starting 3/1; must reply by 5/1 or within 2 week(s) of notification.

**Academics. Special study options:** Accelerated study, combined bachelor's/graduate degree, cross-registration, distance learning, double major, dual enrollment of high school students, ESL, exchange student, honors, independent study, internships, semester at sea, study abroad, teacher certification program, United Nations semester, Washington semester. Baccalaureate/master's degree programs available. **Credit/placement by examination:** AP, CLEP, IB, SAT, ACT, institutional tests. 30 credit hours maximum toward bachelor's degree. **Support services:** Learning center, pre-admission summer program, remedial instruction, study skills assistance, tutoring, writing center.

**Majors. Biology:** General, biochemistry, biophysics, molecular. **Business:** Accounting, business admin, finance, human resources, international, management science, marketing, operations. **Communications:** General. **Computer sciences:** General, information systems. **Conservation:** General. **Education:** Early childhood, elementary, secondary, special. **Engineering:** Electrical. **English:** English lit. **Foreign languages:** Ancient Greek, classics, French, German, Latin, Spanish. **Health:** Clinical lab science, health care admin, nursing (RN). **History:** General. **Interdisciplinary:** Gerontology, neuroscience. **Math:** General. **Philosophy/religion:** Philosophy, religion. **Physical sciences:** Chemistry, physics. **Protective services:** Criminal justice, forensics. **Psychology:** General. **Public administration:** Human services. **Social sciences:** Economics, international relations, political science, sociology. **Visual/performing arts:** Dramatic.

**Most popular majors.** Biology 9%, business/marketing 22%, communications/journalism 7%, education 13%, health sciences 13%, social sciences 9%.

**Computing on campus.** Dormitories wired for high-speed internet access and linked to campus network. Commuter students can connect to campus network. Online course registration, online library, helpline, repair service, student web hosting, wireless network available.

**Student life. Freshman orientation:** Mandatory, $220 fee. Preregistration for classes offered. Overnight program (1.5 days) for students and parents, held between end of June and mid-July. **Housing:** Guaranteed on-campus for all undergraduates. Coed dorms, single-sex dorms, apartments available. $150 nonrefundable deposit, deadline 5/1. Theme houses (French, Spanish, international, service, education, arts) available. **Activities:** Bands, campus ministries, choral groups, dance, drama, international student organizations, literary magazine, music ensembles, radio station, student government, student newspaper, TV station, religious and social service organizations, veterans club, Young Democrats, Young Republicans, professional clubs, collegiate volunteers, multicultural club, debating club.

**Athletics.** NCAA. **Intercollegiate:** Baseball M, basketball, cross-country, field hockey W, golf M, ice hockey M, lacrosse, soccer, softball W, swimming, tennis, volleyball W, wrestling M. **Intramural:** Baseball M, basketball, bowling, cross-country, football (tackle) M, golf, handball, lacrosse, racquetball, rugby, skiing, soccer, softball, swimming, table tennis, tennis, track and field, volleyball, water polo M, wrestling M. **Team name:** Royals.

**Student services.** Adult student services, alcohol/substance abuse counseling, campus ministries, career counseling, student employment services, health services, personal counseling, placement for graduates, veterans' counselor. **Physically disabled:** Services for visually, hearing impaired.

**Contact.** E-mail: admissions@scranton.edu
Phone: (570) 941-7540 Toll-free number: (888) 727-2686
Fax: (570) 941-5928
Joseph Roback, Assistant Vice President for Admissions and Enrollment, University of Scranton, 800 Linden Street, Scranton, PA 18510-4699

## University of the Arts
**Philadelphia, Pennsylvania**
www.uarts.edu

**CB member**
**CB code: 2664**

- Private 4-year visual arts and performing arts college
- Residential campus in very large city
- 2,181 degree-seeking undergraduates
- 48% of applicants admitted
- SAT or ACT (ACT writing optional), application essay required

**General.** Founded in 1870. Regionally accredited. **Degrees:** 399 bachelor's awarded; master's offered. **Calendar:** Semester, limited summer session. **Full-time faculty:** 115 total. **Part-time faculty:** 359 total. **Class size:** 79% < 20, 21% 20-39, less than 1% 50-99. **Special facilities:** Digital multimedia laboratories, Oxberry animation stand, MIDI and recording studios, analog and digital electronic music studios, music calligraphy laboratory, center for publication arts, industrial design computer-aided product design center, genre-specific art galleries.

**Freshman class profile.** 2,470 applied, 1,184 admitted, 567 enrolled.

| Mid 50% test scores | | | |
|---|---|---|---|
| SAT critical reading: | 470-600 | GPA 3.0-3.49: | 26% |
| SAT math: | 450-570 | GPA 2.0-2.99: | 55% |
| SAT writing: | 470-580 | Rank in top quarter: | 32% |
| ACT composite: | 18-25 | Rank in top tenth: | 10% |
| GPA 3.50 or higher: | 17% | Out-of-state: | 61% |
| | | Live on campus: | 87% |

**Basis for selection.** Academic records, art work portfolio, audition very important. SAT or ACT scores considered in relation to the former. Statement of purpose and letters of recommendation also important. Class placement in English composition through SAT/ACT scores. August 15 score deadline for placement, counseling and/or credit. Interview recommended for all; audition required for performing arts programs; portfolio required for multimedia, visual arts, writing programs; essay required for media arts, performing arts, and visual arts programs.

**High school preparation.** Required and recommended units include English 4, mathematics 3, social studies 2, history 2, science 2 and foreign language 2. Coursework in art, dance, music, creative writing, or theater as appropriate for specific programs recommended.

**2008-2009 Annual costs.** Tuition/fees: $30,600. Room only: $8,712. Books/supplies: $2,000. Personal expenses: $2,000.

**Financial aid. Non-need-based:** Scholarships awarded for academics, art, music/drama.

**Application procedures. Admission:** Priority date 3/1; no deadline. $60 fee, may be waived for applicants with need. Admission notification on a rolling basis beginning on or about 11/1. Must reply by May 1 or within 3 week(s) if notified thereafter. **Financial aid:** Priority date 3/1; no closing date. FAFSA required. Applicants notified on a rolling basis starting 3/15; must reply within 2 week(s) of notification.

**Academics.** Credit for course work may be given to entering freshmen by portfolio review (awarded after first year) or audition and placement testing. Art and design students declare major at end of first year, dance students at end of second year. **Special study options:** Accelerated study, cross-registration, double major, dual enrollment of high school students, ESL, exchange student, independent study, internships, study abroad, teacher certification program. **Credit/placement by examination:** AP, CLEP, IB, SAT, ACT, institutional tests. Credit by examination counted toward bachelor's degree varies by program. **Support services:** Learning center, pre-admission summer program, reduced course load, remedial instruction, study skills assistance, tutoring, writing center.

**Majors. Communications:** Digital media. **Education:** Drama/dance. **Visual/performing arts:** Acting, cinematography, crafts, dance, graphic design, illustration, industrial design, multimedia, music performance, music theory/composition, painting, photography, play/screenwriting, printmaking, sculpture, theater design.

**Most popular majors.** Visual/performing arts 95%.

**Computing on campus.** PC or laptop required. 400 workstations in library, computer center, student center. Dormitories wired for high-speed internet access and linked to campus network. Commuter students can connect to campus network. Online course registration, online library, helpline, wireless network available.

**Student life. Freshman orientation:** Available. Preregistration for classes offered. Includes educational sessions on various social issues of university life. **Policies:** Campus code of conduct. **Housing:** Coed dorms, apartments, substance-free housing available. $300 deposit, deadline 6/1. All housing in apartment-style units. **Activities:** Jazz band, choral groups, dance, drama, film society, literary magazine, music ensembles, musical theater, radio station, student government, African American student union, chess club, fencing club, Gallery One, Green Team, Rainbow Connection, Christian Fellowship.

**Athletics. Intramural:** Volleyball.

**Student services.** Adult student services, alcohol/substance abuse counseling, career counseling, services for economically disadvantaged, student employment services, financial aid counseling, health services, personal counseling, placement for graduates, veterans' counselor. **Physically disabled:** Services for visually, speech, hearing impaired.

**Contact.** E-mail: admissions@uarts.edu
Phone: (215) 717-6049 Toll-free number: (800) 616-2787
Fax: (215) 717-6045
Susan Gandy, Director of Admission, University of the Arts, 320 South Broad Street, Philadelphia, PA 19102

# University of the Sciences in Philadelphia
**Philadelphia, Pennsylvania**
www.usp.edu

**CB member**
**CB code: 2663**

- Private 4-year health science and pharmacy college
- Residential campus in very large city
- 2,116 degree-seeking undergraduates: 1% part-time, 59% women, 5% African American, 35% Asian American, 2% Hispanic American, 1% international
- 778 degree-seeking graduate students
- 58% of applicants admitted
- SAT or ACT with writing required
- 62% graduate within 6 years

**General.** Founded in 1821. Regionally accredited. **Degrees:** 183 bachelor's awarded; master's, doctoral, first professional offered. **ROTC:** Army, Air Force. **Calendar:** Semester, limited summer session. **Full-time faculty:** 154 total; 78% have terminal degrees, 14% minority, 44% women. **Part-time faculty:** 101 total; 13% minority, 54% women. **Class size:** 40% < 20, 45% 20-39, 2% 40-49, 5% 50-99, 7% >100. **Special facilities:** History of pharmacy museum, advanced pharmacy studies lab, research labs, science and technology center, wet labs.

**Freshman class profile.** 3,963 applied, 2,307 admitted, 557 enrolled.

| Mid 50% test scores | | | | |
|---|---|---|---|---|
| SAT critical reading: | 530-600 | Rank in top quarter: | 80% |
| SAT math: | 560-660 | Rank in top tenth: | 41% |
| ACT composite: | 23-27 | End year in good standing: | 91% |
| GPA 3.50 or higher: | 61% | Return as sophomores: | 91% |
| GPA 3.0-3.49: | 33% | Out-of-state: | 47% |
| GPA 2.0-2.99: | 6% | Live on campus: | 89% |
| | | International: | 2% |

**Basis for selection.** High school curriculum, GPA, class rank if provided by high school, and SAT or ACT test scores most important criteria. Essay and/or letters of recommendation not required, but reviewed if provided. **Homeschooled:** Transcript of courses and grades, state high school equivalency certificate required. **Learning Disabled:** If admitted under current admission process, students will be provided with necessary additional services to assist in academic success.

**High school preparation.** 19 units required. Required and recommended units include English 4, mathematics 3-4, social studies 1, history 1, science 3-4 (laboratory 3) and academic electives 4.

**2007-2008 Annual costs.** Tuition/fees: $26,930. Tiered cost structure applies to students enrolled in 5- and 6-year programs that lead to professional degrees. Room/board: $10,524. Books/supplies: $1,020. Personal expenses: $2,700.

**2006-2007 Financial aid. Need-based:** 455 full-time freshmen applied for aid; 396 were judged to have need; 396 of these received aid. Average need met was 98%. Average scholarship/grant was $7,815; average loan $2,792. 60% of total undergraduate aid awarded as scholarships/grants, 40% as loans/jobs. **Non-need-based:** Awarded to 549 full-time undergraduates, including 109 freshmen. Scholarships awarded for academics, athletics.

**Application procedures. Admission:** No deadline. $45 fee, may be waived for applicants with need. Application may be submitted online. Admission notification on a rolling basis beginning on or about 10/1. Must reply by May 1 or within 2 week(s) if notified thereafter. **Financial aid:** Closing date 3/15. FAFSA required. Applicants notified on a rolling basis starting 1/15; must reply by 5/1 or within 2 week(s) of notification.

**Academics.** Direct-entry admission for freshman pharmacy, DPT and MPT physical therapy program, occupational therapy and physician assistant programs. Students not required to reapply to professional phase of their majors. **Special study options:** Combined bachelor's/graduate degree, double major, ESL, honors, internships, liberal arts/career combination, teacher certification program. **Credit/placement by examination:** AP, CLEP, IB, SAT, ACT, institutional tests. **Support services:** Learning center, pre-admission summer program, reduced course load, remedial instruction, study skills assistance, tutoring, writing center.

**Majors. Biology:** General, biochemistry, bioinformatics, microbiology, pharmacology/toxicology. **Business:** Marketing. **Computer sciences:** General. **Conservation:** Environmental science. **Health:** Clinical lab science, health services, physician assistant. **Parks/recreation:** Sports admin. **Physical sciences:** Chemistry. **Psychology:** General, medical.

**Most popular majors.** Biology 13%, business/marketing 7%, health sciences 77%.

**Computing on campus.** 190 workstations in dormitories, library, computer center, student center. Dormitories wired for high-speed internet access and linked to campus network. Commuter students can connect to campus network. Online course registration, online library, helpline, repair service, wireless network available.

**Student life. Freshman orientation:** Mandatory. Programs for parents and students; placement testing. **Policies:** Campus alcohol free. **Housing:** Guaranteed on-campus for freshmen. Coed dorms, fraternity/sorority housing, substance-free housing available. $175 nonrefundable deposit, deadline 5/1. Honor halls. **Activities:** Concert band, choral groups, dance, drama, literary magazine, musical theater; student government, student newspaper, professional organizations, Greek letter organizations, religious groups, honor societies, student community involvement program, ethnic/diversity groups, student chapters of scientific organizations, student publications.

**Athletics.** NAIA, NCAA. **Intercollegiate:** Baseball M, basketball, cross-country, golf, rifle, softball W, tennis, volleyball W. **Intramural:** Archery, badminton, basketball, bowling, rifle, table tennis, volleyball. **Team name:** Devils.

**Student services.** Adult student services, alcohol/substance abuse counseling, career counseling, student employment services, financial aid counseling, health services, personal counseling, placement for graduates, veterans' counselor. **Physically disabled:** Services for visually, speech, hearing impaired.

**Contact.** E-mail: admit@usp.edu
Phone: (215) 596-8810 Toll-free number: (888) 996-8747
Fax: (215) 596-8821
Louis Hegyes, Director of Admission, University of the Sciences in Philadelphia, 600 South 43rd Street, Philadelphia, PA 19104-4495

# Ursinus College
**Collegeville, Pennsylvania**
www.ursinus.edu

**CB member**
**CB code: 2931**

- Private 4-year liberal arts college
- Residential campus in small town
- 1,563 degree-seeking undergraduates: 52% women, 6% African American, 5% Asian American, 3% Hispanic American, 1% international
- 53% of applicants admitted
- Application essay required
- 75% graduate within 6 years; 34% enter graduate study

**General.** Founded in 1869. Regionally accredited. All freshmen receive laptop computers (updated at beginning of junior year). **Degrees:** 408 bachelor's awarded. **Location:** 28 miles from Philadelphia. **Calendar:** Semester. **Full-time faculty:** 119 total; 92% have terminal degrees, 9% minority, 45% women. **Part-time faculty:** 40 total; 45% have terminal degrees, 10% minority, 55% women. **Class size:** 77% < 20, 21% 20-39, less than 1% 40-49, less than 1% 50-99, less than 1% >100. **Special facilities:** Performing arts center, art museum, observatory, outdoor sculpture collection, public walking trails.

**Freshman class profile.** 5,141 applied, 2,711 admitted, 468 enrolled.

| Mid 50% test scores | | | | |
|---|---|---|---|---|
| SAT critical reading: | 550-660 | Rank in top tenth: | 40% |
| SAT math: | 560-660 | Return as sophomores: | 88% |
| SAT writing: | 550-660 | Out-of-state: | 45% |
| ACT composite: | 22-29 | Live on campus: | 98% |
| Rank in top quarter: | 74% | Fraternities: | 20% |
| | | Sororities: | 30% |

**Basis for selection.** GED not accepted. Academic achievement most important, including courses taken, grades received. Test scores also important. Motivation and activities considered. Rank in top fifth of class preferred. Alumni children and minorities receive special consideration. SAT/ACT optional for students ranking in top 10% of class, or with minimum 3.5 GPA from non-ranking school. Interview recommended.

**High school preparation.** 17 units required; 20 recommended. Required and recommended units include English 4, mathematics 3-4, social studies 1-3, science 1-3 (laboratory 1), foreign language 2-4 and academic electives 5. Science majors should have minumum of 4 units each in math and science.

**2007-2008 Annual costs.** Tuition/fees: $35,160. Room/board: $8,000. Books/supplies: $1,000. Personal expenses: $1,200.

**2007-2008 Financial aid. Need-based:** 393 full-time freshmen applied for aid; 306 were judged to have need; 306 of these received aid. Average need met was 85%. Average scholarship/grant was $19,726; average loan

$3,203. 73% of total undergraduate aid awarded as scholarships/grants, 27% as loans/jobs. **Non-need-based:** Awarded to 575 full-time undergraduates, including 190 freshmen. Scholarships awarded for academics, alumni affiliation, art, leadership, music/drama.

**Application procedures. Admission:** Closing date 2/15 (receipt date). $50 fee, may be waived for applicants with need. Application may be submitted online. Admission notification 4/1. Must reply by 4/1. Rolling notification for Early Action within 7 weeks of receipt of application. **Financial aid:** Closing date 2/15. FAFSA, CSS PROFILE required. Applicants notified by 3/15; must reply by 5/1.

**Academics.** Summer undergraduate research fellowships available. Independent Learning Experience required of all. Study abroad encouraged. All first-year students complete 2 semester overview of human thought, creativity, culture, history. **Special study options:** Accelerated study, combined bachelor's/graduate degree, double major, dual enrollment of high school students, exchange student, honors, independent study, internships, semester at sea, student-designed major, study abroad, teacher certification program, United Nations semester, Washington semester. Howard University semester. **Credit/placement by examination:** AP, CLEP, IB, institutional tests. **Support services:** Pre-admission summer program, tutoring, writing center.

**Majors. Area/ethnic studies:** American, East Asian. **Biology:** General. **Communications:** General. **Computer sciences:** Computer science. **Conservation:** Environmental studies. **English:** English lit. **Foreign languages:** Classics, French, German, Spanish. **History:** General. **Interdisciplinary:** Biological/physical sciences, neuroscience. **Math:** General. **Parks/recreation:** Health/fitness. **Philosophy/religion:** Philosophy. **Physical sciences:** Chemistry, physics. **Psychology:** General. **Social sciences:** Anthropology, economics, international relations, political science, sociology. **Visual/performing arts:** Art, art history/conservation, dance, dramatic.

**Most popular majors.** Biology 16%, English 7%, parks/recreation 8%, psychology 9%, social sciences 25%.

**Computing on campus.** PC or laptop required. 1,655 workstations in dormitories, library, computer center, student center. Dormitories wired for high-speed internet access and linked to campus network. Commuter students can connect to campus network. Online course registration, online library, helpline, repair service, student web hosting, wireless network available.

**Student life. Freshman orientation:** Mandatory. Preregistration for classes offered. Two-day session in June and 4-day session in August before start of classes. **Policies:** Students may have aquariums in dorm rooms. **Housing:** Guaranteed on-campus for all undergraduates. Coed dorms, single-sex dorms, substance-free housing available. $500 nonrefundable deposit, deadline 5/1. Wellness house, quiet halls and houses; multicultural, community service, art, physical sciences, and literature-themed dorms available. **Activities:** Bands, campus ministries, choral groups, dance, drama, film society, literary magazine, music ensembles, Model UN, musical theater, radio station, student government, student newspaper, TV station, Alternative Spring Break, Association of Latinos Motivated to Achieve, Best Buddies, College Democrats, College Republicans, Hillel, Inter-Faith Outreach, Buddhist meditation group.

**Athletics.** NCAA. **Intercollegiate:** Baseball M, basketball, cross-country, field hockey W, football (tackle) M, golf, gymnastics W, lacrosse, soccer, softball W, swimming, tennis, track and field, volleyball W, wrestling M. **Intramural:** Basketball, football (non-tackle) M, soccer, softball, squash, swimming, tennis, volleyball. **Team name:** Bears.

**Student services.** Adult student services, alcohol/substance abuse counseling, campus ministries, career counseling, student employment services, financial aid counseling, health services, minority student services, personal counseling, placement for graduates. **Physically disabled:** Services for visually, speech, hearing impaired.

**Contact.** E-mail: admissions@ursinus.edu
Phone: (610) 409-3200 Fax: (610) 409-3662
Robert McCullough, Dean of Admission, Ursinus College, PO Box 1000, Collegeville, PA 19426-1000

---

## Valley Forge Christian College
**Phoenixville, Pennsylvania**
www.vfcc.edu                                    CB code: 2579

- Private 4-year liberal arts college affiliated with Assemblies of God
- Residential campus in large town
- 946 degree-seeking undergraduates: 17% part-time, 53% women, 7% African American, 2% Asian American, 8% Hispanic American
- 4 degree-seeking graduate students

---

- 72% of applicants admitted
- SAT or ACT with writing, application essay required
- 45% graduate within 6 years

**General.** Founded in 1938. Regionally accredited. **Degrees:** 182 bachelor's, 4 associate awarded; master's offered. **Location:** 25 miles from Philadelphia. **Calendar:** Semester, limited summer session. **Full-time faculty:** 30 total; 50% have terminal degrees, 7% minority, 37% women. **Part-time faculty:** 35 total; 20% have terminal degrees, 3% minority, 29% women.

**Freshman class profile.** 368 applied, 265 admitted, 166 enrolled.

**End year in good standing:** 100%    **Return as sophomores:** 79%

**Basis for selection.** School achievement record, pastor recommendation, written essay, test scores important. English, math, Bible study skills tests required for all; music, computer tests required for some. Interview recommended. **Homeschooled:** Statement describing homeschool structure and mission required. **Learning Disabled:** Academic recommendation from counselor IEP or other.

**High school preparation.** 16 units recommended. Recommended units include English 4, mathematics 2, social studies 4, science 4 and foreign language 2.

**2008-2009 Annual costs.** Tuition/fees (projected): $12,990. Room/board: $6,570. Books/supplies: $950. Personal expenses: $1,776.

**2007-2008 Financial aid. Need-based:** Average need met was 49%. Average scholarship/grant was $5,894; average loan $3,288. 41% of total undergraduate aid awarded as scholarships/grants, 59% as loans/jobs. **Non-need-based:** Scholarships awarded for academics, leadership, music/drama, religious affiliation, state residency.

**Application procedures. Admission:** Priority date 5/1; deadline 8/1 (receipt date). $25 fee, may be waived for applicants with need. Application may be submitted online. Admission notification 8/15. Admission notification on a rolling basis. **Financial aid:** Priority date 5/1; no closing date. FAFSA required. Applicants notified on a rolling basis starting 3/15; must reply within 3 week(s) of notification.

**Academics. Special study options:** Accelerated study, combined bachelor's/graduate degree, distance learning, dual enrollment of high school students, ESL, independent study, internships, liberal arts/career combination, study abroad, teacher certification program, weekend college. **Credit/placement by examination:** AP, CLEP, SAT, ACT, institutional tests. 30 credit hours maximum toward bachelor's degree. **Support services:** Learning center, pre-admission summer program, reduced course load, remedial instruction, study skills assistance, tutoring.

**Majors. Business:** Business admin. **Education:** Early childhood, elementary, music. **Public administration:** Social work. **Theology:** Bible, missionary, pastoral counseling, religious ed, sacred music, theology. **Visual/performing arts:** Music performance.

**Most popular majors.** Business/marketing 6%, education 21%, psychology 15%, theological studies 56%.

**Computing on campus.** PC or laptop required. 54 workstations in library, computer center. Dormitories wired for high-speed internet access and linked to campus network. Commuter students can connect to campus network. Online course registration, online library, helpline, wireless network available.

**Student life. Freshman orientation:** Mandatory, $55 fee. Preregistration for classes offered. Held weekend prior to beginning of classes. **Policies:** Religious observance required. **Housing:** Guaranteed on-campus for all undergraduates. Single-sex dorms, apartments, substance-free housing available. $100 nonrefundable deposit. **Activities:** Bands, campus ministries, choral groups, drama, music ensembles, student government.

**Athletics.** NCCAA. **Intercollegiate:** Baseball M, basketball, soccer, volleyball W. **Intramural:** Basketball, bowling, football (non-tackle), soccer, softball. **Team name:** Patriots.

**Student services.** Campus ministries, career counseling, student employment services, financial aid counseling, health services, personal counseling, placement for graduates, veterans' counselor.

**Contact.** E-mail: admission@vfcc.edu
Phone: (610) 935-0450 Toll-free number: (800) 432-8322
Fax: (610) 935-9353
William Chenco, Director of Admissions, Valley Forge Christian College, 1401 Charlestown Road, Phoenixville, PA 19460

## Villanova University
**Villanova, Pennsylvania**

www.villanova.edu

CB member

CB code: 2959

- Private 4-year university affiliated with Roman Catholic Church
- Residential campus in small town
- 6,949 degree-seeking undergraduates: 4% part-time, 51% women, 4% African American, 6% Asian American, 6% Hispanic American, 2% international
- 2,925 degree-seeking graduate students
- 42% of applicants admitted
- SAT or ACT with writing, application essay required
- 88% graduate within 6 years; 23% enter graduate study

**General.** Founded in 1842. Regionally accredited. **Degrees:** 1,694 bachelor's, 7 associate awarded; master's, doctoral, first professional offered. **ROTC:** Army, Naval, Air Force. **Location:** 12 miles from Philadelphia. **Calendar:** Semester, extensive summer session. **Full-time faculty:** 570 total; 89% have terminal degrees, 13% minority, 36% women. **Part-time faculty:** 362 total; 38% have terminal degrees, 5% minority, 43% women. **Class size:** 42% < 20, 52% 20-39, 1% 40-49, 4% 50-99, less than 1% >100. **Special facilities:** Astronomy and astrophysics observatories, electron microscope, research with NASA, arboretum, structural engineering teaching and research laboratory.

**Freshman class profile.** 13,760 applied, 5,718 admitted, 1,604 enrolled.

| Mid 50% test scores | | | |
|---|---|---|---|
| SAT critical reading: | 580-680 | Rank in top quarter: | 96% |
| SAT math: | 610-700 | Rank in top tenth: | 54% |
| SAT writing: | 590-680 | End year in good standing: | 98% |
| ACT composite: | 27-31 | Return as sophomores: | 94% |
| GPA 3.50 or higher: | 81% | Out-of-state: | 79% |
| GPA 3.0-3.49: | 18% | Live on campus: | 98% |
| GPA 2.0-2.99: | 1% | International: | 3% |

**Basis for selection.** High school record, class rank, standardized test scores, counselor recommendation, essay, extracurricular activities considered. Interview required for finalists of health affiliation programs and Presidential Scholarship consideration. **Homeschooled:** Objective 3rd party evaluation (state high school association, for example), including syllabi, required.

**High school preparation.** 22 units required; 25 recommended. Required and recommended units include English 4, mathematics 4, science 4 (laboratory 2-3), foreign language 2-4 and academic electives 2. 4 social studies and/or history required. Total units required varies by academic college.

**2007-2008 Annual costs.** Tuition/fees: $34,620. Full-time tuition includes laptop for all freshmen. Room/board: $9,810. Books/supplies: $950. Personal expenses: $950.

**2007-2008 Financial aid. Need-based:** 1,043 full-time freshmen applied for aid; 767 were judged to have need; 763 of these received aid. Average need met was 84%. Average scholarship/grant was $20,714; average loan $4,283. 63% of total undergraduate aid awarded as scholarships/grants, 37% as loans/jobs. **Non-need-based:** Awarded to 1,304 full-time undergraduates, including 304 freshmen. Scholarships awarded for academics, alumni affiliation, athletics, leadership, minority status, religious affiliation, ROTC.

**Application procedures. Admission:** Priority date 12/15; deadline 1/7 (receipt date). $75 fee, may be waived for applicants with need. Application may be submitted online. Admission notification 4/1. Must reply by 5/1. November 1 priority application date for scholarship consideration. Commuting students and nursing majors notified of decisions on a rolling basis beginning January 15. **Financial aid:** Closing date 2/7. FAFSA, institutional form required. Applicants notified by 4/1; must reply by 5/1 or within 2 week(s) of notification.

**Academics. Special study options:** Accelerated study, combined bachelor's/graduate degree, cooperative education, cross-registration, distance learning, double major, dual enrollment of high school students, ESL, exchange student, honors, independent study, internships, study abroad, teacher certification program, Washington semester. Cooperative certification programs in elementary education with Rosemont College. **Credit/placement by examination:** AP, CLEP, IB, institutional tests. 30 credit hours maximum toward bachelor's degree. Deans make decisions regarding prior work and life experiences on individual basis. **Support services:** Reduced course load, study skills assistance, tutoring, writing center.

**Majors. Biology:** General. **Business:** Accounting, business admin, finance, management information systems, managerial economics, marketing. **Communications:** General. **Computer sciences:** General, information systems. **Education:** Elementary, secondary. **Engineering:** Chemical, civil, computer, electrical, mechanical. **English:** English lit. **Foreign languages:** Classics, French, German, Italian, Spanish. **Health:** Nursing (RN), predental, premedicine. **History:** General. **Interdisciplinary:** Biological/physical sciences. **Liberal arts:** Arts/sciences. **Math:** General. **Philosophy/religion:** Philosophy, religion. **Physical sciences:** Astronomy, astrophysics, chemistry, physics. **Protective services:** Law enforcement admin. **Psychology:** General. **Public administration:** Human services. **Social sciences:** Economics, geography, political science, sociology. **Visual/performing arts:** Art history/conservation.

**Most popular majors.** Business/marketing 35%, communications/journalism 7%, engineering/engineering technologies 10%, health sciences 9%, social sciences 11%.

**Computing on campus.** PC or laptop required. 2,530 workstations in dormitories, library, computer center, student center. Dormitories wired for high-speed internet access and linked to campus network. Commuter students can connect to campus network. Online course registration, online library, helpline, repair service, student web hosting, wireless network available.

**Student life. Freshman orientation:** Mandatory, $125 fee. 4-day on-campus program prior to start of fall term. **Housing:** Guaranteed on-campus for freshmen. Coed dorms, single-sex dorms, apartments, substance-free housing available. $700 nonrefundable deposit, deadline 5/1. On-campus housing available for transfer students on space-available basis. **Activities:** Bands, campus ministries, choral groups, dance, drama, international student organizations, literary magazine, music ensembles, musical theater, radio station, student government, student newspaper, symphony orchestra, TV station, Special Olympics, Amnesty International, Villanovans for Life, Black Cultural Society, Big Brother/Sister, Committee for the Homeless, Project Sunshine, Habitat for Humanity, Blue Key Society.

**Athletics.** NCAA. **Intercollegiate:** Baseball M, basketball, bowling W, cheerleading, cross-country, diving, field hockey W, football (tackle) M, golf M, lacrosse, rowing (crew) W, soccer, softball W, swimming, tennis, track and field, volleyball W, water polo W. **Intramural:** Basketball, cross-country, field hockey W, football (non-tackle), skiing, soccer, softball, tennis, volleyball. **Team name:** Wildcats.

**Student services.** Adult student services, alcohol/substance abuse counseling, campus ministries, career counseling, services for economically disadvantaged, student employment services, financial aid counseling, health services, minority student services, personal counseling, placement for graduates. **Physically disabled:** Services for visually, hearing impaired.

**Contact.** E-mail: gotovu@villanova.edu
Phone: (610) 519-4000 Fax: (610) 519-6450
Michael Gaynor, Director of University Admission, Villanova University, 800 Lancaster Avenue, Villanova, PA 19085-1672

## Washington & Jefferson College
**Washington, Pennsylvania**

www.washjeff.edu

CB member

CB code: 2967

- Private 4-year liberal arts college
- Residential campus in large town
- 1,514 degree-seeking undergraduates: 1% part-time, 47% women, 3% African American, 1% Asian American, 1% Hispanic American
- 34% of applicants admitted
- SAT or ACT (ACT writing optional), application essay required
- 71% graduate within 6 years; 35% enter graduate study

**General.** Founded in 1781. Regionally accredited. **Degrees:** 290 bachelor's awarded. **ROTC:** Army, Air Force. **Location:** 27 miles from Pittsburgh. **Calendar:** 4-1-4, limited summer session. **Full-time faculty:** 109 total; 94% have terminal degrees, 9% minority, 37% women. **Part-time faculty:** 45 total; 36% have terminal degrees, 11% minority, 51% women. **Class size:** 72% < 20, 27% 20-39, less than 1% 40-49, less than 1% 50-99. **Special facilities:** Microplate reader, cell culture labs, isolator lab, x-ray diffraction unit, neuropsychology lab, atomic absorption unit, nuclear magnetic resonance (NMR) lab, refrigerated centrifuge, global learning unit, language lab, spectrometers, laser scanning confocal microscope facility.

**Freshman class profile.** 7,377 applied, 2,529 admitted, 407 enrolled.

| Mid 50% test scores | | | |
|---|---|---|---|
| SAT critical reading: | 520-620 | Rank in top quarter: | 76% |
| SAT math: | 530-640 | Rank in top tenth: | 37% |
| ACT composite: | 23-27 | End year in good standing: | 91% |
| GPA 3.50 or higher: | 53% | Return as sophomores: | 84% |
| GPA 3.0-3.49: | 34% | Out-of-state: | 23% |
| GPA 2.0-2.99: | 13% | Live on campus: | 94% |

**Basis for selection.** Entire high school record including difficulty of schedule, GPA, class rank, extracurricular activities, essay, letters of recommendation important. **Homeschooled:** Letter of recommendation (nonparent) required.

**High school preparation.** 15 units required. Required units include English 3, mathematics 3, history 1, foreign language 2 and academic electives 6. Six or more academic elective courses from English, math, foreign language, history, and social or natural history required.

**2007-2008 Annual costs.** Tuition/fees: $29,532. Room/board: $8,030. Books/supplies: $800. Personal expenses: $700.

**2007-2008 Financial aid. Need-based:** 366 full-time freshmen applied for aid; 313 were judged to have need; 313 of these received aid. Average need met was 82%. Average scholarship/grant was $7,557; average loan $3,864. 68% of total undergraduate aid awarded as scholarships/grants, 32% as loans/jobs. **Non-need-based:** Awarded to 1,249 full-time undergraduates, including 374 freshmen. Scholarships awarded for academics, alumni affiliation.

**Application procedures. Admission:** Priority date 1/15; deadline 3/1 (postmark date). $25 fee, may be waived for applicants with need. Application may be submitted online. Admission notification on a rolling basis beginning on or about 10/1. Must reply by May 1 or within 2 week(s) if notified thereafter. **Financial aid:** Priority date 3/1; no closing date. FAFSA required. Applicants notified on a rolling basis starting 3/1.

**Academics. Special study options:** Accelerated study, combined bachelor's/graduate degree, double major, dual enrollment of high school students, honors, independent study, internships, student-designed major, study abroad, teacher certification program, Washington semester. Advanced placement credit. **Credit/placement by examination:** AP, CLEP, IB, institutional tests. 68 credit hours maximum toward bachelor's degree. **Support services:** Learning center, reduced course load, study skills assistance, tutoring.

**Majors. Biology:** General, biochemistry, biophysics, cellular/anatomical. **Business:** General, accounting, international. **Computer sciences:** Information technology. **Conservation:** Environmental studies. **Education:** General, art. **English:** English lit. **Foreign languages:** French, German, Spanish. **History:** General. **Math:** General. **Philosophy/religion:** Philosophy. **Physical sciences:** Chemistry, physics. **Psychology:** General. **Social sciences:** Economics, political science, sociology. **Visual/performing arts:** Art, theater history.

**Most popular majors.** Biology 14%, business/marketing 24%, English 11%, psychology 12%, social sciences 11%.

**Computing on campus.** 450 workstations in library, computer center. Dormitories wired for high-speed internet access and linked to campus network. Commuter students can connect to campus network. Online course registration, online library, helpline, repair service, student web hosting, wireless network available.

**Student life. Freshman orientation:** Mandatory. Preregistration for classes offered. Includes placement tests. **Policies:** All students required to live in campus housing unless granted written approval. Students not permitted to smoke in rooms, hallways, or lounges. **Housing:** Guaranteed on-campus for all undergraduates. Coed dorms, single-sex dorms, special housing for disabled, fraternity/sorority housing, substance-free housing available. Pets allowed in dorm rooms. On-campus suites available. **Activities:** Bands, campus ministries, choral groups, dance, drama, film society, international student organizations, literary magazine, music ensembles, musical theater, radio station, student government, student newspaper, symphony orchestra, Newman Club, Hillel Society, Young Republicans, College Democrats, liberal student union, black student union, Alpha Phi Omega, Get Involved in Volunteer Experiences.

**Athletics.** NCAA. **Intercollegiate:** Baseball M, basketball, cheerleading, cross-country, diving, field hockey W, football (tackle) M, golf, lacrosse, soccer, softball W, swimming, tennis, track and field, volleyball W, water polo, wrestling M. **Intramural:** Basketball, bowling, cross-country, football (non-tackle), racquetball, soccer, softball, table tennis, tennis, volleyball. **Team name:** Presidents.

**Student services.** Adult student services, alcohol/substance abuse counseling, campus ministries, career counseling, student employment services, financial aid counseling, health services, minority student services, personal counseling, placement for graduates.

**Contact.** E-mail: admission@washjeff.edu
Phone: (724) 223-6025 Toll-free number: (888) 926-3529
Fax: (724) 223-6534
Alton Newell, Vice President for Enrollment, Washington & Jefferson College, 60 South Lincoln Street, Washington, PA 15301

---

## Waynesburg University
**Waynesburg, Pennsylvania**  **CB member**
www.waynesburg.edu  **CB code: 2969**

- Private 4-year liberal arts college affiliated with Presbyterian Church (USA)
- Residential campus in small town
- 1,614 degree-seeking undergraduates: 5% part-time, 62% women, 2% African American, 1% Hispanic American
- 662 degree-seeking graduate students
- 66% of applicants admitted
- SAT or ACT with writing required
- 52% graduate within 6 years; 16% enter graduate study

**General.** Founded in 1849. Regionally accredited. Member of the Council for Christian Colleges and Universities. **Degrees:** 355 bachelor's, 7 associate awarded; master's, doctoral offered. **ROTC:** Army. **Location:** 50 miles from Pittsburgh. **Calendar:** Semester, limited summer session. **Full-time faculty:** 65 total; 68% have terminal degrees, 3% minority, 46% women. **Part-time faculty:** 106 total; 18% have terminal degrees, 53% women. **Class size:** 62% < 20, 35% 20-39, 3% 40-49, less than 1% 50-99. **Special facilities:** Geological museum, historical museum, constutional studies and moral leadership center, research and economic development center, service leadership center.

**Freshman class profile.** 1,983 applied, 1,302 admitted, 403 enrolled.

| | | | |
|---|---|---|---|
| GPA 3.50 or higher: | 49% | Rank in top tenth: | 17% |
| GPA 3.0-3.49: | 38% | Return as sophomores: | 74% |
| GPA 2.0-2.99: | 13% | Out-of-state: | 18% |
| Rank in top quarter: | 43% | Live on campus: | 86% |

**Basis for selection.** High school classes taken, grades, test scores, activities, community activities, interview, and recommendations considered. Essay, interview recommended. **Homeschooled:** Statement describing homeschool structure and mission, transcript of courses and grades, state high school equivalency certificate required. College should be apprised if homeschooled applicant enrolled in program approved by state's department of education.

**High school preparation.** 16 units required. Required and recommended units include English 4, mathematics 3, social studies 2, science 2-3, foreign language 2 and academic electives 5.

**2007-2008 Annual costs.** Tuition/fees: $16,420. Room/board: $6,700. Books/supplies: $1,100. Personal expenses: $230.

**2007-2008 Financial aid. Need-based:** Average need met was 89%. Average scholarship/grant was $11,145; average loan $3,785. 66% of total undergraduate aid awarded as scholarships/grants, 34% as loans/jobs. **Non-need-based:** Scholarships awarded for academics, alumni affiliation, job skills, leadership, religious affiliation, state residency.

**Application procedures. Admission:** No deadline. $20 fee, may be waived for applicants with need. Application may be submitted online. Admission notification on a rolling basis. Rolling date as specified in deposit letter. **Financial aid:** Priority date 3/15; no closing date. FAFSA required. Applicants notified on a rolling basis starting 2/15; must reply within 2 week(s) of notification.

**Academics.** Nursing majors must complete 126 credit hours for bachelor of science degree. **Special study options:** Accelerated study, combined bachelor's/graduate degree, distance learning, double major, dual enrollment of high school students, honors, independent study, internships, liberal arts/career combination, study abroad, teacher certification program, Washington semester. 3-2 program in engineering with Case Western Reserve University, Penn State University, Washington University; 3-1 program in marine biology with Florida Institute of Technology; 3-3 law program with Duquesne University. **Credit/placement by examination:** AP, CLEP, IB, SAT, ACT, institutional tests. 15 credit hours maximum toward bachelor's degree. **Support services:** Learning center, reduced course load, study skills assistance, tutoring, writing center.

**Majors. Biology:** General, environmental, marine. **Business:** General, accounting, business admin, finance, international, international marketing. **Communications:** General, advertising, broadcast journalism, digital media, journalism, public relations. **Computer sciences:** General, computer science, information technology, networking. **Education:** Art, biology, chemistry, elementary, English, history, mathematics, science, secondary, social studies, special. **English:** British lit, creative writing, English lit. **Family/consumer sciences:** Family studies. **Health:** Athletic training, nursing (RN), predental, premedicine, preveterinary. **History:** General. **Legal studies:** Prelaw. **Math:** General. **Parks/recreation:** Exercise sciences, sports admin. **Philosophy/religion:** Religion. **Physical sciences:** Chemistry. **Protective services:** Forensics, law enforcement admin. **Psychology:** General. **Public administration:** Human services. **Social sciences:** General, political science, sociology. **Theology:** Theology. **Visual/performing arts:** Art, arts management, commercial/advertising art, music management, theater arts management. **Other:** Forensic accounting.

**Most popular majors.** Business/marketing 18%, communications/journalism 7%, education 6%, health sciences 33%, public administration/social services 12%.

**Computing on campus.** 160 workstations in library, computer center, student center. Dormitories wired for high-speed internet access and linked to campus network. Commuter students can connect to campus network. Online course registration, online library, helpline, wireless network available.

**Student life. Freshman orientation:** Mandatory. Preregistration for classes offered. One-day summer program for parents and students; 2-day program prior to start of classes. **Policies:** No alcohol or drugs permitted on campus. **Housing:** Guaranteed on-campus for all undergraduates. Coed dorms, single-sex dorms, substance-free housing available. $150 partly refundable deposit. **Activities:** Bands, choral groups, dance, drama, international student organizations, literary magazine, music ensembles, musical theater, radio station, student government, student newspaper, TV station, Fellowship of Christian Athletes, Newman Club, black student union, Waynesburg Christian Fellowship, Bonner Scholars (service group), Alpha Phi Omega, Habitat for Humanity, leadership program.

**Athletics. NCAA. Intercollegiate:** Baseball M, basketball, cross-country, football (tackle) M, golf, lacrosse W, soccer, softball W, tennis, track and field, volleyball W, wrestling M. **Intramural:** Basketball, bowling, football (non-tackle), racquetball, softball, table tennis, volleyball W. **Team name:** Yellow Jackets.

**Student services.** Adult student services, campus ministries, career counseling, student employment services, financial aid counseling, health services, minority student services, personal counseling, placement for graduates.

**Contact.** E-mail: admissions@waynesburg.edu
Phone: (724) 852-3248 Toll-free number: (800) 225-7393
Fax: (724) 627-8124
Sarah Szwinger, Director of Admissions, Waynesburg University, 51 West College Street, Waynessburg, PA 15370-1222

---

## West Chester University of Pennsylvania

**West Chester, Pennsylvania** CB member
www.wcupa.edu CB code: 2659

- Public 4-year university
- Commuter campus in large town
- 10,716 degree-seeking undergraduates: 8% part-time, 61% women, 9% African American, 2% Asian American, 3% Hispanic American
- 1,551 degree-seeking graduate students
- 48% of applicants admitted
- SAT or ACT with writing, application essay required
- 64% graduate within 6 years

**General.** Founded in 1871. Regionally accredited. **Degrees:** 2,160 bachelor's awarded; master's offered. **ROTC:** Army, Air Force. **Location:** 23 miles from Philadelphia. **Calendar:** Semester, extensive summer session. **Full-time faculty:** 572 total; 14% minority, 48% women. **Part-time faculty:** 257 total; 5% minority, 59% women. **Special facilities:** Herbarium, 151-acre natural area for environmental studies, planetarium, speech and hearing clinic, autism clinic, center for government and community affairs, mineral museum.

**Freshman class profile.** 12,237 applied, 5,834 admitted, 1,964 enrolled.

| Mid 50% test scores | | | |
|---|---|---|---|
| SAT critical reading: | 480-570 | Rank in top quarter: | 38% |
| SAT math: | 490-580 | Rank in top tenth: | 9% |
| SAT writing: | 480-570 | End year in good standing: | 90% |
| GPA 3.50 or higher: | 40% | Return as sophomores: | 86% |
| GPA 3.0-3.49: | 40% | Out-of-state: | 15% |
| GPA 2.0-2.99: | 19% | Live on campus: | 91% |

**Basis for selection.** College preparatory curriculum in high school, standardized test scores, and personal statement required. Specific course prerequisites depend on major selection. Additional documentation is required of candidates for the summer academic development program. Interview required for athletic training, premedical, and pharmaceutical product development programs. Audition required for music. **Homeschooled:** Students must have work certified by PA Homeschoolers' Association or their high school.

**High school preparation.** 16 units required; 25 recommended. Required and recommended units include English 4, mathematics 3-4, social studies 2, history 2, science 2-3 (laboratory 1-2), foreign language 2, computer science 1, visual/performing arts 1 and academic electives 1-2.

**2007-2008 Annual costs.** Tuition/fees: $6,676; $14,443 out-of-state. Room/board: $6,590. Books/supplies: $1,200. Personal expenses: $1,974.

**2006-2007 Financial aid. Need-based:** 1,511 full-time freshmen applied for aid; 1,044 were judged to have need; 994 of these received aid. Average need met was 54%. Average scholarship/grant was $4,795; average loan $2,691. 33% of total undergraduate aid awarded as scholarships/grants, 67% as loans/jobs. **Non-need-based:** Awarded to 459 full-time undergraduates, including 140 freshmen.

**Application procedures. Admission:** Priority date 1/1; no deadline. $35 fee, may be waived for applicants with need. Application may be submitted online. Admission notification on a rolling basis beginning on or about 10/1. Must reply by May 1 or within 4 week(s) if notified thereafter. **Financial aid:** Priority date 3/1; no closing date. FAFSA required. Must reply within 4 week(s) of notification.

**Academics. Special study options:** Cooperative education, cross-registration, distance learning, double major, dual enrollment of high school students, ESL, exchange student, honors, independent study, internships, liberal arts/career combination, student-designed major, study abroad, teacher certification program, Washington semester. **Credit/placement by examination:** AP, CLEP, IB, SAT, institutional tests. 30 credit hours maximum toward bachelor's degree. **Support services:** Learning center, preadmission summer program, reduced course load, remedial instruction, study skills assistance, tutoring, writing center.

**Majors. Area/ethnic studies:** American, women's. **Biology:** General, biochemistry. **Business:** General, accounting, business admin, finance, managerial economics, sales/distribution. **Communications:** General. **Computer sciences:** General. **Education:** Early childhood, elementary, special. **English:** English lit, speech/rhetoric. **Foreign languages:** French, German, Latin, Russian, Spanish. **Health:** Athletic training, audiology/speech pathology, dietetics, health care admin, nursing (RN), premedicine. **History:** General. **Liberal arts:** Arts/sciences. **Math:** General. **Parks/recreation:** Health/fitness. **Philosophy/religion:** Philosophy. **Physical sciences:** Analytical chemistry, chemistry, geology, physics. **Protective services:** Criminal justice. **Psychology:** General. **Public administration:** Social work. **Social sciences:** Anthropology, geography, political science, sociology. **Visual/performing arts:** Art, dramatic, music performance, studio arts.

**Most popular majors.** Business/marketing 15%, education 17%, English 9%, health sciences 12%, liberal arts 9%, parks/recreation 6%, visual/performing arts 7%.

**Computing on campus.** 1,100 workstations in dormitories, library, computer center, student center. Dormitories wired for high-speed internet access and linked to campus network. Commuter students can connect to campus network. Helpline, wireless network available.

**Student life. Freshman orientation:** Mandatory, $135 fee. Preregistration for classes offered. One-day program in late June/early July followed by 3-day program prior to start of classes. **Policies:** Code of conduct applicable on and off campus. **Housing:** Coed dorms, single-sex dorms, special housing for disabled, apartments, fraternity/sorority housing, substance-free housing available. $100 deposit, deadline 5/1. **Activities:** Bands, campus ministries, choral groups, dance, drama, international student organizations, literary magazine, music ensembles, musical theater, opera, radio station, student government, student newspaper, symphony orchestra, TV station, lesbian, gay, bisexual, and transgender association; Hillel; Newman Club; Crusade for Christ; Black Student Union; Latino American student organization; Asian American organization.

**Athletics.** NCAA. **Intercollegiate:** Baseball M, basketball, cheerleading M, cross-country, diving, field hockey W, football (tackle) M, golf, gymnastics W, lacrosse W, rugby W, soccer, softball W, swimming, tennis, track and field, volleyball W. **Intramural:** Basketball, field hockey, football (nontackle), soccer, softball, tennis, volleyball. **Team name:** Rams.

**Student services.** Adult student services, alcohol/substance abuse counseling, campus ministries, career counseling, services for economically disadvantaged, student employment services, financial aid counseling, health services, legal services, minority student services, on-campus daycare, personal counseling, placement for graduates, women's services. **Physically disabled:** Services for visually, speech, hearing impaired. **Learning disabled:** Comprehensive services available.

**Contact.** E-mail: ugadmiss@wcupa.edu
Phone: (610) 436-3411 Toll-free number: (877) 315-2165
Fax: (610) 436-2907
Marsha Haug, Assistant Vice President for Admissions and Enrollment Services, West Chester University of Pennsylvania, Messikomer Hall, West Chester, PA 19383

---

## Westminster College
**New Wilmington, Pennsylvania**     **CB member**
**www.westminster.edu**     **CB code: 2975**

- Private 4-year liberal arts college affiliated with Presbyterian Church (USA)
- Residential campus in small town
- 1,308 degree-seeking undergraduates
- 71% of applicants admitted
- Application essay required

**General.** Founded in 1852. Regionally accredited. General studies curriculum with a freshman common experience. Semester at Oxford. **Degrees:** 299 bachelor's awarded; master's offered. **ROTC:** Army. **Location:** 60 miles from Pittsburgh; 17 miles from Youngstown, Ohio. **Calendar:** Semester, limited summer session. **Full-time faculty:** 103 total. **Part-time faculty:** 51 total. **Class size:** 63% < 20, 36% 20-39, less than 1% 40-49, less than 1% 50-99. **Special facilities:** Observatory, environmental outdoor laboratory, planetarium, electron microscopes, radar defractor.

**Freshman class profile.** 1,368 applied, 968 admitted, 311 enrolled.

| Mid 50% test scores | | | |
|---|---|---|---|
| SAT critical reading: | 470-580 | GPA 2.0-2.99: | 19% |
| SAT math: | 480-530 | Rank in top quarter: | 59% |
| SAT writing: | 470-570 | Rank in top tenth: | 26% |
| ACT composite: | 20-25 | Out-of-state: | 19% |
| GPA 3.50 or higher: | 49% | Live on campus: | 97% |
| GPA 3.0-3.49: | 32% | Fraternities: | 33% |
| | | Sororities: | 35% |

**Basis for selection.** Class rank most important. Test scores also important. SAT or ACT recommended. Interview recommended for all; audition recommended for music; portfolio recommended for art.

**High school preparation.** 16 units required. Required units include English 4, mathematics 3, social studies 2, history 1, science 2 (laboratory 2), foreign language 2 and academic electives 3.

**2008-2009 Annual costs.** Tuition/fees: $28,100. Room/board: $8,100. Books/supplies: $900. Personal expenses: $685.

**2007-2008 Financial aid. Need-based:** 69% of total undergraduate aid awarded as scholarships/grants, 31% as loans/jobs. **Non-need-based:** Scholarships awarded for academics, athletics.

**Application procedures. Admission:** Closing date 5/1. $35 fee, may be waived for applicants with need. Admission notification on a rolling basis beginning on or about 11/1. Must reply by May 1 or within 2 week(s) if notified thereafter. **Financial aid:** Closing date 5/1. FAFSA, institutional form required. Applicants notified on a rolling basis starting 11/1; must reply by 5/1 or within 3 week(s) of notification.

**Academics. Special study options:** Double major, exchange student, honors, independent study, internships, liberal arts/career combination, semester at sea, student-designed major, study abroad, teacher certification program, Washington semester. 3-2 engineering programs with Case Western Reserve University (OH), Penn State, Washington University (MO), 3-2 law program with Duquesne University. **Credit/placement by examination:** AP, CLEP, institutional tests. **Support services:** Learning center, reduced course load, tutoring.

**Majors. Biology:** General, biochemistry, biophysics, ecology, molecular. **Business:** Accounting, business admin, finance, international, international

---

finance, management science, managerial economics, organizational behavior. **Communications:** Broadcast journalism, public relations. **Computer sciences:** General, computer science, programming. **Education:** General, elementary, English, foreign languages, middle, multi-level teacher, secondary, social studies. **Engineering:** General. **English:** American lit, British lit, creative writing, English lit. **Foreign languages:** General, classics, French, German, Latin, Spanish. **Health:** Predental, premedicine, prepharmacy, preveterinary. **History:** General. **Interdisciplinary:** Biopsychology, math/computer science. **Legal studies:** Prelaw. **Math:** General. **Philosophy/religion:** Philosophy, religion. **Physical sciences:** Chemistry, physics. **Protective services:** Criminal justice. **Psychology:** General. **Public administration:** Social work. **Social sciences:** Economics, international relations, political science, sociology. **Theology:** Religious ed. **Visual/performing arts:** Art, dramatic, music performance, music theory/composition, piano/organ, studio arts, voice/opera.

**Computing on campus.** 160 workstations in library, computer center. Dormitories linked to campus network. Commuter students can connect to campus network. Helpline available.

**Student life. Freshman orientation:** Mandatory, $105 fee. 4-day general social and academic orientation. **Housing:** Guaranteed on-campus for freshmen. Coed dorms, single-sex dorms, special housing for disabled, fraternity/sorority housing available. **Activities:** Bands, campus ministries, choral groups, dance, drama, film society, literary magazine, music ensembles, musical theater, radio station, student government, student newspaper, symphony orchestra, TV station, Fellowship of Christian Athletes, mock convention, service organizations, social awareness and action groups, Students in Action Who Value the Environment, Habitat for Humanity, Alpha Phi Omega.

**Athletics.** NCAA. **Intercollegiate:** Baseball M, basketball, cross-country, football (tackle) M, golf, soccer, softball W, swimming, tennis, track and field, volleyball W. **Intramural:** Archery, badminton, basketball, equestrian, racquetball, rugby M, softball, track and field W, volleyball. **Team name:** Titans.

**Student services.** Adult student services, career counseling, student employment services, health services, personal counseling, placement for graduates.

**Contact.** E-mail: admis@westminster.edu
Phone: (724) 946-7100 Fax: (724) 946-7171
Bradley Tokar, Dean of Admissions, Westminster College, Admissions, Westminster College, New Wilmington, PA 16172-0001

---

## Widener University
**Chester, Pennsylvania**     **CB member**
**www.widener.edu**     **CB code: 2642**

- Private 4-year university
- Residential campus in large town
- 3,213 degree-seeking undergraduates: 18% part-time, 57% women, 13% African American, 3% Asian American, 3% Hispanic American, 2% international
- 2,919 degree-seeking graduate students
- 66% of applicants admitted
- SAT or ACT (ACT writing optional) required
- 52% graduate within 6 years

**General.** Founded in 1821. Regionally accredited. **Degrees:** 576 bachelor's, 11 associate awarded; master's, doctoral, first professional offered. **ROTC:** Army, Naval, Air Force. **Location:** 10 miles from Philadelphia, 10 miles from Wilmington, Delaware. **Calendar:** Semester, limited summer session. **Full-time faculty:** 309 total; 89% have terminal degrees, 11% minority, 50% women. **Part-time faculty:** 348 total; 53% have terminal degrees, 11% minority, 42% women. **Class size:** 61% < 20, 38% 20-39, less than 1% 40-49, less than 1% 50-99. **Special facilities:** Astronomical observatory, rock climbing wall, restaurant lab, executive seminar facility, child development center, recording studio, education lab, commercial graphics lab, physical therapy lab.

**Freshman class profile.** 4,394 applied, 2,913 admitted, 800 enrolled.

| Mid 50% test scores | | | |
|---|---|---|---|
| | | Rank in top tenth: | 9% |
| SAT critical reading: | 440-530 | Return as sophomores: | 76% |
| SAT math: | 460-560 | Out-of-state: | 44% |
| GPA 3.50 or higher: | 41% | Live on campus: | 85% |
| GPA 3.0-3.49: | 32% | International: | 2% |
| GPA 2.0-2.99: | 27% | Fraternities: | 4% |
| Rank in top quarter: | 34% | Sororities: | 3% |

**Basis for selection.** Strength of curriculum, GPA, standardized test scores, class rank most important; recommendations, strength of character important. Interview recommended. **Homeschooled:** Transcript of courses and grades required. Curriculum validation and interview with director of admissions required.

**High school preparation.** 18 units required; 23 recommended. Required and recommended units include English 4, mathematics 3-4, social studies 3-4, science 3-4 (laboratory 2), foreign language 2 and academic electives 3.

**2007-2008 Annual costs.** Tuition/fees: $28,630. $950 additional fee for engineering students; $200 additional fee for junior/senior nursing students. Room/board: $10,240. Books/supplies: $990. Personal expenses: $1,170.

**2007-2008 Financial aid. Need-based:** 692 full-time freshmen applied for aid; 630 were judged to have need; 630 of these received aid. Average need met was 84%. Average scholarship/grant was $8,873; average loan $4,267. 55% of total undergraduate aid awarded as scholarships/grants, 45% as loans/jobs. **Non-need-based:** Awarded to 2,013 full-time undergraduates, including 713 freshmen. Scholarships awarded for academics, leadership, music/drama, ROTC.

**Application procedures. Admission:** Priority date 2/15; no deadline. $35 fee, may be waived for applicants with need. Application may be submitted online. Admission notification on a rolling basis beginning on or about 10/1. Must reply by May 1 or within 2 week(s) if notified thereafter. **Financial aid:** Priority date 2/15; no closing date. FAFSA required. Applicants notified on a rolling basis starting 3/15; must reply within 4 week(s) of notification.

**Academics. Special study options:** Accelerated study, combined bachelor's/graduate degree, cooperative education, distance learning, double major, ESL, honors, independent study, internships, liberal arts/career combination, student-designed major, study abroad, teacher certification program, weekend college. **Credit/placement by examination:** AP, CLEP, IB, institutional tests. Students can earn up to 2 years of credit in some fields via CLEP, challenge exams, and Advanced Placement exams. **Support services:** Learning center, pre-admission summer program, reduced course load, remedial instruction, study skills assistance, tutoring, writing center.

**Majors. Area/ethnic studies:** Women's. **Biology:** General, biochemistry. **Business:** Accounting, business admin, finance, financial planning, hospitality admin, human resources, international, management information systems, managerial economics, operations. **Communications:** General. **Computer sciences:** General, computer science, information systems. **Education:** Early childhood, elementary, science, special. **Engineering:** General, chemical, civil, electrical, mechanical. **English:** Creative writing, English lit. **Foreign languages:** French, Spanish. **Health:** Health services, nursing (RN), predental, premedicine, prenursing, preveterinary. **History:** General. **Legal studies:** Prelaw. **Liberal arts:** Arts/sciences. **Math:** General. **Physical sciences:** Chemistry, physics. **Protective services:** Law enforcement admin. **Psychology:** General. **Public administration:** Social work. **Social sciences:** Anthropology, economics, international relations, political science, sociology. **Visual/performing arts:** Studio arts.

**Most popular majors.** Business/marketing 26%, engineering/engineering technologies 9%, health sciences 21%, psychology 9%, social sciences 6%.

**Computing on campus.** 720 workstations in library, student center. Dormitories wired for high-speed internet access and linked to campus network. Commuter students can connect to campus network. Online course registration, online library, helpline, repair service, student web hosting, wireless network available.

**Student life. Freshman orientation:** Mandatory. Preregistration for classes offered. **Housing:** Guaranteed on-campus for freshmen. Coed dorms, single-sex dorms, apartments, cooperative housing, fraternity/sorority housing, substance-free housing available. $100 nonrefundable deposit. Wellness housing, special interest housing. **Activities:** Bands, campus ministries, choral groups, dance, drama, film society, international student organizations, literary magazine, music ensembles, radio station, student government, student newspaper, TV station, Hillel, black student union, political affairs club, Young Republicans, Young Democrats, environmental society, Widener Big Friends, Crusade for Christ, Alpha Phi Omega, Asian student association, presidential service corps.

**Athletics. NCAA. Intercollegiate:** Baseball M, basketball, cheerleading M, cross-country, field hockey W, football (tackle) M, golf M, lacrosse, soccer, softball W, swimming, track and field, volleyball W. **Intramural:** Basketball, cricket M, football (non-tackle), skiing, soccer, softball, volleyball, water polo M. **Team name:** Pride.

**Student services.** Adult student services, alcohol/substance abuse counseling, campus ministries, career counseling, services for economically disadvantaged, student employment services, financial aid counseling, health services, on-campus daycare, personal counseling, placement for graduates, veterans' counselor, women's services. **Physically disabled:** Services for

visually, speech, hearing impaired. **Learning disabled:** Comprehensive services available.

**Contact.** E-mail: admissions.office@widener.edu
Phone: (610) 499-4126 Toll-free number: (888) 943-3637
Fax: (610) 499-4676
Edwin Wright, Director of Admissions, Widener University, One University Place, Chester, PA 19013

## Wilkes University
**Wilkes-Barre, Pennsylvania**
www.wilkes.edu

CB member
CB code: 2977

- Private 4-year university
- Residential campus in small city
- 2,257 degree-seeking undergraduates: 7% part-time, 50% women, 3% African American, 2% Asian American, 2% Hispanic American, 2% international
- 2,778 degree-seeking graduate students
- 79% of applicants admitted
- SAT or ACT required
- 63% graduate within 6 years

**General.** Founded in 1933. Regionally accredited. **Degrees:** 412 bachelor's awarded; master's, doctoral, first professional offered. **ROTC:** Army, Air Force. **Location:** 100 miles from Philadelphia, 140 miles from New York City. **Calendar:** Semester, extensive summer session. **Full-time faculty:** 137 total; 89% have terminal degrees, 10% minority, 42% women. **Part-time faculty:** 276 total; 44% women. **Class size:** 41% < 20, 49% 20-39, 6% 40-49, 5% 50-99, less than 1% >100. **Special facilities:** Performing arts center, field station, telecommunications center, indoor recreation and athletic center.

**Freshman class profile.** 2,668 applied, 2,102 admitted, 623 enrolled.

| Mid 50% test scores | | | |
|---|---|---|---|
| SAT critical reading: | 460-560 | Rank in top tenth: | 24% |
| SAT math: | 470-600 | Return as sophomores: | 79% |
| SAT writing: | 440-560 | Out-of-state: | 22% |
| Rank in top quarter: | 48% | Live on campus: | 78% |
| | | International: | 3% |

**Basis for selection.** 920 SAT (exclusive of Writing) and/or rank in top 50% of high school class required for unconditional admission. Conditional admission may be offered to some applicants who do not meet these standards; must attend summer program prior to first semester. Interview recommended for all; audition required for theater arts programs.

**High school preparation.** Recommended units include English 4, mathematics 3, social studies 3, science 3 (laboratory 2) and computer science 1.

**2007-2008 Annual costs.** Tuition/fees: $24,080. Room/board: $10,310. Books/supplies: $1,050. Personal expenses: $1,000.

**2007-2008 Financial aid. Need-based:** 580 full-time freshmen applied for aid; 529 were judged to have need; 529 of these received aid. Average need met was 81%. Average scholarship/grant was $15,215; average loan $2,891. 61% of total undergraduate aid awarded as scholarships/grants, 39% as loans/jobs. **Non-need-based:** Scholarships awarded for academics, leadership, minority status, music/drama.

**Application procedures. Admission:** No deadline. $45 fee, may be waived for applicants with need. Application may be submitted online. Admission notification on a rolling basis. Must reply by May 1 or within 2 week(s) if notified thereafter. **Financial aid:** Priority date 3/1; no closing date. FAFSA required. Applicants notified on a rolling basis starting 3/1.

**Academics. Special study options:** Combined bachelor's/graduate degree, cooperative education, cross-registration, distance learning, double major, dual enrollment of high school students, ESL, external degree, honors, independent study, internships, student-designed major, study abroad, teacher certification program, weekend college. **Credit/placement by examination:** AP, CLEP, institutional tests. Credit by examination may be given to within 30 credits of graduation. **Support services:** Learning center, pre-admission summer program, reduced course load, remedial instruction, study skills assistance, tutoring, writing center.

**Majors. Biology:** General, biochemistry. **Business:** Accounting, business admin, entrepreneurial studies. **Communications:** General, digital media. **Computer sciences:** General, information systems. **Education:** Elementary, special. **Engineering:** Electrical, environmental, mechanical. **Engineering technology:** Industrial management. **English:** English lit. **Foreign languages:** French, Spanish. **Health:** Clinical lab science, nursing (RN), pharmaceutical sciences. **History:** General. **Liberal arts:** Arts/sciences. **Math:** General. **Philosophy/religion:** Philosophy. **Physical sciences:** Chemistry, geology. **Protective services:** Criminal justice. **Psychology:** General. **Social sciences:** International relations, political science, sociology. **Visual/performing arts:** Dramatic, music performance.

**Most popular majors.** Biology 9%, business/marketing 16%, communications/journalism 6%, education 10%, English 6%, health sciences 11%, liberal arts 12%, psychology 8%.

**Computing on campus.** 530 workstations in library, computer center, student center. Dormitories wired for high-speed internet access and linked to campus network. Commuter students can connect to campus network. Online course registration, online library, helpline, wireless network available.

**Student life. Freshman orientation:** Mandatory, $125 fee. Preregistration for classes offered. **Housing:** Guaranteed on-campus for all undergraduates. Coed dorms, single-sex dorms, apartments available. $100 nonrefundable deposit. **Activities:** Bands, choral groups, dance, drama, literary magazine, music ensembles, musical theater, radio station, student government, student newspaper, TV station.

**Athletics. NCAA. Intercollegiate:** Baseball M, basketball, field hockey W, football (tackle) M, golf M, lacrosse W, soccer, softball W, tennis, volleyball W, wrestling M. **Intramural:** Basketball M, bowling, football (tackle) M, ice hockey M, racquetball, rowing (crew), rugby M, skiing, softball, table tennis, volleyball. **Team name:** Colonels.

**Student services.** Adult student services, career counseling, student employment services, financial aid counseling, health services, personal counseling, placement for graduates, veterans' counselor. **Physically disabled:** Services for visually, hearing impaired.

**Contact.** E-mail: admissions@wilkes.edu
Phone: (570) 408-4400 Toll-free number: (800) 945-5378
Fax: (570) 408-4904
Michael Frantz, Vice President Enrollment Services, Wilkes University, 84 West South Street, Wilkes-Barre, PA 18766

---

## Williamson Free School of Mechanical Trades
**Media, Pennsylvania**
www.williamson.edu
**CB code: 0765**

▶ Private 3-year technical college for men affiliated with nondenominational tradition
▶ Residential campus in large town
▶ 234 degree-seeking undergraduates
▶ 38% of applicants admitted
▶ Interview required

**General.** Founded in 1888. Accredited by ACCSCT. Discipline-oriented school that prepares students through academic instruction and hands-on training in a structured environment; scholarship-only students. **Degrees:** 62 associate awarded. **Location:** 14 miles from Philadelphia, 14 miles from Wilmington, Delaware. **Calendar:** Semester. **Full-time faculty:** 19 total. **Part-time faculty:** 13 total. **Special facilities:** Natural arboretum.

**Freshman class profile.** 261 applied, 99 admitted, 90 enrolled.

| Out-of-state: | 15% | Live on campus: | 100% |
|---|---|---|---|

**Basis for selection.** Family economic need, high school performance, letters of character reference, interview important. First consideration given to applicants with 2.0 or better average in math, science, and English. Applicant must have reached 16th birthday (but not passed 20th birthday) prior to June of year of admission. Armed Services Vocational Aptitude Battery (ASVAB) required by March 24th. Essay recommended.

**High school preparation.** 7 units required. Required units include English 3, mathematics 2 and science 2. Math units must include algebra I and geometry. Science units should include chemistry and physics.

**2007-2008 Annual costs.** All students receive full scholarships covering tuition, room and board, and textbooks. Required fees vary by program and year, average $995.

**Application procedures. Admission:** Closing date 2/28 (postmark date). No application fee. Admission notification 4/30. Must reply by 5/23. **Financial aid:** No deadline.

**Academics. Special study options:** Cooperative education, internships. **Credit/placement by examination:** CLEP, institutional tests. **Support services:** Pre-admission summer program, tutoring.

---

**Computing on campus.** 35 workstations in library, computer center.

**Student life. Freshman orientation:** Mandatory. Takes place first 3 days of school and includes shop orientation, rules, classroom schedules and math testing. **Policies:** Student life carefully structured, including prescribed daily schedule, dress code, required chapel, and clearly defined privileges and responsibilities. Religious observance required. **Housing:** Guaranteed on-campus for all undergraduates. **Activities:** Jazz band, choral groups, student government, student newspaper, Campus Crusade for Christ, Bible study groups.

**Athletics. NJCAA. Intercollegiate:** Baseball M, basketball M, cross-country M, football (tackle) M, lacrosse M, soccer M, wrestling M. **Intramural:** Archery M, volleyball M. **Team name:** Mechanics.

**Student services.** Alcohol/substance abuse counseling, career counseling, student employment services, health services, personal counseling, placement for graduates.

**Contact.** E-mail: jmerillat@williamson.edu
Phone: (610) 566-1776 ext. 235 Fax: (610) 566-6502
Merillat Jason, Director of Enrollments, Williamson Free School of Mechanical Trades, 106 South New Middletown Road, Media, PA 19063

---

## Wilson College
**Chambersburg, Pennsylvania**
www.wilson.edu
**CB member**
**CB code: 2979**

▶ Private 4-year liberal arts college for women affiliated with Presbyterian Church (USA)
▶ Residential campus in large town
▶ 521 degree-seeking undergraduates: 35% part-time, 96% women, 4% African American, 2% Hispanic American, 7% international
▶ 13 degree-seeking graduate students
▶ 48% of applicants admitted
▶ Application essay required
▶ 63% graduate within 6 years; 30% enter graduate study

**General.** Founded in 1869. Regionally accredited. Men admitted to continuing studies division, adult learning program, associate degree programs, post baccalaureate teacher intern program. Residential program for single mothers with children. **Degrees:** 79 bachelor's, 7 associate awarded; master's offered. **ROTC:** Army. **Location:** 90 miles from Washington, DC; 145 miles from Philadelphia. **Calendar:** 4-1-4, limited summer session. **Full-time faculty:** 39 total; 80% have terminal degrees, 5% minority, 54% women. **Part-time faculty:** 47 total; 21% have terminal degrees, 57% women. **Class size:** 86% < 20, 14% 20-39. **Special facilities:** Equestrian center, sustainable living center, veterinary medical center, archival center.

**Freshman class profile.** 479 applied, 229 admitted, 84 enrolled.

| Mid 50% test scores | | Rank in top quarter: | 33% |
|---|---|---|---|
| SAT critical reading: | 430-540 | Rank in top tenth: | 12% |
| SAT math: | 440-530 | End year in good standing: | 87% |
| SAT writing: | 440-560 | Return as sophomores: | 61% |
| ACT composite: | 21-23 | Out-of-state: | 41% |
| GPA 3.50 or higher: | 34% | Live on campus: | 82% |
| GPA 3.0-3.49: | 43% | International: | 6% |
| GPA 2.0-2.99: | 23% | | |

**Basis for selection.** Admissions based on secondary school record. Class rank, recommendations, character, and personal qualities also important. SAT/ACT optional for students with 3.0 GPA in college prep curriculum from a regionally accredited secondary school. Interview recommended. **Home-schooled:** Transcript of courses and grades, letter of recommendation (non-parent) required.

**High school preparation.** 15 units required. Required units include English 4, mathematics 3, social studies 4, science 2 (laboratory 2) and foreign language 2.

**2008-2009 Annual costs.** Tuition/fees: $25,900. Room/board: $8,630. Books/supplies: $1,000. Personal expenses: $800.

**2007-2008 Financial aid. Need-based:** 73 full-time freshmen applied for aid; 57 were judged to have need; 57 of these received aid. Average need met was 78%. Average scholarship/grant was $15,190; average loan $4,346. 61% of total undergraduate aid awarded as scholarships/grants, 39% as loans/jobs. **Non-need-based:** Scholarships awarded for academics, alumni affiliation, religious affiliation, state residency.

**Application procedures. Admission:** Priority date 4/30; no deadline. $35 fee, may be waived for applicants with need. Application may be submitted online. Admission notification on a rolling basis beginning on or about 9/15. Must reply by May 1 or within 3 week(s) if notified thereafter. **Financial aid:** Priority date 4/30; no closing date. FAFSA, institutional form required. Applicants notified on a rolling basis starting 2/15.

**Academics. Special study options:** Cooperative education, cross-registration, double major, ESL, honors, independent study, internships, liberal arts/career combination, student-designed major, study abroad, teacher certification program, Washington semester. **Credit/placement by examination:** AP, CLEP, IB, SAT, ACT, institutional tests. 4 credit hours maximum toward associate degree, 4 toward bachelor's. **Support services:** Learning center, reduced course load, remedial instruction, study skills assistance, tutoring, writing center.

**Majors. Agriculture:** Equestrian studies. **Biology:** General. **Business:** Accounting, business admin, international, management information systems, managerial economics. **Communications:** Media studies. **Conservation:** Environmental studies. **Education:** Elementary. **English:** English lit. **Foreign languages:** French, Spanish. **Health:** Premedicine, preveterinary, veterinary technology/assistant. **History:** General. **Interdisciplinary:** Behavioral sciences, biopsychology. **Math:** General. **Parks/recreation:** Exercise sciences. **Philosophy/religion:** Religion. **Physical sciences:** Chemistry. **Psychology:** General. **Social sciences:** General, international relations, political science, sociology. **Visual/performing arts:** Art.

**Most popular majors.** Business/marketing 14%, education 15%, health sciences 26%, interdisciplinary studies 6%, visual/performing arts 6%.

**Computing on campus.** 116 workstations in dormitories, library, computer center, student center. Dormitories wired for high-speed internet access and linked to campus network. Commuter students can connect to campus network. Online course registration, online library, helpline, repair service, wireless network available.

**Student life. Freshman orientation:** Mandatory, $250 fee. Preregistration for classes offered. Held in August. **Policies:** Honor principle, shared governance. **Housing:** Guaranteed on-campus for all undergraduates. Substance-free housing available. $300 fully refundable deposit. Pets allowed in dorm rooms. Students of junior standing or above guaranteed single residence hall room. Housing for single mothers with children available. **Activities:** Choral groups, dance, drama, international student organizations, literary magazine, music ensembles, radio station, student government, student newspaper, religious activities committee, language clubs, interfaith support group, black student union, Curran Scholars, Alternative Spring Break, Bible study, Habitat for Humanity.

**Athletics.** NCAA. **Intercollegiate:** Basketball W, field hockey W, gymnastics W, soccer W, softball W. **Team name:** Phoenix.

**Student services.** Adult student services, alcohol/substance abuse counseling, campus ministries, career counseling, student employment services, financial aid counseling, health services, on-campus daycare, personal counseling, placement for graduates, women's services.

**Contact.** E-mail: admissions@wilson.edu
Phone: (717) 262-2002 Toll-free number: (800) 421-8402
Fax: (717) 262-2546
Mary Ann Naso, Vice President for Enrollment and Admissions, Wilson College, 1015 Philadelphia Avenue, Chambersburg, PA 17201-1285

## Yeshivath Beth Moshe
**Scranton, Pennsylvania**

**CB code: 1657**

- Private 4-year rabbinical college for men affiliated with Jewish faith
- Small city
- 60 degree-seeking undergraduates
- 95% graduate within 6 years

**General.** Founded in 1965. Accredited by AARTS. First and second Talmudic degrees offered. Ordination available. **Calendar:** Continuous. **Full-time faculty:** 6 total.

**Basis for selection.** Open admission.

**2007-2008 Annual costs.** Tuition/fees: $9,200. Room/board: $3,900. Books/supplies: $150.

**Application procedures. Admission:** No deadline. No application fee. Admission notification on a rolling basis. **Financial aid:** No deadline. Applicants notified on a rolling basis.

**Academics. Credit/placement by examination:** CLEP.

**Majors. Theology:** Talmudic.

**Student life. Activities:** Choral groups, TV station.

**Contact.** Phone: (717) 346-1747 Fax: (717) 346-2251
Rabbi Chaim Bressler, Admissions Director, Yeshivath Beth Moshe, 930 Hickory Street, Scranton, PA 18505

## York College of Pennsylvania
**York, Pennsylvania**
**www.ycp.edu**

**CB member**
**CB code: 2991**

- Private 4-year liberal arts college
- Residential campus in small city
- 5,219 degree-seeking undergraduates: 11% part-time, 56% women
- 277 degree-seeking graduate students
- 64% of applicants admitted
- SAT or ACT with writing required
- 63% graduate within 6 years

**General.** Founded in 1787. Regionally accredited. **Degrees:** 953 bachelor's, 43 associate awarded; master's offered. **ROTC:** Army. **Location:** 46 miles from Baltimore, 95 miles from Philadelphia. **Calendar:** Semester, extensive summer session. **Full-time faculty:** 155 total; 81% have terminal degrees, 42% women. **Part-time faculty:** 264 total; 20% have terminal degrees, 47% women. **Class size:** 38% < 20, 58% 20-39, 4% 40-49, less than 1% 50-99, less than 1% >100. **Special facilities:** Engineering innovation center, telecommunications center, rare books collection, oral history room, video production studios, nursing education center.

**Freshman class profile.** 7,009 applied, 4,462 admitted, 1,186 enrolled.

| Mid 50% test scores | | | |
|---|---|---|---|
| SAT critical reading: | 490-580 | GPA 2.0-2.99: | 18% |
| SAT math: | 500-600 | Rank in top quarter: | 36% |
| SAT writing: | 480-570 | Rank in top tenth: | 12% |
| ACT composite: | 19-24 | End year in good standing: | 88% |
| GPA 3.50 or higher: | 52% | Return as sophomores: | 77% |
| GPA 3.0-3.49: | 30% | Out-of-state: | 49% |

**Basis for selection.** High school record, standardized test results, and personal qualities most important. Interviews and essays recommended for academically borderline; audition required for music programs; portfolio recommended for art programs. **Homeschooled:** Statement describing homeschool structure and mission, transcript of courses and grades, state high school equivalency certificate, letter of recommendation (nonparent) required. Diploma required from home school association or local school district; portfolio evaluation conducted by certified teacher; syllabus for each course.

**High school preparation.** 15 units required. Required and recommended units include English 4, mathematics 3-4, social studies 3, science 3 and foreign language 2. One biology, 2 chemistry, and 2 algebra required of nursing applicants.

**2008-2009 Annual costs.** Tuition/fees: $13,680. Room/board: $7,800. Books/supplies: $600. Personal expenses: $1,000.

**2007-2008 Financial aid. Need-based:** 1,008 full-time freshmen applied for aid; 644 were judged to have need; 641 of these received aid. Average need met was 77%. Average scholarship/grant was $4,826; average loan $5,444. 51% of total undergraduate aid awarded as scholarships/grants, 49% as loans/jobs. **Non-need-based:** Awarded to 1,259 full-time undergraduates, including 527 freshmen. Scholarships awarded for academics, alumni affiliation, art, music/drama.

**Application procedures. Admission:** No deadline. $30 fee, may be waived for applicants with need. Application may be submitted online. Admission notification on a rolling basis beginning on or about 10/1. **Financial aid:** Priority date 3/1; no closing date. FAFSA required. Applicants notified on a rolling basis starting 2/15; must reply within 4 week(s) of notification.

**Academics. Special study options:** Combined bachelor's/graduate degree, cooperative education, distance learning, double major, dual enrollment of high school students, honors, independent study, internships, student-designed major, study abroad, teacher certification program. **Credit/placement by examination:** AP, CLEP, IB, institutional tests. 30 credit hours maximum toward associate degree, 30 toward bachelor's. **Support services:** Learning center, reduced course load, remedial instruction, study skills assistance, tutoring, writing center.

**Majors.** **Biology:** General. **Business:** General, accounting, business admin, entrepreneurial studies, finance, knowledge management, managerial economics, marketing. **Communications:** General, digital media, media studies, public relations. **Computer sciences:** General, computer science, information systems. **Education:** General, biology, elementary, English, history, mathematics, music, science, secondary, special. **Engineering:** Computer, electrical, mechanical. **Engineering technology:** Industrial management. **English:** English lit, speech/rhetoric, technical writing. **Foreign languages:** Spanish. **Health:** Clinical lab technology, nuclear medical technology, nursing (RN), predental, premedicine, prepharmacy, preveterinary, recreational therapy, respiratory therapy technology. **History:** General. **Interdisciplinary:** Behavioral sciences. **Legal studies:** Prelaw. **Liberal arts:** Arts/sciences, humanities. **Math:** General. **Parks/recreation:** General, facilities management, sports admin. **Physical sciences:** Chemistry. **Protective services:** Corrections, forensics, law enforcement admin, police science, security services. **Psychology:** General. **Public administration:** General. **Social sciences:** General, political science, sociology. **Visual/performing arts:** General, dramatic, graphic design, music performance, studio arts.

**Most popular majors.** Business/marketing 17%, communications/journalism 9%, education 13%, health sciences 12%, parks/recreation 7%, security/protective services 7%, social sciences 11%.

**Computing on campus.** 450 workstations in library, computer center. Dormitories wired for high-speed internet access and linked to campus network. Commuter students can connect to campus network. Online course registration, online library, helpline, wireless network available.

**Student life.** **Freshman orientation:** Mandatory. Preregistration for classes offered. 3-day program prior to fall semester. **Housing:** Guaranteed on-campus for freshmen. Coed dorms, single-sex dorms, special housing for disabled, apartments, substance-free housing available. $200 nonrefundable deposit. Minidorms featuring units of 10 students, suites, sponsored houses, and apartments available. **Activities:** Bands, choral groups, drama, film society, literary magazine, music ensembles, musical theater, radio station, student government, student newspaper, symphony orchestra, TV station, over 80 student organizations.

**Athletics.** NCAA. **Intercollegiate:** Baseball M, basketball, cheerleading, cross-country, field hockey W, golf M, lacrosse, soccer, softball W, swimming, tennis, track and field, volleyball W, wrestling M. **Intramural:** Badminton, basketball, football (non-tackle), lacrosse M, rugby M, skiing, soccer M, softball, swimming, tennis, track and field, volleyball, water polo M, wrestling M. **Team name:** Spartans.

**Student services.** Adult student services, alcohol/substance abuse counseling, campus ministries, career counseling, services for economically disadvantaged, student employment services, financial aid counseling, health services, minority student services, personal counseling, placement for graduates, veterans' counselor. **Physically disabled:** Services for visually, hearing impaired.

**Contact.** E-mail: admissions@ycp.edu
Phone: (717) 849-1600 Toll-free number: (800) 455-8018
Fax: (717) 849-1607
Nancy Spataro, Director of Admissions, York College of Pennsylvania, 441 Country Club Road, York, PA 17403-3651

# Puerto Rico

## American University of Puerto Rico
**Bayamon, Puerto Rico**                          **CB member**
www.aupr.edu                                      **CB code: 0961**

- Private 4-year university and business college
- Commuter campus in large city
- 2,923 undergraduates

**General.** Founded in 1963. Regionally accredited. Branch campus at Manati. **Degrees:** 419 bachelor's, 50 associate awarded; master's offered. **ROTC:** Army. **Location:** 12 miles from San Juan. **Calendar:** Semester, limited summer session. **Full-time faculty:** 85 total. **Part-time faculty:** 125 total. **Special facilities:** Fully computerized classrooms.

**Basis for selection.** Open admission. SAT required for English-speaking applicants and NCAA student athletes. Interview recommended. **Homeschooled:** Transcript of courses and grades, state high school equivalency certificate required.

**High school preparation.** 18 units recommended. Recommended units include English 3, mathematics 2, social studies 2, history 1, science 2, foreign language 3 and academic electives 5.

**2007-2008 Annual costs.** Tuition/fees: $4,630. Books/supplies: $800.

**Financial aid.** All financial aid based on need.

**Application procedures. Admission:** No deadline. $15 fee, may be waived for applicants with need. Admission notification on a rolling basis. **Financial aid:** Priority date 4/30, closing date 5/31. FAFSA, institutional form required. Applicants notified by 6/1; must reply within 2 week(s) of notification.

**Academics. Special study options:** Cooperative education, honors, independent study, internships, liberal arts/career combination. **Credit/placement by examination:** CLEP, institutional tests. **Support services:** Learning center, reduced course load, tutoring.

**Majors. Business:** General, accounting, administrative services, business admin, office technology, office/clerical, purchasing. **Communications:** General. **Communications technology:** General. **Education:** General, business, elementary, ESL, mathematics, physical, secondary, Spanish, special. **Social sciences:** General.

**Computing on campus.** 75 workstations in computer center.

**Student life. Freshman orientation:** Mandatory. Preregistration for classes offered. **Activities:** Student government.

**Athletics.** NCAA. **Intercollegiate:** Basketball, cross-country, swimming, tennis, track and field, volleyball. **Intramural:** Basketball, cross-country, softball M, table tennis, track and field, volleyball. **Team name:** Pirates.

**Student services.** Career counseling, student employment services, health services, personal counseling, veterans' counselor. **Physically disabled:** Services for speech impaired.

**Contact.** E-mail: oficinaadmisiones@aupr.edu
Phone: (787) 620-2040 Fax: (787) 785-7377
Margarita Cruz, Director of Admissions, American University of Puerto Rico, Box 2037, Bayamon, PR 00960-2037

## Atlantic College
**Guaynabo, Puerto Rico**
www.atlanticcollege-pr.com                        **CB code: 7137**

- Private 4-year visual arts, business and liberal arts college
- Commuter campus in small city
- 996 degree-seeking undergraduates

**General.** Founded in 1983. Accredited by ACICS. **Degrees:** 141 bachelor's, 21 associate awarded; master's offered. **Location:** 20 miles from San Juan. **Calendar:** Quarter, extensive summer session. **Full-time faculty:** 22

total. **Part-time faculty:** 24 total. **Special facilities:** Motion caption laboratories, audio laboratories (for study of digital graphic design, computerized animation technology).

**Freshman class profile.** 260 applied, 252 admitted, 242 enrolled.

**Basis for selection.** Open admission.

**High school preparation.** 16 units recommended. Recommended units include English 3, mathematics 2, social studies 1, history 2, science 2, foreign language 3 and academic electives 3.

**2007-2008 Annual costs.** Books/supplies: $500.

**Financial aid.** All financial aid based on need.

**Application procedures. Admission:** No deadline. $30 fee. Admission notification on a rolling basis. **Financial aid:** Closing date 6/30. FAFSA, institutional form required. Applicants notified on a rolling basis starting 4/1; must reply within 2 week(s) of notification.

**Academics. Special study options:** Combined bachelor's/graduate degree, honors, internships, liberal arts/career combination, student-designed major. **Credit/placement by examination:** CLEP. **Support services:** Learning center, pre-admission summer program, remedial instruction, tutoring.

**Majors. Business:** Accounting, administrative services, business admin. **Computer sciences:** Game design, security. **Education:** Early childhood special. **Visual/performing arts:** Commercial/advertising art.

**Most popular majors.** Business/marketing 6%, computer/information sciences 12%, visual/performing arts 74%.

**Computing on campus.** 16 workstations in library, computer center. Online library, repair service, wireless network available.

**Student life. Freshman orientation:** Available. **Activities:** Dance, drama, student government, student newspaper.

**Athletics. Intercollegiate:** Basketball. **Intramural:** Basketball, volleyball.

**Student services.** Alcohol/substance abuse counseling, career counseling, financial aid counseling, health services, personal counseling, placement for graduates. **Physically disabled:** Services for hearing impaired.

**Contact.** E-mail: admisiones@atlanticcollege.edu
Phone: (787) 720-1022 ext. 1027 Fax: (787) 720-1092
Zaida Perez, Director of Admissions, Atlantic College, PO Box 3918, Guaynabo, PR 00970

## Bayamon Central University
**Bayamon, Puerto Rico**                          **CB member**
www.ucb.edu.pr                                    **CB code: 0840**

- Private 4-year university affiliated with Roman Catholic Church
- Commuter campus in large city
- 2,133 degree-seeking undergraduates

**General.** Founded in 1970. Regionally accredited. Member of consortium of U.S. and South American universities. Virtually all students come from Spanish-speaking backgrounds. **Degrees:** 276 bachelor's, 20 associate awarded; master's offered. **ROTC:** Army, Air Force. **Location:** 9 miles from San Juan. **Calendar:** Semester, limited summer session. **Full-time faculty:** 58 total. **Part-time faculty:** 236 total. **Special facilities:** Library of Dominican Order.

**Freshman class profile.** 799 applied, 264 admitted, 223 enrolled.

**Basis for selection.** Open admission, but selective for some programs and for out-of-state students. School achievement record and test scores most important. Minimum 2.0 high school GPA. Fluency in Spanish, basic knowledge of English necessary. Conditional admission to those identified as having underdeveloped academic potential. SAT or ACT accepted from English-speaking students. Score report must be received by 04/15. Essay recommended for all; interview recommended for academically weak. **Homeschooled:** Transcript of courses and grades required.

**High school preparation.** Required units include English 3, mathematics 3, social studies 3 and science 1. 3 units of Spanish required.

**2007-2008 Annual costs.** Tuition/fees: $4,850. Books/supplies: $800. Personal expenses: $1,200.

**Financial aid.** All financial aid based on need.

**Application procedures. Admission:** Priority date 12/6; deadline 4/6 (postmark date). $15 fee, may be waived for applicants with need. Admission notification on a rolling basis beginning on or about 3/4. **Financial aid:** Priority date 5/31, closing date 7/2. FAFSA, institutional form required.

**Academics.** All classroom instruction conducted in Spanish. Core curriculum includes courses in Spanish. Course in methodology of learning must be satisfactorily completed. **Special study options:** Double major, independent study, teacher certification program. **Credit/placement by examination:** AP, CLEP. **Support services:** Learning center, reduced course load, tutoring.

**Majors. Biology:** General. **Business:** General, accounting, administrative services, business admin, finance, human resources, management information systems, management science, marketing. **Communications:** Journalism. **Conservation:** General. **Education:** Early childhood, elementary, English, instructional media, mathematics, physical, science, secondary, Spanish, special. **English:** English lit. **Foreign languages:** Spanish. **Health:** Occupational health. **Interdisciplinary:** Biological/physical sciences, natural sciences. **Philosophy/religion:** Philosophy, religion. **Physical sciences:** Chemistry. **Psychology:** General. **Public administration:** General, social work.

**Computing on campus.** 130 workstations in computer center. Online library available.

**Student life. Freshman orientation:** Mandatory. Preregistration for classes offered. **Activities:** Choral groups, drama, student government, student newspaper, various cultural, religious, and social activities.

**Athletics. Intercollegiate:** Basketball, cross-country, softball, swimming, table tennis, tennis, track and field, volleyball. **Intramural:** Basketball, track and field, volleyball. **Team name:** Halcones.

**Student services.** Career counseling, student employment services, financial aid counseling, health services, on-campus daycare, personal counseling, placement for graduates. **Physically disabled:** Services for visually, hearing impaired.

**Contact.** E-mail: chernandez@ucb.edu.pr
Phone: (787) 786-3030 ext. 2100 Fax: (787) 740-2200
Cristina Hernandez, Director of Admissions, Bayamon Central University, PO Box 1725, Bayamon, PR 00960-1725

---

## Caribbean University
**Bayamon, Puerto Rico**
www.caribbean.edu
**CB member**
**CB code: 0779**

- Private 4-year health science and liberal arts college
- Commuter campus in large city
- 4,464 degree-seeking undergraduates: 100% Hispanic American

**General.** Founded in 1969. Regionally accredited. Extension centers in Carolina, Vega Baja, and Ponce. **Degrees:** 248 bachelor's, 69 associate awarded; master's, first professional offered. **ROTC:** Army. **Location:** 12 miles from San Juan. **Calendar:** Differs by program, limited summer session. **Full-time faculty:** 60 total. **Part-time faculty:** 80 total. **Special facilities:** College-operated museum program at Bayamon campus.

**Basis for selection.** Open admission. School achievement record, test scores important. Interview considered. SAT required of English-speaking applicants. PAA score reports by August 15. Interview recommended for academically weak. **Homeschooled:** State high school equivalency certificate required.

**2007-2008 Annual costs.** Books/supplies: $640. Personal expenses: $1,950.

**Application procedures. Admission:** No deadline. $25 fee, may be waived for applicants with need. Application may be submitted online. Admission notification on a rolling basis beginning on or about 3/1. **Financial aid:** Priority date 7/30; no closing date. FAFSA required. Applicants notified on a rolling basis starting 7/30; must reply within 2 week(s) of notification.

**Academics. Special study options:** Combined bachelor's/graduate degree, honors, liberal arts/career combination, teacher certification program, weekend college. **Credit/placement by examination:** CLEP, institutional tests. **Support services:** Learning center, remedial instruction, tutoring.

**Majors. Biology:** General. **Business:** Accounting, administrative services, business admin. **Computer sciences:** General. **Education:** Business, elementary, English, mathematics, science, secondary, special. **Engineering:** Civil, petroleum. **Foreign languages:** Spanish. **Health:** Nursing (RN), premedicine. **Legal studies:** Prelaw. **Parks/recreation:** General. **Public administration:** Social work. **Social sciences:** General, criminology.

**Computing on campus.** 100 workstations in library, computer center, student center. Online course registration, online library, student web hosting, wireless network available.

**Student life. Freshman orientation:** Mandatory. Preregistration for classes offered. **Activities:** Choral groups, drama, music ensembles, student government, student newspaper.

**Athletics. Intercollegiate:** Cheerleading. **Intramural:** Basketball, cross-country, gymnastics, table tennis, tennis, track and field, volleyball. **Team name:** Gryphoms.

**Student services.** Alcohol/substance abuse counseling, career counseling, services for economically disadvantaged, student employment services, financial aid counseling, health services, personal counseling, placement for graduates, veterans' counselor. **Physically disabled:** Services for visually, speech, hearing impaired.

**Contact.** E-mail: admissiones@caribbean.edu
Phone: (787) 780-0070 ext. 1111 Fax: (787) 785-0101
Roxana Vazquez, Admissions Coordinator, Caribbean University, PO Box 493, Bayamon, PR 00960-0493

---

## Carlos Albizu University: San Juan
**San Juan, Puerto Rico**
www.albizu.edu
**CB code: 2104**

- Private two-year upper-division university
- Large town
- 90% of applicants admitted
- Test scores, application essay, interview required

**General.** Regionally accredited. **Degrees:** 65 bachelor's awarded; master's, doctoral offered. **Calendar:** Semester, limited summer session. **Full-time faculty:** 19 total. **Part-time faculty:** 7 total.

**Student profile.** 192 degree-seeking undergraduates, 697 graduate students. 63 applied as first time-transfer students, 57 admitted, 51 enrolled.

**Basis for selection.** College transcript, application essay, interview, standardized test scores required. Transfer accepted as sophomores.

**2007-2008 Annual costs.** Books/supplies: $2,606. Personal expenses: $3,681.

**Financial aid. Need-based:** 16% of total undergraduate aid awarded as scholarships/grants, 84% as loans/jobs.

**Application procedures. Admission:** $75 fee. Application must be submitted on paper.

**Academics. Special study options:** Combined bachelor's/graduate degree, distance learning. **Credit/placement by examination:** CLEP.

**Majors. Education:** Speech impaired. **Interdisciplinary:** Behavioral sciences.

**Computing on campus.** 30 workstations in computer center.

**Contact.** Phone: (787) 725-6500 ext. 21 Fax: (787) 721-7187
Carlos Rodriguez-Irizarry, Director of Admissions, Carlos Albizu University: San Juan, 151 Tanca Street, San Juan, PR 00902-3711

---

## Colegio Biblico Pentecostal
**Saint Just, Puerto Rico**
www.cbp.edu

- Private 4-year Bible and seminary college
- Small city

**General.** Accredited by ABHE. **Calendar:** Semester.

**Contact.** Phone: (787) 761-0808
Registrar, PO Box 901, Saint Just, PR 00978-0901

---

## Colegio Pentecostal Mizpa
**San Juan, Puerto Rico**
www.colmizpa.edu

- Private 4-year Bible college
- Commuter campus in very large city

- 250 degree-seeking undergraduates: 64% part-time, 46% women
- 64% of applicants admitted
- Interview required

**General.** Accredited by ABHE. **Degrees:** 16 bachelor's, 18 associate awarded. **Calendar:** Semester, limited summer session. **Full-time faculty:** 5 total; 20% have terminal degrees, 20% women. **Part-time faculty:** 16 total; 6% have terminal degrees, 56% women. **Class size:** 100% 50-99.

**Freshman class profile.** 14 applied, 9 admitted, 9 enrolled.

| | | | |
|---|---|---|---|
| GPA 3.50 or higher: | 13% | Return as sophomores: | 2% |
| GPA 3.0-3.49: | 55% | Out-of-state: | 1% |
| GPA 2.0-2.99: | 30% | Live on campus: | 4% |
| End year in good standing: | 100% | | |

**Basis for selection.** Academic GPA, religious affiliation very important, rigor of secondary school record considered. **Homeschooled:** State high school equivalency certificate, interview required. **Learning Disabled:** Certified information concerning disability must be provided by student.

**2007-2008 Annual costs.** Tuition/fees: $2,550. Room/board: $1,250. Books/supplies: $500. Personal expenses: $3,440.

**2006-2007 Financial aid.** All financial aid based on need. 7 full-time freshmen applied for aid; 7 were judged to have need; 7 of these received aid.

**Application procedures. Admission:** No deadline. $40 fee ($40 out-of-state). Application must be submitted on paper. **Financial aid:** No deadline. FAFSA required.

**Academics. Special study options:** External degree. **Credit/placement by examination:** CLEP, institutional tests. **Support services:** Learning center, writing center.

**Majors. Theology:** Bible, pastoral counseling, religious ed.

**Computing on campus.** Online library, wireless network available.

**Student life. Freshman orientation:** Mandatory. Preregistration for classes offered. **Policies:** Religious observance required. **Housing:** Single-sex dorms, substance-free housing available. $125 fully refundable deposit. **Activities:** Radio station, student government.

**Student services.** Campus ministries, career counseling, services for economically disadvantaged, student employment services, financial aid counseling, personal counseling.

**Contact.** E-mail: decanatoestudiante@colmizpa.edu
Phone: (787) 720-4476 Fax: (787) 720-2012
Jorge Burgos, Admissions Director, Colegio Pentecostal Mizpa, PO Box 20966, San Juan, PR 00928-0966

## Columbia Centro Universitario: Caguas
**Caguas, Puerto Rico**
www.columbiaco.edu
CB code: 2315

- For-profit 4-year business and technical college
- Commuter campus in small city
- 791 degree-seeking undergraduates
- Interview required

**General.** Founded in 1966. Accredited by ACICS. **Degrees:** 91 bachelor's, 91 associate awarded; master's offered. **Location:** 15 miles from San Juan. **Calendar:** Differs by program, extensive summer session. **Full-time faculty:** 14 total. **Part-time faculty:** 77 total. **Class size:** 60% < 20, 40% 20-39.

**Basis for selection.** Open admission, but selective for some programs. Parent signature and vaccination certificate required for students under age 21. Portfolio required for adult education students.

**High school preparation.** 15 units required. Required units include English 3, mathematics 2, social studies 2, history 2, science 3 and academic electives 3.

**2007-2008 Annual costs.** Tuition/fees: $3,850. Books/supplies: $441. Personal expenses: $1,684.

**2006-2007 Financial aid.** All financial aid based on need. 185 full-time freshmen applied for aid; 185 were judged to have need; 185 of these received aid. 98% of total undergraduate aid awarded as scholarships/grants, 2% as loans/jobs.

**Application procedures. Admission:** No deadline. $50 fee. Application must be submitted on paper. Admission notification on a rolling basis.

**Academics. Credit/placement by examination:** AP, CLEP. **Support services:** Tutoring.

**Majors. Business:** Business admin. **Health:** Nursing (RN).

**Most popular majors.** Business/marketing 64%, health sciences 36%.

**Computing on campus.** 27 workstations in library, computer center.

**Student life. Freshman orientation:** Mandatory. General orientation lasts about two hours.

**Student services.** Career counseling, student employment services, financial aid counseling, personal counseling, placement for graduates, veterans' counselor.

**Contact.** E-mail: info@columbiaco.edu
Phone: (787) 743-4041 ext. 240 Toll-free number: (800) 981-4877 ext. 240 Fax: (787) 744-7031
Ana Burgos, Marketing, Recruitment and Admissions Coordinator, Columbia Centro Universitario: Caguas, PO Box 8517, Caguas, PR 00726

## Conservatory of Music of Puerto Rico
**San Juan, Puerto Rico**
www.cmpr.edu
CB code: 1115

- Public 4-year music college
- Commuter campus in large city
- 361 degree-seeking undergraduates: 30% part-time, 28% women, 100% Hispanic American
- 28 degree-seeking graduate students
- 70% of applicants admitted
- 48% graduate within 6 years

**General.** Founded in 1959. Regionally accredited. **Degrees:** 35 bachelor's awarded; master's offered. **Calendar:** Semester, limited summer session. **Full-time faculty:** 50 total; 8% have terminal degrees, 94% minority, 22% women. **Part-time faculty:** 23 total; 30% have terminal degrees, 100% minority, 30% women. **Special facilities:** Library with more than 26,000 musical scores, technology lab (computers applied to music), piano lab, theater.

**Freshman class profile.** 110 applied, 77 admitted, 71 enrolled.

| | | | |
|---|---|---|---|
| End year in good standing: | 93% | Return as sophomores: | 93% |

**Basis for selection.** Musical ability very important. School achievement record, test scores important. Recommendations considered. Must take entrance examination in both theory and instrument. SAT is accepted from applicants from US mainland. Audition required for music performance. Essays also required for Music Education. **Homeschooled:** State high school equivalency certificate required.

**High school preparation.** Required and recommended units include English 3, mathematics 3, history 3, science 3, foreign language 3 and academic electives 3.

**2007-2008 Annual costs.** Tuition/fees: $2,292. Books/supplies: $1,650. Personal expenses: $950.

**Financial aid.** All financial aid based on need.

**Application procedures. Admission:** Closing date 2/28 (receipt date). $35 fee. Application must be submitted on paper. Admission notification 5/30. **Financial aid:** Priority date 6/30; no closing date. FAFSA, institutional form required. Applicants notified on a rolling basis starting 8/30.

**Academics. Special study options:** Cross-registration, dual enrollment of high school students, liberal arts/career combination, teacher certification program. **Credit/placement by examination:** AP, CLEP, institutional tests. 12 credit hours maximum toward bachelor's degree. **Support services:** Learning center, pre-admission summer program, reduced course load, remedial instruction, tutoring.

**Majors. Education:** Music. **Visual/performing arts:** Jazz, music performance, piano/organ, stringed instruments, voice/opera.

**Most popular majors.** Education 29%, visual/performing arts 71%.

**Computing on campus.** 17 workstations in library, computer center. Online library, wireless network available.

**Student life. Freshman orientation:** Mandatory. Preregistration for classes offered. **Activities:** Bands, choral groups, music ensembles, opera, student government, symphony orchestra.

**Student services.** Career counseling, student employment services, financial aid counseling, personal counseling, placement for graduates.

**Contact.** E-mail: esantiag@cmpr.gobierno.pr
Phone: (787) 751-0160 ext. 275 Fax: (787) 758-8268
Eutimia Santiago, Director, Admissions Office and Institutional Research, Conservatory of Music of Puerto Rico, Rafael Lamar #350 Esq. Roosevelt, San Juan, PR 00918-2199

## Electronic Data Processing College of Puerto Rico
### Hato Rey, Puerto Rico
### www.edpcollege.edu                    CB code: 2243

- For-profit 4-year business and technical college
- Commuter campus in very large city

**General.** Founded in 1968. Candidate for regional accreditation. **Calendar:** Semester.

**Annual costs/financial aid.** Books/supplies: $465. Personal expenses: $1,455.

**Contact.** Phone: (787) 765-3560
Admissions Director, PO Box 1923, Hato Rey, PR 00919-2303

## Electronic Data Processing College: San Sebastian
### San Sebastian, Puerto Rico
### www.edpcollege.edu                    CB code: 3219

- For-profit 4-year business and health science college
- Commuter campus in small city

**General.** Accredited by ACICS. **Location:** 28 miles from Mayaguez. **Calendar:** Semester.

**Contact.** Phone: (787) 896-2252 ext. 225
Admissions Officer, PO Box 1674, San Sebastian, PR 00685

## Escuela de Artes Plasticas de Puerto Rico
### San Juan, Puerto Rico
### www.eap.edu                    CB code: 7036

- Public 4-year visual arts college
- Commuter campus in large city
- 494 degree-seeking undergraduates
- 74% of applicants admitted
- Interview required

**General.** Founded in 1965. Regionally accredited. **Degrees:** 41 bachelor's awarded. **Location:** In Old San Juan. **Calendar:** Semester, limited summer session. **Full-time faculty:** 16 total. **Part-time faculty:** 60 total. **Class size:** 86% < 20, 14% 20-39.

**Freshman class profile.** 135 applied, 100 admitted, 70 enrolled.

**Basis for selection.** Applicants must complete pre-admissions studio course during the summer. Admissions committee interviews each candidate and reviews portfolio. Test scores and high school GPA very important. SAT for mainland U.S. applicants. Portfolio required.

**2008-2009 Annual costs.** Tuition/fees (projected): $2,923. Books/supplies: $2,250. Personal expenses: $1,750.

**2006-2007 Financial aid.** All financial aid based on need. 99% of total undergraduate aid awarded as scholarships/grants, 1% as loans/jobs.

**Application procedures. Admission:** Closing date 3/3 (receipt date). $20 fee. Admission notification on a rolling basis. **Financial aid:** Priority date 4/25, closing date 5/23. FAFSA, institutional form required. Applicants notified by 7/11.

**Academics. Special study options:** Internships, liberal arts/career combination, teacher certification program. **Credit/placement by examination:**

CLEP. **Support services:** Learning center, pre-admission summer program, reduced course load, study skills assistance, tutoring.

**Majors. Education:** Art. **Visual/performing arts:** General, design, industrial design, painting, printmaking, sculpture.

**Most popular majors.** Education 19%, visual/performing arts 81%.

**Computing on campus.** 22 workstations in library, computer center.

**Student life. Freshman orientation:** Available. Preregistration for classes offered. **Policies:** Policies in effect regarding drugs and alcohol, academic progress, sexual harassment; security workshops; handicap policies. **Activities:** Film society, literary magazine, music ensembles, student government.

**Student services.** Adult student services, alcohol/substance abuse counseling, career counseling, financial aid counseling, personal counseling. **Physically disabled:** Services for speech impaired.

**Contact.** Phone: (787) 725-8120 ext. 233 Fax: (787) 725-8111
Janet Centeno, Director of Admissions, Escuela de Artes Plasticas de Puerto Rico, PO Box 9021112, San Juan, PR 00902-1112

## Inter American University of Puerto Rico: Aguadilla Campus
### Aguadilla, Puerto Rico
### www.aguadilla.inter.edu                    CB code: 2042

- Private 4-year university and liberal arts college
- Commuter campus in small city
- 3,953 degree-seeking undergraduates: 15% part-time, 56% women, 100% Hispanic American
- 175 degree-seeking graduate students
- 93% of applicants admitted
- 18% graduate within 6 years

**General.** Founded in 1957. Regionally accredited. Adult higher education program, continuing education program. **Degrees:** 362 bachelor's, 47 associate awarded; master's offered. **ROTC:** Army, Air Force. **Location:** 10 miles from Aguadilla City, 17 miles from Mayaguez. **Calendar:** Semester, extensive summer session. **Full-time faculty:** 76 total; 28% have terminal degrees, 58% women. **Part-time faculty:** 168 total; 13% have terminal degrees, 55% women. **Special facilities:** Manuel Mendez Bellester special collection.

**Freshman class profile.** 884 applied, 818 admitted, 666 enrolled.

**Basis for selection.** Regular program requires minimum 2.0 GPA from accredited secondary school and combined score of 800 on SAT (exclusive of Writing) or PAA. School achievement record, test scores very important. Pilot Program requires minimum 1.75 GPA from accredited secondary school and College Board examination test. SAT accepted for English-speaking applicants. Interview required for AVANCE, adult higher education, and Educational Services Programs.

**High school preparation.** 18 units required. Required units include English 3, mathematics 2, history 2, science 2, foreign language 3 and academic electives 6.

**2007-2008 Annual costs.** Tuition/fees: $4,874.

**Financial aid. Non-need-based:** Scholarships awarded for academics.

**Application procedures. Admission:** Priority date 5/1; deadline 5/15 (receipt date). No application fee. Application may be submitted online. Admission notification on a rolling basis. **Financial aid:** Closing date 4/30. FAFSA required. Applicants notified by 6/15; must reply by 8/8.

**Academics. Special study options:** Cross-registration, distance learning, dual enrollment of high school students, exchange student, honors, independent study, internships, teacher certification program, Washington semester, weekend college. **Credit/placement by examination:** AP, CLEP. **Support services:** Learning center, remedial instruction, study skills assistance, tutoring.

**Majors. Biology:** General, biotechnology, microbiology. **Business:** Accounting, administrative services, business admin, hotel/motel admin, management information systems, marketing. **Computer sciences:** Computer science, networking. **Education:** Early childhood, elementary, secondary. **Engineering technology:** Electrical. **Health:** Nursing (RN). **Parks/recreation:** Facilities management. **Protective services:** Criminal justice. **Other:** Psychosocial Human Services.

**Most popular majors.** Business/marketing 23%, education 43%, health sciences 7%, public administration/social services 6%, security/protective services 7%.

**Computing on campus.** 493 workstations in library, computer center. Commuter students can connect to campus network. Online course registration, online library, wireless network available.

**Student life. Freshman orientation:** Mandatory. One-day program in August. **Activities:** Choral groups, drama, radio station, student government, Juventud Universitaria Catolica, Asociacion Evangelica Universitaria, Future Teachers Association, Criminal Justice Association, Secretarial Sciences Association, Psychosocial Human Services Association, Hotel Management Association, Marketing Association, Honors Society.

**Athletics. Intercollegiate:** Baseball M, basketball, cheerleading, cross-country, judo, soccer M, softball, table tennis, tennis, track and field, volleyball, weight lifting. **Intramural:** Basketball, cross-country, softball, table tennis, tennis, track and field, volleyball, weight lifting. **Team name:** Tigers.

**Student services.** Adult student services, campus ministries, career counseling, student employment services, financial aid counseling, health services, personal counseling, placement for graduates, veterans' counselor.

**Contact.** Phone: (787) 891-0925 ext. 2101 Fax: (787) 882-3020
Doris Perez, Director of Admissions, Inter American University of Puerto Rico: Aguadilla Campus, Box 20000, Aguadilla, PR 00605

## Inter American University of Puerto Rico: Arecibo Campus
**Arecibo, Puerto Rico**
**www.arecibo.inter.edu**
**CB code: 1411**

- Private 4-year liberal arts college
- Commuter campus in small city
- 4,241 degree-seeking undergraduates

**General.** Founded in 1957. Regionally accredited. **Degrees:** 413 bachelor's, 29 associate awarded; master's offered. **ROTC:** Army. **Location:** 45 miles from San Juan. **Calendar:** Semester, limited summer session. **Full-time faculty:** 88 total. **Part-time faculty:** 209 total.

**Basis for selection.** Minimum 2.0 high school GPA. Test scores important; minimum admission index of 800 required. Special admissions policies apply to adults 21 years or older. SAT required of English-speaking applicants. Score reports by August 3. Interview recommended for academically weak.

**High school preparation.** 15 units required. Required units include English 3, mathematics 3, social studies 3, science 3 and foreign language 3.

**2007-2008 Annual costs.** Tuition/fees: $4,886. Books/supplies: $890. Personal expenses: $880.

**Financial aid. Non-need-based:** Scholarships awarded for academics, athletics.

**Application procedures. Admission:** No application fee. Application may be submitted online. Admission notification on a rolling basis. **Financial aid:** Priority date 4/28; no closing date. FAFSA, institutional form required. Applicants notified on a rolling basis.

**Academics. Special study options:** Cooperative education, distance learning, honors, independent study, internships, study abroad, teacher certification program. **Credit/placement by examination:** AP, CLEP, institutional tests. 15 credit hours maximum toward associate degree, 15 toward bachelor's. **Support services:** Pre-admission summer program, remedial instruction, study skills assistance, tutoring.

**Majors. Biology:** General, bacteriology. **Business:** Accounting, administrative services, business admin, management science. **Computer sciences:** General, computer science. **Education:** Biology, chemistry, early childhood, elementary, secondary, Spanish, special. **Health:** Nursing (RN). **Physical sciences:** Chemistry. **Protective services:** Criminal justice. **Public administration:** Social work.

**Computing on campus.** 350 workstations in library, computer center. Commuter students can connect to campus network. Helpline, wireless network available.

**Student life. Freshman orientation:** Mandatory. **Activities:** Drama, student government, Baptist Unity, Young Catholics Association, Criminal Justice Association, Haziel Evangelical Association, Future Social Workers Association, Bahai Association, Student Counseling Association, Society for Human Resources.

**Athletics. Intercollegiate:** Basketball, soccer, softball, table tennis, tennis, track and field, volleyball. **Intramural:** Basketball, cheerleading, soccer, softball, table tennis, tennis, track and field, volleyball. **Team name:** Tigers.

**Student services.** Adult student services, alcohol/substance abuse counseling, campus ministries, career counseling, student employment services, health services, personal counseling, veterans' counselor. **Physically disabled:** Services for visually, hearing impaired.

**Contact.** E-mail: pmontalvo@arecibo.inter.edu
Phone: (787) 878-5195 Fax: (787) 880-1624
Provi Montalvo, Director of Admissions, Inter American University of Puerto Rico: Arecibo Campus, PO Box 4050, Arecibo, PR 00614-4050

## Inter American University of Puerto Rico: Barranquitas Campus
**Barranquitas, Puerto Rico**
**www.br.inter.edu**
**CB code: 2067**

- Private 4-year university and branch campus college
- Commuter campus in large town
- 2,068 degree-seeking undergraduates: 23% part-time, 60% women
- 106 degree-seeking graduate students

**General.** Founded in 1957. Regionally accredited. **Degrees:** 244 bachelor's, 32 associate awarded; master's offered. **Location:** 35 miles from San Juan. **Calendar:** Semester, extensive summer session. **Full-time faculty:** 41 total. **Part-time faculty:** 105 total. **Special facilities:** Nature preserve, 35 e-classrooms.

**Basis for selection.** 2.0 high school GPA and minimum PAA or SAT score required. Interview, portfolio, essay recommended. **Homeschooled:** Transcript of courses and grades, state high school equivalency certificate required.

**High school preparation.** 15 units required. Required units include English 3, mathematics 2, social studies 2 and science 3. 3 units of Spanish required for Puerto Rican high school graduates, 2 units liberal arts recommended.

**2007-2008 Annual costs.** Tuition/fees: $4,874. Books/supplies: $900. Personal expenses: $2,731.

**Financial aid.** All financial aid based on need.

**Application procedures. Admission:** No deadline. No application fee. Application may be submitted online. Admission notification on a rolling basis. **Financial aid:** Closing date 4/30. FAFSA required. Applicants notified on a rolling basis; must reply within 2 week(s) of notification.

**Academics. Special study options:** Accelerated study, combined bachelor's/graduate degree, cross-registration, distance learning, ESL, honors, independent study, internships, liberal arts/career combination, teacher certification program, Washington semester, weekend college. **Credit/placement by examination:** CLEP. **Support services:** Learning center, pre-admission summer program, remedial instruction, study skills assistance, tutoring.

**Majors. Biology:** General, biotechnology. **Business:** General, accounting, administrative services, business admin. **Computer sciences:** General, computer science, information systems. **Education:** General, biology, early childhood, elementary, English, mathematics, secondary, social studies, Spanish, visually handicapped. **Engineering:** General. **Health:** Audiology/speech pathology, nursing (RN), radiologic technology/medical imaging. **Protective services:** Law enforcement admin.

**Most popular majors.** Business/marketing 16%, education 56%, health sciences 8%, social sciences 11%.

**Computing on campus.** 43 workstations in library, computer center, student center. Commuter students can connect to campus network. Online course registration, online library, helpline, wireless network available.

**Student life. Freshman orientation:** Mandatory. **Activities:** Concert band, dance, drama, literary magazine, musical theater, student government, student newspaper.

**Athletics.** NAIA. **Intercollegiate:** Baseball M, basketball M, cross-country, softball, tennis, volleyball. **Team name:** Tigers.

**Student services.** Adult student services, career counseling, personal counseling, veterans' counselor. **Physically disabled:** Services for visually, speech, hearing impaired.

**Contact.** E-mail: mdiaz@br.inter.edu
Phone: (787) 857-3600 ext. 2011 Fax: (787) 857-2125
Maribel Diaz, Director of Admissions, Inter American University of Puerto Rico: Barranquitas Campus, PO Box 517, Barranquitas, PR 00794

## Inter American University of Puerto Rico: Bayamon Campus
**Bayamon, Puerto Rico**
bc.inter.edu                                              CB code: 2043

- Private 4-year university and engineering college
- Commuter campus in small city
- 4,983 degree-seeking undergraduates: 16% part-time, 50% women, 100% Hispanic American
- 31 degree-seeking graduate students
- 39% of applicants admitted
- 23% graduate within 6 years

**General.** Founded in 1912. Regionally accredited. **Degrees:** 456 bachelor's, 39 associate awarded; master's offered. **ROTC:** Army, Naval, Air Force. **Location:** 15 miles from San Juan. **Calendar:** Semester, limited summer session. **Full-time faculty:** 99 total; 34% have terminal degrees, 48% women. **Part-time faculty:** 215 total; 6% have terminal degrees, 42% women. **Special facilities:** Wetland used as a natural laboratory, mata de platano field station.

**Freshman class profile.** 4,081 applied, 1,609 admitted, 1,178 enrolled.

| GPA 3.50 or higher: | 20% | GPA 2.0-2.99: | 50% |
|---|---|---|---|
| GPA 3.0-3.49: | 27% | | |

**Basis for selection.** High school GPA and test scores most important. Minimum GPA of 2.0, minimum admission index (based on college formula) of 800. Achievement tests required for placement in math, English, and Spanish. Interview recommended.

**High school preparation.** Required units include English 3, mathematics 3, social studies 1, history 2, science 3 and foreign language 3.

**2007-2008 Annual costs.** Tuition/fees: $4,912. Books/supplies: $890.

**2007-2008 Financial aid.** All financial aid based on need. Average need met was 3%. Average scholarship/grant was $284; average loan $303. 25% of total undergraduate aid awarded as scholarships/grants, 75% as loans/jobs.

**Application procedures.** **Admission:** Closing date 5/1 (receipt date). No application fee. Application may be submitted online. Admission notification on a rolling basis. Must reply by 8/1. **Financial aid:** Priority date 6/30; no closing date. FAFSA required. Applicants notified on a rolling basis starting 5/10.

**Academics.** **Special study options:** Accelerated study, cooperative education, distance learning, honors, independent study, internships, study abroad. **Credit/placement by examination:** AP, CLEP. 225 credit hours maximum toward associate degree, 225 toward bachelor's. **Support services:** Learning center, pre-admission summer program, study skills assistance, tutoring.

**Majors.** **Biology:** General, bioinformatics, biomedical sciences, biotechnology, environmental, microbiology. **Business:** Accounting, administrative services, business admin, entrepreneurial studies, executive assistant, finance, human resources, management information systems, management science, managerial economics, marketing, office technology. **Communications technology:** General. **Computer sciences:** Computer science, information systems. **Conservation:** General, environmental science. **Engineering:** General, electrical, industrial, mechanical. **Engineering technology:** Electrical, industrial management. **Interdisciplinary:** Math/computer science. **Math:** General, applied. **Mechanic/repair:** Computer. **Physical sciences:** Chemistry. **Protective services:** Forensics. **Public administration:** General. **Science technology:** Chemical. **Transportation:** Air traffic control, airline/commercial pilot, aviation, aviation management, flight instructor.

**Most popular majors.** Biology 9%, business/marketing 44%, communication technologies 12%, engineering/engineering technologies 14%, trade and industry 11%.

**Computing on campus.** 480 workstations in library, computer center. Commuter students can connect to campus network. Online course registration, online library, repair service, wireless network available.

**Student life.** **Freshman orientation:** Mandatory. Preregistration for classes offered. **Housing:** Substance-free housing available. **Activities:** Concert band, choral groups, drama, student council, business administration students association, Catholic students association, Christian university brotherhood association, society of joined students for science, photography club, AN-CLA group, senior class association, engineering students association.

**Athletics.** **Intercollegiate:** Baseball M, basketball, cross-country, soccer M, softball, swimming, table tennis, tennis, track and field, volleyball, wrestling M. **Intramural:** Basketball, cross-country, softball, swimming, table tennis, tennis, track and field, volleyball, wrestling M. **Team name:** Tigers.

**Student services.** Adult student services, alcohol/substance abuse counseling, campus ministries, career counseling, student employment services, financial aid counseling, health services, on-campus daycare, personal counseling, placement for graduates, veterans' counselor. **Physically disabled:** Services for visually, speech, hearing impaired.

**Contact.** E-mail: calicea@bc.inter.edu
Phone: (787) 279-1912 ext. 2017 Fax: (787) 279-2205
Carlos Alicea, Director of Admissions, Inter American University of Puerto Rico: Bayamon Campus, 500 Dr. John Will Harris Road, Bayamon, PR 00957

## Inter American University of Puerto Rico: Fajardo Campus
**Fajardo, Puerto Rico**
fajardo.inter.edu                                         CB code: 2065

- Private 4-year university and branch campus college
- Commuter campus in large town
- 2,256 undergraduates
- 39% of applicants admitted

**General.** Regionally accredited. **Degrees:** 245 bachelor's, 22 associate awarded; master's offered. **ROTC:** Air Force. **Location:** 34 miles from San Juan. **Calendar:** Semester, limited summer session. **Full-time faculty:** 41 total; 29% have terminal degrees, 56% women. **Part-time faculty:** 121 total; 58% women.

**Freshman class profile.** 1,722 applied, 665 admitted, 532 enrolled.

**Basis for selection.** High school students must have 2.0 GPA and average of 400 on first three parts of PAA. Special admissions policies apply to adults age 21 or older. PAA test required for Spanish-speaking applicants; SAT or ACT required for English-speaking applicants. Interview required for adult education program.

**High school preparation.** 15 units required. Required units include English 3, mathematics 2, social studies 2 and science 3. 3 units Spanish required for Puerto Rican students.

**2007-2008 Annual costs.** Tuition/fees: $4,939. Books/supplies: $686.

**Application procedures.** **Admission:** Closing date 5/15. No application fee. Application may be submitted online. Admission notification on a rolling basis. **Financial aid:** Closing date 4/30. FAFSA, institutional form required. Applicants notified on a rolling basis.

**Academics.** **Special study options:** Cross-registration, distance learning, double major, dual enrollment of high school students, ESL, honors, independent study, internships, Washington semester. Adult education program. **Credit/placement by examination:** CLEP, institutional tests. 15 credit hours maximum toward bachelor's degree. Maximum 24 credit hours counted for adult education students. **Support services:** Tutoring.

**Majors.** **Business:** General, accounting, administrative services, business admin. **Education:** General, biology, early childhood, elementary, ESL, secondary, social studies, Spanish. **Protective services:** Criminal justice.

**Most popular majors.** Business/marketing 41%, computer/information sciences 18%, education 21%, science technologies 10%, social sciences 15%.

**Computing on campus.** 188 workstations in library, computer center. Commuter students can connect to campus network. Online library, wireless network available.

**Student life.** **Freshman orientation:** Mandatory. **Activities:** Dance, student government, student council, young Christian students fraternity, tourism student association, history club, human resources students association, future teachers association, criminal justice student association, multilingual student association, special education students association, computer science student association.

**Athletics. Intramural:** Basketball, softball, table tennis, tennis, track and field, volleyball.

**Student services.** Adult student services, campus ministries, career counseling, student employment services, financial aid counseling, health services, personal counseling, placement for graduates, veterans' counselor.

**Contact.**   E-mail: adcaraba@fajardo.inter.edu
Phone: (787) 860-3100 Fax: (787) 860-3470
Ada Caraballo, Admissions Director, Inter American University of Puerto Rico: Fajardo Campus, Call Box 70003, Fajardo, PR 00738-7003

---

### Inter American University of Puerto Rico: Guayama Campus
**Guayama, Puerto Rico**
www.guayama.inter.edu                     CB code: 2077

▶ Private 4-year university
▶ Commuter campus in large town
▶ 2,151 degree-seeking undergraduates: 22% part-time, 70% women, 100% Hispanic American
▶ 33 degree-seeking graduate students
▶ 84% of applicants admitted
▶ Interview required
▶ 22% graduate within 6 years

**General.** Founded in 1957. Regionally accredited. **Degrees:** 235 bachelor's, 59 associate awarded; master's offered. **ROTC:** Army. **Location:** 18 miles from Ponce. **Calendar:** Semester, limited summer session. **Full-time faculty:** 44 total. **Part-time faculty:** 162 total. **Class size:** 54% < 20, 41% 20-39, 5% 40-49.

**Freshman class profile.** 418 applied, 351 admitted, 292 enrolled.

**Basis for selection.** High school graduates must have 2.0 GPA and 800 admission index.

**2007-2008 Annual costs.** Tuition/fees: $4,874. All undergraduates not already insured pay $240 for health insurance coverage. Books/supplies: $800. Personal expenses: $350.

**2007-2008 Financial aid.** All financial aid based on need. Average need met was 3%. Average scholarship/grant was $159; average loan $489. 17% of total undergraduate aid awarded as scholarships/grants, 83% as loans/jobs.

**Application procedures. Admission:** Priority date 5/15; no deadline. No application fee. Application may be submitted online. Admission notification on a rolling basis beginning on or about 4/1. **Financial aid:** Closing date 4/29. FAFSA, institutional form required. Applicants notified by 6/15; must reply by 7/30.

**Academics. Special study options:** Accelerated study, distance learning, dual enrollment of high school students, exchange student, external degree, honors, internships, study abroad, teacher certification program, weekend college. **Credit/placement by examination:** CLEP. **Support services:** Learning center, remedial instruction, tutoring.

**Majors. Biology:** General, biotechnology. **Business:** Accounting, business admin, human resources, office management. **Education:** Early childhood special, elementary, ESL, kindergarten/preschool, physical. **Health:** Nursing (RN), respiratory therapy technology. **Mechanic/repair:** Computer. **Philosophy/religion:** Religion. **Protective services:** Law enforcement admin.

**Most popular majors.** Business/marketing 37%, computer/information sciences 11%, education 27%, health sciences 10%, security/protective services 10%.

**Computing on campus.** 250 workstations in library, computer center, student center. Online library, wireless network available.

**Student life. Freshman orientation:** Mandatory. **Activities:** Choral groups, dance, student government, religious circle.

**Athletics. Intercollegiate:** Baseball M, basketball, cross-country, soccer M. **Intramural:** Baseball M, basketball, cross-country M, softball, table tennis W, tennis W, track and field.

---

**Student services.** Adult student services, campus ministries, career counseling, student employment services, health services, personal counseling, placement for graduates, veterans' counselor. **Physically disabled:** Services for visually impaired.

**Contact.**   E-mail: lferrer@inter.edu
Phone: (787) 864-7059 Fax: (787) 864-8232
Laura Ferrer-Sanchez, Director of Admissions, Inter American University of Puerto Rico: Guayama Campus, PO Box 10004, Guayama, PR 00785

---

### Inter American University of Puerto Rico: Metropolitan Campus
**San Juan, Puerto Rico**                               CB member
http://metro.inter.edu/                               CB code: 0873

▶ Private 4-year branch campus college
▶ Commuter campus in large city
▶ 6,780 degree-seeking undergraduates: 30% part-time, 54% women, 100% Hispanic American
▶ 3,303 degree-seeking graduate students
▶ 22% of applicants admitted
▶ 20% graduate within 6 years

**General.** Founded in 1962. Regionally accredited. **Degrees:** 793 bachelor's, 44 associate awarded; master's, doctoral offered. **ROTC:** Army, Air Force. **Location:** 9 miles from San Juan. **Calendar:** Semester, limited summer session. **Full-time faculty:** 215 total; 54% have terminal degrees, 54% women. **Part-time faculty:** 369 total; 33% have terminal degrees, 50% women. **Class size:** 48% < 20, 42% 20-39, 7% 40-49, 3% 50-99, less than 1% >100.

**Freshman class profile.** 4,204 applied, 914 admitted, 795 enrolled.

**Basis for selection.** School grade average and test scores important. Minimum GPA of 2.0 plus score average of 400 in SAT. Special admissions policies apply to adults 21 years of age or older. SAT required of English-speaking applicants.

**High school preparation.** Required units include English 3, mathematics 3 and science 3.

**2007-2008 Annual costs.** Tuition/fees: $4,926. Books/supplies: $985. Personal expenses: $3,592.

**2007-2008 Financial aid. Need-based:** 29 full-time freshmen applied for aid; 14 were judged to have need; 11 of these received aid. Average scholarship/grant was $4; average loan $6. 41% of total undergraduate aid awarded as scholarships/grants, 59% as loans/jobs. **Non-need-based:** Awarded to 28 full-time undergraduates, including 1 freshmen.

**Application procedures. Admission:** Closing date 5/15 (receipt date). No application fee. Application may be submitted online. Admission notification on a rolling basis. Must reply by 8/15. **Financial aid:** Closing date 4/30. FAFSA required. Applicants notified on a rolling basis.

**Academics.** Adult education programs available. **Special study options:** Accelerated study, distance learning, ESL, honors, independent study, internships. **Credit/placement by examination:** AP, CLEP. 12 credit hours maximum toward associate degree, 12 toward bachelor's. Departmental convalidation test. **Support services:** Learning center, pre-admission summer program, remedial instruction, study skills assistance, tutoring, writing center.

**Majors. Biology:** General, biomedical sciences. **Business:** Accounting, administrative services, business admin, finance, human resources, management information systems, marketing, office/clerical. **Computer sciences:** General. **Education:** Bilingual, biology, chemistry, early childhood, elementary, English, ESL, history, learning disabled, mathematics, mentally handicapped, multi-level teacher, multiple handicapped, physical, science, secondary, social science, social studies, Spanish, special, speech impaired. **English:** English lit. **Foreign languages:** Spanish. **Health:** Clinical lab science, nursing (RN). **History:** General. **Math:** General. **Physical sciences:** Chemistry. **Protective services:** Criminal justice. **Psychology:** General. **Public administration:** Social work. **Social sciences:** General, anthropology, political science, sociology.

**Computing on campus.** 708 workstations in library, computer center. Commuter students can connect to campus network. Online course registration, online library available.

**Student life. Freshman orientation:** Mandatory. Preregistration for classes offered. Held 2 weeks before regular classes begin. **Activities:** Choral groups, drama, student government, student newspaper, Asociacion Justicia Criminal, Futuros Trabajadores Sociales, Asociacion Cristiana Universitaria, Asociacion Circulo de Psicologia, American Marketing Association, Asociacion

Profesionales de Justicia Criminal, Asociacion Graduados de Psicologia, English Trimestral Association, Asociacion para la Gerencia de los Recursos Humanos, Asociacion Estudiantes de Quimica.

**Athletics. Intercollegiate:** Baseball M, basketball, judo M, softball, swimming, tennis, track and field, volleyball. **Intramural:** Basketball, softball, table tennis, tennis, volleyball. **Team name:** Tigres.

**Student services.** Adult student services, alcohol/substance abuse counseling, campus ministries, career counseling, student employment services, financial aid counseling, health services, on-campus daycare, personal counseling, placement for graduates, veterans' counselor. **Physically disabled:** Services for visually, speech, hearing impaired.

**Contact.** E-mail: jolivieri@metro.inter.edu
Phone: (787) 250-1912 ext. 2188 Fax: (787) 250-1025
Janies Olivieri, Admissions, Inter American University of Puerto Rico: Metropolitan Campus, Box 191293, San Juan, PR 00919-1293

## Inter American University of Puerto Rico: Ponce Campus

**Mercedita, Puerto Rico**

ponce.inter.edu                 CB code: 3531

- Private 4-year university
- Large town
- 5,163 degree-seeking undergraduates: 17% part-time, 63% women, 100% Hispanic American
- 243 degree-seeking graduate students
- 71% of applicants admitted
- 15% graduate within 6 years

**General.** Regionally accredited. **Degrees:** 527 bachelor's, 86 associate awarded; master's offered. **ROTC:** Naval. **Calendar:** Semester. **Full-time faculty:** 87 total; 30% have terminal degrees, 54% women. **Part-time faculty:** 204 total; 6% have terminal degrees, 57% women. **Class size:** 36% <20, 46% 20-39, 13% 40-49, 6% 50-99, less than 1% >100.

**Freshman class profile.** 1,590 applied, 1,124 admitted, 915 enrolled.

**Basis for selection.** 2.0 high school GPA and average of 400 on first three parts of PAA. Interview required for AVANCE program.

**High school preparation.** 18 units required. Required units include English 3, mathematics 3, social studies 1, history 3, science 3 (laboratory 1), foreign language 3 and academic electives 1.

**2007-2008 Annual costs.** Tuition/fees: $4,886. Books/supplies: $921. Personal expenses: $2,831.

**2007-2008 Financial aid.** All financial aid based on need. 1,238 full-time freshmen applied for aid; 1,229 were judged to have need; 984 of these received aid. Average need met was 2%. Average scholarship/grant was $208; average loan $205. 29% of total undergraduate aid awarded as scholarships/grants, 71% as loans/jobs.

**Application procedures. Admission:** Closing date 5/15 (receipt date). No application fee. Admission notification on a rolling basis. **Financial aid:** No deadline. FAFSA required.

**Academics. Special study options:** Cooperative education, distance learning, honors, independent study, internships, study abroad, teacher certification program, weekend college. Adult programs (AVANCE), development programs, PREAD program. **Credit/placement by examination:** CLEP. **Support services:** Learning center, study skills assistance, tutoring.

**Majors. Biology:** General. **Business:** Accounting, administrative services, business admin, finance, hotel/motel admin, human resources, international, management information systems, management science, marketing, office technology, operations, training/development. **Communications:** Journalism, public relations. **Computer sciences:** Computer science, information systems. **Conservation:** General. **Education:** Biology, early childhood, elementary, ESL, secondary, special. **Health:** Nursing (RN). **Protective services:** Law enforcement admin.

**Most popular majors.** Business/marketing 31%, computer/information sciences 8%, education 33%, health sciences 6%, legal studies 12%.

**Computing on campus.** PC or laptop required. 490 workstations in library, computer center, student center. Commuter students can connect to campus network. Online course registration, online library, helpline available.

**Student life. Freshman orientation:** Available. Includes workshops, seminars, and social activities. **Activities:** Concert band, choral groups, dance, student government, student newspaper.

**Athletics. Intercollegiate:** Baseball M, basketball, judo, softball, swimming, table tennis, track and field, triathlon, volleyball, weight lifting, wrestling. **Intramural:** Baseball M, basketball M, softball, table tennis, track and field, volleyball, weight lifting. **Team name:** Tigers.

**Student services.** Adult student services, alcohol/substance abuse counseling, campus ministries, career counseling, student employment services, financial aid counseling, health services, on-campus daycare, personal counseling, placement for graduates, women's services. **Physically disabled:** Services for visually, speech, hearing impaired.

**Contact.** E-mail: fldiaz@poce.inter.edu
Phone: (787) 841-0110 Fax: (787) 841-0103
Franco Diaz Vega, Director of Admissions, Inter American University of Puerto Rico: Ponce Campus, 104 Turpo Industrial Park Road #1, Mercedita, PR 00715-1602

## Inter American University of Puerto Rico: San German Campus

**San German, Puerto Rico**

www.sg.inter.edu                 CB code: 0946

- Private 4-year university
- Commuter campus in large town
- 4,645 degree-seeking undergraduates: 15% part-time, 52% women
- 774 degree-seeking graduate students
- 99% of applicants admitted
- SAT or ACT (ACT writing optional) required
- 5% graduate within 6 years

**General.** Founded in 1912. Regionally accredited. San German Inter American School (pre-school to grade 12). **Degrees:** 531 bachelor's, 33 associate awarded; master's, doctoral offered. **ROTC:** Army, Air Force. **Location:** 14 miles from Mayaguez, 104 miles from San Juan. **Calendar:** Semester, extensive summer session. **Full-time faculty:** 131 total; 46% have terminal degrees, 54% women. **Part-time faculty:** 195 total; 15% have terminal degrees, 57% women. **Class size:** 42% <20, 53% 20-39, 4% 40-49, less than 1% 50-99. **Special facilities:** Nature preserve, botanical garden.

**Freshman class profile.** 1,107 applied, 1,097 admitted, 745 enrolled.

**Basis for selection.** High school GPA and test scores important. SAT required of English-speaking applicants. Essay, interview recommended for all; audition recommended for music; portfolio recommended for art programs. **Homeschooled:** Statement describing homeschool structure and mission required.

**High school preparation.** 11 units required; 18 recommended. Required and recommended units include English 3, mathematics 2-3, social studies 2-3, history 2-3, science 2-3, foreign language 3 and academic electives 3. 3 units of Spanish required of Spanish-speaking students.

**2007-2008 Annual costs.** Tuition/fees: $4,939. Room/board: $2,400. Books/supplies: $890. Personal expenses: $880.

**2006-2007 Financial aid. Need-based:** 1,095 full-time freshmen applied for aid; 1,072 were judged to have need; 884 of these received aid. Average need met was 4%. Average scholarship/grant was $299; average loan $461. 59% of total undergraduate aid awarded as scholarships/grants, 41% as loans/jobs. **Non-need-based:** Awarded to 130 full-time undergraduates, including 27 freshmen. Scholarships awarded for academics, athletics.

**Application procedures. Admission:** Closing date 5/15 (receipt date). No application fee. Application may be submitted online. Admission notification on a rolling basis beginning on or about 2/15. **Financial aid:** Closing date 5/14. FAFSA, institutional form required. Applicants notified on a rolling basis; must reply by 8/1.

**Academics.** Bilingual program enables students to learn English or Spanish while taking courses in their native language. **Special study options:** Accelerated study, cooperative education, cross-registration, distance learning, double major, dual enrollment of high school students, ESL, honors, independent study, internships, liberal arts/career combination, study abroad, teacher certification program. **Credit/placement by examination:** AP, CLEP, institutional tests. 12 credit hours maximum toward associate degree, 18 toward bachelor's. **Support services:** Learning center, reduced course load, remedial instruction, tutoring.

**Majors. Architecture:** Architecture. **Biology:** General. **Business:** Accounting, administrative services, business admin, finance, human resources, management information systems, management science, marketing, office management. **Computer sciences:** General, computer science. **Education:** General, art, biology, chemistry, early childhood, elementary, English, ESL, history, kindergarten/preschool, mathematics, music, physical, secondary, social studies, Spanish, special, voc/tech. **Engineering technology:** Electrical. **English:** English lit. **Health:** Clinical lab science, licensed practical nurse, nursing (RN). **Math:** General. **Parks/recreation:** Health/fitness. **Physical sciences:** Chemistry. **Psychology:** General. **Public administration:** General. **Social sciences:** Political science, sociology. **Visual/performing arts:** General, ceramics, drawing, music performance, painting, photography, sculpture.

**Most popular majors.** Biology 13%, business/marketing 17%, education 36%, psychology 7%.

**Computing on campus.** 800 workstations in dormitories, library, computer center, student center. Dormitories wired for high-speed internet access and linked to campus network. Commuter students can connect to campus network. Online course registration, online library, wireless network available.

**Student life. Freshman orientation:** Mandatory. Preregistration for classes offered. General orientation program offered in spring, summer and fall. **Housing:** Single-sex dorms, apartments, substance-free housing available. $25 fully refundable deposit, deadline 6/30. **Activities:** Bands, choral groups, dance, drama, international student organizations, music ensembles, student government, student newspaper, Bahai association, student bible union, counselors student association, Catholic student organization, bilingual English-Spanish organization.

**Athletics. Intercollegiate:** Baseball M, basketball, cross-country, soccer M, softball, swimming, table tennis, tennis, track and field, volleyball, weight lifting. **Intramural:** Basketball, cross-country, softball, table tennis, tennis, track and field, volleyball. **Team name:** Tigers.

**Student services.** Adult student services, alcohol/substance abuse counseling, campus ministries, career counseling, student employment services, financial aid counseling, health services, on-campus daycare, personal counseling, placement for graduates, veterans' counselor.

**Contact.** E-mail: milcama@sg.inter.edu
Phone: (787) 892-3090 Fax: (787) 892-6350
Mildred Camacho, Director of Admissions, Inter American University of Puerto Rico: San German Campus, Box 5100, San German, PR 00683-9801

---

## Pontifical Catholic University of Puerto Rico

**Ponce, Puerto Rico**
www.pucpr.edu

**CB member**
**CB code: 0910**

- Private 4-year university affiliated with Roman Catholic Church
- Commuter campus in small city
- 5,203 degree-seeking undergraduates
- 82% of applicants admitted
- SAT or ACT (ACT writing optional) required
- 38% graduate within 6 years

**General.** Founded in 1948. Regionally accredited. Branch campuses in Arecibo and Mayaguez. **Degrees:** 704 bachelor's, 11 associate awarded; master's, doctoral, first professional offered. **ROTC:** Army, Air Force. **Location:** 60 miles from San Juan. **Calendar:** Semester, limited summer session. **Full-time faculty:** 192 total. **Part-time faculty:** 188 total.

**Freshman class profile.** 1,694 applied, 1,387 admitted, 1,049 enrolled.

| Mid 50% test scores | | Live on campus: | 4% |
|---|---|---|---|
| SAT critical reading: | 400-530 | Fraternities: | 1% |
| SAT math: | 400-530 | Sororities: | 1% |

**Basis for selection.** School achievement record, test scores important. SAT required of English-speaking applicants. Interview required for special program. **Homeschooled:** Transcript of courses and grades required.

**High school preparation.** 15 units required. Required units include English 4, mathematics 3, history 2, science 2 and foreign language 4. 3 units English, 3 units foreign language, 2 units mathematics, 1 unit science, 1 unit history required for 3-year high schools.

**2007-2008 Annual costs.** Tuition/fees: $5,018. Books/supplies: $600. Personal expenses: $316.

---

**Financial aid. Non-need-based:** Scholarships awarded for academics, athletics.

**Application procedures. Admission:** Priority date 3/15; deadline 7/15 (receipt date). $15 fee, may be waived for applicants with need. Admission notification on a rolling basis beginning on or about 2/15. **Financial aid:** Priority date 5/1; no closing date. FAFSA, institutional form required. Applicants notified by 6/15; must reply within 4 week(s) of notification.

**Academics. Special study options:** Accelerated study, combined bachelor's/graduate degree, double major, dual enrollment of high school students, ESL, exchange student, honors, independent study, internships, liberal arts/career combination, study abroad. **Credit/placement by examination:** AP, CLEP, institutional tests. 30 credit hours maximum toward bachelor's degree. **Support services:** Learning center, pre-admission summer program, reduced course load, remedial instruction, tutoring.

**Majors. Area/ethnic studies:** Hispanic-American/Latino/Chicano. **Biology:** General. **Business:** General, accounting, administrative services, business admin, communications, finance, international, management information systems, managerial economics, marketing, tourism/travel. **Communications:** General. **Conservation:** General, environmental studies. **Education:** Art, biology, business, chemistry, early childhood, elementary, English, ESL, family/consumer sciences, history, mathematics, music, physical lit, science, secondary, social studies, Spanish, special. **English:** English lit. **Family/consumer sciences:** General. **Foreign languages:** Spanish. **Health:** Clinical lab science, health services. **History:** General. **Interdisciplinary:** Gerontology. **Legal studies:** General, prelaw. **Liberal arts:** Arts/sciences. **Math:** General. **Philosophy/religion:** Philosophy. **Physical sciences:** Chemistry, physics. **Psychology:** General. **Public administration:** General, social work. **Social sciences:** Criminology, political science, sociology. **Visual/performing arts:** Studio arts.

**Computing on campus.** 419 workstations in library, computer center, student center. Commuter students can connect to campus network. Online course registration, online library, wireless network available.

**Student life. Freshman orientation:** Mandatory. **Housing:** Single-sex dorms available. $25 nonrefundable deposit. **Activities:** Choral groups, dance, drama, musical theater, radio station, student government, student newspaper, TV station, Pi Gamma Mu, Phi Alpha Theta, Beta Beta Beta, Alpha Beta Chi, Phi Delta Kappa, honor society for business students, Pioneer Students in Christ and Mary, Miles Jesu, Knights of Columbus, Phi Sigma Kappa.

**Athletics. Intercollegiate:** Basketball, cross-country, diving, judo, soccer, softball M, swimming, table tennis, tennis, track and field, volleyball, water polo M, wrestling M. **Intramural:** Archery, basketball, cross-country, diving, softball, swimming, table tennis, tennis, track and field, volleyball, wrestling M. **Team name:** Pioneers.

**Student services.** Campus ministries, career counseling, student employment services, health services, on-campus daycare, personal counseling, placement for graduates, veterans' counselor. **Learning disabled:** Comprehensive services available.

**Contact.** E-mail: admisiones@pucpr.edu
Phone: (787) 841-2000 ext. 1000 Fax: (787) 840-4295
Ana Bonilla, Director of Admissions, Pontifical Catholic University of Puerto Rico, 2250 Las Americas Avenue, Suite 284, Ponce, PR 00717-9777

---

## Turabo University

**Gurabo, Puerto Rico**
www.suagm.edu/ut

**CB code: 0780**

- Private 4-year university and liberal arts college
- Commuter campus in small city
- 12,677 degree-seeking undergraduates: 20% part-time, 60% women, 100% Hispanic American
- 3,219 degree-seeking graduate students
- 18% graduate within 6 years

**General.** Founded in 1972. Regionally accredited. 5 off-campus sites. **Degrees:** 975 bachelor's, 79 associate awarded; master's, doctoral offered. **ROTC:** Army. **Location:** 17 miles from San Juan. **Calendar:** Semester, limited summer session. **Full-time faculty:** 153 total; 40% have terminal degrees, 100% minority, 50% women. **Part-time faculty:** 773 total; 15% have terminal degrees, 100% minority, 52% women. **Class size:** 49% < 20, 47% 20-39, 3% 40-49, less than 1% 50-99. **Special facilities:** Museum.

**Freshman class profile.** 5,986 applied, 3,090 admitted, 2,308 enrolled.

| GPA 3.50 or higher: | 12% | GPA 2.0-2.99: | 55% |
|---|---|---|---|
| GPA 3.0-3.49: | 24% | Return as sophomores: | 72% |

**Basis for selection.** Open admission, but selective for some programs. Minimum 2.0 high school GPA for secretarial applicants, 2.5 for science applicants. SAT required for admission to honors and science programs.

**High school preparation.** 15 units required. Required units include English 3, mathematics 3, social studies 2, science 2 and foreign language 3.

**2007-2008 Annual costs.** Tuition/fees: $4,340. Room/board: $4,993. Books/supplies: $1,500.

**2007-2008 Financial aid.** All financial aid based on need.

**Application procedures. Admission:** No deadline. $15 fee, may be waived for applicants with need. Admission notification on a rolling basis beginning on or about 10/7. **Financial aid:** Priority date 5/30; no closing date. FAFSA required. Applicants notified by 7/30.

**Academics. Special study options:** Accelerated study, combined bachelor's/graduate degree, distance learning, honors, independent study, internships, liberal arts/career combination, weekend college. **Credit/placement by examination:** CLEP, institutional tests. **Support services:** Remedial instruction, study skills assistance, tutoring.

**Majors. Biology:** General. **Business:** Accounting, administrative services, business admin, logistics, management information systems, marketing, office management. **Communications:** General. **Conservation:** Environmental science. **Education:** Biology, chemistry, early childhood, elementary, English, history, mathematics, physical, science, social science, Spanish, special, trade/industrial. **Engineering:** Computer, electrical, mechanical. **Engineering technology:** Architectural drafting, computer systems, electrical, industrial management, mechanical, quality control. **Foreign languages:** Sign language interpretation. **Health:** Clinical nutrition, dietetics, nursing (RN), speech pathology. **Interdisciplinary:** Natural sciences. **Liberal arts:** Humanities. **Physical sciences:** Chemistry. **Psychology:** General. **Public administration:** General, social work. **Social sciences:** General, criminology, sociology. **Visual/performing arts:** Graphic design.

**Most popular majors.** Business/marketing 37%, education 29%, engineering/engineering technologies 7%, health sciences 6%, social sciences 11%.

**Computing on campus.** Commuter students can connect to campus network. Helpline available.

**Student life. Freshman orientation:** Available. Preregistration for classes offered. **Activities:** Choral groups, dance, drama, music ensembles, radio station, student government, student newspaper, TV station.

**Athletics.** NAIA. **Intercollegiate:** Baseball M, basketball, cross-country, judo, soccer M, softball, swimming, tennis, track and field, volleyball, weight lifting. **Intramural:** Basketball, softball, table tennis, tennis W, volleyball, weight lifting. **Team name:** Taínos.

**Student services.** Adult student services, alcohol/substance abuse counseling, career counseling, services for economically disadvantaged, student employment services, financial aid counseling, health services, personal counseling, placement for graduates, veterans' counselor. **Physically disabled:** Services for visually, speech, hearing impaired.

**Contact.** Phone: (787) 746-3009 Toll-free number: (800) 747-8362 Fax: (787) 743-7940
Virginia Gonzalez, Associate Director of Admissions and Financial Aid, Turabo University, PO Box 3030, Gurabo, PR 00778

---

### Universidad Adventista de las Antillas
**Mayaguez, Puerto Rico**
www.uaa.edu                                    CB code: 1020

- Private 4-year university and liberal arts college affiliated with Seventh-day Adventists
- Commuter campus in small city
- 581 degree-seeking undergraduates: 7% part-time, 59% women

**General.** Founded in 1957. Regionally accredited. **Degrees:** 92 bachelor's, 24 associate awarded; master's offered. **Location:** 100 miles from San Juan. **Calendar:** Semester, limited summer session. **Full-time faculty:** 36 total; 22% have terminal degrees, 47% women. **Part-time faculty:** 39 total; 5% have terminal degrees, 49% women. **Class size:** 30% < 20, 49% 20-39, 9% 40-49, 11% 50-99, less than 1% >100.

**Freshman class profile.** 366 applied, 324 admitted, 286 enrolled.

---

**Basis for selection.** Open admission, but selective for some programs. SAT or ACT recommended for English-speaking applicants. Interview required for nursing program. **Homeschooled:** Unless homeschool is accredited, applicant must take GED.

**High school preparation.** 18 units recommended. Recommended units include English 3, mathematics 3, social studies 3, science 3 and academic electives 3. 3 Spanish units recommended.

**2008-2009 Annual costs.** Tuition/fees (projected): $6,892. Tuition for nonresident aliens is the sum of private tuition ($4,500) and the Form I-20 deposit ($5,000); after the first year, these students receive credit refund at registration ($500 per semester). An average of $150 per semester is included in tuition for lab expenses. Room/board: $1,650. Books/supplies: $1,000. Personal expenses: $750.

**Application procedures. Admission:** No deadline. $20 fee, may be waived for applicants with need. Admission notification on a rolling basis. **Financial aid:** No deadline. FAFSA, institutional form required. Applicants notified on a rolling basis starting 8/15; must reply within 3 week(s) of notification.

**Academics. Special study options:** Cooperative education, double major, ESL, internships, liberal arts/career combination, teacher certification program. **Credit/placement by examination:** CLEP, institutional tests. 12 credit hours maximum toward associate degree, 12 toward bachelor's. **Support services:** Learning center, reduced course load, remedial instruction, tutoring.

**Majors. Biology:** General. **Business:** General, administrative services. **Computer sciences:** General, computer science, information systems. **Education:** Elementary, music, secondary. **Foreign languages:** Spanish. **Health:** Respiratory therapy technology. **History:** General. **Physical sciences:** Chemistry. **Psychology:** General. **Theology:** Theology.

**Most popular majors.** Business/marketing 11%, education 15%, health sciences 41%, theological studies 18%.

**Computing on campus.** 62 workstations in library, computer center. Online library, repair service available.

**Student life. Freshman orientation:** Mandatory. Preregistration for classes offered. 2-day program at beginning of each semester. **Policies:** Religious environment designed for Seventh-day Adventist students. **Housing:** Guaranteed on-campus for freshmen. Single-sex dorms, apartments available. **Activities:** Concert band, choral groups, drama, music ensembles, student government, student newspaper, L.I.F.E., S.C.O.R., international club, ministerial club.

**Athletics. Intramural:** Basketball, bowling, gymnastics, soccer, softball M, swimming, table tennis, tennis, track and field, volleyball. **Team name:** Eagles Gym Team.

**Student services.** Alcohol/substance abuse counseling, campus ministries, career counseling, student employment services, financial aid counseling, health services, personal counseling, veterans' counselor.

**Contact.** E-mail: admissions@uaa.edu
Phone: (787) 834-9595 ext. 2208 Fax: (787) 834-9597
Evelyn del Valle, Director of Admissions, Universidad Adventista de las Antillas, PO Box 118, Mayaguez, PR 00681-0118

---

### Universidad Central del Caribe
**Bayamon, Puerto Rico**
www.uccaribe.edu/                              CB code: 1549

- Private 4-year university
- Small city

**General.** Regionally accredited. **Calendar:** Differs by program.

**Contact.** Phone: (787) 740-1611
Decanato de Admisiones y Asuntos Estudiantiles, Bayamon, PR 00960-6032

---

### Universidad del Este
**Carolina, Puerto Rico**                      CB member
www.suagm.edu/une                              CB code: 0883

- Private 4-year university and liberal arts college
- Commuter campus in small city
- 10,471 degree-seeking undergraduates: 28% part-time, 67% women, 100% Hispanic American

♦   822 degree-seeking graduate students

♦   14% graduate within 6 years

**General.** Founded in 1949. Regionally accredited. **Degrees:** 872 bachelor's, 117 associate awarded; master's offered. **ROTC:** Army. **Location:** 5 miles from San Juan. **Calendar:** Semester, limited summer session. **Full-time faculty:** 78 total; 30% have terminal degrees, 100% minority, 60% women. **Part-time faculty:** 811 total; 9% have terminal degrees, 100% minority, 58% women. **Class size:** 49% < 20, 49% 20-39, 2% 40-49.

**Freshman class profile.** 7,931 applied, 3,648 admitted, 2,205 enrolled.

| | | | |
|---|---|---|---|
| GPA 3.50 or higher: | 6% | GPA 2.0-2.99: | 60% |
| GPA 3.0-3.49: | 18% | Return as sophomores: | 64% |

**Basis for selection.** Open admission, but selective for some programs. Special requirements for health and science programs; interview recommended. SAT required of English-speaking freshman applicants.

**2007-2008 Annual costs.** Tuition/fees: $4,340. Room/board: $4,993. Books/supplies: $1,500.

**2007-2008 Financial aid. Non-need-based:** Scholarships awarded for academics, athletics.

**Application procedures. Admission:** Priority date 3/30; no deadline. $15 fee, may be waived for applicants with need. Application may be submitted online. Admission notification on a rolling basis. **Financial aid:** Priority date 5/30; no closing date. FAFSA, institutional form required. Applicants notified by 7/30.

**Academics. Special study options:** Accelerated study, combined bachelor's/graduate degree, distance learning, honors, independent study, internships, liberal arts/career combination, teacher certification program, weekend college. **Credit/placement by examination:** CLEP. **Support services:** Reduced course load, remedial instruction, study skills assistance, tutoring.

**Majors. Biology:** General, biotechnology, microbiology. **Business:** Accounting, administrative services, business admin, hospitality/recreation, hotel/motel admin, insurance, management information systems, marketing. **Education:** Early childhood, health, physical, science. **Family/consumer sciences:** Facilities/event planning. **Health:** Critical care nursing, health care admin, medical radiologic technology/radiation therapy, nursing (RN), radiologic technology/medical imaging, sonography. **Legal studies:** Paralegal. **Personal/culinary services:** Restaurant/catering. **Protective services:** Law enforcement admin. **Psychology:** General. **Public administration:** Social work. **Social sciences:** General, political science.

**Most popular majors.** Business/marketing 45%, education 17%, health sciences 6%, public administration/social services 17%, security/protective services 12%.

**Computing on campus.** Commuter students can connect to campus network. Online library, helpline, repair service, wireless network available.

**Student life. Freshman orientation:** Available. **Activities:** Choral groups, dance, drama, student government, student newspaper, Phi Theta Kappa, Future Secretaries of America, nursing club.

**Athletics. Intercollegiate:** Baseball M, basketball, cross-country, softball W, track and field, volleyball, weight lifting. **Intramural:** Basketball, cross-country, volleyball. **Team name:** Pitirre.

**Student services.** Adult student services, alcohol/substance abuse counseling, career counseling, services for economically disadvantaged, student employment services, financial aid counseling, health services, personal counseling, placement for graduates, veterans' counselor. **Physically disabled:** Services for visually, speech, hearing impaired.

**Contact.**   E-mail: admisiones_une@suagm.edu
Phone: (787) 257-8080 Toll-free number: (800) 981-6570
Fax: (787) 257-8601 ext. 3307
Magda Ostolaza, Director of Marketing and Recruitment, Universidad del Este, PO Box 2010, Carolina, PR 00984-2010

---

## Universidad Metropolitana
### Rio Piedras, Puerto Rico
www.suagm.edu/umet

CB member
CB code: 1519

♦   Private 4-year university and liberal arts college

♦   Commuter campus in large city

♦   9,314 degree-seeking undergraduates: 19% part-time, 68% women, 100% Hispanic American

♦   2,586 degree-seeking graduate students

♦   45% of applicants admitted

♦   15% graduate within 6 years

**General.** Founded in 1985. Regionally accredited. **Degrees:** 708 bachelor's, 79 associate awarded; master's, doctoral offered. **ROTC:** Army, Naval, Air Force. **Location:** 3 miles from San Juan. **Calendar:** Semester, limited summer session. **Full-time faculty:** 96 total; 34% have terminal degrees, 100% minority, 69% women. **Part-time faculty:** 827 total; 16% have terminal degrees, 100% minority, 53% women. **Class size:** 57% < 20, 42% 20-39, less than 1% 40-49, less than 1% 50-99.

**Freshman class profile.** 6,158 applied, 2,761 admitted, 1,587 enrolled.

| | | | |
|---|---|---|---|
| GPA 3.50 or higher: | 8% | GPA 2.0-2.99: | 59% |
| GPA 3.0-3.49: | 19% | Return as sophomores: | 64% |

**Basis for selection.** School achievement record and test scores considered. SAT required of English-speaking applicants. Interview required for academically weak. **Homeschooled:** State high school equivalency certificate required.

**2007-2008 Annual costs.** Tuition/fees: $4,340. Room/board: $4,993. Books/supplies: $1,500.

**Financial aid.** All financial aid based on need.

**Application procedures. Admission:** Closing date 8/15 (receipt date). $15 fee, may be waived for applicants with need. Admission notification on a rolling basis. **Financial aid:** Priority date 5/30; no closing date. FAFSA required. Applicants notified by 7/30.

**Academics.** Flexible admissions policy allows Universidad Metropolitana to accept challenge of providing all students with increased opportunities for success. **Special study options:** Accelerated study, combined bachelor's/graduate degree, distance learning, honors, independent study, internships, liberal arts/career combination, teacher certification program, Washington semester, weekend college. Off-campus full-degree sites. **Credit/placement by examination:** CLEP. **Support services:** Remedial instruction, tutoring.

**Majors. Biology:** General, cellular/anatomical. **Business:** Accounting, banking/financial services, business admin, management information systems, managerial economics, marketing, office management, sales/distribution, special products marketing. **Communications:** General, journalism, public relations. **Computer sciences:** Computer science. **Conservation:** Environmental science, environmental studies, management/policy. **Education:** Biology, early childhood, elementary, English, history, mathematics, multi-level teacher, physical, Spanish, special. **Engineering:** General. **Health:** EMT paramedic, environmental health, nursing (RN), respiratory therapy technology. **Interdisciplinary:** Natural sciences. **Math:** Applied. **Physical sciences:** General, chemistry. **Protective services:** Criminal justice, law enforcement admin. **Psychology:** General. **Public administration:** Social work. **Social sciences:** General.

**Most popular majors.** Business/marketing 43%, education 23%, health sciences 8%, public administration/social services 9%, security/protective services 7%.

**Computing on campus.** Commuter students can connect to campus network. Helpline, repair service available.

**Student life. Freshman orientation:** Mandatory. Preregistration for classes offered. Held 4 weeks before the beginning of the academic year. **Activities:** Choral groups, drama, student government, student newspaper, TV station, Business Students Association, Hermandad, Social Work, Students Association, Communication Students Association.

**Athletics. Intercollegiate:** Baseball, basketball, cross-country, softball, table tennis, tennis, track and field, volleyball, weight lifting M. **Intramural:** Baseball, basketball, cross-country, softball, table tennis, track and field, volleyball. **Team name:** Cocodrilo.

**Student services.** Adult student services, alcohol/substance abuse counseling, career counseling, services for economically disadvantaged, student employment services, financial aid counseling, health services, on-campus daycare, personal counseling, placement for graduates, veterans' counselor, women's services. **Physically disabled:** Services for visually, hearing impaired.

**Contact.**   Phone: (787) 765-6262 Fax: (787) 759-7663
Julio Rodríguez, Director of Admission and Financial Aid, Universidad Metropolitana, Apartado 21150, Rio Piedras, PR 00928

---

## Universidad Politecnica de Puerto Rico
### Hato Rey, Puerto Rico
www.pupr.edu

CB member
CB code: 0614

♦   Private 5-year university and engineering college

♦   Commuter campus in large city

- 5,185 degree-seeking undergraduates: 100% Hispanic American
- 724 graduate students
- 97% of applicants admitted

**General.** Founded in 1966. Regionally accredited. **Degrees:** 470 bachelor's awarded; master's offered. **ROTC:** Army, Air Force. **Location:** 3 miles from San Juan. **Calendar:** Trimester, extensive summer session. **Full-time faculty:** 167 total. **Part-time faculty:** 135 total.

**Freshman class profile.** 973 applied, 948 admitted, 761 enrolled.

**Basis for selection.** Minimum 2.5 high school GPA and PAA combined score of 1300 required. SAT in English or Spanish required. **Homeschooled:** Statement describing homeschool structure and mission, transcript of courses and grades, state high school equivalency certificate required.

**High school preparation.** 15 units required. Required units include English 3, mathematics 3, social studies 3, science 3, foreign language 3 and academic electives 3.

**2007-2008 Annual costs.** Tuition/fees: $6,033. Room/board: $5,355. Books/supplies: $1,727.

**Financial aid. Non-need-based:** Scholarships awarded for academics, music/drama.

**Application procedures. Admission:** Closing date 8/1. $30 fee. Application may be submitted online. Admission notification on a rolling basis. **Financial aid:** Priority date 5/15, closing date 6/30. FAFSA required. Applicants notified by 7/15.

**Academics. Special study options:** Cooperative education, distance learning, honors. **Credit/placement by examination:** AP, CLEP. **Support services:** Pre-admission summer program, remedial instruction, study skills assistance, tutoring.

**Majors. Architecture:** Architecture. **Business:** General, business admin. **Computer sciences:** Computer science. **Engineering:** Chemical, civil, computer, electrical, industrial, mechanical. **Engineering technology:** Surveying.

**Most popular majors.** Engineering/engineering technologies 90%.

**Computing on campus.** 550 workstations in library, computer center. Online library, wireless network available.

**Student life. Freshman orientation:** Available. Preregistration for classes offered. Week-long orientation offered every trimester. **Activities:** Choral groups, drama, student government, TV station, University Bible Association, drugs and alcohol committee.

**Athletics. Intercollegiate:** Baseball M, basketball, cross-country, soccer M, table tennis, tennis, track and field, volleyball. **Intramural:** Basketball, cross-country W, table tennis, tennis, track and field, volleyball. **Team name:** Beavers.

**Student services.** Alcohol/substance abuse counseling, career counseling, services for economically disadvantaged, student employment services, financial aid counseling, health services, personal counseling, placement for graduates, veterans' counselor. **Physically disabled:** Services for hearing impaired.

**Contact.** Phone: (787) 754-8000 ext. 309 Fax: (787) 764-8712 Teresa Cardona, Director of Admissions, Universidad Politecnica de Puerto Rico, PO Box 192017, San Juan, PR 00919-2017

---

## University College of San Juan
San Juan, Puerto Rico
www.cunisanjuan.edu
CB member
CB code: 0391

- Public 4-year community and technical college
- Commuter campus in very large city
- 1,004 degree-seeking undergraduates: 16% part-time, 51% women, 100% Hispanic American
- 88% of applicants admitted

**General.** Founded in 1972. Regionally accredited. **Degrees:** 54 bachelor's, 147 associate awarded. **Calendar:** Semester, limited summer session. **Full-time faculty:** 40 total; 5% have terminal degrees. **Part-time faculty:** 46 total; 2% have terminal degrees. **Class size:** 51% < 20, 48% 20-39, 1% 40-49. **Special facilities:** Language laboratory, learning resource center, amphitheater.

**Freshman class profile.** 346 applied, 304 admitted, 304 enrolled.

**Basis for selection.** Combined College Board PAA test scores of 2000 and 2.0 high school GPA required for regular students. Special consideration and priority to applicants from low-income families. SAT/ACT accepted from US applicants. Interview required for nursing program.

**High school preparation.** 16 units required. Required units include English 3, mathematics 2, social studies 2, history 2, science 1 and academic electives 2. 3 Spanish courses required.

**2007-2008 Annual costs.** Tuition/fees: $2,715. Room/board: $6,350. Books/supplies: $800.

**2006-2007 Financial aid.** All financial aid based on need.

**Application procedures. Admission:** Closing date 5/1. $15 fee. Application may be submitted online. Admission notification 6/1. Admission after July 31 on space-available basis. **Financial aid:** Closing date 9/30. FAFSA, institutional form required. Applicants notified by 10/30.

**Academics. Special study options:** Cooperative education, double major, exchange student, honors, study abroad. **Credit/placement by examination:** AP, CLEP. **Support services:** Remedial instruction, tutoring.

**Majors. Business:** Accounting. **Computer sciences:** General. **Health:** Nursing (RN). **Protective services:** Police science.

**Most popular majors.** Business/marketing 6%, computer/information sciences 35%, health sciences 44%, security/protective services 15%.

**Computing on campus.** 240 workstations in library, computer center. Commuter students can connect to campus network. Online library, wireless network available.

**Student life. Freshman orientation:** Mandatory. One-day program in summer that offers opportunity to meet faculty and staff. **Activities:** Drama, student government.

**Athletics. Intercollegiate:** Basketball M, cross-country, softball, table tennis, tennis, track and field, volleyball, weight lifting. **Intramural:** Basketball, bowling, cross-country, handball, racquetball, softball M, table tennis, tennis, track and field, volleyball. **Team name:** Falcons.

**Student services.** Career counseling, student employment services, health services, personal counseling, placement for graduates, veterans' counselor. **Physically disabled:** Services for visually, speech, hearing impaired.

**Contact.** E-mail: admisiones@cts.sanjuancapital.com
Phone: (787) 250-7375 Fax: (787) 250-7395
Sandra Rivera, Admissions Officer, University College of San Juan, 180 Jose R. Oliver Avenue, San Juan, PR 00918

---

## University of Puerto Rico: Aguadilla
Aguadilla, Puerto Rico
www.uprag.edu
CB code: 0983

- Public 4-year liberal arts and technical college
- Commuter campus in small city
- 2,969 degree-seeking undergraduates: 10% part-time, 63% women
- 96% of applicants admitted

**General.** Founded in 1972. Regionally accredited. **Degrees:** 322 bachelor's, 45 associate awarded. **ROTC:** Army. **Location:** 81 miles from San Juan. **Calendar:** Semester, limited summer session. **Full-time faculty:** 148 total; 19% have terminal degrees. **Part-time faculty:** 13 total; 8% have terminal degrees.

**Freshman class profile.** 949 applied, 908 admitted, 811 enrolled.

**Basis for selection.** Admissions based on secondary school record and standardized test scores. Talent and ability considered. SAT and SAT Subject Tests in Spanish and math level I required of English-speaking applicants. **Homeschooled:** Copy of curriculum required.

**High school preparation.** Recommended units include English 3, mathematics 2 and social studies 2. 3 Spanish recommended.

**2007-2008 Annual costs.** Tuition/fees: $1,692; $3,938 out-of-state. Books/supplies: $1,320. Personal expenses: $1,000.

**2006-2007 Financial aid.** All financial aid based on need. 84% of total undergraduate aid awarded as scholarships/grants, 16% as loans/jobs.

**Application procedures. Admission:** Priority date 11/17; deadline 1/30 (receipt date). $20 fee, may be waived for applicants with need. Application must be submitted on paper. Admission notification 4/2. Admission notification on a rolling basis. Must reply by 4/30. **Financial aid:** Closing date 5/6. FAFSA, institutional form required. Applicants notified on a rolling basis starting 4/1; must reply within 1 week(s) of notification.

**Academics. Special study options:** Honors, liberal arts/career combination, teacher certification program. **Credit/placement by examination:** CLEP, institutional tests. **Support services:** Learning center, remedial instruction, tutoring.

**Majors. Biology:** General. **Business:** General, accounting, executive assistant, finance, human resources, management information systems, marketing. **Education:** Elementary, English. **Engineering technology:** Electrical, environmental, quality control.

**Most popular majors.** Biology 14%, business/marketing 47%, education 24%, engineering/engineering technologies 15%.

**Computing on campus.** 220 workstations in library, computer center, student center. Online library, student web hosting, wireless network available.

**Student life. Freshman orientation:** Available. **Housing:** Family community housing and private guest house available. **Activities:** Concert band, choral groups, drama, student government, Organizacion Juventud en Cristo, Estudiantes Orientadores, Teatro Experimental 80, Bio-Study, Kayukembo Association, Companeros Alertas Ante Un Mundo Buscando Alternativas, alcohol and drug prevention organization, Centro de Reciclaje y Orientación Ambiental.

**Athletics. Intercollegiate:** Baseball M, basketball, cross-country, softball W, table tennis, tennis, track and field, volleyball, weight lifting. **Intramural:** Baseball M, basketball, cross-country, softball W, table tennis, tennis, track and field, volleyball, weight lifting. **Team name:** Tiburones.

**Student services.** Alcohol/substance abuse counseling, career counseling, student employment services, health services, personal counseling, placement for graduates. **Physically disabled:** Services for visually impaired.

**Contact.** E-mail: melba_serrano@hotmail.com
Phone: (787) 890-2681 ext. 280
Melba Serrano, Admissions Officer, University of Puerto Rico: Aguadilla, Box 250160, Aguadilla, PR 00604

---

## University of Puerto Rico: Arecibo
Arecibo, Puerto Rico
www.upra.edu                                    CB code: 0911

‣ Public 4-year university
‣ Commuter campus in small city
‣ 3,868 degree-seeking undergraduates: 10% part-time, 65% women, 100% Hispanic American
‣ 42% of applicants admitted
‣ 39% graduate within 6 years

**General.** Founded in 1967. Regionally accredited. **Degrees:** 493 bachelor's, 52 associate awarded. **ROTC:** Army. **Location:** 48 miles from San Juan. **Calendar:** Semester, limited summer session. **Full-time faculty:** 217 total; 26% have terminal degrees, 55% women. **Part-time faculty:** 60 total; 5% have terminal degrees, 60% women. **Class size:** 25% < 20, 75% 20-39.

**Freshman class profile.** 2,569 applied, 1,084 admitted, 1,021 enrolled.

**Basis for selection.** Admissions considered according to admission index (defined and published for each academic program) based equally on high school GPA and SAT scores. Those who apply for UPR admission must take the Academic Aptitude Test and Achievement Test offered by the College Entrance Examination Board (CEEB). Interviews sometimes required. **Homeschooled:** State high school equivalency certificate required.

**2007-2008 Annual costs.** Tuition/fees: $1,692; $3,938 out-of-state. Books/supplies: $1,320. Personal expenses: $1,000.

**Financial aid.** All financial aid based on need.

**Application procedures. Admission:** Closing date 11/30. $20 fee. Application may be submitted online. Admission notification 3/18. **Financial aid:** Closing date 4/27. FAFSA, institutional form required.

---

**Academics. Special study options:** ESL, exchange student, honors, internships, liberal arts/career combination, study abroad, Washington semester. Evening college, continuing education program, and professional improvement program. **Credit/placement by examination:** AP, CLEP, IB. **Support services:** Learning center, pre-admission summer program, remedial instruction, study skills assistance, tutoring, writing center.

**Majors. Biology:** Bacteriology. **Business:** Accounting, administrative services, business admin, finance, marketing. **Communications:** Radio/tv. **Communications technology:** Radio/tv. **Computer sciences:** Computer science. **Education:** Elementary, physical. **Engineering technology:** Industrial. **Health:** Nursing (RN). **Psychology:** Industrial.

**Most popular majors.** Biology 9%, business/marketing 26%, communications/journalism 15%, education 25%, health sciences 9%, psychology 7%.

**Computing on campus.** 269 workstations in library, computer center. Commuter students can connect to campus network. Online library, student web hosting, wireless network available.

**Student life. Freshman orientation:** Mandatory. Preregistration for classes offered. 4-day program held (mornings) in summer. **Activities:** Concert band, choral groups, dance, drama, film society, music ensembles, student government, student newspaper, Cheerleaders UPRA, Rhythm Busters, Federacion de Estudiantes de Iberoamericana, Asociación de Estudiantes Coro de Concierto, Asociación Nacional de Estudiantes de Educación, writers club, Capítulo de Estudiantes de Microbiología, Asociación Intercesores Cristiana, ACTRE.

**Athletics. Intercollegiate:** Baseball M, basketball, cross-country, judo, softball W, track and field, volleyball, weight lifting, wrestling M. **Intramural:** Basketball, softball W, volleyball. **Team name:** Los Lobos (Wolves).

**Student services.** Alcohol/substance abuse counseling, career counseling, services for economically disadvantaged, student employment services, financial aid counseling, health services, personal counseling, placement for graduates, women's services. **Physically disabled:** Services for visually, hearing impaired.

**Contact.** E-mail: mmendez@upra.edu
Phone: (787) 815-0000 ext. 4110 Fax: (787) 817-3461
Magaly Mendez, Admissions Officer, University of Puerto Rico: Arecibo, PO Box 4010, Arecibo, PR 00614-4010

---

## University of Puerto Rico: Bayamon University College
Bayamon, Puerto Rico
www.uprb.edu                                    CB code: 0852

‣ Public 4-year university and technical college
‣ Commuter campus in small city
‣ 4,916 degree-seeking undergraduates: 18% part-time, 54% women, 100% Hispanic American
‣ 25% of applicants admitted
‣ 32% graduate within 6 years

**General.** Founded in 1971. Regionally accredited. **Degrees:** 479 bachelor's, 58 associate awarded. **ROTC:** Army. **Location:** 9 miles from San Juan. **Calendar:** Semester, limited summer session. **Full-time faculty:** 264 total; 26% have terminal degrees, 100% minority, 54% women. **Part-time faculty:** 45 total; 27% have terminal degrees, 100% minority, 64% women. **Class size:** 76% < 20, 24% 20-39. **Special facilities:** Multimedia laboratory.

**Freshman class profile.** 5,620 applied, 1,430 admitted, 1,283 enrolled.

| | | |
|---|---|---|
| End year in good standing: | 91% | Out-of-state: 1% |
| Return as sophomores: | 85% | |

**Basis for selection.** High school GPA and test scores most important. Higher scores required of applicants to bachelor's programs. Special consideration given to applicants with special talents or handicaps. SAT, SAT Subject Tests recommended. SAT and 2 SAT Subject Tests (Spanish, mathematics) accepted for English-speaking applicants from U.S. mainland. PAA required of Spanish-speaking applicants.

**High school preparation.** 12 units required. Required and recommended units include English 2, mathematics 2, social studies 1-2 and science 1. 3 units Spanish also required.

**2007-2008 Annual costs.** Tuition/fees: $1,692; $3,938 out-of-state. Books/supplies: $800. Personal expenses: $600.

**Financial aid.** All financial aid based on need.

**Application procedures. Admission:** Priority date 12/10; deadline 1/31 (receipt date). $15 fee. Application must be submitted on paper. Admission notification on a rolling basis beginning on or about 4/25. Must reply by 5/30. **Financial aid:** Closing date 6/15. Institutional form required. Applicants notified by 7/12; must reply within 4 week(s) of notification.

**Academics. Special study options:** Cooperative education, cross-registration, double major, ESL, exchange student, honors, internships. **Credit/placement by examination:** AP, CLEP. **Support services:** Pre-admission summer program, reduced course load, study skills assistance, tutoring.

**Majors. Biology:** General. **Business:** Accounting, executive assistant, finance, logistics, marketing. **Computer sciences:** General. **Education:** Multi-level teacher, physically handicapped. **Engineering technology:** Electrical.

**Computing on campus.** 370 workstations in computer center. Commuter students can connect to campus network. Wireless network available.

**Student life. Freshman orientation:** Available. **Activities:** Bands, choral groups, drama, student government, student newspaper, Confraternidad de Cristianos Unidos, Asociacion Juventud Catolica, Society for Human Resource Management, Asociacion de Estudiantes Orientadores, American Marketing Association, Asociacion de Estudiantes de Computadoras, Asociacion de Gerencia de Materiales.

**Athletics.** NCAA. **Intercollegiate:** Baseball M, basketball, cheerleading, cross-country, swimming, table tennis, tennis, track and field, volleyball, weight lifting, wrestling M. **Intramural:** Table tennis, tennis, volleyball. **Team name:** Vaqueros.

**Student services.** Adult student services, career counseling, student employment services, health services, personal counseling, placement for graduates.

**Contact.** E-mail: cmontes@uprb.edu
Phone: (787) 993-8952 Fax: (787) 993-8929
Carmen Montes, Director of Admissions, University of Puerto Rico: Bayamon University College, 174 State Road #170 Parque Industrial Minillas, Bayamon, PR 00959

---

## University of Puerto Rico: Carolina Regional College

**Carolina, Puerto Rico**
www.uprc.edu                    CB code: 3891

- Public 4-year university
- Commuter campus in small city
- 4,236 degree-seeking undergraduates: 28% part-time, 64% women, 100% Hispanic American
- 35% of applicants admitted
- 40% graduate within 6 years

**General.** Founded in 1974. Regionally accredited. **Degrees:** 464 bachelor's, 123 associate awarded. **ROTC:** Army, Air Force. **Location:** 10 miles from San Juan. **Calendar:** Quarter, limited summer session. **Full-time faculty:** 118 total; 30% have terminal degrees, 46% women. **Part-time faculty:** 111 total; 14% have terminal degrees, 40% women.

**Freshman class profile.** 3,766 applied, 1,301 admitted, 1,130 enrolled.

| | | | |
|---|---|---|---|
| GPA 3.50 or higher: | 43% | End year in good standing: | 83% |
| GPA 3.0-3.49: | 35% | Return as sophomores: | 86% |
| GPA 2.0-2.99: | 22% | | |

**Basis for selection.** High school GPA and test scores important. SAT and SAT Subject Tests in Spanish, Math Level 1 required of English-speaking applicants. Interview recommended for those with exceptional ability; portfolio recommended for art.

**High school preparation.** 15 units required; 17 recommended. Required and recommended units include English 3, mathematics 3, social studies 3, history 2, science 2, foreign language 3 and academic electives 1.

**2007-2008 Annual costs.** Tuition/fees: $2,808; $4,109 out-of-state. Books/supplies: $1,980. Personal expenses: $1,000.

**2006-2007 Financial aid.** All financial aid based on need. 687 full-time freshmen applied for aid; 687 were judged to have need; 687 of these received aid. Average need met was 36%. Average scholarship/grant was $381. 88% of total undergraduate aid awarded as scholarships/grants, 12% as loans/jobs.

---

**Application procedures. Admission:** Closing date 1/31 (receipt date). $20 fee ($30 out-of-state). Application must be submitted on paper. Must reply by 6/12. **Financial aid:** Closing date 6/30. FAFSA, institutional form required. Applicants notified by 6/30; Applicants notified on a rolling basis starting 6/10.

**Academics. Special study options:** Honors, internships, liberal arts/career combination, study abroad. **Credit/placement by examination:** AP, CLEP. **Support services:** Learning center, pre-admission summer program, remedial instruction, tutoring.

**Majors. Business:** Administrative services, business admin, finance, hotel/motel admin, tourism promotion. **Communications:** Advertising. **Communications technology:** Graphic/printing. **Protective services:** Forensics, law enforcement admin.

**Most popular majors.** Business/marketing 55%, communications/journalism 14%, communication technologies 7%, security/protective services 23%.

**Computing on campus.** 451 workstations in library, computer center. Commuter students can connect to campus network. Online course registration, wireless network available.

**Student life. Freshman orientation:** Mandatory. Preregistration for classes offered. **Activities:** Bands, choral groups, dance, drama, music ensembles, student government, religious, departmental, and athletic organizations.

**Athletics. Intercollegiate:** Baseball M, basketball, cheerleading, cross-country, soccer M, softball M, table tennis, tennis, track and field, volleyball, weight lifting. **Intramural:** Basketball, cross-country, volleyball.

**Student services.** Alcohol/substance abuse counseling, career counseling, student employment services, financial aid counseling, health services, personal counseling, placement for graduates, veterans' counselor. **Physically disabled:** Services for visually, hearing impaired.

**Contact.** Phone: (787) 757-1485 Fax: (787) 750-7940
Celia Méndez, Admissions Officer, University of Puerto Rico: Carolina Regional College, PO Box 4800, Carolina, PR 00984-4800

---

## University of Puerto Rico: Cayey University College

**Cayey, Puerto Rico**                    CB member
www.cayey.upr.edu                    CB code: 0981

- Public 4-year liberal arts college
- Commuter campus in large town
- 3,562 degree-seeking undergraduates: 11% part-time, 70% women, 100% Hispanic American
- 3,659 graduate students
- 34% of applicants admitted
- 41% graduate within 6 years

**General.** Founded in 1967. Regionally accredited. **Degrees:** 524 bachelor's, 1 associate awarded. **ROTC:** Army. **Location:** 30 miles from San Juan. **Calendar:** Semester, limited summer session. **Full-time faculty:** 139 total; 54% have terminal degrees, 42% women. **Part-time faculty:** 35 total; 23% have terminal degrees, 49% women. **Class size:** 31% < 20, 68% 20-39, less than 1% 40-49. **Special facilities:** Pio Lopez museum, Las Verdes Sombras Eco-Park.

**Freshman class profile.** 2,544 applied, 863 admitted, 800 enrolled.

| | | | |
|---|---|---|---|
| End year in good standing: | 86% | Return as sophomores: | 88% |

**Basis for selection.** School achievement record, test scores most important. SAT required of English-speaking applicants. Audition, portfolio required of all; interview recommended for music, theater programs.

**High school preparation.** 18 units required. Required units include English 3, mathematics 3, social studies 3, history 3, science 2 and academic electives 3. 3 units Spanish required.

**2007-2008 Annual costs.** Tuition/fees: $1,692; $3,938 out-of-state. Books/supplies: $1,520. Personal expenses: $1,000.

**Financial aid.** All financial aid based on need.

**Application procedures. Admission:** Closing date 11/30 (postmark date). $20 fee. Application may be submitted online. Admission notification 4/4. Must reply by 5/4. **Financial aid:** Closing date 6/30. FAFSA required. Applicants notified by 7/30.

**Academics. Special study options:** Accelerated study, combined bachelor's/graduate degree, ESL, exchange student, honors, liberal arts/career combination, study abroad. **Credit/placement by examination:** AP, CLEP, institutional tests. 72 credit hours maximum toward associate degree, 135 toward bachelor's. **Support services:** Pre-admission summer program, remedial instruction, tutoring.

**Majors. Area/ethnic studies:** Hispanic-American/Latino/Chicano. **Biology:** General. **Business:** General, accounting, administrative services, business admin, office management. **Education:** English, history, mathematics, physical, science, social studies, Spanish, special. **English:** English lit. **Foreign languages:** Spanish. **History:** General. **Liberal arts:** Arts/sciences. **Math:** General. **Physical sciences:** Chemistry. **Psychology:** General. **Social sciences:** General, economics, sociology.

**Computing on campus.** 1,000 workstations in library, computer center. Online course registration, wireless network available.

**Student life. Freshman orientation:** Mandatory. Preregistration for classes offered. **Activities:** Concert band, choral groups, drama, music ensembles, student government, student newspaper.

**Athletics.** NCAA. **Intercollegiate:** Baseball M, basketball, cross-country, judo, soccer M, softball, swimming, table tennis, tennis, track and field, volleyball, weight lifting, wrestling M. **Intramural:** Baseball M, basketball, cross-country, soccer M, softball, swimming, table tennis, tennis, track and field, volleyball, weight lifting, wrestling M. **Team name:** Bulls.

**Student services.** Career counseling, services for economically disadvantaged, student employment services, financial aid counseling, health services, on-campus daycare, personal counseling, placement for graduates, veterans' counselor. **Physically disabled:** Services for visually impaired.

**Contact.** E-mail: wilopez@cayey.upr.edu
Phone: (787) 738-5633 Fax: (787) 738-5633
Wilfredo Lopez, Director of Admissions, University of Puerto Rico: Cayey University College, Oficina de Admisiones UPR- Cayey, Cayey, PR 00736

## University of Puerto Rico: Humacao
**Humacao, Puerto Rico**
**www.uprh.edu**                               **CB code: 0874**

- Public 4-year university and liberal arts college
- Commuter campus in small city
- 4,336 degree-seeking undergraduates: 10% part-time, 69% women
- 45% of applicants admitted
- 46% graduate within 6 years

**General.** Founded in 1962. Regionally accredited. **Degrees:** 451 bachelor's, 122 associate awarded. **ROTC:** Army. **Location:** 30 miles from San Juan. **Calendar:** Semester, limited summer session. **Full-time faculty:** 266 total; 42% have terminal degrees, 53% women. **Part-time faculty:** 30 total; 57% women. **Special facilities:** Observatory, census data center, communication competencies center.

**Freshman class profile.** 2,705 applied, 1,204 admitted, 1,105 enrolled.

| Mid 50% test scores | | | |
|---|---|---|---|
| | | GPA 3.0-3.49: | 34% |
| SAT critical reading: | 480-580 | GPA 2.0-2.99: | 9% |
| SAT math: | 480-600 | Return as sophomores: | 89% |
| GPA 3.50 or higher: | 57% | Out-of-state: | 2% |

**Basis for selection.** High school achievement record, test scores important. Non-native speakers of Spanish required to prove fluency through institutional examinations, interviews. Applicants for admission must take the Spanish version of Puerto Rico CEEB of the College Board: aptitude test (verbal and mathematics) and achievement test battery (Spanish, English and mathematics). In lieu of the above, applicants make take SAT and SAT Subject Tests (Spanish Composition and Spanish Reading). SAT and SAT Subject Tests (Spanish and Mathematics Level I) required of English-speaking applicants. **Homeschooled:** Sworn statement indicating that student received formal education at home. **Learning Disabled:** Director of Disabled Students Services Office (SERPI) evaluates learning disabled students to determine if they qualify for special admission.

**High school preparation.** 18 units recommended. Recommended units include English 3, mathematics 3, social studies 1, history 2, science 3, foreign language 3 and academic electives 3. Foreign language must be Spanish.

**2007-2008 Annual costs.** Tuition/fees: $1,692; $3,938 out-of-state. Books/supplies: $1,520. Personal expenses: $1,000.

**Financial aid. Non-need-based:** Scholarships awarded for academics, athletics, music/drama.

**Application procedures. Admission:** Priority date 11/15; deadline 11/30 (receipt date). $20 fee. Application may be submitted online. Admission notification 4/15. Admission notification on a rolling basis. Must reply by 5/1. **Financial aid:** Closing date 7/31. FAFSA, institutional form required. Applicants notified by 9/30.

**Academics.** Course work conducted in Spanish. **Special study options:** Exchange student, honors, internships, teacher certification program. Students can travel to Europe during summer and earn 6 credits in elective courses. **Credit/placement by examination:** AP, CLEP. 40 credit hours maximum toward associate degree, 40 toward bachelor's. **Support services:** Learning center, pre-admission summer program, reduced course load, remedial instruction, study skills assistance, tutoring, writing center.

**Majors. Biology:** General, marine, microbiology. **Business:** General, accounting, administrative services, business admin, human resources, international. **Conservation:** Wildlife. **Education:** Elementary, ESL. **Health:** Nursing (RN). **Math:** Computational. **Physical sciences:** Chemistry, physics. **Public administration:** Social work. **Social sciences:** General.

**Most popular majors.** Biology 14%, business/marketing 39%, education 22%, health sciences 6%, physical sciences 8%, public administration/social services 9%.

**Computing on campus.** 438 workstations in library, computer center. Commuter students can connect to campus network. Online course registration, wireless network available.

**Student life. Freshman orientation:** Available. Preregistration for classes offered. One-day program. **Activities:** Concert band, choral groups, dance, drama, literary magazine, student government, various religious and social service organizations.

**Athletics. Intercollegiate:** Baseball M, basketball, cheerleading, cross-country, judo, softball W, swimming, tennis W, track and field, weight lifting, wrestling M. **Intramural:** Basketball, softball W, volleyball, weight lifting. **Team name:** Buhos.

**Student services.** Alcohol/substance abuse counseling, career counseling, student employment services, health services, legal services, personal counseling, placement for graduates. **Physically disabled:** Services for visually, speech, hearing impaired.

**Contact.** E-mail: m_alvarez@uprh.edu
Phone: (787) 850-0000 ext. 9301 Fax: (787) 850-9428
Milagros Álvarez, Director of Admissions, University of Puerto Rico: Humacao, 100 Road 908 CUH Station, Humacao, PR 00791

## University of Puerto Rico: Mayaguez
**Mayaguez, Puerto Rico**                        **CB member**
**www.uprm.edu**                               **CB code: 0912**

- Public 5-year university
- Commuter campus in small city
- 11,534 degree-seeking undergraduates: 7% part-time, 49% women, 99% Hispanic American, 1% international
- 1,062 degree-seeking graduate students
- 78% of applicants admitted
- 48% graduate within 6 years

**General.** Founded in 1911. Regionally accredited. Most courses conducted in Spanish. Students must have working knowledge of Spanish and English. **Degrees:** 1,446 bachelor's awarded; master's, doctoral offered. **ROTC:** Army, Air Force. **Location:** 100 miles from San Juan. **Calendar:** Semester, limited summer session. **Full-time faculty:** 672 total; 67% have terminal degrees, 96% minority, 33% women. **Part-time faculty:** 42 total; 33% have terminal degrees, 162% minority, 48% women. **Special facilities:** Planetarium, botanical garden, agricultural extension service, agricultural experimental station, natural history collection, resource center for science and engineering.

**Freshman class profile.** 3,290 applied, 2,564 admitted, 2,465 enrolled.

| Mid 50% test scores | | | |
|---|---|---|---|
| | | GPA 3.0-3.49: | 22% |
| SAT critical reading: | 530-630 | GPA 2.0-2.99: | 7% |
| SAT math: | 560-690 | Out-of-state: | 1% |
| GPA 3.50 or higher: | 71% | | |

**Basis for selection.** Applicants must have high school diploma or its equivalent from educational institution duly accredited by Department of Education of Puerto Rico. Prospective applicants must take University Evaluation and Admissions Tests (PEAU in Spanish) administered by the College Board. First-year applicants only considered for admission in August of first semester. Applications should be submitted before November 30 of year prior to admission. SAT and SAT Subject Tests required for English-speaking applicants. Students from Puerto Rico are required to submit scores from the College Board Entrance Examination aptitude tests. **Home-schooled:** Must supply notarized document (sworn statement) that functions as certification of student educated in home.

**High school preparation.** 18 units recommended. Recommended units include English 3, mathematics 2, social studies 2, history 2, science 2, foreign language 3 and academic electives 4.

**2007-2008 Annual costs.** Tuition/fees: $1,692; $3,938 out-of-state. Books/supplies: $1,520. Personal expenses: $1,000.

**2006-2007 Financial aid.** All financial aid based on need. 97% of total undergraduate aid awarded as scholarships/grants, 3% as loans/jobs.

**Application procedures. Admission:** Closing date 12/15 (postmark date). $20 fee. Application may be submitted online. Admission notification on a rolling basis beginning on or about 4/1. Must reply by 4/15. **Financial aid:** Priority date 1/30, closing date 6/30. FAFSA, institutional form required. Applicants notified by 5/30; Applicants notified on a rolling basis starting 5/30.

**Academics.** Online support available. Spanish language skills (reading, writing) required to read most online course materials. **Special study options:** Cooperative education, distance learning, double major, ESL, exchange student, honors, internships, study abroad, teacher certification program. **Credit/placement by examination:** AP, CLEP, institutional tests. 22 credit hours maximum toward bachelor's degree. **Support services:** Reduced course load, remedial instruction, tutoring, writing center.

**Majors. Agriculture:** Agribusiness operations, agronomy, animal sciences, business, economics, education services, horticultural science, plant protection, soil science. **Biology:** General, biotechnology, marine, microbiology. **Business:** Accounting, administrative services, business admin, finance, human resources, marketing, office management, organizational behavior, sales/distribution. **Computer sciences:** General, computer science, systems analysis. **Education:** Agricultural, mathematics, physical. **Engineering:** General, chemical, civil, computer, electrical, industrial, mechanical. **Engineering technology:** Surveying. **English:** English lit. **Foreign languages:** Comparative lit, French, Spanish. **Health:** Athletic training, nursing (RN), premedicine. **History:** General. **Interdisciplinary:** Math/computer science. **Math:** General. **Parks/recreation:** Facilities management, health/fitness. **Philosophy/religion:** Philosophy. **Physical sciences:** General, chemistry, geology, physics. **Psychology:** General. **Social sciences:** General, economics, political science, sociology. **Visual/performing arts:** Art history/conservation, studio arts.

**Most popular majors.** Agriculture 8%, biology 12%, business/marketing 12%, engineering/engineering technologies 40%, social sciences 6%.

**Computing on campus.** 1,000 workstations in library, computer center. Commuter students can connect to campus network. Online library, wireless network available.

**Student life. Freshman orientation:** Mandatory. Orientation session (4 days) held during week preceding classes in the fall semester. **Housing:** Housing available near campus. **Activities:** Bands, choral groups, dance, drama, literary magazine, radio station, student government, student newspaper, international associations, model of United Nations council.

**Athletics.** NCAA. **Intercollegiate:** Baseball M, basketball, cross-country, gymnastics, soccer M, softball W, swimming, table tennis, tennis, track and field, volleyball, water polo M, wrestling M. **Intramural:** Archery, baseball M, basketball, cross-country, racquetball, soccer M, softball, swimming, table tennis, tennis, volleyball, water polo M, wrestling M. **Team name:** Tarzanes "Bulldogs".

**Student services.** Career counseling, student employment services, health services, personal counseling, placement for graduates, veterans' counselor. **Physically disabled:** Services for visually, speech, hearing impaired.

**Contact.** E-mail: admisiones@upr.edu
Phone: (787) 265-3811 Fax: (787) 834-5265
Norma Torres, Director of Admissions, University of Puerto Rico: Mayaguez, Admissions Office, Mayaguez, PR 00681-9021

## University of Puerto Rico: Medical Sciences
**San Juan, Puerto Rico**
**www.rcm.upr.edu**                    CB code: 0631

- Public 4-year university
- Commuter campus in large city

- 414 degree-seeking undergraduates: 17% part-time, 82% women, 100% Hispanic American
- 1,890 degree-seeking graduate students

**General.** Founded in 1950. Regionally accredited. First-time freshmen not admitted. **Degrees:** 133 bachelor's, 39 associate awarded; master's, doctoral, first professional offered. **Calendar:** Differs by program, limited summer session. **Full-time faculty:** 639 total; 58% women. **Part-time faculty:** 180 total; 44% women.

**Basis for selection.** Candidates are admitted on a competitive basis. Applicants must present evidence of successful completion of all admission requirements for the program in which they are interested. In most programs, an admissions committee will also consider nonacademic factors as additional criteria in screening applicants.

**2007-2008 Annual costs.** Tuition/fees: $1,692; $3,938 out-of-state. Books/supplies: $1,200. Personal expenses: $800.

**Financial aid.** All financial aid based on need.

**Application procedures. Admission:** $20 fee. **Financial aid:** Priority date 4/30, closing date 6/15. FAFSA, institutional form required. Applicants notified on a rolling basis starting 8/1; must reply within 2 week(s) of notification.

**Academics. Special study options:** Combined bachelor's/graduate degree, exchange student, honors, internships. **Credit/placement by examination:** CLEP. **Support services:** Tutoring.

**Majors. Health:** Clinical lab science, clinical lab technology, nuclear medical technology, nursing (RN), public health ed, speech pathology, veterinary technology/assistant.

**Computing on campus.** 216 workstations in library, computer center. Commuter students can connect to campus network. Helpline, repair service available.

**Student life. Activities:** Choral groups, dance, drama, student government.

**Athletics. Intramural:** Basketball M, soccer M, softball M, volleyball.

**Student services.** Career counseling, student employment services, financial aid counseling, health services, legal services, personal counseling, women's services. **Physically disabled:** Services for visually impaired.

**Contact.** E-mail: marrivera@rcm.upr.edu
Phone: (787) 758-2525 ext. 5211 Fax: (787) 282-7117
Margarita Rivera, Director, Central Office of Admissions, University of Puerto Rico: Medical Sciences, P.O. Box 365067, San Juan, PR 00936-5067

## University of Puerto Rico: Ponce
**Ponce, Puerto Rico**
**www.uprp.edu**                    CB code: 0836

- Public 4-year university and branch campus college
- Commuter campus in small city
- 2,911 degree-seeking undergraduates: 8% part-time, 62% women
- 40% of applicants admitted
- 35% graduate within 6 years

**General.** Founded in 1970. Regionally accredited. **Degrees:** 372 bachelor's, 74 associate awarded. **ROTC:** Army. **Location:** 68 miles from San Juan, 46 miles from Mayaguez. **Calendar:** Semester, limited summer session. **Full-time faculty:** 157 total; 27% have terminal degrees, 100% minority, 59% women. **Part-time faculty:** 39 total; 3% have terminal degrees, 100% minority, 49% women. **Class size:** 32% < 20, 68% 20-39.

**Freshman class profile.** 2,340 applied, 930 admitted, 783 enrolled.

| | | | |
|---|---|---|---|
| GPA 3.50 or higher: | 66% | End year in good standing: | 43% |
| GPA 3.0-3.49: | 28% | Return as sophomores: | 79% |
| GPA 2.0-2.99: | 6% | | |

**Basis for selection.** Admission based on general application index (GAI), combination of high school GPA and College Board test scores (50% each). Programs have their own GAI requirements. Interview required for academically weak and special ability. **Homeschooled:** State high school equivalency certificate required.

**Four-Year Colleges**

**High school preparation.** 18 units required. Required units include English 3, mathematics 3, social studies 3, science 3 and academic electives 2. 3 units Spanish, 1 unit fine arts.

**2007-2008 Annual costs.** Tuition/fees: $1,692; $3,938 out-of-state. Books/supplies: $1,520. Personal expenses: $800.

**2007-2008 Financial aid.** All financial aid based on need.

**Application procedures. Admission:** Closing date 11/30. $20 fee. Admission notification on a rolling basis beginning on or about 4/15. Must reply by May 1 or within 3 week(s) if notified thereafter. **Financial aid:** Closing date 5/30. FAFSA, institutional form required.

**Academics. Special study options:** Dual enrollment of high school students, honors, internships. **Credit/placement by examination:** CLEP. **Support services:** Remedial instruction, tutoring.

**Majors. Business:** Accounting, administrative services, business admin, finance, marketing. **Computer sciences:** General. **Education:** Elementary. **Health:** Athletic training. **Math:** General. **Protective services:** Forensics. **Psychology:** General.

**Most popular majors.** Biology 9%, business/marketing 28%, education 30%, health sciences 9%, psychology 19%.

**Computing on campus.** 344 workstations in library, computer center, student center. Wireless network available.

**Student life. Freshman orientation:** Mandatory. **Activities:** Bands, choral groups, dance, drama, student government, Christian youth organizations, including those devoted to Catholic and Baptist students.

**Athletics. Intercollegiate:** Basketball, cross-country, softball, table tennis, tennis, track and field, volleyball. **Intramural:** Basketball, cross-country, gymnastics, softball, table tennis, tennis, track and field, volleyball.

**Student services.** Career counseling, student employment services, health services, on-campus daycare, personal counseling, placement for graduates, veterans' counselor. **Physically disabled:** Services for visually impaired.

**Contact.** Phone: (787) 844-8181 ext. 2531 Fax: (787) 840-8108 Acmin Velazquez, Admissions Director, University of Puerto Rico: Ponce, Box 7186, Ponce, PR 00732

---

## University of Puerto Rico: Rio Piedras
**San Juan, Puerto Rico**
**www.rrp.upr.edu**
**CB member**
**CB code: 0979**

- Public 4-year university
- Commuter campus in large city
- 15,094 degree-seeking undergraduates: 15% part-time, 66% women
- 3,678 graduate students
- 38% of applicants admitted
- 47% graduate within 6 years

**General.** Founded in 1903. Regionally accredited. Most courses conducted in Spanish. Students must have working knowledge of Spanish and English. **Degrees:** 2,376 bachelor's awarded; master's, doctoral, first professional offered. **ROTC:** Army, Air Force. **Location:** 10 miles from Rio Piedras. **Calendar:** Semester, limited summer session. **Full-time faculty:** 956 total; 72% have terminal degrees, 50% women. **Part-time faculty:** 324 total; 31% have terminal degrees, 52% women. **Class size:** 43% < 20, 55% 20-39, less than 1% 40-49, less than 1% 50-99, less than 1% >100. **Special facilities:** Museum of history, anthropology and art; theatre; warm-blooded animal house; herbarium; biology museum; high technology mycroscipy; nanotechnology lasers; virtual astronomy lab.

**Freshman class profile.** 7,747 applied, 2,951 admitted, 2,725 enrolled.

| Mid 50% test scores | | | |
|---|---|---|---|
| SAT critical reading: | 540-640 | GPA 3.0-3.49: | 26% |
| SAT math: | 550-670 | GPA 2.0-2.99: | 8% |
| GPA 3.50 or higher: | 66% | Return as sophomores: | 89% |
| | | Live on campus: | 10% |

**Basis for selection.** Admissions based on secondary school record and standardized test scores. Talent and ability considered. Applicants must take Academic Aptitude Test and Achievement Test offered by the College Board. Otherwise, SAT scores must be submitted. **Homeschooled:** State high school equivalency certificate required.

**High school preparation.** Required and recommended units include English 3, mathematics 2, social studies 1, history 1, science 2 and academic electives 6. 3 units Spanish required.

---

**2007-2008 Annual costs.** Tuition/fees: $1,692; $3,938 out-of-state. Room/board: $7,580. Books/supplies: $1,320. Personal expenses: $1,000.

**Financial aid.** All financial aid based on need. **Additional information:** Tuition waived for honor students, athletes, members of chorus, and others with special talents.

**Application procedures. Admission:** Closing date 2/15. $20 fee. Application may be submitted online. Admission notification 5/10. Must reply by 6/15. **Financial aid:** FAFSA required.

**Academics. Special study options:** Combined bachelor's/graduate degree, cooperative education, double major, ESL, exchange student, external degree, honors, internships, liberal arts/career combination, study abroad, Washington semester. Students can study abroad in the United States, Spain, France, Mexico, Costa Rica, Italy, Germany, Japan, China, Argentina, Nicaragua, as well as in other countries. **Credit/placement by examination:** AP, CLEP, institutional tests. 30 credit hours maximum toward bachelor's degree. **Support services:** Learning center, pre-admission summer program, remedial instruction, tutoring.

**Majors. Architecture:** Environmental design, urban/community planning. **Biology:** General. **Business:** General, accounting, administrative services, business admin, finance, human resources, labor relations, management information systems, managerial economics, marketing, operations, statistics. **Communications:** Digital media, journalism, media studies, public relations. **Computer sciences:** Computer science. **Conservation:** General. **Education:** Elementary, family/consumer sciences, secondary. **English:** English lit. **Family/consumer sciences:** General, food/nutrition. **Foreign languages:** General, comparative lit, French, Spanish. **History:** General. **Interdisciplinary:** Intercultural, natural sciences. **Legal studies:** Prelaw. **Liberal arts:** Arts/sciences. **Math:** General. **Philosophy/religion:** Philosophy. **Physical sciences:** Chemistry, physics. **Psychology:** General. **Public administration:** Social work. **Social sciences:** General, anthropology, economics, geography, political science, sociology. **Visual/performing arts:** General, art, art history/conservation, dramatic, drawing, multimedia, painting, sculpture, studio arts.

**Most popular majors.** Business/marketing 20%, communications/journalism 6%, education 21%, interdisciplinary studies 10%, psychology 7%, social sciences 10%.

**Computing on campus.** 154 workstations in dormitories, library, computer center, student center. Dormitories linked to campus network. Commuter students can connect to campus network. Online library, wireless network available.

**Student life. Freshman orientation:** Available. Preregistration for classes offered. 3 days in summer. **Policies:** Students represented in university administration. **Housing:** Coed dorms, substance-free housing available. $35 deposit, deadline 10/29. **Activities:** Jazz band, choral groups, dance, drama, film society, literary magazine, musical theater, radio station, student government, student newspaper, TV station, Club Avanza, Confraternidad Universitaria de Avivamiento, Jovenes Cristianos Universitarios, Juventud Universitaria Popular, Club de la Cruz Roja Americana del Recinto de Rio Piedras.

**Athletics.** NAIA, NCAA. **Intercollegiate:** Basketball, cross-country, gymnastics, soccer M, softball, swimming, table tennis, tennis, track and field, volleyball, water polo M, wrestling M. **Intramural:** Basketball, cross-country, gymnastics, soccer M, softball, swimming, table tennis, tennis, track and field, volleyball, water polo, wrestling M. **Team name:** Gallitos/Jerezanas.

**Student services.** Adult student services, alcohol/substance abuse counseling, career counseling, student employment services, health services, on-campus daycare, personal counseling, placement for graduates, veterans' counselor. **Physically disabled:** Services for visually, speech, hearing impaired.

**Contact.** Phone: (787) 764-7290 Toll-free number: (888) 966-2877 Fax: (787) 763-4265 Cruz Valentin, Director of Admissions, University of Puerto Rico: Rio Piedras, Box 23344, San Juan, PR 00931-3344

---

## University of Puerto Rico: Utuado
**Utuado, Puerto Rico**
**www.uprutuado.edu**
**CB member**
**CB code: 3893**

- Public 4-year agricultural college
- Commuter campus in large town
- 1,527 degree-seeking undergraduates: 7% part-time, 59% women, 100% Hispanic American
- 51% of applicants admitted

♦ Interview required

♦ 35% graduate within 6 years

**General.** Founded in 1979. Regionally accredited. **Degrees:** 97 bachelor's, 46 associate awarded. **ROTC:** Army. **Location:** 20 miles from Arecibo. **Calendar:** Semester, limited summer session. **Full-time faculty:** 74 total; 38% have terminal degrees, 100% minority, 45% women. **Part-time faculty:** 26 total; 4% have terminal degrees, 100% minority, 42% women. **Special facilities:** 118-acre farm.

**Freshman class profile.** 2,018 applied, 1,025 admitted, 599 enrolled.

**Basis for selection.** GED not accepted. High school GPA, test scores important. SAT required of English-speaking students.

**High school preparation.** Required units include English 3, mathematics 2, history 3, science 2 and foreign language 3. 3 fine arts required.

**2007-2008 Annual costs.** Tuition/fees: $1,692; $3,938 out-of-state. Books/supplies: $1,520. Personal expenses: $1,000.

**Financial aid.** All financial aid based on need.

**Application procedures. Admission:** Priority date 11/15; no deadline. $20 fee, may be waived for applicants with need. Must reply by May 1 or within 2 week(s) if notified thereafter. **Financial aid:** Priority date 5/31; no closing date. FAFSA required. Applicants notified on a rolling basis starting 9/30; must reply within 4 week(s) of notification.

**Academics. Special study options:** Cooperative education, honors, internships, teacher certification program. **Credit/placement by examination:** AP, CLEP. **Support services:** Reduced course load, remedial instruction, tutoring.

**Majors. Business:** Accounting, office/clerical. **Education:** Elementary.

**Most popular majors.** Business/marketing 24%, education 63%.

**Computing on campus.** 90 workstations in library, computer center. Online library available.

**Student life. Freshman orientation:** Mandatory. **Housing:** Substance-free housing available. **Activities:** Concert band, choral groups, dance, drama, student government.

**Athletics. Intercollegiate:** Baseball M, basketball, cross-country, softball, tennis, track and field, volleyball, weight lifting. **Intramural:** Baseball M, basketball, cross-country, softball, table tennis, tennis, track and field, volleyball, weight lifting. **Team name:** Guaraguao.

**Student services.** Alcohol/substance abuse counseling, career counseling, financial aid counseling, health services, personal counseling, placement for graduates, veterans' counselor.

**Contact.** Phone: (787) 894-2316 Fax: (787) 894-2891
Maria Robles, Admissions Officer, University of Puerto Rico: Utuado, PO Box 2500, Utuado, PR 00641

---

## University of the Sacred Heart
### Santurce, Puerto Rico
### www.sagrado.edu
**CB member**
**CB code: 0913**

♦ Private 4-year university and liberal arts college affiliated with Roman Catholic Church

♦ Commuter campus in large city

♦ 4,362 degree-seeking undergraduates: 18% part-time, 64% women, 100% Hispanic American

♦ 1,021 degree-seeking graduate students

**General.** Founded in 1935. Regionally accredited. **Degrees:** 542 bachelor's, 3 associate awarded; master's offered. **Calendar:** Semester, extensive summer session. **Full-time faculty:** 122 total. **Part-time faculty:** 236 total. **Special facilities:** Jardin Escultorico, Museo de la Radio, Pabellon de las Artes, Patio de las Artes, Galeria Jose (Pepin) Mendez y Teatro Emilio S. Belaval.

**Freshman class profile.**

| GPA 3.50 or higher: | 20% | Return as sophomores: | 75% |
|---|---|---|---|
| GPA 3.0-3.49: | 29% | Out-of-state: | 2% |
| GPA 2.0-2.99: | 49% | | |

**Basis for selection.** High school GPA and highest score CEEB important. SAT scores accepted in place of CEEB. Interview required for nursing program.

**High school preparation.** 15 units required. Required and recommended units include English 3, mathematics 3, social studies 2, science 3, foreign language 3 and academic electives 3.

**2007-2008 Annual costs.** Tuition/fees: $5,670. Room only: $2,300. Books/supplies: $1,398. Personal expenses: $2,246.

**Financial aid. Non-need-based:** Scholarships awarded for academics, athletics.

**Application procedures. Admission:** Priority date 12/15; deadline 6/30. $15 fee, may be waived for applicants with need. Application may be submitted online. Admission notification on a rolling basis. **Financial aid:** Priority date 4/30, closing date 5/30. FAFSA, institutional form required. Applicants notified on a rolling basis starting 6/15; must reply by 8/30.

**Academics. Special study options:** Combined bachelor's/graduate degree, cooperative education, cross-registration, double major, dual enrollment of high school students, exchange student, external degree, honors, independent study, internships, liberal arts/career combination, semester at sea, teacher certification program. International programs with universities in Mexico and Spain. **Credit/placement by examination:** AP, CLEP, institutional tests. **Support services:** Pre-admission summer program, reduced course load, remedial instruction, tutoring.

**Majors. Biology:** General. **Business:** Accounting, administrative services, business admin, tourism promotion. **Communications:** General, advertising, journalism. **Computer sciences:** Computer science, information systems. **Education:** General, bilingual, elementary, secondary. **English:** English lit. **Foreign languages:** French, Spanish. **Health:** Clinical lab technology, nursing (RN). **History:** General. **Interdisciplinary:** Natural sciences. **Math:** General. **Parks/recreation:** Health/fitness. **Physical sciences:** Chemistry. **Psychology:** General. **Public administration:** Social work. **Social sciences:** General. **Visual/performing arts:** General, dramatic.

**Computing on campus.** 500 workstations in dormitories, library, computer center, student center. Commuter students can connect to campus network. Repair service available.

**Student life. Freshman orientation:** Available. **Housing:** Single-sex dorms available. $125 deposit, deadline 6/15. **Activities:** Choral groups, drama, film society, literary magazine, radio station, student government, student newspaper, TV station, pastoral services organization, health and allied sciences organization, student council, senior class organization, judo club, soccer club, nursing club, Christian club, microbioloby club, psychology club, chemistry club, justice system, telecommunication club.

**Athletics. Intercollegiate:** Basketball M, cross-country, swimming, tennis M, track and field, volleyball, wrestling M. **Intramural:** Basketball M, softball M, swimming, table tennis, volleyball. **Team name:** Dolphins.

**Student services.** Alcohol/substance abuse counseling, career counseling, student employment services, financial aid counseling, health services, personal counseling, placement for graduates, veterans' counselor. **Physically disabled:** Services for visually, hearing impaired.

**Contact.** E-mail: admision@sagrado.edu
Phone: (787) 728-2070 Fax: (787) 728-2066
Luis Henriquez, Director of Admissions and Promotion, University of the Sacred Heart, Universidad del Sagrado Corazon Oficina de Nuevo Ingreso, San Juan, PR 00914-0383

# Rhode Island

## Brown University

Providence, Rhode Island
www.brown.edu

CB member
CB code: 3094

- Private 4-year university and liberal arts college
- Residential campus in small city
- 5,813 degree-seeking undergraduates: 1% part-time, 52% women, 7% African American, 15% Asian American, 8% Hispanic American, 1% Native American, 7% international
- 2,108 degree-seeking graduate students
- 14% of applicants admitted
- SAT and SAT Subject Tests or ACT with writing, application essay required
- 95% graduate within 6 years; 35% enter graduate study

**General.** Founded in 1764. Regionally accredited. **Degrees:** 1,530 bachelor's awarded; master's, doctoral, first professional offered. **ROTC:** Army. **Location:** 45 miles from Boston. **Calendar:** Semester, limited summer session. **Full-time faculty:** 661 total; 95% have terminal degrees, 18% minority, 32% women. **Part-time faculty:** 139 total; 95% have terminal degrees, 18% minority, 43% women. **Special facilities:** Museum of anthropology, observatory, center for the performing arts, center for information technology, institute for education, institute for international studies.

**Freshman class profile.** 19,097 applied, 2,669 admitted, 1,484 enrolled.

| Mid 50% test scores | | | |
|---|---|---|---|
| SAT critical reading: | 660-760 | Rank in top tenth: | 92% |
| SAT math: | 670-770 | Return as sophomores: | 98% |
| SAT writing: | 660-760 | Out-of-state: | 86% |
| ACT composite: | 28-33 | Live on campus: | 100% |
| Rank in top quarter: | 99% | International: | 9% |

**Basis for selection.** GED not accepted. Strength of academic course load and student's achievement in courses most important. Extracurricular activities, recommendations, personal essay important; test scores strongly considered. Students submitting SAT should submit 2 SAT Subject Tests of their choice. ACT with Writing may take place of both SAT and SAT Subject Tests. Portfolio recommended for art, music programs. Alumni interviews are available, but not required, for all applicants. **Learning Disabled:** Untimed standardized tests accepted.

**High school preparation.** 16 units required; 19 recommended. Required and recommended units include English 4, mathematics 3-4, history 2, science 3-4 (laboratory 2-3), foreign language 3-4 and academic electives 1. At least 1 art unit (music or art) recommended. Familiarity with computers recommended. Physics, chemistry, and advanced mathematics recommended for prospective science or engineering majors.

**2007-2008 Annual costs.** Tuition/fees: $36,342. Room/board: $9,606. Books/supplies: $1,184. Personal expenses: $1,528.

**Financial aid.** All financial aid based on need.

**Application procedures. Admission:** Closing date 1/1 (postmark date). $70 fee, may be waived for applicants with need. Application may be submitted online. Admission notification 4/1. Must reply by 5/1. **Financial aid:** Closing date 2/1. FAFSA, CSS PROFILE required. Applicants notified by 4/1; must reply by 5/1.

**Academics.** Students must complete course requirements in major(s) of choice, but are free to choose courses without a core curriculum prior to designating a major. **Special study options:** Accelerated study, combined bachelor's/graduate degree, cross-registration, double major, exchange student, honors, independent study, internships, student-designed major, study abroad, teacher certification program. 8-year medical program, cross-registration with Rhode Island School of Design, early childhood certification (in teaching) program via Wheaton College courses. **Credit/placement by examination:** AP, CLEP, institutional tests. **Support services:** Reduced course load, study skills assistance, tutoring, writing center.

**Majors. Architecture:** History/criticism. **Area/ethnic studies:** African, African-American, American, Asian, East Asian, European, French, German, Hispanic-American/Latino/Chicano, Italian, Latin American, Near/Middle Eastern, Slavic, South Asian, women's. **Biology:** General, aquatic, biochemistry, biophysics, cell/histology, molecular. **Computer sciences:** Computer science. **Conservation:** Environmental science, environmental studies. **Education:** General. **Engineering:** Biomedical, chemical, civil, computer, electrical, materials, mechanical, physics. **English:** American lit, British lit, English lit. **Foreign languages:** Ancient Greek, classics, comparative lit, French, German, Italian, Latin, linguistics, Portuguese, Slavic, Spanish. **Health:** Community health services. **History:** General. **Interdisciplinary:** Ancient studies, biological/physical sciences, cognitive science, math/computer science, medieval/Renaissance, neuroscience. **Math:** General, applied, statistics. **Philosophy/religion:** Judaic, philosophy, religion. **Physical sciences:** Chemical physics, chemistry, geochemistry, geology, geophysics, physics. **Psychology:** General. **Public administration:** Policy analysis. **Social sciences:** Anthropology, archaeology, economics, international economic development, international relations, political science, sociology, urban studies. **Visual/performing arts:** General, art history/conservation, dramatic, musicology, studio arts.

**Most popular majors.** Biology 19%, physical sciences 11%, social sciences 45%.

**Computing on campus.** 500 workstations in dormitories, library, computer center, student center. Dormitories wired for high-speed internet access and linked to campus network. Commuter students can connect to campus network. Online course registration, online library, helpline, repair service, wireless network available.

**Student life. Freshman orientation:** Mandatory. Preregistration for classes offered. 5-day program, beginning Wednesday prior to Labor Day. **Policies:** Students must live in on-campus housing for first 3 years; those entering 7th semester may request off-campus residence. **Housing:** Guaranteed on-campus for all undergraduates. Coed dorms, single-sex dorms, cooperative housing, fraternity/sorority housing, substance-free housing available. Language houses, social dormitories, cultural houses, special program housing (international students, technology students, environmental studies) available. **Activities:** Bands, choral groups, dance, drama, film society, literary magazine, music ensembles, musical theater, radio station, student government, student newspaper, symphony orchestra, TV station, African students association, ACLU, Amnesty International, Asian American students association, Big Brothers, Community Outreach, Catholic Pastoral Council, Latino American students association, International Organization, Canadian club.

**Athletics.** NCAA. **Intercollegiate:** Baseball M, basketball, cross-country, diving, equestrian W, fencing, field hockey W, football (tackle) M, golf, gymnastics W, ice hockey, lacrosse, rowing (crew), skiing W, soccer, softball W, squash, swimming, tennis, track and field, volleyball W, water polo, wrestling M. **Intramural:** Badminton, basketball, fencing, field hockey W, ice hockey, lacrosse, racquetball, rugby, soccer, softball, squash, swimming, tennis, volleyball, water polo. **Team name:** Bears.

**Student services.** Adult student services, alcohol/substance abuse counseling, campus ministries, career counseling, student employment services, financial aid counseling, health services, minority student services, personal counseling, placement for graduates, women's services. **Physically disabled:** Services for visually, hearing impaired.

**Contact.** E-mail: admission_undergraduate@brown.edu
Phone: (401) 863-2378 Fax: (401) 863-9300
James Miller, Director of Admission, Brown University, 45 Prospect Street, Providence, RI 02912

## Bryant University

Smithfield, Rhode Island
www.bryant.edu

CB member
CB code: 3095

- Private 4-year business and liberal arts college
- Residential campus in large town
- 3,328 degree-seeking undergraduates: 4% part-time, 43% women, 3% African American, 3% Asian American, 4% Hispanic American, 3% international
- 368 degree-seeking graduate students
- 44% of applicants admitted
- SAT or ACT (ACT writing optional), application essay required
- 74% graduate within 6 years

**General.** Founded in 1863. Regionally accredited. **Degrees:** 765 bachelor's awarded; master's offered. **ROTC:** Army. **Location:** 12 miles from Providence, 40 miles from Boston. **Calendar:** Semester, extensive summer session. **Full-time faculty:** 155 total; 98% have terminal degrees, 15% minority, 36% women. **Part-time faculty:** 96 total; 8% minority, 46% women.

**Class size:** 22% < 20, 77% 20-39, 2% 40-49. **Special facilities:** Technology center, simulated financial trading floor, digital library, digital TV studio, high speed Unix lab with 20 Sun workstations.

**Freshman class profile.** 5,649 applied, 2,476 admitted, 857 enrolled.

| Mid 50% test scores | | | |
|---|---|---|---|
| SAT critical reading: | 520-600 | GPA 2.0-2.99: | 13% |
| SAT math: | 550-630 | Rank in top quarter: | 64% |
| SAT writing: | 520-600 | Rank in top tenth: | 25% |
| ACT composite: | 22-26 | Return as sophomores: | 88% |
| GPA 3.50 or higher: | 41% | Out-of-state: | 90% |
| GPA 3.0-3.49: | 46% | Live on campus: | 96% |
| | | International: | 5% |

**Basis for selection.** Secondary school curriculum, GPA, guidance counselor's recommendation, personal essay very important, class rank and test scores important. Evidence of math ability is important for consideration to business programs. **Homeschooled:** Must be completing a state-accredited program. Course descriptions and progress reports required as part of application process. **Learning Disabled:** Foreign language requirement may be waived.

**High school preparation.** 16 units required. Required and recommended units include English 4, mathematics 4, history 2-4, science 2 (laboratory 2) and foreign language 2. Mathematics must include a year beyond algebra II, with a preference for pre-calculus or calculus in senior year. History includes social sciences.

**2007-2008 Annual costs.** Tuition/fees: $27,639. Tuition includes cost of laptop computer. $500 non-refundable enrollment commitment deposit is required of both residents and commuters. Room/board: $10,928.

**Financial aid. Non-need-based:** Scholarships awarded for academics, athletics, minority status, ROTC.

**Application procedures. Admission:** Closing date 2/1 (postmark date). $50 fee, may be waived for applicants with need. Application may be submitted online. Admission notification 3/21. **Financial aid:** Priority date 2/15, closing date 2/15. FAFSA required. Applicants notified by 3/24; must reply by 5/1.

**Academics.** Business majors must minor in Arts & Sciences. Arts & Sciences majors must minor in Business. All students may select further minors. New students complete a one credit Foundations for Learning course. International Business majors share residence and must complete 12 credit hours in study abroad. **Special study options:** Distance learning, double major, ESL, honors, independent study, internships, study abroad. **Credit/placement by examination:** AP, CLEP, IB, SAT, ACT, institutional tests. 30 credit hours maximum toward bachelor's degree. **Support services:** Learning center, study skills assistance, tutoring, writing center.

**Majors. Business:** Accounting, accounting technology, actuarial science, business admin, finance, financial planning, international, marketing. **Communications:** General. **Computer sciences:** General, information technology. **English:** English lit. **History:** General. **Psychology:** General. **Social sciences:** Applied economics, economics, international relations, sociology.

**Most popular majors.** Business/marketing 84%, computer/information sciences 6%.

**Computing on campus.** PC or laptop required. 478 workstations in library, computer center. Dormitories wired for high-speed internet access and linked to campus network. Commuter students can connect to campus network. Online course registration, online library, helpline, repair service, student web hosting, wireless network available.

**Student life. Freshman orientation:** Mandatory, $75 fee. Preregistration for classes offered. 2-day program in June during which students and parents/guardians are housed in campus residence halls overnight. Students also take mathematics placement exam and register for elective courses. **Policies:** All residence halls are smoke free; students 21 and over may drink in privacy of room, quiet study hour policy in effect through academic year. **Housing:** Guaranteed on-campus for freshmen. Coed dorms, single-sex dorms, special housing for disabled, fraternity/sorority housing, substance-free housing available. 24 hour quiet, honors, all women (upperclass), international business student housing available. **Activities:** Jazz band, campus ministries, choral groups, dance, drama, international student organizations, literary magazine, Model UN, radio station, student government, student newspaper, Christian fellowship, Hillel, College Democrats and Republicans, multicultural student union, Alliance for Women's Awareness, Amnesty International, Big Brothers/Big Sisters.

**Athletics.** NCAA. **Intercollegiate:** Baseball M, basketball, cross-country, field hockey W, football (tackle) M, golf M, lacrosse, soccer, softball W, swimming, tennis, track and field, volleyball W, wrestling M. **Intramural:** Basketball, football (non-tackle) M, soccer, softball, volleyball. **Team name:** Bulldogs.

**Student services.** Adult student services, alcohol/substance abuse counseling, campus ministries, career counseling, services for economically disadvantaged, student employment services, financial aid counseling, health services, minority student services, personal counseling, placement for graduates, veterans' counselor, women's services. **Physically disabled:** Services for visually, hearing impaired.

**Contact.** E-mail: admission@bryant.edu
Phone: (401) 232-6100 Toll-free number: (800) 622-7001
Fax: (401) 232-6741
Michelle Beauregard, Director of Admission, Bryant University, 1150 Douglas Pike, Smithfield, RI 02917

## Johnson & Wales University: Providence
Providence, Rhode Island      **CB member**
www.jwu.edu      **CB code: 3465**

- Private 4-year university
- Residential campus in small city
- 9,053 degree-seeking undergraduates: 10% part-time, 53% women, 8% African American, 3% Asian American, 7% Hispanic American, 5% international
- 1,052 degree-seeking graduate students
- 72% of applicants admitted

**General.** Founded in 1914. Regionally accredited. **Degrees:** 1,582 bachelor's, 1,617 associate awarded; master's, doctoral offered. **ROTC:** Army. **Location:** 200 miles from New York City, 50 miles from Boston. **Calendar:** Quarter, limited summer session. **Full-time faculty:** 284 total. **Part-time faculty:** 135 total. **Class size:** 36% < 20, 51% 20-39, 13% 40-49, less than 1% 50-99. **Special facilities:** 3 University-operated hotels and restaurants, banquet facilities, information kiosk, culinary archives and museum, equine center.

**Freshman class profile.** 13,617 applied, 9,853 admitted, 2,259 enrolled.

| Mid 50% test scores | | | |
|---|---|---|---|
| SAT critical reading: | 410-520 | Live on campus: | 73% |
| SAT math: | 400-500 | International: | 5% |
| Out-of-state: | 22% | Sororities: | 6% |

**Basis for selection.** Academic record, secondary school curriculum, GPA, class rank, test scores important; student motivation and interest given strong consideration. SAT or ACT recommended. SAT or ACT required for honors, paralegal, and electronics engineering programs. Interview and letter of recommendation generally required of students in bottom quarter of class, essay and interview recommended for all others.

**High school preparation.** 12 units recommended. Recommended units include English 4, mathematics 3, social studies 2 and science 3.

**2007-2008 Annual costs.** Tuition/fees: $21,717. Freshman required fees also include $255 orientation fee. Weekend meal plan is also available for $987. Room/board: $8,550. Books/supplies: $900. Personal expenses: $594.

**2007-2008 Financial aid. Need-based:** 1,729 full-time freshmen applied for aid; 1,517 were judged to have need; 1,512 of these received aid. Average need met was 67%. Average scholarship/grant was $8,460; average loan $3,265. 42% of total undergraduate aid awarded as scholarships/grants, 58% as loans/jobs. **Non-need-based:** Awarded to 4,283 full-time undergraduates, including 1,446 freshmen. Scholarships awarded for academics, alumni affiliation, job skills, leadership, state residency.

**Application procedures. Admission:** No deadline. No application fee. Admission notification on a rolling basis beginning on or about 11/1. **Financial aid:** No deadline. FAFSA required. Applicants notified on a rolling basis starting 3/1; must reply within 2 week(s) of notification.

**Academics. Special study options:** Accelerated study, cooperative education, dual enrollment of high school students, ESL, external degree, honors, independent study, internships, study abroad, weekend college. Externships, practicums (hands-on learning). **Credit/placement by examination:** CLEP, institutional tests. **Support services:** Learning center, pre-admission summer program, reduced course load, remedial instruction, study skills assistance, tutoring, writing center.

**Majors. Agriculture:** Equestrian studies, equine science, farm/ranch. **Business:** Accounting, business admin, entrepreneurial studies, fashion, finance, hospitality admin, hotel/motel admin, international, investments/securities, marketing, public finance, tourism promotion, tourism/travel. **Communications:** General. **Computer sciences:** Information systems, systems analysis, web page design, webmaster. **Engineering:** Computer, systems. **Engineering technology:** Drafting. **Interdisciplinary:** Nutrition sciences. **Legal studies:** Paralegal. **Parks/recreation:** Facilities management, sports admin. **Personal/culinary services:** Baking, chef training, culinary arts, food service, restaurant/catering. **Protective services:** Law enforcement admin.

**Most popular majors.** Business/marketing 46%, computer/information sciences 6%, family/consumer sciences 15%, parks/recreation 6%, personal/culinary services 15%.

**Computing on campus.** 400 workstations in library, computer center. Dormitories wired for high-speed internet access and linked to campus network. Commuter students can connect to campus network. Online library, helpline, wireless network available.

**Student life. Freshman orientation:** Mandatory, $250 fee. Preregistration for classes offered. **Housing:** Guaranteed on-campus for freshmen. Coed dorms, substance-free housing available. $300 deposit. Dormitory for National Student Organization scholarship winners, single rooms, women's floors available. **Activities:** Choral groups, drama, student government, student newspaper, Hillel, Christian student union, ACLU, Latin-American club, Asian club, T.R.U.E. (Together Realizing Unity Can Exist), College Republicans.

**Athletics.** NCAA. **Intercollegiate:** Baseball M, basketball, cross-country, equestrian, golf, ice hockey, soccer, softball W, tennis, volleyball, wrestling M. **Intramural:** Basketball, golf, soccer, softball, tennis. **Team name:** Wildcats.

**Student services.** Career counseling, student employment services, financial aid counseling, health services, personal counseling, placement for graduates, veterans' counselor, women's services. **Physically disabled:** Services for visually, speech, hearing impaired.

**Contact.** E-mail: admissions.pvd@jwu.edu
Phone: (401) 598-2310 Toll-free number: (800) 342-5598
Fax: (401) 598-2948
Maureen Dumas, Dean of Admissions, Johnson & Wales University: Providence, 8 Abbott Park Place, Providence, RI 02903-3703

## New England Institute of Technology
Warwick, Rhode Island
www.neit.edu
CB code: 0339

- Private 4-year technical college
- Commuter campus in small city
- 2,993 degree-seeking undergraduates
- Interview required

**General.** Founded in 1940. Regionally accredited. **Degrees:** 175 bachelor's, 906 associate awarded. **Location:** 10 miles from Providence, 50 miles from Boston. **Calendar:** Quarter, extensive summer session. **Full-time faculty:** 101 total; 10% have terminal degrees. **Part-time faculty:** 185 total; 4% have terminal degrees.

**Basis for selection.** Open admission. Basic skills testing, Ronald P. Carver reading test used for placement. Portfolio recommended for drafting program.

**2008-2009 Annual costs.** Tuition/fees (projected): $17,165. Fees vary from $1,265 to $2,165 according to program. Books/supplies: $600. Personal expenses: $1,440.

**Financial aid. Non-need-based:** Scholarships awarded for academics. **Additional information:** Tuition at time of first enrollment guaranteed all students for 2 years.

**Application procedures. Admission:** No deadline. $25 fee. Application may be submitted online. Admission notification on a rolling basis. Must reply by May 1 or within 4 week(s) if notified thereafter. **Financial aid:** Priority date 6/1; no closing date. FAFSA, institutional form required. Applicants notified on a rolling basis starting 6/15.

**Academics. Special study options:** Accelerated study, cooperative education, distance learning, double major, ESL, internships, student-designed major. **Credit/placement by examination:** AP, CLEP, institutional tests. 51 credit hours maximum toward associate degree. **Support services:** Learning center, pre-admission summer program, reduced course load, remedial instruction, study skills assistance, tutoring, writing center.

**Majors. Business:** General. **Communications technology:** Recording arts. **Computer sciences:** General, computer science, information technology, systems analysis. **Engineering:** Architectural, manufacturing, mechanical.

**Engineering technology:** Electrical, manufacturing. **Visual/performing arts:** Interior design.

**Computing on campus.** 50 workstations in library, computer center. Online course registration, online library, wireless network available.

**Student life. Freshman orientation:** Mandatory. Preregistration for classes offered. **Activities:** Radio station, student newspaper, TV station, international student club.

**Student services.** Career counseling, student employment services, financial aid counseling, personal counseling, placement for graduates, veterans' counselor.

**Contact.** E-mail: neit@neit.edu
Phone: (401) 467-7744 Toll-free number: (800) 736-7744 ext. 3357
Fax: (401) 738-5122
Mark Blondin, Director of Admissions, New England Institute of Technology, 2500 Post Road, Warwick, RI 02886-2286

## Providence College
Providence, Rhode Island
www.providence.edu
CB member
CB code: 3693

- Private 4-year liberal arts college affiliated with Roman Catholic Church
- Residential campus in small city
- 3,959 degree-seeking undergraduates: 56% women, 2% African American, 2% Asian American, 2% Hispanic American, 1% international
- 479 degree-seeking graduate students
- 41% of applicants admitted
- Application essay required
- 87% graduate within 6 years

**General.** Founded in 1917. Regionally accredited. **Degrees:** 1,038 bachelor's, 5 associate awarded; master's offered. **ROTC:** Army. **Location:** 50 miles from Boston, 180 miles from New York City. **Calendar:** Semester, limited summer session. **Full-time faculty:** 291 total; 84% have terminal degrees, 9% minority, 33% women. **Part-time faculty:** 96 total; 33% have terminal degrees, 8% minority, 44% women. **Class size:** 48% < 20, 48% 20-39, 1% 40-49, 3% 50-99, less than 1% >100.

**Freshman class profile.** 9,802 applied, 4,064 admitted, 989 enrolled.

| Mid 50% test scores | | | |
|---|---|---|---|
| SAT critical reading: | 530-630 | Rank in top quarter: | 83% |
| SAT math: | 540-640 | Rank in top tenth: | 45% |
| SAT writing: | 540-650 | End year in good standing: | 96% |
| ACT composite: | 23-28 | Return as sophomores: | 92% |
| GPA 3.50 or higher: | 49% | Out-of-state: | 86% |
| GPA 3.0-3.49: | 45% | Live on campus: | 97% |
| GPA 2.0-2.99: | 6% | International: | 1% |

**Basis for selection.** GED not accepted. Emphasis placed on scholastic ability, motivation, character, and seriousness of purpose. Recommendations and essay considered. Strength of curriculum and grades are the most important factors. Standardized tests scores are optional. Audition recommended for music programs; portfolio recommended for art programs. **Homeschooled:** Statement describing homeschool structure and mission, transcript of courses and grades, state high school equivalency certificate, letter of recommendation (nonparent) required. **Learning Disabled:** Students must provide documentation of disability. Accomodations are then made as deemed appropriate.

**High school preparation.** College-preparatory program required. 16 units required; 18 recommended. Required and recommended units include English 4, mathematics 4, social studies 2, history 2, science 3-4 (laboratory 2) and foreign language 3.

**2007-2008 Annual costs.** Tuition/fees: $29,499. Room/board: $10,335. Books/supplies: $800. Personal expenses: $1,500.

**2007-2008 Financial aid. Need-based:** 716 full-time freshmen applied for aid; 597 were judged to have need; 597 of these received aid. Average need met was 66%. Average scholarship/grant was $15,361; average loan $4,431. 65% of total undergraduate aid awarded as scholarships/grants, 35% as loans/jobs. **Non-need-based:** Awarded to 764 full-time undergraduates, including 173 freshmen. Scholarships awarded for academics, athletics, minority status, ROTC.

**Application procedures. Admission:** Closing date 1/15 (postmark date). $55 fee, may be waived for applicants with need. Application may be submitted online. Admission notification 4/1. Must reply by 5/1. **Financial aid:** Closing date 2/1. FAFSA, CSS PROFILE required. Applicants notified by 4/1; must reply by 5/1.

**Academics. Special study options:** Combined bachelor's/graduate degree, cross-registration, double major, dual enrollment of high school students, honors, independent study, internships, student-designed major, study abroad, teacher certification program, Washington semester. **Credit/placement by examination:** AP, CLEP, IB, SAT, ACT, institutional tests. International Baccalaureate credit restricted to 5-7 higher level exams. **Support services:** Learning center, reduced course load, study skills assistance, tutoring, writing center.

**Majors. Area/ethnic studies:** American. **Biology:** General, biochemistry. **Business:** Accounting, banking/financial services, business admin, finance, labor relations, marketing, organizational behavior. **Computer sciences:** Computer science. **Education:** Music, secondary, special. **Engineering:** Physics, systems. **English:** English lit. **Foreign languages:** French, Italian, Spanish. **Health:** Health care admin. **History:** General. **Interdisciplinary:** Global studies. **Liberal arts:** Arts/sciences, humanities. **Math:** General. **Philosophy/religion:** Philosophy. **Physical sciences:** Chemistry. **Protective services:** Firefighting. **Psychology:** General. **Public administration:** Community org/advocacy, social work. **Social sciences:** General, economics, political science, sociology. **Theology:** Theology. **Visual/performing arts:** General, art history/conservation, ceramics, digital art, drawing, painting, photography, sculpture, studio arts. **Other:** Ministry/divinity, Organization Communication.

**Most popular majors.** Business/marketing 28%, education 9%, English 7%, history 7%, psychology 6%, social sciences 14%.

**Computing on campus.** 278 workstations in dormitories, library, computer center, student center. Dormitories wired for high-speed internet access and linked to campus network. Commuter students can connect to campus network. Online course registration, online library, helpline, repair service, student web hosting, wireless network available.

**Student life. Freshman orientation:** Mandatory. Preregistration for classes offered. 2-day session held in the summer, involves both parents and students. **Housing:** Guaranteed on-campus for freshmen. Coed dorms, single-sex dorms, special housing for disabled, apartments, substance-free housing available. $200 nonrefundable deposit, deadline 5/1. **Activities:** Bands, campus ministries, choral groups, dance, drama, international student organizations, literary magazine, music ensembles, musical theater, radio station, student government, student newspaper, TV station, Afro-American society, Big Brothers and Sisters, Pastoral Service Organization, PC Pals, Best Buddies, College Democrats, College Republicans, Amigos Unidos, Asian American Club.

**Athletics.** NCAA. **Intercollegiate:** Basketball, cross-country, diving, field hockey W, ice hockey, lacrosse M, soccer, softball W, swimming, tennis W, track and field, volleyball W. **Intramural:** Basketball, field hockey W, football (non-tackle), ice hockey, lacrosse, racquetball, soccer, softball, tennis, volleyball. **Team name:** Friars.

**Student services.** Adult student services, alcohol/substance abuse counseling, campus ministries, career counseling, services for economically disadvantaged, student employment services, financial aid counseling, health services, minority student services, personal counseling, placement for graduates. **Physically disabled:** Services for visually, hearing impaired.

**Contact.** E-mail: pcadmiss@providence.edu
Phone: (401) 865-2535 Toll-free number: (800) 721-6444
Fax: (401) 865-2826
Christopher Lydon, Associate Vice President for Admissions and Enrollment Planning, Providence College, Harkins Hall 222, 549 River Avenue, Providence, RI 02918-0001

## Rhode Island College
**Providence, Rhode Island**
www.ric.edu

**CB member**
**CB code: 3724**

- Public 4-year liberal arts college
- Commuter campus in small city
- 7,197 degree-seeking undergraduates: 27% part-time, 68% women, 6% African American, 2% Asian American, 6% Hispanic American
- 733 degree-seeking graduate students
- 72% of applicants admitted
- SAT or ACT with writing, application essay required
- 45% graduate within 6 years

**General.** Founded in 1854. Regionally accredited. **Degrees:** 1,183 bachelor's awarded; master's, doctoral offered. **ROTC:** Army. **Location:** 4 miles from downtown. **Calendar:** Semester, extensive summer session. **Full-time faculty:** 315 total; 91% have terminal degrees, 11% minority, 54% women. **Part-time faculty:** 368 total; 56% women. **Class size:** 40% < 20, 58% 20-39, less than 1% 40-49, 1% 50-99, less than 1% >100. **Special facilities:** Center for the performing arts.

**Freshman class profile.** 3,636 applied, 2,624 admitted, 1,127 enrolled.

| Mid 50% test scores | | | |
|---|---|---|---|
| SAT critical reading: | 430-530 | Rank in top quarter: | 37% |
| SAT math: | 420-530 | Rank in top tenth: | 12% |
| SAT writing: | 430-530 | Return as sophomores: | 75% |
| ACT composite: | 18-22 | Out-of-state: | 18% |
| | | Live on campus: | 48% |

**Basis for selection.** High school academic record and class rank most important, followed by test scores, essay, references. SAT scores required of international students in U.S. over five years. Interview available but not required; audition required for music performance; portfolio required for bachelor of fine arts. **Homeschooled:** Must submit GED scores unless their home school curriculum is provided by an accredited agency.

**High school preparation.** 18 units required. Required units include English 4, mathematics 3, social studies 2, science 2 (laboratory 2), foreign language 2, visual/performing arts .5, academic electives 4.5. .5 unit in the arts (music, art, dance, theatre) is required. Biology and either chemistry or physics are required lab sciences. 2 years of the same foreign language is required. Algebra I, II and geometry required. All units must be college-preparatory.

**2007-2008 Annual costs.** Tuition/fees: $5,256; $13,664 out-of-state. Permanent residents of Massachusetts communities within a 20-mile radius of Providence are eligible for Rhode Island's in-state tuition plus 50% of the in-state rate. Room/board: $7,820. Books/supplies: $850. Personal expenses: $1,000.

**2007-2008 Financial aid. Need-based:** 921 full-time freshmen applied for aid; 647 were judged to have need; 624 of these received aid. Average need met was 42%. Average scholarship/grant was $6,278; average loan $2,997. 48% of total undergraduate aid awarded as scholarships/grants, 52% as loans/jobs. **Non-need-based:** Awarded to 210 full-time undergraduates, including 82 freshmen. Scholarships awarded for academics, alumni affiliation, art, music/drama.

**Application procedures. Admission:** Closing date 5/1 (postmark date). $50 fee, may be waived for applicants with need. Application may be submitted online. Admission notification on a rolling basis beginning on or about 12/15. Must reply by May 1 or within 2 week(s) if notified thereafter. **Financial aid:** Priority date 3/1; no closing date. FAFSA, institutional form required. Applicants notified on a rolling basis starting 3/15; must reply within 3 week(s) of notification.

**Academics. Special study options:** Double major, ESL, exchange student, honors, independent study, internships, student-designed major, study abroad, teacher certification program. **Credit/placement by examination:** AP, CLEP, SAT, ACT, institutional tests. **Support services:** Learning center, pre-admission summer program, reduced course load, remedial instruction, study skills assistance, tutoring, writing center.

**Majors. Area/ethnic studies:** African-American, Latin American, women's. **Biology:** General. **Business:** General, accounting, business admin, finance, labor studies, management information systems, managerial economics, marketing. **Communications:** General. **Computer sciences:** General, computer science. **Education:** Art, biology, chemistry, early childhood, elementary, English, foreign languages, French, geography, health, history, mathematics, multi-level teacher, music, physical, physics, science, secondary, social science, social studies, Spanish, special, technology/industrial arts, voc/tech. **English:** English lit. **Foreign languages:** French, Spanish. **Health:** Clinical lab science, medical radiologic technology/radiation therapy, nursing (RN), predental, premedicine, preveterinary, substance abuse counseling. **History:** General. **Legal studies:** Prelaw. **Liberal arts:** Arts/sciences. **Math:** General. **Philosophy/religion:** Philosophy. **Physical sciences:** Chemistry, physics. **Protective services:** Criminal justice. **Psychology:** General. **Public administration:** General, social work. **Social sciences:** General, anthropology, economics, geography, political science, sociology. **Visual/performing arts:** Art history/conservation, dance, dramatic, film/cinema, music performance, studio arts.

**Most popular majors.** Business/marketing 10%, communications/journalism 7%, education 26%, health sciences 11%, psychology 12%, social sciences 6%, visual/performing arts 7%.

**Computing on campus.** 675 workstations in library, computer center, student center. Dormitories wired for high-speed internet access and linked to campus network. Commuter students can connect to campus network. Online course registration, online library, helpline, repair service, student web hosting, wireless network available.

**Student life. Freshman orientation:** Available, $85 fee. Preregistration for classes offered. Held throughout the month of July in 2 day cycles. Some single days are available. **Housing:** Coed dorms, single-sex dorms, special housing for disabled available. $214 partly refundable deposit, deadline 5/1. **Activities:** Bands, campus ministries, choral groups, dance, drama, film society, international student organizations, literary magazine, music ensembles, musical theater, radio station, student government, student newspaper, symphony orchestra, Catholic and Protestant religious organizations, Amnesty International, Cape Verdean student association, Habitat for Humanity, Intra-Varsity Student Fellowship, Latin American student association, Muslim students, RIC Angels RIC Republicans, Harambee, NAACP.

**Athletics.** NCAA. **Intercollegiate:** Baseball M, basketball, cross-country, golf M, gymnastics W, lacrosse W, soccer, softball W, tennis, track and field, volleyball W, wrestling M. **Intramural:** Basketball, football (non-tackle) M, gymnastics, softball, tennis, volleyball. **Team name:** Anchormen, Anchorwomen.

**Student services.** Adult student services, alcohol/substance abuse counseling, campus ministries, career counseling, student employment services, financial aid counseling, health services, minority student services, on-campus daycare, personal counseling, placement for graduates, veterans' counselor, women's services. **Physically disabled:** Services for visually, speech, hearing impaired. **Learning disabled:** Comprehensive services available.

**Contact.** E-mail: admissions@ric.edu
Phone: (401) 456-8234 Toll-free number: (800) 669-5760
Fax: (401) 456-8817
Holly Shadoian, Director of Admissions, Rhode Island College, 600 Mount Pleasant Avenue, Providence, RI 02908

---

## Rhode Island School of Design
### Providence, Rhode Island
www.risd.edu

CB member
CB code: 3726

- Private 4-year visual arts college
- Residential campus in small city
- 1,927 degree-seeking undergraduates: 67% women, 1% African American, 14% Asian American, 4% Hispanic American, 16% international
- 410 graduate students
- 31% of applicants admitted
- SAT or ACT with writing, application essay required
- 90% graduate within 6 years; 4% enter graduate study

**General.** Founded in 1877. Regionally accredited. **Degrees:** 453 bachelor's awarded; master's offered. **Location:** 52 miles from Boston, 180 miles from New York City. **Calendar:** 4-1-4, limited summer session. **Full-time faculty:** 146 total; 14% minority, 41% women. **Part-time faculty:** 357 total; 7% minority. **Special facilities:** Fine art and design museum, extensive photograph and clipping collections, slide collection, recreational farm on Narragansett Bay, nature laboratory.

**Freshman class profile.** 2,771 applied, 863 admitted, 432 enrolled.

| Mid 50% test scores | | | |
|---|---|---|---|
| SAT critical reading: | 540-650 | Rank in top tenth: | 23% |
| SAT math: | 560-670 | Return as sophomores: | 94% |
| SAT writing: | 540-660 | Out-of-state: | 96% |
| Rank in top quarter: | 58% | Live on campus: | 98% |
| | | International: | 16% |

**Basis for selection.** Academic history, visual portfolio and 3 required drawings most important parts of application. Portfolio required for all applicants. **Homeschooled:** Proof of high school equivalent/GED required.

**High school preparation.** Architecture, interior architecture, landscape architecture, and industrial design applicants must have 2 algebra, .5 trigonometry, 1 science.

**2008-2009 Annual costs.** Tuition/fees (projected): $34,925. Room/board: $10,260. Books/supplies: $2,000.

**Application procedures. Admission:** Closing date 2/15 (receipt date). $60 fee, may be waived for applicants with need. Application may be submitted online. Admission notification 4/1. Must reply by 5/1. **Financial aid:** Closing date 2/15. FAFSA, CSS PROFILE required. Applicants notified by 4/1; must reply by 5/1.

**Academics. Special study options:** Cross-registration, double major, exchange student, independent study, internships, study abroad, teacher certification program. **Credit/placement by examination:** AP, CLEP, IB. **Support services:** Remedial instruction, tutoring, writing center.

---

**Majors. Architecture:** Architecture, interior, landscape. **Visual/performing arts:** Ceramics, cinematography, fashion design, fiber arts, graphic design, illustration, industrial design, metal/jewelry, painting, photography, printmaking, sculpture, studio arts.

**Most popular majors.** Architecture 9%, visual/performing arts 91%.

**Computing on campus.** 425 workstations in dormitories, library, computer center, student center. Dormitories wired for high-speed internet access and linked to campus network. Commuter students can connect to campus network. Online course registration, helpline, repair service, student web hosting, wireless network available.

**Student life. Freshman orientation:** Mandatory. **Housing:** Guaranteed on-campus for freshmen. Coed dorms, apartments, substance-free housing available. $175 nonrefundable deposit, deadline 5/1. **Activities:** Dance, drama, film society, literary magazine, student government, student newspaper, all major religions represented on campus, professional societies, clubs.

**Athletics. Intramural:** Baseball M, basketball, ice hockey, soccer, softball.

**Student services.** Alcohol/substance abuse counseling, campus ministries, career counseling, financial aid counseling, health services, legal services, minority student services, personal counseling, placement for graduates. **Physically disabled:** Services for hearing impaired.

**Contact.** E-mail: admissions@risd.edu
Phone: (401) 454-6300 Toll-free number: (800) 364-7473
Fax: (401) 454-6309
Edward Newhall, Director of Admissions, Rhode Island School of Design, Two College Street, Providence, RI 02903-2791

---

## Roger Williams University
### Bristol, Rhode Island
www.rwu.edu

CB member
CB code: 3729

- Private 4-year university and liberal arts college
- Residential campus in large town
- 4,353 degree-seeking undergraduates: 12% part-time, 49% women, 1% African American, 1% Asian American, 2% Hispanic American, 2% international
- 812 degree-seeking graduate students
- 67% of applicants admitted
- SAT or ACT (ACT writing recommended), application essay required
- 58% graduate within 6 years; 12% enter graduate study

**General.** Founded in 1956. Regionally accredited. Certificate and Associate programs offered only in continuing education. Continuing education in Providence and Bristol. **Degrees:** 886 bachelor's, 11 associate awarded; master's, first professional offered. **ROTC:** Army. **Location:** 18 miles from Providence, 10 miles from Newport. **Calendar:** Semester, limited summer session. **Full-time faculty:** 197 total; 80% have terminal degrees, 12% minority, 43% women. **Part-time faculty:** 319 total; 30% have terminal degrees, 7% minority, 37% women. **Class size:** 54% < 20, 45% 20-39, less than 1% 40-49, less than 1% 50-99. **Special facilities:** Marine and natural sciences building with marine biology wetlab.

**Freshman class profile.** 7,335 applied, 4,884 admitted, 1,045 enrolled.

| Mid 50% test scores | | | |
|---|---|---|---|
| SAT critical reading: | 490-580 | GPA 2.0-2.99: | 32% |
| SAT math: | 510-600 | Rank in top quarter: | 37% |
| SAT writing: | 490-580 | Rank in top tenth: | 14% |
| ACT composite: | 21-25 | Return as sophomores: | 82% |
| GPA 3.50 or higher: | 23% | Out-of-state: | 92% |
| GPA 3.0-3.49: | 45% | Live on campus: | 97% |
| | | International: | 1% |

**Basis for selection.** High school record, standardized test scores, essay, extracurricular activities and achievements most important. Teacher or counselor recommendations considered. Audition required for dance; portfolio required for art, architecture programs. **Homeschooled:** State high school equivalency certificate required. Students must submit portfolio of their work.

**High school preparation.** 22 units required; 26 recommended. Required and recommended units include English 4, mathematics 3-4, social studies 2-3, history 2-3, science 2-4 (laboratory 2), foreign language 2 and academic electives 2-3. Specific subject requirements vary with intended major.

**2007-2008 Annual costs.** Tuition/fees: $25,942. Tuition differential for architecture program. Room/board: $11,240. Books/supplies: $900. Personal expenses: $515.

**2007-2008 Financial aid. Need-based:** 742 full-time freshmen applied for aid; 646 were judged to have need; 643 of these received aid. Average need met was 88%. Average scholarship/grant was $7,608; average loan $4,539. 52% of total undergraduate aid awarded as scholarships/grants, 48% as loans/jobs. **Non-need-based:** Awarded to 1,427 full-time undergraduates, including 510 freshmen. Scholarships awarded for academics, ROTC.

**Application procedures. Admission:** Closing date 2/1. $50 fee. Application must be submitted online. Admission notification on a rolling basis beginning on or about 3/15. Must reply by 5/1. **Financial aid:** Priority date 1/1, closing date 2/1. FAFSA, CSS PROFILE required. Applicants notified on a rolling basis starting 3/20; must reply by 5/1.

**Academics.** All students graduate with two areas of specialization: one in their major and a second in a liberal arts discipline; most students may complete two majors. **Special study options:** Combined bachelor's/graduate degree, cooperative education, distance learning, double major, dual enrollment of high school students, ESL, exchange student, external degree, honors, independent study, internships, liberal arts/career combination, semester at sea, student-designed major, study abroad, teacher certification program, Washington semester. **Credit/placement by examination:** AP, CLEP, IB, SAT, ACT, institutional tests. **Support services:** Learning center, reduced course load, study skills assistance, tutoring, writing center.

**Honors college/program.** Applicants must have minimum SAT score of 1250 (exclusive of Writing) and a 3.3 GPA. (1300/ 3.3 for Architecture and Marine Biology). Application deadline February 1.

**Majors. Architecture:** Architecture, history/criticism. **Area/ethnic studies:** American. **Biology:** General, marine. **Business:** Accounting, business admin, finance, international, management information systems, marketing. **Communications:** Journalism, media studies. **Communications technology:** Graphics. **Computer sciences:** General, computer science. **Conservation:** General. **Construction:** Site management. **Education:** Elementary, secondary. **Engineering:** General. **English:** British lit, creative writing. **Foreign languages:** General. **History:** General. **Interdisciplinary:** Historic preservation. **Legal studies:** General, paralegal. **Math:** General. **Philosophy/religion:** Philosophy. **Physical sciences:** Chemistry. **Protective services:** Law enforcement admin. **Psychology:** General. **Public administration:** General. **Social sciences:** Anthropology, economics, political science, sociology. **Visual/performing arts:** Art history/conservation, dance, dramatic, graphic design, studio arts.

**Most popular majors.** Architecture 7%, business/marketing 24%, communications/journalism 8%, engineering/engineering technologies 7%, psychology 9%, security/protective services 14%.

**Computing on campus.** 540 workstations in dormitories, library, computer center. Dormitories wired for high-speed internet access and linked to campus network. Commuter students can connect to campus network. Online course registration, helpline, repair service available.

**Student life. Freshman orientation:** Mandatory. Preregistration for classes offered. 2-day program with overnight stay on campus during summer. Separate orientations for transfer and international students. **Housing:** Coed dorms, special housing for disabled, apartments, substance-free housing available. $350 fully refundable deposit, deadline 5/1. Special interest academic theme and honors housing available, living/learning. **Activities:** Choral groups, dance, drama, film society, literary magazine, musical theater, radio station, student government, student newspaper, Hillel, Inter-Varsity Christian Fellowship, multicultural student union, College Democrats, College Republicans, environmental and animal rights club, Model UN, Best Buddies of Rhode Island, Habitat for Humanity, student volunteer association.

**Athletics.** NCAA. **Intercollegiate:** Baseball M, basketball, cross-country, diving, equestrian, lacrosse, sailing, soccer, softball W, swimming, tennis, volleyball W, wrestling M. **Intramural:** Basketball, field hockey, football (non-tackle), golf, racquetball, skiing, soccer, softball, squash, tennis, volleyball, water polo. **Team name:** Hawks.

**Student services.** Campus ministries, career counseling, student employment services, financial aid counseling, health services, minority student services, personal counseling, women's services. **Physically disabled:** Services for visually, hearing impaired.

**Contact.** E-mail: admit@rwu.edu
Phone: (401) 254-3500 Toll-free number: (800) 458-7144 ext. 3500
Fax: (401) 254-3557
Didier Bouvet, Executive Director of Undergraduate Admissions, Roger Williams University, One Old Ferry Road, Bristol, RI 02809

---

**Salve Regina University**
Newport, Rhode Island
www.salve.edu
CB member
CB code: 3759

- Private 4-year university and liberal arts college affiliated with Roman Catholic Church
- Residential campus in large town

---

- 2,109 degree-seeking undergraduates: 3% part-time, 69% women, 1% African American, 1% Asian American, 3% Hispanic American, 2% international
- 414 degree-seeking graduate students
- 54% of applicants admitted
- SAT or ACT (ACT writing optional), application essay required
- 65% graduate within 6 years; 20% enter graduate study

**General.** Founded in 1934. Regionally accredited. Affiliated with Religious Sisters of Mercy. **Degrees:** 461 bachelor's, 1 associate awarded; master's, doctoral offered. **ROTC:** Army. **Location:** 30 miles from Providence. **Calendar:** Semester, limited summer session. **Full-time faculty:** 122 total; 77% have terminal degrees, 7% minority, 54% women. **Part-time faculty:** 141 total; 32% have terminal degrees, 52% women. **Class size:** 58% < 20, 41% 20-39, less than 1% 40-49. **Special facilities:** International relations and public policy center.

**Freshman class profile.** 5,801 applied, 3,107 admitted, 560 enrolled.

| Mid 50% test scores | | | |
|---|---|---|---|
| SAT critical reading: | 510-600 | Rank in top quarter: | 52% |
| SAT math: | 510-590 | Rank in top tenth: | 15% |
| SAT writing: | 510-600 | End year in good standing: | 98% |
| ACT composite: | 22-26 | Return as sophomores: | 82% |
| GPA 3.50 or higher: | 38% | Out-of-state: | 90% |
| GPA 3.0-3.49: | 41% | Live on campus: | 99% |
| GPA 2.0-2.99: | 21% | International: | 1% |

**Basis for selection.** High school achievement most important, followed by rank in top half of high school class, test scores, recommendations, essay, activities, interview. Special consideration given to applicants from minority and low-income families. SAT or TOEFL required for international applicants. Audition and portfolio considered. **Homeschooled:** Statement describing homeschool structure and mission, transcript of courses and grades, letter of recommendation (nonparent) required. Require two recommendations, one of which must be academic. Course syllabus required for each course; results of SAT or ACT examinations; portfolio of academic accomplishments including a reading list, course descriptions and list of extracurricular/community involvement.

**High school preparation.** 16 units required. Required units include English 4, mathematics 3, social studies 1, science 2 (laboratory 2), foreign language 2 and academic electives 4. Additional course work may be required of students who have not completed recommended units. Social studies includes history.

**2008-2009 Annual costs.** Tuition/fees: $31,500. Required fees include a one-time laptop fee of $2,350 for all first-year students. Room/board: $10,700. Books/supplies: $900. Personal expenses: $1,000.

**2007-2008 Financial aid. Need-based:** 445 full-time freshmen applied for aid; 369 were judged to have need; 361 of these received aid. Average need met was 74%. Average scholarship/grant was $16,410; average loan $4,870. 65% of total undergraduate aid awarded as scholarships/grants, 35% as loans/jobs. **Non-need-based:** Awarded to 356 full-time undergraduates, including 107 freshmen. Scholarships awarded for academics, ROTC.

**Application procedures. Admission:** Priority date 2/1; no deadline. $40 fee, may be waived for applicants with need. Application may be submitted online. Must reply by May 1 or within 2 week(s) if notified thereafter. **Financial aid:** Priority date 3/1; no closing date. FAFSA, CSS PROFILE required. Applicants notified by 4/1; must reply by 4/15 or within 2 week(s) of notification.

**Academics.** Credit may be awarded for learning associated with life experience. **Special study options:** Accelerated study, combined bachelor's/graduate degree, distance learning, double major, dual enrollment of high school students, ESL, exchange student, honors, independent study, internships, liberal arts/career combination, semester at sea, study abroad, teacher certification program, Washington semester. **Credit/placement by examination:** AP, CLEP, IB, SAT, ACT, institutional tests. **Support services:** Learning center, reduced course load, study skills assistance, tutoring, writing center.

**Majors. Area/ethnic studies:** American. **Biology:** General. **Business:** Accounting, business admin, finance, management science, market research. **Computer sciences:** Information systems. **Education:** Biology, drama/dance, early childhood, elementary, English, French, history, mathematics, music, Spanish, special. **English:** English lit. **Foreign languages:** French, Spanish. **Health:** Nursing (RN). **History:** American, European. **Interdisciplinary:** Historic preservation. **Liberal arts:** Arts/sciences. **Math:** General. **Philosophy/religion:** Philosophy, religion. **Physical sciences:** Chemistry. **Protective services:** Law enforcement admin. **Psychology:** General. **Public**

**administration:** Social work. **Social sciences:** Economics, political science, sociology. **Visual/performing arts:** Art history/conservation, ceramics, dramatic, graphic design, painting, photography, studio arts. **Other:** Interactive Communication Technology.

**Most popular majors.** Business/marketing 19%, education 22%, English 7%, health sciences 11%, security/protective services 11%.

**Computing on campus.** PC or laptop required. 120 workstations in dormitories, library, computer center, student center. Dormitories wired for high-speed internet access and linked to campus network. Commuter students can connect to campus network. Online course registration, online library, helpline, repair service, student web hosting, wireless network available.

**Student life. Freshman orientation:** Mandatory, $300 fee. Preregistration for classes offered. 2 day sessions during June and July for full-time freshmen; separate sessions for international and transfer students. **Housing:** Guaranteed on-campus for freshmen. Coed dorms, single-sex dorms, special housing for disabled, apartments, substance-free housing available. $200 fully refundable deposit, deadline 5/1. Historic and conventional style housing options available on campus. Off-campus housing available to upperclassmen. **Activities:** Bands, campus ministries, choral groups, dance, drama, film society, international student organizations, literary magazine, music ensembles, radio station, student government, student newspaper, The Artist's Guild, The Artist's Sanctuary, Circle K, environmental club, Student Outdoor Adventures, Volunteers Interested in Researching and Guiding, Women's Issues Now, Stagefright Theater Company.

**Athletics.** NCAA. **Intercollegiate:** Baseball M, basketball, cross-country, field hockey W, football (tackle) M, ice hockey, lacrosse, soccer, softball W, tennis, track and field W, volleyball W. **Intramural:** Basketball, field hockey W, football (non-tackle) W, football (tackle) M, racquetball, soccer, softball, tennis, track and field W, volleyball, weight lifting. **Team name:** Seahawks.

**Student services.** Campus ministries, career counseling, financial aid counseling, health services, minority student services, personal counseling, veterans' counselor. **Physically disabled:** Services for visually, hearing impaired.

**Contact.** E-mail: sruadmis@salve.edu
Phone: (401) 341-2908 Toll-free number: (888) 467-2583
Fax: (401) 848-2823
Colleen Emerson, Dean of Undergraduate Admissions, Salve Regina University, 100 Ochre Point Avenue, Newport, RI 02840-4192

---

## University of Rhode Island

**Kingston, Rhode Island**
www.uri.edu

CB member
CB code: 3919

- Public 4-year university
- Commuter campus in small town
- 12,268 degree-seeking undergraduates: 12% part-time, 56% women, 5% African American, 2% Asian American, 5% Hispanic American
- 2,458 degree-seeking graduate students
- 79% of applicants admitted
- SAT or ACT with writing, application essay required
- 58% graduate within 6 years

**General.** Founded in 1892. Regionally accredited. College of Continuing Education in Providence offers credit-bearing courses for degree and non-degree part-time students. **Degrees:** 2,008 bachelor's awarded; master's, doctoral, first professional offered. **ROTC:** Army. **Location:** 30 miles from Providence. **Calendar:** Semester, extensive summer session. **Full-time faculty:** 704 total; 89% have terminal degrees, 13% minority, 39% women. **Part-time faculty:** 28 total; 61% have terminal degrees, 11% minority, 61% women. **Class size:** 36% < 20, 51% 20-39, 6% 40-49, 5% 50-99, 3% >100. **Special facilities:** Center for robotics research, animal science farm, planetarium, Narragansett Bay Campus for Marine Sciences, American historic textiles museum, aquaculture center, fisheries and marine technology laboratory, biotechnology center, human performance laboratory.

**Freshman class profile.** 14,272 applied, 11,300 admitted, 3,189 enrolled.

| Mid 50% test scores | | | |
|---|---|---|---|
| SAT critical reading: | 490-590 | Out-of-state: | 51% |
| SAT math: | 500-600 | Live on campus: | 93% |
| Return as sophomores: | 81% | Fraternities: | 9% |
| | | Sororities: | 8% |

**Basis for selection.** School record primary, test scores secondary; extracurricular activities considered. Economically and socially disadvantaged students from Rhode Island admitted through special program for talent

development. Additional requirement for music and composition performance majors.

**High school preparation.** 18 units required. Required units include English 4, mathematics 3, social studies 2, science 2 (laboratory 1), foreign language 2 and academic electives 5.

**2007-2008 Annual costs.** Tuition/fees: $8,184; $23,038 out-of-state. Room/board: $8,732.

**2007-2008 Financial aid. Need-based:** 2,484 full-time freshmen applied for aid; 1,931 were judged to have need; 1,559 of these received aid. Average need met was 72%. Average scholarship/grant was $7,371; average loan $7,290. 47% of total undergraduate aid awarded as scholarships/grants, 53% as loans/jobs. **Non-need-based:** Awarded to 1,075 full-time undergraduates, including 403 freshmen. Scholarships awarded for academics, alumni affiliation, art, athletics, music/drama, ROTC.

**Application procedures. Admission:** Closing date 2/1. $50 fee, may be waived for applicants with need. Application may be submitted online. Admission notification 3/31. Admission notification on a rolling basis beginning on or about 12/1. Must reply by 5/1. **Financial aid:** Priority date 3/1; no closing date. FAFSA required. Applicants notified on a rolling basis starting 3/31; must reply by 5/1.

**Academics. Special study options:** Combined bachelor's/graduate degree, cooperative education, distance learning, double major, dual enrollment of high school students, exchange student, honors, independent study, internships, semester at sea, study abroad, teacher certification program, Washington semester. **Credit/placement by examination:** AP, CLEP, institutional tests. **Support services:** Learning center, pre-admission summer program, remedial instruction, study skills assistance, tutoring, writing center.

**Honors college/program.** Different admission requirements and different courses offered.

**Majors. Agriculture:** Animal sciences, turf management. **Architecture:** Landscape. **Area/ethnic studies:** African-American, Latin American, women's. **Biology:** General, marine, microbiology, zoology. **Business:** General, accounting, apparel, business admin, finance, international, marketing. **Communications:** General, journalism, public relations. **Computer sciences:** General. **Conservation:** Environmental studies, fisheries, management/policy, water/wetlands/marine, wildlife. **Education:** Elementary, music, physical, secondary. **Engineering:** Biomedical, chemical, civil, computer, electrical, industrial, mechanical, ocean. **English:** English lit. **Family/consumer sciences:** Clothing/textiles, family studies, food/nutrition. **Foreign languages:** Classics, comparative lit, French, German, Italian, Spanish. **Health:** Clinical lab science, communication disorders, dietetics, health care admin, nursing (RN), pharmacy assistant. **History:** General. **Math:** General. **Philosophy/religion:** Philosophy. **Physical sciences:** Chemistry, geology, oceanography, physics. **Psychology:** General. **Public administration:** Policy analysis. **Social sciences:** Anthropology, econometrics, economics, political science, sociology. **Visual/performing arts:** Art history/conservation, cinematography, dramatic, music performance, music theory/composition, studio arts. **Other:** Applied sociology, Kinesiology, Urban horticulture.

**Most popular majors.** Business/marketing 18%, communications/journalism 12%, education 8%, engineering/engineering technologies 7%, health sciences 8%, psychology 7%, social sciences 7%.

**Computing on campus.** 800 workstations in dormitories, library, computer center, student center. Dormitories wired for high-speed internet access and linked to campus network. Commuter students can connect to campus network. Online course registration, online library, helpline, student web hosting, wireless network available.

**Student life. Freshman orientation:** Available, $150 fee. Preregistration for classes offered. Two-day orientation held in late June, early July. **Housing:** Guaranteed on-campus for freshmen. Coed dorms, special housing for disabled, apartments, fraternity/sorority housing available. $100 partly refundable deposit, deadline 5/1. **Activities:** Bands, campus ministries, choral groups, dance, drama, film society, international student organizations, literary magazine, music ensembles, musical theater, radio station, student government, student newspaper, TV station, African awareness association, Asian student association, business students of color, Cape Verdean student association, Italian American organization, French club, the gay, lesbian, bisexual, transgender center, Young Democrats, Young Republicans.

**Athletics.** NCAA. **Intercollegiate:** Baseball M, basketball, cheerleading, cross-country, diving, field hockey W, football (tackle) M, golf M, gymnastics W, rowing (crew) W, soccer, softball W, swimming, tennis, track and field, volleyball W. **Intramural:** Badminton, basketball, bowling, boxing, cross-country, football (non-tackle), golf, soccer, softball, swimming, tennis, volleyball, water polo. **Team name:** Rams.

**Student services.** Adult student services, alcohol/substance abuse counseling, campus ministries, career counseling, services for economically disadvantaged, student employment services, financial aid counseling, health services, legal services, minority student services, on-campus daycare, personal counseling, placement for graduates, veterans' counselor, women's services. **Physically disabled:** Services for visually, speech, hearing impaired.

**Contact.** E-mail: admission@uri.edu
Phone: (401) 874-7000 Fax: (401) 874-5523
Cynthia Bonn, Dean of Admission, University of Rhode Island, 14 Upper College Road, Kingston, RI 02881-1322

---

## Zion Bible College
### Barrington, Rhode Island
**www.zbc.edu**      **CB code: 3942**

- Private 4-year Bible college affiliated with Assemblies of God
- Residential campus in large town
- 251 degree-seeking undergraduates: 12% part-time, 48% women, 11% African American, 2% Asian American, 7% Hispanic American, 3% international
- 90% of applicants admitted
- SAT or ACT with writing, application essay required
- 46% graduate within 6 years; 10% enter graduate study

**General.** Accredited by ABHE. **Degrees:** 36 bachelor's awarded. **ROTC:** Army. **Location:** 10 miles from Providence. **Calendar:** Semester, limited summer session. **Full-time faculty:** 11 total; 46% have terminal degrees, 27% women. **Part-time faculty:** 21 total; 52% women.

**Freshman class profile.** 63 applied, 57 admitted, 48 enrolled.

| Mid 50% test scores | | | |
|---|---|---|---|
| SAT critical reading: | 380-610 | ACT composite: | 14- |
| SAT math: | 390-590 | Return as sophomores: | 75% |
| SAT writing: | 380-580 | Out-of-state: | 93% |

**Basis for selection.** Three references required for admission including a pastoral recommendation. High school transcript, immunizations, health certificate and test scores also required. **Homeschooled:** Transcript of courses and grades required. Applicants must produce diploma and transcript that verifies graduation by the state department of education, local school district or accrediting association. Students who cannot produce this must submit GED.

**2007-2008 Annual costs.** Tuition/fees: $6,805. Room/board: $5,200.

**Financial aid. Non-need-based:** Scholarships awarded for academics, leadership, minority status.

**Application procedures. Admission:** No deadline. $35 fee. Application may be submitted online. Admission notification on a rolling basis. Must reply by May 1 or within 4 week(s) if notified thereafter. Letter of Intent with deposit (tuition and board) required one month after notification.

**Academics. Special study options:** Independent study, internships, weekend college. **Credit/placement by examination:** AP, CLEP, SAT, ACT, institutional tests. **Support services:** Learning center, reduced course load, study skills assistance.

**Majors. Theology:** Bible.

**Computing on campus.** 15 workstations in library, computer center. Online library, wireless network available.

**Student life. Freshman orientation:** Mandatory. Preregistration for classes offered. **Policies:** 10:30 curfew except for Fridays when it is extended to 11:00 p.m. (midnight for senors.) Chapel attendance required Tuesday-Friday. No alcohol, drugs, or smoking permitted on or off campus. Full-time students are assigned to assist in an area church. Religious observance required. **Housing:** Guaranteed on-campus for all undergraduates. Single-sex dorms, apartments available. $50 fully refundable deposit. **Activities:** Concert band, choral groups, music ensembles, student government, student newspaper.

**Student services.** Campus ministries, financial aid counseling.

**Contact.** E-mail: admissions@zbc.edu
Phone: (401) 628-2131 Toll-free number: (800) 356-4014
Fax: (401) 246-0906
Helen Brouillette, Director of Admissions and Records, Zion Bible College, 27 Middle Highway, Barrington, RI 02806

# South Carolina

## Allen University
### Columbia, South Carolina
www.allenuniversity.edu

CB code: 5006

- Private 4-year university and liberal arts college affiliated with African Methodist Episcopal Church
- Residential campus in large city
- 651 degree-seeking undergraduates: 2% part-time, 48% women

**General.** Founded in 1870. Regionally accredited. **Degrees:** 61 bachelor's awarded. **ROTC:** Army. **Location:** 112 miles from Charleston, 72 miles from Charlotte, North Carolina. **Calendar:** Semester, limited summer session. **Full-time faculty:** 35 total; 60% have terminal degrees, 74% minority, 37% women. **Part-time faculty:** 9 total; 33% have terminal degrees, 78% minority, 44% women. **Class size:** 73% < 20, 15% 20-39, 2% 40-49, 3% 50-99, 7% >100.

**Freshman class profile.** 817 applied, 817 admitted, 247 enrolled.

| | | | |
|---|---|---|---|
| GPA 3.50 or higher: | 4% | GPA 2.0-2.99: | 55% |
| GPA 3.0-3.49: | 20% | Return as sophomores: | 90% |

**Basis for selection.** Open admission. Interview, campus visit recommended. **Homeschooled:** Statement describing homeschool structure and mission, transcript of courses and grades, state high school equivalency certificate, interview, letter of recommendation (nonparent) required.

**High school preparation.** Recommended units include English 4, mathematics 4, social studies 3, history 3, science 3 and foreign language 2.

**2008-2009 Annual costs.** Tuition/fees (projected): $9,884. Room/board: $5,240. Books/supplies: $800.

**Financial aid. Non-need-based:** Scholarships awarded for academics, athletics, music/drama, ROTC.

**Application procedures. Admission:** Priority date 6/30; deadline 7/31. No application fee. Application may be submitted online. Admission notification on a rolling basis. **Financial aid:** Priority date 4/15, closing date 7/20. FAFSA required. Applicants notified on a rolling basis starting 4/1; must reply within 2 week(s) of notification.

**Academics. Special study options:** Cooperative education, honors, independent study, internships, teacher certification program, weekend college. Nontraditional program for returning students. **Credit/placement by examination:** CLEP, institutional tests. 3 credit hours maximum toward bachelor's degree. **Support services:** Learning center, pre-admission summer program, reduced course load, study skills assistance, tutoring, writing center.

**Majors. Biology:** General. **Business:** Business admin. **English:** English lit. **Math:** General. **Philosophy/religion:** Religion. **Physical sciences:** Chemistry. **Social sciences:** General.

**Computing on campus.** Dormitories linked to campus network. Commuter students can connect to campus network. Online course registration, online library, helpline, wireless network available.

**Student life. Freshman orientation:** Mandatory. Preregistration for classes offered. Week-long session. Students complete financial aid forms and receive dorm assignments. **Housing:** Guaranteed on-campus for freshmen. Single-sex dorms, apartments available. $50 deposit, deadline 7/31. **Activities:** Choral groups, international student organizations, student government, student newspaper, social science club, NAACP.

**Athletics. Intercollegiate:** Basketball, cross-country M, track and field M, volleyball W. **Team name:** Yellow Jackets.

**Student services.** Adult student services, campus ministries, career counseling, student employment services, financial aid counseling, health services, personal counseling, placement for graduates.

**Contact.** Phone: (803) 376-5735 Toll-free number: (877) 625-5368 Fax: (803) 758-2704
Donna Foster, Director of Admissions, Allen University, 1530 Harden Street, Columbia, SC 29204

## Anderson University
### Anderson, South Carolina
www.andersonuniversity.edu

CB member
CB code: 5008

- Private 4-year liberal arts and teachers college affiliated with Southern Baptist Convention
- Residential campus in large town
- 1,597 degree-seeking undergraduates: 12% part-time, 64% women, 12% African American, 1% Asian American, 2% Hispanic American, 2% international
- 28 degree-seeking graduate students
- 85% of applicants admitted
- SAT or ACT (ACT writing optional) required
- 34% graduate within 6 years

**General.** Founded in 1911. Regionally accredited. **Degrees:** 284 bachelor's awarded; master's offered. **ROTC:** Army, Air Force. **Location:** 32 miles from Greenville, 100 miles from Atlanta. **Calendar:** Semester, limited summer session. **Full-time faculty:** 72 total; 56% have terminal degrees, 7% minority, 49% women. **Part-time faculty:** 75 total; 23% have terminal degrees, 4% minority, 44% women. **Class size:** 51% < 20, 49% 20-39. **Special facilities:** Fine arts center cultural program, on-campus audio recording studio, electronic classrooms.

**Freshman class profile.** 1,191 applied, 1,017 admitted, 436 enrolled.

| Mid 50% test scores | | | |
|---|---|---|---|
| SAT critical reading: | 440-550 | GPA 2.0-2.99: | 17% |
| SAT math: | 450-560 | Rank in top quarter: | 45% |
| SAT writing: | 430-550 | Rank in top tenth: | 17% |
| ACT composite: | 18-23 | Out-of-state: | 16% |
| GPA 3.50 or higher: | 60% | Live on campus: | 94% |
| GPA 3.0-3.49: | 22% | International: | 2% |

**Basis for selection.** High school achievement record, test scores important; recommendations considered. Minimum high school GPA of 2.5 and SAT (exclusive of Writing) combined score of 1000 preferred. Each applicant considered individually. Applicants not meeting these guidelines may be admitted into developmental studies program. Recommendations, further grades or interview may be required for academically weak applicants. Interview recommended for some; audition required for art, music, theater programs. **Learning Disabled:** Applicants with diagnosed learning disabilities must meet regular requirements and supply summary of recent (within 1 year of enrollment) diagnostic testing.

**High school preparation.** 20 units required. Required and recommended units include English 4, mathematics 3-4, social studies 2, history 2, science 3-4 (laboratory 2), foreign language 2 and academic electives 4.

**2007-2008 Annual costs.** Tuition/fees: $17,850. Room/board: $6,750. Books/supplies: $1,650. Personal expenses: $2,450.

**2006-2007 Financial aid. Need-based:** 347 full-time freshmen applied for aid; 267 were judged to have need; 267 of these received aid. Average need met was 90%. Average scholarship/grant was $9,000; average loan $3,100. 70% of total undergraduate aid awarded as scholarships/grants, 30% as loans/jobs. **Non-need-based:** Awarded to 2,231 full-time undergraduates, including 721 freshmen. Scholarships awarded for academics, alumni affiliation, art, athletics, leadership, minority status, music/drama, religious affiliation, state residency.

**Application procedures. Admission:** No deadline. $25 fee, may be waived for applicants with need. Application may be submitted online. Admission notification on a rolling basis beginning on or about 9/1. **Financial aid:** Priority date 3/1, closing date 6/30. FAFSA required. Applicants notified on a rolling basis starting 3/15; must reply within 2 week(s) of notification.

**Academics. Special study options:** Accelerated study, cooperative education, distance learning, double major, dual enrollment of high school students, honors, independent study, internships, liberal arts/career combination, study abroad, teacher certification program, Washington semester. **Credit/placement by examination:** AP, CLEP, IB, institutional tests. 24 credit hours maximum toward bachelor's degree. **Support services:** Learning center, reduced course load, remedial instruction, study skills assistance, tutoring, writing center.

**Majors. Biology:** General. **Business:** General, business admin, finance, human resources, marketing, retailing. **Communications:** General, media studies, public relations. **Computer sciences:** General. **Education:** Art, early childhood, elementary, English, history, mathematics, multi-level teacher, music, physical, science, secondary, social studies, special. **English:** English lit. **Foreign languages:** Spanish. **History:** General. **Math:** General.

**Parks/recreation:** Exercise sciences. **Philosophy/religion:** Religion. **Protective services:** Law enforcement admin. **Psychology:** General. **Public administration:** Human services. **Theology:** Sacred music, theology. **Visual/performing arts:** Art, dramatic, interior design, music performance. **Other:** Christian Ministry, Pre-engineering.

**Most popular majors.** Business/marketing 32%, education 23%, parks/recreation 8%, philosophy/religious studies 6%, psychology 7%, visual/performing arts 10%.

**Computing on campus.** 192 workstations in library, computer center, student center. Dormitories wired for high-speed internet access and linked to campus network. Commuter students can connect to campus network. Online course registration, online library, helpline, wireless network available.

**Student life. Freshman orientation:** Mandatory. Preregistration for classes offered. 2 orientation sessions held during summer. **Housing:** Guaranteed on-campus for freshmen. Single-sex dorms, apartments, substance-free housing available. $250 fully refundable deposit, deadline 5/1. **Activities:** Bands, campus ministries, choral groups, dance, drama, literary magazine, music ensembles, musical theater, student government, student newspaper, symphony orchestra, Gamma Beta Phi, campus activities board, Fellowship of Christian Athletes, Minorities for Change, student alumni council, Reformed University Fellowship, Young Life.

**Athletics.** NCAA. **Intercollegiate:** Baseball M, basketball, cheerleading M, cross-country, golf, soccer, softball W, tennis, track and field, volleyball W, wrestling M. **Intramural:** Basketball, football (non-tackle), racquetball, softball, table tennis, tennis, volleyball, weight lifting M. **Team name:** Trojans.

**Student services.** Adult student services, campus ministries, career counseling, student employment services, financial aid counseling, health services, on-campus daycare, personal counseling, placement for graduates. **Physically disabled:** Services for visually impaired.

**Contact.** E-mail: admissions@andersonuniversity.edu
Phone: (864) 231-2030 Toll-free number: (800) 542-3594
Fax: (864) 231-2033
Pam Bryant, Director of Admissions, Anderson University, 316 Boulevard, Anderson, SC 29621-4002

---

## Benedict College
### Columbia, South Carolina
**www.benedict.edu**

CB member
CB code: 5056

- Private 4-year liberal arts college affiliated with American Baptist Churches in the USA
- Residential campus in very large city
- 2,641 degree-seeking undergraduates: 2% part-time, 51% women, 99% African American, 1% Hispanic American
- 83% of applicants admitted

**General.** Founded in 1870. Regionally accredited. **Degrees:** 303 bachelor's awarded. **ROTC:** Army, Air Force. **Location:** 110 miles from Greenville, 120 miles from Charleston. **Calendar:** Semester, limited summer session. **Full-time faculty:** 117 total; 65% have terminal degrees, 95% minority, 58% women. **Part-time faculty:** 44 total; 84% minority, 57% women. **Class size:** 49% < 20, 33% 20-39, 12% 40-49, 6% 50-99.

**Freshman class profile.** 4,624 applied, 3,833 admitted, 638 enrolled.

| Mid 50% test scores | | | |
|---|---|---|---|
| SAT critical reading: | 320-430 | GPA 2.0-2.99: | 51% |
| SAT math: | 320-430 | Rank in top quarter: | 15% |
| ACT composite: | 13-17 | Rank in top tenth: | 5% |
| GPA 3.50 or higher: | 10% | Return as sophomores: | 53% |
| GPA 3.0-3.49: | 19% | Out-of-state: | 52% |
| | | Live on campus: | 93% |

**High school preparation.** 20 units recommended. Recommended units include English 4, mathematics 3, social studies 3 and science 2.

**2007-2008 Annual costs.** Tuition/fees: $14,010. Room/board: $6,444. Books/supplies: $1,000. Personal expenses: $1,400.

**Application procedures. Admission:** No deadline. $25 fee. Admission notification on a rolling basis. **Financial aid:** Priority date 4/15; no closing date. FAFSA required. Applicants notified on a rolling basis starting 4/15.

**Academics. Special study options:** Accelerated study, double major, dual enrollment of high school students, external degree, honors, internships, teacher certification program, weekend college. **Credit/placement by examination:** AP, CLEP, institutional tests. 24 credit hours maximum toward

---

bachelor's degree. **Support services:** Learning center, pre-admission summer program, reduced course load, remedial instruction, study skills assistance, tutoring, writing center.

**Majors. Biology:** General. **Business:** Accounting, business admin. **Computer sciences:** General, computer science. **Conservation:** Environmental science. **Education:** Early childhood, elementary. **Engineering technology:** Electrical. **English:** English lit. **Family/consumer sciences:** Family studies. **History:** General. **Math:** General. **Parks/recreation:** Health/fitness. **Physical sciences:** Chemistry, physics. **Public administration:** Social work. **Social sciences:** Economics, political science. **Visual/performing arts:** Art, multimedia.

**Most popular majors.** Biology 8%, business/marketing 23%, communications/journalism 6%, computer/information sciences 8%, engineering/engineering technologies 9%, family/consumer sciences 11%, legal studies 8%, parks/recreation 9%, public administration/social services 6%.

**Computing on campus.** 385 workstations in dormitories, library, computer center, student center. Dormitories wired for high-speed internet access and linked to campus network. Commuter students can connect to campus network. Online library, helpline, repair service, wireless network available.

**Student life. Freshman orientation:** Mandatory. Preregistration for classes offered. **Housing:** Guaranteed on-campus for freshmen. Single-sex dorms available. **Activities:** Bands, choral groups, dance, drama, music ensembles, radio station, student government, student newspaper, Gordon-Jenkins Theological Association.

**Athletics.** NAIA. **Intercollegiate:** Baseball M, basketball, cross-country, football (tackle) M, golf, soccer M, softball, tennis, track and field, volleyball W, wrestling M. **Intramural:** Baseball M, basketball, softball W, volleyball W. **Team name:** Tigers.

**Student services.** Adult student services, campus ministries, career counseling, student employment services, financial aid counseling, health services, minority student services, on-campus daycare, personal counseling, placement for graduates, veterans' counselor.

**Contact.** E-mail: admissions@benedict.edu
Phone: (803) 705-4491 Toll-free number: (800) 868-6598
Fax: (803) 253-5167
Phyllis Thompson, Director of Admissions, Benedict College, 1600 Harden Street, Columbia, SC 29204

---

## Charleston Southern University
### Charleston, South Carolina
**www.csuniv.edu**

CB code: 5079

- Private 4-year university and liberal arts college affiliated with Southern Baptist Convention
- Commuter campus in large city
- 2,831 degree-seeking undergraduates: 14% part-time, 62% women, 29% African American, 1% Asian American, 2% Hispanic American, 2% international
- 430 degree-seeking graduate students
- 57% of applicants admitted
- SAT or ACT with writing required

**General.** Founded in 1964. Regionally accredited. **Degrees:** 410 bachelor's awarded; master's offered. **ROTC:** Air Force. **Location:** 15 miles from downtown. **Calendar:** 4-1-4. **Full-time faculty:** 115 total; 56% have terminal degrees, 3% minority, 47% women. **Part-time faculty:** 95 total; 52% women. **Class size:** 46% < 20, 44% 20-39, 5% 40-49, 5% 50-99. **Special facilities:** Earthquake research center.

**Freshman class profile.** 2,941 applied, 1,667 admitted, 687 enrolled.

| Mid 50% test scores | | | |
|---|---|---|---|
| SAT critical reading: | 430-530 | GPA 2.0-2.99: | 27% |
| SAT math: | 430-550 | Rank in top quarter: | 52% |
| ACT composite: | 18-22 | Rank in top tenth: | 21% |
| GPA 3.50 or higher: | 40% | Out-of-state: | 23% |
| GPA 3.0-3.49: | 31% | Live on campus: | 73% |
| | | International: | 1% |

**Basis for selection.** School achievement record, academic coursework, test scores, GPA most important. Interview and recommendations considered. Students may be required to take institutional math test for acceptance and/or placement. Essay, interview recommended for all; audition recommended for music programs. **Learning Disabled:** Special needs allowances require documentation and interview with Director of Special Needs.

**High school preparation.** 23 units required. Required and recommended units include English 4, mathematics 3-4, social studies 2, history 2, science 3 (laboratory 2) and foreign language 2.

**2007-2008 Annual costs.** Tuition/fees: $17,620. Room/board: $6,772.

**Financial aid. Non-need-based:** Scholarships awarded for academics, athletics, religious affiliation, ROTC.

**Application procedures. Admission:** No deadline. $40 fee, may be waived for applicants with need. Application may be submitted online. Admission notification on a rolling basis beginning on or about 9/1. **Financial aid:** Priority date 4/15; no closing date. FAFSA required. Applicants notified on a rolling basis starting 3/1; must reply within 2 week(s) of notification.

**Academics. Special study options:** Accelerated study, combined bachelor's/graduate degree, cooperative education, cross-registration, distance learning, double major, dual enrollment of high school students, honors, internships, study abroad, teacher certification program. **Credit/placement by examination:** AP, CLEP, IB, SAT, ACT, institutional tests. 30 credit hours maximum toward associate degree, 30 toward bachelor's. **Support services:** Learning center, remedial instruction, study skills assistance, tutoring, writing center.

**Majors. Biology:** General, biochemistry. **Business:** Accounting, business admin, finance, management information systems, marketing. **Computer sciences:** Computer science. **Education:** Early childhood, elementary, English, mathematics, multi-level teacher, music, physical, science, social studies, Spanish. **English:** English lit. **Foreign languages:** Spanish. **Health:** Athletic training, music therapy, nursing (RN). **History:** General, American, European. **Liberal arts:** Humanities. **Math:** General, applied. **Parks/recreation:** Health/fitness. **Philosophy/religion:** Religion. **Physical sciences:** Chemistry. **Protective services:** Criminal justice. **Psychology:** General. **Social sciences:** General, economics, political science, sociology. **Theology:** Sacred music, youth ministry. **Visual/performing arts:** Music performance, voice/opera. **Other:** Biological and biomedical sciences, Business administration, management and operations, Dramatic/theatre arts and stagecraft, Science technologies/technicians.

**Most popular majors.** Biology 9%, business/marketing 23%, education 10%, health sciences 7%, psychology 10%, security/protective services 6%, social sciences 8%, visual/performing arts 6%.

**Computing on campus.** 150 workstations in dormitories, library, computer center, student center. Dormitories wired for high-speed internet access. Commuter students can connect to campus network. Online library, helpline, student web hosting, wireless network available.

**Student life. Freshman orientation:** Available. Preregistration for classes offered. **Policies:** Religious observance required. **Housing:** Guaranteed on-campus for freshmen. Single-sex dorms available. $200 fully refundable deposit, deadline 8/15. **Activities:** Bands, choral groups, dance, drama, international student organizations, literary magazine, music ensembles, musical theater, student government, student newspaper, College Republicans, Young Democrats, Afro-American society, Baptist Student Union, Fellowship of Christian Athletes, Campus Crusade, future teachers society.

**Athletics.** NCAA. **Intercollegiate:** Baseball M, basketball, cross-country, football (tackle) M, golf, soccer, softball W, tennis, track and field, volleyball W. **Intramural:** Basketball, soccer, softball, volleyball. **Team name:** Buccaneer.

**Student services.** Adult student services, campus ministries, career counseling, student employment services, financial aid counseling, health services, personal counseling, placement for graduates, veterans' counselor. **Physically disabled:** Services for visually, speech, hearing impaired.

**Contact.** E-mail: enroll@csuniv.edu
Phone: (843) 863-7050 Toll-free number: (800) 947-7474
Fax: (843) 863-7070
Jim Rhoton, Director of Admissions, Charleston Southern University, 9200 University Boulevard, Charleston, SC 29423-8087

---

## The Citadel
**Charleston, South Carolina**
www.citadel.edu

**CB member**
**CB code: 5108**

- Public 4-year military college
- Residential campus in large city
- 2,209 degree-seeking undergraduates: 4% part-time, 7% women, 7% African American, 3% Asian American, 5% Hispanic American, 2% international
- 832 degree-seeking graduate students

- 78% of applicants admitted
- SAT or ACT with writing required
- 71% graduate within 6 years

**General.** Founded in 1842. Regionally accredited. **Degrees:** 510 bachelor's awarded; master's offered. **ROTC:** Army, Naval, Air Force. **Location:** 110 miles from Columbia, 120 miles from Savannah, Georgia. **Calendar:** Semester, extensive summer session. **Full-time faculty:** 167 total; 93% have terminal degrees, 13% minority, 24% women. **Part-time faculty:** 80 total; 41% have terminal degrees, 6% minority, 44% women. **Class size:** 44% < 20, 49% 20-39, 3% 40-49, 4% 50-99. **Special facilities:** Archives museum, beach house, boating center.

**Freshman class profile.** 2,081 applied, 1,629 admitted, 621 enrolled.

| Mid 50% test scores | | | |
|---|---|---|---|
| SAT critical reading: | 490-580 | Rank in top quarter: | 33% |
| SAT math: | 500-600 | Rank in top tenth: | 10% |
| ACT composite: | 20-24 | Return as sophomores: | 81% |
| GPA 3.50 or higher: | 35% | Out-of-state: | 57% |
| GPA 3.0-3.49: | 36% | Live on campus: | 100% |
| GPA 2.0-2.99: | 29% | International: | 2% |

**Basis for selection.** Admissions based on class rank, test scores, GPA, alumni recommendations, extracurricular activities. Interview recommended.

**High school preparation.** 20 units required. Required and recommended units include English 4, mathematics 3-4, social studies 2, history 1, science 3 (laboratory 3), foreign language 2 and academic electives 4. One physical education or ROTC required.

**2007-2008 Annual costs.** Tuition/fees: $7,735; $19,291 out-of-state. Students in Corps of Cadets required to pay $1,000 in fees which include laundry and dry cleaning charges and infirmary fees. Freshmen also pay $5,470 deposit and upperclassmen pay $1,630 deposit for uniforms, books, and supplies. Room/board: $5,390.

**2007-2008 Financial aid. Need-based:** 481 full-time freshmen applied for aid; 362 were judged to have need; 342 of these received aid. Average need met was 62%. Average scholarship/grant was $12,135; average loan $3,384. 54% of total undergraduate aid awarded as scholarships/grants, 46% as loans/jobs. **Non-need-based:** Awarded to 846 full-time undergraduates, including 289 freshmen. Scholarships awarded for academics, alumni affiliation, athletics, leadership, music/drama, religious affiliation, ROTC, state residency.

**Application procedures. Admission:** No deadline. $40 fee, may be waived for applicants with need. Application may be submitted online. Admission notification on a rolling basis beginning on or about 7/15. **Financial aid:** Priority date 2/28; no closing date. FAFSA required. Applicants notified on a rolling basis starting 4/1; must reply within 2 week(s) of notification.

**Academics.** 4 years of ROTC required. **Special study options:** Combined bachelor's/graduate degree, cooperative education, double major, ESL, honors, independent study, internships, study abroad, teacher certification program. **Credit/placement by examination:** AP, CLEP, institutional tests. **Support services:** Learning center, study skills assistance, tutoring, writing center.

**Majors. Biology:** General. **Business:** Business admin. **Computer sciences:** General. **Education:** Physical, secondary. **Engineering:** Civil, electrical. **English:** English lit. **Foreign languages:** General. **History:** General. **Math:** General. **Physical sciences:** Chemistry, physics. **Protective services:** Law enforcement admin. **Psychology:** General. **Social sciences:** Political science.

**Most popular majors.** Business/marketing 32%, education 7%, engineering/engineering technologies 14%, history 7%, security/protective services 12%, social sciences 10%.

**Computing on campus.** 350 workstations in dormitories, library, computer center. Dormitories linked to campus network. Commuter students can connect to campus network. Online course registration, online library, helpline, repair service available.

**Student life. Freshman orientation:** Mandatory. Preregistration for classes offered. **Housing:** Guaranteed on-campus for all undergraduates. Coed dorms available. **Activities:** Bands, choral groups, drama, literary magazine, music ensembles, student government, student newspaper, African American Society, American Society of Civil Engineers, Association for Computing Machinery, Alpha Phi Omega, Summerall Guards, African Methodist Episcopal, Baptist Student Union, Campus Crusade for Christ, Knights of Columbus, Army Aviator Association of America.

**Athletics.** NCAA. **Intercollegiate:** Baseball M, basketball M, cross-country, football (tackle) M, golf W, rifle, soccer, tennis M, track and field, volleyball W, wrestling M. **Intramural:** Badminton, basketball, diving, football (non-tackle), handball, racquetball, rifle, softball, swimming, table tennis, tennis, track and field, triathlon, volleyball, water polo, weight lifting, wrestling. **Team name:** Bulldogs.

**Student services.** Alcohol/substance abuse counseling, campus ministries, career counseling, student employment services, financial aid counseling, health services, minority student services, personal counseling, placement for graduates, veterans' counselor.

**Contact.** E-mail: admissions@citadel.edu
Phone: (843) 953-5230 Toll-free number: (800) 868-1842
Fax: (843) 953-7036
John Powell, Director of Admissions, The Citadel, 171 Moultrie Street, Charleston, SC 29409

---

### Claflin University
**Orangeburg, South Carolina**
www.claflin.edu

**CB member**
**CB code: 5109**

- Private 4-year liberal arts college affiliated with United Methodist Church
- Residential campus in large town
- 1,627 degree-seeking undergraduates: 3% part-time, 68% women, 94% African American, 4% international
- 82 degree-seeking graduate students
- 45% of applicants admitted
- SAT or ACT (ACT writing optional) required
- 55% graduate within 6 years

**General.** Founded in 1869. Regionally accredited. **Degrees:** 273 bachelor's awarded; master's offered. **ROTC:** Army. **Location:** 45 miles from Columbia. **Calendar:** Semester, limited summer session. **Full-time faculty:** 96 total; 78% have terminal degrees, 50% minority, 41% women. **Part-time faculty:** 31 total. **Special facilities:** Center for excellence in science and math, center for excellence in mass communication, nuclear magnetic resonance, leadership development center, museum, internet radio.

**Freshman class profile.** 2,857 applied, 1,294 admitted, 390 enrolled.

| Mid 50% test scores | | | |
|---|---|---|---|
| SAT critical reading: | 420-550 | Rank in top quarter: | 47% |
| SAT math: | 400-500 | Rank in top tenth: | 25% |
| GPA 3.50 or higher: | 18% | Return as sophomores: | 70% |
| GPA 3.0-3.49: | 30% | Out-of-state: | 23% |
| GPA 2.0-2.99: | 50% | Live on campus: | 90% |
| | | International: | 3% |

**Basis for selection.** School achievement record, test scores, recommendation of high school officials, personal background, experience, character traits, educational objectives important. Audition required; essay, interview, portfolio recommended.

**High school preparation.** 20 units required. Required units include English 4, mathematics 3, social studies 2, history 1, (laboratory 2) and academic electives 7. Physical education.

**2007-2008 Annual costs.** Tuition/fees: $12,358. Room/board: $6,640. Books/supplies: $1,200. Personal expenses: $1,600.

**Application procedures. Admission:** Closing date 8/1. $20 fee, may be waived for applicants with need. Application may be submitted online. Admission notification on a rolling basis beginning on or about 10/1. **Financial aid:** Priority date 4/15; no closing date. FAFSA, institutional form required. Applicants notified on a rolling basis starting 5/15; must reply within 2 week(s) of notification.

**Academics. Special study options:** Accelerated study, combined bachelor's/graduate degree, cooperative education, cross-registration, double major, dual enrollment of high school students, honors, independent study, internships, liberal arts/career combination, study abroad, teacher certification program, weekend college. **Credit/placement by examination:** AP, CLEP, institutional tests. 18 credit hours maximum toward bachelor's degree. **Support services:** Learning center, pre-admission summer program, reduced course load, remedial instruction, tutoring, writing center.

**Honors college/program.** 30 to 35 students admitted annually based on academic achievement, leadership, and SAT scores.

**Majors. Area/ethnic studies:** African-American, American. **Biology:** General, biochemistry, bioinformatics, biotechnology. **Business:** Business admin, management information systems, marketing, organizational behavior. **Communications:** Media studies. **Computer sciences:** Computer science.

**Conservation:** Environmental science. **Education:** Art, early childhood, elementary, English, mathematics, middle, music. **Engineering:** Software. **English:** English lit. **History:** General. **Math:** General. **Parks/recreation:** Health/fitness, sports admin. **Philosophy/religion:** Philosophy, religion. **Physical sciences:** Chemistry. **Protective services:** Law enforcement admin. **Social sciences:** Sociology. **Visual/performing arts:** Art.

**Most popular majors.** Biology 8%, business/marketing 26%, communications/journalism 10%, security/protective services 17%, social sciences 14%.

**Computing on campus.** 500 workstations in dormitories, library, computer center, student center. Dormitories wired for high-speed internet access and linked to campus network. Commuter students can connect to campus network. Online course registration, online library, repair service, wireless network available.

**Student life. Freshman orientation:** Mandatory. Preregistration for classes offered. **Housing:** Guaranteed on-campus for freshmen. Single-sex dorms available. $50 deposit, deadline 4/15. **Activities:** Bands, drama, film society, literary magazine, music ensembles, radio station, student government, student newspaper, TV station, Alpha Kappa Mu, Oxford Club, literature, art and film society, Phi Beta Lambda, Esquire XIII, Students in Free Enterprise, NAACP.

**Athletics.** NCAA. **Intercollegiate:** Baseball M, basketball, cross-country, softball W, track and field, volleyball W. **Intramural:** Basketball, softball W, volleyball W. **Team name:** Panthers.

**Student services.** Adult student services, campus ministries, career counseling, student employment services, financial aid counseling, health services, minority student services, personal counseling, placement for graduates, veterans' counselor.

**Contact.** E-mail: mzeigler@claflin.edu
Phone: (803) 535-5340 Toll-free number: (800) 922-1276
Fax: (803) 535-5387
Michael Zeigler, Director of Admissions, Claflin University, 400 Magnolia Street, Orangeburg, SC 29115

---

### Clemson University
**Clemson, South Carolina**
www.clemson.edu

**CB member**
**CB code: 5111**

- Public 4-year university
- Residential campus in large town
- 14,173 degree-seeking undergraduates: 6% part-time, 45% women
- 2,943 degree-seeking graduate students
- 50% of applicants admitted
- SAT or ACT with writing required
- 78% graduate within 6 years

**General.** Founded in 1889. Regionally accredited. **Degrees:** 2,946 bachelor's awarded; master's, doctoral offered. **ROTC:** Army, Air Force. **Location:** 17 miles from Anderson. **Calendar:** Semester, extensive summer session. **Full-time faculty:** 1,086 total; 86% have terminal degrees, 14% minority, 33% women. **Part-time faculty:** 162 total; 45% have terminal degrees, 7% minority, 44% women. **Class size:** 48% < 20, 33% 20-39, 8% 40-49, 8% 50-99, 3% >100. **Special facilities:** Planetarium, agricultural and forestry experimental facilities, geology museum, state botanical gardens, center for sustainable living, John C. Calhoun historical site and home, performing arts center.

**Freshman class profile.** 14,255 applied, 7,154 admitted, 2,762 enrolled.

| Mid 50% test scores | | | |
|---|---|---|---|
| SAT critical reading: | 550-640 | Rank in top tenth: | 56% |
| SAT math: | 580-680 | Return as sophomores: | 89% |
| ACT composite: | 25-30 | Out-of-state: | 34% |
| Rank in top quarter: | 85% | Live on campus: | 97% |

**Basis for selection.** Admission competitive and based largely on high school curriculum, performance in that curriculum, peer comparison, SAT or ACT scores, and choice of major. Campus visit recommended for all. Interview, portfolio recommended for architecture; required for art applicants. Audition required for performing arts program. **Homeschooled:** Include copies of all secondary school transcripts and course descriptions of any courses different from those traditionally offered in public school settings.

**High school preparation.** 19 units required. Required and recommended units include English 4, mathematics 3-4, social studies 3-4, history

1-2, science 3 (laboratory 3-4), foreign language 3-4 and academic electives 2. Also require physical education or ROTC. 3 foreign language units must be in same language.

**2007-2008 Annual costs.** Tuition/fees: $9,870; $21,800 out-of-state. Laptop computer required of all entering new students. This cost has been estimated at $1600. Room/board: $5,992. Books/supplies: $924. Personal expenses: $1,866.

**Financial aid. Non-need-based:** Scholarships awarded for academics, art, athletics, leadership, minority status, music/drama, ROTC, state residency.

**Application procedures. Admission:** Priority date 12/1; deadline 5/1 (postmark date). $50 fee, may be waived for applicants with need. Application may be submitted online. Admission notification on a rolling basis beginning on or about 2/15. Must reply by May 1 or within 3 week(s) if notified thereafter. Scholarship candidates notified on rolling basis, beginning on or about October 1 for fall admission. Preferred application date of December 1. Those who apply by that date, and whose application file is complete, will receive an admission decision on or about February 15. **Financial aid:** Priority date 4/1; no closing date. FAFSA required. Applicants notified on a rolling basis starting 4/1; must reply within 3 week(s) of notification.

**Academics. Special study options:** Combined bachelor's/graduate degree, cooperative education, distance learning, double major, dual enrollment of high school students, exchange student, honors, independent study, internships, study abroad, teacher certification program, Washington semester. **Credit/placement by examination:** AP, CLEP, IB, institutional tests. Challenge examinations offered by each academic department. **Support services:** Learning center, pre-admission summer program, study skills assistance, tutoring, writing center.

**Honors college/program.** Less than 10 percent of freshman class invited to enroll. Minimum peer comparison must show student in top 3 percent of graduating secondary school class.

**Majors. Agriculture:** Agribusiness operations, animal sciences, dairy, economics, farm/ranch, food science, horticultural science, horticulture, plant sciences, poultry, soil science, turf management. **Architecture:** Architecture, landscape. **Biology:** General, bacteriology, biochemistry, genetics, plant pathology. **Business:** Accounting, business admin, international, operations, tourism/travel. **Communications:** General. **Computer sciences:** General, computer science, information systems. **Conservation:** Fisheries, forestry. **Education:** Agricultural, early childhood, elementary, mathematics, science, secondary, special, technology/industrial arts. **Engineering:** Agricultural, biomedical, ceramic, chemical, civil, computer, electrical, mechanical, textile. **English:** English lit, speech/rhetoric. **Foreign languages:** General, French, German, Spanish. **Health:** Clinical lab science, premedicine, prepharmacy, preveterinary. **History:** General. **Interdisciplinary:** Nutrition sciences. **Legal studies:** Prelaw. **Math:** General. **Parks/recreation:** Facilities management. **Philosophy/religion:** Philosophy. **Physical sciences:** Chemistry, geology, physics. **Psychology:** General. **Social sciences:** Economics, political science, sociology. **Visual/performing arts:** Commercial/advertising art, design, directing/producing, industrial design, studio arts.

**Most popular majors.** Biology 9%, business/marketing 18%, education 9%, engineering/engineering technologies 16%, health sciences 7%, social sciences 8%.

**Computing on campus.** PC or laptop required. 875 workstations in library, computer center. Dormitories wired for high-speed internet access and linked to campus network. Commuter students can connect to campus network. Online course registration, online library, helpline, repair service, student web hosting, wireless network available.

**Student life. Freshman orientation:** Mandatory, $55 fee. Preregistration for classes offered. One and 1/2-day sessions held 8 times during June and July. Students must complete online mathematics placement exam prior to participating in orientation. **Housing:** Guaranteed on-campus for freshmen. Coed dorms, single-sex dorms, apartments, fraternity/sorority housing, substance-free housing available. $35 nonrefundable deposit. Housing guaranteed to freshmen and to students continuing in on-campus housing. **Activities:** Bands, choral groups, dance, drama, literary magazine, music ensembles, radio station, student government, student newspaper, symphony orchestra, TV station, religious organizations, Young Democrats, Young Republicans, minority awareness organizations, Blue Key, Alpha Phi Omega, Mortarboard, Hillel, Fellowship of Christian Athletes.

**Athletics.** NCAA. **Intercollegiate:** Baseball M, basketball, cross-country, diving, football (tackle) M, golf M, rowing (crew) W, soccer, swimming, tennis, track and field, volleyball W. **Intramural:** Basketball, diving, fencing, field hockey W, football (non-tackle), golf, racquetball, soccer, softball, table tennis, tennis, track and field, volleyball. **Team name:** Tigers.

**Student services.** Alcohol/substance abuse counseling, campus ministries, career counseling, student employment services, financial aid counseling, health services, minority student services, personal counseling, placement for graduates, veterans' counselor. **Physically disabled:** Services for visually, speech, hearing impaired.

**Contact.** E-mail: cuadmissions@clemson.edu
Phone: (864) 656-2287 Fax: (864) 656-2464
Robert Barkley, Director of Admissions, Clemson University, 105 Sikes Hall, Clemson, SC 29634-5124

---

## Coastal Carolina University
**Conway, South Carolina**
www.coastal.edu

CB member
CB code: 5837

- Public 4-year university
- Commuter campus in small city
- 6,851 degree-seeking undergraduates: 6% part-time, 53% women, 12% African American, 1% Asian American, 2% Hispanic American, 1% international
- 181 degree-seeking graduate students
- 68% of applicants admitted
- SAT or ACT (ACT writing optional) required
- 44% graduate within 6 years

**General.** Founded in 1954. Regionally accredited. Barrier-reef island used for marine science field studies and research. **Degrees:** 1,004 bachelor's awarded; master's offered. **Location:** 9 miles from Myrtle Beach. **Calendar:** Semester, extensive summer session. **Full-time faculty:** 262 total; 82% have terminal degrees, 10% minority, 38% women. **Part-time faculty:** 246 total; 23% have terminal degrees, 6% minority, 58% women. **Class size:** 34% < 20, 48% 20-39, 12% 40-49, 5% 50-99, less than 1% >100.

**Freshman class profile.** 6,618 applied, 4,524 admitted, 1,652 enrolled.

| Mid 50% test scores | | | |
|---|---|---|---|
| SAT critical reading: | 470-550 | Rank in top tenth: | 11% |
| SAT math: | 480-570 | End year in good standing: | 85% |
| ACT composite: | 20-22 | Return as sophomores: | 71% |
| GPA 3.50 or higher: | 41% | Out-of-state: | 53% |
| GPA 3.0-3.49: | 33% | Live on campus: | 78% |
| GPA 2.0-2.99: | 26% | Fraternities: | 6% |
| Rank in top quarter: | 36% | Sororities: | 7% |

**Basis for selection.** Secondary school record and test scores most important; class rank important. Applicants whose native language is not English must take TOEFL. Interview recommended for all. **Homeschooled:** Transcript of courses and grades required. Copy of declaration of intent to home school as filed with local board of education. **Learning Disabled:** To become eligible for support services, students with disabilities must provide documentation of disability to Service for Students with Disabilities Office.

**High school preparation.** 20 units required. Required and recommended units include English 4, mathematics 3-4, social studies 2, history 1, science 3 (laboratory 3), foreign language 2, computer science 1, visual/performing arts 1 and academic electives 4. 1 unit of physical education or ROTC.

**2007-2008 Annual costs.** Tuition/fees: $7,600; $16,590 out-of-state. Room/board: $6,680.

**2006-2007 Financial aid. Need-based:** 1,211 full-time freshmen applied for aid; 858 were judged to have need; 827 of these received aid. Average need met was 51%. Average scholarship/grant was $3,165; average loan $5,928. 32% of total undergraduate aid awarded as scholarships/grants, 68% as loans/jobs. **Non-need-based:** Awarded to 2,545 full-time undergraduates, including 771 freshmen. Scholarships awarded for academics, art, athletics, leadership, music/drama, state residency.

**Application procedures. Admission:** Closing date 8/15. $45 fee, may be waived for applicants with need. Admission notification on a rolling basis beginning on or about 9/15. Must reply by May 1 or within 2 week(s) if notified thereafter. **Financial aid:** Priority date 4/1; no closing date. FAFSA required. Applicants notified on a rolling basis starting 3/1.

**Academics.** Professional golf management option in marketing program, accredited by PGA. Resort and international tourism management options in management program. CPA/CFA option in accounting. **Special study options:** Accelerated study, combined bachelor's/graduate degree, cooperative education, distance learning, double major, dual enrollment of high school students, honors, independent study, internships, liberal arts/career combination, student-designed major, study abroad, teacher certification program. 3-2 engineering program with Clemson University, nursing program with Francis Marion University and Medical University of South Carolina, master of educational administration with University of South Carolina. **Credit/placement by examination:** AP, CLEP, IB, SAT, institutional tests. 30 credit hours maximum toward bachelor's degree. **Support services:** Learning center, reduced course load, tutoring, writing center.

**Majors. Biology:** General. **Business:** Accounting, business admin, finance, managerial economics, marketing, resort management. **Communications:** General. **Computer sciences:** General. **Education:** Early childhood, elementary, middle, physical, special. **English:** English lit. **Foreign languages:** Spanish. **Health:** Public health ed. **History:** General. **Interdisciplinary:** Marine science. **Liberal arts:** Arts/sciences. **Math:** Applied. **Parks/recreation:** Sports admin. **Philosophy/religion:** Philosophy. **Physical sciences:** Chemistry, physics. **Psychology:** General. **Social sciences:** Political science, sociology. **Visual/performing arts:** Dramatic, musical theater, studio arts.

**Most popular majors.** Biology 12%, business/marketing 33%, education 10%, psychology 8%, social sciences 8%, visual/performing arts 6%.

**Computing on campus.** 600 workstations in dormitories, library, computer center, student center. Dormitories wired for high-speed internet access and linked to campus network. Commuter students can connect to campus network. Online library, wireless network available.

**Student life. Freshman orientation:** Mandatory, $90 fee. Preregistration for classes offered. 2-day programs. **Housing:** Coed dorms, special housing for disabled available. $150 partly refundable deposit, deadline 8/15. **Activities:** Bands, choral groups, dance, drama, international student organizations, literary magazine, music ensembles, musical theater, student government, student newspaper, Fellowship of Christian Athletes, African American association, gospel choir, Society for Advancement of Management, Students Taking Active Responsibility, fitness club.

**Athletics. NCAA. Intercollegiate:** Baseball M, basketball, cheerleading, cross-country, football (tackle) M, golf, soccer, softball W, tennis, track and field, volleyball W. **Intramural:** Badminton, basketball, bowling, football (tackle), golf, racquetball, soccer, softball, table tennis, tennis, track and field, volleyball, water polo, weight lifting. **Team name:** Chanticleers.

**Student services.** Adult student services, alcohol/substance abuse counseling, career counseling, student employment services, financial aid counseling, health services, minority student services, personal counseling, placement for graduates, veterans' counselor, women's services. **Physically disabled:** Services for visually, speech, hearing impaired.

**Contact.** E-mail: admissions@coastal.edu
Phone: (843) 349-2026 Toll-free number: (800) 277-7000
Fax: (843) 349-2127
Judy Vogt, Vice President for Enrollment Services, Coastal Carolina University, PO Box 261954, Conway, SC 29528-6054

---

## Coker College
**Hartsville, South Carolina**     CB member
**www.coker.edu**     CB code: 5112

- Private 4-year liberal arts college
- Residential campus in large town
- 635 degree-seeking undergraduates
- 54% of applicants admitted
- SAT or ACT required

**General.** Founded in 1908. Regionally accredited. **Degrees:** 103 bachelor's awarded. **Location:** 70 miles from Columbia, 80 miles from Charlotte, North Carolina. **Calendar:** Semester, limited summer session. **Full-time faculty:** 55 total. **Part-time faculty:** 15 total. **Class size:** 92% < 20, 8% 20-39. **Special facilities:** Botanical gardens.

**Freshman class profile.** 1,322 applied, 711 admitted, 243 enrolled.

| Mid 50% test scores | | ACT composite: | 18-22 |
|---|---|---|---|
| SAT critical reading: | 440-530 | Out-of-state: | 15% |
| SAT math: | 440-540 | Live on campus: | 82% |

**Basis for selection.** Academic record, test scores, interview, school and community activities important. Recommendations also used to determine status. Applicants admitted on basis of test scores and GPA in academic core courses. Special talents and alumni relations important. Essay recommended for all; audition required for dance, music, theater programs; portfolio required for art programs.

**High school preparation.** 19 units required. Required and recommended units include English 4, mathematics 3, social studies 2, history 1, science 3 (laboratory 1), foreign language 3 and academic electives 3. Recommended science units includes 1 physical science, 1 biology.

**2007-2008 Annual costs.** Tuition/fees: $18,552. Room/board: $5,920. Books/supplies: $900. Personal expenses: $550.

**Financial aid. Non-need-based:** Scholarships awarded for academics, art, athletics, music/drama. **Additional information:** Endowed scholarship program for qualified applicants. June 1 deadline for filing South Carolina Tuition Grant forms.

**Application procedures. Admission:** No deadline. $15 fee, may be waived for applicants with need. Application may be submitted online. Admission notification on a rolling basis beginning on or about 6/1. Must reply by May 1 or within 3 week(s) if notified thereafter. Juniors allowed to apply and make admissions decision during summer prior to senior year. **Financial aid:** Priority date 4/1, closing date 6/1. FAFSA required. Applicants notified on a rolling basis starting 12/1; must reply by 5/1 or within 3 week(s) of notification.

**Academics. Special study options:** Cooperative education, double major, dual enrollment of high school students, ESL, honors, independent study, internships, liberal arts/career combination, student-designed major, study abroad, teacher certification program. 2-2 programs with two-year colleges, 3-1 program with regional medical facility. **Credit/placement by examination:** AP, CLEP, IB, institutional tests. Unlimited hours of credit by examination may be counted toward degree. **Support services:** Reduced course load, remedial instruction, study skills assistance, tutoring, writing center.

**Majors. Biology:** General. **Business:** Business admin. **Communications:** General. **Computer sciences:** Computer science. **Education:** General, art, biology, business, chemistry, early childhood, elementary, English, history, mathematics, music, physical. **English:** English lit, technical writing. **Foreign languages:** French, Spanish. **Health:** Clinical lab science, dance therapy, recreational therapy. **History:** General. **Math:** General. **Parks/recreation:** Exercise sciences, sports admin. **Physical sciences:** Chemistry. **Psychology:** General. **Public administration:** Social work. **Social sciences:** Criminology, political science, sociology. **Visual/performing arts:** Acting, art, commercial/advertising art, dance, dramatic, music performance, music theory/composition, photography, piano/organ, studio arts, theater design, voice/opera.

**Computing on campus.** 49 workstations in dormitories, library, computer center, student center. Dormitories wired for high-speed internet access and linked to campus network. Online library, student web hosting available.

**Student life. Freshman orientation:** Mandatory. Preregistration for classes offered. 3-day session held immediately before fall classes begin. **Housing:** Guaranteed on-campus for freshmen. Coed dorms available. $75 deposit, deadline 5/1. **Activities:** Choral groups, dance, drama, literary magazine, musical theater, student government, student newspaper, Campus Crusade, Psi Chi, African American Sisterhood, Helping: Our Way of Life, multicultural affairs committee.

**Athletics. NCAA. Intercollegiate:** Baseball M, basketball, cheerleading, cross-country, golf M, soccer, softball W, tennis, volleyball W. **Intramural:** Badminton, basketball, bowling, cross-country, football (non-tackle), handball, racquetball, rowing (crew) W, sailing, soccer, softball, swimming, table tennis, tennis, track and field, volleyball, water polo, weight lifting. **Team name:** Cobras.

**Student services.** Adult student services, campus ministries, career counseling, student employment services, financial aid counseling, health services, personal counseling, placement for graduates.

**Contact.** E-mail: admissions@coker.edu
Phone: (843) 383-8050 Toll-free number: (800) 950-1908
Fax: (843) 383-8056
Perry Wilson, Director of Admissions, Coker College, 300 East College Avenue, Hartsville, SC 29550

---

## College of Charleston
**Charleston, South Carolina**     CB member
**www.cofc.edu**     CB code: 5113

- Public 4-year liberal arts college
- Residential campus in large city
- 9,499 degree-seeking undergraduates: 6% part-time, 64% women, 6% African American, 2% Asian American, 2% Hispanic American, 1% international
- 481 degree-seeking graduate students
- 65% of applicants admitted
- SAT or ACT (ACT writing optional), application essay required
- 61% graduate within 6 years

**General.** Founded in 1770. Regionally accredited. **Degrees:** 2,145 bachelor's awarded; master's offered. **ROTC:** Air Force. **Calendar:** Semester, limited summer session. **Full-time faculty:** 521 total; 86% have terminal degrees, 10% minority, 42% women. **Part-time faculty:** 378 total; 39% have terminal degrees, 9% minority, 58% women. **Class size:** 34% < 20, 58% 20-39, 4% 40-49, 4% 50-99, less than 1% >100. **Special facilities:** Communications museum, early childhood development center, observatory, marine science laboratory, sculpture studio, sailing center, African-American history and culture research center, bilingual legal interpreting center, media and technology studio, center for entrepreneurship.

**Freshman class profile.** 8,941 applied, 5,775 admitted, 2,064 enrolled.

| Mid 50% test scores | | | |
|---|---|---|---|
| SAT critical reading: | 570-650 | GPA 2.0-2.99: | 3% |
| SAT math: | 570-650 | Rank in top quarter: | 60% |
| ACT composite: | 23-26 | Rank in top tenth: | 27% |
| GPA 3.50 or higher: | 74% | Return as sophomores: | 82% |
| GPA 3.0-3.49: | 23% | Out-of-state: | 45% |
| | | Live on campus: | 88% |

**Basis for selection.** School grades, class rank, curriculum most important, then test scores. Recommendations and activities helpful in borderline cases. Personal essay optional. Writing portion of ACT required only if student does not also submit SAT (with mandatory Writing component). Interview recommended for all. **Homeschooled:** Students should indicate which school district syllabus was followed during home schooling.

**High school preparation.** 20 units required. Required and recommended units include English 4, mathematics 3-4, social studies 3, history 2, science 3-4 (laboratory 3), foreign language 3 and academic electives 4. Mathematics requirement includes 2 algebra. Social science recommendation .5 economics and .5 government. 2 units of same foreign language, 1 additional unit of advanced mathematics, computer science, world history, world geography, or Western civilization required.

**2007-2008 Annual costs.** Tuition/fees: $7,778; $18,732 out-of-state. Room/board: $8,495. Books/supplies: $999. Personal expenses: $2,013.

**2006-2007 Financial aid.** **Need-based:** 1,150 full-time freshmen applied for aid; 678 were judged to have need; 645 of these received aid. Average need met was 66%. Average scholarship/grant was $2,944; average loan $2,737. 47% of total undergraduate aid awarded as scholarships/grants, 53% as loans/jobs. **Non-need-based:** Awarded to 2,382 full-time undergraduates, including 778 freshmen. Scholarships awarded for academics, alumni affiliation, art, athletics, music/drama.

**Application procedures. Admission:** Closing date 4/1. $45 fee, may be waived for applicants with need. Application may be submitted online. Notification sent by mid April. Must reply by 5/1. March 1 application date recommended for residence hall students. Admissions deposit refundable until May 1 for fall semester, December 1 for spring semester. Written notice required. **Financial aid:** Priority date 3/15; no closing date. FAFSA required. Applicants notified on a rolling basis starting 4/10; must reply within 8 week(s) of notification.

**Academics. Special study options:** Accelerated study, combined bachelor's/graduate degree, cooperative education, cross-registration, double major, dual enrollment of high school students, ESL, exchange student, honors, independent study, internships, liberal arts/career combination, semester at sea, study abroad, teacher certification program. Internships and courses in conjunction with Spoleto US (international arts festival); 3-2 engineering program with Case Western Reserve University, Clemson University, University of South Carolina; marine engineering option with University of Michigan. **Credit/placement by examination:** AP, CLEP, IB, institutional tests. 30 credit hours maximum toward bachelor's degree. **Support services:** Learning center, pre-admission summer program, reduced course load, study skills assistance, tutoring, writing center.

**Majors. Area/ethnic studies:** Latin American. **Biology:** General, biochemistry, marine. **Business:** Accounting, business admin, hospitality admin, international. **Communications:** General. **Computer sciences:** General, information systems. **Education:** Early childhood, elementary, middle, physical, special. **English:** English lit. **Foreign languages:** Classics, French, German, Spanish. **Health:** Athletic training, predental, premedicine. **History:** General. **Interdisciplinary:** Historic preservation. **Math:** General. **Philosophy/religion:** Philosophy, religion. **Physical sciences:** Astronomy, astrophysics, chemistry, geology, physics. **Psychology:** General. **Social sciences:** Anthropology, economics, political science, sociology, urban studies. **Visual/performing arts:** Art history/conservation, arts management, dramatic, studio arts. **Other:** Discovery informatics.

**Most popular majors.** Biology 8%, business/marketing 18%, communications/journalism 12%, education 8%, psychology 8%, social sciences 13%, visual/performing arts 10%.

**Computing on campus.** 2,500 workstations in dormitories, library, computer center, student center. Dormitories wired for high-speed internet access and linked to campus network. Commuter students can connect to campus network. Online course registration, helpline, wireless network available.

**Student life. Freshman orientation:** Mandatory. Preregistration for classes offered. **Housing:** Coed dorms, single-sex dorms, special housing for disabled, fraternity/sorority housing available. $200 fully refundable deposit, deadline 5/1. Restored old Charleston houses used as residence halls, some with kitchen facilities in suite. **Activities:** Bands, choral groups, dance, drama, literary magazine, music ensembles, musical theater, radio station, student government, student newspaper, symphony orchestra, over 100 organizations available.

**Athletics.** NCAA. **Intercollegiate:** Baseball M, basketball, cross-country, diving, equestrian W, golf, sailing, soccer, softball W, swimming, tennis, track and field W, volleyball W. **Intramural:** Badminton, basketball, equestrian W, fencing, football (tackle), racquetball, rowing (crew), rugby W, soccer, softball, tennis, volleyball, weight lifting. **Team name:** Cougars.

**Student services.** Adult student services, alcohol/substance abuse counseling, campus ministries, career counseling, student employment services, financial aid counseling, health services, legal services, minority student services, on-campus daycare, personal counseling, placement for graduates, veterans' counselor. **Physically disabled:** Services for visually, speech, hearing impaired.

**Contact.** E-mail: admissions@cofc.edu
Phone: (843) 953-5670 Fax: (843) 953-6322
Suzette Stille, Director of Admission, College of Charleston, Office of Admissions and Adult Student Services, Charleston, SC 29424-0001

## Columbia College
**Columbia, South Carolina**
**www.columbiacollegesc.edu**
**CB member**
**CB code: 5117**

- Private 4-year liberal arts college for women affiliated with United Methodist Church
- Residential campus in large city
- 1,224 degree-seeking undergraduates: 20% part-time, 98% women, 44% African American, 1% Asian American, 2% Hispanic American, 1% international
- 218 degree-seeking graduate students
- 71% of applicants admitted
- SAT or ACT with writing required
- 45% graduate within 6 years

**General.** Founded in 1854. Regionally accredited. **Degrees:** 164 bachelor's awarded; master's offered. **ROTC:** Army. **Location:** 70 miles from Charlotte, North Carolina. **Calendar:** Semester, limited summer session. **Full-time faculty:** 75 total; 80% have terminal degrees, 12% minority, 67% women. **Part-time faculty:** 87 total; 33% have terminal degrees, 5% minority, 64% women. **Class size:** 75% < 20, 25% 20-39. **Special facilities:** Leadership center for women.

**Freshman class profile.** 1,075 applied, 763 admitted, 273 enrolled.

| Mid 50% test scores | | | |
|---|---|---|---|
| SAT critical reading: | 450-540 | Rank in top quarter: | 52% |
| SAT math: | 430-530 | Rank in top tenth: | 15% |
| SAT writing: | 430-540 | End year in good standing: | 78% |
| ACT composite: | 18-23 | Return as sophomores: | 68% |
| GPA 3.50 or higher: | 48% | Out-of-state: | 10% |
| GPA 3.0-3.49: | 30% | Live on campus: | 82% |
| GPA 2.0-2.99: | 22% | International: | 1% |

**Basis for selection.** School record, test scores, recommendations most important. Audition recommended for dance, music programs; portfolio recommended for art programs; essay, interview recommended for borderline applicants.

**High school preparation.** 16 units recommended. Recommended units include English 4, mathematics 3, social studies 2, history 1, science 2 (laboratory 2), foreign language 2 and academic electives 2. 2.5 units in music, dance, art also recommended.

**2007-2008 Annual costs.** Tuition/fees: $21,650. Room/board: $6,232. Books/supplies: $800. Personal expenses: $2,750.

**2006-2007 Financial aid.** **Need-based:** 250 full-time freshmen applied for aid; 216 were judged to have need; 216 of these received aid. Average need met was 81%. Average scholarship/grant was $8,601; average loan $2,593. 62% of total undergraduate aid awarded as scholarships/grants, 38% as loans/jobs. **Non-need-based:** Awarded to 711 full-time undergraduates, including 222 freshmen. Scholarships awarded for academics, alumni affiliation, art, athletics, leadership, music/drama.

**Application procedures. Admission:** No deadline. $25 fee, may be waived for applicants with need. Application may be submitted online. Admission notification on a rolling basis beginning on or about 10/1. Must reply by May 1 or within 4 week(s) if notified thereafter. **Financial aid:** Priority date 4/1; no closing date. FAFSA required. Applicants notified on a rolling basis starting 3/15; must reply within 2 week(s) of notification.

**Academics. Special study options:** Double major, dual enrollment of high school students, exchange student, honors, independent study, internships, student-designed major, study abroad, teacher certification program, Washington semester. **Credit/placement by examination:** AP, CLEP, IB, SAT, ACT, institutional tests. **Support services:** Learning center, reduced course load, remedial instruction, study skills assistance, tutoring, writing center.

**Majors. Biology:** General. **Business:** Accounting, business admin. **Communications:** General, journalism. **Computer sciences:** General. **Education:** Drama/dance, early childhood, elementary, middle, music, special. **English:** English lit. **Family/consumer sciences:** Family studies. **Foreign languages:** French, Spanish. **Health:** Speech pathology. **History:** General. **Liberal arts:** Arts/sciences. **Math:** General. **Philosophy/religion:** Religion. **Physical sciences:** Chemistry. **Psychology:** General. **Public administration:** Social work. **Social sciences:** General, political science. **Theology:** Religious ed. **Visual/performing arts:** Art, dance, music performance, piano/organ, studio arts, voice/opera.

**Most popular majors.** Business/marketing 16%, communications/journalism 9%, education 11%, family/consumer sciences 6%, psychology 7%, public administration/social services 11%, social sciences 8%, visual/performing arts 11%.

**Computing on campus.** 165 workstations in dormitories, library, computer center, student center. Dormitories wired for high-speed internet access and linked to campus network. Online course registration, online library, helpline, repair service, wireless network available.

**Student life. Freshman orientation:** Available, $150 fee. Preregistration for classes offered. 1-day program in June. 4-day program in August where students participate in community service project. **Policies:** All students required to live on campus during first 2 years unless living with parent or guardian. All residence halls nonsmoking. Chapel requirements in place for first-year, sophomore, and junior students. Religious observance required. **Housing:** Guaranteed on-campus for freshmen. Substance-free housing available. $100 deposit, deadline 5/1. **Activities:** Concert band, choral groups, dance, drama, international student organizations, literary magazine, music ensembles, musical theater, student government, student newspaper, Young Republicans, Young Democrats, CC Serves, Sister to Sista, African-American student association, NAACP.

**Athletics.** NAIA. **Intercollegiate:** Basketball W, soccer W, tennis W, volleyball W. **Team name:** Koalas.

**Student services.** Adult student services, campus ministries, career counseling, student employment services, financial aid counseling, health services, personal counseling, placement for graduates, veterans' counselor.

**Contact.** E-mail: admissions@colacoll.edu
Phone: (803) 786-3871 Toll-free number: (800) 277-1301
Fax: (803) 786-3674
Ron White, Vice President of Enrollment Management, Columbia College, 1301 Columbia College Drive, Columbia, SC 29203

---

# Columbia International University
## Columbia, South Carolina
www.ciu.edu                    CB code: 5116

▶ Private 4-year university and Bible college affiliated with multidenominational/evangelical churches
▶ Residential campus in small city
▶ 462 degree-seeking undergraduates: 7% part-time, 54% women
▶ 444 degree-seeking graduate students
▶ 70% of applicants admitted
▶ SAT or ACT (ACT writing optional), application essay required
▶ 48% graduate within 6 years

**General.** Founded in 1923. Regionally accredited; also accredited by ABHE, ATS. **Degrees:** 130 bachelor's, 4 associate awarded; master's, doctoral, first professional offered. **Location:** 75 miles from Charlotte, North Carolina, 225 miles from Atlanta. **Calendar:** Semester, limited summer session. **Full-time faculty:** 25 total. **Part-time faculty:** 26 total. **Class size:** 76% < 20, 15% 20-39, 2% 40-49, 4% 50-99, 3% >100. **Special facilities:** Prayer towers.

**Freshman class profile.** 244 applied, 172 admitted, 95 enrolled.

| Mid 50% test scores | | | |
|---|---|---|---|
| SAT critical reading: | 480-610 | Rank in top quarter: | 47% |
| SAT math: | 440-590 | Rank in top tenth: | 23% |
| ACT composite: | 19-25 | End year in good standing: | 87% |
| GPA 3.50 or higher: | 57% | Return as sophomores: | 71% |
| GPA 3.0-3.49: | 20% | Out-of-state: | 50% |
| GPA 2.0-2.99: | 19% | Live on campus: | 84% |
| | | International: | 1% |

**Basis for selection.** School achievement, recommendations, test scores, essay, school and community activities, religious commitment important. Audition required for church music program. **Homeschooled:** Transcripts should include GPA.

**High school preparation.** Recommended units include English 4, mathematics 2, social studies 2, science 1 and foreign language 2. Thorough background in English grammar and composition required.

**2008-2009 Annual costs.** Tuition/fees (projected): $15,665. Room/board: $5,750. Books/supplies: $700. Personal expenses: $2,000.

**2007-2008 Financial aid. Need-based:** 89 full-time freshmen applied for aid; 69 were judged to have need; 69 of these received aid. Average need met was 89%. Average scholarship/grant was $9,090; average loan $3,321. 73% of total undergraduate aid awarded as scholarships/grants, 27% as loans/jobs. **Non-need-based:** Awarded to 657 full-time undergraduates, including 145 freshmen. Scholarships awarded for academics, leadership, state residency. **Additional information:** Spouse scholarship program; special short quarter scholarships for missionaries on furlough.

**Application procedures. Admission:** Priority date 5/1; deadline 8/1 (postmark date). $45 fee, may be waived for applicants with need. Application may be submitted online. Admission notification on a rolling basis. **Financial aid:** Priority date 1/31; no closing date. FAFSA, institutional form required. Applicants notified on a rolling basis starting 12/18; must reply within 4 week(s) of notification.

**Academics. Special study options:** Combined bachelor's/graduate degree, cross-registration, distance learning, double major, independent study, internships, liberal arts/career combination, study abroad, teacher certification program. **Credit/placement by examination:** AP, CLEP, IB. 15 credit hours maximum toward associate degree, 30 toward bachelor's. **Support services:** Learning center, reduced course load, remedial instruction, study skills assistance, tutoring.

**Majors. Area/ethnic studies:** Near/Middle Eastern. **Business:** Nonprofit/public. **Communications:** General. **Education:** Multi-level teacher. **English:** English lit. **Foreign languages:** Biblical. **Interdisciplinary:** Intercultural. **Liberal arts:** Humanities. **Psychology:** General. **Theology:** Bible, pastoral counseling, religious ed, sacred music, youth ministry.

**Most popular majors.** Communications/journalism 9%, education 6%, interdisciplinary studies 12%, liberal arts 27%, psychology 14%, theological studies 24%.

**Computing on campus.** 46 workstations in library, computer center. Dormitories wired for high-speed internet access and linked to campus network. Online course registration, online library, helpline, repair service available.

**Student life. Freshman orientation:** Mandatory, $40 fee. Preregistration for classes offered. 3 sessions held prior to start of fall semester; 1 session held 3 days prior to start of spring semester. **Policies:** Standards of Christian living are outlined in the Biblical Standards Handbook. Religious observance required. **Housing:** Guaranteed on-campus for all undergraduates. Single-sex dorms available. $100 partly refundable deposit. Mobile home park available for married students. **Activities:** Concert band, choral groups, drama, music ensembles, radio station, student government, student newspaper, symphony orchestra, student missions connection, African-American Fellowship, student senate, student union, grad life council.

**Athletics. Intramural:** Basketball, football (non-tackle), soccer M, softball, table tennis, volleyball.

**Student services.** Campus ministries, career counseling, student employment services, financial aid counseling, health services, personal counseling, placement for graduates, veterans' counselor. **Physically disabled:** Services for visually, hearing impaired. **Learning disabled:** Comprehensive services available.

**Contact.** E-mail: yesciu@ciu.edu
Phone: (803) 754-4100 ext. 5024 Toll-free number: (800) 777-2227
Fax: (803) 786-4209
Michelle MacGregor, Director of Admissions, Columbia International University, PO Box 3122, Columbia, SC 29230-3122

## Converse College
**Spartanburg, South Carolina**
www.converse.edu

CB member
CB code: 5121

- Private 4-year music and liberal arts college for women
- Residential campus in small city
- 730 degree-seeking undergraduates: 13% part-time, 100% women, 12% African American, 1% Asian American, 2% Hispanic American, 1% Native American, 3% international
- 1,144 degree-seeking graduate students
- 73% of applicants admitted
- SAT or ACT (ACT writing optional), application essay required

**General.** Founded in 1889. Regionally accredited. Men admitted to graduate programs. **Degrees:** 182 bachelor's awarded; master's offered. **ROTC:** Army. **Location:** 70 miles from Charlotte, North Carolina. **Calendar:** 4-1-4, limited summer session. **Full-time faculty:** 87 total; 88% have terminal degrees, 6% minority. **Part-time faculty:** 5 total; 60% have terminal degrees. **Class size:** 85% < 20, 15% 20-39. **Special facilities:** Science facility, music library, music and performing arts auditorium.

**Freshman class profile.** 1,299 applied, 943 admitted, 150 enrolled.

| Mid 50% test scores | | | |
|---|---|---|---|
| SAT critical reading: | 510-610 | GPA 2.0-2.99: | 6% |
| SAT math: | 480-590 | Rank in top quarter: | 60% |
| ACT composite: | 20-26 | Rank in top tenth: | 22% |
| GPA 3.50 or higher: | 79% | Return as sophomores: | 71% |
| GPA 3.0-3.49: | 15% | Out-of-state: | 44% |
| | | Live on campus: | 90% |

**Basis for selection.** School record, class rank, test scores, extracurricular activities, school recommendation considered. Interview recommended for all; audition required for music programs. **Homeschooled:** Statement describing homeschool structure and mission, interview, letter of recommendation (nonparent) required.

**High school preparation.** 20 units required. Required and recommended units include English 4, mathematics 3, social studies 1, history 1, science 2 (laboratory 2), foreign language 2 and academic electives 6.

**2007-2008 Annual costs.** Tuition/fees: $23,344. Special fees for laboratory, studio art, computer programming, and other courses requiring special materials. Room/board: $7,190. Books/supplies: $750. Personal expenses: $1,500.

**2007-2008 Financial aid. Need-based:** 137 full-time freshmen applied for aid; 122 were judged to have need; 122 of these received aid. Average need met was 93%. Average scholarship/grant was $19,361; average loan $4,597. 72% of total undergraduate aid awarded as scholarships/grants, 28% as loans/jobs. **Non-need-based:** Awarded to 308 full-time undergraduates, including 88 freshmen. Scholarships awarded for academics, alumni affiliation, art, athletics, leadership, music/drama, ROTC, state residency.

**Application procedures. Admission:** Priority date 4/1; no deadline. No application fee. Application may be submitted online. Admission notification on a rolling basis beginning on or about 10/1. Must reply by May 1 or within 2 week(s) if notified thereafter. **Financial aid:** Closing date 3/1. FAFSA required. Applicants notified on a rolling basis starting 3/1; must reply by 5/1 or within 2 week(s) of notification.

**Academics. Special study options:** Combined bachelor's/graduate degree, cross-registration, double major, ESL, honors, independent study, internships, liberal arts/career combination, student-designed major, study abroad, teacher certification program. Women's leadership program. **Credit/placement by examination:** AP, CLEP, IB, SAT, ACT, institutional tests. 30 credit hours maximum toward bachelor's degree. **Support services:** Learning center, study skills assistance, tutoring, writing center.

**Majors. Biology:** General, biochemistry. **Business:** Accounting, finance, international, managerial economics, marketing, training/development. **Computer sciences:** General. **Education:** General, Deaf/hearing impaired, early childhood, elementary, special. **English:** English lit. **Foreign languages:** General, French, Spanish. **Health:** Art therapy. **History:** General. **Math:** General. **Philosophy/religion:** Religion. **Physical sciences:** Chemistry. **Psychology:** General. **Social sciences:** Economics, political science. **Visual/performing arts:** Art history/conservation, dramatic, interior design, music history, music pedagogy, music performance, music theory/composition, studio arts.

**Most popular majors.** Biology 6%, business/marketing 13%, education 19%, English 6%, history 6%, mathematics 7%, psychology 8%, visual/performing arts 20%.

**Computing on campus.** 75 workstations in dormitories, library, computer center, student center. Dormitories wired for high-speed internet access and linked to campus network. Commuter students can connect to campus network. Online library, helpline, repair service, wireless network available.

**Student life. Freshman orientation:** Mandatory. Preregistration for classes offered. 3-day program. **Policies:** Strong honor tradition based on mutual trust and responsibility. **Housing:** Guaranteed on-campus for all undergraduates. Substance-free housing available. $300 nonrefundable deposit, deadline 5/1. **Activities:** Concert band, campus ministries, choral groups, dance, drama, literary magazine, music ensembles, Model UN, musical theater, opera, student government, student newspaper, symphony orchestra, Student Christian Association, student activities committee, Young Republicans, community service organizations, honor organizations, student volunteer services.

**Athletics.** NCAA. **Intercollegiate:** Basketball W, cross-country W, equestrian W, lacrosse W, soccer W, swimming W, tennis W, volleyball W. **Intramural:** Basketball W, soccer W, softball W, swimming W, synchronized swimming W, volleyball W. **Team name:** Valkyries.

**Student services.** Adult student services, alcohol/substance abuse counseling, campus ministries, career counseling, student employment services, financial aid counseling, health services, personal counseling, placement for graduates. **Physically disabled:** Services for hearing impaired.

**Contact.** E-mail: admissions@converse.edu
Phone: (864) 596-9040 Toll-free number: (800) 766-1125
Fax: (864) 596-9225
Aaron Meis, Dean of Admissions, Converse College, 580 East Main Street, Spartanburg, SC 29302-0006

## Erskine College
**Due West, South Carolina**
www.erskine.edu

CB member
CB code: 5188

- Private 4-year liberal arts and seminary college affiliated with Associate Reformed Presbyterian Church
- Residential campus in rural community
- 567 degree-seeking undergraduates: 2% part-time, 56% women, 7% African American, 1% Asian American, 1% Hispanic American, 1% international
- 308 degree-seeking graduate students
- 66% of applicants admitted
- SAT or ACT with writing required
- 62% graduate within 6 years

**General.** Founded in 1839. Regionally accredited. Affiliated with Erskine Theological Seminary. **Degrees:** 147 bachelor's awarded; master's, doctoral, first professional offered. **Location:** 18 miles from Anderson, 45 miles from Greenville. **Calendar:** 4-1-4, limited summer session. **Full-time faculty:** 40 total; 85% have terminal degrees, 10% minority, 40% women. **Part-time faculty:** 27 total; 33% have terminal degrees, 22% women. **Class size:** 76% < 20, 23% 20-39, less than 1% 40-49. **Special facilities:** Arts center.

**Freshman class profile.** 874 applied, 573 admitted, 165 enrolled.

| Mid 50% test scores | | | |
|---|---|---|---|
| SAT critical reading: | 470-590 | GPA 2.0-2.99: | 8% |
| SAT math: | 500-610 | Rank in top quarter: | 62% |
| SAT writing: | 470-580 | Rank in top tenth: | 34% |
| ACT composite: | 22-25 | End year in good standing: | 78% |
| GPA 3.50 or higher: | 78% | Return as sophomores: | 78% |
| GPA 3.0-3.49: | 14% | Out-of-state: | 23% |
| | | Live on campus: | 95% |

**Basis for selection.** School achievement record, with special emphasis on advanced placement and honor courses, most important. Consider high school courses twice as important as SAT scores. Test scores, counselor recommendations also important. Essay, interview, class rank, activities considered. Special consideration given to members of supporting church and alumni children. Essay recommended for all; interview required for academically weak; audition required for music. **Homeschooled:** High school diploma, GED, or college preparatory diploma certification required. Applicants must also submit portfolio of all high school work and 2 recommendations.

**High school preparation.** 14 units required. Required and recommended units include English 4, mathematics 2-4, social studies 3, science 3 (laboratory 2) and foreign language 2. Biology, chemistry, physics, history highly recommended. Preference given to students with more than minimum preparation.

**2008-2009 Annual costs.** Tuition/fees: $23,165. Room/board: $7,961. Books/supplies: $1,250.

**Financial aid. Non-need-based:** Scholarships awarded for academics, alumni affiliation, art, athletics, leadership, minority status, music/drama, religious affiliation, state residency. **Additional information:** Filing deadline 5/1 for institutional form, 6/30 for state form.

**Application procedures. Admission:** No deadline. $25 fee, may be waived for applicants with need. Application may be submitted online. Admission notification on a rolling basis. **Financial aid:** Priority date 4/1; no closing date. FAFSA, institutional form required. Applicants notified on a rolling basis starting 12/15; must reply within 2 week(s) of notification.

**Academics. Special study options:** Double major, independent study, internships, study abroad, teacher certification program. **Credit/placement by examination:** AP, CLEP, IB, institutional tests. 18 credit hours maximum toward bachelor's degree. **Support services:** Pre-admission summer program, tutoring.

**Majors. Area/ethnic studies:** American. **Biology:** General. **Business:** Business admin. **Education:** Early childhood, elementary, physical, secondary, social studies, special. **English:** English lit. **Foreign languages:** French, Spanish. **Health:** Athletic training, clinical lab technology. **History:** General. **Math:** General. **Parks/recreation:** General, health/fitness, sports admin. **Philosophy/religion:** Philosophy, religion. **Physical sciences:** Chemistry, physics. **Psychology:** General. **Theology:** Religious ed. **Visual/performing arts:** Art.

**Most popular majors.** Biology 14%, business/marketing 19%, education 13%, English 7%, parks/recreation 7%, philosophy/religious studies 12%, physical sciences 6%, psychology 8%.

**Computing on campus.** Dormitories wired for high-speed internet access and linked to campus network. Commuter students can connect to campus network. Helpline, repair service, student web hosting, wireless network available.

**Student life. Freshman orientation:** Mandatory. Preregistration for classes offered. Week-long orientation in August held 1 week prior to first day of classes. **Policies:** Religious observance required. **Housing:** Guaranteed on-campus for all undergraduates. Single-sex dorms, substance-free housing available. $300 deposit. **Activities:** Bands, campus ministries, choral groups, dance, drama, literary magazine, music ensembles, musical theater, radio station, student government, student newspaper, national honor societies for academics, drama, and leadership, association of minority students, denominational organizations, judicial council, Fellowship of Christian Athletes, Habitat for Humanity, council for exceptional children.

**Athletics.** NCAA. **Intercollegiate:** Baseball M, basketball, cross-country, soccer, softball W, tennis. **Intramural:** Basketball, football (non-tackle) W, football (tackle) M, racquetball, soccer, softball, tennis, volleyball. **Team name:** Flying Fleet.

**Student services.** Adult student services, campus ministries, career counseling, financial aid counseling, health services, personal counseling, placement for graduates.

**Contact.** E-mail: admissions@erskine.edu
Phone: (864) 379-8838 Toll-free number: (800) 241-8721
Fax: (864) 379-2167
Bart Walker, Director of Admissions, Erskine College, PO Box 338, Due West, SC 29639-0176

---

## Francis Marion University
**Florence, South Carolina**
www.fmarion.edu

**CB member**
**CB code: 5442**

- Public 4-year university and liberal arts college
- Commuter campus in small city
- 3,231 degree-seeking undergraduates: 6% part-time, 67% women, 44% African American, 1% Asian American, 1% Hispanic American, 1% Native American, 1% international
- 221 degree-seeking graduate students
- 65% of applicants admitted
- SAT or ACT (ACT writing optional) required
- 42% graduate within 6 years

**General.** Founded in 1970. Regionally accredited. **Degrees:** 536 bachelor's awarded; master's offered. **Location:** 7 miles from downtown, 80 miles from Columbia. **Calendar:** Semester, limited summer session. **Full-time faculty:** 202 total; 79% have terminal degrees, 8% minority, 41% women. **Part-time faculty:** 82 total; 32% have terminal degrees, 5% minority, 54% women. **Class size:** 44% < 20, 49% 20-39, 4% 40-49, 4% 50-99. **Special facilities:** Planetarium, observatory, arboretum, hewn timber cabins.

**Freshman class profile.** 2,725 applied, 1,760 admitted, 779 enrolled.

| Mid 50% test scores | | | |
|---|---|---|---|
| SAT critical reading: | 430-520 | Rank in top tenth: | 15% |
| SAT math: | 440-530 | End year in good standing: | 68% |
| SAT writing: | 410-500 | Return as sophomores: | 68% |
| ACT composite: | 18-21 | Out-of-state: | 3% |
| GPA 3.50 or higher: | 46% | Live on campus: | 70% |
| GPA 3.0-3.49: | 33% | International: | 1% |
| GPA 2.0-2.99: | 21% | Fraternities: | 4% |
| Rank in top quarter: | 43% | Sororities: | 4% |

**Basis for selection.** Combination of standardized test scores and high school GPA important. Borderline cases may be admitted provisionally. Proficiency in math and English required. **Learning Disabled:** Accommodations provided with documentation.

**High school preparation.** 20 units required. Required and recommended units include English 4, mathematics 3-4, social studies 3, history 1, science 3 (laboratory 3), foreign language 2 and academic electives 4. Social studies should include 1 history; 2 units of same foreign language required.

**2007-2008 Annual costs.** Tuition/fees: $7,038; $13,841 out-of-state. Room/board: $5,860. Books/supplies: $1,100. Personal expenses: $2,500.

**2007-2008 Financial aid. Need-based:** 684 full-time freshmen applied for aid; 613 were judged to have need; 599 of these received aid. 42% of total undergraduate aid awarded as scholarships/grants, 58% as loans/jobs. **Non-need-based:** Awarded to 1,800 full-time undergraduates, including 310 freshmen. Scholarships awarded for academics, music/drama.

**Application procedures. Admission:** No deadline. $30 fee, may be waived for applicants with need. Application must be submitted on paper. Admission notification on a rolling basis beginning on or about 9/1. April 1 reply date for dormitory students. **Financial aid:** Priority date 3/1; no closing date. FAFSA, institutional form required. Applicants notified on a rolling basis starting 4/15.

**Academics. Special study options:** Double major, dual enrollment of high school students, honors, independent study, internships, study abroad, teacher certification program, Washington semester. **Credit/placement by examination:** AP, CLEP, institutional tests. **Support services:** Reduced course load, tutoring, writing center.

**Majors. Biology:** General. **Business:** Accounting, business admin, finance, management information systems, managerial economics, marketing. **Communications:** Media studies. **Computer sciences:** General. **Education:** Art, early childhood, elementary, English, history, mathematics, secondary, social studies. **English:** English lit. **Foreign languages:** French, German, Spanish. **Health:** Nursing (RN). **History:** General. **Liberal arts:** Arts/sciences. **Math:** General. **Physical sciences:** Chemistry, physics. **Psychology:** General. **Social sciences:** Economics, international relations, political science, sociology. **Visual/performing arts:** Art, dramatic.

**Most popular majors.** Biology 14%, business/marketing 27%, education 8%, psychology 8%, social sciences 11%.

**Computing on campus.** 551 workstations in dormitories, library, computer center, student center. Dormitories wired for high-speed internet access. Online course registration, online library available.

**Student life. Freshman orientation:** Mandatory, $46 fee. Preregistration for classes offered. Held in summer for fall term. Session in January for spring. **Housing:** Single-sex dorms, special housing for disabled, apartments, substance-free housing available. $250 deposit. **Activities:** Jazz band, campus ministries, choral groups, drama, literary magazine, music ensembles, student government, student newspaper, TV station, College Democrats, Young Republicans, NAACP, Rotaract, minority student association, psychology club, education club, First Fellowship.

**Athletics.** NCAA. **Intercollegiate:** Baseball M, basketball, cross-country, golf M, soccer, softball W, tennis, track and field, volleyball W. **Intramural:** Basketball, bowling, football (non-tackle), golf, racquetball, soccer, softball, table tennis, tennis, track and field, volleyball. **Team name:** Patriots.

**Student services.** Adult student services, campus ministries, career counseling, student employment services, health services, minority student services, personal counseling, placement for graduates, veterans' counselor. **Physically disabled:** Services for visually, speech, hearing impaired.

**Contact.** E-mail: admission@fmarion.edu
Phone: (843) 661-1231 Toll-free number: (800) 368-7551
Fax: (843) 661-4635
James Schlimmer, Director of Admissions, Francis Marion University, PO Box 100547, Florence, SC 29501-0547

## Furman University
### Greenville, South Carolina
www.furman.edu

**CB member**
**CB code: 5222**

- Private 4-year liberal arts college
- Residential campus in small city
- 2,737 degree-seeking undergraduates: 4% part-time, 56% women, 7% African American, 2% Asian American, 1% Hispanic American, 2% international
- 86 degree-seeking graduate students
- 56% of applicants admitted
- Application essay required
- 83% graduate within 6 years; 41% enter graduate study

**General.** Founded in 1826. Regionally accredited. Abundant internship and collaborative research opportunities. **Degrees:** 651 bachelor's awarded; master's offered. **ROTC:** Army. **Location:** 100 miles from Charlotte, North Carolina, 140 miles from Atlanta. **Calendar:** Semester, extensive summer session. **Full-time faculty:** 236 total; 96% have terminal degrees, 12% minority, 33% women. **Part-time faculty:** 45 total; 38% have terminal degrees, 13% minority, 69% women. **Class size:** 62% < 20, 38% 20-39, less than 1% 50-99. **Special facilities:** Observatory, center for engaged learning, center for international education, center for collaborative learning and communication.

**Freshman class profile.** 3,879 applied, 2,159 admitted, 700 enrolled.

| Mid 50% test scores | | | |
|---|---|---|---|
| SAT critical reading: | 590-690 | Rank in top tenth: | 63% |
| SAT math: | 590-690 | End year in good standing: | 99% |
| SAT writing: | 580-680 | Return as sophomores: | 90% |
| ACT composite: | 25-30 | Out-of-state: | 72% |
| GPA 3.50 or higher: | 60% | Live on campus: | 98% |
| GPA 3.0-3.49: | 32% | International: | 2% |
| GPA 2.0-2.99: | 8% | Fraternities: | 33% |
| Rank in top quarter: | 85% | Sororities: | 44% |

**Basis for selection.** High school record including courses taken and grades most important, then SAT or ACT scores. Special talents such as fine arts, athletic ability, writing ability considered. Special consideration given to children of alumni and minorities. SAT or ACT recommended. If ACT or SAT score is not submitted, the student must submit either AP, SAT Subject Test or IB scores in both Math and English. Audition required for music scholarship applicants; portfolio required for art scholarship applicants. **Homeschooled:** SAT Subject Tests including math, subject of student's choice recommended. Interview strongly recommended.

**High school preparation.** 14 units required; 18 recommended. Required and recommended units include English 4, mathematics 3-4, social studies 3-4, science 2-3 (laboratory 2-3) and foreign language 2-3.

**2007-2008 Annual costs.** Tuition/fees: $31,560. Room/board: $8,064. Books/supplies: $850. Personal expenses: $776.

**2007-2008 Financial aid. Need-based:** 366 full-time freshmen applied for aid; 290 were judged to have need; 290 of these received aid. Average need met was 90%. Average scholarship/grant was $21,673; average loan $3,600. 76% of total undergraduate aid awarded as scholarships/grants, 24% as loans/jobs. **Non-need-based:** Awarded to 1,916 full-time undergraduates, including 480 freshmen. Scholarships awarded for academics, alumni affiliation, art, athletics, leadership, music/drama, religious affiliation, ROTC, state residency. **Additional information:** 5-point comprehensive education financing plan includes financial aid packaging, money management counseling, debt management counseling, outside scholarship coordination, summer job-match program.

**Application procedures. Admission:** Closing date 1/15 (postmark date). No application fee. Admission notification 3/15. Must reply by 5/1. **Financial aid:** Closing date 1/15. FAFSA, institutional form required. Applicants notified by 3/15; must reply by 5/1.

**Academics.** Strong emphasis on research, internships and other opportunities for engaged, hands-on learning. **Special study options:** Combined bachelor's/graduate degree, double major, independent study, internships, student-designed major, study abroad, teacher certification program, United Nations semester, Washington semester. Undergraduate research program, 3-2 engineering with Auburn University, Clemson University, Georgia Institute of Technology, North Carolina State, Washington University in St. Louis, 3-2 forestry program with Duke University, 3-1 dentistry and medicine programs with any accredited medical or dental school, 3-2 nursing, pharmacy, physical therapy, and physician assistant programs with any accredited medical school. **Credit/placement by examination:** AP, CLEP, IB, institutional

tests. **Support services:** Learning center, reduced course load, study skills assistance, tutoring, writing center.

**Majors. Area/ethnic studies:** Asian. **Biology:** General. **Business:** Accounting, business admin, management information systems. **Communications:** General. **Computer sciences:** Computer science. **Conservation:** Environmental studies. **Education:** General, music. **English:** English lit. **Foreign languages:** Ancient Greek, French, German, Latin, Spanish. **Health:** Predental, premedicine, prenursing, prepharmacy, preveterinary. **History:** General. **Interdisciplinary:** Math/computer science. **Legal studies:** Prelaw. **Liberal arts:** Arts/sciences. **Math:** General. **Parks/recreation:** Health/fitness. **Philosophy/religion:** Philosophy, religion. **Physical sciences:** Chemistry, geology, physics. **Psychology:** General. **Social sciences:** Economics, political science, sociology, urban studies. **Theology:** Sacred music. **Visual/performing arts:** Art, dramatic, music history, music performance, music theory/composition. **Other:** Mathematics Economics.

**Most popular majors.** Biology 6%, business/marketing 12%, communications/journalism 6%, foreign language 8%, history 9%, parks/recreation 7%, philosophy/religious studies 6%, physical sciences 6%, social sciences 14%, visual/performing arts 6%.

**Computing on campus.** 340 workstations in library, computer center, student center. Dormitories wired for high-speed internet access and linked to campus network. Commuter students can connect to campus network. Online course registration, helpline, student web hosting, wireless network available.

**Student life. Freshman orientation:** Mandatory. 5-day orientation session, including academic placement testing, advisory services, entertainment, and recreation. **Housing:** Guaranteed on-campus for freshmen. Coed dorms, single-sex dorms, apartments, substance-free housing available. $400 nonrefundable deposit, deadline 5/1. Language house for students focusing on specific language. Lakeside cottages and environmentally equipped eco-cottage also available. **Activities:** Bands, campus ministries, choral groups, dance, drama, film society, international student organizations, literary magazine, music ensembles, musical theater, opera, radio station, student government, student newspaper, symphony orchestra, TV station, Collegiate Educational Service Corps, Young Democrats, College Republicans, Student League for Black Culture, Fellowship of Christian Athletes, Council for Exceptional Children, Habitat for Humanity, arts students league, Amnesty International.

**Athletics.** NCAA. **Intercollegiate:** Baseball M, basketball, cheerleading, cross-country, football (tackle) M, golf, soccer, softball W, tennis, track and field, volleyball W. **Intramural:** Basketball, bowling, cross-country, football (non-tackle), golf, handball, racquetball, rowing (crew), soccer, softball, swimming, tennis, track and field, volleyball. **Team name:** Paladins.

**Student services.** Adult student services, alcohol/substance abuse counseling, campus ministries, career counseling, student employment services, financial aid counseling, health services, minority student services, personal counseling, placement for graduates, veterans' counselor. **Physically disabled:** Services for visually, hearing impaired.

**Contact.** E-mail: admissions@furman.edu
Phone: (864) 294-2034 Fax: (864) 294-2018
David O'Cain, Director of Admissions, Furman University, 3300 Poinsett Highway, Greenville, SC 29613

## ITT Technical Institute: Greenville
### Greenville, South Carolina
www.itt-tech.edu

**CB code: 2708**

- For-profit 4-year technical college
- Commuter campus in large city

**General.** Accredited by ACICS. **Calendar:** Quarter.

**Annual costs/financial aid.** Tuition varies by program, $260-$368 per credit hour.

**Contact.** Phone: (864) 288-0777
Director of Recruitment, 6 Independence Pointe, Greenville, SC 29615

## Lander University
### Greenwood, South Carolina
www.lander.edu

**CB member**
**CB code: 5363**

- Public 4-year liberal arts and teachers college
- Residential campus in large town
- 2,325 degree-seeking undergraduates: 10% part-time, 66% women
- 27 degree-seeking graduate students

- SAT or ACT (ACT writing optional) required
- 46% graduate within 6 years

**General.** Founded in 1872. Regionally accredited. **Degrees:** 469 bachelor's awarded; master's offered. **ROTC:** Army. **Location:** 55 miles from Greenville, 75 miles from Columbia. **Calendar:** Semester, limited summer session. **Full-time faculty:** 123 total; 68% have terminal degrees, 10% minority, 46% women. **Part-time faculty:** 70 total; 9% minority, 61% women. **Class size:** 60% < 20, 35% 20-39, 4% 40-49, 2% 50-99.

### Freshman class profile.

| Mid 50% test scores | | | |
|---|---|---|---|
| SAT critical reading: | 420-520 | GPA 2.0-2.99: | 25% |
| SAT math: | 420-550 | Return as sophomores: | 59% |
| ACT composite: | 17-21 | Out-of-state: | 4% |
| GPA 3.50 or higher: | 43% | Live on campus: | 80% |
| GPA 3.0-3.49: | 32% | International: | 1% |

**Basis for selection.** Test scores, class rank, curriculum, high school GPA important. Out-of-state students must rank in top half of high school class. Selectivity of students may be based on transcripts and GED score. Audition required for music programs; interview recommended for art, music programs; portfolio recommended for art programs.

**High school preparation.** 20 units recommended. Recommended units include English 4, mathematics 3, social studies 2, history 1, science 3 (laboratory 3), foreign language 2 and academic electives 4. One unit physical education or ROTC also recommended.

**2007-2008 Annual costs.** Tuition/fees: $7,888; $14,776 out-of-state. Room/board: $5,782. Books/supplies: $840. Personal expenses: $2,520.

**Financial aid. Non-need-based:** Scholarships awarded for academics, art, athletics, leadership, music/drama.

**Application procedures. Admission:** No deadline. $35 fee, may be waived for applicants with need. Application may be submitted online. Admission notification on a rolling basis. **Financial aid:** Priority date 4/15; no closing date. FAFSA required. Applicants notified on a rolling basis starting 4/15; must reply within 4 week(s) of notification.

**Academics. Special study options:** Cooperative education, distance learning, double major, dual enrollment of high school students, honors, independent study, internships, liberal arts/career combination, student-designed major, study abroad, teacher certification program. Dual degree in engineering with Clemson University, nursing (RN to BSN completion) offered online, MBA and M.Ed. in counseling/school administration from Clemson University offered on campus. **Credit/placement by examination:** AP, CLEP, IB, institutional tests. 30 credit hours maximum toward bachelor's degree. **Support services:** Learning center, pre-admission summer program, reduced course load, remedial instruction, study skills assistance, tutoring, writing center.

**Majors. Biology:** General. **Business:** Business admin. **Computer sciences:** General. **Conservation:** Environmental science. **Education:** Early childhood, elementary, physical, secondary, special. **English:** English lit. **Foreign languages:** Spanish. **Health:** Athletic training, nursing (RN). **History:** General. **Liberal arts:** Arts/sciences, humanities. **Math:** General. **Parks/recreation:** Exercise sciences. **Physical sciences:** Chemistry. **Psychology:** General. **Social sciences:** Political science, sociology. **Visual/performing arts:** Art.

**Most popular majors.** Business/marketing 23%, education 16%, health sciences 12%, parks/recreation 7%, psychology 9%, social sciences 13%, visual/performing arts 6%.

**Computing on campus.** PC or laptop required. 233 workstations in library, computer center. Dormitories linked to campus network. Commuter students can connect to campus network. Online course registration, online library, helpline, repair service, wireless network available.

**Student life. Freshman orientation:** Mandatory. Preregistration for classes offered. **Housing:** Coed dorms, single-sex dorms available. $175 partly refundable deposit, deadline 4/15. **Activities:** Bands, choral groups, dance, drama, literary magazine, music ensembles, student government, student newspaper, Baptist Student Union, Bible study, Young Democrats, College Republicans, Minorities on the Move, Blue Key and Alpha Kappa Gamma (honor societies).

**Athletics.** NCAA. **Intercollegiate:** Baseball M, basketball, cross-country W, golf M, soccer, softball W, tennis, volleyball W. **Intramural:** Basketball, football (non-tackle), golf, soccer, softball, volleyball. **Team name:** Bearcats.

**Student services.** Adult student services, alcohol/substance abuse counseling, career counseling, student employment services, health services, minority student services, personal counseling, placement for graduates, veterans' counselor. **Physically disabled:** Services for visually, speech, hearing impaired.

**Contact.** E-mail: admissions@lander.edu
Phone: (864) 388-8307 Fax: (864) 388-8125
Bettie Horne, Director of Admissions, Lander University, Stanley Avenue, Greenwood, SC 29649-2099

---

## Limestone College
**Gaffney, South Carolina**
www.limestone.edu
CB code: 5366

- Private 4-year liberal arts college
- Residential campus in large town
- 780 degree-seeking undergraduates: 2% part-time, 43% women, 15% African American, 2% Hispanic American, 6% international
- 59% of applicants admitted
- SAT or ACT (ACT writing optional) required
- 47% graduate within 6 years

**General.** Founded in 1845. Regionally accredited. Evening classes located at 9 sites throughout state. **Degrees:** 107 bachelor's, 2 associate awarded. **ROTC:** Army. **Location:** 25 miles from Spartanburg. **Calendar:** Semester, limited summer session. **Full-time faculty:** 55 total; 74% have terminal degrees, 2% minority, 40% women. **Part-time faculty:** 10 total; 30% have terminal degrees, 10% minority, 70% women. **Class size:** 69% < 20, 28% 20-39, 4% 40-49. **Special facilities:** Computer graphics art lab.

**Freshman class profile.** 1,021 applied, 604 admitted, 190 enrolled.

| Mid 50% test scores | | | |
|---|---|---|---|
| SAT critical reading: | 450-540 | Rank in top quarter: | 23% |
| SAT math: | 460-560 | Rank in top tenth: | 5% |
| ACT composite: | 18-23 | End year in good standing: | 86% |
| GPA 3.50 or higher: | 32% | Return as sophomores: | 52% |
| GPA 3.0-3.49: | 26% | Out-of-state: | 47% |
| GPA 2.0-2.99: | 40% | Live on campus: | 74% |
| | | International: | 7% |

**Basis for selection.** SAT combined score of 890 (exclusive of Writing) and GPA of 2.0. Admissions committee must approve all applicants who do not meet these standards. SAT requirement waived for freshmen 21 or older or in military service. The SAT or ACT requirement is waived for students admitted into the PALS (Program for Alternative Learning Styles) Program. Interview required for lower-ranking applicants; recommended for all others. Audition required of first-time, first-year freshmen for music, music education, theater programs; portfolio required for art education, studio art programs; essay required for honors program. **Learning Disabled:** Documentation required to be eligible for Program for Alternative Learning Styles (PALS).

**High school preparation.** 12 units required. Required units include English 4, mathematics 3, social studies 3, science 2 (laboratory 2).

**2008-2009 Annual costs.** Tuition/fees: $17,300. Room/board: $6,400. Books/supplies: $1,870. Personal expenses: $1,640.

**2006-2007 Financial aid. Need-based:** 134 full-time freshmen applied for aid; 113 were judged to have need; 113 of these received aid. Average need met was 60%. Average scholarship/grant was $9,532; average loan $2,338. 60% of total undergraduate aid awarded as scholarships/grants, 40% as loans/jobs. **Non-need-based:** Awarded to 152 full-time undergraduates, including 71 freshmen. Scholarships awarded for academics, alumni affiliation, art, athletics, job skills, leadership, music/drama, religious affiliation, ROTC, state residency.

**Application procedures. Admission:** Priority date 8/1; deadline 8/26 (receipt date). $25 fee, may be waived for applicants with need. Application may be submitted online. Admission notification on a rolling basis beginning on or about 6/1. **Financial aid:** Priority date 2/1; no closing date. FAFSA required. Applicants notified on a rolling basis starting 1/15; must reply within 3 week(s) of notification.

**Academics. Special study options:** Accelerated study, distance learning, double major, honors, independent study, internships, liberal arts/career combination, student-designed major, teacher certification program. **Credit/placement by examination:** AP, CLEP, institutional tests. 15 credit hours maximum toward associate degree, 30 toward bachelor's. **Support services:** Learning center, reduced course load, remedial instruction, study skills assistance, tutoring, writing center.

**Majors. Biology:** General. **Business:** Accounting, business admin, e-commerce, managerial economics, marketing, training/development. **Computer sciences:** General, computer science, database management, programming, security, system admin, web page design, webmaster. **Education:** General, elementary, English, mathematics, music, physical, secondary. **English:** English lit. **Health:** Athletic training, predental, premedicine, prenursing, prepharmacy, preveterinary. **History:** General. **Legal studies:** Prelaw. **Liberal arts:** Arts/sciences. **Math:** General. **Parks/recreation:** Exercise sciences, health/fitness, sports admin. **Physical sciences:** Chemistry. **Protective services:** Law enforcement admin. **Psychology:** General. **Public administration:** Social work. **Social sciences:** Economics. **Visual/performing arts:** Dramatic, graphic design, jazz, studio arts. **Other:** Pre-Chiropractic.

**Most popular majors.** Business/marketing 23%, education 32%, parks/recreation 9%, visual/performing arts 7%.

**Computing on campus.** 79 workstations in library, computer center. Dormitories wired for high-speed internet access and linked to campus network. Commuter students can connect to campus network. Online library, helpline, repair service, wireless network available.

**Student life. Freshman orientation:** Mandatory. Preregistration for classes offered. 5 days prior to start of semester. **Policies:** Alcohol-free campus. Students must live on campus unless age 21, or have attained 90 credit hours, or live with immediate family within 50 miles of campus. **Housing:** Guaranteed on-campus for freshmen. Single-sex dorms, substance-free housing available. $50 fully refundable deposit. Off-campus apartments available. **Activities:** Bands, choral groups, drama, literary magazine, music ensembles, musical theater, student government, Fellowship of Christian Athletes, student alumni leadership council, student organization of social workers, Students in Free Enterprise, Christian Education and Leadership Program, Chi Alpha Sigma, outdoor recreation and education club.

**Athletics.** NCAA. **Intercollegiate:** Baseball M, basketball, cross-country, golf, lacrosse, soccer, softball W, swimming, tennis, track and field, volleyball W, wrestling M. **Intramural:** Basketball, bowling, softball, table tennis, tennis, volleyball. **Team name:** Saints.

**Student services.** Adult student services, alcohol/substance abuse counseling, campus ministries, career counseling, student employment services, financial aid counseling, health services, personal counseling, placement for graduates, veterans' counselor. **Learning disabled:** Comprehensive services available.

**Contact.** E-mail: cphenicie@limestone.edu
Phone: (864) 488-4554 Toll-free number: (800) 795-7151 ext. 4554
Fax: (864) 487-8706
Chris Phenicie, Vice President for Enrollment Services, Limestone College, 1115 College Drive, Gaffney, SC 29340-3799

---

## Medical University of South Carolina
### Charleston, South Carolina
www.musc.edu                    CB code: 5407

▸ Public two-year upper-division health science and nursing college
▸ Commuter campus in large city

**General.** Founded in 1824. Regionally accredited. **Location:** 350 miles from Atlanta. **Calendar:** Differs by program.

**Annual costs/financial aid.** Tuition and fees for BS in nursing for in-state $11,482, out-of-state $29,842; BS in cardiovascular perfusion for in-state is $11,821, out-of-state $30,491; BS in health professions, in-state $11,536, out-of-state $30,206. Need-based financial aid available to full-time and part-time students.

**Contact.** Phone: (843) 792-3281
Director of Admissions, 41 Bee Street, Charleston, SC 29425

---

## Morris College
### Sumter, South Carolina
www.morris.edu          CB member
                        CB code: 5418

▸ Private 4-year liberal arts college affiliated with Baptist faith
▸ Residential campus in large town
▸ 868 degree-seeking undergraduates: 3% part-time, 57% women, 100% African American
▸ 90% of applicants admitted
▸ 37% graduate within 6 years; 13% enter graduate study

**General.** Founded in 1908. Regionally accredited. **Degrees:** 140 bachelor's awarded. **ROTC:** Army. **Location:** 45 miles from Columbia, 110 miles from Charlotte, North Carolina. **Calendar:** Semester, limited summer session. **Full-time faculty:** 47 total; 68% have terminal degrees, 57% minority, 55% women. **Part-time faculty:** 18 total; 22% have terminal degrees, 83% minority, 39% women. **Class size:** 61% < 20, 34% 20-39, 4% 40-49, less than 1% 50-99. **Special facilities:** Radio station/training lab, electronic learning lab, television production studio.

**Freshman class profile.** 1,457 applied, 1,311 admitted, 295 enrolled.

| | | | |
|---|---|---|---|
| GPA 3.50 or higher: | 3% | End year in good standing: | 62% |
| GPA 3.0-3.49: | 13% | Return as sophomores: | 60% |
| GPA 2.0-2.99: | 49% | Out-of-state: | 17% |
| Rank in top quarter: | 8% | Live on campus: | 93% |
| Rank in top tenth: | 2% | | |

**Basis for selection.** High school record most important. Students with less than 2.0 high school GPA may be admitted on probation but limited to 13-credit-hour load during each of first 2 semesters and required to participate in tutorial and study sessions. SAT or ACT scores must be submitted for all degree-seeking students, except foreign students. Scores are used for informational purposes only. Interview recommended.

**High school preparation.** 24 units required. Required and recommended units include English 4, mathematics 4, social studies 2, history 1, science 3, foreign language 1-2 and academic electives 7. 1 physical education or ROTC, 1 computer science.

**2007-2008 Annual costs.** Tuition/fees: $9,250. Room/board: $4,134. Books/supplies: $1,500. Personal expenses: $1,200.

**2007-2008 Financial aid.** All financial aid based on need. 295 full-time freshmen applied for aid; 290 were judged to have need; 290 of these received aid. Average need met was 78%. Average scholarship/grant was $8,000; average loan $3,500. 63% of total undergraduate aid awarded as scholarships/grants, 37% as loans/jobs. **Additional information:** Students are encouraged to complete FAFSA on the web.

**Application procedures. Admission:** Priority date 7/1; no deadline. $20 fee, may be waived for applicants with need. Application must be submitted on paper. Admission notification on a rolling basis beginning on or about 11/1. **Financial aid:** Priority date 3/30; no closing date. FAFSA, institutional form required. Applicants notified on a rolling basis starting 6/1; must reply within 2 week(s) of notification.

**Academics. Special study options:** Accelerated study, combined bachelor's/graduate degree, cooperative education, double major, honors, internships, liberal arts/career combination, teacher certification program. Adult Degree Program in Organizational Management offered through evening courses; students must be at least 25 years old and have earned 60 credit hours. **Credit/placement by examination:** AP, CLEP. 30 credit hours maximum toward bachelor's degree. **Support services:** Learning center, reduced course load, remedial instruction, study skills assistance, tutoring, writing center.

**Majors. Biology:** General. **Business:** Business admin, operations. **Communications:** Broadcast journalism, journalism, media studies. **Education:** Biology, early childhood, elementary, English, mathematics, social studies. **English:** English lit. **Health:** Community health services. **History:** General. **Liberal arts:** Arts/sciences. **Math:** General. **Parks/recreation:** Facilities management. **Protective services:** Law enforcement admin. **Social sciences:** Political science, sociology. **Theology:** Religious ed, theology.

**Most popular majors.** Business/marketing 25%, communications/journalism 12%, health sciences 12%, parks/recreation 8%, security/protective services 16%, social sciences 14%.

**Computing on campus.** 285 workstations in dormitories, library, computer center. Dormitories wired for high-speed internet access and linked to campus network. Wireless network available.

**Student life. Freshman orientation:** Mandatory. Preregistration for classes offered. Held during first week of fall and spring semesters. **Policies:** College promotes drug-free, alcohol-free campus. Cigarette smoking prohibited in all buildings. **Housing:** Guaranteed on-campus for freshmen. Single-sex dorms, substance-free housing available. $100 fully refundable deposit, deadline 8/1. **Activities:** Choral groups, dance, drama, literary magazine, radio station, student government, student newspaper, Baptist Student Union, NAACP, Alpha Phi Omega, Durham Ministerial Union, National Association of Blacks in Criminal Justice.

**Athletics.** NAIA. **Intercollegiate:** Baseball M, basketball, cheerleading, cross-country, golf M, softball W, tennis, track and field, volleyball W. **Intramural:** Basketball, football (non-tackle), golf M, table tennis, tennis, volleyball. **Team name:** Hornets.

**Student services.** Adult student services, alcohol/substance abuse counseling, campus ministries, career counseling, student employment services, financial aid counseling, health services, personal counseling, placement for graduates, veterans' counselor.

**Contact.** E-mail: dcalhoun@morris.edu
Phone: (803) 934-3225 Toll-free number: (866)·853-1345
Fax: (803) 773-8241
Deborah Calhoun, Director of Admission and Records, Morris College, 100 West College Street, Sumter, SC 29150-3599

## Newberry College
**Newberry, South Carolina**
**www.newberry.edu**

**CB member**
**CB code: 5493**

- Private 4-year liberal arts college affiliated with Evangelical Lutheran Church in America
- Residential campus in small city
- 911 degree-seeking undergraduates: 2% part-time, 41% women, 25% African American, 1% Asian American, 2% Hispanic American, 4% international
- SAT or ACT required
- 43% graduate within 6 years

**General.** Founded in 1856. Regionally accredited. **Degrees:** 135 bachelor's awarded. **ROTC:** Army. **Location:** 40 miles from Columbia. **Calendar:** Semester, limited summer session. **Full-time faculty:** 51 total; 69% have terminal degrees, 8% minority, 43% women. **Part-time faculty:** 36 total; 28% have terminal degrees, 6% minority, 33% women. **Class size:** 60% < 20, 39% 20-39, 1% 40-49, less than 1% 50-99.

**Freshman class profile.**

| Mid 50% test scores | | Return as sophomores: | 60% |
|---|---|---|---|
| SAT critical reading: | 430-530 | Out-of-state: | 20% |
| SAT math: | 440-540 | Live on campus: | 90% |
| ACT composite: | 17-20 | Fraternities: | 14% |
| Rank in top quarter: | 22% | Sororities: | 26% |
| Rank in top tenth: | 6% | | |

**Basis for selection.** High school record and test scores important; recommendations and interview considered. Interview recommended for all; audition required for drama, music programs; portfolio required for art. **Homeschooled:** Submit transcripts from HS or home school association. If unavailable, submit major essays and course descriptions. References necessary from primary instructor and another source.

**High school preparation.** 15 units required. Required units include English 4, mathematics 3, social studies 2, history 1, science 2 (laboratory 2), foreign language 2 and academic electives 1.

**2008-2009 Annual costs.** Tuition/fees: $21,560. Room/board: $7,400. Books/supplies: $1,480. Personal expenses: $1,800.

**2006-2007 Financial aid. Need-based:** 70% of total undergraduate aid awarded as scholarships/grants, 30% as loans/jobs. **Non-need-based:** Scholarships awarded for academics, alumni affiliation, athletics, music/drama, religious affiliation, ROTC, state residency.

**Application procedures. Admission:** Priority date 1/30; no deadline. $30 fee, may be waived for applicants with need. Application may be submitted online. Admission notification on a rolling basis beginning on or about 9/15. Must reply by May 1 or within 3 week(s) if notified thereafter. **Financial aid:** Priority date 3/15; no closing date. FAFSA, institutional form required. Applicants notified on a rolling basis starting 3/1; must reply by 5/1 or within 2 week(s) of notification.

**Academics. Special study options:** Cooperative education, double major, dual enrollment of high school students, external degree, honors, independent study, internships, liberal arts/career combination, student-designed major, study abroad, teacher certification program. Dual degree programs in Engineering with Clemson University, Georgia Institute of Technology. Other dual degree programs with Duke and Medical University of South Carolina. **Credit/placement by examination:** AP, CLEP, IB, institutional tests. 30 credit hours maximum toward bachelor's degree. Sophomore standing available by earning 24 credit hours based on AP exam scores. **Support services:** Learning center, reduced course load, remedial instruction, tutoring, writing center.

**Majors. Biology:** General. **Business:** Business admin. **Communications:** General. **Education:** General, early childhood, elementary, music, physical. **English:** English lit. **History:** General. **Interdisciplinary:** Global studies.

**Legal studies:** Prelaw. **Liberal arts:** Arts/sciences, humanities. **Math:** General. **Parks/recreation:** General, sports admin. **Philosophy/religion:** Philosophy, religion. **Physical sciences:** Chemistry. **Psychology:** General. **Social sciences:** International relations, political science, sociology. **Theology:** Sacred music. **Visual/performing arts:** Art, dramatic, music history, music performance, music theory/composition.

**Most popular majors.** Biology 8%, business/marketing 19%, communications/journalism 7%, education 11%, parks/recreation 19%, psychology 6%, visual/performing arts 7%.

**Computing on campus.** 112 workstations in library, computer center. Dormitories wired for high-speed internet access and linked to campus network. Online library, helpline, repair service, student web hosting, wireless network available.

**Student life. Freshman orientation:** Mandatory, $100 fee. Preregistration for classes offered. 2-day event. Students stay overnight on campus. **Housing:** Guaranteed on-campus for freshmen. Coed dorms, single-sex dorms available. $100 deposit. **Activities:** Bands, choral groups, drama, literary magazine, music ensembles, musical theater, radio station, student government, student newspaper, TV station, Lutheran Student Movement, Baptist student union, Young Republicans, Intervarsity Fellowship of Christian Athletes, Students Organized for Community Service, South Carolina State Student Legislature.

**Athletics.** NCAA. **Intercollegiate:** Baseball M, basketball, cheerleading M, cross-country, football (tackle) M, golf, soccer, softball W, tennis, volleyball W, wrestling M. **Intramural:** Basketball, softball, volleyball W. **Team name:** Indians.

**Student services.** Alcohol/substance abuse counseling, campus ministries, career counseling, student employment services, financial aid counseling, health services, personal counseling, placement for graduates.

**Contact.** E-mail: admissions@newberry.edu
Phone: (803) 321-5127 Toll-free number: (800) 845-4955 ext. 5127
Fax: (803) 321-5138
Michael Robbins, Director of Admissions, Newberry College, 2100 College Street, Newberry, SC 29108

## North Greenville University
**Tigerville, South Carolina**
**www.ngu.edu**

**CB code: 5498**

- Private 4-year liberal arts college affiliated with Southern Baptist Convention
- Residential campus in rural community
- 1,868 degree-seeking undergraduates: 5% part-time, 50% women
- 92 graduate students
- 75% of applicants admitted
- SAT and SAT Subject Tests or ACT (ACT writing optional) required
- 47% graduate within 6 years

**General.** Founded in 1891. Regionally accredited. Off-site recreation and learning center for Outdoor Leadership major. **Degrees:** 304 bachelor's, 14 associate awarded; master's offered. **ROTC:** Army. **Location:** 18 miles from Greenville, 54 miles from Asheville, North Carolina. **Calendar:** Semester, limited summer session. **Full-time faculty:** 103 total; 63% have terminal degrees, 10% minority, 39% women. **Part-time faculty:** 58 total. **Class size:** 65% < 20, 35% 20-39, less than 1% 50-99. **Special facilities:** Bible museum.

**Freshman class profile.** 1,373 applied, 1,031 admitted, 513 enrolled.

| Mid 50% test scores | | GPA 2.0-2.99: | 25% |
|---|---|---|---|
| SAT critical reading: | 440-590 | Rank in top quarter: | 38% |
| SAT math: | 440-570 | Rank in top tenth: | 13% |
| ACT composite: | 18-24 | Out-of-state: | 21% |
| GPA 3.50 or higher: | 41% | Live on campus: | 86% |
| GPA 3.0-3.49: | 32% | | |

**Basis for selection.** High school record, standardized test scores, class rank most important. Require 2 of the following: SAT 820 (exclusive of Writing); ACT 16; GPA 2.0; class rank top 60 percent. Computerized Placement Test required for those with SAT verbal and math scores below 500. Portfolio recommended for all; audition required for music, theater programs; essay required for English-deficient; interview recommended for music, theater programs. **Learning Disabled:** Meet with Director of Disability Services.

**High school preparation.** 12 units required; 18 recommended. Required and recommended units include English 4, mathematics 2-3, social

studies 1, history 1, science 2-3 (laboratory 1), foreign language 2, computer science 1, visual/performing arts 1 and academic electives 2.

**2007-2008 Annual costs.** Tuition/fees: $11,180. Room/board: $6,420. Books/supplies: $1,000. Personal expenses: $2,000.

**Financial aid.** All financial aid based on need.

**Application procedures. Admission:** Priority date 6/1; deadline 8/26. $25 fee, may be waived for applicants with need. Admission notification on a rolling basis. **Financial aid:** Priority date 6/1, closing date 6/30. FAFSA required. Applicants notified on a rolling basis starting 8/1; must reply within 2 week(s) of notification.

**Academics. Special study options:** Cross-registration, double major, dual enrollment of high school students, ESL, honors, independent study, internships, student-designed major, teacher certification program. **Credit/placement by examination:** AP, CLEP, IB, institutional tests. 16 credit hours maximum toward associate degree, 30 toward bachelor's. CLEP and other exam credits cannot exceed 25 percent of hours needed for degree. **Support services:** Learning center, reduced course load, remedial instruction, study skills assistance, tutoring, writing center.

**Majors. Biology:** General. **Business:** General, accounting, business admin, international. **Communications:** General, journalism, media studies, radio/tv. **Education:** Biology, early childhood, elementary, English, music. **English:** English lit. **Health:** Predental, premedicine, prepharmacy. **History:** General. **Interdisciplinary:** Accounting/computer science. **Legal studies:** Prelaw. **Liberal arts:** Arts/sciences. **Math:** General. **Parks/recreation:** General, sports admin. **Philosophy/religion:** Christian. **Physical sciences:** Chemistry, physics. **Psychology:** General. **Social sciences:** Economics. **Theology:** Missionary, sacred music, youth ministry. **Visual/performing arts:** Music history, music performance, music theory/composition, piano/organ, theater arts management, voice/opera.

**Most popular majors.** Business/marketing 21%, communications/journalism 8%, education 17%, liberal arts 12%, parks/recreation 7%, philosophy/religious studies 9%, theological studies 6%.

**Computing on campus.** 75 workstations in library, computer center, student center. Dormitories wired for high-speed internet access. Commuter students can connect to campus network. Helpline, wireless network available.

**Student life. Freshman orientation:** Mandatory. Preregistration for classes offered. Held in August. **Policies:** Religious observance required. **Housing:** Guaranteed on-campus for all undergraduates. Single-sex dorms, special housing for disabled, apartments, substance-free housing available. $100 deposit, deadline 8/26. **Activities:** Bands, campus ministries, choral groups, drama, literary magazine, music ensembles, radio station, student government, student newspaper, symphony orchestra, Baptist student union, athletic ministries, Etude music society, Fellowship of Christians in Service, College Republicans.

**Athletics.** NCAA, NCCAA. **Intercollegiate:** Baseball M, basketball, cheerleading, cross-country, football (tackle) M, golf M, soccer, softball W, tennis, volleyball W. **Intramural:** Basketball, football (non-tackle) M, softball, table tennis, tennis, volleyball. **Team name:** Crusaders.

**Student services.** Campus ministries, career counseling, student employment services, financial aid counseling, health services, on-campus daycare, personal counseling, placement for graduates. **Physically disabled:** Services for visually impaired.

**Contact.** E-mail: admissions@ngc.edu
Phone: (864) 977-7001 Toll-free number: (800) 468-6642
Fax: (864) 977-7177
Keli Sewell, Vice President for Admissions and Financial Aid, North Greenville University, PO Box 1892, Tigerville, SC 29688-1892

---

## Presbyterian College

**Clinton, South Carolina**
**www.presby.edu**

**CB member**
**CB code: 5540**

- Private 4-year liberal arts college affiliated with Presbyterian Church (USA)
- Residential campus in small town
- 1,139 degree-seeking undergraduates: 2% part-time, 50% women, 7% African American, 1% Asian American, 1% Hispanic American
- 71% of applicants admitted
- SAT or ACT with writing, application essay required
- 71% graduate within 6 years; 25% enter graduate study

**General.** Founded in 1880. Regionally accredited. Academic student exchange with Finland, South Korea, and Germany. Study abroad in England, Scotland, Ireland, Austria, France, Spain, Mexico, Germany, Japan, Australia, New Zealand, and China. **Degrees:** 226 bachelor's awarded. **ROTC:** Army. **Location:** 40 miles from Greenville, 35 miles from Spartanburg. **Calendar:** Semester, limited summer session. **Full-time faculty:** 85 total; 95% have terminal degrees, 5% minority, 35% women. **Part-time faculty:** 41 total; 27% have terminal degrees, 12% minority, 49% women. **Class size:** 66% < 20, 33% 20-39, less than 1% 40-49, less than 1% 50-99. **Special facilities:** Scanning electron and transmission microscopes, ecological research center, Southeastern Center for Intercultural Studies.

**Freshman class profile.** 1,138 applied, 807 admitted, 290 enrolled.

| Mid 50% test scores | | | |
|---|---|---|---|
| SAT critical reading: | 500-610 | Rank in top quarter: | 66% |
| SAT math: | 530-640 | Rank in top tenth: | 32% |
| ACT composite: | 22-27 | End year in good standing: | 82% |
| GPA 3.50 or higher: | 49% | Return as sophomores: | 83% |
| GPA 3.0-3.49: | 29% | Out-of-state: | 31% |
| GPA 2.0-2.99: | 22% | Live on campus: | 100% |

**Basis for selection.** Rigor of high school curriculum most important, followed by test scores, high school GPA, and high school recommendation. Extracurricular involvement and interview considered in some cases. Interview recommended. **Homeschooled:** Transcript of courses and grades, state high school equivalency certificate required.

**High school preparation.** 17 units required. Required units include English 4, mathematics 3, history 2, science 2 (laboratory 2), foreign language 2 and academic electives 2. 2 or more units of laboratory science for science majors recommended.

**2008-2009 Annual costs.** Tuition/fees: $27,902. Room/board: $8,064.

**Financial aid. Non-need-based:** Scholarships awarded for academics, alumni affiliation, athletics, job skills, leadership, minority status, music/drama, religious affiliation, ROTC.

**Application procedures. Admission:** Priority date 3/1; deadline 6/1 (postmark date). $40 fee, may be waived for applicants with need. Application may be submitted online. Admission notification on a rolling basis. **Financial aid:** Priority date 3/1; no closing date. FAFSA, institutional form required. Applicants notified on a rolling basis starting 4/1; must reply by 5/1.

**Academics. Special study options:** Accelerated study, combined bachelor's/graduate degree, double major, dual enrollment of high school students, exchange student, honors, independent study, internships, liberal arts/career combination, semester at sea, study abroad, teacher certification program, Washington semester. 3-2 environmental science program, 3-2 engineering program, religious educational program, dual degrees offered with Auburn University (AL), Clemson University, Vanderbilt University (TN). **Credit/placement by examination:** AP, CLEP, IB, SAT, ACT, institutional tests. 40 credit hours maximum toward bachelor's degree. **Support services:** Preadmission summer program, reduced course load, study skills assistance, tutoring, writing center.

**Majors. Biology:** General. **Business:** Accounting, business admin. **Computer sciences:** Computer science. **Education:** Early childhood, middle, music, special. **English:** Creative writing, English lit. **Foreign languages:** General, French, German, Spanish. **History:** General. **Math:** General. **Philosophy/religion:** Philosophy, religion. **Physical sciences:** Chemistry, physics. **Psychology:** General. **Social sciences:** Economics, political science, sociology. **Theology:** Sacred music. **Visual/performing arts:** Art, art history/conservation, dramatic, music performance, studio arts. **Other:** Medical Physics, Religious Education.

**Most popular majors.** Biology 9%, business/marketing 20%, education 6%, English 8%, history 10%, philosophy/religious studies 6%, psychology 8%, social sciences 13%, visual/performing arts 6%.

**Computing on campus.** 120 workstations in dormitories, library, computer center, student center. Dormitories wired for high-speed internet access and linked to campus network. Commuter students can connect to campus network. Online course registration, helpline, student web hosting, wireless network available.

**Student life. Freshman orientation:** Mandatory, $100 fee. Preregistration for classes offered. Orientation includes registration, placement testing and organization fair. **Policies:** Honor code governs conduct inside and outside classroom, on and off campus. Cultural Enrichment Program requires students to attend 40 on-campus cultural events as part of graduation requirement. **Housing:** Guaranteed on-campus for all undergraduates. Coed dorms, single-sex dorms, apartments, fraternity/sorority housing, substance-free housing available. $400 nonrefundable deposit, deadline 5/1. All full-time students, except those commuting daily from family's residence, required to live on campus. Sorority housing not available. **Activities:** Bands, campus ministries, choral groups, dance, drama, international student organizations, literary magazine, music ensembles, musical theater, radio station, student government, student newspaper, symphony orchestra, volunteer organizations, multicultural student union, Young Democrats and Republicans, interdenominational organizations, Habitat for Humanity, Amnesty International, Fellowship of Christian Athletes.

**Athletics.** NCAA. **Intercollegiate:** Baseball M, basketball, cheerleading, cross-country, football (tackle) M, golf, lacrosse, soccer, softball W, tennis, volleyball W. **Intramural:** Basketball, football (non-tackle), golf, soccer, softball, tennis, volleyball. **Team name:** Blue Hose.

**Student services.** Campus ministries, career counseling, student employment services, financial aid counseling, health services, minority student services, personal counseling, placement for graduates.

**Contact.** E-mail: admissions@presby.edu
Phone: (864) 833-8230 Toll-free number: (800) 960-7583
Fax: (864) 833-8195
Leni Patterson, Dean of Admissions and Financial Aid, Presbyterian College, 503 South Broad Street, Clinton, SC 29325-9989

## South Carolina State University

**Orangeburg, South Carolina**   **CB member**
**www.scsu.edu**   **CB code: 5618**

- Public 4-year university
- Residential campus in large town
- 4,289 degree-seeking undergraduates: 6% part-time, 55% women, 97% African American
- 572 degree-seeking graduate students
- 88% of applicants admitted
- SAT or ACT (ACT writing optional) required
- 54% graduate within 6 years; 56% enter graduate study

**General.** Founded in 1896. Regionally accredited. **Degrees:** 474 bachelor's awarded; master's, doctoral offered. **ROTC:** Army, Air Force. **Location:** 40 miles from Columbia, 70 miles from Charleston. **Calendar:** Semester, limited summer session. **Full-time faculty:** 229 total; 89% have terminal degrees, 75% minority, 43% women. **Part-time faculty:** 64 total; 33% have terminal degrees, 91% minority, 48% women. **Special facilities:** Planetarium.

**Freshman class profile.** 3,866 applied, 3,408 admitted, 1,318 enrolled.

| Mid 50% test scores | | | |
|---|---|---|---|
| SAT critical reading: | 360-440 | GPA 3.0-3.49: | 25% |
| SAT math: | 370-450 | GPA 2.0-2.99: | 53% |
| ACT composite: | 15-18 | Return as sophomores: | 65% |
| GPA 3.50 or higher: | 15% | Out-of-state: | 22% |

**Basis for selection.** Admission decisions based primarily on high school record, class rank, and standardized test scores. Audition required for music education program; portfolio required for art education program. **Learning Disabled:** Student must submit documentation, which is sent to Student Health Services Center--Disabled Student Support Services.

**High school preparation.** 20 units required. Required units include English 4, mathematics 3, social studies 3, science 3 (laboratory 3), foreign language 2 and academic electives 4. 1 physical education or ROTC required.

**2007-2008 Annual costs.** Tuition/fees: $7,161; $14,322 out-of-state. Room/board: $5,118. Books/supplies: $1,000. Personal expenses: $700.

**Financial aid. Non-need-based:** Scholarships awarded for academics, athletics, ROTC.

**Application procedures. Admission:** Closing date 7/31 (postmark date). $25 fee, may be waived for applicants with need. Application may be submitted online. Admission notification on a rolling basis. **Financial aid:** Closing date 5/1. FAFSA required. Applicants notified on a rolling basis starting 6/15; must reply by 8/1 or within 4 week(s) of notification.

**Academics. Special study options:** Cooperative education, cross-registration, distance learning, double major, dual enrollment of high school students, exchange student, honors, internships, liberal arts/career combination, study abroad, teacher certification program, Washington semester. **Credit/placement by examination:** AP, CLEP, institutional tests. 30 credit hours maximum toward bachelor's degree. **Support services:** Learning center, remedial instruction, tutoring, writing center.

**Majors. Agriculture:** Agribusiness operations. **Biology:** General. **Business:** Accounting, business admin, managerial economics, marketing. **Computer sciences:** General. **Education:** Art, biology, business, chemistry, drama/dance, early childhood, elementary, emotionally handicapped, English, family/consumer sciences, French, history, learning disabled, mathematics, mentally handicapped, middle, music, physical, social studies, Spanish, special, technology/industrial arts, trade/industrial. **Engineering:** Nuclear. **Engineering technology:** Civil, electrical, industrial, mechanical. **English:** English lit. **Family/consumer sciences:** General, food/nutrition. **Foreign languages:** General. **Health:** Audiology/speech pathology, nursing (RN). **History:** General. **Math:** General. **Parks/recreation:** Health/fitness. **Physical sciences:** Chemistry, physics. **Protective services:** Law enforcement admin. **Psychology:** General. **Public administration:** Social work. **Social sciences:** Political science, sociology. **Visual/performing arts:** Dramatic, music management, music performance, studio arts.

**Most popular majors.** Biology 10%, business/marketing 16%, education 8%, engineering/engineering technologies 9%, family/consumer sciences 14%, psychology 7%, security/protective services 7%.

**Computing on campus.** 300 workstations in dormitories, library, computer center, student center. Dormitories wired for high-speed internet access and linked to campus network. Commuter students can connect to campus network. Online course registration, online library, helpline, repair service, wireless network available.

**Student life. Freshman orientation:** Available. Preregistration for classes offered. **Housing:** Guaranteed on-campus for freshmen. Single-sex dorms, apartments available. $25 deposit. **Activities:** Bands, choral groups, dance, drama, music ensembles, radio station, student government, student newspaper.

**Athletics.** NCAA. **Intercollegiate:** Basketball, bowling W, cross-country, football (tackle) M, golf, soccer W, softball W, tennis, track and field, volleyball W. **Intramural:** Basketball, softball. **Team name:** Bulldogs.

**Student services.** Adult student services, career counseling, health services, personal counseling, placement for graduates, veterans' counselor. **Physically disabled:** Services for speech, hearing impaired.

**Contact.** E-mail: admissions@scsu.edu
Phone: (803) 536-7185 Toll-free number: (800) 260-5956
Fax: (803) 536-8990
Antonio Boyle, AVP, Enrollment Management, South Carolina State University, 300 College Street NE, Orangeburg, SC 29117

## South University

**Columbia, South Carolina**
**www.southuniversity.edu**   **CB code: 5097**

- For-profit 4-year university
- Commuter campus in small city
- 593 degree-seeking undergraduates: 36% part-time, 80% women, 85% African American, 1% Asian American, 2% Hispanic American
- 208 degree-seeking graduate students

**General.** Founded in 1935. Regionally accredited. **Degrees:** 32 bachelor's, 71 associate awarded; master's offered. **Location:** 5 miles from downtown. **Calendar:** Quarter, extensive summer session. **Full-time faculty:** 22 total. **Part-time faculty:** 19 total.

**Basis for selection.** Open admission, but selective for some programs. Special requirements for pharmacy, nursing, physician assistant studies programs. SAT or ACT may be submitted in place of required institutional tests for placement. Score report due by September 15. **Homeschooled:** Transcript of courses and grades required.

**2007-2008 Annual costs.** Tuition/fees: $12,390.

**Financial aid.** All financial aid based on need.

**Application procedures. Admission:** No deadline. $25 fee, may be waived for applicants with need. Application may be submitted online. Admission notification on a rolling basis. **Financial aid:** Priority date 5/30; no closing date. FAFSA required. Applicants notified on a rolling basis starting 5/30.

**Academics. Special study options:** Cooperative education, distance learning, double major, internships, weekend college. **Credit/placement by examination:** AP, CLEP, institutional tests. **Support services:** Reduced course load, remedial instruction, study skills assistance, tutoring, writing center.

**Majors. Business:** Business admin. **Computer sciences:** Information technology. **Health:** Nursing (RN). **Legal studies:** General. **Protective services:** Corrections, juvenile corrections, law enforcement admin, police science.

**Computing on campus.** 40 workstations in library, computer center. Commuter students can connect to campus network. Online library, helpline, wireless network available.

**Student life. Freshman orientation:** Mandatory. Preregistration for classes offered. **Activities:** Literary magazine.

**Student services.** Adult student services, career counseling, student employment services, financial aid counseling, personal counseling, placement for graduates, veterans' counselor. **Physically disabled:** Services for visually, speech, hearing impaired.

**Contact.** Phone: (803) 799-9082 Toll-free number: (866) 629-3031
Fax: (803) 799-9038
Trisha Sherwood, Director of Admissions, South University, 9 Science Court, Columbia, SC 29203

---

## Southern Wesleyan University
### Central, South Carolina
**www.swu.edu**      **CB code: 5896**

- Private 4-year university and liberal arts college affiliated with Wesleyan Church
- Commuter campus in small town
- 1,730 degree-seeking undergraduates: 1% part-time, 63% women, 30% African American, 2% Hispanic American, 1% international
- 700 degree-seeking graduate students
- 95% of applicants admitted
- SAT or ACT (ACT writing optional), application essay required
- 54% graduate within 6 years; 25% enter graduate study

**General.** Founded in 1906. Regionally accredited. **Degrees:** 474 bachelor's, 114 associate awarded; master's offered. **ROTC:** Army, Air Force. **Location:** 25 miles from Greenville. **Calendar:** Semester, limited summer session. **Full-time faculty:** 50 total; 74% have terminal degrees, 10% minority, 28% women. **Part-time faculty:** 184 total; 40% have terminal degrees, 24% minority, 43% women. **Class size:** 81% < 20, 19% 20-39, less than 1% 40-49. **Special facilities:** Electron microscope facility.

**Freshman class profile.** 317 applied, 301 admitted, 158 enrolled.

| Mid 50% test scores | | GPA 2.0-2.99: | 21% |
|---|---|---|---|
| SAT critical reading: | 430-540 | Rank in top quarter: | 31% |
| SAT math: | 430-560 | Rank in top tenth: | 6% |
| SAT writing: | 410-540 | Return as sophomores: | 76% |
| ACT composite: | 18-22 | Out-of-state: | 30% |
| GPA 3.50 or higher: | 51% | Live on campus: | 75% |
| GPA 3.0-3.49: | 28% | International: | 2% |

**Basis for selection.** GPA, class rank, test scores, and religious commitment important. Recommendations considered. Students admitted conditionally if combined SAT score is less than 800 (exclusive of Writing) or high school GPA is less than 2.3, and rank in bottom half of class. Students admitted conditionally take limited number of course hours and are on academic warning. Audition required for music; interview recommended for applicants with special physical, emotional problems.

**High school preparation.** 10 units required. Required units include English 4, mathematics 2, social studies 2 and science 2.

**2007-2008 Annual costs.** Tuition/fees: $17,150. Room/board: $6,200. Books/supplies: $950. Personal expenses: $1,850.

**2007-2008 Financial aid. Need-based:** 150 full-time freshmen applied for aid; 140 were judged to have need; 139 of these received aid. Average need met was 80%. Average scholarship/grant was $12,286; average loan $4,037. 55% of total undergraduate aid awarded as scholarships/grants, 45% as loans/jobs. **Non-need-based:** Scholarships awarded for academics, athletics, music/drama.

**Application procedures. Admission:** Closing date 8/1 (postmark date). $25 fee, may be waived for applicants with need. Application may be submitted online. Admission notification on a rolling basis beginning on or about 10/1. Must reply by 5/1. **Financial aid:** Priority date 3/31, closing date 6/30. FAFSA, institutional form required. Applicants notified on a rolling basis starting 2/1; must reply within 2 week(s) of notification.

**Academics. Special study options:** Cooperative education, cross-registration, distance learning, double major, dual enrollment of high school

students, external degree, honors, independent study, internships, liberal arts/ career combination, student-designed major, study abroad, teacher certification program, Washington semester. **Credit/placement by examination:** AP, CLEP, SAT, ACT, institutional tests. 48 credit hours maximum toward associate degree, 68 toward bachelor's. **Support services:** Learning center, reduced course load, remedial instruction, study skills assistance, tutoring, writing center.

**Majors. Biology:** General. **Business:** Accounting, business admin, e-commerce, human resources. **Communications:** General. **Computer sciences:** General. **Education:** Biology, early childhood, elementary, emotionally handicapped, English, learning disabled, mathematics, mentally handicapped, music, physical, special. **English:** English lit. **Health:** Medical radiologic technology/radiation therapy, predental, premedicine, prenursing. **History:** General. **Math:** General. **Parks/recreation:** General, sports admin. **Philosophy/religion:** Religion. **Physical sciences:** Chemistry. **Protective services:** Criminal justice, forensics. **Psychology:** General. **Public administration:** Human services. **Social sciences:** General. **Other:** Forensic Computer Science.

**Most popular majors.** Business/marketing 73%, education 11%.

**Computing on campus.** 256 workstations in dormitories, library, computer center. Dormitories wired for high-speed internet access and linked to campus network. Commuter students can connect to campus network. Online course registration, online library, helpline, repair service, student web hosting, wireless network available.

**Student life. Freshman orientation:** Mandatory. Preregistration for classes offered. Held at the beginning of fall and spring semesters. **Policies:** Students must agree to abide by lifestyle expectations of university. Religious observance required. **Housing:** Guaranteed on-campus for all undergraduates. Coed dorms, single-sex dorms, special housing for disabled, apartments, substance-free housing available. $200 fully refundable deposit. **Activities:** Bands, choral groups, drama, literary magazine, music ensembles, musical theater, student government, Christian Service Organization, Student Missions Fellowship, Rotaract, Fellowship of Christian Athletes, student activities board, Habitat for Humanity.

**Athletics.** NAIA, NCCAA. **Intercollegiate:** Baseball M, basketball, cross-country, golf M, soccer, softball W, volleyball W. **Intramural:** Basketball, football (non-tackle), soccer, softball, table tennis, tennis, volleyball. **Team name:** Warriors.

**Student services.** Adult student services, alcohol/substance abuse counseling, campus ministries, career counseling, financial aid counseling, health services, minority student services, personal counseling. **Physically disabled:** Services for visually, hearing impaired.

**Contact.** E-mail: admissions@swu.edu
Phone: (864) 644-5550 Toll-free number: (800) 282-8798
Fax: (864) 644-5972
Chad Peters, Director of Admissions, Southern Wesleyan University, PO Box 1020, Central, SC 29630-1020

---

## University of South Carolina
### Columbia, South Carolina      **CB member**
**www.sc.edu**      **CB code: 5818**

- Public 4-year university
- Residential campus in small city
- 18,497 degree-seeking undergraduates: 7% part-time, 55% women, 12% African American, 3% Asian American, 2% Hispanic American, 1% international
- 7,110 degree-seeking graduate students
- 59% of applicants admitted
- SAT or ACT with writing required
- 63% graduate within 6 years

**General.** Founded in 1801. Regionally accredited. **Degrees:** 3,725 bachelor's, 11 associate awarded; master's, doctoral, first professional offered. **ROTC:** Army, Naval, Air Force. **Location:** 70 miles from Charlotte, North Carolina. **Calendar:** Semester, extensive summer session. **Full-time faculty:** 1,250 total; 84% have terminal degrees, 14% minority, 38% women. **Part-time faculty:** 482 total; 39% have terminal degrees, 8% minority, 45% women. **Class size:** 46% < 20, 38% 20-39, 6% 40-49, 7% 50-99, 2% >100. **Special facilities:** Observatory, arboretum, green dorm with learning center focusing on sustainability.

**Freshman class profile.** 14,994 applied, 8,908 admitted, 3,719 enrolled.

| Mid 50% test scores | | | |
|---|---|---|---|
| SAT critical reading: | 530-630 | **Rank in top tenth:** | 29% |
| SAT math: | 550-650 | **Return as sophomores:** | 87% |
| ACT composite: | 23-28 | **Out-of-state:** | 38% |
| GPA 3.50 or higher: | 77% | **Live on campus:** | 94% |
| GPA 3.0-3.49: | 19% | **International:** | 1% |
| GPA 2.0-2.99: | 4% | **Fraternities:** | 4% |
| Rank in top quarter: | 65% | **Sororities:** | 6% |

**Basis for selection.** Admission based on high school curriculum, grades in required high school courses, SAT and ACT scores. **Learning Disabled:** Diagnostic tests required for learning disabled students.

**High school preparation.** 19 units required. Required units include English 4, mathematics 3, social studies 2, history 1, science 3 (laboratory 3), foreign language 2 and academic electives 4. One unit of physical education or ROTC required.

**2007-2008 Annual costs.** Tuition/fees: $8,346; $21,632 out-of-state. Health professions (pharmacy, health, nursing), law and medical professions have higher undergraduate and graduate fees. Room/board: $6,550. Books/supplies: $900. Personal expenses: $2,420.

**2007-2008 Financial aid.** **Need-based:** 2,546 full-time freshmen applied for aid; 1,510 were judged to have need; 1,506 of these received aid. Average need met was 76%. Average scholarship/grant was $4,290; average loan $1,961. 52% of total undergraduate aid awarded as scholarships/grants, 48% as loans/jobs. **Non-need-based:** Awarded to 10,659 full-time undergraduates, including 3,160 freshmen. Scholarships awarded for academics, alumni affiliation, art, athletics, job skills, leadership, minority status, music/drama, religious affiliation, ROTC, state residency.

**Application procedures.** **Admission:** Closing date 12/1. $50 fee, may be waived for applicants with need. Application must be submitted on paper. Admission notification on a rolling basis beginning on or about 3/15. Must reply by May 1 or within 2 week(s) if notified thereafter. **Financial aid:** Priority date 4/1; no closing date. FAFSA required. Applicants notified on a rolling basis starting 4/1.

**Academics.** One-month May term focusing on specialized topics. **Special study options:** Accelerated study, combined bachelor's/graduate degree, co-operative education, cross-registration, distance learning, double major, dual enrollment of high school students, ESL, exchange student, external degree, honors, independent study, internships, student-designed major, study abroad, teacher certification program, weekend college. Alternative Spring Break, Dobson Volunteer Service Program, International Program for Students, Undergraduate Research. **Credit/placement by examination:** AP, CLEP, IB, institutional tests. Maximum number of semester hours of credit by examination allowed varies according to degree and program of study. **Support services:** Learning center, reduced course load, study skills assistance, tutoring, writing center.

**Honors college/program.** To be competitive for admission, students must have an SAT score of at least 1300 (exclusive of Writing) and a high school GPA of at least 3.5. 600 are admitted to yield a freshman class of 275. Academic program consists of 115-125 honors classes per semester across most disciplines and levels.

**Majors.** **Area/ethnic studies:** African-American, European, Latin American, women's. **Biology:** General, marine. **Business:** Accounting, business admin, finance, hospitality admin, insurance, management science, managerial economics, marketing, office management, real estate, retailing. **Communications:** Advertising, broadcast journalism, journalism, media studies, public relations. **Computer sciences:** General. **Education:** Art, early childhood, physical. **Engineering:** Chemical, civil, computer, electrical, mechanical. **English:** English lit. **Foreign languages:** Classics, French, German, Italian, Russian, Spanish. **Health:** Cardiovascular technology, nursing (RN). **History:** General. **Liberal arts:** Arts/sciences. **Math:** General, statistics. **Parks/recreation:** Exercise sciences, sports admin. **Philosophy/religion:** Philosophy, religion. **Physical sciences:** Chemistry, geology, geophysics, physics. **Protective services:** Law enforcement admin. **Psychology:** Experimental. **Social sciences:** Anthropology, economics, geography, international relations, political science, sociology. **Visual/performing arts:** Art history/conservation, dance, dramatic, film/cinema, studio arts. **Other:** Business & technology education, Technology Support and Training Management, Visual Communications.

**Most popular majors.** Biology 7%, business/marketing 25%, communications/journalism 8%, parks/recreation 6%, psychology 6%, social sciences 10%, visual/performing arts 6%.

**Computing on campus.** 2,800 workstations in dormitories, library, computer center, student center. Dormitories wired for high-speed internet access and linked to campus network. Commuter students can connect to campus network. Online course registration, online library, helpline, wireless network available.

**Student life.** **Freshman orientation:** Available, $60 fee. Preregistration for classes offered. Parents may also attend to view campus for $20 fee. **Housing:** Guaranteed on-campus for freshmen. Coed dorms, single-sex dorms, special housing for disabled, apartments, fraternity/sorority housing, substance-free housing available. $145 deposit, deadline 5/1. Honors (undergraduate) and wellness housing, Preston Residential College, communities for pre-medical, engineering, athletic, teaching fellows, global, and environmentally friendly available. **Activities:** Bands, campus ministries, choral groups, dance, drama, film society, international student organizations, literary magazine, music ensembles, Model UN, musical theater, opera, radio station, student government, student newspaper, symphony orchestra, TV station, Baptist Collegiate Ministry, University Ambassadors, Association of African American Students, Habitat for Humanity, Dance Marathon, cultural exchange association, orientation leaders association, Hill of the Lord, BGLSA.

**Athletics.** NCAA. **Intercollegiate:** Baseball M, basketball, cross-country W, diving, equestrian W, football (tackle) M, golf, soccer, softball W, swimming, tennis, track and field, volleyball W. **Intramural:** Badminton, basketball, bowling, golf, racquetball, soccer, softball, swimming, table tennis, tennis, volleyball, weight lifting. **Team name:** Fighting Gamecocks.

**Student services.** Adult student services, alcohol/substance abuse counseling, career counseling, services for economically disadvantaged, student employment services, financial aid counseling, health services, minority student services, personal counseling, placement for graduates, veterans' counselor. **Physically disabled:** Services for visually, speech, hearing impaired. **Learning disabled:** Comprehensive services available.

**Contact.** E-mail: admissions-ugrad@sc.edu
Phone: (803) 777-7700 Toll-free number: (800) 868-5872
Fax: (803) 777-0101
Scott Verzyl, Director of Undergraduate Admissions, University of South Carolina, Office of Undergraduate Admissions, Columbia, SC 29208

---

## University of South Carolina at Aiken

**Aiken, South Carolina**  CB member
**www.usca.edu**  CB code: 5840

- Public 4-year university and liberal arts college
- Commuter campus in large town
- 2,867 degree-seeking undergraduates: 19% part-time, 66% women, 27% African American, 1% Asian American, 2% Hispanic American, 2% international
- 60 degree-seeking graduate students
- 51% of applicants admitted
- SAT or ACT (ACT writing recommended) required
- 41% graduate within 6 years

**General.** Founded in 1961. Regionally accredited. **Degrees:** 538 bachelor's awarded; master's offered. **Location:** 55 miles from Columbia, 15 miles from Augusta, Georgia. **Calendar:** Semester, limited summer session. **Full-time faculty:** 148 total; 72% have terminal degrees, 12% minority, 47% women. **Part-time faculty:** 111 total; 22% have terminal degrees, 11% minority, 55% women. **Class size:** 56% < 20, 44% 20-39, less than 1% 50-99. **Special facilities:** Fine arts center, science center, natatorium, planetarium, convocation center.

**Freshman class profile.** 1,849 applied, 944 admitted, 626 enrolled.

| Mid 50% test scores | | | |
|---|---|---|---|
| SAT critical reading: | 440-540 | **Rank in top quarter:** | 40% |
| SAT math: | 450-550 | **Rank in top tenth:** | 14% |
| SAT writing: | 430-540 | **Return as sophomores:** | 67% |
| ACT composite: | 18-22 | **Out-of-state:** | 10% |
| GPA 3.50 or higher: | 13% | **Live on campus:** | 43% |
| GPA 3.0-3.49: | 28% | **International:** | 1% |
| GPA 2.0-2.99: | 59% | **Fraternities:** | 5% |
| | | **Sororities:** | 9% |

**Basis for selection.** Test scores, high school core GPA important. Admission based on course selection, standardized test scores and a predicted college GPA. Audition, essay, interview, portfolio recommended.

**High school preparation.** 21 units required. Required units include English 4, mathematics 4, social studies 2, history 1, science 3 (laboratory 3), foreign language 2, computer science 1, visual/performing arts 1 and academic electives 4. Elective college preparatory credits from 3 different fields.

**2007-2008 Annual costs.** Tuition/fees: $7,036; $13,952 out-of-state. Room/board: $5,870. Books/supplies: $1,080. Personal expenses: $1,690.

**2006-2007 Financial aid.** **Need-based:** 520 full-time freshmen applied for aid; 281 were judged to have need; 237 of these received aid. Average need met was 61%. Average scholarship/grant was $1,310; average loan

$3,330. **Non-need-based:** Awarded to 663 full-time undergraduates, including 140 freshmen.

**Application procedures. Admission:** Priority date 7/1; deadline 8/1 (postmark date). $45 fee, may be waived for applicants with need. Application may be submitted online. Admission notification on a rolling basis beginning on or about 9/1. Must reply by May 1 or within 3 week(s) if notified thereafter. **Financial aid:** Priority date 3/15; no closing date. FAFSA required. Applicants notified on a rolling basis starting 4/20; must reply within 2 week(s) of notification.

**Academics. Special study options:** Cooperative education, distance learning, double major, dual enrollment of high school students, ESL, honors, independent study, internships, study abroad, teacher certification program. **Credit/placement by examination:** AP, CLEP, institutional tests. 30 credit hours maximum toward bachelor's degree. **Support services:** Study skills assistance, tutoring, writing center.

**Majors. Biology:** General. **Business:** General. **Communications:** General. **Education:** General, early childhood, elementary, English, mathematics, middle, music, science, secondary, social science, social studies, special. **English:** English lit. **Health:** Nursing (RN). **History:** General. **Interdisciplinary:** Math/computer science. **Math:** Applied. **Parks/recreation:** Exercise sciences. **Physical sciences:** Chemistry. **Psychology:** General. **Social sciences:** Political science, sociology. **Visual/performing arts:** Studio arts.

**Most popular majors.** Biology 7%, business/marketing 23%, communications/journalism 7%, education 14%, health sciences 16%, psychology 7%, social sciences 8%.

**Computing on campus.** 802 workstations in dormitories, library, computer center, student center. Dormitories wired for high-speed internet access and linked to campus network. Online course registration, helpline, wireless network available.

**Student life. Freshman orientation:** Mandatory, $75 fee. Preregistration for classes offered. Held in June, July, and August. June and July orientations offer registration. **Housing:** Coed dorms, special housing for disabled, apartments, substance-free housing available. $25 partly refundable deposit. **Activities:** Bands, campus ministries, dance, drama, international student organizations, music ensembles, musical theater, student government, student newspaper, symphony orchestra, Campus Crusade for Christ, honor societies, Association for Women's Issues, Pacer Union Board, High Adventure Club, African American Students' Alliance, Community Action Board, College Republicans.

**Athletics.** NCAA. **Intercollegiate:** Baseball M, basketball, cheerleading, cross-country W, golf M, soccer, softball W, tennis, volleyball W. **Intramural:** Badminton, baseball M, basketball, bowling, golf, soccer, softball, table tennis, tennis, volleyball. **Team name:** Pacers.

**Student services.** Adult student services, alcohol/substance abuse counseling, career counseling, student employment services, financial aid counseling, health services, minority student services, on-campus daycare, personal counseling, placement for graduates, veterans' counselor. **Physically disabled:** Services for visually, speech, hearing impaired.

**Contact.** E-mail: admit@usca.edu
Phone: (803) 641-3366 Toll-free number: (888) 969-8722
Fax: (803) 641-3727
Andrew Hendrix, Director of Admissions, University of South Carolina at Aiken, 471 University Parkway, Aiken, SC 29801

---

## University of South Carolina at Beaufort
**Bluffton, South Carolina**     **CB member**
www.uscb.edu     **CB code: 5845**

- Public 4-year university and liberal arts college
- Commuter campus in large town
- 1,192 degree-seeking undergraduates: 27% part-time, 65% women, 17% African American, 1% Asian American, 3% Hispanic American, 1% Native American, 1% international
- 61% of applicants admitted
- SAT or ACT (ACT writing optional) required

**General.** Founded in 1959. Regionally accredited. **Degrees:** 113 bachelor's, 23 associate awarded. **Location:** 72 miles from Charleston, 42 miles from Savannah, Georgia. **Calendar:** Semester, limited summer session. **Full-time faculty:** 53 total; 77% have terminal degrees, 15% minority, 40% women. **Part-time faculty:** 62 total; 40% have terminal degrees. **Class size:** 59% < 20, 38% 20-39, 2% 40-49, less than 1% 50-99. **Special facilities:** Pritchard's Island, a 1,600-acre undeveloped island used for research, instruction, and as center for Loggerhead Sea Turtle Conservation Project.

**Freshman class profile.** 765 applied, 469 admitted, 288 enrolled.

| Mid 50% test scores | | | |
|---|---|---|---|
| SAT critical reading: | 430-540 | Return as sophomores: | 54% |
| SAT math: | 420-540 | Out-of-state: | 20% |
| ACT composite: | 17-21 | Live on campus: | 40% |

**Basis for selection.** Test scores, rigor of secondary school record important; academic GPA considered.

**High school preparation.** 20 units required. Required units include English 4, mathematics 3, social studies 2, history 1, science 3 (laboratory 3), foreign language 2 and academic electives 5. Electives must be from 3 areas. Computer Science course recommended. 1 PE or ROTC required.

**2007-2008 Annual costs.** Tuition/fees: $6,310; $13,992 out-of-state. Books/supplies: $975. Personal expenses: $1,512.

**Financial aid. Non-need-based:** Scholarships awarded for academics, state residency.

**Application procedures. Admission:** No deadline. $40 fee, may be waived for applicants with need. Application may be submitted online. Admission notification on a rolling basis beginning on or about 2/1. Students may submit application through CollegeNET. **Financial aid:** Priority date 4/15; no closing date. FAFSA required. Applicants notified on a rolling basis starting 5/31; must reply within 2 week(s) of notification.

**Academics. Special study options:** Cooperative education, distance learning, dual enrollment of high school students, independent study, internships, student-designed major, study abroad, teacher certification program. **Credit/placement by examination:** AP, CLEP, institutional tests. 15 credit hours maximum toward associate degree, 30 toward bachelor's. **Support services:** Learning center, reduced course load, study skills assistance, tutoring, writing center.

**Majors. Biology:** General. **Business:** Business admin, hospitality admin. **Education:** Early childhood. **English:** English lit. **Foreign languages:** Spanish. **Health:** Nursing (RN). **History:** General. **Liberal arts:** Arts/sciences. **Psychology:** General. **Social sciences:** General.

**Most popular majors.** Biology 7%, business/marketing 27%, education 16%, English 11%, liberal arts 11%, psychology 10%, social sciences 15%.

**Computing on campus.** 114 workstations in library, computer center. Dormitories wired for high-speed internet access. Online course registration, online library available.

**Student life. Freshman orientation:** Mandatory. Preregistration for classes offered. **Housing:** Special housing for disabled, apartments, substance-free housing available. **Activities:** Drama, literary magazine, musical theater, student government, student newspaper, African American student association, Christian student fellowship, business club, veterans association, education club, Gamma Beta Phi honor society, psychology/sociology/anthropology club.

**Athletics. Intercollegiate:** Baseball M, cross-country, golf. **Intramural:** Football (non-tackle), soccer. **Team name:** Sand Sharks.

**Student services.** Career counseling, services for economically disadvantaged, student employment services, financial aid counseling, personal counseling, veterans' counselor.

**Contact.** E-mail: webbdh@gwm.sc.edu
Phone: (843) 208-8000 Toll-free number: (877) 885-5271
Fax: (843) 208-8290
Donna Webb, Director of Admissions, University of South Carolina at Beaufort, One University Boulevard, Bluffton, SC 29909

---

## University of South Carolina Upstate
**Spartanburg, South Carolina**
www.uscupstate.edu     **CB code: 5850**

- Public 4-year university
- Commuter campus in small city
- 4,752 degree-seeking undergraduates: 16% part-time, 65% women, 25% African American, 2% Asian American, 2% Hispanic American, 2% international
- 19 degree-seeking graduate students
- 54% of applicants admitted
- SAT or ACT (ACT writing optional) required
- 38% graduate within 6 years

**General.** Founded in 1967. Regionally accredited. **Degrees:** 910 bachelor's awarded; master's offered. **ROTC:** Army. **Location:** 30 miles from Greenville, 70 miles from Charlotte, North Carolina. **Calendar:** Semester, extensive summer session. **Full-time faculty:** 235 total; 64% have terminal degrees, 17% minority, 54% women. **Part-time faculty:** 153 total; 21% have terminal degrees, 13% minority, 54% women. **Class size:** 60% < 20, 38% 20-39, 1% 40-49, less than 1% 50-99. **Special facilities:** Recital hall, language laboratory, center for international studies and language services, audiovisual production center, digital lab, watershed ecology center.

**Freshman class profile.** 2,761 applied, 1,492 admitted, 822 enrolled.

| Mid 50% test scores | | | |
|---|---|---|---|
| SAT critical reading: | 440-530 | Rank in top quarter: | 40% |
| SAT math: | 450-540 | Rank in top tenth: | 14% |
| SAT writing: | 430-520 | Return as sophomores: | 62% |
| ACT composite: | 19-22 | Out-of-state: | 6% |
| GPA 3.50 or higher: | 53% | Live on campus: | 53% |
| GPA 3.0-3.49: | 29% | International: | 2% |
| GPA 2.0-2.99: | 18% | Fraternities: | 1% |
| | | Sororities: | 1% |

**Basis for selection.** Cumulative average of C or better in preparatory courses and minimum 850 SAT (exclusive of Writing), or 18 ACT required. Higher grades may offset lower SAT/ACT scores, and higher SAT/ACT scores may offset lower grades. Interviews recommended.

**High school preparation.** 20 units required; 22 recommended. Required and recommended units include English 4, mathematics 3-4, social studies 2, history 1, science 3 (laboratory 3), foreign language 2-3 and academic electives 4. Students who graduated from high school between 1988-2000 must meet above requirements. However, these students need 2 rather than 3 laboratory sciences and 1 rather than 4 electives.

**2007-2008 Annual costs.** Tuition/fees: $7,920; $15,912 out-of-state. Room/board: $6,350. Books/supplies: $1,000. Personal expenses: $200.

**2006-2007 Financial aid. Need-based:** 635 full-time freshmen applied for aid; 480 were judged to have need; 478 of these received aid. Average need met was 34%. Average scholarship/grant was $4,160; average loan $2,456. 39% of total undergraduate aid awarded as scholarships/grants, 61% as loans/jobs. **Non-need-based:** Awarded to 1,223 full-time undergraduates, including 463 freshmen. Scholarships awarded for academics, athletics, minority status, ROTC, state residency. **Additional information:** Out-of-state students who are recipients of financial aid may qualify for out-of-state fee waiver. Educational benefits available to veterans and children of deceased/disabled veterans.

**Application procedures. Admission:** Priority date 8/15; no deadline. $40 fee, may be waived for applicants with need. Application may be submitted online. Admission notification on a rolling basis beginning on or about 9/15. **Financial aid:** Priority date 3/1, closing date 7/15. FAFSA, institutional form required. Applicants notified on a rolling basis starting 5/1; must reply within 2 week(s) of notification.

**Academics. Special study options:** Accelerated study, cross-registration, distance learning, double major, ESL, exchange student, honors, independent study, internships, liberal arts/career combination, student-designed major, study abroad, teacher certification program, Washington semester. **Credit/placement by examination:** AP, CLEP, IB, institutional tests. 30 credit hours maximum toward bachelor's degree. **Support services:** Learning center, reduced course load, remedial instruction, study skills assistance, tutoring, writing center.

**Majors. Biology:** General. **Business:** Business admin. **Communications:** General. **Computer sciences:** General, information systems. **Education:** Early childhood, elementary, physical, secondary, special. **Engineering technology:** Industrial management. **English:** English lit. **Foreign languages:** French, Spanish. **Health:** Nursing (RN). **History:** General. **Interdisciplinary:** Accounting/computer science. **Liberal arts:** Arts/sciences. **Math:** General, applied. **Physical sciences:** Chemistry. **Protective services:** Criminal justice. **Psychology:** General. **Social sciences:** Political science, sociology. **Visual/performing arts:** Commercial/advertising art, design.

**Most popular majors.** Business/marketing 18%, communications/journalism 6%, education 17%, health sciences 24%, liberal arts 9%, psychology 6%.

**Computing on campus.** 600 workstations in dormitories, library, computer center, student center. Dormitories wired for high-speed internet access and linked to campus network. Commuter students can connect to campus network. Online course registration, online library, helpline, repair service, student web hosting, wireless network available.

**Student life. Freshman orientation:** Available. Preregistration for classes offered. **Housing:** Coed dorms, apartments, substance-free housing available. $135 fully refundable deposit, deadline 6/1. **Activities:** Jazz band, choral groups, dance, drama, international student organizations, literary magazine, music ensembles, student government, student newspaper, African-American Association, Baptist student union, Campus Crusade for Christ, College Republicans, Young Democrats, student education association, campus activity board, Association for the Education of Young Children, environmental club, Amnesty International.

**Athletics.** NCAA. **Intercollegiate:** Baseball M, basketball, cheerleading, cross-country, golf, soccer, softball W, tennis, volleyball W. **Intramural:** Basketball, bowling, football (non-tackle), soccer, softball, table tennis, tennis, volleyball. **Team name:** Spartans.

**Student services.** Adult student services, alcohol/substance abuse counseling, campus ministries, career counseling, services for economically disadvantaged, student employment services, financial aid counseling, health services, minority student services, on-campus daycare, personal counseling, placement for graduates, veterans' counselor, women's services. **Physically disabled:** Services for visually, speech, hearing impaired. **Learning disabled:** Comprehensive services available.

**Contact.** E-mail: dstewart@uscupstate.edu
Phone: (864) 503-5246 Toll-free number: (800) 277-8727
Fax: (864) 503-5727
Donette Stewart, Assistant Vice Chancelor for Enrollment Services, University of South Carolina Upstate, 800 University Way, Spartanburg, SC 29303

---

## Voorhees College
**Denmark, South Carolina**
www.voorhees.edu                    CB code: 5863

▶ Private 4-year liberal arts college affiliated with Episcopal Church
▶ Residential campus in small town
▶ 603 degree-seeking undergraduates

**General.** Founded in 1897. Regionally accredited. **Degrees:** 145 bachelor's awarded. **ROTC:** Army. **Location:** 50 miles from Columbia and Augusta, Georgia. **Calendar:** Semester, limited summer session. **Full-time faculty:** 40 total. **Part-time faculty:** 17 total.

**Freshman class profile.**

| Mid 50% test scores | | | |
|---|---|---|---|
| SAT critical reading: | 310-420 | Rank in top quarter: | 10% |
| SAT math: | 310-440 | Rank in top tenth: | 2% |
| ACT composite: | 13-16 | Out-of-state: | 10% |
| | | Live on campus: | 95% |

**Basis for selection.** Secondary school record, GPA (2.0 or above), recommendations, and standardized test scores considered in admissions decisions. Interview required for Project Smart applicants.

**High school preparation.** 20 units recommended. Recommended units include English 4, mathematics 3, social studies 2, science 2, foreign language 2 and academic electives 7.

**2007-2008 Annual costs.** Tuition/fees: $8,984. Room/board: $5,342. Books/supplies: $600. Personal expenses: $1,365.

**Application procedures. Admission:** Priority date 4/15; no deadline. $25 fee, may be waived for applicants with need. Application may be submitted online. Admission notification on a rolling basis beginning on or about 1/15. **Financial aid:** Priority date 4/15; no closing date. FAFSA, institutional form required. Applicants notified on a rolling basis starting 3/1; must reply within 2 week(s) of notification.

**Academics. Special study options:** Accelerated study, combined bachelor's/graduate degree, cooperative education, honors, independent study, internships, liberal arts/career combination, study abroad, weekend college. **Credit/placement by examination:** AP, CLEP, IB, institutional tests. 15 credit hours maximum toward bachelor's degree. **Support services:** Learning center, reduced course load, remedial instruction, study skills assistance, tutoring.

**Majors. Biology:** General. **Business:** General, accounting, accounting/finance, business admin, management information systems, organizational behavior. **Communications:** Broadcast journalism, media studies. **Computer sciences:** General, computer science. **English:** English lit. **Health:** Predental, premedicine, prenursing. **Math:** General. **Parks/recreation:** Health/fitness. **Social sciences:** Sociology.

**Computing on campus.** 175 workstations in dormitories, library, computer center. Dormitories wired for high-speed internet access and linked to campus network. Commuter students can connect to campus network. Online library, helpline, wireless network available.

**Student life. Freshman orientation:** Mandatory. Preregistration for classes offered. One day orientation offered in June and July. One week orientation offered in August. **Housing:** Guaranteed on-campus for all undergraduates. Single-sex dorms available. $60 deposit, deadline 7/31. Accommodations for single mothers. **Activities:** Pep band, choral groups, dance, drama, radio station, student government, student newspaper.

**Athletics.** NAIA. **Intercollegiate:** Baseball M, basketball, cheerleading, cross-country, softball W, track and field, volleyball W. **Intramural:** Baseball M, basketball, softball W. **Team name:** Tigers.

**Student services.** Adult student services, campus ministries, career counseling, student employment services, financial aid counseling, health services, personal counseling, placement for graduates, veterans' counselor.

**Contact.** E-mail: spellman@voorhees.edu
Phone: (803) 780-1031 Toll-free number: (800) 446-6250
Fax: (803) 780-1444
Willie Jefferson, Dean, Enrollment Management, Voorhees College, 213 Wiggins Road, Denmark, SC 29042

---

## W.L. Bonner Bible College
### Columbia, South Carolina

- Private 4-year Bible college
- Small city

**General.** Accredited by ABHE. **Calendar:** Semester.

**Contact.** Phone: (803) 754-3950
4430 Argent Court, Columbia, SC 29203

---

## Winthrop University
### Rock Hill, South Carolina
### www.winthrop.edu

**CB member**
**CB code: 5910**

- Public 4-year university
- Residential campus in small city
- 4,757 degree-seeking undergraduates: 6% part-time, 69% women, 28% African American, 2% Asian American, 2% Hispanic American, 2% international
- 1,213 degree-seeking graduate students
- 70% of applicants admitted
- SAT or ACT (ACT writing optional) required
- 58% graduate within 6 years

**General.** Founded in 1886. Regionally accredited. **Degrees:** 1,014 bachelor's awarded; master's offered. **ROTC:** Army. **Location:** 20 miles from Charlotte, North Carolina. **Calendar:** Semester, extensive summer session. **Full-time faculty:** 282 total; 82% have terminal degrees, 12% minority, 49% women. **Part-time faculty:** 277 total; 21% have terminal degrees, 11% minority, 59% women. **Class size:** 40% < 20, 48% 20-39, 9% 40-49, 4% 50-99. **Special facilities:** Nursery laboratory, music conservatory.

**Freshman class profile.** 3,996 applied, 2,781 admitted, 1,186 enrolled.

| Mid 50% test scores | | | |
|---|---|---|---|
| SAT critical reading: | 470-570 | Rank in top quarter: | 38% |
| SAT math: | 480-570 | Rank in top tenth: | 18% |
| ACT composite: | 20-25 | Return as sophomores: | 72% |
| GPA 3.50 or higher: | 63% | Out-of-state: | 13% |
| GPA 3.0-3.49: | 30% | Live on campus: | 89% |
| GPA 2.0-2.99: | 7% | International: | 2% |
| | | Sororities: | 3% |

**Basis for selection.** School achievement record, test scores, counselor recommendations important, school and community activities considered. Essay, interview recommended for all; audition recommended for dance, music, theater programs.

**High school preparation.** 20 units required. Required units include English 4, mathematics 3, social studies 3, history 1, science 3 (laboratory 3), foreign language 2 and academic electives 4. Physical education or ROTC required.

**2007-2008 Annual costs.** Tuition/fees: $10,210; $19,034 out-of-state. Room/board: $5,800. Books/supplies: $750. Personal expenses: $1,236.

**2006-2007 Financial aid. Need-based:** 981 full-time freshmen applied for aid; 720 were judged to have need; 716 of these received aid. Average need met was 70%. Average scholarship/grant was $7,828; average loan $2,763. 61% of total undergraduate aid awarded as scholarships/grants, 39% as loans/jobs. **Non-need-based:** Awarded to 894 full-time undergraduates,

including 193 freshmen. Scholarships awarded for academics, art, athletics, music/drama, state residency. **Additional information:** Academic scholarships from $1,500 to full tuition and board awarded to approximately one-third of entering freshman class each year.

**Application procedures. Admission:** Closing date 5/1. $40 fee, may be waived for applicants with need. Application must be submitted on paper. Admission notification on a rolling basis beginning on or about 10/21. Must reply by May 1 or within 3 week(s) if notified thereafter. 8 monthly notification dates for fall between October and May on the 21st of the month. **Financial aid:** Priority date 3/1; no closing date. FAFSA required. Applicants notified on a rolling basis starting 4/1; must reply within 2 week(s) of notification.

**Academics. Special study options:** Cooperative education, cross-registration, distance learning, double major, exchange student, honors, independent study, internships, study abroad, teacher certification program, United Nations semester. **Credit/placement by examination:** AP, CLEP, IB, SAT, ACT, institutional tests. 30 credit hours maximum toward bachelor's degree. **Support services:** Pre-admission summer program, study skills assistance, tutoring, writing center.

**Majors. Biology:** General. **Business:** Business admin, e-commerce. **Communications:** Journalism, public relations. **Computer sciences:** General. **Education:** Early childhood, elementary, middle, music, physical, special. **English:** English lit, technical writing. **Family/consumer sciences:** Food/nutrition. **Foreign languages:** General. **Health:** Clinical lab science, communication disorders. **History:** General. **Math:** General. **Parks/recreation:** Sports admin. **Philosophy/religion:** Philosophy, religion. **Physical sciences:** Chemistry. **Psychology:** General. **Public administration:** Social work. **Social sciences:** Political science, sociology. **Visual/performing arts:** Art, art history/conservation, dance, dramatic, studio arts.

**Most popular majors.** Biology 6%, business/marketing 20%, communications/journalism 7%, education 19%, psychology 8%, social sciences 8%, visual/performing arts 14%.

**Computing on campus.** 250 workstations in dormitories, library, computer center, student center. Dormitories linked to campus network. Online course registration, helpline, student web hosting, wireless network available.

**Student life. Freshman orientation:** Available. 3-day session in June. **Policies:** First and second year students are required to live on campus unless living with parents within 50 miles. **Housing:** Guaranteed on-campus for freshmen. Coed dorms, single-sex dorms, apartments, fraternity/sorority housing, substance-free housing available. $100 deposit. **Activities:** Bands, campus ministries, choral groups, dance, drama, international student organizations, literary magazine, music ensembles, Model UN, radio station, student government, student newspaper, symphony orchestra, TV station, 115 clubs and organizations.

**Athletics.** NCAA. **Intercollegiate:** Baseball M, basketball, cross-country, golf, soccer, softball W, tennis, track and field, volleyball W. **Intramural:** Badminton, basketball, cross-country, fencing, football (non-tackle), football (tackle) M, golf, handball, racquetball, soccer, softball, swimming, table tennis, tennis, volleyball. **Team name:** Eagles.

**Student services.** Adult student services, alcohol/substance abuse counseling, career counseling, student employment services, financial aid counseling, health services, minority student services, personal counseling, placement for graduates, veterans' counselor.

**Contact.** E-mail: admissions@winthrop.edu
Phone: (803) 323-2191 Toll-free number: (800) 763-0230
Fax: (803) 323-2137
Debi Barber, Director of Admissions, Winthrop University, 701 Oakland Avenue, Rock Hill, SC 29733

---

## Wofford College
### Spartanburg, South Carolina
### www.wofford.edu

**CB member**
**CB code: 5912**

- Private 4-year liberal arts college affiliated with United Methodist Church
- Residential campus in small city
- 1,316 degree-seeking undergraduates: 1% part-time, 47% women, 6% African American, 2% Asian American, 2% Hispanic American, 1% international
- 53% of applicants admitted
- SAT or ACT with writing, application essay required
- 77% graduate within 6 years; 47% enter graduate study

**General.** Founded in 1854. Regionally accredited. Opportunities for summer research "Community of Scholars," studies abroad, service learning, and environmental studies. **Degrees:** 266 bachelor's awarded. **ROTC:** Army. **Location:** 70 miles from Charlotte, North Carolina, 180 miles from Atlanta. **Calendar:** 4-1-4, limited summer session. **Full-time faculty:** 106 total; 93% have terminal degrees, 8% minority, 39% women. **Part-time faculty:** 27 total; 56% have terminal degrees, 11% minority, 33% women. **Class size:** 64% < 20, 34% 20-39, less than 1% 40-49, 1% 50-99. **Special facilities:** National arboretum, South Carolina Methodist Archives.

**Freshman class profile.** 2,354 applied, 1,256 admitted, 385 enrolled.

| Mid 50% test scores | | Rank in top tenth: | 58% |
|---|---|---|---|
| SAT critical reading: | 560-680 | End year in good standing: | 92% |
| SAT math: | 570-680 | Return as sophomores: | 93% |
| SAT writing: | 560-660 | Out-of-state: | 42% |
| ACT composite: | 22-27 | Live on campus: | 98% |
| GPA 3.50 or higher: | 82% | International: | 1% |
| GPA 3.0-3.49: | 14% | Fraternities: | 40% |
| GPA 2.0-2.99: | 4% | Sororities: | 51% |
| Rank in top quarter: | 87% | | |

**Basis for selection.** High school record, including AP courses, most important. Test scores important. School recommendation, leadership, extracurricular activities considered. Interview recommended.

**High school preparation.** 20 units recommended. Recommended units include English 4, mathematics 4, social studies 2, history 1, (laboratory 3), foreign language 3, computer science 1, visual/performing arts 1 and academic electives 1.

**2007-2008 Annual costs.** Tuition/fees: $27,830. Room/board: $7,705. Books/supplies: $907. Personal expenses: $1,800.

**Financial aid. Non-need-based:** Scholarships awarded for academics, athletics, leadership, music/drama, religious affiliation, ROTC, state residency.

**Application procedures. Admission:** Closing date 2/1 (postmark date). $50 fee, may be waived for applicants with need. Application may be submitted online. Admission notification 3/15. Must reply by 5/1. Must be admitted by December 15 to be eligible for Wofford Scholars (academic merit scholarship) program. **Financial aid:** Priority date 3/15; no closing date. FAFSA required. Applicants notified on a rolling basis starting 3/31; must reply by 5/1.

**Academics.** January interim program devoted to internships, foreign travel, independent study, and other nontraditional academic pursuits. **Special study options:** Accelerated study, combined bachelor's/graduate degree, cross-registration, double major, dual enrollment of high school students, independent study, internships, liberal arts/career combination, student-designed major, study abroad, teacher certification program, Washington semester. **Credit/placement by examination:** AP, CLEP, IB. 30 credit hours maximum toward bachelor's degree. Chemistry majors must validate AP score of 4 in chemistry by successfully passing a departmental test. **Support services:** Tutoring, writing center.

**Majors. Biology:** General. **Business:** Accounting, finance, international, managerial economics. **Computer sciences:** General, computer science. **English:** English lit. **Foreign languages:** Chinese, French, German, Spanish. **History:** General. **Liberal arts:** Arts/sciences. **Math:** General. **Philosophy/religion:** Philosophy, religion. **Physical sciences:** Chemistry, physics. **Psychology:** General. **Social sciences:** Economics, sociology, U.S. government. **Visual/performing arts:** Art history/conservation, theater design.

**Most popular majors.** Biology 19%, business/marketing 23%, English 7%, foreign language 8%, physical sciences 6%, social sciences 15%.

**Computing on campus.** 250 workstations in library, computer center, student center. Dormitories linked to campus network. Commuter students can connect to campus network. Online course registration, online library, helpline, student web hosting, wireless network available.

**Student life. Freshman orientation:** Mandatory. Preregistration for classes offered. **Policies:** Honor code and honor council. **Housing:** Guaranteed on-campus for all undergraduates. Coed dorms, apartments, substance-free housing available. $300 nonrefundable deposit, deadline 5/1. Students not living with immediate family member must secure permission to live off-campus. **Activities:** Bands, campus ministries, choral groups, drama, literary magazine, music ensembles, student government, student newspaper, Fellowship of Christian Athletes, Baptist student union, Association of African-American Students, student volunteer services, College Republicans, College Democrats, Lion's Club, Rotaract Club.

**Athletics.** NCAA. **Intercollegiate:** Baseball M, basketball, cross-country, football (tackle) M, golf, rifle, soccer, tennis, track and field, volleyball W. **Intramural:** Basketball, football (non-tackle), soccer, softball, volleyball. **Team name:** Terriers.

**Student services.** Alcohol/substance abuse counseling, campus ministries, career counseling, student employment services, financial aid counseling, health services, minority student services, personal counseling, placement for graduates. **Physically disabled:** Services for visually, speech, hearing impaired.

**Contact.** E-mail: admission@wofford.edu
Phone: (864) 597-4130 Fax: (864) 597-4147
Jennifer Page, Director of Admission, Wofford College, 429 North Church Street, Spartanburg, SC 29303-3663

# South Dakota

## Augustana College
**Sioux Falls, South Dakota**
www.augie.edu

CB member
CB code: 6015

- Private 4-year liberal arts college affiliated with Evangelical Lutheran Church in America
- Residential campus in small city
- 1,718 degree-seeking undergraduates: 6% part-time, 62% women, 2% African American, 2% Asian American, 1% international
- 27 degree-seeking graduate students
- 82% of applicants admitted
- SAT or ACT (ACT writing optional), application essay required
- 65% graduate within 6 years; 25% enter graduate study

**General.** Founded in 1860. Regionally accredited. **Degrees:** 388 bachelor's awarded; master's offered. **Location:** 160 miles from Omaha, Nebraska, 230 miles from Minneapolis-St. Paul. **Calendar:** 4-1-4, limited summer session. **Full-time faculty:** 118 total; 77% have terminal degrees, 2% minority, 44% women. **Part-time faculty:** 73 total; 18% have terminal degrees, 1% minority, 52% women. **Class size:** 51% < 20, 45% 20-39, less than 1% 40-49, 3% 50-99, less than 1% >100. **Special facilities:** Western studies museum and archives, archeology lab, liturgical art center, prairie garden, ASL laboratory.

**Freshman class profile.** 1,353 applied, 1,106 admitted, 432 enrolled.

| Mid 50% test scores | | | |
|---|---|---|---|
| SAT critical reading: | 490-640 | Rank in top quarter: | 60% |
| SAT math: | 530-630 | Rank in top tenth: | 30% |
| ACT composite: | 22-27 | End year in good standing: | 94% |
| GPA 3.50 or higher: | 67% | Return as sophomores: | 78% |
| GPA 3.0-3.49: | 22% | Out-of-state: | 58% |
| GPA 2.0-2.99: | 10% | Live on campus: | 97% |
| | | International: | 2% |

**Basis for selection.** High school transcript, test scores, 1 recommendation, and writing sample required. Minimum requirements: 20 ACT (or equivalent SAT), 2.75 GPA, class rank at 50% or higher. Interview recommended for all; supplementary essay questions/materials required for students who do not meet minimum admission requirements.

**High school preparation.** 16 units recommended. Recommended units include English 4, mathematics 4, social studies 3, science 4 (laboratory 3) and foreign language 2. 1 unit fine arts and 1/2 unit computer science also recommended.

**2008-2009 Annual costs.** Tuition/fees: $22,452. Room/board: $5,920. Books/supplies: $800. Personal expenses: $800.

**2007-2008 Financial aid. Need-based:** 360 full-time freshmen applied for aid; 290 were judged to have need; 290 of these received aid. Average need met was 97%. Average scholarship/grant was $14,219; average loan $5,374. 64% of total undergraduate aid awarded as scholarships/grants, 36% as loans/jobs. **Non-need-based:** Awarded to 1,697 full-time undergraduates, including 458 freshmen. Scholarships awarded for academics, alumni affiliation, art, athletics, leadership, minority status, music/drama, religious affiliation, state residency.

**Application procedures. Admission:** Priority date 1/15; deadline 9/1. No application fee. Application may be submitted online. Admission notification on a rolling basis beginning on or about 10/1. Must reply by May 1 or within 3 week(s) if notified thereafter. **Financial aid:** Priority date 3/1; no closing date. FAFSA required. Applicants notified on a rolling basis starting 3/15; must reply within 3 week(s) of notification.

**Academics. Special study options:** Combined bachelor's/graduate degree, cross-registration, distance learning, double major, honors, independent study, internships, liberal arts/career combination, student-designed major, study abroad, teacher certification program, urban semester, Washington semester. **Credit/placement by examination:** AP, CLEP, IB, SAT, ACT, institutional tests. 32 credit hours maximum toward bachelor's degree. **Support services:** Learning center, pre-admission summer program, reduced course load, remedial instruction, study skills assistance, tutoring, writing center.

**Majors. Biology:** General. **Business:** General, accounting, business admin, communications, management information systems. **Communications:** General, journalism. **Computer sciences:** Computer science. **Education:** Art, biology, Deaf/hearing impaired, elementary, emotionally handicapped, English, French, German, history, learning disabled, mathematics, mentally handicapped, multicultural, music, physical, physically handicapped, physics, psychology, secondary, social studies, Spanish, special, speech, speech impaired. **Engineering:** Physics. **English:** English lit. **Foreign languages:** General, French, German, sign language interpretation, Spanish. **Health:** Athletic training, audiology/speech pathology, clinical lab science, clinical lab technology, communication disorders, nursing (RN), predental, premedicine, prepharmacy, preveterinary. **History:** General. **Interdisciplinary:** Global studies. **Math:** General. **Parks/recreation:** Exercise sciences, health/fitness, sports admin. **Philosophy/religion:** Philosophy, religion. **Physical sciences:** Chemistry, physics. **Protective services:** Forensics. **Psychology:** General. **Social sciences:** Economics, political science, sociology. **Theology:** Sacred music. **Visual/performing arts:** Art, dramatic.

**Most popular majors.** Biology 8%, business/marketing 17%, education 20%, health sciences 12%, psychology 6%, social sciences 9%.

**Computing on campus.** 255 workstations in dormitories, library, computer center, student center. Dormitories wired for high-speed internet access and linked to campus network. Commuter students can connect to campus network. Online course registration, online library, helpline, repair service, wireless network available.

**Student life. Freshman orientation:** Mandatory. Preregistration for classes offered. Begins on move-in day and extends through first week of class. **Housing:** Guaranteed on-campus for all undergraduates. Coed dorms, special housing for disabled, apartments, substance-free housing available. $100 fully refundable deposit. 14 college-owned theme houses available to upperclassmen. **Activities:** Bands, campus ministries, choral groups, dance, drama, film society, literary magazine, music ensembles, musical theater, opera, radio station, student government, student newspaper, symphony orchestra, Lutheran-ELCA congregation, Fellowship of Christian Athletes, Circle K, Augie Democrats, College Republicans, Augie Green, Catholics in Action, Augustana Coalition for Social Justice.

**Athletics.** NCAA. **Intercollegiate:** Baseball M, basketball, cheerleading M, cross-country, football (tackle) M, golf, soccer W, softball W, tennis, track and field, volleyball W, wrestling M. **Intramural:** Baseball M, basketball, football (non-tackle), golf, racquetball, soccer, softball, triathlon, volleyball. **Team name:** Vikings.

**Student services.** Adult student services, alcohol/substance abuse counseling, campus ministries, career counseling, student employment services, financial aid counseling, health services, on-campus daycare, personal counseling, placement for graduates, veterans' counselor. **Physically disabled:** Services for visually, hearing impaired.

**Contact.** E-mail: admission@augie.edu
Phone: (605) 274-5516 Toll-free number: (800) 727-2844
Fax: (605) 274-5518
Nancy Davidson, Vice President for Enrollment, Augustana College, 2001 South Summit Avenue, Sioux Falls, SD 57197-9990

## Black Hills State University
**Spearfish, South Dakota**
www.bhsu.edu

CB code: 6042

- Public 4-year liberal arts and teachers college
- Commuter campus in small town
- 3,041 degree-seeking undergraduates
- 97% of applicants admitted
- SAT or ACT (ACT writing optional) required

**General.** Founded in 1883. Regionally accredited. Evening degree program available at Ellsworth Air Force Base campus in Rapid City. **Degrees:** 432 bachelor's, 33 associate awarded; master's offered. **ROTC:** Army. **Location:** 45 miles from Rapid City. **Calendar:** Semester, extensive summer session. **Full-time faculty:** 117 total; 71% have terminal degrees, 8% minority, 39% women. **Part-time faculty:** 73 total; 34% have terminal degrees, 6% minority, 48% women. **Class size:** 41% < 20, 49% 20-39, 5% 40-49, 5% 50-99, less than 1% >100.

**Freshman class profile.** 2,142 applied, 2,068 admitted, 1,149 enrolled.

| Mid 50% test scores | | | |
|---|---|---|---|
| | | GPA 2.0-2.99: | 39% |
| ACT composite: | 18-23 | Rank in top quarter: | 24% |
| GPA 3.50 or higher: | 28% | Rank in top tenth: | 6% |
| GPA 3.0-3.49: | 30% | Out-of-state: | 24% |

**Basis for selection.** For bachelor's degree programs, minimum ACT composite score of 18 or class rank in top 60% (in-state applicants), top half (out-of-state applicants), or minimum GPA 2.6 in required courses. Portfolio recommended.

**High school preparation.** 14 units required. Required units include English 4, mathematics 3, social studies 3, science 3 (laboratory 3). One fine arts required.

**2007-2008 Annual costs.** Tuition/fees: $5,441; $6,679 out-of-state. Reciprocity agreements reduce tuition for some out-of-state students . Room/board: $5,226. Books/supplies: $600. Personal expenses: $1,252.

**Financial aid.** All financial aid based on need.

**Application procedures. Admission:** Closing date 7/15. $20 fee. Application may be submitted online. Admission notification on a rolling basis. **Financial aid:** Closing date 2/15. FAFSA required. Applicants notified on a rolling basis starting 5/15; must reply within 3 week(s) of notification.

**Academics. Special study options:** Cooperative education, distance learning, double major, dual enrollment of high school students, honors, independent study, internships, study abroad, teacher certification program. **Credit/placement by examination:** AP, CLEP, ACT, institutional tests. 32 credit hours maximum toward bachelor's degree. **Support services:** Learning center, remedial instruction, study skills assistance, tutoring.

**Majors. Area/ethnic studies:** Native American. **Biology:** General. **Business:** Accounting, business admin, entrepreneurial studies, human resources, marketing, office management, tourism/travel. **Communications:** Media studies. **Education:** Art, biology, business, chemistry, elementary, English, foreign languages, history, kindergarten/preschool, mathematics, middle, music, physical, science, social science, special, speech, technology/industrial arts. **Engineering technology:** Industrial. **English:** English lit, speech/rhetoric. **Foreign languages:** Spanish. **Health:** Facilities admin. **History:** General. **Math:** General. **Parks/recreation:** General, exercise sciences, sports admin. **Physical sciences:** General, chemistry. **Psychology:** General. **Public administration:** Community org/advocacy. **Social sciences:** General, political science, sociology. **Visual/performing arts:** Art, commercial/advertising art.

**Computing on campus.** 500 workstations in dormitories, library, student center. Dormitories wired for high-speed internet access and linked to campus network. Commuter students can connect to campus network. Online course registration, online library, helpline, wireless network available.

**Student life. Freshman orientation:** Available. Preregistration for classes offered. **Housing:** Guaranteed on-campus for freshmen. Coed dorms, single-sex dorms, apartments available. $100 deposit. Married student housing. **Activities:** Bands, choral groups, drama, music ensembles, radio station, student government, student newspaper, TV station, Native American Special Services, Inter-Greek Council, United Ministry, Veterans Club, Young Democrats, Young Republicans.

**Athletics.** NAIA. **Intercollegiate:** Basketball, cross-country, football (tackle) M, golf W, softball W, track and field, volleyball W. **Intramural:** Archery, badminton, basketball, bowling, golf, skiing, soccer, softball, swimming, table tennis, tennis, volleyball. **Team name:** Yellow Jackets.

**Student services.** Campus ministries, career counseling, student employment services, financial aid counseling, health services, on-campus daycare, personal counseling, placement for graduates, veterans' counselor. **Physically disabled:** Services for visually, speech, hearing impaired.

**Contact.** E-mail: admissions@bhsu.edu
Phone: (605) 642-6343 Toll-free number: (800) 255-2478
Fax: (605) 642-6022
Beth Azevedo, Dean of Enrollment, Black Hills State University, University Street Box 9502, Spearfish, SD 57799-9502

## Dakota State University
**Madison, South Dakota**
www.dsu.edu                                    CB code: 6247

- Public 4-year university
- Residential campus in small town
- 1,403 degree-seeking undergraduates: 21% part-time, 49% women, 1% African American, 1% Asian American, 1% Hispanic American, 1% Native American, 1% international
- 184 degree-seeking graduate students
- 97% of applicants admitted
- SAT or ACT (ACT writing optional) required
- 48% graduate within 6 years

**General.** Founded in 1881. Regionally accredited. All degree-seeking undergraduates participate in the Wireless Mobile Computing Initiative. Students are provided with: a TabletPC, licensed software installed, ubiquitous access to wireless network, repair components not covered by warranty or accidental damage protection plan, and access to licensed software installed on Citrix servers - support of graphics/math/analytical applications. Students are assessed a fee each semester for these services. **Degrees:** 209 bachelor's, 37 associate awarded; master's, doctoral offered. **ROTC:** Army, Air Force. **Location:** 45 miles from Sioux Falls. **Calendar:** Semester, limited summer session. **Full-time faculty:** 82 total; 74% have terminal degrees, 6% minority, 33% women. **Part-time faculty:** 31 total; 29% have terminal degrees, 61% women. **Class size:** 58% < 20, 40% 20-39, 1% 40-49, 1% 50-99, less than 1% >100.

**Freshman class profile.** 472 applied, 457 admitted, 236 enrolled.

| Mid 50% test scores | | | |
|---|---|---|---|
| ACT composite: | 18-25 | Rank in top tenth: | 6% |
| GPA 3.50 or higher: | 32% | Return as sophomores: | 71% |
| GPA 3.0-3.49: | 33% | Out-of-state: | 17% |
| GPA 2.0-2.99: | 32% | Live on campus: | 90% |
| Rank in top quarter: | 25% | International: | 1% |

**Basis for selection.** All students must be either in top 60% of class or have minimum ACT composite scores of 18, or have high school minimum GPA of 2.6 in core courses. Underqualified applicants considered. **Home-schooled:** State high school equivalency certificate required.

**High school preparation.** Recommended units include English 4, mathematics 3, social studies 3, science 3 (laboratory 3). 1 fine arts required, 0.5 computer studies.

**2007-2008 Annual costs.** Tuition/fees: $6,045; $7,283 out-of-state. Reciprocity agreements reduce tuition for some out-of-state students. Room/board: $4,374. Books/supplies: $850. Personal expenses: $1,937.

**2006-2007 Financial aid. Need-based:** Average need met was 85%. Average scholarship/grant was $3,184; average loan $3,322. 27% of total undergraduate aid awarded as scholarships/grants, 73% as loans/jobs. **Non-need-based:** Scholarships awarded for academics, alumni affiliation, art, athletics, leadership, minority status, music/drama, state residency. **Additional information:** Application deadline for grants and scholarships March 1. No deadline for loan and job applications.

**Application procedures. Admission:** No deadline. $20 fee. Application may be submitted online. Admission notification on a rolling basis. **Financial aid:** Priority date 3/1; no closing date. FAFSA required. Applicants notified on a rolling basis starting 4/1; must reply within 2 week(s) of notification.

**Academics.** Health information management degree, master of science in information systems, master of science in education in educational technology, and master of science in information assurance offered online. **Special study options:** Cooperative education, cross-registration, distance learning, double major, dual enrollment of high school students, ESL, honors, independent study, internships, teacher certification program. **Credit/placement by examination:** AP, CLEP, SAT, ACT, institutional tests. 16 credit hours maximum toward associate degree, 32 toward bachelor's. **Support services:** Learning center, reduced course load, remedial instruction, study skills assistance, tutoring, writing center.

**Majors. Biology:** General. **Business:** Accounting, business admin, finance, marketing. **Computer sciences:** General, computer graphics, information systems, security. **Education:** Biology, business, computer, elementary, English, mathematics, physical. **English:** English lit. **Health:** Medical records admin, respiratory therapy technology. **Parks/recreation:** Exercise sciences. **Physical sciences:** General. **Science technology:** Chemical. **Other:** Biology for Information Systems, Elementary Educ/Spec Learning Behavior, English for Information Systems, Mathematics for Information Systems.

**Most popular majors.** Business/marketing 24%, computer/information sciences 37%, education 24%.

**Computing on campus.** PC or laptop required. Dormitories wired for high-speed internet access and linked to campus network. Commuter students can connect to campus network. Online course registration, online library, helpline, student web hosting, wireless network available.

**Student life. Freshman orientation:** Mandatory. Preregistration for classes offered. **Housing:** Guaranteed on-campus for freshmen. Coed dorms, single-sex dorms, apartments, substance-free housing available. $50 fully refundable deposit. Apartment style residence halls available. **Activities:** Bands, choral groups, dance, drama, literary magazine, music ensembles, musical theater, radio station, student government, student newspaper.

**Athletics.** NAIA. **Intercollegiate:** Archery M, baseball M, basketball, cheerleading, cross-country, football (tackle) M, soccer, softball W, tennis, track and field, volleyball W. **Intramural:** Racquetball, table tennis, tennis. **Team name:** Trojans.

**Student services.** Alcohol/substance abuse counseling, campus ministries, career counseling, student employment services, financial aid counseling, health services, minority student services, personal counseling, placement for graduates, veterans' counselor. **Physically disabled:** Services for visually, speech, hearing impaired.

**Contact.** E-mail: yourfuture@dsu.edu
Phone: (605) 256-5139 Toll-free number: (888) 378-9988
Fax: (605) 256-5020
Amy Crissinger, Director of Admission, Dakota State University, 820 North Washington Avenue, Madison, SD 57042

## Dakota Wesleyan University
### Mitchell, South Dakota
### www.dwu.edu
**CB code: 6155**

- Private 4-year university and liberal arts college affiliated with United Methodist Church
- Commuter campus in large town
- 756 degree-seeking undergraduates: 4% part-time, 56% women, 4% African American, 1% Asian American, 4% Hispanic American, 3% Native American, 1% international
- 32 degree-seeking graduate students
- 68% of applicants admitted
- SAT or ACT (ACT writing optional) required
- 38% graduate within 6 years

**General.** Founded in 1885. Regionally accredited. **Degrees:** 121 bachelor's, 63 associate awarded; master's offered. **Location:** 70 miles from Sioux Falls. **Calendar:** Semester, limited summer session. **Full-time faculty:** 51 total; 69% have terminal degrees, 55% women. **Part-time faculty:** 45 total; 4% have terminal degrees, 69% women. **Class size:** 70% < 20, 28% 20-39, less than 1% 40-49, less than 1% 50-99. **Special facilities:** Observatory.

**Freshman class profile.** 564 applied, 385 admitted, 156 enrolled.

| Mid 50% test scores | | | |
|---|---|---|---|
| SAT critical reading: | 430-540 | Return as sophomores: | 68% |
| SAT math: | 370-520 | Out-of-state: | 29% |
| ACT composite: | 18-23 | Live on campus: | 87% |
| End year in good standing: | 91% | International: | 7% |

**Basis for selection.** High school record, test scores, school activities, personal interview considered. Recommendations and personal interview used for marginal students. **Homeschooled:** Transcript of courses and grades required. Meeting with an admissions counselor and placement testing when appropriate. **Learning Disabled:** For special assistance, documentation of student's learning disability required.

**High school preparation.** Recommended units include English 4, mathematics 4, social studies 4, history 3, science 3 (laboratory 1) and foreign language 2.

**2007-2008 Annual costs.** Tuition/fees: $17,500. Room/board: $5,180. Books/supplies: $800. Personal expenses: $1,200.

**2007-2008 Financial aid. Need-based:** 55% of total undergraduate aid awarded as scholarships/grants, 45% as loans/jobs. **Non-need-based:** Scholarships awarded for academics, alumni affiliation, art, athletics, leadership, minority status, music/drama, religious affiliation.

**Application procedures. Admission:** Priority date 4/1; deadline 8/25 (receipt date). $25 fee, may be waived for applicants with need. Application may be submitted online. Admission notification on a rolling basis. **Financial aid:** Priority date 4/15; no closing date. FAFSA required. Applicants notified on a rolling basis starting 3/1; must reply within 2 week(s) of notification.

**Academics. Special study options:** Cross-registration, distance learning, double major, dual enrollment of high school students, exchange student, honors, independent study, internships, student-designed major, study abroad, teacher certification program, Washington semester. **Credit/placement by examination:** AP, CLEP, IB, SAT, ACT, institutional tests. 12 credit hours maximum toward associate degree, 63 toward bachelor's. **Support services:** Learning center, pre-admission summer program, reduced course load, remedial instruction, study skills assistance, tutoring, writing center.

**Majors. Biology:** General. **Business:** General, accounting. **Communications:** General, journalism. **Computer sciences:** Web page design. **Conservation:** Wildlife. **Education:** General, art, biology, business, elementary, English, mathematics, music, physical, science, social science, social studies, special. **English:** Creative writing, English lit. **Health:** Athletic training, predental, premedicine, prepharmacy, preveterinary. **History:** General. **Interdisciplinary:** Behavioral sciences. **Legal studies:** Prelaw. **Math:** General. **Parks/recreation:** Exercise sciences, sports admin. **Philosophy/religion:** Religion. **Protective services:** Criminal justice. **Psychology:** General. **Public administration:** Human services. **Social sciences:** General, sociology. **Theology:** Sacred music. **Visual/performing arts:** Art, dramatic. **Other:** Public Service and Leadership.

**Most popular majors.** Biology 9%, business/marketing 27%, education 17%, health sciences 6%, psychology 6%, security/protective services 10%.

**Computing on campus.** 85 workstations in dormitories, library, computer center, student center. Dormitories wired for high-speed internet access and linked to campus network. Commuter students can connect to campus network. Online library, helpline, repair service, student web hosting, wireless network available.

**Student life. Freshman orientation:** Mandatory. Preregistration for classes offered. 2 days, the weekend before fall classes begin. In spring, held first day of finalization. **Housing:** Guaranteed on-campus for freshmen. Coed dorms, single-sex dorms, apartments, substance-free housing available. Honor housing available for upperclassmen; ADA rooms and apartments available. **Activities:** Concert band, choral groups, drama, literary magazine, music ensembles, student government, student newspaper, Variety of religious, ethnic, minority, political, and service groups.

**Athletics.** NAIA. **Intercollegiate:** Baseball M, basketball, cheerleading, cross-country, football (tackle) M, golf, soccer, softball W, track and field, volleyball W, wrestling M. **Intramural:** Basketball, softball, volleyball, weight lifting. **Team name:** Tigers.

**Student services.** Adult student services, alcohol/substance abuse counseling, campus ministries, career counseling, services for economically disadvantaged, student employment services, financial aid counseling, health services, minority student services, on-campus daycare, personal counseling, placement for graduates. **Physically disabled:** Services for visually, hearing impaired.

**Contact.** E-mail: admissions@dwu.edu
Phone: (605) 995-2650 Toll-free number: (800) 333-8506
Fax: (605) 995-2699
Amy Novak, Vice President for Enrollment Management, Dakota Wesleyan University, 1200 West University Avenue, Mitchell, SD 57301-4398

## Mount Marty College
### Yankton, South Dakota
### www.mtmc.edu
**CB code: 6416**

- Private 4-year liberal arts college affiliated with Roman Catholic Church
- Residential campus in large town
- 829 degree-seeking undergraduates: 26% part-time, 64% women
- 134 graduate students
- 68% of applicants admitted
- SAT or ACT (ACT writing optional) required

**General.** Founded in 1936. Regionally accredited. **Degrees:** 112 bachelor's, 28 associate awarded; master's offered. **ROTC:** Army. **Location:** 75 miles from Sioux Falls, 60 miles from Sioux City, Iowa. **Calendar:** Semester, limited summer session. **Full-time faculty:** 47 total; 64% have terminal degrees, 4% minority, 47% women. **Part-time faculty:** 33 total; 3% have terminal degrees, 9% women. **Class size:** 80% < 20, 19% 20-39, less than 1% 40-49, less than 1% 50-99, less than 1% >100.

**Freshman class profile.** 505 applied, 343 admitted, 237 enrolled.

| Mid 50% test scores | | | |
|---|---|---|---|
| SAT critical reading: | 410-540 | Rank in top quarter: | 33% |
| SAT math: | 440-500 | Rank in top tenth: | 14% |
| ACT composite: | 19-25 | End year in good standing: | 97% |
| GPA 3.50 or higher: | 50% | Return as sophomores: | 77% |
| GPA 3.0-3.49: | 25% | Out-of-state: | 60% |
| GPA 2.0-2.99: | 23% | Live on campus: | 95% |

**Basis for selection.** Academic record, test scores, GPA very important. Minimum 2.0 GPA and 18 ACT required for admission consideration. Interview recommended for all; audition required for scholarship recipients, music and theater programs. **Learning Disabled:** Students requesting disability services must submit letter requesting services and documentation to support diagnosed disability.

**2007-2008 Annual costs.** Tuition/fees: $17,468. Room/board: $5,058. Books/supplies: $760. Personal expenses: $1,512.

**Financial aid. Non-need-based:** Scholarships awarded for academics, art, athletics, leadership, music/drama, religious affiliation. **Additional information:** Prestige scholarships application deadline 2/1.

**Application procedures. Admission:** Closing date 8/30 (receipt date). $35 fee, may be waived for applicants with need. Application may be submitted online. Admission notification on a rolling basis. **Financial aid:** Priority date 3/1; no closing date. FAFSA, institutional form required. Applicants notified on a rolling basis starting 3/15; must reply within 2 week(s) of notification.

**Academics. Special study options:** Accelerated study, cooperative education, double major, dual enrollment of high school students, honors, independent study, internships, liberal arts/career combination, student-designed major, teacher certification program, weekend college. **Credit/placement by examination:** AP, CLEP, IB, ACT, institutional tests. 88 credit hours maximum toward associate degree, 24 toward bachelor's. **Support services:** Learning center, reduced course load, remedial instruction, study skills assistance, tutoring, writing center.

**Majors. Biology:** General. **Business:** Accounting, business admin. **Communications:** Digital media. **Computer sciences:** Computer science, information technology, programming. **Education:** Biology, chemistry, elementary, English, health, history, mathematics, middle, music, physical, science, secondary, social science, special. **English:** English lit. **Health:** Clinical lab science, medical radiologic technology/radiation therapy, nursing (RN). **History:** General. **Liberal arts:** Arts/sciences. **Math:** General. **Parks/recreation:** Facilities management. **Philosophy/religion:** Religion. **Physical sciences:** Chemistry. **Protective services:** Criminal justice, forensics. **Psychology:** General. **Social sciences:** General. **Visual/performing arts:** Dramatic. **Other:** Exercise and Wellness, Forensic Accounting, IT Management.

**Most popular majors.** Business/marketing 15%, education 17%, health sciences 23%, liberal arts 10%, social sciences 12%.

**Computing on campus.** PC or laptop required. 53 workstations in dormitories, library, computer center, student center. Dormitories wired for high-speed internet access and linked to campus network. Commuter students can connect to campus network. Online library, helpline, repair service, wireless network available.

**Student life. Freshman orientation:** Mandatory. Preregistration for classes offered. 3-day intensive orientation prior to beginning of fall semester. Orientation programs throughout academic year. **Policies:** Alcohol, tobacco and drug-free campus. Unmarried undergraduates under 21 required to live in college housing unless living with family. **Housing:** Guaranteed on-campus for freshmen. Single-sex dorms, special housing for disabled, substance-free housing available. $50 partly refundable deposit. **Activities:** Bands, campus ministries, choral groups, drama, literary magazine, music ensembles, musical theater, student government, student newspaper, outreach team, Habitat for Humanity, education club, nursing club, English club.

**Athletics.** NAIA. **Intercollegiate:** Baseball M, basketball, cross-country, soccer, softball W, track and field, volleyball W. **Intramural:** Basketball. **Team name:** Lancers.

**Student services.** Adult student services, alcohol/substance abuse counseling, campus ministries, career counseling, student employment services, financial aid counseling, health services, on-campus daycare, personal counseling, placement for graduates, veterans' counselor. **Learning disabled:** Comprehensive services available.

**Contact.** E-mail: mmcadmit@mtmc.edu
Phone: (800) 658-4552 Toll-free number: (800) 658-4552
Fax: (605) 668-1607
Brandi Tschumper, Vice President of Enrollment Management, Mount Marty College, 1105 West Eighth Street, Yankton, SD 57078

---

## National American University: Rapid City
### Rapid City, South Dakota
www.national.edu/rc      **CB code: 6464**

▸ For-profit 4-year business and technical college
▸ Residential campus in small city
▸ 475 degree-seeking undergraduates

**General.** Founded in 1941. Regionally accredited. **Degrees:** 292 bachelor's, 68 associate awarded; master's offered. **ROTC:** Army. **Location:** 400 miles from Denver. **Calendar:** Quarter, extensive summer session. **Full-time faculty:** 13 total; 23% have terminal degrees, 46% women. **Part-time faculty:** 34 total; 15% have terminal degrees, 53% women. **Special facilities:** Animal health laboratories, equine training center, athletic training facility.

**Basis for selection.** Open admission, but selective for some programs. All students required to complete university assessment testing prior to enrollment. Selective admission to equine management program; essay required. TOEFL and/or TWE used for placement. Interview recommended for all. **Homeschooled:** Completion of GED or accredited high school correspondence required.

**High school preparation.** Algebra helpful for computer technology. Science recommended for health program.

**2007-2008 Annual costs.** Tuition/fees: $11,835. Room/board: $4,443. Books/supplies: $400.

**Financial aid.** All financial aid based on need.

**Application procedures. Admission:** No deadline. $25 fee. Application may be submitted online. Admission notification on a rolling basis. **Financial aid:** No deadline. FAFSA, institutional form required. Applicants notified on a rolling basis; must reply within 4 week(s) of notification.

**Academics.** Applied management program for students with associate degree in health or technical fields who desire to continue education in management. **Special study options:** Accelerated study, cooperative education, distance learning, double major, independent study, internships, liberal arts/career combination. **Credit/placement by examination:** AP, CLEP, IB, institutional tests. **Support services:** Learning center, reduced course load, remedial instruction, tutoring.

**Majors. Agriculture:** Animal training. **Business:** Accounting, business admin, management information systems, marketing, personal/financial services. **Computer sciences:** General, LAN/WAN management, programming, systems analysis, web page design, webmaster. **Health:** Athletic training, facilities admin. **Legal studies:** Paralegal, prelaw.

**Most popular majors.** Business/marketing 38%, computer/information sciences 7%, legal studies 6%.

**Computing on campus.** 77 workstations in dormitories, library, computer center. Wireless network available.

**Student life. Freshman orientation:** Mandatory. Preregistration for classes offered. **Housing:** Coed dorms available. $100 deposit. **Activities:** Student government, student newspaper.

**Athletics.** NAIA. **Intercollegiate:** Rodeo, volleyball W. **Intramural:** Basketball, volleyball. **Team name:** Mavericks.

**Student services.** Career counseling, student employment services, financial aid counseling, personal counseling, placement for graduates, veterans' counselor.

**Contact.** E-mail: rcadmissions@national.edu
Phone: (605) 394-48200 Toll-free number: (800) 843-8892
Fax: (605) 394-4871
Angela Beck, Director of Admissions, National American University: Rapid City, 321 Kansas City Street, Rapid City, SD 57701

---

## Northern State University
### Aberdeen, South Dakota
www.northern.edu      **CB code: 6487**

▸ Public 4-year university and liberal arts college
▸ Residential campus in large town
▸ 1,725 degree-seeking undergraduates: 14% part-time, 58% women
▸ 131 degree-seeking graduate students
▸ 89% of applicants admitted
▸ ACT (writing optional) required
▸ 43% graduate within 6 years; 17% enter graduate study

**General.** Founded in 1901. Regionally accredited. Technology proficiency certification available for all degree programs. Emphasis on distance delivery technology in all degree programs, especially in all levels of teacher preparation. **Degrees:** 310 bachelor's, 19 associate awarded; master's offered. **Location:** 285 miles from Minneapolis-St. Paul. **Calendar:** Semester, limited summer session. **Full-time faculty:** 92 total; 82% have terminal degrees, 10% minority, 35% women. **Class size:** 42% < 20, 46% 20-39, 9%

40-49, 3% 50-99, less than 1% >100. **Special facilities:** E-learning center, center of excellence for international business.

**Freshman class profile.** 914 applied, 818 admitted, 347 enrolled.

| Mid 50% test scores | | Return as sophomores: | 62% |
|---|---|---|---|
| ACT composite: | 18-24 | Out-of-state: | 18% |

**Basis for selection.** Applicants to 4-year programs must meet following: GPA in required courses or rank in top 60% of graduating class. Minimum ACT composite score of 18. Minimum GPA 2.6. Applicants lacking required high school units admitted provisionally. Equivalent work must be completed within 2 years. Interview recommended for borderline applicants; portfolio recommended for art program.

**High school preparation.** 13 units required. Required units include English 4, mathematics 3, social studies 3, science 3 (laboratory 3). Mathematics units must be algebra or above; .5 fine arts required.

**2007-2008 Annual costs.** Tuition/fees: $5,280; $6,518 out-of-state. Reciprocity agreements reduce tuition for some out-of-state students . Room/board: $4,155. Books/supplies: $850. Personal expenses: $2,500.

**Financial aid. Non-need-based:** Scholarships awarded for academics, art, athletics, leadership, minority status, music/drama, state residency.

**Application procedures. Admission:** No deadline. $20 fee. Admission notification on a rolling basis. **Financial aid:** Priority date 3/1; no closing date. FAFSA required. Applicants notified by 4/15; must reply within 2 week(s) of notification.

**Academics. Special study options:** Accelerated study, cooperative education, cross-registration, distance learning, double major, dual enrollment of high school students, ESL, exchange student, external degree, honors, independent study, internships, liberal arts/career combination, student-designed major, study abroad, teacher certification program, Washington semester, weekend college. **Credit/placement by examination:** AP, CLEP, IB, institutional tests. 32 credit hours maximum toward bachelor's degree. **Support services:** Learning center, pre-admission summer program, reduced course load, remedial instruction, study skills assistance, tutoring, writing center.

**Majors. Biology:** General, ecology. **Business:** General, accounting, banking/financial services, business admin, finance, international, management information systems, marketing, office/clerical. **Computer sciences:** General. **Education:** General, art, business, early childhood, elementary, English, foreign languages, history, mathematics, multi-level teacher, music, physical, science, social science, special, speech. **English:** English lit. **Foreign languages:** French, German, Spanish. **Health:** Audiology/hearing, audiology/speech pathology, clinical lab science, speech pathology. **History:** General. **Math:** General. **Parks/recreation:** Health/fitness, sports admin. **Physical sciences:** Chemistry. **Psychology:** General. **Public administration:** Community org/advocacy, social work. **Social sciences:** Economics, political science, sociology. **Visual/performing arts:** Art.

**Computing on campus.** 900 workstations in dormitories, library, computer center, student center. Dormitories wired for high-speed internet access and linked to campus network. Commuter students can connect to campus network. Online course registration, online library, helpline, repair service, student web hosting, wireless network available.

**Student life. Freshman orientation:** Mandatory. Preregistration for classes offered. **Housing:** Coed dorms, single-sex dorms, special housing for disabled, apartments available. $50 deposit. Married graduate student housing available for summer session as well. **Activities:** Bands, choral groups, dance, drama, literary magazine, music ensembles, musical theater, student government, student newspaper, symphony orchestra, TV station, over 100 student organizations.

**Athletics.** NCAA. **Intercollegiate:** Baseball M, basketball, cheerleading, cross-country, football (tackle) M, golf, rugby, soccer W, softball W, swimming W, tennis, track and field, volleyball W, wrestling M. **Intramural:** Badminton, baseball M, basketball, field hockey W, softball, swimming, table tennis, tennis, volleyball, weight lifting. **Team name:** Wolves.

**Student services.** Adult student services, alcohol/substance abuse counseling, campus ministries, career counseling, services for economically disadvantaged, student employment services, financial aid counseling, health services, legal services, minority student services, on-campus daycare, personal counseling, placement for graduates, veterans' counselor, women's services. **Physically disabled:** Services for visually, speech, hearing impaired. **Learning disabled:** Comprehensive services available.

**Contact.** E-mail: admissions1@northern.edu
Phone: (605) 626-2544 Toll-free number: (800) 678-5330
Fax: (605) 626-2587
Allan Vogel, Director of Admissions, Northern State University, 1200 South Jay Street, Aberdeen, SD 57401-7198

## Oglala Lakota College
**Kyle, South Dakota**
www.olc.edu     CB code: 1430

- Public 4-year liberal arts and teachers college
- Commuter campus in small town
- 1,362 degree-seeking undergraduates
- 39 graduate students

**General.** Founded in 1971. Regionally accredited. Tribal College and a founding member of the American Indian Higher Education Consortium. **Degrees:** 43 bachelor's, 96 associate awarded; master's offered. **Location:** 90 miles from Rapid City, on Pine Ridge Indian Reservation. **Calendar:** Semester, extensive summer session. **Full-time faculty:** 72 total; 17% have terminal degrees, 33% minority, 49% women. **Part-time faculty:** 117 total; 6% have terminal degrees, 45% minority, 58% women.

**Freshman class profile.** 156 applied, 156 admitted, 156 enrolled.

**Basis for selection.** Open admission. Testing for placement.

**2008-2009 Annual costs.** Tuition/fees (projected): $2,900. Above rates for Native Americans. Non-Native American students pay tuition rate of $2,940 and $98 per credit hour. Books/supplies: $260. Personal expenses: $450.

**Financial aid. Additional information:** Deadline for applications for Bureau of Indian Affairs Higher Education Grants, is March 15; applicants notified early summer.

**Application procedures. Admission:** No deadline. No application fee. Application must be submitted on paper. **Financial aid:** No deadline. Applicants notified on a rolling basis.

**Academics.** College is one of 2 tribally chartered, fully accredited institutions in the United States. **Credit/placement by examination:** CLEP, institutional tests. 13 credit hours maximum toward bachelor's degree. **Support services:** Learning center, reduced course load, remedial instruction, tutoring.

**Majors. Area/ethnic studies:** Native American. **Business:** Accounting, business admin, management information systems. **Computer sciences:** General. **Education:** Elementary. **History:** General. **Liberal arts:** Arts/sciences. **Public administration:** Human services, social work. **Social sciences:** Sociology.

**Computing on campus.** 175 workstations in library, student center. Dormitories wired for high-speed internet access. Wireless network available.

**Student life. Freshman orientation:** Available. Preregistration for classes offered. **Housing:** Coed dorms available. **Activities:** Student government, student newspaper, TV station.

**Athletics.** NJCAA. **Intercollegiate:** Basketball, cross-country, volleyball. **Team name:** Brave Hearts.

**Student services.** Career counseling, personal counseling.

**Contact.** Phone: (605) 455-6000 Fax: (605) 455-2787
Leslie Mesteth, Registrar, Oglala Lakota College, Box 490, Kyle, SD 57752-0490

## Presentation College
**Aberdeen, South Dakota**
www.presentation.edu     CB code: 6582

- Private 4-year business and health science college affiliated with Roman Catholic Church
- Commuter campus in large town
- 700 degree-seeking undergraduates
- SAT or ACT (ACT writing optional) required

**General.** Founded in 1951. Regionally accredited. **Degrees:** 113 bachelor's, 51 associate awarded. **Location:** 200 miles from Sioux Falls, 280 miles from Minneapolis-St. Paul. **Calendar:** Semester, extensive summer session. **Full-time faculty:** 37 total. **Part-time faculty:** 50 total.

## Freshman class profile.

| Mid 50% test scores | | GPA 2.0-2.99: | 33% |
|---|---|---|---|
| ACT composite: | 17-23 | Out-of-state: | 19% |
| GPA 3.50 or higher: | 28% | Live on campus: | 90% |
| GPA 3.0-3.49: | 29% | | |

**Basis for selection.** Academic GPA very important, followed by rigor of secondary school record and standardized test scores. Minimum ACT composite of 18 or combined SAT score of 860 (exclusive of Writing). ACT required for admission to radiologic technology program. COMPASS assessment used for math placement. TOEFL required for ESL students. **Home-schooled:** Official transcript from local schooling guild, detailed course descriptions, and textbooks used required. Letter of academic recommendation from primary educator also required.

**High school preparation.** 16 units recommended. Recommended units include English 4, mathematics 3, social studies 2 and science 2. CPR certificate required of nursing and allied health applicants.

**2007-2008 Annual costs.** Tuition/fees: $13,150. Room/board: $4,875. Books/supplies: $1,300. Personal expenses: $620.

**Application procedures. Admission:** Priority date 4/1; deadline 9/1 (receipt date). $25 fee. Application may be submitted online. Admission notification on a rolling basis. **Financial aid:** Priority date 4/1; no closing date. FAFSA required. Applicants notified on a rolling basis starting 5/1; must reply within 2 week(s) of notification.

**Academics. Special study options:** Distance learning, double major, dual enrollment of high school students, external degree, internships, liberal arts/career combination. **Credit/placement by examination:** CLEP, ACT, institutional tests. 15 credit hours maximum toward associate degree, 30 toward bachelor's. **Support services:** Learning center, reduced course load, remedial instruction, study skills assistance, tutoring.

**Majors. Business:** Business admin. **Communications:** General. **Health:** Health care admin, medical radiologic technology/radiation therapy, nursing (RN). **Parks/recreation:** General. **Public administration:** Social work.

**Computing on campus.** 180 workstations in dormitories, library, computer center. Dormitories wired for high-speed internet access and linked to campus network.

**Student life. Freshman orientation:** Mandatory. Preregistration for classes offered. **Housing:** Coed dorms available. $250 deposit, deadline 7/15. **Activities:** Drama, student government, student newspaper, Native American club.

**Athletics.** NAIA. **Intercollegiate:** Baseball M, basketball, cross-country, golf, soccer, softball W, volleyball W. **Intramural:** Basketball, volleyball W. **Team name:** Saints.

**Student services.** Adult student services, career counseling, student employment services, health services, personal counseling, placement for graduates, veterans' counselor.

**Contact.** E-mail: admit@presentation.edu
Phone: (605) 229-8492 Toll-free number: (800) 437-6060
Fax: (605) 229-8425
JoEllen Lindner, Vice President for Enrollment and Student Retention Services, Presentation College, 1500 North Main Street, Aberdeen, SD 57401

## Sinte Gleska University
**Mission, South Dakota**
www.sintegleska.edu/ CB code: 7328

- Public 4-year university and liberal arts college
- Commuter campus in rural community

**General.** Founded in 1970. Regionally accredited. **Location:** 90 miles from Pierre, 240 miles from Sioux Falls. **Calendar:** Semester.

**Annual costs/financial aid.** Tuition/fees (2007-2008): $3,250. Books/supplies: $500. Personal expenses: $500. Need-based financial aid available to full-time and part-time students.

**Contact.** Phone: (605) 747-2263
Registrar, Box 105, Mission, SD 57555

## South Dakota School of Mines and Technology
**Rapid City, South Dakota**
www.sdsmt.edu CB code: 6652

- Public 4-year university and engineering college
- Residential campus in small city
- 1,578 degree-seeking undergraduates: 12% part-time, 23% women, 1% African American, 1% Asian American, 1% Hispanic American, 3% Native American, 1% international
- 231 degree-seeking graduate students
- 88% of applicants admitted
- SAT or ACT (ACT writing optional) required
- 40% graduate within 6 years

**General.** Founded in 1885. Regionally accredited. **Degrees:** 227 bachelor's, 11 associate awarded; master's, doctoral offered. **ROTC:** Army. **Location:** 222 miles from Cheyenne, Wyoming. **Calendar:** Semester, limited summer session. **Full-time faculty:** 135 total; 74% have terminal degrees, 13% minority, 20% women. **Part-time faculty:** 19 total; 47% have terminal degrees, 5% minority, 42% women. **Class size:** 41% < 20, 45% 20-39, 7% 40-49, 5% 50-99, less than 1% >100. **Special facilities:** Geology/paleontology museum, engineering/mining experiment station, atmospheric science institute, camp-center for advanced manufacturing and production, advanced materials processing and joining lab, analytical characterization and testing laboratory, additive manufacturing laboratory, center for accelerated applications at the nanoscale.

**Freshman class profile.** 814 applied, 720 admitted, 353 enrolled.

| Mid 50% test scores | | Rank in top tenth: | 23% |
|---|---|---|---|
| SAT critical reading: | 480-600 | Return as sophomores: | 76% |
| SAT math: | 540-630 | Out-of-state: | 35% |
| ACT composite: | 23-28 | Live on campus: | 75% |
| GPA 3.50 or higher: | 57% | International: | 2% |
| GPA 3.0-3.49: | 30% | Fraternities: | 19% |
| GPA 2.0-2.99: | 13% | Sororities: | 26% |
| Rank in top quarter: | 54% | | |

**Basis for selection.** Test scores and high school grades or class rank used in selection process. ACT Math and English scores and/or COMPASS math and English placement tests used for initial student placement. **Home-schooled:** Must have completed the GED with a combined score of 225 and a minimum of 40 on each test (paper based); or 2250 combined score and minimum of 410 on each test (computer based); or submit ACT/SAT scores and be reviewed by admissions review committee.

**High school preparation.** 20 units required. Required and recommended units include English 4, mathematics 3, social studies 3, science 3 (laboratory 3) and foreign language 2. One year of fine arts required. Incoming students assessed and found deficient in basic keyboarding/computer skills may be required to complete specific computer skills courses.

**2007-2008 Annual costs.** Tuition/fees: $5,670; $6,910 out-of-state. Reciprocity agreements reduce tuition for some out-of-state students. Room/board: $4,600. Books/supplies: $1,200. Personal expenses: $1,600.

**2006-2007 Financial aid. Need-based:** 263 full-time freshmen applied for aid; 132 were judged to have need; 132 of these received aid. Average need met was 80%. Average scholarship/grant was $3,675; average loan $2,432. 32% of total undergraduate aid awarded as scholarships/grants, 68% as loans/jobs. **Non-need-based:** Awarded to 535 full-time undergraduates, including 185 freshmen. Scholarships awarded for academics, athletics, leadership, ROTC. **Additional information:** Closing date for scholarship applications February 1.

**Application procedures. Admission:** No deadline. $20 fee. Application may be submitted online. Admission notification on a rolling basis beginning on or about 11/1. **Financial aid:** Priority date 3/15; no closing date. FAFSA required. Applicants notified on a rolling basis starting 5/1; must reply within 3 week(s) of notification.

**Academics.** Leading institution in friction stir-welding technology. Undergraduate teams compete in solar vehicle, ChemE Car, unmanned aero vehicle, SAE aero design, ASCE concrete canoe and bridge, SAE Formula SAE, SAE Mini Baja, ASME human-powered vehicle, SAE clean snowmobile challenge and SAMPE Composites national competitions. **Special study options:** Combined bachelor's/graduate degree, cooperative education, cross-registration, distance learning, double major, dual enrollment of high school students, ESL, independent study, internships, liberal arts/career combination, study abroad. Web-based technical management MS program. **Credit/placement by examination:** AP, CLEP, IB, SAT, ACT, institutional tests. 18 credit hours maximum toward associate degree, 36 toward bachelor's.

**Support services:** Learning center, reduced course load, remedial instruction, tutoring.

**Majors. Computer sciences:** Computer science. **Engineering:** Chemical, civil, computer, electrical, geological, industrial, mechanical, metallurgical. **Math:** General. **Physical sciences:** Chemistry, geology, physics.

**Most popular majors.** Computer/information sciences 8%, engineering/engineering technologies 76%, interdisciplinary studies 9%.

**Computing on campus.** 210 workstations in dormitories, library, computer center, student center. Dormitories wired for high-speed internet access and linked to campus network. Commuter students can connect to campus network. Online course registration, online library, helpline, repair service, student web hosting, wireless network available.

**Student life. Freshman orientation:** Available. Preregistration for classes offered. Orientation for students and parents in April and May. Adventure weekends/orientations for various groups in summer including special one for athletes. **Housing:** Guaranteed on-campus for freshmen. Coed dorms, special housing for disabled, fraternity/sorority housing, substance-free housing available. $100 deposit, deadline 8/15. **Activities:** Bands, campus ministries, choral groups, dance, drama, international student organizations, music ensembles, radio station, student government, student newspaper, Circle K, College Republicans, College Democrats, American Indian Science & Engineering Society, Habitat for Humanity, Muslim student association, Intervarsity Christian Fellowship.

**Athletics.** NAIA. **Intercollegiate:** Basketball, cross-country, football (tackle) M, golf, track and field, volleyball W. **Intramural:** Basketball, golf, racquetball, skiing, softball, swimming, track and field, volleyball. **Team name:** Hardrockers.

**Student services.** Adult student services, alcohol/substance abuse counseling, campus ministries, career counseling, student employment services, financial aid counseling, health services, minority student services, on-campus daycare, personal counseling, placement for graduates, veterans' counselor, women's services. **Physically disabled:** Services for visually, speech, hearing impaired.

**Contact.** E-mail: admissions@sdsmt.edu
Phone: (605) 394-2414 Toll-free number: (877) 877-6044
Fax: (605) 394-1979
Tex Claymore, Director of Admissions, South Dakota School of Mines and Technology, 501 East St. Joseph Street, Rapid City, SD 57701

## South Dakota State University
**Brookings, South Dakota**
www.sdstate.edu                                         CB code: 6653

- Public 4-year university
- Commuter campus in large town
- 9,353 degree-seeking undergraduates: 13% part-time, 50% women, 1% African American, 1% Asian American, 1% Hispanic American, 2% Native American, 1% international
- 1,388 graduate students
- 94% of applicants admitted
- SAT or ACT (ACT writing optional) required
- 53% graduate within 6 years

**General.** Founded in 1881. Regionally accredited. **Degrees:** 1,535 bachelor's, 30 associate awarded; master's, doctoral, first professional offered. **ROTC:** Army, Air Force. **Location:** 50 miles from Sioux Falls. **Calendar:** Semester, limited summer session. **Full-time faculty:** 493 total; 77% have terminal degrees, 12% minority, 40% women. **Part-time faculty:** 178 total; 25% have terminal degrees, 4% minority, 67% women. **Class size:** 38% < 20, 42% 20-39, 7% 40-49, 10% 50-99, 3% >100. **Special facilities:** Water resources research center, agricultural experiment station, cooperative extension service, Northern Great Plains biostress center, agricultural heritage museum, animal disease research and diagnostic laboratory, entrepreneur institute, GIS center of excellence, innovation research park, performing arts center.

**Freshman class profile.** 3,738 applied, 3,519 admitted, 2,022 enrolled.

| Mid 50% test scores | | | |
|---|---|---|---|
| ACT composite: | 20-25 | Rank in top tenth: | 14% |
| GPA 3.50 or higher: | 44% | Return as sophomores: | 77% |
| GPA 3.0-3.49: | 30% | Out-of-state: | 33% |
| GPA 2.0-2.99: | 24% | Live on campus: | 97% |
| Rank in top quarter: | 37% | International: | 1% |

**Basis for selection.** School achievement record and test scores most important. ACT not required of first-time freshmen over 24. **Home-schooled:** Transcript of courses and grades required. Must take ACT and receive scores of 18 Comp, 18 English, 20 Math, 17 Social Studies/Reasoning, and 17 Science Reasoning.

**High school preparation.** 14 units required. Required units include English 4, mathematics 3, social studies 3, science 3 (laboratory 3). 1 fine arts required for students graduating from SD high school. Will accept noncredit fine arts activities in out-of-state schools that do not require it.

**2007-2008 Annual costs.** Tuition/fees: $5,373; $6,611 out-of-state. Reduced out-of-state tuition for Minnesota students. Room/board: $5,240. Books/supplies: $976. Personal expenses: $2,004.

**2007-2008 Financial aid. Need-based:** 1,661 full-time freshmen applied for aid; 1,486 were judged to have need; 1,486 of these received aid. Average need met was 87%. Average scholarship/grant was $3,814; average loan $4,534. 32% of total undergraduate aid awarded as scholarships/grants, 68% as loans/jobs. **Non-need-based:** Awarded to 7,322 full-time undergraduates, including 1,660 freshmen. Scholarships awarded for academics, art, athletics, job skills, leadership, minority status, music/drama, ROTC, state residency.

**Application procedures. Admission:** No deadline. $20 fee. Application may be submitted online. Admission notification on a rolling basis. **Financial aid:** Priority date 3/11; no closing date. FAFSA required. Applicants notified on a rolling basis starting 4/1; must reply within 3 week(s) of notification.

**Academics.** Evening, weekend and other condensed degree-awarding classes available at Sioux Falls Center for Public Higher Education. **Special study options:** Accelerated study, combined bachelor's/graduate degree, cooperative education, cross-registration, distance learning, double major, dual enrollment of high school students, exchange student, honors, independent study, internships, liberal arts/career combination, New York semester, study abroad, teacher certification program. **Credit/placement by examination:** AP, CLEP, IB, ACT, institutional tests. 32 credit hours maximum toward bachelor's degree. **Support services:** Pre-admission summer program, reduced course load, remedial instruction, study skills assistance, tutoring, writing center.

**Majors. Agriculture:** General, agribusiness operations, agronomy, animal sciences, dairy, economics, horticulture, landscaping, mechanization, range science. **Biology:** General, biochemistry, microbiology. **Business:** Hotel/motel admin. **Communications:** Journalism. **Computer sciences:** General. **Conservation:** Management/policy, wildlife. **Education:** Agricultural, early childhood, music, secondary, voc/tech. **Engineering:** Agricultural, civil, electrical, mechanical, physics, software. **Engineering technology:** Construction, electrical, GIS, industrial management, industrial safety, manufacturing. **English:** English lit, speech/rhetoric. **Family/consumer sciences:** Apparel marketing, consumer economics, family resources, family studies, food/nutrition. **Foreign languages:** French, German, Spanish. **Health:** Athletic training, clinical lab science, nursing (RN), pharmaceutical sciences. **History:** General. **Interdisciplinary:** Global studies. **Liberal arts:** Arts/sciences. **Math:** General. **Parks/recreation:** Facilities management, health/fitness. **Physical sciences:** Chemistry, physics. **Psychology:** General. **Social sciences:** Economics, geography, political science, sociology. **Transportation:** Aviation, aviation management, flight instructor. **Visual/performing arts:** General, graphic design, interior design, music management. **Other:** Health promotion.

**Most popular majors.** Agriculture 12%, biology 6%, engineering/engineering technologies 11%, health sciences 21%, social sciences 12%.

**Computing on campus.** 728 workstations in dormitories, library, computer center, student center. Dormitories wired for high-speed internet access and linked to campus network. Commuter students can connect to campus network. Online course registration, online library, helpline, repair service, wireless network available.

**Student life. Freshman orientation:** Mandatory. Preregistration for classes offered. 2-day programs in June. 1-day programs later in the summer. **Policies:** Students out of high school for less than 2 years required to live in campus housing unless living with family. **Housing:** Guaranteed on-campus for freshmen. Coed dorms, special housing for disabled, apartments, fraternity/sorority housing, substance-free housing available. $50 fully refundable deposit. Limited single rooms with optional meal plan available for upperclassmen. **Activities:** Bands, choral groups, dance, drama, literary magazine, music ensembles, musical theater, radio station, student government, student newspaper, symphony orchestra, Students' Association, University Program Council, Golden Key Honor Society, Campus Crusade for Christ, Fellowship of Christian Athletes, Native American Club, Circle K International, Black Student Alliance, Geography Club.

**Athletics.** NCAA. **Intercollegiate:** Baseball M, basketball, cross-country, equestrian W, football (tackle) M, golf, soccer W, softball W, swimming, tennis, track and field, volleyball W, wrestling M. **Intramural:** Badminton, basketball, football (non-tackle), golf, racquetball, soccer W, softball, swimming, table tennis, track and field, volleyball, wrestling M. **Team name:** Jackrabbits.

**Student services.** Adult student services, alcohol/substance abuse counseling, campus ministries, career counseling, services for economically disadvantaged, student employment services, financial aid counseling, health services, legal services, minority student services, personal counseling, placement for graduates, veterans' counselor. **Physically disabled:** Services for visually, speech, hearing impaired.

**Contact.** E-mail: SDSU.Admissions@sdstate.edu
Phone: (605) 688-4121 Toll-free number: (800) 952-3541
Fax: (605) 688-6891
Tracy Welsh, Director of Admissions and High School Relations, South Dakota State University, Box 2201 SAD 200, Brookings, SD 57007-0649

## University of Sioux Falls
### Sioux Falls, South Dakota
www.usiouxfalls.edu                                    CB code: 6651

- Private 4-year liberal arts college affiliated with American Baptist Churches in the USA
- Residential campus in small city
- 1,490 degree-seeking undergraduates
- 1,628 graduate students
- 97% of applicants admitted
- SAT or ACT required

**General.** Founded in 1883. Regionally accredited. **Degrees:** 231 bachelor's, 2 associate awarded; master's offered. **Location:** 180 miles from Omaha, Nebraska. **Calendar:** 4-1-4, limited summer session. **Full-time faculty:** 65 total. **Part-time faculty:** 75 total. **Class size:** 58% < 20, 32% 20-39, 5% 40-49, 5% 50-99, less than 1% >100.

**Freshman class profile.** 638 applied, 621 admitted, 356 enrolled.

| Mid 50% test scores | | ACT composite: | 16-26 |
|---|---|---|---|
| SAT critical reading: | 390-480 | Out-of-state: | 40% |
| SAT math: | 430-470 | Live on campus: | 83% |

**Basis for selection.** Test scores, high school record, and rank in top half of graduating class important. Audition required for music, theater programs; portfolio recommended for art program.

**High school preparation.** Recommended units include English 4, mathematics 3, social studies 3, history 3 and science 2. One unit computer science recommended.

**2007-2008 Annual costs.** Tuition/fees: $17,940. Room/board: $5,400. Books/supplies: $640. Personal expenses: $2,000.

**Financial aid. Non-need-based:** Scholarships awarded for academics, alumni affiliation, art, athletics, job skills, leadership, minority status, music/drama, religious affiliation, state residency.

**Application procedures. Admission:** No deadline. $25 fee, may be waived for applicants with need. Admission notification on a rolling basis. **Financial aid:** Priority date 3/1; no closing date. FAFSA required. Applicants notified on a rolling basis starting 3/1; must reply within 2 week(s) of notification.

**Academics.** Degree completion program offered for adults 25 and older with 64 hours previous college education. **Special study options:** Accelerated study, cross-registration, distance learning, double major, dual enrollment of high school students, honors, independent study, internships, liberal arts/career combination, student-designed major, study abroad, teacher certification program, Washington semester. **Credit/placement by examination:** CLEP, institutional tests. 16 credit hours maximum toward bachelor's degree. **Support services:** Pre-admission summer program, reduced course load, remedial instruction, study skills assistance, tutoring, writing center.

**Majors. Biology:** General. **Business:** Accounting, business admin, hospitality admin, organizational behavior. **Communications:** Journalism. **Computer sciences:** General, computer science. **Education:** Art, elementary, health, multi-level teacher, music. **English:** English lit, speech/rhetoric. **History:** General. **Liberal arts:** Arts/sciences. **Math:** General, applied. **Parks/recreation:** Exercise sciences. **Philosophy/religion:** Religion. **Physical sciences:** Chemistry. **Psychology:** General. **Public administration:** Social work. **Social sciences:** General, political science, sociology. **Theology:** Theology. **Visual/performing arts:** Art, dramatic.

**Most popular majors.** Biology 6%, business/marketing 49%, education 18%.

**Computing on campus.** 75 workstations in dormitories, library, computer center, student center. Dormitories wired for high-speed internet access and linked to campus network. Commuter students can connect to campus network. Student web hosting available.

**Student life. Freshman orientation:** Available. Preregistration for classes offered. Held 2 days immediately preceding fall semester. **Policies:** No alcohol at university-sponsored events. **Housing:** Coed dorms, single-sex dorms, apartments available. $100 deposit. Freshmen, sophomores required to live in college housing unless over 20 years of age or given permission by director of residence life. **Activities:** Bands, choral groups, dance, drama, music ensembles, musical theater, opera, radio station, student government, student newspaper, symphony orchestra, TV station, nontraditional student association, student volunteer groups, religious organizations, Fellowship of Christian Athletes.

**Athletics.** NAIA. **Intercollegiate:** Baseball M, basketball, cheerleading M, cross-country, football (tackle) M, golf, soccer, softball W, tennis, track and field, volleyball W, wrestling M. **Intramural:** Basketball, golf, soccer, softball, table tennis, tennis, volleyball. **Team name:** Cougars.

**Student services.** Adult student services, alcohol/substance abuse counseling, campus ministries, career counseling, student employment services, financial aid counseling, health services, personal counseling, placement for graduates, veterans' counselor, women's services. **Physically disabled:** Services for hearing impaired.

**Contact.** E-mail: admissions@usiouxfalls.edu
Phone: (605) 331-6600 Toll-free number: (800) 888-1047
Fax: (605) 331-6615
Greg Fritz, Vice President of Admissions and Marketing, University of Sioux Falls, 1101 West 22nd Street, Sioux Falls, SD 57105-1699

## University of South Dakota
### Vermillion, South Dakota
www.usd.edu                    CB member
                               CB code: 6881

- Public 4-year university
- Residential campus in small town
- 6,046 degree-seeking undergraduates: 27% part-time, 62% women, 1% African American, 1% Asian American, 1% Hispanic American, 2% Native American
- 2,074 degree-seeking graduate students
- 80% of applicants admitted
- SAT and SAT Subject Tests or ACT (ACT writing optional), interview required
- 48% graduate within 6 years; 50% enter graduate study

**General.** Founded in 1862. Regionally accredited. **Degrees:** 764 bachelor's, 319 associate awarded; master's, doctoral, first professional offered. **ROTC:** Army. **Location:** 55 miles from Sioux Falls, 35 miles from Sioux City, Iowa. **Calendar:** Semester, extensive summer session. **Full-time faculty:** 366 total; 82% have terminal degrees, 11% minority, 44% women. **Part-time faculty:** 22 total; 50% have terminal degrees, 4% minority, 73% women. **Class size:** 46% < 20, 43% 20-39, 5% 40-49, 4% 50-99, 3% >100. **Special facilities:** Center for instructional design and delivery, center for disabilities, governmental research bureau, state data center, federal technical procurement center, geological survey, archaeology lab, speech and hearing center, disaster mental health institute.

**Freshman class profile.** 3,517 applied, 2,805 admitted, 1,178 enrolled.

| Mid 50% test scores | | Rank in top quarter: | 35% |
|---|---|---|---|
| SAT critical reading: | 420-540 | Rank in top tenth: | 14% |
| SAT math: | 490-590 | Return as sophomores: | 72% |
| ACT composite: | 20-25 | Out-of-state: | 30% |
| GPA 3.50 or higher: | 40% | Live on campus: | 85% |
| GPA 3.0-3.49: | 30% | Fraternities: | 16% |
| GPA 2.0-2.99: | 29% | Sororities: | 11% |

**Basis for selection.** Admission in good standing granted with 2.0 GPA or higher in required courses or 2.6 overall, rank in top 60% of class, or ACT composite score of 20 or above. Interview recommended for dental hygiene, nursing, physician assistant programs; audition recommended for music, theater programs; portfolio recommended for art progam.

**High school preparation.** 14 units required; 18 recommended. Required and recommended units include English 4, mathematics 3-4, social studies 3, science 3-4 (laboratory 3) and foreign language 2. 1 fine arts required.

**2007-2008 Annual costs.** Tuition/fees: $5,393; $6,631 out-of-state. Reciprocity agreement in place for Minnesota residents. Reduced tuition for

Iowa residents. Room/board: $5,174. Books/supplies: $750. Personal expenses: $2,000.

**2006-2007 Financial aid. Need-based:** 886 full-time freshmen applied for aid; 602 were judged to have need; 543 of these received aid. Average need met was 72%. Average scholarship/grant was $3,700; average loan $2,785. 29% of total undergraduate aid awarded as scholarships/grants, 71% as loans/jobs. **Non-need-based:** Awarded to 1,959 full-time undergraduates, including 606 freshmen. Scholarships awarded for academics, art, athletics, leadership, minority status, music/drama, ROTC.

**Application procedures. Admission:** No deadline. $20 fee. Application may be submitted online. Admission notification on a rolling basis beginning on or about 9/20. February 15 closing date for application to dental hygiene and nursing programs. **Financial aid:** Priority date 3/15; no closing date. FAFSA required. Applicants notified on a rolling basis starting 5/5.

**Academics. Special study options:** Accelerated study, combined bachelor's/graduate degree, cross-registration, distance learning, double major, dual enrollment of high school students, ESL, exchange student, external degree, honors, independent study, internships, liberal arts/career combination, student-designed major, study abroad, teacher certification program. **Credit/placement by examination:** AP, CLEP, institutional tests. 30 credit hours maximum toward bachelor's degree. **Support services:** Pre-admission summer program, reduced course load, remedial instruction, tutoring.

**Honors college/program.** University Honors Program open to students in all majors who displayed potential for honors work in high school through good grades, college preparatory curriculum, high ACT scores, and participation in school and community activities.

**Majors. Area/ethnic studies:** Native American. **Biology:** General. **Business:** Accounting, business admin, finance, managerial economics. **Communications:** General, journalism, media studies. **Computer sciences:** General. **Education:** Biology, chemistry, drama/dance, early childhood, elementary, English, foreign languages, French, German, history, kindergarten/preschool, mathematics, music, physical, physics, science, social science, Spanish, special, speech. **English:** English lit, speech/rhetoric. **Foreign languages:** French, German, Spanish. **Health:** Communication disorders, dental hygiene, health services admin, substance abuse counseling. **History:** General. **Interdisciplinary:** Global studies. **Liberal arts:** Arts/sciences. **Math:** General. **Parks/recreation:** General. **Philosophy/religion:** Philosophy. **Physical sciences:** Chemistry, geology, physics. **Protective services:** Criminal justice. **Psychology:** General. **Public administration:** Social work. **Social sciences:** Anthropology, economics, political science, sociology. **Visual/performing arts:** Art, arts management, dramatic, music performance, studio arts.

**Most popular majors.** Biology 6%, business/marketing 23%, communications/journalism 7%, education 11%, health sciences 11%, psychology 11%, security/protective services 7%, social sciences 7%.

**Computing on campus.** 877 workstations in dormitories, library, computer center, student center. Dormitories wired for high-speed internet access and linked to campus network. Commuter students can connect to campus network. Online course registration, online library, helpline, student web hosting, wireless network available.

**Student life. Freshman orientation:** Mandatory. Preregistration for classes offered. **Policies:** Students required to live in residence halls for first 2 years unless living in fraternity or sorority housing, or commuting from home. **Housing:** Guaranteed on-campus for freshmen. Coed dorms, special housing for disabled, apartments, fraternity/sorority housing, substance-free housing available. $100 partly refundable deposit, deadline 9/1. Apartments available for students with dependent children. **Activities:** Bands, choral groups, dance, drama, international student organizations, literary magazine, music ensembles, musical theater, opera, radio station, student government, student newspaper, symphony orchestra, TV station, Young Democrats, College Republicans, Campus Crusade for Christ, Chinese student association, gay/lesbian/bisexual alliance, Habitat for Humanity, nontraditional student association, political science league.

**Athletics.** NCAA. **Intercollegiate:** Basketball, cross-country, diving, football (tackle) M, golf, soccer W, softball W, swimming, tennis W, track and field. **Intramural:** Badminton, basketball, bowling, cross-country, football (non-tackle), golf, racquetball, soccer, softball, swimming, table tennis, tennis, track and field, volleyball. **Team name:** Coyotes.

**Student services.** Adult student services, alcohol/substance abuse counseling, campus ministries, career counseling, services for economically disadvantaged, student employment services, financial aid counseling, health services, legal services, minority student services, on-campus daycare, personal counseling, placement for graduates, veterans' counselor. **Physically disabled:** Services for visually, speech, hearing impaired.

**Contact.** E-mail: admission@usd.edu
Phone: (605) 677-5434 Toll-free number: (877) 269-6837
Fax: (605) 677-6753
Stephanie Moser, Director, University of South Dakota, 414 East Clark Street, Vermillion, SD 57069-2390

# Tennessee

## American Baptist College of ABT Seminary
**Nashville, Tennessee**
www.abcnash.edu                                    CB code: 2401

- Private 4-year Bible college affiliated with Baptist faith
- Commuter campus in very large city
- 108 degree-seeking undergraduates: 28% part-time, 31% women, 94% African American, 5% international
- Application essay required
- 84% graduate within 6 years; 52% enter graduate study

**General.** Founded in 1924. Accredited by ABHE. **Degrees:** 24 bachelor's, 3 associate awarded. **Calendar:** Semester, limited summer session. **Full-time faculty:** 7 total. **Part-time faculty:** 8 total.

**Freshman class profile.** 51 applied, 15 admitted, 15 enrolled.

| | | | |
|---|---|---|---|
| End year in good standing: | 92% | Live on campus: | 26% |
| Return as sophomores: | 93% | | |

**Basis for selection.** Open admission. Recommendations, personal essay, religious commitment important. Admissions committee selects applicants best qualified to benefit from opportunities offered by college.

**2007-2008 Annual costs.** Tuition/fees: $5,820. Room only: $1,800. Books/supplies: $440.

**Application procedures. Admission:** Closing date 7/1 (receipt date). $20 fee. Admission notification on a rolling basis. **Financial aid:** No deadline. FAFSA required. Applicants notified on a rolling basis; must reply within 2 week(s) of notification.

**Academics.** All students major in Bible studies or theology. Additional major in business administration optional. **Special study options:** Double major. **Credit/placement by examination:** CLEP, institutional tests.

**Majors. Area/ethnic studies:** African-American. **Business:** Business admin. **Education:** General, history, social science. **Liberal arts:** Arts/sciences. **Social sciences:** General. **Theology:** Bible, pastoral counseling, religious ed, theology.

**Computing on campus.** 15 workstations in library.

**Student life. Freshman orientation:** Mandatory. Preregistration for classes offered. **Housing:** Single-sex dorms, apartments available. **Activities:** Student government, student newspaper.

**Contact.** E-mail: mlockhart@abcnash.edu
Phone: (615) 256-1463 Fax: (615) 226-7855
Marcella Lockhart, Director of Enrollment Management, American Baptist College of ABT Seminary, 1800 Baptist World Center Drive, Nashville, TN 37207

## Aquinas College
**Nashville, Tennessee**                            CB member
www.aquinas-tn.edu                                 CB code: 7318

- Private 4-year nursing and liberal arts college affiliated with Roman Catholic Church
- Commuter campus in very large city
- 846 degree-seeking undergraduates
- 59% of applicants admitted

**General.** Founded in 1961. Regionally accredited. **Degrees:** 68 bachelor's, 121 associate awarded. **Location:** 1 mile from downtown, 195 miles from Knoxville. **Calendar:** Semester, limited summer session. **Full-time faculty:** 25 total. **Part-time faculty:** 60 total.

**Freshman class profile.**

| Mid 50% test scores | | SAT writing: | 490-620 |
|---|---|---|---|
| SAT critical reading: | 560-660 | ACT composite: | 18-25 |
| SAT math: | 460-600 | | |

**Basis for selection.** School achievement record, test scores important. **Homeschooled:** Transcript of courses and grades required. Must provide copy of transcript from accredited home school agency along with official ACT Report.

**High school preparation.** 20 units recommended. Recommended units include English 4, mathematics 3, social studies 3, science 3, foreign language 2 and academic electives 5.

**2007-2008 Annual costs.** Tuition/fees: $15,005. Additional $40 per-credit hour for nursing classes. Additional required fees for nursing and teacher education programs. Books/supplies: $1,000. Personal expenses: $1,500.

**Financial aid. Non-need-based:** Scholarships awarded for academics, alumni affiliation, leadership, religious affiliation.

**Application procedures. Admission:** Priority date 3/1; no deadline. $25 fee, may be waived for applicants with need. Application may be submitted online. Admission notification on a rolling basis. **Financial aid:** Priority date 3/1; no closing date. FAFSA required. Applicants notified on a rolling basis starting 3/1; must reply within 2 week(s) of notification.

**Academics. Special study options:** Accelerated study, independent study, liberal arts/career combination, teacher certification program. **Credit/placement by examination:** AP, CLEP, SAT, ACT, institutional tests. 30 credit hours maximum toward associate degree, 30 toward bachelor's. **Support services:** Learning center, reduced course load, remedial instruction, study skills assistance, tutoring, writing center.

**Majors. Business:** Business admin, management information systems. **Education:** Elementary. **Health:** Nursing (RN). **Liberal arts:** Arts/sciences.

**Computing on campus.** 50 workstations in library, computer center. Online library, helpline available.

**Student life. Freshman orientation:** Mandatory. **Policies:** Drug-free/alcohol-free campus. **Activities:** Choral groups, student government, Phi Beta Lambda, Delta Epsilon Sigma, Association of Student Nurses, Association for Supervision and Curriculum Development student chapter, Student Affairs Council, Frassati Society, Sigma Beta Delta,.

**Athletics. Team name:** Cavaliers.

**Student services.** Campus ministries, financial aid counseling.

**Contact.** E-mail: admissions@aquinas-tn.edu
Phone: (615) 297-7545 ext. 460 Toll-free number: (800) 649-9956
Fax: (615) 279-3893
Diane LeJeune, Director of Admissions, Aquinas College, 4210 Harding Road, Nashville, TN 37205-2086

## Austin Peay State University
**Clarksville, Tennessee**                          CB member
www.apsu.edu                                        CB code: 1028

- Public 4-year university and liberal arts college
- Commuter campus in small city
- 8,282 degree-seeking undergraduates: 27% part-time, 62% women, 16% African American, 2% Asian American, 4% Hispanic American, 1% Native American, 2% international
- 728 degree-seeking graduate students
- 91% of applicants admitted
- 33% graduate within 6 years

**General.** Founded in 1927. Regionally accredited. **Degrees:** 1,059 bachelor's, 133 associate awarded; master's offered. **ROTC:** Army, Air Force. **Location:** 45 miles from Nashville. **Calendar:** Semester, limited summer session. **Full-time faculty:** 299 total; 30% minority, 46% women. **Part-time faculty:** 222 total; 13% minority, 54% women. **Class size:** 39% < 20, 53% 20-39, 5% 40-49, 3% 50-99, less than 1% >100. **Special facilities:** Zoological museum.

**Freshman class profile.** 2,575 applied, 2,340 admitted, 1,412 enrolled.

| Mid 50% test scores | | | |
|---|---|---|---|
| SAT critical reading: | 440-550 | Rank in top tenth: | 15% |
| SAT math: | 450-510 | Return as sophomores: | 66% |
| ACT composite: | 19-24 | Out-of-state: | 13% |
| GPA 3.50 or higher: | 26% | Live on campus: | 37% |
| GPA 3.0-3.49: | 32% | International: | 2% |
| GPA 2.0-2.99: | 39% | Fraternities: | 4% |
| Rank in top quarter: | 39% | Sororities: | 3% |

**Basis for selection.** Rigor of secondary school record, GPA, standardized test scores very important. Four available admission categories: Unconditional, Conditional, Admission by Exception, or Admission by Alternative Standards. ACT/SAT is required for all first time freshman applicants under age 21, except for active duty military. All first time freshman applicants 21 years of age and older, except for active duty military, must submit official COMPASS assessment scores prior to admission. **Learning Disabled:** Students with learning disabilities are admitted as regular students.

**High school preparation.** 14 units required. Required units include English 4, mathematics 3, social studies 1, history 1, science 2 (laboratory 1) and foreign language 2. Mathematics units should be algebra I and II, 1 geometry or advanced mathematics. Social science units should be 1 social studies, 1 US history. Foreign language units must be in 1 language. 1 visual and/or performing arts also required.

**2007-2008 Annual costs.** Tuition/fees: $5,238; $15,514 out-of-state. Room/board: $5,510. Books/supplies: $1,404. Personal expenses: $1,575.

**2006-2007 Financial aid. Need-based:** 1,131 full-time freshmen applied for aid; 921 were judged to have need; 913 of these received aid. Average scholarship/grant was $3,996. 44% of total undergraduate aid awarded as scholarships/grants, 56% as loans/jobs. **Non-need-based:** Awarded to 2,762 full-time undergraduates, including 991 freshmen. Scholarships awarded for academics, art, athletics, leadership, music/drama, ROTC, state residency.

**Application procedures. Admission:** Closing date 7/27. $15 fee. Application may be submitted online. Admission notification on a rolling basis. **Financial aid:** Priority date 3/1; no closing date. FAFSA required. Applicants notified on a rolling basis starting 5/1.

**Academics. Special study options:** Accelerated study, cooperative education, distance learning, double major, dual enrollment of high school students, ESL, honors, independent study, internships, study abroad, teacher certification program. Service Members Opportunity College (associate and bachelor's degrees). **Credit/placement by examination:** AP, CLEP, SAT, ACT, institutional tests. 32 credit hours maximum toward associate degree, 64 toward bachelor's. **Support services:** Learning center, remedial instruction, study skills assistance, tutoring, writing center.

**Honors college/program.** Rank in the top 10% of high school class, have a minimum ACT composite score of 26, and have a commendable high school record.

**Majors. Agriculture:** General. **Biology:** General. **Business:** General, nonprofit/public. **Communications:** Media studies. **Computer sciences:** General. **Education:** Health, special. **Engineering technology:** General. **English:** English lit. **Foreign languages:** General, Spanish. **Health:** Clinical lab science, medical radiologic technology/radiation therapy, nursing (RN). **History:** General. **Liberal arts:** Arts/sciences. **Math:** General. **Parks/recreation:** Health/fitness. **Philosophy/religion:** Philosophy. **Physical sciences:** Chemistry, geology, physics. **Protective services:** Law enforcement admin. **Psychology:** General. **Public administration:** Social work. **Social sciences:** Political science, sociology. **Visual/performing arts:** Art.

**Most popular majors.** Business/marketing 20%, communications/journalism 6%, health sciences 12%, interdisciplinary studies 8%, liberal arts 7%, social sciences 6%.

**Computing on campus.** 760 workstations in dormitories, library, computer center, student center. Dormitories wired for high-speed internet access and linked to campus network. Commuter students can connect to campus network. Online course registration, online library, helpline, wireless network available.

**Student life. Freshman orientation:** Mandatory, $60 fee. Preregistration for classes offered. **Policies:** Alcohol not permitted on campus. **Housing:** Coed dorms, single-sex dorms, special housing for disabled, apartments, fraternity/sorority housing available. $100 fully refundable deposit, deadline 8/15. Honors dorm available. **Activities:** Bands, campus ministries, choral groups, dance, drama, literary magazine, music ensembles, musical theater, radio station, student government, student newspaper, TV station, Wesley Foundation, Room In the Inn, Student Organization to Advance Renewable Energy, student art league.

**Athletics.** NCAA. **Intercollegiate:** Baseball M, basketball, cross-country, football (tackle) M, golf, rifle W, soccer W, softball W, tennis, track and field W, volleyball W. **Intramural:** Basketball, football (non-tackle), racquetball, soccer, table tennis, volleyball. **Team name:** Governors.

**Student services.** Adult student services, alcohol/substance abuse counseling, career counseling, student employment services, financial aid counseling, health services, on-campus daycare, personal counseling, veterans' counselor. **Physically disabled:** Services for visually, speech, hearing impaired.

**Contact.** E-mail: admissions@apsu.edu
Phone: (931) 221-7661 Toll-free number: (800) 844-2778
Fax: (931) 221-6168
Ryan Forsythe, Director of Admissions, Austin Peay State University, PO Box 4548, Clarksville, TN 37044

## Baptist College of Health Sciences
### Memphis, Tennessee
### www.bchs.edu

- Private 4-year health science and nursing college affiliated with Baptist faith
- Commuter campus in very large city
- 910 degree-seeking undergraduates: 31% part-time, 88% women, 30% African American, 2% Asian American, 1% Hispanic American
- 31% of applicants admitted
- SAT or ACT (ACT writing optional) required
- 37% graduate within 6 years

**General.** Regionally accredited. **Degrees:** 161 bachelor's awarded. **Calendar:** Trimester, limited summer session. **Full-time faculty:** 60 total. **Part-time faculty:** 30 total. **Class size:** 56% < 20, 43% 20-39, less than 1% 40-49, less than 1% 50-99.

**Freshman class profile.** 187 applied, 58 admitted, 56 enrolled.

| | | | |
|---|---|---|---|
| GPA 3.50 or higher: | 38% | End year in good standing: | 88% |
| GPA 3.0-3.49: | 54% | Return as sophomores: | 88% |
| GPA 2.0-2.99: | 8% | | |

**Basis for selection.** GED not accepted. Standardized test scores, GPA, rigor of secondary school record, recommendations very important. **Homeschooled:** Transcript of courses and grades, letter of recommendation (nonparent) required. A transcript is required from an accredited home school agency showing GPA, high school graduation date, and all courses and grades. **Learning Disabled:** With proper documentation, students may be allowed to take the entrance exam with pencil and paper instead of on computer.

**High school preparation.** 10 units required; 15 recommended. Required and recommended units include English 4, mathematics 2, social studies 1, history 1, science 2 (laboratory 2), foreign language 2 and academic electives 1.

**2008-2009 Annual costs.** Tuition/fees (projected): $9,070.

**2006-2007 Financial aid. Need-based:** 39% of total undergraduate aid awarded as scholarships/grants, 61% as loans/jobs.

**Application procedures. Admission:** Priority date 2/15; deadline 6/1 (postmark date). $25 fee, may be waived for applicants with need. Application may be submitted online. Admission notification on a rolling basis beginning on or about 6/1. Must reply by 7/1.

**Academics. Credit/placement by examination:** AP, CLEP, institutional tests. 15 credit hours maximum toward bachelor's degree. **Support services:** Learning center, tutoring.

**Majors. Health:** Health care admin, medical radiologic technology/radiation therapy, nuclear medical technology, nursing (RN), radiologic technology/medical imaging, respiratory therapy technology, sonography.

**Computing on campus.** Dormitories linked to campus network. Commuter students can connect to campus network. Online course registration, helpline available.

**Student life. Freshman orientation:** Mandatory. Preregistration for classes offered. **Housing:** Coed dorms, substance-free housing available. $100 fully refundable deposit. **Activities:** Student government.

**Student services.** Campus ministries, financial aid counseling, health services, personal counseling.

**Contact.** E-mail: admissions@bchs.edu
Phone: (901) 575-2247 Toll-free number: (866) 575-2247
Fax: (901) 572-2461
Lissa Morgan, Manager, Admissions, Baptist College of Health Sciences,
1003 Monroe Avenue, Memphis, TN 38104

## Belmont University
### Nashville, Tennessee
### www.belmont.edu                    CB code: 1058

- Private 4-year university
- Residential campus in very large city
- 3,979 degree-seeking undergraduates: 8% part-time, 59% women, 4% African American, 2% Asian American, 2% Hispanic American, 1% international
- 704 degree-seeking graduate students
- 61% of applicants admitted
- SAT or ACT (ACT writing optional), interview required
- 65% graduate within 6 years

**General.** Founded in 1951. Regionally accredited. **Degrees:** 794 bachelor's awarded; master's, doctoral offered. **ROTC:** Army, Naval. **Location:** 2 miles from downtown. **Calendar:** Semester, limited summer session. **Full-time faculty:** 239 total; 81% have terminal degrees, 3% minority, 51% women. **Part-time faculty:** 298 total; 23% have terminal degrees, 5% minority, 52% women. **Class size:** 50% < 20, 50% 20-39, less than 1% 40-49. **Special facilities:** 22-track recording studio, Studio B on Music Row, 140-year-old antebellum mansion.

**Freshman class profile.** 2,793 applied, 1,712 admitted, 804 enrolled.

| Mid 50% test scores | | | |
|---|---|---|---|
| SAT critical reading: | 540-630 | Rank in top tenth: | 31% |
| SAT math: | 530-630 | Return as sophomores: | 80% |
| ACT composite: | 23-28 | Out-of-state: | 37% |
| GPA 3.50 or higher: | 53% | Live on campus: | 98% |
| GPA 3.0-3.49: | 38% | International: | 1% |
| GPA 2.0-2.99: | 9% | Fraternities: | 3% |
| Rank in top quarter: | 59% | Sororities: | 4% |

**Basis for selection.** Admissions based on test scores, course selection, GPA, class rank, recommendations, leadership activity. Interview required for music business; audition required for music programs.

**High school preparation.** 18 units required. Required and recommended units include English 4, mathematics 3-4, social studies 2, science 2-3, foreign language 2 and academic electives 5.

**2007-2008 Annual costs.** Tuition/fees: $19,780. Room/board: $7,570. Books/supplies: $1,200. Personal expenses: $1,600.

**2006-2007 Financial aid. Need-based:** 695 full-time freshmen applied for aid; 389 were judged to have need; 389 of these received aid. Average need met was 84%. Average scholarship/grant was $5,295; average loan $2,739. 32% of total undergraduate aid awarded as scholarships/grants, 68% as loans/jobs. **Non-need-based:** Awarded to 2,103 full-time undergraduates, including 644 freshmen. Scholarships awarded for academics, art, athletics, leadership, music/drama, religious affiliation, state residency.

**Application procedures. Admission:** Priority date 12/1; deadline 8/1. $35 fee. Application may be submitted online. Admission notification on a rolling basis beginning on or about 9/1. Must reply by May 1 or within 2 week(s) if notified thereafter. **Financial aid:** Priority date 3/1; no closing date. FAFSA required. Applicants notified on a rolling basis starting 3/15; must reply by 5/1 or within 2 week(s) of notification.

**Academics. Special study options:** Accelerated study, combined bachelor's/graduate degree, cooperative education, distance learning, double major, ESL, honors, independent study, internships, liberal arts/career combination, student-designed major, study abroad, teacher certification program, Washington semester. **Credit/placement by examination:** AP, CLEP, IB, SAT, ACT, institutional tests. 24 credit hours maximum toward bachelor's degree. **Support services:** Learning center, pre-admission summer program, reduced course load, tutoring, writing center.

**Majors. Biology:** General, environmental, molecular, molecular biochemistry. **Business:** General, accounting, entrepreneurial studies, finance, hospitality admin, management information systems, management science, managerial economics, marketing. **Communications:** General, broadcast journalism, journalism, media studies, public relations. **Computer sciences:** Computer science, information systems. **Education:** General, art, biology, chemistry, early childhood, elementary, English, French, health, health occupations, history, mathematics, middle, music, physical, physics, science, secondary,

social science, social studies, Spanish. **English:** English lit, speech/rhetoric. **Family/consumer sciences:** Child care. **Foreign languages:** French, German, Spanish. **Health:** Nursing (RN). **History:** General. **Liberal arts:** Arts/sciences. **Math:** General. **Parks/recreation:** Exercise sciences, health/fitness. **Philosophy/religion:** Philosophy, religion. **Physical sciences:** Chemistry, physics. **Psychology:** General. **Public administration:** Social work. **Social sciences:** Economics, political science, sociology. **Theology:** Sacred music. **Visual/performing arts:** Art, commercial/advertising art, dramatic, music management, music pedagogy, music performance, music theory/composition, piano/organ, voice/opera.

**Most popular majors.** Business/marketing 17%, health sciences 12%, visual/performing arts 40%.

**Computing on campus.** 500 workstations in dormitories, library, computer center, student center. Dormitories wired for high-speed internet access and linked to campus network. Commuter students can connect to campus network. Online course registration, online library, helpline, wireless network available.

**Student life. Freshman orientation:** Mandatory, $60 fee. Preregistration for classes offered. 2-day program in summer or 4-day program in fall before classes start. **Housing:** Guaranteed on-campus for freshmen. Single-sex dorms, apartments, substance-free housing available. $100 nonrefundable deposit, deadline 5/1. **Activities:** Bands, choral groups, dance, drama, international student organizations, literary magazine, music ensembles, musical theater, opera, radio station, student government, student newspaper, symphony orchestra, TV station, Baptist student union, Christian music society, Campus Crusade for Christ, Fellowship of Christian Athletes, Black Student Alliance.

**Athletics.** NCAA. **Intercollegiate:** Baseball M, basketball, cross-country, golf, soccer, softball W, tennis, track and field, volleyball W. **Intramural:** Basketball, bowling, golf M, racquetball, softball, table tennis, tennis, volleyball. **Team name:** Bruins.

**Student services.** Adult student services, alcohol/substance abuse counseling, campus ministries, career counseling, student employment services, financial aid counseling, health services, minority student services, personal counseling, placement for graduates, veterans' counselor.

**Contact.** E-mail: buadmission@mail.belmont.edu
Phone: (615) 460-6785 Fax: (615) 460-5434
Kathy Baugher, Dean of Enrollment Services, Belmont University, 1900 Belmont Boulevard, Nashville, TN 37212-3757

## Bethel College
### McKenzie, Tennessee
### www.bethel-college.edu              CB code: 1063

- Private 4-year liberal arts college affiliated with Presbyterian Church (USA)
- Residential campus in small town
- 1,996 degree-seeking undergraduates
- 159 graduate students
- 57% of applicants admitted
- SAT or ACT (ACT writing optional) required

**General.** Founded in 1842. Regionally accredited. Students are provided with a laptop upon registration. **Degrees:** 388 bachelor's awarded; master's offered. **Location:** 115 miles from Nashville, 120 miles from Memphis. **Calendar:** Semester, limited summer session. **Full-time faculty:** 60 total. **Class size:** 72% < 20, 28% 20-39, less than 1% 40-49, less than 1% 50-99. **Special facilities:** Wildlife agency research laboratory.

**Freshman class profile.**

| Mid 50% test scores | | | |
|---|---|---|---|
| | | ACT composite: | 17-21 |
| SAT critical reading: | 420-470 | Out-of-state: | 7% |
| SAT math: | 390-500 | Live on campus: | 32% |

**Basis for selection.** Counselor recommendation, interview considered for academically marginal applicants. High school GPA and academic units considered. **Homeschooled:** ACT of 19 or above and passing score on GED required.

**High school preparation.** Required units include English 4, mathematics 2, social studies 2 and science 2.

**2007-2008 Annual costs.** Tuition/fees: $11,690. Room/board: $6,472. Books/supplies: $1,000. Personal expenses: $1,750.

**Financial aid. Non-need-based:** Scholarships awarded for academics, athletics, music/drama, religious affiliation, state residency.

**Application procedures. Admission:** Priority date 2/3; no deadline. $30 fee. Application may be submitted online. Admission notification on a rolling basis. **Financial aid:** Priority date 3/3, closing date 6/30. FAFSA, institutional form required. Applicants notified on a rolling basis starting 3/1.

**Academics. Special study options:** Accelerated study, combined bachelor's/graduate degree, double major, internships, liberal arts/career combination, student-designed major, teacher certification program, weekend college. **Credit/placement by examination:** AP, CLEP, SAT, ACT, institutional tests. 30 credit hours maximum toward bachelor's degree. Accepts CLEP, DANTES, institutional exams for credit. **Support services:** Learning center, remedial instruction, study skills assistance, tutoring, writing center.

**Majors. Biology:** General, zoology. **Business:** Accounting, business admin. **Computer sciences:** General. **Education:** Art, elementary, English, health, history, physical, science, secondary, special. **English:** English lit. **History:** General. **Interdisciplinary:** Biological/physical sciences. **Math:** General, applied. **Physical sciences:** Chemistry. **Psychology:** General. **Public administration:** Human services. **Social sciences:** General. **Visual/performing arts:** Dramatic, studio arts.

**Most popular majors.** Business/marketing 78%, education 7%.

**Computing on campus.** PC or laptop required. 650 workstations in dormitories, library. Dormitories wired for high-speed internet access and linked to campus network. Commuter students can connect to campus network. Online library, helpline, repair service, wireless network available.

**Student life. Freshman orientation:** Mandatory. Preregistration for classes offered. One-day orientations held in June, July, August on Saturday. **Housing:** Guaranteed on-campus for freshmen. Single-sex dorms available. $175 deposit. **Activities:** Bands, choral groups, drama, music ensembles, musical theater, student government, Fellowship of Christian Athletes, Christian Fellowship, Black Students United, honor societies, Christian Issues Organization, American Chemical Society, commuter club, business club, Student TN Education Association, wildlife club.

**Athletics.** NAIA. **Intercollegiate:** Baseball M, basketball, cheerleading, cross-country, football (tackle) M, golf, soccer, softball W, tennis, track and field, volleyball W. **Intramural:** Basketball, football (non-tackle), football (tackle), softball, swimming, table tennis, volleyball W. **Team name:** Wildcats.

**Student services.** Adult student services, alcohol/substance abuse counseling, campus ministries, career counseling, student employment services, financial aid counseling, personal counseling, placement for graduates, veterans' counselor. **Physically disabled:** Services for visually, speech, hearing impaired.

**Contact.** E-mail: admissions@bethel-college.edu
Phone: (731) 352-4030 Fax: (731) 352-4069
Tina Hodges, Director of Admission and Retention, Bethel College, 325 Cherry Avenue, McKenzie, TN 38201

---

## Bryan College
**Dayton, Tennessee**
www.bryan.edu                                    CB code: 1908

- Private 4-year liberal arts college affiliated with interdenominational tradition
- Residential campus in small town
- 981 degree-seeking undergraduates
- 71% of applicants admitted
- SAT or ACT (ACT writing recommended), application essay required

**General.** Founded in 1930. Regionally accredited. All courses taught from Christian perspective. All faculty sign statement of faith annually. **Degrees:** 213 bachelor's awarded; master's offered. **Location:** 40 miles from Chattanooga. **Calendar:** Semester, limited summer session. **Full-time faculty:** 33 total; 82% have terminal degrees, 18% women. **Part-time faculty:** 6 total; 17% women. **Special facilities:** Natural history museum.

**Freshman class profile.** 517 applied, 366 admitted, 234 enrolled.

| Mid 50% test scores | | | |
|---|---|---|---|
| | | **ACT composite:** | 21-27 |
| SAT critical reading: | 530-650 | **Out-of-state:** | 60% |
| SAT math: | 520-640 | **Live on campus:** | 92% |
| SAT writing: | 530-640 | | |

**Basis for selection.** High school record, Christian character supported by references, and SAT or ACT scores important. ACT composite score of 23 or SAT equivalent, or Pre-Professional Skills Test required of all teacher education applicants. Interview required for marginal applicants. **Home-schooled:** A detailed high school transcript of courses taken and grades received is required.

**High school preparation.** 20 units recommended. Recommended units include English 4, mathematics 3, social studies 3, science 3 and foreign language 2.

**2007-2008 Annual costs.** Tuition/fees: $16,320. Room/board: $4,770. Books/supplies: $1,000. Personal expenses: $1,000.

**2006-2007 Financial aid. Need-based:** 172 full-time freshmen applied for aid; 150 were judged to have need; 147 of these received aid. Average need met was 70%. Average scholarship/grant was $5,611; average loan $4,220. 53% of total undergraduate aid awarded as scholarships/grants, 47% as loans/jobs. **Non-need-based:** Awarded to 791 full-time undergraduates, including 179 freshmen. Scholarships awarded for academics, alumni affiliation, art, athletics, job skills, leadership, music/drama.

**Application procedures. Admission:** Priority date 5/1; deadline 7/31 (postmark date). $30 fee, may be waived for applicants with need. Application may be submitted online. Admission notification on a rolling basis. Must reply by May 1 or within 2 week(s) if notified thereafter. **Financial aid:** Priority date 2/15; no closing date. FAFSA, institutional form required. Applicants notified on a rolling basis starting 1/1; must reply within 2 week(s) of notification.

**Academics. Special study options:** Combined bachelor's/graduate degree, distance learning, double major, dual enrollment of high school students, honors, internships, study abroad, teacher certification program, Washington semester. Adult degree completion program. **Credit/placement by examination:** AP, CLEP, IB, SAT, ACT, institutional tests. 30 credit hours maximum toward associate degree, 31 toward bachelor's. **Support services:** Reduced course load, remedial instruction, study skills assistance, tutoring, writing center.

**Majors. Biology:** General. **Business:** General, business admin, management information systems. **Communications:** General, political. **Computer sciences:** Computer science. **Education:** General. **English:** English lit. **Foreign languages:** Spanish. **History:** General. **Interdisciplinary:** Math/computer science. **Liberal arts:** Arts/sciences. **Math:** General. **Parks/recreation:** Exercise sciences. **Philosophy/religion:** Christian. **Psychology:** General. **Theology:** Bible, religious ed. **Visual/performing arts:** Music management, music pedagogy, music performance, piano/organ, voice/opera.

**Most popular majors.** Business/marketing 57%, communications/journalism 12%.

**Computing on campus.** 100 workstations in dormitories, library, computer center, student center. Dormitories wired for high-speed internet access and linked to campus network. Commuter students can connect to campus network. Online library, helpline, student web hosting, wireless network available.

**Student life. Freshman orientation:** Mandatory. Preregistration for classes offered. **Policies:** No alcohol, tobacco, drugs. Curfew and dress code enforced. Religious observance required. **Housing:** Guaranteed on-campus for all undergraduates. Single-sex dorms, apartments, substance-free housing available. $100 deposit, deadline 5/1. **Activities:** Campus ministries, choral groups, drama, international student organizations, music ensembles, musical theater, student government, student newspaper, Christian service organizations, community tutoring program, Students for Life, Fellowship of Christian Athletes.

**Athletics.** NAIA, NCCAA. **Intercollegiate:** Baseball M, basketball, cross-country, soccer, volleyball W. **Intramural:** Basketball, football (non-tackle) M, soccer, softball, table tennis, tennis, volleyball. **Team name:** Lions.

**Student services.** Adult student services, campus ministries, career counseling, student employment services, financial aid counseling, health services, personal counseling, placement for graduates.

**Contact.** E-mail: admissions@bryan.edu
Phone: (423) 775-7204 Toll-free number: (800) 277-9522
Fax: (423) 775-7199
Michael Sapienza, Director of Enrollment Management, Bryan College, PO Box 7000, Dayton, TN 37321-7000

---

## Carson-Newman College
**Jefferson City, Tennessee**                    CB member
www.cn.edu                                       CB code: 1102

- Private 4-year liberal arts college affiliated with Southern Baptist Convention
- Residential campus in small town

▶ 1,815 degree-seeking undergraduates: 5% part-time, 58% women, 9% African American, 1% Asian American, 1% Hispanic American, 2% international

▶ 178 degree-seeking graduate students

▶ 62% of applicants admitted

▶ SAT or ACT required

▶ 52% graduate within 6 years

**General.** Founded in 1851. Regionally accredited. **Degrees:** 368 bachelor's awarded; master's offered. **ROTC:** Army, Air Force. **Location:** 30 miles from Knoxville. **Calendar:** Semester, extensive summer session. **Full-time faculty:** 126 total; 69% have terminal degrees. **Part-time faculty:** 86 total. **Class size:** 59% < 20, 38% 20-39, 2% 40-49, less than 1% 50-99. **Special facilities:** Appalachia Museum.

**Freshman class profile.** 3,298 applied, 2,037 admitted, 436 enrolled.

| Mid 50% test scores | | | |
|---|---|---|---|
| | | Rank in top tenth: | 27% |
| ACT composite: | 20-25 | Return as sophomores: | 69% |
| GPA 3.0-3.49: | 68% | Out-of-state: | 32% |
| GPA 2.0-2.99: | 30% | Live on campus: | 90% |
| Rank in top quarter: | 47% | International: | 1% |

**Basis for selection.** Minimum 2.5 high school GPA, minimum ACT composite score of 19 or SAT combined score of 920 (exclusive of Writing), school and community activities, and recommendations important. Rank in top half of class considered. Essay required for marginal students; audition required for music; portfolio required for art; interview recommended for academically weak.

**High school preparation.** 20 units required. Required and recommended units include English 4, mathematics 2-3, social studies 3, history 2, science 2 (laboratory 1) and foreign language 2.

**2007-2008 Annual costs.** Tuition/fees: $16,980. Room/board: $5,360. Books/supplies: $990.

**Financial aid. Non-need-based:** Scholarships awarded for academics, art, athletics, leadership, minority status, music/drama, religious affiliation, ROTC.

**Application procedures. Admission:** Priority date 12/31; deadline 8/1. $25 fee, may be waived for applicants with need. Application may be submitted online. Admission notification on a rolling basis. Must reply by May 1 or within 4 week(s) if notified thereafter. **Financial aid:** Priority date 4/1; no closing date. FAFSA, institutional form required. Applicants notified on a rolling basis starting 2/1; must reply within 2 week(s) of notification.

**Academics.** 3-year pre-engineering programs available. **Special study options:** Accelerated study, double major, dual enrollment of high school students, ESL, exchange student, honors, independent study, internships, liberal arts/career combination, student-designed major, study abroad, teacher certification program, Washington semester, weekend college. **Credit/placement by examination:** AP, CLEP, institutional tests. 32 credit hours maximum toward associate degree, 32 toward bachelor's. **Support services:** Learning center, pre-admission summer program, reduced course load, remedial instruction, tutoring.

**Majors. Biology:** General. **Business:** General, accounting, business admin, managerial economics, small business admin. **Communications:** General, journalism. **Computer sciences:** General, computer science. **Education:** General, early childhood, elementary, family/consumer sciences, music, physical, secondary, special. **English:** English lit, speech/rhetoric. **Family/consumer sciences:** Clothing/textiles, family/community services, food/nutrition. **Foreign languages:** French, German, Spanish. **Health:** Athletic training, clinical lab science, health care admin, nursing (RN), predental, premedicine, prepharmacy. **History:** General. **Liberal arts:** Arts/sciences. **Math:** General. **Parks/recreation:** General, exercise sciences, health/fitness. **Philosophy/religion:** Philosophy, religion. **Physical sciences:** Applied physics, chemistry, physics. **Psychology:** General. **Social sciences:** Economics, international economics, political science, sociology. **Theology:** Sacred music. **Visual/performing arts:** General, art, drawing, interior design, music performance, music theory/composition, painting, photography. **Other:** Applied Physics.

**Most popular majors.** Business/marketing 13%, communications/journalism 6%, education 19%, health sciences 21%, psychology 6%, social sciences 6%.

**Computing on campus.** 100 workstations in dormitories, library, computer center.

**Student life. Freshman orientation:** Available. Preregistration for classes offered. **Policies:** Religious observance required. **Housing:** Guaranteed on-campus for freshmen. Single-sex dorms, apartments available. $50 deposit, deadline 8/1. Honors house available. **Activities:** Bands, choral groups, dance, drama, film society, literary magazine, music ensembles, musical theater,

radio station, student government, student newspaper, TV station, Baptist Student Union, Fellowship of Christian Athletes, honor societies, Appalachian Outreach, Bonners Scholars Community Service.

**Athletics.** NCAA. **Intercollegiate:** Baseball M, basketball, cross-country, football (tackle) M, golf M, soccer, softball W, tennis, track and field, volleyball W, wrestling M. **Intramural:** Badminton, basketball, bowling, golf, racquetball, soccer, softball, swimming, table tennis, tennis, volleyball. **Team name:** Eagles.

**Student services.** Adult student services, career counseling, health services, personal counseling, placement for graduates, veterans' counselor. **Physically disabled:** Services for visually, hearing impaired.

**Contact.** E-mail: thuebner@cn.edu
Phone: (865) 471-3223 Fax: (865) 471-3502
Tom Huebner, Dean of Admissions, Carson-Newman College, 1646 Russell Avenue, Jefferson City, TN 37760

## Christian Brothers University
**Memphis, Tennessee** — CB member
www.cbu.edu — CB code: 1121

▶ Private 4-year university affiliated with Roman Catholic Church

▶ Commuter campus in very large city

▶ 1,430 degree-seeking undergraduates: 16% part-time, 55% women

▶ 400 degree-seeking graduate students

▶ 69% of applicants admitted

▶ SAT or ACT (ACT writing optional), application essay required

▶ 62% graduate within 6 years

**General.** Founded in 1871. Regionally accredited. **Degrees:** 252 bachelor's awarded; master's offered. **ROTC:** Army, Naval, Air Force. **Location:** 200 miles from Nashville, 150 miles from Little Rock, Arkansas. **Calendar:** Semester, limited summer session. **Full-time faculty:** 94 total; 92% have terminal degrees, 18% minority, 33% women. **Part-time faculty:** 64 total; 48% have terminal degrees, 11% minority, 39% women. **Class size:** 66% < 20, 33% 20-39, less than 1% 40-49.

**Freshman class profile.** 1,360 applied, 942 admitted, 321 enrolled.

| Mid 50% test scores | | | |
|---|---|---|---|
| SAT critical reading: | 470-610 | Rank in top tenth: | 29% |
| SAT math: | 480-620 | Return as sophomores: | 80% |
| ACT composite: | 21-26 | Out-of-state: | 17% |
| GPA 3.50 or higher: | 45% | Live on campus: | 61% |
| GPA 3.0-3.49: | 33% | International: | 2% |
| GPA 2.0-2.99: | 22% | Fraternities: | 24% |
| Rank in top quarter: | 62% | Sororities: | 22% |

**Basis for selection.** Graduation from approved secondary school or GED equivalent, GPA of 2.0 and rank in upper 2/3 of graduating class, and satisfactory test scores required. SAT and ACT scores are used for math placement. Audition required for some programs; interview recommended for all. **Homeschooled:** Must have standardized test scores.

**High school preparation.** Recommended units include English 4, mathematics 4 and science 4. College-preparatory program required of engineering applicants.

**2007-2008 Annual costs.** Tuition/fees: $21,360. Room/board: $5,680.

**2007-2008 Financial aid. Need-based:** 296 full-time freshmen applied for aid; 229 were judged to have need; 229 of these received aid. Average need met was 93%. Average scholarship/grant was $6,626; average loan $3,271. 52% of total undergraduate aid awarded as scholarships/grants, 48% as loans/jobs. **Non-need-based:** Awarded to 1,128 full-time undergraduates, including 333 freshmen. Scholarships awarded for academics, alumni affiliation, athletics, music/drama, state residency. **Additional information:** ROTC scholarships available to qualified applicants.

**Application procedures. Admission:** Priority date 12/1; no deadline. $25 fee, may be waived for applicants with need. Application may be submitted online. Admission notification on a rolling basis beginning on or about 12/1. Must reply by May 1 or within 3 week(s) if notified thereafter. **Financial aid:** Priority date 2/15; no closing date. FAFSA required. Applicants notified on a rolling basis starting 3/1; must reply within 2 week(s) of notification.

**Academics. Special study options:** Accelerated study, double major, dual enrollment of high school students, exchange student, honors, independent study, internships, liberal arts/career combination, study abroad, teacher certification program. **Credit/placement by examination:** AP, CLEP, IB, SAT,

ACT, institutional tests. 30 credit hours maximum toward bachelor's degree. **Support services:** Pre-admission summer program, reduced course load, tutoring, writing center.

**Majors. Biology:** General, biomedical sciences. **Business:** General, business admin. **Computer sciences:** Computer science. **Education:** Biology, chemistry, elementary, English, history, mathematics, physics, secondary. **Engineering:** Chemical, civil, computer, electrical, mechanical, physics. **English:** English lit. **History:** General. **Interdisciplinary:** Biological/physical sciences, intercultural, math/computer science, natural sciences. **Liberal arts:** Arts/sciences. **Math:** General. **Philosophy/religion:** Philosophy, religion. **Physical sciences:** General, chemistry, physics. **Psychology:** General. **Visual/performing arts:** Studio arts.

**Most popular majors.** Business/marketing 39%, computer/information sciences 7%, education 7%, engineering/engineering technologies 10%, physical sciences 8%, psychology 19%.

**Computing on campus.** 310 workstations in dormitories, library, computer center, student center. Dormitories wired for high-speed internet access and linked to campus network. Commuter students can connect to campus network. Online course registration, online library, helpline, wireless network available.

**Student life. Freshman orientation:** Mandatory. Preregistration for classes offered. Held Friday through Monday before classes begin in fall. Spring orientation held the morning on the day before classes begin. **Housing:** Guaranteed on-campus for freshmen. Single-sex dorms, apartments available. $300 nonrefundable deposit, deadline 5/1. Juniors and seniors may live in on-campus apartments. All Freshmen and Sophomores whose permanent address is beyond a 30 mile radius are required to live on campus. **Activities:** Choral groups, drama, literary magazine, musical theater, student government, student newspaper, Black Student Association, The Chosen Generation, Intercultural Club, Lasallian Collegians, Student Peace Association, Up 'Til Dawn.

**Athletics.** NCAA. **Intercollegiate:** Baseball M, basketball, cross-country, golf, soccer, softball W, tennis, volleyball W. **Intramural:** Basketball, bowling, football (non-tackle), soccer, softball, swimming, tennis, volleyball. **Team name:** Buccaneers.

**Student services.** Adult student services, alcohol/substance abuse counseling, campus ministries, career counseling, student employment services, financial aid counseling, health services, minority student services, personal counseling, placement for graduates.

**Contact.** E-mail: admissions@cbu.edu
Phone: (901) 321-3205 Toll-free number: (800) 288-7576
Fax: (901) 321-3202
Tracey Dysart-Ford, Dean of Admissions, Christian Brothers University, 650 East Parkway South, Memphis, TN 38104-5519

## Crichton College
**Memphis, Tennessee**
**www.crichton.edu**                                    CB code: 1782

- Private 4-year liberal arts college affiliated with nondenominational tradition
- Commuter campus in very large city
- 906 degree-seeking undergraduates: 36% part-time, 66% women, 69% African American, 1% Hispanic American, 2% international
- SAT or ACT (ACT writing optional), application essay required
- 33% graduate within 6 years

**General.** Founded in 1941. Regionally accredited. **Degrees:** 150 bachelor's awarded. **Location:** 7 miles from downtown. **Calendar:** Semester, limited summer session. **Full-time faculty:** 39 total; 72% have terminal degrees, 28% minority, 36% women. **Part-time faculty:** 36 total; 36% have terminal degrees, 22% minority, 33% women. **Class size:** 70% < 20, 29% 20-39, less than 1% 40-49.

**Freshman class profile.**

| Mid 50% test scores | | End year in good standing: | 57% |
|---|---|---|---|
| ACT composite: | 16-20 | Return as sophomores: | 55% |
| GPA 3.50 or higher: | 10% | Out-of-state: | 15% |
| GPA 3.0-3.49: | 34% | Live on campus: | 43% |
| GPA 2.0-2.99: | 50% | International: | 1% |

**Basis for selection.** School achievement record, test scores, interview, references, and class rank considered. Minimum ACT composite score of 19 or minimum of 900 on SAT (combined math and critical reading) required for regular admission. **Homeschooled:** Transcript of courses and grades required. Homeschooled applicants will be admitted based on homeschool

transcript. Must be accredited or affiliated with an accredited institution in order to be considered for acceptance. **Learning Disabled:** Student is responsible for disclosing information regarding nature of the disability and must register with the Office of Student Success and provide current documentation of the qualified disability.

**High school preparation.** 14 units required. Required units include English 4, mathematics 3, social studies 3, science 3 and academic electives 1.

**2007-2008 Annual costs.** Tuition/fees: $11,256. Room/board: $7,982. Books/supplies: $1,032. Personal expenses: $7,982.

**2007-2008 Financial aid. Need-based:** Average need met was 34%. Average scholarship/grant was $3,044; average loan $3,442. 50% of total undergraduate aid awarded as scholarships/grants, 50% as loans/jobs. **Non-need-based:** Scholarships awarded for academics, alumni affiliation, athletics, leadership, music/drama, religious affiliation.

**Application procedures. Admission:** Priority date 1/1; no deadline. $25 fee, may be waived for applicants with need. Application may be submitted online. Admission notification on a rolling basis. **Financial aid:** Priority date 3/15; no closing date. FAFSA, institutional form required. Applicants notified on a rolling basis starting 3/1; must reply within 2 week(s) of notification.

**Academics. Special study options:** Accelerated study, distance learning, double major, dual enrollment of high school students, honors, independent study, internships, liberal arts/career combination, student-designed major, study abroad, teacher certification program, weekend college. **Credit/placement by examination:** AP, CLEP, IB, SAT, ACT, institutional tests. 30 credit hours maximum toward bachelor's degree. **Support services:** Learning center, pre-admission summer program, reduced course load, remedial instruction, study skills assistance, tutoring.

**Majors. Biology:** General, biomedical sciences. **Business:** Business admin. **Education:** General, biology, business, chemistry, elementary, English, history, mathematics, middle, psychology. **English:** English lit. **History:** General. **Legal studies:** Prelaw. **Liberal arts:** Arts/sciences. **Physical sciences:** Chemistry. **Psychology:** General. **Theology:** Bible, youth ministry.

**Most popular majors.** Business/marketing 46%, education 23%, psychology 10%, theological studies 16%.

**Computing on campus.** 34 workstations in library, computer center. Dormitories wired for high-speed internet access and linked to campus network. Commuter students can connect to campus network. Online library, helpline, repair service, wireless network available.

**Student life. Freshman orientation:** Mandatory, $40 fee. Preregistration for classes offered. 2-day program. **Policies:** Religious observance required. **Housing:** Special housing for disabled, apartments, substance-free housing available. $150 fully refundable deposit, deadline 8/15. **Activities:** Campus ministries, choral groups, dance, drama, film society, musical theater, student government, student newspaper, Christian Responsibility to Engage our World (Community Service), Crichton Christian Fellowship, Campus Crusade for Christ, InterVarsity.

**Athletics.** NAIA. **Intercollegiate:** Baseball M, basketball M, cheerleading M, cross-country, golf, soccer, softball, track and field, volleyball W. **Team name:** Comets.

**Student services.** Adult student services, campus ministries, career counseling, student employment services, financial aid counseling, personal counseling, placement for graduates.

**Contact.** E-mail: info@crichton.edu
Phone: (901) 320-9797 Toll-free number: (800) 960-9777
Fax: (901) 320-9791
Justin Casey, Assistant Director of Admissions, Crichton College, 255 North Highland, Memphis, TN 38111-1375

## Cumberland University
**Lebanon, Tennessee**
**www.cumberland.edu**                                 CB code: 1146

- Private 4-year university and liberal arts college
- Commuter campus in large town
- 994 degree-seeking undergraduates: 9% part-time, 52% women, 11% African American, 1% Asian American, 2% Hispanic American, 1% Native American, 4% international
- 267 degree-seeking graduate students
- 61% of applicants admitted

- ACT (writing optional), application essay required
- 35% graduate within 6 years; 19% enter graduate study

**General.** Founded in 1842. Regionally accredited. **Degrees:** 154 bachelor's, 2 associate awarded; master's offered. **ROTC:** Army. **Location:** 30 miles from Nashville. **Calendar:** Semester, limited summer session. **Full-time faculty:** 48 total; 77% have terminal degrees, 10% minority, 62% women. **Part-time faculty:** 42 total; 29% have terminal degrees, 2% minority, 36% women. **Class size:** 56% < 20, 34% 20-39, 6% 40-49, 4% 50-99.

**Freshman class profile.** 602 applied, 367 admitted, 212 enrolled.

| Mid 50% test scores | | Rank in top tenth: | 15% |
|---|---|---|---|
| SAT critical reading: | 420-510 | Return as sophomores: | 56% |
| SAT math: | 410-520 | Out-of-state: | 12% |
| ACT composite: | 19-23 | Live on campus: | 60% |
| GPA 3.50 or higher: | 38% | International: | 2% |
| GPA 3.0-3.49: | 29% | Fraternities: | 19% |
| GPA 2.0-2.99: | 33% | Sororities: | 12% |
| Rank in top quarter: | 38% | | |

**Basis for selection.** High school academic record and standardized test scores most important. Audition, portfolio required for some programs; interview recommended for academically weak. **Homeschooled:** Transcript of courses and grades required.

**High school preparation.** 16 units required; 19 recommended. Required and recommended units include English 4, mathematics 3-4, social studies 2, history 2, science 3 (laboratory 1-2) and foreign language 2.

**2008-2009 Annual costs.** Tuition/fees (projected): $16,720. Room/board: $6,070. Books/supplies: $1,260. Personal expenses: $2,545.

**2007-2008 Financial aid. Need-based:** 203 full-time freshmen applied for aid; 167 were judged to have need; 167 of these received aid. Average need met was 70%. Average scholarship/grant was $4,034; average loan $2,806. 50% of total undergraduate aid awarded as scholarships/grants, 50% as loans/jobs. **Non-need-based:** Awarded to 686 full-time undergraduates, including 184 freshmen. Scholarships awarded for academics, art, athletics, music/drama.

**Application procedures. Admission:** Priority date 2/15; no deadline. $25 fee, may be waived for applicants with need. Application may be submitted online. Admission notification on a rolling basis beginning on or about 3/1. Permission of high school principal or guidance counselor required for early admission. Housing deposit refundable before August 1. **Financial aid:** Priority date 2/1; no closing date. FAFSA, institutional form required. Applicants notified on a rolling basis starting 5/1; must reply within 2 week(s) of notification.

**Academics.** Selection of major or minor not required. **Special study options:** Accelerated study, combined bachelor's/graduate degree, cooperative education, distance learning, double major, dual enrollment of high school students, honors, independent study, internships, liberal arts/career combination, teacher certification program. **Credit/placement by examination:** AP, CLEP, ACT, institutional tests. 30 credit hours maximum toward bachelor's degree. **Support services:** Learning center, pre-admission summer program, reduced course load, remedial instruction, study skills assistance, tutoring, writing center.

**Honors college/program.** Honors program requires minimum composite ACT score of 25 and consists of about 20 participating students per year.

**Majors. Area/ethnic studies:** American. **Biology:** General. **Business:** General, accounting, management science. **Education:** General, biology, early childhood, elementary, English, history, mathematics, middle, multi-level teacher, music, physical, secondary, social science, special. **English:** English lit. **Health:** Nursing (RN), predental, premedicine, prepharmacy, preveterinary. **History:** General. **Legal studies:** Prelaw. **Liberal arts:** Arts/sciences. **Math:** General. **Parks/recreation:** Health/fitness, sports admin. **Protective services:** Criminal justice. **Psychology:** General. **Public administration:** General. **Social sciences:** General, political science, sociology. **Visual/performing arts:** Studio arts.

**Most popular majors.** Business/marketing 18%, education 23%, health sciences 32%, security/protective services 6%.

**Computing on campus.** 60 workstations in library, computer center. Dormitories linked to campus network. Commuter students can connect to campus network. Online library, helpline, repair service, wireless network available.

**Student life. Freshman orientation:** Mandatory. Preregistration for classes offered. Held on August 27 and 28, 1-1/2 days long. **Housing:** Single-sex dorms, apartments, substance-free housing available. $200 deposit, deadline 8/1. **Activities:** Bands, campus ministries, choral groups, dance, drama, music ensembles, musical theater, radio station, student government, student newspaper, Fellowship of Christian Athletes, African American student association, Campus Crusade for Christ, Champions for Christ.

**Athletics.** NAIA. **Intercollegiate:** Baseball M, basketball, cheerleading, cross-country, football (tackle) M, golf, soccer, softball W, tennis, volleyball W, wrestling M. **Intramural:** Basketball, bowling, football (nontackle) M, softball, table tennis, volleyball. **Team name:** Bulldogs.

**Student services.** Adult student services, campus ministries, career counseling, student employment services, financial aid counseling, health services, personal counseling, placement for graduates. **Physically disabled:** Services for visually impaired.

**Contact.** E-mail: admissions@cumberland.edu
Phone: (615) 444-2562 Toll-free number: (800) 467-0562
Fax: (615) 444-2569
Jason Brewer, Dean of Undergraduate Admissions and First Year Programs, Cumberland University, One Cumberland Square, Lebanon, TN 37087

---

## DeVry University: Memphis
**Memphis, Tennessee**
www.devry.edu

- For-profit 4-year business and technical college
- Very large city
- 38 degree-seeking undergraduates: 42% part-time, 68% women, 79% African American, 3% Asian American
- 18 degree-seeking graduate students

**General.** Regionally accredited. **Calendar:** Semester. **Part-time faculty:** 1 total.

**Basis for selection.** Academic GPA important. Test scores, class rank considered. SAT/ACT tests considered but not required for admission. If applicant chooses not to submit either, he/she must take DeVry-administered admissions test.

**2007-2008 Annual costs.** Books/supplies: $1,300. Personal expenses: $5,082.

**Financial aid. Non-need-based:** Scholarships awarded for academics.

**Application procedures. Admission:** No deadline. $50 fee. Admission notification on a rolling basis. **Financial aid:** No deadline. FAFSA required.

**Academics. Special study options:** Accelerated study, distance learning. **Credit/placement by examination:** CLEP.

**Majors. Business:** Business admin. **Other:** Technical management.

**Contact.** DeVry University: Memphis, 6401 Poplar Avenue, Ste. 600, Memphis, TN 38119

---

## East Tennessee State University
**Johnson City, Tennessee**     **CB member**
www.etsu.edu     **CB code: 1198**

- Public 4-year university
- Commuter campus in small city
- 10,270 degree-seeking undergraduates: 14% part-time, 57% women, 4% African American, 2% Asian American, 1% Hispanic American, 1% Native American, 1% international
- 2,274 degree-seeking graduate students
- 97% of applicants admitted
- SAT or ACT (ACT writing optional) required
- 38% graduate within 6 years

**General.** Founded in 1911. Regionally accredited. Additional campuses in Kingsport, Bristol, and Greeneville. Paramedical center, College of Medicine, College of Pharmacy, pre-professional programs. **Degrees:** 1,698 bachelor's awarded; master's, doctoral, first professional offered. **ROTC:** Army. **Location:** 90 miles from Knoxville, 60 miles from Asheville, North Carolina. **Calendar:** Semester, extensive summer session. **Full-time faculty:** 497 total; 72% have terminal degrees, 5% minority, 44% women. **Part-time faculty:** 287 total; 21% have terminal degrees, 3% minority, 51% women. **Class size:** 44% < 20, 40% 20-39, 7% 40-49, 7% 50-99, 2% >100. **Special facilities:** Appalachian archives, planetarium, observatory, arboretum.

**Freshman class profile.** 2,428 applied, 2,366 admitted, 1,939 enrolled.

| Mid 50% test scores | | | |
|---|---|---|---|
| SAT critical reading: | 440-560 | Rank in top tenth: | 17% |
| SAT math: | 450-560 | End year in good standing: | 80% |
| SAT writing: | 430-550 | Return as sophomores: | 68% |
| ACT composite: | 20-25 | Out-of-state: | 14% |
| GPA 3.50 or higher: | 42% | Live on campus: | 53% |
| GPA 3.0-3.49: | 32% | International: | 1% |
| GPA 2.0-2.99: | 25% | Fraternities: | 5% |
| Rank in top quarter: | 42% | Sororities: | 5% |

**Basis for selection.** Completion of 14 specific high school units required by state. Minimum 2.3 GPA or ACT composite score of 19 or comparable SAT score required. Those with ACT composite scores below 19 or Math or English scores below 19 complete the appropriate assessment (Compass). Interview recommended for dental hygiene, health-related professions, nursing, physical therapy programs; audition required for music; portfolio recommended for art. **Homeschooled:** Transcript of courses and grades required.

**High school preparation.** 14 units required; 16 recommended. Required and recommended units include English 4, mathematics 3-4, social studies 1, history 1, science 2-3 (laboratory 1), foreign language 2 and visual/performing arts 1.

**2007-2008 Annual costs.** Tuition/fees: $4,887; $15,163 out-of-state. Room/board: $5,166. Books/supplies: $1,008. Personal expenses: $2,718.

**2007-2008 Financial aid. Need-based:** 1,655 full-time freshmen applied for aid; 1,241 were judged to have need; 1,211 of these received aid. Average need met was 81%. Average scholarship/grant was $5,022; average loan $1,235. 55% of total undergraduate aid awarded as scholarships/grants, 45% as loans/jobs. **Non-need-based:** Awarded to 2,721 full-time undergraduates, including 601 freshmen. Scholarships awarded for academics, alumni affiliation, art, athletics, job skills, leadership, minority status, music/drama, religious affiliation, ROTC, state residency. **Additional information:** Housing costs payable by installment.

**Application procedures. Admission:** Priority date 7/1; no deadline. $15 fee, may be waived for applicants with need. Application may be submitted online. Admission notification on a rolling basis. **Financial aid:** Priority date 4/15; no closing date. FAFSA required. Applicants notified on a rolling basis starting 4/15; must reply within 2 week(s) of notification.

**Academics. Special study options:** Accelerated study, combined bachelor's/graduate degree, cooperative education, distance learning, double major, dual enrollment of high school students, exchange student, honors, independent study, internships, study abroad, teacher certification program. **Credit/placement by examination:** AP, CLEP, IB, SAT, ACT, institutional tests. **Support services:** Learning center, reduced course load, study skills assistance, tutoring.

**Honors college/program.** Honors program selects 20 new freshmen each year for specifically designed courses. Requires minimum 29 ACT or comparable SAT, 3.5 high school GPA.

**Majors. Biology:** General. **Business:** Accounting, business admin, finance, managerial economics, marketing. **Communications:** Media studies. **Communications technology:** Animation/special effects. **Computer sciences:** General. **Education:** Special. **Engineering technology:** General, surveying. **English:** English lit, speech/rhetoric. **Family/consumer sciences:** General, child development, family studies. **Foreign languages:** General. **Health:** Dental hygiene, environmental health, health services, nursing (RN). **History:** General. **Liberal arts:** Arts/sciences. **Math:** General. **Parks/recreation:** Health/fitness, sports admin. **Philosophy/religion:** Philosophy. **Physical sciences:** Chemistry, physics. **Protective services:** Law enforcement admin. **Psychology:** General. **Public administration:** Social work. **Social sciences:** Economics, geography, political science, sociology. **Visual/performing arts:** Art.

**Most popular majors.** Business/marketing 15%, family/consumer sciences 6%, health sciences 19%, interdisciplinary studies 7%, liberal arts 8%.

**Computing on campus.** 1,400 workstations in dormitories, library, computer center, student center. Dormitories wired for high-speed internet access and linked to campus network. Commuter students can connect to campus network. Online course registration, online library, helpline, repair service, student web hosting, wireless network available.

**Student life. Freshman orientation:** Mandatory. Preregistration for classes offered. 5 sessions during summer for 1-2 days. **Housing:** Coed dorms, single-sex dorms, special housing for disabled, apartments, fraternity/sorority housing, substance-free housing available. $100 fully refundable deposit. **Activities:** Bands, campus ministries, choral groups, drama, international student organizations, literary magazine, music ensembles, radio station, student government, student newspaper, TV station, Baptist Student Union, Campus Crusade, Catholic Center, Christian Student Fellowship, Fellowship of Christian Athletes, Real Life Fellowship, Wesley Foundation, Black Affairs Association.

**Athletics.** NCAA. **Intercollegiate:** Baseball M, basketball, cross-country, golf, soccer, softball W, tennis, track and field, volleyball W. **Intramural:** Basketball, cross-country, football (non-tackle), golf, handball, racquetball, softball, tennis, volleyball W, weight lifting M. **Team name:** Buccaneers.

**Student services.** Adult student services, alcohol/substance abuse counseling, campus ministries, career counseling, services for economically disadvantaged, student employment services, financial aid counseling, health services, legal services, minority student services, on-campus daycare, personal counseling, placement for graduates, veterans' counselor, women's services. **Physically disabled:** Services for visually, speech, hearing impaired.

**Contact.** E-mail: go2etsu@etsu.edu
Phone: (423) 439-4213 Toll-free number: (800) 462-3878
Fax: (423) 439-4630
T Pitts, Director of Admissions, East Tennessee State University, ETSU Box 70731, Johnson City, TN 37614

## Fisk University
**Nashville, Tennessee**
www.fisk.edu

**CB member**
**CB code: 1224**

- Private 4-year liberal arts college affiliated with United Church of Christ
- Residential campus in very large city

**General.** Founded in 1866. Regionally accredited. **Location:** 216 miles from Memphis, 225 miles from Atlanta. **Calendar:** Semester.

**Annual costs/financial aid.** Tuition/fees (2007-2008): $15,620. Room/board: $7,430. Books/supplies: $1,400. Personal expenses: $2,050. Need-based financial aid available to full-time and part-time students.

**Contact.** Phone: (615) 329-8665
Dean of Admissions, 1000 17th Avenue North, Nashville, TN 37208-3051

## Free Will Baptist Bible College
**Nashville, Tennessee**
www.fwbbc.edu

**CB code: 1232**

- Private 4-year Bible and teachers college affiliated with Free Will Baptists
- Residential campus in very large city
- 291 degree-seeking undergraduates: 18% part-time, 53% women, 3% African American
- 47% graduate within 6 years

**General.** Founded in 1942. Regionally accredited; also accredited by ABHE. **Degrees:** 69 bachelor's, 9 associate awarded. **ROTC:** Army, Air Force. **Location:** 3 miles from downtown. **Calendar:** Semester, limited summer session. **Full-time faculty:** 21 total; 33% have terminal degrees, 29% women. **Part-time faculty:** 26 total; 38% have terminal degrees, 27% women. **Class size:** 83% < 20, 16% 20-39, less than 1% 40-49, less than 1% 50-99.

**Freshman class profile.** 161 applied, 161 admitted, 62 enrolled.

| Mid 50% test scores | | | |
|---|---|---|---|
| ACT composite: | 18-25 | GPA 2.0-2.99: | 23% |
| GPA 3.50 or higher: | 52% | Return as sophomores: | 68% |
| GPA 3.0-3.49: | 25% | Out-of-state: | 62% |
| | | Live on campus: | 87% |

**Basis for selection.** Open admission. Applicants without high school diploma or GED must pass GED prior to receiving degree.

**High school preparation.** 22 units recommended. Recommended units include English 4, mathematics 4, social studies 3, history 2, science 4, foreign language 3 and academic electives 2.

**2007-2008 Annual costs.** Tuition/fees: $12,382. Room/board: $4,866. Books/supplies: $600. Personal expenses: $820.

**2006-2007 Financial aid. Need-based:** 37% of total undergraduate aid awarded as scholarships/grants, 63% as loans/jobs. **Non-need-based:** Scholarships awarded for academics, art, music/drama.

**Application procedures. Admission:** Priority date 4/15; no deadline. $35 fee. Application may be submitted online. Admission notification on a rolling basis. **Financial aid:** Priority date 4/15; no closing date. FAFSA, institutional form required. Applicants notified on a rolling basis starting 7/1; must reply within 2 week(s) of notification.

**Academics. Special study options:** Distance learning, double major, independent study, internships, teacher certification program. **Credit/ placement by examination:** AP, CLEP, IB, institutional tests. 16 credit hours maximum toward bachelor's degree. **Support services:** Reduced course load, remedial instruction, tutoring.

**Majors. Business:** Business admin. **Education:** Early childhood, elementary, music, physical, secondary. **English:** English lit. **History:** General. **Parks/recreation:** Exercise sciences. **Psychology:** General. **Theology:** Bible, missionary, religious ed, theology.

**Most popular majors.** Business/marketing 19%, education 18%, English 7%, psychology 15%, theological studies 38%.

**Computing on campus.** 42 workstations in library, computer center, student center. Commuter students can connect to campus network. Online library, repair service, wireless network available.

**Student life. Freshman orientation:** Mandatory. Preregistration for classes offered. **Policies:** Religious observance required. **Housing:** Single-sex dorms, apartments available. $100 deposit, deadline 8/1. Single students required to live on campus unless living with parents or close relatives. **Activities:** Campus ministries, choral groups, drama, music ensembles, musical theater, student government, ministerial and missionary organizations, Christian service assignments, organization for business students, literary societies.

**Athletics.** NCCAA. **Intercollegiate:** Baseball M, basketball, volleyball W. **Intramural:** Basketball, softball, table tennis M, tennis, volleyball. **Team name:** Flames.

**Student services.** Career counseling, student employment services, financial aid counseling, personal counseling, placement for graduates, veterans' counselor.

**Contact.** E-mail: recruit@fwbbc.edu
Phone: (615) 844-5000 Toll-free number: (800) 763-9222
Fax: (615) 269-6028
Jeff Caudill, Director of Enrollment Services, Free Will Baptist Bible College, 3606 West End Avenue, Nashville, TN 37205-2403

---

## Freed-Hardeman University
**Henderson, Tennessee**
www.fhu.edu

**CB member**
**CB code: 1230**

- Private 4-year university and liberal arts college affiliated with Church of Christ
- Residential campus in small town
- 1,428 degree-seeking undergraduates: 4% part-time, 55% women, 4% African American, 1% Hispanic American, 3% international
- 532 graduate students
- SAT or ACT (ACT writing recommended) required
- 58% graduate within 6 years; 33% enter graduate study

**General.** Founded in 1869. Regionally accredited. Henderson Church of Christ facilities adjacent to campus. Campus in Verviers, Belgium. **Degrees:** 302 bachelor's awarded; master's, first professional offered. **Location:** 15 miles from Jackson, 85 miles from Memphis. **Calendar:** Semester, limited summer session. **Full-time faculty:** 108 total; 69% have terminal degrees, 5% minority, 31% women. **Part-time faculty:** 40 total; 45% have terminal degrees, 8% minority, 35% women. **Class size:** 55% < 20, 37% 20-39, 4% 40-49, 4% 50-99. **Special facilities:** Cancer research institute.

**Freshman class profile.** 386 enrolled.

| Mid 50% test scores | | | |
|---|---|---|---|
| SAT critical reading: | 480-640 | Rank in top quarter: | 51% |
| SAT math: | 480-600 | Rank in top tenth: | 25% |
| ACT composite: | 20-26 | Return as sophomores: | 74% |
| GPA 3.50 or higher: | 60% | Out-of-state: | 50% |
| GPA 3.0-3.49: | 27% | Live on campus: | 90% |
| GPA 2.0-2.99: | 13% | International: | 2% |

**Basis for selection.** Admissions based on school achievement record, test scores, references. Applicants without minimum test score or high school GPA may be admitted with restrictions after further evaluation. **Homeschooled:** Applicants expected to take ACT or SAT.

**High school preparation.** 20 units recommended. Recommended units include English 4, mathematics 2, social studies 2, science 2 and academic electives 10. Additional science and mathematics courses recommended.

**2007-2008 Annual costs.** Tuition/fees: $13,192. Room/board: $6,560. Books/supplies: $1,710. Personal expenses: $1,930.

**2007-2008 Financial aid. Need-based:** 329 full-time freshmen applied for aid; 273 were judged to have need; 272 of these received aid. Average need met was 76%. Average scholarship/grant was $10,290; average loan $3,438. 55% of total undergraduate aid awarded as scholarships/grants, 45% as loans/jobs. **Non-need-based:** Awarded to 466 full-time undergraduates, including 143 freshmen. Scholarships awarded for academics, art, athletics, leadership, minority status, music/drama, state residency.

**Application procedures. Admission:** No deadline. No application fee. Application may be submitted online. Admission notification on a rolling basis. Housing deposit refundable up to 30 days prior to term. **Financial aid:** Priority date 3/1; no closing date. FAFSA required. Applicants notified on a rolling basis starting 3/1; must reply within 4 week(s) of notification.

**Academics.** Students enrolled for 12 or more undergraduate hours must register for Bible class. **Special study options:** Accelerated study, combined bachelor's/graduate degree, cooperative education, cross-registration, distance learning, double major, dual enrollment of high school students, honors, independent study, internships, liberal arts/career combination, student-designed major, study abroad, teacher certification program. 3-2 engineering, Honors College, study abroad programs in Belgium and Italy. **Credit/ placement by examination:** AP, CLEP, IB, SAT, ACT, institutional tests. 33 credit hours maximum toward bachelor's degree. **Support services:** Learning center, reduced course load, remedial instruction, study skills assistance, tutoring.

**Honors college/program.** Approximately 5% of freshmen class admitted to honors course work as result of competitive application process.

**Majors. Biology:** General, biochemistry. **Business:** Accounting, business admin, finance, human resources, management information systems, marketing. **Communications:** General, journalism, media studies, public relations. **Computer sciences:** General. **Education:** Art, biology, curriculum, early childhood, elementary, English, history, mathematics, middle, multi-level teacher, music, physical, science, secondary, special. **English:** English lit. **Family/consumer sciences:** Family studies. **Health:** Health care admin. **History:** General. **Liberal arts:** Arts/sciences. **Math:** General. **Parks/ recreation:** Exercise sciences. **Philosophy/religion:** Philosophy. **Physical sciences:** General, chemistry. **Protective services:** Criminal justice. **Psychology:** General. **Public administration:** Social work. **Social sciences:** General. **Theology:** Bible, missionary, theology. **Visual/performing arts:** Acting, art, design, interior design, theater design.

**Most popular majors.** Biology 7%, business/marketing 14%, communications/journalism 13%, interdisciplinary studies 12%, public administration/social services 7%, theological studies 13%, visual/performing arts 8%.

**Computing on campus.** 238 workstations in dormitories, library, computer center, student center. Dormitories wired for high-speed internet access and linked to campus network. Commuter students can connect to campus network. Online course registration, online library, helpline, repair service, wireless network available.

**Student life. Freshman orientation:** Mandatory. Preregistration for classes offered. 4 days prior to start of classes in August. **Policies:** Daily chapel is mandatory. Nightly curfew. Religious observance required. **Housing:** Guaranteed on-campus for freshmen. Single-sex dorms, apartments, substance-free housing available. Some student-teacher housing for education majors. **Activities:** Bands, choral groups, drama, international student organizations, music ensembles, musical theater, radio station, student government, student newspaper, TV station, evangelism forum, preachers club, student-alumni association, university student ambassadors, university program council, youth workers club, Impact Team, Young Republicans, Young Democrats.

**Athletics.** NAIA. **Intercollegiate:** Baseball M, basketball, cheerleading W, soccer, softball W, volleyball W. **Intramural:** Badminton, basketball, cross-country, football (non-tackle), racquetball, soccer, softball, table tennis, tennis, volleyball. **Team name:** Lions.

**Student services.** Alcohol/substance abuse counseling, campus ministries, career counseling, student employment services, financial aid counseling, health services, on-campus daycare, personal counseling, placement for graduates, veterans' counselor. **Physically disabled:** Services for visually, hearing impaired.

**Contact.** E-mail: admissions@fhu.edu
Phone: (731) 989-6651 Toll-free number: (800) 630-3480
Fax: (731) 989-6045
Belinda Anderson, Director of Admissions, Freed-Hardeman University, 158 East Main Street, Henderson, TN 38340

## International Academy of Design and Technology: Nashville
**Nashville, Tennessee**
www.iadtnashville.com

- ◆ For-profit 4-year branch campus and visual arts college
- ◆ Commuter campus in very large city
- ◆ 501 degree-seeking undergraduates

**General.** Accredited by ACICS. **Degrees:** 81 associate awarded. **Calendar:** Quarter, extensive summer session. **Full-time faculty:** 9 total. **Part-time faculty:** 31 total.

**Basis for selection.** Open admission.

**2007-2008 Annual costs.** Tuition/fees: $15,875. Books/supplies: $1,800.

**2006-2007 Financial aid. Need-based:** 33% of total undergraduate aid awarded as scholarships/grants, 67% as loans/jobs.

**Application procedures. Admission:** No deadline. $50 fee. **Financial aid:** No deadline.

**Academics. Credit/placement by examination:** CLEP.

**Majors. Business:** Fashion. **Visual/performing arts:** Fashion design, graphic design, interior design.

**Computing on campus.** Online library available.

**Student life. Freshman orientation:** Available.

**Student services.** Student employment services, financial aid counseling, placement for graduates.

**Contact.** E-mail: admissions@iadtnashville.com
Phone: (866) 302-4238
Bruce Schlee, Admissions Director, International Academy of Design and Technology: Nashville, 1 Bridgestone Park, Nashville, TN 37214

## ITT Technical Institute: Knoxville
**Knoxville, Tennessee**
www.itt-tech.edu                    **CB code: 7139**

- ◆ For-profit 4-year technical college
- ◆ Commuter campus in small city

**General.** Accredited by ACICS. **Calendar:** Quarter.

**Annual costs/financial aid.** Tuition varies by program, $260-$368 per credit hour.

**Contact.** Phone: (865) 671-2800
Director of Recruitment, 10208 Technology Drive, Knoxville, TN 37932

## ITT Technical Institute: Memphis
**Cordova, Tennessee**
www.itt-tech.edu                    **CB code: 2731**

- ◆ For-profit 4-year technical college
- ◆ Commuter campus in very large city

**General.** Accredited by ACICS. **Calendar:** Quarter.

**Annual costs/financial aid.** Tuition varies by program, $260-$368 per credit hour.

**Contact.** Phone: (901) 762-0556
Director of Recruitment, 7260 Goodlett Farms Parkway, Cordova, TN 38016

## ITT Technical Institute: Nashville
**Nashville, Tennessee**
www.itt-tech.edu                    **CB code: 7025**

- ◆ For-profit 4-year technical college
- ◆ Commuter campus in very large city

**General.** Accredited by ACICS. **Calendar:** Quarter.

**Annual costs/financial aid.** Tuition varies by program, $260-$368 per credit hour.

**Contact.** Phone: (615) 889-8700
Director of Recruitment, 2845 Elm Hill Pike, Nashville, TN 37214

## Johnson Bible College
**Knoxville, Tennessee**
www.jbc.edu                    **CB code: 1345**

- ◆ Private 4-year Bible college affiliated with Christian Church
- ◆ Residential campus in small city
- ◆ 768 degree-seeking undergraduates
- ◆ 93% of applicants admitted
- ◆ SAT or ACT (ACT writing recommended), application essay required

**General.** Founded in 1893. Regionally accredited; also accredited by ABHE. **Degrees:** 146 bachelor's, 23 associate awarded; master's offered. **Location:** 7 miles from Knoxville. **Calendar:** Semester, limited summer session. **Full-time faculty:** 29 total. **Part-time faculty:** 36 total. **Class size:** 38% < 20, 31% 20-39, 13% 40-49, 19% 50-99.

**Freshman class profile.**

| Mid 50% test scores | | | |
|---|---|---|---|
| SAT critical reading: | 460-590 | GPA 3.0-3.49: | 30% |
| SAT math: | 460-580 | GPA 2.0-2.99: | 28% |
| SAT writing: | 460-570 | Rank in top quarter: | 46% |
| ACT composite: | 19-26 | Rank in top tenth: | 20% |
| GPA 3.50 or higher: | 42% | Out-of-state: | 83% |
| | | Live on campus: | 96% |

**Basis for selection.** High school transcript and 3 references, 1 from minister required. Combination of high school percentile rank and ACT score determines initial admission criteria. Interview recommended.

**High school preparation.** 16 units required. Required units include academic electives 4. 12 of the 16 units must be content courses such as English, history, mathematics, foreign language, and science.

**2007-2008 Annual costs.** Tuition/fees: $7,180. Part-time students pay mandatory fee of $30.42 per credit hour. Room/board: $4,890. Books/supplies: $900. Personal expenses: $2,060.

**Financial aid. Non-need-based:** Scholarships awarded for academics, leadership, minority status, music/drama, religious affiliation, state residency.

**Application procedures. Admission:** Closing date 7/1 (receipt date). $35 fee. Admission notification 9/1. Admission notification on a rolling basis. **Financial aid:** Priority date 5/1, closing date 8/1. FAFSA, institutional form required. Applicants notified on a rolling basis starting 4/30; must reply within 2 week(s) of notification.

**Academics.** All degree programs have major in Bible. Double majors in Bible and music, Bible and teacher education, Bible and counseling, Bible and preaching, Bible and youth ministry/preaching offered. **Special study options:** Accelerated study, combined bachelor's/graduate degree, cooperative education, distance learning, double major, ESL, honors, independent study, internships, teacher certification program. **Credit/placement by examination:** AP, CLEP, institutional tests. 32 credit hours maximum toward bachelor's degree. **Support services:** Learning center, remedial instruction, study skills assistance, tutoring.

**Majors. Theology:** Bible, sacred music.

**Most popular majors.** Education 13%, philosophy/religious studies 87%.

**Computing on campus.** 35 workstations in library, computer center. Dormitories linked to campus network. Helpline, student web hosting, wireless network available.

**Student life. Freshman orientation:** Mandatory. Preregistration for classes offered. Weekend preceeding first semester. **Policies:** Religious observance required. **Housing:** Single-sex dorms, apartments, substance-free housing available. $100 deposit, deadline 8/1. Mobile homes, duplex houses, and apartments available for family housing. **Activities:** Choral groups, drama, music ensembles, musical theater, radio station, student government.

**Athletics.** NCCAA. **Intercollegiate:** Baseball M, basketball, soccer, volleyball W. **Intramural:** Basketball, softball, tennis, volleyball.

**Student services.** Alcohol/substance abuse counseling, campus ministries, career counseling, student employment services, financial aid counseling, health services, on-campus daycare, personal counseling, placement for graduates.

**Contact.** E-mail: twingfield@jbc.edu
Phone: (865) 251-2233 Toll-free number: (800) 827-2122
Fax: (865) 251-2336
Tim Wingfield, Director of Admissions, Johnson Bible College, 7900
Johnson Drive, Knoxville, TN 37998-0001

## King College
### Bristol, Tennessee
### www.king.edu
**CB member**
**CB code: 1371**

- Private 4-year nursing and liberal arts college affiliated with
  Presbyterian Church (USA)
- Residential campus in large town
- 1,192 degree-seeking undergraduates: 2% part-time, 63% women, 2%
  African American, 1% Asian American, 2% Hispanic American, 3%
  international
- 249 degree-seeking graduate students
- 26% of applicants admitted
- SAT or ACT (ACT writing optional), application essay required
- 53% graduate within 6 years; 3% enter graduate study

**General.** Founded in 1867. Regionally accredited. Christian values emphasized. **Degrees:** 247 bachelor's awarded; master's offered. **Location:** 110
miles from Knoxville, 95 miles from Asheville, North Carolina. **Calendar:**
Semester, limited summer session. **Full-time faculty:** 58 total; 81% have
terminal degrees, 3% minority, 53% women. **Part-time faculty:** 85 total;
59% have terminal degrees, 2% minority. **Class size:** 83% < 20, 16% 20-
39, less than 1% 40-49, less than 1% 50-99. **Special facilities:** Observatory,
nuclear physics laboratory.

**Freshman class profile.** 856 applied, 222 admitted, 184 enrolled.

| Mid 50% test scores | | | |
|---|---|---|---|
| SAT critical reading: | 430-530 | Rank in top quarter: | 49% |
| SAT math: | 450-550 | Rank in top tenth: | 24% |
| ACT composite: | 21-26 | Return as sophomores: | 71% |
| GPA 3.50 or higher: | 49% | Out-of-state: | 50% |
| GPA 3.0-3.49: | 30% | Live on campus: | 86% |
| GPA 2.0-2.99: | 20% | International: | 4% |

**Basis for selection.** Qualified applicants should have a minimum of a
2.4/4.0 GPA and a minimum ACT or SAT composite score of 19 or 890
(exclusive of Writing). Those who do not present this pattern may be conditionally accepted with permission from the Admissions Committee. SAT
or ACT scores must be received by the 1st day of fall classes for fall-term
admission. SAT Writing scores are used for finanaical aid eligibility purposes only. Interview recommended.

**High school preparation.** 19 units required. Required units include English 4, mathematics 3, social studies 2, history 2, science 1 (laboratory 1),
foreign language 2, computer science 1 and academic electives 4. 2 Algebra
(Algebra I and II); one unit of Geometry; 1 Natural Science required.

**2007-2008 Annual costs.** Tuition/fees: $19,262. Room/board: $6,508.
Books/supplies: $800.

**2007-2008 Financial aid. Need-based:** 163 full-time freshmen applied
for aid; 151 were judged to have need; 151 of these received aid. Average
need met was 80%. Average scholarship/grant was $14,147; average loan
$4,010. 64% of total undergraduate aid awarded as scholarships/grants, 36%
as loans/jobs. **Non-need-based:** Awarded to 493 full-time undergraduates,
including 96 freshmen. Scholarships awarded for academics, athletics, music/
drama.

**Application procedures. Admission:** No deadline. $20 fee, may be
waived for applicants with need. Application may be submitted online. Admission notification on a rolling basis. Refund available in full until May 1.
**Financial aid:** Priority date 3/1; no closing date. FAFSA required. Applicants notified on a rolling basis starting 4/1; must reply within 2 week(s) of
notification.

**Academics. Special study options:** Accelerated study, combined bachelor's/
graduate degree, cross-registration, double major, dual enrollment of high
school students, ESL, exchange student, honors, independent study, internships, student-designed major, study abroad, teacher certification program,
Washington semester. **Credit/placement by examination:** AP, CLEP, SAT,
ACT, institutional tests. 30 credit hours maximum toward bachelor's degree. **Support services:** Learning center, reduced course load, remedial instruction, study skills assistance, tutoring, writing center.

**Honors college/program.** Current students may be invited to join the
Jack E. Snider Honors Center by invitation from a faculty member. Prospective students will meet entrance exam requirements.

**Majors. Area/ethnic studies:** American. **Biology:** General, biochemistry,
biophysics. **Business:** Accounting, business admin, management information systems. **Communications:** Digital media. **Education:** Music. **English:** English lit. **Foreign languages:** General, French, Spanish. **Health:**
Athletic training, clinical lab science, nursing (RN). **History:** General. **Math:**
General. **Parks/recreation:** Health/fitness. **Philosophy/religion:** Religion.
**Physical sciences:** Chemistry, physics. **Psychology:** General. **Social sciences:** Economics, political science. **Theology:** Bible, youth ministry. **Visual/
performing arts:** General. **Other:** Applied Science, Engineering.

**Most popular majors.** Business/marketing 18%, health sciences 51%,
psychology 6%.

**Computing on campus.** PC or laptop required. 88 workstations in library, computer center, student center. Dormitories wired for high-speed
internet access and linked to campus network. Commuter students can connect to campus network. Online library, helpline, repair service, wireless
network available.

**Student life. Freshman orientation:** Available. Preregistration for classes
offered. **Policies:** Traditional undergraduate students participate in Chapel
and Convocation series as a part of their service requirements necessary to
fulfill degree requirements. Religious observance required. **Housing:** Guaranteed on-campus for all undergraduates. Single-sex dorms, special housing
for disabled, apartments available. $50 fully refundable deposit. **Activities:**
Bands, campus ministries, choral groups, dance, drama, international student organizations, literary magazine, music ensembles, musical theater, student government, student newspaper, Fellowship of Christian Athletes, Young
Life Leadership, Student Life and Activities Committee at King, Students in
Free Enterprise, King College Republicans, World Christian Fellowship,
literary society.

**Athletics.** NAIA. **Intercollegiate:** Baseball M, basketball, cheerleading,
cross-country, golf, soccer, softball W, tennis, track and field, volleyball W,
wrestling M. **Intramural:** Badminton, basketball, cross-country, football
(non-tackle), golf, soccer, softball W, table tennis, track and field, volleyball. **Team name:** Tornado.

**Student services.** Adult student services, campus ministries, career counseling, student employment services, financial aid counseling, health services, personal counseling, placement for graduates.

**Contact.** E-mail: admissions@king.edu
Phone: (423) 652-4861 Toll-free number: (800) 362-0014
Fax: (423) 652-4727
Melinda Clark, Vice President of Enrollment Management, King College,
1350 King College Road, Bristol, TN 37620-2699

## Lambuth University
### Jackson, Tennessee
### www.lambuth.edu
**CB code: 1394**

- Private 4-year university and liberal arts college affiliated with United
  Methodist Church
- Residential campus in small city
- 721 degree-seeking undergraduates: 2% part-time, 51% women, 19%
  African American, 2% Asian American, 2% Hispanic American, 3%
  international
- 49% of applicants admitted
- SAT or ACT (ACT writing optional), application essay required
- 40% graduate within 6 years; 21% enter graduate study

**General.** Founded in 1843. Regionally accredited. **Degrees:** 153 bachelor's awarded. **Location:** 80 miles from Memphis, 120 miles from Nashville. **Calendar:** Semester, limited summer session. **Full-time faculty:** 67
total; 66% have terminal degrees, 3% minority, 39% women. **Part-time
faculty:** 30 total; 20% have terminal degrees, 7% minority, 33% women.
**Class size:** 77% < 20, 22% 20-39, less than 1% 50-99. **Special facilities:**
Planetarium, art and interior design complex, biological field station, education curriculum lab.

**Freshman class profile.** 826 applied, 407 admitted, 172 enrolled.

| Mid 50% test scores | | | |
|---|---|---|---|
| SAT critical reading: | 450-570 | Rank in top quarter: | 48% |
| SAT math: | 460-570 | Rank in top tenth: | 23% |
| ACT composite: | 20-25 | End year in good standing: | 94% |
| GPA 3.50 or higher: | 37% | Return as sophomores: | 60% |
| GPA 3.0-3.49: | 27% | Out-of-state: | 19% |
| GPA 2.0-2.99: | 34% | Live on campus: | 87% |
| | | International: | 4% |

**Basis for selection.** High school comprehensive record, test scores important. Applicants whose native language is not English need to provide
evidence of English proficiency by results of TOEFL or results of ACT or

SAT. Other approved English proficiency tests may be considered. Audition required for drama, music programs; portfolio recommended for art program; tryouts required for athletes. **Learning Disabled:** Appropriate documentation supporting request for accommodations must be provided to director of student disabilities.

**High school preparation.** 14 units recommended. Recommended units include English 4, mathematics 3, social studies 2, history 1, science 3 and foreign language 1.

**2007-2008 Annual costs.** Tuition/fees: $17,400. Room/board: $7,160. Books/supplies: $1,200. Personal expenses: $1,732.

**2007-2008 Financial aid. Need-based:** 159 full-time freshmen applied for aid; 137 were judged to have need; 135 of these received aid. Average need met was 92%. Average scholarship/grant was $14,484; average loan $5,160. 77% of total undergraduate aid awarded as scholarships/grants, 23% as loans/jobs. **Non-need-based:** Awarded to 265 full-time undergraduates, including 91 freshmen. Scholarships awarded for academics, alumni affiliation, art, athletics, job skills, leadership, music/drama, religious affiliation, state residency. **Additional information:** Part-time students eligible for federal and state aid, but not institutional aid.

**Application procedures. Admission:** No deadline. $25 fee, may be waived for applicants with need. Application may be submitted online. Admission notification on a rolling basis beginning on or about 10/1. Must reply by May 1 or within 2 week(s) if notified thereafter. **Financial aid:** Priority date 2/15; no closing date. FAFSA required. Applicants notified on a rolling basis starting 3/1; must reply by 5/1 or within 2 week(s) of notification.

**Academics.** Math and science study halls are held three nights during the week and are led by professors and peer tutors. **Special study options:** Combined bachelor's/graduate degree, cross-registration, double major, ESL, honors, independent study, internships, liberal arts/career combination, student-designed major, study abroad, teacher certification program, Washington semester. Legislative internships at state and national level. **Credit/placement by examination:** AP, CLEP, IB, SAT, ACT. 32 credit hours maximum toward bachelor's degree. **Support services:** Learning center, reduced course load, remedial instruction, study skills assistance, tutoring.

**Majors. Biology:** General. **Business:** General, accounting, accounting/business management, business admin, fashion, international, management information systems, managerial economics, marketing. **Communications:** General. **Computer sciences:** General. **Conservation:** Environmental science. **Education:** General, art, biology, business, chemistry, Deaf/hearing impaired, developmentally delayed, elementary, English, health, history, mathematics, mentally handicapped, middle, multiple handicapped, music, physical, secondary, special, speech impaired. **English:** English lit. **Family/consumer sciences:** General, clothing/textiles, food/nutrition. **Foreign languages:** General, French, Germanic, Spanish. **Health:** Communication disorders. **History:** General. **Interdisciplinary:** Global studies. **Legal studies:** Prelaw. **Liberal arts:** Arts/sciences. **Math:** General. **Parks/recreation:** Facilities management, health/fitness, sports admin. **Philosophy/religion:** Philosophy, religion. **Physical sciences:** Chemistry. **Protective services:** Law enforcement admin. **Psychology:** General. **Public administration:** Social work. **Social sciences:** International relations, political science, sociology. **Theology:** Sacred music. **Visual/performing arts:** General, art, art history/conservation, design, dramatic, interior design, music performance, piano/organ, studio arts, voice/opera.

**Most popular majors.** Business/marketing 15%, communications/journalism 7%, education 7%, English 6%, parks/recreation 13%, psychology 10%, social sciences 12%, visual/performing arts 7%.

**Computing on campus.** 100 workstations in dormitories, library, computer center, student center. Dormitories wired for high-speed internet access and linked to campus network. Commuter students can connect to campus network. Online library, helpline, repair service, wireless network available.

**Student life. Freshman orientation:** Mandatory, $55 fee. Preregistration for classes offered. Held each summer and one-session several days prior to the beginning of classes. **Policies:** No alcohol regardless of age, no drug paraphernalia, hazing, fireworks, or firearms. **Housing:** Guaranteed on-campus for freshmen. Coed dorms, single-sex dorms, special housing for disabled, apartments, fraternity/sorority housing, substance-free housing available. $100 nonrefundable deposit, deadline 5/1. **Activities:** Bands, campus ministries, choral groups, dance, drama, international student organizations, literary magazine, music ensembles, Model UN, musical theater, student government, student newspaper, Black Student Union, Alpha Omega, Gamma Beta Phi, Fellowship of Christian Athletes, Best Buddies, Phi Sigma Eta, Religious Life Council, Companions in Christ, Discipleship/Accountability groups.

**Athletics.** NAIA. **Intercollegiate:** Baseball M, basketball, cheerleading, cross-country, football (tackle) M, golf, soccer, softball W, swimming, tennis, volleyball W. **Intramural:** Basketball, football (non-tackle), softball, swimming, table tennis, volleyball. **Team name:** Eagles.

**Student services.** Campus ministries, career counseling, student employment services, financial aid counseling, health services, personal counseling, placement for graduates, veterans' counselor. **Physically disabled:** Services for visually, speech, hearing impaired.

**Contact.** E-mail: admit@lambuth.edu
Phone: (731) 425-3223 Toll-free number: (800) 526-2884
Fax: (731) 425-3496
Sharon Handelsman, Interim Vice President for Enrollment, Lambuth University, 705 Lambuth Boulevard, Jackson, TN 38301-5296

## Lane College
**Jackson, Tennessee**
**www.lanecollege.edu**                    **CB code: 1395**

- Private 4-year liberal arts college affiliated with Christian Methodist Episcopal Church
- Residential campus in small city
- 1,766 degree-seeking undergraduates: 1% part-time, 50% women
- 36% of applicants admitted
- SAT or ACT required

**General.** Founded in 1882. Regionally accredited. **Degrees:** 149 bachelor's awarded. **Location:** 80 miles from Memphis, 126 miles from Nashville. **Calendar:** Semester, limited summer session. **Full-time faculty:** 57 total. **Part-time faculty:** 1 total. **Class size:** 33% < 20, 64% 20-39, 3% 40-49. **Special facilities:** The college currently operates a radio from the campus to aid students majoring in mass communication.

**Freshman class profile.** 3,979 applied, 1,438 admitted, 594 enrolled.

| | | | |
|---|---|---|---|
| GPA 3.50 or higher: | 49% | Rank in top tenth: | 28% |
| GPA 3.0-3.49: | 45% | Out-of-state: | 48% |
| Rank in top quarter: | 53% | Live on campus: | 97% |

**Basis for selection.** School achievement record and recommendations most important. TOEFL required to establish language proficiency. Interview, audition recommended.

**High school preparation.** 16 units required. Required and recommended units include English 4, mathematics 2, social studies 2, history 2, science 2 (laboratory 1) and foreign language 2.

**2007-2008 Annual costs.** Tuition/fees: $7,620. Room/board: $5,000. Books/supplies: $1,000. Personal expenses: $675.

**2006-2007 Financial aid.** All financial aid based on need. 52% of total undergraduate aid awarded as scholarships/grants, 48% as loans/jobs.

**Application procedures. Admission:** Priority date 7/1; deadline 8/1 (postmark date). No application fee. Application may be submitted online. Admission notification on a rolling basis beginning on or about 2/1. Must reply by May 1 or within 2 week(s) if notified thereafter. **Financial aid:** Priority date 3/1; no closing date. FAFSA, institutional form required. Applicants notified on a rolling basis starting 3/31; must reply within 2 week(s) of notification.

**Academics. Special study options:** Accelerated study, independent study, internships, study abroad, teacher certification program. **Credit/placement by examination:** AP, CLEP. **Support services:** Study skills assistance, tutoring, writing center.

**Majors. Biology:** General. **Business:** Business admin. **Communications:** General. **Computer sciences:** General. **Education:** Physical. **English:** English lit. **Foreign languages:** French. **History:** General. **Math:** General. **Philosophy/religion:** Religion. **Physical sciences:** Chemistry, physics. **Protective services:** Criminal justice. **Social sciences:** Sociology.

**Most popular majors.** Biology 14%, business/marketing 20%, communications/journalism 9%, computer/information sciences 6%, education 8%, interdisciplinary studies 13%, security/protective services 14%, social sciences 7%.

**Computing on campus.** 470 workstations in library, computer center. Dormitories wired for high-speed internet access and linked to campus network. Online library, helpline, wireless network available.

**Student life. Freshman orientation:** Mandatory. Preregistration for classes offered. Held during weekend in July. **Policies:** Religious observance required. **Housing:** Guaranteed on-campus for all undergraduates. Single-sex dorms available. $50 deposit. **Activities:** Bands, choral groups, dance, drama, music ensembles, student government, student newspaper, Student Ministerial Alliance, Student Christian Association, Pre-Alumni Council.

**Athletics.** NCAA. **Intercollegiate:** Baseball M, basketball, cross-country, football (tackle) M, softball W, tennis, track and field, volleyball W. **Intramural:** Badminton, basketball, softball, swimming, table tennis, volleyball. **Team name:** Dragons.

**Student services.** Alcohol/substance abuse counseling, campus ministries, career counseling, services for economically disadvantaged, student employment services, financial aid counseling, health services, personal counseling, placement for graduates, veterans' counselor.

**Contact.** E-mail: ebrown@lanecollege.edu
Phone: (731) 426-7532 Toll-free number: (800) 960-7533
Fax: (731) 426-7559
Evelyn Brown, Director of Admissions, Lane College, 545 Lane Avenue, Jackson, TN 38301-4598

## Lee University
### Cleveland, Tennessee
### www.leeuniversity.edu
**CB code: 1401**

- Private 4-year university and liberal arts college affiliated with Church of God
- Residential campus in large town
- 3,586 degree-seeking undergraduates: 8% part-time, 56% women, 5% African American, 1% Asian American, 3% Hispanic American, 1% Native American, 6% international
- 316 degree-seeking graduate students
- 50% graduate within 6 years

**General.** Founded in 1918. Regionally accredited. **Degrees:** 661 bachelor's awarded; master's offered. **Location:** 20 miles from Chattanooga, 75 miles from Knoxville. **Calendar:** Semester, limited summer session. **Full-time faculty:** 162 total; 79% have terminal degrees, 14% minority, 32% women. **Part-time faculty:** 167 total; 19% have terminal degrees, 7% minority, 44% women. **Class size:** 53% < 20, 35% 20-39, 7% 40-49, 4% 50-99, 1% >100.

**Freshman class profile.** 1,601 applied, 823 admitted, 792 enrolled.

| Mid 50% test scores | | Rank in top quarter: | 49% |
|---|---|---|---|
| SAT critical reading: | 470-630 | Rank in top tenth: | 23% |
| SAT math: | 450-620 | Return as sophomores: | 71% |
| ACT composite: | 20-27 | Out-of-state: | 62% |
| GPA 3.50 or higher: | 50% | Live on campus: | 95% |
| GPA 3.0-3.49: | 26% | International: | 6% |
| GPA 2.0-2.99: | 22% | | |

**Basis for selection.** Open admission, but selective for some programs. School achievement record and test scores considered. SAT or ACT required for placement only, except for applicants with 16 college semester hours (24 college semester hours for TN residents). Audition required for music program. **Homeschooled:** Must have high school transcript with date of graduation and 17 on ACT or 860 on SAT (exclusive of Writing).

**High school preparation.** 13 units required; 14 recommended. Required and recommended units include English 4, mathematics 3, social studies 2, history 1, science 2, foreign language 1 and computer science 1.

**2007-2008 Annual costs.** Tuition/fees: $10,782. Room/board: $5,276. Books/supplies: $800. Personal expenses: $1,350.

**2007-2008 Financial aid. Need-based:** Average need met was 66%. Average scholarship/grant was $7,625; average loan $3,478. 48% of total undergraduate aid awarded as scholarships/grants, 52% as loans/jobs. **Non-need-based:** Scholarships awarded for academics, alumni affiliation, athletics, leadership, minority status, music/drama, religious affiliation, state residency.

**Application procedures. Admission:** Closing date 9/1 (receipt date). $25 fee. Application may be submitted online. Admission notification on a rolling basis beginning on or about 9/1. **Financial aid:** Priority date 3/15; no closing date. FAFSA required. Applicants notified on a rolling basis starting 2/1; must reply within 3 week(s) of notification.

**Academics. Special study options:** Distance learning, double major, dual enrollment of high school students, ESL, exchange student, external degree, honors, independent study, internships, liberal arts/career combination, study abroad, teacher certification program, Washington semester. **Credit/placement by examination:** AP, CLEP, IB, institutional tests. 32 credit hours maximum toward bachelor's degree. **Support services:** Learning center, pre-admission summer program, reduced course load, remedial instruction, tutoring, writing center.

**Majors. Biology:** General, biochemistry, environmental. **Business:** Accounting, business admin. **Communications:** General, advertising, digital media, journalism, public relations. **Computer sciences:** General. **Education:** General, biology, business, early childhood, elementary, English, foreign languages, health, history, mathematics, music, physical, psychology, secondary, Spanish, special. **English:** English lit. **Family/consumer sciences:** Family studies. **Foreign languages:** French, Spanish. **Health:** Athletic training, health services. **History:** General. **Math:** General. **Parks/recreation:** Health/fitness. **Physical sciences:** Chemistry. **Psychology:** General. **Social sciences:** Anthropology, political science, sociology. **Theology:** Bible, missionary, pastoral counseling, preministerial, religious ed, sacred music, theology, youth ministry. **Visual/performing arts:** Dramatic, music management, music performance. **Other:** Missiology/Intercultural Studies.

**Most popular majors.** Business/marketing 14%, communications/journalism 8%, education 22%, history 9%, psychology 9%, theological studies 18%.

**Computing on campus.** 429 workstations in dormitories, library, computer center, student center. Dormitories wired for high-speed internet access and linked to campus network. Online library, helpline, wireless network available.

**Student life. Freshman orientation:** Mandatory. Preregistration for classes offered. New student and parent orientation held weekend before classes begin. **Policies:** Religious observance required. **Housing:** Guaranteed on-campus for freshmen. Single-sex dorms, apartments, substance-free housing available. $200 fully refundable deposit, deadline 9/1. University leases apartments and houses for students. **Activities:** Bands, choral groups, drama, international student organizations, literary magazine, music ensembles, musical theater, opera, student government, student newspaper, symphony orchestra, Greek councils, student leadership council, Collegiate Sertoma, Married Students Fellowship, Pioneers for Christ, Fellowship of Christian Athletes, Missions Alive, Deaf Ministry Association.

**Athletics.** NAIA, NCCAA. **Intercollegiate:** Baseball M, basketball, cross-country, golf M, soccer, softball W, tennis, volleyball W. **Intramural:** Basketball, bowling, football (non-tackle) M, racquetball, soccer, softball, table tennis, tennis, volleyball. **Team name:** Flames.

**Student services.** Alcohol/substance abuse counseling, campus ministries, career counseling, student employment services, financial aid counseling, health services, personal counseling, placement for graduates, veterans' counselor.

**Contact.** E-mail: admissions@leeuniversity.edu
Phone: (423) 614-8500 Toll-free number: (800) 533-9930
Fax: (423) 614-8533
Phil Cook, Assistant Vice President for Enrollment, Lee University, 1120 North Ocoee Street, Cleveland, TN 37320-3450

## LeMoyne-Owen College
### Memphis, Tennessee
### www.loc.edu
**CB member**
**CB code: 1403**

- Private 4-year liberal arts college affiliated with United Church of Christ and Tennessee Baptist Convention
- Commuter campus in very large city
- 569 degree-seeking undergraduates: 15% part-time, 64% women, 98% African American, 1% international
- 68% of applicants admitted
- SAT or ACT (ACT writing recommended) required

**General.** Founded in 1862. Regionally accredited. **Degrees:** 127 bachelor's awarded. **ROTC:** Army, Air Force. **Calendar:** Semester, extensive summer session. **Full-time faculty:** 50 total; 68% have terminal degrees, 82% minority, 46% women. **Part-time faculty:** 33 total; 6% have terminal degrees, 97% minority, 54% women. **Class size:** 82% < 20, 18% 20-39, less than 1% 40-49.

**Freshman class profile.** 698 applied, 477 admitted, 84 enrolled.

| Mid 50% test scores | | Return as sophomores: | 48% |
|---|---|---|---|
| ACT composite: | 14-17 | Out-of-state: | 5% |
| End year in good standing: | 70% | Live on campus: | 10% |

**Basis for selection.** High school transcript, test scores, letter of recommendation, and interview important. Special consideration given to children of alumni. Essay, interview recommended.

**High school preparation.** 15 units required. Required units include English 4, mathematics 3, history 2, science 3, foreign language 2 and academic electives 1.

**2007-2008 Annual costs.** Tuition/fees: $10,098. Room/board: $4,852. Books/supplies: $750. Personal expenses: $1,800.

**2006-2007 Financial aid. Need-based:** 83 full-time freshmen applied for aid; 78 were judged to have need; 76 of these received aid. Average need met was 47%. Average scholarship/grant was $6,274; average loan $2,226. 62% of total undergraduate aid awarded as scholarships/grants, 38% as loans/jobs. **Non-need-based:** Awarded to 58 full-time undergraduates, including 9 freshmen. Scholarships awarded for academics, athletics, music/ drama.

**Application procedures. Admission:** Closing date 4/15. $25 fee, may be waived for applicants with need. Application may be submitted online. Admission notification on a rolling basis. Must reply by May 1 or within 2 week(s) if notified thereafter. **Financial aid:** Priority date 4/15; no closing date. FAFSA required. Applicants notified on a rolling basis starting 4/1.

**Academics. Special study options:** Accelerated study, cooperative education, cross-registration, distance learning, double major, dual enrollment of high school students, exchange student, honors, internships, liberal arts/ career combination, student-designed major, study abroad, teacher certification program, weekend college. **Credit/placement by examination:** AP, CLEP, IB, ACT, institutional tests. 24 credit hours maximum toward bachelor's degree. **Support services:** Learning center, pre-admission summer program, reduced course load, remedial instruction, tutoring.

**Majors. Biology:** General. **Business:** Business admin. **Computer sciences:** Computer science, information technology. **Education:** Early childhood, English, mathematics, science, social studies, special. **English:** English lit. **History:** General. **Liberal arts:** Humanities. **Math:** General. **Physical sciences:** Chemistry. **Protective services:** Police science. **Public administration:** Social work. **Social sciences:** General, political science, sociology. **Visual/performing arts:** Art.

**Most popular majors.** Biology 8%, business/marketing 39%, education 19%, security/protective services 11%.

**Computing on campus.** 223 workstations in library, computer center. Helpline, repair service available.

**Student life. Freshman orientation:** Mandatory. Preregistration for classes offered. **Housing:** Single-sex dorms, substance-free housing available. $100 deposit. **Activities:** Jazz band, choral groups, dance, drama, music ensembles, student government, student newspaper, NAACP, Social Work Club, Students for Free Enterprise, Pre-Alumni Council, National Student Business Organization.

**Athletics.** NCAA. **Intercollegiate:** Baseball M, basketball, cross-country, golf, soccer, softball W, tennis, volleyball W. **Intramural:** Basketball. **Team name:** Magicians.

**Student services.** Adult student services, career counseling, student employment services, health services, personal counseling, placement for graduates, veterans' counselor.

**Contact.** E-mail: admission@loc.edu
Phone: (901) 435-1500 Fax: (901) 435-1524
June Chinn-Jointer, Director of Admissions/Recruitment, LeMoyne-Owen College, 807 Walker Avenue, Memphis, TN 38126

## Lincoln Memorial University
**Harrogate, Tennessee**
www.lmunet.edu

CB member
CB code: 1408

- Private 4-year university and liberal arts college
- Commuter campus in small town
- 1,481 degree-seeking undergraduates
- 64% of applicants admitted

**General.** Founded in 1897. Regionally accredited. **Degrees:** 140 bachelor's, 163 associate awarded; master's offered. **Location:** 50 miles from Knoxville. **Calendar:** Semester, limited summer session. **Full-time faculty:** 159 total. **Part-time faculty:** 73 total. **Class size:** 71% < 20, 28% 20-39, less than 1% 40-49, less than 1% 50-99, less than 1% >100. **Special facilities:** Abraham Lincoln Library and Museum, Cumberland Mountain Research Center.

**Freshman class profile.** 1,168 applied, 744 admitted, 249 enrolled.

| Mid 50% test scores | | | |
|---|---|---|---|
| SAT critical reading: | 450-540 | Out-of-state: | 52% |
| SAT math: | 450-550 | Live on campus: | 32% |
| ACT composite: | 18-23 | Fraternities: | 5% |
| | | Sororities: | 10% |

**Basis for selection.** Academic record, ACT or SAT, recommendations, interviews for some programs. Specialized programs often have admission requirements in addition to those of the general university. In some programs, specialized admission tests also required. Interviews and essays help candidates seeking academic or talent related scholarships. **Homeschooled:** Must submit SAT or ACT scores.

**High school preparation.** 10 units required; 22 recommended. Required and recommended units include English 4, mathematics 2-3, social studies 1-2, history 1, science 2, foreign language 2 and academic electives 7.

**2007-2008 Annual costs.** Tuition/fees: $14,400. Room/board: $5,380.

**Financial aid. Non-need-based:** Scholarships awarded for academics, athletics, music/drama, state residency.

**Application procedures. Admission:** Priority date 3/1; no deadline. $25 fee, may be waived for applicants with need. Admission notification on a rolling basis beginning on or about 9/1. **Financial aid:** Priority date 4/1; no closing date. FAFSA required. Applicants notified on a rolling basis starting 4/15; must reply within 3 week(s) of notification.

**Academics. Special study options:** Double major, ESL, independent study, internships, liberal arts/career combination, teacher certification program. **Credit/placement by examination:** AP, CLEP, IB, ACT, institutional tests. 16 credit hours maximum toward associate degree, 32 toward bachelor's. **Support services:** Learning center, reduced course load, remedial instruction, study skills assistance, tutoring.

**Majors. Area/ethnic studies:** American. **Biology:** General. **Business:** General, accounting, business admin, management science, managerial economics, office/clerical. **Communications:** General, broadcast journalism. **Computer sciences:** General. **Conservation:** General, fisheries, wildlife. **Education:** General, art, biology, business, chemistry, early childhood, elementary, English, health, history, mathematics, middle, physical, science, secondary, social science, social studies. **English:** English lit. **Health:** Athletic training, clinical lab science, clinical lab technology, nursing (RN), predental, premedicine, prepharmacy, preveterinary, veterinary technology/assistant. **History:** General. **Legal studies:** Prelaw. **Liberal arts:** Arts/sciences. **Math:** General. **Parks/recreation:** Health/fitness. **Physical sciences:** Chemistry. **Psychology:** General. **Public administration:** Social work. **Social sciences:** General. **Visual/performing arts:** General, art.

**Most popular majors.** Business/marketing 16%, computer/information sciences 10%, education 26%, health sciences 13%, history 6%, public administration/social services 8%.

**Computing on campus.** 150 workstations in library, computer center. Dormitories wired for high-speed internet access and linked to campus network. Commuter students can connect to campus network. Online library available.

**Student life. Freshman orientation:** Mandatory. Preregistration for classes offered. 4 sessions over summer proceeding fall semester. **Housing:** Guaranteed on-campus for all undergraduates. Coed dorms, single-sex dorms, apartments available. $100 deposit, deadline 8/1. **Activities:** Choral groups, drama, literary magazine, radio station, student government, student newspaper, TV station, Baptist Student Union, Wesley Foundation.

**Athletics.** NCAA. **Intercollegiate:** Baseball M, basketball, cheerleading, cross-country, golf, soccer, softball W, tennis, volleyball W. **Intramural:** Basketball, soccer M, softball, table tennis, volleyball. **Team name:** Railsplitters.

**Student services.** Alcohol/substance abuse counseling, career counseling, financial aid counseling, on-campus daycare, personal counseling, placement for graduates, veterans' counselor.

**Contact.** E-mail: admissions@lmunet.edu
Phone: (423) 869-3611 ext. 6280 Toll-free
number: (800) 325-0900 ext. 6280 Fax: (423) 869-6250
Conrad Daniels, Dean of Admissions, Lincoln Memorial University, 6965 Cumberland Gap Parkway, Harrogate, TN 37752-1901

## Lipscomb University
**Nashville, Tennessee**
www.lipscomb.edu

CB code: 1161

- Private 4-year Bible and liberal arts college affiliated with Church of Christ
- Residential campus in very large city
- 2,319 degree-seeking undergraduates: 8% part-time, 57% women, 5% African American, 2% Asian American, 2% Hispanic American, 1% international

- 368 degree-seeking graduate students
- 57% of applicants admitted
- SAT or ACT (ACT writing recommended) required
- 57% graduate within 6 years

**General.** Founded in 1891. Regionally accredited. **Degrees:** 477 bachelor's awarded; master's, first professional offered. **ROTC:** Army, Air Force. **Location:** 4 miles from downtown. **Calendar:** Semester, extensive summer session. **Full-time faculty:** 108 total; 85% have terminal degrees, 2% minority, 26% women. **Part-time faculty:** 176 total; 48% have terminal degrees, 5% minority, 42% women. **Class size:** 61% < 20, 33% 20-39, 4% 40-49, 2% 50-99.

**Freshman class profile.** 2,240 applied, 1,274 admitted, 576 enrolled.

| Mid 50% test scores | | | |
|---|---|---|---|
| SAT critical reading: | 500-610 | GPA 2.0-2.99: | 12% |
| SAT math: | 490-620 | Rank in top quarter: | 52% |
| SAT writing: | 490-590 | Rank in top tenth: | 25% |
| ACT composite: | 21-27 | Return as sophomores: | 76% |
| GPA 3.50 or higher: | 52% | Out-of-state: | 35% |
| GPA 3.0-3.49: | 35% | Live on campus: | 90% |
| | | International: | 1% |

**Basis for selection.** School achievement record, test scores, educational and personal references required. Strong moral character desired. Essay recommended for all; audition required for music; portfolio required for art; interview recommended for art, honors, music programs.

**High school preparation.** 14 units required. Required units include English 4, mathematics 2, social studies 2, science 2, foreign language 2 and academic electives 2. Math units preferably Algebra I, II. Foreign language units in the same language. 2 academic electives should be selected from natural sciences, mathematics, foreign languages, or social sciences.

**2007-2008 Annual costs.** Tuition/fees: $16,811. Room/board: $7,070. Books/supplies: $1,000. Personal expenses: $1,250.

**2007-2008 Financial aid. Need-based:** 564 full-time freshmen applied for aid; 347 were judged to have need; 347 of these received aid. Average need met was 69%. Average scholarship/grant was $5,999; average loan $4,138. 63% of total undergraduate aid awarded as scholarships/grants, 37% as loans/jobs. **Non-need-based:** Awarded to 1,482 full-time undergraduates, including 468 freshmen. Scholarships awarded for academics, alumni affiliation, art, athletics, leadership, minority status, music/drama, religious affiliation, state residency.

**Application procedures. Admission:** Priority date 10/31; no deadline. $25 fee, may be waived for applicants with need. Application may be submitted online. Admission notification on a rolling basis beginning on or about 8/15. **Financial aid:** Priority date 3/1; no closing date. FAFSA required. Applicants notified on a rolling basis starting 2/15.

**Academics. Special study options:** Cross-registration, distance learning, double major, dual enrollment of high school students, honors, independent study, internships, study abroad, teacher certification program, weekend college. **Credit/placement by examination:** AP, CLEP, IB, SAT, ACT, institutional tests. 30 credit hours maximum toward bachelor's degree. **Support services:** Learning center, pre-admission summer program, reduced course load, remedial instruction, study skills assistance, tutoring, writing center.

**Majors. Area/ethnic studies:** American. **Biology:** General, biochemistry. **Business:** Accounting, business admin, fashion, human resources, international, management information systems, managerial economics, marketing. **Communications:** Journalism, media studies, organizational, public relations. **Computer sciences:** Computer science, information technology. **Conservation:** Environmental science. **Education:** Art, biology, chemistry, drama/dance, elementary, English, ESL, French, German, history, mathematics, music, physical, physics, Spanish. **Engineering:** Computer, mechanical, mechanics, science. **English:** English lit, speech/rhetoric. **Family/consumer sciences:** General, clothing/textiles, family systems, institutional food production. **Foreign languages:** French, German, Spanish. **Health:** Athletic training, dietetics, nursing (RN), predental, premedicine, prenursing, prepharmacy, preveterinary. **History:** General. **Legal studies:** General, prelaw. **Math:** General. **Parks/recreation:** Exercise sciences. **Philosophy/religion:** Philosophy. **Physical sciences:** Chemistry, physics. **Psychology:** General. **Public administration:** General, social work. **Social sciences:** Political science, urban studies. **Theology:** Bible, missionary, youth ministry. **Visual/performing arts:** Commercial/advertising art, dramatic, music performance, music theory/composition, piano/organ, studio arts, voice/opera. **Other:** Pre-Engineering.

**Most popular majors.** Biology 7%, business/marketing 30%, education 10%, health sciences 9%.

**Computing on campus.** 366 workstations in dormitories, library, computer center, student center. Dormitories wired for high-speed internet access and linked to campus network. Commuter students can connect to campus network. Online course registration, helpline, repair service, wireless network available.

**Student life. Freshman orientation:** Mandatory. Preregistration for classes offered. **Policies:** Daily chapel service and Bible studies required. Religious observance required. **Housing:** Single-sex dorms available. $125 fully refundable deposit. Out-of-town undergraduates required to live on campus, except for seniors, students over age of 21, married students. **Activities:** Bands, campus ministries, choral groups, drama, international student organizations, literary magazine, music ensembles, musical theater, radio station, student government, student newspaper, College Republicans, Young Democrats, honorary societies, multicultural association.

**Athletics.** NCAA. **Intercollegiate:** Baseball M, basketball, cross-country, golf, soccer, softball W, tennis, track and field, volleyball W. **Intramural:** Basketball, football (non-tackle) M, softball, volleyball. **Team name:** Bisons.

**Student services.** Adult student services, career counseling, student employment services, health services, minority student services, personal counseling, placement for graduates. **Physically disabled:** Services for visually, speech, hearing impaired.

**Contact.** E-mail: admissions@lipscomb.edu
Phone: (615) 966-1776 Toll-free number: (877) 582-4766
Fax: (615) 966-1804
Corey Patterson, Senior Director of Enrollment, Lipscomb University, One University Park Drive, Nashville, TN 37204-3951

---

## Martin Methodist College
**Pulaski, Tennessee**
**www.martinmethodist.edu**

**CB code: 1449**

- Private 4-year liberal arts college affiliated with United Methodist Church
- Residential campus in small town
- 286 degree-seeking undergraduates: 66% women
- 52% graduate within 6 years; 10% enter graduate study

**General.** Founded in 1870. Regionally accredited. **Degrees:** 111 bachelor's, 17 associate awarded. **Location:** 70 miles from Nashville, 40 miles from Huntsville, Alabama. **Calendar:** Semester, limited summer session. **Full-time faculty:** 51 total; 53% have terminal degrees, 37% women. **Part-time faculty:** 24 total; 38% have terminal degrees, 33% women. **Class size:** 78% < 20, 21% 20-39, less than 1% 40-49.

**Freshman class profile.**

| Mid 50% test scores | | | |
|---|---|---|---|
| ACT composite: | 17-22 | End year in good standing: | 85% |
| GPA 3.50 or higher: | 30% | Return as sophomores: | 55% |
| GPA 3.0-3.49: | 34% | Out-of-state: | 16% |
| GPA 2.0-2.99: | 32% | Live on campus: | 46% |

**Basis for selection.** Open admission, but selective for some programs. High school record, interview, test scores important. Minimum 2.0 GPA, 18 ACT, or rank in upper 50% of class. Must meet 2 of these 3 criteria for admission or apply for "special circumstances" admission status. Students whose academic record or test scores do not qualify them for admission can be conditionally admitted and offered full enrollment if they complete a semester with a 2.0 GPA. Audition recommended for music; portfolio recommended for art.

**High school preparation.** 13 units required. Required and recommended units include English 4, mathematics 2, social studies 1, history 1, science 2, foreign language 2, computer science 1 and academic electives 4.

**2007-2008 Annual costs.** Tuition/fees: $16,554. Room/board: $5,800. Books/supplies: $750. Personal expenses: $1,200.

**Financial aid. Non-need-based:** Scholarships awarded for academics, art, athletics, leadership, music/drama, religious affiliation, state residency.

**Application procedures. Admission:** Priority date 5/1; deadline 8/1 (postmark date). $25 fee. Application may be submitted online. Admission notification on a rolling basis. **Financial aid:** No deadline. FAFSA, institutional form required. Applicants notified on a rolling basis starting 3/1; must reply within 2 week(s) of notification.

**Academics. Special study options:** Dual enrollment of high school students, ESL, honors, independent study, study abroad. **Credit/placement by examination:** CLEP. 30 credit hours maximum toward associate degree. **Support services:** Learning center, pre-admission summer program, reduced course load, study skills assistance, tutoring.

**Majors. Biology:** General. **Business:** General, accounting, business admin. **Education:** Elementary, middle, secondary. **English:** English lit. **History:** General. **Parks/recreation:** Sports admin. **Philosophy/religion:** Religion.

**Psychology:** General. **Public administration:** Human services. **Other:** History and Political Science, Sport Management.

**Computing on campus.** 150 workstations in library, computer center. Dormitories wired for high-speed internet access and linked to campus network. Online course registration, online library, helpline, wireless network available.

**Student life. Freshman orientation:** Mandatory. Preregistration for classes offered. 3 days prior to other students coming on campus. **Housing:** Guaranteed on-campus for all undergraduates. Single-sex dorms available. $100 fully refundable deposit, deadline 6/1. **Activities:** Choral groups, drama, music ensembles, student government, student newspaper, student Christian association, black student union, Fellowship of Christian Athletes.

**Athletics.** NAIA, NJCAA. **Intercollegiate:** Baseball M, basketball, cross-country, golf M, soccer, softball W, tennis, volleyball W. **Intramural:** Basketball, racquetball, softball, swimming, table tennis, volleyball. **Team name:** RedHawks.

**Student services.** Adult student services, campus ministries, career counseling, student employment services, financial aid counseling, personal counseling, placement for graduates, veterans' counselor.

**Contact.** E-mail: mkelley@martinmethodist.edu
Phone: (931) 363-9868 Toll-free number: (800) 467-1273
Fax: (931) 363-9803
Michael Kelley, Director of Admissions, Martin Methodist College, 433 West Madison, Pulaski, TN 38478-2799

---

### Maryville College
**Maryville, Tennessee**
www.maryvillecollege.edu

CB member
CB code: 1454

♦ Private 4-year liberal arts college affiliated with Presbyterian Church (USA)
♦ Residential campus in small city
♦ 1,176 degree-seeking undergraduates: 1% part-time, 55% women
♦ 76% of applicants admitted
♦ SAT or ACT (ACT writing optional) required
♦ 52% graduate within 6 years; 28% enter graduate study

**General.** Founded in 1819. Regionally accredited. **Degrees:** 201 bachelor's awarded. **Location:** 15 miles from Knoxville. **Calendar:** 4-1-4, limited summer session. **Full-time faculty:** 78 total; 85% have terminal degrees, 6% minority, 53% women. **Part-time faculty:** 41 total; 24% have terminal degrees, 10% minority, 51% women. **Class size:** 68% < 20, 32% 20-39, less than 1% 40-49. **Special facilities:** Science center, fine arts center, Mountain Challenge outdoor program, college woods with ropes courses, equestrian center.

**Freshman class profile.** 1,584 applied, 1,203 admitted, 317 enrolled.

| Mid 50% test scores | | GPA 2.0-2.99: | 15% |
|---|---|---|---|
| SAT critical reading: | 460-600 | Rank in top quarter: | 64% |
| SAT math: | 480-590 | Rank in top tenth: | 28% |
| SAT writing: | 460-600 | End year in good standing: | 87% |
| ACT composite: | 21-27 | Return as sophomores: | 72% |
| GPA 3.50 or higher: | 53% | Out-of-state: | 23% |
| GPA 3.0-3.49: | 32% | Live on campus: | 87% |

**Basis for selection.** Students are admitted based on academic criteria, extracurricular involvement, and personal achievement, without regard to financial need. Successful students typically follow strong college preparatory curriculums in high school and rank in the top 25% of their classes. International students who score at least 525 on TOEFL or 80 on Michigan Test eligible to enroll full time. Others may enroll in limited number of college level courses until they complete international students' orientation. Writing samples are encouraged for assistance in admissions decisions. Essay, interview recommended for all; audition required for music; portfolio recommended for art. **Homeschooled:** Pursue rigorous curriculum that includes strong emphasis on writing and reasoning.

**High school preparation.** 15 units required. Required and recommended units include English 4, mathematics 3, social studies 2, history 1, science 2 (laboratory 1), foreign language 2 and academic electives 1.

**2007-2008 Annual costs.** Tuition/fees: $25,350. Room/board: $7,800. Books/supplies: $850. Personal expenses: $900.

**2007-2008 Financial aid. Need-based:** 262 full-time freshmen applied for aid; 262 were judged to have need; 262 of these received aid. Average need met was 95%. Average scholarship/grant was $14,783; average loan $4,345. 77% of total undergraduate aid awarded as scholarships/grants, 23%

as loans/jobs. **Non-need-based:** Awarded to 757 full-time undergraduates, including 261 freshmen. Scholarships awarded for academics, art, leadership, minority status, music/drama, religious affiliation, state residency.

**Application procedures. Admission:** Priority date 1/15; no deadline. , may be waived for applicants with need. No application fee. Application may be submitted online. Admission notification on a rolling basis beginning on or about 10/1. Must reply by May 1 or within 2 week(s) if notified thereafter. Required enrollment deposit of $200 includes housing deposit, refundable before May 1. **Financial aid:** Priority date 3/1; no closing date. FAFSA required. Applicants notified on a rolling basis starting 3/15; must reply within 4 week(s) of notification.

**Academics.** All students complete 6 credit-hour research project and comprehensive examination in their major area of study. **Special study options:** Combined bachelor's/graduate degree, double major, ESL, honors, independent study, internships, liberal arts/career combination, student-designed major, study abroad, teacher certification program, Washington semester. **Credit/placement by examination:** AP, CLEP, IB, institutional tests. 32 credit hours maximum toward bachelor's degree. Students may petition individual departments for credit by examination. **Support services:** Learning center, reduced course load, remedial instruction, study skills assistance, tutoring, writing center.

**Majors. Biology:** General, biochemistry. **Business:** Business admin, international. **Computer sciences:** General. **Conservation:** Environmental studies. **Education:** General, biology, chemistry, English, ESL, health, history, mathematics, music, physical, social science, social studies, Spanish. **Engineering:** General. **English:** English lit, technical writing. **Foreign languages:** American Sign Language, sign language interpretation, Spanish. **Health:** Nursing (RN), predental, premedicine, prenursing, prepharmacy, preveterinary. **History:** General. **Interdisciplinary:** Math/computer science. **Math:** General. **Parks/recreation:** General, health/fitness. **Philosophy/religion:** Philosophy, religion. **Physical sciences:** Chemical physics, chemistry. **Psychology:** General. **Social sciences:** Economics, international relations, political science, sociology. **Visual/performing arts:** Art, dramatic, music performance, studio arts.

**Most popular majors.** Biology 8%, business/marketing 24%, education 20%, English 6%, psychology 8%, social sciences 10%, visual/performing arts 6%.

**Computing on campus.** 265 workstations in library, computer center. Dormitories wired for high-speed internet access and linked to campus network. Commuter students can connect to campus network. Online course registration, online library, helpline, repair service, wireless network available.

**Student life. Freshman orientation:** Mandatory, $25 fee. Preregistration for classes offered. Includes Mountain Challenge component. Begins several days before registration. Optional 3-day wilderness experience. **Housing:** Guaranteed on-campus for all undergraduates. Coed dorms, single-sex dorms, special housing for disabled, apartments, substance-free housing available. $200 fully refundable deposit, deadline 5/1. **Activities:** Bands, campus ministries, choral groups, dance, drama, film society, international student organizations, literary magazine, music ensembles, Model UN, student government, student newspaper, symphony orchestra, Habitat for Humanity, Literary Corps, Fellowship of Christian Athletes, MC Wellness Council, Student Programming Board, Black student association.

**Athletics.** NCAA. **Intercollegiate:** Baseball M, basketball, cross-country, equestrian, football (tackle) M, soccer, softball W, tennis, volleyball W. **Intramural:** Archery, badminton, baseball M, basketball, bowling, football (non-tackle), golf, racquetball, rugby, skiing, soccer, softball, swimming, table tennis, tennis, track and field, volleyball, water polo. **Team name:** Scots.

**Student services.** Adult student services, alcohol/substance abuse counseling, campus ministries, career counseling, student employment services, financial aid counseling, health services, minority student services, personal counseling, placement for graduates. **Physically disabled:** Services for visually, speech, hearing impaired.

**Contact.** E-mail: admissions@maryvillecollege.edu
Phone: (865) 981-8092 Toll-free number: (800) 597-2687
Fax: (865) 981-8005
Ned Willard, Vice President for Enrollment Management, Maryville College, 502 East Lamar Alexander Parkway, Maryville, TN 37804-5907

---

### Memphis College of Art
**Memphis, Tennessee**
www.mca.edu

CB code: 1511

♦ Private 4-year visual arts college
♦ Residential campus in very large city

- 284 degree-seeking undergraduates: 10% part-time, 55% women, 17% African American, 2% Asian American, 2% Hispanic American, 2% international
- 55 degree-seeking graduate students
- 46% of applicants admitted
- SAT or ACT (ACT writing optional) required
- 46% graduate within 6 years; 23% enter graduate study

**General.** Founded in 1936. Regionally accredited. Situated in 324-acre city park with bicycle trails and golf course. Students have access to Memphis Brooks Museum of Art and Overton Park Zoo. Consortium with four other colleges provides greater selection of liberal studies classes. Mobility program with 30+ other independent colleges of art around the country and in Canada available. **Degrees:** 53 bachelor's awarded; master's offered. **Location:** 500 miles from New Orleans, 700 miles from Dallas. **Calendar:** Semester, limited summer session. **Full-time faculty:** 26 total; 85% have terminal degrees, 12% minority, 54% women. **Part-time faculty:** 20 total; 45% have terminal degrees, 10% minority, 50% women. **Special facilities:** 5 campus galleries for faculty, student and visiting artist exhibitions.

**Freshman class profile.** 474 applied, 219 admitted, 73 enrolled.

| Mid 50% test scores | | Return as sophomores: | 57% |
|---|---|---|---|
| ACT composite: | 21-25 | Out-of-state: | 68% |
| GPA 3.50 or higher: | 30% | Live on campus: | 85% |
| GPA 3.0-3.49: | 38% | International: | 1% |
| GPA 2.0-2.99: | 31% | | |

**Basis for selection.** Art portfolio, high school transcript, test scores required; letter of recommendation from art teacher and essay considered, but not required. Portfolio required; essay, interview recommended for all.

**High school preparation.** Portfolio should include 10 to 20 pieces of work, originals or slides, with focus on direct observational drawing.

**2007-2008 Annual costs.** Tuition/fees: $20,660. Room/board: $7,860. Books/supplies: $1,600. Personal expenses: $1,490.

**2007-2008 Financial aid. Need-based:** 66 full-time freshmen applied for aid; 52 were judged to have need; 52 of these received aid. Average need met was 75%. Average scholarship/grant was $3,567; average loan $3,500. 45% of total undergraduate aid awarded as scholarships/grants, 55% as loans/jobs. **Non-need-based:** Awarded to 228 full-time undergraduates, including 71 freshmen. Scholarships awarded for academics, art. **Additional information:** Students considered for institutional resources through admissions application process.

**Application procedures. Admission:** Priority date 3/31; no deadline. $25 fee, may be waived for applicants with need. Application may be submitted online. Admission notification on a rolling basis beginning on or about 11/15. Must reply by May 1 or within 3 week(s) if notified thereafter. **Financial aid:** Priority date 3/1; no closing date. FAFSA required. Applicants notified on a rolling basis starting 3/15; must reply within 3 week(s) of notification.

**Academics. Special study options:** Combined bachelor's/graduate degree, cross-registration, double major, exchange student, independent study, internships, New York semester, study abroad. New York Studio Exchange Program. Mobility semester exchange at 30+ independent art colleges across the country (AICAD consortium). **Credit/placement by examination:** AP, CLEP, IB, SAT, ACT, institutional tests. 15 credit hours maximum toward bachelor's degree. **Support services:** Reduced course load, remedial instruction, study skills assistance, tutoring, writing center.

**Majors. Computer sciences:** Computer graphics. **Visual/performing arts:** Art, commercial/advertising art, design, digital art, drawing, graphic design, illustration, metal/jewelry, multimedia, painting, photography, printmaking, sculpture, studio arts.

**Computing on campus.** 200 workstations in dormitories, library, computer center. Dormitories wired for high-speed internet access. Wireless network available.

**Student life. Freshman orientation:** Mandatory. Preregistration for classes offered. 4-day session and parent sessions. **Housing:** Coed dorms, apartments, substance-free housing available. $300 deposit. Considerable assistance available in matching roommates and helping students find affordable housing within walking distance. **Activities:** Student government, student newspaper, international student club, photography club, student alliance, multicultural student association.

**Student services.** Adult student services, career counseling, student employment services, financial aid counseling, personal counseling, placement for graduates, veterans' counselor.

**Contact.** E-mail: info@mca.edu
Phone: (901) 272-5151 Toll-free number: (800) 727-1088
Fax: (901) 272-5158
Annette Moore, Director of Admissions, Memphis College of Art, 1930 Poplar Avenue, Memphis, TN 38104-2764

---

## Middle Tennessee State University

**Murfreesboro, Tennessee**   **CB member**
**www.mtsu.edu**   **CB code: 1466**

- Public 4-year university
- Commuter campus in small city
- 19,883 degree-seeking undergraduates: 11% part-time, 55% women
- 2,363 degree-seeking graduate students
- 39% of applicants admitted
- SAT or ACT (ACT writing optional) required

**General.** Founded in 1911. Regionally accredited. **Degrees:** 3,629 bachelor's awarded; master's, doctoral offered. **ROTC:** Army. **Location:** 32 miles from Nashville. **Calendar:** Semester, extensive summer session. **Full-time faculty:** 931 total; 4% have terminal degrees, 16% minority, 44% women. **Part-time faculty:** 336 total; less than 1% have terminal degrees, 10% minority, 53% women. **Special facilities:** 3 recording studios, observatory, flight simulators, weather center, electronic music laboratory, digital audio edit laboratory, satellite mapping equipment, seismograph, 3 television studios, electronic newsroom, Centers for Historic Preservation and Popular Music.

**Freshman class profile.** 14,182 applied, 5,559 admitted, 3,576 enrolled.

| Mid 50% test scores | | Rank in top tenth: | 12% |
|---|---|---|---|
| SAT critical reading: | 450-570 | Live on campus: | 6% |
| SAT math: | 450-550 | Fraternities: | 8% |
| ACT composite: | 19-24 | Sororities: | 6% |
| Rank in top quarter: | 29% | | |

**Basis for selection.** Must meet high school curriculum requirements and have 3.0 high school GPA or ACT composite score of 22 or a combination of a 19 ACT and a 2.7 GPA. Personal statement required of students who do not meet standard requirements.

**High school preparation.** 14 units required. Required units include English 4, mathematics 3, social studies 1, history 1, science 2 (laboratory 1), foreign language 2 and visual/performing arts 1. Foreign language units must be in single language. Mathematics units must include algebra I and II, geometry or other advanced mathematics. 1 US history, 1 global studies also required.

**2007-2008 Annual costs.** Tuition/fees: $5,278; $15,554 out-of-state. Room/board: $6,204. Books/supplies: $1,000. Personal expenses: $1,400.

**Financial aid. Non-need-based:** Scholarships awarded for academics, alumni affiliation, art, athletics, job skills, leadership, minority status, music/drama, religious affiliation, ROTC, state residency. **Additional information:** Application filing deadline for scholarships February 15.

**Application procedures. Admission:** Closing date 7/1 (postmark date). $25 fee. Application may be submitted online. Admission notification on a rolling basis. **Financial aid:** Priority date 5/1; no closing date. FAFSA required. Applicants notified on a rolling basis starting 4/15; must reply within 2 week(s) of notification.

**Academics. Special study options:** Cooperative education, distance learning, double major, dual enrollment of high school students, honors, independent study, internships, study abroad, teacher certification program. Academic basic skills. **Credit/placement by examination:** AP, CLEP, IB, SAT, ACT, institutional tests. 66 credit hours maximum toward bachelor's degree. Up to 66 semester hours from correspondence study, credit-by-examination, credit for service-related experience, and flight training may be counted toward degree. **Support services:** Learning center, pre-admission summer program, reduced course load, remedial instruction, study skills assistance, tutoring, writing center.

**Honors college/program.** Must have minimum ACT composite score of 26 (1170 SAT, exclusive of Writing) and 3.0 GPA or 3.5 GPA and ACT of 22 (950 SAT); returning or transfer students must have overall college GPA of 3.0 or higher.

**Majors. Agriculture:** Agribusiness operations, animal sciences, plant sciences, soil science. **Biology:** General. **Business:** Accounting, business admin, finance, management information systems, managerial economics, marketing, office management, purchasing, sales/distribution. **Communications:**

Media studies. **Computer sciences:** General, computer science. **Education:** Art, business, early childhood, health, kindergarten/preschool, sales/marketing, special, technology/industrial arts. **Engineering technology:** General, architectural, environmental, industrial, industrial management. **English:** English lit. **Family/consumer sciences:** Clothing/textiles, family resources, food/nutrition. **Foreign languages:** General. **Health:** Athletic training, nursing (RN). **History:** General. **Interdisciplinary:** Biological/physical sciences. **Liberal arts:** Arts/sciences. **Math:** General. **Parks/recreation:** Facilities management, health/fitness. **Philosophy/religion:** Philosophy. **Physical sciences:** Chemistry, geology, physics. **Protective services:** Law enforcement admin. **Psychology:** General. **Public administration:** Social work. **Social sciences:** Anthropology, economics, international relations, political science, sociology. **Transportation:** Aviation. **Visual/performing arts:** Art, art history/conservation, dramatic, interior design, music management.

**Most popular majors.** Business/marketing 20%, communications/journalism 9%, interdisciplinary studies 10%, visual/performing arts 11%.

**Computing on campus.** 2,300 workstations in dormitories, library, computer center, student center. Dormitories wired for high-speed internet access and linked to campus network. Commuter students can connect to campus network. Online course registration, online library, helpline, wireless network available.

**Student life. Freshman orientation:** Mandatory, $45 fee. Preregistration for classes offered. Held from mid-June to mid-July. **Policies:** Parents notified when student under age of 21 found responsible for use and/or possession of drugs or alcohol. **Housing:** Single-sex dorms, apartments, fraternity/sorority housing, substance-free housing available. $200 partly refundable deposit. Honors living, learning hall, freshman year experience hall available. **Activities:** Bands, choral groups, dance, drama, international student organizations, literary magazine, music ensembles, Model UN, musical theater, radio station, student government, student newspaper, symphony orchestra, TV station, Golden Key National Honor Society, African American student association, Fellowship of Christian Athletes, Collegiate Women International, Citizens for Action, Baptist Student Union, Aerospace Maintenance Club, agricultural council, Student Tennessee Education Association.

**Athletics.** NCAA. **Intercollegiate:** Baseball M, basketball, cross-country, football (tackle) M, golf, soccer W, softball W, tennis, track and field, volleyball W. **Intramural:** Basketball M, boxing M, equestrian, football (tackle) M, racquetball, rugby M, soccer, softball, swimming, tennis, volleyball. **Team name:** Blue Raiders.

**Student services.** Adult student services, campus ministries, career counseling, student employment services, financial aid counseling, health services, minority student services, on-campus daycare, personal counseling, placement for graduates, veterans' counselor, women's services. **Physically disabled:** Services for visually, speech, hearing impaired.

**Contact.** E-mail: admissions@mtsu.edu
Phone: (615) 898-2111 Fax: (615) 898-5478
Lynn Palmer, Director of Admissions, Middle Tennessee State University, 1301 East Main Street, Murfreesboro, TN 37132

---

## Milligan College
**Milligan College, Tennessee**
www.milligan.edu                                    CB code: 1469

- Private 4-year liberal arts college affiliated with Christian Churches/Churches of Christ
- Residential campus in small city
- 761 degree-seeking undergraduates: 3% part-time, 61% women, 3% African American, 1% Asian American, 2% Hispanic American, 3% international
- 231 graduate students
- 78% of applicants admitted
- SAT or ACT (ACT writing optional), application essay required
- 55% graduate within 6 years

**General.** Founded in 1866. Regionally accredited. Weekly chapels, convocation programs, vespers. **Degrees:** 187 bachelor's awarded; master's offered. **ROTC:** Army. **Location:** 3 miles from Johnson City. **Calendar:** Semester, limited summer session. **Full-time faculty:** 71 total; 73% have terminal degrees, 1% minority, 49% women. **Part-time faculty:** 43 total; 30% have terminal degrees, 2% minority, 42% women. **Class size:** 73% < 20, 25% 20-39, 1% 40-49, 1% >100.

**Freshman class profile.** 552 applied, 428 admitted, 197 enrolled.

| Mid 50% test scores | | | |
|---|---|---|---|
| SAT critical reading: | 470-610 | GPA 3.0-3.49: | 31% |
| SAT math: | 480-610 | GPA 2.0-2.99: | 13% |
| SAT writing: | 460-600 | Return as sophomores: | 77% |
| ACT composite: | 20-26 | Out-of-state: | 83% |
| GPA 3.50 or higher: | 56% | Live on campus: | 85% |
| | | International: | 3% |

**Basis for selection.** Academic work, test scores, and references from minister or church leader and high school principal or counselor required for admission. Audition required for music; interview recommended in some instances.

**High school preparation.** 17 units recommended. Recommended units include English 4, mathematics 3, social studies 2, history 3, science 3 and foreign language 2.

**2007-2008 Annual costs.** Tuition/fees: $19,510. Room/board: $5,390. Books/supplies: $750. Personal expenses: $1,132.

**Financial aid. Non-need-based:** Scholarships awarded for academics, alumni affiliation, art, athletics, job skills, minority status, music/drama, religious affiliation, state residency.

**Application procedures. Admission:** Priority date 4/1; deadline 8/1 (postmark date). $30 fee, may be waived for applicants with need. Application may be submitted online. Admission notification on a rolling basis beginning on or about 10/1. Must reply by May 1 or within 2 week(s) if notified thereafter. Housing deposit is refundable until May 1. **Financial aid:** Priority date 3/1; no closing date. FAFSA required. Applicants notified on a rolling basis starting 3/15; must reply within 2 week(s) of notification.

**Academics. Special study options:** Cross-registration, double major, independent study, internships, study abroad, teacher certification program, Washington semester. American Studies Program in Washington, DC; Australia Studies Center; China Studies Program; Contemporary Music Center in Martha's Vineyard; Latin American Studies Program in Costa Rica; Los Angeles Film Studies Center; Middle East Studies Program in Egypt; Russian Studies Program; Scholars' Semester in Oxford; Uganda Studies Program; Summer Institute of Journalism in Washington, DC; Oxford Summer Programme. **Credit/placement by examination:** AP, CLEP, IB, SAT, ACT, institutional tests. 32 credit hours maximum toward bachelor's degree. Students may not receive credit by examination upon achieving a total of 64 credit hours. **Support services:** Reduced course load, remedial instruction, study skills assistance, tutoring, writing center.

**Majors. Biology:** General. **Business:** Accounting, business admin. **Communications:** General. **Computer sciences:** General. **Education:** General, early childhood, music. **English:** English lit. **Health:** Nursing (RN). **History:** General. **Liberal arts:** Humanities. **Math:** General. **Parks/recreation:** Health/fitness. **Physical sciences:** Chemistry. **Psychology:** General. **Public administration:** Human services. **Social sciences:** Sociology. **Theology:** Bible. **Visual/performing arts:** General.

**Most popular majors.** Biology 8%, business/marketing 19%, education 30%, health sciences 10%, philosophy/religious studies 8%.

**Computing on campus.** 102 workstations in library, computer center. Dormitories wired for high-speed internet access and linked to campus network. Commuter students can connect to campus network. Online library, helpline, repair service, student web hosting, wireless network available.

**Student life. Freshman orientation:** Available, $10 fee. Preregistration for classes offered. Weekend sessions available in April or June for students and parents. Abbreviated version offered weekend prior to first day of fall classes. **Policies:** Smoking and alcoholic beverages are not permitted on campus. Religious observance required. **Housing:** Guaranteed on-campus for all undergraduates. Single-sex dorms, apartments, substance-free housing available. $200 nonrefundable deposit, deadline 8/15. Students must live in college housing unless married or living with members of immediate family. **Activities:** Bands, choral groups, drama, literary magazine, music ensembles, musical theater, radio station, student government, student newspaper, symphony orchestra, Fellowship of Christian Athletes, missions club, service seekers, student government association, Beacon (missions organization), campus ministry team, College Republicans, Habitat for Humanity, political awareness group, Roteract.

**Athletics.** NAIA. **Intercollegiate:** Baseball M, basketball, cross-country, golf M, soccer, softball W, swimming, tennis, track and field, volleyball W. **Intramural:** Basketball, football (non-tackle), softball, table tennis, tennis, volleyball. **Team name:** Buffaloes.

**Student services.** Adult student services, campus ministries, career counseling, financial aid counseling, health services, minority student services, personal counseling, placement for graduates.

**Contact.** E-mail: admissions@milligan.edu
Phone: (423) 461-8730 Toll-free number: (800) 262-8337
Fax: (423) 461-8982
Tracy Brinn, Director of Enrollment Management, Milligan College, Box 210, Milligan College, TN 37682

## O'More College of Design
**Franklin, Tennessee**
www.omorecollege.edu                    CB code: 1545

- Private 4-year visual arts college
- Commuter campus in large town
- 195 degree-seeking undergraduates
- 38% of applicants admitted
- SAT or ACT (ACT writing optional) required

**General.** Founded in 1970. Accredited by ACCSCT. Interior design program accredited by Council for Interior Design Accreditation. **Degrees:** 36 bachelor's awarded. **Location:** 15 miles from Nashville. **Calendar:** Semester, limited summer session. **Full-time faculty:** 12 total; 25% have terminal degrees, 8% minority, 50% women. **Part-time faculty:** 38 total; 53% women.

### Freshman class profile.

| Mid 50% test scores | | | |
|---|---|---|---|
| SAT critical reading: | 470-610 | GPA 3.50 or higher: | 32% |
| SAT math: | 490-620 | GPA 3.0-3.49: | 48% |
| SAT writing: | 500-560 | GPA 2.0-2.99: | 16% |
| ACT composite: | 21-25 | Out-of-state: | 8% |

**Basis for selection.** High school record most important. Test scores, grades given equal weight. Portfolio or departmental home exam may be required. Portfolio of artwork is recommended for students not admitted automatically on the basis of his or her grades or test scores. If student does not have portfolio and does not meet admittance criteria on basis of academic record alone, the student will need to contact chair of department to which he or she seeks admittance for instructions on completing department's home exam.

**High school preparation.** 18 units recommended. Recommended units include English 4, mathematics 3, social studies 1, history 2, science 3, foreign language 2 and academic electives 3. Art, mechanical drawing, and design courses are recommended.

**2007-2008 Annual costs.** Tuition/fees: $15,514. Books/supplies: $750.

**Financial aid.** All financial aid based on need.

**Application procedures. Admission:** Closing date 8/1 (postmark date). $50 fee, may be waived for applicants with need. Application may be submitted online. Admission notification on a rolling basis. **Financial aid:** Priority date 4/1, closing date 7/30. FAFSA required. Applicants notified on a rolling basis starting 8/1.

**Academics. Special study options:** Dual enrollment of high school students, internships, liberal arts/career combination, study abroad. Students may pick a minor at Belmont University. Annual study-abroad program in Ireland, and one every third year in Italy. **Credit/placement by examination:** AP, CLEP, institutional tests. 9 credit hours maximum toward bachelor's degree.

**Majors. Business:** Fashion. **Visual/performing arts:** Commercial/advertising art, interior design.

**Computing on campus.** PC or laptop required. 25 workstations in library, computer center, student center. Student web hosting, wireless network available.

**Student life. Freshman orientation:** Mandatory. Preregistration for classes offered. **Activities:** Student government, student chapter of American Society of Interior Designers, O'More Fashion Merchandisers Association, Student Government Association, American Institute of Graphic Arts, International Interior Design Association.

**Student services.** Career counseling.

**Contact.** E-mail: admissions@omorecollege.edu
Phone: (615) 794-4254 Fax: (615) 790-1662
Christopher Lee, Dean of Enrollment, O'More College of Design, 423 South Margin Street, Franklin, TN 37064-0908

## Rhodes College
**Memphis, Tennessee**                    CB member
www.rhodes.edu                    CB code: 1730

- Private 4-year liberal arts college affiliated with Presbyterian Church (USA)
- Residential campus in very large city
- 1,670 degree-seeking undergraduates: 1% part-time, 58% women, 6% African American, 5% Asian American, 2% Hispanic American
- 13 degree-seeking graduate students
- 51% of applicants admitted
- SAT or ACT (ACT writing optional), application essay required
- 74% graduate within 6 years

**General.** Founded in 1848. Regionally accredited. **Degrees:** 391 bachelor's awarded; master's offered. **ROTC:** Army, Air Force. **Location:** 4 miles from downtown. **Calendar:** Semester. **Full-time faculty:** 137 total; 93% have terminal degrees, 10% minority, 44% women. **Part-time faculty:** 30 total; 67% have terminal degrees, 10% minority, 53% women. **Class size:** 73% < 20, 25% 20-39, less than 1% 40-49, less than 1% 50-99. **Special facilities:** Arboretum, scanning electron microscope, rooftop observatory, cell culture facility, nuclear magnetic resonance instrument.

### Freshman class profile. 3,709 applied, 1,887 admitted, 454 enrolled.

| Mid 50% test scores | | | |
|---|---|---|---|
| SAT critical reading: | 590-690 | Rank in top tenth: | 51% |
| SAT math: | 590-690 | Return as sophomores: | 88% |
| ACT composite: | 26-30 | Out-of-state: | 73% |
| GPA 3.50 or higher: | 75% | Live on campus: | 96% |
| GPA 3.0-3.49: | 20% | International: | 1% |
| GPA 2.0-2.99: | 5% | Fraternities: | 37% |
| Rank in top quarter: | 83% | Sororities: | 48% |

**Basis for selection.** Academic record, standardized test scores, class rank, recommendations, essay, school and community activities important. Applications sought from international students, minorities, and children of alumni. Interview recommended. **Homeschooled:** Applicants must submit two SAT Subject Tests other than mathematics or literature in addition to usual requirements.

**High school preparation.** 16 units required. Required units include English 4, mathematics 3, social studies 2, science 2 (laboratory 2), foreign language 2 and academic electives 3.

**2007-2008 Annual costs.** Tuition/fees: $30,652. Room/board: $7,468. Books/supplies: $904. Personal expenses: $1,295.

**2007-2008 Financial aid. Need-based:** 289 full-time freshmen applied for aid; 197 were judged to have need; 197 of these received aid. Average need met was 88%. Average scholarship/grant was $20,159; average loan $4,151. 81% of total undergraduate aid awarded as scholarships/grants, 19% as loans/jobs. **Non-need-based:** Awarded to 977 full-time undergraduates, including 265 freshmen. Scholarships awarded for academics, art, minority status, music/drama, religious affiliation. **Additional information:** Auditions required for theater and music achievement awards and art achievement awards. Interviews recommended for merit scholarships.

**Application procedures. Admission:** Priority date 1/15; no deadline. $45 fee, may be waived for applicants with need. Application may be submitted online. Admission notification 3/1. Must reply by 5/1. Notification of admissions decision for Bellingrath Scholarship applicants by 03/15; must reply by 05/01. **Financial aid:** Closing date 3/1. FAFSA, CSS PROFILE required. Must reply by 5/1.

**Academics.** Expense-paid summer internships in businesses abroad. Model United Nations program, opportunities for participation in computer-simulated international negotiating, mock trial program. **Special study options:** Combined bachelor's/graduate degree, cooperative education, cross-registration, double major, dual enrollment of high school students, exchange student, honors, independent study, internships, liberal arts/career combination, student-designed major, study abroad, Washington semester. **Credit/placement by examination:** AP, CLEP, IB, institutional tests. 28 credit hours maximum toward bachelor's degree. **Support services:** Tutoring, writing center.

**Majors. Area/ethnic studies:** Latin American, Russian/Slavic. **Biology:** General, Biochemistry/biophysics and molecular biology. **Business:** Business admin, managerial economics. **Computer sciences:** Computer science. **English:** English lit. **Foreign languages:** Classics, French, German, modern Greek, Russian, Spanish. **History:** General. **Math:** General. **Philosophy/religion:** Philosophy, religion. **Physical sciences:** Chemistry, physics. **Psychology:** General. **Social sciences:** Anthropology, economics, international relations, political science, sociology, urban studies. **Visual/performing arts:** Art, dramatic.

**Most popular majors.** Biology 16%, business/marketing 8%, English 11%, history 9%, philosophy/religious studies 8%, psychology 7%, social sciences 24%, visual/performing arts 6%.

**Computing on campus.** 220 workstations in library, computer center, student center. Dormitories wired for high-speed internet access and linked to campus network. Commuter students can connect to campus network. Online course registration, online library, helpline, wireless network available.

**Student life. Freshman orientation:** Mandatory. Preregistration for classes offered. 5-day orientation acquaints students with academic expectations and regulations and gives opportunity to plan program of study with help from advisor. **Policies:** Student-run honor system central to campus life. **Housing:** Guaranteed on-campus for freshmen. Coed dorms, single-sex dorms, apartments, substance-free housing available. Special interest townhouses. **Activities:** Bands, campus ministries, choral groups, dance, drama, film society, international student organizations, literary magazine, music ensembles, Model UN, musical theater, radio station, student government, student newspaper, symphony orchestra, TV station, Black Student Association, Kinney (social service), Inter-Varsity Christian Fellowship, international house, Habitat for Humanity, Interfaith Circle, Diversity Group, College Democrats, College Republicans.

**Athletics. NCAA. Intercollegiate:** Baseball M, basketball, cross-country, field hockey W, football (tackle) M, golf, soccer, softball W, swimming, tennis, track and field, volleyball W. **Intramural:** Basketball, football (non-tackle), football (tackle), racquetball, soccer, squash M, table tennis, tennis, volleyball. **Team name:** Lynx.

**Student services.** Campus ministries, career counseling, student employment services, financial aid counseling, health services, minority student services, personal counseling, placement for graduates. **Physically disabled:** Services for visually, speech, hearing impaired.

**Contact.** E-mail: adminfo@rhodes.edu
Phone: (901) 843-3700 Toll-free number: (800) 844-5969
Fax: (901) 843-3631
David Wottle, Dean of Admissions and Financial Aid, Rhodes College, 2000 North Parkway, Memphis, TN 38112

## South College
### Knoxville, Tennessee
### www.southcollegetn.edu
**CB code: 0711**

- For-profit 4-year liberal arts college
- Commuter campus in small city
- 715 degree-seeking undergraduates
- SAT or ACT with writing, interview required

**General.** Founded in 1882. Regionally accredited. **Degrees:** 28 bachelor's, 54 associate awarded. **Location:** Downtown. **Calendar:** Quarter, extensive summer session. **Full-time faculty:** 75 total. **Part-time faculty:** 25 total.

**Basis for selection.** CPTS examination required. SAT/ACT or CPAT required for admission.

**2007-2008 Annual costs.** Tuition/fees: $14,100. Reported annual costs are for programs in physical therapy assistance, radiography, health science. Costs of other programs vary by program. Books/supplies: $1,300. Personal expenses: $1,200.

**Financial aid.** All financial aid based on need.

**Application procedures. Admission:** No deadline. $40 fee. Admission notification on a rolling basis. **Financial aid:** No deadline. FAFSA, institutional form required. Applicants notified on a rolling basis.

**Academics. Special study options:** Accelerated study, double major, dual enrollment of high school students, internships, teacher certification program. **Credit/placement by examination:** CLEP, institutional tests. **Support services:** Learning center, reduced course load, study skills assistance, tutoring, writing center.

**Majors. Business:** Business admin. **Legal studies:** General.

**Computing on campus.** 85 workstations in library, computer center. Online library, wireless network available.

**Student life. Freshman orientation:** Mandatory. Preregistration for classes offered. **Activities:** Literary magazine, student government, student newspaper, Collegiate Secretaries International, paralegal association, student affairs advisory council, Empowerment Club (business), students of medical assisting, movie club, community service club.

**Student services.** Career counseling, student employment services, financial aid counseling, placement for graduates, veterans' counselor.

**Contact.** E-mail: admissions@southcollegetn.edu
Phone: (865) 251-1800 Fax: (865) 470-8737
Walter Hosea, Admissions Director, South College, 3904 Lonas Drive, Knoxville, TN 37909

## Southern Adventist University
### Collegedale, Tennessee
### www.southern.edu
**CB code: 1727**

- Private 4-year university and liberal arts college affiliated with Seventh-day Adventists
- Residential campus in small town
- 2,353 degree-seeking undergraduates: 10% part-time, 55% women, 11% African American, 5% Asian American, 13% Hispanic American, 6% international
- 163 degree-seeking graduate students
- 68% of applicants admitted
- SAT or ACT (ACT writing optional) required
- 45% graduate within 6 years; 15% enter graduate study

**General.** Founded in 1892. Regionally accredited. **Degrees:** 335 bachelor's, 118 associate awarded; master's offered. **Location:** 18 miles from Chattanooga. **Calendar:** Semester, limited summer session. **Full-time faculty:** 134 total; 69% have terminal degrees, 13% minority, 38% women. **Part-time faculty:** 82 total; 35% have terminal degrees, 11% minority, 43% women. **Class size:** 50% < 20, 34% 20-39, 6% 40-49, 10% 50-99, less than 1% >100. **Special facilities:** Civil War collection, Lincoln collection, Anton Memorial Organ.

**Freshman class profile.** 1,540 applied, 1,054 admitted, 535 enrolled.

| Mid 50% test scores | | | |
|---|---|---|---|
| SAT math: | 440-560 | GPA 2.0-2.99: | 18% |
| ACT composite: | 19-25 | Return as sophomores: | 69% |
| GPA 3.50 or higher: | 50% | Out-of-state: | 76% |
| GPA 3.0-3.49: | 31% | Live on campus: | 89% |
| | | International: | 6% |

**Basis for selection.** School achievement record and test scores are important. Interview recommended for all; audition required for music, gymnastics programs. **Homeschooled:** Transcript of courses and grades required. Home school organization must be academically accredited or student must take GED. GED recommended in all situations. Portfolio required and must include 1) Copy of an original research paper. 2) Written statement reflecting on value student received from the home school experience.

**High school preparation.** 18 units required; 24 recommended. Required and recommended units include English 3-4, mathematics 2-3, social studies 1, history 1-2, science 2-3, foreign language 2 and academic electives 9. One unit chemistry (2.0 GPA or better) required for nursing majors. 2 units foreign language required for BA program applicants. Computer competency strongly recommended.

**2008-2009 Annual costs.** Tuition/fees (projected): $16,560. Room/board: $4,750. Books/supplies: $1,000. Personal expenses: $2,000.

**Financial aid. Non-need-based:** Scholarships awarded for academics, alumni affiliation, art, leadership, music/drama.

**Application procedures. Admission:** Closing date 9/8 (receipt date). $25 fee, may be waived for applicants with need. Application may be submitted online. Admission notification on a rolling basis. Must reply by 9/8. **Financial aid:** Priority date 3/1; no closing date. FAFSA required. Applicants notified on a rolling basis starting 2/15; must reply within 2 week(s) of notification.

**Academics. Special study options:** Combined bachelor's/graduate degree, double major, dual enrollment of high school students, ESL, honors, independent study, internships, study abroad, teacher certification program. **Credit/placement by examination:** AP, CLEP, SAT, ACT, institutional tests. 12 credit hours maximum toward bachelor's degree. **Support services:** Learning center, reduced course load, remedial instruction, study skills assistance, tutoring, writing center.

**Majors. Biology:** General, biochemistry, biophysics. **Business:** Accounting, business admin, finance, human resources, international, management information systems, management science, marketing, nonprofit/public. **Communications:** Advertising, broadcast journalism, journalism, media studies, public relations. **Communications technology:** General. **Computer sciences:** Computer science, programming. **Education:** Art, biology, chemistry, elementary, English, French, history, mathematics, music, physical, physics, Spanish. **English:** English lit. **Family/consumer sciences:** Family systems. **Foreign languages:** General, French, Spanish. **Health:** Art therapy, clinical lab science, health care admin, nursing (RN). **History:** General. **Math:** General. **Parks/recreation:** Exercise sciences, sports admin. **Philosophy/religion:** Religion. **Physical sciences:** Chemistry, physics. **Psychology:** General. **Public administration:** Social work. **Social sciences:** Archaeology. **Theology:** Missionary, pastoral counseling, religious ed, theology. **Visual/performing arts:** Art, cinematography, commercial/advertising art, music performance, music theory/composition, photography. **Other:** Outdoor Education.

**Most popular majors.** Biology 8%, business/marketing 15%, communications/journalism 6%, health sciences 21%, theological studies 6%, visual/performing arts 11%.

**Computing on campus.** 200 workstations in dormitories, library, computer center. Dormitories wired for high-speed internet access and linked to campus network. Commuter students can connect to campus network. Online course registration, online library, repair service, wireless network available.

**Student life. Freshman orientation:** Mandatory. Preregistration for classes offered. Orientation prior to registration for fall term. Includes exams and instruction in course planning as well as social occasions for students to meet faculty and fellow students. **Policies:** Alcohol and drug free. Religious observance required. **Housing:** Guaranteed on-campus for all undergraduates. Single-sex dorms, apartments available. $250 fully refundable deposit, deadline 7/15. **Activities:** Bands, campus ministries, choral groups, drama, film society, music ensembles, radio station, student government, student newspaper, symphony orchestra, TV station, African club, Black Christian Union, Partners at Wellness, Association of South East Asian Nation Students.

**Athletics. Intramural:** Badminton, basketball, racquetball, soccer, softball, table tennis, tennis, volleyball.

**Student services.** Campus ministries, career counseling, student employment services, financial aid counseling, health services, personal counseling, placement for graduates, veterans' counselor.

**Contact.** E-mail: admissions@southern.edu
Phone: (423) 236-2844 Toll-free number: (800) 768-8437
Fax: (423) 236-1844
Marc Grundy, Director of Admissions, Southern Adventist University, Box 370, Collegedale, TN 37315-0370

## Tennessee State University

**Nashville, Tennessee**
www.tnstate.edu

**CB member**
**CB code: 1803**

‣ Public 4-year university
‣ Residential campus in very large city
‣ 6,966 degree-seeking undergraduates: 18% part-time, 65% women, 82% African American, 1% Asian American, 1% Hispanic American, 1% international
‣ 1,665 degree-seeking graduate students
‣ 67% of applicants admitted
‣ SAT or ACT required
‣ 71% graduate within 6 years; 7% enter graduate study

**General.** Founded in 1912. Regionally accredited. **Degrees:** 994 bachelor's, 114 associate awarded; master's, doctoral offered. **ROTC:** Air Force. **Location:** 115 miles from Chattanooga, 195 miles from Memphis. **Calendar:** Semester, limited summer session. **Full-time faculty:** 434 total; 80% have terminal degrees, 61% minority, 43% women. **Part-time faculty:** 167 total; 40% have terminal degrees, 48% minority, 52% women. **Class size:** 45% < 20, 49% 20-39, 4% 40-49, 3% 50-99, less than 1% >100.

**Freshman class profile.** 4,259 applied, 2,842 admitted, 1,228 enrolled.

| Mid 50% test scores | | | |
|---|---|---|---|
| | | GPA 3.0-3.49: | 27% |
| SAT critical reading: | 400-500 | GPA 2.0-2.99: | 55% |
| SAT math: | 410-500 | End year in good standing: | 82% |
| ACT composite: | 16-20 | Out-of-state: | 42% |
| GPA 3.50 or higher: | 15% | Live on campus: | 75% |

**Basis for selection.** School achievement record, test scores important. Interview required for allied health, nursing, physical therapy programs.

**High school preparation.** 14 units required. Required units include English 4, mathematics 3, social studies 2, science 2 (laboratory 1) and foreign language 2. One unit visual and/or performing arts recommended.

**2007-2008 Annual costs.** Tuition/fees: $4,856; $15,132 out-of-state. Room/board: $4,872. Books/supplies: $925. Personal expenses: $2,800.

**2006-2007 Financial aid. Need-based:** 705 full-time freshmen applied for aid; 625 were judged to have need; 615 of these received aid. Average need met was 86%. Average scholarship/grant was $856; average loan $383. 34% of total undergraduate aid awarded as scholarships/grants, 66% as loans/jobs. **Non-need-based:** Awarded to 2,597 full-time undergraduates, including 384 freshmen. Scholarships awarded for academics.

**Application procedures. Admission:** Closing date 8/1. $15 fee. Application must be submitted on paper. Admission notification on a rolling basis. **Financial aid:** Priority date 4/1; no closing date. FAFSA required. Applicants notified on a rolling basis starting 4/15; must reply within 3 week(s) of notification.

**Academics. Special study options:** Combined bachelor's/graduate degree, cooperative education, cross-registration, distance learning, double major, ESL, exchange student, honors, independent study, study abroad, teacher certification program, weekend college. **Credit/placement by examination:** AP, CLEP, SAT, ACT, institutional tests. 33 credit hours maximum toward bachelor's degree. **Support services:** Learning center, remedial instruction, study skills assistance, tutoring, writing center.

**Majors. Agriculture:** Animal sciences. **Architecture:** Architecture. **Biology:** General, biochemistry. **Business:** Accounting, administrative services, business admin, managerial economics. **Communications:** General, journalism. **Computer sciences:** General, programming. **Education:** General, early childhood, physical, secondary, special. **Engineering:** General, architectural, civil, electrical. **English:** English lit. **Family/consumer sciences:** General, clothing/textiles, family studies, food/nutrition. **Foreign languages:** French, Spanish. **Health:** Audiology/speech pathology, dental hygiene, health care admin, medical records admin. **History:** General. **Interdisciplinary:** Biological/physical sciences. **Liberal arts:** Arts/sciences. **Math:** General. **Physical sciences:** Chemistry, physics. **Protective services:** Criminal justice. **Psychology:** General. **Public administration:** Social work. **Social sciences:** General, political science, sociology. **Visual/performing arts:** Art history/conservation, dramatic.

**Most popular majors.** Business/marketing 19%, communications/journalism 7%, education 6%, health sciences 14%, liberal arts 19%, psychology 7%.

**Computing on campus.** 450 workstations in library, computer center, student center. Dormitories linked to campus network. Commuter students can connect to campus network. Online course registration, online library, helpline, student web hosting available.

**Student life. Freshman orientation:** Mandatory. Preregistration for classes offered. **Housing:** Coed dorms, single-sex dorms, apartments available. $50 fully refundable deposit, deadline 4/1. **Activities:** Bands, choral groups, dance, drama, film society, music ensembles, musical theater, radio station, student government, student newspaper, religious organizations, foreign student organization, honor organization, literary organization.

**Athletics. NCAA. Intercollegiate:** Baseball M, basketball, cross-country, football (tackle) M, golf, softball W, tennis, track and field, volleyball W. **Intramural:** Basketball, racquetball, tennis, track and field, volleyball. **Team name:** Tigers.

**Student services.** Career counseling, student employment services, financial aid counseling, health services, minority student services, on-campus daycare, personal counseling, placement for graduates, veterans' counselor. **Physically disabled:** Services for visually, speech, hearing impaired.

**Contact.** E-mail: jcade@tnstate.edu
Phone: (615) 963-5101 Fax: (615) 963-5108
John Cade, Associate Vice President of Enrollment, Tennessee State University, 3500 John A. Merritt Boulevard, Nashville, TN 37209-1561

## Tennessee Technological University

**Cookeville, Tennessee**
www.tntech.edu

**CB member**
**CB code: 1804**

‣ Public 4-year university
‣ Residential campus in large town
‣ 7,875 degree-seeking undergraduates: 9% part-time, 46% women, 4% African American, 1% Asian American, 1% Hispanic American, 2% international

- 1,495 degree-seeking graduate students
- 88% of applicants admitted
- SAT or ACT (ACT writing recommended) required
- 43% graduate within 6 years

**General.** Founded in 1915. Regionally accredited. **Degrees:** 1,354 bachelor's awarded; master's, doctoral offered. **ROTC:** Army, Air Force. **Location:** 80 miles from Nashville, 100 miles from Knoxville. **Calendar:** Semester, extensive summer session. **Full-time faculty:** 388 total; 80% have terminal degrees, 14% minority, 36% women. **Part-time faculty:** 232 total; 27% have terminal degrees, 4% minority, 62% women. **Class size:** 39% < 20, 46% 20-39, 6% 40-49, 6% 50-99, 2% >100. **Special facilities:** Center for crafts, cooperative fishery research unit, agricultural pavilion, center for energy systems research, center for manufacturing research, center for the management, utilization and protection of water resources, childcare resource center.

**Freshman class profile.** 3,790 applied, 3,329 admitted, 1,661 enrolled.

| Mid 50% test scores | | | |
|---|---|---|---|
| SAT critical reading: | 460-620 | Rank in top tenth: | 26% |
| SAT math: | 500-630 | Return as sophomores: | 73% |
| ACT composite: | 20-25 | Out-of-state: | 4% |
| GPA 3.50 or higher: | 38% | Live on campus: | 67% |
| GPA 3.0-3.49: | 30% | International: | 2% |
| GPA 2.0-2.99: | 32% | Fraternities: | 10% |
| Rank in top quarter: | 52% | Sororities: | 10% |

**Basis for selection.** All students must complete 14 specific high school courses. In addition to these required courses, applicants must fall into one of the following two categories to be admitted: 1) have a 19 ACT composite (900 SAT) and a 2.00 high school GPA; 2) have a 17 ACT composite (810 SAT) and a 2.5 high school GPA. Engineering applicants need ACT mathematics score of 20, composite score of 20 and GPA of 2.35. Computer science and mathematics applicants need ACT mathematics score of 21. Nursing applicants need an ACT composite score of 20 and a 3.0 GPA or higher. Pre-professional majors need an ACT composite score of 21, a Mathematics subtest score of 21 and a 3.0 GPA or higher. (SAT and ACT scores are exclusive of the Writing test). Interview recommended for all; audition recommended for music; portfolio recommended for arts, crafts. **Homeschooled:** Must have same core units as high school curriculum, 2.50 GPA and 19 ACT; GED required otherwise.

**High school preparation.** 14 units required. Required units include English 4, mathematics 3, social studies 1, history 1, science 2 (laboratory 1) and foreign language 2. Mathematics units must include algebra I and II and geometry or advanced mathematics course. Science units must be biology, chemistry, or physics with laboratories (can include physical sciences). Foreign language units must be in single language. 1 US history, 1 unit visual and/or performing arts also required. Social studies must be either world, ancient, modern, or European history, or world geography.

**2007-2008 Annual costs.** Tuition/fees: $4,980; $15,256 out-of-state. Room/board: $6,530. Books/supplies: $633. Personal expenses: $840.

**2006-2007 Financial aid. Need-based:** 805 full-time freshmen applied for aid; 523 were judged to have need; 519 of these received aid. Average need met was 87%. Average scholarship/grant was $3,922; average loan $927. 42% of total undergraduate aid awarded as scholarships/grants, 58% as loans/jobs. **Non-need-based:** Awarded to 4,086 full-time undergraduates, including 708 freshmen. Scholarships awarded for academics, alumni affiliation, art, athletics, leadership, minority status, music/drama, ROTC, state residency. **Additional information:** Tuition and/or fee waivers available for children of Tennessee public school teachers.

**Application procedures. Admission:** Priority date 5/1; deadline 8/1 (postmark date). $15 fee, may be waived for applicants with need. Application may be submitted online. Admission notification on a rolling basis. **Financial aid:** Priority date 3/15; no closing date. FAFSA required. Applicants notified on a rolling basis starting 3/15; must reply within 2 week(s) of notification.

**Academics. Special study options:** Accelerated study, cooperative education, distance learning, double major, dual enrollment of high school students, ESL, honors, independent study, internships, liberal arts/career combination, study abroad, teacher certification program. **Credit/placement by examination:** AP, CLEP, IB, institutional tests. 33 credit hours maximum toward bachelor's degree. **Support services:** Learning center, pre-admission summer program, reduced course load, remedial instruction, study skills assistance, tutoring, writing center.

**Majors. Agriculture:** Agribusiness operations, agronomy, animal sciences, horticultural science, horticulture, landscaping, nursery operations, soil science. **Biology:** General, biochemistry. **Business:** General, accounting, finance, labor relations, management science, managerial economics, operations. **Communications:** General, journalism. **Communications technology:** General. **Computer sciences:** General, computer science, web page design. **Conservation:** General, fisheries, wildlife. **Education:** General, agricultural, early childhood, English, health, music, physical, secondary, special. **Engineering:** Chemical, civil, computer, electrical, industrial, mechanical. **Engineering technology:** Manufacturing. **English:** English lit, technical writing. **Family/consumer sciences:** General, clothing/textiles, family/community services, food/nutrition, housing. **Foreign languages:** French, German, Spanish. **Health:** Nursing (RN), predental, premedicine, prepharmacy, preveterinary. **History:** General. **Math:** General. **Parks/recreation:** Health/fitness. **Physical sciences:** Chemistry, geology, physics. **Psychology:** General. **Social sciences:** Economics, political science, sociology. **Visual/performing arts:** Ceramics, drawing, fiber arts, music performance, painting, sculpture, studio arts.

**Most popular majors.** Business/marketing 22%, education 20%, engineering/engineering technologies 15%.

**Computing on campus.** 600 workstations in dormitories, library, computer center. Dormitories wired for high-speed internet access and linked to campus network. Commuter students can connect to campus network. Online course registration, online library, helpline, wireless network available.

**Student life. Freshman orientation:** Mandatory, $45 fee. Preregistration for classes offered. **Housing:** Guaranteed on-campus for freshmen. Coed dorms, single-sex dorms, special housing for disabled, apartments, fraternity/sorority housing available. $50 deposit. **Activities:** Bands, choral groups, dance, drama, literary magazine, music ensembles, musical theater, opera, radio station, student government, student newspaper, symphony orchestra, TV station, more than 190 student organizations.

**Athletics.** NCAA. **Intercollegiate:** Baseball M, basketball, cheerleading, cross-country, football (tackle) M, golf, rifle, soccer W, softball W, tennis, track and field W, volleyball W. **Intramural:** Basketball, bowling, golf M, handball, racquetball, rugby M, soccer, softball, tennis, volleyball, wrestling M. **Team name:** Golden Eagles.

**Student services.** Alcohol/substance abuse counseling, career counseling, student employment services, financial aid counseling, health services, minority student services, on-campus daycare, personal counseling, placement for graduates, veterans' counselor, women's services. **Physically disabled:** Services for visually, speech, hearing impaired. **Learning disabled:** Comprehensive services available.

**Contact.** E-mail: admissions@tntech.edu
Phone: (931) 372-3888 Toll-free number: (800) 255-8881
Fax: (931) 372-6250
Vanessa Palmer, Admissions, Tennessee Technological University, Office of Admissions, Cookeville, TN 38505-0001

---

## Tennessee Temple University
**Chattanooga, Tennessee**
www.tntemple.edu
**CB code: 1818**

- Private 4-year university and Bible college affiliated with Baptist faith
- Residential campus in small city
- 503 undergraduates
- 14% of applicants admitted
- SAT or ACT with writing, application essay required

**General.** Founded in 1946. **Degrees:** 67 bachelor's, 5 associate awarded; master's, doctoral, first professional offered. **Location:** 120 miles from Atlanta. **Calendar:** Semester, limited summer session. **Full-time faculty:** 25 total. **Part-time faculty:** 20 total. **Class size:** 77% < 20, 17% 20-39, 4% 40-49, less than 1% 50-99, less than 1% >100.

**Freshman class profile.**

| Mid 50% test scores | | | |
|---|---|---|---|
| SAT critical reading: | 400-540 | ACT composite: | 17-20 |
| SAT math: | 400-480 | Out-of-state: | 26% |
| | | Live on campus: | 72% |

**Basis for selection.** Test scores, one personal reference, one pastoral reference and a written personal testimony about applicant's faith are required. **Homeschooled:** Relevant experiences that may indicate and support ability to succeed in college work may be substituted for high school diploma or GED. Students should submit a transcript and other supporting information, such as course or curriculum descriptions, grades, graduation date, and the signatures of the instructor. Students should submit official transcripts from other secondary or post secondary institutions attended. Students must submit official scores from the ACT Enhanced Test or SAT Test.

**High school preparation.** 10 units required; 15 recommended. Required and recommended units include English 4, mathematics 2-3, social

studies 2-3, science 2-3 and foreign language 2. Computer fundamentals recommended.

**2007-2008 Annual costs.** Tuition/fees: $9,520. Room/board: $5,930. Books/supplies: $700. Personal expenses: $850.

**Financial aid. Non-need-based:** Scholarships awarded for academics, alumni affiliation, athletics, leadership, music/drama, state residency.

**Application procedures. Admission:** Priority date 3/31; deadline 8/1 (receipt date). $30 fee, may be waived for applicants with need. Application may be submitted online. Admission notification on a rolling basis. **Financial aid:** Priority date 3/31; no closing date. FAFSA required. Applicants notified on a rolling basis starting 2/15; must reply within 2 week(s) of notification.

**Academics. Special study options:** Distance learning, double major, dual enrollment of high school students, external degree, independent study, internships, liberal arts/career combination, teacher certification program, Washington semester. **Credit/placement by examination:** AP, CLEP, IB, institutional tests. 16 credit hours maximum toward associate degree, 32 toward bachelor's. **Support services:** Reduced course load, remedial instruction, study skills assistance, tutoring, writing center.

**Majors. Biology:** General. **Business:** General, administrative services, business admin, office management. **Computer sciences:** Computer science. **Education:** Biology, Deaf/hearing impaired, elementary, English, history, mathematics, music, science, secondary, speech. **English:** English lit, speech/rhetoric. **Health:** Premedicine. **History:** General. **Legal studies:** Prelaw. **Liberal arts:** Arts/sciences. **Math:** General. **Physical sciences:** General. **Psychology:** General. **Social sciences:** Political science. **Theology:** Bible, missionary, religious ed, sacred music, theology.

**Computing on campus.** 105 workstations in dormitories, library, computer center. Dormitories wired for high-speed internet access and linked to campus network. Commuter students can connect to campus network. Wireless network available.

**Student life. Freshman orientation:** Mandatory, $25 fee. Held 2-3 days prior to beginning of classes. **Policies:** Religious observance required. **Housing:** Guaranteed on-campus for all undergraduates. Single-sex dorms, apartments available. $100 deposit, deadline 5/31. **Activities:** Choral groups, drama, music ensembles, radio station, student government, student newspaper, Student Missions Fellowship, Student Preachers Fellowship.

**Athletics.** NCCAA. **Intercollegiate:** Baseball M, basketball, soccer M, volleyball W. **Intramural:** Basketball, football (tackle) M, soccer, softball, table tennis, tennis, volleyball, wrestling M. **Team name:** Crusaders.

**Student services.** Campus ministries, student employment services, financial aid counseling, personal counseling, placement for graduates, veterans' counselor. **Physically disabled:** Services for visually, hearing impaired.

**Contact.** E-mail: ttuinfo@tntemple.edu
Phone: (423) 493-4371 Toll-free number: (800) 553-4050
Fax: (423) 493-4497
Chris Dooley, Director of Enrollment Services, Tennessee Temple University, 1815 Union Avenue, Chattanooga, TN 37404

## Tennessee Wesleyan College
**Athens, Tennessee**
**www.twcnet.edu**                                    **CB code: 1805**

- Private 4-year liberal arts and teachers college affiliated with United Methodist Church
- Commuter campus in large town
- 846 degree-seeking undergraduates: 13% part-time, 63% women
- 79% of applicants admitted
- SAT or ACT (ACT writing optional) required
- 44% graduate within 6 years; 40% enter graduate study

**General.** Founded in 1857. Regionally accredited. Baccalaureate programs in nursing and evening business school through Knoxville campus. **Degrees:** 194 bachelor's awarded. **Location:** 50 miles from Chattanooga and Knoxville. **Calendar:** Semester, extensive summer session. **Full-time faculty:** 44 total. **Part-time faculty:** 44 total. **Class size:** 69% < 20, 26% 20-39, 4% 40-49, 1% 50-99, less than 1% >100.

**Freshman class profile.** 463 applied, 366 admitted, 153 enrolled.

| Mid 50% test scores | | | |
|---|---|---|---|
| SAT critical reading: | 430-570 | Rank in top quarter: | 43% |
| SAT math: | 480-560 | Rank in top tenth: | 18% |
| ACT composite: | 19-24 | Return as sophomores: | 62% |
| GPA 3.50 or higher: | 39% | Out-of-state: | 12% |
| GPA 3.0-3.49: | 28% | Live on campus: | 65% |
| GPA 2.0-2.99: | 32% | International: | 3% |

**Basis for selection.** Test scores, school records, recommendations and GPA very important. ACT and SAT are not required if student is older than 21 or if they have a GED. Essay recommended for all; interview recommended for academically weak; audition required for music and theater. **Homeschooled:** Must take the ACT or SAT before being considered for admission.

**High school preparation.** 10 units recommended. Recommended units include English 4, mathematics 2, social studies 1, history 1 and science 2.

**2008-2009 Annual costs.** Tuition/fees (projected): $17,050. Room/board: $5,830. Books/supplies: $1,000. Personal expenses: $2,000.

**Financial aid. Non-need-based:** Scholarships awarded for academics, alumni affiliation, athletics, job skills, minority status, music/drama, religious affiliation.

**Application procedures. Admission:** Closing date 8/15 (receipt date). $25 fee, may be waived for applicants with need. Application may be submitted online. Admission notification on a rolling basis beginning on or about 9/1. **Financial aid:** No deadline. FAFSA, institutional form required. Applicants notified on a rolling basis starting 2/15; must reply within 2 week(s) of notification.

**Academics.** Study abroad opportunities available for students wishing to extend their learning globally. **Special study options:** Accelerated study, double major, exchange student, honors, independent study, internships, student-designed major, study abroad, teacher certification program. Member of the Private College Consortium for International Studies (semester in London program). **Credit/placement by examination:** AP, CLEP, IB, SAT, ACT, institutional tests. 12 credit hours maximum toward bachelor's degree. **Support services:** Learning center, reduced course load, remedial instruction, study skills assistance, tutoring, writing center.

**Majors. Area/ethnic studies:** American. **Biology:** General. **Business:** Accounting, business admin, finance, human resources. **Computer sciences:** General. **Conservation:** Environmental studies. **Education:** Early childhood, elementary, multi-level teacher, secondary. **English:** English lit. **Health:** Nursing (RN), predental, premedicine, prenursing, prepharmacy, preveterinary. **History:** General. **Interdisciplinary:** Behavioral sciences, global studies, intercultural. **Legal studies:** Prelaw. **Math:** General. **Parks/recreation:** Health/fitness, sports admin. **Philosophy/religion:** Christian. **Physical sciences:** Chemistry. **Psychology:** General. **Public administration:** Human services. **Theology:** Preministerial. **Other:** Pre-Physical Therapy.

**Most popular majors.** Business/marketing 25%, education 26%, health sciences 20%, interdisciplinary studies 6%, parks/recreation 7%.

**Computing on campus.** 133 workstations in dormitories, library, computer center, student center. Dormitories wired for high-speed internet access and linked to campus network. Online library, wireless network available.

**Student life. Freshman orientation:** Mandatory. Preregistration for classes offered. Held in August. Participation in orientation earns students one credit hour. **Policies:** All students are required to live on campus unless they reside with a relative who is within commuting distance, have a child, or are married. Visitation in the dorms by the opposite sex is restricted to the hours of 11AM and Midnight and the visitor must leave an ID with a Resident life staff member while in the building. No alcohol is allowed on campus for any reason. Religious observance required. **Housing:** Guaranteed on-campus for freshmen. Single-sex dorms, apartments, substance-free housing available. **Activities:** Concert band, campus ministries, choral groups, drama, international student organizations, literary magazine, music ensembles, student government, student newspaper, Circle K, Hackberry and Oak Society, The National Student Nurses Association, Student Activities Board, Education Angels, Fellowship of Christian Athletes, Wesleyan Christian Fellowship, College Democrats.

**Athletics.** NAIA. **Intercollegiate:** Baseball M, basketball, cross-country, golf, soccer, softball W, tennis, volleyball W. **Team name:** Bulldogs.

**Student services.** Adult student services, alcohol/substance abuse counseling, campus ministries, career counseling, student employment services, financial aid counseling, personal counseling, placement for graduates, veterans' counselor. **Physically disabled:** Services for visually, hearing impaired.

**Contact.** E-mail: admissions@twcnet.edu
Phone: (423) 745-7504 Toll-free number: (800) 742-5892
Fax: (423) 745-9335
Stan Harrison, Vice President Enrollment Management and Director of Athletics, Tennessee Wesleyan College, 204 East College Street, Athens, TN 37371-0040

## Trevecca Nazarene University
**Nashville, Tennessee**
www.trevecca.edu
CB code: 1809

- Private 4-year university and liberal arts college affiliated with Church of the Nazarene
- Residential campus in very large city
- 1,200 degree-seeking undergraduates: 11% part-time, 56% women, 8% African American, 1% Asian American, 2% Hispanic American, 1% Native American, 2% international
- 1,002 degree-seeking graduate students
- 68% of applicants admitted
- SAT or ACT (ACT writing optional) required
- 49% graduate within 6 years

**General.** Founded in 1901. Regionally accredited. **Degrees:** 350 bachelor's, 1 associate awarded; master's, doctoral offered. **ROTC:** Army. **Location:** 200 miles from Memphis, 175 miles from Knoxville. **Calendar:** Semester, limited summer session. **Full-time faculty:** 76 total; 76% have terminal degrees, 9% minority, 32% women. **Part-time faculty:** 134 total; 47% have terminal degrees, 3% minority, 43% women. **Class size:** 59% < 20, 32% 20-39, 5% 40-49, 5% 50-99.

**Freshman class profile.** 821 applied, 560 admitted, 248 enrolled.

| Mid 50% test scores | | | |
|---|---|---|---|
| SAT critical reading: | 480-600 | GPA 2.0-2.99: | 25% |
| SAT math: | 460-580 | Rank in top quarter: | 43% |
| ACT composite: | 19-25 | Rank in top tenth: | 17% |
| GPA 3.50 or higher: | 35% | Return as sophomores: | 74% |
| GPA 3.0-3.49: | 38% | Out-of-state: | 49% |
| | | Live on campus: | 84% |

**Basis for selection.** Freshmen required to meet one of two conditions: a minimum 18 ACT composite (860 SAT composite, exclusive of Writing) or 2.5 high school GPA based on 4.0 scale. **Homeschooled:** Transcript with all subjects and grades should be provided by the correspondence-school based organization or the parent depending on the method of homeschooling. **Learning Disabled:** Contact Disability Services in the Academic Support Center for information concerning documentation of disability and services available.

**High school preparation.** 15 units recommended. Recommended units include English 4, mathematics 2, social studies 1, history 1, science 1, foreign language 2 and academic electives 4.

**2007-2008 Annual costs.** Tuition/fees: $15,512. Room/board: $6,874.

**2006-2007 Financial aid. Need-based:** 41% of total undergraduate aid awarded as scholarships/grants, 59% as loans/jobs. **Non-need-based:** Scholarships awarded for academics, alumni affiliation, athletics, leadership, minority status, music/drama, religious affiliation.

**Application procedures. Admission:** Priority date 4/1; no deadline. $25 fee. Application may be submitted online. Admission notification on a rolling basis. Enrollment deposit of $200 due by May 1. **Financial aid:** Priority date 3/1; no closing date. FAFSA required. Applicants notified on a rolling basis starting 3/1; must reply by 9/1 or within 2 week(s) of notification.

**Academics. Special study options:** Double major, internships, study abroad, teacher certification program. Adult degree completion program. **Credit/placement by examination:** AP, CLEP, IB, SAT, ACT. 22 credit hours maximum toward associate degree, 45 toward bachelor's. Credit awarded after one semester and tuition paid. **Support services:** Learning center, remedial instruction, study skills assistance, tutoring.

**Majors. Biology:** General. **Business:** Accounting, business admin, e-commerce, management information systems, marketing. **Communications:** General, media studies, organizational. **Computer sciences:** Information technology, web page design. **Education:** Biology, business, chemistry, drama/dance, elementary, English, history, mathematics, music, physical, physics, secondary, special, speech. **English:** English lit. **Health:** Clinical lab science, health services, nursing (RN). **History:** General. **Interdisciplinary:** Behavioral sciences. **Math:** General. **Parks/recreation:** Health/fitness. **Philosophy/religion:** Religion. **Physical sciences:** Chemistry, physics. **Psychology:** General. **Public administration:** Social work. **Social sciences:** General, political science. **Theology:** Preministerial, sacred music. **Visual/**

**performing arts:** Dramatic, music management. **Other:** Christian Ministries, Community Development, Financial Mathematics, General Science, History/Political Science, Interpersonal communications.

**Most popular majors.** Business/marketing 59%, education 6%.

**Computing on campus.** 200 workstations in dormitories, library, computer center, student center. Dormitories linked to campus network. Commuter students can connect to campus network. Wireless network available.

**Student life. Freshman orientation:** Mandatory. Preregistration for classes offered. **Policies:** Religious observance required. **Housing:** Single-sex dorms, apartments available. **Activities:** Bands, campus ministries, choral groups, drama, literary magazine, music ensembles, musical theater, radio station, student government, student newspaper, symphony orchestra, TV station, Mission Club, Trevecca Ministerial Association, Phi Beta Lambda.

**Athletics.** NAIA. **Intercollegiate:** Baseball M, basketball, golf, soccer, softball W, volleyball W. **Intramural:** Badminton, basketball, football (tackle) M, golf, racquetball, softball, table tennis, track and field, volleyball. **Team name:** Trojans.

**Student services.** Campus ministries, career counseling, student employment services, financial aid counseling, health services, personal counseling, placement for graduates.

**Contact.** E-mail: admissions_und@trevecca.edu
Phone: (615) 248-1320 Toll-free number: (888) 210-4868
Fax: (615) 248-7406
Michael Cantrell, Director of Admissions, Trevecca Nazarene University, 333 Murfreesboro Road, Nashville, TN 37210

## Tusculum College
**Greeneville, Tennessee**
www.tusculum.edu
CB member
CB code: 1812

- Private 4-year liberal arts college affiliated with Presbyterian Church (USA)
- Residential campus in large town
- 2,446 degree-seeking undergraduates: 3% part-time, 61% women, 11% African American, 2% Hispanic American, 2% international
- 155 degree-seeking graduate students
- 68% of applicants admitted
- SAT or ACT (ACT writing optional), application essay required
- 40% graduate within 6 years

**General.** Founded in 1794. Regionally accredited. Strong civic arts focus and service-learning curriculum. **Degrees:** 594 bachelor's awarded; master's offered. **Location:** 70 miles from Knoxville, 30 miles from Johnson City. **Calendar:** Differs by program, limited summer session. **Full-time faculty:** 74 total; 66% have terminal degrees, 51% women. **Part-time faculty:** 130 total. **Class size:** 83% < 20, 17% 20-39.

**Freshman class profile.** 1,672 applied, 1,139 admitted, 254 enrolled.

| Mid 50% test scores | | | |
|---|---|---|---|
| SAT critical reading: | 430-510 | Return as sophomores: | 55% |
| SAT math: | 420-480 | Out-of-state: | 30% |
| ACT composite: | 19-24 | Live on campus: | 60% |
| | | International: | 4% |

**Basis for selection.** Admissions based on secondary school record and standardized test scores. Essay also important. Math and English placement tests may be required based on ACT or SAT scores. Interview recommended.

**High school preparation.** 12 units required. Required units include English 4, mathematics 3, social studies 3 and science 2.

**2007-2008 Annual costs.** Tuition/fees: $17,385. Room/board: $6,910. Books/supplies: $955. Personal expenses: $1,300.

**Financial aid. Non-need-based:** Scholarships awarded for academics, athletics, leadership, religious affiliation, state residency.

**Application procedures. Admission:** No deadline. No application fee. Application may be submitted online. Admission notification on a rolling basis. **Financial aid:** Closing date 2/15. FAFSA required. Applicants notified on a rolling basis starting 3/1; must reply within 3 week(s) of notification.

**Academics.** Semesters are comprised of 4 blocks, each 3 1/2 weeks long. Students take one course per block. Students and faculty can concentrate on one course at a time. Intensive 16-month professional studies program designed for non-traditional students also offered. **Special study options:** Accelerated study, double major, honors, independent study, internships, student-designed major, study abroad, teacher certification program. **Credit/placement by examination:** AP, CLEP, institutional tests. 30 credit hours maximum toward bachelor's degree. **Support services:** Learning center, pre-admission summer program, study skills assistance, tutoring, writing center.

**Majors. Biology:** General. **Business:** Accounting, business admin, entrepreneurial studies. **Communications:** Journalism. **Conservation:** General, environmental studies. **Education:** Art, biology, business, early childhood, elementary, English, health, history, mathematics, middle, physical, psychology, secondary, special. **English:** English lit. **Health:** Athletic training, clinical lab science, premedicine, prepharmacy. **History:** General. **Interdisciplinary:** Museum. **Legal studies:** Prelaw. **Math:** General. **Parks/recreation:** Health/fitness, sports admin. **Psychology:** General. **Social sciences:** Political science. **Visual/performing arts:** General.

**Most popular majors.** Business/marketing 71%, education 22%.

**Computing on campus.** 160 workstations in library, computer center, student center. Dormitories wired for high-speed internet access and linked to campus network. Commuter students can connect to campus network. Online library, helpline, repair service available.

**Student life. Freshman orientation:** Mandatory. Preregistration for classes offered. **Housing:** Guaranteed on-campus for freshmen. Single-sex dorms available. $200 nonrefundable deposit, deadline 6/1. **Activities:** Choral groups, drama, literary magazine, radio station, student government, student newspaper, Bonwandi, Campus Activities Board, Fellowship of Christian Athletes.

**Athletics.** NAIA, NCAA. **Intercollegiate:** Baseball M, basketball, cheerleading M, cross-country, football (tackle) M, golf, soccer, softball W, tennis, volleyball W. **Intramural:** Basketball, football (tackle) M, soccer, softball, table tennis, tennis, volleyball. **Team name:** Pioneers.

**Student services.** Adult student services, campus ministries, career counseling, student employment services, health services, personal counseling, placement for graduates, veterans' counselor.

**Contact.** E-mail: mripley@tusculum.edu
Phone: (423) 636-7300 Toll-free number: (800) 729-0256
Fax: (423) 638-7166
Jacqui Elliott, Director of Admissions, Tusculum College, 60 Shiloh Road, Greeneville, TN 37743

## Union University
**Jackson, Tennessee**
**www.uu.edu**                                      **CB code: 1826**

- Private 4-year university and liberal arts college affiliated with Southern Baptist Convention
- Residential campus in small city
- 2,100 degree-seeking undergraduates: 13% part-time, 61% women, 10% African American, 1% Asian American, 1% Hispanic American, 2% international
- 864 degree-seeking graduate students
- 81% of applicants admitted
- 59% graduate within 6 years

**General.** Founded in 1823. Regionally accredited. **Degrees:** 411 bachelor's, 2 associate awarded; master's, doctoral, first professional offered. **Location:** 80 miles from Memphis, 120 miles from Nashville. **Calendar:** Semester, extensive summer session. **Full-time faculty:** 174 total; 82% have terminal degrees, 8% minority, 44% women. **Part-time faculty:** 87 total; 24% have terminal degrees, 10% minority, 74% women. **Class size:** 68% < 20, 28% 20-39, 4% 40-49. **Special facilities:** Aquatic center, creative communications center.

**Freshman class profile.** 1,140 applied, 918 admitted, 450 enrolled.

| Mid 50% test scores | | Rank in top quarter: | 60% |
|---|---|---|---|
| SAT critical reading: | 510-680 | Rank in top tenth: | 35% |
| SAT math: | 510-640 | Out-of-state: | 28% |
| ACT composite: | 22-28 | Live on campus: | 81% |
| GPA 3.50 or higher: | 61% | International: | 4% |
| GPA 3.0-3.49: | 27% | Fraternities: | 10% |
| GPA 2.0-2.99: | 12% | Sororities: | 16% |

**Basis for selection.** School achievement, recommendations, special talents, test scores important. Minimum 22 ACT or 1030 SAT (exclusive of Writing), top 50% of high school class, and 2.5 GPA required. Interview recommended for all; audition required for music; portfolio recommended for art, communications. Essay required for academic and leadership scholarships. **Homeschooled:** If a class rank is unavailable, students may be admitted without conditions provided they meet minimum ACT/SAT scores and GPA requirements.

**High school preparation.** 15 units required; 22 recommended. Required and recommended units include English 4, mathematics 3-4, social studies 2, history 1-2, science 3-4 (laboratory 2), foreign language 1-2, computer science 1, visual/performing arts 1 and academic electives 1-4.

**2007-2008 Annual costs.** Tuition/fees: $18,620. Room/board: $6,500. Books/supplies: $750. Personal expenses: $3,000.

**2006-2007 Financial aid. Need-based:** 367 full-time freshmen applied for aid; 288 were judged to have need; 288 of these received aid. Average need met was 77%. Average scholarship/grant was $4,810; average loan $2,693. 62% of total undergraduate aid awarded as scholarships/grants, 38% as loans/jobs. **Non-need-based:** Awarded to 1,446 full-time undergraduates, including 437 freshmen. Scholarships awarded for academics, alumni affiliation, art, athletics, leadership, minority status, music/drama, religious affiliation, state residency.

**Application procedures. Admission:** Priority date 12/1; deadline 8/1 (postmark date). $35 fee, may be waived for applicants with need. Application may be submitted online. Admission notification on a rolling basis beginning on or about 10/1. Must reply by May 1 or within 2 week(s) if notified thereafter. **Financial aid:** Priority date 2/15, closing date 3/1. FAFSA, institutional form required. Applicants notified on a rolling basis starting 2/15; must reply by 5/1 or within 2 week(s) of notification.

**Academics. Special study options:** Accelerated study, combined bachelor's/graduate degree, cooperative education, cross-registration, distance learning, double major, dual enrollment of high school students, ESL, exchange student, honors, independent study, internships, study abroad, teacher certification program, Washington semester. **Credit/placement by examination:** CLEP, IB, institutional tests. 32 credit hours maximum toward bachelor's degree. **Support services:** Learning center, pre-admission summer program, reduced course load, remedial instruction, study skills assistance, tutoring, writing center.

**Majors. Biology:** General, cellular/molecular, conservation, zoology. **Business:** Accounting, business admin, international, managerial economics, marketing. **Communications:** General, advertising, broadcast journalism, digital media, journalism, public relations. **Computer sciences:** Computer science, web page design. **Education:** General, art, biology, business, chemistry, early childhood special, elementary, English, ESL, foreign languages, French, history, kindergarten/preschool, mathematics, middle, music, physical, science, secondary, Spanish, special. **Engineering:** Electrical, mechanical, physics. **English:** English lit, speech/rhetoric. **Family/consumer sciences:** Family systems. **Foreign languages:** French, Spanish. **Health:** Athletic training, clinical lab science, nursing (RN), preop/surgical nursing. **History:** General. **Interdisciplinary:** Intercultural. **Math:** General. **Parks/recreation:** Exercise sciences, sports admin. **Philosophy/religion:** Christian, ethics, philosophy, religion. **Physical sciences:** General, chemical physics, chemistry, physics. **Psychology:** General. **Public administration:** Social work. **Social sciences:** Economics, political science, sociology. **Theology:** Sacred music, theology, youth ministry. **Visual/performing arts:** Dramatic, music performance, music theory/composition, studio arts.

**Most popular majors.** Business/marketing 10%, education 8%, health sciences 28%, interdisciplinary studies 12%, philosophy/religious studies 7%.

**Computing on campus.** 300 workstations in dormitories, library, computer center, student center. Dormitories wired for high-speed internet access and linked to campus network. Commuter students can connect to campus network. Online course registration, online library, helpline, repair service, wireless network available.

**Student life. Freshman orientation:** Available, $70 fee. Preregistration for classes offered. Held 4 days before classes begin for freshmen and transfer students. **Policies:** Full-time resident students required to attend 14 chapel services per semester. Smoke and alcohol-free campus. Religious observance required. **Housing:** Guaranteed on-campus for all undergraduates. Single-sex dorms, special housing for disabled, apartments available. $100 nonrefundable deposit, deadline 5/1. **Activities:** Bands, choral groups, drama, film society, literary magazine, music ensembles, student government, student newspaper, Fellowship of Christian Athletes, Ministerial Association, student activity council, Mu Kappa, honors student association, Tennessee Intercollegiate State Legislature, international student organization, LIFE Groups, Klemata, weekend ministry teams.

**Athletics.** NAIA. **Intercollegiate:** Baseball M, basketball, cheerleading M, cross-country, golf M, soccer, softball W, tennis, volleyball W. **Intramural:** Basketball, cheerleading W, cross-country, football (non-tackle), golf, racquetball, softball, swimming, table tennis, tennis, volleyball, weight lifting. **Team name:** Bulldogs.

**Student services.** Adult student services, alcohol/substance abuse counseling, campus ministries, career counseling, student employment services, financial aid counseling, health services, personal counseling, placement for graduates, veterans' counselor. **Physically disabled:** Services for visually, speech, hearing impaired.

**Contact.** E-mail: info@uu.edu
Phone: (731) 661-5000 Toll-free number: (800) 338-6466
Fax: (731) 661-5017
Rich Grimm, Vice President for Enrollment Services, Union University, 1050 Union University Drive, Jackson, TN 38305-3697

## University of Memphis
### Memphis, Tennessee
### www.memphis.edu
**CB code: 1459**

- Public 4-year university
- Commuter campus in very large city
- 15,228 degree-seeking undergraduates: 24% part-time, 62% women, 39% African American, 2% Asian American, 2% Hispanic American, 2% international
- 3,521 degree-seeking graduate students
- 66% of applicants admitted
- SAT or ACT (ACT writing optional) required
- 35% graduate within 6 years

**General.** Founded in 1912. Regionally accredited. **Degrees:** 2,482 bachelor's awarded; master's, doctoral, first professional offered. **ROTC:** Army, Naval, Air Force. **Location:** 10 miles from downtown. **Calendar:** Semester, extensive summer session. **Full-time faculty:** 833 total; 80% have terminal degrees, 19% minority, 40% women. **Part-time faculty:** 534 total; 74% have terminal degrees, 20% minority, 55% women. **Class size:** 40% < 20, 46% 20-39, 5% 40-49, 8% 50-99, 2% >100. **Special facilities:** Institute of Egyptian art and archaeology, speech and hearing center, earthquake research and information center, technology institute, Chucalissa Indian village and museum, Confucius institute.

**Freshman class profile.** 6,025 applied, 3,986 admitted, 2,017 enrolled.

| Mid 50% test scores | | GPA 2.0-2.99: | 41% |
|---|---|---|---|
| SAT critical reading: | 460-620 | Rank in top quarter: | 45% |
| SAT math: | 460-580 | Rank in top tenth: | 18% |
| SAT writing: | 460-570 | Return as sophomores: | 73% |
| ACT composite: | 19-25 | Out-of-state: | 9% |
| GPA 3.50 or higher: | 25% | Live on campus: | 45% |
| GPA 3.0-3.49: | 34% | International: | 2% |

**Basis for selection.** High school GPA and test scores are important. An Admissions Index will be calculated for each applicant by first multiplying the cumulative high school GPA by 30 and then adding the ACT composite score. The admission of first-time freshmen is competitive based on the calculated index, and also includes an evaluation of the high school curriculum completed. Interview required for university college; audition required for music; portfolio required for fine arts. **Homeschooled:** Transcript of courses and grades required. Applicants must comply with state law by submitting proof of registration with the local education agency.

**High school preparation.** Required units include English 4, mathematics 3, social studies 2, history 1, science 2 (laboratory 1), foreign language 2 and visual/performing arts 1.

**2007-2008 Annual costs.** Tuition/fees: $5,802; $16,630 out-of-state. Room/board: $5,360. Books/supplies: $1,000. Personal expenses: $3,973.

**2007-2008 Financial aid. Need-based:** 1,805 full-time freshmen applied for aid; 1,263 were judged to have need; 1,187 of these received aid. Average need met was 81%. Average scholarship/grant was $5,472; average loan $1,605. 52% of total undergraduate aid awarded as scholarships/grants, 48% as loans/jobs. **Non-need-based:** Awarded to 6,754 full-time undergraduates, including 1,671 freshmen. Scholarships awarded for academics, alumni affiliation, art, athletics, leadership, minority status, music/drama, ROTC, state residency.

**Application procedures. Admission:** Closing date 7/1 (postmark date). $25 fee. Application may be submitted online. Admission notification on a rolling basis. Must meet registration deadline. **Financial aid:** Priority date 3/1, closing date 6/30. FAFSA required. Applicants notified on a rolling basis starting 3/1; must reply within 2 week(s) of notification.

**Academics.** University enables students to create non-traditional degrees. **Special study options:** Accelerated study, combined bachelor's/graduate

degree, cooperative education, cross-registration, distance learning, double major, dual enrollment of high school students, ESL, exchange student, external degree, honors, independent study, internships, liberal arts/career combination, student-designed major, study abroad, teacher certification program. **Credit/placement by examination:** AP, CLEP, IB, SAT, ACT, institutional tests. 24 credit hours maximum toward bachelor's degree. Number of credits awarded decided by individual departments. **Support services:** Learning center, pre-admission summer program, reduced course load, remedial instruction, study skills assistance, tutoring, writing center.

**Honors college/program.** ACT of 27 or high or a combined SAT score of 1200 or more (exclusive of Writing); 3.5 cumulative high school GPA.

**Majors. Architecture:** Architecture, environmental design. **Area/ethnic studies:** African-American. **Biology:** General, bacteriology. **Business:** Accounting, business admin, finance, hospitality admin, hotel/motel admin, international, logistics, management information systems, managerial economics, marketing, real estate, resort management, sales/distribution, selling. **Communications:** Journalism, media studies. **Computer sciences:** Computer science. **Education:** Elementary, multi-level teacher, physical, special. **Engineering:** Biomedical, civil, computer, electrical, mechanical. **Engineering technology:** Computer, electrical, manufacturing. **English:** English lit. **Family/consumer sciences:** Family studies. **Foreign languages:** General. **Health:** Nursing (RN). **History:** General. **Liberal arts:** Arts/sciences. **Math:** General. **Parks/recreation:** Exercise sciences, sports admin. **Philosophy/religion:** Philosophy. **Physical sciences:** Chemistry, geology, physics. **Protective services:** Law enforcement admin. **Psychology:** General. **Public administration:** Social work. **Social sciences:** Anthropology, economics, geography, international relations, political science, sociology. **Visual/performing arts:** Art, art history/conservation, dramatic, music management. **Other:** Music, Other.

**Most popular majors.** Business/marketing 21%, communications/journalism 7%, education 8%, health sciences 6%, interdisciplinary studies 10%, liberal arts 7%, psychology 6%, social sciences 6%.

**Computing on campus.** 2,000 workstations in dormitories, library, computer center, student center. Dormitories wired for high-speed internet access and linked to campus network. Commuter students can connect to campus network. Online course registration, online library, helpline, repair service, wireless network available.

**Student life. Freshman orientation:** Mandatory. Preregistration for classes offered. One- or 2-day sessions, evening program for adult students. Fees vary by program. **Housing:** Coed dorms, single-sex dorms, special housing for disabled, apartments, fraternity/sorority housing available. $100 fully refundable deposit, deadline 7/1. **Activities:** Bands, choral groups, dance, drama, literary magazine, music ensembles, musical theater, opera, radio station, student government, student newspaper, symphony orchestra.

**Athletics.** NCAA. **Intercollegiate:** Baseball M, basketball, cross-country, football (tackle) M, golf, rifle, soccer, softball W, tennis, track and field, volleyball W. **Intramural:** Basketball, bowling, cross-country, football (non-tackle), golf, racquetball, soccer, softball, table tennis, tennis, volleyball. **Team name:** Tigers.

**Student services.** Adult student services, career counseling, student employment services, health services, minority student services, on-campus daycare, personal counseling, placement for graduates, veterans' counselor, women's services. **Physically disabled:** Services for visually, speech, hearing impaired.

**Contact.** E-mail: recruitment@memphis.edu
Phone: (901) 678-2111 Toll-free number: (800) 669-2678
Fax: (901) 678-3053
David Wallace, Director of Admissions, University of Memphis, 101 Wilder Tower, Memphis, TN 38152

## University of Tennessee Health Science Center
### Memphis, Tennessee
### www.utmem.edu
**CB code: 1850**

- Public two-year upper-division university and health science college
- Commuter campus in very large city
- Test scores, application essay, interview required

**General.** Founded in 1911. Regionally accredited. **Degrees:** 101 bachelor's awarded; master's, doctoral, first professional offered. **Location:** 220 miles from Nashville, 299 miles from St. Louis, Missouri. **Calendar:** Semester, limited summer session. **Full-time faculty:** 1,172 total; 20% minority. **Part-time faculty:** 208 total; 121% minority. **Special facilities:** Computer laboratories, special laboratories for nursing, pharmacy, allied health, and dentistry instruction, simulated patients.

**Student profile.** 294 degree-seeking undergraduates, 2,361 degree-seeking graduate students. 58% entered as juniors, 42% entered as seniors. 58% transferred from two-year, 42% transferred from four-year institutions.

| Women: | 90% | Part-time: | 2% |
|---|---|---|---|

**Basis for selection.** High school transcript, college transcript, application essay, interview, standardized test scores required. Students must have minimum 2 years of college and meet minimum requirements. Admissions based on GPA, test scores, consistency in achievement, course load and content, recommendations, extracurricular performance, motivation and goals, preprofessional evaluation, interview if required by program. Minimum GPA requirements and application closing dates vary by program. Transfer accepted as juniors, seniors.

**2007-2008 Annual costs.** Tuition/fees: $5,194; $11,784 out-of-state. Above cost are for bachelor's program in nursing. Other programs vary by cost. Books/supplies: $1,182.

**Financial aid. Need-based:** Average need met was 42%. 25% of total undergraduate aid awarded as scholarships/grants, 75% as loans/jobs. **Non-need-based:** Scholarships awarded for academics, leadership, minority status, state residency. **Additional information:** Scholarships available to defray out-of-state portion of fees charged to out-of-state minority students.

**Application procedures. Admission:** $50 fee, may be waived for applicants with need. Application may be submitted online. Must reply by 6/1. **Financial aid:** No deadline. Applicants notified on a rolling basis starting 5/1; must reply within 2 weeks of notification. FAFSA required.

**Academics. Special study options:** Accelerated study, combined bachelor's/graduate degree, cooperative education, cross-registration, distance learning, double major, exchange student, independent study, internships. **Credit/placement by examination:** CLEP.

**Honors college/program.** Varies for each undergraduate program.

**Majors. Health:** Clinical lab science, cytotechnology, dental hygiene, medical records admin, nursing (RN), occupational therapy assistant.

**Computing on campus.** 100 workstations in library, computer center. Commuter students can connect to campus network. Online library, helpline, repair service, student web hosting, wireless network available.

**Student life. Housing:** Coed dorms, substance-free housing available. $50 fully refundable deposit. **Activities:** International student organizations, student government, student newspaper, Baptist Student Union, United Methodist Fellowship, Catholic Student Association, Black Student Association.

**Athletics. Intramural:** Badminton, basketball, bowling, golf, handball, racquetball, soccer, softball, squash, swimming, table tennis, tennis, volleyball, water polo.

**Student services.** Adult student services, alcohol/substance abuse counseling, career counseling, services for economically disadvantaged, student employment services, financial aid counseling, health services, legal services, minority student services, personal counseling, placement for graduates, veterans' counselor. **Physically disabled:** Services for visually, speech, hearing impaired. **Learning disabled:** Comprehensive services available.

**Contact.** E-mail: etaylor@utmem.edu
Phone: (901) 448-5562 Fax: (901) 448-7772
Eunice Taylor, Registrar, University of Tennessee Health Science Center, 800 Madison Avenue, Memphis, TN 38163

## University of Tennessee: Chattanooga
**Chattanooga, Tennessee**
**www.utc.edu**                                    CB code: 1831

- Public 4-year university
- Commuter campus in large city
- 7,987 degree-seeking undergraduates: 11% part-time, 56% women, 19% African American, 2% Asian American, 2% Hispanic American, 1% international
- 1,293 degree-seeking graduate students
- 83% of applicants admitted
- SAT or ACT (ACT writing optional) required
- 45% graduate within 6 years

**General.** Founded in 1886. Regionally accredited. **Degrees:** 1,222 bachelor's awarded; master's, doctoral offered. **ROTC:** Army. **Location:** 130 miles from Nashville, 118 miles from Atlanta. **Calendar:** Semester, extensive summer session. **Full-time faculty:** 400 total; 72% have terminal degrees, 13% minority, 46% women. **Part-time faculty:** 296 total; 19% have terminal degrees, 10% minority, 49% women. **Class size:** 46% < 20, 44% 20-39, 9% 40-49, 1% 50-99, less than 1% >100. **Special facilities:** 2 art galleries, theater, observatory.

**Freshman class profile.** 5,210 applied, 4,328 admitted, 1,947 enrolled.

| Mid 50% test scores | | Out-of-state: | 6% |
|---|---|---|---|
| ACT composite: | 19-24 | Live on campus: | 75% |
| GPA 3.50 or higher: | 31% | International: | 1% |
| GPA 3.0-3.49: | 34% | Fraternities: | 20% |
| GPA 2.0-2.99: | 35% | Sororities: | 16% |
| Return as sophomores: | 64% | | |

**Basis for selection.** High school curriculum and GPA (minimum 2.75), test scores, special talents, recommendations, essay or personal statement considered. Conditional admission for GPA between 2.0 and 2.74 and SAT combined score between 640 and 900 (exclusive of Writing) or ACT composite score between 12 and 19. Essay recommended. **Homeschooled:** Transcript of courses and grades required. Entrance requirements for home schooled students: 2.75 HS GPA; 21 ACT or 980 SAT (excluding writing). **Learning Disabled:** Admissions process is the same for all prospective students. Once students with any disability are accepted, they may then choose to register for services with the Office for Students with Disabilities.

**High school preparation.** 14 units required; 15 recommended. Required and recommended units include English 4, mathematics 3, social studies 2, history 1, science 2-4 (laboratory 2) and foreign language 2. Foreign language units must be in same language. Social science units should be US history and world/European history or world geography, one fine arts unit.

**2007-2008 Annual costs.** Tuition/fees: $5,062; $15,024 out-of-state. Room/board: $6,750. Books/supplies: $950. Personal expenses: $1,402.

**2007-2008 Financial aid. Need-based:** 1,802 full-time freshmen applied for aid; 1,114 were judged to have need; 1,091 of these received aid. Average need met was 85%. Average scholarship/grant was $4,199; average loan $3,941. 44% of total undergraduate aid awarded as scholarships/grants, 56% as loans/jobs. **Non-need-based:** Awarded to 3,345 full-time undergraduates, including 1,123 freshmen. Scholarships awarded for academics, alumni affiliation, art, athletics, job skills, leadership, minority status, music/drama, religious affiliation, ROTC, state residency.

**Application procedures. Admission:** Closing date 8/1. $30 fee, may be waived for applicants with need. Application may be submitted online. Admission notification on a rolling basis. **Financial aid:** Priority date 4/1; no closing date. FAFSA, institutional form required. Applicants notified on a rolling basis starting 3/1; must reply within 6 week(s) of notification.

**Academics. Special study options:** Combined bachelor's/graduate degree, cooperative education, cross-registration, distance learning, double major, dual enrollment of high school students, ESL, honors, independent study, internships, study abroad, teacher certification program. Cooperative program in criminal justice with Cleveland State Community College. **Credit/placement by examination:** AP, CLEP, SAT, ACT, institutional tests. 24 credit hours maximum toward bachelor's degree. May only be used for elective credit hours. **Support services:** Learning center, pre-admission summer program, reduced course load, remedial instruction, study skills assistance, tutoring, writing center.

**Majors. Biology:** General. **Business:** Business admin. **Communications:** General. **Computer sciences:** General. **Conservation:** General. **Education:** Art, English, foreign languages, mathematics, middle, music, science, secondary, social studies, special. **Engineering:** General. **Engineering technology:** Industrial management. **English:** English lit. **Family/consumer sciences:** General. **Foreign languages:** Classics, French, Latin, Spanish. **Health:** Nursing (RN). **History:** General. **Legal studies:** Paralegal. **Liberal arts:** Arts/sciences, humanities. **Math:** General, applied. **Parks/recreation:** Exercise sciences. **Physical sciences:** Chemistry, geology, physics. **Protective services:** Law enforcement admin. **Psychology:** General. **Public administration:** Community org/advocacy, social work. **Social sciences:** General, economics, political science, sociology. **Visual/performing arts:** Art, dramatic.

**Most popular majors.** Business/marketing 27%, education 8%, family/consumer sciences 10%, health sciences 6%, psychology 7%.

**Computing on campus.** 1,200 workstations in library, computer center, student center. Dormitories wired for high-speed internet access and linked to campus network. Commuter students can connect to campus network. Online course registration, online library, helpline, repair service, wireless network available.

**Student life. Freshman orientation:** Mandatory, $50 fee. Preregistration for classes offered. Held in summer, 2 days, at 5 different times. **Housing:** Coed dorms, apartments, fraternity/sorority housing, substance-free housing available. $75 partly refundable deposit. **Activities:** Bands, campus ministries, choral groups, dance, drama, film society, international student organizations, music ensembles, radio station, student government, student newspaper, symphony orchestra, several religious, political, ethnic, and social service organizations.

**Athletics.** NCAA. **Intercollegiate:** Basketball, cross-country, football (tackle) M, golf, rowing (crew), soccer W, softball W, tennis, track and field, volleyball W, wrestling M. **Intramural:** Archery, badminton, basketball, bowling, fencing, football (non-tackle), golf, racquetball, soccer, softball W, swimming, table tennis, tennis, track and field, volleyball, weight lifting, wrestling M. **Team name:** Mocs.

**Student services.** Adult student services, campus ministries, career counseling, student employment services, financial aid counseling, health services, minority student services, on-campus daycare, personal counseling, placement for graduates, veterans' counselor, women's services. **Physically disabled:** Services for visually, hearing impaired.

**Contact.** E-mail: yancy-freeman@utc.edu
Phone: (423) 425-4662 Toll-free number: (800) 882-6627
Fax: (423) 425-4157
Yancy Freeman, Director of Student Recruitment and Admissions, University of Tennessee: Chattanooga, 615 McCallie Avenue, Chattanooga, TN 37403

## University of Tennessee: Knoxville

Knoxville, Tennessee                                 CB member
www.tennessee.edu                                    CB code: 1843

▶ Public 4-year university
▶ Residential campus in large city
▶ 21,001 degree-seeking undergraduates: 6% part-time, 51% women, 9% African American, 3% Asian American, 2% Hispanic American, 1% international
▶ 8,177 degree-seeking graduate students
▶ 71% of applicants admitted
▶ SAT or ACT (ACT writing optional) required
▶ 58% graduate within 6 years

**General.** Founded in 1794. Regionally accredited. **Degrees:** 3,681 bachelor's awarded; master's, doctoral, first professional offered. **ROTC:** Army, Air Force. **Location:** 224 miles from Atlanta, 178 miles from Nashville. **Calendar:** Semester, extensive summer session. **Full-time faculty:** 1,550 total; 82% have terminal degrees, 12% minority, 38% women. **Part-time faculty:** 115 total; 70% have terminal degrees, 12% minority, 30% women. **Class size:** 32% < 20, 56% 20-39, 4% 40-49, 5% 50-99, 3% >100. **Special facilities:** 2 theaters, science/engineering research facility, international house, Olympic track, baseball stadium.

**Freshman class profile.** 12,824 applied, 9,136 admitted, 4,351 enrolled.

| Mid 50% test scores | | | | |
|---|---|---|---|---|
| SAT critical reading: | 520-630 | Rank in top tenth: | 39% |
| SAT math: | 530-640 | Return as sophomores: | 84% |
| ACT composite: | 23-28 | Out-of-state: | 14% |
| GPA 3.50 or higher: | 63% | Live on campus: | 96% |
| GPA 3.0-3.49: | 28% | International: | 1% |
| GPA 2.0-2.99: | 8% | Fraternities: | 19% |
| Rank in top quarter: | 69% | Sororities: | 27% |

**Basis for selection.** Admission based on high school grades in core academic subjects and standardized test scores. Other factors that indicate future academic success considered, as are special talents, student statement, extracurricular leadership, community involvement, class rank, and background. Essay required, portfolio recommended for architecture; audition required for music; interview recommended for marginally prepared, reentry.

**High school preparation.** 14 units required. Required units include English 4, mathematics 3, social studies 1, history 1, science 2 (laboratory 1), foreign language 2 and visual/performing arts 1. Social science units must be 1 U.S. history and either world history, European history, or world geography. Mathematics units must include algebra I, algebra II, and 1 unit of either geometry, trigonometry, advanced mathematics, or calculus.

**2007-2008 Annual costs.** Tuition/fees: $5,932; $17,874 out-of-state. Out-of-state students pay additional required fees of $300. Room/board: $6,358. Books/supplies: $1,288. Personal expenses: $2,956.

**2007-2008 Financial aid.** All financial aid based on need. 4,061 full-time freshmen applied for aid; 2,044 were judged to have need; 2,006 of

these received aid. Average need met was 79%. Average scholarship/grant was $2,627; average loan $3,511. 67% of total undergraduate aid awarded as scholarships/grants, 33% as loans/jobs. **Additional information:** Application priority date for scholarships 2/1.

**Application procedures. Admission:** Closing date 12/1 (postmark date). $30 fee, may be waived for applicants with need. Application may be submitted online. Priority applicants notified in January. Regular applicants notified in March. Must reply by 5/1. **Financial aid:** Priority date 3/1; no closing date. FAFSA required. Applicants notified on a rolling basis starting 3/15; must reply within 3 week(s) of notification.

**Academics. Special study options:** Combined bachelor's/graduate degree, cooperative education, distance learning, double major, dual enrollment of high school students, ESL, exchange student, external degree, honors, independent study, internships, liberal arts/career combination, student-designed major, study abroad, teacher certification program. **Credit/placement by examination:** AP, CLEP, IB, institutional tests. Departmental proficiency available. Up to 50 hours of credit awarded for International Baccalaureate. **Support services:** Learning center, study skills assistance, tutoring, writing center.

**Majors. Agriculture:** Animal sciences, economics, food science, ornamental horticulture, plant sciences, soil chem/physics. **Architecture:** Architecture. **Area/ethnic studies:** African-American, American, Asian, Latin American, Russian/Slavic, women's. **Biology:** General. **Business:** General, accounting, business admin, finance, hotel/motel admin, human resources, logistics, managerial economics, marketing, tourism/travel. **Communications:** Advertising, journalism, public relations. **Computer sciences:** Computer science. **Conservation:** Forestry, wildlife. **Education:** Agricultural, art, Deaf/hearing impaired, music, special. **Engineering:** Aerospace, agricultural, biomedical, chemical, civil, computer, electrical, environmental, industrial, materials, materials science, mechanical, nuclear, physics, science. **English:** English lit, speech/rhetoric. **Family/consumer sciences:** Consumer economics, family studies, food/nutrition. **Foreign languages:** Ancient Greek, classics, comparative lit, French, German, Italian, Latin, linguistics, Portuguese, Russian, Spanish. **Health:** Audiology/hearing, clinical lab science, occupational health nursing, predental, premedicine, prepharmacy, preveterinary, speech pathology. **History:** General. **Interdisciplinary:** Medieval/Renaissance. **Legal studies:** Prelaw. **Math:** General, statistics. **Parks/recreation:** General, exercise sciences, sports admin. **Philosophy/religion:** Philosophy, religion. **Physical sciences:** Chemistry, geology, physics. **Protective services:** Criminal justice. **Psychology:** General. **Public administration:** General. **Social sciences:** Anthropology, economics, geography, political science, sociology. **Visual/performing arts:** Art, art history/conservation, commercial/advertising art, dramatic, interior design, music theory/composition, piano/organ, studio arts, voice/opera. **Other:** Journalism & Electronic Media.

**Most popular majors.** Business/marketing 18%, communications/journalism 9%, engineering/engineering technologies 8%, health sciences 7%, psychology 11%, social sciences 11%.

**Computing on campus.** 1,000 workstations in dormitories, library, computer center, student center. Dormitories wired for high-speed internet access and linked to campus network. Commuter students can connect to campus network. Online course registration, online library, helpline, repair service, student web hosting, wireless network available.

**Student life. Freshman orientation:** Mandatory, $99 fee. Preregistration for classes offered. 2 days. Parents may also attend orientation for $20 per parent; fee does not include housing. **Housing:** Guaranteed on-campus for freshmen. Coed dorms, single-sex dorms, special housing for disabled, apartments, fraternity/sorority housing available. $100 fully refundable deposit. Foreign language housing available. Freshmen must live on campus unless residing with parent or legal guardian. Transfer student floors available. **Activities:** Bands, choral groups, dance, drama, film society, literary magazine, music ensembles, musical theater, opera, radio station, student government, student newspaper, symphony orchestra, TV station, Black cultural center, student political, ethnic, social, and service organizations, women's center, various denomination student unions.

**Athletics.** NCAA. **Intercollegiate:** Baseball M, basketball, cricket, cross-country, diving, football (tackle) M, golf, rowing (crew) W, soccer W, softball W, swimming, tennis, track and field, volleyball W. **Intramural:** Badminton, basketball, bowling, cross-country, field hockey, golf, racquetball, skin diving, soccer, softball, swimming, table tennis, tennis, track and field, volleyball. **Team name:** Volunteers.

**Student services.** Adult student services, alcohol/substance abuse counseling, campus ministries, career counseling, student employment services, financial aid counseling, health services, minority student services, on-campus daycare, personal counseling, placement for graduates, veterans' counselor, women's services. **Physically disabled:** Services for visually, speech, hearing impaired.

**Contact.** E-mail: admissions@utk.edu
Phone: (865) 974-2184 Fax: (865) 974-6341
Nancy McGlasson, Director of Admissions, University of Tennessee:
Knoxville, 320 Student Services Building, Knoxville, TN 37996-0230

## University of Tennessee: Martin
### Martin, Tennessee
www.utm.edu       CB code: 1844

- Public 4-year university
- Commuter campus in small town
- 5,827 degree-seeking undergraduates: 10% part-time, 57% women, 16% African American, 1% Asian American, 1% Hispanic American, 2% international
- 366 degree-seeking graduate students
- 77% of applicants admitted
- SAT or ACT (ACT writing optional) required
- 44% graduate within 6 years; 20% enter graduate study

**General.** Founded in 1927. Regionally accredited. Sponsors only collegiate rodeo team in Tennessee; coordinates online education for UT system. **Degrees:** 969 bachelor's awarded; master's offered. **ROTC:** Army. **Location:** 125 miles from Memphis, 150 miles from Nashville. **Calendar:** Semester, extensive summer session. **Full-time faculty:** 258 total; 70% have terminal degrees, 10% minority, 43% women. **Part-time faculty:** 242 total; 24% have terminal degrees, 5% minority, 51% women. **Class size:** 51% < 20, 38% 20-39, 4% 40-49, 7% 50-99, less than 1% >100. **Special facilities:** Center for global studies and international education, four off-campus educational centers, four compressed video classrooms, network of compressed video classes across the state, teacher resource center, 680-acre agriculture, natural resources teaching, demonstration complex, teaching/research facility resort.

**Freshman class profile.** 3,010 applied, 2,318 admitted, 1,311 enrolled.

| Mid 50% test scores | | End year in good standing: | 73% |
|---|---|---|---|
| ACT composite: | 19-24 | Return as sophomores: | 71% |
| GPA 3.50 or higher: | 42% | Out-of-state: | 4% |
| GPA 3.0-3.49: | 35% | Live on campus: | 65% |
| GPA 2.0-2.99: | 23% | International: | 2% |
| Rank in top quarter: | 52% | Fraternities: | 19% |
| Rank in top tenth: | 21% | Sororities: | 13% |

**Basis for selection.** High School GPA of 2.85 and minimum ACT composite score of 18, or GPA of 2.50 and minimum ACT score of 21. Students not meeting regular admission requirements may be considered for conditional admission. **Homeschooled:** 19 ACT and 2.6 GPA.

**High school preparation.** 14 units required. Required units include English 4, mathematics 3, history 2, science 2 (laboratory 1) and foreign language 2. 1 visual and performing arts.

**2007-2008 Annual costs.** Tuition/fees: $5,005; $15,045 out-of-state. Room/board: $4,446. Books/supplies: $1,200. Personal expenses: $2,200.

**2007-2008 Financial aid.** All financial aid based on need. 1,237 full-time freshmen applied for aid; 858 were judged to have need; 848 of these received aid. Average need met was 82%. Average scholarship/grant was $5,402; average loan $3,026. 55% of total undergraduate aid awarded as scholarships/grants, 45% as loans/jobs.

**Application procedures.** Admission: Priority date 2/1; deadline 8/1. $30 fee. Application may be submitted online. Admission notification on a rolling basis beginning on or about 9/1. **Financial aid:** Priority date 3/1; no closing date. FAFSA required. Applicants notified on a rolling basis starting 4/1.

**Academics.** Special study options: Accelerated study, cooperative education, cross-registration, distance learning, double major, dual enrollment of high school students, ESL, exchange student, honors, independent study, internships, student-designed major, study abroad, teacher certification program. 3-1 pharmacy program, 3-1 veterinary medicine program, 3-1 dentistry program, 3-1 medicine program, 3-1 optometry program, 3-1 podiatry program, 3-1 chiropractory program. **Credit/placement by examination:** AP, CLEP, SAT, ACT, institutional tests. 30 credit hours maximum toward bachelor's degree. **Support services:** Learning center, remedial instruction, study skills assistance, tutoring, writing center.

**Majors. Agriculture:** General. **Biology:** General. **Business:** Accounting, business admin, finance, management information systems, managerial economics, marketing. **Communications:** General. **Computer sciences:** Computer science. **Conservation:** Management/policy. **Education:** Biology, business, chemistry, English, French, geography, German, history, mathematics, Spanish, special. **Engineering:** General. **English:** English lit. **Family/**

consumer sciences: General. **Foreign languages:** French, Spanish. **Health:** Health services, nursing (RN). **History:** General. **Math:** General. **Parks/recreation:** Health/fitness. **Philosophy/religion:** Philosophy. **Physical sciences:** Chemistry, geology. **Protective services:** Law enforcement admin. **Psychology:** General. **Public administration:** General, social work. **Social sciences:** International relations, political science, sociology. **Visual/performing arts:** General.

**Most popular majors.** Agriculture 7%, business/marketing 16%, health sciences 6%, interdisciplinary studies 22%.

**Computing on campus.** 234 workstations in dormitories, library, student center. Dormitories wired for high-speed internet access and linked to campus network. Commuter students can connect to campus network. Online course registration, online library, helpline, repair service, student web hosting, wireless network available.

**Student life. Freshman orientation:** Available, $165 fee. Preregistration for classes offered. 4-day program held in August. **Policies:** Freshmen must live on campus. **Housing:** Guaranteed on-campus for freshmen. Coed dorms, single-sex dorms, special housing for disabled, apartments, fraternity/sorority housing, substance-free housing available. $100 fully refundable deposit, deadline 8/1. Honors floors available. **Activities:** Bands, campus ministries, choral groups, dance, drama, international student organizations, literary magazine, music ensembles, opera, radio station, student government, student newspaper, TV station, Panhellenic Council, Reformed University Fellowship, Alpha Phi Omega, Black student association, College Republicans, College Democrats, Rotaract.

**Athletics.** NCAA. **Intercollegiate:** Baseball M, basketball, cheerleading M, cross-country, equestrian W, football (tackle) M, golf M, rifle, rodeo, soccer W, softball W, tennis, volleyball W. **Intramural:** Basketball, football (non-tackle), golf, soccer, softball, tennis, volleyball, water polo. **Team name:** Skyhawks.

**Student services.** Adult student services, alcohol/substance abuse counseling, campus ministries, career counseling, services for economically disadvantaged, student employment services, financial aid counseling, health services, minority student services, on-campus daycare, personal counseling, placement for graduates, veterans' counselor, women's services. **Physically disabled:** Services for visually, speech, hearing impaired. **Learning disabled:** Comprehensive services available.

**Contact.** E-mail: admitme@utm.edu
Phone: (731) 881-7020 Toll-free number: (800) 829-8861
Fax: (731) 881-7029
Judy Rayburn, Director of Admissions, University of Tennessee: Martin, 200 Hall Moody Administration Building, Martin, TN 38238

## University of the South
### Sewanee, Tennessee
www.sewanee.edu       CB member   CB code: 1842

- Private 4-year university affiliated with Episcopal Church
- Residential campus in rural community
- 1,455 degree-seeking undergraduates: 53% women, 4% African American, 2% Asian American, 2% Hispanic American, 1% Native American, 2% international
- 80 degree-seeking graduate students
- 64% of applicants admitted
- Application essay required
- 79% graduate within 6 years

**General.** Founded in 1857. Regionally accredited; also accredited by ATS. **Degrees:** 354 bachelor's awarded; master's, doctoral, first professional offered. **Location:** 45 miles from Chattanooga, 57 miles from Huntsville. **Calendar:** Semester, limited summer session. **Full-time faculty:** 139 total; 94% have terminal degrees, 9% minority, 36% women. **Part-time faculty:** 40 total; 72% have terminal degrees, 5% minority, 42% women. **Class size:** 67% < 20, 31% 20-39, 1% 40-49, less than 1% 50-99. **Special facilities:** Landscape analysis lab, observatory, materials analysis laboratory with electron microscopy, 10,000- acre wooded campus, hiking and horseback riding trails, climbing.

**Freshman class profile.** 2,424 applied, 1,542 admitted, 403 enrolled.

| Mid 50% test scores | | | |
|---|---|---|---|
| SAT critical reading: | 570-680 | Rank in top quarter: | 78% |
| SAT math: | 560-650 | Rank in top tenth: | 47% |
| SAT writing: | 580-670 | Return as sophomores: | 88% |
| ACT composite: | 25-30 | Out-of-state: | 73% |
| GPA 3.50 or higher: | 52% | Live on campus: | 99% |
| GPA 3.0-3.49: | 31% | International: | 1% |
| GPA 2.0-2.99: | 17% | Fraternities: | 65% |
| | | Sororities: | 71% |

**Basis for selection.** GED not accepted. School achievement record, recommendations, extracurricular activities, test scores, essay important. Children of alumni and minority applicants given special consideration. SAT or ACT recommended. Interview recommended.

**High school preparation.** 13 units required; 20 recommended. Required and recommended units include English 4, mathematics 3-4, social studies 1-2, history 1-2, science 2-4 (laboratory 2-3) and foreign language 2-4.

**2007-2008 Annual costs.** Tuition/fees: $30,660. Room/board: $8,780. Books/supplies: $800. Personal expenses: $900.

**2007-2008 Financial aid.** **Need-based:** 243 full-time freshmen applied for aid; 167 were judged to have need; 166 of these received aid. Average need met was 93%. Average scholarship/grant was $22,333; average loan $3,272. 84% of total undergraduate aid awarded as scholarships/grants, 16% as loans/jobs. **Non-need-based:** Awarded to 311 full-time undergraduates, including 67 freshmen. Scholarships awarded for academics, minority status, religious affiliation.

**Application procedures.** **Admission:** Closing date 2/1 (postmark date). $45 fee, may be waived for applicants with need. Application may be submitted online. Admission notification 4/1. Must reply by May 1 or within 2 week(s) if notified thereafter. **Financial aid:** Priority date 3/1; no closing date. FAFSA, institutional form required. Applicants notified by 4/1; must reply within 4 week(s) of notification.

**Academics.** **Special study options:** Double major, independent study, internships, semester at sea, student-designed major, study abroad, teacher certification program, Washington semester. Oak Ridge semester in experimental science, summer science program on St. Catherines Island, Georgia. **Credit/placement by examination:** AP, CLEP, IB, SAT, ACT, institutional tests. 60 credit hours maximum toward bachelor's degree. **Support services:** Tutoring.

**Majors.** **Area/ethnic studies:** American, Asian, French, German, Russian/Slavic. **Biology:** General, biochemistry. **Computer sciences:** General, computer science. **Conservation:** Environmental studies, forestry, management/policy. **English:** English lit. **Foreign languages:** Ancient Greek, comparative lit, French, German, Latin, modern Greek, Russian, Spanish. **History:** General. **Interdisciplinary:** Global studies, math/computer science, medieval/Renaissance. **Math:** General. **Philosophy/religion:** Philosophy, religion. **Physical sciences:** Chemistry, geology, physics. **Psychology:** General. **Social sciences:** Anthropology, economics, political science. **Visual/performing arts:** General, art history/conservation, studio arts.

**Most popular majors.** English 16%, foreign language 8%, history 10%, psychology 9%, social sciences 17%, visual/performing arts 13%.

**Computing on campus.** 200 workstations in dormitories, library, computer center. Dormitories wired for high-speed internet access and linked to campus network. Commuter students can connect to campus network. Online course registration, online library, helpline, repair service, student web hosting, wireless network available.

**Student life.** **Freshman orientation:** Mandatory. Preregistration for classes offered. Several days before the college opens in the fall. Students dine with the faculty advisor, sign the Honor Code, and participate in discussions of the summer reading. **Policies:** Student-administered honor code strictly observed. **Housing:** Guaranteed on-campus for freshmen. Coed dorms, single-sex dorms, special housing for disabled, apartments, fraternity/sorority housing, substance-free housing available. $300 nonrefundable deposit, deadline 5/1. German, French, Spanish, Russian language houses available. **Activities:** Jazz band, campus ministries, choral groups, dance, drama, film society, international student organizations, literary magazine, music ensembles, Model UN, musical theater, radio station, student government, student newspaper, symphony orchestra, tutoring center for disadvantaged youth, religious organizations, Big Brother-Big Sister program.

**Athletics.** NCAA. **Intercollegiate:** Baseball M, basketball, cross-country, diving, equestrian, fencing, field hockey W, football (tackle) M, golf, lacrosse, rowing (crew), rugby M, skiing, soccer, softball W, swimming, tennis, track and field, volleyball W. **Intramural:** Basketball, cross-country, diving, golf, handball, racquetball, skin diving, soccer, softball, swimming, table tennis, tennis, track and field, volleyball, wrestling M. **Team name:** Tigers.

**Student services.** Campus ministries, career counseling, student employment services, health services, minority student services, on-campus daycare, personal counseling, placement for graduates. **Physically disabled:** Services for visually, hearing impaired.

**Contact.** E-mail: admiss@sewanee.edu
Phone: (931) 598-1238 Toll-free number: (800) 522-2234
Fax: (931) 538-3248
David Lesesne, Dean of Admission, University of the South, Office of Admission, Sewanee, TN 37383-1000

## Vanderbilt University
**Nashville, Tennessee**
www.vanderbilt.edu

CB member
CB code: 1871

- Private 4-year university
- Residential campus in very large city
- 6,496 degree-seeking undergraduates: 1% part-time, 53% women, 9% African American, 7% Asian American, 6% Hispanic American, 3% international
- 5,184 degree-seeking graduate students
- 33% of applicants admitted
- SAT or ACT with writing, application essay required
- 91% graduate within 6 years

**General.** Founded in 1873. Regionally accredited. **Degrees:** 1,468 bachelor's awarded; master's, doctoral, first professional offered. **ROTC:** Army, Naval, Air Force. **Location:** 240 miles from Atlanta, 300 miles from St. Louis. **Calendar:** Semester, limited summer session. **Full-time faculty:** 818 total; 16% minority, 32% women. **Class size:** 66% < 20, 24% 20-39, 4% 40-49, 4% 50-99, 2% >100. **Special facilities:** Observatory, free electron laser, electron microscopes, television news archive, national arboretum, video productions, Black cultural center, women's center, cinema and art museum.

**Freshman class profile.** 12,911 applied, 4,238 admitted, 1,673 enrolled.

| Mid 50% test scores | | | |
|---|---|---|---|
| SAT critical reading: | 640-740 | Rank in top quarter: | 95% |
| SAT math: | 660-740 | Rank in top tenth: | 80% |
| SAT writing: | 640-730 | Return as sophomores: | 96% |
| ACT composite: | 29-34 | Out-of-state: | 84% |
| GPA 3.50 or higher: | 73% | Live on campus: | 99% |
| GPA 3.0-3.49: | 23% | International: | 4% |
| GPA 2.0-2.99: | 4% | Fraternities: | 42% |
| | | Sororities: | 53% |

**Basis for selection.** Academic achievement, recommendation, essay, test scores, activities important. SAT Subject Tests recommended. Audition required for music program.

**High school preparation.** 20 units required; 25 recommended. Required and recommended units include English 4, mathematics 3-4, social studies 2-3, history 2, science 3-4 (laboratory 2), foreign language 2-4 and academic electives 2. Additional unit in mathematics and 2 in science recommended for engineering applicants. Blair School of Music does not require 2 units of science. School of Engineering recommends 2 years of language. Peabody College of Education & Human Development does not require language. Blair, Engineering, and Peabody require 1 year of history.

**2007-2008 Annual costs.** Tuition/fees: $35,278. Room/board: $11,446. Books/supplies: $1,140. Personal expenses: $1,902.

**2007-2008 Financial aid.** **Need-based:** 885 full-time freshmen applied for aid; 763 were judged to have need; 761 of these received aid. Average need met was 100%. Average scholarship/grant was $28,838; average loan $3,413. 86% of total undergraduate aid awarded as scholarships/grants, 14% as loans/jobs. **Non-need-based:** Awarded to 2,324 full-time undergraduates, including 728 freshmen. Scholarships awarded for academics, minority status, music/drama, state residency.

**Application procedures.** **Admission:** Closing date 1/3. $50 fee, may be waived for applicants with need. Application may be submitted online. Admission notification 4/1. Must reply by 5/1. **Financial aid:** Priority date 2/1; no closing date. FAFSA, CSS PROFILE required. Applicants notified on a rolling basis starting 4/1.

**Academics.** All undergraduates take portion of coursework in College of Arts and Science. **Special study options:** Accelerated study, combined bachelor's/graduate degree, cooperative education, cross-registration, distance learning, double major, dual enrollment of high school students, ESL, honors, independent study, internships, student-designed major, study abroad, teacher certification program, Washington semester. **Credit/placement by examination:** AP, CLEP, IB, institutional tests. 30 credit hours maximum toward bachelor's degree. **Support services:** Learning center, tutoring.

**Majors. Area/ethnic studies:** African, African-American, American, East Asian, European, Latin American. **Biology:** Molecular. **Business:** Human resources. **Communications:** General. **Computer sciences:** General. **Education:** General, early childhood, elementary, secondary, social studies, special. **Engineering:** Biomedical, chemical, civil, computer, electrical, mechanical, science. **English:** English lit. **Family/consumer sciences:** Family studies. **Foreign languages:** General, classics, French, German, Russian, Spanish. **History:** General. **Math:** General. **Philosophy/religion:** Philosophy, religion. **Physical sciences:** Chemistry, geology, physics. **Psychology:** General. **Social sciences:** Anthropology, economics, political science, sociology, urban studies. **Visual/performing arts:** Dramatic, music performance, music theory/composition, studio arts.

**Most popular majors.** Engineering/engineering technologies 15%, foreign language 7%, psychology 6%, social sciences 29%.

**Computing on campus.** 400 workstations in library, computer center, student center. Dormitories wired for high-speed internet access and linked to campus network. Commuter students can connect to campus network. Online course registration, online library, helpline, repair service, student web hosting, wireless network available.

**Student life. Freshman orientation:** Mandatory. Preregistration for classes offered. **Housing:** Guaranteed on-campus for freshmen. Coed dorms, single-sex dorms, special housing for disabled, apartments, substance-free housing available. Housing for students with interest in foreign languages or philosophy available. **Activities:** Bands, campus ministries, choral groups, dance, drama, film society, literary magazine, music ensembles, Model UN, musical theater, opera, radio station, student government, student newspaper, symphony orchestra, over 200 clubs and organizations.

**Athletics.** NCAA. **Intercollegiate:** Baseball M, basketball, bowling W, cross-country, football (tackle) M, golf, lacrosse W, soccer W, tennis, track and field W. **Intramural:** Badminton, basketball, bowling, football (non-tackle), golf, racquetball, soccer, softball, squash, swimming, table tennis, tennis, track and field, volleyball, water polo, wrestling. **Team name:** Commodores.

**Student services.** Alcohol/substance abuse counseling, campus ministries, career counseling, student employment services, financial aid counseling, health services, minority student services, on-campus daycare, personal counseling, placement for graduates, women's services. **Physically disabled:** Services for visually, speech, hearing impaired.

**Contact.** E-mail: admissions@vanderbilt.edu
Phone: (615) 322-2561 Toll-free number: (800) 288-0432
Fax: (615) 343-7765
Douglas Christiansen, Associate Provost for Enrollment and Dean of Undergraduate Admissions, Vanderbilt University, 2305 West End Avenue, Nashville, TN 37203-1727

## Williamson Christian College
### Franklin, Tennessee
### www.williamsoncc.edu

- Private 4-year liberal arts college affiliated with interdenominational tradition
- Commuter campus in small city
- 65 degree-seeking undergraduates

**General.** Accredited by ABHE. Accelerated degree completion programs available for working adults. **Degrees:** 10 bachelor's, 1 associate awarded. **Location:** 15 miles from downtown. **Calendar:** Semester, limited summer session. **Full-time faculty:** 5 total. **Part-time faculty:** 25 total. **Class size:** 100% < 20.

**Basis for selection.** Open admission, but selective for some programs.

**2007-2008 Annual costs.** Tuition/fees: $9,090. Books/supplies: $800. Personal expenses: $3,800.

**Application procedures. Admission:** No deadline. $25 fee. Application must be submitted on paper. Admission notification on a rolling basis. **Financial aid:** No deadline.

**Academics. Special study options:** Accelerated study, distance learning, liberal arts/career combination, weekend college. **Credit/placement by examination:** AP, CLEP. 15 credit hours maximum toward associate degree, 32 toward bachelor's.

**Majors. Business:** Nonprofit/public. **Philosophy/religion:** Religion.

**Most popular majors.** Business/marketing 50%, philosophy/religious studies 50%.

**Computing on campus.** 3 workstations in computer center. Wireless network available.

**Student life. Freshman orientation:** Mandatory. Preregistration for classes offered. **Activities:** Student government, student newspaper.

**Student services.** Adult student services, campus ministries, financial aid counseling, personal counseling.

**Contact.** E-mail: chris@williamsoncc.edu
Phone: (615) 771-7821 Fax: (615) 771-7810
Steve Smith, Director of Admissions, Williamson Christian College, 200 Seaboard Lane, Franklin, TN 37067

# Texas

## Abilene Christian University
### Abilene, Texas
### www.acu.edu

**CB member**
**CB code: 6001**

- Private 4-year university affiliated with Church of Christ
- Residential campus in small city
- 3,954 degree-seeking undergraduates: 7% part-time, 55% women, 8% African American, 1% Asian American, 6% Hispanic American, 1% Native American, 4% international
- 615 degree-seeking graduate students
- 47% of applicants admitted
- SAT or ACT (ACT writing recommended) required
- 57% graduate within 6 years

**General.** Founded in 1906. Regionally accredited. **Degrees:** 729 bachelor's, 3 associate awarded; master's, doctoral, first professional offered. **Location:** 180 miles from Dallas. **Calendar:** Semester, limited summer session. **Full-time faculty:** 229 total; 79% have terminal degrees, 8% minority, 32% women. **Part-time faculty:** 139 total; 28% have terminal degrees, 3% minority, 42% women. **Class size:** 46% < 20, 40% 20-39, 6% 40-49, 7% 50-99, less than 1% >100. **Special facilities:** Observatory, 3 college farms (for agriculture majors), center for Biblical studies, voice institute.

**Freshman class profile.** 3,900 applied, 1,840 admitted, 890 enrolled.

| Mid 50% test scores | | Rank in top quarter: | 49% |
| --- | --- | --- | --- |
| SAT critical reading: | 480-610 | Rank in top tenth: | 21% |
| SAT math: | 490-620 | Return as sophomores: | 74% |
| ACT composite: | 20-26 | Out-of-state: | 17% |
| GPA 3.50 or higher: | 58% | Live on campus: | 92% |
| GPA 3.0-3.49: | 30% | International: | 2% |
| GPA 2.0-2.99: | 12% | | |

**Basis for selection.** Rank in top half of class and/or 960 SAT (exclusive of Writing) or 20 ACT required. Interview, portfolio recommended for all; audition required for debate, forensics, music, theater programs. **Home-schooled:** Transcript of courses and grades required.

**High school preparation.** 12 units recommended. Recommended units include English 4, mathematics 3, science 3 (laboratory 2) and foreign language 2.

**2007-2008 Annual costs.** Tuition/fees: $17,410. Room/board: $6,350. Books/supplies: $1,100. Personal expenses: $1,740.

**2006-2007 Financial aid. Need-based:** 914 full-time freshmen applied for aid; 587 were judged to have need; 587 of these received aid. Average need met was 68%. Average scholarship/grant was $9,604; average loan $2,648. 68% of total undergraduate aid awarded as scholarships/grants, 32% as loans/jobs. **Non-need-based:** Awarded to 3,320 full-time undergraduates, including 917 freshmen. Scholarships awarded for academics, art, athletics, leadership, minority status, music/drama, religious affiliation, state residency. **Additional information:** Early estimate service available.

**Application procedures. Admission:** Priority date 2/1; deadline 8/1 (postmark date). $25 fee. Application may be submitted online. Admission notification on a rolling basis beginning on or about 8/1. **Financial aid:** Priority date 3/1; no closing date. FAFSA, institutional form required. Applicants notified on a rolling basis starting 4/1.

**Academics. Special study options:** Cross-registration, distance learning, double major, dual enrollment of high school students, ESL, honors, independent study, internships, student-designed major, study abroad, teacher certification program. Campus abroad programs in England, Mexico, Uruguay; pass/fail grading option. **Credit/placement by examination:** AP, CLEP, IB, SAT, ACT, institutional tests. 15 credit hours maximum toward associate degree, 30 toward bachelor's. **Support services:** Pre-admission summer program, reduced course load, remedial instruction, study skills assistance, tutoring.

**Majors. Agriculture:** Agribusiness operations, animal sciences, range science. **Biology:** General, biochemistry. **Business:** Accounting, business admin, finance, management information systems, marketing. **Communications:** General, advertising, digital media, journalism, public relations.

**Computer sciences:** Computer science, information technology. **Conservation:** Environmental science. **Education:** Art, biology, elementary, English, foreign languages, history, mathematics, middle, music, physical, reading, science, secondary, social studies, special. **Engineering:** Physics, science. **English:** English lit, speech/rhetoric. **Family/consumer sciences:** Family studies. **Foreign languages:** Spanish. **Health:** Clinical lab science, dietetics, nursing (RN), ophthalmic lab technology, predental, premedicine, prepharmacy, preveterinary, speech pathology. **History:** General. **Interdisciplinary:** Global studies. **Legal studies:** Prelaw. **Liberal arts:** Arts/sciences. **Math:** General. **Parks/recreation:** Health/fitness, sports admin. **Physical sciences:** Chemistry, physics. **Protective services:** Law enforcement admin. **Psychology:** General. **Public administration:** Social work. **Social sciences:** Political science, sociology. **Theology:** Bible, missionary, pastoral counseling, preministerial, youth ministry. **Visual/performing arts:** Arts management, dramatic, graphic design, interior design, piano/organ, studio arts, voice/opera.

**Most popular majors.** Biology 6%, business/marketing 21%, education 9%, health sciences 7%, interdisciplinary studies 11%, psychology 6%, visual/performing arts 7%.

**Computing on campus.** 650 workstations in dormitories, library, computer center. Dormitories wired for high-speed internet access and linked to campus network. Commuter students can connect to campus network. Online course registration, online library, helpline, student web hosting, wireless network available.

**Student life. Freshman orientation:** Mandatory, $115 fee. Preregistration for classes offered. Overnight program, held twice in summer; includes assessment testing and registration. **Policies:** Religious observance required. **Housing:** Guaranteed on-campus for freshmen. Single-sex dorms, special housing for disabled, apartments available. $100 fully refundable deposit. **Activities:** Bands, campus ministries, choral groups, drama, international student organizations, literary magazine, music ensembles, musical theater, opera, radio station, student government, student newspaper, symphony orchestra, TV station, student association, Seekers of the Word, international student association, campus activities team, Hispanos Unidos, College Democrats, African Missions Fellowship, Essence of Ebony, mission student committee, College Republicans.

**Athletics.** NCAA. **Intercollegiate:** Baseball M, basketball, cross-country, football (tackle) M, golf M, softball W, tennis, track and field, volleyball W. **Intramural:** Badminton, basketball, bowling, cross-country, football (non-tackle), racquetball, soccer, softball, table tennis, tennis, track and field, volleyball, water polo M. **Team name:** Wildcats.

**Student services.** Adult student services, alcohol/substance abuse counseling, campus ministries, career counseling, student employment services, financial aid counseling, health services, minority student services, personal counseling, placement for graduates, veterans' counselor. **Physically disabled:** Services for visually, speech, hearing impaired.

**Contact.** E-mail: info@admissions.acu.edu
Phone: (325) 674-2650 Toll-free number: (800) 460-6228 ext. 2650
Fax: (325) 674-2130
Hayley Webb, Director of Admissions, Abilene Christian University, ACU Box 29000, Abilene, TX 79699

## Amberton University
### Garland, Texas
### www.amberton.edu

**CB code: 6140**

- Private 4-year university affiliated with nondenominational tradition
- Commuter campus in small city
- 465 degree-seeking undergraduates: 48% part-time, 62% women, 28% African American, 2% Asian American, 6% Hispanic American
- 1,121 degree-seeking graduate students

**General.** Founded in 1971. Regionally accredited. Upper level and graduate institution designed for adult students. Must have previous college and be over 21 years old to attend. **Degrees:** 50 bachelor's awarded; master's offered. **Location:** 12 miles from downtown Dallas. **Calendar:** Four 10-week sessions. Extensive summer session. **Full-time faculty:** 15 total; 93% have terminal degrees. **Part-time faculty:** 60 total; 92% have terminal degrees.

**Basis for selection.** All students required to have previously completed college work. No first-time freshmen. Must be at least 21 years of age.

**2007-2008 Annual costs.** Tuition/fees: $6,750. Books/supplies: $500.

**Application procedures. Admission:** No deadline. No application fee. Application must be submitted on paper. Admission notification on a rolling basis. **Financial aid:** No deadline.

**Academics. Special study options:** Distance learning, independent study, weekend college. **Credit/placement by examination:** CLEP. 30 credit hours maximum toward bachelor's degree.

**Majors. Business:** General, accounting, business admin. **Liberal arts:** Arts/sciences.

**Most popular majors.** Business/marketing 90%, liberal arts 10%.

**Computing on campus.** 25 workstations in library, computer center. Online library available.

**Student services.** Adult student services, career counseling, personal counseling, placement for graduates, veterans' counselor.

**Contact.** E-mail: advisor@amberton.edu
Phone: (972) 279-6511 Fax: (972) 279-9773
Don Hebbard, Academic Dean, Amberton University, 1700 Eastgate Drive, Garland, TX 75041-5595

---

## Angelo State University
**San Angelo, Texas**  **CB member**
**www.angelo.edu**  **CB code: 6644**

- Public 4-year university
- Residential campus in small city
- 5,720 degree-seeking undergraduates: 15% part-time, 55% women, 7% African American, 1% Asian American, 24% Hispanic American, 1% Native American, 1% international
- 416 degree-seeking graduate students
- 99% of applicants admitted
- SAT or ACT (ACT writing optional) required
- 34% graduate within 6 years

**General.** Founded in 1928. Regionally accredited. **Degrees:** 822 bachelor's, 90 associate awarded; master's offered. **ROTC:** Air Force. **Location:** 215 miles from San Antonio, 200 miles from Austin. **Calendar:** Semester, extensive summer session. **Full-time faculty:** 240 total; 71% have terminal degrees, 12% minority. **Part-time faculty:** 108 total; 18% have terminal degrees, 12% minority. **Class size:** 25% < 20, 54% 20-39, 10% 40-49, 9% 50-99, less than 1% >100. **Special facilities:** Planetarium, management, instruction, and research center for agriculture, food safety and product development laboratory, West Texas collection, natural history collections.

**Freshman class profile.** 3,268 applied, 3,236 admitted, 1,475 enrolled.

| Mid 50% test scores | | | |
|---|---|---|---|
| SAT critical reading: | 410-520 | Rank in top tenth: | 12% |
| SAT math: | 420-550 | Return as sophomores: | 59% |
| SAT writing: | 400-510 | Out-of-state: | 3% |
| ACT composite: | 17-22 | Live on campus: | 67% |
| Rank in top quarter: | 35% | Fraternities: | 3% |
| | | Sororities: | 4% |

**Basis for selection.** Applicants must graduate from accredited high school and satisfactorily complete recommended high school program or advanced college-prep curriculum, or rank in top half of high school class. If ranked in third quarter, must have 23 ACT or 1030 SAT (exclusive of Writing). If ranked in fourth quarter, must have 30 ACT or 1270 SAT. **Homeschooled:** Transcript of courses and grades required. Recommend that students have completed the equivalent of a high school curriculum.

**High school preparation.** 23 units recommended. Recommended units include English 4, mathematics 3, social studies 3, science 3 and foreign language 2. One computer science recommended.

**2007-2008 Annual costs.** Tuition/fees: $5,111; $13,451 out-of-state. Room/board: $5,621. Books/supplies: $1,000.

**Financial aid. Non-need-based:** Scholarships awarded for academics, athletics, leadership, music/drama, ROTC.

**Application procedures. Admission:** Closing date 8/15 (postmark date). $25 fee. Application may be submitted online. Admission notification on a rolling basis. **Financial aid:** Priority date 5/1; no closing date. FAFSA, institutional form required. Applicants notified on a rolling basis starting 4/1.

**Academics. Special study options:** Combined bachelor's/graduate degree, distance learning, double major, dual enrollment of high school students, honors, independent study, internships, study abroad, teacher certification program. 3-2 engineering-physics and 3-2 agriculture-education programs with Texas A&M and University of Texas El Paso. **Credit/placement by**

examination: AP, CLEP, SAT, ACT. Unlimited credits by examination provided student meets hours required in residence. **Support services:** Learning center, reduced course load, remedial instruction, tutoring, writing center.

**Honors college/program.** Students admitted must have a 3.25 GPA in coursework done at ASU. If enrolling from high school the student must be in the top 10% of their graduating class and have scored a 27 on the ACT or a 1200 on the SAT (exclusive of Writing). Some classes are strictly honors students only. Normal grade level classes can be given honors credit by contract. The student must meet with the professor before the semester and discuss what additional coursework will make it qualify for honors credit.

**Majors. Agriculture:** Animal husbandry, animal sciences. **Biology:** General, biochemistry, evolutionary. **Business:** Accounting, business admin, finance, international, management information systems, marketing, real estate. **Communications:** General, journalism. **Computer sciences:** General. **Conservation:** Management/policy. **English:** English lit. **Family/consumer sciences:** Child development. **Foreign languages:** French, German, Spanish. **Health:** Athletic training, clinical lab science, nursing (RN). **History:** General. **Math:** General. **Parks/recreation:** Health/fitness. **Physical sciences:** Chemistry, physics. **Protective services:** Criminal justice. **Psychology:** General. **Social sciences:** Political science, sociology. **Visual/performing arts:** Art, dramatic, studio arts.

**Most popular majors.** Agriculture 7%, business/marketing 23%, communications/journalism 7%, education 14%, parks/recreation 12%, psychology 12%.

**Computing on campus.** 700 workstations in dormitories, library, computer center, student center. Dormitories wired for high-speed internet access and linked to campus network. Commuter students can connect to campus network. Online course registration, online library, helpline, student web hosting, wireless network available.

**Student life. Freshman orientation:** Available, $25 fee. Preregistration for classes offered. Sessions offered several times during the summer. **Policies:** Single undergraduates with 12-60 semester credit hours of college-level work who do not live with parents required to reside in University-owned housing. **Housing:** Coed dorms, single-sex dorms, special housing for disabled, apartments, substance-free housing available. $100 fully refundable deposit. **Activities:** Bands, campus ministries, choral groups, dance, drama, film society, international student organizations, literary magazine, music ensembles, musical theater, radio station, student government, student newspaper, TV station, College Republicans, Young Democrats, Baptist student union, residence hall association, Block and Bridle, Newman Center, nontraditional student organization.

**Athletics. NCAA. Intercollegiate:** Baseball M, basketball, cross-country, football (tackle) M, soccer W, softball W, track and field, volleyball W. **Intramural:** Badminton, basketball, football (non-tackle), golf, racquetball, soccer, softball, swimming, table tennis, tennis, track and field, volleyball, weight lifting. **Team name:** Rams.

**Student services.** Adult student services, alcohol/substance abuse counseling, campus ministries, career counseling, services for economically disadvantaged, student employment services, financial aid counseling, health services, minority student services, personal counseling, placement for graduates, veterans' counselor. **Physically disabled:** Services for visually, hearing impaired.

**Contact.** E-mail: admissions@angelo.edu
Phone: (325) 942-2185 Toll-free number: (800) 946-8627
Fax: (325) 942-2078
Frederic Dietz, Director of Admissions, Angelo State University, ASU Station #11014, San Angelo, TX 76909-1014

---

## Arlington Baptist College
**Arlington, Texas**
**www.abconline.edu**  **CB code: 6039**

- Private 4-year Bible and teachers college affiliated with Baptist faith
- Residential campus in very large city
- 142 degree-seeking undergraduates: 25% part-time, 47% women, 4% African American, 3% Hispanic American, 4% international
- Application essay required
- 22% graduate within 6 years; 15% enter graduate study

**General.** Founded in 1939. Accredited by ABHE. **Degrees:** 32 bachelor's awarded. **Location:** 10 miles from Fort Worth, 25 miles from Dallas. **Calendar:** Semester, limited summer session. **Full-time faculty:** 8 total; 12% minority, 38% women. **Part-time faculty:** 10 total; 20% have terminal degrees, 30% women. **Class size:** 89% < 20, 11% 20-39.

**Freshman class profile.** 35 applied, 35 admitted, 17 enrolled.

| | | | |
|---|---|---|---|
| GPA 3.50 or higher: | 24% | End year in good standing: | 77% |
| GPA 3.0-3.49: | 50% | Return as sophomores: | 57% |
| GPA 2.0-2.99: | 26% | Out-of-state: | 11% |
| Rank in top quarter: | 17% | Live on campus: | 56% |
| Rank in top tenth: | 8% | International: | 5% |

**Basis for selection.** Open admission. Interview recommended for all; audition required for music. **Homeschooled:** Interview required. Advised to obtain GED.

**High school preparation.** 16 units recommended. Recommended units include English 3, mathematics 2, social studies 3, history 3 and science 1.

**2008-2009 Annual costs.** Tuition/fees (projected): $6,090. Room/board: $4,100. Books/supplies: $750. Personal expenses: $720.

**2006-2007 Financial aid.** All financial aid based on need. 62 full-time freshmen applied for aid; 28 were judged to have need; 28 of these received aid. Average need met was 65%. Average scholarship/grant was $2,809; average loan $5,970. 44% of total undergraduate aid awarded as scholarships/grants, 56% as loans/jobs.

**Application procedures. Admission:** Priority date 8/1; no deadline. $15 fee, may be waived for applicants with need. Application must be submitted on paper. Admission notification on a rolling basis. **Financial aid:** Closing date 8/15. FAFSA required. Applicants notified on a rolling basis.

**Academics. Special study options:** Distance learning, double major, dual enrollment of high school students, teacher certification program. **Credit/placement by examination:** AP, CLEP, institutional tests. 30 credit hours maximum toward bachelor's degree. **Support services:** Reduced course load, remedial instruction.

**Majors. Education:** General, early childhood, elementary, middle, music. **Philosophy/religion:** Religion. **Theology:** Bible, missionary, pastoral counseling, religious ed, sacred music, youth ministry.

**Most popular majors.** Education 31%, theological studies 35%.

**Computing on campus.** 17 workstations in library, computer center.

**Student life. Freshman orientation:** Mandatory. Preregistration for classes offered. Orientation includes placement testing. **Policies:** Religious observance required. **Housing:** Guaranteed on-campus for freshmen. Single-sex dorms, substance-free housing available. $25 nonrefundable deposit. **Activities:** Choral groups, music ensembles, student government, student newspaper, student missionary association, student preachers' fellowship, youth majors organization.

**Athletics.** NCCAA. **Intercollegiate:** Baseball M, basketball, volleyball W. **Team name:** Patriots.

**Student services.** Career counseling, student employment services, financial aid counseling, personal counseling, placement for graduates, veterans' counselor.

**Contact.** E-mail: jtaylor@abconline.org
Phone: (817) 461-8741 ext. 105 Fax: (817) 274-1138
Janie Taylor, Registrar, Arlington Baptist College, 3001 West Division, Arlington, TX 76012

## Art Institute of Dallas
**Dallas, Texas**
www.aid.edu                                          CB code: 2680

- For-profit 4-year visual arts college
- Very large city
- 1,739 degree-seeking undergraduates

**General.** Regionally accredited. **Degrees:** 92 bachelor's, 182 associate awarded. **Calendar:** Quarter. **Full-time faculty:** 60 total. **Part-time faculty:** 41 total.

**Basis for selection.** Open admission, but selective for some programs. Some animation, art and design associate degree programs may require portfolio evaluation.

**2007-2008 Annual costs.** Total program costs vary by program: bachelor's programs $80,952-$83,795; associate's programs $47,650-$49,921. Personal expenses: $2,880.

**Application procedures. Admission:** No deadline. $50 fee. Admission notification on a rolling basis. **Financial aid:** FAFSA required. Applicants notified on a rolling basis.

**Academics. Credit/placement by examination:** CLEP.

**Majors. Visual/performing arts:** Studio arts.

**Contact.** E-mail: cwilliams@aii.edu
Phone: (214) 692-8080 Toll-free number: (800) 275-4243
Myrna Little, Director of Admissions, Art Institute of Dallas, Two North Park, 8080 Park Lane, Dallas, TX 75231

## Art Institute of Houston
**Houston, Texas**
www.artinstitutes.edu/houston              CB code: 8271

- For-profit 4-year culinary school and visual arts college
- Very large city
- 1,793 degree-seeking undergraduates

**General.** Regionally accredited. **Degrees:** 31 bachelor's, 379 associate awarded. **Calendar:** Quarter. **Full-time faculty:** 55 total. **Part-time faculty:** 50 total.

**Basis for selection.** Based on high school record or GED and personal interview with admissions representative; test scores optional but may be considered if submitted. Observes TASP guidelines. ASSET or COMPASS testing may be required. Remediation may be required if test scores fall below required ranges; some remediation available on campus.

**2008-2009 Annual costs.** Tuition and fees vary by program.

**Application procedures. Admission:** No deadline. $50 fee. Admission notification on a rolling basis. **Financial aid:** Priority date 3/1; no closing date. FAFSA, institutional form required.

**Academics. Special study options:** Distance learning, honors, internships, study abroad. **Credit/placement by examination:** CLEP.

**Majors. Visual/performing arts:** Graphic design, interior design.

**Contact.** E-mail: aihadm@aii.edu
Phone: (713) 623-2040 Toll-free number: (800) 275-4244
Fax: (713) 966-2797
Susanne Behrens, Director of Admission, Art Institute of Houston, 1900 Yorktown, Houston, TX 77056-4115

## Austin College
**Sherman, Texas**                          **CB member**
www.austincollege.edu                      **CB code: 6016**

- Private 4-year liberal arts and teachers college affiliated with Presbyterian Church (USA)
- Residential campus in small city
- 1,312 degree-seeking undergraduates: 52% women, 3% African American, 14% Asian American, 8% Hispanic American, 1% Native American, 1% international
- 19 degree-seeking graduate students
- 71% of applicants admitted
- SAT or ACT with writing, application essay required
- 78% graduate within 6 years; 24% enter graduate study

**General.** Founded in 1849. Regionally accredited. **Degrees:** 282 bachelor's awarded; master's offered. **Location:** 60 miles from Dallas. **Calendar:** 4-1-4, limited summer session. **Full-time faculty:** 95 total; 96% have terminal degrees, 8% minority, 30% women. **Part-time faculty:** 42 total; 57% have terminal degrees, 14% minority, 50% women. **Class size:** 64% < 20, 29% 20-39, 5% 40-49, 2% 50-99. **Special facilities:** Environmental research areas totaling 174 acres, lake recreation area, tissue culture facility for study of cellular molecular interactions of eukaryotic cells, high performance numeric and graphics computing facility for advanced scientific computing and 3-D graphics.

**Freshman class profile.** 1,678 applied, 1,190 admitted, 334 enrolled.

| Mid 50% test scores | | Rank in top tenth: | 38% |
|---|---|---|---|
| SAT critical reading: | 560-670 | End year in good standing: | 79% |
| SAT math: | 560-660 | Return as sophomores: | 82% |
| ACT composite: | 23-28 | Out-of-state: | 6% |
| GPA 3.50 or higher: | 49% | Live on campus: | 95% |
| GPA 3.0-3.49: | 39% | International: | 1% |
| GPA 2.0-2.99: | 12% | Fraternities: | 11% |
| Rank in top quarter: | 73% | Sororities: | 18% |

**Basis for selection.** Academic transcript record, test scores, recommendations, extracurricular involvement, essay important. Interview considered. Interview recommended for all; audition recommended for music, theater (required for scholarship consideration); portfolio recommended for art (required for scholarship consideration).

**High school preparation.** Required and recommended units include English 4, mathematics 3-4, social studies 2-3, science 3-4 (laboratory 2-3), foreign language 2-3, visual/performing arts 1-2 and academic electives 1.

**2008-2009 Annual costs.** Tuition/fees: $26,555. Room/board: $8,657. Books/supplies: $1,000. Personal expenses: $750.

**2007-2008 Financial aid. Need-based:** 252 full-time freshmen applied for aid; 201 were judged to have need; 201 of these received aid. Average need met was 99%. Average scholarship/grant was $16,988; average loan $6,044. 68% of total undergraduate aid awarded as scholarships/grants, 32% as loans/jobs. **Non-need-based:** Awarded to 695 full-time undergraduates, including 194 freshmen. Scholarships awarded for academics, alumni affiliation, art, leadership, music/drama, religious affiliation, state residency.

**Application procedures. Admission:** Priority date 1/15; deadline 5/1 (postmark date). $35 fee, may be waived for applicants with need. Application may be submitted online. Notification sent within 4 weeks of application deadline. Must reply by 5/1. **Financial aid:** Priority date 4/1; no closing date. FAFSA, institutional form required. Applicants notified on a rolling basis starting 3/1; must reply by 5/1.

**Academics. Special study options:** Double major, exchange student, honors, independent study, internships, liberal arts/career combination, student-designed major, study abroad, teacher certification program, Washington semester. 3-2 dual degree engineering program with University of Texas Dallas, Washington University in St. Louis, Columbia University, Texas A&M University. **Credit/placement by examination:** AP, CLEP, IB, institutional tests. **Support services:** Learning center, study skills assistance, tutoring.

**Majors. Area/ethnic studies:** American, Latin American. **Biology:** General, biochemistry. **Business:** General. **Communications:** General. **Computer sciences:** Computer science. **Conservation:** Environmental studies. **English:** English lit. **Foreign languages:** Classics, French, German, Latin, Spanish. **History:** General. **Math:** General. **Philosophy/religion:** Philosophy, religion. **Physical sciences:** Chemistry, physics. **Psychology:** General. **Social sciences:** Economics, international economics, international relations, political science, sociology. **Visual/performing arts:** Art.

**Most popular majors.** Biology 6%, business/marketing 12%, education 7%, foreign language 10%, interdisciplinary studies 6%, psychology 12%, social sciences 18%.

**Computing on campus.** 160 workstations in dormitories, library, computer center, student center. Dormitories wired for high-speed internet access and linked to campus network. Commuter students can connect to campus network. Online library, helpline, student web hosting, wireless network available.

**Student life. Freshman orientation:** Mandatory. Preregistration for classes offered. Held the weekend prior to the first day of classes. **Housing:** Guaranteed on-campus for all undergraduates. Coed dorms, single-sex dorms, special housing for disabled, apartments available. Language emphasis residence; suite-style housing for upper-level students with private bedroom, common area, kitchenette. **Activities:** Jazz band, choral groups, dance, drama, international student organizations, literary magazine, music ensembles, musical theater, student government, student newspaper, symphony orchestra, Alpha Phi Omega, Intervarsity Christian Fellowship, Black Expressions, Young Democrats, Service Station, Los Amigos, Habitat for Humanity, Activators, Amnesty International.

**Athletics.** NCAA. **Intercollegiate:** Baseball M, basketball, football (tackle) M, soccer, softball W, swimming, tennis, volleyball W. **Intramural:** Basketball, football (non-tackle), soccer, softball, volleyball. **Team name:** Roos.

**Student services.** Campus ministries, career counseling, student employment services, financial aid counseling, health services, personal counseling.

**Contact.** E-mail: admission@austincollege.edu
Phone: (903) 813-3000 Toll-free number: (800) 526-4276
Fax: (903) 813-3198
Nan Davis, Vice President for Institutional Enrollment, Austin College, 900 North Grand Avenue, Suite 6N, Sherman, TX 75090-4400

## Austin Graduate School of Theology
**Austin, Texas**
**www.austingrad.edu**        **CB code: 4969**

- Private two-year upper-division Bible and seminary college affiliated with Church of Christ
- Commuter campus in large city

**General.** Founded in 1917. Regionally accredited. **Location:** 80 miles from San Antonio, 150 miles from Houston. **Calendar:** Semester.

**Annual costs/financial aid.** Tuition/fees (2007-2008): $6,750. Books/supplies: $400. Personal expenses: $1,764. Need-based financial aid available to full-time and part-time students.

**Contact.** Phone: (512) 476-2772
Director of Admissions, 1909 University Avenue, Austin, TX 78705

## Baptist Missionary Association Theological Seminary
**Jacksonville, Texas**
**www.bmats.edu**        **CB code: 7042**

- Private 4-year Bible and seminary college affiliated with Baptist faith
- Commuter campus in large town

**General.** Founded in 1955. Regionally accredited. **Location:** 120 miles from Dallas. **Calendar:** Semester.

**Annual costs/financial aid.** Tuition/fees (2007-2008): $2,780. Room/board: $2,400.

**Contact.** Phone: (903) 586-2501
Dean/Registrar, 1530 East Pine Street, Jacksonville, TX 75766

## Baptist University of the Americas
**San Antonio, Texas**

- Private 4-year university and Bible college affiliated with Baptist General Convention of Texas
- Commuter campus in very large city
- 157 degree-seeking undergraduates

**General.** Accredited by ABHE. Baptist University of the Americas trains cross-culturally students in Biblical/Theological Studies and Ministry Studies, at a higher education academic level, from a Hispanic context. **Degrees:** 17 bachelor's, 2 associate awarded. **Calendar:** Semester, limited summer session. **Full-time faculty:** 8 total. **Part-time faculty:** 10 total.

**Freshman class profile.** 21 applied, 21 admitted, 21 enrolled.

**Basis for selection.** Open admission. Observes THEA requirements.

**2007-2008 Annual costs.** Tuition/fees: $4,210. Books/supplies: $1,740.

**Application procedures. Admission:** Closing date 2/15. $25 fee. **Financial aid:** No deadline.

**Academics. Credit/placement by examination:** CLEP.

**Majors. Theology:** Bible, theology.

**Student life. Freshman orientation:** Available. **Housing:** $200 deposit.

**Contact.** E-mail: mranjel@bua.edu
Phone: (210) 924-4338
Mary Ranjel, Director of Admissions, Baptist University of the Americas, 8019 South Pan Am Expressway, San Antonio, TX 78224

## Baylor University

Waco, Texas

www.baylor.edu

CB member

CB code: 6032

- Private 4-year university affiliated with Baptist faith
- Residential campus in small city
- 11,851 degree-seeking undergraduates: 2% part-time, 58% women, 8% African American, 7% Asian American, 10% Hispanic American, 1% Native American, 2% international
- 2,272 degree-seeking graduate students
- 68% of applicants admitted
- SAT or ACT with writing, application essay required
- 72% graduate within 6 years

**General.** Founded in 1845. Regionally accredited. **Degrees:** 2,377 bachelor's awarded; master's, doctoral, first professional offered. **ROTC:** Air Force. **Location:** 100 miles from Dallas-Fort Worth, 100 miles from Austin. **Calendar:** Semester, extensive summer session. **Full-time faculty:** 813 total; 81% have terminal degrees, 9% minority, 35% women. **Part-time faculty:** 250 total; 7% minority, 48% women. **Class size:** 39% < 20, 44% 20-39, 8% 40-49, 7% 50-99, 3% >100. **Special facilities:** Museum of natural science, Texas collection library, Armstrong Browning library.

**Freshman class profile.** 17,101 applied, 11,668 admitted, 2,732 enrolled.

| Mid 50% test scores | | | |
|---|---|---|---|
| SAT critical reading: | 550-650 | Rank in top tenth: | 45% |
| SAT math: | 560-660 | End year in good standing: | 91% |
| SAT writing: | 540-640 | Return as sophomores: | 86% |
| ACT composite: | 23-28 | Out-of-state: | 21% |
| Rank in top quarter: | 76% | Live on campus: | 99% |
| | | International: | 1% |

**Basis for selection.** Competitive high school performance and competitive scores on ACT or SAT most important; above-average achievement and potential expected. Audition required for music and theater programs; interview recommended for marginal achievers; portfolio recommended for art. **Homeschooled:** Transcript of courses and grades required. If applicant graduated from home school not officially recognized by state in which school is located, applicant must be 17 before first day of class unless GED certificate submitted prior to registration.

**High school preparation.** Required units include English 4, mathematics 3, social studies 1, history 1, science 3 (laboratory 2) and foreign language 2.

**2008-2009 Annual costs.** Tuition/fees: $26,234. Room/board: $7,608. Books/supplies: $1,634. Personal expenses: $2,120.

**2007-2008 Financial aid. Need-based:** 1,879 full-time freshmen applied for aid; 1,469 were judged to have need; 1,468 of these received aid. Average need met was 71%. Average scholarship/grant was $13,967; average loan $2,213. 60% of total undergraduate aid awarded as scholarships/grants, 40% as loans/jobs. **Non-need-based:** Awarded to 8,667 full-time undergraduates, including 2,557 freshmen. Scholarships awarded for academics, art, athletics, job skills, leadership, music/drama, ROTC.

**Application procedures. Admission:** Closing date 2/1 (postmark date). $50 fee, may be waived for applicants with need. Application must be submitted online. Admission notification 1/15. Must reply by 3/15. $300 enrollment deposit deadline is May 1. **Financial aid:** Priority date 3/1; no closing date. FAFSA required. Applicants notified on a rolling basis starting 3/10; must reply by 5/1 or within 2 week(s) of notification.

**Academics.** Online support (website advising resources and tutoring) is available when success center is closed. **Special study options:** Accelerated study, combined bachelor's/graduate degree, double major, honors, internships, student-designed major, study abroad, teacher certification program. Architecture program with Washington University, forestry with Duke University. **Credit/placement by examination:** AP, CLEP, IB, institutional tests. 60 credit hours maximum toward bachelor's degree. **Support services:** Learning center, pre-admission summer program, reduced course load, remedial instruction, study skills assistance, tutoring, writing center.

**Honors college/program.** All highly qualified and highly motivated students are eligible to apply to join the Honors program as freshmen. While not required, applicants are helped by having SAT or ACT scores at least in the average range set by prior years' Honors freshmen. The cohort entering the program in 2007-2008 averaged around 1350 on the SAT (Math plus Critical Reading) and/or over 31 (Composite) on the ACT.

**Majors. Architecture:** Architecture. **Area/ethnic studies:** American, Asian, Latin American, Slavic. **Biology:** General, biochemistry, bioinformatics, exercise physiology. **Business:** General, accounting, business admin, entrepreneurial studies, fashion, finance, financial planning, human resources, insurance, international, logistics, management information systems, managerial

economics, marketing, real estate, sales/distribution. **Communications:** General, digital media, journalism. **Computer sciences:** Computer science. **Conservation:** Environmental science, environmental studies, forestry. **Education:** General, art, computer, early childhood, elementary, English, health occupations, mathematics, music, physical, science, social studies, special. **Engineering:** General, electrical, mechanical. **English:** Composition, English lit. **Family/consumer sciences:** General, family studies, human nutrition. **Foreign languages:** Ancient Greek, Biblical, classics, French, German, Latin, linguistics, Russian, Spanish. **Health:** Athletic training, clinical lab science, communication disorders, health services, nursing (RN), predental, premedicine, prenursing. **History:** General. **Interdisciplinary:** Museum, neuroscience. **Liberal arts:** Humanities. **Math:** General, applied, statistics. **Parks/recreation:** Health/fitness. **Philosophy/religion:** Philosophy, religion. **Physical sciences:** Chemistry, geology, geophysics, physics. **Protective services:** Forensics. **Psychology:** General. **Public administration:** General, social work. **Social sciences:** Anthropology, archaeology, geography, international relations, political science, sociology. **Theology:** Sacred music. **Transportation:** Airline/commercial pilot. **Visual/performing arts:** Acting, art history/conservation, dramatic, fashion design, interior design, music history, music pedagogy, music performance, music theory/composition, studio arts, theater design.

**Most popular majors.** Biology 8%, business/marketing 26%, communications/journalism 10%, education 7%, health sciences 9%, social sciences 7%.

**Computing on campus.** 1,688 workstations in dormitories, library, computer center, student center. Dormitories wired for high-speed internet access and linked to campus network. Commuter students can connect to campus network. Online course registration, online library, helpline, repair service, student web hosting, wireless network available.

**Student life. Freshman orientation:** Mandatory. Preregistration for classes offered. 10 2-day sessions primarily in June. **Policies:** All students required to participate in chapel-forum for 2 semesters. **Housing:** Guaranteed on-campus for freshmen. Single-sex dorms, special housing for disabled, apartments, substance-free housing available. Brooks Residential College, Honors Residential College, Engineering and Computer Science living-learning center, Outdoor Adventure living-learning center, Leadership living-learning center. **Activities:** Bands, campus ministries, choral groups, dance, drama, film society, international student organizations, literary magazine, music ensembles, Model UN, musical theater, opera, radio station, student government, student newspaper, symphony orchestra, TV station, Campus Crusade for Christ, College Republicans, Young Democrats, association of black students, Hispanic student association, Asian student association, Habitat for Humanity, Alpha Phi Omega, Baylor Chamber of Commerce.

**Athletics.** NCAA. **Intercollegiate:** Baseball M, basketball, cross-country, equestrian W, football (tackle) M, golf, soccer W, softball W, tennis, track and field, volleyball W. **Intramural:** Basketball, bowling, cross-country, equestrian, football (non-tackle), golf, lacrosse, racquetball, soccer, softball, swimming, table tennis, tennis, track and field, volleyball, weight lifting. **Team name:** Bears.

**Student services.** Campus ministries, career counseling, student employment services, financial aid counseling, health services, legal services, personal counseling, placement for graduates. **Physically disabled:** Services for visually, speech, hearing impaired.

**Contact.** E-mail: admissions@baylor.edu
Phone: (254) 710-3435 Toll-free number: (800) 229-5678
Fax: (254) 710-3436
Jennifer Carron, Director of Admissions Services, Baylor University, One Bear Place #97056, Waco, TX 76798-7056

## College of Biblical Studies-Houston

Houston, Texas

www.cbshouston.edu

CB code: 3946

- Private 4-year Bible college
- Commuter campus in very large city
- 574 degree-seeking undergraduates

**General.** Accredited by ABHE. Multidenominational Christian Bible college. **Degrees:** 128 bachelor's, 17 associate awarded. **Calendar:** Trimester, extensive summer session. **Full-time faculty:** 10 total. **Part-time faculty:** 41 total.

**Basis for selection.** Open admission, but selective for some programs. ASSET testing may be required for associate or baccalaureate level programs. **Homeschooled:** State high school equivalency certificate required.

**2007-2008 Annual costs.** Tuition/fees: $4,050.

**Application procedures. Admission:** No deadline. $20 fee. Application must be submitted on paper. Admission notification on a rolling basis. **Financial aid:** No deadline.

**Academics. Special study options:** Accelerated study, dual enrollment of high school students, ESL, independent study. **Credit/placement by examination:** CLEP. **Support services:** Learning center, remedial instruction.

**Majors. Theology:** Bible, preministerial.

**Computing on campus.** 14 workstations in library. Online course registration available.

**Student life. Freshman orientation:** Available. Preregistration for classes offered. 2 sessions lasting 2 hours held week before classes begin; new students requested to attend 1 session. **Policies:** Religious observance required. **Activities:** Student government.

**Student services.** Adult student services, campus ministries, financial aid counseling.

**Contact.** E-mail: cbs@cbshouston.edu
Phone: (713) 785-5995 Fax: (713) 785-5998
Doris Price, Director of Enrollment Management/Registrar, College of Biblical Studies-Houston, 7000 Regency Square Boulevard, #110, Houston, TX 77036-3211

---

## College of Saint Thomas More
**Fort Worth, Texas**
www.cstm.edu      **CB code: 0169**

- Private 4-year liberal arts college affiliated with Roman Catholic Church
- Commuter campus in very large city
- 47 degree-seeking undergraduates
- SAT, interview required

**General.** Regionally accredited. All students take 3 trips: Rome, Greece, and Oxford, England. **Degrees:** 6 bachelor's awarded. **Calendar:** Semester, limited summer session. **Full-time faculty:** 4 total. **Part-time faculty:** 5 total.

**Basis for selection.** Secondary school record, essay, interview, test scores important; 2 letters of recommendation required.

**2007-2008 Annual costs.** Tuition/fees: $12,150. Books/supplies: $500. Personal expenses: $1,575.

**Application procedures. Admission:** No deadline. $35 fee. Admission notification on a rolling basis.

**Academics. Special study options:** Dual enrollment of high school students, study abroad. **Credit/placement by examination:** CLEP. **Support services:** Remedial instruction, study skills assistance, tutoring, writing center.

**Majors. Liberal arts:** Arts/sciences.

**Computing on campus.** 10 workstations in library, student center.

**Student life. Freshman orientation:** Mandatory. Preregistration for classes offered. **Housing:** Apartments available. **Activities:** Student government.

**Student services.** Alcohol/substance abuse counseling, campus ministries, career counseling, financial aid counseling, personal counseling.

**Contact.** E-mail: jpatrick@cstm.edu
Phone: (817) 923-8459 Toll-free number: (800) 583-6489
Fax: (817) 924-3206
James Patrick, Chancellor, College of Saint Thomas More, 3020 Lubbock Avenue, Fort Worth, TX 76109

---

## Concordia University at Austin
**Austin, Texas**
www.concordia.edu      **CB code: 6127**

- Private 4-year university and liberal arts college affiliated with Lutheran Church - Missouri Synod
- Commuter campus in very large city
- 1,090 degree-seeking undergraduates: 25% part-time, 57% women, 10% African American, 1% Asian American, 20% Hispanic American
- 670 degree-seeking graduate students

- 62% of applicants admitted
- SAT or ACT (ACT writing optional) required

**General.** Founded in 1926. Regionally accredited. **Degrees:** 197 bachelor's, 14 associate awarded; master's offered. **ROTC:** Army, Air Force. **Calendar:** Semester, extensive summer session. **Full-time faculty:** 45 total; 76% have terminal degrees, 2% minority, 31% women. **Part-time faculty:** 62 total; 10% minority, 42% women. **Class size:** 81% < 20, 19% 20-39, less than 1% 40-49.

**Freshman class profile.** 691 applied, 428 admitted, 165 enrolled.

| Mid 50% test scores | | | |
|---|---|---|---|
| SAT critical reading: | 420-550 | GPA 3.0-3.49: | 44% |
| SAT math: | 430-560 | GPA 2.0-2.99: | 30% |
| SAT writing: | 420-540 | Rank in top quarter: | 29% |
| ACT composite: | 18-25 | Rank in top tenth: | 7% |
| GPA 3.50 or higher: | 25% | Return as sophomores: | 52% |
| | | Out-of-state: | 8% |

**Basis for selection.** School achievement record, test scores, and 2.5 GPA important. Interview recommended for academically weak.

**High school preparation.** Basic college preparatory program recommended.

**2007-2008 Annual costs.** Tuition/fees: $18,910. Room/board: $7,300. Books/supplies: $1,000. Personal expenses: $1,170.

**Financial aid. Non-need-based:** Scholarships awarded for academics, leadership, music/drama, religious affiliation.

**Application procedures. Admission:** Priority date 5/1; deadline 8/15. $25 fee, may be waived for applicants with need. Application may be submitted online. Admission notification on a rolling basis beginning on or about 8/15. Reply by August 15 if dormitory applicant. **Financial aid:** No deadline. FAFSA, institutional form required. Applicants notified on a rolling basis starting 2/15; must reply within 2 week(s) of notification.

**Academics. Special study options:** Accelerated study, combined bachelor's/graduate degree, double major, dual enrollment of high school students, independent study, internships, study abroad, teacher certification program. Simultaneous enrollment with other institutions of Concordia University System for two semesters. **Credit/placement by examination:** AP, CLEP, IB, SAT, ACT, institutional tests. 15 credit hours maximum toward associate degree, 30 toward bachelor's. **Support services:** Reduced course load, remedial instruction, tutoring.

**Majors. Biology:** General. **Business:** General, business admin, training/development. **Communications:** General. **Computer sciences:** Computer science. **Conservation:** Environmental studies. **Education:** Elementary, secondary. **English:** English lit. **Health:** Health care admin. **History:** General. **Legal studies:** Prelaw. **Liberal arts:** Arts/sciences. **Math:** General. **Parks/recreation:** Exercise sciences. **Philosophy/religion:** Religion. **Protective services:** Law enforcement admin. **Social sciences:** General. **Theology:** Religious ed, sacred music. **Visual/performing arts:** Conducting, piano/organ.

**Most popular majors.** Business/marketing 55%, education 9%, parks/recreation 7%, social sciences 6%, theological studies 7%.

**Computing on campus.** 45 workstations in library, computer center. Dormitories wired for high-speed internet access and linked to campus network. Commuter students can connect to campus network. Helpline, student web hosting available.

**Student life. Freshman orientation:** Mandatory. **Housing:** Guaranteed on-campus for freshmen. Coed dorms, single-sex dorms, special housing for disabled available. $250 deposit, deadline 7/1. **Activities:** Bands, campus ministries, choral groups, drama, literary magazine, music ensembles, student government, student newspaper, Sisters in Christ, Lutheran Student Fellowship, Lutheran Women's Missionary League, Pro Life, College Republicans, Pre-Sem Club (pre-seminary students), Fellowship of Christian Athletes, students active for the environment, writer's guild.

**Athletics.** NCAA. **Intercollegiate:** Baseball M, basketball, cross-country, golf, soccer, softball W, tennis, volleyball W. **Intramural:** Badminton, basketball, bowling, handball, racquetball, softball, table tennis, tennis, volleyball. **Team name:** Tornadoes.

**Student services.** Adult student services, alcohol/substance abuse counseling, campus ministries, career counseling, student employment services, financial aid counseling, personal counseling, placement for graduates, veterans' counselor.

**Contact.** E-mail: admissions@concordia.edu
Phone: (512) 486-2000 Toll-free number: (800) 865-4282
Fax: (512) 459-8517
Kristi Kirk, Associate Director of Admissions, Concordia University at
Austin, 3400 Interstate 35 North, Austin, TX 78705-2799

## Criswell College
### Dallas, Texas
www.criswell.edu                                CB code: 0794

- Private 4-year Bible and seminary college affiliated with Southern
  Baptist Convention
- Commuter campus in very large city
- 125 full-time, degree-seeking undergraduates
- SAT or ACT (ACT writing optional), application essay required

**General.** Founded in 1970. Regionally accredited. **Degrees:** 32 bachelor's,
3 associate awarded; master's offered. **Calendar:** Semester, limited summer
session. **Full-time faculty:** 20 total. **Part-time faculty:** 4 total.

**Basis for selection.** Test scores and 2 letters of recommendation required. School achievement, essay, religious affiliation very important. Interview recommended.

**High school preparation.** Recommended units include English 4, mathematics 2, social studies 2, science 3 and foreign language 2.

**2007-2008 Annual costs.** Tuition/fees: $7,470. Books/supplies: $500.

**Application procedures. Admission:** Priority date 5/1; no deadline. $30
fee, may be waived for applicants with need. Admission notification on a
rolling basis. Must reply by May 1 or within 2 week(s) if notified thereafter.
**Financial aid:** Priority date 6/1; no closing date. CSS PROFILE required.
Applicants notified on a rolling basis.

**Academics. Special study options:** Double major, dual enrollment of
high school students, independent study, internships. **Credit/placement by
examination:** CLEP. **Support services:** Reduced course load, study skills
assistance, tutoring.

**Majors. Philosophy/religion:** Philosophy, religion. **Theology:** Bible, missionary, pastoral counseling, theology.

**Computing on campus.** 25 workstations in computer center. Online
course registration available.

**Student life. Policies:** Religious observance required. **Activities:** Student
government, student newspaper, missionary fellowship, international fellowship, student council.

**Athletics. Intramural:** Basketball, soccer, softball, table tennis, volleyball.

**Student services.** Career counseling, student employment services, personal counseling, veterans' counselor.

**Contact.** E-mail: tccsa@criswell.edu
Phone: (214) 818-1305 Toll-free number: (800) 899-0012
Fax: (214) 818-1310
Danny Blair, Academic and Enrollment Services, Criswell College, 4010
Gaston Avenue, Dallas, TX 75246-1537.

## Dallas Baptist University
### Dallas, Texas                              CB member
www.dbu.edu                                     CB code: 6159

- Private 4-year university affiliated with Baptist faith
- Commuter campus in very large city
- 3,581 degree-seeking undergraduates: 39% part-time, 59% women,
  18% African American, 2% Asian American, 9% Hispanic American,
  1% Native American, 8% international
- 1,663 degree-seeking graduate students
- 52% of applicants admitted
- SAT or ACT with writing, application essay required
- 58% graduate within 6 years

**General.** Founded in 1898. Regionally accredited. **Degrees:** 754 bachelor's, 1 associate awarded; master's, doctoral offered. **ROTC:** Army, Air
Force. **Location:** 13 miles from downtown, 29 miles from Fort Worth. **Calendar:** 4-1-4, extensive summer session. **Full-time faculty:** 112 total; 72%
have terminal degrees, 12% minority, 40% women. **Part-time faculty:** 392

total; 33% have terminal degrees, 9% minority, 46% women. **Class size:**
65% < 20, 32% 20-39, 2% 40-49, less than 1% 50-99, less than 1% >100.

**Freshman class profile.** 1,202 applied, 629 admitted, 329 enrolled.

| Mid 50% test scores | | |
|---|---|---|
| SAT critical reading: | 470-590 | |
| SAT math: | 470-580 | |
| ACT composite: | 19-24 | |
| Rank in top quarter: | 39% | |

| | |
|---|---|
| Rank in top tenth: | 17% |
| Return as sophomores: | 73% |
| Out-of-state: | 8% |
| Live on campus: | 92% |

**Basis for selection.** All factors considered for admission, including test
scores, class rank, essay and GPA. Interview recommended. **Homeschooled:** Transcript of courses and grades required. If student is not in
accredited program, GED required.

**High school preparation.** 16 units recommended. Recommended units
include English 4, mathematics 3, social studies 3, history 2, science 2 and
foreign language 2.

**2007-2008 Annual costs.** Tuition/fees: $14,940. Room/board: $5,148.
Books/supplies: $1,350. Personal expenses: $1,566.

**2007-2008 Financial aid. Need-based:** 294 full-time freshmen applied
for aid; 198 were judged to have need; 196 of these received aid. Average
need met was 80%. Average scholarship/grant was $2,957; average loan
$3,090. 43% of total undergraduate aid awarded as scholarships/grants, 57%
as loans/jobs. **Non-need-based:** Awarded to 1,180 full-time undergraduates, including 304 freshmen. Scholarships awarded for academics, athletics, job skills, leadership, music/drama, religious affiliation.

**Application procedures. Admission:** Priority date 1/15; no deadline.
$25 fee. Application may be submitted online. Admission notification on a
rolling basis. **Financial aid:** Priority date 3/15, closing date 5/1. FAFSA,
institutional form required. Applicants notified on a rolling basis.

**Academics. Special study options:** Accelerated study, combined bachelor's/
graduate degree, distance learning, double major, dual enrollment of high
school students, ESL, honors, independent study, internships, study abroad,
teacher certification program, Washington semester, weekend college. **Credit/
placement by examination:** AP, CLEP, IB, SAT, ACT, institutional tests.
Credit by examination not counted toward residency hours. Credits recorded on permanent record after student has completed minimum of 12
hours in residence. **Support services:** Learning center, pre-admission summer program, remedial instruction, study skills assistance, tutoring, writing
center.

**Majors. Biology:** General. **Business:** General, accounting, business admin,
finance, management information systems, managerial economics, marketing. **Communications:** General. **Computer sciences:** General, computer
science. **Education:** General, early childhood, elementary, music, physical,
science, secondary. **English:** English lit. **Health:** Health care admin. **History:** General. **Liberal arts:** Arts/sciences. **Math:** General. **Philosophy/
religion:** Philosophy. **Protective services:** Criminal justice. **Psychology:**
General. **Social sciences:** Political science, sociology. **Theology:** Bible, pastoral counseling, religious ed, sacred music. **Visual/performing arts:** Art,
music theory/composition, piano/organ, voice/opera.

**Computing on campus.** 220 workstations in dormitories, library, computer center, student center. Dormitories wired for high-speed internet access and linked to campus network. Commuter students can connect to campus network. Online library, helpline, wireless network available.

**Student life. Freshman orientation:** Available. Preregistration for classes
offered. **Policies:** Religious observance required. **Housing:** Single-sex dorms,
special housing for disabled, apartments, substance-free housing available.
$100 fully refundable deposit. **Activities:** Campus ministries, choral groups,
drama, music ensembles, musical theater, opera, student government, College Republicans, Spanish-speaking students association, Chinese student
association, Ministerial Alliance, Japanese student association, Korean student association.

**Athletics.** NCAA, NCCAA. **Intercollegiate:** Baseball M, cross-country,
golf, soccer, tennis, track and field, volleyball W. **Intramural:** Badminton,
basketball, football (non-tackle), golf M, softball, table tennis, tennis, volleyball. **Team name:** Patriots.

**Student services.** Adult student services, alcohol/substance abuse counseling, campus ministries, career counseling, student employment services,
financial aid counseling, health services, personal counseling, placement for
graduates, veterans' counselor. **Physically disabled:** Services for visually,
speech, hearing impaired.

**Contact.** E-mail: admiss@dbu.edu
Phone: (214) 333-5360 Toll-free number: (800) 460-1328
Fax: (214) 333-5447
Erin Spivey, Director of Undergraduate Admissions, Dallas Baptist
University, 3000 Mountain Creek Parkway, Dallas, TX 75211-9299

## Dallas Christian College
**Dallas, Texas**
www.dallas.edu                                       CB code: 0792

- Private 4-year Bible college affiliated with nondenominational tradition
- Commuter campus in very large city
- 327 degree-seeking undergraduates: 31% part-time, 44% women
- 24 degree-seeking graduate students
- 47% of applicants admitted
- SAT or ACT, application essay required

**General.** Founded in 1950. Accredited by ABHE. Special program for
adult, nontraditional students. **Degrees:** 52 bachelor's, 1 associate awarded.
**Location:** 10 miles from downtown. **Calendar:** 4-1-4, limited summer session. **Full-time faculty:** 8 total; 50% have terminal degrees, 25% women.
**Part-time faculty:** 48 total; 23% have terminal degrees, 10% minority, 17%
women.

**Freshman class profile.** 154 applied, 73 admitted, 45 enrolled.

| Mid 50% test scores | | | |
|---|---|---|---|
| | | Rank in top quarter: | 14% |
| SAT critical reading: | 430-560 | Rank in top tenth: | 2% |
| SAT math: | 400-560 | Out-of-state: | 27% |
| ACT composite: | 18-23 | Live on campus: | 98% |

**Basis for selection.** School record and recommendation, followed by
test scores. Class rank also important. Interview recommended.

**2007-2008 Annual costs.** Tuition/fees: $9,720. Room/board: $6,000. Books/
supplies: $600.

**Application procedures. Admission:** Priority date 7/1; deadline 7/15
(postmark date). $40 fee, may be waived for applicants with need. Applica-
tion may be submitted online. Admission notification on a rolling basis.
Must reply by 8/15. **Financial aid:** Closing date 4/15. FAFSA, institutional
form required. Applicants notified on a rolling basis; must reply within 2
week(s) of notification.

**Academics. Special study options:** Distance learning, double major, dual
enrollment of high school students, independent study, internships, liberal
arts/career combination, teacher certification program. Evening degree-
seeking program for adults, online degree program. **Credit/placement by
examination:** AP, CLEP, institutional tests. 30 credit hours maximum toward bachelor's degree. **Support services:** Reduced course load, remedial
instruction, study skills assistance.

**Majors. Business:** Business admin. **Education:** General, early childhood,
elementary, English, history, multi-level teacher, music, secondary. **Liberal
arts:** Arts/sciences. **Psychology:** General. **Theology:** Bible, religious ed,
sacred music, theology.

**Computing on campus.** 16 workstations in library, computer center.
Dormitories wired for high-speed internet access. Commuter students can
connect to campus network. Online library, wireless network available.

**Student life. Freshman orientation:** Mandatory, $100 fee. Preregistra-
tion for classes offered. Held 3 days prior to registration. **Policies:** All resident students and those taking 6 hours or more required to attend campus
chapel services 2 times a week. **Housing:** Guaranteed on-campus for all
undergraduates. Single-sex dorms, substance-free housing available. $50 de-
posit, deadline 8/10. **Activities:** Pep band, campus ministries, choral groups,
drama, music ensembles, student government.

**Athletics.** NCCAA. **Intercollegiate:** Basketball, soccer M, volleyball W.
**Team name:** Crusaders.

**Student services.** Adult student services, campus ministries, student employment services, financial aid counseling, personal counseling, placement
for graduates.

**Contact.** E-mail: dcc@dallas.edu
Phone: (972) 241-3371 ext. 149 Toll-free number: (800) 688-1029
Fax: (972) 241-8021
Eric Hinton, Director of Admissions, Dallas Christian College, 2700
Christian Parkway, Dallas, TX 75234-7299

## DeVry University: Houston
**Houston, Texas**
www.devry.edu                                       CB code: 4132

- For-profit 4-year university
- Commuter campus in very large city
- 926 degree-seeking undergraduates: 36% part-time, 43% women, 35%
  African American, 5% Asian American, 35% Hispanic American, 1%
  international
- 150 degree-seeking graduate students

**General. Degrees:** 117 bachelor's, 39 associate awarded; master's offered.
**Calendar:** Semester. **Full-time faculty:** 22 total; 36% minority, 32% women.
**Part-time faculty:** 48 total; 42% minority, 38% women.

**Freshman class profile.**

| Return as sophomores: | 39% | Out-of-state: | 1% |
|---|---|---|---|

**Basis for selection.** Interview, high school GPA, and test scores most
important. DeVry-administered admissions tests may be submitted in place
of SAT/ACT.

**2007-2008 Annual costs.** Tuition/fees: $13,220. Books/supplies: $1,300.
Personal expenses: $5,082.

**2006-2007 Financial aid. Non-need-based:** Scholarships awarded for
academics.

**Application procedures. Admission:** No deadline. $50 fee. Admission
notification on a rolling basis. **Financial aid:** No deadline. FAFSA required.
Applicants notified on a rolling basis.

**Academics. Special study options:** Accelerated study, distance learning.
**Credit/placement by examination:** CLEP.

**Majors. Business:** Business admin. **Computer sciences:** Systems analysis. **Engineering technology:** Biomedical, computer, electrical. **Other:** Technical management.

**Most popular majors.** Business/marketing 96%.

**Contact.** Phone: (713) 973-3000 Fax: (713) 896-7650
DeVry University: Houston, 11125 Equity Drive, Houston, TX 77041-8217

## DeVry University: Irving
**Dallas, Texas**                                   **CB member**
www.devry.edu                                       CB code: 6180

- For-profit 4-year university
- Commuter campus in small city
- 1,453 degree-seeking undergraduates: 52% part-time, 31% women,
  32% African American, 4% Asian American, 20% Hispanic American,
  1% Native American
- 251 degree-seeking graduate students
- Interview required

**General.** Founded in 1969. Regionally accredited. **Degrees:** 234 bachelor's, 48 associate awarded; master's offered. **Location:** 12 miles from
Dallas. **Calendar:** Semester, extensive summer session. **Full-time faculty:**
39 total; 28% minority, 33% women. **Part-time faculty:** 50 total; 30% minority, 38% women.

**Freshman class profile.**

| Return as sophomores: | 42% | Out-of-state: | 4% |
|---|---|---|---|

**Basis for selection.** Applicants must have a high school diploma or
equivalent or a degree from an accredited postsecondary institution, demonstrating proficiency in basic college-level skills through SAT or ACT scores
or institution-administered placement examinations, and be at least 17 years
of age on the first day of classes. New students may enter at beginning of
any semester. CPT also accepted.

**2007-2008 Annual costs.** Tuition/fees: $13,220. Books/supplies: $1,300.
Personal expenses: $5,082.

**2006-2007 Financial aid.** All financial aid based on need.

**Application procedures. Admission:** No deadline. $50 fee. Applica-
tion may be submitted online. Admission notification on a rolling basis.

**Financial aid:** No deadline. FAFSA required. Applicants notified on a rolling basis.

**Academics. Special study options:** Accelerated study, distance learning. **Credit/placement by examination:** CLEP, institutional tests. No more than 35% of credit toward graduation requirement accepted. **Support services:** Learning center, remedial instruction, tutoring.

**Majors. Biology:** Bioinformatics. **Business:** Business admin. **Computer sciences:** Networking, systems analysis. **Engineering:** Software. **Engineering technology:** Biomedical, computer, electrical. **Health:** Medical records technology.

**Most popular majors.** Business/marketing 65%, computer/information sciences 24%, engineering/engineering technologies 11%.

**Computing on campus.** 450 workstations in library, computer center. Online course registration, online library, helpline available.

**Student life. Freshman orientation:** Mandatory. **Activities:** Student newspaper, Association of Information Technology Professionals, campus Bible study, Christian Students Fellowship, Habitat for Humanity, Institute of Electrical and Electronics Engineers, Institute of Management Accountants, minority student union, National Society of Black Engineers, Society of Women Engineers, Telecommunications Management and Associations, Society of Hispanic Professionals Engineers, gamers.

**Athletics. Intramural:** Basketball, football (tackle) M, volleyball.

**Student services.** Career counseling, student employment services, financial aid counseling, placement for graduates, veterans' counselor. **Physically disabled:** Services for visually, hearing impaired.

**Contact.**  E-mail: cwilliams@mail.dal.devry.edu
Phone: (972) 929-5777 Toll-free number: (800) 633-3879
Fax: (972) 929-2860
Chad Williams, Director of Admissions, DeVry University: Irving, 4800 Regent Boulevard, Dallas, TX 75063-2439

## East Texas Baptist University
Marshall, Texas
www.etbu.edu

CB code: 6187

- Private 4-year university and liberal arts college affiliated with Baptist faith
- Residential campus in large town
- 1,215 degree-seeking undergraduates: 5% part-time, 54% women, 16% African American, 1% Asian American, 4% Hispanic American, 1% Native American, 1% international
- 75% of applicants admitted
- SAT or ACT (ACT writing optional) required
- 34% graduate within 6 years

**General.** Founded in 1912. Regionally accredited. **Degrees:** 221 bachelor's awarded. **Location:** 35 miles from Shreveport, Louisiana, 20 miles from Longview. **Calendar:** 4-1-4, extensive summer session. **Full-time faculty:** 63 total; 79% have terminal degrees, 5% minority, 30% women. **Part-time faculty:** 42 total; 14% have terminal degrees, 5% minority, 55% women. **Class size:** 49% < 20, 42% 20-39, 7% 40-49, 1% 50-99. **Special facilities:** Caddo Lake international wetlands.

**Freshman class profile.** 679 applied, 507 admitted, 313 enrolled.

| Mid 50% test scores | | Rank in top tenth: | 17% |
|---|---|---|---|
| SAT critical reading: | 430-540 | End year in good standing: | 81% |
| SAT math: | 440-560 | Return as sophomores: | 52% |
| ACT composite: | 18-23 | Out-of-state: | 8% |
| GPA 3.50 or higher: | 36% | Live on campus: | 94% |
| GPA 3.0-3.49: | 31% | International: | 1% |
| GPA 2.0-2.99: | 32% | Fraternities: | 3% |
| Rank in top quarter: | 40% | | |

**Basis for selection.** School achievement record and test scores most important. Evidence of good character also important. Applicants should be in top 40% of class. Interview recommended for academically deficient; audition recommended for music, speech, theater arts programs. **Learning Disabled:** Student should provide documentation of learning disability to Office of Student Services, which verifies documentation and assists in acquiring reasonable accommodations.

**High school preparation.** 22 units recommended. Recommended units include English 4, mathematics 3, social studies 2.5, science 2 and academic electives 1. 0.5 economics, 1.5 physical education, 0.5 health education, 1 technology applications, 0.5 speech.

**2008-2009 Annual costs.** Tuition/fees: $16,140. Room/board: $4,913. Books/supplies: $866. Personal expenses: $1,405.

**2007-2008 Financial aid. Need-based:** 294 full-time freshmen applied for aid; 250 were judged to have need; 250 of these received aid. Average need met was 63%. Average scholarship/grant was $7,926; average loan $3,518. 52% of total undergraduate aid awarded as scholarships/grants, 48% as loans/jobs. **Non-need-based:** Awarded to 933 full-time undergraduates, including 297 freshmen. Scholarships awarded for academics, alumni affiliation, leadership, music/drama, religious affiliation.

**Application procedures. Admission:** Priority date 6/1; deadline 8/14 (receipt date). $25 fee. Application may be submitted online. Admission notification on a rolling basis beginning on or about 9/1. **Financial aid:** Priority date 6/1; no closing date. FAFSA, institutional form required. Applicants notified on a rolling basis starting 1/15; must reply within 3 week(s) of notification.

**Academics. Special study options:** Accelerated study, double major, dual enrollment of high school students, exchange student, honors, independent study, internships, liberal arts/career combination, student-designed major, study abroad, teacher certification program, Washington semester. **Credit/placement by examination:** AP, CLEP, IB, SAT, ACT, institutional tests. 30 credit hours maximum toward bachelor's degree. ACT required for placement. Departmental examinations administered on request upon approval of department chair. **Support services:** Learning center, reduced course load, study skills assistance, tutoring, writing center.

**Majors. Biology:** General. **Business:** General, accounting, management information systems. **Communications:** Media studies. **Education:** General, biology, chemistry, drama/dance, elementary, English, history, mathematics, music, physical, social studies, Spanish, speech. **English:** English lit, speech/rhetoric. **Foreign languages:** Spanish. **Health:** Athletic training, nursing (RN). **History:** General. **Interdisciplinary:** Global studies. **Liberal arts:** Arts/sciences. **Math:** General. **Parks/recreation:** Health/fitness. **Philosophy/religion:** Religion. **Physical sciences:** Chemistry. **Psychology:** General, industrial. **Social sciences:** Sociology. **Theology:** Bible, missionary, pastoral counseling, religious ed, sacred music, youth ministry. **Visual/performing arts:** Dramatic, piano/organ, voice/opera. **Other:** University studies.

**Most popular majors.** Business/marketing 12%, education 32%, English 6%, health sciences 8%, psychology 8%, theological studies 7%.

**Computing on campus.** 206 workstations in dormitories, library, computer center, student center. Dormitories wired for high-speed internet access and linked to campus network. Commuter students can connect to campus network. Online course registration, online library, helpline, repair service, student web hosting, wireless network available.

**Student life. Freshman orientation:** Mandatory. Preregistration for classes offered. One week of activities, lectures, seminar sessions, and community service activities. **Policies:** Graded curfew, weekly clean room check. Religious observance required. **Housing:** Guaranteed on-campus for all undergraduates. Single-sex dorms, apartments, substance-free housing available. $100 fully refundable deposit. **Activities:** Bands, campus ministries, choral groups, drama, international student organizations, literary magazine, music ensembles, Model UN, musical theater, student government, student newspaper, symphony orchestra, Fellowship of Christian Athletes, political awareness society, Delta Pi Theta, Pi Sigma, Sigma Sigma Epsilon.

**Athletics.** NCAA. **Intercollegiate:** Baseball M, basketball, cross-country, football (tackle) M, soccer, softball W, volleyball W. **Intramural:** Basketball, football (non-tackle) M, softball, volleyball. **Team name:** Tigers.

**Student services.** Adult student services, campus ministries, career counseling, student employment services, financial aid counseling, health services, personal counseling, placement for graduates, veterans' counselor. **Physically disabled:** Services for hearing impaired.

**Contact.**  E-mail: admissions@etbu.edu
Phone: (903) 923-2000 Toll-free number: (800) 804-3828
Fax: (903) 923-2001
Melissa Fitts, Director of Admissions, East Texas Baptist University, 1209 North Grove, Marshall, TX 75670-1498

## Hardin-Simmons University
Abilene, Texas
www.hsutx.edu

CB member
CB code: 6268

- Private 4-year university affiliated with Baptist faith
- Residential campus in small city

- 1,991 degree-seeking undergraduates: 12% part-time, 57% women, 5% African American, 1% Asian American, 10% Hispanic American, 1% Native American, 1% international
- 405 degree-seeking graduate students
- 36% of applicants admitted
- SAT or ACT with writing required
- 47% graduate within 6 years; 35% enter graduate study

**General.** Founded in 1891. Regionally accredited. Part of 3-member consortium (with Abilene Christian University and McMurry University) comprising Abilene Intercollegiate School of Nursing. **Degrees:** 383 bachelor's awarded; master's, doctoral, first professional offered. **Location:** 150 miles from Fort Worth. **Calendar:** Semester, extensive summer session. **Full-time faculty:** 130 total; 77% have terminal degrees, 2% minority, 35% women. **Part-time faculty:** 70 total; 29% have terminal degrees, 13% minority, 47% women. **Class size:** 58% < 20, 39% 20-39, 2% 40-49, 1% 50-99. **Special facilities:** Rare and fine book room, observatory.

**Freshman class profile.** 1,757 applied, 635 admitted, 465 enrolled.

| Mid 50% test scores | | |
|---|---|---|
| SAT critical reading: | 460-570 | |
| SAT math: | 470-580 | |
| SAT writing: | 450-550 | |
| ACT composite: | 19-25 | |
| GPA 3.50 or higher: | 69% | |
| GPA 3.0-3.49: | 18% | |
| GPA 2.0-2.99: | 12% | |

| | |
|---|---|
| Rank in top quarter: | 54% |
| Rank in top tenth: | 23% |
| End year in good standing: | 79% |
| Return as sophomores: | 66% |
| Out-of-state: | 3% |
| Live on campus: | 88% |
| International: | 2% |

**Basis for selection.** Applicants admitted on basis of acceptable combination of test scores and prior academic record. Special cases considered individually. Non-native speakers of English require score of 550 on TOEFL, unless transferring 24 or more credits. Audition required for music program; interview recommended for special cases. Written essay, interview, and separate application required for honors program. **Homeschooled:** GED scores required only if applicant plans to apply for federal need-based financial aid. **Learning Disabled:** There are no special admission requirements for students with disabilities. Once accepted, there is an application process to the Office for Students with Disabilities.

**High school preparation.** 16 units required. Required units include English 3, mathematics 2, social studies 2, science 2 and academic electives 7. Math must include algebra I and above.

**2008-2009 Annual costs.** Tuition/fees: $18,380. Room/board: $5,180. Books/supplies: $800. Personal expenses: $1,482.

**2007-2008 Financial aid. Need-based:** 459 full-time freshmen applied for aid; 334 were judged to have need; 334 of these received aid. Average need met was 87%. Average scholarship/grant was $7,429; average loan $2,930. 42% of total undergraduate aid awarded as scholarships/grants, 58% as loans/jobs. **Non-need-based:** Awarded to 1,461 full-time undergraduates, including 403 freshmen. Scholarships awarded for academics, art, job skills, leadership, music/drama, religious affiliation.

**Application procedures. Admission:** No deadline. $50 fee, may be waived for applicants with need. Application may be submitted online. Admission notification on a rolling basis beginning on or about 9/1. **Financial aid:** Priority date 3/15; no closing date. FAFSA required. Applicants notified on a rolling basis starting 1/1; must reply within 2 week(s) of notification.

**Academics. Special study options:** Accelerated study, cross-registration, distance learning, double major, dual enrollment of high school students, honors, independent study, internships, New York semester, study abroad, teacher certification program, United Nations semester, Washington semester. **Credit/placement by examination:** AP, CLEP, SAT, ACT, institutional tests. 32 credit hours maximum toward bachelor's degree. Maximum 14 hours in any one discipline. **Support services:** Pre-admission summer program, reduced course load, remedial instruction, study skills assistance, tutoring, writing center.

**Majors. Agriculture:** Agronomy, animal sciences, business. **Biology:** General, Biochemistry/biophysics and molecular biology. **Business:** Accounting, business admin, finance, management science, marketing. **Communications:** General, broadcast journalism, media studies, public relations, radio/tv. **Computer sciences:** Programming. **Conservation:** Environmental science. **Education:** Art, business, computer, drama/dance, early childhood, English, history, mathematics, music, physical, reading, science, social studies, Spanish, speech. **English:** English lit, speech/rhetoric. **Foreign languages:** Spanish. **Health:** Athletic training, audiology/speech pathology, nursing (RN), predental, premedicine. **History:** General. **Legal studies:** Prelaw. **Math:** General. **Parks/recreation:** Exercise sciences, health/fitness. **Philosophy/**

**religion:** Philosophy. **Physical sciences:** Chemistry, geology, physics. **Protective services:** Criminal justice. **Psychology:** General. **Public administration:** Social work. **Social sciences:** Economics, political science, sociology. **Theology:** Bible, missionary, preministerial, sacred music, theology, youth ministry. **Visual/performing arts:** Dramatic, graphic design, music history, music management, music performance, music theory/composition, piano/organ, stringed instruments, studio arts, voice/opera.

**Most popular majors.** Biology 9%, business/marketing 13%, communications/journalism 9%, education 18%, health sciences 9%, parks/recreation 7%, security/protective services 6%.

**Computing on campus.** 225 workstations in dormitories, library, computer center, student center. Dormitories wired for high-speed internet access and linked to campus network. Online library, helpline, wireless network available.

**Student life. Freshman orientation:** Available, $85 fee. Preregistration for classes offered. Held Tuesday through Sunday the week before classes begin. **Policies:** Single, undergraduate students under 21 who have not completed 60 credit hours and are not living at home required to live in residence halls. Religious observance required. **Housing:** Guaranteed on-campus for freshmen. Single-sex dorms, special housing for disabled, apartments, substance-free housing available. $100 fully refundable deposit. Single and duplex housing available with priority given to families. **Activities:** Bands, campus ministries, choral groups, drama, international student organizations, literary magazine, music ensembles, Model UN, musical theater, opera, student government, student newspaper, symphony orchestra, unity group, student foundation, black student fellowship, moot court team, Latin American club, United Mexican American Students, social work club, criminal justice club, Students in Free Enterprise, Collegiates for Racial Harmony.

**Athletics.** NCAA. **Intercollegiate:** Baseball M, basketball, cheerleading, football (tackle) M, golf, soccer, softball W, tennis, volleyball W. **Intramural:** Badminton, basketball, bowling, football (non-tackle), football (tackle), golf, handball, racquetball, soccer, softball, tennis, volleyball. **Team name:** Cowboys/Cowgirls.

**Student services.** Campus ministries, career counseling, student employment services, financial aid counseling, health services, personal counseling, placement for graduates, veterans' counselor. **Physically disabled:** Services for visually, speech, hearing impaired.

**Contact.** E-mail: enroll@hsutx.edu
Phone: (325) 670-1206 Toll-free number: (877) 464-7889
Fax: (325) 671-2115
Vicki House, Director of Admissions and Recruiting, Hardin-Simmons University, PO Box 16050, Abilene, TX 79698-0001

## Houston Baptist University
**Houston, Texas**
**www.hbu.edu**

CB member
CB code: 6282

- Private 4-year university and liberal arts college affiliated with Baptist faith
- Commuter campus in very large city
- 1,992 degree-seeking undergraduates: 10% part-time, 67% women, 19% African American, 16% Asian American, 17% Hispanic American, 6% international
- 317 degree-seeking graduate students
- 48% of applicants admitted
- SAT or ACT with writing, application essay required
- 49% graduate within 6 years

**General.** Founded in 1960. Regionally accredited. **Degrees:** 290 bachelor's, 4 associate awarded; master's offered. **ROTC:** Army, Naval. **Location:** 180 miles from San Antonio. **Calendar:** Semester, extensive summer session. **Full-time faculty:** 118 total; 69% have terminal degrees, 11% minority, 51% women. **Part-time faculty:** 84 total; 34% have terminal degrees, 24% minority, 61% women. **Class size:** 67% < 20, 32% 20-39, less than 1% 40-49, less than 1% 50-99. **Special facilities:** Morris cultural arts center, museum of American architecture and decorative arts, Bible in America museum, museum of southern history.

## Freshman class profile. 4,005 applied, 1,911 admitted, 456 enrolled.

| Mid 50% test scores | | Rank in top tenth: | 21% |
|---|---|---|---|
| SAT critical reading: | 470-590 | Return as sophomores: | 70% |
| SAT math: | 480-590 | Out-of-state: | 3% |
| SAT writing: | 470-580 | Live on campus: | 52% |
| ACT composite: | 19-24 | International: | 4% |
| Rank in top quarter: | 47% | Sororities: | 1% |

**Basis for selection.** School achievement record, test scores, recommendations, class rank, special talents, and skills most important. Audition required for music majors; portfolio required for art majors; interview recommended for academically weak students.

**High school preparation.** 18 units recommended. Recommended units include English 4, mathematics 3, social studies 2, history 2, science 3 (laboratory 1), foreign language 2 and academic electives 2.

**2008-2009 Annual costs.** Tuition/fees: $18,820. Room/board: $4,995. Books/supplies: $1,230. Personal expenses: $1,825.

**2007-2008 Financial aid. Need-based:** 322 full-time freshmen applied for aid; 123 were judged to have need; 123 of these received aid. Average need met was 69%. Average scholarship/grant was $9,941; average loan $3,294. 56% of total undergraduate aid awarded as scholarships/grants, 44% as loans/jobs. **Non-need-based:** Awarded to 1,284 full-time undergraduates, including 397 freshmen. Scholarships awarded for academics, alumni affiliation, art, athletics, leadership, music/drama, religious affiliation.

**Application procedures. Admission:** No deadline. $25 fee, may be waived for applicants with need. Application may be submitted online. Admission notification on a rolling basis. **Financial aid:** Priority date 3/1, closing date 4/15. FAFSA required. Applicants notified on a rolling basis starting 3/10.

**Academics. Special study options:** Accelerated study, combined bachelor's/graduate degree, double major, dual enrollment of high school students, ESL, honors, independent study, internships, liberal arts/career combination, teacher certification program. **Credit/placement by examination:** AP, CLEP, IB, institutional tests. CLEP credit limited to students with 63 or fewer credit hours. **Support services:** Reduced course load, remedial instruction, tutoring, writing center.

**Majors. Biology:** General, molecular. **Business:** General, accounting, business admin, entrepreneurial studies, finance, information resources management, management information systems, managerial economics, marketing. **Communications:** General, media studies. **Education:** Art, early childhood, English, mathematics, middle, music, physical, science, secondary, social studies. **English:** Creative writing, English lit. **Family/consumer sciences:** Child development. **Foreign languages:** Biblical, French, Spanish. **Health:** Nursing (RN). **History:** General. **Interdisciplinary:** Accounting/computer science. **Math:** General. **Parks/recreation:** Exercise sciences, health/fitness. **Philosophy/religion:** Christian. **Physical sciences:** Chemistry, physics. **Psychology:** General. **Social sciences:** Economics, political science, sociology. **Theology:** Pastoral counseling, sacred music. **Visual/performing arts:** Music performance, music theory/composition, studio arts.

**Most popular majors.** Biology 13%, business/marketing 26%, education 11%, health sciences 7%, philosophy/religious studies 7%, psychology 8%.

**Computing on campus.** 95 workstations in dormitories, library, computer center. Dormitories wired for high-speed internet access and linked to campus network. Commuter students can connect to campus network. Online course registration, online library, helpline, repair service, wireless network available.

**Student life. Freshman orientation:** Available. Preregistration for classes offered. 2-and-a-half-day camp held off campus. **Policies:** Spiritual Life Program graduation requirement for all undergraduate students. **Housing:** Guaranteed on-campus for freshmen. Single-sex dorms, apartments, substance-free housing available. $200 deposit. **Activities:** Bands, campus ministries, choral groups, drama, literary magazine, music ensembles, musical theater, opera, student government, student newspaper, symphony orchestra, TV station, Christian Life on Campus, Psi Chi, Nursing Association, international club, Black Student Fellowship, Toastmasters, Digital Eon, Vietnamese Student Association, Indian Student Association, Sisters for the Lord, Brothers Under Christ.

**Athletics.** NAIA. **Intercollegiate:** Baseball M, basketball, cheerleading, softball W, volleyball W. **Intramural:** Badminton, basketball, bowling, football (non-tackle), golf, soccer, softball, table tennis, tennis, volleyball. **Team name:** Huskies.

**Student services.** Adult student services, alcohol/substance abuse counseling, campus ministries, career counseling, student employment services, financial aid counseling, health services, personal counseling, placement for graduates, women's services. **Physically disabled:** Services for visually, speech, hearing impaired.

**Contact.** E-mail: admissions@hbu.edu
Phone: (281) 649-3211 Toll-free number: (800) 969-3210
Fax: (281) 649-3217
James Steen, Vice President of Enrollment Management, Houston Baptist University, 7502 Fondren Road, Houston, TX 77074-3298

---

## Howard Payne University
### Brownwood, Texas
### www.hputx.edu
CB code: 6278

- Private 4-year liberal arts and teachers college affiliated with Baptist faith
- Residential campus in large town
- 1,173 degree-seeking undergraduates: 11% part-time, 47% women
- 15 degree-seeking graduate students
- 62% of applicants admitted
- SAT or ACT with writing required
- 35% graduate within 6 years

**General.** Founded in 1889. Regionally accredited. **Degrees:** 217 bachelor's, 3 associate awarded; master's offered. **Location:** 150 miles from Dallas, 77 miles from Abilene. **Calendar:** Semester, limited summer session. **Full-time faculty:** 78 total; 60% have terminal degrees, 3% minority, 30% women. **Part-time faculty:** 78 total; 18% have terminal degrees, 10% minority, 38% women. **Class size:** 74% < 20, 25% 20-39, less than 1% 40-49, less than 1% 50-99. **Special facilities:** General Douglas MacArthur Academy of Freedom.

**Freshman class profile.** 960 applied, 598 admitted, 276 enrolled.

| Mid 50% test scores | | Rank in top quarter: | 40% |
|---|---|---|---|
| SAT critical reading: | 440-540 | Rank in top tenth: | 18% |
| SAT math: | 440-550 | Return as sophomores: | 51% |
| ACT composite: | 18-23 | Out-of-state: | 2% |
| GPA 3.50 or higher: | 53% | Live on campus: | 91% |
| GPA 3.0-3.49: | 37% | Fraternities: | 15% |
| GPA 2.0-2.99: | 9% | Sororities: | 15% |

**Basis for selection.** Must have 19 ACT or 910 SAT (exclusive of Writing) and B average throughout high school. Those not meeting requirements may be eligible for provisional or conditional admission. ACT/SAT scores used to exempt students from placement tests in English, math, or reading. Interview required for academic program applicants, recommended for all others. Interview may be required by admissions committee. Audition required for music program.

**High school preparation.** 15 units required; 23 recommended. Required and recommended units include English 4, mathematics 3, social studies 2.5, science 2, computer science 1, academic electives 10.5. Remaining credits must be among those listed in approved courses provided by Texas Education Agency.

**2008-2009 Annual costs.** Tuition/fees (projected): $17,400. Room/board: $4,826. Books/supplies: $1,000. Personal expenses: $1,500.

**Financial aid. Non-need-based:** Scholarships awarded for academics, alumni affiliation, art, job skills, music/drama.

**Application procedures. Admission:** Priority date 3/15; no deadline. $25 fee. Application may be submitted online. Admission notification on a rolling basis. **Financial aid:** Priority date 3/1; no closing date. FAFSA, institutional form required. Applicants notified on a rolling basis starting 3/30; must reply within 3 week(s) of notification.

**Academics. Special study options:** Accelerated study, cooperative education, distance learning, double major, dual enrollment of high school students, ESL, honors, independent study, internships, liberal arts/career combination, study abroad, teacher certification program. Extension classes in El Paso, Corpus Christi, Harlingen, Ft. Worth, Midland. **Credit/placement by examination:** AP, CLEP, SAT, ACT, institutional tests. 30 credit hours maximum toward bachelor's degree. **Support services:** Reduced course load, remedial instruction, study skills assistance, tutoring, writing center.

**Majors. Biology:** General. **Business:** General, accounting, business admin, finance, marketing. **Communications:** General, public relations. **Communications technology:** Graphics, radio/tv. **Computer sciences:** Information systems. **Education:** General, art, biology, business, chemistry, drama/dance, elementary, English, history, mathematics, multi-level teacher, music, physical, science, secondary, social science, Spanish, speech. **English:** English lit, speech/rhetoric. **Foreign languages:** Biblical, Spanish. **Health:** Athletic training, premedicine. **History:** General. **Legal studies:** Prelaw.

Liberal arts: Arts/sciences. Math: General. Parks/recreation: General, exercise sciences, health/fitness, sports admin. Philosophy/religion: Philosophy, religion. Physical sciences: Chemistry. Psychology: General. Public administration: Social work. Social sciences: General, political science, sociology. Theology: Bible, religious ed, sacred music, theology, youth ministry. Visual/performing arts: Art, dramatic, music performance, piano/organ, stringed instruments, studio arts, voice/opera.

**Most popular majors.** Business/marketing 14%, communications/journalism 8%, education 17%, psychology 12%, security/protective services 7%, theological studies 12%.

**Computing on campus.** 260 workstations in dormitories, library, computer center, student center. Dormitories wired for high-speed internet access and linked to campus network. Online library, helpline, wireless network available.

**Student life. Freshman orientation:** Available, $50 fee. Preregistration for classes offered. Held the weekend before fall semester classes begin. **Policies:** Religious observance required. **Housing:** Guaranteed on-campus for freshmen. Single-sex dorms, apartments, substance-free housing available. $100 nonrefundable deposit, deadline 8/1. **Activities:** Bands, choral groups, dance, drama, literary magazine, music ensembles, musical theater, opera, radio station, student government, student newspaper, student foundation, ministerial alliance, Fellowship of Christian Athletes.

**Athletics.** NCAA. **Intercollegiate:** Baseball M, basketball, cheerleading, football (tackle) M, soccer, softball W, tennis, track and field, volleyball W. **Intramural:** Basketball, football (non-tackle), softball, table tennis, tennis, volleyball. **Team name:** Yellow Jackets.

**Student services.** Adult student services, campus ministries, career counseling, student employment services, financial aid counseling, health services, personal counseling, placement for graduates.

**Contact.** E-mail: enroll@hputx.edu
Phone: (325) 649-8020 Toll-free number: (800) 880-4478
Fax: (325) 649-8901
Brad Johnson, Vice President for Enrollment & Student Services, Howard Payne University, 1000 Fisk Avenue, Brownwood, TX 76801

## Huston-Tillotson University

**Austin, Texas**                                    **CB member**
www.htu.edu                                          **CB code: 6280**

▶ Private 4-year business and liberal arts college affiliated with United Church of Christ and United Methodist Church

▶ Residential campus in very large city

▶ 724 degree-seeking undergraduates: 6% part-time, 50% women, 76% African American, 1% Asian American, 12% Hispanic American, 2% international

▶ 41 degree-seeking graduate students

▶ 40% of applicants admitted

▶ SAT or ACT required

**General.** Founded in 1876. Regionally accredited. **Degrees:** 94 bachelor's awarded. **ROTC:** Army, Naval, Air Force. **Location:** Downtown. **Calendar:** Semester, extensive summer session. **Full-time faculty:** 34 total; 82% have terminal degrees, 68% minority, 56% women. **Part-time faculty:** 34 total; 26% minority. **Class size:** 63% < 20, 35% 20-39, 1% 40-49, less than 1% 50-99.

**Freshman class profile.** 484 applied, 196 admitted, 194 enrolled.

| Mid 50% test scores | | GPA 2.0-2.99: | 54% |
|---|---|---|---|
| SAT critical reading: | 350-440 | Rank in top quarter: | 23% |
| SAT math: | 360-470 | Rank in top tenth: | 12% |
| ACT composite: | 14-17 | Return as sophomores: | 46% |
| GPA 3.50 or higher: | 16% | Out-of-state: | 7% |
| GPA 3.0-3.49: | 24% | Live on campus: | 84% |

**Basis for selection.** School achievement record important. Test scores and interview considered.

**High school preparation.** 22 units required. Required and recommended units include English 4, mathematics 3, social studies 2.5, science 2, foreign language 2 and academic electives 1.

**2007-2008 Annual costs.** Tuition/fees: $10,038. Room/board: $5,892. Books/supplies: $800. Personal expenses: $1,306.

**2006-2007 Financial aid. Need-based:** 182 full-time freshmen applied for aid; 179 were judged to have need; 179 of these received aid. Average need met was 48%. Average scholarship/grant was $6,689; average loan

$2,703. 51% of total undergraduate aid awarded as scholarships/grants, 49% as loans/jobs. **Non-need-based:** Awarded to 83 full-time undergraduates, including 34 freshmen. Scholarships awarded for academics, alumni affiliation, art, athletics, job skills, leadership, minority status, music/drama, religious affiliation, ROTC, state residency.

**Application procedures. Admission:** Priority date 3/1; deadline 7/1. $25 fee. Admission notification on a rolling basis beginning on or about 1/1. **Financial aid:** Priority date 3/15, closing date 4/1. FAFSA, institutional form required. Applicants notified on a rolling basis starting 4/1; must reply within 4 week(s) of notification.

**Academics. Special study options:** Cross-registration, distance learning, double major, dual enrollment of high school students, external degree, honors, independent study, internships, liberal arts/career combination, study abroad, teacher certification program. 3-2 engineering program with Prairie View A&M University. **Credit/placement by examination:** AP, CLEP, SAT, ACT, institutional tests. 15 credit hours maximum toward bachelor's degree. **Support services:** Learning center, remedial instruction, tutoring, writing center.

**Majors. Biology:** General. **Business:** Accounting, business admin, international, marketing. **Computer sciences:** General, computer science. **Education:** General, physical. **English:** Composition. **History:** General. **Liberal arts:** Arts/sciences. **Math:** General. **Physical sciences:** Chemistry. **Protective services:** Criminal justice. **Psychology:** General. **Social sciences:** General, political science, sociology.

**Most popular majors.** Biology 7%, business/marketing 25%, interdisciplinary studies 14%, social sciences 16%.

**Computing on campus.** 400 workstations in dormitories, library, computer center, student center. Dormitories wired for high-speed internet access and linked to campus network. Commuter students can connect to campus network. Online library, helpline, wireless network available.

**Student life. Freshman orientation:** Mandatory. Preregistration for classes offered. **Housing:** Guaranteed on-campus for all undergraduates. Single-sex dorms, substance-free housing available. **Activities:** Choral groups, literary magazine, music ensembles, student government, student newspaper.

**Athletics.** NAIA. **Intercollegiate:** Baseball M, basketball, golf, soccer M, track and field, volleyball W. **Intramural:** Basketball, soccer M, softball, table tennis, volleyball. **Team name:** Rams.

**Student services.** Adult student services, career counseling, student employment services, financial aid counseling, health services, personal counseling, placement for graduates, veterans' counselor. **Physically disabled:** Services for visually, hearing impaired.

**Contact.** E-mail: slstinson@htu.edu
Phone: (512) 505-3027 Toll-free number: (877) 505-3028
Fax: (512) 505-3190
Shakitha Stinson, Director of Admission, Huston-Tillotson University, 900 Chicon Street, Austin, TX 78702-2795

## Jarvis Christian College

**Hawkins, Texas**
www.jarvis.edu                                       **CB code: 6319**

▶ Private 4-year liberal arts and teachers college affiliated with Christian Church (Disciples of Christ)

▶ Residential campus in rural community

▶ 712 degree-seeking undergraduates: 12% part-time, 50% women

**General.** Founded in 1912. Regionally accredited. **Degrees:** 85 bachelor's awarded. **Location:** 100 miles from Dallas, 100 miles from Shreveport, Louisiana. **Calendar:** Semester, extensive summer session. **Full-time faculty:** 39 total; 31% have terminal degrees, 56% minority, 44% women. **Part-time faculty:** 15 total; 40% have terminal degrees, 67% minority, 47% women. **Class size:** 59% < 20, 32% 20-39, 6% 40-49, 3% 50-99. **Special facilities:** Observatory, natatorium, archives of black Christian church (Disciples of Christ).

**Freshman class profile.** 589 applied, 581 admitted, 214 enrolled.

| GPA 3.50 or higher: | 8% | Out-of-state: | 8% |
|---|---|---|---|
| GPA 3.0-3.49: | 34% | Live on campus: | 93% |
| GPA 2.0-2.99: | 57% | | |

**Basis for selection.** Open admission. **Homeschooled:** State high school equivalency certificate required.

**High school preparation.** 16 units recommended. Recommended units include English 3, mathematics 2, social studies 3, science 1 and academic electives 7.

**2008-2009 Annual costs.** Tuition/fees (projected): $8,208. Room/board: $4,954. Books/supplies: $800. Personal expenses: $950.

**2006-2007 Financial aid. Need-based:** 113 full-time freshmen applied for aid; 96 were judged to have need; 96 of these received aid. Average need met was 97%. Average scholarship/grant was $3,900; average loan $3,100. 53% of total undergraduate aid awarded as scholarships/grants, 47% as loans/jobs. **Non-need-based:** Awarded to 286 full-time undergraduates, including 43 freshmen. Scholarships awarded for academics, athletics, religious affiliation. **Additional information:** High school transcript required for scholarship consideration.

**Application procedures. Admission:** No deadline. $25 fee, may be waived for applicants with need. Application may be submitted online. Admission notification on a rolling basis beginning on or about 4/1. **Financial aid:** Priority date 5/31; no closing date. FAFSA required. Applicants notified on a rolling basis starting 5/1; must reply within 2 week(s) of notification.

**Academics. Special study options:** Accelerated study, combined bachelor's/graduate degree, cooperative education, cross-registration, distance learning, double major, dual enrollment of high school students, ESL, honors, internships, liberal arts/career combination, student-designed major, teacher certification program, Washington semester. **Credit/placement by examination:** AP, CLEP, IB, institutional tests. 18 credit hours maximum toward bachelor's degree. **Support services:** Learning center, reduced course load, remedial instruction, study skills assistance, tutoring, writing center.

**Majors. Biology:** General. **Business:** Business admin. **Communications:** Journalism. **Computer sciences:** General. **Education:** General, biology, business, early childhood, elementary, English, history, mathematics, middle, physical, reading, secondary, special. **English:** English lit. **Health:** Premedicine. **History:** General. **Math:** General. **Philosophy/religion:** Religion. **Physical sciences:** Chemistry. **Protective services:** Criminal justice. **Social sciences:** Sociology.

**Most popular majors.** Biology 9%, business/marketing 25%, education 20%, health sciences 9%, interdisciplinary studies 6%, security/protective services 22%.

**Computing on campus.** 359 workstations in dormitories, library, computer center. Dormitories wired for high-speed internet access and linked to campus network. Online library, helpline, repair service, wireless network available.

**Student life. Freshman orientation:** Mandatory. Preregistration for classes offered. **Policies:** Religious services available, regardless of denomination. Religious observance required. **Housing:** Guaranteed on-campus for all undergraduates. Single-sex dorms, special housing for disabled, apartments, substance-free housing available. $100 nonrefundable deposit, deadline 8/1. Single parents housing available on limited basis. **Activities:** Bands, choral groups, music ensembles, student government, student ministers' association, United Campus Christian Fellowship, pre-law club, National Society of Black Accountants, Student National Educational Association, Students in Free Enterprise, Phi Beta Lambda English Club, college church.

**Athletics.** NAIA. **Intercollegiate:** Baseball M, basketball, cheerleading, volleyball W. **Intramural:** Baseball M, basketball, football (non-tackle), football (tackle) M, golf, soccer, softball, swimming, table tennis, tennis, volleyball, weight lifting, wrestling M. **Team name:** Bulldogs.

**Student services.** Campus ministries, career counseling, services for economically disadvantaged, student employment services, financial aid counseling, health services, personal counseling, placement for graduates, veterans' counselor. **Physically disabled:** Services for visually, speech, hearing impaired.

**Contact.** E-mail: felecia_tyiska@jarvis.edu
Phone: (903) 769-5734 Fax: (903) 769-1282
Felecia Tyiska, Director of Admissions, Jarvis Christian College, PO Box 1470, Hawkins, TX 75765-1470

---

## Lamar University

**Beaumont, Texas**
www.lamar.edu

**CB member**
**CB code: 6360**

- Public 4-year university
- Commuter campus in small city
- 8,428 degree-seeking undergraduates: 13% part-time, 60% women, 28% African American, 3% Asian American, 7% Hispanic American, 1% Native American, 1% international
- 1,412 degree-seeking graduate students
- 68% of applicants admitted
- SAT or ACT required
- 36% graduate within 6 years

**General.** Founded in 1923. Regionally accredited. **Degrees:** 1,248 bachelor's, 30 associate awarded; master's, doctoral offered. **Location:** 75 miles from Houston. **Calendar:** Semester, limited summer session. **Full-time faculty:** 359 total; 72% have terminal degrees, 21% minority, 45% women. **Part-time faculty:** 148 total; 20% have terminal degrees, 18% minority, 47% women. **Class size:** 34% < 20, 48% 20-39, 10% 40-49, 8% 50-99, less than 1% >100. **Special facilities:** Texas Hazardous Waste Research Center, Spindletop/Gladys City Museum, Gulf Coast Hazardous Substance Research Center.

**Freshman class profile.** 3,850 applied, 2,634 admitted, 1,443 enrolled.

| Mid 50% test scores | | End year in good standing: | 73% |
|---|---|---|---|
| SAT critical reading: | 400-520 | Return as sophomores: | 64% |
| SAT math: | 400-530 | Out-of-state: | 1% |
| SAT writing: | 400-510 | Live on campus: | 56% |
| ACT composite: | 16-21 | International: | 1% |
| Rank in top quarter: | 39% | Fraternities: | 5% |
| Rank in top tenth: | 14% | Sororities: | 2% |

**Basis for selection.** Admission decision based on high school class rank, SAT scores, and completion of 14 high school units of college preparatory courses. SAT Subject Tests recommended for students with strong academic background. Interview required of students accepted with GED tests and required for early entry. **Homeschooled:** Transcript of courses and grades required. Must submit SAT and meet state TASP testing requirements.

**High school preparation.** 15 units required. Required and recommended units include English 4, mathematics 3, social studies 3, science 2, foreign language 2 and academic electives 3.

**2007-2008 Annual costs.** Tuition/fees: $5,579; $13,919 out-of-state. Room/board: $5,888. Books/supplies: $1,382. Personal expenses: $2,028.

**2007-2008 Financial aid.** All financial aid based on need. 1,039 full-time freshmen applied for aid; 655 were judged to have need; 608 of these received aid. Average need met was 51%. 54% of total undergraduate aid awarded as scholarships/grants, 46% as loans/jobs.

**Application procedures. Admission:** Closing date 8/1. No application fee. Admission notification on a rolling basis. **Financial aid:** Priority date 4/1; no closing date. FAFSA, institutional form required. Applicants notified on a rolling basis starting 4/1; must reply within 2 week(s) of notification.

**Academics. Special study options:** Accelerated study, cooperative education, distance learning, double major, dual enrollment of high school students, ESL, honors, independent study, internships, study abroad, teacher certification program. **Credit/placement by examination:** AP, CLEP, institutional tests. 15 credit hours maximum toward associate degree, 30 toward bachelor's. **Support services:** Learning center, pre-admission summer program, reduced course load, remedial instruction, study skills assistance, tutoring, writing center.

**Majors. Architecture:** Interior. **Biology:** General, marine. **Business:** General, accounting, business admin, finance, human resources, management information systems, managerial economics, marketing, office management, sales/distribution. **Communications:** General, advertising. **Computer sciences:** General. **Conservation:** General, environmental studies. **Education:** Art, Deaf/hearing impaired, early childhood, elementary, family/consumer sciences, health, mathematics, music, physical, school counseling, science, secondary, social studies, special. **Engineering:** General, chemical, civil, electrical, environmental, industrial, mechanical. **Engineering technology:** Industrial, industrial management. **English:** English lit, speech/rhetoric. **Family/consumer sciences:** General, clothing/textiles, family/community services, food/nutrition. **Foreign languages:** French, Spanish. **Health:** Audiology/speech pathology, clinical lab science, nursing (RN). **History:** General. **Liberal arts:** Arts/sciences. **Math:** General, applied. **Parks/recreation:** Health/fitness. **Physical sciences:** Chemistry, geology, physics, planetary. **Protective services:** Criminal justice. **Psychology:** General. **Public administration:** Social work. **Social sciences:** Economics, political science, sociology. **Visual/performing arts:** Art, commercial/advertising art, dance, dramatic, voice/opera.

**Most popular majors.** Business/marketing 19%, engineering/engineering technologies 7%, health sciences 11%, interdisciplinary studies 16%, liberal arts 11%.

**Computing on campus.** 644 workstations in dormitories, library, computer center, student center. Dormitories wired for high-speed internet access and linked to campus network. Commuter students can connect to campus network. Online course registration, online library, helpline, repair service, student web hosting, wireless network available.

**Student life. Freshman orientation:** Available, $10 fee. Preregistration for classes offered. One-day program available June-August. **Housing:** Guaranteed on-campus for freshmen. Coed dorms, single-sex dorms, special housing for disabled, substance-free housing available. $100 deposit, deadline 8/1. **Activities:** Bands, choral groups, dance, drama, film society, literary magazine, music ensembles, musical theater, opera, radio station, student government, student newspaper, symphony orchestra, TV station, Catholic student union, Church of Latter-day Saints, Episcopal Center, Church of Christ Student Center, Wesley Foundation, Vietnamese student organization.

**Athletics.** NCAA. **Intercollegiate:** Baseball M, basketball, cross-country, golf, soccer W, tennis, track and field, volleyball W. **Intramural:** Badminton, basketball, cross-country, racquetball, soccer, softball, swimming, table tennis, tennis, track and field, volleyball, weight lifting. **Team name:** Cardinals.

**Student services.** Adult student services, career counseling, student employment services, health services, on-campus daycare, personal counseling, placement for graduates, veterans' counselor. **Physically disabled:** Services for visually, speech, hearing impaired.

**Contact.** E-mail: admissions@hal.lamar.edu
Phone: (409) 880-8888 Fax: (409) 880-8463
James Rush, Director of Academic Services, Lamar University, Box 10009, Beaumont, TX 77705

## LeTourneau University
**Longview, Texas**
www.letu.edu                                                    CB code: 6365

- Private 4-year university affiliated with nondenominational tradition
- Residential campus in small city
- 3,552 degree-seeking undergraduates: 12% part-time, 58% women, 22% African American, 2% Asian American, 8% Hispanic American, 1% international
- 324 degree-seeking graduate students
- 70% of applicants admitted
- SAT or ACT with writing, application essay required
- 52% graduate within 6 years

**General.** Founded in 1946. Regionally accredited. Centers in Tyler, Dallas, Houston, Austin, and Bedford. **Degrees:** 584 bachelor's, 4 associate awarded; master's offered. **Location:** 120 miles from Dallas, 60 miles from Shreveport, Louisiana. **Calendar:** Semester, limited summer session. **Full-time faculty:** 74 total; 73% have terminal degrees, 11% minority, 19% women. **Part-time faculty:** 287 total; 42% have terminal degrees, 13% minority, 45% women. **Class size:** 83% < 20, 16% 20-39, 1% 40-49, less than 1% 50-99. **Special facilities:** Microprocessor and robotics laboratory, CAD laboratory, scanning electronic microscope, dynamic simulation laboratory, fleet of nine up-to-date airplanes, biomedical engineering laboratory with motion analysis system.

**Freshman class profile.** 938 applied, 658 admitted, 302 enrolled.

| Mid 50% test scores | | | |
|---|---|---|---|
| SAT critical reading: | 510-640 | GPA 2.0-2.99: | 8% |
| SAT math: | 520-650 | Rank in top quarter: | 58% |
| SAT writing: | 490-610 | Rank in top tenth: | 34% |
| ACT composite: | 22-28 | Return as sophomores: | 78% |
| GPA 3.50 or higher: | 61% | Out-of-state: | 52% |
| GPA 3.0-3.49: | 31% | Live on campus: | 89% |
| | | International: | 1% |

**Basis for selection.** Applicants should rank in top half of high school graduating class, have minimum ACT of 20 or minimum SAT of 950 (exclusive of Writing), and GPA of 2.5. Interview recommended. **Home-schooled:** Require SAT or ACT, transcript; recommend GED and detailed summary of curriculum used.

**High school preparation.** 16 units required. Required and recommended units include English 4, mathematics 3, social studies 2, history 1, science 3 (laboratory 3), foreign language 1 and academic electives 2. 4 math (including trigonometry) recommended for engineering applicants.

**2007-2008 Annual costs.** Tuition/fees: $17,910. Tuition for 1-6 hours is $322 per credit, for 7-11 hours is $707 per credit. Room/board: $6,950. Books/supplies: $1,280. Personal expenses: $1,032.

**Financial aid. Non-need-based:** Scholarships awarded for academics, leadership.

**Application procedures. Admission:** Priority date 12/31; deadline 8/1. $25 fee, may be waived for applicants with need. Application may be submitted online. Admission notification on a rolling basis beginning on or about 8/1. Must reply by 5/1. **Financial aid:** Priority date 2/15; no closing date. FAFSA required. Applicants notified on a rolling basis starting 3/1; must reply within 3 week(s) of notification.

**Academics.** Peer advisers, student resource center, CARE committee, freshman year experience course available. **Special study options:** Accelerated study, cooperative education, distance learning, double major, dual enrollment of high school students, honors, independent study, internships, study abroad, teacher certification program, weekend college. **Credit/placement by examination:** AP, CLEP, IB, SAT, ACT, institutional tests. Credit must be established by end of student's first year at school. **Support services:** Reduced course load, remedial instruction, tutoring.

**Majors. Biology:** General. **Business:** General, accounting, business admin, finance, human resources, international, management information systems, marketing, operations. **Computer sciences:** General, computer science, information systems. **Education:** Business, computer, elementary, English, history, mathematics, middle, multi-level teacher, physical, science, secondary, social studies. **Engineering:** General, biomedical, computer, electrical, mechanical. **Engineering technology:** Aerospace, computer, electrical, mechanical. **English:** English lit. **Health:** Clinical lab science, predental, premedicine, prepharmacy, preveterinary. **History:** General. **Interdisciplinary:** Math/computer science. **Legal studies:** Prelaw. **Math:** General. **Mechanic/repair:** Aircraft, aircraft powerplant. **Parks/recreation:** Exercise sciences, sports admin. **Physical sciences:** Chemistry, physical chemistry. **Psychology:** General. **Social sciences:** Political science. **Theology:** Bible. **Transportation:** Airline/commercial pilot, aviation.

**Most popular majors.** Business/marketing 15%, education 13%, engineering/engineering technologies 36%, history 6%, psychology 6%.

**Computing on campus.** 200 workstations in library, computer center. Dormitories wired for high-speed internet access and linked to campus network. Commuter students can connect to campus network. Online library, helpline, wireless network available.

**Student life. Freshman orientation:** Mandatory, $65 fee. Preregistration for classes offered. 3-day event for students and parents held before classes start. **Policies:** Religious observance required. **Housing:** Guaranteed on-campus for all undergraduates. Single-sex dorms, special housing for disabled, apartments available. $100 deposit, deadline 5/1. Residential societies available. **Activities:** Jazz band, choral groups, drama, music ensembles, student government, student newspaper, international student organization, Fellowship of Christian Athletes, Student Foundation, Habitat for Humanity, summer missions, married student fellowship, student ministries, 2 CARE Council.

**Athletics.** NCAA, NCCAA. **Intercollegiate:** Baseball M, basketball, golf, soccer, softball W, tennis, volleyball W. **Intramural:** Badminton, basketball, cross-country, football (non-tackle), golf, racquetball, soccer, softball, swimming, table tennis, tennis, volleyball. **Team name:** YellowJackets.

**Student services.** Campus ministries, career counseling, student employment services, financial aid counseling, health services, personal counseling, placement for graduates, veterans' counselor. **Physically disabled:** Services for visually, speech, hearing impaired.

**Contact.** E-mail: admissions@letu.edu
Phone: (903) 233-4300 Toll-free number: (800) 759-8811
Fax: (903) 233-4301
James Townsend, Director of Admissions, LeTourneau University, PO Box 7001, Longview, TX 75607-7001

## Lubbock Christian University
**Lubbock, Texas**
www.lcu.edu                                                     CB code: 6378

- Private 4-year university and liberal arts college affiliated with Church of Christ
- Commuter campus in small city
- 1,718 degree-seeking undergraduates: 19% part-time, 57% women, 5% African American, 1% Asian American, 16% Hispanic American, 1% international
- 242 degree-seeking graduate students
- 73% of applicants admitted
- SAT or ACT (ACT writing recommended) required
- 41% graduate within 6 years

**General.** Founded in 1957. Regionally accredited. **Degrees:** 400 bachelor's, 1 associate awarded; master's, first professional offered. **ROTC:** Army. **Location:** 300 miles from Dallas, 325 miles from Albuquerque, New Mexico. **Calendar:** Semester, limited summer session. **Full-time faculty:** 85 total; 62% have terminal degrees, 5% minority, 41% women. **Part-time faculty:**

85 total; 29% have terminal degrees, 11% minority, 46% women. **Class size:** 61% < 20, 33% 20-39, 4% 40-49, 2% 50-99, less than 1% >100. **Special facilities:** 2 farms totaling 450 acres.

**Freshman class profile.** 948 applied, 692 admitted, 305 enrolled.

| Mid 50% test scores | | | |
|---|---|---|---|
| SAT critical reading: | 440-550 | Rank in top quarter: | 40% |
| SAT math: | 450-530 | Rank in top tenth: | 19% |
| SAT writing: | 430-540 | Return as sophomores: | 65% |
| ACT composite: | 17-24 | Out-of-state: | 13% |
| GPA 3.50 or higher: | 50% | Live on campus: | 85% |
| GPA 3.0-3.49: | 38% | Fraternities: | 42% |
| GPA 2.0-2.99: | 10% | Sororities: | 44% |

**Basis for selection.** Standardized test scores and secondary academic record considered. **Homeschooled:** Transcript of courses and grades required. **Learning Disabled:** Applicants accepted for admission who claim disabilities must provide evidence of disabilities to Disability Coordinator.

**High school preparation.** 23 units recommended. Recommended units include English 4, mathematics 3, social studies 2, history 2, science 3 (laboratory 2), foreign language 2, computer science 1 and academic electives 4.

**2007-2008 Annual costs.** Tuition/fees: $14,290. Room/board: $4,750. Books/supplies: $1,032. Personal expenses: $2,008.

**2006-2007 Financial aid. Need-based:** 234 full-time freshmen applied for aid; 200 were judged to have need; 200 of these received aid. Average need met was 74%. Average scholarship/grant was $8,234; average loan $2,941. 43% of total undergraduate aid awarded as scholarships/grants, 57% as loans/jobs. **Non-need-based:** Awarded to 346 full-time undergraduates, including 87 freshmen. Scholarships awarded for academics, athletics, job skills, leadership, music/drama.

**Application procedures. Admission:** Closing date 8/15 (receipt date). $25 fee, may be waived for applicants with need. Application may be submitted online. Admission notification on a rolling basis. **Financial aid:** Priority date 6/1; no closing date. FAFSA, institutional form required. Applicants notified on a rolling basis starting 3/1.

**Academics.** Computer use integrated into the curriculum. **Special study options:** Distance learning, double major, honors, internships, liberal arts/career combination, student-designed major, study abroad, teacher certification program. **Credit/placement by examination:** AP, CLEP, IB, SAT, ACT, institutional tests. 45 credit hours maximum toward bachelor's degree. **Support services:** Learning center, pre-admission summer program, reduced course load, remedial instruction, study skills assistance, tutoring.

**Majors. Agriculture:** General, animal sciences, business, plant sciences. **Biology:** General. **Business:** Accounting, business admin, finance, management information systems, marketing. **Communications:** General, organizational. **Education:** Agricultural, art, biology, business, chemistry, computer, early childhood, elementary, English, history, mathematics, multilevel teacher, music, physical, science, secondary, social studies, Spanish, special, speech. **Engineering:** General. **Family/consumer sciences:** Work/family studies. **Health:** Athletic training, nursing (RN), predental, premedicine, prenursing, prepharmacy, preveterinary. **Liberal arts:** Humanities. **Math:** General. **Parks/recreation:** Exercise sciences, health/fitness, sports admin. **Physical sciences:** Chemistry. **Protective services:** Law enforcement admin. **Psychology:** General. **Public administration:** Social work. **Theology:** Bible, missionary, sacred music, youth ministry. **Visual/performing arts:** Design.

**Most popular majors.** Business/marketing 28%, education 15%, health sciences 11%, parks/recreation 6%, public administration/social services 8%.

**Computing on campus.** 235 workstations in dormitories, library, computer center, student center. Dormitories wired for high-speed internet access and linked to campus network. Commuter students can connect to campus network. Online course registration, online library, helpline, repair service, wireless network available.

**Student life. Freshman orientation:** Available, $145 fee. Preregistration for classes offered. Week-long orientation held the week before fall semester begins. **Policies:** Chapel attendance required for full-time students age 24 or under. Religious observance required. **Housing:** Guaranteed on-campus for freshmen. Single-sex dorms, special housing for disabled, apartments, substance-free housing available. $90 nonrefundable deposit, deadline 8/15. **Activities:** Campus ministries, choral groups, drama, international student organizations, music ensembles, musical theater, student government, student newspaper, Best Friends, Missions Club, Fellowship of Christian Athletes, Students in Free Enterprise, Social Work Outreach Association, social clubs, Organization of Latin American Students.

**Athletics.** NAIA. **Intercollegiate:** Baseball M, basketball, golf, volleyball W. **Intramural:** Badminton, basketball, bowling, football (non-tackle), soccer, softball, table tennis, tennis, volleyball. **Team name:** Chaparrals.

**Student services.** Adult student services, alcohol/substance abuse counseling, campus ministries, career counseling, student employment services, financial aid counseling, health services, personal counseling, placement for graduates, veterans' counselor.

**Contact.** E-mail: admissions@lcu.edu
Phone: (806) 720-7151 Toll-free number: (800) 933-7601 ext. 7151
Fax: (806) 720-7162
Stan Scott, Director of Admissions, Lubbock Christian University, 5601 19th Street, Lubbock, TX 79407

---

## McMurry University
### Abilene, Texas
www.mcm.edu

CB member
CB code: 6402

- Private 4-year university and liberal arts college affiliated with United Methodist Church
- Residential campus in small city
- 1,365 degree-seeking undergraduates: 13% part-time, 50% women, 14% African American, 1% Asian American, 16% Hispanic American, 1% Native American, 1% international
- 53% of applicants admitted
- SAT or ACT (ACT writing recommended), application essay required
- 43% graduate within 6 years; 22% enter graduate study

**General.** Founded in 1923. Regionally accredited. Three-week May term available; additional off-campus extension at Dyess Air Force Base; part of 3-member consortium providing collegiate nursing education in Texas. **Degrees:** 251 bachelor's awarded. **Location:** 155 miles from Fort Worth, 220 miles from Austin. **Calendar:** Semester, extensive summer session. **Full-time faculty:** 75 total; 72% have terminal degrees, 33% women. **Part-time faculty:** 54 total; 20% have terminal degrees, 56% women. **Class size:** 60% < 20, 38% 20-39, less than 1% 40-49, 2% 50-99. **Special facilities:** Buffalo Gap historical village.

**Freshman class profile.** 1,537 applied, 811 admitted, 311 enrolled.

| Mid 50% test scores | | | |
|---|---|---|---|
| SAT critical reading: | 420-530 | Rank in top quarter: | 37% |
| SAT math: | 440-550 | Rank in top tenth: | 14% |
| ACT composite: | 17-22 | End year in good standing: | 81% |
| GPA 3.50 or higher: | 48% | Return as sophomores: | 61% |
| GPA 3.0-3.49: | 32% | Out-of-state: | 3% |
| GPA 2.0-2.99: | 20% | Live on campus: | 83% |
| | | International: | 2% |

**Basis for selection.** Applicants evaluated on basis of ACT or SAT scores, high school rank and GPA, academic preparation, and extracurricular activities; character considered. Interview recommended for all; audition required for music, theater programs; portfolio required for art; interview required for admission to Honors Program. **Learning Disabled:** Appropriate documentation required for students seeking special accommodations.

**High school preparation.** 14 units required; 16 recommended. Required and recommended units include English 4, mathematics 3, social studies 4, science 3 and foreign language 2. 2 units of foreign language strongly recommended; those who enroll with fewer than 2 units required to take 8 hours of foreign language.

**2008-2009 Annual costs.** Tuition/fees (projected): $17,950. Room/board: $6,620. Books/supplies: $1,200. Personal expenses: $1,800.

**2007-2008 Financial aid. Need-based:** 291 full-time freshmen applied for aid; 258 were judged to have need; 258 of these received aid. Average need met was 93%. Average scholarship/grant was $10,788; average loan $3,723. 68% of total undergraduate aid awarded as scholarships/grants, 32% as loans/jobs. **Non-need-based:** Awarded to 680 full-time undergraduates, including 197 freshmen. Scholarships awarded for academics, alumni affiliation, art, music/drama, religious affiliation, ROTC.

**Application procedures. Admission:** Priority date 3/15; deadline 8/15 (receipt date). $20 fee, may be waived for applicants with need. Application may be submitted online. Admission notification on a rolling basis beginning on or about 9/1. Must reply by May 1 or within 2 week(s) if notified thereafter. **Financial aid:** Priority date 3/15; no closing date. FAFSA required. Applicants notified on a rolling basis starting 2/1; must reply within 3 week(s) of notification.

**Academics.** Students receive credit for both nontraditional and traditional courses on and off campus during 3-week May term. Opportunities for bachelor's degree after early admission to dental, medical, or veterinary school.

**Special study options:** Accelerated study, combined bachelor's/graduate degree, cross-registration, double major, dual enrollment of high school students, honors, independent study, internships, liberal arts/career combination, study abroad, teacher certification program. Engineering with Texas A&M University. **Credit/placement by examination:** AP, CLEP, IB, SAT, ACT, institutional tests. 45 credit hours maximum toward bachelor's degree. Special examinations may be given, upon approval of necessary department, for credit in areas not covered by AP or CLEP. **Support services:** Learning center, reduced course load, remedial instruction, study skills assistance, tutoring, writing center.

**Majors.** **Biology:** General, biochemistry. **Business:** General, accounting, business admin, finance, management information systems, marketing. **Computer sciences:** General. **Education:** Art, early childhood, elementary, middle, physical, secondary. **English:** Creative writing, English lit. **Foreign languages:** Spanish. **Health:** Athletic training, nursing (RN). **History:** General. **Math:** General. **Philosophy/religion:** Religion. **Physical sciences:** Chemistry, physics. **Psychology:** General. **Social sciences:** Political science, sociology. **Visual/performing arts:** Dramatic, graphic design, studio arts.

**Most popular majors.** Business/marketing 20%, education 24%, health sciences 13%, social sciences 9%, visual/performing arts 6%.

**Computing on campus.** PC or laptop required. 236 workstations in library, computer center, student center. Dormitories wired for high-speed internet access and linked to campus network. Commuter students can connect to campus network. Online library, helpline, student web hosting, wireless network available.

**Student life. Freshman orientation:** Available, $150 fee. Preregistration for classes offered. Summer weekend orientation plus 4-day orientation before first week of classes. **Housing:** Guaranteed on-campus for all undergraduates. Single-sex dorms, special housing for disabled, apartments, substance-free housing available. $150 partly refundable deposit, deadline 5/1. **Activities:** Bands, choral groups, drama, literary magazine, music ensembles, musical theater, student government, student newspaper, Alpha Phi Omega, Fellowship of Christian Athletes, Religious Life, Servant Leadership, Students in Free Enterprise, West Texas Model United Nations, Kappa Delta Sigma, Association of Information Technology Professionals.

**Athletics.** NCAA. **Intercollegiate:** Baseball M, basketball, cheerleading, cross-country, diving, football (tackle) M, golf, soccer, swimming, tennis, track and field, volleyball W. **Intramural:** Basketball, football (non-tackle), golf, racquetball, soccer, softball, tennis, volleyball.

**Student services.** Alcohol/substance abuse counseling, campus ministries, career counseling, student employment services, financial aid counseling, health services, personal counseling, placement for graduates, veterans' counselor.

**Contact.** E-mail: admissions@mcm.edu
Phone: (325) 793-4700 Toll-free number: (800) 460-2392
Fax: (325) 793-4701
Scott Smiley, Director of Admission, McMurry University, South 14th and Sayles Boulevard, Abilene, TX 79697-0001

---

## Midwestern State University
Wichita Falls, Texas

CB member
CB code: 6408

www.mwsu.edu

- Public 4-year university and liberal arts college
- Commuter campus in small city
- 5,348 degree-seeking undergraduates: 27% part-time, 58% women, 13% African American, 4% Asian American, 9% Hispanic American, 1% Native American, 5% international
- 592 degree-seeking graduate students
- 69% of applicants admitted
- SAT or ACT with writing required

**General.** Founded in 1922. Regionally accredited. **Degrees:** 958 bachelor's, 49 associate awarded; master's offered. **ROTC:** Air Force. **Location:** 130 miles from Dallas-Fort Worth. **Calendar:** Semester, extensive summer session. **Full-time faculty:** 209 total; 68% have terminal degrees, 11% minority, 47% women. **Part-time faculty:** 100 total; 28% have terminal degrees, 2% minority, 57% women. **Class size:** 33% < 20, 49% 20-39, 7% 40-49, 11% 50-99, less than 1% >100. **Special facilities:** Kurzweil reading machine for the blind, greenhouse, 2 biologic study properties.

**Freshman class profile.** 1,538 applied, 1,054 admitted, 762 enrolled.

| Mid 50% test scores | | | |
|---|---|---|---|
| SAT critical reading: | 450-550 | Rank in top quarter: | 38% |
| SAT math: | 460-560 | Rank in top tenth: | 12% |
| SAT writing: | 440-530 | Return as sophomores: | 72% |
| ACT composite: | 19-23 | Out-of-state: | 3% |
| GPA 3.50 or higher: | 38% | Live on campus: | 50% |
| GPA 3.0-3.49: | 36% | International: | 1% |
| GPA 2.0-2.99: | 25% | Fraternities: | 13% |
| | | Sororities: | 14% |

**Basis for selection.** For unconditional admission, students must graduate from accredited high school, meet requirements, submit official transcripts and ACT/SAT scores. Entrance exams determined by class rank. Texas public universities require THEA test score on file prior to enrollment unless student exempt. Audition required for applied music program.

**High school preparation.** 15 units required. Required units include English 4, mathematics 3, science 2 and academic electives 6.

**2007-2008 Annual costs.** Tuition/fees: $5,376; $6,276 out-of-state. Room/board: $5,350. Books/supplies: $1,140. Personal expenses: $1,326.

**2007-2008 Financial aid. Need-based:** Average need met was 73%. Average scholarship/grant was $5,058; average loan $3,349. 37% of total undergraduate aid awarded as scholarships/grants, 63% as loans/jobs. **Non-need-based:** Scholarships awarded for academics, alumni affiliation, art, athletics, leadership, music/drama. **Additional information:** Employees offered educational incentive plan in which tuition reimbursed provided employee meets stated criteria. Additionally, dependents and children of faculty and staff may receive scholarship to defer local tuition and fees.

**Application procedures. Admission:** Priority date 7/1; deadline 8/7 (receipt date). $25 fee. Application may be submitted online. Admission notification on a rolling basis beginning on or about 9/1. **Financial aid:** Priority date 5/1; no closing date. FAFSA, institutional form required. Applicants notified on a rolling basis starting 4/1; must reply within 4 week(s) of notification.

**Academics. Special study options:** Combined bachelor's/graduate degree, distance learning, double major, dual enrollment of high school students, ESL; honors, independent study, internships, liberal arts/career combination, study abroad, teacher certification program. Study abroad in England, France, Spain, and Mexico. **Credit/placement by examination:** AP, CLEP, IB, SAT, ACT, institutional tests. 26 credit hours maximum toward associate degree, 60 toward bachelor's. **Support services:** Learning center, reduced course load, remedial instruction, study skills assistance, tutoring, writing center.

**Majors. Biology:** General. **Business:** General, accounting, business admin, finance, international, management information systems, marketing. **Communications:** Media studies. **Computer sciences:** General. **Conservation:** Environmental science. **Education:** Bilingual, early childhood, English. **Engineering:** General, mechanical. **Engineering technology:** Manufacturing. **English:** English lit. **Foreign languages:** Spanish. **Health:** Athletic training, clinical lab science, dental hygiene, nursing (RN), predental, premedicine, prepharmacy, preveterinary, radiologic technology/medical imaging, respiratory therapy technology. **History:** General. **Interdisciplinary:** Global studies. **Legal studies:** Prelaw. **Liberal arts:** Humanities. **Math:** General. **Parks/recreation:** Exercise sciences, facilities management, health/fitness. **Physical sciences:** General, chemistry, geology, physics. **Protective services:** Criminal justice. **Psychology:** General. **Public administration:** Social work. **Social sciences:** Economics, political science, sociology. **Visual/performing arts:** Art, dramatic, studio arts.

**Most popular majors.** Business/marketing 18%, education 8%, health sciences 21%, interdisciplinary studies 17%.

**Computing on campus.** 429 workstations in dormitories, library, computer center, student center. Dormitories wired for high-speed internet access and linked to campus network. Commuter students can connect to campus network. Online course registration, online library, wireless network available.

**Student life. Freshman orientation:** Mandatory. Preregistration for classes offered. Parents and family welcome to attend orientation events. **Housing:** Guaranteed on-campus for freshmen. Coed dorms, single-sex dorms, special housing for disabled, apartments, substance-free housing available. $100 fully refundable deposit. Cooperative housing units for honors students and biology students. **Activities:** Bands, campus ministries, choral groups, dance, drama, film society, international student organizations, literary magazine, music ensembles, student government, student newspaper, TV station, Methodist student foundation, Baptist student center, Student Ambassadors, black student union, organization of Hispanic students, University Democrats, College Republicans, Amnesty International.

**Athletics.** NCAA. **Intercollegiate:** Basketball, cross-country W, football (tackle) M, rowing (crew) W, soccer, softball W, tennis, volleyball W. **Intramural:** Archery, badminton, basketball, bowling, football (non-tackle), football (tackle) M, golf, soccer, softball, table tennis, tennis, volleyball. **Team name:** Mustangs.

**Student services.** Alcohol/substance abuse counseling, career counseling, student employment services, financial aid counseling, health services, personal counseling, placement for graduates, veterans' counselor. **Physically disabled:** Services for visually, speech, hearing impaired.

**Contact.** E-mail: admissions@mwsu.edu
Phone: (940) 397-4334 Toll-free number: (800) 842-1922
Fax: (940) 397-4672
Barbara Merkle, Director of Admissions, Midwestern State University, 3410 Taft Boulevard, Wichita Falls, TX 76308-2099

## Northwood University: Texas
**Cedar Hill, Texas**
www.northwood.edu                    **CB code: 6499**

- Private 4-year university and business college
- Residential campus in large town
- 526 degree-seeking undergraduates: 5% part-time, 48% women, 15% African American, 4% Asian American, 30% Hispanic American, 1% Native American, 6% international
- 60% of applicants admitted
- SAT or ACT (ACT writing optional), application essay required
- 31% graduate within 6 years

**General.** Founded in 1966. Regionally accredited. Specialty university offering only business degrees in professional management; 3 residential campuses in Michigan, Florida, and Texas; 48 program centers; library center in Maine. **Degrees:** 76 bachelor's, 61 associate awarded. **Location:** 18 miles from Dallas, 28 miles from Fort Worth. **Calendar:** Quarter, limited summer session. **Full-time faculty:** 24 total; 21% have terminal degrees, 12% minority, 29% women. **Class size:** 58% < 20, 41% 20-39, 2% 40-49.

**Freshman class profile.** 581 applied, 350 admitted, 124 enrolled.

| Mid 50% test scores | | | |
|---|---|---|---|
| SAT critical reading: | 410-500 | Rank in top quarter: | 25% |
| SAT math: | 410-520 | Rank in top tenth: | 7% |
| SAT writing: | 380-500 | End year in good standing: | 70% |
| ACT composite: | 18-23 | Return as sophomores: | 78% |
| GPA 3.50 or higher: | 24% | Out-of-state: | 5% |
| GPA 3.0-3.49: | 52% | Live on campus: | 57% |
| GPA 2.0-2.99: | 24% | International: | 3% |

**Basis for selection.** Minimum GPA of 2.0 and strong interest in business or related field. Test scores considered. Students with lower GPA possibly admitted on probation. Interview recommended. **Homeschooled:** Transcript of courses and grades required.

**High school preparation.** 17 units recommended. Recommended units include English 4, mathematics 3, social studies 3, science 3 (laboratory 2), foreign language 1 and computer science 1.

**2007-2008 Annual costs.** Tuition/fees: $16,455. Room/board: $6,888. Books/supplies: $1,404. Personal expenses: $1,395.

**2007-2008 Financial aid. Need-based:** 104 full-time freshmen applied for aid; 88 were judged to have need; 88 of these received aid. Average need met was 59%. Average scholarship/grant was $5,345; average loan $3,259. 61% of total undergraduate aid awarded as scholarships/grants, 39% as loans/jobs. **Non-need-based:** Awarded to 214 full-time undergraduates, including 65 freshmen. Scholarships awarded for academics, alumni affiliation, athletics, leadership, minority status, state residency.

**Application procedures. Admission:** No deadline. $25 fee, may be waived for applicants with need. Application may be submitted online. Admission notification on a rolling basis. **Financial aid:** No deadline. FAFSA required. Applicants notified on a rolling basis starting 3/1.

**Academics. Special study options:** Distance learning, double major, dual enrollment of high school students, honors, independent study, internships, student-designed major, study abroad. **Credit/placement by examination:** AP, CLEP, IB, SAT, ACT, institutional tests. 12 credit hours maximum toward associate degree, 12 toward bachelor's. **Support services:** Learning center, reduced course load, remedial instruction, study skills assistance, tutoring, writing center.

**Majors. Business:** Accounting, banking/financial services, business admin, entrepreneurial studies, fashion, hotel/motel admin, international, management information systems, marketing, vehicle parts marketing. **Communications:** Advertising. **Computer sciences:** General. **Parks/recreation:** Sports admin.

**Most popular majors.** Business/marketing 75%, communications/journalism 8%, parks/recreation 14%.

**Computing on campus.** 50 workstations in library, computer center. Dormitories wired for high-speed internet access and linked to campus network. Commuter students can connect to campus network. Online course registration, online library, helpline, student web hosting, wireless network available.

**Student life. Freshman orientation:** Mandatory, $125 fee. Preregistration for classes offered. 5 days in early September. **Housing:** Guaranteed on-campus for freshmen. Single-sex dorms, apartments, substance-free housing available. $100 fully refundable deposit, deadline 8/1. **Activities:** Choral groups, dance, drama, literary magazine, student government, student newspaper, Christian Fellowship.

**Athletics.** NAIA. **Intercollegiate:** Baseball M, cross-country, golf, soccer, softball W, track and field. **Intramural:** Basketball, volleyball. **Team name:** Knights.

**Student services.** Adult student services, career counseling, student employment services, financial aid counseling, health services, personal counseling, placement for graduates.

**Contact.** E-mail: txadmit@northwood.edu
Phone: (972) 293-5400 Toll-free number: (800) 927-9663
Fax: (972) 291-3824
Sylvia Correa, Director of Admissions, Northwood University: Texas, 1114 West FM 1382, Cedar Hill, TX 75104

## Our Lady of the Lake University of San Antonio
**San Antonio, Texas**                    **CB member**
www.ollusa.edu                    **CB code: 6550**

- Private 4-year university affiliated with Roman Catholic Church
- Commuter campus in very large city
- 1,528 degree-seeking undergraduates: 28% part-time, 76% women, 7% African American, 1% Asian American, 74% Hispanic American, 1% international
- 1,080 degree-seeking graduate students
- 49% of applicants admitted
- SAT or ACT (ACT writing optional) required
- 35% graduate within 6 years

**General.** Founded in 1895. Regionally accredited. **Degrees:** 338 bachelor's awarded; master's, doctoral offered. **ROTC:** Army, Air Force. **Location:** 4 miles from downtown, 80 miles from Austin. **Calendar:** Semester, limited summer session. **Full-time faculty:** 112 total; 39% minority, 55% women. **Part-time faculty:** 142 total; 40% minority, 57% women. **Class size:** 77% < 20, 22% 20-39, less than 1% 40-49. **Special facilities:** International center, international folk culture center, speech and hearing clinic, community counseling center, elementary school, child development center, center for social work research, center for women in church and society.

**Freshman class profile.** 2,572 applied, 1,264 admitted, 285 enrolled.

| Mid 50% test scores | | | |
|---|---|---|---|
| | | GPA 2.0-2.99: | 19% |
| SAT critical reading: | 420-500 | Rank in top quarter: | 51% |
| SAT math: | 410-500 | Rank in top tenth: | 21% |
| ACT composite: | 17-21 | Return as sophomores: | 55% |
| GPA 3.50 or higher: | 37% | Out-of-state: | 2% |
| GPA 3.0-3.49: | 44% | Live on campus: | 69% |

**Basis for selection.** High school academic record and test scores important. **Homeschooled:** Transcript of courses and grades required.

**High school preparation.** 16 units required. Required and recommended units include English 4, mathematics 2-3, social studies 3, science 2 (laboratory 2), foreign language 3 and academic electives 3.

**2007-2008 Annual costs.** Tuition/fees: $19,116. Room/board: $5,838. Books/supplies: $1,000. Personal expenses: $1,850.

**Financial aid. Non-need-based:** Scholarships awarded for academics, alumni affiliation, art, music/drama.

**Application procedures. Admission:** Priority date 5/1; deadline 7/15 (receipt date). $25 fee, may be waived for applicants with need. Application may be submitted online. Admission notification on a rolling basis. **Financial aid:** Priority date 2/28; no closing date. FAFSA required. Applicants notified on a rolling basis starting 4/1; must reply within 2 week(s) of notification.

**Academics. Special study options:** Combined bachelor's/graduate degree, cooperative education, cross-registration, distance learning, double major, dual enrollment of high school students, ESL, honors, independent study, internships, liberal arts/career combination, study abroad, teacher certification program, weekend college. Service learning. **Credit/placement by examination:** AP, CLEP, IB, institutional tests. No limit to number of credit hours that may be awarded through CLEP or that may be counted towards bachelor's degree. **Support services:** Learning center, pre-admission summer program, reduced course load, remedial instruction, study skills assistance, tutoring.

**Majors. Biology:** General. **Business:** Accounting, business admin, human resources, marketing, nonprofit/public. **Communications:** General, broadcast journalism, journalism, public relations. **Computer sciences:** General. **Education:** Kindergarten/preschool, special, speech impaired. **English:** English lit. **Family/consumer sciences:** Business. **Foreign languages:** Spanish. **Health:** Speech pathology. **History:** General. **Interdisciplinary:** Natural sciences. **Liberal arts:** Arts/sciences. **Math:** General. **Philosophy/religion:** Philosophy, religion. **Physical sciences:** Chemistry. **Protective services:** Criminal justice. **Psychology:** General. **Public administration:** Social work. **Social sciences:** General, political science, sociology. **Visual/performing arts:** Art, dramatic.

**Most popular majors.** Biology 8%, business/marketing 20%, education 12%, liberal arts 8%, psychology 12%, public administration/social services 11%, social sciences 6%.

**Computing on campus.** 208 workstations in dormitories, library, computer center, student center. Dormitories wired for high-speed internet access and linked to campus network. Commuter students can connect to campus network. Online course registration, helpline, repair service, wireless network available.

**Student life. Freshman orientation:** Mandatory, $50 fee. Preregistration for classes offered. Overnight program, 4 times during the spring and summer. Familiarity with faculty, staff, campus, and assessment testing. Parent participation encouraged. **Housing:** Guaranteed on-campus for freshmen. Coed dorms, single-sex dorms, special housing for disabled, substance-free housing available. $100 deposit, deadline 8/1. **Activities:** Jazz band, choral groups, dance, drama, music ensembles, musical theater, student government, student newspaper, symphony orchestra, TV station, religious organizations, black and Hispanic clubs, service clubs.

**Athletics. Intercollegiate:** Soccer M, volleyball W. **Intramural:** Basketball, football (non-tackle), golf, racquetball, soccer W, softball, swimming, tennis, volleyball M. **Team name:** Saints.

**Student services.** Adult student services, alcohol/substance abuse counseling, campus ministries, career counseling, student employment services, financial aid counseling, health services, personal counseling, placement for graduates, veterans' counselor, women's services. **Physically disabled:** Services for visually, speech, hearing impaired.

**Contact.** E-mail: admission@lake.ollusa.edu
Phone: (210) 434-6711 ext. 2314 Toll-free number: (800) 436-6558
Fax: (210) 431-4036
Michael Boatner, Dean of Admissions, Our Lady of the Lake University of San Antonio, 411 Southwest 24th Street, San Antonio, TX 78207-4689

## Paul Quinn College
**Dallas, Texas**
www.pqc.edu                                      **CB code: 6577**

- Private 4-year liberal arts college affiliated with African Methodist Episcopal Church
- Residential campus in very large city

**General.** Founded in 1872. Regionally accredited. **Location:** 12 miles from Dallas. **Calendar:** Semester.

**Annual costs/financial aid.** Tuition/fees (2007-2008): $8,930. Room/board: $4,800. Books/supplies: $1,000. Personal expenses: $500.

**Contact.** Phone: (214) 302-3575
Director of Admissions, 3837 Simpson Stuart Road, Dallas, TX 75241

## Prairie View A&M University
**Prairie View, Texas**                          **CB member**
www.pvamu.edu                                    **CB code: 6580**

- Public 4-year university
- Commuter campus in small town
- 6,118 degree-seeking undergraduates
- 2,264 graduate students
- 40% of applicants admitted
- SAT or ACT (ACT writing optional) required
- 39% graduate within 6 years

**General.** Founded in 1876. Regionally accredited. Historically black college. **Degrees:** 839 bachelor's awarded; master's, doctoral offered. **ROTC:** Army, Naval. **Location:** 45 miles from Houston. **Calendar:** Semester, extensive summer session. **Full-time faculty:** 359 total; 78% minority, 34% women. **Part-time faculty:** 128 total; 75% minority, 54% women. **Class size:** 27% < 20, 58% 20-39, 8% 40-49, 7% 50-99, less than 1% >100. **Special facilities:** Nuclear magnetic resonance spectrometric differentiator, scanning calorimeter, high pressure liquid chromatograph, solid state engineering laboratory, computer-aided design and drafting laboratory, center for learning and teaching effectiveness, international dairy goat research center, cooperative agricultural research center, solar observatory.

**Freshman class profile.** 5,899 applied, 2,385 admitted, 1,445 enrolled.

| Mid 50% test scores | | | |
|---|---|---|---|
| SAT critical reading: | 370-460 | GPA 2.0-2.99: | 58% |
| SAT math: | 380-480 | Rank in top quarter: | 19% |
| ACT composite: | 15-19 | Rank in top tenth: | 6% |
| GPA 3.50 or higher: | 9% | End year in good standing: | 71% |
| GPA 3.0-3.49: | 32% | Return as sophomores: | 76% |

**Basis for selection.** Score on institution's entrance examination, personal qualities, high school GPA important. Students may be admitted conditionally if grades or test scores are below minimum requirement.

**High school preparation.** 16 units required; 18 recommended. Required and recommended units include English 4, mathematics 3-4, social studies 2, science 3, foreign language 2 and academic electives 4. Recommend 1 computer science.

**2007-2008 Annual costs.** Tuition/fees: $6,046; $14,386 out-of-state. Room/board: $6,447. Books/supplies: $1,200. Personal expenses: $2,120.

**Financial aid. Non-need-based:** Scholarships awarded for academics, athletics, ROTC.

**Application procedures. Admission:** Closing date 6/1 (postmark date). $25 fee, may be waived for applicants with need. Application may be submitted online. Admission notification on a rolling basis. **Financial aid:** Closing date 3/1. FAFSA, institutional form required. Applicants notified by 6/1; must reply by 8/1.

**Academics. Special study options:** Accelerated study, combined bachelor's/graduate degree, cooperative education, cross-registration, distance learning, double major, dual enrollment of high school students, exchange student, external degree, honors, independent study, internships, liberal arts/career combination, study abroad, teacher certification program, weekend college. **Credit/placement by examination:** AP, CLEP. 30 credit hours maximum toward bachelor's degree. **Support services:** Learning center, pre-admission summer program, reduced course load, remedial instruction, tutoring.

**Majors. Agriculture:** General. **Architecture:** Architecture. **Biology:** General. **Business:** Accounting, business admin, finance, management information systems. **Communications:** General. **Computer sciences:** General. **Engineering:** Chemical, civil, computer, electrical, mechanical. **Engineering technology:** Computer, construction, drafting, electrical, industrial. **English:** English lit. **Family/consumer sciences:** Food/nutrition. **Foreign languages:** Spanish. **Health:** Clinical lab science, health services, nursing (RN). **History:** General. **Math:** General. **Parks/recreation:** Health/fitness. **Physical sciences:** Chemistry, physics. **Protective services:** Criminal justice. **Psychology:** General. **Public administration:** Social work. **Social sciences:** Political science, sociology. **Visual/performing arts:** Dramatic, music performance, piano/organ, voice/opera.

**Computing on campus.** 500 workstations in dormitories, library, computer center, student center. Dormitories wired for high-speed internet access and linked to campus network. Commuter students can connect to campus network. Online library, helpline, wireless network available.

**Student life. Freshman orientation:** Mandatory, $60 fee. Preregistration for classes offered. 1 day for Phase 1; 3 days for Phase 2. **Housing:** Guaranteed on-campus for freshmen. Coed dorms, special housing for disabled, apartments, substance-free housing available. $150 fully refundable deposit. **Activities:** Bands, choral groups, dance, drama, film society, literary magazine, music ensembles, musical theater, radio station, student government, student newspaper, symphony orchestra, College Republicans, Spanish-speaking students association, Baptist student ministry, Chinese student association, ministerial alliance, Japanese student association, Korean student association.

**Athletics.** NAIA, NCAA. **Intercollegiate:** Baseball M, basketball, bowling W, cross-country, football (tackle) M, golf, soccer W, softball W, tennis, track and field, volleyball W. **Intramural:** Basketball, bowling W, golf, soccer W, softball, tennis, track and field, volleyball W. **Team name:** Panthers.

**Student services.** Adult student services, career counseling, student employment services, financial aid counseling, health services, personal counseling, placement for graduates, veterans' counselor. **Physically disabled:** Services for hearing impaired.

**Contact.** E-mail: admissions@pvamu.edu
Phone: (936) 261-1000
Mary Gooch, Assistant Director Admissions, Prairie View A&M University, PO Box 519, MS 1009, Prairie View, TX 77446-0519

## Rice University
**Houston, Texas**
**www.rice.edu**

CB member
CB code: 6609

- Private 4-year university
- Residential campus in very large city
- 3,001 degree-seeking undergraduates: 1% part-time, 48% women, 7% African American, 19% Asian American, 12% Hispanic American, 1% Native American, 5% international
- 2,144 degree-seeking graduate students
- 25% of applicants admitted
- SAT and SAT Subject Tests or ACT with writing, application essay required
- 91% graduate within 6 years

**General.** Founded in 1891. Regionally accredited. Every student member of one of 9 residential colleges. **Degrees:** 1,038 bachelor's awarded; master's, doctoral offered. **ROTC:** Army, Naval, Air Force. **Location:** 2 miles from downtown. **Calendar:** Semester, limited summer session. **Full-time faculty:** 583 total; 94% have terminal degrees, 18% minority, 29% women. **Part-time faculty:** 134 total; 61% have terminal degrees, 4% minority, 42% women. **Class size:** 68% < 20, 20% 20-39, 5% 40-49, 6% 50-99, 1% >100. **Special facilities:** Rice University Art Gallery, wetland center for biochemical research, nanotechnology lab, center for study of languages and culture, civil engineering lab, concert hall with grand organ, institutes for public policy.

**Freshman class profile.** 8,968 applied, 2,251 admitted, 742 enrolled.

| Mid 50% test scores | | | |
|---|---|---|---|
| SAT critical reading: | 640-750 | Rank in top tenth: | 83% |
| SAT math: | 670-780 | End year in good standing: | 96% |
| SAT writing: | 640-730 | Return as sophomores: | 97% |
| ACT composite: | 29-34 | Out-of-state: | 47% |
| Rank in top quarter: | 95% | Live on campus: | 98% |
| | | International: | 7% |

**Basis for selection.** High school course selection and performance, test scores, teacher and counselor recommendations, extracurricular activity, and application answers/essay most important. Two SAT Subject Tests required (recommend subject tests be in subjects related to student's area of interest). Audition required for music; portfolio required for architecture. Interview recommended for all freshman applicants. **Homeschooled:** Statement describing homeschool structure and mission, letter of recommendation (non-parent) required.

**High school preparation.** 16 units required; 20 recommended. Required and recommended units include English 4, mathematics 3-4, social studies 2, science 2-4 (laboratory 2-3), foreign language 2-4 and academic electives 3. Trigonometry (pre-calculus), physics, and chemistry required of engineering and natural science majors, although 2nd year chemistry or biology may replace physics requirement.

**2008-2009 Annual costs.** Tuition/fees: $30,479. Room/board: $10,750. Books/supplies: $800. Personal expenses: $1,550.

**2007-2008 Financial aid. Need-based:** 631 full-time freshmen applied for aid; 291 were judged to have need; 291 of these received aid. Average

need met was 100%. Average scholarship/grant was $24,776; average loan $1,184. 88% of total undergraduate aid awarded as scholarships/grants, 12% as loans/jobs. **Non-need-based:** Awarded to 1,168 full-time undergraduates, including 313 freshmen. Scholarships awarded for academics, art, athletics, leadership, minority status, music/drama, ROTC, state residency.

**Application procedures. Admission:** Closing date 1/2 (postmark date). $60 fee, may be waived for applicants with need. Application may be submitted online. Admission notification 4/1. Must reply by May 1 or within 1 week(s) if notified thereafter. $300 enrollment deposit. **Financial aid:** Priority date 3/1; no closing date. FAFSA, CSS PROFILE required. Applicants notified by 4/15; must reply by 5/1 or within 1 week(s) of notification.

**Academics. Special study options:** Combined bachelor's/graduate degree, cross-registration, double major, dual enrollment of high school students, ESL, exchange student, honors, independent study, internships, liberal arts/career combination, student-designed major, study abroad, teacher certification program. 8-year guaranteed medical school program with Baylor College of Medicine for 15 entering freshmen. **Credit/placement by examination:** AP, CLEP, IB, institutional tests. **Support services:** Study skills assistance, tutoring.

**Majors. Architecture:** Architecture. **Area/ethnic studies:** Asian, German, Hispanic-American/Latino/Chicano, Latin American, Slavic, women's. **Biology:** General, biochemistry, ecology, evolutionary. **Business:** Business admin. **Computer sciences:** Computer science. **Engineering:** Biomedical, chemical, civil, computer, electrical, environmental, materials, mechanical. **English:** English lit. **Foreign languages:** Ancient Greek, classics, French, German, Latin, linguistics, Slavic, Spanish. **History:** General. **Interdisciplinary:** Classical/archaeology, cognitive science, medieval/Renaissance. **Math:** General, applied, statistics. **Parks/recreation:** Exercise sciences. **Philosophy/religion:** Philosophy, religion. **Physical sciences:** Astronomy, astrophysics, chemical physics, chemistry, geology, geophysics, physical chemistry, physics. **Psychology:** General. **Public administration:** Policy analysis. **Social sciences:** General, anthropology, economics, political science, sociology. **Visual/performing arts:** General, art, art history/conservation, music history, music performance, music theory/composition, studio arts.

**Computing on campus.** 523 workstations in dormitories, library, computer center, student center. Dormitories wired for high-speed internet access and linked to campus network. Commuter students can connect to campus network. Online course registration, online library, helpline, student web hosting, wireless network available.

**Student life. Freshman orientation:** Mandatory, $250 fee. Held the week before start of classes. **Policies:** Academic honor code. All undergraduates are granted membership in one of 9 residential college communities and maintains that affiliation for their entire college career. Each college is self governing and designed to facilitate student and faculty networking, leadership development, pre-major advising, and social interaction. **Housing:** Guaranteed on-campus for freshmen. Coed dorms, special housing for disabled, substance-free housing available. $100 deposit, deadline 5/1. **Activities:** Bands, campus ministries, choral groups, dance, drama, film society, international student organizations, literary magazine, music ensembles, Model UN, musical theater, opera, radio station, student government, student newspaper, symphony orchestra, TV station, Hispanic student association, Hillel, black student association, Young Democrats, Young Republicans, Chinese student association, Baptist Student Union, Catholic student center, student volunteer program.

**Athletics.** NCAA. **Intercollegiate:** Baseball M, basketball, cheerleading, cross-country, fencing M, field hockey W, football (tackle) M, golf M, lacrosse, rowing (crew), rugby M, soccer, softball W, swimming W, tennis, track and field, volleyball W. **Intramural:** Badminton, basketball, football (non-tackle), racquetball, softball, swimming, table tennis, tennis, track and field, volleyball. **Team name:** Owls.

**Student services.** Alcohol/substance abuse counseling, campus ministries, career counseling, student employment services, financial aid counseling, health services, minority student services, personal counseling, placement for graduates, women's services. **Physically disabled:** Services for visually, speech, hearing impaired.

**Contact.** E-mail: admission@rice.edu
Phone: (713) 348-7423 Toll-free number: (800) 527-6957
Fax: (713) 348-5952
Keith Todd, Director of Admission, Rice University, 6100 Main Street, Houston, TX 77251-1892

## St. Edward's University
**Austin, Texas**
**www.gotostedwards.com**

CB member
CB code: 6619

- Private 4-year university and liberal arts college affiliated with Roman Catholic Church
- Residential campus in very large city

- 4,312 degree-seeking undergraduates: 23% part-time, 60% women, 5% African American, 2% Asian American, 31% Hispanic American, 1% Native American, 2% international
- 926 degree-seeking graduate students
- 65% of applicants admitted
- SAT or ACT with writing, application essay required
- 53% graduate within 6 years

**General.** Founded in 1885. Regionally accredited. **Degrees:** 837 bachelor's awarded; master's offered. **ROTC:** Army, Air Force. **Location:** 80 miles from San Antonio, 180 miles from Dallas. **Calendar:** Semester, limited summer session. **Full-time faculty:** 180 total; 90% have terminal degrees, 9% minority, 47% women. **Part-time faculty:** 306 total; 49% have terminal-degrees, 13% minority, 49% women. **Class size:** 48% < 20, 52% 20-39, less than 1% 40-49. **Special facilities:** Fine arts facility with photography laboratory; chapel; natural sciences center including laboratories, classrooms and seminar rooms.

**Freshman class profile.** 2,372 applied, 1,544 admitted, 727 enrolled.

| Mid 50% test scores | | | |
|---|---|---|---|
| SAT critical reading: | 520-620 | Rank in top tenth: | 19% |
| SAT math: | 510-600 | End year in good standing: | 93% |
| SAT writing: | 510-610 | Return as sophomores: | 85% |
| ACT composite: | 21-26 | Out-of-state: | 8% |
| Rank in top quarter: | 49% | Live on campus: | 91% |
| | | International: | 1% |

**Basis for selection.** Grades and curriculum, rank in top half of class, test scores in top 50th percentile nationally most important. Extracurricular leadership and service, essay, letter of recommendation also considered. **Homeschooled:** Assessment done on individual basis. **Learning Disabled:** Students may submit learning disability documentation with admission application, if they so choose.

**High school preparation.** 14 units required; 20 recommended. Required and recommended units include English 4, mathematics 3-4, social studies 1, history 2-3, science 2-3 (laboratory 2-3), foreign language 2-3, computer science 1 and academic electives 1.

**2008-2009 Annual costs.** Tuition/fees: $22,150. Room/board: $8,158. Books/supplies: $1,100. Personal expenses: $2,522.

**2007-2008 Financial aid. Need-based:** 579 full-time freshmen applied for aid; 470 were judged to have need; 470 of these received aid. Average need met was 78%. Average scholarship/grant was $10,982; average loan $3,433. 69% of total undergraduate aid awarded as scholarships/grants, 31% as loans/jobs. **Non-need-based:** Awarded to 1,635 full-time undergraduates, including 461 freshmen. Scholarships awarded for academics, art, athletics, leadership, music/drama, state residency.

**Application procedures. Admission:** Priority date 2/1; deadline 5/1 (postmark date). $45 fee, may be waived for applicants with need. Application may be submitted online. Admission notification on a rolling basis beginning on or about 11/1. Must reply by May 1 or within 2 week(s) if notified thereafter. Applicants seeking scholarship consideration must apply by February 1. **Financial aid:** Priority date 3/1, closing date 4/15. FAFSA required. Applicants notified on a rolling basis starting 1/15; must reply by 5/1 or within 2 week(s) of notification.

**Academics. Special study options:** Double major, honors, internships, liberal arts/career combination, semester at sea, study abroad, teacher certification program. **Credit/placement by examination:** AP, CLEP, IB, SAT, ACT, institutional tests. 90 credit hours maximum toward bachelor's degree. **Support services:** Learning center, reduced course load, remedial instruction, study skills assistance, tutoring, writing center.

**Majors. Area/ethnic studies:** Latin American. **Biology:** General, biochemistry, bioinformatics. **Business:** Accounting, accounting technology, business admin, entrepreneurial studies, finance, international, marketing. **Communications:** Digital media, media studies. **Computer sciences:** General, computer science. **Conservation:** Environmental studies. **Education:** Art, biology, chemistry, drama/dance, history, mathematics, multi-level teacher, physical, social studies, Spanish. **English:** Composition, English lit. **Foreign languages:** Spanish. **History:** General. **Interdisciplinary:** Global studies. **Liberal arts:** Arts/sciences. **Math:** General. **Parks/recreation:** General, exercise sciences. **Philosophy/religion:** Philosophy. **Physical sciences:** Chemistry. **Protective services:** Criminal justice, forensics. **Psychology:** General. **Public administration:** Social work. **Social sciences:** Criminology, economics, political science, sociology. **Theology:** Religious ed, theology. **Visual/performing arts:** Art, dramatic, graphic design, photography. **Other:** Environmental chemistry.

**Most popular majors.** Business/marketing 36%, communications/journalism 9%, psychology 8%, social sciences 9%, visual/performing arts 8%.

**Computing on campus.** 642 workstations in dormitories, library, computer center, student center. Dormitories wired for high-speed internet access and linked to campus network. Commuter students can connect to campus network. Online course registration, online library, helpline, student web hosting, wireless network available.

**Student life. Freshman orientation:** Mandatory, $150 fee. Preregistration for classes offered. 2-day sessions held 6 times during summer. **Policies:** Student organizations must receive annual university recognition through office of student life. **Housing:** Guaranteed on-campus for freshmen. Coed dorms, single-sex dorms, special housing for disabled, apartments available. $150 nonrefundable deposit, deadline 5/1. Community-style living in casitas/casas available. Two living-learning communities: Global Understanding and Service/Social Justice. **Activities:** Jazz band, campus ministries, choral groups, dance, drama, international student organizations, literary magazine, music ensembles, musical theater, student government, student newspaper, 85 student groups on campus.

**Athletics.** NCAA. **Intercollegiate:** Baseball M, basketball, cross-country, golf, soccer, softball W, tennis, volleyball W. **Intramural:** Basketball, football (non-tackle), soccer, volleyball. **Team name:** Hilltoppers.

**Student services.** Adult student services, alcohol/substance abuse counseling, campus ministries, career counseling, student employment services, financial aid counseling, health services, personal counseling, placement for graduates, veterans' counselor. **Physically disabled:** Services for visually, speech, hearing impaired.

**Contact.** E-mail: seu.admit@stedwards.edu
Phone: (512) 448-8500 Toll-free number: (800) 555-0164
Fax: (512) 464-8877
Tracy Manier, Dean of Undergraduate Admission, St. Edward's University, 3001 South Congress Avenue, Austin, TX 78704-6425

---

## St. Mary's University
**San Antonio, Texas**
www.stmarytx.edu

**CB member**
**CB code: 6637**

- Private 4-year university affiliated with Roman Catholic Church
- Residential campus in very large city
- 2,412 degree-seeking undergraduates: 8% part-time, 59% women, 4% African American, 3% Asian American, 70% Hispanic American, 3% international
- 1,494 graduate students
- 62% of applicants admitted
- SAT or ACT (ACT writing recommended), application essay required
- 58% graduate within 6 years

**General.** Founded in 1852. Regionally accredited. **Degrees:** 482 bachelor's awarded; master's, doctoral, first professional offered. **ROTC:** Army, Air Force. **Location:** 5 miles from downtown. **Calendar:** Semester, limited summer session. **Full-time faculty:** 187 total; 91% have terminal degrees, 22% minority, 37% women. **Part-time faculty:** 135 total; 53% have terminal degrees, 33% minority, 40% women. **Class size:** 41% < 20, 57% 20-39, 1% 40-49, less than 1% 50-99.

**Freshman class profile.** 2,400 applied, 1,488 admitted, 566 enrolled.

| Mid 50% test scores | | | |
|---|---|---|---|
| SAT critical reading: | 460-570 | GPA 3.0-3.49: | 33% |
| SAT math: | 490-590 | GPA 2.0-2.99: | 14% |
| SAT writing: | 460-560 | Return as sophomores: | 79% |
| ACT composite: | 21-26 | Out-of-state: | 5% |
| GPA 3.50 or higher: | 52% | Live on campus: | 73% |
| | | International: | 2% |

**Basis for selection.** Recommendations, talent/ability, character/personal qualities very important. Secondary school record, class rank, standardized test scores, essay and volunteer work important. Interviews, extracurricular activities, alumni/ae relation, religious affiliation or commitment, and work experience considered.

**High school preparation.** 19 units recommended. Recommended units include English 4, mathematics 3, social studies 3, science 3, foreign language 2 and academic electives 1. Applicants to science and engineering program should complete 4 units of math and 3 units of lab science.

**2008-2009 Annual costs.** Tuition/fees: $21,156. Notebook computer $1,000. Room/board: $6,892. Books/supplies: $1,500. Personal expenses: $1,177.

**Financial aid. Non-need-based:** Scholarships awarded for academics, alumni affiliation, athletics, leadership, music/drama, ROTC.

**Application procedures. Admission:** Priority date 1/15; no deadline. $30 fee, may be waived for applicants with need. Application may be submitted online. Admission notification on a rolling basis beginning on or about 10/20. Must reply by May 1 or within 2 week(s) if notified thereafter. **Financial aid:** Priority date 2/15; no closing date. FAFSA required. Applicants notified on a rolling basis starting 5/1; must reply within 2 week(s) of notification.

**Academics.** Writing across the curriculum program requires students in all undergraduate programs to take writing-intensive courses. **Special study options:** Cooperative education, cross-registration, distance learning, double major, dual enrollment of high school students, exchange student, honors, independent study, internships, liberal arts/career combination, study abroad, teacher certification program, Washington semester. Evening studies program. **Credit/placement by examination:** AP, CLEP, SAT, ACT, institutional tests. 30 credit hours maximum toward bachelor's degree. **Support services:** Learning center, pre-admission summer program, reduced course load, remedial instruction, study skills assistance, tutoring, writing center.

**Majors. Area/ethnic studies:** Latin American. **Biology:** General, biochemistry, biophysics. **Business:** General, accounting, entrepreneurial studies, human resources, international, marketing. **Communications:** General. **Computer sciences:** General, computer science. **Engineering:** Computer, electrical, science. **English:** English lit. **Foreign languages:** French, German, Spanish. **Health:** Clinical lab science. **History:** General. **Liberal arts:** Arts/sciences. **Math:** General. **Parks/recreation:** Exercise sciences. **Philosophy/religion:** Philosophy. **Physical sciences:** Chemistry, geology, physics. **Protective services:** Criminal justice. **Social sciences:** International relations, political science, sociology. **Theology:** Theology.

**Most popular majors.** Biology 13%, business/marketing 25%, communications/journalism 6%, parks/recreation 6%, psychology 8%, social sciences 15%.

**Computing on campus.** PC or laptop required. 100 workstations in dormitories, library, computer center, student center. Dormitories wired for high-speed internet access and linked to campus network. Commuter students can connect to campus network. Online library, helpline, repair service, wireless network available.

**Student life. Freshman orientation:** Available. Preregistration for classes offered. June orientation weekend with residence accommodations for students and parents. **Housing:** Guaranteed on-campus for freshmen. Coed dorms, single-sex dorms, special housing for disabled available. $100 deposit, deadline 5/1. Nontraditional residence halls for students 22 years old or above available. **Activities:** Bands, campus ministries, choral groups, dance, drama, literary magazine, music ensembles, musical theater, student government, student newspaper, We the People, Circle K, Amnesty International, black student union, College Democrats, emerging leaders, environmental rescue, Habitat for Humanity, League of United Latin American Citizens.

**Athletics.** NAIA, NCAA. **Intercollegiate:** Baseball M, basketball, cross-country W, golf, soccer, softball W, tennis, volleyball W. **Intramural:** Badminton, basketball, bowling, cross-country, soccer, softball, swimming, table tennis, tennis, volleyball. **Team name:** Rattlers.

**Student services.** Adult student services, campus ministries, career counseling, student employment services, financial aid counseling, health services, personal counseling, placement for graduates, veterans' counselor. **Physically disabled:** Services for visually, speech, hearing impaired.

**Contact.** E-mail: uadm@stmarytx.edu
Phone: (210) 436-3126 Toll-free number: (800) 367-7868
Fax: (210) 431-6742
Chad Bridwell, Director of Admissions, St. Mary's University, One Camino Santa Maria, San Antonio, TX 78228

---

## Sam Houston State University
### Huntsville, Texas
### www.shsu.edu

**CB member**
**CB code: 6643**

- Public 4-year university
- Residential campus in large town
- 14,149 degree-seeking undergraduates: 16% part-time, 57% women, 15% African American, 1% Asian American, 12% Hispanic American, 1% Native American, 1% international
- 2,034 degree-seeking graduate students
- 80% of applicants admitted
- SAT or ACT (ACT writing optional) required
- 40% graduate within 6 years

**General.** Founded in 1879. Regionally accredited. **Degrees:** 2,547 bachelor's awarded; master's, doctoral offered. **ROTC:** Army. **Location:** 69 miles from Houston, 170 miles from Dallas. **Calendar:** Semester, extensive summer session. **Full-time faculty:** 645 total; 70% have terminal degrees, 16% minority, 45% women. **Part-time faculty:** 297 total; 14% have terminal degrees, 18% minority, 54% women. **Class size:** 31% < 20, 50% 20-39, 9% 40-49, 8% 50-99, 2% >100. **Special facilities:** Sam Houston memorial museum, Huntsville State Park.

**Freshman class profile.** 9,810 applied, 7,822 admitted, 2,260 enrolled.

| Mid 50% test scores | | | |
|---|---|---|---|
| SAT critical reading: | 420-530 | Rank in top tenth: | 13% |
| SAT math: | 430-540 | Return as sophomores: | 70% |
| ACT composite: | 17-22 | Out-of-state: | 1% |
| Rank in top quarter: | 44% | Live on campus: | 84% |
| | | International: | 1% |

**Basis for selection.** Test scores, school achievement records very important. Students graduating in top quarter of accredited high school exempt from test requirements.

**High school preparation.** 22 units required; 26 recommended. Required and recommended units include English 4, mathematics 3-4, social studies 2.5-3.5, history 2.5-3.5, science 2-4 (laboratory 1), foreign language 2, computer science 1, visual/performing arts 1 and academic electives 1.

**2008-2009 Annual costs.** Tuition/fees: $5,910; $14,250 out-of-state. Room/board: $6,046. Books/supplies: $1,038. Personal expenses: $1,816.

**2006-2007 Financial aid. Need-based:** 1,535 full-time freshmen applied for aid; 1,080 were judged to have need; 1,054 of these received aid. Average need met was 38%. Average scholarship/grant was $2,882; average loan $2,184. 57% of total undergraduate aid awarded as scholarships/grants, 43% as loans/jobs. **Non-need-based:** Awarded to 2,264 full-time undergraduates, including 714 freshmen. Scholarships awarded for academics, athletics, ROTC.

**Application procedures. Admission:** Priority date 6/15; deadline 8/1 (postmark date). $40 fee, may be waived for applicants with need. Application may be submitted online. Admission notification on a rolling basis beginning on or about 9/1. **Financial aid:** Priority date 3/31, closing date 5/31. FAFSA, institutional form required. Applicants notified on a rolling basis starting 5/1; must reply within 4 week(s) of notification.

**Academics. Special study options:** Combined bachelor's/graduate degree, distance learning, double major, dual enrollment of high school students, ESL, honors, independent study, internships, liberal arts/career combination, study abroad, teacher certification program, weekend college. **Credit/placement by examination:** AP, CLEP, IB, SAT, ACT, institutional tests. 30 credit hours maximum toward bachelor's degree. **Support services:** Learning center, pre-admission summer program, reduced course load, remedial instruction, study skills assistance, tutoring, writing center.

**Majors. Agriculture:** General, agribusiness operations, animal sciences, horticultural science, mechanization. **Architecture:** Interior. **Biology:** General. **Business:** General, accounting, banking/financial services, business admin, fashion, finance, human resources, international, management information systems, managerial economics, marketing, operations. **Communications:** General, advertising, journalism, media studies, public relations, radio/tv. **Computer sciences:** General, security. **Conservation:** Environmental science. **Engineering technology:** Construction, drafting, electrical, industrial, manufacturing. **English:** English lit, speech/rhetoric. **Family/consumer sciences:** General, food/nutrition, institutional food production. **Foreign languages:** French, Spanish. **Health:** Dietetics, health services, music therapy. **History:** General. **Interdisciplinary:** Biological/physical sciences. **Math:** General. **Parks/recreation:** Health/fitness. **Philosophy/religion:** Philosophy. **Physical sciences:** Chemistry, geology, physics. **Protective services:** Corrections, criminal justice. **Psychology:** General. **Social sciences:** General, geography, political science, sociology. **Visual/performing arts:** Art, commercial/advertising art, dance, dramatic, music theory/composition, photography, studio arts.

**Most popular majors.** Agriculture 7%, business/marketing 14%, health sciences 7%, legal studies 15%.

**Computing on campus.** 552 workstations in library, computer center, student center. Dormitories wired for high-speed internet access and linked to campus network. Commuter students can connect to campus network. Online course registration, online library, helpline, repair service, student web hosting, wireless network available.

**Student life. Freshman orientation:** Available, $125 fee. Preregistration for classes offered. Overnight program throughout summer and before classes commence. Parent participation. **Housing:** Guaranteed on-campus for freshmen. Coed dorms, single-sex dorms, apartments, fraternity/sorority housing, substance-free housing available. $200 deposit. **Activities:** Bands, choral groups, dance, drama, music ensembles, musical theater, radio station, student government, student newspaper, symphony orchestra, TV station, Democratic and Republican student associations, Baptist student ministry, Church of Christ student center, Lutheran student center, Hillel, Muslim students association, student Pagan association, ROTARACT, Habitat for Humanity.

**Athletics.** NCAA. **Intercollegiate:** Baseball M, basketball, cross-country, equestrian, football (tackle) M, golf, rifle, rodeo, soccer, softball W, tennis, track and field, volleyball W. **Intramural:** Basketball, bowling, diving, football (tackle) M, golf, gymnastics W, handball, lacrosse M, racquetball, rugby M, soccer, softball, swimming, tennis, volleyball, water polo. **Team name:** Bearkats.

**Student services.** Alcohol/substance abuse counseling, career counseling, student employment services, financial aid counseling, health services, legal services, minority student services, on-campus daycare, personal counseling, placement for graduates, veterans' counselor. **Physically disabled:** Services for visually impaired.

**Contact.** E-mail: admissions@shsu.edu
Phone: (936) 294-1828 Toll-free number: (866) 232-7528
Fax: (936) 294-3758
Trevor Thorn, Director of Admissions, Sam Houston State University, Box 2418, Huntsville, TX 77341-2418

## Schreiner University
**Kerrville, Texas** — CB member
www.schreiner.edu — CB code: 6647

- Private 4-year liberal arts college affiliated with Presbyterian Church (USA)
- Residential campus in large town
- 926 degree-seeking undergraduates: 5% part-time, 57% women, 3% African American, 1% Asian American, 20% Hispanic American, 1% Native American, 1% international
- 40 degree-seeking graduate students
- 58% of applicants admitted
- SAT or ACT with writing required
- 44% graduate within 6 years

**General.** Founded in 1923. Regionally accredited. **Degrees:** 99 bachelor's, 1 associate awarded; master's offered. **Location:** 60 miles from San Antonio, 80 miles from Austin. **Calendar:** Semester, limited summer session. **Full-time faculty:** 55 total; 66% have terminal degrees, 9% minority, 47% women. **Part-time faculty:** 46 total; 41% have terminal degrees, 9% minority, 33% women. **Class size:** 52% < 20, 48% 20-39.

**Freshman class profile.** 973 applied, 563 admitted, 278 enrolled.

| Mid 50% test scores | | | |
|---|---|---|---|
| SAT critical reading: | 430-540 | Rank in top quarter: | 38% |
| SAT math: | 450-560 | Rank in top tenth: | 16% |
| SAT writing: | 420-430 | Return as sophomores: | 64% |
| ACT composite: | 18-23 | Out-of-state: | 1% |
| GPA 3.50 or higher: | 57% | Live on campus: | 86% |
| GPA 3.0-3.49: | 41% | Fraternities: | 12% |
| GPA 2.0-2.99: | 2% | Sororities: | 20% |

**Basis for selection.** High school courses taken, grades, class rank, extracurricular activities, test scores, recommendations, interviews considered. Students admitted to Learning Support Services program not required to take SAT or ACT. Interview recommended for all; essay required for applicants not meeting certain admissions standards; portfolio recommended for fine arts.

**High school preparation.** 24 units recommended. Recommended units include English 4, mathematics 3, social studies 2, history 2, science 3 (laboratory 2), foreign language 2, computer science 1, visual/performing arts 1 and academic electives 4.

**2007-2008 Annual costs.** Tuition/fees: $16,908. Room/board: $8,822. Books/supplies: $1,000. Personal expenses: $1,000.

**2007-2008 Financial aid. Need-based:** 231 full-time freshmen applied for aid; 190 were judged to have need; 190 of these received aid. Average need met was 73%. Average scholarship/grant was $10,965; average loan $2,980. 66% of total undergraduate aid awarded as scholarships/grants, 34% as loans/jobs. **Non-need-based:** Scholarships awarded for academics, art, job skills, leadership, music/drama, religious affiliation.

**Application procedures. Admission:** Priority date 5/1; deadline 8/1. $25 fee, may be waived for applicants with need. Application may be submitted online. Admission notification on a rolling basis. Must reply by 5/1.

**Financial aid:** Priority date 4/1; no closing date. FAFSA required. Applicants notified on a rolling basis starting 2/20; must reply within 2 week(s) of notification.

**Academics. Special study options:** Accelerated study, double major, dual enrollment of high school students, honors, independent study, internships, liberal arts/career combination, student-designed major, study abroad, teacher certification program, weekend college. **Credit/placement by examination:** AP, CLEP, IB, SAT, ACT, institutional tests. **Support services:** Learning center, reduced course load, remedial instruction, study skills assistance, tutoring, writing center.

**Majors. Biology:** General, biochemistry. **Business:** General, accounting, management information systems. **Education:** General, biology, early childhood, elementary, English, history, mathematics, middle, music, physical, secondary. **Engineering:** General. **English:** English lit. **Health:** Predental. **History:** General. **Interdisciplinary:** Accounting/computer science. **Legal studies:** Prelaw. **Liberal arts:** Arts/sciences, humanities. **Math:** General. **Parks/recreation:** Exercise sciences. **Philosophy/religion:** Religion. **Physical sciences:** Chemistry. **Psychology:** General. **Social sciences:** Political science. **Visual/performing arts:** Dramatic, graphic design.

**Most popular majors.** Biology 12%, business/marketing 17%, education 16%, English 11%, interdisciplinary studies 6%, psychology 8%, visual/performing arts 7%.

**Computing on campus.** 103 workstations in dormitories, library, computer center, student center. Dormitories wired for high-speed internet access and linked to campus network. Commuter students can connect to campus network. Online library, repair service, student web hosting, wireless network available.

**Student life. Freshman orientation:** Mandatory. Preregistration for classes offered. Overnight program before classes begin. **Housing:** Guaranteed on-campus for all undergraduates. Coed dorms, special housing for disabled, apartments, substance-free housing available. $100 nonrefundable deposit, deadline 5/1. **Activities:** Pep band, campus ministries, choral groups, dance, drama, literary magazine, music ensembles, musical theater, student government, student newspaper, symphony orchestra, community outreach program, Best Buddies, BACCHUS (Boosting Alcohol Consciousness Concerning the Health of University Students), Celtic Cross, Episcopal-Lutheran Association, Fellowship of Christian Athletes, Young Catholic Adults, Young Republicans.

**Athletics.** NCAA. **Intercollegiate:** Baseball M, basketball, cheerleading M, golf, soccer, softball W, tennis, volleyball W. **Intramural:** Basketball, football (non-tackle), football (tackle), golf, racquetball, soccer, swimming, table tennis, tennis, volleyball. **Team name:** Mountaineers.

**Student services.** Adult student services, campus ministries, career counseling, student employment services, health services, personal counseling, placement for graduates. **Physically disabled:** Services for visually, speech, hearing impaired. **Learning disabled:** Comprehensive services available.

**Contact.** E-mail: admissions@schreiner.edu
Phone: (830) 792-7217 Toll-free number: (800) 343-4919
Fax: (830) 896-3232
Sandra Speed, Director of Admissions, Schreiner University, 2100 Memorial Boulevard, Kerrville, TX 78028-5697

## Southern Methodist University
**Dallas, Texas** — CB member
www.smu.edu — CB code: 6660

- Private 4-year university affiliated with United Methodist Church
- Residential campus in large town
- 6,081 degree-seeking undergraduates: 4% part-time, 54% women, 5% African American, 6% Asian American, 8% Hispanic American, 1% Native American, 5% international
- 4,290 degree-seeking graduate students
- 50% of applicants admitted
- SAT or ACT (ACT writing optional), application essay required
- 71% graduate within 6 years

**General.** Founded in 1911. Regionally accredited. Courses are also offered at SMU-in-Legacy in Plano and SMU-in-Taos in New Mexico. **Degrees:** 1,661 bachelor's awarded; master's, doctoral, first professional offered. **ROTC:** Army, Air Force. **Location:** 5 miles from downtown. **Calendar:** Semester, limited summer session. **Full-time faculty:** 633 total; 84% have terminal degrees, 16% minority, 34% women. **Part-time faculty:** 350 total; 44% have terminal degrees, 38% women. **Class size:** 58% < 20, 27% 20-39, 6% 40-49, 8% 50-99, 1% >100. **Special facilities:** Film/video archives, New Mexico archeological dig of 13th century Indian pueblo, institute for the study of Earth and man, seismological observatory, electron microscopy laboratory, paleontology museum, business information center.

**Freshman class profile.** 8,253 applied, 4,133 admitted, 1,309 enrolled.

| Mid 50% test scores | | GPA 2.0-2.99: | 10% |
|---|---|---|---|
| SAT critical reading: | 560-660 | Rank in top quarter: | 71% |
| SAT math: | 570-670 | Rank in top tenth: | 40% |
| SAT writing: | 560-650 | Return as sophomores: | 89% |
| ACT composite: | 25-29 | Out-of-state: | 56% |
| GPA 3.50 or higher: | 59% | Live on campus: | 95% |
| GPA 3.0-3.49: | 31% | International: | 3% |

**Basis for selection.** GED not accepted. Students evaluated comprehensively. High school curriculum, GPA, test scores, school/community activities, recommendations, and essay important. Special talents considered. Interview recommended for all; audition required for performing arts; portfolio recommended for studio art. **Homeschooled:** SAT Subject Tests required.

**High school preparation.** 15 units required. Required and recommended units include English 4, mathematics 3-4, social studies 1-2, history 2-3, science 3-4 (laboratory 2-3) and foreign language 2-3.

**2008-2009 Annual costs.** Tuition/fees: $33,170. Room/board: $11,875. Books/supplies: $800. Personal expenses: $1,100.

**2007-2008 Financial aid. Need-based:** 584 full-time freshmen applied for aid; 408 were judged to have need; 408 of these received aid. Average need met was 90%. Average scholarship/grant was $16,282; average loan $2,609. 76% of total undergraduate aid awarded as scholarships/grants, 24% as loans/jobs. **Non-need-based:** Awarded to 3,444 full-time undergraduates, including 960 freshmen. Scholarships awarded for academics, art, athletics, leadership, music/drama, religious affiliation, ROTC, state residency.

**Application procedures. Admission:** Priority date 1/15; deadline 3/15 (postmark date). $60 fee, may be waived for applicants with need. Application may be submitted online. Admission notification on a rolling basis beginning on or about 12/31. Must reply by 5/1. **Financial aid:** Priority date 2/15; no closing date. FAFSA, CSS PROFILE required. Applicants notified on a rolling basis starting 3/15.

**Academics. Special study options:** Accelerated study, combined bachelor's/graduate degree, cooperative education, distance learning, double major, ESL, exchange student, honors, independent study, internships, student-designed major, study abroad, teacher certification program, Washington semester. **Credit/placement by examination:** AP, CLEP, IB, SAT, ACT, institutional tests. No limit on number of AP credits that may be counted toward bachelor's degree. Maximum of 8 hours of International Baccalaureate credits may be counted toward bachelor's degree. **Support services:** Learning center, pre-admission summer program, remedial instruction, study skills assistance, tutoring, writing center.

**Majors. Area/ethnic studies:** African-American, European, German, Hispanic-American/Latino/Chicano, Italian, Latin American. **Biology:** General, biochemistry. **Business:** General, accounting, business admin, finance, financial planning, management information systems, management science, marketing, organizational behavior, real estate. **Communications:** Advertising, journalism, media studies, public relations, radio/tv. **Computer sciences:** Computer science, information systems. **Conservation:** Environmental science. **Education:** Music. **Engineering:** Civil, computer, electrical, environmental, mechanical. **Engineering technology:** Industrial management. **English:** Creative writing, English lit. **Foreign languages:** General, French, German, Italian, Russian, Spanish. **Health:** Music therapy. **History:** General. **Interdisciplinary:** Medieval/Renaissance. **Liberal arts:** Humanities. **Math:** General, statistics. **Philosophy/religion:** Philosophy, religion. **Physical sciences:** Chemistry, geology, geophysics, physics. **Psychology:** General. **Public administration:** Policy analysis. **Social sciences:** General, anthropology, applied economics, econometrics, economics, international relations, political science, sociology. **Visual/performing arts:** Art, art history/conservation, dance, dramatic, film/cinema, music performance, music theory/composition, piano/organ, studio arts, voice/opera.

**Most popular majors.** Business/marketing 26%, communications/journalism 14%, psychology 8%, social sciences 18%, visual/performing arts 8%.

**Computing on campus.** 758 workstations in dormitories, library, computer center, student center. Dormitories wired for high-speed internet access and linked to campus network. Commuter students can connect to campus network. Online course registration, online library, helpline, repair service, student web hosting, wireless network available.

**Student life. Freshman orientation:** Mandatory. **Housing:** Guaranteed on-campus for freshmen. Coed dorms, apartments, fraternity/sorority housing, substance-free housing available. $200 nonrefundable deposit, deadline 5/15. Theme residence halls available. **Activities:** Bands, campus ministries, choral groups, dance, drama, film society, international student organizations, literary magazine, music ensembles, musical theater, opera, radio

station, student government, student newspaper, symphony orchestra, over 130 groups available.

**Athletics.** NCAA. **Intercollegiate:** Basketball, cross-country W, diving, equestrian W, football (tackle) M, golf, rowing (crew) W, soccer, swimming, tennis, track and field W, volleyball W. **Intramural:** Basketball, bowling, golf, racquetball, soccer, softball, swimming, table tennis, tennis, volleyball. **Team name:** Mustangs.

**Student services.** Adult student services, alcohol/substance abuse counseling, campus ministries, career counseling, student employment services, financial aid counseling, health services, on-campus daycare, personal counseling, placement for graduates, women's services. **Physically disabled:** Services for visually, speech, hearing impaired.

**Contact.** E-mail: enrol_serv@smu.edu
Phone: (214) 768-3417 Toll-free number: (800) 323-0672
Fax: (214) 768-0202
Ron Moss, Executive Director of Enrollment Services, Southern Methodist University, PO Box 750181, Dallas, TX 75275-0181

---

## Southwestern Adventist University
**Keene, Texas**
www.swau.edu
CB code: 6671

- Private 4-year university and liberal arts college affiliated with Seventh-day Adventists
- Residential campus in small town
- 820 degree-seeking undergraduates: 15% part-time, 60% women, 13% African American, 9% Asian American, 29% Hispanic American, 1% Native American, 10% international
- 54 graduate students
- 48% of applicants admitted
- 55% graduate within 6 years

**General.** Founded in 1893. Regionally accredited. **Degrees:** 138 bachelor's, 29 associate awarded; master's offered. **Location:** 55 miles from Dallas, 25 miles from Fort Worth. **Calendar:** Semester, limited summer session. **Full-time faculty:** 54 total; 39% women. **Part-time faculty:** 74 total; 38% women. **Class size:** 65% < 20, 24% 20-39, 9% 40-49, 2% 50-99, less than 1% >100. **Special facilities:** Observatory, museum of student life.

**Freshman class profile.** 632 applied, 306 admitted, 210 enrolled.

| Mid 50% test scores | | Return as sophomores: | 68% |
|---|---|---|---|
| SAT critical reading: | 410-530 | Out-of-state: | 44% |
| SAT math: | 410-500 | Live on campus: | 35% |
| ACT composite: | 18-22 | International: | 7% |
| End year in good standing: | 91% | | |

**Basis for selection.** Secondary school record, test scores important. Additional requirements for nursing and education programs. SAT or ACT recommended. SAT preferred for placement. **Homeschooled:** A state high school equivalency certificate is accepted instead of a high school diploma or GED.

**High school preparation.** Recommended units include English 4, mathematics 2, social studies 2.5, science 2 and foreign language 2.

**2007-2008 Annual costs.** Tuition/fees: $14,284. Room/board: $6,424. Books/supplies: $864. Personal expenses: $1,220.

**Financial aid. Non-need-based:** Scholarships awarded for academics, leadership, music/drama.

**Application procedures. Admission:** Closing date 8/31. No application fee. Application may be submitted online. Admission notification on a rolling basis. **Financial aid:** Priority date 3/15; no closing date. FAFSA, institutional form required. Applicants notified on a rolling basis starting 4/15.

**Academics. Special study options:** Accelerated study, combined bachelor's/graduate degree, cooperative education, cross-registration, distance learning, double major, ESL, external degree, honors, independent study, internships, liberal arts/career combination, student-designed major, study abroad, teacher certification program. **Credit/placement by examination:** AP, CLEP, IB, institutional tests. **Support services:** Reduced course load, remedial instruction, tutoring, writing center.

**Majors. Biology:** General, biostatistics. **Business:** Accounting, administrative services, business admin, communications, international, management information systems, management science, office management. **Communications:** General, broadcast journalism, journalism. **Computer sciences:**

General, computer science, information systems. **Education:** Business, elementary. **English:** English lit. **Health:** Clinical lab technology, health care admin, medical secretary, nursing (RN). **History:** General. **Math:** General, applied. **Parks/recreation:** Health/fitness. **Philosophy/religion:** Religion. **Physical sciences:** Chemistry, theoretical physics. **Protective services:** Criminal justice. **Psychology:** General. **Social sciences:** General, international relations. **Theology:** Theology.

**Most popular majors.** Business/marketing 13%, education 24%, liberal arts 9%, psychology 10%, theological studies 11%.

**Computing on campus.** 150 workstations in library, computer center. Dormitories wired for high-speed internet access and linked to campus network. Commuter students can connect to campus network. Helpline, repair service, student web hosting, wireless network available.

**Student life. Freshman orientation:** Mandatory. Preregistration for classes offered. Held the week prior to fall registration. **Housing:** Guaranteed on-campus for all undergraduates. Single-sex dorms, apartments available. $100 fully refundable deposit, deadline 8/31. **Activities:** Concert band, campus ministries, choral groups, drama, international student organizations, music ensembles, musical theater, radio station, student government, student newspaper, symphony orchestra, TV station.

**Athletics. Intramural:** Baseball M, basketball, gymnastics, soccer M, volleyball W.

**Student services.** Adult student services, career counseling, student employment services, financial aid counseling, health services, personal counseling, placement for graduates, veterans' counselor.

**Contact.** E-mail: admissions@swau.edu
Phone: (817) 202-6252 Toll-free number: (800) 433-2240
Fax: (817) 556-4744
Steve Stafford, Enrollment and Marketing Vice President, Southwestern Adventist University, Box 567, Keene, TX 76059

## Southwestern Assemblies of God University
**Waxahachie, Texas**
www.sagu.edu                                    CB code: 6669

- Private 4-year university and Bible college affiliated with Assemblies of God
- Residential campus in large town
- 1,543 degree-seeking undergraduates: 17% part-time, 50% women
- 288 degree-seeking graduate students
- 75% of applicants admitted
- SAT or ACT (ACT writing optional), application essay required

**General.** Founded in 1927. Regionally accredited. **Degrees:** 271 bachelor's, 52 associate awarded; master's offered. **ROTC:** Army. **Location:** 20 miles from Dallas. **Calendar:** Semester, limited summer session. **Full-time faculty:** 60 total. **Part-time faculty:** 54 total.

**Freshman class profile.** 715 applied, 537 admitted, 256 enrolled.

| Mid 50% test scores | | ACT composite: | 16-23 |
|---|---|---|---|
| SAT critical reading: | 420-520 | Out-of-state: | 45% |
| SAT math: | 410-510 | Live on campus: | 80% |

**Basis for selection.** Minister's reference and 1 personal reference required. Interview recommended. **Learning Disabled:** Enrollment with the Achievement Center indicated.

**2007-2008 Annual costs.** Tuition/fees: $11,530. Room/board: $5,282. Books/supplies: $612. Personal expenses: $1,479.

**Application procedures. Admission:** Priority date 7/1; no deadline. $35 fee. Admission notification on a rolling basis beginning on or about 3/1. **Financial aid:** Priority date 3/1, closing date 6/1. FAFSA required. Applicants notified on a rolling basis starting 6/1; must reply within 2 week(s) of notification.

**Academics. Special study options:** Distance learning, double major, dual enrollment of high school students, external degree, independent study, internships, teacher certification program. **Credit/placement by examination:** CLEP, institutional tests. 15 credit hours maximum toward associate degree, 30 toward bachelor's. **Support services:** Learning center, reduced course load, remedial instruction, tutoring.

**Majors. Business:** General, accounting, business admin, marketing. **Education:** Early childhood, elementary, English, music, reading, secondary, social studies. **English:** English lit. **Health:** Clinical pastoral counseling.

**History:** General. **Philosophy/religion:** Christian. **Theology:** Bible, missionary, pastoral counseling, religious ed, sacred music, youth ministry. **Visual/performing arts:** Music performance, piano/organ, voice/opera.

**Computing on campus.** 45 workstations in library, computer center. Dormitories wired for high-speed internet access and linked to campus network. Online library, repair service available.

**Student life. Freshman orientation:** Mandatory. Preregistration for classes offered. **Policies:** Dress code observed. Religious observance required. **Housing:** Guaranteed on-campus for freshmen. Coed dorms, single-sex dorms, apartments available. Unmarried students 23 and under required to live in college housing unless alternative arrangements agreed to upon enrollment. **Activities:** Bands, choral groups, drama, music ensembles, musical theater, student government, student newspaper, prayer groups, ministry labs.

**Athletics.** NAIA, NCCAA. **Intercollegiate:** Baseball M, basketball, cheerleading, football (tackle) M, soccer M, volleyball W. **Intramural:** Basketball, football (non-tackle) W, racquetball, softball, table tennis, volleyball. **Team name:** Lions.

**Student services.** Adult student services, campus ministries, career counseling, student employment services, financial aid counseling, health services, personal counseling, placement for graduates, veterans' counselor.

**Contact.** E-mail: admissions@sagu.edu
Phone: (972) 937-4010 ext. 1125 Toll-free number: (888) 937-7248 ext. 1125 Fax: (972) 923-0006
Pat Thompson, Admissions Counselor, Southwestern Assemblies of God University, 1200 Sycamore Street, Waxahachie, TX 75165

## Southwestern Christian College
**Terrell, Texas**
www.swcc.edu                                    CB code: 6705

- Private 4-year Bible and liberal arts college affiliated with Church of Christ
- Residential campus in large town

**General.** Founded in 1949. Regionally accredited. **Location:** 30 miles from Dallas. **Calendar:** Semester.

**Annual costs/financial aid.** Tuition/fees (2007-2008): $6,182. Room/board: $4,132. Books/supplies: $460. Personal expenses: $400.

**Contact.** Phone: (972) 524-3341
Director of Admissions, Box 10, Terrell, TX 75160

## Southwestern University
**Georgetown, Texas**                          CB member
www.southwestern.edu                           CB code: 6674

- Private 4-year liberal arts college affiliated with United Methodist Church
- Residential campus in large town
- 1,283 degree-seeking undergraduates: 2% part-time, 60% women, 3% African American, 5% Asian American, 14% Hispanic American, 1% Native American
- 67% of applicants admitted
- SAT or ACT with writing, application essay required
- 72% graduate within 6 years; 28% enter graduate study

**General.** Founded in 1840. Regionally accredited. **Degrees:** 296 bachelor's awarded. **Location:** 28 miles from Austin. **Calendar:** Semester, limited summer session. **Full-time faculty:** 122 total; 98% have terminal degrees, 12% minority, 47% women. **Part-time faculty:** 53 total; 49% have terminal degrees, 9% minority, 55% women. **Class size:** 72% < 20, 27% 20-39, less than 1% 40-49.

**Freshman class profile.** 1,916 applied, 1,291 admitted, 371 enrolled.

| Mid 50% test scores | | End year in good standing: | 77% |
|---|---|---|---|
| SAT critical reading: | 560-680 | Return as sophomores: | 87% |
| SAT math: | 570-660 | Out-of-state: | 6% |
| ACT composite: | 24-29 | Live on campus: | 100% |
| Rank in top quarter: | 81% | Fraternities: | 28% |
| Rank in top tenth: | 50% | Sororities: | 27% |

**Basis for selection.** School record, class rank, recommendations, test scores, essay most important. Audition required for music, theater programs; portfolio required for art program.

**High school preparation.** 17 units required; 20 recommended. Required and recommended units include English 4, mathematics 4, social studies 2-3, history 1-2, science 3-4 (laboratory 2-3), foreign language 2-3 and academic electives 1.

**2007-2008 Annual costs.** Tuition/fees: $25,740. Room/board: $7,970. Books/supplies: $1,000. Personal expenses: $870.

**2007-2008 Financial aid.** Need-based: 264 full-time freshmen applied for aid; 197 were judged to have need; 197 of these received aid. Average need met was 88%. Average scholarship/grant was $17,465; average loan $4,617. 67% of total undergraduate aid awarded as scholarships/grants, 33% as loans/jobs. **Non-need-based:** Awarded to 780 full-time undergraduates, including 249 freshmen. Scholarships awarded for academics, art, minority status, music/drama, religious affiliation.

**Application procedures. Admission:** Closing date 2/15 (postmark date). $40 fee, may be waived for applicants with need. Application may be submitted online. Admission notification 4/1. Must reply by 5/1. Applicants accepted after 2/15 if space allows. **Financial aid:** Closing date 3/1. FAFSA required. Applicants notified on a rolling basis starting 3/1; must reply by 5/1 or within 2 week(s) of notification.

**Academics.** Students must demonstrate computer skills and grasp of major through capstone project, course, or examination prior to graduation. **Special study options:** Combined bachelor's/graduate degree, double major, honors, independent study, internships, liberal arts/career combination, New York semester, student-designed major, study abroad, teacher certification program, Washington semester. **Credit/placement by examination:** AP, CLEP, IB, institutional tests. **Support services:** Reduced course load, study skills assistance, tutoring, writing center.

**Majors. Area/ethnic studies:** American, women's. **Biology:** General. **Business:** General, accounting. **Communications:** General. **Computer sciences:** General. **Education:** General, elementary, music, physical. **English:** English lit. **Foreign languages:** Classics, French, German, Latin, Spanish. **Health:** Athletic training. **History:** General. **Math:** General. **Philosophy/religion:** Philosophy, religion. **Physical sciences:** Chemistry, physics. **Psychology:** General. **Social sciences:** General, anthropology, economics, international relations, political science, sociology. **Theology:** Sacred music. **Visual/performing arts:** Art, art history/conservation, dramatic, music history, music performance, studio arts.

**Most popular majors.** Biology 12%, business/marketing 10%, communications/journalism 14%, education 6%, foreign language 8%, psychology 8%, social sciences 14%, visual/performing arts 10%.

**Computing on campus.** 410 workstations in dormitories, library, computer center, student center. Dormitories wired for high-speed internet access and linked to campus network. Online course registration, online library, helpline, repair service, student web hosting, wireless network available.

**Student life. Freshman orientation:** Mandatory. **Housing:** Guaranteed on-campus for freshmen. Coed dorms, single-sex dorms, special housing for disabled, apartments, fraternity/sorority housing available. $250 nonrefundable deposit, deadline 5/1. **Activities:** Bands, choral groups, dance, drama, film society, literary magazine, music ensembles, musical theater, student government, student newspaper, Alpha Phi Omega, Ebony, Mexican American student association, political science society, international club, Equal Voice For Women's Perspective.

**Athletics.** NCAA. **Intercollegiate:** Baseball M, basketball, cross-country, diving, golf, soccer, swimming, tennis, track and field, volleyball W. **Team name:** Bucs/Pirates.

**Student services.** Alcohol/substance abuse counseling, campus ministries, career counseling, student employment services, financial aid counseling, health services, minority student services, personal counseling, placement for graduates. **Physically disabled:** Services for hearing impaired.

**Contact.** E-mail: admission@southwestern.edu
Phone: (512) 863-1200 Toll-free number: (800) 252-3166
Fax: (512) 863-9601
Tom Oliver, Vice President Enrollment Services, Southwestern University, 1001 East University Avenue, Georgetown, TX 78626

---

## Stephen F. Austin State University

**Nacogdoches, Texas**
**www.sfasu.edu**

**CB member**
**CB code: 6682**

- Public 4-year university
- Residential campus in large town
- 10,106 degree-seeking undergraduates: 13% part-time, 59% women, 19% African American, 1% Asian American, 9% Hispanic American, 1% Native American, 1% international

- 1,152 degree-seeking graduate students
- 74% of applicants admitted
- SAT or ACT with writing required
- 38% graduate within 6 years

**General.** Founded in 1923. Regionally accredited. **Degrees:** 1,796 bachelor's awarded; master's, doctoral offered. **ROTC:** Army. **Location:** 140 miles from Houston, 70 miles from Longview. **Calendar:** Semester, extensive summer session. **Full-time faculty:** 453 total; 72% have terminal degrees, 7% minority, 43% women. **Part-time faculty:** 171 total; 40% have terminal degrees, 7% minority, 53% women. **Class size:** 27% < 20, 51% 20-39, 13% 40-49, 7% 50-99, 2% >100. **Special facilities:** Computerized observatory; experimental forest; on-campus arboretum; beef, poultry and swine research facilities; biotechnology/environmental science research center; Stone Fort museum; agricultural pond; forest resources institute; geographic information systems lab; regional geospatial service center.

**Freshman class profile.** 7,409 applied, 5,481 admitted, 2,245 enrolled.

| Mid 50% test scores | | | | |
|---|---|---|---|---|
| SAT critical reading: | 430-540 | Return as sophomores: | 64% |
| SAT math: | 450-550 | Out-of-state: | 1% |
| ACT composite: | 18-23 | Live on campus: | 87% |
| Rank in top quarter: | 45% | International: | 1% |
| Rank in top tenth: | 16% | Fraternities: | 12% |
| | | Sororities: | 9% |

**Basis for selection.** Applicants must complete prescribed high school preparation and submit official high school transcript and SAT or ACT scores. No minimum score required for those ranking in top quartile; those in second quartile must have composite score (exclusive of Writing) of 850 SAT, 18 ACT; third quartile 1050 SAT, 23 ACT; fourth quartile 1250 SAT, 28 ACT. Applicants not meeting rank-in-class and test requirements reviewed on individual basis. SAT or ACT scores must be received by last day of registration for fall term admission. **Homeschooled:** Applicants assessed on individual basis; those whose academic background indicates probability of success may be admitted.

**High school preparation.** 12 units required; 18 recommended. Required and recommended units include English 4, mathematics 3, social studies 3, science 3 and foreign language 2. 1 fine arts, 1 computer science, 1 government/economics recommended.

**2007-2008 Annual costs.** Tuition/fees: $6,162; $14,502 out-of-state. Room/board: $6,885. Books/supplies: $996. Personal expenses: $1,556.

**2006-2007 Financial aid.** Need-based: 1,623 full-time freshmen applied for aid; 1,175 were judged to have need; 1,155 of these received aid. Average need met was 98%. Average scholarship/grant was $4,212; average loan $2,323. 46% of total undergraduate aid awarded as scholarships/grants, 54% as loans/jobs. **Non-need-based:** Awarded to 2,475 full-time undergraduates, including 837 freshmen. Scholarships awarded for academics, alumni affiliation, athletics, leadership, music/drama, state residency.

**Application procedures. Admission:** No deadline. $35 fee, may be waived for applicants with need. Application may be submitted online. Admission notification on a rolling basis beginning on or about 9/1. **Financial aid:** Priority date 4/1; no closing date. FAFSA, institutional form required. Applicants notified on a rolling basis starting 4/10; must reply within 3 week(s) of notification.

**Academics. Special study options:** Accelerated study, combined bachelor's/graduate degree, distance learning, double major, dual enrollment of high school students, honors, independent study, internships, liberal arts/career combination, student-designed major, study abroad, teacher certification program. **Credit/placement by examination:** AP, CLEP, IB, institutional tests. 32 credit hours maximum toward bachelor's degree. **Support services:** Learning center, pre-admission summer program, reduced course load, remedial instruction, study skills assistance, tutoring, writing center.

**Majors. Agriculture:** General, agribusiness operations, agronomy, animal sciences, horticultural science, horticulture, mechanization, poultry, production. **Architecture:** Interior. **Biology:** General, biochemistry. **Business:** General, accounting, business admin, fashion, finance, hospitality admin, international, managerial economics, marketing, office management. **Communications:** General, journalism, radio/tv. **Computer sciences:** General, data processing. **Conservation:** Environmental science, forest management, forestry, wildlife. **English:** Creative writing, English lit, speech/rhetoric. **Family/consumer sciences:** General, family studies, food/nutrition. **Foreign languages:** French, Spanish. **Health:** Audiology/hearing, audiology/speech pathology, clinical lab science, health services, nursing (RN). **History:** General. **Interdisciplinary:** Gerontology. **Legal studies:** Paralegal. **Liberal arts:** Arts/sciences, humanities. **Math:** General. **Parks/recreation:** Facilities management, health/fitness. **Philosophy/religion:** Philosophy. **Physical sciences:** Chemistry, geology, physics. **Protective services:** Corrections, criminal justice, police science. **Psychology:** General. **Public**

administration: General, social work. **Social sciences:** General, economics, geography, political science, sociology. **Visual/performing arts:** Art, art history/conservation, dance, dramatic, music performance.

**Most popular majors.** Business/marketing 22%, communications/journalism 6%, health sciences 9%, interdisciplinary studies 18%, parks/recreation 6%, visual/performing arts 6%.

**Computing on campus.** 1,000 workstations in dormitories, library, computer center, student center. Dormitories wired for high-speed internet access and linked to campus network. Commuter students can connect to campus network. Online course registration, online library, helpline, repair service, student web hosting, wireless network available.

**Student life. Freshman orientation:** Available, $130 fee. Preregistration for classes offered. Five 3-day sessions held each summer for students and parents. **Housing:** Guaranteed on-campus for freshmen. Coed dorms, single-sex dorms, special housing for disabled, apartments, fraternity/sorority housing, substance-free housing available. $100 fully refundable deposit. Students must live in college housing until 60 semester hours completed. Off-campus housing permitted if student is 21 or older, married, commutes from permanent address of parent or relative, or enrolls for 8 hours or less. **Activities:** Bands, campus ministries, choral groups, dance, drama, film society, international student organizations, literary magazine, music ensembles, musical theater, opera, radio station, student government, student newspaper, symphony orchestra, TV station, African American student association, Canterbury Episcopal student association, Campus Crusade for Christ, Jewish Student Fellowship, Habitat for Humanity, SFA Democrats, Young Republicans, social services.

**Athletics.** NCAA. **Intercollegiate:** Baseball M, basketball, cross-country, equestrian W, football (tackle) M, golf M, soccer W, softball W, tennis W, track and field, volleyball W. **Intramural:** Badminton, baseball M, basketball, cross-country, gymnastics, lacrosse M, racquetball, rodeo, rugby, soccer M, softball, table tennis, tennis, volleyball, water polo, wrestling M. **Team name:** Lumberjacks/Ladyjacks.

**Student services.** Adult student services, alcohol/substance abuse counseling, career counseling, student employment services, financial aid counseling, health services, legal services, minority student services, on-campus daycare, personal counseling, placement for graduates, veterans' counselor. **Physically disabled:** Services for visually, speech, hearing impaired.

**Contact.** E-mail: admissions@sfasu.edu
Phone: (936) 468-2504 Fax: (936) 468-3849
Monique Cossich, Executive Director of Enrollment Management, Stephen F. Austin State University, Box 13051, SFA Station, Nacogdoches, TX 75962-3051

---

## Sul Ross State University
**Alpine, Texas**      **CB member**
**www.sulross.edu**      **CB code: 6685**

- Public 4-year university
- Residential campus in small town
- 1,935 degree-seeking undergraduates
- 782 graduate students
- 81% of applicants admitted
- SAT or ACT (ACT writing optional) required

**General.** Founded in 1917. Regionally accredited. Off-campus upper-level and graduate programs available in Del Rio, Eagle Pass, and Uvalde. **Degrees:** 178 bachelor's, 7 associate awarded; master's offered. **Location:** 140 miles from Odessa, 220 miles from El Paso. **Calendar:** Semester, limited summer session. **Full-time faculty:** 106 total. **Part-time faculty:** 28 total. **Class size:** 61% < 20, 33% 20-39, 4% 40-49, 3% 50-99. **Special facilities:** Center for Big Bend studies, materials characterization laboratory.

**Freshman class profile.** 804 applied, 651 admitted, 261 enrolled.

| Mid 50% test scores | | ACT composite: | 15-20 |
|---|---|---|---|
| SAT critical reading: | 390-500 | Out-of-state: | 3% |
| SAT math: | 390-490 | Live on campus: | 74% |

**Basis for selection.** Students must meet one of following criteria: ACT score of 20, SAT score of 800 (exclusive of Writing), or rank in top half of graduating class. Probational admission for all other applicants.

**High school preparation.** 16 units required; 25.5 recommended. Required and recommended units include English 4, mathematics 3-4, social studies 2, history 1-2, science 2-4 (laboratory 2), foreign language 3, academic electives 2.5. 1 fine art, 1 computer science required.

---

**2008-2009 Annual costs.** Tuition/fees: $5,058; $13,398 out-of-state. Room/board: $6,190. Books/supplies: $1,110. Personal expenses: $1,872.

**Financial aid. Non-need-based:** Scholarships awarded for academics, alumni affiliation, leadership.

**Application procedures. Admission:** Priority date 3/1; no deadline. $25 fee, may be waived for applicants with need. Application may be submitted online. Admission notification on a rolling basis. **Financial aid:** Priority date 5/1; no closing date. FAFSA, institutional form required. Applicants notified on a rolling basis starting 5/1; must reply within 2 week(s) of notification.

**Academics. Special study options:** Distance learning, honors, internships, teacher certification program. **Credit/placement by examination:** AP, CLEP, institutional tests. 30 credit hours maximum toward bachelor's degree. **Support services:** Learning center, pre-admission summer program, reduced course load, remedial instruction, study skills assistance, tutoring, writing center.

**Majors. Agriculture:** Agribusiness operations, animal health, animal sciences, equestrian studies, food science, range science. **Biology:** General. **Business:** General, accounting, administrative services, business admin, finance, marketing, office management. **Communications:** General. **Computer sciences:** General. **Conservation:** General, management/policy, wildlife. **Education:** Elementary. **English:** English lit, speech/rhetoric. **Foreign languages:** Spanish. **History:** General. **Math:** General. **Parks/recreation:** Health/fitness. **Physical sciences:** Chemistry, geology. **Protective services:** Criminal justice. **Psychology:** General. **Social sciences:** General, political science. **Visual/performing arts:** Art, dramatic.

**Computing on campus.** 200 workstations in library, computer center. Dormitories wired for high-speed internet access and linked to campus network. Commuter students can connect to campus network. Online library, helpline, repair service, wireless network available.

**Student life. Freshman orientation:** Available, $100 fee. Preregistration for classes offered. **Housing:** Guaranteed on-campus for freshmen. Coed dorms, single-sex dorms, special housing for disabled, apartments available. $100 deposit, deadline 8/1. Students not living with parents must live on campus until they reach 20 years of age and complete 45 semester credit hours. **Activities:** Bands, choral groups, dance, drama, literary magazine, music ensembles, musical theater, radio station, student government, student newspaper, Wesley Foundation, Newman Club, Baptist Student Union, Fellowship of Christian Athletes, Spanish club, rodeo club, black student association, international student association, nontraditional student association.

**Athletics.** NCAA. **Intercollegiate:** Baseball M, basketball, cross-country, football (tackle) M, softball W, tennis, track and field, volleyball W. **Intramural:** Basketball, football (non-tackle), racquetball, soccer, softball, tennis, volleyball, water polo, weight lifting. **Team name:** Lobos.

**Student services.** Alcohol/substance abuse counseling, campus ministries, career counseling, student employment services, financial aid counseling, health services, on-campus daycare, personal counseling, placement for graduates, veterans' counselor. **Physically disabled:** Services for visually, hearing impaired.

**Contact.** E-mail: admissions@sulross.edu
Phone: (432) 837-8050 Toll-free number: (888) 722-7778
Fax: (432) 837-8431
Greg Schwab, Director of Recruiting and Admission, Sul Ross State University, Box C-2, Alpine, TX 79832

---

## Tarleton State University
**Stephenville, Texas**      **CB member**
**www.tarleton.edu**      **CB code: 6817**

- Public 4-year university
- Residential campus in large town
- 7,781 degree-seeking undergraduates: 23% part-time, 57% women, 8% African American, 1% Asian American, 9% Hispanic American, 1% Native American, 1% international
- 1,656 degree-seeking graduate students
- 55% of applicants admitted
- SAT or ACT with writing, application essay required
- 44% graduate within 6 years

**General.** Founded in 1899. Regionally accredited. Graduate courses available at several off-campus locations within 150-mile radius. Upper level/graduate program offered at Tarleton University System Center in Killeen. Educational program for prison inmates offered in Gatesville on Fort Hood

Military Post. **Degrees:** 1,493 bachelor's, 10 associate awarded; master's, doctoral offered. **ROTC:** Army. **Location:** 65 miles from Fort Worth. **Calendar:** Semester, extensive summer session. **Full-time faculty:** 318 total; 67% have terminal degrees, 10% minority, 41% women. **Part-time faculty:** 258 total; 10% have terminal degrees, 9% minority, 48% women. **Class size:** 37% < 20, 49% 20-39, 6% 40-49, 7% 50-99, 1% >100. **Special facilities:** University farm and equine center, planetarium.

**Freshman class profile.** 3,544 applied, 1,932 admitted, 1,216 enrolled.

| Mid 50% test scores | | | |
|---|---|---|---|
| SAT critical reading: | 430-530 | Return as sophomores: | 62% |
| SAT math: | 440-540 | Out-of-state: | 1% |
| SAT writing: | 420-510 | Live on campus: | 73% |
| ACT composite: | 18-23 | International: | 1% |
| Rank in top quarter: | 35% | Fraternities: | 8% |
| Rank in top tenth: | 8% | Sororities: | 7% |

**Basis for selection.** Unconditional admission requires 930 combined SAT (exclusive of Writing) or 20 ACT. Rank in top quarter of class ensures unconditional admission if student has taken 4 years English and 3 years math. **Homeschooled:** Must provide proof of curriculum completed from an agency or teacher. **Learning Disabled:** Contact Director of Disability Services for appropriate accommodation.

**High school preparation.** 19 units required. Required and recommended units include English 4, mathematics 3, social studies 2, history 1, science 2-3 (laboratory 2), foreign language 2 and academic electives 2-4.

**2007-2008 Annual costs.** Tuition/fees: $4,864; $13,204 out-of-state. Distance learning fee additional $40 per credit hour. Room/board: $6,788. Books/supplies: $1,050.

**2006-2007 Financial aid.** **Need-based:** 1,026 full-time freshmen applied for aid; 942 were judged to have need; 680 of these received aid. Average need met was 73%. Average scholarship/grant was $4,158; average loan $2,494. 48% of total undergraduate aid awarded as scholarships/grants, 52% as loans/jobs. **Non-need-based:** Awarded to 2,822 full-time undergraduates, including 720 freshmen. Scholarships awarded for academics, alumni affiliation, art, athletics, leadership, music/drama, ROTC.

**Application procedures.** **Admission:** Priority date 7/1; deadline 8/1 (receipt date). $30 fee. Application may be submitted online. Admission notification on a rolling basis beginning on or about 2/1. Early acceptance available to applicants who rank in top 10% of class; notification on rolling basis beginning January 1. **Financial aid:** Priority date 4/1, closing date 10/15. FAFSA required. Applicants notified on a rolling basis starting 2/1; must reply within 2 week(s) of notification.

**Academics.** **Special study options:** Accelerated study, distance learning, double major, dual enrollment of high school students, honors, internships, study abroad, teacher certification program. Specialized bachelor of applied arts and science degree for students with practical work experience in field of study; cooperative doctoral program in educational administration offered in partnership with Texas A&M University-Commerce; 2-2 engineering with Texas A&M University and University of Texas Arlington. **Credit/placement by examination:** AP, CLEP, SAT, ACT, institutional tests. Students can earn the majority of credits toward their degree by examination. **Support services:** Learning center, pre-admission summer program, reduced course load, remedial instruction, study skills assistance, tutoring, writing center.

**Majors. Agriculture:** General, agribusiness operations, agronomy, animal husbandry, animal sciences, business, economics, livestock, mechanization, ornamental horticulture, supplies. **Biology:** General, zoology. **Business:** General, accounting, business admin, finance, human resources, management information systems, marketing, office management. **Communications:** General. **Computer sciences:** General. **Conservation:** Wildlife. **Education:** Computer, science. **Engineering:** Environmental, physics. **Engineering technology:** General, industrial, manufacturing. **English:** English lit. **Family/consumer sciences:** General. **Foreign languages:** Spanish. **Health:** Clinical lab science, nursing (RN). **History:** General. **Liberal arts:** Arts/sciences. **Math:** General. **Parks/recreation:** Health/fitness. **Physical sciences:** Chemistry, geology, hydrology, physics. **Protective services:** Criminal justice. **Psychology:** General. **Public administration:** Social work. **Social sciences:** Economics, political science, sociology. **Transportation:** Airline/commercial pilot, aviation management. **Visual/performing arts:** Dramatic, studio arts.

**Most popular majors.** Agriculture 11%, business/marketing 30%, interdisciplinary studies 11%, parks/recreation 7%.

**Computing on campus.** 1,600 workstations in dormitories, library, computer center, student center. Dormitories wired for high-speed internet access and linked to campus network. Commuter students can connect to campus network. Online course registration, online library, helpline, repair service, student web hosting, wireless network available.

**Student life. Freshman orientation:** Mandatory, $125 fee. Preregistration for classes offered. Held multiple times during the summer. **Housing:** Guaranteed on-campus for freshmen. Coed dorms, single-sex dorms, apartments, substance-free housing available. $100 fully refundable deposit, deadline 3/1. **Activities:** Bands, campus ministries, choral groups, dance, drama, international student organizations, literary magazine, music ensembles, musical theater, radio station, student government, student newspaper, symphony orchestra, Los Tejanos, Chinese student association, progressive united black student organization, student social work association, Alpha Phi Omega, Circle K, Fellowship of Christian Athletes, Fellowship of Christian Cowboys, College Republicans, Young Democrats.

**Athletics.** NCAA. **Intercollegiate:** Baseball M, basketball, cheerleading, cross-country, football (tackle) M, golf W, rodeo, softball W, tennis W, track and field, volleyball W. **Intramural:** Archery, basketball, football (non-tackle) M, football (tackle), golf, racquetball, rodeo, soccer, softball, table tennis, tennis, volleyball. **Team name:** Texans.

**Student services.** Adult student services, alcohol/substance abuse counseling, campus ministries, career counseling, student employment services, financial aid counseling, health services, legal services, minority student services, on-campus daycare, personal counseling, placement for graduates, veterans' counselor. **Physically disabled:** Services for visually, speech, hearing impaired.

**Contact.** E-mail: uadm@tarleton.edu
Phone: (254) 968-9125 Toll-free number: (800) 687-8236
Fax: (254) 968-9951
Cindy Hess, Director of Admissions, Tarleton State University, Box T-0030, Stephenville, TX 76402

## Texas A&M International University

**Laredo, Texas**
**www.tamiu.edu**
**CB member**
**CB code: 0359**

- Public 4-year university
- Commuter campus in small city
- 4,065 degree-seeking undergraduates: 34% part-time, 63% women, 1% African American, 1% Asian American, 93% Hispanic American, 4% international
- 845 degree-seeking graduate students
- 54% of applicants admitted
- SAT or ACT (ACT writing recommended) required
- 38% graduate within 6 years; 16% enter graduate study

**General.** Founded in 1969. Regionally accredited. **Degrees:** 693 bachelor's awarded; master's, doctoral offered. **Location:** 150 miles from San Antonio and Corpus Christi. **Calendar:** Semester, extensive summer session. **Full-time faculty:** 154 total; 70% have terminal degrees, 42% minority, 38% women. **Part-time faculty:** 129 total; 20% have terminal degrees, 67% minority, 45% women. **Class size:** 39% < 20, 46% 20-39, 6% 40-49, 8% 50-99, less than 1% >100. **Special facilities:** Planetarium.

**Freshman class profile.** 2,183 applied, 1,180 admitted, 694 enrolled.

| Mid 50% test scores | | | |
|---|---|---|---|
| SAT critical reading: | 380-490 | GPA 2.0-2.99: | 3% |
| SAT math: | 410-500 | Rank in top quarter: | 54% |
| SAT writing: | 380-480 | Rank in top tenth: | 22% |
| ACT composite: | 15-20 | End year in good standing: | 65% |
| GPA 3.50 or higher: | 69% | Return as sophomores: | 59% |
| GPA 3.0-3.49: | 26% | International: | 2% |

**Basis for selection.** Students in top half of graduating class admitted with no minimum ACT or SAT score. Students in bottom half need minimum score of 860 on SAT (exclusive of Writing) or 18 on ACT.

**High school preparation.** Required and recommended units include English 4, mathematics 3, history 3, science 2, foreign language 2 and academic electives 2. 1 computer technology, 1 fine arts recommended.

**2007-2008 Annual costs.** Tuition/fees: $5,038; $13,378 out-of-state. Room/board: $6,630.

**Financial aid.** **Non-need-based:** Scholarships awarded for academics.

**Application procedures.** **Admission:** Closing date 7/1. No application fee. Application may be submitted online. Admission notification on a rolling basis beginning on or about 11/1. **Financial aid:** Priority date 3/15; no closing date. FAFSA, institutional form required. Applicants notified on a rolling basis starting 7/15; must reply within 2 week(s) of notification.

**Academics. Special study options:** Cooperative education, cross-registration, double major, dual enrollment of high school students, ESL, honors, independent study, internships, liberal arts/career combination, study abroad, teacher certification program. **Credit/placement by examination:** AP, CLEP, IB, institutional tests. 33 credit hours maximum toward bachelor's degree. **Support services:** Learning center, pre-admission summer program, reduced course load, remedial instruction, study skills assistance, tutoring, writing center.

**Majors. Area/ethnic studies:** Latin American. **Biology:** General. **Business:** Accounting, business admin, finance, management information systems, managerial economics, marketing. **Communications:** General. **Conservation:** General. **Education:** Bilingual, biology, early childhood, elementary, English, history, mathematics, reading, social studies, Spanish, special. **English:** English lit. **Foreign languages:** Spanish. **Health:** Nursing (RN), preop/surgical nursing. **History:** General. **Math:** General. **Parks/recreation:** Health/fitness. **Physical sciences:** Chemistry. **Protective services:** Criminal justice. **Psychology:** General. **Public administration:** Social work. **Social sciences:** General, political science, sociology, urban studies.

**Most popular majors.** Business/marketing 27%, interdisciplinary studies 28%, psychology 8%, security/protective services 8%.

**Computing on campus.** 200 workstations in dormitories, library, computer center. Dormitories wired for high-speed internet access and linked to campus network. Commuter students can connect to campus network.

**Student life. Freshman orientation:** Available. Preregistration for classes offered. Day program offered in May, June, July and August. **Housing:** Apartments available. On-campus housing, not owned by college (private contractor) available. **Activities:** Concert band, choral groups, dance, drama, literary magazine, music ensembles, student government, student newspaper, Student Ambassadors, Association of International Students, Tau Sigma Chi (criminal justice), High Twisters, Ballet Folklorico, Student System Group, Student Finance Society.

**Athletics. Intramural:** Baseball, basketball, soccer, table tennis, volleyball, weight lifting. **Team name:** Dust Devils.

**Student services.** Career counseling, services for economically disadvantaged, student employment services, financial aid counseling, health services, personal counseling, placement for graduates, veterans' counselor. **Physically disabled:** Services for visually, speech, hearing impaired.

**Contact.** E-mail: enroll@tamiu.edu
Phone: (956) 326-2200 Fax: (956) 326-2199
Rosa Dickinson, Director of Admissions, Texas A&M International University, 5201 University Boulevard, Laredo, TX 78041-1900

## Texas A&M University
**College Station, Texas**

**www.tamu.edu**

**CB member**
**CB code: 6003**

- Public 4-year university
- Residential campus in small city
- 37,341 degree-seeking undergraduates: 9% part-time, 48% women, 3% African American, 4% Asian American, 12% Hispanic American, 1% Native American, 1% international
- 8,972 degree-seeking graduate students
- 76% of applicants admitted
- SAT or ACT with writing, application essay required
- 78% graduate within 6 years

**General.** Founded in 1876. Regionally accredited. **Degrees:** 8,133 bachelor's awarded; master's, doctoral, first professional offered. **ROTC:** Army, Naval, Air Force. **Location:** 90 miles from Houston, 100 miles from Austin. **Calendar:** Semester, extensive summer session. **Full-time faculty:** 2,188 total; 92% have terminal degrees, 21% minority, 29% women. **Part-time faculty:** 420 total; 71% have terminal degrees, 15% minority, 38% women. **Class size:** 22% < 20, 47% 20-39, 8% 40-49, 12% 50-99, 11% >100. **Special facilities:** Reactor, cyclotron, observatory, agriculture research property, 18-hole golf course, supercomputer center, oceanographic research vessel, Italian study center, George H. W. Bush Presidential Library and Museum.

**Freshman class profile.** 18,817 applied, 14,380 admitted, 8,094 enrolled.

| Mid 50% test scores | | Rank in top tenth: | 45% |
|---|---|---|---|
| SAT critical reading: | 520-630 | Return as sophomores: | 92% |
| SAT math: | 560-670 | Out-of-state: | 4% |
| SAT writing: | 500-610 | Live on campus: | 68% |
| ACT composite: | 23-28 | Fraternities: | 6% |
| Rank in top quarter: | 76% | Sororities: | 15% |

**Basis for selection.** Automatic admission to applicants in top 10% of Texas high school class (with completed application), as specified by state law. Strong senior year course schedule recommended. Test scores required of all applicants but not used for admission of applicants from top 10% of any Texas high school class. **Learning Disabled:** Must provide documentation of disability from qualified professional licensed or certified to diagnose disability.

**High school preparation.** 17.5 units required; 18.5 recommended. Required and recommended units include English 4, mathematics 3.5, social studies 2, history 1, science 3 (laboratory 2) and foreign language 2. 1 unit computer usage required.

**2007-2008 Annual costs.** Tuition/fees: $7,335; $15,675 out-of-state. Room/board: $7,660. Books/supplies: $1,156. Personal expenses: $2,160.

**2007-2008 Financial aid. Need-based:** 4,781 full-time freshmen applied for aid; 2,841 were judged to have need; 2,772 of these received aid. Average need met was 89.1%. Average scholarship/grant was $9,752; average loan $4,014. 62% of total undergraduate aid awarded as scholarships/grants, 38% as loans/jobs. **Non-need-based:** Awarded to 5,645 full-time undergraduates, including 1,399 freshmen. Scholarships awarded for academics, alumni affiliation, art, athletics, job skills, leadership, music/drama, ROTC, state residency. **Additional information:** Short-term loans available. Out-of-state students awarded academic scholarships of $1,000 or more are eligible for waiver of out-of-state tuition.

**Application procedures. Admission:** Closing date 2/1 (receipt date). $60 fee, may be waived for applicants with need. Application may be submitted online. Admission notification on a rolling basis beginning on or about 9/1. Must reply by 5/1. **Financial aid:** Priority date 3/31; no closing date. FAFSA, institutional form required. Applicants notified on a rolling basis starting 4/1; must reply within 4 week(s) of notification.

**Academics.** Core curriculum requirements in foreign language and computer science may be satisfied by selected high school courses. **Special study options:** Accelerated study, combined bachelor's/graduate degree, cooperative education, distance learning, double major, dual enrollment of high school students, ESL, honors, independent study, internships, liberal arts/career combination, study abroad, teacher certification program. Exchange programs in architecture with Instituto Tecnologico y de Estudios Superiores de Monterrey, King's College London (England), University of Lancaster (England), Denmark's international study program, Ruhr University Bochum (Germany), University of Lausanne (Switzerland). **Credit/placement by examination:** AP, CLEP, IB, institutional tests. **Support services:** Learning center, pre-admission summer program, remedial instruction, tutoring, writing center.

**Majors. Agriculture:** General, agribusiness operations, agronomy, animal husbandry, animal sciences, aquaculture, business, communications, dairy, economics, farm/ranch, food science, horticultural science, horticulture, ornamental horticulture, plant protection, plant sciences, poultry, production, range science, soil science, supplies, turf management. **Architecture:** Architecture, environmental design, landscape. **Area/ethnic studies:** American. **Biology:** General, biochemistry, biomedical sciences, botany, cellular/molecular, entomology, environmental, microbiology, molecular genetics, zoology. **Business:** Accounting, finance, management science, marketing, sales/distribution, tourism promotion, tourism/travel. **Communications:** Digital media, journalism. **Computer sciences:** Computer science. **Conservation:** General, environmental science, environmental studies, forest management, forestry, management/policy, urban forestry, wildlife. **Engineering:** Aerospace, agricultural, biomedical, chemical, civil, computer, electrical, geological, industrial, mechanical, nuclear, ocean, petroleum. **Engineering technology:** General, construction, electrical, manufacturing. **English:** English lit, speech/rhetoric. **Family/consumer sciences:** Food/nutrition. **Foreign languages:** Classics, French, German, Russian, Spanish. **Health:** Community health services, preveterinary. **History:** General. **Interdisciplinary:** Global studies. **Math:** General, applied. **Parks/recreation:** General, facilities management, health/fitness. **Philosophy/religion:** Philosophy. **Physical sciences:** Atmospheric science, chemistry, geology, geophysics, physics. **Protective services:** Forensics. **Psychology:** General. **Public administration:** Community org/advocacy. **Social sciences:** Anthropology, cartography, economics, geography, political science, sociology. **Visual/performing arts:** Dramatic.

**Most popular majors.** Agriculture 13%, biology 10%, business/marketing 16%, engineering/engineering technologies 14%, interdisciplinary studies 10%, parks/recreation 7%, social sciences 8%.

**Computing on campus.** 1,321 workstations in dormitories, library, computer center, student center. Dormitories wired for high-speed internet access and linked to campus network. Commuter students can connect to campus network. Online course registration, online library, helpline, repair service, student web hosting, wireless network available.

**Student life. Freshman orientation:** Mandatory, $35 fee. Preregistration for classes offered. 2 1/2 day program throughout the summer. **Housing:** Coed dorms, single-sex dorms, special housing for disabled, apartments, fraternity/sorority housing, substance-free housing available. $300 fully refundable deposit. Campus housing guaranteed to members of Corps of Cadets and recipients of major 4-year endowed academic scholarships. Freshman honors dorm available. **Activities:** Bands, choral groups, dance, drama, film society, literary magazine, music ensembles, musical theater, radio station, student government, student newspaper, symphony orchestra, TV station, black awareness committee, committee for the awareness of Mexican American culture, student Y association, student conference on national affairs, social service organizations, College Republicans, Aggie Democrats, political forum, united campus ministries, Aggies for Christ.

**Athletics.** NCAA. **Intercollegiate:** Archery W, baseball M, basketball, cross-country, diving, equestrian W, football (tackle) M, golf, soccer W, softball W, swimming, tennis, track and field, volleyball W. **Intramural:** Archery, badminton, basketball, bowling, diving, golf, lacrosse, racquetball, rodeo, soccer, softball, squash, swimming, table tennis, track and field, volleyball. **Team name:** Aggies.

**Student services.** Alcohol/substance abuse counseling, career counseling, student employment services, financial aid counseling, health services, legal services, minority student services, on-campus daycare, personal counseling, placement for graduates, veterans' counselor, women's services. **Physically disabled:** Services for visually, speech, hearing impaired.

**Contact.** E-mail: admissions@tamu.edu
Phone: (979) 845-3741 Fax: (979) 458-1808
Scott McDonald, Director of Admissions, Texas A&M University, PO Box 30014, College Station, TX 77842-3014

---

### Texas A&M University-Baylor College of Dentistry
**Dallas, Texas**
www.bcd.tamhsc.edu                           CB code: 6059

- Public two-year upper-division health science college
- Commuter campus in very large city
- 32% of applicants admitted
- Application essay, interview required

**General.** Founded in 1905. Regionally accredited. **Degrees:** 27 bachelor's awarded; master's, doctoral, first professional offered. **Articulation:** Agreement with Collin Community College District. **Calendar:** Semester. **Full-time faculty:** 118 total; 100% have terminal degrees, 11% minority, 36% women. **Part-time faculty:** 130 total; 100% have terminal degrees, 8% minority, 29% women.

**Student profile.** 60 degree-seeking undergraduates, 401 degree-seeking graduate students. 106 applied as first time-transfer students, 34 admitted, 30 enrolled. 60% transferred from two-year, 40% transferred from four-year institutions.

| | | | |
|---|---|---|---|
| Women: | 100% | Native American: | 2% |
| African American: | 2% | Out-of-state: | 4% |
| Asian American: | 20% | 25 or older: | 25% |
| Hispanic American: | 10% | | |

**Basis for selection.** High school transcript, college transcript, application essay, interview required. School achievement most important. Essay, interview, and recommendations highly considered. Transfer accepted as juniors.

**2007-2008 Annual costs.** Tuition/fees: $5,401; $15,131 out-of-state. Personal expenses: $2,700.

**Financial aid. Need-based:** 41 applied for aid; 37 were judged to have need; 34 of these received aid. Average need met was 42%. 18% of total undergraduate aid awarded as scholarships/grants, 82% as loans/jobs. **Non-need-based:** Awarded to 3 undergraduates. Scholarships awarded for academics.

**Application procedures. Admission:** Priority date 12/31. $35 fee. **Financial aid:** FAFSA, institutional form required.

**Academics.** Participation in research activities under faculty sponsorship and annual research fellowships awarded by college offered. **Special study**

**options:** Combined bachelor's/graduate degree, internships. **Credit/placement by examination:** CLEP.

**Majors. Health:** Dental hygiene.

**Computing on campus.** 25 workstations in library, computer center. Commuter students can connect to campus network. Online library, helpline, wireless network available.

**Student life. Housing:** Baylor Medical Center nursing dormitory housing available. **Activities:** Student government.

**Student services.** Student employment services, financial aid counseling, health services, personal counseling.

**Contact.** Phone: (214) 828-8230 Fax: (214) 828-8346
Barbara Miller, Director, Texas A&M University-Baylor College of Dentistry, PO Box 660677, Dallas, TX 75266-0677

---

### Texas A&M University-Commerce
**Commerce, Texas**                           **CB member**
www.tamu-commerce.edu                         **CB code: 6188**

- Public 4-year university
- Residential campus in small town
- 5,166 degree-seeking undergraduates: 60% part-time, 62% women, 18% African American, 2% Asian American, 10% Hispanic American, 1% Native American, 1% international
- 3,716 degree-seeking graduate students
- 55% of applicants admitted
- SAT or ACT with writing required

**General.** Founded in 1889. Regionally accredited. **Degrees:** 1,303 bachelor's awarded; master's, doctoral offered. **Location:** 60 miles from Dallas. **Calendar:** Semester, extensive summer session. **Full-time faculty:** 271 total; 70% have terminal degrees, 6% minority, 37% women. **Part-time faculty:** 175 total; 27% have terminal degrees, 65% women. **Class size:** 48% < 20, 39% 20-39, 8% 40-49, 5% 50-99, less than 1% >100. **Special facilities:** Instructional university farm, new state-of-the-art science building with planetarium.

**Freshman class profile.** 1,734 applied, 954 admitted, 644 enrolled.

| Mid 50% test scores | | | |
|---|---|---|---|
| SAT critical reading: | 440-550 | Rank in top quarter: | 42% |
| SAT math: | 430-550 | Rank in top tenth: | 16% |
| ACT composite: | 18-23 | International: | 1% |

**Basis for selection.** ACT or SAT scores most important, followed by high school grades and class rank. Students admitted with 20 ACT or 920 SAT (exclusive of Writing). TASP scores may exempt student from SAT or ACT tests. If student is TASP remedial, must take TASP within first semester of enrolling. Portfolio required for advertising art program; audition recommended for music program. **Homeschooled:** Must earn GED and be at least 18 years of age.

**High school preparation.** 12 units required. Required and recommended units include English 4, mathematics 3, science 2 and foreign language 2. 2.5 hours history/social studies required.

**2007-2008 Annual costs.** Tuition/fees: $5,190; $13,440 out-of-state. Room/board: $6,340. Books/supplies: $1,200. Personal expenses: $1,700.

**Financial aid. Non-need-based:** Scholarships awarded for academics, art, athletics, leadership, music/drama. **Additional information:** Work-study also available for full-time students.

**Application procedures. Admission:** Closing date 8/1 (postmark date). $25 fee ($50 out-of-state). Application may be submitted online. Admission notification on a rolling basis beginning on or about 10/1. High school seniors may enroll part-time before graduation with consent of high school principal if they meet requirements. **Financial aid:** Priority date 4/1; no closing date. FAFSA required. Applicants notified on a rolling basis starting 4/1; must reply within 2 week(s) of notification.

**Academics. Special study options:** Combined bachelor's/graduate degree, cooperative education, distance learning, double major, dual enrollment of high school students, external degree, honors, independent study, internships, liberal arts/career combination, study abroad, teacher certification program, weekend college. **Credit/placement by examination:** AP, CLEP, IB, SAT, ACT, institutional tests. 6 credit hours maximum toward bachelor's degree. **Support services:** Learning center, pre-admission summer program, remedial instruction, study skills assistance, tutoring, writing center.

**Majors. Agriculture:** Animal sciences, communications, economics, food science, plant sciences, soil science. **Biology:** General, cell/histology. **Business:** General, accounting, business admin, human resources, management information systems, managerial economics, marketing, office management, office/clerical, operations, public finance. **Communications:** General, advertising, broadcast journalism, digital media, journalism, public relations. **Communications technology:** Graphic/printing. **Computer sciences:** General, computer science, information systems. **Conservation:** General, environmental studies, wildlife. **Construction:** Maintenance. **Education:** Bilingual, biology, chemistry, driver/safety, early childhood, elementary, middle, multi-level teacher, physical, special. **Engineering:** Operations research. **Engineering technology:** Construction, manufacturing. **English:** American lit, British lit, composition, English lit, speech/rhetoric. **Foreign languages:** German, Spanish. **Health:** Athletic training, health care admin, medical records admin, predental, premedicine, prepharmacy, preveterinary. **History:** General. **Interdisciplinary:** Biological/physical sciences. **Legal studies:** Legal secretary, paralegal, prelaw. **Liberal arts:** Arts/sciences, library science. **Math:** General. **Parks/recreation:** Health/fitness. **Physical sciences:** Chemistry, geology, organic chemistry, physics, planetary. **Protective services:** Criminal justice, law enforcement admin. **Psychology:** General. **Public administration:** Social work. **Social sciences:** General, anthropology, criminology, economics, geography, political science, sociology. **Theology:** Preministerial. **Visual/performing arts:** General, art, arts management, ceramics, commercial photography, commercial/advertising art, design, dramatic, industrial design, metal/jewelry, music history, music pedagogy, music performance, music theory/composition, musicology, painting, photography, piano/organ, printmaking, sculpture, voice/opera.

**Computing on campus.** 1,500 workstations in dormitories, library, computer center. Dormitories wired for high-speed internet access and linked to campus network. Commuter students can connect to campus network. Online course registration, online library, helpline, repair service, wireless network available.

**Student life. Freshman orientation:** Mandatory, $100 fee. Preregistration for classes offered. Held throughout summer; includes advising, assessment testing, and parental involvement. **Housing:** Coed dorms, single-sex dorms, special housing for disabled, apartments, fraternity/sorority housing, substance-free housing available. $100 deposit, deadline 7/1. Shared freshman experience housing available. **Activities:** Bands, choral groups, dance, drama, film society, literary magazine, music ensembles, musical theater, opera, radio station, student government, student newspaper, symphony orchestra, TV station, Baptist student union, Church of Christ Bible chair, Newman Club, university Christian center, Young Democrats, association cultural de Hispanos-Americanos, Chinese student association, Muslim society, NAACP, Thai students association, Alpha Phi Omega.

**Athletics.** NCAA. **Intercollegiate:** Basketball, cross-country, football (tackle) M, golf, soccer W, track and field, volleyball W. **Intramural:** Archery, badminton, baseball M, basketball, bowling, cross-country, golf, racquetball, softball, swimming, table tennis, tennis, track and field, volleyball. **Team name:** Lions.

**Student services.** Alcohol/substance abuse counseling, campus ministries, career counseling, student employment services, financial aid counseling, health services, legal services, on-campus daycare, personal counseling, placement for graduates, veterans' counselor. **Physically disabled:** Services for visually, speech, hearing impaired.

**Contact.** E-mail: Jody_Todhunterl@tamu-commerce.edu
Phone: (903) 886-5081 Toll-free number: (888) 886-2682
Fax: (903) 468-6080
Jody Todhunter, Director of Admissions, Texas A&M
University-Commerce, Box 3011, Commerce, TX 75429-3011

---

## Texas A&M University-Corpus Christi

| | |
|---|---|
| **Corpus Christi, Texas** | **CB member** |
| **www.tamucc.edu** | **CB code: 0366** |

- Public 4-year university
- Commuter campus in large city

**General.** Founded in 1947. Regionally accredited. **Location:** 150 miles from San Antonio, 200 miles from Houston. **Calendar:** Semester.

**Annual costs/financial aid.** Tuition/fees (projected): $6,121. Books/supplies: $840. Personal expenses: $1,019. Need-based financial aid available to full-time and part-time students.

**Contact.** Phone: (361) 825-2624
Director of Admissions, 6300 Ocean Drive, Corpus Christi, TX 78412

---

## Texas A&M University-Galveston

| | |
|---|---|
| **Galveston, Texas** | **CB member** |
| **www.tamug.edu** | **CB code: 6835** |

- Public 4-year university and branch campus college
- Residential campus in small city
- 1,565 degree-seeking undergraduates: 7% part-time, 41% women
- 49 degree-seeking graduate students
- 78% of applicants admitted
- SAT or ACT (ACT writing optional), application essay required
- 54% graduate within 6 years; 35% enter graduate study

**General.** Founded in 1962. Regionally accredited. Institution houses Texas Maritime Academy, 1 of 5 seacoast maritime academies in the U.S. preparing graduates for licensing as officers in the Merchant Marine. **Degrees:** 250 bachelor's awarded; master's offered. **ROTC:** Naval. **Location:** 50 miles from Houston. **Calendar:** Semester, limited summer session. **Full-time faculty:** 92 total; 65% have terminal degrees, 13% minority, 20% women. **Part-time faculty:** 78 total; 22% have terminal degrees, 14% minority, 42% women. **Class size:** 67% < 20, 23% 20-39, 4% 40-49, 4% 50-99, 2% >100. **Special facilities:** Fleet of research and training boats, 300-acre wetlands on west Galveston Bay, wetlands research center, ship bridge simulator.

**Freshman class profile.** 1,181 applied, 926 admitted, 465 enrolled.

| Mid 50% test scores | | Rank in top tenth: | 11% |
|---|---|---|---|
| SAT critical reading: | 460-590 | End year in good standing: | 78% |
| SAT math: | 490-600 | Return as sophomores: | 78% |
| ACT composite: | 20-25 | Out-of-state: | 14% |
| Rank in top quarter: | 40% | Live on campus: | 75% |

**Basis for selection.** School achievement record and test scores most important. Adverse circumstances, leadership, exceptional talents, course selections, and references reviewed on individual basis. **Homeschooled:** Transcript of courses and grades, letter of recommendation (nonparent) required.

**High school preparation.** 13 units required; 19 recommended. Required and recommended units include English 4, mathematics 3-4, social studies 3, science 3-4 (laboratory 2) and foreign language 3. 1 unit computer literacy required. Science courses must be selected from biology, chemistry or physics.

**2007-2008 Annual costs.** Tuition/fees: $6,055; $14,395 out-of-state. Room/board: $6,105. Books/supplies: $1,381. Personal expenses: $1,960.

**2006-2007 Financial aid. Need-based:** 245 full-time freshmen applied for aid; 202 were judged to have need; 191 of these received aid. Average need met was 15%. Average scholarship/grant was $4,190; average loan $2,550. 41% of total undergraduate aid awarded as scholarships/grants, 59% as loans/jobs. **Non-need-based:** Awarded to 76 full-time undergraduates, including 16 freshmen. Scholarships awarded for academics, state residency.

**Application procedures. Admission:** No deadline. $45 fee, may be waived for applicants with need. Application may be submitted online. Admission notification on a rolling basis. **Financial aid:** Priority date 4/1; no closing date. FAFSA required. Applicants notified on a rolling basis starting 3/15; must reply within 3 week(s) of notification.

**Academics.** All academic programs are ocean-related. USCG ship officer's license may be earned through license option program. **Special study options:** Accelerated study, combined bachelor's/graduate degree, cooperative education, double major, dual enrollment of high school students, independent study, internships, liberal arts/career combination, semester at sea, study abroad, teacher certification program. Merchant marine licensing program available with marine biology, marine science, marine transportation, and marine engineering technology degrees. **Credit/placement by examination:** AP, CLEP, IB, institutional tests. **Support services:** Learning center, pre-admission summer program, remedial instruction, study skills assistance, tutoring.

**Majors. Agriculture:** Aquaculture. **Biology:** General, aquatic, biomedical sciences, botany, marine, zoology. **Business:** Business admin, international, international finance, tourism/travel, transportation. **Conservation:** General, fisheries. **Education:** Biology, science. **Engineering:** Marine, ocean, systems. **Engineering technology:** Mechanical. **Interdisciplinary:** Biological/physical sciences. **Liberal arts:** Arts/sciences. **Parks/recreation:** General. **Physical sciences:** General, geology, hydrology, oceanography. **Transportation:** General, commercial fishing, maritime/Merchant Marine.

**Most popular majors.** Biology 31%, business/marketing 21%, engineering/engineering technologies 13%, interdisciplinary studies 7%, natural resources/environmental science 11%, trade and industry 12%.

**Computing on campus.** 130 workstations in dormitories, library, computer center. Dormitories wired for high-speed internet access and linked to campus network. Commuter students can connect to campus network. Helpline, repair service available.

**Student life. Freshman orientation:** Mandatory, $50 fee. Preregistration for classes offered. 4 days in June and August. **Housing:** Coed dorms, single-sex dorms, special housing for disabled, apartments, substance-free housing available. $250 fully refundable deposit. **Activities:** Choral groups, dance, drama, literary magazine, student government, student newspaper, Circle K, Campus Crusade for Christ, emergency care team, outdoor and environmental conservation, Catholic student association, SEED (Students Encouraging Ethnic Diversity), Wesley Foundation.

**Athletics. Intercollegiate:** Rowing (crew), sailing. **Intramural:** Basketball, football (non-tackle), racquetball, soccer, softball, tennis, volleyball, water polo. **Team name:** Aggies.

**Student services.** Alcohol/substance abuse counseling, campus ministries, career counseling, student employment services, financial aid counseling, health services, minority student services, personal counseling, placement for graduates, veterans' counselor. **Physically disabled:** Services for hearing impaired.

**Contact.** E-mail: seaaggie@tamug.edu
Phone: (409) 740-4414 Toll-free number: (877) 322-4443
Fax: (409) 740-4731
Cheryl Moon, Executive Director of Enrollment Services, Texas A&M University-Galveston, PO Box 1675, Galveston, TX 77553-1675

## Texas A&M University-Kingsville

**Kingsville, Texas**
**www.tamuk.edu**

CB member
CB code: 6822

- Public 4-year university
- Commuter campus in large town
- 5,009 degree-seeking undergraduates
- 1,538 graduate students

**General.** Founded in 1925. Regionally accredited. **Degrees:** 1,050 bachelor's awarded; master's, doctoral offered. **ROTC:** Army. **Location:** 40 miles from Corpus Christi, 250 miles from Houston. **Calendar:** Semester, extensive summer session. **Full-time faculty:** 275 total. **Part-time faculty:** 147 total. **Class size:** 41% < 20, 51% 20-39, 5% 40-49, 2% 50-99, less than 1% >100. **Special facilities:** Equine facilities, observatory, college-operated farms, research center for citrus.

**Freshman class profile.**

| Mid 50% test scores | | Out-of-state: | 1% |
|---|---|---|---|
| SAT critical reading: | 410-520 | Live on campus: | 60% |
| SAT math: | 410-540 | Fraternities: | 2% |
| ACT composite: | 16-21 | Sororities: | 2% |

**Basis for selection.** Open admission, but selective for some programs. Audition required, portfolio recommended for music program.

**High school preparation.** 24 units recommended. Recommended units include English 4, mathematics 3, social studies 4, history 3, science 3, foreign language 3 and academic electives 3. One fine arts, 1 computer recommended.

**2007-2008 Annual costs.** Tuition/fees: $4,878; $13,218 out-of-state. Room/board: $4,654. Books/supplies: $614. Personal expenses: $2,108.

**Financial aid. Non-need-based:** Scholarships awarded for academics, leadership.

**Application procedures. Admission:** No deadline. $15 fee, may be waived for applicants with need. Admission notification on a rolling basis. **Financial aid:** FAFSA required. Applicants notified on a rolling basis.

**Academics. Special study options:** Cooperative education, distance learning, double major, ESL, honors, internships, study abroad, teacher certification program. **Credit/placement by examination:** AP, CLEP.

**Majors. Agriculture:** Agribusiness operations, animal sciences, business, food science, plant sciences, range science. **Architecture:** Interior. **Biology:** General. **Business:** General, accounting, finance, international, management information systems, management science, managerial economics. **Communications:** General. **Conservation:** Wildlife. **Education:** General, agricultural, art, bilingual, elementary, family/consumer sciences, health, music, physical, secondary. **Engineering:** Chemical, civil, computer, electrical, mechanical, petroleum. **Engineering technology:** Industrial management. **English:** English lit. **Family/consumer sciences:** General, clothing/textiles,

family studies, food/nutrition. **Foreign languages:** Spanish. **Health:** Speech pathology. **History:** General. **Math:** General. **Physical sciences:** Chemistry, geology, physics. **Psychology:** General. **Social sciences:** Anthropology, political science, sociology. **Visual/performing arts:** Dramatic, interior design, studio arts.

**Student life. Freshman orientation:** Mandatory. **Housing:** Guaranteed on-campus for freshmen. Coed dorms, single-sex dorms, apartments available. **Activities:** Bands, choral groups, dance, drama, music ensembles, musical theater, radio station, student government, student newspaper, TV station, Muslim student association, Baptist student associates, black student union, La Barraca Tejana, American Society of Women Engineers, Society of Hispanic Professional Engineers, pre-law society.

**Athletics. NCAA. Intercollegiate:** Baseball M, basketball, cross-country, football (tackle) M, softball W, tennis, track and field, volleyball W. **Intramural:** Archery, bowling, equestrian, golf, racquetball, softball, volleyball.

**Student services.** Adult student services, career counseling, student employment services, health services, on-campus daycare, personal counseling, placement for graduates, veterans' counselor. **Physically disabled:** Services for visually, speech, hearing impaired.

**Contact.** E-mail: ksossrx@tamuk.edu
Phone: (361) 593-2315 Toll-free number: (800) 687-6000
Fax: (361) 593-2195
Laura Knippers, Director of Admissions and Registrar, Texas A&M University-Kingsville, MSC 105, Kingsville, TX 78363-8201

## Texas A&M University-Texarkana

**Texarkana, Texas**
**www.tamut.edu**

CB code: 6206

- Public two-year upper-division university
- Commuter campus in small city
- 59% of applicants admitted
- Test scores required

**General.** Founded in 1971. Regionally accredited. **Degrees:** 322 bachelor's awarded; master's offered. **Articulation:** Agreements with Texarkana College, Northeast Texas Community College, Panola College, Paris Junior College, Cossatot College, Rich Mountain College, University of Arkansas Community College at Hope. **Location:** 180 miles from Dallas, 145 miles from Little Rock, Arkansas. **Calendar:** Semester, limited summer session. **Full-time faculty:** 47 total; 15% minority. **Part-time faculty:** 53 total; 6% minority.

**Student profile.** 1,003 degree-seeking undergraduates, 532 degree-seeking graduate students. 454 applied as first time-transfer students, 269 admitted, 231 enrolled.

| | | | |
|---|---|---|---|
| Women: | 73% | Native American: | 1% |
| African American: | 15% | Part-time: | 57% |
| Asian American: | 1% | Out-of-state: | 25% |
| Hispanic American: | 5% | 25 or older: | 60% |

**Basis for selection.** Open admission. College transcript, standardized test scores required. Minimum 2.0 GPA for 75 hours or more; 1.75 GPA for less than 75 hours; must satisfy Texas Success Initiative. Transfer accepted as sophomores, juniors, seniors.

**2007-2008 Annual costs.** Tuition/fees: $3,721; $12,061 out-of-state. Books/supplies: $968. Personal expenses: $1,574.

**Financial aid. Non-need-based:** Scholarships awarded for academics, leadership, state residency.

**Application procedures. Admission:** Rolling admission. No application fee. Application may be submitted online. **Financial aid:** Applicants notified on a rolling basis; must reply within 10 weeks of notification. Must have completed minimum of 54 semester hours of transferable college credit to apply for financial aid. Notified applicants must reply within 45 days from date of award letter. Exceptions made on individual basis. April 1 financial aid deadline for scholarships.

**Academics. Special study options:** Combined bachelor's/graduate degree, cross-registration, distance learning, dual enrollment of high school students, independent study, internships, liberal arts/career combination, student-designed major, teacher certification program. **Credit/placement by examination:** AP, CLEP, IB, institutional tests. BAAS degree limits credit by exam to 18 semester credit hours. **Support services:** Tutoring, writing center.

**Majors. Biology:** General. **Business:** General, accounting, business admin, finance, human resources, international, management information systems, marketing. **Communications:** Media studies. **Computer sciences:** General. **English:** English lit. **Health:** Nursing (RN). **History:** General. **Math:** General. **Protective services:** Criminal justice. **Psychology:** General. **Social sciences:** Political science.

**Most popular majors.** Business/marketing 22%, interdisciplinary studies 34%, liberal arts 15%, psychology 7%.

**Computing on campus.** 119 workstations in library, computer center. Commuter students can connect to campus network. Online library, wireless network available.

**Student life. Activities:** Student government, student newspaper, multicultural association.

**Student services.** Career counseling, student employment services, financial aid counseling, personal counseling, placement for graduates, veterans' counselor. **Physically disabled:** Services for visually, hearing impaired.

**Contact.** E-mail: admissions@tamut.edu
Phone: (903) 223-3069 Fax: (903) 223-3140
Patricia Black, Director of Admissions and Registrar, Texas A&M University-Texarkana, 2600 North Robinson Road, Texarkana, TX 75505-5518

---

## Texas Christian University

Fort Worth, Texas — CB member
www.tcu.edu — CB code: 6820

- Private 4-year university affiliated with Christian Church (Disciples of Christ)
- Residential campus in large city
- 7,264 degree-seeking undergraduates: 4% part-time, 59% women, 5% African American, 3% Asian American, 8% Hispanic American, 5% international
- 1,271 degree-seeking graduate students
- 49% of applicants admitted
- SAT or ACT with writing, application essay required
- 69% graduate within 6 years

**General.** Founded in 1873. Regionally accredited. 2 comprehensive leadership programs offered. Leadership center, information and resources related to leadership development and training. **Degrees:** 1,624 bachelor's awarded; master's, doctoral offered. **ROTC:** Army, Air Force. **Location:** 3 miles from downtown, 29 miles from Dallas. **Calendar:** Semester, limited summer session. **Full-time faculty:** 479 total; 86% have terminal degrees, 12% minority, 43% women. **Part-time faculty:** 317 total; 27% have terminal degrees, 9% minority, 47% women. **Class size:** 46% < 20, 38% 20-39, 10% 40-49, 5% 50-99, 2% >100. **Special facilities:** Geological center for remote sensing, nuclear magnetic resonance facility, observatory, film library, performance complex, behavioral research institute, meteorite collection, lab school, speech and hearing clinic.

**Freshman class profile.** 11,888 applied, 5,812 admitted, 1,644 enrolled.

| Mid 50% test scores | | | |
|---|---|---|---|
| SAT critical reading: | 530-620 | End year in good standing: | 87% |
| SAT math: | 530-640 | Return as sophomores: | 86% |
| SAT writing: | 530-620 | Out-of-state: | 23% |
| ACT composite: | 23-28 | Live on campus: | 93% |
| Rank in top quarter: | 64% | International: | 5% |
| Rank in top tenth: | 30% | Fraternities: | 39% |
| | | Sororities: | 42% |

**Basis for selection.** GED not accepted. Academic credentials most important; talents, leadership potential, and applicant's determination to make difference considered. Audition, portfolio required for fine arts students; interview recommended for all. **Homeschooled:** Interview with admissions officer recommended, additional weight may be placed on SAT/ACT scores in admissions process.

**High school preparation.** 17 units required; 24 recommended. Required and recommended units include English 4, mathematics 3-4, social studies 3-4, science 3-4, foreign language 2-4 and academic electives 2-4.

**2008-2009 Annual costs.** Tuition/fees: $26,948. Room/board: $9,600. Books/supplies: $880. Personal expenses: $1,500.

**2007-2008 Financial aid. Need-based:** 799 full-time freshmen applied for aid; 611 were judged to have need; 607 of these received aid. Average need met was 78%. Average scholarship/grant was $12,529; average loan $8,667. 41% of total undergraduate aid awarded as scholarships/grants, 59%

as loans/jobs. **Non-need-based:** Awarded to 3,291 full-time undergraduates, including 866 freshmen. Scholarships awarded for academics, alumni affiliation, art, leadership, minority status, music/drama, religious affiliation, ROTC, state residency.

**Application procedures. Admission:** Priority date 11/15; deadline 2/15 (postmark date). $40 fee, may be waived for applicants with need. Application may be submitted online. Admission notification 4/1. Admission notification on a rolling basis. Must reply by 5/1. **Financial aid:** Closing date 5/1. FAFSA required. Applicants notified on a rolling basis starting 3/15; must reply by 5/1 or within 2 week(s) of notification.

**Academics.** Premajor option and accompanying special academic advising for entering students unsure of major; can be used for up to 4 semesters. **Special study options:** Accelerated study, combined bachelor's/graduate degree, cross-registration, distance learning, double major, ESL, honors, independent study, internships, liberal arts/career combination, semester at sea, study abroad, teacher certification program, Washington semester. **Credit/placement by examination:** AP, CLEP, IB, institutional tests. **Support services:** Study skills assistance, tutoring, writing center.

**Majors. Biology:** General, biochemistry. **Business:** Accounting, business admin, e-commerce, fashion, finance, international, international finance, international marketing, management science, marketing, real estate. **Communications:** General, advertising, broadcast journalism, journalism, radio/tv. **Computer sciences:** General, information technology. **Conservation:** Environmental science. **Education:** Art, Deaf/hearing impaired, early childhood, English, mathematics, music, physical, science, secondary, social studies. **Engineering:** General. **English:** English lit. **Foreign languages:** French, German, Japanese, Spanish. **Health:** Athletic training, dietetics, movement therapy, nursing (RN), speech pathology. **History:** General. **Interdisciplinary:** Neuroscience. **Liberal arts:** Arts/sciences. **Math:** General. **Parks/recreation:** Health/fitness. **Personal/culinary services:** Food service. **Philosophy/religion:** Philosophy, religion. **Physical sciences:** Chemistry, geology, physics. **Protective services:** Criminal justice. **Psychology:** General. **Public administration:** Social work. **Social sciences:** Anthropology, economics, geography, international economics, international relations, political science, sociology. **Theology:** Sacred music. **Visual/performing arts:** Acting, art history/conservation, ballet, ceramics, dance, directing/producing, dramatic, film/cinema, graphic design, interior design, music performance, music theory/composition, painting, photography, piano/organ, printmaking, sculpture, studio arts, theater design. **Other:** Writing.

**Most popular majors.** Business/marketing 23%, communications/journalism 19%, education 8%, health sciences 10%, social sciences 8%.

**Computing on campus.** Dormitories wired for high-speed internet access and linked to campus network. Commuter students can connect to campus network. Online course registration, online library, helpline, repair service, wireless network available.

**Student life. Freshman orientation:** Mandatory, $115 fee. Preregistration for classes offered. 2 or 3 day program for students and parents. **Housing:** Guaranteed on-campus for freshmen. Coed dorms, single-sex dorms, apartments, fraternity/sorority housing, substance-free housing available. $250 partly refundable deposit, deadline 5/1. Designated rooms available for ADA needs. **Activities:** Bands, campus ministries, choral groups, dance, drama, international student organizations, literary magazine, music ensembles, musical theater, opera, radio station, student government, student newspaper, TV station, over 190 social, religious, service, academic, and preprofessional organizations.

**Athletics.** NCAA. **Intercollegiate:** Baseball M, basketball, cross-country, diving, equestrian W, football (tackle) M, golf, rifle W, soccer W, swimming, tennis, track and field, volleyball W. **Team name:** Horned Frogs.

**Student services.** Adult student services, alcohol/substance abuse counseling, campus ministries, career counseling, student employment services, financial aid counseling, health services, minority student services, personal counseling, placement for graduates, veterans' counselor, women's services. **Physically disabled:** Services for visually, speech, hearing impaired.

**Contact.** E-mail: frogmail@tcu.edu
Phone: (817) 257-7490 Toll-free number: (800) 828-3764
Fax: (817) 257-7268
Raymond Brown, Dean of Admissions, Texas Christian University, TCU Box 297013, Fort Worth, TX 76129

---

## Texas College

Tyler, Texas
www.texascollege.edu — CB code: 6821

- Private 4-year liberal arts college affiliated with Christian Methodist Episcopal Church
- Residential campus in small city

◆ 741 degree-seeking undergraduates: 3% part-time, 42% women, 87% African American, 9% Hispanic American

◆ 33 degree-seeking graduate students

**General.** Founded in 1894. Regionally accredited. **Degrees:** 76 bachelor's, 1 associate awarded. **Location:** 90 miles from Dallas, 100 miles from Shreveport, Louisiana. **Calendar:** Semester, limited summer session. **Full-time faculty:** 36 total; 50% have terminal degrees, 67% minority, 33% women. **Part-time faculty:** 15 total; 53% have terminal degrees, 73% minority, 53% women. **Class size:** 60% < 20, 22% 20-39, 12% 40-49, 6% 50-99, less than 1% >100.

**Freshman class profile.** 218 enrolled.

**Basis for selection.** Open admission. Students admitted based on completion of minimum of 16 high school units and submission of official high school transcript or GED test scores. SAT/ACT recommended for scholarships and placement.

**High school preparation.** 16 units required. Required units include English 4, mathematics 2, social studies 2, science 2 and academic electives 6.

**2007-2008 Annual costs.** Tuition/fees: $8,746. Room/board: $5,600. Books/supplies: $800. Personal expenses: $1,500.

**2006-2007 Financial aid. Need-based:** 185 full-time freshmen applied for aid; 181 were judged to have need; 177 of these received aid. Average need met was 61%. Average scholarship/grant was $6,268; average loan $2,053. 58% of total undergraduate aid awarded as scholarships/grants, 42% as loans/jobs. **Non-need-based:** Awarded to 272 full-time undergraduates, including 57 freshmen.

**Application procedures. Admission:** No deadline. $20 fee, may be waived for applicants with need. Application must be submitted on paper. Admission notification on a rolling basis. **Financial aid:** Priority date 6/1; no closing date. FAFSA, institutional form required. Applicants notified on a rolling basis starting 4/15; must reply within 2 week(s) of notification.

**Academics. Special study options:** Accelerated study, distance learning, double major, dual enrollment of high school students, independent study, internships, teacher certification program. **Credit/placement by examination:** AP, CLEP, institutional tests. 32 credit hours maximum toward bachelor's degree. **Support services:** Learning center, reduced course load, remedial instruction, study skills assistance, tutoring.

**Majors. Biology:** General. **Business:** Business admin. **Computer sciences:** General. **Education:** Art, biology, elementary, history, mathematics, middle, music, physical. **English:** English lit. **History:** General. **Liberal arts:** Arts/sciences. **Math:** General. **Parks/recreation:** Health/fitness. **Philosophy/religion:** Religion. **Protective services:** Law enforcement admin. **Public administration:** Social work. **Social sciences:** Political science, sociology. **Visual/performing arts:** Studio arts.

**Most popular majors.** Biology 12%, business/marketing 58%, public administration/social services 8%.

**Computing on campus.** 200 workstations in dormitories, library, computer center. Dormitories wired for high-speed internet access and linked to campus network. Commuter students can connect to campus network. Online library, helpline, repair service, student web hosting, wireless network available.

**Student life. Freshman orientation:** Mandatory. Preregistration for classes offered. Held first week of school. **Policies:** Students required to attend weekly religious-natured assembly program twice a month. Religious observance required. **Housing:** Guaranteed on-campus for freshmen. Single-sex dorms, substance-free housing available. $150 nonrefundable deposit, deadline 8/15. Housing for students in single parent program. **Activities:** Bands, choral groups, dance, music ensembles, student government, Young Adults for Christ, NAACP, Fellowship of Christian Athletes, criminal justice association, Students in Free Enterprise, student ministerial alliance, pre-alumni council, Young Republicans.

**Athletics.** NAIA. **Intercollegiate:** Baseball M, basketball, cheerleading, football (tackle) M, soccer, softball W, track and field, volleyball W. **Intramural:** Basketball, football (non-tackle) M, softball W, volleyball W. **Team name:** Steers.

**Student services.** Adult student services, alcohol/substance abuse counseling, campus ministries, career counseling, student employment services, financial aid counseling, health services, on-campus daycare, personal counseling.

**Contact.** E-mail: rbrazzle@texascollege.edu
Phone: (903) 593-8311 ext. 2297 Toll-free number: (800) 306-6299
Fax: (903) 526-7879
Reggie Brazzle, Director of Enrollment Services, Texas College, 2404 North Grand Avenue, Tyler, TX 75712-4500

---

### Texas Lutheran University
Seguin, Texas
www.tlu.edu

CB member
CB code: 6823

◆ Private 4-year university and liberal arts college affiliated with Evangelical Lutheran Church in America

◆ Residential campus in large town

◆ 1,334 degree-seeking undergraduates: 2% part-time, 52% women, 9% African American, 1% Asian American, 19% Hispanic American, 1% international

◆ 63% of applicants admitted

◆ SAT or ACT (ACT writing optional), application essay required

◆ 55% graduate within 6 years

**General.** Founded in 1891. Regionally accredited. **Degrees:** 260 bachelor's awarded. **ROTC:** Army, Air Force. **Location:** 30 miles from San Antonio, 55 miles from Austin. **Calendar:** Semester, limited summer session. **Full-time faculty:** 66 total; 79% have terminal degrees, 14% minority, 42% women. **Part-time faculty:** 66 total; 39% have terminal degrees, 17% minority, 42% women. **Class size:** 50% < 20, 48% 20-39, 3% 40-49. **Special facilities:** Biology field station, Mexican-American study center, life enrichment center, geological museum.

**Freshman class profile.** 1,166 applied, 735 admitted, 365 enrolled.

| Mid 50% test scores | | | |
|---|---|---|---|
| SAT critical reading: | 450-550 | GPA 2.0-2.99: | 21% |
| SAT math: | 460-580 | Rank in top quarter: | 51% |
| SAT writing: | 440-530 | Rank in top tenth: | 21% |
| ACT composite: | 19-24 | Return as sophomores: | 64% |
| GPA 3.50 or higher: | 51% | Out-of-state: | 2% |
| GPA 3.0-3.49: | 26% | Live on campus: | 88% |

**Basis for selection.** Quality of academic curriculum pursued and class rank most important. Academic record and test scores also important. Interview recommended. **Homeschooled:** Transcript of courses and grades, letter of recommendation (nonparent) required. Greater emphasis placed on SAT or ACT scores.

**High school preparation.** 17 units required; 23 recommended. Required and recommended units include English 4, mathematics 3-4, social studies 3-4, history 2, science 3-4 (laboratory 2), foreign language 2-3, computer science 1 and academic electives 1.

**2007-2008 Annual costs.** Tuition/fees: $20,060. Room/board: $5,860. Books/supplies: $740. Personal expenses: $1,100.

**2006-2007 Financial aid. Need-based:** 378 full-time freshmen applied for aid; 281 were judged to have need; 281 of these received aid. Average need met was 41%. Average scholarship/grant was $11,431; average loan $3,174. 65% of total undergraduate aid awarded as scholarships/grants, 35% as loans/jobs. **Non-need-based:** Awarded to 382 full-time undergraduates, including 132 freshmen. Scholarships awarded for academics, alumni affiliation, art, job skills, leadership, music/drama, religious affiliation.

**Application procedures. Admission:** Priority date 5/6; deadline 8/6 (postmark date). $25 fee, may be waived for applicants with need. Application may be submitted online. Admission notification on a rolling basis beginning on or about 10/1. **Financial aid:** Priority date 4/1; no closing date. FAFSA required. Applicants notified on a rolling basis starting 3/1; must reply within 2 week(s) of notification.

**Academics. Special study options:** Combined bachelor's/graduate degree, double major, dual enrollment of high school students, honors, independent study, internships, liberal arts/career combination, study abroad, teacher certification program, Washington semester. International studies curriculum, dual BS program in applied science and engineering in conjunction with Texas state institutions. **Credit/placement by examination:** AP, CLEP, IB, institutional tests. 30 credit hours maximum toward bachelor's degree. **Support services:** Study skills assistance, tutoring, writing center.

**Majors. Biology:** General, molecular. **Business:** General, accounting, business admin. **Communications:** General. **Computer sciences:** General, computer science, information systems. **Education:** Elementary, English, history, mathematics, middle, multi-level teacher, music, physical, reading, social studies. **English:** English lit. **Foreign languages:** Spanish. **Health:** Athletic training. **History:** General, public archives. **Math:** General. **Parks/

**recreation:** Exercise sciences, health/fitness, sports admin. **Philosophy/ religion:** Philosophy. **Physical sciences:** Chemistry, physics. **Psychology:** General. **Social sciences:** Economics, political science, sociology. **Theology:** Preministerial, youth ministry. **Visual/performing arts:** General, art, dramatic, music history, music performance. **Other:** Pre-engineering/ applied science.

**Most popular majors.** Biology 10%, business/marketing 22%, education 11%, parks/recreation 13%, physical sciences 6%, psychology 6%, social sciences 6%.

**Computing on campus.** 48 workstations in dormitories, library, computer center, student center. Dormitories wired for high-speed internet access and linked to campus network. Commuter students can connect to campus network. Online library, helpline, wireless network available.

**Student life. Freshman orientation:** Mandatory. Preregistration for classes offered. Held 2 days prior to start of fall semester. **Housing:** Guaranteed on-campus for freshmen. Coed dorms, single-sex dorms, apartments available. $200 fully refundable deposit, deadline 8/6. **Activities:** Bands, choral groups, dance, drama, literary magazine, music ensembles, musical theater, student government, student newspaper, symphony orchestra, black student union, Mexican American student association, Young Democrats, College Republicans, Fellowship of Christian Athletes, Students Make a Difference, Lutheran student movement, Canterbury, Catholic student organization, international student association.

**Athletics.** NCAA. **Intercollegiate:** Baseball M, basketball, cross-country W, football (tackle) M, golf, soccer, softball W, tennis, track and field W, volleyball W. **Intramural:** Basketball, bowling, football (non-tackle), handball, racquetball, softball, swimming, tennis, volleyball. **Team name:** Bulldogs.

**Student services.** Alcohol/substance abuse counseling, campus ministries, career counseling, student employment services, financial aid counseling, health services, personal counseling, placement for graduates, veterans' counselor.

**Contact.** E-mail: admissions@tlu.edu
Phone: (830) 372-8050 Toll-free number: (800) 771-8521
Fax: (830) 372-8096
Jamie Kocian, Director of Admissions, Texas Lutheran University, 1000 West Court Street, Seguin, TX 78155-5999

---

## Texas Southern University
**Houston, Texas**  **CB member**
www.tsu.edu  **CB code: 6824**

- Public 4-year university
- Commuter campus in very large city
- 7,572 degree-seeking undergraduates: 20% part-time, 59% women, 90% African American, 3% Asian American, 4% Hispanic American, 3% international
- 1,918 degree-seeking graduate students

**General.** Founded in 1947. Regionally accredited. **Degrees:** 780 bachelor's awarded; master's, doctoral, first professional offered. **ROTC:** Army. **Location:** 2 miles from downtown. **Calendar:** Semester, extensive summer session. **Full-time faculty:** 342 total; 85% minority, 42% women. **Part-time faculty:** 191 total; 91% minority, 52% women. **Class size:** 36% < 20, 44% 20-39, 14% 40-49, 5% 50-99, less than 1% >100. **Special facilities:** University museum.

**Freshman class profile.** 7,098 applied, 6,952 admitted, 1,266 enrolled.

| Mid 50% test scores | | End year in good standing: | 65% |
|---|---|---|---|
| ACT composite: | 14-19 | Return as sophomores: | 50% |
| GPA 3.50 or higher: | 10% | Out-of-state: | 22% |
| GPA 3.0-3.49: | 18% | Live on campus: | 21% |
| GPA 2.0-2.99: | 55% | International: | 3% |
| Rank in top quarter: | 25% | Fraternities: | 3% |
| Rank in top tenth: | 7% | Sororities: | 1% |

**Basis for selection.** Open admission, but selective for some programs. Special requirements for pharmacy, law, accounting, marketing, and computer science programs. For selective programs high school achievement, interview, essay important; test scores, individual abilities, high school activities considered.

**High school preparation.** Recommended units include English 4, mathematics 3, social studies 4, science 2, foreign language 2 and academic electives 6.

**2007-2008 Annual costs.** Tuition/fees: $5,878; $14,128 out-of-state. Room/ board: $6,664. Books/supplies: $1,200. Personal expenses: $2,025.

---

**Financial aid.** All financial aid based on need.

**Application procedures. Admission:** Priority date 7/31; deadline 8/15 (postmark date). $42 fee, may be waived for applicants with need. Application may be submitted online. Admission notification on a rolling basis. Must reply by 7/31. **Financial aid:** Priority date 5/1; no closing date. FAFSA required. Applicants notified on a rolling basis starting 6/1.

**Academics. Special study options:** Cooperative education, distance learning, double major, ESL, honors, internships, teacher certification program, weekend college. **Credit/placement by examination:** CLEP, institutional tests. **Support services:** Learning center, pre-admission summer program, remedial instruction, study skills assistance, tutoring.

**Majors. Biology:** General. **Business:** Accounting, banking/financial services, business admin, management information systems, marketing, operations. **Communications:** General, journalism, radio/tv. **Computer sciences:** General. **Conservation:** Environmental studies. **Education:** Health, physical. **Engineering technology:** Civil, electrical, industrial. **English:** English lit, speech/rhetoric. **Family/consumer sciences:** General, child development, food/nutrition. **Foreign languages:** French, Spanish. **Health:** Clinical lab science, dietetics, environmental health, health care admin, health services, medical records admin, nursing (RN), prepharmacy, respiratory therapy technology. **History:** General. **Math:** General. **Parks/recreation:** Health/fitness. **Physical sciences:** Chemistry, physics. **Protective services:** Law enforcement admin. **Psychology:** General. **Public administration:** General, social work. **Social sciences:** Economics, political science, sociology. **Transportation:** Aviation, aviation management. **Visual/performing arts:** Dramatic, fashion design, studio arts.

**Most popular majors.** Biology 11%, business/marketing 25%, health sciences 12%, security/protective services 7%.

**Computing on campus.** 500 workstations in library, computer center, student center. Online course registration, online library, wireless network available.

**Student life. Freshman orientation:** Mandatory. Preregistration for classes offered. Two-day orientation held every semester during registration week. First-time freshmen and transfer students participate in seminars, meet with academic advisors, complete course selection/registration, and take placement test. **Housing:** Guaranteed on-campus for freshmen. Single-sex dorms, apartments available. $300 deposit, deadline 6/1. **Activities:** Bands, choral groups, drama, film society, music ensembles, musical theater, opera, radio station, student government, student newspaper, symphony orchestra, TV station, Alpha Phi Omega, Campus Crusade for Christ, health information management association, sociology club, political science club, student psychological club, NAACP.

**Athletics.** NCAA. **Intercollegiate:** Baseball M, basketball, bowling W, cross-country, football (tackle) M, golf, soccer W, softball W, tennis, track and field, volleyball W. **Intramural:** Basketball, bowling W, cheerleading, softball W, tennis, track and field, volleyball W. **Team name:** Tigers.

**Student services.** Alcohol/substance abuse counseling, campus ministries, career counseling, student employment services, financial aid counseling, health services, on-campus daycare, personal counseling, placement for graduates, veterans' counselor. **Physically disabled:** Services for speech impaired.

**Contact.** E-mail: admissions@tsu.edu
Phone: (713) 313-7472 Toll-free number: (866) 878-4968
Fax: (713) 313-7851
Brian Armstrong, Director of Recruitment and Retention, Texas Southern University, 3100 Cleburne Street, Houston, TX 77004

---

## Texas State University: San Marcos
**San Marcos, Texas**  **CB member**
www.txstate.edu  **CB code: 6667**

- Public 4-year university
- Commuter campus in large town
- 24,038 degree-seeking undergraduates: 18% part-time, 55% women, 5% African American, 2% Asian American, 22% Hispanic American, 1% Native American, 1% international
- 3,484 degree-seeking graduate students
- 71% of applicants admitted
- SAT or ACT with writing, application essay required
- 55% graduate within 6 years; 27% enter graduate study

**General.** Founded in 1899. Regionally accredited. **Degrees:** 4,673 bachelor's awarded; master's, doctoral, first professional offered. **ROTC:** Army, Air Force. **Location:** 30 miles from Austin, 49 miles from San Antonio.

**Calendar:** Semester, extensive summer session. **Full-time faculty:** 897 total; 70% have terminal degrees, 19% minority, 45% women. **Part-time faculty:** 418 total; 30% have terminal degrees, 10% minority, 54% women. **Class size:** 16% < 20, 55% 20-39, 9% 40-49, 13% 50-99, 7% >100. **Special facilities:** Ranch, natural spring with unique aquatic plants and animals, Southwestern writers collection (original manuscripts), observatory with 17-inch telescope, archeological forensic laboratory.

**Freshman class profile.** 10,869 applied, 7,710 admitted, 3,065 enrolled.

| Mid 50% test scores | | Rank in top tenth: | 14% |
| --- | --- | --- | --- |
| SAT critical reading: | 480-580 | End year in good standing: | 88% |
| SAT math: | 500-590 | Return as sophomores: | 75% |
| SAT writing: | 470-560 | Out-of-state: | 1% |
| ACT composite: | 21-25 | Live on campus: | 89% |
| Rank in top quarter: | 55% | International: | 1% |

**Basis for selection.** Applicants who rank in top 10% of high school class have no minimum test score requirements. Otherwise score requirements are as follows: rank in next 15%, 920 SAT or 20 ACT; rank in second quarter, 1010 SAT, 22 ACT; rank in third quarter, 1180 SAT, 26 ACT; rank in bottom quarter, 1270 SAT, 29 ACT. (SAT scores exclusive of Writing). SAT Subject Tests required for placement in certain higher level courses. SAT Subject Tests required for placement in certain higher level courses. Audition required for music program. **Homeschooled:** Transcript of courses and grades required. Minimum 26 ACT or 1180 SAT (exclusive of Writing) and admissions essay.

**High school preparation.** 24 units required; 26 recommended. Required and recommended units include English 4, mathematics 3-4, social studies 3.5, science 3-4 (laboratory 2), foreign language 2-3, computer science 1, visual/performing arts 1, academic electives 3.5. 1.5 physical education, 1 computer literacy, 1 fine arts, 0.5 economics, 0.5 speech required, 0.5 health education required.

**2008-2009 Annual costs.** Tuition/fees: $6,994; $15,424 out-of-state. Room/board: $6,012. Books/supplies: $1,000. Personal expenses: $2,550.

**2007-2008 Financial aid. Need-based:** 1,991 full-time freshmen applied for aid; 1,353 were judged to have need; 1,294 of these received aid. Average need met was 66%. Average scholarship/grant was $4,534; average loan $3,085. 47% of total undergraduate aid awarded as scholarships/grants, 53% as loans/jobs. **Non-need-based:** Awarded to 1,814 full-time undergraduates, including 656 freshmen. Scholarships awarded for academics, art, athletics, leadership, music/drama, ROTC, state residency.

**Application procedures. Admission:** Closing date 5/1 (receipt date). $40 fee, may be waived for applicants with need. Application may be submitted online. Admission notification on a rolling basis beginning on or about 9/15. Applicants to the McCoy College of Business must have their application in by March 15 for Summer and Fall Admission and October 15 for Spring admission. Applicants to the Department of Communication Design must have application in by March 15 for fall admission and October 15 for Spring admission. **Financial aid:** Priority date 4/1; no closing date. FAFSA required. Applicants notified on a rolling basis starting 5/1; must reply within 3 week(s) of notification.

**Academics. Special study options:** Accelerated study, combined bachelor's/graduate degree, distance learning, double major, dual enrollment of high school students, ESL, exchange student, honors, independent study, internships, study abroad, teacher certification program, Washington semester, weekend college. **Credit/placement by examination:** AP, CLEP, IB, institutional tests. Credit hours earned by exam do not count as credit earned in residence. **Support services:** Learning center, remedial instruction, study skills assistance, tutoring, writing center.

**Majors. Agriculture:** General, agribusiness operations, animal sciences. **Architecture:** Urban/community planning. **Area/ethnic studies:** American, Asian, European, Near/Middle Eastern, Russian/Slavic. **Biology:** General, animal physiology, aquatic, biochemistry, botany, microbiology, wildlife, zoology. **Business:** Accounting, business admin, fashion, finance, management information systems, managerial economics, marketing. **Communications:** Advertising, journalism, media studies, public relations, radio/tv. **Communications technology:** Desktop publishing, recording arts. **Computer sciences:** General. **Conservation:** Environmental science, water/wetlands/marine. **Engineering:** Electrical, industrial, manufacturing. **Engineering technology:** General, construction, industrial, manufacturing. **English:** English lit, speech/rhetoric. **Family/consumer sciences:** General, family studies, food/nutrition. **Foreign languages:** French, German, Spanish. **Health:** Athletic training, audiology/speech pathology, clinical lab science, health care admin, health services, medical radiologic technology/radiation therapy, medical records admin, respiratory therapy technology. **History:** General. **Interdisciplinary:** Global studies. **Math:** General, applied. **Parks/recreation:** Facilities management, health/fitness, sports admin. **Philosophy/religion:** Philosophy. **Physical sciences:** Chemistry, physics. **Protective services:** Corrections, criminal justice, police science.

**Psychology:** General. **Public administration:** General, social work. **Social sciences:** Anthropology, cartography, economics, geography, international relations, political science, sociology. **Visual/performing arts:** Art, dance, dramatic, graphic design, interior design, jazz, music performance, studio arts.

**Most popular majors.** Business/marketing 20%, communications/journalism 7%, English 6%, interdisciplinary studies 12%, parks/recreation 6%, social sciences 7%, visual/performing arts 7%.

**Computing on campus.** 1,480 workstations in dormitories, library, computer center, student center. Dormitories wired for high-speed internet access and linked to campus network. Commuter students can connect to campus network. Online course registration, helpline, repair service, student web hosting, wireless network available.

**Student life. Freshman orientation:** Mandatory, $25 fee. Preregistration for classes offered. 2-day program combined with welcome week prior to start of semester. **Policies:** All unmarried students under 21 with fewer than 56 credit hours must live in university housing. **Housing:** Guaranteed on-campus for freshmen. Coed dorms, single-sex dorms, apartments, fraternity/sorority housing, substance-free housing available. $100 fully refundable deposit. **Activities:** Bands, campus ministries, choral groups, dance, drama, film society, international student organizations, literary magazine, music ensembles, Model UN, musical theater, opera, radio station, student government, student newspaper, symphony orchestra, over 250 social, service, religious, political, and professional organizations.

**Athletics.** NCAA. **Intercollegiate:** Baseball M, basketball, cheerleading, cross-country, football (tackle) M, golf, soccer W, softball W, tennis W, track and field, volleyball W. **Intramural:** Basketball, bowling, football (non-tackle), golf, racquetball, soccer, softball, tennis, volleyball. **Team name:** Bobcats.

**Student services.** Adult student services, alcohol/substance abuse counseling, campus ministries, career counseling, student employment services, financial aid counseling, health services, legal services, minority student services, personal counseling, placement for graduates, veterans' counselor. **Physically disabled:** Services for visually, speech, hearing impaired.

**Contact.** E-mail: admissions@txstate.edu
Phone: (512) 245-2364 Fax: (512) 245-8044
Christie Kangas, Director of Admissions, Texas State University: San Marcos, 429 North Guadalupe Street, San Marcos, TX 78666-5709

---

## Texas Tech University
Lubbock, Texas
www.ttu.edu

CB member
CB code: 6827

- Public 4-year university
- Commuter campus in small city
- 22,996 degree-seeking undergraduates: 8% part-time, 44% women, 4% African American, 3% Asian American, 13% Hispanic American, 1% Native American, 1% international
- 4,961 degree-seeking graduate students
- 77% of applicants admitted
- SAT or ACT with writing required
- 56% graduate within 6 years

**General.** Founded in 1923. Regionally accredited. **Degrees:** 4,673 bachelor's awarded; master's, doctoral, first professional offered. **ROTC:** Army, Air Force. **Location:** 320 miles from Dallas, 320 miles from Albuquerque, New Mexico. **Calendar:** Semester, extensive summer session. **Full-time faculty:** 1,078 total; 6% have terminal degrees, 15% minority, 35% women. **Part-time faculty:** 96 total; 7% have terminal degrees, 10% minority, 52% women. **Class size:** 24% < 20, 42% 20-39, 13% 40-49, 14% 50-99, 8% >100. **Special facilities:** Museum, national fanching heritage center, special collections library, archaeological dig/state park, international cultural center, international textile research center, science research laboratory, arid and semi-arid land studies center, seismological observatory, child development research center, institutes for environmental and human health, Vietnam center, Moody planetarium.

**Freshman class profile.** 13,976 applied, 10,759 admitted, 4,496 enrolled.

| Mid 50% test scores | | End year in good standing: | 85% |
|---|---|---|---|
| SAT critical reading: | 480-580 | Return as sophomores: | 83% |
| SAT math: | 500-610 | Out-of-state: | 4% |
| SAT writing: | 460-560 | Live on campus: | 90% |
| ACT composite: | 21-26 | International: | 1% |
| Rank in top quarter: | 48% | Fraternities: | 12% |
| Rank in top tenth: | 18% | Sororities: | 21% |

**Basis for selection.** Class rank and test scores considered first, and students meeting the following score requirements (exclusive of Writing) eligible for unconditional admission: class rank in top 10%, no minimum test scores; rank in next 15%, with 1140 SAT or 25 ACT; rank in second quarter, with 1230 SAT or 28 ACT; rank in lower half, with 1270 SAT or 29 ACT. Applicants who do not meet assured admission criteria will have records reviewed in holistic manner. Auditions and portfolios required for admission to some programs.

**High school preparation.** 11 units required. Required units include English 4, mathematics 3, science 2 (laboratory 2) and foreign language 2. Algebra I, geometry, and algebra II recommended for required math units. Biology I, chemistry I or physics I recommended for science units. If 2 years of foreign language not completed in high school, at least 2 semesters of single foreign language will be required at college level.

**2007-2008 Annual costs.** Tuition/fees: $6,783; $15,123 out-of-state. Students from adjacent counties in New Mexico and Oklahoma pay in-state tuition rates; students from all other counties in New Mexico and Oklahoma pay reduced out-of-state tuition rates. Room/board: $7,460. Books/supplies: $845. Personal expenses: $1,926.

**2006-2007 Financial aid. Need-based:** 2,731 full-time freshmen applied for aid; 1,462 were judged to have need; 1,434 of these received aid. Average need met was 52%. Average scholarship/grant was $5,794; average loan $3,048. 46% of total undergraduate aid awarded as scholarships/grants, 54% as loans/jobs. **Non-need-based:** Awarded to 3,033 full-time undergraduates, including 1,002 freshmen. Scholarships awarded for academics, art, athletics, job skills, leadership, music/drama, ROTC.

**Application procedures. Admission:** Closing date 5/1 (receipt date). $50 fee, may be waived for applicants with need. Application may be submitted online. Admission notification on a rolling basis. **Financial aid:** Priority date 4/15; no closing date. FAFSA required. Applicants notified on a rolling basis; must reply within 2 week(s) of notification.

**Academics. Special study options:** Accelerated study, combined bachelor's/graduate degree, cooperative education, distance learning, double major, dual enrollment of high school students, ESL, external degree, honors, independent study, internships, liberal arts/career combination, semester at sea, student-designed major, study abroad, teacher certification program. **Credit/placement by examination:** AP, CLEP, IB, SAT, ACT, institutional tests. **Support services:** Learning center, pre-admission summer program, remedial instruction, study skills assistance, tutoring, writing center.

**Honors college/program.** Requires separate application, minimum 1200 SAT (exclusive of Writing) or 26 ACT, or top 10% class rank, essays, 2 teacher recommendations. 245 freshmen admitted. Average SAT score: 1304; total enrollment 801. 2 tracks offered to students: nondegree program working with all colleges and majors to provide honors academic, co-curricular and social program; and interdisciplinary degree program for bachelor of arts degree in natural history and humanities or Honors Arts and Letters.

**Majors. Agriculture:** General, agronomy, animal sciences, business, communications, economics, food science, horticulture, range science. **Architecture:** Architecture, interior, landscape. **Area/ethnic studies:** Latin American, Russian/Slavic. **Biology:** General, biochemistry, cellular/molecular, microbiology, zoology. **Business:** General, accounting, business admin, fashion, finance, hotel/motel admin, international, management information systems, marketing. **Communications:** Advertising, journalism, photojournalism, public relations, radio/tv. **Computer sciences:** General. **Conservation:** General, fisheries, wildlife. **Engineering:** General, chemical, civil, computer, electrical, environmental, industrial, mechanical, petroleum, physics. **Engineering technology:** General, architectural, electrical, mechanical. **English:** English lit, speech/rhetoric, technical writing. **Family/consumer sciences:** General, child development, clothing/textiles, family studies, family systems, family/community services, food/nutrition, work/family studies. **Foreign languages:** Classics, French, German, Spanish. **Health:** Dietetics, health services. **History:** General. **Interdisciplinary:** Biological/physical sciences. **Liberal arts:** Arts/sciences. **Math:** General. **Parks/recreation:** Health/fitness. **Philosophy/religion:** Philosophy. **Physical sciences:** Chemistry, geology, geophysics, physics. **Psychology:** General. **Public administration:** Social work. **Social sciences:** Anthropology, economics, geography, political science, sociology. **Visual/performing arts:** Acting, art, art history/conservation, dance, dramatic, fashion design, graphic design, music performance, music theory/composition, studio arts, theater design. **Other:** Energy commerce, Multidisciplinary studies/ University studies.

**Most popular majors.** Business/marketing 27%, communications/journalism 7%, engineering/engineering technologies 9%, family/consumer sciences 12%.

**Computing on campus.** 3,000 workstations in dormitories, library, computer center, student center. Dormitories wired for high-speed internet access and linked to campus network. Commuter students can connect to campus network. Online course registration, online library, helpline, repair service, student web hosting, wireless network available.

**Student life. Freshman orientation:** Mandatory, $55 fee. Preregistration for classes offered. Two- or three-day sessions held in January, April, May, June and July. **Policies:** Freshmen required to live on campus. **Housing:** Guaranteed on-campus for freshmen. Coed dorms, single-sex dorms, special housing for disabled, apartments, substance-free housing available. $50 nonrefundable deposit, deadline 5/1. Special interest housing: honors, intensive study, learning communities, upperclass-graduate areas. **Activities:** Bands, campus ministries, choral groups, dance, drama, international student organizations, literary magazine, music ensembles, musical theater, radio station, student government, student newspaper, symphony orchestra, TV station, College Republicans, Wesley Foundation, black student association, Hispanic student society, Alpha Phi Omega, women's service organization, University Democrats, Campus Crusade for Christ.

**Athletics.** NCAA. **Intercollegiate:** Baseball M, basketball, cross-country, football (tackle) M, golf, soccer W, softball W, tennis, track and field, volleyball W. **Intramural:** Badminton, baseball, basketball, bowling, football (non-tackle), golf, racquetball, soccer, softball, swimming, table tennis, tennis, volleyball, water polo, weight lifting. **Team name:** Red Raiders/ Lady Raiders.

**Student services.** Alcohol/substance abuse counseling, career counseling, student employment services, financial aid counseling, health services, legal services, personal counseling, placement for graduates, veterans' counselor. **Physically disabled:** Services for visually, speech, hearing impaired. **Learning disabled:** Comprehensive services available.

**Contact.** E-mail: admissions@ttu.edu
Phone: (806) 742-1480 Fax: (806) 742-0062
Robert Shindell, Associate Vice President of Recruitment and Admissions, Texas Tech University, Box 45005, Lubbock, TX 79409-5005

## Texas Tech University Health Sciences Center
### Lubbock, Texas
www.ttuhsc.edu

CB code: 3423

▶ Public two-year upper-division university
▶ Commuter campus in small city

**General.** Founded in 1969. Regionally accredited. **Degrees:** 526 bachelor's awarded; master's, doctoral, first professional offered. **Calendar:** Semester. **Full-time faculty:** 750 total; 81% have terminal degrees, 14% minority, 41% women. **Part-time faculty:** 69 total; 83% have terminal degrees, 12% minority, 35% women.

**Student profile.** 608 degree-seeking undergraduates, 2,008 degree-seeking graduate students.

| Women: | 86% | Hispanic American: | 12% |
|---|---|---|---|
| African American: | 5% | International: | 1% |
| Asian American: | 4% | Part-time: | 10% |

**Basis for selection.** Transfer accepted as juniors.

**2007-2008 Annual costs.** Tuition and fees vary by school and program: $126 per-credit-hour in-state for School of Allied Health Sciences or $404 out-of-state.

**Application procedures. Admission:** $40 fee.

**Academics. Special study options:** Combined bachelor's/graduate degree, distance learning. **Credit/placement by examination:** CLEP.

**Majors. Health:** Clinical lab science, communication disorders, health care admin, health services, nursing (RN).

**Student services. Physically disabled:** Services for visually, speech, hearing impaired.

**Contact.** Phone: (806) 743-2300
Texas Tech University Health Sciences Center, 3601 Fourth Street, Lubbock, TX 79430

## Texas Wesleyan University
### Fort Worth, Texas
www.txwes.edu                                    CB code: 6828

▶ Private 4-year university affiliated with United Methodist Church
▶ Commuter campus in large city
▶ 1,422 degree-seeking undergraduates: 23% part-time, 66% women, 19% African American, 2% Asian American, 20% Hispanic American
▶ 1,444 degree-seeking graduate students
▶ 61% of applicants admitted
▶ SAT or ACT (ACT writing optional) required

**General.** Founded in 1890. Regionally accredited. **Degrees:** 225 bachelor's awarded; master's, first professional offered. **ROTC:** Army, Air Force. **Location:** 2 miles from downtown. **Calendar:** Semester, limited summer session. **Full-time faculty:** 154 total; 79% have terminal degrees, 13% minority, 49% women. **Class size:** 62% < 20, 36% 20-39, 1% 40-49, less than 1% 50-99.

**Freshman class profile.** 745 applied, 456 admitted, 211 enrolled.

| Mid 50% test scores | | | |
|---|---|---|---|
| SAT critical reading: | 450-550 | End year in good standing: | 70% |
| SAT math: | 430-550 | Return as sophomores: | 59% |
| ACT composite: | 17-23 | Live on campus: | 6% |

**Basis for selection.** Regular freshmen admission requires minimum 2.5 high school GPA, 19 ACT or 920 SAT combined score (exclusive of Writing), top 50% ranking in senior class. **Homeschooled:** Transcript of courses and grades required.

**High school preparation.** 20 units recommended. Recommended units include English 4, mathematics 4, social studies 3, science 3, foreign language 1 and academic electives 7.

**2008-2009 Annual costs.** Tuition/fees: $16,730. Room/board: $6,100. Books/supplies: $1,020. Personal expenses: $1,863.

**Financial aid.** All financial aid based on need.

**Application procedures. Admission:** No deadline. $25 fee, may be waived for applicants with need. Application may be submitted online. Admission notification on a rolling basis. **Financial aid:** Priority date 4/15; no closing date. FAFSA, institutional form required. Applicants notified on a rolling basis starting 4/15; must reply within 2 week(s) of notification.

**Academics. Special study options:** Accelerated study, combined bachelor's/graduate degree, distance learning, double major, dual enrollment of high school students, ESL, exchange student, independent study, internships, liberal arts/career combination, study abroad, teacher certification program, weekend college. 3-2 engineering programs with Case Western Reserve University and Southern Methodist University. **Credit/placement by examination:** AP, CLEP, institutional tests. 30 credit hours maximum toward bachelor's degree. **Support services:** Learning center, pre-admission summer program, reduced course load, remedial instruction, study skills assistance, tutoring, writing center.

**Majors. Biology:** General, biochemistry. **Business:** Accounting, business admin, finance, international marketing, management science, office technology. **Communications:** General, journalism, public relations, radio/tv. **Computer sciences:** General, computer science, information systems. **Education:** General, bilingual, biology, business, chemistry, early childhood, elementary, English, history, mathematics, multi-level teacher, music, physical, reading, secondary, social science, social studies, Spanish. **English:** English lit. **Foreign languages:** Spanish. **Health:** Athletic training, predental, premedicine. **History:** General. **Legal studies:** Paralegal, prelaw. **Math:** General. **Parks/recreation:** Facilities management, health/fitness. **Physical sciences:** Chemistry. **Psychology:** General. **Social sciences:** General, political science. **Theology:** Religious ed. **Visual/performing arts:** General, art, dramatic.

**Most popular majors.** Business/marketing 16%, education 29%, interdisciplinary studies 12%, psychology 9%, social sciences 8%.

**Computing on campus.** 306 workstations in library, computer center. Dormitories wired for high-speed internet access and linked to campus network. Online library, wireless network available.

**Student life. Freshman orientation:** Mandatory. Preregistration for classes offered. **Policies:** Resident chaplain on staff. **Housing:** Coed dorms, single-sex dorms, apartments, substance-free housing available. $150 deposit. **Activities:** Bands, choral groups, drama, literary magazine, music ensembles, musical theater, opera, student government, student newspaper, Methodist and Baptist student unions, Student Foundation, Alpha Phi Omega, Fellowship of Christian Athletes.

**Athletics.** NAIA. **Intercollegiate:** Baseball M, basketball, golf M, soccer, softball W, table tennis M, volleyball W. **Intramural:** Badminton, basketball, bowling, diving, golf M, soccer, softball, swimming, table tennis, tennis W, volleyball. **Team name:** Rams.

**Student services.** Adult student services, alcohol/substance abuse counseling, campus ministries, career counseling, student employment services, financial aid counseling, health services, personal counseling, placement for graduates, veterans' counselor.

**Contact.** E-mail: admission@txwes.edu
Phone: (817) 531-4422 Toll-free number: (800) 580-8980
Fax: (817) 531-7515
Holly Kiser, Director of Freshman Admissions, Texas Wesleyan University, 1201 Wesleyan Street, Fort Worth, TX 76105-1536

## Texas Woman's University
### Denton, Texas
www.twu.edu                          CB member
                                      CB code: 6826

▶ Public 4-year university
▶ Commuter campus in small city
▶ 6,986 degree-seeking undergraduates: 28% part-time, 93% women, 21% African American, 7% Asian American, 17% Hispanic American, 1% Native American, 2% international
▶ 4,656 degree-seeking graduate students
▶ 88% of applicants admitted
▶ SAT or ACT (ACT writing optional) required
▶ 42% graduate within 6 years

**General.** Founded in 1901. Regionally accredited. Primarily women's university. **Degrees:** 1,311 bachelor's awarded; master's, doctoral offered. **ROTC:** Army, Air Force. **Location:** 35 miles from Dallas and Fort Worth. **Calendar:** Semester, extensive summer session. **Full-time faculty:** 372 total; 15% minority, 69% women. **Part-time faculty:** 299 total; 15% minority, 75% women. **Class size:** 51% < 20, 39% 20-39, 5% 40-49, 4% 50-99, 1% >100. **Special facilities:** History of Texas women collection, DAR museum.

**Freshman class profile.** 2,190 applied, 1,924 admitted, 786 enrolled.

| Mid 50% test scores | | | |
|---|---|---|---|
| SAT critical reading: | 450-550 | Rank in top tenth: | 18% |
| SAT math: | 450-550 | End year in good standing: | 56% |
| ACT composite: | 19-24 | Return as sophomores: | 69% |
| GPA 3.50 or higher: | 42% | Out-of-state: | 1% |
| GPA 3.0-3.49: | 40% | Live on campus: | 78% |
| GPA 2.0-2.99: | 18% | International: | 1% |
| Rank in top quarter: | 42% | Sororities: | 3% |

**Basis for selection.** School achievement record and test scores most important: Texas Academic Skills Program, SAT of 950 (exclusive of Writing) or ACT of 20. Interview and audition required for drama and music programs; interview required and portfolio recommended for art program.

**High school preparation.** 22 units required. Required units include English 4, mathematics 3, social studies 2, science 2 and academic electives 11.

**2007-2008 Annual costs.** Tuition/fees: $5,467; $13,807 out-of-state. Room/board: $5,846. Books/supplies: $948. Personal expenses: $1,854.

**Application procedures. Admission:** Priority date 2/1; deadline 7/1 (receipt date). $30 fee, may be waived for applicants with need. Application may be submitted online. Admission notification on a rolling basis beginning on or about 3/1. **Financial aid:** Priority date 4/1; no closing date. FAFSA, institutional form required. Applicants notified on a rolling basis starting 3/1; must reply within 2 week(s) of notification.

**Academics. Special study options:** Accelerated study, combined bachelor's/graduate degree, cooperative education, cross-registration, distance learning, double major, dual enrollment of high school students, honors, independent study, internships, liberal arts/career combination, study abroad, teacher certification program, weekend college. **Credit/placement by examination:** AP, CLEP, SAT, ACT, institutional tests. 30 credit hours maximum toward bachelor's degree. **Support services:** Learning center, pre-admission summer program, reduced course load, remedial instruction, study skills assistance, tutoring, writing center.

**Majors. Biology:** General, biochemistry, zoology. **Business:** Accounting, administrative services, business admin, fashion, finance, marketing. **Computer sciences:** General. **English:** English lit. **Family/consumer sciences:** General, child development, family studies, food/nutrition. **Health:** Audiology/speech pathology, clinical lab science, dental hygiene, dietetics, health services, music therapy, nursing (RN). **History:** General. **Interdisciplinary:** Nutrition sciences. **Legal studies:** Paralegal. **Math:** General. **Parks/recreation:** Health/fitness. **Physical sciences:** Chemistry. **Protective services:** Criminal justice. **Psychology:** General. **Public administration:** Social work. **Social sciences:** Political science, sociology. **Visual/performing arts:** Art, dance, dramatic, fashion design. **Other:** Interdisciplinary Studies.

**Most popular majors.** Business/marketing 8%, health sciences 38%, interdisciplinary studies 12%, liberal arts 7%, psychology 6%.

**Computing on campus.** 1,000 workstations in dormitories, library, computer center, student center. Dormitories linked to campus network. Commuter students can connect to campus network. Online course registration, helpline available.

**Student life. Freshman orientation:** Mandatory, $25 fee. Preregistration for classes offered. One-day event. **Housing:** Guaranteed on-campus for all undergraduates. Coed dorms, single-sex dorms, special housing for disabled, apartments, cooperative housing, fraternity/sorority housing, substance-free housing available. $100 deposit. Family housing, honors students housing, theme floors available. **Activities:** Jazz band, campus ministries, choral groups, dance, drama, international student organizations, music ensembles, musical theater, opera, student government, student newspaper, Alpha Theta Omega, LULAC, multicultural African organization, NAACP, Alpha Kappa Alpha Sorority, Delta Sigma Theta Sorority, Zeta Phi Beta Sorority, Golden Key international honor society.

**Athletics. NCAA. Intercollegiate:** Basketball W, gymnastics W, soccer W, softball W, volleyball W. **Intramural:** Basketball, football (non-tackle), golf, racquetball, soccer, softball, swimming, table tennis M, tennis, volleyball, weight lifting. **Team name:** Pioneers.

**Student services.** Adult student services, alcohol/substance abuse counseling, career counseling, student employment services, financial aid counseling, health services, minority student services, on-campus daycare, personal counseling, veterans' counselor, women's services. **Physically disabled:** Services for visually, speech, hearing impaired.

**Contact.** E-mail: admissions@twu.edu
Phone: (940) 898-3188 Toll-free number: (866) 809-6130
Fax: (940) 898-3081
Erma Nieto, Director of Admissions, Texas Woman's University, Box 425589, Denton, TX 76204-5589

## Trinity University

**San Antonio, Texas**
**www.trinity.edu**

**CB member**
**CB code: 6831**

- Private 4-year liberal arts college affiliated with Presbyterian Church (USA)
- Residential campus in very large city
- 2,464 degree-seeking undergraduates: 1% part-time, 54% women, 4% African American, 6% Asian American, 11% Hispanic American, 1% Native American, 5% international
- 200 degree-seeking graduate students
- 52% of applicants admitted
- SAT or ACT (ACT writing optional), application essay required
- 79% graduate within 6 years

**General.** Founded in 1869. Regionally accredited. **Degrees:** 552 bachelor's awarded; master's offered. **ROTC:** Air Force. **Location:** 3 miles from downtown. **Calendar:** Semester, limited summer session. **Full-time faculty:** 221 total; 5% have terminal degrees, 11% minority, 36% women. **Part-time faculty:** 66 total. **Class size:** 57% < 20, 39% 20-39, 2% 40-49, 2% 50-99, less than 1% >100.

**Freshman class profile.** 4,511 applied, 2,324 admitted, 632 enrolled.

| Mid 50% test scores | | | |
|---|---|---|---|
| SAT critical reading: | 600-690 | Rank in top quarter: | 85% |
| SAT math: | 610-690 | Rank in top tenth: | 53% |
| ACT composite: | 27-31 | Return as sophomores: | 90% |
| GPA 3.50 or higher: | 60% | Out-of-state: | 33% |
| GPA 3.0-3.49: | 32% | Live on campus: | 100% |
| GPA 2.0-2.99: | 8% | International: | 6% |

**Basis for selection.** GPA, high school rank, test scores, essay, interview, recommendations, extracurricular involvement, and achievement important.

**Homeschooled:** At least 3 SAT Subject Tests recommended, including natural science and foreign language.

**High school preparation.** 15 units required; 19 recommended. Required and recommended units include English 4, mathematics 3, social studies 3, science 3 (laboratory 2-3), foreign language 2-3 and academic electives 3.

**2008-2009 Annual costs.** Tuition/fees: $27,699. Room/board: $8,822. Books/supplies: $950. Personal expenses: $1,050.

**2007-2008 Financial aid. Need-based:** 371 full-time freshmen applied for aid; 259 were judged to have need; 259 of these received aid. Average need met was 92%. Average scholarship/grant was $14,832; average loan $5,189. 74% of total undergraduate aid awarded as scholarships/grants, 26% as loans/jobs. **Non-need-based:** Awarded to 1,308 full-time undergraduates, including 325 freshmen. Scholarships awarded for academics, leadership, music/drama.

**Application procedures. Admission:** Closing date 2/1 (postmark date). $50 fee, may be waived for applicants with need. Application may be submitted online. Admission notification 4/1. Admission notification on a rolling basis. Must reply by 5/1. **Financial aid:** Priority date 2/1, closing date 4/1. FAFSA required. Must reply by 5/1 or within 4 week(s) of notification.

**Academics. Special study options:** Accelerated study, combined bachelor's/graduate degree, double major, honors, independent study, internships, liberal arts/career combination, New York semester, semester at sea, student-designed major, study abroad, teacher certification program, United Nations semester, urban semester, Washington semester. **Credit/placement by examination:** AP, CLEP, IB, institutional tests. 36 credit hours maximum toward bachelor's degree. **Support services:** Writing center.

**Majors. Area/ethnic studies:** Asian, European, Latin American. **Biology:** General, biochemistry. **Business:** Accounting, business admin, finance, international, management science, marketing. **Communications:** General. **Computer sciences:** General. **Education:** Elementary. **Engineering:** Science. **English:** English lit, speech/rhetoric. **Foreign languages:** Chinese, classics, French, German, Russian, Spanish. **History:** General. **Math:** General. **Philosophy/religion:** Philosophy, religion. **Physical sciences:** Chemistry, geology, physics. **Psychology:** General. **Social sciences:** Anthropology, economics, political science, sociology, urban studies. **Visual/performing arts:** Art, art history/conservation, dramatic, music performance, music theory/composition, theater design, voice/opera.

**Most popular majors.** Business/marketing 21%, communications/journalism 7%, English 8%, foreign language 10%, history 6%, social sciences 18%, visual/performing arts 6%.

**Computing on campus.** 400 workstations in library, computer center, student center. Dormitories wired for high-speed internet access and linked to campus network. Commuter students can connect to campus network. Online course registration, online library, helpline, student web hosting, wireless network available.

**Student life. Freshman orientation:** Available. **Housing:** Coed dorms available. $500 nonrefundable deposit, deadline 5/1. **Activities:** Bands, campus ministries, choral groups, dance, drama, film society, literary magazine, music ensembles, Model UN, musical theater, opera, radio station, student government, student newspaper, symphony orchestra, TV station, Phi Beta Kappa, academic honor societies, activities council, Young Democrats, Young Republicans, association of student representatives, Alpha Phi Omega, religious organizations, minority student organizations (Trinity Multicultural Network).

**Athletics. NCAA. Intercollegiate:** Baseball M, basketball, cross-country, diving, football (tackle) M, golf, soccer, softball W, swimming, tennis, track and field, volleyball W. **Intramural:** Basketball, cross-country, fencing, football (non-tackle), golf, racquetball, soccer, softball, swimming, table tennis, tennis, track and field, volleyball, water polo, wrestling. **Team name:** Tigers.

**Student services.** Campus ministries, career counseling, student employment services, financial aid counseling, health services, personal counseling, placement for graduates, veterans' counselor. **Physically disabled:** Services for visually, hearing impaired.

**Contact.** E-mail: admissions@trinity.edu
Phone: (210) 999-7207 Toll-free number: (800) 874-6489
Fax: (210) 999-8164
Christopher Ellertson, Dean of Admissions and Financial Aid, Trinity University, One Trinity Place, San Antonio, TX 78212-7200

## University of Dallas
### Irving, Texas
www.udallas.edu

CB member
CB code: 6868

- Private 4-year university and liberal arts college affiliated with Roman Catholic Church
- Residential campus in small city
- 1,222 degree-seeking undergraduates: 2% part-time, 54% women, 1% African American, 6% Asian American, 16% Hispanic American, 1% international
- 1,627 degree-seeking graduate students
- 75% of applicants admitted
- SAT or ACT with writing, application essay required
- 63% graduate within 6 years; 59% enter graduate study

**General.** Founded in 1956. Regionally accredited. Additional campus in Rome, Italy. **Degrees:** 254 bachelor's awarded; master's, doctoral offered. **ROTC:** Army, Air Force. **Location:** 5 miles from Dallas. **Calendar:** Semester, limited summer session. **Full-time faculty:** 125 total; 88% have terminal degrees, 8% minority, 30% women. **Part-time faculty:** 113 total; 29% have terminal degrees, 11% minority, 24% women. **Class size:** 54% < 20, 41% 20-39, 4% 40-49, 1% 50-99.

**Freshman class profile.** 1,161 applied, 868 admitted, 363 enrolled.

| Mid 50% test scores | | | |
|---|---|---|---|
| SAT critical reading: | 550-680 | Rank in top quarter: | 61% |
| SAT math: | 520-650 | Rank in top tenth: | 33% |
| SAT writing: | 530-660 | End year in good standing: | 88% |
| ACT composite: | 24-29 | Return as sophomores: | 79% |
| GPA 3.50 or higher: | 65% | Out-of-state: | 53% |
| GPA 3.0-3.49: | 25% | Live on campus: | 93% |
| GPA 2.0-2.99: | 10% | International: | 2% |

**Basis for selection.** Sufficient academic preparation and ability to do the work required along with evidence of good character. Critical writing and composition skills important. Interview recommended for academically marginal; audition recommended for theater program; portfolio recommended for art program.

**High school preparation.** Recommended units include English 4, mathematics 4, social studies 4, history 4, science 3 (laboratory 3), foreign language 2 and visual/performing arts 2.

**2007-2008 Annual costs.** Tuition/fees: $23,267. Room/board: $7,615. Books/supplies: $1,500. Personal expenses: $1,500.

**2006-2007 Financial aid. Need-based:** 263 full-time freshmen applied for aid; 202 were judged to have need; 202 of these received aid. Average need met was 85%. Average scholarship/grant was $14,886; average loan $6,297. 82% of total undergraduate aid awarded as scholarships/grants, 18% as loans/jobs. **Non-need-based:** Awarded to 460 full-time undergraduates, including 130 freshmen. Scholarships awarded for academics, alumni affiliation, art, leadership, music/drama.

**Application procedures. Admission:** Priority date 1/15; deadline 8/1 (postmark date). $40 fee, may be waived for applicants with need. Application may be submitted online. Admission notification on a rolling basis beginning on or about 2/1. Must reply by May 1 or within 4 week(s) if notified thereafter. **Financial aid:** Priority date 3/1, closing date 7/1. FAFSA required. Applicants notified on a rolling basis starting 3/1; must reply by 5/1 or within 2 week(s) of notification.

**Academics.** 80% of undergraduates spend semester of sophomore year at university's campus in Rome, Italy. Optional credit-bearing intersession available. **Special study options:** Combined bachelor's/graduate degree, double major, dual enrollment of high school students, independent study, internships, liberal arts/career combination, student-designed major, study abroad, teacher certification program. Intensive honors chemistry summer program for entering freshmen. **Credit/placement by examination:** AP, CLEP, IB, institutional tests. 32 credit hours maximum toward bachelor's degree. **Support services:** Pre-admission summer program, reduced course load, tutoring, writing center.

**Majors. Biology:** General, biochemistry. **Business:** Business admin. **Education:** General, elementary. **English:** English lit. **Foreign languages:** Classics, French, German, Spanish. **History:** General. **Math:** General. **Philosophy/religion:** Philosophy. **Physical sciences:** Chemistry, physics. **Psychology:** General. **Social sciences:** Economics, political science. **Theology:** Preministerial, theology. **Visual/performing arts:** Art history/conservation, ceramics, dramatic, painting, printmaking, sculpture.

**Most popular majors.** Biology 11%, business/marketing 13%, education 8%, English 13%, foreign language 6%, history 8%, psychology 8%, social sciences 10%, theological studies 7%, visual/performing arts 8%.

**Computing on campus.** 125 workstations in library, computer center, student center. Dormitories wired for high-speed internet access and linked to campus network. Commuter students can connect to campus network. Online library, helpline, wireless network available.

**Student life. Freshman orientation:** Mandatory. One-day program prior to fall semester. **Housing:** Guaranteed on-campus for freshmen. Coed dorms, single-sex dorms, apartments available. $100 fully refundable deposit, deadline 8/1. **Activities:** Campus ministries, choral groups, dance, drama, film society, international student organizations, literary magazine, music ensembles, musical theater, radio station, student government, student newspaper, Best Buddies, Society of St. Vincent de Paul, Alpha Phi Omega, Crusaders for Life, Asian student organization, Latin American student association.

**Athletics.** NCAA. **Intercollegiate:** Baseball M, basketball, cross-country, golf M, lacrosse W, soccer, softball W, track and field, volleyball W. **Intramural:** Basketball M, football (non-tackle), soccer, softball, volleyball. **Team name:** Crusaders.

**Student services.** Campus ministries, career counseling, student employment services, financial aid counseling, health services, personal counseling, placement for graduates. **Physically disabled:** Services for visually impaired.

**Contact.** E-mail: ugadmis@udallas.edu
Phone: (972) 721-5266 Toll-free number: (800) 628-6999
Fax: (972) 721-5017
Curt Eley, Dean of Enrollment Management, University of Dallas, 1845 East Northgate Drive, Irving, TX 75062-4736

## University of Houston
### Houston, Texas
www.uh.edu

CB member
CB code: 6870

- Public 4-year university
- Commuter campus in very large city
- 26,495 degree-seeking undergraduates: 27% part-time, 51% women, 15% African American, 22% Asian American, 22% Hispanic American, 4% international
- 7,091 degree-seeking graduate students
- 77% of applicants admitted
- SAT or ACT (ACT writing optional) required
- 43% graduate within 6 years

**General.** Founded in 1927. Regionally accredited. Research university with highly diverse student population. **Degrees:** 4,810 bachelor's awarded; master's, doctoral, first professional offered. **ROTC:** Army, Naval, Air Force. **Location:** 2 miles from downtown Houston. **Calendar:** Semester, extensive summer session. **Full-time faculty:** 1,209 total; 81% have terminal degrees, 21% minority, 34% women. **Part-time faculty:** 500 total; 52% have terminal degrees, 19% minority, 39% women. **Class size:** 29% < 20, 38% 20-39, 9% 40-49, 14% 50-99, 10% >100. **Special facilities:** Theater complex, observatory, opera house, coastal center, underground satellite center, wellness and recreation center.

**Freshman class profile.** 10,984 applied, 8,466 admitted, 3,508 enrolled.

| Mid 50% test scores | | | |
|---|---|---|---|
| SAT critical reading: | 460-570 | Rank in top tenth: | 20% |
| SAT math: | 490-600 | Return as sophomores: | 77% |
| ACT composite: | 19-24 | Out-of-state: | 3% |
| GPA 3.50 or higher: | 42% | Live on campus: | 24% |
| GPA 3.0-3.49: | 39% | International: | 2% |
| GPA 2.0-2.99: | 18% | Fraternities: | 2% |
| Rank in top quarter: | 52% | Sororities: | 3% |

**Basis for selection.** Freshmen applicants ranked in top 20% of class are automatically accepted. Applicants in next 30% with minimum score of 1000 SAT (exclusive of Writing) or 21 ACT will be admitted. After that, applicants individually reviewed. SAT Subject Tests recommended. Freshmen applicants who do not rank in top 20% of their class will have test scores reviewed. Top 20% applicants are automatically admitted regardless of test scores. Audition required for music program; essay recommended for honors college and individual review. **Homeschooled:** Must submit minimum SAT score of 1180 (exclusive of Writing) and transcript (can be created by parent). In order to qualify for financial aid, must pass GED exam.

SAT not recognized by financial aid department. **Learning Disabled:** Intake appointment with counselor scheduled upon receipt of required documentation indicating that disability substantially limits some major life activity.

**High school preparation.** Required and recommended units include English 4, mathematics 3, social studies 2, history 2, science 2 (laboratory 2) and foreign language 2. 1 chemistry, 1 physics, 1 mechanical drawing recommended for engineering and science applicants.

**2007-2008 Annual costs.** Tuition/fees: $7,450; $15,790 out-of-state. Room/board: $6,651. Books/supplies: $1,100. Personal expenses: $3,024.

**2007-2008 Financial aid. Need-based:** 2,279 full-time freshmen applied for aid; 1,932 were judged to have need; 1,811 of these received aid. Average need met was 68%. Average scholarship/grant was $6,875; average loan $3,739. 45% of total undergraduate aid awarded as scholarships/grants, 55% as loans/jobs. **Non-need-based:** Awarded to 1,265 full-time undergraduates, including 403 freshmen. Scholarships awarded for academics, alumni affiliation, art, athletics, job skills, leadership, music/drama, ROTC, state residency.

**Application procedures. Admission:** Closing date 4/1. $50 fee ($75 out-of-state), may be waived for applicants with need. Application may be submitted online. Admission notification on a rolling basis beginning on or about 9/1. **Financial aid:** Priority date 4/1; no closing date. FAFSA required. Applicants notified on a rolling basis starting 5/1; must reply within 4 week(s) of notification.

**Academics. Special study options:** Accelerated study, cooperative education, cross-registration, distance learning, double major, dual enrollment of high school students, ESL, exchange student, honors, independent study, internships, semester at sea, study abroad, teacher certification program, Washington semester, weekend college. Academic enrichment programs, certification programs and affiliated studies. **Credit/placement by examination:** AP, CLEP, IB, SAT, ACT, institutional tests. **Support services:** Learning center, reduced course load, remedial instruction, study skills assistance, tutoring, writing center.

**Majors. Architecture:** Architecture, environmental design, interior. **Area/ethnic studies:** German, Russian/Slavic. **Biology:** General, biochemistry, biophysics. **Business:** Accounting, communications, entrepreneurial studies, finance, human resources, management information systems, managerial economics, marketing, merchandising, operations, organizational behavior, personal/financial services, sales/distribution, statistics. **Communications:** General, journalism, public relations, radio/tv. **Computer sciences:** General, information science, systems analysis. **Education:** Health, physical, trade/industrial. **Engineering:** Chemical, civil, computer, electrical, mechanical. **Engineering technology:** Architectural, civil, construction, electrical, industrial, industrial management, manufacturing. **English:** English lit, speech/rhetoric. **Family/consumer sciences:** General, business, family studies, food/nutrition. **Foreign languages:** Classics, French, German, Italian, Latin, Spanish. **Health:** Audiology/speech pathology, clinical lab science, communication disorders, kinesiotherapy, nuclear medical technology, optician, prepharmacy. **History:** General. **Math:** General, applied. **Parks/recreation:** Exercise sciences, health/fitness, sports admin. **Philosophy/religion:** Philosophy. **Physical sciences:** Chemistry, geology, geophysics, physics, planetary. **Psychology:** General. **Social sciences:** Anthropology, economics, political science, sociology, urban studies. **Visual/performing arts:** Art, art history/conservation, ceramics, commercial/advertising art, dance, dramatic, graphic design, industrial design, interior design, metal/jewelry, music performance, music theory/composition, painting, photography, printmaking, sculpture, studio arts.

**Most popular majors.** Biology 6%, business/marketing 32%, communications/journalism 6%, engineering/engineering technologies 9%, psychology 8%, social sciences 8%.

**Computing on campus.** 625 workstations in dormitories, library, computer center, student center. Dormitories wired for high-speed internet access and linked to campus network. Commuter students can connect to campus network. Online library, helpline, repair service, student web hosting, wireless network available.

**Student life. Freshman orientation:** Mandatory, $90 fee. Preregistration for classes offered. Two-day conferences include advising, phone registration, placement testing, textbook orders. **Housing:** Coed dorms, special housing for disabled, apartments, fraternity/sorority housing available. $100 fully refundable deposit, deadline 4/1. **Activities:** Bands, campus ministries, choral groups, dance, drama, film society, international student organizations, literary magazine, music ensembles, musical theater, opera, radio station, student government, student newspaper, symphony orchestra, TV station, Asian student association, Hispanic student association, Habitat for Humanity, Hillel, College Republicans/Democrats, NAACP, Green Party, Indian student association, Muslim students association, Bahai student association.

**Athletics.** NCAA. **Intercollegiate:** Baseball M, basketball, cross-country, diving W, football (tackle) M, golf M, soccer W, softball W, swimming W, tennis W, track and field, volleyball W. **Intramural:** Badminton, basketball, bowling, cross-country, diving, football (tackle) M, golf, racquetball, soccer, softball, swimming, table tennis, tennis, track and field, volleyball, water polo. **Team name:** Cougars.

**Student services.** Adult student services, campus ministries, career counseling, student employment services, financial aid counseling, health services, on-campus daycare, personal counseling, placement for graduates, veterans' counselor, women's services. **Physically disabled:** Services for visually, speech, hearing impaired.

**Contact.** E-mail: admissions@uh.edu
Phone: (713) 743-1010 Fax: (713) 743-9633
Josie Anderson, Director of Admissions, University of Houston, 122 East Cullen Building, Houston, TX 77204-2023

## University of Houston: Clear Lake
**Houston, Texas**                                              **CB member**
**www.uhcl.edu**                                              **CB code: 6916**

◆ Public two-year upper-division university
◆ Commuter campus in very large city

**General.** Founded in 1971. Regionally accredited. Upper level university for undergraduates. Located 3 miles from NASA. **Degrees:** 1,117 bachelor's awarded; master's offered. **Articulation:** Agreements with all community colleges in Houston metropolitan area, Houston CC, North Harris CC, San Jacinto College, Brazosport College, Galveston College, Alvin CC, Lee College, College of the Mainland, Kingwood College, Montgomery College, Tomball College, Wharton County JC. **Location:** 21 miles from Houston. **Calendar:** Semester, limited summer session. **Full-time faculty:** 195 total. **Part-time faculty:** 407 total. **Class size:** 47% < 20, 44% 20-39, 5% 40-49, 2% 50-99, less than 1% >100.

**Student profile.** 4,280 degree-seeking undergraduates, 3,240 graduate students. 82% entered as juniors, 18% entered as seniors.

| | | | |
|---|---|---|---|
| Out-of-state: | 1% | 25 or older: | 57% |
| Live on campus: | 2% | | |

**Basis for selection.** College transcript required. Students with 54 hours of credit with grades 2.0 or better (exclusive of remedial or development or repeated courses) from regionally accredited institution will be admitted. Students must also have completed college algebra or higher mathematics course and have passing scores on THEA. Students must be eligible to return to last institution attended. Transfer accepted as juniors, seniors.

**2007-2008 Annual costs.** Tuition/fees: $5,194; $13,954 out-of-state. Room only: $6,912.

**Financial aid. Non-need-based:** Scholarships awarded for state residency.

**Application procedures. Admission:** Priority date 6/2. $35 fee. Application may be submitted online. **Financial aid:** Priority date 4/1, no deadline. Applicants notified on a rolling basis starting 5/15; must reply within 4 weeks of notification. FAFSA, institutional form required.

**Academics. Special study options:** Combined bachelor's/graduate degree, cooperative education, distance learning, double major, dual enrollment of high school students, independent study, internships, student-designed major, study abroad, teacher certification program, weekend college. **Credit/placement by examination:** AP, CLEP. 18 credit hours maximum toward bachelor's degree.

**Majors. Biology:** General. **Business:** General, accounting, business admin, finance, management information systems, marketing. **Communications:** General. **Computer sciences:** General, computer science. **Conservation:** General, environmental science, environmental studies. **Education:** General. **Engineering:** Computer. **English:** English lit. **Health:** Health care admin. **History:** General. **Interdisciplinary:** Behavioral sciences, math/computer science. **Legal studies:** Prelaw. **Liberal arts:** Arts/sciences, humanities. **Math:** General. **Parks/recreation:** Health/fitness. **Physical sciences:** Chemistry. **Psychology:** General. **Public administration:** Policy analysis, social work. **Social sciences:** Anthropology, criminology, geography, political science, sociology. **Visual/performing arts:** Art.

**Computing on campus.** 715 workstations in library, computer center. Commuter students can connect to campus network. Online course registration, online library, helpline, wireless network available.

**Student life. Housing:** Limited apartments on campus. **Activities:** Campus ministries, film society, international student organizations, literary magazine, student government, student newspaper, Black student association, Chinese Christian student fellowship, Hispanic advancement in culture and education, student organization for Native American studies, student council for exceptional children, clinical psychology club, Muslim student association.

**Student services.** Alcohol/substance abuse counseling, career counseling, student employment services, financial aid counseling, health services, minority student services, personal counseling, placement for graduates, veterans' counselor, women's services. **Physically disabled:** Services for visually, speech, hearing impaired.

**Contact.** E-mail: admissions@uhcl.edu
Phone: (281) 283-2521 Fax: (281) 283-2530
Rauchelle Jones, Director of Admissions, University of Houston: Clear Lake, 2700 Bay Area Boulevard, Houston, TX 77058-1098

## University of Houston: Downtown
Houston, Texas        CB member
www.uhd.edu        CB code: 6922

- Public 4-year university
- Commuter campus in very large city
- 11,670 degree-seeking undergraduates: 48% part-time, 59% women, 27% African American, 10% Asian American, 36% Hispanic American, 3% international
- 123 degree-seeking graduate students

**General.** Founded in 1974. Regionally accredited. Distance education locations in Sugar Land, Cinco Ranch, The Woodlands, Cy-Fair. **Degrees:** 1,949 bachelor's awarded; master's offered. **ROTC:** Army. **Calendar:** Semester, limited summer session. **Full-time faculty:** 286 total; 78% have terminal degrees, 32% minority, 46% women. **Part-time faculty:** 277 total; 35% have terminal degrees, 39% minority, 45% women. **Class size:** 24% < 20, 63% 20-39, 10% 40-49, 3% 50-99, less than 1% >100.

**Freshman class profile.** 1,968 applied, 1,957 admitted, 1,014 enrolled.

| | | | |
|---|---|---|---|
| **Return as sophomores:** | 56% | **International:** | 3% |
| **Out-of-state:** | 2% | | |

**Basis for selection.** Open admission. **Homeschooled:** Transcript of courses and grades required.

**High school preparation.** 25 units recommended. Recommended units include English 4, mathematics 3, social studies 3.5, science 3, foreign language 3 and academic electives 1. 7.5 units fine arts, speech, technology, health education, economics, and physical education recommended.

**2007-2008 Annual costs.** Tuition/fees: $4,832; $13,172 out-of-state. Books/supplies: $1,044. Personal expenses: $3,800.

**2007-2008 Financial aid. Need-based:** 664 full-time freshmen applied for aid; 629 were judged to have need; 614 of these received aid. Average need met was 51%. Average scholarship/grant was $5,693; average loan $3,264. 36% of total undergraduate aid awarded as scholarships/grants, 64% as loans/jobs. **Non-need-based:** Awarded to 323 full-time undergraduates, including 126 freshmen. Scholarships awarded for academics, leadership, state residency.

**Application procedures. Admission:** Closing date 7/15 (postmark date). $35 fee, may be waived for applicants with need. Application may be submitted online. Notification within 3-5 business days after all items received by college. **Financial aid:** Priority date 4/1; no closing date. FAFSA required. Applicants notified on a rolling basis starting 1/2; must reply within 8 week(s) of notification.

**Academics. Special study options:** Cooperative education, distance learning, dual enrollment of high school students, ESL, honors, independent study, internships, study abroad, teacher certification program, weekend college. **Credit/placement by examination:** AP, CLEP, institutional tests. 24 credit hours maximum toward bachelor's degree. **Support services:** Learning center, reduced course load, remedial instruction, study skills assistance, tutoring, writing center.

**Majors. Biology:** General, microbiology. **Business:** General, accounting, business admin, finance, international, management information systems, marketing, purchasing. **Computer sciences:** General. **Engineering technology:** Civil, computer, industrial safety, mechanical, occupational safety. **English:** English lit, speech/rhetoric, technical writing. **Foreign languages:** Spanish. **History:** General. **Interdisciplinary:** Biological/physical sciences. **Liberal arts:** Arts/sciences, humanities. **Math:** Applied. **Philosophy/**

**religion:** Philosophy. **Physical sciences:** Chemistry. **Protective services:** Criminal justice. **Psychology:** General. **Social sciences:** General, political science, sociology. **Other:** Industrial chemistry.

**Most popular majors.** Business/marketing 41%, English 6%, interdisciplinary studies 9%, liberal arts 20%, psychology 6%, security/protective services 9%.

**Computing on campus.** 1,250 workstations in library, computer center, student center. Commuter students can connect to campus network. Online course registration, online library, helpline, student web hosting, wireless network available.

**Student life. Freshman orientation:** Mandatory, $20 fee. Preregistration for classes offered. One-day program. **Activities:** Jazz band, drama, literary magazine, student government, student newspaper, African student association, Christ Over Life, Central American student association, League of United Latin American Citizens, Muslim student association, NAACP, Caribbean students association, College Democrats.

**Athletics. Intramural:** Badminton, basketball, bowling, football (non-tackle) M, soccer, softball, tennis, volleyball, weight lifting. **Team name:** Gator.

**Student services.** Alcohol/substance abuse counseling, career counseling, student employment services, financial aid counseling, health services, personal counseling, placement for graduates, veterans' counselor. **Physically disabled:** Services for visually, hearing impaired.

**Contact.** E-mail: uhdadmit@uhd.edu
Phone: (713) 221-8522
Jose Cantu, Director of Admissions, University of Houston: Downtown, One Main Street, Suite 350-S, Houston, TX 77002

## University of Houston: Victoria
Victoria, Texas
www.uhv.edu        CB code: 6917

- Public two-year upper-division university
- Commuter campus in small city
- 66% of applicants admitted
- Test scores required

**General.** Founded in 1973. Regionally accredited. **Degrees:** 350 bachelor's awarded; master's offered. **Articulation:** Agreements with Bee County College, Victoria College, Wharton County Junior College, Blinn College. **Location:** 100 miles from Houston and San Antonio. **Calendar:** Semester, limited summer session. **Full-time faculty:** 81 total; 98% have terminal degrees, 28% minority, 41% women. **Part-time faculty:** 73 total; 42% have terminal degrees, 14% minority, 48% women.

**Student profile.** 1,386 degree-seeking undergraduates, 1,316 degree-seeking graduate students. 863 applied as first time-transfer students, 567 admitted, 405 enrolled. 90% entered as juniors, 10% entered as seniors.

| | | | |
|---|---|---|---|
| **Women:** | 74% | **Native American:** | 1% |
| **African American:** | 9% | **Part-time:** | 63% |
| **Asian American:** | 4% | **25 or older:** | 60% |
| **Hispanic American:** | 22% | | |

**Basis for selection.** College transcript, standardized test scores required. Minimum of 54 semester hours in non-remedial college-level coursework from an institution accredited by one of the recognized regional accrediting associations is required for unconditional admission. Student must have earned minimum 2.0 (A-4.0) GPA and have passed all parts (reading, writing and mathematics) of TASP/THEA exam. Transfer accepted as juniors, seniors.

**2007-2008 Annual costs.** Tuition/fees: $5,055; $13,395 out-of-state.

**Financial aid. Need-based:** 584 applied for aid; 285 were judged to have need; 266 of these received aid. Average need met was 52%. 43% of total undergraduate aid awarded as scholarships/grants, 57% as loans/jobs. **Non-need-based:** Awarded to 45 undergraduates. Scholarships awarded for academics, athletics, leadership, state residency. **Additional information:** Short-term loans available at registration.

**Application procedures. Admission:** Rolling admission. No application fee. Application must be submitted online. **Financial aid:** No deadline. Applicants notified on a rolling basis; must reply within 3 weeks of notification. FAFSA required.

**Academics.** Online course support. **Special study options:** Distance learning, double major, independent study, internships, study abroad, teacher certification program. **Credit/placement by examination:** CLEP.

**Majors. Biology:** General. **Business:** General, accounting, business admin, marketing. **Communications:** General. **Computer sciences:** General, information systems. **Education:** General. **English:** English lit, speech/rhetoric. **Health:** Nursing (RN). **History:** General. **Math:** General. **Protective services:** Law enforcement admin. **Psychology:** General.

**Most popular majors.** Biology 8%, business/marketing 15%, computer/information sciences 6%, education 31%, psychology 7%.

**Computing on campus.** 250 workstations in library, computer center, student center. Commuter students can connect to campus network. Online library, helpline, repair service, wireless network available.

**Student life. Activities:** Student government, student newspaper.

**Athletics.** NAIA. **Intercollegiate:** Baseball M, softball W. **Team name:** Jaguares.

**Student services.** Career counseling, student employment services, financial aid counseling, placement for graduates, veterans' counselor. **Physically disabled:** Services for visually, hearing impaired.

**Contact.** E-mail: admission@uhv.edu
Phone: (361) 570-4110 Toll-free number: (877) 970-4848 ext. 110
Fax: (361) 570-4114
Trudy Wortham, Director of Admissions; University of Houston: Victoria, 3007 North Ben Wilson, Victoria, TX 77901-4450

---

## University of Mary Hardin-Baylor

| Belton, Texas | CB member |
| --- | --- |
| www.umhb.edu | CB code: 6396 |

- Private 4-year university affiliated with Baptist faith
- Residential campus in large town
- 2,481 degree-seeking undergraduates: 10% part-time, 63% women, 12% African American, 2% Asian American, 12% Hispanic American, 1% Native American, 1% international
- 156 degree-seeking graduate students
- 76% of applicants admitted
- SAT or ACT with writing required
- 42% graduate within 6 years

**General.** Founded in 1845. Regionally accredited. Information, counseling, and administrative services, as well as limited number of undergraduate and graduate level evening courses, offered at Fort Hood. Affiliated with Baptist General Convention of Texas. **Degrees:** 541 bachelor's awarded; master's, doctoral offered. **ROTC:** Air Force. **Location:** 60 miles from Austin. **Calendar:** Semester, limited summer session. **Full-time faculty:** 141 total; 67% have terminal degrees, 57% women. **Part-time faculty:** 91 total; 24% have terminal degrees, 41% women. **Class size:** 53% < 20, 42% 20-39, 4% 40-49, 1% 50-99.

**Freshman class profile.** 1,258 applied, 962 admitted, 482 enrolled.

| Mid 50% test scores | | End year in good standing: | 70% |
| --- | --- | --- | --- |
| SAT critical reading: | 450-560 | Return as sophomores: | 60% |
| SAT math: | 460-570 | Out-of-state: | 1% |
| SAT writing: | 440-550 | Live on campus: | 90% |
| ACT composite: | 20-24 | | |

**Basis for selection.** School achievement record and test scores important. Must either rank in top 10% of graduating class; rank in the top half of class and score 950 SAT or 20 ACT; or rank in lower half of class and score 990 SAT or 21 ACT (all SAT scores exclusive of Writing). Academically deficient students may be accepted on individual basis by approval of admissions committee. Interview recommended for academically marginal; audition recommended for music. **Homeschooled:** Transcript of courses and grades required. Admission based on ACT or SAT test scores.

**High school preparation.** 22 units required. Required units include English 4, mathematics 3, social studies 2.5.

**2007-2008 Annual costs.** Tuition/fees: $17,760. Room/board: $4,700. Books/supplies: $1,200. Personal expenses: $1,684.

**2007-2008 Financial aid. Need-based:** 395 full-time freshmen applied for aid; 337 were judged to have need; 337 of these received aid. Average need met was 64%. Average scholarship/grant was $8,888; average loan $3,911. 56% of total undergraduate aid awarded as scholarships/grants, 44% as loans/jobs. **Non-need-based:** Awarded to 406 full-time undergraduates, including 100 freshmen. Scholarships awarded for academics, art, leadership, music/drama, religious affiliation.

---

**Application procedures. Admission:** No deadline. $35 fee, may be waived for applicants with need. Application may be submitted online. Admission notification on a rolling basis. Must reply by May 1 or within 2 week(s) if notified thereafter. **Financial aid:** Priority date 3/1; no closing date. FAFSA, institutional form required. Applicants notified on a rolling basis starting 2/1; must reply within 2 week(s) of notification.

**Academics. Special study options:** Accelerated study, combined bachelor's/graduate degree, double major, dual enrollment of high school students, ESL, honors, independent study, internships, study abroad, teacher certification program. Servicemember Opportunity Colleges (SOC) programs, military degree completion programs, tuition exchange program with other participating universities. **Credit/placement by examination:** AP, CLEP, IB, institutional tests. 31 credit hours maximum toward bachelor's degree. No more than one-fourth of total credit hours required for degree may be earned through credit by examination. **Support services:** Learning center, preadmission summer program, reduced course load, remedial instruction, study skills assistance, tutoring.

**Majors. Area/ethnic studies:** American. **Biology:** Biomedical sciences. **Business:** General, accounting, business admin, finance, management information systems, marketing. **Communications:** General. **Computer sciences:** General, computer graphics, computer science, information systems. **Education:** Chemistry, elementary, English, mathematics, music, physical, science, social studies, special. **English:** English lit. **Foreign languages:** Spanish. **Health:** Athletic training, clinical lab science, nursing (RN). **History:** General. **Math:** General. **Parks/recreation:** General, sports admin. **Philosophy/religion:** Christian, religion. **Physical sciences:** Chemistry. **Protective services:** Law enforcement admin. **Psychology:** General. **Public administration:** Social work. **Social sciences:** Political science, sociology. **Theology:** Bible, pastoral counseling, sacred music, theology. **Visual/performing arts:** Dramatic, music performance, music theory/composition, studio arts.

**Most popular majors.** Business/marketing 14%, computer/information sciences 7%, education 15%, health sciences 12%, liberal arts 9%, psychology 9%.

**Computing on campus.** 275 workstations in dormitories, library, computer center, student center. Dormitories wired for high-speed internet access and linked to campus network. Online course registration, online library, helpline, wireless network available.

**Student life. Freshman orientation:** Available, $30 fee. Preregistration for classes offered. One-day orientation in summer for students and parents. Full-week orientation for students only before start of classes. **Policies:** Religious observance required. **Housing:** Guaranteed on-campus for freshmen. Single-sex dorms, special housing for disabled, apartments, substance-free housing available. $300 partly refundable deposit. **Activities:** Bands, campus ministries, choral groups, drama, international student organizations, literary magazine, music ensembles, musical theater, opera, student government, student newspaper, symphony orchestra, Catholic student organization, College Democrats, College Republicans, Crusaders for Christ, Fellowship of Christian Athletes, Focus (community-wide worship), Habitat for Humanity.

**Athletics.** NCAA. **Intercollegiate:** Baseball M, basketball, football (tackle) M, golf, soccer, softball W, tennis, volleyball W. **Intramural:** Basketball, football (non-tackle), golf, soccer, softball, table tennis, volleyball, weight lifting. **Team name:** Crusaders.

**Student services.** Alcohol/substance abuse counseling, campus ministries, career counseling, student employment services, financial aid counseling, health services, personal counseling, placement for graduates, veterans' counselor. **Physically disabled:** Services for visually, speech, hearing impaired.

**Contact.** E-mail: admissions@umhb.edu
Phone: (254) 295-4520 Toll-free number: (800) 727-8642 ext. 4520
Fax: (254) 295-5049
Robbin Steen, Director of Admissions and Recruiting, University of Mary Hardin-Baylor, 900 College Street, Belton, TX 76513

---

## University of North Texas

| Denton, Texas | CB member |
| --- | --- |
| www.unt.edu | CB code: 6481 |

- Public 4-year university and liberal arts college
- Residential campus in small city
- 27,242 degree-seeking undergraduates: 21% part-time, 55% women, 13% African American, 5% Asian American, 12% Hispanic American, 1% Native American, 2% international
- 6,911 degree-seeking graduate students
- 65% of applicants admitted

◆ SAT or ACT (ACT writing recommended) required

◆ 45% graduate within 6 years

**General.** Founded in 1890. Regionally accredited. **Degrees:** 4,870 bachelor's awarded; master's, doctoral offered. **ROTC:** Army, Air Force. **Location:** 35 miles from Dallas and Fort Worth. **Calendar:** Semester, extensive summer session. **Full-time faculty:** 936 total; 89% have terminal degrees, 17% minority, 35% women. **Part-time faculty:** 727 total; 21% minority, 56% women. **Class size:** 20% < 20, 44% 20-39, 12% 40-49, 11% 50-99, 13% >100. **Special facilities:** Laser, observatory, accelerators, environmental science facility, planetarium.

**Freshman class profile.** 12,387 applied, 8,099 admitted, 3,721 enrolled.

| Mid 50% test scores | | Return as sophomores: | 75% |
|---|---|---|---|
| SAT critical reading: | 490-600 | Out-of-state: | 3% |
| SAT math: | 500-600 | Live on campus: | 73% |
| ACT composite: | 20-25 | International: | 2% |
| Rank in top quarter: | 49% | Fraternities: | 1% |
| Rank in top tenth: | 19% | Sororities: | 1% |
| End year in good standing: | 79% | | |

**Basis for selection.** It is recommended that students apply well in advance of stated application deadlines. School achievement record most important. Test score minimums vary with class rank: top 10% no minimum. Students seeking early admission before high school graduation must be in top quarter of class with strong B average, complete 3 units of English and 2 each of math, social science, natural science; present minimum SAT score of 1180 (exclusive of Writing) or ACT 27. On an individual basis, UNT may admit high school students to the freshman class after completion of the junior year of high school. To be considered, students must be ranked in the top quarter of their class, have a strong B average, completed 3 units of English and 2 units each of solid mathematics, social sciences and natural sciences, present minimum combined SAT (critical reading + math) score of 1180 or ACT composite of 26, submit letters from high school counselor or principal recommending early admission, submit a letter from parents or guardians stating they approve, and arrange an interview in the Office of Admissions. Audition required for music program. **Homeschooled:** Statement describing homeschool structure and mission, transcript of courses and grades required. An interview, essay and letters of recommendation may be required after a review of the application.

**High school preparation.** 24 units required. Required units include English 4, mathematics 4, social studies 2, history 2, science 3, foreign language 3, academic electives 2.5, 0.5 health, 1.5 physical education, 0.5-1 computer sciences, 1 fine arts recommended.

**2008-2009 Annual costs.** Tuition/fees: $6,767; $15,107 out-of-state. Room/board: $6,026. Books/supplies: $1,210. Personal expenses: $1,200.

**2007-2008 Financial aid. Need-based:** 2,358 full-time freshmen applied for aid; 1,571 were judged to have need; 1,539 of these received aid. Average need met was 71%. Average scholarship/grant was $4,788; average loan $2,890. 36% of total undergraduate aid awarded as scholarships/grants, 64% as loans/jobs. **Non-need-based:** Awarded to 3,586 full-time undergraduates, including 909 freshmen. Scholarships awarded for academics.

**Application procedures. Admission:** Closing date 6/16 (postmark date). $40 fee, may be waived for applicants with need. Application may be submitted online. Admission notification on a rolling basis beginning on or about 10/1. **Financial aid:** Priority date 6/1; no closing date. FAFSA required. Applicants notified on a rolling basis starting 4/1.

**Academics. Special study options:** Accelerated study, combined bachelor's/graduate degree, cooperative education, cross-registration, distance learning, double major, dual enrollment of high school students, ESL, exchange student, external degree, honors, independent study, internships, study abroad, teacher certification program, weekend college. **Credit/placement by examination:** AP, CLEP, IB, institutional tests. 30 credit hours maximum toward bachelor's degree. **Support services:** Learning center, study skills assistance, tutoring, writing center.

**Majors. Architecture:** Interior. **Biology:** General, biochemistry. **Business:** General, accounting, banking/financial services, e-commerce, fashion, financial planning, hospitality admin, insurance, logistics, management information systems, managerial economics, marketing, operations, organizational behavior, real estate, sales/distribution, special products marketing. **Communications:** Broadcast journalism, journalism, radio/tv. **Computer sciences:** General, information systems. **Engineering:** Computer, electrical, materials science, mechanical. **Engineering technology:** Construction, electrical, manufacturing, mechanical. **English:** English lit, speech/rhetoric. **Family/consumer sciences:** Family studies. **Foreign languages:** French, German, Spanish. **Health:** Audiology/speech pathology, clinical lab science, cytotechnology, health services, vocational rehab counseling. **History:** General. **Interdisciplinary:** Behavioral sciences, gerontology, global studies. **Math:**

General. **Parks/recreation:** Facilities management, health/fitness. **Philosophy/religion:** Philosophy. **Physical sciences:** Chemistry, physics. **Protective services:** Criminal justice. **Psychology:** General. **Public administration:** General, social work. **Science technology:** Nuclear power. **Social sciences:** General, anthropology, economics, geography, political science, sociology. **Visual/performing arts:** Art, art history/conservation, commercial/advertising art, dance, dramatic, fashion design, jazz, music history, music performance, music theory/composition, studio arts. **Other:** Applied Arts & Sciences, Engineering Physics, Rehabilitation Studies.

**Most popular majors.** Business/marketing 21%, communications/journalism 7%, education 12%, interdisciplinary studies 14%, social sciences 11%, visual/performing arts 9%.

**Computing on campus.** 705 workstations in dormitories, library, computer center, student center. Dormitories wired for high-speed internet access and linked to campus network. Commuter students can connect to campus network. Online course registration, online library, helpline, student web hosting, wireless network available.

**Student life. Freshman orientation:** Mandatory, $169 fee. Preregistration for classes offered. Eight sessions during June and July; each 2 nights and 3 days. **Housing:** Guaranteed on-campus for freshmen. Coed dorms, single-sex dorms, special housing for disabled, apartments, fraternity/sorority housing, substance-free housing available. $400 fully refundable deposit. **Activities:** Bands, choral groups, dance, drama, film society, literary magazine, music ensembles, musical theater, opera, radio station, student government, student newspaper, symphony orchestra, TV station, honorary societies; religious, ethnic, and social service organizations.

**Athletics.** NCAA. **Intercollegiate:** Basketball, cross-country, diving W, football (tackle) M, golf, soccer W, softball, swimming W, tennis W, track and field, volleyball W. **Intramural:** Basketball, bowling, football (nontackle), golf, racquetball, soccer, softball, table tennis, tennis, volleyball. **Team name:** Mean Green.

**Student services.** Adult student services, alcohol/substance abuse counseling, career counseling, student employment services, financial aid counseling, health services, legal services, minority student services, on-campus daycare, personal counseling, placement for graduates, veterans' counselor, women's services. **Physically disabled:** Services for visually, speech, hearing impaired.

**Contact.** E-mail: undergrad@unt.edu
Phone: (940) 565-2681 Toll-free number: (800) 868-8211
Fax: (940) 565-2408
Marcilla Collinsworth, Director of Admissions, University of North Texas, 1401 West Prairie, Suite 309, Denton, TX 76203

---

### University of St. Thomas
**Houston, Texas**
**www.stthom.edu**
**CB member**
**CB code: 6880**

◆ Private 4-year university and liberal arts college affiliated with Roman Catholic Church

◆ Commuter campus in very large city

◆ 1,609 degree-seeking undergraduates: 20% part-time, 60% women, 5% African American, 11% Asian American, 30% Hispanic American, 1% Native American, 4% international

◆ 1,137 degree-seeking graduate students

◆ 84% of applicants admitted

◆ SAT or ACT with writing required

◆ 55% graduate within 6 years

**General.** Founded in 1947. Regionally accredited. **Degrees:** 302 bachelor's awarded; master's, doctoral, first professional offered. **ROTC:** Army, Air Force. **Location:** 3 miles from downtown. **Calendar:** Semester, limited summer session. **Full-time faculty:** 131 total; 91% have terminal degrees, 10% minority, 37% women. **Part-time faculty:** 144 total; 52% have terminal degrees, 12% minority, 52% women. **Class size:** 62% < 20, 38% 20-39, less than 1% 40-49, less than 1% 50-99. **Special facilities:** Chapel of St. Basil, archaeology gallery.

**Freshman class profile.** 861 applied, 720 admitted, 294 enrolled.

| Mid 50% test scores | | | |
|---|---|---|---|
| SAT critical reading: | 510-630 | **Rank in top quarter:** | 51% |
| SAT math: | 530-630 | **Rank in top tenth:** | 27% |
| SAT writing: | 510-610 | **End year in good standing:** | 79% |
| ACT composite: | 21-27 | **Return as sophomores:** | 68% |
| GPA 3.50 or higher: | 51% | **Out-of-state:** | 3% |
| GPA 3.0-3.49: | 26% | **Live on campus:** | 47% |
| GPA 2.0-2.99: | 23% | **International:** | 9% |

**Basis for selection.** School achievement record, test scores, and graded essay most important. Cumulative high school GPA of 2.5 or higher in a minimum of 18 college preparatory units required, as well as minimum 1020 SAT (exclusive of Writing) or 22 ACT. High school class rank in the upper 50% required, if high school attended ranks graduates. Audition required for applied music, drama, voice programs; portfolio required for art program.

**High school preparation.** 18 units required. Required units include English 4, mathematics 3, social studies 2, history 1, science 3 (laboratory 2), foreign language 2 and academic electives 3.

**2007-2008 Annual costs.** Tuition/fees: $19,070. Room/board: $7,300.

**2007-2008 Financial aid. Need-based:** 192 full-time freshmen applied for aid; 163 were judged to have need; 163 of these received aid. Average need met was 77%. Average scholarship/grant was $12,446; average loan $3,470. 74% of total undergraduate aid awarded as scholarships/grants, 26% as loans/jobs. **Non-need-based:** Awarded to 428 full-time undergraduates, including 131 freshmen. Scholarships awarded for academics, athletics.

**Application procedures. Admission:** No deadline. $25 fee, may be waived for applicants with need. Application may be submitted online. Admission notification on a rolling basis beginning on or about 9/15. Must reply by May 1 or within 2 week(s) if notified thereafter. **Financial aid:** No deadline. FAFSA required. Applicants notified on a rolling basis starting 3/22; must reply within 2 week(s) of notification.

**Academics. Special study options:** Combined bachelor's/graduate degree, distance learning, double major, honors, independent study, internships, study abroad. First-year experiences, learning communities, service learning, senior capstone or culminating academic experiences, undergraduate research/creative projects. **Credit/placement by examination:** AP, CLEP, IB, SAT, ACT, institutional tests. 30 credit hours maximum toward bachelor's degree. Validation of credit by examination contingent upon completion of at least 24 semester hours in residence at institution. **Support services:** Learning center, reduced course load, remedial instruction, study skills assistance, tutoring, writing center.

**Majors. Biology:** General, bioinformatics. **Business:** Accounting, business admin, finance, marketing. **Communications:** General. **Conservation:** Environmental studies. **Education:** General, elementary, music, secondary. **English:** English lit. **Foreign languages:** French, Spanish. **History:** General. **Liberal arts:** Arts/sciences. **Math:** General. **Philosophy/religion:** Philosophy. **Physical sciences:** Chemistry. **Psychology:** General. **Social sciences:** Economics, international relations, political science. **Theology:** Pastoral counseling, theology. **Visual/performing arts:** Dramatic, studio arts.

**Most popular majors.** Business/marketing 23%, English 6%, liberal arts 18%, psychology 6%, social sciences 15%, visual/performing arts 6%.

**Computing on campus.** 156 workstations in dormitories, library, computer center, student center. Dormitories wired for high-speed internet access. Online library, helpline, wireless network available.

**Student life. Freshman orientation:** Available. Preregistration for classes offered. Held in August and January. **Housing:** Coed dorms available. $300 fully refundable deposit. Pets allowed in dorm rooms. Houses and living-learning center available. **Activities:** Jazz band, campus ministries, choral groups, drama, international student organizations, literary magazine, music ensembles, musical theater, student government, student newspaper, Best Buddies, Black student union, Muslim student association, Society of St. Vincent de Paul, student organization of Latinos, Vietnamese student association, Filipino student association.

**Athletics.** NAIA. **Intercollegiate:** Soccer M, volleyball W. **Intramural:** Basketball, golf, racquetball, table tennis, tennis, volleyball. **Team name:** Celts.

**Student services.** Adult student services, campus ministries, career counseling, student employment services, financial aid counseling, health services, personal counseling, placement for graduates.

**Contact.** E-mail: admissions@stthom.edu
Phone: (713) 525-3500 Toll-free number: (800) 856-8565
Fax: (713) 525-3558
David Melton, Assistant Vice President of University Admissions, University of St. Thomas, 3800 Montrose Boulevard, Houston, TX 77006-4626

## University of Texas at Arlington
**Arlington, Texas**      **CB member**
**www.uta.edu**      **CB code: 6013**

- Public 4-year university
- Large city
- 18,489 degree-seeking undergraduates: 31% part-time, 52% women
- 5,556 degree-seeking graduate students
- 77% of applicants admitted
- SAT or ACT with writing required
- 42% graduate within 6 years

**General.** Founded in 1895. Regionally accredited. **Degrees:** 3,833 bachelor's awarded; master's, doctoral offered. **ROTC:** Army, Air Force. **Location:** 15 miles from Dallas and Fort Worth. **Calendar:** 4-1-4-1. Extensive summer session. **Full-time faculty:** 794 total; less than 1% have terminal degrees, 24% minority, 37% women. **Part-time faculty:** 602 total; 9% have terminal degrees, 16% minority, 48% women. **Class size:** 28% < 20, 41% 20-39, 8% 40-49, 18% 50-99, 5% >100. **Special facilities:** Robotics center, observatory, planetarium, maps collection, minority cultures collection, cartographic history library, library of Texana and Mexican War material.

**Freshman class profile.** 5,811 applied, 4,447 admitted, 2,162 enrolled.

| Mid 50% test scores | | | |
|---|---|---|---|
| SAT critical reading: | 450-560 | **Return as sophomores:** | 61% |
| SAT math: | 480-590 | **Out-of-state:** | 2% |
| ACT composite: | 19-23 | **Live on campus:** | 50% |
| | | **International:** | 3% |
| **Rank in top quarter:** | 63% | **Fraternities:** | 11% |
| **Rank in top tenth:** | 22% | **Sororities:** | 7% |

**Basis for selection.** GED not accepted. Admission based on test scores and high school rank. Fourth quarter of high school class must be approved by director of admissions or associate director. SAT or ACT math scores used for placement for students majoring in architecture, engineering, biology, biochemistry, chemistry, math, physics and students majoring in the BS geology or BS psychology program. Interview recommended for academically weak; audition recommended for music; portfolio recommended for art, architecture programs. **Homeschooled:** Transcript of courses and grades, letter of recommendation (nonparent) required.

**High school preparation.** 20 units required. Required and recommended units include English 4, mathematics 3-4, social studies 3-4, science 3, foreign language 2-3 and academic electives 5. 1 computing proficiency, 1 fine arts, 1 music/theatre art recommended.

**2007-2008 Annual costs.** Tuition/fees: $7,194; $15,534 out-of-state. Room/board: $6,170. Books/supplies: $840. Personal expenses: $1,418.

**2007-2008 Financial aid. Need-based:** Average need met was 71%. Average scholarship/grant was $4,969; average loan $2,873. 42% of total undergraduate aid awarded as scholarships/grants, 58% as loans/jobs.

**Application procedures. Admission:** Priority date 6/1; no deadline. $35 fee ($50 out-of-state), may be waived for applicants with need. Application may be submitted online. Admission notification on a rolling basis. **Financial aid:** Priority date 5/15; no closing date. FAFSA required. Applicants notified on a rolling basis starting 4/1; must reply within 3 week(s) of notification.

**Academics. Special study options:** Combined bachelor's/graduate degree, cross-registration, distance learning, double major, dual enrollment of high school students, ESL, honors, independent study, internships, student-designed major, study abroad, teacher certification program. **Credit/placement by examination:** AP, CLEP, IB, institutional tests. Credit by exam does not count as credit earned in residence. **Support services:** Learning center, reduced course load, remedial instruction, study skills assistance, tutoring, writing center.

**Majors. Architecture:** Architecture, interior. **Biology:** General, biochemistry, microbiology. **Business:** Accounting, banking/financial services, business admin, international, management information systems, managerial economics, marketing, real estate. **Communications:** Advertising, digital media, journalism, public relations, radio/tv. **Computer sciences:** Computer science. **Engineering:** Aerospace, civil, computer, electrical, industrial, mechanical, software. **English:** English lit, speech/rhetoric. **Family/consumer sciences:** Child development. **Foreign languages:** General, classics, French,

German, Russian, Spanish. **Health:** Athletic training, clinical lab science, nursing (RN). **History:** General. **Math:** General. **Parks/recreation:** Health/fitness. **Philosophy/religion:** Philosophy. **Physical sciences:** Chemistry, geology, physics. **Protective services:** Criminal justice. **Psychology:** General. **Public administration:** Social work. **Social sciences:** Anthropology, economics, political science, sociology. **Visual/performing arts:** Art, art history/conservation, dramatic, studio arts.

**Most popular majors.** Biology 8%, business/marketing 25%, communications/journalism 6%, engineering/engineering technologies 8%, health sciences 8%, interdisciplinary studies 12%.

**Computing on campus.** 1,000 workstations in dormitories, library, computer center, student center. Dormitories wired for high-speed internet access and linked to campus network. Commuter students can connect to campus network. Online course registration, online library, helpline, student web hosting, wireless network available.

**Student life. Freshman orientation:** Mandatory. Preregistration for classes offered. One-and-a-half-day sessions held in June, July, August. Students stay in residence halls. **Housing:** Coed dorms, single-sex dorms, apartments, fraternity/sorority housing available. $350 partly refundable deposit. Priority given to students with dependent children. **Activities:** Bands, choral groups, dance, drama, film society, international student organizations, literary magazine, music ensembles, opera, radio station, student government, student newspaper, symphony orchestra, University Democrats, Baptist student ministry, international students organization, association of Mexican American students, Vietnamese student association, Wesley Foundation, Mavericks for Christ, Business Beta Gamana Sigma, College Republicans, Business Delta Sigma Pi.

**Athletics.** NCAA. **Intercollegiate:** Baseball M, basketball, cross-country, golf M, softball W, tennis, track and field, volleyball W. **Intramural:** Badminton, basketball, bowling, football (non-tackle), golf, racquetball, soccer, softball, squash, swimming, table tennis, tennis, track and field, volleyball, weight lifting. **Team name:** Mavericks.

**Student services.** Alcohol/substance abuse counseling, campus ministries, career counseling, services for economically disadvantaged, student employment services, financial aid counseling, health services, legal services, minority student services, on-campus daycare, personal counseling, placement for graduates, veterans' counselor. **Physically disabled:** Services for visually, hearing impaired.

**Contact.** E-mail: admissions@uta.edu
Phone: (817) 272-6287 Fax: (817) 272-3435
Hans Gatterdam, Director of Admissions & Records, University of Texas at Arlington, Box 19111, Arlington, TX 76019

---

## University of Texas at Austin

**Austin, Texas**
www.utexas.edu

**CB member**
**CB code: 6882**

- Public 4-year university
- Commuter campus in very large city
- 36,881 degree-seeking undergraduates: 7% part-time, 52% women, 5% African American, 17% Asian American, 18% Hispanic American, 4% international
- 12,710 degree-seeking graduate students
- 51% of applicants admitted
- SAT or ACT with writing, application essay required
- 78% graduate within 6 years

**General.** Founded in 1883. Regionally accredited. **Degrees:** 8,521 bachelor's awarded; master's, doctoral, first professional offered. **ROTC:** Army, Naval, Air Force. **Location:** 70 miles from San Antonio, 163 miles from Houston. **Calendar:** Semester, extensive summer session. **Full-time faculty:** 2,599 total; 19% minority, 36% women. **Part-time faculty:** 273 total; 14% minority, 44% women. **Class size:** 35% < 20, 36% 20-39, 6% 40-49, 14% 50-99, 9% >100. **Special facilities:** Humanities and scientific research centers, observatory, marine science institute, fusion reactor, presidential library and museum, performing arts center.

**Freshman class profile.** 27,237 applied, 13,800 admitted, 7,478 enrolled.

| Mid 50% test scores | | End year in good standing: | 92% |
|---|---|---|---|
| SAT critical reading: | 540-670 | Return as sophomores: | 92% |
| SAT math: | 570-700 | Out-of-state: | 6% |
| SAT writing: | 540-660 | Live on campus: | 57% |
| ACT composite: | 23-29 | International: | 3% |
| Rank in top quarter: | 94% | Fraternities: | 13% |
| Rank in top tenth: | 69% | Sororities: | 10% |

**Basis for selection.** Applicants from top 10% of class from accredited Texas high school automatically admitted with completed application. Off-campus coordinated admission program available for Texans who complete all required high school units and apply immediately upon high school graduation, but are not otherwise eligible for regular admission. Audition required, interview recommended for music program; interview recommended for art, liberal arts honors program.

**High school preparation.** College-preparatory program recommended. 15.5 units required; 19 recommended. Required and recommended units include English 4, mathematics 3-4, social studies 3, science 2-3 (laboratory 2-3), foreign language 2-3 and academic electives 1. Foreign language must be same language; .5 fine arts elective strongly recommended.

**2007-2008 Annual costs.** Tuition/fees: $7,670; $24,544 out-of-state. Room/board: $8,576. Books/supplies: $800. Personal expenses: $2,300.

**2007-2008 Financial aid. Need-based:** 5,100 full-time freshmen applied for aid; 4,200 were judged to have need; 4,200 of these received aid. Average need met was 89%. Average scholarship/grant was $6,800; average loan $3,800. 58% of total undergraduate aid awarded as scholarships/grants, 42% as loans/jobs. **Non-need-based:** Awarded to 10,000 full-time undergraduates, including 1,250 freshmen. Scholarships awarded for academics, art, athletics, leadership, music/drama, ROTC, state residency.

**Application procedures. Admission:** Closing date 2/1 (receipt date). $60 fee, may be waived for applicants with need. Application may be submitted online. Admission notification 4/1. Admission notification on a rolling basis beginning on or about 11/15. Must reply by May 1 or within 2 week(s) if notified thereafter. **Financial aid:** Priority date 4/1; no closing date. FAFSA required. Applicants notified on a rolling basis starting 3/15; must reply within 4 week(s) of notification.

**Academics. Special study options:** Accelerated study, combined bachelor's/graduate degree, cooperative education, distance learning, double major, dual enrollment of high school students, ESL, honors, independent study, internships, liberal arts/career combination, student-designed major, study abroad, teacher certification program, Washington semester. **Credit/placement by examination:** AP, CLEP, IB, institutional tests. **Support services:** Learning center, reduced course load, remedial instruction, study skills assistance, tutoring, writing center.

**Majors. Architecture:** Architecture. **Area/ethnic studies:** American, Asian, Latin American, Near/Middle Eastern, Russian/Slavic. **Biology:** General, biochemistry, botany, ecology, microbiology, zoology. **Business:** General, accounting, business admin, finance, management information systems, marketing. **Communications:** General, advertising, journalism, public relations, radio/tv. **Computer sciences:** General. **Engineering:** Aerospace, architectural, biomedical, chemical, civil, electrical, mechanical, petroleum. **English:** English lit. **Family/consumer sciences:** General, clothing/textiles, family studies, food/nutrition. **Foreign languages:** General, ancient Greek, Arabic, classics, Czech, East Asian, French, German, Hebrew, Italian, Latin, linguistics, Persian, Portuguese, Russian, Scandinavian, Semitic, Spanish, Turkish. **Health:** Athletic training, clinical lab science, communication disorders, health services, nursing (RN). **History:** General. **Interdisciplinary:** Ancient studies. **Liberal arts:** Arts/sciences, humanities. **Math:** General. **Parks/recreation:** Health/fitness, sports admin. **Philosophy/religion:** Islamic, Judaic, philosophy, religion. **Physical sciences:** Astronomy, chemistry, geology, geophysics, hydrology, physics. **Psychology:** General. **Public administration:** Social work. **Social sciences:** Anthropology, archaeology, economics, geography, political science, sociology, urban studies. **Visual/performing arts:** General, art, art history/conservation, dance, design, dramatic, interior design, music history, music performance, music theory/composition, studio arts.

**Most popular majors.** Biology 8%, business/marketing 12%, communications/journalism 13%, engineering/engineering technologies 11%, social sciences 14%.

**Computing on campus.** 500 workstations in dormitories, library, computer center, student center. Dormitories wired for high-speed internet access and linked to campus network. Commuter students can connect to campus network. Online course registration, online library, helpline, repair service, student web hosting, wireless network available.

**Student life. Freshman orientation:** Available, $105 fee. Held during summer. **Housing:** Coed dorms, single-sex dorms, apartments available. $300 nonrefundable deposit. Honors residence, living-learning centers available for first-time freshmen. **Activities:** Bands, campus ministries, choral groups, dance, drama, film society, international student organizations, literary magazine, music ensembles, musical theater, opera, radio station, student government, student newspaper, symphony orchestra, TV station, wide variety of religious, political, ethnic, and social service organizations.

**Athletics.** NCAA. **Intercollegiate:** Baseball M, basketball, cross-country, diving, football (tackle) M, golf, rowing (crew) W, soccer W, softball W, swimming, tennis, track and field, volleyball W. **Intramural:** Badminton, basketball, bowling, football (non-tackle), golf, handball, racquetball, soccer, softball, squash, swimming, table tennis, tennis, track and field, volleyball, weight lifting. **Team name:** Longhorns.

**Student services.** Adult student services, alcohol/substance abuse counseling, campus ministries, career counseling, services for economically disadvantaged, student employment services, financial aid counseling, health services, legal services, minority student services, on-campus daycare, personal counseling, placement for graduates, veterans' counselor, women's services. **Physically disabled:** Services for visually, speech, hearing impaired. **Learning disabled:** Comprehensive services available.

**Contact.**  Phone: (512) 475-7399
Bruce Walker, Vice Provost and Director of Admissions, University of Texas at Austin, PO Box 8058, Austin, TX 78713-8058

---

### University of Texas at Brownsville

| Brownsville, Texas | CB member |
| --- | --- |
| www.utb.edu | CB code: 2054 |

- Public 4-year university and community college
- Commuter campus in small city
- 9,724 undergraduates
- 780 graduate students

**General.** Founded in 1977. Regionally accredited. Campus has both lower and upper division students. Close association with Texas Southmost College, which shares campus. **Degrees:** 919 bachelor's awarded; master's offered. **Calendar:** Semester, extensive summer session. **Full-time faculty:** 384 total. **Part-time faculty:** 247 total. **Class size:** 59% < 20, 32% 20-39, 3% 40-49, 5% 50-99, less than 1% >100.

#### Freshman class profile.

| | | | |
| --- | --- | --- | --- |
| Rank in top quarter: | 29% | Out-of-state: | 1% |
| Rank in top tenth: | 16% | Live on campus: | 1% |

**Basis for selection.** Open admission, but selective for some programs. Special requirements for nursing and allied health programs.

**2007-2008 Annual costs.** Tuition/fees: $4,665; $13,005 out-of-state. Books/supplies: $601. Personal expenses: $2,465.

**Application procedures.** **Admission:** Priority date 3/1; deadline 7/1 (receipt date). No application fee. Application may be submitted online. Admission notification on a rolling basis. **Financial aid:** Priority date 4/1, closing date 8/15. FAFSA required. Applicants notified on a rolling basis; must reply within 4 week(s) of notification.

**Academics.** **Special study options:** Combined bachelor's/graduate degree, cooperative education, cross-registration, distance learning, double major, dual enrollment of high school students, ESL, independent study, internships, liberal arts/career combination, teacher certification program. **Credit/placement by examination:** AP, CLEP, IB, institutional tests. **Support services:** Learning center, pre-admission summer program, reduced course load, remedial instruction, study skills assistance, tutoring.

**Majors.** **Biology:** General. **Business:** General, accounting, business admin, finance, marketing. **Communications:** General. **Computer sciences:** General, information systems. **Engineering:** Physics. **Engineering technology:** Electrical, industrial, manufacturing, mechanical. **English:** English lit. **Foreign languages:** Spanish. **Health:** Health services, nursing (RN). **History:** General. **Liberal arts:** Arts/sciences. **Math:** General. **Parks/recreation:** Health/fitness. **Physical sciences:** Chemistry, physics. **Protective services:** Corrections, law enforcement admin. **Psychology:** General. **Social sciences:** Political science, sociology. **Visual/performing arts:** Art.

**Computing on campus.** 650 workstations in dormitories, library, computer center. Dormitories wired for high-speed internet access and linked to campus network. Commuter students can connect to campus network. Online course registration, online library, helpline, repair service, student web hosting, wireless network available.

**Student life.** **Freshman orientation:** Available. **Housing:** Coed dorms, substance-free housing available. **Activities:** Jazz band, choral groups, dance, music ensembles, student government, student newspaper.

**Athletics.** NJCAA. **Intercollegiate:** Baseball M, golf, volleyball W. **Team name:** Scorpions.

**Student services.** Career counseling, services for economically disadvantaged, student employment services, financial aid counseling, health services, minority student services, on-campus daycare, personal counseling, placement for graduates, veterans' counselor. **Physically disabled:** Services for visually, hearing impaired.

**Contact.**  E-mail: admissions@utb.edu
Phone: (956) 882-8295 Toll-free number: (800) 850-0160
Fax: (956) 882-7810
Rene Villarreal, Director of Admissions, University of Texas at Brownsville, 80 Fort Brown, Brownsville, TX 78520

---

### University of Texas at Dallas

| Richardson, Texas | CB member |
| --- | --- |
| www.utdallas.edu | CB code: 6897 |

- Public 4-year university
- Commuter campus in very large city
- 9,096 degree-seeking undergraduates: 27% part-time, 46% women, 7% African American, 20% Asian American, 11% Hispanic American, 1% Native American, 4% international
- 4,763 degree-seeking graduate students
- 56% of applicants admitted
- SAT or ACT with writing required
- 55% graduate within 6 years

**General.** Founded in 1969. Regionally accredited. Established internships in industrial practice positions with over 200 advanced technology firms located near the university. **Degrees:** 2,334 bachelor's awarded; master's, doctoral offered. **ROTC:** Army, Air Force. **Location:** 18 miles from downtown Dallas. **Calendar:** Semester, extensive summer session. **Full-time faculty:** 495 total; 91% have terminal degrees, 28% minority, 26% women. **Part-time faculty:** 201 total; 57% have terminal degrees, 15% minority, 45% women. **Class size:** 31% < 20, 32% 20-39, 9% 40-49, 22% 50-99, 6% >100. **Special facilities:** Geological information library, history of aviation library, rare book library, philatelic research library, center for communications disorders, Holocaust collection, translation library.

**Freshman class profile.** 4,198 applied, 2,336 admitted, 1,057 enrolled.

| Mid 50% test scores | | | |
| --- | --- | --- | --- |
| SAT critical reading: | 540-670 | Rank in top tenth: | 43% |
| SAT math: | 580-690 | End year in good standing: | 80% |
| SAT writing: | 530-640 | Return as sophomores: | 81% |
| ACT composite: | 24-29 | Out-of-state: | 6% |
| GPA 3.50 or higher: | 73% | Live on campus: | 60% |
| GPA 3.0-3.49: | 23% | International: | 3% |
| GPA 2.0-2.99: | 4% | Fraternities: | 6% |
| Rank in top quarter: | 74% | Sororities: | 7% |

**Basis for selection.** 1140 SAT (exclusive of Writing) or 25 ACT, rank in top 25% of class, completion of required high school course work required for automatic admission. All others reviewed for admission. In-state high school students finishing in top 10% of class automatically admitted to state public universities. Texas Higher Education Assessment test required for some based on high school performance.

**High school preparation.** 18 units required; 24 recommended. Required and recommended units include English 4, mathematics 3.5-4, social studies 3-4, science 3 (laboratory 3), foreign language 2-3, computer science 1, visual/performing arts .5-1, academic electives 1.5-2.5. 0.5 health, 1.5 physical education recommended.

**2007-2008 Annual costs.** Tuition/fees: $8,554; $17,854 out-of-state. Room/board: $6,671. Books/supplies: $1,200. Personal expenses: $1,885.

**2007-2008 Financial aid.** **Need-based:** 629 full-time freshmen applied for aid; 442 were judged to have need; 440 of these received aid. Average need met was 84%. Average scholarship/grant was $6,288; average loan $2,648. 37% of total undergraduate aid awarded as scholarships/grants, 63% as loans/jobs. **Non-need-based:** Awarded to 3,402 full-time undergraduates, including 729 freshmen. Scholarships awarded for academics.

**Application procedures. Admission:** Closing date 7/1 (postmark date). $50 fee, may be waived for applicants with need. Application may be submitted online. Admission notification on a rolling basis. **Financial aid:** Priority date 3/31, closing date 4/12. FAFSA required. Applicants notified on a rolling basis starting 3/1; must reply within 2 week(s) of notification.

**Academics. Special study options:** Accelerated study, combined bachelor's/graduate degree, cooperative education, cross-registration, distance learning, double major, dual enrollment of high school students, honors, independent study, internships, student-designed major, study abroad, teacher certification program, Washington semester, weekend college. 3-2 engineering and 2-2 transfer programs. **Credit/placement by examination:** AP, CLEP, IB, institutional tests. 30 credit hours maximum toward bachelor's degree. No limit on lower-level courses, 6 hours limit on upper-level courses. SAT Subject Tests in Math Levels I and II accepted for advanced placement. **Support services:** Learning center, pre-admission summer program, reduced course load, remedial instruction, study skills assistance, tutoring, writing center.

**Majors. Area/ethnic studies:** American, women's. **Biology:** General, biochemistry, molecular. **Business:** General, accounting, finance. **Computer sciences:** General. **Engineering:** Computer, electrical, software. **Foreign languages:** Comparative lit. **Health:** Audiology/speech pathology. **History:** General. **Interdisciplinary:** Cognitive science, neuroscience. **Liberal arts:** Arts/sciences. **Math:** General, applied, statistics. **Physical sciences:** Chemistry, geology, physics. **Psychology:** General. **Public administration:** General. **Social sciences:** Criminology, economics, geography, political science, sociology. **Visual/performing arts:** General, studio arts.

**Most popular majors.** Biology 7%, business/marketing 33%, computer/information sciences 6%, engineering/engineering technologies 7%, interdisciplinary studies 14%, psychology 8%, social sciences 8%.

**Computing on campus.** 630 workstations in library, computer center. Dormitories linked to campus network. Commuter students can connect to campus network. Online course registration, online library, helpline, wireless network available.

**Student life. Freshman orientation:** Available, $100 fee. Preregistration for classes offered. Family 1-day sessions and student 2-day sessions held in April, July and August. **Housing:** Apartments available. $100 partly refundable deposit, deadline 6/30. Pets allowed in dorm rooms. Living-learning communities for freshmen. **Activities:** Dance, drama, radio station, student government, student newspaper, College Republicans, campus Hispanic association, African American student alliance, Friendship Association of Chinese Students and Visiting Scholars, Indian students association, multicultural association, Campus Crusade for Christ, Muslim students association, Pacific Asian student association.

**Athletics.** NCAA. **Intercollegiate:** Baseball M, basketball, cross-country, golf, soccer, softball W, tennis, volleyball W. **Intramural:** Basketball, bowling, cheerleading, football (non-tackle), golf, racquetball, soccer, softball, squash, tennis, volleyball, weight lifting. **Team name:** Comets.

**Student services.** Alcohol/substance abuse counseling, career counseling, student employment services, financial aid counseling, health services, legal services, minority student services, on-campus daycare, personal counseling, placement for graduates, veterans' counselor, women's services. **Physically disabled:** Services for visually, speech, hearing impaired.

**Contact.** E-mail: interest@utdallas.edu
Phone: (972) 883-2270 Toll-free number: (800) 889-2443
Fax: (972) 883-2599
Sheila Pineres, Director of Enrollment Services, University of Texas at Dallas, Office of Admissions, Richardson, TX 75083-0688

---

## University of Texas at El Paso

El Paso, Texas                              **CB member**
www.utep.edu                                **CB code: 6829**

▸ Public 4-year university
▸ Commuter campus in very large city
▸ 16,658 degree-seeking undergraduates: 34% part-time, 55% women, 3% African American, 1% Asian American, 77% Hispanic American, 10% international
▸ 2,723 degree-seeking graduate students
▸ 99% of applicants admitted
▸ 31% graduate within 6 years

**General.** Founded in 1913. Regionally accredited. Bilingual community, programs, and student body. Located within 100 yards of Mexico. **Degrees:** 2,463 bachelor's awarded; master's, doctoral offered. **ROTC:** Army, Air Force. **Calendar:** Semester, extensive summer session. **Full-time faculty:** 662 total; 19% minority, 38% women. **Part-time faculty:** 435 total; 23%

minority, 45% women. **Class size:** 31% < 20, 49% 20-39, 8% 40-49, 9% 50-99, 3% >100. **Special facilities:** Solar energy facility.

**Freshman class profile.** 5,147 applied, 5,098 admitted, 2,309 enrolled.

| Mid 50% test scores | | | |
|---|---|---|---|
| SAT critical reading: | 390-510 | Rank in top tenth: | 18% |
| SAT math: | 410-530 | Return as sophomores: | 68% |
| ACT composite: | 16-21 | Out-of-state: | 3% |
| Rank in top quarter: | 43% | International: | 9% |

**Basis for selection.** Minimum GED score of 45, or top half of high school class with 20 ACT or 920 SAT (exclusive of Writing). Provisional admission for in-state residents not meeting these criteria. For students in top quarter of high school class, any score acceptable. SAT or ACT, when required, may be used for counseling. Credit may be given for selected SAT Subject Tests.

**High school preparation.** 21 units recommended. Recommended units include English 4, mathematics 3, social studies 2, history 2, science 3 and foreign language 2. 1 additional math for science and engineering majors.

**2007-2008 Annual costs.** Tuition/fees: $5,610; $13,950 out-of-state. Mexican citizens who show need may qualify for in-state tuition. Room/board: $7,696. Books/supplies: $900. Personal expenses: $1,780.

**2006-2007 Financial aid. Need-based:** 1,723 full-time freshmen applied for aid; 1,356 were judged to have need; 1,344 of these received aid. Average need met was 80%. Average scholarship/grant was $6,494; average loan $2,827. 42% of total undergraduate aid awarded as scholarships/grants, 58% as loans/jobs. **Non-need-based:** Awarded to 1,651 full-time undergraduates, including 384 freshmen. Scholarships awarded for academics, alumni affiliation, art, athletics, job skills, leadership, minority status, music/drama, religious affiliation, ROTC, state residency. **Additional information:** Emergency loans available.

**Application procedures. Admission:** Priority date 5/1; deadline 7/31 (postmark date). No application fee. Application may be submitted online. Admission notification on a rolling basis. Notification of early action applicants when admission file is complete. **Financial aid:** Closing date 3/15. FAFSA, institutional form required. Applicants notified by 6/30; must reply within 2 week(s) of notification.

**Academics. Special study options:** Accelerated study, combined bachelor's/graduate degree, cooperative education, cross-registration, distance learning, double major, dual enrollment of high school students, ESL, exchange student, honors, independent study, internships, study abroad, teacher certification program, weekend college. **Credit/placement by examination:** AP, CLEP, IB, SAT, institutional tests. **Support services:** Learning center, pre-admission summer program, reduced course load, remedial instruction, study skills assistance, tutoring, writing center.

**Majors. Area/ethnic studies:** Hispanic-American/Latino/Chicano, Latin American. **Biology:** General, microbiology. **Business:** General, accounting, business admin, finance, management information systems, managerial economics, marketing, operations. **Communications:** General, advertising, journalism, media studies, public relations. **Computer sciences:** General. **Conservation:** Environmental science. **Education:** General, elementary, middle, special. **Engineering:** General, civil, electrical, industrial, mechanical, metallurgical. **English:** Creative writing. **Foreign languages:** Comparative lit, French, German, linguistics, Spanish. **Health:** Audiology/speech pathology, clinical lab science, community health services, health services, nursing (RN). **History:** General. **Interdisciplinary:** Biological/physical sciences. **Liberal arts:** Arts/sciences. **Math:** General, applied, statistics. **Parks/recreation:** Health/fitness. **Philosophy/religion:** Philosophy. **Physical sciences:** General, chemistry, geology, geophysics, physics. **Protective services:** Criminal justice. **Psychology:** General. **Public administration:** Social work. **Social sciences:** Anthropology, political science, sociology. **Visual/performing arts:** Art, ceramics, dance, dramatic, drawing, graphic design, metal/jewelry, music performance, music theory/composition, painting, piano/organ, printmaking, sculpture, studio arts, voice/opera.

**Most popular majors.** Biology 6%, business/marketing 17%, engineering/engineering technologies 9%, health sciences 9%, interdisciplinary studies 29%.

**Computing on campus.** 2,500 workstations in library, computer center, student center. Dormitories wired for high-speed internet access. Commuter students can connect to campus network. Online course registration, online library, helpline, student web hosting, wireless network available.

**Student life. Freshman orientation:** Available. Preregistration for classes offered. 3-5 day program. **Housing:** Special housing for disabled, apartments available. **Activities:** Bands, choral groups, dance, drama, film society, literary magazine, music ensembles, musical theater, opera, radio station, student government, student newspaper, symphony orchestra, black student coalition, Mexican student organizations, Society of Hispanic Professional Engineers.

**Athletics.** NCAA. **Intercollegiate:** Basketball, cross-country, football (tackle) M, golf, rifle, soccer W, softball W, tennis, track and field, volleyball W. **Intramural:** Badminton, baseball M, basketball, bowling, fencing, football (tackle) M, golf, gymnastics, handball, racquetball, skiing, soccer, softball, squash, swimming, table tennis, tennis, track and field, volleyball, water polo, wrestling M. **Team name:** Miners.

**Student services.** Alcohol/substance abuse counseling, campus ministries, career counseling, student employment services, financial aid counseling, health services, on-campus daycare, personal counseling, placement for graduates, veterans' counselor, women's services. **Physically disabled:** Services for visually, speech, hearing impaired.

**Contact.** E-mail: futureminer@utep.edu
Phone: (915) 747-5890 Fax: (915) 747-8893
Gustavo Monzon, Associate Director, University of Texas at El Paso, 500 West University Avenue, El Paso, TX 79968-0510

---

## University of Texas at San Antonio
**San Antonio, Texas**  **CB member**
**www.utsa.edu**  **CB code: 6919**

- Public 4-year university
- Commuter campus in very large city
- 24,280 degree-seeking undergraduates: 23% part-time, 51% women, 8% African American, 6% Asian American, 44% Hispanic American, 2% international
- 3,828 graduate students
- 93% of applicants admitted
- SAT or ACT with writing required

**General.** Founded in 1969. Regionally accredited. Second campus in downtown area. **Degrees:** 3,649 bachelor's awarded; master's, doctoral offered. **ROTC:** Army, Air Force. **Location:** 15 miles from downtown. **Calendar:** Semester, limited summer session. **Full-time faculty:** 917 total; 72% have terminal degrees, 36% minority, 41% women. **Part-time faculty:** 226 total; 42% have terminal degrees, 30% minority, 45% women. **Class size:** 25% < 20, 44% 20-39, 8% 40-49, 14% 50-99, 9% >100. **Special facilities:** Institute of Texan cultures, center for archaelogical research, neuroscience research center, center for water research, center for lasers and materials science, center for economic development, culture and policy institute, institute for music research, center for professional excellence.

**Freshman class profile.** 10,929 applied, 10,163 admitted, 4,928 enrolled.

| Mid 50% test scores | | Return as sophomores: | 59% |
|---|---|---|---|
| SAT critical reading: | 440-550 | Out-of-state: | 1% |
| SAT math: | 460-570 | Live on campus: | 43% |
| SAT writing: | 430-530 | International: | 3% |
| ACT composite: | 18-23 | Fraternities: | 2% |
| Rank in top quarter: | 31% | Sororities: | 1% |
| Rank in top tenth: | 10% | | |

**Basis for selection.** Texas residents who graduate in top 10% of high school graduating class admitted, regardless of ACT or SAT scores. Those not in top 10% must meet appropriate ACT or SAT scores based on class rank. If test score/rank criteria not met, additional factors may be taken into consideration. Out-of-state applicants must graduate in top half of graduating class in addition to meeting corresponding ACT or SAT score requirements. **Homeschooled:** Conditional admissions decision based on SAT score over 970 (exclusive of Writing) plus high school educational record (courses taken and grades earned) signed and dated by person responsible for conducting educational program. Upon high school graduation, final high school record indicating graduation date signed and dated by responsible educator must be submitted.

**High school preparation.** 16.5 units recommended. Recommended units include English 4, mathematics 3, social studies 3.5, science 3 and foreign language 2. 1 or more fine arts recommended.

**2007-2008 Annual costs.** Tuition/fees: $6,677; $14,927 out-of-state. Room/board: $7,542. Books/supplies: $1,000. Personal expenses: $2,202.

**2006-2007 Financial aid.** **Need-based:** 3,488 full-time freshmen applied for aid; 2,317 were judged to have need; 2,198 of these received aid. Average need met was 50%. Average scholarship/grant was $4,636; average loan $2,431. 44% of total undergraduate aid awarded as scholarships/grants, 56% as loans/jobs. **Non-need-based:** Awarded to 2,637 full-time undergraduates, including 1,023 freshmen. Scholarships awarded for academics, alumni

affiliation, art, athletics, job skills, leadership, music/drama, ROTC, state residency.

**Application procedures.** **Admission:** Priority date 4/1; deadline 7/1 (receipt date). $40 fee, may be waived for applicants with need. Application may be submitted online. Admission notification on a rolling basis beginning on or about 10/1. **Financial aid:** Priority date 3/31; no closing date. FAFSA, institutional form required. Applicants notified on a rolling basis starting 4/1; must reply within 4 week(s) of notification.

**Academics.** Freshman Initiative includes learning communities and freshman seminar program, enhancing academic services for new students in order to increase retention and success in college. **Special study options:** Accelerated study, cooperative education, distance learning, double major, dual enrollment of high school students, ESL, exchange student, honors, independent study, internships, study abroad, teacher certification program. 2-2 programs with Alamo Community College District, Southwest Texas Junior College, Laredo Junior College, Victoria College, Del Mar College, Coastal Bend Community College, Austin Community College; telecampus agreement with UT System. **Credit/placement by examination:** AP, CLEP, institutional tests. Some departments have limits on number of credits earned by examination. **Support services:** Learning center, pre-admission summer program, remedial instruction, study skills assistance, tutoring, writing center.

**Majors.** **Architecture:** Architecture, interior. **Area/ethnic studies:** American, Hispanic-American/Latino/Chicano. **Biology:** General. **Business:** General, accounting, actuarial science, business admin, finance, human resources, international, management information systems, management science, managerial economics, marketing, operations, sales/distribution, tourism/travel. **Communications:** General, media studies, public relations. **Computer sciences:** General, security. **Conservation:** Environmental science. **Engineering:** Civil, electrical, mechanical. **English:** English lit, speech/rhetoric, technical writing. **Foreign languages:** Classics, French, German, Spanish. **Health:** Clinical lab science, health services. **History:** General. **Interdisciplinary:** Biological/physical sciences. **Liberal arts:** Humanities. **Math:** General, statistics. **Parks/recreation:** Health/fitness. **Philosophy/religion:** Philosophy. **Physical sciences:** General, chemistry, geology, physics. **Protective services:** Criminal justice. **Psychology:** General. **Social sciences:** General, anthropology, geography, political science, sociology. **Visual/performing arts:** Art, art history/conservation, music management, music performance, music theory/composition, studio arts.

**Most popular majors.** Biology 8%, business/marketing 28%, interdisciplinary studies 14%, psychology 7%.

**Computing on campus.** 550 workstations in dormitories, library, computer center, student center. Dormitories wired for high-speed internet access and linked to campus network. Commuter students can connect to campus network. Online course registration, online library, helpline, repair service, student web hosting, wireless network available.

**Student life.** **Freshman orientation:** Mandatory, $55 fee. Preregistration for classes offered. One-day sessions held throughout the year; optional 2-day camp held in August. **Housing:** Coed dorms, apartments available. $200 partly refundable deposit. **Activities:** Bands, choral groups, dance, drama, film society, literary magazine, music ensembles, radio station, student government, student newspaper, IDS student association, pre-med society, Golden Key national honor society, Intervarsity Christian Fellowship, S/B Alpha Chi national honor society, Catholic student association, Mortar Board national college senior honor society, Texas Association of Chicanos in Higher Education.

**Athletics.** NCAA. **Intercollegiate:** Baseball M, basketball, cross-country, golf, soccer W, softball W, tennis, track and field, volleyball W. **Intramural:** Badminton, basketball, bowling, football (non-tackle), golf, racquetball, soccer, softball, table tennis, tennis, volleyball, weight lifting. **Team name:** Roadrunners.

**Student services.** Career counseling, student employment services, financial aid counseling, health services, personal counseling, placement for graduates, veterans' counselor. **Physically disabled:** Services for visually, speech, hearing impaired.

**Contact.** E-mail: prospects@utsa.edu
Phone: (210) 458-8000 Toll-free number: (800) 669-0919
Fax: (210) 458-2001
George Norton, Director of Admissions, University of Texas at San Antonio, One UTSA Circle, San Antonio, TX 78249-0617

---

## University of Texas at Tyler
**Tyler, Texas**  **CB member**
**www.uttyler.edu**  **CB code: 0389**

- Public 4-year university
- Commuter campus in small city

- 4,938 degree-seeking undergraduates: 22% part-time, 60% women, 9% African American, 2% Asian American, 7% Hispanic American, 1% Native American, 1% international
- 961 degree-seeking graduate students
- 80% of applicants admitted
- SAT or ACT (ACT writing optional) required
- 37% graduate within 6 years

**General.** Founded in 1971. Regionally accredited. Off-campus sites at Palestine and Longview. Internet courses and telecampus available. **Degrees:** 899 bachelor's awarded; master's, doctoral offered. **Location:** 80 miles from Dallas. **Calendar:** Semester, limited summer session. **Full-time faculty:** 250 total; 72% have terminal degrees, 10% minority, 50% women. **Part-time faculty:** 131 total; 28% have terminal degrees, 5% minority, 50% women. **Class size:** 36% < 20, 43% 20-39, 7% 40-49, 12% 50-99, 2% >100. **Special facilities:** Desktop manufacturing lab, computer-based virtual lab instruments.

**Freshman class profile.** 1,475 applied, 1,180 admitted, 621 enrolled.

| Mid 50% test scores | | | |
|---|---|---|---|
| SAT critical reading: | 460-580 | Return as sophomores: | 68% |
| SAT math: | 490-590 | Out-of-state: | 1% |
| SAT writing: | 440-570 | Live on campus: | 66% |
| ACT composite: | 20-25 | Fraternities: | 3% |
| | | Sororities: | 2% |

**Basis for selection.** Top 10% accepted automatically, others admitted based on ACT/SAT scores and high school preparation.

**High school preparation.** Required and recommended units include English 4, mathematics 3-4, social studies 3, science 3 (laboratory 1-3) and foreign language 2. Math requirement must be algebra I and higher. 4 mathematics recommended for science, engineering, and other technical fields.

**2007-2008 Annual costs.** Tuition/fees: $5,382; $13,722 out-of-state. Room/board: $6,586. Books/supplies: $900. Personal expenses: $1,148.

**2006-2007 Financial aid. Need-based:** 389 full-time freshmen applied for aid; 245 were judged to have need; 245 of these received aid. Average need met was 51%. Average scholarship/grant was $5,050; average loan $2,164. 39% of total undergraduate aid awarded as scholarships/grants, 61% as loans/jobs. **Non-need-based:** Awarded to 393 full-time undergraduates, including 88 freshmen. Scholarships awarded for academics, art, music/drama. **Additional information:** Apply early for all programs.

**Application procedures. Admission:** No deadline. $25 fee, may be waived for applicants with need. Application may be submitted online. Admission notification on a rolling basis beginning on or about 9/1. Must reply by May 1 or within 4 week(s) if notified thereafter. **Financial aid:** Priority date 4/1; no closing date. FAFSA, institutional form required. Applicants notified on a rolling basis starting 4/15; must reply within 2 week(s) of notification.

**Academics. Special study options:** Cooperative education, distance learning, double major, independent study, internships, student-designed major, teacher certification program. **Credit/placement by examination:** AP, CLEP, IB, SAT, ACT, institutional tests. AP, CLEP and International Baccalaureate awarded transfer credit with no maximum limit. **Support services:** Learning center, remedial instruction, study skills assistance, tutoring, writing center.

**Majors. Biology:** General. **Business:** Accounting, business admin, finance, managerial economics, marketing, sales/distribution. **Communications:** Journalism. **Computer sciences:** General. **Engineering:** Civil, electrical, mechanical. **Engineering technology:** General, industrial, occupational safety. **English:** English lit, speech/rhetoric. **Foreign languages:** General, Spanish. **Health:** Clinical lab science, community health services, nursing (RN). **History:** General. **Math:** General. **Parks/recreation:** Health/fitness. **Physical sciences:** Chemistry. **Protective services:** Criminal justice. **Psychology:** General. **Social sciences:** Political science, sociology. **Visual/performing arts:** Art.

**Most popular majors.** Business/marketing 19%, engineering/engineering technologies 6%, health sciences 23%, interdisciplinary studies 15%, science technologies 6%.

**Computing on campus.** 175 workstations in dormitories, library, computer center, student center. Dormitories wired for high-speed internet access and linked to campus network. Commuter students can connect to campus network. Online course registration, online library, wireless network available.

**Student life. Freshman orientation:** Mandatory, $35 fee. Preregistration for classes offered. One-day orientation in summer for students and parents. **Housing:** Coed dorms, apartments available. **Activities:** Bands, campus ministries, choral groups, international student organizations, literary magazine,

music ensembles, Model UN, musical theater, opera, student government, student newspaper, Bible study fellowship, University Democrats, University Republicans, criminal justice club, Nurses Christian Fellowship, foreign language club, Webb Historical Society, press club.

**Athletics.** NCAA. **Intercollegiate:** Baseball M, basketball, cheerleading, cross-country, golf, soccer, softball W, tennis, volleyball W. **Intramural:** Baseball M, basketball, bowling, football (non-tackle), football (tackle), golf, racquetball, soccer, softball, swimming, table tennis, tennis, volleyball W. **Team name:** Patriots.

**Student services.** Adult student services, alcohol/substance abuse counseling, career counseling, student employment services, financial aid counseling, health services, personal counseling, veterans' counselor. **Physically disabled:** Services for visually, speech, hearing impaired.

**Contact.** E-mail: admissions@mail.uttyl.edu
Phone: (903) 566-7202 Toll-free number: (800) 888-9537
Fax: (903) 566-7068
Jim Hutto, Dean of Enrollment Management, University of Texas at Tyler, 3900 University Boulevard, Tyler, TX 75799

---

## University of Texas Health Science Center at Houston
Houston, Texas
www.uth.tmc.edu     CB code: 6888

- Public two-year upper-division university and health science college
- Commuter campus in very large city

**General.** Founded in 1972. Regionally accredited. **Location:** 5 miles from downtown. **Calendar:** Semester.

**Annual costs/financial aid.** Tuition/fees (2007-2008): $4,415; $13,055 out-of-state. Cost above are for RN-BSN nursing program. Nursing program students must attend for full calendar year (fall, spring, summer semesters). Books/supplies: $1,050. Need-based financial aid available to full-time and part-time students.

**Contact.** Phone: (713) 500-3361
Associate Registrar, Box 20036, Houston, TX 77225

---

## University of Texas Health Science Center at San Antonio
San Antonio, Texas     CB member
www.uthscsa.edu     CB code: 6908

- Public two-year upper-division university and health science college
- Commuter campus in very large city

**General.** Founded in 1969. Regionally accredited. Located in South Texas Medical Center. **Degrees:** 350 bachelor's awarded; master's, doctoral, first professional offered. **Location:** 10 miles from downtown. **Calendar:** Semester, limited summer session. **Full-time faculty:** 1,154 total. **Part-time faculty:** 355 total.

**Student profile.** 683 degree-seeking undergraduates, 2,173 graduate students. 99% entered as juniors, 1% entered as seniors.

**Basis for selection.** High school transcript, college transcript required. Admission varies with each program. In many cases, academic records and interview required. Application closing and priority dates vary with each program. Transfer accepted as juniors.

**2007-2008 Annual costs.** Tuition/fees: $5,420; $15,500 out-of-state. Tuition and fees vary by program. Books/supplies: $850. Personal expenses: $1,100.

**Financial aid. Additional information:** Students strongly advised to provide parental information on need analysis form regardless of dependency status.

**Application procedures. Admission:** Application fees vary from $10 to $55 depending on program. **Financial aid:** FAFSA, institutional form required.

**Academics. Special study options:** Combined bachelor's/graduate degree, cross-registration, internships. Pharmacy program with University of Texas-Austin; joint degree program with University of Texas-San Antonio allied health sciences; joint PhD nursing program with Texas Tech University. **Credit/placement by examination:** CLEP, institutional tests.

**Majors. Health:** Clinical lab science, dental hygiene, dental lab technology, nursing (RN), physician assistant, respiratory therapy technology.

**Computing on campus.** 50 workstations in library. Commuter students can connect to campus network. Helpline, wireless network available.

**Student life. Activities:** Student government, student newspaper, Texas Association of Mexican-American Medical Students, Latin-American Nursing Student Association, Diversified Dental Students.

**Athletics. Intramural:** Baseball M, basketball, softball, tennis, volleyball.

**Student services.** Financial aid counseling, health services, personal counseling.

**Contact.** E-mail: registrars@uthscsa.edu
Phone: (210) 567-2621 Fax: (210) 567-2685
Debra Goode, Registrar, University of Texas Health Science Center at San Antonio, 7703 Floyd Curl Drive, San Antonio, TX 78229

## University of Texas Medical Branch at Galveston
### Galveston, Texas
www.utmb.edu                                    CB code: 6887

◗ Public two-year upper-division health science and nursing college
◗ Commuter campus in small city

**General.** Founded in 1881. Regionally accredited. **Degrees:** 221 bachelor's awarded; master's, doctoral, first professional offered. **Location:** 50 miles from Houston. **Calendar:** Semester, limited summer session.

**Student profile.** 562 degree-seeking undergraduates, 1,860 degree-seeking graduate students.

| | | | |
|---|---|---|---|
| Women: | 80% | Out-of-state: | 1% |
| Part-time: | 46% | 25 or older: | 57% |

**Basis for selection.** College transcript required. Students with 60 hours from accredited college or university considered. Nonresident enrollment limited by legislature to not more than 10% of any class. Transfer decisions based on competitive comparison of transcripts, allied health experience, departmental testing, and personal interviews. Specific prerequisites and application closing dates vary by program. Transfer accepted as juniors, seniors.

**2007-2008 Annual costs.** Tuition/fees: $5,278; $13,618 out-of-state. Tuition and fees vary by program.

**Financial aid. Non-need-based:** Scholarships awarded for academics, minority status, state residency.

**Application procedures. Admission:** Rolling admission. $30 fee. Application may be submitted online. Application closing dates vary with school and program. **Financial aid:** FAFSA required.

**Academics.** Institution located in a medical complex. Curriculum provides clinical experience in 6 hospitals, 85 clinics, Shriners Burn Institute, and school for children with cerebral palsy. **Special study options:** Distance learning, independent study, internships. **Credit/placement by examination:** CLEP, IB. 30 credit hours maximum toward bachelor's degree. **Support services:** Learning center, pre-admission summer program, reduced course load, remedial instruction, study skills assistance, tutoring.

**Majors. Health:** Clinical lab science, nursing (RN), respiratory therapy technology.

**Computing on campus.** Dormitories wired for high-speed internet access and linked to campus network. Commuter students can connect to campus network. Online library, helpline, repair service, wireless network available.

**Student life. Housing:** Coed dorms, apartments, fraternity/sorority housing available. **Activities:** Campus ministries, student government, student newspaper, Wesley Foundation, Newman Center, sports clubs, Christian Medical and Dental Society, Jewish student and faculty organization, multicultural awareness council, student national medical association, Texas Association of Latin American Medical Students.

**Athletics. Intramural:** Basketball, football (non-tackle), soccer, softball, volleyball.

**Student services.** Alcohol/substance abuse counseling, campus ministries, career counseling, student employment services, financial aid counseling, health services, legal services, on-campus daycare, personal counseling, veterans' counselor, women's services. **Physically disabled:** Services for visually, speech, hearing impaired.

**Contact.** E-mail: enrollment.services@utmb.edu
Phone: (409) 772-1215 Fax: (409) 772-4466
Vicki Brewer, Registrar, University of Texas Medical Branch at Galveston, 301 University Boulevard, Galveston, TX 77555-1305

## University of Texas of the Permian Basin
### Odessa, Texas                                    CB member
www.utpb.edu                                        CB code: 0448

◗ Public 4-year university
◗ Commuter campus in small city
◗ 2,634 degree-seeking undergraduates: 26% part-time, 61% women, 5% African American, 2% Asian American, 41% Hispanic American, 1% Native American
◗ 626 degree-seeking graduate students
◗ 50% of applicants admitted
◗ SAT or ACT (ACT writing optional) required

**General.** Founded in 1969. Regionally accredited. **Degrees:** 532 bachelor's awarded; master's offered. **Location:** 150 miles from Lubbock, 350 miles from Dallas. **Calendar:** Semester, extensive summer session. **Full-time faculty:** 104 total. **Part-time faculty:** 118 total. **Class size:** 38% < 20, 44% 20-39, 6% 40-49, 10% 50-99, less than 1% >100.

**Freshman class profile.** 1,403 applied, 701 admitted, 362 enrolled.

| Mid 50% test scores | | GPA 2.0-2.99: | 19% |
|---|---|---|---|
| SAT critical reading: | 420-530 | Rank in top quarter: | 52% |
| SAT math: | 440-530 | Rank in top tenth: | 18% |
| ACT composite: | 18-22 | Out-of-state: | 1% |
| GPA 3.50 or higher: | 38% | Live on campus: | 38% |
| GPA 3.0-3.49: | 42% | International: | 1% |

**Basis for selection.** Secondary school record, class rank, test scores important. Foreign students whose native language is not English must take TOEFL. Requirement may be waived for non-English speakers transferring from a U.S. college or high school.

**High school preparation.** 24 units required. Required units include English 4, mathematics 3, social studies 3.5, science 3 (laboratory 3), foreign language 2, computer science 1, visual/performing arts 1, academic electives 3.5. 1 English unit in developmental writing recommended.

**2007-2008 Annual costs.** Tuition/fees: $4,849; $13,189 out-of-state. New Mexico residents living in areas contiguous to Texas border pay in-district rate; other New Mexico residents pay $5,749 for tuition plus fees. Books/supplies: $555. Personal expenses: $1,375.

**2006-2007 Financial aid. Need-based:** 65 full-time freshmen applied for aid; 48 were judged to have need; 48 of these received aid. Average need met was 65%. Average scholarship/grant was $5,394; average loan $1,977. 62% of total undergraduate aid awarded as scholarships/grants, 38% as loans/jobs. **Non-need-based:** Awarded to 859 full-time undergraduates, including 36 freshmen. Scholarships awarded for academics.

**Application procedures. Admission:** Closing date 7/14. No application fee. Admission notification on a rolling basis. **Financial aid:** Priority date 5/1; no closing date. FAFSA required. Applicants notified on a rolling basis starting 6/1; must reply within 2 week(s) of notification.

**Academics. Special study options:** Distance learning, double major, independent study, internships, teacher certification program. **Credit/placement by examination:** AP, CLEP, institutional tests. 28 credit hours maximum toward bachelor's degree. Credit/placement awarded on AP or CLEP exams, special exams administered by School of Business. **Support services:** Learning center, reduced course load, remedial instruction, study skills assistance, writing center.

**Majors. Biology:** General. **Business:** Accounting, business admin, finance, managerial economics, marketing. **Communications:** General. **Computer sciences:** General, information systems. **Conservation:** Environmental studies. **Engineering technology:** Industrial. **English:** English lit. **Family/consumer sciences:** Family studies. **Foreign languages:** Spanish. **History:** General. **Interdisciplinary:** Biological/physical sciences. **Liberal arts:** Arts/sciences. **Math:** General. **Parks/recreation:** Health/fitness. **Physical sciences:** Chemistry, geology. **Protective services:** Criminal justice. **Psychology:** General. **Public administration:** Social work. **Social sciences:**

Criminology, political science, sociology. **Visual/performing arts:** Art. **Other:** Leadership studies.

**Most popular majors.** Business/marketing 19%, English 7%, family/consumer sciences 11%, history 8%, parks/recreation 7%, psychology 8%, social sciences 8%.

**Computing on campus.** 50 workstations in dormitories, library, computer center, student center. Dormitories linked to campus network. Commuter students can connect to campus network. Online course registration, student web hosting, wireless network available.

**Student life. Freshman orientation:** Available. Preregistration for classes offered. 3 separate sessions in June, July and August, lasting at least 2 days with some meals, refreshments provided. Limited lodging for out-of-town students. **Housing:** Special housing for disabled, apartments available. $100 deposit. **Activities:** Dance, literary magazine, student government, student newspaper, Baptist student ministries, Genesis Bible study, political science club, black student organization, students in philanthropy, Catholic student organization.

**Athletics.** NAIA. **Intercollegiate:** Basketball, cheerleading W, soccer, softball W, swimming, volleyball W. **Intramural:** Badminton, baseball M, basketball, bowling, golf, handball, racquetball, rugby M, soccer, softball, swimming, table tennis, tennis, volleyball, weight lifting. **Team name:** Falcons.

**Student services.** Campus ministries, career counseling, student employment services, financial aid counseling, personal counseling, placement for graduates, veterans' counselor. **Physically disabled:** Services for visually, speech, hearing impaired.

**Contact.** E-mail: admissions@utpb.edu
Phone: (432) 552-2605 Toll-free number: (866) 552-8872
Fax: (432) 552-3605
Trey Wetendorf, Director of Admissions, University of Texas of the Permian Basin, 4901 East University Boulevard, Odessa, TX 79762

## University of Texas Southwestern Medical Center at Dallas
**Dallas, Texas**
www.utsouthwestern.edu                      CB code: 0273

- Public two-year upper-division university and health science college
- Commuter campus in very large city
- 42% of applicants admitted
- Application essay required

**General.** Founded in 1943. Regionally accredited. Four teaching hospitals adjoin campus. **Degrees:** 48 bachelor's awarded; master's, doctoral, first professional offered. **Articulation:** Agreements with Dallas County Community College District, Collin County Community College, Tarrant County College District. **Location:** 3 miles from downtown. **Calendar:** Semester, limited summer session. **Full-time faculty:** 1,464 total. **Part-time faculty:** 402 total. **Class size:** 88% < 20, 12% 20-39.

**Student profile.** 118 degree-seeking undergraduates, 2,302 degree-seeking graduate students. 88 applied as first time-transfer students, 37 admitted, 37 enrolled. 92% entered as juniors, 8% entered as seniors.

| Women: | 75% | Out-of-state: | 10% |
|---|---|---|---|
| Part-time: | 12% | 25 or older: | 63% |

**Basis for selection.** College transcript, application essay required. Application closing dates vary by program. No limit on transferable credits. Students must complete prescribed professional curriculum and be Texas Core Curriculum complete. Transfer accepted as juniors, seniors.

**2007-2008 Annual costs.** Tuition/fees: $4,140; $12,380 out-of-state. Tuition and fees are based on Allied Health program. Books/supplies: $775.

**Financial aid. Need-based:** 90 applied for aid; 86 were judged to have need; 86 of these received aid. Average need met was 86%. 19% of total undergraduate aid awarded as scholarships/grants, 81% as loans/jobs. **Non-need-based:** Awarded to 5 undergraduates.

**Application procedures. Admission:** Rolling admission. $10 fee. Application may be submitted online. **Financial aid:** Priority date 3/1. Applicants notified on a rolling basis starting 4/1; must reply within 3 weeks of notification.

**Academics.** Offers 2-year upper division baccalaureate and master's programs in allied health professions. **Special study options:** Cross-registration, distance learning, independent study, internships. **Credit/placement by examination:** CLEP, institutional tests. Credit granted in English,

government and history via advanced standing exams. Cannot exceed 3 semester hours in each subject.

**Majors. Health:** Clinical lab science, dietetics, orthotics/prosthetics.

**Computing on campus.** 150 workstations in library, computer center. Commuter students can connect to campus network. Online library, helpline available.

**Student life. Activities:** Student Dietetic Association, student membership in American Physical Therapy Association, American Academy of Physician Assistants, American Dietetic Association, American Society for Medical Technology, National Rehabilitation Association, American Society of Allied Health Professions.

**Athletics. Intramural:** Basketball, golf, softball, table tennis, tennis, volleyball.

**Student services.** Career counseling, financial aid counseling, health services, personal counseling, placement for graduates, veterans' counselor.

**Contact.** E-mail: admissions@utsouthwestern.edu
Phone: (214) 648-5617 Fax: (214) 648-3289
Wes Norred, Vice President Student and Alumni Affairs, University of Texas Southwestern Medical Center at Dallas, 5323 Harry Hines Boulevard, Dallas, TX 75390-9162

## University of Texas: Pan American
**Edinburg, Texas**                           CB member
www.utpa.edu                                 CB code: 6570

- Public 4-year university
- Commuter campus in small city
- 14,995 degree-seeking undergraduates: 25% part-time, 58% women, 1% African American, 1% Asian American, 88% Hispanic American, 5% international
- 2,195 degree-seeking graduate students
- 62% of applicants admitted
- SAT or ACT (ACT writing optional) required
- 33% graduate within 6 years

**General.** Founded in 1927. Regionally accredited. Hispanic serving institution. **Degrees:** 2,404 bachelor's awarded; master's, doctoral offered. **ROTC:** Army. **Location:** 250 miles from San Antonio, 300 miles from Austin. **Calendar:** Semester, extensive summer session. **Full-time faculty:** 633 total; 40% minority, 40% women. **Part-time faculty:** 127 total; 67% minority, 50% women. **Class size:** 16% < 20, 56% 20-39, 10% 40-49, 16% 50-99, 2% >100. **Special facilities:** Coastal studies laboratory on South Padre Island.

**Freshman class profile.** 6,884 applied, 4,266 admitted, 2,626 enrolled.

| Mid 50% test scores | | Return as sophomores: | 68% |
|---|---|---|---|
| SAT critical reading: | 400-510 | Out-of-state: | 1% |
| SAT math: | 420-540 | Live on campus: | 9% |
| SAT writing: | 410-520 | International: | 8% |
| ACT composite: | 17-21 | Fraternities: | 3% |
| Rank in top quarter: | 45% | Sororities: | 2% |
| Rank in top tenth: | 16% | | |

**Basis for selection.** For regular admission, rank in top quartile of class or acceptable ACT/SAT scores required. Students who do not meet criteria for regular or clear admission placed in PEP (Provisional Enrollment Program).

**High school preparation.** 24 units required. Required units include English 4, mathematics 3, social studies 3.5, science 3, foreign language 2, academic electives 3.5, .5 economics, .5 health education, 1 fine arts, .5 speech, 1 technology required, 1.5 physical education required.

**2007-2008 Annual costs.** Tuition/fees: $4,613; $12,953 out-of-state. Mexican citizens may be eligible for in-state tuition rates. Room/board: $5,930. Books/supplies: $1,000. Personal expenses: $1,800.

**2006-2007 Financial aid. Need-based:** 2,036 full-time freshmen applied for aid; 1,910 were judged to have need; 1,879 of these received aid. Average need met was 68%. Average scholarship/grant was $7,753; average loan $2,292. 66% of total undergraduate aid awarded as scholarships/grants, 34% as loans/jobs. **Non-need-based:** Awarded to 826 full-time undergraduates, including 194 freshmen. Scholarships awarded for academics, alumni affiliation, art, athletics, leadership, music/drama, ROTC, state residency.

**Application procedures. Admission:** Priority date 2/1; deadline 8/11 (receipt date). No application fee. Application may be submitted online. Admission notification on a rolling basis. **Financial aid:** Closing date 3/1. FAFSA required. Applicants notified on a rolling basis starting 3/15; must reply within 2 week(s) of notification.

**Academics. Special study options:** Accelerated study, combined bachelor's/graduate degree, cooperative education, distance learning, double major, dual enrollment of high school students, ESL, exchange student, honors, independent study, internships, study abroad, teacher certification program, weekend college. Concurrent enrollment (high school students taking limited number of college classes either on campus or through distance learning). **Credit/placement by examination:** AP, CLEP, IB, institutional tests. 45 credit hours maximum toward bachelor's degree. **Support services:** Learning center, pre-admission summer program, remedial instruction, study skills assistance, tutoring, writing center.

**Majors. Area/ethnic studies:** American, Hispanic-American/Latino/Chicano. **Biology:** General. **Business:** Accounting, business admin, finance, international, management information systems, marketing. **Communications:** General, journalism. **Computer sciences:** General, computer science. **Engineering:** Electrical, industrial, manufacturing, mechanical. **English:** English lit. **Foreign languages:** French, Spanish. **Health:** Audiology/speech pathology, clinical lab science, dietetics, health services, nursing (RN), physician assistant, substance abuse counseling, vocational rehab counseling. **History:** General. **Legal studies:** Prelaw. **Math:** General. **Parks/recreation:** Health/fitness. **Philosophy/religion:** Philosophy. **Physical sciences:** Chemistry, physics. **Protective services:** Law enforcement admin. **Psychology:** General. **Public administration:** Social work. **Social sciences:** General, anthropology, economics, political science, sociology. **Visual/performing arts:** Dance, dramatic, studio arts. **Other:** Applied Arts and Sciences, Rehabilitation Services.

**Most popular majors.** Biology 6%, business/marketing 18%, English 7%, health sciences 11%, interdisciplinary studies 17%, security/protective services 6%.

**Computing on campus.** 900 workstations in dormitories, library, computer center. Dormitories wired for high-speed internet access and linked to campus network. Commuter students can connect to campus network. Online course registration, online library, helpline, student web hosting, wireless network available.

**Student life. Freshman orientation:** Mandatory, $15 fee. Preregistration for classes offered. Several 1-day sessions held prior to beginning of semester. **Housing:** Coed dorms, single-sex dorms, apartments, substance-free housing available. $75 fully refundable deposit. **Activities:** Bands, campus ministries, choral groups, dance, drama, international student organizations, music ensembles, musical theater, student government, student newspaper, symphony orchestra, Episcopal Canterbury Association, Latter-day Saints student association, Baha'i association, Baptist student union, Campus Crusade for Christ, Fellowship of Christian Athletes, Asian American students association, Society of Hispanic Professional Engineers.

**Athletics. NCAA. Intercollegiate:** Baseball M, basketball, cross-country, golf, tennis, track and field, volleyball W. **Intramural:** Badminton, basketball, bowling, cheerleading, football (non-tackle), golf, racquetball, soccer, softball, tennis, volleyball. **Team name:** Broncs/Lady Broncs.

**Student services.** Alcohol/substance abuse counseling, career counseling, services for economically disadvantaged, student employment services, financial aid counseling, health services, on-campus daycare, personal counseling, placement for graduates, veterans' counselor, women's services. **Physically disabled:** Services for visually, speech, hearing impaired.

**Contact.** E-mail: admissions@utpa.edu
Phone: (956) 381-2201 Toll-free number: (866) 441-8872
Fax: (956) 381-2212
Magdalena Hinojosa, Dean of Admissions & Enrollment Services, University of Texas: Pan American, 1201 West University Drive, Edinburg, TX 78541-2999

---

## University of the Incarnate Word
**San Antonio, Texas**   **CB member**
www.uiw.edu   **CB code: 6303**

◆ Private 4-year university and liberal arts college affiliated with Roman Catholic Church
◆ Commuter campus in very large city
◆ 4,666 degree-seeking undergraduates: 38% part-time, 68% women
◆ 1,054 degree-seeking graduate students
◆ 80% of applicants admitted
◆ SAT or ACT (ACT writing optional) required
◆ 39% graduate within 6 years

**General.** Founded in 1881. Regionally accredited. Off-campus courses available at US Automobile Association, Randolph Air Force Base, City Public Service Board, Santa Rosa Hospital, Northeast Campus, San Antonio College, Delmar Campus. **Degrees:** 681 bachelor's, 7 associate awarded; master's, doctoral, first professional offered. **ROTC:** Army. **Location:** 5 miles from downtown. **Calendar:** Semester, extensive summer session. **Full-time faculty:** 183 total; 74% have terminal degrees, 26% minority, 56% women. **Part-time faculty:** 321 total; 29% minority, 50% women. **Class size:** 61% < 20, 37% 20-39, 1% 40-49, less than 1% 50-99. **Special facilities:** Teaching theater.

**Freshman class profile.** 1,982 applied, 1,589 admitted, 718 enrolled.

| Mid 50% test scores | | | |
|---|---|---|---|
| SAT critical reading: | 420-530 | Rank in top quarter: | 41% |
| SAT math: | 410-530 | Rank in top tenth: | 15% |
| SAT writing: | 410-510 | End year in good standing: | 81% |
| ACT composite: | 16-22 | Out-of-state: | 2% |
| GPA 3.50 or higher: | 43% | Live on campus: | 51% |
| GPA 3.0-3.49: | 46% | International: | 1% |
| GPA 2.0-2.99: | 10% | | |

**Basis for selection.** Test scores and school achievement record most important. Interview helpful. Rolling policy for submission of test scores. Interview recommended for academically weak. **Homeschooled:** Statement describing homeschool structure and mission, transcript of courses and grades required. Interview, letters, and testing may be necessary for some students.

**High school preparation.** 16 units required; 18 recommended. Required and recommended units include English 4, mathematics 3-4, social studies 3-4, science 3, foreign language 2 and visual/performing arts 1.

**2008-2009 Annual costs.** Tuition/fees: $20,260. Room/board: $7,380. Books/supplies: $1,000. Personal expenses: $1,560.

**2007-2008 Financial aid. Need-based:** 699 full-time freshmen applied for aid; 550 were judged to have need; 550 of these received aid. Average need met was 63%. Average scholarship/grant was $6,970; average loan $3,558. 58% of total undergraduate aid awarded as scholarships/grants, 42% as loans/jobs. **Non-need-based:** Awarded to 2,139 full-time undergraduates, including 693 freshmen. Scholarships awarded for academics, alumni affiliation, art, athletics, leadership, music/drama, religious affiliation, ROTC, state residency. **Additional information:** Students encouraged to pursue outside scholarship programs.

**Application procedures. Admission:** Priority date 2/1; no deadline. $20 fee, may be waived for applicants with need. Application may be submitted online. Notification approximately 2 weeks following submission. Response by May 1 encouraged. **Financial aid:** Priority date 4/1; no closing date. FAFSA required. Applicants notified on a rolling basis starting 2/15; must reply within 2 week(s) of notification.

**Academics. Special study options:** Accelerated study, combined bachelor's/graduate degree, cross-registration, distance learning, double major, dual enrollment of high school students, ESL, independent study, internships, study abroad, teacher certification program, weekend college. Adult Degree Completion Program: accelerated 8-week term program. **Credit/placement by examination:** AP, CLEP, SAT, ACT, institutional tests. 30 credit hours maximum toward bachelor's degree. **Support services:** Learning center, reduced course load, remedial instruction, study skills assistance, tutoring, writing center.

**Majors. Area/ethnic studies:** Native American. **Biology:** General. **Business:** Business admin, human resources, organizational behavior. **Communications:** Media studies. **Computer sciences:** Information technology. **Conservation:** Environmental science. **Education:** Elementary. **English:** English lit. **Family/consumer sciences:** Child development. **Foreign languages:** Spanish. **Health:** Athletic training, music therapy, nuclear medical technology, nursing (RN). **History:** General. **Interdisciplinary:** Nutrition sciences. **Liberal arts:** Arts/sciences. **Math:** General. **Parks/recreation:** Exercise sciences. **Philosophy/religion:** Philosophy, religion. **Physical sciences:** Chemistry, meteorology. **Psychology:** General. **Social sciences:** Political science, sociology. **Visual/performing arts:** Art, design, dramatic, interior design. **Other:** Engineering Management.

**Most popular majors.** Business/marketing 47%, communications/journalism 6%, health sciences 11%, liberal arts 6%, visual/performing arts 7%.

**Computing on campus.** PC or laptop required. Dormitories wired for high-speed internet access and linked to campus network. Commuter students can connect to campus network. Online course registration, online library, helpline, repair service, wireless network available.

**Student life. Freshman orientation:** Mandatory, $200 fee. Preregistration for classes offered. Overnight program for out-of-towners and 1-day session for local students. Parents encouraged to participate. **Housing:** Guaranteed on-campus for freshmen. Coed dorms, single-sex dorms, special housing for disabled, apartments, substance-free housing available. $250 fully refundable deposit. **Activities:** Bands, campus ministries, choral groups, dance, drama, international student organizations, literary magazine, music ensembles, musical theater, radio station, student government, student newspaper, Hispanic student association, black student association, international student association, student ambassadors, Crusaders for Christ.

**Athletics.** NCAA. **Intercollegiate:** Baseball M, basketball, cross-country, golf, soccer, softball W, swimming, synchronized swimming W, tennis, track and field, volleyball W. **Intramural:** Basketball, football (non-tackle), racquetball, soccer, softball, swimming, tennis, volleyball. **Team name:** Cardinals.

**Student services.** Campus ministries, career counseling, student employment services, financial aid counseling, health services, personal counseling, placement for graduates.

**Contact.** E-mail: admis@uiwtx.edu
Phone: (210) 829-6005 Toll-free number: (800) 749-9673
Fax: (210) 829-3921
Andrea Cyterski-Acosta, Director of Admissions, University of the Incarnate Word, 4301 Broadway, San Antonio, TX 78209-6397

---

## Wayland Baptist University

Plainview, Texas — CB member
www.wbu.edu — CB code: 6930

- Private 4-year university and liberal arts college affiliated with Southern Baptist Convention
- Residential campus in large town
- 934 degree-seeking undergraduates: 11% part-time, 55% women, 4% African American, 1% Asian American, 25% Hispanic American, 1% Native American, 2% international
- 171 degree-seeking graduate students
- 80% of applicants admitted
- SAT or ACT (ACT writing optional) required
- 39% graduate within 6 years

**General.** Founded in 1908. Regionally accredited. Off-campus sites in Amarillo, Lubbock, San Antonio, Wichita Falls, Alaska, Arizona, Hawaii, Oklahoma, New Mexico. **Degrees:** 134 bachelor's, 3 associate awarded; master's offered. **ROTC:** Army, Air Force. **Location:** 50 miles from Lubbock, 70 miles from Amarillo. **Calendar:** Semester, limited summer session. **Full-time faculty:** 76 total; 70% have terminal degrees, 4% minority, 28% women. **Part-time faculty:** 39 total; 18% have terminal degrees, 3% minority, 44% women. **Class size:** 69% < 20, 31% 20-39, less than 1% 40-49. **Special facilities:** Museum of the Llano Estacado.

**Freshman class profile.** 416 applied, 331 admitted, 252 enrolled.

| Mid 50% test scores | | Rank in top quarter: | 41% |
|---|---|---|---|
| SAT critical reading: | 390-550 | Rank in top tenth: | 14% |
| SAT math: | 410-570 | Return as sophomores: | 64% |
| SAT writing: | 380-540 | Out-of-state: | 6% |
| ACT composite: | 17-22 | Live on campus: | 75% |
| GPA 3.50 or higher: | 57% | International: | 3% |
| GPA 3.0-3.49: | 21% | Fraternities: | 2% |
| GPA 2.0-2.99: | 21% | Sororities: | 1% |

**Basis for selection.** Regular freshman admission is based on a combination of class rank and the score on either the ACT composite or SAT. Interview, audition recommended.

**High school preparation.** 9 units required. Required and recommended units include English 3, mathematics 2-3, social studies 2 and science 2-3.

**2007-2008 Annual costs.** Tuition/fees: $11,250. Room/board: $3,584. Books/supplies: $1,200. Personal expenses: $2,314.

**2007-2008 Financial aid. Need-based:** 204 full-time freshmen applied for aid; 162 were judged to have need; 161 of these received aid. Average need met was 72%. Average scholarship/grant was $7,685; average loan $2,886. 61% of total undergraduate aid awarded as scholarships/grants, 39% as loans/jobs. **Non-need-based:** Awarded to 305 full-time undergraduates, including 92 freshmen. Scholarships awarded for academics, alumni affiliation, art, athletics, job skills, leadership, minority status, music/drama, religious affiliation, state residency.

**Application procedures. Admission:** Priority date 8/1; no deadline. $35 fee. Application may be submitted online. Admission notification on a rolling basis beginning on or about 3/1. **Financial aid:** Priority date 5/1; no

closing date. FAFSA, institutional form required. Applicants notified on a rolling basis starting 2/15; must reply within 3 week(s) of notification.

**Academics. Special study options:** Accelerated study, distance learning, double major, dual enrollment of high school students, external degree, honors, internships, teacher certification program. **Credit/placement by examination:** AP, CLEP, IB, SAT, ACT, institutional tests. 30 credit hours maximum toward bachelor's degree. **Support services:** Learning center, reduced course load, remedial instruction, study skills assistance, tutoring.

**Majors. Biology:** General. **Business:** Business admin. **Communications:** Media studies. **Education:** Elementary, music, physical, technology/industrial arts, trade/industrial. **English:** English lit. **Foreign languages:** Spanish. **Health:** Nursing (RN). **History:** General. **Math:** General. **Philosophy/religion:** Christian. **Physical sciences:** General, chemistry. **Protective services:** Criminal justice. **Psychology:** General. **Public administration:** Human services. **Social sciences:** Political science, sociology. **Theology:** Religious ed, sacred music. **Visual/performing arts:** Art, dramatic.

**Most popular majors.** Biology 6%, business/marketing 14%, communications/journalism 6%, education 27%, history 8%, psychology 6%, public administration/social services 8%, visual/performing arts 7%.

**Computing on campus.** 203 workstations in library, computer center. Dormitories linked to campus network. Commuter students can connect to campus network. Helpline, wireless network available.

**Student life. Freshman orientation:** Mandatory, $15 fee. Preregistration for classes offered. Entry seminar course designed to help students succeed academically, socially, and spiritually. Taken during initial term of enrollment. **Policies:** Religious observance required. **Housing:** Guaranteed on-campus for freshmen. Single-sex dorms, apartments, substance-free housing available. $100 fully refundable deposit. **Activities:** Bands, choral groups, drama, music ensembles, musical theater, radio station, student government, student newspaper, TV station, Over 20 religious, service, and special interest organizations available.

**Athletics.** NAIA. **Intercollegiate:** Baseball M, basketball, cross-country, golf M, soccer W, track and field, volleyball W. **Intramural:** Basketball, football (non-tackle), softball, volleyball. **Team name:** Pioneers, Flying Queens.

**Student services.** Campus ministries, career counseling, student employment services, financial aid counseling, health services, personal counseling, placement for graduates.

**Contact.** E-mail: admityou@wbu.edu
Phone: (806) 291-3500 Toll-free number: (800) 588-1928
Fax: (806) 291-1960
Director of Admissions, Wayland Baptist University, 1900 West Seventh Street, CMB #712, Plainview, TX 79072

---

## West Texas A&M University

Canyon, Texas — CB member
www.wtamu.edu — CB code: 6938

- Public 4-year university
- Residential campus in large town
- 5,849 degree-seeking undergraduates: 24% part-time, 55% women, 5% African American, 2% Asian American, 18% Hispanic American, 1% Native American, 2% international
- 1,522 degree-seeking graduate students
- 71% of applicants admitted
- SAT or ACT (ACT writing optional) required
- 37% graduate within 6 years

**General.** Founded in 1909. Regionally accredited. **Degrees:** 1,081 bachelor's awarded; master's, doctoral offered. **Location:** 17 miles from Amarillo. **Calendar:** Semester, limited summer session. **Full-time faculty:** 238 total; 66% have terminal degrees, 10% minority, 44% women. **Part-time faculty:** 72 total; 18% have terminal degrees, 6% minority, 58% women. **Class size:** 35% < 20, 46% 20-39, 9% 40-49, 9% 50-99, less than 1% >100. **Special facilities:** 24,000-acre farm and ranch, alternative energy institute, historical museum, event center.

**Freshman class profile.** 2,340 applied, 1,660 admitted, 960 enrolled.

| Mid 50% test scores | | Return as sophomores: | 67% |
|---|---|---|---|
| SAT critical reading: | 440-580 | Out-of-state: | 9% |
| SAT math: | 440-560 | Live on campus: | 76% |
| ACT composite: | 18-23 | International: | 1% |
| Rank in top quarter: | 49% | Fraternities: | 2% |
| Rank in top tenth: | 15% | Sororities: | 2% |

**Basis for selection.** Freshman applicants must be in top half of graduating class, have minimum 950 SAT (exclusive of writing) or 20 ACT, or attend a summer provisional term. Texas Success Initiative Testing required of all incoming students before entrance. Audition required for music program; portfolio recommended for art, theater programs.

**High school preparation.** 24 units required. Required and recommended units include English 4, mathematics 3, social studies 3.5, science 3 and foreign language 2.

**2007-2008 Annual costs.** Tuition/fees: $4,920; $13,260 out-of-state. Out-of-district students from border counties pay in-state tuition. Tuition reduction plan available to students from border states. Room/board: $5,627. Books/supplies: $900. Personal expenses: $1,668.

**Financial aid. Non-need-based:** Scholarships awarded for academics, art, athletics, leadership, music/drama, state residency. **Additional information:** Scholarship deadline February 1.

**Application procedures. Admission:** Priority date 7/20; no deadline. $25 fee, may be waived for applicants with need. Application may be submitted online. Admission notification on a rolling basis. **Financial aid:** Priority date 4/15; no closing date. FAFSA required. Applicants notified on a rolling basis starting 3/1; must reply within 2 week(s) of notification.

**Academics. Special study options:** Combined bachelor's/graduate degree, cooperative education, distance learning, double major, ESL, honors, independent study, internships, liberal arts/career combination, study abroad, teacher certification program, Washington semester. **Credit/placement by examination:** AP, CLEP, IB, institutional tests. Only 6 of a student's last 30 hours can come from CLEP. **Support services:** Learning center, remedial instruction, study skills assistance, tutoring, writing center.

**Majors. Agriculture:** General, agribusiness operations, animal sciences, business, equestrian studies, plant protection, plant sciences. **Biology:** General, biotechnology. **Business:** General, accounting, business admin, finance, management information systems, managerial economics, marketing. **Communications:** Advertising, broadcast journalism, journalism. **Computer sciences:** General. **Conservation:** Environmental science, wildlife. **Engineering:** Mechanical. **Engineering technology:** Industrial. **English:** English lit, speech/rhetoric. **Foreign languages:** Spanish. **Health:** Athletic training, clinical lab science, communication disorders, music therapy, nursing (RN). **History:** General. **Legal studies:** Prelaw. **Math:** General. **Parks/recreation:** Health/fitness. **Physical sciences:** Chemistry, geology, physics. **Protective services:** Law enforcement admin. **Psychology:** General. **Public administration:** General, social work. **Social sciences:** General, economics, geography, political science, sociology. **Visual/performing arts:** Art, dance, dramatic, graphic design, music performance, music theory/composition, studio arts.

**Most popular majors.** Business/marketing 16%, health sciences 12%, interdisciplinary studies 18%, liberal arts 15%.

**Computing on campus.** 1,800 workstations in dormitories, library, computer center, student center. Dormitories wired for high-speed internet access and linked to campus network. Commuter students can connect to campus network. Online course registration, online library, helpline, student web hosting, wireless network available.

**Student life. Freshman orientation:** Available, $50 fee. Preregistration for classes offered. 2-day summer orientation and preregistration and 3-day orientation before school starts. **Policies:** Students with fewer than 60 semester hours accumulated, enrolled in 9 or more semester hours, and under 21 on first day of class each semester required to live in university residence halls. **Housing:** Guaranteed on-campus for all undergraduates. Coed dorms, single-sex dorms, special housing for disabled, fraternity/sorority housing available. $100 fully refundable deposit. Honors hall for students in honors program available. **Activities:** Bands, campus ministries, choral groups, dance, drama, international student organizations, literary magazine, music ensembles, musical theater, opera, radio station, student government, student newspaper, symphony orchestra, Chinese student association, Hispanic association, agriculture organizations, Students in Free Enterprise, pre-professional organizations, Black students association, College Republicans, Catholic student association.

**Athletics.** NCAA. **Intercollegiate:** Baseball M, basketball, cross-country, equestrian W, football (tackle) M, golf, soccer, softball W, volleyball W. **Intramural:** Archery, badminton, basketball, bowling, football (non-tackle), golf, racquetball, rodeo, soccer, softball, swimming, table tennis, tennis, volleyball. **Team name:** Buffaloes.

**Student services.** Alcohol/substance abuse counseling, career counseling, services for economically disadvantaged, student employment services, financial aid counseling, health services, on-campus daycare, personal counseling, placement for graduates, veterans' counselor. **Physically disabled:** Services for visually, speech, hearing impaired.

**Contact.** E-mail: admissions@mail.wtamu.edu
Phone: (806) 651-2020 Toll-free number: (800) 999-8268
Fax: (806) 651-5268
Shawn Thomas, Director of Admissions, West Texas A&M University, 2501 Fourth Avenue, WTAMU Box 60907, Canyon, TX 79016-0001

## Wiley College
**Marshall, Texas**      **CB member**
www.wileyc.edu      **CB code: 6940**

- Private 4-year liberal arts college affiliated with United Methodist Church
- Residential campus in large town
- 922 degree-seeking undergraduates

**General.** Founded in 1873. Regionally accredited. **Degrees:** 161 bachelor's awarded. **Location:** 40 miles from Shreveport, Louisiana, 150 miles from Dallas. **Calendar:** Semester, extensive summer session. **Full-time faculty:** 51 total. **Part-time faculty:** 20 total. **Class size:** 60% < 20, 35% 20-39, 3% 40-49, 2% 50-99. **Special facilities:** Nature trail.

**Freshman class profile.**

| Mid 50% test scores | | Rank in top quarter: | 15% |
|---|---|---|---|
| SAT critical reading: | 320-430 | Rank in top tenth: | 3% |
| SAT math: | 320-430 | Out-of-state: | 38% |
| ACT composite: | 13-17 | Live on campus: | 90% |

**Basis for selection.** Open admission, but selective for some programs.

**High school preparation.** 16 units recommended. Recommended units include English 4, mathematics 2, social studies 2, science 2 and academic electives 6.

**2007-2008 Annual costs.** Tuition/fees: $9,150. Reported tuition includes cost of books. Room/board: $5,300. Books/supplies: $1,320. Personal expenses: $1,002.

**Financial aid.** All financial aid based on need.

**Application procedures. Admission:** Priority date 8/15; no deadline. $25 fee. Admission notification on a rolling basis. **Financial aid:** No deadline. FAFSA, institutional form required. Applicants notified on a rolling basis.

**Academics. Special study options:** Accelerated study, cross-registration, distance learning, double major, dual enrollment of high school students, honors, independent study, internships, liberal arts/career combination, study abroad, teacher certification program, weekend college. **Credit/placement by examination:** AP, CLEP, institutional tests. **Support services:** Learning center, reduced course load, remedial instruction, study skills assistance, tutoring.

**Majors. Biology:** General. **Business:** Accounting, business admin, operations. **Communications:** Journalism. **Computer sciences:** Computer science. **Education:** Elementary, physical, secondary. **English:** English lit. **History:** General. **Math:** General. **Physical sciences:** Chemistry. **Protective services:** Law enforcement admin. **Social sciences:** Sociology.

**Most popular majors.** Business/marketing 66%, education 6%.

**Computing on campus.** 177 workstations in dormitories, library, computer center. Dormitories wired for high-speed internet access and linked to campus network. Commuter students can connect to campus network. Online course registration, online library, helpline, wireless network available.

**Student life. Freshman orientation:** Mandatory. Preregistration for classes offered. **Policies:** Religious observance required. **Housing:** Single-sex dorms, substance-free housing available. $50 deposit. **Activities:** Choral groups, drama, music ensembles, radio station, student government, student newspaper, national service fraternity, interdenominational student movement, religion majors club.

**Athletics.** NAIA. **Intercollegiate:** Baseball M, basketball, cross-country, softball W, track and field, volleyball W. **Intramural:** Baseball M, basketball, cheerleading, softball, table tennis, tennis, track and field, volleyball, weight lifting M. **Team name:** Wildcats.

**Student services.** Adult student services, campus ministries, career counseling, services for economically disadvantaged, student employment services, financial aid counseling, health services, personal counseling, placement for graduates, veterans' counselor.

**Contact.**  E-mail: admissions@wileyc.edu
Phone: (903) 927-3311 Toll-free number: (800) 658-6889
Fax: (903) 927-3366
Alvena Jones, Director of Admissions and Recruitmen, Wiley College, 711
Wiley Avenue, Marshall, TX 75670

# Utah

## Brigham Young University

**Provo, Utah**      **CB member**
**www.byu.edu**      **CB code: 4019**

- Private 4-year university affiliated with Church of Jesus Christ of Latter-day Saints
- Residential campus in small city
- 30,873 degree-seeking undergraduates: 10% part-time, 49% women, 3% Asian American, 3% Hispanic American, 1% Native American, 4% international
- 3,301 graduate students
- 74% of applicants admitted
- ACT (writing recommended), application essay, interview required
- 78% graduate within 6 years

**General.** Founded in 1875. Regionally accredited. Additional educational center in Salt Lake City. **Degrees:** 7,142 bachelor's awarded; master's, doctoral, first professional offered. **ROTC:** Army, Air Force. **Location:** 45 miles from Salt Lake City. **Calendar:** Semester, limited summer session. **Full-time faculty:** 1,305 total; 82% have terminal degrees, 6% minority, 20% women. **Part-time faculty:** 466 total; 28% have terminal degrees, 6% minority, 60% women. **Class size:** 47% < 20, 37% 20-39, 6% 40-49, 7% 50-99, 3% >100. **Special facilities:** Aquatic ecology laboratory, science and anthropological museums, veterinary pathology laboratory, fine arts museum, reading and writing laboratories, mathematics and language computer laboratories, supercomputer.

**Freshman class profile.** 9,979 applied, 7,384 admitted, 5,716 enrolled.

| Mid 50% test scores | | | |
|---|---|---|---|
| SAT critical reading: | 550-670 | Rank in top quarter: | 83% |
| SAT math: | 570-680 | Rank in top tenth: | 49% |
| ACT composite: | 25-30 | Return as sophomores: | 84% |
| GPA 3.50 or higher: | 87% | Out-of-state: | 65% |
| GPA 3.0-3.49: | 12% | Live on campus: | 71% |
| GPA 2.0-2.99: | 1% | International: | 3% |

**Basis for selection.** School achievement record, test scores, endorsements and recommendations important. Students must maintain ideals and standards in harmony with The Church of Jesus Christ of Latter-day Saints. Interview is ecclesiastical. **Homeschooled:** Portfolio not considered in placement. **Learning Disabled:** Untimed ACT accepted.

**High school preparation.** Required and recommended units include English 4, mathematics 3-4, history 2, science 2-3 (laboratory 2-3), foreign language 2-4, computer science 1 and visual/performing arts 1. 2 units of literature/writing required.

**2007-2008 Annual costs.** Tuition/fees: $3,840. Undergraduate 2-semester tuition $7,680 for nonmembers of The Church of Jesus Christ of Latter-day Saints. Undergraduate per-credit-hour charge $394 for nonmembers. Room/board: $6,460. Books/supplies: $1,170. Personal expenses: $2,064.

**2006-2007 Financial aid. Need-based:** 2,083 full-time freshmen applied for aid; 1,312 were judged to have need; 1,125 of these received aid. Average need met was 21%. Average scholarship/grant was $1,579; average loan $733. 62% of total undergraduate aid awarded as scholarships/grants, 38% as loans/jobs. **Non-need-based:** Awarded to 15,672 full-time undergraduates, including 2,976 freshmen. Scholarships awarded for academics, art, athletics, leadership, minority status, music/drama, religious affiliation, ROTC, state residency. **Additional information:** Students notified of scholarships on or about April 20th.

**Application procedures. Admission:** Closing date 2/1 (receipt date). $30 fee, may be waived for applicants with need. Application may be submitted online. Admission notification on a rolling basis. **Financial aid:** Priority date 4/15; no closing date. FAFSA required. Applicants notified on a rolling basis starting 4/1.

**Academics. Special study options:** Accelerated study, combined bachelor's/graduate degree, cooperative education, cross-registration, distance learning, double major, ESL, external degree, honors, independent study, internships, liberal arts/career combination, study abroad, teacher certification program, Washington semester. **Credit/placement by examination:** AP, CLEP, IB,

ACT, institutional tests. **Support services:** Learning center, pre-admission summer program, reduced course load, remedial instruction, study skills assistance, tutoring, writing center.

**Majors. Agriculture:** Crop production, food processing, food science, landscaping, soil science. **Area/ethnic studies:** American, Asian, Latin American. **Biology:** General, biochemistry, bioinformatics, biophysics, biostatistics, biotechnology, botany, microbiology, molecular, physiology. **Business:** General, accounting, actuarial science, business admin, construction management, entrepreneurial studies, finance, financial planning, information resources management, logistics, management information systems, marketing, statistics. **Communications:** Journalism. **Communications technology:** Animation/special effects. **Computer sciences:** Computer science, information technology. **Conservation:** Wildlife. **Education:** Chemistry, drama/dance, early childhood, elementary, English, family/consumer sciences, French, German, health, history, Latin, mathematics, music, physical, physics, science, social science, special, speech, technology/industrial arts. **Engineering:** Chemical, civil, computer, electrical, manufacturing, mechanical. **English:** English lit, speech/rhetoric. **Family/consumer sciences:** General, family resources, family studies. **Foreign languages:** General, ancient Greek, Biblical, Chinese, classics, comparative lit, French, German, Italian, Japanese, Korean, Latin, linguistics, Portuguese, Russian, Spanish, translation. **Health:** Athletic training, audiology/speech pathology, clinical lab science, dietetics, nursing (RN), recreational therapy. **History:** General. **Interdisciplinary:** Biological/physical sciences, neuroscience, nutrition sciences. **Liberal arts:** Arts/sciences, humanities. **Math:** General, statistics. **Parks/recreation:** General, health/fitness. **Philosophy/religion:** Philosophy. **Physical sciences:** Astronomy, chemistry, geology, hydrology, physics. **Psychology:** General. **Public administration:** Social work. **Social sciences:** Anthropology, archaeology, cartography, economics, geography, international relations, political science, sociology. **Visual/performing arts:** Acting, art, art history/conservation, ballet, dance, design, dramatic, film/cinema, graphic design, illustration, industrial design, jazz, music history, music performance, music theory/composition, photography, piano/organ, stringed instruments, studio arts, voice/opera.

**Most popular majors.** Biology 9%, business/marketing 16%, education 12%, engineering/engineering technologies 6%, foreign language 6%, social sciences 10%, visual/performing arts 6%.

**Computing on campus.** 2,000 workstations in dormitories, library, computer center, student center. Dormitories wired for high-speed internet access and linked to campus network. Commuter students can connect to campus network. Online course registration, online library, helpline, repair service, student web hosting, wireless network available.

**Student life. Freshman orientation:** Available. Preregistration for classes offered. **Policies:** Honor code enforced. Religious observance required. **Housing:** Single-sex dorms, special housing for disabled, apartments, substance-free housing available. $100 fully refundable deposit. Language houses available. **Activities:** Bands, choral groups, dance, drama, film society, literary magazine, music ensembles, musical theater, opera, radio station, student government, student newspaper, symphony orchestra, TV station, College Republicans, College Democrats, African American club, Black Student Union, Latin American student association, international student association, Intercollegiate Knights, Circle-K International, Southeast Asian club, Baptist Student Union.

**Athletics.** NCAA. **Intercollegiate:** Baseball M, basketball, cheerleading, cross-country, diving, football (tackle) M, golf, gymnastics W, soccer W, softball W, swimming, tennis, track and field, volleyball. **Intramural:** Badminton, basketball, football (non-tackle), football (tackle), golf, racquetball, soccer, softball, tennis, volleyball, water polo, wrestling M. **Team name:** Cougars.

**Student services.** Campus ministries, career counseling, services for economically disadvantaged, student employment services, financial aid counseling, health services, minority student services, personal counseling, placement for graduates, veterans' counselor, women's services. **Physically disabled:** Services for visually, speech, hearing impaired.

**Contact.** E-mail: admissions@byu.edu
Phone: (801) 422-2507 Fax: (801) 422-0005
Tom Gourley, Director of Admissions, Brigham Young University, A-153 ASB, BYU, Provo, UT 84602

## DeVry University: Sandy
**Sandy, Utah**

- For-profit 4-year college
- Small city
- 39 degree-seeking undergraduates: 77% part-time, 44% women, 3% African American, 10% Hispanic American
- 16 degree-seeking graduate students

**General.** Regionally accredited. **Calendar:** Semester. **Part-time faculty:** 11 total; 27% minority, 54% women.

**Freshman class profile.** 2 enrolled.

**Basis for selection.** Applicants must have high school diploma or equivalent, or degree from accredited post-secondary institution, demonstrate proficiency in basic college-level skills through SAT or ACT scores or institution-administered placement examinations, and be at least 17 years of age. DeVry-administered admissions test required if SAT or ACT test scores are not submitted. .

**2007-2008 Annual costs.** Books/supplies: $1,300. Personal expenses: $5,082.

**Financial aid. Non-need-based:** Scholarships awarded for academics.

**Application procedures. Admission:** No deadline. $50 fee. Admission notification on a rolling basis. **Financial aid:** No deadline. FAFSA required. Applicants notified on a rolling basis.

**Academics. Special study options:** Accelerated study, distance learning. **Credit/placement by examination:** CLEP.

**Contact.** DeVry University: Sandy, 9350 South 150 East, Suite 420, Sandy, UT 84070

## Dixie State College of Utah
### St. George, Utah
www.dixie.edu                                          CB code: 4283

- Public 4-year-technical college
- Commuter campus in small city
- 4,607 degree-seeking undergraduates: 34% part-time, 53% women
- 33% graduate within 6 years

**General.** Founded in 1911. Regionally accredited. Bachelor's and master's degree course work from Utah's 4-year universities presented over distance-learning media and on-campus instruction. Four-year programs in business admin, computer tech, communications media, elem education, biology, English and nursing offered by DSC on campus. **Degrees:** 134 bachelor's, 864 associate awarded. **ROTC:** Army. **Location:** 300 miles from Salt Lake City, 120 miles from Las Vegas. **Calendar:** Semester, extensive summer session. **Full-time faculty:** 113 total; 60% have terminal degrees, 7% minority, 35% women. **Part-time faculty:** 206 total; 9% have terminal degrees, 2% minority, 52% women. **Class size:** 45% < 20, 43% 20-39, 8% 40-49, 3% 50-99, less than 1% >100.

**Freshman class profile.** 2,777 applied, 1,995 admitted, 1,270 enrolled.

| Mid 50% test scores | | | |
|---|---|---|---|
| SAT critical reading: | 420-550 | GPA 3.0-3.49: | 33% |
| SAT math: | 423-480 | GPA 2.0-2.99: | 26% |
| SAT writing: | 400-490 | Rank in top quarter: | 30% |
| ACT composite: | 18-23 | Rank in top tenth: | 10% |
| GPA 3.50 or higher: | 38% | Return as sophomores: | 49% |
| | | Out-of-state: | 4% |

**Basis for selection.** Open admission, but selective for some programs. Some health occupation programs require prerequisites before admission into program. Those applying for bachelor degrees in elementary education and nursing must have associate degree. Some courses use test score combined with high school GPA as prerequisite. CPT (computerized placement test) or COMPASS may be taken in lieu of ACT/SAT. **Homeschooled:** Letter from parent certifying that student has completed equivalent of high school diploma and letter from high school counselor or secondary school district documenting student is no longer required to attend secondary school.

**High school preparation.** 16 units recommended. Recommended units include English 4, mathematics 4, history 3, science 3 (laboratory 1) and foreign language 2. One computer literacy unit recommended.

**2007-2008 Annual costs.** Tuition/fees: $2,728; $9,460 out-of-state. Room/board: $3,098.

**Financial aid. Non-need-based:** Scholarships awarded for academics, alumni affiliation, art, athletics, leadership, minority status, music/drama.

**Application procedures. Admission:** No deadline. $35 fee. Application may be submitted online. Admission notification on a rolling basis. **Financial aid:** Priority date 4/1; no closing date. FAFSA required. Applicants notified on a rolling basis starting 5/1; must reply within 2 week(s) of notification.

**Academics. Special study options:** Cooperative education, distance learning, dual enrollment of high school students, ESL, honors, independent study,

teacher certification program. **Credit/placement by examination:** AP, CLEP, SAT, ACT, institutional tests. 32 credit hours maximum toward associate degree. **Support services:** Learning center, remedial instruction, study skills assistance, tutoring, writing-center.

**Majors. Biology:** General. **Business:** Accounting, business admin. **Communications:** General, digital media, journalism, media studies, organizational, public relations. **Computer sciences:** General, computer science, information technology, web page design. **Education:** Elementary. **English:** English lit. **Health:** Nursing (RN).

**Most popular majors.** Business/marketing 41%, computer/information sciences 14%, education 36%, health sciences 8%.

**Computing on campus.** 400 workstations in dormitories, library, computer center, student center. Dormitories wired for high-speed internet access and linked to campus network. Commuter students can connect to campus network. Online course registration, online library, helpline, repair service available.

**Student life. Freshman orientation:** Mandatory. Preregistration for classes offered. 4- hour program held in summer. **Policies:** Stringent drug and alcohol policies. **Housing:** Coed dorms, single-sex dorms, apartments, substance-free housing available. $100 nonrefundable deposit, deadline 7/1. **Activities:** Bands, choral groups, dance, drama, international student organizations, literary magazine, music ensembles, musical theater, radio station, student government, student newspaper, symphony orchestra, TV station, international club, religious groups, Native American club, polynesian club, political clubs, Diversity Club, Phi Beta Lambda.

**Athletics.** NCAA. **Intercollegiate:** Baseball M, basketball, cross-country, football (tackle) M, golf M, soccer, softball W, tennis W, volleyball W. **Intramural:** Badminton, basketball, bowling, football (non-tackle), golf, racquetball, soccer, softball, swimming, tennis, volleyball, water polo, weight lifting, wrestling M. **Team name:** Rebels.

**Student services.** Adult student services, alcohol/substance abuse counseling, campus ministries, career counseling, services for economically disadvantaged, student employment services, financial aid counseling, health services, minority student services, personal counseling, placement for graduates, veterans' counselor. **Physically disabled:** Services for visually, speech, hearing impaired.

**Contact.** E-mail: admissions@dixie.edu
Phone: (435) 652-7706 Toll-free number: (888) 462-3494
Fax: (435) 656-4005
Brandon Boulter, Director of Admissions, Dixie State College of Utah, 225 South 700 East, St. George, UT 84770-3876

## Independence University
### Salt Lake City, Utah
www.independence.edu

- For-profit 4-year health science college
- Commuter campus in small city

**General.** Founded in 1975. Accredited by DETC. **Calendar:** Continuous.

**Annual costs/financial aid.** Per-credit-hour charges vary: certificate $350/semester credit, associate degree $295/semester credit, bachelor's degree $350/semester credit. Course materials/textbook fee $125/course. Required credits may vary by individual program within degree levels.

**Contact.** Phone: (800) 972-5149
5295 South Commerce Drive Suite G-50, Salt Lake City, UT 84107

## ITT Technical Institute: Murray
### Murray, Utah
www.itt-tech.edu                                          CB code: 3601

- For-profit 4-year technical college
- Commuter campus in small city

**General.** Founded in 1984. Accredited by ACICS. **Location:** 10 miles from Salt Lake City. **Calendar:** Quarter.

**Annual costs/financial aid.** Tuition varies by program, $260-$368 per credit hour.

**Contact.** Phone: (801) 263-3313
Director of Recruitment, 920 West LeVoy Drive, Murray, UT 84123

## Neumont University
### South Jordan, Utah
**www.neumont.edu** CB code: 4516

- For-profit 4-year engineering and technical college
- Residential campus in very large city
- 295 degree-seeking undergraduates
- SAT or ACT (ACT writing optional), application essay, interview required

**General.** Accredited by ACICS. **Degrees:** 105 bachelor's awarded; master's offered. **Location:** 20 miles from Salt Lake City. **Calendar:** Quarter, extensive summer session. **Full-time faculty:** 18 total; 22% have terminal degrees. **Part-time faculty:** 5 total.

**Freshman class profile.**

Out-of-state: 50% Live on campus: 50%

**Basis for selection.** Open admission, but selective for some programs. Academic potential, computer experience, and interest and motivation for the program all considered. **Homeschooled:** State high school equivalency certificate required.

**2007-2008 Annual costs.** Tuition/fees: $28,275.

**Application procedures. Admission:** No deadline. $35 fee, may be waived for applicants with need. Application may be submitted online. Admission notification on a rolling basis. **Financial aid:** No deadline.

**Academics. Special study options:** Accelerated study, internships. **Credit/placement by examination:** AP, CLEP. **Support services:** Remedial instruction, study skills assistance, tutoring.

**Majors. Computer sciences:** Computer science.

**Computing on campus.** PC or laptop required. Commuter students can connect to campus network. Online library, helpline, repair service, student web hosting, wireless network available.

**Student life. Freshman orientation:** Mandatory. Preregistration for classes offered. **Housing:** Apartments available. $275 deposit.

**Student services.** Career counseling, financial aid counseling, placement for graduates.

**Contact.** E-mail: info@neumont.edu
Phone: (801) 302-2800 Toll-free number: (866) 622-3448
Fax: (801) 302-2880
Brock Holmes, Vice President of Enrollment, Neumont University, 10701 South River Front Parkway, Suite 300, South Jordan, UT 84095

## Southern Utah University
### Cedar City, Utah
**www.suu.edu** CB member
CB code: 4092

- Public 4-year university
- Residential campus in large town
- 5,329 degree-seeking undergraduates: 14% part-time, 56% women, 1% African American, 2% Asian American, 4% Hispanic American, 2% Native American, 1% international
- 568 degree-seeking graduate students
- 84% of applicants admitted
- SAT or ACT (ACT writing optional) required
- 42% graduate within 6 years

**General.** Founded in 1897. Regionally accredited. **Degrees:** 886 bachelor's, 168 associate awarded; master's offered. **ROTC:** Army. **Location:** 265 miles from Salt Lake City, 160 miles from Las Vegas. **Calendar:** Semester, extensive summer session. **Full-time faculty:** 222 total; 8% have terminal degrees, 14% minority, 32% women. **Part-time faculty:** 94 total; 2% minority, 54% women. **Class size:** 45% < 20, 39% 20-39, 7% 40-49, 7% 50-99, 1% >100. **Special facilities:** Natural life museum, observatory, Shakespearean theater.

**Freshman class profile.** 2,774 applied, 2,336 admitted, 1,214 enrolled.

| Mid 50% test scores | | | |
|---|---|---|---|
| SAT critical reading: | 430-540 | Rank in top tenth: | 27% |
| SAT math: | 440-560 | Return as sophomores: | 66% |
| ACT composite: | 18-24 | Out-of-state: | 21% |
| GPA 3.50 or higher: | 54% | Live on campus: | 41% |
| GPA 3.0-3.49: | 29% | International: | 1% |
| GPA 2.0-2.99: | 17% | Fraternities: | 4% |
| Rank in top quarter: | 53% | Sororities: | 4% |

**Basis for selection.** Admission is based on high school GPA and ACT/SAT scores.

**High school preparation.** Recommended units include English 4, mathematics 3, social studies 3, science 3 (laboratory 1) and foreign language 2. 1 unit of social studies must be U.S. history and government; 2 math units must be elementary algebra or above; English units should have a composition and literature emphasis.

**2007-2008 Annual costs.** Tuition/fees: $3,796; $11,327 out-of-state. Room/board: $4,922.

**2006-2007 Financial aid. Need-based:** Average need met was 76%. Average scholarship/grant was $3,952; average loan $2,560. 49% of total undergraduate aid awarded as scholarships/grants, 51% as loans/jobs. **Non-need-based:** Scholarships awarded for academics, alumni affiliation, art, athletics, job skills, leadership, minority status, music/drama, state residency.

**Application procedures. Admission:** Closing date 8/1. $40 fee. Admission notification on a rolling basis. Early action notification is done when decision is made. **Financial aid:** No deadline. FAFSA, institutional form required. Applicants notified by 11/6.

**Academics. Special study options:** Combined bachelor's/graduate degree, cooperative education, distance learning, double major, ESL, honors, independent study, internships, liberal arts/career combination, teacher certification program, weekend college. **Credit/placement by examination:** AP, CLEP, ACT. 25 credit hours maximum toward associate degree, 25 toward bachelor's. **Support services:** Learning center, pre-admission summer program, reduced course load, remedial instruction, study skills assistance, tutoring, writing center.

**Majors. Agriculture:** Business. **Biology:** General, botany, zoology. **Business:** Accounting, business admin, finance, management information systems, managerial economics, marketing. **Communications:** General, advertising, journalism, public relations. **Computer sciences:** Computer science, information systems. **Construction:** Maintenance. **Education:** General, art, biology, business, chemistry, drama/dance, elementary, English, family/consumer sciences, foreign languages, French, German, history, learning disabled, mathematics, music, science, secondary, social science, Spanish, special, speech, technology/industrial arts, trade/industrial. **Engineering:** General. **English:** British lit, English lit, speech/rhetoric. **Family/consumer sciences:** General. **Foreign languages:** General, French, German, Spanish. **Health:** Nursing (RN), predental, premedicine, prepharmacy, preveterinary. **History:** General. **Interdisciplinary:** Behavioral sciences. **Legal studies:** Prelaw. **Math:** General, statistics. **Philosophy/religion:** Philosophy. **Physical sciences:** Chemistry, geology, planetary. **Protective services:** Criminal justice. **Psychology:** General. **Social sciences:** General, economics, political science, sociology. **Visual/performing arts:** Art, commercial/advertising art, dance, dramatic.

**Most popular majors.** Biology 8%, business/marketing 16%, communications/journalism 6%, education 21%, health sciences 10%, psychology 6%.

**Computing on campus.** 300 workstations in dormitories, library, computer center. Dormitories wired for high-speed internet access and linked to campus network. Commuter students can connect to campus network. Online library, helpline, wireless network available.

**Student life. Freshman orientation:** Mandatory. Preregistration for classes offered. One-day program held throughout the summer. Parents are welcome and encouraged to attend. **Housing:** Coed dorms, single-sex dorms, special housing for disabled, apartments, fraternity/sorority housing available. $200 fully refundable deposit. **Activities:** Bands, choral groups, dance, drama, literary magazine, music ensembles, musical theater, opera, radio station, student government, student newspaper, symphony orchestra, TV station, intercultural club, LDSSA, Newman Club, Campus Christian Fellowship, College Republicans, College Democrats.

**Athletics.** NAIA, NCAA. **Intercollegiate:** Badminton, baseball M, basketball, cross-country, football (tackle) M, golf M, gymnastics W, rodeo, soccer W, softball W, tennis W, track and field. **Intramural:** Badminton, basketball, golf, soccer, tennis, volleyball. **Team name:** Thunderbirds.

**Student services.** Career counseling, student employment services, health services, minority student services, personal counseling, placement for graduates, veterans' counselor. **Physically disabled:** Services for speech impaired.

**Contact.** E-mail: adminfo@suu.edu
Phone: (435) 586-7740 Fax: (435) 865-8223
Stephen Allen, Director of Admissions, Southern Utah University, 351 West Center Street, Cedar City, UT 84720

## Stevens-Henager College: Logan
**Logan, Utah**
www.stevenshenager.edu

▸ For-profit 4-year business and technical college
▸ Large town

**General.** Accredited by ACCSCT. **Calendar:** Continuous.

**Annual costs/financial aid.** Tuition/fees (2007-2008): $16,350. Tuition and fees can vary by program.

**Contact.** Phone: (435) 713-4777
755 South Highway 89-91, Logan, UT 84321

## Stevens-Henager College: Murray
**Salt Lake City, Utah**
www.stevenshenager.edu

▸ For-profit 4-year business and health science college
▸ Commuter campus in large town
▸ 401 degree-seeking undergraduates
▸ Interview required

**General.** Accredited by ACCSCT. **Degrees:** 62 bachelor's, 92 associate awarded; master's offered. **Location:** 5 Miles from Salt Lake City. **Calendar:** Continuous. **Full-time faculty:** 9 total. **Part-time faculty:** 20 total.

**Basis for selection.** Open admission, but selective for some programs. Consideration given to secondary school record, GPA, recommendations, test scores, interview, residency and level of interest. **Homeschooled:** State high school equivalency certificate required.

**2007-2008 Annual costs.** Tuition/fees: $16,350. Tuition and fees can vary by program.

**Financial aid. Additional information:** Financial aid application must be completed prior to enrollment.

**Application procedures. Admission:** No deadline. No application fee. **Financial aid:** No deadline.

**Academics. Credit/placement by examination:** CLEP.

**Majors. Business:** Accounting technology, business admin. **Computer sciences:** General. **Health:** Health care admin.

**Computing on campus.** Commuter students can connect to campus network. Online library available.

**Student life. Freshman orientation:** Mandatory.

**Student services.** Adult student services, career counseling, financial aid counseling, placement for graduates.

**Contact.** Phone: (800) 622-2640 Fax: (801) 262-7660
Ken Reynolds, Admissions Director, Stevens-Henager College: Murray, 383 West Vine Street, Salt Lake City, UT 84123

## Stevens-Henager College: Ogden
**Ogden, Utah**
www.stevenshenager.edu                    **CB code: 4751**

▸ For-profit 4-year liberal arts college
▸ Commuter campus in small city
▸ 425 degree-seeking undergraduates
▸ Interview required

**General.** Accredited by ACCSCT. **Degrees:** 62 bachelor's, 51 associate awarded. **Location:** 35 miles from Salt Lake City. **Calendar:** Continuous. **Full-time faculty:** 15 total. **Part-time faculty:** 15 total.

**Freshman class profile.** 1,400 applied, 1,380 admitted, 1,370 enrolled.

**Basis for selection.** Open admission, but selective for some programs. Special requirements for surgical technology program.

**High school preparation.** Required units include history 4.

**2008-2009 Annual costs.** Tuition/fees (projected): $19,933. Tuition and fees can vary by program. Personal expenses: $4,000.

**Application procedures. Admission:** No deadline. No application fee. Application must be submitted on paper. Admission notification on a rolling basis.

**Academics. Special study options:** Accelerated study, cooperative education, distance learning, liberal arts/career combination. **Credit/placement by examination:** AP, CLEP. **Support services:** Tutoring.

**Majors. Business:** Accounting, business admin. **Computer sciences:** General. **Health:** Health care admin.

**Computing on campus.** 15 workstations in library, computer center. Commuter students can connect to campus network. Online library available.

**Student life. Freshman orientation:** Mandatory. **Housing:** Single-sex dorms available. $100 deposit.

**Student services.** Financial aid counseling, placement for graduates.

**Contact.** Phone: (801) 394-7791 Fax: (801) 621-0853
Cynthia Williams, Director of Admissions, Stevens-Henager College: Ogden, 1890 South 1350 West, Ogden, UT 84401

## Stevens-Henager College: Orem
**Orem, Utah**
www.stevenshenager.edu

▸ For-profit 4-year business and health science college
▸ Large city

**General.** Founded in 1891. Accredited by ACCSCT. **Location:** In the heart of Orem which abuts Provo city, and approximately 35 miles south of Salt Lake City. **Calendar:** Continuous.

**Annual costs/financial aid.** Tuition/fees (2007-2008): $16,350. Tuition and fees vary by program. Personal expenses: $2,123.

**Contact.** Phone: (801) 375-5455
Director of Admissions, 1476 South Sand Hill Road, Orem, UT 84058

## University of Utah
**Salt Lake City, Utah**                   **CB member**
www.utah.edu                              **CB code: 4853**

▸ Public 4-year university
▸ Commuter campus in large city
▸ 20,560 degree-seeking undergraduates: 30% part-time, 45% women, 1% African American, 6% Asian American, 5% Hispanic American, 1% Native American, 3% international
▸ 6,604 degree-seeking graduate students
▸ 82% of applicants admitted
▸ SAT and SAT Subject Tests or ACT (ACT writing optional) required
▸ 56% graduate within 6 years

**General.** Founded in 1850. Regionally accredited. **Degrees:** 6,892 bachelor's awarded; master's, doctoral, first professional offered. **ROTC:** Army, Naval, Air Force. **Location:** 2 miles from downtown. **Calendar:** Semester, limited summer session. **Full-time faculty:** 1,248 total; 84% have terminal degrees, 12% minority, 38% women. **Part-time faculty:** 622 total; 40% have terminal degrees, 6% minority, 45% women. **Class size:** 40% < 20, 36% 20-39, 6% 40-49, 13% 50-99, 4% >100. **Special facilities:** Arboretum, fine arts museum, natural history museum, architecture exhibition hall, Olympic Cauldron Park, cancer research institute.

**Freshman class profile.** 7,123 applied, 5,833 admitted, 2,743 enrolled.

| Mid 50% test scores | | | |
|---|---|---|---|
| SAT critical reading: | 490-630 | Rank in top tenth: | 23% |
| SAT math: | 490-630 | End year in good standing: | 82% |
| ACT composite: | 21-27 | Return as sophomores: | 80% |
| GPA 3.50 or higher: | 59% | Out-of-state: | 30% |
| GPA 3.0-3.49: | 29% | Live on campus: | 34% |
| GPA 2.0-2.99: | 12% | International: | 2% |
| Rank in top quarter: | 50% | Fraternities: | 2% |
| | | Sororities: | 4% |

**Basis for selection.** High school course requirements, admissions index using high school GPA and test scores important. Recommendations and extracurricular activities considered. Audition required for dance, drama, music programs; portfolio required for art program. **Homeschooled:** ACT score of 23 or SAT score of 1060 (exclusive of Writing), official high school transcript, GED composite scores of at least 550. **Learning Disabled:** Disclosure of learning disabilities not part of admission application; however, the University's Center for Disability Services assists students with disabilities in the admission process.

**High school preparation.** 16 units required. Required units include English 4, mathematics 2, history 1, science 3 (laboratory 2), foreign language 2 and academic electives 4. 4 units from at least 2 of the following: history, English, mathematics beyond algebra, laboratory science, foreign language, social science, fine arts.

**2007-2008 Annual costs.** Tuition/fees: $4,987; $15,662 out-of-state. Room/board: $5,778. Books/supplies: $1,080. Personal expenses: $4,032.

**2007-2008 Financial aid. Need-based:** 968 full-time freshmen applied for aid; 666 were judged to have need; 658 of these received aid. Average need met was 60%. Average scholarship/grant was $5,530; average loan $3,344. 41% of total undergraduate aid awarded as scholarships/grants, 59% as loans/jobs. **Non-need-based:** Awarded to 580 full-time undergraduates, including 244 freshmen. Scholarships awarded for academics, alumni affiliation, art, athletics, leadership, minority status, music/drama, ROTC, state residency.

**Application procedures. Admission:** Priority date 2/15; deadline 4/1 (postmark date). $35 fee. Application may be submitted online. Admission notification on a rolling basis. **Financial aid:** Closing date 3/15. FAFSA, institutional form required. Applicants notified on a rolling basis starting 4/15; must reply within 6 week(s) of notification.

**Academics. Special study options:** Accelerated study, combined bachelor's/graduate degree, cooperative education, distance learning, double major, ESL, exchange student, honors, independent study, internships, liberal arts/career combination, student-designed major, study abroad, teacher certification program, Washington semester. **Credit/placement by examination:** AP, CLEP, IB, SAT, ACT, institutional tests. 32 credit hours maximum toward bachelor's degree. **Support services:** Learning center, pre-admission summer program, reduced course load, remedial instruction, study skills assistance, tutoring, writing center.

**Majors. Architecture:** Architecture. **Area/ethnic studies:** Asian, Near/Middle Eastern, women's. **Biology:** General, anatomy, biochemistry, cell/histology, cellular/molecular, human/medical genetics, neurobiology/physiology, oncology, pathology, physiology. **Business:** General, accounting, business admin, entrepreneurial studies, finance, management information systems, marketing. **Communications:** General, media studies. **Computer sciences:** Computer science. **Conservation:** Environmental science, environmental studies. **Education:** Art, biology, chemistry, drama/dance, elementary, English, foreign languages, French, geography, German, health, history, mathematics, multi-level teacher, music, psychology, science, social science, social studies, Spanish, special, speech. **Engineering:** General, biomedical, chemical, civil, computer, electrical, environmental, geological, materials, mechanical, metallurgical, mining, nuclear, petroleum. **English:** English lit. **Family/consumer sciences:** Consumer economics, family resources, family studies. **Foreign languages:** General, Arabic, Chinese, classics, French, German, Hebrew, Japanese, linguistics, Persian, Russian, Spanish. **Health:** Audiology/hearing, audiology/speech pathology, clinical lab science, health services, medical records technology, nursing (RN), predental, premedicine, prenursing, prepharmacy, public health ed. **History:** General. **Interdisciplinary:** Global studies, math/computer science. **Legal studies:** Prelaw. **Liberal arts:** Humanities. **Math:** General. **Parks/recreation:** General, exercise sciences, health/fitness. **Philosophy/religion:** Philosophy. **Physical sciences:** General, chemistry, geology, geophysics, meteorology, molecular physics, physics. **Psychology:** General. **Public administration:** Social work. **Social sciences:** General, anthropology, economics, geography, political science, sociology, urban studies. **Visual/performing arts:** General, art, art history/conservation, ballet, dance, dramatic, film/cinema. **Other:** 51.2002 Pharmacy Administration.

**Most popular majors.** Business/marketing 12%, communications/journalism 9%, engineering/engineering technologies 6%, health sciences 8%, social sciences 19%, visual/performing arts 6%.

**Computing on campus.** 8,800 workstations in dormitories, library, computer center, student center. Dormitories wired for high-speed internet access and linked to campus network. Commuter students can connect to campus network. Online course registration, online library, helpline, repair service, student web hosting, wireless network available.

**Student life. Freshman orientation:** Mandatory. Preregistration for classes offered. 1-day, 2-day, and 4-day programs offered before fall semester. Late orientations offered in August and mini-orientations held the first day of class. Some orientation options have nominal fees. **Housing:** Single-sex dorms, special housing for disabled, apartments, fraternity/sorority housing, substance-free housing available. $75 fully refundable deposit, deadline 3/28. Theme, limited visitation, 24-hour quiet housing available. **Activities:** Bands, choral groups, dance, drama, film society, literary magazine, music ensembles, musical theater, opera, radio station, student government, student newspaper, symphony orchestra, TV station, political and religious groups, ethnic clubs, outdoor clubs, community service organization.

**Athletics.** NCAA. **Intercollegiate:** Baseball M, basketball, cheerleading, cross-country W, diving, football (tackle) M, golf M, gymnastics W, skiing, soccer W, softball W, swimming, tennis, track and field W, volleyball W. **Intramural:** Fencing, lacrosse, racquetball, rugby M, soccer M, volleyball M, water polo M. **Team name:** Utes.

**Student services.** Adult student services, alcohol/substance abuse counseling, campus ministries, career counseling, student employment services, financial aid counseling, health services, minority student services, on-campus daycare, personal counseling, placement for graduates, veterans' counselor, women's services. **Physically disabled:** Services for visually, speech, hearing impaired.

**Contact.** E-mail: admissions@sa.utah.edu
Phone: (801) 581-7281 Fax: (801) 585-7864
Timothy Ebner, Associate Vice President of Enrollment Management, University of Utah, 201 South 1460 East, Room 250 S, Salt Lake City, UT 84112-9057

## Utah Career College
**West Jordan, Utah**
www.utahcollege.edu                          CB code: 2892

- For-profit 4-year technical college
- Commuter campus in small city
- 689 degree-seeking undergraduates
- Interview required

**General.** Accredited by ACCSCT. **Degrees:** 159 associate awarded. **Location:** 8 miles from Salt Lake City. **Calendar:** Quarter, extensive summer session. **Full-time faculty:** 20 total. **Part-time faculty:** 55 total.

**Freshman class profile.** 210 applied, 204 admitted, 118 enrolled.

**Basis for selection.** Open admission, but selective for some programs. Interview and institutional testing required. **Homeschooled:** GED certificate and documentation required.

**2007-2008 Annual costs.** Tuition/fees: $15,075. Nursing program courses $450 per credit hour.

**Financial aid.** All financial aid based on need.

**Application procedures. Admission:** No deadline. No application fee. Application must be submitted on paper. Admission notification on a rolling basis. **Financial aid:** No deadline. FAFSA, institutional form required. Applicants notified on a rolling basis starting 7/1; must reply within 2 week(s) of notification.

**Academics. Special study options:** Distance learning, liberal arts/career combination. **Credit/placement by examination:** AP, CLEP. Credits for prior work experience and examination may not exceed 75% of total credits required to complete student's program. **Support services:** Reduced course load, study skills assistance, tutoring.

**Majors. Computer sciences:** Information technology. **Legal studies:** Paralegal. **Parks/recreation:** Exercise sciences.

**Most popular majors.** Legal studies 50%, parks/recreation 50%.

**Computing on campus.** 90 workstations in library, computer center.

**Student life. Freshman orientation:** Mandatory. Preregistration for classes offered. **Policies:** Drug and alcohol free campus.

**Student services.** Career counseling, student employment services, financial aid counseling, placement for graduates, veterans' counselor.

**Contact.** E-mail: admissions@utahcollege.edu
Phone: (801) 304-4224 Toll-free number: (866) 304-4224
Fax: (801) 304-4229
Director of Admissions, Utah Career College, 1902 West 7800 South, West Jordan, UT 84088

## Utah State University
### Logan, Utah
www.usu.edu CB code: 4857

- Public 4-year university
- Residential campus in small city
- 12,995 degree-seeking undergraduates: 16% part-time, 48% women, 1% African American, 1% Asian American, 2% Hispanic American, 4% international
- 1,609 degree-seeking graduate students
- 98% of applicants admitted
- SAT or ACT (ACT writing optional) required
- 48% graduate within 6 years; 23% enter graduate study

**General.** Founded in 1888. Regionally accredited. **Degrees:** 2,853 bachelor's, 24 associate awarded; master's, doctoral offered. **ROTC:** Army, Air Force. **Location:** 80 miles from Salt Lake City. **Calendar:** Semester, extensive summer session. **Full-time faculty:** 692 total; 88% have terminal degrees, 5% minority, 30% women. **Part-time faculty:** 47 total; 47% have terminal degrees, 2% minority, 68% women. **Class size:** 39% < 20, 38% 20-39, 8% 40-49, 9% 50-99, 6% >100. **Special facilities:** Agricultural experiment stations, water research laboratory, space shuttle experiments, forestry research facility, botanical gardens, teaching greenhouse, research park, laboratory school, off-campus theater performance lab, anthropology museum.

**Freshman class profile.** 6,045 applied, 5,907 admitted, 2,842 enrolled.

| Mid 50% test scores | | Rank in top quarter: | 49% |
| --- | --- | --- | --- |
| SAT critical reading: | 470-600 | Rank in top tenth: | 21% |
| SAT math: | 490-620 | Out-of-state: | 17% |
| ACT composite: | 20-27 | International: | 3% |
| GPA 3.50 or higher: | 63% | Fraternities: | 2% |
| GPA 3.0-3.49: | 25% | Sororities: | 2% |
| GPA 2.0-2.99: | 12% | | |

**Basis for selection.** High school record, test scores most important. Audition required for music; portfolio required for art. **Homeschooled:** Early entry policy applies: junior equivalent, ACT, letters of approval. **Learning Disabled:** Recent documentation/diagnosis required for special consideration.

**High school preparation.** Required and recommended units include English 4, mathematics 3, history 1, science 3 (laboratory 1), foreign language 2 and academic electives 4. Some social studies electives required.

**2007-2008 Annual costs.** Tuition/fees: $4,199; $12,224 out-of-state. Room/board: $4,580.

**2006-2007 Financial aid. Need-based:** 1,002 full-time freshmen applied for aid; 751 were judged to have need; 744 of these received aid. Average need met was 61%. Average scholarship/grant was $3,153; average loan $2,749. 51% of total undergraduate aid awarded as scholarships/grants, 49% as loans/jobs. **Non-need-based:** Awarded to 2,028 full-time undergraduates, including 632 freshmen. Scholarships awarded for academics, alumni affiliation, art, athletics, leadership, minority status, music/drama, religious affiliation, ROTC.

**Application procedures. Admission:** Priority date 4/1; no deadline. $40 fee. Application may be submitted online. Admission notification on a rolling basis. **Financial aid:** No deadline. FAFSA required. Applicants notified on a rolling basis starting 4/1; must reply within 4 week(s) of notification.

**Academics. Special study options:** Accelerated study, cooperative education, cross-registration, distance learning, double major, dual enrollment of high school students, ESL, exchange student, honors, independent study, internships, liberal arts/career combination, student-designed major, study abroad, teacher certification program, weekend college. **Credit/placement by examination:** AP, CLEP, IB, SAT, ACT, institutional tests. 16 credits of lower division course work per language. **Support services:** Learning center, pre-admission summer program, reduced course load, remedial instruction, study skills assistance, tutoring, writing center.

**Majors. Agriculture:** Agronomy, animal sciences, business, dairy, economics, equipment technology, food science, horticultural science, ornamental horticulture, range science, soil science. **Architecture:** Landscape. **Area/**

ethnic studies: American, Asian. **Biology:** General, botany, ecology, entomology, zoology. **Business:** General, accounting, administrative services, business admin, fashion, finance, human resources, marketing, operations. **Communications:** Journalism. **Computer sciences:** General, information systems. **Conservation:** Forestry, wildlife. **Education:** Agricultural, biology, business, chemistry, early childhood, elementary, family/consumer sciences, health, mathematics, multi-level teacher, music, physical, physics, sales/marketing, science, secondary, social studies, special, technology/industrial arts, voc/tech. **Engineering:** General, aerospace, agricultural, civil, computer, electrical, environmental, mechanical. **Engineering technology:** Electrical. **English:** English lit, speech/rhetoric. **Family/consumer sciences:** Clothing/textiles, family studies, food/nutrition, housing. **Foreign languages:** French, German, Spanish. **Health:** Audiology/speech pathology, clinical lab science, music therapy, predental, premedicine, preveterinary. **History:** General. **Legal studies:** Prelaw. **Liberal arts:** Arts/sciences. **Math:** General, statistics. **Mechanic/repair:** Aircraft. **Parks/recreation:** General, facilities management. **Philosophy/religion:** Philosophy. **Physical sciences:** Chemistry, geology, hydrology, physics. **Psychology:** General. **Public administration:** Social work. **Social sciences:** Anthropology, economics, geography, political science, sociology. **Visual/performing arts:** Art, dance, dramatic, interior design.

**Most popular majors.** Business/marketing 16%, education 16%, engineering/engineering technologies 7%, social sciences 8%, visual/performing arts 6%.

**Computing on campus.** 910 workstations in dormitories, library, computer center, student center. Dormitories wired for high-speed internet access and linked to campus network. Commuter students can connect to campus network. Online course registration, helpline, repair service, student web hosting available.

**Student life. Freshman orientation:** Mandatory, $25 fee. Preregistration for classes offered. Half-day, 1, 2 and 4-day orientation sessions available in June and July for fall semester, half-day session in November for spring semester, and half-day session in March for summer semester. **Housing:** Coed dorms, single-sex dorms, special housing for disabled, apartments, fraternity/sorority housing, substance-free housing available. $150 deposit, deadline 7/1. Mobile home park available. **Activities:** Bands, choral groups, drama, music ensembles, musical theater, opera, student government, student newspaper, symphony orchestra, Latter-day Saints, Catholic, Lutheran, Baptist student organizations, Crusade for Christ, Christian Fellowship, black student union, Hispanic student union, Native American student union, Polynesian student union, Asian American student union.

**Athletics.** NCAA. **Intercollegiate:** Basketball, cross-country, football (tackle) M, golf M, gymnastics W, soccer W, softball W, tennis, track and field, volleyball W. **Intramural:** Badminton, basketball, cross-country, football (non-tackle), golf, racquetball, soccer, softball, table tennis, tennis, triathlon, volleyball. **Team name:** Aggies.

**Student services.** Adult student services, alcohol/substance abuse counseling, career counseling, student employment services, financial aid counseling, health services, minority student services, on-campus daycare, personal counseling, placement for graduates, veterans' counselor, women's services. **Physically disabled:** Services for visually, speech, hearing impaired.

**Contact.** E-mail: admit@usu.edu
Phone: (435) 797-1079 Toll-free number: (800) 488-8108
Fax: (435) 797-3708
Jenn Putnam, Director of Admissions, Utah State University, 0160 Old Main Hill, Logan, UT 84322-0160

## Utah Valley State College
### Orem, Utah
www.uvsc.edu CB code: 4870

- Public 4-year university and technical college
- Commuter campus in small city
- 20,159 degree-seeking undergraduates: 45% part-time, 41% women, 1% African American, 3% Asian American, 5% Hispanic American, 1% Native American, 1% international
- 37% graduate within 6 years

**General.** Founded in 1941. Regionally accredited. Access to libraries at Brigham Young University. Over 50 four-year bachelor degree programs available. **Degrees:** 1,479 bachelor's, 1,781 associate awarded. **ROTC:** Army, Air Force. **Location:** 45 miles from Salt Lake City. **Calendar:** Semester, limited summer session. **Full-time faculty:** 456 total; 3% have terminal degrees, 8% minority, 33% women. **Part-time faculty:** 1,041 total; less than 1% have terminal degrees, 5% minority, 30% women. **Class size:** 45% < 20, 47% 20-39, 4% 40-49, 3% 50-99, less than 1% >100. **Special facilities:** Provo airport campus.

**Freshman class profile.** 4,715 applied, 4,715 admitted, 3,581 enrolled.

| Mid 50% test scores | | Rank in top quarter: | 28% |
|---|---|---|---|
| SAT math: | 420-530 | Rank in top tenth: | 10% |
| ACT composite: | 18-23 | End year in good standing: | 83% |
| GPA 3.50 or higher: | 39% | Return as sophomores: | 43% |
| GPA 3.0-3.49: | 30% | Out-of-state: | 19% |
| GPA 2.0-2.99: | 29% | International: | 1% |

**Basis for selection.** Open admission. Students admitted without ACT/SAT scores, but all students under 21 must complete ACT/SAT prior to registration. ACT/SAT score minimums (ACT English and Math 19, SAT Verbal and Math 500) required or must take New Student Assessment prior to being cleared for registrations. Interviews, auditions, portfolios, and essays are not required for admission. **Homeschooled:** State high school equivalency certificate required. **Learning Disabled:** Students with learning disabilities may apply for reasonable accommodations and assistance through the Accessibility Services Department.

**2007-2008 Annual costs.** Tuition/fees: $3,528; $11,028 out-of-state. Books/supplies: $1,562. Personal expenses: $2,914.

**2007-2008 Financial aid. Need-based:** 1,358 full-time freshmen applied for aid; 1,165 were judged to have need; 764 of these received aid. Average need met was 51%. Average scholarship/grant was $3,670; average loan $3,277. 36% of total undergraduate aid awarded as scholarships/grants, 64% as loans/jobs. **Non-need-based:** Awarded to 2,467 full-time undergraduates, including 621 freshmen. Scholarships awarded for academics, alumni affiliation, art, athletics, leadership, minority status, music/drama.

**Application procedures. Admission:** No deadline. $35 fee, may be waived for applicants with need. Application may be submitted online. Admission notification on a rolling basis. 3-5 business days after application is received. **Financial aid:** Priority date 5/1; no closing date. FAFSA, institutional form required. Applicants notified on a rolling basis starting 1/1; must reply within 2 week(s) of notification.

**Academics. Special study options:** Accelerated study, cooperative education, cross-registration, distance learning, double major, dual enrollment of high school students, ESL, honors, independent study, internships, liberal arts/career combination, student-designed major, study abroad, teacher certification program, weekend college, evening school, internet programs. **Credit/placement by examination:** AP, CLEP, IB, SAT, ACT, institutional tests. 16 credit hours maximum toward associate degree, 16 toward bachelor's. No more than 25% of credits applied toward associate degree, diploma, or certificate may be awarded through challenge credit. Regardless of certificate, diploma, or degree (to include a BS degree), maximum 16 credit hours of challenge credit. **Support services:** Learning center, reduced course load, remedial instruction, study skills assistance, tutoring, writing center.

**Majors. Biology:** General, biotechnology. **Business:** Accounting, business admin, hospitality admin, operations. **Communications:** General. **Computer sciences:** General, computer science, data processing, web page design. **Education:** Biology, business, chemistry, drama/dance, early childhood, elementary, English, health, history, kindergarten/preschool, mathematics, music, physical, science, Spanish. **English:** English lit. **Foreign languages:** American Sign Language, Spanish. **Health:** Community health, nursing (RN). **History:** General. **Legal studies:** Paralegal. **Math:** General. **Parks/recreation:** Health/fitness. **Philosophy/religion:** Philosophy. **Physical sciences:** Chemistry, physics. **Protective services:** Fire services admin, forensics, law enforcement admin. **Psychology:** General. **Social sciences:** Economics, political science. **Transportation:** Airline/commercial pilot. **Visual/performing arts:** Dance, design, dramatic.

**Most popular majors.** Business/marketing 30%, computer/information sciences 9%, education 15%, psychology 14%, trade and industry 8%.

**Computing on campus.** 1,000 workstations in library, computer center, student center. Commuter students can connect to campus network. Online course registration, online library, helpline, repair service, wireless network available.

**Student life. Freshman orientation:** Mandatory. 3-day adventure session in mountain setting with river rafting, rock climbing. On-campus session also available. **Activities:** Bands, choral groups, dance, drama, international student organizations, literary magazine, music ensembles, musical theater, student government, student newspaper, symphony orchestra, TV station, Baptist student union, Black student union, German Club, international student council, Japan club, Latin American club, Latter-day Saint student association, Multi-Cultural Voices, Native Sun, Russian club.

**Athletics.** NCAA. **Intercollegiate:** Baseball M, basketball, cross-country, golf, soccer W, softball W, track and field, volleyball W, wrestling M. **Intramural:** Football (tackle). **Team name:** Wolverines.

**Student services.** Adult student services, alcohol/substance abuse counseling, career counseling, services for economically disadvantaged, student employment services, financial aid counseling, health services, legal services, minority student services, on-campus daycare, personal counseling, placement for graduates, veterans' counselor, women's services. **Physically disabled:** Services for visually, speech, hearing impaired.

**Contact.** E-mail: info@uvsc.edu
Phone: (801) 863-8466 Fax: (801) 225-4677
Liz Childs, Director of Admissions, Utah Valley State College, 800 West University Parkway, Orem, UT 84058-5999

---

## Weber State University
**Ogden, Utah**
www.weber.edu

**CB member**
**CB code: 4941**

- Public 4-year university
- Commuter campus in small city
- 17,617 degree-seeking undergraduates: 46% part-time, 51% women
- 464 degree-seeking graduate students

**General.** Founded in 1889. Regionally accredited. **Degrees:** 1,940 bachelor's, 1,630 associate awarded; master's offered. **ROTC:** Army, Naval, Air Force. **Location:** 35 miles from Salt Lake City. **Calendar:** Semester, extensive summer session. **Full-time faculty:** 461 total; 86% have terminal degrees, 9% minority, 40% women. **Part-time faculty:** 446 total. **Class size:** 51% < 20, 41% 20-39, 4% 40-49, 4% 50-99, less than 1% >100. **Special facilities:** Museum of natural history, planetarium, aerospace technology center.

**Freshman class profile.** 4,221 applied, 4,221 admitted, 2,186 enrolled.

| Mid 50% test scores | | Rank in top quarter: | 52% |
|---|---|---|---|
| ACT composite: | 18-24 | Out-of-state: | 2% |
| GPA 3.50 or higher: | 41% | Live on campus: | 4% |
| GPA 3.0-3.49: | 27% | Fraternities: | 1% |
| GPA 2.0-2.99: | 27% | Sororities: | 1% |

**Basis for selection.** Open admission, but selective for some programs. Special requirements for nursing, dental health, health professions. Based on test scores, freshmen placed on college or university tier; students with higher scores have fewer restrictions on courses. General aptitude test battery required for nursing, dental health, and health professions programs. If student has not taken SAT or ACT, ACT will be administered upon enrollment.

**High school preparation.** 15 units recommended. Recommended units include English 4, mathematics 2, history 1, science 2, foreign language 2 and academic electives 4. 4 additional courses, at least 2 of which should be from the following: history, English, mathematics beyond algebra, laboratory science, fine arts and computer science.

**2007-2008 Annual costs.** Tuition/fees: $3,664; $11,135 out-of-state. Room/board: $6,634. Books/supplies: $1,200. Personal expenses: $2,892.

**2006-2007 Financial aid.** All financial aid based on need. 44% of total undergraduate aid awarded as scholarships/grants, 56% as loans/jobs.

**Application procedures. Admission:** Closing date 8/22. $45 fee. Application may be submitted online. Admission notification on a rolling basis. **Financial aid:** Priority date 3/1; no closing date. FAFSA, institutional form required. Applicants notified on a rolling basis starting 3/15; must reply within 2 week(s) of notification.

**Academics.** Students apply for upper-division courses in junior year. **Special study options:** Accelerated study, cooperative education, distance learning, double major, dual enrollment of high school students, ESL, exchange student, external degree, honors, independent study, internships, New York semester, semester at sea, student-designed major, study abroad, teacher certification program, United Nations semester, Washington semester. First-year experience. **Credit/placement by examination:** AP, CLEP, IB, institutional tests. 30 credit hours maximum toward bachelor's degree. **Support services:** Learning center, pre-admission summer program, reduced course load, remedial instruction, study skills assistance, tutoring, writing center.

**Majors. Area/ethnic studies:** African-American, Hispanic-American/Latino/Chicano, Native American. **Biology:** Bacteriology, botany, zoology. **Business:** Accounting, administrative services, business admin, finance, human resources, logistics, management information systems, managerial economics, marketing, office management. **Communications:** Broadcast journalism, journalism, public relations. **Computer sciences:** General, computer science, information systems, networking. **Construction:** Maintenance. **Education:** Art, bilingual, biology, business, chemistry, drama/dance, early childhood, elementary, English, French, German, history, mathematics, music, physical, physics, science, secondary, social science, social studies, Spanish. **Engineering technology:** Electrical. **English:** Technical writing. **Family/consumer sciences:** Family studies. **Foreign languages:** French, German,

1227

Spanish. **Health:** Athletic training, clinical lab science, dental hygiene, health care admin, medical radiologic technology/radiation therapy, nuclear medical technology, nursing (RN), respiratory therapy technology, sonography. **History:** General. **Interdisciplinary:** Gerontology. **Liberal arts:** Arts/sciences. **Math:** General, applied. **Military:** General. **Parks/recreation:** Exercise sciences, health/fitness. **Physical sciences:** Chemistry, geology, physics. **Protective services:** Corrections, criminal justice, police science. **Psychology:** General. **Public administration:** Social work. **Social sciences:** Economics, geography, political science, sociology. **Visual/performing arts:** General, art, commercial/advertising art, dance, design, dramatic, music performance, photography, piano/organ, studio arts, voice/opera.

**Most popular majors.** Business/marketing 20%, computer/information sciences 6%, education 11%, health sciences 18%, security/protective services 7%.

**Computing on campus.** 558 workstations in dormitories, library, computer center, student center. Dormitories wired for high-speed internet access and linked to campus network. Commuter students can connect to campus network. Online course registration, online library, helpline, repair service, student web hosting, wireless network available.

**Student life. Freshman orientation:** Available. Preregistration for classes offered. April 19 through 25, 4 hours in length. **Housing:** Single-sex dorms, special housing for disabled, apartments, substance-free housing available. $175 partly refundable deposit, deadline 8/1. **Activities:** Bands, choral groups, dance, drama, film society, literary magazine, music ensembles, musical theater, opera, radio station, student government, student newspaper, symphony orchestra, TV station, Latter-day Saint Student Association, Newman Center, Black Scholars United, international student association, physically challenged student association.

**Athletics.** NCAA. **Intercollegiate:** Basketball, cross-country, football (tackle) M, golf, soccer W, tennis, track and field, volleyball W. **Intramural:** Baseball M, basketball, bowling, racquetball, soccer, softball, tennis, track and field, volleyball. **Team name:** Wildcats.

**Student services.** Adult student services, alcohol/substance abuse counseling, campus ministries, career counseling, services for economically disadvantaged, student employment services, financial aid counseling, health services, legal services, minority student services, on-campus daycare, personal counseling, placement for graduates, veterans' counselor, women's services. **Physically disabled:** Services for visually, speech, hearing impaired.

**Contact.** E-mail: admissions@weber.edu
Phone: (801) 626-6744 Toll-free number: (800) 848-7770
Fax: (801) 626-6747
Christopher Rivera, Director of Admissions, Weber State University, 1137 University Circle, Ogden, UT 84408-1137

## Western Governors University
**Salt Lake City, Utah**
**www.wgu.edu**

▶ Private 4-year virtual college
▶ Very large city

**General.** Candidate for regional accreditation. **Calendar:** Continuous.

**Annual costs/financial aid.** Tuition/fees (2007-2008): $5,670. Tuition is based on 6 month terms.

**Contact.** Phone: (801) 274-3280
Director of Enrollment, 4001 South 700 East, Suite 700, Salt Lake City, UT 84107

## Westminster College
**Salt Lake City, Utah**
**www.westminstercollege.edu**      CB code: 4948

▶ Private 4-year liberal arts college
▶ Commuter campus in very large city
▶ 2,020 degree-seeking undergraduates: 10% part-time, 58% women, 1% African American, 3% Asian American, 6% Hispanic American, 1% Native American, 2% international
▶ 611 degree-seeking graduate students
▶ 86% of applicants admitted
▶ SAT or ACT (ACT writing recommended), application essay required
▶ 53% graduate within 6 years; 19% enter graduate study

**General.** Founded in 1875. Regionally accredited. Curriculum combines professional and liberal arts study. **Degrees:** 437 bachelor's awarded; master's offered. **ROTC:** Army, Naval, Air Force. **Location:** 6 miles from downtown. **Calendar:** 4-1-4, limited summer session. **Full-time faculty:** 130 total; 94% have terminal degrees, 3% minority, 51% women. **Part-time faculty:** 156 total; 35% have terminal degrees, 3% minority, 55% women. **Class size:** 65% < 20, 33% 20-39, 2% 40-49, less than 1% 50-99. **Special facilities:** Meade Lx200 telescope, elevated soccer/lacrosse field, health,wellness and athletics center.

**Freshman class profile.** 1,146 applied, 987 admitted, 452 enrolled.

| Mid 50% test scores | | | |
|---|---|---|---|
| SAT critical reading: | 490-630 | Rank in top quarter: | 56% |
| SAT math: | 480-610 | Rank in top tenth: | 29% |
| ACT composite: | 21-27 | End year in good standing: | 91% |
| GPA 3.50 or higher: | 61% | Return as sophomores: | 77% |
| GPA 3.0-3.49: | 27% | Out-of-state: | 30% |
| GPA 2.0-2.99: | 12% | Live on campus: | 59% |
| | | International: | 2% |

**Basis for selection.** Academic performance in high school and GPA are important. SAT or ACT scores must be received by the last day to add and drop classes, approximately 09/11. Interviews are recommended.

**High school preparation.** Required and recommended units include English 4, mathematics 2-3, social studies 2, history 1, science 3, foreign language 2-3 and academic electives 2-3.

**2008-2009 Annual costs.** Tuition/fees: $23,790. Room/board: $6,672. Books/supplies: $1,000. Personal expenses: $1,225.

**2007-2008 Financial aid. Need-based:** 307 full-time freshmen applied for aid; 248 were judged to have need; 247 of these received aid. Average need met was 90%. Average scholarship/grant was $11,350; average loan $3,590. 62% of total undergraduate aid awarded as scholarships/grants, 38% as loans/jobs. **Non-need-based:** Awarded to 865 full-time undergraduates, including 252 freshmen. Scholarships awarded for academics, alumni affiliation, art, athletics, leadership, minority status, music/drama, religious affiliation, ROTC.

**Application procedures. Admission:** Priority date 4/15; no deadline. $40 fee, may be waived for applicants with need. Application may be submitted online. Admission notification on a rolling basis beginning on or about 10/1. Must reply by May 1 or within 3 week(s) if notified thereafter. **Financial aid:** Priority date 4/15; no closing date. FAFSA required. Applicants notified on a rolling basis starting 3/15; must reply by 5/1 or within 3 week(s) of notification.

**Academics. Special study options:** Accelerated study, combined bachelor's/graduate degree, cooperative education, double major, dual enrollment of high school students, honors, independent study, internships, liberal arts/career combination, semester at sea, student-designed major, study abroad, teacher certification program, weekend college. **Credit/placement by examination:** AP, CLEP, IB, SAT, ACT, institutional tests. 40 credit hours maximum toward bachelor's degree. **Support services:** Remedial instruction, study skills assistance, tutoring, writing center.

**Honors college/program.** 35 freshman per year, admission by invitation.

**Majors. Biology:** General. **Business:** General, accounting, business admin, entrepreneurial studies, finance, human resources, information resources management, international, management information systems, management science, managerial economics, marketing. **Communications:** General. **Computer sciences:** Computer science. **Education:** General, early childhood, elementary, secondary, special. **English:** English lit. **Health:** Nurse anesthetist, nursing (RN). **History:** General. **Math:** General. **Philosophy/religion:** Philosophy. **Physical sciences:** Chemistry, physics. **Psychology:** General. **Social sciences:** General, political science, sociology. **Transportation:** Aviation, aviation management. **Visual/performing arts:** Art, arts management.

**Most popular majors.** Business/marketing 34%, health sciences 18%, psychology 7%.

**Computing on campus.** 412 workstations in dormitories, library, computer center, student center. Dormitories wired for high-speed internet access and linked to campus network. Commuter students can connect to campus network. Online course registration, online library, helpline, student web hosting, wireless network available.

**Student life. Freshman orientation:** Mandatory. Preregistration for classes offered. **Housing:** Guaranteed on-campus for freshmen. Coed dorms, single-sex dorms, special housing for disabled, apartments available. $200 nonrefundable deposit, deadline 6/1. **Activities:** Jazz band, campus ministries, choral groups, dance, drama, film society, international student organizations, literary magazine, music ensembles, musical theater, student government, student newspaper, symphony orchestra, College Democrats, College

Republicans, Habitat for Humanity, Earth Effort, Latter-day Saint Student Association, Native American Club, Volunteer Club, Pride Club.

**Athletics.** NAIA. **Intercollegiate:** Basketball, cross-country, golf, lacrosse M, soccer, volleyball W. **Intramural:** Basketball, football (nontackle), volleyball. **Team name:** Griffins.

**Student services.** Alcohol/substance abuse counseling, campus ministries, career counseling, student employment services, financial aid counseling, health services, minority student services, personal counseling, placement for graduates, veterans' counselor. **Physically disabled:** Services for visually, speech, hearing impaired.

**Contact.** E-mail: admission@westminstercollege.edu
Phone: (801) 832-2200 Toll-free number: (800) 748-4753
Fax: (801) 832-3101
Christina Twelves, Director of Undergraduate Admissions, Westminster College, 1840 South 1300 East, Salt Lake City, UT 84105

# Vermont

## Bennington College

**Bennington, Vermont**
www.bennington.edu

**CB member**
**CB code: 3080**

- Private 4-year liberal arts college
- Residential campus in large town
- 583 degree-seeking undergraduates: 68% women, 2% African American, 2% Asian American, 2% Hispanic American, 3% international
- 140 degree-seeking graduate students
- 63% of applicants admitted
- Application essay required
- 57% graduate within 6 years

**General.** Founded in 1932. Regionally accredited. **Degrees:** 134 bachelor's awarded; master's offered. **Location:** 40 miles from Albany, New York, 150 miles from Boston. **Calendar:** 15-week fall and spring terms; 7-week winter field work term. **Full-time faculty:** 60 total; 73% have terminal degrees, 13% minority, 45% women. **Part-time faculty:** 32 total; 38% have terminal degrees, 12% minority, 34% women. **Class size:** 86% < 20, 13% 20-39, less than 1% 50-99. **Special facilities:** Digital arts lab, architecture, drawing, painting, printmaking, and sculpture studios, ceramics studio and kilns, color and black-and-white photography darkrooms, film and video editing studio, fully equipped professional theaters, scripts library, dance studios and archives, electronic music and sound recording studios, music practice rooms and music library, observatory, greenhouse.

**Freshman class profile.** 1,011 applied, 632 admitted, 204 enrolled.

| Mid 50% test scores | | | |
|---|---|---|---|
| SAT critical reading: | 580-700 | Rank in top quarter: | 70% |
| SAT math: | 540-630 | Rank in top tenth: | 28% |
| SAT writing: | 580-690 | End year in good standing: | 95% |
| ACT composite: | 24-30 | Return as sophomores: | 81% |
| GPA 3.50 or higher: | 50% | Out-of-state: | 96% |
| GPA 3.0-3.49: | 31% | Live on campus: | 100% |
| GPA 2.0-2.99: | 19% | International: | 4% |

**Basis for selection.** Admissions decisions based upon strength of applicant's academic record and extracurricular activities, quality of ideas expressed in application, and support of teachers and guidance counselor in discussing student's performance in school. SAT and SAT Subject Tests or ACT recommended. TOEFL or SAT is required for international students. Interviews strongly encouraged. Portfolio reviews not offered or required, but supplemental materials to application welcome. **Homeschooled:** Statement describing homeschool structure and mission, transcript of courses and grades, state high school equivalency certificate, letter of recommendation (nonparent) required. Documentation of academic work (course descriptions and a reading list) required. Strongly encourage standardized test, SAT or ACT.

**High school preparation.** 21 units recommended. Recommended units include English 4, mathematics 4, social studies 4, history 4, science 3 and foreign language 2.

**2007-2008 Annual costs.** Tuition/fees: $36,800. Room/board: $9,380. Books/supplies: $800. Personal expenses: $1,700.

**2007-2008 Financial aid.** **Need-based:** 159 full-time freshmen applied for aid; 145 were judged to have need; 145 of these received aid. Average need met was 83%. Average scholarship/grant was $25,065; average loan $2,930. 81% of total undergraduate aid awarded as scholarships/grants, 19% as loans/jobs. **Non-need-based:** Awarded to 67 full-time undergraduates, including 29 freshmen. Scholarships awarded for academics, art, leadership, music/drama. **Additional information:** All applicants for undergraduate admission considered for scholarships based on quality of overall application.

**Application procedures. Admission:** Closing date 1/3 (postmark date). $60 fee, may be waived for applicants with need. Application may be submitted online. Admission notification 4/1. Must reply by May 1 or within 2 week(s) if notified thereafter. **Financial aid:** Priority date 3/1; no closing date. FAFSA, institutional form required. CSS PROFILE required of early decision applicants only. Applicants notified by 4/1; must reply by 5/1 or within 2 week(s) of notification.

**Academics.** Internships and field work required. **Special study options:** Accelerated study, combined bachelor's/graduate degree, cross-registration, double major, ESL, independent study, internships, student-designed major, study abroad, teacher certification program. Postbaccalaureate program in preparation for medical or allied health school graduate programs. **Credit/placement by examination:** AP, CLEP, IB. **Support services:** Reduced course load, study skills assistance, tutoring, writing center.

**Majors. Architecture:** Architecture. **Area/ethnic studies:** American, Asian, European, gay/lesbian, women's. **Biology:** General, botany, cellular/molecular, ecology, environmental, evolutionary, zoology. **Communications:** Journalism. **Communications technology:** Animation/special effects. **Computer sciences:** General, computer science. **Conservation:** Environmental science, environmental studies. **Education:** General, early childhood, elementary, middle, secondary. **English:** American lit, British lit, composition, creative writing, English lit. **Family/consumer sciences:** Child development. **Foreign languages:** General, Chinese, French, Germanic, Italian, Japanese, Spanish. **Health:** Premedicine. **History:** General, American, European. **Interdisciplinary:** Global studies, math/computer science, peace/conflict. **Legal studies:** Prelaw. **Liberal arts:** Arts/sciences, humanities. **Math:** General. **Philosophy/religion:** Philosophy. **Physical sciences:** General, astronomy, chemistry, physics. **Psychology:** General, social. **Social sciences:** General, anthropology, international relations, political science, sociology, U.S. government. **Visual/performing arts:** General, acting, ceramics, cinematography, dance, design, directing/producing, dramatic, drawing, film/cinema, jazz, multimedia, music history, music performance, music theory/composition, musicology, painting, photography, piano/organ, play/screenwriting, printmaking, sculpture, stringed instruments, studio arts, theater design, theater history, voice/opera.

**Most popular majors.** English 14%, foreign language 7%, liberal arts 6%, visual/performing arts 56%.

**Computing on campus.** 90 workstations in library, computer center. Dormitories wired for high-speed internet access and linked to campus network. Commuter students can connect to campus network. Online library, helpline, repair service, wireless network available.

**Student life. Freshman orientation:** Available. Preregistration for classes offered. 6-day orientation program prior to start of fall classes. International students have 1 extra day. Students may also participate in pre-orientation service or camping trips run by Outing Club. **Housing:** Guaranteed on-campus for all undergraduates. Coed dorms, special housing for disabled, cooperative housing, substance-free housing available. **Activities:** Jazz band, choral groups, dance, drama, film society, international student organizations, literary magazine, music ensembles, musical theater, opera, radio station, student government, student newspaper.

**Athletics. Intramural:** Badminton, basketball, bowling, skiing, soccer, softball, table tennis, tennis, volleyball.

**Student services.** Alcohol/substance abuse counseling, career counseling, student employment services, financial aid counseling, health services, minority student services, on-campus daycare, personal counseling, placement for graduates, women's services. **Physically disabled:** Services for hearing impaired.

**Contact.** E-mail: admissions@bennington.edu
Phone: (802) 440-4312 Toll-free number: (800) 833-6845
Fax: (802) 440-4320
Ken Himmelman, Dean of Admissions and Financial Aid, Bennington College, One College Drive, Bennington, VT 05201-6003

## Burlington College

**Burlington, Vermont**
www.burlington.edu

**CB code: 1119**

- Private 4-year liberal arts college
- Commuter campus in small city
- 172 degree-seeking undergraduates: 30% part-time, 44% women, 3% African American, 1% Asian American, 1% Hispanic American, 2% Native American, 2% international
- 62% of applicants admitted
- Application essay, interview required

**General.** Founded in 1972. Regionally accredited. **Degrees:** 42 bachelor's, 4 associate awarded. **Location:** 90 miles from Montreal, 160 miles from Boston. **Calendar:** Semester, limited summer session. **Full-time faculty:** 5 total; 40% have terminal degrees, 60% women. **Part-time faculty:** 44 total; 32% have terminal degrees, 48% women. **Class size:** 100% < 20. **Special facilities:** Film production facilities.

**Freshman class profile.** 69 applied, 43 admitted, 25 enrolled.

| | | | |
|---|---|---|---|
| End year in good standing: | 67% | Live on campus: | 44% |
| Return as sophomores: | 79% | International: | 4% |
| Out-of-state: | 68% | | |

**Basis for selection.** Application essay and interview very important, followed by recommendations and test scores. Writing samples needed for independent degree program. Two letters of recommendation. SAT or ACT scores not required, but students must take assessments for math, writing, and computer literacy. **Homeschooled:** Portfolio-style transcripts accepted.

**High school preparation.** 24 units recommended. Recommended units include English 4, mathematics 3, social studies 4, history 3, science 3 (laboratory 1), foreign language 2 and academic electives 4.

**2008-2009 Annual costs.** Tuition/fees: $19,640. Room only: $6,095. Books/supplies: $1,075. Personal expenses: $1,800.

**2007-2008 Financial aid. Need-based:** 19 full-time freshmen applied for aid; 17 were judged to have need; 16 of these received aid. Average need met was 49%. Average scholarship/grant was $5,394; average loan $4,967. 32% of total undergraduate aid awarded as scholarships/grants, 68% as loans/jobs.

**Application procedures. Admission:** No deadline. $50 fee, may be waived for applicants with need. Application may be submitted online. Admission notification on a rolling basis. Must confirm by registration period. Application fee may be deferred until enrollment for qualified financial aid applicants. **Financial aid:** No deadline. FAFSA required. Applicants notified on a rolling basis.

**Academics. Special study options:** Cross-registration, distance learning, double major, dual enrollment of high school students, external degree, honors, independent study, internships, liberal arts/career combination, student-designed major, study abroad. Flexible, self-designed degree programs, independent study options. **Credit/placement by examination:** AP, CLEP, IB, institutional tests. 45 credit hours maximum toward associate degree, 90 toward bachelor's. **Support services:** Reduced course load, study skills assistance, tutoring, writing center.

**Majors. Area/ethnic studies:** Latin American. **English:** English lit. **Legal studies:** General. **Psychology:** General. **Public administration:** Human services. **Visual/performing arts:** Film/cinema, photography, studio arts. **Other:** Gender Studies, Inidividualized/Multidisciplinary Studies, Transpersonal Psychology.

**Most popular majors.** English 21%, interdisciplinary studies 29%, psychology 14%, public administration/social services 7%, visual/performing arts 24%.

**Computing on campus.** 21 workstations in library, computer center, student center. Commuter students can connect to campus network. Online library, wireless network available.

**Student life. Freshman orientation:** Mandatory, $150 fee. Preregistration for classes offered. Held over 2-3 days. **Housing:** Apartments, cooperative housing available. **Activities:** Drama, film society, literary magazine, student government, student newspaper, Institute for Civic Engagement, community garden.

**Student services.** Adult student services, career counseling, financial aid counseling, legal services, personal counseling.

**Contact.** E-mail: admissions@burlington.edu
Phone: (802) 862-9616 ext. 104 Toll-free number: (800) 862-9616 ext. 104
Fax: (802) 660-4331
Joshua Doyle, Admissions Director, Burlington College, 95 North Avenue, Burlington, VT 05401

---

## Castleton State College
**Castleton, Vermont**
**www.castleton.edu**

**CB member**
**CB code: 3765**

- Public 4-year liberal arts college
- Residential campus in small town
- 1,873 degree-seeking undergraduates: 10% part-time, 55% women, 1% African American, 1% Asian American, 2% Hispanic American, 1% Native American
- 32 degree-seeking graduate students
- 71% of applicants admitted
- SAT or ACT with writing, application essay required
- 38% graduate within 6 years

**General.** Founded in 1787. Regionally accredited. **Degrees:** 271 bachelor's, 76 associate awarded; master's offered. **ROTC:** Army. **Location:** 12 miles from Rutland. **Calendar:** Semester, limited summer session. **Full-time faculty:** 88 total; 93% have terminal degrees, 7% minority, 48% women. **Part-time faculty:** 120 total; 26% have terminal degrees, 39% women. **Class size:** 72% < 20, 27% 20-39, less than 1% 40-49, 1% 50-99, less than 1% >100. **Special facilities:** Medical society museum, outdoor classroom.

**Freshman class profile.** 1,828 applied, 1,303 admitted, 418 enrolled.

| Mid 50% test scores | | | |
|---|---|---|---|
| SAT critical reading: | 440-530 | GPA 2.0-2.99: | 58% |
| SAT math: | 450-530 | Rank in top quarter: | 18% |
| ACT composite: | 18-22 | Rank in top tenth: | 4% |
| GPA 3.50 or higher: | 14% | Return as sophomores: | 66% |
| GPA 3.0-3.49: | 28% | Out-of-state: | 40% |
| | | Live on campus: | 88% |

**Basis for selection.** School achievement record, test scores, essay, recommendations, class rank very important. Interview recommended for all; audition recommended for music.

**High school preparation.** College-preparatory program required. 14 units required; 16 recommended. Required and recommended units include English 4, mathematics 3, social studies 3-4, science 3-4 (laboratory 2) and foreign language 2.

**2007-2008 Annual costs.** Tuition/fees: $7,244; $15,428 out-of-state. New England Board of Higher Education rate for students from other New England states: 150% of Vermont resident tuition. Available to degree candidates in academic areas not offered by educational institutions in their home states. Room/board: $7,220. Books/supplies: $800. Personal expenses: $600.

**2006-2007 Financial aid. Need-based:** 30% of total undergraduate aid awarded as scholarships/grants, 70% as loans/jobs. **Non-need-based:** Scholarships awarded for academics, alumni affiliation, art, leadership, music/drama, state residency.

**Application procedures. Admission:** No deadline. $35 fee, may be waived for applicants with need. Admission notification on a rolling basis beginning on or about 12/1. **Financial aid:** Priority date 2/15; no closing date. FAFSA required. Applicants notified on a rolling basis starting 1/1; must reply by 5/1 or within 2 week(s) of notification.

**Academics. Special study options:** Combined bachelor's/graduate degree, cooperative education, cross-registration, double major, dual enrollment of high school students, honors, independent study, internships, liberal arts/career combination, student-designed major, study abroad, teacher certification program. 5-year MBA with Clarkson University, 7-year physical therapy with Sage Graduate School, 6-year occupational therapy with Sage Graduate School. **Credit/placement by examination:** AP, CLEP, SAT, ACT, institutional tests. 30 credit hours maximum toward associate degree, 60 toward bachelor's. **Support services:** Learning center, reduced course load, remedial instruction, study skills assistance, tutoring, writing center.

**Majors. Biology:** General. **Business:** General, accounting, business admin, management science, marketing. **Communications:** Digital media, journalism, media studies. **Computer sciences:** General. **Conservation:** Environmental science. **Education:** Art, biology, chemistry, drama/dance, elementary, English, foreign languages, history, mathematics, middle, music, physical, physics, science, secondary, social science, social studies, Spanish. **English:** American lit, English lit. **Foreign languages:** Spanish. **Health:** Athletic training. **History:** General. **Interdisciplinary:** Biological/physical sciences, math/computer science, natural sciences. **Math:** General, statistics. **Parks/recreation:** Exercise sciences, health/fitness, sports admin. **Philosophy/religion:** Philosophy. **Physical sciences:** Geology. **Protective services:** Criminal justice. **Psychology:** General. **Public administration:** Social work. **Social sciences:** General, criminology, sociology. **Visual/performing arts:** General, art, dramatic.

**Most popular majors.** Business/marketing 30%, communications/journalism 10%, interdisciplinary studies 6%, parks/recreation 6%, psychology 10%, security/protective services 6%, social sciences 6%, visual/performing arts 6%.

**Computing on campus.** 200 workstations in dormitories, library, computer center. Dormitories wired for high-speed internet access and linked to campus network. Commuter students can connect to campus network. Repair service, wireless network available.

**Student life. Freshman orientation:** Mandatory. Preregistration for classes offered. 2 and a half day program. **Housing:** Guaranteed on-campus for freshmen. Coed dorms, substance-free housing available. $100 nonrefundable deposit, deadline 5/1. **Activities:** Jazz band, choral groups, dance, drama, literary magazine, music ensembles, musical theater, radio station, student government, student newspaper, TV station, Christian fellowships, political discussion group, Spanish club, social issues club, community service club, women's issues group.

**Athletics.** NCAA. **Intercollegiate:** Baseball M, basketball, cross-country, field hockey W, golf M, ice hockey, lacrosse, skiing, soccer, softball W, tennis, volleyball W. **Intramural:** Basketball, football (non-tackle), racquetball, soccer, softball, swimming, table tennis, tennis, volleyball. **Team name:** Spartans.

**Student services.** Adult student services, alcohol/substance abuse counseling, career counseling, services for economically disadvantaged, student employment services, financial aid counseling, health services, personal counseling, placement for graduates.

**Contact.** E-mail: info@castleton.edu
Phone: (802) 468-1213 Toll-free number: (800) 639-8521
Fax: (802) 468-1476
Maurice Ouimet, Director of Admissions, Castleton State College, Seminary Street, Castleton, VT 05735

## Champlain College

| Burlington, Vermont | |
| --- | --- |
| www.champlain.edu | **CB member** |
| | **CB code: 3291** |

- Private 4-year business and liberal arts college
- Residential campus in small city
- 2,493 degree-seeking undergraduates: 20% part-time, 44% women, 1% African American, 1% Asian American, 1% Hispanic American
- 109 degree-seeking graduate students
- 59% of applicants admitted
- SAT or ACT (ACT writing optional), application essay required
- 70% graduate within 6 years; 8% enter graduate study

**General.** Founded in 1878. Regionally accredited. **Degrees:** 392 bachelor's, 102 associate awarded; master's offered. **ROTC:** Army. **Location:** 200 miles from Boston, 90 miles from Montreal. **Calendar:** Semester, limited summer session. **Full-time faculty:** 82 total; 42% have terminal degrees, 1% minority, 35% women. **Part-time faculty:** 250 total; 18% have terminal degrees, 3% minority, 45% women. **Class size:** 55% < 20, 45% 20-39, less than 1% 40-49.

**Freshman class profile.** 2,723 applied, 1,602 admitted, 475 enrolled.

| Mid 50% test scores | | | |
| --- | --- | --- | --- |
| SAT critical reading: | 500-600 | Rank in top tenth: | 10% |
| SAT math: | 510-600 | End year in good standing: | 84% |
| ACT composite: | 20-26 | Return as sophomores: | 84% |
| Rank in top quarter: | 31% | Out-of-state: | 73% |
| | | Live on campus: | 90% |

**Basis for selection.** GPA, level of difficulty of high school curriculum, essay, interview, counselor recommendations most important. Waiting list for Radiography and Electronic Gaming and Interactive Design programs only. Interview strongly recommended. **Homeschooled:** GED or 2 SAT Subject Tests required.

**High school preparation.** 20 units required. Required and recommended units include English 4, mathematics 3-4, social studies 2, history 4, science 3-4 (laboratory 2-3), foreign language 2 and academic electives 4.

**2007-2008 Annual costs.** Tuition/fees: $22,550. Room/board: $10,910. Books/supplies: $600. Personal expenses: $600.

**2007-2008 Financial aid. Need-based:** 419 full-time freshmen applied for aid; 349 were judged to have need; 349 of these received aid. Average need met was 60%. Average scholarship/grant was $6,000; average loan $4,290. 46% of total undergraduate aid awarded as scholarships/grants, 54% as loans/jobs. **Non-need-based:** Awarded to 1,544 full-time undergraduates, including 247 freshmen. Scholarships awarded for academics, leadership.

**Application procedures. Admission:** Closing date 1/31. $50 fee, may be waived for applicants with need. Application may be submitted online. Admission notification on a rolling basis beginning on or about 3/25. Must reply by 5/1. Housing deposit refundable prior to 5/1 only. **Financial aid:** Closing date 3/1. FAFSA required. Applicants notified by 3/19; must reply by 5/1.

**Academics.** 96% of majors include required internship. **Special study options:** Accelerated study, combined bachelor's/graduate degree, cooperative education, cross-registration, distance learning, double major, honors, independent study, internships, liberal arts/career combination, study abroad, teacher certification program. Clinical internships at Fletcher Allen Medical Center. **Credit/placement by examination:** AP, CLEP, IB, institutional tests. 30 credit hours maximum toward associate degree, 75 toward bachelor's. **Support services:** Reduced course load, study skills assistance, tutoring, writing center.

**Majors. Business:** General, accounting, accounting/business management, accounting/finance, business admin, communications, e-commerce, hospitality admin, hospitality/recreation, hotel/motel admin, human resources, international, marketing, organizational behavior, restaurant/food services, small business admin, tourism promotion, tourism/travel, travel services. **Communications:** Digital media, journalism, media studies, organizational, public relations. **Communications technology:** Animation/special effects, graphics. **Computer sciences:** General, computer graphics, computer science, information systems, LAN/WAN management, networking, security, system admin, systems analysis, web page design, webmaster. **Education:** General, early childhood, elementary, kindergarten/preschool, middle, secondary. **Engineering:** Software. **English:** Composition, creative writing, technical writing. **Family/consumer sciences:** Family/community services. **Legal studies:** Paralegal, prelaw. **Liberal arts:** Arts/sciences. **Personal/culinary services:** Restaurant/catering. **Protective services:** Criminal justice, forensics, law enforcement admin, security management, security services. **Psychology:** General. **Public administration:** Human services, social work. **Visual/performing arts:** Cinematography, design, graphic design, multimedia.

**Computing on campus.** 260 workstations in library, computer center, student center. Dormitories wired for high-speed internet access and linked to campus network. Commuter students can connect to campus network. Online course registration, online library, helpline, wireless network available.

**Student life. Freshman orientation:** Available, $60 fee. Preregistration for classes offered. 4-day program. **Policies:** No alcohol permitted on campus. **Housing:** Guaranteed on-campus for freshmen. Coed dorms, single-sex dorms, substance-free housing available. $150 nonrefundable deposit, deadline 5/1. Wellness, music-focus, and community service theme dorms available. **Activities:** Choral groups, dance, drama, literary magazine, musical theater, radio station, student government, student newspaper, cultural diversity committee, GET REAL community service, international club, outing club, Champlain Heritage Society, Reader's Exchange, flash animation club, Intercollegiate Writers Exchange.

**Athletics. Intramural:** Basketball, bowling, golf, ice hockey, skiing, soccer, volleyball.

**Student services.** Adult student services, alcohol/substance abuse counseling, career counseling, student employment services, financial aid counseling, health services, minority student services, personal counseling, placement for graduates. **Physically disabled:** Services for visually, hearing impaired.

**Contact.** E-mail: admission@champlain.edu
Phone: (802) 860-2727 Toll-free number: (800) 570-5858
Fax: (802) 860-2767
Laryn Runco, Director of Admissions, Champlain College, 163 South Willard Street, Burlington, VT 05402-0670

## College of St. Joseph in Vermont

| Rutland, Vermont | |
| --- | --- |
| www.csj.edu | **CB member** |
| | **CB code: 3297** |

- Private 4-year liberal arts and teachers college affiliated with Roman Catholic Church
- Residential campus in large town
- 209 degree-seeking undergraduates: 23% part-time, 55% women, 4% African American, 1% Asian American, 5% Hispanic American, 1% Native American
- 162 degree-seeking graduate students
- 88% of applicants admitted
- SAT or ACT (ACT writing optional), application essay required
- 58% graduate within 6 years

**General.** Founded in 1950. Regionally accredited. **Degrees:** 52 bachelor's, 11 associate awarded; master's offered. **Location:** 70 miles from Burlington, 100 miles from Albany, New York. **Calendar:** Semester, extensive summer session. **Full-time faculty:** 15 total; 53% have terminal degrees, 40% women. **Part-time faculty:** 50 total; 24% have terminal degrees, 2% minority, 42% women. **Class size:** 92% < 20, 8% 20-39. **Special facilities:** Photography and ceramics studios.

**Freshman class profile.** 101 applied, 89 admitted, 34 enrolled.

| Mid 50% test scores | | | |
| --- | --- | --- | --- |
| SAT critical reading: | 410-530 | GPA 2.0-2.99: | 76% |
| SAT math: | 390-490 | Rank in top quarter: | 4% |
| SAT writing: | 410-480 | End year in good standing: | 85% |
| ACT composite: | 17-23 | Return as sophomores: | 76% |
| GPA 3.0-3.49: | 21% | Out-of-state: | 59% |
| | | Live on campus: | 71% |

1232

**Basis for selection.** Decisions based on high school course selection, minimum 2.0 out of 4.0 high school GPA in college preparatory coursework, 2 academic letters of recommendation, essay, ACT or SAT scores; and extracurricular activities are considered. CSJ only accepts the GED for students age 22 and over. Interview recommended. **Homeschooled:** Transcript of courses and grades, interview, letter of recommendation (nonparent) required.

**High school preparation.** 16 units required. Required and recommended units include English 4, mathematics 3, social studies 2, science 2, foreign language 2 and academic electives 5.

**2008-2009 Annual costs.** Tuition/fees (projected): $15,760. Room/board: $7,600. Books/supplies: $650. Personal expenses: $900.

**2007-2008 Financial aid. Need-based:** 30 full-time freshmen applied for aid; 28 were judged to have need; 28 of these received aid. Average need met was 76%. Average scholarship/grant was $11,224; average loan $3,306. 55% of total undergraduate aid awarded as scholarships/grants, 45% as loans/jobs. **Non-need-based:** Awarded to 12 full-time undergraduates, including 2 freshmen. Scholarships awarded for academics, athletics. **Additional information:** Instructors at local Catholic schools are granted a tuition reduction.

**Application procedures. Admission:** Priority date 3/1; no deadline. $25 fee, may be waived for applicants with need. Application may be submitted online. Admission notification on a rolling basis. Must reply by May 1 or within 2 week(s) if notified thereafter. **Financial aid:** Priority date 3/1; no closing date. FAFSA, institutional form required. Applicants notified on a rolling basis starting 3/15.

**Academics.** Experiential educational options including internships available. **Special study options:** Accelerated study, double major, dual enrollment of high school students, independent study, internships, liberal arts/career combination, teacher certification program. **Credit/placement by examination:** AP, CLEP, IB, institutional tests. 12 credit hours maximum toward associate degree, 12 toward bachelor's. **Support services:** Learning center, reduced course load, study skills assistance, tutoring, writing center.

**Majors. Business:** General, accounting, business admin, management science, operations. **Education:** Elementary, English, history, middle, multilevel teacher, secondary, social studies. **English:** English lit. **History:** General. **Liberal arts:** Arts/sciences. **Parks/recreation:** Sports admin. **Psychology:** General. **Public administration:** Human services. **Other:** Alcohol and Substance Abuse Counseling.

**Most popular majors.** Business/marketing 40%, education 21%, liberal arts 12%, psychology 15%.

**Computing on campus.** 34 workstations in library, computer center, student center. Dormitories wired for high-speed internet access and linked to campus network. Commuter students can connect to campus network. Online library, repair service, wireless network available.

**Student life. Freshman orientation:** Mandatory, $125 fee. Preregistration for classes offered. 5-day orientation before upperclassmen move into dorms. **Housing:** Guaranteed on-campus for all undergraduates. Single-sex dorms available. $200 nonrefundable deposit, deadline 5/1. Some single rooms available. **Activities:** Campus ministries, choral groups, drama, literary magazine, student government, student newspaper, student ambassadors, human services club, education club, honor societies.

**Athletics.** NAIA. **Intercollegiate:** Baseball M, basketball, soccer, softball W. **Intramural:** Bowling, weight lifting. **Team name:** Fighting Saints.

**Student services.** Adult student services, alcohol/substance abuse counseling, campus ministries, career counseling, student employment services, financial aid counseling, personal counseling, placement for graduates, veterans' counselor. **Physically disabled:** Services for visually, speech, hearing impaired.

**Contact.** E-mail: admissions@csj.edu
Phone: (802) 773-5900 ext. 3286 Toll-free number: (877) 270-9998
Fax: (802) 776-5258
Tracy Gallipo, Director of Admissions, College of St. Joseph in Vermont, 71 Clement Road, Rutland, VT 05701-3899

## Goddard College
**Plainfield, Vermont**
**www.goddard.edu**                    **CB code: 3416**

- Private 4-year liberal arts college
- Rural community
- 242 degree-seeking undergraduates: 71% women
- 430 graduate students
- Application essay, interview required

**General.** Founded in 1938. Regionally accredited. Nontraditional institution; independent study programs designed for working adults. Short residencies required two times a year on campus. MFA in Creative Writing and MFA in Interdisciplinary Arts offered in Port Townsend, WA as well as Plainfield, VT. **Degrees:** 44 bachelor's awarded; master's offered. **Location:** 10 miles from Montpelier. **Calendar:** Semester. **Full-time faculty:** 5 total; 60% women. **Part-time faculty:** 98 total; 72% women.

**Freshman class profile.** 8 applied, 8 admitted, 8 enrolled.

**Basis for selection.** Open admission, but selective for some programs. Academic potential, maturity, ability to work independently, personal statement, and interview important. SAT/ACT scores optional. Students encouraged to include portfolio with application. **Homeschooled:** GED recommended.

**2007-2008 Annual costs.** Annual tuition for distance learning Bachelor of Arts is $12,130. Books/supplies: $765. Personal expenses: $1,127.

**2007-2008 Financial aid. Need-based:** Average need met was 40%. Average scholarship/grant was $4,630; average loan $4,591. 26% of total undergraduate aid awarded as scholarships/grants, 74% as loans/jobs. **Non-need-based:** Scholarships awarded for academics, art, job skills, leadership, music/drama, state residency.

**Application procedures. Admission:** $40 fee, may be waived for applicants with need. Application may be submitted online. Admission notification on a rolling basis. Must reply by May 1 or within 4 week(s) if notified thereafter. **Financial aid:** FAFSA required. Applicants notified on a rolling basis starting 4/15; must reply within 4 week(s) of notification.

**Academics.** Written evaluations replace grades. Individually designed majors at bachelor's and master's levels. Students design programs of study in collaboration with faculty mentor. Students on campus for 8 days at beginning of each semester and then work from home following study plan designed in collaboration with adviser. **Special study options:** Distance learning, external degree, independent study, internships, liberal arts/career combination, student-designed major, study abroad, teacher certification program. **Credit/placement by examination:** AP, CLEP, IB. 30 credit hours maximum toward bachelor's degree.

**Majors. Area/ethnic studies:** African-American, American, European, Latin American, Native American, Near/Middle Eastern, women's. **Biology:** General, ecology. **Business:** Business admin. **Conservation:** Environmental studies. **Education:** General, art, early childhood, elementary, English, middle, secondary, social studies. **English:** Creative writing, English lit. **History:** General. **Interdisciplinary:** Peace/conflict. **Liberal arts:** Arts/sciences. **Philosophy/religion:** Judaic, philosophy, religion. **Psychology:** General. **Public administration:** Community org/advocacy, social work. **Social sciences:** General. **Visual/performing arts:** General, crafts, studio arts.

**Computing on campus.** PC or laptop required. 100 workstations in dormitories, library, computer center, student center. Dormitories wired for high-speed internet access and linked to campus network. Commuter students can connect to campus network. Online library, helpline, wireless network available.

**Student life. Freshman orientation:** Mandatory, $105 fee. Held day before registration. **Housing:** Substance-free housing available. Housing available 8 days per semester. **Activities:** Radio station.

**Contact.** E-mail: admissions@goddard.edu
Phone: (802) 454-8311 ext. 243 Toll-free number: (800) 906-8312 ext. 243
Fax: (802) 454-1029
Brenda Hawkins, Director of Admissions, Goddard College, 123 Pitkin Road, Plainfield, VT 05667

## Green Mountain College
**Poultney, Vermont**                    **CB member**
**www.greenmtn.edu**                    **CB code: 3418**

- Private 4-year liberal arts college affiliated with United Methodist Church
- Residential campus in small town
- 759 degree-seeking undergraduates: 1% part-time, 48% women, 3% African American, 1% Asian American, 2% Hispanic American, 1% Native American
- 53 degree-seeking graduate students
- 77% of applicants admitted
- Application essay required

**General.** Founded in 1834. Regionally accredited. **Degrees:** 110 bachelor's awarded; master's offered. **Location:** 20 miles from Rutland, 35 miles from Killington. **Calendar:** Differs by program. **Full-time faculty:** 45 total; 84% have terminal degrees, 4% minority, 29% women. **Part-time faculty:** 25 total; 24% have terminal degrees, 44% women. **Class size:** 51% < 20, 49% 20-39. **Special facilities:** Student-operated organically managed farm, ropes course, 80-acre nature preserve, collection of Welsh artifacts and literature, collection of early American decoration, art collection.

**Freshman class profile.** 1,287 applied, 991 admitted, 255 enrolled.

| | | | |
|---|---|---|---|
| Out-of-state: | 85% | Live on campus: | 96% |

**Basis for selection.** Academic achievement, recommendations, interview, essay, test scores, personal statement, school and community activities important. SAT or ACT recommended. Interview recommended; audition recommended for theater or music; portfolio recommended for art. **Homeschooled:** Statement describing homeschool structure and mission, transcript of courses and grades, state high school equivalency certificate, letter of recommendation (nonparent) required. Applicants advised to develop thorough portfolio of all work completed. Students highly encouraged to interview on campus.

**High school preparation.** 21 units required. Required and recommended units include English 4, mathematics 3-4, social studies 3, history 1-2, science 3-4 (laboratory 2), foreign language 2-3 and academic electives 5.

**2007-2008 Annual costs.** Tuition/fees: $24,565. Room/board: $8,982. Books/supplies: $1,000. Personal expenses: $770.

**2007-2008 Financial aid. Need-based:** Average need met was 71%. Average scholarship/grant was $16,071; average loan $4,380. 66% of total undergraduate aid awarded as scholarships/grants, 34% as loans/jobs. **Non-need-based:** Scholarships awarded for academics, alumni affiliation, art, leadership, music/drama, religious affiliation. **Additional information:** Service/recognition awards available to all students.

**Application procedures. Admission:** Priority date 3/1; no deadline. $30 fee, may be waived for applicants with need. Application may be submitted online. Admission notification on a rolling basis beginning on or about 9/1. Must reply by May 1 or within 2 week(s) if notified thereafter. **Financial aid:** Priority date 3/1; no closing date. FAFSA required. CSS PROFILE is recommended to receive an earlier financial aid package. Applicants notified on a rolling basis starting 1/1; must reply by 5/1 or within 4 week(s) of notification.

**Academics.** Environmental core curriculum. **Special study options:** Accelerated study, double major, ESL, exchange student, honors, independent study, internships, liberal arts/career combination, student-designed major, study abroad, teacher certification program. Exchange programs at Aberystwyth University (Wales), Hannam University (Korea), Nogoya University (Japan). Credit granted for programs of National Outdoor Leadership School. Member of Eco-League Consortium; students can spend up to 2 semesters at one of 5 other schools: Alaska Pacific University, Antioch University, College of the Atlantic, Northand College, Prescott College. **Credit/placement by examination:** AP, CLEP, IB, SAT, ACT, institutional tests. **Support services:** Learning center, pre-admission summer program, reduced course load, remedial instruction, study skills assistance, tutoring, writing center.

**Majors. Biology:** General. **Business:** Business admin, hospitality admin, hospitality/recreation, resort management. **Communications:** General, journalism. **Conservation:** General, environmental studies, management/policy. **Education:** Art, elementary, English, middle, secondary, social studies, special. **English:** Creative writing, English lit. **History:** General. **Liberal arts:** Arts/sciences. **Parks/recreation:** General, facilities management. **Philosophy/religion:** Philosophy. **Psychology:** General. **Social sciences:** Anthropology, sociology. **Visual/performing arts:** Art, studio arts. **Other:** Environmental Management.

**Computing on campus.** 60 workstations in dormitories, library, computer center, student center. Dormitories wired for high-speed internet access and linked to campus network. Commuter students can connect to campus network. Online course registration, online library, helpline, wireless network available.

**Student life. Freshman orientation:** Mandatory, $100 fee. Preregistration for classes offered. Orientation held week before classes begin in August and January. Students also may opt to come to campus on specified days during summer. **Housing:** Guaranteed on-campus for all undergraduates. Coed dorms, substance-free housing available. Theme floors including substance-free, sustainable living, adventure recreation, creative arts, quiet floor, honors floor available. **Activities:** Bands, choral groups, drama, film society, literary magazine, music ensembles, radio station, student government, student newspaper, outdoor adventure programs, Poultney Partners Mentoring Program, environmental volunteer and research groups, African American Culture Club, diversity club, UNICEF.

**Athletics.** NCAA. **Intercollegiate:** Basketball, cross-country, golf M, lacrosse, skiing, soccer, softball W, tennis, volleyball W. **Intramural:** Basketball, football (non-tackle), skiing, soccer, softball, table tennis, tennis, volleyball. **Team name:** Eagles.

**Student services.** Alcohol/substance abuse counseling, campus ministries, career counseling, student employment services, financial aid counseling, health services, personal counseling, placement for graduates.

**Contact.** E-mail: admiss@greenmtn.edu
Phone: (802) 287-8207 Toll-free number: (800) 776-6675
Fax: (802) 287-8099
Sandra Bartholomew, Dean of Enrollment Management, Green Mountain College, One College Circle, Poultney, VT 05764

---

## Johnson State College
**Johnson, Vermont**
www.jsc.vsc.edu

**CB member**
**CB code: 3766**

- Public 4-year liberal arts college
- Residential campus in rural community
- 1,470 degree-seeking undergraduates
- SAT or ACT (ACT writing optional), application essay required

**General.** Founded in 1828. Regionally accredited. Special tuition rate for New England residents who apply to selected fields of study. **Degrees:** 296 bachelor's, 16 associate awarded; master's offered. **ROTC:** Army. **Location:** 50 miles from Burlington, 90 miles from Montreal. **Calendar:** Semester, limited summer session. **Full-time faculty:** 56 total. **Part-time faculty:** 87 total. **Class size:** 72% < 20, 28% 20-39. **Special facilities:** 1,000-acre nature preserve, visual arts center, human performance laboratory, interactive multimedia math and science laboratory, recording studio, community service learning center, Vermont Interactive Television site, snowboard park.

**Freshman class profile.**

| Mid 50% test scores | | | |
|---|---|---|---|
| | | ACT composite: | 20-28 |
| SAT critical reading: | 430-550 | Out-of-state: | 29% |
| SAT math: | 430-550 | Live on campus: | 90% |

**Basis for selection.** High school transcript, GPA, SAT or ACT scores, class rank, recommendations, and essay important. Tests not required for any student who graduated high school at least one year ago, or for students taking the GED. Interview recommended. **Homeschooled:** SAT required. Applicants encouraged to complete GED or other state certified achievement test to demonstrate aptitude.

**High school preparation.** 9 units required; 15 recommended. Required and recommended units include English 4, mathematics 3-4, social studies 2, history 2, science 2-3 (laboratory 1-2) and foreign language 2. Mathematics units to include algebra II.

**2007-2008 Annual costs.** Tuition/fees: $7,244; $15,428 out-of-state. New England Board of Higher Education rate for students from other New England states: 150% of Vermont resident tuition. Available to degree candidates in academic areas not offered by educational institutions in their home states. Room/board: $7,220. Books/supplies: $800. Personal expenses: $650.

**Financial aid. Non-need-based:** Scholarships awarded for academics.

**Application procedures. Admission:** Priority date 3/1; no deadline. $35 fee, may be waived for applicants with need. Application may be submitted online. Admission notification on a rolling basis beginning on or about 12/1. Must reply by May 1 or within 2 week(s) if notified thereafter. Although students are admitted and notified on a rolling basis, we strongly recommend students apply for admission before March 1 in order to insure optimal financial aid consideration. **Financial aid:** Priority date 3/1; no closing date. FAFSA required. Applicants notified on a rolling basis starting 4/1; must reply within 3 week(s) of notification.

**Academics.** Transition program for students who show potential academic success but may be unprepared academically and/or socially. **Special study options:** Accelerated study, cross-registration, distance learning, double major, dual enrollment of high school students, ESL, exchange student, external degree, independent study, internships, study abroad, teacher certification program. **Credit/placement by examination:** AP, CLEP, institutional tests. **Support services:** Learning center, pre-admission summer program, reduced course load, remedial instruction, study skills assistance, tutoring, writing center.

**Majors. Biology:** General, cell/histology, molecular. **Business:** General, business admin, hospitality admin, tourism/travel. **Communications:** Journalism. **Conservation:** General, environmental studies, management/policy.

**Education:** General, art, biology, drama/dance, elementary, English, history, mathematics, middle, multi-level teacher, music, physical, science, secondary, social science, social studies. **English:** English lit. **Foreign languages:** Comparative lit. **Health:** Athletic training, premedicine. **History:** General. **Liberal arts:** Arts/sciences. **Math:** General. **Parks/recreation:** General, exercise sciences, health/fitness, sports admin. **Psychology:** General. **Social sciences:** General, anthropology, political science, sociology. **Visual/performing arts:** General, art, dance, dramatic, jazz, music history, music performance, music theory/composition, musical theater, piano/organ, studio arts, theater design, voice/opera. **Other:** Wellness and alternative medicine.

**Most popular majors.** Business/marketing 13%, education 15%, history 6%, liberal arts 21%, psychology 17%, visual/performing arts 11%.

**Computing on campus.** 131 workstations in library, computer center. Dormitories wired for high-speed internet access and linked to campus network. Commuter students can connect to campus network. Online course registration, helpline, wireless network available.

**Student life. Freshman orientation:** Mandatory, $182 fee. Preregistration for classes offered. Held prior to start of semester. **Housing:** Guaranteed on-campus for all undergraduates. Coed dorms, apartments, substance-free housing available. $300 nonrefundable deposit, deadline 5/1. Alcohol and Drug Free Dorm. **Activities:** Bands, choral groups, dance, drama, film society, international student organizations, literary magazine, music ensembles, musical theater, radio station, student government, student newspaper, behavioral science club, Christian Fellowship Club, diversity committee, political awareness club, Little Brother/Little Sister, Habitat for Humanity, Native American club, Students Enriching and Responding Through Volunteer Efforts, earth awareness club.

**Athletics.** NCAA. **Intercollegiate:** Basketball, cross-country, lacrosse M, rugby, soccer, softball W, tennis. **Intramural:** Badminton, basketball, bowling, cross-country, football (non-tackle), golf, lacrosse, racquetball, rugby, soccer, softball, swimming, table tennis, tennis, volleyball, water polo, weight lifting. **Team name:** Badgers.

**Student services.** Adult student services, alcohol/substance abuse counseling, career counseling, services for economically disadvantaged, student employment services, financial aid counseling, health services, on-campus daycare, personal counseling, placement for graduates. **Physically disabled:** Services for visually, hearing impaired.

**Contact.** E-mail: jscadmissions@jsc.vsc.edu
Phone: (802) 635-1219 Toll-free number: (800) 635-2356 ext. 1
Fax: (802) 635-1230
Penny Howrigan, Associate Dean of Enrollment Services, Johnson State College, 337 College Hill, Johnson, VT 05656

## Lyndon State College
**Lyndonville, Vermont**
**www.lyndonstate.edu**

**CB member**
**CB code: 3767**

♦ Public 4-year liberal arts and teachers college
♦ Residential campus in small town
♦ 1,371 degree-seeking undergraduates: 12% part-time, 47% women
♦ 44 degree-seeking graduate students
♦ 89% of applicants admitted
♦ SAT or ACT with writing, application essay required
♦ 38% graduate within 6 years

**General.** Founded in 1911. Regionally accredited. **Degrees:** 174 bachelor's, 40 associate awarded; master's offered. **ROTC:** Air Force. **Location:** 10 miles from St. Johnsbury, 85 miles from Burlington. **Calendar:** Semester, limited summer session. **Full-time faculty:** 58 total; 91% have terminal degrees, 40% women. **Part-time faculty:** 109 total; 43% have terminal degrees, 2% minority, 44% women. **Class size:** 75% < 20, 25% 20-39, less than 1% 40-49. **Special facilities:** Meteorology laboratory, ropes course.

**Freshman class profile.** 1,171 applied, 1,039 admitted, 406 enrolled.

| Mid 50% test scores | | | |
|---|---|---|---|
| | | ACT composite: | 18-21 |
| SAT critical reading: | 400-510 | Return as sophomores: | 53% |
| SAT math: | 400-510 | Out-of-state: | 58% |
| SAT writing: | 400-500 | Live on campus: | 65% |

**Basis for selection.** High school courses and grades most important, then class rank (top half preferred), recommendations, and test scores. Interview recommended. **Learning Disabled:** Required to meet with our Learning Specialist.

**High school preparation.** Required and recommended units include English 4, mathematics 3-4, social studies 2, history 1, science 2-4 (laboratory 2) and foreign language 2. Physics and advanced mathematics for meteorology and computer science recommended.

**2007-2008 Annual costs.** Tuition/fees: $7,244; $15,428 out-of-state. New England Board of Higher Education rate for students from other New England states: 150% of Vermont resident tuition. Available to degree candidates in academic areas not offered by educational institutions in their home states. Room/board: $7,220. Books/supplies: $600. Personal expenses: $900.

**Financial aid. Non-need-based:** Scholarships awarded for academics, leadership.

**Application procedures. Admission:** Priority date 5/1; no deadline. $36 fee, may be waived for applicants with need. Application may be submitted online. Admission notification on a rolling basis beginning on or about 11/1. **Financial aid:** Priority date 2/1; no closing date. FAFSA required. Applicants notified on a rolling basis starting 4/1; must reply within 2 week(s) of notification.

**Academics. Special study options:** Accelerated study, combined bachelor's/graduate degree, cooperative education, double major, dual enrollment of high school students, honors, internships, liberal arts/career combination, student-designed major, study abroad, teacher certification program. **Credit/placement by examination:** AP, CLEP, IB. 60 credit hours maximum toward bachelor's degree. **Support services:** Learning center, reduced course load, remedial instruction, study skills assistance, tutoring, writing center.

**Majors. Business:** Accounting, business admin, entrepreneurial studies. **Communications:** General, journalism, radio/tv. **Communications technology:** General. **Computer sciences:** General. **Education:** General, early childhood, elementary, English, physical, science, social science, special. **English:** English lit. **Health:** Athletic training. **Interdisciplinary:** Biological/physical sciences. **Liberal arts:** Arts/sciences. **Math:** General. **Parks/recreation:** Facilities management. **Physical sciences:** Atmospheric science. **Psychology:** General. **Public administration:** Human services. **Social sciences:** General. **Visual/performing arts:** Graphic design.

**Most popular majors.** Business/marketing 16%, health sciences 9%, liberal arts 7%, psychology 21%, visual/performing arts 9%.

**Computing on campus.** 50 workstations in library, computer center. Dormitories wired for high-speed internet access and linked to campus network. Commuter students can connect to campus network. Online library, helpline available.

**Student life. Freshman orientation:** Mandatory. Preregistration for classes offered. Held weekend before classes start. **Housing:** Guaranteed on-campus for freshmen. Coed dorms, single-sex dorms, special housing for disabled, substance-free housing available. $100 deposit, deadline 5/1. All students under 23 years of age must live on campus for four full semesters unless residing with parents or must live within 45-mile commuting distance. **Activities:** Choral groups, dance, drama, radio station, student government, student newspaper, symphony orchestra, TV station, American Meteorological Society (student chapter), community service learning group.

**Athletics.** NAIA. **Intercollegiate:** Baseball M, basketball, cross-country, ice hockey, soccer, softball W, tennis. **Intramural:** Basketball, cross-country, handball, ice hockey, lacrosse, racquetball, rugby, soccer, softball, squash, swimming, table tennis, tennis, track and field, volleyball, water polo M, weight lifting. **Team name:** Hornets.

**Student services.** Alcohol/substance abuse counseling, career counseling, student employment services, financial aid counseling, health services, personal counseling, placement for graduates, veterans' counselor. **Physically disabled:** Services for visually, hearing impaired.

**Contact.** E-mail: admissions@lyndonstate.edu
Phone: (802) 626-6413 Toll-free number: (800) 225-1998
Fax: (802) 626-6335
Bernard Hartshorn, Associate Director of Admissions, Lyndon State College, 1001 College Road, Lyndonville, VT 05851

## Marlboro College
**Marlboro, Vermont**
**www.marlboro.edu**

**CB member**
**CB code: 3509**

♦ Private 4-year liberal arts college
♦ Residential campus in rural community
♦ 330 degree-seeking undergraduates: 4% part-time, 52% women
♦ 70% of applicants admitted
♦ Application essay required
♦ 50% graduate within 6 years

**General.** Founded in 1946. Regionally accredited. **Degrees:** 77 bachelor's awarded; master's offered. **Location:** 12 miles from Brattleboro, 70 miles from Albany, New York. **Calendar:** Semester. **Full-time faculty:** 40 total; 75% have terminal degrees, 8% minority, 48% women. **Part-time faculty:** 13 total; 69% have terminal degrees, 8% minority, 54% women. **Special facilities:** Aviary, observatory, darkroom, theater 3/4 round, robotics lab, DNA lab, nature preserve, organic campus farm.

**Freshman class profile.** 327 applied, 230 admitted, 66 enrolled.

| Mid 50% test scores | | Return as sophomores: | 75% |
|---|---|---|---|
| SAT critical reading: | 590-690 | Out-of-state: | 90% |
| SAT math: | 510-650 | Live on campus: | 98% |
| ACT composite: | 24-32 | | |

**Basis for selection.** Academic ability, intellectual potential, writing skills, demonstrated leadership qualities, and potential to offer contribution to college community most important considerations. SAT or ACT recommended. Selected applicants may be required to interview at discretion of admission committee. **Homeschooled:** Statement describing homeschool structure and mission, letter of recommendation (nonparent) required. Provide documentation of home school curriculum and projects. List of textbooks preferred. Writing sample required. **Learning Disabled:** Additional documentation may be required.

**High school preparation.** Recommended units include English 4, mathematics 3, social studies 2, history 2, science 3 (laboratory 3), foreign language 3 and academic electives 5. Advanced electives in area of interest and in performing and/or visual arts also recommended.

**2007-2008 Annual costs.** Tuition/fees: $30,680. Room/board: $8,860. Books/supplies: $800. Personal expenses: $400.

**2007-2008 Financial aid. Need-based:** 67% of total undergraduate aid awarded as scholarships/grants, 33% as loans/jobs. **Non-need-based:** Scholarships awarded for academics, leadership.

**Application procedures. Admission:** Priority date 1/15; deadline 2/15 (postmark date). $50 fee, may be waived for applicants with need. Application may be submitted online. Admission notification 4/15. Admission notification on a rolling basis beginning on or about 2/1. Must reply by May 1 or within 2 week(s) if notified thereafter. **Financial aid:** Closing date 3/1. FAFSA required. Applicants notified on a rolling basis starting 2/15; must reply by 5/1 or within 2 week(s) of notification.

**Academics.** Students self-design field of study, often interdisciplinary in nature. They work closely with faculty to determine concentration and have formal review in senior year by internal and external faculty. **Special study options:** Double major, dual enrollment of high school students, independent study, internships, student-designed major, study abroad. World Studies Program: opportunity to integrate study-abroad experience and/or internship in undergraduate course of study. **Credit/placement by examination:** AP, CLEP, IB, institutional tests. **Support services:** Learning center, reduced course load, study skills assistance, tutoring, writing center.

**Majors. Area/ethnic studies:** American, Asian, Central/Eastern European, East Asian, European, Latin American, Near/Middle Eastern, Russian/Slavic, South Asian, Southeast Asian, Western European. **Biology:** General, biochemistry, botany, cell/histology, ecology, genetics, molecular, plant physiology. **Computer sciences:** General, computer science. **Conservation:** General, environmental studies. **English:** American lit, British lit, composition, creative writing, English lit. **Foreign languages:** General, comparative lit, linguistics, Spanish, translation. **History:** General. **Interdisciplinary:** Biological/physical sciences, global studies, math/computer science, peace/conflict. **Legal studies:** Prelaw. **Liberal arts:** Arts/sciences. **Math:** General. **Philosophy/religion:** Philosophy, religion. **Physical sciences:** Astronomy, chemistry, organic chemistry, physics, theoretical physics. **Psychology:** General. **Social sciences:** General, anthropology, economics, political science, sociology. **Visual/performing arts:** General, art, art history/conservation, ceramics, cinematography, dance, dramatic, drawing, film/cinema, music history, painting, photography, play/screenwriting, sculpture, studio arts, theater design, theater history.

**Computing on campus.** 45 workstations in dormitories, library, computer center. Dormitories wired for high-speed internet access and linked to campus network. Commuter students can connect to campus network. Online library, helpline, student web hosting, wireless network available.

**Student life. Freshman orientation:** Mandatory. 5-day program in late August, option to go on pre-orientation outdoor trips during week prior to on-campus orientation and student enrollment. **Policies:** Self-governing community based on old-fashioned, historical New England-style town meeting. Students, faculty, and staff have equal vote. Elected community court enforces bylaws. **Housing:** Guaranteed on-campus for freshmen. Coed dorms, single-sex dorms, apartments, substance-free housing available. $300 nonrefundable deposit, deadline 5/1. **Activities:** Dance, drama, film society,

literary magazine, music ensembles, musical theater, student government, student newspaper, Amnesty International, animal rights, gay/lesbian and bisexual group, Committee on Environmental Quality, fire and safety commission.

**Athletics. Intercollegiate:** Soccer. **Intramural:** Basketball, fencing, soccer, softball, swimming, table tennis, volleyball. **Team name:** Fighting Dead Trees.

**Student services.** Alcohol/substance abuse counseling, career counseling, financial aid counseling, health services, personal counseling. **Physically disabled:** Services for visually impaired.

**Contact.** E-mail: admissions@marlboro.edu
Phone: (802) 258-9236 Toll-free number: (800) 343-0049
Fax: (802) 451-7555
Alan Young, Dean of Enrollment and Financial Aid, Marlboro College, PO Box A, Marlboro, VT 05344-0300

## Middlebury College
**Middlebury, Vermont**
**www.middlebury.edu**

**CB member**
**CB code: 3526**

- Private 4-year liberal arts college
- Residential campus in small town
- 2,475 degree-seeking undergraduates: 1% part-time, 51% women, 3% African American, 8% Asian American, 6% Hispanic American, 10% international
- 21% of applicants admitted
- SAT and SAT Subject Tests or ACT (ACT writing optional), application essay required
- 94% graduate within 6 years

**General.** Founded in 1800. Regionally accredited. Affiliated with Monterey Institute of International Studies. **Degrees:** 648 bachelor's awarded; master's, doctoral offered. **ROTC:** Army. **Location:** 200 miles from Boston, 250 miles from New York City. **Calendar:** 4-1-4, limited summer session. **Full-time faculty:** 249 total; 97% have terminal degrees, 12% minority, 38% women. **Part-time faculty:** 56 total; 75% have terminal degrees, 7% minority, 45% women. **Class size:** 71% < 20, 20% 20-39, 5% 40-49, 4% 50-99. **Special facilities:** Observatory, fine arts center, downhill and cross country ski areas, interactive language laboratories, 18-hole golf course.

**Freshman class profile.** 7,180 applied, 1,479 admitted, 644 enrolled.

| Mid 50% test scores | | Rank in top quarter: | 97% |
|---|---|---|---|
| SAT critical reading: | 650-750 | Rank in top tenth: | 82% |
| SAT math: | 650-740 | Out-of-state: | 94% |
| SAT writing: | 650-730 | Live on campus: | 100% |
| ACT composite: | 29-33 | International: | 10% |

**Basis for selection.** School record most important (including course selection and course load), followed by class rank, extracurricular activities, letters of recommendation and test scores. Requirement may be met by submitting ACT, SAT, or 3 exams in different areas of study, which may be selected from SAT Subject Tests, AP exams, or International Baccalaureate exams.

**High school preparation.** Recommended units include English 4, mathematics 4, social studies 3, science 3 (laboratory 3) and foreign language 4. Music, art, or drama recommended.

**2007-2008 Annual costs.** Comprehensive fee: $46,910. Books/supplies: $750. Personal expenses: $1,000.

**2006-2007 Financial aid.** All financial aid based on need. 333 full-time freshmen applied for aid; 255 were judged to have need; 255 of these received aid. Average need met was 100%. Average scholarship/grant was $29,097; average loan $3,386. 88% of total undergraduate aid awarded as scholarships/grants, 12% as loans/jobs. **Additional information:** College maintains need-blind admissions policy and meets full demonstrated financial need of students who qualify for admission, to degree resources permit.

**Application procedures. Admission:** Closing date 1/1 (postmark date). $65 fee, may be waived for applicants with need. Application may be submitted online. Admission notification 4/1. Must reply by 5/1. **Financial aid:** Priority date 11/15, closing date 1/1. FAFSA, institutional form, CSS PROFILE required. Applicants notified by 4/1; must reply by 5/1.

**Academics. Special study options:** Accelerated study, double major, exchange student, honors, independent study, internships, semester at sea, student-designed major, study abroad, teacher certification program, Washington semester. Williams College-Mystic Seaport Program in American Maritime Studies, Oxford University summer program, independent scholar program, exchange programs with Berea College and Swarthmore College, 3-year international major. **Credit/placement by examination:** AP, CLEP, IB, institutional tests. **Support services:** Learning center, pre-admission summer program, reduced course load, study skills assistance, tutoring, writing center.

**Majors. Area/ethnic studies:** African, American, Central/Eastern European, East Asian, European, Latin American, Near/Middle Eastern, Russian/Slavic, Southeast Asian, women's. **Biology:** General, biochemistry, molecular. **Computer sciences:** Computer science. **Conservation:** Environmental studies. **English:** American lit, English lit. **Foreign languages:** Chinese, classics, French, German, Italian, Japanese, Russian, Spanish. **History:** General. **Interdisciplinary:** Neuroscience. **Liberal arts:** Arts/sciences. **Math:** General. **Philosophy/religion:** Philosophy, religion. **Physical sciences:** Chemistry, geology, physics. **Psychology:** General. **Social sciences:** Economics, geography, international relations, political science, sociology. **Visual/performing arts:** Art history/conservation, cinematography, dance, dramatic, studio arts.

**Most popular majors.** Area/ethnic studies 8%, English 11%, foreign language 6%, history 11%, interdisciplinary studies 8%, natural resources/environmental science 7%, psychology 6%, social sciences 26%.

**Computing on campus.** 494 workstations in dormitories, library, computer center, student center. Dormitories wired for high-speed internet access and linked to campus network. Commuter students can connect to campus network. Online course registration, online library, helpline, repair service, student web hosting, wireless network available.

**Student life. Freshman orientation:** Mandatory. Elective portion of orientation carries cost of $150. **Housing:** Guaranteed on-campus for all undergraduates. Coed dorms, special housing for disabled, apartments, substance-free housing available. $200 deposit, deadline 5/1. Multicultural, environmental, foreign language, and 5 social houses available. Commons System organizes residence halls into 5 groups, each with own budget, government, faculty, and staff associates. **Activities:** Jazz band, choral groups, dance, drama, film society, international student organizations, literary magazine, music ensembles, musical theater, radio station, student government, student newspaper, symphony orchestra, African-American Alliance, Alianza Latinoamerica y Caribena, Asian students organization, environmental quality, Hillel, Gay Lesbian Bisexual Alliance, mountain club, volunteer service program, women's organization.

**Athletics.** NCAA. **Intercollegiate:** Baseball M, basketball, cross-country, diving, field hockey W, football (tackle) M, golf, ice hockey, lacrosse, skiing, soccer, softball W, squash W, swimming, tennis, track and field, volleyball W. **Intramural:** Badminton, basketball, cross-country, diving, football (non-tackle), golf, ice hockey, lacrosse, skiing, soccer, softball, squash W, swimming, table tennis, tennis, triathlon, volleyball. **Team name:** Panthers.

**Student services.** Alcohol/substance abuse counseling, campus ministries, career counseling, student employment services, financial aid counseling, health services, minority student services, personal counseling, placement for graduates, women's services. **Physically disabled:** Services for visually, speech, hearing impaired.

**Contact.** E-mail: admissions@middlebury.edu
Phone: (802) 443-3000 Fax: (802) 443-0258
Robert Clagett, Dean of Admissions, Middlebury College, The Emma Willard House, Middlebury, VT 05753-6002

## Norwich University
**Northfield, Vermont**
www.norwich.edu

**CB member**
**CB code: 3669**

♦ Private 4-year university and military college
♦ Residential campus in small town
♦ 1,995 degree-seeking undergraduates
♦ 58% of applicants admitted
♦ SAT or ACT (ACT writing optional) required

**General.** Founded in 1819. Regionally accredited. Oldest private military college in U.S. Adult programs, baccalaureate and masters, are self-designed, individually mentored programs. Both military and civilian students accepted. **Degrees:** 355 bachelor's awarded; master's offered. **ROTC:** Army, Naval, Air Force. **Location:** 50 miles from Burlington, 180 miles from Boston. **Calendar:** Semester, limited summer session. **Full-time faculty:** 125 total. **Part-time faculty:** 137 total. **Special facilities:** Museum.

**Freshman class profile.** 2,941 applied, 1,703 admitted, 668 enrolled.

| Mid 50% test scores | | ACT composite: | 19-24 |
|---|---|---|---|
| SAT critical reading: | 470-600 | Out-of-state: | 80% |
| SAT math: | 480-600 | Live on campus: | 98% |

**Basis for selection.** High school record, recommendations, activities, honors, awards, test scores important. Class rank considered in admissions decisions and will be criterion for financial aid awarding.

**High school preparation.** 18 units recommended. Recommended units include English 4, mathematics 3, social studies 2, science 1 and foreign language 2.

**2007-2008 Annual costs.** Tuition/fees: $24,430. Military students pay an additional $1,500 per year for cadet uniform for first and second years. Room/board: $8,522. Books/supplies: $500. Personal expenses: $400.

**Financial aid. Non-need-based:** Scholarships awarded for academics, leadership, music/drama, ROTC. **Additional information:** Winners of ROTC scholarships receive full room and board; must maintain 2.75 GPA. Renewable up to 4 years.

**Application procedures. Admission:** Priority date 5/1; no deadline. $35 fee, may be waived for applicants with need. Application may be submitted online. Admission notification on a rolling basis beginning on or about 11/30. Must reply by May 1 or within 3 week(s) if notified thereafter. **Financial aid:** Priority date 3/1; no closing date. FAFSA, institutional form, CSS PROFILE required. Applicants notified on a rolling basis starting 12/15.

**Academics. Special study options:** Accelerated study, combined bachelor's/graduate degree, distance learning, double major, external degree, honors, independent study, internships, liberal arts/career combination, student-designed major, study abroad, teacher certification program. **Credit/placement by examination:** AP, CLEP, institutional tests. **Support services:** Learning center, pre-admission summer program, reduced course load, remedial instruction, tutoring.

**Majors. Biology:** General, biochemistry, biomedical sciences. **Business:** Accounting, business admin. **Communications:** General. **Computer sciences:** General, computer science. **Conservation:** General. **Education:** Physical. **Engineering:** Civil, electrical, mechanical. **English:** English lit. **Health:** Athletic training. **History:** General. **Interdisciplinary:** Peace/conflict. **Legal studies:** Prelaw. **Liberal arts:** Arts/sciences. **Math:** General. **Physical sciences:** Chemistry, geology, physics. **Protective services:** Criminal justice. **Psychology:** General. **Social sciences:** Economics, international relations, political science.

**Computing on campus.** 150 workstations in library, computer center. Dormitories linked to campus network. Commuter students can connect to campus network. Helpline available.

**Student life. Freshman orientation:** Available, $10 fee. Preregistration for classes offered. Wednesday through Sunday, including 1-day cruise dinner included. **Housing:** Guaranteed on-campus for all undergraduates. Coed dorms available. $250 deposit, deadline 5/1. ROTC participants must live in dormitories. **Activities:** Bands, choral groups, drama, international student organizations, literary magazine, music ensembles, musical theater, radio station, student government, student newspaper, symphony orchestra, Arnold Air Society, Special Operations Company Association of the United States Army, Norwich University Volunteer Organization, Norwich Christian Fellowship, ambulance rescue squad, Young Republicans, Square and Compass.

**Athletics.** NCAA. **Intercollegiate:** Baseball M, basketball, cross-country, diving, football (tackle) M, golf, ice hockey M, lacrosse, rifle, rugby W, soccer, softball W, swimming, tennis, track and field, wrestling M. **Intramural:** Basketball, cross-country, fencing, football (tackle) M, ice hockey M, lacrosse M, racquetball, skiing, soccer, softball, tennis, track and field, volleyball. **Team name:** Cadets.

**Student services.** Adult student services, career counseling, student employment services, health services, personal counseling, placement for graduates, veterans' counselor.

**Contact.** E-mail: nuadm@norwich.edu
Phone: (802) 485-2002 Toll-free number: (800) 468-6679
Fax: (802) 485-2002
Karen McGrath, Dean of Enrollment, Norwich University, 158 Harmon Drive, Northfield, VT 05663

## St. Michael's College
**Colchester, Vermont**
www.smcvt.edu

**CB member**
**CB code: 3757**

♦ Private 4-year liberal arts college affiliated with Roman Catholic Church
♦ Residential campus in large town

- 1,980 degree-seeking undergraduates: 1% part-time, 53% women, 1% African American, 1% Asian American, 1% Hispanic American, 1% international
- 280 degree-seeking graduate students
- 69% of applicants admitted
- SAT or ACT with writing, application essay required
- 80% graduate within 6 years; 17% enter graduate study

**General.** Founded in 1904. Regionally accredited. **Degrees:** 441 bachelor's awarded; master's offered. **ROTC:** Army, Air Force. **Location:** 3 miles from Burlington, 95 miles from Montreal, Canada. **Calendar:** Semester, limited summer session. **Full-time faculty:** 154 total; 85% have terminal degrees, 7% minority, 44% women. **Part-time faculty:** 58 total; 38% have terminal degrees, 3% minority, 53% women. **Class size:** 57% < 20, 41% 20-39, 1% 40-49, 1% 50-99, less than 1% >100. **Special facilities:** Observatory.

**Freshman class profile.** 3,504 applied, 2,423 admitted, 532 enrolled.

| Mid 50% test scores | | | |
|---|---|---|---|
| SAT critical reading: | 520-620 | Rank in top quarter: | 50% |
| SAT math: | 520-610 | Rank in top tenth: | 23% |
| SAT writing: | 520-620 | End year in good standing: | 91% |
| ACT composite: | 22-26 | Return as sophomores: | 90% |
| GPA 3.50 or higher: | 48% | Out-of-state: | 77% |
| GPA 3.0-3.49: | 29% | Live on campus: | 99% |
| GPA 2.0-2.99: | 23% | International: | 1% |

**Basis for selection.** Test scores, curriculum important. Essay, recommendations, and activities also important. College administers language placement tests during academic orientation prior to beginning of each semester. **Homeschooled:** Statement describing homeschool structure and mission, transcript of courses and grades, state high school equivalency certificate required. Standardized tests (SAT or ACT) take on additional emphasis.

**High school preparation.** 16 units required; 20 recommended. Required and recommended units include English 4, mathematics 3-4, social studies 3-4, science 3-4 (laboratory 2-3) and foreign language 3-4. Physics, mathematics, chemistry, biology emphasized for science applicants. History courses fulfill social studies requirement.

**2008-2009 Annual costs.** Tuition/fees: $31,940. Room/board: $7,960. Books/supplies: $1,200. Personal expenses: $310.

**2007-2008 Financial aid. Need-based:** 390 full-time freshmen applied for aid; 296 were judged to have need; 296 of these received aid. Average need met was 75%. Average scholarship/grant was $13,095; average loan $4,652. 65% of total undergraduate aid awarded as scholarships/grants, 35% as loans/jobs. **Non-need-based:** Awarded to 581 full-time undergraduates, including 195 freshmen. Scholarships awarded for academics, athletics, ROTC.

**Application procedures. Admission:** Priority date 11/1; deadline 2/1 (postmark date). $50 fee, may be waived for applicants with need. Application may be submitted online. Admission notification 4/1. Must reply by May 1 or within 2 week(s) if notified thereafter. 2 Early Action deadlines: November 1 and December 1. Corresponding Early Action notification of admission decision dates January 1 and February 1. **Financial aid:** Priority date 3/15; no closing date. FAFSA required. CSS PROFILE should be submitted by students who apply for early action and want early estimate on aid. Applicants notified on a rolling basis starting 2/1; must reply by 5/1 or within 2 week(s) of notification.

**Academics.** All students must achieve second-language proficiency. **Special study options:** Combined bachelor's/graduate degree, cross-registration, double major, ESL, honors, independent study, internships, semester at sea, student-designed major, study abroad, teacher certification program, Washington semester. 3-2 engineering with University of Vermont and Clarkson University, 4-1 MBA with Clarkson University, international exchange student program. **Credit/placement by examination:** AP, CLEP, IB, institutional tests. 30 credit hours maximum toward bachelor's degree. **Support services:** Learning center, reduced course load, study skills assistance, tutoring, writing center.

**Majors. Area/ethnic studies:** American. **Biology:** General, biochemistry. **Business:** Accounting, business admin. **Communications:** Journalism. **Computer sciences:** Computer science, information systems. **Conservation:** Environmental science. **Education:** Art, elementary. **Engineering:** General. **English:** English lit. **Foreign languages:** General, classics, French, Latin, Spanish. **History:** General. **Math:** General. **Philosophy/religion:** Philosophy, religion. **Physical sciences:** General, chemistry, physics. **Psychology:** General. **Social sciences:** Anthropology, economics, political science, sociology. **Visual/performing arts:** Art, dramatic, studio arts. **Other:** Gender Studies.

**Most popular majors.** Biology 6%, business/marketing 25%, English 11%, psychology 13%, social sciences 14%.

**Computing on campus.** 375 workstations in dormitories, library, computer center, student center. Dormitories wired for high-speed internet access and linked to campus network. Commuter students can connect to campus network. Online course registration, online library, helpline, student web hosting, wireless network available.

**Student life. Freshman orientation:** Mandatory. Preregistration for classes offered. One-day academic orientation held in July. Off-campus weekend experience during summer offered to all new students. **Policies:** Limited number of parking permits available for first-time, first-year students to have cars on campus during spring semester. **Housing:** Guaranteed on-campus for all undergraduates. Coed dorms, single-sex dorms, special housing for disabled, apartments, substance-free housing available. $500 nonrefundable deposit, deadline 5/1. Theme housing available. **Activities:** Bands, campus ministries, choral groups, dance, drama, international student organizations, literary magazine, music ensembles, musical theater, radio station, student government, student newspaper, fire and rescue squad, Mobilization of Volunteer Efforts, Martin Luther King Society, diversity coalition, political science club, Alianza Society, Peace and Justice, Student Global AIDS Campaign.

**Athletics.** NCAA. **Intercollegiate:** Baseball M, basketball, cross-country, diving, field hockey W, golf M, ice hockey, lacrosse, skiing, soccer, softball W, swimming, tennis, volleyball W. **Intramural:** Badminton, basketball, bowling, football (non-tackle), ice hockey, racquetball, soccer, softball, squash, table tennis, volleyball. **Team name:** Purple Knights.

**Student services.** Alcohol/substance abuse counseling, campus ministries, career counseling, student employment services, financial aid counseling, health services, minority student services, on-campus daycare, personal counseling, placement for graduates, women's services. **Physically disabled:** Services for visually, speech, hearing impaired.

**Contact.** E-mail: admission@smcvt.edu
Phone: (802) 654-3000 Toll-free number: (800) 762-8000
Fax: (802) 654-2906
Jacqueline Murphy, Director of Admissions, St. Michael's College, One Winooski Park, Colchester, VT 05439

## Southern Vermont College
**Bennington, Vermont**
**www.svc.edu**                    **CB code: 3796**

- Private 4-year liberal arts college
- Residential campus in large town
- 406 degree-seeking undergraduates: 17% part-time, 68% women, 6% African American, 2% Asian American, 2% Hispanic American, 2% international
- 65% of applicants admitted
- SAT or ACT with writing, application essay required
- 47% graduate within 6 years

**General.** Founded in 1926. Regionally accredited. **Degrees:** 52 bachelor's, 31 associate awarded. **Location:** 40 miles from Albany, New York, 90 miles from Springfield, Massachusetts. **Calendar:** Semester, limited summer session. **Full-time faculty:** 16 total. **Part-time faculty:** 15 total. **Class size:** 70% < 20, 30% 20-39. **Special facilities:** 25 miles of trails, 2 natural ponds, 27-room Edwardian mansion.

**Freshman class profile.** 566 applied, 368 admitted, 149 enrolled.

| Mid 50% test scores | | | |
|---|---|---|---|
| SAT critical reading: | 420-500 | Rank in top quarter: | 4% |
| SAT math: | 400-480 | End year in good standing: | 85% |
| ACT composite: | 14-21 | Return as sophomores: | 59% |
| GPA 3.50 or higher: | 2% | Out-of-state: | 72% |
| GPA 3.0-3.49: | 30% | Live on campus: | 83% |
| GPA 2.0-2.99: | 67% | International: | 3% |

**Basis for selection.** Potential for academic achievement most important. Test scores, interview, personal references important. None of admissions criteria intended as absolute cut-offs, but students failing to meet these standards must demonstrate potential for academic success in other ways. Interview strongly recommended.

**High school preparation.** Required and recommended units include English 4, mathematics 3, social studies 4, history 4, science 4, foreign language 2 and academic electives 4.

**2008-2009 Annual costs.** Tuition/fees (projected): $16,800. Health insurance, if applicable, $650 per year. Room/board: $8,100.

**Financial aid. Non-need-based:** Scholarships awarded for academics, leadership.

**Application procedures. Admission:** No deadline. $30 fee, may be waived for applicants with need. Application may be submitted online. Admission notification on a rolling basis. Must reply by May 1 or within 2 week(s) if notified thereafter. High school seniors may take up to six credits per semester. They must fill out a contract and meet all other requirements. **Financial aid:** No deadline. FAFSA, institutional form required. Applicants notified on a rolling basis.

**Academics.** Students can receive free walk-in tutoring, individualized tutoring, study group sessions, workshops for skill review, proofreading, and note-taking. Disabilities Support Program. **Special study options:** Combined bachelor's/graduate degree, double major, independent study, internships, liberal arts/career combination. **Credit/placement by examination:** CLEP, SAT, ACT. **Support services:** Learning center, reduced course load, remedial instruction, study skills assistance, tutoring, writing center.

**Majors. Business:** Business admin, nonprofit/public. **Communications:** General. **English:** Creative writing, English lit. **Health:** Nursing (RN). **Legal studies:** Prelaw. **Liberal arts:** Arts/sciences. **Protective services:** Police science. **Psychology:** General. **Other:** History and Politics, Professional Studies.

**Most popular majors.** Business/marketing 27%, communications/journalism 12%, English 6%, health sciences 14%, liberal arts 6%, psychology 10%, security/protective services 14%.

**Computing on campus.** 43 workstations in library, computer center. Dormitories wired for high-speed internet access and linked to campus network. Commuter students can connect to campus network. Online library, repair service, student web hosting, wireless network available.

**Student life. Freshman orientation:** Mandatory. 4-day experience held with 3-part theme: academics, student life, outdoor recreation. Outdoor component parallels what students encounter during first semester: learning to adapt to unfamiliar environment. **Housing:** Guaranteed on-campus for freshmen. Coed dorms, substance-free housing available. $200 deposit. Quiet, substance-free, non-smoking, and freshman residence halls available. **Activities:** Drama, international student organizations, literary magazine, radio station, student government, student newspaper, criminal justice club, Everyone's Earth, community action program.

**Athletics.** NCAA. **Intercollegiate:** Baseball M, basketball, cross-country, rugby, soccer, softball W, volleyball, wrestling M. **Intramural:** Basketball, ice hockey, skiing, soccer, tennis, volleyball. **Team name:** Mountaineers.

**Student services.** Adult student services, alcohol/substance abuse counseling, career counseling, student employment services, financial aid counseling, health services, personal counseling, placement for graduates. **Physically disabled:** Services for visually, hearing impaired.

**Contact.** E-mail: admis@svc.edu
Phone: (802) 447-6304 Toll-free number: (800) 378-2782
Fax: (802) 447-4695
Joel Wincowski, Dean of Enrollment Management, Southern Vermont College, 982 Mansion Drive, Bennington, VT 05201

---

## Sterling College
**Craftsbury Common, Vermont**
www.sterlingcollege.edu

**CB member**
**CB code: 3752**

- Private 4-year agricultural and liberal arts college
- Residential campus in rural community
- 104 degree-seeking undergraduates: 2% part-time, 45% women, 2% Hispanic American
- 76% of applicants admitted
- Application essay required
- 56% graduate within 6 years; 30% enter graduate study

**General.** Founded in 1958. Regionally accredited. Global Field Studies in Nepal, Labrador, Scotland, Newfoundland, Iceland, Canada, Japan, India, Belize, Mexico, and Scandinavian countries. Member of National Work Colleges Consortium. Special accreditation through the Association of Experiential Educators. **Degrees:** 16 bachelor's, 12 associate awarded. **Location:** 40 miles from Montpelier, 70 miles from Burlington. **Calendar:** Semester, limited summer session. **Full-time faculty:** 14 total; 29% have terminal degrees, 50% women. **Part-time faculty:** 19 total; 32% have terminal degrees, 5% minority, 74% women. **Class size:** 98% < 20, 2% 20-39. **Special facilities:** Managed woodlots, livestock farm, extensive cross-country ski trails, back-country recreation, solar and wind powered barns, organic gardens, greenhouse, 32-foot climbing wall, low and high ropes challenge course, sugar house, 350-acre educational Bear Swamp (boreal forest and muskeg).

**Freshman class profile.** 97 applied, 74 admitted, 30 enrolled.

| | | | |
|---|---|---|---|
| GPA 3.50 or higher: | 20% | End year in good standing: | 100% |
| GPA 3.0-3.49: | 30% | Return as sophomores: | 67% |
| GPA 2.0-2.99: | 45% | Out-of-state: | 77% |
| Rank in top quarter: | 40% | Live on campus: | 97% |
| Rank in top tenth: | 10% | | |

**Basis for selection.** Demonstrated interest in programs, motivation, interview, academic record, recommendations important; test scores considered if submitted. Admissions interview is highly recommended. **Homeschooled:** Transcript of courses and grades required. Portfolio of educational and life experience may be submitted in lieu of diploma or equivalency. Students must meet home school requirements for their particular state of residence.

**High school preparation.** Required and recommended units include English 4, mathematics 3-4, social studies 2, history 2, science 2-3 (laboratory 2-3) and foreign language 2.

**2008-2009 Annual costs.** Tuition/fees: $21,655. Students receive $1,550 tuition and book credit in exchange for work done on campus. Room/board: $7,192. Books/supplies: $750. Personal expenses: $600.

**Financial aid. Non-need-based:** Scholarships awarded for academics, leadership, state residency.

**Application procedures. Admission:** Priority date 2/15; deadline 4/1 (postmark date). $35 fee, may be waived for applicants with need. Application may be submitted online. Admission notification 4/1. Must reply by May 1 or within 2 week(s) if notified thereafter. **Financial aid:** Priority date 3/15; no closing date. FAFSA, institutional form required. Applicants notified on a rolling basis starting 2/1; must reply by 5/1 or within 2 week(s) of notification.

**Academics. Special study options:** Double major, dual enrollment of high school students, exchange student, independent study, internships, liberal arts/career combination, semester at sea, student-designed major, study abroad, urban semester. 2-week Global Field Studies. **Credit/placement by examination:** AP, CLEP, institutional tests. **Support services:** Learning center, reduced course load, remedial instruction, study skills assistance, tutoring, writing center.

**Majors. Agriculture:** General. **Biology:** Conservation, ecology, environmental, wildlife. **Conservation:** General, environmental studies, forest management, forestry, water/wetlands/marine, wildlife. **Education:** Agricultural, curriculum. **Liberal arts:** Arts/sciences. **Parks/recreation:** General. **Other:** Circumpolar studies/Northern studies, Environmental education, Sustainable agriculture.

**Most popular majors.** Agriculture 19%, area/ethnic studies 25%, biology 19%, liberal arts 25%, parks/recreation 12%.

**Computing on campus.** 20 workstations in library, computer center, student center. Dormitories wired for high-speed internet access and linked to campus network. Commuter students can connect to campus network. Online library, helpline, repair service, wireless network available.

**Student life. Freshman orientation:** Mandatory. All entering freshmen participate in series of adventure challenge and academic activities. **Housing:** Guaranteed on-campus for all undergraduates. Coed dorms, apartments, substance-free housing available. Pets allowed in dorm rooms. **Activities:** Literary magazine, music ensembles, student government.

**Athletics. Intramural:** Archery, badminton, baseball, basketball, bowling, boxing, cross-country, equestrian, fencing, ice hockey, rifle, skiing, soccer, softball, swimming, table tennis, volleyball, weight lifting.

**Student services.** Adult student services, alcohol/substance abuse counseling, career counseling, student employment services, financial aid counseling, health services, personal counseling, placement for graduates, veterans' counselor.

**Contact.** E-mail: admissions@sterlingcollege.edu
Phone: (802) 586-7711 ext. 100 Toll-free number: (800) 648-3591
Fax: (802) 586-2596
Gwyn Harris, Director of Admissions, Sterling College, PO Box 72, Craftsbury Common, VT 05827-0072

---

## University of Vermont
**Burlington, Vermont**
www.uvm.edu

**CB member**
**CB code: 3920**

- Public 4-year university
- Residential campus in large town

- 9,454 degree-seeking undergraduates: 3% part-time, 55% women, 1% African American, 2% Asian American, 2% Hispanic American
- 1,705 degree-seeking graduate students
- 70% of applicants admitted
- SAT or ACT with writing, application essay required
- 72% graduate within 6 years; 21% enter graduate study

**General.** Founded in 1791. Regionally accredited. **Degrees:** 1,913 bachelor's awarded; master's, doctoral, first professional offered. **ROTC:** Army. **Location:** 225 miles from Boston, 100 miles from Montreal. **Calendar:** Semester, extensive summer session. **Full-time faculty:** 586 total; 84% have terminal degrees, 12% minority, 41% women. **Part-time faculty:** 183 total; 36% have terminal degrees, 5% minority, 57% women. **Class size:** 50% < 20, 33% 20-39, 5% 40-49, 6% 50-99, 5% >100. **Special facilities:** Horse farm, dairy farm, geology museum, natural areas, science center, research vessel on Lake Champlain, ecosystem science laboratory on Lake Champlain, art and anthropology museum, maple research facility.

**Freshman class profile.** 18,814 applied, 13,079 admitted, 2,450 enrolled.

| Mid 50% test scores | | | |
|---|---|---|---|
| SAT critical reading: | 540-630 | **Rank in top tenth:** | 23% |
| SAT math: | 540-640 | **End year in good standing:** | 88% |
| SAT writing: | 530-630 | **Return as sophomores:** | 86% |
| ACT composite: | 23-28 | **Out-of-state:** | 74% |
| **Rank in top quarter:** | 61% | **Live on campus:** | 98% |

**Basis for selection.** School achievement record of primary importance; test scores also important. Essay, extracurricular activities considered. Letter of recommendation required. Special consideration to Vermont residents, children of alumni, minority students, and foreign students. Informational interview recommended. Music applicants must present audition tape or CD. **Homeschooled:** Transcript of courses and grades, state high school equivalency certificate, letter of recommendation (nonparent) required. Applicants must provide proof of completion of minimum entrance requirements and completion of GED.

**High school preparation.** 16 units required. Required units include English 4, mathematics 3, social studies 3, science 2 (laboratory 1) and foreign language 2. Additional mathematics and/or science units required in engineering, business, health science programs.

**2007-2008 Annual costs.** Tuition/fees: $12,054; $27,938 out-of-state. Additional $24 fee for on-campus students. Room/board: $8,024. Books/supplies: $936. Personal expenses: $1,136.

**2006-2007 Financial aid. Need-based:** 1,574 full-time freshmen applied for aid; 1,199 were judged to have need; 1,195 of these received aid. Average need met was 80%. Average scholarship/grant was $11,313; average loan $5,764. 66% of total undergraduate aid awarded as scholarships/grants, 34% as loans/jobs. **Non-need-based:** Awarded to 1,931 full-time undergraduates, including 766 freshmen. Scholarships awarded for academics, art, athletics, ROTC.

**Application procedures. Admission:** Closing date 1/15 (postmark date). $45 fee, may be waived for applicants with need. Application may be submitted online. Admission notification 3/31. Must reply by May 1 or within 3 week(s) if notified thereafter. Waitlist admits have 2 days to reply. Early action candidates may have final decision deferred until completion of fall semester review. **Financial aid:** Priority date 2/10; no closing date. FAFSA required. Applicants notified on a rolling basis starting 3/15; must reply within 4 week(s) of notification.

**Academics. Special study options:** Combined bachelor's/graduate degree, cooperative education, distance learning, double major, dual enrollment of high school students, exchange student, honors, independent study, internships, liberal arts/career combination, student-designed major, study abroad, teacher certification program, Washington semester. Evening university option in several programs, limited English as a second language. **Credit/placement by examination:** AP, CLEP, IB, institutional tests. Half of major and half of minor requirements must be completed in residence. **Support services:** Learning center, pre-admission summer program, reduced course load, study skills assistance, tutoring, writing center.

**Honors college/program.** All first-year applicants automatically considered for Honors College. Admission considerations include excellent SAT and/or ACT scores, high school rank, challenging high school course work, and an ability to overcome obstacles; about 100 admitted each year.

**Majors. Agriculture:** General, agronomy, animal sciences, horticultural science. **Area/ethnic studies:** Asian, Canadian, European, Italian, Latin American, Russian/Slavic, women's. **Biology:** General, biochemistry, botany, microbiology, molecular, wildlife, zoology. **Business:** Business admin, entrepreneurial studies. **Computer sciences:** Computer science, systems analysis.

**Conservation:** General, environmental science, environmental studies, forestry. **Education:** General, art, early childhood, early childhood special, elementary, English, family/consumer sciences, foreign languages, mathematics, middle, music, physical, science, secondary, social studies. **Engineering:** Civil, electrical, environmental, industrial, mechanical. **English:** English lit. **Family/consumer sciences:** Family studies. **Foreign languages:** Ancient Greek, Chinese, classics, French, German, Japanese, Latin, Russian, Spanish. **Health:** Athletic training, clinical lab science, communication disorders, dietetics, medical radiologic technology/radiation therapy, nuclear medical technology, nursing (RN). **History:** General. **Interdisciplinary:** Nutrition sciences. **Liberal arts:** Arts/sciences. **Math:** General, statistics. **Parks/recreation:** Exercise sciences, facilities management. **Philosophy/religion:** Philosophy, religion. **Physical sciences:** Chemistry, geology, physics. **Psychology:** General. **Public administration:** Social work. **Social sciences:** Anthropology, economics, geography, international economic development, political science, sociology. **Visual/performing arts:** Art history/conservation, dramatic, film/cinema, music performance, studio arts.

**Most popular majors.** Biology 6%, business/marketing 11%, education 8%, English 6%, health sciences 7%, natural resources/environmental science 7%, psychology 8%, social sciences 17%.

**Computing on campus.** 685 workstations in dormitories, library, computer center, student center. Dormitories wired for high-speed internet access and linked to campus network. Commuter students can connect to campus network. Online course registration, online library, helpline, repair service, wireless network available.

**Student life. Freshman orientation:** Mandatory. Preregistration for classes offered. 2-day sessions offered at various times in June. For those who cannot attend in June, a session is offered prior to the start of the fall term in August. **Policies:** Student code of conduct. **Housing:** Guaranteed on-campus for freshmen. Coed dorms, apartments, fraternity/sorority housing, substance-free housing available. **Activities:** Bands, campus ministries, choral groups, dance, drama, film society, international student organizations, literary magazine, music ensembles, musical theater, radio station, student government, student newspaper, TV station, Hillel, black student union, Asian American student union, gay/lesbian/bisexual/transgender alliance, Alianza Latina, Catholic center, Volunteers in Action, Vermont student environmental program.

**Athletics.** NCAA. **Intercollegiate:** Baseball M, basketball, cross-country, diving W, field hockey W, ice hockey, lacrosse, skiing, soccer, softball W, swimming W, track and field. **Intramural:** Basketball, bowling, cricket, football (non-tackle), football (tackle), ice hockey, racquetball, soccer, softball, table tennis, tennis, volleyball, water polo. **Team name:** Catamounts.

**Student services.** Alcohol/substance abuse counseling, campus ministries, career counseling, services for economically disadvantaged, student employment services, financial aid counseling, health services, minority student services, on-campus daycare, personal counseling, placement for graduates, veterans' counselor, women's services. **Physically disabled:** Services for visually, speech, hearing impaired. **Learning disabled:** Comprehensive services available.

**Contact.** E-mail: admissions@uvm.edu
Phone: (802) 656-3370 Fax: (802) 656-8611
Susan Wertheimer, Admission and Enrollment Planning, University of Vermont, 194 South Prospect Street, Burlington, VT 05401-3596

## Vermont Technical College
**Randolph Center, Vermont**
www.vtc.edu

CB member
CB code: 3941

- Public 4-year technical college
- Residential campus in small town
- 1,378 degree-seeking undergraduates: 16% part-time, 40% women, 1% African American, 2% Asian American, 1% Hispanic American, 1% Native American
- 57% of applicants admitted
- 54% graduate within 6 years

**General.** Founded in 1866. Regionally accredited. Some classes offered on Vermont Interactive Television and broadcast to 12 locations in Vermont. Vermont Academy of Science and Technology enrolls high school seniors who excel in math/science to complete last year of high school and first year of college simultaneously. **Degrees:** 63 bachelor's, 323 associate awarded. **ROTC:** Army. **Location:** 20 miles from Montpelier, 50 miles from Burlington. **Calendar:** Semester, limited summer session. **Full-time faculty:** 79 total; 80% have terminal degrees, 47% women. **Part-time faculty:** 77 total; 58% have terminal degrees, 46% women. **Special facilities:** 500-acre farmstead and orchard, lighted ski hill, nursing laboratory.

**Freshman class profile.** 920 applied, 529 admitted, 284 enrolled.

| Mid 50% test scores | | | |
|---|---|---|---|
| SAT critical reading: | 410-520 | Rank in top quarter: | 27% |
| SAT math: | 450-560 | Rank in top tenth: | 8% |
| SAT writing: | 410-520 | End year in good standing: | 50% |
| GPA 3.50 or higher: | 13% | Return as sophomores: | 65% |
| GPA 3.0-3.49: | 33% | Out-of-state: | 18% |
| GPA 2.0-2.99: | 51% | Live on campus: | 80% |

**Basis for selection.** School achievement record most important, followed by test scores, recommendations, interview. Interview and essay required for veterinary applicants. Entrance exam required for nursing applicants. Veterinary technology, dental hygiene and nursing programs highly selective. SAT or ACT not required of nursing applicants or non-traditional students. Interview is required in some cases, but always strongly encouraged. Post-application essay is required during placement testing. **Homeschooled:** Statement describing homeschool structure and mission required. May choose affiliated Vermont Academy of Science and Technology to get high school diploma and first year of college simultaneously.

**High school preparation.** College-preparatory program recommended. 16 units required. Required and recommended units include English 4, mathematics 3-4, social studies 2, history 2, science 2-3 (laboratory 1-2), foreign language 2 and academic electives 2.

**2007-2008 Annual costs.** Tuition/fees: $9,148; $17,092 out-of-state. New England Board of Higher Education rate for students from other New England states: 150% of Vermont resident tuition. Available to degree candidates in academic areas not offered by educational institutions in their home states. Room/board: $7,220. Books/supplies: $1,000. Personal expenses: $650.

**Financial aid. Non-need-based:** Scholarships awarded for academics.

**Application procedures. Admission:** Priority date 3/1; no deadline. $36 fee, may be waived for applicants with need. Application may be submitted online. Admission notification on a rolling basis beginning on or about 12/15. Must reply by May 1 or within 4 week(s) if notified thereafter. **Financial aid:** Priority date 3/1; no closing date. FAFSA required. Applicants notified on a rolling basis starting 3/15; must reply within 2 week(s) of notification.

**Academics.** 3-year preparatory program options for students planning engineering programs. **Special study options:** Accelerated study, distance learning, double major, dual enrollment of high school students, ESL, honors, independent study, internships. Vermont Academy of Science and Technology program combines senior year of high school and first year of college. **Credit/placement by examination:** CLEP, institutional tests. 36 credit hours maximum toward associate degree, 60 toward bachelor's. **Support services:** Learning center, pre-admission summer program, reduced course load, remedial instruction, study skills assistance, tutoring, writing center.

**Majors. Business:** General, business admin. **Computer sciences:** General, information technology, LAN/WAN management, networking, programming, security, system admin, web page design, webmaster. **Engineering:** Architectural, computer, software. **Engineering technology:** Architectural. **Health:** Dental hygiene.

**Computing on campus.** 250 workstations in dormitories, library, computer center. Dormitories wired for high-speed internet access and linked to campus network. Commuter students can connect to campus network. Online library, helpline, repair service, student web hosting, wireless network available.

**Student life. Freshman orientation:** Mandatory, $60 fee. Preregistration for classes offered. 2 days prior to start of classes. **Housing:** Coed dorms, special housing for disabled, substance-free housing available. $100 deposit, deadline 6/1. Theme housing available. **Activities:** Drama, international student organizations, radio station, student government, student newspaper, TV station, national student chapters of: American Institute of Architects, American Society of Civil Engineers, Institute of Electrical and Electronic Engineers, Society of Manufacturing Engineers, Society of Women Engineers, National Association of Veterinary Technicians, Women Issues Christian Fellowship, Phi Theta Kappa, Tau Alpha Pi.

**Athletics.** NAIA, USCAA. **Intercollegiate:** Baseball M, basketball, cross-country, golf, soccer, volleyball. **Intramural:** Basketball, football (non-tackle), golf, ice hockey, racquetball, skiing, soccer, softball, swimming, table tennis, tennis, volleyball, water polo. **Team name:** Knights.

**Student services.** Alcohol/substance abuse counseling, career counseling, services for economically disadvantaged, student employment services, financial aid counseling, health services, minority student services, personal counseling, placement for graduates, veterans' counselor, women's services. **Physically disabled:** Services for visually, hearing impaired.

**Contact.** E-mail: admissions@vtc.edu
Phone: (802) 728-1242 Toll-free number: (800) 442-8821
Fax: (802) 728-1390
Dwight Cross, Assistant Dean of Enrollment, Vermont Technical College, PO Box 500, Randolph Center, VT 05061-0500

## Woodbury College
### Montpelier, Vermont
**www.woodbury-college.edu** **CB code: 2600**

- Private 4-year technical and career college
- Commuter campus in small town
- 70 degree-seeking undergraduates: 24% part-time, 96% women, 3% Asian American, 1% Hispanic American
- 22 degree-seeking graduate students
- Application essay, interview required
- 64% graduate within 6 years

**General.** Regionally accredited. Woodbury's Dispute Resolution Center provides mediation and facilitation services to the community, and serves as a learning laboratory for mediation and conflict management students. **Degrees:** 27 bachelor's, 11 associate awarded; master's offered. **Location:** 38 miles from Burlington. **Calendar:** Trimester. **Part-time faculty:** 26 total; 27% have terminal degrees, 4% minority, 58% women. **Class size:** 100% < 20.

**Freshman class profile.**

| End year in good standing: | 67% | Return as sophomores: | 67% |
|---|---|---|---|

**Basis for selection.** Open admission, but selective for some programs. All certificate programs require associate degree as minimum qualification. Master's program requires bachelor's degree as minimum qualification. **Homeschooled:** State high school equivalency certificate required.

**2007-2008 Annual costs.** Tuition/fees: $16,050. Books/supplies: $600. Personal expenses: $2,400.

**2006-2007 Financial aid. Need-based:** 2 full-time freshmen applied for aid; 2 were judged to have need; 2 of these received aid. Average need met was 48%. Average scholarship/grant was $8,330; average loan $3,500.

**Application procedures. Admission:** No deadline. $30 fee, may be waived for applicants with need. Application must be submitted on paper. Admission notification on a rolling basis. **Financial aid:** No deadline. FAFSA required.

**Academics. Special study options:** Cooperative education, distance learning, double major, independent study, internships, liberal arts/career combination, student-designed major, weekend college. **Credit/placement by examination:** CLEP, institutional tests. 30 credit hours maximum toward associate degree, 90 toward bachelor's. Credit by examination treated like transfer credits. **Support services:** Reduced course load, remedial instruction, study skills assistance, tutoring.

**Majors. Legal studies:** General, paralegal, prelaw. **Public administration:** Community org/advocacy.

**Most popular majors.** Interdisciplinary studies 12%, legal studies 52%, public administration/social services 36%.

**Computing on campus.** 18 workstations in library, computer center. Commuter students can connect to campus network. Online library, wireless network available.

**Student life. Freshman orientation:** Mandatory. Preregistration for classes offered.

**Student services.** Adult student services, career counseling, financial aid counseling, personal counseling.

**Contact.** E-mail: admiss@woodbury-college.edu
Phone: (802) 229-0516 ext. 232 Toll-free number: (800) 639-6039 ext. 232
Fax: (802) 229-2141
Denise MacMartin, Director of Admissions, Woodbury College, 660 Elm Street, Montpelier, VT 05602

# Virginia

## Art Institute of Washington
**Arlington, Virginia**
www.aiw.artinstitutes.edu
CB code: 3836

- For-profit 4-year culinary school and visual arts college
- Commuter campus in small city
- 1,700 degree-seeking undergraduates
- Application essay, interview required

**General.** Regionally accredited. **Degrees:** 132 bachelor's, 47 associate awarded. **Location:** One mile from Washington, DC. **Calendar:** Quarter, extensive summer session. **Full-time faculty:** 50 total. **Part-time faculty:** 50 total.

**Basis for selection.** Secondary school record, essay, placement test scores, interview most important; portfolio also considered. Students may take math and English placement test at the college, free of charge, in lieu of SAT or ACT. **Homeschooled:** Transcript of courses and grades required.

**2008-2009 Annual costs.** Tuition/fees (projected): $20,880. Room only: $8,370.

**Application procedures. Admission:** No deadline. $50 fee. Application may be submitted online. Admission notification on a rolling basis. **Financial aid:** FAFSA, institutional form required.

**Academics. Special study options:** Accelerated study, independent study, internships, study abroad. **Credit/placement by examination:** AP, CLEP, IB, SAT, ACT. **Support services:** Learning center, pre-admission summer program, reduced course load, remedial instruction, study skills assistance, tutoring, writing center.

**Majors. Communications:** Advertising, digital media. **Communications technology:** Animation/special effects, graphics, recording arts. **Computer sciences:** Game design, web page design. **Personal/culinary services:** Baking, chef training, culinary arts, restaurant/catering. **Visual/performing arts:** Graphic design, interior design.

**Computing on campus.** Online course registration, online library, student web hosting, wireless network available.

**Student life. Freshman orientation:** Mandatory. Preregistration for classes offered. **Housing:** Coed dorms available. $250 partly refundable deposit.

**Student services.** Adult student services, alcohol/substance abuse counseling, career counseling, student employment services, financial aid counseling. **Physically disabled:** Services for visually, speech, hearing impaired. **Learning disabled:** Comprehensive services available.

**Contact.** E-mail: aiwadm@aii.edu
Phone: (703) 358-9550 Fax: (703) 358-9759
Sara Cruley, Director of Admissions, Art Institute of Washington, 1820 North Fort Myer Drive, Arlington, VA 22209-1802

## Averett University
**Danville, Virginia**
www.averett.edu
CB member
CB code: 5017

- Private 4-year university and liberal arts college
- Residential campus in small city
- 790 degree-seeking undergraduates: 4% part-time, 44% women, 28% African American, 1% Asian American, 4% Hispanic American, 1% Native American, 2% international
- 44 degree-seeking graduate students
- 90% of applicants admitted
- SAT or ACT (ACT writing optional) required
- 40% graduate within 6 years

**General.** Founded in 1859. Regionally accredited. **Degrees:** 169 bachelor's awarded; master's offered. **Location:** 45 miles from Greensboro, North Carolina, 150 miles from Richmond. **Calendar:** Semester, limited summer

session. **Full-time faculty:** 54 total; 78% have terminal degrees, 4% minority, 39% women. **Part-time faculty:** 53 total; 30% have terminal degrees, 4% minority, 55% women. **Class size:** 69% < 20, 31% 20-39. **Special facilities:** 100-acre equestrian center, flight center.

**Freshman class profile.** 1,173 applied, 1,052 admitted, 238 enrolled.

| Mid 50% test scores | | | |
|---|---|---|---|
| SAT critical reading: | 410-450 | Rank in top tenth: | 7% |
| SAT math: | 420-460 | End year in good standing: | 92% |
| ACT composite: | 16-19 | Return as sophomores: | 56% |
| GPA 3.50 or higher: | 18% | Out-of-state: | 53% |
| GPA 3.0-3.49: | 27% | Live on campus: | 85% |
| GPA 2.0-2.99: | 53% | International: | 2% |
| Rank in top quarter: | 21% | Fraternities: | 1% |
| | | Sororities: | 1% |

**Basis for selection.** Rigor of secondary school record and GPA very important; standardized test scores important. Recommendations, essay, interview, extracurricular activities, talent/ability/alumni/ae relation, volunteer work, work experience and level of interest all considered. Auditions required for music program; portfolios for art recommended. Essay recommended. **Homeschooled:** Transcript of courses and grades, state high school equivalency certificate required. **Learning Disabled:** Documentation of neuropsychological or comprehensive psychoeducational evaluation required for access to learning disabled services. Minimum SAT requirements may be waived.

**High school preparation.** 16 units required; 25 recommended. Required and recommended units include English 4, mathematics 3-4, social studies 3-4, science 3-4 (laboratory 3), foreign language 3, computer science 2, visual/performing arts 1 and academic electives 3.

**2007-2008 Annual costs.** Tuition/fees: $20,512. Room/board: $7,100.

**2006-2007 Financial aid. Need-based:** 151 full-time freshmen applied for aid; 124 were judged to have need; 124 of these received aid. Average need met was 74%. Average scholarship/grant was $9,211; average loan $4,367. 65% of total undergraduate aid awarded as scholarships/grants, 35% as loans/jobs. **Non-need-based:** Awarded to 645 full-time undergraduates, including 154 freshmen. Scholarships awarded for academics, alumni affiliation, art, leadership, minority status, music/drama, state residency.

**Application procedures. Admission:** Priority date 5/1; deadline 7/1 (receipt date). No application fee. Application may be submitted online. Admission notification on a rolling basis. Must reply by May 1 or within 2 week(s) if notified thereafter. Deferred admission is up to 1 year. **Financial aid:** Priority date 4/1; no closing date. FAFSA required. Applicants notified on a rolling basis starting 2/15; must reply within 2 week(s) of notification.

**Academics. Special study options:** Accelerated study, cooperative education, cross-registration, double major, dual enrollment of high school students, exchange student, honors, independent study, internships, student-designed major, study abroad, teacher certification program, Washington semester. Undergraduates may take graduate level classes. **Credit/placement by examination:** AP, CLEP, IB, SAT, ACT, institutional tests. 27 credit hours maximum toward associate degree, 90 toward bachelor's. **Support services:** Learning center, reduced course load, remedial instruction, study skills assistance, tutoring, writing center.

**Majors. Agriculture:** Equestrian studies. **Biology:** General, ecology. **Business:** Accounting, business admin, finance, management science, marketing. **Communications:** Journalism. **Computer sciences:** Information systems. **Conservation:** Environmental science. **Education:** Art, biology, chemistry, English, health, mathematics, multi-level teacher, social studies. **English:** English lit. **Health:** Athletic training, clinical lab science, medical radiologic technology/radiation therapy, premedicine. **History:** General. **Interdisciplinary:** Biological/physical sciences. **Legal studies:** Prelaw. **Liberal arts:** Arts/sciences. **Math:** General. **Parks/recreation:** Health/fitness, sports admin. **Philosophy/religion:** Religion. **Physical sciences:** Chemistry. **Protective services:** Law enforcement admin. **Psychology:** Clinical, cognitive, industrial, psychobiology. **Social sciences:** Political science, sociology. **Transportation:** Airline/commercial pilot, aviation, aviation management. **Visual/performing arts:** Art, dramatic, theater history. **Other:** Criminal justice/aerospace management, English theater, History and politics, Math decision science, Wellness/sports medicine.

**Most popular majors.** Business/marketing 11%, education 9%, health sciences 8%, liberal arts 9%, parks/recreation 14%, psychology 7%, security/protective services 12%, social sciences 6%.

**Computing on campus.** 150 workstations in library, computer center, student center. Dormitories wired for high-speed internet access. Online course registration, online library, helpline, student web hosting, wireless network available.

**Student life. Freshman orientation:** Mandatory, $50 fee. Preregistration for classes offered. 11-day orientation; begins on Saturday and lasts until classes start. **Policies:** No alcohol on campus, no smoking in dorms. **Housing:** Guaranteed on-campus for all undergraduates. Coed dorms, single-sex dorms, apartments available. $400 deposit, deadline 5/1. Coed housing by floor or suite. **Activities:** Campus ministries, choral groups, drama, international student organizations, literary magazine, Model UN, musical theater, student government, student newspaper, Alpha Beta Rho, Brothers and Sisters in Christ, campus activities board, Christian Student Union, Fellowship of Christian Athletes, multicultural student association, Phi Sigma Sigma, Phi Kappa Phi.

**Athletics.** NCAA. **Intercollegiate:** Baseball M, basketball, cross-country, equestrian, football (tackle) M, golf M, lacrosse W, soccer, softball W, tennis, volleyball W. **Intramural:** Basketball, cheerleading, football (non-tackle) M, softball. **Team name:** Cougars.

**Student services.** Adult student services, alcohol/substance abuse counseling, career counseling, student employment services, financial aid counseling, personal counseling, placement for graduates, veterans' counselor. **Physically disabled:** Services for visually, speech, hearing impaired.

**Contact.** E-mail: admit@averett.edu
Phone: (434) 791-4996 Toll-free number: (800) 283-7388
Fax: (434) 797-2784
Kathie Tune, Dean of Admissions, Averett University, 420 West Main Street, Danville, VA 24541

---

## Bluefield College
**Bluefield, Virginia**
www.bluefield.edu                                    **CB code: 5063**

- Private 4-year liberal arts college affiliated with Baptist faith
- Residential campus in small town
- 761 degree-seeking undergraduates: 16% part-time, 60% women, 19% African American, 1% Hispanic American
- 52% of applicants admitted
- SAT or ACT (ACT writing optional) required
- 42% graduate within 6 years

**General.** Founded in 1920. Regionally accredited. **Degrees:** 275 bachelor's awarded. **Location:** 90 miles from Roanoke. **Calendar:** Semester, limited summer session. **Full-time faculty:** 34 total; 65% have terminal degrees, 38% women. **Part-time faculty:** 70 total; 39% have terminal degrees, 6% minority, 30% women. **Class size:** 87% < 20, 13% 20-39.

**Freshman class profile.** 556 applied, 288 admitted, 108 enrolled.

| Mid 50% test scores | | | |
|---|---|---|---|
| SAT critical reading: | 420-530 | End year in good standing: | 82% |
| SAT math: | 420-500 | Return as sophomores: | 64% |
| ACT composite: | 17-21 | Out-of-state: | 19% |
| GPA 3.50 or higher: | 43% | Live on campus: | 67% |
| GPA 3.0-3.49: | 21% | Fraternities: | 7% |
| GPA 2.0-2.99: | 33% | Sororities: | 10% |

**Basis for selection.** Students must have minimum 2.0 GPA, 18 ACT or SAT equivalent, and rank in upper 50% of graduating class. **Home-schooled:** Must supply written description and transcript of home school curriculum.

**High school preparation.** 22 units required. Required units include English 4, mathematics 3, social studies 3, science 3 (laboratory 1) and academic electives 6. 2 units of health and physical education; 1 unit of fine arts.

**2008-2009 Annual costs.** Tuition/fees: $15,640. Room/board: $6,560. Books/supplies: $1,100. Personal expenses: $1,500.

**2007-2008 Financial aid.** **Need-based:** Average need met was 81%. Average scholarship/grant was $10,055; average loan $3,162. 46% of total undergraduate aid awarded as scholarships/grants, 54% as loans/jobs. **Non-need-based:** Scholarships awarded for academics, art, athletics, leadership, music/drama, religious affiliation, state residency.

**Application procedures.** **Admission:** Closing date 8/1 (postmark date). $30 fee, may be waived for applicants with need. Application may be submitted online. Admission notification on a rolling basis beginning on or about 9/1. Must reply by May 1 or within 3 week(s) if notified thereafter. **Financial aid:** Priority date 3/15; no closing date. FAFSA required. Applicants notified on a rolling basis starting 3/1; must reply within 3 week(s) of notification.

**Academics.** **Special study options:** Double major, honors, internships, liberal arts/career combination, study abroad, teacher certification program.

---

**Credit/placement by examination:** AP, CLEP, IB, SAT, ACT, institutional tests. 30 credit hours maximum toward bachelor's degree. **Support services:** Learning center, reduced course load, remedial instruction, study skills assistance, tutoring, writing center.

**Majors.** **Biology:** General, exercise physiology. **Business:** General, accounting, business admin, e-commerce, marketing. **Communications:** General. **Communications technology:** Graphics. **Computer sciences:** Information technology. **Education:** General, art, biology, business, chemistry, elementary, English, health, history, mathematics, middle, multi-level teacher, music, physical, secondary, social studies. **English:** English lit. **History:** General. **Interdisciplinary:** Behavioral sciences. **Liberal arts:** Arts/sciences. **Math:** General. **Parks/recreation:** Exercise sciences. **Philosophy/religion:** Christian. **Physical sciences:** Chemistry. **Protective services:** Forensics, law enforcement admin, police science. **Psychology:** General. **Social sciences:** General. **Theology:** Bible, preministerial, sacred music, theology, youth ministry. **Visual/performing arts:** Art, design, dramatic, music performance, piano/organ, voice/opera.

**Most popular majors.** Business/marketing 39%, psychology 25%, security/protective services 22%.

**Computing on campus.** 100 workstations in dormitories, library, computer center, student center. Dormitories wired for high-speed internet access and linked to campus network. Commuter students can connect to campus network. Online library, wireless network available.

**Student life.** **Freshman orientation:** Available. Preregistration for classes offered. Held in June or July. **Policies:** Weekly convocation attendance required. Limited visitation hours in dormitories. Religious observance required. **Housing:** Guaranteed on-campus for freshmen. Coed dorms, single-sex dorms, apartments, substance-free housing available. $100 fully refundable deposit. **Activities:** Campus ministries, choral groups, drama, film society, literary magazine, music ensembles, musical theater, opera, student government, student newspaper, Fellowship of Christian Athletes, Alpha Delta, Phi Mu Delta, Kappa Psi Omicron, Sigma Alpha Alpha.

**Athletics.** NAIA. **Intercollegiate:** Baseball M, basketball, cross-country, golf M, soccer, softball W, tennis, volleyball W. **Intramural:** Badminton, basketball, bowling, football (non-tackle), softball, table tennis, tennis, volleyball. **Team name:** Rams.

**Student services.** Adult student services, campus ministries, career counseling, financial aid counseling, health services, personal counseling, placement for graduates, veterans' counselor.

**Contact.** E-mail: admissions@bluefield.edu
Phone: (276) 326-4602 Toll-free number: (800) 872-0175
Fax: (276) 326-4288
George Campbell, Director of Traditional Admissions, Bluefield College, 3000 College Drive, Bluefield, VA 24605

---

## Bridgewater College
**Bridgewater, Virginia**                              **CB member**
www.bridgewater.edu                                    **CB code: 5069**

- Private 4-year liberal arts college affiliated with Church of the Brethren
- Residential campus in small town
- 1,527 degree-seeking undergraduates: 57% women, 7% African American, 1% Asian American, 2% Hispanic American, 1% Native American
- 84% of applicants admitted
- SAT or ACT (ACT writing optional) required
- 66% graduate within 6 years

**General.** Founded in 1880. Regionally accredited. **Degrees:** 301 bachelor's awarded. **Location:** 8 miles from Harrisonburg, 130 miles from Washington, DC. **Calendar:** 4-1-4, limited summer session. **Full-time faculty:** 96 total; 79% have terminal degrees, 2% minority, 38% women. **Part-time faculty:** 31 total; 36% have terminal degrees, 10% minority, 58% women. **Class size:** 51% < 20, 46% 20-39, 2% 40-49, less than 1% 50-99. **Special facilities:** 75-acre equestrian center for equestrian competitions and boarding of College- and student-owned horses.

**Freshman class profile.** 1,537 applied, 1,290 admitted, 445 enrolled.

| Mid 50% test scores | | | |
|---|---|---|---|
| SAT critical reading: | 450-560 | GPA 2.0-2.99: | 25% |
| SAT math: | 460-570 | Rank in top quarter: | 39% |
| SAT writing: | 450-550 | Rank in top tenth: | 15% |
| ACT composite: | 18-23 | Return as sophomores: | 76% |
| GPA 3.50 or higher: | 42% | Out-of-state: | 19% |
| GPA 3.0-3.49: | 33% | Live on campus: | 94% |

**Basis for selection.** High school GPA most important, followed by test scores and letters of recommendation. Prefer applicants in top half of high school class. Consider those in bottom half with strong compensating qualities. Interview required for some, recommended for all. **Homeschooled:** GED required for students applying for Title IV financial aid.

**High school preparation.** 15 units required; 22 recommended. Required and recommended units include English 4, mathematics 3-4, science 2-4 (laboratory 2), foreign language 3 and academic electives 4. Social studies and history: 2 required, 3 recommended.

**2008-2009 Annual costs.** Tuition/fees: $23,090. Room/board: $9,900. Books/supplies: $1,050. Personal expenses: $1,080.

**2007-2008 Financial aid. Need-based:** 389 full-time freshmen applied for aid; 328 were judged to have need; 328 of these received aid. Average need met was 85%. Average scholarship/grant was $4,669; average loan $4,867. 72% of total undergraduate aid awarded as scholarships/grants, 28% as loans/jobs. **Non-need-based:** Awarded to 1,386 full-time undergraduates, including 379 freshmen. Scholarships awarded for academics, music/drama, religious affiliation.

**Application procedures. Admission:** No deadline. $30 fee, may be waived for applicants with need. Application may be submitted online. Admission notification on a rolling basis beginning on or about 9/1. Must reply by May 1 or within 2 week(s) if notified thereafter. **Financial aid:** Priority date 3/1; no closing date. FAFSA required. Applicants notified on a rolling basis starting 3/15; must reply within 2 week(s) of notification.

**Academics. Special study options:** Combined bachelor's/graduate degree, double major, honors, independent study, internships, liberal arts/career combination, study abroad, teacher certification program, Washington semester. 3-2 engineering with George Washington University (BA/BA) and 3-2 engineering with Virginia Tech (BA/BA), 3-2 forestry with Duke University (BA/MS), 3-2 nursing with Vanderbilt University (BA/MN), 3-2 physical therapy with George Washington University (BA/MPT), 3-4 physical therapy with Shenandoah University (BA/DPT), 3-4 veterinary medicine with Virginia Tech (BA/DVM). **Credit/placement by examination:** AP, CLEP, IB, institutional tests. **Support services:** Reduced course load, study skills assistance, tutoring, writing center.

**Majors. Biology:** General. **Business:** Business admin, management information systems. **Communications:** Media studies. **Computer science:** Computer science. **Conservation:** Environmental science. **Education:** Family/consumer sciences, physical. **English:** English lit. **Family/consumer sciences:** General, food/nutrition. **Foreign languages:** French, Spanish. **Health:** Athletic training, clinical lab science. **History:** General. **Liberal arts:** Arts/sciences. **Math:** General. **Parks/recreation:** Exercise sciences, health/fitness. **Philosophy/religion:** Philosophy, religion. **Physical sciences:** Chemistry, physics. **Psychology:** General. **Social sciences:** Economics, international relations, political science, sociology. **Visual/performing arts:** Music history, studio arts.

**Most popular majors.** Biology 11%, business/marketing 19%, communications/journalism 9%, education 9%, family/consumer sciences 6%, parks/recreation 16%, psychology 6%.

**Computing on campus.** 187 workstations in library. Dormitories wired for high-speed internet access and linked to campus network. Commuter students can connect to campus network. Online course registration, online library, helpline, repair service, student web hosting, wireless network available.

**Student life. Freshman orientation:** Mandatory. Preregistration for classes offered. Students may choose from 2 spring 2-day sessions. One-day summer session also available. Further orientation activities 2 days preceding classes. Parents included in spring and summer orientations. **Policies:** Alcoholic beverages not permitted on campus. Co-ed visitation hours. Smoking and other tobacco products permitted only in designated areas minimum of 20 feet from residence hall. Unmarried students under age 23 must live on campus unless living with parents. **Housing:** Guaranteed on-campus for all undergraduates. Single-sex dorms, special housing for disabled, apartments, substance-free housing available. Honor housing available. **Activities:** Bands, campus ministries, choral groups, dance, drama, international student organizations, literary magazine, music ensembles, musical theater, radio station, student government, student newspaper, Brethren Student Fellowship,

College Republicans, Young Democrats, Black Student Association, Fellowship of Christian Athletes, Amnesty International, Habitat for Humanity.

**Athletics.** NCAA. **Intercollegiate:** Baseball M, basketball, cross-country, equestrian, field hockey W, football (tackle) M, golf M, lacrosse W, soccer, softball W, swimming W, tennis, track and field, volleyball W. **Intramural:** Badminton, basketball, bowling, football (non-tackle), golf, racquetball, soccer, softball, table tennis, tennis, volleyball. **Team name:** Eagles.

**Student services.** Campus ministries, career counseling, student employment services, financial aid counseling, health services, minority student services, personal counseling, placement for graduates. **Physically disabled:** Services for visually impaired.

**Contact.** E-mail: admissions@bridgewater.edu
Phone: (540) 828-5375 Toll-free number: (800) 759-8328
Fax: (540) 828-5481
Linda Stout, Director of Enrollment Operations, Bridgewater College, 402 East College Street, Bridgewater, VA 22812-1599

---

## Catholic Distance University
Hamilton, Virginia
www.cdu.edu

- Private two-year upper-division virtual university
- Rural community

**General.** Accredited by DETC. **Calendar:** Differs by program.

**Annual costs/financial aid.** Tuition/fees (2007-2008): $6,960.

**Contact.** Phone: (540) 338-2700 ext. 710
Director of Admissions, 120 East Colonial Highway, Hamilton, VA 20158-9012

---

## Christendom College
Front Royal, Virginia
www.christendom.edu          CB code: 5691

- Private 4-year liberal arts college affiliated with Roman Catholic Church
- Residential campus in large town
- 397 degree-seeking undergraduates: 2% part-time, 54% women, 2% Asian American, 3% Hispanic American, 3% international
- 68 degree-seeking graduate students
- 81% of applicants admitted
- SAT or ACT (ACT writing optional), application essay required
- 69% graduate within 6 years

**General.** Founded in 1977. Regionally accredited. **Degrees:** 69 bachelor's, 2 associate awarded; master's offered. **Location:** 70 miles from Washington, DC. **Calendar:** Semester, limited summer session. **Full-time faculty:** 20 total; 65% have terminal degrees, 10% women. **Part-time faculty:** 21 total; 29% have terminal degrees, 38% women. **Class size:** 64% < 20, 35% 20-39, 2% 40-49.

**Freshman class profile.** 254 applied, 206 admitted, 93 enrolled.

| Mid 50% test scores | | | |
|---|---|---|---|
| SAT critical reading: | 590-690 | Rank in top quarter: | 63% |
| SAT math: | 500-630 | Rank in top tenth: | 40% |
| SAT writing: | 560-660 | End year in good standing: | 98% |
| ACT composite: | 22-28 | Return as sophomores: | 88% |
| GPA 3.50 or higher: | 62% | Out-of-state: | 85% |
| GPA 3.0-3.49: | 31% | Live on campus: | 98% |
| GPA 2.0-2.99: | 7% | International: | 1% |

**Basis for selection.** Secondary school record, essay, test scores, class rank, GPA, recommendations important. Applicants can present additional material and explain scores, evaluations, etc. which they believe do not adequately reflect their abilities. Interview recommended. **Homeschooled:** Transcript forms required (available from college).

**High school preparation.** 14 units recommended. Recommended units include English 4, mathematics 2, social studies 1, history 2, science 2, foreign language 2 and academic electives 1.

**2008-2009 Annual costs.** Tuition/fees: $18,806. Room/board: $6,688. Books/supplies: $500. Personal expenses: $300.

**2007-2008 Financial aid. Need-based:** 65 full-time freshmen applied for aid; 43 were judged to have need; 43 of these received aid. Average need met was 90%. Average scholarship/grant was $6,130; average loan $4,825. 52% of total undergraduate aid awarded as scholarships/grants, 48% as loans/jobs. **Non-need-based:** Awarded to 86 full-time undergraduates, including 24 freshmen. Scholarships awarded for academics, alumni affiliation. **Additional information:** Christendom accepts no direct federal aid, nor does it participate in indirect programs of federal aid.

**Application procedures. Admission:** Priority date 3/1; no deadline. $25 fee. Application may be submitted online. Admission notification on a rolling basis. **Financial aid:** Priority date 4/1, closing date 6/1. Institutional form required. Applicants notified on a rolling basis starting 2/1; must reply within 4 week(s) of notification.

**Academics. Special study options:** Double major, honors, independent study, internships, study abroad. Junior semester in Rome. **Credit/placement by examination:** AP, CLEP, institutional tests. **Support services:** Pre-admission summer program, reduced course load, writing center.

**Majors. English:** English lit. **Foreign languages:** Classics. **History:** General. **Philosophy/religion:** Philosophy. **Social sciences:** Political science.

**Most popular majors.** English 10%, foreign language 7%, history 29%, philosophy/religious studies 30%, social sciences 10%, theological studies 15%.

**Computing on campus.** 70 workstations in library. Online course registration available.

**Student life. Freshman orientation:** Mandatory. Preregistration for classes offered. Orientation held weekend before school starts. **Policies:** Although no student is required to participate, college encourages religious activities. **Housing:** Guaranteed on-campus for all undergraduates. Single-sex dorms, substance-free housing available. $250 deposit, deadline 3/15. **Activities:** Choral groups, drama, film society, literary magazine, musical theater, student government, student newspaper, Legion of Mary, Shield of Roses, St. Genesius Society, Holy Rood Guild, College Republicans, works of mercy group.

**Athletics. USCAA. Intercollegiate:** Baseball M, basketball, rugby M, soccer, volleyball W. **Intramural:** Basketball, cross-country, fencing, football (non-tackle), handball, racquetball, skiing, soccer, softball, table tennis, tennis, volleyball. **Team name:** Crusaders.

**Student services.** Campus ministries, career counseling, financial aid counseling, health services, personal counseling, placement for graduates.

**Contact.** E-mail: admissions@christendom.edu
Phone: (540) 636-2900 Toll-free number: (800) 877-5456
Fax: (540) 636-1655
Thomas McFadden, Director of Admissions, Christendom College, 134 Christendom Drive, Front Royal, VA 22630

---

## Christopher Newport University

**Newport News, Virginia**
**www.cnu.edu**

**CB member**
**CB code: 5128**

- Public 4-year university and liberal arts college
- Residential campus in small city
- 4,663 degree-seeking undergraduates: 4% part-time, 55% women, 7% African American, 3% Asian American, 3% Hispanic American, 1% Native American
- 128 degree-seeking graduate students
- 54% of applicants admitted
- SAT or ACT (ACT writing optional) required
- 52% graduate within 6 years

**General.** Founded in 1960. Regionally accredited. **Degrees:** 892 bachelor's awarded; master's offered. **ROTC:** Army. **Location:** 20 miles from Norfolk, 70 miles from Richmond. **Calendar:** Semester, limited summer session. **Full-time faculty:** 226 total; 84% have terminal degrees, 15% minority, 44% women. **Part-time faculty:** 136 total; 26% have terminal degrees, 18% minority, 38% women. **Class size:** 33% < 20, 57% 20-39, 8% 40-49, 2% 50-99, less than 1% >100.

**Freshman class profile.** 6,694 applied, 3,639 admitted, 1,242 enrolled.

| Mid 50% test scores | | | |
|---|---|---|---|
| SAT critical reading: | 550-630 | Rank in top quarter: | 56% |
| SAT math: | 540-620 | Rank in top tenth: | 20% |
| ACT composite: | 22-25 | End year in good standing: | 83% |
| GPA 3.50 or higher: | 50% | Return as sophomores: | 82% |
| GPA 3.0-3.49: | 46% | Out-of-state: | 6% |
| GPA 2.0-2.99: | 4% | Live on campus: | 97% |
| | | International: | 1% |

**Basis for selection.** Minimum 3.0 GPA, rank in top half of class. Type of diploma and difficulty of classes taken considered. Test scores required for all freshman applicants who graduated from high school within past 2 years. Audition required for music; interview recommended for marginal; portfolio recommended for art. **Homeschooled:** Applicants should submit copy of high school transcript and descriptions, along with ACT or SAT score.

**High school preparation.** 23 units required. Required and recommended units include English 4, mathematics 4, history 3-4, science 3-4 and foreign language 3.

**2008-2009 Annual costs.** Tuition/fees (projected): $7,050; $14,150 out-of-state. Room/board: $8,500. Books/supplies: $870. Personal expenses: $2,011.

**2007-2008 Financial aid. Need-based:** Average need met was 79%. Average scholarship/grant was $4,890; average loan $3,060. 51% of total undergraduate aid awarded as scholarships/grants, 49% as loans/jobs. **Non-need-based:** Scholarships awarded for academics, art, leadership, music/drama, ROTC, state residency.

**Application procedures. Admission:** Closing date 3/1 (receipt date). $45 fee, may be waived for applicants with need. Application may be submitted online. Admission notification on a rolling basis beginning on or about 12/1. Must reply by May 1 or within 2 week(s) if notified thereafter. **Financial aid:** Priority date 3/1; no closing date. FAFSA required. Applicants notified on a rolling basis starting 2/21; must reply within 2 week(s) of notification.

**Academics.** Special programs for Leadership, Honors and freshman learning communities. **Special study options:** Cross-registration, double major, dual enrollment of high school students, honors, independent study, internships, student-designed major, study abroad. Member of Virginia Tidewater Consortium, Freshman Learning Communities. **Credit/placement by examination:** AP, CLEP, IB, institutional tests. **Support services:** Study skills assistance, tutoring, writing center.

**Majors. Agriculture:** Ornamental horticulture. **Biology:** General. **Business:** Accounting, business admin, finance, managerial economics, marketing. **Communications:** General. **Computer sciences:** Computer science, information systems. **Conservation:** Environmental studies. **Engineering:** Computer. **English:** English lit. **Foreign languages:** French, German, Spanish. **History:** General. **Math:** General. **Philosophy/religion:** Philosophy. **Physical sciences:** Chemistry, physics. **Psychology:** General. **Public administration:** Social work. **Social sciences:** Political science, sociology. **Visual/performing arts:** Dramatic, music performance, studio arts.

**Most popular majors.** Biology 11%, business/marketing 21%, communications/journalism 9%, English 8%, history 6%, psychology 11%, social sciences 18%, visual/performing arts 6%.

**Computing on campus.** 325 workstations in dormitories, library, computer center, student center. Dormitories wired for high-speed internet access and linked to campus network. Commuter students can connect to campus network. Online course registration, online library, helpline, student web hosting, wireless network available.

**Student life. Freshman orientation:** Mandatory, $175 fee. Preregistration for classes offered. 2 programs required: 1.5-day program with overnight stay in residence halls, offered June-July, and welcome week program prior to start of classes in fall. **Policies:** Alcohol not permitted in residence halls; 1st and 2nd year students required to live on campus unless they reside with their parents or legal guardians in Gloucester, Hampton, Isle of Wight, James City County, Matthews County, Newport News, Poquoson, Williamsburg or York County (of Virginia). **Housing:** Guaranteed on-campus for freshmen. Coed dorms, apartments, fraternity/sorority housing, substance-free housing available. $250 partly refundable deposit, deadline 5/1. Learning communities available. **Activities:** Bands, campus ministries, choral groups, dance, drama, international student organizations, literary magazine, music ensembles, Model UN, musical theater, opera, radio station, student government, student newspaper, symphony orchestra, TV station, Baptist Student Union, Intervarsity Christian Fellowship, Lutheran student association, various honor societies, Young Life.

**Athletics. NCAA. Intercollegiate:** Baseball M, basketball, cheerleading, cross-country, equestrian, field hockey W, football (tackle) M, golf M, lacrosse, sailing, soccer, softball W, tennis, track and field, volleyball W. **Intramural:** Badminton, basketball, football (non-tackle) M, soccer, softball, tennis, volleyball. **Team name:** Captains.

**Student services.** Campus ministries, career counseling, student employment services, financial aid counseling,. health services, minority student services, personal counseling, placement for graduates, veterans' counselor. **Physically disabled:** Services for visually, speech, hearing impaired.

**Contact.** E-mail: admit@cnu.edu
Phone: (757) 594-7015 Toll-free number: (800) 333-4268
Fax: (757) 594-7333
Patricia Patten, Dean of Admissions, Christopher Newport University, 1 University Place, Newport News, VA 23606

## College of William and Mary
**Williamsburg, Virginia**
www.wm.edu

CB member
CB code: 5115

▶ Public 4-year university
▶ Residential campus in large town
▶ 5,706 degree-seeking undergraduates: 1% part-time, 54% women, 7% African American, 8% Asian American, 6% Hispanic American, 1% Native American
▶ 1,930 degree-seeking graduate students
▶ 34% of applicants admitted
▶ SAT or ACT (ACT writing optional), application essay required
▶ 91% graduate within 6 years; 28% enter graduate study

**General.** Founded in 1693. Regionally accredited. **Degrees:** 1,769 bachelor's awarded; master's, doctoral, first professional offered. **ROTC:** Army. **Location:** 50 miles from Richmond, 50 miles from Norfolk. **Calendar:** Semester, extensive summer session. **Full-time faculty:** 600 total. **Part-time faculty:** 150 total. **Class size:** 47% < 20, 39% 20-39, 7% 40-49, 4% 50-99, 3% >100. **Special facilities:** Observatory, continuous beam accelerator, 3 interdisciplinary centers in humanities, international studies, writing resources, marine science institute, materials processes research center, public policy research center.

**Freshman class profile.** 10,853 applied, 3,655 admitted, 1,346 enrolled.

| Mid 50% test scores | | Rank in top quarter: | 97% |
|---|---|---|---|
| SAT critical reading: | 630-740 | Rank in top tenth: | 79% |
| SAT math: | 620-710 | Return as sophomores: | 95% |
| SAT writing: | 620-710 | Out-of-state: | 66% |
| ACT composite: | 27-32 | Live on campus: | 100% |
| GPA 3.50 or higher: | 87% | Fraternities: | 14% |
| GPA 3.0-3.49: | 12% | Sororities: | 21% |
| GPA 2.0-2.99: | 1% | | |

**Basis for selection.** GED not accepted. Academic preparation most important, with particular emphasis on course selection and grades, test scores, special talents and abilities. Special consideration given to children of alumni. Preference given to Virginia residents. Diverse backgrounds, special abilities, unique interests and experiences preferred. Applications evaluated on own merits without specific course requirements. Most candidates present as strong a college preparatory program as possible. Advanced placement, honors, accelerated courses strongly weighed in evaluation process.

**High school preparation.** 20 units recommended. Recommended units include English 4, mathematics 4, social studies 4, science 4 (laboratory 3) and foreign language 4. Recommend most demanding high school course available.

**2007-2008 Annual costs.** Tuition/fees: $9,164; $26,725 out-of-state. Room/board: $7,385. Books/supplies: $800. Personal expenses: $970.

**2007-2008 Financial aid. Need-based:** 883 full-time freshmen applied for aid; 397 were judged to have need; 397 of these received aid. Average need met was 85%. Average scholarship/grant was $12,376; average loan $2,330. 75% of total undergraduate aid awarded as scholarships/grants, 25% as loans/jobs. **Non-need-based:** Awarded to 1,103 full-time undergraduates, including 282 freshmen. Scholarships awarded for academics, athletics, leadership, ROTC.

**Application procedures. Admission:** Closing date 1/1 (postmark date). $60 fee, may be waived for applicants with need. Application may be submitted online. Admission notification 4/1. Must reply by 5/1. Housing deposit due with reply. **Financial aid:** Priority date 2/15, closing date 3/15. FAFSA required. CSS PROFILE required of early decision applicants only. Applicants notified on a rolling basis starting 3/15; must reply by 5/1 or within 2 week(s) of notification.

**Academics. Special study options:** Accelerated study, combined bachelor's/graduate degree, double major, dual enrollment of high school students, exchange student, honors, independent study, internships, semester at sea,

student-designed major, study abroad, teacher certification program, Washington semester. Early assurance program with Eastern Virginia Medical School. **Credit/placement by examination:** AP, CLEP, IB, institutional tests. **Support services:** Pre-admission summer program, reduced course load, study skills assistance, tutoring, writing center.

**Majors. Area/ethnic studies:** African, African-American, American, East Asian, European, Latin American, Near/Middle Eastern, Russian/Slavic, women's. **Biology:** General. **Business:** Business admin. **Computer sciences:** General. **Conservation:** Environmental studies. **English:** English lit. **Foreign languages:** Ancient Greek, classics, French, German, Latin, linguistics, Spanish. **History:** General. **Interdisciplinary:** Biopsychology, medieval/Renaissance, neuroscience. **Math:** General. **Parks/recreation:** Health/fitness. **Philosophy/religion:** Philosophy, religion. **Physical sciences:** Chemistry, geology, physics. **Psychology:** General. **Public administration:** Policy analysis. **Social sciences:** Anthropology, economics, international relations, political science, sociology. **Visual/performing arts:** Art, art history/conservation, dramatic, studio arts.

**Most popular majors.** Biology 6%, business/marketing 11%, English 9%, history 8%, interdisciplinary studies 9%, mathematics 7%, psychology 8%, social sciences 24%.

**Computing on campus.** PC or laptop required. 350 workstations in dormitories, library, computer center, student center. Dormitories wired for high-speed internet access and linked to campus network. Commuter students can connect to campus network. Online course registration, online library, helpline, repair service, student web hosting, wireless network available.

**Student life. Freshman orientation:** Mandatory, $83 fee. Preregistration for classes offered. 5-day program. **Policies:** Honor system in effect. **Housing:** Guaranteed on-campus for freshmen. Coed dorms, single-sex dorms, apartments, fraternity/sorority housing available. $200 nonrefundable deposit, deadline 5/1. Special interest housing (Italian, French, German, Asian, Russian, Spanish, Project Plus, international studies, ecology) available. **Activities:** Bands, choral groups, dance, drama, film society, international student organizations, literary magazine, music ensembles, musical theater, opera, radio station, student government, student newspaper, symphony orchestra, TV station, Black student organization, College Republicans, Young Democrats, women's issues group, College Partnerships for Kids, Student Environmental Action Coalition, ecumenical council, Asian student union, Hispanic cultural organization.

**Athletics.** NCAA. **Intercollegiate:** Baseball M, basketball, cross-country, diving, field hockey W, football (tackle) M, golf, gymnastics, lacrosse W, soccer, swimming, tennis, track and field, volleyball W. **Intramural:** Badminton, baseball M, basketball, cross-country, golf, racquetball, soccer, softball, tennis, track and field, wrestling M. **Team name:** Tribe.

**Student services.** Alcohol/substance abuse counseling, campus ministries, career counseling, student employment services, financial aid counseling, health services, legal services, minority student services, on-campus daycare, personal counseling, placement for graduates. **Physically disabled:** Services for visually, hearing impaired.

**Contact.** E-mail: admission@wm.edu
Phone: (757) 221-4223 Fax: (757) 221-1242
Henry Broaddus, Dean of Admissions, College of William and Mary, PO Box 8795, Williamsburg, VA 23187-8795

## DeVry University: Arlington
**Arlington, Virginia**
www.devry.edu

CB code: 3813

▶ For-profit 4-year university
▶ Commuter campus in very large city
▶ 550 degree-seeking undergraduates: 40% part-time, 27% women, 48% African American, 4% Asian American, 10% Hispanic American, 1% Native American, 1% international
▶ 128 degree-seeking graduate students
▶ Interview required

**General. Degrees:** 72 bachelor's, 8 associate awarded; master's offered. **Calendar:** Semester, extensive summer session. **Full-time faculty:** 19 total; 42% minority, 21% women. **Part-time faculty:** 14 total; 71% minority, 21% women.

**Freshman class profile.**

| Return as sophomores: | 51% | International: | 1% |
|---|---|---|---|
| Out-of-state: | 67% | | |

**Basis for selection.** Applicant must have high school diploma or equivalent, degree from an accredited postsecondary institution, or submit acceptable test scores and be at least 17 years of age. CPT also accepted.

**High school preparation.** Required units include mathematics 1. Math unit must be algebra or higher.

**2007-2008 Annual costs.** Tuition/fees: $14,640. Books/supplies: $1,300. Personal expenses: $3,152.

**Financial aid.** All financial aid based on need.

**Application procedures. Admission:** No deadline. $50 fee. Application may be submitted online. Admission notification on a rolling basis. **Financial aid:** No deadline. FAFSA required. Applicants notified on a rolling basis starting 7/1.

**Academics. Special study options:** Accelerated study, cooperative education, distance learning. **Credit/placement by examination:** CLEP. **Support services:** Learning center, remedial instruction, tutoring.

**Majors. Business:** Business admin. **Computer sciences:** Game design, information systems, networking. **Engineering:** Software. **Engineering technology:** General, construction, electrical. **Other:** Technical management.

**Most popular majors.** Business/marketing 57%, computer/information sciences 25%, engineering/engineering technologies 18%.

**Computing on campus.** Online course registration, online library, helpline available.

**Student life. Freshman orientation:** Mandatory. **Activities:** Linux users' group.

**Athletics. Intramural:** Basketball, volleyball.

**Student services.** Career counseling, student employment services, financial aid counseling, placement for graduates, veterans' counselor. **Physically disabled:** Services for visually, hearing impaired.

**Contact.** E-mail: admissions@crys.devry.edu
Phone: (703) 414-4100 Toll-free number: (866) 338-7932
Fax: (703) 414-4040
Bob Pavlovics, Director of Admissions, DeVry University: Arlington, 2450 Crystal Drive, Arlington, VA 22202

---

## Eastern Mennonite University

**Harrisonburg, Virginia**
www.emu.edu

**CB member**
**CB code: 5181**

- Private 4-year university and liberal arts college affiliated with Mennonite Church
- Residential campus in large town
- 953 degree-seeking undergraduates: 1% part-time, 62% women, 8% African American, 2% Asian American, 3% Hispanic American, 4% international
- 253 degree-seeking graduate students
- 71% of applicants admitted
- SAT or ACT with writing required
- 61% graduate within 6 years; 7% enter graduate study

**General.** Founded in 1917. Regionally accredited. **Degrees:** 284 bachelor's awarded; master's, first professional offered. **Location:** 110 miles from Richmond, 110 miles from Washington, DC. **Calendar:** Semester, limited summer session. **Full-time faculty:** 118 total; 65% have terminal degrees, 3% minority, 53% women. **Part-time faculty:** 39 total; 28% have terminal degrees, 15% minority, 33% women. **Class size:** 64% < 20, 31% 20-39, 3% 40-49, 2% 50-99, less than 1% >100. **Special facilities:** Museum of natural history, arboretum, student-run coffee shop.

**Freshman class profile.** 740 applied, 525 admitted, 203 enrolled.

| Mid 50% test scores | | | |
|---|---|---|---|
| SAT critical reading: | 450-600 | Rank in top quarter: | 45% |
| SAT math: | 470-600 | Rank in top tenth: | 22% |
| SAT writing: | 430-580 | End year in good standing: | 77% |
| ACT composite: | 19-27 | Return as sophomores: | 76% |
| GPA 3.50 or higher: | 53% | Out-of-state: | 53% |
| GPA 3.0-3.49: | 25% | Live on campus: | 96% |
| GPA 2.0-2.99: | 21% | International: | 6% |

**Basis for selection.** 2.2 high school GPA required. SAT score of 920 (exclusive of Writing) or ACT minimum composite score of 20 required.

---

Conditional admission possible for motivated applicants who fail to reach minimum admissions requirements. Interviews recommended. **Home-schooled:** Detailed record of coursework completed for grades 9-12, SAT or ACT required. **Learning Disabled:** Interview recommended for learning disabled; meet with academic support center personnel.

**High school preparation.** 21 units recommended. Recommended units include English 4, mathematics 3, social studies 3, science 3 (laboratory 3), foreign language 2 and academic electives 6.

**2007-2008 Annual costs.** Tuition/fees: $21,960. Room/board: $6,900. Books/supplies: $1,000. Personal expenses: $780.

**Financial aid. Non-need-based:** Scholarships awarded for academics, alumni affiliation, art, leadership, religious affiliation, state residency.

**Application procedures. Admission:** No deadline. $25 fee, may be waived for applicants with need. Application may be submitted online. Admission notification on a rolling basis. **Financial aid:** Priority date 3/1; no closing date. FAFSA required. Applicants notified on a rolling basis starting 3/1; must reply within 4 week(s) of notification.

**Academics.** Missions programs available. Cross-cultural education component required in 3-week or 3-month assignments to locations around the world. **Special study options:** Double major, ESL, honors, independent study, internships, liberal arts/career combination, study abroad, teacher certification program, Washington semester. **Credit/placement by examination:** AP, CLEP, IB, SAT, ACT, institutional tests. **Support services:** Learning center, reduced course load, remedial instruction, study skills assistance, tutoring, writing center.

**Majors. Biology:** General, biochemistry. **Business:** Accounting, business admin, international, organizational behavior. **Communications:** General, digital media. **Computer sciences:** Computer science. **Conservation:** Environmental science. **Education:** Physical. **English:** English lit. **Foreign languages:** French, Spanish. **Health:** Clinical lab science, nursing (RN), predental, premedicine, preveterinary. **History:** General. **Interdisciplinary:** Peace/conflict. **Liberal arts:** Arts/sciences. **Math:** General. **Parks/recreation:** Sports admin. **Physical sciences:** Chemistry. **Psychology:** General. **Public administration:** Social work. **Social sciences:** General, economics, international economic development, sociology. **Theology:** Bible, preministerial, theology. **Visual/performing arts:** Art, dramatic, photography. **Other:** Camping, Recreation, and Outdoor Ministries, Congregational and Youth Ministries, Philosophy and Theology.

**Most popular majors.** Business/marketing 20%, health sciences 26%, liberal arts 15%.

**Computing on campus.** 100 workstations in library, computer center, student center. Dormitories wired for high-speed internet access and linked to campus network. Commuter students can connect to campus network. Online library, helpline, student web hosting, wireless network available.

**Student life. Freshman orientation:** Mandatory. Preregistration for classes offered. One-week orientation begins 5 days before fall semester. **Policies:** Alcohol and drug use by students prohibited. Chapel attendance expected. Students must sign and adhere to Community Lifestyle Commitment. Emphasis on justice and peacemaking. **Housing:** Guaranteed on-campus for freshmen. Coed dorms, single-sex dorms, special housing for disabled, apartments, substance-free housing available. Intentional communities available. **Activities:** Bands, campus ministries, choral groups, dance, drama, film society, international student organizations, literary magazine, music ensembles, musical theater, student government, student newspaper, symphony orchestra, Young People's Christian Association, Peace Fellowship, Black student union, Latino student alliance, Earth Keepers, Social Work is People, A Safe Place, Alpha Omega Steppers For Christ.

**Athletics.** NCAA. **Intercollegiate:** Baseball M, basketball, cross-country, field hockey W, soccer, softball W, track and field, volleyball. **Intramural:** Basketball, football (tackle) M, golf, soccer, table tennis, tennis, volleyball. **Team name:** Royals.

**Student services.** Adult student services, alcohol/substance abuse counseling, campus ministries, career counseling, student employment services, financial aid counseling, health services, minority student services, personal counseling, placement for graduates. **Physically disabled:** Services for visually, speech, hearing impaired.

**Contact.** E-mail: admiss@emu.edu
Phone: (540) 432-4118 Toll-free number: (800) 368-2665
Fax: (540) 432-4444
Stephanie Shafer, Director of Admissions, Eastern Mennonite University, 1200 Park Road, Harrisonburg, VA 22802-2462

## ECPI College of Technology: Newport News
Newport News, Virginia
www.ecpi.edu

- For-profit 4-year business and technical college
- Very large city

**General.** Regionally accredited. **Calendar:** Continuous.

**Annual costs/financial aid.** Tuition/fees (2007-2008): $10,150.

**Contact.** 1001 Omni Boulevard Suite 105, Newport News, VA 23662

## ECPI College of Technology: Virginia Beach
Virginia Beach, Virginia
www.ecpi.edu                                                    CB code: 7140

- For-profit 4-year health science and technical college
- Commuter campus in very large city
- 6,100 degree-seeking undergraduates
- Interview required

**General.** Founded in 1966. Regionally accredited. **Degrees:** 23 bachelor's, 1,100 associate awarded. **Calendar:** Continuous, extensive summer session. **Full-time faculty:** 300 total. **Part-time faculty:** 200 total. **Class size:** 80% < 20, 20% 20-39.

**Basis for selection.** Requirements include interview and program specific admissions test. No special considerations given. SAT or ACT recommended. **Learning Disabled:** Consideration may be given on case-by-case basis.

**High school preparation.** Recommended units include English 4, mathematics 2, social studies 2, history 2 and science 2.

**2008-2009 Annual costs.** Tuition/fees: $10,300. Personal expenses: $1,710.

**Financial aid. Non-need-based:** Scholarships awarded for academics.

**Application procedures. Admission:** No deadline. $75 fee. Application may be submitted online. Admission notification on a rolling basis. **Financial aid:** No deadline. Institutional form required. Applicants notified on a rolling basis.

**Academics. Special study options:** Accelerated study, cooperative education, distance learning, double major, dual enrollment of high school students, independent study, internships. **Credit/placement by examination:** AP, CLEP, ACT, institutional tests. 18 credit hours maximum toward associate degree, 33 toward bachelor's. **Support services:** Learning center, remedial instruction, study skills assistance, tutoring, writing center.

**Majors. Computer sciences:** General.

**Computing on campus.** 2,800 workstations in library, computer center, student center. Commuter students can connect to campus network. Online course registration, online library, helpline, wireless network available.

**Student life. Freshman orientation:** Mandatory. Preregistration for classes offered. Half-day orientation held day prior to each term start. **Housing:** Substance-free housing available. Student housing assistance provided at Virginia Beach campus. **Activities:** Student government, student newspaper, student electronic technicians association, information technology exchange, accounting society, International Association of Administrative Professionals, Phi Theta Kappa.

**Student services.** Adult student services, alcohol/substance abuse counseling, career counseling, services for economically disadvantaged, student employment services, financial aid counseling, personal counseling, placement for graduates, veterans' counselor.

**Contact.** Phone: (757) 671-7171 Toll-free number: (800) 986-1200 Fax: (757) 671-8661
Jeff Marcus, Director of Admissions, ECPI College of Technology: Virginia Beach, 5555 Greenwich Road, Suite 300, Virginia Beach, VA 23462-6542

## ECPI Technical College: Glen Allen
Glen Allen, Virginia
www.ecpitech.edu

- For-profit 4-year technical college
- Commuter campus in large town

- 370 degree-seeking undergraduates
- Interview required

**General.** Accredited by ACCSCT. **Degrees:** 144 associate awarded. **Calendar:** Semester, extensive summer session. **Full-time faculty:** 21 total. **Part-time faculty:** 10 total.

**Basis for selection.** Program specific admission test required.

**2007-2008 Annual costs.** Tuition/fees: $10,150.

**Application procedures. Admission:** No deadline. $50 fee. Admission notification on a rolling basis.

**Academics. Special study options:** Distance learning, internships, study abroad. **Credit/placement by examination:** AP, CLEP, institutional tests. **Support services:** Remedial instruction, tutoring.

**Majors. Computer sciences:** General.

**Computing on campus.** 300 workstations in library, computer center. Online library available.

**Student life. Freshman orientation:** Mandatory. Preregistration for classes offered.

**Student services.** Adult student services, career counseling, student employment services, financial aid counseling, placement for graduates, veterans' counselor.

**Contact.** Phone: (804) 934-0100
Sharon Fitzgerald, Admissions, ECPI Technical College: Glen Allen, 4305 Cox Road, Glen Allen, VA 23060

## Emory & Henry College
Emory, Virginia
www.ehc.edu                                    CB member
                                                CB code: 5185

- Private 4-year liberal arts college affiliated with United Methodist Church
- Residential campus in rural community
- 977 degree-seeking undergraduates: 50% women
- 49 degree-seeking graduate students
- 72% of applicants admitted
- SAT or ACT (ACT writing optional) required

**General.** Founded in 1836. Regionally accredited. Partnership with Barter Theatre (state theater of Virginia), extensive Lyceum/cultural program, ScienceFest. **Degrees:** 222 bachelor's awarded; master's offered. **Location:** 25 miles from Bristol. **Calendar:** Semester, limited summer session. **Full-time faculty:** 75 total; 83% have terminal degrees, 7% minority, 37% women. **Part-time faculty:** 46 total; 15% have terminal degrees, 2% minority, 46% women. **Class size:** 76% < 20, 23% 20-39, less than 1% 40-49. **Special facilities:** Observatory, 1912 art depot, outdoor leadership center, disc golf course, golf course.

**Freshman class profile.** 1,455 applied, 1,048 admitted, 257 enrolled.

| Mid 50% test scores | | | |
|---|---|---|---|
| SAT critical reading: | 470-590 | GPA 2.0-2.99: | 21% |
| SAT math: | 480-570 | Rank in top quarter: | 47% |
| ACT composite: | 20-26 | Rank in top tenth: | 20% |
| GPA 3.50 or higher: | 46% | Out-of-state: | 34% |
| GPA 3.0-3.49: | 33% | Live on campus: | 91% |

**Basis for selection.** School achievement record, test scores, involvement in extracurricular and community activities, class rank, recommendations used. Audition required for preprofessional degrees in acting, directing, musical theater, and design/production. Auditions required for performance and teacher preparation tracks within music program. Portfolio recommended for art program.

**High school preparation.** 13 units required. Required units include English 4, mathematics 3, social studies 2, science 2 (laboratory 2) and foreign language 2. 1 fine arts recommended.

**2007-2008 Annual costs.** Tuition/fees: $22,320. Room/board: $7,670. Books/supplies: $700. Personal expenses: $1,000.

**2007-2008 Financial aid. Need-based:** 73% of total undergraduate aid awarded as scholarships/grants, 27% as loans/jobs. **Non-need-based:** Scholarships awarded for academics, art, leadership, minority status, music/

drama, religious affiliation, state residency. **Additional information:** Virginia residents eligible for additional in-state tuition grants.

**Application procedures. Admission:** No deadline. $30 fee, may be waived for applicants with need. Application may be submitted online. Admission notification on a rolling basis beginning on or about 8/1. **Financial aid:** Priority date 4/1, closing date 8/1. FAFSA required. Applicants notified on a rolling basis starting 2/1; must reply within 4 week(s) of notification.

**Academics. Special study options:** Double major, dual enrollment of high school students, honors, independent study, internships, liberal arts/career combination, student-designed major, study abroad, teacher certification program. **Credit/placement by examination:** AP, CLEP, IB, SAT, ACT, institutional tests. **Support services:** Learning center, pre-admission summer program, reduced course load, study skills assistance, tutoring, writing center.

**Majors. Area/ethnic studies:** East Asian, European, French, Near/Middle Eastern, Spanish/Iberian. **Biology:** General. **Business:** Accounting, business admin, international. **Communications:** General. **Computer sciences:** General, computer science. **Conservation:** Environmental science, environmental studies. **Education:** Art, biology, business, chemistry, English, French, physical, Spanish. **English:** Creative writing, English lit. **Foreign languages:** French, Spanish. **Health:** Athletic training. **History:** General, public archives. **Math:** General. **Parks/recreation:** Health/fitness, sports admin. **Philosophy/religion:** Philosophy, religion. **Physical sciences:** Chemistry, physics. **Psychology:** General. **Public administration:** Community org/advocacy. **Social sciences:** Anthropology, economics, geography, political science, sociology, U.S. government. **Visual/performing arts:** Acting, art, directing/producing, dramatic, graphic design, music performance.

**Most popular majors.** Biology 6%, business/marketing 9%, communications/journalism 6%, education 7%, history 7%, parks/recreation 8%, psychology 6%, social sciences 14%, visual/performing arts 7%.

**Computing on campus.** 174 workstations in dormitories, library, computer center, student center. Dormitories wired for high-speed internet access and linked to campus network. Commuter students can connect to campus network. Online library, helpline, wireless network available.

**Student life. Freshman orientation:** Mandatory. Preregistration for classes offered. Orientation occurs before registration. Students participate in community service activity and attend fine arts event following weekend as part of extended orientation. **Housing:** Guaranteed on-campus for all undergraduates. Coed dorms, single-sex dorms, special housing for disabled, substance-free housing available. $400 fully refundable deposit, deadline 8/1. Religious life, honor houses, and environmentally conscious house available. **Activities:** Bands, choral groups, dance, drama, literary magazine, music ensembles, musical theater, radio station, student government, student newspaper, TV station, Young Democrats, Young Republicans, Alpha Phi Omega, Fellowship of Christian Athletes, outdoor leadership program, Habitat for Humanity, Campus Christian Fellowship, multicultural student association.

**Athletics.** NCAA. **Intercollegiate:** Baseball M, basketball, cheerleading M, cross-country, football (tackle) M, golf M, soccer, softball W, swimming W, tennis, volleyball W. **Intramural:** Badminton, basketball, football (non-tackle), golf, soccer, softball, swimming, table tennis, tennis, volleyball, water polo. **Team name:** Wasps.

**Student services.** Alcohol/substance abuse counseling, campus ministries, career counseling, student employment services, financial aid counseling, health services, on-campus daycare, personal counseling, placement for graduates, veterans' counselor. **Physically disabled:** Services for visually, hearing impaired. **Learning disabled:** Comprehensive services available.

**Contact.** E-mail: ehadmiss@ehc.edu
Phone: (276) 944-6133 Toll-free number: (800) 848-5493
Fax: (276) 944-6935
David Hawsey, Vice President of Enrollment Management, Emory & Henry College, Box 10, Emory, VA 24327

---

## Ferrum College
Ferrum, Virginia
www.ferrum.edu

**CB member**
**CB code: 5213**

- Private 4-year liberal arts college affiliated with United Methodist Church
- Residential campus in rural community
- 1,240 degree-seeking undergraduates: 2% part-time, 44% women
- 78% of applicants admitted
- SAT or ACT (ACT writing recommended) required

---

**General.** Founded in 1913. Regionally accredited. **Degrees:** 157 bachelor's awarded. **Location:** 35 miles from Roanoke, 65 miles from Greensboro, North Carolina. **Calendar:** Semester, limited summer session. **Full-time faculty:** 69 total; 68% have terminal degrees, 42% women. **Part-time faculty:** 45 total; 9% have terminal degrees, 56% women. **Class size:** 71% < 20, 29% 20-39. **Special facilities:** Blue Ridge Institute and Farm Museum, State Center for Blue Ridge Folklore, forest and agricultural acreage used as outdoor labs in science, high and low ropes courses.

**Freshman class profile.** 2,009 applied, 1,570 admitted, 546 enrolled.

| Mid 50% test scores | | | |
|---|---|---|---|
| SAT critical reading: | 390-480 | GPA 2.0-2.99: | 61% |
| SAT math: | 390-490 | Rank in top quarter: | 15% |
| ACT composite: | 14-18 | Rank in top tenth: | 5% |
| GPA 3.50 or higher: | 14% | Return as sophomores: | 60% |
| GPA 3.0-3.49: | 18% | Out-of-state: | 15% |
| | | Live on campus: | 97% |

**Basis for selection.** High school record most important, followed by test scores, counselor recommendations, areas of intended college study, and extracurricular activities. Essay and interview recommended. **Home-schooled:** Transcript of courses and grades required. **Learning Disabled:** Submit current disability documentation to Director of Disability Services.

**High school preparation.** Recommended units include English 4, mathematics 3, social studies 3, science 2 (laboratory 1), foreign language 2 and academic electives 2.

**2007-2008 Annual costs.** Tuition/fees: $20,885. Room/board: $6,700. Books/supplies: $800. Personal expenses: $1,300.

**2007-2008 Financial aid. Need-based:** 66% of total undergraduate aid awarded as scholarships/grants, 34% as loans/jobs. **Non-need-based:** Scholarships awarded for academics, job skills, leadership, religious affiliation, state residency.

**Application procedures. Admission:** Priority date 3/1; deadline 8/15 (postmark date). $25 fee, may be waived for applicants with need. Application may be submitted online. Admission notification on a rolling basis. Must reply no later than 30 days after receiving official acceptance letter. **Financial aid:** Priority date 4/1; no closing date. FAFSA required. Applicants notified on a rolling basis starting 3/1.

**Academics.** Field experiences and internships emphasized. Academic services/support available fall and spring academic semesters. **Special study options:** Double major, dual enrollment of high school students, exchange student, honors, independent study, internships, liberal arts/career combination, student-designed major, study abroad, teacher certification program. **Credit/placement by examination:** AP, CLEP, IB, SAT, ACT, institutional tests. 12 credit hours maximum toward bachelor's degree. **Support services:** Learning center, pre-admission summer program, reduced course load, remedial instruction, study skills assistance, tutoring, writing center.

**Majors. Agriculture:** Business, horticultural science. **Biology:** General. **Business:** Accounting, business admin, finance, management information systems, marketing. **Computer sciences:** Computer science, information systems. **Conservation:** Environmental science. **Education:** General. **English:** English lit. **Foreign languages:** Russian, Spanish. **Health:** Clinical lab science, health services. **History:** General. **Liberal arts:** Arts/sciences. **Math:** General. **Parks/recreation:** General, health/fitness, sports admin. **Philosophy/religion:** Philosophy, religion. **Physical sciences:** Chemistry. **Protective services:** Criminal justice. **Psychology:** General. **Public administration:** Social work. **Social sciences:** General, international relations, political science. **Visual/performing arts:** General, art, dramatic.

**Most popular majors.** Business/marketing 22%, liberal arts 10%, parks/recreation 11%, security/protective services 11%.

**Computing on campus.** PC or laptop required. 600 workstations in dormitories, library, computer center, student center. Dormitories wired for high-speed internet access and linked to campus network. Commuter students can connect to campus network. Online course registration, online library, helpline, repair service, student web hosting, wireless network available.

**Student life. Freshman orientation:** Mandatory. Preregistration for classes offered. 2-day student orientation held immediately prior to fall semester. **Housing:** Guaranteed on-campus for all undergraduates. Coed dorms, single-sex dorms, apartments, substance-free housing available. $200 deposit. Housing substance-free; no alcohol or tobacco products allowed. **Activities:** Jazz band, choral groups, dance, drama, literary magazine, music ensembles, musical theater, radio station, student government, student newspaper, Environmental Action Coalition, Big Buddy/Little Buddy, African American student association, Bonner Scholars, Student Christian Fellowship, Kappa Delta Chi, Habitat for Humanity, Colleges Against Cancer, Alpha Phi Omega.

**Athletics.** NCAA. **Intercollegiate:** Baseball M, basketball, cheerleading, cross-country, football (tackle) M, golf M, lacrosse W, soccer, softball W, tennis, volleyball W. **Intramural:** Basketball, bowling, football (non-tackle) M, racquetball, softball, swimming, table tennis, tennis, volleyball. **Team name:** Panthers.

**Student services.** Adult student services, alcohol/substance abuse counseling, campus ministries, career counseling, student employment services, financial aid counseling, health services, minority student services, personal counseling, placement for graduates, veterans' counselor.

**Contact.** E-mail: admissions@ferrum.edu
Phone: (540) 365-4290 Toll-free number: (800) 868-9797
Fax: (540) 365-4266
Gilda Woods, Director of Admissions, Ferrum College, Spilman-Daniel House, Ferrum, VA 24088

## George Mason University
**Fairfax, Virginia**
www.gmu.edu

**CB member**
**CB code: 5827**

- Public 4-year university
- Residential campus in large town
- 17,983 degree-seeking undergraduates: 23% part-time, 54% women, 8% African American, 16% Asian American, 7% Hispanic American, 4% international
- 9,612 degree-seeking graduate students
- 56% of applicants admitted
- Application essay required
- 59% graduate within 6 years

**General.** Founded in 1972. Regionally accredited. **Degrees:** 3,715 bachelor's awarded; master's, doctoral, first professional offered. **ROTC:** Army, Air Force. **Location:** 15 miles from Washington, DC. **Calendar:** Semester, extensive summer session. **Full-time faculty:** 1,055 total. **Part-time faculty:** 985 total. **Special facilities:** Library of Congress Federal Theater Project collection, arts center, observatory, the National Zoo's conservation and research center.

**Freshman class profile.** 13,327 applied, 7,436 admitted, 2,229 enrolled.

| Mid 50% test scores | | | |
|---|---|---|---|
| SAT critical reading: | 480-600 | **GPA 2.0-2.99:** | 5% |
| SAT math: | 490-610 | **Rank in top quarter:** | 54% |
| SAT writing: | 470-590 | **Rank in top tenth:** | 18% |
| ACT composite: | 20-25 | **End year in good standing:** | 85% |
| GPA 3.50 or higher: | 44% | **Return as sophomores:** | 85% |
| GPA 3.0-3.49: | 51% | **International:** | 2% |

**Basis for selection.** Test scores, class rank, academic record with emphasis on courses taken, and GPA most important. Special talents and abilities and counselor recommendations also important. SAT Subject Tests recommended. Audition required for dance, music applicants. Portfolio required for BFA art and visual technology applicants.

**High school preparation.** 18 units required; 23 recommended. Required and recommended units include English 4, mathematics 3-4, social studies 3-4, science 3-4 (laboratory 3-4), foreign language 2-3 and academic electives 3-5. Additional mathematics and science units required for engineering, mathematics, and computer science applicants.

**2007-2008 Annual costs.** Tuition/fees: $6,840; $19,728 out-of-state. Room/board: $7,020.

**2006-2007 Financial aid. Need-based:** 1,522 full-time freshmen applied for aid; 894 were judged to have need; 834 of these received aid. Average need met was 68%. Average scholarship/grant was $5,141; average loan $2,763. 43% of total undergraduate aid awarded as scholarships/grants, 57% as loans/jobs. **Non-need-based:** Awarded to 1,399 full-time undergraduates, including 400 freshmen. Scholarships awarded for academics, athletics, minority status, music/drama, ROTC, state residency.

**Application procedures. Admission:** Priority date 12/1; deadline 1/15 (postmark date). $70 fee, may be waived for applicants with need. Application may be submitted online. Admission notification 4/1. Must reply by May 1 or within 3 week(s) if notified thereafter. **Financial aid:** Priority date 3/1; no closing date. FAFSA required. Applicants notified on a rolling basis starting 4/1; must reply within 3 week(s) of notification.

**Academics. Special study options:** Accelerated study, combined bachelor's/graduate degree, cooperative education, cross-registration, distance learning, double major, dual enrollment of high school students, ESL, exchange student, external degree, honors, independent study, internships, liberal arts/ career combination, student-designed major, study abroad, teacher certification program. **Credit/placement by examination:** AP, CLEP, IB, institutional tests. 30 credit hours maximum toward bachelor's degree. **Support services:** Learning center, study skills assistance, tutoring, writing center.

**Majors. Area/ethnic studies:** Latin American, Russian/Slavic. **Biology:** General. **Business:** Accounting, business admin, finance, marketing. **Computer sciences:** General. **Education:** Health, physical. **Engineering:** Computer, electrical, systems. **English:** English lit, speech/rhetoric. **Foreign languages:** General. **Health:** Athletic training, clinical lab science, nursing (RN). **History:** General. **Interdisciplinary:** Math/computer science, neuroscience, peace/conflict. **Liberal arts:** Arts/sciences. **Math:** General. **Parks/recreation:** General, health/fitness. **Philosophy/religion:** Philosophy, religion. **Physical sciences:** Astronomy, chemistry, geology, physics. **Protective services:** Police science. **Psychology:** General. **Public administration:** General, social work. **Social sciences:** Anthropology, economics, geography, international relations, political science, sociology. **Visual/performing arts:** General, art, cinematography, dance, dramatic, music performance. **Other:** Decision Science and Operations Management, Electronics and Communications Engineering, Global and Environmental Change, Health Science.

**Computing on campus.** 1,500 workstations in dormitories, library, computer center, student center. Dormitories wired for high-speed internet access and linked to campus network. Commuter students can connect to campus network. Online course registration, online library, helpline, repair service, student web hosting, wireless network available.

**Student life. Freshman orientation:** Mandatory, $160 fee. Preregistration for classes offered. Held at the beginning of the fall and spring semesters. **Housing:** Guaranteed on-campus for freshmen. Coed dorms, single-sex dorms, special housing for disabled, apartments, substance-free housing available. $300 nonrefundable deposit, deadline 5/1. **Activities:** Bands, choral groups, dance, drama, film society, literary magazine, music ensembles, musical theater, opera, radio station, student government, student newspaper, symphony orchestra, TV station.

**Athletics.** NCAA. **Intercollegiate:** Baseball M, basketball, cross-country, diving, golf M, lacrosse W, rowing (crew) W, soccer, softball W, swimming, tennis, track and field, volleyball, wrestling M. **Intramural:** Basketball, soccer, tennis, volleyball. **Team name:** Patriots.

**Student services.** Alcohol/substance abuse counseling, campus ministries, career counseling, student employment services, financial aid counseling, health services, minority student services, on-campus daycare, personal counseling, placement for graduates, veterans' counselor, women's services. **Physically disabled:** Services for visually, hearing impaired.

**Contact.** E-mail: admissions@gmu.edu
Phone: (703) 993-2400 Fax: (703) 993-4622
Andrew Flagel, Associate Vice President, Enrollment Development / Dean of Admissions, George Mason University, 4400 University Drive, MSN 3A4, Fairfax, VA 22030-4444

## Gibbs College: Vienna
**Vienna, Virginia**
www.gibbsva.edu

**CB code: 5655**

- For-profit 4-year business and technical college
- Large city

**General.** Accredited by ACICS. **Calendar:** Quarter.

**Contact.** Phone: (703) 556-8888
1980 Gallows Road, Vienna, VA 22182

## Hampden-Sydney College
**Hampden-Sydney, Virginia**
www.hsc.edu

**CB member**
**CB code: 5291**

- Private 4-year liberal arts college for men affiliated with Presbyterian Church (USA)
- Residential campus in rural community
- 1,122 degree-seeking undergraduates: 5% African American, 1% Asian American, 1% Hispanic American, 2% international
- 67% of applicants admitted
- SAT or ACT with writing, application essay required
- 68% graduate within 6 years; 33% enter graduate study

**General.** Founded in 1776. Regionally accredited. **Degrees:** 220 bachelor's awarded. **ROTC:** Army. **Location:** 60 miles from Richmond, 69 miles from Charlottesville. **Calendar:** Semester, limited summer session. **Full-time faculty:** 97 total; 53% have terminal degrees, 6% minority, 29% women.

**Part-time faculty:** 36 total; 28% have terminal degrees, 8% minority, 22% women. **Class size:** 69% < 20, 31% 20-39. **Special facilities:** International communications center, observatory, college operated museum, Athlete Hall of Fame museum, hiking trail.

**Freshman class profile.** 1,470 applied, 984 admitted, 334 enrolled.

| Mid 50% test scores | | | |
|---|---|---|---|
| SAT critical reading: | 510-600 | Rank in top quarter: | 38% |
| SAT math: | 520-630 | Rank in top tenth: | 13% |
| SAT writing: | 480-590 | End year in good standing: | 86% |
| ACT composite: | 20-26 | Return as sophomores: | 77% |
| GPA 3.50 or higher: | 38% | Out-of-state: | 33% |
| GPA 3.0-3.49: | 35% | Live on campus: | 100% |
| GPA 2.0-2.99: | 27% | International: | 1% |
| | | Fraternities: | 34% |

**Basis for selection.** High school academic record most important. Recommendations, test scores, extracurricular activities, essay also important. SAT Subject Tests recommended. SAT Subject Test in Math Level 1 recommended. Interview recommended.

**High school preparation.** 16 units required. Required and recommended units include English 4, mathematics 3-4, social studies 1, science 2-3 (laboratory 1), foreign language 2-3 and academic electives 3.

**2007-2008 Annual costs.** Tuition/fees: $27,732. Fees are same for in-state and out-of-state students. Room/board: $8,712. Books/supplies: $1,000. Personal expenses: $1,200.

**2007-2008 Financial aid. Need-based:** Average need met was 86%. Average scholarship/grant was $17,219; average loan $4,099. 76% of total undergraduate aid awarded as scholarships/grants, 24% as loans/jobs. **Non-need-based:** Scholarships awarded for academics, leadership, religious affiliation, ROTC, state residency.

**Application procedures. Admission:** Closing date 3/1 (postmark date). $30 fee, may be waived for applicants with need. Application must be submitted on paper. Admission notification 4/15. Must reply by 5/1. **Financial aid:** Priority date 3/1; no closing date. FAFSA, CSS PROFILE required. Applicants notified on a rolling basis starting 2/1; must reply by 5/1 or within 2 week(s) of notification.

**Academics.** Public service concentration for men interested in government involves classwork and internship followed by paper presented and defended publicly. **Special study options:** Cross-registration, double major, dual enrollment of high school students, exchange student, honors, independent study, internships, semester at sea, study abroad, Washington semester, Appalachian semester, junior year exchange program with members of Virginia consortium. **Credit/placement by examination:** AP, CLEP, IB, SAT, ACT, institutional tests. **Support services:** Reduced course load, study skills assistance, tutoring, writing center.

**Majors. Biology:** General, biochemistry, biophysics. **Business:** Managerial economics. **Computer sciences:** Computer science. **English:** English lit. **Foreign languages:** Ancient Greek, classics, French, German, Latin, Spanish. **History:** General. **Interdisciplinary:** Math/computer science. **Liberal arts:** Humanities. **Math:** General, applied. **Philosophy/religion:** Philosophy, religion. **Physical sciences:** Chemistry, physics. **Psychology:** General. **Social sciences:** Econometrics, economics, international relations, political science. **Visual/performing arts:** Studio arts.

**Most popular majors.** Biology 11%, business/marketing 31%, history 19%, social sciences 19%.

**Computing on campus.** 98 workstations in dormitories, library, computer center. Dormitories wired for high-speed internet access and linked to campus network. Commuter students can connect to campus network. Online course registration, online library, helpline, repair service, wireless network available.

**Student life. Freshman orientation:** Mandatory, $150 fee. Preregistration for classes offered. 4-day program before start of classes. **Housing:** Guaranteed on-campus for all undergraduates. Apartments, fraternity/sorority housing available. $300 deposit, deadline 5/1. **Activities:** Pep band, campus ministries, choral groups, drama, international student organizations, literary magazine, music ensembles, radio station, student government, student newspaper, Inter-Varsity Christian Fellowship, Republican Society, volunteer fire department, Good Men and Good Citizens (community service), Student Environmental Action Coalition, museum board, Fellowship of Christian Athletes, Minority Student Union, Young Democrats.

**Athletics.** NCAA. **Intercollegiate:** Baseball M, basketball M, cross-country M, football (tackle) M, golf M, lacrosse M, soccer M, tennis M. **Intramural:** Basketball M, racquetball M, rugby M, soccer M, softball M, volleyball M. **Team name:** Tigers.

**Student services.** Alcohol/substance abuse counseling, campus ministries, career counseling, student employment services, financial aid counseling, health services, minority student services, personal counseling, placement for graduates.

**Contact.** E-mail: hsapp@hsc.edu
Phone: (434) 223-6120 Toll-free number: (800) 755-0733
Fax: (434) 223-6346
Anita Garland, Dean of Admissions, Hampden-Sydney College, Box 667, Hampden-Sydney, VA 23943

## Hampton University
**Hampton, Virginia**
www.hamptonu.edu

**CB member**
**CB code: 5292**

- Private 4-year university
- Residential campus in small city
- 4,874 degree-seeking undergraduates: 6% part-time, 64% women
- 770 graduate students
- 49% of applicants admitted
- SAT or ACT, application essay required

**General.** Founded in 1868. Regionally accredited. **Degrees:** 860 bachelor's, 4 associate awarded; master's, doctoral, first professional offered. **ROTC:** Army, Naval. **Location:** 10 miles from Norfolk. **Calendar:** Semester, extensive summer session. **Full-time faculty:** 325 total. **Part-time faculty:** 125 total. **Class size:** 51% < 20, 38% 20-39, 7% 40-49, 4% 50-99, less than 1% >100. **Special facilities:** African American literature and history collection, university archives, North American Indian, African, Oceanic and Black American art collections.

**Freshman class profile.** 8,707 applied, 4,231 admitted, 1,145 enrolled.

| Mid 50% test scores | | | |
|---|---|---|---|
| SAT critical reading: | 470-620 | GPA 2.0-2.99: | 40% |
| SAT math: | 470-580 | Out-of-state: | 68% |
| ACT composite: | 17-26 | Live on campus: | 71% |
| GPA 3.50 or higher: | 19% | Fraternities: | 5% |
| GPA 3.0-3.49: | 41% | Sororities: | 4% |

**Basis for selection.** Academic record, rank in top half of graduating class, personal references, intended major, test scores and personal statement important. Extracurricular activities, essay, school recommendation considered. Audition required for music. **Homeschooled:** Transcript of courses and grades required. Must present secondary school record if it exists, GED test scores, verification by state/regional official, SAT or ACT results.

**High school preparation.** 17 units required. Required and recommended units include English 4, mathematics 3, social studies 2, science 2 (laboratory 2), foreign language 2 and academic electives 6. One chemistry, biology with lab, algebra I and II, geometry required.

**2007-2008 Annual costs.** Tuition/fees: $15,610. Room/board: $7,086. Books/supplies: $750. Personal expenses: $1,103.

**Financial aid. Non-need-based:** Scholarships awarded for academics, athletics, leadership, music/drama, ROTC.

**Application procedures. Admission:** Priority date 12/1; deadline 3/1 (postmark date). $35 fee. Application may be submitted online. Admission notification on a rolling basis beginning on or about 12/15. Must reply by 5/1. **Financial aid:** Priority date 3/1; no closing date. FAFSA required. Applicants notified on a rolling basis starting 4/15; must reply within 2 week(s) of notification.

**Academics.** Students who have completed one semester with minimum 3.2 GPA may apply to honors program. Academic skills workshops held throughout year available for all students. Students may take courses at other Tidewater consortium schools. **Special study options:** Accelerated study, combined bachelor's/graduate degree, cooperative education, cross-registration, distance learning, double major, dual enrollment of high school students, honors, independent study, internships, study abroad, teacher certification program. Grad level programs for undergraduates, coop programs in arts, business, education, engineering, social/behavioral science. **Credit/placement by examination:** AP, CLEP, IB, institutional tests. 30 credit hours maximum toward bachelor's degree. **Support services:** Learning center, pre-admission summer program, reduced course load, remedial instruction, tutoring, writing center.

**Majors. Architecture:** Architecture. **Biology:** General, marine, molecular. **Business:** Accounting, banking/financial services, business admin, finance, management information systems, managerial economics, marketing. **Communications:** Advertising, broadcast journalism, journalism, media studies, public relations. **Computer sciences:** General, computer science, networking. **Conservation:** Environmental science. **Education:** General, health, physical, special. **Engineering:** General, chemical, computer, electrical. **English:** English lit, speech/rhetoric. **Foreign languages:** Spanish. **Health:** Audiology/speech pathology, communication disorders, nursing (RN). **History:** General. **Legal studies:** Paralegal, prelaw. **Liberal arts:** Arts/sciences. **Math:** General. **Parks/recreation:** General, facilities management, sports admin. **Physical sciences:** Chemistry, physics. **Protective services:** Fire services admin, law enforcement admin. **Psychology:** General. **Social sciences:** Political science, sociology. **Theology:** Theology. **Transportation:** Aviation management. **Visual/performing arts:** Art, commercial/advertising art, dramatic, music performance.

**Computing on campus.** 1,500 workstations in dormitories, library, computer center, student center. Dormitories wired for high-speed internet access and linked to campus network. Commuter students can connect to campus network. Online course registration, online library, helpline, repair service, student web hosting, wireless network available.

**Student life. Freshman orientation:** Mandatory. Preregistration for classes offered. One-week orientation held in August. **Housing:** Guaranteed on-campus for freshmen. Coed dorms, single-sex dorms, substance-free housing available. $500 deposit, deadline 5/1. **Activities:** Bands, choral groups, dance, drama, international student organizations, music ensembles, musical theater, opera, radio station, student government, student newspaper, symphony orchestra, TV station, Christian student association, Big Brothers/Big Sisters, political science/pre-law club, Women in Communications, Muslim student fellowship, service learning and leadership organizations, National Leadership of Black Journalists.

**Athletics.** NCAA. **Intercollegiate:** Basketball, bowling W, cheerleading M, cross-country, football (tackle) M, golf, sailing, softball W, tennis, track and field, volleyball W. **Intramural:** Basketball, bowling W, softball W, swimming. **Team name:** Pirates.

**Student services.** Campus ministries, career counseling, services for economically disadvantaged, student employment services, financial aid counseling, health services, on-campus daycare, personal counseling, placement for graduates, veterans' counselor. **Physically disabled:** Services for visually, speech, hearing impaired.

**Contact.** E-mail: admit@hamptonu.edu
Phone: (757) 727-5328 Toll-free number: (800) 624-3328
Fax: (757) 727-5095
Angela Boyd, Director of Admissions, Hampton University, Office of Admissions, Hampton, VA 23668

---

## Hollins University
**Roanoke, Virginia**
www.hollins.edu

**CB member**
**CB code: 5294**

- Private 4-year university and liberal arts college for women
- Residential campus in small city
- 772 degree-seeking undergraduates: 3% part-time, 100% women, 8% African American, 2% Asian American, 3% Hispanic American, 1% Native American, 3% international
- 240 degree-seeking graduate students
- 88% of applicants admitted
- SAT or ACT (ACT writing optional), application essay required
- 70% graduate within 6 years

**General.** Founded in 1842. Regionally accredited. **Degrees:** 182 bachelor's awarded; master's offered. **Location:** 175 miles from Richmond, 250 miles from Washington, DC. **Calendar:** 4-1-4, limited summer session. **Full-time faculty:** 72 total; 96% have terminal degrees, 8% minority, 50% women. **Part-time faculty:** 36 total; 39% have terminal degrees, 11% minority, 69% women. **Class size:** 86% < 20, 13% 20-39, less than 1% 40-49. **Special facilities:** Electron microscope facilities, EEG and biofeedback equipment, research facilities for chromatography, spectrophotometry, electrochemistry, gas kinetics, centrifugation.

**Freshman class profile.** 632 applied, 559 admitted, 206 enrolled.

| Mid 50% test scores | | | |
|---|---|---|---|
| SAT critical reading: | 520-650 | GPA 2.0-2.99: | 17% |
| SAT math: | 470-580 | Rank in top quarter: | 56% |
| SAT writing: | 520-630 | Rank in top tenth: | 20% |
| ACT composite: | 20-27 | Return as sophomores: | 68% |
| GPA 3.50 or higher: | 52% | Out-of-state: | 58% |
| GPA 3.0-3.49: | 31% | Live on campus: | 98% |
| | | International: | 3% |

**Basis for selection.** School achievement record, school recommendation, and test scores very important. Essay, talent/ability important. Interview, class rank, character, alumni relation, extracurricular activities, volunteer work, work experience considered. Interview recommended. **Homeschooled:** Applicants encouraged to take 3 SAT Subject Tests.

**High school preparation.** 16 units required. Required units include English 4, mathematics 3, social studies 3, science 3 and foreign language 3.

**2007-2008 Annual costs.** Tuition/fees: $25,645. Room/board: $9,140. Books/supplies: $800. Personal expenses: $850.

**2007-2008 Financial aid. Need-based:** Average loan was $3,389. 68% of total undergraduate aid awarded as scholarships/grants, 32% as loans/jobs. **Non-need-based:** Scholarships awarded for academics, alumni affiliation, art, leadership, music/drama, state residency.

**Application procedures. Admission:** Priority date 2/1; no deadline. $35 fee, may be waived for applicants with need. Application may be submitted online. Admission notification on a rolling basis beginning on or about 12/15. Must reply by May 1 or within 2 week(s) if notified thereafter. **Financial aid:** Priority date 2/15; no closing date. FAFSA required. Applicants notified on a rolling basis starting 3/1; must reply by 5/1.

**Academics. Special study options:** Accelerated study, combined bachelor's/graduate degree, cooperative education, cross-registration, double major, dual enrollment of high school students, exchange student, independent study, internships, liberal arts/career combination, student-designed major, study abroad, teacher certification program. Numerous college exchange programs, 5- and 6-year dual degree programs in engineering with Washington University in St. Louis and Virginia Tech, Louis D. Rubin, Jr., Semester in Creative Writing. **Credit/placement by examination:** AP, CLEP, IB, institutional tests. **Support services:** Tutoring, writing center.

**Majors. Area/ethnic studies:** Women's. **Biology:** General, environmental. **Business:** General. **Communications:** General. **Conservation:** Environmental studies. **English:** Creative writing, English lit. **Foreign languages:** Classics, French, German, Spanish. **History:** General. **Interdisciplinary:** Global studies. **Math:** General. **Philosophy/religion:** Philosophy, religion. **Physical sciences:** Chemistry, physics. **Psychology:** General. **Social sciences:** Economics, political science, sociology. **Visual/performing arts:** Art history/conservation, dance, dramatic, studio arts.

**Most popular majors.** Business/marketing 10%, communications/journalism 7%, English 18%, foreign language 8%, psychology 7%, social sciences 13%, visual/performing arts 19%.

**Computing on campus.** 100 workstations in dormitories, library, computer center, student center. Dormitories wired for high-speed internet access and linked to campus network. Commuter students can connect to campus network. Online course registration, online library, helpline, wireless network available.

**Student life. Freshman orientation:** Mandatory. 5-day program includes mini-classes and community service. **Housing:** Guaranteed on-campus for all undergraduates. Special housing for disabled, apartments, substance-free housing available. $400 nonrefundable deposit. Special interest housing. **Activities:** Choral groups, dance, drama, film society, literary magazine, music ensembles, Model UN, musical theater, student government, student newspaper, TV station, religious life association, Black student alliance, College Democrats, College Republicans, Colleges Against Cancer, Student Health Advisory Board, Students Helping Achieve Rewarding Experiences, Mujeres Unidas, Circle K.

**Athletics.** NCAA. **Intercollegiate:** Basketball W, equestrian W, field hockey W, golf W, lacrosse W, soccer W, swimming W, tennis W, volleyball W.

**Student services.** Adult student services, alcohol/substance abuse counseling, campus ministries, career counseling, student employment services, financial aid counseling, health services, minority student services, personal counseling, placement for graduates, women's services. **Physically disabled:** Services for visually, hearing impaired.

**Contact.** E-mail: huadm@hollins.edu
Phone: (540) 362-6401 Toll-free number: (800) 456-9595
Fax: (540) 362-6218
Rebecca Eckstein, Dean of Admissions, Hollins University, PO Box 9707, Roanoke, VA 24020-1707

---

## ITT Technical Institute: Chantilly
**Chantilly, Virginia**

**CB code: 4086**

- For-profit 4-year technical college
- Commuter campus in large town

**General.** Accredited by ACICS. **Calendar:** Quarter.

**Annual costs/financial aid.** Tuition varies by program, $260-$368 per credit hour.

**Contact.** Phone: (703) 263-2541
Director of Recruitment, 14420 Albemarle Point Place, Chantilly, VA 20151

## ITT Technical Institute: Norfolk
**Norfolk, Virginia**
www.itt-tech.edu                    CB code: 2737

- For-profit 4-year technical college
- Commuter campus in large city

**General.** Accredited by ACICS. **Location:** 81 miles from Richmond, 145 miles from Washington, DC. **Calendar:** Quarter.

**Annual costs/financial aid.** Tuition varies by program, $260-$368 per credit hour.

**Contact.** Phone: (757) 466-1260
Director of Recruitment, 863 Glenrock Road, Norfolk, VA 23502

## ITT Technical Institute: Richmond
**Richmond, Virginia**
www.itt-tech.edu                    CB code: 2748

- For-profit 4-year technical college
- Commuter campus in small city

**General.** Accredited by ACICS. **Location:** 98 miles from Washington, DC. **Calendar:** Quarter.

**Annual costs/financial aid.** Tuition varies by program, $260-$368 per credit hour. Books/supplies: $3,100.

**Contact.** Phone: (804) 330-4992
Director of Recruitment, 300 Gateway Centre Parkway, Richmond, VA 23235

## ITT Technical Institute: Springfield
**Springfield, Virginia**

- For-profit 4-year technical college
- Commuter campus in large town

**General.** Accredited by ACICS. **Calendar:** Quarter.

**Annual costs/financial aid.** Tuition varies by program, $260-$368 per credit hour.

**Contact.** Phone: (703) 440-9535
Director of Recruitment, 7300 Boston Boulevard, Springfield, VA 22153

## James Madison University
**Harrisonburg, Virginia**                    CB member
www.jmu.edu                                   CB code: 5392

- Public 4-year university
- Residential campus in large town
- 16,108 degree-seeking undergraduates: 3% part-time, 60% women, 4% African American, 5% Asian American, 2% Hispanic American, 1% international
- 1,266 degree-seeking graduate students
- 64% of applicants admitted
- SAT or ACT (ACT writing optional) required
- 81% graduate within 6 years

**General.** Founded in 1908. Regionally accredited. **Degrees:** 3,475 bachelor's awarded; master's, doctoral offered. **ROTC:** Army, Air Force. **Location:** 123 miles from Washington, DC. **Calendar:** Semester, extensive summer session. **Full-time faculty:** 854 total; 80% have terminal degrees, 7% minority, 44% women. **Part-time faculty:** 398 total; 28% have terminal degrees, 3% minority, 50% women. **Class size:** 31% < 20, 48% 20-39, 7% 40-49, 10% 50-99, 4% >100. **Special facilities:** Arboretum, observatory, planetarium, mineral museum, science on a sphere (SOS).

**Freshman class profile.** 18,352 applied, 11,660 admitted, 3,867 enrolled.

| Mid 50% test scores | | | |
|---|---|---|---|
| SAT critical reading: | 520-610 | Rank in top tenth: | 29% |
| SAT math: | 530-620 | End year in good standing: | 90% |
| SAT writing: | 520-610 | Return as sophomores: | 91% |
| ACT composite: | 22-26 | Out-of-state: | 35% |
| GPA 3.50 or higher: | 71% | Live on campus: | 99% |
| GPA 3.0-3.49: | 27% | International: | 1% |
| GPA 2.0-2.99: | 2% | Fraternities: | 6% |
| Rank in top quarter: | 75% | Sororities: | 6% |

**Basis for selection.** Rigor of high school curriculum, as shown by the quantity and quality of courses, most important. Class rank or GPA, test scores, extracurricular activities, special skills or talents important. Counselor recommendation considered. Applicants with solid achievement in 5 or more academic courses in each of 4 years of high school have decided advantage in admissions process. Audition required for dance, music, theater programs; portfolio and interview required for art. Nursing, justice studies, media arts and design, political science, psychology, and social work students must apply to their applicable departments in addition to applying for undergraduate admission. **Homeschooled:** Statement describing home-school structure and mission required.

**High school preparation.** Required and recommended units include English 4, mathematics 4, social studies 3-4, science 3-4 (laboratory 3-4) and foreign language 3. 3 of same foreign language recommended, or 2 of one language and 2 of another. Social studies may include units in history.

**2007-2008 Annual costs.** Tuition/fees: $6,666; $17,386 out-of-state. Room/board: $7,108. Books/supplies: $838. Personal expenses: $1,794.

**2007-2008 Financial aid. Need-based:** 2,719 full-time freshmen applied for aid; 1,439 were judged to have need; 1,218 of these received aid. Average need met was 45%. Average scholarship/grant was $6,497; average loan $3,615. 40% of total undergraduate aid awarded as scholarships/grants; 60% as loans/jobs. **Non-need-based:** Awarded to 1,718 full-time undergraduates, including 678 freshmen. Scholarships awarded for academics, alumni affiliation, art, athletics, leadership, minority status, music/drama, state residency.

**Application procedures. Admission:** Priority date 11/1; deadline 1/15 (postmark date). $40 fee, may be waived for applicants with need. Application may be submitted online. Admission notification 4/1. Must reply by 5/1. Housing deposit may be refunded only for personal illness certified by a physician or other extenuating circumstances approved by the assistant vice president for finance. **Financial aid:** Priority date 3/1; no closing date. FAFSA required. Applicants notified on a rolling basis starting 4/1; must reply within 4 week(s) of notification.

**Academics. Special study options:** Accelerated study, combined bachelor's/graduate degree, distance learning, double major, honors, independent study, internships, study abroad, teacher certification program, Washington semester. Continuing education programs offered on campus. **Credit/placement by examination:** AP, CLEP, IB, institutional tests. 8 credit hours maximum toward bachelor's degree. CLEP credit awarded only to students seeking bachelor's in individualized study. **Support services:** Learning center, study skills assistance, tutoring, writing center.

**Majors. Biology:** General, biotechnology. **Business:** Accounting, business admin, finance, hospitality admin, international, managerial economics, marketing. **Communications:** General. **Computer sciences:** General, information systems. **Engineering:** General. **English:** English lit, technical writing. **Family/consumer sciences:** Food/nutrition. **Foreign languages:** General. **Health:** Athletic training, community health services, health care admin, nursing (RN), speech pathology. **History:** General. **Interdisciplinary:** Science/society, systems science. **Liberal arts:** Arts/sciences. **Math:** General. **Parks/recreation:** Health/fitness. **Physical sciences:** Chemistry, geology, physics. **Psychology:** General. **Public administration:** General, social work. **Social sciences:** General, anthropology, economics, geography, international relations, political science, sociology. **Visual/performing arts:** Art, art history/conservation, dramatic, music performance. **Other:** Justice Studies, Philosophy and religion, Quantitative finance.

**Most popular majors.** Business/marketing 22%, communications/journalism 8%, English 6%, health sciences 10%, parks/recreation 6%, psychology 6%, social sciences 10%, visual/performing arts 6%.

**Computing on campus.** 1,583 workstations in dormitories, library, computer center. Dormitories wired for high-speed internet access and linked to campus network. Commuter students can connect to campus network. Online course registration, online library, helpline, repair service, student web hosting, wireless network available.

**Student life. Freshman orientation:** Mandatory, $140 fee. Preregistration for classes offered. One-day orientation in June or July, plus 5-day program in August prior to the beginning of classes. **Housing:** Guaranteed on-campus for freshmen. Coed dorms, apartments, fraternity/sorority housing, substance-free housing available. $250 nonrefundable deposit, deadline 5/1. Theme housing communities available: Madison international community, learning community, substance-free community and second-year experience; Students must apply. Fraternities located off campus. **Activities:** Bands, campus ministries, choral groups, dance, drama, international student organizations, literary magazine, music ensembles, musical theater, opera, radio station, student government, student newspaper, symphony orchestra, 328 student organizations and clubs.

**Athletics.** NCAA. **Intercollegiate:** Baseball M, basketball, cheerleading, cross-country W, diving W, field hockey W, football (tackle) M, golf, lacrosse W, soccer, softball W, swimming W, tennis, track and field W, volleyball W. **Intramural:** Basketball, bowling, football (non-tackle), golf, racquetball, soccer, softball, table tennis, tennis, volleyball. **Team name:** Dukes.

**Student services.** Adult student services, alcohol/substance abuse counseling, campus ministries, career counseling, student employment services, health services, minority student services, personal counseling, placement for graduates. **Physically disabled:** Services for visually, speech, hearing impaired.

**Contact.** E-mail: admissions@jmu.edu
Phone: (540) 568-5681 Fax: (540) 568-3332
Michael Walsh, Director of Admissions, James Madison University, Sonner Hall, MSC 0101, Harrisonburg, VA 22807

## Jefferson College of Health Sciences
Roanoke, Virginia
www.jchs.edu                                    CB code: 5099

- Private 4-year health science and nursing college
- Commuter campus in small city
- 927 degree-seeking undergraduates: 29% part-time, 83% women, 13% African American, 1% Asian American, 1% Hispanic American
- 32 degree-seeking graduate students
- 43% of applicants admitted
- SAT or ACT (ACT writing recommended) required

**General.** Founded in 1982. Regionally accredited. Access to educational seminars broadcast live by American Hospital Association, Hospital Satellite network, and other networks. One of 50 demonstration centers nationwide for interactive video in nursing education. Part of Carilion system. **Degrees:** 85 bachelor's, 195 associate awarded; master's offered. **Calendar:** Semester, limited summer session. **Full-time faculty:** 62 total; 26% have terminal degrees, 66% women. **Part-time faculty:** 38 total; 18% have terminal degrees, 66% women. **Class size:** 46% < 20, 50% 20-39, 4% 40-49.

**Freshman class profile.** 554 applied, 237 admitted, 91 enrolled.

| Mid 50% test scores | | | |
|---|---|---|---|
| SAT critical reading: | 400-500 | GPA 3.0-3.49: | 31% |
| SAT math: | 410-500 | GPA 2.0-2.99: | 42% |
| SAT writing: | 390-490 | End year in good standing: | 83% |
| ACT composite: | 18-21 | Return as sophomores: | 66% |
| GPA 3.50 or higher: | 21% | Out-of-state: | 4% |
| | | Live on campus: | 32% |

**Basis for selection.** Certification required for some programs. Emergency health sciences program requires emergency medical technician ambulance certification prior to entering program.

**High school preparation.** 16 units required. Required units include English 4, mathematics 2 and science 2.

**2007-2008 Annual costs.** Tuition/fees: $15,500. Tuition for physician assistant program: $48,860 for full 2-year program. Room/board: $6,310. Books/supplies: $800. Personal expenses: $2,100.

**2006-2007 Financial aid. Need-based:** 136 full-time freshmen applied for aid; 122 were judged to have need; 122 of these received aid. Average need met was 52%. Average scholarship/grant was $3,121; average loan $4,479. 18% of total undergraduate aid awarded as scholarships/grants, 82% as loans/jobs. **Non-need-based:** Awarded to 564 full-time undergraduates, including 99 freshmen. Scholarships awarded for academics.

**Application procedures. Admission:** No deadline. $35 fee, may be waived for applicants with need. Application may be submitted online. Admission notification on a rolling basis. Must reply by May 1 or within 2 week(s) if notified thereafter. **Financial aid:** No deadline. FAFSA, institutional form required. Applicants notified on a rolling basis; must reply within 2 week(s) of notification.

**Academics. Special study options:** Accelerated study, cross-registration, distance learning, double major, independent study, internships, liberal arts/career combination. **Credit/placement by examination:** AP, CLEP, IB, institutional tests. Maximum of 18 credit hours may be satisfied by CLEP/DANTES examinations. **Support services:** Learning center, pre-admission summer program, tutoring.

**Majors. Biology:** Biomedical sciences. **Health:** Athletic training, health care admin, nursing (RN), physician assistant, premedicine, prenursing, prepharmacy. **Parks/recreation:** Exercise sciences. **Psychology:** Medical.

**Most popular majors.** Health sciences 95%.

**Computing on campus.** 56 workstations in library, computer center. Dormitories wired for high-speed internet access. Online library, helpline, repair service available.

**Student life. Freshman orientation:** Mandatory. Preregistration for classes offered. One-day orientation held multiple times during summer. **Housing:** Coed dorms available. $250 nonrefundable deposit. **Activities:** Campus ministries, choral groups, student government, student newspaper, student nurse association, student occupational therapy association, student physical therapy assistant assembly, Good Samaritan Club, Habitat for Humanity, Hands of Healing.

**Student services.** Adult student services, career counseling, student employment services, financial aid counseling, health services, personal counseling, placement for graduates.

**Contact.** E-mail: jmckeon@jchs.edu
Phone: (540) 985-8483 Toll-free number: (888) 985-8483
Fax: (540) 985-9773
Judith McKeon, Director of Admissions, Jefferson College of Health Sciences, Box 13186, Roanoke, VA 24031-3186

## Liberty University
Lynchburg, Virginia                              CB member
www.liberty.edu                                  CB code: 5385

- Private 4-year university and seminary college affiliated with Baptist faith
- Residential campus in small city
- 18,475 degree-seeking undergraduates: 30% part-time, 52% women, 12% African American, 1% Asian American, 4% Hispanic American, 1% Native American, 3% international
- 8,334 degree-seeking graduate students
- 94% of applicants admitted
- SAT or ACT (ACT writing optional), application essay required

**General.** Founded in 1971. Regionally accredited. **Degrees:** 1,773 bachelor's, 129 associate awarded; master's, doctoral, first professional offered. **ROTC:** Army, Air Force. **Location:** 120 miles from Richmond, 150 miles from Raleigh, North Carolina. **Calendar:** Semester, limited summer session. **Full-time faculty:** 340 total; 10% minority, 29% women. **Part-time faculty:** 485 total; 5% minority, 40% women. **Class size:** 29% < 20, 54% 20-39, 4% 40-49, 7% 50-99, 6% >100. **Special facilities:** Ice rink, running and hiking trails.

**Freshman class profile.** 5,776 applied, 5,415 admitted, 3,438 enrolled.

| Mid 50% test scores | | | |
|---|---|---|---|
| SAT critical reading: | 440-550 | GPA 2.0-2.99: | 36% |
| SAT math: | 420-540 | Rank in top quarter: | 13% |
| ACT composite: | 18-24 | Rank in top tenth: | 4% |
| GPA 3.50 or higher: | 33% | Out-of-state: | 67% |
| GPA 3.0-3.49: | 30% | Live on campus: | 84% |
| | | International: | 5% |

**Basis for selection.** Secondary school record, standardized test scores, and essay most important. Applicants who fail to meet the minimum required GPA may be admitted on academic warning status and will be limited to 13 semester hours of coursework. TOEFL required for international students.

**High school preparation.** 17 units recommended. Recommended units include English 4, mathematics 3, social studies 2, science 2 (laboratory 2), foreign language 2 and academic electives 4.

**2007-2008 Annual costs.** Tuition/fees: $15,800. Room/board: $5,400. Books/supplies: $1,400. Personal expenses: $1,400.

**Financial aid. Non-need-based:** Scholarships awarded for academics, alumni affiliation, athletics, leadership, music/drama, religious affiliation, ROTC, state residency.

**Application procedures. Admission:** Priority date 6/30; no deadline. $40 fee, may be waived for applicants with need. Application may be submitted online. Admission notification on a rolling basis. Must reply by May 1 or within 2 week(s) if notified thereafter. **Financial aid:** Closing date 3/1. FAFSA required. Applicants notified on a rolling basis starting 3/15; must reply within 3 week(s) of notification.

**Academics. Special study options:** Accelerated study, cooperative education, distance learning, double major, dual enrollment of high school students, ESL, external degree, honors, independent study, internships, student-designed major, teacher certification program, weekend college. Associate school of the Institute of Holy Land Studies in Jerusalem. **Credit/placement by examination:** AP, CLEP, IB, SAT, ACT, institutional tests. 30 credit hours maximum toward bachelor's degree. **Support services:** Learning center, reduced course load, remedial instruction, study skills assistance, tutoring.

**Majors. Biology:** General, biochemistry. **Business:** General, accounting, management information systems. **Communications:** General. **Computer sciences:** General, web page design. **Education:** ESL. **Engineering:** Computer, electrical, industrial, software, systems. **English:** English lit. **Family/consumer sciences:** General, clothing/textiles. **Foreign languages:** Spanish. **Health:** Athletic training, community health, nursing (RN), public health ed. **History:** General. **Liberal arts:** Arts/sciences. **Math:** General. **Parks/recreation:** Exercise sciences, health/fitness, sports admin. **Philosophy/religion:** Philosophy, religion. **Protective services:** Criminal justice. **Psychology:** General. **Social sciences:** General, political science. **Theology:** Bible, missionary, pastoral counseling, sacred music, youth ministry. **Transportation:** Aviation. **Visual/performing arts:** Design, dramatic.

**Most popular majors.** Business/marketing 17%, communications/journalism 6%, health sciences 7%, interdisciplinary studies 13%, philosophy/religious studies 17%, psychology 12%.

**Computing on campus.** 406 workstations in library, computer center, student center. Dormitories wired for high-speed internet access and linked to campus network. Commuter students can connect to campus network. Online course registration, online library, helpline, repair service, wireless network available.

**Student life. Freshman orientation:** Mandatory. Preregistration for classes offered. **Policies:** All students involved in Christian or community service. **Housing:** Guaranteed on-campus for all undergraduates. Single-sex dorms, special housing for disabled, apartments, substance-free housing available. $250 nonrefundable deposit. Students required to live on campus unless living with parents, over age 21, or married. **Activities:** Bands, campus ministries, choral groups, drama, music ensembles, musical theater, opera, radio station, student government, student newspaper, TV station, Circle K, Youthquest, Light Ministries, Fellowship of Christian Athletes, Students Teaching Elementary School, College Republicans, Campus SERVE.

**Athletics.** NCAA. **Intercollegiate:** Baseball M, basketball, cheerleading, cross-country, football (tackle) M, golf M, soccer, softball W, tennis, track and field, volleyball W. **Intramural:** Basketball, football (non-tackle), soccer, softball, tennis, volleyball. **Team name:** Flames.

**Student services.** Campus ministries, career counseling, student employment services, financial aid counseling, health services, minority student services, personal counseling, placement for graduates, veterans' counselor, women's services. **Physically disabled:** Services for hearing impaired.

**Contact.** E-mail: admissions@liberty.edu
Phone: (434) 582-5985 Toll-free number: (800) 543-5317
Fax: (800) 542-2311
Paul Clark, Director of Residential Admissions, Liberty University, 1971 University Boulevard, Lynchburg, VA 24502

## Longwood University

**Farmville, Virginia**
**www.whylongwood.com**

**CB member**
**CB code: 5368**

- Public 4-year university
- Residential campus in small town
- 3,932 degree-seeking undergraduates: 3% part-time, 65% women, 7% African American, 2% Asian American, 2% Hispanic American
- 412 degree-seeking graduate students
- 66% of applicants admitted
- SAT or ACT (ACT writing optional), application essay required
- 65% graduate within 6 years

**General.** Founded in 1839. Regionally accredited. **Degrees:** 669 bachelor's awarded; master's offered. **ROTC:** Army. **Location:** 65 miles from Richmond, 60 miles from Charlottesville. **Calendar:** Semester, limited summer session. **Full-time faculty:** 208 total; 80% have terminal degrees, 7%

minority, 46% women. **Part-time faculty:** 39 total; 18% minority, 67% women. **Special facilities:** Golf course, flora collection, visual arts center, greenhouse.

**Freshman class profile.** 4,352 applied, 2,872 admitted, 988 enrolled.

| Mid 50% test scores | | | |
|---|---|---|---|
| SAT critical reading: | 480-570 | Rank in top quarter: | 35% |
| SAT math: | 480-560 | Rank in top tenth: | 9% |
| SAT writing: | 460-550 | Return as sophomores: | 79% |
| ACT composite: | 21-25 | Out-of-state: | 10% |
| GPA 3.50 or higher: | 31% | Live on campus: | 97% |
| GPA 3.0-3.49: | 48% | International: | 1% |
| GPA 2.0-2.99: | 21% | Fraternities: | 2% |
| | | Sororities: | 2% |

**Basis for selection.** Rank in top half of class, combined SAT score (exclusive of Writing) of 1000 minimum and cumulative GPA of 2.7 minimum in college preparatory courses required. Extracurricular activities and recommendations also considered. For Early Action consideration, applicants must have 3.0 high school grade point average and 1000 on SAT (exclusive of Writing). Modern language majors required to take SAT subject test in intended language of study for placement. Audition required for music. **Homeschooled:** Statement describing homeschool structure and mission, interview, letter of recommendation (nonparent) required. Applications reviewed on case-by-case basis.

**High school preparation.** 24 units required. Required units include English 4, mathematics 3, social studies 2, history 2, science 3 (laboratory 2), foreign language 2 and visual/performing arts 1.

**2007-2008 Annual costs.** Tuition/fees: $8,058; $16,259 out-of-state. Required laptop computer for first year students $1,200. Room/board: $6,740. Books/supplies: $800. Personal expenses: $1,200.

**2007-2008 Financial aid. Need-based:** 686 full-time freshmen applied for aid; 427 were judged to have need; 427 of these received aid. Average need met was 74%. Average scholarship/grant was $5,053; average loan $3,184. 52% of total undergraduate aid awarded as scholarships/grants, 48% as loans/jobs. **Non-need-based:** Awarded to 1,306 full-time undergraduates, including 372 freshmen. Scholarships awarded for academics, alumni affiliation, art, athletics, leadership, music/drama, ROTC, state residency.

**Application procedures. Admission:** Priority date 3/1; no deadline. $40 fee, may be waived for applicants with need. Application may be submitted online. Admission notification on a rolling basis beginning on or about 1/15. Must reply by May 1 or within 1 week(s) if notified thereafter. **Financial aid:** Priority date 3/1; no closing date. FAFSA required. Applicants notified on a rolling basis starting 4/10.

**Academics. Special study options:** Accelerated study, combined bachelor's/graduate degree, cross-registration, distance learning, double major, dual enrollment of high school students, ESL, exchange student, honors, independent study, internships, liberal arts/career combination, study abroad, teacher certification program. Summer field programs in archaeology and botany. **Credit/placement by examination:** AP, CLEP, IB, institutional tests. **Support services:** Learning center, reduced course load, study skills assistance, tutoring, writing center.

**Majors. Biology:** General. **Business:** General, accounting, business admin, finance, management information systems, management science, marketing, retailing. **Communications:** General. **Computer sciences:** General, computer science. **Education:** General, art, biology, business, chemistry, early childhood, elementary, English, French, German, health, history, mathematics, middle, multi-level teacher, music, physical, physics, science, social studies, Spanish, special, speech impaired. **English:** Creative writing, English lit. **Foreign languages:** French, German, Spanish. **Health:** Athletic training, predental, premedicine, prepharmacy, preveterinary, recreational therapy. **History:** General, public archives. **Legal studies:** Prelaw. **Liberal arts:** Arts/sciences. **Math:** General. **Parks/recreation:** Exercise sciences, health/fitness. **Physical sciences:** Chemistry, physics. **Protective services:** Criminal justice. **Psychology:** General. **Public administration:** Social work. **Social sciences:** Anthropology, criminology, economics, political science, sociology. **Visual/performing arts:** General, art, art history/conservation, commercial/advertising art, dramatic, music performance, studio arts.

**Computing on campus.** PC or laptop required. 197 workstations in dormitories, library, computer center, student center. Dormitories wired for high-speed internet access and linked to campus network. Commuter students can connect to campus network. Online course registration, online library, helpline, repair service, student web hosting, wireless network available.

**Student life. Freshman orientation:** Mandatory, $75 fee. Preregistration for classes offered. One-day orientation held during spring and summer. **Housing:** Guaranteed on-campus for freshmen. Coed dorms, single-sex dorms, special housing for disabled, apartments, fraternity/sorority housing, substance-free housing available. $400 nonrefundable deposit, deadline 5/1. Honor student housing available. **Activities:** Bands, campus ministries, choral groups, dance, drama, literary magazine, music ensembles, opera, radio station, student government, student newspaper, College Democrats, unity alliance, interfraternity council, Habitat for Humanity, Alpha Phi Omega, Students Educating for Active Leadership, College Republicans, Peer Helpers, Big Sibling Program.

**Athletics.** NCAA. **Intercollegiate:** Baseball M, basketball, cheerleading, cross-country, field hockey W, golf, soccer, softball W, tennis. **Intramural:** Basketball, bowling, football (non-tackle), soccer, softball, tennis, volleyball. **Team name:** Lancers.

**Student services.** Adult student services, alcohol/substance abuse counseling, career counseling, student employment services, financial aid counseling, health services, minority student services, personal counseling, placement for graduates, women's services. **Physically disabled:** Services for visually, speech, hearing impaired.

**Contact.** E-mail: admissions@longwood.edu
Phone: (434) 395-2060 Toll-free number: (800) 281-4677 ext. 2
Fax: (434) 395-2332
Robert Chonko, Dean of Admissions, Longwood University, 201 High Street, Farmville, VA 23909-1898

---

## Lynchburg College
**Lynchburg, Virginia**
**www.lynchburg.edu**

**CB member**
**CB code: 5372**

- Private 4-year liberal arts college affiliated with Christian Church (Disciples of Christ)
- Residential campus in small city
- 2,046 degree-seeking undergraduates: 3% part-time, 59% women, 7% African American, 2% Asian American, 2% Hispanic American, 1% international
- 376 degree-seeking graduate students
- 69% of applicants admitted
- SAT or ACT (ACT writing optional) required
- 53% graduate within 6 years; 18% enter graduate study

**General.** Founded in 1903. Regionally accredited. **Degrees:** 461 bachelor's awarded; master's offered. **Location:** 180 miles from Washington, DC, 60 miles from Roanoke. **Calendar:** Semester, extensive summer session. **Full-time faculty:** 157 total; 76% have terminal degrees, 10% minority, 49% women. **Part-time faculty:** 57 total; 44% have terminal degrees, 2% minority, 60% women. **Class size:** 60% < 20, 40% 20-39, less than 1% 40-49. **Special facilities:** Nature study center, center for media development, geographic information system labs, forensic cadaver lab, astronomical observatory.

**Freshman class profile.** 4,248 applied, 2,934 admitted, 601 enrolled.

| Mid 50% test scores | | | |
|---|---|---|---|
| SAT critical reading: | 460-560 | GPA 2.0-2.99: | 40% |
| SAT math: | 460-570 | Rank in top quarter: | 37% |
| SAT writing: | 450-550 | Rank in top tenth: | 13% |
| ACT composite: | 18-22 | End year in good standing: | 65% |
| GPA 3.50 or higher: | 28% | Return as sophomores: | 73% |
| GPA 3.0-3.49: | 31% | Out-of-state: | 44% |
| | | Live on campus: | 95% |

**Basis for selection.** School record, test scores, school and community involvement, recommendation, academic quality of secondary school attended, essay, interview important. Audition recommended for music, theater arts programs; portfolio recommended for studio art. Essay or personal statement strongly encouraged, but not formally required. **Learning Disabled:** Documentation must be received no later than 45 days prior to the first day of class.

**High school preparation.** 16 units required; 20 recommended. Required and recommended units include English 4, mathematics 3-4, social studies 2, history 2, science 3-4 (laboratory 2), foreign language 2-3 and academic electives 1.

**2008-2009 Annual costs.** Tuition/fees: $27,565. Room/board: $7,000. Books/supplies: $600. Personal expenses: $200.

**2007-2008 Financial aid.** Need-based: 473 full-time freshmen applied for aid; 396 were judged to have need; 396 of these received aid. Average need met was 93%. Average scholarship/grant was $17,717; average loan $3,579. 80% of total undergraduate aid awarded as scholarships/grants, 20% as loans/jobs. **Non-need-based:** Awarded to 1,521 full-time undergraduates, including 429 freshmen. Scholarships awarded for academics, art, leadership, music/drama, state residency.

---

**Application procedures. Admission:** No deadline. $30 fee, may be waived for applicants with need. Application may be submitted online. Admission notification on a rolling basis beginning on or about 9/1. Must reply by May 1 or within 2 week(s) if notified thereafter. **Financial aid:** Priority date 3/1; no closing date. FAFSA required. Applicants notified on a rolling basis starting 3/5; must reply by 5/1 or within 2 week(s) of notification.

**Academics. Special study options:** Accelerated study, cross-registration, double major, dual enrollment of high school students, honors, independent study, internships, study abroad, teacher certification program. **Credit/placement by examination:** AP, CLEP, IB, institutional tests. **Support services:** Study skills assistance, tutoring, writing center.

**Majors. Biology:** General, ecology, exercise physiology. **Business:** Accounting, business admin, international, marketing. **Communications:** General. **Computer sciences:** General. **Conservation:** Environmental science. **Education:** Elementary, health, physical. **English:** English lit. **Family/consumer sciences:** Family studies. **Foreign languages:** Comparative lit, French, Spanish. **Health:** Athletic training, nursing (RN). **History:** General. **Math:** General. **Parks/recreation:** Health/fitness, sports admin. **Philosophy/religion:** Philosophy, religion. **Physical sciences:** Chemistry, physics. **Psychology:** General. **Social sciences:** Economics, international relations, political science, sociology. **Visual/performing arts:** Art, dramatic.

**Most popular majors.** Biology 9%, business/marketing 12%, communications/journalism 6%, education 13%, health sciences 12%, parks/recreation 7%, psychology 6%, social sciences 13%, visual/performing arts 7%.

**Computing on campus.** 360 workstations in dormitories, library, computer center, student center. Dormitories wired for high-speed internet access and linked to campus network. Online library, repair service, wireless network available.

**Student life. Freshman orientation:** Mandatory. Preregistration for classes offered. Held during summer for fall semester students and in January for spring semester students. Separate but concurrent orientation programs available to parents and other guests of new students. **Policies:** Honor system promoted and adhered to. **Housing:** Guaranteed on-campus for all undergraduates. Coed dorms, single-sex dorms, special housing for disabled, fraternity/sorority housing, substance-free housing available. $200 nonrefundable deposit, deadline 5/1. College-owned townhomes, houses, and special interest houses available. **Activities:** Bands, choral groups, dance, drama, film society, literary magazine, music ensembles, student government, student newspaper, TV station, over 50 clubs and organizations.

**Athletics.** NCAA. **Intercollegiate:** Baseball M, basketball, cross-country, equestrian, field hockey W, golf M, lacrosse, soccer, softball W, tennis, track and field, volleyball W. **Intramural:** Basketball, field hockey W, lacrosse M, soccer, softball, volleyball. **Team name:** Hornets.

**Student services.** Adult student services, campus ministries, career counseling, student employment services, financial aid counseling, health services, minority student services, personal counseling. **Physically disabled:** Services for visually, hearing impaired.

**Contact.** E-mail: admissions@lynchburg.edu
Phone: (434) 544-8300 Toll-free number: (800) 426-8101 ext. 8300
Fax: (434) 544-8653
Sharon Walters-Bower, Director of Recruitment, Lynchburg College, 1501 Lakeside Drive, Lynchburg, VA 24501-3199

---

## Mary Baldwin College
**Staunton, Virginia**
**www.mbc.edu**

**CB member**
**CB code: 5397**

- Private 4-year liberal arts college for women affiliated with Presbyterian Church (USA)
- Residential campus in large town
- 1,369 degree-seeking undergraduates: 27% part-time, 95% women, 19% African American, 3% Asian American, 4% Hispanic American, 1% Native American, 1% international
- 170 degree-seeking graduate students
- 74% of applicants admitted
- SAT or ACT (ACT writing optional), interview required
- 51% graduate within 6 years; 18% enter graduate study

**General.** Founded in 1842. Regionally accredited. Bachelor's degree available for younger women (13-15) in program for exceptionally gifted. Adult degree program available on main campus and at several satellite campuses throughout Virginia. Men admitted to adult program. The Virginia Women's Institute for Leadership program. **Degrees:** 249 bachelor's awarded; master's offered. **ROTC:** Army, Naval, Air Force. **Location:** 100 miles from

Richmond, 150 miles from Washington, DC. **Calendar:** 4-4-1 semester system for traditional students. **Full-time faculty:** 74 total; 97% have terminal degrees, 10% minority, 51% women. **Part-time faculty:** 70 total; 14% minority, 59% women. **Class size:** 66% < 20, 34% 20-39. **Special facilities:** Electron microscope, gas chromatoscope.

**Freshman class profile.** 1,464 applied, 1,090 admitted, 268 enrolled.

| Mid 50% test scores | | | |
|---|---|---|---|
| SAT critical reading: | 470-580 | Rank in top quarter: | 37% |
| SAT math: | 440-550 | Rank in top tenth: | 12% |
| SAT writing: | 460-570 | End year in good standing: | 93% |
| ACT composite: | 20-29 | Return as sophomores: | 66% |
| GPA 3.50 or higher: | 36% | Out-of-state: | 13% |
| GPA 3.0-3.49: | 40% | Live on campus: | 92% |
| GPA 2.0-2.99: | 24% | International: | 1% |

**Basis for selection.** School achievement record most important; test scores, involvement in school or civic groups also important; recommendations considered; 3.0 GPA recommended. Portfolio recommended for art majors.

**High school preparation.** Required and recommended units include English 4, mathematics 3, social studies 3, science 2 (laboratory 1), foreign language 2-3 and academic electives 2. Higher requirements for Virginia Women's Institute for Leadership.

**2008-2009 Annual costs.** Tuition/fees: $23,645. Room/board: $6,730. Books/supplies: $900. Personal expenses: $915.

**2006-2007 Financial aid. Need-based:** Average need met was 93%. Average scholarship/grant was $10,502; average loan $1,886. 73% of total undergraduate aid awarded as scholarships/grants, 27% as loans/jobs. **Non-need-based:** Scholarships awarded for academics, leadership, state residency.

**Application procedures. Admission:** No deadline. $35 fee, may be waived for applicants with need. Application may be submitted online. Admission notification on a rolling basis beginning on or about 9/1. Regular admission notification within 48 hours of receipt of all necessary materials. It is recommended for International Students to get applications in by June 1 to allow time to get a visa. **Financial aid:** Priority date 5/15; no closing date. FAFSA required. Applicants notified on a rolling basis starting 2/1.

**Academics.** Students complete requirements in experiential education, international education, women's studies. May term offers opportunity for individualized programming, externships, study abroad. Institute combines academics, physical training and leadership development in rigorous 4-year bachelor's program. **Special study options:** Accelerated study, combined bachelor's/graduate degree, cooperative education, cross-registration, distance learning, double major, dual enrollment of high school students, ESL, exchange student, external degree, honors, independent study, internships, liberal arts/career combination, semester at sea, student-designed major, study abroad, teacher certification program. Summer exchange program with Doshisha Women's College in Kyoto, Japan. **Credit/placement by examination:** AP, CLEP, IB, institutional tests. 25% of required credits may be counted toward bachelor's degree. **Support services:** Learning center, reduced course load, study skills assistance, tutoring, writing center.

**Honors college/program.** Minimum SAT score of 1150 (exclusive of Writing) or ACT score of 25, minimum 3.5 high school GPA, essay, interview required for admission. About 36 freshmen admitted.

**Majors. Area/ethnic studies:** Asian. **Biology:** General, biochemistry. **Business:** Business admin. **Communications:** General. **Computer sciences:** General, computer science, information systems. **English:** English lit. **Foreign languages:** French, Spanish. **Health:** Clinical lab science, health care admin. **History:** General. **Math:** General, applied. **Philosophy/religion:** Philosophy, religion. **Physical sciences:** Chemistry, physics. **Psychology:** General. **Public administration:** Social work. **Social sciences:** Economics, international relations, political science, sociology. **Visual/performing arts:** Art, arts management, dramatic.

**Most popular majors.** Business/marketing 15%, communications/journalism 6%, history 10%, psychology 17%, social sciences 17%, visual/performing arts 10%.

**Computing on campus.** 244 workstations in dormitories, library, computer center. Dormitories wired for high-speed internet access and linked to campus network. Commuter students can connect to campus network. Online course registration, online library, helpline, repair service, wireless network available.

**Student life. Freshman orientation:** Mandatory. Preregistration for classes offered. **Policies:** College prohibits drinking under age 21. Honor code observed. **Housing:** Guaranteed on-campus for all undergraduates. Apartments, substance-free housing available. $300 partly refundable deposit. Special interest houses focusing on Japan, honors, leadership, and community

service available. **Activities:** Marching band, choral groups, dance, drama, film society, literary magazine, music ensembles, musical theater, radio station, student government, student newspaper, TV station, Circle K, Habitat for Humanity, College Republicans, College Democrats, Black Student Alliance, Latinas Unidas, Christian Student Union, Campus Crusade for Christ, Anointed Voices of Praise Gospel Choir.

**Athletics.** NCAA. **Intercollegiate:** Basketball W, cross-country W, field hockey W, soccer W, softball W, swimming W, tennis W, volleyball W. **Team name:** Squirrels.

**Student services.** Adult student services, campus ministries, career counseling, student employment services, health services, minority student services, personal counseling, placement for graduates, women's services. **Physically disabled:** Services for visually, hearing impaired.

**Contact.** E-mail: admit@mbc.edu
Phone: (540) 887-7019 Toll-free number: (800) 468-2262
Fax: (540) 887-7279
Lisa Branson, Associate Vice President for Enrollment Management, Mary Baldwin College, Office of Admissions, Staunton, VA 24401

## Marymount University
**Arlington, Virginia**
www.marymount.edu

CB member
CB code: 5405

- Private 4-year university affiliated with Roman Catholic Church
- Residential campus in small city
- 2,199 degree-seeking undergraduates: 13% part-time, 75% women, 15% African American, 8% Asian American, 12% Hispanic American, 1% Native American, 6% international
- 1,288 degree-seeking graduate students
- 81% of applicants admitted
- SAT or ACT (ACT writing optional) required
- 51% graduate within 6 years; 30% enter graduate study

**General.** Founded in 1950. Regionally accredited. Classes available in government sites including Office of Naval Research and Navy Federal Credit Union. Extensive utilization of local resources in Washington, DC area, including placement in senior internships. **Degrees:** 512 bachelor's, 33 associate awarded; master's, doctoral offered. **ROTC:** Army. **Location:** 7 miles from Washington, DC. **Calendar:** Semester, extensive summer session. **Full-time faculty:** 138 total; 89% have terminal degrees, 5% minority, 74% women. **Part-time faculty:** 183 total; 51% have terminal degrees, 4% minority, 53% women. **Class size:** 46% < 20, 51% 20-39, 3% 40-49, less than 1% 50-99, less than 1% >100.

**Freshman class profile.** 1,904 applied, 1,541 admitted, 400 enrolled.

| Mid 50% test scores | | | |
|---|---|---|---|
| SAT critical reading: | 450-560 | Rank in top quarter: | 41% |
| SAT math: | 450-550 | Rank in top tenth: | 15% |
| SAT writing: | 450-550 | End year in good standing: | 88% |
| ACT composite: | 18-24 | Return as sophomores: | 71% |
| GPA 3.50 or higher: | 26% | Out-of-state: | 52% |
| GPA 3.0-3.49: | 33% | Live on campus: | 69% |
| GPA 2.0-2.99: | 41% | International: | 5% |

**Basis for selection.** GPA in academic courses and test scores most important. Class rank, recommendations from guidance counselors and teachers also important. Essay, interview recommended.

**High school preparation.** 15 units required. Required and recommended units include English 4, mathematics 3, social studies 3, science 2 and foreign language 3.

**2008-2009 Annual costs.** Tuition/fees: $21,528. Room/board: $9,190. Books/supplies: $800. Personal expenses: $900.

**2006-2007 Financial aid. Need-based:** 287 full-time freshmen applied for aid; 234 were judged to have need; 230 of these received aid. Average need met was 81%. Average scholarship/grant was $7,929; average loan $2,590. 57% of total undergraduate aid awarded as scholarships/grants, 43% as loans/jobs. **Non-need-based:** Awarded to 1,171 full-time undergraduates, including 274 freshmen. Scholarships awarded for academics, alumni affiliation, leadership, ROTC, state residency.

**Application procedures. Admission:** Priority date 5/1; no deadline. $40 fee, may be waived for applicants with need. Application may be submitted online. Admission notification on a rolling basis. Must reply by May 1 or within 3 week(s) if notified thereafter. **Financial aid:** Priority date 3/1; no closing date. FAFSA required. Applicants notified on a rolling basis starting 3/15; must reply within 2 week(s) of notification.

**Academics.** All undergraduates complete internship before graduation. **Special study options:** Accelerated study, combined bachelor's/graduate degree, cross-registration, distance learning, double major, ESL, honors, independent study, internships, student-designed major, study abroad, teacher certification program. Member of the Consortium of Universities of the Washington, DC metropolitan area. **Credit/placement by examination:** AP, CLEP, IB, institutional tests. 30 credit hours maximum toward associate degree, 30 toward bachelor's. Credit for prior work/life experience available through Portfolio Assessment and Credit by Examination program. **Support services:** Learning center, reduced course load, tutoring.

**Honors college/program.** Admission competitive and limited to 20 students each year. Minimum high school or college GPA of 3.5, minimum composite SAT score of 1200 (exclusive of Writing) or ACT of 26, minimum TOEFL score of 617 (paper) or 260 (computer) for international students, composition proficiency as demonstrated by credit for English 101 (AP or transfer), satisfactory score on the MU writing test recommended.

**Majors. Biology:** General, cellular/molecular. **Business:** Business admin, fashion, human resources. **Communications:** General. **Computer sciences:** Information systems. **English:** English lit. **Health:** Nursing (RN). **History:** General. **Liberal arts:** Arts/sciences. **Math:** General. **Parks/recreation:** Exercise sciences. **Philosophy/religion:** Philosophy, religion. **Protective services:** Criminal justice. **Psychology:** General. **Social sciences:** Criminology, economics, political science, sociology. **Visual/performing arts:** Fashion design, graphic design, interior design, studio arts.

**Most popular majors.** Business/marketing 15%, communications/journalism 8%, health sciences 20%, liberal arts 6%, psychology 9%, social sciences 7%, visual/performing arts 17%.

**Computing on campus.** 270 workstations in dormitories, library, computer center. Dormitories wired for high-speed internet access and linked to campus network. Commuter students can connect to campus network. Online course registration, helpline, wireless network available.

**Student life. Freshman orientation:** Mandatory. Preregistration for classes offered. 3 weekend orientation sessions in summer. **Housing:** Guaranteed on-campus for freshmen. Coed dorms, single-sex dorms available. $300 nonrefundable deposit, deadline 5/1. **Activities:** Campus ministries, choral groups, dance, drama, international student organizations, literary magazine, student government, student newspaper, Black student alliance, Students in Free Enterprise, College Democrats/College Republicans, Best Buddies.

**Athletics.** NCAA. **Intercollegiate:** Basketball, cross-country, golf M, lacrosse, soccer, swimming, volleyball W. **Intramural:** Basketball, football (non-tackle), golf M, soccer, softball, swimming, volleyball, water polo, weight lifting. **Team name:** Saints.

**Student services.** Campus ministries, career counseling, student employment services, financial aid counseling, health services, personal counseling. **Physically disabled:** Services for visually, speech, hearing impaired.

**Contact.** E-mail: admissions@marymount.edu
Phone: (703) 284-1500 Toll-free number: (800) 548-7638
Fax: (703) 522-0349
Chris Domes, Vice President for Enrollment and Student Services, Marymount University, 2807 North Glebe Road, Arlington, VA 22207-4299

## National College: Roanoke Valley

**Roanoke, Virginia**
www.national-college.edu
**CB code: 5502**

- For-profit 4-year business college
- Commuter campus in large city
- 599 degree-seeking undergraduates
- Interview required

**General.** Founded in 1886. Accredited by ACICS. **Degrees:** 34 bachelor's, 104 associate awarded; master's offered. **Calendar:** Quarter, limited summer session. **Full-time faculty:** 16 total. **Part-time faculty:** 50 total.

**Basis for selection.** Open admission.

**2008-2009 Annual costs.** Tuition/fees: $9,585.

**Financial aid.** All financial aid based on need.

**Application procedures. Admission:** Closing date 9/1 (receipt date). $30 fee, may be waived for applicants with need. Application may be submitted online. Admission notification on a rolling basis. **Financial aid:** No deadline. FAFSA required. Applicants notified on a rolling basis.

**Academics. Special study options:** Double major, internships. **Credit/placement by examination:** CLEP, institutional tests. **Support services:** Tutoring.

**Majors. Business:** Accounting, business admin.

**Computing on campus.** 35 workstations in library, computer center.

**Student life. Freshman orientation:** Mandatory. Preregistration for classes offered. **Housing:** Coed dorms available. Hotel accommodations available. **Activities:** Student government.

**Student services.** Career counseling, financial aid counseling, placement for graduates.

**Contact.** Phone: (540) 986-1800 Fax: (540) 444-4198
Larry Steele, Vice President of Admissions, National College: Roanoke Valley, PO Box 6400, Roanoke, VA 24017-0400

## Norfolk State University

**Norfolk, Virginia**
www.nsu.edu
**CB member**
**CB code: 5864**

- Public 4-year university
- Commuter campus in small city
- 5,259 degree-seeking undergraduates: 18% part-time, 63% women, 88% African American, 1% Asian American, 2% Hispanic American, 1% international
- 637 degree-seeking graduate students
- 68% of applicants admitted
- SAT or ACT (ACT writing optional) required
- 30% graduate within 6 years

**General.** Founded in 1935. Regionally accredited. **Degrees:** 709 bachelor's, 52 associate awarded; master's, doctoral offered. **ROTC:** Army, Naval. **Location:** 5 miles from downtown. **Calendar:** Semester, extensive summer session. **Full-time faculty:** 272 total; 70% have terminal degrees, 72% minority, 48% women. **Part-time faculty:** 105 total. **Class size:** 54% < 20, 38% 20-39, 6% 40-49, 2% 50-99. **Special facilities:** Planetarium, crystal laboratory, laser laboratory, nuclear magnetic resonance laboratory, institute for service learning, literacy center for entrepreneurial studies, center for materials research, institute for minorities in applied sciences, assistive technology laboratory.

**Freshman class profile.** 4,584 applied, 3,095 admitted, 995 enrolled.

| Mid 50% test scores | | Rank in top tenth: | 6% |
|---|---|---|---|
| SAT critical reading: | 400-480 | Return as sophomores: | 70% |
| SAT math: | 400-470 | Out-of-state: | 28% |
| ACT composite: | 16-20 | Live on campus: | 78% |
| GPA 3.50 or higher: | 6% | International: | 1% |
| GPA 3.0-3.49: | 20% | Fraternities: | 10% |
| GPA 2.0-2.99: | 73% | Sororities: | 10% |
| Rank in top quarter: | 23% | | |

**Basis for selection.** Combination of academic preparation, aptitude, achievements, and motivation predict a reasonable probability of success are most important. Interview recommended for electronics, engineering, nursing programs; audition recommended for music; portfolio recommended for art. **Homeschooled:** Transcript of courses and grades required.

**High school preparation.** 22 units required. Required units include English 4, mathematics 3, history 3, science 3 and academic electives 9. 2 science required for nursing applicants: 1 chemistry, 1 biology, 2 high school math (1 algebra), 2 science required for business applicants. 1 geometry, 2 algebra recommended for mathematics applicants. 2 mathematics must include algebra for computer science applicants.

**2007-2008 Annual costs.** Tuition/fees: $5,322; $16,242 out-of-state. Room/board: $6,996. Books/supplies: $1,000. Personal expenses: $1,400.

**Financial aid. Non-need-based:** Scholarships awarded for academics, alumni affiliation, athletics, leadership, music/drama, ROTC, state residency.

**Application procedures. Admission:** Closing date 5/31 (postmark date). $25 fee, may be waived for applicants with need. Application may be submitted online. Admission notification on a rolling basis. Must reply by May 1 or within 2 week(s) if notified thereafter. **Financial aid:** Priority date 5/31; no closing date. FAFSA required. Applicants notified on a rolling basis starting 4/1; must reply within 2 week(s) of notification.

**Academics.** **Special study options:** Combined bachelor's/graduate degree, cooperative education, cross-registration, distance learning, double major, dual enrollment of high school students, ESL, honors, independent study, internships, liberal arts/career combination, teacher certification program. **Credit/placement by examination:** AP, CLEP, SAT, ACT, institutional tests. No limit on number of credits university will accept, as long as student passes exam and has departmental approval. **Support services:** Learning center, reduced course load, study skills assistance, tutoring, writing center.

**Majors.** **Biology:** General. **Business:** General, accounting, hospitality admin. **Communications:** Journalism, media studies. **Computer sciences:** General. **Education:** Business, kindergarten/preschool, special, trade/industrial. **Engineering:** Electrical. **Engineering technology:** CAD/CADD, computer, construction, electrical. **English:** English lit. **Health:** Clinical lab science, health care admin, medical records admin, nursing (RN). **History:** General. **Math:** General. **Parks/recreation:** Exercise sciences. **Physical sciences:** Chemistry, optics, physics. **Psychology:** General. **Public administration:** Social work. **Social sciences:** Political science, sociology. **Visual/performing arts:** Art.

**Computing on campus.** 1,028 workstations in dormitories, library, computer center. Dormitories linked to campus network. Online library, helpline available.

**Student life.** **Freshman orientation:** Mandatory. Preregistration for classes offered. Held during June, July and August. **Housing:** Single-sex dorms, special housing for disabled, substance-free housing available. $300 nonrefundable deposit, deadline 5/31. **Activities:** Bands, choral groups, dance, drama, music ensembles, radio station, student government, student newspaper, symphony orchestra, TV station, Beta Psi Club, Omega Psi Phi, Alpha Kappa Alpha, Delta Sigma Theta, Alpha Delta Mu, Young Democrats, Young Republicans, Alpha Phi Alpha, Kappa Alpha Psi.

**Athletics.** NCAA. **Intercollegiate:** Baseball M, basketball, bowling W, cross-country, football (tackle) M, softball W, tennis, track and field, volleyball W. **Intramural:** Basketball, bowling, cheerleading, football (nontackle) M, soccer M, softball, swimming, table tennis, tennis, volleyball. **Team name:** Spartans.

**Student services.** Adult student services, alcohol/substance abuse counseling, campus ministries, career counseling, student employment services, financial aid counseling, health services, on-campus daycare, personal counseling, placement for graduates, veterans' counselor, women's services. **Physically disabled:** Services for visually, speech, hearing impaired.

**Contact.** E-mail: admissions@nsu.edu
Phone: (757) 823-8396 Fax: (757) 823-2078
Michelle Marable, Director of Admissions, Norfolk State University, 700 Park Avenue, Norfolk, VA 23504

---

## Old Dominion University

Norfolk, Virginia
www.odu.edu

CB member
CB code: 5126

- Public 4-year university
- Commuter campus in small city
- 15,655 degree-seeking undergraduates: 26% part-time, 58% women, 22% African American, 6% Asian American, 4% Hispanic American, 1% Native American, 2% international
- 4,077 degree-seeking graduate students
- 74% of applicants admitted
- SAT or ACT with writing required
- 49% graduate within 6 years

**General.** Founded in 1930. Regionally accredited. 4 regional Centers of Higher Education, distance learning network TELETECHNET, includes more than 40 sites across Virginia, Georgia, Illinois, Arizona, Washington, the Bahamas and the District of Columbia, along with U.S. Navy ships at sea. **Degrees:** 2,832 bachelor's awarded; master's, doctoral offered. **ROTC:** Army, Naval. **Location:** 2 miles from downtown, 200 miles from Washington, DC. **Calendar:** Semester, extensive summer session. **Full-time faculty:** 686 total; 79% have terminal degrees, 22% minority, 40% women. **Part-time faculty:** 418 total; 15% minority, 57% women. **Class size:** 38% < 20, 43% 20-39, 8% 40-49, 7% 50-99, 4% >100. **Special facilities:** Student art gallery, centers for urban research/service, economic education and child study centers, laser optics lab, planetarium, robotics lab, sub-/super-sonic wind tunnels, marine science research vessel, random wave pool.

**Freshman class profile.** 8,504 applied, 6,321 admitted, 2,571 enrolled.

| Mid 50% test scores | | | |
|---|---|---|---|
| SAT critical reading: | 480-570 | Rank in top tenth: | 15% |
| SAT math: | 480-580 | End year in good standing: | 75% |
| SAT writing: | 470-560 | Return as sophomores: | 73% |
| ACT composite: | 18-22 | Out-of-state: | 11% |
| GPA 3.50 or higher: | 29% | Live on campus: | 67% |
| GPA 3.0-3.49: | 45% | International: | 2% |
| GPA 2.0-2.99: | 26% | Fraternities: | 5% |
| Rank in top quarter: | 46% | Sororities: | 4% |

**Basis for selection.** Students who submit acceptable GPA and SAT/ACT scores are admitted. Those who do not meet acceptable GPA or SAT scores are reviewed by admissions committee. Committee looks at grades in core curriculum courses, student essay, student activity, resume/letters of recommendation, high school attended, IB and AP courses taken, etc. Audition required for music; portfolio required for art. **Homeschooled:** Scores from SAT or ACT must be submitted. GED not required. Students not attending program that requires regular curriculum review and submission of test scores to local school board must submit Stanford 9 results. **Learning Disabled:** Documentation of disabilities must be submitted before receiving services from Office of Disability Services.

**High school preparation.** 16 units required. Required units include English 4, mathematics 3, social studies 3, science 3 and foreign language 3.

**2008-2009 Annual costs.** Tuition/fees (projected): $6,608; $17,748 out-of-state. Room/board: $7,100. Books/supplies: $1,000. Personal expenses: $1,875.

**2007-2008 Financial aid.** **Need-based:** 1,861 full-time freshmen applied for aid; 1,669 were judged to have need; 1,485 of these received aid. Average need met was 85%. Average scholarship/grant was $4,557; average loan $3,393. 48% of total undergraduate aid awarded as scholarships/grants, 52% as loans/jobs. **Non-need-based:** Awarded to 1,831 full-time undergraduates, including 646 freshmen. Scholarships awarded for academics, alumni affiliation, art, athletics, leadership, music/drama, ROTC, state residency.

**Application procedures.** **Admission:** Priority date 12/1; deadline 3/15 (receipt date). $40 fee, may be waived for applicants with need. Application may be submitted online. Admission notification on a rolling basis beginning on or about 1/15. Students required to submit following: $40 application fee, high school transcripts, application, SAT or ACT scores, 1-3 letters of recommendation, one essay, one student activity resume. **Financial aid:** Priority date 2/15, closing date 3/15. FAFSA required. Applicants notified on a rolling basis starting 2/1; must reply within 2 week(s) of notification.

**Academics.** Guaranteed work or internship experience for credit in all fields of study. **Special study options:** Accelerated study, combined bachelor's/graduate degree, cooperative education, cross-registration, distance learning, double major, dual enrollment of high school students, ESL, exchange student, honors, independent study, internships, liberal arts/career combination, student-designed major, study abroad, teacher certification program, weekend college. Experiential learning. **Credit/placement by examination:** AP, CLEP, IB, institutional tests. 60 credit hours maximum toward bachelor's degree. Work life credits awarded through certification or department evaluations. Essay required to receive CLEP credit in American History I and II, Analysis and Interpretation of Literature, and Western Civilization I and II. **Support services:** Learning center, pre-admission summer program, reduced course load, study skills assistance, tutoring, writing center.

**Majors.** **Area/ethnic studies:** Asian, women's. **Biology:** General, biochemistry, marine. **Business:** Accounting, business admin, finance, international, management information systems, managerial economics, marketing. **Communications:** General. **Computer sciences:** General. **Education:** Art, biology, chemistry, drama/dance, English, foreign languages, French, geography, German, history, mathematics, music, physical, physics, sales/marketing, Spanish, technology/industrial arts. **Engineering:** Civil, computer, electrical, environmental, mechanical. **Engineering technology:** General, civil, computer, electrical, mechanical, nuclear. **English:** English lit, speech/rhetoric. **Foreign languages:** General, French, German, Spanish. **Health:** Audiology/speech pathology, clinical lab science, community health services, cytotechnology, dental hygiene, environmental health, health services, nuclear medical technology, nursing (RN), ophthalmic technology. **History:** General. **Math:** General. **Parks/recreation:** Exercise sciences, facilities management, sports admin. **Philosophy/religion:** Philosophy. **Physical sciences:** Chemistry, geology, oceanography, physics. **Psychology:** General. **Social sciences:** Criminology, economics, geography, international relations, political science, sociology. **Visual/performing arts:** Acting, art, art history/conservation, dance, dramatic, graphic design, music performance, studio arts.

**Most popular majors.** Business/marketing 19%, education 6%, engineering/engineering technologies 12%, English 8%, health sciences 17%, interdisciplinary studies 8%, psychology 6%, social sciences 11%.

**Computing on campus.** 2,035 workstations in library, computer center, student center. Dormitories wired for high-speed internet access and linked to campus network. Commuter students can connect to campus network. Online course registration, online library, helpline, repair service, wireless network available.

**Student life. Freshman orientation:** Mandatory, $100 fee. Preregistration for classes offered. Consists of campus tours available Monday through Friday and Saturday mornings. Summer orientation programs available. **Housing:** Coed dorms, special housing for disabled, apartments, substance-free housing available. $150 fully refundable deposit. **Activities:** Bands, choral groups, dance, drama, film society, international student organizations, literary magazine, music ensembles, musical theater, radio station, student government, student newspaper, TV station, approximately 200 student clubs and organizations available.

**Athletics.** NCAA. **Intercollegiate:** Baseball M, basketball, diving, field hockey W, golf, lacrosse W, sailing, soccer, tennis, wrestling M. **Intramural:** Badminton, basketball, bowling, cross-country, football (non-tackle), golf, sailing M, soccer, softball, table tennis, tennis, volleyball. **Team name:** Monarchs.

**Student services.** Adult student services, alcohol/substance abuse counseling, campus ministries, career counseling, services for economically disadvantaged, student employment services, financial aid counseling, health services, minority student services, on-campus daycare, personal counseling, placement for graduates, veterans' counselor, women's services. **Physically disabled:** Services for visually, speech, hearing impaired. **Learning disabled:** Comprehensive services available.

**Contact.** E-mail: admit@odu.edu
Phone: (757) 683-3685 Toll-free number: (800) 348-7926
Fax: (757) 683-3255
Alice McAdory, Director of Admissions, Old Dominion University, 108 Rollins Hall, 5115 Hampton Boulevard, Norfolk, VA 23529

## Potomac College
### Herndon, Virginia
### www.potomac.edu

- For-profit 4-year business college
- Residential campus in large town
- 300 degree-seeking undergraduates

**General. Degrees:** 40 bachelor's, 10 associate awarded. **Location:** 30 miles from Washington, DC. **Calendar:** Continuous, extensive summer session. **Full-time faculty:** 1 total. **Part-time faculty:** 4 total.

**Basis for selection.** Open admission.

**2007-2008 Annual costs.** Tuition/fees: $13,480. Upper division tuition and fees vary.

**Application procedures. Admission:** No deadline. $15 fee, may be waived for applicants with need. Admission notification on a rolling basis.

**Academics. Special study options:** Accelerated study, independent study. **Credit/placement by examination:** CLEP, institutional tests.

**Majors. Business:** Business admin. **Computer sciences:** General, information technology.

**Computing on campus.** 16 workstations in library, computer center. Wireless network available.

**Student life. Freshman orientation:** Mandatory. Preregistration for classes offered.

**Contact.** Phone: (703) 709-5875 Fax: (703) 709-8972
Marcus Palmore, Admissions Director, Potomac College, 1029 Herndon Parkway, Herndon, VA 20170

## Radford University
### Radford, Virginia
### www.radford.edu
**CB member**
**CB code: 5565**

- Public 4-year university
- Residential campus in large town
- 7,982 degree-seeking undergraduates: 4% part-time, 58% women, 6% African American, 2% Asian American, 2% Hispanic American, 1% international
- 948 degree-seeking graduate students

- 78% of applicants admitted
- SAT or ACT (ACT writing optional) required
- 56% graduate within 6 years; 22% enter graduate study

**General.** Founded in 1910. Regionally accredited. **Degrees:** 1,992 bachelor's awarded; master's, doctoral offered. **ROTC:** Army. **Location:** 36 miles from Roanoke. **Calendar:** Semester, limited summer session. **Full-time faculty:** 397 total; 84% have terminal degrees, 11% minority, 47% women. **Part-time faculty:** 203 total; 6% minority, 64% women. **Class size:** 36% < 20, 51% 20-39, 10% 40-49, 4% 50-99, less than 1% >100. **Special facilities:** Planetarium, greenhouse, nature and recreational conservatory, technology and learning center, museum of the earth sciences.

**Freshman class profile.** 7,046 applied, 5,466 admitted, 1,841 enrolled.

| Mid 50% test scores | | | |
|---|---|---|---|
| SAT critical reading: | 450-550 | GPA 2.0-2.99: | 37% |
| SAT math: | 460-550 | Rank in top quarter: | 25% |
| SAT writing: | 450-540 | Rank in top tenth: | 6% |
| ACT composite: | 20-24 | Return as sophomores: | 77% |
| GPA 3.50 or higher: | 18% | Out-of-state: | 9% |
| GPA 3.0-3.49: | 45% | Live on campus: | 96% |
| | | International: | 1% |

**Basis for selection.** Students selected on basis of high school records, standardized test scores, optional student essay, and evidence of interest and motivation as indicated in supplied materials. Audition required for music, theater, dance programs; portfolio required for art. **Homeschooled:** Must take either ACT or SAT and SAT Subject Tests.

**High school preparation.** 24 units recommended. Recommended units include English 4, mathematics 4, social studies 2, history 2, science 4 (laboratory 3), foreign language 3 and academic electives 5. Pre-nursing students should complete units in both biology and chemistry.

**2007-2008 Annual costs.** Tuition/fees: $6,176; $14,510 out-of-state. Room/board: $6,490. Books/supplies: $800. Personal expenses: $1,600.

**2006-2007 Financial aid. Need-based:** 1,108 full-time freshmen applied for aid; 608 were judged to have need; 578 of these received aid. Average need met was 76%. Average scholarship/grant was $5,656; average loan $2,581. 45% of total undergraduate aid awarded as scholarships/grants, 55% as loans/jobs. **Non-need-based:** Awarded to 1,057 full-time undergraduates, including 334 freshmen. Scholarships awarded for academics, alumni affiliation, art, athletics, leadership, music/drama, ROTC, state residency. **Additional information:** Student's need and grades considered. Top consideration given to those with greatest need and who apply by deadline.

**Application procedures. Admission:** Closing date 2/1 (postmark date). $50 fee, may be waived for applicants with need. Application may be submitted online. Admission notification 3/20. Admission notification on a rolling basis beginning on or about 1/9. Must reply by May 1 or within 2 week(s) if notified thereafter. **Financial aid:** Priority date 3/1; no closing date. FAFSA required. Applicants notified on a rolling basis starting 4/15; must reply within 2 week(s) of notification.

**Academics. Special study options:** Accelerated study, cross-registration, distance learning, double major, dual enrollment of high school students, honors, independent study, internships, student-designed major, study abroad, teacher certification program. **Credit/placement by examination:** AP, CLEP, IB. **Support services:** Learning center, study skills assistance, tutoring, writing center.

**Majors. Biology:** General. **Business:** Accounting, business admin, finance, marketing. **Communications:** General, journalism. **Computer sciences:** Computer science, information systems. **Education:** Health, physical. **English:** English lit. **Family/consumer sciences:** Food/nutrition. **Foreign languages:** General. **Health:** Clinical lab science, nursing (RN). **History:** General. **Math:** General. **Parks/recreation:** General. **Physical sciences:** Chemistry, geology, physics. **Protective services:** Criminal justice. **Psychology:** General. **Public administration:** Social work. **Social sciences:** General, anthropology, economics, geography, political science, sociology. **Visual/performing arts:** Art, dance, design, dramatic, studio arts.

**Most popular majors.** Business/marketing 18%, communications/journalism 11%, health sciences 6%, interdisciplinary studies 12%, security/protective services 6%, social sciences 7%, visual/performing arts 9%.

**Computing on campus.** 710 workstations in dormitories, library, computer center, student center. Dormitories wired for high-speed internet access and linked to campus network. Commuter students can connect to campus network. Online course registration, online library, helpline, repair service, student web hosting, wireless network available.

**Student life. Freshman orientation:** Available, $200 fee. Preregistration for classes offered. 5 2-day sessions in June or August. **Policies:** Honor code enforced. **Housing:** Guaranteed on-campus for freshmen. Coed dorms, special housing for disabled, apartments, substance-free housing available. $200 nonrefundable deposit, deadline 5/1. **Activities:** Bands, choral groups, dance, drama, literary magazine, music ensembles, musical theater, radio station, student government, student newspaper, TV station, Campus Crusade for Christ, Hillel B'nai B'rith, gospel choir, Alpha Phi Omega, American Red Cross, Habitat for Humanity, Educated Women of Color, NAACP, Hispanic and Asian American student association, Legislative Action Committee.

**Athletics.** NCAA. **Intercollegiate:** Baseball M, basketball, cross-country, diving W, field hockey W, golf, soccer, softball W, swimming W, tennis, track and field, volleyball W. **Intramural:** Basketball, bowling, cross-country, football (non-tackle), racquetball, soccer, softball, table tennis, tennis, volleyball, weight lifting. **Team name:** Highlanders.

**Student services.** Adult student services, alcohol/substance abuse counseling, campus ministries, career counseling, services for economically disadvantaged, student employment services, financial aid counseling, health services, minority student services, personal counseling, placement for graduates, veterans' counselor, women's services. **Physically disabled:** Services for visually, speech, hearing impaired.

**Contact.** E-mail: ruadmiss@radford.edu
Phone: (540) 831-5371 Toll-free number: (800) 890-4265
Fax: (540) 831-5038
David Kraus, Director of Admissions, Radford University, 209 Martin Hall, Radford, VA 24142

---

## Randolph College
**Lynchburg, Virginia**
www.randolphcollege.edu

**CB member**
**CB code: 5567**

- Private 4-year liberal arts college affiliated with United Methodist Church
- Residential campus in small city
- 618 degree-seeking undergraduates: 1% part-time, 89% women, 9% African American, 3% Asian American, 6% Hispanic American, 1% Native American, 12% international
- 7 degree-seeking graduate students
- 83% of applicants admitted
- SAT or ACT (ACT writing optional), application essay required
- 62% graduate within 6 years; 27% enter graduate study

**General.** Founded in 1891. Regionally accredited. **Degrees:** 138 bachelor's awarded; master's offered. **Location:** 60 miles from Roanoke and Charlottesville. **Calendar:** Semester, limited summer session. **Full-time faculty:** 75 total; 92% have terminal degrees, 12% minority, 56% women. **Part-time faculty:** 18 total; 39% have terminal degrees, 78% women. **Class size:** 85% < 20, 15% 20-39. **Special facilities:** Observatory, 3 nature preserves, botanical garden, 100-acre equestrian center, museum of American art, science and mathematics resource center, learning resources center, writing lab.

**Freshman class profile.** 1,222 applied, 1,018 admitted, 178 enrolled.

| Mid 50% test scores | | Rank in top quarter: | 59% |
|---|---|---|---|
| SAT critical reading: | 510-640 | Rank in top tenth: | 30% |
| SAT math: | 500-610 | Return as sophomores: | 70% |
| ACT composite: | 21-29 | Out-of-state: | 51% |
| GPA 3.50 or higher: | 48% | Live on campus: | 98% |
| GPA 3.0-3.49: | 39% | International: | 14% |
| GPA 2.0-2.99: | 13% | | |

**Basis for selection.** Rigor of high school curriculum and achievement most important, followed by teacher and counselor recommendations, test scores, activities, personal achievement. International students may submit SAT or ACT in lieu of TOEFL. Interview recommended. Essay submission may be essay written on topic of applicant's choice or copy of graded essay written by applicant in 11th or 12th grade. **Learning Disabled:** Submit documentation to Director of the Learning Resources Center, who will work in consultation with Office of the Dean of the College and faculty to determine reasonable and appropriate accommodations.

**High school preparation.** 16 units required. Required and recommended units include English 4, mathematics 3, history 2, science 2 (laboratory 2), foreign language 3-4 and academic electives 1-2. 3 years of one foreign language recommended, but applicants may offer 2 units of each of 2 languages instead. Student must have successfully completed or be enrolled in algebra II senior year in order for application to be considered.

**2008-2009 Annual costs.** Tuition/fees: $27,890. Room and board charges include free use of laundry facilities. Room/board: $9,310. Books/supplies: $800. Personal expenses: $1,000.

**2007-2008 Financial aid. Need-based:** 143 full-time freshmen applied for aid; 118 were judged to have need; 118 of these received aid. Average need met was 84%. Average scholarship/grant was $16,467; average loan $4,947. 70% of total undergraduate aid awarded as scholarships/grants, 30% as loans/jobs. **Non-need-based:** Awarded to 262 full-time undergraduates, including 78 freshmen. Scholarships awarded for academics, alumni affiliation, art, leadership, minority status, music/drama, religious affiliation, state residency. **Additional information:** College offers approximately $2 million annually to incoming first-year students. Grants range up to full tuition. Students must reapply each year.

**Application procedures. Admission:** Closing date 3/1 (postmark date). $35 fee, may be waived for applicants with need. Application may be submitted online. Admission notification on a rolling basis beginning on or about 11/1. Must reply by May 1 or within 2 week(s) if notified thereafter. **Financial aid:** Priority date 3/1; no closing date. FAFSA required. Applicants notified on a rolling basis starting 3/1; must reply by 5/1 or within 2 week(s) of notification.

**Academics.** Honor system includes self-scheduled examinations. **Special study options:** Accelerated study, combined bachelor's/graduate degree, cross-registration, double major, dual enrollment of high school students, exchange student, honors, independent study, internships, liberal arts/career combination, student-designed major, study abroad, teacher certification program, Washington semester. 7-college exchange with Washington and Lee University, Hollins University, Hampden-Sydney College, Mary Baldwin College, Sweet Briar College, Randolph-Macon College; junior year abroad program at University of Reading, England; affiliate abroad programs in Greece, France, Denmark, Japan, Italy, Ireland, Mexico, Spain; assistance with non-affiliated abroad programs; Marine Biological Laboratory Semester in Environmental Science; American Culture program (1-semester program including study on-site at key locations in and near Virginia), Tri-College Consortium with Lynchburg College and Sweet Briar College. **Credit/placement by examination:** AP, CLEP, IB, SAT, ACT, institutional tests. Applicants with scores at or above 50th percentile awarded credit for CLEP subject examinations in subject areas offered by college. However, subject tests in foreign languages granted credit only if they represent achievement beyond that of previous high school or college preparation. **Support services:** Learning center, reduced course load, study skills assistance, tutoring, writing center.

**Majors. Biology:** General. **Business:** General. **Communications:** General. **Conservation:** Environmental studies. **Engineering:** Physics. **English:** British lit, creative writing, English lit. **Foreign languages:** Ancient Greek, classics, French, Latin, Spanish. **Health:** Health services. **History:** General. **Interdisciplinary:** Global studies, museum. **Math:** General. **Philosophy/religion:** Philosophy, religion. **Physical sciences:** Chemistry, physics. **Psychology:** General. **Social sciences:** Economics, political science, sociology. **Visual/performing arts:** Art history/conservation, dance, dramatic, music history, music performance, music theory/composition, studio arts.

**Most popular majors.** Biology 8%, English 8%, foreign language 6%, history 7%, interdisciplinary studies 8%, philosophy/religious studies 8%, psychology 8%, social sciences 17%, visual/performing arts 9%.

**Computing on campus.** 155 workstations in dormitories, library, computer center, student center. Dormitories wired for high-speed internet access and linked to campus network. Commuter students can connect to campus network. Online course registration, online library, helpline, student web hosting, wireless network available.

**Student life. Freshman orientation:** Mandatory, $125 fee. Preregistration for classes offered. 5 days before start of classes. **Policies:** The Honor code has been fundamental to the conduct and governance of the College since its opening in 1893. **Housing:** Guaranteed on-campus for all undergraduates. Coed dorms, single-sex dorms, substance-free housing available. $300 nonrefundable deposit, deadline 5/1. All students under 24 years of age required to live in college housing unless living with family. **Activities:** Choral groups, dance, drama, film society, international student organizations, literary magazine, music ensembles, Model UN, radio station, student government, student newspaper, Young Democrats, College Republicans, black women's alliance, women's organizations, Christian Fellowship, language clubs, volunteer service organizations.

**Athletics.** NCAA. **Intercollegiate:** Basketball, cross-country, equestrian, lacrosse W, soccer, softball W, swimming W, tennis, volleyball W. **Intramural:** Basketball, softball, table tennis. **Team name:** Wildcats.

**Student services.** Adult student services, alcohol/substance abuse counseling, campus ministries, career counseling, student employment services, financial aid counseling, health services, minority student services, personal counseling, placement for graduates, women's services. **Physically disabled:** Services for visually, hearing impaired.

**Contact.** E-mail: admissions@randolphcollege.edu
Phone: (434) 947-8100 Toll-free number: (800) 745-7692
Fax: (434) 947-8996
Dean of Admissions and Student Financial Services, Randolph College,
2500 Rivermont Avenue, Lynchburg, VA 24503-1555

## Randolph-Macon College
### Ashland, Virginia
**CB member**
**www.rmc.edu**
**CB code: 5566**

♦ Private 4-year liberal arts college affiliated with United Methodist Church
♦ Residential campus in small town
♦ 1,166 degree-seeking undergraduates: 1% part-time, 54% women, 9% African American, 2% Asian American, 2% Hispanic American, 1% Native American, 2% international
♦ 61% of applicants admitted
♦ SAT or ACT (ACT writing recommended), application essay required
♦ 52% graduate within 6 years; 28% enter graduate study

**General.** Founded in 1830. Regionally accredited. **Degrees:** 231 bachelor's awarded. **ROTC:** Army. **Location:** 15 miles from Richmond, 90 miles from Washington, DC. **Calendar:** 4-1-4, limited summer session. **Full-time faculty:** 91 total; 92% have terminal degrees, 7% minority, 38% women. **Part-time faculty:** 68 total; 34% have terminal degrees, 3% minority, 53% women. **Class size:** 73% < 20, 27% 20-39. **Special facilities:** Observatory with 12-inch reflecting telescope and 3-meter radio telescope, 6 historic buildings, greenhouse.

**Freshman class profile.** 3,177 applied, 1,953 admitted, 392 enrolled.

| Mid 50% test scores | | | |
|---|---|---|---|
| SAT critical reading: | 490-580 | Rank in top quarter: | 46% |
| SAT math: | 500-590 | Rank in top tenth: | 17% |
| SAT writing: | 490-570 | End year in good standing: | 92% |
| GPA 3.50 or higher: | 37% | Return as sophomores: | 72% |
| GPA 3.0-3.49: | 33% | Out-of-state: | 30% |
| GPA 2.0-2.99: | 30% | Live on campus: | 95% |
| | | International: | 1% |

**Basis for selection.** School achievement record, class rank, and test scores most important. Personal recommendations, leadership skills and participation considered. Interview recommended. **Homeschooled:** Statement describing homeschool structure and mission, transcript of courses and grades, letter of recommendation (nonparent) required. **Learning Disabled:** Students with learning disabilities encouraged to meet with director of disability support services.

**High school preparation.** 16 units required; 22 recommended. Required and recommended units include English 4, mathematics 3-4, social studies 1-2, history 2, science 3-4 (laboratory 2-4), foreign language 2-4 and academic electives 1-2.

**2007-2008 Annual costs.** Tuition/fees: $26,830. Room/board: $8,180. Books/supplies: $1,000. Personal expenses: $720.

**2007-2008 Financial aid. Need-based:** 301 full-time freshmen applied for aid; 242 were judged to have need; 242 of these received aid. Average need met was 86%. Average scholarship/grant was $16,112; average loan $5,217. 71% of total undergraduate aid awarded as scholarships/grants, 29% as loans/jobs. **Non-need-based:** Awarded to 568 full-time undergraduates, including 182 freshmen. Scholarships awarded for academics, alumni affiliation, minority status, religious affiliation, state residency.

**Application procedures. Admission:** Priority date 2/1; deadline 3/1 (postmark date). $30 fee, may be waived for applicants with need. Application may be submitted online. Admission notification 4/1. Must reply by May 1 or within 2 week(s) if notified thereafter. Applications accepted after March 1 on space-available basis. **Financial aid:** Priority date 2/1, closing date 3/1. FAFSA required. Applicants notified by 3/15; must reply by 5/1 or within 2 week(s) of notification.

**Academics.** Comprehensive liberal arts core curriculum. All students must complete an internship, study abroad, or original research project for graduation. Interdisciplinary First-Year Experience for all freshmen. **Special study options:** Accelerated study, combined bachelor's/graduate degree, cross-registration, double major, dual enrollment of high school students, exchange student, honors, independent study, internships, liberal arts/career combination, study abroad, teacher certification program, United Nations semester, Washington semester. Member of Seven College consortium, 3-2 program in engineering with Columbia University and University of Virginia, 3-2 in forestry with Duke University, 4-1 in accounting with Virginia Commonwealth University. **Credit/placement by examination:** AP, CLEP, IB, institutional tests. 75 credit hours maximum toward bachelor's degree.

At least one-half major course of study must be completed at Randolph-Macon College. **Support services:** Learning center, reduced course load, study skills assistance, tutoring, writing center.

**Majors. Area/ethnic studies:** Women's. **Biology:** General. **Business:** Accounting, managerial economics. **Computer sciences:** General. **Conservation:** Environmental studies. **English:** English lit. **Foreign languages:** Ancient Greek, classics, French, German, Latin, Spanish. **History:** General. **Interdisciplinary:** Global studies. **Math:** General. **Philosophy/religion:** Philosophy, religion. **Physical sciences:** Chemistry, physics. **Psychology:** General. **Social sciences:** Economics, political science, sociology. **Visual/performing arts:** Art history/conservation, arts management, dramatic, studio arts.

**Most popular majors.** Biology 7%, business/marketing 20%, English 11%, history 7%, psychology 9%, social sciences 24%.

**Computing on campus.** 350 workstations in library, computer center, student center. Dormitories wired for high-speed internet access and linked to campus network. Commuter students can connect to campus network. Online course registration, online library, helpline, repair service, student web hosting, wireless network available.

**Student life. Freshman orientation:** Mandatory, $100 fee. Preregistration for classes offered. 4-day program held for students and parents prior to start of fall classes. **Housing:** Guaranteed on-campus for all undergraduates. Coed dorms, single-sex dorms, special housing for disabled, apartments, fraternity/sorority housing, substance-free housing available. Honors house, special interest housing available. **Activities:** Bands, choral groups, dance, drama, film society, literary magazine, musical theater, radio station, student government, student newspaper, TV station, over 100 clubs and organizations.

**Athletics.** NCAA. **Intercollegiate:** Baseball M, basketball, field hockey W, football (tackle) M, golf M, lacrosse, soccer, softball W, swimming W, tennis, volleyball W. **Intramural:** Basketball, football (non-tackle), lacrosse, racquetball, rugby, soccer, softball, table tennis, tennis, volleyball. **Team name:** Yellow Jackets.

**Student services.** Alcohol/substance abuse counseling, campus ministries, career counseling, student employment services, financial aid counseling, health services, minority student services, personal counseling, placement for graduates, women's services. **Physically disabled:** Services for visually, speech, hearing impaired.

**Contact.** E-mail: admissions@rmc.edu
Phone: (804) 752-7305 Toll-free number: (800) 888-1762
Fax: (804) 752-4707
Steven Nape, Dean of Admissions and Financial Aid, Randolph-Macon College, PO Box 5005, Ashland, VA 23005-5505

## Regent University
### Virginia Beach, Virginia
**www.regent.edu**
**CB code: 4452**

♦ Private 4-year university affiliated with interdenominational tradition
♦ Commuter campus in large city
♦ 1,177 degree-seeking undergraduates: 51% part-time, 70% women
♦ 2,910 degree-seeking graduate students
♦ 53% of applicants admitted
♦ SAT or ACT (ACT writing optional), application essay required

**General.** Founded in 1977. Regionally accredited. **Degrees:** 153 bachelor's awarded; master's, doctoral, first professional offered. **Location:** 8 miles from Norfolk. **Calendar:** Semester, extensive summer session. **Full-time faculty:** 181 total; 16% minority, 36% women. **Part-time faculty:** 448 total; 17% minority, 46% women. **Class size:** 82% < 20, 18% 20-39. **Special facilities:** Communication and performing arts center.

**Freshman class profile.** 1,256 applied, 670 admitted, 152 enrolled.

| Mid 50% test scores | | | |
|---|---|---|---|
| SAT critical reading: | 480-640 | GPA 3.0-3.49: | 23% |
| SAT math: | 450-570 | GPA 2.0-2.99: | 30% |
| SAT writing: | 470-560 | End year in good standing: | 74% |
| ACT composite: | 20-24 | Return as sophomores: | 67% |
| GPA 3.50 or higher: | 42% | Out-of-state: | 56% |
| | | International: | 1% |

**Basis for selection.** Academic GPA, test scores, and essay very important. **Homeschooled:** Transcript of courses and grades required.

**High school preparation.** Recommended units include English 4, mathematics 3, social studies 2, history 1, science 3 and foreign language 3.

**2007-2008 Annual costs.** Tuition/fees: $12,600. Books/supplies: $1,000.

**2006-2007 Financial aid. Need-based:** 92 full-time freshmen applied for aid; 92 were judged to have need; 92 of these received aid. Average need met was 36%. Average scholarship/grant was $4,203; average loan $3,564. 7% of total undergraduate aid awarded as scholarships/grants, 93% as loans/jobs. **Non-need-based:** Awarded to 266 full-time undergraduates, including 58 freshmen. Scholarships awarded for academics, leadership.

**Application procedures. Admission:** Closing date 8/13 (receipt date). $50 fee. Application may be submitted online. Admission notification on a rolling basis. Must reply by 8/15. **Financial aid:** Priority date 3/15; no closing date. FAFSA, institutional form required. Applicants notified on a rolling basis starting 3/1; must reply within 2 week(s) of notification.

**Academics. Special study options:** Combined bachelor's/graduate degree, distance learning, double major, dual enrollment of high school students, study abroad, teacher certification program. **Credit/placement by examination:** AP, CLEP, IB. 30 credit hours maximum toward bachelor's degree. **Support services:** Remedial instruction, study skills assistance, tutoring, writing center.

**Majors. Business:** Business admin, international, organizational behavior. **Communications:** General, journalism. **Communications technology:** Animation/special effects. **Education:** General. **English:** English lit. **Philosophy/religion:** Religion. **Psychology:** General. **Social sciences:** Political science. **Visual/performing arts:** Cinematography, theater arts management.

**Most popular majors.** Business/marketing 36%, communications/journalism 14%, interdisciplinary studies 12%, philosophy/religious studies 12%, psychology 25%.

**Computing on campus.** 130 workstations in library, computer center, student center. Dormitories wired for high-speed internet access and linked to campus network. Online course registration, online library, helpline, wireless network available.

**Student life. Freshman orientation:** Mandatory. Preregistration for classes offered. **Activities:** Concert band, choral groups, drama, international student organizations, student government, student newspaper, Association of Black Psychologists, College Republicans, undergraduate student advisory council, Newman Club, Regent Students for Life, Students in Free Enterprise, student alumni association, student advisory leadership team.

**Student services.** Campus ministries, career counseling, financial aid counseling.

**Contact.** E-mail: admissions@regent.edu
Phone: (757) 226-4127 Toll-free number: (800) 373-5504
Fax: (757) 226-4381
Ken Baker, Director of Admissions, Regent University, 1000 Regent University Drive, SC 218, Virginia Beach, VA 23464-9800

## Roanoke College

Salem, Virginia      CB member
www.roanoke.edu      CB code: 5571

- Private 4-year liberal arts college affiliated with Evangelical Lutheran Church in America
- Residential campus in large town
- 1,945 degree-seeking undergraduates: 3% part-time, 57% women, 3% African American, 1% Asian American, 2% Hispanic American, 1% international
- 73% of applicants admitted
- SAT or ACT (ACT writing optional) required
- 65% graduate within 6 years; 20% enter graduate study

**General.** Founded in 1842. Regionally accredited. **Degrees:** 417 bachelor's awarded. **Location:** 7 miles from Roanoke. **Calendar:** Semester, extensive summer session. **Full-time faculty:** 157 total; 78% have terminal degrees, 10% minority, 49% women. **Part-time faculty:** 33 total; 18% have terminal degrees, 9% minority, 52% women. **Class size:** 60% < 20, 40% 20-39, less than 1% 40-49. **Special facilities:** Fine arts center with 3 galleries, multimedia classrooms, greenhouse, nuclear magnetic resonance equipment, center for community research, center for church and society, center for teaching and learning.

**Freshman class profile.** 3,258 applied, 2,385 admitted, 566 enrolled.

| Mid 50% test scores | | | |
|---|---|---|---|
| SAT critical reading: | 500-600 | Rank in top tenth: | 21% |
| SAT math: | 500-590 | Return as sophomores: | 74% |
| SAT writing: | 480-570 | Out-of-state: | 51% |
| GPA 3.50 or higher: | 36% | Live on campus: | 93% |
| GPA 3.0-3.49: | 34% | International: | 1% |
| GPA 2.0-2.99: | 30% | Fraternities: | 14% |
| Rank in top quarter: | 54% | Sororities: | 18% |

**Basis for selection.** School achievement record and class rank most important. Essay, interview recommended for all; audition recommended for music; portfolio recommended for graphic arts. **Homeschooled:** Transcript of courses and grades required. **Learning Disabled:** Documentation of learning disability needed for special services after enrollment.

**High school preparation.** 18 units required. Required and recommended units include English 4, mathematics 3, social studies 2, science 2 (laboratory 2), foreign language 4 and academic electives 5. Mathematics must include algebra II.

**2008-2009 Annual costs.** Tuition/fees: $27,935. Room/board: $9,285. Books/supplies: $850. Personal expenses: $750.

**2007-2008 Financial aid. Need-based:** 436 full-time freshmen applied for aid; 432 were judged to have need; 432 of these received aid. Average need met was 92%. Average scholarship/grant was $18,963; average loan $3,912. 70% of total undergraduate aid awarded as scholarships/grants, 30% as loans/jobs. **Non-need-based:** Awarded to 1,347 full-time undergraduates, including 388 freshmen. Scholarships awarded for academics, minority status, music/drama, religious affiliation.

**Application procedures. Admission:** Closing date 3/15 (postmark date). $30 fee, may be waived for applicants with need. Application may be submitted online. Admission notification 4/1. Must reply by May 1 or within 2 week(s) if notified thereafter. **Financial aid:** Priority date 3/1; no closing date. FAFSA required. Applicants notified on a rolling basis starting 11/1; must reply within 2 week(s) of notification.

**Academics. Special study options:** Accelerated study, combined bachelor's/graduate degree, cross-registration, double major, dual enrollment of high school students, ESL, honors, independent study, internships, liberal arts/career combination, study abroad, teacher certification program, Washington semester. **Credit/placement by examination:** AP, CLEP, IB, institutional tests. 27 credit hours maximum toward bachelor's degree. **Support services:** Learning center, reduced course load, study skills assistance, tutoring, writing center.

**Majors. Biology:** General, biochemistry. **Business:** Business admin. **Computer sciences:** General, computer science, information systems. **Conservation:** Environmental science, management/policy. **Education:** Physical. **English:** English lit. **Foreign languages:** French, Spanish. **Health:** Athletic training, clinical lab science. **History:** General. **Math:** General. **Parks/recreation:** Health/fitness. **Philosophy/religion:** Philosophy, religion. **Physical sciences:** Chemistry, physics. **Protective services:** Criminal justice. **Psychology:** General. **Social sciences:** Economics, international relations, political science, sociology. **Theology:** Theology. **Visual/performing arts:** Art, art history/conservation, dramatic.

**Most popular majors.** Business/marketing 24%, English 8%, history 12%, psychology 8%, social sciences 15%, visual/performing arts 6%.

**Computing on campus.** 185 workstations in library, computer center, student center. Dormitories wired for high-speed internet access and linked to campus network. Commuter students can connect to campus network. Online course registration, online library, helpline, repair service, student web hosting, wireless network available.

**Student life. Freshman orientation:** Mandatory, $125 fee. Preregistration for classes offered. **Housing:** Guaranteed on-campus for freshmen. Coed dorms, single-sex dorms, apartments, fraternity/sorority housing, substance-free housing available. $300 deposit, deadline 5/1. Theme houses for a variety of student interests available. **Activities:** Bands, campus ministries, choral groups, dance, drama, film society, literary magazine, music ensembles, Model UN, musical theater, radio station, student government, student newspaper, Alpha Phi Omega, Earthbound, Fellowship of Christian Athletes, Habitat for Humanity, Lutheran Student Movement, Baptist Student Union, Shades of Maroon.

**Athletics.** NCAA. **Intercollegiate:** Baseball M, basketball, cross-country, field hockey W, golf M, lacrosse, soccer, softball W, tennis, track and field, volleyball W. **Intramural:** Badminton, baseball M, basketball, field hockey W, football (non-tackle), golf W, racquetball, soccer, softball, table tennis, tennis, volleyball. **Team name:** Maroons.

**Student services.** Adult student services, alcohol/substance abuse counseling, campus ministries, career counseling, student employment services, financial aid counseling, health services, minority student services, personal counseling, placement for graduates.

**Contact.** E-mail: admissions@roanoke.edu
Phone: (540) 375-2270 Toll-free number: (800) 388-2276
Fax: (540) 375-2267
Brenda Poggendorf, Vice President of Enrollment, Roanoke College, 221 College Lane, Salem, VA 24153-3794

## St. Paul's College
**Lawrenceville, Virginia**

www.saintpauls.edu

CB member

CB code: 5604

◆ Private 4-year liberal arts college affiliated with Episcopal Church
◆ Residential campus in small town
◆ 687 degree-seeking undergraduates: 3% part-time, 51% women
◆ 86% of applicants admitted
◆ SAT or ACT (ACT writing optional), application essay required

**General.** Founded in 1888. Regionally accredited. **Degrees:** 137 bachelor's awarded. **ROTC:** Army. **Location:** 80 miles from Richmond. **Calendar:** Semester, limited summer session. **Full-time faculty:** 28 total; 61% have terminal degrees, 75% minority, 39% women. **Part-time faculty:** 10 total; 70% minority, 50% women. **Class size:** 67% < 20, 23% 20-39, 8% 40-49, 3% 50-99, less than 1% >100.

**Freshman class profile.** 496 applied, 426 admitted, 252 enrolled.

| Mid 50% test scores | | | |
|---|---|---|---|
| SAT critical reading: | 310-410 | GPA 2.0-2.99: | 57% |
| SAT math: | 300-410 | Rank in top quarter: | 10% |
| ACT composite: | 13-16 | Rank in top tenth: | 3% |
| GPA 3.50 or higher: | 2% | Return as sophomores: | 46% |
| GPA 3.0-3.49: | 7% | Out-of-state: | 24% |
| | | Live on campus: | 93% |

**Basis for selection.** School achievement record most important. School recommendations considered. Rank in top half of class important. 3.0 GPA recommended. Interview recommended.

**High school preparation.** 10 units required. Required units include English 4, mathematics 2, social studies 2 and science 2.

**2007-2008 Annual costs.** Tuition/fees: $12,020. Room/board: $6,190. Books/supplies: $1,400. Personal expenses: $2,620.

**2006-2007 Financial aid. Need-based:** 246 full-time freshmen applied for aid; 246 were judged to have need; 246 of these received aid. Average need met was 90%. Average scholarship/grant was $10,900. 68% of total undergraduate aid awarded as scholarships/grants, 32% as loans/jobs. **Non-need-based:** Awarded to 63 full-time undergraduates, including 6 freshmen. Scholarships awarded for academics, athletics, leadership, ROTC.

**Application procedures. Admission:** No deadline. $20 fee, may be waived for applicants with need. Application may be submitted online. Admission notification on a rolling basis. Must reply by May 1 or within 2 week(s) if notified thereafter. **Financial aid:** No deadline. FAFSA required. Applicants notified on a rolling basis starting 1/15; must reply by 7/1 or within 4 week(s) of notification.

**Academics. Special study options:** Accelerated study, cooperative education, cross-registration, double major, exchange student, honors, independent study, internships, teacher certification program. Organizational Management Program for adults 25 and older. **Credit/placement by examination:** AP, CLEP, institutional tests. 24 credit hours maximum toward bachelor's degree. **Support services:** Learning center, pre-admission summer program, reduced course load, remedial instruction, tutoring.

**Majors. Biology:** General, marine. **Business:** Accounting, administrative services, business admin, management information systems, operations. **Computer sciences:** General. **Conservation:** General. **Education:** Business. **English:** English lit. **Math:** General. **Philosophy/religion:** Philosophy, religion. **Protective services:** Criminal justice. **Social sciences:** General, political science, sociology.

**Most popular majors.** Business/marketing 77%.

**Computing on campus.** 100 workstations in dormitories, library, computer center, student center. Dormitories wired for high-speed internet access and linked to campus network. Commuter students can connect to campus network. Helpline, repair service, wireless network available.

**Student life. Freshman orientation:** Mandatory. Preregistration for classes offered. **Housing:** Single-sex dorms available. $50 nonrefundable deposit.

**Activities:** Choral groups, dance, student government, Altar Guild, veterans club, Canterbury club, NAACP, single parent support system.

**Athletics.** NCAA. **Intercollegiate:** Baseball M, basketball, bowling, cross-country, football (tackle) M, golf, softball W, tennis, track and field, volleyball W. **Intramural:** Basketball, softball, volleyball. **Team name:** Tigers.

**Student services.** Adult student services, career counseling, student employment services, financial aid counseling, health services, on-campus daycare, personal counseling, placement for graduates, veterans' counselor.

**Contact.** E-mail: admissions@saintpauls.edu
Phone: (434) 848-3111 Toll-free number: (800) 678-7071
Fax: (434) 848-1846
Rosemary Lewis, Director of Admissions, St. Paul's College, 115 College Drive, Lawrenceville, VA 23868

## Shenandoah University
**Winchester, Virginia**

www.su.edu

CB member

CB code: 5613

◆ Private 4-year university affiliated with United Methodist Church
◆ Residential campus in small city
◆ 1,587 degree-seeking undergraduates: 5% part-time, 57% women, 6% African American, 2% Asian American, 1% Hispanic American, 3% international
◆ 1,389 degree-seeking graduate students
◆ 88% of applicants admitted
◆ SAT or ACT (ACT writing optional) required
◆ 46% graduate within 6 years

**General.** Founded in 1875. Regionally accredited. **Degrees:** 372 bachelor's, 2 associate awarded; master's, doctoral, first professional offered. **Location:** 100 miles from Baltimore, 75 miles from Washington, DC. **Calendar:** Differs by program, limited summer session. **Full-time faculty:** 196 total; 80% have terminal degrees, 9% minority, 50% women. **Part-time faculty:** 217 total; 27% have terminal degrees, 5% minority, 65% women. **Class size:** 80% < 20, 18% 20-39, 1% 40-49, less than 1% 50-99, less than 1% >100. **Special facilities:** Arts and media centers, conservatory, recording studio.

**Freshman class profile.** 1,281 applied, 1,132 admitted, 398 enrolled.

| Mid 50% test scores | | | |
|---|---|---|---|
| SAT critical reading: | 440-560 | GPA 2.0-2.99: | 38% |
| SAT math: | 440-560 | End year in good standing: | 94% |
| ACT composite: | 17-23 | Return as sophomores: | 65% |
| GPA 3.50 or higher: | 33% | Out-of-state: | 38% |
| GPA 3.0-3.49: | 29% | Live on campus: | 95% |
| | | International: | 2% |

**Basis for selection.** Applicants evaluated on basis of GPA and standardized test scores along with recommendation. Audition required for Conservatory applicants. Nursing applicants must take ATI Test of Essential Academic Skills. In-house English proficiency tests administered. Interview recommended for all; audition required for dance, music, and theater programs. **Homeschooled:** Transcript of courses and grades, letter of recommendation (nonparent) required. May request GED score. Applicants must submit written documentation of local school district approval of the homeschool arrangement if available.

**High school preparation.** 15 units required. Required units include English 4, mathematics 3, social studies 2, science 2 (laboratory 1) and foreign language 2.

**2007-2008 Annual costs.** Tuition/fees: $22,340. Room/board: $7,990. Books/supplies: $1,000. Personal expenses: $1,500.

**2006-2007 Financial aid. Need-based:** 325 full-time freshmen applied for aid; 325 were judged to have need; 325 of these received aid. Average need met was 86%. Average scholarship/grant was $15,022; average loan $4,229. 15% of total undergraduate aid awarded as scholarships/grants, 85% as loans/jobs. **Non-need-based:** Awarded to 793 full-time undergraduates, including 172 freshmen. Scholarships awarded for academics, job skills, music/drama, religious affiliation, state residency.

**Application procedures. Admission:** Priority date 3/1; deadline 8/29. $30 fee, may be waived for applicants with need. Application may be submitted online. Admission notification on a rolling basis beginning on or about 10/1. Must reply by May 1 or within 2 week(s) if notified thereafter. **Financial aid:** Closing date 3/2. FAFSA required. Applicants notified on a rolling basis starting 3/15; must reply within 2 week(s) of notification.

**Academics. Special study options:** Accelerated study, combined bachelor's/graduate degree, distance learning, double major, dual enrollment of high school students, ESL, internships, study abroad, teacher certification program, weekend college. **Credit/placement by examination:** AP, CLEP, IB, SAT, ACT, institutional tests. AP placement grade may be higher for exams taken in student's major. CEEB, CLEP, academic department exams used. **Support services:** Learning center, reduced course load, remedial instruction, study skills assistance, tutoring, writing center.

**Majors. Area/ethnic studies:** American. **Biology:** General. **Business:** Business admin. **Communications:** General. **Communications technology:** Recording arts. **Computer sciences:** General. **Conservation:** General. **Education:** Computer, drama/dance, elementary, ESL, music, physical. **English:** English lit. **Foreign languages:** Spanish. **Health:** Music therapy, nursing (RN), respiratory therapy technology. **History:** General. **Liberal arts:** Arts/sciences. **Math:** General. **Philosophy/religion:** Religion. **Physical sciences:** Chemistry. **Protective services:** Law enforcement admin. **Psychology:** General. **Public administration:** General. **Social sciences:** Sociology. **Visual/performing arts:** General, acting, arts management, dance, dramatic, music performance, music theory/composition, piano/organ, theater design.

**Computing on campus.** 175 workstations in dormitories, library, computer center, student center. Dormitories wired for high-speed internet access and linked to campus network. Commuter students can connect to campus network. Online course registration, online library, helpline, repair service, wireless network available.

**Student life. Freshman orientation:** Mandatory. Preregistration for classes offered. One week; week before start of classes. **Policies:** All first and second year undergraduate students required to live in on-campus housing. **Housing:** Guaranteed on-campus for freshmen. Coed dorms, special housing for disabled, substance-free housing available. $100 nonrefundable deposit, deadline 7/1. **Activities:** Bands, choral groups, dance, drama, literary magazine, music ensembles, musical theater, opera, radio station, student government, student newspaper, symphony orchestra, TV station, Circle K, Alpha Chi Honor Society, Alpha Lambda Delta, freshman honor society, nursing honor society, Christian Pharmacists Fellowship International, Omicron Delta Kappa, College Democrats, College Republicans.

**Athletics.** NCAA. **Intercollegiate:** Baseball M, basketball, cross-country, field hockey W, football (tackle) M, golf M, lacrosse, soccer, softball W, tennis, volleyball W. **Intramural:** Basketball, cheerleading, football (non-tackle), soccer, softball, tennis, track and field, volleyball. **Team name:** Hornets.

**Student services.** Adult student services, alcohol/substance abuse counseling, campus ministries, career counseling, student employment services, financial aid counseling, health services, minority student services, personal counseling, placement for graduates, veterans' counselor. **Physically disabled:** Services for visually, speech, hearing impaired.

**Contact.** E-mail: admit@su.edu
Phone: (540) 665-4581 Toll-free number: (800) 432-2266
Fax: (540) 665-4627
David Anthony, Dean of Admissions, Shenandoah University, 1460 University Drive, Winchester, VA 22601-5195

---

## Southern Virginia University

**Buena Vista, Virginia**            **CB member**
**www.svu.edu**                      **CB code: 5625**

- Private 4-year liberal arts college affiliated with Church of Jesus Christ of Latter-day Saints
- Residential campus in small town
- 698 degree-seeking undergraduates: 4% part-time, 57% women, 3% African American, 3% Asian American, 3% Hispanic American, 2% international
- 96% of applicants admitted
- SAT or ACT (ACT writing optional) required

**General. Degrees:** 82 bachelor's awarded. **ROTC:** Army. **Location:** 60 miles from Roanoke, 60 miles from Charlottesville. **Calendar:** Semester, limited summer session. **Full-time faculty:** 38 total; 74% have terminal degrees, 40% women. **Part-time faculty:** 41 total; 32% have terminal degrees, 24% women. **Class size:** 64% < 20, 34% 20-39, less than 1% 40-49, less than 1% 50-99, less than 1% >100.

**Freshman class profile.** 647 applied, 620 admitted, 238 enrolled.

| Mid 50% test scores | | Rank in top quarter: | 36% |
|---|---|---|---|
| SAT critical reading: | 440-580 | Rank in top tenth: | 2% |
| SAT math: | 430-570 | Return as sophomores: | 34% |
| ACT composite: | 19-26 | Out-of-state: | 81% |
| GPA 3.50 or higher: | 36% | Live on campus: | 88% |
| GPA 3.0-3.49: | 30% | International: | 1% |
| GPA 2.0-2.99: | 33% | | |

**Basis for selection.** GPA, test scores, interview, religious affiliation or commitment all important. **Homeschooled:** Transcript of courses and grades required.

**High school preparation.** Recommended units include English 4, mathematics 2, social studies 2, history 2, science 2 (laboratory 2), foreign language 2 and academic electives 1.

**2007-2008 Annual costs.** Tuition/fees: $16,500. Room/board: $4,900. Books/supplies: $1,000. Personal expenses: $400.

**2006-2007 Financial aid. Need-based:** 307 full-time freshmen applied for aid; 275 were judged to have need; 275 of these received aid. Average need met was 41%. Average scholarship/grant was $6,475; average loan $2,075. 65% of total undergraduate aid awarded as scholarships/grants, 35% as loans/jobs. **Non-need-based:** Awarded to 315 full-time undergraduates, including 127 freshmen. Scholarships awarded for academics, art, athletics, leadership, music/drama.

**Application procedures. Admission:** Closing date 7/31. $35 fee, may be waived for applicants with need. **Financial aid:** FAFSA required. Applicants notified on a rolling basis starting 2/1; must reply by 5/1 or within 3 week(s) of notification.

**Academics. Special study options:** Double major, independent study, internships, liberal arts/career combination, study abroad. **Credit/placement by examination:** AP, CLEP, IB, SAT, ACT, institutional tests. **Support services:** Learning center, study skills assistance, tutoring.

**Majors. Biology:** General. **Business:** Business admin. **Computer sciences:** General. **English:** English lit. **Family/consumer sciences:** Family systems. **Foreign languages:** Spanish. **History:** General. **Liberal arts:** Arts/sciences. **Philosophy/religion:** Philosophy. **Visual/performing arts:** Art, dramatic.

**Most popular majors.** Business/marketing 20%, English 11%, family/consumer sciences 17%, history 9%, liberal arts 15%, parks/recreation 11%, visual/performing arts 9%.

**Computing on campus.** 37 workstations in library, computer center. Dormitories wired for high-speed internet access and linked to campus network. Commuter students can connect to campus network. Online course registration, helpline, repair service, wireless network available.

**Student life. Freshman orientation:** Mandatory. Preregistration for classes offered. **Policies:** Students are responsible for familiarizing themselves with and abiding by the honor code, the dress and grooming standards, and the residential living policies. **Housing:** Guaranteed on-campus for freshmen. Single-sex dorms, apartments, substance-free housing available. $250 fully refundable deposit, deadline 9/6. **Activities:** Pep band, choral groups, dance, drama, literary magazine, music ensembles, musical theater, student government, student newspaper, symphony orchestra.

**Athletics. Intercollegiate:** Baseball M, basketball M, cheerleading, cross-country, football (tackle) M, golf, soccer, softball W, tennis M, track and field, volleyball W. **Team name:** Knights.

**Student services.** Campus ministries, career counseling, financial aid counseling, personal counseling.

**Contact.** E-mail: admissions@svu.edu
Phone: (540) 261-2756 Toll-free number: (800) 229-8420
Tony Caputo, Dean of Admissions, Southern Virginia University, One University Hill Drive, Buena Vista, VA 24416

---

## Stratford University: Falls Church

**Falls Church, Virginia**
**www.stratford.edu**               **CB code: 3778**

- For-profit 4-year university
- Small city

**General.** Accredited by ACICS. **Calendar:** Quarter.

**Annual costs/financial aid.** Tuition/fees (2007-2008): $10,620.

**Contact.** Phone: (703) 821-8570
Director of Admissions, 7777 Leesburg Pike, Falls Church, VA 22043

## Stratford University: Woodbridge
**Woodbridge, Virginia**
**www.stratford.edu**

▶ For-profit 4-year university
▶ Large town

**General.** Accredited by ACICS. **Calendar:** Quarter.

**Annual costs/financial aid.** Tuition/fees (2007-2008): $10,620.

**Contact.** Phone: (703) 897-1982
Director of Admissions, 13576 Minnieville Road, Woodbridge, VA 22192

## Sweet Briar College
**Sweet Briar, Virginia**                          CB member
**www.sbc.edu**                                    CB code: 5634

▶ Private 4-year liberal arts college for women
▶ Residential campus in rural community
▶ 636 degree-seeking undergraduates: 1% part-time, 100% women, 3% African American, 1% Asian American, 3% Hispanic American, 1% Native American, 1% international
▶ 11 degree-seeking graduate students
▶ 81% of applicants admitted
▶ SAT or ACT with writing, application essay required
▶ 71% graduate within 6 years; 24% enter graduate study

**General.** Founded in 1901. Regionally accredited. Studio art building houses 4 large studios for painting, drawing and printmaking, photo studio and darkroom, and faculty offices. **Degrees:** 102 bachelor's awarded; master's offered. **Location:** 12 miles from Lynchburg, 166 miles from Washington, DC. **Calendar:** Semester, limited summer session. **Full-time faculty:** 65 total. **Part-time faculty:** 30 total. **Special facilities:** Indoor and outdoor riding facilities, 3 nature sanctuaries, college-run nursery school and kindergarten for student teaching, observatory, environmental education and nature center.

**Freshman class profile.** 619 applied, 504 admitted, 202 enrolled.

| Mid 50% test scores | | Rank in top quarter: | 56% |
|---|---|---|---|
| SAT critical reading: | 510-620 | Rank in top tenth: | 22% |
| SAT math: | 480-590 | Return as sophomores: | 75% |
| ACT composite: | 21-26 | Out-of-state: | 43% |
| GPA 3.50 or higher: | 43% | Live on campus: | 95% |
| GPA 3.0-3.49: | 26% | International: | 1% |
| GPA 2.0-2.99: | 31% | | |

**Basis for selection.** High school curriculum and grades are of primary importance, followed by school and teacher recommendations, test scores, and writing ability as demonstrated by essay or personal statement. Interview, extracurricular activities, and personal characteristics are also considered. **Learning Disabled:** Applicant must submit written request for accommodated admissions review to Office of Admissions and enclose appropriate documentation with request.

**High school preparation.** 16 units required; 20 recommended. Required and recommended units include English 4, mathematics 3-4, social studies 3-4, science 3-4 (laboratory 2-3) and foreign language 2-4. Mathematics preparation must be at least through Algebra II. Foreign language must include 2 consecutive years of same language.

**2007-2008 Annual costs.** Tuition/fees: $25,015. Room/board: $10,040. Books/supplies: $600. Personal expenses: $750.

**2007-2008 Financial aid. Need-based:** 140 full-time freshmen applied for aid; 107 were judged to have need; 105 of these received aid. Average need met was 73%. Average scholarship/grant was $16,470; average loan $7,667. 68% of total undergraduate aid awarded as scholarships/grants, 32% as loans/jobs. **Non-need-based:** Scholarships awarded for academics, art, leadership, music/drama, state residency.

**Application procedures. Admission:** Closing date 2/1 (postmark date). $40 fee, may be waived for applicants with need. Application may be submitted online. Admission notification 3/15. Must reply by 5/1. **Financial aid:** Priority date 3/1; no closing date. FAFSA required. Applicants notified on a rolling basis starting 3/1; must reply by 5/1 or within 2 week(s) of notification.

**Academics.** General Education Program: students complete requirements that involve communication and quantitative reasoning skills; rationale for broad liberal arts background; emphasis on internships; regular progress self-assessments. Summer research program provides opportunities for high-level work with faculty. **Special study options:** Accelerated study, combined bachelor's/graduate degree, cross-registration, double major, dual enrollment of high school students, exchange student, honors, independent study, internships, liberal arts/career combination, student-designed major, study abroad, teacher certification program, Washington semester. **Credit/placement by examination:** AP, CLEP, IB, institutional tests. Exemption from 1 or more of degree requirements and/or admission to advanced courses may be granted on basis of Advanced Placement Exams, International Baccalaureate Program, transfer credit, or, in some cases, placement tests taken at college. **Support services:** Learning center, study skills assistance, tutoring, writing center.

**Majors. Area/ethnic studies:** German, Italian. **Biology:** General. **Business:** General. **Computer sciences:** Computer science. **Conservation:** Environmental science, environmental studies. **Engineering:** Science. **Engineering technology:** Industrial management. **English:** Creative writing, English lit. **Foreign languages:** General, classics, French, German, Spanish. **History:** General. **Liberal arts:** Arts/sciences. **Math:** General. **Philosophy/religion:** Philosophy, religion. **Physical sciences:** Chemistry, physics, theoretical physics. **Psychology:** General. **Social sciences:** Anthropology, economics, international relations, political science, sociology. **Visual/performing arts:** Art history/conservation, dance, dramatic, studio arts. **Other:** Biochemistry and molecular biology, Multi-/interdisciplinary studies, Spanish business.

**Most popular majors.** Biology 8%, business/marketing 15%, foreign language 8%, history 6%, psychology 8%, social sciences 23%, visual/performing arts 9%.

**Computing on campus.** 117 workstations in library, computer center. Dormitories wired for high-speed internet access and linked to campus network. Commuter students can connect to campus network. Online course registration, online library, helpline, repair service, student web hosting, wireless network available.

**Student life. Freshman orientation:** Mandatory. Preregistration for classes offered. Begins on a Saturday in August through the following Thursday, which is the official beginning of classes. **Policies:** Self-governing student body; honor system observed. **Housing:** Guaranteed on-campus for all undergraduates. Substance-free housing available. $500 deposit, deadline 5/1. **Activities:** Campus ministries, choral groups, dance, drama, film society, literary magazine, music ensembles, musical theater, radio station, student government, student newspaper, symphony orchestra, TV station, Campus Christian Fellowship, campus spirituality coalition, College Republicans, College Democrats, Circle K, Habitat for Humanity, student environmental organization, Vixen PAWS, Newman Club.

**Athletics.** NCAA. **Intercollegiate:** Field hockey W, lacrosse W, soccer W, softball W, swimming W, tennis W, volleyball W. **Team name:** Vixens.

**Student services.** Alcohol/substance abuse counseling, campus ministries, career counseling, student employment services, financial aid counseling, health services, personal counseling, placement for graduates, women's services. **Physically disabled:** Services for hearing impaired.

**Contact.** E-mail: admissions@sbc.edu
Phone: (434) 381-6142 Toll-free number: (800) 381-6142
Fax: (434) 381-6152
Ken Huus, Dean of Admissions, Sweet Briar College, PO Box B, Sweet Briar, VA 24595

## University of Management and Technology
**Arlington, Virginia**
**www.umtweb.edu**

▶ For-profit 4-year business and engineering college
▶ Very large city

**General.** Accredited by DETC. **Calendar:** Continuous.

**Annual costs/financial aid.** Tuition/fees (2007-2008): $11,700.

**Contact.** Phone: (703) 516-0035
1901 N Fort Myer Drive/Suite 700, Arlington, VA 22209

# University of Mary Washington

**Fredericksburg, Virginia**
www.umw.edu

**CB member**
**CB code: 5398**

- Public 4-year university and liberal arts college
- Residential campus in small city
- 4,117 degree-seeking undergraduates: 12% part-time, 66% women, 3% African American, 4% Asian American, 3% Hispanic American
- 647 degree-seeking graduate students
- 80% of applicants admitted
- SAT or ACT (ACT writing optional), application essay required
- 76% graduate within 6 years

**General.** Founded in 1908. Regionally accredited. UMW graduate campus located approximately 8 miles away. **Degrees:** 930 bachelor's awarded; master's offered. **Location:** 50 miles from Richmond, 50 miles from Washington, DC. **Calendar:** Semester, limited summer session. **Full-time faculty:** 251 total; 90% have terminal degrees, 11% minority, 45% women. **Part-time faculty:** 120 total; 11% minority, 54% women. **Class size:** 49% < 20, 47% 20-39, 1% 40-49, 3% 50-99, less than 1% >100. **Special facilities:** Center for historic preservation, computer access center for visually impaired, James Monroe museum, center for Asian studies.

**Freshman class profile.** 4,475 applied, 3,590 admitted, 973 enrolled.

| Mid 50% test scores | | | |
|---|---|---|---|
| SAT critical reading: | 560-660 | Rank in top quarter: | 83% |
| SAT math: | 530-630 | Rank in top tenth: | 38% |
| SAT writing: | 550-650 | Return as sophomores: | 87% |
| ACT composite: | 23-27 | Out-of-state: | 36% |
| GPA 3.50 or higher: | 50% | Live on campus: | 97% |
| GPA 3.0-3.49: | 44% | | |

GPA 2.0-2.99: 6%

**Basis for selection.** Rigor of high school program most important, followed by GPA, standardized test scores, activities, essays, recommendations. SAT Subject Tests recommended. SAT Subject Tests recommended including mathematics. **Homeschooled:** Students strongly advised to take 3 SAT Subject Tests: math and 2 other subject areas of choice.

**High school preparation.** Required and recommended units include English 4, mathematics 3-4, social studies 2, history 1-2, science 3-4 (laboratory 3-4) and foreign language 2-4.

**2008-2009 Annual costs.** Tuition/fees (projected): $7,200; $18,600 out-of-state. Room/board: $7,500. Books/supplies: $1,200. Personal expenses: $1,700.

**2006-2007 Financial aid. Need-based:** 591 full-time freshmen applied for aid; 252 were judged to have need; 219 of these received aid. Average need met was 50%. Average scholarship/grant was $5,590; average loan $2,640. 47% of total undergraduate aid awarded as scholarships/grants, 53% as loans/jobs. **Non-need-based:** Awarded to 420 full-time undergraduates, including 171 freshmen. Scholarships awarded for academics, art, leadership, music/drama, state residency.

**Application procedures. Admission:** Priority date 1/15; deadline 2/1 (postmark date). $45 fee, may be waived for applicants with need. Application may be submitted online. Admission notification 4/1. Admission notification on a rolling basis. Must reply by 5/1. Applicants for regular admission who complete application by January 15 eligible for honor admission (early notification). **Financial aid:** Closing date 3/1. FAFSA, institutional form required. Applicants notified by 4/15; must reply by 5/1 or within 2 week(s) of notification.

**Academics.** College provides grants for undergraduate research program enabling students to work individually with faculty members. **Special study options:** Combined bachelor's/graduate degree, double major, independent study, internships, semester at sea, student-designed major, study abroad, teacher certification program, Washington semester. **Credit/placement by examination:** AP, CLEP, IB, institutional tests. Credit from CLEP scores applicable to adult degree program only. **Support services:** Pre-admission summer program, study skills assistance, tutoring, writing center.

**Majors. Area/ethnic studies:** American. **Biology:** General. **Business:** Business admin. **Computer sciences:** Computer science. **Conservation:** General. **English:** English lit. **Foreign languages:** Classics, French, German, Latin, Spanish. **History:** General. **Interdisciplinary:** Historic preservation. **Math:** General. **Philosophy/religion:** Philosophy, religion. **Physical sciences:** Chemistry, geology, physics. **Psychology:** General. **Social sciences:** Anthropology, economics, geography, international relations, political science, sociology. **Visual/performing arts:** Art history/conservation, dramatic, music history, music performance, studio arts.

**Most popular majors.** Biology 8%, business/marketing 13%, English 12%, interdisciplinary studies 9%, liberal arts 8%, psychology 9%, public administration/social services 16%.

**Computing on campus.** 306 workstations in library, computer center, student center. Dormitories wired for high-speed internet access and linked to campus network. Commuter students can connect to campus network. Online course registration, online library, helpline, repair service, wireless network available.

**Student life. Freshman orientation:** Mandatory. Preregistration for classes offered. 5-day freshmen/transfer orientation held in August prior to start of classes. **Policies:** Honor system. **Housing:** Guaranteed on-campus for freshmen. Coed dorms, single-sex dorms, special housing for disabled, apartments, substance-free housing available. $250 nonrefundable deposit, deadline 5/1. Special interest housing options include foreign language and leadership/service living areas. Guaranteed on-campus housing for freshmen and sophomores. **Activities:** Bands, choral groups, dance, drama, film society, literary magazine, music ensembles, musical theater, radio station, student government, student newspaper, symphony orchestra, Amnesty International, Baptist Student Union, Catholic Student Union, Hillel, Hispanic student association, Model UN, Asian student association, Young Democrats, Campus Christian Community, College Republicans.

**Athletics.** NCAA. **Intercollegiate:** Baseball M, basketball, cross-country, equestrian, field hockey W, lacrosse, rowing (crew), soccer, softball W, swimming, tennis, track and field, volleyball W. **Intramural:** Basketball, football (non-tackle) M, golf, ice hockey, racquetball, soccer, softball, volleyball, water polo. **Team name:** Eagles.

**Student services.** Adult student services, campus ministries, career counseling, services for economically disadvantaged, student employment services, financial aid counseling, health services, minority student services, personal counseling, placement for graduates, veterans' counselor, women's services. **Physically disabled:** Services for visually, speech, hearing impaired.

**Contact.** E-mail: admit@umw.edu
Phone: (540) 654-2000 Toll-free number: (800) 468-5614
Fax: (540) 654-1857
Martin Wilder, Vice-President for Enrollment and Communications, University of Mary Washington, 1301 College Avenue, Fredericksburg, VA 22401-5358

# University of Northern Virginia

**Manassas, Virginia**
www.unva.edu

- For-profit 4-year university and business college
- Large town
- 40 degree-seeking undergraduates
- 810 graduate students
- Interview required

**General.** Accredited by ACICS. Branch campuses in London, Hong Kong, Prague, and Cyprus. **Degrees:** 10 bachelor's awarded; master's, doctoral offered. **Location:** 25 miles from Washington, DC. **Calendar:** Quadmester. Extensive summer session. **Full-time faculty:** 9 total; 67% have terminal degrees, 89% minority, 22% women. **Part-time faculty:** 40 total; 38% have terminal degrees, 75% minority, 5% women. **Class size:** 100% < 20.

**Basis for selection.** Level of interest most important.

**2008-2009 Annual costs.** Tuition/fees: $14,000. Books/supplies: $920.

**Application procedures. Admission:** Closing date 8/10. $60 fee, may be waived for applicants with need. Admission notification on a rolling basis.

**Academics. Special study options:** Accelerated study, combined bachelor's/graduate degree, cooperative education, cross-registration, distance learning, double major, ESL, exchange student, external degree, independent study, internships, study abroad, teacher certification program. **Credit/placement by examination:** AP, CLEP, IB, institutional tests. **Support services:** Learning center, reduced course load, tutoring, writing center.

**Majors. Business:** Business admin, international, marketing. **Computer sciences:** General, information technology.

**Most popular majors.** Business/marketing 40%, computer/information sciences 60%.

**Computing on campus.** 78 workstations in library, computer center. Commuter students can connect to campus network. Online library, helpline, repair service, student web hosting, wireless network available.

**Student life. Freshman orientation:** Mandatory, $225 fee. Preregistration for classes offered. **Activities:** Student government.

**Student services.** Career counseling, personal counseling.

**Contact.** E-mail: ibehery.admin@unva.edu
Phone: (703) 392-0771 ext. 2104 Fax: (703) 392-0756
Irena Behery, Admissions Manager, University of Northern Virginia, 10021 Balls Ford Road, Manassas, VA 20109

---

## University of Richmond
### University of Richmond, Virginia
www.richmond.edu

CB member
CB code: 5569

- Private 4-year university and liberal arts college
- Residential campus in very large city
- 2,719 degree-seeking undergraduates: 1% part-time, 49% women, 6% African American, 4% Asian American, 3% Hispanic American, 5% international
- 650 degree-seeking graduate students
- 40% of applicants admitted
- SAT or ACT (ACT writing optional), application essay required
- 86% graduate within 6 years

**General.** Founded in 1830. Regionally accredited. **Degrees:** 790 bachelor's awarded; master's, first professional offered. **ROTC:** Army. **Location:** 6 miles from Richmond, 100 miles from Washington, DC. **Calendar:** Semester, limited summer session. **Full-time faculty:** 286 total; 92% have terminal degrees, 10% minority, 39% women. **Part-time faculty:** 75 total; 63% have terminal degrees, 9% minority, 53% women. **Class size:** 60% < 20, 39% 20-39, less than 1% 40-49, less than 1% 50-99, less than 1% >100. **Special facilities:** Greenhouse, electron microscope, radionuclide complex, print study center, natural sciences museum, neuroscience research laboratory, music technology laboratory, art technology laboratory, foundry, herbarium, computer connection to the Jefferson Lab's particle accelerator.

**Freshman class profile.** 6,649 applied, 2,654 admitted, 810 enrolled.

| Mid 50% test scores | | | |
|---|---|---|---|
| SAT critical reading: | 590-690 | Rank in top tenth: | 62% |
| SAT math: | 610-690 | Return as sophomores: | 91% |
| SAT writing: | 590-690 | Out-of-state: | 84% |
| ACT composite: | 27-31 | Live on campus: | 99% |
| Rank in top quarter: | 89% | International: | 5% |

**Basis for selection.** Students evaluated on high school transcript, test scores, essay, GPA and letter of reference. Campus visits recommended; interviews not offered. SAT Subject Tests in foreign languages may be used for placement, but not required. January SAT and SAT Subject Test date and February ACT test date are last acceptable testing dates for fall admission. Character statement required. **Homeschooled:** Statement describing homeschool structure and mission, interview required. Applicant must submit narrative description of home schooling environment. 2 SAT Subject Tests in history and natural science strongly recommended.

**High school preparation.** 16 units required; 20 recommended. Required and recommended units include English 4, mathematics 3-4, history 2-4, science 2-4 (laboratory 2-4) and foreign language 2-4.

**2007-2008 Annual costs.** Tuition/fees: $37,610. Room/board: $7,200.

**2007-2008 Financial aid. Need-based:** 440 full-time freshmen applied for aid; 344 were judged to have need; 344 of these received aid. Average need met was 100%. Average scholarship/grant was $29,533; average loan $3,127. 91% of total undergraduate aid awarded as scholarships/grants, 9% as loans/jobs. **Non-need-based:** Scholarships awarded for academics, art, athletics, leadership, minority status, music/drama, ROTC, state residency. **Additional information:** Early decision: Financial aid package estimated using historical data; applicant still required to submit all financial aid forms.

**Application procedures. Admission:** Closing date 1/15 (postmark date). $50 fee, may be waived for applicants with need. Application may be submitted online. Admission notification 4/1. Admission notification on a rolling basis. Must reply by May 1 or within 2 week(s) if notified thereafter. **Financial aid:** Closing date 2/15. FAFSA, institutional form required. Applicants notified by 4/1; must reply by 5/1 or within 4 week(s) of notification.

**Academics. Special study options:** Accelerated study, cross-registration, distance learning, double major, ESL, exchange student, honors, independent study, internships, student-designed major, study abroad, teacher certification program, Washington semester. 86 different study abroad programs in over 30 different countries. **Credit/placement by examination:** AP, CLEP,

IB, institutional tests. 30 credit hours maximum toward bachelor's degree. School of Continuing Studies follows different guidelines and credit granting procedures. **Support services:** Learning center, study skills assistance, tutoring, writing center.

**Majors. Area/ethnic studies:** African, American, Asian, European, German, Latin American, Russian/Slavic, women's. **Biology:** General, molecular biochemistry. **Business:** Accounting, business admin, human resources, organizational behavior. **Communications:** Journalism. **Computer sciences:** General, information technology. **Conservation:** Environmental studies. **English:** English lit, speech/rhetoric. **Foreign languages:** Ancient Greek, French, Latin, Spanish. **History:** General. **Interdisciplinary:** Ancient studies, cognitive science. **Liberal arts:** Humanities. **Math:** General. **Philosophy/religion:** Philosophy, religion. **Physical sciences:** Chemistry, physics. **Protective services:** Criminal justice. **Psychology:** General. **Public administration:** Human services. **Social sciences:** Anthropology, economics, international economics, international relations, political science, sociology. **Visual/performing arts:** Art history/conservation, dramatic, studio arts. **Other:** Mathematical Economics.

**Most popular majors.** Biology 7%, business/marketing 25%, English 9%, foreign language 8%, social sciences 20%.

**Computing on campus.** 600 workstations in dormitories, library, computer center. Dormitories wired for high-speed internet access and linked to campus network. Commuter students can connect to campus network. Online course registration, helpline, repair service, student web hosting, wireless network available.

**Student life. Freshman orientation:** Mandatory. 3 days before upperclassmen arrive in the fall. **Policies:** Undergraduate students become members of residential colleges: Richmond College (men) and Westhampton College (women). Classes and extracurricular activities co-educational. Separate student governments, honor/judicial councils and deans. **Housing:** Coed dorms, single-sex dorms, special housing for disabled, apartments, substance-free housing available. $300 nonrefundable deposit, deadline 5/1. Theme housing available. **Activities:** Bands, campus ministries, choral groups, dance, drama, film society, international student organizations, literary magazine, music ensembles, Model UN, musical theater, radio station, student government, student newspaper, symphony orchestra, over 200 organizations.

**Athletics.** NCAA. **Intercollegiate:** Baseball M, basketball, cross-country, diving W, field hockey W, football (tackle) M, golf, lacrosse W, soccer, swimming W, tennis, track and field. **Intramural:** Badminton, basketball, golf, handball, racquetball, soccer, softball, squash, swimming, synchronized swimming W, table tennis, tennis, volleyball, water polo M, wrestling M. **Team name:** Spiders.

**Student services.** Alcohol/substance abuse counseling, campus ministries, career counseling, student employment services, financial aid counseling, health services, minority student services, personal counseling, placement for graduates, veterans' counselor. **Physically disabled:** Services for visually, speech, hearing impaired.

**Contact.** E-mail: admissions@richmond.edu
Phone: (804) 289-8640 Toll-free number: (800) 700-1662
Fax: (804) 289-6003
Pamela Spence, Dean of Admissions, University of Richmond, 28 Westhampton Way, University of Richmond, VA 23173

---

## University of Virginia
### Charlottesville, Virginia
www.virginia.edu

CB member
CB code: 5820

- Public 4-year university
- Residential campus in small city
- 13,726 degree-seeking undergraduates: 2% part-time, 56% women, 9% African American, 11% Asian American, 4% Hispanic American, 5% international
- 6,532 degree-seeking graduate students
- 35% of applicants admitted
- SAT or ACT with writing, application essay required
- 93% graduate within 6 years

**General.** Founded in 1819. Regionally accredited. **Degrees:** 3,367 bachelor's awarded; master's, doctoral, first professional offered. **ROTC:** Army, Naval, Air Force. **Location:** 70 miles from Richmond, 120 miles from Washington, DC. **Calendar:** Semester, extensive summer session. **Full-time faculty:** 1,253 total; 92% have terminal degrees, 11% minority, 32% women. **Part-time faculty:** 87 total; 58% have terminal degrees, 5% minority, 46% women. **Class size:** 49% < 20, 31% 20-39, 5% 40-49, 8% 50-99, 6% >100. **Special facilities:** Observatory, center for biological timing, experimental farm.

**Freshman class profile.** 17,798 applied, 6,273 admitted, 3,248 enrolled.

| Mid 50% test scores | | | |
|---|---|---|---|
| SAT critical reading: | 590-700 | Rank in top quarter: | 96% |
| SAT math: | 610-720 | Rank in top tenth: | 87% |
| SAT writing: | 600-710 | End year in good standing: | 98% |
| GPA 3.50 or higher: | 94% | Return as sophomores: | 97% |
| GPA 3.0-3.49: | 5% | Out-of-state: | 28% |
| GPA 2.0-2.99: | 1% | Live on campus: | 100% |
| | | International: | 5% |

**Basis for selection.** School achievement record, class rank, test scores most important. Extracurricular activities and interests, quality of writing, recommendation also important. Special consideration for minorities, children of alumni, and in-state students. School diploma may be waived for especially qualified applicants. Following international tests accepted: International Baccalaureate, German Abitur, British AICE, French Baccalaureate, Swiss Federal Maturity Certificate. SAT Subject Tests recommended.

**High school preparation.** 16 units required. Required and recommended units include English 4, mathematics 4-5, social studies 1-4, science 2-4 and foreign language 2-5. 3 units of science (1 chemistry, 1 physics) required if applying to the School of Engineering and Applied Science.

**2007-2008 Annual costs.** Tuition/fees: $8,500; $27,515 out-of-state. Room/board: $7,435. Books/supplies: $1,100. Personal expenses: $1,760.

**2007-2008 Financial aid. Need-based:** 1,787 full-time freshmen applied for aid; 839 were judged to have need; 806 of these received aid. Average need met was 94%. Average scholarship/grant was $13,433; average loan $4,065. 78% of total undergraduate aid awarded as scholarships/grants, 22% as loans/jobs. **Non-need-based:** Awarded to 321 full-time undergraduates, including 112 freshmen. Scholarships awarded for academics, athletics, leadership, minority status, music/drama, state residency. **Additional information:** Access UVA program offers loan-free packages for low-income students, caps on need-based loans for all other students, and commitment to meet 100 percent of need for every student.

**Application procedures. Admission:** Closing date 1/2 (postmark date). $60 fee, may be waived for applicants with need. Application may be submitted online. Admission notification 4/1. Must reply by May 1 or within 2 week(s) if notified thereafter. Deferred admission maximum postponement is one year. **Financial aid:** Priority date 3/1; no closing date. FAFSA, institutional form required. Applicants notified by 4/5.

**Academics. Special study options:** Accelerated study, combined bachelor's/graduate degree, cooperative education, double major, ESL, exchange student, honors, independent study, internships, liberal arts/career combination, semester at sea, student-designed major, study abroad, teacher certification program. Echols and Rodman Scholar programs for highest-achieving high school students. **Credit/placement by examination:** AP, CLEP, IB, institutional tests. **Support services:** Learning center, pre-admission summer program, reduced course load, study skills assistance, tutoring, writing center.

**Majors. Architecture:** Architecture, history/criticism, urban/community planning. **Area/ethnic studies:** African-American, Latin American. **Biology:** General. **Business:** General. **Computer sciences:** General. **Conservation:** Environmental science. **Education:** Physical. **Engineering:** General, aerospace, biomedical, chemical, civil, computer, electrical, mechanical, systems. **English:** English lit. **Foreign languages:** Classics, comparative lit, French, German, Italian, Slavic, Spanish. **Health:** Audiology/speech pathology, nursing (RN). **History:** General. **Liberal arts:** Arts/sciences. **Math:** General. **Philosophy/religion:** Philosophy, religion. **Physical sciences:** Astronomy, chemistry, physics. **Psychology:** General. **Social sciences:** Anthropology, economics, international relations, political science, sociology. **Visual/performing arts:** Art, dramatic.

**Most popular majors.** Business/marketing 8%, engineering/engineering technologies 10%, English 6%, foreign language 6%, history 7%, liberal arts 7%, psychology 8%, social sciences 21%.

**Computing on campus.** Dormitories wired for high-speed internet access and linked to campus network. Commuter students can connect to campus network. Online course registration, online library, helpline, repair service, student web hosting, wireless network available.

**Student life. Freshman orientation:** Mandatory, $190 fee. Preregistration for classes offered. 2-day program held in July; August session held for international students. **Housing:** Guaranteed on-campus for freshmen. Coed dorms, apartments, fraternity/sorority housing available. French, German, Russian and Spanish language houses, 3 residential colleges available. **Activities:** Bands, choral groups, dance, drama, film society, literary magazine, music ensembles, musical theater, opera, radio station, student government, student newspaper, symphony orchestra, TV station, community service group, Black Student Alliance, general clubs and religious organizations, political organizations, service fraternities and sororities, debating union.

**Athletics.** NCAA. **Intercollegiate:** Baseball M, basketball, cross-country, diving, field hockey W, football (tackle) M, golf, lacrosse, rowing (crew) W, soccer, softball W, swimming, tennis, track and field, volleyball W, wrestling M. **Intramural:** Basketball, field hockey W, football (non-tackle), golf, racquetball, rowing (crew), soccer, softball, tennis, volleyball, water polo. **Team name:** Cavaliers.

**Student services.** Alcohol/substance abuse counseling, career counseling, student employment services, financial aid counseling, health services, legal services, minority student services, on-campus daycare, personal counseling, placement for graduates, veterans' counselor, women's services. **Physically disabled:** Services for visually, speech, hearing impaired.

**Contact.** E-mail: undergradadmission@virginia.edu
Phone: (434) 982-3200 Fax: (434) 924-3587
John Blackburn, Dean of Admission, University of Virginia, Box 400160, Charlottesville, VA 22904-4160

---

## University of Virginia's College at Wise

Wise, Virginia — CB member
www.uvawise.edu — CB code: 5124

- Public 4-year liberal arts college
- Commuter campus in small town
- 1,657 degree-seeking undergraduates: 10% part-time, 50% women, 8% African American, 1% Asian American, 2% Hispanic American, 1% international
- 80% of applicants admitted
- SAT or ACT (ACT writing recommended) required
- 39% graduate within 6 years

**General.** Founded in 1954. Regionally accredited. **Degrees:** 287 bachelor's awarded. **Location:** 60 miles from Bristol. **Calendar:** Semester, limited summer session. **Full-time faculty:** 95 total; 70% have terminal degrees, 1% minority, 38% women. **Part-time faculty:** 65 total; 15% have terminal degrees, 2% minority, 52% women. **Class size:** 71% < 20, 27% 20-39, less than 1% 40-49, 1% 50-99. **Special facilities:** Observatory, scanning electron microscope, oral communication center, nursing assessment stations.

**Freshman class profile.** 1,121 applied, 893 admitted, 401 enrolled.

| Mid 50% test scores | | | |
|---|---|---|---|
| SAT critical reading: | 420-510 | Rank in top quarter: | 23% |
| SAT math: | 430-530 | Rank in top tenth: | 14% |
| SAT writing: | 420-510 | Return as sophomores: | 72% |
| ACT composite: | 17-22 | Out-of-state: | 6% |
| GPA 3.50 or higher: | 39% | Live on campus: | 46% |
| GPA 3.0-3.49: | 24% | Fraternities: | 2% |
| GPA 2.0-2.99: | 36% | Sororities: | 1% |

**Basis for selection.** Applications reviewed on rolling basis. Emphasis given to academic courses and grades earned in those courses. Interview required for marginal applicants.

**High school preparation.** 18 units required. Required units include English 4, mathematics 3, social studies 1, history 1, science 2 (laboratory 2), foreign language 2 and academic electives 5. 1 American history, 1 world history required.

**2007-2008 Annual costs.** Tuition/fees: $6,151; $17,715 out-of-state. Room/board: $6,984. Books/supplies: $700. Personal expenses: $890.

**2007-2008 Financial aid. Need-based:** 328 full-time freshmen applied for aid; 256 were judged to have need; 256 of these received aid. Average need met was 94%. Average scholarship/grant was $5,041; average loan $2,301. 62% of total undergraduate aid awarded as scholarships/grants, 38% as loans/jobs. **Non-need-based:** Awarded to 1,087 full-time undergraduates, including 412 freshmen. Scholarships awarded for academics, alumni affiliation, art, athletics, job skills, leadership, music/drama, religious affiliation, state residency.

**Application procedures. Admission:** Priority date 12/1; deadline 8/15 (postmark date). $25 fee, may be waived for applicants with need. Application may be submitted online. Admission notification 8/20. Admission notification on a rolling basis beginning on or about 8/15. Must reply by May 1 or within 2 week(s) if notified thereafter. Early action notification on a rolling basis. **Financial aid:** Priority date 4/1; no closing date. FAFSA required. Applicants notified on a rolling basis starting 2/15; must reply within 4 week(s) of notification.

**Academics. Special study options:** Accelerated study, cooperative education, distance learning, double major, dual enrollment of high school students, honors, independent study, internships, liberal arts/career combination, student-designed major, study abroad, teacher certification program. **Credit/placement by examination:** AP, CLEP, IB, institutional tests. **Support services:** Learning center, reduced course load, remedial instruction, study skills assistance, tutoring, writing center.

**Majors. Biology:** General. **Business:** Accounting, business admin, management information systems. **Communications:** General. **Computer sciences:** Computer science. **Conservation:** Environmental studies. **Engineering technology:** Software. **English:** English lit. **Foreign languages:** General, French, Spanish. **Health:** Clinical lab science, nursing (RN). **History:** General. **Liberal arts:** Arts/sciences. **Math:** General. **Physical sciences:** Chemistry. **Protective services:** Criminal justice. **Psychology:** General. **Public administration:** General. **Social sciences:** Economics, political science, sociology. **Visual/performing arts:** Art, dramatic.

**Computing on campus.** 300 workstations in dormitories, library, computer center. Dormitories wired for high-speed internet access and linked to campus network. Commuter students can connect to campus network. Helpline, repair service, student web hosting available.

**Student life. Freshman orientation:** Mandatory, $45 fee. Preregistration for classes offered. 2-day program held for students and parents. Dormitory space available (free for students, $35 per night for parents). **Housing:** Coed dorms, single-sex dorms, special housing for disabled, apartments available. $150 deposit, deadline 5/1. **Activities:** Concert band, choral groups, dance, drama, international student organizations, literary magazine, music ensembles, musical theater, radio station, student government, student newspaper, TV station, Young Republicans, Young Democrats, multicultural alliance, honors societies, professional organizations, student activities board, Baptist Student Union, Wesley Foundation.

**Athletics.** NAIA. **Intercollegiate:** Baseball M, basketball, cross-country, football (tackle) M, golf M, softball W, tennis, track and field, volleyball W. **Intramural:** Badminton, basketball, football (non-tackle), racquetball, soccer, softball, table tennis, tennis, volleyball, water polo. **Team name:** Cavaliers.

**Student services.** Alcohol/substance abuse counseling, campus ministries, career counseling, services for economically disadvantaged, student employment services, financial aid counseling, health services, minority student services, personal counseling, placement for graduates. **Physically disabled:** Services for visually, speech, hearing impaired.

**Contact.** E-mail: admissions@uvawise.edu
Phone: (276) 328-0102 Toll-free number: (888) 282-9324
Fax: (276) 328-0251
Russell Necessary, Vice Chancellor of Enrollment Management, University of Virginia's College at Wise, 1 College Avenue, Wise, VA 24293-4412

---

# Virginia Commonwealth University
**Richmond, Virginia**
www.vcu.edu

**CB member**
**CB code: 5570**

- Public 4-year university
- Commuter campus in small city
- 20,232 degree-seeking undergraduates: 14% part-time, 59% women, 21% African American, 11% Asian American, 4% Hispanic American, 1% Native American, 3% international
- 7,074 degree-seeking graduate students
- 62% of applicants admitted
- SAT or ACT (ACT writing optional), application essay required
- 45% graduate within 6 years

**General.** Founded in 1838. Regionally accredited. **Degrees:** 3,322 bachelor's awarded; master's, doctoral, first professional offered. **ROTC:** Army. **Location:** 100 miles from Washington, DC. **Calendar:** Semester, extensive summer session. **Full-time faculty:** 1,888 total; 19% minority, 42% women. **Part-time faculty:** 1,101 total; 15% minority, 53% women. **Class size:** 44% < 20, 39% 20-39, 6% 40-49, 6% 50-99, 5% >100. **Special facilities:** Center for environmental life sciences, School of Engineering cleanrooms.

**Freshman class profile.** 15,160 applied, 9,331 admitted, 3,882 enrolled.

| Mid 50% test scores | | | |
|---|---|---|---|
| SAT critical reading: | 480-590 | Rank in top quarter: | 42% |
| SAT math: | 480-580 | Rank in top tenth: | 15% |
| SAT writing: | 460-570 | End year in good standing: | 79% |
| ACT composite: | 19-24 | Return as sophomores: | 82% |
| GPA 3.50 or higher: | 30% | Out-of-state: | 9% |
| GPA 3.0-3.49: | 40% | International: | 3% |
| GPA 2.0-2.99: | 30% | Fraternities: | 4% |
| | | Sororities: | 5% |

**Basis for selection.** Applicants considered primarily based on strength of high school record, grades in those courses, and SAT or ACT scores. **Homeschooled:** Transcript of courses and grades required.

**High school preparation.** 20 units required; 24 recommended. Required and recommended units include English 4, mathematics 3-4, social studies 1, history 2-3, science 3-4 (laboratory 1), foreign language 2-3, visual/performing arts 1 and academic electives 5.

**2007-2008 Annual costs.** Tuition/fees: $6,196; $18,572 out-of-state. Room/board: $7,567.

**2007-2008 Financial aid. Need-based:** 2,521 full-time freshmen applied for aid; 1,866 were judged to have need; 1,866 of these received aid. Average need met was 69%. Average scholarship/grant was $5,061; average loan $4,116. 48% of total undergraduate aid awarded as scholarships/grants, 52% as loans/jobs. **Non-need-based:** Awarded to 2,085 full-time undergraduates, including 376 freshmen. Scholarships awarded for academics, art, athletics, leadership, music/drama.

**Application procedures. Admission:** Priority date 2/1; no deadline. $40 fee, may be waived for applicants with need. Application may be submitted online. Admission notification on a rolling basis beginning on or about 11/1. Must reply by May 1 or within 4 week(s) if notified thereafter. **Financial aid:** Priority date 3/1; no closing date. FAFSA required. Applicants notified on a rolling basis starting 3/15; must reply by 5/1 or within 3 week(s) of notification.

**Academics. Special study options:** Accelerated study, cooperative education, distance learning, double major, dual enrollment of high school students, ESL, exchange student, honors, independent study, internships, liberal arts/career combination, student-designed major, study abroad, teacher certification program. **Credit/placement by examination:** AP, CLEP, IB, institutional tests. **Support services:** Learning center, reduced course load, study skills assistance, tutoring, writing center.

**Majors. Area/ethnic studies:** African-American, women's. **Biology:** General, bioinformatics. **Business:** Accounting, business admin, managerial economics, marketing. **Communications:** Media studies. **Computer sciences:** General, information systems. **Conservation:** Environmental studies. **Education:** Art, health. **Engineering:** Biomedical, chemical, computer, electrical, mechanical. **English:** English lit. **Foreign languages:** General. **Health:** Clinical lab science, dental hygiene, nursing (RN), radiologic technology/medical imaging. **History:** General. **Interdisciplinary:** Biological/physical sciences, global studies. **Math:** General. **Parks/recreation:** General. **Philosophy/religion:** Philosophy, religion. **Physical sciences:** Chemistry, physics. **Protective services:** Emergency management/homeland security, forensics, law enforcement admin. **Psychology:** General. **Public administration:** Social work. **Social sciences:** Anthropology, political science, sociology, urban studies. **Visual/performing arts:** Art history/conservation, cinematography, crafts, dance, dramatic, fashion design, graphic design, illustration, interior design, music performance, painting, photography, sculpture. **Other:** Kinetic imaging.

**Most popular majors.** Business/marketing 14%, communications/journalism 6%, health sciences 10%, psychology 11%, security/protective services 8%, visual/performing arts 15%.

**Computing on campus.** PC or laptop required. 2,000 workstations in dormitories, library, computer center, student center. Dormitories wired for high-speed internet access and linked to campus network. Commuter students can connect to campus network. Online course registration, online library, helpline, repair service, student web hosting, wireless network available.

**Student life. Freshman orientation:** Mandatory, $40 fee. Preregistration for classes offered. **Policies:** Most events open to VCU students with ID. Events sponsored by activity fees. **Housing:** Guaranteed on-campus for freshmen. Coed dorms, special housing for disabled, apartments, substance-free housing available. $250 fully refundable deposit, deadline 6/1. Special housing for honors program and engineering. Suites for upperclassmen. **Activities:** Bands, campus ministries, choral groups, dance, drama, international student organizations, literary magazine, music ensembles, opera, radio station, student government, student newspaper, symphony orchestra, College Republicans, Young Democrats, NAACP, Black Student Alliance, activities programming board, Sexual Minority Student Alliance, Chinese students, scholars association.

**Athletics.** NAIA, NCAA. **Intercollegiate:** Baseball M, basketball, field hockey W, golf M, soccer, tennis, track and field, volleyball W. **Intramural:** Badminton, basketball, football (non-tackle), golf, handball, racquetball, soccer, softball, table tennis, tennis, volleyball, water polo. **Team name:** Rams.

**Student services.** Adult student services, alcohol/substance abuse counseling, career counseling, student employment services, financial aid counseling, health services, on-campus daycare, personal counseling, placement for graduates, veterans' counselor. **Physically disabled:** Services for visually, speech, hearing impaired.

**Contact.** E-mail: ugrad@vcu.edu
Phone: (804) 828-1222 Toll-free number: (800) 841-3638
Fax: (804) 828-1899
Sybil Halloran, Director of Admissions, Virginia Commonwealth University, Box 842526, Richmond, VA 23284-2526

## Virginia Intermont College
### Bristol, Virginia
**www.vic.edu**                              **CB code: 5857**

▶ Private 4-year liberal arts college affiliated with Baptist faith

▶ Residential campus in small city

▶ 627 degree-seeking undergraduates: 16% part-time, 74% women, 5% African American, 1% Hispanic American, 2% international

▶ 69% of applicants admitted

▶ SAT or ACT (ACT writing recommended) required

**General.** Founded in 1884. Regionally accredited. Adult degree studies program available for working adults; limited majors available. **Degrees:** 261 bachelor's, 7 associate awarded. **Location:** 144 miles from Roanoke, 114 miles from Knoxville, Tennessee. **Calendar:** Semester, limited summer session. **Full-time faculty:** 39 total; 80% have terminal degrees, 5% minority, 44% women. **Part-time faculty:** 42 total; 40% have terminal degrees, 2% minority, 57% women. **Class size:** 96% < 20, 4% 20-39, less than 1% 40-49. **Special facilities:** 120-acre riding center with 2 indoor riding arenas.

**Freshman class profile.** 672 applied, 466 admitted, 134 enrolled.

| Mid 50% test scores | | | |
|---|---|---|---|
| SAT critical reading: | 400-550 | GPA 3.0-3.49: | 38% |
| SAT math: | 380-540 | GPA 2.0-2.99: | 21% |
| ACT composite: | 17-24 | Out-of-state: | 58% |
| GPA 3.50 or higher: | 40% | Live on campus: | 78% |

**Basis for selection.** School achievement record, SAT or ACT scores, school and community activities important. Essay, interview recommended for all; audition recommended for dance, equine studies, performing arts; portfolio recommended for art, photography. **Homeschooled:** Transcript of courses and grades, state high school equivalency certificate required. **Learning Disabled:** Students admitted conditionally, restricted to 12 credit hours in first semester.

**High school preparation.** 15 units required. Required units include English 4, mathematics 2, social studies 2, (laboratory 1) and academic electives 6.

**2007-2008 Annual costs.** Tuition/fees: $19,366. Room/board: $6,495. Books/supplies: $1,000. Personal expenses: $2,190.

**2006-2007 Financial aid. Need-based:** 83 full-time freshmen applied for aid; 69 were judged to have need; 68 of these received aid. Average need met was 53%. Average scholarship/grant was $8,962; average loan $2,795. 49% of total undergraduate aid awarded as scholarships/grants, 51% as loans/jobs. **Non-need-based:** Awarded to 297 full-time undergraduates, including 79 freshmen. Scholarships awarded for art, athletics, music/drama, religious affiliation, state residency.

**Application procedures. Admission:** No deadline. $25 fee, may be waived for applicants with need. Application may be submitted online. Admission notification on a rolling basis. **Financial aid:** Priority date 3/1, closing date 6/1. FAFSA required. Applicants notified on a rolling basis starting 2/15; must reply within 3 week(s) of notification.

**Academics. Special study options:** Accelerated study, cross-registration, distance learning, double major, honors, independent study, internships, teacher certification program. **Credit/placement by examination:** AP, CLEP, IB, institutional tests. No maximums for prior work or credit by examination; no cumulative restrictions imposed upon hours earned toward elective credits. Students must complete at least one half of major and take minimum of

25% of classes at school to meet minimum residency requirement. **Support services:** Learning center, reduced course load, study skills assistance, tutoring, writing center.

**Majors. Agriculture:** Equestrian studies. **Biology:** General. **Business:** Business admin, international, marketing. **Computer sciences:** General. **Conservation:** Environmental studies. **Education:** General, art, biology, elementary, English, physical, secondary, social studies, special. **English:** English lit. **Health:** Premedicine, preveterinary. **History:** General. **Legal studies:** General, paralegal, prelaw. **Liberal arts:** Arts/sciences. **Parks/recreation:** Health/fitness, sports admin. **Philosophy/religion:** Religion. **Protective services:** Law enforcement admin. **Psychology:** General. **Public administration:** General, social work. **Social sciences:** Political science. **Visual/performing arts:** Art, dance, dramatic, photography.

**Most popular majors.** Agriculture 13%, business/marketing 12%, education 40%, parks/recreation 7%, public administration/social services 6%, visual/performing arts 9%.

**Computing on campus.** 100 workstations in dormitories, library, computer center. Dormitories wired for high-speed internet access and linked to campus network. Commuter students can connect to campus network. Online library, helpline, wireless network available.

**Student life. Freshman orientation:** Mandatory. Preregistration for classes offered. **Policies:** Alcohol and tobacco use prohibited on campus. No open flame items or cooking appliances other than microwave ovens. (Juniors and seniors may live off campus, but all other students under 21 years of age not living with parents must live on campus.). **Housing:** Guaranteed on-campus for freshmen. Coed dorms, single-sex dorms, apartments, substance-free housing available. $200 deposit. **Activities:** Campus ministries, choral groups, dance, drama, international student organizations, music ensembles, musical theater, student government, Christian student union, Cardinal Key, social work action group, Fellowship of Christian Athletes, Alpha Phi Omega.

**Athletics.** NAIA. **Intercollegiate:** Baseball M, basketball, cheerleading M, equestrian, golf M, softball W, volleyball W. **Intramural:** Basketball, football (non-tackle), golf, softball, table tennis, volleyball. **Team name:** Cobras.

**Student services.** Adult student services, alcohol/substance abuse counseling, campus ministries, career counseling, student employment services, financial aid counseling, health services, minority student services, personal counseling, placement for graduates. **Physically disabled:** Services for visually, hearing impaired.

**Contact.** E-mail: viadmit@vic.edu
Phone: (276) 466-7856 Toll-free number: (800) 451-1842
Fax: (276) 466-7855
Tony England, Vice President of Enrollment, Virginia Intermont College, 1013 Moore Street, Bristol, VA 24201

## Virginia Military Institute
### Lexington, Virginia                    **CB member**
**www.vmi.edu**                          **CB code: 5858**

▶ Public 4-year liberal arts and military college

▶ Residential campus in small town

▶ 1,378 degree-seeking undergraduates: 8% women, 6% African American, 4% Asian American, 3% Hispanic American, 2% international

▶ 54% of applicants admitted

▶ SAT or ACT (ACT writing optional) required

**General.** Founded in 1839. Regionally accredited. Mandatory ROTC classes and optional commissioning in the Army, Air Force, Navy, or Marines. **Degrees:** 325 bachelor's awarded. **ROTC:** Army, Naval, Air Force. **Location:** 55 miles from Roanoke, 140 miles from Richmond. **Calendar:** Semester, limited summer session. **Full-time faculty:** 117 total; 98% have terminal degrees, 8% minority, 16% women. **Part-time faculty:** 49 total; 41% have terminal degrees, 6% minority, 29% women. **Class size:** 72% < 20, 28% 20-39, less than 1% 40-49. **Special facilities:** Historical museums, research library, observatory, particle accelerator.

**Freshman class profile.** 1,704 applied, 926 admitted, 463 enrolled.

| Mid 50% test scores | | | |
|---|---|---|---|
| SAT critical reading: | 510-610 | GPA 2.0-2.99: | 20% |
| SAT math: | 520-620 | Rank in top quarter: | 39% |
| SAT writing: | 480-580 | Rank in top tenth: | 14% |
| ACT composite: | 21-25 | Return as sophomores: | 80% |
| GPA 3.50 or higher: | 38% | Out-of-state: | 38% |
| GPA 3.0-3.49: | 42% | Live on campus: | 100% |
| | | International: | 2% |

**Basis for selection.** GED not accepted. Admissions based on secondary school record, class rank, standardized test scores, character, and personal qualities. Interview, extracurricular activities, state residency, minority status, and volunteer work also important. **Homeschooled:** Require transcript with list of texts used or group affiliation.

**High school preparation.** Required and recommended units include English 4, mathematics 3-4, science 3 (laboratory 3) and foreign language 3-4.

**2007-2008 Annual costs.** Tuition/fees: $10,048; $25,892 out-of-state. Room/board: $6,108. Books/supplies: $775. Personal expenses: $1,500.

**2006-2007 Financial aid. Need-based:** 295 full-time freshmen applied for aid; 216 were judged to have need; 215 of these received aid. Average need met was 85%. Average scholarship/grant was $9,397; average loan $2,972. 80% of total undergraduate aid awarded as scholarships/grants, 20% as loans/jobs. **Non-need-based:** Awarded to 466 full-time undergraduates, including 147 freshmen. Scholarships awarded for academics, athletics, leadership, music/drama, ROTC.

**Application procedures. Admission:** Closing date 2/15 (postmark date). $35 fee, may be waived for applicants with need. Application may be submitted online. Admission notification on a rolling basis beginning on or about 1/1. Must reply by May 1 or within 2 week(s) if notified thereafter. **Financial aid:** Priority date 3/1; no closing date. FAFSA, institutional form required. Applicants notified on a rolling basis starting 3/15; must reply by 5/1.

**Academics. Special study options:** Accelerated study, double major, exchange student, honors, independent study, internships, study abroad, teacher certification program. Summer Transition program: Optional for incoming freshmen. **Credit/placement by examination:** AP, CLEP, IB, institutional tests. No policy, but it is unlikely any student would receive more than 36 hours credit. **Support services:** Learning center, pre-admission summer program, study skills assistance, tutoring, writing center.

**Majors. Biology:** General. **Computer sciences:** Computer science. **Engineering:** Civil, electrical, mechanical. **English:** English lit. **Foreign languages:** General. **History:** General. **Interdisciplinary:** Global studies. **Math:** General. **Physical sciences:** Chemistry, physics. **Psychology:** General. **Social sciences:** Economics.

**Most popular majors.** Biology 6%, engineering/engineering technologies 21%, history 18%, psychology 11%, social sciences 28%.

**Computing on campus.** PC or laptop required. 200 workstations in library, computer center. Dormitories wired for high-speed internet access and linked to campus network. Online course registration, online library, helpline, repair service, wireless network available.

**Student life. Freshman orientation:** Mandatory. 8 days before beginning of fall classes. Optional month-long summer orientation program coincides with summer academic session, and participants can complete 1 freshman course. **Policies:** Student-run honor system integral part of institution. **Housing:** Guaranteed on-campus for all undergraduates. Barracks house 3-5 students per room. **Activities:** Bands, choral groups, drama, literary magazine, music ensembles, musical theater, student government, student newspaper, more than 50 clubs and student organizations available.

**Athletics.** NCAA. **Intercollegiate:** Baseball M, basketball M, cross-country, diving M, football (tackle) M, golf M, lacrosse M, rifle M, soccer, swimming, tennis M, track and field, wrestling M. **Intramural:** Basketball, football (non-tackle), soccer, softball. **Team name:** Keydets.

**Student services.** Alcohol/substance abuse counseling, campus ministries, career counseling, student employment services, financial aid counseling, health services, personal counseling, placement for graduates.

**Contact.** E-mail: admissions@vmi.edu
Phone: (540) 464-7211 Toll-free number: (800) 767-4207
Fax: (540) 464-7746
Col. Vernon Beitzel, Director of Admissions, Virginia Military Institute, 319 Letcher Avenue, Lexington, VA 24450-9967

## Virginia Polytechnic Institute and State University
**Blacksburg, Virginia**                    **CB member**
**www.vt.edu**                              **CB code: 5859**

- Public 4-year university
- Residential campus in large town
- 22,940 degree-seeking undergraduates: 2% part-time, 42% women, 4% African American, 7% Asian American, 3% Hispanic American, 2% international

- 6,848 degree-seeking graduate students
- 67% of applicants admitted
- SAT or ACT with writing required
- 78% graduate within 6 years

**General.** Founded in 1872. Regionally accredited. Option of enrolling as member of cadet corps. **Degrees:** 4,887 bachelor's, 48 associate awarded; master's, doctoral, first professional offered. **ROTC:** Army, Naval, Air Force. **Location:** 38 miles from Roanoke. **Calendar:** Semester, limited summer session. **Full-time faculty:** 1,371 total; 89% have terminal degrees, 14% minority, 30% women. **Part-time faculty:** 231 total; 7% minority, 42% women. **Class size:** 23% < 20, 45% 20-39, 11% 40-49, 13% 50-99, 8% >100. **Special facilities:** Natural history, geology and art museums, observatory, wind tunnel, Black cultural center, digital music center, robotics laboratory, multimedia laboratory, media center, women's center, math emporium, advanced communications/information technology center, teaching forest.

**Freshman class profile.** 19,429 applied, 13,031 admitted, 5,122 enrolled.

| Mid 50% test scores | | | |
|---|---|---|---|
| SAT critical reading: | 530-630 | Rank in top quarter: | 82% |
| SAT math: | 570-670 | Rank in top tenth: | 40% |
| SAT writing: | 530-630 | Return as sophomores: | 93% |
| GPA 3.50 or higher: | 80% | Out-of-state: | 30% |
| GPA 3.0-3.49: | 18% | Live on campus: | 98% |
| GPA 2.0-2.99: | 2% | International: | 2% |
| | | Fraternities: | 7% |

**Basis for selection.** High school course work, grades, test scores most important. Prospective students encouraged to pursue rigorous preparatory course of study through senior year. Students from other than accredited schools must take, in addition to SAT (including mandatory Writing component) or ACT (including Writing component), SAT Subject Tests in Math (Level Ic or IIc) and second area of study to be chosen by applicant. SAT Subject Tests may not be required if student has dual-enrollment or AP credit. Audition required for music. **Homeschooled:** Transcript of courses and grades required. Must submit standardized test scores; statement describing homeschool structure and mission recommended but not required.

**High school preparation.** 18 units required. Required and recommended units include English 4, mathematics 3-4, social studies 1, history 1, science 2-3 (laboratory 2), foreign language 3 and academic electives 4. Preference given to applicants with mathematics beyond Algebra II. 4 mathematics required for general engineering, biochemistry, chemistry, computer science, math, physics and statistics. 3 science including physics required for engineering and recommended for all science-related majors.

**2007-2008 Annual costs.** Tuition/fees: $7,397; $19,605 out-of-state. Room/board: $5,106. Books/supplies: $1,024. Personal expenses: $1,431.

**2006-2007 Financial aid. Need-based:** 3,541 full-time freshmen applied for aid; 2,083 were judged to have need; 1,762 of these received aid. Average need met was 61%. Average scholarship/grant was $5,569; average loan $3,500. 53% of total undergraduate aid awarded as scholarships/grants, 47% as loans/jobs. **Non-need-based:** Awarded to 3,570 full-time undergraduates, including 1,205 freshmen. Scholarships awarded for art, athletics, ROTC.

**Application procedures. Admission:** Closing date 1/15 (postmark date). $50 fee, may be waived for applicants with need. Application may be submitted online. Admission notification 4/1. Must reply by 5/1. $400 matriculation deposit required. **Financial aid:** Priority date 3/11; no closing date. FAFSA required. Applicants notified on a rolling basis starting 3/30; must reply by 5/1 or within 4 week(s) of notification.

**Academics. Special study options:** Accelerated study, combined bachelor's/graduate degree, cooperative education, distance learning, double major, dual enrollment of high school students, ESL, honors, independent study, internships, study abroad, teacher certification program, Washington semester. **Credit/placement by examination:** AP, CLEP, IB, institutional tests. 12 credit hours maximum toward associate degree, 12 toward bachelor's. **Support services:** Learning center, pre-admission summer program, study skills assistance, tutoring, writing center.

**Majors. Agriculture:** General, agronomy, animal sciences, dairy, economics, food science, horticultural science. **Architecture:** Architecture, landscape. **Biology:** General, biochemistry. **Business:** Accounting, business admin, construction management, finance, hospitality admin, management science, managerial economics, marketing. **Communications:** General. **Computer sciences:** General. **Conservation:** Environmental science, environmental studies, forestry. **Education:** Secondary. **Engineering:** Aerospace, agricultural, chemical, civil, computer, construction, electrical, industrial, materials, mechanical, mechanics, mining. **English:** English lit. **Family/consumer sciences:** Business, family studies, food/nutrition. **Foreign languages:** General. **History:** General. **Interdisciplinary:** Science/society. **Liberal arts:** Arts/sciences. **Math:** General, statistics. **Philosophy/religion:** Philosophy.

**Physical sciences:** Chemistry, geology, physics. **Psychology:** General. **Public administration:** Policy analysis. **Social sciences:** Economics, geography, international relations, political science, sociology. **Visual/performing arts:** Art, dramatic, industrial design, interior design.

**Most popular majors.** Biology 8%, business/marketing 21%, engineering/engineering technologies 20%, family/consumer sciences 9%, social sciences 7%.

**Computing on campus.** PC or laptop required. 1,050 workstations in dormitories, library, computer center, student center. Dormitories wired for high-speed internet access and linked to campus network. Commuter students can connect to campus network. Online course registration, online library, helpline, repair service, student web hosting, wireless network available.

**Student life. Freshman orientation:** Available, $120 fee. Preregistration for classes offered. Day and a half long program held in July. **Policies:** Freshmen required to live on campus, unless living with parents or close relatives, married, veteran, or at least 21 years old. Honor system in force. **Housing:** Guaranteed on-campus for freshmen. Coed dorms, single-sex dorms, special housing for disabled, fraternity/sorority housing, substance-free housing available. Cadets live in cadet residence halls. Foreign language hall and academic success hall available. **Activities:** Bands, choral groups, dance, drama, literary magazine, music ensembles, musical theater, radio station, student government, student newspaper, 400 clubs and organizations available.

**Athletics.** NCAA. **Intercollegiate:** Baseball M, basketball, cheerleading, cross-country, diving, football (tackle) M, golf M, lacrosse W, soccer, softball W, swimming, tennis, track and field, volleyball W, wrestling M. **Intramural:** Basketball, bowling, football (non-tackle), golf, racquetball, soccer, softball, squash, swimming, table tennis, tennis, volleyball, water polo. **Team name:** Hokies.

**Student services.** Alcohol/substance abuse counseling, campus ministries, career counseling, student employment services, financial aid counseling, health services, legal services, minority student services, personal counseling, placement for graduates, veterans' counselor, women's services. **Physically disabled:** Services for visually, hearing impaired.

**Contact.** E-mail: vtadmiss@vt.edu
Phone: (540) 231-6267 Fax: (540) 231-3242
Norrine Spencer, Associate Provost and Director of Undergraduate Admissions, Virginia Polytechnic Institute and State University, 201 Burruss Hall, Blacksburg, VA 24061-0202

---

## Virginia State University
**Petersburg, Virginia**  **CB member**
**www.vsu.edu**  **CB code: 5860**

- Public 4-year university
- Residential campus in large town
- 4,195 degree-seeking undergraduates: 6% part-time, 61% women, 95% African American, 1% Hispanic American
- 389 degree-seeking graduate students
- 58% of applicants admitted
- SAT or ACT (ACT writing optional) required
- 43% graduate within 6 years

**General.** Founded in 1882. Regionally accredited. **Degrees:** 716 bachelor's, 4 associate awarded; master's, doctoral offered. **ROTC:** Army. **Location:** 25 miles from Richmond. **Calendar:** Semester, limited summer session. **Full-time faculty:** 263 total; 69% minority, 40% women. **Part-time faculty:** 125 total; 47% women. **Class size:** 35% < 20, 52% 20-39, 7% 40-49, 5% 50-99, less than 1% >100.

**Freshman class profile.** 4,481 applied, 2,590 admitted, 1,042 enrolled.

| Mid 50% test scores | | | |
|---|---|---|---|
| SAT critical reading: | 400-470 | Rank in top quarter: | 23% |
| SAT math: | 390-470 | Rank in top tenth: | 7% |
| SAT writing: | 380-460 | Return as sophomores: | 74% |
| GPA 3.50 or higher: | 10% | Out-of-state: | 41% |
| GPA 3.0-3.49: | 24% | Live on campus: | 89% |
| GPA 2.0-2.99: | 66% | | |

**Basis for selection.** School achievement record most important; recommendation required. Essay recommended for all; audition required for music; portfolio recommended for art.

**High school preparation.** 11 units required. Required and recommended units include English 4, mathematics 3, social studies 2, science 2 (laboratory 1) and foreign language 2. Mathematics requirement must include algebra I.

---

**2007-2008 Annual costs.** Tuition/fees: $5,655; $13,185 out-of-state. Out of state students pay an additional fee. Room/board: $7,340. Books/supplies: $900. Personal expenses: $675.

**Financial aid. Non-need-based:** Scholarships awarded for academics, alumni affiliation, art, athletics, job skills, leadership, music/drama, religious affiliation, ROTC. **Additional information:** Strongly recommend that students apply for scholarship assistance through federal, state, local and private agencies.

**Application procedures. Admission:** Priority date 3/31; deadline 5/1 (postmark date). $25 fee, may be waived for applicants with need. Application may be submitted online. Admission notification on a rolling basis. Must reply by May 1 or within 2 week(s) if notified thereafter. **Financial aid:** Priority date 3/31, closing date 5/1. FAFSA, institutional form required. Applicants notified on a rolling basis starting 5/1; must reply within 2 week(s) of notification.

**Academics. Special study options:** Cooperative education, double major, dual enrollment of high school students, exchange student, honors, independent study, internships, teacher certification program. **Credit/placement by examination:** AP, CLEP, institutional tests. 12 credit hours maximum toward bachelor's degree. **Support services:** Study skills assistance, tutoring, writing center.

**Majors. Agriculture:** General. **Biology:** General. **Business:** Accounting, business admin, hospitality admin, managerial economics, marketing. **Communications:** Media studies. **Computer sciences:** Computer science, information technology. **Education:** Business, physical, trade/industrial. **Engineering:** Computer, manufacturing. **Engineering technology:** General, electrical, mechanical. **English:** English lit. **Family/consumer sciences:** Communication. **History:** General. **Liberal arts:** Arts/sciences. **Math:** General. **Physical sciences:** Chemistry, physics. **Protective services:** Criminal justice. **Psychology:** General. **Public administration:** General, social work. **Social sciences:** Political science, sociology. **Visual/performing arts:** General, music performance.

**Most popular majors.** Business/marketing 19%, communications/journalism 7%, computer/information sciences 7%, education 13%, interdisciplinary studies 8%, liberal arts 6%, psychology 6%, security/protective services 7%, social sciences 6%.

**Computing on campus.** 750 workstations in dormitories, library, student center. Dormitories wired for high-speed internet access and linked to campus network. Commuter students can connect to campus network. Online course registration, online library, helpline, repair service available.

**Student life. Freshman orientation:** Mandatory, $75 fee. Preregistration for classes offered. Two-day orientation held at various times in the summer. **Housing:** Guaranteed on-campus for freshmen. Coed dorms, single-sex dorms, apartments, substance-free housing available. $150 deposit. **Activities:** Bands, campus ministries, choral groups, dance, drama, literary magazine, music ensembles, radio station, student government, student newspaper, TV station, NAACP, Black Students Against Drugs, Muslim student organization, peer mediators, Betterment of Brothers and Sisters, Caribbean students association, Institute for Leadership Development.

**Athletics.** NCAA. **Intercollegiate:** Baseball M, basketball, bowling W, cheerleading, cross-country, football (tackle) M, golf, softball W, tennis, track and field, volleyball W. **Intramural:** Basketball, football (tackle) M, swimming, table tennis, tennis, track and field, volleyball W. **Team name:** Trojans.

**Student services.** Alcohol/substance abuse counseling, campus ministries, career counseling, services for economically disadvantaged, student employment services, financial aid counseling, health services, personal counseling, placement for graduates, veterans' counselor. **Physically disabled:** Services for visually, hearing impaired.

**Contact.** E-mail: admiss@vsu.edu
Phone: (804) 524-5902 Toll-free number: (800) 871-7611
Fax: (804) 524-5055
Irene Logan, Director of Admissions, Virginia State University, One Hayden Street, Petersburg, VA 23806

---

## Virginia Union University
**Richmond, Virginia**  **CB member**
**www.vuu.edu**  **CB code: 5862**

- Private 4-year university and liberal arts college affiliated with Baptist faith
- Residential campus in small city
- 1,194 degree-seeking undergraduates

♦ 342 graduate students

♦ SAT or ACT (ACT writing recommended) required

**General.** Founded in 1865. Regionally accredited. **Degrees:** 198 bachelor's awarded; master's, doctoral, first professional offered. **ROTC:** Army. **Location:** 90 miles from Norfolk, 100 miles from Washington, DC. **Calendar:** Semester, limited summer session. **Full-time faculty:** 85 total. **Part-time faculty:** 20 total. **Special facilities:** Police academy, learning resource center.

### Freshman class profile.

| Mid 50% test scores | | | |
|---|---|---|---|
| SAT critical reading: | 350-420 | **GPA 2.0-2.99:** | 70% |
| SAT math: | 320-410 | **Rank in top quarter:** | 12% |
| ACT composite: | 13-17 | **Rank in top tenth:** | 4% |
| **GPA 3.50 or higher:** | 4% | **Out-of-state:** | 46% |
| **GPA 3.0-3.49:** | 8% | **Live on campus:** | 79% |

**Basis for selection.** Secondary school record, test scores, extracurricular activities most important. Essay, interview, and talent or ability also important. Essay recommended for all. Interview recommended for academically weak. Audition required for band, choir, music, university players.

**High school preparation.** 16 units required. Required units include English 4, mathematics 3, social studies 2, science 2, foreign language 2 and academic electives 3.

**2007-2008 Annual costs.** Tuition/fees: $13,394. Room/board: $6,054. Books/supplies: $500. Personal expenses: $1,000.

**Financial aid. Non-need-based:** Scholarships awarded for academics, athletics, ROTC, state residency.

**Application procedures. Admission:** Priority date 6/30; no deadline. $25 fee, may be waived for applicants with need. Application may be submitted online. Admission notification on a rolling basis. **Financial aid:** Priority date 4/27; no closing date. FAFSA required. Applicants notified on a rolling basis starting 5/1; must reply within 2 week(s) of notification.

**Academics. Special study options:** Cooperative education, honors, independent study, internships, liberal arts/career combination, teacher certification program. **Credit/placement by examination:** AP, CLEP, IB, institutional tests. 18 credit hours maximum toward bachelor's degree. **Support services:** Learning center, reduced course load, remedial instruction, tutoring, writing center.

**Majors. Biology:** General. **Business:** Accounting, business admin, finance, management information systems, sales/distribution. **Communications:** Journalism. **Computer sciences:** General. **Education:** Multi-level teacher. **English:** English lit. **History:** General. **Interdisciplinary:** Natural sciences. **Math:** General. **Philosophy/religion:** Religion. **Physical sciences:** Chemistry. **Psychology:** General. **Public administration:** Social work. **Social sciences:** Political science, sociology. **Visual/performing arts:** Art, dramatic, music theory/composition, piano/organ, voice/opera.

**Most popular majors.** Business/marketing 14%, education 9%, psychology 8%, social sciences 11%, theological studies 42%.

**Computing on campus.** PC or laptop required. 148 workstations in library, computer center. Dormitories linked to campus network. Online course registration, wireless network available.

**Student life. Freshman orientation:** Mandatory. **Housing:** Coed dorms, single-sex dorms available. $250 deposit, deadline 7/1. **Activities:** Bands, choral groups, dance, drama, music ensembles, musical theater, opera, student government, student newspaper, social work club, sociology club, student education association, Ministers Alliance.

**Athletics.** NCAA. **Intercollegiate:** Basketball, bowling W, cross-country, football (tackle) M, golf, softball W, tennis, track and field, volleyball W. **Intramural:** Basketball, football (non-tackle) M, softball, table tennis. **Team name:** Panthers.

**Student services.** Career counseling, student employment services, health services, personal counseling, placement for graduates.

**Contact.** E-mail: admissions@vuu.edu
Phone: (804) 342-3570 Toll-free number: (800) 368-3227
Fax: (804) 342-3511
Delores Scott, Vice President of Student Affairs, Virginia Union University, 1500 North Lombardy Street, Richmond, VA 23220

---

# Virginia Wesleyan College
**Norfolk, Virginia**
**www.vwc.edu**

**CB member**
**CB code: 5867**

♦ Private 4-year liberal arts college affiliated with United Methodist Church

♦ Residential campus in large city

♦ 1,379 degree-seeking undergraduates: 13% part-time, 63% women, 19% African American, 2% Asian American, 4% Hispanic American

♦ 90% of applicants admitted

♦ SAT or ACT (ACT writing optional), application essay required

♦ 41% graduate within 6 years

**General.** Founded in 1961. Regionally accredited. **Degrees:** 277 bachelor's awarded. **ROTC:** Army. **Location:** 8 miles from downtown. **Calendar:** 4-1-4, limited summer session. **Full-time faculty:** 85 total; 84% have terminal degrees, 8% minority, 41% women. **Part-time faculty:** 44 total; 23% minority, 57% women. **Class size:** 82% < 20, 18% 20-39. **Special facilities:** 46 foot research vessel, center for sacred music, greenhouse, center for study of religious freedom, 142-acre woodlands, rock climbing wall.

**Freshman class profile.** 1,502 applied, 1,359 admitted, 362 enrolled.

| Mid 50% test scores | | | |
|---|---|---|---|
| SAT critical reading: | 430-540 | **GPA 2.0-2.99:** | 39% |
| SAT math: | 430-540 | **Rank in top quarter:** | 35% |
| ACT composite: | 17-21 | **Rank in top tenth:** | 11% |
| **GPA 3.50 or higher:** | 27% | **Return as sophomores:** | 71% |
| **GPA 3.0-3.49:** | 33% | **Out-of-state:** | 30% |
| | | **Live on campus:** | 75% |

**Basis for selection.** Above average grades in solid college-preparatory curriculum, SAT scores, campus interview, personal statement, extracurricular activities important. **Homeschooled:** Transcript of courses and grades required.

**High school preparation.** 12 units required; 16 recommended. Required and recommended units include English 4, mathematics 3, history 1, science 2 (laboratory 2), foreign language 2 and academic electives 4.

**2007-2008 Annual costs.** Tuition/fees: $24,515. Damage deposit of $150 for residents. Room/board: $6,900. Books/supplies: $900. Personal expenses: $1,800.

**2006-2007 Financial aid. Need-based:** 409 full-time freshmen applied for aid; 306 were judged to have need; 304 of these received aid. Average need met was 68%. Average scholarship/grant was $3,322; average loan $2,958. 32% of total undergraduate aid awarded as scholarships/grants, 68% as loans/jobs. **Non-need-based:** Awarded to 1,134 full-time undergraduates, including 403 freshmen. Scholarships awarded for academics, art, leadership, music/drama, religious affiliation, state residency.

**Application procedures. Admission:** Priority date 3/1; no deadline. $40 fee, may be waived for applicants with need. Application may be submitted online. Admission notification on a rolling basis beginning on or about 9/15. Must reply by May 1 or within 2 week(s) if notified thereafter. **Financial aid:** Priority date 3/1; no closing date. FAFSA required. Applicants notified on a rolling basis starting 2/15; must reply by 5/1 or within 2 week(s) of notification.

**Academics. Special study options:** Accelerated study, cross-registration, double major, honors, independent study, internships, liberal arts/career combination, student-designed major, study abroad, teacher certification program. Externships; 4-year competitive honors program integrates liberal arts and experiential learning. **Credit/placement by examination:** AP, CLEP, IB, institutional tests. 64 credit hours maximum toward bachelor's degree. **Support services:** Learning center, reduced course load, remedial instruction, study skills assistance, tutoring, writing center.

**Majors. Area/ethnic studies:** Women's. **Biology:** General. **Business:** Business admin. **Communications:** General. **Computer sciences:** Computer science. **Conservation:** Environmental studies. **Education:** Art. **English:** English lit. **Foreign languages:** General, French, German, Spanish. **Health:** Predental, premedicine, prepharmacy, preveterinary. **History:** General. **Interdisciplinary:** Global studies, math/computer science, natural sciences. **Liberal arts:** Arts/sciences, humanities. **Math:** General. **Parks/recreation:** General. **Philosophy/religion:** Philosophy, religion. **Physical sciences:** Chemistry. **Protective services:** Criminal justice. **Psychology:** General. **Public administration:** Human services. **Social sciences:** General, international relations, political science, sociology. **Visual/performing arts:** Art, dramatic, theater history.

**Most popular majors.** Business/marketing 19%, communications/ journalism 8%, interdisciplinary studies 14%, legal studies 10%, parks/ recreation 8%, social sciences 11%.

**Computing on campus.** 99 workstations in library, computer center, student center. Dormitories wired for high-speed internet access and linked to campus network. Online course registration, online library, helpline, repair service, student web hosting, wireless network available.

**Student life. Freshman orientation:** Mandatory, $100 fee. Preregistration for classes offered. 2-day event scheduled twice in July; multi-day academic-related orientation in August. **Housing:** Guaranteed on-campus for freshmen. Coed dorms, single-sex dorms, special housing for disabled, apartments, fraternity/sorority housing, substance-free housing available. $300 nonrefundable deposit, deadline 5/1. Pets allowed in dorm rooms. Coed dorms house men and women on alternating floors. Honors and scholars hall, townhouse style dorms available. Wellness hall available: substance-free hall providing special programs focusing on social, physical, spiritual, emotional, and intellectual wellness. **Activities:** Campus ministries, choral groups, dance, drama, international student organizations, literary magazine, Model UN, musical theater, radio station, student government, student newspaper, political science association, Habitat for Humanity, Black student union, Holy Fire, Honors & Scholars, Campus Kaleidoscope, SALSA, activities council.

**Athletics.** NCAA. **Intercollegiate:** Baseball M, basketball, cheerleading M, cross-country, field hockey W, golf M, lacrosse, soccer, softball W, tennis, track and field, volleyball W. **Intramural:** Basketball, field hockey W, football (non-tackle), racquetball, soccer, table tennis, volleyball. **Team name:** Marlins.

**Student services.** Adult student services, alcohol/substance abuse counseling, campus ministries, career counseling, student employment services, financial aid counseling, health services, minority student services, personal counseling, veterans' counselor, women's services. **Physically disabled:** Services for visually, hearing impaired.

**Contact.** E-mail: admissions@vwc.edu
Phone: (757) 455-3208 Toll-free number: (800) 737-8684
Fax: (757) 461-5238
Richard Hinshaw, Vice President for Enrollment Management and Dean of Admissions, Virginia Wesleyan College, 1584 Wesleyan Drive, Norfolk, VA 23502-5599

## Washington and Lee University
**Lexington, Virginia**
www.wlu.edu

**CB member**
**CB code: 5887**

- Private 4-year university and liberal arts college
- Residential campus in small town
- 1,774 degree-seeking undergraduates: 50% women, 4% African American, 4% Asian American, 2% Hispanic American, 4% international
- 403 degree-seeking graduate students
- 27% of applicants admitted
- SAT and SAT Subject Tests or ACT with writing, application essay required
- 89% graduate within 6 years; 33% enter graduate study

**General.** Founded in 1749. Regionally accredited. Front campus and Lee Chapel designated as National Historic Landmark. **Degrees:** 425 bachelor's awarded; master's, first professional offered. **ROTC:** Army. **Location:** 50 miles from Roanoke, 60 miles from Charlottesville. **Calendar:** 4-4-2. **Full-time faculty:** 212 total; 95% have terminal degrees, 8% minority, 32% women. **Part-time faculty:** 2 total; 100% women. **Class size:** 64% < 20, 35% 20-39, 1% 40-49. **Special facilities:** Asian export pottery center, Asian art pavilion, performing arts center, university special collections, multimedia center, archaeology museum.

**Freshman class profile.** 3,719 applied, 1,018 admitted, 462 enrolled.

| Mid 50% test scores | | | |
|---|---|---|---|
| SAT critical reading: | 650-740 | Return as sophomores: | 95% |
| SAT math: | 650-730 | Out-of-state: | 85% |
| ACT composite: | 28-31 | Live on campus: | 100% |
| Rank in top quarter: | 99% | International: | 5% |
| Rank in top tenth: | 81% | Fraternities: | 81% |
| End year in good standing: | 99% | Sororities: | 77% |

**Basis for selection.** School achievement record most important, followed closely by test scores, school and community activities, recommendations and personal qualities. Special consideration given to children of alumni and applicants from minorities and low-income families. 2 unrelated SAT Subject Tests required. Interview recommended. **Homeschooled:** Recommend taking 5 SAT Subject Tests in unrelated fields, interview with admissions officer. Require documentation of reading lists and syllabi.

**High school preparation.** 16 units required. Required and recommended units include English 4, mathematics 3-4, social studies 1, history 1-2, science 1-3 (laboratory 1), foreign language 3 and academic electives 4.

**2007-2008 Annual costs.** Tuition/fees: $35,445. Room/board: $8,725. Books/supplies: $1,400. Personal expenses: $1,730.

**2006-2007 Financial aid.** **Need-based:** 251 full-time freshmen applied for aid; 171 were judged to have need; 171 of these received aid. Average need met was 99%. Average scholarship/grant was $27,360; average loan $3,088. 87% of total undergraduate aid awarded as scholarships/grants, 13% as loans/jobs. **Non-need-based:** Awarded to 710 full-time undergraduates, including 148 freshmen. Scholarships awarded for academics.

**Application procedures. Admission:** Closing date 1/15 (postmark date). $50 fee, may be waived for applicants with need. Application may be submitted online. Admission notification 4/1. Admission notification on a rolling basis. Must reply by 5/1. **Financial aid:** Closing date 2/1. FAFSA, CSS PROFILE required. Applicants notified by 4/1; must reply by 5/1.

**Academics. Special study options:** Combined bachelor's/graduate degree, double major, exchange student, honors, independent study, internships, liberal arts/career combination, student-designed major, study abroad, teacher certification program, Washington semester. Member Seven College Consortium, professional ethics seminars in business, law, medicine, journalism. **Credit/placement by examination:** AP, CLEP, IB, institutional tests. **Support services:** Study skills assistance, tutoring, writing center.

**Majors. Area/ethnic studies:** East Asian, Russian/Slavic. **Biology:** General, biochemistry. **Business:** Accounting, business admin. **Communications:** Journalism. **Computer sciences:** General. **Engineering:** Chemical, physics. **English:** English lit. **Foreign languages:** General, classics, French, German, Spanish. **History:** General. **Interdisciplinary:** Medieval/Renaissance, neuroscience. **Math:** General. **Philosophy/religion:** Philosophy, religion. **Physical sciences:** Chemistry, geology, physics. **Psychology:** General. **Public administration:** Policy analysis. **Social sciences:** Anthropology, archaeology, economics, political science, sociology. **Visual/performing arts:** Art history/conservation, dramatic, studio arts.

**Most popular majors.** Area/ethnic studies 8%, biology 6%, business/marketing 7%, English 7%, history 9%, social sciences 24%, visual/performing arts 14%.

**Computing on campus.** 410 workstations in dormitories, library, computer center, student center. Dormitories wired for high-speed internet access and linked to campus network. Commuter students can connect to campus network. Online course registration, online library, helpline, repair service, wireless network available.

**Student life. Freshman orientation:** Mandatory. Preregistration for classes offered. 4 days prior to beginning of fall term. **Policies:** Student-run honor system, observed with single sanction. **Housing:** Guaranteed on-campus for freshmen. Coed dorms, apartments, fraternity/sorority housing available. $150 nonrefundable deposit, deadline 5/1. Outing Club House, Spanish House, Chavis House available. **Activities:** Bands, choral groups, dance, drama, film society, international student organizations, literary magazine, music ensembles, radio station, student government, student newspaper, symphony orchestra, TV station, Alpha Phi Omega, Christian fellowship, service league, Hillel, Habitat for Humanity, minority student association, outing club.

**Athletics.** NCAA. **Intercollegiate:** Baseball M, basketball, cross-country, equestrian W, field hockey W, football (tackle) M, golf M, lacrosse, soccer, swimming, tennis, track and field, volleyball W, wrestling M. **Intramural:** Badminton, basketball, football (non-tackle), soccer, softball, swimming, table tennis, tennis, volleyball, water polo, wrestling M. **Team name:** Generals.

**Student services.** Alcohol/substance abuse counseling, campus ministries, career counseling, student employment services, health services, personal counseling, placement for graduates. **Physically disabled:** Services for visually, hearing impaired.

**Contact.** E-mail: admissions@wlu.edu
Phone: (540) 458-8710 Fax: (540) 458-8062
William Hartog, Dean of Admissions and Financial Aid, Washington and Lee University, 204 West Washington Street, Lexington, VA 24450-2116

## World College
**Virginia Beach, Virginia**
www.cie-wc.edu

**CB code: 3970**

- For-profit 4-year technical college
- Large city
- 445 degree-seeking undergraduates

**General.** Accredited by DETC. Affiliated with Cleveland Institute of Electronics. **Degrees:** 10 bachelor's awarded. **Calendar:** Continuous. **Full-time faculty:** 3 total. **Part-time faculty:** 3 total.

**Basis for selection.** Open admission, but selective for some programs.

**2008-2009 Annual costs.** Tuition/fees (projected): $3,540.

**Application procedures. Admission:** No deadline. No application fee. Admission notification on a rolling basis.

**Academics. Credit/placement by examination:** CLEP.

**Majors. Computer sciences:** Security. **Engineering technology:** Electrical.

**Computing on campus.** PC or laptop required.

**Contact.**  E-mail: instruct@cie-wc.edu
Phone: (800) 696-7532 Toll-free number: (800) 696-7532
World College, Lake Shore Plaza, 5193 Shore Drive, Suite 105, Virginia Beach, VA 23455-2500

# Washington

## Antioch University Seattle
**Seattle, Washington**
www.antiochsea.edu                    CB code: 3070

◗ Private two-year upper-division university and liberal arts college
◗ Commuter campus in very large city
◗ Application essay, interview required

**General.** Founded in 1976. Regionally accredited. Individualized degree programs offered on both graduate and undergraduate levels. **Degrees:** 86 bachelor's awarded; master's offered. **Calendar:** Quarter, extensive summer session. **Full-time faculty:** 10 total. **Part-time faculty:** 10 total.

**Student profile.** 250 degree-seeking undergraduates.

**Basis for selection.** High school transcript, college transcript, application essay, interview required. Transfer accepted as juniors, seniors.

**2007-2008 Annual costs.** Tuition/fees: $20,310. For BA with Teacher Prep program, $18,900 per year, $420 per credit hour. Books/supplies: $918. Personal expenses: $555.

**Application procedures. Admission:** Rolling admission. $50 fee. **Financial aid:** FAFSA, institutional form required.

**Academics.** Bachelor's program is a completion program only. Students generally transfer in with at least 90 credits. **Special study options:** Cross-registration, independent study, student-designed major, teacher certification program. **Credit/placement by examination:** CLEP. **Support services:** Tutoring.

**Majors. Liberal arts:** Arts/sciences.

**Computing on campus.** 16 workstations in library, computer center. Commuter students can connect to campus network.

**Student life. Activities:** Student government, student newspaper.

**Student services.** Career counseling, financial aid counseling, personal counseling, veterans' counselor. **Physically disabled:** Services for visually impaired.

**Contact.** E-mail: admissions@antiochsea.edu
Phone: (206) 441-5352 ext. 5201 Toll-free number: (888) 268-4477
Fax: (206) 441-3307
Doug Arnold, Director of Admissions, Antioch University Seattle, 2326 Sixth Avenue, Seattle, WA 98121-1814

## Art Institute of Seattle
**Seattle, Washington**
www.ais.edu                    CB code: 4805

◗ For-profit 4-year visual arts and technical college
◗ Commuter campus in very large city
◗ 2,261 degree-seeking undergraduates: 32% part-time, 52% women, 4% African American, 14% Asian American, 6% Hispanic American, 2% Native American, 6% international
◗ 81% of applicants admitted
◗ Application essay, interview required

**General.** Founded in 1982. Regionally accredited. **Degrees:** 89 bachelor's, 387 associate awarded. **Location:** Downtown. **Calendar:** Quarter, extensive summer session. **Full-time faculty:** 54 total; 24% have terminal degrees, 4% minority, 33% women. **Part-time faculty:** 93 total; 9% have terminal degrees, 18% minority, 39% women. **Class size:** 8% < 20, 89% 20-39, 3% 40-49, less than 1% 50-99. **Special facilities:** Gallery with rotating art/design shows.

**Freshman class profile.** 779 applied, 632 admitted, 527 enrolled.

| | | | |
|---|---|---|---|
| Out-of-state: | 40% | International: | 8% |
| Live on campus: | 20% | | |

**Basis for selection.** Secondary school record, essay, interview most important; recommendations, academic records, test scores required. SAT or ACT recommended. Some programs require a portfolio. **Learning Disabled:** Admissions notifies counselors of students who disclose learning disabilities and special needs. Counselor determines eligibility.

**2008-2009 Annual costs.** Tuition/fees (projected): $20,565. Room/board: $10,684. Books/supplies: $975. Personal expenses: $2,265.

**2007-2008 Financial aid. Need-based:** 26% of total undergraduate aid awarded as scholarships/grants, 74% as loans/jobs. **Non-need-based:** Scholarships awarded for academics, art.

**Application procedures. Admission:** No deadline. $50 fee. Application may be submitted online. Admission notification on a rolling basis. **Financial aid:** Priority date 4/15; no closing date. FAFSA required. Applicants notified on a rolling basis; must reply within 4 week(s) of notification.

**Academics. Special study options:** Distance learning, ESL, independent study, internships, study abroad. **Credit/placement by examination:** AP, CLEP, IB, institutional tests. 6 credit hours maximum toward associate degree, 6 toward bachelor's. Course waived by proficiency exam; credit does not count toward degree. **Support services:** Learning center, reduced course load, remedial instruction, study skills assistance, tutoring.

**Majors. Computer sciences:** Game design, web page design. **Visual/performing arts:** General, cinematography, fashion design, graphic design, interior design. **Other:** Fashion marketing.

**Computing on campus.** 494 workstations in library, computer center, student center. Dormitories wired for high-speed internet access. Online course registration, online library, helpline, student web hosting, wireless network available.

**Student life. Freshman orientation:** Available. Preregistration for classes offered. 1 to 4-day program held 3 weeks before start of the quarter. **Housing:** Guaranteed on-campus for all undergraduates. Coed dorms available. $200 deposit. AIS housing located 1 mile from campus. Students share 1 bedroom and studio apartments in secured apartment complexes. **Activities:** Student government, student newspaper.

**Athletics. Intramural:** Soccer, softball.

**Student services.** Adult student services, career counseling, student employment services, financial aid counseling, personal counseling, placement for graduates, veterans' counselor. **Physically disabled:** Services for visually, speech, hearing impaired.

**Contact.** E-mail: aisadm@aii.edu
Phone: (206) 448-6600 Toll-free number: (800) 275-2471
Fax: (206) 269-0275
Brian Cicero, Director of Admissions, Art Institute of Seattle, 2323 Elliott Avenue, Seattle, WA 98121-1622

## Bastyr University
**Kenmore, Washington**
www.bastyr.edu                    CB code: 0181

◗ Private two-year upper-division university and health science college
◗ Commuter campus in small city
◗ Application essay required

**General.** Founded in 1978. Regionally accredited. **Degrees:** 93 bachelor's awarded; master's, doctoral, first professional offered. **Location:** 16 miles from Seattle. **Calendar:** Quarter, limited summer session. **Full-time faculty:** 54 total; 74% have terminal degrees, 18% minority, 56% women. **Part-time faculty:** 97 total; 82% have terminal degrees, 13% minority, 62% women. **Special facilities:** Gourmet vegetarian cafeteria, research center, medicinal herb and culinary garden.

**Student profile.** 213 degree-seeking undergraduates, 867 degree-seeking graduate students. 94 applied as first time-transfer students. 100% entered as juniors. 80% transferred from two-year, 20% transferred from four-year institutions.

| | | | |
|---|---|---|---|
| Women: | 83% | Live on campus: | 5% |
| Part-time: | 8% | 25 or older: | 85% |
| Out-of-state: | 50% | | |

**Basis for selection.** College transcript, application essay required. Transfer accepted as juniors, seniors.

**2007-2008 Annual costs.** Tuition/fees: $17,040. Room/board: $3,650. Books/supplies: $1,125.

**Financial aid. Need-based:** Average need met was 50%. 77% of total undergraduate aid awarded as scholarships/grants, 23% as loans/jobs. **Non-need-based:** Scholarships awarded for academics.

**Application procedures. Admission:** Priority date 3/15. $60 fee. Application may be submitted online. **Financial aid:** Priority date 5/1, no deadline. Applicants notified on a rolling basis; must reply within 3 weeks of notification. FAFSA, institutional form required.

**Academics. Special study options:** Double major, internships. Selected tracks within major. **Credit/placement by examination:** AP, CLEP.

**Majors. Health:** Acupuncture, Chinese medicine/herbology, herbalism. **Interdisciplinary:** Nutrition sciences. **Parks/recreation:** Exercise sciences. **Psychology:** General.

**Computing on campus.** 44 workstations in library, computer center. Dormitories wired for high-speed internet access and linked to campus network. Online library, helpline, wireless network available.

**Student life. Housing:** Coed dorms, substance-free housing available. **Activities:** Student government, student newspaper, Student Physicians for Social Responsibility, Herbal Ways, Nature Cure club, Africana student association, Christian Fellowship, pediatrics club, Student Association of Nutrition & Dietetics, Toastmasters.

**Athletics. Intramural:** Basketball, soccer.

**Student services.** Career counseling, financial aid counseling, health services, on-campus daycare, personal counseling, placement for graduates. **Physically disabled:** Services for visually impaired.

**Contact.** E-mail: admissions@bastyr.edu
Phone: (425) 602-3330 Fax: (425) 602-3090
Ted Olsen, Director of Admissions, Bastyr University, 14500 Juanita Drive, NE, Kenmore, WA 98028

---

## Central Washington University
**Ellensburg, Washington**      **CB member**
**www.cwu.edu**      **CB code: 4044**

- Public 4-year university
- Residential campus in large town
- 9,463 degree-seeking undergraduates: 10% part-time, 52% women, 3% African American, 7% Asian American, 8% Hispanic American, 2% Native American, 2% international
- 429 degree-seeking graduate students
- 80% of applicants admitted
- SAT or ACT (ACT writing optional) required
- 50% graduate within 6 years

**General.** Founded in 1890. Regionally accredited. **Degrees:** 2,113 bachelor's awarded; master's offered. **ROTC:** Army, Air Force. **Location:** 105 miles from Seattle. **Calendar:** Quarter, limited summer session. **Full-time faculty:** 396 total; 16% minority, 38% women. **Part-time faculty:** 182 total; 6% minority, 54% women. **Class size:** 35% < 20, 51% 20-39, 9% 40-49, 5% 50-99, less than 1% >100. **Special facilities:** Chimpanzee and Human Communication Institute, geodesy lab, data analysis center, education technology center, Northwest Native American and Circum-Pacific artifacts museum.

**Freshman class profile.** 4,602 applied, 3,688 admitted, 1,473 enrolled.

| Mid 50% test scores | | | |
|---|---|---|---|
| SAT critical reading: | 430-550 | GPA 2.0-2.99: | 33% |
| SAT math: | 440-550 | Rank in top quarter: | 27% |
| ACT composite: | 18-23 | Rank in top tenth: | 8% |
| GPA 3.50 or higher: | 23% | Out-of-state: | 3% |
| GPA 3.0-3.49: | 44% | Live on campus: | 97% |

**Basis for selection.** Admission generally based on weighted combination of test scores and GPA. Interview, essay, and recommendations required for students whose grades or test scores do not reflect their potential for success. Additional academic support provided within alternate admission program. ACT COMPASS may be substituted for SAT or ACT. **Home-schooled:** Must submit transcripts for any periods enrolled in secondary school, submit ACT or SAT scores, write substantial essay about applicant's

preparation for college and how schooling meets or parallels core requirements.

**High school preparation.** 15 units required; 17 recommended. Required and recommended units include English 4, mathematics 3, social studies 3, science 2-3 (laboratory 1) and foreign language 2. One year of a performing or fine art or additional year of study in any main subject area is also required. Coursework in U.S. history and U.S. government recommended and will count toward social studies requirements.

**2007-2008 Annual costs.** Tuition/fees: $5,493; $14,894 out-of-state. Room/board: $7,418. Books/supplies: $924. Personal expenses: $1,683.

**Financial aid. Non-need-based:** Scholarships awarded for academics, alumni affiliation, art, athletics, job skills, leadership, minority status, music/drama, religious affiliation, ROTC, state residency.

**Application procedures. Admission:** Closing date 4/1 (receipt date). $50 fee, may be waived for applicants with need. Application may be submitted online. Admission notification on a rolling basis beginning on or about 12/1. **Financial aid:** Priority date 3/1; no closing date. FAFSA required. Applicants notified on a rolling basis starting 4/15; must reply within 4 week(s) of notification.

**Academics.** Extended degree programs at locations in Yakima, Wenatchee, and greater Seattle area. **Special study options:** Cooperative education, distance learning, double major, dual enrollment of high school students, ESL, exchange student, honors, independent study, internships, liberal arts/career combination, student-designed major, study abroad, teacher certification program. **Credit/placement by examination:** AP, CLEP, IB, SAT, ACT, institutional tests. 45 credit hours maximum toward bachelor's degree. **Support services:** Learning center, reduced course load, remedial instruction, study skills assistance, tutoring, writing center.

**Honors college/program.** General education program emphasizes history, philosophy, literature. Applicants should score in upper 10 percent on SAT and ACT Verbal Composite and Quantitative Composite. 3.0 GPA required. 25 freshmen generally admitted.

**Majors. Area/ethnic studies:** Asian. **Biology:** General. **Business:** Accounting, business admin, construction management, fashion, office management. **Communications:** General, journalism, public relations. **Computer sciences:** General. **Education:** Art, biology, business, chemistry, drama/dance, early childhood, elementary, English, family/consumer sciences, foreign languages, French, German, health, history, mathematics, music, physical, science, social science, Spanish, special, technology/industrial arts, trade/industrial. **Engineering technology:** Construction, electrical, industrial, mechanical. **English:** English lit. **Family/consumer sciences:** General, food/nutrition. **Foreign languages:** Chinese, French, German, Japanese, Russian, Spanish. **Health:** Occupational health. **History:** General. **Interdisciplinary:** Gerontology. **Math:** General. **Parks/recreation:** General, sports admin. **Philosophy/religion:** Philosophy, religion. **Physical sciences:** Chemistry, geology, physics, planetary. **Protective services:** Criminal justice. **Psychology:** General. **Public administration:** Human services, policy analysis. **Social sciences:** General, anthropology, economics, geography, political science, sociology. **Transportation:** Aviation. **Visual/performing arts:** Art, commercial/advertising art, dramatic, music management, music performance, music theory/composition, piano/organ, stringed instruments, studio arts, voice/opera.

**Most popular majors.** Business/marketing 28%, education 20%, security/protective services 9%, social sciences 9%.

**Computing on campus.** 700 workstations in dormitories, library, computer center, student center. Dormitories wired for high-speed internet access and linked to campus network. Commuter students can connect to campus network. Online course registration, online library, helpline, student web hosting, wireless network available.

**Student life. Freshman orientation:** Mandatory. Preregistration for classes offered. 2-day introduction to campus held for students and parents. **Housing:** Guaranteed on-campus for freshmen. Coed dorms, single-sex dorms, special housing for disabled, apartments, substance-free housing available. $200 partly refundable deposit, deadline 6/1. Academic interests, upperclassmen, over 21 housing available. **Activities:** Bands, campus ministries, choral groups, dance, drama, film society, international student organizations, literary magazine, music ensembles, musical theater, opera, radio station, student government, student newspaper, symphony orchestra, TV station, religious, political, ethnic, minority student organizations, professional societies, major field clubs available.

**Athletics.** NAIA, NCAA. **Intercollegiate:** Baseball M, basketball, cheerleading, cross-country, football (tackle) M, soccer W, softball W, track and field, volleyball W. **Intramural:** Badminton, basketball, football (non-tackle), soccer, softball, tennis, volleyball. **Team name:** Wildcats.

**Student services.** Adult student services, alcohol/substance abuse counseling, campus ministries, career counseling, services for economically disadvantaged, student employment services, financial aid counseling, health services, minority student services, on-campus daycare, personal counseling, placement for graduates, veterans' counselor, women's services. **Physically disabled:** Services for visually, speech, hearing impaired.

**Contact.** E-mail: cwuadmis@cwu.edu
Phone: (509) 963-1211 Toll-free number: (866) 298-4968
Fax: (509) 963-3022
Lisa Garcia-Hanson, Director of Admissions, Central Washington University, 400 East University Way, Ellensburg, WA 98926-7463

## City University of Seattle
### Bellevue, Washington
www.cityu.edu                              CB code: 4042

◗ Private two-year upper-division university
◗ Commuter campus in very large city

**General.** Founded in 1973. Regionally accredited. University maintains satellite sites in Renton, Everett, North Seattle, Tacoma, and Vancouver, Washington; Victoria, Vancouver, Edmonton, and Calgary, Canada; Trencin and Bratislava, Slovakia; Prague, Czech Republic; Sophia and Pratvetz, Bulgaria; Athens, Greece; and Beijing, China. **Degrees:** 728 bachelor's, 17 associate awarded; master's offered. **Location:** 12 miles from Seattle. **Calendar:** Quarter, extensive summer session. **Full-time faculty:** 25 total. **Part-time faculty:** 1,231 total. **Class size:** 96% < 20, 4% 20-39.

**Student profile.** 1,443 degree-seeking undergraduates, 1,551 graduate students.

| Women: | 61% | Out-of-state: | 15% |
|---|---|---|---|
| Part-time: | 44% | 25 or older: | 81% |

**Basis for selection.** Open admission. High school transcript, college transcript required. Based on course content equivalency and grade point average. Transfer accepted as sophomores, juniors, seniors.

**2007-2008 Annual costs.** Tuition/fees: $13,275. Books/supplies: $860.

**Financial aid. Non-need-based:** Scholarships awarded for academics. **Additional information:** All degree programs approved for veteran's administration educational benefits.

**Application procedures. Admission:** Rolling admission. $50 fee. Application may be submitted online. **Financial aid:** FAFSA, institutional form required.

**Academics. Special study options:** Accelerated study, distance learning, double major, dual enrollment of high school students, ESL, external degree, internships, student-designed major, study abroad, teacher certification program, weekend college. **Credit/placement by examination:** CLEP, IB. 45 credit hours maximum toward associate degree, 90 toward bachelor's.

**Majors. Business:** Accounting, business admin, international, management information systems, marketing. **Communications:** General. **Computer sciences:** Programming. **Education:** Elementary, middle, special. **Liberal arts:** Arts/sciences. **Psychology:** General.

**Most popular majors.** Business/marketing 45%, computer/information sciences 21%, education 22%, liberal arts 7%.

**Computing on campus.** PC or laptop required. 150 workstations in library, computer center. Commuter students can connect to campus network. Online library, helpline, wireless network available.

**Student services.** Adult student services, career counseling, financial aid counseling, personal counseling, veterans' counselor. **Physically disabled:** Services for visually, hearing impaired.

**Contact.** E-mail: info@cityu.edu
Phone: (425) 637-1010 Toll-free number: (888) 422-4898
Fax: (425) 709-5361
Melissa Mecham, Vice President Admissions/Student Affairs, City University of Seattle, 11900 NE First Street, Bellevue, WA 98005

## Cornish College of the Arts
### Seattle, Washington
www.cornish.edu                              CB code: 0058

◗ Private 4-year visual arts and performing arts college
◗ Commuter campus in very large city

◗ 800 degree-seeking undergraduates
◗ Application essay required

**General.** Founded in 1914. Regionally accredited. **Degrees:** 162 bachelor's awarded. **Calendar:** Semester, limited summer session. **Full-time faculty:** 55 total. **Part-time faculty:** 95 total. **Class size:** 87% < 20, 13% 20-39. **Special facilities:** Electronic music laboratory, experimental books laboratory, music listening center, costumemaking facilities, video editing facilities.

**Freshman class profile.** 290 enrolled.

**Basis for selection.** Portfolio (for visual artists) or audition (for performing artists), academic achievement history, creative ability, and artistic goals considered. SAT or ACT recommended. Interview recommended for all; audition required for dance, music, theater; portfolio required for art, design, performance production. Alternative audition and portfolio arrangements for long-distance applicants. **Homeschooled:** Transcript of courses and grades, state high school equivalency certificate required.

**High school preparation.** Required and recommended units include English 4, mathematics 2-4, social studies 3, science 2-4 (laboratory 1) and foreign language 2.

**2007-2008 Annual costs.** Tuition/fees: $24,100. Design majors required to have laptop computer and Adobe software, estimated cost $3,000. Books/supplies: $1,800. Personal expenses: $2,000.

**2007-2008 Financial aid. Need-based:** Average need met was 59%. Average scholarship/grant was $7,664; average loan $3,653. 45% of total undergraduate aid awarded as scholarships/grants, 55% as loans/jobs. **Non-need-based:** Scholarships awarded for academics.

**Application procedures. Admission:** Priority date 2/1; deadline 8/15 (receipt date). $35 fee, may be waived for applicants with need. Application may be submitted online. Admission notification on a rolling basis beginning on or about 1/1. Must reply by May 1 or within 2 week(s) if notified thereafter. **Financial aid:** Priority date 2/15; no closing date. FAFSA, institutional form required. Applicants notified on a rolling basis starting 4/15; must reply by 5/1 or within 2 week(s) of notification.

**Academics. Special study options:** Cooperative education, independent study, internships, study abroad. **Credit/placement by examination:** AP, CLEP, institutional tests. 30 credit hours maximum toward bachelor's degree. A total of 30 credits through a combination of prior work experience and credit by exam allowed. **Support services:** Remedial instruction, study skills assistance, tutoring, writing center.

**Majors. Visual/performing arts:** General, acting, art, cinematography, commercial/advertising art, dance, design, directing/producing, dramatic, drawing, graphic design, illustration, interior design, jazz, music performance, music theory/composition, painting, photography, piano/organ, play/screenwriting, printmaking, sculpture, stringed instruments, studio arts, theater design, voice/opera.

**Computing on campus.** 91 workstations in library, computer center, student center. Online library, helpline, wireless network available.

**Student life. Freshman orientation:** Mandatory. Preregistration for classes offered. Begins one week before class starts each fall. Students will meet the Chair of their department and register for classes. **Activities:** Bands, choral groups, dance, drama, film society, literary magazine, music ensembles, musical theater, opera, student government, student newspaper, art history club, Birds and Whistles, Black student alliance, bowling club, digital illustration club, Inform the Misinformed Campaign/Corporate Watchdogs, movie club, Salt and Light (Bible study), sports/intramural club.

**Student services.** Adult student services, alcohol/substance abuse counseling, career counseling, student employment services, financial aid counseling, personal counseling, placement for graduates. **Physically disabled:** Services for visually impaired.

**Contact.** E-mail: admissions@cornish.edu
Phone: (206) 726-5016 Toll-free number: (800) 726-2787
Fax: (206) 720-1011
Sharon Sterling, Director of Admissions, Cornish College of the Arts, 1000 Lenora Street, Seattle, WA 98121

## Crown College
### Tacoma, Washington
www.crowncollege.edu                              CB code: 3129

◗ For-profit 4-year business college
◗ Commuter campus in large city

**General.** Accredited by ACCSCT. **Location:** 30 miles from Seattle. **Calendar:** Continuous.

**Annual costs/financial aid.** Tuition/fees (2007-2008): $8,085. Need-based financial aid available for full-time students.

**Contact.** Phone: (253) 531-3123
Director of Admissions, 8739 South Hosmer Street, Tacoma, WA 98444-1836

## DeVry University: Federal Way
**Federal Way, Washington**
www.devry.edu                          CB code: 3696

♦ For-profit 4-year university
♦ Commuter campus in large city
♦ 661 degree-seeking undergraduates: 32% part-time, 27% women, 9% African American, 11% Asian American, 7% Hispanic American, 1% Native American
♦ 106 degree-seeking graduate students
♦ Interview required

**General. Degrees:** 151 bachelor's, 11 associate awarded; master's offered. **ROTC:** Army. **Calendar:** Semester, extensive summer session. **Full-time faculty:** 23 total; 30% minority, 22% women. **Part-time faculty:** 30 total; 20% minority, 23% women.

**Freshman class profile.** 119 enrolled.

| | | | |
|---|---|---|---|
| **Return as sophomores:** | 50% | **Out-of-state:** | 13% |

**Basis for selection.** Applicants must have high school diploma or equivalent, or a degree from an accredited postsecondary institution. Must demonstrate proficiency in basic college level skills through test scores and/or institutionally-administered placement exams, and be at least 17 years of age on the first day of classes. New students may enter at the beginning of any semester. CPT also accepted.

**High school preparation.** Required units include mathematics 1. Math unit must be algebra or higher.

**2007-2008 Annual costs.** Tuition/fees: $14,640. Books/supplies: $1,300. Personal expenses: $5,082.

**Financial aid.** All financial aid based on need.

**Application procedures. Admission:** No deadline. $50 fee. Application may be submitted online. Admission notification on a rolling basis. **Financial aid:** No deadline. FAFSA required. Applicants notified on a rolling basis.

**Academics. Special study options:** Accelerated study, distance learning. **Credit/placement by examination:** CLEP. **Support services:** Learning center, remedial instruction, tutoring.

**Majors. Business:** General, business admin. **Computer sciences:** Game design, information technology, security, systems analysis. **Engineering technology:** Computer, electrical.

**Most popular majors.** Business/marketing 60%, computer/information sciences 27%, engineering/engineering technologies 14%.

**Computing on campus.** 335 workstations in library, computer center. Online course registration, online library, helpline available.

**Student life. Freshman orientation:** Mandatory. **Housing:** Private apartments, student-plan housing, private rooms. **Activities:** Student government, student newspaper, alternative sports, business & technology club, gaming, robotics, Institution of Electrical and Electronic Engineers, network gaming.

**Student services.** Career counseling, student employment services, financial aid counseling, placement for graduates, veterans' counselor. **Physically disabled:** Services for visually, hearing impaired.

**Contact.** E-mail: admissions@sea.devry.edu
Phone: (253) 943-2810 Toll-free number: (877) 923-3879
Fax: (253) 943-3291
Fred Pressel, Director of Admissions, DeVry University: Federal Way, 3600 South 344th Way, Federal Way, WA 98001-9558

## DigiPen Institute of Technology
**Redmond, Washington**
www.digipen.edu                        CB code: 4138

♦ For-profit 4-year visual arts and engineering college
♦ Residential campus in large town
♦ 812 degree-seeking undergraduates
♦ 58 graduate students
♦ SAT or ACT (ACT writing optional), application essay required

**General.** Accredited by ACCSCT. Comprised of two campuses, the main campus and the art campus. **Degrees:** 76 bachelor's, 11 associate awarded; master's offered. **Location:** 20 miles from downtown Seattle. **Calendar:** Semester, limited summer session. **Full-time faculty:** 40 total; 28% women. **Part-time faculty:** 21 total; 14% women. **Class size:** 41% < 20, 32% 20-39, 12% 40-49, 14% 50-99.

**Freshman class profile.**

| Mid 50% test scores | | | |
|---|---|---|---|
| **SAT critical reading:** | 530-640 | **SAT writing:** | 480-580 |
| **SAT math:** | 560-680 | **ACT composite:** | 23-28 |
| | | **Out-of-state:** | 56% |

**Basis for selection.** Applicants must submit official transcripts, test scores, recommendation letters, a personal statement, and an art portfolio when applying to the animation program. Non-native English speakers must provide a minimum TOEFL iBT score of 80. Animation applicants who have already graduated from high school and have at least one year of college experience not required to submit SAT/ACT scores. Portfolios of 10-20 pieces of work required for art program applicants. **Homeschooled:** Applicants who have completed an accredited high school curriculum may submit official transcripts as proof of their high school equivalence. Applicants who did not complete an accredited program must take an official high school equivalence test, such as the GED, and submit those scores. **Learning Disabled:** Students desiring special needs should contact the Disability Support Services Coordinator to arrange accommodations.

**High school preparation.** Recommended units include English 4, mathematics 4, science 4, computer science 1 and visual/performing arts 1. Applicants for the BFA program are recommended to take as many art classes as possible and BS applicants are encouraged to take classes in computer science and physics.

**2008-2009 Annual costs.** Full-time tuition for academic year (based on 20 hours per term), $19,040; required fees, $160; per-credit-hour charge, $476. Full-time tuition for non-resident aliens for academic year (based on 20 hours per term), $24,840; per-credit-hour charge, $621. Books/supplies: $924.

**Financial aid. Non-need-based:** Scholarships awarded for job skills, leadership, minority status. **Additional information:** Many aid programs are on a first-come, first-serve basis.

**Application procedures. Admission:** Priority date 2/1; no deadline. $75 fee, may be waived for applicants with need. Application may be submitted online. Admission notification on a rolling basis. Applicants must respond by the date listed on their individual acceptance letters. **Financial aid:** Priority date 4/15; no closing date. FAFSA, institutional form required. Applicants notified on a rolling basis starting 1/1; must reply within 4 week(s) of notification.

**Academics. Special study options:** Accelerated study, independent study, internships. **Credit/placement by examination:** AP, CLEP, IB, institutional tests. **Support services:** Reduced course load, study skills assistance, tutoring.

**Majors. Visual/performing arts:** Multimedia. **Other:** Production animation.

**Computing on campus.** Online course registration, helpline, wireless network available.

**Student life. Freshman orientation:** Mandatory. Preregistration for classes offered. 3-4 day orientation is held the week before classes begin. **Housing:** All housing is off campus. Most students live in co-ed situations with 2-4 students in an apartment. Plenty of housing options near campus. Most students relocate to Redmond, WA. **Activities:** International student organizations, student government.

**Student services.** Career counseling, student employment services, financial aid counseling, personal counseling, veterans' counselor. **Physically disabled:** Services for hearing impaired.

**Contact.** E-mail: admissions@digipen.edu
Phone: (425) 558-0299 Toll-free number: (866) 478-5236
Fax: (425) 558-0378
Angela Kugler, Director of Admissions, DigiPen Institute of Technology, 5001-150th Avenue Northeast, Redmond, WA 98052

## Eastern Washington University
**Cheney, Washington**        **CB member**
**www.ewu.edu**        **CB code: 4301**

- Public 4-year university
- Commuter campus in large town

**General.** Founded in 1882. Regionally accredited. **Location:** 17 miles from Spokane, 200 miles from Seattle. **Calendar:** Quarter.

**Annual costs/financial aid.** Tuition/fees (2007-2008): $4,847; $13,718 out-of-state. Room/board: $6,433. Books/supplies: $690. Personal expenses: $1,908. Need-based financial aid available to full-time and part-time students.

**Contact.** Phone: (509) 359-2397
Director of Admissions, 101 Sutton Hall, Cheney, WA 99004-2447

## Evergreen State College
**Olympia, Washington**        **CB member**
**www.evergreen.edu**        **CB code: 4292**

- Public 4-year college
- Commuter campus in small city
- 4,135 degree-seeking undergraduates: 8% part-time, 55% women, 4% African American, 5% Asian American, 5% Hispanic American, 4% Native American
- 279 degree-seeking graduate students
- 97% of applicants admitted
- SAT or ACT (ACT writing optional) required
- 58% graduate within 6 years; 22% enter graduate study

**General.** Founded in 1967. Regionally accredited. **Degrees:** 1,114 bachelor's awarded; master's offered. **Location:** 6 miles from downtown, 60 miles from Seattle. **Calendar:** Quarter, limited summer session. **Full-time faculty:** 158 total; 89% have terminal degrees, 27% minority, 49% women. **Part-time faculty:** 84 total; 44% have terminal degrees, 19% minority, 51% women. **Class size:** 43% < 20, 40% 20-39, 8% 40-49, 9% 50-99, less than 1% >100. **Special facilities:** Organic farm and community gardens, Longhouse Education and Cultural Center, animation and design studio, ceramics studio, metal shop, wood shop, photography studios and darkrooms, 3,000 feet of waterfront property on Puget Sound.

**Freshman class profile.** 1,806 applied, 1,750 admitted, 686 enrolled.

| Mid 50% test scores | | | |
|---|---|---|---|
| SAT critical reading: | 520-640 | GPA 2.0-2.99: | 43% |
| SAT math: | 460-590 | Rank in top quarter: | 29% |
| ACT composite: | 21-26 | Rank in top tenth: | 10% |
| GPA 3.50 or higher: | 20% | Return as sophomores: | 68% |
| GPA 3.0-3.49: | 36% | Out-of-state: | 43% |
| | | Live on campus: | 79% |

**Basis for selection.** School achievement record, test scores, strength of curriculum taken in high school, personal statement, and understanding of interdisciplinary study. Official TOEFL test scores are required for most students whose native language is not English. Essay recommended. Interviews optional (by appointment for non-residents.). **Homeschooled:** Transcript of courses and grades required.

**High school preparation.** 15 units required. Required units include English 4, mathematics 3, social studies 3, science 2 (laboratory 1), foreign language 2 and academic electives 1. One fine, visual, or performing arts elective or other college prep elective from the areas above required.

**2007-2008 Annual costs.** Tuition/fees: $5,145; $15,489 out-of-state. Room/board: $6,541. Books/supplies: $900. Personal expenses: $1,890.

**2006-2007 Financial aid. Need-based:** 384 full-time freshmen applied for aid; 255 were judged to have need; 241 of these received aid. Average need met was 55%. Average scholarship/grant was $5,716; average loan $2,845. 56% of total undergraduate aid awarded as scholarships/grants, 44% as loans/jobs. **Non-need-based:** Awarded to 420 full-time undergraduates, including 160 freshmen. Scholarships awarded for academics, art, athletics. **Additional information:** Application deadline for merit and cultural diversity scholarships February 1. Minority students may apply for tuition and fee waiver scholarships; amount of award equal to in-state tuition and fees.

Discount waiver for employees. To meet priority deadline for required financial aid forms, official results of FAFSA must be received by March 15.

**Application procedures. Admission:** Priority date 3/1; no deadline. $50 fee, may be waived for applicants with need. Application may be submitted online. Admission notification on a rolling basis beginning on or about 12/1. Must reply by May 1 or within 4 week(s) if notified thereafter. **Financial aid:** Priority date 3/15; no closing date. FAFSA, institutional form required. Applicants notified on a rolling basis starting 4/15; must reply within 4 week(s) of notification.

**Academics. Special study options:** Accelerated study, double major, exchange student, independent study, internships, student-designed major, study abroad, teacher certification program, weekend college. **Credit/placement by examination:** AP, CLEP, IB. 135 credit hours maximum toward bachelor's degree. **Support services:** Learning center, reduced course load, study skills assistance, tutoring, writing center.

**Majors. Agriculture:** General. **Area/ethnic studies:** Native American. **Biology:** General. **Business:** Business admin. **Communications:** General, journalism. **Computer sciences:** General. **Conservation:** General, environmental science, environmental studies. **Education:** General. **English:** English lit. **Foreign languages:** General, classics, linguistics. **Health:** Health services. **Interdisciplinary:** Biological/physical sciences, global studies, intercultural, natural sciences. **Liberal arts:** Arts/sciences, humanities. **Math:** Probability. **Philosophy/religion:** Philosophy, religion. **Physical sciences:** General. **Psychology:** General. **Public administration:** General. **Social sciences:** General, political science, sociology. **Visual/performing arts:** General, art, cinematography, dramatic, film/cinema, multimedia, studio arts.

**Most popular majors.** Interdisciplinary studies 12%, liberal arts 88%.

**Computing on campus.** 375 workstations in dormitories, library, computer center. Dormitories wired for high-speed internet access and linked to campus network. Commuter students can connect to campus network. Online course registration, online library, helpline, student web hosting, wireless network available.

**Student life. Freshman orientation:** Mandatory. Preregistration for classes offered. Week-long orientation offers academic and social events to familiarize students with teaching, learning, and resources at campus. **Housing:** Guaranteed on-campus for freshmen. Coed dorms, special housing for disabled, apartments, substance-free housing available. $250 fully refundable deposit, deadline 7/15. Apartment-style housing, freshmen halls, freshmen quiet, community action, sustainability, apartment-style quiet, substance free housing available. **Activities:** Choral groups, dance, drama, film society, literary magazine, music ensembles, radio station, student government, student newspaper, TV station, Developing Ecological Agricultural Practices, queer alliance, Women of Color Coalition, Students for Christ, MEChA, women's resource center, political information center, Students at Evergreen for Ecological Design, Geoduck Union.

**Athletics.** NAIA. **Intercollegiate:** Basketball, cross-country, soccer, track and field, volleyball W. **Intramural:** Badminton, basketball, racquetball, soccer, softball, tennis. **Team name:** Geoducks.

**Student services.** Adult student services, alcohol/substance abuse counseling, career counseling, services for economically disadvantaged, student employment services, financial aid counseling, health services, minority student services, on-campus daycare, personal counseling, placement for graduates, veterans' counselor, women's services. **Physically disabled:** Services for visually, speech, hearing impaired.

**Contact.** E-mail: admissions@evergreen.edu
Phone: (360) 867-6170 Fax: (360) 867-5114
Doug Scrima, Director of Admissions, Evergreen State College, 2700 Evergreen Parkway NW, Olympia, WA 98505

## Gonzaga University
**Spokane, Washington**        **CB member**
**www.gonzaga.edu**        **CB code: 4330**

- Private 4-year university and liberal arts college affiliated with Roman Catholic Church
- Residential campus in large city
- 4,318 degree-seeking undergraduates: 2% part-time, 53% women, 1% African American, 5% Asian American, 4% Hispanic American, 1% Native American, 2% international
- 2,344 degree-seeking graduate students
- 69% of applicants admitted
- SAT or ACT (ACT writing optional), application essay required
- 80% graduate within 6 years

**General.** Founded in 1887. Regionally accredited. **Degrees:** 929 bachelor's awarded; master's, doctoral, first professional offered. **ROTC:** Army. **Location:** 300 miles from Seattle. **Calendar:** Semester, extensive summer session. **Full-time faculty:** 351 total; 86% have terminal degrees, 10% minority, 35% women. **Part-time faculty:** 342 total; 2% have terminal degrees. **Class size:** 44% < 20, 50% 20-39, 4% 40-49, 1% 50-99. **Special facilities:** 2 electron microscopes.

**Freshman class profile.** 5,744 applied, 3,961 admitted, 1,036 enrolled.

| Mid 50% test scores | | Rank in top quarter: | 76% |
|---|---|---|---|
| SAT critical reading: | 530-640 | Rank in top tenth: | 42% |
| SAT math: | 540-650 | End year in good standing: | 98% |
| ACT composite: | 24-29 | Return as sophomores: | 91% |
| GPA 3.50 or higher: | 76% | Out-of-state: | 54% |
| GPA 3.0-3.49: | 22% | Live on campus: | 95% |
| GPA 2.0-2.99: | 2% | International: | 2% |

**Basis for selection.** GED not accepted. Academic achievement, scholastic aptitude, personal characteristics important. GPA below 3.0 reevaluated to include only grades in academic subjects. Course content and test scores important. Interview recommended for all; audition recommended for music. **Homeschooled:** Test scores, interview by admissions representative required.

**High school preparation.** Required and recommended units include English 4, mathematics 3-4, social studies 2-3, history 2-3, science 3-4 (laboratory 3-4), foreign language 3-4 and academic electives 3. Algebra, geometry, trigonometry required of engineering applicants. Of 6 additional electives 4 must be from subjects mentioned and the arts.

**2007-2008 Annual costs.** Tuition/fees: $26,538. Room/board: $7,270. Books/supplies: $750. Personal expenses: $1,700.

**2006-2007 Financial aid. Need-based:** 807 full-time freshmen applied for aid; 567 were judged to have need; 566 of these received aid. Average need met was 88%. Average scholarship/grant was $14,902; average loan $4,135. 65% of total undergraduate aid awarded as scholarships/grants, 35% as loans/jobs. **Non-need-based:** Awarded to 1,622 full-time undergraduates, including 625 freshmen. Scholarships awarded for academics, alumni affiliation, athletics, leadership, minority status, music/drama, ROTC.

**Application procedures. Admission:** Closing date 2/1 (postmark date). $45 fee, may be waived for applicants with need. Application may be submitted online. Admission notification 3/15. Must reply by 5/1. **Financial aid:** Priority date 2/1, closing date 6/30. FAFSA required. Applicants notified on a rolling basis starting 3/1; must reply by 5/1 or within 3 week(s) of notification.

**Academics. Special study options:** Accelerated study, combined bachelor's/graduate degree, double major, ESL, exchange student, honors, internships, semester at sea, study abroad, teacher certification program, Washington semester, weekend college. **Credit/placement by examination:** AP, CLEP, IB, SAT, ACT. 32 credit hours maximum toward bachelor's degree. **Support services:** Pre-admission summer program, study skills assistance, writing center.

**Majors. Area/ethnic studies:** Asian, European, Latin American, women's. **Biology:** General, biochemistry. **Business:** Accounting, banking/financial services, business admin, international, management information systems, managerial economics. **Communications:** Broadcast journalism, journalism, public relations. **Computer sciences:** Computer science. **Education:** Music, physical, special. **Engineering:** General, civil, computer, electrical, mechanical. **English:** English lit, speech/rhetoric. **Foreign languages:** Comparative lit, French, Italian, Spanish. **Health:** Preop/surgical nursing. **History:** General. **Liberal arts:** Arts/sciences. **Math:** General. **Parks/recreation:** Sports admin. **Philosophy/religion:** Philosophy, religion. **Physical sciences:** Chemistry, physics. **Protective services:** Criminal justice. **Psychology:** General. **Social sciences:** Economics, international relations, political science, sociology. **Visual/performing arts:** Dramatic, music performance, studio arts.

**Most popular majors.** Biology 6%, business/marketing 27%, communications/journalism 9%, engineering/engineering technologies 7%, psychology 7%, social sciences 11%.

**Computing on campus.** 560 workstations in library, computer center. Dormitories wired for high-speed internet access and linked to campus network. Commuter students can connect to campus network. Online course registration, online library, helpline, repair service, student web hosting, wireless network available.

**Student life. Freshman orientation:** Mandatory, $60 fee. Preregistration for classes offered. **Housing:** Guaranteed on-campus for freshmen. Coed dorms, single-sex dorms, special housing for disabled, apartments, substance-free housing available. $200 fully refundable deposit, deadline 5/1. International students, freshmen and sophomores under 21 must live on campus, unless living at home. **Activities:** Bands, choral groups, dance, drama, literary magazine, music ensembles, radio station, student government, student newspaper, symphony orchestra, TV station, 102 student clubs and service organizations.

**Athletics.** NCAA. **Intercollegiate:** Baseball M, basketball, cross-country, golf, rowing (crew), soccer, tennis, track and field, volleyball W. **Intramural:** Badminton, basketball, racquetball, soccer, softball, tennis, volleyball, weight lifting, wrestling M. **Team name:** Bulldogs.

**Student services.** Adult student services, alcohol/substance abuse counseling, campus ministries, career counseling, student employment services, financial aid counseling, health services, minority student services, personal counseling, veterans' counselor. **Physically disabled:** Services for visually, speech, hearing impaired.

**Contact.** E-mail: mcculloh@gu.gonzaga.edu
Phone: (509) 323-6572 Toll-free number: (800) 322-2584
Fax: (509) 323-5780
Julie McCulloh, Dean of Admissions, Gonzaga University, 502 East Boone Avenue, Spokane, WA 99258-0001

## Heritage University
### Toppenish, Washington
### www.heritage.edu                                    CB code: 4344

- Private 4-year liberal arts and teachers college affiliated with interdenominational tradition
- Commuter campus in small town
- 788 degree-seeking undergraduates: 31% part-time, 76% women
- 400 degree-seeking graduate students

**General.** Founded in 1982. Regionally accredited. **Degrees:** 109 bachelor's, 16 associate awarded; master's offered. **Location:** 165 miles from Seattle, 20 miles from Yakima. **Calendar:** Semester, limited summer session. **Full-time faculty:** 47 total; 38% have terminal degrees, 23% minority, 49% women. **Part-time faculty:** 140 total; 17% have terminal degrees, 19% minority, 39% women. **Class size:** 76% < 20, 24% 20-39. **Special facilities:** Solar telescope, portable planetarium.

**Freshman class profile.** 93 enrolled.

**Basis for selection.** Open admission. All students take institutional placement test. **Homeschooled:** State high school equivalency certificate required.

**High school preparation.** Recommended units include English 3, mathematics 2, history 3, science 1 (laboratory 1) and academic electives 4.

**2007-2008 Annual costs.** Tuition/fees: $11,300. Books/supplies: $1,125. Personal expenses: $2,904.

**2007-2008 Financial aid. Need-based:** Average need met was 75%. Average scholarship/grant was $9,914; average loan $2,697. 58% of total undergraduate aid awarded as scholarships/grants, 42% as loans/jobs. **Non-need-based:** Scholarships awarded for academics, leadership, minority status.

**Application procedures. Admission:** Priority date 3/15; no deadline. No application fee. Application must be submitted on paper. Admission notification on a rolling basis. **Financial aid:** Priority date 2/10; no closing date. FAFSA, institutional form required. Applicants notified on a rolling basis; must reply within 2 week(s) of notification.

**Academics. Special study options:** Cooperative education, distance learning, double major, dual enrollment of high school students, ESL, honors, independent study, internships, liberal arts/career combination, student-designed major, teacher certification program. **Credit/placement by examination:** AP, CLEP, institutional tests. 14 credit hours maximum toward associate degree, 30 toward bachelor's. **Support services:** Learning center, reduced course load, remedial instruction, study skills assistance, tutoring, writing center.

**Majors. Agriculture:** Horticulture. **Area/ethnic studies:** American. **Biology:** General. **Business:** General, accounting, business admin, entrepreneurial studies, human resources, marketing. **Computer sciences:** General. **Conservation:** General, environmental science. **Education:** General, bilingual, biology, chemistry, computer, early childhood, elementary, English, ESL, history, mathematics, middle, reading, science, secondary, Spanish, special. **English:** English lit. **Health:** Health care admin. **Interdisciplinary:** Math/computer science, natural sciences. **Math:** General. **Physical sciences:** General, chemistry. **Psychology:** General. **Public administration:** Social work.

**Most popular majors.** Business/marketing 7%, computer/information sciences 6%, education 53%, public administration/social services 16%.

**Computing on campus.** 160 workstations in library, computer center. Commuter students can connect to campus network. Online library, wireless network available.

**Student life. Freshman orientation:** Available. Preregistration for classes offered. Typically held one day during the week before classes start for the fall and spring semesters. **Activities:** Dance, drama, literary magazine, music ensembles, student government, student newspaper, Native American, Heritage Community Volunteers in Action, Heritage Educators Association, social work club, Nursing students club.

**Student services.** Adult student services, career counseling, services for economically disadvantaged, student employment services, financial aid counseling, on-campus daycare, personal counseling, placement for graduates, veterans' counselor.

**Contact.** E-mail: Admissions@heritage.edu
Phone: (509) 865-8508 Toll-free number: (888) 272-6190
Fax: (509) 865-8659
MIguel Puente, Director of Admissions, Heritage University, 3240 Fort Road, Toppenish, WA 98948-9599

## International Academy of Design and Technology: Seattle
**Seattle, Washington**
**www.iadtseattle.com**

- For-profit 4-year university
- Very large city
- 562 degree-seeking undergraduates
- 100% of applicants admitted

**General.** Accredited by ACICS. **Degrees:** 3 bachelor's, 29 associate awarded. **Calendar:** Quarter. **Full-time faculty:** 10 total. **Part-time faculty:** 34 total.

**Freshman class profile.** 90 applied, 90 admitted, 74 enrolled.

**2007-2008 Annual costs.** Tuition/fees: $15,300.

**Application procedures. Admission:** No deadline. $50 fee. **Financial aid:** No deadline.

**Academics. Credit/placement by examination:** CLEP.

**Contact.** Phone: (888) 424-8111
Lynette Rickman, Director of Admissions, International Academy of Design and Technology: Seattle, 645 Andover Park West, Seattle, WA 98188

## ITT Technical Institute: Everett
**Everett, Washington**
**www.itt-tech.edu**   CB code: 2697

- For-profit 4-year technical college
- Commuter campus in large town

**General.** Accredited by ACICS. **Calendar:** Quarter.

**Annual costs/financial aid.** Tuition varies by program, $260-$368 per credit hour.

**Contact.** Phone: (425) 485-0303
Director of Recruitment, 1615 75th Street, S.W., Everett, WA 98203

## ITT Technical Institute: Seattle
**Seattle, Washington**
**www.itt-tech.edu**   CB code: 3599

- For-profit 4-year technical college
- Commuter campus in very large city

**General.** Founded in 1932. Accredited by ACICS. **Location:** 12 miles from downtown. **Calendar:** Quarter.

**Annual costs/financial aid.** Tuition varies by program, $260-$368 per credit hour.

**Contact.** Phone: (206) 244-3300
Director of Recruitment, 12720 Gateway Drive, Suite 100, Seattle, WA 98168

## ITT Technical Institute: Spokane
**Spokane Valley, Washington**
**www.itt-tech.edu**   CB code: 7027

- For-profit 4-year technical college
- Commuter campus in small city

**General.** Accredited by ACICS. **Location:** 5 miles from downtown. **Calendar:** Quarter.

**Annual costs/financial aid.** Tuition varies by program, $260-$368 per credit hour.

**Contact.** Phone: (509) 926-2900
Director of Recruitment, 13518 East Indiana Avenue, Spokane Valley, WA 99216

## Northwest College of Art
**Poulsbo, Washington**
**www.nca.edu**   CB code: 2432

- For-profit 4-year visual arts college
- Commuter campus in small town
- 97 full-time, degree-seeking undergraduates
- Application essay, interview required

**General.** Founded in 1982. Accredited by ACCSCT. **Degrees:** 24 bachelor's awarded. **Location:** 30 miles from Seattle, 60 miles from Tacoma. **Calendar:** Semester, extensive summer session. **Part-time faculty:** 15 total; 27% have terminal degrees, 40% women. **Class size:** 98% < 20, 2% 20-39.

**Basis for selection.** Requirements include minimum 2.5 GPA, 2 interviews, 3 letters of recommendation, 2-3 page typed essay, portfolio. TOEFL test required for international students from non-english speaking countries. SAT required for students with a GED. Portfolio required. **Homeschooled:** GED required except when homeschool programs show proof of school or program accreditation.

**2008-2009 Annual costs.** Tuition/fees: $15,300.

**Financial aid. Non-need-based:** Scholarships awarded for academics, art, state residency.

**Application procedures. Admission:** Priority date 3/1; deadline 6/1 (postmark date). $50 fee. Application must be submitted on paper. Admission notification on a rolling basis. **Financial aid:** Priority date 3/1, closing date 6/1. FAFSA required. Applicants notified on a rolling basis.

**Academics. Special study options:** Double major, internships. **Credit/placement by examination:** AP, CLEP.

**Majors. Visual/performing arts:** Design, studio arts.

**Student life. Freshman orientation:** Mandatory, $15 fee. Preregistration for classes offered.

**Student services.** Adult student services, career counseling, student employment services, financial aid counseling, personal counseling, placement for graduates, veterans' counselor.

**Contact.** E-mail: kperigard@nca.edu
Phone: (360) 779-9993 Toll-free number: (800) 769-2787
Fax: (360) 779-9933
Mark Stoddard, Northwest College of Art, Northwest College of Art, 16301 Creative Drive NE, Poulsbo, WA 98370

## Northwest University
**Kirkland, Washington**
**www.northwestu.edu**   CB code: 4541

- Private 4-year university and liberal arts college affiliated with Assemblies of God
- Residential campus in small city
- 1,053 degree-seeking undergraduates: 5% part-time, 60% women, 3% African American, 6% Asian American, 4% Hispanic American, 1% Native American, 2% international
- 116 degree-seeking graduate students
- 79% of applicants admitted

◗ SAT or ACT (ACT writing optional), application essay required

◗ 46% graduate within 6 years

**General.** Founded in 1934. Regionally accredited. **Degrees:** 247 bachelor's, 6 associate awarded; master's offered. **ROTC:** Army. **Location:** 10 miles from Seattle. **Calendar:** Semester, limited summer session. **Full-time faculty:** 54 total; 65% have terminal degrees, 9% minority, 39% women. **Part-time faculty:** 51 total; 12% have terminal degrees, 4% minority, 59% women.

**Freshman class profile.** 372 applied, 295 admitted, 163 enrolled.

| Mid 50% test scores | | | |
|---|---|---|---|
| SAT critical reading: | 460-600 | GPA 3.0-3.49: | 32% |
| SAT math: | 440-560 | GPA 2.0-2.99: | 27% |
| SAT writing: | 450-580 | Return as sophomores: | 65% |
| ACT composite: | 18-26 | Out-of-state: | 26% |
| GPA 3.50 or higher: | 41% | International: | 2% |

**Basis for selection.** Entire application reviewed: includes essay, references, transcript, SAT or ACT. GPA of 2.3 required: those with GPA below 2.3 but greater than 2.0 admitted on academic probation if space available. TOEFL (minimum score 500) required for non-native speakers of English. Audition recommended for music and drama scholarships. **Learning Disabled:** Interview with Director of Student Success.

**High school preparation.** 16 units recommended. Recommended units include English 4, mathematics 3, social studies 2, history 2, science 2, foreign language 2 and academic electives 3.

**2008-2009 Annual costs.** Tuition/fees (projected): $20,790. Room/board: $6,578. Books/supplies: $900. Personal expenses: $1,600.

**2007-2008 Financial aid. Need-based:** 134 full-time freshmen applied for aid; 120 were judged to have need; 120 of these received aid. Average need met was 75%. Average scholarship/grant was $11,168; average loan $3,682. 54% of total undergraduate aid awarded as scholarships/grants, 46% as loans/jobs. **Non-need-based:** Awarded to 176 full-time undergraduates, including 34 freshmen. Scholarships awarded for academics, art, athletics, leadership, music/drama, religious affiliation.

**Application procedures. Admission:** Priority date 3/1; deadline 8/1 (postmark date). $30 fee, may be waived for applicants with need. Application may be submitted online. Admission notification on a rolling basis beginning on or about 10/1. **Financial aid:** Priority date 3/1, closing date 8/1. FAFSA, institutional form required. Applicants notified by 3/31; Applicants notified on a rolling basis starting 3/3; must reply within 4 week(s) of notification.

**Academics. Special study options:** Accelerated study, double major, dual enrollment of high school students, ESL, independent study, internships, student-designed major, study abroad, teacher certification program, Washington semester. **Credit/placement by examination:** AP, CLEP, IB, SAT, ACT, institutional tests. 30 credit hours maximum toward associate degree, 30 toward bachelor's. **Support services:** Learning center, reduced course load, remedial instruction, study skills assistance, tutoring, writing center.

**Majors. Biology:** General. **Business:** Business admin. **Communications:** General, media studies, organizational. **Conservation:** Environmental science. **Education:** Elementary, middle, secondary. **English:** English lit. **Health:** Nursing (RN), premedicine. **History:** General. **Math:** General. **Philosophy/religion:** Philosophy. **Psychology:** General. **Social sciences:** Political science. **Theology:** Bible, missionary, pastoral counseling, sacred music, theology, youth ministry. **Other:** Communications/drama.

**Most popular majors.** Business/marketing 25%, communications/journalism 6%, education 10%, health sciences 13%, psychology 8%, theological studies 21%.

**Computing on campus.** 135 workstations in dormitories, library, computer center, student center. Dormitories wired for high-speed internet access and linked to campus network. Commuter students can connect to campus network. Online course registration, online library, helpline, repair service, student web hosting, wireless network available.

**Student life. Freshman orientation:** Mandatory. Held end of August, one week before start of classes. **Policies:** Religious observance required. **Housing:** Guaranteed on-campus for all undergraduates. Single-sex dorms, apartments available. $300 fully refundable deposit, deadline 5/1. **Activities:** Bands, choral groups, drama, music ensembles, musical theater, radio station, student government, student newspaper, community outreach groups, Psi Chi Honor Society (psychology), Association of International Students, Environmental Stewardship Club, Students in Free Enterprise.

**Athletics.** NAIA, NCCAA. **Intercollegiate:** Basketball, cross-country, soccer, track and field, volleyball W. **Intramural:** Football (non-tackle). **Team name:** Eagles.

**Student services.** Adult student services, alcohol/substance abuse counseling, campus ministries, career counseling, student employment services, financial aid counseling, health services, personal counseling, veterans' counselor. **Physically disabled:** Services for visually impaired.

**Contact.** E-mail: admissions@northwestu.edu
Phone: (425) 889-5231 Toll-free number: (800) 669-3781
Fax: (425) 889-5224
Rose-mary Smith, Assistant Vice President, Enrollment, Northwest University, 5520 108th Avenue, NE, Kirkland, WA 98083-0579

## Pacific Lutheran University
Tacoma, Washington
www.plu.edu

**CB member**
**CB code: 4597**

◗ Private 4-year university affiliated with Evangelical Lutheran Church in America

◗ Residential campus in large city

◗ 3,271 degree-seeking undergraduates: 5% part-time, 63% women, 2% African American, 7% Asian American, 2% Hispanic American, 1% Native American, 5% international

◗ 304 degree-seeking graduate students

◗ 76% of applicants admitted

◗ SAT or ACT (ACT writing recommended), application essay required

◗ 66% graduate within 6 years

**General.** Founded in 1890. Regionally accredited. **Degrees:** 793 bachelor's awarded; master's offered. **ROTC:** Army. **Location:** 7 miles from Tacoma, 30 miles from Seattle. **Calendar:** 4-1-4, extensive summer session. **Full-time faculty:** 240 total; 82% have terminal degrees, 12% minority, 47% women. **Part-time faculty:** 15 total; 73% have terminal degrees, 7% minority, 53% women. **Class size:** 44% < 20, 50% 20-39, 3% 40-49, 3% 50-99, less than 1% >100. **Special facilities:** Herbarium, invertebrate and vertebrate museums, greenhouse, field station and boat equipped for studies of Puget Sound, Scandinavian cultural center, observatory, performing arts center.

**Freshman class profile.** 2,236 applied, 1,707 admitted, 715 enrolled.

| Mid 50% test scores | | | |
|---|---|---|---|
| SAT critical reading: | 500-620 | GPA 2.0-2.99: | 8% |
| SAT math: | 490-610 | Rank in top quarter: | 66% |
| SAT writing: | 480-600 | Rank in top tenth: | 36% |
| ACT composite: | 22-28 | Return as sophomores: | 84% |
| GPA 3.50 or higher: | 67% | Out-of-state: | 28% |
| GPA 3.0-3.49: | 25% | Live on campus: | 90% |
| | | International: | 3% |

**Basis for selection.** Grades, test scores, essay, recommendations, service, leadership. Admission on rolling basis until class is full. Interview recommended for borderline, exceptional; audition required for music, forensics, theater; portfolio recommended for art. **Homeschooled:** Must provide proof of high-school equivalency.

**High school preparation.** 17 units required. Required and recommended units include English 4, mathematics 2-3, social studies 2, science 2 (laboratory 2), foreign language 2, visual/performing arts 1 and academic electives 3. Computer science, speech, debate, music also recommended. 2 years visual or performing arts recommended.

**2008-2009 Annual costs.** Tuition/fees (projected): $26,800. Room/board: $8,200. Books/supplies: $924. Personal expenses: $2,094.

**2007-2008 Financial aid. Need-based:** 636 full-time freshmen applied for aid; 512 were judged to have need; 510 of these received aid. Average need met was 92%. Average scholarship/grant was $16,116; average loan $5,715. 59% of total undergraduate aid awarded as scholarships/grants, 41% as loans/jobs. **Non-need-based:** Awarded to 2,275 full-time undergraduates, including 600 freshmen. Scholarships awarded for academics, alumni affiliation, art, leadership, music/drama, religious affiliation, ROTC.

**Application procedures. Admission:** Priority date 2/15; no deadline. $40 fee, may be waived for applicants with need. Application may be submitted online. Admission notification on a rolling basis beginning on or about 10/1. Must reply by May 1 or within 2 week(s) if notified thereafter. Housing deposit is refundable only through May 1. **Financial aid:** Priority date 1/31; no closing date. FAFSA required. Applicants notified on a rolling basis starting 3/15; must reply by 5/1 or within 4 week(s) of notification.

**Academics.** Freshman year program includes topic-oriented writing and critical conversation classes. **Special study options:** Combined bachelor's/graduate degree, cooperative education, cross-registration, double major, dual enrollment of high school students, ESL, exchange student, honors, independent study, internships, liberal arts/career combination, student-designed major, study abroad, teacher certification program. **Credit/placement by examination:** AP, CLEP, IB, institutional tests. 30 credit hours maximum toward bachelor's degree. **Support services:** Pre-admission summer program, reduced course load, study skills assistance, tutoring, writing center.

**Majors. Area/ethnic studies:** Scandinavian, women's. **Biology:** General. **Business:** Business admin. **Communications:** General. **Computer sciences:** Computer science. **Conservation:** Environmental science. **Education:** Elementary, secondary. **Engineering:** Computer, science. **English:** English lit. **Foreign languages:** Chinese, classics, French, German, Norwegian, Spanish. **Health:** Nursing (RN). **History:** General. **Interdisciplinary:** Global studies. **Math:** General. **Parks/recreation:** General, health/fitness. **Philosophy/religion:** Philosophy, religion. **Physical sciences:** Chemistry, geology, physics. **Psychology:** General. **Public administration:** Social work. **Social sciences:** Anthropology, economics, political science, sociology. **Visual/performing arts:** Art, studio arts, theater arts management.

**Most popular majors.** Business/marketing 14%, education 7%, health sciences 10%, psychology 6%, social sciences 11%, visual/performing arts 6%.

**Computing on campus.** 250 workstations in library, student center. Dormitories wired for high-speed internet access and linked to campus network. Commuter students can connect to campus network. Helpline, student web hosting available.

**Student life. Freshman orientation:** Available. Preregistration for classes offered. **Policies:** All single, full-time students must live in university housing, unless student lives at home with parent or legal guardian, is 20 years of age or older on or before a specific college-designated date, or has achieved junior status. **Housing:** Guaranteed on-campus for all undergraduates. Coed dorms, single-sex dorms, special housing for disabled, apartments, cooperative housing, substance-free housing available. $200 deposit, deadline 5/1. **Activities:** Bands, campus ministries, choral groups, dance, drama, film society, international student organizations, literary magazine, music ensembles, musical theater, opera, radio station, student government, student newspaper, symphony orchestra, TV station, Intervarsity Christian Fellowship, Advocates for Social Justice, Asian & Pacific Islanders club, B.L.A.C.K. at PLU, environmental action, Puentes, social work organization, Amnesty International, Habitat for Humanity, Young Life.

**Athletics.** NCAA. **Intercollegiate:** Baseball M, basketball, cheerleading, cross-country, football (tackle) M, golf, rowing (crew), soccer, softball W, swimming, tennis, track and field, volleyball W. **Intramural:** Badminton, basketball, bowling, cross-country, football (non-tackle), golf, handball, racquetball, soccer, softball, squash, table tennis, tennis, track and field, volleyball. **Team name:** Lutes.

**Student services.** Adult student services, campus ministries, career counseling, student employment services, financial aid counseling, health services, minority student services, personal counseling, placement for graduates, veterans' counselor, women's services. **Physically disabled:** Services for visually, speech, hearing impaired.

**Contact.** E-mail: admission@plu.edu
Phone: (253) 535-7151 Toll-free number: (800) 274-6758
Fax: (253) 536-5136
Karl Stumo, Dean of Admission and Financial Aid, Pacific Lutheran University, Office of Admissions, Tacoma, WA 98447-0003

## Saint Martin's University
**Lacey, Washington**
**www.stmartin.edu**

**CB member**
**CB code: 4674**

- Private 4-year liberal arts college affiliated with Roman Catholic Church
- Commuter campus in large town
- 1,245 degree-seeking undergraduates: 15% part-time, 56% women, 7% African American, 11% Asian American, 6% Hispanic American, 2% Native American, 4% international
- 271 degree-seeking graduate students
- 93% of applicants admitted
- SAT or ACT with writing, application essay required
- 41% graduate within 6 years

**General.** Founded in 1895. Regionally accredited. Campus is home to Benedictine Monastery where 40 monks live and work. **Degrees:** 298 bachelor's awarded; master's offered. **ROTC:** Army, Air Force. **Location:** 3 miles from Olympia, 60 miles from Seattle. **Calendar:** Semester, limited summer session. **Full-time faculty:** 70 total; 81% have terminal degrees,

21% minority, 37% women. **Part-time faculty:** 119 total; 12% have terminal degrees, 4% minority, 37% women. **Class size:** 73% < 20, 27% 20-39, less than 1% 40-49.

**Freshman class profile.** 657 applied, 611 admitted, 245 enrolled.

| Mid 50% test scores | | | |
|---|---|---|---|
| SAT critical reading: | 440-540 | GPA 3.0-3.49: | 33% |
| SAT math: | 440-560 | GPA 2.0-2.99: | 35% |
| SAT writing: | 420-540 | End year in good standing: | 85% |
| ACT composite: | 19-23 | Return as sophomores: | 77% |
| GPA 3.50 or higher: | 32% | Out-of-state: | 14% |
| | | Live on campus: | 82% |

**Basis for selection.** School achievement record most important. Test scores important. 3.0 GPA required for regular admittance. Interview recommended. **Learning Disabled:** Recommend students self-identify to Director of Access Services for information on support services.

**High school preparation.** 14 units recommended. Recommended units include English 4, mathematics 3, social studies 2, science 3 (laboratory 1), foreign language 2 and academic electives 3.

**2008-2009 Annual costs.** Tuition/fees: $24,110. Room/board: $8,040. Books/supplies: $1,000. Personal expenses: $1,000.

**2006-2007 Financial aid. Need-based:** 198 full-time freshmen applied for aid; 174 were judged to have need; 172 of these received aid. Average need met was 81%. Average scholarship/grant was $14,580; average loan $2,690. 57% of total undergraduate aid awarded as scholarships/grants, 43% as loans/jobs. **Non-need-based:** Awarded to 269 full-time undergraduates, including 85 freshmen. Scholarships awarded for academics, alumni affiliation, athletics, leadership, music/drama, religious affiliation, ROTC, state residency.

**Application procedures. Admission:** Priority date 3/1; no deadline. $35 fee, may be waived for applicants with need. Application may be submitted online. Admission notification on a rolling basis. Must reply by May 1 or within 3 week(s) if notified thereafter. **Financial aid:** Priority date 3/1; no closing date. FAFSA required. Applicants notified on a rolling basis starting 2/15.

**Academics. Special study options:** Distance learning, double major, ESL, exchange student, independent study, internships, study abroad, teacher certification program, Washington semester. **Credit/placement by examination:** AP, CLEP, IB, SAT, ACT, institutional tests. 32 credit hours maximum toward associate degree, 64 toward bachelor's. **Support services:** Learning center, pre-admission summer program, reduced course load, remedial instruction, study skills assistance, tutoring, writing center.

**Majors. Biology:** General. **Business:** Accounting, business admin. **Computer sciences:** General, computer science. **Education:** Elementary, special. **Engineering:** Civil, mechanical. **English:** English lit. **Health:** Predental, premedicine, prepharmacy, preveterinary. **History:** General. **Liberal arts:** Humanities. **Math:** General. **Philosophy/religion:** Philosophy, religion. **Physical sciences:** Chemistry. **Protective services:** Criminal justice. **Psychology:** General. **Public administration:** Community org/advocacy. **Social sciences:** Political science, sociology. **Visual/performing arts:** Dramatic.

**Most popular majors.** Business/marketing 33%, education 9%, engineering/engineering technologies 10%, psychology 20%, security/protective services 10%, social sciences 8%.

**Computing on campus.** 140 workstations in library, computer center. Dormitories wired for high-speed internet access and linked to campus network. Commuter students can connect to campus network. Online library, helpline, wireless network available.

**Student life. Freshman orientation:** Mandatory, $150 fee. Preregistration for classes offered. Occurs the 5 days prior to fall classes. **Policies:** Dry campus. **Housing:** Guaranteed on-campus for freshmen. Coed dorms, special housing for disabled, apartments, substance-free housing available. $325 partly refundable deposit, deadline 7/1. **Activities:** Bands, campus ministries, choral groups, dance, drama, international student organizations, Model UN, musical theater, student government, student newspaper, Circle K, Hawaiian Club, nontraditional student group, social action club, Young Republicans, women's club, Gay/Straight Alliance, Democratic club.

**Athletics.** NCAA. **Intercollegiate:** Baseball M, basketball, cross-country, golf, soccer, softball W, track and field, volleyball W. **Intramural:** Basketball, bowling, soccer, softball, tennis, volleyball. **Team name:** Saints.

**Student services.** Adult student services, alcohol/substance abuse counseling, campus ministries, career counseling, student employment services, financial aid counseling, personal counseling, placement for graduates, veterans' counselor. **Physically disabled:** Services for visually, hearing impaired.

**Contact.** E-mail: admissions@stmartin.edu
Phone: (360) 438-4311 Toll-free number: (800) 368-8803
Fax: (360) 412-6189
Eric Pedersen, Dean of Enrollment and Financial Aid, Saint Martin's University, 5300 Pacific Avenue SE, Lacey, WA 98503-7500

## Seattle Pacific University

### Seattle, Washington.
### www.spu.edu

**CB member**
**CB code: 4694**

- Private 4-year university affiliated with Free Methodist Church of North America
- Residential campus in very large city
- 3,015 degree-seeking undergraduates: 4% part-time, 67% women, 2% African American, 7% Asian American, 3% Hispanic American, 1% Native American, 1% international
- 711 degree-seeking graduate students
- 85% of applicants admitted
- SAT or ACT (ACT writing recommended), application essay required
- 66% graduate within 6 years

**General.** Founded in 1891. Regionally accredited. **Degrees:** 721 bachelor's awarded; master's, doctoral offered. **ROTC:** Army, Naval, Air Force. **Location:** 3 miles from downtown. **Calendar:** Quarter, limited summer session. **Full-time faculty:** 186 total; 86% have terminal degrees, 8% minority, 40% women. **Part-time faculty:** 138 total; 12% have terminal degrees, 5% minority, 59% women. **Class size:** 50% < 20, 36% 20-39, 8% 40-49, 5% 50-99, less than 1% >100. **Special facilities:** 2 island campuses used for biological studies.

**Freshman class profile.** 2,055 applied, 1,756 admitted, 716 enrolled.

| Mid 50% test scores | | | |
|---|---|---|---|
| SAT critical reading: | 520-640 | GPA 3.0-3.49: | 32% |
| SAT math: | 510-640 | GPA 2.0-2.99: | 5% |
| SAT writing: | 620-620 | Return as sophomores: | 86% |
| ACT composite: | 22-28 | Out-of-state: | 55% |
| GPA 3.50 or higher: | 63% | Live on campus: | 98% |
| | | International: | 1% |

**Basis for selection.** Admission decisions based primarily based on grades, grade trend, test scores, essays, letters of recommendation and extracurricular activities. Audition required for music, performing art workshop; portfolio required for fine art scholarship.

**High school preparation.** Required units include English 4, mathematics 3, social studies 3, history 2, science 2 and foreign language 3.

**2007-2008 Annual costs.** Tuition/fees: $25,128. Room/board: $8,082. Books/supplies: $849. Personal expenses: $1,707.

**2007-2008 Financial aid. Need-based:** 586 full-time freshmen applied for aid; 463 were judged to have need; 462 of these received aid. Average need met was 83%. Average scholarship/grant was $18,303; average loan $5,757. 60% of total undergraduate aid awarded as scholarships/grants, 40% as loans/jobs. **Non-need-based:** Awarded to 857 full-time undergraduates, including 214 freshmen. Scholarships awarded for academics, alumni affiliation, art, athletics, leadership, minority status, music/drama, religious affiliation, ROTC.

**Application procedures. Admission:** Priority date 11/15; deadline 2/1. $45 fee, may be waived for applicants with need. Application may be submitted online. Admission notification 4/1. Must reply by May 1 or within 2 week(s) if notified thereafter. **Financial aid:** Priority date 4/1; no closing date. FAFSA required. Applicants notified on a rolling basis starting 3/15; must reply by 5/1 or within 4 week(s) of notification.

**Academics. Special study options:** Cooperative education, cross-registration, distance learning, double major, ESL, exchange student, external degree, honors, independent study, internships, liberal arts/career combination, student-designed major, study abroad, teacher certification program, Washington semester, weekend college. **Credit/placement by examination:** AP, CLEP, IB, SAT, ACT, institutional tests. 45 credit hours maximum toward bachelor's degree. **Support services:** Learning center, reduced course load, remedial instruction, tutoring, writing center.

**Majors. Area/ethnic studies:** European, Latin American. **Biology:** General, biochemistry. **Business:** Accounting. **Communications:** General. **Education:** Art, English, mathematics, music, science, special. **Engineering:** Computer, electrical, science. **English:** English lit. **Family/consumer sciences:** Clothing/textiles, food/nutrition. **Foreign languages:** Classics, French, German, Latin, Russian, Spanish. **Health:** Nursing (RN). **History:** General. **Legal studies:** Prelaw. **Math:** General. **Parks/recreation:** Exercise sciences. **Philosophy/religion:** Philosophy. **Physical sciences:** Chemistry, physics. **Psychology:** General. **Social sciences:** Economics, political science,

sociology. **Theology:** Religious ed. **Visual/performing arts:** General, art, dramatic.

**Most popular majors.** Biology 6%, business/marketing 13%, communications/journalism 6%, English 6%, family/consumer sciences 11%, health sciences 8%, psychology 10%, social sciences 12%, visual/performing arts 6%.

**Computing on campus.** 150 workstations in dormitories, library, computer center, student center. Dormitories wired for high-speed internet access and linked to campus network. Commuter students can connect to campus network. Online course registration, online library, helpline, repair service, wireless network available.

**Student life. Freshman orientation:** Mandatory. Preregistration for classes offered. **Policies:** Religious observance required. **Housing:** Coed dorms, apartments, substance-free housing available. $300 fully refundable deposit, deadline 6/1. Theme housing. **Activities:** Bands, campus ministries, choral groups, drama, literary magazine, music ensembles, musical theater, radio station, student government, student newspaper, symphony orchestra, more than 25 clubs and organizations.

**Athletics.** NCAA. **Intercollegiate:** Basketball, cross-country, gymnastics W, rowing (crew), soccer, track and field, volleyball W. **Intramural:** Badminton, basketball, bowling, cross-country, football (tackle) M, golf, skiing, soccer, softball, swimming, table tennis, tennis, track and field, volleyball, wrestling M. **Team name:** Falcons.

**Student services.** Adult student services, campus ministries, career counseling, student employment services, health services, personal counseling, placement for graduates, veterans' counselor. **Physically disabled:** Services for visually, hearing impaired.

**Contact.** E-mail: admissions@spu.edu
Phone: (206) 281-2021 Toll-free number: (800) 366-3344
Fax: (206) 281-2544
Jobe Nice, Director of Undergraduate Admissions, Seattle Pacific University, 3307 Third Avenue West, Seattle, WA 98119-1997

## Seattle University

### Seattle, Washington
### www.seattleu.edu

**CB member**
**CB code: 4695**

- Private 4-year university affiliated with Roman Catholic Church
- Residential campus in very large city
- 4,234 degree-seeking undergraduates: 7% part-time, 61% women, 5% African American, 20% Asian American, 7% Hispanic American, 1% Native American, 8% international
- 3,240 degree-seeking graduate students
- 64% of applicants admitted
- SAT or ACT (ACT writing optional), application essay required
- 68% graduate within 6 years

**General.** Founded in 1891. Regionally accredited. Courses also offered at Bellevue Campus. **Degrees:** 1,032 bachelor's awarded; master's, doctoral, first professional offered. **ROTC:** Army, Naval, Air Force. **Location:** One mile from downtown. **Calendar:** Quarter, extensive summer session. **Full-time faculty:** 426 total; 82% have terminal degrees, 16% minority, 49% women. **Part-time faculty:** 219 total; 65% have terminal degrees, 6% minority, 50% women. **Class size:** 55% < 20, 42% 20-39, 2% 40-49, 1% 50-99. **Special facilities:** Design center (where engineering students work with major companies in the area), observatory.

**Freshman class profile.** 4,918 applied, 3,131 admitted, 768 enrolled.

| Mid 50% test scores | | | |
|---|---|---|---|
| SAT critical reading: | 520-640 | GPA 2.0-2.99: | 4% |
| SAT math: | 530-630 | Rank in top quarter: | 63% |
| SAT writing: | 510-620 | Rank in top tenth: | 32% |
| ACT composite: | 23-28 | Return as sophomores: | 86% |
| GPA 3.50 or higher: | 57% | Out-of-state: | 48% |
| GPA 3.0-3.49: | 39% | Live on campus: | 89% |
| | | International: | 4% |

**Basis for selection.** 2.75 GPA minimum, higher for some programs. Secondary school record, recommendations, test scores most important. Essay, school, community activities also important. Applicants must submit one test with a writing component. The ACT writing component is required if the applicant does not submit the SAT Reasoning scores. Interview recommended for marginal students.

**High school preparation.** 16 units required. Required and recommended units include English 4, mathematics 3-4, science 2-3 (laboratory 2), foreign language 2 and academic electives 3.

**2007-2008 Annual costs.** Tuition/fees: $26,325. $200 enrollment deposit, $95 matriculation fee required. $95 per-credit-hour charge for credit by examination. $95 per-credit-hour charge for validation of field experience. Room/board: $7,860. Books/supplies: $945. Personal expenses: $1,878.

**2007-2008 Financial aid. Need-based:** 662 full-time freshmen applied for aid; 472 were judged to have need; 468 of these received aid. Average need met was 80%. Average scholarship/grant was $6,420; average loan $4,452. 63% of total undergraduate aid awarded as scholarships/grants, 37% as loans/jobs. **Non-need-based:** Awarded to 1,758 full-time undergraduates, including 295 freshmen. Scholarships awarded for academics, alumni affiliation, athletics, leadership, minority status, music/drama, ROTC, state residency.

**Application procedures. Admission:** Priority date 2/1; no deadline. $45 fee, may be waived for applicants with need. Application may be submitted online. Admission notification on a rolling basis beginning on or about 2/1. Must reply by May 1 or within 4 week(s) if notified thereafter. **Financial aid:** Priority date 2/1; no closing date. FAFSA required. Applicants notified by 3/21; Applicants notified on a rolling basis starting 3/21; must reply by 5/1 or within 2 week(s) of notification.

**Academics. Special study options:** Combined bachelor's/graduate degree, cooperative education, cross-registration, double major, honors, independent study, internships, liberal arts/career combination, student-designed major, study abroad, teacher certification program. **Credit/placement by examination:** AP, CLEP, IB, institutional tests. 45 credit hours maximum toward bachelor's degree. Special arrangements for nursing majors who take NLN exams. 50 credits maximum. **Support services:** Learning center, reduced course load, study skills assistance, tutoring, writing center.

**Majors. Area/ethnic studies:** Asian, women's. **Biology:** General, biochemistry. **Business:** General, accounting, business admin, e-commerce, finance, international, managerial economics, marketing. **Communications:** Journalism, media studies, public relations. **Computer sciences:** Computer science. **Conservation:** General. **Engineering:** Civil, electrical, mechanical. **English:** Creative writing, English lit. **Foreign languages:** General, French, Spanish. **Health:** Clinical lab science, medical records admin, nurse practitioner, nursing (RN), public health nursing, sonography. **History:** General. **Interdisciplinary:** Global studies. **Liberal arts:** Arts/sciences, humanities. **Math:** General. **Philosophy/religion:** Philosophy, religion. **Physical sciences:** General, chemistry, physics. **Protective services:** Criminal justice, criminalistics. **Psychology:** General. **Public administration:** General, social work. **Social sciences:** Economics, political science, sociology. **Visual/performing arts:** General, art history/conservation, dramatic.

**Most popular majors.** Business/marketing 21%, English 6%, health sciences 14%, liberal arts 7%, psychology 6%, social sciences 7%.

**Computing on campus.** 401 workstations in dormitories, library, computer center, student center. Dormitories wired for high-speed internet access and linked to campus network. Commuter students can connect to campus network. Helpline, student web hosting available.

**Student life. Freshman orientation:** Mandatory. Preregistration for classes offered. 3 days prior to start of classes. **Housing:** Guaranteed on-campus for freshmen. Coed dorms, apartments, substance-free housing available. $300 nonrefundable deposit, deadline 5/1. Single-gender floors available. **Activities:** Bands, campus ministries, choral groups, dance, drama, international student organizations, literary magazine, music ensembles, musical theater, radio station, student government, student newspaper, 65 clubs available.

**Athletics.** NCAA. **Intercollegiate:** Basketball, cross-country, soccer, softball W, swimming, tennis W, track and field, volleyball W. **Intramural:** Basketball, football (non-tackle), soccer, softball, tennis, volleyball. **Team name:** Redhawks.

**Student services.** Adult student services, alcohol/substance abuse counseling, campus ministries, career counseling, student employment services, financial aid counseling, health services, minority student services, personal counseling, placement for graduates, veterans' counselor, women's services. **Physically disabled:** Services for visually, speech, hearing impaired.

**Contact.** E-mail: admissions@seattleu.edu
Phone: (206) 296-2000 Toll-free number: (800) 426-7123
Fax: (206) 296-5656
Michael McKeon, Dean of Admissions, Seattle University, 901 12th Avenue, Seattle, WA 98122-4340

## South Seattle Community College
**Seattle, Washington**
**www.southseattle.edu**　　　　**CB code: 4759**

- Public 4-year community college
- Commuter campus in very large city
- 3,230 degree-seeking undergraduates

**General.** Founded in 1969. Regionally accredited. Culturally diverse campus with over 35 languages spoken. **Degrees:** 351 associate awarded. **Location:** 10 minutes from downtown. **Calendar:** Quarter, limited summer session. **Full-time faculty:** 79 total; 11% have terminal degrees, 27% minority. **Part-time faculty:** 260 total; 19% minority. **Special facilities:** College operated bakery and restaurants, arboretum; Seattle Chinese Garden.

**Basis for selection.** Open admission, but selective for some programs. COMPASS, ESL COMPASS tests used for placement and counseling. **Learning Disabled:** Referred to Educational Support Services Office.

**2007-2008 Annual costs.** Tuition/fees: $2,897; $8,105 out-of-state. Books/supplies: $924. Personal expenses: $1,590.

**2006-2007 Financial aid. Need-based:** 94% of total undergraduate aid awarded as scholarships/grants, 6% as loans/jobs. **Non-need-based:** Scholarships awarded for academics, state residency.

**Application procedures. Admission:** No deadline. No application fee. Application may be submitted online. Admission notification on a rolling basis. **Financial aid:** Priority date 4/16; no closing date. FAFSA, institutional form required. Applicants notified on a rolling basis starting 7/1.

**Academics. Special study options:** Combined bachelor's/graduate degree, cross-registration, distance learning, dual enrollment of high school students, ESL, independent study, internships, study abroad, teacher certification program. Concurrent enrollment agreements with other colleges in vicinity; university partners offer bachelor's degrees on campus. **Credit/placement by examination:** CLEP, IB, institutional tests. Credit awarded for CLEP applies only to electives category of Associate of Arts degree. **Support services:** Learning center, remedial instruction, study skills assistance, tutoring, writing center.

**Majors. Business:** Hospitality admin.

**Computing on campus.** 700 workstations in library, computer center, student center. Online course registration, online library, wireless network available.

**Student life. Freshman orientation:** Available. **Policies:** Enrollment in 10 or more credits and 2.5 cumulative GPA required to serve as student government representative. **Activities:** Choral groups, international student organizations, literary magazine, student government, student newspaper, Vietnamese student club, Black student union, Cambodian club, Gay Straight Alliance, engineering club, Aviation Technician Association.

**Athletics. Intramural:** Basketball, soccer. **Team name:** Storm.

**Student services.** Adult student services, career counseling, services for economically disadvantaged, student employment services, financial aid counseling, minority student services, on-campus daycare, personal counseling, placement for graduates, veterans' counselor, women's services. **Physically disabled:** Services for visually, speech, hearing impaired.

**Contact.** E-mail: SSCCAdmissions@sccd.ctc.edu
Phone: (206) 768-7943 Fax: (206) 764-7947
Rosanette Rimando, Director of Student Outreach, Admissions and Recruitment, South Seattle Community College, 6000 16th Avenue, SW, Seattle, WA 98106-1499

## Trinity Lutheran College
**Issaquah, Washington**
**www.tlc.edu**　　　　**CB code: 4408**

- Private 4-year Bible and liberal arts college affiliated with Lutheran Church
- Residential campus in small city
- 103 degree-seeking undergraduates
- 78% of applicants admitted
- SAT or ACT (ACT writing optional) required

**General.** Founded in 1944. Regionally accredited. All students participate in off-campus service learning practicums. **Degrees:** 32 bachelor's, 3 associate awarded. **Location:** 30 miles from Seattle. **Calendar:** 4-1-4. **Full-time faculty:** 13 total. **Part-time faculty:** 18 total. **Special facilities:** Children, youth and family resource center; preschool and Christian school.

**Freshman class profile.** 100 applied, 78 admitted, 47 enrolled.

**Basis for selection.** High school GPA, test scores, 1 recommendation. Interview considered. **Homeschooled:** Statement describing homeschool structure and mission, transcript of courses and grades, letter of recommendation (nonparent) required.

**High school preparation.** Recommended units include English 3, mathematics 2, history 2, science 2 and foreign language 1.

**2007-2008 Annual costs.** Tuition/fees: $14,170. Room/board: $6,078. Books/supplies: $642. Personal expenses: $1,818.

**Financial aid. Non-need-based:** Scholarships awarded for academics, alumni affiliation, art, leadership, music/drama.

**Application procedures. Admission:** Priority date 3/1; deadline 8/25 (receipt date). $30 fee, may be waived for applicants with need. Application may be submitted online. Admission notification on a rolling basis beginning on or about 10/1. Must reply by May 1 or within 2 week(s) if notified thereafter. **Financial aid:** Priority date 3/1; no closing date. FAFSA, institutional form required. Applicants notified on a rolling basis starting 3/15; must reply within 2 week(s) of notification.

**Academics. Special study options:** Combined bachelor's/graduate degree, cooperative education, dual enrollment of high school students, independent study, internships, liberal arts/career combination, student-designed major, study abroad, urban semester. Study trips to Holy Lands, Italy, Greece, Africa. **Credit/placement by examination:** AP, CLEP, IB, institutional tests. 8 credit hours maximum toward associate degree, 8 toward bachelor's. **Support services:** Reduced course load, remedial instruction, study skills assistance, tutoring, writing center.

**Majors. Business:** Business admin, nonprofit/public. **Communications:** Media studies. **Education:** Early childhood, elementary. **Philosophy/religion:** Christian, religion. **Psychology:** General. **Public administration:** Social work. **Theology:** Bible, missionary, sacred music, theology, youth ministry.

**Computing on campus.** 15 workstations in dormitories, library, computer center, student center. Dormitories wired for high-speed internet access and linked to campus network. Commuter students can connect to campus network. Online library, helpline, wireless network available.

**Student life. Freshman orientation:** Mandatory. Preregistration for classes offered. **Housing:** Guaranteed on-campus for all undergraduates. Single-sex dorms, special housing for disabled, apartments, substance-free housing available. $75 partly refundable deposit, deadline 5/1. **Activities:** Choral groups, drama, music ensembles, musical theater, student government, student newspaper, Student learning practicums, Global Concerns Mission, Worship Commission, Environmental Commission.

**Athletics. Intramural:** Basketball, football (non-tackle), soccer, softball, table tennis, tennis, volleyball. **Team name:** Eagles.

**Student services.** Adult student services, campus ministries, career counseling, student employment services, financial aid counseling, health services, personal counseling, placement for graduates. **Physically disabled:** Services for visually impaired.

**Contact.** E-mail: admission@tlc.edu
Phone: (425) 961-5510 Toll-free number: (800) 843-5659
Fax: (425) 392-0404
Trinity Lutheran College, 4221 228th Avenue Southeast, Issaquah, WA 98029

---

## University of Puget Sound

Tacoma, Washington
www.ups.edu

CB member
CB code: 4067

- Private 4-year university and liberal arts college
- Residential campus in small city
- 2,527 degree-seeking undergraduates: 1% part-time, 58% women, 3% African American, 9% Asian American, 4% Hispanic American, 1% Native American
- 235 degree-seeking graduate students
- 66% of applicants admitted
- SAT or ACT (ACT writing recommended), application essay required
- 7.7% graduate within 6 years; 25% enter graduate study

**General.** Founded in 1888. Regionally accredited. **Degrees:** 566 bachelor's awarded; master's, first professional offered. **ROTC:** Army. **Location:** 35 miles from Seattle, 28 miles from Olympia. **Calendar:** Semester, limited summer session. **Full-time faculty:** 224 total; 88% have terminal degrees, 9% minority, 46% women. **Part-time faculty:** 55 total; 29% have terminal degrees, 7% minority, 49% women. **Class size:** 58% < 20, 40% 20-39, 1% 40-49. **Special facilities:** Natural history museum, arboretum, x-ray laboratory, electron microscope lab, observatory, concert hall, sculpture building, greenhouse, sedimentology lab, rock and mineral collection, exercise science lab, physiology labs.

**Freshman class profile.** 5,273 applied, 3,502 admitted, 644 enrolled.

| Mid 50% test scores | | | |
|---|---|---|---|
| SAT critical reading: | 570-690 | GPA 2.0-2.99: | 8% |
| SAT math: | 550-660 | Rank in top quarter: | 69% |
| SAT writing: | 560-660 | Rank in top tenth: | 40% |
| ACT composite: | 25-30 | End year in good standing: | 94% |
| GPA 3.50 or higher: | 59% | Return as sophomores: | 86% |
| GPA 3.0-3.49: | 33% | Out-of-state: | 78% |
| | | Live on campus: | 98% |

**Basis for selection.** High school record most important followed by test scores. Writing ability as demonstrated through the essay and short answer questions. Recommendations and activities important. If applicants have taken both SAT and ACT, they should submit all scores. Interview recommended for all; audition required for music; portfolio recommended for art; audition recommended for theater. **Homeschooled:** Applicants should show work in writing, critical reading, mathematics, history; and social, physical, and natural sciences. Foreign language recommended.

**High school preparation.** 19 units recommended. Recommended units include English 4, mathematics 4, social studies 3, history 3, science 4 (laboratory 4), foreign language 3 and visual/performing arts 1. One fine, visual or performing art recommended.

**2008-2009 Annual costs.** Tuition/fees: $33,975. Room/board: $8,760. Books/supplies: $1,000. Personal expenses: $1,800.

**2007-2008 Financial aid. Need-based:** 466 full-time freshmen applied for aid; 393 were judged to have need; 393 of these received aid. Average need met was 86%. Average scholarship/grant was $20,462; average loan $4,655. 67% of total undergraduate aid awarded as scholarships/grants, 33% as loans/jobs. **Non-need-based:** Awarded to 747 full-time undergraduates, including 174 freshmen. Scholarships awarded for academics, alumni affiliation, art, leadership, music/drama, religious affiliation. **Additional information:** Cooperative education allows qualified upperclassmen to alternate semesters of full-time study and full-time work.

**Application procedures. Admission:** Closing date 2/1 (postmark date). $40 fee, may be waived for applicants with need. Application may be submitted online. Admission notification 4/1. Must reply by May 1 or within 2 week(s) if notified thereafter. **Financial aid:** Priority date 2/1; no closing date. FAFSA required. Students applying for Early Decision must complete the CSS PROFILE for notification of need-based financial aid eligibility. Applicants notified on a rolling basis starting 3/15; must reply by 5/1 or within 2 week(s) of notification.

**Academics.** All students complete core curriculum, including courses in writing and rhetoric, scholarly and creative inquiry, fine arts, humanistic, mathematical, natural scientific and social scientific approaches, and a connections course intended to develop an understanding of the interrelationship of fields of knowledge. **Special study options:** Combined bachelor's/graduate degree, cooperative education, double major, honors, independent study, internships, student-designed major, study abroad, teacher certification program. Institution also offers community service opportunities, forensics & debate, diversity & leadership training, multiple speaker/lecturer programs, year of study in Asia, 3-2 engineering program, business leadership program. **Credit/placement by examination:** AP, CLEP, IB, institutional tests. **Support services:** Learning center, reduced course load, study skills assistance, tutoring, writing center.

**Majors. Area/ethnic studies:** Asian. **Biology:** General, biochemistry, cellular/molecular. **Business:** Business admin. **Communications:** General. **Computer sciences:** General, computer science. **Education:** Music. **English:** English lit. **Foreign languages:** Classics, French, German, Spanish. **History:** General. **Interdisciplinary:** Natural sciences, science/society. **Math:** General. **Parks/recreation:** Exercise sciences. **Philosophy/religion:** Philosophy, religion. **Physical sciences:** Chemistry, geology, physics. **Psychology:** General. **Social sciences:** Economics, international economics, political science, sociology. **Visual/performing arts:** Art, dramatic, music management, music performance.

**Most popular majors.** Biology 8%, business/marketing 16%, English 8%, foreign language 9%, psychology 8%, social sciences 19%, visual/performing arts 9%.

**Computing on campus.** 324 workstations in dormitories, library, computer center, student center. Dormitories wired for high-speed internet access and linked to campus network. Commuter students can connect to campus network. Online course registration, online library, helpline, repair service, student web hosting, wireless network available.

**Student life. Freshman orientation:** Available. 9-day introduction to academic life and campus community. **Housing:** Guaranteed on-campus for freshmen. Coed dorms, single-sex dorms, special housing for disabled, fraternity/sorority housing, substance-free housing available. $200 nonrefundable deposit, deadline 5/1. 56 university-owned homes on campus. Variety of theme houses and residence hall theme floors. **Activities:** Bands, choral groups, dance, drama, film society, literary magazine, music ensembles, musical theater, opera, radio station, student government, student newspaper, symphony orchestra, Black student union, Hui-o-Hawaii, Circle K, Jewish student organization, Bisexuals, Gays, Lesbians, and Allies for Diversity, Pacific American student union, Students for Peace and Justice, First Nations, Habitat for Humanity, film and theatre society.

**Athletics.** NCAA. **Intercollegiate:** Baseball M, basketball, cheerleading, cross-country, football (tackle) M, golf, lacrosse W, rowing (crew), soccer, softball W, swimming, tennis, track and field, volleyball W. **Intramural:** Basketball, football (non-tackle), soccer, softball, tennis, volleyball. **Team name:** Loggers.

**Student services.** Alcohol/substance abuse counseling, campus ministries, career counseling, student employment services, financial aid counseling, health services, legal services, minority student services, personal counseling, placement for graduates. **Physically disabled:** Services for visually, speech, hearing impaired.

**Contact.** E-mail: admission@ups.edu
Phone: (253) 879-3211 Toll-free number: (800) 396-7191
Fax: (253) 879-3993
George Mills, Vice President for Enrollment, University of Puget Sound, 1500 North Warner Street, Tacoma, WA 98416-1062

## University of Washington

| Seattle, Washington | CB member |
| --- | --- |
| www.washington.edu | CB code: 4854 |

- Public 4-year university
- Residential campus in very large city
- 26,509 degree-seeking undergraduates: 9% part-time, 52% women, 3% African American, 28% Asian American, 5% Hispanic American, 1% Native American, 4% international
- 11,648 degree-seeking graduate students
- 65% of applicants admitted
- SAT or ACT with writing, application essay required
- 75% graduate within 6 years

**General.** Founded in 1861. Regionally accredited. **Degrees:** 7,024 bachelor's awarded; master's, doctoral, first professional offered. **ROTC:** Army, Naval, Air Force. **Location:** 5 miles from downtown. **Calendar:** Quarter, extensive summer session. **Full-time faculty:** 2,640 total; 89% have terminal degrees, 17% minority, 36% women. **Part-time faculty:** 656 total; 83% have terminal degrees, 14% minority, 47% women. **Class size:** 35% < 20, 40% 20-39, 8% 40-49, 9% 50-99, 7% >100. **Special facilities:** Arboretum, observatory, anthropological museum, applied physics laboratory, planetarium.

**Freshman class profile.** 17,877 applied, 11,568 admitted, 5,338 enrolled.

| Mid 50% test scores | | | |
| --- | --- | --- | --- |
| SAT critical reading: | 530-650 | Rank in top quarter: | 97% |
| SAT math: | 560-670 | Rank in top tenth: | 86% |
| SAT writing: | 520-630 | Return as sophomores: | 92% |
| ACT composite: | 23-29 | Out-of-state: | 16% |
| GPA 3.50 or higher: | 80% | Live on campus: | 63% |
| GPA 3.0-3.49: | 19% | International: | 3% |
| GPA 2.0-2.99: | 1% | Fraternities: | 10% |
| | | Sororities: | 9% |

**Basis for selection.** Applicants evaluated and ranked on completion of core subject requirements, grades and test scores and supplemental factors including personal statement, completion of substantial number of courses beyond minimum, grades in college-preparatory courses, enrollment in AP or honors courses, cultural diversity and documented evidence of exceptional artistic talent. Auditions are required for admission to performing arts programs. Application interviews are not available, only informational appointments. **Homeschooled:** Each applicant is reviewed case-by-case. To confirm successful completion of certain core subject requirements or levels, applicants may be asked to provide additional documentation or placement testing information. **Learning Disabled:** Applicants with documented disabilities are not expected to disclose them at the time of application, but are welcome do so in the applicant's own written materials, or via relevant documentation or letters. Students are encouraged to first speak with an admissions counselor.

**High school preparation.** 15 units required; 20 recommended. Required and recommended units include English 4, mathematics 3-4, social studies 3-4, history 1, science 2-3 (laboratory 1-3), foreign language 2-3, computer science 1, visual/performing arts .5-1. One semester (.5) elective from required subjects list and .5 fine arts course.

**2007-2008 Annual costs.** Tuition/fees: $6,385; $22,131 out-of-state. Room/board: $9,198. Books/supplies: $1,008. Personal expenses: $2,265.

**2007-2008 Financial aid. Need-based:** Average need met was 88%. Average scholarship/grant was $5,300; average loan $3,650. 60% of total undergraduate aid awarded as scholarships/grants, 40% as loans/jobs. **Non-need-based:** Scholarships awarded for academics, alumni affiliation, art, athletics, leadership, music/drama, ROTC. **Additional information:** Tuition not due until third week of term.

**Application procedures. Admission:** Priority date 12/1; deadline 1/15 (postmark date). $50 fee, may be waived for applicants with need. Application may be submitted online. Admission notification 4/15. Admission notification on a rolling basis beginning on or about 12/1. Must reply by 5/1. Applications accepted after closing date on space-available basis. **Financial aid:** Priority date 2/28; no closing date. FAFSA required. Applicants notified by 3/31; must reply within 3 week(s) of notification.

**Academics. Special study options:** Combined bachelor's/graduate degree, cooperative education, distance learning, double major, ESL, exchange student, honors, independent study, internships, student-designed major, study abroad, teacher certification program, Washington semester. Quarter at Friday Harbor Laboratories, San Juan Islands. **Credit/placement by examination:** AP, CLEP, IB, institutional tests. 90 credit hours maximum toward bachelor's degree. **Support services:** Learning center, pre-admission summer program, reduced course load, remedial instruction, study skills assistance, tutoring, writing center.

**Majors. Architecture:** Architecture, landscape, urban/community planning. **Area/ethnic studies:** African, African-American, Asian, Asian-American, Canadian, Central/Eastern European, Chinese, European, French, German, Hispanic-American/Latino/Chicano, Italian, Japanese, Korean, Latin American, Native American, Near/Middle Eastern, Russian/Slavic, Scandinavian, Slavic, South Asian, Southeast Asian, women's. **Biology:** General, bacteriology, biochemistry, botany, ecology, marine, microbiology, zoology. **Business:** Accounting, business admin, construction management, finance, human resources, international, management information systems, organizational behavior. **Communications:** General. **Computer sciences:** General, computer science, information systems, information technology. **Conservation:** General, fisheries, forest resources, forestry, wildlife. **Education:** Music. **Engineering:** General, aerospace, biomedical, ceramic, chemical, civil, computer, electrical, environmental, forest, industrial, materials, materials science, mechanical, metallurgical. **English:** English lit, speech/rhetoric, technical writing. **Foreign languages:** Ancient Greek, Arabic, Chinese, classics, comparative lit, Danish, East Asian, French, German, Germanic, Hebrew, Italian, Japanese, Korean, Latin, linguistics, Norwegian, Russian, Scandinavian, South Asian, Southeast Asian, Spanish, Swedish, Turkish, Ukrainian. **Health:** Audiology/speech pathology, clinical lab science, dental hygiene, environmental health, nursing (RN), orthotics/prosthetics, physician assistant. **History:** General. **Interdisciplinary:** Peace/conflict. **Liberal arts:** Arts/sciences. **Math:** General, applied. **Philosophy/religion:** Judaic, philosophy, religion. **Physical sciences:** Astronomy, astrophysics, atmospheric science, chemistry, geology, oceanography, physics, planetary. **Psychology:** General. **Public administration:** Social work. **Social sciences:** General, anthropology, economics, geography, international relations, political science, sociology. **Visual/performing arts:** Art, art history/conservation, ceramics, commercial/advertising art, dance, dramatic, fiber arts, industrial design, metal/jewelry, music history, music performance, music theory/composition, musicology, painting, photography, piano/organ, printmaking, sculpture, stringed instruments, voice/opera.

**Most popular majors.** Biology 10%, business/marketing 10%, communications/journalism 6%, engineering/engineering technologies 9%, psychology 6%, social sciences 19%.

**Computing on campus.** 1,500 workstations in dormitories, library, computer center, student center. Dormitories wired for high-speed internet access and linked to campus network. Commuter students can connect to campus network. Online course registration, online library, helpline, repair service, student web hosting, wireless network available.

**Student life. Freshman orientation:** Mandatory, $250 fee. Preregistration for classes offered. Advising and registration throughout the summer. **Housing:** Guaranteed on-campus for freshmen. Coed dorms, special housing for disabled, apartments, cooperative housing, fraternity/sorority housing, substance-free housing available. $500 deposit, deadline 5/1. Special interest houses available. **Activities:** Bands, campus ministries, choral groups, dance, drama, film society, international student organizations, literary magazine, music ensembles, Model UN, musical theater, opera, radio station, student government, student newspaper, symphony orchestra, TV station, over 500 student organizations.

**Athletics.** NCAA. **Intercollegiate:** Baseball M, basketball, cheerleading, cross-country, football (tackle) M, golf, gymnastics W, rowing (crew), soccer, softball W, swimming, tennis, track and field, volleyball W. **Intramural:** Basketball, bowling, football (non-tackle), racquetball, rowing (crew), soccer, softball, swimming, tennis, volleyball. **Team name:** Huskies.

**Student services.** Alcohol/substance abuse counseling, career counseling, services for economically disadvantaged, student employment services, financial aid counseling, health services, legal services, minority student services, on-campus daycare, personal counseling, placement for graduates, veterans' counselor, women's services. **Physically disabled:** Services for visually, speech, hearing impaired.

**Contact.** Phone: (206) 543-9686 Fax: (206) 685-3655
Philip Ballinger, Director of Admissions, University of Washington, 1410 Northeast Campus Parkway, Box 355852, Seattle, WA 98195-5852

## Walla Walla University
**College Place, Washington**
**www.wallawalla.edu**                                    CB code: 4940

- Private 4-year university and liberal arts college affiliated with Seventh-day Adventists
- Residential campus in large town
- 1,586 degree-seeking undergraduates: 5% part-time, 48% women, 3% African American, 6% Asian American, 9% Hispanic American, 1% Native American, 1% international
- 218 degree-seeking graduate students
- 93% of applicants admitted
- SAT or ACT (ACT writing optional) required
- 51% graduate within 6 years

**General.** Founded in 1892. Regionally accredited. Branch campus in Portland, Oregon, for final two years of nursing program. Summer biology courses offered at marine research facility near Anacortes. Graduate social work program in Billings and Missoula, Montana. **Degrees:** 317 bachelor's, 5 associate awarded; master's offered. **Location:** 270 miles from Seattle, 250 miles from Portland, Oregon. **Calendar:** Quarter, extensive summer session. **Full-time faculty:** 117 total; 69% have terminal degrees, 5% minority, 35% women. **Part-time faculty:** 87 total; 13% have terminal degrees, 3% minority, 62% women. **Class size:** 67% < 20, 24% 20-39, 5% 40-49, 3% 50-99, less than 1% >100. **Special facilities:** Marine biological research facility, observatory.

**Freshman class profile.** 374 applied, 347 admitted, 346 enrolled.

| Mid 50% test scores | | Rank in top quarter: | 26% |
|---|---|---|---|
| ACT composite: | 20-26 | Rank in top tenth: | 12% |
| GPA 3.50 or higher: | 42% | Return as sophomores: | 73% |
| GPA 3.0-3.49: | 20% | Out-of-state: | 64% |
| GPA 2.0-2.99: | 24% | International: | 1% |

**Basis for selection.** Must have a combined 2.0 high school GPA. If entering with GED must have an average score of 500 or higher and each test must be 450 or higher. Official TOEFL scores required for prospective students whose first language is not English. ACT recommended. Audition recommended. **Homeschooled:** May be admitted by acceptable score on ACT test, GED test, or transcript from accredited home school organization.

**High school preparation.** 11 units required; 16 recommended. Required and recommended units include English 4, mathematics 3-4, social studies 1, history 2, science 2-3 (laboratory 2) and foreign language 2. Mathematics units must be algebra and geometry. 2 laboratory units recommended.

**2008-2009 Annual costs.** Tuition/fees (projected): $21,945. Room/board: $5,055. Books/supplies: $1,014. Personal expenses: $1,746.

**2006-2007 Financial aid. Need-based:** 302 full-time freshmen applied for aid; 216 were judged to have need; 216 of these received aid. Average need met was 90%. Average scholarship/grant was $6,429; average loan $6,374. 53% of total undergraduate aid awarded as scholarships/grants, 47% as loans/jobs. **Non-need-based:** Awarded to 984 full-time undergraduates, including 291 freshmen. Scholarships awarded for academics, leadership, music/drama.

**Application procedures. Admission:** Priority date 9/1; no deadline. $40 fee, may be waived for applicants with need. Application may be submitted online. Admission notification on a rolling basis beginning on or about 9/5. **Financial aid:** No deadline. FAFSA, institutional form required. Applicants notified on a rolling basis starting 3/15.

**Academics. Special study options:** Combined bachelor's/graduate degree, cooperative education, distance learning, double major, honors, independent study, internships, liberal arts/career combination, study abroad, teacher certification program. **Credit/placement by examination:** AP, CLEP,

IB, SAT, ACT, institutional tests. 12 credit hours maximum toward associate degree, 24 toward bachelor's. **Support services:** Learning center, preadmission summer program, reduced course load, remedial instruction, study skills assistance, tutoring, writing center.

**Majors. Biology:** General, biochemistry, biophysics. **Business:** Accounting, business admin, finance, human resources, international, management science. **Communications:** General, journalism, media studies. **Communications technology:** Graphic/printing. **Computer sciences:** General, computer graphics, computer science, data processing, information systems. **Education:** General, business, elementary, music, physical, special, voc/tech. **Engineering:** General, biomedical, civil, computer, electrical, mechanical. **English:** English lit. **Foreign languages:** French, German, Spanish. **Health:** Nursing (RN). **History:** General. **Liberal arts:** Arts/sciences. **Math:** General. **Mechanic/repair:** Automotive. **Philosophy/religion:** Religion. **Physical sciences:** Chemistry, physics. **Psychology:** General. **Public administration:** Social work. **Social sciences:** Sociology. **Theology:** Theology. **Visual/performing arts:** Art, music performance.

**Computing on campus.** 105 workstations in dormitories, library, computer center. Dormitories wired for high-speed internet access and linked to campus network. Commuter students can connect to campus network. Online course registration, online library, helpline, repair service, student web hosting, wireless network available.

**Student life. Freshman orientation:** Mandatory. Preregistration for classes offered. Held during week before classes begin. **Policies:** Chapel requirement once a week; worship policy for resident students. Religious observance required. **Housing:** Guaranteed on-campus for all undergraduates. Single-sex dorms, special housing for disabled, apartments available. **Activities:** Concert band, campus ministries, choral groups, drama, international student organizations, music ensembles, radio station, student government, student newspaper, symphony orchestra, TV station, student entepeneur group, student missionary groups, drama, foreign student organizations, academic department clubs, service clubs, music groups.

**Athletics.** NCCAA. **Intercollegiate:** Basketball, golf, ice hockey M, soccer M, softball W, volleyball. **Intramural:** Badminton, basketball, football (non-tackle), racquetball, soccer, softball, table tennis, tennis, volleyball. **Team name:** Wolves.

**Student services.** Campus ministries, career counseling, student employment services, financial aid counseling, health services, minority student services, on-campus daycare, personal counseling, placement for graduates, veterans' counselor. **Physically disabled:** Services for visually, speech, hearing impaired.

**Contact.** E-mail: info@wallawalla.edu
Phone: (509) 527-2327 Toll-free number: (800) 541-8900
Fax: (509) 527-2397
Dallas Weis, Vice President for Admissions and Marketing, Walla Walla University, 204 South College Avenue, College Place, WA 99324-3000

## Washington State University
**Pullman, Washington**                                    CB member
**www.wsu.edu**                                            CB code: 4705

- Public 4-year university
- Residential campus in large town
- 19,822 degree-seeking undergraduates: 13% part-time, 51% women, 2% African American, 6% Asian American, 5% Hispanic American, 1% Native American, 2% international
- 4,114 degree-seeking graduate students
- 76% of applicants admitted
- SAT or ACT (ACT writing optional), application essay required
- 63% graduate within 6 years

**General.** Founded in 1890. Regionally accredited. Regional campuses in Spokane, Tri-Cities, and Vancouver. **Degrees:** 4,797 bachelor's awarded; master's, doctoral, first professional offered. **ROTC:** Army, Naval, Air Force. **Location:** 80 miles from Spokane. **Calendar:** Semester, extensive summer session. **Full-time faculty:** 1,178 total; 91% have terminal degrees, 12% minority, 39% women. **Part-time faculty:** 474 total; 44% have terminal degrees, 6% minority, 48% women. **Class size:** 40% < 20, 35% 20-39, 7% 40-49, 12% 50-99, 7% >100. **Special facilities:** Anthropology museum, art museum, creamery, ecological reserve, geological collections, historic textiles and costume collection, entomological collection, observatory, planetarium, herbarium and mycological herbarium, soil monolith collection, veterinary anatomy teaching museum, laboratory for atmospheric research, laboratory for biotechnology and bioanalysis, electron microscopy center, environmental research center, geoanalytical laboratory, nuclear radiation center, social and economic sciences research center, state of Washington water research center, center for spectroscopy, music recording studio, center for teaching, learning and technology, vet teaching hospital, center for undergraduate research.

**Freshman class profile.** 10,853 applied, 8,240 admitted, 3,477 enrolled.

| Mid 50% test scores | | | |
|---|---|---|---|
| SAT critical reading: | 490-600 | End year in good standing: | 88% |
| SAT math: | 510-610 | Return as sophomores: | 84% |
| GPA 3.50 or higher: | 47% | Out-of-state: | 11% |
| GPA 3.0-3.49: | 38% | Live on campus: | 99% |
| GPA 2.0-2.99: | 15% | International: | 2% |
| Rank in top quarter: | 57% | Fraternities: | 16% |
| Rank in top tenth: | 36% | Sororities: | 23% |

**Basis for selection.** Admission based on combination of high school GPA and SAT or ACT scores, completion of course work, and personal statement. Special circumstances, community activities and recommendations considered in some cases. An appeal process is available for those denied admission. **Homeschooled:** Official transcripts from GED exam or an academic resume that provides documentation of all subjects studied, or proof that the home based instruction fulfills our core requirements must be provided. **Learning Disabled:** Upon acceptance student can opt to notify Disability Services of desire to have assistance with their disability.

**High school preparation.** 16 units required. Required and recommended units include English 4, mathematics 3-4, social studies 2, history 1, science 2 (laboratory 1), foreign language 2, visual/performing arts 1 and academic electives 1. Mathematics units must include one year each, algebra, geometry, and advanced algebra. Foreign language must be 2 years of single language (Native American or American Sign Language are accepted). One unit fine/performing arts or additional academic elective.

**2007-2008 Annual costs.** Tuition/fees: $6,866; $17,180 out-of-state. Room/board: $7,316. Books/supplies: $912. Personal expenses: $2,108.

**2006-2007 Financial aid. Need-based:** 2,281 full-time freshmen applied for aid; 1,218 were judged to have need; 1,212 of these received aid. Average need met was 75%. Average scholarship/grant was $5,747; average loan $3,005. 53% of total undergraduate aid awarded as scholarships/grants, 47% as loans/jobs. **Non-need-based:** Awarded to 3,932 full-time undergraduates, including 994 freshmen. Scholarships awarded for academics, alumni affiliation, art, athletics, job skills, leadership, minority status, music/drama, religious affiliation, ROTC, state residency.

**Application procedures. Admission:** Priority date 1/31; no deadline. $50 fee, may be waived for applicants with need. Application may be submitted online. Admission notification on a rolling basis beginning on or about 12/1. Must reply by May 1 or within 3 week(s) if notified thereafter. Applications accepted after May 1 and later if space is still available. **Financial aid:** Priority date 3/1; no closing date. FAFSA required. Applicants notified on a rolling basis starting 4/15.

**Academics. Special study options:** Accelerated study, combined bachelor's/graduate degree, cross-registration, distance learning, double major, dual enrollment of high school students, ESL, exchange student, honors, independent study, internships, liberal arts/career combination, student-designed major, study abroad, teacher certification program. **Credit/placement by examination:** AP, CLEP, IB, SAT, ACT, institutional tests. 60 credit hours maximum toward bachelor's degree. **Support services:** Learning center, study skills assistance, tutoring, writing center.

**Honors college/program.** Acceptance into the Honors College is competitive, and spaces are limited. Selection is based on GPA and SAT/ACT scores, essay responses, strength of high school curriculum, Running Start credits, AP/IP programs, honors courses, 2 letters of recommendation, one from a math or science teacher and one from an English teacher, and overall motivation, organizational skills, and a desire for challenge.

**Majors. Agriculture:** General, agronomy, animal sciences, business, communications, crop production, economics, horticultural science, mechanization, plant protection, soil science. **Architecture:** Architecture, landscape. **Area/ethnic studies:** American, Asian, women's. **Biology:** General, biochemistry, biomedical sciences, biotechnology, entomology, genetics, microbiology, molecular genetics, zoology. **Business:** General, accounting, business admin, construction management, e-commerce, entrepreneurial studies, finance, hospitality admin, human resources, insurance, international, management information systems, management science, managerial economics, marketing, real estate. **Communications:** Digital media, media studies. **Computer sciences:** General, computer science. **Conservation:** General, environmental science, forestry, wildlife. **Education:** General, agricultural, bilingual, biology, chemistry, early childhood, elementary, English, ESL, family/consumer sciences, foreign languages, French, German, health, history, kindergarten/preschool, mathematics, multi-level teacher, music, physical,

physics, reading, science, secondary, social studies, Spanish, special. **Engineering:** Agricultural, biomedical, chemical, civil, computer, electrical, manufacturing, materials, mechanical. **English:** English lit. **Family/consumer sciences:** General, clothing/textiles, family studies, food/nutrition, human nutrition. **Foreign languages:** General, French, German, linguistics, Russian, Spanish. **Health:** Athletic training, audiology/speech pathology, nursing (RN), premedicine. **History:** General. **Interdisciplinary:** Biological/physical sciences, global studies, neuroscience. **Legal studies:** Prelaw. **Liberal arts:** Arts/sciences, humanities. **Math:** General, applied. **Parks/recreation:** General, exercise sciences, sports admin. **Philosophy/religion:** Philosophy, religion. **Physical sciences:** General, chemistry, geology, physics. **Protective services:** Police science. **Psychology:** General. **Public administration:** Policy analysis. **Social sciences:** General, anthropology, economics, political science, sociology. **Visual/performing arts:** Art, dramatic, interior design, music performance, music theory/composition, studio arts. **Other:** Comparative ethnic studies.

**Most popular majors.** Biology 6%, business/marketing 18%, communications/journalism 9%, engineering/engineering technologies 6%, health sciences 7%, social sciences 15%.

**Computing on campus.** 2,500 workstations in dormitories, library, computer center, student center. Dormitories wired for high-speed internet access and linked to campus network. Commuter students can connect to campus network. Online course registration, online library, helpline, repair service, student web hosting, wireless network available.

**Student life. Freshman orientation:** Available, $150 fee. Preregistration for classes offered. Two-and-a half day program for students and families during the summer. **Housing:** Guaranteed on-campus for freshmen. Coed dorms, single-sex dorms, apartments, fraternity/sorority housing, substance-free housing available. $200 fully refundable deposit, deadline 6/1. Single undergraduate freshmen under 20 required to live on campus. **Activities:** Bands, choral groups, dance, drama, film society, literary magazine, music ensembles, opera, radio station, student government, student newspaper, symphony orchestra, TV station, Over 200 clubs and special interest groups.

**Athletics.** NCAA. **Intercollegiate:** Baseball M, basketball, cross-country, football (tackle) M, golf, rowing (crew) W, soccer W, swimming W, tennis W, track and field, volleyball W. **Intramural:** Badminton, basketball, football (non-tackle), golf, racquetball, soccer, softball, table tennis, tennis, volleyball, wrestling. **Team name:** Cougars.

**Student services.** Alcohol/substance abuse counseling, campus ministries, career counseling, student employment services, financial aid counseling, health services, legal services, minority student services, on-campus daycare, personal counseling, placement for graduates, veterans' counselor, women's services. **Physically disabled:** Services for visually, speech, hearing impaired.

**Contact.** E-mail: admiss2@wsu.edu
Phone: (509) 335-5586 Toll-free number: (888) 468-6978
Fax: (509) 335-4902
Wendy Peterson, Director of Admissions, Washington State University, 370 Lighty Student Services Bldg, Pullman, WA 99164-1067

---

## Western Washington University
**Bellingham, Washington**
www.wwu.edu

**CB member**
**CB code: 4947**

- Public 4-year university
- Residential campus in small city
- 12,967 degree-seeking undergraduates: 8% part-time, 55% women, 3% African American, 9% Asian American, 4% Hispanic American, 2% Native American
- 1,177 graduate students
- 73% of applicants admitted
- SAT or ACT (ACT writing optional), application essay required
- 64% graduate within 6 years

**General.** Founded in 1893. Regionally accredited. **Degrees:** 3,036 bachelor's awarded; master's offered. **Location:** 90 miles from Seattle. **Calendar:** Quarter, extensive summer session. **Full-time faculty:** 505 total; 90% have terminal degrees, 14% minority, 39% women. **Part-time faculty:** 232 total; 24% have terminal degrees, 9% minority, 57% women. **Class size:** 54% < 20, 33% 20-39, 3% 40-49, 7% 50-99, 2% >100. **Special facilities:** Wind tunnel, electron microscope, neutron generator laboratory, planetarium, air pollution laboratory, motor vehicle research laboratory, electronic music studio, 11-acre recreational park on lake, marine laboratory, intergrated laboratory network.

**Freshman class profile.** 8,850 applied, 6,447 admitted, 2,585 enrolled.

| Mid 50% test scores | | | |
|---|---|---|---|
| SAT critical reading: | 490-610 | GPA 2.0-2.99: | 5% |
| SAT math: | 500-610 | Rank in top quarter: | 60% |
| SAT writing: | 480-590 | Rank in top tenth: | 26% |
| ACT composite: | 21-26 | Return as sophomores: | 84% |
| GPA 3.50 or higher: | 53% | Out-of-state: | 9% |
| GPA 3.0-3.49: | 42% | Live on campus: | 87% |

**Basis for selection.** Academic achievement most significant factor. Curriculum rigor (level and difficulty of courses), grade trends, school, community activities, special talent, multicultural experience, personal circumstances considered. All students encouraged to take courses beyond minimums. Consideration given to motivation, achievements outside of classroom, multicultural experience, and attributes that will enhance institution's learning community. Audition recommended for music; portfolio required for art.

**High school preparation.** 16 units required. Required units include English 4, mathematics 3, social studies 3, science 2 (laboratory 1), foreign language 2, visual/performing arts .5, academic electives 0.5. Mathematics requirement includes 2 algebra. Sciences include 1 algebra-based chemistry or physics. Foreign language should be in 1 language. .5 fine arts and .5 academic elective required.

**2007-2008 Annual costs.** Tuition/fees: $5,301; $16,375 out-of-state. Room/board: $7,090. Books/supplies: $924. Personal expenses: $1,854.

**2007-2008 Financial aid. Need-based:** 1,783 full-time freshmen applied for aid; 943 were judged to have need; 912 of these received aid. Average need met was 90%. Average scholarship/grant was $6,816; average loan $3,255. 56% of total undergraduate aid awarded as scholarships/grants, 44% as loans/jobs. **Non-need-based:** Awarded to 496 full-time undergraduates, including 111 freshmen. Scholarships awarded for academics, alumni affiliation, art, athletics, job skills, leadership, minority status, music/drama, state residency. **Additional information:** Short-term student loans ranging from $100 to $1,000 available on a quarterly basis.

**Application procedures. Admission:** Closing date 3/1 (postmark date). $50 fee, may be waived for applicants with need. Application may be submitted online. Admission notification on a rolling basis beginning on or about 12/1. Must reply by May 1 or within 2 week(s) if notified thereafter. **Financial aid:** Priority date 2/15; no closing date. FAFSA required. Applicants notified on a rolling basis starting 3/20; must reply within 3 week(s) of notification.

**Academics. Special study options:** Distance learning, double major, ESL, exchange student, honors, independent study, internships, student-designed major, study abroad, teacher certification program. **Credit/placement by examination:** AP, CLEP, IB, institutional tests. 135 credit hours maximum toward bachelor's degree. **Support services:** Learning center, study skills assistance, tutoring, writing center.

**Majors. Area/ethnic studies:** American, Canadian, East Asian. **Biology:** General, biochemistry, botany, cell/histology, cellular/molecular, ecology, evolutionary, marine, zoology. **Business:** Accounting, business admin, finance, human resources, international, management information systems, marketing, operations. **Communications:** General, journalism. **Computer sciences:** General. **Conservation:** Environmental science, environmental studies. **Education:** Art, biology, chemistry, drama/dance, elementary, English, German, history, mathematics, music, physical, science, social science, social studies, Spanish, special, speech, technology/industrial arts. **Engineering technology:** Electrical, industrial, manufacturing, plastics. **English:** Creative writing, English lit. **Family/consumer sciences:** Child development. **Foreign languages:** General, French, German, linguistics, Spanish. **Health:** Audiology/speech pathology, community health services. **History:** General. **Interdisciplinary:** Accounting/computer science, biological/physical sciences. **Liberal arts:** Humanities. **Math:** General, applied. **Parks/recreation:** General, health/fitness. **Philosophy/religion:** Philosophy. **Physical sciences:** Chemistry, geology, geophysics, physics. **Psychology:** General, developmental. **Public administration:** Human services. **Social sciences:** Anthropology, archaeology, economics, geography, political science, sociology. **Visual/performing arts:** General, art, art history/conservation, ceramics, commercial/advertising art, dance, design, dramatic, drawing, fiber arts, graphic design, industrial design, multimedia, music history, music performance, music theory/composition, painting, photography, printmaking, sculpture.

**Most popular majors.** Business/marketing 13%, English 6%, psychology 6%, social sciences 14%.

**Computing on campus.** 2,132 workstations in dormitories, library, computer center, student center. Dormitories wired for high-speed internet access and linked to campus network. Commuter students can connect to campus network. Online course registration, online library, helpline, repair service, student web hosting, wireless network available.

**Student life. Freshman orientation:** Available. Preregistration for classes offered. 6 programs offered for students and family members, early-mid August. Program 1-2 days, based on housing needs. **Housing:** Coed dorms, special housing for disabled, apartments, substance-free housing available. $200 partly refundable deposit, deadline 6/15. Wellness floors, multicultural floors available. **Activities:** Bands, campus ministries, choral groups, dance, drama, film society, international student organizations, literary magazine, music ensembles, musical theater, opera, radio station, student government, student newspaper, symphony orchestra, TV station, Campus Christian Fellowship, veteran's outreach center, volunteer services and resources, international student club, The Inn (nondenominational), ethnic student center, Mecha, Circle K, American Red Cross chapter.

**Athletics.** NCAA. **Intercollegiate:** Basketball, cross-country, football (tackle) M, golf, rowing (crew), soccer, softball W, track and field, volleyball W. **Intramural:** Badminton, basketball, football (non-tackle), golf, racquetball, soccer, softball, table tennis, tennis, volleyball. **Team name:** Vikings.

**Student services.** Adult student services, alcohol/substance abuse counseling, campus ministries, career counseling, student employment services, financial aid counseling, health services, minority student services, on-campus daycare, personal counseling, placement for graduates, veterans' counselor. **Physically disabled:** Services for visually, speech, hearing impaired.

**Contact.** E-mail: admit@wwu.edu
Phone: (360) 650-3440 Fax: (360) 650-7369
Karen Copetas, Director of Admissions and Enrollment Planning, Western Washington University, 516 High Street, Bellingham, WA 98225-9009

## Whitman College
**Walla Walla, Washington**
**www.whitman.edu**

CB member
CB code: 4951

- Private 4-year liberal arts college
- Residential campus in large town
- 1,455 degree-seeking undergraduates: 1% part-time, 56% women, 2% African American, 10% Asian American, 5% Hispanic American, 1% Native American, 3% international
- 48% of applicants admitted
- SAT or ACT with writing, application essay required
- 86% graduate within 6 years

**General.** Founded in 1883. Regionally accredited. **Degrees:** 361 bachelor's awarded. **Location:** 150 miles from Spokane, 235 miles from Portland, Oregon. **Calendar:** Semester. **Full-time faculty:** 127 total; 96% with terminal degrees, 16% minority, 43% women. **Part-time faculty:** 56 total; 45% have terminal degrees, 4% minority, 54% women. **Class size:** 74% < 20, 24% 20-39, 2% 40-49, less than 1% 50-99. **Special facilities:** Asian art collection, natural history museum, planetarium, 2 electron microscopes, outdoor observatory, indoor and outdoor rock-climbing walls, outdoor sculpture walk, organic garden.

**Freshman class profile.** 2,892 applied, 1,398 admitted, 400 enrolled.

| Mid 50% test scores | | | |
|---|---|---|---|
| SAT critical reading: | 620-730 | Rank in top tenth: | 61% |
| SAT math: | 620-700 | End year in good standing: | 97% |
| SAT writing: | 610-700 | Return as sophomores: | 94% |
| ACT composite: | 27-32 | Out-of-state: | 63% |
| GPA 3.50 or higher: | 88% | Live on campus: | 100% |
| GPA 3.0-3.49: | 11% | International: | 3% |
| GPA 2.0-2.99: | 1% | Fraternities: | 34% |
| Rank in top quarter: | 91% | Sororities: | 28% |

**Basis for selection.** Scholastic record, quality of written expression, and level of motivation are very important. Evidence of talent, imagination, creativity, leadership, responsibility, and maturity are also considered. Writing for all students. TOEFL, ELPT, or APIEL accepted as language proficiency exams. Interview recommended.

**High school preparation.** 16 units recommended. Recommended units include English 4, mathematics 4, social studies 2, history 2, science 3 (laboratory 2), foreign language 2 and visual/performing arts 1.

**2008-2009 Annual costs.** Tuition/fees: $35,192. Room/board: $8,820. Books/supplies: $1,400.

**2007-2008 Financial aid. Need-based:** 248 full-time freshmen applied for aid; 191 were judged to have need; 191 of these received aid. Average need met was 95%. Average scholarship/grant was $22,650; average loan $4,013. 79% of total undergraduate aid awarded as scholarships/grants, 21% as loans/jobs. **Non-need-based:** Awarded to 493 full-time undergraduates,

including 111 freshmen. Scholarships awarded for academics, art, leadership, minority status, music/drama, religious affiliation, state residency.

**Application procedures. Admission:** Priority date 11/15; deadline 1/15 (postmark date). $45 fee, may be waived for applicants with need. Application may be submitted online. Admission notification 4/1. Must reply by May 1 or within 2 week(s) if notified thereafter. **Financial aid:** Priority date 11/15, closing date 2/1. FAFSA, CSS PROFILE required. Applicants notified on a rolling basis starting 12/20; must reply within 2 week(s) of notification.

**Academics.** Library open 24 hours, seven days a week during academic year. **Special study options:** Accelerated study, combined bachelor's/graduate degree, cooperative education, cross-registration, double major, dual enrollment of high school students, exchange student, honors, independent study, liberal arts/career combination, student-designed major, study abroad, urban semester, Washington semester. Study abroad opportunities in over 20 countries; Whitman-In-China allows recent graduates to spend a year teaching English in one of 3 Chinese universities; 3-2 engineering and computer science programs with California Institute of Technology, Columbia University (NY), Duke University (NC), Washington University (MO) and University of Washington; 3-2 oceanography and biology or geology program with University of Washington; 3-3 law program with Columbia University; 3-2 program with Monterey Institute of International Studies; 4-1 program with Bank Street College of Education; undergraduate research conference; semester in the West field study. **Credit/placement by examination:** AP, CLEP, IB, institutional tests. 30 credit hours maximum toward bachelor's degree. **Support services:** Learning center, reduced course load, study skills assistance, tutoring, writing center.

**Majors. Area/ethnic studies:** Asian, Latin American. **Biology:** General, Biochemistry/biophysics and molecular biology. **Conservation:** Environmental studies. **English:** English lit. **Foreign languages:** Classics, French, German, Spanish. **History:** General. **Math:** General. **Philosophy/religion:** Philosophy, religion. **Physical sciences:** Astronomy, chemistry, geology, physics. **Psychology:** General. **Social sciences:** Anthropology, economics, political science, sociology. **Visual/performing arts:** Art history/conservation, dramatic, film/cinema, studio arts. **Other:** Race and ethnic studies.

**Most popular majors.** Biology 15%, English 7%, history 9%, physical sciences 7%, psychology 8%, social sciences 26%, visual/performing arts 11%.

**Computing on campus.** 410 workstations in dormitories, library, computer center, student center. Dormitories wired for high-speed internet access and linked to campus network. Commuter students can connect to campus network. Online library, helpline, student web hosting available.

**Student life. Freshman orientation:** Available. **Housing:** Guaranteed on-campus for freshmen. Coed dorms, single-sex dorms, apartments, fraternity/sorority housing available. $300 nonrefundable deposit, deadline 5/1. German, French, Spanish, Japanese language houses. Asian Studies, multiethnic, environmental, fine arts, community service, writing, global awareness houses available, college-owned rentals. **Activities:** Bands, campus ministries, choral groups, dance, drama, film society, literary magazine, music ensembles, musical theater, radio station, student government, student newspaper, symphony orchestra, multiethnic cultural association, community service, political organizations, environmental groups, sexual-assault prevention educators.

**Athletics.** NCAA. **Intercollegiate:** Baseball M, basketball, cross-country, golf, skiing, soccer, swimming, tennis, volleyball W. **Intramural:** Basketball, bowling, football (non-tackle), soccer, tennis, triathlon, volleyball. **Team name:** Missionaries.

**Student services.** Adult student services, alcohol/substance abuse counseling, career counseling, student employment services, financial aid counseling, health services, minority student services, on-campus daycare, personal counseling, placement for graduates, veterans' counselor, women's services. **Physically disabled:** Services for visually, speech, hearing impaired.

**Contact.** E-mail: admission@whitman.edu
Phone: (509) 527-5176 Toll-free number: (877) 462-9448
Fax: (509) 527-4967
Tony Cabasco, Dean of Admission and Financial Aid, Whitman College, 345 Boyer Avenue, Walla Walla, WA 99362-2046

---

## Whitworth University
**Spokane, Washington**
www.whitworth.edu

**CB member**
**CB code: 4953**

- Private 4-year liberal arts college affiliated with Presbyterian Church (USA)
- Residential campus in large city

---

- 2,310 degree-seeking undergraduates: 12% part-time, 59% women, 2% African American, 3% Asian American, 3% Hispanic American, 1% Native American, 1% international
- 246 degree-seeking graduate students
- 49% of applicants admitted
- Application essay required
- 74% graduate within 6 years

**General.** Founded in 1890. Regionally accredited. **Degrees:** 506 bachelor's awarded; master's offered. **ROTC:** Army. **Location:** 6 miles from downtown, 280 miles from Seattle. **Calendar:** 4-1-4, limited summer session. **Full-time faculty:** 123 total; 74% have terminal degrees, 10% minority, 42% women. **Part-time faculty:** 165 total; 10% minority. **Class size:** 58% < 20, 35% 20-39, 4% 40-49, 2% 50-99, less than 1% >100.

**Freshman class profile.** 5,062 applied, 2,490 admitted, 533 enrolled.

| Mid 50% test scores | | | |
|---|---|---|---|
| SAT critical reading: | 550-650 | GPA 2.0-2.99: | 4% |
| SAT math: | 560-650 | End year in good standing: | 97% |
| SAT writing: | 540-640 | Return as sophomores: | 87% |
| ACT composite: | 25-29 | Out-of-state: | 45% |
| GPA 3.50 or higher: | 78% | Live on campus: | 96% |
| GPA 3.0-3.49: | 18% | International: | 1% |

**Basis for selection.** School achievement, extracurricular activities, recommendations most important. SAT or ACT recommended. Interview recommended.

**High school preparation.** College-preparatory program recommended. 18 units recommended. Recommended units include English 4, mathematics 3, social studies 3, history 3, science 3 (laboratory 2) and foreign language 2.

**2008-2009 Annual costs.** Tuition/fees: $27,420. Room/board: $7,700. Books/supplies: $912. Personal expenses: $1,682.

**2007-2008 Financial aid. Need-based:** 438 full-time freshmen applied for aid; 353 were judged to have need; 353 of these received aid. Average need met was 86%. Average scholarship/grant was $14,871; average loan $4,755. 66% of total undergraduate aid awarded as scholarships/grants, 34% as loans/jobs. **Non-need-based:** Awarded to 743 full-time undergraduates, including 201 freshmen. Scholarships awarded for academics, art, music/drama, ROTC.

**Application procedures. Admission:** Closing date 3/1 (postmark date). No application fee. Application may be submitted online. Admission notification on a rolling basis beginning on or about 12/20. Must reply by 5/1. **Financial aid:** Priority date 3/1; no closing date. FAFSA required. Applicants notified on a rolling basis starting 3/1; must reply by 5/1 or within 4 week(s) of notification.

**Academics. Special study options:** Accelerated study, cross-registration, distance learning, double major, dual enrollment of high school students, ESL, independent study, internships, student-designed major, study abroad, teacher certification program, Washington semester. 3-2 engineering programs. **Credit/placement by examination:** AP, CLEP, IB, SAT, ACT, institutional tests. 32 credit hours maximum toward bachelor's degree. **Support services:** Learning center, reduced course load, study skills assistance, tutoring, writing center.

**Majors. Area/ethnic studies:** American. **Biology:** General. **Business:** Accounting, business admin, international, marketing. **Communications:** General, journalism. **Computer sciences:** General, computer science. **Education:** General, biology, chemistry, elementary, ESL, French, history, mathematics, middle, multi-level teacher, music, physical, physics, secondary, Spanish, special, speech. **Engineering:** General. **English:** English lit. **Foreign languages:** French, Spanish. **Health:** Athletic training, nursing (RN). **History:** General. **Interdisciplinary:** Peace/conflict. **Liberal arts:** Arts/sciences. **Math:** General, applied. **Parks/recreation:** Health/fitness. **Philosophy/religion:** Philosophy. **Physical sciences:** Chemistry, physics. **Psychology:** General. **Social sciences:** General, economics, international relations, political science, sociology. **Theology:** Theology. **Visual/performing arts:** General, art, jazz, music performance, piano/organ, theater history, voice/opera.

**Most popular majors.** Business/marketing 20%, education 10%, liberal arts 7%, social sciences 8%, theological studies 7%, visual/performing arts 7%.

**Computing on campus.** 150 workstations in library, computer center, student center. Dormitories wired for high-speed internet access and linked to campus network. Commuter students can connect to campus network. Online course registration, helpline, repair service available.

**Student life. Freshman orientation:** Mandatory. Preregistration for classes offered. **Housing:** Guaranteed on-campus for freshmen. Coed dorms, single-sex dorms, special housing for disabled, apartments available. $100 partly refundable deposit, deadline 5/1. Theme houses. **Activities:** Bands, campus ministries, choral groups, dance, drama, international student organizations, literary magazine, music ensembles, Model UN, musical theater, radio station, student government, student newspaper, symphony orchestra, Black Student Union, Fellowship of Christian Athletes, international club, Hawaiian club, political activist club, Native American club, Amnesty International, Habitat for Humanity, Asian American club, Circle-K International.

**Athletics.** NCAA. **Intercollegiate:** Baseball M, basketball, cross-country, football (tackle) M, golf, soccer, softball W, swimming, tennis, track and field, volleyball W. **Intramural:** Basketball, soccer, softball, table tennis, tennis, volleyball. **Team name:** Pirates.

**Student services.** Adult student services, campus ministries, career counseling, student employment services, financial aid counseling, health services, minority student services, personal counseling, placement for graduates, veterans' counselor. **Physically disabled:** Services for visually, speech, hearing impaired.

**Contact.** E-mail: admissions@whitworth.edu
Phone: (509) 777-4786 Toll-free number: (800) 533-4668
Fax: (509) 777-3758
Fred Pfursich, Dean of Enrollment Services, Whitworth University, 300 West Hawthorne Road, Spokane, WA 99251-0002

# West Virginia

## Alderson-Broaddus College
**Philippi, West Virginia**
www.ab.edu                                    CB code: 5005

- Private 4-year liberal arts college affiliated with American Baptist Churches in the USA
- Commuter campus in small town
- 616 degree-seeking undergraduates: 7% part-time, 68% women, 5% African American, 2% Asian American, 1% Hispanic American, 1% international
- 117 degree-seeking graduate students
- 70% of applicants admitted
- SAT and SAT Subject Tests or ACT (ACT writing optional) required
- 49% graduate within 6 years; 15% enter graduate study

**General.** Founded in 1871. Regionally accredited. **Degrees:** 130 bachelor's, 10 associate awarded; master's offered. **Location:** 100 miles from Charleston, 125 miles from Pittsburgh. **Calendar:** Semester, limited summer session. **Full-time faculty:** 58 total; 48% have terminal degrees, 12% minority, 60% women. **Part-time faculty:** 38 total; 34% have terminal degrees, 8% minority, 42% women. **Class size:** 80% < 20, 16% 20-39, 4% 40-49. **Special facilities:** Gross anatomy laboratory, hydro-therapy pool.

**Freshman class profile.** 671 applied, 471 admitted, 153 enrolled.

| Mid 50% test scores | | | |
|---|---|---|---|
| SAT critical reading: | 440-530 | Rank in top quarter: | 50% |
| SAT math: | 430-530 | Rank in top tenth: | 19% |
| SAT writing: | 430-510 | End year in good standing: | 84% |
| ACT composite: | 19-23 | Return as sophomores: | 68% |
| GPA 3.50 or higher: | 40% | Out-of-state: | 17% |
| GPA 3.0-3.49: | 37% | Live on campus: | 76% |
| GPA 2.0-2.99: | 22% | International: | 1% |

**Basis for selection.** High school record, rank in top half of class, test scores, interview very important. Physician's assistant and nursing applicants should have strong background in science. Interview required for physician's assistant applicants, recommended for all others. Audition required for music. **Homeschooled:** ACT/SAT and results from Iowa Tests required.

**High school preparation.** College-preparatory program recommended. 10 units required; 15 recommended. Required and recommended units include English 4, mathematics 3, social studies 2, history 2, science 3 (laboratory 3) and foreign language 1.

**2008-2009 Annual costs.** Tuition/fees: $21,020. Room/board: $6,798. Books/supplies: $800. Personal expenses: $1,500.

**2006-2007 Financial aid. Need-based:** 138 full-time freshmen applied for aid; 133 were judged to have need; 133 of these received aid. Average need met was 82%. Average scholarship/grant was $14,793; average loan $3,464. 61% of total undergraduate aid awarded as scholarships/grants, 39% as loans/jobs. **Non-need-based:** Awarded to 107 full-time undergraduates, including 25 freshmen. Scholarships awarded for academics, athletics, music/drama.

**Application procedures. Admission:** No deadline. $25 fee, may be waived for applicants with need. Application may be submitted online. Admission notification on a rolling basis. **Financial aid:** Priority date 3/1; no closing date. FAFSA required. Applicants notified on a rolling basis starting 2/15; must reply within 2 week(s) of notification.

**Academics. Special study options:** Double major, honors, independent study, internships, liberal arts/career combination, study abroad, teacher certification program. Business department offers an on-line certificate program. **Credit/placement by examination:** AP, CLEP, SAT, ACT, institutional tests. 40 credit hours maximum toward associate degree, 60 toward bachelor's. **Support services:** Learning center, reduced course load, remedial instruction, study skills assistance, tutoring.

**Majors. Biology:** General. **Business:** Accounting, business admin, marketing. **Communications:** General. **Computer sciences:** Computer science. **Conservation:** Environmental science. **Education:** Elementary, music, physical, secondary. **English:** Creative writing, English lit. **Family/consumer sciences:** Family systems. **Health:** Health services, medical radiologic technology/radiation therapy, nursing (RN), physician assistant, recreational therapy. **History:** General. **Liberal arts:** Arts/sciences. **Math:** Applied. **Parks/recreation:** Facilities management, sports admin. **Philosophy/religion:** Christian. **Physical sciences:** Chemistry. **Psychology:** General. **Social sciences:** Political science. **Visual/performing arts:** Dramatic, music performance, studio arts. **Other:** Natural science.

**Most popular majors.** Biology 6%, business/marketing 14%, education 9%, health sciences 46%, visual/performing arts 6%.

**Computing on campus.** 95 workstations in dormitories, library, student center. Dormitories wired for high-speed internet access and linked to campus network. Commuter students can connect to campus network. Online library, helpline, student web hosting, wireless network available.

**Student life. Freshman orientation:** Available. Preregistration for classes offered. On Saturday prior to start of fall classes. **Policies:** Participation in campus activities stressed. Voluntary weekly chapel service offered. **Housing:** Guaranteed on-campus for all undergraduates. Coed dorms, single-sex dorms, special housing for disabled, apartments, substance-free housing available. $100 fully refundable deposit. **Activities:** Bands, campus ministries, choral groups, dance, drama, literary magazine, music ensembles, musical theater, opera, radio station, student government, student newspaper, TV station, A-B Collegiate 4-H, association of women's studies, College Players, Fellowship of Christian Athletes, Students in Free Enterprise, Students Learning in Community Education, A-B mission team.

**Athletics.** NCAA. **Intercollegiate:** Baseball M, basketball, cross-country, soccer M, softball W, track and field, volleyball W. **Intramural:** Basketball, football (non-tackle), racquetball, soccer, softball W, tennis, volleyball. **Team name:** Battlers.

**Student services.** Adult student services, alcohol/substance abuse counseling, campus ministries, career counseling, financial aid counseling, health services, personal counseling, placement for graduates, veterans' counselor. **Physically disabled:** Services for visually, hearing impaired.

**Contact.** E-mail: admissions@ab.edu
Phone: (304) 457-6256 Toll-free number: (800) 263-1549
Fax: (304) 457-6239
Kimberly Klaus, Director of Admissions, Alderson-Broaddus College, 101 College Hill Drive, Philippi, WV 26416

## American Public University System
**Charles Town, West Virginia**
www.apus.edu

- For-profit 4-year virtual university and liberal arts college
- Small town
- 20,201 degree-seeking undergraduates
- 7,523 graduate students

**General.** Accredited by DETC. Regionally and nationally accredited online institution serving military and public service communities through the American Military University and American Public University. **Degrees:** 562 bachelor's, 165 associate awarded; master's offered. **Location:** Online university. **Calendar:** Continuous. **Full-time faculty:** 97 total. **Part-time faculty:** 325 total.

**Basis for selection.** Open admission.

**2007-2008 Annual costs.** Tuition/fees: $7,500. Distance learning only. Personal expenses: $1,840.

**Financial aid. Additional information:** Students should complete a Federal Student Aid Intent Form and register for classes at least 37 days prior to start to allow sufficient time for financial aid process.

**Application procedures. Admission:** No deadline. No application fee. Application must be submitted online. Admission notification on a rolling basis. **Financial aid:** No deadline. FAFSA, institutional form required. Applicants notified on a rolling basis; must reply within 14 week(s) of notification.

**Academics. Credit/placement by examination:** CLEP. **Support services:** Remedial instruction, study skills assistance, tutoring.

**Majors. Area/ethnic studies:** African-American, Asian, Near/Middle Eastern. **Business:** Business admin, hospitality admin, marketing. **Computer sciences:** Information technology. **Conservation:** Environmental studies. **English:** English lit. **Family/consumer sciences:** Child development, family systems. **History:** General. **Legal studies:** General. **Parks/recreation:** Sports admin. **Philosophy/religion:** Philosophy, religion. **Protective services:** Emergency management/homeland security, fire services admin, law enforcement admin, security management. **Psychology:** General. **Social sciences:** International relations, political science, sociology. **Transportation:** Aviation. **Other:** International peace and conflict resolution, Military history, Transportation and logistics management.

**Most popular majors.** Business/marketing 23%, military 20%, security/protective services 27%, social sciences 6%.

**Computing on campus.** PC or laptop required. Online library available.

**Student life. Freshman orientation:** Mandatory. Preregistration for classes offered.

**Contact.** E-mail: info@apus.edu
Phone: (877) 468-6268 Toll-free number: (877) 468-6268
Fax: (304) 724-3787
Terry Grant, Director of Admissions, American Public University System, 111 West Congress Street, Charles Town, WV 25414

## Appalachian Bible College
**Bradley, West Virginia**
**www.abc.edu**                                              CB code: 7305

- Private 4-year Bible college affiliated with nondenominational tradition
- Residential campus in rural community
- 223 degree-seeking undergraduates: 6% part-time, 44% women
- 62% of applicants admitted
- SAT or ACT (ACT writing optional), application essay required

**General.** Founded in 1950. Regionally accredited; also accredited by ABHE. **Degrees:** 41 bachelor's, 12 associate awarded; master's offered. **Location:** 5 miles from Beckley. **Calendar:** Semester, limited summer session. **Full-time faculty:** 10 total. **Part-time faculty:** 5 total.

**Freshman class profile.** 117 applied, 73 admitted, 58 enrolled.

| Mid 50% test scores | | | |
|---|---|---|---|
| | | ACT composite: | 19-26 |
| SAT critical reading: | 440-610 | Out-of-state: | 64% |
| SAT math: | 430-580 | Live on campus: | 89% |

**Basis for selection.** Profession of Jesus Christ as Savior, essential agreement with doctrinal statement of college, approved character very important. Minimum 2.0 GPA, test scores, achievement and potential in English also considered. If no scores are submitted, student must test on first available test date after enrollment and must take developmental English. Interview recommended. **Homeschooled:** Must provide accurate record of curriculum used, subjects studied, grades earned for grade levels 9-12.

**High school preparation.** Recommended units include English 4, mathematics 3, social studies 3, history 3, science 3, foreign language 1 and academic electives 4.

**2007-2008 Annual costs.** Tuition/fees: $9,270. Room/board: $4,920. Books/supplies: $1,100. Personal expenses: $1,115.

**2007-2008 Financial aid.** All financial aid based on need. 76% of total undergraduate aid awarded as scholarships/grants, 24% as loans/jobs.

**Application procedures. Admission:** No deadline. $20 fee, may be waived for applicants with need. Application may be submitted online. Admission notification on a rolling basis. **Financial aid:** Closing date 6/15. FAFSA, institutional form required. Applicants notified on a rolling basis starting 6/15; must reply by 8/1 or within 4 week(s) of notification.

**Academics. Special study options:** Cooperative education, dual enrollment of high school students, independent study, internships, teacher certification program. **Credit/placement by examination:** AP, CLEP, SAT, ACT, institutional tests. 29 credit hours maximum toward bachelor's degree. **Support services:** Reduced course load, remedial instruction, study skills assistance, tutoring.

**Majors. Theology:** Bible.

**Computing on campus.** 10 workstations in library. Dormitories wired for high-speed internet access and linked to campus network. Commuter students can connect to campus network. Online library, repair service available.

**Student life. Freshman orientation:** Mandatory. Preregistration for classes offered. Held for 3 days immediately prior to beginning of semester. **Policies:** Chapel held three times a week. Annual Spiritual Life Conference,

Distinguished Christian Lecture Series, Bible and missions conferences. Religious observance required. **Housing:** Single-sex dorms, apartments, substance-free housing available. $25 nonrefundable deposit. **Activities:** Choral groups, drama, music ensembles, student government.

**Athletics.** NCCAA. **Intercollegiate:** Basketball, soccer M, volleyball W. **Intramural:** Basketball, soccer M, table tennis, tennis, volleyball. **Team name:** Warriors.

**Student services.** Career counseling, financial aid counseling, health services, personal counseling, placement for graduates, veterans' counselor.

**Contact.** E-mail: admissions@abc.edu
Phone: (304) 877-6428 ext. 3213 Toll-free number: (800) 678-9222
Fax: (304) 877-5082
Karen Nelson, Director of Admissions, Appalachian Bible College, PO Box ABC, Bradley, WV 25818-1353

## Bethany College
**Bethany, West Virginia**                                   CB member
**www.bethanywv.edu**                                        CB code: 5060

- Private 4-year liberal arts college affiliated with Christian Church (Disciples of Christ)
- Residential campus in rural community
- 815 degree-seeking undergraduates: 54% women
- 60% of applicants admitted
- SAT or ACT (ACT writing recommended), application essay required
- 70% graduate within 6 years; 37% enter graduate study

**General.** Founded in 1840. Regionally accredited. Center for Spirituality; Center for Global Initiatives. **Degrees:** 197 bachelor's awarded. **Location:** 14 miles from Wheeling, 40 miles from Pittsburgh. **Calendar:** Semester. **Full-time faculty:** 51 total; 72% have terminal degrees, 10% minority, 29% women. **Part-time faculty:** 39 total; 10% have terminal degrees, 62% women. **Class size:** 79% < 20, 18% 20-39, 2% 40-49, 2% 50-99. **Special facilities:** 1300 acres of nature preserves, 5 national historic sites, equestrian center adjacent to campus.

**Freshman class profile.** 1,328 applied, 802 admitted, 249 enrolled.

| Mid 50% test scores | | | |
|---|---|---|---|
| | | GPA 2.0-2.99: | 34% |
| SAT critical reading: | 440-570 | Rank in top quarter: | 31% |
| SAT math: | 440-550 | Rank in top tenth: | 12% |
| SAT writing: | 430-550 | End year in good standing: | 82% |
| ACT composite: | 18-24 | Return as sophomores: | 66% |
| GPA 3.50 or higher: | 28% | Live on campus: | 98% |
| GPA 3.0-3.49: | 37% | | |

**Basis for selection.** Rank in top half of graduating class, test scores, interview, activities, and recommendations important. Interviews are strongly reccommended, but not required. **Homeschooled:** Statement describing homeschool structure and mission required. **Learning Disabled:** Submit official diagnosis of learning disability after acceptance.

**High school preparation.** 15 units required. Required and recommended units include English 4, mathematics 3, social studies 3, science 3 (laboratory 1), foreign language 2 and academic electives 2.

**2007-2008 Annual costs.** Tuition/fees: $18,205. Room/board: $7,777. Books/supplies: $600. Personal expenses: $900.

**Financial aid. Non-need-based:** Scholarships awarded for academics, alumni affiliation, art, leadership, music/drama, religious affiliation. **Additional information:** Scholarships available for travel program.

**Application procedures. Admission:** Priority date 4/1; no deadline. $25 fee, may be waived for applicants with need. Application may be submitted online. Admission notification on a rolling basis beginning on or about 10/1. Must reply by May 1 or within 3 week(s) if notified thereafter. **Financial aid:** Priority date 3/1, closing date 5/1. FAFSA required. Applicants notified on a rolling basis starting 2/1; must reply within 3 week(s) of notification.

**Academics.** Students with learning disabilities must apply by Febuary 15 for priority consideration in limited-enrollment learning disabled program. **Special study options:** Accelerated study, combined bachelor's/graduate degree, double major, dual enrollment of high school students, ESL, independent study, internships, liberal arts/career combination, student-designed major, study abroad, teacher certification program, United Nations semester, Washington semester. **Credit/placement by examination:** AP, CLEP, IB, SAT, ACT, institutional tests. 80 credit hours maximum toward bachelor's degree. **Support services:** Learning center, remedial instruction, study skills assistance, tutoring, writing center.

**Majors. Biology:** General, biochemistry. **Business:** General, accounting, finance, international, international finance. **Communications:** General, advertising, broadcast journalism, journalism, public relations, radio/tv. **Communications technology:** Graphics. **Computer sciences:** General, computer science. **Conservation:** Environmental studies. **Education:** General, art, biology, chemistry, elementary, English, foreign languages, French, German, history, learning disabled, mathematics, multi-level teacher, multiple handicapped, physical, secondary, social studies, Spanish, special. **English:** English lit. **Foreign languages:** French, German, Spanish. **History:** General. **Interdisciplinary:** Biological/physical sciences, global studies, math/computer science. **Math:** General. **Parks/recreation:** Health/fitness, sports admin. **Philosophy/religion:** Philosophy, religion. **Physical sciences:** Chemistry, physics. **Psychology:** General. **Public administration:** Social work. **Social sciences:** Economics, international relations, political science. **Visual/performing arts:** General, art, design, dramatic, studio arts.

**Most popular majors.** Biology 7%, business/marketing 10%, communications/journalism 15%, education 14%, interdisciplinary studies 10%, psychology 15%.

**Computing on campus.** 145 workstations in dormitories, library, computer center, student center. Dormitories wired for high-speed internet access and linked to campus network. Commuter students can connect to campus network. Online library, helpline, repair service, student web hosting, wireless network available.

**Student life. Freshman orientation:** Mandatory, $100 fee. Preregistration for classes offered. Summer registration and orientation to campus and facilities and/or pre-college orientation in late August for students who cannot participate in summer programs. **Housing:** Guaranteed on-campus for all undergraduates. Coed dorms, single-sex dorms, special housing for disabled, apartments, fraternity/sorority housing available. Off-campus housing available in the village of Bethany for students who meet requirements. **Activities:** Bands, choral groups, dance, drama, film society, international student organizations, literary magazine, music ensembles, Model UN, musical theater, radio station, student government, student newspaper, TV station, community service organization, ecumenical religious organization, multicultural students club, advertising club, social work club, Amnesty International, Coalition for Christian Outreach, Circle K, equestrian club.

**Athletics.** NCAA. **Intercollegiate:** Baseball M, basketball, cheerleading, cross-country, diving, football (tackle) M, golf M, soccer, softball W, swimming, tennis, track and field, volleyball W. **Intramural:** Basketball, football (non-tackle) M, handball, racquetball, soccer, softball, swimming, tennis, volleyball. **Team name:** Bison.

**Student services.** Alcohol/substance abuse counseling, campus ministries, career counseling, student employment services, financial aid counseling, health services, minority student services, personal counseling, placement for graduates, women's services. **Physically disabled:** Services for visually, speech, hearing impaired. **Learning disabled:** Comprehensive services available.

**Contact.** E-mail: kwilson@bethanywv.edu
Phone: (304) 829-7611 Toll-free number: (800) 922-7611
Fax: (304) 829-7142
Kevin Wilson, Director of Admission, Bethany College, Office of Admission, Bethany, WV 26032-0428

## Bluefield State College
**Bluefield, West Virginia**
www.bluefieldstate.edu                CB code: 5064

- Public 4-year liberal arts and technical college
- Commuter campus in large town
- 1,693 degree-seeking undergraduates: 16% part-time, 60% women, 12% African American, 1% Asian American, 1% international
- 91% of applicants admitted
- SAT or ACT with writing required

**General.** Founded in 1895. Regionally accredited. Off-campus locations at Lewisburg, Welch, Beckley, and Summersville. **Degrees:** 223 bachelor's, 105 associate awarded. **Location:** 100 miles from Charleston, 100 miles from Roanoke, Virginia. **Calendar:** Semester, limited summer session. **Full-time faculty:** 85 total; 47% have terminal degrees, 9% minority, 49% women. **Part-time faculty:** 60 total; 8% have terminal degrees, 7% minority, 62% women. **Class size:** 63% < 20, 35% 20-39, 3% 40-49. **Special facilities:** Instructional technology center.

**Freshman class profile.** 445 applied, 404 admitted, 319 enrolled.

| Mid 50% test scores | | | |
|---|---|---|---|
| SAT critical reading: | 380-520 | GPA 2.0-2.99: | 28% |
| SAT math: | 400-540 | Return as sophomores: | 62% |
| ACT composite: | 17-21 | Out-of-state: | 15% |
| GPA 3.50 or higher: | 35% | Fraternities: | 1% |
| GPA 3.0-3.49: | 35% | Sororities: | 1% |

**Basis for selection.** 2.5 minimum GPA, college preparatory program, test scores required for applicants to health, teacher education, humanities, social science and business administration programs. High school requirements not necessary for associate's program.

**High school preparation.** 17 units required. Required units include English 4, mathematics 4, social studies 3, history 1, science 3 (laboratory 2), foreign language 2 and academic electives 1.

**2007-2008 Annual costs.** Tuition/fees: $3,984; $8,160 out-of-state. Tuition for students residing in border counties will pay $5,720. Books/supplies: $1,600. Personal expenses: $2,840.

**2007-2008 Financial aid. Need-based:** Average need met was 70%. Average scholarship/grant was $3,000; average loan $3,300. 54% of total undergraduate aid awarded as scholarships/grants, 46% as loans/jobs. **Non-need-based:** Scholarships awarded for academics, alumni affiliation, art, athletics, job skills, leadership, minority status, music/drama, state residency.

**Application procedures. Admission:** No deadline. No application fee. Application may be submitted online. Admission notification on a rolling basis. **Financial aid:** Closing date 3/1. FAFSA, institutional form required. Applicants notified by 5/1.

**Academics. Special study options:** Distance learning, honors, internships, liberal arts/career combination, student-designed major, teacher certification program. **Credit/placement by examination:** AP, CLEP, IB, ACT, institutional tests. **Support services:** Learning center, pre-admission summer program, reduced course load, remedial instruction, study skills assistance, tutoring, writing center.

**Majors. Business:** Accounting, business admin. **Computer sciences:** General. **Education:** Elementary, middle. **Engineering technology:** Architectural, civil, electrical, mechanical, mining. **Health:** Medical radiologic technology/radiation therapy, nursing (RN). **Interdisciplinary:** Biological/physical sciences. **Liberal arts:** Arts/sciences. **Protective services:** Criminal justice. **Social sciences:** General.

**Most popular majors.** Business/marketing 26%, computer/information sciences 13%, education 15%, engineering/engineering technologies 19%, health sciences 13%, liberal arts 15%.

**Computing on campus.** 358 workstations in library, computer center. Online library, helpline, student web hosting, wireless network available.

**Student life. Freshman orientation:** Available. Preregistration for classes offered. One day in July or August. **Housing:** Off-campus housing services provided. **Activities:** Campus ministries, choral groups, international student organizations, Model UN, radio station, student government, student newspaper, Minorities on the Move, student nurses association.

**Athletics.** NCAA. **Intercollegiate:** Baseball M, basketball, cheerleading, cross-country, golf M, softball W, tennis, volleyball W. **Intramural:** Badminton, basketball, bowling, football (non-tackle) M, golf, racquetball, softball, swimming, table tennis, tennis, volleyball. **Team name:** Big Blues.

**Student services.** Career counseling, student employment services, financial aid counseling, health services, minority student services, personal counseling, placement for graduates, veterans' counselor. **Physically disabled:** Services for visually, speech, hearing impaired.

**Contact.** E-mail: bscadmit@bluefieldstate.edu
Phone: (304) 327-4065 Toll-free number: (800) 654-7798
Fax: (304) 325-7747
John Cardwell, Director of Enrollment Management, Bluefield State College, 219 Rock Street, Bluefield, WV 24701

## Concord University
**Athens, West Virginia**
www.concord.edu                CB member
                               CB code: 5120

- Public 4-year university
- Residential campus in small town
- 2,671 degree-seeking undergraduates: 17% part-time, 59% women

♦  23 graduate students
♦  69% of applicants admitted
♦  SAT or ACT (ACT writing optional) required

**General.** Founded in 1872. Regionally accredited. **Degrees:** 403 bachelor's, 2 associate awarded; master's offered. **Location:** 5 miles from Princeton, 80 miles from Charleston. **Calendar:** Semester, extensive summer session. **Full-time faculty:** 104 total; 61% have terminal degrees, 44% women. **Part-time faculty:** 88 total; 16% have terminal degrees, 54% women. **Class size:** 60% < 20, 32% 20-39, 5% 40-49, 3% 50-99, less than 1% >100. **Special facilities:** Southern West Virginia technology center.

**Freshman class profile.** 1,975 applied, 1,359 admitted, 628 enrolled.

| Mid 50% test scores | | | |
|---|---|---|---|
| SAT critical reading: | 410-540 | ACT composite: | 18-24 |
| SAT math: | 390-540 | Return as sophomores: | 63% |

**Basis for selection.** 2.0 high school GPA and 810 SAT (exclusive of Writing) required. **Homeschooled:** Statement describing homeschool structure and mission, transcript of courses and grades required.

**High school preparation.** Required units include English 4, mathematics 3, social studies 2, history 1, science 1 (laboratory 2). Mathematics courses must include algebra I and another higher level course. Social science requirement includes 1 US history.

**2007-2008 Annual costs.** Tuition/fees: $4,414; $9,806 out-of-state. Room/board: $6,280. Books/supplies: $1,500. Personal expenses: $2,169.

**2006-2007 Financial aid. Need-based:** 41% of total undergraduate aid awarded as scholarships/grants, 59% as loans/jobs. **Non-need-based:** Scholarships awarded for academics, alumni affiliation, art, athletics, job skills, leadership, minority status, music/drama, state residency. **Additional information:** Room and board may be paid in 2 installments each semester: 60% at registration, 40% six weeks later. March 1 is priority deadline for state forms. April 15 is priority deadline for FAFSA.

**Application procedures. Admission:** No deadline. No application fee. Admission notification on a rolling basis beginning on or about 9/1. **Financial aid:** FAFSA, institutional form required. Applicants notified on a rolling basis starting 3/1; must reply within 2 week(s) of notification.

**Academics. Special study options:** Cooperative education, distance learning, double major, dual enrollment of high school students, ESL, honors, internships, liberal arts/career combination, student-designed major, study abroad, teacher certification program. English as a second language program for foreign students, mentoring programs for pre-law and pre-med students. **Credit/placement by examination:** AP, CLEP, SAT, ACT, institutional tests. **Support services:** Learning center, reduced course load, remedial instruction, study skills assistance, tutoring, writing center.

**Majors. Biology:** General, genetics. **Business:** General, accounting, business admin, finance, hospitality admin, hospitality/recreation, hotel/motel admin, human resources, managerial economics, marketing, resort management, restaurant/food services, tourism promotion, tourism/travel. **Communications:** General, advertising, broadcast journalism, journalism, public relations. **Computer sciences:** General, computer science. **Education:** General, art, biology, business, chemistry, early childhood, elementary, English, health, learning disabled, mathematics, mentally handicapped, music, physical, science, social studies, speech. **English:** British lit, composition, English lit. **Health:** Athletic training, clinical lab science, predental, premedicine, prepharmacy, preveterinary. **History:** General. **Interdisciplinary:** Global studies. **Legal studies:** Prelaw. **Liberal arts:** Arts/sciences, library science. **Math:** General. **Parks/recreation:** General, facilities management, health/fitness, sports admin. **Personal/culinary services:** Restaurant/catering. **Physical sciences:** Chemistry, geology. **Psychology:** General. **Public administration:** General, social work. **Social sciences:** Geography, political science, sociology. **Visual/performing arts:** Art, commercial/advertising art, dramatic, graphic design, studio arts.

**Most popular majors.** Biology 7%, business/marketing 25%, education 27%, liberal arts 9%, social sciences 7%.

**Computing on campus.** 250 workstations in dormitories, library, computer center, student center. Dormitories wired for high-speed internet access. Online library, helpline, repair service, wireless network available.

**Student life. Freshman orientation:** Mandatory, $40 fee. Preregistration for classes offered. **Housing:** Guaranteed on-campus for all undergraduates. Coed dorms, single-sex dorms, special housing for disabled, apartments, fraternity/sorority housing, substance-free housing available. $50 deposit. **Activities:** Bands, choral groups, dance, drama, film society, literary magazine, music ensembles, radio station, student government, student newspaper, TV station, over 50 clubs and organizations.

**Athletics.** NCAA. **Intercollegiate:** Baseball M, basketball, cross-country, football (tackle) M, golf, soccer, softball W, tennis, track and field, volleyball W. **Intramural:** Archery, badminton, basketball, bowling, football (tackle) M, golf, handball, racquetball, soccer W, softball, swimming, tennis, track and field, volleyball, water polo. **Team name:** Mountain Lions.

**Student services.** Career counseling, student employment services, financial aid counseling, health services, on-campus daycare, personal counseling, placement for graduates, veterans' counselor. **Learning disabled:** Comprehensive services available.

**Contact.** E-mail: admissions@concord.edu
Phone: (304) 384-5248 Toll-free number: (888) 384-5249
Fax: (304) 384-3218
Kent Gamble, Director of Enrollment, Concord University, PO Box 1000, Athens, WV 24712-1000

---

## Davis and Elkins College
**Elkins, West Virginia**  CB member
**www.davisandelkins.edu**  CB code: 5151

♦  Private 4-year liberal arts college affiliated with Presbyterian Church (USA)
♦  Residential campus in small town
♦  599 degree-seeking undergraduates: 5% part-time, 65% women, 4% African American, 1% Asian American, 2% Hispanic American, 1% Native American, 6% international
♦  75% of applicants admitted
♦  SAT or ACT (ACT writing optional) required
♦  47% graduate within 6 years; 13% enter graduate study

**General.** Founded in 1904. Regionally accredited. **Degrees:** 73 bachelor's, 44 associate awarded. **Location:** 130 miles from Pittsburgh, 200 miles from Washington, DC. **Calendar:** 4-1-4, extensive summer session. **Full-time faculty:** 44 total; 75% have terminal degrees, 11% minority, 48% women. **Part-time faculty:** 20 total; 25% have terminal degrees, 5% minority, 45% women. **Class size:** 78% < 20, 17% 20-39, 5% 40-49. **Special facilities:** Pearl S. Buck collection, observatory, greenhouse, planetarium, 8 buildings on the national historic registry.

**Freshman class profile.** 351 applied, 264 admitted, 117 enrolled.

| Mid 50% test scores | | | |
|---|---|---|---|
| SAT critical reading: | 420-530 | Rank in top tenth: | 11% |
| SAT math: | 400-510 | End year in good standing: | 92% |
| SAT writing: | 410-530 | Return as sophomores: | 66% |
| ACT composite: | 17-22 | Out-of-state: | 44% |
| GPA 3.50 or higher: | 25% | Live on campus: | 79% |
| GPA 3.0-3.49: | 22% | International: | 7% |
| GPA 2.0-2.99: | 43% | Fraternities: | 10% |
| Rank in top quarter: | 28% | Sororities: | 14% |

**Basis for selection.** Admission is based on school achievement record (minimum cumulative GPA of 2.0), test scores, and extracurricular activities. Recommended interview also important. Tests are required for admission and must be submitted before application can be evaluated. Essay, academic/personal recommendations recommended for all applicants; audition required for musicians and theater students; portfolio required for art students. **Homeschooled:** Transcript of courses and grades required. **Learning Disabled:** Must complete a separate application for the Supported Learning Program.

**High school preparation.** 14 units required. Required and recommended units include English 4, mathematics 3-4, social studies 3-4, science 3-4 (laboratory 1-2), foreign language 1-2 and academic electives 4. Mathematics units must include Algebra I or Algebra II, and Geometry.

**2007-2008 Annual costs.** Tuition/fees: $18,746. Room/board: $6,350. Books/supplies: $800.

**2006-2007 Financial aid. Need-based:** 100 full-time freshmen applied for aid; 83 were judged to have need; 83 of these received aid. Average need met was 76%. Average scholarship/grant was $4,220; average loan $4,435. 49% of total undergraduate aid awarded as scholarships/grants, 51% as loans/jobs. **Non-need-based:** Awarded to 674 full-time undergraduates, including 157 freshmen. Scholarships awarded for academics, alumni affiliation, art, athletics, leadership, minority status, music/drama, religious affiliation.

**Application procedures. Admission:** Priority date 5/1; no deadline. $35 fee, may be waived for applicants with need. Application may be submitted online. Admission notification on a rolling basis beginning on or about 9/30.

**Financial aid:** Priority date 3/1; no closing date. FAFSA required. Applicants notified on a rolling basis starting 5/1; must reply within 2 week(s) of notification.

**Academics. Special study options:** Combined bachelor's/graduate degree, cooperative education, cross-registration, distance learning, double major, dual enrollment of high school students, external degree, honors, independent study, internships, liberal arts/career combination, student-designed major, study abroad, teacher certification program, Washington semester. **Credit/placement by examination:** AP, CLEP, IB, institutional tests. Hours of credit by examination is limited only by the circumstances of the individual student. **Support services:** Learning center, reduced course load, remedial instruction, study skills assistance, tutoring, writing center.

**Majors. Biology:** General. **Business:** General, accounting, business admin, hospitality admin, international, marketing, office management, tourism/travel. **Computer sciences:** Applications programming, computer science. **Conservation:** General, environmental studies. **Education:** General, elementary, secondary. **English:** English lit. **Foreign languages:** General, Spanish. **Health:** Health care admin, predental, premedicine, prepharmacy, preveterinary. **History:** General. **Math:** General. **Parks/recreation:** Exercise sciences, sports admin. **Philosophy/religion:** Philosophy, religion. **Physical sciences:** Chemistry. **Psychology:** General. **Social sciences:** Political science, sociology. **Visual/performing arts:** Dramatic, music management, voice/opera.

**Most popular majors.** Business/marketing 23%, education 14%, history 10%, parks/recreation 14%, psychology 7%, theological studies 7%, visual/performing arts 8%.

**Computing on campus.** 80 workstations in library, computer center. Dormitories wired for high-speed internet access and linked to campus network. Commuter students can connect to campus network. Helpline, repair service, wireless network available.

**Student life. Freshman orientation:** Mandatory. Preregistration for classes offered. Various options available. **Housing:** Guaranteed on-campus for all undergraduates. Coed dorms, single-sex dorms, fraternity/sorority housing, substance-free housing available. $200 nonrefundable deposit, deadline 5/1. **Activities:** Bands, choral groups, drama, international student organizations, literary magazine, music ensembles, musical theater, radio station, student government, student newspaper, Black Student Assembly, Common Ground, Food For Thought.

**Athletics.** NCAA. **Intercollegiate:** Baseball M, basketball, cross-country, golf M, skiing, soccer, softball W, volleyball W. **Intramural:** Basketball, soccer, tennis, volleyball. **Team name:** Senators.

**Student services.** Alcohol/substance abuse counseling, campus ministries, career counseling, student employment services, financial aid counseling, health services, personal counseling, placement for graduates, veterans' counselor. **Learning disabled:** Comprehensive services available.

**Contact.** E-mail: admiss@davisandelkins.edu
Phone: (304) 637-1230 Toll-free number: (800) 624-3157 ext. 1230
Fax: (304) 637-1800
Renee Heckel, Director of Enrollment Management, Davis and Elkins College, 100 Campus Drive, Elkins, WV 26241

---

## Fairmont State University
**Fairmont, West Virginia**
www.fairmontstate.edu
**CB code: 5211**

- Public 4-year university and technical college
- Commuter campus in large town
- 6,227 degree-seeking undergraduates: 18% part-time, 57% women, 4% African American, 1% Hispanic American, 1% international
- 342 degree-seeking graduate students
- SAT or ACT required
- 36% graduate within 6 years; 16% enter graduate study

**General.** Founded in 1865. Regionally accredited. **Degrees:** 663 bachelor's, 324 associate awarded; master's offered. **ROTC:** Army, Air Force. **Location:** 90 miles from Pittsburgh. **Calendar:** Semester, limited summer session. **Full-time faculty:** 232 total; 48% have terminal degrees, 6% minority, 45% women. **Part-time faculty:** 263 total; 28% have terminal degrees, 5% minority, 55% women. **Class size:** 55% <20, 37% 20-39, 3% 40-49, 5% 50-99, less than 1% >100. **Special facilities:** Student life center, folk-life center.

**Freshman class profile.** 3,400 applied, 2,692 admitted, 1,220 enrolled.

| Mid 50% test scores | | | |
|---|---|---|---|
| SAT critical reading: | 400-510 | Rank in top tenth: | 7% |
| SAT math: | 390-500 | End year in good standing: | 88% |
| ACT composite: | 17-22 | Return as sophomores: | 70% |
| GPA 3.50 or higher: | 23% | Out-of-state: | 8% |
| GPA 3.0-3.49: | 31% | Live on campus: | 35% |
| GPA 2.0-2.99: | 40% | Fraternities: | 3% |
| Rank in top quarter: | 24% | Sororities: | 2% |

**Basis for selection.** Open admission, but selective for some programs. 2.5 high school GPA and a minimum 17 ACT or 830 SAT equivalent required for bachelor's programs. For associate degree programs, SAT or ACT required for placement but not admission. **Homeschooled:** GED required.

**High school preparation.** 24 units required. Required and recommended units include English 4, mathematics 3, social studies 2, history 1, science 3 (laboratory 2), foreign language 2 and academic electives 11. 1 unit U.S. history required. Mathematics must include algebra and at least 1 higher unit. 2 units lab science required for biology, chemistry, and physics majors.

**2007-2008 Annual costs.** Tuition/fees: $4,614; $9,960 out-of-state. Room/board: $6,684. Books/supplies: $900. Personal expenses: $950.

**Financial aid.** All financial aid based on need.

**Application procedures. Admission:** Priority date 3/1; deadline 8/15 (postmark date). No application fee. Application may be submitted online. Admission notification on a rolling basis beginning on or about 10/1. **Financial aid:** Closing date 2/1. FAFSA required. Applicants notified on a rolling basis starting 4/15; must reply within 2 week(s) of notification.

**Academics. Special study options:** Cooperative education, distance learning, double major, dual enrollment of high school students, ESL, exchange student, honors, internships, liberal arts/career combination, study abroad, teacher certification program, Washington semester, weekend college. **Credit/placement by examination:** AP, CLEP, IB, institutional tests. 28 credit hours maximum toward bachelor's degree. **Support services:** Learning center, reduced course load, remedial instruction, study skills assistance, tutoring.

**Majors. Biology:** General. **Business:** General, accounting, banking/financial services, business admin, management information systems, management science, office management. **Communications:** General. **Communications technology:** Graphic/printing. **Computer sciences:** General, computer science. **Education:** General, art, biology, business, chemistry, early childhood, elementary, emotionally handicapped, English, family/consumer sciences, gifted/talented, history, mathematics, mentally handicapped, middle, music, physical, physics, science, secondary, social studies, speech, technology/industrial arts, trade/industrial. **Engineering technology:** Aerospace, architectural, civil, construction, drafting, electrical, mechanical, occupational safety. **English:** English lit. **Family/consumer sciences:** General. **Foreign languages:** French, Spanish. **Health:** Health care admin, nursing (RN). **History:** General. **Math:** General. **Parks/recreation:** Exercise sciences, health/fitness. **Physical sciences:** Chemistry. **Protective services:** Criminal justice, forensics, law enforcement admin. **Psychology:** General. **Social sciences:** Political science, sociology. **Transportation:** Aviation, aviation management. **Visual/performing arts:** Commercial/advertising art, dramatic.

**Most popular majors.** Business/marketing 24%, education 20%, engineering/engineering technologies 9%, liberal arts 7%, psychology 8%, security/protective services 9%.

**Computing on campus.** 950 workstations in dormitories, library, computer center, student center. Dormitories wired for high-speed internet access and linked to campus network. Commuter students can connect to campus network. Online library, helpline, student web hosting, wireless network available.

**Student life. Freshman orientation:** Available. Preregistration for classes offered. 2 days in fall, one day in spring. **Policies:** Alcohol not allowed. **Housing:** Guaranteed on-campus for freshmen. Coed dorms, single-sex dorms, apartments available. $200 fully refundable deposit, deadline 6/15. **Activities:** Bands, campus ministries, choral groups, dance, drama, literary magazine, music ensembles, musical theater, student government, student newspaper, symphony orchestra, Black Student Union, Circle K, Disabled Students Society, International Relations Society, Society of Non-Traditional Students.

**Athletics.** NCAA. **Intercollegiate:** Baseball M, basketball, cheerleading M, cross-country, football (tackle) M, golf, softball W, swimming, tennis, volleyball W. **Intramural:** Archery, badminton W, basketball, bowling, cross-country, field hockey W, football (tackle) M, golf, gymnastics, racquetball, softball, swimming, table tennis, tennis, track and field, volleyball, wrestling M. **Team name:** Falcons.

**Student services.** Adult student services, career counseling, student employment services, financial aid counseling, health services, on-campus daycare, personal counseling, placement for graduates, veterans' counselor. **Physically disabled:** Services for visually, hearing impaired.

**Contact.** E-mail: admit@fairmontstate.edu
Phone: (304) 367-4892 Toll-free number: (800) 641-5678
Fax: (304) 367-4789
Steve Leadman, Executive Director of Enrollment Services, Fairmont State University, 1201 Locust Avenue, Fairmont, WV 26554-2470

## Glenville State College
**Glenville, West Virginia**
**www.glenville.edu**

**CB member**
**CB code: 5254**

- Public 4-year liberal arts and teachers college
- Commuter campus in rural community
- 1,155 degree-seeking undergraduates: 7% part-time, 50% women
- SAT or ACT (ACT writing optional) required
- 36% graduate within 6 years

**General.** Founded in 1872. Regionally accredited. **Degrees:** 182 bachelor's, 32 associate awarded. **Location:** 87 miles from Charleston, 86 miles from Morgantown. **Calendar:** Semester, limited summer session. **Full-time faculty:** 57 total; 61% have terminal degrees, 4% minority, 35% women. **Part-time faculty:** 28 total; 18% have terminal degrees, 7% minority, 57% women. **Class size:** 56% < 20, 40% 20-39, 3% 40-49, 2% 50-99. **Special facilities:** Law enforcement teaching and training center.

**Freshman class profile.** 1,143 applied, 1,143 admitted, 291 enrolled.

| Mid 50% test scores | | Rank in top quarter: | 25% |
|---|---|---|---|
| SAT critical reading: | 380-460 | Rank in top tenth: | 8% |
| SAT math: | 340-460 | End year in good standing: | 59% |
| ACT composite: | 16-22 | Return as sophomores: | 72% |
| GPA 3.50 or higher: | 25% | Out-of-state: | 12% |
| GPA 3.0-3.49: | 26% | Live on campus: | 70% |
| GPA 2.0-2.99: | 43% | | |

**Basis for selection.** Open admission, but selective for some programs. Students must have graduated from an accredited high school with at least a 2.0 average or an ACT composite score of at least 17 or an SAT of 820 (exclusive of Writing). Associate degree programs open to all students who have graduated from any high school or hold a GED. Students who want to pursue a bachelor's degree program, but who do not meet the admissions requirements outlined above, may enter a two-year program and later transfer into a bachelor's degree program. Audition required for music education only. **Homeschooled:** GED required. **Learning Disabled:** Must provide documentation of disability for services of disabilities coordinator.

**High school preparation.** 28 units required. Required and recommended units include English 4, mathematics 3, social studies 3, science 3 (laboratory 2), foreign language 2 and academic electives 15. Mathematics should be algebra and higher. The laboratory science units should be from coordinated and thematic science, biology, chemistry, physics and other courses with a strong laboratory orientation. Social studies should include U.S. history. English should include courses in grammar, composition and literature.

**2007-2008 Annual costs.** Tuition/fees: $4,147; $9,990 out-of-state. Room/board: $5,800. Books/supplies: $900. Personal expenses: $1,906.

**2006-2007 Financial aid. Need-based:** 250 full-time freshmen applied for aid; 222 were judged to have need; 220 of these received aid. Average need met was 70%. Average scholarship/grant was $4,463; average loan $2,334. 57% of total undergraduate aid awarded as scholarships/grants, 43% as loans/jobs. **Non-need-based:** Awarded to 510 full-time undergraduates, including 173 freshmen. Scholarships awarded for academics, athletics, music/drama, state residency.

**Application procedures. Admission:** No deadline. $10 fee, may be waived for applicants with need. Application may be submitted online. Admission notification on a rolling basis. **Financial aid:** Priority date 2/1; no closing date. Applicants notified on a rolling basis starting 4/1; must reply within 2 week(s) of notification.

**Academics.** Credit for employment, military, and life experience awarded only in nontraditional Regents Bachelor of Arts degree program (designed for adult students). **Special study options:** Accelerated study, cooperative education, distance learning, double major, ESL, honors, internships, student-designed major, study abroad, teacher certification program, Washington

semester. **Credit/placement by examination:** AP, CLEP, SAT, ACT, institutional tests. Unlimited number of hours of credit may be counted for degree. **Support services:** Remedial instruction, study skills assistance, tutoring, writing center.

**Majors. Biology:** General. **Business:** Business admin. **Conservation:** Management/policy. **Education:** Elementary, kindergarten/preschool, secondary, special. **English:** English lit. **Health:** Nursing (RN). **History:** General. **Interdisciplinary:** Behavioral sciences. **Physical sciences:** Chemistry. **Visual/performing arts:** Music performance.

**Most popular majors.** Business/marketing 20%, education 28%, health sciences 7%, liberal arts 9%, natural resources/environmental science 6%, social sciences 15%.

**Computing on campus.** 175 workstations in library, computer center, student center. Dormitories wired for high-speed internet access and linked to campus network. Commuter students can connect to campus network. Online course registration, online library, helpline, repair service, wireless network available.

**Student life. Freshman orientation:** Mandatory, $80 fee. Preregistration for classes offered. Held immediately preceding the start of classes each semester, assists students in becoming acclimated to campus. Addresses transitional issues critical to first year success. **Policies:** All unmarried students who have earned less than 58 credit hours are required to reside on campus so long as space is available. Alcoholic beverages, tobacco and controlled substances are not permitted on campus. All students are required to adhere to the Student Code of Conduct. Community service required of student organizations. **Housing:** Guaranteed on-campus for freshmen. Single-sex dorms, special housing for disabled, apartments, substance-free housing available. $75 partly refundable deposit, deadline 4/1. **Activities:** Bands, choral groups, drama, literary magazine, music ensembles, student government, student newspaper, Fellowship of Christian Athletes, environmental organization, students in free enterprise, Student National Education Association, student athlete advisory committee, student awareness organization, Music Educators National Conference, Kappa Delta Pi.

**Athletics.** NCAA. **Intercollegiate:** Basketball, cross-country, football (tackle) M, golf, softball W, track and field, volleyball W. **Intramural:** Basketball, fencing, football (non-tackle), soccer, softball, table tennis, tennis, track and field, volleyball, weight lifting, wrestling. **Team name:** Pioneers.

**Student services.** Adult student services, alcohol/substance abuse counseling, career counseling, services for economically disadvantaged, student employment services, financial aid counseling, health services, personal counseling, placement for graduates, veterans' counselor. **Physically disabled:** Services for visually, speech, hearing impaired.

**Contact.** E-mail: admissions@glenville.edu
Phone: (304) 462-4128 Toll-free number: (800) 924-2010
Fax: (304) 462-8619
Donald Chapman, Vice President for Enrollment Services, Glenville State College, 200 High Street, Glenville, WV 26351-1292

## Marshall University
**Huntington, West Virginia**
**www.marshall.edu**

**CB member**
**CB code: 5396**

- Public 4-year university
- Commuter campus in small city
- 8,904 degree-seeking undergraduates: 12% part-time, 55% women, 6% African American, 1% Asian American, 1% Hispanic American, 1% international
- 3,441 degree-seeking graduate students
- SAT or ACT (ACT writing optional) required
- 48% graduate within 6 years

**General.** Founded in 1837. Regionally accredited. **Degrees:** 1,389 bachelor's, 96 associate awarded; master's, doctoral, first professional offered. **ROTC:** Army. **Location:** 126 miles from Lexington, Kentucky, 160 miles from Columbus, Ohio. **Calendar:** Semester, limited summer session. **Full-time faculty:** 463 total; 81% have terminal degrees, 12% minority, 40% women. **Part-time faculty:** 239 total; 9% have terminal degrees, 4% minority, 48% women. **Class size:** 41% < 20, 46% 20-39, 9% 40-49, 4% 50-99, less than 1% >100. **Special facilities:** Confederate history collection, superconducting nuclear magnetic resonance spectrometer.

**Freshman class profile.** 2,405 applied, 2,059 admitted, 1,688 enrolled.

| Mid 50% test scores | | | |
|---|---|---|---|
| SAT critical reading: | 450-570 | GPA 3.0-3.49: | 28% |
| SAT math: | 440-560 | GPA 2.0-2.99: | 26% |
| SAT writing: | 450-560 | Return as sophomores: | 71% |
| ACT composite: | 20-25 | Out-of-state: | 26% |
| GPA 3.50 or higher: | 45% | International: | 1% |

**Basis for selection.** Open admission, but selective for some programs and for out-of-state students. Full admission requires a 2.0 GPA and ACT 19 or SAT 910 (exclusive of Writing). Conditional admission is granted below a 2.0 GPA or the above scores, on a limited, first-come, first-served basis. Programs and colleges may have different requirements for admissions. Audition required for music majors; interview recommended for academically weak, learning disabled; portfolio recommended. **Home-schooled:** Applicants should apply early and have home schooling well documented.

**High school preparation.** 20 units required. Required units include English 4, mathematics 4, social studies 3, science 3 (laboratory 3), foreign language 2 and visual/performing arts 1.

**2007-2008 Annual costs.** Tuition/fees: $4,360; $11,264 out-of-state. Room/board: $6,818. Books/supplies: $1,000. Personal expenses: $2,540.

**2007-2008 Financial aid. Need-based:** 1,075 full-time freshmen applied for aid; 738 were judged to have need; 727 of these received aid. Average need met was 57%. Average scholarship/grant was $5,291; average loan $4,345. 41% of total undergraduate aid awarded as scholarships/grants, 59% as loans/jobs. **Non-need-based:** Awarded to 3,329 full-time undergraduates, including 853 freshmen. Scholarships awarded for academics, art, athletics, minority status, music/drama, ROTC, state residency.

**Application procedures. Admission:** No deadline. $30 fee, may be waived for applicants with need. Application may be submitted online. Admission notification on a rolling basis beginning on or about 9/1. **Financial aid:** Priority date 3/1; no closing date. FAFSA required. Applicants notified on a rolling basis starting 5/1; must reply within 2 week(s) of notification.

**Academics. Special study options:** Accelerated study, combined bachelor's/graduate degree, cooperative education, cross-registration, distance learning, double major, ESL, exchange student, honors, independent study, internships, study abroad, teacher certification program, Washington semester. 2-2 preengineering program, 3-2 program in forestry with Duke University. **Credit/placement by examination:** AP, CLEP, IB, institutional tests. **Support services:** Learning center, pre-admission summer program, reduced course load, remedial instruction, study skills assistance, tutoring, writing center.

**Majors. Biology:** General. **Business:** Accounting, business admin, finance, management information systems, managerial economics, marketing. **Communications:** Journalism. **Computer sciences:** General. **Conservation:** Environmental science. **Education:** Elementary, physical, school counseling, secondary. **Engineering:** General. **Engineering technology:** Occupational safety. **English:** English lit, speech/rhetoric. **Family/consumer sciences:** General. **Foreign languages:** General. **Health:** Clinical lab science, cytotechnology, dietetics, nursing (RN), respiratory therapy technology, speech pathology. **History:** General. **Interdisciplinary:** Systems science. **Liberal arts:** Humanities. **Math:** General. **Parks/recreation:** Facilities management. **Physical sciences:** Chemistry, geology, physics. **Protective services:** Criminal justice. **Psychology:** General. **Public administration:** Social work. **Social sciences:** Economics, geography, international relations, political science, sociology. **Visual/performing arts:** Art, fashion design.

**Most popular majors.** Biology 7%, business/marketing 19%, education 20%, health sciences 8%, liberal arts 14%, security/protective services 6%.

**Computing on campus.** 1,461 workstations in dormitories, library, computer center, student center. Dormitories wired for high-speed internet access and linked to campus network. Commuter students can connect to campus network. Online course registration, online library, helpline, student web hosting available.

**Student life. Freshman orientation:** Available. Preregistration for classes offered. One-day programs in June, July, August. **Housing:** Guaranteed on-campus for freshmen. Coed dorms, single-sex dorms, special housing for disabled, apartments, fraternity/sorority housing, substance-free housing available. $150 deposit. **Activities:** Bands, campus ministries, choral groups, drama, literary magazine, music ensembles, musical theater, opera, radio station, student government, student newspaper, symphony orchestra, TV station, Black United Students, College Republicans, Lambda Society, Habitat for Humanity, Student Organization for Alumni Relations.

**Athletics.** NCAA. **Intercollegiate:** Baseball M, basketball, cross-country, football (tackle) M, golf, soccer, softball W, swimming W, tennis W, track

and field, volleyball W. **Intramural:** Basketball, bowling, football (tackle), golf, racquetball, soccer, softball, swimming, tennis, track and field, volleyball. **Team name:** Thundering Herd.

**Student services.** Adult student services, alcohol/substance abuse counseling, campus ministries, career counseling, student employment services, health services, minority student services, on-campus daycare, personal counseling, placement for graduates, veterans' counselor, women's services. **Physically disabled:** Services for visually, speech, hearing impaired.

**Contact.** E-mail: admissions@marshall.edu
Phone: (304) 696-3160 Toll-free number: (800) 642-3499
Fax: (304) 696-3135
Tammy Johnson, Director of Admissions, Marshall University, One John Marshall Drive, Huntington, WV 25755

## Mountain State University

| **Beckley, West Virginia** | **CB member** |
|---|---|
| **www.mountainstate.edu** | **CB code: 5054** |

- Private 4-year university and health science college
- Commuter campus in large town
- 4,053 degree-seeking undergraduates: 26% part-time, 64% women, 8% African American, 3% Asian American, 2% Hispanic American, 1% Native American, 3% international
- 678 degree-seeking graduate students

**General.** Founded in 1933. Regionally accredited. **Degrees:** 703 bachelor's, 170 associate awarded; master's offered. **Location:** 55 miles from Charleston. **Calendar:** Semester, limited summer session. **Full-time faculty:** 96 total; 32% have terminal degrees, 10% minority, 66% women. **Part-time faculty:** 268 total; 22% have terminal degrees, 4% minority, 51% women. **Class size:** 78% < 20, 20% 20-39, less than 1% 40-49, 1% 50-99. **Special facilities:** YMCA, medicinal botanical garden, greenhouse.

**Freshman class profile.** 1,652 applied, 1,652 admitted, 540 enrolled.

| | | | |
|---|---|---|---|
| GPA 3.50 or higher: | 21% | Return as sophomores: | 52% |
| GPA 3.0-3.49: | 35% | Out-of-state: | 21% |
| GPA 2.0-2.99: | 34% | Live on campus: | 1% |
| Rank in top quarter: | 26% | International: | 9% |
| Rank in top tenth: | 7% | Fraternities: | 1% |
| End year in good standing: | 38% | | |

**Basis for selection.** Open admission, but selective for some programs. Special requirements for health science programs. ACT or SAT scores required for nursing and physician's assistant programs. **Homeschooled:** Provide official academic records.

**High school preparation.** 13 units required; 15 recommended. Required and recommended units include English 4, mathematics 2, social studies 3, history 2, science 2 (laboratory 2).

**2007-2008 Annual costs.** Tuition/fees: $8,100. Certain programs require additional costs: health science and culinary/hospitality are $300 per credit hour. Room/board: $5,854. Books/supplies: $1,300.

**2006-2007 Financial aid. Need-based:** 213 full-time freshmen applied for aid; 184 were judged to have need; 184 of these received aid. Average need met was 31%. Average scholarship/grant was $3,377; average loan $2,344. 40% of total undergraduate aid awarded as scholarships/grants, 60% as loans/jobs. **Non-need-based:** Awarded to 123 full-time undergraduates, including 23 freshmen. Scholarships awarded for academics, alumni affiliation, athletics, leadership, minority status.

**Application procedures. Admission:** No deadline. $25 fee, may be waived for applicants with need. Application may be submitted online. Admission notification on a rolling basis. **Financial aid:** No deadline. FAFSA required. Applicants notified on a rolling basis starting 4/1.

**Academics. Special study options:** Accelerated study, combined bachelor's/graduate degree, cooperative education, cross-registration, distance learning, double major, dual enrollment of high school students, ESL, independent study, internships, liberal arts/career combination, student-designed major, weekend college. Degree completion program, credit for prior learning (challenge exam and portfolio assessment). **Credit/placement by examination:** AP, CLEP, IB, institutional tests. 32 credit hours maximum toward associate degree, 64 toward bachelor's. CLEP, DANTES and Challenge exams available. **Support services:** Learning center, reduced course load, remedial instruction, study skills assistance, tutoring, writing center.

**Majors. Biology:** General. **Business:** General, accounting, business admin, e-commerce, entrepreneurial studies, financial planning, hospitality admin, hospitality/recreation, human resources, international, logistics, management science, marketing, nonprofit/public, office management, organizational behavior, tourism/travel. **Communications:** Media studies. **Computer sciences:** Computer science, information systems, LAN/WAN management, networking, webmaster. **Conservation:** General, environmental studies. **English:** English lit. **Health:** Health care admin, health services, nursing (RN), occupational health, premedicine, public health ed, respiratory therapy assistant, respiratory therapy technology, sonography. **Interdisciplinary:** Accounting/computer science, behavioral sciences, biological/physical sciences, math/computer science. **Legal studies:** General. **Liberal arts:** Arts/sciences, humanities, library science. **Personal/culinary services:** Chef training. **Philosophy/religion:** Religion. **Physical sciences:** General. **Protective services:** Correctional facilities, corrections, criminal justice, emergency management/homeland security, forensics, law enforcement admin, security management. **Psychology:** General. **Public administration:** Social work. **Transportation:** Aviation management. **Other:** Health education and wellness, Organizational leadership.

**Most popular majors.** Biology 7%, business/marketing 28%, health sciences 40%, interdisciplinary studies 6%, security/protective services 14%.

**Computing on campus.** 90 workstations in library, computer center. Dormitories wired for high-speed internet access and linked to campus network. Commuter students can connect to campus network. Online course registration, online library, helpline, repair service, student web hosting, wireless network available.

**Student life. Freshman orientation:** Available. Preregistration for classes offered. One-day orientation during summer. Special sessions for parents. **Housing:** Guaranteed on-campus for freshmen. Coed dorms, substance-free housing available. $150 fully refundable deposit. Handicapped-accessible dorms, off-campus housing for athletes available. **Activities:** Pep band, choral groups, drama, international student organizations, student government, student newspaper, Christian student organization, American Association of Medical Assistants, criminal justice association, forensic club, legal club, student association for respiratory care, student nursing association, Students in Free Enterprise, student social work organization.

**Athletics.** NAIA. **Intercollegiate:** Basketball M, cheerleading, soccer, softball W, volleyball W. **Intramural:** Basketball, football (non-tackle), football (tackle), soccer, softball, table tennis, volleyball. **Team name:** Cougars.

**Student services.** Adult student services, alcohol/substance abuse counseling, career counseling, student employment services, financial aid counseling, health services, on-campus daycare, personal counseling, placement for graduates, veterans' counselor.

**Contact.** E-mail: gomsu@mountainstate.edu
Phone: (304) 929-1433 Toll-free number: (800) 766-6067
Fax: (304) 253-3463
Tammy Toney, Director of the Admissions Process, Mountain State University, 609 South Kanawha Street, Beckley, WV 25802-9003

## Ohio Valley University
**Vienna, West Virginia**
www.ovu.edu
CB code: 5519

- Private 4-year university and liberal arts college affiliated with Church of Christ
- Residential campus in small city
- 526 degree-seeking undergraduates: 4% part-time, 54% women, 6% African American, 2% Hispanic American, 7% international
- 56% of applicants admitted
- SAT or ACT (ACT writing optional) required

**General.** Founded in 1960. Regionally accredited. **Degrees:** 125 bachelor's, 36 associate awarded. **Location:** 95 miles from Columbus, 120 miles from Pittsburgh. **Calendar:** Semester, limited summer session. **Full-time faculty:** 26 total; 38% have terminal degrees, 35% women. **Part-time faculty:** 40 total; 20% have terminal degrees, 28% women. **Class size:** 78% < 20, 22% 20-39.

**Freshman class profile.** 493 applied, 277 admitted, 121 enrolled.

| Mid 50% test scores | | | |
|---|---|---|---|
| SAT critical reading: | 440-570 | Rank in top quarter: | 25% |
| SAT math: | 430-550 | Rank in top tenth: | 8% |
| SAT writing: | 410-540 | End year in good standing: | 87% |
| ACT composite: | 18-24 | Return as sophomores: | 63% |
| GPA 3.50 or higher: | 26% | Out-of-state: | 12% |
| GPA 3.0-3.49: | 27% | Live on campus: | 90% |
| GPA 2.0-2.99: | 45% | International: | 10% |

**Basis for selection.** School achievement record, test scores and reference considered. Essay, interview recommended.

**High school preparation.** 12 units recommended. Recommended units include English 3, mathematics 3, social studies 2, history 1, science 3 (laboratory 1).

**2007-2008 Annual costs.** Tuition/fees: $15,120. Room/board: $6,140. Books/supplies: $1,000. Personal expenses: $800.

**2007-2008 Financial aid. Need-based:** Average need met was 66%. Average scholarship/grant was $8,600; average loan $3,401. 31% of total undergraduate aid awarded as scholarships/grants, 69% as loans/jobs. **Non-need-based:** Scholarships awarded for academics, alumni affiliation, athletics, job skills, leadership, music/drama.

**Application procedures. Admission:** No deadline. $20 fee, may be waived for applicants with need. Application may be submitted online. Admission notification on a rolling basis. **Financial aid:** Priority date 2/15; no closing date. FAFSA required. Applicants notified on a rolling basis starting 3/15; must reply within 4 week(s) of notification.

**Academics.** Full-time students required to take a Bible course each semester. **Special study options:** Cooperative education, double major, dual enrollment of high school students, ESL, honors, independent study, internships, student-designed major, teacher certification program, weekend college. Degree completion programs and special certifications. **Credit/placement by examination:** AP, CLEP, IB, SAT, ACT, institutional tests. 30 credit hours maximum toward associate degree, 30 toward bachelor's. Challenge course testing. **Support services:** Learning center, pre-admission summer program, reduced course load, remedial instruction, study skills assistance, tutoring.

**Majors. Business:** Accounting, business admin, human resources, nonprofit/public. **Computer sciences:** Information technology. **Education:** General, elementary, English, mathematics, multi-level teacher, physical, science, secondary, social studies. **Liberal arts:** Arts/sciences. **Philosophy/religion:** Religion. **Psychology:** General. **Theology:** Bible.

**Computing on campus.** 44 workstations in dormitories, library, computer center. Dormitories wired for high-speed internet access and linked to campus network. Commuter students can connect to campus network. Online library, repair service, wireless network available.

**Student life. Freshman orientation:** Mandatory. Preregistration for classes offered. Orientation programs held in the summer and fall are designed to integrate incoming students into the campus community. **Policies:** Chapel/Assembly attendance required three times a week. Religious observance required. **Housing:** Guaranteed on-campus for all undergraduates. Single-sex dorms, apartments, substance-free housing available. $150 deposit, deadline 8/20. **Activities:** Bands, choral groups, drama, literary magazine, music ensembles, musical theater, student government, student newspaper, symphony orchestra, prospective ministers and prospective missionaries clubs, women's club, diversity at the university.

**Athletics.** NCAA. **Intercollegiate:** Baseball M, basketball, cross-country, golf, soccer, softball W, volleyball W. **Intramural:** Basketball, bowling, cross-country, football (non-tackle), soccer, softball, table tennis, track and field, volleyball. **Team name:** Fighting Scots.

**Student services.** Adult student services, alcohol/substance abuse counseling, campus ministries, career counseling, student employment services, financial aid counseling, health services, minority student services, personal counseling, placement for graduates.

**Contact.** E-mail: admissions@ovu.edu
Phone: (304) 865-6200 Toll-free number: (877) 446-8668
Fax: (304) 865-6175
Rob Dudley, Associate Vice President for Enrollment, Ohio Valley University, One Campus View Drive, Vienna, WV 26105

## Salem International University
**Salem, West Virginia**
www.salemu.edu
CB code: 5608

- For-profit 4-year university and liberal arts college
- Residential campus in rural community
- 342 degree-seeking undergraduates: 41% women
- 178 degree-seeking graduate students

**General.** Founded in 1888. Regionally accredited. **Degrees:** 71 bachelor's awarded; master's offered. **Location:** 12 miles from Clarksburg, 125 miles from Pittsburgh. **Calendar:** Modular; 12 modules of 4 weeks, divided into 3 terms. Limited summer session. **Full-time faculty:** 13 total; 46% have terminal degrees, 8% minority, 23% women. **Part-time faculty:** 3 total; 67% women. **Class size:** 77% < 20, 17% 20-39, 6% 40-49.

**Freshman class profile.**

| | | | |
|---|---|---|---|
| Out-of-state: | 32% | **Fraternities:** | 5% |
| Live on campus: | 90% | **Sororities:** | 8% |

**Basis for selection.** School achievement record, test scores, counselor recommendations most important. SAT or ACT recommended. Essay, interview recommended. **Homeschooled:** State high school equivalency certificate required.

**High school preparation.** 16 units recommended. Recommended units include English 4, mathematics 2, social studies 3, science 2 and foreign language 2. 16 required units should be in academic areas.

**2007-2008 Annual costs.** Tuition/fees: $13,950. Room/board: $5,420. Books/supplies: $660. Personal expenses: $320.

**Financial aid. Non-need-based:** Scholarships awarded for academics.

**Application procedures. Admission:** No deadline. $25 fee, may be waived for applicants with need. Application may be submitted online. Admission notification on a rolling basis. **Financial aid:** Priority date 4/15; no closing date. FAFSA required. Applicants notified on a rolling basis starting 2/15; must reply within 4 week(s) of notification.

**Academics.** In keeping with college's mission to foster global awareness, all students required to complete international core curriculum. **Special study options:** Accelerated study, distance learning, double major, dual enrollment of high school students, independent study, internships, liberal arts/career combination, student-designed major, study abroad, teacher certification program, Washington semester. **Credit/placement by examination:** AP, CLEP, IB, institutional tests. 24 credit hours maximum toward bachelor's degree. **Support services:** Learning center, reduced course load, remedial instruction, study skills assistance, tutoring, writing center.,

**Majors. Biology:** General. **Business:** Business admin. **Computer sciences:** General, computer science. **Education:** General, multi-level teacher, secondary. **Liberal arts:** Arts/sciences. **Protective services:** Criminal justice.

**Computing on campus.** 50 workstations in library, computer center. Dormitories wired for high-speed internet access and linked to campus network. Commuter students can connect to campus network. Online library, helpline, wireless network available.

**Student life. Freshman orientation:** Available, $30 fee. Preregistration for classes offered. Program includes introduction to international aspects of college. Special orientation for international students with U.S. life-skills training. **Policies:** Unless local resident, freshmen and sophomores required to live on-campus. **Housing:** Guaranteed on-campus for all undergraduates. Coed dorms, single-sex dorms, substance-free housing available. $50 fully refundable deposit. Private rooms subject to availability. **Activities:** Campus ministries, international student organizations, student government, student newspaper, Gamma Beta Phi Honor Society, Alpha Phi Omega fraternity service organization, Campus Crusade for Christ, Rainbow Alliance, International Woman's Alliance, Christian Student Fellowship, Indian student association, Chinese student association.

**Athletics.** NCAA. **Intercollegiate:** Baseball M, basketball, golf, soccer, softball W, tennis M, volleyball W. **Intramural:** Basketball, football (non-tackle), racquetball, skiing M, soccer, swimming, table tennis, tennis, volleyball. **Team name:** Tigers.

**Contact.** E-mail: admissions@salemu.edu
Phone: (888) 235-5024 Toll-free number: (888) 359-5782
Fax: (304) 326-1592
Gina Cossey, Vice Presdent, Recruiting and Marketing, Salem International University, 223 West Main Street, Salem, WV 26426

---

## Shepherd University

**Shepherdstown, West Virginia**
www.shepherd.edu

**CB member**
**CB code: 5615**

- Public 4-year university
- Commuter campus in small town
- 3,548 degree-seeking undergraduates: 12% part-time, 59% women, 6% African American, 1% Asian American, 3% Hispanic American, 1% international
- 154 degree-seeking graduate students
- 88% of applicants admitted

---

- SAT or ACT (ACT writing recommended) required
- 35% graduate within 6 years; 28% enter graduate study

**General.** Founded in 1871. Regionally accredited. **Degrees:** 589 bachelor's awarded; master's offered. **ROTC:** Air Force. **Location:** 8 miles from Martinsburg, 70 miles from Washington, DC. **Calendar:** Semester, extensive summer session. **Full-time faculty:** 116 total; 81% have terminal degrees, 11% minority, 42% women. **Part-time faculty:** 198 total; 22% have terminal degrees, 4% minority, 47% women. **Class size:** 42% < 20, 55% 20-39, 2% 40-49, 1% 50-99. **Special facilities:** Creative arts center with computer-controlled theater, recital hall with concert grand piano, recording studio, nursery school, 3 theaters, Civil War center, observatory, center for legislative studies, nursing building.

**Freshman class profile.** 1,611 applied, 1,418 admitted, 706 enrolled.

| Mid 50% test scores | | | |
|---|---|---|---|
| SAT critical reading: | 450-560 | GPA 2.0-2.99: | 42% |
| SAT math: | 460-540 | End year in good standing: | 63% |
| ACT composite: | 19-24 | Return as sophomores: | 67%. |
| GPA 3.50 or higher: | 28% | Out-of-state: | 41% |
| GPA 3.0-3.49: | 28% | Live on campus: | 58% |

**Basis for selection.** Minimum 2.0 academic GPA and 19 ACT or 910 SAT (exclusive of Writing) required. Essays and recommendations are optional but important. Interview required for honors program and nursing applicants; recommended for others. Audition required for music; portfolio required for art majors. **Homeschooled:** ACT and/or SAT test scores, portfolio of work completed.

**High school preparation.** 21 units required. Required units include English 4, mathematics 4, social studies 3, history 1, science 3 (laboratory 3), foreign language 2 and academic electives 6. History unit must include US history; science unit must include biology. All science courses must be college preparatory laboratory sciences.

**2007-2008 Annual costs.** Tuition/fees: $4,564; $12,036 out-of-state. Room/board: $6,714. Books/supplies: $1,100. Personal expenses: $1,500.

**2007-2008 Financial aid. Need-based:** 595 full-time freshmen applied for aid; 361 were judged to have need; 344 of these received aid. Average need met was 79%. Average scholarship/grant was $4,205; average loan $3,202. 43% of total undergraduate aid awarded as scholarships/grants, 57% as loans/jobs. **Non-need-based:** Awarded to 1,170 full-time undergraduates, including 334 freshmen. Scholarships awarded for academics, art, athletics, job skills, leadership, minority status, music/drama, state residency.

**Application procedures. Admission:** Priority date 2/1; no deadline. $35 fee, may be waived for applicants with need. Application may be submitted online. Admission notification on a rolling basis beginning on or about 9/1. Must reply by May 1 or within 3 week(s) if notified thereafter. **Financial aid:** Priority date 3/1; no closing date. FAFSA required. Applicants notified on a rolling basis starting 3/15; must reply within 3 week(s) of notification.

**Academics. Special study options:** Cooperative education, double major, honors, independent study, internships, liberal arts/career combination, teacher certification program, Washington semester. **Credit/placement by examination:** AP, CLEP, IB, SAT, ACT, institutional tests. 32 credit hours maximum toward bachelor's degree. No limit for students pursuing Regents' Bachelor of Arts degree. **Support services:** Learning center, pre-admission summer program, reduced course load, remedial instruction, study skills assistance, tutoring, writing center.

**Majors. Biology:** General. **Business:** Accounting, business admin. **Communications:** General. **Computer sciences:** General, applications programming. **Conservation:** General, environmental studies. **Education:** Elementary, secondary. **English:** English lit. **Family/consumer sciences:** General. **Foreign languages:** Spanish. **Health:** Nursing (RN). **History:** General. **Math:** General. **Parks/recreation:** General. **Physical sciences:** Chemistry. **Psychology:** General. **Public administration:** Social work. **Social sciences:** Economics, political science, sociology. **Visual/performing arts:** Art.

**Most popular majors.** Business/marketing 15%, education 15%, health sciences 6%, liberal arts 15%, parks/recreation 7%, social sciences 7%, visual/performing arts 8%.

**Computing on campus.** 350 workstations in library, computer center, student center. Dormitories wired for high-speed internet access and linked to campus network. Commuter students can connect to campus network. Online course registration, helpline, student web hosting, wireless network available.

**Student life. Freshman orientation:** Mandatory, $75 fee. Preregistration for classes offered. 2-day sessions held in June and July for students and parents. August orientation conducted on the Thursday and/or Friday and Saturday prior to the first day of classes. **Housing:** Guaranteed on-campus for all undergraduates. Coed dorms, apartments, substance-free housing available. $200 partly refundable deposit, deadline 6/1. Living/learning center, honors housing, freshmen housing available. Housing guaranteed if deadlines met. **Activities:** Bands, choral groups, dance, drama, international student organizations, literary magazine, music ensembles, musical theater, radio station, student government, student newspaper, symphony orchestra, College Republicans, College Democrats, Christians in Action, NAACP, United Brothers, Shepherd Greens, Allies, Sistaz, student community services.

**Athletics.** NCAA. **Intercollegiate:** Baseball M, basketball, football (tackle) M, golf M, soccer, softball W, tennis, volleyball W. **Intramural:** Basketball, bowling, football (non-tackle), racquetball, soccer, softball, swimming, table tennis, tennis, volleyball, weight lifting, wrestling. **Team name:** Rams.

**Student services.** Adult student services, alcohol/substance abuse counseling, career counseling, student employment services, financial aid counseling, health services, minority student services, personal counseling, placement for graduates, veterans' counselor. **Physically disabled:** Services for visually, speech, hearing impaired.

**Contact.** E-mail: admissions@shepherd.edu
Phone: (304) 876-5212 Toll-free number: (800) 344-5231 ext. 5212
Fax: (304) 876-5165
Kimberly Scranage, Director of Admissions, Shepherd University, PO Box 3210, Shepherdstown, WV 25443-3210

## University of Charleston
**Charleston, West Virginia**
www.ucwv.edu

**CB member**
**CB code: 5419**

- Private 4-year university and liberal arts college
- Residential campus in small city
- 1,134 degree-seeking undergraduates: 4% part-time, 60% women, 5% African American, 1% Asian American, 1% Hispanic American, 10% international
- 227 degree-seeking graduate students
- 67% of applicants admitted
- SAT or ACT (ACT writing optional) required
- 41% graduate within 6 years

**General.** Founded in 1888. Regionally accredited. **Degrees:** 145 bachelor's, 23 associate awarded; master's, doctoral offered. **ROTC:** Army. **Location:** 200 miles from Pittsburgh, 200 miles from Charlotte, North Carolina. **Calendar:** Semester, limited summer session. **Full-time faculty:** 59 total; 46% have terminal degrees, 7% minority, 56% women. **Part-time faculty:** 31 total; 10% have terminal degrees, 6% minority, 52% women. **Class size:** 68% < 20, 28% 20-39, 2% 40-49, 2% 50-99. **Special facilities:** Sports medicine clinic, clinics at nearby hospital, entrepreneurship center.

**Freshman class profile.** 1,451 applied, 966 admitted, 328 enrolled.

| Mid 50% test scores | | | |
|---|---|---|---|
| SAT critical reading: | 430-560 | Rank in top quarter: | 58% |
| SAT math: | 460-550 | Rank in top tenth: | 29% |
| ACT composite: | 20-25 | Return as sophomores: | 70% |
| GPA 3.50 or higher: | 51% | Out-of-state: | 32% |
| GPA 3.0-3.49: | 28% | Live on campus: | 71% |
| GPA 2.0-2.99: | 21% | Fraternities: | 6% |
| | | Sororities: | 13% |

**Basis for selection.** School achievement record and courses taken most important. Test scores, school recommendation, school and community activities, class rank, and interview also considered. High school GPA recomputed to reflect performance in academic subjects only. Essay, interview, portfolio recommended for all; audition required for music. **Homeschooled:** If part of diploma-granting organization, list of coursework completed and level of performance required. Otherwise, detailed portfolio required and essay, 3 letters of reference, on-campus interview recommended. **Learning Disabled:** Documentation from a professional within last 2 years required.

**High school preparation.** 16 units recommended. Recommended units include English 4, mathematics 3, social studies 3, history 2, science 3 and foreign language 1. Chemistry, algebra required for 4-year nursing program.

**2008-2009 Annual costs.** Tuition/fees: $23,150. Tuition for pharmacy students: $25,224. Room/board: $8,325. Books/supplies: $1,000. Personal expenses: $500.

**2007-2008 Financial aid. Need-based:** Average need met was 80%. Average scholarship/grant was $4,500; average loan $6,900. 54% of total undergraduate aid awarded as scholarships/grants, 46% as loans/jobs. **Non-need-based:** Scholarships awarded for academics, alumni affiliation, athletics, leadership, music/drama, state residency.

**Application procedures. Admission:** Priority date 5/1; no deadline. $25 fee, may be waived for applicants with need. Application may be submitted online. Admission notification on a rolling basis. For most health science programs, application deadline is January 15, early decision recommended. **Financial aid:** Priority date 3/1, closing date 8/30. FAFSA, institutional form required. Applicants notified on a rolling basis starting 4/1; must reply by 5/1 or within 4 week(s) of notification.

**Academics.** Students can fulfill course requirements at their own pace. **Special study options:** Accelerated study, combined bachelor's/graduate degree, cooperative education, double major, dual enrollment of high school students, ESL, exchange student, independent study, internships, liberal arts/career combination, student-designed major, study abroad, teacher certification program, Washington semester. **Credit/placement by examination:** AP, CLEP, IB, SAT, ACT, institutional tests. 30 credit hours maximum toward associate degree, 60 toward bachelor's. **Support services:** Learning center, reduced course load, remedial instruction, study skills assistance, tutoring, writing center.

**Majors. Biology:** General. **Business:** Accounting, business admin, finance. **Communications:** Media studies. **Education:** General, biology, elementary, English, health, physical, science, secondary, social studies, special. **Health:** Athletic training, nursing (RN), predental, premedicine, prepharmacy, preveterinary, radiologic technology/medical imaging. **Parks/recreation:** Sports admin. **Physical sciences:** Chemistry. **Psychology:** General. **Public administration:** Policy analysis. **Visual/performing arts:** Art, interior design.

**Most popular majors.** Business/marketing 19%, health sciences 30%, parks/recreation 9%, psychology 6%, visual/performing arts 10%.

**Computing on campus.** 65 workstations in dormitories, library, computer center, student center. Dormitories wired for high-speed internet access and linked to campus network. Commuter students can connect to campus network. Online library, helpline, student web hosting, wireless network available.

**Student life. Freshman orientation:** Mandatory. Preregistration for classes offered. **Policies:** On-campus housing required for dependent freshmen and sophomores not living with parents or legal guardian in local area. **Housing:** Guaranteed on-campus for freshmen. Coed dorms, special housing for disabled, substance-free housing available. $100 fully refundable deposit. Single rooms and suites available. **Activities:** Pep band, campus ministries, choral groups, drama, international student organizations, musical theater, student government, student newspaper, honorary fraternities, Fellowship Christian Athletes, Young Republicans, College Democrats.

**Athletics.** NCAA. **Intercollegiate:** Baseball M, basketball, cheerleading, cross-country, football (tackle) M, golf M, rowing (crew) W, soccer, softball W, tennis, track and field W, volleyball W. **Intramural:** Basketball, bowling, football (non-tackle) M, tennis, volleyball. **Team name:** Golden Eagles.

**Student services.** Career counseling, student employment services, financial aid counseling, personal counseling, placement for graduates.

**Contact.** E-mail: admissions@ucwv.edu
Phone: (304) 357-4750 Toll-free number: (800) 995-4682
Fax: (304) 357-4781
Brad Parrish, Vice President for Enrollment, University of Charleston, 2300 MacCorkle Avenue, SE, Charleston, WV 25304

## West Liberty State College
**West Liberty, West Virginia**
www.westliberty.edu

**CB code: 5901**

- Public 4-year liberal arts college
- Residential campus in rural community
- 2,236 degree-seeking undergraduates: 8% part-time, 56% women
- 3 graduate students
- 83% of applicants admitted
- SAT or ACT with writing required
- 44% graduate within 6 years

**General.** Founded in 1837. Regionally accredited. **Degrees:** 374 bachelor's, 33 associate awarded. **Location:** 10 miles from Wheeling, 50 miles from Pittsburgh. **Calendar:** Semester, limited summer session. **Full-time faculty:** 99 total; 60% have terminal degrees, 1% minority, 40% women. **Part-time faculty:** 64 total; 48% women. **Class size:** 62% < 20, 31% 20-39, 6% 40-49, less than 1% 50-99. **Special facilities:** Media arts center, rare book room, rare sheet music collection.

**Freshman class profile.** 1,524 applied, 1,262 admitted, 474 enrolled.

| Mid 50% test scores | | Rank in top quarter: | 30% |
|---|---|---|---|
| SAT critical reading: | 400-530 | Rank in top tenth: | 12% |
| SAT math: | 400-520 | Return as sophomores: | 65% |
| ACT composite: | 17-22 | Out-of-state: | 9% |
| GPA 3.50 or higher: | 30% | Live on campus: | 81% |
| GPA 3.0-3.49: | 30% | Fraternities: | 2% |
| GPA 2.0-2.99: | 38% | Sororities: | 2% |

**Basis for selection.** Minimum 2.0 high school GPA required or 17 on enhanced ACT or 810 (exclusive of Writing) on SAT. Audition required for music education; portfolio recommended for art.

**High school preparation.** 15 units required. Required and recommended units include English 4, mathematics 3, social studies 2, history 1, science 3 (laboratory 2) and foreign language 2. Mathematics must be algebra I and higher. Social science must include American history.

**2007-2008 Annual costs.** Tuition/fees: $4,172; $10,192 out-of-state. Room/board: $5,984. Books/supplies: $1,000. Personal expenses: $1,000.

**2007-2008 Financial aid. Need-based:** 48% of total undergraduate aid awarded as scholarships/grants, 52% as loans/jobs. **Non-need-based:** Scholarships awarded for academics, alumni affiliation, art, athletics, leadership, music/drama. **Additional information:** Non-need based student employment available at food service, college union, bookstore, and tutoring office. Resident assistant and campus security jobs also available.

**Application procedures. Admission:** No deadline. No application fee. Application may be submitted online. Admission notification on a rolling basis beginning on or about 9/1. **Financial aid:** Priority date 3/1; no closing date. FAFSA required. Applicants notified on a rolling basis starting 2/15; must reply within 2 week(s) of notification.

**Academics.** Freshman experience course available. **Special study options:** Accelerated study, distance learning, double major, dual enrollment of high school students, external degree, honors, independent study, internships, liberal arts/career combination, student-designed major, study abroad, teacher certification program, Washington semester. **Credit/placement by examination:** AP, CLEP, SAT, ACT, institutional tests. **Support services:** Reduced course load, remedial instruction, tutoring.

**Majors. Biology:** General, bacteriology, biotechnology. **Business:** General, accounting, banking/financial services, business admin, managerial economics, tourism promotion, tourism/travel. **Communications:** General. **Computer sciences:** Information systems. **Education:** Art, biology, chemistry, early childhood, elementary, English, health, mathematics, mentally handicapped, music, physical, science, secondary, social science, special. **English:** English lit. **Health:** Clinical lab science, dental hygiene. **History:** General. **Liberal arts:** Arts/sciences. **Math:** General. **Parks/recreation:** Exercise sciences. **Physical sciences:** Chemistry. **Protective services:** Criminal justice. **Psychology:** General. **Social sciences:** General, political science, sociology. **Visual/performing arts:** Commercial/advertising art.

**Most popular majors.** Business/marketing 26%, education 22%, health sciences 11%, liberal arts 12%, security/protective services 6%.

**Computing on campus.** 300 workstations in dormitories, library, computer center, student center. Dormitories wired for high-speed internet access and linked to campus network. Commuter students can connect to campus network. Online course registration, helpline, repair service available.

**Student life. Freshman orientation:** Mandatory, $30 fee. Preregistration for classes offered. Held Friday through Sunday before first day of classes. **Housing:** Guaranteed on-campus for all undergraduates. Coed dorms, single-sex dorms, special housing for disabled, apartments available. $100 fully refundable deposit, deadline 6/1. Honors residence for students who meet criteria specifications. **Activities:** Bands, choral groups, drama, international student organizations, literary magazine, music ensembles, musical theater, radio station, student government, student newspaper, TV station, Amnesty International, WLSC Students for Life, B-Pride, Electric Square, non-traditional student support group, Students in Free Enterprise, Students for Unity and Understanding.

**Athletics.** NCAA. **Intercollegiate:** Baseball M, basketball, cross-country, football (tackle) M, golf, softball W, tennis, track and field, volleyball W, wrestling M. **Intramural:** Basketball, golf, handball M, racquetball, softball, table tennis, tennis, volleyball. **Team name:** Hilltoppers.

**Student services.** Alcohol/substance abuse counseling, campus ministries, career counseling, student employment services, financial aid counseling, health services, minority student services, personal counseling, placement for graduates, veterans' counselor. **Physically disabled:** Services for visually, hearing impaired.

**Contact.** E-mail: wladmsn1@wlsc.edu
Phone: (304) 336-8076 Toll-free number: (800) 732-6204
Fax: (304) 336-8403
Brenda King, Director of Admissions & Recruitment, West Liberty State College, Box 295, West Liberty, WV 26074-0295

## West Virginia State University

**Institute, West Virginia**
www.wvstateu.edu

**CB member**
**CB code: 5903**

- Public 4-year liberal arts and teachers college
- Commuter campus in small town

**General.** Founded in 1891. Regionally accredited. **Location:** 8 miles from Charleston. **Calendar:** Semester.

**Annual costs/financial aid.** Tuition/fees (2007-2008): $4,136; $9,718 out-of-state. Room/board: $5,600. Books/supplies: $948. Personal expenses: $2,951. Need-based financial aid available to full-time and part-time students.

**Contact.** Phone: (304) 766-3221
Director, Campus Box 197, Institute, WV 25112-1000

## West Virginia University

**Morgantown, West Virginia**
www.wvu.edu

**CB member**
**CB code: 5904**

- Public 4-year university
- Residential campus in small city
- 21,145 degree-seeking undergraduates: 7% part-time, 46% women, 3% African American, 2% Asian American, 2% Hispanic American, 2% international
- 6,968 degree-seeking graduate students
- 89% of applicants admitted
- SAT or ACT with writing required
- 55% graduate within 6 years

**General.** Founded in 1867. Regionally accredited. Regional centers at Charleston, Clarksburg, Parkersburg, Potomac State College in Keyser, Shepherdstown, WVU Institute of Technology, and West Liberty. Health Sciences Center operates division in Charleston. **Degrees:** 3,620 bachelor's awarded; master's, doctoral, first professional offered. **ROTC:** Army, Air Force. **Location:** 70 miles from Pittsburgh, 200 miles from Baltimore. **Calendar:** Semester, extensive summer session. **Full-time faculty:** 802 total; 80% have terminal degrees, 11% minority, 35% women. **Part-time faculty:** 350 total; 29% have terminal degrees, 5% minority, 55% women. **Class size:** 34% < 20, 39% 20-39, 9% 40-49, 11% 50-99, 8% >100. **Special facilities:** Personal rapid transit system (PRT), arboretum, planetarium, herbarium, pharmacy museum, 2 art galleries, 7 experimental farms, 3 forests, software development center, mineral and energy resources museum, center for Black culture and research.

**Freshman class profile.** 13,634 applied, 12,200 admitted, 4,731 enrolled.

| Mid 50% test scores | | Rank in top tenth: | 18% |
|---|---|---|---|
| SAT critical reading: | 470-560 | Return as sophomores: | 79% |
| SAT math: | 490-590 | Out-of-state: | 50% |
| ACT composite: | 21-26 | Live on campus: | 84% |
| GPA 3.50 or higher: | 41% | International: | 1% |
| GPA 3.0-3.49: | 32% | Fraternities: | 10% |
| GPA 2.0-2.99: | 27% | Sororities: | 12% |
| Rank in top quarter: | 43% | | |

**Basis for selection.** High school GPA and SAT or ACT scores most important. Minimum 2.0 GPA and SAT of 910 (exclusive of Writing) or ACT of 19 required of state residents. Minimum 2.25 GPA and SAT of 950 or ACT of 20 required of nonresidents. Applicants with high GPA, high test scores, or special talents (athletics or the arts) who do not meet all admissions criteria may be considered on individual basis. Up to 5% of each incoming class may be admitted under this special policy. Internal placement test for math, chemistry, and foreign languages. Interview required for dental hygiene; audition required for drama, music; portfolio required for art. Essay required for some programs. **Homeschooled:** Students should submit ACT or SAT scores, transcript or descriptions of class background and/or experience.

**High school preparation.** 17 units required. Required units include English 4, mathematics 4, social studies 3, science 3 (laboratory 3), foreign language 2 and visual/performing arts 1. 4 units of English including grammar, composition, and literature; 3 units of social studies including US history; 4 units of college preparatory mathematics including algebra I and II, plane geometry; 2 units of the same language and 1 unit of fine arts required.

**2007-2008 Annual costs.** Tuition/fees: $4,722; $14,600 out-of-state. Room/board: $7,046. Books/supplies: $900. Personal expenses: $1,316.

**2007-2008 Financial aid. Need-based:** 2,099 full-time freshmen applied for aid; 1,658 were judged to have need; 1,310 of these received aid. Average need met was 75%. Average scholarship/grant was $3,598; average loan $4,413. 42% of total undergraduate aid awarded as scholarships/grants, 58% as loans/jobs. **Non-need-based:** Awarded to 11,399 full-time undergraduates, including 1,944 freshmen. Scholarships awarded for academics, alumni affiliation, art, athletics, job skills, leadership, minority status, music/drama, state residency. **Additional information:** February 1 closing date for freshman scholarships.

**Application procedures. Admission:** Priority date 3/1; deadline 8/1. $25 fee ($40 out-of-state), may be waived for applicants with need. Application may be submitted online. Admission notification on a rolling basis beginning on or about 9/15. **Financial aid:** Closing date 3/1. FAFSA required. Applicants notified on a rolling basis starting 3/15; must reply within 4 week(s) of notification.

**Academics. Special study options:** Accelerated study, combined bachelor's/graduate degree, cooperative education, distance learning, double major, ESL, exchange student, external degree, honors, independent study, internships, semester at sea, student-designed major, study abroad, teacher certification program, Washington semester. **Credit/placement by examination:** AP, CLEP, IB, SAT, ACT, institutional tests. 38 credit hours maximum toward bachelor's degree. **Support services:** Learning center, pre-admission summer program, reduced course load, remedial instruction, study skills assistance, tutoring, writing center.

**Majors. Agriculture:** Agronomy, animal sciences, business, economics, horticultural science, plant sciences, soil science. **Architecture:** Landscape. **Biology:** General, biochemistry, exercise physiology. **Business:** Accounting, business admin, finance, management information systems, managerial economics, marketing. **Communications:** General, advertising, broadcast journalism, journalism, media studies, public relations. **Computer sciences:** Computer science. **Conservation:** Forest management, wildlife, wood science. **Education:** Agricultural, physical. **Engineering:** Aerospace, chemical, civil, computer, electrical, industrial, mechanical, mining, petroleum. **English:** English lit. **Family/consumer sciences:** General, child development, clothing/textiles, family/community services, food/nutrition. **Foreign languages:** General. **Health:** Athletic training, audiology/speech pathology, clinical lab science, dental hygiene, nursing (RN), prenursing, prepharmacy. **History:** General. **Liberal arts:** Arts/sciences. **Math:** General. **Parks/recreation:** Exercise sciences, facilities management, health/fitness, sports admin. **Philosophy/religion:** Philosophy. **Physical sciences:** Chemistry, geology, physics. **Protective services:** Criminalistics, forensics. **Psychology:** General. **Public administration:** Social work. **Social sciences:** Economics, geography, political science, sociology. **Visual/performing arts:** General, art, art history/conservation, dramatic, theater history. **Other:** Biometric systems.

**Most popular majors.** Biology 6%, business/marketing 12%, communications/journalism 10%, engineering/engineering technologies 10%, health sciences 8%, interdisciplinary studies 8%, liberal arts 7%, social sciences 8%.

**Computing on campus.** 2,500 workstations in dormitories, library, computer center, student center. Dormitories wired for high-speed internet access and linked to campus network. Commuter students can connect to campus network. Online course registration, online library, helpline, repair service, student web hosting, wireless network available.

**Student life. Freshman orientation:** Available, $45 fee. Preregistration for classes offered. Held during summer; several options ranging in length and fees. **Policies:** Anti-hazing, affirmative action and nondiscrimination policies. Mandatory freshmen housing program places faculty residence hall leaders adjacent to residence halls. **Housing:** Guaranteed on-campus for freshmen. Coed dorms, single-sex dorms, special housing for disabled, apartments, fraternity/sorority housing, substance-free housing available. $200 partly refundable deposit, deadline 5/1. Special interest floors available. **Activities:** Bands, campus ministries, choral groups, dance, drama, international student organizations, literary magazine, music ensembles, musical theater, radio station, student government, student newspaper, symphony orchestra, TV station, Sierra student coalition, Hillel House, Zeta Delat Phi, Circle K, Campus Crusade for Christ, College Republicans, Muslim student association.

**Athletics.** NCAA. **Intercollegiate:** Baseball M, basketball, cross-country W, diving, football (tackle) M, gymnastics W, rifle, rowing (crew) W, soccer, swimming, tennis W, track and field W, volleyball W, wrestling M.

**Intramural:** Badminton, basketball, bowling, football (non-tackle), racquetball, soccer, tennis W, volleyball. **Team name:** Mountaineers.

**Student services.** Adult student services, alcohol/substance abuse counseling, campus ministries, career counseling, services for economically disadvantaged, student employment services, financial aid counseling, health services, legal services, minority student services, personal counseling, placement for graduates, veterans' counselor, women's services. **Physically disabled:** Services for visually, speech, hearing impaired.

**Contact.** E-mail: go2wvu@mail.wvu.edu
Phone: (304) 293-2121 Toll-free number: (800) 344-9881
Fax: (304) 293-3080
Cheng Khoo, Director of Admissions and Records, West Virginia University, Admissions and Records Office, Morgantown, WV 26506-6009

## West Virginia University at Parkersburg
**Parkersburg, West Virginia**
www.wvup.edu
CB code: 5932

- Public 4-year branch campus and community college
- Commuter campus in large town
- 3,141 degree-seeking undergraduates: 30% part-time, 64% women, 1% African American, 1% Asian American, 1% Hispanic American
- 35% graduate within 6 years; 15% enter graduate study

**General.** Founded in 1971. Regionally accredited. Regional campus of West Virginia University. **Degrees:** 149 bachelor's, 345 associate awarded. **Location:** 80 miles from Charleston, 110 miles from Columbus, Ohio. **Calendar:** Semester, limited summer session. **Full-time faculty:** 86 total; 17% have terminal degrees, 5% minority, 48% women. **Part-time faculty:** 163 total; 5% have terminal degrees, 2% minority, 48% women. **Class size:** 55% < 20, 41% 20-39, 2% 40-49, 1% 50-99.

**Freshman class profile.** 622 applied, 622 admitted, 622 enrolled.

| Mid 50% test scores | | | |
|---|---|---|---|
| ACT composite: | 16-21 | | |
| GPA 3.50 or higher: | 20% | | |
| GPA 3.0-3.49: | 30% | | |

| | |
|---|---|
| GPA 2.0-2.99: | 45% |
| End year in good standing: | 71% |
| Return as sophomores: | 55% |
| Out-of-state: | 1% |

**Basis for selection.** Open admission, but selective for some programs. Special requirements for nursing, surgical technology, and bachelor's degree programs. SAT or ACT scores required but not used in admission decisions; ACT preferred. Interview required for nursing program.

**High school preparation.** 16 units recommended. Recommended units include English 4, mathematics 3, social studies 4, science 3 (laboratory 2). Social studies recommendations may be fulfilled with history units.

**2007-2008 Annual costs.** Tuition/fees: $1,824; $6,460 out-of-state. Books/supplies: $1,000. Personal expenses: $1,400.

**2007-2008 Financial aid. Need-based:** 460 full-time freshmen applied for aid; 430 were judged to have need; 430 of these received aid. Average need met was 77%. Average scholarship/grant was $5,400; average loan $3,000. 97% of total undergraduate aid awarded as scholarships/grants, 3% as loans/jobs. **Non-need-based:** Awarded to 700 full-time undergraduates, including 260 freshmen. Scholarships awarded for academics, state residency.

**Application procedures. Admission:** No deadline. No application fee. Application may be submitted online. Admission notification on a rolling basis. **Financial aid:** Priority date 3/1; no closing date. FAFSA required. Applicants notified on a rolling basis; must reply within 2 week(s) of notification.

**Academics. Special study options:** Cooperative education, cross-registration, distance learning, dual enrollment of high school students, ESL, external degree, honors, independent study, internships, teacher certification program. **Credit/placement by examination:** AP, CLEP, institutional tests. **Support services:** Learning center, reduced course load, remedial instruction, study skills assistance, tutoring.

**Majors. Business:** Business admin. **Education:** Elementary. **Engineering technology:** Industrial management.

**Most popular majors.** Business/marketing 28%, education 21%, engineering/engineering technologies 11%, liberal arts 40%.

**Computing on campus.** 435 workstations in library, computer center. Online course registration, wireless network available.

**Student life. Freshman orientation:** Available. Preregistration for classes offered. Held several weeks prior to the start of classes. **Activities:** Choral groups, drama, student government, student newspaper, Campus Christian Fellowship, criminal justice organization, social service organization.

**Athletics. Intramural:** Basketball, bowling, softball, table tennis, volleyball.

**Student services.** Adult student services, career counseling, services for economically disadvantaged, student employment services, financial aid counseling, health services, on-campus daycare, placement for graduates, veterans' counselor. **Physically disabled:** Services for visually, speech, hearing impaired.

**Contact.** E-mail: info@mail.wvup.edu
Phone: (304) 424-8220 Fax: (304) 424-8332
Cecelia Malhotra, Registrar, West Virginia University at Parkersburg, 300 Campus Drive, Parkersburg, WV 26104-8647

## West Virginia University Institute of Technology
**Montgomery, West Virginia**
www.wvutech.edu                                   CB code: 5902

- Public 4-year engineering and technical college
- Commuter campus in small town

**General.** Founded in 1895. Regionally accredited. **Location:** 30 miles from Charleston. **Calendar:** Semester.

**Annual costs/financial aid.** Tuition/fees (2007-2008): $4,598; $11,808 out-of-state. Room/board: $5,900. Books/supplies: $800. Personal expenses: $1,600. Need-based financial aid available for full-time students.

**Contact.** Phone: (304) 442-3167
Director of Admissions, 405 Fayette Pike, Montgomery, WV 25136-2436

## West Virginia Wesleyan College
**Buckhannon, West Virginia**                      CB member
www.wvwc.edu                                        CB code: 5905

- Private 4-year liberal arts college affiliated with United Methodist Church
- Residential campus in small town
- 1,210 degree-seeking undergraduates: 1% part-time, 54% women, 3% African American, 1% Hispanic American, 4% international
- 39 degree-seeking graduate students
- 77% of applicants admitted
- SAT or ACT (ACT writing optional) required
- 55% graduate within 6 years; 36% enter graduate study

**General.** Founded in 1890. Regionally accredited. **Degrees:** 308 bachelor's awarded; master's offered. **Location:** 115 miles from Charleston, 135 miles from Pittsburgh. **Calendar:** Semester, limited summer session. **Full-time faculty:** 69 total; 74% have terminal degrees, 3% minority, 45% women. **Part-time faculty:** 69 total; 13% have terminal degrees, 3% minority, 61% women. **Class size:** 63% < 20, 35% 20-39, 2% 40-49, less than 1% 50-99. **Special facilities:** Planetarium, botany museum, herbarium, greenhouse.

**Freshman class profile.** 1,388 applied, 1,065 admitted, 402 enrolled.

| Mid 50% test scores | | Rank in top quarter: | 57% |
|---|---|---|---|
| SAT critical reading: | 420-550 | Rank in top tenth: | 29% |
| SAT math: | 430-560 | End year in good standing: | 70% |
| SAT writing: | 430-550 | Return as sophomores: | 75% |
| ACT composite: | 20-26 | Out-of-state: | 39% |
| GPA 3.50 or higher: | 44% | Live on campus: | 90% |
| GPA 3.0-3.49: | 26% | International: | 3% |
| GPA 2.0-2.99: | 29% | | |

**Basis for selection.** School achievement record and test scores required. Essay, interview recommended for all; audition recommended for drama, music; portfolio recommended for art. **Homeschooled:** Transcript of courses and grades, state high school equivalency certificate required.

**High school preparation.** 15 units recommended. Recommended units include English 4, mathematics 2, social studies 2, history 2, science 2 (laboratory 2), foreign language 1, computer science 1 and visual/performing arts 1.

**2007-2008 Annual costs.** Tuition/fees: $21,830. Room/board: $6,160. Books/supplies: $2,500. Personal expenses: $2,500.

**2007-2008 Financial aid. Need-based:** 363 full-time freshmen applied for aid; 318 were judged to have need; 318 of these received aid. Average need met was 84.4%. Average scholarship/grant was $17,627; average loan $3,144. 82% of total undergraduate aid awarded as scholarships/grants, 18% as loans/jobs. **Non-need-based:** Awarded to 649 full-time undergraduates, including 202 freshmen. Scholarships awarded for academics, alumni affiliation, art, athletics, leadership, music/drama, religious affiliation.

**Application procedures. Admission:** Priority date 3/1; no deadline. $35 fee, may be waived for applicants with need. Application may be submitted online. Admission notification on a rolling basis beginning on or about 9/15. Must reply by May 1 or within 5 week(s) if notified thereafter. **Financial aid:** Priority date 2/15; no closing date. FAFSA required. Applicants notified on a rolling basis starting 3/15; must reply within 4 week(s) of notification.

**Academics. Special study options:** Combined bachelor's/graduate degree, double major, ESL, exchange student, honors, independent study, internships, liberal arts/career combination, student-designed major, study abroad, teacher certification program, Washington semester. **Credit/placement by examination:** AP, CLEP, IB, SAT, ACT, institutional tests. 60 credit hours maximum toward bachelor's degree. **Support services:** Learning center, reduced course load, remedial instruction, study skills assistance, tutoring, writing center.

**Majors. Biology:** General. **Business:** Accounting, business admin, finance, international, managerial economics, marketing. **Communications:** General, public relations. **Computer sciences:** General, computer science, information systems. **Conservation:** Environmental science. **Education:** General, art, biology, chemistry, elementary, English, health, history, kindergarten/preschool, learning disabled, mathematics, music, physical, science, secondary, social studies, special. **Engineering:** General. **English:** Creative writing, English lit. **Health:** Athletic training, predental, premedicine, prepharmacy, preveterinary. **History:** General. **Legal studies:** Prelaw. **Math:** General. **Parks/recreation:** Exercise sciences, health/fitness. **Philosophy/religion:** Philosophy, religion. **Physical sciences:** Chemistry, physics. **Protective services:** Law enforcement admin. **Psychology:** General. **Social sciences:** Economics, international relations, political science, sociology. **Theology:** Religious ed. **Visual/performing arts:** Art, arts management, ceramics, dramatic, drawing, graphic design, painting, studio arts, theater arts management.

**Most popular majors.** Biology 6%, business/marketing 20%, communications/journalism 6%, education 13%, health sciences 8%, social sciences 9%.

**Computing on campus.** PC or laptop required. Dormitories wired for high-speed internet access and linked to campus network. Commuter students can connect to campus network. Online library, helpline, repair service, wireless network available.

**Student life. Freshman orientation:** Mandatory, $200 fee. Preregistration for classes offered. Held weekend before fall class registration; provides programs for new students and parents. Full semester 4 credit freshmen seminar required of all first-time, full-time freshmen. **Housing:** Guaranteed on-campus for all undergraduates. Coed dorms, single-sex dorms, special housing for disabled, apartments, fraternity/sorority housing, substance-free housing available. $200 deposit. Full-time students required to live on campus unless married, living with parents, or have received written permission from the Housing Committee to live off campus. **Activities:** Bands, campus ministries, choral groups, dance, drama, international student organizations, literary magazine, music ensembles, musical theater, radio station, student government, student newspaper, TV station, Christian Life Council, Fellowship of Christian Athletes, Alpha Phi Omega service fraternity, Black Student Union, College Republicans, Young Democrats, Green Club, Wesleyan service corps.

**Athletics.** NCAA. **Intercollegiate:** Baseball M, basketball, cross-country, football (tackle) M, golf, soccer, softball W, swimming, tennis, track and field, volleyball W. **Intramural:** Basketball, football (non-tackle), racquetball, softball, table tennis, volleyball, water polo M. **Team name:** Bobcats.

**Student services.** Alcohol/substance abuse counseling, campus ministries, career counseling, financial aid counseling, health services, minority student services, personal counseling, placement for graduates. **Physically disabled:** Services for visually, speech, hearing impaired.

**Contact.** E-mail: admission@wvwc.edu
Phone: (304) 473-8510 Toll-free number: (800) 722-9933
Fax: (304) 473-8108
Chris Coons, Director of Admission, West Virginia Wesleyan College, 59 College Avenue, Buckhannon, WV 26201-2998

## Wheeling Jesuit University
**Wheeling, West Virginia**                         CB member
www.wju.edu                                          CB code: 5906

- Private 4-year university and liberal arts college affiliated with Roman Catholic Church
- Residential campus in small city

- 1,093 degree-seeking undergraduates: 12% part-time, 61% women, 3% African American, 1% Asian American, 1% Hispanic American, 3% international
- 221 degree-seeking graduate students
- 69% of applicants admitted
- SAT or ACT (ACT writing optional), application essay required
- 59% graduate within 6 years

**General.** Founded in 1954. Regionally accredited. **Degrees:** 258 bachelor's awarded; master's, doctoral offered. **Location:** 55 miles from Pittsburgh, 125 miles from Columbus, Ohio. **Calendar:** Semester, limited summer session. **Full-time faculty:** 78 total; 70% have terminal degrees, 6% minority, 41% women. **Part-time faculty:** 60 total; 25% have terminal degrees, 53% women. **Class size:** 58% < 20, 42% 20-39, less than 1% 40-49. **Special facilities:** NASA Classroom of the Future.

**Freshman class profile.** 1,370 applied, 950 admitted, 240 enrolled.

| Mid 50% test scores | | Rank in top quarter: | 49% |
|---|---|---|---|
| SAT critical reading: | 460-540 | Rank in top tenth: | 22% |
| SAT math: | 450-570 | End year in good standing: | 89% |
| ACT composite: | 20-25 | Return as sophomores: | 76% |
| GPA 3.50 or higher: | 55% | Out-of-state: | 59% |
| GPA 3.0-3.49: | 32% | Live on campus: | 85% |
| GPA 2.0-2.99: | 13% | International: | 4% |

**Basis for selection.** High school GPA, quality of courses taken, and test scores most important. Some exception made to minimum when warranted by high school record. Personal recommendations and extracurricular activities important. In-state and out-of-state applicants treated equally. Interview recommended. **Learning Disabled:** Students need to submit written documentation of disability.

**High school preparation.** 15 units required. Required and recommended units include English 4, mathematics 2, social studies 2, history 2, science 1 (laboratory 1), foreign language 2 and academic electives 6. Applicants for programs in the natural sciences should have 1 unit of biology and 1 of chemistry. Applicants preparing for future study in the physical therapy doctorate program should have a minimum of 3 years of college preparatory math and 3 years of lab science, including physics.

**2008-2009 Annual costs.** Tuition/fees (projected): $24,390. Room/board: $7,650. Books/supplies: $800. Personal expenses: $600.

**2007-2008 Financial aid. Need-based:** 225 full-time freshmen applied for aid; 207 were judged to have need; 207 of these received aid. Average need met was 89%. Average scholarship/grant was $6,236; average loan $4,165. 53% of total undergraduate aid awarded as scholarships/grants, 47% as loans/jobs. **Non-need-based:** Awarded to 953 full-time undergraduates, including 245 freshmen. Scholarships awarded for academics, alumni affiliation, athletics, leadership, music/drama.

**Application procedures. Admission:** No deadline. $25 fee, may be waived for applicants with need. Application may be submitted online. Admission notification on a rolling basis beginning on or about 9/1. Must reply by May 1 or within 2 week(s) if notified thereafter. **Financial aid:** Priority date 2/15; no closing date. FAFSA required. Applicants notified on a rolling basis starting 3/15; must reply within 2 week(s) of notification.

**Academics. Special study options:** Combined bachelor's/graduate degree, distance learning, double major, ESL, honors, independent study, internships, liberal arts/career combination, semester at sea, student-designed major, study abroad, teacher certification program, United Nations semester, Washington semester. **Credit/placement by examination:** AP, CLEP, SAT, ACT. 30 credit hours maximum toward bachelor's degree. **Support services:** Learning center, remedial instruction, study skills assistance, tutoring, writing center.

**Majors. Biology:** General. **Business:** Accounting, business admin, international. **Computer science:** Computer science. **Education:** Science. **English:** Creative writing, English lit. **Foreign languages:** French, Spanish. **Health:** Health care admin, nuclear medical technology, respiratory therapy technology. **History:** General. **Liberal arts:** Arts/sciences. **Math:** General. **Philosophy/religion:** Philosophy. **Physical sciences:** Chemistry, physics. **Protective services:** Criminal justice. **Psychology:** General. **Social sciences:** International relations, political science. **Theology:** Theology. **Other:** Political and economic philosophy.

**Computing on campus.** 243 workstations in dormitories, library, computer center, student center. Dormitories wired for high-speed internet access and linked to campus network. Commuter students can connect to campus network. Online library, helpline, student web hosting, wireless network available.

**Student life. Freshman orientation:** Available. Preregistration for classes offered. 3 day orientation for freshmen and transfer students prior to the beginning of the fall semester. **Housing:** Guaranteed on-campus for all undergraduates. Coed dorms, single-sex dorms, apartments available. $100 fully refundable deposit. **Activities:** Pep band, campus ministries, choral groups, dance, drama, international student organizations, literary magazine, student government, student newspaper, TV station, social service outreach organization, academic clubs, leadership development group.

**Athletics.** NCAA. **Intercollegiate:** Baseball M, basketball, cheerleading, cross-country, golf, lacrosse M, soccer, softball W, swimming, track and field, volleyball W. **Intramural:** Basketball, soccer, softball, tennis, volleyball. **Team name:** Cardinals.

**Student services.** Adult student services, alcohol/substance abuse counseling, campus ministries, career counseling, student employment services, financial aid counseling, health services, minority student services, personal counseling, placement for graduates, veterans' counselor.

**Contact.** E-mail: admiss@wju.edu
Phone: (304) 243-2359 Toll-free number: (800) 624-6992
Fax: (304) 243-2397
Denny Bardos, Dean of Enrollment, Wheeling Jesuit University, 316 Washington Avenue, Wheeling, WV 26003-6295

# Wisconsin

## Alverno College
### Milwaukee, Wisconsin
### www.alverno.edu
**CB member**
**CB code: 1012**

- Private 4-year liberal arts college for women affiliated with Roman Catholic Church
- Commuter campus in very large city
- 2,251 degree-seeking undergraduates: 26% part-time, 100% women, 17% African American, 4% Asian American, 12% Hispanic American, 1% Native American, 1% international
- 273 degree-seeking graduate students
- 87% of applicants admitted
- SAT or ACT (ACT writing optional), application essay required
- 42% graduate within 6 years; 14% enter graduate study

**General.** Founded in 1887. Regionally accredited. **Degrees:** 296 bachelor's, 6 associate awarded; master's offered. **ROTC:** Army, Air Force. **Location:** 5 miles from downtown. **Calendar:** Semester, limited summer session. **Full-time faculty:** 110 total; 90% have terminal degrees, 8% minority, 76% women. **Part-time faculty:** 118 total; 58% have terminal degrees, 10% minority, 81% women. **Class size:** 52% < 20, 47% 20-39, less than 1% 40-49. **Special facilities:** Multimedia productions facility, independent science research areas, native prairie, clinical nursing resource center.

**Freshman class profile.** 484 applied, 419 admitted, 290 enrolled.

| Mid 50% test scores | | Return as sophomores: | 73% |
|---|---|---|---|
| ACT composite: | 17-22 | Out-of-state: | 1% |
| GPA 3.50 or higher: | 17% | Live on campus: | 30% |
| GPA 3.0-3.49: | 31% | Sororities: | 2% |
| GPA 2.0-2.99: | 47% | | |

**Basis for selection.** Review of high school transcripts including GPA, academic units completed, standardized test scores, essay, Communication Placement Assessment results. Audition required for music therapy; portfolio required for studio art. **Homeschooled:** Letter of recommendation (non-parent) required. Portfolio of work required.

**High school preparation.** College-preparatory program required. 17 units required. Required and recommended units include English 4, mathematics 3, social studies 3, science 3 and foreign language 2.

**2007-2008 Annual costs.** Tuition/fees: $17,296. Tuition and fees may vary by program. Room/board: $6,106. Books/supplies: $1,050. Personal expenses: $1,620.

**2007-2008 Financial aid. Need-based:** 254 full-time freshmen applied for aid; 232 were judged to have need; 232 of these received aid. Average scholarship/grant was $10,708; average loan $3,393. 62% of total undergraduate aid awarded as scholarships/grants, 38% as loans/jobs. **Non-need-based:** Awarded to 188 full-time undergraduates, including 28 freshmen. Scholarships awarded for academics, alumni affiliation, leadership.

**Application procedures. Admission:** No deadline. $20 fee, may be waived for applicants with need. Application may be submitted online. Admission notification on a rolling basis beginning on or about 9/1. Must reply by May 1 or within 2 week(s) if notified thereafter. **Financial aid:** Priority date 2/15; no closing date. FAFSA, institutional form required. Applicants notified on a rolling basis starting 3/15; must reply within 2 week(s) of notification.

**Academics.** Required internships in all majors provide research opportunities through federal government, local organizations and businesses. Students in every major area spend from 8 to 12 hours per week for one semester in field internship. Students also have opportunities to do service learning through individual courses. Degrees with honor awarded based on outstanding achievement and application of learning in service to others. **Special study options:** Double major, independent study, internships, semester at sea, student-designed major, study abroad, teacher certification program, Washington semester, weekend college. **Credit/placement by examination:** AP, CLEP, IB, institutional tests. **Support services:** Learning center, pre-admission summer program, reduced course load, remedial instruction, study skills assistance, tutoring, writing center.

**Majors. Biology:** General, molecular. **Business:** Business admin, international. **Communications:** General. **Computer sciences:** General. **Conservation:** Environmental science. **Education:** General, art, elementary, English, middle, music, science, social studies. **English:** English lit. **Health:** Art therapy, music therapy, nursing (RN). **History:** General. **Liberal arts:** Arts/sciences. **Math:** General. **Philosophy/religion:** Philosophy, religion. **Physical sciences:** Chemistry. **Psychology:** General. **Public administration:** Community org/advocacy. **Social sciences:** General, international relations, political science, sociology. **Visual/performing arts:** Art. **Other:** Communication management and technology, Interactive media design.

**Most popular majors.** Business/marketing 19%, communications/journalism 8%, education 8%, health sciences 29%, psychology 7%.

**Computing on campus.** 500 workstations in dormitories, library, computer center. Dormitories wired for high-speed internet access and linked to campus network. Commuter students can connect to campus network. Online library, student web hosting, wireless network available.

**Student life. Freshman orientation:** Mandatory. Preregistration for classes offered. Overnight program held during the summer. **Housing:** Guaranteed on-campus for all undergraduates. $100 partly refundable deposit. Smoke-free areas available, semi-apartment living within residence halls available to older students. **Activities:** Campus ministries, choral groups, dance, drama, international student organizations, literary magazine, music ensembles, student newspaper, Alliance of the Sciences, Alverno College Entrepreneurs, Alverno Student Education Organization, Artourage, Circle K, Hispanic Women of Alverno, Student Nurses Association, Students in Free Enterprise, Women in Communications, Inc., Women of Asian Ethnicity.

**Athletics.** NCAA. **Intercollegiate:** Basketball W, cross-country W, soccer W, softball W, volleyball W. **Intramural:** Basketball W, volleyball W. **Team name:** Alverno Inferno.

**Student services.** Adult student services, campus ministries, career counseling, financial aid counseling, health services, on-campus daycare, personal counseling. **Physically disabled:** Services for visually, speech, hearing impaired.

**Contact.** E-mail: admissions@alverno.edu
Phone: (414) 382-6101 Toll-free number: (800) 933-3401
Fax: (414) 382-6055
Kim Wankowski, Director of Admissions for Information Processing, Alverno College, 3400 South 43rd Street, Milwaukee, WI 53234-3922

## Bellin College of Nursing
### Green Bay, Wisconsin
### www.bcon.edu
**CB code: 1046**

- Private 4-year nursing college
- Commuter campus in small city
- 259 degree-seeking undergraduates
- 45 graduate students
- 30% of applicants admitted
- ACT (writing optional), interview required
- 61% graduate within 6 years

**General.** Founded in 1909. Regionally accredited. **Degrees:** 58 bachelor's awarded; master's offered. **ROTC:** Army. **Location:** 120 miles from Milwaukee. **Calendar:** Semester, limited summer session. **Full-time faculty:** 17 total; 24% have terminal degrees, 100% women. **Part-time faculty:** 3 total; 33% have terminal degrees, 100% women. **Class size:** 11% < 20, 59% 20-39, 30% 50-99. **Special facilities:** Associated with a health system and hospital.

**Freshman class profile.** 92 applied, 28 admitted, 27 enrolled.

| Mid 50% test scores | | GPA 3.0-3.49: | 30% |
|---|---|---|---|
| ACT composite: | 22-25 | End year in good standing: | 100% |
| GPA 3.50 or higher: | 70% | Return as sophomores: | 87% |

**Basis for selection.** 23 ACT and 3.25 GPA required, although students with 21-22 ACT will be reviewed for admission. Personal interview very important. Three references required, including 1 academic and 1 from employer if working.

**High school preparation.** 13 units required. Required units include English 4, mathematics 3, social studies 3 and science 3. Math must include 1 algebra and 2 advanced math. Sciences must include 1 chemistry, 1 biology, and 1 advanced science.

**2007-2008 Annual costs.** Tuition/fees: $16,839. Books/supplies: $875. Personal expenses: $665.

**Financial aid. Non-need-based:** Scholarships awarded for academics. **Additional information:** Freshmen and sophomores receive aid through University of Wisconsin-Green Bay. Juniors and seniors receive aid through Bellin College of Nursing.

**Application procedures. Admission:** Priority date 9/1; no deadline. $30 fee. Application may be submitted online. Admission notification on a rolling basis beginning on or about 9/1. Must reply by May 1 or within 3 week(s) if notified thereafter. Limited freshman applications accepted. **Financial aid:** Priority date 3/1; no closing date. FAFSA required. Applicants notified on a rolling basis starting 4/1; must reply within 2 week(s) of notification.

**Academics.** Students fulfill liberal education requirements at University of Wisconsin-Green Bay/St Norbert College or another accredited college or university of their choice while enrolled at Bellin College of Nursing. **Special study options:** Accelerated study, independent study. **Credit/placement by examination:** AP, CLEP. **Support services:** Study skills assistance, tutoring.

**Majors. Health:** Nursing (RN).

**Computing on campus.** 18 workstations in computer center. Commuter students can connect to campus network.

**Student life. Freshman orientation:** Mandatory. Preregistration for classes offered. One-day session in early summer and half-day session within a week prior to fall semester. **Housing:** Students may live in dorms in which they are dually enrolled, such as on the University of Wisconsin-Green Bay or St. Norbert College campus. **Activities:** Student government, student nurses association, ambassadors club, honor society, student senate.

**Student services.** Financial aid counseling, health services, personal counseling.

**Contact.** E-mail: admissons@bcon.edu
Phone: (920) 433-5803 ext. 5803 Toll-free number: (800) 236-8707
Fax: (920) 433-7416
Carol Rafferty, Director of Admissions, Bellin College of Nursing, PO Box 23400, Green Bay, WI 54305-3400

---

**Beloit College**
Beloit, Wisconsin                                CB member
www.beloit.edu                                   CB code: 1059

- Private 4-year liberal arts college
- Residential campus in large town
- 1,286 degree-seeking undergraduates: 57% women, 4% African American, 4% Asian American, 3% Hispanic American, 1% Native American, 5% international
- 60% of applicants admitted
- SAT or ACT (ACT writing optional), application essay required
- 79% graduate within 6 years

**General.** Founded in 1846. Regionally accredited. **Degrees:** 336 bachelor's awarded. **Location:** 60 miles from Madison, 90 miles from Chicago. **Calendar:** Semester, limited summer session. **Full-time faculty:** 120 total; 94% have terminal degrees, 13% minority, 44% women. **Part-time faculty:** 10 total; 80% have terminal degrees, 10% minority, 30% women. **Class size:** 76% < 20, 23% 20-39, less than 1% 40-49. **Special facilities:** LEED-certified science center, anthropology museum, art museum, observatory, 2 nature preserves, social science research laboratory, immunology laboratory, 2 electron microscopes, superconducting NMR, ICAP spectrometer, marketing research center, center for entrepreneurial leadership.

**Freshman class profile.** 2,157 applied, 1,304 admitted, 329 enrolled.

| Mid 50% test scores | | Rank in top quarter: | 68% |
|---|---|---|---|
| SAT critical reading: | 620-710 | Rank in top tenth: | 31% |
| SAT math: | 590-670 | End year in good standing: | 97% |
| ACT composite: | 25-29 | Return as sophomores: | 89% |
| GPA 3.50 or higher: | 44% | Out-of-state: | 78% |
| GPA 3.0-3.49: | 41% | Live on campus: | 98% |
| GPA 2.0-2.99: | 15% | International: | 4% |

**Basis for selection.** Rigor of high school curriculum and high school record are most important. Test scores, recommendations, essays, interviews, extracurricular activities also very important. Interview recommended. **Homeschooled:** Letter of recommendation (nonparent) required.

**High school preparation.** Recommended units include English 4, mathematics 4, social studies 4, science 3 and foreign language 2.

**2008-2009 Annual costs.** Tuition/fees: $31,540. Room/board: $6,696. Books/supplies: $400. Personal expenses: $900.

**2007-2008 Financial aid. Need-based:** 262 full-time freshmen applied for aid; 206 were judged to have need; 206 of these received aid. Average need met was 97%. Average scholarship/grant was $19,818; average loan $3,312. 67% of total undergraduate aid awarded as scholarships/grants, 33% as loans/jobs. **Non-need-based:** Awarded to 768 full-time undergraduates, including 204 freshmen. Scholarships awarded for academics, leadership, minority status, music/drama.

**Application procedures. Admission:** Priority date 1/15; no deadline. $35 fee, may be waived for applicants with need. Application may be submitted online. Admission notification on a rolling basis beginning on or about 2/15. Must reply by May 1 or within 2 week(s) if notified thereafter. **Financial aid:** Closing date 3/1. FAFSA, institutional form required. Applicants notified on a rolling basis starting 4/1; must reply by 5/1 or within 2 week(s) of notification.

**Academics.** Heavy emphasis placed on international education, interdisciplinary study, and experiential learning. **Special study options:** Combined bachelor's/graduate degree, double major, ESL, exchange student, independent study, internships, liberal arts/career combination, student-designed major, study abroad, teacher certification program, urban semester, Washington semester. Field schools in archeology and geology, Center for Language Studies, intensive summer foreign language program, reserved admission to Medical College of Wisconsin. 3-2 programs in engineering, nursing, med tech and forestry. **Credit/placement by examination:** AP, CLEP, IB. 32 credit hours maximum toward bachelor's degree. **Support services:** Learning center, study skills assistance, tutoring, writing center.

**Majors. Area/ethnic studies:** Women's. **Biology:** General, biochemistry, cellular/molecular, environmental, molecular. **Business:** Business admin, managerial economics. **Computer sciences:** Computer science. **Conservation:** Environmental science, forestry. **Education:** General, art, science. **Engineering:** General. **English:** Creative writing, English lit, speech/rhetoric. **Foreign languages:** General, classics, comparative lit, East Asian, French, German, Russian, Spanish. **Health:** Nursing (RN). **History:** General. **Interdisciplinary:** Science/society. **Liberal arts:** Arts/sciences. **Math:** General. **Philosophy/religion:** Philosophy, religion. **Physical sciences:** Chemistry, geology, physics. **Psychology:** General. **Social sciences:** Anthropology, economics, international relations, political science, sociology. **Visual/performing arts:** Art history/conservation, dance, dramatic. **Other:** Health and Society.

**Most popular majors.** English 10%, foreign language 11%, physical sciences 7%, psychology 7%, social sciences 28%, visual/performing arts 11%.

**Computing on campus.** 270 workstations in dormitories, library, computer center, student center. Dormitories wired for high-speed internet access and linked to campus network. Commuter students can connect to campus network. Helpline, student web hosting, wireless network available.

**Student life. Freshman orientation:** Mandatory. Preregistration for classes offered. First year initiatives begins 10 days before start of fall semester. **Policies:** Residence hall system is student managed. **Housing:** Guaranteed on-campus for all undergraduates. Coed dorms, single-sex dorms, apartments, cooperative housing, fraternity/sorority housing, substance-free housing available. Special-interest housing subject to change and includes: Anthropology house, French house, Spanish house, German house, Russian house, arts co-op, and women's center. Available to students that have completed at least one semester. **Activities:** Jazz band, campus ministries, choral groups, dance, drama, film society, international student organizations, literary magazine, music ensembles, musical theater, radio station, student government, student newspaper, symphony orchestra, TV station, volunteer community tutoring service, women's center program, Gay Alliance, Young Republicans, Young Democrats, Science Fiction and Fantasy Association, Voces Latinas, Black Students United, fencing club.

**Athletics.** NCAA. **Intercollegiate:** Baseball M, basketball, cross-country, diving, football (tackle) M, golf, soccer, softball W, swimming, tennis, track and field, volleyball W. **Intramural:** Basketball, fencing, handball, ice hockey M, racquetball, rugby M, sailing, soccer, softball, swimming, tennis, volleyball, water polo. **Team name:** Bucs.

**Student services.** Campus ministries, career counseling, services for economically disadvantaged, student employment services, financial aid counseling, health services, minority student services, on-campus daycare, personal counseling, placement for graduates, women's services. **Physically disabled:** Services for visually, hearing impaired.

**Contact.** E-mail: admiss@beloit.edu
Phone: (608) 363-2500 Toll-free number: (800) 923-5648
Fax: (608) 363-2075
Nancy Benedict, Vice President of Enrollment Services, Beloit College, 700 College Street, Beloit, WI 53511-5595

## Cardinal Stritch University
**Milwaukee, Wisconsin**
www.ThisIsStritch.com                CB code: 1100

- Private 4-year university affiliated with Roman Catholic Church
- Commuter campus in very large city
- 3,180 degree-seeking undergraduates: 6% part-time, 69% women, 22% African American, 1% Asian American, 3% Hispanic American, 1% Native American, 2% international
- 2,763 degree-seeking graduate students
- 93% of applicants admitted
- SAT or ACT (ACT writing optional), application essay required
- 68% graduate within 6 years

**General.** Founded in 1937. Regionally accredited. **Degrees:** 564 bachelor's, 278 associate awarded; master's, doctoral offered. **Location:** 7 miles from downtown, 85 miles from Chicago. **Calendar:** Semester, limited summer session. **Full-time faculty:** 98 total; 56% have terminal degrees, 10% minority, 62% women. **Part-time faculty:** 360 total; 19% minority, 51% women. **Class size:** 97% < 20, 3% 20-39, less than 1% 40-49, less than 1% 50-99.

**Freshman class profile.** 734 applied, 681 admitted, 195 enrolled.

| Mid 50% test scores | | Out-of-state: | 20% |
|---|---|---|---|
| SAT critical reading: | 460-510 | Live on campus: | 63% |
| SAT math: | 470-540 | International: | 6% |
| ACT composite: | 19-24 | | |

**Basis for selection.** High school GPA of 2.0, minimum ACT test score of 20 or SAT combined score of 840 (exclusive of Writing). Interview, activities, recommendations considered. Conditional admission available to applicants not meeting all admissions criteria. Institutional tests used for admission of academically weak students. Interview recommended for all; portfolio recommended for art; audition recommended for music and theatre.

**High school preparation.** 16 units required; 18 recommended. Required and recommended units include English 4, mathematics 2-3, social studies 1, history 1, science 2-3, foreign language 2 and academic electives 4.

**2007-2008 Annual costs.** Tuition/fees: $19,074. Additional $55 per credit for the nursing program. Room/board: $5,750. Books/supplies: $500. Personal expenses: $1,200.

**Financial aid. Non-need-based:** Scholarships awarded for academics, art, athletics, music/drama.

**Application procedures. Admission:** Priority date 4/1; no deadline. $25 fee, may be waived for applicants with need. Application may be submitted online. Admission notification on a rolling basis beginning on or about 9/1. **Financial aid:** Priority date 4/15; no closing date. FAFSA, institutional form required. Applicants notified on a rolling basis starting 3/1; must reply within 3 week(s) of notification.

**Academics. Special study options:** Accelerated study, distance learning, double major, exchange student, independent study, internships, student-designed major, study abroad, teacher certification program. **Credit/placement by examination:** AP, CLEP, IB, institutional tests. 30 credit hours maximum toward associate degree, 60 toward bachelor's. **Support services:** Learning center, reduced course load, remedial instruction, study skills assistance, tutoring, writing center.

**Majors. Biology:** General. **Business:** General, accounting, business admin, international, management information systems. **Communications:** General. **Computer sciences:** Computer science. **Education:** General, special. **English:** Creative writing, English lit. **Foreign languages:** Spanish. **Health:** Nursing (RN). **History:** General. **Interdisciplinary:** Math/computer science. **Legal studies:** Prelaw. **Math:** General. **Parks/recreation:** Sports admin. **Philosophy/religion:** Religion. **Physical sciences:** Chemistry. **Psychology:** General. **Social sciences:** General, political science, sociology. **Theology:** Pastoral counseling, youth ministry. **Visual/performing arts:** Art, commercial/advertising art, dramatic, music performance, photography, studio arts.

**Most popular majors.** Business/marketing 75%, education 6%.

**Computing on campus.** 236 workstations in dormitories, library, computer center, student center. Dormitories wired for high-speed internet access and linked to campus network. Commuter students can connect to campus network. Online library, helpline, wireless network available.

**Student life. Freshman orientation:** Mandatory. Preregistration for classes offered. One week long program prior to first week of classes. **Housing:** Coed dorms available. $50 fully refundable deposit. **Activities:** Bands, campus ministries, choral groups, dance, drama, literary magazine, music ensembles, Model UN, musical theater, radio station, student government, student newspaper, Students for Political Awareness, multicultural committee, Asian club, Black student union, United Latino Organization, Fellowship of Christian Students, service corps, peer helpers.

**Athletics.** NAIA. **Intercollegiate:** Baseball M, basketball, cross-country, soccer, softball W, volleyball. **Intramural:** Basketball, volleyball. **Team name:** Wolves.

**Student services.** Adult student services, alcohol/substance abuse counseling, campus ministries, career counseling, student employment services, financial aid counseling, health services, personal counseling, placement for graduates, veterans' counselor. **Physically disabled:** Services for hearing impaired.

**Contact.** E-mail: admityou@stritch.edu
Phone: (414) 410-4040 Toll-free number: (800) 347-8822 ext. 4040
Fax: (414) 410-4058
Kirk Messer, Director of Admission, Cardinal Stritch University, 6801 North Yates Road, Box 516, Milwaukee, WI 53217-7516

## Carroll College
**Waukesha, Wisconsin**
www.cc.edu                CB code: 1101

- Private 4-year liberal arts college affiliated with Presbyterian Church (USA)
- Residential campus in small city
- 2,925 degree-seeking undergraduates: 15% part-time, 68% women, 2% African American, 1% Asian American, 3% Hispanic American, 2% international
- 265 degree-seeking graduate students
- 72% of applicants admitted
- SAT or ACT (ACT writing recommended) required
- 59% graduate within 6 years

**General.** Founded in 1846. Regionally accredited. **Degrees:** 489 bachelor's awarded; master's, doctoral offered. **ROTC:** Army, Air Force. **Location:** 15 miles from Milwaukee. **Calendar:** Semester, extensive summer session. **Full-time faculty:** 121 total; 63% have terminal degrees, 2% minority, 46% women. **Part-time faculty:** 168 total; 17% have terminal degrees, 65% women. **Class size:** 53% < 20, 41% 20-39, 3% 40-49, 4% 50-99. **Special facilities:** Scientific study and conservancy, trout stream, wetland and upland habitats.

**Freshman class profile.** 2,728 applied, 1,975 admitted, 679 enrolled.

| Mid 50% test scores | | End year in good standing: | 79% |
|---|---|---|---|
| ACT composite: | 20-25 | Return as sophomores: | 74% |
| GPA 3.50 or higher: | 44% | Out-of-state: | 26% |
| GPA 3.0-3.49: | 36% | Live on campus: | 85% |
| GPA 2.0-2.99: | 20% | International: | 1% |
| Rank in top quarter: | 55% | Fraternities: | 4% |
| Rank in top tenth: | 21% | Sororities: | 9% |

**Basis for selection.** School achievement record most important, followed by test scores. Recommendations, essay, interview considered. Essay, interview recommended for all; audition recommended for music, theater; portfolio recommended for art. **Homeschooled:** Transcript of courses and grades required.

**High school preparation.** 17 units recommended. Recommended units include English 4, mathematics 4, social studies 3, history 3, science 3 (laboratory 2).

**2008-2009 Annual costs.** Tuition/fees: $21,926. Room/board: $6,694. Books/supplies: $1,060. Personal expenses: $1,291.

**2007-2008 Financial aid. Need-based:** 587 full-time freshmen applied for aid; 458 were judged to have need; 458 of these received aid. Average need met was 100%. Average scholarship/grant was $11,969; average loan $2,453. 71% of total undergraduate aid awarded as scholarships/grants, 29% as loans/jobs. **Non-need-based:** Awarded to 2,116 full-time undergraduates, including 577 freshmen. Scholarships awarded for academics, alumni affiliation, art, leadership, music/drama, ROTC.

**Application procedures. Admission:** Priority date 3/15; no deadline. No application fee. Application may be submitted online. Admission notification on a rolling basis. **Financial aid:** No deadline. FAFSA required. Applicants notified on a rolling basis starting 2/15; must reply by 5/1 or within 2 week(s) of notification.

**Academics.** Education majors must maintain 2.75 GPA in major and teaching minors. Nursing students must maintain 2.75 GPA. Six majors available for pre-physical therapy programs. **Special study options:** Combined bachelor's/graduate degree, distance learning, double major, exchange student, honors, independent study, internships, liberal arts/career combination, student-designed major, study abroad, teacher certification program, United Nations semester, Washington semester. **Credit/placement by examination:** AP, CLEP, IB, institutional tests. **Support services:** Learning center, pre-admission summer program, reduced course load, study skills assistance, tutoring, writing center.

**Majors. Area/ethnic studies:** European. **Biology:** General, animal behavior, biochemistry. **Business:** Accounting, actuarial science, business admin, finance, human resources, management information systems, marketing, organizational behavior, small business admin. **Communications:** General, journalism, organizational, public relations. **Communications technology:** Graphics, printing management. **Computer sciences:** General, information systems. **Conservation:** General, environmental science. **Education:** General, art, biology, chemistry, early childhood, elementary, English, foreign languages, geography, health, history, mathematics, middle, music, physical, psychology, science, social science, social studies, Spanish. **Engineering:** Physics, software. **English:** Creative writing, English lit. **Foreign languages:** Spanish. **Health:** Athletic training, clinical lab science, nursing (RN), predental, premedicine, prepharmacy, preveterinary. **History:** General, European. **Math:** General, applied. **Parks/recreation:** Exercise sciences, facilities management, health/fitness. **Philosophy/religion:** Religion. **Physical sciences:** Chemistry. **Protective services:** Criminal justice, forensics. **Psychology:** General. **Social sciences:** International relations, political science, sociology. **Visual/performing arts:** Art, commercial/advertising art, dramatic, photography, studio arts.

**Most popular majors.** Biology 7%, business/marketing 16%, computer/information sciences 6%, education 12%, health sciences 14%, psychology 10%, social sciences 8%, visual/performing arts 6%.

**Computing on campus.** 250 workstations in dormitories, library, computer center, student center. Dormitories wired for high-speed internet access and linked to campus network. Commuter students can connect to campus network. Online library, helpline, student web hosting, wireless network available.

**Student life. Freshman orientation:** Mandatory. Preregistration for classes offered. **Housing:** Guaranteed on-campus for freshmen. Coed dorms, single-sex dorms, apartments available. $200 nonrefundable deposit. **Activities:** Bands, choral groups, dance, drama, international student organizations, literary magazine, music ensembles, radio station, student government, student newspaper, College Democrats, Bible study group, Intervarsity Christian Fellowship, black student union, Colleges Against Cancer, Habitat for Humanity, Latin American student organization, Circle K.

**Athletics.** NCAA. **Intercollegiate:** Baseball M, basketball, cross-country, football (tackle) M, golf, soccer, swimming, tennis, track and field, volleyball W. **Intramural:** Basketball, bowling, cheerleading, football (non-tackle), soccer, tennis, volleyball. **Team name:** Pioneers.

**Student services.** Adult student services, campus ministries, career counseling, student employment services, financial aid counseling, health services, minority student services, personal counseling, placement for graduates. **Physically disabled:** Services for visually, hearing impaired.

**Contact.** E-mail: ccinfo@cc.edu
Phone: (262) 524-7220 Toll-free number: (800) 227-7655
Fax: (262) 951-3037
Jim Wiseman, Vice President for Enrollment, Carroll College, 100 North East Avenue, Waukesha, WI 53186-9988

---

## Carthage College
### Kenosha, Wisconsin
### www.carthage.edu

**CB member**
**CB code: 1103**

- Private 4-year liberal arts college affiliated with Evangelical Lutheran Church in America
- Residential campus in small city
- 2,372 degree-seeking undergraduates: 6% part-time, 57% women
- 73 degree-seeking graduate students
- 77% of applicants admitted
- SAT or ACT (ACT writing optional) required
- 54% graduate within 6 years

**General.** Founded in 1847. Regionally accredited. **Degrees:** 469 bachelor's awarded; master's offered. **ROTC:** Army, Air Force. **Location:** 60 miles from Chicago, 30 miles from Milwaukee. **Calendar:** 4-1-4, limited summer session. **Full-time faculty:** 137 total. **Class size:** 54% < 20, 45%

20-39, 1% 40-49. **Special facilities:** Planetarium, paleontology institute, center for children's literature, undergraduate science research laboratory, computer/mathematics research laboratory, greenhouse, arboretum, Audubon sanctuary, geographic information systems (GIS) lab, 24-hour cyber-cafe.

**Freshman class profile.** 4,687 applied, 3,619 admitted, 686 enrolled.

| Mid 50% test scores | | | |
|---|---|---|---|
| SAT critical reading: | 500-620 | GPA 3.0-3.49: | 29% |
| SAT math: | 500-620 | GPA 2.0-2.99: | 31% |
| ACT composite: | 21-26 | End year in good standing: | 91% |
| GPA 3.50 or higher: | 40% | Return as sophomores: | 75% |
| | | Out-of-state: | 72% |

**Basis for selection.** High school GPA (calculated based on academic courses) and test scores most important. Interview recommended; audition recommended for music and theater. **Homeschooled:** Transcript of courses and grades required.

**High school preparation.** 18 units recommended. Recommended units include English 4, mathematics 3, social studies 3, science 3 (laboratory 2), foreign language 2 and academic electives 3.

**2008-2009 Annual costs.** Tuition/fees: $26,500. Room/board: $7,500. Books/supplies: $1,200. Personal expenses: $1,500.

**2007-2008 Financial aid. Need-based:** 67% of total undergraduate aid awarded as scholarships/grants, 33% as loans/jobs. **Non-need-based:** Scholarships awarded for academics, alumni affiliation, art, leadership, minority status, music/drama, religious affiliation.

**Application procedures. Admission:** No deadline. $25 fee, may be waived for applicants with need. Application may be submitted online. Admission notification on a rolling basis. Must reply by May 1 or within 2 week(s) if notified thereafter. **Financial aid:** Priority date 2/15; no closing date. FAFSA required. Applicants notified on a rolling basis starting 3/1.

**Academics.** All students take the Heritage Seminar Series, a 2-course combination of oral and written communication skills and cross-cultural studies. Students must also complete a Carthage symposium and a senior thesis in their major. **Special study options:** Accelerated study, combined bachelor's/graduate degree, cross-registration, double major, dual enrollment of high school students, honors, independent study, internships, liberal arts/career combination, student-designed major, study abroad, teacher certification program, Washington semester. **Credit/placement by examination:** AP, CLEP, IB, institutional tests. 32 credit hours maximum toward bachelor's degree. **Support services:** Pre-admission summer program, reduced course load, study skills assistance, tutoring, writing center.

**Majors. Area/ethnic studies:** Asian. **Biology:** General. **Business:** Accounting, business admin, management information systems, marketing. **Communications technology:** Graphics. **Computer sciences:** Computer science. **Conservation:** Environmental science. **Education:** Elementary, physical, special. **English:** English lit. **Foreign languages:** Classics, French, German, Spanish. **Health:** Athletic training. **History:** General. **Interdisciplinary:** Neuroscience. **Liberal arts:** Humanities. **Math:** General. **Parks/recreation:** Exercise sciences. **Philosophy/religion:** Philosophy, religion. **Physical sciences:** Chemistry, physics. **Protective services:** Correctional facilities, police science. **Psychology:** General. **Public administration:** Social work. **Social sciences:** General, economics, geography, international economics, political science, sociology. **Visual/performing arts:** Art history/conservation, dramatic, studio arts, theater design. **Other:** Communications and media studies.

**Most popular majors.** Business/marketing 23%, education 9%, social sciences 7%, visual/performing arts 7%.

**Computing on campus.** 275 workstations in dormitories, library, computer center, student center. Dormitories wired for high-speed internet access and linked to campus network. Commuter students can connect to campus network. Online library, helpline, repair service, student web hosting, wireless network available.

**Student life. Freshman orientation:** Mandatory. Preregistration for classes offered. Held for a few days immediately prior to start of fall classes. **Housing:** Guaranteed on-campus for freshmen. Coed dorms, single-sex dorms, apartments, fraternity/sorority housing, substance-free housing available. $300 deposit, deadline 5/1. **Activities:** Bands, campus ministries, choral groups, dance, drama, film society, international student organizations, literary magazine, music ensembles, Model UN, musical theater, opera, radio station, student government, student newspaper, symphony orchestra, Black Student Union, International Friendship Society, United Women of Color, Carthage Christian Fellowship, Latinos Unidos, Circle K International, College Republicans, Young Democrats.

**Athletics.** NCAA. **Intercollegiate:** Baseball M, basketball, cross-country, football (tackle) M, golf, soccer, softball W, swimming, tennis, track and field, volleyball, water polo W. **Intramural:** Basketball, football (non-tackle), racquetball, soccer, softball, volleyball. **Team name:** Red Men, Lady Reds.

**Student services.** Adult student services, alcohol/substance abuse counseling, campus ministries, career counseling, student employment services, financial aid counseling, health services, personal counseling, placement for graduates, veterans' counselor.

**Contact.** E-mail: admissions@carthage.edu
Phone: (262) 551-6000 Toll-free number: (800) 351-4058
Fax: (262) 551-5762
Bradley Andrews, Vice President for Enrollment and Student Life, Carthage College, 2001 Alford Park Drive, Kenosha, WI 53140-1994

## Columbia College of Nursing
**Milwaukee, Wisconsin**
www.ccon.edu                                          CB code: 3409

▶ Private 4-year nursing college
▶ Commuter campus in very large city
▶ 218 degree-seeking undergraduates: 10% African American, 5% Asian American, 5% Hispanic American, 1% Native American, 1% international

**General.** Founded in 1901. Regionally accredited. Joint bachelor's degree in nursing awarded with Mount Mary College. **Degrees:** 55 bachelor's awarded. **Location:** 90 miles from Chicago, 70 miles from Madison. **Calendar:** Semester, limited summer session. **Full-time faculty:** 17 total; 12% have terminal degrees, 94% women. **Part-time faculty:** 8 total; 12% have terminal degrees, 75% women. **Class size:** 23% < 20, 15% 20-39, 38% 40-49, 23% 50-99.

**Basis for selection.** Admission to Mount Mary college required. Admission to nursing major occurs in sophomore year. 2.8 GPA and all prerequisites required.

**High school preparation.** 3 units required. Required and recommended units include English 4, mathematics 1-2, science 2-3 and foreign language 2. Algebra required. Chemistry, biology required as science units.

**2007-2008 Annual costs.** Tuition/fees: $18,938. Room/board: $5,400. Books/supplies: $734. Personal expenses: $1,234.

**Financial aid. Non-need-based:** Scholarships awarded for academics. **Additional information:** Students must apply to and meet financial aid requirements of Mount Mary College.

**Application procedures. Admission:** Closing date 3/1 (receipt date). Application may be submitted online. Admission notification on a rolling basis. **Financial aid:** No deadline. FAFSA required. Applicants notified on a rolling basis starting 2/15; must reply by 5/1 or within 2 week(s) of notification.

**Academics.** Students generally complete first 2 years on Mt. Mary campus and last 2 years on Columbia campus. **Special study options:** Combined bachelor's/graduate degree, double major, ESL, honors, independent study, study abroad. Cultural immersion options. **Credit/placement by examination:** CLEP. **Support services:** Learning center, remedial instruction, study skills assistance, tutoring, writing center.

**Majors. Health:** Nursing (RN).

**Computing on campus.** 20 workstations in library, computer center. Online library, helpline available.

**Student life. Freshman orientation:** Mandatory. **Housing:** Guaranteed on-campus for freshmen. Coed dorms, apartments, substance-free housing available. **Activities:** Student newspaper, student nursing organization, nursing honor society.

**Student services.** Alcohol/substance abuse counseling, campus ministries, career counseling, financial aid counseling, health services, minority student services, personal counseling, placement for graduates.

**Contact.** E-mail: admiss@mtmary.edu
Phone: (414) 256-1219 Toll-free number: (800) 321-6265
Fax: (414) 256-0180
Brooke Konapacki, Dean of Enrollment, Mount Mary College, Columbia College of Nursing, Mount Mary College Enrollment Office, Milwaukee, WI 53222-4597

## Concordia University Wisconsin
**Mequon, Wisconsin**
www.cuw.edu                                          CB code: 1139

▶ Private 4-year university and liberal arts college affiliated with Lutheran Church - Missouri Synod
▶ Residential campus in large town
▶ 3,356 degree-seeking undergraduates: 42% part-time, 63% women, 12% African American, 1% Asian American, 2% Hispanic American, 1% Native American, 1% international
▶ 1,985 degree-seeking graduate students
▶ 66% of applicants admitted
▶ ACT (writing optional) required
▶ 64% graduate within 6 years

**General.** Founded in 1881. Regionally accredited. **Degrees:** 564 bachelor's, 27 associate awarded; master's, doctoral offered. **Location:** 15 miles from Milwaukee. **Calendar:** 4-1-4, limited summer session. **Full-time faculty:** 96 total; 68% have terminal degrees, 6% minority, 47% women. **Part-time faculty:** 135 total; 19% have terminal degrees, 58% women. **Class size:** 49% < 20, 47% 20-39, 3% 40-49, 2% 50-99. **Special facilities:** Access to Lake Michigan.

**Freshman class profile.** 2,112 applied, 1,397 admitted, 425 enrolled.

| Mid 50% test scores | | | |
|---|---|---|---|
| ACT composite: | 19-25 | Rank in top tenth: | 13% |
| GPA 3.50 or higher: | 38% | Return as sophomores: | 77% |
| GPA 3.0-3.49: | 30% | Out-of-state: | 40% |
| GPA 2.0-2.99: | 32% | Live on campus: | 90% |
| Rank in top quarter: | 33% | International: | 1% |

**Basis for selection.** School achievement record and test scores important. Essay, interview recommended; audition recommended for music.

**High school preparation.** 16 units required. Required and recommended units include English 3-4, mathematics 2-3, social studies 2, science 2, foreign language 2 and academic electives 5. Two liberal arts required.

**2007-2008 Annual costs.** Tuition/fees: $19,040. Room/board: $7,200. Books/supplies: $1,100. Personal expenses: $1,950.

**2007-2008 Financial aid. Need-based:** 407 full-time freshmen applied for aid; 340 were judged to have need; 335 of these received aid. Average need met was 80%. Average scholarship/grant was $10,802; average loan $5,419. 56% of total undergraduate aid awarded as scholarships/grants, 44% as loans/jobs. **Non-need-based:** Scholarships awarded for academics, religious affiliation.

**Application procedures. Admission:** Priority date 5/1; deadline 8/15. $35 fee, may be waived for applicants with need. Application may be submitted online. Admission notification on a rolling basis beginning on or about 10/15. **Financial aid:** Priority date 4/1; no closing date. FAFSA required. Applicants notified on a rolling basis starting 3/1; must reply within 3 week(s) of notification.

**Academics. Special study options:** Accelerated study, combined bachelor's/graduate degree, cross-registration, distance learning, double major, dual enrollment of high school students, ESL, exchange student, independent study, internships, liberal arts/career combination, student-designed major, study abroad, teacher certification program, weekend college. Cooperative programs with Cardinal Stritch University, Marquette University, and Milwaukee Institute of Art and Design. **Credit/placement by examination:** AP, CLEP, IB, ACT, institutional tests. 15 credit hours maximum toward associate degree, 30 toward bachelor's. **Support services:** Learning center, reduced course load, remedial instruction, tutoring, writing center.

**Majors. Biology:** General, exercise physiology. **Business:** General, accounting, actuarial science, business admin, finance, international finance, marketing. **Communications:** General, broadcast journalism, digital media, media studies. **Computer sciences:** General. **Conservation:** Environmental studies. **Education:** General, art, biology, business, early childhood, elementary, English, health, history, kindergarten/preschool, mathematics, middle, multi-level teacher, music, physical, science, secondary, social science, social studies, Spanish. **English:** English lit. **Foreign languages:** Biblical, German, Spanish. **Health:** Athletic training, clinical/medical social work, health services, medical radiologic technology/radiation therapy, nursing (RN). **History:** General. **Legal studies:** Prelaw. **Liberal arts:** Arts/sciences, humanities. **Math:** General. **Philosophy/religion:** Religion. **Protective services:** Criminal justice. **Psychology:** General. **Public administration:** Social work. **Social sciences:** Economics. **Theology:** Bible, missionary, pastoral counseling, preministerial, religious ed, sacred music, theology, youth ministry. **Visual/performing arts:** Art, commercial/advertising art, graphic design, illustration, interior design, music performance, photography, piano/organ. **Other:** Business communication, Rehabilitative science.

**Most popular majors.** Business/marketing 37%, education 15%, health sciences 16%, security/protective services 10%.

**Computing on campus.** 200 workstations in dormitories, library, computer center, student center. Dormitories wired for high-speed internet access and linked to campus network. Commuter students can connect to campus network. Online library, helpline, repair service available.

**Student life. Freshman orientation:** Available. Preregistration for classes offered. Held before start of fall semester, includes sessions for parents. **Policies:** Lutheran church services available every Sunday. Chapel services held daily. **Housing:** Single-sex dorms, substance-free housing available. $160 deposit, deadline 4/15. **Activities:** Bands, campus ministries, choral groups, dance, drama, international student organizations, music ensembles, musical theater, radio station, student government, student newspaper, Jeremiah Project, Servant Events.

**Athletics.** NCAA. **Intercollegiate:** Baseball M, basketball, cross-country, football (tackle) M, golf, soccer, softball W, tennis, track and field, volleyball, wrestling M. **Intramural:** Basketball, soccer, softball, table tennis, tennis, volleyball. **Team name:** Falcons.

**Student services.** Adult student services, alcohol/substance abuse counseling, campus ministries, career counseling, student employment services, financial aid counseling, health services, minority student services, personal counseling, placement for graduates, veterans' counselor. **Physically disabled:** Services for hearing impaired.

**Contact.** E-mail: admission@cuw.edu
Phone: (262) 243-5700 Toll-free number: (888) 628-9472
Fax: (262) 243-4545
Kenneth Gaschk, Vice President of Enrollment Services, Concordia University Wisconsin, 12800 North Lake Shore Drive, Mequon, WI 53097

## DeVry University: Milwaukee
### Milwaukee, Wisconsin
### www.devry.edu

- For-profit 4-year university
- Commuter campus in very large city
- 108 degree-seeking undergraduates: 61% part-time, 65% women, 48% African American, 3% Asian American, 10% Hispanic American
- 98 degree-seeking graduate students
- Interview required

**General. Degrees:** 10 bachelor's awarded; master's offered. **Calendar:** Semester. **Part-time faculty:** 4 total; 25% women.

**Basis for selection.** Interview important.

**2007-2008 Annual costs.** Tuition/fees: $13,020. Books/supplies: $1,300. Personal expenses: $5,082.

**2006-2007 Financial aid. Non-need-based:** Scholarships awarded for academics.

**Application procedures. Admission:** No deadline. $50 fee. Admission notification on a rolling basis. **Financial aid:** No deadline. FAFSA required. Applicants notified on a rolling basis.

**Academics. Special study options:** Accelerated study, distance learning. **Credit/placement by examination:** CLEP.

**Majors. Business:** Business admin. **Computer sciences:** General. **Other:** Technical management.

**Contact.** Phone: (414) 278-7677
DeVry University: Milwaukee, 100 East Wisconsin Avenue, Suite 2550, Milwaukee, WI 53202

## Edgewood College
### Madison, Wisconsin
### www.edgewood.edu
**CB member**
**CB code: 1202**

- Private 4-year liberal arts college affiliated with Roman Catholic Church
- Commuter campus in small city

- 1,860 degree-seeking undergraduates
- 80% of applicants admitted
- SAT or ACT required

**General.** Founded in 1927. Regionally accredited. **Degrees:** 360 bachelor's awarded; master's, doctoral offered. **Location:** 82 miles from Milwaukee, 140 miles from Chicago. **Calendar:** 4-1-4, limited summer session. **Full-time faculty:** 106 total. **Part-time faculty:** 169 total. **Class size:** 69% < 20, 30% 20-39, less than 1% 40-49, less than 1% 50-99. **Special facilities:** Science center, biological research station, nursery school.

**Freshman class profile.** 1,104 applied, 886 admitted, 302 enrolled.

| Mid 50% test scores | | Rank in top quarter: | 34% |
|---|---|---|---|
| ACT composite: | 20-24 | Rank in top tenth: | 11% |
| GPA 3.50 or higher: | 39% | Out-of-state: | 8% |
| GPA 3.0-3.49: | 34% | Live on campus: | 71% |
| GPA 2.0-2.99: | 27% | | |

**Basis for selection.** High school transcript and test scores most important.

**High school preparation.** 16 units recommended. Recommended units include English 4, mathematics 2, social studies 2, history 1, science 2 (laboratory 1) and foreign language 2.

**2008-2009 Annual costs.** Tuition/fees (projected): $20,040. Room/board: $6,570. Books/supplies: $750. Personal expenses: $1,968.

**2006-2007 Financial aid. Need-based:** 51% of total undergraduate aid awarded as scholarships/grants, 49% as loans/jobs. **Non-need-based:** Scholarships awarded for academics, alumni affiliation, art, leadership, minority status, music/drama, religious affiliation. **Additional information:** Auditions required for music scholarships, portfolios required for fine arts scholarships, essays required for a number of institutional scholarships, including AHANA Student Advancement Award, Alumni Association Scholarship, O'Connor Memorial Scholarship.

**Application procedures. Admission:** Priority date 3/1; deadline 8/21 (receipt date). $25 fee, may be waived for applicants with need. Application may be submitted online. Admission notification on a rolling basis beginning on or about 9/1. **Financial aid:** Priority date 3/1; no closing date. FAFSA, institutional form required. Applicants notified on a rolling basis starting 3/30; must reply within 2 week(s) of notification.

**Academics. Special study options:** Accelerated study, cross-registration, distance learning, double major, dual enrollment of high school students, honors, independent study, internships, liberal arts/career combination, student-designed major, study abroad, teacher certification program, weekend college. **Credit/placement by examination:** AP, CLEP, IB, institutional tests. 30 credit hours maximum toward associate degree, 60 toward bachelor's. **Support services:** Learning center, reduced course load, remedial instruction, study skills assistance, tutoring, writing center.

**Majors. Area/ethnic studies:** American. **Biology:** General. **Business:** General, accounting, business admin, finance, management information systems, market research. **Communications:** Media studies. **Communications technology:** Graphics. **Computer sciences:** General, information systems. **Education:** General, art, biology, business, chemistry, early childhood, elementary, English, foreign languages, French, history, kindergarten/preschool, mathematics, middle, music, science, secondary, social science, Spanish, special. **English:** English lit. **Foreign languages:** French, Spanish. **Health:** Art therapy, cytotechnology, nursing (RN). **History:** General. **Interdisciplinary:** Natural sciences. **Liberal arts:** Arts/sciences. **Math:** General. **Philosophy/religion:** Religion. **Physical sciences:** Chemistry. **Protective services:** Criminal justice. **Psychology:** General. **Social sciences:** General, economics, international relations, political science, sociology. **Theology:** Religious ed. **Visual/performing arts:** General, art, commercial/advertising art.

**Most popular majors.** Business/marketing 18%, education 25%, health sciences 13%, psychology 11%, visual/performing arts 9%.

**Computing on campus.** 100 workstations in dormitories, library, computer center, student center. Dormitories wired for high-speed internet access and linked to campus network. Commuter students can connect to campus network. Online course registration, online library, helpline available.

**Student life. Freshman orientation:** Available. Preregistration for classes offered. Three-day program held in fall. **Housing:** Coed dorms, single-sex dorms, special housing for disabled, apartments available. $150 deposit. Student leadership house. **Activities:** Bands, choral groups, drama, international student organizations, literary magazine, music ensembles, musical theater, student government, student newspaper, symphony orchestra, student business association, student nurse association, Amnesty International, Habitat for Humanity, student association of various ethnicities.

**Athletics.** NCAA. **Intercollegiate:** Baseball M, basketball, cross-country, golf, soccer, softball W, tennis, volleyball W. **Intramural:** Basketball, bowling, diving, skiing, softball, swimming, table tennis, volleyball, weight lifting. **Team name:** Eagles.

**Student services.** Campus ministries, career counseling, student employment services, financial aid counseling, health services, minority student services, personal counseling, placement for graduates, veterans' counselor.

**Contact.** E-mail: admissions@edgewood.edu
Phone: (608) 663-2294 Toll-free number: (800) 444-4861 ext. 2294
Fax: (608) 663-3291
Christine Benedict, Director of Undergraduate Admissions, Edgewood College, 1000 Edgewood College Drive, Madison, WI 53711-1997

## Herzing College
### Madison, Wisconsin
### www.herzing.edu/madison
**CB code: 0388**

- For-profit 3-year business and technical college
- Commuter campus in small city
- 900 degree-seeking undergraduates
- Interview required

**General.** Founded in 1948. Regionally accredited. **Degrees:** 113 bachelor's, 131 associate awarded. **Location:** 90 miles from Milwaukee, 150 miles from Chicago. **Calendar:** Continuous, extensive summer session. **Full-time faculty:** 15 total. **Part-time faculty:** 30 total.

**Basis for selection.** Open admission, but selective for some programs. Interview and placement test required prior to acceptance. Application process varies by program. **Homeschooled:** State high school equivalency certificate required. **Learning Disabled:** Must provide documentation to admissions advisor prior to starting classes.

**2007-2008 Annual costs.** Tuition is $335 per credit hour for most on-campus courses; $375 for on-line courses. Book use included in tuition.

**Application procedures. Admission:** No deadline. No application fee. Application may be submitted online. Admission notification on a rolling basis. **Financial aid:** No deadline. FAFSA, institutional form required. Applicants notified on a rolling basis.

**Academics.** Bachelors degree may be acquired in 3 years, associate degree in 1 year, 8 months. **Special study options:** Combined bachelor's/graduate degree, cooperative education, distance learning, double major, honors, independent study, internships, liberal arts/career combination, study abroad. **Credit/placement by examination:** AP, CLEP, institutional tests. **Support services:** Learning center, pre-admission summer program, reduced course load, remedial instruction, study skills assistance, tutoring, writing center.

**Majors. Business:** Accounting, accounting/business management, accounting/finance, business admin, finance, human resources, office management, office technology, office/clerical. **Communications technology:** Animation/special effects. **Computer sciences:** General, applications programming, computer graphics, computer science, game design, information systems, information technology, LAN/WAN management, networking, programming. **Engineering:** Software. **Engineering technology:** Architectural drafting, CAD/CADD, civil, civil drafting, computer, computer hardware, computer systems, drafting, electrical, electrical drafting, mechanical drafting, software, telecommunications. **Health:** Facilities admin, health care admin, medical records admin, medical records technology, office admin, ward clerk, ward supervisor. **Legal studies:** General. **Mechanic/repair:** Communications systems, computer, electronics/electrical, industrial electronics. **Protective services:** Emergency management/homeland security. **Visual/performing arts:** Graphic design. **Other:** Electronics engineering technology.

**Computing on campus.** 450 workstations in library, computer center, student center. Commuter students can connect to campus network. Online library, helpline, repair service, wireless network available.

**Student life. Freshman orientation:** Mandatory. **Activities:** Student government, student newspaper.

**Student services.** Adult student services, career counseling, student employment services, financial aid counseling, personal counseling, placement for graduates. **Physically disabled:** Services for visually, speech, hearing impaired.

**Contact.** E-mail: info@msn.herzing.edu
Phone: (608) 249-6611 Toll-free number: (800) 582-1227
Fax: (608) 249-8593
Rebecca Abrams, Director of Admissions, Herzing College, 5218 East Terrace Drive, Madison, WI 53718

## ITT Technical Institute: Green Bay
### Green Bay, Wisconsin
### www.itt-tech.edu

- For-profit 4-year technical college
- Small city

**General.** Accredited by ACICS. **Calendar:** Trimester.

**Annual costs/financial aid.** Tuition varies by program, $260-$368 per credit hour.

**Contact.** Phone: (920) 662-9000
Director of Recruitment, 470 Security Boulevard, Green Bay, WI 54313

## ITT Technical Institute: Greenfield
### Greenfield, Wisconsin
### www.itt-tech.edu
**CB code: 2706**

- For-profit 4-year technical college
- Commuter campus in large town

**General.** Accredited by ACICS. **Calendar:** Quarter.

**Annual costs/financial aid.** Tuition varies by program, $260-$368 per credit hour.

**Contact.** Phone: (414) 282-9494
Director of Recruitment, 6300 West Layton Avenue, Greenfield, WI 53220-4612

## Lakeland College
### Sheboygan, Wisconsin
### www.lakeland.edu
**CB code: 1393**

- Private 4-year liberal arts college affiliated with United Church of Christ
- Residential campus in small city
- 2,918 degree-seeking undergraduates: 64% part-time, 63% women, 6% African American, 3% Asian American, 2% Hispanic American, 1% Native American, 4% international
- 820 degree-seeking graduate students
- 67% of applicants admitted
- SAT or ACT (ACT writing recommended) required
- 39% graduate within 6 years; 25% enter graduate study

**General.** Founded in 1862. Regionally accredited. Evening, online, and graduate classes offered for nontraditional students at 7 in-state sites. Associate program available at Tokyo, Japan campus. **Degrees:** 722 bachelor's, 24 associate awarded; master's offered. **Location:** 60 miles from Milwaukee, 60 miles from Green Bay. **Calendar:** 4-4-1. Limited summer session. **Full-time faculty:** 66 total; 59% have terminal degrees, 8% minority, 46% women. **Part-time faculty:** 248 total; 13% minority, 48% women. **Class size:** 69% < 20, 30% 20-39, 1% 40-49.

**Freshman class profile.** 898 applied, 602 admitted, 202 enrolled.

| Mid 50% test scores | | | |
|---|---|---|---|
| SAT critical reading: | 360-550 | Rank in top tenth: | 8% |
| SAT math: | 430-630 | Return as sophomores: | 71% |
| ACT composite: | 17-23 | Out-of-state: | 15% |
| GPA 3.50 or higher: | 19% | Live on campus: | 90% |
| GPA 3.0-3.49: | 29% | International: | 3% |
| GPA 2.0-2.99: | 49% | Fraternities: | 3% |
| Rank in top quarter: | 24% | Sororities: | 3% |

**Basis for selection.** Applicants with 19 ACT, 2.0 GPA and rank in the top half of class admitted. Essays are recommended. **Homeschooled:** Transcript of courses and grades, state high school equivalency certificate required.

**High school preparation.** Recommended units include English 4, mathematics 2, social studies 2, history 2, science 2, foreign language 2 and academic electives 2.

**2008-2009 Annual costs.** Tuition/fees: $18,435. Room/board: $6,360. Books/supplies: $900. Personal expenses: $750.

**2007-2008 Financial aid. Need-based:** 181 full-time freshmen applied for aid; 180 were judged to have need; 178 of these received aid. Average need met was 75%. Average scholarship/grant was $10,395; average loan $3,527. 50% of total undergraduate aid awarded as scholarships/grants, 50% as loans/jobs. **Non-need-based:** Awarded to 295 full-time undergraduates, including 102 freshmen. Scholarships awarded for academics.

**Application procedures. Admission:** No deadline. $20 fee, may be waived for applicants with need. Application may be submitted online. Admission notification on a rolling basis. **Financial aid:** Priority date 3/31, closing date 7/1. FAFSA, institutional form required. Applicants notified on a rolling basis starting 2/1; must reply within 2 week(s) of notification.

**Academics.** Applicants whose test scores reflect weakness in basic skills must take basic skills courses in freshman year. **Special study options:** Combined bachelor's/graduate degree, cooperative education, distance learning, double major, dual enrollment of high school students, ESL, honors, independent study, internships, liberal arts/career combination, study abroad, teacher certification program. Engineering program with University of Wisconsin-Madison, nursing program with Bellin College of Nursing. **Credit/placement by examination:** AP, CLEP, IB, institutional tests. 30 credit hours maximum toward bachelor's degree. **Support services:** Learning center, reduced course load, remedial instruction, study skills assistance, tutoring, writing center.

**Majors. Biology:** General, biochemistry. **Business:** Accounting, business admin, international, marketing, nonprofit/public, resort management. **Computer sciences:** Computer science. **Education:** Elementary, kindergarten/preschool, middle, secondary. **English:** Composition, English lit. **Foreign languages:** German, Spanish. **History:** General. **Math:** General. **Philosophy/religion:** Religion. **Physical sciences:** Chemistry. **Protective services:** Law enforcement admin. **Psychology:** General. **Social sciences:** Sociology. **Visual/performing arts:** Art.

**Most popular majors.** Business/marketing 68%, computer/information sciences 19%, education 11%.

**Computing on campus.** 218 workstations in dormitories, library, computer center, student center. Dormitories wired for high-speed internet access and linked to campus network. Commuter students can connect to campus network. Online course registration, online library, helpline, wireless network available.

**Student life. Freshman orientation:** Mandatory. Preregistration for classes offered. **Housing:** Guaranteed on-campus for freshmen. Coed dorms, single-sex dorms, special housing for disabled, apartments available. $50 deposit. Honor apartments and apartments for students with senior standing available. **Activities:** Concert band, choral groups, drama, music ensembles, student government, student newspaper, campus activities board, student association, black student union, Mortar Board, global students association, business fraternity, Inter-Greek Council.

**Athletics.** NCAA. **Intercollegiate:** Baseball M, basketball, cross-country, football (tackle) M, golf, soccer, softball W, tennis, track and field, volleyball W, wrestling M. **Team name:** Muskies.

**Student services.** Alcohol/substance abuse counseling, campus ministries, career counseling, services for economically disadvantaged, student employment services, financial aid counseling, health services, on-campus daycare, personal counseling, placement for graduates, veterans' counselor. **Physically disabled:** Services for visually impaired.

**Contact.** E-mail: admissions@lakeland.edu
Phone: (920) 565-1217 Toll-free number: (800) 242-3347
Fax: (920) 565-1206
Nathan Dehne, Director of Admissions, Lakeland College, Box 359, Sheboygan, WI 53082-0359

---

## Lawrence University
**Appleton, Wisconsin**

CB member
CB code: 1398

www.lawrence.edu

▸ Private 4-year music and liberal arts college
▸ Residential campus in small city
▸ 1,400 degree-seeking undergraduates: 2% part-time, 54% women, 2% African American, 3% Asian American, 2% Hispanic American, 7% international
▸ 56% of applicants admitted
▸ Application essay required
▸ 79% graduate within 6 years; 17% enter graduate study

**General.** Founded in 1847. Regionally accredited. **Degrees:** 316 bachelor's awarded. **Location:** 100 miles from Milwaukee, 30 miles from Green Bay. **Calendar:** Trimester. **Full-time faculty:** 153 total; 95% have terminal degrees, 9% minority, 34% women. **Part-time faculty:** 37 total; 38% have terminal degrees, 8% minority, 43% women. **Class size:** 72% < 20, 21% 20-39, 4% 40-49, 3% 50-99. **Special facilities:** Laser physics laboratory, 250 MHz nuclear magnetic resonance spectrometer, physics/computational graphics laboratory, Bjorklunden-425 acre lakefront retreat center.

**Freshman class profile.** 2,599 applied, 1,445 admitted, 357 enrolled.

| Mid 50% test scores | | | |
|---|---|---|---|
| SAT critical reading: | 610-730 | GPA 2.0-2.99: | 4% |
| SAT math: | 590-700 | Rank in top quarter: | 71% |
| SAT writing: | 600-700 | Rank in top tenth: | 39% |
| ACT composite: | 27-31 | Return as sophomores: | 88% |
| GPA 3.50 or higher: | 72% | Out-of-state: | 65% |
| GPA 3.0-3.49: | 24% | Live on campus: | 99% |
| | | International: | 10% |

**Basis for selection.** GED not accepted. Strength of curriculum, school achievement record most important. Recommendations, out-of-class activities, test scores considered. Music applicants judged on musicianship, teacher's recommendations, and academic ability. Interview recommended; portfolio recommended for studio art. Audition required for conservatory of music study. **Homeschooled:** Require some standardized test results, evidence of coursework completed and level of performance, letters of recommendation, and GED if applicable.

**High school preparation.** 16 units required. Required and recommended units include English 4, mathematics 3, social studies 2, history 2, science 3 and foreign language 2. Strong musical preparation required of music applicants.

**2007-2008 Annual costs.** Tuition/fees: $31,080. Room/board: $6,690. Books/supplies: $600. Personal expenses: $1,005.

**2007-2008 Financial aid. Need-based:** 273 full-time freshmen applied for aid; 211 were judged to have need; 211 of these received aid. Average need met was 91%. Average scholarship/grant was $18,100; average loan $5,000. 66% of total undergraduate aid awarded as scholarships/grants, 34% as loans/jobs. **Non-need-based:** Awarded to 298 full-time undergraduates, including 84 freshmen. Scholarships awarded for academics, alumni affiliation, minority status, music/drama, state residency. **Additional information:** The first $1,000 (aggregate) of independently-sponsored scholarships received by a needy student will reduce student's loan or work-study commitment. Half of scholarships in excess of $1,000 will offset loan or work-study and the other half will reduce institutional grant funding.

**Application procedures. Admission:** Closing date 1/15 (postmark date). $40 fee, may be waived for applicants with need. Application may be submitted online. Admission notification 4/1. Must reply by 5/1. **Financial aid:** Priority date 3/15; no closing date. FAFSA, institutional form required. Applicants notified on a rolling basis starting 3/15; must reply by 5/1 or within 2 week(s) of notification.

**Academics.** As an adjunct to a major, students may pursue 1 interdisciplinary area of study: biomedical ethics, international studies, neuroscience, or cognitive science. **Special study options:** Combined bachelor's/graduate degree, double major, independent study, internships, student-designed major, study abroad, teacher certification program, urban semester, Washington semester. Study abroad programs in 27 countries; marine biology term, marine geology term, Oak Ridge science semester; urban semester in Chicago; Newberry Library Program in humanities; environmental studies and forestry programs with Duke University; occupational therapy program with Washington University, St. Louis. **Credit/placement by examination:** AP, CLEP, IB, institutional tests. 30 credit hours maximum toward bachelor's degree. Course credit awarded for scores of at least 5 on International Baccalaureate examinations. Sophomore status granted for completion of full IB diploma. **Support services:** Learning center, reduced course load, study skills assistance, tutoring, writing center.

**Majors. Area/ethnic studies:** Chinese, East Asian, Japanese, Russian/Slavic. **Biology:** General. **Computer sciences:** General. **Conservation:** Environmental studies. **Education:** Music. **English:** English lit. **Foreign languages:** Ancient Greek, Chinese, classics, East Asian, French, German, Japanese, Latin, linguistics, Russian, Spanish. **History:** General. **Interdisciplinary:** Cognitive science, global studies, math/computer science, natural sciences, neuroscience. **Math:** General. **Philosophy/religion:** Philosophy, religion. **Physical sciences:** Chemistry, geology, physics. **Psychology:** General. **Social sciences:** Anthropology, economics, political science. **Visual/performing arts:** Art, art history/conservation, dramatic, music performance, music theory/composition, studio arts.

**Most popular majors.** Biology 10%, English 8%, foreign language 8%, interdisciplinary studies 8%, psychology 6%, social sciences 15%, visual/performing arts 22%.

**Computing on campus.** 175 workstations in dormitories, library, computer center. Dormitories wired for high-speed internet access and linked to

campus network. Commuter students can connect to campus network. On-line course registration, online library, helpline, repair service, wireless network available.

**Student life. Freshman orientation:** Mandatory. Preregistration for classes offered. New student orientation held 5 days prior to start of fall classes. **Policies:** Honor code in effect. All single students are required to live in university residence halls for 4 years. **Housing:** Guaranteed on-campus for all undergraduates. Coed dorms, single-sex dorms, apartments, substance-free housing available. 14 theme/group houses available. **Activities:** Bands, campus ministries, choral groups, dance, drama, film society, international student organizations, literary magazine, music ensembles, musical theater, opera, radio station, student government, student newspaper, symphony orchestra, Chavurah, Black Organization of Students, Latin American student organization, social service groups, political and academic clubs, professional sororities and fraternities.

**Athletics. NCAA. Intercollegiate:** Baseball M, basketball, cross-country, diving, fencing, football (tackle) M, golf M, ice hockey M, lacrosse, soccer, softball W, swimming, tennis, track and field, volleyball W, wrestling M. **Intramural:** Badminton, basketball, bowling, fencing, football (non-tackle), golf, handball, lacrosse, racquetball, soccer, softball, squash, table tennis, tennis, volleyball, water polo. **Team name:** Vikings.

**Student services.** Alcohol/substance abuse counseling, career counseling, student employment services, financial aid counseling, health services, minority student services, personal counseling, placement for graduates. **Physically disabled:** Services for visually, speech, hearing impaired.

**Contact.** E-mail: excel@lawrence.edu
Phone: (920) 832-6500 Toll-free number: (800) 227-0982
Fax: (920) 832-6782
Steven Syverson, Vice President for Enrollment Management, Lawrence University, Box 599, Appleton, WI 54912-0599

## Maranatha Baptist Bible College
**Watertown, Wisconsin**
**www.mbbc.edu**                                **CB code: 2732**

- Private 4-year Bible college affiliated with Baptist faith
- Residential campus in large town
- 829 degree-seeking undergraduates: 4% part-time, 55% women, 1% African American, 1% Asian American, 1% Hispanic American
- 37 degree-seeking graduate students
- 68% of applicants admitted
- ACT (writing optional), application essay required
- 50% graduate within 6 years; 18% enter graduate study

**General.** Founded in 1968. Regionally accredited. **Degrees:** 116 bachelor's, 21 associate awarded; master's offered. **ROTC:** Army, Air Force. **Location:** 45 miles from Milwaukee, 38 miles from Madison. **Calendar:** Semester, limited summer session. **Full-time faculty:** 44 total; 27% have terminal degrees, 4% minority, 25% women. **Part-time faculty:** 29 total; 10% have terminal degrees, 7% minority, 45% women. **Class size:** 63% < 20, 26% 20-39, 4% 40-49, 6% 50-99, 2% >100.

**Freshman class profile.** 331 applied, 226 admitted, 222 enrolled.

| Mid 50% test scores | | Return as sophomores: | 78% |
|---|---|---|---|
| ACT composite: | 20-25 | Out-of-state: | 76% |
| End year in good standing: | 75% | Live on campus: | 76% |

**Basis for selection.** Recommendations, religious commitment most important. Secondary school record, test scores, character also important. Class rank, essay considered. At-risk students placed on admissions probation. Audition required for fine arts.

**High school preparation.** College-preparatory program recommended. 18 units recommended. Recommended units include English 4, mathematics 3, social studies 3, history 3, science 3 and foreign language 2. Two units of physical education and one unit of word processing recommended.

**2007-2008 Annual costs.** Tuition/fees: $9,486. Room/board: $5,500. Books/supplies: $840. Personal expenses: $1,890.

**2006-2007 Financial aid. Need-based:** 202 full-time freshmen applied for aid; 172 were judged to have need; 172 of these received aid. Average need met was 40%. Average scholarship/grant was $3,396; average loan $2,296. 28% of total undergraduate aid awarded as scholarships/grants, 72% as loans/jobs. **Non-need-based:** Awarded to 59 full-time undergraduates, including 15 freshmen. Scholarships awarded for academics.

**Application procedures. Admission:** No deadline. $50 fee. Application may be submitted online. Admission notification on a rolling basis.

**Financial aid:** Priority date 3/1; no closing date. FAFSA required. Applicants notified on a rolling basis starting 2/1; must reply within 2 week(s) of notification.

**Academics.** Hands-on ministerial work available. **Special study options:** Distance learning, double major, independent study, internships, liberal arts/career combination, study abroad, teacher certification program. **Credit/placement by examination:** AP, CLEP, ACT, institutional tests. 12 credit hours maximum toward associate degree, 12 toward bachelor's. Only 6 credits may be counted in any one field of study. **Support services:** Reduced course load, remedial instruction, study skills assistance, tutoring, writing center.

**Majors. Area/ethnic studies:** Women's. **Biology:** General. **Business:** Accounting/business management, business admin, management information systems, marketing, office management. **Education:** General, business, early childhood, elementary, English, history, mathematics, music, physical, science, secondary, social studies. **English:** English lit. **Health:** Nursing (RN). **Liberal arts:** Humanities. **Theology:** Bible, missionary, pastoral counseling, sacred music, youth ministry. **Visual/performing arts:** Music pedagogy, music performance, piano/organ.

**Most popular majors.** Business/marketing 10%, education 43%, liberal arts 10%, philosophy/religious studies 31%.

**Computing on campus.** 120 workstations in dormitories, library, computer center. Dormitories wired for high-speed internet access and linked to campus network. Online library, repair service, student web hosting, wireless network available.

**Student life. Freshman orientation:** Mandatory. Preregistration for classes offered. Held Saturday through Monday before classes begin. **Policies:** Religious observance required. **Housing:** Guaranteed on-campus for all undergraduates. Single-sex dorms, substance-free housing available. $175 nonrefundable deposit. **Activities:** Bands, campus ministries, choral groups, drama, music ensembles, musical theater, student government, symphony orchestra.

**Athletics. NCAA, NCCAA. Intercollegiate:** Baseball M, basketball, cross-country, football (tackle) M, soccer, softball W, volleyball W, wrestling M. **Intramural:** Basketball, soccer W, volleyball. **Team name:** Crusaders.

**Student services.** Campus ministries, career counseling, financial aid counseling, health services, on-campus daycare, personal counseling, placement for graduates, veterans' counselor.

**Contact.** E-mail: admissions@mbbc.edu
Phone: (920) 261-9300 Toll-free number: (800) 611-1947
Fax: (920) 261-9109
James Harrison, Director of Admissions, Maranatha Baptist Bible College, 745 West Main Street, Watertown, WI 53094

## Marian College of Fond du Lac
**Fond du Lac, Wisconsin**                        **CB member**
**www.mariancollege.edu**                          **CB code: 1443**

- Private 4-year liberal arts college affiliated with Roman Catholic Church
- Residential campus in large town
- 1,958 degree-seeking undergraduates: 28% part-time, 74% women, 4% African American, 1% Asian American, 2% Hispanic American, 1% Native American, 1% international
- 717 degree-seeking graduate students
- 85% of applicants admitted
- SAT or ACT (ACT writing optional) required
- 50% graduate within 6 years

**General.** Founded in 1936. Regionally accredited. **Degrees:** 365 bachelor's awarded; master's, doctoral offered. **ROTC:** Army. **Location:** 60 miles from Milwaukee, 65 miles from Green Bay. **Calendar:** Semester, extensive summer session. **Full-time faculty:** 86 total; 65% have terminal degrees, 6% minority, 51% women. **Part-time faculty:** 183 total; 19% have terminal degrees, 2% minority, 49% women. **Class size:** 75% < 20, 24% 20-39, 1% 40-49.

**Freshman class profile.** 747 applied, 633 admitted, 267 enrolled.

| Mid 50% test scores | | | |
|---|---|---|---|
| ACT composite: | 18-22 | Return as sophomores: | 76% |
| GPA 3.50 or higher: | 27% | Out-of-state: | 10% |
| GPA 3.0-3.49: | 28% | Live on campus: | 74% |
| GPA 2.0-2.99: | 42% | International: | 3% |
| Rank in top quarter: | 29% | Fraternities: | 9% |
| Rank in top tenth: | 9% | Sororities: | 6% |

**Basis for selection.** School achievement record most important, followed by test scores. Applicants must meet 2 of following 3 criteria: 2.0 GPA, top half of class, 18 ACT. Special admissions procedures required for nursing and education divisions. If admission criteria not met, students may be admitted on provisional basis. Interview, audition recommended.

**High school preparation.** Required and recommended units include English 4, mathematics 2-3, history 1, science 1-2 (laboratory 1) and foreign language 2. Biology and chemistry prerequisite for nursing program.

**2007-2008 Annual costs.** Tuition/fees: $18,665. Room/board: $5,220. Books/supplies: $700. Personal expenses: $1,420.

**2007-2008 Financial aid. Need-based:** 253 full-time freshmen applied for aid; 221 were judged to have need; 221 of these received aid. Average need met was 87%. Average scholarship/grant was $10,478; average loan $4,491. 53% of total undergraduate aid awarded as scholarships/grants, 47% as loans/jobs. **Non-need-based:** Awarded to 1,120 full-time undergraduates, including 242 freshmen. Scholarships awarded for academics, ROTC, state residency.

**Application procedures. Admission:** Priority date 4/1; no deadline. $20 fee, may be waived for applicants with need. Application may be submitted online. Admission notification on a rolling basis. Must reply by May 1 or within 4 week(s) if notified thereafter. **Financial aid:** Priority date 3/1; no closing date. FAFSA, institutional form required. Applicants notified on a rolling basis starting 3/1; must reply within 4 week(s) of notification.

**Academics. Special study options:** Accelerated study, cooperative education, distance learning, double major, dual enrollment of high school students, honors, independent study, internships, liberal arts/career combination, student-designed major, study abroad, teacher certification program. Accelerated programs for adults in business, nursing, operation management, radiologic technology, administration of justice. **Credit/placement by examination:** AP, CLEP, IB, institutional tests. 30 credit hours maximum toward bachelor's degree. Writing sample required for placement and counseling. **Support services:** Learning center, pre-admission summer program, reduced course load, remedial instruction, study skills assistance, tutoring, writing center.

**Honors college/program.** Unrestricted admissions with 25 ACT, 3.5 GPA, positive recommendation, application essay.

**Majors. Biology:** General. **Business:** General, accounting, business admin, human resources, managerial economics, marketing, operations. **Communications:** General, organizational. **Computer sciences:** Information technology. **Education:** General, art, biology, chemistry, early childhood, elementary, English, history, mathematics, music, science, secondary, social studies, Spanish. **English:** British lit, composition, English lit. **Foreign languages:** Spanish. **Health:** Art therapy, cytotechnology, nursing (RN), radiologic technology/medical imaging. **History:** General. **Liberal arts:** Arts/sciences. **Math:** General. **Parks/recreation:** Sports admin. **Physical sciences:** Chemistry. **Protective services:** Law enforcement admin. **Psychology:** General. **Public administration:** Social work. **Visual/performing arts:** Graphic design, music management, studio arts.

**Most popular majors.** Business/marketing 32%, education 9%, health sciences 27%, security/protective services 10%.

**Computing on campus.** 300 workstations in dormitories, library, computer center, student center. Dormitories wired for high-speed internet access and linked to campus network. Commuter students can connect to campus network. Online course registration, online library, helpline, wireless network available.

**Student life. Freshman orientation:** Mandatory. Preregistration for classes offered. **Policies:** Emphasis on community volunteer activity. Service transcript available for graduates. **Housing:** Guaranteed on-campus for all undergraduates. Coed dorms, special housing for disabled, apartments, fraternity/sorority housing, substance-free housing available. $100 deposit. Townhouses, penthouses and residential suites available. **Activities:** Bands, campus ministries, choral groups, drama, international student organizations, literary magazine, music ensembles, Model UN, student government, student newspaper, symphony orchestra, Circle K, eco club, social justice committee, African American student union.

**Athletics. NCAA. Intercollegiate:** Baseball M, basketball, cross-country, golf, ice hockey M, soccer, softball W, tennis, volleyball W. **Intramural:** Badminton, basketball, bowling, football (non-tackle) M, skiing, softball M, tennis, volleyball. **Team name:** Sabre Cats.

**Student services.** Adult student services, alcohol/substance abuse counseling, campus ministries, career counseling, services for economically disadvantaged, student employment services, financial aid counseling, health services, minority student services, on-campus daycare, personal counseling, placement for graduates, women's services. **Physically disabled:** Services for visually, speech, hearing impaired.

**Contact.** E-mail: admissions@mariancollege.edu
Phone: (920) 923-7650 Toll-free number: (800) 262-7426
Fax: (920) 923-8755
Stacey Akey, Vice President for Enrollment and Marketing, Marian College of Fond du Lac, 45 South National Avenue, Fond du Lac, WI 54935-4699

## Marquette University
**Milwaukee, Wisconsin**
**www.marquette.edu**

CB member
CB code: 1448

- Private 4-year university affiliated with Roman Catholic Church
- Residential campus in very large city
- 7,742 degree-seeking undergraduates: 3% part-time, 54% women, 5% African American, 5% Asian American, 5% Hispanic American, 1% international
- 3,328 degree-seeking graduate students
- 67% of applicants admitted
- SAT or ACT (ACT writing recommended), application essay required
- 75% graduate within 6 years

**General.** Founded in 1881. Regionally accredited. **Degrees:** 1,745 bachelor's awarded; master's, doctoral, first professional offered. **ROTC:** Army, Naval, Air Force. **Location:** Downtown. **Calendar:** Semester, extensive summer session. **Full-time faculty:** 609 total; 89% have terminal degrees, 14% minority, 37% women. **Part-time faculty:** 467 total; 48% have terminal degrees, 9% minority, 41% women. **Class size:** 38% < 20, 43% 20-39, 7% 40-49, 8% 50-99, 4% >100. **Special facilities:** 15th century St. Joan of Arc chapel.

**Freshman class profile.** 13,375 applied, 9,005 admitted, 1,820 enrolled.

| Mid 50% test scores | | | |
|---|---|---|---|
| SAT critical reading: | 540-630 | Rank in top tenth: | 34% |
| SAT math: | 550-660 | Return as sophomores: | 89% |
| SAT writing: | 530-640 | Out-of-state: | 57% |
| ACT composite: | 24-29 | Live on campus: | 92% |
| Rank in top quarter: | 64% | International: | 2% |

**Basis for selection.** High school course selection, trend of performance, test scores and class rank most important. Essay, leadership, community service and extracurricular activities considered. **Homeschooled:** Provide detailed list of curriculum and bibliography. Personal interview may be required.

**High school preparation.** 16 units required; 22 recommended. Required and recommended units include English 4, mathematics 2-4, social studies 2-3, science 2-3 (laboratory 2-3), foreign language 2 and academic electives 2-5. Algebra, geometry, and intermediate algebra required for arts & sciences, business administration and health sciences. Algebra and geometry required for nursing. 3 years of science recommended for premedical, predental and science majors. Students interested in international business strongly urged to complete 4 units of single foreign language.

**2007-2008 Annual costs.** Tuition/fees: $26,678. Room/board: $8,820. Books/supplies: $900. Personal expenses: $1,350.

**2007-2008 Financial aid. Need-based:** 1,391 full-time freshmen applied for aid; 1,050 were judged to have need; 1,049 of these received aid. Average need met was 84%. Average scholarship/grant was $14,214; average loan $5,304. 60% of total undergraduate aid awarded as scholarships/grants, 40% as loans/jobs. **Non-need-based:** Awarded to 2,520 full-time undergraduates, including 504 freshmen. Scholarships awarded for academics, athletics, leadership, music/drama, ROTC.

**Application procedures. Admission:** Closing date 12/1 (postmark date). $30 fee, may be waived for applicants with need. Application may be submitted online. Admission notification 1/31. Admission notification on a rolling basis. Must reply by May 1 or within 2 week(s) if notified thereafter. Application closing date for physical therapy and athletic training programs is 12/1 for direct admits. **Financial aid:** Priority date 2/1; no closing date.

FAFSA required. Applicants notified on a rolling basis starting 3/20; must reply by 5/1 or within 3 week(s) of notification.

**Academics. Special study options:** Accelerated study, combined bachelor's/graduate degree, cooperative education, cross-registration, double major, dual enrollment of high school students, honors, internships, student-designed major, study abroad, teacher certification program, Washington semester, weekend college. **Credit/placement by examination:** AP, CLEP, IB, institutional tests. 30 credit hours maximum toward bachelor's degree. **Support services:** Learning center, pre-admission summer program, reduced course load, study skills assistance, tutoring, writing center.

**Majors. Area/ethnic studies:** African-American, women's. **Biology:** General, biochemistry, molecular. **Business:** Accounting, accounting technology, business admin, e-commerce, finance, human resources, international, management information systems, managerial economics, marketing. **Communications:** General, advertising, broadcast journalism, journalism, media studies, public relations. **Computer sciences:** Computer science, information systems. **Education:** Elementary, English, foreign languages, mathematics, middle, science, secondary, social science, social studies. **Engineering:** General, biomedical, civil, computer, electrical, environmental, manufacturing, mechanical. **Engineering technology:** Industrial management. **English:** Creative writing, English lit, speech/rhetoric. **Foreign languages:** Classics, French, German, Spanish. **Health:** Athletic training, audiology/speech pathology, clinical lab technology, nursing (RN), predental, premedicine. **History:** General. **Interdisciplinary:** Global studies, intercultural, math/computer science. **Legal studies:** Prelaw. **Math:** General, computational, statistics. **Parks/recreation:** Exercise sciences. **Philosophy/religion:** Philosophy, religion. **Physical sciences:** Chemistry, physics. **Psychology:** General. **Social sciences:** General, anthropology, criminology, economics, international relations, political science, sociology. **Visual/performing arts:** Dramatic.

**Most popular majors.** Biology 7%, business/marketing 23%, communications/journalism 12%, engineering/engineering technologies 8%, health sciences 9%, social sciences 11%.

**Computing on campus.** 1,200 workstations in dormitories, library, computer center, student center. Dormitories wired for high-speed internet access and linked to campus network. Commuter students can connect to campus network. Online course registration, online library, helpline, student web hosting, wireless network available.

**Student life. Freshman orientation:** Available. Preregistration for classes offered. 4 day session held week before classes begin in fall; June program also available. **Policies:** Written policies concerning racial and sexual harassment, alcohol, drugs and safety. Students provided materials detailing policies and programs. **Housing:** Guaranteed on-campus for freshmen. Coed dorms, single-sex dorms, special housing for disabled, apartments, fraternity/sorority housing available. $200 nonrefundable deposit, deadline 5/1. Special housing for engineering, nursing, and honor students. **Activities:** Bands, campus ministries, choral groups, dance, drama, international student organizations, literary magazine, music ensembles, Model UN, musical theater, radio station, student government, student newspaper, symphony orchestra, TV station, JUSTICE, College Republicans, College Democrats, Campus Crusade for Christ, Intervarsity, Latin American student organization.

**Athletics.** NCAA. **Intercollegiate:** Basketball, cheerleading, cross-country, golf M, soccer, tennis, track and field, volleyball W. **Intramural:** Badminton, basketball, football (tackle), golf, racquetball, soccer, softball, squash, tennis, track and field, volleyball, water polo, weight lifting. **Team name:** Golden Eagles.

**Student services.** Adult student services, alcohol/substance abuse counseling, campus ministries, career counseling, services for economically disadvantaged, student employment services, financial aid counseling, health services, minority student services, on-campus daycare, personal counseling, placement for graduates. **Physically disabled:** Services for visually, speech, hearing impaired.

**Contact.** E-mail: admissions@marquette.edu
Phone: (414) 288-7302 Toll-free number: (800) 222-6544
Fax: (414) 288-3764
Robert Blust, Dean of Undergraduate Admissions, Marquette University, PO Box 1881, Milwaukee, WI 53201-1881

## Milwaukee Institute of Art & Design
**Milwaukee, Wisconsin**
www.miad.edu                                          CB code: 1506

- Private 4-year visual arts college
- Commuter campus in very large city
- 636 degree-seeking undergraduates
- Application essay, interview required

**General.** Founded in 1974. Regionally accredited. **Degrees:** 120 bachelor's awarded. **Location:** 90 miles from Chicago. **Calendar:** Semester, limited summer session. **Full-time faculty:** 33 total; 67% have terminal degrees, 6% minority, 42% women. **Part-time faculty:** 86 total; 2% minority, 42% women. **Class size:** 87% < 20, 13% 20-39, less than 1% 40-49. **Special facilities:** Design center, advertising and design museum, gallery of industrial design, Riverwalk (public art project), art galleries, foundry, 3-D lab.

**Freshman class profile.**

| | | | |
|---|---|---|---|
| GPA 3.50 or higher: | 23% | Rank in top tenth: | 6% |
| GPA 3.0-3.49: | 32% | Out-of-state: | 46% |
| GPA 2.0-2.99: | 43% | Live on campus: | 65% |
| Rank in top quarter: | 25% | | |

**Basis for selection.** Portfolio and interview most important. 3.0 GPA in high school art curriculum recommended. Portfolio of 15-20 pieces of artwork required. **Homeschooled:** Transcript of courses and grades required.

**High school preparation.** 4 years high school visual art study highly recommended.

**2007-2008 Annual costs.** Tuition/fees: $24,900. Room/board: $7,200. Books/supplies: $1,625. Personal expenses: $1,624.

**Financial aid. Non-need-based:** Scholarships awarded for academics, art, leadership.

**Application procedures. Admission:** Priority date 2/15; no deadline. $25 fee, may be waived for applicants with need. Application may be submitted online. Admission notification on a rolling basis beginning on or about 5/1. Must reply by May 1 or within 2 week(s) if notified thereafter. **Financial aid:** Priority date 3/1; no closing date. FAFSA required. Applicants notified on a rolling basis starting 4/1; must reply by 5/1 or within 4 week(s) of notification.

**Academics. Special study options:** Double major, exchange student, independent study, internships, liberal arts/career combination, New York semester, study abroad. **Credit/placement by examination:** AP, CLEP. **Support services:** Learning center, reduced course load, remedial instruction, study skills assistance, tutoring, writing center.

**Majors. Visual/performing arts:** Commercial/advertising art, drawing, industrial design, interior design, painting, photography, printmaking, sculpture.

**Computing on campus.** 175 workstations in library, computer center, student center. Commuter students can connect to campus network. Wireless network available.

**Student life. Freshman orientation:** Mandatory. Held before each semester for 2 days. **Housing:** Coed dorms available. $175 nonrefundable deposit, deadline 5/1. **Activities:** Drama, literary magazine, student government, minority student organization, Interior Design Society of America, National Industrial Design Society, student activities committee.

**Student services.** Alcohol/substance abuse counseling, career counseling, student employment services, financial aid counseling, health services, minority student services, personal counseling, placement for graduates, veterans' counselor.

**Contact.** E-mail: admissions@miad.edu
Phone: (414) 291-8070 Toll-free number: (888) 749-6423
Fax: (414) 291-8077
Mark Fetherson, Director of Admissions, Milwaukee Institute of Art & Design, 273 East Erie Street, Milwaukee, WI 53202

## Milwaukee School of Engineering
**Milwaukee, Wisconsin**                               **CB member**
www.msoe.edu                                          **CB code: 1476**

- Private 4-year university
- Residential campus in very large city
- 2,317 degree-seeking undergraduates: 11% part-time, 19% women, 4% African American, 3% Asian American, 3% Hispanic American, 1% Native American, 2% international
- 199 degree-seeking graduate students
- 65% of applicants admitted
- SAT or ACT (ACT writing optional) required
- 52% graduate within 6 years; 39% enter graduate study

**General.** Founded in 1903. Regionally accredited. **Degrees:** 384 bachelor's awarded; master's offered. **ROTC:** Army, Naval, Air Force. **Location:** 72 miles from Chicago. **Calendar:** Quarter, limited summer session. **Full-time faculty:** 119 total; 70% have terminal degrees, 9% minority, 24% women. **Part-time faculty:** 116 total; 27% have terminal degrees, 10% minority, 34% women. **Class size:** 42% < 20, 58% 20-39, less than 1% 40-49. **Special facilities:** Museum, teaching and research laboratories for fluid power motion control, construction engineering, energy systems, rapid prototyping, software development, health and wellness facility with indoor ice hockey arena.

**Freshman class profile.** 2,732 applied, 1,767 admitted, 575 enrolled.

| Mid 50% test scores | | End year in good standing: | 80% |
|---|---|---|---|
| SAT critical reading: | 520-630 | Return as sophomores: | 73% |
| SAT math: | 590-690 | Out-of-state: | 29% |
| ACT composite: | 23-28 | Live on campus: | 82% |
| GPA 3.50 or higher: | 51% | International: | 1% |
| GPA 3.0-3.49: | 38% | Fraternities: | 4% |
| GPA 2.0-2.99: | 11% | Sororities: | 8% |

**Basis for selection.** Admissions based on secondary school record and standardized test scores. **Homeschooled:** Transcript of courses and grades required. **Learning Disabled:** Untimed standardized tests required.

**High school preparation.** 10 units required. Required and recommended units include English 4, mathematics 4, science 2 (laboratory 2). For business and technical communication, math units should include 1 algebra. For biomedical engineering, science units should include 1 biological science.

**2008-2009 Annual costs.** Tuition/fees: $27,300. $1,140 technology package required for all full-time first-year students. Includes laptop computer, software, Internet, insurance and repairs; upgrade every two years, wireless access, training and support, and compatibility computing throughout campus. Room/board: $6,825. Books/supplies: $1,500. Personal expenses: $3,140.

**2006-2007 Financial aid.** **Need-based:** 501 full-time freshmen applied for aid; 429 were judged to have need; 429 of these received aid. Average need met was 68%. Average scholarship/grant was $14,289; average loan $1,768. 68% of total undergraduate aid awarded as scholarships/grants, 32% as loans/jobs. **Non-need-based:** Awarded to 507 full-time undergraduates, including 167 freshmen. Scholarships awarded for academics, ROTC.

**Application procedures. Admission:** Priority date 2/1; no deadline. $25 fee, may be waived for applicants with need. Application may be submitted online. Admission notification on a rolling basis beginning on or about 10/1. **Financial aid:** Priority date 3/15; no closing date. FAFSA required. Applicants notified on a rolling basis starting 3/1; must reply within 2 week(s) of notification.

**Academics.** Average of 600 hours of laboratory experience for each program. **Special study options:** Accelerated study, combined bachelor's/graduate degree, distance learning, double major, dual enrollment of high school students, ESL, internships, study abroad. Bachelor of Science in business, mechanical engineering, and in electrical engineering with Lubeck University of Applied Sciences, Germany; exchange program with Czech Technical University, bachelor's or master's option in an engineering discipline and master's in environmental engineering. **Credit/placement by examination:** AP, CLEP, IB, SAT, ACT. **Support services:** Learning center, pre-admission summer program, reduced course load, study skills assistance, tutoring, writing center.

**Majors. Business:** General, business admin, construction management, international, management information systems. **Communications:** General. **Engineering:** General, architectural, biomedical, computer, electrical, industrial, mechanical, software. **Engineering technology:** Electrical, mechanical. **English:** Technical writing. **Health:** Nursing (RN).

**Most popular majors.** Business/marketing 20%, engineering/engineering technologies 74%.

**Computing on campus.** PC or laptop required. 150 workstations in dormitories, library, computer center, student center. Dormitories wired for high-speed internet access and linked to campus network. Commuter students can connect to campus network. Online course registration, online library, helpline, repair service, student web hosting, wireless network available.

**Student life. Freshman orientation:** Available. Preregistration for classes offered. Three- to 4-day program prior to start of classes. **Policies:** Smoke-free campus and residential facilities. **Housing:** Guaranteed on-campus for freshmen. Coed dorms, special housing for disabled, substance-free housing available. $75 nonrefundable deposit, deadline 6/1. **Activities:** Bands, campus ministries, dance, drama, film society, international student organizations, literary magazine, radio station, student government, student newspaper, symphony orchestra, residence hall association, Circle-K, Asian Student

Organization, Society of Hispanic Professional Engineers, National Society of Black Engineers, National Student Nurses Association.

**Athletics.** NCAA. **Intercollegiate:** Baseball M, basketball, cheerleading, cross-country, golf, ice hockey M, rowing (crew) M, soccer, softball W, tennis, track and field, volleyball, wrestling M. **Intramural:** Basketball, football (non-tackle), soccer, softball, volleyball. **Team name:** Raiders.

**Student services.** Adult student services, alcohol/substance abuse counseling, campus ministries, career counseling, services for economically disadvantaged, student employment services, financial aid counseling, health services, minority student services, personal counseling, placement for graduates, veterans' counselor, women's services. **Physically disabled:** Services for visually, speech, hearing impaired. **Learning disabled:** Comprehensive services available.

**Contact.** E-mail: explore@msoe.edu
Phone: (414) 277-6763 Toll-free number: (800) 332-6763
Fax: (414) 277-7475
Paul Borens, Director, Admission, Milwaukee School of Engineering, 1025 North Broadway, Milwaukee, WI 53202-3109

---

## Mount Mary College
### Milwaukee, Wisconsin
### www.mtmary.edu
**CB code: 1490**

▸ Private 4-year liberal arts college for women affiliated with Roman Catholic Church
▸ Commuter campus in very large city
▸ 1,203 degree-seeking undergraduates: 33% part-time, 99% women, 19% African American, 4% Asian American, 6% Hispanic American, 2% Native American, 1% international
▸ 300 degree-seeking graduate students
▸ 59% of applicants admitted
▸ SAT or ACT (ACT writing optional) required
▸ 33% graduate within 6 years

**General.** Founded in 1913. Regionally accredited. Open to all faiths. Small number of men admitted as part-time non-degree-seeking students and for joint nursing students with Columbia College of Nursing. **Degrees:** 164 bachelor's awarded; master's offered. **ROTC:** Army, Naval. **Location:** 7 miles from downtown. **Calendar:** Semester, limited summer session. **Full-time faculty:** 66 total; 62% have terminal degrees, 85% women. **Part-time faculty:** 137 total; 25% have terminal degrees, 76% women. **Class size:** 84% < 20, 15% 20-39, less than 1% 40-49. **Special facilities:** Historic costume collection, labyrinth.

**Freshman class profile.** 482 applied, 284 admitted, 126 enrolled.

| GPA 3.50 or higher: | 23% | Return as sophomores: | 68% |
|---|---|---|---|
| GPA 3.0-3.49: | 31% | Out-of-state: | 6% |
| GPA 2.0-2.99: | 41% | Live on campus: | 44% |
| Rank in top quarter: | 35% | International: | 2% |
| Rank in top tenth: | 16% | | |

**Basis for selection.** Academic record, test scores and supplemental information are reviewed. Class rank, core curriculum, test scores and GPA important. Interview recommended and essay required for students who do not meet direct admission requirements. **Homeschooled:** Transcript of courses and grades required. **Learning Disabled:** Students encouraged to talk with Disabilities Coordinator, at least one semester prior to enrollment, to determine if reasonable accommodations can be made.

**High school preparation.** 16 units required. Required and recommended units include English 4, mathematics 2-3, social studies 2, history 2, science 2 (laboratory 2), foreign language 2 and academic electives 4.

**2008-2009 Annual costs.** Tuition/fees: $20,350. Room/board: $6,994. Books/supplies: $1,100. Personal expenses: $1,562.

**2007-2008 Financial aid. Need-based:** Average need met was 58%. Average scholarship/grant was $9,065; average loan $3,885. 56% of total undergraduate aid awarded as scholarships/grants, 44% as loans/jobs. **Non-need-based:** Scholarships awarded for academics, alumni affiliation, art, leadership, music/drama.

**Application procedures. Admission:** No deadline. $25 fee, may be waived for applicants with need. Application may be submitted online. Admission notification on a rolling basis beginning on or about 9/15. Must reply by May 1 or within 2 week(s) if notified thereafter. **Financial aid:** Priority date 3/11; no closing date. FAFSA required. Applicants notified on a rolling basis starting 1/1; must reply within 2 week(s) of notification.

**Academics.** **Special study options:** Accelerated study, combined bachelor's/graduate degree, double major, honors, independent study, internships, liberal arts/career combination, student-designed major, study abroad, teacher certification program. **Credit/placement by examination:** AP, CLEP, IB, ACT, institutional tests. Maximum of 24 credits earned through a combination of credit exams, credit from life experience, directed and independent study. **Support services:** Learning center, reduced course load, remedial instruction, study skills assistance, tutoring.

**Majors.** **Biology:** General. **Business:** Accounting, business admin, fashion, marketing. **Communications:** General, public relations. **Computer sciences:** Computer graphics, computer science. **Education:** General, art, biology, business, chemistry, early childhood, elementary, English, foreign languages, French, history, mathematics, music, science, secondary, social studies, Spanish. **English:** English lit, technical writing. **Foreign languages:** French, Spanish. **Health:** Art therapy, dietetics, nursing (RN), predental, premedicine, preveterinary. **History:** General. **Interdisciplinary:** Behavioral sciences, biological/physical sciences. **Legal studies:** Prelaw. **Math:** General. **Philosophy/religion:** Philosophy, religion. **Physical sciences:** Chemistry. **Protective services:** Criminal justice. **Psychology:** General. **Public administration:** Social work. **Social sciences:** General, international relations. **Theology:** Religious ed. **Visual/performing arts:** Art, commercial/advertising art, fashion design, interior design.

**Most popular majors.** Business/marketing 14%, health sciences 35%, psychology 6%, visual/performing arts 19%.

**Computing on campus.** 313 workstations in dormitories, library, computer center, student center. Dormitories wired for high-speed internet access and linked to campus network. Commuter students can connect to campus network. Helpline available.

**Student life.** **Freshman orientation:** Mandatory. Preregistration for classes offered. **Policies:** No overnight male visitation. **Housing:** Guaranteed on-campus for freshmen. $100 nonrefundable deposit, deadline 5/1. **Activities:** Campus ministries, choral groups, international student organizations, literary magazine, music ensembles, student government, student newspaper, commuter council, hall council, gospel choir, programming and activities council, student athletes, department-affiliated clubs.

**Athletics.** NCAA. **Intercollegiate:** Basketball W, soccer W, softball W, tennis W, volleyball W. **Intramural:** Basketball W, bowling W, cross-country W, golf W, skiing W, soccer W, swimming W, tennis W, track and field W, volleyball W. **Team name:** Blue Angels.

**Student services.** Campus ministries, career counseling, student employment services, financial aid counseling, minority student services, on-campus daycare, personal counseling. **Physically disabled:** Services for visually impaired.

**Contact.** E-mail: admiss@mtmary.edu
Phone: (414) 256-1219 Toll-free number: (800) 321-6265
Fax: (414) 256-0180
Brooke Konopacki, Dean of Enrollment, Mount Mary College, 2900 North Menomonee River Parkway, Milwaukee, WI 53222

---

## Northland College

**Ashland, Wisconsin**
**www.northland.edu**

**CB member**
**CB code: 1561**

- Private 4-year liberal arts college affiliated with United Church of Christ
- Residential campus in small town
- 656 degree-seeking undergraduates: 6% part-time, 55% women, 1% African American, 1% Asian American, 3% Hispanic American, 2% Native American, 2% international
- 71% of applicants admitted
- SAT or ACT (ACT writing optional), application essay required
- 47% graduate within 6 years

**General.** Founded in 1892. Regionally accredited. **Degrees:** 128 bachelor's awarded. **Location:** 220 miles from Minneapolis-St. Paul, 65 miles from Duluth, Minnesota. **Calendar:** 4-1-4, limited summer session. **Full-time faculty:** 38 total; 76% have terminal degrees, 5% minority, 21% women. **Part-time faculty:** 58 total; 28% have terminal degrees, 14% minority, 34% women. **Class size:** 65% < 20, 32% 20-39, 2% 40-49, less than 1% 50-99. **Special facilities:** Field stations for natural science courses, atmospheric and environmental satellite links.

**Freshman class profile.** 1,243 applied, 883 admitted, 153 enrolled.

| Mid 50% test scores | | | |
|---|---|---|---|
| SAT critical reading: | 530-620 | Rank in top quarter: | 50% |
| SAT math: | 480-620 | Rank in top tenth: | 27% |
| ACT composite: | 21-27 | Return as sophomores: | 71% |
| GPA 3.50 or higher: | 47% | Out-of-state: | 43% |
| GPA 3.0-3.49: | 30% | Live on campus: | 96% |
| GPA 2.0-2.99: | 23% | International: | 3% |

**Basis for selection.** High school curriculum evaluation, class rank, guidance counselor recommendation, GPA, and test scores considered. Audition, portfolio recommended; interview required for borderline applicants.

**High school preparation.** 18 units required; 21 recommended. Required and recommended units include English 4, mathematics 3, social studies 3, science 3 (laboratory 2), foreign language 2 and academic electives 3-4.

**2008-2009 Annual costs.** Tuition/fees: $23,101. Room/board: $6,440. Books/supplies: $800. Personal expenses: $1,500.

**2007-2008 Financial aid.** **Need-based:** 140 full-time freshmen applied for aid; 128 were judged to have need; 128 of these received aid. Average need met was 87%. Average scholarship/grant was $15,049; average loan $3,995. 70% of total undergraduate aid awarded as scholarships/grants, 30% as loans/jobs. **Non-need-based:** Awarded to 99 full-time undergraduates, including 25 freshmen. Scholarships awarded for academics, alumni affiliation, art, job skills, leadership, minority status, music/drama, religious affiliation, state residency.

**Application procedures.** **Admission:** Priority date 12/1; no deadline. $25 fee, may be waived for applicants with need. Admission notification on a rolling basis beginning on or about 9/1. Must reply by May 1 or within 2 week(s) if notified thereafter. **Financial aid:** Priority date 4/15; no closing date. FAFSA required. Applicants notified on a rolling basis starting 3/1; must reply by 5/1 or within 4 week(s) of notification.

**Academics.** Accelerated evening degree completion business program offered; classes meet one night a week over 16-month period. Accelerated Bachelor of Nursing for students who have an earned RN. **Special study options:** Combined bachelor's/graduate degree, distance learning, double major, exchange student, honors, independent study, internships, student-designed major, teacher certification program. 3-2 cooperative degree programs in environmental engineering and forestry with Michigan Technological University. Ecoleague exchange with Antioch, Alaska Pacific, Green Mountain, Prescott, College of the Atlantic. **Credit/placement by examination:** AP, CLEP, IB, SAT, ACT, institutional tests. 30 credit hours maximum toward bachelor's degree. **Support services:** Learning center, reduced course load, study skills assistance, tutoring, writing center.

**Majors.** **Architecture:** Urban/community planning. **Area/ethnic studies:** Native American. **Biology:** General, biochemistry, ecology. **Business:** General, accounting, business admin, management science. **Conservation:** General, environmental studies, fisheries, forestry, management/policy, wildlife. **Education:** Elementary. **English:** Creative writing, English lit. **Health:** Health care admin, predental, premedicine, prepharmacy, preveterinary, recreational therapy. **History:** General. **Interdisciplinary:** Biological/physical sciences, global studies, natural sciences, peace/conflict. **Legal studies:** Prelaw. **Liberal arts:** Arts/sciences. **Math:** General. **Parks/recreation:** General. **Philosophy/religion:** Religion. **Physical sciences:** Atmospheric science, chemistry, geology, planetary. **Psychology:** General. **Public administration:** Policy analysis. **Social sciences:** General, sociology. **Theology:** Preministerial. **Visual/performing arts:** Art, music performance, studio arts. **Other:** Veterinary life science.

**Most popular majors.** Biology 13%, business/marketing 11%, education 19%, health sciences 6%, interdisciplinary studies 11%, natural resources/environmental science 11%, physical sciences 7%, psychology 6%.

**Computing on campus.** 125 workstations in dormitories, library, computer center, student center. Dormitories wired for high-speed internet access and linked to campus network. Commuter students can connect to campus network. Online course registration, online library, helpline, repair service, wireless network available.

**Student life.** **Freshman orientation:** Mandatory. Preregistration for classes offered. Outdoor orientation or North County orientation. **Housing:** Guaranteed on-campus for freshmen. Coed dorms, single-sex dorms, apartments, substance-free housing available. $200 nonrefundable deposit. Environmental living and learning residential hall available. **Activities:** Bands, choral groups, dance, drama, international student organizations, music ensembles, radio station, student government, student newspaper, symphony orchestra, Native American Council, veterans organization, environmental group, ecology club.

**Athletics.** NAIA, NCAA. **Intercollegiate:** Baseball M, basketball, cross-country, ice hockey M, soccer, softball W, volleyball W. **Intramural:** Archery, badminton, basketball, football (non-tackle), ice hockey, racquetball, rugby, skiing, soccer, softball, table tennis, tennis, volleyball. **Team name:** Lumberjacks, Lumberjills.

**Student services.** Adult student services, alcohol/substance abuse counseling, campus ministries, career counseling, services for economically disadvantaged, student employment services, financial aid counseling, health services, minority student services, personal counseling, placement for graduates, women's services. **Physically disabled:** Services for visually, hearing impaired.

**Contact.** E-mail: admit@northland.edu
Phone: (715) 682-1224 Toll-free number: (800) 753-1840
Fax: (715) 682-1258
Susan Greenwald, Director of Admission, Northland College, 1411 Ellis Avenue, Ashland, WI 54806

---

## Ripon College
**Ripon, Wisconsin**
www.ripon.edu

**CB member**
**CB code: 1664**

- Private 4-year liberal arts college
- Residential campus in small town
- 977 degree-seeking undergraduates: 1% part-time, 52% women, 2% African American, 1% Asian American, 3% Hispanic American, 1% Native American, 1% international
- 80% of applicants admitted
- SAT or ACT (ACT writing optional), application essay required
- 73% graduate within 6 years; 25% enter graduate study

**General.** Founded in 1851. Regionally accredited. **Degrees:** 210 bachelor's awarded. **ROTC:** Army. **Location:** 80 miles from Milwaukee, 80 miles from Madison. **Calendar:** Semester. **Full-time faculty:** 52 total; 96% have terminal degrees, 8% minority, 44% women. **Part-time faculty:** 38 total; 55% have terminal degrees, 3% minority, 37% women. **Class size:** 52% < 20, 42% 20-39, 3% 40-49, 3% 50-99. **Special facilities:** Woodland preservation area with outdoor classroom.

**Freshman class profile.** 974 applied, 775 admitted, 262 enrolled.

| Mid 50% test scores | | Rank in top tenth: | 21% |
|---|---|---|---|
| SAT critical reading: | 440-610 | End year in good standing: | 95% |
| SAT math: | 480-650 | Return as sophomores: | 86% |
| ACT composite: | 21-27 | Out-of-state: | 23% |
| GPA 3.50 or higher: | 42% | Live on campus: | 98% |
| GPA 3.0-3.49: | 39% | International: | 2% |
| GPA 2.0-2.99: | 19% | Fraternities: | 36% |
| Rank in top quarter: | 51% | Sororities: | 18% |

**Basis for selection.** School achievement record, interview, class rank, test scores, recommendations, extracurricular or community activities important. **Homeschooled:** Transcript of courses and grades required.

**High school preparation.** 17 units required. Required and recommended units include English 4, mathematics 2-4, social studies 2-4, science 2-4 and foreign language 2. Math must include 1 algebra and geometry. 7 units chosen from additional units in math, science, social science, foreign language.

**2008-2009 Annual costs.** Tuition/fees: $24,245. Room/board: $6,770. Books/supplies: $1,000. Personal expenses: $800.

**2007-2008 Financial aid. Need-based:** 248 full-time freshmen applied for aid; 215 were judged to have need; 215 of these received aid. Average need met was 96%. Average scholarship/grant was $16,333; average loan $4,716. 74% of total undergraduate aid awarded as scholarships/grants, 26% as loans/jobs. **Non-need-based:** Awarded to 347 full-time undergraduates, including 88 freshmen. Scholarships awarded for academics, alumni affiliation, art, leadership, minority status, music/drama, religious affiliation, ROTC, state residency.

**Application procedures. Admission:** Priority date 3/15; no deadline. $30 fee, may be waived for applicants with need. Application may be submitted online. Admission notification on a rolling basis beginning on or about 9/15. Must reply by May 1 or within 2 week(s) if notified thereafter. **Financial aid:** Priority date 3/1; no closing date. FAFSA required. Applicants notified on a rolling basis starting 3/1; must reply within 2 week(s) of notification.

**Academics. Special study options:** Accelerated study, combined bachelor's/graduate degree, double major, exchange student, internships, liberal arts/

career combination, student-designed major, study abroad, teacher certification program, urban semester, Washington semester. Domestic and international off-campus study programs. **Credit/placement by examination:** AP, CLEP, IB, institutional tests. Amount of credit and placement for AP exams subject to departmental approval. **Support services:** Learning center, study skills assistance, tutoring.

**Majors. Area/ethnic studies:** Latin American, women's. **Biology:** General, biochemistry. **Business:** Business admin. **Communications:** General. **Computer sciences:** Computer science. **Conservation:** Environmental studies. **Education:** General. **English:** English lit. **Foreign languages:** General, classics, French, German, Spanish. **Health:** Predental, premedicine, prenursing, prepharmacy, preveterinary. **History:** General. **Interdisciplinary:** Biopsychology, global studies. **Legal studies:** Prelaw. **Math:** General. **Parks/recreation:** Exercise sciences. **Philosophy/religion:** Philosophy, religion. **Physical sciences:** General, chemistry, physics. **Psychology:** General. **Social sciences:** Anthropology, economics, political science, sociology. **Visual/performing arts:** Art, art history/conservation, dramatic.

**Most popular majors.** Biology 15%, business/marketing 15%, education 8%, English 6%, foreign language 7%, history 10%, psychology 7%, social sciences 12%.

**Computing on campus.** 150 workstations in dormitories, library, computer center. Dormitories linked to campus network. Commuter students can connect to campus network. Helpline, student web hosting available.

**Student life. Freshman orientation:** Mandatory, $45 fee. Preregistration for classes offered. 2-day overnight orientation held in late June for students and family. **Housing:** Guaranteed on-campus for all undergraduates. Coed dorms, single-sex dorms, fraternity/sorority housing, substance-free housing available. $200 nonrefundable deposit, deadline 8/15. **Activities:** Bands, choral groups, dance, drama, film society, international student organizations, literary magazine, music ensembles, musical theater, radio station, student government, student newspaper, symphony orchestra, Christian Fellowship, Big Brother/Big Sister, multicultural club, romance language club, environmental group, Feminists for Equality, College Democrats, College Republicans.

**Athletics.** NCAA. **Intercollegiate:** Baseball M, basketball, cross-country, diving, football (tackle) M, golf, soccer, softball W, swimming, tennis, track and field, volleyball W. **Intramural:** Basketball, bowling, fencing, football (non-tackle), golf, racquetball, soccer, softball, table tennis, tennis, volleyball, water polo. **Team name:** Red Hawks.

**Student services.** Career counseling, student employment services, financial aid counseling, health services, personal counseling, placement for graduates.

**Contact.** E-mail: adminfo@ripon.edu
Phone: (920) 748-8114 Toll-free number: (800) 947-4766
Fax: (920) 748-8335
Leigh Mlodzik, Director of Admission, Ripon College, 300 Seward Street, Ripon, WI 54971-0248

---

## St. Norbert College
**De Pere, Wisconsin**
www.snc.edu

**CB member**
**CB code: 1706**

- Private 4-year liberal arts college affiliated with Roman Catholic Church
- Residential campus in large town
- 2,045 degree-seeking undergraduates: 1% part-time, 57% women, 1% African American, 1% Asian American, 3% Hispanic American, 1% Native American, 3% international
- 42 degree-seeking graduate students
- 87% of applicants admitted
- SAT or ACT (ACT writing optional) required
- 70% graduate within 6 years; 13% enter graduate study

**General.** Founded in 1898. Regionally accredited. Study abroad strongly supported, and students are allowed to apply all of their financial aid to their study abroad program costs; student/faculty collaborative research. **Degrees:** 399 bachelor's awarded; master's offered. **ROTC:** Army. **Location:** 5 miles from Green Bay. **Calendar:** Semester, limited summer session. **Full-time faculty:** 109 total; 93% have terminal degrees, 6% minority, 36% women. **Part-time faculty:** 67 total; 48% have terminal degrees, 6% minority, 45% women. **Special facilities:** Marina, on-campus hotel and conference center, fine and performing arts centers, art galleries, center for international education, peace and justice center, center for leadership and service, center for adaptive education and assistive technology, children's center, women's center, men's center, prayer and reflection spaces, survey center, center for Norbertine studies.

**Freshman class profile.** 1,789 applied, 1,562 admitted, 543 enrolled.

| Mid 50% test scores | | | |
|---|---|---|---|
| ACT composite: | 22-27 | Rank in top tenth: | 27% |
| GPA 3.50 or higher: | 55% | Return as sophomores: | 85% |
| GPA 3.0-3.49: | 29% | Out-of-state: | 32% |
| GPA 2.0-2.99: | 16% | Live on campus: | 99% |
| Rank in top quarter: | 58% | International: | 4% |

**Basis for selection.** High school record, rigor of courses, and grades earned important. Preference given to students successfully completing challenging courses. Counselor and teacher recommendations, community service considered. Students not in college preparatory programs may be offered admission if test results, class rank, and grades demonstrate aptitude for college work. Essay, interview recommended for all; audition recommended for music. **Learning Disabled:** Students should submit documentation of specific disability to receive proper level of support from institution.

**High school preparation.** 16 units recommended. Recommended units include English 4, mathematics 3, social studies 3, history 3, science 3 (laboratory 3) and foreign language 2. As many college-prep elective units as possible.

**2008-2009 Annual costs.** Tuition/fees: $25,926. Room/board: $6,781. Books/supplies: $500. Personal expenses: $750.

**2006-2007 Financial aid. Need-based:** 441 full-time freshmen applied for aid; 340 were judged to have need; 340 of these received aid. Average need met was 89%. Average scholarship/grant was $13,493; average loan $3,466. 59% of total undergraduate aid awarded as scholarships/grants, 41% as loans/jobs. **Non-need-based:** Awarded to 638 full-time undergraduates, including 168 freshmen. Scholarships awarded for academics, art, leadership, minority status, music/drama, ROTC, state residency.

**Application procedures. Admission:** Priority date 4/1; no deadline. $25 fee, may be waived for applicants with need. Application may be submitted online. Admission notification on a rolling basis beginning on or about 9/15. Must reply by May 1 or within 3 week(s) if notified thereafter. **Financial aid:** Priority date 3/1; no closing date. FAFSA required. Applicants notified on a rolling basis starting 3/15; must reply within 2 week(s) of notification.

**Academics. Special study options:** Double major, dual enrollment of high school students, ESL, honors, independent study, internships, student-designed major, study abroad, teacher certification program, Washington semester. Foundation for International Education (London) Internship. **Credit/placement by examination:** AP, CLEP, IB, institutional tests. **Support services:** Learning center, reduced course load, remedial instruction, study skills assistance, tutoring, writing center.

**Majors. Biology:** General. **Business:** General, accounting, international. **Communications:** General, media studies. **Computer sciences:** Computer science. **Conservation:** Environmental science. **Education:** Early childhood, elementary, music. **English:** Creative writing, English lit. **Foreign languages:** French, German, Spanish. **Health:** Predental, premedicine, prenursing, prepharmacy, preveterinary. **History:** General. **Interdisciplinary:** Biological/physical sciences. **Legal studies:** Prelaw. **Liberal arts:** Humanities. **Math:** General. **Philosophy/religion:** Philosophy, religion. **Physical sciences:** Chemistry, geology, physics. **Psychology:** General. **Social sciences:** Economics, international economics, international relations, political science, sociology. **Visual/performing arts:** Art, commercial/advertising art, dramatic, graphic design.

**Most popular majors.** Business/marketing 25%, communications/journalism 10%, education 15%, social sciences 12%, visual/performing arts 6%.

**Computing on campus.** 221 workstations in dormitories, library, computer center, student center. Dormitories wired for high-speed internet access and linked to campus network. Commuter students can connect to campus network. Online course registration, online library, helpline, repair service, wireless network available.

**Student life. Freshman orientation:** Mandatory. Preregistration for classes offered. 2-day summer program for students and parents. **Housing:** Guaranteed on-campus for all undergraduates. Coed dorms, single-sex dorms, special housing for disabled, apartments, fraternity/sorority housing, substance-free housing available. $100 nonrefundable deposit, deadline 5/1. Townhouses and college-owned houses near campus also available. **Activities:** Bands, campus ministries, choral groups, drama, film society, international student organizations, literary magazine, music ensembles, musical theater, radio station, student government, student newspaper, TV station, InterVarsity Christian Fellowship, Amnesty International, Unity Among Friends, Japan club, Discoveries International, Circle K, Athletes for Life.

**Athletics.** NCAA. **Intercollegiate:** Baseball M, basketball, cross-country, football (tackle) M, golf, ice hockey M, soccer, softball W, swimming W, tennis, track and field, volleyball W. **Intramural:** Basketball, football (non-tackle), softball, volleyball. **Team name:** Green Knights.

**Student services.** Alcohol/substance abuse counseling, campus ministries, career counseling, student employment services, financial aid counseling, health services, minority student services, on-campus daycare, personal counseling, placement for graduates, veterans' counselor, women's services. **Physically disabled:** Services for visually, speech, hearing impaired.

**Contact.** E-mail: admit@snc.edu
Phone: (920) 403-3005 Toll-free number: (800) 236-4878
Fax: (920) 403-4072
Bridget O'Connor, Enrollment Management and Communications, St. Norbert College, 100 Grant Street, De Pere, WI 54115-2099

## Sanford-Brown College: Milwaukee
**West Allis, Wisconsin**
**www.sbcmilwaukee.com**

❱ For-profit 4-year business and health science college
❱ Commuter campus in small city

**General.** Accredited by ACICS. **Calendar:** Continuous.

**Annual costs/financial aid.** Criminal Justice Associate and Bachelor degree $3750 per term (12 credits), Business Associate and Bachelor degree $3250 per term (12 credits), Medical Assistant Associate degree $3250 per term (12 credits), Medical Assistant diploma program $2750 per term (12 credits), Medical Coding and Billing diploma program $2750 per term (12 credits).

**Contact.** Phone: (414) 771-2200
6737 West Washington Street, Suite 2355, West Allis, WI 53214

## Silver Lake College
**Manitowoc, Wisconsin**
**www.sl.edu** — CB code: 1300

❱ Private 4-year business and liberal arts college affiliated with Roman Catholic Church
❱ Commuter campus in large town
❱ 380 degree-seeking undergraduates: 54% part-time, 75% women, 1% African American, 1% Hispanic American, 6% Native American, 2% international
❱ 137 degree-seeking graduate students
❱ 63% of applicants admitted
❱ SAT or ACT (ACT writing optional) required
❱ 48% graduate within 6 years; 8% enter graduate study

**General.** Founded in 1935. Regionally accredited. **Degrees:** 113 bachelor's awarded; master's offered. **Location:** 80 miles from Milwaukee, 30 miles from Green Bay. **Calendar:** Semester, extensive summer session. **Full-time faculty:** 30 total; 47% have terminal degrees, 7% minority, 63% women. **Part-time faculty:** 214 total; 7% have terminal degrees, 64% women. **Class size:** 97% < 20, 3% 20-39. **Special facilities:** Nature preserve.

**Freshman class profile.** 167 applied, 105 admitted, 38 enrolled.

| Mid 50% test scores | | | |
|---|---|---|---|
| ACT composite: | 16-22 | End year in good standing: | 70% |
| GPA 3.50 or higher: | 25% | Return as sophomores: | 70% |
| GPA 3.0-3.49: | 33% | Out-of-state: | 10% |
| GPA 2.0-2.99: | 39% | Live on campus: | 70% |
| Rank in top quarter: | 21% | International: | 3% |

**Basis for selection.** Admission based on formula of GPA x ACT x 10. Those below 300 will be denied admission, 301-449 granted provisional admission, and 450 and above accepted. Audition required, interview recommended for music; portfolio, interview recommended for art. **Home-schooled:** Transcript of courses and grades required. **Learning Disabled:** Provide IEP information to Director of Learning Resources.

**High school preparation.** 21 units required. Required and recommended units include English 4, mathematics 2, social studies 2, history 2, science 2 (laboratory 2), foreign language 1 and academic electives 8.

**2008-2009 Annual costs.** Tuition/fees: $19,194. Room/board: $7,150. Books/supplies: $890. Personal expenses: $1,200.

**2007-2008 Financial aid. Need-based:** 35 full-time freshmen applied for aid; 34 were judged to have need; 34 of these received aid. Average

need met was 78%. Average scholarship/grant was $10,737; average loan $3,398. 49% of total undergraduate aid awarded as scholarships/grants, 51% as loans/jobs. **Non-need-based:** Awarded to 22 full-time undergraduates, including 2 freshmen. Scholarships awarded for academics, art, athletics, leadership, music/drama, religious affiliation, state residency.

**Application procedures. Admission:** Priority date 8/1; no deadline. $35 fee, may be waived for applicants with need. Application may be submitted online. Admission notification on a rolling basis beginning on or about 9/1. **Financial aid:** Priority date 3/15; no closing date. FAFSA required. Applicants notified on a rolling basis starting 3/15; must reply within 2 week(s) of notification.

**Academics. Special study options:** Accelerated study, combined bachelor's/graduate degree, distance learning, double major, dual enrollment of high school students, independent study, internships, liberal arts/career combination, student-designed major, teacher certification program. **Credit/placement by examination:** AP, CLEP, IB, SAT, ACT, institutional tests. 30 credit hours maximum toward associate degree, 60 toward bachelor's. **Support services:** Learning center, reduced course load, remedial instruction, study skills assistance, tutoring.

**Majors. Biology:** General. **Business:** Accounting, business admin, human resources. **Computer sciences:** Computer science, information systems. **Education:** Art, early childhood, elementary, learning disabled, mentally handicapped, music. **English:** English lit. **History:** General. **Math:** General. **Psychology:** General. **Public administration:** General. **Theology:** Theology. **Visual/performing arts:** Art.

**Most popular majors.** Business/marketing 55%, education 21%, psychology 9%.

**Computing on campus.** 40 workstations in library, computer center, student center. Commuter students can connect to campus network. Online course registration, online library, wireless network available.

**Student life. Freshman orientation:** Mandatory. Preregistration for classes offered. **Housing:** Apartments, substance-free housing available. $100 non-refundable deposit, deadline 8/1. Men's and women's housing available, located off campus. **Activities:** Jazz band, choral groups, dance, literary magazine, music ensembles, student government, student newspaper, campus ministry, student forum, student Wisconsin Education Association, student Wisconsin Early Childhood Association, student council for exceptional children, music educators national conference for students.

**Athletics.** USCAA. **Intercollegiate:** Basketball, cross-country, golf. **Intramural:** Table tennis, volleyball. **Team name:** Lakers.

**Student services.** Adult student services, alcohol/substance abuse counseling, campus ministries, career counseling, student employment services, financial aid counseling, health services, personal counseling, placement for graduates.

**Contact.** E-mail: admslc@silver.sl.edu
Phone: (920) 686-6175 Toll-free number: (800) 236-4752 ext. 175
Fax: (920) 684-7082
Jane Bishop, Dean of Enrollment Management, Silver Lake College, 2406 South Alverno Road, Manitowoc, WI 54220-9319

## University of Wisconsin-Eau Claire
**Eau Claire, Wisconsin**
www.uwec.edu                                    CB code: 1913

- Public 4-year university
- Residential campus in small city
- 9,947 degree-seeking undergraduates: 5% part-time, 59% women, 3% Asian American, 1% Hispanic American, 1% Native American, 1% international
- 416 degree-seeking graduate students
- 69% of applicants admitted
- SAT or ACT (ACT writing optional) required
- 60% graduate within 6 years; 10% enter graduate study

**General. Founded** in 1916. Regionally accredited. **Degrees:** 1,926 bachelor's, 9 associate awarded; master's offered. **ROTC:** Army. **Location:** 90 miles from Minneapolis-St. Paul. **Calendar:** Semester, extensive summer session. **Full-time faculty:** 413 total; 82% have terminal degrees, 11% minority, 44% women. **Part-time faculty:** 117 total; 36% have terminal degrees, 4% minority, 68% women. **Class size:** 28% < 20, 50% 20-39, 9% 40-49, 10% 50-99, 2% >100. **Special facilities:** Observatories, planetarium, bird museum, 200-acre reserve for study of flora and fauna, collections of Native American materials.

**Freshman class profile.** 7,446 applied, 5,142 admitted, 2,034 enrolled.

| Mid 50% test scores | | | |
|---|---|---|---|
| SAT critical reading: | 530-680 | Rank in top tenth: | 26% |
| SAT math: | 550-680 | End year in good standing: | 92% |
| SAT writing: | 530-630 | Return as sophomores: | 81% |
| ACT composite: | 22-26 | Out-of-state: | 24% |
| Rank in top quarter: | 59% | Live on campus: | 81% |

**Basis for selection.** Applicants must present required combination of rank and test scores. Special consideration to disadvantaged, veterans, and minority applicants. Applicants with rank in top 50% and/or ACT score of 23 or better given first priority. Some applicants not admitted to the fall semester may be considered for admission to the following spring semester. Wisconsin residents required to take ACT; non-residents may submit SAT. Audition required for music programs.

**High school preparation.** 17 units required. Required units include English 4, mathematics 3, social studies 3, science 3, foreign language 2 and academic electives 2. 3 units English must be composition and/or literature. One of the 3 social studies units must be world or U.S. history.

**2007-2008 Annual costs.** Tuition/fees: $5,841; $13,414 out-of-state. Minnesota reciprocity tuition: $223 per credit hour. Room/board: $5,150. Books/supplies: $460. Personal expenses: $1,780.

**2006-2007 Financial aid. Need-based:** 1,523 full-time freshmen applied for aid; 834 were judged to have need; 825 of these received aid. Average need met was 95%. Average scholarship/grant was $4,444; average loan $4,210. 34% of total undergraduate aid awarded as scholarships/grants, 66% as loans/jobs. **Non-need-based:** Awarded to 919 full-time undergraduates, including 356 freshmen. Scholarships awarded for academics, art, leadership, minority status, music/drama, state residency.

**Application procedures. Admission:** Priority date 12/1; no deadline. $35 fee, may be waived for applicants with need. Application may be submitted online. Admission notification on a rolling basis beginning on or about 9/15. Must reply by May 1 or within 2 week(s) if notified thereafter. Closing and priority dates vary. **Financial aid:** Priority date 4/15; no closing date. FAFSA required. Applicants notified on a rolling basis starting 4/15.

**Academics.** Baccalaureate degree includes service-learning requirement, freshman seminars, capstone courses, internships in most majors, and opportunities for students to collaborate with faculty on research and scholarly projects. **Special study options:** Accelerated study, cooperative education, distance learning, double major, dual enrollment of high school students, ESL, exchange student, external degree, honors, independent study, internships, study abroad, teacher certification program. **Credit/placement by examination:** AP, CLEP, IB, institutional tests. 15 credit hours maximum toward associate degree, 30 toward bachelor's. **Support services:** Learning center, pre-admission summer program, reduced course load, remedial instruction, study skills assistance, tutoring, writing center.

**Majors. Area/ethnic studies:** Latin American, Native American, women's. **Biology:** General, biomedical sciences, molecular. **Business:** Accounting, business admin, finance, information resources management, marketing. **Communications:** General, journalism, media studies. **Computer sciences:** General. **Education:** Elementary, science, social studies, special. **English:** English lit. **Foreign languages:** French, Germanic, Spanish. **Health:** Athletic training, communication disorders, environmental health, health care admin, music therapy, nursing (RN). **History:** General. **Math:** General. **Parks/recreation:** Exercise sciences. **Philosophy/religion:** Philosophy, religion. **Physical sciences:** Chemistry, geology, physics. **Protective services:** Criminal justice. **Psychology:** General. **Public administration:** Social work. **Social sciences:** Economics, geography, political science, sociology. **Visual/performing arts:** Art, dramatic. **Other:** Chemistry with business emphasis.

**Most popular majors.** Biology 6%, business/marketing 24%, communications/journalism 8%, education 10%, health sciences 11%, security/protective services 6%, social sciences 6%.

**Computing on campus.** 1,150 workstations in dormitories, library, computer center, student center. Dormitories wired for high-speed internet access and linked to campus network. Commuter students can connect to campus network. Online course registration, online library, helpline, wireless network available.

**Student life. Freshman orientation:** Mandatory, $100 fee. Preregistration for classes offered. **Housing:** Guaranteed on-campus for freshmen. Coed dorms, single-sex dorms, apartments, substance-free housing available. $75 fully refundable deposit. **Activities:** Bands, choral groups, dance, drama, film society, literary magazine, music ensembles, musical theater, opera, radio station, student government, student newspaper, symphony orchestra, TV station, College Republicans, College Democrats, Newman Student Association, ecumenical religious center student association, Alpha Phi Omega service fraternity, Mortar Board, Black student organization, Native American student organization, Hmong student association.

**Athletics.** NCAA. **Intercollegiate:** Basketball, cross-country, diving, football (tackle) M, golf, gymnastics W, ice hockey, soccer W, softball W, swimming, tennis, track and field, volleyball W, wrestling M. **Intramural:** Badminton, baseball M, basketball, bowling, diving, football (tackle), golf, ice hockey, racquetball, rugby, skiing, soccer, softball, swimming, table tennis, tennis, volleyball, water polo M, weight lifting. **Team name:** Blugolds.

**Student services.** Adult student services, alcohol/substance abuse counseling, campus ministries, career counseling, services for economically disadvantaged, student employment services, financial aid counseling, health services, legal services, minority student services, on-campus daycare, personal counseling, placement for graduates, veterans' counselor, women's services. **Physically disabled:** Services for visually, speech, hearing impaired.

**Contact.** E-mail: admissions@uwec.edu
Phone: (715) 836-5415 Fax: (715) 836-2409
Kristina Anderson, Executive Director, Enrollment Services & Admissions, University of Wisconsin-Eau Claire, 112 Schofield Hall, Eau Claire, WI 54701

## University of Wisconsin-Green Bay

**Green Bay, Wisconsin**
www.uwgb.edu

**CB member**
**CB code: 1859**

- Public 4-year university and liberal arts college
- Residential campus in small city
- 5,546 degree-seeking undergraduates: 17% part-time, 65% women, 1% African American, 3% Asian American, 1% Hispanic American, 2% Native American, 1% international
- 141 degree-seeking graduate students
- 71% of applicants admitted
- SAT or ACT (ACT writing optional) required
- 53% graduate within 6 years; 15% enter graduate study

**General.** Founded in 1965. Regionally accredited. **Degrees:** 993 bachelor's, 1 associate awarded; master's offered. **ROTC:** Army. **Location:** 80 miles from Milwaukee. **Calendar:** Semester, limited summer session. **Full-time faculty:** 180 total; 82% have terminal degrees, 12% minority, 39% women. **Part-time faculty:** 103 total; 4% minority, 57% women. **Class size:** 27% < 20, 45% 20-39, 12% 40-49, 11% 50-99, 4% >100. **Special facilities:** Natural history museum, herbarium, 290-acre arboretum, performing arts center.

**Freshman class profile.** 3,452 applied, 2,461 admitted, 1,000 enrolled.

| Mid 50% test scores | | Return as sophomores: | 75% |
|---|---|---|---|
| ACT composite: | 20-25 | Out-of-state: | 5% |
| GPA 3.50 or higher: | 33% | Live on campus: | 74% |
| GPA 3.0-3.49: | 41% | International: | 1% |
| GPA 2.0-2.99: | 26% | Fraternities: | 1% |
| End year in good standing: | 80% | Sororities: | 1% |

**Basis for selection.** ACT score, high school GPA and extracurricular or community involvement very important. Priority given to students with 23 ACT or 3.25 GPA. Students not meeting standard admission requirements (17 ACT and 2.25 GPA) may be considered on individual basis. ACT requirement may be waived for international students at application. ACT reports should be supplied prior to receiving admission. Interview may be requested of borderline applicants; audition required for music.

**High school preparation.** College-preparatory program required. 17 units required; 19 recommended. Required and recommended units include English 4, mathematics 3, social studies 3, science 3 (laboratory 1), foreign language 2 and academic electives 4. Math must include algebra or more advanced course. 2 of the 4 required academic electives must be from English, math, science, social studies, or foreign language.

**2007-2008 Annual costs.** Tuition/fees: $5,959; $13,532 out-of-state. Room/board: $5,200. Books/supplies: $800. Personal expenses: $1,920.

**2007-2008 Financial aid. Need-based:** 848 full-time freshmen applied for aid; 570 were judged to have need; 546 of these received aid. Average need met was 77%. Average scholarship/grant was $4,685; average loan $3,526. 44% of total undergraduate aid awarded as scholarships/grants, 56% as loans/jobs. **Non-need-based:** Awarded to 1,058 full-time undergraduates, including 207 freshmen. Scholarships awarded for academics, art, athletics, leadership, minority status, music/drama. **Additional information:** Auditions required for music and theater scholarships. Tuition is waived for children of Wisconsin soldiers and policemen who were slain in the line of duty. Tuition is also waived for all veterans.

**Application procedures. Admission:** Priority date 1/1; no deadline. $35 fee, may be waived for applicants with need. Application may be submitted online. Admission notification on a rolling basis beginning on or about 9/15. **Financial aid:** Priority date 4/15; no closing date. FAFSA required. Applicants notified on a rolling basis starting 11/1; must reply within 3 week(s) of notification.

**Academics.** Minimum credit hours required in major for bachelor's degree varies depending on field. Teacher certification available in conjunction with bachelor's degree. **Special study options:** Combined bachelor's/graduate degree, distance learning, double major, dual enrollment of high school students, exchange student, external degree, independent study, internships, liberal arts/career combination, student-designed major, study abroad, teacher certification program. **Credit/placement by examination:** AP, CLEP, IB, ACT, institutional tests. 47 credit hours maximum toward associate degree, 93 toward bachelor's. **Support services:** Pre-admission summer program, reduced course load, remedial instruction, study skills assistance, tutoring, writing center.

**Majors. Area/ethnic studies:** Native American, women's. **Biology:** General. **Business:** Accounting, business admin. **Communications:** General. **Computer sciences:** Computer science, information systems. **Conservation:** Environmental science, environmental studies. **Education:** Elementary. **English:** English lit. **Foreign languages:** French, German, Spanish. **Health:** Nursing (RN). **History:** General. **Interdisciplinary:** Biological/physical sciences. **Liberal arts:** Arts/sciences, humanities. **Math:** General. **Philosophy/religion:** Philosophy. **Physical sciences:** Chemistry, physics. **Psychology:** General. **Public administration:** General, social work. **Social sciences:** Economics, political science, sociology, urban studies. **Visual/performing arts:** General, art, dramatic.

**Most popular majors.** Biology 11%, business/marketing 18%, communications/journalism 7%, education 7%, psychology 17%, public administration/social services 7%, social sciences 7%.

**Computing on campus.** 600 workstations in dormitories, library, computer center, student center. Dormitories wired for high-speed internet access and linked to campus network. Commuter students can connect to campus network. Online course registration, online library, helpline, repair service, wireless network available.

**Student life. Freshman orientation:** Available, $200 fee. Preregistration for classes offered. Orientation takes place the week before fall classes begin; combines academic, social and small group activities. **Housing:** Coed dorms, apartments, substance-free housing available. $225 fully refundable deposit. Suite-style apartments with private bathrooms. **Activities:** Bands, choral groups, dance, drama, film society, literary magazine, music ensembles, Model UN, musical theater, radio station, student government, student newspaper, TV station, College Republicans, College Democrats, Habitat for Humanity, Circle K, Ten Percent Society, Athletes in Action, American Marketing Association, psychology and human development club, student government association, Wisconsin Education Assocation Council.

**Athletics.** NCAA. **Intercollegiate:** Basketball, cheerleading, cross-country, diving, golf, skiing, soccer, softball W, swimming, tennis, volleyball W. **Intramural:** Basketball, football (non-tackle), golf, racquetball, soccer, softball, tennis, volleyball. **Team name:** Phoenix.

**Student services.** Adult student services, alcohol/substance abuse counseling, career counseling, student employment services, financial aid counseling, health services, minority student services, personal counseling, placement for graduates, veterans' counselor. **Physically disabled:** Services for visually, hearing impaired.

**Contact.** E-mail: admissions@uwgb.edu
Phone: (920) 465-2111 Fax: (920) 465-5754
Pam Harvey-Jacobs, Director of Admissions, University of Wisconsin-Green Bay, 2420 Nicolet Drive, Green Bay, WI 54311-7001

## University of Wisconsin-La Crosse

**La Crosse, Wisconsin**
www.uwlax.edu

**CB code: 1914**

- Public 4-year university
- Residential campus in small city
- 8,358 degree-seeking undergraduates: 4% part-time, 58% women, 1% African American, 3% Asian American, 1% Hispanic American, 1% Native American, 2% international
- 1,294 degree-seeking graduate students
- 65% of applicants admitted
- SAT or ACT (ACT writing optional) required
- 67% graduate within 6 years; 21% enter graduate study

**General.** Founded in 1909. Regionally accredited. **Degrees:** 1,552 bachelor's awarded; master's, first professional offered. **ROTC:** Army. **Location:** 140 miles from Madison, 160 miles from Minneapolis-St. Paul. **Calendar:** Semester, limited summer session. **Full-time faculty:** 346 total; 73% have terminal degrees, 11% minority, 38% women. **Part-time faculty:** 100 total; 14% have terminal degrees, 2% minority, 51% women. **Class size:** 36% < 20, 46% 20-39, 10% 40-49, 6% 50-99, 2% >100. **Special facilities:** Greenhouse, planetarium, nuclear radiation laboratory, river studies center, archaeology center.

**Freshman class profile.** 6,777 applied, 4,411 admitted, 1,753 enrolled.

| Mid 50% test scores | | Return as sophomores: | 87% |
|---|---|---|---|
| SAT critical reading: | 500-600 | Out-of-state: | 17% |
| SAT math: | 500-580 | Live on campus: | 94% |
| ACT composite: | 23-26 | International: | 3% |
| Rank in top quarter: | 83% | Fraternities: | 1% |
| Rank in top tenth: | 31% | Sororities: | 1% |
| End year in good standing: | 79% | | |

**Basis for selection.** Applicants should rank in top 25% of class, minimum ACT composite score of 23 (or rank in upper 30% of class with score of 26), and complete a rigorous college prep curriculum. ACT preferred, but SAT also accepted. Interviews not required, but may be considered in admission decision. Auditions may be required for some scholarships. Portfolios and essays may be included with application and will be considered in admission decision. **Homeschooled:** Interview may be required. **Learning Disabled:** Information regarding a learning disability may be considered in admission decision.

**High school preparation.** 17 units required; 21 recommended. Required and recommended units include English 4, mathematics 3-4, social studies 3-4, science 3-4 (laboratory 2), foreign language 3 and academic electives 4.

**2007-2008 Annual costs.** Tuition/fees: $5,850; $13,423 out-of-state. Room/board: $5,130. Books/supplies: $300. Personal expenses: $2,000.

**2006-2007 Financial aid. Need-based:** 1,333 full-time freshmen applied for aid; 740 were judged to have need; 679 of these received aid. Average need met was 70%. Average scholarship/grant was $4,937; average loan $2,753. 33% of total undergraduate aid awarded as scholarships/grants, 67% as loans/jobs. **Non-need-based:** Awarded to 466 full-time undergraduates, including 118 freshmen. Scholarships awarded for academics, alumni affiliation, art, leadership, minority status, music/drama, ROTC.

**Application procedures. Admission:** Priority date 2/1; no deadline. $35 fee, may be waived for applicants with need. Application may be submitted online. Admission notification on a rolling basis beginning on or about 9/15. **Financial aid:** Priority date 3/15; no closing date. FAFSA, institutional form required. Applicants notified on a rolling basis starting 3/10; must reply by 5/10 or within 3 week(s) of notification.

**Academics. Special study options:** Cooperative education, cross-registration, distance learning, double major, dual enrollment of high school students, ESL, honors, independent study, internships, study abroad, teacher certification program. **Credit/placement by examination:** AP, CLEP, IB, SAT, ACT, institutional tests. 16 credit hours maximum toward associate degree, 32 toward bachelor's. **Support services:** Learning center, pre-admission summer program, reduced course load, remedial instruction, study skills assistance, tutoring, writing center.

**Majors. Biology:** General, biochemistry, microbiology. **Business:** Accounting, business admin, finance, international, management information systems, marketing. **Communications:** General. **Computer sciences:** General. **Education:** Elementary, health, science, social studies. **English:** English lit. **Foreign languages:** French, German, Spanish. **Health:** Athletic training, clinical lab science, community health, nuclear medical technology, physician assistant, recreational therapy. **History:** General. **Math:** General. **Parks/recreation:** Exercise sciences, facilities management. **Philosophy/religion:** Philosophy. **Physical sciences:** Chemistry, physics. **Psychology:** General. **Social sciences:** Archaeology, economics, geography, political science, sociology. **Visual/performing arts:** Art, dramatic.

**Most popular majors.** Biology 10%, business/marketing 21%, education 16%, health sciences 9%, psychology 8%, social sciences 11%.

**Computing on campus.** 600 workstations in dormitories, library, computer center, student center. Dormitories wired for high-speed internet access and linked to campus network. Commuter students can connect to campus network. Online course registration, online library, helpline, wireless network available.

**Student life. Freshman orientation:** Available. Preregistration for classes offered. Held week prior to classes. **Housing:** Coed dorms, special housing for disabled, fraternity/sorority housing, substance-free housing available.

$75 fully refundable deposit, deadline 5/1. First Year Experience housing available. **Activities:** Bands, campus ministries, choral groups, dance, drama, literary magazine, music ensembles, musical theater, radio station, student government, student newspaper, symphony orchestra, TV station, Black Students Unity, Native American Council, Hispanic student organization, Asian association, Amnesty International, Newman Club, hall councils, Intervarsity Christian Fellowship, Campus Crusade.

**Athletics.** NAIA, NCAA. **Intercollegiate:** Baseball M, basketball, cross-country, diving, football (tackle) M, gymnastics W, soccer W, softball W, swimming, tennis, track and field, volleyball W, wrestling M. **Intramural:** Badminton, basketball, football (non-tackle), golf M, racquetball, soccer, softball, tennis, volleyball. **Team name:** Eagles.

**Student services.** Adult student services, alcohol/substance abuse counseling, campus ministries, career counseling, services for economically disadvantaged, student employment services, financial aid counseling, health services, legal services, minority student services, on-campus daycare, personal counseling, placement for graduates, veterans' counselor, women's services. **Physically disabled:** Services for visually, speech, hearing impaired.

**Contact.** E-mail: admissions@uwlax.edu
Phone: (608) 785-8939 Fax: (608) 785-8940
Kathryn Kiefer, Associate Director of Admissions, University of Wisconsin-La Crosse, 1725 State Street, Room 115 Main Hall, La Crosse, WI 54601

## University of Wisconsin-Madison

**Madison, Wisconsin**
**www.wisc.edu**

**CB member**
**CB code: 1846**

- ▶ Public 4-year university
- ▶ Residential campus in small city
- ▶ 28,999 degree-seeking undergraduates: 5% part-time, 53% women, 3% African American, 6% Asian American, 3% Hispanic American, 1% Native American, 4% international
- ▶ 11,423 degree-seeking graduate students
- ▶ 56% of applicants admitted
- ▶ SAT or ACT with writing, application essay required
- ▶ 80% graduate within 6 years

**General.** Founded in 1849. Regionally accredited. **Degrees:** 6,040 bachelor's awarded; master's, doctoral, first professional offered. **ROTC:** Army, Naval, Air Force. **Location:** 90 miles from Milwaukee, 150 miles from Chicago. **Calendar:** Semester, extensive summer session. **Full-time faculty:** 2,388 total; 91% have terminal degrees, 16% minority, 34% women. **Part-time faculty:** 512 total; 62% have terminal degrees, 8% minority, 48% women. **Class size:** 44% < 20, 33% 20-39, 5% 40-49, 8% 50-99, 10% >100. **Special facilities:** Teaching nuclear reactor, biotron for simulating environments, nature preserve, observatory.

**Freshman class profile.** 24,870 applied, 13,977 admitted, 5,996 enrolled.

| Mid 50% test scores | | Rank in top tenth: | 60% |
|---|---|---|---|
| SAT critical reading: | 560-670 | End year in good standing: | 93% |
| SAT math: | 620-710 | Return as sophomores: | 93% |
| SAT writing: | 560-670 | Out-of-state: | 39% |
| ACT composite: | 26-30 | Live on campus: | 84% |
| GPA 3.50 or higher: | 77% | International: | 5% |
| GPA 3.0-3.49: | 18% | Fraternities: | 9% |
| GPA 2.0-2.99: | 5% | Sororities: | 8% |
| Rank in top quarter: | 93% | | |

**Basis for selection.** Secondary school record, including grades and/or rank, test scores most important. Candidate statement, recommendations, extracurricular activities and community service also important. Audition required for music; portfolio recommended for fine arts.

**High school preparation.** 17 units required; 20 recommended. Required and recommended units include English 4, mathematics 3-4, social studies 3-4, science 3-4, foreign language 2-4 and academic electives 2. Math units must include 1 each algebra and geometry, plus 1 year advanced math. Computer science or statistics will not fulfill math requirement. Applicants strongly advised to present academic credentials well in excess of minimum units.

**2007-2008 Annual costs.** Tuition/fees: $7,188; $21,438 out-of-state. Room/board: $7,390.

**Financial aid. Non-need-based:** Scholarships awarded for academics, alumni affiliation, art, athletics, job skills, leadership, minority status, music/drama, religious affiliation, ROTC, state residency.

**Application procedures. Admission:** Closing date 2/1 (postmark date). $44 fee, may be waived for applicants with need. Application may be submitted online. Admission notification on a rolling basis beginning on or about 10/1. Must reply by May 1 or within 3 week(s) if notified thereafter. **Financial aid:** No deadline. FAFSA, institutional form required. Applicants notified on a rolling basis starting 4/1; must reply within 9 week(s) of notification.

**Academics. Special study options:** Accelerated study, combined bachelor's/graduate degree, cooperative education, distance learning, double major, dual enrollment of high school students, ESL, honors, independent study, internships, liberal arts/career combination, student-designed major, study abroad, teacher certification program. **Credit/placement by examination:** AP, CLEP, IB, institutional tests. **Support services:** Learning center, pre-admission summer program, reduced course load, remedial instruction, study skills assistance, tutoring, writing center.

**Majors. Agriculture:** Agronomy, animal sciences, business, communications, dairy, economics, food science, horticultural science, poultry, soil science. **Area/ethnic studies:** African-American, Asian, Latin American, Scandinavian, South Asian, women's. **Biology:** General, bacteriology, biochemistry, botany, conservation, entomology, genetics, microbiology, molecular, pharmacology/toxicology, plant pathology, zoology. **Business:** General, accounting, actuarial science, business admin, finance, insurance, international, management information systems, marketing, operations, real estate. **Communications:** General, journalism. **Computer sciences:** General. **Conservation:** Forest sciences, wildlife. **Education:** Agricultural, art, elementary, family/consumer sciences, music, social studies, special. **Engineering:** Agricultural, biomedical, chemical, civil, computer, electrical, geological, industrial, marine, materials, mechanical, mechanics, nuclear, physics. **English:** English lit. **Family/consumer sciences:** General, clothing/textiles, communication, consumer economics, family studies, merchandising. **Foreign languages:** Ancient Greek, Chinese, classics, comparative lit, French, Germanic, Hebrew, Italian, Japanese, Latin, linguistics, Polish, Portuguese, Romance, Russian, Spanish. **Health:** Audiology/speech pathology, clinical lab science, communication disorders, nursing (RN), physician assistant, vocational rehab counseling. **History:** General, science/technology. **Interdisciplinary:** Behavioral sciences, global studies. **Legal studies:** General. **Math:** General, applied, statistics. **Parks/recreation:** Exercise sciences, facilities management. **Philosophy/religion:** Philosophy, religion. **Physical sciences:** Astronomy, astrophysics, atmospheric science, chemistry, geology, geophysics, physics, planetary. **Protective services:** Criminal justice. **Psychology:** General. **Public administration:** Social work. **Social sciences:** Anthropology, cartography, economics, geography, political science, sociology. **Visual/performing arts:** Art, art history/conservation, ceramics, cinematography, commercial/advertising art, conducting, dance, design, dramatic, fashion design, fiber arts, film/cinema, interior design, jazz, metal/jewelry, music history, music performance, music theory/composition, painting, piano/organ, printmaking, sculpture, theater design, voice/opera.

**Most popular majors.** Biology 12%, business/marketing 9%, communications/journalism 6%, engineering/engineering technologies 11%, social sciences 14%.

**Computing on campus.** 3,350 workstations in dormitories, library, computer center, student center. Dormitories wired for high-speed internet access and linked to campus network. Commuter students can connect to campus network. Online course registration, online library, helpline, repair service, student web hosting, wireless network available.

**Student life. Freshman orientation:** Mandatory, $85 fee. Preregistration for classes offered. **Housing:** Coed dorms, single-sex dorms, apartments, cooperative housing, fraternity/sorority housing, substance-free housing available. $50 nonrefundable deposit. Residential learning communities available. **Activities:** Bands, choral groups, dance, drama, film society, literary magazine, music ensembles, musical theater, opera, radio station, student government, student newspaper, symphony orchestra, TV station.

**Athletics.** NCAA. **Intercollegiate:** Basketball, cheerleading, cross-country, football (tackle) M, golf, ice hockey, rowing (crew), soccer, softball W, swimming, tennis, track and field, volleyball W, wrestling M. **Team name:** Badgers.

**Student services.** Adult student services, alcohol/substance abuse counseling, career counseling, services for economically disadvantaged, student employment services, financial aid counseling, health services, minority student services, personal counseling, placement for graduates, veterans' counselor, women's services. **Physically disabled:** Services for visually, speech, hearing impaired.

**Contact.** E-mail: onwisconsin@admissions.wisc.edu
Phone: (608) 262-3961 Fax: (608) 262-7706
Robert Seltzer, Director of Admissions, University of Wisconsin-Madison, Armory & Gymnasium, Madison, WI 53706-1481

---

## University of Wisconsin-Milwaukee

**Milwaukee, Wisconsin** — CB member
www.uwm.edu — CB code: 1473

- Public 4-year university
- Commuter campus in very large city
- 22,937 degree-seeking undergraduates: 13% part-time, 51% women, 7% African American, 5% Asian American, 4% Hispanic American, 1% Native American, 1% international
- 4,427 degree-seeking graduate students
- 83% of applicants admitted
- SAT or ACT (ACT writing optional) required

**General.** Founded in 1956. Regionally accredited. **Degrees:** 3,769 bachelor's awarded; master's, doctoral offered. **ROTC:** Army, Air Force. **Location:** 90 miles from Chicago. **Calendar:** Semester, extensive summer session. **Full-time faculty:** 738 total; 26% minority, 40% women. **Part-time faculty:** 59 total; 20% minority, 48% women. **Class size:** 38% < 20, 42% 20-39, 6% 40-49, 8% 50-99, 7% >100. **Special facilities:** Planetarium, geological museum, American Geological Society Collection.

**Freshman class profile.** 12,555 applied, 10,385 admitted, 4,535 enrolled.

| Mid 50% test scores | | | |
|---|---|---|---|
| SAT critical reading: | 470-610 | GPA 2.0-2.99: | 43% |
| SAT math: | 500-630 | Rank in top quarter: | 25% |
| SAT writing: | 460-600 | Rank in top tenth: | 7% |
| ACT composite: | 19-25 | Out-of-state: | 4% |
| GPA 3.50 or higher: | 20% | Live on campus: | 50% |
| GPA 3.0-3.49: | 35% | International: | 1% |

**Basis for selection.** High school academic record and class rank (top half) important. If applicant ranks in lower half of class, minimum 21 ACT required. ACT (or equivalent SAT score) for out-of-state residents required. Additional requirements for architecture. Students who do not meet standard admission requirements may apply through Academic Opportunity Program Office. SAT and ACT may be accepted for foreign students in lieu of other criteria. Some applicants must also take placement tests in chemistry and/or foreign language. Audition required for dance, music, theater.

**High school preparation.** 17 units required; 20 recommended. Required and recommended units include English 4, mathematics 3, social studies 3, science 3 (laboratory 1) and academic electives 2. Math includes algebra, geometry, and beyond.

**2007-2008 Annual costs.** Tuition/fees: $6,958; $16,686 out-of-state. Room/board: $6,950. Books/supplies: $700. Personal expenses: $1,388.

**2007-2008 Financial aid. Need-based:** 3,249 full-time freshmen applied for aid; 2,503 were judged to have need; 2,415 of these received aid. Average need met was 48%. Average scholarship/grant was $5,479; average loan $4,081. 37% of total undergraduate aid awarded as scholarships/grants, 63% as loans/jobs. **Non-need-based:** Awarded to 1,850 full-time undergraduates, including 507 freshmen. Scholarships awarded for academics, art, athletics.

**Application procedures. Admission:** Priority date 5/1; deadline 7/1. $35 fee, may be waived for applicants with need. Application may be submitted online. Admission notification on a rolling basis beginning on or about 9/15. **Financial aid:** Priority date 3/1; no closing date. FAFSA required. Applicants notified on a rolling basis starting 3/1.

**Academics. Special study options:** Accelerated study, cooperative education, cross-registration, distance learning, double major, dual enrollment of high school students, ESL, external degree, honors, independent study, internships, liberal arts/career combination, student-designed major, study abroad, teacher certification program, United Nations semester, Washington semester. **Credit/placement by examination:** AP, CLEP, institutional tests. **Support services:** Learning center, pre-admission summer program, reduced course load, remedial instruction, tutoring, writing center.

**Majors. Architecture:** Architecture. **Area/ethnic studies:** African-American, women's. **Biology:** General, biochemistry, conservation, microbiology. **Business:** Accounting, actuarial science, finance, human resources, management information systems, marketing, operations, real estate, training/development. **Communications:** General, journalism, media studies. **Computer sciences:** General, computer science. **Conservation:** Environmental science. **Education:** General, art, music. **Engineering:** Civil, computer, electrical, manufacturing, materials, mechanical. **English:** English lit. **Foreign languages:** Classics, comparative lit, French, German, Hebrew, Italian, linguistics, Russian, Spanish. **Health:** Clinical lab science, communication disorders, facilities admin, nursing (RN), predental, premedicine, prepharmacy, preveterinary, recreational therapy. **History:** General. **Interdisciplinary:**

Global studies. **Legal studies:** Prelaw. **Math:** General, applied. **Parks/recreation:** General, exercise sciences. **Philosophy/religion:** Judaic, philosophy, religion. **Physical sciences:** Atmospheric physics, chemistry, geology, physics. **Protective services:** Criminal justice. **Psychology:** General. **Public administration:** Social work. **Social sciences:** General, anthropology, economics, geography, political science, sociology, urban studies. **Visual/performing arts:** Art, art history/conservation, dance, dramatic, film/cinema, multimedia.

**Most popular majors.** Business/marketing 21%, communications/journalism 8%, education 10%, health sciences 9%, social sciences 6%, visual/performing arts 8%.

**Computing on campus.** 1,255 workstations in dormitories, library, computer center, student center. Dormitories wired for high-speed internet access and linked to campus network. Commuter students can connect to campus network. Online course registration, online library, helpline, repair service, student web hosting, wireless network available.

**Student life. Housing:** Coed dorms, special housing for disabled, apartments available. $300 partly refundable deposit. **Activities:** Bands, choral groups, dance, drama, film society, literary magazine, music ensembles, musical theater, radio station, student government, student newspaper, symphony orchestra.

**Athletics.** NCAA. **Intercollegiate:** Baseball M, basketball, cross-country, diving, soccer, swimming, tennis, track and field, volleyball. **Intramural:** Badminton, baseball M, basketball, bowling, diving, fencing, football (tackle) M, golf, handball, racquetball, rugby, sailing, skiing, soccer, softball, swimming, tennis, volleyball, water polo, wrestling M. **Team name:** Panthers.

**Student services.** Adult student services, career counseling, student employment services, health services, on-campus daycare, personal counseling, placement for graduates, veterans' counselor. **Physically disabled:** Services for visually, speech, hearing impaired.

**Contact.** E-mail: uwmlook@uwm.edu
Phone: (414) 229-2222 Fax: (414) 229-6940
Beth Weckmueller, Executive Director of Enrollment Services and Registrar, University of Wisconsin-Milwaukee, Box 749, Milwaukee, WI 53201

## University of Wisconsin-Oshkosh
**Oshkosh, Wisconsin** — CB member
www.uwosh.edu — CB code: 1916

- Public 4-year university
- Residential campus in small city
- 9,844 degree-seeking undergraduates: 12% part-time, 59% women, 1% African American, 3% Asian American, 2% Hispanic American, 1% Native American, 1% international
- 1,111 degree-seeking graduate students
- 79% of applicants admitted
- ACT (writing optional) required
- 47% graduate within 6 years

**General.** Founded in 1871. Regionally accredited. **Degrees:** 1,714 bachelor's awarded; master's offered. **ROTC:** Army. **Location:** 90 miles from Milwaukee. **Calendar:** Semester, limited summer session. **Full-time faculty:** 379 total; 79% have terminal degrees, 14% minority, 42% women. **Part-time faculty:** 185 total; 23% have terminal degrees, 5% minority, 61% women. **Class size:** 30% < 20, 55% 20-39, 4% 40-49, 7% 50-99, 3% >100. **Special facilities:** Planetarium.

**Freshman class profile.** 5,056 applied, 4,017 admitted, 1,763 enrolled.

| Mid 50% test scores | | | |
|---|---|---|---|
| ACT composite: | 20-24 | End year in good standing: | 85% |
| GPA 3.50 or higher: | 32% | Return as sophomores: | 73% |
| GPA 3.0-3.49: | 46% | Out-of-state: | 3% |
| GPA 2.0-2.99: | 22% | Live on campus: | 85% |
| Rank in top quarter: | 40% | International: | 1% |
| Rank in top tenth: | 9% | Fraternities: | 6% |
| | | Sororities: | 5% |

**Basis for selection.** Students must rank in top half of high school class or have 22 ACT if rank is in third quartile. Out-of-state applicants may submit SAT scores. Interview recommended for all; audition required for music.

**High school preparation.** 17 units required. Required and recommended units include English 4, mathematics 3-4, social studies 3, science 3-4 (laboratory 3-4), foreign language 2 and academic electives 4. Social studies must include 1 history.

**2007-2008 Annual costs.** Tuition/fees: $5,689; $13,262 out-of-state. Minnesota reciprocity tuition: $223 per credit hour. Room/board: $5,392. Books/supplies: $800. Personal expenses: $2,214.

**2006-2007 Financial aid. Need-based:** 1,125 full-time freshmen applied for aid; 765 were judged to have need; 765 of these received aid. Average need met was 40%. Average scholarship/grant was $1,700; average loan $3,000. 36% of total undergraduate aid awarded as scholarships/grants, 64% as loans/jobs. **Non-need-based:** Awarded to 1,100 full-time undergraduates, including 650 freshmen. Scholarships awarded for academics, alumni affiliation, art, leadership, minority status, music/drama, state residency.

**Application procedures. Admission:** No deadline. $44 fee, may be waived for applicants with need. Application may be submitted online. Admission notification on a rolling basis. **Financial aid:** Priority date 3/15; no closing date. FAFSA required. Applicants notified on a rolling basis starting 4/15; must reply within 2 week(s) of notification.

**Academics. Special study options:** Accelerated study, cooperative education, cross-registration, distance learning, double major, dual enrollment of high school students, ESL, exchange student, honors, independent study, internships, liberal arts/career combination, student-designed major, study abroad, teacher certification program, weekend college. **Credit/placement by examination:** AP, CLEP, IB, institutional tests. 32 credit hours maximum toward bachelor's degree. **Support services:** Learning center, pre-admission summer program, reduced course load, study skills assistance, tutoring, writing center.

**Majors. Biology:** General, bacteriology. **Business:** Accounting, finance, human resources, management information systems, operations. **Communications:** General, broadcast journalism, journalism. **Computer sciences:** Computer science. **Education:** Elementary, emotionally handicapped, learning disabled, mentally handicapped, music, physical, science, secondary, social science, special. **English:** English lit. **Foreign languages:** French, German, Spanish. **Health:** Clinical lab technology, nursing (RN), predental, premedicine, prepharmacy, preveterinary. **History:** General. **Legal studies:** Prelaw. **Liberal arts:** Arts/sciences. **Math:** General. **Philosophy/religion:** Philosophy, religion. **Physical sciences:** Chemistry, geology, physics. **Psychology:** General. **Public administration:** Human services, social work. **Social sciences:** Anthropology, economics, geography, political science, sociology, urban studies. **Visual/performing arts:** Art, cinematography, dramatic, studio arts.

**Most popular majors.** Business/marketing 18%, communications/journalism 8%, education 17%, health sciences 12%, public administration/social services 6%, social sciences 7%.

**Computing on campus.** 475 workstations in dormitories, library, computer center, student center. Dormitories wired for high-speed internet access and linked to campus network. Commuter students can connect to campus network. Online course registration, helpline, wireless network available.

**Student life. Freshman orientation:** Available. **Policies:** Select group of freshmen take part in residential college experience for more individualized instruction. **Housing:** Guaranteed on-campus for freshmen. Coed dorms, single-sex dorms available. $125 deposit, deadline 6/15. **Activities:** Bands, campus ministries, choral groups, dance, drama, film society, literary magazine, music ensembles, musical theater, opera, radio station, student government, student newspaper, symphony orchestra, TV station, black student union, Asian student association, American Indian student association, Hispanic Cultures United, InterVarsity Christian Fellowship, Athletes in Action, community involvement program, Habitat for Humanity.

**Athletics.** NCAA. **Intercollegiate:** Baseball M, basketball, cross-country, diving, football (tackle) M, golf W, gymnastics W, rifle, soccer, softball W, swimming, tennis, track and field, volleyball W, wrestling M. **Intramural:** Basketball, racquetball, skiing, soccer, softball, volleyball. **Team name:** Titans.

**Student services.** Adult student services, alcohol/substance abuse counseling, career counseling, services for economically disadvantaged, student employment services, financial aid counseling, health services, minority student services, on-campus daycare, personal counseling, placement for graduates, veterans' counselor, women's services. **Physically disabled:** Services for visually, speech, hearing impaired.

**Contact.** E-mail: oshadmuw@uwosh.edu
Phone: (920) 424-0202 Fax: (920) 424-1098
Jill Endries, Director of Admissions, University of Wisconsin-Oshkosh, 800 Algoma Boulevard, Oshkosh, WI 54901-8602

## University of Wisconsin-Parkside
**Kenosha, Wisconsin** — CB member
www.uwp.edu — CB code: 1860

- Public 4-year university
- Commuter campus in small city

- 4,624 degree-seeking undergraduates: 23% part-time, 55% women, 11% African American, 3% Asian American, 7% Hispanic American, 1% Native American, 1% international
- 98 degree-seeking graduate students
- 76% of applicants admitted
- 37% graduate within 6 years

**General.** Founded in 1968. Regionally accredited. **Degrees:** 593 bachelor's awarded; master's offered. **ROTC:** Army. **Location:** 30 miles from Milwaukee, 60 miles from Chicago. **Calendar:** Semester, extensive summer session. **Full-time faculty:** 174 total; 73% have terminal degrees, 23% minority, 44% women. **Part-time faculty:** 100 total; 22% have terminal degrees, 11% minority, 45% women. **Class size:** 52% < 20, 35% 20-39, 6% 40-49, 7% 50-99, less than 1% >100. **Special facilities:** Communication arts building.

**Freshman class profile.** 2,493 applied, 1,902 admitted, 949 enrolled.

| Mid 50% test scores | | Out-of-state: | 7% |
|---|---|---|---|
| ACT composite: | 17-22 | Live on campus: | 49% |
| Rank in top quarter: | 24% | International: | 1% |
| Rank in top tenth: | 7% | Fraternities: | 2% |
| Return as sophomores: | 60% | Sororities: | 2% |

**Basis for selection.** Rank in top half of graduating class with specified distribution of high school units for standard admission. Students can be admitted on conditional status if in top 65% of class or with 18 ACT. Scores also used for placement in English and math courses. Audition required for theater, recommended for music; portfolio recommended for art. **Homeschooled:** Applicants reviewed on an individual basis.

**High school preparation.** 17 units required; 21 recommended. Required and recommended units include English 4, mathematics 3-4, social studies 3, science 3-4 (laboratory 1-2), foreign language 2, visual/performing arts 2 and academic electives 2.

**2007-2008 Annual costs.** Tuition/fees: $5,759; $13,332 out-of-state. Minnesota Reciprocity tuition and fees: $6,298 full-time; $223 per credit hour. Room/board: $5,890. Books/supplies: $800. Personal expenses: $1,564.

**2006-2007 Financial aid. Need-based:** 52% of total undergraduate aid awarded as scholarships/grants, 48% as loans/jobs. **Non-need-based:** Scholarships awarded for academics, art, athletics, minority status, music/drama, state residency.

**Application procedures. Admission:** Priority date 3/1; deadline 8/1 (postmark date). $35 fee, may be waived for applicants with need. Application may be submitted online. Admission notification on a rolling basis beginning on or about 9/15. **Financial aid:** Priority date 3/15; no closing date. FAFSA required. Applicants notified on a rolling basis starting 4/1; must reply within 2 week(s) of notification.

**Academics. Special study options:** Accelerated study, distance learning, double major, dual enrollment of high school students, exchange student, honors, independent study, internships, liberal arts/career combination, study abroad, teacher certification program, weekend college. Cooperative nursing program with University of Wisconsin-Milwaukee. **Credit/placement by examination:** AP, CLEP, IB, SAT, ACT, institutional tests. 30 credit hours maximum toward bachelor's degree. Retroactive credit policy for foreign language study. **Support services:** Learning center, reduced course load, remedial instruction, study skills assistance, tutoring, writing center.

**Majors. Area/ethnic studies:** French, German. **Biology:** General, molecular. **Business:** General, accounting, business admin, finance, human resources, management information systems. **Communications:** General. **Computer sciences:** Computer science. **English:** English lit. **Foreign languages:** French, German, Spanish. **Health:** Predental, premedicine, preveterinary. **History:** General. **Interdisciplinary:** Math/computer science. **Legal studies:** Prelaw. **Liberal arts:** Arts/sciences. **Math:** General. **Parks/recreation:** Sports admin. **Philosophy/religion:** Philosophy. **Physical sciences:** Chemistry, geology, physics. **Protective services:** Criminal justice. **Psychology:** General. **Social sciences:** Economics, geography, political science, sociology. **Visual/performing arts:** Art, dramatic.

**Most popular majors.** Biology 7%, business/marketing 20%, communications/journalism 9%, English 7%, history 6%, parks/recreation 6%, psychology 6%, public administration/social services 11%, social sciences 7%, visual/performing arts 6%.

**Computing on campus.** 225 workstations in dormitories, library, computer center, student center. Dormitories wired for high-speed internet access and linked to campus network. Commuter students can connect to campus network. Online course registration, online library, helpline, student web hosting, wireless network available.

**Student life. Freshman orientation:** Mandatory, $52 fee. Preregistration for classes offered. Day-long session offered several times throughout summer before fall semester. **Housing:** Coed dorms, special housing for disabled, apartments, substance-free housing available. $50 fully refundable deposit. **Activities:** Bands, choral groups, dance, drama, international student organizations, literary magazine, music ensembles, musical theater, radio station, student government, student newspaper, symphony orchestra, Campus Crusade for Christ, Intervarsity Christian Fellowship, Parkside Ethnic Organization, Amnesty International, Black Student Union, activities board.

**Athletics.** NCAA. **Intercollegiate:** Baseball M, basketball, cross-country, golf M, soccer, softball W, track and field, volleyball W, wrestling M. **Intramural:** Basketball, racquetball, soccer, softball, table tennis, tennis, volleyball. **Team name:** Rangers.

**Student services.** Adult student services, alcohol/substance abuse counseling, career counseling, services for economically disadvantaged, student employment services, financial aid counseling, health services, minority student services, on-campus daycare, personal counseling, placement for graduates, veterans' counselor, women's services. **Physically disabled:** Services for visually, speech, hearing impaired.

**Contact.** E-mail: matthew.jensen@uwp.edu
Phone: (262) 595-2355 Fax: (262) 595-2008
Matthew Jensen, Director of Admissions, University of Wisconsin-Parkside, PO Box 2000, Kenosha, WI 53141-2000

## University of Wisconsin-Platteville

| Platteville, Wisconsin | CB member |
|---|---|
| www.uwplatt.edu | CB code: 1917 |

- Public 4-year university
- Residential campus in large town
- 6,252 degree-seeking undergraduates: 9% part-time, 36% women, 2% African American, 1% Asian American, 1% Hispanic American
- 560 degree-seeking graduate students
- 85% of applicants admitted
- SAT or ACT (ACT writing optional) required
- 53% graduate within 6 years

**General.** Founded in 1866. Regionally accredited. **Degrees:** 1,039 bachelor's, 3 associate awarded; master's offered. **ROTC:** Army. **Location:** 25 miles from Dubuque, Iowa, 75 miles from Madison. **Calendar:** Semester, limited summer session. **Full-time faculty:** 285 total; 79% have terminal degrees, 15% minority, 33% women. **Part-time faculty:** 82 total; 21% have terminal degrees, 6% minority, 46% women. **Class size:** 32% < 20, 53% 20-39, 9% 40-49, 4% 50-99, 1% >100.

**Freshman class profile.** 3,519 applied, 2,978 admitted, 1,467 enrolled.

| Mid 50% test scores | | Return as sophomores: | 75% |
|---|---|---|---|
| ACT composite: | 20-25 | Out-of-state: | 21% |
| Rank in top quarter: | 33% | Live on campus: | 91% |
| Rank in top tenth: | 9% | Fraternities: | 7% |
| End year in good standing: | 98% | Sororities: | 7% |

**Basis for selection.** School record, class rank, and test scores most important. Competency Based Admission requirements. Audition required for music scholarships.

**High school preparation.** 17 units required. Required units include English 4, mathematics 3, social studies 3, science 3 (laboratory 2) and academic electives 4. 3 units natural science (2 from biology, chemistry, or physics), 3 units algebra I, geometry, algebra II, or higher.

**2007-2008 Annual costs.** Tuition/fees: $5,746; $13,319 out-of-state. Minnesota reciprocity tuition: $223 per credit hour. Room/board: $5,420. Books/supplies: $300. Personal expenses: $1,170.

**Financial aid.** All financial aid based on need.

**Application procedures. Admission:** Priority date 1/1; no deadline. $35 fee, may be waived for applicants with need. Application may be submitted online. Admission notification on a rolling basis beginning on or about 9/15. **Financial aid:** Priority date 3/15; no closing date. FAFSA required. Applicants notified on a rolling basis starting 6/1; must reply within 2 week(s) of notification.

**Academics.** Tri-State Initiative offers Illinois and Iowa students a discounted out-of-state rate for attending UWP in select majors. **Special study options:** Combined bachelor's/graduate degree, cooperative education, distance learning, double major, dual enrollment of high school students, ESL, exchange student, external degree, honors, independent study, internships, liberal arts/career combination, student-designed major, study abroad, teacher certification program. **Credit/placement by examination:** AP, CLEP, institutional tests. 30 credit hours maximum toward bachelor's degree. **Support services:** Learning center, study skills assistance, tutoring, writing center.

**Majors. Agriculture:** Agribusiness operations, agronomy, animal sciences, economics. **Biology:** General. **Business:** General, accounting, business admin, entrepreneurial studies, finance, human resources, investments/securities, organizational behavior. **Communications:** General. **Computer sciences:** Computer science. **Conservation:** General. **Construction:** Maintenance. **Education:** Agricultural, art, biology, chemistry, early childhood, elementary, English, German, history, mathematics, science, social science, social studies, Spanish, speech, technology/industrial arts, voc/tech. **Engineering:** Civil, electrical, mechanical, physics. **English:** English lit. **Foreign languages:** German, Spanish. **History:** General. **Math:** General. **Parks/recreation:** Health/fitness. **Philosophy/religion:** Philosophy. **Physical sciences:** Chemistry. **Protective services:** Law enforcement admin. **Psychology:** General. **Social sciences:** General, economics, geography, political science, sociology. **Visual/performing arts:** Art, commercial/advertising art, dramatic.

**Most popular majors.** Agriculture 6%, business/marketing 14%, education 12%, engineering/engineering technologies 31%.

**Computing on campus.** 483 workstations in dormitories, library, computer center. Dormitories wired for high-speed internet access and linked to campus network. Commuter students can connect to campus network. Online course registration, online library, helpline, repair service, student web hosting available.

**Student life. Freshman orientation:** Available. **Housing:** Guaranteed on-campus for freshmen. Coed dorms, single-sex dorms, special housing for disabled, fraternity/sorority housing available. $100 partly refundable deposit. All residence halls have connections to campus computer network in every room. **Activities:** Bands, campus ministries, choral groups, drama, international student organizations, literary magazine, music ensembles, musical theater, radio station, student government, student newspaper, symphony orchestra, TV station, black student union, ASIA student group, Hmong club, inter-tribal council, Young Democrats, College Republicans, Circle K.

**Athletics.** NCAA. **Intercollegiate:** Baseball M, basketball, cross-country, football (tackle) M, golf W, soccer, softball W, track and field, volleyball W, wrestling M. **Intramural:** Basketball, bowling, football (tackle), racquetball, soccer, softball, tennis, volleyball, water polo. **Team name:** Pioneers.

**Student services.** Adult student services, alcohol/substance abuse counseling, campus ministries, career counseling, student employment services, financial aid counseling, health services, minority student services, on-campus daycare, personal counseling, placement for graduates, veterans' counselor, women's services. **Physically disabled:** Services for visually, speech, hearing impaired.

**Contact.** E-mail: admit@uwplatt.edu
Phone: (608) 342-1125 Toll-free number: (800) 362-5515
Fax: (608) 342-1122
Angela Udelhofen, Dean of Admissions and Enrollment Management, University of Wisconsin-Platteville, One University Plaza, Platteville, WI 53818

---

## University of Wisconsin-River Falls
**River Falls, Wisconsin**
www.uwrf.edu                                    **CB code: 1918**

- Public 4-year university and liberal arts college
- Residential campus in large town
- 6,007 degree-seeking undergraduates: 58% women, 1% African American, 3% Asian American, 1% Hispanic American, 1% international
- 445 graduate students
- 83% of applicants admitted
- ACT (writing optional), application essay required
- 54% graduate within 6 years

**General.** Founded in 1874. Regionally accredited. **Degrees:** 1,067 bachelor's awarded; master's offered. **ROTC:** Army. **Location:** 30 miles from Minneapolis-St. Paul. **Calendar:** Semester, limited summer session. **Full-time faculty:** 235 total. **Part-time faculty:** 95 total. **Class size:** 10% < 20, 55% 20-39, 17% 40-49, 15% 50-99, 2% >100. **Special facilities:** 2 laboratory farms, 20-inch reflecting telescope, USDA-approved food science laboratory, computerized greenhouse, 42-foot rappelling and climbing wall, indoor track and field house, ice arena, electron microscope, observatory, education regional archive collection.

**Freshman class profile.** 3,152 applied, 2,613 admitted, 1,287 enrolled.

| Mid 50% test scores | | Out-of-state: | 54% |
|---|---|---|---|
| ACT composite: | 19-24 | Live on campus: | 90% |
| Rank in top quarter: | 33% | International: | 1% |
| Rank in top tenth: | 12% | Fraternities: | 5% |
| End year in good standing: | 92% | Sororities: | 5% |
| Return as sophomores: | 75% | | |

**Basis for selection.** Rank in top 40% of class with 18 ACT, or rank in top 60% with 22 ACT. Minority student applications given special consideration. Elementary education applicants must rank in the top 40% of class and 24 ACT.

**High school preparation.** 17 units required. Required and recommended units include English 4, mathematics 3-4, social studies 3-4, science 3-4, foreign language 1 and academic electives 4. Vocational agriculture units also recommended for applicants to College of Agriculture. Wisconsin residents who receive GED must also complete Wisconsin high school equivalency diploma.

**2007-2008 Annual costs.** Tuition/fees: $5,885; $13,458 out-of-state. Minnesota reciprocity tuition and fees: $6,660 full-time, $223 per credit hour. Room/board: $4,964. Books/supplies: $200. Personal expenses: $1,550.

**Financial aid.** All financial aid based on need.

**Application procedures. Admission:** Priority date 2/1; no deadline. $35 fee, may be waived for applicants with need. Application may be submitted online. Admission notification on a rolling basis beginning on or about 9/15. Late applicants considered on individual basis through appeal procedure. **Financial aid:** Priority date 3/15; no closing date. FAFSA required. Applicants notified on a rolling basis starting 4/1; must reply within 4 week(s) of notification.

**Academics. Special study options:** Accelerated study, combined bachelor's/graduate degree, cooperative education, cross-registration, distance learning, double major, dual enrollment of high school students, ESL, exchange student, honors, independent study, internships, liberal arts/career combination, student-designed major, study abroad, teacher certification program. **Credit/placement by examination:** AP, CLEP, IB, ACT, institutional tests. 27 credit hours maximum toward bachelor's degree. Placement in English, foreign languages, and math based on university system placement exams. **Support services:** Learning center, reduced course load, remedial instruction, study skills assistance, tutoring, writing center.

**Majors. Agriculture:** General, agronomy, animal sciences, business, crop production, dairy, dairy husbandry, equestrian studies, equine science, equipment technology, food science, greenhouse operations, horticultural science, horticulture, landscaping, products processing, soil science. **Biology:** General, biochemistry, biotechnology. **Business:** Accounting, business admin. **Communications:** General, journalism. **Computer sciences:** General. **Conservation:** General, environmental science, management/policy. **Education:** Agricultural, art, elementary, ESL, music, physical, speech impaired. **English:** English lit, speech/rhetoric. **Foreign languages:** French, German, Spanish. **Health:** Communication disorders. **History:** General. **Interdisciplinary:** Biological/physical sciences, global studies. **Math:** General. **Physical sciences:** Chemistry, geology, organic chemistry, physics, planetary, polymer chemistry. **Psychology:** General. **Public administration:** Social work. **Social sciences:** General, economics, geography, political science, sociology. **Visual/performing arts:** Art, studio arts.

**Most popular majors.** Agriculture 16%, biology 8%, business/marketing 20%, education 20%, psychology 8%, science technologies 10%.

**Computing on campus.** 700 workstations in dormitories, library, computer center, student center. Dormitories wired for high-speed internet access and linked to campus network. Commuter students can connect to campus network. Online course registration, online library, helpline, repair service, student web hosting, wireless network available.

**Student life. Freshman orientation:** Mandatory. Preregistration for classes offered. Held weekend prior to classes starting. **Policies:** Freshmen and sophomores must live in residence halls unless they reside with parents. **Housing:** Guaranteed on-campus for freshmen. Coed dorms, single-sex dorms, apartments, fraternity/sorority housing, substance-free housing available. $125 partly refundable deposit. **Activities:** Bands, campus ministries, choral groups, dance, drama, international student organizations, literary magazine, music ensembles, musical theater, radio station, student government, student newspaper, symphony orchestra, TV station, African American Alliance, Hispanic Student Coalition, Native American Council, Hmong student association, Habitat for Humanity, Fellowship of Christian Athletes, Young Democrats, Young Republicans, Young Life, Intervarsity Christian Fellowship.

**Athletics.** NCAA. **Intercollegiate:** Basketball, cross-country, diving, football (tackle) M, golf W, ice hockey, soccer W, softball W, swimming, tennis

W, track and field, volleyball W. **Intramural:** Badminton, basketball, bowling, cheerleading, football (non-tackle), golf, handball, ice hockey, racquetball, softball, swimming, tennis, volleyball, water polo. **Team name:** Falcons.

**Student services.** Adult student services, alcohol/substance abuse counseling, campus ministries, career counseling, services for economically disadvantaged, student employment services, financial aid counseling, health services, minority student services, on-campus daycare, personal counseling, placement for graduates, veterans' counselor, women's services. **Physically disabled:** Services for visually, speech, hearing impaired.

**Contact.** E-mail: admit@uwrf.edu
Phone: (715) 425-3500 Fax: (715) 425-0676
Mark Meydam, Director of Admission, University of Wisconsin-River Falls, 410 South 3rd Street, River Falls, WI 54022-5001

## University of Wisconsin-Stevens Point
**Stevens Point, Wisconsin**                    CB member
www.uwsp.edu                                    CB code: 1919

- Public 4-year university
- Residential campus in large town
- 8,621 degree-seeking undergraduates: 6% part-time, 53% women, 1% African American, 2% Asian American, 1% Hispanic American, 1% Native American, 2% international
- 246 degree-seeking graduate students
- 74% of applicants admitted
- SAT or ACT (ACT writing optional) required
- 59% graduate within 6 years; 13% enter graduate study

**General.** Founded in 1894. Regionally accredited. **Degrees:** 1,587 bachelor's, 18 associate awarded; master's, doctoral offered. **ROTC:** Army. **Location:** 110 miles from Madison, 240 miles from Chicago. **Calendar:** Semester, extensive summer session. **Full-time faculty:** 396 total; 78% have terminal degrees, 8% minority, 41% women. **Part-time faculty:** 84 total; 26% have terminal degrees, 7% minority, 46% women. **Special facilities:** Natural history museum, planetarium and observatory, nature preserve, Foucault pendulum, electron microscope, 1,000-acre natural resources summer camp, fire science center, multicultural center.

**Freshman class profile.** 5,123 applied, 3,779 admitted, 1,618 enrolled.

| Mid 50% test scores | | Rank in top quarter: | 46% |
|---|---|---|---|
| SAT critical reading: | 440-610 | Rank in top tenth: | 14% |
| SAT math: | 460-610 | End year in good standing: | 92% |
| SAT writing: | 440-640 | Out-of-state: | 6% |
| ACT composite: | 21-25 | Live on campus: | 90% |
| GPA 3.50 or higher: | 42% | International: | 3% |
| GPA 3.0-3.49: | 44% | Fraternities: | 1% |
| GPA 2.0-2.99: | 14% | Sororities: | 1% |

**Basis for selection.** Applicants must rank in top 25% of high school class or have 21 ACT/990 SAT (exclusive of Writing) and rank in top 50% of class or have 3.25 GPA. Campus visit recommended.

**High school preparation.** 17 units required. Required and recommended units include English 4, mathematics 3, social studies 3-4, science 3-4 and foreign language 2. Additional 2 units from English, math, social sciences, sciences, or foreign language and 2 units from above areas or fine arts, computer science, or other academic areas.

**2007-2008 Annual costs.** Tuition/fees: $5,834; $13,407 out-of-state. Minnesota reciprocity tuition and fees: $6,377 full-year or $223 per credit hour. Room/board: $4,832. Books/supplies: $450. Personal expenses: $1,730.

**2006-2007 Financial aid.** **Need-based:** 1,390 full-time freshmen applied for aid; 765 were judged to have need; 727 of these received aid. Average need met was 96%. Average scholarship/grant was $4,466; average loan $3,215. 36% of total undergraduate aid awarded as scholarships/grants, 64% as loans/jobs. **Non-need-based:** Awarded to 1,023 full-time undergraduates, including 183 freshmen. Scholarships awarded for academics, alumni affiliation, art, music/drama, ROTC. **Additional information:** Tuition discounts offered to qualified residents from other states.

**Application procedures.** **Admission:** No deadline. $35 fee, may be waived for applicants with need. Application may be submitted online. Admission notification on a rolling basis beginning on or about 10/1. **Financial aid:** Priority date 3/15, closing date 6/15. FAFSA required. Applicants notified on a rolling basis starting 5/1; must reply within 4 week(s) of notification.

**Academics.** **Special study options:** Accelerated study, cooperative education, distance learning, double major, dual enrollment of high school students, ESL, independent study, internships, student-designed major, study abroad, teacher certification program. Cooperative program with University of Wisconsin: Eau Claire and St. Joseph's Hospital; collaborative degree program with University of Wisconsin-Marshfield, University of Wisconsin-Marathon and University of Wisconsin-Marinette. **Credit/placement by examination:** AP, CLEP, IB, institutional tests. 16 credit hours maximum toward associate degree, 32 toward bachelor's. **Support services:** Learning center, pre-admission summer program, reduced course load, remedial instruction, study skills assistance, tutoring, writing center.

**Majors.** **Agriculture:** Soil science. **Architecture:** Interior. **Biology:** General. **Business:** Accounting, business admin. **Communications:** General. **Computer sciences:** General, web page design. **Conservation:** General, fisheries, forestry, water/wetlands/marine, wildlife, wood science. **Education:** Early childhood, elementary, family/consumer sciences, music, physical, secondary. **English:** English lit. **Foreign languages:** French, German, Spanish. **Health:** Athletic training, audiology/speech pathology, clinical lab science. **History:** General. **Interdisciplinary:** Biological/physical sciences. **Liberal arts:** Arts/sciences. **Math:** General. **Parks/recreation:** Health/fitness. **Philosophy/religion:** Philosophy. **Physical sciences:** Chemistry, physics. **Psychology:** General. **Public administration:** General. **Social sciences:** General, economics, geography, political science, sociology. **Visual/performing arts:** General, art, arts management, dance, dramatic, interior design, music history, music performance.

**Most popular majors.** Biology 9%, business/marketing 9%, communications/journalism 6%, education 9%, family/consumer sciences 6%, natural resources/environmental science 13%, psychology 7%, social sciences 10%, visual/performing arts 7%.

**Computing on campus.** 634 workstations in dormitories, library, computer center, student center. Dormitories wired for high-speed internet access and linked to campus network. Commuter students can connect to campus network. Online course registration, online library, helpline, student web hosting, wireless network available.

**Student life.** **Freshman orientation:** Mandatory, $35 fee. **Policies:** Non-smoking policy for all campus buildings. **Housing:** Coed dorms, single-sex dorms, substance-free housing available. $125 partly refundable deposit. Intercultural program hall, language hall, quiet wings/floors, upper class/nontraditional hall, eco hall, well emphasis program hall, alcohol-free living community options. **Activities:** Bands, campus ministries, choral groups, dance, drama, film society, international student organizations, literary magazine, music ensembles, Model UN, musical theater, radio station, student government, student newspaper, symphony orchestra, TV station, American Indians Reaching for Opportunities, black student union, College Republicans, College Democrats, Lutheran Collegians, Association for Community Tasks, Newman Catholic student association, Habitat for Humanity, gay-straight alliance.

**Athletics.** NCAA. **Intercollegiate:** Baseball M, basketball, cross-country, diving, football (tackle) M, golf W, ice hockey, soccer W, softball W, swimming, tennis W, track and field, volleyball W, wrestling M. **Intramural:** Badminton, basketball, football (non-tackle), football (tackle) M, golf, ice hockey, racquetball, soccer, softball, tennis, volleyball. **Team name:** Pointers.

**Student services.** Adult student services, alcohol/substance abuse counseling, career counseling, services for economically disadvantaged, student employment services, financial aid counseling, health services, minority student services, on-campus daycare, personal counseling, placement for graduates, veterans' counselor, women's services. **Physically disabled:** Services for visually, speech, hearing impaired.

**Contact.** E-mail: admiss@uwsp.edu
Phone: (715) 346-2441 Fax: (715) 346-3296
Catherine Glennon, Director of Admissions, University of Wisconsin-Stevens Point, Student Services Center, Stevens Point, WI 54481

## University of Wisconsin-Stout
**Menomonie, Wisconsin**
www.uwstout.edu                                 CB code: 1740

- Public 4-year university
- Residential campus in large town
- 7,429 degree-seeking undergraduates: 11% part-time, 49% women, 1% African American, 3% Asian American, 1% Hispanic American, 1% Native American, 1% international
- 667 degree-seeking graduate students
- 79% of applicants admitted

- SAT or ACT (ACT writing optional) required
- 48% graduate within 6 years

**General.** Founded in 1891. Regionally accredited. **Degrees:** 1,182 bachelor's awarded; master's offered. **Location:** 60 miles from Minneapolis-St. Paul. **Calendar:** 4-1-4, limited summer session. **Full-time faculty:** 324 total; 75% have terminal degrees, 11% minority, 44% women. **Part-time faculty:** 88 total; 32% have terminal degrees, 6% minority, 51% women. **Class size:** 34% < 20, 57% 20-39, 3% 40-49, 5% 50-99, 1% >100. **Special facilities:** Teleproduction center, technology transfer institute, vocational rehabilitation institute.

**Freshman class profile.** 3,948 applied, 3,106 admitted, 1,486 enrolled.

| Mid 50% test scores | | Return as sophomores: | 70% |
|---|---|---|---|
| ACT composite: | 19-23 | Out-of-state: | 35% |
| GPA 3.50 or higher: | 26% | Live on campus: | 95% |
| GPA 3.0-3.49: | 41% | International: | 1% |
| GPA 2.0-2.99: | 33% | Fraternities: | 5% |
| Rank in top quarter: | 25% | Sororities: | 12% |
| Rank in top tenth: | 6% | | |

**Basis for selection.** Rank in top half of high school class or 22 ACT required. Rolling admissions with limited enrollment in all programs. Art-graphic design deadline of November 1; not all qualified applicants will be admitted. Applied science and manufacturing engineering require upper 40% of class or 22 ACT, along with 22 ACT-Math score. **Learning Disabled:** Current IEP may be submitted with application.

**High school preparation.** Required and recommended units include English 4, mathematics 3, social studies 3, science 3, foreign language 2 and academic electives 4. Electives in English, math, social sciences, and sciences, technology business, fine art, family & consumer education, sciences.

**2007-2008 Annual costs.** Tuition/fees: $7,272; $15,018 out-of-state. Laptop computer included in the cost of tuition. Room/board: $4,994. Books/supplies: $306. Personal expenses: $1,620.

**2007-2008 Financial aid. Need-based:** 1,175 full-time freshmen applied for aid; 766 were judged to have need; 766 of these received aid. Average need met was 86%. Average scholarship/grant was $4,892; average loan $4,169. 32% of total undergraduate aid awarded as scholarships/grants, 68% as loans/jobs. **Non-need-based:** Awarded to 785 full-time undergraduates, including 318 freshmen. Scholarships awarded for academics.

**Application procedures. Admission:** Priority date 1/1; no deadline. $35 fee, may be waived for applicants with need. Application may be submitted online. Admission notification on a rolling basis beginning on or about 9/15. Enrollment limited. Early application recommended. **Financial aid:** Priority date 3/15; no closing date. FAFSA required. Applicants notified on a rolling basis starting 4/1; must reply within 4 week(s) of notification.

**Academics. Special study options:** Accelerated study, cooperative education, cross-registration, distance learning, double major, dual enrollment of high school students, exchange student, external degree, honors, independent study, internships, study abroad, teacher certification program. **Credit/placement by examination:** AP, CLEP, IB, institutional tests. **Support services:** Learning center, pre-admission summer program, reduced course load, remedial instruction, study skills assistance, tutoring, writing center.

**Majors. Business:** Business admin, customer service, golf management, hospitality admin, operations, sales/distribution. **Communications technology:** Printing management. **Computer sciences:** Networking. **Education:** Art, early childhood, family/consumer sciences, mentally handicapped, sales/marketing, technology/industrial arts, voc/tech. **Engineering:** Manufacturing. **Engineering technology:** General, construction. **English:** Technical writing. **Family/consumer sciences:** Clothing/textiles, family studies, institutional food production. **Health:** Dietetics, vocational rehab counseling. **Math:** Applied. **Psychology:** General. **Other:** Applied Science, Art, Information and Communications Technology, Packaging.

**Most popular majors.** Business/marketing 43%, education 13%, engineering/engineering technologies 8%, family/consumer sciences 11%, visual/performing arts 8%.

**Computing on campus.** 590 workstations in dormitories, library, computer center, student center. Dormitories wired for high-speed internet access and linked to campus network. Commuter students can connect to campus network. Online course registration, helpline, repair service, student web hosting, wireless network available.

**Student life. Freshman orientation:** Available. One-day program with additional activities week immediately before classes begin. **Housing:** Guaranteed on-campus for freshmen. Coed dorms, special housing for disabled,

apartments, substance-free housing available. $125 partly refundable deposit. Freshman housing, smoke-free housing, upperclass/graduate housing, alcohol-free housing available. **Activities:** Bands, choral groups, drama, film society, literary magazine, music ensembles, radio station, student government, student newspaper, black student union, Hmong Stout student organization, Lutheran student fellowship, College Democrats, College Republicans, Chi Alpha Christians in Action, single parent association, Club Los Hispanos.

**Athletics.** NCAA. **Intercollegiate:** Baseball M, basketball, cross-country, football (tackle) M, gymnastics W, ice hockey M, soccer W, softball W, tennis W, track and field, volleyball W. **Intramural:** Baseball M, basketball, golf, ice hockey, racquetball, soccer, softball, volleyball. **Team name:** Blue Devils.

**Student services.** Campus ministries, career counseling, student employment services, health services, on-campus daycare, personal counseling, placement for graduates, veterans' counselor. **Physically disabled:** Services for visually, speech, hearing impaired.

**Contact.** E-mail: admissions@uwstout.edu
Phone: (715) 232-1411 Toll-free number: (800) 447-8688
Fax: (715) 232-1667
Cindy Gilberts, Executive Director of Enrollment Services, University of Wisconsin-Stout, 1 Clocktower Plaza, Menomonie, WI 54751

## University of Wisconsin-Superior
**Superior, Wisconsin**
**www.uwsuper.edu**                                    **CB code: 1920**

- Public 4-year university and liberal arts college
- Commuter campus in large town
- 2,450 degree-seeking undergraduates: 17% part-time, 57% women, 2% African American, 1% Asian American, 1% Hispanic American, 3% Native American, 4% international
- 213 degree-seeking graduate students
- 74% of applicants admitted
- SAT or ACT (ACT writing optional) required
- 43% graduate within 6 years

**General.** Founded in 1893. Regionally accredited. **Degrees:** 444 bachelor's, 5 associate awarded; master's offered. **ROTC:** Air Force. **Location:** 2 miles from Duluth, Minnesota, 150 miles from Minneapolis-St. Paul. **Calendar:** Semester, limited summer session. **Full-time faculty:** 116 total; 79% have terminal degrees, 9% minority, 44% women. **Part-time faculty:** 59 total; 29% have terminal degrees, 12% minority, 42% women. **Class size:** 54% < 20, 40% 20-39, 4% 40-49, 2% 50-99, less than 1% >100. **Special facilities:** Observatory, wetlands, research vessel on Lake Superior.

**Freshman class profile.** 919 applied, 679 admitted, 350 enrolled.

| Mid 50% test scores | | Return as sophomores: | 63% |
|---|---|---|---|
| ACT composite: | 20-24 | Out-of-state: | 41% |
| Rank in top quarter: | 39% | Live on campus: | 60% |
| Rank in top tenth: | 14% | International: | 5% |
| End year in good standing: | 93% | Sororities: | 5% |

**Basis for selection.** Admissions based on secondary school record and class rank. Standardized test scores also important. Essay, audition, portfolio, interview recommended. **Homeschooled:** Statement describing home-school structure and mission, transcript of courses and grades required.

**High school preparation.** 17 units required. Required and recommended units include English 4, mathematics 3-4, social studies 3-4, science 3-4, foreign language 2 and academic electives 4.

**2007-2008 Annual costs.** Tuition/fees: $5,907; $13,480 out-of-state. Minnesota reciprocity tuition: $223 per credit hour. Room/board: $4,720. Books/supplies: $860. Personal expenses: $1,800.

**2007-2008 Financial aid. Need-based:** 252 full-time freshmen applied for aid; 199 were judged to have need; 194 of these received aid. Average scholarship/grant was $5,650; average loan $3,058. 43% of total undergraduate aid awarded as scholarships/grants, 57% as loans/jobs. **Non-need-based:** Awarded to 368 full-time undergraduates, including 109 freshmen. Scholarships awarded for academics, alumni affiliation, art, leadership, minority status, music/drama, ROTC, state residency. **Additional information:** Tuition Assistance Program (TAP) available to non-resident students on limited basis.

**Application procedures. Admission:** Priority date 4/1; no deadline. $35 fee, may be waived for applicants with need. Application may be submitted online. Admission notification on a rolling basis beginning on or about 10/1. Must reply by May 1 or within 4 week(s) if notified thereafter. **Financial**

**aid:** Priority date 4/1; no closing date. FAFSA required. Applicants notified on a rolling basis starting 3/15; must reply by 5/1 or within 4 week(s) of notification.

**Academics.** Post-bachelor's certificates offered in early childhood education, counseling, and secondary education. Post-master's certificate offered in library science. **Special study options:** Combined bachelor's/graduate degree, cooperative education, cross-registration, distance learning, double major, dual enrollment of high school students, ESL, exchange student, external degree, independent study, internships, liberal arts/career combination, student-designed major, study abroad, teacher certification program. Engineering with University of Wisconsin-Madison and Michigan Technological University, Forestry with Michigan Technological University. **Credit/placement by examination:** AP, CLEP, IB, ACT, institutional tests. 32 credit hours maximum toward associate degree, 32 toward bachelor's. **Support services:** Learning center, pre-admission summer program, reduced course load, remedial instruction, study skills assistance, tutoring, writing center.

**Majors. Biology:** General, aquatic, botany, cell/histology, ecology, environmental, molecular. **Business:** General, accounting, business admin, finance, international, management information systems, marketing. **Communications:** General, broadcast journalism, journalism, media studies. **Computer sciences:** Computer science. **Education:** Art, biology, chemistry, elementary, English, history, mathematics, multi-level teacher, music, physical, science, social science, social studies. **English:** English lit, speech/rhetoric. **Health:** Art therapy. **History:** General. **Interdisciplinary:** Biological/physical sciences. **Legal studies:** General, prelaw. **Liberal arts:** Arts/sciences. **Math:** General. **Physical sciences:** Chemistry. **Protective services:** Criminal justice, police science. **Psychology:** General. **Public administration:** General, policy analysis, social work. **Social sciences:** General, economics, political science, sociology. **Transportation:** General. **Visual/performing arts:** General, art, art history/conservation, dramatic, music performance, studio arts.

**Most popular majors.** Business/marketing 18%, communications/journalism 8%, education 23%, interdisciplinary studies 7%, social sciences 9%, visual/performing arts 8%.

**Computing on campus.** 340 workstations in dormitories, library, computer center, student center. Dormitories wired for high-speed internet access and linked to campus network. Commuter students can connect to campus network. Online course registration, online library, helpline, repair service, student web hosting, wireless network available.

**Student life. Freshman orientation:** Mandatory, $70 fee. Preregistration for classes offered. Sessions held in spring and summer; 2 1/2 day program just prior to classes beginning. **Housing:** Guaranteed on-campus for freshmen. Coed dorms, single-sex dorms, special housing for disabled, substance-free housing available. $125 partly refundable deposit, deadline 7/1. Suites available in nontraditional residence halls for married students. Single parents have access to student residences. **Activities:** Bands, choral groups, dance, drama, international student organizations, music ensembles, radio station, student government, student newspaper, symphony orchestra, TV station, criminal justice association, black student union, College Democrats, social work student association, College Republicans, intervarsity Christian fellowship.

**Athletics.** NCAA. **Intercollegiate:** Baseball M, basketball, cross-country, golf W, ice hockey, soccer, softball W, track and field, volleyball W. **Intramural:** Badminton, basketball, bowling, cheerleading, football (nontackle), golf, ice hockey, racquetball, rifle, skiing, soccer, softball, swimming, table tennis, tennis, volleyball. **Team name:** Yellowjackets.

**Student services.** Adult student services, alcohol/substance abuse counseling, campus ministries, career counseling, services for economically disadvantaged, student employment services, financial aid counseling, health services, minority student services, on-campus daycare, personal counseling, placement for graduates, veterans' counselor, women's services. **Physically disabled:** Services for visually, hearing impaired.

**Contact.** E-mail: admissions@uwsuper.edu
Phone: (715) 394-8230 Fax: (715) 394-8407
Lee Parker, Freshmen Admissions Advisor, University of Wisconsin-Superior, Belknap and Catlin, PO Box 2000, Superior, WI 54880

## University of Wisconsin-Whitewater
**Whitewater, Wisconsin**
www.uww.edu                                    CB code: 1921

- Public 4-year university
- Residential campus in large town
- 9,180 degree-seeking undergraduates: 8% part-time, 49% women, 4% African American, 2% Asian American, 2% Hispanic American, 1% international

- 1,329 graduate students
- 75% of applicants admitted

**General.** Founded in 1868. Regionally accredited. **Degrees:** 1,766 bachelor's, 8 associate awarded; master's offered. **ROTC:** Army, Air Force. **Location:** 40 miles from Madison, 50 miles from Milwaukee. **Calendar:** Semester, extensive summer session. **Full-time faculty:** 383 total; 84% have terminal degrees, 19% minority, 44% women. **Part-time faculty:** 121 total; 35% have terminal degrees, 9% minority, 49% women. **Class size:** 35% < 20, 50% 20-39, 10% 40-49, 4% 50-99, less than 1% >100. **Special facilities:** Observatory, nature preserve and recreation area, weather station.

**Freshman class profile.** 6,212 applied, 4,667 admitted, 2,050 enrolled.

| Mid 50% test scores | | Rank in top tenth: | 9% |
|---|---|---|---|
| SAT critical reading: | 470-610 | End year in good standing: | 92% |
| SAT math: | 480-600 | Return as sophomores: | 76% |
| ACT composite: | 20-24 | Out-of-state: | 7% |
| GPA 3.50 or higher: | 29% | Live on campus: | 90% |
| GPA 3.0-3.49: | 42% | International: | 1% |
| GPA 2.0-2.99: | 29% | Fraternities: | 7% |
| Rank in top quarter: | 31% | Sororities: | 6% |

**Basis for selection.** College prep curriculum and rank in top 40% of high school class important. SAT or ACT recommended. Audition required for music; portfolio recommended for art. **Homeschooled:** Transcript of courses and grades required. **Learning Disabled:** Disability should be referenced in essay and include review by Center for Students with Disabilities. Medical documentation may be requested.

**High school preparation.** 17 units required; 20 recommended. Required and recommended units include English 4, mathematics 3-4, social studies 3-4, science 3-4 (laboratory 1), foreign language 2 and academic electives 4.

**2007-2008 Annual costs.** Tuition/fees: $5,858; $13,431 out-of-state. Room/board: $4,474. Books/supplies: $170. Personal expenses: $1,650.

**Financial aid. Non-need-based:** Scholarships awarded for academics, alumni affiliation, art, leadership, minority status, music/drama, ROTC, state residency.

**Application procedures. Admission:** Priority date 1/1; deadline 5/1 (postmark date). $35 fee, may be waived for applicants with need. Application may be submitted online. Admission notification on a rolling basis beginning on or about 9/15. **Financial aid:** Priority date 3/15; no closing date. FAFSA required. Applicants notified on a rolling basis starting 4/1; must reply within 3 week(s) of notification.

**Academics. Special study options:** Accelerated study, combined bachelor's/graduate degree, cooperative education, cross-registration, distance learning, double major, dual enrollment of high school students, ESL, exchange student, external degree, honors, independent study, internships, liberal arts/career combination, student-designed major, study abroad, teacher certification program, weekend college. **Credit/placement by examination:** AP, CLEP, IB, SAT, ACT, institutional tests. 30 credit hours maximum toward associate degree, 60 toward bachelor's. **Support services:** Learning center, pre-admission summer program, reduced course load, remedial instruction, study skills assistance, tutoring, writing center.

**Majors. Area/ethnic studies:** Women's. **Biology:** General. **Business:** General, accounting, business admin, finance, human resources, managerial economics, marketing, nonprofit/public, office/clerical, operations. **Communications:** General, broadcast journalism, journalism. **Computer sciences:** General, information technology, systems analysis, web page design. **Education:** General, art, biology, business, chemistry, computer, drama/dance, early childhood, elementary, English, French, German, history, learning disabled, mathematics, music, physical, sales/marketing, science, secondary, social science, social studies, Spanish, special, speech. **Engineering technology:** Occupational safety. **English:** Creative writing, English lit, speech/rhetoric. **Foreign languages:** French, German, Spanish. **Health:** Speech pathology. **History:** General. **Interdisciplinary:** Global studies. **Legal studies:** Prelaw. **Liberal arts:** Arts/sciences. **Math:** General. **Physical sciences:** Chemistry, physics. **Psychology:** General. **Public administration:** General, policy analysis, social work. **Social sciences:** General, economics, geography, political science, sociology. **Visual/performing arts:** Art, art history/conservation, dance, dramatic, music theory/composition, theater arts management, theater history. **Other:** Integrated Science/Business.

**Most popular majors.** Business/marketing 28%, communications/journalism 10%, education 17%, public administration/social services 6%, social sciences 9%.

**Computing on campus.** 1,373 workstations in dormitories, library, computer center, student center. Dormitories wired for high-speed internet access and linked to campus network. Commuter students can connect to campus network. Online course registration, online library, helpline, repair service, student web hosting, wireless network available.

**Student life. Freshman orientation:** Mandatory, $55 fee. Preregistration for classes offered. Full-day program held in summer. **Housing:** Guaranteed on-campus for freshmen. Coed dorms, single-sex dorms, special housing for disabled, substance-free housing available. $125 partly refundable deposit. **Activities:** Bands, choral groups, dance, drama, literary magazine, music ensembles, musical theater, opera, radio station, student government, student newspaper, symphony orchestra, TV station, Campus Crusade for Christ, Diamond Way Buddhist, College Democrats, College Republicans, Arabic club, Black Student Union, Adopt-A-School Program, America Reads.

**Athletics.** NCAA. **Intercollegiate:** Baseball M, basketball, bowling W, cross-country, diving, football (tackle) M, golf W, gymnastics W, soccer, softball W, swimming, tennis, track and field, volleyball W, wrestling M. **Intramural:** Badminton, basketball, bowling, football (non-tackle), golf, racquetball, soccer, softball, table tennis, tennis, volleyball. **Team name:** Warhawks.

**Student services.** Adult student services, alcohol/substance abuse counseling, campus ministries, career counseling, services for economically disadvantaged, student employment services, financial aid counseling, health services, legal services, minority student services, on-campus daycare, personal counseling, placement for graduates, veterans' counselor, women's services. **Physically disabled:** Services for visually, speech, hearing impaired. **Learning disabled:** Comprehensive services available.

**Contact.** E-mail: uwwadmit@uww.edu
Phone: (262) 472-1440 Fax: (262) 472-1515
Stephen McKellips, Director of Admissions, University of
Wisconsin-Whitewater, 800 West Main Street, Whitewater, WI 53190-1790

---

## Viterbo University
La Crosse, Wisconsin

CB member
www.viterbo.edu — CB code: 1878

- Private 4-year university and liberal arts college affiliated with Roman Catholic Church
- Residential campus in small city
- 1,922 degree-seeking undergraduates: 22% part-time, 71% women, 1% African American, 1% Asian American, 1% Hispanic American, 1% Native American, 1% international
- 555 degree-seeking graduate students
- 88% of applicants admitted
- ACT (writing optional) required
- 48% graduate within 6 years; 7% enter graduate study

**General.** Founded in 1890. Regionally accredited. **Degrees:** 397 bachelor's, 6 associate awarded; master's offered. **ROTC:** Army. **Location:** 150 miles from Minneapolis-St. Paul, 150 miles from Madison. **Calendar:** Semester, limited summer session. **Full-time faculty:** 109 total; 60% have terminal degrees, 5% minority, 57% women. **Part-time faculty:** 116 total; 27% have terminal degrees, 2% minority, 62% women. **Class size:** 70% < 20, 29% 20-39, 1% 50-99. **Special facilities:** Center for ethics, science and technology; fine arts center; center for recreation and education in conjunction with Boys and Girls Club of America.

**Freshman class profile.** 1,148 applied, 1,013 admitted, 368 enrolled.

| Mid 50% test scores | | Rank in top tenth: | 13% |
|---|---|---|---|
| ACT composite: | 20-24 | End year in good standing: | 86% |
| GPA 3.50 or higher: | 43% | Return as sophomores: | 74% |
| GPA 3.0-3.49: | 30% | Out-of-state: | 22% |
| GPA 2.0-2.99: | 26% | Live on campus: | 83% |
| Rank in top quarter: | 39% | International: | 1% |

**Basis for selection.** High school GPA and ACT score most important, then placement testing. Auditions and portfolio reviews required for students applying to School of Fine Arts (music, theater, art, dance). Interview required for students not meeting admission requirements. **Homeschooled:** Transcript of courses and grades required. **Learning Disabled:** All students encouraged to file ADA petition for reasonable accommodations, preferably 8 weeks prior to start of classes.

**High school preparation.** 16 units required; 19 recommended. Required and recommended units include English 3-4, mathematics 2, social studies 2, history 2, science 2 (laboratory 2), foreign language 2 and academic electives 5. Chemistry required for nursing, dietetics, natural sciences, allied health preprofessional students. Portfolios or auditions required for fine arts students.

**2008-2009 Annual costs.** Tuition/fees: $19,490. Additional fees for some art, dietetics, science courses, and nursing clinicals. Room/board: $6,380. Books/supplies: $850. Personal expenses: $1,600.

**Financial aid. Non-need-based:** Scholarships awarded for academics, alumni affiliation, art, athletics, leadership, minority status, music/drama, ROTC.

**Application procedures. Admission:** Priority date 8/1; no deadline. $25 fee, may be waived for applicants with need. Application may be submitted online. Admission notification on a rolling basis. Must reply by May 1 or within 2 week(s) if notified thereafter. **Financial aid:** Priority date 3/15; no closing date. FAFSA, institutional form required. Applicants notified on a rolling basis starting 4/1; must reply within 3 week(s) of notification.

**Academics.** Learning Center offers individual and small group tutoring in all subject areas daily. Library services available daily, on weekends and evenings. **Special study options:** Accelerated study, cross-registration, distance learning, double major, dual enrollment of high school students, honors, independent study, internships, liberal arts/career combination, student-designed major, study abroad, teacher certification program, urban semester, Washington semester, weekend college. Weekend college is basically at Master's level. **Credit/placement by examination:** AP, CLEP, IB, ACT, institutional tests. 30 credit hours maximum toward bachelor's degree. 16 hours awarded for military services. **Support services:** Learning center, reduced course load, remedial instruction, study skills assistance, tutoring, writing center.

**Majors. Biology:** General, biochemistry. **Business:** Accounting, business admin, management information systems, marketing. **Computer sciences:** General. **Education:** Art, biology, business, chemistry, drama/dance, elementary, English, mathematics, music, science, secondary, social studies, Spanish, technology/industrial arts. **English:** English lit. **Foreign languages:** Spanish. **Health:** Dietetics, health services, nursing (RN). **Interdisciplinary:** Biological/physical sciences. **Liberal arts:** Arts/sciences. **Math:** General. **Philosophy/religion:** Religion. **Physical sciences:** Chemistry. **Protective services:** Criminal justice. **Psychology:** General. **Public administration:** Social work. **Social sciences:** General, sociology. **Visual/performing arts:** General, art, arts management, design, dramatic, graphic design, music pedagogy, music performance, studio arts. **Other:** English and theatre arts, Individualized learning, Organizational management, Religious studies/philosophy.

**Most popular majors.** Business/marketing 16%, education 10%, health sciences 37%, interdisciplinary studies 6%, visual/performing arts 7%.

**Computing on campus.** 396 workstations in dormitories, library, computer center, student center. Dormitories wired for high-speed internet access and linked to campus network. Commuter students can connect to campus network. Online course registration, online library, helpline, wireless network available.

**Student life. Freshman orientation:** Mandatory. Preregistration for classes offered. One-day program offered 4 times in the summer for incoming freshmen and parents. **Policies:** Standards of conduct, sexual harassment code, anti-hazing initiation policy, academic honesty policy, academic due process, campus security policy, residence hall terms and conditions, alcohol and drug policy, student event policies. **Housing:** Guaranteed on-campus for freshmen. Coed dorms, apartments, substance-free housing available. $100 fully refundable deposit, deadline 8/1. University-owned theme houses, theme floors. **Activities:** Pep band, choral groups, dance, drama, literary magazine, music ensembles, musical theater, opera, student government, student newspaper, campus ministry, Connect, Students in Free Enterprise, Circle K, student nurses association, education club, Sigma Pi Delta, CREW, Global Rhythms, psychology club.

**Athletics.** NAIA. **Intercollegiate:** Baseball M, basketball, cross-country, golf, soccer, softball W, volleyball W. **Intramural:** Badminton, basketball, bowling, cross-country, golf, handball, racquetball, rugby, skiing, soccer, softball, table tennis, tennis, volleyball. **Team name:** V-Hawks.

**Student services.** Adult student services, alcohol/substance abuse counseling, campus ministries, career counseling, services for economically disadvantaged, student employment services, financial aid counseling, health services, personal counseling, placement for graduates, women's services. **Physically disabled:** Services for visually, hearing impaired.

**Contact.** E-mail: admission@viterbo.edu
Phone: (608) 796-3010 Toll-free number: (800) 848-3726
Fax: (608) 796-3020
Roland Nelson, Vice President for Enrollment, Viterbo University, 900 Viterbo Drive, La Crosse, WI 54601-8804

---

## Wisconsin Lutheran College
Milwaukee, Wisconsin
www.wlc.edu — CB code: 1513

- Private 4-year liberal arts college affiliated with Wisconsin Evangelical Lutheran Synod
- Residential campus in very large city

▶ 692 degree-seeking undergraduates
▶ SAT or ACT (ACT writing optional) required

**General.** Founded in 1973. Regionally accredited. Challenging academic program in a conservative Christian environment. **Degrees:** 158 bachelor's awarded. **ROTC:** Army, Naval, Air Force. **Calendar:** Semester, limited summer session. **Full-time faculty:** 58 total. **Part-time faculty:** 42 total.

**Freshman class profile.**

| Mid 50% test scores | | | |
|---|---|---|---|
| SAT critical reading: | 450-650 | SAT math: | 560-660 |
| | | ACT composite: | 22-27 |

**Basis for selection.** Test scores, class rank, GPA most important. Interview recommended for some; audition required for music scholarships.

**High school preparation.** 16 units required; 20 recommended. Required and recommended units include English 4, mathematics 3-4, history 2, science 2-3 (laboratory 1-2), foreign language 2-4 and academic electives 3. Mathematics or science majors should complete 4 units of mathematics and 3-4 units of appropriate science courses.

**2007-2008 Annual costs.** Tuition/fees: $19,564. Room/board: $6,910. Books/supplies: $700. Personal expenses: $1,470.

**Financial aid. Non-need-based:** Scholarships awarded for academics, art, leadership, minority status, music/drama, state residency.

**Application procedures. Admission:** Priority date 3/1; no deadline. $20 fee, may be waived for applicants with need. Application may be submitted online. Admission notification on a rolling basis beginning on or about 9/1. Must reply by May 1 or within 2 week(s) if notified thereafter. **Financial aid:** Priority date 3/1; no closing date. FAFSA, institutional form required. Applicants notified on a rolling basis starting 3/15; must reply within 2 week(s) of notification.

**Academics.** Special graduation requirements include freshman seminar. **Special study options:** Double major, dual enrollment of high school students, independent study, internships, student-designed major, study abroad, teacher certification program. **Credit/placement by examination:** AP, CLEP, institutional tests. **Support services:** Learning center, reduced course load, study skills assistance, tutoring, writing center.

**Majors. Biology:** General, biochemistry. **Business:** Managerial economics. **Communications:** General. **Education:** Elementary. **English:** English lit. **Foreign languages:** Spanish. **History:** General. **Math:** General. **Physical sciences:** Chemistry. **Psychology:** General. **Social sciences:** General, political science. **Theology:** Theology. **Visual/performing arts:** Art, dramatic.

**Computing on campus.** 200 workstations in dormitories, library, computer center, student center. Dormitories wired for high-speed internet access and linked to campus network. Commuter students can connect to campus network. Online library, helpline, repair service, wireless network available.

**Student life. Freshman orientation:** Mandatory. Preregistration for classes offered. 2-day program held week before start of fall semester. **Policies:** Drug free campus program. No alcohol on campus. Smoking permitted outside only. **Housing:** Guaranteed on-campus for all undergraduates. Single-sex dorms, apartments available. $100 deposit, deadline 5/1. All traditional age, unmarried students less than 5 years out of high school must live in college housing. Upperclassmen eligible for college apartments. **Activities:** Bands, choral groups, dance, drama, music ensembles, student government, student newspaper.

**Athletics.** NCAA. **Intercollegiate:** Baseball M, basketball, cross-country, football (tackle) M, golf, soccer, softball W, tennis W, track and field, volleyball W. **Intramural:** Basketball, football (tackle), softball, volleyball. **Team name:** Warriors.

**Student services.** Adult student services, campus ministries, career counseling, student employment services, financial aid counseling, health services, personal counseling, placement for graduates. **Physically disabled:** Services for visually, hearing impaired.

**Contact.** E-mail: admissions@wlc.edu
Phone: (414) 443-8811 Toll-free number: (888) 947-5884
Fax: (414) 443-8514
Craig Swiontek, Director of Admissions, Wisconsin Lutheran College, 8800 West Bluemound Road, Milwaukee, WI 53226-4699

# Wyoming

## University of Wyoming

Laramie, Wyoming
www.uwyo.edu

**CB member**
**CB code: 4855**

‣ Public 4-year university
‣ Residential campus in large town
‣ 9,140 degree-seeking undergraduates: 15% part-time, 52% women, 1% African American, 1% Asian American, 3% Hispanic American, 1% Native American, 2% international
‣ 2,261 degree-seeking graduate students
‣ 96% of applicants admitted
‣ SAT or ACT (ACT writing optional) required
‣ 56% graduate within 6 years

**General.** Founded in 1886. Regionally accredited. Undergraduate and graduate degree programs offered in Casper. Extension classes available in off-campus locations throughout the state. Online classes offered nationally. **Degrees:** 1,687 bachelor's awarded; master's, doctoral, first professional offered. **ROTC:** Army, Air Force. **Location:** 45 miles from Cheyenne, 130 miles from Denver. **Calendar:** Semester, extensive summer session. **Full-time faculty:** 692 total; 86% have terminal degrees, 8% minority, 35% women. **Part-time faculty:** 48 total; 48% have terminal degrees, 4% minority, 56% women. **Class size:** 40% < 20, 43% 20-39, 7% 40-49, 6% 50-99, 4% >100. **Special facilities:** Museums (art, geological, anthropology, entomology), range herbarium, Rocky Mountain herbarium/mycological herbarium, spatial data and visualization center, botany conservatory, zoological center, learning resource center, meteorological station, National Park research center in Grand Teton National Park, planetarium, veterinary laboratory, materials characterization lab, biological research facility, on-site elementary school, infrared telescope observatory, survey research center, institute of environment & natural resources, fishery and wildlife research unit, American heritage center, insect galleries.

**Freshman class profile.** 3,350 applied, 3,205 admitted, 1,643 enrolled.

| Mid 50% test scores | | | |
|---|---|---|---|
| SAT critical reading: | 480-610 | Rank in top quarter: | 50% |
| SAT math: | 500-630 | Rank in top tenth: | 20% |
| ACT composite: | 21-26 | Return as sophomores: | 74% |
| GPA 3.50 or higher: | 53% | Out-of-state: | 57% |
| GPA 3.0-3.49: | 30% | Live on campus: | 88% |
| GPA 2.0-2.99: | 17% | International: | 1% |

**Basis for selection.** GPA, ACT or SAT scores and completion of 13 required units in pre-college curriculum most important. Test scores not required for non-degree-seeking students. **Homeschooled:** Homeschool credit evaluation form completed by homeschool instructor required. **Learning Disabled:** Must present documentation of disability in order to receive assistance from University Disability Support Services.

**High school preparation.** 13 units required; 19 recommended. Required and recommended units include English 4, mathematics 3-4, science 3-4 (laboratory 3) and foreign language 2. 3 cultural context electives required. 3 behavioral or social sciences, 3 visual or performing arts, and 3 humanities or earth/space sciences recommended.

**2007-2008 Annual costs.** Tuition/fees: $3,554; $10,394 out-of-state. International students must pay an additional $35 fee per semester. Room/board: $7,274.

**2006-2007 Financial aid. Need-based:** 1,233 full-time freshmen applied for aid; 706 were judged to have need; 695 of these received aid. Average need met was 66%. Average scholarship/grant was $3,001; average loan $2,810. 35% of total undergraduate aid awarded as scholarships/grants, 65% as loans/jobs. **Non-need-based:** Awarded to 4,595 full-time undergraduates, including 1,094 freshmen. Scholarships awarded for alumni affiliation, art, athletics, leadership, music/drama, ROTC, state residency.

**Application procedures. Admission:** Priority date 3/1; deadline 8/10 (postmark date). $40 fee, may be waived for applicants with need. Application may be submitted online. Admission notification on a rolling basis. Early application recommended for students seeking financial aid and university housing preferences. **Financial aid:** Priority date 3/1; no closing date. FAFSA required. Applicants notified on a rolling basis starting 3/1.

**Academics.** Remedial instruction offered on campus through Laramie County Community College. **Special study options:** Accelerated study, distance learning, double major, ESL, exchange student, external degree, honors, independent study, internships, New York semester, semester at sea, student-designed major, study abroad, teacher certification program, Washington semester. **Credit/placement by examination:** AP, CLEP, IB, SAT, ACT, institutional tests. Individual departments may also allow additional tests on case-by-case basis. **Support services:** Learning center, pre-admission summer program, reduced course load, study skills assistance, tutoring, writing center.

**Majors. Agriculture:** Agribusiness operations, animal sciences, communications, plant sciences, range science. **Area/ethnic studies:** American, women's. **Biology:** General, botany, microbiology, molecular, wildlife, zoology. **Business:** Accounting, business admin, finance, management science, managerial economics, marketing. **Communications:** General, journalism. **Computer sciences:** Computer science. **Conservation:** Environmental studies. **Education:** Agricultural, elementary, music, physical, secondary, special, technology/industrial arts, trade/industrial. **Engineering:** Architectural, chemical, civil, computer, electrical, mechanical, petroleum. **English:** English lit. **Family/consumer sciences:** General. **Foreign languages:** French, German, Russian, Spanish. **Health:** Audiology/speech pathology, health care, health services, nursing (RN). **History:** General. **Liberal arts:** Humanities. **Math:** General, applied, statistics. **Parks/recreation:** Exercise sciences. **Philosophy/religion:** Philosophy. **Physical sciences:** General, chemistry, geology, physics. **Protective services:** Criminal justice. **Psychology:** General. **Public administration:** Social work. **Social sciences:** General, anthropology, geography, international relations, political science, sociology. **Visual/performing arts:** Art, dramatic, music performance, music theory/composition.

**Most popular majors.** Agriculture 6%, biology 6%, business/marketing 16%, education 15%, engineering/engineering technologies 10%, health sciences 8%, social sciences 8%.

**Computing on campus.** 1,269 workstations in dormitories, library, computer center, student center. Dormitories wired for high-speed internet access and linked to campus network. Commuter students can connect to campus network. Online course registration, online library, helpline, student web hosting, wireless network available.

**Student life. Freshman orientation:** Available, $60 fee. Preregistration for classes offered. Nine 2-day sessions held in June. **Policies:** New freshmen subject to live-in policy. **Housing:** Guaranteed on-campus for all undergraduates. Coed dorms, special housing for disabled, apartments, fraternity/sorority housing, substance-free housing available. $100 partly refundable deposit. Floor-specific living plans in residence halls and health sciences living house. **Activities:** Bands, choral groups, dance, drama, literary magazine, music ensembles, musical theater, opera, radio station, student government, student newspaper, symphony orchestra, TV station, black student leaders, local church organizations, College Republicans, Rocky Mountain Democrats, Fellowship of Christian Athletes, Amnesty International, lesbian/gay/bisexual/transgendered association, Movimiento Estudiantil Chicanos de Atzlan, student health advisory council.

**Athletics.** NCAA. **Intercollegiate:** Basketball, cheerleading, cross-country, diving, football (tackle) M, golf, soccer W, swimming, tennis W, track and field, volleyball W, wrestling M. **Intramural:** Badminton, basketball, bowling, football (non-tackle), golf, racquetball, soccer, softball, swimming, table tennis, tennis, track and field, volleyball, water polo, wrestling. **Team name:** Cowboys, Cowgirls.

**Student services.** Adult student services, alcohol/substance abuse counseling, campus ministries, career counseling, services for economically disadvantaged, student employment services, financial aid counseling, health services, legal services, minority student services, on-campus daycare, personal counseling, placement for graduates, veterans' counselor, women's services. **Physically disabled:** Services for visually, speech, hearing impaired. **Learning disabled:** Comprehensive services available.

**Contact.** E-mail: why-wyo@uwyo.edu
Phone: (307) 766-5160 Toll-free number: (800) 342-5996
Fax: (307) 766-4042
Noah Buckley, Director of Admissions, University of Wyoming, 1000 East University Avenue/Department 3435, Laramie, WY 82071

# Guam

# Virgin Islands, U.S.

## University of Guam
Mangilao, Guam
www.uog.edu                                      CB code: 0959

- Public 4-year university
- Large town
- 2,897 degree-seeking undergraduates: 26% part-time, 62% women, 1% African American, 91% Asian American, 1% Hispanic American, 1% international
- 262 degree-seeking graduate students

**General.** Founded in 1952. Regionally accredited. **Degrees:** 266 bachelor's awarded; master's offered. **ROTC:** Army. **Calendar:** Semester, limited summer session. **Full-time faculty:** 190 total. **Part-time faculty:** 50 total. **Special facilities:** University-operated athletic center, planetarium, marine lab, Pacific and Micronesian library resources.

**Freshman class profile.** 680 applied, 650 admitted, 572 enrolled.

| Out-of-state: | 35% | International: | 2% |
|---|---|---|---|

**Basis for selection.** Open admission, but selective for some programs.

**2007-2008 Annual costs.** Tuition/fees: $5,160; $14,460 out-of-state. Room only: $1,940. Books/supplies: $705. Personal expenses: $1,830.

**2007-2008 Financial aid.** **Need-based:** 93% of total undergraduate aid awarded as scholarships/grants, 7% as loans/jobs.

**Application procedures.** **Admission:** Closing date 6/7. $49 fee. Admission notification on a rolling basis. **Financial aid:** Priority date 4/15; no closing date. FAFSA required. Applicants notified on a rolling basis starting 6/1; must reply within 2 week(s) of notification.

**Academics.** **Special study options:** Double major, internships. **Credit/placement by examination:** CLEP, institutional tests. **Support services:** Reduced course load, remedial instruction, tutoring.

**Majors.** **Biology:** General. **Business:** Accounting, business admin, finance, international. **Communications:** General. **Computer sciences:** General. **Education:** Bilingual, early childhood, elementary, physical, secondary, special. **English:** English lit. **Family/consumer sciences:** General. **Health:** Nursing (RN). **History:** General. **Math:** General. **Physical sciences:** Chemistry. **Protective services:** Criminal justice. **Psychology:** General. **Public administration:** General, social work. **Social sciences:** Anthropology, economics, political science, sociology. **Visual/performing arts:** Art.

**Computing on campus.** Dormitories linked to campus network. Commuter students can connect to campus network. Wireless network available.

**Student life.** **Housing:** Single-sex dorms available. **Activities:** Choral groups, dance, drama, musical theater, student government, student newspaper.

**Athletics.** **Intercollegiate:** Archery, badminton, baseball M, basketball, bowling, boxing M, cross-country, diving, equestrian, fencing, field hockey W, football (tackle) M, golf, gymnastics, handball, ice hockey, lacrosse, racquetball, rifle, rowing (crew), rugby, sailing, skiing, soccer, softball, squash, swimming, table tennis, tennis, track and field, volleyball, water polo, wrestling M. **Intramural:** Archery, badminton, baseball M, basketball, bowling, boxing M, cross-country, diving, equestrian, fencing, field hockey W, football (tackle) M, golf, gymnastics, handball, ice hockey, lacrosse, racquetball, rifle, rowing (crew), rugby, sailing, skiing, skin diving, soccer, softball, squash, swimming, table tennis, tennis, track and field, volleyball, water polo, wrestling M. **Team name:** Tritons.

**Student services.** Student employment services, health services, on-campus daycare, personal counseling, placement for graduates.

**Contact.** E-mail: admitme@uog.edu
Phone: (671) 735-2201
Deborah Leon Guerrero, Registrar, University of Guam, UOG Station, Mangilao, GU 96923

## University of the Virgin Islands
St. Thomas, Virgin Islands, U.S.               CB member
www.uvi.edu                                      CB code: 0879

- Public 4-year university
- Commuter campus in small city
- 2,128 degree-seeking undergraduates: 41% part-time, 75% women, 76% African American, 1% Asian American, 6% Hispanic American, 6% international
- 200 degree-seeking graduate students
- 97% of applicants admitted
- SAT or ACT (ACT writing optional) required
- 31% graduate within 6 years

**General.** Founded in 1962. Regionally accredited. Additional campus on St. Croix. Housing available on St. Thomas and St. Croix. **Degrees:** 200 bachelor's, 82 associate awarded; master's offered. **ROTC:** Army. **Location:** 45 miles from San Juan, Puerto Rico. **Calendar:** Semester, limited summer session. **Full-time faculty:** 100 total; 75% have terminal degrees, 55% minority, 47% women. **Part-time faculty:** 125 total; 18% have terminal degrees, 75% minority, 50% women. **Class size:** 77% < 20, 22% 20-39, less than 1% 40-49, less than 1% 50-99. **Special facilities:** Outdoor amphitheater, Caribbean collection, African art collection.

**Freshman class profile.** 913 applied, 884 admitted, 418 enrolled.

| Mid 50% test scores | | GPA 3.0-3.49: | 24% |
|---|---|---|---|
| SAT critical reading: | 350-460 | GPA 2.0-2.99: | 62% |
| SAT math: | 330-430 | End year in good standing: | 95% |
| SAT writing: | 350-470 | Return as sophomores: | 79% |
| ACT composite: | 13-19 | Out-of-state: | 3% |
| GPA 3.50 or higher: | 9% | International: | 2% |

**Basis for selection.** Secondary school record very important. Must have at least a 2.0 GPA. Nursing Aptitude Test required of nursing applicants.

**High school preparation.** 11 units required. Required units include English 4, mathematics 2, social studies 2, science 2 and foreign language 1.

**2007-2008 Annual costs.** Tuition/fees: $3,726; $10,326 out-of-state. Room/board: $7,550. Books/supplies: $1,500. Personal expenses: $1,800.

**2006-2007 Financial aid.** **Need-based:** 267 full-time freshmen applied for aid; 238 were judged to have need; 216 of these received aid. Average scholarship/grant was $3,457; average loan $2,171. 67% of total undergraduate aid awarded as scholarships/grants, 33% as loans/jobs. **Non-need-based:** Awarded to 201 full-time undergraduates, including 69 freshmen. Scholarships awarded for academics, art, athletics.

**Application procedures.** **Admission:** Priority date 2/1; deadline 4/30 (postmark date). $30 fee. Admission notification on a rolling basis. Must reply by 6/30. **Financial aid:** Closing date 3/1. FAFSA required. Applicants notified on a rolling basis starting 4/1; must reply within 2 week(s) of notification.

**Academics.** **Special study options:** Combined bachelor's/graduate degree, distance learning, exchange student, external degree, independent study, internships. **Credit/placement by examination:** AP, CLEP, SAT, ACT, institutional tests. **Support services:** Learning center, pre-admission summer program, reduced course load, remedial instruction, study skills assistance, tutoring.

**Majors.** **Biology:** General, marine. **Business:** Accounting, business admin. **Computer sciences:** Computer science. **Education:** Elementary, music, trade/industrial. **English:** English lit. **Liberal arts:** Arts/sciences. **Math:** General. **Physical sciences:** Chemistry. **Psychology:** General. **Social sciences:** General.

**Most popular majors.** Biology 7%, business/marketing 47%, education 11%, health sciences 6%, psychology 12%.

**Computing on campus.** 50 workstations in library, computer center. Dormitories linked to campus network. Online course registration, helpline, wireless network available.

**Student life. Freshman orientation:** Mandatory, $50 fee. **Housing:** Single-sex dorms available., $100 partly refundable deposit, deadline 6/1. **Activities:** Jazz band, choral groups, drama, music ensembles, student government, student newspaper, political clubs, president's club, Future Business Leaders of America, explorer's club, Virgin Islands student association, British Virgin Islands student association, Baptist Student Union, environment association, peer health educators.

**Athletics.** NCAA. **Intercollegiate:** Basketball, cross-country, tennis, volleyball. **Intramural:** Archery, badminton, basketball, fencing, golf, gymnastics, racquetball, softball, swimming, table tennis, tennis, track and field, volleyball. **Team name:** Bucs.

**Student services.** Career counseling, student employment services, health services, personal counseling, placement for graduates. **Physically disabled:** Services for visually, speech, hearing impaired.

**Contact.**  E-mail: admissions@uvi.edu
Phone: (340) 693-1150 Fax: (340) 693-1155
Edward Alexander, Director of Admissions, University of the Virgin Islands, No. 2 John Brewers Bay, St. Thomas, VI 00802-9990

# Bolivia

## Universidad Privada Boliviana
### Cochabamba, Bolivia
www.upb.edu                    CB code: 0856

- Private 4-year university, business and engineering college
- Very large city

**General.** Founded in 1992. **Location:** 4 miles from Cochabamba City. **Calendar:** Semester.

**Annual costs/financial aid.** Books/supplies: $400.

**Contact.**  Phone: (4) 426-8287 ext. 255
Director of Admissions, Km 6.5 camimo antiguo a Quillacollo Casilla: 3967, Cochabamba, BO

# Canada

## Acadia University
### Wolfville, Canada                    CB member
www.acadiau.ca                    CB code: 0901

- Public 4-year university
- Residential campus in small town
- 3,083 degree-seeking undergraduates
- SAT required

**General.** Regionally accredited. Acadia Advantage program provides each student with notebook computer. **Degrees:** 854 bachelor's awarded; master's, first professional offered. **Location:** 60 miles from Halifax. **Calendar:** Semester, limited summer session. **Full-time faculty:** 211 total. **Part-time faculty:** 37 total. **Special facilities:** Environmental science center and botanical gardens.

**Basis for selection.** GED not accepted. Academic record and recommendations most important. Class rank and standardized test scores also important. **Homeschooled:** Applicants considered on a case-by-case basis.

**High school preparation.** Required and recommended units include English 3, mathematics 2, history 2 and science 2.

**2007-2008 Annual costs.** Costs reported in Canadian dollars: $14,349 annually for tuition/fees for international students and $8,062 annually for Canadian students (non-Nova Scotia residents); $7,698 for room & board; $800 health/dental insurance fee for non-Canadian international students, $306 for Canadian students. Books/supplies: $1,300.

**Financial aid. Non-need-based:** Scholarships awarded for academics, athletics.

**Application procedures. Admission:** Priority date 3/1; no deadline. $25 fee, may be waived for applicants with need. Application may be submitted online. Admission notification on a rolling basis beginning on or about 10/1.

**Academics. Special study options:** Combined bachelor's/graduate degree, cooperative education, distance learning, double major, ESL, exchange student, honors, independent study, internships, liberal arts/career combination, semester at sea, study abroad, teacher certification program. **Credit/placement by examination:** AP, CLEP, IB. **Support services:** Remedial instruction, study skills assistance, tutoring, writing center.

**Majors. Area/ethnic studies:** Canadian. **Biology:** General. **Business:** General. **Computer sciences:** General. **Conservation:** Environmental science. **Education:** General. **English:** English lit. **Family/consumer sciences:** Food/nutrition. **Foreign languages:** General. **History:** General. **Math:** General. **Parks/recreation:** General, exercise sciences. **Philosophy/religion:** Philosophy. **Physical sciences:** Chemistry, geology, physics. **Psychology:** General. **Social sciences:** Economics, political science, sociology. **Theology:** Theology. **Visual/performing arts:** Art, dramatic.

**Computing on campus.** PC or laptop required. Dormitories wired for high-speed internet access and linked to campus network. Commuter students can connect to campus network. Online course registration, online library, helpline, repair service, student web hosting, wireless network available.

**Student life. Freshman orientation:** Available. Preregistration for classes offered. **Housing:** Guaranteed on-campus for all undergraduates. Coed dorms, single-sex dorms, special housing for disabled, substance-free housing available. $100 deposit. **Activities:** Bands, choral groups, dance, drama, literary magazine, music ensembles, musical theater, opera, radio station, student government, student newspaper, symphony orchestra.

**Athletics. Intercollegiate:** Basketball, cross-country W, football (tackle) M, ice hockey M, rugby W, soccer, volleyball W. **Intramural:** Badminton, baseball, basketball, cheerleading, football (non-tackle) M, football (tackle) M, ice hockey, rugby, soccer, softball, track and field, volleyball. **Team name:** Axemen/Axewomen.

**Student services.** Campus ministries, career counseling, student employment services, financial aid counseling, health services, legal services, minority student services, personal counseling, women's services. **Physically disabled:** Services for visually, hearing impaired.

**Contact.**  E-mail: admissions@acadiau.ca
Phone: (902) 585-1016 Fax: (902) 585-1092
Anne Scott, Manager of Admissions, Acadia University, Box 7, Wolfville, CN B4P-2R6

## McGill University
### Montreal, Canada                    CB member
www.mcgill.ca                    CB code: 0935

- Public 4-year university
- Commuter campus in very large city
- 20,459 degree-seeking undergraduates: 12% part-time, 60% women, 17% international
- 8,460 degree-seeking graduate students
- 54% of applicants admitted
- 86% graduate within 6 years

**General.** Founded in 1821. In addition to main campus, McGill maintains Macdonald Campus (20 miles west of downtown Montreal campus), which occupies 1,600 acres on western tip of island. **Degrees:** 4,333 bachelor's awarded; master's, doctoral, first professional offered. **Calendar:** Semester, limited summer session. **Full-time faculty:** 1,680 total; 95% have terminal degrees, 29% women. **Part-time faculty:** 859 total; 40% have terminal degrees, 47% women. **Class size:** 36% < 20, 28% 20-39, 7% 40-49, 19% 50-99, 11% >100. **Special facilities:** Museum of Canadian history, museum of natural history, entomological museum and research laboratory, ecomuseum, Canadian architecture collection, arboretum, nature reserve, herbarium, Canadian history archives, arctic research station, subarctic research station, sound recording studio.

**Freshman class profile.** 20,391 applied, 11,082 admitted, 4,921 enrolled.

| Mid 50% test scores | | | |
|---|---|---|---|
| SAT critical reading: | 640-740 | GPA 3.0-3.49: | 44% |
| SAT math: | 640-720 | GPA 2.0-2.99: | 1% |
| SAT writing: | 650-720 | Return as sophomores: | 92% |
| ACT composite: | 29-31 | Out-of-state: | 39% |
| GPA 3.50 or higher: | 55% | Live on campus: | 48% |
| | | International: | 18% |

**Basis for selection.** GED not accepted. School achievement record, grades in prerequisite courses, test scores most important. Advanced Placement (AP) results, class rank, recommendations also considered. Generally, minimum of 3.3 high school GPA required. For demonstration of English proficiency, TOEFL, Michigan, or IELTS acceptable. SAT or ACT required for U.S. students, optional for Canadian. Audition required of music majors. Portfolio required of architecture majors. Language tests required for TESL education programs. **Homeschooled:** Statement describing homeschool structure and mission, transcript of courses and grades, letter of recommendation (nonparent) required. Description should include comprehensive list of all texts (and editions) studied, personal statement from applicant and separate statement from home educator. In some cases, further information and/or interview(s) with admissions officer, associate dean, or program director may be required. **Learning Disabled:** No special admission requirements, no specific allowances. Students not asked questions about disabilities in admissions application. Students free to add extenuating circumstances information with application.

**High school preparation.** 15 units recommended. Recommended units include English 4, mathematics 4, social studies 1, history 1, science 3 (laboratory 3) and foreign language 3. 15-20 total recommended academic units; 3 or more combined recommended units for social studies and history. High school requirements vary according to program.

**2007-2008 Annual costs.** Costs reported in Canadian dollars. Full-time tuition for Quebec residents $1,768, for other Canadian students $5,141, for international students $13,965 to $15,420 depending on program. Required fees start at $1,232 and range upward depending on program. Room and board $8,796 to $11,770. Per-credit-hour charges for Quebec residents $59, for other Canadian students $171, for international students $466 to $514 depending on program. Compulsory health insurance for international students $639 (single), $1,794 (dependent), and $3,408 (family). Books and supplies $1,000 and transportation (public transit system) $396. Other expenses estimated at $2,000.

**2006-2007 Financial aid.** All financial aid based on need. 36% of total undergraduate aid awarded as scholarships/grants, 64% as loans/jobs. **Additional information:** McGill offers awards ranging in value from $3,000 renewable to $10,000 renewable and based on outstanding academic achievement or combination of outstanding academic achievement and leadership qualities. Finalists for scholarships valued at over $5,000 may be interviewed. Students who meet following eligibility conditions may apply for entrance awards: must be entering a university for the first time to undertake full-time undergraduate degree program; must be in top 5% of class based on last 2 years of full-time studies.

**Application procedures. Admission:** Closing date 1/15 (postmark date). $80 fee. Application may be submitted online. Admission notification on a rolling basis beginning on or about 1/15. Must reply by May 1 or within 3 week(s) if notified thereafter. Reply by dates are later for CEGEP and Canadian high schools. **Financial aid:** Closing date 6/30. Institutional form required. Applicants notified on a rolling basis starting 3/1; must reply within 4 week(s) of notification.

**Academics.** Students permitted to submit papers and exams in French. **Special study options:** Accelerated study, combined bachelor's/graduate degree, cooperative education, cross-registration, distance learning, double major, ESL, exchange student, honors, independent study, internships, study abroad, teacher certification program, Washington semester. **Credit/placement by examination:** AP, CLEP, IB, institutional tests. 30 credit hours maximum toward bachelor's degree. Maximum 30 AP credits on 120-credit program. **Support services:** Learning center, pre-admission summer program, reduced course load, remedial instruction, study skills assistance, tutoring, writing center.

**Majors. Agriculture:** General, agronomy, animal sciences, business, economics, food science, horticulture, plant sciences, soil science. **Architecture:** Architecture. **Area/ethnic studies:** African, Canadian, Caribbean, East Asian, German, Hispanic-American/Latino/Chicano, Italian, Latin American, Near/Middle Eastern, regional, Russian/Slavic, Spanish/Iberian, women's. **Biology:** General, anatomy, animal behavior, aquatic, bacteriology, biochemistry, biomedical sciences, botany, cell/histology, cellular/anatomical, ecology, environmental, genetics, marine, microbiology, molecular, neuroanatomy, physiology, wildlife, zoology. **Business:** General, accounting, accounting/finance, entrepreneurial studies, finance, human resources, international, international finance, labor relations, management science, managerial economics, marketing, operations, organizational behavior. **Computer sciences:** General, computer science. **Conservation:** General, economics, environmental science, environmental studies, management/policy,

wildlife. **Education:** General, bilingual, biology, chemistry, early childhood, elementary, English, ESL, French, geography, health, history, mathematics, music, physical, physics, science, secondary, social science, social studies. **Engineering:** Agricultural, chemical, civil, computer, electrical, materials, mechanical, metallurgical, mining, software. **English:** English lit. **Family/consumer sciences:** Food/nutrition, human nutrition. **Foreign languages:** Classics, East Asian, French, German, Italian, linguistics, Russian, Spanish, translation. **Health:** Nursing (RN). **History:** General, Asian, Canadian history, European. **Interdisciplinary:** Biological/physical sciences, cognitive science, math/computer science, natural sciences, nutrition sciences. **Legal studies:** General. **Liberal arts:** Humanities. **Math:** General, applied, probability, statistics. **Parks/recreation:** Exercise sciences, health/fitness. **Philosophy/religion:** Judaic, philosophy, religion. **Physical sciences:** Analytical chemistry, atmospheric physics, atmospheric science, chemistry, geology, geophysics, hydrology, inorganic chemistry, organic chemistry, physics, planetary. **Psychology:** General. **Public administration:** Social work. **Social sciences:** Anthropology, economics, geography, international economic development, political science, sociology, urban studies. **Theology:** Religious ed, sacred music, theology. **Visual/performing arts:** Art history/conservation, dramatic, jazz, music history, music pedagogy, music performance, music theory/composition, piano/organ, stringed instruments, voice/opera.

**Most popular majors.** Biology 13%, business/marketing 12%, education 7%, engineering/engineering technologies 9%, health sciences 7%, psychology 6%, social sciences 16%.

**Computing on campus.** 3,797 workstations in dormitories, library, computer center, student center. Dormitories wired for high-speed internet access and linked to campus network. Commuter students can connect to campus network. Online course registration, online library, helpline, repair service, wireless network available.

**Student life. Freshman orientation:** Available. One-day campus-wide orientation session held at end of August; new students meet administrators, senior students from their programs. **Housing:** Guaranteed on-campus for freshmen. Coed dorms, single-sex dorms, apartments, substance-free housing available. $1,000 partly refundable deposit, deadline 6/15. Shared facilities houses: similar to cooperative housing but chores and costs not shared among students. **Activities:** Bands, choral groups, dance, drama, film society, international student organizations, literary magazine, music ensembles, musical theater, opera, radio station, student government, student newspaper, symphony orchestra, TV station, over 100 clubs, service groups, and independent student organizations with interests that include sports, social activities, religion and politics.

**Athletics. Intercollegiate:** Badminton, baseball M, basketball, cheerleading, cross-country, fencing, field hockey W, football (tackle) M, golf, ice hockey, lacrosse, rowing (crew), rugby, sailing, skiing, soccer, squash, swimming, synchronized swimming W, tennis, track and field, volleyball, wrestling. **Intramural:** Badminton, basketball, football (non-tackle), football (tackle) M, ice hockey, soccer, squash, table tennis, tennis, volleyball. **Team name:** Redmen, Martlets.

**Student services.** Adult student services, alcohol/substance abuse counseling, campus ministries, career counseling, services for economically disadvantaged, student employment services, financial aid counseling, health services, legal services, minority student services, on-campus daycare, personal counseling, placement for graduates, women's services. **Physically disabled:** Services for visually, speech, hearing impaired.

**Contact.** E-mail: admissions@mcgill.ca
Phone: (514) 398-3910 Fax: (514) 398-4193
Kim Bartlett, Director, Admissions and Recruitment, McGill University, 845 Sherbrooke Street West, Montreal, CN H3A-2T5

---

## Memorial University of Newfoundland

St. John's, Newfoundland, Canada     **CB member**
www.mun.ca     **CB code: 0885**

- Public 4-year university
- Commuter campus in small city
- 14,702 degree-seeking undergraduates: 14% part-time, 61% women
- 3,172 graduate students

**General.** Founded in 1925. Additional campus (Sir Wilfred Grenfell College) in Corner Brook, Newfoundland; campus in Harow, England. **Degrees:** 2,360 bachelor's awarded; master's, doctoral, first professional offered. **Calendar:** Trimester, limited summer session. **Full-time faculty:** 1,180 total; 34% women. **Part-time faculty:** 46 total; 30% women. **Special facilities:** Center for cold ocean resources engineering, botanical gardens, archaeology unit, ocean sciences center, flume tank, center for fisheries innovation.

**Basis for selection.** GED not accepted. School achievement in a university preparatory high school program most important. Non-native speakers of English must submit TOEFL, Michigan Test of English Proficiency (minimum score of 85), or other acceptable test, unless graduating from English-language high school. Interviews, auditions, and essay required of music, theater, and visual arts majors. Portfolio required of visual arts majors.

**High school preparation.** 16 units required. Required units include English 3, mathematics 3, social studies 1, science 2, foreign language 1 and academic electives 6.

**2007-2008 Annual costs.** Costs reported in Canadian dollars. Annual tuition for Canadians $2,550; for non-Canadians $8,800. Required fees $193. Room and board $5,936. Books/supplies: $700.

**Application procedures. Admission:** Closing date 3/1 (receipt date). $40 fee. Application may be submitted online. Admission notification on a rolling basis beginning on or about 4/30. Application fee $40 CAD for in-province residents, $80 CAD for out-of-province and international students. Housing deposit $200 CAD. **Financial aid:** Priority date 3/15; no closing date.

**Academics.** 3-year diplomas in fisheries and nautical science available from Marine Institute. **Special study options:** Accelerated study, cooperative education, distance learning, double major, ESL, exchange student, honors, internships, liberal arts/career combination, study abroad, teacher certification program. **Credit/placement by examination:** AP, CLEP, IB. **Support services:** Learning center, reduced course load, remedial instruction, study skills assistance, tutoring, writing center.

**Majors. Area/ethnic studies:** Canadian, regional, Russian/Slavic, women's. **Biology:** General, bacteriology, biochemistry, cell/histology, ecology, entomology, marine, parasitology. **Business:** Business admin, marketing. **Computer sciences:** General, computer science. **Conservation:** General, environmental studies, forestry. **Education:** General, adult/continuing, bilingual, biology, chemistry, curriculum, early childhood, elementary, French, history, music, physical, physics, reading, science, secondary, social science, social studies, special. **Engineering:** General, civil, electrical, marine, mechanical, ocean. **English:** Composition, English lit. **Foreign languages:** Classics, French, German, linguistics, Spanish. **Health:** Preop/surgical nursing. **History:** General. **Interdisciplinary:** Math/computer science, medieval/Renaissance, neuroscience, nutrition sciences. **Liberal arts:** Arts/sciences, humanities. **Math:** General, applied, statistics. **Parks/recreation:** General, facilities management. **Philosophy/religion:** Philosophy, religion. **Physical sciences:** Chemistry, geology, oceanography, physics. **Psychology:** General. **Social sciences:** Anthropology, archaeology, demography, economics, geography, political science, sociology. **Visual/performing arts:** General, dramatic, music history, music performance, music theory/composition, studio arts, theater design.

**Most popular majors.** Biology 6%, business/marketing 12%, education 21%, engineering/engineering technologies 6%, health sciences 11%, science technologies 7%.

**Computing on campus.** 850 workstations in dormitories, library, computer center. Dormitories wired for high-speed internet access and linked to campus network. Commuter students can connect to campus network. Online course registration, helpline, repair service, student web hosting, wireless network available.

**Student life. Freshman orientation:** Mandatory. Held a few days prior to start of classes. **Housing:** Coed dorms, single-sex dorms, special housing for disabled, apartments available. $500 nonrefundable deposit, deadline 5/31. **Activities:** Bands, choral groups, dance, drama, literary magazine, music ensembles, musical theater, radio station, student government, student newspaper, symphony orchestra, numerous clubs and societies available.

**Athletics. Intercollegiate:** Basketball, cross-country, diving, fencing, field hockey W, soccer, swimming, volleyball. **Intramural:** Badminton, basketball, boxing, cheerleading, cross-country, diving, fencing, field hockey W, ice hockey M, judo, racquetball, rifle, soccer, softball, squash, swimming, table tennis, tennis, volleyball, water polo, weight lifting M, wrestling. **Team name:** Seahawks.

**Student services.** Campus ministries, career counseling, student employment services, health services, on-campus daycare, personal counseling, placement for graduates, women's services. **Physically disabled:** Services for visually, speech, hearing impaired.

**Contact.** E-mail: admissions@mun.ca
Phone: (709) 737-4431 Fax: (709) 737-4893
Glenn Collins, Registrar, Memorial University of Newfoundland, Memorial University of Newfoundland, Admissions Office-Arts and Admin. Bldg. St. John's, Newfoundland, Canada, CN A1C-S7

## Simon Fraser University
**Burnaby, Canada**
www.sfu.ca

**CB member**
**CB code: 0999**

- Public 4-year university
- Commuter campus in very large city
- 21,796 degree-seeking undergraduates
- 5,044 graduate students
- SAT or ACT (ACT writing recommended) required
- 56% graduate within 6 years

**General.** Founded in 1965. Regionally accredited. Harbour Centre campus in downtown Vancouver; Surrey campus in Surrey, British Columbia. **Degrees:** 4,310 bachelor's awarded; master's, doctoral offered. **Location:** 9 miles from Vancouver, British Columbia. **Calendar:** Semester, extensive summer session. **Full-time faculty:** 911 total; 88% have terminal degrees, 34% women. **Class size:** 18% < 20, 40% 20-39, 12% 40-49, 15% 50-99, 14% >100. **Special facilities:** Climbing wall, child care facility, hyperbaric chamber, underwater laboratory, combative room, apiary, archaeology museum.

**Basis for selection.** GED not accepted. American high school students must have graduated with a GPA of 3.2 or higher, based on a combination of grade 11 and 12 academic courses and test scores; SAT score of 1200 (verbal and math), or ACT score of 26 with a minimum writing/essay subscore of 10. Other factors will be considered, such as rank in class and advanced academic courses. Those who meet our minimum admission standards and have demonstrated commitment or excellence in other endeavours, or who have succeeded in their studies in spite of difficult circumstances, may also gain admission via the Diverse Qualifications process. Applicants who have been required to withdraw from a recognized university are not eligible to apply. Campus visit recommended. Academic background, especially GPA, rank in class, and test scores most important. Canadian residents not required to submit SAT or ACT. Audition/interview may be required for school of contemporary arts. Applicants may submit personal information profile and at least one letter of reference. **Homeschooled:** Applicants must meet state high school graduation requirements.

**High school preparation.** 13 units required. Required units include English 4, mathematics 3, social studies 1, history 1, science 2 and foreign language 2.

**2007-2008 Annual costs.** Costs reported in Canadian dollars. Tuition per year for Canadian students $4,533; for non-Canadian students $14,532. Required fees $516. Per-credit-hour charges for Canadian students $151; for non-Canadian students $484. Full-time students may opt to attend 2 or 3 semesters in academic year. Room only is $3,808 to $4,738 (two semesters) depending on accommodation.

**Financial aid. Non-need-based:** Scholarships awarded for academics, art, athletics, leadership, minority status, music/drama, state residency.

**Application procedures. Admission:** Priority date 2/28; deadline 4/30 (receipt date). $45 fee ($100 out-of-state). Application must be submitted online. Admission notification 6/30. Admission notification on a rolling basis beginning on or about 1/15. Must reply by May 1 or within 3 week(s) if notified thereafter. Application fee of $100 (Canadian) if academic records originate outside of Canada. **Financial aid:** Priority date 7/1, closing date 11/15. Institutional form required.

**Academics. Special study options:** Cooperative education, distance learning, double major, exchange student, honors, independent study, study abroad, teacher certification program. **Credit/placement by examination:** AP, CLEP, IB. 60 credit hours maximum toward bachelor's degree. **Support services:** Learning center, study skills assistance, writing center.

**Majors. Area/ethnic studies:** Canadian, women's. **Biology:** General, biochemistry, molecular. **Business:** Actuarial science, business admin, management information systems. **Communications:** General. **Computer sciences:** General, information systems, programming. **Conservation:** General, environmental science, environmental studies. **Education:** General. **Engineering:** Science. **English:** English lit. **Foreign languages:** French, linguistics. **Health:** International public health. **History:** General. **Interdisciplinary:** Cognitive science, math/computer science, systems science. **Liberal arts:** Arts/sciences. **Math:** General, applied, statistics. **Parks/recreation:** Exercise sciences. **Philosophy/religion:** Philosophy. **Physical sciences:** Chemistry, physics, planetary. **Psychology:** General. **Social sciences:** Anthropology, archaeology, criminology, economics, geography, political science, sociology. **Visual/performing arts:** General, cinematography, dance, design, dramatic.

**Computing on campus.** 900 workstations in library, computer center, student center. Dormitories wired for high-speed internet access. Commuter students can connect to campus network. Online course registration, helpline, repair service, wireless network available.

**Student life. Freshman orientation:** Available, $20 fee. Depending on type of program, 1 or 2 days. **Housing:** Coed dorms, single-sex dorms, special housing for disabled, apartments available. $450 nonrefundable deposit. **Activities:** Dance, drama, film society, international student organizations, radio station, student government, student newspaper, First Nations student center, center for students with disabilities, crisis line, public interest research group, women's center, interfaith center, harassment resolution office, Canadian Federation of Students, student society.

**Athletics.** NAIA. **Intercollegiate:** Basketball, cross-country, diving, field hockey W, football (tackle) M, soccer, softball W, swimming, track and field, volleyball W, wrestling. **Intramural:** Badminton, basketball, football (non-tackle), soccer, softball, tennis, volleyball. **Team name:** The Clan.

**Student services.** Alcohol/substance abuse counseling, campus ministries, career counseling, financial aid counseling, health services, legal services, minority student services, on-campus daycare, personal counseling, women's services. **Physically disabled:** Services for visually, speech, hearing impaired.

**Contact.** E-mail: undergraduate-admissions@sfu.ca
Phone: (604) 291-3224 Fax: (778) 782-4969
Mehran Kiai, Director, Enrolment Services, Simon Fraser University, 8888 University Drive, Burnaby, CN

## University of Alberta
Edmonton, Canada

**CB member**
www.ualberta.ca

**CB code: 0963**

- Public 4-year university
- Commuter campus in very large city
- 30,579 degree-seeking undergraduates
- 6,369 graduate students

**General.** Founded in 1906. Regionally accredited. **Degrees:** 6,686 bachelor's awarded; master's, doctoral, first professional offered. **Location:** 180 miles from Calgary. **Calendar:** Semester, extensive summer session. **Full-time faculty:** 1,600 total. **Part-time faculty:** 1,000 total. **Special facilities:** Fine arts center, botanical gardens, research farm (including several agricultural research stations), field mission scanning electron microscope, professional development center, National Institute for Nanotechnology, heart institute.

**Basis for selection.** GED not accepted. Admission is based on completion of five appropriate Grade 12 subjects (faculty/program specific), including English. Applicant must present a competitive average for admission, with a minimum grade of 50% in each subject. Competitive averages range from 70-85%. SAT Subject Tests recommended. Auditions, portfolios, letters of intent/essays or interviews are required for several programs; however, admission to most programs is based solely on academic merit.

**High school preparation.** 3 units required. Required and recommended units include English 3, mathematics 3, social studies 3, history 3, science 3 (laboratory 3), foreign language 3 and academic electives 3. Specific course requirements vary depending on program.

**2007-2008 Annual costs.** Undergraduate tuition and required fees (most degree programs), Canadian citizens and permanent residents: $5,400. Undergraduate tuition and required fees (most degree programs) for non-Canadian citizens: $16,900. Standard double-occupancy on-campus room: $2,232; board (19 meals per week): $3,990. Figures, which cover expenses for full academic year, are in Canadian dollars. Books/supplies: $1,200. Personal expenses: $1,000.

**2006-2007 Financial aid. Additional information:** American students may use U.S. federal aid and student loans towards university tuition, but must apply for that aid in United States prior to attending university.

**Application procedures. Admission:** Closing date 5/1 (postmark date). $100 fee. Application may be submitted online. Admission notification on a rolling basis beginning on or about 7/1. Must reply by 8/15. **Financial aid:** Closing date 5/1. Institutional form required. Applicants notified on a rolling basis; must reply by 8/15.

**Academics. Special study options:** Combined bachelor's/graduate degree, cooperative education, distance learning, double major, ESL, exchange student, honors, internships, student-designed major, study abroad, teacher certification program. **Credit/placement by examination:** AP, CLEP, IB. **Support services:** Learning center, pre-admission summer program, reduced course load, remedial instruction, study skills assistance, tutoring, writing center.

**Majors. Agriculture:** General, animal sciences, business, crop production, economics, food science, horticultural science. **Area/ethnic studies:** African, Central/Eastern European, East Asian, Latin American, Near/Middle Eastern, Scandinavian, Southeast Asian, women's. **Biology:** General, animal physiology, biochemistry, bioinformatics, botany, cell/histology, environmental, microbiology, molecular genetics, neurobiology/physiology, pharmacology, physiology, plant molecular, zoology. **Business:** General, accounting, actuarial science, business admin, communications, entrepreneurial studies, finance, human resources, international, international finance, management information systems, marketing, operations, organizational behavior, retailing, sales/distribution. **Computer sciences:** Computer science, programming. **Conservation:** General, forestry, wildlife. **Education:** Agricultural, art, biology, comparative, computer, drama/dance, early childhood, English, ESL, foreign languages, French, mathematics, middle, music, physical, physics, science, social studies, special, trade/industrial. **Engineering:** General, chemical, civil, computer, electrical, materials, mechanical, mechanics, mining, petroleum, physics, software. **English:** English lit. **Family/consumer sciences:** Clothing/textiles, family/community services, food/nutrition. **Foreign languages:** General, Chinese, classics, French, German, Italian, Japanese, Latin, linguistics, modern Greek, Romance, Scandinavian, Spanish. **Health:** Athletic training, clinical lab technology, dental hygiene, hematology, nursing (RN), occupational therapy assistant, predental, premedicine, preop/surgical nursing, prepharmacy, preveterinary. **History:** General. **Legal studies:** General. **Math:** General, computational, statistics. **Parks/recreation:** General, exercise sciences, sports admin. **Philosophy/religion:** Philosophy, religion. **Physical sciences:** Atmospheric science, chemistry, physics. **Protective services:** Criminal justice. **Psychology:** General. **Social sciences:** Anthropology, criminology, economics, geography, international relations, political science, sociology. **Visual/performing arts:** Dramatic, film/cinema, metal/jewelry, music history, music theory/composition, printmaking, studio arts, theater design.

**Most popular majors.** Business/marketing 10%, education 19%, engineering/engineering technologies 9%, health sciences 16%, liberal arts 19%, physical sciences 15%.

**Computing on campus.** 1,200 workstations in dormitories, library, computer center, student center. Dormitories wired for high-speed internet access and linked to campus network. Commuter students can connect to campus network. Online course registration, online library, helpline, wireless network available.

**Student life. Freshman orientation:** Available. Preregistration for classes offered. Two-day program includes peer advice presentations and campus tour. **Housing:** Coed dorms, single-sex dorms, special housing for disabled, apartments, fraternity/sorority housing available. $175 deposit. **Activities:** Bands, choral groups, dance, drama, film society, literary magazine, music ensembles, musical theater, opera, radio station, student government, student newspaper, symphony orchestra, more than 300 clubs available.

**Athletics. Intercollegiate:** Basketball, cross-country, field hockey W, football (tackle) M, gymnastics, ice hockey, soccer, swimming, tennis, track and field, volleyball, wrestling. **Intramural:** Badminton, baseball, basketball, cross-country, diving, football (tackle) M, gymnastics, ice hockey, judo, racquetball, rugby, skiing, soccer, squash, swimming, tennis, track and field, volleyball, water polo, wrestling. **Team name:** Golden Bears, Pandas.

**Student services.** Adult student services, alcohol/substance abuse counseling, campus ministries, career counseling, services for economically disadvantaged, student employment services, financial aid counseling, health services, legal services, minority student services, on-campus daycare, personal counseling, placement for graduates, women's services. **Physically disabled:** Services for visually, speech, hearing impaired. **Learning disabled:** Comprehensive services available.

**Contact.** Phone: (780) 492-3113 Fax: (780) 492-7172
Ada Schmude, Interim Associate Registrar, University of Alberta, Administration Building, Room 120, Edmonton, CN T6G 2-M7

## University of British Columbia
Vancouver, Canada

**CB member**
www.welcome.ubc.ca

**CB code: 0965**

- Public 4-year university
- Commuter campus in very large city
- 27,598 degree-seeking undergraduates: 29% part-time, 54% women
- 13,550 graduate students
- 60% of applicants admitted
- 70% graduate within 6 years

**General.** Founded in 1915. UBC comprises 18 faculties, 14 schools and 3 colleges across two major campuses (UBC Vancouver & UBC Okanagan) and two satellite campuses. Undergraduate students may study abroad at any one of 155 partner institutions in 42 countries. **Degrees:** 5,701 bachelor's awarded; master's, doctoral, first professional offered. **Location:** 6 miles from downtown Vancouver (Vancouver campus), 5 miles from downtown Kelowna (Okanagan campus). **Calendar:** Semester, limited summer session. **Full-time faculty:** 2,363 total. **Class size:** 33% < 20, 30% 20-39, 9% 40-49, 17% 50-99, 12% >100. **Special facilities:** Museum of anthropology (Canada's largest teaching museum), museum of geological sciences, botany collection and herbarium, botanical garden, Japanese garden, two astronomical observatories, performing arts centre, global issues centre, winter sports centre (venue for events of the 2010 Olympic Winter Games), world's largest cyclatron.

**Freshman class profile.** 18,773 applied, 11,343 admitted, 5,050 enrolled.

**Basis for selection.** GED not accepted. Admission competitive, with academic averages most important. Minimum requirement is strong B+ average; for science and engineering-based programs, strong A average likely to be required. Evaluation of those from American curriculum will be made on best 8 academic courses from junior and senior years. Applicants schooled out of Canada are encouraged to submit a Broader Based Admission package (including personal statement, references, and special academic and extracurricular achievements). Applicants must also meet specific program requirements. Additional criteria may be considered for secondary-school applicants who have studied outside Canada for at least 1 year before applying. Encourages applications from students completing enriched secondary school programs such as International Baccalaureate (IB), Advanced Placement (AP), General Certificate of Education (GCE), and French Baccalaureate. Generous first-year credit offered to students with high academic achievement in these programs. Standardized achievement test results must be submitted by applicants following US curriculum. Exceptions may be granted for countries where tests not available. Minimum scores for admissions consideration combined SAT score of 1500, or ACT Composite score of 24 (plus 8 on the Writing section). Interviews generally not required. Exceptions at UBC Vancouver are applications to School of Music (interview, audition, and/or portfolio required) and School of Business (supplemental application demonstrating documented leadership and accomplishment required). At UBC Okanagan application to Fine Arts program requires portfolio and letter of intent.

**High school preparation.** 8 units required. Required units include English 4, mathematics 3 and academic electives 16.

**2008-2009 Annual costs.** Tuition for international students (those who are not Canadian citizens or permanent residents) is $644 per credit for most programs. Tuition for Canadian citizens is $142 per credit for most programs. Student fees vary according to program, but are generally $650 to $750, which includes a transit pass for all local public transit. On-campus room and board varies according to accommodation selected, but costs an average of $7,500 per academic year. Amounts shown are in Canadian dollars. Books/supplies: $1,500.

**Financial aid. Non-need-based:** Scholarships awarded for academics, athletics. **Additional information:** Need-based financial aid from public funds is available only to Canadian citizens or permanent residents of Canada. Need-based financial aid to international students is limited.

**Application procedures. Admission:** Closing date 2/28 (postmark date). $60 fee. Application may be submitted online. Admission notification on a rolling basis beginning on or about 1/30. Students applying for on-campus student housing must accept offer of admission by May 31 in order to retain offer of housing placement. Students not required to accept admission offers by May 1. However, applicants receive admissions decision by May 1 deadline provided they submit all required supporting documents by March 31. **Financial aid:** Closing date 2/28. Institutional form required. Applicants notified by 4/14.

**Academics.** Several cross-disciplinary options available in first-year study. Undergraduate students encouraged to engage in research projects supported by annual Undergraduate Research Conference. **Special study options:** Combined bachelor's/graduate degree, cooperative education, cross-registration, distance learning, double major, dual enrollment of high school students, ESL, exchange student, honors, internships, liberal arts/career combination, student-designed major, study abroad, teacher certification program. **Credit/placement by examination:** AP, CLEP, IB. **Support services:** Learning center, pre-admission summer program, reduced course load, study skills assistance, tutoring, writing center.

**Majors. Agriculture:** General, agronomy, animal sciences, aquaculture, economics, food processing, food science, horticultural science, plant sciences, soil science. **Architecture:** Environmental design. **Area/ethnic studies:** Asian, Canadian, Central/Eastern European, East Asian, European, German, Hispanic-American/Latino/Chicano, Italian, Latin American, Russian/Slavic, Slavic, South Asian, Southeast Asian, Western European, women's. **Biology:** General, anatomy, animal physiology, bacteriology, biochemistry, biophysics, biotechnology, cell/histology, conservation, ecology, environmental, epidemiology, evolutionary, genetics, molecular, molecular biochemistry, pathology, pharmacology/toxicology, physiology, reproductive. **Business:** General, accounting, business admin, finance, human resources, international, international finance, international marketing, investments/securities, labor relations, management information systems, management science, managerial economics, marketing, operations, real estate, transportation. **Computer sciences:** General, a.i./robotics, computer science. **Conservation:** General, economics, environmental science, environmental studies, forest management, forest resources, forest sciences, forestry, management/policy, wood science. **Education:** General, elementary, middle, multi-level teacher, Native American, physical, secondary. **Engineering:** General, biomedical, chemical, civil, computer, electrical, environmental, forest, geological, materials, materials science, mechanical, mechanics, metallurgical, mining, operations research, physics, software. **English:** British lit, Canadian lit, creative writing, English lit. **Family/consumer sciences:** General, family/community services, food/nutrition, human nutrition. **Foreign languages:** Chinese, classics, French, German, Germanic, Italian, Japanese, Korean, Latin, linguistics, Native American, Portuguese, Romance, Slavic, South Asian, Spanish, Urdu. **Health:** Athletic training, clinical lab assistant, community health, dental hygiene, nurse midwife, nursing (RN), occupational health, preveterinary. **History:** General. **Interdisciplinary:** Ancient studies, biological/physical sciences, classical/archaeology, cognitive science, medieval/Renaissance, neuroscience, nutrition sciences. **Legal studies:** General. **Math:** General, applied, statistics. **Parks/recreation:** Exercise sciences, facilities management, health/fitness, sports admin. **Philosophy/religion:** Philosophy, religion. **Physical sciences:** Astronomy, atmospheric science, chemistry, geology, geophysics, oceanography, physics, planetary, theoretical physics. **Psychology:** General. **Public administration:** Social work. **Science technology:** Biological. **Social sciences:** Anthropology, archaeology, Canadian government, economics, geography, international relations, political science, sociology. **Transportation:** General. **Visual/performing arts:** General, art, art history/conservation, cinematography, conducting, dramatic, film/cinema, music history, music performance, music theory/composition, musicology, piano/organ, stringed instruments, theater arts management, theater design, voice/opera.

**Computing on campus.** Dormitories wired for high-speed internet access and linked to campus network. Commuter students can connect to campus network. Online course registration, online library, helpline, repair service, wireless network available.

**Student life. Freshman orientation:** Available. Preregistration for classes offered. 3 different orientation programs: GALA International Orientation, 3-day event held during week before start of winter term; Parents Orientation, on Sunday before start of term; IMAGINE UBC (Vancouver) and CREATE (UBC Okanagan), official welcome and orientation experience, on first day of winter term. **Housing:** Guaranteed on-campus for freshmen. Coed dorms, single-sex dorms, apartments, fraternity/sorority housing available. $50 deposit, deadline 5/1. Cultural theme houses in partnership with universities in Japan, Korea, and Mexico available. **Activities:** Bands, choral groups, dance, drama, film society, literary magazine, music ensembles, musical theater, opera, radio station, student government, student newspaper, symphony orchestra, TV station, over 250 clubs, societies, and other groups.

**Athletics.** NAIA. **Intercollegiate:** Baseball M, basketball, cross-country, field hockey, football (tackle) M, golf, ice hockey, rowing (crew), rugby, soccer, swimming, track and field, volleyball. **Intramural:** Badminton, basketball, cheerleading, cross-country, football (non-tackle), ice hockey, judo, racquetball, skiing, soccer, softball, squash, swimming, tennis, triathlon, volleyball, water polo, wrestling M. **Team name:** Thunderbirds.

**Student services.** Alcohol/substance abuse counseling, campus ministries, career counseling, student employment services, financial aid counseling, health services, minority student services, on-campus daycare, personal counseling, placement for graduates, women's services. **Physically disabled:** Services for visually, speech, hearing impaired.

**Contact.** Phone: (604) 822-8999 Toll-free number: (877) 272-1422 Fax: (604) 822-9858
Denise Lauritano, Assistant Registrar, International Undergraduate Admissions, University of British Columbia, 2016 - 1874 East Mall, Vancouver, CN V6T 1-1

---

## University of Manitoba
**Winnipeg, Canada**
www.umanitoba.ca

CB member
CB code: 0973

- Public 4-year university
- Commuter campus in very large city
- 23,062 degree-seeking undergraduates

**General.** Founded in 1877. **Degrees:** 4,165 bachelor's awarded; master's, doctoral, first professional offered. **Location:** 10 miles from downtown Winnipeg. **Calendar:** Semester, limited summer session. **Full-time faculty:** 1,300 total. **Part-time faculty:** 1,600 total. **Special facilities:** Planetarium.

**Freshman class profile.** 8,300 applied, 6,860 admitted, 4,830 enrolled.

**Basis for selection.** Open admission, but selective for some programs.

**High school preparation.** 28 units required.

**2007-2008 Annual costs.** Typically, Canadian residents pay $111 per credit hour, while non-residents pay $306; however, per-credit-hour charges vary depending upon area of study. Figures are reported in Canadian dollars.

**Application procedures. Admission:** Priority date 12/3; deadline 2/22. $90 fee. Application may be submitted online.

**Academics. Special study options:** Combined bachelor's/graduate degree, cooperative education, distance learning, double major, ESL, honors, independent study, internships, liberal arts/career combination, study abroad, teacher certification program, weekend college. **Credit/placement by examination:** CLEP, IB. 30 credit hours maximum toward bachelor's degree. **Support services:** Learning center, reduced course load, study skills assistance.

**Majors. Agriculture:** General, agribusiness operations, agronomy, animal health, animal nutrition, animal sciences, business, dairy, economics, farm/ranch, food science, horticultural science, ornamental horticulture, plant breeding, plant protection, plant sciences, poultry, soil science. **Architecture:** Environmental design. **Area/ethnic studies:** Asian, Canadian, Central/Eastern European, Latin American, Near/Middle Eastern, Russian/Slavic, women's. **Biology:** Bacteriology, biochemistry, botany, cell/histology, ecology, entomology, genetics, molecular, pathology, pharmacology, plant pathology, plant physiology, zoology. **Business:** Accounting, actuarial science, business admin, finance, international, labor relations, market research. **Computer sciences:** General, computer science, data processing, information systems, programming, systems analysis. **Conservation:** General, environmental studies. **Education:** General, adult ed admin, business, curriculum, early childhood, elementary, ESL, family/consumer sciences, foundations, instructional media, leadership, middle, multi-level teacher, music, physical, secondary, special, technology/industrial arts. **Engineering:** General, agricultural, civil, computer, electrical, materials science, mechanical. **English:** American lit, British lit, composition, creative writing, English lit. **Family/consumer sciences:** General, clothing/textiles, family/community services, food/nutrition. **Foreign languages:** Biblical, classics, comparative lit, French, German, Hebrew, Italian, linguistics, modern Greek, Russian, Spanish. **Health:** Athletic training, dental hygiene, nursing (RN), occupational therapy, physical therapy. **History:** General. **Interdisciplinary:** Behavioral sciences, gerontology, global studies, math/computer science, medieval/Renaissance, nutrition sciences. **Legal studies:** General. **Math:** General, applied, statistics. **Parks/recreation:** General, exercise sciences, health/fitness, sports admin. **Philosophy/religion:** Judaic, philosophy, religion. **Physical sciences:** Astronomy, chemistry, geology, physics. **Psychology:** General, clinical, counseling, educational. **Public administration:** General, social work. **Social sciences:** Anthropology, criminology, economics, geography, political science, sociology. **Visual/performing arts:** Art, art history/conservation, commercial/advertising art, dramatic, film/cinema, interior design, music history, music performance, music theory/composition, piano/organ, studio arts, theater history, voice/opera.

**Computing on campus.** 392 workstations in library, computer center. Commuter students can connect to campus network. Online course registration, online library, helpline, repair service, student web hosting available.

**Student life. Freshman orientation:** Mandatory. **Activities:** Bands, choral groups, dance, drama, music ensembles, radio station, student government, student newspaper, symphony orchestra.

**Athletics. Intercollegiate:** Basketball, cross-country, diving, field hockey W, football (tackle) M, gymnastics, ice hockey, skiing, swimming, synchronized swimming W, tennis, track and field, volleyball, weight lifting M, wrestling. **Intramural:** Archery, basketball, cross-country, diving, field hockey W, football (non-tackle) M, handball, ice hockey, judo M, racquetball, soccer, squash, swimming, tennis, volleyball. **Team name:** Bisons.

**Student services.** Adult student services, alcohol/substance abuse counseling, campus ministries, career counseling, student employment services, financial aid counseling, health services, legal services, on-campus daycare, personal counseling, placement for graduates. **Physically disabled:** Services for visually, speech, hearing impaired.

**Contact.** E-mail: admissions@umanitoba.ca
Phone: (204) 474-8808 Fax: (204) 474-7554
Iris Tougas, Director of Admissions, University of Manitoba, 424
University Centre, Winnipeg, CN R3T 2-N2

## University of Toronto
Toronto, Canada
www.utoronto.ca/         CB member

- Public 4-year university
- Commuter campus in very large city
- 58,182 undergraduates
- 17,267 graduate students
- 67% of applicants admitted
- SAT or ACT with writing, SAT Subject Tests, application essay required
- 86% graduate within 6 years

**General. Degrees:** 8,053 bachelor's awarded; master's, doctoral, first professional offered. **Location:** 95 miles from Buffalo, NY. **Calendar:** Semester, limited summer session. **Full-time faculty:** 2,719 total; 87% have terminal degrees, 32% women. **Part-time faculty:** 288 total. **Special facilities:** Greenhouses, observatory, university-operated art galleries and theatres, teaching hospitals, and 150-acre farm.

**Freshman class profile.** 59,943 applied, 39,948 admitted, 12,423 enrolled.

**Basis for selection.** Typically, applicants who are competitive for admission to the University of Toronto are among the top third of their class. Only those applicants who have attained a high level of academic achievement in these qualifications and who present credits to satisfy any prerequisites of specific courses or programs in which they intend to enroll will be admitted. The Faculty of Arts and Science St. George campus, University of Toronto Mississauga, University of Toronto Scarborough, the Faculty of Music, and the Faculty of Physical Education and Health/Kinesiology will consider applications from students in the USA and other countries who have completed or who are completing 12th grade in an accredited high school; such applicants must present high scores in SAT Reasoning or ACT examinations including the Writing Test component and at least three SAT Subject Tests or AP/IB subjects appropriate to their proposed area of study. Scores below 500 in any part of the SAT Reasoning or SAT Subject Tests are not acceptable. Many programs require higher scores. Students seeking admission to science or business/commerce programs are strongly advised to complete AP Calculus (AB or BC) or IB Mathematics (HL or SL or Math Methods with Calculus option). Student profiles required for some programs. **Homeschooled:** Statement describing homeschool structure and mission, transcript of courses and grades required. Application should include course outlines, textbooks and method of evaluation used, samples of written work, relevant details of any independent evaluations or assessments; results of standardized tests may also be considered. **Learning Disabled:** Students can send a letter with supporting documentation.

**2007-2008 Annual costs.** Tuition/fees: $18,640. Books/supplies: $1,000.

**Financial aid.** All financial aid based on need.

**Application procedures. Admission:** Closing date 3/1 (receipt date). $105 fee. Application may be submitted online. Admission notification 5/1. Admission notification on a rolling basis beginning on or about 3/1. Must reply by 5/28. Application deadlines vary by program.

**Academics. Special study options:** Combined bachelor's/graduate degree, cooperative education, double major, ESL, exchange student, honors, independent study, internships, student-designed major, study abroad, teacher certification program. **Credit/placement by examination:** AP, CLEP, IB, SAT, ACT, institutional tests. **Support services:** Learning center, preadmission summer program, reduced course load, study skills assistance, tutoring, writing center.

**Majors. Agriculture:** Animal sciences, food science, plant sciences. **Architecture:** Architecture, environmental design, history/criticism, interior, landscape, urban/community planning. **Area/ethnic studies:** African, African-American, American, Asian, Canadian, Caribbean, Central/Eastern European, Chinese, East Asian, European, French, gay/lesbian, German, Italian, Latin American, Native American, Near/Middle Eastern, Polish, Russian/Slavic, Slavic, Spanish/Iberian, Ukraine, women's. **Biology:** General, anatomy, animal behavior, animal physiology, biochemistry, Biochemistry/biophysics and molecular biology, biomedical sciences, biophysics, biotechnology, botany, cell physiology, cellular/anatomical, ecology, genetics, microbiology, molecular, molecular biochemistry, molecular biophysics, molecular pharmacology, neurobiology/physiology, pharmacology, pharmacology/toxicology, plant pathology, plant physiology, toxicology, zoology. **Business:** General. **Communications:** General, digital media, health, journalism, media studies, organizational. **Communications technology:** General. **Computer sciences:** General, a.i./robotics, applications programming, computer graphics, computer science, data entry, data processing, information systems, information technology, networking, programming, security, systems analysis, vendor certification, web page design, webmaster. **Conservation:** General, environmental science, environmental studies. **Education:** General, adult/continuing, art, biology, business, chemistry, computer, drama/dance, elementary, English, ESL, foreign languages, French, geography, German, gifted/talented, health, health occupations, history, kindergarten/preschool, Latin, mathematics, middle, multi-level teacher, music, physical, physics, science, secondary, social science, social studies, Spanish, speech, teacher assistance. **Engineering:** General, aerospace, agricultural, biomedical, chemical, civil, computer, environmental, industrial, materials, mechanical, mechanics, physics, science. **English:** American lit, British lit, Canadian lit, creative writing, English lit. **Foreign languages:** General, African, ancient Greek, Arabic, Biblical, Celtic, Chinese, classics, comparative lit, Czech, East Asian, French, German, Germanic, Hebrew, Hindi, Italian, Japanese, Korean, Latin, linguistics, Polish, Portuguese, Romance, Russian, Serbo-Croatian, Slavic, Slovak, South Asian, Southeast Asian, Spanish, Ukrainian. **Interdisciplinary:** Accounting/computer science, ancient studies, behavioral sciences, biological/physical sciences, classical/archaeology, cognitive science, global studies, intercultural, math/computer science, medieval/Renaissance, natural sciences, neuroscience, nutrition sciences, peace/conflict. **Liberal arts:** Arts/sciences, humanities. **Math:** General, probability, statistics. **Parks/recreation:** Exercise sciences, health/fitness. **Philosophy/religion:** Buddhist, Christian, ethics, Islamic, Judaic, philosophy, religion. **Physical sciences:** General, applied physics, astronomy, astrophysics, chemistry, forensic chemistry, organic chemistry, paleontology, physics, planetary. **Psychology:** General, child, clinical, cognitive, community, comparative, developmental, educational, environmental, family, forensic, medical, social. **Social sciences:** General, anthropology, applied economics, archaeology, Canadian government, criminology, economics, geography, international economic development, international economics, international relations, physical anthropology, political science, sociology, U.S. government, urban studies. **Theology:** Religious ed, theology. **Visual/performing arts:** General, acting, art, art history/conservation, dramatic, film/cinema, jazz, music history, music performance, music theory/composition, play/screenwriting, stringed instruments, studio arts, theater history, voice/opera.

**Computing on campus.** Dormitories wired for high-speed internet access and linked to campus network. Commuter students can connect to campus network. Online course registration, online library, helpline, repair service, student web hosting, wireless network available.

**Student life. Freshman orientation:** Available, $100 fee. Usually held the week before classes begin. **Housing:** Guaranteed on-campus for freshmen. Coed dorms, single-sex dorms, special housing for disabled, apartments, cooperative housing, substance-free housing available. $600 nonrefundable deposit, deadline 6/15. **Activities:** Bands, campus ministries, choral groups, dance, drama, film society, international student organizations, literary magazine, music ensembles, Model UN, musical theater, opera, radio station, student government, student newspaper, symphony orchestra, TV station.

**Athletics. Intercollegiate:** Badminton, baseball M, basketball, cross-country, fencing, field hockey W, football (non-tackle) M, football (tackle) M, golf, ice hockey, lacrosse, rowing (crew), rugby M, skiing, soccer, softball W, swimming, synchronized swimming W, tennis, track and field, volleyball, water polo, wrestling M. **Intramural:** Badminton, baseball M, basketball, cross-country, fencing, field hockey W, football (non-tackle) M, football (tackle) M, golf, ice hockey, lacrosse, rowing (crew) M, rugby M, skiing, soccer, softball W, swimming, tennis, track and field, volleyball, water polo, wrestling M. **Team name:** Varsity Blues.

**Student services.** Adult student services, alcohol/substance abuse counseling, campus ministries, career counseling, services for economically disadvantaged, student employment services, financial aid counseling, health services, legal services, minority student services, on-campus daycare, personal counseling, placement for graduates, women's services. **Physically disabled:** Services for visually, speech, hearing impaired. **Learning disabled:** Comprehensive services available.

**Contact.** Phone: (416) 978-8342
University of Toronto, 315 Bloor Street West, Toronto, CN

# Egypt

---

**American University in Cairo**
Cairo, Egypt
www.aucegypt.edu

CB member
CB code: 0903

- Private 4-year university
- Commuter campus in very large city
- 4,229 degree-seeking undergraduates: 10% part-time, 52% women
- 1,093 degree-seeking graduate students
- 60% of applicants admitted
- Application essay required
- 83% graduate within 6 years

**General.** Founded in 1919. Regionally accredited. Language of instruction is English; 75% of degree-seeking students must be of Egyptian nationality. **Degrees:** 833 bachelor's awarded; master's offered. **Location:** Center of Cairo. **Calendar:** Semester, extensive summer session. **Full-time faculty:** 352 total; 67% have terminal degrees, 49% women. **Part-time faculty:** 298 total; 59% have terminal degrees, 49% women. **Class size:** 59% < 20, 35% 20-39, 5% 40-49, less than 1% 50-99. **Special facilities:** Located near Cairo Museum (world's largest collection of Egyptian antiquities); many historical sites representing Pharonic, Greco-Roman, Coptic (early Christian) and early Moslem periods in the immediate vicinity.

**Freshman class profile.** 2,323 applied, 1,385 admitted, 1,046 enrolled.

| Mid 50% test scores | | | |
|---|---|---|---|
| SAT critical reading: | 400-500 | GPA 3.50 or higher: | 51% |
| SAT math: | 500-600 | GPA 3.0-3.49: | 25% |
| SAT writing: | 460-550 | GPA 2.0-2.99: | 24% |
| | | Return as sophomores: | 93% |

**Basis for selection.** Undergraduate degree applicants from the United States expected to have completed college preparatory (academic) high school program and to have taken SAT; minimum combined score of 1000 (exclusive of Writing) required. Arab students must take Thanawiya 'Amma; minimum score of 75% required. CE/GCSE/IGCSE certificates will also be considered for admission. SAT Subject Tests required for applicants who have graduated from American-style high schools with less than 3 semesters in residence. **Homeschooled:** Statement describing homeschool structure and mission, transcript of courses and grades, state high school equivalency certificate required.

**High school preparation.** Recommended units include English 3, mathematics 3, social studies 3, science 2 and foreign language 2. One unit fine arts recommended.

**2007-2008 Annual costs.** Tuition/fees: $16,674. Room only: $3,400. Books/supplies: $700. Personal expenses: $2,200.

**2007-2008 Financial aid. Need-based:** 615 full-time freshmen applied for aid; 500 were judged to have need; 368 of these received aid. **Non-need-based:** Scholarships awarded for academics, art, athletics, leadership, music/drama, state residency. **Additional information:** Up to 15 fellowships awarded annually in teaching English as a foreign language. To facilitate attendance of year-abroad U.S. students from state universities, tuition equivalent to difference between university's tuition and out-of-state tuition offered. Up to 20 graduate fellowships for qualified applicants from African countries. On-campus jobs paid at local (Egyptian) wage scale. Non-Egyptian nationals placing in top quarter of applicant pool for the year may receive $4,000 per year Academic Achievement Scholarship; those in the second or third quartile may receive $2,000 per year.

**Application procedures. Admission:** Priority date 3/1; deadline 5/15 (receipt date). $50 fee. Application may be submitted online. Admission notification on a rolling basis beginning on or about 7/7. **Financial aid:** Closing date 5/15. Institutional form required. Applicants notified by 10/15.

**Academics. Special study options:** Double major, ESL, independent study, liberal arts/career combination, study abroad. **Credit/placement by examination:** CLEP, IB, SAT, institutional tests. 30 credit hours maximum toward bachelor's degree. **Support services:** Learning center, reduced course load, remedial instruction, study skills assistance, writing center.

**Majors. Area/ethnic studies:** Near/Middle Eastern. **Biology:** General. **Business:** Accounting, actuarial science, business admin. **Communications:** Journalism. **Computer sciences:** General. **Engineering:** Architectural, computer, construction, electrical, mechanical, petroleum. **English:** English lit. **Foreign languages:** Arabic, comparative lit. **History:** General, Asian. **Math:** General. **Philosophy/religion:** Philosophy. **Physical sciences:** Chemistry, physics. **Psychology:** General. **Social sciences:** Anthropology, archaeology, economics, political science, sociology. **Visual/performing arts:** Art, dramatic.

**Most popular majors.** Business/marketing 22%, communications/journalism 22%, computer/information sciences 8%, engineering/engineering technologies 17%, social sciences 20%.

**Computing on campus.** 840 workstations in dormitories, library, computer center. Dormitories wired for high-speed internet access and linked to campus network. Commuter students can connect to campus network. On-line course registration, online library, helpline, repair service available.

**Student life. Freshman orientation:** Available. **Policies:** Non-smoking campus. **Housing:** Single-sex dorms available. $300 deposit, deadline 6/30. 536 spaces available for international students; preference given to female students. **Activities:** Choral groups, dance, drama, film society, literary magazine, music ensembles, radio station, student government, student newspaper, African students association, community service society, Model United Nations, Model Arab League.

**Athletics. Intercollegiate:** Basketball, diving W, fencing, gymnastics, handball, rowing (crew), soccer M, squash, swimming, table tennis, tennis, track and field, volleyball, water polo M, wrestling M. **Intramural:** Basketball, soccer M, table tennis, tennis, volleyball.

**Student services.** Adult student services, career counseling, health services, personal counseling, placement for graduates.

**Contact.** E-mail: diskaros@aucnyo.edu
Phone: (212) 730-8800 ext. 223 Fax: (212) 730-1600
Ghada Hazem, Director of Admissions, American University in Cairo, 420 Fifth Avenue, Third Floor, New York, NY 10018-2729

# France

## American University of Paris

Paris, France
www.aup.edu                                    CB code: 0866

- Private 4-year university and liberal arts college
- Commuter campus in very large city
- 745 degree-seeking undergraduates: 5% part-time, 67% women
- 145 degree-seeking graduate students
- 69% of applicants admitted
- Application essay required
- 54% graduate within 6 years

**General.** Founded in 1962. Regionally accredited. **Degrees:** 170 bachelor's awarded; master's offered. **Calendar:** Semester, extensive summer session. **Full-time faculty:** 60 total; 80% have terminal degrees, 43% women. **Part-time faculty:** 70 total; 50% women. **Class size:** 60% < 20, 40% 20-39.

**Freshman class profile.** 565 applied, 388 admitted, 203 enrolled.

| Mid 50% test scores | | SAT math: | 520-640 |
|---|---|---|---|
| SAT critical reading: | 550-660 | Return as sophomores: | 70% |

**Basis for selection.** Applicants evaluated on basis of academic performance. Most important sources of information about academic achievements include academic transcripts of all secondary and/or university-level coursework, as well as applicable test scores such as SAT, ACT, and national exams. Non-English speakers are required to take TOEFL or TOEIC or IELTS. **Homeschooled:** Statement describing homeschool structure and mission, transcript of courses and grades, state high school equivalency certificate, interview, letter of recommendation (nonparent) required.

**High school preparation.** 18 units recommended. Recommended units include English 4, mathematics 3, social studies 3, history 2, science 2 (laboratory 1) and foreign language 3.

**2007-2008 Annual costs.** Full-time tuition for academic year: 22,200 euros; housing costs vary, and all accommodations are off-campus. Books/supplies: $1,200.

**2006-2007 Financial aid. Need-based:** 84% of total undergraduate aid awarded as scholarships/grants, 16% as loans/jobs. **Non-need-based:** Scholarships awarded for academics.

**Application procedures. Admission:** Closing date 3/15 (postmark date). $65 fee. Application may be submitted online. Admission notification on a rolling basis. Must reply by May 1 or within 2 week(s) if notified thereafter. **Financial aid:** No deadline. FAFSA, institutional form required.

**Academics. Special study options:** Cooperative education, cross-registration, double major, exchange student, honors, independent study, internships, study abroad. **Credit/placement by examination:** AP, CLEP, IB, institutional tests. 30 credit hours maximum toward bachelor's degree. **Support services:** Reduced course load, study skills assistance, tutoring, writing center.

**Majors. Area/ethnic studies:** European, French. **Business:** Finance, international. **Communications:** General. **Computer sciences:** General, computer science. **Foreign languages:** General, comparative lit, French. **History:** General. **Psychology:** General. **Social sciences:** Economics, international relations. **Visual/performing arts:** Art history/conservation, film/cinema.

**Most popular majors.** Business/marketing 25%, communications/journalism 24%, social sciences 25%, visual/performing arts 7%.

**Computing on campus.** 120 workstations in library, computer center, student center. Online library, wireless network available.

**Student life. Freshman orientation:** Mandatory, $480 fee. Held week before classes begin. Students assisted in housing process, receive academic advising, attend workshops on living in Paris. **Housing:** $550 nonrefundable deposit, deadline 5/1. **Activities:** Choral groups, dance, drama, film society, literary magazine, music ensembles, musical theater, student government, student newspaper.

**Student services.** Career counseling, financial aid counseling, personal counseling.

**Contact.** E-mail: usoffice@aup.edu
Phone: (303) 757-6333 Fax: (303) 757-6444
Candace McLaughlin, Vice President and Dean of Student Services, American University of Paris, 950 South Cherry Street, Suite 210, Denver, CO 80246

## Parsons Paris School of Design

Paris, France
www.parsons-paris.com

- Private 4-year visual arts and business college
- Very large city
- 134 degree-seeking undergraduates: 87% women

**General.** While the legal structure of the school is that of an independent organization, the academic program of Parsons Paris is coordinated with that of Parsons The New School for Design in New York. **Degrees:** 21 bachelor's awarded. **Calendar:** Semester, limited summer session. **Full-time faculty:** 2 total. **Part-time faculty:** 70 total.

**Basis for selection.** A large part of the Admissions Committee's decision is based upon evaluation of the portfolio and home exam. A prospective student's potential for artistic achievement is one of the most important criteria in evaluating candidates for admission.

**2007-2008 Annual costs.** Tuition/fees: $28,332.

**Application procedures. Admission:** Closing date 7/1. $75 fee. **Financial aid:** Closing date 5/1.

**Academics. Credit/placement by examination:** CLEP.

**Majors. Visual/performing arts:** Design, fashion design, illustration, photography, studio arts.

**Contact.** E-mail: admissions@parsons-paris.com
Sara Krauskopf, Director of Admissions, Parsons Paris School of Design, 14 rue Letellier, Paris, FR

# Germany

## University of Karlsruhe
### Karlsruhe, Germany
www.university-karlsruhe.de

**CB member**
**CB code: 3592**

- Public 3-year university
- Small city
- 17,500 undergraduates
- 1,100 graduate students
- Application essay, interview required

**General.** Partnerships with industry; special internship arrangement and placement for graduates. **Calendar:** Semester, limited summer session. **Full-time faculty:** 300 total; 100% have terminal degrees, 3% women.

**Basis for selection.** GED not accepted. SAT or ACT recommended. **Homeschooled:** Statement describing homeschool structure and mission, transcript of courses and grades, state high school equivalency certificate, interview, letter of recommendation (nonparent) required. SAT is not mandatory, yet applicants might enhance their chances by adding this element to their application package. **Learning Disabled:** Successful completion of entrance examination prior to official enrollment.

**High school preparation.** Required units include mathematics 4, science 4 and computer science 4.

**Application procedures. Admission:** Priority date 4/15; deadline 7/15 (receipt date). No application fee. Admission notification 6/1. Admission notification on a rolling basis beginning on or about 3/1. Must reply by 7/31. Must reply by May 1 or within 4 week(s) if notified thereafter. Complete application file should be submitted by June 1st. After review of file, candidate is invited for interview; letters of admission are usually sent within four weeks following interview. The final enrollment decision is based on entrance examination. A preparatory course is offered starting mid-August of each year.

**Academics. Special study options:** Double major, dual enrollment of high school students, exchange student, internships, study abroad. **Credit/placement by examination:** CLEP, institutional tests. **Support services:** Pre-admission summer program, study skills assistance, tutoring, writing center.

**Majors. Architecture:** Architecture. **Biology:** General. **Communications:** Journalism. **Computer sciences:** General, information technology. **Engineering:** Electrical, mechanical. **Physical sciences:** Chemistry, geology, physics. **Social sciences:** Economics.

**Computing on campus.** PC or laptop required. 20 workstations in computer center. Dormitories wired for high-speed internet access and linked to campus network. Wireless network available.

**Student life. Freshman orientation:** Available. **Housing:** $400 fully refundable deposit, deadline 8/15.

**Contact.** E-mail: kappes@id.uni-karlsruhe.de
Phone: (721) 608-7880
Birgitta Kappes, Admissions Director, University of Karlsruhe, Schlossplatz 19, Karlsruhe, GE 76128

# Guatemala

## Universidad del Valle de Guatemala
### Guatemala City, Guatemala
www.uvg.edu.gt

**CB member**
**CB code: 3875**

- Private 5-year university and engineering college
- Commuter campus in very large city

**General. Calendar:** Semester.

**Annual costs/financial aid.** Need-based financial aid available to full-time and part-time students.

**Contact.** Phone: (502) 364-0336 ext. 453
Secretaria General, 18 Avenida 11-95 zona 15, Vista Hermosa III, Guatemala City, GT 01015

# Lebanon

## American University of Beirut
### Beirut, Lebanon
www.aub.edu.lb

**CB member**
**CB code: 0902**

- Private 4-year university
- Commuter campus in very large city
- 5,961 degree-seeking undergraduates: 2% part-time, 49% women
- 1,243 degree-seeking graduate students
- 74% of applicants admitted
- SAT required
- 84% graduate within 6 years; 15% enter graduate study

**General.** Regionally accredited. Most students are from the Arab world. **Degrees:** 1,328 bachelor's awarded; master's, doctoral, first professional offered. **Location:** In Beirut City. **Calendar:** Semester, extensive summer session. **Full-time faculty:** 406 total; 88% have terminal degrees, 37% women. **Part-time faculty:** 229 total; 36% have terminal degrees, 48% women. **Class size:** 32% < 20, 54% 20-39, 4% 40-49, 6% 50-99, 3% >100. **Special facilities:** Archaeological museum, geological museum, rare biological collection.

**Freshman class profile.** 3,556 applied, 2,635 admitted, 1,715 enrolled.

| Mid 50% test scores | | | |
|---|---|---|---|
| SAT critical reading: | 420-530 | GPA 2.0-2.99: | 42% |
| SAT math: | 560-670 | Rank in top quarter: | 54% |
| SAT writing: | 440-540 | Rank in top tenth: | 29% |
| GPA 3.50 or higher: | 17% | End year in good standing: | 90% |
| GPA 3.0-3.49: | 30% | Return as sophomores: | 92% |
| | | Live on campus: | 15% |

**Basis for selection.** Admission based on composite scores: 50% SAT (25% verbal, 25% math) and 50% standardized school grades. Holders of Lebanese, French and International Baccalaureate, among other regional governmental secondary diplomas, will be admittted directly into the sophomore class. SAT must be taken before January of the year preceding admissions. **Homeschooled:** Most applicants must take 3 SAT Subject Tests.

**2007-2008 Annual costs.** Tuition/fees: $11,093. Room only: $2,700. Books/supplies: $300. Personal expenses: $100.

**2006-2007 Financial aid. Need-based:** Average scholarship/grant was $2,449. 83% of total undergraduate aid awarded as scholarships/grants, 17% as loans/jobs. **Non-need-based:** Scholarships awarded for academics.

**Application procedures. Admission:** Priority date 11/30; deadline 1/15 (receipt date). $50 fee. Application may be submitted online. Admission notification on a rolling basis beginning on or about 4/30. Must reply by 7/27. Early action applicants must have a minimum SAT and must have been in top 40th percentile of their class for the past two years. **Financial aid:** Closing date 2/2. Institutional form required. Applicants notified by 5/30.

**Academics. Special study options:** Cross-registration, ESL, exchange student, honors, independent study, internships, liberal arts/career combination, study abroad, teacher certification program. **Credit/placement by examination:** AP, CLEP, IB, SAT, institutional tests. **Support services:** Learning center, remedial instruction, study skills assistance, tutoring, writing center.

**Majors. Agriculture:** General, food science, landscaping. **Architecture:** Architecture. **Biology:** General. **Business:** Business admin. **Computer sciences:** Computer science. **Education:** Elementary. **Engineering:** Civil, computer, electrical, mechanical. **Engineering technology:** Petroleum. **English:** English lit. **Foreign languages:** Arabic. **Health:** Clinical lab technology, dietetics, environmental health, nursing (RN). **History:** General. **Math:** General, statistics. **Philosophy/religion:** Philosophy. **Physical sciences:** Chemistry, geology, physics. **Psychology:** General. **Public administration:** General. **Social sciences:** Anthropology, archaeology, economics, political science, sociology. **Visual/performing arts:** Art history/conservation, graphic design, studio arts.

**Most popular majors.** Biology 12%, business/marketing 30%, engineering/engineering technologies 15%, social sciences 7%.

**Computing on campus.** 885 workstations in dormitories, library, computer center, student center. Dormitories wired for high-speed internet access and linked to campus network. Commuter students can connect to campus network. Online course registration, online library, helpline, repair service, student web hosting, wireless network available.

**Student life. Freshman orientation:** Mandatory. Preregistration for classes offered. Week-long program held in September, ten days before classes begin. **Policies:** Student code of conduct. Violations may be of an academic or non-academic nature. **Housing:** Guaranteed on-campus for freshmen. Single-sex dorms, substance-free housing available. $67 nonrefundable deposit, deadline 8/31. **Activities:** Choral groups, dance, drama, film society, international student organizations, music ensembles, Model UN, student government, student newspaper, Gulf club, Palestinian cultural club, Syrian cultural club, Jordanian cultural club, Lebanese Armenian heritage club, Lebanese Red Cross club, human rights & peace club, special support club for special people, women-s rights club, debate club.

**Athletics. Intercollegiate:** Badminton, basketball, boxing, cross-country, handball, rugby M, skiing, soccer, squash, swimming, table tennis, tennis, track and field, triathlon, volleyball, water polo M. **Intramural:** Badminton, basketball, boxing, cheerleading W, cross-country, handball, soccer, squash, swimming, table tennis, tennis, volleyball, weight lifting.

**Student services.** Alcohol/substance abuse counseling, career counseling, student employment services, financial aid counseling, health services, personal counseling, placement for graduates. **Physically disabled:** Services for visually, hearing impaired.

**Contact.** E-mail: admissions@aub.edu.lb
Phone: (961) 137-4374 ext. 2590 Fax: (961) 175-0775
Salim Kanaan, Director of Admissions, American University of Beirut, PO Box 11-0236, Beirut, LB

# Mexico

---

### Instituto Tecnologico Autonomo de Mexico
**Mexico City, Mexico**          **CB member**
www.itam.mx                      **CB code: 7144**

- Private 4-year university, business and engineering college
- Commuter campus in very large city
- 4,718 degree-seeking undergraduates

**General. Degrees:** 465 bachelor's awarded; master's, doctoral, first professional offered. **Location:** Southern part of Mexico City. **Calendar:** Semester, limited summer session. **Full-time faculty:** 479 total. **Part-time faculty:** 409 total.

**Basis for selection.** Open admission. High school records and admission test mandatory. **Homeschooled:** Complete high school diploma, minimum GPA, and admission test.

**2007-2008 Annual costs.** Undergraduates pay approximately 118,657 Mexican pesos for academic year.

**Application procedures. Admission:** No deadline. $54 fee, may be waived for applicants with need. Application must be submitted on paper. Admission notification on a rolling basis.

**Academics. Special study options:** Combined bachelor's/graduate degree, double major, exchange student, liberal arts/career combination, study abroad. **Credit/placement by examination:** AP, CLEP, IB, institutional tests. **Support services:** Writing center.

**Majors. Business:** Accounting, accounting/business management, actuarial science, business admin. **Communications:** Digital media. **Communications technology:** Computer typography. **Computer sciences:** General. **Engineering:** Computer. **Engineering technology:** General. **Interdisciplinary:** Science/society. **Legal studies:** General, prelaw. **Math:** Applied. **Social sciences:** Economics, international relations, political science.

**Computing on campus.** 140 workstations in computer center. Online library, wireless network available.

**Student life. Activities:** Choral groups, dance, drama, literary magazine, radio station, student newspaper.

**Athletics. Intercollegiate:** Baseball M, basketball, soccer, volleyball. **Team name:** Dragones.

**Student services.** Student employment services.

**Contact.** E-mail: admisiones@itam.mx
Phone: (5) 556-284156 Fax: (5) 554-904655
Cynthia Figueroa, Jefe de Admisiones, Instituto Tecnologico Autonomo de Mexico, Rio Hondo 1, Colonia Progreso Tizapan, Mexico City, MX

---

### Instituto Tecnologico y de Estudios Superiores de Occidente
**Tlaquepaque, Mexico**          **CB member**
www.iteso.mx                     **CB code: 7145**

- Private 4-year university, business and engineering college affiliated with Roman Catholic Church
- Commuter campus in very large city

**General. Location:** In metropolitan Guadalajara. **Calendar:** Semester.

**Annual costs/financial aid.** Tuition ranges from 880 to 904 Mexican pesos per credit hour.

**Contact.** Phone: (52) 333-6693535
Chief of the Admission Office, AP 31-175, Zapopan, MX 45090

---

### Universidad Anahuac
**México City, Mexico**          **CB member**
www.anahuac.mx                   **CB code: 7146**

- Private 6-year university affiliated with Roman Catholic Church
- Commuter campus in small city

**General. Founded** in 1964. **Location:** 5 miles from Mexico City. **Calendar:** Semester.

**Annual costs/financial aid.** Tuition per-credit-hour charge for most programs is $1,001, with required fees of $16,905 per semester; tuition per-credit-hour charge for degrees in tourism management, restaurant management, gastronomy and international hotel administration is $1,001, with required fees of $19,875 per semester. Tuition for programs in medicine and nutrition is $19,875 per semester, with required fees of $14,780 per semester. All figures are in Mexican pesos. Books/supplies: $200. Personal expenses: $550.

**Contact.** Phone: (5) 627-0210 ext. 8458
Director of Admissions, Av. Lomas Anahuac s/n, Mexico City, MX

---

### Universidad Autonoma de Aguascalientes
**Aguascalientes, Mexico**          **CB member**
www.uaa.mx                       **CB code: 7147**

- Public 4-year university
- Residential campus in very large city

**General. Founded** in 1974. Regionally accredited. **Location:** 319 miles from Mexico City. **Calendar:** Semester.

**Annual costs/financial aid.** Tuition and fee costs: 676 pesos for non-U.S. students; 17,424 pesos for U.S. students. Need-based financial aid available for full-time students.

**Contact.** Phone: (449) 910-7422
Jefe de Departamento de Control Escolar, Av. Universidad No. 940, Aguascalientes, MX 20100

## Universidad Autonoma de Coahuila
**Saltillo, Mexico**        **CB member**
**www.uadec.mx**        **CB code: 7148**

- Public 4-year university
- Very large city

**General. Calendar:** Semester.

**Annual costs/financial aid.** Tuition for residents, $780. Tuition for non-resident aliens, $1,710.

**Contact.** Phone: (844) 4-3-81729
Rector, Boulevard V. Carranza y Gonzalez, 25280 Saltillo, Coahuila, Mexico, MX

## Universidad de Monterrey
**San Pedro Garza Garcia, Mexico**
**www.udem.edu.mx**
       **CB member**

- Private 4-year university affiliated with Roman Catholic Church
- Residential campus in very large city
- 7,088 degree-seeking undergraduates: 57% women, 100% Hispanic American
- 416 degree-seeking graduate students
- 88% of applicants admitted
- SAT, application essay, interview required
- 54% graduate within 6 years; 2% enter graduate study

**General. Degrees:** 1,174 bachelor's awarded; master's, first professional offered. **Calendar:** Semester, limited summer session.

**Freshman class profile.** 3,359 applied, 2,970 admitted, 1,635 enrolled.

End year in good standing:    88%      **Return as sophomores:**    88%

**Basis for selection.** GED not accepted. High school record and standardized test scores most important. Minimum PAA score of 1000, with neither portion below 450. English, computer tests required. **Homeschooled:** Interview required.

**High school preparation.** PAA score of 1000 required, plus tests in English and computer literacy. Interview required for psychology, law, medical programs. Essay required of prospective law students.

**2007-2008 Annual costs.** Tuition for full semester: 37,620 Mexican pesos, plus required fees of 2,540 pesos for insurance. Non-Mexican applicants are subject to an additional fee of 5,643 pesos.

**Application procedures. Admission:** Closing date 8/1. $120 fee, may be waived for applicants with need. Application may be submitted online. Admission notification on a rolling basis.

**Academics. Special study options:** Distance learning. Business administration cooperative program in partnership with Athabasca University (Canada). **Credit/placement by examination:** CLEP.

**Majors. Architecture:** Architecture. **Business:** General, accounting, international, international finance, international marketing. **Communications:** General. **Computer sciences:** Information technology. **Education:** General. **Engineering:** Computer, industrial, mechanical, systems. **Liberal arts:** Humanities. **Psychology:** General. **Public administration:** General. **Social sciences:** General, economics, international relations, political science. **Visual/performing arts:** General, graphic design, industrial design.

**Student life. Activities:** Misiones al sur de Nuevo León (Galeana, Iturbide y Aramberri), Pasa tiempo con niños especiales, Sobrevive (Campamento extremo), Misiones solidarias, UDEM en el campo, UDEM en la Tarahumara, Misiones en Schoenstatt, Voluntariado, Misiones en Familia, Misiones para profesionistas.

**Contact.** E-mail: admisiones@udem.edu.mx
Phone: (81) 821-51010 Fax: (81) 821-51013
Jose Alvarez, Dean of Admissions, Universidad de Monterrey, Avenida Ignacio Morones Prieto, 4500 Pte., San Pedro Garza Garcia, NL, MX 66238

# Monaco

## International University of Monaco
**Monte-Carlo, Monaco**
**www.monaco.edu**

- For-profit 4-year university and business college
- Commuter campus in small city
- 143 degree-seeking undergraduates
- Application essay required

**General.** IUM comprises more than 50 nationalities among its students and faculty and has received top rankings for student diversity. **Degrees:** 61 bachelor's awarded; master's, doctoral offered. **Location:** 12 miles from Nice, France. **Calendar:** Trimester, limited summer session. **Full-time faculty:** 45 total. **Part-time faculty:** 29 total. **Special facilities:** Principality of Monaco features high-quality sports facilities, museums and other leisure activities.

**Freshman class profile.** 131 enrolled.

**Basis for selection.** IUM seeks to enroll students from wide range of backgrounds and nationalities. Students who show clear commitment to international education (may be demonstrated by travel experience or languages spoken) and leadership potential given priority. Students should also have high level of math preparation as degree programs require excellent quantitative skills. **Homeschooled:** Interview, letter of recommendation (non-parent) required.

**High school preparation.** Recommended units include mathematics 4 and foreign language 4.

**2007-2008 Annual costs.** Flat fee for all nationalities of 12,800 euros per academic year, over 3 years. One-time enrollment fee of 1,500 (euros) for freshmen. Housing costs range from 500 to 950 (euros) per month. If students live and pay rent in France, it is possible to receive housing subsidy from French government (approximately 120 euros per month). Books/supplies: $1,000.

**Financial aid. Non-need-based:** Scholarships awarded for academics, leadership.

**Application procedures. Admission:** Priority date 1/2; deadline 6/15 (postmark date). $150 fee. Application must be submitted on paper. Admission notification on a rolling basis. Admission must be accepted within 14 days of receiving offer.

**Academics.** One-on-one personalized academic counseling session with academic adviser before each term; high faculty to student ratio (1:8); small class size (fewer than 15 students per class). **Special study options:** Accelerated study, ESL, exchange student, internships, study abroad. **Credit/placement by examination:** CLEP. **Support services:** Reduced course load, study skills assistance, tutoring.

**Majors. Business:** Business admin.

**Computing on campus.** 100 workstations in library, computer center, student center. Commuter students can connect to campus network. Online library, helpline, repair service, wireless network available.

**Student life. Freshman orientation:** Mandatory. Preregistration for classes offered. Orientation held each year at Club Med, Opio, France. Students taken by bus to resort for intensive 3-day teambuilding session. **Housing:** Apartments available. **Activities:** Student government.

**Athletics. Intramural:** Basketball, golf, sailing, soccer, tennis.

**Student services.** Career counseling, student employment services, placement for graduates.

**Contact.** E-mail: info@monaco.edu
Phone: (377) 979-86994 Fax: (377) 920-52830
Gisele Dudognon, Director of Admissions, International University of Monaco, Admissions, Monte-Carlo, MC 98000

# Republic of Korea

**Contact.** E-mail: ysadms@yonsei.ac.kr
Phone: (822) 212-34131 Fax: (822) 364-2364
Eunkyung Kim, Admissions Officer, Yonsei University, 134 Shinchon-dong, Seodaemun-gu, Seoul, KR

# Singapore

## Yonsei University
Seoul, Republic of Korea
www.yonsei.ac.kr

**CB member**
**CB code: 9893**

- Private 4-year university
- Commuter campus in very large city
- 25,353 degree-seeking undergraduates
- 8,867 graduate students
- 14% of applicants admitted
- Application essay, interview required

**General. Degrees:** 4,224 bachelor's awarded; master's, doctoral offered. **ROTC:** Army. **Calendar:** Semester, limited summer session. **Full-time faculty:** 1,725 total. **Part-time faculty:** 2,137 total.

**Freshman class profile.** 30,018 applied, 4,186 admitted, 3,895 enrolled.

| Mid 50% test scores | | | |
|---|---|---|---|
| SAT critical reading: | 640-750 | SAT math: | 720-790 |
| | | SAT writing: | 660-730 |

**Basis for selection.** Admission based on two stages: (1) high school and junior high school academic performance, foreign language proficiency certification, teachers' recommendations, personal statement, and other application information; (2) candidates selected from 1st stage in admission process will proceed to interview, and each candidate will be scored for interview evaluation. Final admission granted to top scoring candidates based on combined scores from 1st and 2nd rounds of selection process. **Homeschooled:** State high school equivalency certificate required.

**2007-2008 Annual costs.** Per-semester charges: $3,172 (tuition), $1,643 (on-campus room/board); books and miscellaneous expenses, $710.

**Application procedures. Admission:** Closing date 5/15 (postmark date). $200 fee. Application may be submitted online.

**Academics. Special study options:** Accelerated study, combined bachelor's/graduate degree, cooperative education, cross-registration, double major, dual enrollment of high school students, study abroad, teacher certification program. **Credit/placement by examination:** AP, CLEP, institutional tests. **Support services:** Learning center, pre-admission summer program, study skills assistance, tutoring, writing center.

**Majors. Architecture:** Architecture, urban/community planning. **Biology:** General, biochemistry. **Business:** General. **Communications:** Media studies. **Computer sciences:** General, information technology. **Education:** General. **Engineering:** Ceramic, chemical, civil, computer, electrical, metallurgical. **Engineering technology:** Electrical. **English:** English lit. **Foreign languages:** Chinese, French, German, Korean, Russian. **Health:** Nursing (RN), predental, premedicine. **History:** General. **Legal studies:** General. **Liberal arts:** Library science. **Math:** General, statistics. **Philosophy/religion:** Philosophy. **Physical sciences:** Chemistry. **Psychology:** General. **Public administration:** General. **Social sciences:** Economics. **Theology:** Theology.

**Computing on campus.** 1,050 workstations in dormitories, library, computer center, student center. Dormitories wired for high-speed internet access. Commuter students can connect to campus network. Online course registration, online library, helpline, repair service, student web hosting, wireless network available.

**Student life. Freshman orientation:** Available. **Housing:** Coed dorms available. **Activities:** Bands, campus ministries, choral groups, dance, drama, film society, international student organizations, literary magazine, music ensembles, Model UN, musical theater, opera, radio station, student government, student newspaper, symphony orchestra, TV station.

**Student services.** Campus ministries, career counseling, services for economically disadvantaged, student employment services, financial aid counseling, health services, minority student services, personal counseling, placement for graduates, women's services. **Physically disabled:** Services for visually, speech, hearing impaired. **Learning disabled:** Comprehensive services available.

## Singapore Management University
Singapore, Singapore
www.smu.edu.sg

**CB member**
**CB code: 3873**

- Private 4-year university
- Very large city
- 5,200 degree-seeking undergraduates
- 25% of applicants admitted
- SAT or ACT required

**General. Degrees:** 344 bachelor's awarded; master's, doctoral offered. **Calendar:** Semester. **Full-time faculty:** 233 total. **Part-time faculty:** 262 total.

**Freshman class profile.** 13,000 applied, 3,219 admitted, 1,537 enrolled.

**Basis for selection.** Holistic selection approach used. SAT scores required for international applicants. Local students may submit SAT scores for consideration along with other credentials.

**2007-2008 Annual costs.** Tuition for international students admitted into a non-Law program is $21,950 (Singapore dollars) for the first year and $22,830 SGD for subsequent years; the cost for international students admitted into the Law program is $23,600 SGD per year. Successfully enrolled students are eligible for a tuition grant offered by the Singapore government. This grant provides qualified international students with a subsidy worth approximately 40% of academic year tuition expenses. Students who opt for this benefit will be bonded to work in any Singapore-registered company upon graduation and for a minimum of three years.

**Application procedures. Admission:** Closing date 4/1. $15 fee. Admission notification 7/1. Admission notification on a rolling basis beginning on or about 5/1. **Financial aid:** No deadline.

**Academics. Special study options:** Cooperative education, double major, exchange student, honors, internships, study abroad. **Credit/placement by examination:** CLEP.

**Majors. Business:** Accounting, business admin, communications, finance, marketing, operations, organizational behavior. **Computer sciences:** Information systems. **Legal studies:** General. **Psychology:** General. **Social sciences:** General, economics, political science, sociology.

**Student life. Activities:** Bands, choral groups, dance, drama, film society, literary magazine, music ensembles, musical theater, radio station, student government, student newspaper, symphony orchestra.

**Athletics. Intramural:** Archery, badminton, basketball, bowling, cricket, cross-country, fencing, football (non-tackle), golf, handball, judo, rugby, sailing, soccer M, squash, swimming, table tennis, tennis, track and field, volleyball, water polo.

**Student services.** Personal counseling.

**Contact.** E-mail: admissions@smu.edu.sg
Phone: (65) 682-80305 Fax: (65) 682-80303
Alan Goh, Director of Undergraduate Admissions, Singapore Management University, 81 Victoria Street, Singapore, SG 25975

# Switzerland

## Franklin College: Switzerland

| Lugano, Switzerland | CB member |
| --- | --- |
| www.fc.edu | CB code: 0922 |

- Private 4-year liberal arts college
- Residential campus in small city
- 361 degree-seeking undergraduates: 2% part-time, 64% women
- 72% of applicants admitted
- SAT or ACT with writing, application essay required
- 47% graduate within 6 years

**General.** Founded in 1969. Regionally accredited. Undergraduate degree programs are accredited in United States and in Switzerland. Instruction in English. Students from 50 nations. **Degrees:** 75 bachelor's, 1 associate awarded. **Location:** 60 miles from Milan, Italy, 80 miles from Lucerne. **Calendar:** Semester, extensive summer session. **Full-time faculty:** 22 total; 73% have terminal degrees, 23% women. **Part-time faculty:** 20 total; 55% have terminal degrees, 30% women.

**Freshman class profile.** 622 applied, 446 admitted, 134 enrolled.

| Mid 50% test scores | | | |
| --- | --- | --- | --- |
| SAT critical reading: | 540-650 | GPA 3.0-3.49: | 36% |
| SAT math: | 510-620 | GPA 2.0-2.99: | 34% |
| SAT writing: | 540-640 | End year in good standing: | 89% |
| ACT composite: | 23-27 | Return as sophomores: | 69% |
| GPA 3.50 or higher: | 30% | Live on campus: | 99% |

**Basis for selection.** High school academic record, recommendations, extracurricular participation most important. Essay, test scores, interview also important. TOEFL required for students whose first language is not English. SAT Subject Tests recommended. Essay and personal statement required. Interview recommended for all. **Homeschooled:** Statement describing homeschool structure and mission, letter of recommendation (nonparent) required.

**High school preparation.** 19 units recommended. Recommended units include English 4, mathematics 3, social studies 1, history 3, science 3, foreign language 3 and academic electives 2. Electives include computer science, art, music.

**2007-2008 Annual costs.** Tuition/fees: $30,860. Room/board: $10,500. Books/supplies: $1,000. Personal expenses: $2,000.

**Financial aid.** All financial aid based on need.

**Application procedures. Admission:** Priority date 3/15; no deadline. $85 fee. Application may be submitted online. Admission notification on a rolling basis beginning on or about 12/15. Must reply by May 1 or within 2 week(s) if notified thereafter. **Financial aid:** Priority date 2/15, closing date 3/30. FAFSA, institutional form required. CSS PROFILE preferred. Applicants notified on a rolling basis starting 2/15; must reply by 5/1 or within 3 week(s) of notification.

**Academics.** 2-week credit-bearing academic travel program required each semester. **Special study options:** Double major, ESL, exchange student, honors, independent study, internships, semester at sea, study abroad, Washington semester. Sophomore and junior year abroad programs with cooperating colleges/universities. **Credit/placement by examination:** AP, CLEP, IB, institutional tests. 15 credit hours maximum toward associate degree, 30 toward bachelor's. **Support services:** Reduced course load, study skills assistance, tutoring, writing center.

**Majors. Area/ethnic studies:** European. **Communications:** General. **Conservation:** Environmental science. **English:** Creative writing, English lit. **Foreign languages:** General, comparative lit, French, Italian. **History:** General. **Social sciences:** International economics, international relations. **Visual/performing arts:** General, art history/conservation. **Other:** International management.

**Most popular majors.** Business/marketing 32%, communications/journalism 19%, interdisciplinary studies 6%, social sciences 27%, visual/performing arts 9%.

**Computing on campus.** 57 workstations in library, computer center, student center. Dormitories wired for high-speed internet access and linked to campus network. Commuter students can connect to campus network. Online library, repair service, student web hosting, wireless network available.

**Student life. Freshman orientation:** Mandatory, $265 fee. **Policies:** All students live within the Lugano community; 55% from United States. **Housing:** Guaranteed on-campus for freshmen. Coed dorms, single-sex dorms, apartments, substance-free housing available. $315 partly refundable deposit, deadline 6/15. College-owned and leased apartments on and adjacent to campus and in Lugano; freshmen and sophomores must live in college housing. **Activities:** Dance, drama, literary magazine, student government, student newspaper, international business club, language clubs, numerous sports clubs, international relations club, cultural clubs, booster club, film society, Amnesty International, Far Lawn Club.

**Athletics. Intramural:** Basketball, soccer, tennis, volleyball. **Team name:** Falcons.

**Student services.** Alcohol/substance abuse counseling, career counseling, student employment services, financial aid counseling, health services, personal counseling, placement for graduates, women's services.

**Contact.** E-mail: info@fc.edu
Phone: (718) 335-6800 Fax: (718) 335-6733
Karen Ballard, Director of Admissions, Franklin College: Switzerland, 91-31 Queens Boulevard, Suite 411, Elmhurst, NY 11373

# United Arab Emirates

## American University in Dubai - United Arab Emirates

| Dubai, United Arab Emirates | CB member |
| --- | --- |
| www.aud.edu | CB code: 2688 |

- Private 4-year university
- Commuter campus in very large city
- 2,429 degree-seeking undergraduates
- 46% of applicants admitted
- Application essay required

**General.** Regionally accredited. **Degrees:** 342 bachelor's awarded; master's offered. **Calendar:** Semester, extensive summer session. **Full-time faculty:** 80 total. **Part-time faculty:** 72 total.

**Freshman class profile.** 976 applied, 450 admitted, 380 enrolled.

**Basis for selection.** GED not accepted. Applications reviewed on a rolling basis. Students will be notified of their admissions status within two weeks after applying. Students can sit for the Math placement test at AUD or submit an acceptable SAT score. All Engineering applicants must take SAT. Combined score of 1090 (exclusive of Writing) is required for admissions to the program. **Learning Disabled:** Student should declare disability upon applying. Student services provides support on a case by case basis.

**2007-2008 Annual costs.** Tuition/fees: $14,769. Room only: $3,870. Books/supplies: $600.

**Application procedures. Admission:** Closing date 8/20. $50 fee. Application must be submitted on paper. Admission notification on a rolling basis.

**Academics. Special study options:** Combined bachelor's/graduate degree, ESL, internships, study abroad. **Credit/placement by examination:** AP, CLEP, IB, SAT, institutional tests. **Support services:** Pre-admission summer program, reduced course load, study skills assistance, tutoring.

**Majors. Business:** General, accounting, banking/financial services, e-commerce, management science, marketing. **Communications:** Media studies. **Communications technology:** Graphics. **Computer sciences:** Information technology. **Engineering:** Civil, computer, electrical. **Visual/performing arts:** Commercial/advertising art, graphic design, illustration, interior design, photography.

**Computing on campus.** 65 workstations in library, computer center. Dormitories wired for high-speed internet access. Commuter students can connect to campus network. Online library, helpline, repair service, wireless network available.

**Student life. Freshman orientation:** Mandatory. **Policies:** Dress code; no alcohol and no drugs on campus. **Housing:** Single-sex dorms, special housing for disabled, substance-free housing available. $680 deposit, deadline 6/2. **Activities:** Dance, drama, international student organizations, student government, student newspaper, African, Egyptian, Indian cultural clubs; Khaleej, Lebanese, Palestinian, and Pakistani student associations; Syrian and Islamic awareness club.

**Athletics. Intercollegiate:** Basketball, soccer, swimming, tennis, track and field, volleyball. **Intramural:** Soccer, table tennis, volleyball, water polo.

**Student services.** Alcohol/substance abuse counseling, career counseling, student employment services, health services, on-campus daycare, personal counseling, placement for graduates. **Physically disabled:** Services for visually, speech, hearing impaired.

**Contact.** E-mail: admissions@aud.edu
Phone: (4) 399-9000 Fax: (4) 399-8899
Carol Maalouf, Director of Admissions, American University in Dubai - United Arab Emirates, PO Box 28282, Dubai, AE

# United Kingdom

## Richmond, The American International University in London

**Richmond-upon-Thames, United Kingdom**   **CB member**
**www.richmond.ac.uk**   **CB code: 0823**

- Private 4-year university and liberal arts college
- Residential campus in very large city
- 703 degree-seeking undergraduates: 1% part-time, 61% women
- 10 degree-seeking graduate students
- Application essay required
- 49% graduate within 6 years

**General.** Founded in 1972. Regionally accredited. International student body with over 110 countries represented. Students spend their first two years on the Richmond Hill campus and the second two on the Kensington campus in London. Study centers in Florence and Rome, Italy. Degrees accredited in the both the US and the UK. **Degrees:** 169 bachelor's awarded; master's offered. **Calendar:** Semester, extensive summer session. **Full-time faculty:** 43 total. **Part-time faculty:** 69 total. **Class size:** 68% < 20, 32% 20-39, less than 1% 40-49. **Special facilities:** The Richmond Hill campus is next to Richmond Park, the largest of the Royal Parks and Europe's largest urban walled park.

**Freshman class profile.** 189 enrolled.

| | | | |
|---|---|---|---|
| End year in good standing: | 78% | Live on campus: | 82% |
| Return as sophomores: | 65% | | |

**Basis for selection.** Open admission, but selective for some programs. School achievement record most important. Letters of recommendation and personal statement considered. SAT/ACT scores also considered but not required. SAT or ACT recommended.

**High school preparation.** 19 units required. Required and recommended units include English 4, mathematics 3-4, social studies 1, history 1, science 3-4 (laboratory 1), foreign language 2-3, computer science 1, visual/performing arts 1 and academic electives 2-4.

**2007-2008 Annual costs.** Tuition/fees: $25,000. Room/board: $11,000. Books/supplies: $600. Personal expenses: $4,500.

**Financial aid. Non-need-based:** Scholarships awarded for academics. **Additional information:** U.S. government loan programs available for eligible U.S. citizens/students.

**Application procedures. Admission:** Priority date 3/1; no deadline. $50 fee, may be waived for applicants with need. Application may be submitted online. Admission notification on a rolling basis. Must reply by May 1 or within 4 week(s) if notified thereafter. **Financial aid:** Priority date 3/15, closing date 8/1. FAFSA required. Applicants notified on a rolling basis starting 3/1; must reply by 5/1 or within 4 week(s) of notification.

**Academics.** English language development programs for non-native English speakers. **Special study options:** Combined bachelor's/graduate degree, cross-registration, double major, ESL, independent study, internships, liberal arts/career combination, study abroad. Joint engineering program with George Washington University. **Credit/placement by examination:** AP, CLEP, IB, institutional tests. **Support services:** Reduced course load, remedial instruction, study skills assistance, tutoring, writing center.

**Majors. Business:** Finance, international, marketing. **Communications:** Media studies. **Computer sciences:** General. **Engineering:** General, computer. **English:** English lit. **History:** General. **Liberal arts:** Arts/sciences. **Psychology:** General. **Social sciences:** Economics, international relations, political science. **Visual/performing arts:** Design, studio arts.

**Most popular majors.** Business/marketing 35%, communications/journalism 20%, computer/information sciences 9%, psychology 6%, social sciences 18%, visual/performing arts 6%.

**Computing on campus.** 250 workstations in library, computer center, student center. Online library, helpline, wireless network available.

**Student life. Freshman orientation:** Mandatory. **Housing:** Guaranteed on-campus for all undergraduates. Coed dorms, single-sex dorms, apartments, substance-free housing available. $600 nonrefundable deposit, deadline 5/1. **Activities:** Choral groups, dance, drama, literary magazine, music ensembles, musical theater, student government, student newspaper, Community Outreach Club, Amnesty International, Pan-African Club, Middle Eastern Society, Literary Society, International Night, Student Ambassadors, Kuwaiti United, History/Politics Society, Royal United Services Institute for Defense and Security Studies (RUSI for Richmond University).

**Student services.** Alcohol/substance abuse counseling, career counseling, financial aid counseling, health services, minority student services, personal counseling, placement for graduates.

**Contact.** E-mail: enroll@richmond.ac.uk
Phone: (617) 450-5617 Fax: (617) 450-5601
Brian Davis, Director, US Office of Admissions, Richmond, The American International University in London, 343 Congress Street, Suite 3100, Boston, MA 02210-1214

# Two-year colleges

## Alabama

### Alabama Southern Community College
Monroeville, Alabama
www.ascc.edu      CB code: 1644

◗ Public 2-year community and junior college
◗ Commuter campus in small town

**General.** Founded in 1965. Regionally accredited. **Location:** 85 miles from Mobile. **Calendar:** Semester.

**Annual costs/financial aid.** Tuition/fees (2007-2008): $2,700; $4,830 out-of-state. Books/supplies: $750.

**Contact.** Phone: (251) 575-3156
Dean of Students, Box 2000, Monroeville, AL 36461

### Bevill State Community College
Sumiton, Alabama
www.bscc.edu      CB code: 0723

◗ Public 2-year community college
◗ Commuter campus in small town

**General.** Founded in 1969. Regionally accredited. Sumiton (main), Fayette, Hamilton, and Jasper campuses. Learning site in Carrollton. **Enrollment:** 3,805 degree-seeking undergraduates. **Degrees:** 437 associate awarded. **Location:** 25 miles from Birmingham. **Calendar:** Semester, limited summer session. **Full-time faculty:** 121 total; 7% minority, 54% women. **Part-time faculty:** 182 total. **Special facilities:** Observatory, simulated underground mine.

**Student profile.** Among degree-seeking undergraduates, 56% enrolled in a transfer program, 44% enrolled in a vocational program, 1% already have a bachelor's degree or higher, 965 enrolled as first-time, first-year students.

| | | | |
|---|---|---|---|
| Part-time: | 45% | Hispanic American: | 1% |
| Women: | 67% | Live on campus: | 1% |
| African American: | 15% | | |

**Basis for selection.** Open admission, but selective for some programs. Admission to nursing programs competitive and limited. High school diploma not required in some technical programs. COMPASS required for placement. **Homeschooled:** State high school equivalency certificate required.

**2007-2008 Annual costs.** Tuition/fees: $2,700; $4,830 out-of-state. Per-credit charge: $71 in-state; $142 out-of-state. Room-only rates for Bevill campuses: $1,350. Books/supplies: $1,200. Personal expenses: $2,500.

**Financial aid. Need-based:** Need-based aid available for part-time students. **Non-need-based:** Scholarships awarded for academics, athletics, leadership, music/drama.

**Application procedures. Admission:** No deadline. No application fee. Admission notification on a rolling basis beginning on or about 7/1. **Financial aid:** Priority date 5/1; no closing date. FAFSA required. Applicants notified on a rolling basis starting 7/1.

**Academics. Special study options:** Accelerated study, cooperative education, distance learning, dual enrollment of high school students, honors, weekend college. License preparation in nursing, paramedic. **Credit/placement by examination:** AP, CLEP, institutional tests. Only 25% of program credits can be awarded through nontraditional means. **Support services:** GED preparation and test center, learning center, reduced course load, remedial instruction, tutoring, writing center.

**Majors. Business:** Administrative services. **Computer sciences:** General, computer science. **Construction:** Electrician. **Engineering technology:** Drafting, heat/ac/refrig. **Family/consumer sciences:** Child care. **Health:** EMT paramedic, nursing (RN). **Legal studies:** Paralegal. **Liberal arts:** Arts/sciences. **Mechanic/repair:** Industrial electronics. **Personal/culinary services:** Cosmetic. **Production:** Tool and die.

**Computing on campus.** 1,200 workstations in library, computer center, student center. Dormitories wired for high-speed internet access and linked to campus network. Online course registration, online library, helpline, wireless network available.

**Student life. Freshman orientation:** Mandatory, $30 fee. Preregistration for classes offered. **Housing:** Coed dorms, substance-free housing available. Housing for student athletes available. **Activities:** Bands, choral groups, dance, drama, music ensembles, student government, Inter-Varsity Christian Fellowship, Black Student Union, Circle-K.

**Athletics.** NJCAA. **Intercollegiate:** Baseball M, basketball, cheerleading, cross-country W, softball W, volleyball W. **Intramural:** Basketball, boxing, football (non-tackle), softball, table tennis. **Team name:** Bears.

**Student services.** Campus ministries, career counseling, services for economically disadvantaged, student employment services, financial aid counseling, on-campus daycare, placement for graduates, veterans' counselor. **Physically disabled:** Services for visually, speech, hearing impaired. **Transfer:** Transfer adviser, college fairs on campus for students transferring to 4-year colleges.

**Contact.** E-mail: msellers@bscc.edu
Phone: (205) 648-3271 ext. 5400 Toll-free
number: (800) 648-3271 ext. 5400 Fax: (205) 648-3311
Melissa Stowe, Assistant to the Dean of Student Services, Bevill State Community College, Box 800, Sumiton, AL 35148

### Bishop State Community College
Mobile, Alabama
www.bishop.edu      CB code: 1517

◗ Public 2-year community college
◗ Commuter campus in small city

**General.** Founded in 1963. Regionally accredited. 4 off-campus sites for technical and health-related programs. **Enrollment:** 2,812 degree-seeking undergraduates. **Degrees:** 333 associate awarded. **ROTC:** Army, Air Force. **Calendar:** Semester, limited summer session. **Full-time faculty:** 110 total. **Part-time faculty:** 15 total. **Partnerships:** Training for business and industry, JTPA Assessment Center, formal partnership with Mobile County public school system.

**Basis for selection.** Open admission.

**2007-2008 Annual costs.** Tuition/fees: $2,700; $4,830 out-of-state. Per-credit charge: $71 in-state; $142 out-of-state. Books/supplies: $700. Personal expenses: $1,033.

**Financial aid. Non-need-based:** Scholarships awarded for academics, athletics.

**Application procedures. Admission:** No deadline. No application fee. Admission notification on a rolling basis. **Financial aid:** Priority date 4/1; no closing date. FAFSA, institutional form required. Applicants notified on a rolling basis; must reply within 2 week(s) of notification.

**Academics.** Students must complete 112 credit hours for graduation from technical programs. **Special study options:** Accelerated study, cooperative education, cross-registration, dual enrollment of high school students, honors, internships, weekend college. Degree programs available in allied health through University of Alabama at Birmingham. License preparation in nursing. **Credit/placement by examination:** CLEP. **Support services:** Learning center, pre-admission summer program, reduced course load, remedial instruction, tutoring.

**Majors. Business:** Accounting, administrative services, business admin. **Computer sciences:** General. **Education:** General. **Engineering technology:** Civil, drafting. **Health:** Medical records technology, nursing (RN), physical therapy assistant. **Liberal arts:** Arts/sciences. **Mechanic/repair:** Electronics/electrical. **Personal/culinary services:** Culinary arts, mortuary science. **Protective services:** Fire services admin, law enforcement admin.

**Computing on campus.** 71 workstations in library, computer center.

**Student life. Freshman orientation:** Available. **Activities:** Bands, choral groups, dance, drama, music ensembles, radio station, student government, student newspaper, social service organization, Baptist Student Union, Young Democrats.

**Athletics.** NJCAA. **Intercollegiate:** Baseball M, basketball, softball W. **Team name:** Wildcats.

**Student services.** Adult student services, career counseling, student employment services, health services, on-campus daycare, personal counseling, placement for graduates, veterans' counselor. **Physically disabled:** Services for visually, speech, hearing impaired. **Transfer:** Transfer adviser for students transferring to 4-year colleges.

**Contact.** Phone: (251) 690-6801 Fax: (251) 438-5403
Wanda Daniels, Director of Admissions, Bishop State Community College, 351 North Broad Street, Mobile, AL 36603-5898

---

## Calhoun Community College
**Decatur, Alabama**                    **CB member**
**www.calhoun.edu**                    **CB code: 1356**

◆ Public 2-year community and junior college
◆ Commuter campus in small city

**General.** Founded in 1963. Regionally accredited. Satellite campuses at Research Park in Huntsville and at Redstone Arsenal. **Enrollment:** 9,228 degree-seeking undergraduates. **Degrees:** 807 associate awarded. **Location:** 20 miles from Huntsville. **Calendar:** Semester, limited summer session. **Full-time faculty:** 129 total. **Part-time faculty:** 289 total. **Partnerships:** Formal partnership with Boeing.

**Transfer out. Colleges most students transferred to 2007:** Athens State University, University of North Alabama, Wallace State Community College, Auburn University, University of Alabama.

**Basis for selection.** Open admission, but selective for some programs. Selective admission to nursing program. SAT/ACT scores used for placement. Students from unaccredited high schools are required to have a minimum ACT score of 16 or SAT score of 790 (exclusive of Writing). Portfolio recommended for art majors. **Homeschooled:** Must have ACT score of at least 16, SAT score of 790 (exclusive of Writing), successfully complete GED or high school graduation examination.

**High school preparation.** 26 units recommended. Recommended units include English 4, mathematics 4, social studies 4, science 4, foreign language 2 and academic electives 10. In-state high school graduates must pass state high school competency examination.

**2007-2008 Annual costs.** Tuition/fees: $2,850; $4,980 out-of-state. Per-credit charge: $71 in-state; $142 out-of-state. Books/supplies: $1,500. Personal expenses: $1,000.

**Financial aid. Need-based:** Work-study available for part-time students. **Non-need-based:** Scholarships awarded for academics.

**Application procedures. Admission:** No deadline. No application fee. Application must be submitted on paper. Admission notification on a rolling basis. **Financial aid:** Priority date 5/1; no closing date. FAFSA, institutional form required. Applicants notified on a rolling basis starting 7/1; must reply within 2 week(s) of notification.

**Academics.** Numerous courses available online and by videocassette. **Special study options:** Accelerated study, distance learning, dual enrollment of high school students, liberal arts/career combination, weekend college. License preparation in dental hygiene, nursing, paramedic, real estate. **Credit/placement by examination:** AP, CLEP, institutional tests. 30 credit hours maximum toward associate degree. AP Exam credit limited to 18 semester hours. **Support services:** GED preparation and test center, reduced course load, remedial instruction, tutoring, writing center.

**Majors. Agriculture:** General. **Biology:** General. **Business:** Accounting, business admin. **Communications technology:** General, photo/film/video. **Computer sciences:** General, applications programming, computer graphics, programming. **Construction:** Electrician. **Education:** General, early childhood, elementary, secondary. **Engineering technology:** Aerospace, drafting, heat/ac/refrig. **English:** English lit. **Family/consumer sciences:** Child care, child development. **Health:** Cytogenetics, dental assistant, EMT paramedic, nursing (RN), predental, premedicine, prenursing, prepharmacy, preveterinary. **History:** General. **Legal studies:** Paralegal, prelaw. **Liberal arts:** Arts/sciences. **Math:** General. **Mechanic/repair:** Heating/ac/refrig. **Parks/recreation:** Health/fitness. **Physical sciences:** Chemistry. **Production:** Machine tool, tool and die. **Social sciences:** General. **Transportation:** Aviation. **Visual/performing arts:** Commercial/advertising art, photography, theater arts management. **Other:** Aerospace technology, Family financial planning and counseling, Missile and munitions technology, Music industry communications.

**Most popular majors.** Business/marketing 22%, computer/information sciences 6%, education 10%, health sciences 25%, liberal arts 22%, military 14%.

**Computing on campus.** 166 workstations in library, student center. Commuter students can connect to campus network. Online course registration, wireless network available.

**Student life. Freshman orientation:** Mandatory, $95 fee. Preregistration for classes offered. Class held the first semester of attendance. **Activities:** Jazz band, choral groups, drama, music ensembles, student government, student newspaper, TV station, BACCHUS/SADD, campus ministries, Black Students Alliance Club, criminal justice club, Native American club, Phi Theta Kappa, Allied Health Students Association, The Centurians.

**Athletics.** NJCAA. **Intercollegiate:** Baseball M, softball W. **Intramural:** Basketball, volleyball. **Team name:** Warhawks.

**Student services.** Career counseling, financial aid counseling, minority student services, on-campus daycare, veterans' counselor. **Transfer:** Transfer adviser, college fairs on campus for students transferring to 4-year colleges.

**Contact.** E-mail: sjl@calhoun.edu
Phone: (256) 306-2593 Toll-free number: (800) 626-3628
Fax: (256) 306-2941
M. Tosh, Director of Admissions and Registrar, Calhoun Community College, Box 2216, Decatur, AL 35609-2216

---

## Central Alabama Community College
**Childersburg, Alabama**
**www.cacc.cc.al.us**                    **CB code: 0715**

◆ Public 2-year community college
◆ Commuter campus in large town

**General.** Founded in 1965. Regionally accredited. 2 campuses: Childersburg, predominantly for technical courses, and Alexander City, predominantly for transfer courses. **Enrollment:** 2,180 degree-seeking undergraduates. **Degrees:** 211 associate awarded. **Location:** 50 miles from Montgomery, 35 miles from Birmingham. **Calendar:** Semester, extensive summer session. **Full-time faculty:** 56 total. **Part-time faculty:** 68 total. **Special facilities:** Wildlife museum, wellness center, pioneer village.

**Student profile.**

| | | | |
|---|---|---|---|
| Out-of-state: | 1% | 25 or older: | 48% |

**Basis for selection.** Open admission, but selective for some programs. Graduates of non-accredited high schools and certain nursing applicants may be required to take SAT or ACT.

**2007-2008 Annual costs.** Tuition/fees: $2,700; $4,830 out-of-state. Per-credit charge: $71 in-state; $142 out-of-state. Books/supplies: $300. Personal expenses: $500.

**Financial aid. Non-need-based:** Scholarships awarded for academics, athletics, state residency.

**Application procedures. Admission:** Closing date 8/21. No application fee. Admission notification on a rolling basis. **Financial aid:** Priority date 7/15; no closing date. FAFSA, institutional form required. Applicants notified on a rolling basis.

**Academics. Special study options:** Cooperative education, dual enrollment of high school students, independent study. **Credit/placement by examination:** CLEP, institutional tests. 48 credit hours maximum toward associate degree. **Support services:** GED preparation and test center, learning center, remedial instruction, study skills assistance, tutoring.

**Majors. Agriculture:** Business. **Business:** General, administrative services, business admin, management information systems. **Computer sciences:** General. **Education:** General. **Engineering:** General. **Engineering technology:** Drafting, electrical. **Health:** Clinical lab science, EMT paramedic, health services, medical assistant, medical radiologic technology/radiation therapy, medical records technology, occupational therapy assistant, physical therapy assistant, respiratory therapy technology. **Liberal arts:** Arts/sciences. **Protective services:** Criminal justice, firefighting, police science.

**Computing on campus.** 45 workstations in library, computer center, student center.

**Student life. Freshman orientation:** Mandatory. **Activities:** Jazz band, choral groups, dance, drama, radio station, student government.

**Athletics.** NJCAA. **Intercollegiate:** Baseball M, golf M, softball W, tennis, volleyball W. **Team name:** Trojans.

**Student services.** Career counseling, personal counseling, veterans' counselor. **Transfer:** Pre-admission transcript evaluation for new students. Transfer adviser, college fairs on campus for students transferring to 4-year colleges.

**Contact.** Phone: (256) 215-4255 Toll-free number: (800) 643-2657 Amanda Harkins, Dean of Students, Central Alabama Community College, 34091 US Highway 280 South, Childersburg, AL 35044

---

### Chattahoochee Valley Community College
**Phenix City, Alabama**
www.cv.edu                                    CB code: 1187

♦ Public 2-year community college
♦ Commuter campus in small city

**General.** Founded in 1974. Regionally accredited. **Enrollment:** 1,929 degree-seeking undergraduates. **Degrees:** 228 associate awarded. **ROTC:** Army. **Location:** 2 miles from Columbus, Georgia. **Calendar:** Semester, extensive summer session. **Full-time faculty:** 36 total. **Part-time faculty:** 75 total.

**Transfer out. Colleges most students transferred to 2007:** Columbus State University, Auburn University, Columbus Technical College, Southern Union State Community College, Troy State University.

**Basis for selection.** Open admission, but selective for some programs. Additional requirements for health occupation programs. SAT and ACT considered if submitted. ASSET waived for students submitting appropriate ACT/SAT scores. **Homeschooled:** State high school equivalency certificate required. Program must be accredited by a state or federal department of education.

**2007-2008 Annual costs.** Tuition/fees: $2,700; $4,830 out-of-state. Per-credit charge: $71 in-state; $142 out-of-state. Books/supplies: $800. Personal expenses: $750.

**2006-2007 Financial aid. Need-based:** Need-based aid available for part-time students. Work-study available nights, weekends and for part-time students. **Non-need-based:** Scholarships awarded for academics, art, athletics, leadership, music/drama.

**Application procedures. Admission:** Priority date 7/15; no deadline. No application fee. Admission notification on a rolling basis. **Financial aid:** Priority date 7/1; no closing date. FAFSA required. Applicants notified on a rolling basis; must reply within 1 week(s) of notification.

**Academics. Special study options:** Accelerated study, distance learning, dual enrollment of high school students, honors, independent study, liberal arts/career combination. License preparation in nursing. **Credit/placement by examination:** CLEP, institutional tests. 18 credit hours maximum toward associate degree. **Support services:** GED test center, learning center, reduced course load, remedial instruction.

**Majors. Biology:** General. **Business:** Accounting, administrative services, business admin. **Computer sciences:** General, data processing. **Conservation:** Forestry. **Education:** Business, elementary, physical, secondary. **Engineering:** General. **Health:** Medical records technology, nursing (RN). **Liberal arts:** Arts/sciences. **Math:** General. **Parks/recreation:** Health/fitness. **Physical sciences:** Chemistry, physics. **Protective services:** Criminal justice, firefighting. **Visual/performing arts:** Art history/conservation, dramatic.

**Computing on campus.** 150 workstations in library, computer center. Online library available.

**Student life. Freshman orientation:** Available. Preregistration for classes offered. **Activities:** Choral groups, drama, music ensembles, musical theater, student government, student newspaper.

**Athletics.** NJCAA. **Intercollegiate:** Baseball M, basketball, softball W. **Team name:** Pirates.

**Student services.** Adult student services, career counseling, personal counseling, placement for graduates, veterans' counselor. **Physically disabled:** Services for visually, hearing impaired.

**Contact.** Phone: (334) 291-4929 Fax: (334) 291-4994 David Hodge, Dean of Student and Administrative Services, Chattahoochee Valley Community College, 2602 College Drive, Phenix City, AL 36869

---

### Community College of the Air Force
**Maxwell Air Force Base, Alabama**                CB member
www.au.af.mil/au/ccaf                              CB code: 1175

♦ Public 2-year community and technical college
♦ Commuter campus in small city
♦ Interview required

**General.** Founded in 1972. Regionally accredited. Multicampus, worldwide, for United States Air Force enlisted personnel. Administrative offices at Maxwell Air Force Base. Primary campuses are technical training centers located at 5 Air Force bases in 3 states. Other campuses include USAF PME Centers, USAF Command Sponsored Schools, and Field Training Detachments. **Enrollment:** 332,853 degree-seeking undergraduates. **Degrees:** 17,056 associate awarded. **Location:** 160 miles from Atlanta, 90 miles from Birmingham. **Calendar:** Continuous, extensive summer session. **Full-time faculty:** 5,900 total.

**Basis for selection.** Open admission. All USAF enlisted personnel automatically registered upon completion of basic military training and assignment to an Air Force career field. All applicants must take the Armed Services Vocational Aptitude Battery.

**High school preparation.** 16 units recommended. Recommended units include English 4, mathematics 3, social studies 3, science 2 and foreign language 2.

**2007-2008 Annual costs.** Students pay no tuition or fees.

**Financial aid. Additional information:** Air Force Tuition Assistance program available for general and technical education courses taken at civilian colleges and universities. Pays 75% of tuition costs.

**Application procedures. Admission:** No deadline. No application fee. Admission notification on a rolling basis. **Financial aid:** No deadline.

**Academics. Special study options:** Accelerated study, distance learning, independent study, internships, liberal arts/career combination. License preparation in aviation, physical therapy, radiology. **Credit/placement by examination:** AP, CLEP, institutional tests. 30 credit hours maximum toward associate degree. **Support services:** Reduced course load, remedial instruction, tutoring.

**Majors. Business:** Human resources, management information systems, office management, operations, purchasing. **Communications:** Public relations. **Communications technology:** General. **Computer sciences:** General, networking. **Education:** Technology/industrial arts. **Engineering technology:** Construction, electrical. **Health:** Cardiovascular technology, dental assistant, dental lab technology, health care admin, health services, histologic assistant, medical assistant, nuclear medical technology, ophthalmic lab technology, pharmacy assistant, physical therapy assistant, radiologic technology/medical imaging, sonography, surgical technology. **History:** General, public archives. **Interdisciplinary:** Nutrition sciences. **Legal studies:** Paralegal. **Mechanic/repair:** Aircraft, electronics/electrical, heating/ac/refrig, industrial. **Military:** General. **Parks/recreation:** General, **Physical sciences:** Atmospheric science. **Protective services:** Criminal justice, fire safety technology. **Public administration:** Social work. **Transportation:** General, air traffic control, aviation, aviation management.

**Student life. Policies:** Air Force bases provide housing, student services, activities, and athletics. **Housing:** Coed dorms, single-sex dorms, apartments available.

**Athletics. Intramural:** Badminton, baseball M, basketball, bowling, boxing M, cross-country, golf, handball, racquetball, rifle, soccer M, softball, squash, swimming, table tennis, tennis, track and field, volleyball, weight lifting.

**Student services.** Adult student services, alcohol/substance abuse counseling, career counseling, financial aid counseling, health services, legal services, on-campus daycare, personal counseling, veterans' counselor. **Transfer:** Transfer center, transfer adviser, college fairs on campus for students transferring to 4-year colleges.

**Contact.** E-mail: registrar.ccat@maxwell.af.mil
Phone: (334) 953-2794 Fax: (334) 953-5231
Terry Amatuzzi, Director of Admissions, Community College of the Air Force, 130 West Maxwell Boulevard, Maxwell Air Force Base, AL 36112-6613

## Enterprise-Ozark Community College
Enterprise, Alabama
www.eocc.edu
CB code: 1213

- Public 2-year community college
- Commuter campus in large town

**General.** Founded in 1963. Regionally accredited. **Location:** 85 miles from Montgomery. **Calendar:** Semester.

**Annual costs/financial aid.** Tuition/fees (2007-2008): $2,700; $4,830 out-of-state. Books/supplies: $500. Personal expenses: $500.

**Contact.** Phone: (334) 347-2623 ext. 2234
Registrar, Box 1300, Enterprise, AL 36331

## Faulkner State Community College
Bay Minette, Alabama
www.faulknerstate.edu
CB code: 1939

- Public 2-year community college
- Commuter campus in large town

**General.** Founded in 1965. Regionally accredited. Branch campuses in Fairhope and Gulf Shores. **Enrollment:** 3,403 degree-seeking undergraduates. **Degrees:** 260 associate awarded. **Location:** 35 miles from Mobile. **Calendar:** Semester, extensive summer session. **Full-time faculty:** 68 total. **Part-time faculty:** 110 total.

**Transfer out. Colleges most students transferred to 2007:** University of Alabama, Auburn University, University of South Alabama.

**Basis for selection.** Open admission, but selective for some programs. Students applying for dental assisting program must take and pass Health Occupations Aptitude exam. Audition recommended for music majors, portfolio for art majors. **Homeschooled:** If school nonaccredited, ACT Composite of 16 or better or GED required.

**2007-2008 Annual costs.** Tuition/fees: $2,790; $4,920 out-of-state. Per-credit charge: $71 in-state; $142 out-of-state. Room/board: $4,050. Books/supplies: $450. Personal expenses: $800.

**Application procedures. Admission:** No deadline. No application fee. Admission notification on a rolling basis. **Financial aid:** Priority date 7/1, closing date 8/1. FAFSA, institutional form required. Applicants notified on a rolling basis starting 8/1.

**Academics. Special study options:** Accelerated study, cooperative education, distance learning, double major, dual enrollment of high school students, honors, independent study, internships. **Credit/placement by examination:** CLEP. 20 credit hours maximum toward associate degree. **Support services:** GED preparation and test center, learning center, remedial instruction, tutoring.

**Majors. Agriculture:** General, business, landscaping. **Biology:** General. **Business:** Administrative services, business admin, finance, hospitality admin, office technology. **Communications:** Journalism. **Computer sciences:** General, computer graphics, systems analysis. **Conservation:** Forestry. **Education:** Business, early childhood, elementary, physical. **Engineering technology:** Hazardous materials. **English:** English lit. **Family/consumer sciences:** General. **Health:** Clinical lab science, clinical lab technology, dental assistant, EMT paramedic, medical secretary, predental, premedicine, prenursing, prepharmacy, preveterinary. **Legal studies:** Court reporting, legal secretary, paralegal. **Liberal arts:** Arts/sciences. **Math:** General. **Parks/recreation:** Facilities management. **Personal/culinary services:** Culinary arts. **Physical sciences:** Chemistry. **Social sciences:** General. **Visual/performing arts:** General, art, commercial/advertising art, studio arts.

**Computing on campus.** 16 workstations in library, computer center.

**Student life. Freshman orientation:** Available. **Housing:** Single-sex dorms available. $35 deposit. **Activities:** Jazz band, choral groups, drama, music ensembles, student government, student newspaper, Pow-wow leadership, Phi Beta Lambda, Baptist Campus Ministries, Phi Theta Kappa, Psi Beta, association of computational machinery.

**Athletics.** NJCAA. **Intercollegiate:** Baseball M, basketball, cheerleading, golf, softball W, tennis, volleyball. **Intramural:** Basketball M, bowling, racquetball, softball, volleyball W. **Team name:** Sun Chiefs.

**Student services.** Career counseling, student employment services, health services, personal counseling, placement for graduates, veterans' counselor. **Physically disabled:** Services for visually impaired. **Transfer:** Transfer adviser for students transferring to 4-year colleges.

**Contact.** E-mail: pduck@faulknerstate.edu
Phone: (251) 580-2111 Toll-free number: (800) 231-3752
Fax: (251) 580-2285
Betty Shefield, Director of Admissions, Faulkner State Community College, 1900 Highway 31 South, Bay Minette, AL 36507

## Gadsden State Community College
Gadsden, Alabama
www.gadsdenstate.edu
CB code: 1262

- Public 2-year community and technical college
- Commuter campus in large town

**General.** Founded in 1985. Regionally accredited. Off-campus sites include Ayers Campus, McClellan Campus and Cherokee County Center. **Enrollment:** 5,516 degree-seeking undergraduates. **Degrees:** 479 associate awarded. **ROTC:** Army. **Location:** 60 miles from Birmingham. **Calendar:** Semester, limited summer session. **Full-time faculty:** 142 total. **Part-time faculty:** 121 total. **Special facilities:** Advanced technology center, language institute, aquaculture education.

**Student profile.** Among degree-seeking undergraduates, 59% enrolled in a transfer program, 41% enrolled in a vocational program, 1,430 enrolled as first-time, first-year students.

| | | | |
|---|---|---|---|
| Part-time: | 44% | Native American: | 1% |
| Out-of-state: | 2% | International: | 3% |
| Women: | 61% | 25 or older: | 30% |
| African American: | 20% | Live on campus: | 4% |
| Hispanic American: | 2% | | |

**Transfer out. Colleges most students transferred to 2007:** Jacksonville State University, Auburn University, University of Alabama, University of Alabama at Birmingham, University of Alabama at Huntsville.

**Basis for selection.** Open admission, but selective for some programs. Special requirements for health-related programs. Career Program Assessment Test required for some programs. Interview recommended for computer technology, court reporting, and most health science majors. **Homeschooled:** Transcript of courses and grades required. An ACT score of 16 or a SAT score 790.

**High school preparation.** 27 units recommended. Recommended units include English 4, mathematics 4, social studies 4, science 4 (laboratory 2) and academic electives 9. Electives must include .5 unit computer, .5 unit of fine arts.

**2007-2008 Annual costs.** Tuition/fees: $2,700; $4,830 out-of-state. Per-credit charge: $71 in-state; $142 out-of-state. Room/board: $2,800. Books/supplies: $800. Personal expenses: $825.

**2006-2007 Financial aid. Need-based:** Average scholarship/grant was $1,923. 95% of total undergraduate aid awarded as scholarships/grants, 5% as loans/jobs. Need-based aid available for part-time students. Work-study available for part-time students. **Non-need-based:** Scholarships awarded for academics, alumni affiliation, art, athletics, leadership, minority status, music/drama, state residency.

**Application procedures. Admission:** No deadline. No application fee. Application may be submitted online. Admission notification on a rolling basis. **Financial aid:** Priority date 4/15; no closing date. FAFSA, institutional form required. Applicants notified on a rolling basis starting 6/10; must reply within 2 week(s) of notification.

**Academics. Special study options:** Accelerated study, cooperative education, cross-registration, distance learning, dual enrollment of high school students, ESL, honors, independent study, internships, weekend college. License preparation in nursing, paramedic. **Credit/placement by examination:** CLEP, institutional tests. 20 credit hours maximum toward associate degree. **Support services:** GED preparation and test center, remedial instruction, study skills assistance, tutoring, writing center.

**Majors. Agriculture:** General. **Area/ethnic studies:** American. **Biology:** General. **Business:** Accounting technology, administrative services, business admin, sales/distribution. **Communications:** General. **Communications technology:** General, graphics. **Computer sciences:** General, computer science, information systems, information technology, LAN/WAN management, networking, programming. **Conservation:** Forestry. **Education:** General, early childhood, elementary, kindergarten/preschool, mathematics. **Engineering:** General. **Engineering technology:** Civil, civil drafting, computer systems, electrical, heat/ac/refrig, industrial, mechanical, mechanical drafting, telecommunications. **English:** English lit. **Family/consumer sciences:** Child development. **Health:** Clinical lab assistant, clinical lab technology, EMT paramedic, medical radiologic technology/radiation therapy, medical records technology, nursing (RN), predental, premedicine, prenursing, prepharmacy, preveterinary, substance abuse counseling. **History:** General. **Legal studies:** Court reporting, paralegal, prelaw. **Liberal arts:** Arts/sciences. **Math:** General. **Mechanic/repair:** Electronics/electrical, heating/ac/refrig, industrial. **Parks/recreation:** Health/fitness. **Philosophy/religion:** Religion. **Physical sciences:** Chemistry. **Protective services:** Law enforcement admin. **Psychology:** General. **Social sciences:** Sociology. **Visual/performing arts:** Art.

**Computing on campus.** 250 workstations in library, computer center, student center. Dormitories wired for high-speed internet access. Online course registration, online library available.

**Student life. Freshman orientation:** Mandatory, $90 fee. Preregistration for classes offered. **Housing:** Coed dorms, substance-free housing available. **Activities:** Bands, choral groups, dance, drama, student government, Circle-K, International Club, Baptist Student Union, Phi Beta Lambda.

**Athletics.** NJCAA. **Intercollegiate:** Baseball M, basketball, cross-country W, golf M, softball W, volleyball W. **Team name:** Cardinals.

**Student services.** Adult student services, career counseling, services for economically disadvantaged, student employment services, personal counseling, placement for graduates, veterans' counselor. **Physically disabled:** Services for visually, speech, hearing impaired. **Transfer:** Pre-admission transcript evaluation for new students. Transfer adviser, college fairs on campus for students transferring to 4-year colleges.

**Contact.** E-mail: info@gadsdenstate.edu
Phone: (256) 549-8210 Toll-free number: (800) 226-5563
Fax: (256) 549-8205
Teresa Rhea, Associate Dean of Student Services and Registrar, Gadsden State Community College, 1001 George Wallace Drive, Gadsden, AL 35902-0227

## George C. Wallace Community College at Dothan
**Dothan, Alabama**
www.wallace.edu                                    CB code: 1264

▶ Public 2-year community college
▶ Commuter campus in small city

**General.** Founded in 1949. Regionally accredited. Additional campuses in Eufaula and Ft. Rucker. **Enrollment:** 3,708 degree-seeking undergraduates. **Degrees:** 445 associate awarded. **Calendar:** Semester, extensive summer session. **Full-time faculty:** 128 total. **Part-time faculty:** 110 total.

**Student profile.**

| | | | |
|---|---|---|---|
| Out-of-state: | 4% | 25 or older: | 43% |

**Transfer out. Colleges most students transferred to 2007:** University of Alabama, Auburn University, University of Alabama at Birmingham.

**Basis for selection.** Open admission, but selective for some programs. Additional requirements for allied health and nursing programs. National League for Nursing examination required for nursing applicants. Interview required of nursing majors.

**2007-2008 Annual costs.** Tuition/fees: $2,700; $4,830 out-of-state. Per-credit charge: $72 in-state; $143 out-of-state. Books/supplies: $900. Personal expenses: $500.

**Financial aid. Need-based:** Work-study available for part-time students. **Non-need-based:** Scholarships awarded for academics, athletics, leadership.

**Application procedures. Admission:** No deadline. No application fee. Admission notification on a rolling basis. **Financial aid:** Priority date 5/1; no closing date. FAFSA required. Applicants notified on a rolling basis.

**Academics. Special study options:** Accelerated study, cooperative education, cross-registration, distance learning, dual enrollment of high school students, ESL, honors, weekend college. License preparation in nursing, paramedic, physical therapy, radiology. **Credit/placement by examination:** AP, CLEP, institutional tests. 48 credit hours maximum toward associate degree. **Support services:** GED preparation and test center, learning center, pre-admission summer program, remedial instruction, study skills assistance, tutoring.

**Majors. Business:** Administrative services. **Computer sciences:** General. **Construction:** Electrician. **Engineering technology:** Drafting. **Health:** EMT paramedic, medical assistant, medical radiologic technology/radiation therapy, respiratory therapy technology. **Liberal arts:** Arts/sciences. **Mechanic/repair:** Electronics/electrical.

**Student life. Freshman orientation:** Mandatory. Preregistration for classes offered. **Activities:** Jazz band, choral groups, drama, music ensembles, student government, student newspaper, Association of Student Practical Nursing, Diplomats, Elite Club, National Vocational-Technical Honor Society, Phi Theta Kappa, Phi Beta Lambda, Respiratory Therapy Association for Better Breathing.

**Athletics.** NJCAA. **Intercollegiate:** Baseball M, softball W. **Team name:** Govs (M), Lady Govs (W).

**Student services.** Adult student services, career counseling, services for economically disadvantaged, student employment services, financial aid counseling, personal counseling, placement for graduates, veterans' counselor. **Learning disabled:** Comprehensive services available. **Transfer:** Transfer adviser, college fairs on campus for students transferring to 4-year colleges.

**Contact.** E-mail: bbarnes@wallace.edu
Phone: (334) 983-3521 Toll-free number: (800) 543-2426
Fax: (334) 983-6066
Brenda Barnes, Assistant Dean of Student Affairs, George C. Wallace Community College at Dothan, 1141 Wallace Drive, Dothan, AL 36303-0943

## George C. Wallace State Community College at Selma
**Selma, Alabama**
www.wccs.edu                                    CB code: 3146

▶ Public 2-year community and technical college
▶ Commuter campus in large town

**General.** Founded in 1963. Regionally accredited. **Location:** 50 miles from Montgomery, 90 miles from Birmingham. **Calendar:** Semester.

**Annual costs/financial aid.** Tuition/fees (2007-2008): $2,700; $4,830 out-of-state. Books/supplies: $690. Personal expenses: $976.

**Contact.** Phone: (334) 876-9295
Director of Admissions, PO Box 2530, Selma, AL 36702-2530

## J. F. Drake State Technical College
**Huntsville, Alabama**
www.drakestate.edu                                CB code: 2108

▶ Public 2-year technical college
▶ Commuter campus in small city

**General.** Founded in 1961. Regionally accredited. **Enrollment:** 675 degree-seeking undergraduates; 16 non-degree-seeking students. **Degrees:** 60 associate awarded. **Location:** 100 miles from Birmingham, 200 miles from Atlanta. **Calendar:** Semester. **Full-time faculty:** 24 total. **Part-time faculty:** 50 total. **Class size:** 65% < 20, 29% 20-39, 4% 40-49, 2% 50-99.

**Student profile.** Among degree-seeking undergraduates, 196 enrolled as first-time, first-year students.

| | | | |
|---|---|---|---|
| Part-time: | 38% | Women: | 52% |
| Out-of-state: | 2% | 25 or older: | 53% |

**Basis for selection.** Open admission, but selective for some programs. Nursing applicants must pass pre-entrance examination. COMPASS required for all students for placement only.

**2007-2008 Annual costs.** Tuition/fees: $2,700; $4,830 out-of-state. Per-credit charge: $71 in-state; $142 out-of-state.

**Financial aid. Need-based:** Need-based aid available for part-time students. Work-study available for part-time students. **Non-need-based:** Scholarships awarded for academics, state residency.

**Application procedures. Admission:** Priority date 6/30; no deadline. No application fee. Admission notification on a rolling basis. **Financial aid:** Priority date 7/1; no closing date. FAFSA required. Applicants notified on a rolling basis.

**Academics. Special study options:** Cooperative education, dual enrollment of high school students, internships. License preparation in nursing. **Credit/placement by examination:** CLEP, institutional tests. **Support services:** GED preparation, learning center, reduced course load, remedial instruction, tutoring.

**Majors. Business:** Accounting, administrative services. **Communications technology:** Graphic/printing. **Computer sciences:** Data processing, programming. **Engineering technology:** Drafting. **Mechanic/repair:** Electronics/electrical. **Production:** Machine tool.

**Computing on campus.** 130 workstations in library, computer center, student center. Online library, repair service available.

**Student life. Freshman orientation:** Available. Preregistration for classes offered. One-day program includes a study skills seminar. **Activities:** Student government, student newspaper, Phi Beta Lambda, VICA, National Vocational Technical Honor Society.

**Student services.** Career counseling, services for economically disadvantaged, student employment services, financial aid counseling, personal counseling, placement for graduates, veterans' counselor. **Physically disabled:** Services for hearing impaired. **Transfer:** Pre-admission transcript evaluation for new students. Transfer adviser for students transferring to 4-year colleges.

**Contact.** E-mail: sudeall@drakestate.edu
Phone: (256) 551-3109 Toll-free number: (888) 413-7253
Fax: (256) 539-6439
Monica Sudeall, Director of Admissions, J. F. Drake State Technical College, 3421 Meridian Street North, Huntsville, AL 35811

## Jefferson Davis Community College
**Brewton, Alabama**
**www.jdcc.edu**        **CB code: 1355**

▶ Public 2-year nursing and community college
▶ Commuter campus in small town

**General.** Founded in 1965. Regionally accredited. **Enrollment:** 1,085 degree-seeking undergraduates; 155 non-degree-seeking students. **Degrees:** 153 associate awarded. **Location:** 60 miles from Pensacola, Florida. **Calendar:** Semester, limited summer session. **Full-time faculty:** 42 total; 24% minority, 50% women. **Part-time faculty:** 41 total. **Class size:** 63% < 20, 37% 20-39. **Special facilities:** Museum, golf course, telecommunications center.

**Student profile.** Among degree-seeking undergraduates, 54% enrolled in a transfer program, 46% enrolled in a vocational program, 2% already have a bachelor's degree or higher, 360 enrolled as first-time, first-year students, 425 transferred in from other institutions.

| | | | |
|---|---|---|---|
| Part-time: | 42% | Hispanic American: | 1% |
| Out-of-state: | 8% | Native American: | 4% |
| Women: | 54% | 25 or older: | 48% |
| African American: | 29% | Live on campus: | 6% |
| Asian American: | 1% | | |

**Basis for selection.** Open admission, but selective for some programs. Special admissions requirements for nursing program. **Homeschooled:** ACT score of 16 or higher required.

**High school preparation.** 24 units recommended. Recommended units include English 4, mathematics 4, social studies 4, science 4 and academic electives 8.

**2007-2008 Annual costs.** Tuition/fees: $2,700; $4,830 out-of-state. Per-credit charge: $71 in-state; $142 out-of-state. Room only-Apartments $2800; Suite $3600. Room only: $2,800. Books/supplies: $800. Personal expenses: $400.

**2006-2007 Financial aid. Need-based:** 105 full-time freshmen applied for aid; 80 were judged to have need; 71 of these received aid. Average

need met was 53%. Average scholarship/grant was $600. 89% of total undergraduate aid awarded as scholarships/grants, 11% as loans/jobs. Need-based aid available for part-time students. Work-study available nights and for part-time students. **Non-need-based:** Awarded to 82 full-time undergraduates, including 23 freshmen. Scholarships awarded for academics, athletics, leadership.

**Application procedures. Admission:** No deadline. No application fee. Application may be submitted online. Admission notification on a rolling basis. **Financial aid:** Priority date 5/8; no closing date. FAFSA required. Applicants notified on a rolling basis; must reply within 2 week(s) of notification.

**Academics. Special study options:** Cooperative education, distance learning, dual enrollment of high school students, ESL, honors, independent study. Bachelor's degree programs available on campus. License preparation in nursing, paramedic. **Credit/placement by examination:** AP, CLEP. **Support services:** GED preparation and test center, learning center, remedial instruction, study skills assistance, tutoring.

**Majors. Business:** Administrative services. **Engineering technology:** Drafting. **Health:** Nursing (RN). **Liberal arts:** Arts/sciences.

**Most popular majors.** Health sciences 34%, liberal arts 60%.

**Computing on campus.** 420 workstations in library, computer center. Online course registration, wireless network available.

**Student life. Freshman orientation:** Mandatory. Preregistration for classes offered. New student orientation is held during the summer. Mandatory for all students attending JDCC for the first time. **Housing:** Coed dorms, substance-free housing available. $150 partly refundable deposit. **Activities:** Campus ministries, student government, student newspaper, Baptist student union, Phi Theta Kappa, Phi Beta Lambda, Psi Beta.

**Athletics.** NJCAA. **Intercollegiate:** Baseball M, basketball M, softball W, volleyball W. **Team name:** Warhawks.

**Student services.** Adult student services, campus ministries, career counseling, services for economically disadvantaged, financial aid counseling, personal counseling, veterans' counselor. **Physically disabled:** Services for visually impaired. **Transfer:** Pre-admission transcript evaluation for new students. Transfer adviser, college fairs on campus for students transferring to 4-year colleges.

**Contact.** Phone: (251) 809-1594 Fax: (251) 809-1593
Robin Sessions, Registrar, Jefferson Davis Community College, PO Box 958, Brewton, AL 36427

## Jefferson State Community College
**Birmingham, Alabama**
**www.jeffstateonline.com**        **CB code: 1352**

▶ Public 2-year community college
▶ Commuter campus in large city

**General.** Founded in 1963. Regionally accredited. **Enrollment:** 6,070 degree-seeking undergraduates; 1,434 non-degree-seeking students. **Degrees:** 595 associate awarded. **ROTC:** Army, Air Force. **Location:** 12 miles from downtown. **Calendar:** Semester, extensive summer session. **Full-time faculty:** 124 total; 18% have terminal degrees, 20% minority, 70% women. **Part-time faculty:** 300 total; 12% have terminal degrees, 17% minority, 53% women. **Class size:** 59% < 20, 38% 20-39, 3% 40-49. **Special facilities:** Learning success center, nature trail.

**Student profile.** Among degree-seeking undergraduates, 52% enrolled in a transfer program, 48% enrolled in a vocational program, 1,269 enrolled as first-time, first-year students, 693 transferred in from other institutions.

| | | | |
|---|---|---|---|
| Part-time: | 53% | Asian American: | 2% |
| Out-of-state: | 1% | Hispanic American: | 1% |
| Women: | 64% | International: | 2% |
| African American: | 21% | 25 or older: | 39% |

**Transfer out. Colleges most students transferred to 2007:** University of Alabama at Birmingham, University of Alabama, Auburn University.

**Basis for selection.** Open admission, but selective for some programs. Special requirements for allied health programs. Applicants from non-accredited high schools admitted with high school diploma and minimum ACT score of 16 or equivalent SAT score. Students registering for five (plus) hours of credit must take ACT ASSET or ACT COMPASS prior to registration. Placement test exemptions are given for students who have completed college level math or English courses, or students who have equivalent ACT scores. **Adult students:** SAT/ACT scores not required. **Home-schooled:** Must have minimum ACT score of 16 or pass Alabama Public High School Graduation Exam.

**High school preparation.** Recommended units include English 4, mathematics 4, social studies 2, science 3 and foreign language 2.

**2007-2008 Annual costs.** Tuition/fees: $3,060; $5,190 out-of-state. Per-credit charge: $71 in-state; $142 out-of-state. Books/supplies: $1,372. Personal expenses: $3,796.

**Financial aid. Need-based:** Need-based aid available for part-time students. Work-study available nights and for part-time students. **Non-need-based:** Scholarships awarded for academics, art, athletics, leadership, music/drama. **Additional information:** Any Alabama resident over age 60 may attend classes tuition free, on a space available basis.

**Application procedures. Admission:** No deadline. No application fee. Application may be submitted online. Admission notification on a rolling basis. **Financial aid:** Priority date 5/1; no closing date. FAFSA, institutional form required. Applicants notified on a rolling basis starting 6/1.

**Academics. Special study options:** Accelerated study, distance learning, dual enrollment of high school students, ESL, honors, independent study, internships. Bachelor's degree programs available on campus. License preparation in paramedic, real estate. **Credit/placement by examination:** AP, CLEP, IB, institutional tests. 20 credit hours maximum toward associate degree. **Support services:** GED preparation and test center, learning center, reduced course load, remedial instruction, study skills assistance, tutoring.

**Majors. Agriculture:** Business. **Business:** General, accounting technology, administrative services, banking/financial services, hospitality admin. **Communications technology:** Radio/tv. **Computer sciences:** General. **Engineering technology:** General, construction, manufacturing. **Family/consumer sciences:** Child care, home furnishings. **Health:** Clinical lab technology, EMT paramedic, medical radiologic technology/radiation therapy, nursing (RN), physical therapy assistant, veterinary technology/assistant. **Liberal arts:** Arts/sciences. **Personal/culinary services:** Mortuary science. **Protective services:** Fire services admin, police science.

**Most popular majors.** Business/marketing 16%, family/consumer sciences 6%, health sciences 36%, liberal arts 29%.

**Computing on campus.** 232 workstations in library, computer center. Commuter students can connect to campus network. Online course registration, online library, helpline available.

**Student life. Freshman orientation:** Available. Preregistration for classes offered. **Activities:** Campus ministries, choral groups, drama, literary magazine, music ensembles, musical theater, radio station, student government, student newspaper, senior adult student club, African American Society, BACCHUS, students in free enterprise, Ambassadors.

**Athletics.** NJCAA. **Intercollegiate:** Baseball M, softball W. **Intramural:** Basketball, football (non-tackle), softball, volleyball. **Team name:** Pioneers.

**Student services.** Adult student services, career counseling, student employment services, financial aid counseling, placement for graduates, veterans' counselor, women's services. **Physically disabled:** Services for visually, speech, hearing impaired. **Transfer:** Transfer adviser, college fairs on campus for students transferring to 4-year colleges.

**Contact.** E-mail: help@jeffstateonline.com
Phone: (205) 856-7704 Toll-free number: (800) 239-5900
Fax: (205) 856-6070
Lillian Owens, Director, Admissions & Retention, Jefferson State Community College, 2601 Carson Road, Birmingham, AL 35215-3098

## Lawson State Community College
**Birmingham, Alabama**
www.lawsonstate.edu

**CB member**
**CB code: 1933**

▶ Public 2-year community college
▶ Commuter campus in small city

**General.** Founded in 1949. Regionally accredited. **Enrollment:** 3,173 degree-seeking undergraduates; 152 non-degree-seeking students. **Degrees:** 191 associate awarded. **Calendar:** Semester, limited summer session. **Full-time faculty:** 100 total. **Part-time faculty:** 121 total. **Class size:** 100% >100.

**Student profile.** Among degree-seeking undergraduates, 819 enrolled as first-time, first-year students, 388 transferred in from other institutions.

| | | | |
|---|---|---|---|
| Part-time: | 46% | Women: | 65% |
| Out-of-state: | 1% | Live on campus: | 2% |

**Transfer out. Colleges most students transferred to 2007:** Miles College, University of Alabama at Birmingham, Alabama A&M University, Alabama State University, Jefferson State Community College.

**Basis for selection.** Open admission, but selective for some programs. Advanced placement option for licensed practical nurses (LPN) and nursing education. Nursing students must pass nursing entrance exam or have composite ACT of 20 or comparable SAT.

**2007-2008 Annual costs.** Tuition/fees: $3,000; $5,130 out-of-state. Per-credit charge: $71 in-state; $142 out-of-state. Books/supplies: $1,390. Personal expenses: $920.

**2007-2008 Financial aid.** All financial aid based on need. 94% of total undergraduate aid awarded as scholarships/grants, 6% as loans/jobs. Need-based aid available for part-time students. Work-study available nights and for part-time students.

**Application procedures. Admission:** No deadline. No application fee. Admission notification on a rolling basis. **Financial aid:** Priority date 6/1; no closing date. FAFSA required. Applicants notified on a rolling basis starting 8/1; must reply within 2 week(s) of notification.

**Academics. Special study options:** Accelerated study, double major, dual enrollment of high school students, internships, liberal arts/career combination, student-designed major. License preparation in dental hygiene, nursing, real estate. **Credit/placement by examination:** AP, CLEP, institutional tests. **Support services:** GED preparation and test center, learning center, reduced course load, remedial instruction, tutoring.

**Majors. Biology:** General. **Business:** Accounting, administrative services, business admin, office management, office technology, operations. **Computer sciences:** Computer science. **Construction:** General. **Education:** General, early childhood, health, health occupations, multi-level teacher, physical, social studies. **Engineering:** General, electrical. **Engineering technology:** Architectural, automotive, construction, drafting, electrical, mechanical drafting. **English:** English lit. **Health:** Medical secretary, nursing (RN). **History:** General. **Legal studies:** Legal secretary, prelaw. **Liberal arts:** Arts/sciences. **Math:** General. **Mechanic/repair:** Auto body. **Parks/recreation:** Health/fitness. **Protective services:** Criminal justice. **Psychology:** General. **Public administration:** Social work. **Social sciences:** Economics, political science, sociology.

**Most popular majors.** Business/marketing 19%, computer/information sciences 10%, engineering/engineering technologies 14%, health sciences 16%, liberal arts 30%.

**Computing on campus.** 421 workstations in library, computer center, student center. Online course registration, online library available.

**Student life. Freshman orientation:** Mandatory. Preregistration for classes offered. **Activities:** Jazz band, choral groups, dance, drama, music ensembles, radio station, student government, student newspaper, TV station, Scholars Bowl Team, Sophist Club.

**Athletics.** NJCAA. **Intercollegiate:** Baseball M, basketball, track and field M, volleyball W. **Intramural:** Baseball M, basketball. **Team name:** Cougars.

**Student services.** Adult student services, career counseling, services for economically disadvantaged, student employment services, financial aid counseling, health services, on-campus daycare, personal counseling, placement for graduates, veterans' counselor. **Physically disabled:** Services for hearing impaired. **Transfer:** College fairs on campus for students transferring to 4-year colleges.

**Contact.** E-mail: dallen@lawsonstate.edu
Phone: (205) 929-6309 Fax: (205) 923-7106
Jeff Shelley, Director of Admissions, Lawson State Community College, 3060 Wilson Road SW, Birmingham, AL 35221-1717

## Lurleen B. Wallace Community College
**Andalusia, Alabama**
www.lbwcc.edu

**CB code: 1429**

▶ Public 2-year junior college
▶ Commuter campus in small town

**General.** Founded in 1969. Regionally accredited. MacArthur campus in Opp and Greenville campus in Greenville. **Enrollment:** 1,370 degree-seeking undergraduates. **Degrees:** 191 associate awarded. **Location:** 90 miles from Montgomery. **Calendar:** Semester, limited summer session. **Full-time faculty:** 50 total. **Part-time faculty:** 60 total. **Special facilities:** Nature trail.

**Transfer out. Colleges most students transferred to 2007:** Troy State University, Auburn University, Auburn University in Montgomery.

**Basis for selection.** Open admission. COMPASS required for placement unless student scores 20 or higher in math and English on ACT.

**2007-2008 Annual costs.** Tuition/fees: $2,700; $4,830 out-of-state. Per-credit charge: $71 in-state; $142 out-of-state. Books/supplies: $450. Personal expenses: $600.

**Financial aid. Non-need-based:** Scholarships awarded for academics, art, athletics, leadership, music/drama, state residency.

**Application procedures. Admission:** No deadline. No application fee. Admission notification on a rolling basis. **Financial aid:** Priority date 5/1; no closing date. Applicants notified on a rolling basis starting 7/1; must reply within 2 week(s) of notification.

**Academics. Special study options:** Accelerated study, cooperative education, dual enrollment of high school students, honors. License preparation in paramedic. **Credit/placement by examination:** CLEP, institutional tests. 30 credit hours maximum toward associate degree. **Support services:** GED preparation and test center, learning center, reduced course load, remedial instruction, tutoring.

**Majors. Conservation:** Forest resources. **Health:** EMT paramedic. **Liberal arts:** Arts/sciences.

**Most popular majors.** Liberal arts 87%.

**Computing on campus.** 50 workstations in computer center.

**Student life. Freshman orientation:** Available, $10 fee. **Activities:** Jazz band, choral groups, drama, music ensembles, musical theater, student government, student newspaper, Collegiate Civitan Club, Circle-K, Christian Student Union, adult re-entry club.

**Athletics.** NJCAA. **Intercollegiate:** Baseball M, basketball, cross-country, softball W. **Team name:** Saints.

**Student services.** Career counseling, student employment services, personal counseling, placement for graduates, veterans' counselor. **Transfer:** Transfer adviser, college fairs on campus for students transferring to 4-year colleges.

**Contact.** Phone: (334) 222-6591 ext. 271 Fax: (334) 222-0136
Mackie Stephens, Director of Admissions, Lurleen B. Wallace Community College, Box 1418, Andalusia, AL 36420-1418

---

## Marion Military Institute
### Marion, Alabama
### www.marionmilitary.edu
**CB code: 1447**

- Public 2-year junior and military college
- Residential campus in small town
- SAT or ACT (ACT writing optional) required

**General.** Founded in 1842. Regionally accredited. **Enrollment:** 389 degree-seeking undergraduates. **Degrees:** 29 associate awarded. **ROTC:** Army, Air Force. **Location:** 70 miles from Birmingham, 52 miles from Tuscaloosa. **Calendar:** Semester. **Full-time faculty:** 15 total; 27% have terminal degrees, 13% minority, 40% women. **Part-time faculty:** 3 total; 67% have terminal degrees, 67% minority, 33% women. **Class size:** 48% < 20, 37% 20-39, 6% 40-49, 6% 50-99, 3% >100. **Special facilities:** Alabama Military Hall of Honor, golf course, bird sanctuary.

**Student profile.** Among degree-seeking undergraduates, 224 enrolled as first-time, first-year students, 11 transferred in from other institutions.

| | | | |
|---|---|---|---|
| Part-time: | 12% | Women: | 22% |
| Out-of-state: | 58% | Live on campus: | 100% |

**Transfer out.** 75% of students enrolled in the transfer program go on to 4-year colleges. **Colleges most students transferred to 2007:** University of Alabama, Auburn University, University of Arkansas.

**Basis for selection.** Academic record, recommendations, test scores, character and personal qualities important. Extracurricular activities and alumni

relation also important. Interview recommended. **Homeschooled:** Applicants must have been enrolled in approved programs.

**High school preparation.** 25 units required. Required and recommended units include English 4, mathematics 4, social studies 1, history 3, science 4, foreign language 2 and academic electives 8.

**2007-2008 Annual costs.** Tuition/fees: $6,796; $12,796 out-of-state. Room/board: $3,450.

**Financial aid. Need-based:** Need-based aid available for part-time students. **Non-need-based:** Scholarships awarded for academics, alumni affiliation, athletics, leadership, music/drama, ROTC.

**Application procedures. Admission:** Closing date 8/15 (receipt date). $40 fee, may be waived for applicants with need. Application may be submitted online. Admission notification on a rolling basis. Must reply by 8/15. **Financial aid:** No deadline. FAFSA required. Applicants notified on a rolling basis starting 6/15; must reply within 6 week(s) of notification.

**Academics.** Special preparation for national service academies. **Special study options:** Cross-registration, dual enrollment of high school students, ESL. Students have option to participate in precision drill team, orienteering team, and United States Army Ranger-type training. **Credit/placement by examination:** AP, CLEP, SAT, ACT, institutional tests. **Support services:** Reduced course load, remedial instruction, study skills assistance, tutoring.

**Majors. Liberal arts:** Arts/sciences.

**Computing on campus.** 41 workstations in library. Dormitories wired for high-speed internet access. Online library, helpline, wireless network available.

**Student life. Freshman orientation:** Mandatory. Preregistration for classes offered. **Policies:** Structured military school environment. **Housing:** Guaranteed on-campus for all undergraduates. Single-sex dorms, substance-free housing available. $200 nonrefundable deposit, deadline 8/15. Students must live on campus. **Activities:** Bands, choral groups, drama, music ensembles, musical theater, student government, Normandy Society.

**Athletics.** NJCAA. **Intercollegiate:** Basketball M, soccer M, softball W, tennis W. **Intramural:** Basketball, cross-country, diving, golf, handball, rifle, swimming, track and field, volleyball, weight lifting. **Team name:** Tigers.

**Student services.** Adult student services, campus ministries, career counseling, student employment services, financial aid counseling, health services, personal counseling, veterans' counselor. **Transfer:** Transfer adviser for students transferring to 4-year colleges.

**Contact.** E-mail: admissions@marionmilitary.edu
Phone: (334) 683-2305 Toll-free number: (800) 664-1842
Fax: (334) 683-2383
SGM. Dennis Hastings, Director of Enrollment Management, Marion Military Institute, 1101 Washington Street, Marion, AL 36756-0420

---

## Northeast Alabama Community College
### Rainsville, Alabama
### www.nacc.edu
**CB code: 1576**

- Public 2-year community college
- Commuter campus in rural community

**General.** Founded in 1963. Regionally accredited. **Enrollment:** 2,014 degree-seeking undergraduates. **Degrees:** 229 associate awarded. **Location:** 55 miles from Huntsville, 110 miles from Birmingham. **Calendar:** Semester, extensive summer session. **Full-time faculty:** 45 total. **Special facilities:** Community theater, lakeside walking trail.

**Transfer out. Colleges most students transferred to 2007:** Jacksonville State University, University of Alabama: Huntsville, Athens State University, University of Alabama, Auburn University.

**Basis for selection.** Open admission, but selective for some programs. **Homeschooled:** Must provide official transcript and have ACT score of 16. **Learning Disabled:** Students who may require accommodations are encouraged to communicate with Disability Services.

**High school preparation.** 24 units recommended. Recommended units include English 4, mathematics 4, social studies 2, history 2, science 4 (laboratory 2), foreign language 2 and academic electives 4.

**2007-2008 Annual costs.** Tuition/fees: $2,850; $4,980 out-of-state. Per-credit charge: $71 in-state; $142 out-of-state. In-state costs apply to on-campus or distance-learning courses. Out-of-state distance-learning students pay $5,400 for academic year (or $180 per-credit-hour). Personal expenses: $1,500.

**Financial aid. Need-based:** Need-based aid available for part-time students. Work-study available for part-time students. **Non-need-based:** Scholarships awarded for academics, art, leadership, minority status, music/drama.

**Application procedures. Admission:** No deadline. No application fee. Application may be submitted online. Admission notification on a rolling basis. **Financial aid:** No deadline. FAFSA required. Applicants notified on a rolling basis.

**Academics. Special study options:** Accelerated study, distance learning, dual enrollment of high school students, ESL. 2-year degree programs in allied health available requiring 1 year study at Wallace State Community College at Hanceville. Bachelor's degree programs available on campus. License preparation in nursing, paramedic. **Credit/placement by examination:** AP, CLEP, institutional tests. 16 credit hours maximum toward associate degree. **Support services:** GED preparation and test center, learning center, remedial instruction, study skills assistance, tutoring, writing center.

**Majors. Business:** General, administrative services, banking/financial services, business admin, office management. **Computer sciences:** General, computer science. **Engineering technology:** CAD/CADD, electrical. **English:** English lit. **Health:** EMT paramedic, nursing (RN). **Legal studies:** Paralegal.

**Computing on campus.** 321 workstations in library, computer center. Commuter students can connect to campus network. Online course registration, online library, helpline, wireless network available.

**Student life. Freshman orientation:** Available. Preregistration for classes offered. Groups of 100 meet for an afternoon. **Activities:** Bands, campus ministries, choral groups, drama, literary magazine, music ensembles, musical theater, student government.

**Athletics. Intramural:** Basketball. **Team name:** Mustangs.

**Student services.** Career counseling, student employment services, financial aid counseling, personal counseling, placement for graduates, veterans' counselor. **Physically disabled:** Services for visually, speech, hearing impaired. **Transfer:** Pre-admission transcript evaluation for new students. Transfer adviser, college fairs on campus for students transferring to 4-year colleges.

**Contact.** E-mail: yatesw@nacc.edu
Phone: (256) 228-6001 ext. 222 Fax: (256) 638-6043
Tonie Niblett, Dean of Student Services, Northeast Alabama Community College, Admissions Office, NACC, Rainsville, AL 35986-0159

## Northwest-Shoals Community College
**Muscle Shoals, Alabama**
www.nwscc.edu                                    **CB code: 0188**

- Public 2-year community and technical college
- Commuter campus in large town

**General.** Founded in 1966. Regionally accredited. Two campuses: Phil Campbell and Muscle Shoals. **Enrollment:** 3,108 degree-seeking undergraduates. **Degrees:** 279 associate awarded. **ROTC:** Army. **Location:** 120 miles from Birmingham, 134 miles from Memphis, Tennessee. **Calendar:** Semester, extensive summer session. **Full-time faculty:** 87 total; 7% have terminal degrees, 8% minority, 52% women. **Part-time faculty:** 155 total; 4% have terminal degrees, 12% minority, 54% women. **Class size:** 13% < 20, 37% 20-39, 13% 40-49, 37% 50-99. **Partnerships:** Formal agreement with high schools for Tech prep articulation programs.

**Student profile.** Among degree-seeking undergraduates, 850 enrolled as first-time, first-year students.

| | | | |
|---|---|---|---|
| Part-time: | 37% | Hispanic American: | 1% |
| Out-of-state: | 1% | Native American: | 1% |
| Women: | 59% | 25 or older: | 35% |
| African American: | 11% | Live on campus: | 2% |
| Asian American: | 1% | | |

**Transfer out. Colleges most students transferred to 2007:** University of North Alabama, University of Alabama, Athens State University, University of Alabama at Huntsville.

**Basis for selection.** Open admission, but selective for some programs. Additional requirements for health occupation programs. **Homeschooled:** Equivalent number of required units for graduation and ACT score of 16 or SAT score of 790 (exclusive of Writing) required.

**High school preparation.** 22 units recommended. Recommended units include English 4, mathematics 2, social studies 3 and science 4.

**2007-2008 Annual costs.** Tuition/fees: $2,880; $5,010 out-of-state. Per-credit charge: $71 in-state; $142 out-of-state. Room only: $1,600. Books/supplies: $1,190.

**2006-2007 Financial aid. Need-based:** 49% of total undergraduate aid awarded as scholarships/grants, 51% as loans/jobs. Need-based aid available for part-time students. Work-study available nights, weekends and for part-time students. **Non-need-based:** Scholarships awarded for academics, art, athletics, leadership, minority status, music/drama.

**Application procedures. Admission:** No deadline. No application fee. Admission notification on a rolling basis. **Financial aid:** Priority date 4/1; no closing date. FAFSA, institutional form required. Applicants notified on a rolling basis; must reply within 2 week(s) of notification.

**Academics. Special study options:** Accelerated study, cooperative education, cross-registration, distance learning, dual enrollment of high school students, independent study, internships, liberal arts/career combination, weekend college. License preparation in nursing, paramedic. **Credit/placement by examination:** AP, CLEP, institutional tests. 30 credit hours maximum toward associate degree. **Support services:** GED preparation and test center, learning center, pre-admission summer program, remedial instruction, tutoring.

**Majors. Business:** Accounting technology, administrative services. **Computer sciences:** General, applications programming, data processing, information systems, information technology, programming. **Conservation:** Environmental studies. **Engineering technology:** CAD/CADD, drafting, electrical, environmental. **Family/consumer sciences:** Child care. **Health:** EMT paramedic, nursing (RN). **Liberal arts:** Arts/sciences. **Mechanic/repair:** Industrial. **Protective services:** Police science.

**Most popular majors.** Business/marketing 10%, health sciences 22%, interdisciplinary studies 6%, liberal arts 48%.

**Computing on campus.** 650 workstations in library, computer center, student center. Online course registration, online library, helpline, repair service, wireless network available.

**Student life. Freshman orientation:** Mandatory, $10 fee. Preregistration for classes offered. Program includes components for developing research skills and good study habits. Occupational students also receive orientation to work ethics and workplace readiness. **Housing:** Coed dorms, substance-free housing available. $75 fully refundable deposit. **Activities:** Bands, campus ministries, choral groups, music ensembles, student government, Phi Theta Kappa, Ambassadors, Fellowship of Christian Athletes, Music Educators National Conference, student government association, college bowl team, science club, American Society of Heating, Refrigerating and Air Conditioning Engineers.

**Athletics.** NJCAA. **Intercollegiate:** Baseball M, basketball, cheerleading, cross-country M, golf M, tennis W, volleyball W. **Intramural:** Basketball, softball, table tennis, tennis. **Team name:** Patriots.

**Student services.** Career counseling, student employment services, on-campus daycare, personal counseling, placement for graduates, veterans' counselor. **Physically disabled:** Services for hearing impaired. **Transfer:** Pre-admission transcript evaluation for new students. Transfer adviser, college fairs on campus for students transferring to 4-year colleges.

**Contact.** Phone: (256) 331-5363 Fax: (256) 331-5366
Karen Berryhill, Vice President for Student Development Services, Northwest-Shoals Community College, PO Box 2545, Muscle Shoals, AL 35662

## Prince Institute of Professional Studies
**Montgomery, Alabama**
www.princeinstitute.edu                          **CB code: 3450**

- For-profit 2-year technical college
- Commuter campus in large city

**General.** Accredited by ACICS. **Calendar:** Quarter.

**Annual costs/financial aid.** Tuition/fees (2007-2008): $6,895. Additional required fees vary per program. Books/supplies: $272. Personal expenses: $1,674. Need-based financial aid available to full-time and part-time students.

**Contact.** Phone: (334) 271-1670
Admissions Director, 7735 Atlanta Highway, Montgomery, AL 36117-4231

## Remington College: Mobile
### Mobile, Alabama
www.educationamerica.com          CB code: 3157

▶ Private 2-year technical college
▶ Commuter campus in large city

**General.** Accredited by ACCSCT. **Enrollment:** 147 degree-seeking undergraduates. **Degrees:** 85 associate awarded. **Calendar:** Quarter, extensive summer session. **Full-time faculty:** 30 total. **Part-time faculty:** 15 total.

**Basis for selection.** Open admission. **Homeschooled:** Must take CDAT Test.

**2007-2008 Annual costs.** Bachelor programs $32,050. Associate programs $39,650. Diploma programs (Allied Health) $13,050. Cost includes tuition, fees and books.

**Financial aid.** All financial aid based on need. Work-study available nights.

**Application procedures. Admission:** No deadline. $50 fee. **Financial aid:** FAFSA required.

**Academics. Special study options:** Cooperative education, honors, liberal arts/career combination. Bachelor's degree programs available on campus. **Credit/placement by examination:** CLEP. **Support services:** Tutoring.

**Majors. Business:** Business admin. **Computer sciences:** General. **Engineering:** Electrical. **Engineering technology:** Drafting.

**Computing on campus.** PC or laptop required. Helpline, repair service available.

**Student life. Freshman orientation:** Available. Preregistration for classes offered. Held the week before class for 2 1/2 hours.

**Student services.** Career counseling, financial aid counseling, placement for graduates. **Transfer:** Pre-admission transcript evaluation for new students.

**Contact.** Phone: (251) 343-8200 Toll-free number: (800) 866-0850
Fax: (251) 343-8200
David Helveston, Director of Admissions, Remington College: Mobile, 828 Downtowner Loop West, Mobile, AL 36609-5404

## Shelton State Community College
### Tuscaloosa, Alabama
www.sheltonstate.edu          CB code: 3338

▶ Public 2-year community and technical college
▶ Commuter campus in small city

**General.** Founded in 1963. Regionally accredited. Designated as Alabama's Community College of the Fine Arts; includes C.A. Fredd campus, an Historically Black College. **Enrollment:** 5,328 degree-seeking undergraduates. **Degrees:** 261 associate awarded. **ROTC:** Army, Air Force. **Location:** 60 miles from Birmingham. **Calendar:** Semester, extensive summer session. **Full-time faculty:** 78 total; 13% have terminal degrees, 19% minority, 58% women. **Part-time faculty:** 168 total; 5% have terminal degrees, 23% minority, 59% women. **Class size:** 42% < 20, 48% 20-39, 10% 40-49, less than 1% 50-99. **Special facilities:** Observatories, wellness center, community theatre.

**Student profile.**

| | | | |
|---|---|---|---|
| Out-of-state: | 5% | 25 or older: | 32% |

**Transfer out. Colleges most students transferred to 2007:** University of Alabama, Auburn University, Stillman College, University of Alabama at Birmingham.

**Basis for selection.** Open admission. COMPASS test required of all first-time freshmen for placement unless students have taken ACT.

**2007-2008 Annual costs.** Tuition/fees: $2,700; $4,830 out-of-state. Books/supplies: $750. Personal expenses: $200.

**Financial aid.** All financial aid based on need. Need-based aid available for part-time students. Work-study available nights.

**Application procedures. Admission:** No deadline. No application fee. Application may be submitted online. Admission notification on a rolling basis. **Financial aid:** Priority date 6/30; no closing date. FAFSA required. Applicants notified on a rolling basis starting 7/30.

**Academics. Special study options:** Accelerated study, distance learning, double major, dual enrollment of high school students, honors, liberal arts/career combination. License preparation in nursing, real estate. **Credit/placement by examination:** AP, CLEP, IB, institutional tests. 20 credit hours maximum toward associate degree. **Support services:** GED preparation and test center, learning center, reduced course load, remedial instruction, study skills assistance, tutoring.

**Majors. Architecture:** Technology. **Business:** Administrative services. **Construction:** Electrician. **Education:** General, music, secondary. **Engineering:** General. **Engineering technology:** Drafting, heat/ac/refrig. **Health:** Nursing (RN), respiratory therapy technology. **Liberal arts:** Arts/sciences. **Math:** General. **Mechanic/repair:** Industrial electronics. **Production:** General, tool and die. **Public administration:** Social work. **Visual/performing arts:** Studio arts.

**Most popular majors.** Business/marketing 25%, health sciences 26%, liberal arts 33%, trade and industry 11%.

**Computing on campus.** 300 workstations in library, computer center. Commuter students can connect to campus network. Online course registration, wireless network available.

**Student life. Freshman orientation:** Mandatory. Preregistration for classes offered. **Activities:** Jazz band, choral groups, dance, drama, music ensembles, musical theater, student government, student newspaper, Phi Theta Kappa, Circle K.

**Athletics.** NJCAA. **Intercollegiate:** Baseball M, basketball, cheerleading, soccer W, softball W. **Team name:** Buccaneers.

**Student services.** Career counseling, student employment services, financial aid counseling, personal counseling, placement for graduates, veterans' counselor. **Transfer:** College fairs on campus for students transferring to 4-year colleges.

**Contact.** Phone: (205) 391-2214 Fax: (205) 391-3910
Tommy Taylor, Dean of Student Services, Shelton State Community College, 9500 Old Greensboro Road, Tuscaloosa, AL 35405-8522

## Snead State Community College
### Boaz, Alabama
www.snead.edu          CB code: 1721

▶ Public 2-year community college
▶ Commuter campus in small town

**General.** Founded in 1898. Regionally accredited. Upper-level courses offered on campus through Athens State University and distance learning. **Enrollment:** 2,158 degree-seeking undergraduates. **Degrees:** 240 associate awarded. **Location:** 65 miles from Birmingham. **Calendar:** Semester, extensive summer session. **Full-time faculty:** 34 total; 24% have terminal degrees, 3% minority, 68% women. **Part-time faculty:** 59 total. **Special facilities:** Museum, state diagnostic lab. **Partnerships:** Partnership with Marshall County Tech Prep Consortium (grant writer and fiscal agent for eight secondary schools).

**Student profile.** Among degree-seeking undergraduates, 60% enrolled in a transfer program, 40% enrolled in a vocational program.

| | | | |
|---|---|---|---|
| Out-of-state: | 2% | Live on campus: | 4% |
| 25 or older: | 33% | | |

**Transfer out.** 58% of students enrolled in the transfer program go on to 4-year colleges. **Colleges most students transferred to 2007:** Jacksonville State University, Auburn University, University of Alabama, University of Alabama at Birmingham, University of Alabama in Huntsville.

**Basis for selection.** Open admission, but selective for some programs. Nursing students must submit an application package. Minimum ACT score of 16 or equivalent score on SAT required for high school graduates from non-accredited schools and for those receiving occupational diplomas.

**High school preparation.** 24 units recommended. Recommended units include English 4, mathematics 4, social studies 4, science 4, foreign language 2 and academic electives 8. Half unit fine arts, 1/2 computer applications, 5 1/2 electives recommended.

**2007-2008 Annual costs.** Tuition/fees: $2,820; $4,950 out-of-state. Per-credit charge: $71 in-state; $142 out-of-state. Room/board: $2,400. Books/supplies: $1,050. Personal expenses: $1,200.

**Financial aid. Need-based:** Need-based aid available for part-time students. Work-study available nights and for part-time students. **Non-need-based:** Scholarships awarded for academics, alumni affiliation, art, athletics, leadership, music/drama.

**Application procedures. Admission:** Closing date 8/14 (postmark date). No application fee. Application must be submitted on paper. Admission notification on a rolling basis. **Financial aid:** Priority date 4/15; no closing date. FAFSA required. Applicants notified on a rolling basis starting 4/15.

**Academics. Special study options:** Accelerated study, distance learning, dual enrollment of high school students, independent study, internships, student-designed major. **Credit/placement by examination:** AP, CLEP, institutional tests. 20 credit hours maximum toward associate degree. **Support services:** GED preparation and test center, learning center, remedial instruction, study skills assistance, tutoring, writing center.

**Majors. Business:** Administrative services. **Computer sciences:** General. **Engineering:** General. **Engineering technology:** General. **Family/consumer sciences:** Child care. **Health:** Nursing (RN). **Liberal arts:** Arts/sciences. **Personal/culinary services:** Cosmetic.

**Computing on campus.** 350 workstations in library, computer center, student center. Online course registration, online library available.

**Student life. Freshman orientation:** Available, $94 fee. Preregistration for classes offered. Orientation offered as one credit-hour course on 2 consecutive Fridays or Saturdays. **Housing:** Coed dorms available. $25 deposit. **Activities:** Jazz band, choral groups, music ensembles, student government, student newspaper, Baptist Campus Ministry, Ambassadors, Snead Agricultural Organization, Phi Beta Lambda, Phi Theta Kappa, student government association, College Republicans, Civitans.

**Athletics.** NJCAA. **Intercollegiate:** Baseball M, basketball, softball W, tennis W. **Intramural:** Basketball, softball, table tennis, volleyball. **Team name:** Parsons.

**Student services.** Campus ministries, career counseling, services for economically disadvantaged, student employment services, financial aid counseling, personal counseling, placement for graduates, veterans' counselor. **Physically disabled:** Services for visually, speech, hearing impaired. **Transfer:** Pre-admission transcript evaluation for new students. Transfer center, transfer adviser, college fairs on campus for students transferring to 4-year colleges.

**Contact.** E-mail: mbuchanan@snead.edu
Phone: (256) 593-5120 ext. 207 Fax: (256) 593-7180
Martha Buchanan, Admissions and Records Director, Snead State Community College, PO Box 734, Boaz, AL 35957-0734

## Southern Union State Community College
**Wadley, Alabama**
**www.suscc.edu**                                    CB code: 1728

▸ Public 2-year community and technical college
▸ Commuter campus in small city

**General.** Founded in 1963. Regionally accredited. In addition to the main campus in Wadley, there are two branch campuses in Opelika and a campus in Valley, Alabama. **Enrollment:** 4,796 degree-seeking undergraduates. **Degrees:** 416 associate awarded. **Location:** 90 miles from Atlanta, 90 miles from Birmingham. **Calendar:** Semester, extensive summer session. **Full-time faculty:** 85 total. **Part-time faculty:** 240 total.

### Student profile.

| | | | |
|---|---|---|---|
| Out-of-state: | 20% | Live on campus: | 4% |
| 25 or older: | 25% | | |

**Basis for selection.** Open admission, but selective for some programs. Criteria for some health sciences programs include test scores.

**2007-2008 Annual costs.** Tuition/fees: $2,700; $4,830 out-of-state. Per-credit charge: $71 in-state; $142 out-of-state. Room/board: $2,400. Books/supplies: $400. Personal expenses: $1,100.

**Financial aid. Need-based:** Need-based aid available for part-time students.

**Application procedures. Admission:** No deadline. No application fee. Admission notification on a rolling basis. **Financial aid:** Priority date 7/1; no closing date. FAFSA required. Applicants notified on a rolling basis.

**Academics. Special study options:** Accelerated study, distance learning, dual enrollment of high school students. License preparation in nursing, paramedic, radiology. **Credit/placement by examination:** CLEP. **Support services:** GED preparation and test center, remedial instruction, tutoring.

**Majors. Biology:** General. **Business:** Accounting, office management. **Communications:** General. **Computer sciences:** General. **Construction:** Carpentry. **Education:** Physical. **Engineering technology:** Drafting. **Health:** EMT paramedic, insurance coding, nursing (RN), radiologic technology/medical imaging. **Mechanic/repair:** Heating/ac/refrig. **Physical sciences:** Chemistry, theoretical physics. **Social sciences:** General.

**Student life. Freshman orientation:** Available. Preregistration for classes offered. Held during June and July. **Housing:** Single-sex dorms, substance-free housing available. **Activities:** Choral groups, dance, drama, musical theater, student government, student newspaper, Student Government Association, Association of Radiologic Students, Baptist Campus Ministries, Global Environmental Organization of Students, Music Club, Letterman's Club, National Student Nurses' Association, Phi Beta Lambda, Phi Theta Kappa, Southern Union Players.

**Athletics.** NJCAA. **Intercollegiate:** Baseball M, basketball, cheerleading, cross-country, softball W, volleyball W. **Team name:** Bisons.

**Student services.** Adult student services, career counseling, financial aid counseling.

**Contact.** E-mail: cstringfellow@suscc.edu
Phone: (256) 395-2211 Fax: (256) 395-2215
Cathryn Stringfellow, Registrar, Southern Union State Community College, 750 Roberts Street, Wadley, AL 36276

## Virginia College at Mobile
**Mobile, Alabama**
**www.vc.edu/mobile**

▸ For-profit 2-year technical college
▸ Commuter campus in large city

**General.** Accredited by ACICS. **Calendar:** Continuous.

**Annual costs/financial aid.** Most students pay $4,000 per quarter; additional fees vary according to program of study.

**Contact.** Phone: (251) 343-7227
Director of Admissions, 2970 Cottage Hill Road, Mobile, AL 36606

## Wallace State Community College at Hanceville
**Hanceville, Alabama**
**www.wallacestate.edu**                        CB code: 0528

▸ Public 2-year health science and community college
▸ Commuter campus in rural community

**General.** Founded in 1966. Regionally accredited. **Location:** 35 miles from Birmingham, 50 miles from Huntsville. **Calendar:** Semester.

**Annual costs/financial aid.** Tuition/fees (2007-2008): $2,700; $4,830 out-of-state. Room only–Dorms $1550; House $1100. Room: $1,450. Books/supplies: $700. Personal expenses: $2,650. Need-based financial aid available to full-time and part-time students.

**Contact.** Phone: (256) 352-8236
Director of Admissions/Registrar, PO Box 2000, Hanceville, AL 35077-2000

# Alaska

## Ilisagvik College
### Barrow, Alaska
www.ilisagvik.cc      **CB code: 0469**

▶ Public 2-year tribal college
▶ Rural community

**General. Enrollment:** 476 degree-seeking undergraduates. **Degrees:** 7 associate awarded. **Location:** 500 miles from Fairbanks. **Calendar:** Semester, limited summer session. **Full-time faculty:** 14 total. **Part-time faculty:** 17 total.

**Basis for selection.** Open admission.

**2007-2008 Annual costs.** $9868 per year includes tuition, fees, room and board.

**Application procedures. Admission:** No deadline. No application fee. **Financial aid:** No deadline.

**Academics.** Many Inupiat Eskimo traditional courses offered. **Credit/placement by examination:** CLEP.

**Majors. Business:** Management science. **Construction:** General.

**Student life. Freshman orientation:** Available.

**Contact.** E-mail: patty.stith@ilisagvik.cc
Phone: (907) 852-1763 Toll-free number: (907) 478-7337 ext. 1784
Fax: (907) 852-1784
Patty Stith, Registrar, Ilisagvik College, 100 Stevenson Road, Barrow, AK 99723

## Prince William Sound Community College
### Valdez, Alaska
www.pwscc.edu      **CB code: 4636**

▶ Public 2-year community college
▶ Commuter campus in small town

**General.** Founded in 1978. Regionally accredited. Service area of 44,000 square miles. Full schedule of courses plus live video and audio conferencing for students in remote areas. Off-campus centers at Cordova and Glennallen offer credit-bearing courses. **Enrollment:** 150 degree-seeking undergraduates. **Degrees:** 16 associate awarded. **Location:** 300 miles from Anchorage. **Calendar:** Semester, limited summer session. **Full-time faculty:** 7 total. **Part-time faculty:** 55 total. **Class size:** 94% < 20, 5% 20-39, less than 1% 40-49, less than 1% 50-99, less than 1% >100. **Special facilities:** Alaska native museum.

**Transfer out. Colleges most students transferred to 2007:** University of Alaska - Anchorage.

**Basis for selection.** Open admission. **Homeschooled:** Statement describing homeschool structure and mission required.

**2007-2008 Annual costs.** Tuition/fees: $3,660. Per-credit charge: $110. Books/supplies: $600.

**Financial aid. Need-based:** Need-based aid available for part-time students. **Non-need-based:** Scholarships awarded for state residency.

**Application procedures. Admission:** No deadline. $10 fee. Application must be submitted on paper. Admission notification on a rolling basis. **Financial aid:** Priority date 6/30; no closing date. FAFSA required. Applicants notified on a rolling basis.

**Academics. Special study options:** Distance learning, double major, dual enrollment of high school students, ESL, external degree, honors, independent study, internships. Bachelor's degree programs available on campus. **Credit/placement by examination:** AP, CLEP, IB, institutional tests. **Support services:** GED preparation and test center, learning center, reduced course load, remedial instruction, study skills assistance, tutoring.

**Majors. Business:** Office management. **Engineering technology:** Electrical. **Liberal arts:** Arts/sciences.

**Computing on campus.** 50 workstations in dormitories, library, computer center. Online library, helpline available.

**Student life. Freshman orientation:** Available. Preregistration for classes offered. **Housing:** Coed dorms, apartments, substance-free housing available. $200 deposit. **Activities:** Drama, film society, student government.

**Student services.** Adult student services, career counseling, financial aid counseling, veterans' counselor. **Transfer:** Transfer adviser, college fairs on campus for students transferring to 4-year colleges.

**Contact.** E-mail: sfoster@pwscc.edu
Phone: (907) 834-1632 Toll-free number: (800) 478-8800
Fax: (907) 834-1635
Shannon Foster, Registrar, Prince William Sound Community College, Box 97, Valdez, AK 99686

# Arizona

## Arizona Automotive Institute
### Glendale, Arizona
### www.aai.edu                                    CB code: 2127

▶ For-profit 2-year technical college
▶ Commuter campus in small city

**General.** Founded in 1967. Accredited by ACCSCT. **Enrollment:** 540 degree-seeking undergraduates. **Degrees:** 320 associate awarded. **Location:** 3 miles from Phoenix. **Calendar:** Quarter, extensive summer session. **Full-time faculty:** 25 total. **Part-time faculty:** 5 total.

**Student profile.**

| Out-of-state: | 36% | 25 or older: | 25% |
|---|---|---|---|

**Basis for selection.** Open admission. Interview highly recommended.

**2007-2008 Annual costs.** Total cost of associate degree program is $26,110 including tuition, books, supplies, tools. Cost of diploma is $17,440.

**Application procedures. Admission:** No deadline. $100 fee. Admission notification on a rolling basis. **Financial aid:** No deadline. FAFSA, institutional form required. Applicants notified on a rolling basis.

**Academics. Special study options:** Double major. **Credit/placement by examination:** CLEP.

**Majors. Mechanic/repair:** Automotive, diesel.

**Computing on campus.** 15 workstations in computer center.

**Student life. Housing:** Apartments available.

**Athletics. Intramural:** Basketball M, bowling, football (tackle) M, softball, volleyball.

**Student services.** Career counseling, student employment services, personal counseling, placement for graduates, veterans' counselor.

**Contact.** E-mail: info@azautoinst.com
Phone: (623) 934-7273 Toll-free number: (800) 528-0717
Fax: (623) 930-4948
Norman Dom, Director of Admissions, Arizona Automotive Institute, 6829 North 46th Avenue, Glendale, AZ 85301

## Arizona Western College
### Yuma, Arizona                                  CB member
### www.azwestern.edu                              CB code: 4013

▶ Public 2-year community college
▶ Commuter campus in small city

**General.** Founded in 1963. Regionally accredited. Satellite sites in Parker, San Luis-Somerton, Wellton. Campus shared with Northern Arizona University, which offers completion of bachelor's, master's and doctoral programs. **Enrollment:** 6,056 degree-seeking undergraduates; 897 non-degree-seeking students. **Degrees:** 492 associate awarded. **Location:** 7 miles from Yuma. **Calendar:** Semester, limited summer session. **Full-time faculty:** 110 total. **Part-time faculty:** 234 total. **Class size:** 54% < 20, 45% 20-39, less than 1% 40-49, less than 1% 50-99, less than 1% >100. **Partnerships:** Formal partnerships with Yuma Educational Consortium and Yuma Regional Medical Center.

**Student profile.** Among degree-seeking undergraduates, 65% enrolled in a transfer program, 29% enrolled in a vocational program, 4% already have a bachelor's degree or higher, 185 enrolled as first-time, first-year students.

| Part-time: | 58% | Hispanic American: | 55% |
|---|---|---|---|
| Out-of-state: | 14% | Native American: | 2% |
| Women: | 60% | International: | 13% |
| African American: | 3% | 25 or older: | 31% |
| Asian American: | 2% | | |

**Transfer out.** 40% of students enrolled in the transfer program go on to 4-year colleges. **Colleges most students transferred to 2007:** Northern Arizona University at Yuma, Arizona State University, University of Arizona.

**Basis for selection.** Open admission, but selective for some programs. Out-of-state applicants screened for social or disciplinary problems. Special requirements for nursing program. Mandatory testing for placement.

**2007-2008 Annual costs.** Tuition/fees: $1,380; $5,940 out-of-state. Per-credit charge: $46 in-state; $52 out-of-state. Room/board: $4,630. Books/supplies: $1,240. Personal expenses: $2,895.

**Financial aid. Need-based:** Need-based aid available for part-time students. Work-study available nights, weekends and for part-time students. **Non-need-based:** Scholarships awarded for academics, athletics.

**Application procedures. Admission:** No deadline. No application fee. Application may be submitted online. Admission notification on a rolling basis. **Financial aid:** Priority date 4/1; no closing date. FAFSA, institutional form required. Applicants notified on a rolling basis starting 5/1.

**Academics. Special study options:** Accelerated study, cooperative education, distance learning, dual enrollment of high school students, ESL, honors, independent study, internships, study abroad, teacher certification program, weekend college. License preparation in nursing, occupational therapy, paramedic, radiology. **Credit/placement by examination:** AP, CLEP, IB, institutional tests. 24 credit hours maximum toward associate degree. **Support services:** GED preparation, learning center, reduced course load, remedial instruction, study skills assistance, tutoring, writing center.

**Majors. Agriculture:** General, plant sciences. **Biology:** General. **Business:** General, business admin, hospitality admin, marketing, office management. **Communications:** General, radio/tv. **Communications technology:** Radio/tv. **Computer sciences:** General, computer graphics, data entry. **Conservation:** Environmental science. **Education:** General, early childhood, elementary, secondary. **Engineering:** General. **Engineering technology:** CAD/CADD, industrial, water quality. **English:** English lit. **Family/consumer sciences:** General, child development. **Foreign languages:** Spanish. **Health:** EMT paramedic, health services, massage therapy, nursing (RN), nursing admin, radiologic technology/medical imaging. **History:** General. **Math:** General. **Mechanic/repair:** Automotive, heating/ac/refrig. **Parks/recreation:** Health/fitness. **Personal/culinary services:** Restaurant/catering. **Philosophy/religion:** Philosophy. **Physical sciences:** Chemistry, oceanography, physics. **Production:** Welding. **Protective services:** Firefighting, law enforcement admin, police science. **Public administration:** Human services. **Social sciences:** General, political science. **Visual/performing arts:** Dramatic, multimedia, studio arts. **Other:** Electical/Electronics maintenance and repair technology, Management sciences and quantitative methods.

**Computing on campus.** 270 workstations in dormitories, library, computer center, student center. Dormitories wired for high-speed internet access and linked to campus network. Commuter students can connect to campus network. Online course registration, online library, helpline, repair service, student web hosting, wireless network available.

**Student life. Freshman orientation:** Available. Preregistration for classes offered. **Housing:** Guaranteed on-campus for all undergraduates. Coed dorms, single-sex dorms, special housing for disabled, substance-free housing available. $100 nonrefundable deposit. **Activities:** Bands, choral groups, dance, drama, literary magazine, music ensembles, radio station, student government, student newspaper, TV station, AACHE, Phi Theta Kappa, Native American club, Hispanic students club, international students club.

**Athletics.** NJCAA. **Intercollegiate:** Baseball M, basketball, football (tackle) M, soccer M, softball W, volleyball W. **Team name:** Matadors.

**Student services.** Adult student services, career counseling, services for economically disadvantaged, student employment services, financial aid counseling, health services, minority student services, on-campus daycare, personal counseling, placement for graduates, veterans' counselor, women's services. **Physically disabled:** Services for visually, hearing impaired. **Transfer:** Pre-admission transcript evaluation for new students. Transfer center, transfer adviser, college fairs on campus for students transferring to 4-year colleges.

**Contact.** E-mail: veronica.garcia@azwestern.edu
Phone: (928) 317-6000 Toll-free number: (888) 293-0392
Fax: (928) 344-7543
Bryan Doak, Associate Dean of Enrollment Services, Arizona Western College, PO Box 929, Yuma, AZ 85366-0929

## Bryman School
### Phoenix, Arizona
### www.brymanschool.edu
CB code: 3040

- For-profit 2-year health science college
- Very large city

**General.** Accredited by ACCSCT. **Calendar:** Continuous.

**Annual costs/financial aid.** Diploma programs range in price from $10,750 to $21,950 ($9,050 to $19,850 for agency) and $22,950 to $26,250 for degree ($18,100 to $22,000 for agency). Registration fee of $50.00. Books/supplies: $424. Personal expenses: $3,360.

**Contact.** Phone: (602) 274-4300
Director of Admissions, 2250 West Peoria Ave, Phoenix, AZ 85029-4919

## Central Arizona College
### Coolidge, Arizona
### www.centralaz.edu/
CB code: 4122

- Public 2-year community college
- Commuter campus in rural community

**General.** Founded in 1962. Regionally accredited. **Enrollment:** 4,951 degree-seeking undergraduates. **Degrees:** 295 associate awarded. **Location:** 45 miles from Phoenix. **Calendar:** Semester, limited summer session. **Full-time faculty:** 97 total. **Part-time faculty:** 256 total. **Special facilities:** Observatory. **Partnerships:** Formal partnership with CAVIT.

**Student profile.**

| | | | |
|---|---|---|---|
| Out-of-state: | 2% | Live on campus: | 4% |
| 25 or older: | 65% | | |

**Transfer out. Colleges most students transferred to 2007:** Arizona State University, Northern Arizona University, University of Arizona.

**Basis for selection.** Open admission, but selective for some programs. Special requirements for nursing programs. Placement tests required of all degree-seeking students. **Learning Disabled:** Contact special needs coordinator.

**2007-2008 Annual costs.** Tuition/fees: $1,622; $7,154 out-of-state. Per-credit charge: $57 in-state; $114 out-of-state. Room/board: $4,560. Books/supplies: $1,050. Personal expenses: $1,350.

**Financial aid. Need-based:** Need-based aid available for part-time students. Work-study available nights, weekends and for part-time students.

**Application procedures. Admission:** No deadline. $22 fee. Application may be submitted online. Admission notification on a rolling basis. **Financial aid:** Priority date 5/1, closing date 7/15. FAFSA required. Applicants notified by 5/30; must reply within 3 week(s) of notification.

**Academics. Special study options:** Distance learning, dual enrollment of high school students, ESL, honors, independent study, liberal arts/career combination, student-designed major. Bachelor's degree programs available on campus. License preparation in nursing, radiology, real estate. **Credit/placement by examination:** AP, CLEP, institutional tests. 30 credit hours maximum toward associate degree. **Support services:** GED preparation and test center, learning center, pre-admission summer program, reduced course load, remedial instruction, study skills assistance, tutoring, writing center.

**Majors. Agriculture:** Business. **Biology:** General. **Business:** General, accounting, administrative services, business admin, hospitality/recreation, management information systems, office technology. **Communications:** Journalism. **Computer sciences:** General, applications programming, data processing, programming. **Education:** General, early childhood, elementary, multi-level teacher, special. **Engineering:** General, civil, mechanical, mechanics. **Engineering technology:** Electrical, industrial management, manufacturing. **English:** Composition, English lit. **Family/consumer sciences:** Family studies. **Health:** EMT paramedic, medical assistant, medical secretary, medical transcription, nursing (RN), pharmacy assistant, preveterinary. **Interdisciplinary:** Biological/physical sciences. **Legal studies:** Legal secretary. **Liberal arts:** Arts/sciences, humanities. **Math:** General. **Mechanic/repair:** Automotive, diesel, industrial. **Parks/recreation:** Exercise sciences. **Personal/culinary services:** Culinary arts. **Physical sciences:** Chemistry. **Protective services:** Corrections, criminal justice, firefighting. **Psychology:** General. **Social sciences:** General, criminology. **Visual/performing arts:** General, art, dramatic.

**Computing on campus.** 500 workstations in dormitories, library, computer center, student center. Dormitories wired for high-speed internet access. Commuter students can connect to campus network. Online course registration, helpline, wireless network available.

**Student life. Freshman orientation:** Available. Preregistration for classes offered. **Policies:** Student code of conduct. **Housing:** Coed dorms, special housing for disabled, substance-free housing available. $100 fully refundable deposit. **Activities:** Bands, choral groups, drama, music ensembles, musical theater, student government, student newspaper, Phi Theta Kappa/Lamba, art club, Playmasters, Campus Crusade For Christ, international club, Native American club, rodeo club, We Can Do It club, Student Nurses Association of Arizona.

**Athletics.** NJCAA. **Intercollegiate:** Baseball M, basketball, cross-country, rodeo, softball W, track and field. **Team name:** Vaqueros.

**Student services.** Adult student services, alcohol/substance abuse counseling, career counseling, student employment services, financial aid counseling, on-campus daycare, personal counseling, placement for graduates. **Physically disabled:** Services for visually, hearing impaired. **Transfer:** Re-entry adviser, pre-admission transcript evaluation for new students. Transfer center, transfer adviser, college fairs on campus for students transferring to 4-year colleges.

**Contact.** E-mail: admissions@centralaz.edu
Phone: (520) 494-5260 Toll-free number: (800) 237-9814
Fax: (520) 494-5083
James Smalley, District-wide Registrar, Central Arizona College, 8470 North Overfield Road, Coolidge, AZ 85228-9778

## Chandler-Gilbert Community College: Pecos
### Chandler, Arizona
### www.cgc.maricopa.edu
CB code: 0535

- Public 2-year community college
- Commuter campus in small city

**General.** Regionally accredited. **Enrollment:** 1,471 degree-seeking undergraduates; 7,949 non-degree-seeking students. **Degrees:** 349 associate awarded. **Location:** 20 miles from Phoenix. **Calendar:** Semester, limited summer session. **Full-time faculty:** 116 total. **Part-time faculty:** 314 total. **Class size:** 43% < 20, 47% 20-39, 8% 40-49, less than 1% 50-99.

**Student profile.** Among degree-seeking undergraduates, 75% enrolled in a transfer program, 18% enrolled in a vocational program, 4% already have a bachelor's degree or higher, 567 enrolled as first-time, first-year students.

| | | | |
|---|---|---|---|
| Part-time: | 54% | 25 or older: | 28% |
| Out-of-state: | 5% | Live on campus: | 2% |
| Women: | 61% | | |

**Transfer out. Colleges most students transferred to 2007:** Arziona State University, Northern Arizona University, University of Arizona.

**Basis for selection.** Open admission.

**2007-2008 Annual costs.** Tuition/fees: $1,965; $8,415 out-of-state. Per-credit charge: $65 in-state; $280 out-of-state. Books/supplies: $1,064. Personal expenses: $4,878.

**Financial aid. Need-based:** Work-study available nights, weekends and for part-time students.

**Application procedures. Admission:** No deadline. No application fee. Application may be submitted online.

**Academics. Special study options:** Distance learning, dual enrollment of high school students, ESL, honors, independent study, weekend college. License preparation in aviation, nursing. **Credit/placement by examination:** AP, CLEP, IB, institutional tests. 30 credit hours maximum toward associate degree. **Support services:** Learning center, reduced course load, remedial instruction, study skills assistance, tutoring, writing center.

**Majors. Business:** General, accounting, nonprofit/public, office technology. **Computer sciences:** General, computer science, data entry, information technology, networking, system admin, vendor certification. **Education:** Elementary. **Health:** Clinical nutrition, dietetic technician, massage therapy, nursing assistant. **Visual/performing arts:** Music management. **Other:** Automated manufacturing systems, Retail management.

**Most popular majors.** Computer/information sciences 17%, education 8%, history 7%, liberal arts 62%.

**Computing on campus.** 140 workstations in library, computer center. Commuter students can connect to campus network. Online course registration, online library, wireless network available.

**Student life. Freshman orientation:** Available. Preregistration for classes offered. Sessions are held at the beginning of the term (two days are available from which to choose, offering a weekend day and weeknight evening). **Housing:** Coed dorms available. Student housing for CGCC students is available on-campus only at the Williams campus in cooperation with Arizona State University Polytechnic. CGCC students attending any of the college's campuses can apply for student housing at the Williams campus. **Activities:** Bands, choral groups, dance, drama, music ensembles, musical theater, student government, political science organization, Christians in Action, Latter Day Saints student association, intercultural exchange club, Wall Street club, Phi Theta Kappa, Black Student Union, Hispanic student organization.

**Athletics.** NJCAA. **Intercollegiate:** Baseball M, basketball, golf, soccer, softball W, volleyball W. **Team name:** Coyotes.

**Student services.** Adult student services, alcohol/substance abuse counseling, career counseling, services for economically disadvantaged, student employment services, financial aid counseling, personal counseling, placement for graduates, veterans' counselor. **Physically disabled:** Services for visually, speech, hearing impaired. **Transfer:** Pre-admission transcript evaluation for new students. Transfer center, transfer adviser, college fairs on campus for students transferring to 4-year colleges.

**Contact.** Phone: (480) 732-7320
Douglas Bullock, Dean Enrollment Services, Chandler-Gilbert Community College: Pecos, 2626 East Pecos Road, Chandler, AZ 85225

---

## Chandler-Gilbert Community College: Sun Lakes Education Center

**Sun Lakes, Arizona**
www.cgc.maricopa.edu                    CB code: 3826

- Public 2-year community college
- Commuter campus in small town

**General.** Regionally accredited. **Location:** 25 miles from Phoenix. **Calendar:** Semester.

**Annual costs/financial aid.** Tuition/fees (2007-2008): $1,965; $8,415 out-of-state. Books/supplies: $1,064. Personal expenses: $4,878.

**Contact.** Phone: (480) 857-5500
Supervisor of Admissions Records and Registration, 25105 South Alma School Road, Sun Lakes, AZ 85248-7158

---

## Chandler-Gilbert Community College: Williams Campus

**Mesa, Arizona**
www.cgc.maricopa.edu                    CB code: 3827

- Public 2-year community college
- Commuter campus in large city

**General.** Regionally accredited. **Location:** 33 miles from Phoenix. **Calendar:** Semester.

**Annual costs/financial aid.** Tuition/fees (2007-2008): $1,980; $8,430 out-of-state. Room/board: $7,368. Books/supplies: $1,064.

**Contact.** Phone: (480) 732-7320
Supervisor of Admissions, Records and Registration, 2626 East Pecos Road, Chandler, AZ 85225-2499

---

## Cochise College

**Douglas, Arizona**                    CB member
www.cochise.edu                         CB code: 4097

- Public 2-year community college
- Commuter campus in large town

**General.** Founded in 1962. Regionally accredited. Courses offered at 2 campuses; 4 extended learning centers located in 2 counties and online. **Enrollment:** 3,113 degree-seeking undergraduates; 1,381 non-degree-seeking students. **Degrees:** 1,030 associate awarded. **Location:** 120 miles

from Tucson. **Calendar:** Semester, limited summer session. **Full-time faculty:** 96 total; 16% minority. **Part-time faculty:** 258 total; 17% minority. **Class size:** 88% < 20, 12% 20-39, less than 1% 40-49, less than 1% 50-99. **Special facilities:** Asian art collection, college airport.

**Student profile.** Among degree-seeking undergraduates, 23% enrolled in a transfer program, 46% enrolled in a vocational program, 741 enrolled as first-time, first-year students, 1,271 transferred in from other institutions.

| | | | |
|---|---|---|---|
| Part-time: | 71% | Hispanic American: | 40% |
| Out-of-state: | 4% | Native American: | 1% |
| Women: | 59% | 25 or older: | 45% |
| African American: | 6% | Live on campus: | 3% |
| Asian American: | 3% | | |

**Transfer out. Colleges most students transferred to 2007:** University of Arizona, Arizona State University, Northern Arizona University, Western New Mexico University.

**Basis for selection.** Open admission, but selective for some programs. Special requirements for air transportation (professional pilot, aviation maintenance) and nursing programs; interview required. Walk-in admission available.

**2008-2009 Annual costs.** Tuition/fees: $1,540; $7,330 out-of-state. Room/board: $4,380. Books/supplies: $1,000. Personal expenses: $1,350.

**2006-2007 Financial aid. Need-based:** 359 full-time freshmen applied for aid; 304 were judged to have need; 288 of these received aid. Average scholarship/grant was $2,614; average loan $2,114. 74% of total undergraduate aid awarded as scholarships/grants, 26% as loans/jobs. Need-based aid available for part-time students. Work-study available for part-time students. **Non-need-based:** Awarded to 305 full-time undergraduates, including 135 freshmen. Scholarships awarded for academics, athletics.

**Application procedures. Admission:** No deadline. No application fee. Application may be submitted online. Admission notification on a rolling basis. **Financial aid:** Closing date 4/15. FAFSA, institutional form required. Applicants notified on a rolling basis starting 6/15; must reply within 2 week(s) of notification.

**Academics. Special study options:** Cooperative education, distance learning, double major, dual enrollment of high school students, ESL, honors, independent study, internships, teacher certification program, weekend college. License preparation in aviation, nursing, paramedic, real estate. **Credit/placement by examination:** AP, CLEP, institutional tests. 30 credit hours maximum toward associate degree. Student must complete at least one Cochise College course before credit may be granted for CLEP/DANTES. **Support services:** GED preparation, learning center, reduced course load, remedial instruction, tutoring, writing center.

**Majors. Agriculture:** Business. **Biology:** General. **Business:** Administrative services, business admin, management information systems. **Communications:** General. **Computer sciences:** Computer science, data processing, information systems, networking, security. **Construction:** General. **Education:** Art, biology, chemistry, early childhood, English, foreign languages, history, mathematics, music, physical. **Engineering:** Manufacturing. **Engineering technology:** CAD/CADD, electrical. **English:** English lit. **Foreign languages:** General, sign language interpretation, Spanish, translation. **Health:** Health services, nursing (RN), prenursing. **History:** General. **Legal studies:** Legal secretary. **Liberal arts:** Arts/sciences, humanities. **Math:** General. **Mechanic/repair:** Aircraft. **Military:** General. **Parks/recreation:** Health/fitness. **Personal/culinary services:** Chef training. **Physical sciences:** Chemistry, physics. **Protective services:** Police science. **Psychology:** General. **Public administration:** Human services. **Social sciences:** Anthropology, economics, geography, political science, sociology. **Transportation:** Airline/commercial pilot. **Visual/performing arts:** Art.

**Most popular majors.** Liberal arts 17%, military 56%.

**Computing on campus.** 571 workstations in dormitories, library, computer center. Dormitories wired for high-speed internet access. Online course registration, online library, wireless network available.

**Student life. Freshman orientation:** Available. Preregistration for classes offered. **Housing:** Single-sex dorms, apartments available. $100 partly refundable deposit. **Activities:** Choral groups, drama, film society, literary magazine, music ensembles, student government, Alpha Delta Omega, Alpha Eta Rho, armed forces communication and electronics association, aviation maintenance specialist club, campus activities board, ECO club, Vocational Industrial Clubs of America, Future Teacher's club, Phi Beta Lambda, Phi Theta Kappa.

**Athletics.** NJCAA. **Intercollegiate:** Baseball M, basketball, rodeo, soccer W. **Intramural:** Basketball. **Team name:** Apaches.

**Student services.** Career counseling, student employment services, financial aid counseling, health services, personal counseling, placement for graduates, veterans' counselor. **Physically disabled:** Services for visually, hearing impaired. **Transfer:** Transfer adviser, college fairs on campus for students transferring to 4-year colleges.

**Contact.** E-mail: admissions@cochise.edu
Phone: (520) 515-5412 Toll-free number: (800) 593-9567
Fax: (520) 515-5452
Debbie Quick, Director of Admissions, Cochise College, 901 North Colombo Avenue, Sierra Vista, AZ 85635

---

## Coconino County Community College
**Flagstaff, Arizona**
www.coconino.edu

**CB member**
**CB code: 1712**

- Public 2-year community college
- Commuter campus in small city

**General.** Regionally accredited. **Enrollment:** 2,700 degree-seeking undergraduates; 1,183 non-degree-seeking students. **Degrees:** 165 associate awarded. **ROTC:** Army, Air Force. **Location:** 140 miles from Phoenix. **Calendar:** Semester, limited summer session. **Full-time faculty:** 38 total; 55% women. **Part-time faculty:** 220 total; 52% women.

**Student profile.** Among degree-seeking undergraduates, 35% enrolled in a transfer program, 19% enrolled in a vocational program, 7% already have a bachelor's degree or higher, 879 enrolled as first-time, first-year students, 61 transferred in from other institutions.

| | | | |
|---|---|---|---|
| Part-time: | 72% | Asian American: | 1% |
| Out-of-state: | 5% | Hispanic American: | 11% |
| Women: | 57% | Native American: | 29% |
| African American: | 1% | | |

**Transfer out.** 47% of students enrolled in the transfer program go on to 4-year colleges. **Colleges most students transferred to 2007:** Northern Arizona University, Arizona State University, University of Arizona.

**Basis for selection.** Open admission, but selective for some programs. Special requirements for nursing program. High school students must complete additional paperwork.

**2007-2008 Annual costs.** Tuition/fees: $1,690; $8,450 out-of-state. Per-credit charge: $65 in-state; $325 out-of-state. Books/supplies: $1,000. Personal expenses: $3,222.

**Application procedures. Admission:** No deadline. No application fee. Application must be submitted on paper. Admission notification on a rolling basis. **Financial aid:** Priority date 4/15, closing date 6/30.

**Academics.** The writing center, learning center and tutoring are free to all students. The writing center and math tutoring are offered online and in-person. **Special study options:** Distance learning, dual enrollment of high school students, honors, internships. License preparation in nursing, paramedic, real estate. **Credit/placement by examination:** CLEP. **Support services:** GED preparation and test center, learning center, remedial instruction, study skills assistance, tutoring, writing center.

**Majors. Architecture:** Technology. **Business:** General, accounting, business admin, construction management, finance, hospitality admin, marketing. **Computer sciences:** System admin. **Conservation:** Environmental science. **Construction:** Carpentry. **Education:** General, early childhood, elementary. **Engineering:** General. **Engineering technology:** Architectural drafting, CAD/CADD, computer systems, construction, software, solar energy. **Health:** Medical secretary, nursing assistant. **Interdisciplinary:** Biological/physical sciences. **Legal studies:** Paralegal. **Physical sciences:** Geochemistry. **Protective services:** Criminal justice, firefighting. **Psychology:** General. **Public administration:** Social work. **Social sciences:** Anthropology, sociology. **Visual/performing arts:** Art. **Other:** Colorado plateau studies.

**Computing on campus.** 100 workstations in library, computer center, student center. Online course registration, online library, helpline available.

**Student life. Freshman orientation:** Available. Preregistration for classes offered. **Housing:** Some dorm opportunities may be available through Northern Arizona University. **Activities:** Jazz band, dance, symphony orchestra.

**Student services.** Adult student services, career counseling, financial aid counseling, on-campus daycare, veterans' counselor. **Physically disabled:** Services for visually, speech, hearing impaired. **Transfer:** Pre-admission transcript evaluation for new students. Transfer adviser, college fairs on campus for students transferring to 4-year colleges.

**Contact.** E-mail: admissions&registration@coconino.edu
Phone: (928) 527-1222 ext. 4299 Toll-free
number: (800) 350-7122 ext. 4299 Fax: (928) 226-4110
Liz Gallegos, Co-interim Registrar/Director for Admissions, Coconino County Community College, 2800 S Lone Tree Road, Flagstaff, AZ 86001

---

## Dine College
**Tsaile, Arizona**
www.dinecollege.edu

**CB member**
**CB code: 4550**

- Public 2-year community college
- Residential campus in rural community

**General.** Founded in 1968. Regionally accredited. The first tribally controlled community college in the United States; chartered by the Navajo Nation. **Enrollment:** 927 degree-seeking undergraduates. **Degrees:** 212 associate awarded. **Location:** 55 miles from Window Rock. **Calendar:** Semester, limited summer session. **Full-time faculty:** 61 total; 43% women. **Part-time faculty:** 73 total; 48% women. **Special facilities:** Museum.

**Student profile.**

| | | | |
|---|---|---|---|
| Out-of-state: | 15% | Live on campus: | 20% |
| 25 or older: | 49% | | |

**Transfer out. Colleges most students transferred to 2007:** Northern Arizona University, Arizona State University, Fort Lewis College, University of Arizona, University of New Mexico.

**Basis for selection.** Open admission. **Homeschooled:** Statement describing homeschool structure and mission, transcript of courses and grades, state high school equivalency certificate required.

**2007-2008 Annual costs.** Tuition/fees: $850. Per-credit charge: $30. Room/board: $3,764. Books/supplies: $950. Personal expenses: $2,500.

**Financial aid.** All financial aid based on need. Need-based aid available for part-time students.

**Application procedures. Admission:** No deadline. $20 fee. Application must be submitted on paper. Admission notification on a rolling basis. **Financial aid:** Priority date 4/15; no closing date. FAFSA, institutional form required. Applicants notified on a rolling basis starting 5/1; must reply within 4 week(s) of notification.

**Academics. Special study options:** Cooperative education, distance learning, double major, independent study. **Credit/placement by examination:** CLEP, institutional tests. 12 credit hours maximum toward associate degree. **Support services:** Learning center, pre-admission summer program, remedial instruction, tutoring.

**Majors. Area/ethnic studies:** Native American. **Biology:** General. **Business:** Administrative services, business admin, office/clerical. **Computer sciences:** General, computer science. **Conservation:** Environmental science. **Education:** General. **Foreign languages:** Native American. **Health:** Public health ed. **Liberal arts:** Arts/sciences. **Psychology:** General. **Social sciences:** General. **Visual/performing arts:** Studio arts. **Other:** Pre-Engineering.

**Computing on campus.** 104 workstations in dormitories, library, computer center, student center. Dormitories wired for high-speed internet access and linked to campus network. Online library, helpline, repair service, wireless network available.

**Student life. Freshman orientation:** Available. Preregistration for classes offered. **Housing:** Coed dorms, single-sex dorms, substance-free housing available. **Activities:** Student government, Red Dawn Indian club.

**Athletics.** NJCAA. **Intercollegiate:** Archery, cross-country, rodeo. **Intramural:** Archery, cross-country, rodeo. **Team name:** Warrior.

**Student services.** Alcohol/substance abuse counseling, career counseling, personal counseling, veterans' counselor. **Transfer:** Pre-admission transcript evaluation for new students. Transfer adviser, college fairs on campus for students transferring to 4-year colleges.

**Contact.** Phone: (928) 724-6630 Fax: (928) 724-3349
Louise Litzin, Registrar, Dine College, Box 67, Tsaile, AZ 86556

---

## Eastern Arizona College
**Thatcher, Arizona**
www.eac.edu

**CB code: 4297**

- Public 2-year community college
- Commuter campus in large town

**General.** Founded in 1888. Regionally accredited. Near archaeological sites. Several continuing education centers within 165 miles of campus. **Enrollment:** 3,058 degree-seeking undergraduates; 2,252 non-degree-seeking students. **Degrees:** 283 associate awarded. **Location:** 160 miles from Phoenix, 130 miles from Tucson. **Calendar:** Semester, limited summer session. **Full-time faculty:** 92 total; 14% have terminal degrees, 12% minority, 33% women. **Part-time faculty:** 188 total; 2% have terminal degrees, 14% minority, 55% women. **Class size:** 81% < 20, 16% 20-39, less than 1% 40-49, less than 1% 50-99, less than 1% >100. **Special facilities:** Observatory, golf course, wilderness area. **Partnerships:** Formal partnerships with local high schools allow high school students to obtain degrees in areas such as office technology and drafting.

**Student profile.** Among degree-seeking undergraduates, 66% enrolled in a transfer program, 33% enrolled in a vocational program, 615 enrolled as first-time, first-year students, 44 transferred in from other institutions.

| | | | |
|---|---|---|---|
| Part-time: | 55% | Hispanic American: | 18% |
| Out-of-state: | 5% | Native American: | 11% |
| Women: | 58% | International: | 1% |
| African American: | 3% | 25 or older: | 51% |
| Asian American: | 1% | Live on campus: | 6% |

**Basis for selection.** Open admission, but selective for some programs. Special requirements for nursing and several paramedical programs.

**High school preparation.** 15 units recommended. Recommended units include English 4, mathematics 4, social studies 1, history 1, science 3 (laboratory 3) and foreign language 2.

**2007-2008 Annual costs.** Tuition/fees: $1,300; $6,540 out-of-state. Per-credit charge: $55 in-state; $110 out-of-state. Room/board: $4,320. Books/supplies: $800. Personal expenses: $1,722.

**2007-2008 Financial aid. Need-based:** Average scholarship/grant was $4,247. 92% of total undergraduate aid awarded as scholarships/grants, 8% as loans/jobs. Need-based aid available for part-time students. Work-study available nights, weekends and for part-time students. **Non-need-based:** Scholarships awarded for academics, art, athletics, leadership, music/drama, state residency. **Additional information:** Limited number of tuition waivers for New Mexico residents. Unlimited number of waivers for those meeting WUE requirements.

**Application procedures. Admission:** No deadline. No application fee. Application may be submitted online. Admission notification on a rolling basis. **Financial aid:** Priority date 3/1; no closing date. FAFSA, institutional form required. Applicants notified on a rolling basis starting 3/15.

**Academics. Special study options:** Cooperative education, distance learning, double major, dual enrollment of high school students, independent study. Bachelor's degree programs available on campus. License preparation in nursing, paramedic. **Credit/placement by examination:** AP, CLEP, IB, institutional tests. 48 credit hours maximum toward associate degree. **Support services:** GED preparation and test center, learning center, reduced course load, remedial instruction, study skills assistance, tutoring, writing center.

**Majors. Agriculture:** Agribusiness operations. **Biology:** General, environmental, wildlife. **Business:** Administrative services, business admin, entrepreneurial studies, office technology. **Computer sciences:** Information systems, system admin. **Conservation:** Forestry. **Education:** Art, business, elementary, secondary, technology/industrial arts. **Engineering technology:** Civil, drafting, mining. **English:** English lit. **Foreign languages:** General. **Health:** EMT paramedic, nursing (RN), pharmacy assistant, premedicine, prepharmacy. **History:** General. **Legal studies:** Prelaw. **Liberal arts:** Arts/sciences. **Math:** General. **Mechanic/repair:** Automotive. **Parks/recreation:** Health/fitness. **Personal/culinary services:** Cosmetic. **Physical sciences:** Chemistry, geology, physics. **Protective services:** Law enforcement admin, police science. **Psychology:** General. **Social sciences:** Anthropology, political science, sociology. **Visual/performing arts:** Art, commercial/advertising art, dramatic, studio arts.

**Most popular majors.** Education 11%, health sciences 28%, liberal arts 33%, security/protective services 18%.

**Computing on campus.** 564 workstations in library, computer center. Dormitories wired for high-speed internet access and linked to campus network. Online course registration, online library, wireless network available.

**Student life. Freshman orientation:** Available. Preregistration for classes offered. Half-day session given the week prior to beginning of classes each semester and weekly during summer months. **Housing:** Single-sex dorms, substance-free housing available. $150 fully refundable deposit. **Activities:** Bands, choral groups, dance, drama, literary magazine, music ensembles, musical theater, student government, symphony orchestra, Latter-Day-Saints student association, Newman club, drama club, Hispanic Leaders,

Intertribal club, Phi Theta Kappa, Spanish Club, Gila Force, Rowdy Reptiles.

**Athletics.** NJCAA. **Intercollegiate:** Baseball M, basketball, football (tackle) M, golf M, softball W, tennis W, volleyball W. **Intramural:** Basketball, soccer, swimming, tennis, volleyball. **Team name:** Gila Monsters.

**Student services.** Adult student services, alcohol/substance abuse counseling, career counseling, services for economically disadvantaged, student employment services, financial aid counseling, minority student services, personal counseling, placement for graduates, veterans' counselor, women's services. **Physically disabled:** Services for visually, speech, hearing impaired. **Transfer:** Re-entry adviser, pre-admission transcript evaluation for new students. Transfer adviser, college fairs on campus for students transferring to 4-year colleges.

**Contact.** E-mail: admissions@eac.edu
Phone: (928) 428-8272 Toll-free number: (800) 678-3808
Fax: (928) 428-8462
Erik Lehmann, Admissions Counselor, Eastern Arizona College, 615 North Stadium Avenue, Thatcher, AZ 85552-0769

---

## Estrella Mountain Community College
**Avondale, Arizona**
**www.estrellamountain.edu**      **CB code: 3810**

▶ Public 2-year community college
▶ Commuter campus in small city

**General.** Regionally accredited. **Enrollment:** 2,133 degree-seeking undergraduates. **Degrees:** 348 associate awarded. **ROTC:** Air Force. **Location:** 15 miles from Phoenix. **Calendar:** Semester, limited summer session. **Full-time faculty:** 70 total. **Part-time faculty:** 347 total.

**Student profile.**

| | | | |
|---|---|---|---|
| Out-of-state: | 1% | 25 or older: | 46% |

**Transfer out. Colleges most students transferred to 2007:** Arizona State University.

**Basis for selection.** Open admission.

**2007-2008 Annual costs.** Tuition/fees: $1,965; $8,415 out-of-state. Per-credit charge: $65 in-state; $280 out-of-state. Books/supplies: $1,104. Personal expenses: $2,718.

**2006-2007 Financial aid. Need-based:** 77% of total undergraduate aid awarded as scholarships/grants, 23% as loans/jobs. Need-based aid available for part-time students. Work-study available nights and for part-time students. **Non-need-based:** Scholarships awarded for leadership.

**Application procedures. Admission:** Closing date 3/1. $5 fee. Application may be submitted online. **Financial aid:** Priority date 4/1; no closing date. Applicants notified on a rolling basis starting 4/15.

**Academics. Special study options:** Accelerated study, dual enrollment of high school students, ESL, honors, independent study, weekend college. **Credit/placement by examination:** CLEP, IB. 30 credit hours maximum toward associate degree. **Support services:** GED test center, learning center, pre-admission summer program, reduced course load, remedial instruction, study skills assistance, tutoring, writing center.

**Majors. Business:** Business admin, hotel/motel admin, organizational behavior. **Computer sciences:** Applications programming, data entry, LAN/WAN management, vendor certification. **Education:** General, elementary, secondary, teacher assistance. **Liberal arts:** Arts/sciences. **Personal/culinary services:** Chef training, culinary arts. **Protective services:** Criminal justice. **Psychology:** General. **Public administration:** Social work.

**Computing on campus.** 185 workstations in library, computer center. Online course registration, online library, helpline, wireless network available.

**Student life. Freshman orientation:** Available. Preregistration for classes offered. **Activities:** Literary magazine, student government.

**Student services.** Adult student services, alcohol/substance abuse counseling, career counseling, financial aid counseling, personal counseling, veterans' counselor. **Physically disabled:** Services for visually, speech, hearing impaired. **Transfer:** Pre-admission transcript evaluation for new students. College fairs on campus for students transferring to 4-year colleges.

**Contact.** Phone: (623) 935-8000
Frank Amparo, Director of Admission and Records, Estrella Mountain Community College, 3000 North Dysart Road, Avondale, AZ 85392

## Everest College: Phoenix
**Phoenix, Arizona**
www.everest-college.com          **CB code: 2172**

- For-profit 2-year business and technical college
- Commuter campus in very large city
- Interview required

**General.** Founded in 1982. Regionally accredited. **Enrollment:** 2,766 degree-seeking undergraduates. **Degrees:** 16 bachelor's, 117 associate awarded. **Location:** 10 miles from downtown Phoenix. **Calendar:** Differs by program, extensive summer session. **Full-time faculty:** 8 total; 12% have terminal degrees, 38% minority, 62% women. **Part-time faculty:** 48 total; 12% have terminal degrees, 21% minority, 58% women.

**Student profile.** Among degree-seeking undergraduates, 2,766 enrolled as first-time, first-year students.

| | | | |
|---|---|---|---|
| Part-time: | 76% | Women: | 82% |
| Out-of-state: | 5% | 25 or older: | 65% |

**Transfer out. Colleges most students transferred to 2007:** Arizona State University, Northern Arizona University, University of Phoenix.

**Basis for selection.** Interview very important.

**2007-2008 Annual costs.** Per-credit charge: $272. Full-time tuition for traditional students is $9,792; on-line students pay $12,582 for academic year. All students pay $75 per year in required fees. Books/supplies: $975.

**Application procedures. Admission:** No deadline. No application fee. Application may be submitted online. Admission notification on a rolling basis. **Financial aid:** No deadline. FAFSA required. Applicants notified on a rolling basis.

**Academics. Special study options:** Cooperative education, distance learning, independent study, internships, weekend college. Bachelor's degree programs available on campus. License preparation in nursing. **Credit/placement by examination:** AP, CLEP, institutional tests. 68 credit hours maximum toward associate degree, 136 toward bachelor's. **Support services:** Reduced course load, remedial instruction, study skills assistance, tutoring.

**Majors. Business:** Accounting, business admin, office management. **Health:** Health services, nursing (RN). **Legal studies:** Paralegal. **Protective services:** Criminal justice.

**Most popular majors.** Business/marketing 21%, legal studies 85%.

**Computing on campus.** 120 workstations in library, computer center. Online course registration, online library, helpline available.

**Student life. Freshman orientation:** Mandatory.

**Student services.** Career counseling, student employment services, financial aid counseling, personal counseling, placement for graduates, veterans' counselor. **Transfer:** Pre-admission transcript evaluation for new students. Transfer adviser for students transferring to 4-year colleges.

**Contact.** E-mail: jaskins@cci.edu
Phone: (602) 942-4141 Toll-free number: (888) 741-4271
Fax: (602) 943-0960
Jim Askins, Director of Admissions, Everest College: Phoenix, 10400 North 25th Avenue Suite 190, Phoenix, AZ 85021

## Gateway Community College
**Phoenix, Arizona**
www.gatewaycc.edu/          **CB code: 0455**

- Public 2-year community and technical college
- Commuter campus in very large city

**General.** Founded in 1968. Regionally accredited. **Enrollment:** 6,313 degree-seeking undergraduates. **Degrees:** 435 associate awarded. **ROTC:** Army, Naval, Air Force. **Calendar:** Semester, extensive summer session. **Full-time faculty:** 98 total; 55% minority, 63% women. **Part-time faculty:** 266 total; 57% women. **Partnerships:** Formal partnerships with Intel, Johnson Control, Toyota, Motorola.

**Student profile.** Among degree-seeking undergraduates, 2% enrolled in a transfer program, 85% enrolled in a vocational program. Of all enrolled students, 10% already have a bachelor's degree or higher.

| | | | |
|---|---|---|---|
| Out-of-state: | 5% | 25 or older: | 80% |

**Transfer out. Colleges most students transferred to 2007:** Arizona State Unversity, Northern Arizona University, University of Arizona.

**Basis for selection.** Open admission, but selective for some programs. Special requirements for nursing and some allied health programs. General Aptitude Test Battery required of health science applicants.

**2007-2008 Annual costs.** Tuition/fees: $1,965; $7,905 out-of-state. Per-credit charge: $65 in-state; $263 out-of-state.

**Financial aid. Need-based:** Need-based aid available for part-time students. Work-study available nights, weekends and for part-time students. **Non-need-based:** Scholarships awarded for athletics.

**Application procedures. Admission:** No deadline. No application fee. Application may be submitted online. Admission notification on a rolling basis. **Financial aid:** Priority date 4/15; no closing date. FAFSA, institutional form required. Applicants notified on a rolling basis starting 7/1; must reply within 4 week(s) of notification.

**Academics. Special study options:** Accelerated study, combined bachelor's/graduate degree, cooperative education, cross-registration, distance learning, double major, dual enrollment of high school students, ESL, honors, independent study, internships, liberal arts/career combination, study abroad, teacher certification program. License preparation in nursing, physical therapy, radiology. **Credit/placement by examination:** AP, CLEP, IB, institutional tests. 30 credit hours maximum toward associate degree. **Support services:** GED test center, learning center, reduced course load, remedial instruction, study skills assistance, tutoring, writing center.

**Majors. Business:** General, accounting, administrative services, banking/financial services, international, office management. **Computer sciences:** General, information systems, LAN/WAN management, networking, system admin, systems analysis. **Construction:** Carpentry, electrician, maintenance, masonry, pipefitting, power transmission. **Education:** General, elementary. **Engineering:** General, aerospace, water resource. **Engineering technology:** Aerospace, hazardous materials, manufacturing, occupational safety, water quality. **Health:** Health care admin, medical radiologic technology/radiation therapy, medical transcription, nuclear medical technology, nursing (RN), physical therapy assistant, respiratory therapy technology, sonography, surgical technology. **Legal studies:** Court reporting. **Liberal arts:** Arts/sciences. **Mechanic/repair:** Automotive, electronics/electrical, heating/ac/refrig. **Social sciences:** Sociology.

**Most popular majors.** Health sciences 67%, liberal arts 23%.

**Computing on campus.** 100 workstations in library, computer center, student center. Commuter students can connect to campus network. Online course registration, online library, helpline, wireless network available.

**Student life. Freshman orientation:** Available. Preregistration for classes offered. **Activities:** Film society, student government, student newspaper, Newman Club, MEHCA, Indian Tribal Club, Single Parents Association, VA Club, internatilonal student club, women's club, health sciences club, business club.

**Athletics.** NJCAA. **Intercollegiate:** Cross-country, golf, tennis. **Team name:** Geckos.

**Student services.** Adult student services, alcohol/substance abuse counseling, career counseling, services for economically disadvantaged, student employment services, financial aid counseling, minority student services, on-campus daycare, personal counseling, placement for graduates, veterans' counselor, women's services. **Physically disabled:** Services for visually, speech, hearing impaired. **Learning disabled:** Comprehensive services available. **Transfer:** Re-entry adviser, pre-admission transcript evaluation for new students. Transfer center, transfer adviser, college fairs on campus for students transferring to 4-year colleges.

**Contact.** E-mail: cathy.gibson@gwmail.maricopa.edu
Phone: (602) 286-8200 Fax: (602) 286-8072
Cathy Gibson, Director Admissions and Records, Gateway Community College, 108 North 40th Street, Phoenix, AZ 85034

## Glendale Community College
**Glendale, Arizona**
www.gccaz.edu/          **CB code: 4338**

- Public 2-year community college
- Commuter campus in small city

**General.** Founded in 1965. Regionally accredited. Extension site at Glendale Community College North in Peoria. **Enrollment:** 4,446 degree-seeking undergraduates; 14,687 non-degree-seeking students. **Degrees:** 946 associate awarded. **Location:** 17 miles from Phoenix. **Calendar:** Semester, extensive summer session. **Full-time faculty:** 252 total; 18% minority, 51% women. **Part-time faculty:** 837 total; 29% minority, 48% women. **Class size:** 52% < 20, 46% 20-39, 2% 40-49, less than 1% 50-99, less than 1% >100. **Special facilities:** Performing arts center, high-technology centers, international student center. **Partnerships:** Formal partnerships with General Motors, Ford, Chrysler, Best Western, and John Deere.

**Student profile.** Among degree-seeking undergraduates, 31% enrolled in a transfer program, 6% already have a bachelor's degree or higher.

| | | | |
|---|---|---|---|
| Part-time: | 61% | Hispanic American: | 24% |
| Out-of-state: | 4% | Native American: | 2% |
| Women: | 56% | International: | 1% |
| African American: | 7% | 25 or older: | 39% |
| Asian American: | 3% | | |

**Transfer out. Colleges most students transferred to 2007:** Arizona State University, Arizona State University West, University of Arizona, Grand Canyon University.

**Basis for selection.** Open admission, but selective for some programs. Special requirements for nursing, basic emergency medical technology, General Motors and Ford automotive programs, international students. **Home-schooled:** If under 18, special admissions required.

**2007-2008 Annual costs.** Tuition/fees: $1,960; $8,410 out-of-state. Per-credit charge: $65 in-state; $280 out-of-state. Books/supplies: $1,064. Personal expenses: $2,616.

**Financial aid. Need-based:** Need-based aid available for part-time students. Work-study available nights, weekends and for part-time students.

**Application procedures. Admission:** No deadline. No application fee. Application may be submitted online. Admission notification on a rolling basis. **Financial aid:** Priority date 4/30, closing date 8/1. FAFSA required. Applicants notified on a rolling basis starting 6/1.

**Academics. Special study options:** Cooperative education, distance learning, dual enrollment of high school students, ESL, honors, independent study, internships, weekend college. ACE Plus (Achieving College Education), a high school bridge program, intensive English program. License preparation in nursing, paramedic. **Credit/placement by examination:** AP, CLEP, institutional tests. 30 credit hours maximum toward associate degree. **Support services:** GED preparation and test center, learning center, remedial instruction, study skills assistance, tutoring, writing center.

**Majors. Agriculture:** Landscaping, supplies. **Biology:** Biotechnology. **Business:** General, accounting technology, administrative services, business admin, finance, marketing, real estate. **Communications:** Public relations. **Communications technology:** Radio/tv. **Computer sciences:** General, data entry, networking, security, systems analysis. **Education:** Elementary, trade/industrial. **Engineering technology:** Architectural drafting, computer, electrical, energy systems. **Family/consumer sciences:** Child care, family studies, human nutrition. **Health:** Clinical nurse specialist, EMT paramedic, health services, nursing (RN). **Interdisciplinary:** Behavioral sciences. **Liberal arts:** Arts/sciences. **Mechanic/repair:** Automotive. **Parks/recreation:** Exercise sciences. **Physical sciences:** General. **Protective services:** Criminal justice, firefighting, security services. **Psychology:** General. **Public administration:** Social work. **Visual/performing arts:** General, commercial/advertising art, dramatic, music management, studio arts.

**Most popular majors.** Business/marketing 15%, education 6%, health sciences 8%, liberal arts 50%, physical sciences 6%.

**Computing on campus.** 1,500 workstations in library, computer center, student center. Commuter students can connect to campus network. Online course registration, online library, helpline, student web hosting, wireless network available.

**Student life. Freshman orientation:** Available. Preregistration for classes offered. **Activities:** Bands, choral groups, dance, drama, literary magazine, music ensembles, musical theater, opera, student government, student newspaper.

**Athletics.** NJCAA. **Intercollegiate:** Baseball M, basketball, cheerleading, cross-country, football (tackle) M, golf M, soccer, softball W, tennis, track and field, volleyball W. **Team name:** Gauchos.

**Student services.** Adult student services, campus ministries, career counseling, student employment services, financial aid counseling, minority student services, on-campus daycare, veterans' counselor. **Physically disabled:** Services for visually, speech, hearing impaired. **Transfer:** Transfer adviser, college fairs on campus for students transferring to 4-year colleges.

**Contact.** E-mail: info@gcmail.maricopa.edu
Phone: (623) 845-3300 Fax: (623) 845-3303
Mary Massal, Dean, Enrollment Services, Glendale Community College, 6000 West Olive Avenue, Glendale, AZ 85302

## Golf Academy of Arizona
**Scottsdale, Arizona**
www.sdga.edu/locations_arizona.php          CB code: 3460

- For-profit 2-year college of golf course management
- Small city

**General.** Accredited by ACICS. **Enrollment:** 238 undergraduates. **Degrees:** 132 associate awarded. **Calendar:** Semester. **Full-time faculty:** 5 total. **Part-time faculty:** 10 total.

**Basis for selection.** Open admission.

**2007-2008 Annual costs.** Tuition/fees: $9,850. Books/supplies: $700. Personal expenses: $2,862.

**Application procedures. Admission:** No deadline.

**Academics. Credit/placement by examination:** CLEP.

**Majors. Business:** Business admin. **Parks/recreation:** Facilities management.

**Contact.** E-mail: sdga@sdgagolf.com
Phone: (480) 905-9288 Toll-free number: (800) 342-7342
Fax: (480) 905-8705
Golf Academy of Arizona, 7373 North Scottsdale Road, Suite B-100, Scottsdale, AZ 85253

## High-Tech Institute
**Phoenix, Arizona**
www.hightechinstitute.edu          CB code: 3170

- For-profit 2-year technical college
- Commuter campus in very large city

**General.** Accredited by ACCSCT. **Calendar:** Continuous.

**Annual costs/financial aid.** Total costs of associate degrees vary by program and range from $22,950 to $29,350. Total costs of diplomas vary by program and range from $10,750 to $17,550. Personal expenses: $205. Need-based financial aid available for full-time students.

**Contact.** Phone: (602) 279-9700
Director of Admissions, 1515 East Indian School Road, Phoenix, AZ 85014-4901

## Lamson College
**Tempe, Arizona**
www.lamsoncollege.com          CB code: 1899

- For-profit 2-year junior and technical college
- Commuter campus in very large city

**General.** Founded in 1889. Accredited by ACICS. **Calendar:** Quarter.

**Annual costs/financial aid.** Per-credit-hour charges vary according to program: $215 to $275; cost of books and supplies ranges from $890 to $3,000, depending on program of study. Need-based financial aid available to full-time and part-time students.

**Contact.** Phone: (480) 898-7000
Director of Admission, 1126 North Scottsdale Road, Suite 17, Tempe, AZ 85281-1700

## Long Technical College
**Phoenix, Arizona**
www.kc-phoenix.com          CB code: 3052

- For-profit 2-year technical college
- Residential campus in very large city
- Interview required

**General.** Accredited by ACICS, ACCSCT. **Enrollment:** 322 undergraduates. **Degrees:** 102 associate awarded. **Calendar:** Continuous. **Full-time faculty:** 40 total.

**Basis for selection.** Open admission, but selective for some programs. Entrance exam (Wonderlic) required.

**2007-2008 Annual costs.** Tuition and fees vary by degree program. Prices range from $11,976 - $35,064.

**Application procedures. Admission:** No deadline. $25 fee.

**Academics. Credit/placement by examination:** CLEP. **Support services:** Learning center, tutoring.

**Majors. Health:** Respiratory therapy technology.

**Student life. Freshman orientation:** Mandatory.

**Contact.** E-mail: mcrance@kaplan.edu
Phone: (602) 548-1955 ext. 1366 Toll-free
number: (877) 548-1955 ext. 1366 Fax: (602) 548-1956
Michael Crance, Director of Admissions, Long Technical College, 13610 North Black Canyon Highway, Suite 104, Phoenix, AZ 85029

## Mesa Community College
**Mesa, Arizona**
**www.mc.maricopa.edu**                    **CB code: 4513**

- Public 2-year community college
- Commuter campus in very large city

**General.** Founded in 1965. Regionally accredited. **Enrollment:** 2,656 degree-seeking undergraduates. **Degrees:** 1,625 associate awarded. **ROTC:** Army, Naval, Air Force. **Location:** 12 miles from Phoenix. **Calendar:** Semester, extensive summer session. **Full-time faculty:** 300 total. **Part-time faculty:** 900 total.

**Student profile.** Among degree-seeking undergraduates, 63% enrolled in a transfer program, 27% enrolled in a vocational program.

**Transfer out.** 63% of students enrolled in the transfer program go on to 4-year colleges.

**Basis for selection.** Open admission, but selective for some programs. General education requirements and minimum 2.5 GPA required for nursing, mortuary science, and fire academy.

**2007-2008 Annual costs.** Tuition/fees: $1,980; $8,430 out-of-state. Per-credit charge: $65 in-state; $280 out-of-state. Books/supplies: $500.

**Financial aid. Non-need-based:** Scholarships awarded for academics, athletics. **Additional information:** Awards available for Maricopa County residents.

**Application procedures. Admission:** No deadline. No application fee. Admission notification on a rolling basis. Diploma or GED required for applicants under 18. **Financial aid:** Priority date 5/1; no closing date. Institutional form required. Applicants notified on a rolling basis starting 7/1.

**Academics.** Associate of General Studies degree allows students to take half of credits in required courses, and dictate own program of electives. **Special study options:** Cooperative education, cross-registration, distance learning, dual enrollment of high school students, ESL, exchange student, honors, independent study, internships, liberal arts/career combination, student-designed major, study abroad, teacher certification program, weekend college. License preparation in dental hygiene, nursing, real estate. **Credit/ placement by examination:** CLEP, IB, institutional tests. 30 credit hours maximum toward associate degree. **Support services:** GED preparation and test center, learning center, remedial instruction, study skills assistance, tutoring, writing center.

**Honors college/program.** Honors courses open to all students with minimum 3.5 GPA.

**Majors. Agriculture:** Agribusiness operations, horticulture, landscaping. **Business:** Accounting, business admin, fashion, marketing, office management, office/clerical. **Communications:** Journalism. **Computer sciences:** General, applications programming, computer science, networking. **Education:** Teacher assistance. **Engineering:** General. **Engineering technology:** Architectural. **Family/consumer sciences:** Clothing/textiles, food/nutrition. **Health:** Nursing (RN). **Liberal arts:** Library assistant. **Visual/performing arts:** Interior design.

**Computing on campus.** 1,000 workstations in library, computer center, student center. Commuter students can connect to campus network. Online course registration, online library, helpline, repair service, student web hosting, wireless network available.

**Student life. Freshman orientation:** Available. **Housing:** Coed dorms, apartments available. Housing available at Williams campus. **Activities:** Jazz band, choral groups, dance, drama, music ensembles, musical theater, student government, student newspaper.

**Athletics.** NJCAA. **Intercollegiate:** Baseball M, basketball, cross-country, football (tackle) M, golf, gymnastics W, soccer, softball W, swimming M, track and field, volleyball W, wrestling M. **Intramural:** Basketball, bowling, cross-country, football (tackle) M, softball, track and field, volleyball, wrestling M. **Team name:** Thunderbirds.

**Student services.** Adult student services, alcohol/substance abuse counseling, career counseling, services for economically disadvantaged, student employment services, financial aid counseling, legal services, on-campus daycare, personal counseling, placement for graduates, veterans' counselor. **Physically disabled:** Services for visually, speech, hearing impaired. **Transfer:** Transfer adviser for students transferring to 4-year colleges.

**Contact.** E-mail: admissions@mc.maricopa.edu
Phone: (480) 461-7000 Fax: (480) 461-7805
Linda Shaw, Director of Admissions, Mesa Community College, 1833 West Southern Avenue, Mesa, AZ 85202

## Mohave Community College
**Kingman, Arizona**
**www.mohave.edu**                    **CB code: 0443**

- Public 2-year community college
- Commuter campus in small city

**General.** Founded in 1971. Regionally accredited. **Enrollment:** 2,975 degree-seeking undergraduates. **Degrees:** 287 associate awarded. **Location:** 200 miles from Phoenix, 100 miles from Las Vegas. **Calendar:** Semester, limited summer session. **Full-time faculty:** 61 total. **Part-time faculty:** 409 total.

**Transfer out. Colleges most students transferred to 2007:** Northern Arizona University, University of Arizona, Arizona State University.

**Basis for selection.** Open admission, but selective for some programs. Special requirements for nursing, dental hygiene and EMT/paramedic programs.

**2007-2008 Annual costs.** Tuition/fees: $1,620; $4,860 out-of-state. Per-credit charge: $54 in-state; $162 out-of-state.

**Financial aid. Need-based:** Need-based aid available for part-time students. Work-study available nights and for part-time students.

**Application procedures. Admission:** No deadline. No application fee. Application may be submitted online. **Financial aid:** Priority date 4/15; no closing date. FAFSA, institutional form required. Applicants notified on a rolling basis starting 5/1; must reply within 2 week(s) of notification.

**Academics. Special study options:** Distance learning, dual enrollment of high school students, ESL, independent study, internships, liberal arts/ career combination, student-designed major. License preparation in dental hygiene, nursing, paramedic, physical therapy. **Credit/placement by examination:** CLEP, IB, institutional tests. 20 credit hours maximum toward associate degree. **Support services:** GED preparation and test center, learning center, reduced course load, remedial instruction, study skills assistance, tutoring.

**Majors. Business:** Administrative services, business admin. **Computer sciences:** General. **Education:** General. **English:** English lit. **Health:** Dental hygiene, nursing (RN). **Liberal arts:** Arts/sciences. **Mechanic/repair:** Automotive, heating/ac/refrig. **Protective services:** Firefighting, police science. **Other:** Chemical dependency therapy.

**Computing on campus.** 300 workstations in library, computer center. Commuter students can connect to campus network. Online course registration, online library, helpline, wireless network available.

**Student life. Freshman orientation:** Available. Preregistration for classes offered. **Activities:** Bands, choral groups, dance, drama, music ensembles, musical theater, student government, symphony orchestra.

**Student services.** Adult student services, career counseling, student employment services, financial aid counseling, veterans' counselor. **Physically**

**disabled:** Services for visually, speech, hearing impaired. **Transfer:** Transfer adviser for students transferring to 4-year colleges.

**Contact.** E-mail: johwil@mohave.edu
Phone: (928) 757-0847 Toll-free number: (866) 664-2832
Fax: (928) 757-0808
John Wilson, Director of Admissions, Mohave Community College, 1971 Jagerson Avenue, Kingman, AZ 86409

## Northland Pioneer College
### Holbrook, Arizona
www.npc.edu                                      CB code: 0325

- Public 2-year community and technical college
- Commuter campus in small town

**General.** Founded in 1973. Regionally accredited. 10 locations in Navajo and Apache Counties. **Enrollment:** 1,942 degree-seeking undergraduates. **Degrees:** 164 associate awarded. **Location:** 200 miles from Phoenix, 90 miles from Flagstaff. **Calendar:** Semester, limited summer session. **Full-time faculty:** 85 total. **Part-time faculty:** 260 total.

**Student profile.**

Out-of-state:          5%          25 or older:          51%

**Transfer out. Colleges most students transferred to 2007:** Northern Arizona University, University of Arizona, Arizona State University, Western New Mexico University, Brigham Young University.

**Basis for selection.** Open admission, but selective for some programs. Limited admission for nursing and cosmetology.

**2007-2008 Annual costs.** Tuition/fees: $1,056; $6,900 out-of-state. Per-credit charge: $44 in-state; $76 out-of-state. Books/supplies: $580.

**Financial aid. Need-based:** Need-based aid available for part-time students. Work-study available nights, weekends and for part-time students. **Non-need-based:** Scholarships awarded for academics, art, job skills, leadership, minority status, music/drama, state residency.

**Application procedures. Admission:** No deadline. No application fee. Admission notification on a rolling basis. **Financial aid:** Priority date 6/1; no closing date. FAFSA, institutional form required. Applicants notified on a rolling basis starting 5/15; must reply within 2 week(s) of notification.

**Academics. Special study options:** Cooperative education, distance learning, dual enrollment of high school students, honors, independent study, internships, liberal arts/career combination. License preparation in nursing, paramedic, real estate. **Credit/placement by examination:** AP, CLEP, IB, institutional tests. 52 credit hours maximum toward associate degree. **Support services:** GED preparation and test center, learning center, remedial instruction, study skills assistance, tutoring, writing center.

**Honors college/program.** Competitive admission to President's Scholars Program based on recommendations and high school achievement.

**Majors. Agriculture:** Turf management. **Business:** General, accounting, administrative services, business admin. **Communications technology:** General. **Computer sciences:** General, computer graphics, data processing, networking. **Construction:** General, carpentry, electrician, plumbing. **Engineering technology:** Electrical. **Family/consumer sciences:** Child care. **Health:** EMT paramedic, medical assistant, medical transcription, nursing (RN). **Interdisciplinary:** Biological/physical sciences. **Liberal arts:** Arts/sciences, library assistant. **Mechanic/repair:** Automotive, heating/ac/refrig, industrial. **Parks/recreation:** General. **Personal/culinary services:** Cosmetic. **Protective services:** Criminal justice, firefighting. **Transportation:** Heavy/earthmoving equipment.

**Computing on campus.** 120 workstations in library, computer center. Helpline, wireless network available.

**Student life. Activities:** Jazz band, choral groups, drama, literary magazine, musical theater, student government, symphony orchestra, National Honor Society, Phi Theta Kappa.

**Athletics.** NJCAA. **Team name:** Golden Eagles.

**Student services.** Career counseling, services for economically disadvantaged, student employment services, financial aid counseling, placement for graduates, veterans' counselor. **Physically disabled:** Services for visually impaired. **Transfer:** Transfer adviser, college fairs on campus for students transferring to 4-year colleges.

**Contact.** E-mail: admissions@npc.edu
Phone: (928) 536-6257 Toll-free number: (800) 266-7845
Fax: (928) 524-7612
Ann Hess, Director of Marketing and Recruitment, Northland Pioneer College, PO Box 610, Holbrook, AZ 86025-0610

## Paradise Valley Community College
### Phoenix, Arizona                              CB member
www.pvc.maricopa.edu                             CB code: 2179

- Public 2-year community college
- Commuter campus in very large city

**General.** Founded in 1985. Regionally accredited. **Enrollment:** 3,100 degree-seeking undergraduates. **Degrees:** 517 associate awarded. **ROTC:** Army. **Calendar:** Semester, limited summer session. **Full-time faculty:** 98 total; 20% minority, 50% women. **Part-time faculty:** 275 total. **Special facilities:** Studio theater, performing arts center.

**Student profile.**

Out-of-state:          3%          25 or older:          50%

**Transfer out. Colleges most students transferred to 2007:** Arizona State University, Arizona State University West, Northern Arizona University, University of Arizona.

**Basis for selection.** Open admission.

**2007-2008 Annual costs.** Tuition/fees: $1,980; $8,430 out-of-state. Per-credit charge: $65 in-state; $280 out-of-state. Books/supplies: $700. Personal expenses: $1,185.

**Financial aid. Need-based:** Need-based aid available for part-time students.

**Application procedures. Admission:** No deadline. No application fee. Admission notification on a rolling basis. **Financial aid:** No deadline. FAFSA required. Applicants notified on a rolling basis starting 6/1.

**Academics. Special study options:** Accelerated study, cooperative education, cross-registration, distance learning, ESL, honors, independent study, internships, teacher certification program, weekend college. License preparation in nursing, paramedic. **Credit/placement by examination:** AP, CLEP, institutional tests. 30 credit hours maximum toward associate degree. **Support services:** Learning center, remedial instruction, study skills assistance, tutoring, writing center.

**Majors. Business:** General, accounting, administrative services, international, office technology, office/clerical, organizational behavior. **Computer sciences:** General, word processing. **Engineering technology:** Hazardous materials. **Liberal arts:** Arts/sciences. **Visual/performing arts:** Music.

**Computing on campus.** 600 workstations in library, computer center, student center. Commuter students can connect to campus network. Online course registration, helpline, wireless network available.

**Student life. Freshman orientation:** Mandatory. **Activities:** Jazz band, choral groups, dance, drama, international student organizations, literary magazine, music ensembles, musical theater, opera, student government, student newspaper, Phi Theta Kappa, student Christian association, human service club, Returning Adults to Education, environmental club, Latter Day Saints student association, recreational outdoor club.

**Athletics.** NJCAA. **Intercollegiate:** Cross-country, golf, soccer, softball W, tennis, track and field. **Team name:** Pumas.

**Student services.** Adult student services, career counseling, student employment services, financial aid counseling, minority student services, on-campus daycare, personal counseling, placement for graduates, veterans' counselor. **Physically disabled:** Services for visually, speech, hearing impaired. **Transfer:** Transfer adviser, college fairs on campus for students transferring to 4-year colleges.

**Contact.** Phone: (602) 787-7020 Fax: (602) 787-6625
Shirley Green, Associate Dean Student Services, Paradise Valley Community College, 18401 North 32nd Street, Phoenix, AZ 85032

## Paralegal Institute
### Glendale, Arizona
www.theparalegalinstitute.edu                    CB code: 3888

- For-profit 2-year virtual community and career college
- Very large city

**General.** Accredited by DETC. **Enrollment:** 315 degree-seeking undergraduates. **Degrees:** 60 associate awarded. **Calendar:** Continuous, extensive summer session. **Full-time faculty:** 2 total. **Part-time faculty:** 2 total.

**Student profile.** Among degree-seeking undergraduates, 65% enrolled in a vocational program, 10% already have a bachelor's degree or higher.

**Basis for selection.** Open admission.

**2008-2009 Annual costs.** Tuition/fees (projected): $7,500. Per-credit charge: $125.

**Application procedures. Admission:** No deadline. No application fee. Application must be submitted on paper.

**Academics. Credit/placement by examination:** CLEP.

**Majors. Legal studies:** Paralegal.

**Student life. Freshman orientation:** Available. Preregistration for classes offered.

**Student services. Transfer:** Pre-admission transcript evaluation for new students.

**Contact.** E-mail: kallen@theparalegalinstitute.edu
Phone: (602) 212-0501 Toll-free number: (800) 354-1254
Fax: (602) 212-0502
Paralegal Institute, 18275 North 59th Avenue, Suite 186 Building N, Glendale, AZ 85308

## Penn Foster College
### Scottsdale, Arizona
### www.pennfostercollege.edu
### CB code: 7313

▶ For-profit 2-year virtual college
▶ Commuter campus in small city

**General.** Founded in 1975. Accredited by DETC. All courses are offered via distance learning. **Enrollment:** 25,000 undergraduates. **Degrees:** 169 associate awarded. **Calendar:** Continuous. **Full-time faculty:** 26 total. **Part-time faculty:** 51 total.

**Basis for selection.** Open admission. **Homeschooled:** Copy of completion document from a school or copy of standardized tests required.

**2007-2008 Annual costs.** Cost of degree programs range from $3,840 to $4,790 depending on program. Additional costs to fulfill resident laboratory requirement in technology programs.

**Application procedures. Admission:** No deadline. $200 fee. Application may be submitted online. Admission notification on a rolling basis.

**Academics.** Students allowed 12 months to complete semester (15-20 credit hours). **Special study options:** Distance learning, external degree, independent study. **Credit/placement by examination:** CLEP. **Support services:** Remedial instruction, tutoring.

**Majors. Business:** General, accounting, finance, hospitality admin, marketing. **Computer sciences:** General. **Education:** Early childhood. **Engineering technology:** Civil, electrical, industrial, mechanical. **Health:** Medical records technology. **Legal studies:** Paralegal. **Protective services:** Police science.

**Most popular majors.** Business/marketing 69%, computer/information sciences 16%, engineering/engineering technologies 7%.

**Student life. Freshman orientation:** Mandatory.

**Student services. Transfer:** Pre-admission transcript evaluation for new students.

**Contact.** Phone: (800) 275-4410 Toll-free number: (800) 275-4410
Linda Smith, Manager, DP Services, Penn Foster College, 14300 North Northsight Boulevard, Suite 111, Scottsdale, AZ 85254

## Phoenix College
### Phoenix, Arizona
### www.pc.maricopa.edu
### CB code: 4606

▶ Public 2-year community college
▶ Commuter campus in very large city

**General.** Founded in 1920. Regionally accredited. **Enrollment:** 2,573 full-time, degree-seeking students. **Degrees:** 1,183 associate awarded. **ROTC:** Army, Air Force. **Calendar:** Semester, limited summer session. **Full-time faculty:** 146 total. **Part-time faculty:** 450 total.

**Student profile.**

| Out-of-state: | 2% | 25 or older: | 53% |
|---|---|---|---|

**Basis for selection.** Open admission, but selective for some programs. ASSET, COMPASS and Celsa test scores used for placement.

**2007-2008 Annual costs.** Tuition/fees: $1,980; $8,130 out-of-state. Per-credit charge: $65 in-state; $270 out-of-state. Books/supplies: $700. Personal expenses: $3,654.

**Financial aid. Need-based:** Work-study available weekends.

**Application procedures. Admission:** No deadline. No application fee. Application may be submitted online. Admission notification on a rolling basis. **Financial aid:** Priority date 6/30; no closing date. FAFSA required. Applicants notified on a rolling basis starting 5/1.

**Academics. Special study options:** Cooperative education, cross-registration, distance learning, dual enrollment of high school students, ESL, honors, independent study, internships, liberal arts/career combination, study abroad. License preparation in nursing. **Credit/placement by examination:** CLEP, institutional tests. 30 credit hours maximum toward associate degree. **Support services:** GED test center, learning center, reduced course load, remedial instruction, tutoring.

**Honors college/program.** Requires 3.0 GPA.

**Majors. Architecture:** Interior. **Business:** General, accounting, banking/financial services, business admin, management information systems, management science, marketing, tourism promotion, tourism/travel. **Communications:** General. **Computer sciences:** General, computer graphics, information systems. **Education:** General, family/consumer sciences. **Engineering:** General, software. **Engineering technology:** Civil. **Family/consumer sciences:** General, child care, institutional food production. **Foreign languages:** Sign language interpretation. **Health:** Clinical lab science, dental assistant, dental hygiene, EMT paramedic, medical records technology, medical transcription, nursing (RN), premedicine. **Legal studies:** Legal secretary, paralegal. **Liberal arts:** Arts/sciences. **Physical sciences:** Chemistry. **Protective services:** Firefighting, police science. **Visual/performing arts:** Art, commercial/advertising art, interior design.

**Computing on campus.** Online course registration, helpline, wireless network available.

**Student life. Freshman orientation:** Available. Preregistration for classes offered. **Activities:** Bands, choral groups, dance, drama, music ensembles, musical theater, opera, student newspaper, symphony orchestra, TV station.

**Athletics.** NJCAA. **Intercollegiate:** Baseball M, basketball, cross-country, football (tackle) M, golf M, soccer M, softball W, tennis, track and field, volleyball W. **Team name:** PC Bears.

**Student services.** Adult student services, career counseling, services for economically disadvantaged, student employment services, legal services, on-campus daycare, personal counseling, placement for graduates, veterans' counselor. **Physically disabled:** Services for visually, speech, hearing impaired. **Transfer:** Re-entry adviser, pre-admission transcript evaluation for new students. Transfer adviser, college fairs on campus for students transferring to 4-year colleges.

**Contact.** E-mail: info@pcmail.maricopa.edu
Phone: (602) 285-7502 Fax: (602) 285-7813
Kathy French, Director of Admissions and Records, Phoenix College, 1202 West Thomas Road, Phoenix, AZ 85013

## Pima Community College
### Tucson, Arizona
### www.pima.edu
### CB member
### CB code: 4623

▶ Public 2-year community and technical college
▶ Commuter campus in very large city

**General.** Founded in 1966. Regionally accredited. 6 campuses, 3 centers and Public Safety Institute serve Tucson metropolitan area. **Enrollment:** 27,191 degree-seeking undergraduates. **Degrees:** 2,081 associate awarded. **ROTC:** Army, Naval, Air Force. **Location:** 120 miles from Phoenix. **Calendar:** Semester, limited summer session. **Full-time faculty:** 325 total. **Part-time faculty:** 1,157 total. **Special facilities:** Arts center.

**Student profile.** Among degree-seeking undergraduates, 47% enrolled in a transfer program, 23% enrolled in a vocational program, 4% already have a bachelor's degree or higher.

| | | | |
|---|---|---|---|
| Out-of-state: | 5% | 25 or older: | 41% |

**Transfer out. Colleges most students transferred to 2007:** University of Arizona, Arizona State University, Northern Arizona University, University of Phoenix.

**Basis for selection.** Open admission, but selective for some programs. Special requirements for nursing, dental hygiene, and pharmacy technology.

**2007-2008 Annual costs.** Tuition/fees: $1,565; $7,235 out-of-state. Per-credit charge: $47 in-state; $80 out-of-state. Books/supplies: $2,000. Personal expenses: $2,520.

**Financial aid. Need-based:** Need-based aid available for part-time students. **Non-need-based:** Scholarships awarded for academics, alumni affiliation, art, athletics, minority status, music/drama.

**Application procedures. Admission:** No deadline. No application fee. Application may be submitted online. Admission notification on a rolling basis. **Financial aid:** Priority date 3/15; no closing date. FAFSA required. Applicants notified on a rolling basis starting 7/1; must reply within 2 week(s) of notification.

**Academics. Special study options:** Accelerated study, cooperative education, distance learning, double major, dual enrollment of high school students, ESL, honors, independent study, internships, student-designed major, teacher certification program, weekend college. License preparation in dental hygiene, nursing, radiology. **Credit/placement by examination:** AP, CLEP, institutional tests. 30 credit hours maximum toward associate degree. **Support services:** GED preparation and test center, learning center, remedial instruction, study skills assistance, tutoring.

**Majors. Area/ethnic studies:** Native American. **Business:** Accounting, administrative services, business admin, hospitality admin, international, tourism/travel. **Communications:** Radio/tv. **Communications technology:** Animation/special effects, graphics. **Computer sciences:** General, networking, systems analysis. **Construction:** Maintenance. **Education:** General, adult/continuing. **Engineering technology:** Architectural drafting, construction, environmental, laser/optical. **Family/consumer sciences:** Child development. **Foreign languages:** Sign language interpretation. **Health:** Clinical lab technology, dental hygiene, dental lab technology, EMT paramedic, histologic assistant, massage therapy, medical records admin, medical records technology, nursing (RN), pharmacy assistant, radiologic technology/medical imaging, respiratory therapy technology, substance abuse counseling, veterinary technology/assistant. **Legal studies:** Paralegal. **Liberal arts:** Arts/sciences. **Mechanic/repair:** Aircraft powerplant, automotive, industrial electronics. **Personal/culinary services:** Restaurant/catering. **Production:** Machine shop technology, welding. **Protective services:** Criminal justice, firefighting, police science. **Social sciences:** Anthropology, archaeology, political science, sociology. **Visual/performing arts:** General, art, design, dramatic.

**Most popular majors.** Business/marketing 12%, health sciences 16%, liberal arts 54%.

**Computing on campus.** 1,500 workstations in library, computer center. Commuter students can connect to campus network. Online course registration, online library available.

**Student life. Freshman orientation:** Mandatory. Orientation programs based on majors. **Activities:** Bands, choral groups, dance, drama, literary magazine, music ensembles, student government, student newspaper, TV station, forensics activities, speech communication program, clubs for various student groups.

**Athletics.** NJCAA. **Intercollegiate:** Baseball M, basketball, cross-country, football (tackle) M, golf, soccer, softball W, tennis, track and field, volleyball W. **Intramural:** Badminton, baseball M, basketball, cross-country, football (non-tackle) M, golf, racquetball, tennis, track and field, volleyball. **Team name:** Aztecs.

**Student services.** Career counseling, student employment services, health services, minority student services, on-campus daycare, personal counseling, placement for graduates, veterans' counselor. **Physically disabled:** Services for visually, speech, hearing impaired. **Transfer:** Transfer adviser, college fairs on campus for students transferring to 4-year colleges.

**Contact.** E-mail: coadmit@pima.edu
Phone: (520) 206-4643 Fax: (520) 206-4790
Michael Tulino, Enrollment Services/Registrar, Pima Community College, 4905B East Broadway, Tucson, AZ 85709-1120

---

## Refrigeration School
**Phoenix, Arizona**
www.rsiaz.edu                                    **CB code: 2888**

- For-profit 1-year technical college
- Very large city
- Interview required

**General.** Accredited by ACCSCT. **Enrollment:** 45 degree-seeking undergraduates. **Degrees:** 30 associate awarded. **Calendar:** 3, 6 or 8 month programs. **Full-time faculty:** 12 total. **Part-time faculty:** 14 total.

**Basis for selection.** Open admission. **Homeschooled:** State high school equivalency certificate required.

**2007-2008 Annual costs.** Costs of entire programs range from $6,500 to $19,800; includes books and supplies.

**Application procedures. Admission:** No deadline. No application fee.

**Academics. Credit/placement by examination:** CLEP. **Support services:** Tutoring.

**Majors. Engineering technology:** Energy systems. **Mechanic/repair:** Heating/ac/refrig.

**Computing on campus.** 4 workstations in library.

**Contact.** Phone: (602) 275-7133 Toll-free number: (877) 477-4669
Fax: (602) 267-4805
Mary Simmons, Admissions Director, Refrigeration School, 4210 East Washington Street, Phoenix, AZ 85034-1816

---

## Rio Salado College
**Tempe, Arizona**                               **CB member**
www.riosalado.edu                                **CB code: 0997**

- Public 2-year virtual community college
- Commuter campus in very large city

**General.** Founded in 1978. Regionally accredited. Access to libraries at Arizona State University and 10 Maricopa County community colleges. **Enrollment:** 1,193 degree-seeking undergraduates. **Degrees:** 357 associate awarded. **Location:** 120 miles from Tucson, 10 miles from Phoenix. **Calendar:** Semester, extensive summer session. **Full-time faculty:** 31 total. **Part-time faculty:** 982 total. **Special facilities:** Public radio stations.

**Student profile.**

| | | | |
|---|---|---|---|
| Out-of-state: | 5% | 25 or older: | 46% |

**Transfer out. Colleges most students transferred to 2007:** Arizona State University, University of Arizona, Northern Arizona University.

**Basis for selection.** Open admission, but selective for some programs. GPA requirements for dental hygiene program. **Adult students:** SAT/ACT scores not required.

**2007-2008 Annual costs.** Tuition/fees: $1,980; $8,430 out-of-state. Per-credit charge: $65 in-state; $280 out-of-state. Books/supplies: $1,024. Personal expenses: $2,616.

**Financial aid.** All financial aid based on need. Need-based aid available for part-time students.

**Application procedures. Admission:** No deadline. No application fee. Application may be submitted online. Admission notification on a rolling basis. **Financial aid:** Priority date 6/30; no closing date. FAFSA, institutional form required. Applicants notified on a rolling basis starting 6/30.

**Academics.** Agreement with Army allows military personnel to take Internet courses. Online Nursing and Clinical Dental Assisting programs. **Special study options:** Accelerated study, cooperative education, cross-registration, distance learning, double major, dual enrollment of high school students, ESL, honors, independent study, internships, liberal arts/career combination, weekend college. License preparation in dental hygiene. **Credit/placement by examination:** AP, CLEP, institutional tests. 30 credit hours maximum toward associate degree. Placement testing required for students taking English, reading, and mathematics courses. **Support services:** GED preparation, learning center, remedial instruction, study skills assistance, tutoring, writing center.

**Majors. Business:** General, accounting, banking/financial services, business admin, international, office management. **Computer sciences:** General. **Engineering technology:** Water quality. **Health:** Dental hygiene, nursing assistant, substance abuse counseling. **Protective services:** Law enforcement admin. **Public administration:** General.

**Computing on campus.** 500 workstations in library, computer center. Commuter students can connect to campus network. Online course registration, online library, helpline, wireless network available.

**Student life. Activities:** Radio station, Phi Theta Kappa.

**Student services.** Adult student services, career counseling, student employment services, financial aid counseling, personal counseling, veterans' counselor. **Physically disabled:** Services for visually, speech, hearing impaired. **Transfer:** Re-entry adviser, pre-admission transcript evaluation for new students. Transfer adviser for students transferring to 4-year colleges.

**Contact.** E-mail: admissions@email.rio.maricopa.edu
Phone: (480) 517-8150 Toll-free number: (800) 729-1197
Fax: (480) 517-8199
Ruby Miller, Director of Registration and Records, Rio Salado College, 2323 West 14th Street, Tempe, AZ 85281

## Scottsdale Community College
### Scottsdale, Arizona
### www.scottsdalecc.edu
**CB code: 4755**

- Public 2-year community college
- Commuter campus in small city

**General.** Founded in 1969. Regionally accredited. **Enrollment:** 3,038 degree-seeking undergraduates. **Degrees:** 682 associate awarded. **Location:** 10 miles from Tempe. **Calendar:** Semester, limited summer session. **Full-time faculty:** 173 total; 26% have terminal degrees, 14% minority, 51% women. **Part-time faculty:** 495 total; 8% have terminal degrees, 11% minority, 52% women. **Class size:** 57% < 20, 40% 20-39, 1% 40-49, 1% 50-99, less than 1% >100. **Special facilities:** Student-operated restaurant associated with school of culinary arts.

**Student profile.**

| Out-of-state: | 5% | 25 or older: | 39% |
|---|---|---|---|

**Basis for selection.** Open admission.

**High school preparation.** 16 units recommended. Recommended units include English 4, mathematics 4, social studies 2, history 1, science 3 and foreign language 2.

**2007-2008 Annual costs.** Tuition/fees: $2,010; $8,460 out-of-state. Per-credit charge: $65 in-state; $280 out-of-state. Books/supplies: $848. Personal expenses: $4,194.

**Financial aid. Non-need-based:** Scholarships awarded for academics, athletics. **Additional information:** Athletic scholarships offered in rodeo. All athletic scholarships limited to county residents.

**Application procedures. Admission:** No deadline. No application fee. Application may be submitted online. Admission notification on a rolling basis. **Financial aid:** Priority date 6/30; no closing date. FAFSA, institutional form required. Applicants notified on a rolling basis starting 4/1; must reply by 7/15 or within 3 week(s) of notification.

**Academics. Special study options:** Cooperative education, cross-registration, distance learning, dual enrollment of high school students, ESL, honors, internships, study abroad. **Credit/placement by examination:** AP, CLEP, institutional tests. 52 credit hours maximum toward associate degree. **Support services:** Learning center, remedial instruction, tutoring, writing center.

**Majors. Agriculture:** Equestrian studies. **Architecture:** Environmental design. **Area/ethnic studies:** Native American. **Business:** General, accounting, administrative services, fashion, hospitality admin, international, management information systems, retailing. **Communications:** Public relations. **Communications technology:** Radio/tv. **Computer sciences:** General, information systems. **Construction:** Building inspection. **Education:** Early childhood. **Engineering technology:** Architectural drafting. **Family/consumer sciences:** Child care. **Health:** EMT paramedic, medical radiologic technology/radiation therapy, nursing (RN). **Liberal arts:** Arts/sciences. **Parks/recreation:** General. **Personal/culinary services:** Culinary arts. **Physical sciences:** General. **Protective services:** Criminal justice, firefighting, law enforcement admin. **Visual/performing arts:** General, cinematography, dance, dramatic, interior design, studio arts.

**Most popular majors.** Business/marketing 6%, communication technologies 7%, health sciences 19%, liberal arts 48%, visual/performing arts 8%.

**Computing on campus.** 998 workstations in library, computer center, student center. Commuter students can connect to campus network. Online course registration, online library, helpline, repair service, wireless network available.

**Student life. Freshman orientation:** Available. Preregistration for classes offered. **Activities:** Bands, choral groups, dance, drama, music ensembles, student government, student newspaper, symphony orchestra, TV station.

**Athletics.** NAIA, NJCAA. **Intercollegiate:** Baseball M, basketball, cross-country, football (tackle) M, golf M, soccer M, softball W, tennis, track and field, volleyball W. **Intramural:** Baseball M. **Team name:** Artichokes.

**Student services.** Adult student services, alcohol/substance abuse counseling, career counseling, student employment services, financial aid counseling, on-campus daycare, personal counseling, placement for graduates, veterans' counselor. **Physically disabled:** Services for visually, speech, hearing impaired. **Transfer:** Transfer adviser, college fairs on campus for students transferring to 4-year colleges.

**Contact.** E-mail: admissions@sccmail.maricopa.edu
Phone: (480) 423-6100 Fax: (480) 423-6200
Fran Watkins, Director of Admissions and Records, Scottsdale Community College, 9000 East Chaparral Road, Scottsdale, AZ 85256-2626

## Scottsdale Culinary Institute
### Scottsdale, Arizona
### www.scichefs.com
**CB code: 3028**

- For-profit 2-year culinary school and technical college
- Commuter campus in large city

**General.** Accredited by ACCSCT. **Location:** 2 miles from downtown. **Calendar:** Continuous.

**Annual costs/financial aid.** Tuition and fees vary by degree and by program. Total costs of programs (includes fees and books): certificate programs start at $21,350; Associate degree programs start at $35,100; Bachelor's degree programs start at $61,400. Books/supplies: $910. Personal expenses: $2,275.

**Contact.** Phone: (480) 990-3773
Director of Admissions, 8100 East Camelback Road, Suite 1001, Scottsdale, AZ 85251

## South Mountain Community College
### Phoenix, Arizona
### www.smc.maricopa.edu
**CB code: 4734**

- Public 2-year community college
- Commuter campus in very large city

**General.** Founded in 1979. Regionally accredited. Learning Center in Guadalupe, Arizona. Arizona Agribusiness Equine Charter. **Enrollment:** 210 full-time, degree-seeking undergraduates. **Degrees:** 293 associate awarded. **Location:** 8 miles from downtown Phoenix. **Calendar:** Semester, limited summer session. **Full-time faculty:** 52 total. **Part-time faculty:** 125 total. **Partnerships:** Agribusiness charter school on campus.

**Student profile.**

| Out-of-state: | 2% | 25 or older: | 45% |
|---|---|---|---|

**Basis for selection.** Open admission. ASSET used for placement in math, reading, and English.

**2007-2008 Annual costs.** Tuition/fees: $1,980; $8,430 out-of-state. Per-credit charge: $65 in-state; $280 out-of-state. Books/supplies: $760. Personal expenses: $1,250.

**Financial aid. Need-based:** Need-based aid available for part-time students. Work-study available nights, weekends and for part-time students. **Non-need-based:** Scholarships awarded for academics, athletics, minority status, music/drama.

**Application procedures. Admission:** No deadline. No application fee. Application may be submitted online. Admission notification on a rolling basis. **Financial aid:** Priority date 5/1; no closing date. FAFSA required. Applicants notified on a rolling basis starting 5/15; must reply within 3 week(s) of notification.

**Academics. Special study options:** Cooperative education, cross-registration, dual enrollment of high school students, ESL, honors, independent study. **Credit/placement by examination:** CLEP, IB, institutional tests. 30 credit hours maximum toward associate degree. **Support services:** GED preparation and test center, learning center, remedial instruction, tutoring.

**Majors. Biology:** General. **Business:** Administrative services, business admin, international, logistics, office technology. **Computer sciences:** General, information systems, security, system admin, systems analysis. **Education:** General, early childhood, music, physical. **Engineering technology:** Software. **English:** English lit. **Family/consumer sciences:** General. **History:** General. **Liberal arts:** Arts/sciences. **Math:** General. **Physical sciences:** General, chemistry, physics. **Psychology:** General. **Social sciences:** Political science, sociology. **Visual/performing arts:** Art, music.

**Most popular majors.** Computer/information sciences 6%, liberal arts 83%.

**Computing on campus.** 125 workstations in library, computer center.

**Student life. Freshman orientation:** Available. **Activities:** Concert band, choral groups, dance, drama, music ensembles, student government, student newspaper, African-American Unity Coalition, Society of Hispanic Engineers and Scientists, Christian Student Club, Star Native American Club, forensic club, music club, volunteers program, Phi Theta Kappa.

**Athletics.** NJCAA. **Intercollegiate:** Baseball M, basketball, golf, soccer M, softball W, tennis, volleyball W. **Team name:** Cougars.

**Student services.** Career counseling, student employment services, on-campus daycare, personal counseling, veterans' counselor. **Transfer:** Re-entry adviser, pre-admission transcript evaluation for new students. Transfer adviser, college fairs on campus for students transferring to 4-year colleges.

**Contact.** Phone: (602) 243-8123 Fax: (602) 243-8199
Raul Sandoval, Associate Dean of Student Services, South Mountain Community College, 7050 South 24th Street, Phoenix, AZ 85042

## Tohono O'odham Community College
### Sells, Arizona
### www.tocc.cc.az.us

- Public 2-year community college
- Commuter campus in rural community

**General.** TOCC is a Tribal College. **Enrollment:** 96 degree-seeking undergraduates; 58 non-degree-seeking students. **Degrees:** 23 associate awarded. **Location:** 60 miles from Tucson. **Calendar:** Semester, limited summer session. **Full-time faculty:** 14 total; 21% have terminal degrees. **Part-time faculty:** 15 total. **Class size:** 98% < 20, 2% 20-39.

**Student profile.** Among degree-seeking undergraduates, 4% enrolled in a transfer program, 12% enrolled in a vocational program, 5% already have a bachelor's degree or higher, 11 enrolled as first-time, first-year students, 4 transferred in from other institutions.

| | | | |
|---|---|---|---|
| Part-time: | 72% | Native American: | 99% |
| Women: | 71% | 25 or older: | 81% |
| Asian American: | 1% | | |

**Basis for selection.** Open admission. **Homeschooled:** Transcript of courses and grades, state high school equivalency certificate required.

**2007-2008 Annual costs.** Tuition/fees: $1,270; $6,340 out-of-state. Per-credit charge: $42 in-state; $72 out-of-state. Books/supplies: $750.

**2006-2007 Financial aid.** All financial aid based on need. 96% of total undergraduate aid awarded as scholarships/grants, 4% as loans/jobs. Need-based aid available for part-time students. Work-study available for part-time students.

**Application procedures. Admission:** No deadline. No application fee. **Financial aid:** No deadline. FAFSA, institutional form required. Applicants notified on a rolling basis.

**Academics. Special study options:** Distance learning, dual enrollment of high school students, independent study. **Credit/placement by examination:** CLEP. **Support services:** GED preparation, learning center, remedial instruction, study skills assistance, tutoring, writing center.

**Majors. Agriculture:** Production. **Business:** Business admin. **Computer sciences:** System admin. **Construction:** Carpentry, electrician, painting, plumbing, site management. **Education:** Early childhood special, elementary. **Liberal arts:** Arts/sciences. **Social sciences:** General.

**Most popular majors.** Business/marketing 17%, education 33%, interdisciplinary studies 33%, public administration/social services 17%.

**Student life. Freshman orientation:** Mandatory. Preregistration for classes offered. Orientation class offers information on student services and academic support services. **Activities:** Student government.

**Student services.** Adult student services, career counseling, student employment services, financial aid counseling, personal counseling, placement for graduates. **Transfer:** Re-entry adviser, pre-admission transcript evaluation for new students. College fairs on campus for students transferring to 4-year colleges.

**Contact.** E-mail: lluna@tocc.cc.az.us
Phone: (520) 383-8401 ext. 35 Fax: (520) 383-0029
Leslie Luna, Registar, Tohono O'odham Community College, PO Box 3129, Sells, AZ 85634-3129

## Universal Technical Institute
### Avondale, Arizona
### www.uticorp.com
### CB code: 2504

- For-profit 2-year technical college
- Commuter campus in small city

**General.** Founded in 1965. Accredited by ACCSCT. **Enrollment:** 1,761 degree-seeking undergraduates; 13 non-degree-seeking students. **Degrees:** 1,639 associate awarded. **Location:** 17 miles from Phoenix, 11 miles from Glendale. **Calendar:** Continuous, extensive summer session. **Full-time faculty:** 80 total; 2% women.

**Student profile.** Among degree-seeking undergraduates, 100% enrolled in a vocational program, 664 enrolled as first-time, first-year students.

| | | | |
|---|---|---|---|
| Out-of-state: | 65% | Women: | 2% |

**Basis for selection.** Open admission. **Homeschooled:** Must pass the Wonderlic Scholastic Level Exam. **Learning Disabled:** Students seeking accommodations must provide the school with a copy of an IEP from high school and/or medical documentation. They must also complete paperwork requesting the accommodation and meet with the School Counselor or Student Services Director prior to starting school.

**2008-2009 Annual costs.** Tuition/fees (projected): $15,130. Tuition varies by program and by campus.

**Application procedures. Admission:** No deadline. No application fee. Application may be submitted online. Admission notification on a rolling basis. **Financial aid:** No deadline. FAFSA required.

**Academics. Special study options:** Accelerated study. **Credit/placement by examination:** CLEP. **Support services:** Tutoring.

**Majors. Mechanic/repair:** Automotive, diesel.

**Student life. Freshman orientation:** Mandatory.

**Student services.** Career counseling, services for economically disadvantaged, student employment services, financial aid counseling, veterans' counselor.

**Contact.** E-mail: info@uticorp.com
Phone: (623) 245-4600 Toll-free number: (800) 859-1202
Fax: (602) 245-4601
Bruce Trexler, Campus Admissions Director, Universal Technical Institute, 10695 West Pierce Street, Avondale, AZ 85323

## Yavapai College
### Prescott, Arizona
### www.yc.edu
### CB code: 4996

- Public 2-year community college
- Commuter campus in large town

**General.** Founded in 1966. Regionally accredited. Classes offered at branch campus in Clarkdale and several locations in Yavapai County. **Enrollment:** 4,718 degree-seeking undergraduates; 4,345 non-degree-seeking students. **Degrees:** 333 associate awarded. **ROTC:** Army, Air Force. **Location:** 100 miles from Phoenix. **Calendar:** Semester, limited summer session. **Full-time faculty:** 98 total; 9% minority, 45% women. **Part-time faculty:** 309 total; 16% minority, 52% women. **Special facilities:** Solar laboratory, solar greenhouse, performance hall, career technical educational center.

**Student profile.** Among degree-seeking undergraduates, 764 enrolled as first-time, first-year students.

| | | | |
|---|---|---|---|
| Part-time: | 71% | 25 or older: | 24% |
| Out-of-state: | 6% | Live on campus: | 10% |
| Women: | 61% | | |

**Transfer out. Colleges most students transferred to 2007:** Arizona State University, Northern Arizona University, University of Arizona, Old Dominion University.

**Basis for selection.** Open admission, but selective for some programs. Limited admission for registered nursing, gunsmithing, and independent filmmaking. Interview required of nursing majors. Essay for independent filmmaking.

**2007-2008 Annual costs.** Tuition/fees: $1,470; $8,140 out-of-state. Per-credit charge: $49 in-state; $327 out-of-state. Room/board: $4,350. Books/supplies: $900. Personal expenses: $1,500.

**Financial aid. Need-based:** Need-based aid available for part-time students. **Non-need-based:** Scholarships awarded for academics, athletics.

**Application procedures. Admission:** No deadline. No application fee. Application may be submitted online. Admission notification on a rolling basis. **Financial aid:** Priority date 4/1; no closing date. FAFSA required. Applicants notified on a rolling basis.

**Academics. Special study options:** Accelerated study, distance learning, dual enrollment of high school students, ESL, honors, independent study, internships, liberal arts/career combination, teacher certification program, weekend college. 2-2 program with Northern Arizona University for bachelor degree in education and business, program with Old Dominion University offering bachelor degree completion. Bachelor's degree programs available on campus. License preparation in nursing, paramedic, real estate. **Credit/placement by examination:** AP, CLEP, IB, institutional tests. 30 credit hours maximum toward associate degree. **Support services:** GED preparation and test center, learning center, pre-admission summer program, reduced course load, remedial instruction, study skills assistance, tutoring, writing center.

**Majors. Agriculture:** Business. **Architecture:** Environmental design. **Business:** Accounting, administrative services, business admin, office management, office technology. **Computer sciences:** General. **Construction:** Maintenance. **Education:** Early childhood. **Engineering technology:** Manufacturing. **Health:** Medical secretary, nursing (RN). **Legal studies:** Legal secretary, paralegal. **Liberal arts:** Arts/sciences. **Mechanic/repair:** Automotive, gunsmithing. **Protective services:** Firefighting, law enforcement admin. **Visual/performing arts:** Commercial/advertising art, industrial design.

**Computing on campus.** 1,609 workstations in dormitories, library, computer center. Dormitories wired for high-speed internet access and linked to campus network. Online course registration, online library, wireless network available.

**Student life. Freshman orientation:** Available. Preregistration for classes offered. **Housing:** Coed dorms, special housing for disabled, substance-free housing available. $150 deposit. **Activities:** Bands, choral groups, dance, drama, literary magazine, music ensembles, musical theater, student government, student newspaper, nursing association, Native American club, international student club, Hispanic Club, Campus Crusade for Christ, Bahai Club, PTK, Veterans' Club.

**Athletics.** NJCAA. **Intercollegiate:** Baseball M, basketball, soccer M, volleyball W. **Team name:** Roughriders.

**Student services.** Adult student services, career counseling, student employment services, financial aid counseling, health services, personal counseling, placement for graduates, veterans' counselor. **Physically disabled:** Services for visually, hearing impaired. **Transfer:** College fairs on campus for students transferring to 4-year colleges.

**Contact.** E-mail: registration@yc.edu
Phone: (928) 445-7300 ext. 2148 Toll-free number: (800) 922-6787
Fax: (928) 776-2151
David Van Ness, Registrar, Yavapai College, 1100 East Sheldon Street, Prescott, AZ 86301

# Arkansas

## Arkansas Northeastern College
**Blytheville, Arkansas**
www.anc.edu                    CB code: 1267

▪ Public 2-year community college
▪ Commuter campus in large town

**General.** Founded in 1974. Regionally accredited. **Enrollment:** 1,360 degree-seeking undergraduates. **Degrees:** 202 associate awarded. **Location:** 65 miles from Memphis, Tennessee. **Calendar:** Semester, limited summer session. **Full-time faculty:** 78 total. **Part-time faculty:** 95 total. **Class size:** 66% < 20, 32% 20-39, less than 1% 40-49, 1% 50-99. **Partnerships:** Formal partnership with Tech Prep for business and technical courses.

**Student profile.**
Out-of-state:          18%    25 or older:         50%

**Transfer out. Colleges most students transferred to 2007:** Arkansas State University, Southeast Missouri State University.

**Basis for selection.** Open admission, but selective for some programs. Entrance exam required for nursing program.

**High school preparation.** Recommended units include English 4, mathematics 4, social studies 1, history 2, science 3 (laboratory 3).

**2007-2008 Annual costs.** Tuition/fees: $1,690; $1,990 out-of-district; $3,490 out-of-state. Per-credit charge: $49 in-district; $59 out-of-district; $109 out-of-state. Books/supplies: $1,000. Personal expenses: $4,188.

**Financial aid. Need-based:** Need-based aid available for part-time students. Work-study available nights and for part-time students. **Non-need-based:** Scholarships awarded for academics, minority status, music/drama, state residency.

**Application procedures. Admission:** No deadline. No application fee. Admission notification on a rolling basis. **Financial aid:** Priority date 4/15; no closing date. FAFSA, institutional form required. Applicants notified on a rolling basis starting 5/1; must reply within 2 week(s) of notification.

**Academics. Special study options:** Distance learning, double major, dual enrollment of high school students, weekend college. Bachelor's degree programs available on campus. License preparation in nursing, paramedic. **Credit/placement by examination:** CLEP, institutional tests. 15 credit hours maximum toward associate degree. Placement tests required for algebra, English composition. **Support services:** GED preparation and test center, learning center, reduced course load, remedial instruction, study skills assistance, tutoring, writing center.

**Majors. Agriculture:** Food science, horticulture. **Business:** General, administrative services, management information systems. **Education:** Middle. **Engineering technology:** Metallurgical. **Health:** Nursing (RN). **Liberal arts:** Arts/sciences. **Mechanic/repair:** Industrial. **Protective services:** Police science.

**Most popular majors.** Business/marketing 12%, education 8%, health sciences 12%, liberal arts 58%.

**Computing on campus.** 400 workstations in library, computer center. Commuter students can connect to campus network. Online library available.

**Student life. Freshman orientation:** Available. Preregistration for classes offered. **Activities:** Choral groups, music ensembles, student newspaper, Cultural Diversity Association, Baptist College Ministry, Adult Student Association.

**Student services.** Adult student services, career counseling, services for economically disadvantaged, student employment services, financial aid counseling, on-campus daycare, personal counseling, placement for graduates, veterans' counselor. **Physically disabled:** Services for visually, speech, hearing impaired. **Transfer:** Pre-admission transcript evaluation for new students. Transfer adviser, college fairs on campus for students transferring to 4-year colleges.

**Contact.** E-mail: jwalters@anc.edu
Phone: (870) 762-1020 ext. 1114 Fax: (870) 763-1654
June Walters, Vice President for Student Services and Registrar, Arkansas Northeastern College, Box 1109, Blytheville, AR 72316-1109

## Arkansas State University: Beebe
**Beebe, Arkansas**
www.asub.edu                    CB code: 0782

▪ Public 2-year branch campus and community college
▪ Commuter campus in small town

**General.** Founded in 1927. Regionally accredited. Approved as Serviceman's Opportunity College. **Enrollment:** 3,310 degree-seeking undergraduates. **Degrees:** 533 associate awarded. **Location:** 35 miles from Little Rock. **Calendar:** Semester, extensive summer session. **Full-time faculty:** 99 total. **Part-time faculty:** 167 total.

**Student profile.**
Out-of-state:        1%      Live on campus:        4%

**Basis for selection.** Open admission.

**High school preparation.** 15 units recommended. Recommended units include English 3, mathematics 1, social studies 2 and science 2.

**2007-2008 Annual costs.** Tuition/fees: $2,715; $4,400 out-of-state. Per-credit charge: $75 in-state; $122 out-of-state. Room/board: $2,680. Books/supplies: $800. Personal expenses: $1,900.

**2007-2008 Financial aid. Need-based:** 21% of total undergraduate aid awarded as scholarships/grants, 79% as loans/jobs. Need-based aid available for part-time students. Work-study available nights, weekends and for part-time students. **Non-need-based:** Scholarships awarded for academics, leadership, minority status, music/drama.

**Application procedures. Admission:** No deadline. No application fee. Admission notification on a rolling basis beginning on or about 8/1. **Financial aid:** Priority date 6/1; no closing date. FAFSA, institutional form required. Applicants notified on a rolling basis starting 6/1; must reply within 2 week(s) of notification.

**Academics. Special study options:** Accelerated study, double major, dual enrollment of high school students, honors, independent study. **Credit/placement by examination:** CLEP. 30 credit hours maximum toward associate degree. **Support services:** Learning center, reduced course load, remedial instruction, tutoring.

**Majors. Agriculture:** Business. **Biology:** General, botany, zoology. **Business:** General, administrative services, business admin, office management, office technology. **Computer sciences:** General. **Education:** General, music. **Engineering technology:** Drafting, electrical. **English:** English lit, speech/rhetoric. **History:** General. **Liberal arts:** Arts/sciences. **Math:** General. **Social sciences:** General, sociology.

**Student life. Freshman orientation:** Available. Preregistration for classes offered. **Housing:** Single-sex dorms available. **Activities:** Choral groups, drama, student government, student newspaper, Gamma Beta Phi.

**Athletics.** NJCAA. **Intramural:** Archery, badminton, basketball, bowling, softball, table tennis, tennis, track and field, volleyball.

**Student services.** Career counseling, personal counseling, veterans' counselor. **Transfer:** Transfer adviser, college fairs on campus for students transferring to 4-year colleges.

**Contact.** E-mail: rahayes@asub.edu
Phone: (501) 882-8260 Toll-free number: (800) 632-9985
Fax: (501) 882-8370
Robin Hayes, Registrar and Director of Admissions, Arkansas State University: Beebe, PO Box 1000, Beebe, AR 72012-1000

## Arkansas State University: Mountain Home
**Mountain Home, Arkansas**
www.asumh.edu                    CB code: 6057

▪ Public 1-year community and technical college
▪ Commuter campus in large town

**General. Enrollment:** 1,055 degree-seeking undergraduates; 124 non-degree-seeking students. **Degrees:** 171 associate awarded. **Location:** 130 miles north of Little Rock. **Calendar:** Semester, limited summer session.

**Full-time faculty:** 44 total; 25% have terminal degrees, 4% minority, 61% women. **Part-time faculty:** 23 total; 4% have terminal degrees, 48% women. **Class size:** 73% < 20, 27% 20-39.

**Student profile.** Among degree-seeking undergraduates, 23% enrolled in a transfer program, 2% enrolled in a vocational program, 252 enrolled as first-time, first-year students, 216 transferred in from other institutions.

| | | | |
|---|---|---|---|
| Part-time: | 48% | Women: | 63% |
| Out-of-state: | 3% | 25 or older: | 46% |

**Transfer out. Colleges most students transferred to 2007:** Arkansas State University-Jonesboro, University of Central Arkansas-Conway, University of Arkansas-Fayetteville.

**Basis for selection.** Open admission, but selective for some programs. Additional requirements for practical nursing program, respiratory care program, and phlebotomy program. **Homeschooled:** Statement describing homeschool structure and mission, transcript of courses and grades, state high school equivalency certificate required. **Learning Disabled:** Students with learning disabilities must document them with disability coordinator.

**High school preparation.** Recommended units include English 4, mathematics 4, social studies 3 and science 4.

**2007-2008 Annual costs.** Tuition/fees: $2,370; $3,900 out-of-state. Per-credit charge: $71 in-state; $122 out-of-state. Books/supplies: $800.

**Financial aid. Need-based:** Need-based aid available for part-time students. **Non-need-based:** Scholarships awarded for academics, state residency.

**Application procedures. Admission:** Closing date 8/15 (receipt date). No application fee. Application must be submitted on paper. Admission notification on a rolling basis. **Financial aid:** Priority date 7/1; no closing date. FAFSA, institutional form required. Applicants notified on a rolling basis starting 5/1; must reply within 2 week(s) of notification.

**Academics. Special study options:** Cooperative education, distance learning, dual enrollment of high school students, honors, independent study, liberal arts/career combination. License preparation in funeral sciences; AAS in Hearing Healthcare or Opticianry is online. Bachelor's degree programs available on campus. License preparation in nursing, paramedic, radiology. **Credit/placement by examination:** AP, CLEP. 15 credit hours maximum toward associate degree, 15 toward bachelor's. **Support services:** GED preparation and test center, learning center, remedial instruction, study skills assistance, tutoring, writing center.

**Majors. Business:** Administrative services. **Computer sciences:** Information systems. **Education:** Middle. **Health:** EMT paramedic, optician, respiratory therapy technology. **Liberal arts:** Arts/sciences. **Mechanic/repair:** Industrial. **Personal/culinary services:** Mortuary science. **Protective services:** Forensics, law enforcement admin.

**Most popular majors.** Business/marketing 8%, computer/information sciences 8%, liberal arts 59%, personal/culinary services 12%.

**Computing on campus.** 50 workstations in library, computer center. Commuter students can connect to campus network. Online course registration, online library, wireless network available.

**Student life. Freshman orientation:** Available. Preregistration for classes offered. **Activities:** Campus ministries, choral groups, drama, literary magazine, student government, Circle K, criminal justice club, mortuary science club, student ambassadors, student practical nurses association, Phi Beta Lambda, Phi Delta Kappa, Phi Theta Kappa, Rotaract.

**Student services.** Adult student services, campus ministries, career counseling, financial aid counseling, veterans' counselor. **Physically disabled:** Services for visually, hearing impaired. **Transfer:** Pre-admission transcript evaluation for new students. College fairs on campus for students transferring to 4-year colleges.

**Contact.**   E-mail: rblagg@asumh.edu
Phone: (870) 508-6104 Fax: (870) 508-6287
Rosalyn Blagg, Assistant Vice Chancellor for Enrollment, Arkansas State University: Mountain Home, 1600 South College Street, Mountain Home, AR 72653

## Arkansas State University: Newport
**Newport, Arkansas**
**www.asun.edu**

- Public 2-year community and liberal arts college
- Commuter campus in small town

**General. Enrollment:** 399 full-time, degree-seeking students. **Degrees:** 61 associate awarded. **Location:** 100 miles from Little Rock. **Calendar:** Semester, limited summer session. **Full-time faculty:** 37 total. **Part-time faculty:** 44 total.

**Transfer out. Colleges most students transferred to 2007:** University of Central Arkansas.

**Basis for selection.** Open admission. **Homeschooled:** Transcript of courses and grades required.

**2007-2008 Annual costs.** Tuition/fees: $2,340; $3,930 out-of-state. Per-credit charge: $73 in-state; $126 out-of-state.

**Application procedures. Admission:** No deadline. No application fee. Application may be submitted online. Admission notification on a rolling basis.

**Academics. Special study options:** Cooperative education, distance learning, dual enrollment of high school students, independent study, internships, liberal arts/career combination, study abroad, teacher certification program. License preparation in nursing. **Credit/placement by examination:** AP, CLEP, institutional tests. 30 credit hours maximum toward associate degree. **Support services:** GED preparation and test center, learning center, remedial instruction, study skills assistance, tutoring.

**Majors. Business:** General, management information systems. **Education:** Middle. **Engineering technology:** Computer. **Health:** EMT paramedic. **Liberal arts:** Arts/sciences.

**Computing on campus.** Commuter students can connect to campus network. Online course registration, online library, helpline, repair service, wireless network available.

**Student life. Activities:** Drama, student government.

**Student services. Transfer:** Re-entry adviser, pre-admission transcript evaluation for new students. Transfer adviser, college fairs on campus for students transferring to 4-year colleges.

**Contact.**   E-mail: tbyrd@asun.edu
Phone: (870) 512-7800 Toll-free number: (800) 976-1676
Fax: (870) 512-7825
Tara Byrd, Registrar/Director of Admissions, Arkansas State University: Newport, 7648 Victory Boulevard, Newport, AR 72112

## Black River Technical College
**Pocahontas, Arkansas**
**www.blackrivertech.org**          CB code: 3879

- Public 2-year technical college
- Large town
- SAT or ACT (ACT writing optional) required

**General.** Regionally accredited. **Enrollment:** 1,590 degree-seeking undergraduates. **Degrees:** 193 associate awarded. **Calendar:** Semester. **Full-time faculty:** 55 total. **Part-time faculty:** 59 total.

**Basis for selection.** High school transcript and standardized test scores most important.

**2007-2008 Annual costs.** Tuition/fees: $2,052; $5,412 out-of-state. Per-credit charge: $66 in-state; $178 out-of-state.

**Application procedures. Admission:** No deadline. No application fee. **Financial aid:** Priority date 4/1, closing date 6/30.

**Academics. Credit/placement by examination:** CLEP.

**Majors. Business:** Accounting, business admin, management information systems. **Education:** Early childhood, elementary. **English:** English lit. **Foreign languages:** German. **Math:** General. **Protective services:** Criminal justice. **Social sciences:** Economics. **Visual/performing arts:** Art.

**Contact.**   E-mail: elisec@blackrivertech.org
Phone: (870) 248-4000
Mary Anderson, Director of Admissions, Black River Technical College, Highway 304 East, Pocahontas, AR 72455

## Cossatot Community College of the University of Arkansas
**De Queen, Arkansas**
www.cccua.edu    CB code: 3613

◆ Public 2-year community college
◆ Commuter campus in small town

**General.** Regionally accredited. **Location:** 60 miles from Texarkana. **Calendar:** Semester.

**Annual costs/financial aid.** Tuition/fees (2007-2008): $1,650; $1,950 out-of-district; $5,250 out-of-state. Residents of bordering out-of-state counties may qualify for in-state tuition. Books/supplies: $1,100. Personal expenses: $1,564. Need-based financial aid available to full-time and part-time students.

**Contact.** Phone: (870) 584-4471 ext. 344
Dean of Student Services, 183 Highway 399, De Queen, AR 71832

## Crowley's Ridge College
**Paragould, Arkansas**
www.crowleysridgecollege.edu    CB code: 6131

◆ Private 2-year junior college affiliated with Church of Christ
◆ Commuter campus in large town

**General.** Regionally accredited. **Enrollment:** 118 degree-seeking undergraduates. **Degrees:** 16 associate awarded. **Location:** 23 miles from Jonesboro. **Calendar:** Semester, limited summer session. **Full-time faculty:** 8 total. **Part-time faculty:** 13 total.

**Transfer out. Colleges most students transferred to 2007:** Arkansas State University, Williams Baptist College, Harding University, Freed-Hardeman University.

**Basis for selection.** Open admission. Placement in freshman composition and algebra determined by ACT and ASSET scores. Development courses required for students with ACT score under 19.

**2008-2009 Annual costs.** Tuition/fees (projected): $8,410. Per-credit charge: $245. Room/board: $5,300. Books/supplies: $550.

**2007-2008 Financial aid. Need-based:** 91% of total undergraduate aid awarded as scholarships/grants, 9% as loans/jobs. Work-study available nights and weekends. **Non-need-based:** Scholarships awarded for academics, leadership, music/drama.

**Application procedures. Admission:** No deadline. No application fee. Admission notification on a rolling basis. **Financial aid:** No deadline. FAFSA required.

**Academics. Special study options:** Dual enrollment of high school students, independent study. **Credit/placement by examination:** CLEP. 34 credit hours maximum toward associate degree. **Support services:** Remedial instruction, study skills assistance, tutoring.

**Majors. Liberal arts:** Arts/sciences. **Philosophy/religion:** Religion.

**Computing on campus.** 15 workstations in dormitories, library, computer center. Dormitories linked to campus network.

**Student life. Freshman orientation:** Available. Preregistration for classes offered. Takes place first week of August. **Policies:** Chapel attendance required. **Housing:** Guaranteed on-campus for all undergraduates. Single-sex dorms available. $100 deposit. **Activities:** Choral groups, music ensembles, student government.

**Athletics. Intercollegiate:** Baseball M, basketball, volleyball W. **Intramural:** Basketball, softball, tennis, volleyball. **Team name:** Pioneers.

**Student services.** Campus ministries, financial aid counseling. **Transfer:** Pre-admission transcript evaluation for new students. College fairs on campus for students transferring to 4-year colleges.

**Contact.** E-mail: njoneshill@crowleysridgecollege.edu
Phone: (870) 236-6901 ext. 14 Toll-free number: (800) 264-1096
Fax: (870) 236-7748
Nancy Joneshill, Admissions Director, Crowley's Ridge College, 100 College Drive, Paragould, AR 72450

## East Arkansas Community College
**Forrest City, Arkansas**
www.eacc.edu    CB code: 0847

◆ Public 2-year community college
◆ Commuter campus in large town

**General.** Founded in 1973. Regionally accredited. **Enrollment:** 1,121 degree-seeking undergraduates; 426 non-degree-seeking students. **Degrees:** 143 associate awarded. **Location:** 40 miles from Memphis, Tennessee. **Calendar:** Semester, limited summer session. **Full-time faculty:** 35 total; 9% minority, 63% women. **Part-time faculty:** 58 total; 22% minority, 59% women.

**Student profile.** Among degree-seeking undergraduates, 40% enrolled in a transfer program, 50% enrolled in a vocational program, 277 enrolled as first-time, first-year students.

| | | | |
|---|---|---|---|
| Part-time: | 32% | Asian American: | 1% |
| Out-of-state: | 1% | Hispanic American: | 1% |
| Women: | 72% | 25 or older: | 47% |
| African American: | 44% | | |

**Transfer out. Colleges most students transferred to 2007:** Arkansas State University.

**Basis for selection.** Open admission. ASSET may be substituted for ACT or SAT for placement. Interview required of Allied Health majors. **Homeschooled:** Transcript of courses and grades, state high school equivalency certificate required.

**2007-2008 Annual costs.** Tuition/fees: $1,770; $2,010 out-of-district; $2,370 out-of-state. Per-credit charge: $51 in-district; $59 out-of-district; $71 out-of-state. Books/supplies: $700. Personal expenses: $1,000.

**Financial aid.** All financial aid based on need. Need-based aid available for part-time students.

**Application procedures. Admission:** No deadline. No application fee. Application must be submitted on paper. Admission notification on a rolling basis. **Financial aid:** Priority date 3/1, closing date 7/1. FAFSA required. Applicants notified on a rolling basis starting 5/15; must reply within 2 week(s) of notification.

**Academics. Special study options:** Cooperative education, distance learning, dual enrollment of high school students, honors, internships, liberal arts/career combination. License preparation in nursing, paramedic, radiology. **Credit/placement by examination:** AP, CLEP, institutional tests. 12 credit hours maximum toward associate degree. **Support services:** Learning center, remedial instruction, tutoring.

**Majors. Agriculture:** General. **Business:** Administrative services, business admin, finance, management information systems. **Computer sciences:** Web page design. **Education:** Middle. **Engineering technology:** CAD/CADD, environmental. **Family/consumer sciences:** Child care. **Health:** EMT paramedic, medical radiologic technology/radiation therapy, nursing (RN). **Mechanic/repair:** Industrial. **Protective services:** Police science.

**Most popular majors.** Business/marketing 11%, health sciences 28%, liberal arts 54%, security/protective services 6%.

**Computing on campus.** 35 workstations in library, computer center. Commuter students can connect to campus network.

**Student life. Freshman orientation:** Available. Preregistration for classes offered. **Activities:** Choral groups, student government, student newspaper.

**Athletics. Intramural:** Basketball, softball, tennis, volleyball.

**Student services.** Career counseling, student employment services, health services, personal counseling, placement for graduates, veterans' counselor. **Physically disabled:** Services for visually, hearing impaired. **Transfer:** Transfer adviser, college fairs on campus for students transferring to 4-year colleges.

**Contact.** E-mail: dadams@eacc.edu
Phone: (870) 633-4480 ext. 300 Toll-free number: (877) 797-3222
Fax: (870) 633-3840
DeAnna Adams, Director of Enrollment Management/Institutional Research, East Arkansas Community College, 1700 Newcastle Road, Forrest City, AR 72335-9598

## Mid-South Community College
**West Memphis, Arkansas**
www.midsouthcc.edu

**CB code: 3880**

▶ Public 2-year community and junior college
▶ Commuter campus in large town

**General.** Regionally accredited. **Enrollment:** 1,005 degree-seeking undergraduates; 646 non-degree-seeking students. **Degrees:** 88 associate awarded. **Location:** 8 miles from Memphis, Tennessee. **Calendar:** Semester, limited summer session. **Full-time faculty:** 45 total; 2% have terminal degrees, 33% minority, 42% women. **Part-time faculty:** 68 total; 6% have terminal degrees, 34% minority, 69% women. **Class size:** 77% < 20, 23% 20-39.

**Student profile.** Among degree-seeking undergraduates, 36% enrolled in a transfer program, 27% enrolled in a vocational program, 289 enrolled as first-time, first-year students, 108 transferred in from other institutions.

| | | | |
|---|---|---|---|
| Part-time: | 62% | Asian American: | 1% |
| Out-of-state: | 10% | Hispanic American: | 1% |
| Women: | 72% | 25 or older: | 53% |
| African American: | 55% | | |

**Transfer out. Colleges most students transferred to 2007:** Arkansas State University, University of Memphis.

**Basis for selection.** Open admission. **Homeschooled:** Transcript of courses and grades required.

**2007-2008 Annual costs.** Tuition/fees: $1,800; $2,100 out-of-district; $3,600 out-of-state. Per-credit charge: $50 in-district; $60 out-of-district; $110 out-of-state. Books/supplies: $1,000. Personal expenses: $5,500.

**Financial aid. Need-based:** Need-based aid available for part-time students. Work-study available nights and for part-time students. **Non-need-based:** Scholarships awarded for academics, state residency.

**Application procedures. Admission:** No deadline. No application fee. Application must be submitted on paper. Admission notification on a rolling basis. **Financial aid:** No deadline. FAFSA, institutional form required. Applicants notified on a rolling basis starting 6/1; must reply within 2 week(s) of notification.

**Academics. Special study options:** Cooperative education, distance learning, dual enrollment of high school students, liberal arts/career combination. **Credit/placement by examination:** AP, CLEP, institutional tests. 18 credit hours maximum toward associate degree. **Support services:** GED preparation and test center, learning center, reduced course load, remedial instruction, study skills assistance, tutoring, writing center.

**Majors. Agriculture:** General. **Business:** Office technology. **Computer sciences:** General. **Education:** Middle. **Liberal arts:** Arts/sciences. **Protective services:** Forensics, law enforcement admin.

**Computing on campus.** 250 workstations in library, computer center, student center. Commuter students can connect to campus network. Online course registration, online library available.

**Student life. Freshman orientation:** Available. Preregistration for classes offered. **Activities:** Jazz band, choral groups, TV station.

**Student services.** Adult student services, career counseling, services for economically disadvantaged, student employment services, financial aid counseling, minority student services, veterans' counselor. **Physically disabled:** Services for visually, speech, hearing impaired. **Transfer:** Transfer adviser, college fairs on campus for students transferring to 4-year colleges.

**Contact.** E-mail: admission@midsouthcc.edu
Phone: (870) 733-6728 Fax: (870) 733-6719
Jeremy Reece, Director of Admissions and Recruiting, Mid-South Community College, 2000 West Broadway, West Memphis, AR 72301

## National Park Community College
**Hot Springs, Arkansas**
www.npcc.edu

**CB code: 6243**

▶ Public 2-year liberal arts and technical college
▶ Commuter campus in large town

**General.** Founded in 1973. Regionally accredited. Located in the Hot Springs National Park. **Enrollment:** 2,503 degree-seeking undergraduates; 441 non-degree-seeking students. **Degrees:** 307 associate awarded. **Location:** 53 miles

from Little Rock. **Calendar:** Semester, extensive summer session. **Full-time faculty:** 64 total. **Part-time faculty:** 105 total. **Class size:** 63% < 20, 37% 20-39, less than 1% 40-49, less than 1% 50-99.

**Student profile.** Among degree-seeking undergraduates, 436 enrolled as first-time, first-year students.

| | | | |
|---|---|---|---|
| Part-time: | 48% | Women: | 66% |
| Out-of-state: | 1% | 25 or older: | 56% |

**Transfer out. Colleges most students transferred to 2007:** Henderson State University, Arkadelphia-University of Arkansas, University of Arkansas-Little Rock, University of Arkansas-Fayetteville.

**Basis for selection.** Open admission, but selective for some programs. Limited admission to allied health programs and nursing. Interview required for some health-related majors.

**High school preparation.** 18 units recommended. Recommended units include English 4, mathematics 4, social studies 3, history 2, science 3 (laboratory 3) and foreign language 2.

**2007-2008 Annual costs.** Tuition/fees: $1,740; $2,040 out-of-district; $3,960 out-of-state. Per-credit charge: $56 in-district; $66 out-of-district; $130 out-of-state. Books/supplies: $700. Personal expenses: $1,420.

**Financial aid. Need-based:** Need-based aid available for part-time students. Work-study available nights, weekends and for part-time students. **Non-need-based:** Scholarships awarded for academics, minority status, music/drama, state residency.

**Application procedures. Admission:** No deadline. No application fee. Application may be submitted online. Admission notification on a rolling basis beginning on or about 3/1. **Financial aid:** Priority date 7/1; no closing date. FAFSA, institutional form required. Applicants notified on a rolling basis starting 3/1.

**Academics. Special study options:** Cooperative education, cross-registration, distance learning, double major, dual enrollment of high school students, honors, independent study, internships, liberal arts/career combination, student-designed major. Bachelor's degree programs available on campus. License preparation in aviation, nursing, paramedic, radiology, real estate. **Credit/placement by examination:** AP, CLEP, institutional tests. 18 credit hours maximum toward associate degree. **Support services:** Learning center, reduced course load, remedial instruction, study skills assistance, tutoring, writing center.

**Majors. Business:** Accounting, hospitality admin, hospitality/recreation, office management, office technology. **Computer sciences:** General, applications programming, computer graphics. **Engineering technology:** Electrical. **Health:** Clinical lab technology, EMT paramedic, medical assistant, medical radiologic technology/radiation therapy, medical records technology, medical secretary, nursing (RN). **Liberal arts:** Arts/sciences. **Parks/recreation:** General. **Visual/performing arts:** Commercial/advertising art.

**Computing on campus.** 470 workstations in library, computer center, student center. Online library available.

**Student life. Freshman orientation:** Mandatory. Preregistration for classes offered. 2-day orientation, held one week prior to beginning of classes. **Activities:** Choral groups, dance, literary magazine, music ensembles, student government, student newspaper, Baptist Student Union, Black Awareness, Association for Barrier Awareness.

**Athletics. Intramural:** Baseball, basketball, bowling, skin diving, softball, table tennis, tennis, volleyball.

**Student services.** Adult student services, career counseling, services for economically disadvantaged, student employment services, financial aid counseling, health services, personal counseling, placement for graduates, veterans' counselor. **Physically disabled:** Services for visually, speech, hearing impaired. **Learning disabled:** Comprehensive services available. **Transfer:** Pre-admission transcript evaluation for new students. Transfer adviser, college fairs on campus for students transferring to 4-year colleges.

**Contact.** E-mail: admissions@npcc.edu
Phone: (501) 767-4222 Toll-free number: (800) 761-1825
Fax: (501) 760-4100
Nancy Happy, Director of Admissions, National Park Community College, 101 College Drive, Hot Springs, AR 71913

## North Arkansas College
**Harrison, Arkansas**
www.northark.edu

**CB code: 1423**

▶ Public 2-year community and technical college
▶ Commuter campus in large town

**General.** Founded in 1974. Regionally accredited. **Enrollment:** 1,664 degree-seeking undergraduates. **Degrees:** 256 associate awarded. **Location:** 75 miles from Fayetteville. **Calendar:** Semester, limited summer session. **Full-time faculty:** 64 total. **Part-time faculty:** 77 total. **Class size:** 70% < 20, 28% 20-39, less than 1% 40-49, less than 1% 50-99.

**Student profile.**

| | | | |
|---|---|---|---|
| Out-of-state: | 4% | 25 or older: | 42% |

**Transfer out. Colleges most students transferred to 2007:** Arkansas Tech University, College of the Ozarks, University of Arkansas, University of Central Arkansas, Southwest Missouri State University.

**Basis for selection.** Open admission, but selective for some programs. Allied health programs require separate application. Regarding CLEP examinations, to receive college credit, a student must score at the 50th percentile or higher, based on national norms, and may not have earned college credit nor have ever been enrolled in the course for which he/she is writing the test.

**High school preparation.** 14 units recommended. Recommended units include English 4, mathematics 4, social studies 1, history 2, science 3 (laboratory 3).

**2007-2008 Annual costs.** Tuition/fees: $1,710; $2,340 out-of-district; $4,470 out-of-state. Per-credit charge: $57 in-district; $78 out-of-district; $149 out-of-state. Books/supplies: $882. Personal expenses: $1,897.

**Financial aid. Need-based:** Need-based aid available for part-time students. Work-study available nights and for part-time students. **Non-need-based:** Scholarships awarded for academics, athletics, state residency.

**Application procedures. Admission:** No deadline. No application fee. Application must be submitted on paper. Admission notification on a rolling basis. **Financial aid:** Priority date 5/1; no closing date. FAFSA, institutional form required. Applicants notified on a rolling basis starting 5/1.

**Academics. Special study options:** Distance learning, dual enrollment of high school students, ESL, honors, independent study, internships, student-designed major. Bachelor's degree programs available on campus. License preparation in nursing, paramedic, radiology, real estate. **Credit/placement by examination:** AP, CLEP, institutional tests. 20 credit hours maximum toward associate degree. Only one-third of the credit hours for a degree can be from Advanced Placement, CLEP, the College Now Program, Challenge Test, various other examinations, or independent studies. Credit for Advanced Placement, CLEP, or Professional Certification Examinations will not be posted to an academic record until the student has successfully completed at least 12 semester credit hours of work. **Support services:** GED preparation and test center, learning center, remedial instruction, study skills assistance, tutoring, writing center.

**Majors. Agriculture:** General, business. **Business:** General, administrative services, hotel/motel admin, management information systems. **Computer sciences:** General. **Education:** Middle. **Engineering technology:** Biomedical, drafting, electrical, electromechanical. **Health:** Clinical lab technology, EMT paramedic, medical radiologic technology/radiation therapy, nursing (RN), surgical technology. **Liberal arts:** Arts/sciences. **Mechanic/repair:** Automotive, communications systems, industrial electronics. **Personal/culinary services:** Institutional food service. **Production:** Machine tool, welding. **Protective services:** Forensics, law enforcement admin, police science. **Other:** General Technology.

**Most popular majors.** Business/marketing 17%, computer/information sciences 8%, health sciences 34%, liberal arts 36%.

**Computing on campus.** 250 workstations in library, computer center. Online course registration, online library, repair service, wireless network available.

**Student life. Activities:** Choral groups, drama, student government, Baptist Student Union, Future Farmers of America, Health Occupations Students of America, Phi Beta Lambda, Phi Theta Kappa, Pioneer Hands club, Rad Tech club, Skills USA, student nurses association.

**Athletics.** NJCAA. **Intercollegiate:** Baseball M, basketball, softball W. **Intramural:** Archery, badminton, basketball, football (non-tackle) M, golf, racquetball, softball, table tennis, volleyball. **Team name:** Pioneers.

**Student services.** Adult student services, alcohol/substance abuse counseling, career counseling, student employment services, financial aid counseling, placement for graduates, veterans' counselor. **Physically disabled:** Services for visually, speech, hearing impaired. **Transfer:** Pre-admission transcript evaluation for new students. Transfer adviser, college fairs on campus for students transferring to 4-year colleges.

**Contact.** E-mail: charlam@northark.edu
Phone: (870) 391-3505 Toll-free number: (800) 679-6622
Fax: (870) 391-3339
Charla Jennings, Director of Admissions, North Arkansas College, 1515 Pioneer Drive, Harrison, AR 72601

## Northwest Arkansas Community College
### Bentonville, Arkansas
www.nwacc.edu      CB code: 7101

- Public 2-year community college
- Commuter campus in small city

**General.** Regionally accredited. **Enrollment:** 5,600 degree-seeking undergraduates; 870 non-degree-seeking students. **Degrees:** 307 associate awarded. **ROTC:** Army, Air Force. **Location:** 30 miles from Fayetteville. **Calendar:** Semester, extensive summer session. **Full-time faculty:** 108 total. **Part-time faculty:** 216 total. **Class size:** 41% < 20, 59% 20-39, less than 1% 40-49.

**Student profile.** Among degree-seeking undergraduates, 55% enrolled in a transfer program, 45% enrolled in a vocational program, 1,148 enrolled as first-time, first-year students, 941 transferred in from other institutions.

| | | | |
|---|---|---|---|
| Part-time: | 62% | Women: | 60% |
| Out-of-state: | 1% | 25 or older: | 20% |

**Transfer out. Colleges most students transferred to 2007:** University of Arkansas.

**Basis for selection.** Open admission, but selective for some programs. Additional requirements for nursing, physical therapy, respiratory therapy, emergency medical technician/paramedic programs.

**High school preparation.** 22 units recommended. Recommended units include English 4, mathematics 3, social studies 1, history 1, science 2, foreign language 1 and academic electives 10.

**2007-2008 Annual costs.** Tuition/fees: $2,125; $3,085 out-of-district; $4,195 out-of-state. Per-credit charge: $58 in-district; $90 out-of-district; $127 out-of-state. Books/supplies: $973.

**Financial aid. Need-based:** Need-based aid available for part-time students. Work-study available nights, weekends and for part-time students. **Non-need-based:** Scholarships awarded for academics, leadership, music/drama, state residency.

**Application procedures. Admission:** No deadline. $10 fee. Application may be submitted online. Admission notification on a rolling basis. **Financial aid:** Priority date 4/1; no closing date. FAFSA, institutional form required. Applicants notified on a rolling basis starting 4/1; must reply within 2 week(s) of notification.

**Academics. Special study options:** Distance learning, dual enrollment of high school students, ESL, honors, independent study, internships, liberal arts/career combination, weekend college. Bachelor's degree programs available on campus. License preparation in aviation, nursing, paramedic, physical therapy. **Credit/placement by examination:** AP, CLEP. 15 credit hours maximum toward associate degree. **Support services:** GED preparation and test center, learning center, remedial instruction, study skills assistance, tutoring, writing center.

**Majors. Business:** Accounting, administrative services, banking/financial services, business admin. **Computer sciences:** General, LAN/WAN management, programming, webmaster. **Engineering:** Environmental. **Engineering technology:** Drafting, electrical. **Family/consumer sciences:** Child care. **Health:** EMT paramedic, nursing (RN), physical therapy assistant, respiratory therapy technology. **Legal studies:** Paralegal. **Liberal arts:** Arts/sciences. **Mechanic/repair:** Aircraft. **Protective services:** Firefighting, law enforcement admin. **Transportation:** Aviation. **Visual/performing arts:** Commercial/advertising art.

**Most popular majors.** Health sciences 26%, liberal arts 54%.

**Computing on campus.** 75 workstations in library, computer center, student center. Commuter students can connect to campus network. Online course registration, online library available.

**Student life. Freshman orientation:** Available. Preregistration for classes offered. **Activities:** Choral groups, drama, literary magazine, music ensembles, musical theater, student government, student newspaper, symphony orchestra.

**Athletics. Intramural:** Archery, basketball, bowling, golf, soccer, softball, table tennis, volleyball.

**Student services.** Adult student services, alcohol/substance abuse counseling, career counseling, financial aid counseling, personal counseling, placement for graduates, veterans' counselor. **Transfer:** Transfer center, transfer adviser, college fairs on campus for students transferring to 4-year colleges.

**Contact.** E-mail: askregistration@nwacc.edu
Phone: (479) 619-4398 Toll-free number: (800) 995-6922
Fax: (479) 619-2229
John Honey, Director of Admissions, Northwest Arkansas Community College, One College Drive, Bentonville, AR 72712

## Ouachita Technical College
**Malvern, Arkansas**
**www.otcweb.edu**                                    **CB code: 3619**

♦ Public 2-year community and technical college
♦ Commuter campus in small town

**General.** Regionally accredited. **Enrollment:** 851 degree-seeking undergraduates. **Degrees:** 78 associate awarded. **ROTC:** Army. **Location:** 45 miles from Little Rock. **Calendar:** Semester, limited summer session. **Full-time faculty:** 34 total. **Part-time faculty:** 68 total.

**Student profile.** Among degree-seeking undergraduates, 114 transferred in from other institutions.

| Out-of-state: | 1% | 25 or older: | 28% |
|---|---|---|---|

**Transfer out. Colleges most students transferred to 2007:** Henderson State University, University of Central Arkansas.

**Basis for selection.** Open admission, but selective for some programs. Admission to practical nursing and cosmetology programs based on test scores.

**2007-2008 Annual costs.** Tuition/fees: $2,040; $3,630 out-of-state. Per-credit charge: $53 in-state; $106 out-of-state. Books/supplies: $1,834. Personal expenses: $1,202.

**Financial aid. Need-based:** Need-based aid available for part-time students. Work-study available nights.

**Application procedures. Admission:** No deadline. No application fee. Application may be submitted online. **Financial aid:** Closing date 6/30. FAFSA required. Applicants notified on a rolling basis starting 7/1; must reply within 6 week(s) of notification.

**Academics.** Associate of Arts in General Education and Associate of Applied Science in Criminal Justice offered online. **Special study options:** Distance learning, dual enrollment of high school students, independent study, internships, liberal arts/career combination. License preparation in nursing. **Credit/placement by examination:** AP, CLEP, institutional tests. **Support services:** GED preparation and test center, learning center, remedial instruction, study skills assistance, tutoring.

**Majors. Business:** General, business admin. **Computer sciences:** General. **Education:** Early childhood. **Family/consumer sciences:** Child care. **Health:** Nursing (RN). **Liberal arts:** Arts/sciences. **Production:** General. **Protective services:** Criminal justice, forensics.

**Most popular majors.** Business/marketing 18%, computer/information sciences 13%, family/consumer sciences 8%, liberal arts 42%, trade and industry 13%.

**Computing on campus.** 150 workstations in library, computer center. Online library, helpline, wireless network available.

**Student life. Freshman orientation:** Mandatory. Preregistration for classes offered. Mandatory orientation can be completed online. Optional orientation offered on-campus. **Activities:** Student government.

**Student services.** Adult student services, alcohol/substance abuse counseling, campus ministries, career counseling, services for economically disadvantaged, student employment services, financial aid counseling, personal counseling, placement for graduates, veterans' counselor. **Physically disabled:** Services for visually, speech, hearing impaired. **Transfer:** Pre-admission transcript evaluation for new students. College fairs on campus for students transferring to 4-year colleges.

**Contact.** E-mail: info@otcweb.edu
Phone: (501) 337-5000 ext. 1118 Fax: (501) 337-9382
Linda Johnson, Registrar, Ouachita Technical College, One College Circle, Malvern, AR 72104

## Ozarka College
**Melbourne, Arkansas**
**www.ozarka.edu**                                    **CB code: 3621**

♦ Public 2-year community and technical college
♦ Commuter campus in rural community

**General.** Regionally accredited. **Enrollment:** 806 degree-seeking undergraduates. **Degrees:** 72 associate awarded. **Location:** 125 miles from Little Rock, 160 miles from Memphis, Tennessee. **Calendar:** Semester, limited summer session. **Full-time faculty:** 37 total. **Part-time faculty:** 50 total.

**Transfer out. Colleges most students transferred to 2007:** Arkansas State University, Lyon College, University of Arkansas, University of Central Arkansas, Williams Baptist College.

**Basis for selection.** Open admission, but selective for some programs. Admission to licensed practical nursing, Registered Nursing, and culinary arts programs based on test scores, and/or essay, interview. **Adult students:** ACT/ASSET/COMPASS/SAT are accepted for placement in math and English. **Homeschooled:** Transcript of courses and grades required.

**2007-2008 Annual costs.** Tuition/fees: $2,285; $5,375 out-of-state. Per-credit charge: $65 in-state; $168 out-of-state. Books/supplies: $800. Personal expenses: $1,800.

**Financial aid. Need-based:** Need-based aid available for part-time students.

**Application procedures. Admission:** No deadline. No application fee. Application may be submitted online. Admission notification on a rolling basis. **Financial aid:** No deadline. FAFSA required. Applicants notified on a rolling basis; must reply within 2 week(s) of notification.

**Academics. Special study options:** Combined bachelor's/graduate degree, cooperative education, distance learning, dual enrollment of high school students, liberal arts/career combination. Bachelor's degree programs available on campus. License preparation in nursing. **Credit/placement by examination:** AP, CLEP, institutional tests. 36 credit hours maximum toward associate degree. **Support services:** GED preparation and test center, learning center, remedial instruction, study skills assistance, tutoring.

**Majors. Business:** Business admin, information resources management. **Education:** General, elementary, middle. **Engineering technology:** General. **Health:** Licensed practical nurse, medical transcription. **Liberal arts:** Arts/sciences. **Mechanic/repair:** Automotive. **Personal/culinary services:** Culinary arts. **Protective services:** Law enforcement admin.

**Computing on campus.** 175 workstations in library, computer center. Commuter students can connect to campus network. Online course registration, helpline, wireless network available.

**Student life. Freshman orientation:** Mandatory. **Activities:** Student government.

**Athletics. Team name:** Eagles.

**Student services.** Campus ministries, career counseling, services for economically disadvantaged, financial aid counseling, on-campus daycare, veterans' counselor, women's services. **Transfer:** Pre-admission transcript evaluation for new students. College fairs on campus for students transferring to 4-year colleges.

**Contact.** E-mail: zwilkerson@ozarka.edu
Phone: (870) 368-2028 Toll-free number: (800) 821-4335 ext. 2028
Fax: (870) 368-2091
Zeda Wilkerson, Director of Admissions, Ozarka College, 218 College Drive, Melbourne, AR 72556-0010

## Phillips Community College of the University of Arkansas
**Helena, Arkansas**
**www.pccua.edu**                                    **CB code: 6583**

♦ Public 2-year community college
♦ Commuter campus in large town

**General.** Founded in 1965. Regionally accredited. Campuses in Helena, Phillips County and Stuttgart and DeWitt in Arkansas county. **Enrollment:** 1,507 degree-seeking undergraduates. **Degrees:** 153 associate awarded. **Location:** 117 miles from Little Rock, 70 miles from Memphis, Tennessee. **Calendar:** Semester, limited summer session. **Full-time faculty:** 111 total.

**Part-time faculty:** 173 total. **Class size:** 78% < 20, 22% 20-39, less than 1% 50-99. **Special facilities:** Performing arts center.

**Basis for selection.** Open admission, but selective for some programs. Additional requirements for nursing program. Interview required of applicants with no high school transcript or test scores. **Adult students:** ASSET or COMPASS test required for students taking English or math. **Home-schooled:** Transcript of courses and grades, state high school equivalency certificate required.

**2007-2008 Annual costs.** Tuition/fees: $1,910; $2,180 out-of-district; $3,320 out-of-state. Per-credit charge: $52 in-district; $61 out-of-district; $99 out-of-state. Books/supplies: $1,200. Personal expenses: $3,660.

**Financial aid.** All financial aid based on need. Need-based aid available for part-time students. Work-study available nights and for part-time students. **Additional information:** Tuition waivers are given to firefighters and law enforcement officers.

**Application procedures. Admission:** No deadline. No application fee. Admission notification on a rolling basis. **Financial aid:** Priority date 4/1, closing date 6/30. FAFSA required. Applicants notified on a rolling basis starting 4/1; must reply within 2 week(s) of notification.

**Academics. Special study options:** Distance learning, dual enrollment of high school students, honors, independent study, internships, weekend college. Bachelor's degree programs available on campus. License preparation in nursing. **Credit/placement by examination:** CLEP, institutional tests. 30 credit hours maximum toward associate degree. **Support services:** GED preparation and test center, learning center, remedial instruction, study skills assistance, tutoring.

**Majors. Biology:** General. **Business:** General, business admin, office technology. **Communications technology:** Graphic/printing. **Computer sciences:** Computer science, information technology, LAN/WAN management. **Education:** General, early childhood, elementary. **Engineering:** General. **Engineering technology:** Biomedical, drafting, manufacturing. **English:** English lit, speech/rhetoric. **Health:** Nursing (RN), phlebotomy. **Legal studies:** Prelaw. **Liberal arts:** Arts/sciences. **Math:** General. **Mechanic/repair:** Industrial. **Physical sciences:** Chemistry, physics. **Psychology:** General. **Social sciences:** General. **Visual/performing arts:** Printmaking.

**Computing on campus.** 275 workstations in library, computer center. Commuter students can connect to campus network. Online course registration, wireless network available.

**Student life. Freshman orientation:** Available. Preregistration for classes offered. **Activities:** Choral groups, dance, drama, musical theater, Baptist Collegiate Ministries, Phi Theta Kappa, Arkansas Licensed Practical Nurses Association, National Student Nurses Association.

**Athletics. Intramural:** Archery, badminton, basketball, football (non-tackle) M, golf, soccer, softball, table tennis, tennis, volleyball.

**Student services.** Adult student services, career counseling, services for economically disadvantaged, student employment services, financial aid counseling, personal counseling, placement for graduates, veterans' counselor. **Physically disabled:** Services for visually, hearing impaired. **Transfer:** Transfer adviser, college fairs on campus for students transferring to 4-year colleges.

**Contact.** E-mail: lboone@pccua.edu
Phone: (870) 338-6474 ext. 1336 Fax: (870) 338-7542
Lynn Boone, Vice Chancellor for Student Services/Registrar, Phillips Community College of the University of Arkansas, 1000 Campus Drive, Helena, AR 72342

---

## Pulaski Technical College
**North Little Rock, Arkansas**
**www.pulaskitech.edu**                         CB code: 3622

◆  Public 2-year community and technical college
◆  Commuter campus in small city

**General.** Regionally accredited. **Enrollment:** 7,606 degree-seeking undergraduates; 1,162 non-degree-seeking students. **Degrees:** 607 associate awarded. **Location:** 4 miles from Little Rock. **Calendar:** Semester, extensive summer session. **Full-time faculty:** 147 total; 3% have terminal degrees, 5% minority, 45% women. **Part-time faculty:** 380 total; 18% minority, 56% women. **Class size:** 53% < 20, 47% 20-39.

**Student profile.** Among degree-seeking undergraduates, 60% enrolled in a transfer program, 28% enrolled in a vocational program, 1% already have

a bachelor's degree or higher, 1,278 enrolled as first-time, first-year students, 330 transferred in from other institutions.

| | | | |
|---|---|---|---|
| Part-time: | 48% | Asian American: | 1% |
| Women: | 71% | Hispanic American: | 2% |
| African American: | 53% | 25 or older: | 57% |

**Transfer out. Colleges most students transferred to 2007:** University of Arkansas at Little Rock, University of Central Arkansas.

**Basis for selection.** Open admission, but selective for some programs. Additional requirements for dental assisting, practical nursing, respiratory therapy, occupational therapy assistant and military technology programs. **Adult students:** COMPASS or ACT scores may be used for placement.

**2007-2008 Annual costs.** Tuition/fees: $2,480; $3,970 out-of-state. Per-credit charge: $74 in-state; $123 out-of-state. Books/supplies: $1,200. Personal expenses: $2,732.

**Financial aid. Need-based:** Need-based aid available for part-time students. Work-study available for part-time students.

**Application procedures. Admission:** No deadline. No application fee. Admission notification on a rolling basis. **Financial aid:** Priority date 5/15; no closing date. FAFSA, institutional form required. Applicants notified on a rolling basis starting 5/1; must reply within 2 week(s) of notification.

**Academics. Special study options:** Cooperative education, distance learning, dual enrollment of high school students, external degree, internships, liberal arts/career combination, weekend college. License preparation in aviation, dental hygiene, nursing. **Credit/placement by examination:** AP, CLEP, institutional tests. **Support services:** Learning center, pre-admission summer program, remedial instruction, study skills assistance, tutoring.

**Majors. Business:** General, management information systems. **Construction:** General. **Education:** Early childhood. **Engineering technology:** Drafting, environmental, industrial, manufacturing. **Family/consumer sciences:** Child care. **Health:** Occupational therapy assistant, respiratory therapy technology. **Legal studies:** Paralegal. **Liberal arts:** Arts/sciences. **Mechanic/repair:** Aircraft powerplant, electronics/electrical, heating/ac/refrig. **Military:** General. **Personal/culinary services:** Chef training. **Protective services:** Forensics, law enforcement admin. **Transportation:** Airline/commercial pilot. **Other:** General technologies.

**Most popular majors.** Business/marketing 17%, liberal arts 66%.

**Computing on campus.** 233 workstations in library, computer center, student center. Commuter students can connect to campus network. Online course registration, online library, helpline, wireless network available.

**Student life. Freshman orientation:** Available. Preregistration for classes offered. Online Orientation. **Activities:** Campus ministries, choral groups, literary magazine, student government, Metro Student Ministries, Culture Shock, Philoshophy Club, Student Ambassadors, Phi Theta Kappa.

**Student services.** Adult student services, career counseling, services for economically disadvantaged, student employment services, financial aid counseling, personal counseling, veterans' counselor. **Physically disabled:** Services for visually, hearing impaired. **Learning disabled:** Comprehensive services available. **Transfer:** Transfer adviser, college fairs on campus for students transferring to 4-year colleges.

**Contact.** E-mail: admissions@pulaskitech.edu
Phone: (501) 812-2231 Fax: (501) 812-2316
Clark Atkins, Director of Admissions, Pulaski Technical College, 3000 West Scenic Drive, North Little Rock, AR 72118-3347

---

## Remington College: Little Rock
**Little Rock, Arkansas**
**www.remingtoncollege.edu**

◆  For-profit 2-year technical college
◆  Commuter campus in very large city

**General.** Accredited by ACCSCT. **Calendar:** Quarter.

**Annual costs/financial aid.** Costs of entire programs leading to certificate, associate degree, bachelor's degree range from $13,000 to $36,009; includes books and supplies.

**Contact.** Phone: (501) 312-0007
Director of Admissions, 19 Remington Drive, Little Rock, AR 72204

## Rich Mountain Community College
Mena, Arkansas
www.rmcc.edu                                          CB code: 0226

▶ Public 2-year community college
▶ Commuter campus in small town

**General.** Founded in 1983. Regionally accredited. **Enrollment:** 565 degree-seeking undergraduates. **Degrees:** 55 associate awarded. **Location:** 85 miles from Fort Smith, 80 miles from Hot Springs. **Calendar:** Semester, limited summer session. **Full-time faculty:** 21 total. **Part-time faculty:** 38 total.

**Student profile.**

| | | | |
|---|---|---|---|
| Out-of-state: | 25% | **25 or older:** | 51% |

**Transfer out. Colleges most students transferred to 2007:** Henderson State University, Arkansas Tech University, Westark College, Cossatot Community College.

**Basis for selection.** Open admission, but selective for some programs. Limited admission to licensed practical nurse program.

**High school preparation.** 18 units recommended. Recommended units include English 4, mathematics 3, social studies 2 and science 4.

**2007-2008 Annual costs.** Tuition/fees: $1,440; $2,160 out-of-district; $5,190 out-of-state. Per-credit charge: $45 in-district; $69 out-of-district; $170 out-of-state. Books/supplies: $800. Personal expenses: $3,000.

**Financial aid. Need-based:** Need-based aid available for part-time students. Work-study available for part-time students. **Non-need-based:** Scholarships awarded for academics.

**Application procedures. Admission:** No deadline. No application fee. Admission notification on a rolling basis. **Financial aid:** Priority date 7/1; no closing date. FAFSA, institutional form required. Applicants notified on a rolling basis starting 6/1; must reply within 2 week(s) of notification.

**Academics.** MBA, masters in education leadership offered on campus by Henderson State University. **Special study options:** Cooperative education, distance learning, dual enrollment of high school students, external degree, internships, student-designed major. License preparation in nursing. **Credit/placement by examination:** AP, CLEP, institutional tests. 30 credit hours maximum toward associate degree. **Support services:** GED preparation and test center, pre-admission summer program, remedial instruction, study skills assistance, tutoring.

**Majors. Agriculture:** General. **Business:** Administrative services, business admin, management information systems. **Computer sciences:** General, information systems, LAN/WAN management, programming, systems analysis. **Education:** General. **Engineering technology:** Computer hardware. **Liberal arts:** Arts/sciences. **Production:** Machine tool.

**Most popular majors.** Business/marketing 17%, liberal arts 78%.

**Computing on campus.** 73 workstations in library, computer center. Commuter students can connect to campus network.

**Student life. Freshman orientation:** Available. Preregistration for classes offered. **Activities:** Radio station, student government, TV station, Baptist student union.

**Student services.** Adult student services, career counseling, services for economically disadvantaged, financial aid counseling, personal counseling, veterans' counselor. **Physically disabled:** Services for visually, hearing impaired. **Transfer:** Pre-admission transcript evaluation for new students. Transfer adviser, college fairs on campus for students transferring to 4-year colleges.

**Contact.** Phone: (501) 394-7622 ext. 1410 Fax: (501) 394-2760 Tammy Young, Dean of Students, Rich Mountain Community College, 1100 College Drive, Mena, AR 71953

## South Arkansas Community College
El Dorado, Arkansas
www.southark.edu                                      CB code: 1550

▶ Public 2-year community and junior college
▶ Commuter campus in large town

**General.** Founded in 1975. Regionally accredited. **Enrollment:** 1,214 degree-seeking undergraduates. **Degrees:** 130 associate awarded. **Location:** 115

miles from Little Rock. **Calendar:** Semester, limited summer session. **Full-time faculty:** 58 total. **Part-time faculty:** 46 total.

**Transfer out. Colleges most students transferred to 2007:** Southern Arkansas University, Louisiana Tech.

**Basis for selection.** Open admission. ACT, ASSET or COMPASS required for placement. **Homeschooled:** Transcript of courses and grades, state high school equivalency certificate required.

**High school preparation.** Recommended units include English 4, mathematics 3, social studies 3 and science 4.

**2007-2008 Annual costs.** Tuition/fees: $1,990; $2,230 out-of-district; $3,880 out-of-state. Per-credit charge: $60 in-district; $68 out-of-district; $123 out-of-state. $25 lab fee for most courses. Books/supplies: $600. Personal expenses: $550.

**Financial aid. Need-based:** Need-based aid available for part-time students.

**Application procedures. Admission:** Priority date 7/31; no deadline. No application fee. Admission notification on a rolling basis. **Financial aid:** Priority date 7/1; no closing date. FAFSA, institutional form required. Applicants notified on a rolling basis starting 7/1; must reply within 2 week(s) of notification.

**Academics. Special study options:** Dual enrollment of high school students, liberal arts/career combination. License preparation in nursing, occupational therapy, paramedic, physical therapy, radiology, real estate. **Credit/placement by examination:** AP, CLEP, IB, institutional tests. 30 credit hours maximum toward associate degree. **Support services:** GED preparation and test center, learning center, reduced course load, remedial instruction, tutoring.

**Majors. Business:** General, administrative services, business admin. **Communications:** Digital media. **Communications technology:** Desktop publishing. **Computer sciences:** General, applications programming, computer graphics, computer science, information technology, programming. **Conservation:** General. **Education:** General, early childhood, elementary, kindergarten/preschool, middle, multi-level teacher, secondary. **Family/consumer sciences:** Child care. **Health:** Clinical lab technology, EMT paramedic, medical radiologic technology/radiation therapy, nursing (RN), occupational therapy assistant, physical therapy assistant, radiologic technology/medical imaging. **Liberal arts:** Arts/sciences. **Mechanic/repair:** Automotive, industrial. **Protective services:** Police science. **Visual/performing arts:** Commercial/advertising art.

**Computing on campus.** 250 workstations in library, computer center, student center. Online course registration, student web hosting available.

**Student life. Freshman orientation:** Available. Preregistration for classes offered. **Activities:** Choral groups, literary magazine, Phi Beta Lambda, Phi Theta Kappa, student leadership group.

**Athletics. Intramural:** Basketball, tennis, volleyball.

**Student services.** Adult student services, career counseling, services for economically disadvantaged, student employment services, financial aid counseling, personal counseling, placement for graduates, veterans' counselor. **Physically disabled:** Services for visually, hearing impaired. **Transfer:** Transfer adviser, college fairs on campus for students transferring to 4-year colleges.

**Contact.** E-mail: registrar@southark.edu
Phone: (870) 862-8131 Toll-free number: (800) 955-2289
Fax: (870) 864-7137
Dean Inman, Director of Enrollment Services, South Arkansas Community College, Box 7010, El Dorado, AR 71731-7010

## Southeast Arkansas College
Pine Bluff, Arkansas
www.seark.edu                                         CB code: 3624

▶ Public 2-year community and technical college
▶ Commuter campus in small city

**General.** Regionally accredited. **Enrollment:** 1,710 degree-seeking undergraduates; 434 non-degree-seeking students. **Degrees:** 189 associate awarded. **Location:** 42 miles from Little Rock. **Calendar:** Semester, limited summer session. **Full-time faculty:** 51 total. **Part-time faculty:** 83 total. **Class size:** 64% < 20, 36% 20-39, less than 1% 40-49.

**Student profile.** Among degree-seeking undergraduates, 77% enrolled in a vocational program, 264 enrolled as first-time, first-year students, 39 transferred in from other institutions.

| Part-time: | 43% | **Women:** | 75% |
|---|---|---|---|

**Transfer out. Colleges most students transferred to 2007:** University of Arkansas at Pine Bluff, University of Arkansas at Monticello, University of Arkansas at Little Rock.

**Basis for selection.** Open admission, but selective for some programs. Additional requirements for some health programs. ACT, ASSET or COMPASS required for placement.

**High school preparation.** Recommended units include English 4, mathematics 2, social studies 2, history 2, science 2 and foreign language 1.

**2007-2008 Annual costs.** Tuition/fees: $1,720; $3,220 out-of-state. Per-credit charge: $50 in-state; $100 out-of-state. $5 per credit hour technology fee. $5 assessment fee. $2 per hour services fee. Books/supplies: $700. Personal expenses: $2,450.

**Financial aid. Need-based:** Need-based aid available for part-time students. Work-study available nights, weekends and for part-time students. **Non-need-based:** Scholarships awarded for academics, leadership, state residency.

**Application procedures. Admission:** No deadline. No application fee. **Financial aid:** Priority date 6/1; no closing date. FAFSA required. Applicants notified on a rolling basis starting 5/1; must reply within 2 week(s) of notification.

**Academics. Special study options:** Cooperative education, distance learning, independent study, internships. License preparation in nursing, paramedic, real estate. **Credit/placement by examination:** AP, CLEP. 15 credit hours maximum toward associate degree. Credit awarded through challenge exams. **Support services:** GED preparation and test center, learning center, remedial instruction, tutoring.

**Majors. Biology:** Biotechnology. **Business:** General. **Computer sciences:** General, networking, web page design, webmaster. **Engineering technology:** Drafting. **Family/consumer sciences:** Child care. **Health:** EMT paramedic, medical assistant, medical radiologic technology/radiation therapy, nursing (RN), surgical technology. **Legal studies:** Paralegal. **Liberal arts:** Arts/sciences. **Mechanic/repair:** Electronics/electrical, industrial. **Protective services:** Criminal justice, firefighting.

**Most popular majors.** Business/marketing 14%, health sciences 23%, legal studies 17%, liberal arts 35%.

**Computing on campus.** PC or laptop required. 500 workstations in library, computer center.

**Student life. Freshman orientation:** Available. Preregistration for classes offered. 1-hour program held Sunday afternoon before start of classes. **Activities:** Student government.

**Student services.** Adult student services, alcohol/substance abuse counseling, career counseling, services for economically disadvantaged, student employment services, financial aid counseling, personal counseling, placement for graduates, veterans' counselor. **Physically disabled:** Services for visually, speech, hearing impaired. **Learning disabled:** Comprehensive services available. **Transfer:** Pre-admission transcript evaluation for new students. College fairs on campus for students transferring to 4-year colleges.

**Contact.** E-mail: hpost@seark.edu
Phone: (870) 543-5908 Fax: (870) 543-5956
Barbara Dunn, Admissions and Enrollment Management Coordinator, Southeast Arkansas College, 1900 Hazel Street, Pine Bluff, AR 71603

---

## Southern Arkansas University Tech
**Camden, Arkansas**
www.sautech.edu                    CB code: 6704

- Public 2-year community and technical college
- Commuter campus in large town

**General.** Founded in 1967. Regionally accredited. **Enrollment:** 787 degree-seeking undergraduates; 1,324 non-degree-seeking students. **Degrees:** 96 associate awarded. **Location:** 90 miles from Little Rock. **Calendar:** Semester, limited summer session. **Full-time faculty:** 34 total; 3% have terminal degrees, 6% minority, 50% women. **Part-time faculty:** 77 total; 4% have terminal degrees, 17% minority, 47% women. **Class size:** 68% < 20, 28%

20-39, less than 1% 40-49, 4% 50-99. **Special facilities:** Fire training academy, environmental science academy, law enforcement academy, career academy, business and industry center. **Partnerships:** Formal partnerships with area businesses/industries and high schools.

**Student profile.** Among degree-seeking undergraduates, 22% enrolled in a vocational program, 216 enrolled as first-time, first-year students, 185 transferred in from other institutions.

| Part-time: | 32% | **Hispanic American:** | 1% |
|---|---|---|---|
| Out-of-state: | 2% | **Native American:** | 1% |
| Women: | 52% | **International:** | 1% |
| African American: | 30% | **25 or older:** | 45% |

**Transfer out.** 95% of students enrolled in the transfer program go on to 4-year colleges. **Colleges most students transferred to 2007:** Southern Arkansas University, Henderson State University, University of Arkansas at Monticello, University of Central Arkansas, South Arkansas Community College.

**Basis for selection.** Open admission, but selective for some programs. Additional requirements for nursing program. **Homeschooled:** State high school equivalency certificate required. Applicants must take the GED test.

**High school preparation.** 23 units recommended. Recommended units include English 4, mathematics 4, social studies 2, history 2, science 3, foreign language 2 and academic electives 6.

**2007-2008 Annual costs.** Tuition/fees: $2,419; $3,049 out-of-state. Per-credit charge: $63 in-state; $84 out-of-state. Books/supplies: $700. Personal expenses: $3,500.

**2006-2007 Financial aid. Need-based:** Need-based aid available for part-time students. Work-study available for part-time students. **Non-need-based:** Scholarships awarded for academics, state residency.

**Application procedures. Admission:** Priority date 7/15; deadline 6/1 (postmark date). No application fee. Application may be submitted online. Admission notification on a rolling basis. **Financial aid:** Priority date 6/1; no closing date. FAFSA required. Applicants notified on a rolling basis starting 5/1.

**Academics. Special study options:** Distance learning, double major, dual enrollment of high school students, honors, independent study, internships. Articulation agreements for Nursing Assistant and Practical Nursing programs. Bachelor's degree programs available on campus. License preparation in aviation, nursing. **Credit/placement by examination:** AP, CLEP, institutional tests. 15 credit hours maximum toward associate degree. **Support services:** GED preparation and test center, learning center, pre-admission summer program, remedial instruction, study skills assistance, tutoring, writing center.

**Majors. Business:** Business admin, office management. **Computer sciences:** Computer science, networking, programming. **Education:** Instructional media, multi-level teacher. **Engineering technology:** Computer systems, environmental, industrial. **Mechanic/repair:** Aircraft powerplant, industrial. **Protective services:** Fire services admin, firefighting. **Other:** Technology.

**Most popular majors.** Business/marketing 20%, computer/information sciences 21%, engineering/engineering technologies 25%, liberal arts 18%, security/protective services 9%.

**Computing on campus.** 250 workstations in library, computer center. Dormitories wired for high-speed internet access and linked to campus network. Commuter students can connect to campus network. Online course registration, online library, helpline, repair service, wireless network available.

**Student life. Freshman orientation:** Mandatory. Preregistration for classes offered. One-day program in late July or early August. **Housing:** Apartments, substance-free housing available. $100 deposit, deadline 7/15. Off-campus housing is available. **Activities:** Campus ministries, radio station, student government, TV station, Multi-Cultural Club, Aviation Club, IMEDIO (multimedia graphics, audio/video) CCUB, Computer Club, Electronics Club, Phi Beta Lambda, Phi Theta Kappa, SAU Tech Ambassadors, Allied Health Student Club, Student Advisers.

**Athletics. Intramural:** Basketball, football (non-tackle), soccer, softball, tennis, volleyball, weight lifting. **Team name:** Varmits.

**Student services.** Adult student services, campus ministries, career counseling, services for economically disadvantaged, student employment services, financial aid counseling, on-campus daycare, personal counseling, placement for graduates, veterans' counselor. **Physically disabled:** Services for visually, speech, hearing impaired. **Transfer:** Re-entry adviser, pre-admission transcript evaluation for new students. Transfer center, transfer adviser, college fairs on campus for students transferring to 4-year colleges.

**Contact.** E-mail: bclark@sautech.edu
Phone: (870) 574-4558 Fax: (870) 574-4478
Patricia Sindle, Director, Enrollment Services, Southern Arkansas
University Tech, PO Box 3499, Camden, AR 71711-1599

## University of Arkansas Community College at Morrilton
### Morrilton, Arkansas
www.uaccm.edu                                    CB code: 3881

- Public 2-year community college
- Commuter campus in small town

**General.** Regionally accredited. **Enrollment:** 1,726 degree-seeking undergraduates; 83 non-degree-seeking students. **Degrees:** 174 associate awarded. **Location:** 26 miles from Russellville. **Calendar:** Semester, limited summer session. **Full-time faculty:** 58 total; 2% have terminal degrees, 57% women. **Part-time faculty:** 46 total; 6% have terminal degrees, 2% minority, 63% women.

**Student profile.** Among degree-seeking undergraduates, 45% enrolled in a transfer program, 54% enrolled in a vocational program, 549 enrolled as first-time, first-year students.

| | | | |
|---|---|---|---|
| Part-time: | 29% | Hispanic American: | 3% |
| Women: | 61% | Native American: | 1% |
| African American: | 7% | 25 or older: | 42% |
| Asian American: | 1% | | |

**Transfer out. Colleges most students transferred to 2007:** University of Central Arkansas, Arkansas Tech University, University of Arkansas at Fayetteville, University of Arkansas at Little Rock.

**Basis for selection.** Open admission. ASSET or COMPASS test scores required for placement. **Homeschooled:** Transcript of courses and grades required.

**2007-2008 Annual costs.** Tuition/fees: $2,430; $2,610 out-of-district; $3,570 out-of-state. Per-credit charge: $64 in-district; $70 out-of-district; $102 out-of-state. Books/supplies: $900.

**2007-2008 Financial aid. Need-based:** Average need met was 47%. Average scholarship/grant was $4,412; average loan $1,210. 74% of total undergraduate aid awarded as scholarships/grants, 26% as loans/jobs. Need-based aid available for part-time students. Work-study available nights and for part-time students. **Non-need-based:** Awarded to 17 full-time undergraduates, including 13 freshmen. Scholarships awarded for academics, leadership, state residency.

**Application procedures. Admission:** No deadline. No application fee. Application may be submitted online. Admission notification on a rolling basis. **Financial aid:** Priority date 7/1; no closing date. FAFSA, institutional form, CSS PROFILE required. Applicants notified by 5/1.

**Academics. Special study options:** Distance learning, internships, liberal arts/career combination. License preparation in nursing. **Credit/placement by examination:** AP, CLEP, institutional tests. **Support services:** GED preparation and test center, learning center, remedial instruction, study skills assistance, tutoring, writing center.

**Majors. Business:** General, finance. **Education:** Multi-level teacher. **Engineering technology:** General, computer systems, drafting, petroleum, surveying. **Family/consumer sciences:** Child development. **Health:** Nursing (RN). **Liberal arts:** Arts/sciences. **Mechanic/repair:** Auto body, automotive, heating/ac/refrig. **Protective services:** Forensics, law enforcement admin.

**Student life. Freshman orientation:** Available. Preregistration for classes offered. **Activities:** Choral groups, drama, student government, student newspaper.

**Athletics.** NJCAA. **Intercollegiate:** Golf M. **Intramural:** Basketball, football (non-tackle), table tennis, volleyball. **Team name:** Timberwolves.

**Student services.** Career counseling, financial aid counseling, on-campus daycare, placement for graduates. **Physically disabled:** Services for visually, speech, hearing impaired. **Transfer:** College fairs on campus for students transferring to 4-year colleges.

**Contact.** E-mail: adm@uaccm.edu
Phone: (501) 977-2053 Toll-free number: (800) 264-1094
Fax: (501) 977-2123
Susan Dewey, Director of Admissions, University of Arkansas Community College at Morrilton, 1537 University Boulevard, Morrilton, AR 72110

## University of Arkansas: Community College at Batesville
### Batesville, Arkansas
www.uaccb.edu                                    CB code: 3628

- Public 2-year community college
- Commuter campus in small town

**General.** Regionally accredited. **Location:** 90 miles from Little Rock. **Calendar:** Semester.

**Annual costs/financial aid.** Tuition/fees (2007-2008): $1,990; $2,290 out-of-district; $4,090 out-of-state. Books/supplies: $700. Personal expenses: $2,100. Need-based financial aid available for full-time students.

**Contact.** Phone: (870) 612-2010
Admissions and Student Activities Coordinator, Box 3350, Batesville, AR 72503

## University of Arkansas: Community College at Hope
### Hope, Arkansas
www.uacch.edu                                    CB code: 3629

- Public 2-year community and technical college
- Commuter campus in small town

**General.** Regionally accredited. **Enrollment:** 966 degree-seeking undergraduates. **Degrees:** 128 associate awarded. **Location:** 30 miles from Texarkana. **Calendar:** Semester, limited summer session. **Full-time faculty:** 38 total; 5% have terminal degrees, 8% minority, 45% women. **Part-time faculty:** 23 total; 48% women.

**Basis for selection.** Open admission, but selective for some programs. Additional requirements for nursing, funeral services, respiratory therapy programs.

**High school preparation.** 15 units recommended. Recommended units include English 4, mathematics 3, social studies 1, history 2, science 3 and academic electives 2.

**2007-2008 Annual costs.** Tuition/fees: $1,790; $1,940 out-of-district; $3,620 out-of-state. Per-credit charge: $54 in-district; $59 out-of-district; $115 out-of-state. Books/supplies: $900. Personal expenses: $500.

**Financial aid. Need-based:** Need-based aid available for part-time students. Work-study available nights and for part-time students. **Non-need-based:** Scholarships awarded for academics.

**Application procedures. Admission:** No deadline. No application fee. Application may be submitted online. Admission notification on a rolling basis. **Financial aid:** Priority date 7/6; no closing date. FAFSA, institutional form required. Applicants notified on a rolling basis starting 1/1; must reply within 4 week(s) of notification.

**Academics. Special study options:** Distance learning, double major, dual enrollment of high school students, ESL, independent study, liberal arts/career combination. Bachelor's degree programs available on campus. License preparation in nursing, paramedic. **Credit/placement by examination:** AP, CLEP, institutional tests. **Support services:** GED test center, remedial instruction, study skills assistance, tutoring.

**Majors. Agriculture:** General. **Business:** General. **Education:** Middle. **Family/consumer sciences:** Child care. **Health:** Respiratory therapy technology. **Legal studies:** Paralegal. **Liberal arts:** Arts/sciences. **Personal/culinary services:** Mortuary science. **Protective services:** Forensics, law enforcement admin, police science.

**Most popular majors.** Business/marketing 7%, health sciences 9%, legal studies 6%, liberal arts 62%, personal/culinary services 7%.

**Computing on campus.** 20 workstations in library. Commuter students can connect to campus network. Online course registration, online library, helpline, wireless network available.

**Student life. Freshman orientation:** Available. **Activities:** Jazz band, choral groups, drama, music ensembles, student government, student newspaper.

**Student services.** Adult student services, alcohol/substance abuse counseling, campus ministries, career counseling, services for economically disadvantaged, student employment services, financial aid counseling, personal counseling, placement for graduates, veterans' counselor. **Physically**

**disabled:** Services for visually, speech, hearing impaired. **Transfer:** Pre-admission transcript evaluation for new students. College fairs on campus for students transferring to 4-year colleges.

**Contact.** E-mail: dormand@uacch.edu
Phone: (870) 777-5722 Fax: (870) 722-6630
Judy Anderson, Director for Enrollment Services, University of Arkansas: Community College at Hope, 2500 South Main, Hope, AR 71802-0140

**Two-Year Colleges**

# California

## Allan Hancock College
Santa Maria, California
www.hancockcollege.edu                    CB code: 4002

▶ Public 2-year community college
▶ Commuter campus in small city

**General.** Founded in 1920. Regionally accredited. **Enrollment:** 6,095 degree-seeking undergraduates. **Degrees:** 1,173 associate awarded. **Location:** 70 miles from Santa Barbara, 175 miles from Los Angeles. **Calendar:** Semester, extensive summer session. **Full-time faculty:** 158 total. **Part-time faculty:** 450 total.

**Transfer out. Colleges most students transferred to 2007:** California Polytechnic State University, San Luis Obispo; UC Santa Barbara, CSU, San Diego; CSU, Northridge; CSU, Fresno.

**Basis for selection.** Open admission, but selective for some programs. Special requirements for allied health and drama programs. Students required to make separate application for admission to nursing, drama, police academy programs. Interviews required for allied health applicants. Auditions required for drama applicants. **Adult students:** SAT/ACT scores not required.

**2007-2008 Annual costs.** Tuition/fees: $642; $5,832 out-of-state. Per-credit charge: $20 in-state; $193 out-of-state. Books/supplies: $1,422. Personal expenses: $2,924.

**Financial aid.** All financial aid based on need. Need-based aid available for part-time students. Work-study available for part-time students.

**Application procedures. Admission:** No deadline. No application fee. Application may be submitted online. Admission notification on a rolling basis. **Financial aid:** Priority date 5/1; no closing date. FAFSA required. Applicants notified on a rolling basis starting 6/1.

**Academics. Special study options:** Accelerated study, cooperative education, distance learning, double major, dual enrollment of high school students, ESL, honors, independent study, internships, liberal arts/career combination, study abroad, weekend college. Bachelor's degree programs available on campus. License preparation in dental hygiene, nursing, paramedic, real estate. **Credit/placement by examination:** AP, CLEP, institutional tests. 30 credit hours maximum toward associate degree. **Support services:** GED preparation and test center, learning center, reduced course load, remedial instruction, study skills assistance, tutoring, writing center.

**Majors. Agriculture:** Agribusiness operations. **Architecture:** Technology. **Biology:** General. **Business:** General, accounting, administrative services, business admin, international marketing, management information systems, management science, office technology, office/clerical. **Communications technology:** Animation/special effects, graphic/printing, graphics, photo/film/video. **Computer sciences:** General, computer science, information technology. **Conservation:** Environmental studies. **Education:** Early childhood, elementary, physical. **Engineering:** General. **Engineering technology:** General, architectural, civil, electrical, electromechanical, environmental, robotics. **English:** English lit. **Family/consumer sciences:** General, fashion consultant, housing. **Foreign languages:** Spanish. **Health:** Dental assistant, health services, licensed practical nurse, medical assistant, medical records admin, medical records technology, nursing (RN), physical therapy assistant. **Legal studies:** Legal secretary. **Liberal arts:** Arts/sciences. **Math:** General, computational. **Mechanic/repair:** General, auto body, automotive, diesel, electronics/electrical. **Parks/recreation:** General. **Personal/culinary services:** Chef training, cosmetic. **Physical sciences:** Chemistry, physics. **Protective services:** Fire safety technology. **Psychology:** General. **Public administration:** Human services. **Social sciences:** General, international relations. **Visual/performing arts:** Art, commercial photography, commercial/advertising art, dance, design, fashion design, film/cinema, interior design, photography.

**Most popular majors.** Health sciences 9%, liberal arts 58%, security/protective services 12%.

**Computing on campus.** 180 workstations in library, computer center. Online library, wireless network available.

**Student life. Freshman orientation:** Available. **Activities:** Bands, choral groups, dance, drama, film society, literary magazine, music ensembles, musical theater, student government, student newspaper.

**Athletics. Intercollegiate:** Baseball M, basketball, cross-country, football (tackle) M, golf, soccer, tennis, track and field, volleyball W. **Team name:** Bulldogs.

**Student services.** Adult student services, career counseling, services for economically disadvantaged, student employment services, health services, on-campus daycare, personal counseling, placement for graduates, veterans' counselor. **Physically disabled:** Services for visually, hearing impaired. **Transfer:** Pre-admission transcript evaluation for new students. Transfer center, transfer adviser, college fairs on campus for students transferring to 4-year colleges.

**Contact.** Phone: (805) 922-6966 ext. 3248 Fax: (805) 922-3477 Adela Esquivel-Swinson, Director, Admissions and Records, Allan Hancock College, 800 South College Drive, Santa Maria, CA 93454-6399

## American Academy of Dramatic Arts: West
Los Angeles, California
www.aada.org                              CB code: 7024

▶ Private 2-year performing arts college
▶ Commuter campus in very large city
▶ Application essay, interview required

**General.** Founded in 1974. Regionally accredited. **Enrollment:** 250 degree-seeking undergraduates. **Degrees:** 17 associate awarded. **Calendar:** Semester. **Full-time faculty:** 1 total; 100% women. **Part-time faculty:** 27 total; 11% minority, 63% women. **Class size:** 93% < 20, 7% 20-39. **Special facilities:** Performance theater.

**Student profile.**

| | | | |
|---|---|---|---|
| Out-of-state: | 25% | 25 or older: | 20% |

**Basis for selection.** Student attitude, seriousness of intent, and potential as professional actor as indicated by written recommendations, interview, and audition. All applicants must have full command of English language. Auditions required.

**2008-2009 Annual costs.** Tuition/fees: $20,000. Books/supplies: $600. Personal expenses: $1,232.

**Financial aid. Non-need-based:** Scholarships awarded for academics, music/drama.

**Application procedures. Admission:** No deadline. $50 fee. Application may be submitted online. Admission notification on a rolling basis. SAT or ACT recommended for applicants attending directly from high school. **Financial aid:** Priority date 7/1; no closing date. Institutional form required. Applicants notified on a rolling basis starting 6/1; must reply within 3 week(s) of notification.

**Academics.** Select group of students invited to return for additional year of study and performance after graduation in repertory situation. **Special study options:** Cross-registration, exchange student. Students may study 1 year in each of 2 campuses (NY and CA). **Credit/placement by examination:** AP, CLEP. **Support services:** Pre-admission summer program, tutoring, writing center.

**Majors. Visual/performing arts:** Acting.

**Computing on campus.** 10 workstations in computer center.

**Student life. Freshman orientation:** Mandatory. **Activities:** Student government.

**Student services.** Alcohol/substance abuse counseling, career counseling, financial aid counseling, personal counseling, veterans' counselor.

**Contact.** Phone: (323) 464-2777 ext. 109 Toll-free number: (800) 222-2867 Fax: (323) 464-1250 Karen Higginbotham, Director of Admissions, American Academy of Dramatic Arts: West, 1336 N. La Brea Avenue, Los Angeles, CA 90028

## American River College
Sacramento, California
www.arc.losrios.edu                       CB code: 4004

▶ Public 2-year community college
▶ Commuter campus in large city

**General.** Founded in 1955. Regionally accredited. **Enrollment:** 20,828 degree-seeking undergraduates. **Degrees:** 1,736 associate awarded. **Location:** 10 miles from downtown. **Calendar:** Semester, limited summer session. **Full-time faculty:** 380 total. **Part-time faculty:** 605 total.

**Basis for selection.** Open admission, but selective for some programs. Limited admission to nursing program. **Homeschooled:** Transcript of courses and grades, interview, letter of recommendation (nonparent) required.

**2007-2008 Annual costs.** Tuition/fees: $632; $5,822 out-of-state. Per-credit charge: $20 in-state; $193 out-of-state. Books/supplies: $1,386. Personal expenses: $2,126.

**Financial aid.** All financial aid based on need. Need-based aid available for part-time students.

**Application procedures. Admission:** No deadline. No application fee in-state; $173 out-of-state. Application must be submitted online. Admission notification on a rolling basis beginning on or about 7/1. **Financial aid:** Priority date 3/2; no closing date. FAFSA required. Applicants notified on a rolling basis starting 7/1; must reply within 2 week(s) of notification.

**Academics. Special study options:** Accelerated study, cooperative education, cross-registration, distance learning, ESL, honors, independent study, liberal arts/career combination, study abroad, weekend college. **Credit/placement by examination:** AP, CLEP, IB. 15 credit hours maximum toward associate degree. **Support services:** Learning center, pre-admission summer program, reduced course load, remedial instruction, study skills assistance, tutoring, writing center.

**Majors. Architecture:** Landscape. **Business:** Accounting, administrative services, fashion, hospitality/recreation, management information systems, office/clerical, real estate. **Communications:** Journalism. **Communications technology:** Graphic/printing. **Computer sciences:** General, database management, networking, programming. **Conservation:** General. **Education:** Teacher assistance. **Engineering technology:** General, biomedical, drafting, electrical, GIS. **Family/consumer sciences:** General, child care, institutional food production. **Health:** Health services, nursing (RN), respiratory therapy technology. **Interdisciplinary:** Biological/physical sciences, gerontology. **Legal studies:** Paralegal. **Liberal arts:** Arts/sciences. **Mechanic/repair:** Automotive. **Parks/recreation:** General. **Personal/culinary services:** Culinary arts, mortuary science, restaurant/catering. **Protective services:** Fire safety technology, police science. **Visual/performing arts:** Dramatic, interior design.

**Computing on campus.** Online course registration, helpline available.

**Student life. Freshman orientation:** Available. **Activities:** Bands, choral groups, dance, drama, literary magazine, music ensembles, musical theater, student government, student newspaper, symphony orchestra.

**Athletics. Intercollegiate:** Baseball M, basketball, cross-country, football (tackle) M, golf, soccer, softball W, swimming, tennis, track and field, volleyball W, water polo M. **Team name:** Beavers.

**Student services.** Adult student services, career counseling, services for economically disadvantaged, student employment services, financial aid counseling, health services, minority student services, on-campus daycare, personal counseling, placement for graduates, veterans' counselor. **Physically disabled:** Services for visually, speech, hearing impaired. **Learning disabled:** Comprehensive services available.

**Contact.** Phone: (916) 484-8261 Fax: (916) 484-8864
Robin Neal, Dean of Enrollment Services, American River College, 4700 College Oak Drive, Sacramento, CA 95841

---

## Antelope Valley College
**Lancaster, California**
www.avc.edu                         CB code: 4005

▸ Public 2-year community college
▸ Commuter campus in large city

**General.** Founded in 1929. Regionally accredited. Shares campus with Cal State Bakersfield. **Enrollment:** 9,300 degree-seeking undergraduates. **Degrees:** 923 associate awarded. **ROTC:** Air Force. **Location:** 50 miles from Los Angeles. **Calendar:** Semester, limited summer session. **Full-time faculty:** 180 total. **Part-time faculty:** 495 total. **Class size:** 27% < 20, 63% 20-39, 6% 40-49, 3% 50-99, less than 1% >100. **Partnerships:** Formal partnerships with local high schools to provide paraprofessional teacher training; Department of Labor grant provides aerospace worker training for Lockheed Martin and Boeing.

**Transfer out.** Colleges most students transferred to 2007: California State University: Northridge, California State University: Bakersfield, University of California: Los Angeles.

**Basis for selection.** Open admission, but selective for some programs. High school graduate, GED or 18 years of age.

**2007-2008 Annual costs.** Tuition/fees: $602; $5,792 out-of-state. Per-credit charge: $20 in-state; $193 out-of-state. Books/supplies: $1,386. Personal expenses: $2,898.

**Financial aid. Need-based:** Need-based aid available for part-time students. Work-study available for part-time students.

**Application procedures. Admission:** No deadline. No application fee in-state; $175 out-of-state. Application may be submitted online. Admission notification on a rolling basis. **Financial aid:** Priority date 3/2; no closing date. FAFSA, institutional form required. Applicants notified on a rolling basis starting 7/15; must reply within 2 week(s) of notification.

**Academics. Special study options:** Accelerated study, cooperative education, distance learning, double major, dual enrollment of high school students, ESL, honors, independent study, internships, study abroad, teacher certification program, weekend college. Bachelor's degree programs available on campus. License preparation in aviation, nursing, real estate. **Credit/placement by examination:** AP, CLEP, institutional tests. Maximum of 4 courses allowed. **Support services:** GED preparation, learning center, reduced course load, remedial instruction, study skills assistance, tutoring, writing center.

**Majors. Agriculture:** Landscaping, ornamental horticulture. **Biology:** General. **Business:** General, administrative services, business admin, real estate. **Communications technology:** Graphic/printing. **Computer sciences:** General, computer graphics, computer science, data processing, information systems, programming. **Education:** Teacher assistance. **Engineering:** General. **Engineering technology:** Aerospace, construction, drafting. **Family/consumer sciences:** General, child care, child development, clothing/textiles, communication, family resources, food/nutrition, home furnishings. **Foreign languages:** American Sign Language. **Health:** Medical assistant, medical secretary, nursing (RN), office assistant. **Liberal arts:** Arts/sciences. **Math:** General. **Mechanic/repair:** Aircraft, auto body, automotive, electronics/electrical. **Parks/recreation:** Health/fitness. **Production:** Welding. **Protective services:** Fire safety technology. **Visual/performing arts:** General, cinematography, interior design, multimedia, photography.

**Computing on campus.** 300 workstations in library, computer center, student center. Online course registration, online library available.

**Student life. Freshman orientation:** Available. Preregistration for classes offered. Online orientation available. **Activities:** Bands, choral groups, dance, drama, music ensembles, musical theater, student government, student newspaper, symphony orchestra.

**Athletics. NCAA. Intercollegiate:** Baseball M, basketball, cheerleading, cross-country, football (tackle) M, golf, soccer W, softball W, track and field, volleyball W. **Intramural:** Basketball, tennis, volleyball W. **Team name:** Marauders.

**Student services.** Adult student services, career counseling, services for economically disadvantaged, student employment services, financial aid counseling, health services, minority student services, on-campus daycare, personal counseling, veterans' counselor. **Physically disabled:** Services for visually, speech, hearing impaired. **Learning disabled:** Comprehensive services available. **Transfer:** Re-entry adviser for new students. Transfer center, transfer adviser, college fairs on campus for students transferring to 4-year colleges.

**Contact.** Phone: (661) 722-6332 Fax: (661) 722-6531
LaDonna Trimble, Dean of Enrollment Services, Antelope Valley College, 3041 West Avenue K, Lancaster, CA 93536-5426

---

## Art Institute of California: Los Angeles
**Santa Monica, California**
www.artinstitutes.edu/losangeles          CB code: 2490

▸ For-profit 2-year visual arts college
▸ Commuter campus in small city
▸ Application essay, interview required

**General.** Accredited by ACICS. **Enrollment:** 2,149 degree-seeking undergraduates; 2 non-degree-seeking students. **Degrees:** 282 bachelor's, 99 associate awarded. **Calendar:** Continuous. **Full-time faculty:** 64 total. **Part-time faculty:** 63 total. **Class size:** 57% < 20, 43% 20-39.

**Student profile.** Among degree-seeking undergraduates, 561 enrolled as first-time, first-year students.

| | | | |
|---|---|---|---|
| Part-time: | 35% | Live on campus: | 20% |
| Women: | 36% | | |

**Basis for selection.** High school record and general appropriateness of educational background to specific program applied for most important. Portfolio, interview, standardized test scores also important. SAT or ACT recommended.

**2007-2008 Annual costs.** Tuition/fees: $22,322. Per-credit charge: $464. Apartment-style housing offered costing $2663/quarter for 2-bedroom, $3227/quarter for 1-bedroom housing. Books/supplies: $1,733. Personal expenses: $1,500.

**2007-2008 Financial aid. Need-based:** Need-based aid available for part-time students. Work-study available nights, weekends and for part-time students. **Non-need-based:** Scholarships awarded for academics.

**Application procedures. Admission:** No deadline. $50 fee. Application may be submitted online. Admission notification on a rolling basis. **Financial aid:** No deadline. FAFSA required. Applicants notified on a rolling basis.

**Academics. Special study options:** Independent study, internships, study abroad. Bachelor's degree programs available on campus. **Credit/placement by examination:** AP, CLEP, SAT, ACT, institutional tests. **Support services:** Reduced course load, tutoring, writing center.

**Majors. Computer sciences:** Computer graphics, web page design. **Personal/culinary services:** Chef training, culinary arts, food prep. **Visual/performing arts:** Cinematography, commercial/advertising art, design, graphic design.

**Computing on campus.** 250 workstations in library, computer center. Student web hosting available.

**Student life. Freshman orientation:** Mandatory. Preregistration for classes offered. One day program before start of quarter. **Housing:** Guaranteed on-campus for all undergraduates. Apartments available. $250 deposit. **Activities:** Literary magazine, gay, lesbian, straight alliance.

**Athletics. Intramural:** Basketball, softball, volleyball.

**Student services.** Alcohol/substance abuse counseling, career counseling, student employment services, financial aid counseling, personal counseling, placement for graduates.

**Contact.** E-mail: ailaadm@aii.edu
Phone: (310) 752-4700 Toll-free number: (888) 646-4610
Fax: (310) 752-4708
Paul Sallenbach, Director of Admissions, Art Institute of California: Los Angeles, 2900 31st Street, Santa Monica, CA 90405-3035

---

## Bakersfield College
**Bakersfield, California**
**www.bakersfieldcollege.edu**
**CB code: 4015**

- Public 2-year community college
- Commuter campus in small city

**General.** Founded in 1913. Regionally accredited. **Enrollment:** 10,843 degree-seeking undergraduates. **Degrees:** 994 associate awarded. **Location:** 114 miles from Los Angeles. **Calendar:** Semester, limited summer session. **Full-time faculty:** 255 total. **Part-time faculty:** 250 total. **Special facilities:** Planetarium.

**Basis for selection.** Open admission, but selective for some programs. Nursing and other allied health programs have additional admission requirements including required coursework.

**2007-2008 Annual costs.** Tuition/fees: $638; $6,338 out-of-state. Per-credit charge: $20 in-state; $210 out-of-state. Books/supplies: $1,314. Personal expenses: $1,656.

**Application procedures. Admission:** No deadline. No application fee. **Financial aid:** Priority date 3/2; no closing date. FAFSA required. Applicants notified on a rolling basis starting 6/1; must reply within 2 week(s) of notification.

**Academics. Special study options:** Double major, dual enrollment of high school students. **Credit/placement by examination:** CLEP, institutional tests. 12 credit hours maximum toward associate degree. **Support**

---

**services:** Learning center, pre-admission summer program, reduced course load, remedial instruction, tutoring.

**Majors. Agriculture:** Agribusiness operations, animal sciences, horticulture, ornamental horticulture. **Biology:** General, bacteriology. **Business:** Accounting, administrative services, business admin, management information systems, office technology, office/clerical, real estate. **Communications:** Broadcast journalism, journalism. **Communications technology:** General, graphic/printing. **Computer sciences:** Applications programming, data processing. **Conservation:** Forestry. **Construction:** Carpentry, masonry, pipefitting, power transmission. **Engineering technology:** Aerospace, drafting. **English:** English lit. **Family/consumer sciences:** General, food/nutrition, institutional food production. **Foreign languages:** German, Spanish. **Health:** Dental assistant, EMT paramedic, licensed practical nurse, medical radiologic technology/radiation therapy, nursing (RN), predental, premedicine, prepharmacy, preveterinary. **History:** General. **Legal studies:** Prelaw. **Liberal arts:** Arts/sciences. **Math:** General. **Mechanic/repair:** Automotive. **Parks/recreation:** General. **Personal/culinary services:** Culinary arts. **Philosophy/religion:** Philosophy. **Physical sciences:** Chemistry, geology, physics. **Production:** Woodworking. **Protective services:** Fire safety technology, police science. **Psychology:** General. **Social sciences:** Anthropology, criminology, economics, geography, political science, sociology. **Visual/performing arts:** Interior design, photography.

**Student life. Activities:** Bands, choral groups, dance, drama, literary magazine, music ensembles, radio station, student government, student newspaper.

**Athletics. Intercollegiate:** Baseball M, basketball, cross-country, diving, football (tackle) M, golf M, softball W, swimming, tennis, track and field, volleyball W, wrestling M. **Team name:** Renegades.

**Student services.** Career counseling, student employment services, health services, on-campus daycare. **Physically disabled:** Services for visually, speech, hearing impaired.

**Contact.** Phone: (661) 395-4301
Sue Vaughn, Director of Enrollment Services, Bakersfield College, 1801 Panorama Drive, Bakersfield, CA 93305

---

## Barstow Community College
**Barstow, California**
**www.barstow.edu**
**CB code: 4020**

- Public 2-year community college
- Commuter campus in large town

**General.** Founded in 1959. Regionally accredited. **Enrollment:** 1,797 degree-seeking undergraduates. **Degrees:** 287 associate awarded. **Location:** 70 miles from San Bernardino. **Calendar:** Semester, limited summer session. **Full-time faculty:** 35 total. **Part-time faculty:** 70 total.

**Basis for selection.** Open admission.

**2007-2008 Annual costs.** Tuition/fees: $600; $5,790 out-of-state. Per-credit charge: $20 in-state; $193 out-of-state. Books/supplies: $1,422. Personal expenses: $2,394.

**2007-2008 Financial aid.** All financial aid based on need. Need-based aid available for part-time students.

**Application procedures. Admission:** Priority date 8/22; no deadline. No application fee. Admission notification on a rolling basis. **Financial aid:** Closing date 5/22. FAFSA required. Applicants notified on a rolling basis starting 7/1.

**Academics. Special study options:** Accelerated study, cooperative education, distance learning, double major, dual enrollment of high school students, ESL, independent study, liberal arts/career combination. **Credit/placement by examination:** AP, CLEP, institutional tests. 30 credit hours maximum toward associate degree. **Support services:** Learning center, reduced course load, remedial instruction, study skills assistance, tutoring.

**Majors. Biology:** General. **Business:** General, accounting, administrative services, business admin, management information systems, managerial economics, office management, office technology, office/clerical, real estate. **Communications:** General. **Computer sciences:** General, applications programming, programming. **Education:** General, elementary, teacher assistance. **English:** English lit. **Family/consumer sciences:** Child care. **Liberal arts:** Arts/sciences. **Math:** General. **Production:** Welding. **Protective services:** Fire safety technology, police science. **Psychology:** General. **Social sciences:** General. **Visual/performing arts:** Dramatic, studio arts.

**Computing on campus.** 40 workstations in library, computer center.

**Student life. Activities:** Bands, choral groups, dance, drama, music ensembles, musical theater, student government, Christian club, Alpha Gamma Sigma, Phi Theta Kappa.

**Athletics.** NJCAA. **Intercollegiate:** Baseball M, basketball M, cross-country, golf, soccer, tennis, volleyball W. **Intramural:** Badminton, baseball M, basketball, bowling, soccer, softball, swimming, tennis, volleyball. **Team name:** Vikings.

**Student services.** Adult student services, career counseling, student employment services, personal counseling, placement for graduates, veterans' counselor. **Physically disabled:** Services for visually, speech, hearing impaired. **Transfer:** Transfer center, transfer adviser, college fairs on campus for students transferring to 4-year colleges.

**Contact.** E-mail: admit@barstow.edu
Phone: (760) 252-2411 Fax: (760) 252-1875
Heather Porter, Admissions, Records and Financial Aid Manager, Barstow Community College, 2700 Barstow Road, Barstow, CA 92311-9984

## Berkeley City College
**Berkeley, California**
**www.berkeleycitycollege.edu**     CB code: 7711

- Public 2-year community college
- Commuter campus in small city

**General.** Founded in 1974. Regionally accredited. Noncampus college in 125 locations located in 6 cities adjacent to Berkeley. Access to other Peralta community college district libraries, as well as Berkeley Public Library and University of California at Berkeley libraries. **Enrollment:** 5,420 undergraduates. **Degrees:** 120 associate awarded. **Location:** 15 miles from San Francisco. **Calendar:** Semester, limited summer session. **Full-time faculty:** 49 total. **Part-time faculty:** 137 total.

**Student profile.**

| | | | |
|---|---|---|---|
| Out-of-state: | 1% | 25 or older: | 55% |

**Basis for selection.** Open admission.

**2007-2008 Annual costs.** Tuition/fees: $600; $5,790 out-of-state. Per-credit charge: $20 in-state; $193 out-of-state. Books/supplies: $1,422. Personal expenses: $2,502.

**Financial aid.** All financial aid based on need. Need-based aid available for part-time students. Work-study available for part-time students.

**Application procedures. Admission:** No deadline. No application fee. Application may be submitted online. Admission notification on a rolling basis. **Financial aid:** No deadline. Applicants notified on a rolling basis.

**Academics. Special study options:** Accelerated study, cooperative education, cross-registration, distance learning, dual enrollment of high school students, ESL, independent study, liberal arts/career combination, study abroad, weekend college. **Credit/placement by examination:** CLEP, institutional tests. 6 credit hours maximum toward associate degree. **Support services:** Learning center, reduced course load, remedial instruction, study skills assistance, tutoring, writing center.

**Majors. Biology:** Biotechnology. **Business:** Business admin, office/clerical, small business admin. **Computer sciences:** General. **English:** English lit. **Foreign languages:** Sign language interpretation. **Visual/performing arts:** Art.

**Computing on campus.** Commuter students can connect to campus network. Online course registration, online library, wireless network available.

**Student life. Freshman orientation:** Mandatory. Preregistration for classes offered. Assessments and orientations scheduled several times before the beginning of the semester. **Activities:** Literary magazine, student government, Phi Theta Kappa, Spanish Club, X Club, Bahai Club.

**Student services.** Adult student services, career counseling, services for economically disadvantaged, student employment services, financial aid counseling, veterans' counselor. **Physically disabled:** Services for visually, speech, hearing impaired. **Learning disabled:** Comprehensive services available. **Transfer:** Transfer center, transfer adviser, college fairs on campus for students transferring to 4-year colleges.

**Contact.** Phone: (510) 981-2805 Fax: (510) 841-7333
Loretta Newsom, Admissions and Records Specialist, Berkeley City College, 2050 Center Street, Berkeley, CA 94704

## Brooks College
**Long Beach, California**
**www.brookscollege.edu**     CB code: 1263

- For-profit 2-year technical college
- Residential campus in very large city
- Interview required

**General.** Founded in 1971. Regionally accredited. Campuses in Long Beach, Sunnyvale. **Enrollment:** 266 degree-seeking undergraduates. **Degrees:** 231 associate awarded. **Location:** 15 miles from Los Angeles. **Calendar:** Quarter, extensive summer session. **Full-time faculty:** 4 total. **Part-time faculty:** 29 total. **Special facilities:** Antique clothing collection.

**Basis for selection.** Open admission. **Homeschooled:** Transcript of courses and grades, state high school equivalency certificate, interview required.

**2007-2008 Annual costs.** Tuition $15,000 for animation, graphic design, multimedia, fashion design, fashion merchandising, and interior design programs. Books/supplies: $1,500. Personal expenses: $1,100.

**Financial aid. Non-need-based:** Scholarships awarded for academics.

**Application procedures. Admission:** No deadline. $50 fee, may be waived for applicants with need. Admission notification on a rolling basis. **Financial aid:** No deadline. FAFSA required. Applicants notified on a rolling basis starting 5/1; must reply within 2 week(s) of notification.

**Academics.** Curriculum is designed to prepare students for profession in fashion merchandising, fashion design, interior design, multimedia, and graphic design. **Special study options:** Cooperative education, ESL, internships. **Credit/placement by examination:** CLEP, IB. **Support services:** Learning center, remedial instruction, tutoring.

**Majors. Business:** Fashion. **Visual/performing arts:** Commercial/advertising art, fashion design, interior design.

**Computing on campus.** 30 workstations in library, computer center. Dormitories linked to campus network.

**Student life. Freshman orientation:** Mandatory. Held within 3 days of beginning of classes. **Housing:** Single-sex dorms available. **Activities:** Drama, student government, student newspaper, international club.

**Athletics. Intramural:** Softball, volleyball.

**Student services.** Adult student services, alcohol/substance abuse counseling, career counseling, services for economically disadvantaged, student employment services, financial aid counseling, placement for graduates, veterans' counselor.

**Contact.** Phone: (562) 498-2441 Fax: (562) 597-7412
Christine Varon, Dean of Admissions, Brooks College, 4825 East Pacific Coast Highway, Long Beach, CA 90804

## Brooks College: Sunnyvale
**Sunnyvale, California**
**www.brooks-sv.com**

- For-profit 2-year technical college
- Residential campus in very large city

**General.** Regionally accredited. **Location:** 45 miles south of San Francisco. **Calendar:** Quarter.

**Annual costs/financial aid.** Tuition $15,000 for animation, graphic design, multimedia, fashion design, fashion merchandising, and interior design programs.

**Contact.** Phone: (408) 328-5700
Director of Admissions, 1120 Kifer Road, Sunnyvale, CA 94086

## Bryan College: Los Angeles
**Los Angeles, California**
**www.bryancollege.edu**

- For-profit 2-year virtual technical college
- Very large city

**General.** Regionally accredited; also accredited by ACICS. **Enrollment:** 385 degree-seeking undergraduates. **Calendar:** Quarter. **Full-time faculty:** 21 total. **Part-time faculty:** 5 total.

**Student profile.** Of all enrolled students, 5% already have a bachelor's degree or higher.

**Basis for selection.** Open admission, but selective for some programs.

**2007-2008 Annual costs.** Tuition/fees: $3,400.

**Application procedures. Admission:** $100 fee, may be waived for applicants with need.

**Academics. Credit/placement by examination:** CLEP. **Support services:** Learning center, remedial instruction, study skills assistance, tutoring.

**Contact.** Phone: (877) 484-8850 Fax: (213) 483-3936
Bryan College: Los Angeles, 3580 Wilshire Boulevard, Suite 400, Los Angeles, CA 90010

## Bryan College: Sacramento
### Gold River, California
### www.bryancollege.com

♦ For-profit 2-year technical college
♦ Very large city
♦ Interview required

**General.** Accredited by ACCSCT. **Enrollment:** 235 degree-seeking undergraduates. **Degrees:** 32 associate awarded. **Location:** 10 miles from downtown Sacramento. **Calendar:** Continuous, limited summer session. **Full-time faculty:** 25 total. **Part-time faculty:** 10 total.

**Basis for selection.** Interview, interest important.

**2007-2008 Annual costs.** Tuition/fees: $17,507. AOS Massage: $18,613, AOS Massage/Fitness: $21,971, AOS Exercise Science: $21,335, AAS Court Reporting: $51,057. Price does not include books, supplies, testing.

**Application procedures. Admission:** No deadline. $35 fee.

**Academics. Special study options:** Massage therapy students get hands-on experience in public massage clinic. Personal training students work with fitness professionals to gain field experience. **Credit/placement by examination:** CLEP.

**Majors. Biology:** Exercise physiology. **Health:** Massage therapy. **Legal studies:** Court reporting.

**Contact.** E-mail: admissions@bryancollege.com
Phone: (916) 649-2400 Toll-free number: (866) 649-2400
Fax: (916) 641-8649
Eric Lopez, Director of Admissions, Bryan College: Sacramento, 2317 Gold Meadow Way, Gold River, CA 95670

## Butte College
### Oroville, California
### www.butte.edu
**CB code: 4226**

♦ Public 2-year community college
♦ Commuter campus in small city

**General.** Founded in 1966. Regionally accredited. **Enrollment:** 7,385 degree-seeking undergraduates. **Degrees:** 925 associate awarded. **Location:** 100 miles from Sacramento. **Calendar:** Semester, extensive summer session. **Full-time faculty:** 130 total. **Part-time faculty:** 470 total. **Special facilities:** 900-acre wild game refuge, nature trails.

**Basis for selection.** Open admission, but selective for some programs. Nursing, allied health programs have special requirements. Interviews required for allied health applicants.

**2007-2008 Annual costs.** Tuition/fees: $776; $6,326 out-of-state. Per-credit charge: $20 in-state; $205 out-of-state. Books/supplies: $1,324. Personal expenses: $1,954.

**Application procedures. Admission:** No deadline. No application fee. Admission notification on a rolling basis. **Financial aid:** Priority date 5/1; no closing date. FAFSA required. Applicants notified on a rolling basis starting 8/1.

**Academics. Special study options:** Cooperative education, cross-registration, distance learning, double major, dual enrollment of high school students, ESL, honors, independent study, study abroad. License preparation in nursing, paramedic, real estate. **Credit/placement by examination:** CLEP, institutional tests. 9 credit hours maximum toward associate degree. **Support services:** Learning center, remedial instruction, study skills assistance, tutoring.

**Majors. Agriculture:** Agronomy, animal sciences, business, horticulture, ornamental horticulture. **Business:** General, accounting, administrative services, business admin, fashion, management information systems, marketing, office technology, real estate, tourism promotion. **Communications:** Broadcast journalism, journalism. **Communications technology:** General, graphic/printing. **Computer sciences:** General, applications programming, networking. **Construction:** Maintenance. **Education:** General, bilingual, early childhood, physical. **Engineering technology:** Civil, construction, drafting, electrical. **English:** English lit. **Family/consumer sciences:** General, child care. **Health:** Cardiovascular technology, EMT paramedic, licensed practical nurse, medical assistant, medical secretary, nursing (RN), respiratory therapy technology, substance abuse counseling. **Legal studies:** Court reporting, legal secretary, paralegal, prelaw. **Liberal arts:** Arts/sciences. **Math:** General. **Mechanic/repair:** Automotive. **Parks/recreation:** Facilities management. **Personal/culinary services:** Cosmetic. **Production:** Welding. **Protective services:** Fire safety technology, police science. **Social sciences:** General. **Visual/performing arts:** Ceramics, commercial photography, commercial/advertising art, fashion design, photography, studio arts.

**Computing on campus.** 200 workstations in library, computer center. Wireless network available.

**Student life. Activities:** Bands, drama, film society, music ensembles, radio station, student government, student newspaper, symphony orchestra, TV station.

**Athletics.** NJCAA. **Intercollegiate:** Baseball M, basketball, cross-country, field hockey W, football (tackle) M, golf, soccer, softball W, tennis, track and field, volleyball W. **Team name:** Roadrunners.

**Student services.** Adult student services, career counseling, student employment services, health services, on-campus daycare, personal counseling, placement for graduates, veterans' counselor. **Physically disabled:** Services for visually, speech, hearing impaired. **Transfer:** Re-entry adviser for new students. Transfer center, transfer adviser for students transferring to 4-year colleges.

**Contact.** E-mail: admissions@butte.edu
Phone: (530) 895-2361 Fax: (530) 895-2411
Clinton Slaughter, Director of Admissions and Records, Butte College, 3536 Butte Campus Drive, Oroville, CA 95965

## Cabrillo College
### Aptos, California
### www.cabrillo.edu
**CB code: 4084**

♦ Public 2-year community college
♦ Commuter campus in large town

**General.** Founded in 1959. Regionally accredited. **Enrollment:** 7,010 degree-seeking undergraduates. **Degrees:** 755 associate awarded. **Location:** 25 miles from San Jose. **Calendar:** Semester, extensive summer session. **Full-time faculty:** 219 total. **Part-time faculty:** 372 total. **Special facilities:** Observatory, planetarium, horticulture garden.

**Student profile.**

| | | | |
|---|---|---|---|
| Out-of-state: | 2% | 25 or older: | 50% |

**Transfer out. Colleges most students transferred to 2007:** University of California-Santa Cruz, San Jose State University, California State University-Monterey Bay.

**Basis for selection.** Open admission, but selective for some programs. Special prerequisite requirements for nursing, dental hygiene, and radiologic technology. International applicants have special admission requirements.

**2007-2008 Annual costs.** Tuition/fees: $638; $5,858 out-of-state. Per-credit charge: $20 in-state; $194 out-of-state. Books/supplies: $1,242. Personal expenses: $2,700.

**Financial aid. Need-based:** Need-based aid available for part-time students.

**Application procedures. Admission:** No deadline. No application fee. Application may be submitted online. Admission notification on a rolling

basis beginning on or about 6/1. **Financial aid:** No deadline. FAFSA, institutional form required. Applicants notified on a rolling basis starting 7/31; must reply within 3 week(s) of notification.

**Academics. Special study options:** Dual enrollment of high school students, honors, independent study, internships, liberal arts/career combination, study abroad. License preparation in dental hygiene, nursing, radiology. **Credit/placement by examination:** AP, CLEP, institutional tests. **Support services:** Learning center, pre-admission summer program, reduced course load, remedial instruction, tutoring.

**Majors. Agriculture:** Ornamental horticulture. **Area/ethnic studies:** Asian. **Biology:** General. **Business:** General, accounting, banking/financial services, business admin, construction management, entrepreneurial studies, office technology, real estate. **Communications:** Journalism. **Computer sciences:** General, data processing. **Engineering technology:** Hazardous materials, solar energy. **English:** English lit, speech/rhetoric. **Family/consumer sciences:** General, child care. **Foreign languages:** General, Chinese, French, German, Italian, Japanese, Spanish. **Health:** Dental hygiene, licensed practical nurse, medical assistant, medical radiologic technology/radiation therapy, nursing (RN). **History:** General. **Liberal arts:** Arts/sciences, library science. **Math:** General. **Mechanic/repair:** Industrial. **Physical sciences:** Chemistry, physics. **Protective services:** Firefighting, police science. **Psychology:** General. **Social sciences:** General, anthropology, economics, geography, political science, sociology. **Visual/performing arts:** General, art, dance, studio arts.

**Computing on campus.** 350 workstations in library, computer center.

**Student life. Freshman orientation:** Available. Preregistration for classes offered. **Activities:** Bands, choral groups, dance, drama, music ensembles, musical theater, student government, student newspaper, various clubs, literacy, recreational, cultural and/or ethnic organizations.

**Athletics. Intercollegiate:** Baseball M, basketball, cross-country, diving, football (tackle) M, golf M, soccer M, softball W, swimming, tennis, track and field, volleyball W, water polo M. **Team name:** Seahawks.

**Student services.** Adult student services, career counseling, student employment services, health services, personal counseling, placement for graduates, veterans' counselor. **Physically disabled:** Services for visually, speech, hearing impaired. **Transfer:** Transfer center, transfer adviser for students transferring to 4-year colleges.

**Contact.** Phone: (831) 479-6201 Fax: (831) 479-5782
Esperanza Nee, Interim Director, Cabrillo College, 6500 Soquel Drive, Aptos, CA 95003

## California Culinary Academy
### San Francisco, California
### www.caculinary.edu
**CB code: 2209**

- For-profit 2-year culinary school and career college
- Commuter campus in very large city
- Interview required

**General.** Founded in 1977. Accredited by ACCSCT. All programs offered sanctioned by Le Cordon Bleu. **Enrollment:** 150 degree-seeking undergraduates. **Degrees:** 964 associate awarded. **Location:** Downtown. **Calendar:** Continuous. **Full-time faculty:** 53 total. **Part-time faculty:** 4 total. **Special facilities:** Student-staffed public restaurant, mixology lab, gaming room, professional production kitchens, demonstration kitchens, pastry kitchens, confisseries, butchary lab, culinary library.

**Basis for selection.** The school has an open enrollment policy but the student needs to complete an interview with an admissions representative, pass a short entrance exam, have a High School diploma or equivalent before starting school. Wonderlic testing required for all programs.

**2008-2009 Annual costs.** Tuition/fees: $28,000. Room only: $600.

**Application procedures. Admission:** No deadline. $65 fee. Application may be submitted online. Admission notification on a rolling basis. **Financial aid:** No deadline. FAFSA required. Applicants notified on a rolling basis; must reply within 1 week(s) of notification.

**Academics. Special study options:** Internships. **Credit/placement by examination:** CLEP. **Support services:** Study skills assistance, tutoring.

**Majors. Personal/culinary services:** Culinary arts, restaurant/catering.

**Computing on campus.** Student web hosting, wireless network available.

**Student life. Freshman orientation:** Mandatory. **Housing:** Coed dorms available. $600 fully refundable deposit. **Activities:** Brewing arts association, Cuisine Des Femmes, Asian food club, baking and pastry arts club, dinner club, wine club.

**Student services.** Career counseling, student employment services, financial aid counseling, placement for graduates. **Transfer:** Re-entry adviser, pre-admission transcript evaluation for new students.

**Contact.** E-mail: admissions@caculinary.edu
Phone: (415) 771-3500 Toll-free number: (800) 229-2433
Fax: (415) 621-5625
Sanjay Ketty, Director of Admissions, California Culinary Academy, 350 Rhode Island, San Francisco, CA 94103

## California School of Culinary Arts
### Pasadena, California
### www.csca.edu

- For-profit 2-year culinary school
- Commuter campus in very large city
- Interview required

**General.** Accredited by ACICS. Le Cordon Bleu college. **Enrollment:** 1,586 degree-seeking undergraduates. **Degrees:** 745 associate awarded. **Location:** 15 miles from downtown Los Angeles. **Calendar:** Continuous, extensive summer session. **Full-time faculty:** 80 total; 1% have terminal degrees, 30% minority, 38% women. **Part-time faculty:** 11 total; 36% minority, 54% women. **Special facilities:** Fine-dining restaurant and casual cafe where students gain practical work experience.

**Basis for selection.** Open admission. High school diploma/GED, entrance examination required. Students whose first language is not English are required to submit evidence of English Proficiency. This may be done by submitting a TOEFL test score of 500 or higher (for the CPT version, a score of 150 or higher). Entrance Test is required by state agency (BPPVE) for diploma programs. CSCA utilizes the Wonderlic SLE Exam to comply with these regulations. **Learning Disabled:** Students requesting special needs and services required to submit Application for Auxiliary Aid request. Application must include supporting documentation as evidence of disability.

**2007-2008 Annual costs.** Diploma programs vary in cost. Associate of occupational studies in culinary arts program tuition: $43,950, fees $3,000. Associate of occupational students in hospitality/restaurant management tuition: $31,000, fees $4,015. Books/supplies: $1,500. Personal expenses: $1,347.

**Financial aid. Need-based:** Need-based aid available for part-time students. Work-study available nights and weekends.

**Application procedures. Admission:** No deadline. $100 fee. Application may be submitted online. Admission notification on a rolling basis. **Financial aid:** No deadline. FAFSA required. Applicants notified on a rolling basis.

**Academics. Special study options:** Honors. **Credit/placement by examination:** AP, CLEP. **Support services:** Learning center, study skills assistance, tutoring.

**Majors. Personal/culinary services:** Chef training, restaurant/catering.

**Computing on campus.** 40 workstations in library, computer center, student center. Commuter students can connect to campus network. Online library available.

**Student life. Freshman orientation:** Mandatory. Preregistration for classes offered. **Activities:** Student newspaper.

**Student services.** Adult student services, career counseling, financial aid counseling, placement for graduates. **Transfer:** Re-entry adviser, pre-admission transcript evaluation for new students.

**Contact.** E-mail: Admissionsinfo@csca.edu
Phone: (626) 229-1300 Toll-free number: (888) 900-2433
Fax: (626) 403-4835
Martin Yousef, Vice President of Admissions, California School of Culinary Arts, 530 East Colorado Boulevard, Pasadena, CA 91101

## Canada College
### Redwood City, California
### www.canadacollege.edu
**CB code: 4109**

- Public 2-year community college
- Commuter campus in small city

**General.** Founded in 1968. Regionally accredited. **Enrollment:** 2,794 degree-seeking undergraduates. **Degrees:** 159 associate awarded. **Location:** 20 miles from San Francisco. **Calendar:** Semester, limited summer session. **Full-time faculty:** 65 total. **Part-time faculty:** 182 total.

**Transfer out. Colleges most students transferred to 2007:** San Francisco State, San Jose State, College of Notre de Namur, California State University-East Bay.

**Basis for selection.** Open admission, but selective for some programs. Special admission to radiologic technology programs.

**2007-2008 Annual costs.** Tuition/fees: $648; $6,168 out-of-state. Per-credit charge: $20 in-state; $204 out-of-state. Books/supplies: $1,260. Personal expenses: $2,376.

**Application procedures. Admission:** No deadline. No application fee. Admission notification on a rolling basis. **Financial aid:** Priority date 5/1; no closing date. FAFSA required. Applicants notified on a rolling basis starting 7/15; must reply within 2 week(s) of notification.

**Academics. Special study options:** Cooperative education, cross-registration, distance learning, double major, dual enrollment of high school students, ESL, independent study, internships, study abroad. Bachelor's degree programs available on campus. **Credit/placement by examination:** AP, CLEP, IB, institutional tests. 12 credit hours maximum toward associate degree. **Support services:** Learning center, reduced course load, remedial instruction, study skills assistance, tutoring, writing center.

**Majors. Biology:** General. **Business:** General, accounting, administrative services, banking/financial services, business admin, fashion, management information systems, management science, office technology, office/clerical, tourism/travel. **Communications:** Journalism. **Computer sciences:** General, applications programming, programming. **Education:** Early childhood. **Engineering technology:** Computer hardware. **English:** English lit. **Family/consumer sciences:** General, child care. **Foreign languages:** French, Spanish. **Health:** Medical radiologic technology/radiation therapy, ophthalmic lab technology. **History:** General. **Legal studies:** Paralegal. **Liberal arts:** Arts/sciences. **Math:** General. **Philosophy/religion:** Philosophy. **Physical sciences:** Chemistry, physics. **Psychology:** General. **Public administration:** Human services. **Social sciences:** General, anthropology, geography, political science. **Visual/performing arts:** Art, dramatic, interior design, multimedia.

**Computing on campus.** 300 workstations in library, computer center. Online course registration, wireless network available.

**Student life. Freshman orientation:** Available. Preregistration for classes offered. **Activities:** Concert band, choral groups, dance, drama, music ensembles, student government, symphony orchestra, Latin American club, Rotarians, international student club, black student union.

**Athletics. NJCAA. Intercollegiate:** Baseball M, basketball M, golf M, soccer, tennis M. **Team name:** Colts.

**Student services.** Adult student services, career counseling, health services, personal counseling, veterans' counselor. **Physically disabled:** Services for visually, hearing impaired. **Transfer:** Transfer center, transfer adviser, college fairs on campus for students transferring to 4-year colleges.

**Contact.** Phone: (650) 306-3226 Fax: (650) 306-3113
Ruth Miller, Assistant Registrar, Canada College, 4200 Farm Hill Boulevard, Redwood City, CA 94061

## Cerritos College
**Norwalk, California**
www.cerritos.edu

**CB member**
**CB code: 4083**

- Public 2-year community college
- Commuter campus in large city

**General.** Founded in 1955. Regionally accredited. **Enrollment:** 15,718 degree-seeking undergraduates. **Degrees:** 1,161 associate awarded. **Location:** 15 miles from Los Angeles. **Calendar:** Semester, limited summer session. **Full-time faculty:** 285 total. **Part-time faculty:** 585 total. **Special facilities:** Health occupations lab.

**Basis for selection.** Open admission, but selective for some programs. Limited admissions to nursing program.

**2007-2008 Annual costs.** Tuition/fees: $628; $5,818 out-of-state. Per-credit charge: $20 in-state; $193 out-of-state. Books/supplies: $648. Personal expenses: $1,710.

**Application procedures. Admission:** No deadline. No application fee. Admission notification on a rolling basis. **Financial aid:** Priority date 5/8; no closing date. FAFSA required. Applicants notified on a rolling basis; must reply within 2 week(s) of notification.

**Academics. Special study options:** Cooperative education, distance learning, dual enrollment of high school students, honors. Bachelor's degree programs available on campus. License preparation in dental hygiene, nursing, physical therapy. **Credit/placement by examination:** CLEP, institutional tests. 12 credit hours maximum toward associate degree. **Support services:** Learning center, remedial instruction, tutoring.

**Majors. Agriculture:** Ornamental horticulture. **Area/ethnic studies:** Hispanic-American/Latino/Chicano. **Biology:** General, bacteriology, biomedical sciences, botany, zoology. **Business:** General, accounting, administrative services, banking/financial services, business admin, human resources, logistics, office management, office/clerical, real estate. **Communications:** Journalism. **Computer sciences:** General, applications programming, data processing, programming, systems analysis. **Conservation:** Wildlife. **Education:** Bilingual, early childhood, special, teacher assistance. **Engineering technology:** Drafting, electrical, manufacturing, plastics, robotics. **English:** English lit, speech/rhetoric. **Family/consumer sciences:** General, clothing/textiles, institutional food production. **Foreign languages:** French, German, Spanish. **Health:** Dental assistant, dental hygiene, licensed practical nurse, medical assistant, medical records technology, nursing (RN), physical therapy assistant. **History:** General. **Legal studies:** Court reporting, paralegal. **Liberal arts:** Arts/sciences. **Math:** General. **Mechanic/repair:** General, auto body, electronics/electrical. **Parks/recreation:** General. **Philosophy/religion:** Philosophy. **Physical sciences:** Chemistry, geology, physics, planetary. **Protective services:** Police science. **Psychology:** General. **Social sciences:** Anthropology, economics, geography, political science, sociology. **Visual/performing arts:** Art, dramatic, interior design, photography.

**Computing on campus.** 100 workstations in computer center.

**Student life. Activities:** Bands, choral groups, dance, drama, film society, literary magazine, music ensembles, musical theater, radio station, student government, student newspaper, symphony orchestra, Ahora, Indian club, Vietnamese club, Black Student Union.

**Athletics. NJCAA. Intercollegiate:** Baseball M, basketball, cross-country, diving, football (tackle) M, golf M, soccer M, softball W, swimming, tennis, track and field, volleyball W, water polo M, wrestling M. **Team name:** Falcons.

**Student services.** Adult student services, career counseling, financial aid counseling, health services, on-campus daycare, personal counseling, veterans' counselor, women's services. **Physically disabled:** Services for visually, speech, hearing impaired. **Transfer:** Transfer adviser, college fairs on campus for students transferring to 4-year colleges.

**Contact.** Phone: (562) 860-2451 ext. 2211 Fax: (562) 860-9680
Stephanie Murguia, Dean, Admissions and Records, Cerritos College, 11110 Alondra Boulevard, Norwalk, CA 90650

## Cerro Coso Community College
**Ridgecrest, California**
www.cerrocoso.edu

**CB code: 4027**

- Public 2-year community college
- Commuter campus in large town

**General.** Founded in 1973. Regionally accredited. **Enrollment:** 2,101 degree-seeking undergraduates. **Degrees:** 203 associate awarded. **Location:** 120 miles from Bakersfield. **Calendar:** Semester, limited summer session. **Full-time faculty:** 55 total; 27% have terminal degrees. **Part-time faculty:** 140 total. **Class size:** 44% < 20, 52% 20-39, 3% 40-49, 1% 50-99. **Special facilities:** Nature preserve, sculpture garden.

**Student profile.**

| | | | |
|---|---|---|---|
| Out-of-state: | 2% | 25 or older: | 63% |

**Basis for selection.** Open admission. Interview required of nursing majors.

**2007-2008 Annual costs.** Tuition/fees: $600; $6,300 out-of-state. Per-credit charge: $20 in-state; $210 out-of-state. Books/supplies: $1,314. Personal expenses: $1,656.

**Financial aid. Need-based:** Need-based aid available for part-time students. Work-study available nights and for part-time students.

**Application procedures. Admission:** No deadline. No application fee. Application may be submitted online. Admission notification on a rolling

basis. **Financial aid:** Priority date 5/15; no closing date. FAFSA required. Applicants notified on a rolling basis starting 6/1; must reply within 2 week(s) of notification.

**Academics. Special study options:** Cooperative education, distance learning, double major, dual enrollment of high school students, ESL, honors, independent study, internships, study abroad. License preparation in nursing. **Credit/placement by examination:** AP, CLEP. 30 credit hours maximum toward associate degree. **Support services:** GED preparation and test center, learning center, remedial instruction, study skills assistance, tutoring.

**Majors. Business:** General, administrative services, business admin, office management, office technology, office/clerical. **Computer sciences:** General. **Education:** Early childhood. **Engineering technology:** General, drafting, electrical. **Family/consumer sciences:** Child care. **Health:** Licensed practical nurse. **Interdisciplinary:** Biological/physical sciences. **Liberal arts:** Arts/sciences. **Mechanic/repair:** Auto body, heating/ac/refrig. **Parks/recreation:** Facilities management. **Physical sciences:** General. **Protective services:** Fire safety technology, police science. **Social sciences:** General. **Visual/performing arts:** Art.

**Most popular majors.** Business/marketing 18%, computer/information sciences 6%, health sciences 6%, liberal arts 52%, social sciences 13%.

**Computing on campus.** Online course registration, online library available.

**Student life. Freshman orientation:** Available. **Activities:** Bands, choral groups, drama, literary magazine, student government, student newspaper, symphony orchestra.

**Athletics. Intercollegiate:** Baseball M, basketball W, softball W, volleyball W. **Team name:** Coyotes.

**Student services.** Career counseling, student employment services, financial aid counseling, on-campus daycare, personal counseling, placement for graduates, veterans' counselor. **Physically disabled:** Services for visually, speech, hearing impaired. **Learning disabled:** Comprehensive services available. **Transfer:** Transfer adviser, college fairs on campus for students transferring to 4-year colleges.

**Contact.** E-mail: jboard@cerrocoso.edu
Phone: (760) 384-6357 Fax: (760) 384-6377
Dave Cornell, Director of Admission and Records, Cerro Coso Community College, 3000 College Heights Boulevard, Ridgecrest, CA 93555-7777

---

## Chabot College
### Hayward, California
### www.chabotcollege.edu
**CB code: 4725**

▶ Public 2-year community college
▶ Commuter campus in large city

**General.** Founded in 1961. Regionally accredited. **Enrollment:** 8,830 degree-seeking undergraduates. **Degrees:** 685 associate awarded. **ROTC:** Army, Air Force. **Location:** 30 miles from San Francisco, 15 miles from Berkeley. **Calendar:** Semester, extensive summer session. **Full-time faculty:** 191 total; 27% minority, 53% women. **Part-time faculty:** 321 total; 29% minority, 44% women. **Special facilities:** Planetarium. **Partnerships:** Formal partnership with Lawrence Livermore National Lab.

**Student profile.**

| | | | |
|---|---|---|---|
| Out-of-state: | 1% | 25 or older: | 45% |

**Transfer out. Colleges most students transferred to 2007:** CSU: East Bay, San Jose State University, UC: Berkeley, San Francisco State University, UC: Davis.

**Basis for selection.** Open admission, but selective for some programs. All applicants must be 18 years of age or high school graduates. Selective admission to nursing, dental hygiene, and paramedic programs.

**2007-2008 Annual costs. Tuition/fees:** $626; $5,726 out-of-state. Per-credit charge: $20 in-state; $190 out-of-state. Books/supplies: $1,332. Personal expenses: $2,430.

**Financial aid. Need-based:** Work-study available nights, weekends and for part-time students. **Additional information:** Tuition and/or fee waivers for low-income students.

**Application procedures. Admission:** No deadline. No application fee. Application may be submitted online. Admission notification on a rolling basis. Early action available for local high school students only. **Financial**

---

**aid:** Priority date 8/1; no closing date. FAFSA, institutional form required. Applicants notified on a rolling basis.

**Academics. Special study options:** Cooperative education, cross-registration, distance learning, double major, dual enrollment of high school students, ESL, independent study, internships, liberal arts/career combination, student-designed major, study abroad, weekend college. License preparation in dental hygiene, nursing, real estate. **Credit/placement by examination:** CLEP, institutional tests. 15 credit hours maximum toward associate degree. English and math tests required for placement. **Support services:** Learning center, pre-admission summer program, reduced course load, remedial instruction, study skills assistance, tutoring, writing center.

**Majors. Biology:** General. **Business:** General, accounting, administrative services, banking/financial services, logistics, management information systems, management science, office management, office technology, office/clerical, real estate, sales/distribution, tourism/travel. **Communications:** Broadcast journalism, journalism. **Communications technology:** General, radio/tv. **Computer sciences:** General, applications programming, computer science, data processing, information systems, programming. **Construction:** Maintenance, power transmission. **Education:** Early childhood, teacher assistance. **Engineering:** General. **Engineering technology:** Architectural, civil, drafting, electrical, surveying. **English:** English lit, speech/rhetoric. **Family/consumer sciences:** Child care, clothing/textiles. **Foreign languages:** French, German, Italian, Portuguese, Spanish. **Health:** Clinical lab technology, dental hygiene, medical assistant, medical records admin, medical records technology, nursing (RN), predental, premedicine, prepharmacy, preveterinary. **History:** General. **Legal studies:** Court reporting, legal secretary, prelaw. **Liberal arts:** Arts/sciences, library assistant. **Math:** General. **Mechanic/repair:** Auto body, automotive, electronics/electrical. **Parks/recreation:** General. **Personal/culinary services:** General. **Philosophy/religion:** Philosophy. **Physical sciences:** Physics. **Production:** Welding. **Protective services:** Firefighting, police science. **Psychology:** General. **Social sciences:** General, criminology, geography, political science, sociology. **Transportation:** Aviation, flight attendant. **Visual/performing arts:** Art, ceramics, commercial/advertising art, dance, dramatic, drawing, music performance, painting, photography, sculpture, studio arts.

**Most popular majors.** Business/marketing 10%, health sciences 15%, liberal arts 50%.

**Student life. Freshman orientation:** Available. Introduction to college experience, programs, services, and registration process. **Activities:** Bands, choral groups, drama, film society, literary magazine, musical theater, radio station, student government, student newspaper, TV station, various religious, political, ethnic, and social service organizations.

**Athletics.** NJCAA. **Intercollegiate:** Baseball M, basketball, cross-country, football (tackle) M, golf M, soccer, softball W, swimming, tennis, track and field, volleyball W, water polo W, wrestling M. **Intramural:** Archery, badminton, basketball, bowling, handball, racquetball, soccer, softball, table tennis, tennis, volleyball. **Team name:** Gladiators.

**Student services.** Adult student services, career counseling, student employment services, on-campus daycare, personal counseling, placement for graduates. **Physically disabled:** Services for visually, speech, hearing impaired. **Transfer:** Re-entry adviser for new students. Transfer center, college fairs on campus for students transferring to 4-year colleges.

**Contact.** E-mail: jyoung@chabotcollege.edu
Phone: (510) 723-6700 Fax: (510) 723-7510
Judy Young, Registrar, Chabot College, 25555 Hesperian Boulevard, Hayward, CA 94545

---

## Chaffey College
### Rancho Cucamonga, California
### www.chaffey.edu
**CB code: 4046**

▶ Public 2-year community college
▶ Commuter campus in small city

**General.** Founded in 1883. Regionally accredited. **Enrollment:** 12,564 degree-seeking undergraduates. **Degrees:** 1,371 associate awarded. **Location:** 50 miles from Los Angeles. **Calendar:** Semester, limited summer session. **Special facilities:** Nature preserve, natural history collection, planetarium, 2 swimming pools, children's center.

**Transfer out. Colleges most students transferred to 2007:** CSU San Bernardino, California State Polytechnic University: Pomona, CSU Fullerton, University of LaVerne, Loma Linda University.

**Basis for selection.** Open admission. Assessment testing is recommended.

**2007-2008 Annual costs.** Tuition/fees: $630; $5,820 out-of-state. Per-credit charge: $20 in-state; $193 out-of-state. Books/supplies: $1,386. Personal expenses: $2,898.

**Financial aid. Need-based:** Need-based aid available for part-time students. Work-study available for part-time students. **Non-need-based:** Scholarships awarded for academics. **Additional information:** State of California Board of Governors fee waivers to qualified state residents. Criteria for eligibility: households which receive public assistance, meet state's low income guidelines, and demonstrate need as defined by Title IV programs.

**Application procedures. Admission:** No deadline. No application fee. Admission notification on a rolling basis. **Financial aid:** No deadline. FAFSA required. Applicants notified on a rolling basis starting 7/15; must reply within 2 week(s) of notification.

**Academics. Special study options:** Accelerated study, cooperative education, dual enrollment of high school students, ESL, honors, independent study, internships, liberal arts/career combination, study abroad, weekend college. License preparation in aviation, nursing. **Credit/placement by examination:** CLEP, institutional tests. **Support services:** GED preparation, learning center, remedial instruction, tutoring, writing center.

**Majors. Biology:** General. **Business:** Accounting, administrative services, business admin, fashion, office management, sales/distribution. **Communications:** General, broadcast journalism. **Computer sciences:** General, applications programming. **Conservation:** Environmental studies. **Education:** General, early childhood, physical. **Engineering:** General. **Engineering technology:** Architectural, drafting. **English:** English lit. **Family/consumer sciences:** General, child care. **Foreign languages:** French, German, Spanish. **Health:** Dental assistant, medical radiologic technology/radiation therapy, nursing (RN). **History:** General. **Interdisciplinary:** Gerontology, science/society. **Liberal arts:** Arts/sciences. **Math:** General. **Mechanic/repair:** Aircraft, auto body, automotive, electronics/electrical. **Philosophy/religion:** Philosophy, religion. **Physical sciences:** Chemistry, geology, physics, planetary. **Psychology:** General. **Social sciences:** General, anthropology, economics, geography, political science, sociology. **Visual/performing arts:** Art, commercial/advertising art, dance, design, dramatic, fashion design, graphic design, interior design, multimedia, photography, studio arts.

**Computing on campus.** 950 workstations in library, computer center. Repair service available.

**Student life. Freshman orientation:** Mandatory. 3-hour session covers registration procedures, fees, financial aid, programs and services, counseling, course descriptions. **Activities:** Bands, choral groups, dance, drama, film society, music ensembles, musical theater, student government, student newspaper, multicultural organizations, Model United Nations, Vietnamese club, MECHA, Alpha Gamma Sigma, Black Student Union, ski club, religious organizations, French club, German club, Spanish club, Lambda.

**Athletics. Intercollegiate:** Baseball M, basketball, diving, football (tackle) M, softball W, swimming, volleyball W, water polo M. **Team name:** Panthers.

**Student services.** Alcohol/substance abuse counseling, career counseling, services for economically disadvantaged, student employment services, financial aid counseling, health services, on-campus daycare, personal counseling, veterans' counselor. **Physically disabled:** Services for visually, speech, hearing impaired. **Transfer:** Pre-admission transcript evaluation for new students. Transfer center, transfer adviser, college fairs on campus for students transferring to 4-year colleges.

**Contact.** Phone: (909) 652-6600 Fax: (909) 652-6006
Cecilia Carrera, Director of Admissions, Chaffey College, 5885 Haven Avenue, Rancho Cucamonga, CA 91701-3002

---

## Citrus College
### Glendora, California
### www.citruscollege.edu
**CB code: 4051**

♦ Public 2-year community college
♦ Commuter campus in large town

**General.** Founded in 1915. Regionally accredited. **Enrollment:** 13,095 undergraduates. **Degrees:** 778 associate awarded. **Location:** 25 miles from Los Angeles. **Calendar:** Semester, limited summer session. **Full-time faculty:** 190 total. **Part-time faculty:** 290 total. **Special facilities:** Performing arts center, golf driving range.

**Student profile.**

| | | | |
|---|---|---|---|
| Out-of-state: | 3% | 25 or older: | 29% |

**Basis for selection.** Open admission.

**2007-2008 Annual costs.** Tuition/fees: $631; $5,911 out-of-state. Per-credit charge: $20 in-state; $196 out-of-state. Books/supplies: $1,332. Personal expenses: $2,340.

**Financial aid. Need-based:** Need-based aid available for part-time students. Work-study available nights, weekends and for part-time students.

**Application procedures. Admission:** No deadline. No application fee. Application must be submitted on paper. Admission notification on a rolling basis. **Financial aid:** Priority date 3/1; no closing date. FAFSA required. Applicants notified on a rolling basis; must reply within 2 week(s) of notification.

**Academics. Special study options:** Cooperative education, distance learning, double major, dual enrollment of high school students, ESL, honors, independent study, study abroad. License preparation in nursing. **Credit/placement by examination:** AP, CLEP. 30 credit hours maximum toward associate degree. **Support services:** Learning center, remedial instruction, tutoring.

**Majors. Biology:** Botany, zoology. **Business:** General, management information systems, office management, office/clerical. **Computer sciences:** General, data processing. **Conservation:** Forestry. **Engineering:** General. **Engineering technology:** Drafting. **English:** English lit. **Foreign languages:** French, German, Japanese, Spanish. **Health:** Dental assistant, licensed practical nurse, medical assistant. **Interdisciplinary:** Biological/physical sciences. **Liberal arts:** Arts/sciences, library assistant, library science. **Math:** General. **Mechanic/repair:** Automotive, diesel, electronics/electrical, heating/ac/refrig. **Parks/recreation:** Health/fitness. **Personal/culinary services:** Cosmetic. **Physical sciences:** Chemistry, physics. **Protective services:** Criminal justice, law enforcement admin. **Psychology:** General. **Social sciences:** General. **Visual/performing arts:** Art, photography, studio arts.

**Most popular majors.** Business/marketing 17%, English 6%, interdisciplinary studies 15%, liberal arts 13%, social sciences 33%, visual/performing arts 9%.

**Computing on campus.** 1,100 workstations in library, computer center. Online course registration available.

**Student life. Freshman orientation:** Available. **Activities:** Jazz band, dance, drama, literary magazine, music ensembles, musical theater, student government, student newspaper, African American Student Alliance, European Heritage Club, Get Real Christian Fellowship, International Students Club, Latinos Unidos Student Association, Latter Day Saints Students Association, Natives of the Americas Student Association, Students United for Societal Change.

**Athletics. Intercollegiate:** Baseball M, basketball, cross-country, football (tackle) M, golf, soccer, softball W, swimming, tennis, track and field, volleyball W, water polo. **Team name:** Owls.

**Student services.** Career counseling, services for economically disadvantaged, student employment services, financial aid counseling, health services, legal services, minority student services, on-campus daycare, personal counseling, placement for graduates, veterans' counselor. **Physically disabled:** Services for visually, speech, hearing impaired.

**Contact.** E-mail: admissions@citruscollege.edu
Phone: (626) 914-8511 Fax: (626) 914-8613
Lois Papner, Associate Dean of Admissions & Financial Aid, Citrus College, 1000 West Foothill Boulevard, Glendora, CA 91741-1899

---

## City College of San Francisco
### San Francisco, California
### www.ccsf.edu
**CB member**
**CB code: 4052**

♦ Public 2-year community college
♦ Commuter campus in very large city

**General.** Founded in 1935. Regionally accredited. **Enrollment:** 22,332 degree-seeking undergraduates; 11,197 non-degree-seeking students. **Degrees:** 1,246 associate awarded. **ROTC:** Army. **Location:** Downtown. **Calendar:** Semester, extensive summer session. **Full-time faculty:** 741 total; 39% minority. **Part-time faculty:** 1,184 total; 34% minority. **Special facilities:** Observatory.

**Student profile.** Among degree-seeking undergraduates, 20% already have a bachelor's degree or higher, 2,700 enrolled as first-time, first-year students.

| | | | |
|---|---|---|---|
| Part-time: | 67% | Hispanic American: | 16% |
| Out-of-state: | 3% | Native American: | 1% |
| Women: | 55% | International: | 5% |
| African American: | 9% | 25 or older: | 65% |
| Asian American: | 30% | | |

**Transfer out. Colleges most students transferred to 2007:** San Francisco State University, CSU: East Bay, San Jose State University, UC: Berkeley, UC: Davis.

**Basis for selection.** Open admission, but selective for some programs. If applicant lacks high school diploma or equivalent, must be 18 or older and demonstrate ability to benefit. Program for registered nursing and a few other programs have a competitive/ special admissions process. All students entering the credit program are tested for placement into English or ESL and mathematics courses. **Adult students:** SAT/ACT scores not required. Credit programs require placement tests in English or ESL and mathematics. Free noncredit classes require placement tests depending on intended course of study.

**2007-2008 Annual costs.** Tuition/fees: $632; $5,732 out-of-state. Per-credit charge: $20 in-state; $190 out-of-state. Books/supplies: $1,385. Personal expenses: $2,527.

**Financial aid. Need-based:** Work-study available nights, weekends and for part-time students. **Additional information:** Board of Governor fee waiver for low income students.

**Application procedures. Admission:** No deadline. $3 fee. Application may be submitted online. Admission notification on a rolling basis. **Financial aid:** Priority date 3/1; no closing date. FAFSA required. Applicants notified on a rolling basis starting 7/1.

**Academics.** Free, noncredit classes offered in some subjects. Working Adults Degree Program. Bookloan program for low-income students. Intercollegiate Speech and Debate. Learning assistance, diversity, and student success programs. **Special study options:** Accelerated study, distance learning, dual enrollment of high school students, ESL, honors, independent study, internships, liberal arts/career combination, study abroad, weekend college. Credit is available for service-learning. License preparation in dental hygiene, nursing, paramedic, radiology. **Credit/placement by examination:** AP, CLEP, institutional tests. 45 credit hours maximum toward associate degree. Various limitations and stipulations on credit by examination. **Support services:** GED preparation and test center, learning center, pre-admission summer program, remedial instruction, study skills assistance, tutoring, writing center.

**Majors. Agriculture:** Floriculture, landscaping, nursery operations, ornamental horticulture. **Architecture:** Environmental design, interior. **Biology:** General. **Business:** Accounting, administrative services, business admin, fashion, hospitality/recreation, human resources, management information systems, marketing, office technology, office/clerical, operations, real estate, tourism promotion, tourism/travel. **Communications:** Journalism. **Communications technology:** General, graphic/printing. **Computer sciences:** General, computer science. **Construction:** Site management. **Education:** Teacher assistance. **Engineering:** General, mechanical. **Engineering technology:** General, mechanical. **Family/consumer sciences:** Child development. **Health:** Clinical lab science, dental assistant, EMT paramedic, medical assistant, medical radiologic technology/radiation therapy, medical records admin, medical records technology, medical secretary, nursing (RN), office admin, office assistant, physician assistant, ward clerk. **Legal studies:** Legal secretary, paralegal. **Liberal arts:** Library science. **Mechanic/repair:** Aircraft. **Personal/culinary services:** Chef training, restaurant/catering. **Physical sciences:** Chemistry. **Protective services:** Fire safety technology, police science. **Transportation:** Aviation. **Visual/performing arts:** Cinematography, graphic design, interior design, photography, printmaking.

**Computing on campus.** 750 workstations in library, computer center, student center. Commuter students can connect to campus network. Online course registration, online library, helpline, wireless network available.

**Student life. Freshman orientation:** Mandatory. Mandatory for degree-seeking students taking 9 or more credit units. **Activities:** Jazz band, choral groups, dance, drama, film society, literary magazine, music ensembles, musical theater, opera, radio station, student government, student newspaper, symphony orchestra, TV station, City College Press Club; Cartoon Illustration and Art; La Raza Unida; Chinese Culture Club; Christian Fellowship Club; Le Cercle Francais; African American Changing Times; LBGTstr8 Alliance; Students Linking Education and Activism; Women of Color Organization.

**Athletics.** NJCAA. **Intercollegiate:** Badminton W, baseball M, basketball, cheerleading, cross-country, football (tackle) M, judo W, soccer, softball W, tennis, track and field, volleyball W. **Intramural:** Archery, badminton, baseball, basketball, cheerleading, fencing, football (non-tackle), golf,

gymnastics, judo, racquetball, soccer, swimming, tennis, volleyball, weight lifting. **Team name:** Rams.

**Student services.** Adult student services, alcohol/substance abuse counseling, career counseling, services for economically disadvantaged, student employment services, financial aid counseling, health services, minority student services, on-campus daycare, personal counseling, placement for graduates, veterans' counselor, women's services. **Physically disabled:** Services for visually, speech, hearing impaired. **Transfer:** Transfer adviser, college fairs on campus for students transferring to 4-year colleges.

**Contact.** E-mail: admits@ccsf.edu
Phone: (415) 239-3285 Fax: (415) 239-3936
MaryLou Leyba-Frank, Dean of Admissions and Records, City College of San Francisco, Office of Admissions and Records E-107, San Francisco, CA 94112

---

## Coastline Community College
### Fountain Valley, California
www.coastline.edu

**CB member**
**CB code: 0933**

- Public 2-year community college
- Commuter campus in small city

**General.** Founded in 1976. Regionally accredited. Classes held at community-based sites during the daytime, evenings, weekends, and through extensive distance learning education. **Enrollment:** 5,874 degree-seeking undergraduates. **Degrees:** 1,468 associate awarded. **Location:** 30 miles from Los Angeles. **Calendar:** Semester, limited summer session. **Full-time faculty:** 45 total. **Part-time faculty:** 220 total. **Class size:** 45% < 20, 40% 20-39, 6% 40-49, 6% 50-99, 2% >100. **Special facilities:** Computer commons at Garden Grove center for all students. One-stop center in Costa Mesa prepares and gears students to the workplace.

**Student profile.**

| | | | |
|---|---|---|---|
| Out-of-state: | 1% | 25 or older: | 73% |

**Transfer out. Colleges most students transferred to 2007:** California State University: Long Beach, University of California: Irvine, California State University: Fullerton, National University.

**Basis for selection.** Open admission. College administered English and math tests used for placement.

**2007-2008 Annual costs.** Tuition/fees: $658; $5,848 out-of-state. Per-credit charge: $20 in-state; $193 out-of-state. Books/supplies: $648. Personal expenses: $1,566.

**Financial aid.** All financial aid based on need. Need-based aid available for part-time students. **Additional information:** Board of Governor's Grant: statewide fee waiver program for students or dependents receiving HFOL/TANF, SSI, General Relief, or whose income meets set standards or who are considered eligible through Federal needs analysis.

**Application procedures. Admission:** No deadline. No application fee. Application may be submitted online. Admission notification on a rolling basis. **Financial aid:** Priority date 3/2; no closing date. FAFSA, institutional form required. Applicants notified on a rolling basis starting 8/1; must reply within 2 week(s) of notification.

**Academics. Special study options:** Accelerated study, cooperative education, distance learning, dual enrollment of high school students, ESL, independent study, liberal arts/career combination, study abroad, weekend college. Midnight college via telecourse delivery. License preparation in physical therapy, real estate. **Credit/placement by examination:** AP, CLEP. 30 credit hours maximum toward associate degree. If submitted, SAT/ACT used for placement and counseling. **Support services:** GED preparation, reduced course load, remedial instruction, tutoring.

**Majors. Business:** General, accounting, business admin, entrepreneurial studies, management science, office technology, real estate. **Computer sciences:** General. **Liberal arts:** Arts/sciences. **Mechanic/repair:** Electronics/electrical.

**Computing on campus.** 100 workstations in computer center.

**Student life. Freshman orientation:** Available. Preregistration for classes offered. **Activities:** Choral groups, dance, student government.

**Student services.** Career counseling, services for economically disadvantaged, student employment services, financial aid counseling, health services, personal counseling, veterans' counselor. **Physically disabled:** Services for hearing impaired. **Transfer:** Transfer center, transfer adviser, college fairs on campus for students transferring to 4-year colleges.

**Contact.** E-mail: jmcdonald@cccd.edu
Phone: (714) 241-6176 Fax: (714) 241-6288
Jennifer McDonald, Director of Admissions and Records, Coastline
Community College, 11460 Warner Avenue, Fountain Valley, CA 92708

## Coleman College: San Marcos
San Marcos, California
www.coleman.edu

- For-profit 2-year technical college
- Commuter campus in small city

**General.** Accredited by ACICS. Branch campus of Coleman College, La
Mesa. **Enrollment:** 24 degree-seeking undergraduates. **Degrees:** 40 associate awarded. **Calendar:** Continuous. **Full-time faculty:** 6 total. **Part-time
faculty:** 12 total.

**2007-2008 Annual costs.** Per-credit charge: $255. Tuition $27,540 for
13-month associate degree program; costs vary by program.

**Academics. Credit/placement by examination:** CLEP.

**Majors. Biology:** Bioinformatics. **Computer sciences:** Programming. **Visual/
performing arts:** Graphic design.

**Contact.** Phone: (760) 747-3990
Coleman College: San Marcos, 1284 West San Marcos Boulevard, Suite
110, San Marcos, CA 92069

## College of Alameda
Alameda, California
alameda.peralta.edu                    CB code: 4118

- Public 2-year community college
- Commuter campus in small city

**General.** Founded in 1970. Regionally accredited. **Enrollment:** 6,501 undergraduates. **Degrees:** 278 associate awarded. **Calendar:** Semester, limited summer session. **Full-time faculty:** 80 total. **Part-time faculty:** 120
total.

**Student profile.**

| | | | |
|---|---|---|---|
| Out-of-state: | 2% | 25 or older: | 54% |

**Basis for selection.** Open admission.

**2007-2008 Annual costs.** Tuition/fees: $604; $5,794 out-of-state. Per-
credit charge: $20 in-state; $193 out-of-state. Books/supplies: $1,022. Per-
sonal expenses: $2,430.

**Application procedures. Admission:** No deadline. No application fee.
Application may be submitted online. Admission notification on a rolling
basis. **Financial aid:** Priority date 3/2; no closing date. FAFSA required.
Applicants notified on a rolling basis starting 7/1; must reply within 2 week(s)
of notification.

**Academics. Special study options:** Cooperative education, cross-
registration, dual enrollment of high school students, honors, independent
study, liberal arts/career combination. License preparation in aviation. **Credit/
placement by examination:** CLEP, institutional tests. **Support services:**
Learning center, remedial instruction, tutoring.

**Majors. Area/ethnic studies:** African-American. **Biology:** General. **Business:** General, accounting, administrative services, business admin, entrepreneurial studies, fashion, marketing, office/clerical. **Education:** Teacher
assistance. **English:** English lit. **Foreign languages:** Spanish. **Health:** Dental assistant, health aide. **History:** General. **Liberal arts:** Arts/sciences. **Math:**
General. **Mechanic/repair:** Aircraft. **Philosophy/religion:** Philosophy. **Psychology:** General. **Social sciences:** General, anthropology, economics, geography, political science, sociology, urban studies. **Transportation:** Aviation management. **Visual/performing arts:** General, studio arts.

**Computing on campus.** Online course registration available.

**Student life. Freshman orientation:** Available. **Activities:** Jazz band,
choral groups, dance, drama, student government, student newspaper.

**Athletics. Intercollegiate:** Basketball, bowling, cross-country M, fencing,
golf, soccer M, tennis, track and field, volleyball. **Intramural:** Golf, sailing, softball W.

**Student services.** Adult student services, career counseling, services for
economically disadvantaged, student employment services, health services,
on-campus daycare, personal counseling, placement for graduates, veterans'
counselor. **Physically disabled:** Services for visually, speech, hearing impaired. **Transfer:** Transfer adviser, college fairs on campus for students
transferring to 4-year colleges.

**Contact.** E-mail: admissions@peralta.edu
Phone: (510) 748-2228 Fax: (510) 748-5227
Howard Perdue, Associate Vice Chancellor, Admissions, Records and
Student Services, College of Alameda, 555 Ralph Appezzato Memorial
Parkway, Alameda, CA 94501

## College of Marin: Kentfield
Kentfield, California
www.marin.edu                    CB code: 4061

- Public 2-year community college
- Commuter campus in small town

**General.** Founded in 1926. Regionally accredited. Additional campus at
Indian Valley - Novato, CA. **Enrollment:** 2,768 degree-seeking undergraduates. **Degrees:** 45 associate awarded. **Location:** 15 miles from San Francisco. **Calendar:** Semester. **Full-time faculty:** 135 total. **Part-time faculty:** 160 total.

**Transfer out. Colleges most students transferred to 2007:** University of
California: Berkeley, San Francisco State, University of California: Davis.

**Basis for selection.** Open admission. Limited admissions to nursing programs. **Adult students:** SAT/ACT scores not required.

**2007-2008 Annual costs.** Tuition/fees: $630; $6,000 out-of-state. Per-
credit charge: $20 in-state; $199 out-of-state. Books/supplies: $650. Per-
sonal expenses: $2,021.

**Financial aid. Need-based:** Need-based aid available for part-time students.

**Application procedures. Admission:** No deadline. No application fee.
Application may be submitted online. Admission notification on a rolling
basis. **Financial aid:** Priority date 3/1; no closing date. FAFSA required.
Applicants notified on a rolling basis starting 5/15.

**Academics. Special study options:** Distance learning, ESL. **Credit/
placement by examination:** CLEP, institutional tests. **Support services:**
Remedial instruction, study skills assistance, tutoring, writing center.

**Majors. Agriculture:** Landscaping, nursery operations. **Architecture:** Environmental design. **Biology:** General, environmental. **Business:** General,
accounting, real estate. **Communications:** General, broadcast journalism,
public relations. **Computer sciences:** General, programming, systems analysis. **English:** English lit. **Foreign languages:** General, French, Spanish. **History:** General. **Legal studies:** Court reporting. **Liberal arts:** Arts/sciences.
**Math:** General. **Mechanic/repair:** Auto body. **Physical sciences:** General,
chemistry, physics. **Psychology:** General. **Visual/performing arts:** Studio
arts.

**Student life. Activities:** Student government, student newspaper.

**Athletics. Intercollegiate:** Baseball M, basketball, cross-country, diving,
football (tackle) M, soccer, softball, squash, tennis, track and field. **Intramural:** Cross-country, softball, swimming.

**Student services. Transfer:** Transfer center, transfer adviser, college
fairs on campus for students transferring to 4-year colleges.

**Contact.** Phone: (415) 485-9412
Robert Balestreri, Inteim Dean of Enrollment Services, College of Marin:
Kentfield, 835 College Avenue, Kentfield, CA 94904

## College of San Mateo
San Mateo, California
www.collegeofsanmateo.edu                    CB code: 4070

- Public 2-year community college
- Commuter campus in small city

**General.** Founded in 1922. Regionally accredited. **Enrollment:** 5,547 degree-
seeking undergraduates. **Degrees:** 373 associate awarded. **ROTC:** Army,
Air Force. **Location:** 15 miles from San Francisco. **Calendar:** Semester,
limited summer session. **Full-time faculty:** 350 total. **Part-time faculty:**
200 total. **Special facilities:** Planetarium.

## Student profile.

| | | | |
|---|---|---|---|
| Out-of-state: | 2% | 25 or older: | 51% |

**Basis for selection.** Open admission, but selective for some programs. Nursing program has separate requirements.

**2007-2008 Annual costs.** Tuition/fees: $628; $6,148 out-of-state. Per-credit charge: $20 in-state; $204 out-of-state.

**Application procedures. Admission:** No deadline. No application fee. Application may be submitted online. Admission notification on a rolling basis. Completion of CSM Placement tests for English, reading and mathematics recommmended prior to counseling session. **Financial aid:** Priority date 3/2; no closing date. FAFSA, institutional form required. Applicants notified on a rolling basis starting 6/15.

**Academics. Special study options:** Cooperative education, cross-registration, distance learning, double major, dual enrollment of high school students, ESL, honors, independent study, liberal arts/career combination, study abroad, weekend college. License preparation in dental hygiene, nursing, real estate. **Credit/placement by examination:** AP, CLEP, IB, institutional tests. 12 credit hours maximum toward associate degree. **Support services:** Learning center, reduced course load, remedial instruction, study skills assistance, tutoring, writing center.

**Majors. Agriculture:** Horticulture, ornamental horticulture. **Biology:** General, biomedical sciences. **Business:** General, accounting, entrepreneurial studies, fashion, logistics, management information systems, office/clerical, real estate. **Communications:** Advertising, broadcast journalism. **Communications technology:** General. **Computer sciences:** General, web page design. **Construction:** Pipefitting. **Engineering:** General. **Engineering technology:** Drafting, electrical. **English:** English lit, speech/rhetoric. **Foreign languages:** French, German, Spanish. **Health:** Dental assistant, medical assistant, nursing (RN), substance abuse counseling. **Legal studies:** Legal secretary. **Liberal arts:** Arts/sciences. **Math:** General. **Mechanic/repair:** Aircraft, heating/ac/refrig. **Personal/culinary services:** General. **Physical sciences:** Chemistry, geology, physics. **Protective services:** Fire safety technology. **Social sciences:** General. **Transportation:** Airline/commercial pilot, aviation. **Visual/performing arts:** Cinematography, commercial/advertising art, painting, photography, studio arts.

**Computing on campus.** 150 workstations in library, computer center, student center. Online course registration, wireless network available.

**Student life. Freshman orientation:** Available. **Activities:** Bands, choral groups, dance, literary magazine, radio station, student government, student newspaper, symphony orchestra, TV station, Asian student union, Christian Fellowship, ethnic studies society, international students union, Latin American student organization, Arts in Recovery, Ballet Folklorico de CSM, Earth Preservation Committee, Peace Action, Unity Among Brothers.

**Athletics.** NCAA. **Intercollegiate:** Baseball M, basketball W, cross-country, football (tackle) M, softball W, swimming, tennis W, track and field, water polo. **Team name:** Bulldogs.

**Student services.** Adult student services, alcohol/substance abuse counseling, career counseling, services for economically disadvantaged, student employment services, financial aid counseling, health services, minority student services, on-campus daycare, personal counseling, veterans' counselor. **Physically disabled:** Services for visually, speech, hearing impaired. **Learning disabled:** Comprehensive services available. **Transfer:** Pre-admission transcript evaluation for new students. Transfer center, transfer adviser, college fairs on campus for students transferring to 4-year colleges.

**Contact.** E-mail: villarealh@smccd.net
Phone: (650) 574-6165 Fax: (650) 574-6506
Henry Villareal, Dean of Admissions and Records, College of San Mateo, 1700 West Hillsdale Boulevard, San Mateo, CA 94402-3784

## College of the Canyons

Santa Clarita, California
www.canyons.edu

**CB code: 4117**

♦ Public 2-year community college
♦ Commuter campus in small city

**General.** Founded in 1967. Regionally accredited. **Enrollment:** 7,860 degree-seeking undergraduates. **Degrees:** 875 associate awarded. **Location:** 15 miles from Los Angeles. **Calendar:** Semester, extensive summer session. **Full-time faculty:** 184 total. **Part-time faculty:** 427 total. **Class size:** 39% < 20, 53% 20-39, 7% 40-49, less than 1% 50-99, less than 1% >100. **Special facilities:** Performing arts center, proscenium performing arts stage, experimental "black box" theater, university center for access to upper-division and graduate programs.

**Student profile.** Among degree-seeking undergraduates, 42% enrolled in a transfer program, 2% enrolled in a vocational program, 11% already have a bachelor's degree or higher, 516 transferred in from other institutions.

| | | | |
|---|---|---|---|
| Out-of-state: | 4% | Native American: | 1% |
| African American: | 4% | International: | 1% |
| Asian American: | 9% | 25 or older: | 31% |
| Hispanic American: | 24% | | |

**Transfer out. Colleges most students transferred to 2007:** California State University: Northridge, University of California: Los Angeles, San Diego State University, University of California: Santa Barbara, California State University: Long Beach.

**Basis for selection.** Open admission, but selective for some programs. Limited admission to nursing program. **Homeschooled:** Transcript of courses and grades required. Home school affidavit.

**2007-2008 Annual costs.** Tuition/fees: $638; $5,168 out-of-state. Per-credit charge: $20 in-state; $171 out-of-state. Books/supplies: $1,422. Personal expenses: $2,502.

**2006-2007 Financial aid. Need-based:** 75% of total undergraduate aid awarded as scholarships/grants, 25% as loans/jobs. Need-based aid available for part-time students. Work-study available nights and for part-time students. **Non-need-based:** Scholarships awarded for academics, alumni affiliation, art, leadership, music/drama. **Additional information:** Enrollment fees waived for students enrolled concurrently in high school and COC. School has own payment plan.

**Application procedures. Admission:** No deadline. No application fee. Application may be submitted online. Admission notification on a rolling basis. **Financial aid:** Closing date 3/2. FAFSA required. Applicants notified on a rolling basis starting 6/1; must reply within 4 week(s) of notification.

**Academics. Special study options:** Accelerated study, cooperative education, distance learning, dual enrollment of high school students, ESL, honors, independent study, internships, liberal arts/career combination, study abroad, weekend college. Bachelor's degree programs available on campus. License preparation in nursing, real estate. **Credit/placement by examination:** AP, CLEP, institutional tests. 18 credit hours maximum toward associate degree. Applicants must take institutional English, ESL, chemistry, and mathematics placement tests. **Support services:** Learning center, remedial instruction, study skills assistance, tutoring.

**Majors. Business:** Accounting, administrative services, business admin, hospitality admin, hotel/motel admin, office technology, real estate, sales/distribution, small business admin. **Communications:** Digital media, journalism, radio/tv. **Communications technology:** Animation/special effects. **Computer sciences:** Computer science, networking. **Construction:** Site management. **Engineering:** General. **Engineering technology:** Architectural drafting, drafting, manufacturing, mechanical drafting, surveying, water quality. **English:** English lit. **Family/consumer sciences:** Child development. **Foreign languages:** French, German, sign language interpretation, Spanish. **Health:** Nursing (RN). **History:** General. **Interdisciplinary:** Biological/physical sciences. **Legal studies:** Paralegal. **Liberal arts:** Arts/sciences, library assistant. **Math:** General. **Mechanic/repair:** General, automotive, electronics/electrical. **Parks/recreation:** General, health/fitness. **Personal/culinary services:** Restaurant/catering. **Production:** Welding. **Protective services:** Firefighting, police science. **Social sciences:** General. **Visual/performing arts:** Art, cinematography, graphic design, interior design, jazz, multimedia, music theory/composition, photography, voice/opera.

**Most popular majors.** Business/marketing 13%, health sciences 9%, liberal arts 45%, social sciences 9%.

**Computing on campus.** 1,648 workstations in library, computer center, student center. Online course registration, online library, helpline, wireless network available.

**Student life. Freshman orientation:** Available. **Activities:** Jazz band, choral groups, dance, drama, music ensembles, musical theater, student government, student newspaper, symphony orchestra, TV station, Quest Campus Crusade for Christ, COC Bible Study club, Latter-day Saint Student Association, Model U.N., Speech & Debate, OLAS, Armenian Student Association.

**Athletics. Intercollegiate:** Baseball M, basketball, cross-country, football (tackle) M, golf, soccer, softball W, swimming, track and field, volleyball W, water polo W. **Team name:** Cougars.

**Student services.** Adult student services, career counseling, services for economically disadvantaged, student employment services, financial aid counseling, health services, on-campus daycare, personal counseling, placement for graduates, veterans' counselor. **Physically disabled:** Services for visually, speech, hearing impaired. **Learning disabled:** Comprehensive services available. **Transfer:** Pre-admission transcript evaluation for new students. Transfer center, transfer adviser, college fairs on campus for students transferring to 4-year colleges.

**Contact.** E-mail: jasmine.ruys@canyons.edu
Phone: (661) 362-3280 Fax: (661) 259-8302
Jasmine Ruys, Director, Admissions, Records and Online Services, College of the Canyons, 26455 Rockwell Canyon Road, Santa Clarita, CA 91355

---

## College of the Desert
**Palm Desert, California**                     CB member
**www.collegeofthedesert.edu**                  CB code: 4085

- Public 2-year community college
- Commuter campus in small city

**General.** Founded in 1958. Regionally accredited. **Enrollment:** 5,333 degree-seeking undergraduates. **Degrees:** 533 associate awarded. **Location:** 20 miles from Palm Springs, 120 miles from Los Angeles. **Calendar:** Semester, limited summer session. **Full-time faculty:** 108 total; 19% have terminal degrees, 18% minority, 49% women. **Part-time faculty:** 317 total. **Special facilities:** Performing arts center, golf institute, public safety academy.

**Student profile.** Among degree-seeking undergraduates, 316 transferred in from other institutions.

| | | | |
|---|---|---|---|
| Out-of-state: | 3% | Native American: | 1% |
| African American: | 4% | International: | 3% |
| Asian American: | 5% | 25 or older: | 40% |
| Hispanic American: | 49% | | |

**Basis for selection.** Open admission, but selective for some programs. Separate application requirements for nursing and golf management and public safety academy. Interviews required for nursing/allied health majors. **Adult students:** SAT/ACT scores not required. **Learning Disabled:** Participation is voluntary. Interested students must meet with the appropriate Disabled Students Programs and Services counselor to apply for these programs.

**2007-2008 Annual costs.** Tuition/fees: $630; $5,490 out-of-state. Per-credit charge: $20 in-state; $182 out-of-state. Books/supplies: $1,314. Personal expenses: $2,826.

**2006-2007 Financial aid.** All financial aid based on need. 92% of total undergraduate aid awarded as scholarships/grants, 8% as loans/jobs. Need-based aid available for part-time students. Work-study available weekends and for part-time students.

**Application procedures.** **Admission:** Priority date 5/1; deadline 9/4 (receipt date). No application fee. Application must be submitted online. Admission notification on a rolling basis. **Financial aid:** Priority date 3/2; no closing date. FAFSA required. Applicants notified on a rolling basis starting 7/1.

**Academics.** **Special study options:** Cooperative education, distance learning, double major, dual enrollment of high school students, ESL, honors, independent study, liberal arts/career combination. License preparation in nursing. **Credit/placement by examination:** CLEP, institutional tests. **Support services:** GED preparation and test center, learning center, remedial instruction, study skills assistance, tutoring, writing center.

**Majors.** **Agriculture:** Business, ornamental horticulture, plant sciences, turf management. **Architecture:** Technology. **Biology:** General. **Business:** Business admin, construction management, golf management, hotel/motel admin, managerial economics, office management, restaurant/food services. **Communications:** General, journalism, media studies, organizational. **Computer sciences:** General, computer science. **Conservation:** General, environmental science, environmental studies. **Engineering technology:** Architectural, architectural drafting, drafting, heat/ac/refrig. **English:** American lit, composition, English lit, speech/rhetoric. **Family/consumer sciences:** Food/nutrition, human nutrition. **Foreign languages:** French, German, Italian, Spanish. **Health:** Dietetic technician, licensed practical nurse, nursing (RN). **History:** General. **Interdisciplinary:** Biological/physical sciences. **Liberal arts:** Arts/sciences. **Math:** General. **Mechanic/repair:** Heating/ac/refrig. **Parks/recreation:** General, facilities management. **Personal/culinary services:** Restaurant/catering. **Philosophy/religion:** Philosophy. **Physical sciences:** Chemistry, geology, physics. **Protective services:** Fire safety technology, law enforcement admin. **Psychology:** General. **Social sciences:** General, anthropology, economics, geography, political science, sociology. **Visual/performing arts:** Acting, art, art history/conservation, dance, dramatic, drawing, graphic design, painting, photography, printmaking, studio arts, theater history.

**Most popular majors.** Business/marketing 7%, health sciences 22%, liberal arts 44%, visual/performing arts 7%.

**Computing on campus.** 125 workstations in library, computer center, student center. Online course registration, online library, wireless network available.

**Student life.** **Freshman orientation:** Mandatory. **Activities:** Choral groups, dance, drama, international student organizations, music ensembles, musical theater, opera, student government, student newspaper.

**Athletics.** **Intercollegiate:** Baseball M, basketball, cheerleading, cross-country, fencing, football (tackle) M, golf, soccer, softball W, tennis, volleyball W. **Team name:** Roadrunners.

**Student services.** Adult student services, career counseling, services for economically disadvantaged, student employment services, financial aid counseling, health services, minority student services, on-campus daycare, personal counseling, placement for graduates, veterans' counselor. **Physically disabled:** Services for visually, speech, hearing impaired. **Learning disabled:** Comprehensive services available. **Transfer:** Re-entry adviser, pre-admission transcript evaluation for new students. Transfer center, transfer adviser, college fairs on campus for students transferring to 4-year colleges.

**Contact.** Phone: (760) 773-2516 Fax: (760) 862-1379
John Loera, Dean of Enrollment Services, College of the Desert, 43-500 Monterey Avenue, Palm Desert, CA 92260

---

## College of the Redwoods
**Eureka, California**                          CB member
**www.redwoods.edu**                            CB code: 4100

- Public 2-year community college
- Commuter campus in large town

**General.** Founded in 1964. Regionally accredited. Centers at Fort Bragg and Crescent City; instructional sites in Hoopa, Klamath, downtown Eureka, and Arcata. **Enrollment:** 4,516 degree-seeking undergraduates; 1,695 non-degree-seeking students. **Degrees:** 409 associate awarded. **Location:** 275 miles from San Francisco. **Calendar:** Semester, limited summer session. **Full-time faculty:** 95 total. **Part-time faculty:** 310 total. **Class size:** 19% < 20, 64% 20-39, 12% 40-49, 5% 50-99. **Special facilities:** Observatories, fish hatchery, working organic farm.

**Student profile.** Among degree-seeking undergraduates, 912 enrolled as first-time, first-year students.

| | | | |
|---|---|---|---|
| Part-time: | 53% | Hispanic American: | 8% |
| Out-of-state: | 4% | Native American: | 8% |
| Women: | 58% | 25 or older: | 43% |
| African American: | 3% | Live on campus: | 1% |
| Asian American: | 4% | | |

**Transfer out.** **Colleges most students transferred to 2007:** Humboldt State University, California State University: Chico.

**Basis for selection.** Open admission, but selective for some programs. Admission for nursing applicants based on school record and test scores. **Homeschooled:** Must submit a copy of affidavit filed with County Office of Education.

**2007-2008 Annual costs.** Tuition/fees: $624; $7,104 out-of-state. Per-credit charge: $20 in-state; $236 out-of-state. Room/board: $5,900. Books/supplies: $1,330. Personal expenses: $1,476.

**2007-2008 Financial aid.** **Need-based:** 75% of total undergraduate aid awarded as scholarships/grants, 25% as loans/jobs. Need-based aid available for part-time students. Work-study available for part-time students.

**Application procedures.** **Admission:** Priority date 8/14; no deadline. No application fee. Admission notification on a rolling basis. **Financial aid:** Priority date 4/15; no closing date. FAFSA, institutional form required. Applicants notified on a rolling basis starting 5/1; must reply within 6 week(s) of notification.

**Academics.** **Special study options:** Cooperative education, cross-registration, distance learning, double major, dual enrollment of high school students, ESL, honors, independent study, teacher certification program. License preparation in nursing. **Credit/placement by examination:** CLEP, institutional tests. **Support services:** GED preparation and test center, learning center, pre-admission summer program, remedial instruction, tutoring, writing center.

**Majors. Agriculture:** Agribusiness operations, animal sciences, plant sciences. **Business:** General, administrative services, hospitality admin, managerial economics, office technology, real estate. **Communications:** Journalism. **Computer sciences:** General. **Conservation:** Fisheries, forestry. **Construction:** Maintenance. **Education:** Early childhood. **Engineering:** Electrical. **Engineering technology:** Construction, drafting. **Legal studies:** Legal secretary, paralegal. **Liberal arts:** Arts/sciences. **Physical sciences:** Planetary. **Protective services:** Law enforcement admin. **Visual/performing arts:** Commercial/advertising art.

**Most popular majors.** Health sciences 14%, liberal arts 65%.

**Computing on campus.** 578 workstations in dormitories, library, computer center, student center. Dormitories wired for high-speed internet access. Online course registration, online library available.

**Student life. Freshman orientation:** Available. Preregistration for classes offered. **Housing:** Coed dorms available. Limited housing also available for police academy students. **Activities:** Jazz band, choral groups, dance, student government, student newspaper, Native American club, international students club, apologetics club, Bible study, Latter-day Saints club, veterans club, EOPS club.

**Athletics. Intercollegiate:** Baseball M, basketball, cross-country, football (tackle) M, golf M, soccer W, track and field, volleyball W. **Intramural:** Badminton, bowling, diving, golf, gymnastics, soccer, volleyball, water polo. **Team name:** Corsairs.

**Student services.** Career counseling, services for economically disadvantaged, student employment services, financial aid counseling, health services, on-campus daycare, personal counseling, placement for graduates, veterans' counselor. **Physically disabled:** Services for visually, speech, hearing impaired. **Transfer:** Transfer center, transfer adviser, college fairs on campus for students transferring to 4-year colleges.

**Contact.** E-mail: admissions@redwoods.edu
Phone: (707) 476-4200 Toll-free number: (800) 641-0400
Fax: (707) 476-4406
Kathy Goodlive, Manager, Admissions and Records, College of the Redwoods, 7351 Tompkins Hill Road, Eureka, CA 95501-9300

---

## College of the Sequoias
**Visalia, California**
www.cos.edu

CB code: 4071

▶ Public 2-year agricultural and community college
▶ Commuter campus in small city

**General.** Founded in 1925. Regionally accredited. Affiliated with University of California at Davis School of Veterinary Medicine in Tulare. **Enrollment:** 7,425 degree-seeking undergraduates. **Degrees:** 754 associate awarded. **ROTC:** Air Force. **Location:** 45 miles from Fresno. **Calendar:** Semester, limited summer session. **Full-time faculty:** 176 total. **Part-time faculty:** 278 total. **Special facilities:** Self-sufficient farm.

**Student profile.**

| | | | |
|---|---|---|---|
| Out-of-state: | 3% | 25 or older: | 39% |

**Transfer out. Colleges most students transferred to 2007:** California State University: Fresno, California State University: Bakersfield, California Polytechnic State University: San Luis Obispo, California State University: Long Beach.

**Basis for selection.** Open admission, but selective for some programs. Limited admission to nursing program. Interviews required for work program, nursing majors. Auditions required for music majors.

**2007-2008 Annual costs.** Tuition/fees: $642; $6,672 out-of-state. Per-credit charge: $20 in-state; $221 out-of-state. Books/supplies: $1,386. Personal expenses: $2,898.

**Application procedures. Admission:** No deadline. No application fee. Admission notification on a rolling basis. **Financial aid:** Priority date 3/2; no closing date. FAFSA, institutional form required. Applicants notified on a rolling basis starting 6/1; must reply within 2 week(s) of notification.

**Academics. Special study options:** Dual enrollment of high school students, ESL, honors, independent study, internships, student-designed major, study abroad. License preparation in nursing. **Credit/placement by examination:** CLEP, institutional tests. 12 credit hours maximum toward associate degree. **Support services:** Learning center, pre-admission summer program, reduced course load, remedial instruction, study skills assistance, tutoring, writing center.

---

**Majors. Agriculture:** Agribusiness operations, landscaping, ornamental horticulture. **Business:** General, accounting, administrative services, management information systems, office/clerical, real estate, sales/distribution. **Communications:** General, journalism. **Computer sciences:** Computer science. **Construction:** Carpentry, maintenance. **Education:** Adult/continuing, physical. **Engineering:** General. **Engineering technology:** Architectural, construction, drafting, electrical, industrial, manufacturing. **English:** English lit, speech/rhetoric. **Family/consumer sciences:** General, child care. **Foreign languages:** General, French. **Health:** Nursing (RN). **Interdisciplinary:** Biological/physical sciences. **Legal studies:** Paralegal. **Liberal arts:** Arts/sciences. **Math:** General. **Mechanic/repair:** Electronics/electrical. **Parks/recreation:** Facilities management. **Personal/culinary services:** Cosmetic. **Protective services:** Fire safety technology, law enforcement admin. **Public administration:** Human services. **Social sciences:** General. **Visual/performing arts:** Art, commercial/advertising art, dramatic, multimedia, studio arts, theater design.

**Computing on campus.** 325 workstations in library, computer center. Online course registration available.

**Student life. Freshman orientation:** Mandatory. **Activities:** Bands, choral groups, dance, drama, music ensembles, musical theater, student government, student newspaper, symphony orchestra.

**Athletics. Intercollegiate:** Baseball M, basketball, cross-country, diving, football (tackle) M, golf M, soccer W, softball W, swimming, tennis, track and field, volleyball W. **Team name:** Giants.

**Student services.** Adult student services, alcohol/substance abuse counseling, career counseling, services for economically disadvantaged, student employment services, financial aid counseling, health services, minority student services, on-campus daycare, personal counseling, veterans' counselor. **Physically disabled:** Services for visually, speech, hearing impaired. **Transfer:** Transfer adviser, college fairs on campus for students transferring to 4-year colleges.

**Contact.** Phone: (559) 730-3727 Fax: (559) 730-3894
Don Mast, Dean of Student Services, College of the Sequoias, 915 South Mooney Boulevard, Visalia, CA 93277

---

## College of the Siskiyous
**Weed, California**
www.siskiyous.edu

CB code: 4087

▶ Public 2-year community and junior college
▶ Commuter campus in small town

**General.** Founded in 1957. Regionally accredited. **Enrollment:** 1,336 degree-seeking undergraduates; 1,392 non-degree-seeking students. **Degrees:** 176 associate awarded. **Location:** 285 miles from San Francisco, 80 miles from Medford, Oregon. **Calendar:** Semester, limited summer session. **Full-time faculty:** 50 total; 16% have terminal degrees, 10% minority, 36% women. **Part-time faculty:** 150 total; 8% have terminal degrees, 10% minority, 36% women. **Class size:** 57% < 20, 35% 20-39, 3% 40-49, 4% 50-99, less than 1% >100. **Special facilities:** Fire science burn tower and flashover unit, welding lab.

**Student profile.** Among degree-seeking undergraduates, 51% enrolled in a transfer program, 49% enrolled in a vocational program, 5% already have a bachelor's degree or higher, 671 enrolled as first-time, first-year students, 232 transferred in from other institutions.

| | | | |
|---|---|---|---|
| Part-time: | 36% | 25 or older: | 39% |
| Out-of-state: | 27% | Live on campus: | 14% |
| Women: | 55% | | |

**Transfer out.** 51% of students enrolled in the transfer program go on to 4-year colleges. **Colleges most students transferred to 2007:** California State University: Chico, Southern Oregon University, University of California: Davis, Simpson University, Humboldt State University.

**Basis for selection.** Open admission, but selective for some programs. **Adult students:** SAT/ACT scores not required. SAT/ACT scores not required if out of high school 1 year(s) or more.

**2007-2008 Annual costs.** Tuition/fees: $624; $6,174 out-of-state. Per-credit charge: $20 in-state; $205 out-of-state. Oregon residents with interstate exchange program: $42 per unit (no enrollment fee). Room/board: $7,550. Books/supplies: $1,350. Personal expenses: $2,000.

**Financial aid.** All financial aid based on need. Need-based aid available for part-time students. Work-study available nights, weekends and for part-time students.

**Application procedures. Admission:** No deadline. No application fee. Application may be submitted online. **Financial aid:** Priority date 4/30; no closing date. FAFSA required. Applicants notified on a rolling basis starting 6/1; must reply within 2 week(s) of notification.

**Academics. Special study options:** Combined bachelor's/graduate degree, cooperative education, distance learning, dual enrollment of high school students, ESL, exchange student, independent study, internships, liberal arts/career combination, student-designed major, study abroad. Bachelor's degree programs available on campus. License preparation in nursing, paramedic. **Credit/placement by examination:** AP, CLEP, institutional tests. 48 credit hours maximum toward associate degree. **Support services:** GED preparation, learning center, pre-admission summer program, reduced course load, remedial instruction, study skills assistance, tutoring, writing center.

**Majors. Biology:** General. **Business:** General, accounting, accounting technology, administrative services, business admin, management information systems, office management, office/clerical. **Communications:** General, broadcast journalism, digital media, media studies, radio/tv. **Communications technology:** General, graphics, radio/tv. **Computer sciences:** General, applications programming, computer science, programming. **Education:** General, early childhood special. **Engineering:** General. **English:** Composition, English lit. **Family/consumer sciences:** Child care, child development, family studies, family/community services. **Foreign languages:** Spanish. **Health:** EMT paramedic, licensed practical nurse, nursing (RN), predental, premedicine, prenursing, prepharmacy, preveterinary, substance abuse counseling. **History:** General. **Interdisciplinary:** Accounting/computer science, behavioral sciences, biological/physical sciences, natural sciences. **Legal studies:** Prelaw. **Liberal arts:** Arts/sciences, humanities. **Math:** General. **Parks/recreation:** Health/fitness. **Philosophy/religion:** Philosophy. **Physical sciences:** General, chemistry, geology, physics. **Production:** Welding. **Protective services:** Criminal justice, fire safety technology, fire services admin, firefighting, law enforcement admin, police science. **Psychology:** General. **Public administration:** Human services. **Social sciences:** General, anthropology. **Visual/performing arts:** General, acting, art, digital art, directing/producing, dramatic, graphic design, music performance, studio arts, theater arts management, voice/opera. **Other:** Alcohol and Drug Studies, Early Childhood Education, Office Assistant.

**Most popular majors.** Liberal arts 89%, security/protective services 9%.

**Computing on campus.** 260 workstations in dormitories, library, computer center. Dormitories wired for high-speed internet access and linked to campus network. Commuter students can connect to campus network. Online course registration, online library, helpline, repair service, wireless network available.

**Student life. Freshman orientation:** Available. Preregistration for classes offered. Held three months prior to the start of the semester. **Housing:** Guaranteed on-campus for freshmen. Coed dorms, substance-free housing available. $100 fully refundable deposit. **Activities:** Bands, choral groups, dance, drama, international student organizations, music ensembles, musical theater, student government, student newspaper, symphony orchestra, TV station, Latino Student Union, Black Student Union, Phi Theta Kappa honor society, intercultural club, American Indian Alliance, intervarsity club, speech club, chess club, disabled student aliance, speech and forensics club.

**Athletics. Intercollegiate:** Baseball M, basketball, cross-country, football (tackle) M, skiing, softball W, track and field, volleyball W. **Intramural:** Badminton, basketball, bowling, boxing, golf, skiing, softball, tennis, volleyball. **Team name:** Eagles.

**Student services.** Adult student services, alcohol/substance abuse counseling, career counseling, services for economically disadvantaged, student employment services, financial aid counseling, health services, legal services, on-campus daycare, personal counseling, veterans' counselor. **Physically disabled:** Services for visually, speech, hearing impaired. **Learning disabled:** Comprehensive services available. **Transfer:** Re-entry adviser, pre-admission transcript evaluation for new students. Transfer center, transfer adviser, college fairs on campus for students transferring to 4-year colleges.

**Contact.** E-mail: registration@siskiyous.edu
Phone: (530) 938-5555 Toll-free number: (888) 397-4339
Fax: (530) 938-5367
Teresa Winkelman, Director of Admissions & Records, College of the Siskiyous, 800 College Avenue, Weed, CA 96094-2899

---

## Columbia College
**Sonora, California**
**www.gocolumbia.org**                          **CB code: 4108**

▶ Public 2-year community college
▶ Commuter campus in small town

---

**General.** Founded in 1968. Regionally accredited. **Enrollment:** 3,368 undergraduates. **Degrees:** 204 associate awarded. **Location:** 150 miles from Sacramento. **Calendar:** Semester, limited summer session. **Full-time faculty:** 45 total. **Part-time faculty:** 80 total. **Special facilities:** Jogging/fitness trail, arboretum, astronomy dome, seismograph.

**Basis for selection.** Open admission. Institution uses own assessment test for placement only.

**2007-2008 Annual costs.** Tuition/fees: $642; $5,832 out-of-state. Per-credit charge: $20 in-state; $193 out-of-state. Books/supplies: $882. Personal expenses: $1,656.

**Financial aid. Need-based:** Need-based aid available for part-time students. **Non-need-based:** Scholarships awarded for academics.

**Application procedures. Admission:** No deadline. No application fee. Application may be submitted online. Admission notification on a rolling basis. Matriculation procedures required before new or returning students may register. Early application assures accommodation to new student priority registration periods. **Financial aid:** Priority date 3/2, closing date 12/15. FAFSA, institutional form required. Applicants notified on a rolling basis starting 6/15; must reply within 2 week(s) of notification.

**Academics. Special study options:** Cooperative education, double major, ESL, independent study, internships, liberal arts/career combination. License preparation in paramedic. **Credit/placement by examination:** AP, CLEP, institutional tests. 12 credit hours maximum toward associate degree. **Support services:** GED preparation and test center, learning center, remedial instruction, study skills assistance, tutoring, writing center.

**Majors. Biology:** General. **Business:** General, administrative services, business admin, hospitality admin. **Computer sciences:** General, programming. **Conservation:** General, forestry, management/policy. **English:** English lit, speech/rhetoric. **Family/consumer sciences:** Child development. **Interdisciplinary:** Natural sciences. **Liberal arts:** Arts/sciences. **Math:** General. **Mechanic/repair:** Automotive. **Parks/recreation:** Health/fitness. **Personal/culinary services:** Culinary arts. **Physical sciences:** Chemistry, physics, planetary. **Protective services:** Fire safety technology. **Social sciences:** General. **Visual/performing arts:** Art, photography.

**Computing on campus.** 60 workstations in library, computer center.

**Student life. Freshman orientation:** Mandatory. 1-hour session prior to registration. **Housing:** Coed dorms, special housing for disabled, apartments available. Privately owned apartments on campus available to single students. **Activities:** Bands, choral groups, dance, music ensembles, student government, student newspaper, symphony orchestra.

**Athletics. Intercollegiate:** Basketball M, volleyball W. **Team name:** Claim Jumpers.

**Student services.** Adult student services, alcohol/substance abuse counseling, career counseling, services for economically disadvantaged, student employment services, financial aid counseling, health services, on-campus daycare, personal counseling, placement for graduates, veterans' counselor. **Physically disabled:** Services for visually, speech, hearing impaired. **Transfer:** Re-entry adviser for new students. Transfer center, transfer adviser, college fairs on campus for students transferring to 4-year colleges.

**Contact.** Phone: (209) 588-5250 Fax: (209) 588-5337
Kathy Smith, Director of Student Success/Matriculation, Columbia College, 11600 Columbia College Drive, Sonora, CA 95370

---

## Concorde Career College: Garden Grove
**Garden Grove, California**
**www.concorde.edu**

▶ For-profit 2-year health science and technical college
▶ Small city

---

**General.** Regionally accredited; also accredited by ACCSCT. **Enrollment:** 145 full-time, degree-seeking students. **Degrees:** 90 associate awarded. **Calendar:** Continuous. **Full-time faculty:** 40 total.

**Academics. Credit/placement by examination:** CLEP.

**Majors. Health:** Respiratory therapy technology.

**Contact.** E-mail: agueco@concorde.edu
Phone: (714) 703-1900
Cary Kaplan, Director of Admissions, Concorde Career College: Garden Grove, 12951 Euclid Street, #101, Garden Grove, CA 92840

## Concorde Career College: North Hollywood
North Hollywood, California
www.concordecareercolleges.com

- For-profit 2-year health science college
- Large city

**General.** Accredited by ACCSCT. **Enrollment:** 100 degree-seeking undergraduates. **Degrees:** 84 associate awarded. **Calendar:** Continuous. **Full-time faculty:** 35 total. **Part-time faculty:** 15 total.

**Basis for selection.** Institutional exam scores important. CPAT, Wonderlic used.

**2007-2008 Annual costs.** Cost quoted representative annual cost; individual cost may vary by program.

**Application procedures. Admission:** No deadline. No application fee. Admission notification on a rolling basis.

**Academics. Credit/placement by examination:** CLEP.

**Majors. Health:** Respiratory therapy technology.

**Contact.** Phone: (818) 766-8151 Toll-free number: (800) 464-1212 Fax: (818) 766-1587
Concorde Career College: North Hollywood, 12412 Victory Boulevard, North Hollywood, CA 91606

## Concorde Career College: San Bernardino
San Bernardino, California
www.concorde.edu

- For-profit 2-year technical college
- Small city

**General.** Regionally accredited; also accredited by ACCSCT. **Enrollment:** 130 degree-seeking undergraduates. **Degrees:** 91 associate awarded. **Calendar:** Continuous. **Full-time faculty:** 52 total. **Part-time faculty:** 15 total.

**Application procedures. Financial aid:** Closing date 3/2.

**Academics. Credit/placement by examination:** CLEP.

**Majors. Health:** Respiratory therapy technology.

**Contact.** Concorde Career College: San Bernardino, 201 East Airport Dr., San Bernardino, CA 92408

## Concorde Career College: San Diego
San Diego, California
www.concorde.edu

- For-profit 2-year health science and nursing college
- Very large city

**General.** Regionally accredited; also accredited by ACCSCT. **Enrollment:** 550 degree-seeking undergraduates. **Calendar:** Differs by program. **Full-time faculty:** 83 total. **Part-time faculty:** 3 total.

**Academics. Credit/placement by examination:** CLEP.

**Majors. Health:** Respiratory therapy assistant.

**Contact.** E-mail: creese@concorde.edu
Charlie Reese, Director of Admissions, Concorde Career College: San Diego, 4393 Imperial Avenue, San Diego, CA 92113

## Contra Costa College
San Pablo, California
www.contracosta.edu                    CB code: 4943

- Public 2-year community college
- Large town

**General.** Founded in 1948. Regionally accredited. Middle College High School on-campus. 100% pass rate on NCLEX for nursing program graduates. **Enrollment:** 8,574 undergraduates. **Degrees:** 406 associate awarded.

**ROTC:** Naval. **Location:** 20 miles from San Francisco. **Calendar:** Semester, limited summer session. **Full-time faculty:** 110 total. **Part-time faculty:** 225 total. **Special facilities:** Center for scientific excellence.

**Transfer out. Colleges most students transferred to 2007:** California State University: East Bay, California State University: San Francisco, University of California: Davis, San Jose State University, University of California: Berkeley.

**Basis for selection.** Open admission.

**2007-2008 Annual costs.** Tuition/fees: $600; $5,700 out-of-state. Per-credit charge: $20 in-state; $190 out-of-state.

**Application procedures. Admission:** No deadline. No application fee. Admission notification on a rolling basis. **Financial aid:** Priority date 3/2; no closing date. FAFSA required. Applicants notified on a rolling basis; must reply within 2 week(s) of notification.

**Academics. Special study options:** Cross-registration, dual enrollment of high school students, honors, independent study. **Credit/placement by examination:** CLEP, institutional tests. 12 credit hours maximum toward associate degree. **Support services:** Learning center, remedial instruction, tutoring.

**Majors. Area/ethnic studies:** African-American, Hispanic-American/Latino/Chicano. **Biology:** General. **Business:** Administrative services, office/clerical, real estate. **Computer sciences:** General, applications programming. **Education:** Bilingual, teacher assistance. **Engineering:** General. **Engineering technology:** Architectural, drafting. **English:** English lit. **Family/consumer sciences:** Institutional food production. **Health:** Dental assistant, medical assistant, nursing (RN). **History:** General. **Liberal arts:** Arts/sciences. **Math:** General. **Mechanic/repair:** Auto body. **Personal/culinary services:** Cosmetic. **Physical sciences:** Chemistry, physics. **Protective services:** Police science. **Psychology:** General. **Social sciences:** Geography, sociology. **Visual/performing arts:** Dramatic, interior design.

**Most popular majors.** Business/marketing 11%, health sciences 20%, liberal arts 48%.

**Student life. Activities:** Jazz band, student newspaper, TV station.

**Athletics. Intercollegiate:** Baseball M, basketball, football (tackle) M, tennis, track and field.

**Student services.** Career counseling, student employment services, health services, personal counseling. **Transfer:** Re-entry adviser for new students. Transfer center, transfer adviser, college fairs on campus for students transferring to 4-year colleges.

**Contact.** Phone: (510) 235-7800 ext. 4210 Fax: (510) 236-6768
Ken Blustajn, Director of Admission and Records, Contra Costa College, 2600 Mission Bell Drive, San Pablo, CA 94806

## Copper Mountain College
Joshua Tree, California
www.cmccd.edu                    CB code: 3889

- Public 2-year community college
- Commuter campus in small town

**General.** Regionally accredited. **Enrollment:** 1,866 undergraduates. **Degrees:** 155 associate awarded. **Location:** 120 miles from Los Angeles, 45 miles from Palm Springs. **Calendar:** Semester, limited summer session. **Full-time faculty:** 40 total. **Part-time faculty:** 115 total.

**Transfer out. Colleges most students transferred to 2007:** California State University: San Bernardino.

**Basis for selection.** Open admission. Limited admission to some allied health programs.

**2007-2008 Annual costs.** Tuition/fees: $602; $5,792 out-of-state. Per-credit charge: $20 in-state; $193 out-of-state. Books/supplies: $1,386. Personal expenses: $3,898.

**Financial aid. Need-based:** Need-based aid available for part-time students.

**Application procedures. Admission:** No deadline. No application fee. Application must be submitted online. Admission notification on a rolling basis. **Financial aid:** Priority date 3/2; no closing date. FAFSA required.

**Academics. Special study options:** Distance learning, dual enrollment of high school students, ESL, independent study, study abroad. License preparation in nursing, paramedic. **Credit/placement by examination:** AP, CLEP. **Support services:** GED preparation and test center, remedial instruction, study skills assistance, tutoring.

**Majors. Business:** Business admin. **Communications:** General. **Computer sciences:** General, computer science. **English:** English lit. **Foreign languages:** Spanish. **Health:** Licensed practical nurse. **History:** General. **Liberal arts:** Arts/sciences. **Math:** General. **Mechanic/repair:** Automotive. **Philosophy/religion:** Philosophy. **Protective services:** Fire safety technology, law enforcement admin. **Psychology:** General. **Social sciences:** General, anthropology, economics, political science. **Visual/performing arts:** Art.

**Computing on campus.** 40 workstations in library, computer center.

**Student life. Freshman orientation:** Mandatory. Preregistration for classes offered. 1.5 hour group orientation offered about 16 times prior to each semester. **Activities:** Literary magazine, student government.

**Student services.** Adult student services, career counseling, services for economically disadvantaged, student employment services, financial aid counseling, veterans' counselor. **Physically disabled:** Services for visually, speech, hearing impaired. **Transfer:** Pre-admission transcript evaluation for new students. Transfer center, transfer adviser, college fairs on campus for students transferring to 4-year colleges.

**Contact.** Phone: (760) 366-3791 ext. 4232 Toll-free number: (866) 366-3791 ext. 4232 Fax: (760) 366-5257 Gregory Brown, Vice President of Student Services, Copper Mountain College, 6162 Rotary Way, Joshua Tree, CA 92252

## Cosumnes River College
Sacramento, California
www.crc.losrios.edu
**CB code: 4121**

- Public 2-year junior college
- Commuter campus in large city

**General.** Founded in 1970. Regionally accredited. Classes offered at Folsom Lake Center, El Dorado Center and Folsom Prison. **Enrollment:** 9,241 degree-seeking undergraduates. **Degrees:** 556 associate awarded. **Location:** 12 miles from downtown. **Calendar:** Semester, limited summer session. **Full-time faculty:** 175 total. **Part-time faculty:** 200 total.

**Basis for selection.** Open admission.

**2007-2008 Annual costs.** Tuition/fees: $632; $5,822 out-of-state. Per-credit charge: $20 in-state; $193 out-of-state. Books/supplies: $1,386. Personal expenses: $2,126.

**Application procedures. Admission:** No deadline. No application fee. Admission notification on a rolling basis beginning on or about 3/1. First-time students encouraged to participate in orientation and matriculation sessions. English and mathematics tests for placement recommended. **Financial aid:** Priority date 5/1; no closing date. FAFSA required. Applicants notified on a rolling basis starting 7/20; must reply within 4 week(s) of notification.

**Academics. Special study options:** Cooperative education, distance learning, double major, dual enrollment of high school students, ESL, honors, independent study, internships, study abroad. **Credit/placement by examination:** CLEP. 15 credit hours maximum toward associate degree. **Support services:** Learning center, reduced course load, remedial instruction, tutoring.

**Majors. Agriculture:** Animal sciences, business, equestrian studies, horticultural science, plant sciences. **Architecture:** Environmental design, interior, landscape. **Area/ethnic studies:** American, women's. **Business:** General, accounting, business admin, entrepreneurial studies, finance, real estate. **Communications:** Advertising, broadcast journalism, journalism, public relations. **Communications technology:** General. **Computer sciences:** Information systems, programming. **Construction:** Maintenance. **Education:** Early childhood. **Engineering technology:** Drafting. **Health:** Medical assistant, medical records technology. **Interdisciplinary:** Gerontology. **Liberal arts:** Arts/sciences. **Protective services:** Fire safety technology, law enforcement admin. **Social sciences:** Sociology. **Visual/performing arts:** Art, art history/conservation, cinematography, commercial photography, dramatic, interior design, photography, studio arts.

**Most popular majors.** Business/marketing 8%, health sciences 6%, liberal arts 52%, trade and industry 6%.

**Student life. Activities:** Bands, choral groups, drama, radio station, student government, student newspaper, TV station, African-American Students Association, Hispanic/Latino Scholars, Asian American Club, Christian Club, earth club.

**Athletics. Intercollegiate:** Baseball M, basketball, soccer, softball W, tennis, track and field, volleyball W. **Intramural:** Badminton, bowling, fencing, golf, racquetball, skiing, swimming, tennis, track and field, volleyball.

**Student services.** Adult student services, career counseling, student employment services, health services, on-campus daycare, personal counseling, placement for graduates, veterans' counselor. **Physically disabled:** Services for hearing impaired. **Transfer:** Transfer adviser for students transferring to 4-year colleges.

**Contact.** Phone: (916) 691-7410 Fax: (916) 691-7467 Celia Esposito-Noy, Vice President, Student Services and Enrollment Management, Cosumnes River College, 8401 Center Parkway, Sacramento, CA 95823

## Crafton Hills College
Yucaipa, California
www.craftonhills.edu
**CB code: 4126**

- Public 2-year community college
- Commuter campus in large town

**General.** Founded in 1972. Regionally accredited. **Enrollment:** 3,470 degree-seeking undergraduates. **Degrees:** 330 associate awarded. **Location:** 12 miles from San Bernardino. **Calendar:** Semester, limited summer session. **Full-time faculty:** 60 total. **Part-time faculty:** 160 total. **Special facilities:** Golf course, walking trails.

**Basis for selection.** Open admission.

**2007-2008 Annual costs.** Tuition/fees: $642; $5,892 out-of-state. Per-credit charge: $20 in-state; $195 out-of-state. Books/supplies: $630. Personal expenses: $1,440.

**Financial aid.** All financial aid based on need. Need-based aid available for part-time students. Work-study available nights and for part-time students.

**Application procedures. Admission:** No deadline. No application fee. Application may be submitted online. Students under 18 admitted with special permission. **Financial aid:** Priority date 4/15, closing date 6/2. FAFSA, institutional form required. Applicants notified on a rolling basis starting 7/31; must reply within 2 week(s) of notification.

**Academics. Special study options:** Cooperative education, cross-registration, distance learning, dual enrollment of high school students, weekend college. **Credit/placement by examination:** AP, CLEP, institutional tests. 36 credit hours maximum toward associate degree. **Support services:** Learning center, remedial instruction, study skills assistance, tutoring.

**Majors. Biology:** General, bacteriology. **Business:** Administrative services, business admin, office/clerical. **Computer sciences:** General, programming. **Education:** Early childhood, health occupations. **English:** English lit. **Foreign languages:** General, French, Spanish. **Health:** EMT paramedic, medical radiologic technology/radiation therapy, respiratory therapy technology. **History:** General. **Liberal arts:** Arts/sciences. **Math:** General. **Physical sciences:** Chemistry, geology, physics. **Protective services:** Fire-fighting, law enforcement admin. **Psychology:** General. **Social sciences:** General, anthropology, economics, geography, political science, sociology. **Visual/performing arts:** Art, dramatic.

**Computing on campus.** 172 workstations in library, computer center.

**Student life. Freshman orientation:** Mandatory. **Activities:** Jazz band, drama, music ensembles, musical theater, student government, student newspaper.

**Athletics. Intercollegiate:** Golf, tennis, volleyball, weight lifting.

**Student services.** Career counseling, student employment services, health services, on-campus daycare, personal counseling, placement for graduates, veterans' counselor. **Physically disabled:** Services for visually, speech, hearing impaired. **Transfer:** Pre-admission transcript evaluation for new students. Transfer center, transfer adviser, college fairs on campus for students transferring to 4-year colleges.

**Contact.** E-mail: admissions@craftonhills.edu Phone: (909) 389-3372 Fax: (909) 389-9141 Joe Cabrales, Dean, Student Services, Student Development, Crafton Hills College, 11711 Sand Canyon Road, Yucaipa, CA 92399-1799

## Cuesta College
**San Luis Obispo, California**
www.cuesta.org                    CB code: 4101

- Public 2-year community college
- Commuter campus in large town

**General.** Founded in 1964. Regionally accredited. Additional North County Campus in Paso Robles and South County Center(s) in Arroyo Grande and Nipomo. **Enrollment:** 12,157 undergraduates. **Degrees:** 704 associate awarded. **Location:** 200 miles from Los Angeles, 6 miles from San Luis Obispo. **Calendar:** Semester, extensive summer session. **Full-time faculty:** 145 total. **Part-time faculty:** 315 total. **Special facilities:** Adobe museum (Chumash Indian).

**Student profile.**

Out-of-state:              3%      25 or older:              33%

**Transfer out. Colleges most students transferred to 2007:** California Polytechnic State University: San Luis Obispo, CSU: Chico, San Francisco State University, California State Polytechnic University: Pomona.

**Basis for selection.** Open admission, but selective for some programs. Nursing program requires critical thinking and math assessments. Prerequisite courses evaluated. **Learning Disabled:** No special admission but must be assessed and qualified to receive services.

**2007-2008 Annual costs.** Tuition/fees: $660; $5,850 out-of-state. Per-credit charge: $20 in-state; $193 out-of-state. Books/supplies: $1,386. Personal expenses: $2,520.

**Financial aid. Need-based:** Work-study available for part-time students.

**Application procedures. Admission:** No deadline. No application fee. Admission notification on a rolling basis. **Financial aid:** Priority date 3/2; no closing date. FAFSA required. Applicants notified on a rolling basis starting 4/15.

**Academics. Special study options:** Cooperative education, distance learning, double major, ESL, honors, independent study, student-designed major, study abroad, weekend college. Bachelor's degree programs available on campus. **Credit/placement by examination:** CLEP, institutional tests. 12 credit hours maximum toward associate degree. **Support services:** Learning center, remedial instruction, study skills assistance, tutoring, writing center.

**Majors. Biology:** General. **Business:** General, real estate. **Communications:** General, broadcast journalism, journalism. **Computer sciences:** Computer science. **Education:** Art, early childhood, mathematics, physical, special. **Engineering:** Electrical. **Health:** Nursing (RN). **Liberal arts:** Arts/sciences, library assistant. **Math:** General. **Mechanic/repair:** Auto body. **Physical sciences:** Chemistry, physics. **Protective services:** Law enforcement admin. **Visual/performing arts:** Interior design.

**Computing on campus.** 300 workstations in library, computer center, student center. Online course registration, online library available.

**Student life. Freshman orientation:** Available. **Activities:** Jazz band, choral groups, dance, drama, music ensembles, musical theater, radio station, student government, student newspaper, TV station, Alpha Gamma Sigma (honor society).

**Athletics. Intercollegiate:** Baseball M, basketball, cross-country, diving, soccer W, softball W, swimming, tennis W, track and field, volleyball W, water polo, wrestling M.

**Student services.** Adult student services, career counseling, student employment services, financial aid counseling, health services, legal services, on-campus daycare, personal counseling, veterans' counselor. **Physically disabled:** Services for visually, speech, hearing impaired. **Transfer:** Re-entry adviser for new students. Transfer center, transfer adviser, college fairs on campus for students transferring to 4-year colleges.

**Contact.** E-mail: admit@bass.cuesta.cc.ca.us
Phone: (805) 546-3140 Fax: (805) 546-3975
Joy Chambers, Director of Admissions and Records, Cuesta College, Box 8106, San Luis Obispo, CA 93403

## Cuyamaca College
**El Cajon, California**
www.cuyamaca.net                    CB code: 4252

- Public 2-year community college
- Small city

**General.** Founded in 1978. Regionally accredited. **Enrollment:** 4,951 degree-seeking undergraduates. **Degrees:** 362 associate awarded. **ROTC:** Army, Air Force. **Location:** 18 miles from San Diego. **Calendar:** Semester, limited summer session. **Full-time faculty:** 70 total. **Part-time faculty:** 311 total. **Special facilities:** Automotive technology facility, water gardens, child care facility, museum.

**Transfer out. Colleges most students transferred to 2007:** San Diego State University, National University.

**Basis for selection.** Open admission, but selective for some programs.

**2007-2008 Annual costs.** Tuition/fees: $638; $5,528 out-of-state. Per-credit charge: $20 in-state; $183 out-of-state. Books/supplies: $1,200. Personal expenses: $1,500.

**Financial aid. Need-based:** Work-study available nights, weekends and for part-time students.

**Application procedures. Admission:** Closing date 8/22. No application fee in-state; $163 out-of-state. Application may be submitted online. Admission notification on a rolling basis. **Financial aid:** Priority date 3/2; no closing date. FAFSA required. Applicants notified on a rolling basis; must reply within 2 week(s) of notification.

**Academics. Special study options:** Cooperative education, cross-registration, distance learning, double major, dual enrollment of high school students, ESL, honors, independent study, internships, study abroad, weekend college. License preparation in real estate. **Credit/placement by examination:** AP, CLEP, institutional tests. **Support services:** Remedial instruction, tutoring.

**Majors. Agriculture:** Ornamental horticulture. **Business:** Accounting, business admin, real estate. **Engineering technology:** Architectural, computer systems, drafting, electrical, surveying. **Family/consumer sciences:** Child care. **Liberal arts:** Arts/sciences.

**Most popular majors.** Business/marketing 15%, computer/information sciences 6%, education 7%, liberal arts 48%.

**Computing on campus.** Online course registration available.

**Student life. Freshman orientation:** Available. **Activities:** Dance, student government, student newspaper, African American student union, Christian club, Cuyamaca College Spanish club, MECHA, Phi Theta Kappa.

**Athletics. Intercollegiate:** Basketball, cross-country, golf M, soccer, tennis W, track and field, volleyball W. **Team name:** Coyotes.

**Student services.** Adult student services, career counseling, student employment services, financial aid counseling, health services, on-campus daycare, personal counseling, veterans' counselor. **Physically disabled:** Services for visually, speech, hearing impaired. **Transfer:** Pre-admission transcript evaluation for new students. Transfer center, transfer adviser, college fairs on campus for students transferring to 4-year colleges.

**Contact.** Phone: (619) 660-4275 Fax: (619) 660-4575
Cuyamaca College, 900 Rancho San Diego Parkway, El Cajon, CA 92019-4304

## Cypress College
**Cypress, California**
www.cypresscollege.edu                    CB code: 4104

- Public 2-year community college
- Commuter campus in small city

**General.** Founded in 1966. Regionally accredited. **Enrollment:** 9,330 degree-seeking undergraduates. **Degrees:** 775 associate awarded. **Location:** 30 miles from Los Angeles. **Calendar:** Semester, limited summer session. **Full-time faculty:** 190 total. **Part-time faculty:** 220 total.

**Student profile.**

Out-of-state:              5%      **25 or older:**              44%

**Basis for selection.** Open admission. College administered English and math placement exams used for placement.

**2007-2008 Annual costs.** Tuition/fees: $628; $5,488 out-of-state. Per-credit charge: $20 in-state; $182 out-of-state. Books/supplies: $1,386. Personal expenses: $1,898.

**Application procedures. Admission:** No deadline. No application fee. Application may be submitted online. Admission notification on a rolling

basis. **Financial aid:** Priority date 5/31; no closing date. FAFSA required. Applicants notified on a rolling basis starting 8/1; must reply within 2 week(s) of notification.

**Academics. Special study options:** Distance learning, dual enrollment of high school students, ESL, honors, independent study, internships, liberal arts/career combination, study abroad. License preparation in aviation, dental hygiene, nursing, real estate. **Credit/placement by examination:** CLEP, institutional tests. 12 credit hours maximum toward associate degree. **Support services:** Learning center, reduced course load, remedial instruction, study skills assistance, tutoring, writing center.

**Majors. Area/ethnic studies:** Asian, Latin American. **Business:** General, accounting, administrative services, business admin, hospitality/recreation, management information systems, management science, office technology, office/clerical, tourism promotion. **Communications:** Journalism. **Computer sciences:** General, data processing, information systems. **Conservation:** Forestry. **Education:** General, elementary, physical, secondary, technology/industrial arts. **Engineering:** General. **English:** English lit, speech/rhetoric. **Family/consumer sciences:** Institutional food production. **Foreign languages:** French, German, Spanish. **Health:** Dental assistant, dental hygiene, dental lab technology, health services, medical assistant, medical radiologic technology/radiation therapy, medical records admin, medical records technology, nursing (RN), predental, premedicine, prepharmacy, preveterinary. **History:** General. **Legal studies:** Court reporting, legal secretary, pre-law. **Liberal arts:** Arts/sciences. **Math:** General. **Mechanic/repair:** Aircraft, auto body, automotive, electronics/electrical, heating/ac/refrig. **Parks/recreation:** General. **Personal/culinary services:** Culinary arts, mortuary science. **Philosophy/religion:** Philosophy. **Physical sciences:** Chemistry, geology, physics. **Psychology:** General. **Public administration:** Human services. **Social sciences:** Anthropology, economics, geography, political science, sociology. **Transportation:** Airline/commercial pilot, aviation, aviation management, flight attendant. **Visual/performing arts:** General, art, commercial/advertising art, dance, dramatic, music performance, theater design.

**Computing on campus.** 800 workstations in library, computer center, student center.

**Student life. Freshman orientation:** Available. **Activities:** Bands, choral groups, dance, drama, literary magazine, music ensembles, musical theater, student government, student newspaper.

**Athletics. NJCAA. Intercollegiate:** Baseball M, basketball, diving, golf, soccer, softball W, swimming, tennis, volleyball W, water polo, wrestling M. **Intramural:** Badminton, baseball M, basketball, softball, volleyball. **Team name:** Chargers.

**Student services.** Career counseling, student employment services, health services, on-campus daycare, personal counseling, veterans' counselor. **Physically disabled:** Services for visually, speech, hearing impaired. **Transfer:** Re-entry adviser, pre-admission transcript evaluation for new students. Transfer center, transfer adviser, college fairs on campus for students transferring to 4-year colleges.

**Contact.** Phone: (714) 484-7346 Fax: (714) 484-7446
Dave Wassenaar, Dean of Admissions and Records, Cypress College, 9200 Valley View Street, Cypress, CA 90630

## De Anza College
**Cupertino, California**
**www.deanza.edu**
**CB code: 4286**

- Public 2-year community college
- Commuter campus in large town

**General.** Founded in 1967. Regionally accredited. **Enrollment:** 16,921 degree-seeking undergraduates. **Degrees:** 1,071 associate awarded. **ROTC:** Army, Air Force. **Location:** 5 miles from San Jose, 40 miles from San Francisco. **Calendar:** Quarter, extensive summer session. **Full-time faculty:** 300 total. **Part-time faculty:** 540 total. **Special facilities:** Planetarium, California history center, environmental studies area, advanced technology center.

**Transfer out. Colleges most students transferred to 2007:** University of California: Davis, San Jose State, San Francisco State, University of California: Berkeley, University of California: Santa Cruz.

**Basis for selection.** Open admission, but selective for some programs. Limited admission for nursing and physical therapist assistant applicants.

**2007-2008 Annual costs.** Tuition/fees: $621; $5,346 out-of-state. Per-credit charge: $13 in-state; $118 out-of-state.

**Financial aid.** All financial aid based on need. Need-based aid available for part-time students.

**Application procedures. Admission:** No deadline. No application fee. Application may be submitted online. Admission notification on a rolling basis. **Financial aid:** No deadline. FAFSA required. Applicants notified on a rolling basis starting 5/15; must reply within 2 week(s) of notification.

**Academics. Special study options:** Cooperative education, cross-registration, distance learning, dual enrollment of high school students, ESL, honors, independent study, internships, study abroad, weekend college. License preparation in nursing. **Credit/placement by examination:** CLEP, institutional tests. 45 credit hours maximum toward associate degree. **Support services:** Learning center, pre-admission summer program, remedial instruction, tutoring.

**Majors. Area/ethnic studies:** African-American, Asian-American, Hispanic-American/Latino/Chicano, Latin American, Native American. **Biology:** General. **Business:** Accounting, administrative services, business admin, marketing, purchasing, real estate, taxation. **Communications:** General. **Computer sciences:** General, applications programming, computer science, programming, systems analysis. **Education:** Early childhood. **Engineering:** General, computer, electrical, mechanical. **Engineering technology:** Drafting. **English:** English lit, technical writing. **Foreign languages:** French, German, Spanish. **Health:** Medical assistant, nursing (RN). **History:** General. **Legal studies:** Paralegal. **Liberal arts:** Arts/sciences. **Math:** General. **Philosophy/religion:** Philosophy. **Physical sciences:** Astronomy, chemistry, geology, physics. **Protective services:** Law enforcement admin, security services. **Psychology:** General. **Science technology:** Biological. **Social sciences:** Anthropology, economics, geography, political science, sociology. **Visual/performing arts:** Art, art history/conservation, ceramics, cinematography, commercial/advertising art, painting, photography, printmaking, sculpture.

**Computing on campus.** 300 workstations in library, computer center, student center. Online course registration available.

**Student life. Freshman orientation:** Available. Two day counseling course for new, incoming students. **Activities:** Bands, choral groups, dance, drama, literary magazine, music ensembles, student government, student newspaper, symphony orchestra, TV station.

**Athletics. Intercollegiate:** Baseball M, basketball, cross-country, diving, football (tackle) M, golf, soccer, softball W, swimming, tennis, track and field, volleyball, water polo M. **Intramural:** Badminton, baseball M, basketball, bowling, fencing, gymnastics, racquetball, soccer W, swimming, tennis, volleyball. **Team name:** Dons.

**Student services.** Adult student services, alcohol/substance abuse counseling, career counseling, services for economically disadvantaged, student employment services, financial aid counseling, health services, legal services, minority student services, on-campus daycare, personal counseling, placement for graduates, veterans' counselor. **Physically disabled:** Services for visually, speech, hearing impaired. **Transfer:** Re-entry adviser for new students. Transfer center, transfer adviser, college fairs on campus for students transferring to 4-year colleges.

**Contact.** E-mail: webreg@fhda.edu
Phone: (408) 864-5300 Fax: (408) 864-8329
Kathleen Moberg, Dean of Admissions and Records, De Anza College, 21250 Stevens Creek Boulevard, Cupertino, CA 95014

## Deep Springs College
**Dyer, Nevada**
**www.deepsprings.edu**
**CB code: 4281**

- Private 2-year liberal arts college for men
- Residential campus in rural community
- SAT or ACT (ACT writing optional), application essay, interview required

**General.** Founded in 1917. Regionally accredited. **Enrollment:** 25 degree-seeking undergraduates. **Degrees:** 13 associate awarded. **Location:** 45 miles from Bishop. **Calendar:** Continuous, limited summer session. **Full-time faculty:** 4 total; 75% have terminal degrees, 25% women. **Part-time faculty:** 2 total; 100% have terminal degrees. **Class size:** 100% < 20. **Special facilities:** Student-operated 2,600-acre cattle and alfalfa ranch, dairy.

**Student profile.** Among degree-seeking undergraduates, 2 transferred in from other institutions.

**Out-of-state:** 100%  **Live on campus:** 100%

**Transfer out.** 95% of students enrolled in the transfer program go on to 4-year colleges. **Colleges most students transferred to 2007:** Harvard University, University of Chicago, Oxford University, Stanford University, Yale University.

**Basis for selection.** Essays most important. School achievement record, interview, extracurricular activities, and recommendations strongly considered. Admissions process created and run by student committee. SAT Subject Tests recommended. International students who cannot take SAT or who have taken equivalent standardized test evaluated on case-by-case basis. 2-round application process: in first round, 3 essays are required. If accepted into second round, additional 4 essays and 3- to 4-day campus visit and interview required.

**2007-2008 Annual costs.** All students receive full scholarship covering tuition, room, and board. Books/supplies: $1,500.

**Financial aid. Need-based:** Work-study available nights and weekends. **Non-need-based:** Scholarships awarded for academics.

**Application procedures. Admission:** Closing date 11/15 (postmark date). No application fee. Admission notification 4/15. Must reply by 5/1. Approximately 40 applicants are invited to complete part II of application process between January and March. This includes a 3-day campus visit, interview, and writing 4 additional essays. Foreign students and those with economic hardship may be exempt from the visit upon request. **Financial aid:** No deadline.

**Academics.** Students required to take 3 classes: composition, public speaking, and summer seminar (interdisciplinary course broadly oriented around questions of political theory). **Special study options:** Independent study. **Credit/placement by examination:** CLEP.

**Majors. Liberal arts:** Arts/sciences.

**Computing on campus.** 7 workstations in library, computer center. Helpline, repair service available.

**Student life. Freshman orientation:** Mandatory. **Policies:** All students work on jobs running college or ranch. Student committees organize all community events as well as handle admissions, faculty hiring, public relations, and review/reinvitation process. Students also self-govern, managing community issues and each other's conduct. Student-formulated isolation and drug/alcohol policies: drugs prohibited, students prohibited from leaving valley during term, guests prohibited from visiting. **Housing:** Guaranteed on-campus for all undergraduates. Pets allowed in dorm rooms. **Activities:** Jazz band, dance, drama, film society, literary magazine, music ensembles, musical theater, radio station, student government, student newspaper.

**Athletics. Intramural:** Basketball M, cross-country M, equestrian M, football (non-tackle) M, football (tackle) M, rifle M, rodeo M, skiing M, soccer M, swimming M, table tennis M, track and field M, weight lifting M, wrestling M.

**Student services.** Career counseling, health services, personal counseling, placement for graduates. **Transfer:** Transfer adviser for students transferring to 4-year colleges.

**Contact.** E-mail: apcom@deepsprings.edu
Phone: (760) 872-2000 Fax: (760) 872-4466
Sam Allen, Chair, Applications Committee, Deep Springs College, Applications Committee, Dyer, NV 89010-9803

---

## Diablo Valley College
**Pleasant Hill, California**
www.dvc.edu                                    **CB code: 4295**

▸ Public 2-year community college
▸ Commuter campus in large town

**General.** Founded in 1948. Regionally accredited. **Enrollment:** 11,363 degree-seeking undergraduates. **Degrees:** 605 associate awarded. **ROTC:** Army, Naval. **Location:** 25 miles from San Francisco. **Calendar:** Semester, extensive summer session. **Full-time faculty:** 242 total. **Part-time faculty:** 599 total. **Class size:** 24% < 20, 57% 20-39, 17% 40-49, 3% 50-99, less than 1% >100. **Partnerships:** Formal partnerships with Wells Fargo, Chevron, Pacific Bell, City of San Ramon, Telecommunication Incubator.

**Student profile.**

| | | | |
|---|---|---|---|
| Out-of-state: | 1% | 25 or older: | 38% |

**Transfer out. Colleges most students transferred to 2007:** University of California: Berkeley, San Francisco State, University of California: East Bay, California State University: Sacramento, University of California: Davis.

**Basis for selection.** Open admission. Open to all applicants with high school diploma (or equivalent) or no longer in high school and over 18 years of age. **Adult students:** SAT/ACT scores not required. **Home-schooled:** Applicants must supply a copy of their private school affidavit.

---

**2007-2008 Annual costs.** Tuition/fees: $610; $5,500 out-of-state. Per-credit charge: $20 in-state; $183 out-of-state. Books/supplies: $1,332. Personal expenses: $2,430.

**Financial aid. Need-based:** Need-based aid available for part-time students.

**Application procedures. Admission:** Priority date 4/1; no deadline. No application fee. Application may be submitted online. Admission notification on a rolling basis beginning on or about 4/1. **Financial aid:** Priority date 3/2, closing date 5/1. FAFSA, institutional form required. Applicants notified on a rolling basis starting 6/1; must reply within 2 week(s) of notification.

**Academics.** The college offers a comprehensive educational program that includes courses in general education, transfer, vocational, basic skills, and life-long learning. These courses are offered in flexible formats that include different hours, days, term length, and a variety of instructional delivery methods (classroom and on-line). **Special study options:** Accelerated study, cooperative education, cross-registration, distance learning, dual enrollment of high school students, ESL, honors, independent study, internships, liberal arts/career combination, study abroad, weekend college. License preparation in dental hygiene. **Credit/placement by examination:** AP, CLEP, institutional tests. **Support services:** Learning center, pre-admission summer program, reduced course load, remedial instruction, study skills assistance, tutoring, writing center.

**Majors. Computer sciences:** General, computer science, networking. **Education:** Physical, special. **Health:** Athletic training. **Liberal arts:** Arts/sciences.

**Most popular majors.** Liberal arts 98%.

**Computing on campus.** 1,000 workstations in library, computer center, student center. Commuter students can connect to campus network. Online course registration, online library, helpline, repair service available.

**Student life. Freshman orientation:** Mandatory. **Policies:** No smoking except in designated areas. **Activities:** Bands, choral groups, dance, drama, film society, literary magazine, music ensembles, musical theater, student government, student newspaper, symphony orchestra, TV station, Afghan club, Alpha Gamma Sigma, Asian student union, DVC Republicans, student health improvement project, Black student union, Latino students' alliance, Muslim student association, Christian Science organization, horticulture club.

**Athletics.** NJCAA. **Intercollegiate:** Baseball M, basketball, cross-country, football (tackle) M, soccer W, softball W, swimming, tennis, track and field, volleyball W, water polo. **Team name:** Vikings.

**Student services.** Adult student services, career counseling, services for economically disadvantaged, student employment services, financial aid counseling, on-campus daycare, personal counseling, placement for graduates, women's services. **Physically disabled:** Services for visually, speech, hearing impaired. **Learning disabled:** Comprehensive services available. **Transfer:** Re-entry adviser for new students. Transfer center, transfer adviser, college fairs on campus for students transferring to 4-year colleges.

**Contact.** E-mail: informationcenter@dvc.edu
Phone: (925) 685-1310 Fax: (925) 685-1551
Cheryll LeMay, Director of Admissions and Records, Diablo Valley College, 321 Golf Club Road, Pleasant Hill, CA 94523

---

## East Los Angeles College
**Monterey Park, California**                  **CB member**
www.elac.edu                                   **CB code: 4296**

▸ Public 2-year community college
▸ Commuter campus in very large city

**General.** Founded in 1945. Regionally accredited. **Enrollment:** 10,030 degree-seeking undergraduates. **Degrees:** 1,219 associate awarded. **Location:** 5 miles from downtown. **Calendar:** Semester, limited summer session. **Full-time faculty:** 244 total. **Part-time faculty:** 494 total.

**Basis for selection.** Open admission, but selective for some programs. Limited admission to nursing and allied health associate programs. Institution uses Assessment Placement Test for English and mathematics placement. Interview required for nursing, respiratory technology majors.

**2007-2008 Annual costs.** Tuition/fees: $622; $5,812 out-of-state. Per-credit charge: $20 in-state; $193 out-of-state.

**Financial aid. Need-based:** Need-based aid available for part-time students. **Non-need-based:** Scholarships awarded for academics. **Additional**

**information:** Need-based enrollment fee waivers available through a state aid program.

**Application procedures. Admission:** No deadline. No application fee. Application may be submitted online. **Financial aid:** Closing date 3/2. FAFSA required. Applicants notified on a rolling basis; must reply within 2 week(s) of notification.

**Academics.** Plan A major requires 18 credits in major; Plan B major requires 36 credits in major. **Special study options:** Accelerated study, co-operative education, cross-registration, distance learning, double major, dual enrollment of high school students, ESL, honors, independent study, study abroad, weekend college. Program for Adult College Education (PACE), ITV and Saturday classes. **Credit/placement by examination:** AP, CLEP. 15 credit hours maximum toward associate degree. **Support services:** GED preparation, learning center, pre-admission summer program, reduced course load, remedial instruction, study skills assistance, tutoring, writing center.

**Majors. Architecture:** Landscape, urban/community planning. **Area/ ethnic studies:** African-American. **Business:** Accounting, administrative services, business admin, international marketing, managerial economics, office technology, office/clerical, real estate. **Communications:** Journalism. **Computer sciences:** General, programming. **Engineering:** General, architectural, civil, electrical, mechanics. **Engineering technology:** Architectural. **Health:** Electrocardiograph technology, medical assistant, nursing (RN), respiratory therapy technology. **History:** General. **Legal studies:** Legal secretary. **Mechanic/repair:** Automotive. **Parks/recreation:** Health/fitness. **Philosophy/religion:** Philosophy. **Physical sciences:** Chemistry, geology, physics. **Protective services:** Police science. **Psychology:** General. **Social sciences:** General, anthropology, economics, geography, political science, sociology. **Visual/performing arts:** Art, dramatic, photography.

**Computing on campus.** 200 workstations in library, computer center, student center. Online course registration, wireless network available.

**Student life. Freshman orientation:** Available. **Activities:** Jazz band, choral groups, dance, drama, music ensembles, student government, student newspaper, Associated Students Organization, engineering club, Spanish club, Chicanos for Creative Medicine, MESA, American Society of Engineers and Architects.

**Athletics.** NJCAA. **Intercollegiate:** Baseball M, basketball, cross-country, diving, football (tackle) M, soccer, softball W, swimming, track and field, volleyball W, wrestling M. **Team name:** Huskies.

**Student services.** Adult student services, career counseling, student employment services, health services, on-campus daycare, personal counseling. **Physically disabled:** Services for visually, hearing impaired. **Transfer:** Pre-admission transcript evaluation for new students. Transfer center, transfer adviser, college fairs on campus for students transferring to 4-year colleges.

**Contact.** Phone: (323) 265-8712 Fax: (323) 265-8688
Jeremy Allred, Associate Dean of Admissions, East Los Angeles College, 1301 Avenida Cesar Chavez, Monterey Park, CA 91754

---

## El Camino College
### Torrance, California
### www.elcamino.edu
**CB code: 4302**

◆ Public 2-year community college
◆ Commuter campus in very large city

**General.** Founded in 1947. Regionally accredited. **Enrollment:** 13,184 degree-seeking undergraduates. **Degrees:** 1,107 associate awarded. **ROTC:** Army. **Location:** 15 miles from Los Angeles. **Calendar:** Semester, limited summer session. **Full-time faculty:** 312 total. **Part-time faculty:** 743 total. **Special facilities:** Anthropology museum, planetarium, conference center, computer/media center, child development center.

**Transfer out. Colleges most students transferred to 2007:** California State University: Long Beach, California State University: Dominguez Hills, California State University: Northridge, University of California: Los Angeles.

**Basis for selection.** Open admission, but selective for some programs. Allied health programs require completion of preparatory courses (anatomy, microbiology, college-level English and mathematics). Interview required for nursing, honors program, x-ray technician, respiratory care majors. **Homeschooled:** Home school must be registered with state of California.

**2007-2008 Annual costs.** Tuition/fees: $629; $5,819 out-of-state. Per-credit charge: $20 in-state; $193 out-of-state. Books/supplies: $630. Personal expenses: $2,160.

**Financial aid. Need-based:** Work-study available for part-time students. **Non-need-based:** Scholarships awarded for academics, art, leadership, music/drama. **Additional information:** Students may apply for Pell grants until May 1.

**Application procedures. Admission:** No deadline. No application fee. Admission notification on a rolling basis beginning on or about 8/20. **Financial aid:** Closing date 5/1. FAFSA, institutional form required. Applicants notified on a rolling basis starting 7/15.

**Academics. Special study options:** Cooperative education, cross-registration, distance learning, double major, dual enrollment of high school students, ESL, honors, independent study, liberal arts/career combination, study abroad, weekend college. **Credit/placement by examination:** CLEP, IB, institutional tests. 15 credit hours maximum toward associate degree. **Support services:** Learning center, remedial instruction, study skills assistance, tutoring, writing center.

**Majors. Agriculture:** Ornamental horticulture. **Area/ethnic studies:** African-American, American, Asian-American, Hispanic-American/Latino/Chicano, Native American. **Biology:** General, botany, zoology. **Business:** General, administrative services, business admin, office management, real estate, sales/distribution. **Communications:** Journalism. **Communications technology:** General. **Computer sciences:** General, computer science. **Construction:** Maintenance. **Education:** Early childhood. **Engineering:** General. **Engineering technology:** Architectural, construction, drafting. **English:** English lit, speech/rhetoric. **Family/consumer sciences:** General. **Foreign languages:** French, German, Japanese, Spanish. **Health:** Licensed practical nurse, medical radiologic technology/radiation therapy, nursing (RN), predental, premedicine, prepharmacy, respiratory therapy technology. **History:** General. **Legal studies:** Paralegal. **Math:** General. **Mechanic/repair:** Auto body, automotive, electronics/electrical, heating/ac/refrig. **Parks/recreation:** Health/fitness. **Personal/culinary services:** Cosmetic. **Philosophy/religion:** Philosophy. **Physical sciences:** Astronomy, chemistry, geology, physics. **Protective services:** Fire safety technology, law enforcement admin, police science. **Psychology:** General. **Social sciences:** Anthropology, economics, geography, political science, sociology. **Visual/performing arts:** Art, dance, dramatic, photography, studio arts.

**Most popular majors.** Business/marketing 13%, health sciences 11%, liberal arts 37%, social sciences 6%.

**Student life. Freshman orientation:** Available. **Activities:** Bands, choral groups, dance, drama, literary magazine, music ensembles, musical theater, student government, student newspaper, symphony orchestra, approximately 60 service, special interest, activist and religious clubs.

**Athletics.** NJCAA. **Intercollegiate:** Badminton W, baseball M, basketball, cross-country, football (tackle) M, golf M, soccer, softball W, swimming, tennis, track and field, volleyball, water polo. **Team name:** Warriors.

**Student services.** Adult student services, career counseling, student employment services, health services, on-campus daycare, personal counseling, placement for graduates, veterans' counselor. **Physically disabled:** Services for visually, speech, hearing impaired. **Transfer:** Re-entry adviser, pre-admission transcript evaluation for new students. Transfer center, transfer adviser, college fairs on campus for students transferring to 4-year colleges.

**Contact.** E-mail: admissionshelp@elcamino.edu
Phone: (310) 532-3670 Toll-free number: (866) 352-2646
Bill Mulrooney, Director of Admissions and Records, El Camino College, 16007 Crenshaw Boulevard, Torrance, CA 90506

---

## El Camino College: Compton Center
### Compton, California
### www.compton.edu
**CB member**
**CB code: 4078**

◆ Public 2-year community college
◆ Commuter campus in small city

**General.** Founded in 1927. Regionally accredited. **Enrollment:** 1,994 degree-seeking undergraduates. **Degrees:** 26 associate awarded. **Location:** 25 miles from Los Angeles. **Calendar:** Semester, limited summer session. **Full-time faculty:** 84 total. **Part-time faculty:** 71 total.

**Transfer out. Colleges most students transferred to 2007:** California State University: Dominguez Hills.

**Basis for selection.** Open admission, but selective for some programs and for out-of-state students. If under 18, applicant must have graduated from high school and passed the California High School Certificate of Proficiency test. Selective admission to nursing programs.

**2007-2008 Annual costs.** Tuition/fees: $629; $5,819 out-of-state. Per-credit charge: $20 in-state; $193 out-of-state. Books/supplies: $650.

**Application procedures. Admission:** No deadline. No application fee. Admission notification on a rolling basis. **Financial aid:** Closing date 5/15. FAFSA required. Applicants notified on a rolling basis starting 5/15.

**Academics. Special study options:** Accelerated study, cooperative education, cross-registration, honors. **Credit/placement by examination:** CLEP, institutional tests. 12 credit hours maximum toward associate degree. **Support services:** Learning center, reduced course load, remedial instruction, tutoring.

**Majors. Area/ethnic studies:** Women's. **Biology:** General, bacteriology, botany. **Business:** Accounting, administrative services, banking/financial services, business admin, entrepreneurial studies, management information systems, office technology, office/clerical, real estate. **Communications:** Journalism. **Communications technology:** Graphics. **Computer sciences:** General, applications programming, data processing. **Education:** Bilingual, physical, special, teacher assistance. **Engineering:** Computer. **Engineering technology:** Construction, drafting, electrical. **English:** English lit, speech/rhetoric. **Family/consumer sciences:** General, child care, clothing/textiles. **Foreign languages:** French, German, Spanish. **Health:** EMT paramedic, licensed practical nurse, medical assistant, medical radiologic technology/radiation therapy, nursing (RN), premedicine, preop/surgical nursing, respiratory therapy technology. **History:** General. **Legal studies:** Paralegal. **Liberal arts:** Arts/sciences. **Math:** General. **Mechanic/repair:** General, auto body, automotive, small engine. **Parks/recreation:** General. **Personal/culinary services:** Cosmetic. **Philosophy/religion:** Philosophy. **Physical sciences:** Astronomy, chemistry, geology, physics. **Production:** Woodworking. **Protective services:** Firefighting, police science. **Psychology:** General. **Social sciences:** General, geography, political science, sociology. **Visual/performing arts:** Art, commercial/advertising art, dance, dramatic.

**Computing on campus.** 35 workstations in computer center.

**Student life. Activities:** Bands, choral groups, dance, drama, music ensembles, musical theater, student government, student newspaper, TV station, Christian club, Moslem student association.

**Athletics. Intercollegiate:** Baseball M, basketball, cross-country, football (tackle) M, tennis M, track and field. **Intramural:** Basketball, tennis.

**Student services.** Career counseling, student employment services, on-campus daycare, personal counseling, placement for graduates, veterans' counselor. **Physically disabled:** Services for visually, speech, hearing impaired. **Transfer:** Transfer adviser, college fairs on campus for students transferring to 4-year colleges.

**Contact.** Phone: (310) 900-1600 ext. 2043 Fax: (310) 900-1695
Hal Bateman, Director of Enrollment Management, El Camino College: Compton Center, 1111 East Artesia Boulevard, Compton, CA 90221

## Empire College
**Santa Rosa, California**
www.empcol.edu　　　　　**CB code: 4275**

- For-profit 2-year business college
- Commuter campus in small city
- Interview required

**General.** Accredited by ACICS. **Enrollment:** 87 degree-seeking undergraduates; 189 non-degree-seeking students. **Degrees:** 89 associate awarded. **Location:** 55 miles from San Francisco. **Calendar:** Continuous. **Full-time faculty:** 30 total; 63% women. **Part-time faculty:** 6 total; 50% women. **Special facilities:** Law library.

**Student profile.** Among degree-seeking undergraduates, 87 enrolled as first-time, first-year students.

| | | | |
|---|---|---|---|
| Women: | 74% | 25 or older: | 50% |

**Transfer out. Colleges most students transferred to 2007:** Santa Rosa Junior College.

**Basis for selection.** Open admission. Scholastic Level Exam (SLE) administered during admission process. Some programs also have typing speed requirement for entrance.

**2008-2009 Annual costs.** Tuition/fees (projected): $8,625. Books/supplies: $1,500. Personal expenses: $201.

**Financial aid.** All financial aid based on need.

**Application procedures. Admission:** No deadline. $75 fee. Admission notification on a rolling basis. No fall term, ongoing 5-week application/entry. **Financial aid:** No deadline. FAFSA required. Applicants notified on a rolling basis.

**Academics. Special study options:** Accelerated study, double major, internships. **Credit/placement by examination:** CLEP. **Support services:** Tutoring.

**Majors. Business:** Accounting, administrative services. **Computer sciences:** Information systems. **Health:** Medical secretary. **Legal studies:** Paralegal.

**Computing on campus.** 375 workstations in computer center. Online library, student web hosting, wireless network available.

**Student life. Freshman orientation:** Mandatory. **Activities:** Student newspaper.

**Student services.** Student employment services, financial aid counseling, placement for graduates. **Transfer:** Re-entry adviser, pre-admission transcript evaluation for new students.

**Contact.** E-mail: dahnja@empirecollege.com
Phone: (707) 546-4000 ext. 238 Fax: (707) 546-4058
Dahnja Straub, Director of Admissions, Empire College, 3035 Cleveland Avenue, Santa Rosa, CA 95403-2100

## Evergreen Valley College
**San Jose, California**
www.evc.edu　　　　　**CB code: 4273**

- Public 2-year community and junior college
- Commuter campus in very large city

**General.** Founded in 1975. Regionally accredited. **Enrollment:** 5,126 degree-seeking undergraduates. **Degrees:** 490 associate awarded. **Location:** 7 miles from downtown. **Calendar:** Semester, extensive summer session. **Full-time faculty:** 100 total; 40% have terminal degrees. **Special facilities:** Hiking trails, parks, observatory, natural habitat (used in natural science and biology course work), cross-country course.

**Transfer out. Colleges most students transferred to 2007:** San Jose State.

**Basis for selection.** Open admission, but selective for some programs. Limited admission for nursing and criminal justice programs. **Home-schooled:** Interview required. Must complete form R-42 and state affidavit.

**2007-2008 Annual costs.** Tuition/fees: $628; $6,118 out-of-state. Per-credit charge: $20 in-state; $203 out-of-state. Books/supplies: $700.

**Application procedures. Admission:** No deadline. No application fee. Application may be submitted online. Admission notification on a rolling basis. **Financial aid:** Priority date 5/31; no closing date. FAFSA required. Applicants notified on a rolling basis.

**Academics. Special study options:** Accelerated study, cooperative education, cross-registration, distance learning, double major, dual enrollment of high school students, ESL, honors, independent study, internships, liberal arts/career combination, weekend college. License preparation in nursing, paramedic. **Credit/placement by examination:** AP, CLEP, institutional tests. 12 credit hours maximum toward associate degree. Assessment testing as prescribed by California law required for placement in English and mathematics. **Support services:** Learning center, reduced course load, remedial instruction, study skills assistance, tutoring, writing center.

**Majors. Business:** Administrative services, fashion, management information systems, office technology, office/clerical. **Computer sciences:** General, applications programming. **Engineering technology:** Drafting. **Health:** Nursing (RN). **Liberal arts:** Arts/sciences. **Protective services:** Police science. **Visual/performing arts:** Commercial/advertising art.

**Computing on campus.** 800 workstations in library, computer center, student center.

**Student life. Freshman orientation:** Mandatory. Preregistration for classes offered. **Activities:** Choral groups, dance, drama, literary magazine, music ensembles, musical theater, student government, student newspaper, Black Students Union, ASPIRE, Enlace, AFFIRM.

**Athletics. NJCAA. Intercollegiate:** Soccer, track and field, volleyball W, wrestling M. **Intramural:** Basketball, football (non-tackle) M. **Team name:** Hawks.

**Student services.** Alcohol/substance abuse counseling, career counseling, services for economically disadvantaged, student employment services, financial aid counseling, health services, minority student services, on-campus daycare, personal counseling, veterans' counselor. **Physically disabled:** Services for visually, speech, hearing impaired. **Transfer:** Transfer center, transfer adviser, college fairs on campus for students transferring to 4-year colleges.

**Contact.** E-mail: lynn.gulkin@evc.edu
Phone: (408) 270-6441 Fax: (408) 223-9351
Octavio Cruz, Interim Director of Admissions and Records, Evergreen Valley College, 3095 Yerba Buena Road, San Jose, CA 95135

## Fashion Careers College
**San Diego, California**
www.fashioncareerscollege.com                CB code: 3494

- Private 2-year business college
- Commuter campus in very large city
- Application essay, interview required

**General.** Accredited by ACICS. **Enrollment:** 85 degree-seeking undergraduates. **Degrees:** 40 associate awarded. **Calendar:** Quarter. **Part-time faculty:** 10 total; 100% women.

**Basis for selection.** Exam score, essay, interview important. Wonderlic test used for admission.

**2007-2008 Annual costs.** Tuition/fees: $17,400.

**Application procedures. Admission:** No deadline. $25 fee. Admission notification on a rolling basis. **Financial aid:** No deadline. FAFSA required.

**Academics. Credit/placement by examination:** CLEP.

**Majors. Business:** Fashion. **Visual/performing arts:** Fashion design.

**Most popular majors.** Business/marketing 50%, visual/performing arts 50%.

**Computing on campus.** 23 workstations in computer center. Repair service available.

**Student life. Freshman orientation:** Mandatory. Held 1 week before classes start.

**Student services.** Career counseling, financial aid counseling, placement for graduates.

**Contact.** E-mail: info@fashioncareerscollege.com
Phone: (619) 275-4700 Toll-free number: (888) 322-2999
Fax: (619) 275-0635
Fashion Careers College, 1923 Morena Boulevard, San Diego, CA 92110

## Fashion Institute of Design and Merchandising: Los Angeles
**Los Angeles, California**            CB member
www.fidm.edu                          CB code: 4457

- For-profit 2-year visual arts and business college
- Commuter campus in very large city
- Application essay, interview required

**General.** Founded in 1969. Regionally accredited. Branch campuses in Orange County, San Francisco and San Diego. **Enrollment:** 4,457 degree-seeking undergraduates. **Degrees:** 18 bachelor's, 1,621 associate awarded. **Calendar:** Quarter, extensive summer session. **Full-time faculty:** 60 total; 23% minority, 57% women. **Part-time faculty:** 232 total; 16% minority, 62% women. **Class size:** 77% < 20, 23% 20-39. **Special facilities:** Hollywood costume collection, costume museum, textile museum, fragrance bottle collection, fashion library.

**Student profile.** Among degree-seeking undergraduates, 1,125 enrolled as first-time, first-year students.

| | | | |
|---|---|---|---|
| Part-time: | 16% | Asian American: | 16% |
| Out-of-state: | 32% | Hispanic American: | 20% |
| Women: | 90% | International: | 7% |
| African American: | 5% | 25 or older: | 19% |

**Basis for selection.** Open admission. High school record, institutional test scores, references, and evidence of interest in major area through work

experience, high school preparation, or extracurricular activities considered. Portfolio required for fashion design, interior design, and visual presentation majors. Out-of-state applicants interviewed by telephone. Projects are required of all students. **Homeschooled:** Transcript of courses and grades, state high school equivalency certificate, interview required.

**2008-2009 Annual costs.** Tuition/fees: $19,700. Tuition and fees may vary depending on program. Books/supplies: $2,060.

**Financial aid. Non-need-based:** Scholarships awarded for academics. **Additional information:** Tuition/fee expenses may be reduced by applying for admission by December 31 of year before student plans to attend.

**Application procedures. Admission:** No deadline. $25 fee. Application may be submitted online. Admission notification on a rolling basis. **Financial aid:** Priority date 3/1; no closing date. FAFSA, institutional form required. Applicants notified on a rolling basis starting 3/15; must reply within 3 week(s) of notification.

**Academics.** Faculty and staff come from related industries. Project-oriented courses give students hands-on experience. **Special study options:** Exchange student, independent study, internships, study abroad. **Credit/placement by examination:** AP, CLEP, IB, institutional tests. 15 credit hours maximum toward associate degree. **Support services:** Learning center, reduced course load, remedial instruction, study skills assistance, tutoring, writing center.

**Majors. Business:** Fashion, marketing, operations, sales/distribution. **Family/consumer sciences:** Apparel marketing, clothing/textiles, fashion consultant, merchandising, textile manufacture, textile science. **Visual/performing arts:** Design, fashion design, fiber arts, graphic design, interior design, metal/jewelry, theater design.

**Most popular majors.** Business/marketing 36%, visual/performing arts 14%.

**Computing on campus.** 350 workstations in library, computer center, student center. Commuter students can connect to campus network. Online course registration, online library, helpline, wireless network available.

**Student life. Freshman orientation:** Mandatory. **Activities:** International student organizations, student government, student newspaper, honor society, Association of Manufacturing Students, visual design forum, student activities committee, ASID, design council, Phi Theta Kappa.

**Student services.** Adult student services, career counseling, student employment services, personal counseling, placement for graduates. **Physically disabled:** Services for visually, hearing impaired. **Transfer:** Pre-admission transcript evaluation for new students. Transfer adviser for students transferring to 4-year colleges.

**Contact.** E-mail: admissionsdirector@fidm.edu
Phone: (213) 624-1200 Toll-free number: (800) 624-1200
Fax: (213) 624-4799
Susan Aronson, Director of Admission, Fashion Institute of Design and Merchandising: Los Angeles, 919 South Grand Avenue, Los Angeles, CA 90015

## Fashion Institute of Design and Merchandising: San Diego
**San Diego, California**
www.fidm.edu                          CB code: 2949

- For-profit 2-year visual arts and business college
- Commuter campus in very large city
- Application essay, interview required

**General.** Regionally accredited. **Enrollment:** 260 degree-seeking undergraduates. **Degrees:** 54 associate awarded. **Calendar:** Quarter, extensive summer session. **Full-time faculty:** 3 total; 67% women. **Part-time faculty:** 24 total; 29% minority, 88% women. **Class size:** 76% < 20, 22% 20-39. **Special facilities:** Branch level access to Hollywood costume collection, perfume collection, fashion library.

**Student profile.** Among degree-seeking undergraduates, 108 enrolled as first-time, first-year students.

| | | | |
|---|---|---|---|
| Part-time: | 19% | Hispanic American: | 15% |
| Women: | 94% | Native American: | 1% |
| African American: | 6% | International: | 3% |
| Asian American: | 18% | 25 or older: | 19% |

**Basis for selection.** Open admission. Out-of-state applicants interviewed by telephone. Portfolio required for fashion design, interior design, and visual presentation majors. **Homeschooled:** Transcript of courses and grades, state high school equivalency certificate, interview required.

**2008-2009 Annual costs.** Tuition/fees: $19,700. Tuition and fees vary by program. Books/supplies: $2,060.

**Financial aid. Non-need-based:** Scholarships awarded for academics.

**Application procedures. Admission:** No deadline. $25 fee. Application may be submitted online. Admission notification on a rolling basis. **Financial aid:** No deadline. FAFSA, institutional form required. Applicants notified on a rolling basis; must reply within 3 week(s) of notification.

**Academics. Special study options:** Distance learning, ESL, independent study. **Credit/placement by examination:** AP, CLEP, IB, institutional tests. 15 credit hours maximum toward associate degree. **Support services:** Learning center, reduced course load, remedial instruction, study skills assistance, tutoring, writing center.

**Majors. Business:** Fashion, marketing. **Family/consumer sciences:** Apparel marketing, clothing/textiles, fashion consultant, merchandising, textile manufacture, textile science. **Visual/performing arts:** Design, fashion design, fiber arts, graphic design, interior design, theater design.

**Computing on campus.** 45 workstations in library, computer center, student center. Commuter students can connect to campus network. Online course registration, online library, helpline, wireless network available.

**Student life. Freshman orientation:** Mandatory. **Activities:** International student organizations, honor students society, Association of Manufacturing Students, alumni association, ASID student chapter, Design Council, Phi Theta Kappa, student activities committee.

**Student services.** Adult student services, career counseling, student employment services, financial aid counseling, personal counseling, placement for graduates. **Physically disabled:** Services for visually, hearing impaired. **Transfer:** Transfer adviser for students transferring to 4-year colleges.

**Contact.** E-mail: admissionsdirector@fidm.edu
Phone: (619) 235-2049 Toll-free number: (800) 243-3436
Fax: (619) 232-4322
Susan Aronson, Director of Admissions, Fashion Institute of Design and Merchandising: San Diego, 1010 Second Avenue, Suite 2000, San Diego, CA 92101

## Fashion Institute of Design and Merchandising: San Francisco

**San Francisco, California**
www.fidm.com                    CB code: 4988

▶ For-profit 2-year visual arts and business college
▶ Commuter campus in very large city
▶ Application essay, interview required

**General.** Founded in 1969. Regionally accredited. **Enrollment:** 959 degree-seeking undergraduates. **Degrees:** 363 associate awarded. **Location:** Downtown. **Calendar:** Quarter, extensive summer session. **Full-time faculty:** 13 total; 8% minority, 69% women. **Part-time faculty:** 57 total; 18% minority, 68% women. **Class size:** 77% < 20, 23% 20-39. **Special facilities:** Branch level access to Hollywood costume collection, costume museum, textiles museum, perfume collection, fashion library.

**Student profile.** Among degree-seeking undergraduates, 272 enrolled as first-time, first-year students.

| | | | |
|---|---|---|---|
| Part-time: | 18% | Hispanic American: | 15% |
| Out-of-state: | 8% | Native American: | 1% |
| Women: | 93% | International: | 3% |
| African American: | 6% | 25 or older: | 14% |
| Asian American: | 18% | | |

**Basis for selection.** Open admission. Out-of-state applicants interviewed by telephone. Portfolio required for fashion design, interior design, design and visual presentation majors. Projects required for all students.

**2008-2009 Annual costs.** Tuition/fees: $19,700. Tuition and fees vary by program. Books/supplies: $2,060.

**Financial aid. Non-need-based:** Scholarships awarded for academics.

**Application procedures. Admission:** No deadline. $25 fee. Application may be submitted online. Admission notification on a rolling basis. **Financial aid:** No deadline. FAFSA, institutional form required. Applicants

notified on a rolling basis starting 3/15; must reply within 3 week(s) of notification.

**Academics. Special study options:** Distance learning, exchange student, internships, study abroad. **Credit/placement by examination:** AP, CLEP, IB, institutional tests. 15 credit hours maximum toward associate degree. **Support services:** Learning center, reduced course load, remedial instruction, study skills assistance, tutoring, writing center.

**Majors. Business:** Fashion. **Computer sciences:** Computer graphics, webmaster. **Family/consumer sciences:** Apparel marketing, clothing/textiles, fashion consultant, merchandising, textile manufacture, textile science. **Visual/performing arts:** General, commercial/advertising art, design, fashion design, graphic design, interior design, theater design.

**Most popular majors.** Business/marketing 36%, visual/performing arts 64%.

**Computing on campus.** 100 workstations in library, computer center. Commuter students can connect to campus network. Online course registration, online library, helpline, wireless network available.

**Student life. Freshman orientation:** Mandatory. **Activities:** International student organizations, student newspaper, honor students society, Association of Manufacturing Students, alumni association, ASID student chapter, DECA, visual design forum, student activities committee, design council, Phi Theta Kappa.

**Student services.** Adult student services, career counseling, student employment services, personal counseling, placement for graduates. **Physically disabled:** Services for visually, hearing impaired. **Transfer:** Transfer adviser for students transferring to 4-year colleges.

**Contact.** E-mail: admissionsdirector@fidm.edu
Phone: (415) 675-5200 Toll-free number: (800) 422-3436
Fax: (415) 394-9700
Sheryl Badalamente, Director of Admissions, Fashion Institute of Design and Merchandising: San Francisco, 55 Stockton Street, San Francisco, CA 94108-5805

## Feather River College

**Quincy, California**
www.frc.edu                    CB code: 4318

▶ Public 2-year community and liberal arts college
▶ Residential campus in small town

**General.** Founded in 1968. Regionally accredited. **Enrollment:** 627 degree-seeking undergraduates. **Degrees:** 143 associate awarded. **Location:** 150 miles from Sacramento, 80 miles from Reno, Nevada. **Calendar:** Semester, limited summer session. **Full-time faculty:** 25 total. **Part-time faculty:** 85 total. **Class size:** 54% < 20, 46% 20-39. **Special facilities:** Fish hatchery, horse boarding facility, state wildlife preserve.

**Student profile.**

| | | | |
|---|---|---|---|
| Out-of-state: | 30% | Live on campus: | 10% |
| 25 or older: | 35% | | |

**Transfer out. Colleges most students transferred to 2007:** California State University: Chico, Humboldt State University, University of Nevada: Reno, California Polytechnic State University: San Luis Obispo, University of California: Davis.

**Basis for selection.** Open admission. Institute's own test required of all students for placement purposes. **Learning Disabled:** Placement tests in English and Math are required for new students with no college experience.

**2007-2008 Annual costs.** Tuition/fees: $654; $6,054 out-of-state. Per-credit charge: $20 in-state; $200 out-of-state. Room only: $4,208. Books/supplies: $1,386.

**Financial aid. Need-based:** Need-based aid available for part-time students. Work-study available nights, weekends and for part-time students.

**Application procedures. Admission:** No deadline. No application fee. Application may be submitted online. **Financial aid:** No deadline. FAFSA required. Applicants notified on a rolling basis starting 7/30; must reply within 3 week(s) of notification.

**Academics.** General education/core courses are offered that satisfy all lower division requirements of California State University, University of California, and University of Nevada system. **Special study options:** Cooperative education, cross-registration, distance learning, double major, dual enrollment of high school students, ESL, honors, independent study, liberal arts/career combination. License preparation in nursing, paramedic. **Credit/placement by examination:** AP, CLEP, IB, institutional tests. 12 credit hours maximum toward associate degree. **Support services:** GED preparation and test center, learning center, reduced course load, remedial instruction, study skills assistance, tutoring.

**Majors. Agriculture:** Agribusiness operations, business, equestrian studies, equine science, farm/ranch. **Biology:** General, wildlife. **Business:** Business admin, office/clerical. **Computer sciences:** Computer science. **Conservation:** General, environmental studies, fisheries, forest technology, forestry, management/policy, wildlife. **Construction:** Carpentry, maintenance. **Education:** General, early childhood. **Engineering technology:** Construction. **English:** English lit. **Family/consumer sciences:** Child care. **Health:** Licensed practical nurse. **History:** General. **Liberal arts:** Arts/sciences. **Math:** General. **Parks/recreation:** Exercise sciences, health/fitness, sports admin. **Protective services:** Law enforcement admin. **Social sciences:** General, criminology. **Visual/performing arts:** Art. **Other:** Outdoor recreation leadership.

**Most popular majors.** Agriculture 15%, business/marketing 8%, liberal arts 70%.

**Computing on campus.** 120 workstations in dormitories, library, computer center, student center. Dormitories wired for high-speed internet access. Online library available.

**Student life. Freshman orientation:** Mandatory, $26 fee. 2-day, 1-night orientation held in fall and spring. **Housing:** Apartments available. **Activities:** Choral groups, drama, literary magazine, musical theater, student government, Phi Theta Kappa.

**Athletics.** NJCAA. **Intercollegiate:** Baseball M, basketball, football (tackle) M, rodeo, soccer, softball W, volleyball W. **Intramural:** Basketball, equestrian, skiing, softball, volleyball. **Team name:** Golden Eagles.

**Student services.** Adult student services, career counseling, services for economically disadvantaged, student employment services, financial aid counseling, health services, on-campus daycare, personal counseling, placement for graduates, veterans' counselor. **Physically disabled:** Services for visually, speech, hearing impaired. **Transfer:** Re-entry adviser, pre-admission transcript evaluation for new students. Transfer center, transfer adviser, college fairs on campus for students transferring to 4-year colleges.

**Contact.** Phone: (530) 283-0202 ext. 285 Toll-free number: (800) 442-9799 ext. 285 Fax: (530) 283-3757 Tama Bolton, Registrar, Feather River College, 570 Golden Eagle Avenue, Quincy, CA 95971

## Folsom Lake College
**Folsom, California**
www.flc.losrios.edu

CB code: 4462

- Public 2-year community college
- Commuter campus in large town

**General.** Regionally accredited. **Enrollment:** 5,216 degree-seeking undergraduates. **Degrees:** 507 associate awarded. **Location:** 25 miles from Sacramento. **Calendar:** Semester, limited summer session. **Full-time faculty:** 80 total. **Part-time faculty:** 180 total. **Special facilities:** Community park, observatory.

**Transfer out. Colleges most students transferred to 2007:** California State University: Sacramento, University of California: Davis.

**Basis for selection.** Open admission. **Adult students:** SAT/ACT scores not required.

**2007-2008 Annual costs.** Tuition/fees: $632; $225 out-of-district; $5,822 out-of-state. Per-credit charge: $20 in-state; $193 out-of-state. Books/supplies: $1,386. Personal expenses: $2,126.

**Application procedures. Admission:** No deadline. No application fee. Application may be submitted online.

**Academics. Special study options:** Distance learning, ESL, study abroad. **Credit/placement by examination:** CLEP, institutional tests. **Support services:** Study skills assistance, tutoring, writing center.

**Majors. Biology:** General. **Business:** General, accounting, administrative services, finance, management science, marketing, real estate, small business admin. **Communications:** General, organizational. **Computer sciences:** General. **Education:** Early childhood. **Liberal arts:** Arts/sciences. **Math:** General. **Psychology:** General. **Public administration:** Human services. **Visual/performing arts:** Art.

**Computing on campus.** Online course registration, wireless network available.

**Student life. Freshman orientation:** Available. **Activities:** Choral groups, dance, drama, international student organizations, literary magazine, music ensembles, student government.

**Athletics. Team name:** Falcons.

**Student services.** Services for economically disadvantaged, financial aid counseling, on-campus daycare, veterans' counselor. **Physically disabled:** Services for visually, speech, hearing impaired. **Transfer:** Transfer center, transfer adviser, college fairs on campus for students transferring to 4-year colleges.

**Contact.** Phone: (916) 608-6500 Fax: (916) 608-6569 Christine Wurzer, Admissions and Records Supervisor, Folsom Lake College, 10 College Parkway, Folsom, CA 95630

## Foothill College
**Los Altos Hills, California**
www.foothill.edu

CB code: 4315

- Public 2-year community college
- Commuter campus in large town

**General.** Founded in 1958. Regionally accredited. **Enrollment:** 7,844 degree-seeking undergraduates. **Degrees:** 521 associate awarded. **ROTC:** Army, Naval, Air Force. **Calendar:** Quarter, limited summer session. **Full-time faculty:** 205 total; 58% women. **Part-time faculty:** 452 total. **Special facilities:** Center for innovation, Japanese cultural center, observatory, bamboo garden, dental health clinic travel careers computer lab, math center.

**Student profile.** Among degree-seeking undergraduates, 3,183 transferred in from other institutions.

**Transfer out. Colleges most students transferred to 2007:** San Jose State, University of California: Berkeley, University of California: Santa Cruz, University of California: Los Angeles, University of California: Davis.

**Basis for selection.** Open admission, but selective for some programs. Allied health programs have special prerequisites: using point system to rank required college-level and general education classes, top 20-40 students selected for admission. Must be 2-year transfer.

**2007-2008 Annual costs.** Tuition/fees: $625; $5,350 out-of-state. Per-credit charge: $13 in-state; $118 out-of-state. Books/supplies: $1,314. Personal expenses: $2,466.

**Financial aid.** All financial aid based on need. Need-based aid available for part-time students.

**Application procedures. Admission:** No deadline. No application fee. Application may be submitted online. Admission notification on a rolling basis. **Financial aid:** Priority date 3/30; no closing date. FAFSA, institutional form required. Applicants notified on a rolling basis; must reply within 2 week(s) of notification.

**Academics.** NASA Ames Research Center internships available. **Special study options:** Cooperative education, cross-registration, distance learning, ESL, exchange student, honors, independent study, internships, liberal arts/career combination, study abroad, weekend college. License preparation in dental hygiene, paramedic, radiology, real estate. **Credit/placement by examination:** AP, CLEP, institutional tests. 20 credit hours maximum toward associate degree. **Support services:** Learning center, remedial instruction, study skills assistance, tutoring, writing center.

**Honors college/program.** Continuing students should have minimum 3.3 cumulative GPA in 10 or more units completed at Foothill College. New students must have minimum 3.5 cumulative high school GPA or SAT total of at least 2100 or Enhanced ACT Composite of 26 or minimum 3.3 cumulative GPA in 10 or more units completed at another accredited college or university. Minimum AP English score of 3 or 2, minimum score on assessment test of ENGL Reading 93 and ENGL Writing 111 or completion of English 1A with a grade of B or better. Letter of recommendation and personal statement required.

**Majors. Agriculture:** Landscaping, nursery operations, ornamental horticulture. **Area/ethnic studies:** American, women's. **Biology:** General, bioinformatics, biotechnology. **Business:** Accounting, business admin, international, office technology, real estate, tourism promotion. **Communications:** General, broadcast journalism, media studies, radio/tv. **Computer sciences:** General, computer graphics, computer science, database management, information technology, LAN/WAN management, programming. **Construction:** Electrician. **Education:** Early childhood. **Engineering:** General, software.

**Engineering technology:** Biomedical, electrical. **English:** Creative writing, English lit, speech/rhetoric. **Family/consumer sciences:** Child development. **Foreign languages:** Chinese, French, Japanese, linguistics, Spanish. **Health:** Athletic training, dental assistant, dental hygiene, medical radiologic technology/radiation therapy, pharmacy assistant, physician assistant, predental, premedicine, prepharmacy, preveterinary, radiologic technology/medical imaging, respiratory therapy assistant, respiratory therapy technology, sonography, veterinary technology/assistant. **History:** General. **Interdisciplinary:** Intercultural. **Legal studies:** Prelaw. **Liberal arts:** Arts/sciences, library assistant. **Math:** General. **Mechanic/repair:** Aircraft. **Philosophy/religion:** Philosophy. **Physical sciences:** Chemistry, geology, physics. **Psychology:** General. **Science technology:** Biological. **Social sciences:** General, anthropology, economics, geography, political science, sociology. **Visual/performing arts:** Art, art history/conservation, commercial/advertising art, dramatic, photography, studio arts, theater design. **Other:** Informatics, Nanoscience.

**Most popular majors.** Business/marketing 15%, health sciences 28%, interdisciplinary studies 8%, social sciences 16%.

**Computing on campus.** 200 workstations in library, computer center, student center. Commuter students can connect to campus network. Online course registration, online library, wireless network available.

**Student life. Freshman orientation:** Available. **Activities:** Bands, choral groups, dance, drama, film society, music ensembles, musical theater, radio station, student government, student newspaper, symphony orchestra, TV station, 32 different multicultural/ethnic campus clubs.

**Athletics. Intercollegiate:** Basketball, diving, football (tackle) M, golf, soccer, softball W, swimming, tennis, volleyball W, water polo W. **Intramural:** Basketball, cheerleading, football (non-tackle), soccer, softball, volleyball. **Team name:** Owls.

**Student services.** Adult student services, alcohol/substance abuse counseling, career counseling, services for economically disadvantaged, student employment services, financial aid counseling, health services, legal services, minority student services, personal counseling, placement for graduates, veterans' counselor. **Physically disabled:** Services for visually, speech, hearing impaired. **Transfer:** Transfer adviser, college fairs on campus for students transferring to 4-year colleges.

**Contact.** Phone: (650) 949-7325 Fax: (650) 949-7048
Jerry Cellilo, Interim Dean Counseling and Matriculation, Foothill College, 12345 El Monte Road, Los Altos Hills, CA 94022

---

## Fremont College
**Cerritos, California**
**www.fremont.edu**                                **CB code: 3007**

- For-profit 2-year health science and career college
- Commuter campus in very large city
- Application essay, interview required

**General.** Accredited by ACCSCT. Year-round program with starts every 5 weeks. **Enrollment:** 93 degree-seeking undergraduates. **Degrees:** 36 associate awarded. **Location:** 20 miles from Los Angeles. **Calendar:** Continuous. **Full-time faculty:** 2 total. **Part-time faculty:** 10 total. **Class size:** 58% < 20, 42% 20-39.

**Student profile.** Among degree-seeking undergraduates, 93% enrolled in a vocational program.

**Basis for selection.** Open admission, but selective for some programs. High school diploma or GED and successful completion of CPAt required. **Homeschooled:** State high school equivalency certificate required.

**2008-2009 Annual costs.** Paralegal: $24,811. Sports therapy: $22,411. Business administration: $25,375.

**2006-2007 Financial aid.** All financial aid based on need. 47% of total undergraduate aid awarded as scholarships/grants, 53% as loans/jobs.

**Application procedures. Admission:** No deadline. $85 fee. **Financial aid:** FAFSA, institutional form required.

**Academics. Special study options:** Accelerated study. **Credit/placement by examination:** CLEP. **Support services:** Tutoring.

**Majors. Business:** Banking/financial services, real estate. **English:** English lit. **Legal studies:** Paralegal. **Parks/recreation:** Exercise sciences.

**Computing on campus.** 30 workstations in library, computer center.

---

**Student life. Freshman orientation:** Available. Preregistration for classes offered.

**Student services.** Financial aid counseling, placement for graduates. **Transfer:** Pre-admission transcript evaluation for new students.

**Contact.** E-mail: leads@fremont.edu
Phone: (562) 809-5100 Toll-free number: (877) 344-2345
Fax: (562) 809-7100
Admissions Director, Fremont College, 18000 Studebaker Road, 900A, Cerritos, CA 90703-5342

---

## Fresno City College
**Fresno, California**                              **CB member**
**www.fresnocitycollege.edu**                       **CB code: 4311**

- Public 2-year community and liberal arts college
- Commuter campus in large city

**General.** Founded in 1910. Regionally accredited. **Enrollment:** 10,693 degree-seeking undergraduates. **Degrees:** 1,203 associate awarded. **ROTC:** Army, Air Force. **Location:** 185 miles from San Francisco. **Calendar:** Semester, extensive summer session. **Full-time faculty:** 309 total; 29% minority, 47% women. **Part-time faculty:** 742 total; 22% minority, 43% women. **Class size:** 28% < 20, 59% 20-39, 7% 40-49, 4% 50-99, 3% >100. **Special facilities:** Anthropology museum, greenhouse and koi pond, high-tech laboratory for disabled students.

**Student profile.**

| Out-of-state: | 2% | 25 or older: | 39% |
|---|---|---|---|

**Transfer out. Colleges most students transferred to 2007:** California State University: Fresno, University of Phoenix, National University, Fresno Pacific University.

**Basis for selection.** Open admission, but selective for some programs. Limited admission to allied health programs, police academy, and apprenticeship programs.

**2007-2008 Annual costs.** Tuition/fees: $630; $5,820 out-of-state. Per-credit charge: $20 in-state; $193 out-of-state. Books/supplies: $1,206. Personal expenses: $1,710.

**Financial aid.** All financial aid based on need. Need-based aid available for part-time students. Work-study available for part-time students. **Additional information:** Board of Governors Grant Program to offset enrollment fees based on untaxed income, low income, or calculated need. Students qualifying for program also automatically exempt from health fees. March 2 application deadline for California grants.

**Application procedures. Admission:** No deadline. No application fee. Application may be submitted online. Admission notification on a rolling basis. **Financial aid:** Priority date 4/15; no closing date. FAFSA required. Applicants notified on a rolling basis starting 4/1.

**Academics. Special study options:** Accelerated study, cross-registration, distance learning, double major, dual enrollment of high school students, ESL, honors, independent study, internships, study abroad, weekend college. License preparation in dental hygiene, nursing, radiology, real estate. **Credit/placement by examination:** AP, CLEP, institutional tests. 48 credit hours maximum toward associate degree. **Support services:** Learning center, pre-admission summer program, reduced course load, remedial instruction, study skills assistance, tutoring, writing center.

**Majors. Agriculture:** General, food science. **Area/ethnic studies:** African-American, Hispanic-American/Latino/Chicano, Native American, women's. **Business:** General, accounting, administrative services, banking/financial services, business admin, fashion, insurance, office/clerical, purchasing, real estate. **Communications:** General, journalism. **Communications technology:** Graphic/printing. **Computer sciences:** General, computer science, data processing, information systems, programming. **Conservation:** General. **Construction:** Carpentry, electrician, maintenance, pipefitting, power transmission. **Education:** Bilingual, early childhood, multi-level teacher. **Engineering:** General. **Engineering technology:** Drafting. **English:** English lit, speech/rhetoric. **Family/consumer sciences:** General, child care, clothing/textiles, food/nutrition, institutional food production. **Foreign languages:** General, Spanish. **Health:** Clinical lab technology, dental hygiene, medical assistant, medical radiologic technology/radiation therapy, medical records technology, medical secretary, medical transcription, nursing (RN), respiratory therapy technology, substance abuse counseling. **History:** General. **Interdisciplinary:** Biological/physical sciences. **Legal studies:** Legal secretary, paralegal. **Liberal arts:** Arts/sciences, library science. **Math:** General. **Mechanic/repair:** General, auto body, automotive, electronics/electrical, heating/ac/refrig, industrial. **Parks/recreation:** General, facilities management. **Physical sciences: Chemistry. **Protective services:** Corrections, firefighting, law enforcement admin, police science. **Psychology:** General. **Public administration:** General, social work. **Social sciences:** General, anthropology, criminology, geography, sociology. **Transportation:** General. **Visual/performing arts:** General, art, crafts, dance, dramatic, music management, photography, piano/organ, printmaking, theater design, voice/opera.

**Most popular majors.** Health sciences 30%, liberal arts 55%.

**Computing on campus.** 400 workstations in library, computer center. Commuter students can connect to campus network. Online course registration, online library, wireless network available.

**Student life. Freshman orientation:** Available. **Activities:** Bands, choral groups, dance, drama, film society, international student organizations, literary magazine, music ensembles, musical theater, student government, student newspaper, symphony orchestra, TV station, Christian Athletes in Acting, MECHA, Pan American Association, Alpha Gamma Sigma, Phi Theta Kappa.

**Athletics.** NJCAA. **Intercollegiate:** Badminton, baseball M, basketball, cheerleading, cross-country, football (tackle) M, golf, soccer, softball W, tennis, track and field, volleyball W, wrestling M. **Intramural:** Basketball, football (non-tackle), soccer, softball, table tennis, volleyball, weight lifting. **Team name:** Rams.

**Student services.** Adult student services, career counseling, services for economically disadvantaged, student employment services, financial aid counseling, health services, minority student services, on-campus daycare, personal counseling, placement for graduates, veterans' counselor. **Physically disabled:** Services for visually, speech, hearing impaired. **Transfer:** Transfer center, transfer adviser, college fairs on campus for students transferring to 4-year colleges.

**Contact.** E-mail: info@scccd.com
Phone: (559) 442-4600 Toll-free number: (866) 245-3276
Fax: (559) 237-4232
John Cummings, District Dean of Admissions, Records and Institutional Research, Fresno City College, 1101 East University Avenue, Fresno, CA 93741

## Fullerton College
**Fullerton, California**
**www.fullcoll.edu**
CB code: 4314

- Public 2-year community and technical college
- Commuter campus in small city

**General.** Founded in 1913. Regionally accredited. **Enrollment:** 20,136 undergraduates. **Degrees:** 960 associate awarded. **ROTC:** Naval. **Location:** 35 miles from Los Angeles. **Calendar:** Semester, extensive summer session. **Full-time faculty:** 315 total. **Part-time faculty:** 480 total.

**Basis for selection.** Open admission. College-administered English, reading, and math exams used for placement.

**2007-2008 Annual costs.** Tuition/fees: $628; $5,488 out-of-state. Per-credit charge: $20 in-state; $182 out-of-state. Books/supplies: $648. Personal expenses: $1,818.

**Application procedures. Admission:** No deadline. No application fee. Admission notification on a rolling basis. **Financial aid:** No deadline. FAFSA required. Applicants notified on a rolling basis.

**Academics. Special study options:** Distance learning, double major, dual enrollment of high school students, ESL, independent study, internships, study abroad. **Credit/placement by examination:** AP, CLEP, institutional tests. 15 credit hours maximum toward associate degree. **Support services:** Learning center, remedial instruction, tutoring.

**Majors. Agriculture:** Horticulture, nursery operations. **Architecture:** Landscape. **Area/ethnic studies:** Latin American. **Biology:** General, bacteriology, zoology. **Business:** Accounting, administrative services, business admin, fashion, international, management information systems, purchasing, real estate, tourism promotion. **Communications:** General, broadcast journalism, journalism. **Communications technology:** Graphic/printing. **Computer sciences:** General, applications programming, data processing. **Conservation:** General, fisheries, forestry. **Construction:** Carpentry, maintenance. **Education:** Business, trade/industrial. **Engineering:** General. **Engineering technology:** Drafting, electrical. **English:** English lit, speech/rhetoric. **Family/consumer sciences:** General, child care, family studies. **Foreign languages:** General. **Health:** Clinical lab science, prenursing. **History:** General. **Legal studies:** Legal secretary, paralegal. **Liberal arts:** Arts/sciences, library assistant. **Math:** General. **Mechanic/repair:** Auto body. **Parks/recreation:** General. **Personal/culinary services:** Cosmetic. **Philosophy/**

religion: Philosophy. **Physical sciences:** Astronomy, chemistry, geology, physics. **Protective services:** Police science. **Psychology:** General. **Social sciences:** Anthropology, economics, geography, political science, sociology. **Visual/performing arts:** General, art, commercial/advertising art, dance, design, dramatic, fashion design.

**Student life. Activities:** Bands, choral groups, dance, drama, film society, literary magazine, music ensembles, musical theater, radio station, student government, student newspaper, symphony orchestra, TV station, volunteer bureau, Movimiento Estudiantil Chicano de Aztlan.

**Athletics. Intercollegiate:** Badminton, baseball M, basketball, cross-country, diving, football (tackle) M, golf M, gymnastics, soccer, softball W, swimming, tennis, track and field, volleyball, water polo M. **Team name:** Hornets.

**Student services.** Adult student services, career counseling, student employment services, health services, on-campus daycare, personal counseling, placement for graduates, veterans' counselor. **Physically disabled:** Services for visually, speech, hearing impaired. **Transfer:** Transfer adviser for students transferring to 4-year colleges.

**Contact.** E-mail: admissions@fullcoll.edu
Phone: (714) 992-7568
Peter Fong, Vice President, Student Services, Fullerton College, 321 East Chapman Avenue, Fullerton, CA 92832-2095

## Gavilan College
**Gilroy, California**
**www.gavilan.edu**
CB code: 4678

- Public 2-year community college
- Large town

**General.** Founded in 1919. Regionally accredited. **Enrollment:** 3,115 degree-seeking undergraduates. **Degrees:** 264 associate awarded. **Location:** 35 miles from San Jose. **Calendar:** Semester, limited summer session. **Full-time faculty:** 71 total; 11% have terminal degrees. **Part-time faculty:** 116 total; 3% have terminal degrees. **Special facilities:** Golf course, hiking trails.

**Student profile.**

| | | | |
|---|---|---|---|
| African American: | 2% | Native American: | 1% |
| Asian American: | 5% | 25 or older: | 50% |
| Hispanic American: | 48% | | |

**Transfer out. Colleges most students transferred to 2007:** San Jose State, California State University: Monterey Bay, University of California: Santa Cruz.

**Basis for selection.** Open admission.

**2007-2008 Annual costs.** Tuition/fees: $638; $6,128 out-of-state. Per-credit charge: $20 in-state; $203 out-of-state. Books/supplies: $1,332. Personal expenses: $2,430.

**Application procedures. Admission:** No deadline. No application fee. Application must be submitted on paper. Admission notification on a rolling basis. **Financial aid:** Priority date 6/30; no closing date. FAFSA required. Applicants notified on a rolling basis starting 7/15; must reply within 2 week(s) of notification.

**Academics. Special study options:** Distance learning, dual enrollment of high school students, ESL, honors, independent study, internships, liberal arts/career combination, study abroad. License preparation in aviation, nursing. **Credit/placement by examination:** AP, CLEP, institutional tests. **Support services:** Learning center, reduced course load, remedial instruction, study skills assistance, tutoring, writing center.

**Majors. Biology:** General, ecology. **Business:** General. **Communications:** General, journalism. **Computer sciences:** General, computer graphics. **English:** English lit. **Foreign languages:** Spanish. **Health:** Nursing (RN). **History:** General. **Liberal arts:** Arts/sciences. **Math:** General. **Mechanic/repair:** Aircraft. **Personal/culinary services:** Cosmetic. **Philosophy/religion:** Philosophy. **Physical sciences:** Astronomy, chemistry, geology. **Protective services:** Corrections. **Psychology:** General. **Social sciences:** General, anthropology, economics, geography, political science, sociology. **Visual/performing arts:** Art, art history/conservation, dramatic, music performance, studio arts, theater design.

**Most popular majors.** Education 6%, health sciences 18%, liberal arts 61%, security/protective services 6%.

**Computing on campus.** 600 workstations in library, computer center. Wireless network available.

**Student life. Freshman orientation:** Mandatory. **Activities:** Choral groups, drama, literary magazine, music ensembles, musical theater, student government, student newspaper, symphony orchestra, TV station.

**Athletics. Intercollegiate:** Baseball M, basketball, football (tackle) M, golf, soccer W, softball W, tennis, volleyball W. **Team name:** Rams.

**Student services.** Adult student services, career counseling, services for economically disadvantaged, financial aid counseling, health services, on-campus daycare, personal counseling, veterans' counselor. **Physically disabled:** Services for visually, speech, hearing impaired. **Learning disabled:** Comprehensive services available. **Transfer:** Transfer center, transfer adviser, college fairs on campus for students transferring to 4-year colleges.

**Contact.** Phone: (408) 848-4735 Fax: (408) 848-4940
Joy Parker, Director of Admissions and Records, Gavilan College, 5055 Santa Teresa Boulevard, Gilroy, CA 95020

---

## Glendale Community College

| | |
|---|---|
| Glendale, California | **CB member** |
| www.glendale.edu | **CB code: 4327** |

◆ Public 2-year community college
◆ Commuter campus in small city

**General.** Founded in 1927. Regionally accredited. **Enrollment:** 11,651 degree-seeking undergraduates. **Degrees:** 787 associate awarded. **Location:** 10 miles from Los Angeles. **Calendar:** Semester, limited summer session. **Full-time faculty:** 250 total. **Part-time faculty:** 610 total. **Class size:** 35% < 20, 50% 20-39, 10% 40-49, 5% 50-99, less than 1% >100. **Special facilities:** Science center with planetarium, Baja California (Mexico) field station.

**Student profile.** Among degree-seeking undergraduates, 71% enrolled in a transfer program, 7% enrolled in a vocational program, 9% already have a bachelor's degree or higher.

| | | | |
|---|---|---|---|
| Out-of-state: | 1% | Hispanic American: | 23% |
| African American: | 3% | International: | 21% |
| Asian American: | 10% | 25 or older: | 41% |

**Transfer out. Colleges most students transferred to 2007:** California State University: Northridge, University of California: Los Angeles, California State University: Los Angeles, University of Southern California.

**Basis for selection.** Open admission, but selective for some programs. Nursing program has special requirements.

**2007-2008 Annual costs.** Tuition/fees: $633; $5,583 out-of-state. Per-credit charge: $20 in-state; $185 out-of-state. Books/supplies: $1,332. Personal expenses: $2,340.

**Financial aid.** All financial aid based on need. Need-based aid available for part-time students. Work-study available nights, weekends and for part-time students.

**Application procedures. Admission:** Priority date 4/15; no deadline. No application fee. Application may be submitted online. Admission notification on a rolling basis. **Financial aid:** Priority date 4/15; no closing date. FAFSA, institutional form required. Applicants notified on a rolling basis starting 6/15; must reply within 2 week(s) of notification.

**Academics. Special study options:** Cooperative education, distance learning, dual enrollment of high school students, ESL, honors, independent study, internships, study abroad. License preparation in aviation, nursing, real estate. **Credit/placement by examination:** AP, CLEP, institutional tests. 12 credit hours maximum toward associate degree. **Support services:** GED preparation and test center, learning center, remedial instruction, study skills assistance, tutoring, writing center.

**Honors college/program.** Scholars program admits academically accomplished students and offers priority transfer opportunites at UCLA, USC, Pepperdine, and others.

**Majors. Biology:** General. **Business:** General, accounting, administrative services, hospitality/recreation, office management, real estate. **Communications:** Broadcast journalism, journalism. **Computer sciences:** General. **Education:** Early childhood, multi-level teacher. **Engineering technology:** Drafting. **English:** Composition, English lit. **Family/consumer sciences:** General, child care, clothing/textiles, food/nutrition. **Foreign languages:** General, French, Spanish. **Health:** Licensed practical nurse, medical assistant, medical secretary, nursing (RN). **History:** General. **Interdisciplinary:** Biological/physical sciences. **Legal studies:** Legal secretary, paralegal. **Liberal arts:** Arts/sciences, humanities. **Math:** General. **Mechanic/repair:** Aircraft. **Parks/recreation:** General. **Personal/culinary services:** Cosmetic,

culinary arts. **Philosophy/religion:** Philosophy. **Physical sciences:** Chemistry, physics. **Protective services:** Fire safety technology, law enforcement admin, police science. **Psychology:** General. **Social sciences:** General, anthropology, economics, sociology. **Visual/performing arts:** General, commercial/advertising art, dance, theater design.

**Most popular majors.** Business/marketing 15%, English 7%, health sciences 11%, liberal arts 52%, social sciences 6%.

**Computing on campus.** 1,000 workstations in library, computer center. Online course registration, helpline, repair service, wireless network available.

**Student life. Freshman orientation:** Available. **Activities:** Bands, choral groups, dance, drama, literary magazine, music ensembles, musical theater, radio station, student government, student newspaper, TV station, International Student Association, Armenian Student Association, Korean Christian Club, Organization of Latin for Higher Education, Association of Latin American Students.

**Athletics. Intercollegiate:** Baseball M, basketball, cross-country, football (tackle) M, soccer M, tennis, track and field, volleyball W. **Team name:** Vaqueros.

**Student services.** Adult student services, career counseling, services for economically disadvantaged, student employment services, financial aid counseling, health services, on-campus daycare, personal counseling, placement for graduates, veterans' counselor. **Physically disabled:** Services for visually, speech, hearing impaired. **Learning disabled:** Comprehensive services available. **Transfer:** Re-entry adviser for new students. Transfer center, transfer adviser, college fairs on campus for students transferring to 4-year colleges.

**Contact.** E-mail: info@glendale.edu
Phone: (818) 240-1000 ext. 5901 Fax: (818) 549-9436
Sharon Combs, Dean of Admissions and Records, Glendale Community College, 1500 North Verdugo Road, Glendale, CA 91208-2809

---

## Golden West College

| | |
|---|---|
| **Huntington Beach, California** | |
| www.goldenwestcollege.edu | **CB code: 4339** |

◆ Public 2-year community college
◆ Commuter campus in small city

**General.** Founded in 1966. Regionally accredited. **Enrollment:** 9,607 degree-seeking undergraduates. **Degrees:** 769 associate awarded. **Location:** 40 miles from Los Angeles. **Calendar:** Semester, extensive summer session. **Full-time faculty:** 190 total. **Part-time faculty:** 300 total. **Special facilities:** Outdoor amphitheatre, California native garden.

**Transfer out. Colleges most students transferred to 2007:** California State University: Long Beach, California State University: Dominguez Hills, California State University: Fullerton, University of California: Irvine, University of California: Los Angeles.

**Basis for selection.** Open admission, but selective for some programs. Any student at least 18 years of age eligible for admission. Limited admission to police academy and nursing program. Nursing applicants accepted on basis of prerequisite courses completed and GPA. SAT or ACT scores can be used for counseling and placement in lieu of institutional placement exams.

**2007-2008 Annual costs.** Tuition/fees: $658; $5,848 out-of-state. Per-credit charge: $20 in-state; $193 out-of-state. Books/supplies: $810. Personal expenses: $1,530.

**Financial aid. Non-need-based:** Scholarships awarded for academics.

**Application procedures. Admission:** Priority date 4/1; no deadline. No application fee. Admission notification on a rolling basis. **Financial aid:** Priority date 6/1; no closing date. FAFSA, institutional form required. Applicants notified on a rolling basis starting 7/1; must reply within 3 week(s) of notification.

**Academics. Special study options:** Accelerated study, cooperative education, cross-registration, distance learning, double major, dual enrollment of high school students, ESL, honors, independent study, study abroad, weekend college. License preparation in nursing, real estate. **Credit/placement by examination:** AP, CLEP, institutional tests. 6 credit hours maximum toward associate degree. **Support services:** Learning center, pre-admission summer program, remedial instruction, tutoring, writing center.

**Majors. Agriculture:** Horticultural science. **Biology:** General. **Business:** General, accounting, administrative services, business admin, office management, office technology, office/clerical, real estate, sales/distribution. **Communications:** Broadcast journalism, journalism, public relations. **Computer sciences:** General. **Education:** Physical. **Engineering technology:** Architectural, drafting. **English:** English lit, speech/rhetoric. **Foreign languages:** General, French, German, sign language interpretation, Spanish. **Health:** Nursing (RN), predental, premedicine, prepharmacy, preveterinary. **History:** General. **Interdisciplinary:** Biological/physical sciences. **Legal studies:** Legal secretary, prelaw. **Liberal arts:** Arts/sciences. **Math:** General. **Mechanic/repair:** Auto body, automotive, diesel. **Personal/culinary services:** Cosmetic. **Philosophy/religion:** Philosophy. **Physical sciences:** Astronomy, chemistry, geology. **Protective services:** Criminal justice, law enforcement admin. **Psychology:** General. **Social sciences:** General, anthropology, economics, political science, sociology. **Visual/performing arts:** Art, commercial/advertising art, dance, dramatic, music performance, music theory/composition, photography, studio arts.

**Computing on campus.** Online course registration, online library, wireless network available.

**Student life. Freshman orientation:** Mandatory. Preregistration for classes offered. Program held prior to enrollment. **Activities:** Bands, choral groups, dance, drama, film society, literary magazine, music ensembles, musical theater, radio station, student government, student newspaper, symphony orchestra, TV station, honor society, student nurses, cosmetology club, French club, international club, Circle K, Women of Action.

**Athletics.** NJCAA. **Intercollegiate:** Baseball M, basketball, cross-country, football (tackle) M, golf M, soccer, softball W, swimming, tennis, track and field, volleyball, water polo M, wrestling M. **Team name:** Rustlers.

**Student services.** Adult student services, career counseling, services for economically disadvantaged, student employment services, health services, on-campus daycare, personal counseling, placement for graduates, veterans' counselor. **Physically disabled:** Services for visually, speech, hearing impaired. **Transfer:** Transfer center, transfer adviser, college fairs on campus for students transferring to 4-year colleges.

**Contact.** Phone: (714) 895-8306 Fax: (714) 895-8960
Shirley Donnelly, Director Enrollment Services, Golden West College, 15744 Golden West Street, Box 2748, Huntington Beach, CA 92647-2748

---

## Golf Academy of San Diego
### Vista, California
### www.sdgagolf.com
CB code: 3495

▶ For-profit 2-year college of golf course management
▶ Small city

**General.** Accredited by ACICS. **Calendar:** Semester.

**Annual costs/financial aid.** Books/supplies: $700.

**Contact.** Phone: (760) 734-1208
1910 Shadowridge Drive, Suite 111, Vista, CA 92081

---

## Grossmont College
### El Cajon, California
### www.grossmont.edu
CB code: 4334

▶ Public 2-year community college
▶ Commuter campus in small city

**General.** Founded in 1961. Regionally accredited. **Enrollment:** 12,592 degree-seeking undergraduates. **Degrees:** 1,158 associate awarded. **Location:** 25 miles from San Diego. **Calendar:** Semester, extensive summer session. **Full-time faculty:** 180 total. **Part-time faculty:** 550 total.

**Transfer out. Colleges most students transferred to 2007:** San Diego State University.

**Basis for selection.** Open admission, but selective for some programs. Limited admission to health professions programs.

**2007-2008 Annual costs.** Tuition/fees: $630; $5,520 out-of-state. Per-credit charge: $20 in-state; $183 out-of-state. Books/supplies: $850. Personal expenses: $1,100.

**2006-2007 Financial aid.** All financial aid based on need. 89% of total undergraduate aid awarded as scholarships/grants, 11% as loans/jobs. Need-based aid available for part-time students. Work-study available nights, weekends and for part-time students.

**Application procedures. Admission:** Priority date 8/22; no deadline. No application fee. Application may be submitted online. Admission notification on a rolling basis. **Financial aid:** Priority date 2/1; no closing date. FAFSA required. Applicants notified on a rolling basis starting 7/15; must reply within 2 week(s) of notification.

**Academics. Special study options:** Accelerated study, cross-registration, distance learning, double major, dual enrollment of high school students, ESL, independent study, internships, student-designed major, study abroad. License preparation in nursing. **Credit/placement by examination:** AP, CLEP. Students may earn a maximum of 18 units on the CLEP general examinations. **Support services:** Learning center, reduced course load, remedial instruction, tutoring, writing center.

**Majors. Area/ethnic studies:** Native American. **Biology:** General. **Business:** General, administrative services, business admin, executive assistant, hospitality admin, international, management science, marketing, sales/distribution, tourism promotion, tourism/travel. **Communications:** General, broadcast journalism, digital media, journalism. **Computer sciences:** General, applications programming, computer science, LAN/WAN management, programming, webmaster. **English:** Creative writing, English lit, speech/rhetoric. **Family/consumer sciences:** Child care, child development. **Foreign languages:** American Sign Language, Arabic, French, German, Japanese, Russian, Spanish. **Health:** Athletic training, cardiovascular technology, nursing (RN), respiratory therapy technology. **History:** General. **Liberal arts:** Arts/sciences. **Math:** General. **Parks/recreation:** Exercise sciences. **Personal/culinary services:** Baking, culinary arts, restaurant/catering. **Philosophy/religion:** Philosophy. **Physical sciences:** Chemistry, geology, physics. **Protective services:** Corrections, forensics, police science, security services. **Social sciences:** Economics, geography, political science. **Visual/performing arts:** Acting, art history/conservation, ceramics, cinematography, dance, digital art, drawing, jazz, musical theater, painting, photography, sculpture, theater design. **Other:** Speech-Language Pathology Assistant.

**Computing on campus.** 500 workstations in library, computer center. Online course registration, wireless network available.

**Student life. Freshman orientation:** Available. **Activities:** Bands, choral groups, dance, drama, music ensembles, musical theater, radio station, student government, student newspaper, symphony orchestra.

**Athletics. Intercollegiate:** Baseball M, basketball, football (tackle) M, soccer W, softball W, swimming, tennis, volleyball, water polo. **Team name:** Griffins.

**Student services.** Adult student services, alcohol/substance abuse counseling, career counseling, services for economically disadvantaged, student employment services, financial aid counseling, health services, on-campus daycare, personal counseling, placement for graduates. **Physically disabled:** Services for visually, speech, hearing impaired. **Transfer:** Transfer center, transfer adviser, college fairs on campus for students transferring to 4-year colleges.

**Contact.** Phone: (619) 644-7186 Fax: (619) 644-7933
Brad Tiffany, Dean of Admissions and Records, Grossmont College, 8800 Grossmont College Drive, El Cajon, CA 92020

---

## Hartnell College
### Salinas, California
### www.hartnell.edu
CB code: 4340

▶ Public 2-year community college
▶ Commuter campus in small city

**General.** Founded in 1920. Regionally accredited. **Enrollment:** 9,869 undergraduates. **Degrees:** 499 associate awarded. **Location:** 110 miles from San Francisco, 65 miles from San Jose. **Calendar:** Semester, limited summer session. **Full-time faculty:** 115 total. **Part-time faculty:** 250 total.

**Basis for selection.** Open admission, but selective for some programs. Limited admission to nursing programs and animal health technology. Interview required for nursing, physician's assistant, animal health technician majors.

**2007-2008 Annual costs.** Tuition/fees: $608; $5,888 out-of-state. Per-credit charge: $20 in-state; $196 out-of-state. Books/supplies: $800. Personal expenses: $1,800.

**Application procedures. Admission:** No deadline. No application fee. Admission notification on a rolling basis. **Financial aid:** Priority date 8/1; no closing date. FAFSA required. Applicants notified on a rolling basis.

**Academics. Special study options:** Cooperative education. **Credit/ placement by examination:** CLEP. **Support services:** Learning center, remedial instruction, tutoring.

**Majors. Agriculture:** General, agribusiness operations. **Biology:** General. **Business:** Administrative services, banking/financial services, business admin, real estate. **Communications:** Digital media. **Computer sciences:** Information technology, programming, system admin, web page design. **Construction:** Site management. **Education:** Teacher assistance. **Engineering:** General. **Engineering technology:** General, drafting, hazardous materials, mechanical, water quality. **English:** English lit. **Family/consumer sciences:** Child development. **Health:** Clinical lab technology, dental hygiene, nursing (RN), physician assistant, substance abuse counseling, veterinary technology/assistant. **History:** General. **Liberal arts:** Arts/sciences. **Math:** General. **Mechanic/repair:** Auto body, automotive, diesel, electronics/ electrical. **Physical sciences:** Chemistry, geology, physics. **Protective services:** Corrections, firefighting, law enforcement admin. **Psychology:** General. **Social sciences:** General. **Visual/performing arts:** Art, dramatic, photography.

**Student life. Activities:** Bands, choral groups, drama, music ensembles, musical theater, student government, student newspaper.

**Athletics. Intercollegiate:** Baseball M, basketball, cross-country M, football (tackle) M, soccer M.

**Student services.** Career counseling, student employment services, personal counseling, placement for graduates.

**Contact.** Phone: (831) 755-6711 Fax: (831) 759-6014
Cheri Gray, Director of Matriculation and Enrollment Services, Hartnell College, 156 Homestead Avenue, Salinas, CA 93901

## Heald College: Concord
**Concord, California**
www.heald.edu                              CB code: 0235

- Private 2-year business college
- Commuter campus in small city
- Interview required

**General.** Founded in 1863. Regionally accredited. **Enrollment:** 682 degree-seeking undergraduates. **Degrees:** 280 associate awarded. **Location:** 25 miles from San Francisco. **Calendar:** Quarter. **Full-time faculty:** 18 total. **Part-time faculty:** 16 total.

**Basis for selection.** Institutional admissions examination and personal interview. Institutionally designed test used for admissions.

**2008-2009 Annual costs.** Tuition/fees (projected): $10,800. Books/ supplies: $1,500.

**Financial aid.** All financial aid based on need. Need-based aid available for part-time students. Work-study available nights, weekends and for part-time students.

**Application procedures. Admission:** No deadline. No application fee. Admission notification on a rolling basis. **Financial aid:** No deadline. FAFSA required. Applicants notified on a rolling basis.

**Academics. Special study options:** Cooperative education, internships. **Credit/placement by examination:** CLEP. **Support services:** Learning center, remedial instruction, study skills assistance, tutoring.

**Majors. Business:** Business admin. **Health:** Dental assistant, office admin.

**Computing on campus.** Online library available.

**Student services.** Placement for graduates, veterans' counselor.

**Contact.** E-mail: info@heald.edu
Phone: (925) 288-5800 Toll-free number: (800) 755-3550
Fax: (925) 288-5896
Keith Woodman, Admissions Director, Heald College: Concord, 5130 Commercial Circle, Concord, CA 94520

## Heald College: Fresno
**Fresno, California**
www.heald.edu                              CB code: 2119

- Private 2-year business and technical college
- Commuter campus in small city
- Interview required

**General.** Founded in 1863. Regionally accredited. **Enrollment:** 800 degree-seeking undergraduates. **Degrees:** 239 associate awarded. **Location:** 200 miles from San Francisco. **Calendar:** Quarter. **Full-time faculty:** 23 total. **Part-time faculty:** 2 total. **Class size:** 46% < 20, 54% 20-39.

**Transfer out. Colleges most students transferred to 2007:** California State University: Fresno, Fresno City College, National University.

**Basis for selection.** CPAT entrance exam.

**2008-2009 Annual costs.** Tuition/fees (projected): $10,800. Books/ supplies: $1,500.

**Application procedures. Admission:** No deadline. No application fee. Admission notification on a rolling basis. **Financial aid:** No deadline. FAFSA required. Applicants notified on a rolling basis.

**Academics. Special study options:** Liberal arts/career combination. **Credit/ placement by examination:** CLEP. **Support services:** Tutoring.

**Majors. Business:** Accounting, business admin, management information systems, office technology, office/clerical. **Computer sciences:** Data processing. **Legal studies:** Legal secretary.

**Student life. Freshman orientation:** Mandatory.

**Student services.** Adult student services, career counseling, student employment services, placement for graduates.

**Contact.** E-mail: info@heald.edu
Phone: (559) 438-4222 Toll-free number: (800) 755-3550
Fax: (559) 438-0948
Tina Mathis, Admissions Director, Heald College: Fresno, 255 West Bullard, Fresno, CA 93704-1706

## Heald College: Hayward
**Hayward, California**
www.heald.edu                              CB code: 7106

- Private 2-year technical college
- Commuter campus in small city

**General.** Regionally accredited. **Enrollment:** 1,017 degree-seeking undergraduates. **Degrees:** 385 associate awarded. **Calendar:** Quarter. **Full-time faculty:** 23 total. **Part-time faculty:** 11 total.

**Basis for selection.** Admission based on high school diploma/GED equivalent, entrance placement assessment, recommendation of admissions adviser.

**2008-2009 Annual costs.** Tuition/fees (projected): $10,800. Books/ supplies: $1,500.

**Financial aid.** All financial aid based on need. Need-based aid available for part-time students. Work-study available nights, weekends and for part-time students.

**Application procedures. Admission:** No deadline. No application fee. **Financial aid:** No deadline. FAFSA required.

**Academics. Special study options:** Cooperative education, internships. **Credit/placement by examination:** CLEP. **Support services:** Learning center, remedial instruction, study skills assistance, tutoring.

**Majors. Business:** Business admin. **Health:** Dental assistant, office admin.

**Computing on campus.** Online library available.

**Student services.** Career counseling, student employment services, financial aid counseling, placement for graduates.

**Contact.** Phone: (510) 783-2100 Toll-free number: (800) 755-3550
Fax: (510) 783-3287
Cheryl Valente, Admissions Director, Heald College: Hayward, 25500 Industrial Boulevard, Hayward, CA 94545

## Heald College: Rancho Cordova
Rancho Cordova, California
www.heald.edu                    CB code: 7105

- Private 2-year technical college
- Commuter campus in large city
- Interview required

**General.** Regionally accredited. **Enrollment:** 507 degree-seeking undergraduates. **Degrees:** 134 associate awarded. **Calendar:** Quarter. **Full-time faculty:** 18 total. **Part-time faculty:** 4 total.

**Basis for selection.** Institutional admissions test and interview very important.

**2008-2009 Annual costs.** Tuition/fees (projected): $10,800. Books/supplies: $1,500.

**Financial aid.** All financial aid based on need. Need-based aid available for part-time students. Work-study available nights, weekends and for part-time students.

**Application procedures. Admission:** No deadline. No application fee. Application may be submitted online. **Financial aid:** No deadline. FAFSA required.

**Academics. Special study options:** Cooperative education, internships. **Credit/placement by examination:** CLEP. **Support services:** Learning center, remedial instruction, study skills assistance, tutoring.

**Majors. Business:** Accounting, hospitality admin, office technology. **Computer sciences:** Networking. **Health:** Medical secretary. **Legal studies:** Legal secretary.

**Computing on campus.** Online library available.

**Student services.** Career counseling, student employment services, financial aid counseling, placement for graduates.

**Contact.** E-mail: info@heald.edu
Phone: (916) 638-1616 Toll-free number: (800) 884-323
Fax: (916) 638-1580
Cindi Stevens, Director of Admissions, Heald College: Rancho Cordova, 2910 Prospect Park Drive, Rancho Cordova, CA 95670

## Heald College: Roseville
Roseville, California
www.heald.edu                    CB code: 4145

- Private 2-year business and junior college
- Commuter campus in small city
- Interview required

**General.** Regionally accredited. **Enrollment:** 520 degree-seeking undergraduates. **Degrees:** 202 associate awarded. **Calendar:** Quarter. **Full-time faculty:** 19 total. **Part-time faculty:** 6 total.

**Basis for selection.** Institutional placement assessment, interview considered.

**2008-2009 Annual costs.** Tuition/fees (projected): $10,800. Books/supplies: $1,500.

**Financial aid.** All financial aid based on need. Need-based aid available for part-time students. Work-study available nights, weekends and for part-time students.

**Application procedures. Admission:** No deadline. No application fee. Application may be submitted online. **Financial aid:** No deadline. FAFSA required. .

**Academics. Special study options:** Cooperative education, internships. **Credit/placement by examination:** CLEP. **Support services:** Learning center, remedial instruction, study skills assistance, tutoring.

**Majors. Business:** Accounting, business admin.

**Computing on campus.** Online library available.

**Student services.** Career counseling, student employment services, financial aid counseling, placement for graduates.

**Contact.** E-mail: rosevilleinfo@heald.edu
Phone: (916) 789-8600 Toll-free number: (800) 755-3550
Fax: (916) 789-8616
Vickie McDougal, Admissions Director, Heald College: Roseville, 7 Sierra Gate Plaza, Roseville, CA 95678

## Heald College: Salinas
Salinas, California
www.heald.edu                    CB code: 7107

- Private 2-year business college
- Commuter campus in small city
- Interview required

**General.** Regionally accredited. **Enrollment:** 479 degree-seeking undergraduates. **Degrees:** 101 associate awarded. **Location:** 62 miles from San Jose. **Calendar:** Quarter. **Full-time faculty:** 12 total. **Part-time faculty:** 11 total.

**Basis for selection.** Entrance placement assessment, interview important.

**2008-2009 Annual costs.** Tuition/fees (projected): $10,800. Books/supplies: $1,500. Personal expenses: $1,400.

**Financial aid.** All financial aid based on need. Need-based aid available for part-time students. Work-study available nights, weekends and for part-time students.

**Application procedures. Admission:** No deadline. No application fee. **Financial aid:** No deadline. FAFSA required.

**Academics. Special study options:** Cooperative education, internships. **Credit/placement by examination:** CLEP. **Support services:** Learning center, remedial instruction, study skills assistance, tutoring.

**Majors. Business:** General, accounting, administrative services. **Health:** Medical secretary. **Protective services:** Law enforcement admin.

**Computing on campus.** Online library available.

**Student services.** Career counseling, student employment services, financial aid counseling, placement for graduates.

**Contact.** Phone: (831) 443-1700 Toll-free number: (800) 755-3550
Fax: (831) 443-1050
Dan Ujueta, Admissions Director, Heald College: Salinas, 1450 North Main Street, Salinas, CA 93906

## Heald College: San Francisco
San Francisco, California
www.heald.edu                    CB code: 7109

- Private 2-year business college
- Commuter campus in very large city
- Interview required

**General.** Regionally accredited. **Enrollment:** 447 degree-seeking undergraduates. **Degrees:** 121 associate awarded. **Calendar:** Quarter. **Full-time faculty:** 17 total. **Part-time faculty:** 18 total.

**Basis for selection.** Admission based on high school diploma/GED equivalent, entrance placement assessment, recommendation of admissions adviser.

**2008-2009 Annual costs.** Tuition/fees (projected): $10,800. Books/supplies: $1,500.

**Financial aid.** All financial aid based on need. Need-based aid available for part-time students. Work-study available nights, weekends and for part-time students.

**Application procedures. Admission:** No deadline. No application fee. **Financial aid:** No deadline. FAFSA required.

**Academics. Special study options:** Cooperative education, internships. **Credit/placement by examination:** CLEP. **Support services:** Learning center, remedial instruction, study skills assistance, tutoring.

**Majors. Business:** Business admin. **Engineering technology:** Computer. **Health:** Medical secretary.

**Computing on campus.** Online library available.

**Student services.** Career counseling, student employment services, financial aid counseling, placement for graduates.

**Contact.** Phone: (415) 808-3000 Toll-free number: (800) 755-3550
Fax: (418) 808-3005
Edward Lubin, Admissions Director, Heald College: San Francisco, 350
Mission Street, San Francisco, CA 94103

## Heald College: San Jose
**Milpitas, California**
www.heald.edu                                    CB code: 0405

- Private 2-year business college
- Commuter campus in very large city
- Interview required

**General.** Founded in 1863. Regionally accredited. **Enrollment:** 673 degree-seeking undergraduates. **Degrees:** 277 associate awarded. **Location:** 45 miles from San Francisco. **Calendar:** Quarter. **Full-time faculty:** 19 total. **Part-time faculty:** 12 total.

**Basis for selection.** Institutional admissions test and personal interview most important.

**2008-2009 Annual costs.** Tuition/fees (projected): $10,800. Books/supplies: $1,500.

**Financial aid.** All financial aid based on need. Need-based aid available for part-time students. Work-study available nights, weekends and for part-time students.

**Application procedures. Admission:** No deadline. No application fee. Admission notification on a rolling basis. **Financial aid:** No deadline. FAFSA required. Applicants notified on a rolling basis starting 6/15; must reply within 2 week(s) of notification.

**Academics. Special study options:** Cooperative education, internships. **Credit/placement by examination:** CLEP, institutional tests. 45 credit hours maximum toward associate degree. **Support services:** Learning center, reduced course load, remedial instruction, tutoring.

**Majors. Business:** Accounting, business admin, office management. **Health:** Office admin. **Legal studies:** Legal secretary.

**Computing on campus.** Online library available.

**Student services.** Career counseling, student employment services, financial aid counseling, placement for graduates.

**Contact.** E-mail: sanjoseinfo@heald.edu
Phone: (408) 934-4900 Toll-free number: (800) 755-3550
Fax: (415) 934-7777
Clarence Hardiman, Director of Admissions, Heald College: San Jose, 341
Great Mall Parkway, Milpitas, CA 95035

## Heald College: Stockton
**Stockton, California**
www.heald.edu                                    CB code: 7108

- Private 2-year business college
- Large city

**General.** Regionally accredited. **Enrollment:** 755 degree-seeking undergraduates. **Degrees:** 181 associate awarded. **Calendar:** Quarter. **Full-time faculty:** 17 total. **Part-time faculty:** 10 total.

**Basis for selection.** Open admission. Interview, entrance placement assessment considered.

**2008-2009 Annual costs.** Tuition/fees (projected): $10,800. Books/supplies: $1,500.

**Financial aid. Need-based:** Work-study available for part-time students.

**Application procedures. Admission:** No deadline. $40 fee. **Financial aid:** No deadline. FAFSA required.

**Academics. Credit/placement by examination:** CLEP.

**Majors. Business:** Accounting, office technology. **Computer sciences:** Data entry, vendor certification.

**Contact.** Phone: (209) 473-5200 Toll-free number: (800) 755-3550
Fax: (209) 477-2739
Ezra Salas, Admissions Director, Heald College: Stockton, 1605 East
March Lane, Stockton, CA 95210

## High-Tech Institute
**Sacramento, California**
www.hightechinstitute.edu                        CB code: 3041

- For-profit 2-year technical college
- Commuter campus in very large city
- Interview required

**General.** Accredited by ACCSCT. **Enrollment:** 474 undergraduates. **Calendar:** Continuous. **Full-time faculty:** 26 total. **Part-time faculty:** 1 total.

**Basis for selection.** Open admission. All applicants must achieve minimum passing score on school's entrance test.

**2007-2008 Annual costs.** $17,700 for medical assistant program, $21,110 for dental assistant program, $37,300 for surgical technologist program, $32,500 for computer networking and information technology program, $19,900 for medical billing and coding program, $18,500 for massage therapy, $20,700 for pharmacy technician. Includes tuition, fees, book, supplies, and uniform.

**Application procedures. Admission:** No application fee. **Financial aid:** No deadline. FAFSA required. Applicants notified on a rolling basis.

**Academics. Special study options:** License preparation in dental hygiene. **Credit/placement by examination:** CLEP. **Support services:** GED preparation.

**Contact.** Phone: (916) 929-9700
Sonya French, Admissions Director, High-Tech Institute, 9738 Lincoln
Village Drive, Sacramento, CA 95827

## Imperial Valley College
**Imperial, California**                          CB member
www.imperial.edu                                  CB code: 4358

- Public 2-year community college
- Commuter campus in rural community

**General.** Founded in 1922. Regionally accredited. **Enrollment:** 5,876 degree-seeking undergraduates. **Degrees:** 664 associate awarded. **Location:** 6 miles from El Centro. **Calendar:** Semester, limited summer session. **Full-time faculty:** 158 total. **Part-time faculty:** 180 total.

**Transfer out. Colleges most students transferred to 2007:** San Diego State University, California State Polytechnic University: Pomona, California State University: San Marcos, California State University: San Bernardino, California State University: Long Beach.

**Basis for selection.** Open admission, but selective for some programs. Limited admission for nursing programs.

**2007-2008 Annual costs.** Tuition/fees: $630; $5,820 out-of-state. Per-credit charge: $20 in-state; $193 out-of-state. Books/supplies: $1,422. Personal expenses: $2,862.

**Application procedures. Admission:** No deadline. No application fee. Application must be submitted online. Admission notification on a rolling basis. **Financial aid:** Priority date 3/2; no closing date. FAFSA required. Applicants notified on a rolling basis.

**Academics. Special study options:** Distance learning, double major, dual enrollment of high school students, ESL, liberal arts/career combination. License preparation in nursing, paramedic, real estate. **Credit/placement by examination:** AP, CLEP, institutional tests. 25 credit hours maximum toward associate degree. **Support services:** GED test center, learning center, reduced course load, remedial instruction, study skills assistance, tutoring, writing center.

**Majors. Agriculture:** Business. **Business:** Administrative services, banking/financial services, business admin, office management, office technology, office/clerical, real estate. **Communications:** Journalism. **Computer sciences:** General. **Education:** Bilingual, early childhood, elementary. **Engineering:** General, agricultural. **English:** English lit. **Family/consumer sciences:** Child care. **Foreign languages:** General, French, Spanish. **Health:** Health care admin, licensed practical nurse, nursing (RN), substance abuse counseling. **Legal studies:** Paralegal. **Liberal arts:** Arts/sciences. **Math:**

General. **Mechanic/repair:** General, auto body. **Parks/recreation:** Health/fitness. **Protective services:** Corrections, firefighting, law enforcement admin. **Psychology:** General. **Social sciences:** General, anthropology. **Visual/performing arts:** Art.

**Computing on campus.** 90 workstations in library, computer center, student center.

**Student life. Freshman orientation:** Available. **Activities:** Jazz band, choral groups, drama, music ensembles, student government, student newspaper, Christian club, Movimiento Estudiantil Chicano de Aztlan, Upward Bound club, French club, spirit club.

**Athletics. Intercollegiate:** Baseball M, basketball, soccer, softball W, tennis, volleyball W. **Team name:** Arabs.

**Student services.** Career counseling, services for economically disadvantaged, student employment services, financial aid counseling, minority student services, on-campus daycare, personal counseling, veterans' counselor. **Physically disabled:** Services for visually, speech, hearing impaired. **Transfer:** Transfer center, transfer adviser, college fairs on campus for students transferring to 4-year colleges.

**Contact.** Phone: (760) 352-8320 Fax: (760) 355-2663
Kathie Westerfield, Associate Dean, Admissions & Records, Imperial Valley College, Box 158, Imperial, CA 92251-0158

## Irvine Valley College
### Irvine, California
www.ivc.edu
CB code: 3356

- Public 2-year community college
- Commuter campus in small city

**General.** Regionally accredited. **Enrollment:** 1,053 degree-seeking undergraduates. **Degrees:** 346 associate awarded. **ROTC:** Air Force. **Location:** 50 miles from Los Angeles. **Calendar:** Semester, extensive summer session. **Full-time faculty:** 115 total. **Part-time faculty:** 304 total. **Special facilities:** Dance studio, Microsoft Office user specialist testing site, telescope, performing arts center.

**Transfer out. Colleges most students transferred to 2007:** University of California: Irvine, California State University: Fullerton.

**Basis for selection.** Open admission.

**2007-2008 Annual costs.** Tuition/fees: $632; $5,822 out-of-state. Per-credit charge: $20 in-state; $193 out-of-state. Books/supplies: $1,260. Personal expenses: $3,708.

**Financial aid.** All financial aid based on need. Need-based aid available for part-time students. Work-study available nights and for part-time students.

**Application procedures. Admission:** No deadline. No application fee. Application may be submitted online. Admission notification on a rolling basis. **Financial aid:** No deadline. FAFSA, institutional form required. Applicants notified on a rolling basis starting 4/30.

**Academics. Special study options:** Accelerated study, cooperative education, cross-registration, distance learning, double major, dual enrollment of high school students, ESL, honors, independent study, internships, study abroad, weekend college. **Credit/placement by examination:** CLEP, institutional tests. 12 credit hours maximum toward associate degree. Minimum 2.0 GPA in at least 12 units completed at IVC required to enroll in credit by examination. **Support services:** Learning center, remedial instruction, study skills assistance, tutoring, writing center.

**Majors. Area/ethnic studies:** Women's. **Biology:** General, ecology. **Business:** General, accounting, business admin, office management, office technology, real estate. **Communications:** Advertising. **Computer sciences:** General, applications programming, networking, programming, systems analysis. **Conservation:** General. **Education:** Early childhood, physical. **Engineering technology:** Drafting, electrical, manufacturing. **English:** British lit, composition, speech/rhetoric. **Foreign languages:** French, Spanish. **History:** General. **Liberal arts:** Arts/sciences. **Math:** General. **Parks/recreation:** Health/fitness. **Philosophy/religion:** Philosophy. **Physical sciences:** Chemistry, geology. **Protective services:** Law enforcement admin, police science. **Psychology:** General. **Social sciences:** Anthropology, economics, geography, political science, sociology. **Visual/performing arts:** General, art, dance, dramatic, photography, studio arts, theater design.

**Most popular majors.** Business/marketing 9%, liberal arts 77%.

**Computing on campus.** 250 workstations in library, computer center. Commuter students can connect to campus network. Online course registration, online library, helpline available.

**Student life. Freshman orientation:** Mandatory. **Housing:** Homestay referral for international students. **Activities:** Bands, choral groups, dance, drama, literary magazine, music ensembles, musical theater, student government, student newspaper, symphony orchestra, administration of justice club, Phi Theta Kappa honor society, Muslim Student Association, biology society, dance club, geology club, health sciences society, journalism club, Phi Theta Kappa, Psi Beta, student liberties club, computer science society.

**Athletics. Intercollegiate:** Badminton W, baseball M, basketball, cross-country, golf, soccer, softball W, tennis, volleyball. **Intramural:** Basketball, soccer, tennis, volleyball. **Team name:** Lasers.

**Student services.** Adult student services, career counseling, services for economically disadvantaged, student employment services, financial aid counseling, health services, on-campus daycare, personal counseling, placement for graduates, veterans' counselor, women's services. **Physically disabled:** Services for visually, speech, hearing impaired. **Transfer:** Re-entry adviser for new students. Transfer center, transfer adviser, college fairs on campus for students transferring to 4-year colleges.

**Contact.** E-mail: admissions@ivc.edu
Phone: (949) 451-5461 Fax: (949) 451-5443
Ruben Guzmann, Director of Admissions and Records, Irvine Valley College, 5500 Irvine Center Drive, Irvine, CA 92618-4399

## Lake Tahoe Community College
### South Lake Tahoe, California
www.ltcc.edu
CB code: 4420

- Public 2-year community college
- Commuter campus in large town

**General.** Founded in 1975. Regionally accredited. **Enrollment:** 2,620 degree-seeking undergraduates. **Degrees:** 165 associate awarded. **Location:** 55 miles from Reno, Nevada, 110 miles from Sacramento. **Calendar:** Quarter, limited summer session. **Full-time faculty:** 50 total. **Part-time faculty:** 180 total.

**Transfer out. Colleges most students transferred to 2007:** California State University, University of California, University of Nevada: Reno.

**Basis for selection.** Open admission. **Learning Disabled:** Assistance is available through the Disability Resource Center.

**2007-2008 Annual costs.** Tuition/fees: $597; $6,222 out-of-state. Per-credit charge: $13 in-state; $138 out-of-state. $28 per credit hour for Nevada residents. Books/supplies: $1,422. Personal expenses: $2,502.

**Application procedures. Admission:** No deadline. No application fee. Application may be submitted online. Admission notification on a rolling basis. **Financial aid:** Priority date 5/1; no closing date. FAFSA required. Applicants notified on a rolling basis starting 7/1; must reply within 2 week(s) of notification.

**Academics. Special study options:** Cooperative education, distance learning, double major, dual enrollment of high school students, ESL, internships, study abroad. License preparation in real estate. **Credit/placement by examination:** CLEP, institutional tests. 4 credit hours maximum toward associate degree. **Support services:** GED preparation, learning center, remedial instruction, study skills assistance, tutoring, writing center.

**Majors. Business:** General, accounting, administrative services, entrepreneurial studies, finance, marketing, office management, office/clerical, real estate. **Education:** Early childhood. **English:** English lit. **Foreign languages:** Spanish. **Health:** Medical assistant, medical records admin. **Interdisciplinary:** Natural sciences. **Legal studies:** Legal secretary. **Liberal arts:** Arts/sciences. **Parks/recreation:** Health/fitness. **Personal/culinary services:** Culinary arts. **Protective services:** Firefighting, law enforcement admin. **Psychology:** General. **Social sciences:** General. **Visual/performing arts:** Art, dance, dramatic, studio arts.

**Computing on campus.** 155 workstations in library, computer center, student center. Online course registration, online library, wireless network available.

**Student life. Freshman orientation:** Available. **Activities:** Choral groups, dance, drama, music ensembles, musical theater, student government, Alpha Gamma Sigma, associated student council, international club.

**Athletics.** NJCAA. **Intercollegiate:** Cross-country, volleyball W.

**Student services.** Career counseling, services for economically disadvantaged, student employment services, financial aid counseling, minority student services, on-campus daycare, personal counseling, placement for graduates, veterans' counselor. **Physically disabled:** Services for visually, speech, hearing impaired. **Learning disabled:** Comprehensive services available. **Transfer:** Transfer center, transfer adviser, college fairs on campus for students transferring to 4-year colleges.

**Contact.** E-mail: admissions@ltcc.edu
Phone: (530) 541-4660 ext. 211 Fax: (530) 542-1781
Cheri Jones, Director of Admissions & Records, Lake Tahoe Community College, One College Drive, South Lake Tahoe, CA 96150-4524

## Laney College
### Oakland, California
### laney.peralta.edu                              CB code: 4406

- Public 2-year community college
- Commuter campus in large city

**General.** Founded in 1953. Regionally accredited. Vocational programs include programs with PGE and a solar program with UC Lawrence Laboratories. **Enrollment:** 12,754 undergraduates. **Degrees:** 397 associate awarded. **Location:** 10 miles from San Francisco. **Calendar:** Semester, extensive summer session. **Full-time faculty:** 135 total. **Part-time faculty:** 303 total. **Special facilities:** CAD laboratory.

**Student profile.**

| | | | |
|---|---|---|---|
| Out-of-state: | 2% | 25 or older: | 61% |

**Transfer out. Colleges most students transferred to 2007:** California State University: East Bay, San Francisco State, University of California: Berkeley.

**Basis for selection.** Open admission.

**2007-2008 Annual costs.** Tuition/fees: $604; $5,794 out-of-state. Per-credit charge: $20 in-state; $193 out-of-state. Books/supplies: $648. Personal expenses: $1,620.

**Application procedures. Admission:** No deadline. No application fee. Application may be submitted online. Admission notification on a rolling basis. **Financial aid:** Priority date 4/1; no closing date. FAFSA, institutional form required. Applicants notified on a rolling basis; must reply within 2 week(s) of notification.

**Academics. Special study options:** Cooperative education, distance learning, dual enrollment of high school students, ESL, honors, independent study, liberal arts/career combination, weekend college. **Credit/placement by examination:** CLEP, institutional tests. **Support services:** Learning center, remedial instruction, study skills assistance, tutoring.

**Majors. Area/ethnic studies:** African-American, Asian, Latin American. **Business:** General, accounting, administrative services, banking/financial services, management information systems, office technology, office/clerical, operations, sales/distribution. **Communications:** Broadcast journalism, journalism. **Communications technology:** General, graphic/printing. **Computer sciences:** General, information systems. **Construction:** Carpentry, maintenance. **Education:** General. **Engineering technology:** Architectural. **English:** English lit. **Interdisciplinary:** Biological/physical sciences. **Liberal arts:** Arts/sciences. **Math:** General. **Mechanic/repair:** Heating/ac/refrig. **Personal/culinary services:** Cosmetic, culinary arts. **Production:** Woodworking. **Social sciences:** General. **Visual/performing arts:** Art, ceramics, commercial/advertising art, dance, design, dramatic.

**Computing on campus.** 400 workstations in library, computer center, student center. Online course registration, online library available.

**Student life. Freshman orientation:** Mandatory. Preregistration for classes offered. **Activities:** Pep band, dance, drama, literary magazine, musical theater, student government, student newspaper, TV station.

**Athletics. Intercollegiate:** Badminton W, baseball M, basketball M, football (tackle) M, softball W, swimming, track and field W, volleyball W, water polo W. **Team name:** Eagles.

**Student services.** Adult student services, career counseling, services for economically disadvantaged, student employment services, financial aid counseling, health services, minority student services, on-campus daycare, personal counseling, placement for graduates. **Physically disabled:** Services for visually, speech, hearing impaired. **Transfer:** Re-entry adviser for new students. Transfer center, transfer adviser, college fairs on campus for students transferring to 4-year colleges.

**Contact.** E-mail: admissions@peralta.edu
Phone: (510) 464-3121 Fax: (510) 464-3240
Howard Perdue, Director of Admissions and Records, Laney College, 900 Fallon Street, Oakland, CA 94607

## Las Positas College
### Livermore, California
### www.laspositascollege.edu                     CB code: 6507

- Public 2-year community college
- Commuter campus in small city

**General.** Founded in 1991. Regionally accredited. **Enrollment:** 5,411 degree-seeking undergraduates. **Degrees:** 431 associate awarded. **Location:** 43 miles from San Francsico, 39 miles from San Jose. **Calendar:** Semester, limited summer session. **Full-time faculty:** 101 total. **Part-time faculty:** 250 total.

**Transfer out. Colleges most students transferred to 2007:** California State University: East Bay.

**Basis for selection.** Open admission. High school diploma or GED required for student under 18 years.

**2007-2008 Annual costs.** Tuition/fees: $626; $5,726 out-of-state. Per-credit charge: $20 in-state; $190 out-of-state. Books/supplies: $1,332. Personal expenses: $2,331.

**Application procedures. Admission:** No deadline. No application fee. Admission notification on a rolling basis. **Financial aid:** Priority date 5/1; no closing date. Institutional form required. Applicants notified on a rolling basis starting 7/1; must reply within 2 week(s) of notification.

**Academics. Special study options:** Accelerated study, distance learning, dual enrollment of high school students, ESL, independent study, internships, student-designed major. **Credit/placement by examination:** CLEP. **Support services:** Learning center, remedial instruction, tutoring.

**Majors. Agriculture:** Ornamental horticulture. **Biology:** General. **Business:** Office management, sales/distribution. **Communications technology:** Graphic/printing. **Computer sciences:** General, computer science. **Engineering technology:** Drafting. **English:** Speech/rhetoric. **Family/consumer sciences:** Child care. **Health:** Environmental health. **Liberal arts:** Arts/sciences. **Mechanic/repair:** Electronics/electrical. **Physical sciences:** Chemistry, physics. **Protective services:** Firefighting. **Social sciences:** General, international relations, sociology. **Visual/performing arts:** Commercial/advertising art, dramatic, interior design, studio arts.

**Most popular majors.** Business/marketing 26%, computer/information sciences 10%, liberal arts 55%.

**Computing on campus.** 285 workstations in library, computer center.

**Student life. Freshman orientation:** Available. **Activities:** Choral groups, dance, drama, literary magazine, music ensembles, musical theater, student government, student newspaper, TV station.

**Athletics. Intercollegiate:** Cross-country, soccer. **Intramural:** Basketball, bowling, fencing, handball M, racquetball, skin diving, soccer, volleyball.

**Student services.** Adult student services, career counseling, student employment services, financial aid counseling, health services, personal counseling, veterans' counselor. **Learning disabled:** Comprehensive services available. **Transfer:** Transfer center, transfer adviser, college fairs on campus for students transferring to 4-year colleges.

**Contact.** Phone: (925) 424-1000 Fax: (925) 443-0742
Sylvia Rodriguez, Registrar, Las Positas College, 3033 Collier Canyon Road, Livermore, CA 94551

## Lassen College
### Susanville, California
### www.lassencollege.edu                         CB code: 4383

- Public 2-year community college
- Small town

**General.** Founded in 1925. Regionally accredited. **Enrollment:** 857 degree-seeking undergraduates. **Degrees:** 91 associate awarded. **Location:** 100 miles from Chico, 84 miles from Reno, Nevada. **Calendar:** Semester, limited summer session. **Full-time faculty:** 40 total. **Part-time faculty:** 120 total.

## Student profile.

| | | | |
|---|---|---|---|
| Out-of-state: | 7% | Live on campus: | 3% |

**Basis for selection.** Open admission, but selective for some programs. Limited admission to nursing program.

**2007-2008 Annual costs.** Tuition/fees: $615; $6,105 out-of-state. Per-credit charge: $20 in-state; $203 out-of-state. Nevada residents pay $42 per-credit-hour with good neighbor policy. Room/board: $4,100.

**Financial aid. Additional information:** Board of Governors Grant: low-income California residents can have registration fees waived.

**Application procedures. Admission:** No application fee. Admission notification on a rolling basis. Institutional placement tests recommended. **Financial aid:** Priority date 7/1; no closing date. FAFSA required. Applicants notified on a rolling basis starting 7/1; must reply within 2 week(s) of notification.

**Academics.** Gunsmithing and summer NRA programs offered. **Special study options:** Cooperative education, distance learning, dual enrollment of high school students, honors, independent study, internships. **Credit/placement by examination:** AP, CLEP, institutional tests. 15 credit hours maximum toward associate degree. **Support services:** Learning center, pre-admission summer program, reduced course load, remedial instruction, tutoring.

**Majors. Business:** General, accounting, administrative services, business admin, management information systems, office technology, office/clerical, real estate. **Communications:** Journalism. **Computer sciences:** General, applications programming. **Construction:** Maintenance. **Education:** General, early childhood, physical. **Health:** Nursing (RN), nursing assistant. **Interdisciplinary:** Biological/physical sciences. **Liberal arts:** Arts/sciences. **Math:** General. **Mechanic/repair:** Auto body, automotive. **Protective services:** Corrections, law enforcement admin, police science. **Social sciences:** General. **Visual/performing arts:** Art.

**Computing on campus.** 40 workstations in computer center.

**Student life. Housing:** Coed dorms available. **Activities:** Choral groups, drama, film society, student government, student newspaper, over 20 student organizations and clubs.

**Athletics.** NJCAA. **Intercollegiate:** Baseball M, basketball, cross-country, golf, rifle, softball W, track and field, volleyball W, wrestling M. **Intramural:** Skiing.

**Student services.** Career counseling, health services, on-campus daycare, personal counseling, veterans' counselor. **Physically disabled:** Services for visually, speech, hearing impaired. **Transfer:** Transfer adviser, college fairs on campus for students transferring to 4-year colleges.

**Contact.** Phone: (530) 251-8808 Fax: (530) 257-8964
Chris Alberico, Registrar and Admissions Director, Lassen College, Box 3000, Susanville, CA 96130

---

### Long Beach City College
**Long Beach, California**
www.lbcc.edu                    **CB code: 4388**

- Public 2-year community college
- Commuter campus in large city

**General.** Founded in 1927. Regionally accredited. **Enrollment:** 10,533 degree-seeking undergraduates. **Degrees:** 874 associate awarded. **Location:** 20 miles from downtown Los Angeles. **Calendar:** Semester, limited summer session. **Full-time faculty:** 356 total. **Part-time faculty:** 623 total. **Class size:** 35% < 20, 47% 20-39, 10% 40-49, 7% 50-99, 1% >100.

### Student profile.

| | | | |
|---|---|---|---|
| Out-of-state: | 1% | 25 or older: | 51% |

**Transfer out. Colleges most students transferred to 2007:** California State University: Long Beach, California State University: Dominguez Hills, California State University: Fullerton, University of California: Irvine.

**Basis for selection.** Open admission.

**2007-2008 Annual costs.** Tuition/fees: $628; $5,848 out-of-state. Per-credit charge: $20 in-state; $194 out-of-state. Books/supplies: $1,784. Personal expenses: $2,898.

**Financial aid.** All financial aid based on need. Need-based aid available for part-time students. Work-study available for part-time students.

**Application procedures. Admission:** No deadline. No application fee. Admission notification on a rolling basis. **Financial aid:** Priority date 5/6; no closing date. FAFSA, institutional form required. Applicants notified on a rolling basis starting 7/6; must reply within 2 week(s) of notification.

**Academics. Special study options:** Accelerated study, cooperative education, cross-registration, distance learning, dual enrollment of high school students, ESL, honors, independent study, internships, liberal arts/career combination, study abroad, weekend college. License preparation in aviation, nursing, radiology, real estate. **Credit/placement by examination:** AP, CLEP, IB, institutional tests. 40 credit hours maximum toward associate degree. Students must first complete 12 units in residence. **Support services:** GED preparation and test center, learning center, pre-admission summer program, remedial instruction, study skills assistance, tutoring, writing center.

**Majors. Agriculture:** Ornamental horticulture. **Biology:** General. **Business:** General, accounting, administrative services, business admin, fashion, hotel/motel admin, office technology, office/clerical, real estate, restaurant/food services, sales/distribution, tourism promotion, tourism/travel. **Communications:** Advertising, broadcast journalism, journalism, public relations, publishing. **Communications technology:** General, desktop publishing, graphic/printing. **Computer sciences:** Applications programming, data processing, word processing. **Construction:** Carpentry. **Education:** Teacher assistance. **Engineering:** General. **Engineering technology:** Architectural, architectural drafting, drafting, heat/ac/refrig. **English:** English lit, speech/rhetoric. **Family/consumer sciences:** General, child care, child development, consumer economics, family resources, institutional food production. **Foreign languages:** General, Spanish. **Health:** Dietetic technician, licensed practical nurse, medical assistant, medical radiologic technology/radiation therapy, nursing (RN). **Legal studies:** Legal secretary. **Liberal arts:** Arts/sciences. **Math:** General. **Mechanic/repair:** General, aircraft powerplant, alternative fuel vehicle, auto body, automotive, diesel, electronics/electrical. **Parks/recreation:** Health/fitness. **Personal/culinary services:** Baking, culinary arts, restaurant/catering. **Physical sciences:** General. **Production:** Cabinetmaking/millwright, machine shop technology, machine tool, welding. **Protective services:** Fire safety technology, law enforcement admin. **Public administration:** General, human services. **Social sciences:** General. **Transportation:** Aviation. **Visual/performing arts:** Art, commercial photography, commercial/advertising art, dance, design, dramatic, drawing, fashion design, film/cinema, interior design, multimedia, printmaking, sculpture, theater design.

**Most popular majors.** Business/marketing 7%, health sciences 19%, liberal arts 44%, security/protective services 7%.

**Computing on campus.** 500 workstations in library, computer center, student center. Helpline available.

**Student life. Freshman orientation:** Available. Preregistration for classes offered. **Activities:** Bands, campus ministries, choral groups, dance, drama, international student organizations, literary magazine, music ensembles, musical theater, radio station, student government, student newspaper, symphony orchestra, TV station, College Republicans, Students for a Democratic Society.

**Athletics.** NJCAA. **Intercollegiate:** Baseball M, basketball, cross-country, football (tackle) M, golf, soccer, softball W, swimming, tennis, track and field, volleyball, water polo. **Intramural:** Archery, badminton, basketball, bowling, golf, racquetball, soccer, softball, swimming, table tennis, tennis, track and field, volleyball, wrestling M. **Team name:** Vikings.

**Student services.** Career counseling, student employment services, health services, on-campus daycare, personal counseling, veterans' counselor. **Physically disabled:** Services for visually, speech, hearing impaired. **Transfer:** Re-entry adviser for new students. Transfer center, transfer adviser, college fairs on campus for students transferring to 4-year colleges.

**Contact.** Phone: (562) 938-4139 Fax: (562) 938-4858
Ross Miyashiro, Dean of Admissions and Records, Long Beach City College, 4901 East Carson Street, Long Beach, CA 90808

---

### Los Angeles City College
**Los Angeles, California**
www.lacitycollege.edu           **CB code: 4391**

- Public 2-year community college
- Very large city

**General.** Founded in 1929. Regionally accredited. **Enrollment:** 2,833 degree-seeking undergraduates. **Degrees:** 691 associate awarded. **ROTC:** Army, Naval, Air Force. **Location:** 5 miles from downtown. **Calendar:** Semester, limited summer session. **Full-time faculty:** 210 total; 35% minority, 42% women. **Part-time faculty:** 379 total; 31% minority, 48% women.

**Student profile.**

| | | | |
|---|---|---|---|
| Part-time: | 66% | Women: | 57% |
| Out-of-state: | 10% | | |

**Basis for selection.** Open admission. Auditions required of theater academy, music majors.

**2007-2008 Annual costs.** Tuition/fees: $622; $5,812 out-of-state. Per-credit charge: $20 in-state; $193 out-of-state. Books/supplies: $840. Personal expenses: $2,040.

**2006-2007 Financial aid.** All financial aid based on need. 88% of total undergraduate aid awarded as scholarships/grants, 12% as loans/jobs. Need-based aid available for part-time students. **Additional information:** Fee waivers available for public assistance and Social Security insurance recipients; fee credits available for low income families.

**Application procedures. Admission:** Closing date 9/1. No application fee. Admission notification on a rolling basis beginning on or about 4/30. **Financial aid:** Priority date 3/2; no closing date. FAFSA required. Applicants notified by 7/6; Applicants notified on a rolling basis starting 7/6; must reply within 2 week(s) of notification.

**Academics. Special study options:** Accelerated study, cross-registration, dual enrollment of high school students, ESL, honors, independent study. License preparation in dental hygiene, nursing, radiology. **Credit/placement by examination:** CLEP, institutional tests. 15 credit hours maximum toward associate degree. **Support services:** Learning center, remedial instruction, tutoring.

**Majors. Area/ethnic studies:** African-American, Asian-American. **Biology:** General. **Business:** Accounting, administrative services, banking/financial services, business admin, entrepreneurial studies, management information systems, office technology, office/clerical, real estate, tourism promotion, tourism/travel. **Communications:** Advertising, broadcast journalism, journalism, public relations. **Communications technology:** General. **Computer sciences:** General, applications programming. **Engineering:** General, software. **Engineering technology:** Biomedical, drafting, electrical. **English:** English lit. **Family/consumer sciences:** General, child care. **Foreign languages:** Chinese, French, German, Italian, Japanese, Spanish. **Health:** Dental lab technology, health services, medical radiologic technology/radiation therapy, medical records technology, medical secretary. **Legal studies:** Legal secretary, paralegal. **Liberal arts:** Arts/sciences. **Math:** General. **Mechanic/repair:** Electronics/electrical. **Physical sciences:** Chemistry, physics. **Protective services:** Police science. **Psychology:** General. **Visual/performing arts:** Art, cinematography, commercial/advertising art, dramatic, film/cinema, photography.

**Computing on campus.** 200 workstations in library, computer center.

**Student life. Activities:** Bands, choral groups, dance, drama, film society, literary magazine, music ensembles, musical theater, radio station, student government, student newspaper, TV station, religious, political, ethnic, and foreign student clubs.

**Athletics.** NJCAA. **Intercollegiate:** Baseball M, basketball M, cross-country, track and field.

**Student services.** Career counseling, student employment services, health services, on-campus daycare, personal counseling, veterans' counselor. **Physically disabled:** Services for visually, speech, hearing impaired. **Transfer:** Transfer adviser, college fairs on campus for students transferring to 4-year colleges.

**Contact.** Phone: (323) 953-4381 Fax: (323) 953-4013
William Marmolejo, Dean of Admissions, Los Angeles City College, 855 North Vermont Avenue, Los Angeles, CA 90029-3589

---

## Los Angeles County College of Nursing and Allied Health
### Los Angeles, California
### www.ladhs.org/lacusc/lacnah

- Public 2-year nursing and community college
- Very large city

**General.** Clinical component of studies undertaken in cooperation with municipal medical centers in Los Angeles County. **Enrollment:** 290 degree-seeking undergraduates. **Degrees:** 117 associate awarded. **Calendar:** Semester. **Full-time faculty:** 40 total.

**Basis for selection.** Admissions criteria include high school diploma or equivalency, prior college experience, California Achievement Test. Geographical residency in Los Angeles County considered.

**2007-2008 Annual costs.** Tuition/fees: $2,400.

**Application procedures. Admission:** Closing date 3/1. $5 fee.

**Academics. Credit/placement by examination:** CLEP.

**Majors. Health:** Nursing (RN).

**Contact.** Phone: (323) 226-4911
Maria Caballero, Dean of Admissions and Student Services, Los Angeles County College of Nursing and Allied Health, 1237 North Mission Road, Los Angeles, CA 90033-1084

---

## Los Angeles Harbor College
### Wilmington, California
### www.lahc.edu
**CB code: 4395**

- Public 2-year community college
- Commuter campus in small city

**General.** Founded in 1949. Regionally accredited. **Enrollment:** 4,973 degree-seeking undergraduates. **Degrees:** 569 associate awarded. **Location:** 15 miles from downtown. **Calendar:** Semester, limited summer session. **Full-time faculty:** 75 total. **Part-time faculty:** 295 total. **Special facilities:** Observatory, nature museum.

**Transfer out. Colleges most students transferred to 2007:** California State University: Long Beach, California State University: Dominguez Hills.

**Basis for selection.** Open admission.

**High school preparation.** 10 units recommended. Recommended units include English 4, mathematics 3, science 2 (laboratory 1). Nursing program requires high school diploma with chemistry and algebra, or college equivalent.

**2007-2008 Annual costs.** Tuition/fees: $622; $5,812 out-of-state. Per-credit charge: $20 in-state; $193 out-of-state. Books/supplies: $1,314. Personal expenses: $2,826.

**Financial aid.** All financial aid based on need. Need-based aid available for part-time students. Work-study available nights, weekends and for part-time students.

**Application procedures. Admission:** No deadline. No application fee. Application may be submitted online. Admission notification on a rolling basis. High school students accepted on part-time basis. **Financial aid:** Priority date 3/2; no closing date. FAFSA, institutional form required. Applicants notified on a rolling basis; must reply within 2 week(s) of notification.

**Academics.** Transfer-Alliance Honors Program with UCLA. **Special study options:** Accelerated study, cooperative education, cross-registration, distance learning, double major, dual enrollment of high school students, ESL, honors, independent study, liberal arts/career combination, study abroad, weekend college. License preparation in nursing, paramedic, physical therapy, real estate. **Credit/placement by examination:** AP, CLEP. **Support services:** GED preparation, learning center, remedial instruction, study skills assistance, tutoring, writing center.

**Majors. Architecture:** Technology. **Business:** General, accounting, administrative services, business admin, management information systems, office management, office technology, office/clerical, real estate. **Computer sciences:** General, applications programming, data entry, information systems. **Engineering:** Electrical. **Engineering technology:** Architectural, computer systems, drafting, electrical. **Family/consumer sciences:** Child care. **Health:** Medical secretary, nursing (RN). **Legal studies:** Legal secretary. **Liberal arts:** Arts/sciences, library science. **Mechanic/repair:** Automotive, electronics/electrical. **Protective services:** Firefighting, police science. **Psychology:** General. **Visual/performing arts:** Art, interior design.

**Most popular majors.** Health sciences 14%, liberal arts 75%.

**Computing on campus.** 660 workstations in library, computer center, student center. Commuter students can connect to campus network. Online course registration, online library, wireless network available.

**Student life. Freshman orientation:** Available. **Activities:** Bands, choral groups, dance, drama, literary magazine, music ensembles, musical theater, student government, student newspaper, TV station, Equal Opportunity Program Student Association.

Two-Year Colleges

**Athletics.** NJCAA. **Intercollegiate:** Baseball M, basketball, football (tackle) M, soccer, volleyball W. **Team name:** Seahawks.

**Student services.** Adult student services, career counseling, student employment services, health services, legal services, on-campus daycare, personal counseling, placement for graduates, veterans' counselor. **Physically disabled:** Services for visually, speech, hearing impaired. **Transfer:** Transfer center, transfer adviser, college fairs on campus for students transferring to 4-year colleges.

**Contact.**   Phone: (310) 233-5090 Fax: (310) 233-4223
David Ching, Dean of Admissions and Records, Los Angeles Harbor College, 1111 Figueroa Place, Wilmington, CA 90744-2397

## Los Angeles Mission College
### Sylmar, California
www.lamission.edu                                    CB code: 4404

◗   Public 2-year community college
◗   Large town

**General.** Founded in 1974. Regionally accredited. College serves nontraditional student body. **Enrollment:** 1,308 degree-seeking undergraduates. **Degrees:** 378 associate awarded. **ROTC:** Army, Air Force. **Location:** 20 miles from Los Angeles. **Calendar:** Semester, limited summer session. **Full-time faculty:** 60 total. **Part-time faculty:** 125 total.

**Basis for selection.** Open admission.

**2007-2008 Annual costs.** Tuition/fees: $622; $5,812 out-of-state. Per-credit charge: $20 in-state; $193 out-of-state.

**Financial aid.** **Additional information:** Board of Governors Grant available to those in receipt of AFDC, Social Security Insurance, or General Relief. If not in receipt of program, may qualify based on income.

**Application procedures.** **Admission:** Priority date 4/20; no deadline. No application fee. Admission notification on a rolling basis. **Financial aid:** Priority date 8/1; no closing date. FAFSA required. Applicants notified on a rolling basis starting 8/15.

**Academics.** Bilingual instruction available. **Special study options:** Accelerated study, cooperative education, dual enrollment of high school students, independent study. **Credit/placement by examination:** CLEP, institutional tests. 15 credit hours maximum toward associate degree. **Support services:** Learning center, remedial instruction, tutoring.

**Majors.** **Business:** Accounting, administrative services, business admin, management science, market research, office management, office/clerical, real estate. **Computer sciences:** General. **Education:** Teacher assistance. **English:** English lit. **Family/consumer sciences:** Clothing/textiles, food/nutrition, institutional food production. **Foreign languages:** Spanish. **Legal studies:** Paralegal. **Liberal arts:** Arts/sciences. **Math:** General. **Mechanic/repair:** Electronics/electrical. **Personal/culinary services:** Culinary arts. **Philosophy/religion:** Philosophy. **Protective services:** Criminal justice. **Psychology:** General. **Visual/performing arts:** Art, interior design.

**Computing on campus.** 10 workstations in library.

**Student life.** **Activities:** Choral groups, drama, student government.

**Athletics.** **Intercollegiate:** Baseball M, cross-country, golf M, soccer M.

**Student services.** Career counseling, on-campus daycare, personal counseling, placement for graduates, veterans' counselor. **Physically disabled:** Services for speech, hearing impaired.

**Contact.**   Phone: (818) 364-7661
Joe Ramirez, Vice President, Los Angeles Mission College, 13356 Eldridge Avenue, Sylmar, CA 91342-3245

## Los Angeles Pierce College
### Woodland Hills, California                  CB member
www.piercecollege.edu                             CB code: 4398

◗   Public 2-year community college
◗   Commuter campus in very large city

**General.** Founded in 1947. Regionally accredited. **Enrollment:** 9,971 degree-seeking undergraduates. **Degrees:** 1,030 associate awarded. **Location:** 27 miles from downtown. **Calendar:** Semester, extensive summer session. **Full-time faculty:** 196 total. **Part-time faculty:** 531 total. **Special facilities:**

Braille nature trail, life science museum, nature center, weather station, working farm, botanical garden.

**Transfer out. Colleges most students transferred to 2007:** California State University: Northridge, University of California: Los Angeles.

**Basis for selection.** Open admission, but selective for some programs. Limited admission to nursing and animal health technology programs. All students required to take English and math placement tests prior to course registration.

**2007-2008 Annual costs.** Tuition/fees: $626; $5,816 out-of-state. Per-credit charge: $20 in-state; $193 out-of-state. Books/supplies: $1,422. Personal expenses: $2,826.

**Financial aid.** All financial aid based on need. Need-based aid available for part-time students.

**Application procedures.** **Admission:** Closing date 9/10 (receipt date). No application fee. Application may be submitted online. Admission notification on a rolling basis. **Financial aid:** Priority date 5/1; no closing date. FAFSA, institutional form required. Applicants notified on a rolling basis starting 8/1.

**Academics.** **Special study options:** Cooperative education, distance learning, dual enrollment of high school students, honors, student-designed major, study abroad. **Credit/placement by examination:** CLEP, institutional tests. 15 credit hours maximum toward associate degree. **Support services:** GED preparation, learning center, remedial instruction, tutoring.

**Majors.** **Agriculture:** Animal health, animal sciences, business, dairy, equestrian studies, equine science, greenhouse operations, horticultural science, horticulture, landscaping, ornamental horticulture. **Area/ethnic studies:** Latin American. **Business:** General, accounting, business admin, management science, marketing. **Communications:** Journalism. **Computer sciences:** General, applications programming, computer science, programming. **Conservation:** Management/policy. **Engineering:** General. **Engineering technology:** Construction, drafting. **Foreign languages:** French, Italian, sign language interpretation, Spanish. **Health:** Nursing (RN), preveterinary. **Liberal arts:** Arts/sciences. **Mechanic/repair:** Auto body, automotive. **Philosophy/religion:** Religion. **Visual/performing arts:** Commercial/advertising art, industrial design, photography, studio arts.

**Computing on campus.** Online course registration available.

**Student life.** **Activities:** Bands, choral groups, dance, drama, literary magazine, music ensembles, student government, student newspaper, symphony orchestra, international students association, Bible Fellowship, Alpha Gamma Sigma honor society, Phi Theta Kappa honor society, Phi Beta Lambda business association, Hillel, Union of African American Students, Muslim students association.

**Athletics.** NJCAA. **Intercollegiate:** Baseball M, basketball W, cheerleading, diving, football (tackle) M, soccer W, softball W, swimming, tennis, volleyball. **Team name:** Brahmas.

**Student services.** Adult student services, career counseling, services for economically disadvantaged, student employment services, health services, on-campus daycare, personal counseling, placement for graduates, veterans' counselor. **Physically disabled:** Services for visually, speech, hearing impaired. **Transfer:** Transfer center, transfer adviser, college fairs on campus for students transferring to 4-year colleges.

**Contact.**   E-mail: pierceinfo@piercecollege.edu
Phone: (818) 719-6448 Fax: (818) 716-1087
Shelley Gerstl, Dean of Admissions and Records, Los Angeles Pierce College, 6201 Winnetka Avenue, Woodland Hills, CA 91371

## Los Angeles Southwest College
### Los Angeles, California
www.lasc.edu                                        CB code: 4409

◗   Public 2-year community college
◗   Commuter campus in very large city

**General.** Founded in 1967. Regionally accredited. Awards associate degrees in 34 disciplines with occupational certificates in 47 disciplines. It offers wide range of programs to meet community needs - college transfer, occupational, general education, transitional, continuing, community services and joint programs to diverse population. Campus is site of Middle College High School, enabling high school students to take college courses for credit. **Enrollment:** 6,034 undergraduates. **Degrees:** 372 associate awarded. **Calendar:** Semester, limited summer session. **Full-time faculty:** 75 total. **Part-time faculty:** 180 total. **Special facilities:** Career services center, art gallery.

**Basis for selection.** Open admission, but selective for some programs. Limited admission to nursing and allied health programs.

**2007-2008 Annual costs.** Tuition/fees: $622; $5,812 out-of-state. Per-credit charge: $20 in-state; $193 out-of-state.

**Financial aid. Need-based:** Need-based aid available for part-time students. **Additional information:** Board of Governors Enrollment Fee Waiver available to students receiving AFDC, SSI/SSP, or General Assistance. May also qualify on basis of income.

**Application procedures. Admission:** No deadline. No application fee. Late registration allowed through third week of classes, if permitted by instructor. **Financial aid:** No deadline. FAFSA required. Applicants notified on a rolling basis; must reply within 2 week(s) of notification.

**Academics. Special study options:** Accelerated study, cooperative education, cross-registration, double major, dual enrollment of high school students, ESL, honors, independent study, liberal arts/career combination, study abroad, weekend college. **Credit/placement by examination:** CLEP, institutional tests. 15 credit hours maximum toward associate degree. **Support services:** Learning center, reduced course load, remedial instruction, tutoring.

**Majors. Area/ethnic studies:** African-American. **Biology:** General, molecular. **Business:** General, accounting, administrative services, banking/financial services, business admin, insurance, management information systems, office technology, office/clerical, real estate. **Communications:** Advertising, journalism. **Communications technology:** General. **Computer sciences:** General, applications programming, computer graphics, computer science, programming. **Education:** General, early childhood, foreign languages, mathematics, music, teacher assistance. **Engineering:** General, electrical. **Engineering technology:** Drafting, electrical. **English:** English lit. **Family/consumer sciences:** Child care. **Foreign languages:** General, French, Spanish. **Health:** Clinical lab technology, nursing (RN), respiratory therapy technology. **History:** General. **Legal studies:** Paralegal. **Liberal arts:** Arts/sciences. **Math:** General. **Parks/recreation:** General. **Philosophy/religion:** Philosophy. **Physical sciences:** Chemistry, geology, physics. **Psychology:** General. **Social sciences:** Geography, political science, sociology. **Visual/performing arts:** Art, art history/conservation, commercial/advertising art, dramatic, fashion design, photography.

**Computing on campus.** Helpline, repair service available.

**Student life. Activities:** Bands, choral groups, dance, drama, literary magazine, musical theater, student government, student newspaper.

**Athletics.** NJCAA. **Intercollegiate:** Basketball M, cross-country, football (tackle) M, tennis W, track and field. **Intramural:** Baseball M, basketball, bowling, golf, softball, tennis, track and field, volleyball. **Team name:** Cougars.

**Student services.** Career counseling, student employment services, on-campus daycare, personal counseling, placement for graduates. **Transfer:** Transfer adviser for students transferring to 4-year colleges.

**Contact.** Phone: (323) 241-5321
Linda Daniels, Associate Dean of Admissions, Los Angeles Southwest College, 1600 West Imperial Highway, Los Angeles, CA 90047-4899

---

## Los Angeles Trade and Technical College
**Los Angeles, California**
www.lattc.edu                                    **CB code: 4400**

▶  Public 2-year community and technical college
▶  Commuter campus in very large city

**General.** Founded in 1925. Regionally accredited. Specialized culinary arts program, fashion, cosmetology, nursing programs. **Enrollment:** 12,973 undergraduates. **Degrees:** 501 associate awarded. **Calendar:** Semester, limited summer session. **Full-time faculty:** 185 total. **Part-time faculty:** 285 total. **Class size:** 46% < 20, 38% 20-39, 9% 40-49, 4% 50-99, 4% >100.

**Student profile.**

Out-of-state:            8%      25 or older:            60%

**Transfer out. Colleges most students transferred to 2007:** University of California: Los Angeles, California State University: Los Angeles, California State University: Dominguez Hills, University of Southern California.

**Basis for selection.** Open admission. Limited admission to nursing program. Portfolio recommended of commercial art majors.

---

**2007-2008 Annual costs.** Tuition/fees: $622; $5,812 out-of-state. Per-credit charge: $20 in-state; $193 out-of-state.

**Financial aid.** All financial aid based on need. Need-based aid available for part-time students. Work-study available nights, weekends and for part-time students.

**Application procedures. Admission:** No deadline. No application fee. Application may be submitted online. Admission notification on a rolling basis. **Financial aid:** Priority date 5/1; no closing date. FAFSA required. Applicants notified on a rolling basis.

**Academics. Special study options:** Accelerated study, cooperative education, distance learning, dual enrollment of high school students, ESL, independent study, liberal arts/career combination, study abroad, weekend college. License preparation in nursing. **Credit/placement by examination:** CLEP, institutional tests. 15 credit hours maximum toward associate degree. **Support services:** GED preparation, learning center, pre-admission summer program, reduced course load, remedial instruction, study skills assistance, tutoring, writing center.

**Majors. Business:** General, accounting, administrative services, business admin, entrepreneurial studies, fashion, hospitality/recreation, labor relations, office/clerical, real estate. **Communications:** Journalism. **Communications technology:** General, graphic/printing. **Computer sciences:** General, computer science. **Construction:** Carpentry, electrician, maintenance, pipefitting, power transmission. **Engineering:** General. **Engineering technology:** Architectural, drafting, electrical. **Family/consumer sciences:** Clothing/textiles, institutional food production. **Health:** Health services, licensed practical nurse. **Liberal arts:** Arts/sciences. **Mechanic/repair:** Auto body, diesel, electronics/electrical, heating/ac/refrig. **Personal/culinary services:** Culinary arts. **Public administration:** Community org/advocacy. **Visual/performing arts:** Commercial/advertising art, fashion design, photography.

**Most popular majors.** Computer/information sciences 11%, health sciences 11%, liberal arts 34%, trade and industry 30%, visual/performing arts 8%.

**Computing on campus.** 550 workstations in library, computer center. Commuter students can connect to campus network. Online course registration, wireless network available.

**Student life. Freshman orientation:** Available. **Activities:** Dance, student government, student newspaper, political organizations.

**Athletics.** NJCAA. **Intercollegiate:** Basketball, cross-country, tennis, track and field. **Intramural:** Golf, swimming. **Team name:** Beaver.

**Student services.** Adult student services, career counseling, services for economically disadvantaged, student employment services, financial aid counseling, health services, minority student services, on-campus daycare, personal counseling, placement for graduates, veterans' counselor. **Physically disabled:** Services for visually, speech, hearing impaired. **Transfer:** Transfer adviser, college fairs on campus for students transferring to 4-year colleges.

**Contact.** Phone: (213) 763-7000
Ester Usaha, Registrar, Los Angeles Trade and Technical College, 400 West Washington Boulevard, Los Angeles, CA 90015-4181

---

## Los Angeles Valley College
**Valley Glen, California**
www.lavc.edu                                    **CB code: 5546**

▶  Public 2-year community college
▶  Commuter campus in very large city

**General.** Founded in 1949. Regionally accredited. **Enrollment:** 8,678 degree-seeking undergraduates. **Degrees:** 785 associate awarded. **Location:** 15 miles from downtown. **Calendar:** Semester, limited summer session. **Full-time faculty:** 240 total. **Part-time faculty:** 285 total. **Special facilities:** Planetarium.

**Student profile.**

Out-of-state:            2%      25 or older:            69%

**Basis for selection.** Open admission, but selective for some programs. Registered nursing program has competitive admission based on points accumulated for prerequisite courses, grades, and placement test scores. Institutional placement tests required of all students.

**2007-2008 Annual costs.** Tuition/fees: $624; $5,814 out-of-state. Per-credit charge: $60 in-state; $193 out-of-state.

**Financial aid.** All financial aid based on need. Need-based aid available for part-time students.

**Application procedures. Admission:** No deadline. No application fee. Application may be submitted online. Admission notification on a rolling basis. **Financial aid:** Priority date 6/12; no closing date. FAFSA required. Applicants notified on a rolling basis.

**Academics. Special study options:** Cooperative education, dual enrollment of high school students, honors, independent study. License preparation in nursing, paramedic. **Credit/placement by examination:** AP, CLEP, IB, institutional tests. 15 credit hours maximum toward associate degree. **Support services:** Learning center, remedial instruction, study skills assistance, tutoring, writing center.

**Majors. Area/ethnic studies:** American. **Biology:** General. **Business:** General, administrative services, fashion, hospitality/recreation, management information systems, office technology, office/clerical. **Communications:** Broadcast journalism, journalism. **Computer sciences:** Applications programming, data processing. **Engineering technology:** Electrical. **English:** English lit. **Family/consumer sciences:** General. **Foreign languages:** French, German, Italian, Spanish. **Health:** Nursing (RN), respiratory therapy technology. **History:** General. **Liberal arts:** Arts/sciences. **Math:** General. **Parks/recreation:** General. **Philosophy/religion:** Philosophy. **Physical sciences:** Chemistry, geology, physics, planetary. **Protective services:** Police science. **Psychology:** General. **Social sciences:** Economics, geography, political science, sociology. **Visual/performing arts:** Art, art history/conservation, commercial/advertising art.

**Computing on campus.** 300 workstations in library, computer center, student center. Online course registration, wireless network available.

**Student life. Freshman orientation:** Available. Preregistration for classes offered. **Activities:** Bands, choral groups, dance, drama, film society, literary magazine, music ensembles, musical theater, radio station, student government, student newspaper, symphony orchestra.

**Athletics.** NJCAA. **Intercollegiate:** Baseball M, basketball, cross-country, diving, football (tackle) M, soccer W, softball W, swimming, track and field, water polo M. **Team name:** Monarchs.

**Student services.** Career counseling, student employment services, health services, on-campus daycare, personal counseling, placement for graduates, veterans' counselor. **Physically disabled:** Services for visually, speech, hearing impaired. **Learning disabled:** Comprehensive services available. **Transfer:** Transfer adviser, college fairs on campus for students transferring to 4-year colleges.

**Contact.** E-mail: trudgej@lavc.edu
Phone: (818) 947-2553 Fax: (818) 947-2501
Florentino Manzano, Dean of Enrollment Management, Los Angeles Valley College, 5800 Fulton Avenue, Valley Glen, CA 91401-4096

---

## Los Medanos College
**Pittsburg, California**
www.losmedanos.edu                    CB code: 4396

- Public 2-year community college
- Commuter campus in small city

**General.** Founded in 1973. Regionally accredited. **Enrollment:** 9,000 undergraduates. **Degrees:** 255 associate awarded. **Location:** 45 miles from San Francisco. **Calendar:** Semester. **Full-time faculty:** 104 total. **Part-time faculty:** 195 total.

**Student profile.**

| | | | |
|---|---|---|---|
| Out-of-state: | 1% | 25 or older: | 53% |

**Basis for selection.** Open admission.

**2007-2008 Annual costs.** Tuition/fees: $610; $5,710 out-of-state. Per-credit charge: $20 in-state; $190 out-of-state.

**Application procedures. Admission:** No deadline. Admission notification on a rolling basis. **Financial aid:** Priority date 3/2; no closing date. FAFSA required. Applicants notified on a rolling basis starting 7/1; must reply within 2 week(s) of notification.

**Academics. Special study options:** Cooperative education, cross-registration, independent study, study abroad. **Credit/placement by examination:** CLEP, institutional tests. 20 credit hours maximum toward associate degree. **Support services:** Learning center, remedial instruction, tutoring.

**Majors. Biology:** General. **Business:** Accounting, entrepreneurial studies, labor relations, office management, real estate, tourism promotion. **Communications:** Journalism. **Family/consumer sciences:** Child care. **Health:** EMT paramedic, nursing (RN). **Liberal arts:** Arts/sciences. **Math:** General. **Mechanic/repair:** Electronics/electrical, small engine. **Physical sciences:** Chemistry. **Protective services:** Firefighting. **Psychology:** General. **Social sciences:** Anthropology, sociology. **Visual/performing arts:** Commercial/advertising art, music performance, studio arts.

**Most popular majors.** Business/marketing 7%, health sciences 18%, liberal arts 60%.

**Computing on campus.** 150 workstations in computer center.

**Student life. Activities:** Bands, choral groups, drama, music ensembles, student government, student newspaper.

**Athletics. Intercollegiate:** Baseball M, basketball, football (tackle) M, soccer M, softball W, volleyball W. **Intramural:** Basketball, softball, tennis.

**Student services.** Career counseling, student employment services, on-campus daycare, personal counseling, placement for graduates. **Physically disabled:** Services for visually, speech, hearing impaired. **Transfer:** Transfer adviser, college fairs on campus for students transferring to 4-year colleges.

**Contact.** Phone: (925) 439-2181 ext. 7500 Fax: (925) 427-6351
John Mullen, Director, Admissions and Records, Los Medanos College, 2700 East Leland Road, Pittsburg, CA 94565

---

## Maric College
**San Diego, California**
www.mariccollege.edu                    CB code: 3064

- For-profit 2-year business and health science college
- Commuter campus in very large city

**General.** Accredited by ACCSCT. **Calendar:** Continuous.

**Annual costs/financial aid.** Tuition varies by program and ranges from $172 per unit to $400 per unit. Program lengths vary.

**Contact.** Phone: (858) 279-4500
9055 Balboa Avenue, San Diego, CA 92123

---

## Maric College: Palm Springs
**Palm Springs, California**
www.mariccollege.edu

- For-profit 2-year health science and technical college
- Commuter campus in large town

**General.** Accredited by ACCSCT. **Enrollment:** 55 degree-seeking undergraduates. **Degrees:** 13 associate awarded. **Calendar:** Continuous. **Full-time faculty:** 12 total. **Part-time faculty:** 8 total.

**Academics. Credit/placement by examination:** CLEP.

**Majors. Legal studies:** Paralegal.

**Contact.** Phone: (760) 327-4562
Maric College: Palm Springs, 2475 East Tahquitz Canyon Way, Palm Springs, CA 92262

---

## Maric College: Panorama City
**Panorama City, California**
www.mariccollege.edu                    CB code: 3541

- For-profit 2-year junior and technical college
- Commuter campus in very large city
- Interview required

**General.** Accredited by ACICS. **Enrollment:** 90 degree-seeking undergraduates. **Degrees:** 46 associate awarded. **Location:** 15 miles from Los Angeles. **Calendar:** Continuous. **Full-time faculty:** 13 total. **Class size:** 76% < 20, 24% 20-39.

**Basis for selection.** Open admission. **Homeschooled:** Interview required.

**2007-2008 Annual costs.** Tuition/fees: $11,845. Books/supplies: $1,600. Personal expenses: $2,520.

**Financial aid.** All financial aid based on need. Work-study available nights.

**Application procedures. Admission:** No deadline. No application fee. Application must be submitted on paper. **Financial aid:** No deadline. FAFSA, institutional form required.

**Academics. Special study options:** Internships, liberal arts/career combination. **Credit/placement by examination:** AP, CLEP. **Support services:** Learning center, study skills assistance, tutoring.

**Majors. Business:** Accounting, accounting technology, accounting/business management, business admin, office management. **Computer sciences:** Information technology, LAN/WAN management, system admin. **Legal studies:** Court reporting, paralegal.

**Most popular majors.** Business/marketing 17%, computer/information sciences 35%, legal studies 46%.

**Computing on campus.** 20 workstations in library, computer center. Online library available.

**Student life. Freshman orientation:** Mandatory. **Activities:** Student newspaper.

**Student services.** Career counseling, student employment services, financial aid counseling, placement for graduates.

**Contact.** E-mail: lking@mariccollege.edu
Phone: (818) 672-3000 Toll-free number: (800) 206-0095
Fax: (818) 672-8919
Linda King, Director of Admissions, Maric College: Panorama City, 14355 Roscoe Boulevard, Panorama City, CA 91402

## Maric College: Sacramento
### Sacramento, California
### www.mariccollege.edu

- For-profit 2-year business and technical college
- Commuter campus in large city

**General.** Accredited by ACICS. **Calendar:** Continuous.

**Annual costs/financial aid.** Tuition varies by program from $7,600 to $10,249. Required fees $100; per-credit-hour charge varies from $197 to $227.

**Contact.** Phone: (916) 649-8168
Admissions Director, 4330 Watt Avenue, Suite 400, Sacramento, CA 95821

## Maric College: Salida
### Salida, California
### www.mariccollege.edu

- For-profit 2-year health science and technical college
- Commuter campus in small city
- Interview required

**General.** Accredited by ACCSCT. **Enrollment:** 882 degree-seeking undergraduates. **Degrees:** 105 associate awarded. **Calendar:** Continuous. **Full-time faculty:** 25 total. **Part-time faculty:** 10 total.

**Basis for selection.** Open admission. **Homeschooled:** Transcript of courses and grades required.

**Application procedures. Admission:** No deadline. $20 fee. Application must be submitted on paper.

**Academics. Credit/placement by examination:** CLEP.

**Majors. Health:** Respiratory therapy assistant, surgical technology.

**Most popular majors.** Health sciences 64%.

**Computing on campus.** 90 workstations in computer center.

**Student life. Freshman orientation:** Mandatory.

**Student services.** Adult student services, career counseling, financial aid counseling, placement for graduates, veterans' counselor.

**Contact.** E-mail: wtriplett@mariccollege.edu
Phone: (209) 543-7000
Willie Triplett, Director of Admissions, Maric College: Salida, 5172 Kiernan Court, Salida, CA 95368

## Maric College: Vista
### Vista, California
### www.mariccollege.edu

- For-profit 2-year technical college
- Commuter campus in small city

**General.** Accredited by ACCSCT. **Enrollment:** 840 degree-seeking undergraduates. **Degrees:** 55 associate awarded. **Calendar:** Continuous. **Full-time faculty:** 20 total. **Part-time faculty:** 33 total.

**Basis for selection.** Institutional entrance exam important. High school diploma/GED required for some programs. Timed institutional examination administered onsite.

**2007-2008 Annual costs.** Associate degree program costs range from $23,567-$27,620.

**Application procedures. Admission:** No deadline. $20 fee.

**Academics. Credit/placement by examination:** CLEP.

**Majors. Computer sciences:** LAN/WAN management. **Legal studies:** Paralegal. **Protective services:** Criminal justice.

**Contact.** Phone: (760) 630-1555 Fax: (760) 630-1656
Renee Codner, Director of Admissions, Maric College: Vista, 2022 University Drive, Vista, CA 92083

## Marymount College
### Rancho Palos Verdes, California
### www.marymountpv.edu

**CB member**
**CB code: 4515**

- Private 2-year junior and liberal arts college affiliated with Roman Catholic Church
- Residential campus in large town

**General.** Founded in 1933. Regionally accredited. **Enrollment:** 674 degree-seeking undergraduates. **Degrees:** 159 associate awarded. **Location:** 30 miles from Los Angeles. **Calendar:** Semester, limited summer session. **Full-time faculty:** 39 total; 62% have terminal degrees, 13% minority, 51% women. **Part-time faculty:** 46 total; 17% have terminal degrees, 11% minority, 65% women. **Class size:** 64% < 20, 35% 20-39, less than 1% 40-49.

**Student profile.** Among degree-seeking undergraduates, 395 enrolled as first-time, first-year students, 57 transferred in from other institutions.

| | | | |
|---|---|---|---|
| Part-time: | 3% | Hispanic American: | 18% |
| Out-of-state: | 17% | Native American: | 1% |
| Women: | 54% | International: | 10% |
| African American: | 6% | Live on campus: | 58% |
| Asian American: | 7% | | |

**Transfer out.** 90% of students enrolled in the transfer program go on to 4-year colleges. **Colleges most students transferred to 2007:** University of Southern California, Loyola Marymount University, University of California, California State University, Chapman University.

**Basis for selection.** High school record, quality of academic preparation, recommendations, student's personal statement all considered. SAT or ACT recommended. ACCUPLACER used for placement. Interview and essay recommended. **Homeschooled:** Transcript of courses and grades, letter of recommendation (nonparent) required. General syllabus of all coursework completed or private tutoring received, statement explaining why family chose home schooling and its advantages and disadvantages required. SAT or ACT scores and state H.S. equivalency certificate recommended.

**High school preparation.** 13 units recommended. Recommended units include English 4, mathematics 3, social studies 2, science 2 (laboratory 1) and foreign language 2.

**2008-2009 Annual costs.** Tuition/fees: $23,548. Room/board: $10,290. Books/supplies: $1,242. Personal expenses: $3,533.

**2006-2007 Financial aid. Need-based:** 137 full-time freshmen applied for aid; 122 were judged to have need; 122 of these received aid. Average need met was 60%. Average scholarship/grant was $12,752; average loan

$2,475. 83% of total undergraduate aid awarded as scholarships/grants, 17% as loans/jobs. **Non-need-based:** Awarded to 93 full-time undergraduates, including 54 freshmen. Scholarships awarded for academics.

**Application procedures. Admission:** Priority date 3/2; no deadline. $35 fee, may be waived for applicants with need. Application may be submitted online. Admission notification on a rolling basis beginning on or about 12/15. Must reply by May 1 or within 4 week(s) if notified thereafter. **Financial aid:** Priority date 3/1; no closing date. FAFSA required. Applicants notified on a rolling basis starting 2/1; must reply by 5/1 or within 4 week(s) of notification.

**Academics. Special study options:** Cooperative education, dual enrollment of high school students, ESL, honors, independent study, internships, study abroad, urban semester, weekend college. **Credit/placement by examination:** AP, CLEP, IB, institutional tests. 15 credit hours maximum toward associate degree. **Support services:** Learning center, pre-admission summer program, reduced course load, remedial instruction, study skills assistance, tutoring.

**Majors. English:** English lit. **Liberal arts:** Arts/sciences.

**Computing on campus.** 77 workstations in library, computer center. Dormitories wired for high-speed internet access and linked to campus network. Commuter students can connect to campus network. Online library, helpline, repair service, wireless network available.

**Student life. Freshman orientation:** Mandatory, $125 fee. Preregistration for classes offered. **Housing:** Guaranteed on-campus for freshmen. Apartments available. $400 deposit, deadline 7/1. Housing available through volunteers in the community. **Activities:** Campus ministries, choral groups, dance, drama, international student organizations, music ensembles, musical theater, radio station, student government, volunteer club, philosophy discussion club, pre-med club, student integrity council, yoga/meditation club, Phi Theta Kappa, Latinos Unidos, black student union.

**Athletics. NJCAA. Intramural:** Basketball, golf, skiing, soccer, softball, swimming, tennis. **Team name:** Mariners.

**Student services.** Adult student services, alcohol/substance abuse counseling, campus ministries, career counseling, student employment services, financial aid counseling, health services, personal counseling. **Physically disabled:** Services for hearing impaired. **Transfer:** Pre-admission transcript evaluation for new students. Transfer center, transfer adviser, college fairs on campus for students transferring to 4-year colleges.

**Contact.** E-mail: admissions@marymountpv.edu
Phone: (310) 377-5501 ext. 208 Fax: (310) 265-0962
Nina Lococo, Dean of Admissions, Marymount College, 30800 Palos Verdes Drive East, Rancho Palos Verdes, CA 90275-6299

## Mendocino College
**Ukiah, California**
www.mendocino.edu                 CB code: 4517

◆ Public 2-year community college
◆ Commuter campus in large town

**General.** Founded in 1973. Regionally accredited. **Enrollment:** 1,405 degree-seeking undergraduates; 3,715 non-degree-seeking students. **Degrees:** 317 associate awarded. **Location:** 60 miles from Santa Rosa, 110 miles from San Francisco. **Calendar:** Semester, limited summer session. **Full-time faculty:** 37 total; 24% have terminal degrees, 49% women. **Part-time faculty:** 120 total. **Class size:** 46% < 20, 14% 20-39, less than 1% 40-49, less than 1% 50-99, less than 1% >100. **Special facilities:** Gallery and theater complex.

**Student profile.** Among degree-seeking undergraduates, 54% enrolled in a transfer program, 27% enrolled in a vocational program, 16% already have a bachelor's degree or higher, 297 enrolled as first-time, first-year students, 404 transferred in from other institutions.

| | | | |
|---|---|---|---|
| Part-time: | 74% | Asian American: | 2% |
| Out-of-state: | 5% | Hispanic American: | 16% |
| Women: | 68% | Native American: | 8% |
| African American: | 2% | 25 or older: | 60% |

**Transfer out.** 20% of students enrolled in the transfer program go on to 4-year colleges. **Colleges most students transferred to 2007:** Sonoma State University, University of California.

**Basis for selection.** Open admission.

**2007-2008 Annual costs.** Tuition/fees: $634; $6,184 out-of-state. Per-credit charge: $20 in-state; $205 out-of-state. Books/supplies: $630. Personal expenses: $1,584.

**2006-2007 Financial aid. Need-based:** Average scholarship/grant was $2,046; average loan $1,750. 85% of total undergraduate aid awarded as scholarships/grants, 15% as loans/jobs. Need-based aid available for part-time students. Work-study available for part-time students. **Non-need-based:** Scholarships awarded for academics, leadership, state residency.

**Application procedures. Admission:** Priority date 5/1; no deadline. No application fee. Application may be submitted online. Admission notification on a rolling basis beginning on or about 7/1. **Financial aid:** Priority date 5/31; no closing date. FAFSA required. Applicants notified on a rolling basis starting 7/1; must reply within 2 week(s) of notification.

**Academics. Special study options:** Accelerated study, distance learning, double major, dual enrollment of high school students, ESL, independent study, student-designed major. License preparation in nursing, paramedic, real estate. **Credit/placement by examination:** AP, CLEP, institutional tests. 12 credit hours maximum toward associate degree. **Support services:** GED test center, learning center, remedial instruction, tutoring.

**Majors. Agriculture:** Plant sciences. **Biology:** General. **Business:** General, accounting, administrative services, business admin, entrepreneurial studies. **Computer sciences:** General. **English:** English lit, speech/rhetoric. **Foreign languages:** French, Spanish. **Health:** Substance abuse counseling. **Liberal arts:** Arts/sciences. **Math:** General. **Mechanic/repair:** Auto body, electronics/electrical. **Parks/recreation:** Sports admin. **Protective services:** Law enforcement admin. **Psychology:** General. **Social sciences:** General. **Visual/performing arts:** Art, dramatic.

**Most popular majors.** Business/marketing 19%, health sciences 10%, liberal arts 48%, psychology 6%.

**Computing on campus.** 100 workstations in library, computer center, student center. Online library, wireless network available.

**Student life. Freshman orientation:** Available. **Activities:** Bands, choral groups, dance, drama, music ensembles, musical theater, radio station, student government, student newspaper, symphony orchestra.

**Athletics. NJCAA. Intercollegiate:** Baseball M, basketball, cheerleading M, football (tackle) M, soccer, softball W, track and field, volleyball W. **Intramural:** Basketball, bowling, softball, volleyball. **Team name:** Eagles.

**Student services.** Career counseling, services for economically disadvantaged, student employment services, financial aid counseling, on-campus daycare, personal counseling, placement for graduates, veterans' counselor. **Physically disabled:** Services for visually, speech, hearing impaired. **Transfer:** Transfer adviser, college fairs on campus for students transferring to 4-year colleges.

**Contact.** Phone: (707) 468-3101 Fax: (707) 468-3120
Kristie Anderson, Director of Admissions and Records, Mendocino College, 1000 Hensley Creek/Box 3000, Ukiah, CA 95482

## Merced College
**Merced, California**
www.mccd.edu                 CB code: 4500

◆ Public 2-year community college
◆ Commuter campus in small city

**General.** Founded in 1962. Regionally accredited. Off-campus centers at Los Banos. **Enrollment:** 5,866 degree-seeking undergraduates. **Degrees:** 439 associate awarded. **Location:** 50 miles from Fresno. **Calendar:** Semester, limited summer session. **Full-time faculty:** 120 total. **Part-time faculty:** 479 total.

**Transfer out. Colleges most students transferred to 2007:** CSU Stanislaus, CSU Fresno.

**Basis for selection.** Open admission. Institutional placement tests used.

**2007-2008 Annual costs.** Tuition/fees: $628; $5,818 out-of-state. Per-credit charge: $20 in-state; $193 out-of-state. Books/supplies: $650. Personal expenses: $1,750.

**Financial aid. Non-need-based:** Scholarships awarded for academics.

**Application procedures. Admission:** No deadline. No application fee. Application must be submitted on paper. Admission notification on a rolling basis. Must reply by May 1 or within 4 week(s) if notified thereafter. **Financial aid:** Priority date 6/1; no closing date. FAFSA required. Applicants

notified on a rolling basis starting 1/2; must reply within 3 week(s) of notification.

**Academics. Special study options:** Cooperative education, distance learning, dual enrollment of high school students, honors, internships, study abroad. License preparation in nursing, radiology, real estate. **Credit/placement by examination:** AP, CLEP, institutional tests. 12 credit hours maximum toward associate degree. **Support services:** Learning center, pre-admission summer program, remedial instruction, tutoring.

**Majors. Agriculture:** Agronomy, animal sciences, business, equestrian studies, horticulture, ornamental horticulture, soil science. **Biology:** General. **Business:** General, accounting, administrative services, banking/financial services, business admin, entrepreneurial studies, management information systems, office management, office/clerical, real estate. **Communications:** General, journalism. **Computer sciences:** General, applications programming, computer science, information systems, programming. **Education:** General, early childhood. **Engineering:** General, aerospace. **Engineering technology:** Drafting, electrical. **English:** English lit, speech/rhetoric. **Family/consumer sciences:** General, family studies, institutional food production. **Foreign languages:** French, German, Spanish. **Health:** Licensed practical nurse, medical assistant, medical radiologic technology/radiation therapy, medical secretary, nursing (RN), substance abuse counseling. **History:** General. **Legal studies:** Legal secretary. **Liberal arts:** Arts/sciences. **Math:** General. **Mechanic/repair:** Auto body, diesel, industrial. **Parks/recreation:** Health/fitness. **Philosophy/religion:** Philosophy. **Physical sciences:** Chemistry, physics. **Protective services:** Firefighting, police science. **Psychology:** General. **Public administration:** Social work. **Social sciences:** General, anthropology, archaeology, economics, geography, political science, sociology. **Visual/performing arts:** General, commercial/advertising art, dramatic, photography, studio arts.

**Computing on campus.** 400 workstations in library, computer center. Commuter students can connect to campus network. Online library, helpline available.

**Student life. Freshman orientation:** Available. **Activities:** Bands, choral groups, dance, drama, international student organizations, music ensembles, musical theater, student government, student newspaper, symphony orchestra, black student union, Movimiento Estudiantil Chicano de Aztlan, Intervarsity Christian group, Rotaract.

**Athletics.** NJCAA. **Intercollegiate:** Baseball M, basketball, cross-country, diving, football (tackle) M, golf, softball W, swimming, tennis, track and field, volleyball W, water polo. **Team name:** Blue Devils.

**Student services.** Alcohol/substance abuse counseling, career counseling, services for economically disadvantaged, student employment services, financial aid counseling, health services, on-campus daycare, personal counseling, placement for graduates, veterans' counselor. **Physically disabled:** Services for visually, speech, hearing impaired. **Transfer:** Transfer center, transfer adviser, college fairs on campus for students transferring to 4-year colleges.

**Contact.** Phone: (209) 384-6187 Fax: (209) 384-6339
Betsy Donovan, Dean of Student Services, Merced College, Administration Building Box #14, Merced, CA 95348

## Merritt College
Oakland, California
www.merritt.edu
**CB code: 4502**

- Public 2-year community college
- Large city

**General.** Founded in 1953. Regionally accredited. **Enrollment:** 7,409 undergraduates. **Degrees:** 420 associate awarded. **Location:** 15 miles from San Francisco. **Calendar:** Semester, extensive summer session. **Full-time faculty:** 90 total. **Part-time faculty:** 215 total. **Special facilities:** Anthropology museum, landscape/horticulture complex.

**Student profile.**

| | | | |
|---|---|---|---|
| Out-of-state: | 5% | 25 or older: | 60% |

**Basis for selection.** Open admission.

**2007-2008 Annual costs.** Tuition/fees: $604; $5,794 out-of-state. Per-credit charge: $20 in-state; $193 out-of-state. Books/supplies: $1,332. Personal expenses: $2,430.

**Financial aid. Need-based:** Need-based aid available for part-time students.

**Application procedures. Admission:** No deadline. No application fee. Admission notification on a rolling basis. **Financial aid:** Priority date 4/1,

closing date 6/30. FAFSA, institutional form required. Applicants notified on a rolling basis starting 6/1.

**Academics. Special study options:** Cooperative education, cross-registration, distance learning, dual enrollment of high school students, honors, independent study. **Credit/placement by examination:** CLEP, institutional tests. 15 credit hours maximum toward associate degree. **Support services:** Learning center, pre-admission summer program, reduced course load, remedial instruction, tutoring.

**Majors. Agriculture:** Horticultural science, landscaping. **Area/ethnic studies:** African-American. **Business:** General, real estate. **Computer sciences:** General. **Education:** General, business, early childhood. **Engineering:** Electrical. **English:** English lit. **Family/consumer sciences:** Child care, family/community services. **Foreign languages:** French, Spanish. **Health:** Licensed practical nurse, medical radiologic technology/radiation therapy, nursing (RN). **Legal studies:** Paralegal. **Liberal arts:** Arts/sciences. **Math:** General. **Parks/recreation:** General. **Public administration:** Community org/advocacy. **Social sciences:** General.

**Computing on campus.** 200 workstations in library, computer center, student center.

**Student life. Activities:** Choral groups, dance, student government, student newspaper, Merritt Christian Fellowship, LaRaza Student Union, Native American Association, Black Student Union, Asian Student Union, Ecology Action Club, Disabled Students Coalition.

**Athletics. Intercollegiate:** Basketball, cross-country, track and field. **Intramural:** Badminton, golf, tennis, volleyball.

**Student services.** Adult student services, career counseling, student employment services, health services, on-campus daycare, personal counseling, placement for graduates, veterans' counselor. **Physically disabled:** Services for visually, speech, hearing impaired. **Transfer:** Transfer adviser, college fairs on campus for students transferring to 4-year colleges.

**Contact.** E-mail: admissions@peralta.edu
Phone: (510) 436-2487
Howard Perdue, Dean of Admissions and Records, Merritt College, 12500 Campus Drive, Oakland, CA 94619

## MiraCosta College
Oceanside, California
www.miracosta.edu
**CB code: 4582**

- Public 2-year community college
- Commuter campus in large city

**General.** Founded in 1934. Regionally accredited. Study abroad programs in Japan, Mexico, Costa Rica and several countries in Europe. **Enrollment:** 7,834 degree-seeking undergraduates. **Degrees:** 526 associate awarded. **ROTC:** Army, Air Force. **Location:** 35 miles from San Diego. **Calendar:** Semester, limited summer session. **Full-time faculty:** 115 total; 26% minority, 50% women. **Part-time faculty:** 332 total; 19% minority, 59% women. **Class size:** 20% < 20, 64% 20-39, 8% 40-49, 2% 50-99, less than 1% >100. **Special facilities:** Bioprocessing training facility, music recording studios. **Partnerships:** Formal partnerships with local high schools providing tech-prep programs, Cisco Academy providing network and router training.

**Transfer out.** 29% of students enrolled in the transfer program go on to 4-year colleges. **Colleges most students transferred to 2007:** San Diego State University, Cal State: San Marcos, University of California: San Diego.

**Basis for selection.** Open admission, but selective for some programs. Open enrollment is for all 18 yrs of age or high school graduates. High school students require principal and parental permission with grade level limitations. Nursing programs require special application with course and GPA requirements. Locally administered tests may be used for placement and counseling. **Learning Disabled:** Students with learning disabilities are encouraged to contact Disabled Students Programs & Services for assistance if accommodations are needed.

**2007-2008 Annual costs.** Tuition/fees: $638; $5,528 out-of-state. Per-credit charge: $20 in-state; $183 out-of-state. Books/supplies: $1,566. Personal expenses: $2,754.

**2006-2007 Financial aid. Need-based:** 12% of total undergraduate aid awarded as scholarships/grants, 88% as loans/jobs. Need-based aid available for part-time students. Work-study available nights and for part-time students. **Additional information:** Waiver of in-state fees for eligible low-income students.

**Application procedures. Admission:** No deadline. No application fee. Application may be submitted online. Admission notification on a rolling basis. **Financial aid:** Priority date 4/8; no closing date. FAFSA, institutional form required. Applicants notified on a rolling basis; must reply within 4 week(s) of notification.

**Academics. Special study options:** Accelerated study, cooperative education, distance learning, double major, dual enrollment of high school students, ESL, exchange student, honors, independent study, internships, liberal arts/career combination, student-designed major, study abroad, teacher certification program, weekend college. License preparation in nursing, real estate. **Credit/placement by examination:** AP, CLEP, IB, institutional tests. 15 credit hours maximum toward associate degree. **Support services:** GED preparation and test center, learning center, pre-admission summer program, reduced course load, remedial instruction, study skills assistance, tutoring, writing center.

**Honors college/program.** Students wanting to study at the honors level contract for an honors option in designated courses.

**Majors. Agriculture:** Business, floriculture, landscaping, nursery operations, turf management. **Architecture:** Landscape. **Biology:** General. **Business:** Accounting, administrative services, business admin, hospitality admin, office management, office/clerical, real estate, tourism/travel. **Communications:** General. **Computer sciences:** General, computer graphics, computer science, LAN/WAN management, programming. **Education:** Early childhood. **Engineering technology:** Drafting. **English:** English lit. **Family/consumer sciences:** Child care. **Foreign languages:** General, French, German, Japanese, Spanish. **Health:** Licensed practical nurse, premedicine, preveterinary. **History:** General. **Interdisciplinary:** Behavioral sciences, gerontology. **Legal studies:** Prelaw. **Liberal arts:** Arts/sciences. **Math:** General. **Mechanic/repair:** Auto body, automotive. **Personal/culinary services:** Cosmetic. **Philosophy/religion:** Philosophy. **Physical sciences:** Chemistry, geology, physics. **Protective services:** Police science. **Psychology:** General. **Science technology:** Biological. **Social sciences:** General, economics, geography, political science, sociology. **Visual/performing arts:** Art, art history/conservation, commercial/advertising art, dance, dramatic, theater design.

**Most popular majors.** Business/marketing 8%, liberal arts 60%, visual/performing arts 8%.

**Computing on campus.** 1,000 workstations in library, computer center, student center. Online course registration, online library, student web hosting available.

**Student life. Freshman orientation:** Available. One-hour session offered 9 times prior to classes each semester. **Activities:** Bands, choral groups, dance, drama, music ensembles, musical theater, student government, student newspaper, symphony orchestra, MECHA/Latina organization, Black Student Union, women's issues and studies group, Phi Theta Kappa, Future Educators, international club, National Science club, Allied Health club, Behavioral Science club, Creative Entertainers, Japanese club, Intervarsity Christian Fellowship, Latina Leadership Network.

**Athletics. Intercollegiate:** Basketball, soccer. **Intramural:** Soccer, track and field, volleyball. **Team name:** Spartans.

**Student services.** Alcohol/substance abuse counseling, career counseling, services for economically disadvantaged, student employment services, financial aid counseling, health services, on-campus daycare, personal counseling, placement for graduates. **Physically disabled:** Services for visually, speech, hearing impaired. **Learning disabled:** Comprehensive services available. **Transfer:** Transfer center, transfer adviser, college fairs on campus for students transferring to 4-year colleges.

**Contact.** E-mail: admissions@miracosta.edu
Phone: (760) 795-6620 Toll-free number: (888) 201-8480
Fax: (760) 795-6626
Alicia Terry, Director of Admissions and Records, MiraCosta College, One Barnard Drive, Oceanside, CA 92056-3899

---

## Mission College
### Santa Clara, California
### www.missioncollege.org
**CB code: 7587**

- Public 2-year community college
- Small city

**General.** Founded in 1975. Regionally accredited. **Enrollment:** 4,990 degree-seeking undergraduates. **Degrees:** 522 associate awarded. **ROTC:** Naval, Air Force. **Location:** 8 miles from San Jose. **Calendar:** Semester, limited summer session. **Full-time faculty:** 150 total. **Part-time faculty:** 270 total.

**Transfer out. Colleges most students transferred to 2007:** San Jose State.

**Basis for selection.** Open admission, but selective for some programs. Limited admission to vocational nursing and allied health. Interviews required of nursing, psychiatric technician majors.

**2007-2008 Annual costs.** Tuition/fees: $654; $5,844 out-of-state. Per-credit charge: $20 in-state; $193 out-of-state. Books/supplies: $2,172. Personal expenses: $2,898.

**Application procedures. Admission:** No deadline. No application fee. Admission notification on a rolling basis. **Financial aid:** Priority date 5/1; no closing date. Applicants notified on a rolling basis starting 8/1; must reply within 2 week(s) of notification.

**Academics. Special study options:** Cooperative education, dual enrollment of high school students, honors, independent study, weekend college. **Credit/placement by examination:** CLEP, institutional tests. 12 credit hours maximum toward associate degree. **Support services:** Learning center, remedial instruction, tutoring.

**Majors. Agriculture:** Food science. **Biology:** General. **Business:** General, accounting, administrative services, banking/financial services, business admin, management information systems, management science, office management, office/clerical, real estate. **Communications technology:** Graphic/printing. **Computer sciences:** Applications programming, computer science, information systems. **Engineering:** General. **Engineering technology:** Drafting. **Health:** Health services, licensed practical nurse, nursing (RN). **Liberal arts:** Arts/sciences. **Math:** General. **Physical sciences:** Chemistry, physics. **Protective services:** Fire safety technology. **Social sciences:** General. **Visual/performing arts:** Art, commercial/advertising art.

**Student life. Freshman orientation:** Available. **Activities:** Bands, music ensembles, musical theater, TV station.

**Athletics. Intercollegiate:** Baseball M, basketball W, soccer M, softball W, tennis. **Team name:** Saints.

**Student services.** Adult student services, career counseling, student employment services, health services, on-campus daycare, personal counseling, placement for graduates, veterans' counselor. **Transfer:** Transfer center, transfer adviser, college fairs on campus for students transferring to 4-year colleges.

**Contact.** Phone: (408) 988-2200 Fax: (408) 980-8980
Arlene Atondo, Director of Admissions, Mission College, 3000 Mission College Boulevard, Santa Clara, CA 95054-1897

---

## Modesto Junior College
### Modesto, California
### www.mjc.edu
**CB code: 4486**

- Public 2-year community college
- Commuter campus in small city

**General.** Founded in 1921. Regionally accredited. **Enrollment:** 19,236 undergraduates. **Degrees:** 1,188 associate awarded. **Location:** 90 miles from San Francisco. **Calendar:** Semester, limited summer session. **Full-time faculty:** 283 total. **Part-time faculty:** 251 total. **Special facilities:** Natural history museum.

**Transfer out. Colleges most students transferred to 2007:** California State University: Stanislaus, California State University: Fresno, California State University: Sacramento, University of California: Davis, University of California: San Diego.

**Basis for selection.** Open admission, but selective for some programs. Limited admission offered to nursing (RN), dental assisting, medical assisting, and related majors. Selective admission to fire academy.

**High school preparation.** Certain programs require specific courses.

**2007-2008 Annual costs.** Tuition/fees: $640; $5,830 out-of-state. Per-credit charge: $20 in-state; $193 out-of-state. Books/supplies: $1,386. Personal expenses: $2,898.

**Financial aid.** All financial aid based on need. Need-based aid available for part-time students. Work-study available nights, weekends and for part-time students. **Additional information:** Modesto Junior College scholarship priority deadline 12/15.

**Application procedures. Admission:** No deadline. No application fee. Application may be submitted online. Admission notification on a rolling

basis. **Financial aid:** Priority date 3/2; no closing date. FAFSA, institutional form required. Applicants notified on a rolling basis starting 5/1; must reply within 2 week(s) of notification.

**Academics. Special study options:** Cooperative education, distance learning, double major, dual enrollment of high school students, ESL, honors, independent study, internships, liberal arts/career combination, study abroad, weekend college. License preparation in nursing, real estate. **Credit/placement by examination:** AP, CLEP, institutional tests. 30 credit hours maximum toward associate degree. **Support services:** GED preparation, learning center, pre-admission summer program, remedial instruction, study skills assistance, tutoring, writing center.

**Majors. Agriculture:** Agronomy, animal breeding, animal sciences, business, dairy, food science, landscaping, ornamental horticulture, plant sciences, poultry, soil science, supplies. **Architecture:** Landscape, urban/community planning. **Business:** General, accounting, administrative services, business admin, fashion, finance, management information systems, marketing, real estate. **Communications:** General, broadcast journalism, journalism. **Communications technology:** Graphic/printing. **Computer sciences:** General, computer graphics, computer science, programming. **Conservation:** General, forestry, wildlife. **Construction:** Electrician, maintenance, pipefitting. **Engineering:** General, electrical. **Engineering technology:** Architectural, drafting. **English:** English lit, speech/rhetoric. **Family/consumer sciences:** General, child care, clothing/textiles, family/community services, food/nutrition. **Foreign languages:** General, French, German, Spanish. **Health:** Dental assistant, licensed practical nurse, medical assistant, nursing (RN), nursing assistant, respiratory therapy technology. **Liberal arts:** Arts/sciences. **Math:** General. **Mechanic/repair:** General, auto body, automotive, electronics/electrical, heating/ac/refrig. **Parks/recreation:** General, health/fitness. **Protective services:** Criminal justice, firefighting, law enforcement admin, police science. **Public administration:** Human services. **Social sciences:** General. **Visual/performing arts:** General, art, cinematography, commercial photography, commercial/advertising art, dramatic, fashion design, interior design, photography, studio arts.

**Computing on campus.** 95 workstations in library, computer center, student center. Commuter students can connect to campus network. Online course registration available.

**Student life. Freshman orientation:** Available. One hour, held during registration. **Activities:** Bands, choral groups, dance, drama, film society, music ensembles, opera, radio station, student government, student newspaper, symphony orchestra, TV station, Christian Collegiate Fellowship; Able-Disabled Association; foreign, ethnic, minority student and women re-entry clubs; Young Farmers; other special interest and concern groups.

**Athletics. NJCAA. Intercollegiate:** Baseball M, basketball, cross-country, diving, football (tackle) M, golf, soccer, softball W, swimming, tennis, track and field, volleyball W, water polo, wrestling M. **Intramural:** Basketball, football (tackle) M, softball W, table tennis, tennis, volleyball. **Team name:** Pirates.

**Student services.** Adult student services, career counseling, services for economically disadvantaged, student employment services, financial aid counseling, health services, minority student services, on-campus daycare, personal counseling, placement for graduates, veterans' counselor. **Physically disabled:** Services for visually, speech, hearing impaired. **Learning disabled:** Comprehensive services available. **Transfer:** Re-entry adviser for new students. Transfer center, transfer adviser, college fairs on campus for students transferring to 4-year colleges.

**Contact.** Phone: (209) 575-6013 Fax: (209) 575-6859
Susie Agostini, Dean, Matriculation and Enrollment Services, Modesto Junior College, 435 College Avenue, Modesto, CA 95350-5800

---

**Monterey Peninsula College**
Monterey, California
www.mpc.edu                    CB code: 4490

- Public 2-year community college
- Commuter campus in large town

**General.** Founded in 1947. Regionally accredited. **Enrollment:** 3,596 degree-seeking undergraduates. **Degrees:** 379 associate awarded. **Location:** 120 miles from San Francisco. **Calendar:** Semester, limited summer session. **Full-time faculty:** 120 total. **Part-time faculty:** 170 total.

**Basis for selection.** Open admission, but selective for some programs. Additional requirements, including interview, for dental assistant, nursing, administrative justice and police academy programs.

---

**2007-2008 Annual costs.** Tuition/fees: $660; $5,850 out-of-state. Per-credit charge: $20 in-state; $193 out-of-state. Books/supplies: $846. Personal expenses: $1,719.

**Financial aid. Need-based:** Need-based aid available for part-time students.

**Application procedures. Admission:** No deadline. No application fee. Application may be submitted online. Admission notification on a rolling basis. **Financial aid:** Priority date 3/2; no closing date. FAFSA, institutional form required. Applicants notified on a rolling basis starting 6/1.

**Academics. Special study options:** Cooperative education, cross-registration, distance learning, double major, dual enrollment of high school students, ESL, independent study, weekend college. **Credit/placement by examination:** CLEP, institutional tests. 30 credit hours maximum toward associate degree. **Support services:** Learning center, remedial instruction, tutoring.

**Majors. Agriculture:** Ornamental horticulture. **Area/ethnic studies:** Women's. **Biology:** General. **Business:** General, accounting, business admin, hospitality admin, hospitality/recreation, international, office/clerical, real estate. **Communications:** General. **Computer sciences:** General, data processing, LAN/WAN management, programming, web page design, word processing. **Engineering technology:** Drafting. **English:** English lit. **Family/consumer sciences:** General, child development, clothing/textiles, family/community services, fashion consultant, institutional food production. **Foreign languages:** General. **Health:** Dental assistant, medical assistant, nursing (RN), predental, premedicine, prepharmacy, preveterinary. **History:** General. **Liberal arts:** Arts/sciences. **Math:** General. **Philosophy/religion:** Philosophy. **Physical sciences:** Chemistry, physics. **Protective services:** Fire safety technology, law enforcement admin. **Psychology:** General. **Social sciences:** Anthropology, economics, political science, sociology. **Visual/performing arts:** Acting, art, art history/conservation, ceramics, dance, directing/producing, dramatic, drawing, graphic design, interior design, metal/jewelry, painting, photography, printmaking, sculpture, studio arts.

**Student life. Activities:** Bands, choral groups, dance, drama, music ensembles, musical theater, opera, student government.

**Athletics. NJCAA. Intercollegiate:** Baseball M, basketball, cross-country, football (tackle) M, golf, softball W, swimming, tennis W, track and field, volleyball W. **Team name:** Lobos.

**Student services.** Career counseling, student employment services, health services, on-campus daycare, personal counseling. **Physically disabled:** Services for visually, speech, hearing impaired. **Transfer:** Transfer center, transfer adviser, college fairs on campus for students transferring to 4-year colleges.

**Contact.** Phone: (831) 646-4002 Fax: (831) 646-4015
Vera Coleman, Director of Admissions and Records, Monterey Peninsula College, 980 Fremont Street, Monterey, CA 93940-4799

---

**Moorpark College**
Moorpark, California
www.moorparkcollege.edu              CB code: 4512

- Public 2-year community college
- Commuter campus in large town

**General.** Founded in 1963. Regionally accredited. **Enrollment:** 10,003 degree-seeking undergraduates. **Degrees:** 1,141 associate awarded. **Location:** 50 miles from Los Angeles. **Calendar:** Semester, limited summer session. **Full-time faculty:** 176 total. **Part-time faculty:** 401 total. **Special facilities:** Exotic animal compound and teaching zoo, observatory.

**Transfer out. Colleges most students transferred to 2007:** California State University, University of Southern California, University of California: Los Angeles, UC Santa Barbara.

**Basis for selection.** Open admission, but selective for some programs. Limited admission to nursing program, exotic animal training management program, radiologic technology.

**2007-2008 Annual costs.** Tuition/fees: $644; $5,894 out-of-state. Per-credit charge: $20 in-state; $195 out-of-state. Books/supplies: $1,386. Personal expenses: $2,898.

**Application procedures. Admission:** Priority date 7/30; no deadline. No application fee. Application may be submitted online. Admission notification on a rolling basis. **Financial aid:** Priority date 5/14; no closing date. FAFSA required. Applicants notified on a rolling basis starting 6/15; must reply within 2 week(s) of notification.

**Academics. Special study options:** Cooperative education, distance learning, honors, independent study, internships, study abroad. **Credit/placement by examination:** AP, CLEP. 12 credit hours maximum toward associate degree. **Support services:** Learning center, remedial instruction, tutoring.

**Majors. Agriculture:** Animal sciences. **Biology:** General. **Business:** Accounting, administrative services, business admin, management information systems, office management, real estate. **Communications:** General, broadcast journalism. **Communications technology:** General, graphic/printing. **Computer sciences:** General, applications programming, information systems. **Engineering technology:** Electrical. **Family/consumer sciences:** General, child care, family studies. **Health:** Medical radiologic technology/radiation therapy, nursing (RN). **Liberal arts:** Arts/sciences. **Math:** General. **Physical sciences:** Chemistry, geology, physics. **Protective services:** Police science. **Social sciences:** General. **Visual/performing arts:** General, cinematography, commercial/advertising art, dramatic, interior design, photography, studio arts.

**Most popular majors.** Agriculture 10%, health sciences 9%, liberal arts 66%.

**Computing on campus.** 75 workstations in computer center. Online course registration, wireless network available.

**Student life. Freshman orientation:** Available. Online orientation. **Activities:** Bands, choral groups, dance, drama, film society, music ensembles, musical theater, opera, radio station, student government, student newspaper, TV station, Mexican-American club, Black student Union, Alpha Gamma Sigma, Muslim Student Association.

**Athletics. Intercollegiate:** Baseball M, basketball, cheerleading M, cross-country, football (tackle) M, golf M, softball W, tennis W, track and field, volleyball, wrestling M. **Team name:** Raiders.

**Student services.** Career counseling, services for economically disadvantaged, student employment services, financial aid counseling, health services, legal services, on-campus daycare, personal counseling, veterans' counselor. **Physically disabled:** Services for visually, speech, hearing impaired. **Transfer:** Transfer center, transfer adviser, college fairs on campus for students transferring to 4-year colleges.

**Contact.** E-mail: mcadmissions@vcccd.net
Phone: (805) 378-1429 Fax: (805) 378-1499
Katherine Colborn, Registrar, Moorpark College, 7075 Campus Road, Moorpark, CA 93021

---

## Mount San Antonio College
**Walnut, California**
**www.mtsac.edu**                          CB code: 4494

- Public 2-year community college
- Commuter campus in small city

**General.** Founded in 1946. Regionally accredited. **Enrollment:** 21,447 degree-seeking undergraduates. **Degrees:** 2,214 associate awarded. **ROTC:** Air Force. **Location:** 30 miles from Los Angeles. **Calendar:** Semester, extensive summer session. **Full-time faculty:** 360 total. **Part-time faculty:** 750 total. **Special facilities:** Planetarium, wildlife sanctuary.

**Transfer out. Colleges most students transferred to 2007:** California State Polytechnic University: Pomona, California State University: Los Angeles, California State University: Fullerton.

**Basis for selection.** Open admission.

**2007-2008 Annual costs.** Tuition/fees: $630; $5,820 out-of-state. Per-credit charge: $20 in-state; $193 out-of-state. Books/supplies: $1,386. Personal expenses: $2,200.

**Financial aid.** All financial aid based on need. Need-based aid available for part-time students.

**Application procedures. Admission:** No deadline. No application fee. Admission notification on a rolling basis. **Financial aid:** No deadline. FAFSA, institutional form required. Applicants notified on a rolling basis starting 6/1; must reply within 4 week(s) of notification.

**Academics. Special study options:** Cooperative education, cross-registration, distance learning, dual enrollment of high school students, ESL, honors, internships, study abroad, teacher certification program, weekend college. License preparation in aviation, nursing, paramedic, radiology, real

---

estate. **Credit/placement by examination:** CLEP. 12 credit hours maximum toward associate degree. **Support services:** GED preparation, learning center, pre-admission summer program, remedial instruction, study skills assistance, tutoring.

**Majors. Agriculture:** Animal sciences, business, horticulture. **Biology:** General, marine. **Business:** General, accounting, administrative services, banking/financial services, business admin, entrepreneurial studies, fashion, office/clerical, real estate. **Communications:** Advertising, broadcast journalism, journalism. **Communications technology:** General. **Computer sciences:** Data processing. **Conservation:** General, forestry. **Engineering:** General. **Engineering technology:** Architectural, drafting, electrical. **Family/consumer sciences:** General, clothing/textiles. **Foreign languages:** Sign language interpretation. **Health:** EMT paramedic, health services, medical radiologic technology/radiation therapy, medical secretary, nursing (RN), respiratory therapy technology. **Legal studies:** Paralegal. **Liberal arts:** Arts/sciences. **Mechanic/repair:** Aircraft, electronics/electrical, heating/ac/refrig. **Parks/recreation:** General, facilities management. **Protective services:** Firefighting, police science. **Transportation:** Air traffic control, aviation, flight attendant. **Visual/performing arts:** Design, interior design, photography.

**Computing on campus.** 600 workstations in library, computer center, student center. Commuter students can connect to campus network. Online course registration, helpline available.

**Student life. Freshman orientation:** Mandatory. Preregistration for classes offered. **Activities:** Bands, choral groups, dance, drama, film society, literary magazine, music ensembles, musical theater, radio station, student government, student newspaper, symphony orchestra, TV station, Asian student association, Chinese club, Black student alliance, Indo-Pak club, Democratic club, Republican club, sign language club, MECHA, Muslim student association.

**Athletics. Intercollegiate:** Badminton W, baseball M, basketball, cross-country, diving, football (tackle) M, golf, soccer, softball W, swimming, tennis, track and field, volleyball, water polo M, wrestling M. **Team name:** Mounties.

**Student services.** Adult student services, alcohol/substance abuse counseling, career counseling, services for economically disadvantaged, student employment services, financial aid counseling, health services, minority student services, on-campus daycare, personal counseling, placement for graduates, veterans' counselor. **Physically disabled:** Services for visually, speech, hearing impaired. **Transfer:** Re-entry adviser, pre-admission transcript evaluation for new students. Transfer center, transfer adviser, college fairs on campus for students transferring to 4-year colleges.

**Contact.** Phone: (909) 594-5611 ext. 4415 Fax: (909) 468-4068
Patty Montoya, Director of Admissions and Records, Mount San Antonio College, 1100 North Grand Avenue, Walnut, CA 91789

---

## Mount San Jacinto College
**San Jacinto, California**
**www.msjc.edu**                          CB code: 4501

- Public 2-year community college
- Commuter campus in small city

**General.** Founded in 1962. Regionally accredited. **Enrollment:** 6,687 degree-seeking undergraduates. **ROTC:** Army, Air Force. **Location:** 35 miles from Riverside, 45 miles from Palm Springs. **Calendar:** Semester, limited summer session. **Full-time faculty:** 110 total. **Part-time faculty:** 400 total. **Class size:** 38% < 20, 54% 20-39, 7% 40-49, less than 1% 50-99.

**Transfer out. Colleges most students transferred to 2007:** California State University: San Bernardino, University of California: Riverside, California State University: San Marcos, Azusa Pacific University.

**Basis for selection.** Open admission, but selective for some programs. Special requirements for nursing program. Interview required of nursing majors. Audition recommended of performing arts majors.

**2007-2008 Annual costs.** Tuition/fees: $600; $5,790 out-of-state. Per-credit charge: $20 in-state; $193 out-of-state. Books/supplies: $1,386. Personal expenses: $2,250.

**Financial aid.** All financial aid based on need. Need-based aid available for part-time students. Work-study available nights and for part-time students. **Additional information:** Board of Governors Grant Program for state residents to defray cost of enrollment fee.

**Application procedures. Admission:** Closing date 8/20. No application fee. Application may be submitted online. Admission notification on a rolling basis beginning on or about 4/1. All students admitted, but nursing students have additional admissions policies. **Financial aid:** Priority date 3/2; no closing date. FAFSA, institutional form required. Applicants notified on a rolling basis starting 5/1; must reply within 3 week(s) of notification.

**Academics. Special study options:** Cooperative education, cross-registration, distance learning, double major, dual enrollment of high school students, ESL, honors, independent study, internships, weekend college. License preparation in nursing, paramedic, real estate. **Credit/placement by examination:** AP, CLEP, institutional tests. 12 credit hours maximum toward associate degree. **Support services:** Learning center, reduced course load, remedial instruction, study skills assistance, tutoring, writing center.

**Majors. Agriculture:** Turf management. **Business:** Business admin, real estate. **Computer sciences:** General. **Education:** Early childhood, physical. **Health:** Nursing (RN), substance abuse counseling. **Interdisciplinary:** Behavioral sciences. **Liberal arts:** Arts/sciences. **Math:** General. **Mechanic/repair:** Automotive. **Protective services:** Police science. **Social sciences:** General. **Visual/performing arts:** Art, dance, dramatic, photography.

**Computing on campus.** 120 workstations in library, computer center, student center. Commuter students can connect to campus network. Online course registration available.

**Student life. Freshman orientation:** Mandatory. 2-hour orientation. **Activities:** Bands, dance, drama, musical theater, student government, Campus Crusade, MECHA, Black Students Union.

**Athletics. Intercollegiate:** Baseball M, basketball, football (tackle) M, golf, soccer W, softball W, tennis, volleyball W. **Intramural:** Volleyball W. **Team name:** Eagles.

**Student services.** Adult student services, career counseling, services for economically disadvantaged, student employment services, financial aid counseling, on-campus daycare, personal counseling, veterans' counselor. **Physically disabled:** Services for visually, speech, hearing impaired. **Transfer:** Pre-admission transcript evaluation for new students. Transfer center, transfer adviser, college fairs on campus for students transferring to 4-year colleges.

**Contact.** E-mail: enrollsvcs@msjc.edu
Phone: (951) 487-3215 Fax: (951) 654-6738
Susan Loomis, Director, Enrollment Services, Mount San Jacinto College, 1499 North State Street, San Jacinto, CA 92583

## MTI College
### Sacramento, California
www.mticollege.edu

**CB code: 3543**

- For-profit 2-year business and technical college
- Commuter campus in large city
- Interview required

**General.** Regionally accredited. **Enrollment:** 297 degree-seeking undergraduates. **Degrees:** 121 associate awarded. **Calendar:** Continuous, extensive summer session. **Full-time faculty:** 10 total. **Part-time faculty:** 61 total.

**Transfer out. Colleges most students transferred to 2007:** University of Phoenix, Golden Gate University.

**Basis for selection.** Interview, talent, ability, character and personal qualities important.

**2008-2009 Annual costs.** Tuition/fees: $11,025. Books/supplies: $1,386. Personal expenses: $322.

**Financial aid. Need-based:** Work-study available nights.

**Application procedures. Admission:** No deadline. $50 fee. Admission notification on a rolling basis.

**Academics. Special study options:** Cooperative education, distance learning, internships, liberal arts/career combination. **Credit/placement by examination:** CLEP, institutional tests. **Support services:** Learning center, reduced course load, remedial instruction, study skills assistance, tutoring.

**Majors. Business:** Business admin. **Computer sciences:** System admin, systems analysis. **Legal studies:** Paralegal.

**Most popular majors.** Business/marketing 9%, computer/information sciences 27%, legal studies 64%.

**Computing on campus.** 300 workstations in library, computer center.

**Student life. Freshman orientation:** Mandatory.

**Student services.** Adult student services, career counseling, financial aid counseling, placement for graduates, veterans' counselor. **Transfer:** Pre-admission transcript evaluation for new students. College fairs on campus for students transferring to 4-year colleges.

**Contact.** E-mail: webmaster@mticollege.edu
Phone: (916) 339-1500 Fax: (916) 339-0305
Eric Patterson, Director of Admissions, MTI College, 5221 Madison Avenue, Sacramento, CA 95841

## Napa Valley College
### Napa, California
www.napavalley.edu

**CB code: 4530**

- Public 2-year community college
- Commuter campus in small city

**General.** Founded in 1940. Regionally accredited. **Enrollment:** 7,052 undergraduates. **Degrees:** 608 associate awarded. **Location:** 50 miles from San Francisco. **Calendar:** Semester, limited summer session. **Full-time faculty:** 106 total. **Part-time faculty:** 210 total. **Special facilities:** Nature preserve, working vineyard, telecommunications laboratory.

**Basis for selection.** Open admission, but selective for some programs. Special admission requirements for health occupations programs and athletic program applicants.

**2007-2008 Annual costs.** Tuition/fees: $626; $5,426 out-of-state. Per-credit charge: $20 in-state; $180 out-of-state. Books/supplies: $630. Personal expenses: $1,476.

**Application procedures. Admission:** No deadline. No application fee. Admission notification on a rolling basis. College-administered placement tests recommended for students enrolling in English or mathematics. **Financial aid:** Priority date 4/1; no closing date. FAFSA required. Applicants notified on a rolling basis starting 6/1; must reply within 3 week(s) of notification.

**Academics.** Culinary arts program available. **Special study options:** Cooperative education, distance learning, double major, dual enrollment of high school students, ESL, honors, independent study, internships, study abroad, weekend college. Exchange program with Tafe College, Tasmania. **Credit/placement by examination:** CLEP, institutional tests. 12 credit hours maximum toward associate degree. **Support services:** Learning center, remedial instruction, tutoring, writing center.

**Majors. Agriculture:** General. **Business:** General, accounting, administrative services, real estate. **Communications technology:** General. **Computer sciences:** General. **Conservation:** Wildlife. **Education:** General, early childhood. **Engineering technology:** Biomedical, drafting, electrical. **English:** English lit. **Health:** Health services, licensed practical nurse, nursing (RN), respiratory therapy technology. **Legal studies:** Paralegal. **Liberal arts:** Arts/sciences. **Protective services:** Police science. **Social sciences:** General.

**Computing on campus.** 30 workstations in library, computer center.

**Student life. Activities:** Bands, choral groups, dance, drama, music ensembles, musical theater, student government, student newspaper, symphony orchestra, various religious, ethnic, social service, and special interest organizations including International Student Club, Amnesty International, Hispano-Americano Club.

**Athletics.** NJCAA. **Intercollegiate:** Baseball M, basketball, diving, golf, soccer M, softball W, swimming, tennis, volleyball W. **Intramural:** Volleyball. **Team name:** Storm.

**Student services.** Adult student services, career counseling, student employment services, on-campus daycare, personal counseling, veterans' counselor. **Physically disabled:** Services for visually, speech, hearing impaired. **Transfer:** Re-entry adviser for new students. Transfer center, transfer adviser, college fairs on campus for students transferring to 4-year colleges.

**Contact.** Phone: (707) 253-3000 Fax: (707) 253-3064
Beth Hauscarriague, Director of Admissions, Napa Valley College, 2277 Napa-Vallejo Highway, Napa, CA 94558

## National Polytechnic College of Science
### Wilmington, California
www.natpoly.edu

**CB code: 1243**

- For-profit 2-year technical and maritime college
- Commuter campus in small city

**General.** Founded in 1969. Regionally accredited. Provides underwater training for offshore oil industry, coastal and inland water and harbors. All classes near or on water. Campuses also located in San Diego and Hawaii. **Enrollment:** 500 degree-seeking undergraduates. **Degrees:** 18 associate awarded. **Location:** 30 miles from Los Angeles, 5 miles from Long Beach. **Calendar:** Continuous. **Full-time faculty:** 10 total. **Part-time faculty:** 10 total. **Special facilities:** Bell saturation barge, welding pier, hemidome.

**Basis for selection.** Must be medically approved to dive. Applicants who do not have high school diploma or GED must prove their ability to benefit from program. Students expected to have mechanical aptitude and, if possible, experience in construction-related field. Interviews recommended.

**2007-2008 Annual costs.** Associate degree program charge (covering 12 months), $17,360; per-credit-hour charge, $280. Academic year is comprised of 30 weeks (36 quarter credits), with courses offered in five-week sessions. Undergraduate courses are scheduled, typically, for eight to ten hours per day (two days each week, five-week period). Some courses require basic supplies (e.g., wet suit, fins, weights, work boots) that are not covered by tuition; additional cost of these supplies could amount to $500 or more.

**Financial aid.** Additional information: Work-study programs available.

**Application procedures.** Admission: No deadline. $60 fee. Admission notification on a rolling basis. **Financial aid:** No deadline. FAFSA, institutional form required. Applicants notified on a rolling basis; must reply within 3 week(s) of notification.

**Academics.** Special programs prepare students for work as underwater welders, diver medical technicians, and topside/underwater nondestructive testing/inspection personnel. **Credit/placement by examination:** CLEP, institutional tests. 20 credit hours maximum toward associate degree. **Support services:** Remedial instruction, tutoring.

**Majors. Transportation:** Diver. **Other:** Homeland security, Hyperbaric medical technology.

**Student services.** Career counseling, student employment services, personal counseling, placement for graduates, veterans' counselor. **Transfer:** Transfer adviser for students transferring to 4-year colleges.

**Contact.** Phone: (310) 834-2501 Fax: (310) 834-7132
Shelly Mitchell, Director of Admissions, National Polytechnic College of Science, 272 South Fries Avenue, Wilmington, CA 90744

## Ohlone College
**Fremont, California**
**www.ohlone.edu**
**CB code: 4579**

▶ Public 2-year community college
▶ Commuter campus in large city

**General.** Founded in 1966. Regionally accredited. **Enrollment:** 4,526 degree-seeking undergraduates. **Degrees:** 403 associate awarded. **ROTC:** Air Force. **Location:** 15 miles from San Jose, 40 miles from San Francisco. **Calendar:** Semester, extensive summer session. **Full-time faculty:** 154 total. **Part-time faculty:** 358 total. **Class size:** 54% < 20, 40% 20-39, 2% 40-49, 2% 50-99, less than 1% >100. **Special facilities:** Fine and performing arts center, business and technology center. **Partnerships:** Formal partnerships with Sun Microsystems, Metatec Inc., Washington Hospital, Fremont Unified School District, Newark Unified School District.

**Student profile.**

| | | |
|---|---|---|
| Out-of-state: | 1% | 25 or older: | 45% |

**Transfer out.** Colleges most students transferred to 2007: California State University: East Bay, San Jose State University.

**Basis for selection.** Open admission, but selective for some programs. Nursing, respiratory therapy and physical therapy assisting programs require basic competence in reading comprehension and English skills, basic knowledge of related sciences. All candidates who achieve minimum standards selected by lottery. High school diploma or equivalent not required if applicant is 18 years of age or older.

**High school preparation.** Nursing and physical therapy assisting programs require anatomy and physiology. Respiratory therapy program requires algebra and physics 103.

**2007-2008 Annual costs.** Tuition/fees: $652; $5,842 out-of-state. Per-credit charge: $20 in-state; $193 out-of-state. Books/supplies: $810. Personal expenses: $2,616.

**Financial aid. Need-based:** Need-based aid available for part-time students. Work-study available for part-time students. **Non-need-based:** Scholarships awarded for academics.

**Application procedures. Admission:** No deadline. No application fee. **Financial aid:** Priority date 7/1; no closing date. FAFSA, institutional form required. Applicants notified on a rolling basis starting 7/30; must reply within 2 week(s) of notification.

**Academics. Special study options:** Cooperative education, cross-registration, distance learning, double major, dual enrollment of high school students, ESL, independent study, internships, liberal arts/career combination, study abroad, weekend college. License preparation in nursing, physical therapy. **Credit/placement by examination:** CLEP, IB, institutional tests. 10 credit hours maximum toward associate degree. **Support services:** Learning center, pre-admission summer program, reduced course load, remedial instruction, study skills assistance, tutoring, writing center.

**Majors. Biology:** General. **Business:** General, accounting, administrative services, business admin, marketing, office management, office technology, office/clerical, real estate, receptionist, small business admin. **Communications:** Broadcast journalism, digital media, journalism. **Communications technology:** Desktop publishing. **Computer sciences:** Computer graphics, information systems, LAN/WAN management, programming, system admin. **Education:** Early childhood. **Engineering technology:** CAD/CADD, electrical, electromechanical. **Family/consumer sciences:** Child care, food/nutrition, institutional food production. **Foreign languages:** American Sign Language. **Health:** Medical assistant, nursing (RN), physical therapy assistant, respiratory therapy technology. **Interdisciplinary:** Biological/physical sciences, natural sciences. **Liberal arts:** Arts/sciences. **Mechanic/repair:** Electronics/electrical. **Protective services:** Law enforcement admin. **Social sciences:** General. **Visual/performing arts:** Commercial/advertising art, graphic design, interior design, multimedia, studio arts, theater design.

**Most popular majors.** Biological/life sciences 21%, business/marketing 10%, health sciences 18%, liberal arts 38%.

**Computing on campus.** 450 workstations in library, computer center. Online library available.

**Student life. Freshman orientation:** Mandatory. **Activities:** Bands, choral groups, dance, drama, literary magazine, music ensembles, musical theater, radio station, student government, student newspaper, symphony orchestra, TV station, Abundant Life Christian Fellowship, Afghan Students Association, Asian Pacific Islanders Club, Chinese Culture Club, Muslim Student Association, Alpha Gamma Sigma Honor Society, Ohlone Women Engineers and Physical Scientists, Theater and Dance Alliance.

**Athletics. Intercollegiate:** Baseball M, basketball, soccer, softball W, swimming, volleyball, water polo. **Team name:** Renegades.

**Student services.** Adult student services, career counseling, services for economically disadvantaged, student employment services, financial aid counseling, health services, on-campus daycare, personal counseling, placement for graduates, veterans' counselor. **Physically disabled:** Services for visually, hearing impaired. **Transfer:** Pre-admission transcript evaluation for new students. Transfer center, transfer adviser, college fairs on campus for students transferring to 4-year colleges.

**Contact.** E-mail: admissions@ohlone.edu
Phone: (510) 659-6100 Fax: (510) 659-7231
Kimberly Robbie, Registrar, Ohlone College, 43600 Mission Boulevard, Fremont, CA 94539-0390

## Orange Coast College
**Costa Mesa, California**
**www.orangecoastcollege.edu**
**CB code: 4584**

▶ Public 2-year community college
▶ Commuter campus in small city

**General.** Founded in 1947. Regionally accredited. **Enrollment:** 19,025 degree-seeking undergraduates. **Degrees:** 1,282 associate awarded. **Location:** 40 miles from Los Angeles. **Calendar:** Semester, extensive summer session. **Full-time faculty:** 300 total. **Part-time faculty:** 550 total. **Class size:** 28% < 20, 51% 20-39, 11% 40-49, 7% 50-99, 4% >100. **Special facilities:** Planetarium, plastination lab, sailing academy, international center, art gallery.

## Student profile.

| | | | |
|---|---|---|---|
| Out-of-state: | 3% | **Native American:** | 1% |
| African American: | 2% | **International:** | 2% |
| Asian American: | 26% | **25 or older:** | 30% |
| Hispanic American: | 19% | | |

**Transfer out. Colleges most students transferred to 2007:** University of California: Irvine, California State University: Fullerton, California State University: Long Beach.

**Basis for selection.** Open admission.

**2007-2008 Annual costs.** Tuition/fees: $658; $5,848 out-of-state. Per-credit charge: $20 in-state; $193 out-of-state. Books/supplies: $1,422. Personal expenses: $2,830.

**2006-2007 Financial aid. Need-based:** 908 full-time freshmen applied for aid; 890 were judged to have need; 882 of these received aid. Average need met was 38%. Average scholarship/grant was $3,473; average loan $1,884. 84% of total undergraduate aid awarded as scholarships/grants, 16% as loans/jobs. Need-based aid available for part-time students. Work-study available for part-time students. **Non-need-based:** Awarded to 55 full-time undergraduates, including 15 freshmen. Scholarships awarded for academics.

**Application procedures. Admission:** No deadline. No application fee. Admission notification on a rolling basis. Admission opens first working day in April for fall semester, first working day in October for spring semester; dates establish registration priority. **Financial aid:** Priority date 3/2, closing date 5/31. FAFSA, institutional form required. Applicants notified on a rolling basis; must reply within 2 week(s) of notification.

**Academics. Special study options:** Cooperative education, cross-registration, distance learning, ESL, honors, independent study, internships, liberal arts/career combination, student-designed major, study abroad, weekend college. License preparation in aviation, radiology, real estate. **Credit/placement by examination:** AP, CLEP, institutional tests. 12 credit hours maximum toward associate degree. **Support services:** Learning center, pre-admission summer program, reduced course load, remedial instruction, study skills assistance, tutoring, writing center.

**Honors college/program.** Students complete a minimum of 18 units in honors courses for program certification.

**Majors. Agriculture:** Ornamental horticulture. **Biology:** General, ecology. **Business:** General, accounting, administrative services, fashion, hospitality/recreation, international, management information systems, office technology, office/clerical. **Communications:** Advertising, broadcast journalism. **Computer sciences:** General, computer graphics, data entry, information systems. **Construction:** Maintenance, pipefitting, power transmission. **Education:** Early childhood. **Engineering technology:** Architectural, drafting, electrical. **English:** English lit, speech/rhetoric, technical writing. **Family/consumer sciences:** General, child care, food/nutrition. **Foreign languages:** French, German, Italian, Japanese, Spanish. **Health:** Athletic training, cardiovascular technology, dental assistant, electroencephalograph technology, medical assistant, medical radiologic technology/radiation therapy, medical records technology, respiratory therapy technology, sonography. **History:** General. **Liberal arts:** Arts/sciences. **Math:** General. **Mechanic/repair:** Aircraft, electronics/electrical, heating/ac/refrig. **Parks/recreation:** Exercise sciences. **Personal/culinary services:** Culinary arts. **Philosophy/religion:** Philosophy, religion. **Physical sciences:** Astronomy, chemistry, geology, physics. **Psychology:** General. **Social sciences:** Anthropology, economics, geography, political science, sociology. **Transportation:** Aviation, flight attendant. **Visual/performing arts:** Art, cinematography, commercial/advertising art, dance, dramatic, fashion design, film/cinema, interior design, photography, studio arts.

**Computing on campus.** 1,500 workstations in library, computer center. Online course registration, wireless network available.

**Student life. Freshman orientation:** Available. 3-hour sessions given year round. **Activities:** Bands, choral groups, dance, drama, film society, music ensembles, musical theater, student government, student newspaper, symphony orchestra, Buddhists Crusade for Christ, Christian Fellowship, COPTIC, Hillel.

**Athletics. Intercollegiate:** Badminton W, baseball M, basketball, cross-country, diving, football (tackle) M, golf, rowing (crew), soccer, softball W, swimming, tennis, track and field, volleyball, water polo. **Team name:** Pirates.

**Student services.** Adult student services, alcohol/substance abuse counseling, career counseling, services for economically disadvantaged, student employment services, financial aid counseling, health services, minority student services, on-campus daycare, personal counseling, placement for graduates, veterans' counselor. **Physically disabled:** Services for visually, speech,

hearing impaired. **Learning disabled:** Comprehensive services available. **Transfer:** Re-entry adviser for new students. Transfer center, transfer adviser, college fairs on campus for students transferring to 4-year colleges.

**Contact.** E-mail: kclark@occ.cccd.edu
Phone: (714) 432-5072
Kristin Clark, Dean of Enrollment Services, Orange Coast College, 2701 Fairview Road, Costa Mesa, CA 92628-5005

## Oxnard College
**Oxnard, California**
**www.oxnardcollege.edu**     **CB code: 4591**

- Public 2-year community college
- Small city

**General.** Founded in 1975. Regionally accredited. **Enrollment:** 6,763 undergraduates. **Degrees:** 469 associate awarded. **Location:** 60 miles from Los Angeles. **Calendar:** Semester, limited summer session. **Full-time faculty:** 99 total. **Part-time faculty:** 170 total.

**Basis for selection.** Open admission.

**2007-2008 Annual costs.** Tuition/fees: $644; $5,934 out-of-state. Per-credit charge: $20 in-state; $195 out-of-state. Books/supplies: $1,386. Personal expenses: $2,898.

**Application procedures. Admission:** No deadline. No application fee. Admission notification on a rolling basis. **Financial aid:** Priority date 7/1; no closing date. FAFSA required. Applicants notified on a rolling basis; must reply within 2 week(s) of notification.

**Academics. Special study options:** Accelerated study, distance learning, dual enrollment of high school students, independent study, study abroad. First 2 years of bilingual (English-Spanish) teacher preparatory program. **Credit/placement by examination:** CLEP, institutional tests. 12 credit hours maximum toward associate degree. **Support services:** Learning center, remedial instruction, tutoring.

**Majors. Biology:** Bacteriology, marine. **Computer sciences:** General. **Health:** Medical records admin. **Liberal arts:** Arts/sciences.

**Student life. Freshman orientation:** Available. **Activities:** Jazz band, choral groups, drama, student government, student newspaper, TV station, veterans club, Mini Corps Club, Vietnamese Club, Latino Club, ceramics club, Black Student Union, international students club.

**Athletics. Intercollegiate:** Baseball M, basketball, cross-country, soccer, softball W, track and field. **Team name:** Condors.

**Student services.** Career counseling, student employment services, health services, on-campus daycare, personal counseling, veterans' counselor. **Physically disabled:** Services for visually, speech, hearing impaired. **Transfer:** Transfer adviser, college fairs on campus for students transferring to 4-year colleges.

**Contact.** E-mail: ocadmissions@vcccd.edu
Phone: (805) 986-5810 Fax: (805) 986-5943
Susan Cabral, Director of Admissions, Oxnard College, 4000 South Rose Avenue, Oxnard, CA 93033

## Palo Verde College
**Blythe, California**
**www.paloverde.edu**     **CB code: 4603**

- Public 2-year community college
- Commuter campus in large town

**General.** Founded in 1947. Regionally accredited. **Enrollment:** 1,286 degree-seeking undergraduates. **Degrees:** 138 associate awarded. **Location:** 160 miles from Riverside. **Calendar:** Semester. **Full-time faculty:** 42 total. **Part-time faculty:** 98 total.

**Transfer out. Colleges most students transferred to 2007:** Coastline Community College, College of the Desert, Mohave Community College, Fresno Pacific College, Riverside Community College.

**Basis for selection.** Open admission, but selective for some programs. Limited admission to nursing program.

**2007-2008 Annual costs.** Tuition/fees: $600; $5,790 out-of-state. Per-credit charge: $20 in-state; $193 out-of-state. Books/supplies: $1,386. Personal expenses: $2,000.

**Financial aid.** All financial aid based on need. Need-based aid available for part-time students. Work-study available nights and for part-time students.

**Application procedures. Admission:** No deadline. No application fee. Application must be submitted on paper. Admission notification on a rolling basis. SAT or ACT recommended for placement. **Financial aid:** No deadline. FAFSA, institutional form required. Applicants notified on a rolling basis starting 7/1; must reply within 4 week(s) of notification.

**Academics. Special study options:** Cooperative education, distance learning, dual enrollment of high school students, ESL, independent study. **Credit/placement by examination:** AP, CLEP, institutional tests. 12 credit hours maximum toward associate degree. **Support services:** GED test center, learning center, remedial instruction, study skills assistance, tutoring, writing center.

**Majors. Agriculture:** General. **Business:** Accounting, business admin, office/clerical, real estate. **English:** English lit. **History:** General. **Liberal arts:** Arts/sciences. **Mechanic/repair:** Automotive. **Protective services:** Firefighting, law enforcement admin.

**Most popular majors.** Business/marketing 17%, liberal arts 79%.

**Computing on campus.** 125 workstations in library, computer center.

**Student life. Freshman orientation:** Mandatory. Preregistration for classes offered. **Activities:** Literary magazine, student government.

**Athletics. Intramural:** Soccer.

**Student services.** Career counseling, services for economically disadvantaged, student employment services, financial aid counseling, personal counseling, placement for graduates. **Physically disabled:** Services for visually, speech, hearing impaired. **Transfer:** Transfer center, transfer adviser, college fairs on campus for students transferring to 4-year colleges.

**Contact.** E-mail: mwalnoha@paloverde.edu
Phone: (760) 921-5500
Melinda Walnoha, Registrar, Palo Verde College, One College Drive, Blythe, CA 92225

---

## Palomar College
**San Marcos, California**
**www.palomar.edu**   **CB code: 4602**

- Public 2-year community college
- Commuter campus in large town

**General.** Founded in 1946. Regionally accredited. Off-campus sites located throughout North County area. **Enrollment:** 15,362 degree-seeking undergraduates. **Degrees:** 1,373 associate awarded. **Location:** 40 miles from San Diego. **Calendar:** Semester, extensive summer session. **Full-time faculty:** 310 total. **Part-time faculty:** 1,100 total. **Special facilities:** Arboretum, observatory.

**Basis for selection.** Open admission, but selective for some programs. ASSET mathematics and English tests required for nursing applicants. **Adult students:** SAT/ACT scores not required.

**2007-2008 Annual costs.** Tuition/fees: $630; $5,520 out-of-state. Per-credit charge: $20 in-state; $183 out-of-state. Books/supplies: $648. Personal expenses: $1,620.

**Financial aid.** All financial aid based on need. Need-based aid available for part-time students. Work-study available nights and for part-time students.

**Application procedures. Admission:** Priority date 6/9; no deadline. No application fee. Application may be submitted online. Application deadlines for nursing program April 1 for fall semester, November 1 for spring semester. **Financial aid:** Priority date 4/1; no closing date. FAFSA, institutional form required. Applicants notified on a rolling basis starting 6/1.

**Academics. Special study options:** Cooperative education, distance learning, dual enrollment of high school students, ESL, internships, liberal arts/career combination, study abroad, weekend college. **Credit/placement by examination:** AP, CLEP, institutional tests. 15 credit hours maximum toward associate degree. **Support services:** Learning center, pre-admission summer program, reduced course load, remedial instruction, tutoring, writing center.

**Majors. Biology:** General, zoology. **Business:** General, accounting, administrative services, banking/financial services, business admin, fashion, international, management science, office/clerical, operations, real estate, tourism promotion. **Communications:** Advertising, journalism. **Communications technology:** General, graphic/printing. **Computer sciences:** General, computer science, information systems. **Construction:** Carpentry, maintenance, masonry, pipefitting, power transmission. **Education:** Early childhood. **Engineering:** General. **Engineering technology:** Drafting, surveying. **English:** Speech/rhetoric. **Family/consumer sciences:** Child care, institutional food production. **Foreign languages:** Sign language interpretation. **Health:** Dental assistant, EMT paramedic, medical assistant, medical records admin, medical secretary, nursing (RN). **Legal studies:** Legal secretary, paralegal. **Liberal arts:** Arts/sciences, library science. **Math:** General. **Mechanic/repair:** General, auto body, diesel, electronics/electrical. **Parks/recreation:** General, facilities management, health/fitness. **Physical sciences:** Astronomy, chemistry, geology. **Production:** Woodworking. **Protective services:** Firefighting, law enforcement admin, police science, security services. **Public administration:** General. **Social sciences:** Archaeology, economics. **Transportation:** Aviation. **Visual/performing arts:** Art, ceramics, commercial/advertising art, crafts, dance, dramatic, fashion design, film/cinema, interior design, metal/jewelry, painting, photography, printmaking, sculpture.

**Most popular majors.** Health sciences 6%, liberal arts 61%, social sciences 7%, trade and industry 6%.

**Computing on campus.** 922 workstations in library, computer center, student center. Online course registration, online library, wireless network available.

**Student life. Freshman orientation:** Available. **Activities:** Bands, choral groups, dance, drama, literary magazine, music ensembles, musical theater, radio station, student government, student newspaper, symphony orchestra, TV station.

**Athletics.** NJCAA. **Intercollegiate:** Baseball M, basketball, football (tackle) M, golf M, soccer, softball W, swimming, tennis, volleyball, water polo M, wrestling M. **Intramural:** Volleyball W. **Team name:** Comets.

**Student services.** Career counseling, student employment services, financial aid counseling, health services, on-campus daycare, personal counseling, placement for graduates, veterans' counselor. **Physically disabled:** Services for visually, speech, hearing impaired. **Transfer:** Transfer center, transfer adviser, college fairs on campus for students transferring to 4-year colleges.

**Contact.** E-mail: admissions@palomar.edu
Phone: (760) 744-1150 ext. 2164 Fax: (760) 761-3536
Herman Lee, Director of Enrollment Services, Palomar College, 1140 West Mission Road, San Marcos, CA 92069-1487

---

## Pasadena City College
**Pasadena, California**   **CB member**
**www.pasadena.edu**   **CB code: 4604**

- Public 2-year community college
- Commuter campus in small city

**General.** Founded in 1924. Regionally accredited. **Enrollment:** 19,799 degree-seeking undergraduates. **Degrees:** 1,670 associate awarded. **Location:** 10 miles from downtown Los Angeles. **Calendar:** Semester, limited summer session. **Full-time faculty:** 320 total; 30% have terminal degrees. **Part-time faculty:** 740 total; 14% have terminal degrees. **Class size:** 6% < 20, 66% 20-39, 25% 40-49, 2% 50-99, 1% >100. **Special facilities:** Observatory.

**Student profile.**

| | | | |
|---|---|---|---|
| Out-of-state: | 3% | 25 or older: | 36% |

**Transfer out. Colleges most students transferred to 2007:** California State University: Los Angeles, Long Beach, Northridge; California State Polytechnic Institute: Pomona.

**Basis for selection.** Open admission, but selective for some programs. Admission to RN, LVN, dental hygiene programs based on test scores, interview, high school record; minimum 2.0 high school GPA required. School and College Ability Tests, SAT, ACT, or California Achievement Test scores used for admission to some programs. Interview required of dental hygiene majors. Audition required of music majors.

**2007-2008 Annual costs.** Tuition/fees: $628; $5,818 out-of-state. Per-credit charge: $20 in-state; $193 out-of-state. Books/supplies: $1,500. Personal expenses: $2,214.

**Financial aid.** All financial aid based on need.

**Application procedures. Admission:** Closing date 8/11. No application fee. Admission notification on a rolling basis beginning on or about 3/1. **Financial aid:** Priority date 5/13; no closing date. FAFSA required. Applicants notified on a rolling basis starting 6/1; must reply within 2 week(s) of notification.

**Academics. Special study options:** Accelerated study, distance learning, dual enrollment of high school students, honors, independent study, internships, liberal arts/career combination, study abroad. **Credit/placement by examination:** CLEP, institutional tests. 12 credit hours maximum toward associate degree. **Support services:** Learning center, pre-admission summer program, reduced course load, remedial instruction, study skills assistance, tutoring, writing center.

**Majors. Biology:** General. **Business:** General, accounting, administrative services, banking/financial services, entrepreneurial studies, fashion, hospitality/recreation, management information systems, office/clerical, real estate, sales/distribution, tourism promotion. **Communications:** General, broadcast journalism, journalism. **Communications technology:** General. **Computer sciences:** Applications programming, data processing, programming. **Construction:** Carpentry, maintenance. **Education:** Early childhood. **Engineering technology:** Drafting. **English:** Speech/rhetoric. **Health:** Clinical lab technology, dental assistant, dental hygiene, dental lab technology, licensed practical nurse, medical assistant, medical radiologic technology/radiation therapy, medical secretary, nursing (RN). **Legal studies:** Legal secretary, paralegal. **Liberal arts:** Arts/sciences, library assistant. **Mechanic/repair:** Auto body. **Parks/recreation:** General. **Protective services:** Firefighting, police science. **Psychology:** General. **Social sciences:** General. **Visual/performing arts:** Ceramics, commercial photography, commercial/advertising art, crafts, drawing, painting, printmaking, sculpture, studio arts.

**Computing on campus.** 300 workstations in computer center, student center.

**Student life. Freshman orientation:** Available. **Activities:** Bands, choral groups, dance, drama, film society, literary magazine, music ensembles, musical theater, radio station, student government, student newspaper, symphony orchestra, TV station, wide variety of religious, political, ethnic, and social service organizations.

**Athletics. Intercollegiate:** Badminton W, baseball M, basketball, cross-country, football (tackle) M, soccer, softball W, swimming, tennis W, track and field, volleyball W, water polo W. **Team name:** Lancers.

**Student services.** Career counseling, student employment services, health services, personal counseling, placement for graduates. **Physically disabled:** Services for visually, speech, hearing impaired. **Transfer:** Transfer center, transfer adviser, college fairs on campus for students transferring to 4-year colleges.

**Contact.** Phone: (626) 578-7396 Fax: (626) 585-7912
Margaret Ramey, Associate Dean of Admissions and Records, Pasadena City College, 1570 East Colorado Boulevard, Pasadena, CA 91106

## Platt College: Huntington Beach
**Huntington Beach, California**
www.plattcollege.edu          CB code: 3004

- For-profit 2-year visual arts and technical college
- Commuter campus in large city
- Application essay, interview required

**General.** Accredited by ACCSCT. **Enrollment:** 95 degree-seeking undergraduates. **Degrees:** 24 bachelor's, 22 associate awarded. **Calendar:** Continuous. **Full-time faculty:** 3 total. **Class size:** 86% < 20, 14% 20-39.

**Basis for selection.** Standardized test scores, essay, interview most important. Talent, personal qualities, work experience may also be admissions criteria.

**2007-2008 Annual costs.** Full academic program tuition ranges from $28,000 to $59,820.

**Financial aid. Need-based:** Need-based aid available for part-time students. Work-study available nights.

**Application procedures. Admission:** No deadline. $75 fee. Admission notification on a rolling basis. **Financial aid:** Priority date 3/2; no closing date. FAFSA, institutional form required. Applicants notified on a rolling basis starting 1/1.

**Academics. Special study options:** Accelerated study, cooperative education, internships. **Credit/placement by examination:** CLEP, institutional

tests. 48 credit hours maximum toward associate degree. **Support services:** Tutoring.

**Majors. Computer sciences:** Computer graphics, information technology. **Visual/performing arts:** General, commercial/advertising art.

**Most popular majors.** Computer/information sciences 22%, visual/performing arts 78%.

**Computing on campus.** 10 workstations in library.

**Student life. Freshman orientation:** Mandatory. Preregistration for classes offered. Two-hour orientation held on or around first day of classes.

**Student services.** Adult student services, career counseling, student employment services, financial aid counseling, placement for graduates. **Transfer:** Re-entry adviser, pre-admission transcript evaluation for new students. Transfer adviser for students transferring to 4-year colleges.

**Contact.** Phone: (949) 833-2300 Toll-free number: (866) 752-8848 Fax: (949) 833-0269
Joe Brickman, Admissions Director, Platt College: Huntington Beach, 7755 Center Avenue, Suite 400, Huntington Beach, CA 92647

## Platt College: Los Angeles
**Alhambra, California**
www.plattcollege.edu          CB code: 3014

- For-profit 2-year visual arts and technical college
- Commuter campus in very large city
- Application essay, interview required

**General.** Accredited by ACCSCT. **Enrollment:** 135 degree-seeking undergraduates. **Degrees:** 3 bachelor's, 18 associate awarded. **Location:** 10 miles from dowtown Los Angeles. **Calendar:** Continuous. **Full-time faculty:** 25 total. **Class size:** 85% < 20, 15% 20-39.

**Transfer out. Colleges most students transferred to 2007:** University of LaVerne, University of Phoenix.

**Basis for selection.** Must score at least 126 on CPAT for admissions. Multimedia program requires degree. MCSE program requires computer background. **Learning Disabled:** Students with learning disabilities allowed 30 extra minutes on CPAT examination.

**2007-2008 Annual costs.** Varies by program: associate degree cost range $26,780 (paralegal) to $28,370 (information technology).

**Financial aid. Need-based:** Need-based aid available for part-time students. Work-study available nights.

**Application procedures. Admission:** No deadline. $75 fee. Application may be submitted online. Admission notification on a rolling basis. **Financial aid:** Priority date 3/2; no closing date. FAFSA, institutional form required. Applicants notified on a rolling basis starting 1/1.

**Academics. Special study options:** Accelerated study, cooperative education, internships. **Credit/placement by examination:** CLEP, institutional tests. 48 credit hours maximum toward associate degree. **Support services:** Tutoring.

**Majors. Computer sciences:** General, computer graphics. **Visual/performing arts:** General, commercial/advertising art.

**Computing on campus.** 60 workstations in library.

**Student life. Freshman orientation:** Mandatory. Preregistration for classes offered. 2-hour program on or around first day of classes.

**Student services.** Adult student services, career counseling, student employment services, financial aid counseling, placement for graduates. **Transfer:** Re-entry adviser, pre-admission transcript evaluation for new students. Transfer adviser for students transferring to 4-year colleges.

**Contact.** Phone: (626) 300-5444 Toll-free number: (866) 752-8852 Fax: (626) 300-3978
Steven Hinojosa, Admissions Director, Platt College: Los Angeles, 1000 South Fremont Avenue A9W, Alhambra, CA 91803

## Porterville College
**Porterville, California**
www.portervillecollege.edu          CB code: 4608

- Public 2-year community college
- Commuter campus in large town

**General.** Founded in 1927. Regionally accredited. **Enrollment:** 2,039 degree-seeking undergraduates. **Degrees:** 235 associate awarded. **Location:** 75 miles from Fresno, 50 miles from Bakersfield. **Calendar:** Semester, limited summer session. **Full-time faculty:** 80 total. **Part-time faculty:** 1,510 total. **Special facilities:** Anthropology library.

**Basis for selection.** Open admission.

**2007-2008 Annual costs.** Tuition/fees: $634; $6,334 out-of-state. Per-credit charge: $20 in-state; $190 out-of-state.

**Application procedures. Admission:** No deadline. No application fee. Admission notification on a rolling basis. **Financial aid:** Priority date 3/1; no closing date. FAFSA required. Applicants notified on a rolling basis; must reply within 2 week(s) of notification.

**Academics. Special study options:** Double major, dual enrollment of high school students. **Credit/placement by examination:** CLEP, institutional tests. 30 credit hours maximum toward associate degree. **Support services:** Learning center, reduced course load, remedial instruction, tutoring.

**Majors. Biology:** General. **Business:** General, administrative services, banking/financial services, business admin, office/clerical, real estate. **Computer sciences:** General. **Construction:** Carpentry. **Education:** General. **Engineering technology:** Drafting. **English:** English lit. **Family/consumer sciences:** Child care. **Health:** Licensed practical nurse. **Interdisciplinary:** Biological/physical sciences. **Liberal arts:** Arts/sciences. **Math:** General. **Mechanic/repair:** Auto body. **Physical sciences:** Chemistry. **Protective services:** Police science. **Social sciences:** General, criminology. **Visual/performing arts:** General, commercial/advertising art, studio arts.

**Computing on campus.** 25 workstations in library, computer center.

**Student life. Activities:** Choral groups, drama, music ensembles, musical theater, student government, Mexican-American Student Association.

**Athletics.** NJCAA. **Intercollegiate:** Baseball M, basketball, tennis, volleyball W. **Team name:** Pirates.

**Student services.** Career counseling, student employment services, health services, on-campus daycare, personal counseling, placement for graduates, veterans' counselor. **Physically disabled:** Services for visually, speech, hearing impaired. **Transfer:** Transfer adviser for students transferring to 4-year colleges.

**Contact.** Phone: (209) 791-2220 Fax: (209) 784-4779
Virginia Gurrola, Vice President Student Services and Enrollment, Porterville College, 100 East College Avenue, Porterville, CA 93257

## Professional Golfers Career College
### Temecula, California
www.golfcollege.edu                CB code: 3548

‣ For-profit 2-year golf academy
‣ Residential campus in small city

**General.** Accredited by ACICS. **Enrollment:** 150 degree-seeking undergraduates. **Degrees:** 88 associate awarded. **Calendar:** Semester. **Part-time faculty:** 26 total.

**Basis for selection.** Handicap of 20 or below, 3 letters of personal character reference, 1 letter of recommendation attesting to golf ability required. **Homeschooled:** Transcript of courses and grades, letter of recommendation (nonparent) required.

**2007-2008 Annual costs.** Tuition $5,090/semester; program lasts 4 semesters. Books/supplies: $200.

**Application procedures. Admission:** No deadline. $75 fee. Application must be submitted on paper. Admission notification on a rolling basis.

**Academics. Credit/placement by examination:** CLEP.

**Majors. Parks/recreation:** Facilities management.

**Computing on campus.** Online library, wireless network available.

**Student life. Freshman orientation:** Mandatory. **Housing:** Single-sex dorms, apartments, substance-free housing available. $400 nonrefundable deposit.

**Student services.** Alcohol/substance abuse counseling, career counseling, financial aid counseling, personal counseling, placement for graduates, veterans' counselor.

**Contact.** E-mail: admin@progolfed.com
Phone: (951) 719-2994 Toll-free number: (800) 877-4380
Fax: (951) 719-1643
Mark Bland, Admissions Director, Professional Golfers Career College, PO Box 892319, Temecula, CA 92589-2319

## Reedley College
### Reedley, California
www.reedleycollege.edu                CB code: 4655

‣ Public 2-year community college
‣ Commuter campus in large town

**General.** Founded in 1926. Regionally accredited. Courses also offered at community campus sites in Madera, Clovis, Sanger, Easton, Selma, Kerman, Oakhurst, Parlier, Fowler, Orange Cove, Dinuba, Kingsburg, and Sunnyside. **Enrollment:** 6,472 degree-seeking undergraduates. **Degrees:** 728 associate awarded. **Location:** 25 miles from Fresno. **Calendar:** Semester, extensive summer session. **Full-time faculty:** 80 total. **Part-time faculty:** 190 total.

**Student profile.**

| | | | |
|---|---|---|---|
| **25 or older:** | 35% | **Live on campus:** | 4% |

**Transfer out. Colleges most students transferred to 2007:** California State University: Fresno, California State University: Long Beach.

**Basis for selection.** Open admission. **Homeschooled:** If under 18, a letter from parent required.

**2007-2008 Annual costs.** Tuition/fees: $628; $5,818 out-of-state. Per-credit charge: $20 in-state; $193 out-of-state. Room/board: $4,880. Books/supplies: $1,260. Personal expenses: $1,550.

**Financial aid.** All financial aid based on need. Need-based aid available for part-time students. Work-study available for part-time students. **Additional information:** Board of Governors fee waiver available for low-income students. Book voucher available for EOPS students.

**Application procedures. Admission:** No deadline. No application fee. Application may be submitted online. Admission notification on a rolling basis. **Financial aid:** Priority date 3/2; no closing date. FAFSA required. Applicants notified on a rolling basis starting 3/2; must reply within 3 week(s) of notification.

**Academics. Special study options:** Cooperative education, cross-registration, distance learning, double major, dual enrollment of high school students, ESL, honors, independent study, study abroad, weekend college. License preparation in aviation, dental hygiene. **Credit/placement by examination:** AP, CLEP. 48 credit hours maximum toward associate degree. **Support services:** Learning center, pre-admission summer program, reduced course load, remedial instruction, study skills assistance, tutoring, writing center.

**Majors. Agriculture:** Business, plant sciences. **Biology:** General. **Business:** Accounting. **Computer sciences:** General, computer science, information systems. **Conservation:** Forestry. **Education:** Early childhood, physical. **English:** English lit. **Foreign languages:** General. **Health:** Dental assistant. **Liberal arts:** Arts/sciences. **Math:** General. **Social sciences:** General. **Visual/performing arts:** Art, dramatic.

**Most popular majors.** Interdisciplinary studies 80%.

**Computing on campus.** 140 workstations in dormitories, library, computer center. Dormitories wired for high-speed internet access and linked to campus network. Commuter students can connect to campus network. Online course registration, online library available.

**Student life. Freshman orientation:** Available. Preregistration for classes offered. **Housing:** Single-sex dorms available. $125 deposit. **Activities:** Bands, choral groups, drama, music ensembles, musical theater, student government, student newspaper, symphony orchestra.

**Athletics.** NJCAA. **Intercollegiate:** Baseball M, basketball, equestrian, football (tackle) M, golf, softball W, tennis, track and field, volleyball W. **Team name:** Tigers.

**Student services.** Adult student services, alcohol/substance abuse counseling, career counseling, services for economically disadvantaged, student employment services, financial aid counseling, health services, minority student services, on-campus daycare, personal counseling, placement for graduates, veterans' counselor, women's services. **Physically disabled:** Services for visually, speech, hearing impaired. **Transfer:** Transfer adviser, college fairs on campus for students transferring to 4-year colleges.

**Contact.** Phone: (559) 638-0323 Fax: (559) 638-5040
John Cummings, District Dean of Admissions and Records, Reedley
College, 995 North Reed Avenue, Reedley, CA 93654

## Rio Hondo College
### Whittier, California
www.riohondo.edu                    **CB code: 4663**

♦ Public 2-year community college
♦ Commuter campus in small city

**General.** Founded in 1960. Regionally accredited. **Enrollment:** 8,862 degree-seeking undergraduates. **Degrees:** 767 associate awarded. **Location:** 15 miles from Los Angeles. **Calendar:** Semester, extensive summer session. **Full-time faculty:** 184 total; 40% minority, 47% women. **Part-time faculty:** 288 total; 36% minority, 46% women. **Special facilities:** Observatory.

**Student profile.** Among degree-seeking undergraduates, 1,049 transferred in from other institutions.

**Transfer out. Colleges most students transferred to 2007:** Cal State Los Angeles, Cal State Long Beach, Cal State Fullerton, Cal State Polytech, University of California-Los Angeles.

**Basis for selection.** Open admission, but selective for some programs. Nursing program has special requirements. **Learning Disabled:** Disabled Services Program available to stuents with disabilities.

**2007-2008 Annual costs.** Tuition/fees: $626; $5,816 out-of-state. Per-credit charge: $20 in-state; $193 out-of-state. Books/supplies: $1,442. Personal expenses: $2,898.

**2006-2007 Financial aid. Need-based:** 91% of total undergraduate aid awarded as scholarships/grants, 9% as loans/jobs. Need-based aid available for part-time students.

**Application procedures. Admission:** No deadline. No application fee. Admission notification on a rolling basis. **Financial aid:** Priority date 7/15; no closing date. FAFSA required. Applicants notified on a rolling basis.

**Academics. Special study options:** Dual enrollment of high school students, honors, independent study, study abroad, weekend college. **Credit/placement by examination:** CLEP, institutional tests. 12 credit hours maximum toward associate degree. **Support services:** Learning center, remedial instruction, tutoring.

**Majors. Business:** Accounting, administrative services, office/clerical, real estate. **Communications technology:** General, graphic/printing. **Engineering technology:** Drafting. **Health:** Dental assistant, health services, licensed practical nurse, nursing (RN), respiratory therapy technology. **Liberal arts:** Arts/sciences, library assistant. **Mechanic/repair:** Automotive. **Protective services:** Fire safety technology, police science.

**Most popular majors.** Business/marketing 9%, education 12%, health sciences 13%, liberal arts 41%.

**Computing on campus.** Wireless network available.

**Student life. Freshman orientation:** Available. **Activities:** Jazz band, choral groups, dance, drama, film society, literary magazine, music ensembles, musical theater, radio station, student government, student newspaper, TV station.

**Athletics.** NJCAA. **Intercollegiate:** Baseball M, basketball, diving, golf, softball W, swimming, tennis, volleyball W, water polo, wrestling M. **Team name:** Roadrunners.

**Student services.** Career counseling, student employment services, health services, on-campus daycare, personal counseling, veterans' counselor. **Physically disabled:** Services for visually, speech, hearing impaired. **Transfer:** Transfer center, transfer adviser, college fairs on campus for students transferring to 4-year colleges.

**Contact.** Phone: (562) 908-3415 Fax: (562) 692-8318
Judy Pearson, Director of Admissions and Records, Rio Hondo College, 3600 Workman Mill Road, Whittier, CA 90601-1699

## Riverside Community College
### Riverside, California
www.rcc.edu                    **CB member**
                               **CB code: 4658**

♦ Public 2-year community college
♦ Commuter campus in large city

**General.** Founded in 1916. Regionally accredited. **Enrollment:** 14,882 degree-seeking undergraduates. **Degrees:** 1,820 associate awarded. **ROTC:** Army, Naval, Air Force. **Location:** 60 miles from Los Angeles. **Calendar:** Semester, limited summer session. **Full-time faculty:** 266 total; 29% minority, 50% women. **Part-time faculty:** 1,187 total; 27% minority, 46% women. **Class size:** 49% < 20, 44% 20-39, 4% 40-49, 2% 50-99, less than 1% >100. **Special facilities:** Planetarium.

**Student profile.**

| | | | |
|---|---|---|---|
| Out-of-state: | 1% | Hispanic American: | 37% |
| African American: | 13% | Native American: | 1% |
| Asian American: | 11% | 25 or older: | 36% |

**Transfer out. Colleges most students transferred to 2007:** University of California: Riverside, California State University: San Bernardino.

**Basis for selection.** Open admission, but selective for some programs. Limited admission to nursing program.

**2007-2008 Annual costs.** Tuition/fees: $648; $5,838 out-of-state. Per-credit charge: $20 in-state; $193 out-of-state. Books/supplies: $1,386. Personal expenses: $2,520.

**Financial aid. Need-based:** Need-based aid available for part-time students. Work-study available nights, weekends and for part-time students. **Non-need-based:** Scholarships awarded for academics, alumni affiliation, art, leadership, minority status, music/drama, state residency.

**Application procedures. Admission:** No deadline. No application fee. Application may be submitted online. Admission notification on a rolling basis. **Financial aid:** Priority date 3/1; no closing date. FAFSA, institutional form required. Applicants notified on a rolling basis starting 7/1.

**Academics.** Honor Society (Alpha Gamma Sigma) for freshmen with 3.0 GPA. **Special study options:** Cooperative education, distance learning, double major, dual enrollment of high school students, ESL, honors, internships, study abroad, weekend college. License preparation in nursing. **Credit/placement by examination:** AP, CLEP, institutional tests. 30 credit hours maximum toward associate degree. **Support services:** GED preparation, learning center, remedial instruction, tutoring, writing center.

**Majors. Business:** General, accounting, administrative services, business admin, marketing, office technology, real estate. **Communications technology:** Graphic/printing. **Computer sciences:** General, programming. **Construction:** Maintenance. **Education:** Early childhood. **Engineering:** General. **Engineering technology:** Construction, drafting, electrical. **Family/consumer sciences:** General, food/nutrition. **Foreign languages:** Sign language interpretation. **Health:** Dental lab technology, licensed practical nurse, medical assistant, medical secretary, medical transcription, nursing (RN). **Legal studies:** Legal secretary. **Mechanic/repair:** General, auto body, automotive, heating/ac/refrig. **Personal/culinary services:** Cosmetic. **Protective services:** Fire safety technology. **Public administration:** Human services. **Social sciences:** Cartography. **Visual/performing arts:** Commercial/advertising art, photography.

**Most popular majors.** Business/marketing 33%, interdisciplinary studies 31%, liberal arts 22%.

**Computing on campus.** 200 workstations in library, computer center. Online library, helpline, repair service available.

**Student life. Freshman orientation:** Available. **Activities:** Bands, choral groups, dance, drama, literary magazine, music ensembles, musical theater, student government, student newspaper, College Democrats, MECHA, Latter-day Saints student association, multicultural advisory council, African American student union.

**Athletics. Intercollegiate:** Baseball M, basketball, cross-country, diving, football (tackle) M, golf, soccer, softball W, swimming, tennis, track and field, volleyball W, water polo. **Intramural:** Badminton, baseball M, basketball, bowling, golf, racquetball, soccer, tennis, volleyball. **Team name:** Tigers.

**Student services.** Adult student services, career counseling, services for economically disadvantaged, student employment services, financial aid counseling, health services, on-campus daycare, personal counseling, placement for graduates, veterans' counselor. **Physically disabled:** Services for visually, speech, hearing impaired. **Transfer:** Transfer center, transfer adviser, college fairs on campus for students transferring to 4-year colleges.

**Contact.** E-mail: webmstr@rcc.edu
Phone: (951) 222-8600 Fax: (951) 222-8028
Lorraine Anderson, District Dean, Admissions and Records, Riverside Community College, 4800 Magnolia Avenue, Riverside, CA 92506

## Sacramento City College
### Sacramento, California
www.scc.losrios.edu

CB code: 4670

Two-Year Colleges

▶ Public 2-year community college
▶ Commuter campus in large city

**General.** Founded in 1916. Regionally accredited. **Enrollment:** 15,574 degree-seeking undergraduates. **Degrees:** 1,069 associate awarded. **ROTC:** Army, Naval, Air Force. **Location:** 75 miles from San Francisco. **Calendar:** Semester, extensive summer session. **Full-time faculty:** 290 total. **Part-time faculty:** 140 total. **Special facilities:** Observatory.

**Student profile.**

Out-of-state: 5%   25 or older: 68%

**Basis for selection.** Open admission.

**2007-2008 Annual costs.** Tuition/fees: $632; $5,822 out-of-state. Per-credit charge: $20 in-state; $193 out-of-state. Books/supplies: $1,386. Personal expenses: $2,126.

**Financial aid. Need-based:** Need-based aid available for part-time students. Work-study available nights, weekends and for part-time students.

**Application procedures. Admission:** Priority date 7/28; no deadline. No application fee. Admission notification on a rolling basis. **Financial aid:** Priority date 3/2; no closing date. FAFSA required. Applicants notified on a rolling basis starting 7/1; must reply within 2 week(s) of notification.

**Academics. Special study options:** Accelerated study, cooperative education, cross-registration, distance learning, double major, dual enrollment of high school students, ESL, honors, independent study, internships, study abroad, weekend college. License preparation in aviation, dental hygiene, nursing, physical therapy, real estate. **Credit/placement by examination:** CLEP, institutional tests. 15 credit hours maximum toward associate degree. **Support services:** Learning center, remedial instruction, study skills assistance, tutoring, writing center.

**Majors. Area/ethnic studies:** Women's. **Business:** General, accounting, administrative services, international marketing, management information systems, office/clerical, real estate. **Communications:** Journalism. **Communications technology:** Graphic/printing. **Computer sciences:** General. **Education:** Bilingual, special. **Engineering technology:** Drafting. **Family/consumer sciences:** General, child care, clothing/textiles, family/community services. **Health:** Dental assistant, dental hygiene, licensed practical nurse, medical secretary, nursing (RN), occupational therapy assistant, physical therapy assistant. **Legal studies:** Legal secretary. **Liberal arts:** Arts/sciences, library assistant. **Math:** General. **Mechanic/repair:** Aircraft, electronics/electrical, heating/ac/refrig. **Personal/culinary services:** Cosmetic. **Protective services:** Corrections, police science. **Social sciences:** General. **Visual/performing arts:** General, commercial photography, dramatic, music management, studio arts.

**Computing on campus.** 350 workstations in library, computer center. Online course registration available.

**Student life. Freshman orientation:** Available. **Activities:** Bands, choral groups, dance, drama, literary magazine, music ensembles, musical theater, student government, student newspaper, minority groups, professional associations, Bible club, gay and lesbian student alliance, special interest groups.

**Athletics. Intercollegiate:** Baseball M, basketball, cross-country, football (tackle) M, golf W, soccer W, softball W, swimming, tennis, track and field, volleyball W, water polo W, wrestling M. **Intramural:** Badminton, baseball M, basketball, bowling, boxing M, fencing, football (tackle) M, golf, handball, racquetball, softball, swimming, table tennis, tennis, volleyball. **Team name:** Panthers.

**Student services.** Adult student services, career counseling, services for economically disadvantaged, student employment services, financial aid counseling, health services, on-campus daycare, personal counseling, placement for graduates, veterans' counselor. **Physically disabled:** Services for visually, speech, hearing impaired. **Transfer:** Transfer center, transfer adviser, college fairs on campus for students transferring to 4-year colleges.

**Contact.** E-mail: sccaeinfo@scc.losrios.edu
Phone: (916) 558-2351 Fax: (916) 558-2190
Sam Sandusky, Dean of Admissions, Sacramento City College, 3835 Freeport Boulevard, Sacramento, CA 95822

## Saddleback College
### Mission Viejo, California
www.saddleback.edu

CB code: 4747

▶ Public 2-year community college
▶ Commuter campus in small city

**General.** Founded in 1967. Regionally accredited. **Enrollment:** 9,479 degree-seeking undergraduates. **Degrees:** 977 associate awarded. **Location:** 55 miles from Los Angeles and San Diego. **Calendar:** Semester, limited summer session. **Full-time faculty:** 223 total. **Part-time faculty:** 509 total. **Special facilities:** Solar observatory, outdoor environmental laboratory, golf driving range, computer/technology centers, greenhouse.

**Basis for selection.** Open admission, but selective for some programs. Nursing candidates must complete core curriculum with 2.5 GPA or better before screening process. SAT/ACT recommended for placement and counseling.

**High school preparation.** 10 units recommended. Recommended units include English 3, mathematics 2, social studies 3 and science 2.

**2007-2008 Annual costs.** Tuition/fees: $628; $5,818 out-of-state. Per-credit charge: $20 in-state; $193 out-of-state. Books/supplies: $1,386. Personal expenses: $2,898.

**2006-2007 Financial aid.** All financial aid based on need. 70% of total undergraduate aid awarded as scholarships/grants, 30% as loans/jobs. Need-based aid available for part-time students. Work-study available for part-time students.

**Application procedures. Admission:** No deadline. No application fee. Application may be submitted online. Admission notification on a rolling basis. **Financial aid:** Closing date 6/30. FAFSA required. Applicants notified on a rolling basis starting 4/1.

**Academics. Special study options:** Cooperative education, cross-registration, distance learning, double major, dual enrollment of high school students, ESL, honors, independent study, internships, student-designed major, study abroad, weekend college. License preparation in nursing, paramedic, real estate. **Credit/placement by examination:** AP, CLEP, institutional tests. 30 credit hours maximum toward associate degree. **Support services:** Learning center, pre-admission summer program, reduced course load, remedial instruction, study skills assistance, tutoring, writing center.

**Honors college/program.** Overall GPA of 3.25 in all academic work required.

**Majors. Agriculture:** Ornamental horticulture. **Area/ethnic studies:** Women's. **Biology:** General. **Business:** General, accounting, administrative services, business admin, fashion, marketing, office management, real estate, tourism/travel. **Communications:** Broadcast journalism, journalism. **Computer sciences:** General, computer science, programming. **Conservation:** General, environmental studies. **Education:** Early childhood, family/consumer sciences, mathematics, music, physical, social science. **Engineering:** General. **Engineering technology:** Drafting. **English:** British lit, English lit, speech/rhetoric. **Family/consumer sciences:** General, food/nutrition. **Foreign languages:** General, sign language interpretation. **Health:** Medical assistant, nursing (RN), surgical technology. **History:** General. **Interdisciplinary:** Natural sciences. **Legal studies:** Legal secretary, paralegal. **Liberal arts:** Arts/sciences. **Math:** General. **Parks/recreation:** Health/fitness. **Philosophy/religion:** Philosophy. **Physical sciences:** Astronomy, chemistry, geology, physics. **Psychology:** General. **Social sciences:** General, anthropology, economics, geography, international relations, political science, sociology. **Visual/performing arts:** Art, commercial photography, commercial/advertising art, dance, design, dramatic, fashion design, interior design, photography, studio arts.

**Most popular majors.** Business/marketing 13%, health sciences 11%, liberal arts 42%.

**Computing on campus.** 1,030 workstations in library, computer center, student center. Commuter students can connect to campus network. Online course registration, online library, wireless network available.

**Student life. Activities:** Bands, choral groups, dance, drama, literary magazine, music ensembles, musical theater, radio station, student government, student newspaper, symphony orchestra, TV station, Democratic Club, Republican Club, Christian Club, Black United Students, Hillel, Gay and Lesbian Club, Amnesty International, Muslim Student Union, environmental awareness, sign language club.

**Athletics.** NJCAA. **Intercollegiate:** Baseball M, basketball, cheerleading M, cross-country, diving, football (tackle) M, golf, soccer W, softball W, swimming, tennis, track and field, volleyball W, water polo. **Team name:** Gauchos.

**Student services.** Adult student services, alcohol/substance abuse counseling, career counseling, services for economically disadvantaged, student employment services, health services, on-campus daycare, personal counseling, placement for graduates, veterans' counselor, women's services. **Physically disabled:** Services for visually, speech, hearing impaired. **Transfer:** Re-entry adviser for new students. Transfer center, transfer adviser, college fairs on campus for students transferring to 4-year colleges.

**Contact.** E-mail: scadmissions@saddleback.edu
Phone: (949) 582-4555 Fax: (949) 347-8315
Jane Rosenkrans, Director, Admissions, Records and Enrollment Services, Saddleback College, 28000 Marguerite Parkway, Mission Viejo, CA 92692

## Sage College
### Moreno Valley, California
### www.sagecollege.edu

- For-profit 2-year technical college
- Commuter campus in large city

**General.** Accredited by ACICS. **Enrollment:** 440 degree-seeking undergraduates. **Degrees:** 7 associate awarded. **Calendar:** Quarter. **Full-time faculty:** 13 total. **Part-time faculty:** 15 total.

**Basis for selection.** Satisfactory performance on institutional examination required. **Homeschooled:** State high school equivalency certificate required.

**2007-2008 Annual costs.** Tuition/fees: $7,675.

**Application procedures. Admission:** No deadline. $100 fee. Admission notification on a rolling basis.

**Academics. Credit/placement by examination:** CLEP.

**Majors. Legal studies:** Court reporting, paralegal.

**Student life. Freshman orientation:** Mandatory.

**Student services.** Career counseling, financial aid counseling, placement for graduates.

**Contact.** E-mail: admissions@sagecollege.edu
Phone: (951) 781-2727
Lauren Somma, Executive Director, Sage College, 12125 Day Street, Building L, Moreno Valley, CA 92557-6720

## Salvation Army College for Officer Training at Crestmont
### Rancho Palos Verdes, California
### www.crestmont.edu
CB code: 3890

- Private 2-year seminary college
- Residential campus in small city

**General.** Regionally accredited. **Calendar:** Semester.

**Annual costs/financial aid.** Comprehensive fee (2007-2008): $11,500.

**Contact.** Phone: (310) 377-0481
Director of Admissions, 30840 Hawthorne Boulevard, Rancho Palos Verdes, CA 90275

## San Bernardino Valley College
### San Bernardino, California
### www.valleycollege.edu
CB code: 4679

- Public 2-year community college
- Small city

**General.** Founded in 1926. Regionally accredited. **Enrollment:** 12,550 undergraduates. **Degrees:** 706 associate awarded. **Location:** 60 miles from Los Angeles. **Calendar:** Semester, limited summer session. **Full-time faculty:** 160 total. **Part-time faculty:** 355 total. **Special facilities:** Planetarium.

**Basis for selection.** Open admission, but selective for some programs. Special requirements for nursing program. **Homeschooled:** Transcript of courses and grades required.

**2007-2008 Annual costs.** Tuition/fees: $634; $5,434 out-of-state. Per-credit charge: $20 in-state; $180 out-of-state. Books/supplies: $1,113. Personal expenses: $2,250.

**Application procedures. Admission:** No deadline. No application fee. **Financial aid:** Priority date 5/25; no closing date. Applicants notified on a rolling basis starting 5/1; must reply within 2 week(s) of notification.

**Academics. Special study options:** Cooperative education, cross-registration, distance learning, double major, dual enrollment of high school students, ESL, honors, independent study, internships, liberal arts/career combination, weekend college. Service Members Opportunity College. **Credit/placement by examination:** AP, CLEP, institutional tests. **Support services:** GED preparation, learning center, pre-admission summer program, reduced course load, remedial instruction, study skills assistance, tutoring, writing center.

**Majors. Biology:** General. **Business:** Accounting, business admin, real estate. **Communications:** General. **Computer sciences:** Computer science, systems analysis. **Engineering technology:** Electrical. **Liberal arts:** Arts/sciences, library science. **Math:** General. **Mechanic/repair:** Automotive, diesel, electronics/electrical, heating/ac/refrig. **Physical sciences:** Astronomy, chemistry, geology, physics. **Protective services:** Law enforcement admin. **Psychology:** General. **Public administration:** Social work. **Social sciences:** Geography. **Transportation:** Aviation management. **Visual/performing arts:** Commercial/advertising art.

**Computing on campus.** 180 workstations in library, computer center, student center.

**Student life. Freshman orientation:** Available. **Activities:** Choral groups, drama, literary magazine, music ensembles, musical theater, radio station, student government, student newspaper, TV station, Campus Crusade for Christ, Newman Club, Baptist Student Union, Movimiento Estudiantil Chicano de Aztlan, Black Student Union, Young Democrats, Young Republicans.

**Athletics.** NCAA. **Intercollegiate:** Baseball M, basketball, cross-country, football (tackle) M, soccer, softball W, track and field, volleyball W. **Team name:** Wolverines.

**Student services.** Adult student services, career counseling, services for economically disadvantaged, student employment services, financial aid counseling, health services, on-campus daycare, personal counseling, placement for graduates, veterans' counselor. **Physically disabled:** Services for visually, speech, hearing impaired. **Transfer:** Pre-admission transcript evaluation for new students.

**Contact.** E-mail: admissions@valleycollege.edu
Phone: (909) 384-4401
Dan Angelo, Associate Dean of Enrollment, San Bernardino Valley College, 701 South Mount Vernon Avenue, San Bernardino, CA 92410

## San Diego City College
### San Diego, California
### www.sdccd.edu
CB code: 4681

- Public 2-year community college
- Commuter campus in very large city

**General.** Founded in 1914. Regionally accredited. **Enrollment:** 6,186 degree-seeking undergraduates. **Degrees:** 685 associate awarded. **ROTC:** Army, Air Force. **Location:** Downtown. **Calendar:** Semester, extensive summer session. **Full-time faculty:** 160 total. **Part-time faculty:** 325 total. **Special facilities:** Computerized independent study and learning laboratories, vocational training centers.

**Student profile.** Among degree-seeking undergraduates, 10% already have a bachelor's degree or higher, 5,299 transferred in from other institutions.

| | | | |
|---|---|---|---|
| Out-of-state: | 8% | 25 or older: | 49% |

**Basis for selection.** Open admission. High school students seeking college admission must submit an approved application certifed by parents, principal, registrar, or school district official.

**2007-2008 Annual costs.** Tuition/fees: $626; $5,516 out-of-state. Per-credit charge: $20 in-state; $180 out-of-state. Books/supplies: $1,422. Personal expenses: $2,826.

**2006-2007 Financial aid.** All financial aid based on need. 80% of total undergraduate aid awarded as scholarships/grants, 20% as loans/jobs. Need-based aid available for part-time students. Work-study available for part-time students.

**Application procedures. Admission:** No deadline. No application fee. Application may be submitted online. **Financial aid:** Priority date 4/15; no closing date. FAFSA required. Applicants notified on a rolling basis starting 7/1; must reply within 4 week(s) of notification.

**Academics. Special study options:** Accelerated study, cooperative education, cross-registration, double major, dual enrollment of high school students, honors, independent study, internships, liberal arts/career combination, student-designed major, study abroad, teacher certification program, weekend college. **Credit/placement by examination:** AP, CLEP, institutional tests. 15 credit hours maximum toward associate degree. **Support services:** Learning center, pre-admission summer program, reduced course load, remedial instruction, tutoring, writing center.

**Majors. Area/ethnic studies:** African, African-American, Latin American. **Biology:** General. **Business:** General, accounting, administrative services, business admin, labor relations, management information systems, management science, office technology, office/clerical, operations, purchasing, real estate, tourism promotion. **Communications:** Broadcast journalism. **Communications technology:** General. **Computer sciences:** General, applications programming, data entry, data processing, information systems, systems analysis. **Construction:** Pipefitting, power transmission. **Education:** Bilingual. **Engineering:** General. **Engineering technology:** Drafting, electrical, manufacturing. **English:** English lit, speech/rhetoric. **Family/consumer sciences:** Child care. **Foreign languages:** General, French, Italian, Spanish. **Health:** Nursing (RN), substance abuse counseling. **History:** General. **Interdisciplinary:** Behavioral sciences. **Legal studies:** Paralegal, prelaw. **Liberal arts:** Arts/sciences. **Math:** General, applied. **Mechanic/repair:** Heating/ac/refrig. **Parks/recreation:** Health/fitness. **Philosophy/religion:** Philosophy. **Physical sciences:** Chemistry, geology, physics. **Psychology:** General. **Science technology:** Biological. **Social sciences:** General, anthropology, geography, political science. **Visual/performing arts:** General, art history/conservation, commercial/advertising art, dramatic, photography, studio arts.

**Most popular majors.** Business/marketing 8%, health sciences 8%, interdisciplinary studies 9%, liberal arts 40%.

**Computing on campus.** 150 workstations in library, computer center, student center. Online course registration, online library, helpline, repair service available.

**Student life. Freshman orientation:** Available. **Activities:** Jazz band, choral groups, dance, drama, film society, musical theater, radio station, student government, student newspaper, symphony orchestra, TV station, Arabic club, Italian club, MECHA, National Society of Black Engineers, Society of Hispanic Professional Engineers, California Coalition Against Poverty, students for labor and solidarity, lesbian, gay, bisexual and transsexual student union.

**Athletics. Intercollegiate:** Baseball, basketball M, cross-country, football (tackle) M, golf, soccer, softball W, tennis, track and field, volleyball. **Intramural:** Archery, badminton, baseball M, basketball, bowling, racquetball, soccer, tennis, track and field, volleyball, weight lifting. **Team name:** Knights.

**Student services.** Adult student services, career counseling, student employment services, health services, on-campus daycare, personal counseling, placement for graduates, veterans' counselor. **Physically disabled:** Services for visually, speech, hearing impaired. **Transfer:** Pre-admission transcript evaluation for new students. Transfer center, transfer adviser, college fairs on campus for students transferring to 4-year colleges.

**Contact.** Phone: (619) 388-3475 Fax: (619) 388-3505
Lou Humphries, Director, Admissions and Records, San Diego City College, 1313 Park Boulevard, San Diego, CA 92101-4787

**Student profile.**

| | | | |
|---|---|---|---|
| Out-of-state: | 1% | 25 or older: | 43% |

**Transfer out. Colleges most students transferred to 2007:** San Diego State University, University of California: San Diego.

**Basis for selection.** Open admission. Students without high school diploma or equivalent admitted provisionally. **Learning Disabled:** Disabled Student Service Program (DSPS) available.

**2007-2008 Annual costs.** Tuition/fees: $626; $5,516 out-of-state. Per-credit charge: $20 in-state; $183 out-of-state. Books/supplies: $1,422. Personal expenses: $1,584.

**Application procedures. Admission:** No deadline. No application fee. Application may be submitted online. Admission notification on a rolling basis. Applications not accepted by mail. **Financial aid:** Priority date 3/2; no closing date. FAFSA required. Applicants notified on a rolling basis starting 6/15; must reply within 3 week(s) of notification.

**Academics. Special study options:** Accelerated study, distance learning, double major, dual enrollment of high school students, honors, independent study, internships, liberal arts/career combination, student-designed major, study abroad, teacher certification program. License preparation in dental hygiene, physical therapy, real estate. **Credit/placement by examination:** CLEP, institutional tests. 15 credit hours maximum toward associate degree. Institutional test required for placement and counseling. **Support services:** Learning center, reduced course load, remedial instruction, study skills assistance, tutoring.

**Majors. Agriculture:** Animal health. **Architecture:** Landscape. **Area/ethnic studies:** African, African-American, Hispanic-American/Latino/Chicano. **Biology:** General. **Business:** General, accounting, business admin, fashion, hotel/motel admin, real estate, tourism/travel. **Computer sciences:** Programming, web page design. **Education:** Physical, sales/marketing, speech. **Engineering:** General. **Engineering technology:** Construction, water quality. **Family/consumer sciences:** Child development. **Foreign languages:** American Sign Language, French, Spanish. **Health:** Dental assistant, dental lab technology, medical assistant, medical radiologic technology/radiation therapy, physical therapy assistant. **Liberal arts:** Arts/sciences. **Math:** General. **Personal/culinary services:** Culinary arts. **Philosophy/religion:** Philosophy. **Physical sciences:** Chemistry, physics. **Psychology:** General. **Social sciences:** General, anthropology, sociology. **Visual/performing arts:** Art, dramatic, interior design, studio arts.

**Most popular majors.** Business/marketing 10%, liberal arts 20%.

**Computing on campus.** Commuter students can connect to campus network. Online library available.

**Student life. Freshman orientation:** Available. **Activities:** Concert band, choral groups, dance, drama, music ensembles, student government, student newspaper.

**Athletics. Intercollegiate:** Badminton W, baseball M, basketball, cross-country, diving, football (tackle) M, soccer, softball W, swimming, tennis, track and field, volleyball, water polo. **Team name:** Olympians.

**Student services.** Adult student services, career counseling, health services, on-campus daycare, personal counseling, placement for graduates, veterans' counselor. **Physically disabled:** Services for visually, speech, hearing impaired. **Transfer:** Transfer center, transfer adviser, college fairs on campus for students transferring to 4-year colleges.

**Contact.** E-mail: csawyer@sdccd.edu
Phone: (619) 388-2682 Fax: (619) 388-2960
Ivonne Alvarez, Director of Admissions and Records, San Diego Mesa College, 7250 Mesa College Drive, San Diego, CA 92111

---

## San Diego Mesa College
San Diego, California
www.sandiegomesacollege.edu

CB member
CB code: 4735

- Public 2-year community college
- Commuter campus in very large city

**General.** Founded in 1964. Regionally accredited. **Enrollment:** 20,444 undergraduates. **Degrees:** 1,055 associate awarded. **Calendar:** Semester, limited summer session. **Full-time faculty:** 320 total. **Part-time faculty:** 599 total. **Special facilities:** Anthropology museum.

---

## San Diego Miramar College
San Diego, California
www.miramarcollege.net

CB code: 4728

- Public 2-year community college
- Commuter campus in very large city

**General.** Founded in 1969. Regionally accredited. **Enrollment:** 9,020 undergraduates. **Degrees:** 468 associate awarded. **Location:** 9 miles from downtown. **Calendar:** Semester, limited summer session. **Full-time faculty:** 91 total.

## Student profile.

Out-of-state: 1%    25 or older: 64%

**Basis for selection.** Open admission.

**2007-2008 Annual costs.** Tuition/fees: $626; $5,516 out-of-state. Per-credit charge: $20 in-state; $183 out-of-state. Books/supplies: $1,422. Personal expenses: $1,503.

**Financial aid. Need-based:** Need-based aid available for part-time students. **Additional information:** Private scholarships available.

**Application procedures. Admission:** No deadline. No application fee. Admission notification on a rolling basis. **Financial aid:** Priority date 3/2; no closing date. FAFSA required. Applicants notified on a rolling basis; must reply within 3 week(s) of notification.

**Academics. Special study options:** Accelerated study, cross-registration, dual enrollment of high school students, honors, independent study, weekend college. **Credit/placement by examination:** CLEP. Institutional placement tests required. **Support services:** Learning center, remedial instruction, tutoring.

**Majors. Biology:** General, biomedical sciences. **Business:** Accounting, administrative services, business admin, marketing, office/clerical. **Computer sciences:** General. **Education:** Early childhood. **English:** English lit, speech/rhetoric. **Foreign languages:** French, Spanish. **Health:** Occupational health. **History:** General. **Legal studies:** Paralegal. **Liberal arts:** Arts/sciences. **Math:** General, applied. **Mechanic/repair:** Aircraft. **Parks/recreation:** Health/fitness. **Philosophy/religion:** Philosophy. **Physical sciences:** Chemistry, physics. **Protective services:** Criminal justice, law enforcement admin. **Psychology:** General. **Social sciences:** General, anthropology, geography, political science, sociology. **Visual/performing arts:** Art, studio arts.

**Most popular majors.** Business/marketing 14%, legal studies 6%, liberal arts 29%, security/protective services 30%.

**Computing on campus.** 10 workstations in library, computer center.

**Student life. Activities:** Student government, student newspaper, international club, Filipino-American association.

**Student services.** Career counseling, services for economically disadvantaged, on-campus daycare, personal counseling, veterans' counselor. **Physically disabled:** Services for visually, hearing impaired. **Transfer:** Transfer adviser, college fairs on campus for students transferring to 4-year colleges.

**Contact.** Phone: (858) 536-7844
Peter White, Vice President of Student Services, San Diego Miramar College, 10440 Black Mountain Road, San Diego, CA 92126-2999

### San Joaquin Delta College
**Stockton, California**
**www.deltacollege.edu**          CB code: 4706

- Public 2-year community college
- Commuter campus in large city

**General.** Founded in 1935. Regionally accredited. 14 off-campus sites located in service district. **Enrollment:** 12,237 degree-seeking undergraduates. **Degrees:** 3,806 associate awarded. **Location:** 45 miles from Sacramento. **Calendar:** Semester, extensive summer session. **Full-time faculty:** 215 total. **Part-time faculty:** 355 total. **Class size:** 5% < 20, 4% 20-39, less than 1% 40-49, less than 1% 50-99, less than 1% >100. **Special facilities:** Planetarium, electron microscopy laboratory, farm laboratory, natural resources laboratory, 3 theaters. **Partnerships:** Nissan, General Motors, Caterpillar.

**Transfer out. Colleges most students transferred to 2007:** California State University: Stanislaus, California State University: Sacramento, University of the Pacific, California State Polytechnic University, University of California: Davis.

**Basis for selection.** Open admission, but selective for some programs. Limited admission to registered nursing, psychiatric technician, licensed vocational nursing, radiological technician, and police academy programs.

**2007-2008 Annual costs.** Tuition/fees: $600; $5,790 out-of-state. Per-credit charge: $20 in-state; $193 out-of-state. Books/supplies: $1,386. Personal expenses: $2,898.

**Financial aid. Need-based:** Need-based aid available for part-time students. Work-study available nights, weekends and for part-time students.

**Non-need-based:** Scholarships awarded for academics, athletics. **Additional information:** Enrollment fee waivers available for low-income California residents.

**Application procedures. Admission:** No deadline. No application fee. Admission notification on a rolling basis beginning on or about 6/5. **Financial aid:** Priority date 4/15; no closing date. FAFSA, institutional form required. Applicants notified on a rolling basis starting 5/1; must reply within 3 week(s) of notification.

**Academics. Special study options:** Cooperative education, distance learning, dual enrollment of high school students, ESL, internships, liberal arts/career combination, study abroad, weekend college. License preparation in nursing, real estate. **Credit/placement by examination:** AP, CLEP, IB, institutional tests. 15 credit hours maximum toward associate degree. All students taking more than one course must take ASSET or COMPASS for placement. AP and CLEP credit granted after 12 semester hours in residence completed. **Support services:** GED preparation, learning center, reduced course load, remedial instruction, study skills assistance, tutoring, writing center.

**Majors. Agriculture:** Agribusiness operations, agronomy, animal sciences, business, economics, food science, horticulture, ornamental horticulture, plant protection, plant sciences, soil science. **Architecture:** Landscape. **Biology:** General, botany, zoology. **Business:** General, accounting, administrative services, business admin, fashion, management information systems, managerial economics, office technology, office/clerical, real estate. **Communications:** Broadcast journalism, journalism. **Communications technology:** Graphic/printing. **Computer sciences:** General, computer science, data processing, database management, programming. **Conservation:** General, wildlife. **Construction:** Carpentry, maintenance, power transmission. **Engineering:** General, architectural. **Engineering technology:** Architectural, drafting, electrical, software. **English:** American lit, English lit, speech/rhetoric. **Family/consumer sciences:** General, child care, food/nutrition, institutional food production. **Foreign languages:** French, German, Spanish. **Health:** EMT paramedic, medical radiologic technology/radiation therapy, mental health services, nursing (RN). **Interdisciplinary:** Natural sciences. **Legal studies:** Prelaw. **Liberal arts:** Arts/sciences. **Math:** General. **Mechanic/repair:** Heavy equipment, locksmithing. **Personal/culinary services:** Culinary arts. **Physical sciences:** Astronomy, chemistry, geology, physics. **Production:** Woodworking. **Protective services:** Fire safety technology, police science. **Psychology:** General. **Public administration:** General. **Social sciences:** General, anthropology. **Visual/performing arts:** General, crafts, fashion design, interior design, photography, studio arts.

**Computing on campus.** 220 workstations in library, computer center. Commuter students can connect to campus network. Online course registration, online library, helpline, wireless network available.

**Student life. Freshman orientation:** Available. **Activities:** Bands, choral groups, dance, drama, literary magazine, music ensembles, musical theater, radio station, student government, student newspaper, symphony orchestra, African-American Student Union, Movimiento Estudiantil Chicano de Aztlan, Vietnamese and Asian student clubs, International Student Association.

**Athletics.** NJCAA. **Intercollegiate:** Baseball M, basketball, cross-country, diving, football (tackle) M, golf M, soccer, softball W, swimming, tennis, track and field, volleyball W, water polo, wrestling M. **Intramural:** Baseball M, basketball, bowling, diving, fencing, golf, softball, swimming, tennis, track and field, volleyball. **Team name:** Mustangs.

**Student services.** Adult student services, alcohol/substance abuse counseling, career counseling, services for economically disadvantaged, student employment services, financial aid counseling, health services, legal services, minority student services, on-campus daycare, personal counseling, placement for graduates, veterans' counselor. **Physically disabled:** Services for visually, hearing impaired. **Transfer:** Re-entry adviser for new students. Transfer center, transfer adviser, college fairs on campus for students transferring to 4-year colleges.

**Contact.** Phone: (209) 954-5635 Fax: (209) 954-5644
Catherine Mooney, Registrar, San Joaquin Delta College, 5151 Pacific Avenue, Stockton, CA 95207-6370

### San Joaquin Valley College
**Visalia, California**
**www.sjvc.edu**          CB code: 2052

- For-profit 2-year junior college
- Commuter campus in small city
- Application essay, interview required

**General.** Regionally accredited. Additional campuses in Bakersfield, Fresno, Hanford, Modesto, Sacramento and Rancho Cucamonga. Aviation campus located in Fresno. **Enrollment:** 1,040 undergraduates. **Degrees:** 458 associate awarded. **Calendar:** Semester, extensive summer session. **Full-time faculty:** 80 total. **Part-time faculty:** 40 total.

**Basis for selection.** Open admission, but selective for some programs. Limited admission to nursing and some health related programs. ACCUPLACER for placement in Math and English.

**2007-2008 Annual costs.** Costs may vary with program, annual tuition includes textbooks and supplies.

**Application procedures. Admission:** No deadline. No application fee. Admission notification on a rolling basis. **Financial aid:** No deadline. FAFSA, institutional form required.

**Academics. Special study options:** Independent study, internships, liberal arts/career combination. License preparation in aviation, dental hygiene, nursing. **Credit/placement by examination:** CLEP. **Support services:** Learning center, remedial instruction, study skills assistance, tutoring.

**Majors. Business:** Administrative services, business admin, hospitality admin. **Computer sciences:** General, applications programming, information systems, information technology, networking, programming. **Engineering technology:** Electrical. **Health:** Dental assistant, dental hygiene, EMT paramedic, health care admin, insurance coding, licensed practical nurse, medical assistant, medical records admin, medical secretary, office assistant, pharmacy assistant, surgical technology, veterinary technology/assistant. **Mechanic/repair:** Aircraft, heating/ac/refrig. **Protective services:** Corrections.

**Computing on campus.** 100 workstations in library, computer center.

**Student life. Freshman orientation:** Mandatory. Preregistration for classes offered. Full day on Friday prior to start of classes, continues through first week. **Activities:** Student government, student newspaper.

**Student services.** Adult student services, career counseling, services for economically disadvantaged, student employment services, financial aid counseling, personal counseling, placement for graduates. **Transfer:** Pre-admission transcript evaluation for new students.

**Contact.** Phone: (559) 651-2500 Fax: (559) 651-0574
Susie Topjian, Enrollment Services Director, San Joaquin Valley College, 8400 West Mineral King Avenue, Visalia, CA 93291-9283

## San Jose City College
San Jose, California
www.sjcc.edu                                    CB code: 4686

▶ Public 2-year community college
▶ Commuter campus in very large city

**General.** Founded in 1921. Regionally accredited. **Enrollment:** 5,892 degree-seeking undergraduates. **Degrees:** 265 associate awarded. **Location:** 55 miles from San Francisco. **Calendar:** Semester, limited summer session. **Full-time faculty:** 170 total. **Part-time faculty:** 230 total. **Partnerships:** Formal partnerships with Intel (Manufacturing Technology program), Laser Electro-Optics Manufacturing Association (Laser Technology program), IntelSemiconductor (Mask Design Technology program).

**Transfer out. Colleges most students transferred to 2007:** San Jose State University, California State University: East Bay.

**Basis for selection.** Open admission.

**2007-2008 Annual costs.** Tuition/fees: $628; $6,118 out-of-state. Per-credit charge: $20 in-state; $203 out-of-state. Books/supplies: $712.

**Financial aid.** All financial aid based on need. **Additional information:** Board of Governors Grant (fee waivers) available to all qualified applicants.

**Application procedures. Admission:** No deadline. No application fee. Application may be submitted online. **Financial aid:** Priority date 5/31; no closing date. FAFSA required. Applicants notified on a rolling basis; must reply within 4 week(s) of notification.

**Academics. Special study options:** Accelerated study, cooperative education, dual enrollment of high school students, honors, independent study, weekend college. License preparation in real estate. **Credit/placement by examination:** CLEP, IB, institutional tests. 30 credit hours maximum toward associate degree. **Support services:** Learning center, pre-admission summer program, reduced course load, remedial instruction, tutoring.

**Majors. Business:** Accounting, administrative services, banking/financial services, entrepreneurial studies, labor studies, marketing, office technology, office/clerical, real estate. **Communications technology:** General. **Computer sciences:** General, applications programming, data entry, networking, programming. **Construction:** General, power transmission. **Education:** Early childhood. **Engineering technology:** Drafting, electrical, heat/ac/refrig, laser/optical. **Health:** Dental assistant, substance abuse counseling. **Liberal arts:** Arts/sciences. **Mechanic/repair:** Electronics/electrical, heating/ac/refrig. **Personal/culinary services:** Cosmetic, hair styling. **Production:** Machine tool. **Protective services:** Law enforcement admin. **Psychology:** General. **Social sciences:** General. **Visual/performing arts:** Studio arts.

**Computing on campus.** 250 workstations in library, computer center. Commuter students can connect to campus network. Online course registration available.

**Student life. Freshman orientation:** Available. **Activities:** Bands, choral groups, dance, drama, music ensembles, musical theater, radio station, student government, student newspaper, symphony orchestra.

**Athletics. Intercollegiate:** Baseball M, basketball, cross-country, football (tackle) M, golf M, softball W, track and field, volleyball W. **Team name:** Jaguars.

**Student services.** Career counseling, services for economically disadvantaged, student employment services, health services, minority student services, on-campus daycare, personal counseling, veterans' counselor. **Physically disabled:** Services for visually, speech, hearing impaired. **Transfer:** Transfer center, transfer adviser, college fairs on campus for students transferring to 4-year colleges.

**Contact.** Phone: (408) 288-3700 Fax: (408) 298-1935
Carlo Santos, Director of Admissions and Records, San Jose City College, 2100 Moorpark Avenue, San Jose, CA 95128-2798

## Santa Ana College
Santa Ana, California                           CB member
www.sac.edu                                     CB code: 4689

▶ Public 2-year community college
▶ Commuter campus in large city

**General.** Founded in 1915. Regionally accredited. **Enrollment:** 12,741 degree-seeking undergraduates. **Degrees:** 1,295 associate awarded. **Location:** 40 miles from Los Angeles. **Calendar:** Semester, extensive summer session. **Full-time faculty:** 263 total; 35% minority, 59% women. **Part-time faculty:** 1,001 total; 29% minority, 41% women. **Special facilities:** Planetarium.

**Student profile.**

| | | | |
|---|---|---|---|
| Out-of-state: | 2% | Hispanic American: | 51% |
| African American: | 3% | Native American: | 1% |
| Asian American: | 14% | 25 or older: | 37% |

**Transfer out. Colleges most students transferred to 2007:** California State University - Fullerton, California State University - Long Beach, California State University - Irvine.

**Basis for selection.** Open admission. All students 18 years and older who can benefit from instruction are admitted. **Adult students:** SAT/ACT scores not required.

**2007-2008 Annual costs.** Tuition/fees: $628; $5,818 out-of-state. Per-credit charge: $20 in-state; $193 out-of-state. Books/supplies: $1,260. Personal expenses: $2,300.

**Application procedures. Admission:** Priority date 4/1; no deadline. No application fee. Application may be submitted online. Admission notification on a rolling basis. **Financial aid:** Priority date 6/30; no closing date. FAFSA required. Applicants notified on a rolling basis starting 6/1; must reply within 2 week(s) of notification.

**Academics. Special study options:** Cooperative education, distance learning, double major, dual enrollment of high school students, ESL, honors, independent study, internships, liberal arts/career combination, study abroad, weekend college. **Credit/placement by examination:** AP, CLEP, institutional tests. 30 credit hours maximum toward associate degree. **Support services:** GED preparation, learning center, pre-admission summer program, reduced course load, remedial instruction, study skills assistance, tutoring.

**Majors. Area/ethnic studies:** African-American, Hispanic-American/Latino/Chicano, women's. **Biology:** General. **Business:** Accounting, business admin, entrepreneurial studies, fashion, insurance, international, management science, marketing, real estate, tourism promotion. **Communications:** General, advertising, broadcast journalism, journalism. **Computer sciences:** General, computer science, data processing. **Education:** Early childhood. **Engineering:** General. **Engineering technology:** Drafting. **English:** English lit. **Family/consumer sciences:** Family/community services, food/nutrition. **Foreign languages:** General. **Health:** Medical assistant, nursing (RN), occupational therapy assistant, pharmacy assistant. **History:** General. **Legal studies:** Paralegal. **Liberal arts:** Arts/sciences, library science. **Math:** General. **Mechanic/repair:** Automotive, diesel. **Parks/recreation:** Exercise sciences. **Philosophy/religion:** Philosophy. **Physical sciences:** Chemistry, geology, physics. **Production:** Welding. **Protective services:** Fire safety technology, fire services admin, firefighting, police science. **Psychology:** General. **Social sciences:** General, anthropology, economics, geography, political science, sociology. **Visual/performing arts:** General, commercial/advertising art, dance, dramatic, fashion design, photography. **Other:** Ethnic Studies.

**Most popular majors.** Business/marketing 9%, health sciences 11%, liberal arts 58%, security/protective services 10%.

**Computing on campus.** 66 workstations in library, computer center.

**Student life. Freshman orientation:** Available. **Activities:** Bands, choral groups, dance, drama, literary magazine, music ensembles, musical theater, student government, student newspaper, TV station.

**Athletics.** NJCAA. **Intercollegiate:** Baseball M, basketball, cross-country, football (tackle) M, soccer, softball W, track and field, volleyball, water polo, wrestling M. **Team name:** Dons.

**Student services.** Adult student services, alcohol/substance abuse counseling, career counseling, services for economically disadvantaged, student employment services, health services, on-campus daycare, personal counseling, veterans' counselor, women's services. **Physically disabled:** Services for visually, speech, hearing impaired. **Transfer:** Re-entry adviser, preadmission transcript evaluation for new students. Transfer center, transfer adviser, college fairs on campus for students transferring to 4-year colleges.

**Contact.** E-mail: adm_records@rsccd.org
Phone: (714) 564-6042 Fax: (714) 564-6455
Arleen Elseroad, Associate Dean, Admissions and Records, Santa Ana College, 1530 West 17th Street, Santa Ana, CA 92706

## Santa Barbara Business College
### Santa Barbara, California
### www.sbbcollege.edu

- For-profit 2-year junior college
- Large city
- Interview required

**General.** Accredited by ACICS. Campuses located in Santa Barbara, Ventura, Santa Maria, Bakersfield, Palm Desert and On-Line. **Enrollment:** 90 degree-seeking undergraduates. **Degrees:** 50 associate awarded. **Location:** 90 miles from Los Angeles. **Calendar:** Terms begin every 10 weeks. **Full-time faculty:** 5 total. **Part-time faculty:** 10 total.

**Student profile.** Among degree-seeking undergraduates, 100% enrolled in a vocational program. Of all enrolled students, 5% already have a bachelor's degree or higher.

**Basis for selection.** Admission decisions based on Wonderlic assessment and interview to determine interest and motivation of prospective student. **Homeschooled:** Transcript of courses and grades required. Need to take ATB proctored test if unable to supply an official transcript.

**2007-2008 Annual costs.** Costs for full programs as follows: medical assistant diploma, $17,805; medical assistant associate degree, $29,599; business administration associate degree, $29,848; massage therapy, $15,881; fitness trainer, $14,653. Tuition, fees, books, supplies, equipment included in program costs.

**Application procedures. Admission:** No deadline. $25 fee. **Financial aid:** FAFSA required. Applicants notified on a rolling basis.

**Academics. Special study options:** License preparation in nursing. **Credit/placement by examination:** CLEP. **Support services:** Remedial instruction, study skills assistance, tutoring.

**Majors. Business:** General. **Health:** Office assistant, pharmacy assistant. **Legal studies:** Paralegal. **Protective services:** Criminal justice.

**Computing on campus.** Online library available.

**Student life. Freshman orientation:** Mandatory.

**Contact.** Phone: (805) 967-9677 Fax: (805) 967-4248
Holly Ortiz, Director of Admissions, Santa Barbara Business College, 506 Chapala Street, Santa Barbara, CA 93101

## Santa Barbara Business College: Bakersfield
### Bakersfield, California
### www.sbbcollege.edu

- For-profit 2-year business college
- Large city

**General.** Accredited by ACICS. **Enrollment:** 300 degree-seeking undergraduates. **Degrees:** 250 associate awarded. **Calendar:** Modules begin every 6 weeks. **Full-time faculty:** 10 total. **Part-time faculty:** 20 total.

**Basis for selection.** Admissions decisions based on Wonderlic assessment and interview to determine interest and motivation of prospective student.

**2007-2008 Annual costs.** Costs for full programs as follows: medical office systems diploma, $18,042; medical assistant diploma, $17,799; medical assistant associate degree, $29,588; business administration diploma, $18,333; business administration associate degree, $29,836; criminal justice associate degree, $27,781; network systems administration diploma, $19,222; network systems administration associate degree, $27,773; paralegal diploma for students with 2 or 4-year degree in field, $19,703; paralegal associate degree, $29,768; pharmacy technician diploma, $18,685; pharmacy technician associate degree, $26,762; vocational nursing, $26,232; fitness trainer, $14,648; massage therapy, $15,874 (starting in January 2008). Tuition, fees, books, supplies, equipment included in program costs.

**Application procedures. Admission:** No deadline. $25 fee. **Financial aid:** FAFSA required. Applicants notified on a rolling basis.

**Academics. Credit/placement by examination:** CLEP.

**Majors. Business:** General. **Computer sciences:** LAN/WAN management. **Health:** Office assistant, pharmacy assistant. **Legal studies:** Paralegal. **Protective services:** Criminal justice.

**Contact.** Phone: (866) 749-7222
Holly Ortiz, Director of Admissions, Santa Barbara Business College: Bakersfield, 211 South Real Road, Bakersfield, CA 93309

## Santa Barbara Business College: Santa Maria
### Santa Maria, California
### www.sbbcollege.edu

- For-profit 2-year business and career college
- Small city

**General.** Accredited by ACICS. **Enrollment:** 182 degree-seeking undergraduates. **Degrees:** 100 associate awarded. **Calendar:** Quarter, limited summer session. **Full-time faculty:** 8 total. **Part-time faculty:** 12 total.

**Basis for selection.** Admissions decisions based on Wonderlic assessment and interview to determine interest and motivation of prospective student.

**2007-2008 Annual costs.** Costs for full programs as follows: medical office systems diploma, $18,049; medical assistant diploma, $17,805; medical assistant associate degree, $29,599; business administration diploma, $18,339; business administration associate degree, $29,848; criminal justice associate degree, $27,792; paralegal diploma for students with 2 or 4-year degree in field, $19,711; paralegal associate degree, $29,780; pharmacy technician diploma, $18,691; pharmacy technician associate degree, $26,771; vocational nursing, $26,236. Tuition, fees, books, supplies, equipment included in program costs.

**Application procedures. Admission:** No deadline. $25 fee. **Financial aid:** Applicants notified on a rolling basis.

**Academics. Credit/placement by examination:** CLEP.

**Majors. Business:** General. **Health:** Office assistant, pharmacy assistant. **Legal studies:** Paralegal. **Protective services:** Criminal justice.

**Contact.** Phone: (866) 749-7222 Toll-free number: (866) 749-7222
Fax: (805) 346-1862
Holly Ortiz, Director of Admissions, Santa Barbara Business College: Santa Maria, 303 East Plaza Drive, Santa Maria, CA 93454

## Santa Barbara Business College: Ventura
Ventura, California
www.sbbcollege.edu

- For-profit 2-year business and career college
- Commuter campus in small city
- Interview required

**General.** Accredited by ACICS. **Enrollment:** 200 degree-seeking undergraduates. **Degrees:** 100 associate awarded. **Location:** 40 miles from Los Angeles. **Calendar:** Quarter. **Full-time faculty:** 4 total. **Part-time faculty:** 27 total.

**Basis for selection.** Decisions based on Wonderlic assessment and interview to determine interest and motivation of prospective student. Wonderlic Basic Skills Test required.

**2007-2008 Annual costs.** Costs for full programs as follows: medical assistant diploma, $17,799; medical assistant associate degree, $29,588; business administration diploma, $18,333; business administration associate degree, $29,836; criminal justice associate degree, $27,781; paralegal diploma for students with 2 or 4-year degree in field, $19,703; paralegal associate degree, $29,768; pharmacy technician diploma, $18,685; pharmacy technician associate degree, $26,232; fitness trainer, $14,648; massage therapy, $15,874. Tuition, fees, books, supplies, equipment included in program costs.

**Application procedures. Admission:** No deadline. $25 fee. Application must be submitted on paper.

**Academics. Credit/placement by examination:** CLEP. **Support services:** Learning center, study skills assistance.

**Majors. Business:** Business admin. **Health:** Office assistant, pharmacy assistant. **Legal studies:** Paralegal. **Protective services:** Criminal justice.

**Computing on campus.** Online library available.

**Contact.** E-mail: hollyo@sbbcollege.edu
Phone: (866) 749-7222 Fax: (805) 339-2994
Holly Ortiz, Director of Admissions, Santa Barbara Business College: Ventura, 4839 Market Street, Ventura, CA 93003

## Santa Barbara City College
Santa Barbara, California
www.sbcc.edu      CB code: 4690

- Public 2-year community college
- Commuter campus in small city

**General.** Founded in 1908. Regionally accredited. **Enrollment:** 7,771 degree-seeking undergraduates; 8,646 non-degree-seeking students. **Degrees:** 1,180 associate awarded. **Location:** 90 miles from Los Angeles. **Calendar:** Semester, limited summer session. **Full-time faculty:** 259 total; 17% minority, 52% women. **Part-time faculty:** 598 total; 14% minority, 56% women. **Class size:** 18% < 20, 66% 20-39, 10% 40-49, 5% 50-99, 2% >100.

**Student profile.** Among degree-seeking undergraduates, 80% enrolled in a transfer program, 5% enrolled in a vocational program, 12% already have a bachelor's degree or higher, 1,782 enrolled as first-time, first-year students, 685 transferred in from other institutions.

| | | | |
|---|---|---|---|
| Part-time: | 43% | Hispanic American: | 25% |
| Out-of-state: | 7% | Native American: | 1% |
| Women: | 52% | International: | 9% |
| African American: | 3% | 25 or older: | 25% |
| Asian American: | 6% | | |

**Transfer out. Colleges most students transferred to 2007:** University of California: Santa Barbara, California State University: Northridge, San Francisco State University, San Diego State University, University of California: Los Angeles.

**Basis for selection.** Open admission, but selective for some programs. Special requirements for hotel/restaurant/culinary, nursing, radiography, early childhood education, cosmetology, marine diving technology programs. Criteria vary by program. Interview required of nursing, hotel and restaurant management, marine technology majors. Audition required of some music and theater majors. **Adult students:** English assessment test required for placement.

**2007-2008 Annual costs.** Tuition/fees: $670; $5,860 out-of-state. Per-credit charge: $20 in-state; $193 out-of-state. Books/supplies: $1,386. Personal expenses: $2,898.

**Financial aid. Need-based:** Need-based aid available for part-time students. **Additional information:** California residents may qualify for Board of Governor's Financial Assistance Program, which will allow institutions to waive enrollment fee.

**Application procedures. Admission:** Priority date 2/1; deadline 8/22 (receipt date). No application fee. Application may be submitted online. Admission notification on a rolling basis beginning on or about 3/1. **Financial aid:** No deadline. FAFSA required. Applicants notified on a rolling basis starting 5/1; must reply within 2 week(s) of notification.

**Academics. Special study options:** Cooperative education, cross-registration, distance learning, double major, dual enrollment of high school students, ESL, honors, independent study, internships, study abroad. License preparation in nursing, paramedic, radiology, real estate. **Credit/placement by examination:** AP, CLEP, IB, institutional tests. 12 credit hours maximum toward associate degree. **Support services:** Learning center, pre-admission summer program, reduced course load, remedial instruction, study skills assistance, tutoring, writing center.

**Majors. Agriculture:** Horticulture, landscaping, ornamental horticulture. **Area/ethnic studies:** African-American, Hispanic-American/Latino/Chicano, Native American. **Biology:** General. **Business:** General, accounting, accounting technology, administrative services, banking/financial services, business admin, finance, hospitality/recreation, international, marketing, office management, real estate, sales/distribution, selling, small business admin. **Communications:** General, digital media. **Communications technology:** General, computer typography. **Computer sciences:** General, computer science, data processing. **Conservation:** Environmental studies. **Education:** Early childhood, kindergarten/preschool, physical. **Engineering:** General, computer, marine. **Engineering technology:** General, automotive, biomedical, computer, drafting, electrical. **English:** English lit, speech/rhetoric. **Family/consumer sciences:** Child care, institutional food production. **Foreign languages:** French, Spanish. **Health:** Athletic training, licensed practical nurse, medical radiologic technology/radiation therapy, nursing (RN), recreational therapy, sonography, substance abuse counseling. **History:** General. **Legal studies:** General. **Liberal arts:** Arts/sciences. **Math:** General. **Mechanic/repair:** Automotive, electronics/electrical. **Parks/recreation:** General, exercise sciences, health/fitness. **Personal/culinary services:** Cosmetic, culinary arts, institutional food service. **Philosophy/religion:** Philosophy. **Physical sciences:** Chemistry, geology, physics. **Protective services:** Law enforcement admin. **Psychology:** General. **Public administration:** General. **Science technology:** Biological. **Social sciences:** Anthropology, economics, geography, political science, sociology. **Transportation:** Diver. **Visual/performing arts:** Art, art history/conservation, commercial/advertising art, dramatic, film/cinema, interior design, multimedia, studio arts, theater design.

**Most popular majors.** Health sciences 10%, liberal arts 61%.

**Computing on campus.** 1,399 workstations in library, computer center, student center. Commuter students can connect to campus network. Online library, helpline, wireless network available.

**Student life. Freshman orientation:** Mandatory. Preregistration for classes offered. 2-hour on-campus or on-line orientation. **Activities:** Bands, choral groups, dance, drama, literary magazine, music ensembles, musical theater, student government, student newspaper, symphony orchestra, Black Student Union, College Republicans, EOPS, Hillel Club, Latter Day Saint Student Association, Phi Theta Kappa, Shodo Japanese Calligraphy Club, Special Abilities Club, Students Left Alliance Party, Student Sustainability Club, Vaquero Christian Fellowship.

**Athletics. Intercollegiate:** Baseball M, basketball, cross-country, football (tackle) M, golf, soccer, softball W, tennis, track and field, volleyball. **Team name:** Vaqueros.

**Student services.** Adult student services, alcohol/substance abuse counseling, career counseling, services for economically disadvantaged, student employment services, financial aid counseling, health services, minority student services, on-campus daycare, personal counseling, placement for graduates, veterans' counselor, women's services. **Physically disabled:** Services for visually, speech, hearing impaired. **Learning disabled:** Comprehensive services available. **Transfer:** Transfer center, transfer adviser, college fairs on campus for students transferring to 4-year colleges.

**Contact.** E-mail: admissions@sbcc.edu
Phone: (805) 965-0581 ext. 2200 Fax: (805) 963-7222
Allison Curtis, Director of Admissions and Records, Santa Barbara City College, 721 Cliff Drive, Santa Barbara, CA 93109-2394

## Santa Monica College
Santa Monica, California
www.smc.edu      CB member
     CB code: 4691

- Public 2-year community college
- Commuter campus in small city

**General.** Founded in 1929. Regionally accredited. Off-campus program at Santa Monica College of Design. **Enrollment:** 20,248 degree-seeking undergraduates. **Degrees:** 1,467 associate awarded. **Location:** 18 miles from Los Angeles. **Calendar:** Semester, extensive summer session. **Full-time faculty:** 318 total; 23% minority, 55% women. **Part-time faculty:** 900 total; 15% minority, 54% women. **Special facilities:** Planetarium, photo gallery, humanities center, entertainment technology academy. **Partnerships:** Formal partnerships with DreamWorks, Disney Channel, Sony, 20th Century Fox, and other entertainment industry leaders (for Academy of Entertainment Technology students).

**Transfer out. Colleges most students transferred to 2007:** University of California at Los Angeles, California State University-Northridge, University of Southern California.

**Basis for selection.** Open admission, but selective for some programs. Music, theater arts, entertainment technology are competitive with various requirements. Nursing program has course requirements for admission. Audition and portfolio required for music, theater arts.

**2007-2008 Annual costs.** Tuition/fees: $632; $5,372 out-of-state. Per-credit charge: $20 in-state; $178 out-of-state.

**Financial aid. Need-based:** Need-based aid available for part-time students.

**Application procedures. Admission:** No deadline. No application fee. Admission notification on a rolling basis. **Financial aid:** No deadline. FAFSA, institutional form required. Applicants notified on a rolling basis starting 7/1; must reply within 2 week(s) of notification.

**Academics. Special study options:** Accelerated study, cooperative education, distance learning, dual enrollment of high school students, ESL, honors, independent study, internships, study abroad, weekend college. License preparation in nursing. **Credit/placement by examination:** AP, CLEP, institutional tests. 30 credit hours maximum toward associate degree. Math and English placement tests required for some students. **Support services:** Learning center, pre-admission summer program, remedial instruction, study skills assistance, tutoring, writing center.

**Majors. Business:** General, accounting, business admin, entrepreneurial studies, office/clerical, real estate. **Communications:** Journalism. **Communications technology:** General. **Computer sciences:** Data processing, information systems, programming. **Construction:** Maintenance. **Engineering technology:** Architectural, drafting, electrical. **English:** English lit. **Family/consumer sciences:** General. **History:** General. **Liberal arts:** Arts/sciences. **Mechanic/repair:** Auto body. **Parks/recreation:** General. **Physical sciences:** Chemistry, geology, physics. **Protective services:** Firefighting, law enforcement admin, police science. **Social sciences:** General, political science. **Visual/performing arts:** Commercial photography, commercial/advertising art, dance, dramatic, photography, studio arts.

**Most popular majors.** Communications/journalism 20%, computer/information sciences 17%, health sciences 53%, physical sciences 96%.

**Computing on campus.** 600 workstations in library, computer center, student center. Commuter students can connect to campus network. Help-line available.

**Student life. Freshman orientation:** Mandatory. **Activities:** Concert band, choral groups, dance, drama, literary magazine, music ensembles, musical theater, opera, radio station, student government, student newspaper.

**Athletics.** NJCAA. **Intercollegiate:** Basketball, cross-country M, diving, football (tackle) M, swimming, tennis, track and field, volleyball, water polo M. **Intramural:** Badminton. **Team name:** Corsairs.

**Student services.** Adult student services, career counseling, services for economically disadvantaged, student employment services, financial aid counseling, health services, minority student services, on-campus daycare, personal counseling, placement for graduates, veterans' counselor. **Physically disabled:** Services for visually, speech, hearing impaired. **Learning disabled:** Comprehensive services available. **Transfer:** Transfer center, transfer adviser, college fairs on campus for students transferring to 4-year colleges.

**Contact.** Phone: (310) 434-4380 Fax: (310) 434-3645
Teresita Rodriguez, Dean of Enrollment Services, Santa Monica College, 1900 Pico Boulevard, Santa Monica, CA 90405-1628

## Santa Rosa Junior College
**Santa Rosa, California**
www.santarosa.edu                    **CB code: 4692**

- Public 2-year community college
- Commuter campus in small city

**General.** Founded in 1918. Regionally accredited. **Enrollment:** 25,734 degree-seeking undergraduates. **Degrees:** 1,055 associate awarded. **Location:** 55 miles from San Francisco. **Calendar:** Semester, extensive summer session. **Full-time faculty:** 301 total; 15% have terminal degrees, 15% minority, 58% women. **Part-time faculty:** 1,191 total; 11% have terminal degrees, 11% minority, 58% women. **Special facilities:** Native American art museum, farm, summer repertory theater, planetarium.

**Student profile.**

| | | | |
|---|---|---|---|
| Out-of-state: | 2% | 25 or older: | 56% |

**Transfer out. Colleges most students transferred to 2007:** Sonoma State University, San Francisco State University, University of California: Davis, California State University: Chico, California State University: Sacramento.

**Basis for selection.** Open admission. Audition recommended of music performance, some physical education, some communications majors.

**2007-2008 Annual costs.** Tuition/fees: $628; $5,818 out-of-state. Per-credit charge: $20 in-state; $193 out-of-state. Books/supplies: $1,566. Personal expenses: $3,024.

**2006-2007 Financial aid. Need-based:** 82% of total undergraduate aid awarded as scholarships/grants, 18% as loans/jobs. Need-based aid available for part-time students. Work-study available nights, weekends and for part-time students. **Non-need-based:** Scholarships awarded for academics, art, leadership, music/drama. **Additional information:** California's Board of Governors Program (BOG) provides fee waivers for applicants with need, welfare recipients, and families with low income.

**Application procedures. Admission:** No deadline. No application fee. Application may be submitted online. **Financial aid:** Priority date 3/1; no closing date. FAFSA required. Applicants notified on a rolling basis starting 4/5.

**Academics. Special study options:** Cooperative education, cross-registration, distance learning, dual enrollment of high school students, ESL, independent study, internships, liberal arts/career combination, study abroad, weekend college. License preparation in dental hygiene, nursing, paramedic, radiology, real estate. **Credit/placement by examination:** AP, CLEP, IB, institutional tests. **Support services:** GED preparation and test center, learning center, pre-admission summer program, reduced course load, remedial instruction, study skills assistance, tutoring.

**Majors. Agriculture:** Agribusiness operations, equestrian studies, equine science. **Area/ethnic studies:** Latin American. **Biology:** General, physiology. **Business:** Business admin. **Computer sciences:** Computer science. **Conservation:** General, environmental studies. **Education:** General, early childhood. **Engineering:** General. **Engineering technology:** Civil, electrical. **English:** English lit. **Foreign languages:** Portuguese. **Health:** Dental assistant, dental hygiene, EMT paramedic, licensed practical nurse, medical radiologic technology/radiation therapy, mental health services, nursing (RN), nursing assistant, pharmacy assistant. **History:** General. **Interdisciplinary:** Natural sciences. **Liberal arts:** Arts/sciences. **Math:** General. **Parks/recreation:** General. **Philosophy/religion:** Philosophy. **Physical sciences:** Chemistry, physics. **Protective services:** Firefighting, police science. **Psychology:** General. **Social sciences:** Anthropology, economics, geography, political science, sociology. **Visual/performing arts:** Art, commercial/advertising art, dramatic, fashion design.

**Most popular majors.** Health sciences 13%, liberal arts 61%, social sciences 9%.

**Computing on campus.** 1,736 workstations in library, computer center. Commuter students can connect to campus network.

**Student life. Freshman orientation:** Available. Preregistration for classes offered. **Activities:** Jazz band, choral groups, dance, drama, film society, music ensembles, musical theater, student government, student newspaper, symphony orchestra, various clubs and organizations.

**Athletics. Intercollegiate:** Badminton W, baseball M, basketball, cross-country, diving, football (tackle) M, golf M, soccer, softball W, swimming, tennis, track and field, volleyball W, water polo, wrestling M. **Team name:** Bear Cubs.

**Student services.** Adult student services, career counseling, student employment services, financial aid counseling, health services, on-campus daycare, personal counseling, placement for graduates, veterans' counselor. **Physically disabled:** Services for visually, speech, hearing impaired. **Transfer:** Re-entry adviser, pre-admission transcript evaluation for new students. Transfer center, transfer adviser, college fairs on campus for students transferring to 4-year colleges.

**Contact.** Phone: (707) 527-4685 Toll-free number: (800) 564-7752
Fax: (707) 527-4798
Diane Traversi, Director of Enrollment Services, Santa Rosa Junior
College, 1501 Mendocino Avenue, Santa Rosa, CA 95401

## Santiago Canyon College
### Orange, California
### www.sccollege.edu

CB code: 2830

- Public 2-year community college
- Commuter campus in small city

**General.** Regionally accredited. **Enrollment:** 8,685 degree-seeking undergraduates. **Degrees:** 683 associate awarded. **Location:** 30 miles from Los
Angeles. **Calendar:** Semester, extensive summer session. **Full-time faculty:** 117 total; 33% minority, 68% women. **Part-time faculty:** 375 total;
24% minority, 46% women.

**Student profile.** Among degree-seeking undergraduates, 7% already have
a bachelor's degree or higher, 6,310 transferred in from other institutions.

| African American: | 2% | Native American: | 1% |
| Asian American: | 9% | 25 or older: | 40% |
| Hispanic American: | 37% | | |

**Transfer out. Colleges most students transferred to 2007:** California
State University: Fullerton, California State University: Long Beach, Chapman University, University of California: Irvine.

**Basis for selection.** Open admission. **Adult students:** SAT/ACT scores
not required. Placement tests for English, math, reading, and chemistry.
**Homeschooled:** Statement describing homeschool structure and mission required. Must show private school affidavit confirmation from the California
Department of Education.

**2007-2008 Annual costs. Tuition/fees:** $628; $6,148 out-of-state. Per-
credit charge: $20 in-state; $204 out-of-state.

**Financial aid.** All financial aid based on need. Need-based aid available
for part-time students.

**Application procedures. Admission:** No application fee. Application
may be submitted online. **Financial aid:** Priority date 6/1; no closing date.
FAFSA, institutional form required. Applicants notified by 6/1; Applicants
notified on a rolling basis.

**Academics. Special study options:** Accelerated study, cooperative education, distance learning, double major, dual enrollment of high school students, ESL, honors, weekend college. License preparation in real estate.
**Credit/placement by examination:** CLEP, institutional tests. **Support services:** GED preparation and test center, learning center, remedial instruction, study skills assistance, tutoring, writing center.

**Majors. Biology:** General. **Business:** Accounting, business admin, managerial economics, marketing, selling, tourism/travel. **Communications:** General. **Communications technology:** Graphics, photo/film/video. **Computer
sciences:** Computer science, information systems, web page design. **Construction:** Carpentry, electrician. **Engineering:** General. **Engineering technology:** Drafting. **English:** English lit, speech/rhetoric. **Family/consumer
sciences:** General. **Foreign languages:** General, American Sign Language,
French, Italian, Spanish. **Health:** Medical assistant. **History:** General. **Legal studies:** Paralegal. **Liberal arts:** Arts/sciences, library science. **Math:**
General. **Mechanic/repair:** Automotive. **Personal/culinary services:** Cosmetic. **Philosophy/religion:** Philosophy. **Physical sciences:** Chemistry, geology, hydrology, physics. **Protective services:** Fire safety technology. **Psychology:** General. **Social sciences:** General, anthropology, economics,
geography, political science, sociology. **Visual/performing arts:** Art, com-
mercial/advertising art, crafts, dance, fashion design, metal/jewelry.

**Most popular majors.** Business/marketing 6%, liberal arts 84%.

**Computing on campus.** Online course registration, wireless network
available.

**Student life. Freshman orientation:** Available. **Activities:** Bands, choral
groups, dance, drama, music ensembles, student government, student newspaper, TV station.

**Athletics. Intercollegiate:** Cross-country, golf, soccer, track and field. **Intramural:** Softball, track and field. **Team name:** Hawks.

**Student services.** Adult student services, alcohol/substance abuse counseling, career counseling, services for economically disadvantaged, student

employment services, financial aid counseling, health services, minority student services, on-campus daycare, personal counseling, placement for graduates, veterans' counselor, women's services. **Physically disabled:** Services
for visually, hearing impaired. **Learning disabled:** Comprehensive services
available. **Transfer:** Re-entry adviser, pre-admission transcript evaluation
for new students. Transfer center, transfer adviser, college fairs on campus
for students transferring to 4-year colleges.

**Contact.** Phone: (714) 628-4978 Fax: (714) 628-4723
Linda Miskovic, Associate Dean of Admissions, Santiago Canyon College,
8045 East Chapman Avenue, Orange, CA 92869

## Shasta College
### Redding, California
### www.shastacollege.edu

CB code: 4696

- Public 2-year community college
- Commuter campus in small city

**General.** Founded in 1948. Regionally accredited. **Enrollment:** 5,021 degree-
seeking undergraduates. **Degrees:** 610 associate awarded. **Location:** 160
miles from Sacramento. **Calendar:** Semester, limited summer session. **Full-
time faculty:** 130 total. **Part-time faculty:** 370 total. **Class size:** 58% < 20,
38% 20-39, 2% 40-49, 2% 50-99, less than 1% >100.

**Student profile.**

| Out-of-state: | 3% | Live on campus: | 1% |
| 25 or older: | 46% | | |

**Basis for selection.** Open admission, but selective for some programs.
Applicants to nursing program must be high school graduates, take National
League for Nursing examination, and complete series of courses outlined in
college catalog.

**2007-2008 Annual costs. Tuition/fees:** $673; $5,653 out-of-state. Per-
credit charge: $20 in-state; $186 out-of-state. Room only: $2,610. Books/
supplies: $1,300. Personal expenses: $2,000.

**Financial aid.** All financial aid based on need. Need-based aid available
for part-time students.

**Application procedures. Admission:** No deadline. No application fee.
Admission notification on a rolling basis. **Financial aid:** Priority date 3/2;
no closing date. FAFSA, institutional form required. Applicants notified on
a rolling basis starting 7/1.

**Academics.** On-campus programs leading to bachelor's degree from California State University: Chico offered. **Special study options:** Cooperative
education, distance learning, double major, dual enrollment of high school
students, ESL, honors, independent study, internships, weekend college. License preparation in dental hygiene, nursing, occupational therapy, paramedic, physical therapy, real estate. **Credit/placement by examination:**
CLEP, institutional tests. 12 credit hours maximum toward associate degree.
**Support services:** Learning center, reduced course load, remedial instruction, tutoring, writing center.

**Majors. Agriculture:** General, agribusiness operations, business, equestrian studies, ornamental horticulture. **Business:** General, accounting, administrative services, business admin, entrepreneurial studies, executive assistant, fashion, management information systems, office management, office
technology, office/clerical, sales/distribution. **Communications:** General, journalism. **Computer sciences:** General, applications programming. **Construction:** Carpentry. **Education:** Early childhood, teacher assistance. **Engineering:** General, civil. **Engineering technology:** Architectural drafting, civil,
construction, electrical. **Family/consumer sciences:** General, child care, institutional food production. **Health:** Nursing (RN). **Legal studies:** Legal
secretary, paralegal. **Mechanic/repair:** General, aircraft, automotive, diesel,
heating/ac/refrig. **Personal/culinary services:** Culinary arts. **Production:**
Welding. **Protective services:** Fire safety technology, police science. **Public administration:** Human services. **Visual/performing arts:** Art, commercial/
advertising art, dramatic, studio arts.

**Computing on campus.** 141 workstations in library, computer center.
Online library available.

**Student life. Freshman orientation:** Mandatory. **Housing:** Single-sex dorms
available. **Activities:** Bands, choral groups, dance, drama, literary magazine, music ensembles, musical theater, student government, student newspaper, symphony orchestra, Environmental Resources Leadership Club, LEAF,
Ornamental Horticulture club, jazz choir, science club, Veteran's Club, dorm
club.

**Athletics.** NJCAA. **Intercollegiate:** Baseball M, basketball, cross-country, football (tackle) M, golf, soccer, softball W, swimming, tennis, track and field, volleyball W, wrestling M. **Team name:** Knights.

**Student services.** Adult student services, career counseling, services for economically disadvantaged, student employment services, financial aid counseling, health services, minority student services, on-campus daycare, personal counseling, veterans' counselor. **Physically disabled:** Services for visually, speech, hearing impaired. **Transfer:** Transfer center, transfer adviser, college fairs on campus for students transferring to 4-year colleges.

**Contact.** E-mail: cryan@shastacollege.edu
Phone: (530) 225-4841 Fax: (530) 225-4995
Kevin O'Rorke, Dean of Enrollment Services, Shasta College, Box 496006, Redding, CA 96049-6006

---

## Sierra College
**Rocklin, California**
**www.sierracollege.edu**                    **CB code: 4697**

▶ Public 2-year community college
▶ Commuter campus in large town

**General.** Founded in 1914. Regionally accredited. **Enrollment:** 12,281 degree-seeking undergraduates. **Degrees:** 2,385 associate awarded. **Location:** 25 miles from Sacramento. **Calendar:** Semester, extensive summer session. **Full-time faculty:** 210 total. **Part-time faculty:** 770 total. **Class size:** 30% < 20, 58% 20-39, 10% 40-49, 2% 50-99, less than 1% >100. **Special facilities:** Nature trail, planetarium, science museum displays, learning resource center.

**Student profile.**

| | | | |
|---|---|---|---|
| Out-of-state: | 1% | Live on campus: | 6% |

**Transfer out. Colleges most students transferred to 2007:** California State University: Sacramento, University of California: Davis, California State University: Chico, University of California: Berkeley.

**Basis for selection.** Open admission.

**2007-2008 Annual costs.** Tuition/fees: $640; $5,830 out-of-state. Per-credit charge: $20 in-state; $193 out-of-state. Room/board: $7,090. Books/supplies: $1,332. Personal expenses: $1,638.

**Financial aid. Need-based:** Need-based aid available for part-time students. Work-study available nights, weekends and for part-time students.

**Application procedures. Admission:** No deadline. No application fee. Applicants notified within 4 working days. **Financial aid:** Priority date 3/2, closing date 4/22. FAFSA required. Applicants notified on a rolling basis starting 5/15.

**Academics. Special study options:** Cooperative education, cross-registration, distance learning, double major, dual enrollment of high school students, ESL, honors, independent study, internships, study abroad, weekend college. License preparation in nursing, real estate. **Credit/placement by examination:** AP, CLEP, institutional tests. 15 credit hours maximum toward associate degree. **Support services:** Learning center, remedial instruction, study skills assistance, tutoring, writing center.

**Majors. Agriculture:** General, animal husbandry, equestrian studies, horticulture. **Biology:** General. **Business:** General, accounting, administrative services, business admin, real estate, sales/distribution, small business admin. **Communications:** Digital media. **Computer sciences:** Data entry, information technology, networking, programming, system admin, web page design, webmaster. **Conservation:** Forestry. **Construction:** Carpentry, maintenance. **Education:** Early childhood, teacher assistance. **Engineering:** General. **Engineering technology:** Architectural drafting, hazardous materials, mechanical drafting. **English:** Speech/rhetoric. **Family/consumer sciences:** General, child care, institutional food production. **Foreign languages:** American Sign Language. **Health:** Licensed practical nurse, medical secretary, nursing (RN). **Legal studies:** Legal secretary. **Liberal arts:** Arts/sciences, library assistant, library science. **Math:** General. **Mechanic/repair:** Automotive, electronics/electrical. **Parks/recreation:** Health/fitness. **Philosophy/religion:** Philosophy. **Physical sciences:** Chemistry, geology. **Production:** Woodworking. **Protective services:** Criminal justice, fire safety technology, firefighting, police science, security services. **Visual/performing arts:** Art, music performance, photography, studio arts. **Other:** Embedded systems.

**Computing on campus.** 300 workstations in dormitories, library, computer center. Dormitories linked to campus network. Commuter students can connect to campus network. Online course registration, online library, wireless network available.

---

**Student life. Freshman orientation:** Mandatory. **Housing:** Coed dorms available. **Activities:** Concert band, choral groups, drama, music ensembles, student government, student newspaper.

**Athletics. Intercollegiate:** Baseball M, basketball, cross-country W, diving, football (tackle) M, golf, soccer W, softball W; swimming, tennis, track and field W, volleyball W, water polo W, wrestling M. **Intramural:** Archery, badminton, basketball, cheerleading W, football (non-tackle), golf, softball, tennis, volleyball. **Team name:** Wolverines.

**Student services.** Adult student services, alcohol/substance abuse counseling, career counseling, services for economically disadvantaged, student employment services, financial aid counseling, health services, on-campus daycare, personal counseling, veterans' counselor. **Physically disabled:** Services for visually, speech, hearing impaired. **Transfer:** Pre-admission transcript evaluation for new students. Transfer center, transfer adviser, college fairs on campus for students transferring to 4-year colleges.

**Contact.** Phone: (916) 781-0430 Toll-free number: (800) 242-4004
Fax: (916) 781-0403
Gail Modder, Admissions and Records Program Manager, Sierra College, 5000 Rocklin Road, Rocklin, CA 95677

---

## Skyline College
**San Bruno, California**
**www.skylinecollege.edu**                    **CB code: 4746**

▶ Public 2-year community college
▶ Commuter campus in small city

**General.** Founded in 1969. Regionally accredited. **Enrollment:** 4,924 degree-seeking undergraduates. **Degrees:** 450 associate awarded. **Location:** 15 miles from San Francisco. **Calendar:** Semester, limited summer session. **Full-time faculty:** 105 total. **Part-time faculty:** 200 total.

**Student profile.**

| | | | |
|---|---|---|---|
| Out-of-state: | 1% | 25 or older: | 49% |

**Transfer out. Colleges most students transferred to 2007:** San Francisco State University, San Jose State University, California State University: Hayward.

**Basis for selection.** Open admission, but selective for some programs. Additional requirements for applicants to automotive technology, cosmetology, and respiratory therapy programs, and for participants in concurrent enrollment. SAT/ACT may be substituted for institutional placement tests. Interview required of respiratory therapy majors. Essay required of full-time international student applicants.

**2007-2008 Annual costs.** Tuition/fees: $628; $6,148 out-of-state. Per-credit charge: $20 in-state; $204 out-of-state. Books/supplies: $1,260. Personal expenses: $2,376.

**Financial aid. Need-based:** Need-based aid available for part-time students.

**Application procedures. Admission:** Priority date 7/1; deadline 8/1 (receipt date). No application fee. Admission notification on a rolling basis. **Financial aid:** Priority date 3/2; no closing date. FAFSA, institutional form required. Applicants notified on a rolling basis starting 5/1; must reply within 2 week(s) of notification.

**Academics.** Classes given on Sundays. **Special study options:** Cooperative education, cross-registration, dual enrollment of high school students, ESL, honors, study abroad. **Credit/placement by examination:** CLEP, institutional tests. 12 credit hours maximum toward associate degree. **Support services:** Learning center, study skills assistance, tutoring.

**Majors. Business:** Accounting, administrative services, business admin, hospitality admin, management information systems, office/clerical. **Communications technology:** General. **Computer sciences:** General, computer science, data processing, information systems, webmaster. **Education:** Early childhood. **English:** English lit, speech/rhetoric. **Family/consumer sciences:** General, business. **Foreign languages:** Spanish. **Health:** Medical secretary, medical transcription, respiratory therapy technology, surgical technology. **Interdisciplinary:** Global studies. **Legal studies:** Legal secretary, paralegal. **Liberal arts:** Arts/sciences. **Math:** General. **Mechanic/repair:** Automotive. **Personal/culinary services:** Cosmetic. **Protective services:** Law enforcement admin. **Psychology:** General. **Science technology:** Biological. **Visual/performing arts:** General, art, dance.

**Most popular majors.** Business/marketing 13%, health sciences 11%, liberal arts 53%.

**Computing on campus.** 220 workstations in library, computer center, student center. Online course registration, helpline, repair service available.

**Student life. Freshman orientation:** Available. **Activities:** Bands, choral groups, dance, literary magazine, student government, student newspaper.

**Athletics.** NJCAA. **Intercollegiate:** Baseball M, basketball M, cross-country, soccer M, softball W, track and field, volleyball W, wrestling M. **Team name:** Trojans.

**Student services.** Career counseling, services for economically disadvantaged, student employment services, health services, minority student services, on-campus daycare, personal counseling, veterans' counselor, women's services. **Physically disabled:** Services for visually, speech, hearing impaired. **Transfer:** Transfer center, transfer adviser, college fairs on campus for students transferring to 4-year colleges.

**Contact.** E-mail: skyadmissions@smccd.edu
Phone: (650) 738-4252 Fax: (650) 738-4200
Sherri Hancock, Dean of Enrollment Services, Skyline College, 3300 College Drive, San Bruno, CA 94066

## Solano Community College
### Fairfield, California
### www.solano.edu
CB code: 4930

- Public 2-year community college
- Commuter campus in small city

**General.** Founded in 1945. Regionally accredited. Classes offered in Vallejo and Vacaville. **Enrollment:** 7,552 degree-seeking undergraduates. **Degrees:** 887 associate awarded. **ROTC:** Air Force. **Location:** 11 miles from Vallejo. **Calendar:** Semester, extensive summer session. **Full-time faculty:** 160 total. **Part-time faculty:** 275 total.

**Basis for selection.** Open admission, but selective for some programs. Special requirements for nursing program.

**2007-2008 Annual costs.** Tuition/fees: $637; $5,827 out-of-state. Per-credit charge: $20 in-state; $193 out-of-state. Books/supplies: $810. Personal expenses: $2,599.

**Application procedures. Admission:** No deadline. No application fee. Application may be submitted online. Admission notification on a rolling basis. **Financial aid:** Priority date 3/1; no closing date. FAFSA required. Applicants notified on a rolling basis starting 7/1.

**Academics. Special study options:** Cooperative education, cross-registration, distance learning, double major, dual enrollment of high school students, honors, independent study, internships, study abroad, weekend college. **Credit/placement by examination:** AP, CLEP, institutional tests. 15 credit hours maximum toward associate degree. **Support services:** Reduced course load, remedial instruction, tutoring, writing center.

**Majors. Agriculture:** Landscaping, ornamental horticulture. **Area/ethnic studies:** African-American, Asian-American, Hispanic-American/Latino/Chicano, Native American. **Biology:** General. **Business:** Accounting, administrative services, banking/financial services, business admin, office management, real estate. **Communications:** General, journalism. **Computer sciences:** General, programming. **Education:** Early childhood. **Engineering technology:** Aerospace, drafting, electrical, water quality. **English:** English lit. **Family/consumer sciences:** General. **Foreign languages:** General, French, German, Spanish. **Health:** Medical secretary, nursing (RN). **History:** General. **Interdisciplinary:** Biological/physical sciences. **Legal studies:** Legal secretary. **Liberal arts:** Arts/sciences. **Math:** General. **Mechanic/repair:** Aircraft, appliance, auto body, computer. **Parks/recreation:** Health/fitness, sports admin. **Personal/culinary services:** Cosmetic. **Physical sciences:** Chemistry, physics. **Production:** Welding. **Protective services:** Firefighting, police science. **Psychology:** General. **Public administration:** Human services. **Science technology:** Biological. **Social sciences:** General, international relations, political science. **Visual/performing arts:** Commercial photography, commercial/advertising art, dramatic, drawing, interior design, painting, sculpture, studio arts.

**Computing on campus.** 240 workstations in library, computer center.

**Student life. Freshman orientation:** Available. **Activities:** Bands, choral groups, drama, musical theater, student government, student newspaper, symphony orchestra, Black Student Union, women's change, veterans organization, Sierra club, student nurses, Filipino club, Democratic club, Mathematics, Engineering & Science Achievement club, Asian-Pacific Islander club.

**Athletics. Intercollegiate:** Baseball M, basketball, cross-country, diving, football (tackle) M, soccer W, softball W, swimming, track and field, volleyball W, water polo M. **Intramural:** Table tennis, tennis. **Team name:** Falcons.

**Student services.** Career counseling, student employment services, financial aid counseling, health services, on-campus daycare, personal counseling, placement for graduates, veterans' counselor. **Physically disabled:** Services for visually, speech, hearing impaired. **Transfer:** Transfer center for students transferring to 4-year colleges.

**Contact.** E-mail: admissions@solano.edu
Phone: (707) 864-7171 Fax: (707) 864-7175
Catherine Fites, Dean of Admissions and Records, Solano Community College, 4000 Suisun Valley Road, Fairfield, CA 94534-3197

## South Coast College
### Orange, California
### www.southcoastcollege.com

- For-profit 2-year business college
- Small city

**General.** Accredited by ACICS. **Calendar:** Quarter.

**Annual costs/financial aid.** Registration fee varies from $74 to $99 depending on program; monthly program cost $900/month.

**Contact.** Phone: (714) 867-5009
Dean of Admissions and Marketing, 2011 West Chapman Avenue, Orange, CA 92868

## Southwestern College
### Chula Vista, California
### www.swccd.edu
CB code: 4726

- Public 2-year community college
- Commuter campus in small city

**General.** Founded in 1961. Regionally accredited. Medical occupation programs accredited by the National League for Nursing Accrediting Commission Inc. (NLNAC). **Enrollment:** 19,839 undergraduates. **Degrees:** 1,082 associate awarded. **Location:** 10 miles from San Diego. **Calendar:** Semester, extensive summer session. **Full-time faculty:** 80 total. **Part-time faculty:** 120 total. **Class size:** 36% < 20, 49% 20-39, 13% 40-49, 3% 50-99.

**Transfer out. Colleges most students transferred to 2007:** San Diego State University, University of California: San Diego.

**Basis for selection.** Open admission, but selective for some programs. Limited admission to nursing and dental hygiene programs.

**2007-2008 Annual costs.** Tuition/fees: $624; $5,514 out-of-state. Per-credit charge: $20 in-state; $183 out-of-state. Books/supplies: $1,224.

**Financial aid. Need-based:** Need-based aid available for part-time students. Work-study available nights, weekends and for part-time students.

**Application procedures. Admission:** No deadline. No application fee. Application may be submitted online. Admission notification on a rolling basis. **Financial aid:** Closing date 3/2. FAFSA required. Applicants notified on a rolling basis starting 7/1.

**Academics.** Broad offerings of online and traditional courses. Online credit and non-credit courses available. **Special study options:** Cooperative education, cross-registration, distance learning, double major, dual enrollment of high school students, ESL, honors, independent study, internships, study abroad, weekend college. License preparation in dental hygiene, nursing, paramedic, real estate. **Credit/placement by examination:** AP, CLEP, IB, institutional tests. 15 credit hours maximum toward associate degree. In-house placement test required for some. **Support services:** Learning center, pre-admission summer program, remedial instruction, study skills assistance, tutoring, writing center.

**Majors. Agriculture:** Floriculture, greenhouse operations, landscaping, nursery operations, ornamental horticulture, turf management. **Architecture:** Landscape, technology. **Area/ethnic studies:** African-American, American, Asian-American, Hispanic-American/Latino/Chicano, women's. **Biology:** General, biotechnology. **Business:** Accounting, business admin, construction management, entrepreneurial studies, finance, financial planning, international, market research, office management, office/clerical, real estate, tourism promotion, tourism/travel. **Communications:** General, broadcast journalism, journalism. **Communications technology:** General, radio/tv, recording arts.

**Computer sciences:** General, applications programming, computer science, information systems, information technology, networking, programming, web page design, webmaster. **Conservation:** Environmental studies. **Construction:** Building inspection, maintenance. **Education:** General, early childhood, elementary, kindergarten/preschool, physical. **Engineering:** General. **Engineering technology:** CAD/CADD, computer, drafting, occupational safety, telecommunications. **English:** English lit. **Family/consumer sciences:** Child care, child development. **Foreign languages:** French, Spanish. **Health:** Dental hygiene, EMT paramedic, insurance coding, licensed practical nurse, medical records admin, medical records technology, medical transcription, nursing (RN), prenursing, surgical technology. **History:** General. **Legal studies:** General, legal secretary, paralegal. **Liberal arts:** Arts/sciences, humanities. **Math:** General. **Mechanic/repair:** Automotive, electronics/electrical, small engine. **Parks/recreation:** General, health/fitness. **Philosophy/religion:** Philosophy. **Physical sciences:** Astronomy, chemistry, geology, physics. **Protective services:** Criminal justice, firefighting, forensics, law enforcement admin. **Psychology:** General. **Public administration:** Social work. **Social sciences:** Anthropology, economics, geography, political science, sociology. **Visual/performing arts:** Art, cinematography, dance, dramatic, graphic design, photography.

**Computing on campus.** 1,360 workstations in library, computer center. Online course registration, online library, helpline, repair service, student web hosting, wireless network available.

**Student life. Freshman orientation:** Available. Preregistration for classes offered. **Activities:** Jazz band, choral groups, dance, drama, literary magazine, music ensembles, musical theater, student government, student newspaper, over 40 student clubs and organizations available.

**Athletics. Intercollegiate:** Baseball M, basketball, cross-country, football (tackle) M, soccer, softball W, tennis, track and field, volleyball W, water polo. **Team name:** Jaguars.

**Student services.** Career counseling, services for economically disadvantaged, student employment services, financial aid counseling, health services, legal services, on-campus daycare, personal counseling, veterans' counselor, women's services. **Physically disabled:** Services for visually, speech, hearing impaired. **Transfer:** Pre-admission transcript evaluation for new students. Transfer center, transfer adviser, college fairs on campus for students transferring to 4-year colleges.

**Contact.** Phone: (619) 421-6700 ext. 5215 Fax: (619) 482-6489 Michael Kerns, Dean, Student Affairs, Southwestern College, 900 Otay Lakes Road, Chula Vista, CA 91910-7297

---

## Taft College
### Taft, California
**www.taftcollege.edu**  CB code: 4820

- Public 2-year community college
- Commuter campus in small town

**General.** Founded in 1922. Regionally accredited. **Enrollment:** 1,684 degree-seeking undergraduates. **Degrees:** 196 associate awarded. **Location:** 35 miles from Bakersfield. **Calendar:** Semester, limited summer session. **Full-time faculty:** 40 total. **Part-time faculty:** 55 total.

**Transfer out. Colleges most students transferred to 2007:** California State University: Bakersfield, California State University: Fresno, California Polytechnic State University: San Luis Obispo, University of La Verne.

**Basis for selection.** Open admission. **Adult students:** SAT/ACT scores not required.

**2007-2008 Annual costs.** Tuition/fees: $600; $5,790 out-of-state. Per-credit charge: $20 in-state; $193 out-of-state. Room/board: $3,468. Books/supplies: $1,260. Personal expenses: $220.

**Financial aid. Need-based:** Need-based aid available for part-time students. Work-study available nights and for part-time students. **Non-need-based:** Scholarships awarded for academics.

**Application procedures. Admission:** No deadline. No application fee. Application may be submitted online. Admission notification on a rolling basis. **Financial aid:** No deadline. FAFSA, institutional form required. Applicants notified on a rolling basis; must reply within 4 week(s) of notification.

**Academics. Special study options:** Distance learning, ESL, independent study. License preparation in dental hygiene. **Credit/placement by examination:** AP, CLEP, institutional tests. 12 credit hours maximum toward associate degree. **Support services:** GED preparation and test center, learning center, pre-admission summer program, reduced course load, remedial instruction, study skills assistance, tutoring.

**Majors. Business:** General, accounting, administrative services, business admin, management information systems, office/clerical. **Communications:** Journalism. **Computer sciences:** General, computer science, information systems. **Education:** General, early childhood, physical, social science. **Engineering:** General. **Engineering technology:** Automotive, CAD/CADD, electrical, petroleum. **English:** English lit. **Health:** Dental hygiene. **Liberal arts:** Arts/sciences. **Math:** General. **Mechanic/repair:** Automotive, industrial. **Parks/recreation:** General. **Physical sciences:** General. **Protective services:** Corrections, criminal justice. **Social sciences:** General. **Visual/performing arts:** Art.

**Computing on campus.** 121 workstations in dormitories, library, computer center, student center. Dormitories wired for high-speed internet access. Online course registration, online library, helpline available.

**Student life. Freshman orientation:** Available. Offered online or by video. **Housing:** Single-sex dorms, special housing for disabled available. $125 fully refundable deposit. **Activities:** Student government, student newspaper, International club, Rotary club, MECHA club, Best Buddies.

**Athletics. Intercollegiate:** Baseball M, basketball W, soccer, softball W, volleyball W. **Team name:** Cougars.

**Student services.** Adult student services, career counseling, student employment services, on-campus daycare, personal counseling, veterans' counselor. **Physically disabled:** Services for visually, speech, hearing impaired. **Learning disabled:** Comprehensive services available. **Transfer:** Re-entry adviser for new students. Transfer center, transfer adviser, college fairs on campus for students transferring to 4-year colleges.

**Contact.** E-mail: hrussell@taft.org Phone: (661) 763-7741 Toll-free number: (800) 379-6784 Fax: (661) 763-7758 Brian McKee, Registrar and Director of Admissions, Taft College, 29 Emmons Park Drive, Taft, CA 93268

---

## Ventura College
### Ventura, California
**www.venturacollege.edu**  CB code: 4931

- Public 2-year community college
- Small city

**General.** Founded in 1925. Regionally accredited. **Enrollment:** 2,841 full-time, degree-seeking students. **Degrees:** 896 associate awarded. **ROTC:** Air Force. **Location:** 60 miles from Los Angeles. **Calendar:** Semester, limited summer session. **Full-time faculty:** 136 total. **Part-time faculty:** 386 total.

**Basis for selection.** Open admission, but selective for some programs. Limited admission to nursing program.

**2007-2008 Annual costs.** Tuition/fees: $642; $5,892 out-of-state. Per-credit charge: $20 in-state; $195 out-of-state. Books/supplies: $1,386. Personal expenses: $2,898.

**Application procedures. Admission:** No deadline. No application fee. Application may be submitted online. Admission notification on a rolling basis. **Financial aid:** Priority date 3/2; no closing date. FAFSA required. Applicants notified on a rolling basis.

**Academics. Special study options:** Cross-registration, dual enrollment of high school students, ESL, independent study, study abroad. **Credit/placement by examination:** AP, CLEP, institutional tests. 12 credit hours maximum toward associate degree. **Support services:** Learning center, reduced course load, remedial instruction, tutoring.

**Majors. Agriculture:** Agribusiness operations, agronomy, animal sciences, horticulture, ornamental horticulture, plant protection, plant sciences, soil science. **Area/ethnic studies:** African-American, Hispanic-American/Latino/Chicano. **Biology:** General, botany, zoology. **Business:** General, accounting, administrative services, business admin, fashion, human resources, management information systems, management science, managerial economics, marketing, office/clerical, real estate. **Communications:** General, journalism. **Communications technology:** General, graphic/printing. **Computer sciences:** General, applications programming, data processing, information systems, programming. **Construction:** Maintenance, masonry, pipefitting. **Education:** General, bilingual, early childhood. **Engineering:** General. **Engineering technology:** Architectural, civil, drafting, electrical. **English:** English lit, speech/rhetoric. **Family/consumer sciences:** General, child care, food/nutrition. **Foreign languages:** French, German, Spanish. **Health:** EMT paramedic, health services, licensed practical nurse, medical records technology, medical secretary, nursing (RN), predental, premedicine, prepharmacy, preveterinary. **History:** General. **Legal studies:** Legal secretary, prelaw. **Liberal arts:** Arts/sciences. **Math:** General. **Mechanic/**

1453

**repair:** Automotive. **Parks/recreation:** Facilities management. **Philosophy/religion:** Philosophy. **Physical sciences:** Chemistry, geology, physics. **Production:** Welding. **Protective services:** Criminal justice, police science. **Psychology:** General. **Social sciences:** General, anthropology, economics, geography, political science, sociology. **Visual/performing arts:** Ceramics, commercial photography, dramatic, fashion design, interior design, photography, studio arts.

**Computing on campus.** Online course registration available.

**Student life. Freshman orientation:** Available. **Housing:** Student housing available off-campus at nearby apartments. **Activities:** Student newspaper, religious, ethnic, political, special interest organizations, international student club.

**Athletics. Intercollegiate:** Baseball M, basketball, cross-country, diving, football (tackle) M, golf M, rifle M, softball W, swimming, tennis, track and field, volleyball M, water polo M. **Team name:** Pirates.

**Student services.** Adult student services, career counseling, student employment services, health services, on-campus daycare, personal counseling, placement for graduates, veterans' counselor. **Transfer:** Transfer center, transfer adviser, college fairs on campus for students transferring to 4-year colleges.

**Contact.** Phone: (805) 654-6457 Fax: (805) 654-6357
Susan Bricker, Registrar, Ventura College, 4667 Telegraph Road, Ventura, CA 93003

---

## Victor Valley College
**Victorville, California**
**www.vvc.edu**
**CB code: 4932**

- Public 2-year community college
- Small city

**General.** Founded in 1960. Regionally accredited. **Enrollment:** 4,472 degree-seeking undergraduates. **Degrees:** 995 associate awarded. **Location:** 38 from San Bernardino. **Calendar:** Semester, limited summer session. **Full-time faculty:** 136 total. **Part-time faculty:** 379 total. **Special facilities:** Planetarium, mock archaeological dig site.

**Student profile.**

| | | | |
|---|---|---|---|
| Out-of-state: | 1% | 25 or older: | 40% |

**Transfer out. Colleges most students transferred to 2007:** California State University: San Bernardino.

**Basis for selection.** Open admission, but selective for some programs. **Adult students:** SAT/ACT scores not required. **Homeschooled:** Must complete concurrent enrollment form with parent signature.

**2007-2008 Annual costs.** Tuition/fees: $610; $5,800 out-of-state. Per-credit charge: $20 in-state; $193 out-of-state. Nevada residents pay $71 per unit which includes enrollment fee as part of Good Neighbor policy. Books/supplies: $1,026. Personal expenses: $2,340.

**Financial aid. Need-based:** Need-based aid available for part-time students. Work-study available for part-time students. **Additional information:** Board of Governors grant pays enrollment fee in full for low-income students.

**Application procedures. Admission:** No deadline. No application fee. Application may be submitted online. Admission notification on a rolling basis. **Financial aid:** Priority date 3/2; no closing date. FAFSA, institutional form, CSS PROFILE required. Applicants notified on a rolling basis starting 8/1; must reply within 4 week(s) of notification.

**Academics. Special study options:** Cooperative education, distance learning, double major, dual enrollment of high school students, ESL, honors, independent study, semester at sea, study abroad. License preparation in nursing, paramedic. **Credit/placement by examination:** CLEP, institutional tests. 32 credit hours maximum toward associate degree. **Support services:** Learning center, pre-admission summer program, reduced course load, remedial instruction, study skills assistance, tutoring, writing center.

**Majors. Agriculture:** Ornamental horticulture. **Business:** General, administrative services, business admin, real estate. **Construction:** Carpentry. **Health:** EMT paramedic, medical assistant, nursing (RN), respiratory therapy technology. **Liberal arts:** Arts/sciences. **Math:** General. **Mechanic/repair:** Automotive, electronics/electrical, industrial electronics. **Production:** Welding. **Protective services:** Fire safety technology, law enforcement admin. **Visual/performing arts:** Art.

---

**Most popular majors.** Business/marketing 12%, health sciences 9%, interdisciplinary studies 18%, liberal arts 48%.

**Computing on campus.** 350 workstations in computer center, student center. Online course registration, online library, helpline available.

**Student life. Freshman orientation:** Available. **Activities:** Jazz band, choral groups, dance, drama, music ensembles, musical theater, student government, student newspaper, symphony orchestra.

**Athletics.** NJCAA. **Intercollegiate:** Baseball M, basketball, cross-country, football (tackle) M, golf M, soccer, softball W, tennis, track and field, volleyball W, wrestling M. **Team name:** Rams.

**Student services.** Career counseling, services for economically disadvantaged, student employment services, financial aid counseling, health services, on-campus daycare, personal counseling, placement for graduates, veterans' counselor. **Physically disabled:** Services for visually, speech, hearing impaired. **Transfer:** Re-entry adviser, pre-admission transcript evaluation for new students. College fairs on campus for students transferring to 4-year colleges.

**Contact.** Phone: (760) 245-4271 ext. 2280 Fax: (760) 843-7707
Greta Moon, Director, Admissions and Records, Victor Valley College, 18422 Bear Valley Road, Victorville, CA 92392-5849

---

## West Hills College: Coalinga
**Coalinga, California**
**www.westhillscollege.com**
**CB code: 4056**

- Public 2-year community college
- Commuter campus in small town

**General.** Founded in 1932. Regionally accredited. 2 campuses in district: West Hills College-Coalinga, West Hills College-Lemore. **Enrollment:** 1,371 degree-seeking undergraduates; 1,189 non-degree-seeking students. **Degrees:** 192 associate awarded. **Location:** 60 miles from Fresno. **Calendar:** Semester, limited summer session. **Full-time faculty:** 85 total. **Part-time faculty:** 190 total.

**Student profile.** Among degree-seeking undergraduates, 60% enrolled in a transfer program, 40% enrolled in a vocational program, 2% already have a bachelor's degree or higher, 325 enrolled as first-time, first-year students.

| | | | |
|---|---|---|---|
| Part-time: | 43% | Women: | 60% |
| Out-of-state: | 15% | 25 or older: | 48% |

**Transfer out.** 20% of students enrolled in the transfer program go on to 4-year colleges. **Colleges most students transferred to 2007:** California State University: Fresno, California Polytechnic University.

**Basis for selection.** Open admission. K-12 students admitted with parental permission and principal of the educational insitution recommendation as special admit students. **Adult students:** SAT/ACT scores not required. **Homeschooled:** Students must petition President of College in writing for admittance.

**2007-2008 Annual costs.** Tuition/fees: $600; $5,790 out-of-state. Per-credit charge: $20 in-state; $193 out-of-state. Additional $250 refundable deposit for room and boad plan. Room/board: $5,171. Books/supplies: $630. Personal expenses: $1,602.

**Financial aid. Need-based:** Need-based aid available for part-time students.

**Application procedures. Admission:** No deadline. No application fee. Application must be submitted online. Admission notification on a rolling basis. **Financial aid:** Priority date 3/2; no closing date. FAFSA required. Applicants notified on a rolling basis starting 6/1.

**Academics. Special study options:** Cooperative education, distance learning, dual enrollment of high school students, ESL, honors, independent study, study abroad. **Credit/placement by examination:** AP, CLEP, institutional tests. 15 credit hours maximum toward associate degree. **Support services:** Learning center, reduced course load, remedial instruction, tutoring.

**Majors. Agriculture:** General, animal sciences, business. **Business:** General, accounting, administrative services, business admin, management information systems, office technology, office/clerical. **Computer sciences:** General, applications programming. **Education:** Early childhood. **Health:** Health services, psychiatric nursing. **Liberal arts:** Arts/sciences. **Protective services:** Police science. **Psychology:** General. **Social sciences:** General, criminology, geography. **Visual/performing arts:** Art, commercial/advertising art, studio arts.

**Most popular majors.** Business/marketing 9%, health sciences 7%, liberal arts 65%.

**Computing on campus.** 40 workstations in dormitories, library, computer center. Dormitories wired for high-speed internet access. Online course registration, helpline available.

**Student life. Freshman orientation:** Mandatory. Preregistration for classes offered. **Housing:** Single-sex dorms, substance-free housing available. $500 fully refundable deposit. **Activities:** Dance, drama, musical theater, student government.

**Athletics.** NJCAA. **Intercollegiate:** Baseball M, basketball M, cross-country M, football (tackle) M, rodeo, soccer, softball W, tennis W, volleyball W. **Team name:** Falcons.

**Student services.** Adult student services, career counseling, services for economically disadvantaged, student employment services, on-campus daycare, personal counseling, veterans' counselor. **Physically disabled:** Services for visually, speech, hearing impaired. **Transfer:** Transfer center, transfer adviser for students transferring to 4-year colleges.

**Contact.** E-mail: sandradagnino@westhillscollege.com
Phone: (559) 934-2302 Toll-free number: (800) 266-1114
Fax: (559) 935-2788
Darlene Georgatos, District Director, Enrollment Services, West Hills College: Coalinga, 300 Cherry Lane, Coalinga, CA 93210

## West Hills College: Lemoore
**Lemoore, California**
**www.westhillscollege.com**

- Public 2-year community college
- Large town

**General.** Candidate for regional accreditation. 2 campuses in district: West Hills College Coalinga and West Hills College Lemoore. **Enrollment:** 3,619 undergraduates. **Degrees:** 349 associate awarded. **Location:** 20 miles from Fresno. **Calendar:** Semester, limited summer session.

**Student profile.** 60% enrolled in a transfer program, 40% enrolled in a vocational program, 2% already have a bachelor's degree or higher.

**Transfer out. Colleges most students transferred to 2007:** California State University Fresno, California State University Bakersfield, California State University Chico.

**Basis for selection.** Open admission. K-12 students admitted with parental and pirincipal of the educational institution recommendation as special admit students required. **Adult students:** SAT/ACT scores not required. **Homeschooled:** Statement describing homeschool structure and mission required. Parent or guardian must petition the President of West Hills College Lemoore in writing.

**Application procedures. Admission:** No deadline. No application fee. Application must be submitted online. Admission notification on a rolling basis.

**Academics. Special study options:** Cooperative education, distance learning, dual enrollment of high school students, ESL, honors, independent study, study abroad. **Credit/placement by examination:** AP, CLEP. 15 credit hours maximum toward associate degree. **Support services:** Learning center, reduced course load, remedial instruction, tutoring.

**Majors. Business:** General, business admin. **Math:** General. **Protective services:** Law enforcement admin. **Psychology:** General. **Visual/performing arts:** General.

**Most popular majors.** Business/marketing 11%, liberal arts 59%, security/protective services 8%.

**Computing on campus.** Online course registration available.

**Student life. Freshman orientation:** Mandatory. Preregistration for classes offered. **Activities:** Student newspaper.

**Athletics. Intercollegiate:** Golf, soccer, wrestling M. **Team name:** Golden Eagles.

**Student services. Transfer:** Transfer center, transfer adviser for students transferring to 4-year colleges.

**Contact.** E-mail: admissions@westhillscollege.com
Phone: (559) 925-3317 Toll-free number: (800) 266-1114
Fax: (559) 925-3837
Darlene Georgatos, District Director, Enrollment Services, West Hills College: Lemoore, 555 College Avenue, Lemoore, CA 93245

## West Los Angeles College
**Culver City, California**
**www.wlac.edu**                                      CB code: 4964

- Public 2-year community college
- Large town

**General.** Founded in 1968. Regionally accredited. **Enrollment:** 9,261 undergraduates. **Degrees:** 316 associate awarded. **Location:** 10 miles from Civic Center. **Calendar:** Semester, limited summer session. **Full-time faculty:** 105 total. **Part-time faculty:** 200 total.

**Basis for selection.** Open admission.

**2007-2008 Annual costs.** Tuition/fees: $624; $5,814 out-of-state. Per-credit charge: $20 in-state; $193 out-of-state. Books/supplies: $1,314. Personal expenses: $2,826.

**Financial aid.** All financial aid based on need. Need-based aid available for part-time students. Work-study available for part-time students. **Additional information:** California residents may qualify for Board of Governor's Grant Program.

**Application procedures. Admission:** No deadline. No application fee. Admission notification on a rolling basis. **Financial aid:** No deadline. FAFSA required. Applicants notified on a rolling basis; must reply within 4 week(s) of notification.

**Academics. Special study options:** Cooperative education, dual enrollment of high school students, honors, independent study, student-designed major, study abroad. **Credit/placement by examination:** CLEP, institutional tests. 15 credit hours maximum toward associate degree. **Support services:** Learning center, remedial instruction, tutoring.

**Majors. Biology:** General. **Business:** General, accounting, administrative services, business admin, real estate. **Engineering:** General. **English:** English lit, speech/rhetoric. **Foreign languages:** French, Spanish. **Health:** Dental hygiene. **History:** General. **Legal studies:** Paralegal. **Liberal arts:** Arts/sciences. **Mechanic/repair:** Aircraft. **Parks/recreation:** Health/fitness. **Philosophy/religion:** Philosophy. **Physical sciences:** Chemistry, geology, physics. **Psychology:** General. **Social sciences:** Anthropology, economics, geography, political science, sociology. **Visual/performing arts:** Art, ceramics.

**Student life. Freshman orientation:** Available. 2 hour session prior to start of each semester. **Activities:** Bands, choral groups, dance, drama, film society, student government, student newspaper, TV station.

**Athletics. Intercollegiate:** Baseball M, basketball M, football (tackle) M, tennis, track and field. **Team name:** Oilers.

**Student services.** Adult student services, career counseling, services for economically disadvantaged, student employment services, financial aid counseling, health services, on-campus daycare, personal counseling, placement for graduates, veterans' counselor. **Physically disabled:** Services for visually, speech, hearing impaired.

**Contact.** Phone: (310) 287-4501
Len Isakson, West Los Angeles College, 9000 Overland Avenue, Culver City, CA 90230

## West Valley College
**Saratoga, California**
**www.westvalley.edu**                                CB code: 4958

- Public 2-year community college
- Large town

**General.** Founded in 1963. Regionally accredited. **Enrollment:** 14,615 undergraduates. **Degrees:** 688 associate awarded. **ROTC:** Army, Air Force. **Location:** 13 miles from San Jose. **Calendar:** Semester, limited summer session. **Full-time faculty:** 200 total. **Part-time faculty:** 250 total. **Special facilities:** Planetarium, wireless campus center.

**Transfer out. Colleges most students transferred to 2007:** University of California: Davis, San Jose State University.

**Basis for selection.** Open admission.

**2007-2008 Annual costs.** Tuition/fees: $654; $5,844 out-of-state. Per-credit charge: $20 in-state; $193 out-of-state. Books/supplies: $1,422. Personal expenses: $2,898.

**Financial aid.** All financial aid based on need. Need-based aid available for part-time students.

**Application procedures. Admission:** Priority date 4/21; no deadline. No application fee. Admission notification on a rolling basis. **Financial aid:** Priority date 5/31; no closing date. FAFSA required. Applicants notified on a rolling basis starting 7/1.

**Academics. Special study options:** Distance learning, double major, dual enrollment of high school students, ESL, honors, independent study, teacher certification program. **Credit/placement by examination:** CLEP, institutional tests. 12 credit hours maximum toward associate degree. **Support services:** Learning center, pre-admission summer program, remedial instruction, tutoring.

**Majors. Architecture:** Landscape. **Area/ethnic studies:** Women's. **Biology:** General. **Business:** General, accounting, administrative services, business admin, fashion, office management, office technology, office/clerical, real estate. **Computer sciences:** General, programming. **Construction:** Maintenance. **Education:** Early childhood. **Engineering:** General. **Engineering technology:** Drafting, electrical. **English:** English lit, speech/rhetoric. **Family/consumer sciences:** Child care. **Foreign languages:** General. **Health:** Medical assistant. **History:** General. **Legal studies:** Court reporting, paralegal. **Liberal arts:** Arts/sciences. **Math:** General. **Parks/recreation:** Facilities management. **Physical sciences:** Chemistry, geology, physics. **Protective services:** Criminal justice. **Psychology:** General. **Social sciences:** General, sociology. **Visual/performing arts:** Art, dramatic, fashion design, interior design.

**Computing on campus.** 150 workstations in library, computer center. Commuter students can connect to campus network. Online course registration, online library, repair service available.

**Student life. Freshman orientation:** Available. **Activities:** Bands, choral groups, drama, music ensembles, student government, student newspaper, symphony orchestra, TV station, Vietnamese student association, Unlimited Horizons (handicapped), Descendants of Africa, Latin American student association, Alpha Gamma Sigma, Latter-Day Saints, fashion design, Puente, JC Ministries (Christian).

**Athletics. Intercollegiate:** Baseball M, basketball, cross-country, field hockey W, football (tackle) M, gymnastics W, soccer M, softball W, swimming, tennis, track and field, volleyball, water polo M, wrestling M. **Intramural:** Badminton, basketball, bowling, swimming, tennis, volleyball. **Team name:** Vikings.

**Student services.** Adult student services, career counseling, student employment services, health services, on-campus daycare, personal counseling, veterans' counselor. **Physically disabled:** Services for visually, speech, hearing impaired. **Transfer:** Re-entry adviser for new students. Transfer center, transfer adviser, college fairs on campus for students transferring to 4-year colleges.

**Contact.** Phone: (408) 741-2001 Fax: (408) 867-5033
Paula Prichett, Director of Admissions, West Valley College, 14000 Fruitvale Avenue, Saratoga, CA 95070-5698

## Western Career College: Antioch
**Antioch, California**
www.westerncollege.edu          CB code: 3033

- For-profit 2-year technical college
- Commuter campus in small city

**General.** Regionally accredited. **Enrollment:** 60 degree-seeking undergraduates. **Degrees:** 12 associate awarded. **Calendar:** Continuous. **Full-time faculty:** 16 total. **Part-time faculty:** 10 total.

**Basis for selection.** CPAT results important.

**2007-2008 Annual costs.** Tuition and fees range from $14,955 to $41,267 depending on program; certificate program length 30 weeks to 2 years, associate degree slightly over 2 years.

**Application procedures. Admission:** No deadline. $100 fee. Admission notification on a rolling basis. **Financial aid:** No deadline.

**Academics. Credit/placement by examination:** CLEP.

**Majors. Health:** Licensed practical nurse, massage therapy, medical assistant, medical records technology, pharmacy assistant. **Protective services:** Law enforcement admin.

**Contact.** Phone: (925) 280-0235 Fax: (925) 280-0267
Mitch Charles, Director of Admissions, Western Career College: Antioch, 2157 Country Hills Road, Antioch, CA 94531

## Western Career College: Pleasant Hill
**Pleasant Hill, California**
www.westerncollege.com          CB code: 2922

- For-profit 2-year health science and technical college
- Commuter campus in small city

**General.** Regionally accredited. **Calendar:** Continuous.

**Annual costs/financial aid.** Tuition $18,830; books, supplies, uniform expenses for medical billing $1,727, medical administrative assistant $1,402, medical assisting $1,515, dental assisting program $1,229, massage therapy $1,927. Tuition for pharmacy technology $20,125; books, supplies, uniform expenses $1,468. Program length ranges from 15 to 19 months. Registration fee $100.

**Contact.** Phone: (925) 609-6650
Admissions Director, 380 Civic Drive, Suite 300, Pleasant Hill, CA 94523

## Western Career College: Sacramento
**Sacramento, California**
www.westerncollege.com          CB code: 2917

- For-profit 2-year health science and technical college
- Commuter campus in large city

**General.** Regionally accredited. **Calendar:** Continuous.

**Annual costs/financial aid.** Tuition for 15-month associate science degree program: veterinary technology $20,251; dental assisting $18,918; medical assisting $19,204; medical billing $19,446; medical administrative assisting $19,091; pharmacy tech $20,425; massage therapy $19,616; vocational nursing $30,533. Tuition for 10-month certificate program: dental assisting $11,717; medical assisting $12,003; massage therapy $12,414; vocational nursing $24,852. Books, supplies, uniform, fees included. Books/supplies: $448. Personal expenses: $1,686.

**Contact.** Phone: (916) 361-1660
8909 Folsom Boulevard, Sacramento, CA 95826-9823

## Western Career College: San Jose
**San Jose, California**
www.svcollege.com

- For-profit 2-year technical college
- Commuter campus in very large city

**General.** Regionally accredited. **Calendar:** Continuous.

**Contact.** Phone: (408) 360-0840
Admissions Director, 6201 San Ignacio Avenue, San Jose, CA 95119

## Western Career College: San Leandro
**San Leandro, California**
www.westerncollege.edu          CB code: 2918

- For-profit 2-year health science and technical college
- Commuter campus in small city

**General.** Regionally accredited. **Calendar:** Continuous.

**Annual costs/financial aid.** All programs require $100 registration fee. Associate in Criminal Justice (60 weeks): tuition, $22,701; books and uniform, $1,787. Associate in Pharmacy Technology (60 to 80 weeks): tuition, $22,701; books and uniform, $1,554. Associate in Veterinary Technology (86 weeks): tuition, $27,573; books and uniform, $1,663. Students in certificate programs have option to continue and complete associate degree. Following certificate programs are 36 weeks with tuition of $15,192: Dental Assisting (books and uniform, $277); Health Care Administration (books and uniform, $685); Health Information Technology (books and uniform, $1,059). Certificate in Medical Assisting (42 to 50 weeks): tuition, $15,192;

books and uniform, $382. Certificate in Massage Therapy (34 weeks): tuition, $13,926; books and uniform, $1,246. Certificate in Vocational Nursing (67 weeks): tuition, $39,845; books and uniform, $1,221. Books/supplies: $448. Personal expenses: $1,686.

**Contact.** Phone: (510) 276-3888
1555 East 14th Street Suite 500, San Leandro, CA 94578

## Western Career College: Stockton
### Stockton, California
### www.westerncollege.edu

- For-profit 2-year health science, technical and career college
- Small city

**General.** Regionally accredited. **Enrollment:** 160 degree-seeking undergraduates. **Degrees:** 80 associate awarded. **Location:** 40 miles from Sacramento. **Calendar:** Continuous. **Full-time faculty:** 14 total. **Part-time faculty:** 7 total.

**Student profile.** Among degree-seeking undergraduates, 100% enrolled in a vocational program.

**Basis for selection.** Admissions decisions are based upon high school diploma (GED or ATB) formal interview with applicant, a completed application and a passing score on an entrance exam.

**2007-2008 Annual costs.** All programs require $100 registration fee. Associate in Criminal Justice (60 weeks): tuition, $22,701; books and uniform, $1,787. Associate in Pharmacy Technology (60 to 80 weeks): tuition, $22,701; books and uniform, $1,554. Associate in Veterinary Technology (86 weeks): tuition, $27,573; books and uniform, $1,663. Students in certificate programs have option to continue and complete associate degree. Certificate in Health Care Administration (36 weeks); tuition, $15,192; books and uniform, $685; Certificate in Medical Assisting (42 to 50 weeks): tuition, $15,192; books and uniform, $382. Certificate in Massage Therapy (34 weeks): tuition, $13,926; books and uniform, $1,246. An Associate degree option on any of the certificate program (36 weeks); tuition, $10,725; books $1,162.

**Application procedures. Admission:** No deadline. $100 fee.

**Academics. Special study options:** Accelerated study. Bachelor's degree programs available on campus. **Credit/placement by examination:** CLEP. **Support services:** Learning center, tutoring.

**Majors. Health:** Health care admin, massage therapy, medical assistant, pharmacy assistant, veterinary technology/assistant. **Protective services:** Police science.

**Computing on campus.** 25 workstations in library, computer center. Online library available.

**Student life. Freshman orientation:** Mandatory. **Activities:** Student newspaper.

**Contact.** Tiffany Rhodes, Director of Admissions, Western Career College: Stockton, 1313 West Robinhood Drive Suite B, Stockton, CA 95207

## Westwood College: Los Angeles
### Los Angeles, California
### www.westwood.edu

- For-profit 2-year technical college
- Very large city

**General.** Accredited by ACICS. **Enrollment:** 963 degree-seeking undergraduates. **Degrees:** 178 bachelor's, 6 associate awarded; master's offered. **Calendar:** 10-week terms throughout year. **Full-time faculty:** 12 total. **Part-time faculty:** 47 total.

**Basis for selection.** Open admission. Accuplacer required.

**2007-2008 Annual costs.** Tuition/fees: $13,245. Per-credit charge: $304.

**Application procedures. Admission:** No deadline. $100 fee. Admission notification on a rolling basis. **Financial aid:** FAFSA required. Applicants notified on a rolling basis.

**Academics. Credit/placement by examination:** CLEP.

**Majors. Business:** Fashion. **Computer sciences:** Programming. **Engineering:** Computer. **Visual/performing arts:** Fashion design, graphic design.

**Contact.** Phone: (213) 739-9999
Guy Lopatin, Director of Admissions, Westwood College: Los Angeles, 3250 Wilshire Boulevard, Suite 400, Los Angeles, CA 90010

## WyoTech: Fremont
### Fremont, California
### www.wyotech.com — CB code: 3030

- For-profit 2-year technical college
- Small city
- Interview required

**General.** Accredited by ACCSCT. **Enrollment:** 1,054 degree-seeking undergraduates. **Degrees:** 167 associate awarded. **Calendar:** Continuous. **Full-time faculty:** 74 total.

**Basis for selection.** Satisfactory performance on state-mandated entrance exam required.

**2007-2008 Annual costs.** Tuition ranges from $12,776 to $32,156 depending on programs. Tuition includes books, training materials and supplies. Tools are loaned to students for their use during school enrollment. A $50 refundable tool deposit is required.

**Application procedures. Admission:** No deadline. No application fee. **Financial aid:** FAFSA required.

**Academics. Credit/placement by examination:** CLEP. **Support services:** Learning center.

**Majors. Mechanic/repair:** General, heating/ac/refrig.

**Contact.** Phone: (510) 490-6900 Toll-free number: (800) 248-8585 Fax: (510) 490-8599
Corey Faria, Director of Admissions, WyoTech: Fremont, 200 Whitney Place, Fremont, CA 94539

## WyoTech: Long Beach
### Long Beach, California
### www.nitschools.com — CB code: 3162

- For-profit 2-year health science and technical college
- Commuter campus in large city

**General.** Accredited by ACCSCT. **Enrollment:** 1,190 degree-seeking undergraduates. **Calendar:** Continuous. **Full-time faculty:** 62 total. **Part-time faculty:** 16 total.

**Basis for selection.** Institutional placement assessment examination, interview important.

**2007-2008 Annual costs.** Costs vary by program. Full program costs: automotive $21,206, electrical $16,173, HVAC $14,079, IET $21,025, massage therapy $14,352, medical assistant $12,235, plumbing $15,288.

**Application procedures. Admission:** No deadline. No application fee. Application fee varies by program.

**Academics. Credit/placement by examination:** CLEP.

**Majors. Construction:** Electrician.

**Contact.** Phone: (562) 624-9530 Toll-free number: (888) 741-4271 Fax: (562) 437-8111
Claudia Fimbres, Senior Admissions Representative, WyoTech: Long Beach, 2161 Technology Place, Long Beach, CA 90810

## Yuba Community College District
### Marysville, California
### www.yccd.edu — CB code: 4994

- Public 2-year community college
- Commuter campus in small city

**General.** Founded in 1927. Regionally accredited. **Enrollment:** 6,099 degree-seeking undergraduates. **Degrees:** 705 associate awarded. **Location:** 56 miles from Sacramento. **Calendar:** Semester, limited summer session. **Full-time**

**faculty:** 135 total. **Part-time faculty:** 375 total. **Special facilities:** Veterinary technical training clinic, manufacturing technology facilities (factory), measurement science/scale repair training facilities. **Partnerships:** Formal partnerships with numerous local businesses.

**Transfer out. Colleges most students transferred to 2007:** California State University: Sacramento, California State University: Chico, University of California: Davis.

**Basis for selection.** Open admission, but selective for some programs. Limited admission to allied health programs. CPT tests recommended for counseling.

**2007-2008 Annual costs.** Tuition/fees: $612; $5,952 out-of-state. Per-credit charge: $20 in-state; $198 out-of-state. Books/supplies: $1,260.

**Financial aid. Need-based:** Need-based aid available for part-time students. Work-study available for part-time students. **Non-need-based:** Scholarships awarded for academics, athletics, job skills, minority status, music/drama. **Additional information:** Tuition fee waiver based on Board of Governors Grant.

**Application procedures. Admission:** No deadline. No application fee. Admission notification on a rolling basis beginning on or about 6/1. **Financial aid:** Closing date 3/1. FAFSA required. Applicants notified on a rolling basis starting 4/1.

**Academics. Special study options:** Cooperative education, distance learning, ESL. License preparation in nursing, radiology. **Credit/placement by examination:** CLEP, institutional tests. **Support services:** Learning center, remedial instruction, tutoring.

**Majors. Agriculture:** Business, landscaping, mechanization, ornamental horticulture. **Business:** Accounting, administrative services, business admin, entrepreneurial studies, human resources, taxation. **Communications:** Journalism, media studies. **Computer sciences:** General, computer science. **Education:** Early childhood, physical. **Engineering technology:** Electrical, water quality. **English:** English lit. **Family/consumer sciences:** Family/community services. **Health:** Medical radiologic technology/radiation therapy, medical transcription, nursing (RN), substance abuse counseling, veterinary technology/assistant. **History:** General. **Liberal arts:** Arts/sciences. **Math:** General. **Mechanic/repair:** General, automotive, electronics/electrical. **Personal/culinary services:** Cosmetology. **Production:** General, sheet metal. **Protective services:** Criminal justice, fire safety technology, police science. **Social sciences:** General. **Visual/performing arts:** Art, dramatic, photography, studio arts.

**Most popular majors.** Education 31%.

**Computing on campus.** 300 workstations in library.

**Student life. Freshman orientation:** Available. **Activities:** Bands, choral groups, drama, music ensembles, musical theater, student government, student newspaper, symphony orchestra, AD Nursing Students Association, Care Club, EOP&S Club DECA/Marketing Club, Christian Students Association, Green Society, Future Teachers of America, Speech Team, Photography Guild, Veterinary Technicians Association.

**Athletics. Intercollegiate:** Baseball M, basketball, cross-country, football (tackle) M, soccer, softball W, tennis, track and field, volleyball W. **Team name:** 49'ers.

**Student services.** Adult student services, career counseling, services for economically disadvantaged, student employment services, financial aid counseling, health services, minority student services, on-campus daycare, personal counseling, placement for graduates, veterans' counselor, women's services. **Physically disabled:** Services for visually, speech, hearing impaired. **Transfer:** Transfer adviser, college fairs on campus for students transferring to 4-year colleges.

**Contact.** E-mail: kpope@yccd.edu
Phone: (530) 741-6720 Fax: (530) 741-6872
Connie Elder, Admissions Registrar, Yuba Community College District, 2088 North Beale Road, Marysville, CA 95901

# Colorado

## Aims Community College

**Greeley, Colorado**
www.aims.edu

**CB member**
**CB code: 4204**

◗ Public 2-year community college
◗ Commuter campus in small city

**General.** Founded in 1967. Regionally accredited. **Enrollment:** 3,384 degree-seeking undergraduates. **Degrees:** 414 associate awarded. **ROTC:** Air Force. **Location:** 55 miles from Denver. **Calendar:** Quarter, extensive summer session. **Full-time faculty:** 90 total. **Part-time faculty:** 157 total.

**Student profile.**

| Out-of-state: | 2% | 25 or older: | 80% |

**Basis for selection.** Open admission, but selective for some programs. Special requirements for radiologic technology, police academy and biofeedback programs based on test scores. All students must meet assessment requirement by taking computerized placement test, submitting ACT/SAT scores or showing proof of previous college experience. Interview required of radiologic technology, police academy, biofeedback majors.

**2007-2008 Annual costs.** Tuition/fees: $2,165; $2,945 out-of-district; $10,685 out-of-state. Per-credit charge: $52 in-district; $78 out-of-district; $336 out-of-state. Books/supplies: $600. Personal expenses: $450.

**Application procedures. Admission:** No deadline. No application fee. Admission notification on a rolling basis. **Financial aid:** Priority date 4/15; no closing date. FAFSA required. Applicants notified on a rolling basis starting 6/1.

**Academics. Special study options:** Cooperative education, double major, dual enrollment of high school students, independent study, internships, weekend college. **Credit/placement by examination:** AP, CLEP, institutional tests. 48 credit hours maximum toward associate degree. **Support services:** Learning center, remedial instruction, tutoring.

**Majors. Agriculture:** General, supplies. **Business:** Accounting, administrative services, management information systems, marketing. **Communications technology:** Graphic/printing. **Engineering technology:** Electrical. **Family/consumer sciences:** Child care. **Health:** Medical radiologic technology/radiation therapy. **Liberal arts:** Arts/sciences. **Mechanic/repair:** Auto body. **Protective services:** Fire safety technology, law enforcement admin. **Transportation:** Aviation.

**Computing on campus.** 500 workstations in computer center, student center.

**Student life. Activities:** Concert band, dance, drama, literary magazine, musical theater, student government, student newspaper.

**Athletics. Intramural:** Basketball, volleyball.

**Student services.** Career counseling, student employment services, on-campus daycare, placement for graduates, veterans' counselor. **Physically disabled:** Services for visually, speech, hearing impaired. **Transfer:** Transfer adviser, college fairs on campus for students transferring to 4-year colleges.

**Contact.** E-mail: admissions.records@aims.edu
Phone: (970) 339-6440 Toll-free number: (800) 301-5388
Stuart Thomas, Director of Admissions, Aims Community College, 5401 West 20th Street, Greeley, CO 80632

## Arapahoe Community College

**Littleton, Colorado**
www.arapahoe.edu

**CB code: 4014**

◗ Public 2-year community college
◗ Commuter campus in small city

**General.** Founded in 1965. Regionally accredited. **Enrollment:** 5,318 degree-seeking undergraduates; 1,600 non-degree-seeking students. **Degrees:** 536

associate awarded. **ROTC:** Army, Air Force. **Location:** 10 miles from Denver. **Calendar:** Semester, limited summer session. **Full-time faculty:** 98 total; 7% minority, 66% women. **Part-time faculty:** 400 total. **Class size:** 71% < 20, 28% 20-39, less than 1% 40-49, less than 1% 50-99, less than 1% >100. **Partnerships:** Formal partnerships with National Cable Telecommunications Institute, Swedish Medical Center, Porter Adventist Hospital and Skyridge Medical Center.

**Student profile.** Among degree-seeking undergraduates, 1,451 enrolled as first-time, first-year students, 677 transferred in from other institutions.

| Part-time: | 66% | Asian American: | 4% |
| Out-of-state: | 4% | Hispanic American: | 10% |
| Women: | 65% | Native American: | 1% |
| African American: | 4% | 25 or older: | 51% |

**Transfer out. Colleges most students transferred to 2007:** University of Colorado at Denver, Colorado State University, University of Northern Colorado, Colorado School of Mines, Adams State College.

**Basis for selection.** Open admission, but selective for some programs. Allied health, nursing, automotive, legal assistant, and law enforcement programs require interviews and/or test scores. SAT or ACT scores considered for placement if submitted.

**2007-2008 Annual costs.** Tuition/fees: $2,486; $10,889 out-of-state. Per-credit charge: $77 in-state; $357 out-of-state. In-state tuition based upon assumption of Colorado Opportunity Fund waiver of $89 per-credit-hour. Books/supplies: $850.

**Financial aid. Need-based:** Need-based aid available for part-time students. Work-study available nights, weekends and for part-time students. **Non-need-based:** Scholarships awarded for academics, leadership, state residency.

**Application procedures. Admission:** No deadline. No application fee. Application may be submitted online. Admission notification on a rolling basis. Closing date for nursing applicants February 4. **Financial aid:** Priority date 5/1; no closing date. FAFSA, institutional form required. Applicants notified on a rolling basis starting 5/1; must reply within 3 week(s) of notification.

**Academics. Special study options:** Accelerated study, cooperative education, distance learning, double major, dual enrollment of high school students, ESL, independent study, internships, weekend college. License preparation in nursing, occupational therapy, paramedic, physical therapy, real estate. **Credit/placement by examination:** AP, CLEP, institutional tests. No more than half of required credit can be fulfilled through credit for prior learning. **Support services:** GED preparation and test center, learning center, reduced course load, remedial instruction, study skills assistance, tutoring, writing center.

**Majors. Business:** Accounting technology, administrative services, banking/financial services, hospitality admin, international, management information systems, marketing, office management, selling. **Communications technology:** General. **Computer sciences:** Data entry, LAN/WAN management, networking, web page design. **Construction:** General, building inspection. **Engineering technology:** General, architectural, computer, electrical, manufacturing. **Family/consumer sciences:** Child development. **Health:** Clinical lab technology, medical records technology, nursing (RN), occupational therapy assistant, office admin, physical therapy assistant. **Legal studies:** Paralegal. **Liberal arts:** Arts/sciences. **Mechanic/repair:** Automotive. **Parks/recreation:** Health/fitness. **Personal/culinary services:** Mortuary science. **Protective services:** Law enforcement admin. **Visual/performing arts:** Graphic design, interior design.

**Computing on campus.** 110 workstations in library, computer center, student center. Commuter students can connect to campus network. Online course registration, online library, helpline, wireless network available.

**Student life. Freshman orientation:** Mandatory. Preregistration for classes offered. **Activities:** Bands, choral groups, drama, music ensembles, student government, student newspaper, Phi Theta Kappa, Diversity Council, Ron Paul Society.

**Athletics. Team name:** Coyotes.

**Student services.** Adult student services, career counseling, services for economically disadvantaged, student employment services, financial aid counseling, minority student services, on-campus daycare, placement for graduates, veterans' counselor. **Physically disabled:** Services for visually, speech, hearing impaired. **Learning disabled:** Comprehensive services available. **Transfer:** Pre-admission transcript evaluation for new students. Transfer adviser, college fairs on campus for students transferring to 4-year colleges.

Two-Year Colleges

**Contact.** E-mail: admissions@arapahoe.edu
Phone: (303) 797-5621 Fax: (303) 797-5970
Darcy Briggs-Jackson, Director of Admissions and Records, Arapahoe Community College, PO Box 9002, Littleton, CO 80160-9002

## Bel-Rea Institute of Animal Technology
### Denver, Colorado
www.bel-rea.com                                    CB code: 0928

- For-profit 2-year technical college
- Commuter campus in very large city

**General.** Accredited by ACCSCT. **Enrollment:** 650 degree-seeking undergraduates. **Degrees:** 260 associate awarded. **Calendar:** Continuous. **Full-time faculty:** 25 total. **Part-time faculty:** 5 total.

**Transfer out. Colleges most students transferred to 2007:** University of Denver.

**Basis for selection.** Interview most important, followed by school achievement record. Recommendations considered. Minimum 2.5 GPA or GED required. Applicants with below 2.5 GPA or without GED must take entrance exam.

**High school preparation.** As much science and math as possible recommended. Algebra and chemistry recommended.

**2007-2008 Annual costs.** Tuition for full associate program $20,750 including fees. Books/supplies: $1,500. Personal expenses: $1,100.

**Financial aid.** All financial aid based on need.

**Application procedures. Admission:** No deadline. No application fee. Admission notification on a rolling basis. **Financial aid:** Priority date 8/31; no closing date. FAFSA required. Applicants notified on a rolling basis starting 8/15.

**Academics.** Students intern at college-affiliated emergency veterinary hospital. **Special study options:** Internships. **Credit/placement by examination:** CLEP. **Support services:** Reduced course load, study skills assistance, tutoring.

**Majors. Health:** Veterinary technology/assistant.

**Computing on campus.** PC or laptop required. 20 workstations in student center.

**Student life. Freshman orientation:** Available. **Activities:** Student government.

**Student services.** Career counseling, student employment services, personal counseling, placement for graduates, veterans' counselor.

**Contact.** E-mail: kaufman@bel-rea.com
Phone: (303) 751-8700 Toll-free number: (800) 950-8001
Fax: (303) 751-9969
Paulette Kaufman, Director, Bel-Rea Institute of Animal Technology, 1681 South Dayton Street, Denver, CO 80247

## Boulder College of Massage Therapy
### Boulder, Colorado
www.bcmt.org

- Private 1-year health science college
- Residential campus in small city

**General.** Accredited by ACCSCT. **Location:** 30 miles from Denver. **Calendar:** Quarter.

**Annual costs/financial aid.** Programs range from $13,160-$16,450. Need-based financial aid available to full-time and part-time students.

**Contact.** Phone: (303) 530-2100
Director of Marketing and Admissions, 6255 Longbow Drive, Boulder, CO 80301

## Cambridge College
### Aurora, Colorado
www.cambridgecollege.com                        CB code: 3201

- For-profit 2-year technical college
- Commuter campus in small city
- Interview required

**General.** Accredited by ACCSCT. **Enrollment:** 585 full-time, degree-seeking students. **Degrees:** 171 associate awarded. **Calendar:** Continuous, extensive summer session. **Full-time faculty:** 35 total.

**Basis for selection.** Interview most important. Entrance exam required for students out of high school more than 6 months.

**2007-2008 Annual costs.** Tuition for full associate degree programs ranges from $16,550 to $24,500 depending on program; tuition for diploma programs ranges from $7,950 to $10,150. Books and supplies included. Housing provided by private company.

**Financial aid.** All financial aid based on need.

**Application procedures. Admission:** No deadline. $50 fee ($150 out-of-state). Admission notification on a rolling basis. **Financial aid:** No deadline. FAFSA, institutional form required. Applicants notified on a rolling basis.

**Academics. Special study options:** License preparation in radiology. **Credit/placement by examination:** CLEP. **Support services:** GED preparation.

**Majors. Computer sciences:** General. **Health:** Massage therapy, medical assistant, radiologic technology/medical imaging, surgical technology.

**Student life. Freshman orientation:** Mandatory.

**Student services.** Adult student services, career counseling, student employment services, financial aid counseling, placement for graduates.

**Contact.** Phone: (720) 859-7900 Toll-free number: (800) 322-4132
Fax: (303) 338-9701
Stacey Keele, Director of Admissions, Cambridge College, 350 Blackhawk Street, Aurora, CO 80011

## CollegeAmerica: Denver
### Denver, Colorado
www.collegeamerica.com

- For-profit 2-year technical college
- Commuter campus in very large city
- Application essay, interview required

**General.** Accredited by ACCSCT. **Enrollment:** 455 degree-seeking undergraduates. **Degrees:** 69 bachelor's, 99 associate awarded. **Calendar:** Continuous, extensive summer session. **Full-time faculty:** 8 total; 12% have terminal degrees, 25% minority, 50% women. **Part-time faculty:** 19 total; 5% have terminal degrees, 16% minority, 58% women. **Class size:** 91% < 20, 9% 20-39.

**Basis for selection.** Open admission. **Homeschooled:** Transcript of courses and grades, state high school equivalency certificate required.

**2007-2008 Annual costs.** Tuition, fees, books, and supplies: $29,950 for Associate degree programs; $54,900 for Bachelor's degree programs. Books/supplies: $101. Personal expenses: $1,000.

**Financial aid.** All financial aid based on need.

**Application procedures. Admission:** No deadline. $50 fee, may be waived for applicants with need. Application must be submitted on paper. Admission notification on a rolling basis. **Financial aid:** No deadline. FAFSA, institutional form required. Applicants notified on a rolling basis; must reply within 4 week(s) of notification.

**Academics. Special study options:** Accelerated study, distance learning. Bachelor's degree programs available on campus. License preparation in radiology. **Credit/placement by examination:** AP, CLEP. **Support services:** Tutoring.

**Majors. Business:** Accounting/business management, business admin. **Computer sciences:** Computer graphics, networking, programming. **Health:** Health services.

**Most popular majors.** Business/marketing 10%, computer/information sciences 10%, health sciences 80%.

**Computing on campus.** 50 workstations in library, computer center. Commuter students can connect to campus network. Online course registration, online library, repair service, wireless network available.

**Student life. Freshman orientation:** Mandatory.

**Student services.** Career counseling, services for economically disadvantaged, student employment services, financial aid counseling, placement for graduates.

**Contact.** Phone: (303) 691-9756 Toll-free number: (800) 977-5455 Mary Nebel, Director of Admissions, CollegeAmerica: Denver, 1385 South Colorado Boulevard, 5th Floor, Denver, CO 80222-1912

## Colorado Mountain College
### Glenwood Springs, Colorado
**www.coloradomtn.edu**  CB code: 4112

- Public 2-year community and liberal arts college
- Residential campus in small town

**General.** Founded in 1965. Regionally accredited. Total of 12 campuses. Three residential campuses are Alpine Campus in Steamboat Springs, Spring Valley Campus in Glenwood Springs, and Timberline Campus in Leadville. Commuter campuses in Aspen, Summit, Vail-Eagle Valley in Edwards, Rifle, Breckinridge, Buena Vista. **Enrollment:** 4,940 degree-seeking undergraduates. **Degrees:** 303 associate awarded. **Location:** 160 miles from Denver. **Calendar:** Semester, limited summer session. **Full-time faculty:** 80 total. **Part-time faculty:** 270 total. **Special facilities:** Outdoor education center, farm for veterinarian technician program, hot springs, climbing wall, ice wall, community theatre.

**Student profile.**

| | | | |
|---|---|---|---|
| Out-of-state: | 9.7% | 25 or older: | 68% |

**Transfer out. Colleges most students transferred to 2007:** University of Colorado-Boulder, Colorado State University, Mesa State University, Western State College, Fort Lewis College.

**Basis for selection.** Open admission, but selective for some programs. Special requirements for nursing applicants. Testing requirements for veterinary technology, photography, outdoor recreation leadership, culinary arts, paramedic, and ski area operations. SAT or ACT recommended for placement and counseling. College placement test may be used in place of SAT or ACT.

**2007-2008 Annual costs.** Tuition/fees: $1,490; $2,360 out-of-district; $7,130 out-of-state. Per-credit charge: $43 in-district; $72 out-of-district; $231 out-of-state. Room/board: $6,866. Books/supplies: $650. Personal expenses: $2,050.

**Financial aid.** All financial aid based on need. Need-based aid available for part-time students. Work-study available nights, weekends and for part-time students.

**Application procedures. Admission:** No deadline. No application fee. Application must be submitted on paper. Admission notification on a rolling basis. **Financial aid:** Priority date 3/31; no closing date. FAFSA required. Applicants notified on a rolling basis starting 5/15; must reply within 4 week(s) of notification.

**Academics. Special study options:** Distance learning, dual enrollment of high school students, independent study, internships, liberal arts/career combination, study abroad. License preparation in nursing. **Credit/placement by examination:** AP, CLEP, IB, institutional tests. 30 credit hours maximum toward associate degree. Also recognize and accept exam results for DANTES, Excelsior, Institutional Challenge Exams, and credit for life experiences. **Support services:** GED preparation and test center, learning center, reduced course load, remedial instruction, study skills assistance, tutoring.

**Majors. Agriculture:** Animal health, food processing, food science, soil science. **Biology:** General. **Business:** General, accounting, business admin, hospitality admin, hotel/motel admin, management information systems, real estate, resort management. **Communications:** Photojournalism. **Communications technology:** Animation/special effects, graphic/printing, graphics, photo/film/video. **Computer sciences:** General, applications programming, computer graphics, information technology, networking, programming. **Conservation:** General, forestry, management/policy. **Education:** General, bilingual. **Engineering:** General, mechanical. **English:** English lit, speech/rhetoric. **Health:** Nursing (RN), prenursing, veterinary technology/assistant. **Interdisciplinary:** Accounting/computer science, biological/physical sciences, natural sciences, science/society. **Legal studies:** Prelaw. **Liberal arts:** Arts/sciences. **Math:** General. **Parks/recreation:** General, facilities management. **Personal/culinary services:** General, chef training, culinary arts, food prep, restaurant/catering. **Physical sciences:** Chemistry, geology. **Protective services:** Criminal justice, firefighting. **Social sciences:** General. **Visual/performing arts:** General, art, commercial photography, commercial/advertising art, design, dramatic, graphic design, photography.

**Computing on campus.** 30 workstations in dormitories, library, computer center, student center. Dormitories wired for high-speed internet access and linked to campus network. Online library, helpline, wireless network available.

**Student life. Freshman orientation:** Available. Preregistration for classes offered. Fee charged for some orientation activities. **Policies:** All students living on-campus must follow housing policies. **Housing:** Guaranteed on-campus for freshmen. Coed dorms, special housing for disabled, substance-free housing available. $300 partly refundable deposit, deadline 7/1. **Activities:** Dance, drama, musical theater, student government, student newspaper.

**Athletics.** NJCAA. **Intercollegiate:** Skiing, soccer. **Intramural:** Basketball, cross-country, skiing, soccer, softball, volleyball. **Team name:** Eagles.

**Student services.** Adult student services, career counseling, student employment services, financial aid counseling, health services, personal counseling, placement for graduates, veterans' counselor. **Physically disabled:** Services for visually, speech, hearing impaired. **Transfer:** Transfer center, transfer adviser, college fairs on campus for students transferring to 4-year colleges.

**Contact.** E-mail: joinus@coloradomtn.edu
Phone: (970) 947-8327 Toll-free number: (800) 621-8559 ext. 8327
Fax: (970) 947-8324
Bill Sommers, Director of Pre-Enrollment Services, Collegewide, Colorado Mountain College, 831 Grand Avenue, Glenwood Springs, CO 81601

## Colorado Northwestern Community College
### Rangely, Colorado
**www.cncc.edu**  CB code: 4665

- Public 2-year community college
- Residential campus in small town

**General.** Founded in 1962. Regionally accredited. Courses also offered at campus in Craig and 3 off-campus sites in Meeker, Hayden, Oak Creek. **Enrollment:** 1,003 degree-seeking undergraduates. **Degrees:** 115 associate awarded. **Location:** 300 miles from Denver, 90 miles from Grand Junction. **Calendar:** Semester, limited summer session. **Full-time faculty:** 34 total. **Part-time faculty:** 69 total. **Class size:** 87% < 20; 13% 20-39. **Special facilities:** Flight simulator, firearms training simulator, cadaver lab.

**Student profile.**

| | | | |
|---|---|---|---|
| Out-of-state: | 16% | Live on campus: | 45% |
| 25 or older: | 25% | | |

**Transfer out. Colleges most students transferred to 2007:** University of Northern Colorado, Colorado State University, Mesa State College.

**Basis for selection.** Open admission, but selective for some programs. Selective admissions to dental hygiene and nursing. Both programs have application deadline and pre-requisite requirements. Students not submitting ACT/SAT must take institutional placement tests in English, math, reading. Interview required of dental hygiene majors.

**High school preparation.** Biological science and/or chemistry required for dental hygiene. Math/science desirable for aviation technology and aviation maintenance.

**2007-2008 Annual costs.** Tuition/fees: $2,548; $5,218 out-of-state. Per-credit charge: $77 in-state; $166 out-of-state. In-state tuition based upon assumption of Colorado Oppurtunity Fund waiver of $86 per-credit-hour. Room/board: $5,650. Books/supplies: $1,000. Personal expenses: $1,650.

**Financial aid. Need-based:** Need-based aid available for part-time students. Work-study available nights, weekends and for part-time students. **Non-need-based:** Scholarships awarded for academics, athletics, state residency.

**Application procedures. Admission:** No deadline. No application fee. Application may be submitted online. Admission notification on a rolling basis. Application closing date for dental hygiene program 2/15. **Financial aid:** Priority date 5/1; no closing date. FAFSA, institutional form required. Applicants notified on a rolling basis starting 5/15; must reply within 4 week(s) of notification.

**Academics. Special study options:** Distance learning, dual enrollment of high school students, independent study, internships, student-designed major. Bachelor's degree programs available on campus. License preparation in aviation, dental hygiene, nursing. **Credit/placement by examination:** AP, CLEP, institutional tests. 30 credit hours maximum toward associate degree. **Support services:** GED preparation and test center, learning center, remedial instruction, study skills assistance, tutoring, writing center.

**Majors. Business:** Entrepreneurial studies, management information systems, office management. **Family/consumer sciences:** Child care. **Health:** Dental hygiene. **Legal studies:** Paralegal. **Liberal arts:** Arts/sciences. **Mechanic/repair:** Aircraft. **Protective services:** Law enforcement admin. **Transportation:** Aviation.

**Computing on campus.** 54 workstations in dormitories, library, computer center. Dormitories wired for high-speed internet access and linked to campus network. Online course registration, online library, wireless network available.

**Student life. Freshman orientation:** Mandatory, $45 fee. Preregistration for classes offered. Two sessions in July, one in August. **Housing:** Guaranteed on-campus for freshmen. Coed dorms, special housing for disabled, apartments available. $100 deposit. **Activities:** Concert band, choral groups, drama, music ensembles, musical theater, student government, student newspaper.

**Athletics.** NJCAA. **Intercollegiate:** Baseball M, basketball, cross-country, softball W, volleyball W. **Intramural:** Basketball, football (non-tackle), golf, racquetball, soccer, softball, table tennis, tennis, track and field, volleyball. **Team name:** Spartans.

**Student services.** Adult student services, alcohol/substance abuse counseling, career counseling, student employment services, financial aid counseling, personal counseling, placement for graduates, veterans' counselor. **Physically disabled:** Services for visually, hearing impaired. **Transfer:** Preadmission transcript evaluation for new students. Transfer adviser, college fairs on campus for students transferring to 4-year colleges.

**Contact.** E-mail: lisa.lefevre@cncc.edu
Phone: (970) 675-3218 Toll-free number: (800) 562-1105
Fax: (970) 975-3343
Tresa England, Director of Student Services/Registrar, Colorado Northwestern Community College, 500 Kennedy Drive, Rangely, CO 81648

## Colorado School of Healing Arts
**Lakewood, Colorado**
**www.csha.net**

- For-profit 2-year health science college
- Commuter campus in small city
- Application essay, interview required

**General.** Accredited by ACCSCT. **Enrollment:** 240 degree-seeking undergraduates; 1 non-degree-seeking students. **Degrees:** 27 associate awarded. **Location:** 7 miles from Denver. **Calendar:** Quarter, extensive summer session. **Part-time faculty:** 41 total. **Class size:** 79% < 20, 21% 20-39.

**Student profile.** Among degree-seeking undergraduates, 100% enrolled in a vocational program, 20% already have a bachelor's degree or higher, 64 enrolled as first-time, first-year students.

| | | | |
|---|---|---|---|
| Part-time: | 36% | Asian American: | 2% |
| Out-of-state: | 1% | Hispanic American: | 15% |
| Women: | 83% | Native American: | 1% |
| African American: | 2% | International: | 1% |

**Basis for selection.** Open admission. **Homeschooled:** Interview required.

**2008-2009 Annual costs.** Tuition/fees (projected): $10,959. Per-credit charge: $150. Books, massage table package, materials fees, and insurance are included in required fees. Books/supplies: $1,164. Personal expenses: $300..

**Financial aid.** All financial aid based on need. Need-based aid available for part-time students.

**Application procedures. Admission:** No deadline. $50 fee. Application must be submitted on paper. Admission notification on a rolling basis. **Financial aid:** No deadline. FAFSA required.

**Academics. Special study options:** Accelerated study. **Credit/placement by examination:** CLEP. **Support services:** Learning center, tutoring.

**Majors. Health:** Massage therapy.

**Computing on campus.** 2 workstations in library.

**Student life. Freshman orientation:** Mandatory. Preregistration for classes offered. 4 hour program prior to start of each quarter.

**Student services.** Career counseling, financial aid counseling.

**Contact.** E-mail: maureen@csha.net
Phone: (303) 986-2320 Toll-free number: (800) 233-7114
Fax: (303) 980-6594
Maureen Thurston, Admissions Representative, Colorado School of Healing Arts, 7655 West Mississippi, Suite 100, Lakewood, CO 80226

## Colorado School of Trades
**Lakewood, Colorado**
**www.schooloftrades.com**          **CB code: 3211**

- For-profit 2-year technical college
- Small city

**General.** Accredited by ACCSCT. **Enrollment:** 135 degree-seeking undergraduates. **Degrees:** 127 associate awarded. **Calendar:** Continuous. **Full-time faculty:** 10 total. **Part-time faculty:** 3 total.

**Basis for selection.** Open admission.

**2007-2008 Annual costs.** For gunsmithing program: tuition and fees, $16,200; books and supplies, $2,500; other expenses, $180. For farrier science program: tuition and fees, $6,150. Books/supplies: $3,000. Personal expenses: $1,260.

**Application procedures. Admission:** No deadline. $25 fee. Admission notification on a rolling basis. **Financial aid:** FAFSA, institutional form required.

**Academics. Credit/placement by examination:** CLEP.

**Majors. Education:** Trade/industrial. **Mechanic/repair:** General.

**Contact.** Phone: (303) 233-4697 Toll-free number: (800) 234-4594
Sunny Duvont-Holt, Director of Admissions, Colorado School of Trades, 1575 Hoyt Street, Lakewood, CO 80215

## Community College of Aurora
**Aurora, Colorado**
**www.ccaurora.edu**          **CB code: 0969**

- Public 2-year community college
- Commuter campus in large city

**General.** Founded in 1983. Regionally accredited. **Enrollment:** 1,294 full-time, degree-seeking students. **Degrees:** 346 associate awarded. **Calendar:** Semester, extensive summer session. **Full-time faculty:** 40 total. **Part-time faculty:** 300 total.

**Student profile.**

| | | | |
|---|---|---|---|
| Out-of-state: | 3% | Live on campus: | 2% |
| 25 or older: | 60% | | |

**Transfer out. Colleges most students transferred to 2007:** Metropolitan State University, University of Colorado Denver, Colorado State University, University of Northern Colorado.

**Basis for selection.** Open admission.

**2007-2008 Annual costs.** Tuition/fees: $2,429; $10,832 out-of-state. Per-credit charge: $77 in-state; $357 out-of-state. In-state tuition based upon assumption of Colorado Oppurtunity Fund waiver of $89 per-credit-hour. Books/supplies: $400.

**Financial aid. Need-based:** Need-based aid available for part-time students. Work-study available nights and for part-time students.

**Application procedures. Admission:** No deadline. No application fee. Application may be submitted online. Admission notification on a rolling basis. **Financial aid:** Priority date 6/1; no closing date. FAFSA, institutional form required. Applicants notified on a rolling basis starting 7/15.

**Academics. Special study options:** Cooperative education, cross-registration, distance learning, ESL, internships, study abroad, weekend college. License preparation in paramedic. **Credit/placement by examination:** CLEP, IB. 30 credit hours maximum toward associate degree. **Support services:** GED preparation, learning center, remedial instruction, tutoring.

**Majors. Business:** General, accounting, administrative services, banking/financial services, business admin, management information systems, marketing, office technology, sales/distribution. **Communications technology:** Graphic/printing. **Computer sciences:** General, information systems. **Construction:** Carpentry, power transmission. **Education:** Early childhood. **Engineering technology:** Drafting, electrical. **Family/consumer sciences:** Child care. **Health:** Medical secretary. **Legal studies:** Legal secretary, paralegal. **Mechanic/repair:** Heating/ac/refrig. **Personal/culinary services:** Culinary arts. **Protective services:** Criminal justice, law enforcement admin.

**Computing on campus.** 210 workstations in dormitories, library, computer center, student center. Dormitories wired for high-speed internet access and linked to campus network. Commuter students can connect to campus network. Online course registration, online library, repair service available.

**Student life. Freshman orientation:** Available. Preregistration for classes offered. **Housing:** Guaranteed on-campus for freshmen. Coed dorms available. $150 deposit. **Activities:** Dance, drama, music ensembles, musical theater, student government, student newspaper, black student alliance, Lazos Culturales, Phi Theta Kappa, Phi Alpha Omega, Campus Crusade for Christ.

**Athletics. Intramural:** Basketball, softball, tennis, volleyball.

**Student services.** Career counseling, student employment services, financial aid counseling, personal counseling, veterans' counselor. **Physically disabled:** Services for visually, speech, hearing impaired. **Transfer:** Transfer adviser, college fairs on campus for students transferring to 4-year colleges.

**Contact.** Phone: (303) 360-4700 Fax: (303) 361-7432
Kristen Cusack, Registrar, Community College of Aurora, 16000 East CentreTech Parkway, Aurora, CO 80011-9036

## Community College of Denver
**Denver, Colorado**
**www.ccd.edu**                     CB code: 4137

- Public 2-year community college
- Commuter campus in very large city

**General.** Founded in 1970. Regionally accredited. Library, student center and physical education facilities shared with Metropolitan State College at Denver and University of Colorado/Health Sciences Center at Denver. **Enrollment:** 5,566 degree-seeking undergraduates; 3,343 non-degree-seeking students. **Degrees:** 413 associate awarded. **ROTC:** Army. **Calendar:** Semester, limited summer session. **Full-time faculty:** 65 total. **Part-time faculty:** 380 total. **Class size:** 53% < 20, 46% 20-39, less than 1% 40-49, less than 1% 50-99.

**Student profile.** Among degree-seeking undergraduates, 6% enrolled in a transfer program, 12% enrolled in a vocational program, 1,127 enrolled as first-time, first-year students.

| | | | |
|---|---|---|---|
| Part-time: | 65% | Hispanic American: | 26% |
| Out-of-state: | 5% | Native American: | 2% |
| Women: | 66% | International: | 6% |
| African American: | 17% | 25 or older: | 51% |
| Asian American: | 6% | | |

**Transfer out. Colleges most students transferred to 2007:** Metropolitan State College of Denver, University of Colorado at Denver.

**Basis for selection.** Open admission, but selective for some programs. Special requirements for health occupations and computer information systems programs. State of Colorado requires ACT of high school juniors, but institution does not require or recommend it. ACT used for placement if submitted.

**2007-2008 Annual costs.** Tuition/fees: $2,954; $11,357 out-of-state. Per-credit charge: $77 in-state; $345 out-of-state. In-state tuition based upon assumption of Colorado Opportunity Fund waiver of $89 per-credit-hour. Books/supplies: $1,163. Personal expenses: $2,547.

**2006-2007 Financial aid. Need-based:** 69% of total undergraduate aid awarded as scholarships/grants, 31% as loans/jobs. Need-based aid available for part-time students. **Non-need-based:** Scholarships awarded for academics, leadership, state residency.

**Application procedures. Admission:** Priority date 8/1; no deadline. No application fee. Application may be submitted online. Admission notification on a rolling basis. **Financial aid:** Priority date 3/1; no closing date. FAFSA, institutional form required.

**Academics. Special study options:** Accelerated study, cooperative education, cross-registration, distance learning, double major, dual enrollment of high school students, ESL, independent study, internships, liberal arts/career combination, study abroad, weekend college. **Credit/placement by examination:** AP, CLEP, institutional tests. 45 credit hours maximum toward associate degree. **Support services:** GED preparation and test center, learning center, pre-admission summer program, reduced course load, remedial instruction, study skills assistance, tutoring, writing center.

**Majors. Biology:** Biomedical sciences. **Business:** Accounting technology, administrative services, business admin, management information systems. **Computer sciences:** General, applications programming. **Education:** Teacher assistance. **Engineering technology:** Drafting, heat/ac/refrig. **Family/consumer sciences:** Child development. **Health:** Dental hygiene, electroencephalograph technology, health aide, nursing (RN), radiologic technology/medical imaging, veterinary technology/assistant. **Legal studies:** Paralegal. **Liberal arts:** Arts/sciences. **Parks/recreation:** General, health/fitness. **Production:** Welding. **Protective services:** Security services. **Public administration:** Human services. **Visual/performing arts:** Graphic design.

**Most popular majors.** Business/marketing 16%, health sciences 26%, liberal arts 46%.

**Computing on campus.** 1,032 workstations in computer center. Commuter students can connect to campus network. Online course registration available.

**Student life. Freshman orientation:** Mandatory. **Housing:** Dormitory housing available at Lowry campus through cooperative agreement. **Activities:** Choral groups, drama, student government, student newspaper, Mexican-American student organization, African-American student organization, Amnesty International, nursing club.

**Student services.** Adult student services, career counseling, services for economically disadvantaged, student employment services, financial aid counseling, health services, legal services, minority student services, on-campus daycare, personal counseling, placement for graduates, veterans' counselor, women's services. **Physically disabled:** Services for visually, hearing impaired. **Transfer:** Re-entry adviser, pre-admission transcript evaluation for new students. Transfer center, transfer adviser, college fairs on campus for students transferring to 4-year colleges.

**Contact.** E-mail: enrollment_services@ccd.edu
Phone: (303) 556-2420 Fax: (303) 556-2431
Paula Martinez, Associate Director, Enrollment Services, Community College of Denver, Campus Box 201, PO Box 173363, Denver, CO 80217-3363

## Concorde Career College: Aurora
**Aurora, Colorado**
**www.concorde.edu/denver**

- For-profit 2-year health science college
- Large city

**General.** Accredited by ACCSCT. **Calendar:** Continuous.

**Contact.** Phone: (303) 861-1151
Director of Admissions, 111 North Havana Street, Aurora, CO 80010

## Denver Academy of Court Reporting
**Denver, Colorado**
**www.dacr.org**                     CB code: 3561

- For-profit 2-year college of court reporting
- Large city
- Interview required

**General.** Accredited by ACICS. **Enrollment:** 138 degree-seeking undergraduates. **Degrees:** 11 associate awarded. **Calendar:** Quarter, extensive summer session. **Full-time faculty:** 10 total. **Part-time faculty:** 10 total.

**Student profile.** Among degree-seeking undergraduates, 100% enrolled in a vocational program.

| | | | |
|---|---|---|---|
| Women: | 94% | 25 or older: | 50% |

**Basis for selection.** Open admission. Must meet with an admissions representative, tour the facility, and inspect the equipment used in the training program.

**2008-2009 Annual costs.** Tuition/fees (projected): $7,470. Day program tuition $2,300 per quarter, evening program $2,200 per quarter. $150 enrollment fee. $190 per quarter technology fee. Books/supplies: $450.

**Application procedures. Admission:** No deadline. $175 fee.

**Academics. Special study options:** Internships. **Credit/placement by examination:** CLEP.

**Majors. Legal studies:** Court reporting.

**Computing on campus.** Online library, wireless network available.

**Student life. Freshman orientation:** Mandatory.

**Student services. Transfer:** Pre-admission transcript evaluation for new students.

**Contact.** E-mail: info@dacr.org
Phone: (303) 427-5292 Fax: (303) 427-5383
Director of Admissions, Denver Academy of Court Reporting, 9051 Harlan Street, Unit #20, Westminster, CO 80031

## Everest College: Aurora
Aurora, Colorado
www.cci.edu                                          CB code: 3568

- For-profit 2-year branch campus and technical college
- Commuter campus in large city
- Interview required

**General.** Accredited by ACICS. Small interactive learning environment. **Enrollment:** 61 degree-seeking undergraduates; 293 non-degree-seeking students. **Degrees:** 96 associate awarded. **Location:** 15 miles from Denver. **Calendar:** Continuous, extensive summer session. **Full-time faculty:** 11 total. **Part-time faculty:** 15 total.

**Student profile.** Among degree-seeking undergraduates, 61 enrolled as first-time, first-year students.

| | | | |
|---|---|---|---|
| Part-time: | 15% | Women: | 59% |

**Transfer out. Colleges most students transferred to 2007:** University of Phoenix, Florida Metropolitan University.

**Basis for selection.** Open admission. **Homeschooled:** Students without a high school diploma or equivalent may enroll, but must receive a specific score on an admissions test. **Learning Disabled:** Must provide documentation of disability.

**2007-2008 Annual costs.** $287 per credit hour for all linear programs; $25 registration fee and tech fee per quarter. Books/supplies: $900.

**Financial aid.** All financial aid based on need. Need-based aid available for part-time students. Work-study available nights and for part-time students.

**Application procedures. Admission:** No deadline. No application fee. Application may be submitted online. Admission notification on a rolling basis. **Financial aid:** No deadline. FAFSA, institutional form required. Applicants notified on a rolling basis; must reply within 4 week(s) of notification.

**Academics. Special study options:** Accelerated study, cooperative education, distance learning, double major, honors, independent study, internships, liberal arts/career combination. **Credit/placement by examination:** AP, CLEP. 48 credit hours maximum toward associate degree. **Support services:** Learning center, reduced course load, remedial instruction, study skills assistance, tutoring.

**Majors. Business:** Accounting, business admin. **Computer sciences:** General. **Legal studies:** General, paralegal. **Protective services:** Criminal justice.

**Most popular majors.** Business/marketing 48%, computer/information sciences 14%, legal studies 39%.

**Computing on campus.** 6 workstations in library. Commuter students can connect to campus network. Online library, repair service available.

**Student life. Freshman orientation:** Mandatory. Preregistration for classes offered. **Activities:** Student newspaper.

**Student services.** Career counseling, student employment services, financial aid counseling, placement for graduates. **Physically disabled:** Services for speech, hearing impaired. **Transfer:** Re-entry adviser, pre-admission transcript evaluation for new students. Transfer adviser for students transferring to 4-year colleges.

**Contact.** E-mail: Phardy@cci.edu
Phone: (303) 745-6244 Fax: (303) 745-6245
John Heckman, Director of Admissions, Everest College: Aurora, 14280 East Jewell Suite 100, Aurora, CO 80012

## Everest College: Colorado Springs
Colorado Springs, Colorado
www.cci.edu                                          CB code: 0934

- For-profit 2-year business and junior college
- Commuter campus in large city
- Interview required

**General.** Founded in 1897. Accredited by ACICS. **Enrollment:** 400 degree-seeking undergraduates. **Degrees:** 106 associate awarded. **Location:** 70 miles from Denver. **Calendar:** Quarter, extensive summer session. **Full-time faculty:** 8 total. **Part-time faculty:** 25 total.

**Basis for selection.** Admissions based on high school diploma, GED, or ATB. 120 CPAt required for diploma or GED holders; 128 CPAt required for ATB candidates. 15 ACT or 700 SAT (exclusive of Writing) also accepted.

**2007-2008 Annual costs.** $298 per credit hour for all linear programs; $150 in required fees. Books/supplies: $1,025.

**Financial aid. Need-based:** Need-based aid available for part-time students. Work-study available nights and for part-time students.

**Application procedures. Admission:** No deadline. No application fee. Application must be submitted on paper. Admission notification on a rolling basis. **Financial aid:** No deadline. FAFSA, institutional form required. Applicants notified on a rolling basis starting 7/1.

**Academics. Special study options:** Distance learning, double major, dual enrollment of high school students, independent study, internships, liberal arts/career combination. **Credit/placement by examination:** AP, CLEP, institutional tests. **Support services:** Tutoring.

**Majors. Business:** Accounting, business admin. **Computer sciences:** General, LAN/WAN management, networking. **Health:** Medical assistant, medical secretary. **Legal studies:** Legal secretary, paralegal. **Protective services:** Criminal justice.

**Most popular majors.** Business/marketing 42%, computer/information sciences 15%, health sciences 27%, legal studies 16%.

**Computing on campus.** PC or laptop required. 174 workstations in library, computer center.

**Student life. Freshman orientation:** Mandatory. Preregistration for classes offered. **Activities:** Student newspaper.

**Student services.** Career counseling, student employment services, financial aid counseling, personal counseling, placement for graduates, veterans' counselor. **Transfer:** Pre-admission transcript evaluation for new students.

**Contact.** E-mail: afi@cci.edu
Phone: (719) 638-6580 Fax: (719) 574-4493
Don Webb, Director of Admissions, Everest College: Colorado Springs, 1815 Jet Wing Drive, Colorado Springs, CO 80916

## Front Range Community College
Westminster, Colorado
www.frontrange.edu                                   CB code: 4119

- Public 2-year community college
- Commuter campus in large city

**General.** Founded in 1968. Regionally accredited. Additional campuses in Brighton, Boulder County, and Larimer County. **Enrollment:** 12,537 degree-seeking undergraduates; 2,212 non-degree-seeking students. **Degrees:** 1,075 associate awarded. **ROTC:** Army, Air Force. **Location:** 12 miles from Denver. **Calendar:** Semester, limited summer session. **Full-time faculty:** 196 total; 2% have terminal degrees, 9% minority, 59% women. **Part-time faculty:** 795 total; 2% have terminal degrees, 6% minority, 57% women. **Class size:** 51% < 20, 49% 20-39, less than 1% 40-49. **Special facilities:** Observatory (Larimer campus), city libraries (Larimer and Westminster campuses). **Partnerships:** Formal partnerships with local workforce centers for career training or retraining.

**Student profile.** Among degree-seeking undergraduates, 75% enrolled in a transfer program, 25% enrolled in a vocational program, 4% already have a bachelor's degree or higher, 4,143 enrolled as first-time, first-year students, 1,494 transferred in from other institutions.

| | | | |
|---|---|---|---|
| Part-time: | 63% | Asian American: | 4% |
| Out-of-state: | 2% | Hispanic American: | 12% |
| Women: | 60% | Native American: | 1% |
| African American: | 1% | 25 or older: | 38% |

**Transfer out. Colleges most students transferred to 2007:** University of Northern Colorado, University of Colorado at Denver, University of Colorado at Boulder, Metropolitan State College, Colorado State University.

**Basis for selection.** Open admission.

**High school preparation.** 13 units recommended. Recommended units include English 4, mathematics 3, history 3, science 2 (laboratory 1).

**2007-2008 Annual costs.** Tuition/fees: $2,599; $11,002 out-of-state. Per-credit charge: $77 in-state; $357 out-of-state. In-state tuition based upon assumption of Colorado Oppurtunity Fund waiver of $89 per-credit-hour. Books/supplies: $1,198.

**2006-2007 Financial aid. Need-based:** 40% of total undergraduate aid awarded as scholarships/grants, 60% as loans/jobs. Need-based aid available for part-time students. Work-study available nights, weekends and for part-time students. **Non-need-based:** Scholarships awarded for academics, job skills, leadership, state residency.

**Application procedures. Admission:** No deadline. No application fee. Application may be submitted online. Admission notification on a rolling basis. **Financial aid:** Priority date 5/1; no closing date. FAFSA, institutional form required. Applicants notified on a rolling basis starting 7/1; must reply within 3 week(s) of notification.

**Academics. Special study options:** Cooperative education, cross-registration, distance learning, double major, dual enrollment of high school students, ESL, honors, independent study, internships, liberal arts/career combination, study abroad, teacher certification program, weekend college. License preparation in dental hygiene, nursing, paramedic, real estate. **Credit/placement by examination:** CLEP, institutional tests. 30 credit hours maximum toward associate degree. **Support services:** GED preparation and test center, learning center, remedial instruction, study skills assistance, tutoring.

**Majors. Agriculture:** Horticulture. **Business:** Accounting technology, administrative services, hospitality admin, management information systems, office management. **Communications technology:** Animation/special effects. **Conservation:** Wildlife. **Construction:** Masonry. **Engineering technology:** Architectural, drafting, electrical, heat/ac/refrig, manufacturing. **Family/consumer sciences:** Child care. **Foreign languages:** Sign language interpretation. **Health:** Dietician assistant, electroencephalograph technology, nursing (RN), office admin, veterinary technology/assistant. **Liberal arts:** Arts/sciences. **Mechanic/repair:** Automotive. **Production:** Machine shop technology, welding. **Visual/performing arts:** Interior design. **Other:** Applied technology.

**Most popular majors.** Business/marketing 8%, health sciences 24%, liberal arts 57%.

**Computing on campus.** 175 workstations in library, computer center. Online course registration, helpline available.

**Student life. Freshman orientation:** Available. Preregistration for classes offered. **Activities:** Jazz band, choral groups, drama, literary magazine, student government, student newspaper, Student Colorado Registry of Interpreters for the Deaf, Hispanic club, black student alliance.

**Student services.** Career counseling, student employment services, financial aid counseling, minority student services, on-campus daycare, personal counseling, placement for graduates, veterans' counselor, women's services. **Physically disabled:** Services for visually, speech, hearing impaired. **Transfer:** Transfer center, college fairs on campus for students transferring to 4-year colleges.

**Contact.** Phone: (303) 404-5414 Fax: (303) 404-5150
Yolonda Espinoza, Registrar, Front Range Community College, 3645 West 112th Avenue, Westminster, CO 80031

## Heritage College: Denver
**Denver, Colorado**
**www.heritage-education.com**

⬧ For-profit 2-year health science college
⬧ Very large city

**General.** Accredited by ACCSCT. **Calendar:** Continuous.

**Annual costs/financial aid.** Need-based financial aid available for full-time students.

**Contact.** Phone: (303) 477-7240
Director of Admissions, 12 Lakeside Lane, Denver, CO 80212-7413

## Institute of Business & Medical Careers
**Fort Collins, Colorado**
**www.ibmc.edu**                                    CB code: 3566

⬧ For-profit 2-year technical college
⬧ Residential campus in small city
⬧ Application essay, interview required

**General.** Accredited by ACICS. **Enrollment:** 365 degree-seeking undergraduates. **Degrees:** 88 associate awarded. **Location:** 60 miles from Denver, 45 miles from Cheyenne, WY. **Calendar:** Continuous. **Full-time faculty:** 20 total; 15% minority, 85% women. **Part-time faculty:** 55 total; 6% minority, 73% women.

**Transfer out. Colleges most students transferred to 2007:** Colorado Christian University, Front Range Community College, Aims Community College.

**Basis for selection.** Open admission, but selective for some programs. Institutional entrance exam required for placement. **Homeschooled:** State high school equivalency certificate required.

**2007-2008 Annual costs.** Tuition/fees: $12,375. Per-credit charge: $275. Books/supplies: $1,400.

**Application procedures. Admission:** No deadline. $75 fee. Admission notification on a rolling basis.

**Academics. Credit/placement by examination:** AP, CLEP, institutional tests. Up to 50% of total progam credits may be obtained through transfer or test out. **Support services:** Learning center, reduced course load, study skills assistance, tutoring.

**Majors. Business:** Business admin.

**Computing on campus.** 4 workstations in library, student center. Commuter students can connect to campus network. Wireless network available.

**Student life. Freshman orientation:** Available.

**Student services.** Career counseling, student employment services, financial aid counseling, placement for graduates. **Transfer:** Pre-admission transcript evaluation for new students.

**Contact.** E-mail: info@ibmc.edu
Phone: (970) 223-2669 Toll-free number: (800) 495-2669
Steven Steele, President of Operations, Institute of Business & Medical Careers, 1609 Oakridge Drive, Fort Collins, CO 80525

## IntelliTec College
**Colorado Springs, Colorado**
**www.intelliteccollege.com**                        CB code: 2500

⬧ For-profit 2-year technical college
⬧ Commuter campus in large city

**General.** Founded in 1965. Accredited by ACCSCT. **Enrollment:** 500 degree-seeking undergraduates. **Degrees:** 131 associate awarded. **Location:** 68 miles from Denver. **Calendar:** 6-week cycle. Extensive summer session. **Full-time faculty:** 14 total; 7% women. **Part-time faculty:** 10 total; 20% women.

**Student profile.** Among degree-seeking undergraduates, 100% enrolled in a vocational program.

**Transfer out. Colleges most students transferred to 2007:** Pikes Peak Community College, Denver Technical College.

**Basis for selection.** Open admission.

**2007-2008 Annual costs.** Books/supplies: $1,200.

**Financial aid.** All financial aid based on need. Need-based aid available for part-time students. Work-study available nights.

**Application procedures. Admission:** No deadline. No application fee. Admission notification on a rolling basis. **Financial aid:** No deadline. FAFSA, institutional form required. Applicants notified on a rolling basis.

**Academics. Special study options:** Accelerated study, liberal arts/career combination. **Credit/placement by examination:** AP, CLEP. Maximum 50% of required credits may be awarded for prior work and/or life experience. Pre-admission interview required for placement into program. **Support services:** Learning center, tutoring.

**Majors. Computer sciences:** General, computer science, systems analysis. **Engineering technology:** Drafting. **Mechanic/repair:** Electronics/electrical, heating/ac/refrig.

**Computing on campus.** 125 workstations in library, computer center. Online library, repair service available.

**Student life. Freshman orientation:** Available. Preregistration for classes offered. **Activities:** Student newspaper.

**Student services.** Adult student services, career counseling, student employment services, financial aid counseling, personal counseling, placement for graduates, veterans' counselor. **Transfer:** Pre-admission transcript evaluation for new students.

**Contact.** E-mail: admcs@intelliteccollege.com
Phone: (719) 632-7626 Toll-free number: (800) 748-2282
Fax: (719) 632-7451
Michael Schranz, Director of Admissions, IntelliTec College, 2315 East Pikes Peak Avenue, Colorado Springs, CO 80909

## IntelliTec College: Grand Junction
**Grand Junction, Colorado**
**www.intelliteccollege.edu**          CB code: 2489

◆ For-profit 2-year technical college
◆ Commuter campus in small city
◆ Interview required

**General.** Accredited by ACCSCT. **Enrollment:** 250 degree-seeking undergraduates. **Degrees:** 104 associate awarded. **Location:** 250 miles from Denver, 300 miles from Salt Lake City. **Calendar:** Continuous, extensive summer session. **Full-time faculty:** 20 total. **Part-time faculty:** 10 total.

**Basis for selection.** Open admission.

**2007-2008 Annual costs.** Tuition/fees: $17,000. Books/supplies: $1,500.

**Financial aid.** All financial aid based on need.

**Application procedures. Admission:** No deadline. No application fee. Admission notification on a rolling basis. **Financial aid:** No deadline. FAFSA required. Applicants notified on a rolling basis.

**Academics. Special study options:** Cooperative education. **Credit/placement by examination:** CLEP. **Support services:** Tutoring.

**Majors. Business:** Accounting/business management. **Engineering:** Electrical. **Engineering technology:** Architectural drafting, computer hardware, mechanical drafting, software. **Health:** Medical assistant. **Mechanic/repair:** Automotive.

**Computing on campus.** 64 workstations in library, computer center.

**Student services.** Career counseling, student employment services, on-campus daycare, placement for graduates.

**Contact.** Phone: (970) 245-8101 Fax: (970) 243-8074
Carol Earnshaw, Director of Admissions, IntelliTec College: Grand Junction, 772 Horizon Drive, Grand Junction, CO 81506

## Kaplan College: Denver
**Thornton, Colorado**
**www.kaplancollege.com**

◆ For-profit 2-year technical and career college
◆ Very large city

**General.** Accredited by ACCSCT. **Enrollment:** 210 degree-seeking undergraduates. **Degrees:** 25 associate awarded. **Calendar:** Quarter, extensive summer session.

**Basis for selection.** Open admission, but selective for some programs.

**Application procedures. Admission:** No deadline. $20 fee. **Financial aid:** FAFSA required.

**Academics.** Paralegal program is ABA certified. **Special study options:** Accelerated study, independent study. **Credit/placement by examination:** CLEP. **Support services:** GED preparation, learning center, study skills assistance, tutoring.

**Majors. Legal studies:** Paralegal. **Protective services:** Law enforcement admin.

**Computing on campus.** 50 workstations in library, computer center.

**Student life. Freshman orientation:** Mandatory. Preregistration for classes offered.

**Student services.** Alcohol/substance abuse counseling, personal counseling, women's services.

**Contact.** Phone: (303) 295-0550 Toll-free number: (800) 848-0550
Fax: (303) 295-0102
Kristine Conlin, Executive Director, Kaplan College: Denver, 500 East 84th Avenue, Suite W-200, Thornton, CO 80229

## Lamar Community College
**Lamar, Colorado**
**www.lamarcc.edu**          CB code: 4382

◆ Public 2-year community college
◆ Commuter campus in large town

**General.** Founded in 1937. Regionally accredited. **Enrollment:** 500 degree-seeking undergraduates. **Degrees:** 81 associate awarded. **Location:** 117 miles from Pueblo. **Calendar:** Semester, limited summer session. **Full-time faculty:** 30 total. **Part-time faculty:** 60 total.

**Student profile.**

| | | | |
|---|---|---|---|
| Out-of-state: | 10% | Live on campus: | 50% |
| 25 or older: | 75% | | |

**Basis for selection.** Open admission, but selective for some programs. Admission criteria for horse training management based on riding skills; admission to nursing based on test scores. Interview required of horse training and management, practical nursing majors.

**2007-2008 Annual costs.** Tuition/fees: $2,639; $5,309 out-of-state. Per-credit charge: $77 in-state; $166 out-of-state. In-state tuition based upon assumption of Colorado Oppurtunity Fund waiver of $89 per-credit-hour. Room/board: $4,757. Books/supplies: $1,163. Personal expenses: $420.

**Financial aid. Need-based:** Need-based aid available for part-time students.

**Application procedures. Admission:** No deadline. No application fee. Admission notification on a rolling basis. Applicants to horse training and management and LPN nursing program encouraged to apply early. **Financial aid:** Priority date 4/1; no closing date. FAFSA, institutional form required. Applicants notified on a rolling basis starting 7/1.

**Academics. Special study options:** Cooperative education, dual enrollment of high school students, ESL, independent study, internships, student-designed major. **Credit/placement by examination:** CLEP, institutional tests. 16 credit hours maximum toward associate degree. **Support services:** Learning center, pre-admission summer program, remedial instruction, tutoring.

**Majors. Agriculture:** Agronomy, animal sciences, business, equestrian studies, range science. **Biology:** General. **Business:** General, accounting, administrative services, banking/financial services, business admin, office management. **Communications:** General. **Computer sciences:** Computer science, information systems. **Education:** General. **English:** English lit. **Family/consumer sciences:** Child care. **Health:** Medical secretary, predental, prepharmacy, preveterinary. **History:** General. **Legal studies:** Legal secretary, prelaw. **Liberal arts:** Arts/sciences. **Math:** General. **Psychology:** General. **Public administration:** Social work. **Social sciences:** General. **Visual/performing arts:** Art.

**Computing on campus.** 65 workstations in dormitories, library, computer center.

**Student life. Policies:** All single freshmen under age 21 not living with parent, guardian, or relatives must live in dormitory. **Housing:** Guaranteed on-campus for freshmen. Coed dorms, single-sex dorms available. **Activities:** Choral groups, dance, drama, student government, student newspaper,

Christian athletes, horse and rodeo club, Kosmetiques, LPN association, Phi Beta Lambda, nontraditional students club.

**Athletics.** NJCAA. **Intercollegiate:** Baseball M, basketball M, volleyball W. **Intramural:** Bowling, golf, softball, tennis, volleyball.

**Student services.** Career counseling, student employment services, personal counseling. **Transfer:** Transfer adviser, college fairs on campus for students transferring to 4-year colleges.

**Contact.**  E-mail: admissions@lamarcc.edu
Phone: (719) 336-1590
Angela Woodward, Director of Admissions, Lamar Community College, 2401 South Main Street, Lamar, CO 81052-3999

---

## Lincoln College of Technology: Denver
**Denver, Colorado**
www.dadc.com                    CB code: 3133

- For-profit 2-year technical college
- Very large city

**General.** Accredited by ACCSCT. **Calendar:** Continuous.

**Annual costs/financial aid.** 18-month automotive technology program $16,650. 19.5-month diesel technology program $18,000. One time $75 uniform cost required of all students. Books/supplies: $360. Personal expenses: $1,967.

**Contact.**  Phone: (303) 722-5724
Director of Admissions, 460 South Lipan Street, Denver, CO 80223-9366

---

## Morgan Community College
**Fort Morgan, Colorado**
www.morgancc.edu                CB code: 0444

- Public 2-year community college
- Commuter campus in large town

**General.** Founded in 1967. Regionally accredited. **Enrollment:** 528 degree-seeking undergraduates. **Degrees:** 112 associate awarded. **Location:** 81 miles from Denver. **Calendar:** Semester, limited summer session. **Full-time faculty:** 35 total. **Part-time faculty:** 107 total. **Class size:** 69% < 20, 31% 20-39.

**Student profile.**

| | | | |
|---|---|---|---|
| Out-of-state: | 3% | 25 or older: | 46% |

**Basis for selection.** Open admission, but selective for some programs. Special requirements for physical therapist assistant, occupational therapy assistant, and nursing programs. Interview required of allied health majors.

**2007-2008 Annual costs.** Tuition/fees: $2,479; $10,882 out-of-state. Per-credit charge: $77 in-state; $357 out-of-state. In-state tuition based upon assumption of Colorado Oppurtunity Fund waiver of $89 per-credit-hour. Books/supplies: $675.

**2007-2008 Financial aid. Need-based:** 68% of total undergraduate aid awarded as scholarships/grants, 32% as loans/jobs. Need-based aid available for part-time students. Work-study available nights, weekends and for part-time students.

**Application procedures. Admission:** No deadline. No application fee. Admission notification on a rolling basis. **Financial aid:** Priority date 6/1; no closing date. FAFSA required. Applicants notified on a rolling basis.

**Academics. Special study options:** Distance learning, double major, dual enrollment of high school students, ESL, independent study, internships, liberal arts/career combination, student-designed major, teacher certification program, weekend college. **Credit/placement by examination:** AP, CLEP, institutional tests. 31 credit hours maximum toward associate degree. **Support services:** GED preparation and test center, learning center, reduced course load, remedial instruction, study skills assistance, tutoring.

**Majors. Business:** General, accounting. **Computer sciences:** Webmaster. **Education:** General. **Health:** Nursing (RN), occupational therapy assistant, physical therapy assistant. **Interdisciplinary:** Biological/physical sciences. **Liberal arts:** Arts/sciences. **Mechanic/repair:** Auto body, automotive. **Visual/performing arts:** Art. **Other:** Agricultural business planning and financial records.

---

**Computing on campus.** 50 workstations in library, computer center, student center. Commuter students can connect to campus network. Online course registration available.

**Student life. Activities:** Student newspaper, TV station, occupational therapy association, vocational industrial collusion association, Phi Theta Kappa, science club, history club, student nursing association, Phi Beta Lambda, health occupation student organization, physical therapy association.

**Student services.** Career counseling. **Transfer:** Pre-admission transcript evaluation for new students.

**Contact.**  Phone: (970) 542-3156 Fax: (970) 867-6608
Sally Nestor, Director of Admissions, Morgan Community College, 920 Barlow Road, Fort Morgan, CO 80701

---

## Northeastern Junior College
**Sterling, Colorado**
www.njc.edu                     CB code: 4537

- Public 2-year junior college
- Commuter campus in large town

**General.** Founded in 1941. Regionally accredited. **Enrollment:** 1,082 degree-seeking undergraduates. **Degrees:** 149 associate awarded. **Location:** 125 miles from Denver. **Calendar:** Semester, limited summer session. **Full-time faculty:** 51 total; 4% have terminal degrees, 2% minority, 55% women. **Part-time faculty:** 75 total; 1% minority, 73% women. **Class size:** 79% < 20, 20% 20-39, less than 1% 40-49, less than 1% 50-99. **Special facilities:** Equine center, greenhouse, college farm.

**Student profile.** Among degree-seeking undergraduates, 82% enrolled in a transfer program, 13% enrolled in a vocational program, 444 enrolled as first-time, first-year students, 58 transferred in from other institutions.

| | | | |
|---|---|---|---|
| Part-time: | 23% | Hispanic American: | 10% |
| Out-of-state: | 8% | Native American: | 1% |
| Women: | 54% | 25 or older: | 20% |
| African American: | 8% | Live on campus: | 40% |

**Transfer out. Colleges most students transferred to 2007:** Colorado State University, University of Northern Colorado, University of Colorado, University of Wyoming, Oklahoma State University.

**Basis for selection.** Open admission, but selective for some programs. Qualifications for programs with limited space, such as licensed practical nursing program, set individually by department. Cooperative admission program with Colorado State University. SAT or ACT required for some technical vocational programs. Assessment required by ACCUPLACER, minimum ACT or SAT scores in subject areas, or proof of previous successful college experience. **Adult students:** Accuplacer required.

**2007-2008 Annual costs.** Tuition/fees: $2,909; $5,579 out-of-state. Per-credit charge: $77 in-state; $166 out-of-state. In-state tuition based upon assumption of Colorado Oppurtunity Fund waiver of $89 per-credit-hour. Room/board: $5,316. Books/supplies: $1,698. Personal expenses: $2,997.

**2006-2007 Financial aid. Need-based:** 58% of total undergraduate aid awarded as scholarships/grants, 42% as loans/jobs. Need-based aid available for part-time students. **Non-need-based:** Scholarships awarded for academics, alumni affiliation, art, athletics, job skills, leadership, music/drama, state residency. **Additional information:** Need-based financial aid available to part-time students taking 6 credits or more per semester.

**Application procedures. Admission:** No deadline. No application fee. Application may be submitted online. Admission notification on a rolling basis. **Financial aid:** Priority date 3/1; no closing date. FAFSA, institutional form required. Applicants notified on a rolling basis starting 4/15; must reply within 3 week(s) of notification.

**Academics. Special study options:** Cooperative education, distance learning, dual enrollment of high school students, ESL, honors, independent study, internships. License preparation in nursing. **Credit/placement by examination:** AP, CLEP, institutional tests. 45 credit hours maximum toward associate degree. **Support services:** GED preparation and test center, learning center, remedial instruction, study skills assistance, tutoring.

**Majors. Agriculture:** Agribusiness operations, farm/ranch, horticulture, mechanization, ornamental horticulture, production. **Business:** Accounting technology, management information systems. **Education:** Early childhood. **Family/consumer sciences:** Child development. **Health:** EMT paramedic, nursing (RN). **Liberal arts:** Arts/sciences. **Mechanic/repair:** Automotive, diesel. **Protective services:** Law enforcement admin.

**Most popular majors.** Agriculture 34%, business/marketing 10%, liberal arts 51%.

**Computing on campus.** 302 workstations in library, computer center, student center. Dormitories wired for high-speed internet access. Online course registration, helpline, repair service available.

**Student life. Freshman orientation:** Mandatory. Preregistration for classes offered. **Housing:** Coed dorms, single-sex dorms, substance-free housing available. $125 fully refundable deposit. Honors house available. **Activities:** Bands, choral groups, dance, drama, literary magazine, music ensembles, musical theater, student government, student newspaper, campus Christian fellowship.

**Athletics.** NJCAA. **Intercollegiate:** Baseball M, basketball, rodeo, volleyball W. **Intramural:** Badminton, basketball, football (non-tackle) M, tennis, volleyball. **Team name:** Plainswomen, Plainsmen.

**Student services.** Adult student services, alcohol/substance abuse counseling, career counseling, student employment services, financial aid counseling, health services, on-campus daycare, personal counseling, placement for graduates, veterans' counselor. **Physically disabled:** Services for hearing impaired. **Transfer:** Pre-admission transcript evaluation for new students. Transfer adviser, college fairs on campus for students transferring to 4-year colleges.

**Contact.** E-mail: tina.joyce@njc.edu
Phone: (970) 521-6600 Toll-free number: (800) 626-4367 ext. 7000
Fax: (970) 521-6715
Tina Joyce, Director of Admissions, Northeastern Junior College, 100 College Avenue, Sterling, CO 80751

## Otero Junior College
### La Junta, Colorado
www.ojc.edu                                    CB code: 4588

- Public 2-year community and junior college
- Commuter campus in small town

**General.** Founded in 1941. Regionally accredited. **Enrollment:** 1,250 degree-seeking undergraduates. **Degrees:** 137 associate awarded. **Location:** 60 miles from Pueblo, 100 miles from Colorado Springs. **Calendar:** Semester, limited summer session. **Full-time faculty:** 33 total. **Part-time faculty:** 14 total. **Class size:** 74% < 20, 21% 20-39, 2% 40-49, 3% 50-99. **Special facilities:** Koshare Indian kiva museum.

**Student profile.**

| | | | |
|---|---|---|---|
| Out-of-state: | 7% | Live on campus: | 10% |
| 25 or older: | 33% | | |

**Basis for selection.** Open admission, but selective for some programs. Special admission requirements for nursing program.

**2007-2008 Annual costs.** Tuition/fees: $2,509; $5,179 out-of-state. Per-credit charge: $77 in-state; $166 out-of-state. In-state tuition based upon assumption of Colorado Opportunity Fund waiver of $89 per-credit-hour. Room/board: $4,692. Books/supplies: $1,100. Personal expenses: $2,500.

**Financial aid. Need-based:** Need-based aid available for part-time students. Work-study available nights, weekends and for part-time students. **Non-need-based:** Scholarships awarded for academics, athletics, state residency.

**Application procedures. Admission:** No deadline. No application fee. Admission notification on a rolling basis. **Financial aid:** Priority date 4/15; no closing date. FAFSA required. Applicants notified on a rolling basis starting 4/15; must reply within 2 week(s) of notification.

**Academics. Special study options:** Dual enrollment of high school students. Bachelor's degree programs available on campus. **Credit/placement by examination:** AP, CLEP, institutional tests. 30 credit hours maximum toward associate degree. **Support services:** GED preparation and test center, learning center, reduced course load, remedial instruction, study skills assistance, tutoring.

**Majors. Biology:** General. **Business:** Administrative services, business admin. **Computer sciences:** General. **Education:** General, early childhood, elementary, secondary, teacher assistance. **Health:** Medical secretary, nursing (RN), pharmacy assistant, predental, premedicine, prepharmacy, preveterinary, veterinary technology/assistant. **History:** General. **Legal studies:** Legal secretary, prelaw. **Liberal arts:** Arts/sciences. **Math:** General. **Physical sciences:** Chemistry. **Psychology:** General. **Social sciences:** Political science. **Visual/performing arts:** Dramatic.

**Computing on campus.** 100 workstations in library, computer center, student center. Dormitories linked to campus network.

**Student life. Freshman orientation:** Available. Preregistration for classes offered. **Housing:** Single-sex dorms available. **Activities:** Dance, drama, student government.

**Athletics.** NJCAA. **Intercollegiate:** Baseball M, basketball, golf, softball W, volleyball W. **Intramural:** Basketball, volleyball. **Team name:** Rattlers.

**Student services.** Career counseling, student employment services, on-campus daycare, personal counseling, placement for graduates, veterans' counselor. **Physically disabled:** Services for visually, hearing impaired. **Transfer:** Pre-admission transcript evaluation for new students. Transfer adviser, college fairs on campus for students transferring to 4-year colleges.

**Contact.** E-mail: jan.schiro@ojc.edu
Phone: (719) 384-6831 Fax: (719) 384-6933
Jan Schiro, Admissions Coordinator, Otero Junior College, 1802 Colorado Avenue, La Junta, CO 81050

## Pikes Peak Community College
### Colorado Springs, Colorado
www.ppcc.edu                                   CB code: 4291

- Public 2-year community college
- Commuter campus in large city

**General.** Founded in 1967. Regionally accredited. **Enrollment:** 10,797 degree-seeking undergraduates; 702 non-degree-seeking students. **Degrees:** 646 associate awarded. **Location:** 70 miles from Denver. **Calendar:** Semester, extensive summer session. **Full-time faculty:** 158 total. **Part-time faculty:** 508 total. **Class size:** 59% < 20, 41% 20-39, less than 1% 40-49, less than 1% 50-99, less than 1% >100. **Partnerships:** Formal partnership with Cheyenne Mountain Zoo.

**Student profile.** Among degree-seeking undergraduates, 2,614 enrolled as first-time, first-year students.

| | | | |
|---|---|---|---|
| Part-time: | 63% | Asian American: | 4% |
| Out-of-state: | 17% | Hispanic American: | 13% |
| Women: | 60% | Native American: | 1% |
| African American: | 9% | 25 or older: | 49% |

**Basis for selection.** Open admission.

**2007-2008 Annual costs.** Tuition/fees: $2,578; $10,981 out-of-state. Per-credit charge: $77 in-state; $357 out-of-state. In-state tuition eligible for Colorado Oppurtunity Fund (COF) waiver, currently $89 per credit hour. Books/supplies: $1,163. Personal expenses: $2,547.

**Financial aid. Need-based:** Need-based aid available for part-time students. Work-study available nights and for part-time students.

**Application procedures. Admission:** No deadline. No application fee. Application may be submitted online. Admission notification on a rolling basis. **Financial aid:** Priority date 7/1; no closing date. FAFSA required. Applicants notified on a rolling basis starting 8/1; must reply within 2 week(s) of notification.

**Academics. Special study options:** Cooperative education, distance learning, double major, dual enrollment of high school students, ESL, external degree, independent study, internships, study abroad, weekend college. License preparation in nursing, real estate. **Credit/placement by examination:** CLEP, IB, institutional tests. **Support services:** GED test center, learning center, remedial instruction, study skills assistance, tutoring, writing center.

**Majors. Biology:** General. **Business:** General, accounting, accounting technology, business admin, executive assistant, financial planning, international, management information systems, marketing. **Communications technology:** Graphics, radio/tv. **Computer sciences:** General, computer science, LAN/WAN management, networking. **Conservation:** Management/policy. **Construction:** Maintenance. **Engineering technology:** Architectural, CAD/CADD, drafting, electrical, robotics. **English:** American lit, English lit, technical writing. **Family/consumer sciences:** Child development. **Foreign languages:** General, sign language interpretation. **Health:** Dental assistant, EMT paramedic, mental health services, nursing (RN), office admin, premedicine. **History:** General. **Legal studies:** Paralegal. **Liberal arts:** Arts/sciences, humanities. **Math:** General. **Mechanic/repair:** Auto body, automotive. **Personal/culinary services:** Culinary arts. **Philosophy/religion:** Philosophy. **Physical sciences:** Chemistry, geology, physics. **Production:** Machine shop technology, welding. **Protective services:** Emergency management/homeland security, fire safety technology, firefighting, law enforcement admin. **Social sciences:** Anthropology, geography, political science, sociology. **Visual/performing arts:** Dance, dramatic, interior design, music, studio arts.

**Most popular majors.** Health sciences 11%, liberal arts 53%, security/protective services 13%.

**Computing on campus.** 180 workstations in library, computer center. Commuter students can connect to campus network. Online course registration, wireless network available.

**Student life. Freshman orientation:** Available. **Policies:** Dormitory housing available through agreement with the University of Colorado, Colorado Springs. **Activities:** Choral groups, dance, drama, radio station, student government, student newspaper, Phi Theta Kappa.

**Athletics. Team name:** Aardvarks.

**Student services.** Adult student services, alcohol/substance abuse counseling, career counseling, services for economically disadvantaged, student employment services, financial aid counseling, on-campus daycare, personal counseling, placement for graduates, veterans' counselor. **Physically disabled:** Services for visually, speech, hearing impaired. **Learning disabled:** Comprehensive services available. **Transfer:** Re-entry adviser, pre-admission transcript evaluation for new students. Transfer adviser, college fairs on campus for students transferring to 4-year colleges.

**Contact.** E-mail: admissions@ppcc.edu
Phone: (719) 502-3000 Toll-free number: (800) 456-6847
Steve Ochsner, Admissions, Pikes Peak Community College, 5675 South Academy Boulevard, Colorado Springs, CO 80906-5498

## Pueblo Community College
**Pueblo, Colorado**
www.pueblocc.edu                          CB code: 4634

- Public 2-year community college
- Commuter campus in small city

**General.** Founded in 1933. Regionally accredited. **Enrollment:** 4,150 degree-seeking undergraduates. **Degrees:** 532 associate awarded. **Location:** 50 miles from Colorado Springs, 100 miles from Denver. **Calendar:** Semester, extensive summer session. **Full-time faculty:** 75 total. **Part-time faculty:** 300 total. **Special facilities:** Advanced technology centers.

**Basis for selection.** Open admission, but selective for some programs. Admission to health programs based on GPA, high school courses, and test scores. ACT required of dental hygiene applicants; score report by May 1. Interview required of allied health majors.

**2007-2008 Annual costs.** Tuition/fees: $2,578; $10,981 out-of-state. Per-credit charge: $77 in-state; $357 out-of-state. In-state tuition based upon assumption of Colorado Oppurtunity Fund waiver of $89 per-credit-hour. Books/supplies: $1,162. Personal expenses: $1,600.

**Financial aid. Need-based:** Need-based aid available for part-time students. Work-study available for part-time students. **Non-need-based:** Scholarships awarded for academics, state residency.

**Application procedures. Admission:** Priority date 8/1; no deadline. No application fee. Application may be submitted online. Admission notification on a rolling basis. Foreign applicants must pay for 1 full academic year before acceptance. Application closing date for allied health programs, April 1. **Financial aid:** Priority date 3/15; no closing date. FAFSA, institutional form required. Applicants notified on a rolling basis starting 4/15.

**Academics. Special study options:** Accelerated study, cooperative education, distance learning, double major, dual enrollment of high school students, honors, independent study, internships, liberal arts/career combination, weekend college. License preparation in aviation, dental hygiene, nursing, occupational therapy, paramedic, physical therapy, radiology, real estate. **Credit/placement by examination:** AP, CLEP, institutional tests. All but 15 hours residence requirement for either certificate or associate degree may be from credit for prior learning. **Support services:** GED preparation and test center, learning center, reduced course load, remedial instruction, study skills assistance, tutoring, writing center.

**Majors. Business:** Accounting, administrative services, banking/financial services, business admin, hospitality admin, office technology, office/clerical, tourism promotion, tourism/travel. **Communications:** Broadcast journalism. **Computer sciences:** General, computer graphics. **Education:** Early childhood. **Engineering technology:** Architectural, civil, drafting, electrical, manufacturing. **Family/consumer sciences:** Child care, institutional food production. **Health:** Dental assistant, dental hygiene, EMT paramedic, medical radiologic technology/radiation therapy, medical secretary, nursing (RN), occupational therapy assistant, optician, physical therapy assistant, radiologic technology/medical imaging, respiratory therapy assistant, respiratory therapy technology, sonography. **Legal studies:** Legal secretary, paralegal. **Liberal arts:** Arts/sciences, library assistant. **Mechanic/repair:** Auto body,

automotive, industrial, watch/jewelry. **Personal/culinary services:** Culinary arts. **Production:** Machine tool, welding. **Protective services:** Corrections, law enforcement admin, police science. **Visual/performing arts:** Design, metal/jewelry. **Other:** Digital media, Healthcare support technician.

**Computing on campus.** Online course registration, helpline available.

**Student life. Freshman orientation:** Available. **Activities:** Choral groups, drama, radio station, student government, student newspaper, TV station.

**Athletics. Team name:** Panthers.

**Student services.** Adult student services, career counseling, student employment services, financial aid counseling, on-campus daycare, personal counseling, placement for graduates, veterans' counselor. **Physically disabled:** Services for visually, speech, hearing impaired. **Transfer:** Transfer center, transfer adviser, college fairs on campus for students transferring to 4-year colleges.

**Contact.** E-mail: admissions@pueblocc.edu
Phone: (719) 549-3010 Toll-free number: (888) 642-6017
Fax: (719) 549-3012
Mary Santoro, Director of Admissions and Records, Pueblo Community College, 900 West Orman Avenue, Pueblo, CO 81004-1499

## Red Rocks Community College
**Lakewood, Colorado**
www.rrcc.edu                          CB code: 4130

- Public 2-year community college
- Commuter campus in small city

**General.** Founded in 1969. Regionally accredited. **Enrollment:** 5,065 degree-seeking undergraduates; 1,662 non-degree-seeking students. **Degrees:** 423 associate awarded. **ROTC:** Army. **Location:** 10 miles from Denver. **Calendar:** Semester, extensive summer session. **Full-time faculty:** 59 total; 20% have terminal degrees, 7% minority, 59% women. **Part-time faculty:** 355 total; 6% minority, 59% women. **Class size:** 70% < 20, 30% 20-39, less than 1% 50-99. **Partnerships:** Formal partnerships with Coors, Microsoft, Apple, Oracle.

**Student profile.** Among degree-seeking undergraduates, 1,865 enrolled as first-time, first-year students, 192 transferred in from other institutions.

| | | | |
|---|---|---|---|
| Part-time: | 65% | Asian American: | 3% |
| Out-of-state: | 9% | Hispanic American: | 12% |
| Women: | 51% | Native American: | 2% |
| African American: | 2% | 25 or older: | 52% |

**Transfer out. Colleges most students transferred to 2007:** Metropolitan State College of Denver, Regis, Colorado School of Mines, University of Colorado at Boulder, Colorado State University.

**Basis for selection.** Open admission. Degree-seeking students can fulfill assessment requirement by providing test scores.

**2007-2008 Annual costs.** Tuition/fees: $2,587; $10,990 out-of-state. Per-credit charge: $77 in-state; $357 out-of-state. In-state tuition based upon assumption of Colorado Oppurtunity Fund waiver of $89 per-credit-hour. Books/supplies: $1,698. Personal expenses: $2,853.

**Financial aid. Need-based:** Need-based aid available for part-time students. Work-study available nights, weekends and for part-time students.

**Application procedures. Admission:** No deadline. No application fee. Application may be submitted online. Admission notification on a rolling basis. **Financial aid:** Priority date 4/1; no closing date. FAFSA, institutional form required. Applicants notified on a rolling basis starting 6/1; must reply within 2 week(s) of notification.

**Academics.** Students in advanced ESL classes may begin some college level courses early. Scholarships offered for outstanding ESL performance when funds are available. **Special study options:** Accelerated study, cross-registration, distance learning, dual enrollment of high school students, ESL, honors, independent study, internships, liberal arts/career combination, student-designed major, study abroad, teacher certification program, weekend college. License preparation in paramedic, radiology, real estate. **Credit/placement by examination:** AP, CLEP, IB, institutional tests. 45 credit hours maximum toward associate degree. **Support services:** GED preparation and test center, learning center, reduced course load, remedial instruction, study skills assistance, tutoring, writing center.

**Majors. Biology:** General, biotechnology. **Business:** Accounting technology, administrative services, banking/financial services, management information systems, marketing, office technology, real estate. **Communications**

technology: Animation/special effects. **Conservation:** Forest technology. **Construction:** General, carpentry, electrician, masonry, plumbing. **Education:** Teacher assistance. **Engineering technology:** Drafting, electrical, heat/ac/refrig, industrial, manufacturing, surveying, water quality. **English:** English lit. **Family/consumer sciences:** Child development. **Foreign languages:** French, German, Spanish. **Health:** EMT paramedic, nursing (RN), office admin, radiologic technology/medical imaging, sonography. **Liberal arts:** Arts/sciences. **Mechanic/repair:** Auto body, automotive. **Personal/culinary services:** Chef training. **Production:** Machine shop technology, welding, woodworking. **Protective services:** Emergency management/homeland security, fire safety technology, law enforcement admin. **Visual/performing arts:** Cinematography, theater design. **Other:** Applied technology, Business-interdisciplinary.

**Most popular majors.** Health sciences 8%, liberal arts 53%, security/protective services 18%, trade and industry 7%.

**Computing on campus.** 175 workstations in library, computer center, student center. Online course registration, online library, wireless network available.

**Student life. Freshman orientation:** Available. **Activities:** Choral groups, dance, drama, literary magazine, musical theater, student government, student newspaper, Phi Theta Kappa, environment club, international club.

**Athletics.** NJCAA.

**Student services.** Adult student services, career counseling, student employment services, health services, on-campus daycare, personal counseling, placement for graduates, veterans' counselor. **Physically disabled:** Services for visually, speech, hearing impaired. **Transfer:** Transfer adviser, college fairs on campus for students transferring to 4-year colleges.

**Contact.** E-mail: admissions@rrcc.edu
Phone: (303) 914-6351 Fax: (303) 989-6919
Dean Rathe, Director of Enrollment Services, Red Rocks Community College, 13300 West Sixth Avenue, Lakewood, CO 80228-1255

## Redstone College
### Broomfield, Colorado
www.redstonecollege.com          CB code: 2230

◆ For-profit 2-year technical college
◆ Commuter campus in small city

**General.** Accredited by ACCSCT. **Enrollment:** 535 degree-seeking undergraduates. **Degrees:** 231 associate awarded. **Location:** 15 miles from Denver and Boulder. **Calendar:** Continuous. **Full-time faculty:** 22 total. **Part-time faculty:** 6 total.

**Basis for selection.** Open admission.

**2007-2008 Annual costs.** Tuition for entire associate degree ranges from $13,239 to $32,378 depending on program of study.

**Financial aid.** All financial aid based on need.

**Application procedures. Admission:** No deadline. $100 fee. Admission notification on a rolling basis. **Financial aid:** No deadline. FAFSA required. Applicants notified on a rolling basis; must reply within 2 week(s) of notification.

**Academics. Special study options:** License preparation in aviation. **Credit/placement by examination:** CLEP. **Support services:** Learning center, tutoring.

**Majors. Mechanic/repair:** Aircraft, electronics/electrical.

**Computing on campus.** 8 workstations in computer center.

**Student life. Housing:** Apartments available.

**Student services.** Career counseling, student employment services, placement for graduates, veterans' counselor.

**Contact.** Phone: (303) 466-1714 Toll-free number: (800) 460-0592
Fax: (303) 469-3797
Cate Clark, Director of Admissions, Redstone College, 10851 West 120th Avenue, Broomfield, CO 80021-3401

## Remington College: Colorado Springs
### Colorado Springs, Colorado
www.remingtoncollege.com          CB code: 3565

◆ For-profit 2-year technical college
◆ Commuter campus in very large city
◆ Interview required

**General.** Accredited by ACICS. **Enrollment:** 175 degree-seeking undergraduates. **Degrees:** 16 bachelor's, 28 associate awarded. **Location:** 60 miles from Denver. **Calendar:** Quarter, extensive summer session. **Full-time faculty:** 5 total; 60% women. **Part-time faculty:** 15 total; 20% have terminal degrees, 7% minority, 40% women. **Class size:** 100% < 20.

**Basis for selection.** Open admission, but selective for some programs. Non-GED or HS programs applicants required to pass Wonderlic assessment.

**2007-2008 Annual costs.** Tuition varies by program and ranges from $13,000 to $13,860.

**Financial aid.** All financial aid based on need. Need-based aid available for part-time students.

**Application procedures. Admission:** No deadline. $50 fee. Admission notification on a rolling basis. **Financial aid:** No deadline. FAFSA required. Applicants notified on a rolling basis; must reply within 3 week(s) of notification.

**Academics. Special study options:** Accelerated study. Bachelor's degree programs available on campus. **Credit/placement by examination:** AP, CLEP. **Support services:** Tutoring.

**Majors. Computer sciences:** System admin. **Protective services:** Criminal justice.

**Computing on campus.** 34 workstations in library, computer center. Online library, helpline, repair service available.

**Student life. Freshman orientation:** Mandatory. Preregistration for classes offered.

**Student services.** Alcohol/substance abuse counseling, career counseling, student employment services, financial aid counseling, personal counseling, placement for graduates, veterans' counselor. **Transfer:** Pre-admission transcript evaluation for new students.

**Contact.** E-mail: Larry.schafer@remingtoncollege.edu
Phone: (719) 532-1234 Toll-free number: (866) 803-0808
Fax: (719) 264-1234
Larry Schafer, Director of Recruitment, Remington College: Colorado Springs, 6050 Erin Park Drive, Colorado Springs, CO 80918

## Trinidad State Junior College
### Trinidad, Colorado
www.trinidadstate.edu          CB code: 4821

◆ Public 2-year community and junior college
◆ Commuter campus in small town

**General.** Founded in 1925. Regionally accredited. **Enrollment:** 1,276 degree-seeking undergraduates. **Degrees:** 199 associate awarded. **Location:** 90 miles from Pueblo. **Calendar:** Semester, limited summer session. **Full-time faculty:** 37 total; 11% have terminal degrees, 57% women. **Part-time faculty:** 117 total; 5% have terminal degrees, 58% women. **Class size:** 96% < 20, 4% 20-39, less than 1% 50-99. **Special facilities:** Museum of anthropology and geology, gunsmithing laboratory, gun range.

**Student profile.**

| | | | |
|---|---|---|---|
| Out-of-state: | 13% | Live on campus: | 30% |
| 25 or older: | 57% | | |

**Transfer out. Colleges most students transferred to 2007:** Colorado State University, Pueblo, Adams State College, Colorado State University, Northern Colorado University.

**Basis for selection.** Open admission, but selective for some programs. Special requirements for nursing program. Interview recommended for nursing majors.

**2007-2008 Annual costs.** Tuition/fees: $2,622; $5,292 out-of-state. Per-credit charge: $77 in-state; $166 out-of-state. In-state tuition based upon assumption of Colorado Oppurtunity Fund waiver of $86 per-credit-hour. Room/board: $4,555. Books/supplies: $800. Personal expenses: $972.

**2006-2007 Financial aid. Need-based:** 72% of total undergraduate aid awarded as scholarships/grants, 28% as loans/jobs. Need-based aid available for part-time students. Work-study available nights and for part-time students. **Non-need-based:** Scholarships awarded for academics, athletics, state residency.

**Application procedures. Admission:** No deadline. No application fee. Application may be submitted online. Admission notification on a rolling basis. **Financial aid:** Priority date 5/1; no closing date. FAFSA, institutional form required. Applicants notified on a rolling basis starting 6/15.

**Academics. Special study options:** Accelerated study, cooperative education, distance learning, double major, dual enrollment of high school students, ESL, independent study, liberal arts/career combination. Bachelor's degree programs available on campus. License preparation in nursing. **Credit/placement by examination:** AP, CLEP, institutional tests. 45 credit hours maximum toward associate degree. **Support services:** GED preparation and test center, learning center, pre-admission summer program, reduced course load, remedial instruction, study skills assistance, tutoring, writing center.

**Majors. Biology:** General. **Business:** General, accounting, business admin. **Communications:** Advertising, journalism. **Computer sciences:** General, computer science, programming, word processing. **Conservation:** General, fisheries. **Education:** General, physical, social studies. **Engineering:** General. **Engineering technology:** Civil, construction, drafting. **Foreign languages:** Spanish. **Legal studies:** Prelaw. **Liberal arts:** Arts/sciences. **Math:** General. **Mechanic/repair:** Auto body, automotive, diesel. **Parks/recreation:** Health/fitness. **Personal/culinary services:** Cosmetic. **Philosophy/religion:** Philosophy. **Physical sciences:** Chemistry. **Protective services:** Criminal justice, law enforcement admin, police science. **Psychology:** General. **Social sciences:** Criminology. **Visual/performing arts:** Commercial/advertising art.

**Most popular majors.** Business/marketing 6%, education 8%, health sciences 21%, liberal arts 45%, security/protective services 6%, trade and industry 6%.

**Computing on campus.** 260 workstations in dormitories, library. Dormitories wired for high-speed internet access and linked to campus network. Online course registration, wireless network available.

**Student life. Freshman orientation:** Available. Preregistration for classes offered. **Housing:** Single-sex dorms available. $150 partly refundable deposit. **Activities:** Pep band, campus ministries, choral groups, drama, music ensembles, student government, student newspaper, TV station, MECHA (for students of Chicano and Hispanic descent), Black Student Alliance.

**Athletics.** NJCAA. **Intercollegiate:** Baseball M, basketball M, golf, softball W, volleyball W. **Intramural:** Baseball M, basketball, rifle, softball, table tennis, tennis, volleyball. **Team name:** Trojans.

**Student services.** Adult student services, alcohol/substance abuse counseling, career counseling, student employment services, financial aid counseling, on-campus daycare, personal counseling, placement for graduates, veterans' counselor. **Physically disabled:** Services for visually, speech, hearing impaired. **Transfer:** Transfer adviser, college fairs on campus for students transferring to 4-year colleges.

**Contact.** E-mail: johnny.noel@trinidadstate.edu
Phone: (719) 846-5622 Toll-free number: (800) 621-8752
Fax: (719) 846-5620
Sandra Veltri, Vice President of Student and Academic Affairs, Trinidad State Junior College, 600 Prospect Street, Trinidad, CO 81082

# Connecticut

## Asnuntuck Community College

**Enfield, Connecticut**
www.acc.commnet.edu

**CB member**
**CB code: 3656**

▶ Public 2-year community and technical college
▶ Commuter campus in large town

**General.** Founded in 1972. Regionally accredited. **Enrollment:** 1,042 degree-seeking undergraduates. **Degrees:** 155 associate awarded. **Location:** 15 miles from Hartford, 10 miles from Springfield, Massachusetts. **Calendar:** Semester, extensive summer session. **Full-time faculty:** 25 total. **Part-time faculty:** 96 total. **Class size:** 47% < 20, 52% 20-39, less than 1% 40-49.

**Student profile.**

| | | | |
|---|---|---|---|
| Out-of-state: | 4% | 25 or older: | 45% |

**Transfer out. Colleges most students transferred to 2007:** Eastern Connecticut State University, Central Connecticut State University, University of Connecticut, Western New England College.

**Basis for selection.** Open admission.

**2008-2009 Annual costs.** Tuition/fees (projected): $2,984; $8,264 out-of-state. Per-credit charge: $110 in-state; $330 out-of-state. Books/supplies: $1,000. Personal expenses: $1,230.

**Financial aid.** All financial aid based on need. Need-based aid available for part-time students. Work-study available nights, weekends and for part-time students.

**Application procedures. Admission:** No deadline. $20 fee, may be waived for applicants with need. Application may be submitted online. Admission notification on a rolling basis. **Financial aid:** Priority date 6/1; no closing date. FAFSA, institutional form required. Applicants notified on a rolling basis starting 7/1; must reply within 2 week(s) of notification.

**Academics.** On-line tutoring available. **Special study options:** Cooperative education, cross-registration, distance learning, double major, dual enrollment of high school students, independent study, internships, liberal arts/career combination, weekend college. License preparation in paramedic, real estate. **Credit/placement by examination:** AP, CLEP, institutional tests. 48 credit hours maximum toward associate degree. **Support services:** Learning center, remedial instruction, study skills assistance, tutoring.

**Majors. Business:** Accounting technology, administrative services, business admin, fashion, management information systems. **Communications technology:** General, radio/tv. **Engineering technology:** Industrial, manufacturing. **Family/consumer sciences:** Child care. **Health:** Mental health services. **Liberal arts:** Arts/sciences. **Protective services:** Police science.

**Most popular majors.** Business/marketing 31%, family/consumer sciences 7%, liberal arts 47%, security/protective services 7%.

**Computing on campus.** 111 workstations in library, computer center. Online course registration, online library available.

**Student life. Freshman orientation:** Available. **Activities:** Drama, literary magazine, radio station, student government, human services club, Phi Theta Kappa.

**Student services.** Career counseling, student employment services, financial aid counseling, on-campus daycare, personal counseling, placement for graduates, veterans' counselor. **Physically disabled:** Services for visually, speech, hearing impaired. **Transfer:** Pre-admission transcript evaluation for new students. Transfer adviser, college fairs on campus for students transferring to 4-year colleges.

**Contact.** E-mail: dshaw@acc.commnet.edu
Phone: (860) 253-3010 Toll-free number: (800) 501-3967
Fax: (860) 253-3014
Donna Shaw, Director of Admissions and Marketing, Asnuntuck Community College, 170 Elm Street, Enfield, CT 06082

## Capital Community College

**Hartford, Connecticut**
www.ccc.commnet.edu

**CB code: 3421**

▶ Public 2-year community and technical college
▶ Commuter campus in small city

**General.** Founded in 1946. Regionally accredited. **Enrollment:** 3,177 degree-seeking undergraduates; 549 non-degree-seeking students. **Degrees:** 276 associate awarded. **ROTC:** Army, Naval, Air Force. **Calendar:** Semester, limited summer session. **Full-time faculty:** 66 total. **Part-time faculty:** 147 total. **Special facilities:** Mathematics development center, computerized English as a Second Language laboratory, interactive videodisc instruction for nursing students, learning/writing center. **Partnerships:** Formal partnerships with high schools for Tech Prep program.

**Student profile.** Among degree-seeking undergraduates, 617 enrolled as first-time, first-year students.

| | | | |
|---|---|---|---|
| Part-time: | 69% | 25 or older: | 57% |
| Women: | 72% | | |

**Transfer out. Colleges most students transferred to 2007:** University of Connecticut, Central Connecticut State University, University of Hartford, Eastern Connecticut State University.

**Basis for selection.** Open admission, but selective for some programs. SAT scores used to satisfy admission criteria for nursing, physical therapist assistant, and radiologic technology programs.

**High school preparation.** Algebra, biology, and chemistry required for nursing program. Physical therapy assistant, radiologic technology, and pre-nursing programs also have specific course requirements. Paramedic program has specific educational and training requirements.

**2007-2008 Annual costs.** Tuition/fees: $2,828; $8,444 out-of-state. Per-credit charge: $104 in-state; $312 out-of-state. Books/supplies: $850. Personal expenses: $1,965.

**Financial aid.** All financial aid based on need. Need-based aid available for part-time students. Work-study available nights, weekends and for part-time students.

**Application procedures. Admission:** No deadline. $20 fee, may be waived for applicants with need. Application may be submitted online. Admission notification on a rolling basis. **Financial aid:** Closing date 7/15. FAFSA required. Applicants notified on a rolling basis starting 7/15; must reply within 2 week(s) of notification.

**Academics. Special study options:** Accelerated study, cross-registration, distance learning, double major, dual enrollment of high school students, ESL, independent study, internships, weekend college. Interdisciplinary summer program with Smith College. License preparation in nursing, paramedic, radiology. **Credit/placement by examination:** AP, CLEP, institutional tests. **Support services:** GED preparation, learning center, pre-admission summer program, remedial instruction, study skills assistance, tutoring, writing center.

**Majors. Business:** Accounting, administrative services, business admin. **Computer sciences:** General. **Education:** Early childhood. **Engineering:** Electrical. **Engineering technology:** Architectural. **Health:** EMT paramedic, medical assistant, medical radiologic technology/radiation therapy, mental health services, nursing (RN), physical therapy assistant. **Liberal arts:** Arts/sciences, library assistant. **Protective services:** Fire safety technology.

**Most popular majors.** Business/marketing 18%, health sciences 40%, liberal arts 26%, public administration/social services 6%.

**Computing on campus.** 500 workstations in library, computer center, student center. Online course registration, online library available.

**Student life. Freshman orientation:** Available. Preregistration for classes offered. 3 day program held prior to start of semester. **Policies:** Policies against drugs and alcohol, violence, weapons, and sexual harassment on campus. **Activities:** Choral groups, dance, drama, literary magazine, student government, TV station, Latin American students association, senior renewal club, early childhood club, pre-professional club, Phi Theta Kappa, nursing club, Black student union, student senate.

**Student services.** Campus ministries, career counseling, services for economically disadvantaged, student employment services, financial aid counseling, minority student services, on-campus daycare, personal counseling, placement for graduates, veterans' counselor, women's services. **Physically**

**disabled:** Services for visually, speech, hearing impaired. **Learning disabled:** Comprehensive services available. **Transfer:** College fairs on campus for students transferring to 4-year colleges.

**Contact.** E-mail: MBall-davis@ccc.commnet.edu
Phone: (860) 906-5126 Toll-free number: (800) 894-6126
Marsha Ball-Davis, Director of Admissions, Capital Community College, 950 Main Street, Hartford, CT 06103-1207

## Clemens College
### Suffield, Connecticut
www.clemenscollege.edu          CB code: 3615

- For-profit 2-year culinary school and business college
- Residential campus in small town
- Application essay, interview required

**General.** Regionally accredited. Transfer to sister schools in Switzerland or Australia for second year possible. Students can complete a degree program in an 18-month accelerated format. Cost of attendance includes 6-month paid internship. **Enrollment:** 57 degree-seeking undergraduates. **Degrees:** 16 associate awarded. **Location:** 50 miles from Hartford. **Calendar:** Continuous. 11-week accelerated terms. Limited summer session. **Full-time faculty:** 6 total. **Part-time faculty:** 7 total. **Class size:** 95% < 20, 5% 20-39.

**Student profile.**

| | | | |
|---|---|---|---|
| Out-of-state: | 90% | Live on campus: | 90% |
| 25 or older: | 40% | | |

**Transfer out. Colleges most students transferred to 2007:** University Center Cesar Ritz (Switzerland), Institut Hotelier Cesar Ritz (Switzerland).

**Basis for selection.** Recommendations and interview are important. Visa required for international students.

**2007-2008 Annual costs.** Tuition/fees: $19,770. International students who have no health insurance are required to purchase it for $350 per 11-week term. Culinary students pay an extra $667.80 for cutlery and tools. Room/board: $5,690.

**Financial aid. Need-based:** Need-based aid available for part-time students. Work-study available nights, weekends and for part-time students. **Non-need-based:** Scholarships awarded for academics.

**Application procedures. Admission:** Priority date 1/15; no deadline. $40 fee, may be waived for applicants with need. Application may be submitted online. Admission notification on a rolling basis. **Financial aid:** No deadline. Applicants notified on a rolling basis starting 1/1.

**Academics. Special study options:** Accelerated study, cooperative education, internships, liberal arts/career combination, study abroad. **Credit/placement by examination:** AP, CLEP, institutional tests. 18 credit hours maximum toward associate degree. **Support services:** Learning center, remedial instruction, study skills assistance, tutoring, writing center.

**Majors. Business:** Hospitality admin. **Personal/culinary services:** Culinary arts.

**Computing on campus.** 38 workstations in dormitories, library, computer center, student center. Dormitories wired for high-speed internet access and linked to campus network. Online library, helpline, wireless network available.

**Student life. Freshman orientation:** Mandatory. Preregistration for classes offered. Half of the first week is devoted to orientation. **Housing:** Guaranteed on-campus for freshmen. Coed dorms, substance-free housing available. $500 deposit. **Activities:** Film society, student government, Ritz Guild.

**Athletics. Intramural:** Basketball, soccer, table tennis, tennis, volleyball, weight lifting.

**Student services.** Adult student services, alcohol/substance abuse counseling, career counseling, student employment services, financial aid counseling, health services, placement for graduates. **Transfer:** Pre-admission transcript evaluation for new students.

**Contact.** E-mail: admissions@clemenscollege.edu
Phone: (860) 668-3515 ext. 228 Toll-free number: (800) 955-0809
Fax: (860) 668-7369
Jolie Swanson, Director of Admissions, Clemens College, 1760 Mapleton Avenue, Suffield, CT 06078

## Gateway Community College
### New Haven, Connecticut          CB member
www.gwcc.commnet.edu          CB code: 3425

- Public 2-year community college
- Commuter campus in small city

**General.** Founded in 1992. Regionally accredited. **Enrollment:** 4,787 degree-seeking undergraduates; 1,178 non-degree-seeking students. **Degrees:** 456 associate awarded. **Location:** 75 miles from New York City, 130 miles from Boston. **Calendar:** Semester, limited summer session. **Full-time faculty:** 87 total; 17% have terminal degrees, 22% minority, 58% women. **Part-time faculty:** 237 total; 16% minority, 54% women. **Class size:** 34% < 20, 62% 20-39, 4% 40-49, less than 1% 50-99. **Special facilities:** Early childhood learning center, day care center, student operated cafe, student art museum.

**Student profile.** Among degree-seeking undergraduates, 7% enrolled in a transfer program, 18% enrolled in a vocational program, 1% already have a bachelor's degree or higher, 1,178 enrolled as first-time, first-year students.

| | | | |
|---|---|---|---|
| Part-time: | 56% | Asian American: | 4% |
| Out-of-state: | 1% | Hispanic American: | 12% |
| Women: | 62% | International: | 2% |
| African American: | 27% | 25 or older: | 32% |

**Transfer out. Colleges most students transferred to 2007:** Southern Connecticut State University, University of New Haven, Quinnipiac College.

**Basis for selection.** Open admission, but selective for some programs. Special requirements for radiology, nursing, nuclear medicine technology, diagnostic medical sonography, drug and alcohol rehabilitation counselor. ACCUPLACER/LOPE required for placement. Interview required of radiology, drug and alcohol counseling, nuclear medicine technology, diagnostic medical sonography, nursing majors. **Homeschooled:** Transcript of courses and grades required.

**2007-2008 Annual costs.** Tuition/fees: $2,828; $8,444 out-of-state. Per-credit charge: $104 in-state; $312 out-of-state. Books/supplies: $1,200. Personal expenses: $1,100.

**Financial aid.** All financial aid based on need. Need-based aid available for part-time students. Work-study available nights, weekends and for part-time students.

**Application procedures. Admission:** Priority date 6/1; deadline 9/1. $20 fee, may be waived for applicants with need. Application may be submitted online. Admission notification on a rolling basis beginning on or about 2/1. **Financial aid:** No deadline. FAFSA, institutional form required. Applicants notified on a rolling basis; must reply within 2 week(s) of notification.

**Academics. Special study options:** Accelerated study, cross-registration, distance learning, dual enrollment of high school students, ESL, independent study, internships, liberal arts/career combination. License preparation in nursing, radiology. **Credit/placement by examination:** AP, CLEP, institutional tests. 30 credit hours maximum toward associate degree. **Support services:** GED preparation, learning center, pre-admission summer program, reduced course load, remedial instruction, study skills assistance, tutoring, writing center.

**Majors. Business:** Accounting, administrative services, business admin, fashion, hotel/motel admin, office/clerical, restaurant/food services, sales/distribution. **Computer sciences:** Computer science, information systems, programming, word processing. **Conservation:** General, environmental science. **Education:** Early childhood, special. **Engineering:** Science. **Engineering technology:** Biomedical, electrical, manufacturing. **Family/consumer sciences:** Aging, food/nutrition, institutional food production. **Health:** Medical radiologic technology/radiation therapy, medical secretary, nuclear medical technology, nursing (RN), pharmacy assistant, sonography, substance abuse counseling. **Legal studies:** Legal secretary. **Liberal arts:** Arts/sciences. **Math:** General. **Mechanic/repair:** General, automotive. **Personal/culinary services:** Chef training, food prep, restaurant/catering. **Protective services:** Fire services admin. **Visual/performing arts:** Graphic design, studio arts.

**Most popular majors.** Business/marketing 15%, engineering/engineering technologies 9%, family/consumer sciences 9%, health sciences 26%, liberal arts 36%.

**Computing on campus.** 650 workstations in library, computer center. Online library, helpline, wireless network available.

**Student life. Freshman orientation:** Available. **Activities:** Choral groups, drama, international student organizations, literary magazine, music ensembles, student government, student newspaper, Spanish-American club, math/science club, Phi Theta Kappa, art club, athletic club, veteran's club, biology club, Theater Goers, Black Student Union.

**Athletics.** NJCAA. **Intercollegiate:** Baseball M, basketball. **Team name:** Ravens.

**Student services.** Adult student services, career counseling, student employment services, financial aid counseling, health services, on-campus daycare, personal counseling, placement for graduates, veterans' counselor, women's services. **Physically disabled:** Services for visually, speech, hearing impaired. **Transfer:** Transfer adviser for students transferring to 4-year colleges.

**Contact.** E-mail: KShea@gwcc.commnet.edu
Phone: (203) 285-2010 Toll-free number: (800) 390-7723
Fax: (203) 285-2018
Shea Kim, Director of Admissions, Gateway Community College, 60 Sargent Drive, New Haven, CT 06511-5970

## Goodwin College
**East Hartford, Connecticut**
**www.goodwin.edu**                    **CB member**

- Private 2-year health science and junior college
- Commuter campus in small city

**General. Enrollment:** 1,419 degree-seeking undergraduates; 21 non-degree-seeking students. **Degrees:** 154 associate awarded. **Location:** 5 miles from Hartford. **Calendar:** Semester, extensive summer session. **Full-time faculty:** 25 total; 20% minority, 76% women. **Part-time faculty:** 49 total.

**Student profile.** Among degree-seeking undergraduates, 253 enrolled as first-time, first-year students.

**Part-time:**          86%     **Women:**          88%

**Transfer out. Colleges most students transferred to 2007:** Manchester Community College, Capital Community College, University of Connecticut, Central Connecticut State University, Tunxis Community College.

**Basis for selection.** Open admission, but selective for some programs. Applicants to the nursing, respiratory therapist, and histology technician programs must have successfully completed pre-requisite courses prior to application and submit a completed application to program desired. Interviews may be required for some programs. **Homeschooled:** State high school equivalency certificate required.

**2007-2008 Annual costs.** Tuition/fees: $13,820. Per-credit charge: $425.

**Application procedures. Admission:** No deadline. $50 fee, may be waived for applicants with need. Application may be submitted online. Admission notification on a rolling basis.

**Academics. Special study options:** Cooperative education, distance learning, ESL, internships. License preparation in nursing, paramedic. **Credit/placement by examination:** AP, CLEP. **Support services:** Remedial instruction, tutoring.

**Majors. Business:** General, administrative services. **Computer sciences:** General. **Education:** Teacher assistance. **Family/consumer sciences:** Child care, child development. **Health:** Histologic assistant, medical assistant, nursing (RN), office assistant, respiratory therapy assistant. **Protective services:** Emergency management/homeland security. **Public administration:** Human services, youth services.

**Computing on campus.** Online library, repair service available.

**Student life. Freshman orientation:** Mandatory. **Activities:** Student government, student newspaper.

**Athletics. Intramural:** Bowling, golf.

**Student services.** Career counseling, student employment services, financial aid counseling.

**Contact.** E-mail: dnoonan@goodwin.edu
Phone: (860) 528-4111 Toll-free number: (800) 889-3282
Fax: (860) 291-9550
Daniel Noonan, Director of Enrollment, Goodwin College, 745 Burnside Avenue, East Hartford, CT 06108

## Housatonic Community College
**Bridgeport, Connecticut**             **CB member**
**www.hcc.commnet.edu**                **CB code: 3446**

- Public 2-year community college
- Commuter campus in small city

**General.** Founded in 1966. Regionally accredited. **Enrollment:** 3,894 degree-seeking undergraduates. **Degrees:** 350 associate awarded. **Location:** 60 miles from Hartford, 60 miles from New York City. **Calendar:** Semester, extensive summer session. **Full-time faculty:** 90 total. **Part-time faculty:** 195 total. **Class size:** 45% < 20, 53% 20-39, 2% 40-49, less than 1% 50-99.

**Basis for selection.** Open admission, but selective for some programs. Special requirements for clinical lab science, physical therapist assistant, occupational therapy assistant, nursing programs. Interview required of allied health, computer program majors.

**2007-2008 Annual costs.** Tuition/fees: $2,828; $8,444 out-of-state. Per-credit charge: $104 in-state; $312 out-of-state. Books/supplies: $700.

**Financial aid.** All financial aid based on need. Need-based aid available for part-time students.

**Application procedures. Admission:** No deadline. $20 fee, may be waived for applicants with need. Admission notification on a rolling basis. Application period ends one week after start of classes. **Financial aid:** Priority date 11/1, closing date 5/1. FAFSA required. Applicants notified on a rolling basis starting 6/1.

**Academics. Special study options:** Cooperative education, distance learning, double major, dual enrollment of high school students, ESL, honors, independent study, internships, weekend college. **Credit/placement by examination:** CLEP, institutional tests. 30 credit hours maximum toward associate degree. New Jersey Basic Skills Placement Test and/or AC-CUPLACER used for advising and placement. **Support services:** GED preparation, learning center, reduced course load, remedial instruction, study skills assistance, tutoring, writing center.

**Majors. Business:** General, accounting, administrative services, business admin. **Computer sciences:** General. **Education:** Early childhood. **Family/consumer sciences:** Child care. **Health:** Mental health services, nursing (RN), physical therapy assistant, substance abuse counseling. **Liberal arts:** Arts/sciences. **Mechanic/repair:** Aircraft. **Protective services:** Police science. **Public administration:** Human services. **Visual/performing arts:** Commercial/advertising art, studio arts.

**Computing on campus.** 140 workstations in library, computer center.

**Student life. Freshman orientation:** Available. Preregistration for classes offered. **Activities:** Drama, literary magazine, student government, student newspaper.

**Student services.** Adult student services, career counseling, services for economically disadvantaged, student employment services, financial aid counseling, health services, on-campus daycare, personal counseling, placement for graduates, veterans' counselor. **Transfer:** Transfer adviser, college fairs on campus for students transferring to 4-year colleges.

**Contact.** Phone: (203) 332-5100 Fax: (203) 332-5123
Deloris Curtis, Director of Admissions, Housatonic Community College, 900 Lafayette Boulevard, Bridgeport, CT 06604-4704

## Manchester Community College
**Manchester, Connecticut**
**www.mcc.commnet.edu**                **CB code: 3544**

- Public 2-year community college
- Commuter campus in small city

**General.** Founded in 1963. Regionally accredited. **Enrollment:** 5,420 degree-seeking undergraduates; 1,064 non-degree-seeking students. **Degrees:** 556 associate awarded. **Location:** 8 miles from Hartford. **Calendar:** Semester, extensive summer session. **Full-time faculty:** 104 total; 19% minority, 60% women. **Part-time faculty:** 293 total; 27% minority, 50% women. **Class size:** 21% < 20, 70% 20-39, 8% 40-49.

**Student profile.** Among degree-seeking undergraduates, 1,464 enrolled as first-time, first-year students, 793 transferred in from other institutions.

| | | | |
|---|---|---|---|
| Part-time: | 50% | Hispanic American: | 11% |
| Women: | 54% | International: | 1% |
| African American: | 14% | 25 or older: | 32% |
| Asian American: | 4% | | |

**Transfer out. Colleges most students transferred to 2007:** Central Connecticut State University, University of Connecticut, Eastern Connecticut State University.

**Basis for selection.** Open admission, but selective for some programs. 2.0 school GPA, minimum SAT combined score of 800 (exclusive of writing), rank in top half of class considered for admission to allied health programs. SAT required for admission to allied health programs. Interview required of allied health, drug and alcohol rehabilitation counselor majors.

**High school preparation.** 2 units mathematics and 1 unit laboratory science required of allied health applicants.

**2008-2009 Annual costs.** Tuition/fees (projected): $2,828; $7,820 out-of-state. Per-credit charge: $104 in-district; $104 out-of-district; $312 out-of-state. Books/supplies: $800. Personal expenses: $3,032.

**2006-2007 Financial aid. Need-based:** 94% of total undergraduate aid awarded as scholarships/grants, 6% as loans/jobs. Need-based aid available for part-time students.

**Application procedures. Admission:** No deadline. $20 fee, may be waived for applicants with need. Application may be submitted online. Admission notification on a rolling basis beginning on or about 5/1. **Financial aid:** Priority date 5/15; no closing date. FAFSA required. Applicants notified on a rolling basis starting 5/1; must reply within 2 week(s) of notification.

**Academics. Special study options:** Cooperative education, cross-registration, distance learning, double major, dual enrollment of high school students, ESL, independent study, internships, semester at sea, student-designed major, weekend college. **Credit/placement by examination:** AP, CLEP, institutional tests. 45 credit hours maximum toward associate degree. **Support services:** Learning center, reduced course load, remedial instruction, study skills assistance, tutoring, writing center.

**Majors. Area/ethnic studies:** Women's. **Business:** Accounting, administrative services, business admin, hospitality/recreation, management information systems. **Communications:** Digital media, journalism. **Computer sciences:** Data entry, information systems, networking. **Education:** Early childhood, teacher assistance. **Engineering:** Science. **Engineering technology:** Manufacturing. **Family/consumer sciences:** Institutional food production. **Health:** Clinical lab technology, occupational therapy assistant, pharmacy assistant, physical therapy assistant, respiratory therapy technology, substance abuse counseling, surgical technology. **Legal studies:** Paralegal. **Liberal arts:** Arts/sciences. **Parks/recreation:** Exercise sciences. **Public administration:** Community org/advocacy. **Visual/performing arts:** Commercial/advertising art.

**Most popular majors.** Business/marketing 14%, education 11%, family/consumer sciences 15%, health sciences 11%, legal studies 7%, security/protective services 35%.

**Computing on campus.** 310 workstations in library, computer center. Online course registration available.

**Student life. Freshman orientation:** Available. **Activities:** Choral groups, dance, drama, student government, student newspaper, minority student alliance, Hispanic cultural club, Upper Room Christian Fellowship, voluntary action program.

**Athletics.** NJCAA. **Intercollegiate:** Baseball, basketball M, soccer. **Intramural:** Softball M. **Team name:** Cougars.

**Student services.** Adult student services, career counseling, student employment services, health services, on-campus daycare, personal counseling, placement for graduates, veterans' counselor. **Physically disabled:** Services for visually impaired. **Transfer:** Transfer adviser, college fairs on campus for students transferring to 4-year colleges.

**Contact.** Phone: (860) 512-3210 Fax: (860) 512-3221
Peter Harris, Director of Admissions, Manchester Community College, Great Path PO Box 1046, MS 12, Manchester, CT 06040-1046

---

## Middlesex Community College
**Middletown, Connecticut**
www.mxcc.commnet.edu

**CB member**
**CB code: 3551**

▶ Public 2-year community college
▶ Commuter campus in large town

**General.** Founded in 1966. **Enrollment:** 1,849 degree-seeking undergraduates; 774 non-degree-seeking students. **Degrees:** 226 associate awarded. **Location:** 20 miles from Hartford and New Haven. **Calendar:** Semester, limited summer session. **Full-time faculty:** 39 total; 15% minority, 51% women. **Part-time faculty:** 132 total; 3% minority, 57% women.

**Student profile.** Among degree-seeking undergraduates, 32% enrolled in a transfer program, 39% enrolled in a vocational program, 497 enrolled as first-time, first-year students, 213 transferred in from other institutions.

| | | | |
|---|---|---|---|
| Part-time: | 50% | Asian American: | 3% |
| Out-of-state: | 1% | Hispanic American: | 13% |
| Women: | 62% | 25 or older: | 65% |
| African American: | 10% | | |

**Transfer out.** 45% of students enrolled in the transfer program go on to 4-year colleges.

**Basis for selection.** Open admission, but selective for some programs. Special requirements for radiology technician, broadcast communications, human services, and drug and alcohol rehabilitation counselor programs. Interview recommended of mental health, radiology, drug and alcohol counseling program majors.

**2007-2008 Annual costs.** Tuition/fees: $2,828; $8,444 out-of-state. Per-credit charge: $109 in-state; $316 out-of-state. Out-of-state tuition includes fees. Books/supplies: $400. Personal expenses: $700.

**Financial aid.** All financial aid based on need. Need-based aid available for part-time students. Work-study available for part-time students. **Additional information:** Tuition and/or fee waiver for veterans.

**Application procedures. Admission:** Priority date 7/1; deadline 8/1 (postmark date). $20 fee, may be waived for applicants with need. Application may be submitted online. Admission notification on a rolling basis beginning on or about 1/1. **Financial aid:** Priority date 6/1; no closing date. FAFSA, institutional form required. Applicants notified on a rolling basis starting 7/1; must reply within 2 week(s) of notification.

**Academics. Special study options:** Cross-registration, dual enrollment of high school students, ESL, independent study, internships, student-designed major. License preparation in radiology. **Credit/placement by examination:** CLEP, institutional tests. 48 credit hours maximum toward associate degree. **Support services:** Pre-admission summer program, reduced course load, remedial instruction, tutoring.

**Majors. Business:** Accounting, administrative services, business admin, marketing. **Communications:** General, broadcast journalism. **Computer sciences:** Information systems. **Conservation:** General. **Education:** Early childhood. **Health:** Medical radiologic technology/radiation therapy, medical secretary, nuclear medical technology, ophthalmic lab technology, optician, substance abuse counseling. **Legal studies:** Legal secretary. **Liberal arts:** Arts/sciences. **Public administration:** Human services. **Visual/performing arts:** Metal/jewelry, studio arts.

**Most popular majors.** Business/marketing 30%, health sciences 25%, liberal arts 35%.

**Computing on campus.** Online library, helpline available.

**Student life. Freshman orientation:** Available. **Activities:** Concert band, drama, literary magazine, radio station, student government, student newspaper, TV station, Black Student Alliance, national scholastic honor society, student guild, radio/TV club, Collegiate Secretaries International, Minority Opportunities in Education Club, art club, human services organization.

**Student services.** Career counseling, student employment services, on-campus daycare, personal counseling, placement for graduates, veterans' counselor. **Physically disabled:** Services for visually, hearing impaired. **Transfer:** Transfer adviser, college fairs on campus for students transferring to 4-year colleges.

**Contact.** E-mail: mshabazz@mxcc.commnet.edu
Phone: (860) 343-5719 Toll-free number: (800) 818-5501
Fax: (860) 344-7488
Mensimah Shabazz, Director of Admissions, Middlesex Community College, 100 Training Hill Road, Middletown, CT 06457

## Naugatuck Valley Community College

Waterbury, Connecticut
www.nvcc.commnet.edu

CB member
CB code: 3550

- Public 2-year community and technical college
- Commuter campus in small city

**General.** Founded in 1992. Regionally accredited. **Enrollment:** 4,964 degree-seeking undergraduates; 1,002 non-degree-seeking students. **Degrees:** 490 associate awarded. **Location:** 32 miles from Hartford, 2 miles from Waterbury. **Calendar:** Semester, limited summer session. **Full-time faculty:** 103 total; 10% minority, 55% women. **Part-time faculty:** 327 total. **Class size:** 25% < 20, 74% 20-39, less than 1% 40-49, less than 1% >100. **Special facilities:** Observatory, fine arts center, automotive technology center, culinary arts facility. **Partnerships:** Formal partnerships with Disney.

**Student profile.** Among degree-seeking undergraduates, 35% enrolled in a transfer program, 49% enrolled in a vocational program, 2% already have a bachelor's degree or higher, 1,205 enrolled as first-time, first-year students, 727 transferred in from other institutions.

| | | | |
|---|---|---|---|
| Part-time: | 52% | Asian American: | 3% |
| Out-of-state: | 1% | Hispanic American: | 13% |
| Women: | 59% | International: | 1% |
| African American: | 8% | 25 or older: | 38% |

**Transfer out.** 35% of students enrolled in the transfer program go on to 4-year colleges. **Colleges most students transferred to 2007:** Western Connecticut State University, Southern Connecticut State University, Central Connecticut State University, University of Connecticut, Post University.

**Basis for selection.** Open admission, but selective for some programs. Admission to nursing, physical therapy assistant, radiology, respiratory care programs based on school achievement, recommendations, test scores, maturity of student, motivation. Levels of English Proficiency (LOEP) used for ESL population. Interview required of physical therapy majors. Audition recommended of music majors. Portfolio recommended of art majors. **Homeschooled:** Statement describing homeschool structure and mission, interview required. Placement test and interview required.

**High school preparation.** Recommended units include English 4, mathematics 3, social studies 2, history 2 and science 1. Most allied health programs require high school algebra, biology, chemistry. Engineering technologies require 2 years algebra, 1 year laboratory science (preferably physics or chemistry), and some computer literacy.

**2007-2008 Annual costs.** Tuition/fees: $2,828; $8,444 out-of-state. Per-credit charge: $104 in-state; $312 out-of-state. Books/supplies: $1,200. Personal expenses: $1,486.

**Financial aid.** All financial aid based on need. Need-based aid available for part-time students. Work-study available for part-time students.

**Application procedures.** Admission: Priority date 6/1; no deadline. $20 fee, may be waived for applicants with need. Application may be submitted online. Admission notification on a rolling basis beginning on or about 9/1. **Financial aid:** Priority date 4/1; no closing date. FAFSA required. Applicants notified on a rolling basis starting 6/1.

**Academics.** Composition, technical writing, literature, computer information systems, math, business law, psychology, astronomy, biology and criminal justice courses available through distance learning. **Special study options:** Cooperative education, cross-registration, distance learning, double major, dual enrollment of high school students, ESL, independent study, internships, study abroad. License preparation in aviation, nursing, physical therapy, radiology, real estate. **Credit/placement by examination:** AP, CLEP, institutional tests. 45 credit hours maximum toward associate degree. **Support services:** Learning center, reduced course load, remedial instruction, study skills assistance, tutoring, writing center.

**Majors. Agriculture:** Horticulture. **Business:** Accounting technology, administrative services, banking/financial services, business admin, hotel/motel admin, merchandising. **Computer sciences:** General, networking, web page design. **Conservation:** Environmental science. **Education:** Early childhood. **Engineering technology:** General, CAD/CADD, electrical, energy systems, industrial management, manufacturing, mechanical, plastics, quality control. **Family/consumer sciences:** Institutional food production. **Health:** Medical radiologic technology/radiation therapy, mental health services, nursing (RN), physical therapy assistant, respiratory therapy technology, substance abuse counseling. **Legal studies:** Legal secretary, paralegal. **Liberal arts:** Arts/sciences. **Mechanic/repair:** Automotive. **Personal/culinary services:** Food service. **Protective services:** Fire safety technology, police science. **Psychology:** General. **Public administration:** Human services, social work. **Transportation:** Aviation. **Visual/performing arts:** Art, dance, dramatic, multimedia.

**Most popular majors.** Business/marketing 13%, health sciences 26%, liberal arts 27%, public administration/social services 6%.

**Computing on campus.** 1,000 workstations in library, computer center. Online course registration, online library, helpline, repair service, wireless network available.

**Student life. Freshman orientation:** Available. Preregistration for classes offered. **Activities:** Bands, choral groups, dance, drama, international student organizations, literary magazine, music ensembles, musical theater, student government, student newspaper, symphony orchestra, Black student union, Hispanic student union, human services club, Phi Theta Kappa, Alpha Beta Gamma, agro-bio club, student nurses clubs, book club.

**Student services.** Adult student services, career counseling, student employment services, financial aid counseling, health services, personal counseling, placement for graduates, veterans' counselor. **Physically disabled:** Services for visually, speech, hearing impaired. **Learning disabled:** Comprehensive services available. **Transfer:** Pre-admission transcript evaluation for new students. Transfer adviser, college fairs on campus for students transferring to 4-year colleges.

**Contact.** E-mail: nvcc@nvcc.commnet.edu
Phone: (203) 575-8078 Fax: (203) 596-8766
James Daniels, Dean of Student Services, Naugatuck Valley Community College, 750 Chase Parkway, Waterbury, CT 06708-3089

## Northwestern Connecticut Community College

Winsted, Connecticut
www.nwcc.commnet.edu

CB member
CB code: 3652

- Public 2-year community and technical college
- Commuter campus in large town

**General.** Founded in 1965. Regionally accredited. **Enrollment:** 1,196 degree-seeking undergraduates; 436 non-degree-seeking students. **Degrees:** 134 associate awarded. **Location:** 25 miles from Hartford, 25 miles from Waterbury. **Calendar:** Semester, limited summer session. **Full-time faculty:** 28 total. **Part-time faculty:** 102 total. **Class size:** 54% < 20, 43% 20-39, 1% 40-49, 2% 50-99. **Special facilities:** Computer graphics multimedia laboratory.

**Student profile.** Among degree-seeking undergraduates, 258 enrolled as first-time, first-year students, 109 transferred in from other institutions.

| | | | |
|---|---|---|---|
| Part-time: | 55% | Asian American: | 2% |
| Out-of-state: | 1% | Hispanic American: | 4% |
| Women: | 65% | 25 or older: | 34% |
| African American: | 2% | | |

**Basis for selection.** Open admission, but selective for some programs. Special requirements for drug and alcohol rehabilitation counseling, adventure education, physical therapy assistant, and dialysis patient care programs. New Jersey Placement Test required of all first-time freshmen.

**2007-2008 Annual costs.** Tuition/fees: $2,828; $8,444 out-of-state. Per-credit charge: $104 in-state; $312 out-of-state. Books/supplies: $600. Personal expenses: $1,000.

**Financial aid. Non-need-based:** Scholarships awarded for academics, art, state residency.

**Application procedures.** Admission: No deadline. $20 fee, may be waived for applicants with need. Admission notification on a rolling basis. **Financial aid:** Priority date 6/1; no closing date. FAFSA required. Applicants notified on a rolling basis starting 6/1.

**Academics.** Career education for the deaf program offers full range of services and participation in all majors by deaf and hearing impaired students. Interpreting major prepares hearing students for National Registry test for interpreters for the deaf. **Special study options:** Cooperative education, cross-registration, distance learning, double major, dual enrollment of high school students, ESL, independent study, internships. **Credit/placement by examination:** AP, CLEP, institutional tests. 48 credit hours maximum toward associate degree. **Support services:** Learning center, reduced course load, remedial instruction, tutoring.

**Majors. Business:** Accounting, administrative services, business admin, management information systems, marketing. **Computer sciences:** Information systems, programming. **Education:** General, early childhood. **English:** English lit. **Foreign languages:** Sign language interpretation. **Health:** Medical assistant, physical therapy assistant, recreational therapy, substance abuse counseling, veterinary technology/assistant. **Interdisciplinary:** Behavioral sciences. **Liberal arts:** Arts/sciences. **Math:** General. **Parks/recreation:** General, facilities management. **Protective services:** Law enforcement admin. **Public administration:** Human services. **Social sciences:** General. **Visual/performing arts:** Commercial/advertising art, design, studio arts.

**Most popular majors.** Business/marketing 13%, engineering/engineering technologies 7%, foreign language 10%, health sciences 15%, liberal arts 33%, security/protective services 7%, visual/performing arts 7%.

**Computing on campus.** 80 workstations in library, computer center.

**Student life. Housing:** Dormitory for hearing impaired and interpreting students available in Winsted. **Activities:** Literary magazine, student government, student newspaper, Spectrum, community service club, Signs of our Times.

**Student services.** Career counseling, student employment services, on-campus daycare, personal counseling, veterans' counselor. **Physically disabled:** Services for hearing impaired. **Transfer:** Transfer adviser, college fairs on campus for students transferring to 4-year colleges.

**Contact.** E-mail: dmartineau@nwcc.commnet.edu
Phone: (860) 738-6330 Fax: (860) 379-4465
Beverly Chrzan, Director of Admissions, Northwestern Connecticut Community College, Park Place East, Winsted, CT 06098

## Norwalk Community College
**Norwalk, Connecticut**
www.ncc.commnet.edu                     **CB code: 3677**

▶ Public 2-year community and technical college
▶ Commuter campus in small city

**General.** Founded in 1961. Regionally accredited. Non-credit courses offered through continuing education department. Lifetime Learners Institute for senior citizens. **Enrollment:** 2,000 full-time, degree-seeking students. **Degrees:** 430 associate awarded. **Location:** 45 miles from New York City. **Calendar:** Semester, extensive summer session. **Full-time faculty:** 100 total. **Part-time faculty:** 250 total. **Special facilities:** Theater, rotating art and cultural exhibits, culinary arts facility, early childhood education lab/preschool.

**Student profile.**

| Out-of-state: | 1% | 25 or older: | 52% |
|---|---|---|---|

**Basis for selection.** Open admission, but selective for some programs. Special requirements for nursing, legal assistant, respiratory care programs. ACCUPLACER placement test required of all entering, first-time students in English and math. ESL test required of non-native English speakers.

**High school preparation.** Recommended units include English 4, mathematics 3 and science 2. Chemistry, biology and algebra required for nursing and respiratory therapy applicants. Nursing applicants must have taken chemistry within past 5 years.

**2007-2008 Annual costs.** Tuition/fees: $2,828; $8,444 out-of-state. Per-credit charge: $162 in-state; $448 out-of-state. New England Regional Student Program: $241.25 per credit-hour. Books/supplies: $1,200. Personal expenses: $1,751.

**Financial aid. Need-based:** Need-based aid available for part-time students. Work-study available for part-time students. **Non-need-based:** Scholarships awarded for academics, alumni affiliation.

**Application procedures. Admission:** No deadline. $20 fee, may be waived for applicants with need. Admission notification on a rolling basis. Applicants to nursing program should apply by February 1. **Financial aid:** Priority date 7/1; no closing date. FAFSA, institutional form required. Applicants notified on a rolling basis starting 7/1; must reply within 2 week(s) of notification.

**Academics.** Special 10-week sessions with longer class hours per day let students finish courses more quickly during fall and spring. **Special study options:** Cooperative education, cross-registration, double major, dual enrollment of high school students, ESL, honors, internships, liberal arts/career combination, weekend college. Early childhood education credential training program. License preparation in nursing, paramedic, real estate. **Credit/placement by examination:** AP, CLEP, IB, institutional tests. 45 credit hours maximum toward associate degree. **Support services:** Learning center, pre-admission summer program, reduced course load, remedial instruction, study skills assistance, tutoring, writing center.

**Majors. Business:** Accounting, business admin, finance, hospitality admin, management information systems, marketing, office management, office technology. **Communications:** Journalism. **Communications technology:** General. **Computer sciences:** General, applications programming, data processing, information systems, programming, systems analysis. **Education:** Early childhood. **Engineering:** General, architectural, science. **Engineering technology:** Architectural, construction. **Health:** Nursing (RN), recreational therapy, respiratory therapy technology. **Legal studies:** Legal secretary, paralegal. **Liberal arts:** Arts/sciences. **Math:** General. **Parks/recreation:** General. **Protective services:** Fire safety technology, fire services admin, law enforcement admin. **Public administration:** Human services. **Visual/performing arts:** Art, commercial/advertising art, studio arts.

**Computing on campus.** 90 workstations in library, computer center, student center. Commuter students can connect to campus network. Online library, helpline available.

**Student life. Freshman orientation:** Available. One-day orientation for new students before start of semester. **Activities:** Choral groups, drama, international student organizations, literary magazine, student government, student newspaper, TV station, African culture club, Hay Motivo, Phi Theta Kappa, legal assistants club, early childhood education club, French club, Haitian student association, criminal justice club.

**Student services.** Adult student services, career counseling, services for economically disadvantaged, student employment services, financial aid counseling, on-campus daycare, placement for graduates, veterans' counselor, women's services. **Physically disabled:** Services for visually, speech, hearing impaired. **Transfer:** Re-entry adviser, pre-admission transcript evaluation for new students. Transfer adviser, college fairs on campus for students transferring to 4-year colleges.

**Contact.** E-mail: admissions@ncc.commnet.edu
Phone: (203) 857-7060 Fax: (203) 857-3335
Kimberlee Csapo-Ebert, Director of Enrollment Management, Norwalk Community College, 188 Richards Avenue, Norwalk, CT 06854-1655

## Quinebaug Valley Community College
**Danielson, Connecticut**                     **CB member**
www.qvcc.commnet.edu                          **CB code: 3716**

▶ Public 2-year community and technical college
▶ Commuter campus in large town

**General.** Founded in 1971. Regionally accredited. **Enrollment:** 1,595 degree-seeking undergraduates; 251 non-degree-seeking students. **Degrees:** 169 associate awarded. **Location:** 50 miles from Hartford, 25 miles from Providence, Rhode Island. **Calendar:** Semester, limited summer session. **Full-time faculty:** 29 total; 17% have terminal degrees, 10% minority, 55% women. **Part-time faculty:** 107 total; 11% have terminal degrees, 5% minority, 54% women. **Class size:** 51% < 20, 49% 20-39. **Special facilities:** Plastics laboratory, college-operated art gallery.

**Student profile.** Among degree-seeking undergraduates, 30% enrolled in a transfer program, 60% enrolled in a vocational program, 1% already have a bachelor's degree or higher, 393 enrolled as first-time, first-year students, 207 transferred in from other institutions.

| Part-time: | 60% | Asian American: | 2% |
|---|---|---|---|
| Out-of-state: | 1% | Hispanic American: | 10% |
| Women: | 38% | 25 or older: | 44% |
| African American: | 3% | | |

**Transfer out. Colleges most students transferred to 2007:** Eastern Connecticut State University, University of Connecticut, Worcester State College.

**Basis for selection.** Open admission, but selective for some programs. Interview recommended. **Learning Disabled:** Recommend meeting with the Coordinator of Learning Disability Services.

**2007-2008 Annual costs.** Tuition/fees: $2,828; $8,444 out-of-state. Per-credit charge: $104 in-state; $312 out-of-state. Books/supplies: $1,250. Personal expenses: $1,000.

**2007-2008 Financial aid.** All financial aid based on need. 95% of total undergraduate aid awarded as scholarships/grants, 5% as loans/jobs. Need-based aid available for part-time students. Work-study available nights, weekends and for part-time students.

**Application procedures. Admission:** No deadline. $20 fee, may be waived for applicants with need. Application may be submitted online. Admission notification on a rolling basis. **Financial aid:** Closing date 10/1. FAFSA required. Applicants notified on a rolling basis starting 5/1.

**Academics. Special study options:** Distance learning, double major, dual enrollment of high school students, ESL, independent study, internships. License preparation in real estate. **Credit/placement by examination:** AP, CLEP, institutional tests. 30 credit hours maximum toward associate degree. **Support services:** Learning center, pre-admission summer program, reduced course load, remedial instruction, study skills assistance, tutoring, writing center.

**Majors. Business:** Accounting, administrative services, business admin, office management, office technology. **Computer sciences:** General. **Construction:** General. **Education:** Early childhood. **Engineering:** Polymer. **Engineering technology:** Plastics. **Health:** Medical assistant. **Liberal arts:** Arts/sciences. **Mechanic/repair:** Aircraft. **Public administration:** Human services. **Visual/performing arts:** Studio arts.

**Most popular majors.** Business/marketing 18%, liberal arts 61%, visual/performing arts 9%.

**Computing on campus.** 115 workstations in library, computer center. Commuter students can connect to campus network. Online course registration, online library, wireless network available.

**Student life. Freshman orientation:** Available. **Activities:** Student government, medical assisting association, Phi Theta Kappa, Alpha Beta Gamma, book club.

**Student services.** Career counseling, student employment services, financial aid counseling, on-campus daycare, placement for graduates, veterans' counselor. **Physically disabled:** Services for visually, speech, hearing impaired. **Transfer:** Pre-admission transcript evaluation for new students. Transfer adviser, college fairs on campus for students transferring to 4-year colleges.

**Contact.** E-mail: qv_lsd@commnet.edu
Phone: (860) 412-7380 Fax: (860) 774-7768
Toni Moumouris, Enrollment and Transition Counselor, Quinebaug Valley Community College, 742 Upper Maple Street, Danielson, CT 06239-1440

## St. Vincent's College
**Bridgeport, Connecticut**
www.stvincentscollege.edu
**CB code: 3789**

- Private 2-year health science and junior college
- Commuter campus in small city
- SAT or ACT with writing, application essay required

**General.** Regionally accredited. **Enrollment:** 400 degree-seeking undergraduates. **Degrees:** 86 associate awarded. **Calendar:** Semester, limited summer session. **Full-time faculty:** 12 total. **Part-time faculty:** 32 total.

**Basis for selection.** Nursing program deadline February 15th. All other degree programs July 1 deadline. **Adult students:** SAT/ACT scores not required if out of high school 1 year(s) or more. **Homeschooled:** Transcript of courses and grades, letter of recommendation (nonparent) required.

**High school preparation.** 16 units required. Required units include English 4, mathematics 2, social studies 2, science 2 and academic electives 6.

**2007-2008 Annual costs.** Tuition/fees: $10,750. Per-credit charge: $345.

**Application procedures. Admission:** Closing date 2/15. $50 fee, may be waived for applicants with need. Application may be submitted online. Admission notification on a rolling basis beginning on or about 4/1. Must reply by 5/1.

**Academics. Credit/placement by examination:** AP, CLEP, institutional tests. 18 credit hours maximum toward associate degree. **Support services:** Learning center, reduced course load, remedial instruction, study skills assistance, tutoring, writing center.

**Majors. Health:** Cardiovascular technology, medical assistant, nursing (RN), radiologic technology/medical imaging.

**Computing on campus.** 40 workstations in computer center, student center. Commuter students can connect to campus network. Online library available.

**Student life. Freshman orientation:** Mandatory. Held each spring and fall. **Activities:** Student government, student newspaper.

**Student services.** Campus ministries, career counseling, student employment services, financial aid counseling, health services.

**Contact.** E-mail: admissions@stvincentscollege.edu
Phone: (203) 576-5513 Fax: (203) 576-5318
Joseph Marrone, Admissions Director, St. Vincent's College, 2800 Main Street, Bridgeport, CT 06606

## Three Rivers Community College
**Norwich, Connecticut**
www.trcc.commnet.edu
**CB member**
**CB code: 3558**

- Public 2-year community and technical college
- Commuter campus in large town

**General.** Founded in 1969. Regionally accredited. **Enrollment:** 3,445 degree-seeking undergraduates; 413 non-degree-seeking students. **Degrees:** 388 associate awarded. **Location:** 45 miles from Hartford. **Calendar:** Semester, limited summer session. **Full-time faculty:** 78 total; 10% have terminal degrees, 9% minority, 55% women. **Part-time faculty:** 136 total; 51% women. **Special facilities:** Nuclear reactor simulator.

**Student profile.** Among degree-seeking undergraduates, 16% enrolled in a transfer program, 46% enrolled in a vocational program, 1% already have a bachelor's degree or higher, 857 enrolled as first-time, first-year students, 295 transferred in from other institutions.

| | | | |
|---|---|---|---|
| Part-time: | 63% | Asian American: | 3% |
| Out-of-state: | 1% | Hispanic American: | 8% |
| Women: | 62% | Native American: | 1% |
| African American: | 8% | 25 or older: | 52% |

**Transfer out.** 8% of students enrolled in the transfer program go on to 4-year colleges. **Colleges most students transferred to 2007:** Eastern Connecticut State University, University of Connecticut, Central Connecticut State University, Southern Illinois University, Sacred Heart University.

**Basis for selection.** Open admission, but selective for some programs. Selective admission for nursing program based on successful performance on Nursing Aptitude Exam, completion of prerequisite courses, and GPA of 2.5 or higher. **Adult students:** SAT/ACT scores not required. Basic skills placement tests in Math and English required unless students have completed a college level Math and English course. **Homeschooled:** Student may take Ability to Benefit Test if standard documentation requirements are not met.

**High school preparation.** One unit chemistry, biology, and algebra required for nursing program.

**2007-2008 Annual costs.** Tuition/fees: $2,828; $8,444 out-of-state. Per-credit charge: $104 in-state; $312 out-of-state. Out-of-state required fees: $992. Books/supplies: $1,200. Personal expenses: $1,304.

**2006-2007 Financial aid.** All financial aid based on need. 290 full-time freshmen applied for aid; 285 were judged to have need; 204 of these received aid. Average need met was 45%. Average scholarship/grant was $3,465; average loan $2,805. 72% of total undergraduate aid awarded as scholarships/grants, 28% as loans/jobs. Need-based aid available for part-time students.

**Application procedures. Admission:** No deadline. $20 fee, may be waived for applicants with need. Application may be submitted online. Admission notification on a rolling basis beginning on or about 3/30. **Financial aid:** Priority date 7/15; no closing date. FAFSA required. Applicants notified on a rolling basis; must reply within 2 week(s) of notification.

**Academics. Special study options:** Cooperative education, cross-registration, double major, dual enrollment of high school students, ESL, independent study, internships, liberal arts/career combination, study abroad. License preparation in nursing. **Credit/placement by examination:** AP, CLEP, institutional tests. 45 credit hours maximum toward associate degree. **Support services:** Reduced course load, remedial instruction, study skills assistance, tutoring, writing center.

**Majors. Business:** Accounting, business admin, hospitality admin, management information systems, office technology, tourism/travel. **Computer sciences:** General, applications programming, information systems. **Education:** Early childhood, special. **Engineering technology:** Architectural, civil, drafting, electrical, manufacturing, water quality. **Health:** Medical secretary, mental health services, substance abuse counseling. **Legal studies:** Legal secretary. **Liberal arts:** Arts/sciences. **Mechanic/repair:** General. **Physical sciences:** General. **Protective services:** Criminal justice, fire safety technology, police science. **Public administration:** General, human services, policy analysis. **Transportation:** Aviation.

**Most popular majors.** Business/marketing 18%, engineering/engineering technologies 15%, health sciences 19%, liberal arts 39%.

**Computing on campus.** 300 workstations in library, computer center. Online course registration, online library, helpline available.

**Student life. Freshman orientation:** Available. **Policies:** Student government controls student activity fees. **Activities:** Drama, literary magazine, student government, student newspaper, Spanish-American Association, Afro-American Association, student chapters of professional organizations, Gay-Straight Alliance, Get Involved in Volunteer Efforts, golf club, Student Nurses Association, Three Rivers United Environmentalists, Senior Student Ambassadors.

**Athletics.** NJCAA. **Intercollegiate:** Golf. **Intramural:** Basketball, bowling, skiing, table tennis, volleyball.

**Student services.** Adult student services, career counseling, student employment services, on-campus daycare, personal counseling, placement for graduates, veterans' counselor. **Physically disabled:** Services for visually, hearing impaired. **Transfer:** Re-entry adviser for new students. Transfer adviser, college fairs on campus for students transferring to 4-year colleges.

**Contact.** E-mail: admissions@trcc.commnet.edu
Phone: (860) 383-5260 Fax: (860) 885-1684
Gayla Holmes, Director of Admissions, Three Rivers Community College, 7 Mahan Drive, Norwich, CT 06360-2479

---

## Tunxis Community College
**Farmington, Connecticut**
www.tunxis.commnet.edu

**CB member**
**CB code:** 3897

- Public 2-year community college
- Commuter campus in large town

**General.** Founded in 1970. Regionally accredited. **Enrollment:** 2,951 degree-seeking undergraduates; 885 non-degree-seeking students. **Degrees:** 233 associate awarded. **ROTC:** Army, Naval, Air Force. **Location:** 15 miles from Hartford. **Calendar:** Semester, limited summer session. **Full-time faculty:** 67 total. **Part-time faculty:** 186 total. **Class size:** 29% < 20, 70% 20-39, less than 1% 40-49. **Special facilities:** Early childhood center.

**Student profile.** Among degree-seeking undergraduates, 624 enrolled as first-time, first-year students, 600 transferred in from other institutions.

| | | | |
|---|---|---|---|
| Part-time: | 52% | Women: | 62% |
| Out-of-state: | 1% | 25 or older: | 38% |

**Transfer out. Colleges most students transferred to 2007:** Central Connecticut State University, Charter Oak College, St. Joseph College.

**Basis for selection.** Open admission, but selective for some programs. Special requirements for dental hygiene, drug and alcohol rehabilitation counselor, physical therapist assistant, technological studies: television operations option, dental assisting, criminal justice command institute: supervisory leadership programs, and correction pre-service certification. ESL placement test required on non-native English speakers. Interview required of dental hygiene, drug and alcohol rehabilitation counselor majors. **Learning Disabled:** Contact Academic Support Center prior to placement testing if accommodations are necessary.

**2007-2008 Annual costs.** Tuition/fees: $2,828; $8,444 out-of-state. Per-credit charge: $104 in-state; $312 out-of-state. Books/supplies: $420. Personal expenses: $1,210.

**2006-2007 Financial aid. Need-based:** 80% of total undergraduate aid awarded as scholarships/grants, 20% as loans/jobs. Need-based aid available for part-time students. Work-study available nights, weekends and for part-time students. **Non-need-based:** Scholarships awarded for academics, leadership. **Additional information:** Financial aid available to all students showing need. Part-time students encouraged to apply.

**Application procedures. Admission:** No deadline. $20 fee, may be waived for applicants with need. Application may be submitted online. Admission notification on a rolling basis. Dental hygiene program closing date 01/01, notification by 03/01. Drug and alcohol rehabilitation counselor program closing date 02/01. **Financial aid:** Priority date 6/1; no closing date. FAFSA required. Applicants notified on a rolling basis starting 3/1.

**Academics. Special study options:** Cross-registration, distance learning, double major, dual enrollment of high school students, ESL, independent study, internships, liberal arts/career combination. License preparation in dental hygiene, physical therapy. **Credit/placement by examination:** CLEP, institutional tests. 30 credit hours maximum toward associate degree. **Support services:** Learning center, pre-admission summer program, reduced course load, remedial instruction, tutoring.

**Majors. Business:** Accounting, administrative services, business admin, fashion, finance, office/clerical. **Computer sciences:** Applications programming, computer graphics. **Education:** Early childhood. **Engineering:** Science. **Engineering technology:** Manufacturing. **Health:** Dental hygiene,

medical secretary, substance abuse counseling. **Legal studies:** Legal secretary. **Liberal arts:** Arts/sciences. **Public administration:** Human services. **Visual/performing arts:** General, commercial/advertising art.

**Computing on campus.** 200 workstations in library, computer center. Commuter students can connect to campus network.

**Student life. Freshman orientation:** Available. Preregistration for classes offered. Held once a week during the month before start of classes. **Activities:** Jazz band, literary magazine, student government, student newspaper, Minority Student Alliance, human services club, criminal justice club, dental hygiene group.

**Student services.** Career counseling, student employment services, financial aid counseling, health services, minority student services, on-campus daycare, personal counseling, placement for graduates. **Physically disabled:** Services for visually impaired. **Transfer:** Transfer adviser, college fairs on campus for students transferring to 4-year colleges.

**Contact.** E-mail: tx-admissions@txcc.commnet.edu
Phone: (860) 255-3555 Fax: (860) 255-3559
Peter McCluskey, Director of Admissions, Tunxis Community College, 271 Scott Swamp Road, Farmington, CT 06032-3187

# Delaware

## Delaware College of Art and Design
### Wilmington, Delaware
www.dcad.edu                    CB code: 5161

▶ Private 2-year visual arts college
▶ Large city

**General.** Regionally accredited. **Calendar:** Semester.

**Annual costs/financial aid.** Tuition/fees: $17,300. Room: $6,400.

**Contact.** Phone: (302) 622-8867 ext. 118
Director of Admissions, 600 North Market Street, Wilmington, DE 19801

## Delaware Technical and Community College: Owens
### Georgetown, Delaware
www.dtcc.edu                    CB code: 5169

▶ Public 2-year community and technical college
▶ Commuter campus in rural community

**General.** Founded in 1967. Regionally accredited. **Location:** 80 miles from Wilmington. **Calendar:** Semester.

**Annual costs/financial aid.** Tuition/fees (2007-2008): $2,422; $5,681 out-of-state. Books/supplies: $800. Personal expenses: $400. Need-based financial aid available to full-time and part-time students.

**Contact.** Phone: (302) 856-5400
Admissions Coordinator, Box 610, Georgetown, DE 19947

## Delaware Technical and Community College: Stanton/Wilmington
### Newark, Delaware
www.dtcc.edu                    CB code: 5154

▶ Public 2-year community and technical college
▶ Commuter campus in small city

**General.** Founded in 1967. Regionally accredited. **Location:** 30 miles from Philadelphia. **Calendar:** Semester.

**Annual costs/financial aid.** Tuition/fees (2007-2008): $2,422; $5,681 out-of-state. Books/supplies: $800. Personal expenses: $400. Need-based financial aid available to full-time and part-time students.

**Contact.** Phone: (302) 454-3954
Admissions Representative, 400 Stanton-Christiana Road, Newark, DE 19713

## Delaware Technical and Community College: Terry
### Dover, Delaware                    CB member
www.dtcc.edu                    CB code: 5201

▶ Public 2-year community and technical college
▶ Commuter campus in large town

**General.** Founded in 1972. Regionally accredited. **Location:** 90 miles from Baltimore, 75 miles from Philadelphia. **Calendar:** Semester.

**Annual costs/financial aid.** Tuition/fees (2007-2008): $2,422; $5,681 out-of-state. Books/supplies: $800. Personal expenses: $400. Need-based financial aid available to full-time and part-time students.

**Contact.** Phone: (302) 857-1020
Admissions Coordinator, 100 Campus Drive, Dover, DE 19901

# Florida

## ATI Career Training Center: Ft. Lauderdale

**Ft. Lauderdale, Florida**
www.aticareertraining.edu                    CB code: 2945

- For-profit 2-year technical college
- Small city

**General.** Accredited by ACCSCT. **Calendar:** Continuous.

**Annual costs/financial aid.** Full program costs: $25,440 for electronics, $23,140 for medical, $20,500 for Network Administration, $19,300 for drafting. Costs include all tuition, fees and supplies.

**Contact.** Phone: (954) 973-4760
2890 NW 62nd Street, Fort Lauderdale, FL 33309-9731

## ATI Career Training Center: Oakland Park

**Oakland Park, Florida**
www.aticareertraining.edu                    CB code: 3182

- For-profit 2-year technical college
- Large town

**General.** Accredited by ACCSCT. **Calendar:** Continuous.

**Annual costs/financial aid.** Tuition and fees entire AC/refrigeration program $17,776; for entire automotive service technician program $18,000.

**Contact.** Phone: (954) 563-5899
Director of Admission, 3501 NW 9th Avenue, Oakland Park, FL 33309

## ATI College of Health

**Miami, Florida**
www.aticareertraining.edu                    CB code: 3183

- For-profit 2-year health science and technical college
- Very large city

**General.** Accredited by ACCSCT. **Calendar:** Semester.

**Annual costs/financial aid.** $19,380 tuition for medical assistant program and pharmacy technician program; $40,381 tuition for diagnostic ultrasound program and respiratory therapist program; $31,102 for dental and health information technology. Personal expenses: $2,064. Need-based financial aid available to full-time and part-time students.

**Contact.** Phone: (305) 628-1000
1395 NW 167th Street, Miami, FL 33169-5745

## Brevard Community College

**Cocoa, Florida**                              CB member
www.brevardcc.edu                              CB code: 5073

- Public 2-year community college
- Commuter campus in large town

**General.** Founded in 1960. Regionally accredited. Additional campuses in Cocoa, Melbourne, Palm Bay, Titusville. Aerospace technology courses taught at the Kennedy Space Center. **Enrollment:** 13,024 degree-seeking undergraduates; 1,164 non-degree-seeking students. **Degrees:** 1,969 associate awarded. **ROTC:** Army, Air Force. **Location:** 50 miles from Orlando. **Calendar:** Semester, extensive summer session. **Full-time faculty:** 220 total; 20% have terminal degrees, 11% minority, 52% women. **Part-time faculty:** 572 total; 15% minority, 72% women. **Class size:** 34% < 20, 66% 20-39, less than 1% 40-49, less than 1% 50-99. **Special facilities:** Planetarium, observatory, playhouse, WBCC-TV, performing arts center, multicultural center.

**Student profile.** Among degree-seeking undergraduates, 2,651 enrolled as first-time, first-year students.

| | | | |
|---|---|---|---|
| Part-time: | 57% | Hispanic American: | 8% |
| Out-of-state: | 2% | Native American: | 1% |
| Women: | 59% | International: | 1% |
| African American: | 11% | 25 or older: | 34% |
| Asian American: | 3% | | |

**Transfer out.** 70% of students enrolled in the transfer program go on to 4-year colleges. **Colleges most students transferred to 2007:** University of Central Florida.

**Basis for selection.** Open admission, but selective for some programs. Additional application and requirements for health science, law enforcement and corrections programs. CPT required for admission but scores not used. SAT or ACT may be submitted instead of CPT. California Achievement Tests, Stanford Test of Academic Skills, Test of Adult Basic Education required for health program applicants. **Homeschooled:** Affidavit of home school completion required. **Learning Disabled:** Students may self-disclose with Office for Students with Disabilities.

**2007-2008 Annual costs.** Tuition/fees: $2,027; $6,990 out-of-state. Per-credit charge: $55 in-state; $220 out-of-state. Books/supplies: $800. Personal expenses: $1,224.

**Financial aid. Need-based:** Need-based aid available for part-time students. **Non-need-based:** Scholarships awarded for academics, athletics.

**Application procedures. Admission:** Closing date 8/8 (receipt date). $30 fee. Application may be submitted online. Admission notification on a rolling basis. **Financial aid:** Priority date 4/15, closing date 6/30. FAFSA required. Applicants notified on a rolling basis starting 6/1; must reply within 2 week(s) of notification.

**Academics. Special study options:** Accelerated study, cooperative education, cross-registration, distance learning, double major, dual enrollment of high school students, ESL, honors, independent study, internships, student-designed major, study abroad, teacher certification program, weekend college. Bachelor's degree programs available on campus. License preparation in dental hygiene, nursing, paramedic, radiology, real estate. **Credit/placement by examination:** AP, CLEP, IB, institutional tests. 45 credit hours maximum toward associate degree. **Support services:** Learning center, reduced course load, remedial instruction, study skills assistance, tutoring, writing center.

**Majors. Business:** Administrative services, business admin, management information systems, office management. **Computer sciences:** Programming, systems analysis. **Education:** Early childhood. **Engineering:** General, computer. **Engineering technology:** Drafting, electrical. **Health:** Clinical lab technology, dental hygiene, EMT paramedic, medical radiologic technology/radiation therapy, nursing (RN). **Legal studies:** Court reporting, legal secretary, paralegal. **Protective services:** Firefighting, police science. **Visual/performing arts:** Commercial/advertising art.

**Computing on campus.** 1,800 workstations in library, computer center, student center. Commuter students can connect to campus network. Online course registration, online library, helpline, student web hosting, wireless network available.

**Student life. Freshman orientation:** Mandatory. **Activities:** Concert band, campus ministries, choral groups, dance, drama, international student organizations, literary magazine, music ensembles, musical theater, student government, TV station, Student Nurses Association of Florida, Phi Theta Kappa, African American student association, Phi Mu Alpha.

**Athletics.** NJCAA. **Intercollegiate:** Baseball M, basketball, golf M, softball W, volleyball W. **Team name:** Titans.

**Student services.** Adult student services, career counseling, student employment services, financial aid counseling, minority student services, on-campus daycare, veterans' counselor. **Physically disabled:** Services for visually, speech, hearing impaired. **Learning disabled:** Comprehensive services available. **Transfer:** College fairs on campus for students transferring to 4-year colleges.

**Contact.** Phone: (321) 632-1111 Toll-free number: (888) 747-2802 Fax: (321) 433-7357
Donald Astrab, Executive Vice President, Chief Learning Officer, Brevard Community College, 1519 Clearlake Road, Cocoa, FL 32922-9987

## Broward Community College

**Fort Lauderdale, Florida**                    CB member
www.broward.edu                                CB code: 5074

- Public 2-year community college
- Commuter campus in small city

**General.** Founded in 1959. Regionally accredited. Multilocation institution. North campus located in Coconut Creek, central campus in Davie, south campus in Pembroke Pines. Credit courses also offered at corporate sites (Ft. Lauderdale Center). **Enrollment:** 26,028 degree-seeking undergraduates; 5,702 non-degree-seeking students. **Degrees:** 3,567 associate awarded. **ROTC:** Army, Air Force. **Location:** 20 miles from Miami. **Calendar:** Semester, extensive summer session. **Full-time faculty:** 342 total; 31% minority, 51% women. **Part-time faculty:** 1,011 total; 26% minority, 48% women. **Class size:** 40% < 20, 58% 20-39, 1% 40-49, less than 1% 50-99, less than 1% >100. **Special facilities:** Concert hall, planetarium, golf course.

**Student profile.** Among degree-seeking undergraduates, 75% enrolled in a transfer program, 25% enrolled in a vocational program, 5,181 enrolled as first-time, first-year students, 1,791 transferred in from other institutions.

| | | | |
|---|---|---|---|
| Part-time: | 63% | Asian American: | 3% |
| Out-of-state: | 2% | Hispanic American: | 28% |
| Women: | 61% | International: | 8% |
| African American: | 29% | 25 or older: | 43% |

**Transfer out. Colleges most students transferred to 2007:** Florida Atlantic University, Florida International University.

**Basis for selection.** Open admission, but selective for some programs. Limited access programs require secondary application process. SAT or ACT may be used for placement in lieu of Florida CPT. **Homeschooled:** Transcript of courses and grades required.

**2007-2008 Annual costs.** Tuition/fees: $2,004; $7,172 out-of-state. Books/supplies: $1,000. Personal expenses: $1,590.

**2006-2007 Financial aid. Need-based:** 75% of total undergraduate aid awarded as scholarships/grants, 25% as loans/jobs. Need-based aid available for part-time students. Work-study available nights, weekends and for part-time students. **Non-need-based:** Scholarships awarded for academics, athletics, leadership, state residency.

**Application procedures. Admission:** No deadline. $35 fee, may be waived for applicants with need. Application may be submitted online. Admission notification on a rolling basis beginning on or about 2/15. Returning students who have not attended BCC for two or more major semesters (not including summer term) must submit a re-entry application. **Financial aid:** Priority date 4/15, closing date 7/1. FAFSA, institutional form required. Applicants notified on a rolling basis starting 7/15.

**Academics. Special study options:** Accelerated study, cooperative education, distance learning, dual enrollment of high school students, exchange student, honors, independent study, internships, study abroad, weekend college. License preparation in aviation, dental hygiene, nursing, paramedic, physical therapy, real estate. **Credit/placement by examination:** AP, CLEP, IB, institutional tests. 30 credit hours maximum toward associate degree. **Support services:** Learning center, pre-admission summer program, remedial instruction, study skills assistance, tutoring, writing center.

**Majors. Architecture:** Landscape. **Biology:** General. **Business:** General, accounting, business admin, finance, hospitality admin, international, international marketing, management science, office/clerical, tourism/travel. **Communications:** Broadcast journalism, journalism. **Computer sciences:** General, computer graphics, computer science, data processing, information systems, programming, systems analysis. **Conservation:** Environmental science. **Education:** General, early childhood, elementary, mathematics, music, science, special. **Engineering:** General, civil, computer, electrical, software. **Engineering technology:** Civil. **English:** English lit. **Family/consumer sciences:** Child care, food/nutrition. **Foreign languages:** General. **Health:** Athletic training, cardiovascular technology, clinical lab assistant, clinical lab technology, dental hygiene, EMT paramedic, health care admin, medical radiologic technology/radiation therapy, medical records admin, nuclear medical technology, nursing (RN), ophthalmic lab technology, physical therapy assistant, predental, premedicine, prenursing, prepharmacy, preveterinary, recreational therapy, respiratory therapy technology, sonography. **History:** General. **Legal studies:** Court reporting, legal secretary, paralegal, prelaw. **Liberal arts:** Arts/sciences. **Math:** General. **Mechanic/repair:** Automotive. **Parks/recreation:** General. **Philosophy/religion:** Religion. **Physical sciences:** Chemistry, physics. **Protective services:** Criminal justice, firefighting, security services. **Psychology:** General. **Public administration:** Social work. **Social sciences:** Anthropology, economics, geography, political science, sociology. **Transportation:** Aviation, aviation management. **Visual/performing arts:** Art, dramatic, interior design, music history.

**Computing on campus.** 3,856 workstations in library, computer center, student center. Commuter students can connect to campus network. Online course registration, online library, helpline, wireless network available.

**Student life. Freshman orientation:** Available. Preregistration for classes offered. **Activities:** Bands, choral groups, dance, drama, literary magazine, music ensembles, musical theater, opera, student government, student newspaper, symphony orchestra, Phi Theta Kappa, Phi Beta Lambda, African

American student union, American Institute of Architecture Students, Catholic club, chess club, HIV peer educators, film club, French club.

**Athletics.** NCAA. **Intercollegiate:** Baseball M, basketball, diving M, softball W, tennis W, volleyball W. **Intramural:** Basketball, bowling, football (non-tackle) M, soccer M, swimming, tennis. **Team name:** Seahawks.

**Student services.** Adult student services, alcohol/substance abuse counseling, career counseling, student employment services, financial aid counseling, health services, on-campus daycare, personal counseling, placement for graduates, veterans' counselor. **Physically disabled:** Services for visually, speech, hearing impaired.

**Contact.** Phone: (954) 201-7541 Fax: (954) 201-7466
Willie Alexander, Associate Vice President for Student Affairs and Registrar, Broward Community College, 225 East Las Olas Boulevard, Fort Lauderdale, FL 33301

## Brown Mackie College: Miami
**Miami, Florida**
**www.cbcaec.com**

- For-profit 2-year business and career college
- Very large city

**General.** Accredited by ACICS. **Enrollment:** 517 degree-seeking undergraduates; 17 non-degree-seeking students. **Degrees:** 51 associate awarded. **Location:** Downtown. **Calendar:** Quarter, extensive summer session. **Full-time faculty:** 10 total; 70% minority, 50% women. **Part-time faculty:** 17 total; 76% minority, 53% women. **Class size:** 17% < 20, 83% 20-39.

**Student profile.** Among degree-seeking undergraduates, 362 enrolled as first-time, first-year students.

| | | | |
|---|---|---|---|
| Women: | 70% | 25 or older: | 28% |

**Transfer out.** 40% of students enrolled in the transfer program go on to 4-year colleges.

**Basis for selection.** Open admission. **Homeschooled:** Transcript of courses and grades, state high school equivalency certificate, interview required.

**2007-2008 Annual costs.** Tuition/fees: $11,472.

**Academics. Special study options:** Double major. **Credit/placement by examination:** CLEP, institutional tests. **Support services:** Remedial instruction, study skills assistance, tutoring.

**Majors. Business:** Accounting, business admin. **Engineering technology:** Software. **Health:** Medical secretary. **Legal studies:** Paralegal. **Protective services:** Law enforcement admin.

**Computing on campus.** 125 workstations in library, computer center. Dormitories wired for high-speed internet access. Commuter students can connect to campus network. Online library available.

**Student life. Freshman orientation:** Mandatory. **Activities:** Student newspaper.

**Athletics. Team name:** The Lions.

**Student services. Transfer:** Re-entry adviser, pre-admission transcript evaluation for new students. Transfer adviser, college fairs on campus for students transferring to 4-year colleges.

**Contact.** E-mail: bmmiadm@brownmackie.edu
Phone: (305) 341-6600 Toll-free number: (866) 505-0335
Maria Koontz, Director of Admissions, Brown Mackie College: Miami, 1501 Biscayne Boulevard, Miami, FL 33132

## Central Florida College
**Winter Park, Florida**
**www.centralfloridacollege.edu**

- For-profit 2-year technical college
- Very large city
- Interview required

**General.** Accredited by ACCSCT. **Enrollment:** 450 degree-seeking undergraduates. **Degrees:** 45 associate awarded. **Calendar:** Continuous, extensive summer session. **Full-time faculty:** 18 total. **Part-time faculty:** 20 total.

**Basis for selection.** Open admission.

**2007-2008 Annual costs.** Certificate and diploma programs range from $10,690 to $15,225. Associate of Science degrees range from $21,995 to $24,995; including books.

**Financial aid.** All financial aid based on need.

**Application procedures. Admission:** No deadline. $50 fee. Admission notification on a rolling basis. **Financial aid:** No deadline. FAFSA required.

**Academics. Special study options:** Distance learning, liberal arts/career combination. **Credit/placement by examination:** CLEP. **Support services:** Study skills assistance.

**Majors. Business:** Accounting, business admin. **Health:** Insurance specialist, medical assistant, medical records technology. **Personal/culinary services:** Cosmetic. **Protective services:** Police science.

**Most popular majors.** Business/marketing 13%, health sciences 80%.

**Computing on campus.** 64 workstations in library, computer center. Online library available.

**Contact.** E-mail: admissions@centralfloridacollege.edu
Phone: (407) 843-3984
Roger Buck, Coporate Operations Director, Central Florida College, 1573 West Fairbanks Avenue, Winter Park, FL 32789

---

## Central Florida Community College
### Ocala, Florida
**www.cf.edu**  CB code: 5127

- Public 2-year community college
- Commuter campus in small city

**General.** Founded in 1957. Regionally accredited. **Enrollment:** 5,615 degree-seeking undergraduates; 595 non-degree-seeking students. **Degrees:** 804 associate awarded. **Location:** 72 miles from Orlando. **Calendar:** Semester, extensive summer session. **Full-time faculty:** 110 total; 20% have terminal degrees, 6% minority, 52% women. **Part-time faculty:** 497 total; 15% minority, 50% women. **Special facilities:** Art museum. **Partnerships:** Formal partnership with Emergency One Corporation.

**Student profile.** Among degree-seeking undergraduates, 1,114 enrolled as first-time, first-year students.

| | | | |
|---|---|---|---|
| Part-time: | 55% | Women: | 62% |
| Out-of-state: | 1% | 25 or older: | 34% |

**Transfer out. Colleges most students transferred to 2007:** University of Florida, University of Central Florida, Florida State University.

**Basis for selection.** Open admission, but selective for some programs. Special requirements for registered nursing, dental assisting, physical therapy assistant, child care, criminal justice, practical nursing, surgical technology programs.

**High school preparation.** Recommended units include English 4, mathematics 3, social studies 3 and science 3.

**2007-2008 Annual costs.** Tuition/fees: $2,038; $7,382 out-of-state. Books/supplies: $1,230. Personal expenses: $3,386.

**Financial aid. Need-based:** Need-based aid available for part-time students. **Non-need-based:** Scholarships awarded for academics, athletics, minority status, music/drama, state residency.

**Application procedures. Admission:** $20 fee, may be waived for applicants with need. Application must be submitted on paper. Admission notification on a rolling basis. **Financial aid:** No deadline. FAFSA required.

**Academics. Special study options:** Accelerated study, cooperative education, distance learning, dual enrollment of high school students, ESL, honors, independent study, internships, liberal arts/career combination, teacher certification program. Bachelor's degrees available through on-campus University Center. Corporate training available through CFCC Institute. Bachelor's degree programs available on campus. License preparation in real estate. **Credit/placement by examination:** AP, CLEP, IB, institutional tests. 21 credit hours maximum toward associate degree. ACT, SAT, CPT are authorized placement tests for community colleges in Florida. **Support services:** GED preparation and test center, learning center, pre-admission summer program, reduced course load, remedial instruction, study skills assistance, tutoring, writing center.

**Majors. Agriculture:** Equestrian studies, horticulture, landscaping. **Business:** Accounting, accounting technology, business admin, executive assistant, restaurant/food services. **Computer sciences:** System admin. **Education:** Early childhood, elementary. **Engineering technology:** Architectural drafting. **Health:** EMT paramedic, licensed practical nurse, medical records technology, nursing (RN), physical therapy assistant. **Legal studies:** Paralegal. **Liberal arts:** Arts/sciences. **Mechanic/repair:** Automotive. **Personal/culinary services:** Chef training. **Protective services:** Fire safety technology, law enforcement admin. **Public administration:** Human services.

**Most popular majors.** Business/marketing 6%, health sciences 14%, liberal arts 75%.

**Computing on campus.** 2,200 workstations in library, computer center, student center. Online library, helpline available.

**Student life. Freshman orientation:** Mandatory. Preregistration for classes offered. Program held prior to beginning of term; also available online. **Housing:** College Square Student Residence Center owned and operated by Central Florida Community College Foundation near campus. **Activities:** Bands, campus ministries, choral groups, dance, drama, literary magazine, music ensembles, musical theater, student government, student newspaper, symphony orchestra, Afro-student union, Hispanic club, Phi Theta Kappa, Community of Scholars, Brain Bowl, Phi Beta Lambda, gay/straight alliance, peer educators.

**Athletics.** NJCAA. **Intercollegiate:** Baseball M, basketball, softball W, tennis W. **Team name:** Patriots.

**Student services.** Adult student services, career counseling, services for economically disadvantaged, student employment services, financial aid counseling, on-campus daycare, personal counseling, placement for graduates, veterans' counselor. **Physically disabled:** Services for visually, speech, hearing impaired. **Transfer:** Transfer adviser, college fairs on campus for students transferring to 4-year colleges.

**Contact.** Phone: (352) 873-5801 Fax: (352) 873-5875
Christy Jones, Registrar, Central Florida Community College, 3001 SW College Road, Ocala, FL 34474-4415

---

## City College: Casselberry
### Casselberry, Florida

- For-profit 2-year community college
- Large town
- Interview required

**General.** Accredited by ACICS. **Enrollment:** 110 degree-seeking undergraduates. **Degrees:** 40 associate awarded. **Calendar:** Semester. **Full-time faculty:** 4 total. **Part-time faculty:** 19 total.

**Basis for selection.** Applicant must pass the college's entrance examination and interview.

**2008-2009 Annual costs.** Tuition/fees: $9,675. Per-credit charge: $215.

**Application procedures. Admission:** No deadline. $25 fee. **Financial aid:** No deadline.

**Academics. Credit/placement by examination:** CLEP.

**Majors. Business:** Business admin, marketing. **Computer sciences:** General. **Health:** Health services. **Protective services:** Security management.

**Contact.** Phone: (407) 831-8466 Fax: (407) 831-1147
I Cruz, Director of Admissions, City College: Casselberry, 853 State Road 436, Suite 200, Casselberry, FL 32707-5353

---

## City College: Gainesville
### Gainesville, Florida
**www.citycollege.edu**  CB code: 3579

- For-profit 2-year business and health science college
- Small city

**General.** Accredited by ACICS. **Enrollment:** 228 degree-seeking undergraduates. **Degrees:** 11 bachelor's, 70 associate awarded. **Calendar:** Continuous.

**Basis for selection.** Open admission.

**2007-2008 Annual costs.** Tuition/fees: $10,075. Per-credit charge: $195. Books/supplies: $1,044. Personal expenses: $1,692.

**Academics. Credit/placement by examination:** CLEP.

**Majors. Business:** Business admin. **Computer sciences:** General. **Legal studies:** General.

**Contact.**   E-mail: kcartier@citycollege.edu
Phone: (352) 335-4000 Fax: (352) 335-4303
Kelly Cartier, Registrar, City College: Gainesville, 2400 SW 13th Street, Gainesville, FL 32608

## College of Business and Technology: Flagler
**Miami, Florida**
**www.cbt.edu**

- Private 2-year junior and technical college
- Commuter campus in very large city
- Interview required

**General.** Accredited by ACICS. **Enrollment:** 153 degree-seeking undergraduates. **Calendar:** Semester. **Full-time faculty:** 8 total. **Part-time faculty:** 12 total.

**Student profile.** Among degree-seeking undergraduates, 10% enrolled in a transfer program, 60% enrolled in a vocational program, 77 enrolled as first-time, first-year students, 20 transferred in from other institutions.

**Transfer out.** 70% of students enrolled in the transfer program go on to 4-year colleges. **Colleges most students transferred to 2007:** Jones College, Carlos Albizu University.

**Basis for selection.** Open admission. **Homeschooled:** Transcript of courses and grades required.

**2007-2008 Annual costs.** Tuition/fees: $11,772. Per-credit charge: $322. Books/supplies: $1,350.

**Financial aid.** All financial aid based on need. Need-based aid available for part-time students. Work-study available nights and for part-time students.

**Application procedures. Admission:** No deadline. $25 fee. Application may be submitted online. **Financial aid:** No deadline. FAFSA required.

**Academics. Special study options:** Distance learning, ESL. **Credit/placement by examination:** CLEP. **Support services:** Tutoring.

**Majors. Business:** Accounting, business admin. **Computer sciences:** Networking, web page design. **Health:** Medical assistant, office admin. **Mechanic/repair:** Heating/ac/refrig.

**Computing on campus.** PC or laptop required. 100 workstations in library. Online library, repair service, wireless network available.

**Student life. Freshman orientation:** Mandatory.

**Student services.** Career counseling, student employment services, financial aid counseling.

**Contact.**   E-mail: admissions@cbt.edu
Phone: (305) 273-4499 ext. 2203 Fax: (305) 485-4411
Margarita Velez, Director of Admission, College of Business and Technology: Flagler, 8230 West Flagler Street, Miami, FL 33144

## College of Business and Technology: Hialeah
**Hialeah, Florida**
**www.cbt.edu**

- For-profit 2-year business and technical college
- Small city

**General.** Accredited by ACICS. **Calendar:** Continuous.

**Annual costs/financial aid.** Tuition/fees (2007-2008): $11,772.

**Contact.**   Phone: (786) 693-8842
Admissions Director, 935 West 49th Street Suite 203, Hialeah, FL 33012-3436

## College of Business and Technology: Kendall
**Miami, Florida**
**www.cbt.edu**

- Private 2-year health science and junior college
- Very large city

**General.** Accredited by ACICS. **Enrollment:** 93 degree-seeking undergraduates. **Degrees:** 23 associate awarded. **Calendar:** Semester. **Full-time faculty:** 12 total. **Part-time faculty:** 6 total.

**Basis for selection.** Open admission.

**2007-2008 Annual costs.** Tuition/fees: $11,772. Per-credit charge: $322.

**Academics. Credit/placement by examination:** CLEP.

**Majors. Business:** Accounting, business admin. **Computer sciences:** LAN/WAN management. **Health:** Medical assistant, office admin. **Mechanic/repair:** Heating/ac/refrig. **Visual/performing arts:** Graphic design.

**Contact.**   E-mail: admissions@cbt.edu
Phone: (305) 273-4499
Margarita Velez, Director of Admissions, College of Business and Technology: Kendall, 8991 SW 107 Avenue, Miami, FL 33176

## Daytona Beach Community College
**Daytona Beach, Florida**
**www.dbc.edu**                                      CB code: 5159

- Public 2-year community and technical college
- Commuter campus in large city

**General.** Founded in 1958. Regionally accredited. **Enrollment:** 12,111 degree-seeking undergraduates. **Degrees:** 6 bachelor's, 1,560 associate awarded. **ROTC:** Army, Air Force. **Location:** 90 miles from Jacksonville, 65 miles from Orlando. **Calendar:** Semester, limited summer session. **Full-time faculty:** 301 total. **Part-time faculty:** 799 total. **Special facilities:** Museum of photography, interactive TV system.

**Student profile.**

| | | | |
|---|---|---|---|
| Out-of-state: | 6% | 25 or older: | 26% |

**Transfer out. Colleges most students transferred to 2007:** University of Central Florida.

**Basis for selection.** Open admission, but selective for some programs. Special requirements for nursing, allied health, and public service programs.

**High school preparation.** Recommended units include mathematics 3 and science 3.

**2007-2008 Annual costs.** Tuition/fees: $2,083; $8,225 out-of-state. Books/supplies: $800. Personal expenses: $2,624.

**2006-2007 Financial aid. Need-based:** 67% of total undergraduate aid awarded as scholarships/grants, 33% as loans/jobs. Need-based aid available for part-time students. Work-study available for part-time students. **Non-need-based:** Scholarships awarded for athletics, leadership, music/drama.

**Application procedures. Admission:** No deadline. No application fee. Application may be submitted online. Admission notification on a rolling basis. **Financial aid:** No deadline. FAFSA required. Applicants notified on a rolling basis starting 2/15.

**Academics. Special study options:** Cooperative education, distance learning, dual enrollment of high school students, ESL, honors, independent study, internships, liberal arts/career combination, study abroad, weekend college. Bachelor's degree programs available on campus. License preparation in dental hygiene, nursing, paramedic, physical therapy. **Credit/placement by examination:** AP, CLEP, IB, institutional tests. 45 credit hours maximum toward associate degree. **Support services:** GED preparation and test center, learning center, pre-admission summer program, remedial instruction, tutoring.

**Majors. Agriculture:** Turf management. **Architecture:** Interior. **Business:** Accounting, banking/financial services, business admin, hospitality admin, marketing, office management, office technology, tourism/travel. **Computer sciences:** General, information systems, programming. **Education:** General, Deaf/hearing impaired. **Engineering:** General, computer. **Engineering**

technology: Architectural, automotive, civil, computer systems, construction, drafting, electrical. **Family/consumer sciences:** Child care. **Health:** EMT paramedic, health services, medical radiologic technology/radiation therapy, medical records technology, medical secretary, respiratory therapy technology. **Legal studies:** Court reporting, legal secretary, paralegal. **Liberal arts:** Arts/sciences. **Protective services:** Firefighting, police science. **Visual/performing arts:** Commercial/advertising art, interior design, photography.

**Most popular majors.** Health sciences 17%, liberal arts 66%.

**Computing on campus.** 752 workstations in library, computer center. Online course registration available.

**Student life. Freshman orientation:** Available. Preregistration for classes offered. **Housing:** Assistance in locating off-campus housing available to international students. **Activities:** Bands, campus ministries, choral groups, dance, drama, music ensembles, musical theater, opera, student government, student newspaper, symphony orchestra, TV station, Amnesty International, human services paraprofessional organization, African American student union.

**Athletics.** NJCAA. **Intercollegiate:** Baseball M, basketball, golf W, softball W. **Intramural:** Basketball, bowling, fencing, racquetball, soccer, table tennis, tennis, volleyball. **Team name:** Falcons.

**Student services.** Career counseling, student employment services, on-campus daycare, personal counseling, placement for graduates, veterans' counselor, women's services. **Physically disabled:** Services for visually, speech, hearing impaired. **Transfer:** Transfer adviser, college fairs on campus for students transferring to 4-year colleges.

**Contact.** E-mail: admissions@dbc.edu
Phone: (386) 506-3000 ext. 3059 Fax: (386) 506-4489
Karen Sanders, Director of Admissions, Daytona Beach Community College, DBCC Admissions Office, Daytona Beach, FL 32114-2811

## Florida Career College: Hialeah
Hialeah, Florida
www.careercollege.edu

◆ For-profit 2-year junior and technical college
◆ Commuter campus in very large city
◆ Interview required

**General.** Accredited by ACICS. **Enrollment:** 215 degree-seeking undergraduates. **Degrees:** 45 associate awarded. **Calendar:** Quarter, limited summer session. **Full-time faculty:** 14 total. **Part-time faculty:** 3 total. **Class size:** 69% < 20, 31% 20-39.

**Basis for selection.** Open admission.

**2007-2008 Annual costs.** Per-credit charge: $370. Tuition varies by length of program and is $370 per credit hour. Books/supplies: $1,000.

**Application procedures. Admission:** No deadline. No application fee. Application must be submitted on paper. Admission notification on a rolling basis.

**Academics. Special study options:** Accelerated study, internships. **Credit/ placement by examination:** CLEP. Up to 50% of program credits can be earned through a combination of transfer and/or credit by examination. **Support services:** Learning center, tutoring.

**Majors. Computer sciences:** Programming, webmaster. **Engineering:** Computer. **Health:** Office admin.

**Computing on campus.** 250 workstations in library, computer center. Commuter students can connect to campus network. Online course registration, online library available.

**Student life. Freshman orientation:** Available.

**Student services.** Financial aid counseling, placement for graduates.

**Contact.** Phone: (305) 825-3231 Fax: (305) 825-3436
Martin Najarro, Director of Admissions, Florida Career College: Hialeah, 3750 West 18th Avenue, Hialeah, FL 33012

## Florida Career College: Lauderdale Lakes
Lauderdale Lakes, Florida
lauderdalelakes.college-info.com

◆ For-profit 2-year technical college
◆ Large town

**General.** Accredited by ACICS. **Calendar:** Quarter.

**Annual costs/financial aid.** Tuition varies by length of program and is $370 per credit hour.

**Contact.** Phone: (954) 535-8700
Director of Admissions, 3383 North State Road 7, Lauderdale Lakes, FL 33319

## Florida Career College: Miami
Miami, Florida
www.careercollege.edu                    CB code: 3581

◆ For-profit 2-year business and technical college
◆ Large city

**General.** Accredited by ACICS. **Enrollment:** 180 degree-seeking undergraduates. **Degrees:** 100 associate awarded. **Calendar:** Continuous. **Full-time faculty:** 12 total. **Part-time faculty:** 11 total.

**Basis for selection.** Open admission.

**2007-2008 Annual costs.** Per-credit charge: $370. Tuition varies by length of program and is $370 per credit hour.

**Application procedures. Admission:** No deadline. No application fee.

**Academics. Credit/placement by examination:** CLEP.

**Majors. Computer sciences:** General, webmaster. **Engineering:** Computer. **Health:** Office admin. **Mechanic/repair:** General.

**Contact.** Phone: (305) 553-6065
Martin Najarro, Director of Admission, Florida Career College: Miami, 1321 SW 107 Avenue, Suite 201B, Miami, FL 3317-521

## Florida Career College: Pembroke Pines
Pembroke Pines, Florida
www.careercollege.edu

◆ For-profit 2-year business and technical college
◆ Small city

**General.** Accredited by ACICS. **Enrollment:** 500 degree-seeking undergraduates. **Degrees:** 60 associate awarded. **Calendar:** Continuous. **Full-time faculty:** 20 total. **Part-time faculty:** 9 total.

**Basis for selection.** Open admission.

**2007-2008 Annual costs.** Per-credit charge: $370. Tuition varies by length of program and is $370 per credit hour.

**Application procedures. Admission:** No deadline. No application fee.

**Academics. Credit/placement by examination:** CLEP.

**Majors. Computer sciences:** Programming, webmaster. **Engineering:** Computer. **Health:** Office admin.

**Contact.** E-mail: info@careercollege.edu
Phone: (954) 965-7272 Fax: (954) 983-2707
Martin Najarro, Director of Admission, Florida Career College: Pembroke Pines, 7891 Pines Boulevard, Pembroke Pines, FL 33024

## Florida Career College: West Palm Beach
West Palm Beach, Florida

◆ For-profit 2-year technical college
◆ Commuter campus in small city

**General.** Accredited by ACICS. **Enrollment:** 520 degree-seeking undergraduates. **Degrees:** 95 associate awarded. **Calendar:** Continuous. **Full-time faculty:** 20 total. **Part-time faculty:** 15 total.

**Basis for selection.** Open admission.

**2007-2008 Annual costs.** Per-credit charge: $370. Tuition varies by length of program and is $370 per credit hour.

**Application procedures. Admission:** No deadline. No application fee.

**Academics. Credit/placement by examination:** CLEP.

**Majors. Computer sciences:** General. **Engineering:** Computer. **Health:** Office admin.

**Contact.** Phone: (561) 689-0550 Toll-free number: (888) 852-7272 Fax: (561) 689-0739
Martin Najarro, Director of Admissions, Florida Career College: West Palm Beach, 6065 Okeechobee Boulevard West, West Palm Beach, FL 33417

## Florida College of Natural Health: Bradenton
**Bradenton, Florida**
www.fcnh.com                                    CB code: 5024

- For-profit 2-year health science and career college
- Commuter campus in small city

**General.** Accredited by ACCSCT. **Enrollment:** 62 degree-seeking undergraduates. **Degrees:** 46 associate awarded. **Location:** 40 miles from Tampa. **Calendar:** Continuous, extensive summer session. **Full-time faculty:** 6 total; 67% women. **Part-time faculty:** 7 total; 57% women.

**Student profile.** Among degree-seeking undergraduates, 60% enrolled in a vocational program.

**Basis for selection.** Open admission, but selective for some programs. Passing score on college entrance exam (OLSAT) or 800 SAT (exclusive of Writing) or 17 ACT required of degree-seeking applicants.

**2007-2008 Annual costs.** 4 degree programs with $335 per credit hour charge. 2 diploma programs with flat rate: therapeutic massage 6-month training program, $9,720; skincare 4-to 5-month training program, $4,650.

**Financial aid.** All financial aid based on need.

**Application procedures. Admission:** No deadline. No application fee. Admission notification on a rolling basis. **Financial aid:** No deadline. FAFSA required. Applicants notified on a rolling basis.

**Academics. Credit/placement by examination:** CLEP.

**Majors. Health:** Massage therapy.

**Computing on campus.** 2 workstations in library.

**Student life. Freshman orientation:** Mandatory.

**Student services.** Financial aid counseling, placement for graduates.

**Contact.** E-mail: sarasota@fcnh.com
Phone: (941) 744-1244 Toll-free number: (800) 966-7117
Fax: (941) 744-1242
Rose Steptoe, Campus Director, Florida College of Natural Health: Bradenton, 616 67th Street Circle East, Bradenton, FL 34208

## Florida College of Natural Health: Maitland
**Maitland, Florida**
www.fcnh.com                                    CB code: 5239

- For-profit 2-year health science and junior college
- Large town

**General.** Accredited by ACCSCT. **Calendar:** Continuous.

**Annual costs/financial aid.** Tuition for paramedical skin care program: $18,600. 5-month therapeutic massage training diploma program: $8,100. Books/supplies: $1,340. Personal expenses: $1,647. Need-based financial aid available for full-time students.

**Contact.** Phone: (407) 261-0319
Director of Marketing, 2600 Lake Lucien Drive; Suite 240, Maitland, FL 32751

## Florida College of Natural Health: Miami
**Miami, Florida**
www.fcnh.com                                    CB code: 5231

- For-profit 2-year branch campus and community college
- Very large city

**General.** Accredited by ACCSCT. **Calendar:** Continuous.

**Annual costs/financial aid.** Tuition for paramedical skin care program: $18,600. 5-month therapeutic massage training diploma program: $8,100. Books/supplies: $1,340. Personal expenses: $1,647. Need-based financial aid available for full-time students.

**Contact.** Phone: (305) 597-9599
Director of Marketing, 7925 Northwest 12th Street, Suite 201, Miami, FL 33126

## Florida College of Natural Health: Pompano Beach
**Pompano Beach, Florida**
www.fcnh.com                                    CB code: 5238

- For-profit 2-year junior college
- Very large city

**General.** Accredited by ACCSCT. **Calendar:** Continuous.

**Annual costs/financial aid.** Tuition varies per program. Books/supplies: $2,525. Need-based financial aid available for full-time students.

**Contact.** Phone: (954) 975-6400
Chief Operating Officer, 2001 West Sample Road, Suite 100, Pompano Beach, FL 33064

## Florida Community College at Jacksonville
**Jacksonville, Florida**
www.fccj.edu                                    CB code: 5232

- Public 2-year community college
- Commuter campus in very large city

**General.** Founded in 1963. Regionally accredited. 4 campus locations and 6 center sites. **Enrollment:** 19,016 degree-seeking undergraduates; 5,923 non-degree-seeking students. **Degrees:** 3,042 associate awarded. **ROTC:** Naval. **Location:** Downtown. **Calendar:** Semester, extensive summer session. **Full-time faculty:** 384 total; 25% have terminal degrees, 18% minority, 59% women. **Part-time faculty:** 790 total; 5% have terminal degrees, 21% minority, 49% women. **Class size:** 51% < 20, 49% 20-39, less than 1% 40-49, less than 1% 50-99. **Special facilities:** Performing arts theater, computer support wing, allied health building, criminal justice center. **Partnerships:** Formal partnerships with Florida Construction Institute, Florida Home Builders Association, Navy Contracts, GM/ASEP contracts for non-credit (Education-To-Go), NE Florida Credit Union Association, Aviation Professional/Pilot Contract, Cisco Agreement with 2 schools in midwest.

**Student profile.** Among degree-seeking undergraduates, 2,962 enrolled as first-time, first-year students.

| | | | |
|---|---|---|---|
| Part-time: | 66% | Women: | 63% |
| Out-of-state: | 2% | 25 or older: | 43% |

**Transfer out. Colleges most students transferred to 2007:** University of North Florida, Jacksonville University, University of Florida, Florida State University, Central Florida University.

**Basis for selection.** Open admission, but selective for some programs. Special requirements for some associate of science degree programs. Some require specific application in addition to school application. SAT or ACT can be used to satisfy CPT test requirement for placement. **Homeschooled:** Transcript of courses and grades required. Student required to fill out form (home-school letter) and provide high school transcript. **Learning Disabled:** Medical documentation required.

**High school preparation.** 24 units recommended. Recommended units include English 4, mathematics 3, social studies 3, science 3 (laboratory 2), foreign language 2 and academic electives 9. One algebra strongly recommended. 3 social studies recommended: include .5 U.S. government, .5 economics, 1 U.S. history, 1 world history.

**2007-2008 Annual costs.** Tuition/fees: $1,949; $7,452 out-of-state. Books/supplies: $900. Personal expenses: $812.

**2007-2008 Financial aid. Need-based:** 58% of total undergraduate aid awarded as scholarships/grants, 42% as loans/jobs. Need-based aid available for part-time students. Work-study available nights, weekends and for part-time students. **Non-need-based:** Scholarships awarded for academics, alumni affiliation, art, athletics, job skills, leadership, minority status, music/drama.

Two-Year Colleges

**Application procedures. Admission:** Priority date 8/17; no deadline. $15 fee. Application may be submitted online. Admission notification on a rolling basis. **Financial aid:** Priority date 8/1; no closing date. FAFSA, institutional form required. Applicants notified by 7/1.

**Academics. Special study options:** Accelerated study, cooperative education, cross-registration, distance learning, double major, dual enrollment of high school students, ESL, exchange student, external degree, honors, independent study, internships, liberal arts/career combination, study abroad, weekend college. Bachelor's degree programs available on campus. License preparation in aviation, dental hygiene, nursing, paramedic, physical therapy, radiology, real estate. **Credit/placement by examination:** AP, CLEP, institutional tests. 45 credit hours maximum toward associate degree. **Support services:** GED preparation and test center, learning center, reduced course load, remedial instruction, study skills assistance, tutoring.

**Majors. Architecture:** Environmental design, interior. **Biology:** Biomedical sciences. **Business:** Accounting, administrative services, banking/financial services, business admin, fashion, financial planning, hospitality admin, insurance, management information systems, office management, office technology, sales/distribution, tourism/travel. **Communications technology:** Graphic/printing. **Computer sciences:** General, applications programming, computer graphics, data processing, information systems, networking, programming, systems analysis. **Construction:** Maintenance. **Education:** Elementary. **Engineering:** General, biomedical, civil, computer. **Engineering technology:** Architectural, civil, construction, drafting, electrical. **Family/consumer sciences:** Clothing/textiles. **Foreign languages:** Sign language interpretation. **Health:** Clinical lab technology, dental hygiene, EMT paramedic, medical radiologic technology/radiation therapy, medical records technology, medical secretary, nursing (RN), physical therapy assistant, respiratory therapy technology, sonography, substance abuse counseling. **Legal studies:** Paralegal. **Mechanic/repair:** Automotive. **Military:** General. **Personal/culinary services:** Culinary arts, mortuary science. **Protective services:** Criminal justice, fire safety technology, fire services admin, firefighting, law enforcement admin. **Public administration:** Human services. **Transportation:** Air traffic control, aviation, aviation management. **Visual/performing arts:** General, cinematography, commercial/advertising art, design, dramatic, interior design, theater design.

**Computing on campus.** 2,500 workstations in library, computer center, student center. Commuter students can connect to campus network. Online course registration, online library, helpline, repair service, student web hosting, wireless network available.

**Student life. Freshman orientation:** Mandatory. Preregistration for classes offered. Program is for degree seeking students only. **Housing:** Housing assistance available to qualified Talent Grant students. **Activities:** Bands, choral groups, dance, drama, international student organizations, literary magazine, music ensembles, musical theater, radio station, student government, student newspaper, TV station, forensic team, brain bowl team, Phi Theta Kappa.

**Athletics. NJCAA. Intercollegiate:** Baseball M, basketball, softball W, tennis W, volleyball W. **Intramural:** Badminton, basketball, bowling, football (non-tackle), golf, soccer, softball, table tennis, tennis, volleyball. **Team name:** Stars.

**Student services.** Adult student services, career counseling, services for economically disadvantaged, student employment services, financial aid counseling, minority student services, on-campus daycare, personal counseling, placement for graduates, veterans' counselor, women's services. **Physically disabled:** Services for visually, speech, hearing impaired. **Transfer:** Transfer adviser, college fairs on campus for students transferring to 4-year colleges.

**Contact.** E-mail: info@fccj.edu
Phone: (904) 632-3100 Fax: (904) 632-5105
Rosalind Harris, Associate Director of Admissions, Florida Community College at Jacksonville, 501 West State Street, Jacksonville, FL 32202

## Florida Keys Community College
**Key West, Florida**
**www.fkcc.edu**                                    CB code: 5236

- Public 2-year community college
- Commuter campus in large town

**General.** Founded in 1965. Regionally accredited. 2-year AA and AS programs offered at the main campus in Key West, Coral Shores and Marathon branch campuses. **Enrollment:** 898 degree-seeking undergraduates. **Degrees:** 143 associate awarded. **Location:** 154 miles from Miami. **Calendar:** Semester, limited summer session. **Full-time faculty:** 26 total. **Part-time faculty:** 111 total. **Special facilities:** Fine arts center and theater, marine propulsion technology center, welding lab, aquatic center, diving program underwater education complex, ceramics studio.

**Student profile.**

| Out-of-state: | 2% | 25 or older: | 55% |
|---|---|---|---|

**Transfer out. Colleges most students transferred to 2007:** University of Central Florida, Florida International University, University of Florida, Florida State University, St. Leo's College.

**Basis for selection.** Open admission, but selective for some programs. Special application, placement examination, physical examination, and interview required for nursing technology applicants. Admission based on objective points system.

**High school preparation.** Recommended units include English 4, mathematics 3, social studies 3 and science 3.

**2007-2008 Annual costs.** Tuition/fees: $2,125; $8,069 out-of-state. Books/supplies: $2,300. Personal expenses: $1,000.

**Financial aid. Need-based:** Need-based aid available for part-time students. Work-study available for part-time students. **Non-need-based:** Scholarships awarded for academics, art, leadership, minority status.

**Application procedures. Admission:** No deadline. $20 fee. Admission notification on a rolling basis. **Financial aid:** Priority date 5/1; no closing date. FAFSA, institutional form required. Applicants notified on a rolling basis starting 6/15; must reply within 2 week(s) of notification.

**Academics. Special study options:** Distance learning, double major, dual enrollment of high school students, ESL, independent study, semester at sea, teacher certification program. Bachelor's degree programs available on campus. License preparation in nursing, paramedic, real estate. **Credit/placement by examination:** AP, CLEP, IB, institutional tests. 45 credit hours maximum toward associate degree. Students taking Florida College Entry Level Placement Test prior to registering do not need SAT or ACT. **Support services:** Learning center, reduced course load, remedial instruction, tutoring.

**Majors. Biology:** Marine. **Business:** Business admin. **Computer sciences:** General, programming. **Health:** Nursing (RN). **Interdisciplinary:** Marine science. **Mechanic/repair:** Marine. **Public administration:** General. **Transportation:** Diver, maritime/Merchant Marine.

**Computing on campus.** 25 workstations in library, computer center.

**Student life. Freshman orientation:** Available. Preregistration for classes offered. **Activities:** Choral groups, student government, nurses pinning club, Florida nurses student association, Mud-Pi ceramics club, Phi Theta Kappa, cyber league, photo guild club, wreckers club, propmasters club.

**Athletics. Team name:** Wreckers.

**Student services.** Adult student services, career counseling, student employment services, financial aid counseling, placement for graduates, veterans' counselor. **Physically disabled:** Services for visually, speech, hearing impaired. **Transfer:** Pre-admission transcript evaluation for new students. Transfer adviser, college fairs on campus for students transferring to 4-year colleges.

**Contact.** E-mail: malsheim_c@firn.edu
Phone: (305) 809-3188 Fax: (305) 292-5155
Cheryl Malsheimer, Director of Enrollment Services, Florida Keys Community College, 5901 College Road, Key West, FL 33040

## Florida National College
**Hialeah, Florida**
**www.fnc.edu**                                    CB code: 2057

- For-profit 2-year community and junior college
- Commuter campus in very large city

**General.** Regionally accredited. **Enrollment:** 2,058 degree-seeking undergraduates. **Degrees:** 338 associate awarded. **Location:** 12 miles from Miami. **Calendar:** Semester. **Full-time faculty:** 43 total. **Part-time faculty:** 46 total. **Class size:** 100% 20-39.

**Transfer out. Colleges most students transferred to 2007:** Nova Southeastern University, Florida International University, American Intercontinental University, Miami Institute of Psychology.

**Basis for selection.** Open admission, but selective for some programs.

**2008-2009 Annual costs.** Tuition/fees: $12,594. Per-credit charge: $400. Books/supplies: $1,000.

**2006-2007 Financial aid.** All financial aid based on need. Need-based aid available for part-time students.

**Application procedures. Admission:** No deadline. No application fee. Admission notification on a rolling basis beginning on or about 7/15. **Financial aid:** No deadline. FAFSA, institutional form required.

**Academics. Special study options:** Cooperative education, dual enrollment of high school students, ESL, student-designed major. **Credit/placement by examination:** AP, CLEP, institutional tests. 9 credit hours maximum toward associate degree. **Support services:** GED preparation, reduced course load, remedial instruction, tutoring.

**Majors. Business:** Accounting, business admin, tourism promotion, tourism/travel. **Computer sciences:** General, programming, system admin, web page design. **Education:** General. **Engineering technology:** Computer hardware. **Health:** Dental lab technology, medical assistant. **Legal studies:** Paralegal. **Protective services:** Criminal justice.

**Most popular majors.** Business/marketing 19%, computer/information sciences 12%, health sciences 46%, legal studies 18%.

**Student life. Freshman orientation:** Available. **Activities:** Student government, student newspaper.

**Student services.** Career counseling, student employment services, financial aid counseling, personal counseling.

**Contact.** E-mail: admissions@fnc.edu
Phone: (305) 821-3333 Fax: (305) 362-0595
Guillermo Araya, Admissions, Florida National College, 4425 West 20th Avenue, Hialeah, FL 33012

## Florida Technical College: Auburndale
**Lakeland, Florida**
**www.flatech.edu**                                    **CB code: 3432**

- For-profit 2-year business and junior college
- Large town

**General.** Accredited by ACICS. **Calendar:** Continuous.

**Annual costs/financial aid.** Tuition, including cost of books and supplies, ranges from $3,333 to $3,666 per quarter. Fees, $490. Need-based financial aid available to full-time and part-time students.

**Contact.** Phone: (863) 967-8822
School Director, 4715 South Florida Avenue, Lakeland, FL 33813

## Florida Technical College: Deland
**Deland, Florida**
**www.flatech.edu**                                    **CB code: 3589**

- For-profit 2-year junior and technical college
- Small city
- Interview required

**General.** Accredited by ACICS. **Enrollment:** 230 degree-seeking undergraduates. **Degrees:** 179 associate awarded. **Location:** 30 miles from Orlando, 20 miles from Daytona Beach. **Calendar:** Quarter, extensive summer session. **Full-time faculty:** 13 total; 38% minority, 23% women. **Part-time faculty:** 2 total. **Class size:** 100% < 20. **Partnerships:** Formal partnerships with Microsoft, Pearson Vue testing center, NCCT testing center.

**Basis for selection.** Open admission.

**2007-2008 Annual costs.** $4,347 tuition per quarter for paralegal, medical assistant, business, computer drafting & design, electronics/computer technology; $4,713 tuition per quarter for network hardware, network administration/programming, e-commerce, web-design and graphics design. $3650 per quarter for Criminal Justice and $3667 per quarter for Network Administration/Hardware with Wirelss technology. Required fees $100. Tuition includes cost of books and supplies.

**Financial aid.** All financial aid based on need. Need-based aid available for part-time students. Work-study available nights and for part-time students.

**Application procedures. Admission:** No deadline. $25 fee. Admission notification on a rolling basis. **Financial aid:** No deadline. FAFSA required. Applicants notified on a rolling basis.

**Academics. Credit/placement by examination:** CLEP, institutional tests. Credit by examination will be charged $50 per quarter credit not covered by financial aid. Tests must be passed with 70% or higher percentile. May not test out of lab-based classes.

**Majors. Business:** Business admin. **Computer sciences:** General, networking, programming, systems analysis. **Engineering technology:** Drafting. **Health:** Medical assistant, medical secretary, office admin. **Legal studies:** Paralegal. **Mechanic/repair:** Electronics/electrical.

**Computing on campus.** 90 workstations in library, computer center. Online library, wireless network available.

**Student life. Freshman orientation:** Mandatory.

**Student services.** Career counseling, financial aid counseling, placement for graduates.

**Contact.** Phone: (386) 734-3303 Toll-free number: (888) 724-6441
Fax: (386) 734-5150
Dane Boothe, Director of Admissions, Florida Technical College: Deland, 1199 South Woodland Boulevard, Deland, FL 32720

## Florida Technical College: Jacksonville
**Jacksonville, Florida**
**www.flatech.edu**                                    **CB code: 3590**

- For-profit 2-year technical college
- Very large city

**General.** Accredited by ACICS. **Calendar:** Continuous.

**Annual costs/financial aid.** Network administration/programming $12,100 annually. Tuition includes cost of books and supplies.

**Contact.** Phone: (904) 724-2229
Campus Director, 8711 Lone Star Road, Jacksonville, FL 32211

## Florida Technical College: Orlando
**Orlando, Florida**
**www.flatech.edu**                                    **CB code: 3588**

- For-profit 2-year technical college
- Commuter campus in large city

**General.** Accredited by ACICS. **Enrollment:** 163 degree-seeking undergraduates. **Degrees:** 117 associate awarded. **Calendar:** Continuous, extensive summer session. **Full-time faculty:** 12 total. **Part-time faculty:** 3 total. **Class size:** 100% < 20.

**Basis for selection.** Open admission.

**2008-2009 Annual costs.** Network administration/hardware with wireless technology, $22,000 annually. Tuition includes cost of books and supplies.

**Financial aid.** All financial aid based on need. Need-based aid available for part-time students.

**Application procedures. Admission:** No deadline. $25 fee. Admission notification on a rolling basis. **Financial aid:** No deadline. FAFSA, institutional form required. Applicants notified on a rolling basis.

**Academics. Credit/placement by examination:** CLEP, institutional tests. **Support services:** Tutoring.

**Majors. Business:** Business admin. **Communications technology:** General. **Computer sciences:** General, computer science, data processing. **Engineering:** Electrical. **Health:** Medical assistant, medical secretary.

**Computing on campus.** 100 workstations in library, computer center.

**Student life. Freshman orientation:** Mandatory. **Activities:** Student newspaper.

**Student services.** Adult student services, career counseling, student employment services, financial aid counseling, personal counseling.

**Contact.** E-mail: ggarces@flatech.edu
Phone: (407) 447-7300 Fax: (407) 447-7301
Gabe Garces, Director, Florida Technical College: Orlando, 12689 Challenger Parkway, #130, Orlando, FL 32826-2707

## Full Sail University
**Winter Park, Florida**
www.fullsail.com
**CB code: 3164**

- For-profit 2-year visual arts and technical college
- Commuter campus in very large city

**General.** Accredited by ACCSCT. **Enrollment:** 5,697 degree-seeking undergraduates. **Degrees:** 2,143 bachelor's, 1,301 associate awarded; master's offered. **Location:** 8 miles from Orlando. **Calendar:** Continuous. **Full-time faculty:** 560 total. **Part-time faculty:** 23 total. **Special facilities:** Recording studios, production suites, sound stages.

**Student profile.**

| | | | |
|---|---|---|---|
| Out-of-state: | 75% | 25 or older: | 20% |

**Basis for selection.** Open admission, but selective for some programs. Applicants for game design and development bachelor's degree program must have A average in Algebra II. Geometry, physics and programming experience also recommended. **Homeschooled:** Diplomas recognized if applicant's state board of education recognizes them. **Learning Disabled:** Require documentation, not more than 3 years old, describing learning disabilities.

**2007-2008 Annual costs.** Annual tuition for associate and bachelor degree programs range from $13,000 to $16,000. Includes books and supplies.

**Financial aid. Need-based:** Work-study available nights and weekends.

**Application procedures. Admission:** No deadline. $150 fee. Application may be submitted online. Admission notification on a rolling basis. **Financial aid:** No deadline. FAFSA required. Applicants notified on a rolling basis; must reply within 2 week(s) of notification.

**Academics.** Cognitive development course offered at no charge. Tutoring offered through federal work study program. **Special study options:** Cooperative education, internships. Bachelor's degree programs available on campus. **Credit/placement by examination:** AP, CLEP, institutional tests. Students may take test-out exam in each course for which credit is being sought. If credit earned, tuition and program hours reduced accordingly. Minimum of 25% of degree program's semester hours or equivalent must be earned in residence to receive degree. **Support services:** Study skills assistance, tutoring.

**Majors. Communications technology:** Recording arts. **Computer sciences:** Web page design. **Other:** Show Production and Touring.

**Computing on campus.** 56 workstations in library, computer center. Online library, wireless network available.

**Student life. Freshman orientation:** Mandatory. **Policies:** Alcohol and drug free facility.

**Student services.** Financial aid counseling, placement for graduates.

**Contact.** E-mail: admissions@fullsail.com
Phone: (407) 679-6333 Toll-free number: (800) 226-7625
Fax: (407) 678-0070
MaryBeth Plank-Mezo, Director of Admissions, Full Sail University, 3300 University Boulevard, Winter Park, FL 32792-7429

## Golf Academy of the South
**Altamonte Springs, Florida**
www.sdgagolf.com

- For-profit 2-year community college
- Large town

**General.** Accredited by ACICS. **Calendar:** Semester.

**Annual costs/financial aid.** Tuition/fees (2007-2008): $9,995. Books/supplies: $700.

**Contact.** Phone: (480) 905-9288
7373 North Scottsdale Road, Suite B-100, Scottsdale, AZ 85253

## Gulf Coast College
**Tampa, Florida**
www.gulfcoastcollege.com
**CB code: 3448**

- For-profit 2-year technical college
- Large city

**General.** Accredited by ACICS. **Calendar:** Quarter.

**Annual costs/financial aid.** Personal expenses: $2,856.

**Contact.** Phone: (813) 620-1446
Director of Admissions, 3910 U.S. Highway 301 North, Suite 200, Tampa, FL 33619-1290

## Gulf Coast Community College
**Panama City, Florida**
www.gulfcoast.edu
**CB code: 5271**

- Public 2-year community college
- Commuter campus in small city

**General.** Founded in 1957. Regionally accredited. **Enrollment:** 7,251 degree-seeking undergraduates. **Degrees:** 650 associate awarded. **Location:** 100 miles from Tallahassee, 100 miles from Pensacola. **Calendar:** Semester, limited summer session. **Full-time faculty:** 120 total. **Part-time faculty:** 375 total. **Partnerships:** Training programs with local businesses, high school teacher training.

**Student profile.**

| | | | |
|---|---|---|---|
| Part-time: | 68% | Women: | 58% |
| Out-of-state: | 6% | 25 or older: | 42% |

**Transfer out. Colleges most students transferred to 2007:** Florida State University, University of Florida, University of Central Florida, University of West Florida.

**Basis for selection.** Open admission, but selective for some programs. Admission to health science programs determined through high school transcripts, placement test performance and other admissions criteria. Interview required of allied health applicants. Audition recommended for music majors. **Homeschooled:** Home School Affidavit must be submitted with parent's signature and notarized.

**High school preparation.** 13 units recommended. Recommended units include English 4, mathematics 3, social studies 3 and science 3.

**2007-2008 Annual costs.** Tuition/fees: $1,968; $7,109 out-of-state. Books/supplies: $800. Personal expenses: $1,500.

**Financial aid. Need-based:** Need-based aid available for part-time students. Work-study available nights, weekends and for part-time students. **Non-need-based:** Scholarships awarded for academics, athletics, job skills, leadership, minority status, music/drama, state residency.

**Application procedures. Admission:** No deadline. No application fee. Admission notification on a rolling basis. Application deadline for nursing program February 28; dental hygiene April 1; EMT and paramedic June 1; radiography May 15; physical therapist assistant April 1; surgical technology October 21. **Financial aid:** Priority date 4/1, closing date 7/1. FAFSA required. Applicants notified on a rolling basis starting 7/1.

**Academics. Special study options:** Accelerated study, cooperative education, distance learning, dual enrollment of high school students, ESL, honors, independent study, internships, teacher certification program, weekend college. License preparation in dental hygiene, nursing, paramedic, radiology, real estate. **Credit/placement by examination:** AP, CLEP, IB, institutional tests. 45 credit hours maximum toward associate degree. **Support services:** GED preparation, learning center, reduced course load, remedial instruction, study skills assistance, tutoring.

**Majors. Agriculture:** Landscaping, ornamental horticulture. **Biology:** General, marine. **Business:** Accounting, banking/financial services, business admin, communications, marketing, office/clerical, real estate. **Communications:** General, advertising, broadcast journalism, journalism, public relations. **Computer sciences:** General, applications programming, computer science, programming, systems analysis. **Conservation:** General, forestry. **Education:** Biology, chemistry, elementary, family/consumer sciences, health, mathematics, physics, sales/marketing, science, social studies, special. **Engineering:** General, electrical, marine. **Engineering technology:** Architectural, civil, construction, electrical. **English:** English lit, speech/rhetoric. **Family/consumer sciences:** General, institutional food production. **Foreign languages:** General, translation. **Health:** Dental hygiene, EMT paramedic, health services, medical radiologic technology/radiation therapy, medical records admin, nursing (RN), optician, physical therapy assistant, physics/radiologic health, predental, premedicine, prepharmacy, preveterinary, respiratory therapy technology. **History:** General. **Legal studies:** General, paralegal, prelaw. **Liberal arts:** Arts/sciences, library science. **Math:** General. **Parks/recreation:** General, health/fitness. **Personal/culinary services:** Culinary arts. **Philosophy/religion:** Philosophy, religion. **Physical sciences:**

Atmospheric science, chemistry, geology, oceanography, physics. **Protective services:** Criminal justice, fire safety technology, firefighting, law enforcement admin. **Psychology:** General. **Public administration:** Human services, social work. **Social sciences:** Anthropology, archaeology, criminology, economics, political science, sociology. **Visual/performing arts:** Art, dramatic.

**Computing on campus.** 560 workstations in library, computer center. Commuter students can connect to campus network. Online course registration, online library, helpline, wireless network available.

**Student life. Freshman orientation:** Available. Preregistration for classes offered. Orientation programs also available on the Internet. **Activities:** Bands, campus ministries, choral groups, dance, drama, international student organizations, literary magazine, music ensembles, musical theater, radio station, student government, student newspaper, African-American student union.

**Athletics.** NJCAA. **Intercollegiate:** Baseball M, basketball, softball W, volleyball W. **Intramural:** Basketball. **Team name:** Commodores.

**Student services.** Adult student services, career counseling, services for economically disadvantaged, student employment services, financial aid counseling, minority student services, personal counseling, veterans' counselor, women's services. **Physically disabled:** Services for visually, speech, hearing impaired. **Learning disabled:** Comprehensive services available. **Transfer:** Pre-admission transcript evaluation for new students. Transfer adviser, college fairs on campus for students transferring to 4-year colleges.

**Contact.** Phone: (850) 872-3892 Toll-free number: (800) 311-3685 Fax: (850) 913-3308
Sharon Todd, Director of Enrollment Services and Institutional Research, Gulf Coast Community College, 5230 West Highway 98, Panama City, FL 32401-1041

## Heritage Institute: Fort Myers
**Fort Myers, Florida**
www.heritage-education.com

- For-profit 2-year health science and technical college
- Large town

**General.** Accredited by ACCSCT. **Calendar:** Continuous.

**Contact.** Phone: (239) 936-5822
6811-1 Palisades Park Court, Suite 1, Fort Myers, FL 33912

## Heritage Institute: Jacksonville
**Jacksonville, Florida**
www.heritage-education.com

- Private 2-year health science and career college
- Very large city
- Application essay, interview required

**General.** Accredited by ACCSCT. **Enrollment:** 260 degree-seeking undergraduates. **Degrees:** 124 associate awarded. **Calendar:** Continuous. **Full-time faculty:** 6 total. **Part-time faculty:** 4 total.

**Basis for selection.** Open admission.

**2007-2008 Annual costs.** Total cost of occupational associate degree program: $16,550; includes tuition, fees, books and supplies.

**Application procedures. Admission:** No deadline. No application fee. Application must be submitted on paper. Admission notification on a rolling basis. **Financial aid:** No deadline. FAFSA required. Applicants notified on a rolling basis.

**Academics. Special study options:** Occupational Associate of Science Degrees in Massage Therapy, X-Ray Medical Technician, and Esthetics. **Credit/placement by examination:** CLEP. **Support services:** Remedial instruction, study skills assistance, tutoring.

**Majors. Health:** Occupational therapy assistant.

**Computing on campus.** 10 workstations in library. Online library available.

**Student life. Freshman orientation:** Mandatory.

**Student services. Transfer:** Pre-admission transcript evaluation for new students.

**Contact.** Phone: (904) 332-0910 ext. 121
Chris Allsup, Senior Admissions Manager, Heritage Institute: Jacksonville, 4130 Salisbury Road North, Suite 1100, Jacksonville, FL 32216

## Herzing College
**Winter Park, Florida**
www.herzing.edu

**CB code: 3438**

- For-profit 2-year business and health science college
- Commuter campus in very large city

**General.** Regionally accredited. **Calendar:** Semester.

**Annual costs/financial aid.** Tuition/fees (2007-2008): $10,800. Reported annual tuition is representative. Actual costs vary by program.

**Contact.** Phone: (407) 478-0500
Director of Admissions, 1595 South Semoran Boulevard, Suite 1501, Winter Park, FL 32792-5509

## High-Tech Institute
**Orlando, Florida**
www.hightechinstitute.edu

- For-profit 2-year health science and technical college
- Commuter campus in large city

**General.** Accredited by ACCSCT. **Calendar:** Continuous.

**Contact.** Phone: (407) 893-7400
Admissions Director, 3710 Maguire Boulevard, Orlando, FL 32803

## Hillsborough Community College
**Tampa, Florida**
www.hccfl.edu

**CB member**
**CB code: 5304**

- Public 2-year community college
- Commuter campus in large city

**General.** Founded in 1968. Regionally accredited. **Enrollment:** 17,487 degree-seeking undergraduates; 5,134 non-degree-seeking students. **Degrees:** 906 associate awarded. **ROTC:** Army, Air Force. **Calendar:** Semester, limited summer session. **Full-time faculty:** 262 total; 25% have terminal degrees, 20% minority, 54% women. **Part-time faculty:** 887 total; 9% have terminal degrees, 19% minority, 45% women. **Class size:** 50% < 20, 48% 20-39, less than 1% 40-49, less than 1% 50-99, less than 1% >100. **Special facilities:** Environmental study centers at English Creek, Florida Studies Center (site of International Wetlands Conference).

**Student profile.** Among degree-seeking undergraduates, 69% enrolled in a transfer program, 30% enrolled in a vocational program, 3,226 enrolled as first-time, first-year students.

| Part-time: | 62% | Women: | 58% |
|---|---|---|---|

**Transfer out. Colleges most students transferred to 2007:** University of South Florida, Florida State University, University of Florida, University of Central Florida.

**Basis for selection.** Open admission, but selective for some programs. Limited access programs in certain health programs.

**High school preparation.** 24 units recommended. Recommended units include English 4, mathematics 3, science 3, foreign language 2 and academic electives 8.

**2007-2008 Annual costs.** Tuition/fees: $2,091; $7,468 out-of-state. Per-credit charge: $70 in-state; $249 out-of-state. Books/supplies: $1,950. Personal expenses: $2,676.

**Financial aid. Need-based:** Need-based aid available for part-time students. Work-study available nights, weekends and for part-time students.

**Application procedures. Admission:** No deadline. $20 fee, may be waived for applicants with need. Application may be submitted online. Admission notification on a rolling basis. **Financial aid:** Closing date 6/30. FAFSA, institutional form required. Applicants notified on a rolling basis.

**Academics. Special study options:** Accelerated study, cross-registration, distance learning, double major, dual enrollment of high school students, ESL, honors, internships, liberal arts/career combination, study abroad, teacher certification program, weekend college. License preparation in dental hygiene, nursing, paramedic. **Credit/placement by examination:** AP, CLEP, IB, institutional tests. Approval required. **Support services:** GED preparation, learning center, remedial instruction, study skills assistance, tutoring, writing center.

**Majors. Agriculture:** Aquaculture, landscaping. **Biology:** Biomedical sciences. **Business:** Accounting, accounting technology, business admin, executive assistant, hospitality admin, management information systems, operations, restaurant/food services. **Communications technology:** Radio/tv. **Computer sciences:** Applications programming, systems analysis. **Education:** Deaf/hearing impaired. **Engineering technology:** Architectural, biomedical, computer systems, electrical, environmental, industrial management, manufacturing. **Family/consumer sciences:** Child care, food/nutrition. **Health:** Dental hygiene, EMT paramedic, medical radiologic technology/radiation therapy, mental health services, nuclear medical technology, nursing (RN), optician, optometric assistant, respiratory therapy technology, sonography, veterinary technology/assistant. **Legal studies:** Paralegal. **Liberal arts:** Arts/sciences. **Personal/culinary services:** Restaurant/catering. **Protective services:** Fire safety technology, law enforcement admin. **Visual/performing arts:** Cinematography.

**Computing on campus.** 2,014 workstations in library, computer center, student center. Commuter students can connect to campus network. Online course registration, online library, helpline, wireless network available.

**Student life. Freshman orientation:** Mandatory. Preregistration for classes offered. Held approximately 2 hours prior to registration. **Activities:** Bands, choral groups, dance, drama, literary magazine, music ensembles, radio station, student government, student newspaper, African-American student union, American Sign Language club, aquaculture club, Arete club, Association of Professional Scholastic Opticians, College Republicans, computer club, Democrats, dive club.

**Athletics.** NJCAA. **Intercollegiate:** Baseball M, basketball, softball W, tennis W, volleyball W. **Team name:** Hawks.

**Student services.** Career counseling, services for economically disadvantaged, student employment services, financial aid counseling, on-campus daycare. **Physically disabled:** Services for visually, speech, hearing impaired. **Learning disabled:** Comprehensive services available. **Transfer:** Transfer center, transfer adviser, college fairs on campus for students transferring to 4-year colleges.

**Contact.** Phone: (813) 253-7004 Toll-free number: (866) 253-7077 Fax: (813) 253-7196
Kathy Cecil, Admissions, Registration and Records Officer, Hillsborough Community College, Box 31127, Tampa, FL 33631-3127

---

## Indian River Community College
**Fort Pierce, Florida**
www.ircc.edu

**CB member**
**CB code: 5322**

- Public 2-year community college
- Commuter campus in small city

**General.** Founded in 1960. Regionally accredited. Branch campuses in Vero Beach, Stuart, Okeechobee, Port St. Lucie; Criminal Justice Academy, Marine Center in Fort Pierce. **Enrollment:** 7,885 degree-seeking undergraduates. **Degrees:** 1,364 associate awarded. **Location:** 65 miles from West Palm Beach. **Calendar:** Semester, limited summer session. **Full-time faculty:** 170 total. **Part-time faculty:** 700 total. **Special facilities:** Olympic-size pool complex, fine arts center, planetarium.

**Student profile.**

| | | | |
|---|---|---|---|
| Out-of-state: | 2% | 25 or older: | 42% |

**Transfer out. Colleges most students transferred to 2007:** University of Central Florida, University of South Florida, University of Florida, Florida State University, Florida Atlantic University.

**Basis for selection.** Open admission, but selective for some programs. Testing and academic records determine admission to health science programs. SAT or ACT recommended for placement.

**High school preparation.** 24 units recommended. Recommended units include English 4, mathematics 3, social studies 3, history 2, science 3, foreign language 2 and academic electives 7.

**2007-2008 Annual costs.** Tuition/fees: $1,980; $7,295 out-of-state. Books/supplies: $700. Personal expenses: $856.

**2006-2007 Financial aid. Need-based:** Need-based aid available for part-time students. Work-study available for part-time students. **Non-need-based:** Scholarships awarded for academics, athletics, minority status, music/drama, state residency.

**Application procedures. Admission:** No deadline. No application fee. Admission notification on a rolling basis. **Financial aid:** Priority date 7/18; no closing date. FAFSA, institutional form required. Applicants notified on a rolling basis starting 5/15.

**Academics. Special study options:** Accelerated study, distance learning, dual enrollment of high school students, weekend college. License preparation in paramedic, real estate. **Credit/placement by examination:** AP, CLEP, IB, institutional tests. 45 credit hours maximum toward associate degree. Degree-seeking students must achieve state-designated cutoff scores on placement test to enter college-level programs, or complete sequence of developmental courses. **Support services:** GED preparation and test center, learning center, pre-admission summer program, reduced course load, remedial instruction, study skills assistance, tutoring.

**Majors. Agriculture:** Business technology, turf management. **Biology:** General. **Business:** Accounting, administrative services, business admin, hospitality admin, management information systems, office management, sales/distribution. **Communications:** Public relations. **Communications technology:** Graphic/printing. **Computer sciences:** General, applications programming, computer graphics, information technology, programming, systems analysis, web page design. **Conservation:** Environmental studies. **Education:** General, early childhood, elementary, secondary. **Engineering:** General. **Engineering technology:** Architectural drafting, civil, construction, electrical. **English:** English lit. **Foreign languages:** General. **Health:** Clinical lab technology, dental hygiene, dental lab technology, EMT paramedic, medical radiologic technology/radiation therapy, medical records admin, medical records technology, medical transcription, nursing (RN), physical therapy assistant, predental, premedicine, prepharmacy, preveterinary, respiratory therapy technology. **History:** General. **Legal studies:** Legal secretary, paralegal, prelaw. **Liberal arts:** Arts/sciences, library assistant. **Math:** General. **Mechanic/repair:** Automotive, heating/ac/refrig. **Personal/culinary services:** Restaurant/catering. **Philosophy/religion:** Philosophy. **Physical sciences:** Chemistry, physics. **Protective services:** Criminal justice, fire safety technology. **Psychology:** General. **Public administration:** Human services. **Social sciences:** Anthropology, economics, political science, sociology. **Visual/performing arts:** Art, commercial/advertising art, dance, dramatic, interior design.

**Computing on campus.** Online course registration, online library available.

**Student life. Freshman orientation:** Available. **Housing:** Apartments available. **Activities:** Bands, choral groups, dance, drama, international student organizations, literary magazine, music ensembles, musical theater, radio station, student government, symphony orchestra, Distributive Education Clubs of America, Vocational International Clubs of America, cultural exchange club, human services club, ambassador club, Bacchus Club, Phi Beta Lambda.

**Athletics.** NJCAA. **Intercollegiate:** Baseball M, basketball, cheerleading W, diving, softball W, swimming, volleyball W. **Team name:** Pioneers.

**Student services.** Alcohol/substance abuse counseling, career counseling, services for economically disadvantaged, student employment services, financial aid counseling, health services, minority student services, on-campus daycare, placement for graduates, veterans' counselor, women's services. **Physically disabled:** Services for visually, speech, hearing impaired. **Transfer:** Transfer adviser, college fairs on campus for students transferring to 4-year colleges.

**Contact.** Phone: (772) 462-4740 Toll-free number: (866) 866-4722 Fax: (772) 462-4699
Karen Chapdelaine, Director of Admissions, Indian River Community College, 3209 Virginia Avenue, Fort Pierce, FL 34981-5596

---

## Keiser Career College: Greenacres
**Greenacres, Florida**

- For-profit 2-year business and health science college
- Commuter campus in small city

**General.** Accredited by ACCSCT. **Calendar:** Continuous.

**Contact.** Phone: (561) 433-2330
6812 Forest Hill Boulevard, Greenacres, FL 33413

## Keiser Career College: Miami Lakes
### Miami Lakes, Florida

- For-profit 2-year business and health science college
- Commuter campus in large town

**General.** Accredited by ACCSCT. **Calendar:** Continuous.

**Contact.** Phone: (305) 820-5003
17395 NW 59th Avenue, Miami Lakes, FL 33015

## Keiser Career College: Port St. Lucie
### Port St. Lucie, Florida
**CB code: 5355**

- For-profit 2-year business and health science college
- Commuter campus in large town

**General.** Accredited by ACCSCT. **Calendar:** Continuous.

**Contact.** Phone: (772) 398-9990
9468 South US I, Port St. Lucie, FL 34952

## Key College
### Dania Beach, Florida
### www.keycollege.edu
**CB code: 3577**

- For-profit 2-year business and technical college
- Commuter campus in very large city
- Interview required

**General.** Accredited by ACICS. **Enrollment:** 181 degree-seeking undergraduates. **Degrees:** 9 associate awarded. **Calendar:** Quarter, extensive summer session. **Full-time faculty:** 6 total. **Part-time faculty:** 11 total.

**Student profile.**

| | | | |
|---|---|---|---|
| Out-of-state: | 6% | Hispanic American: | 17% |
| African American: | 23% | 25 or older: | 67% |
| Asian American: | 3% | | |

**Basis for selection.** Open admission, but selective for some programs. Entrance exam required. Career Placement Assessment Test (CPAT) used in institution's admissions procedures; SAT or ACT scores may be submitted in lieu of CPAT. **Homeschooled:** State high school equivalency certificate required.

**2008-2009 Annual costs.** Tuition/fees: $9,210. Books/supplies: $1,050.

**Financial aid. Need-based:** Work-study available nights and for part-time students. **Additional information:** Federal Supplemental Educational Opportunities Grant (FSEOG), PELL grant, FFEL (federal loan program) available; direct loans offered.

**Application procedures. Admission:** No deadline. $35 fee. Application must be submitted on paper. Admission notification on a rolling basis. **Financial aid:** No deadline.

**Academics. Credit/placement by examination:** CLEP, institutional tests. **Support services:** Remedial instruction, study skills assistance.

**Majors. Engineering technology:** Drafting. **Legal studies:** Court reporting, paralegal.

**Computing on campus.** 65 workstations in library, computer center.

**Student life. Freshman orientation:** Mandatory. Held one week prior to beginning of classes for approximately 3 hours. **Activities:** Student newspaper.

**Student services.** Career counseling, financial aid counseling, personal counseling, veterans' counselor.

**Contact.** E-mail: admissions@keycollege.edu
Phone: (954) 923-4440 Toll-free number: (800) 581-8292
Fax: (954) 583-9458
Sandra Gabriel, Director of Admissions, Key College, 225 Dania Beach Boulevard, Dania Beach, FL 33004

## Lake City Community College
### Lake City, Florida
### www.lakecitycc.edu
**CB member**
**CB code: 5377**

- Public 2-year community college
- Commuter campus in large town

**General.** Founded in 1947. Regionally accredited. **Enrollment:** 2,723 degree-seeking undergraduates; 126 non-degree-seeking students. **Degrees:** 317 associate awarded. **Location:** 60 miles from Jacksonville, 45 miles from Gainesville. **Calendar:** Semester, limited summer session. **Full-time faculty:** 55 total. **Part-time faculty:** 110 total. **Special facilities:** Performing arts center, arboretum.

**Student profile.** Among degree-seeking undergraduates, 57% enrolled in a transfer program, 43% enrolled in a vocational program, 668 enrolled as first-time, first-year students.

| | | | |
|---|---|---|---|
| Part-time: | 57% | Asian American: | 1% |
| Out-of-state: | 3% | Hispanic American: | 2% |
| Women: | 67% | 25 or older: | 30% |
| African American: | 11% | Live on campus: | 1% |

**Basis for selection.** Open admission, but selective for some programs. Selective to allied health programs. Locally administered CPT test may be used in place of SAT or ACT. Interview recommended for most allied health programs and all golf course operations programs.

**High school preparation.** 13 units recommended. Recommended units include English 4, mathematics 3, social studies 3 and science 3. Applicants to forest management should have good mathematics background.

**2007-2008 Annual costs.** Tuition/fees: $1,986; $7,638 out-of-state. Room/board: $5,395. Books/supplies: $800. Personal expenses: $750.

**Financial aid. Need-based:** Need-based aid available for part-time students. Work-study available for part-time students. **Non-need-based:** Scholarships awarded for academics, athletics.

**Application procedures. Admission:** Priority date 8/1; no deadline. $15 fee. Application must be submitted on paper. Admission notification on a rolling basis. Some technical programs reach maximum enrollment and are closed prior to August 1. **Financial aid:** Priority date 6/1; no closing date. FAFSA, institutional form required. Applicants notified on a rolling basis starting 6/1; must reply within 2 week(s) of notification.

**Academics. Special study options:** Accelerated study, cooperative education, distance learning, dual enrollment of high school students, exchange student, independent study, internships, study abroad, teacher certification program, weekend college. Bachelor's degree programs available on campus. License preparation in nursing, paramedic, physical therapy. **Credit/placement by examination:** CLEP, IB, institutional tests. 30 credit hours maximum toward associate degree. **Support services:** GED preparation and test center, learning center, reduced course load, remedial instruction, study skills assistance, tutoring.

**Majors. Agriculture:** Agribusiness operations, landscaping. **Architecture:** Landscape. **Business:** General, administrative services, business admin, office/clerical. **Communications:** General. **Computer sciences:** General, information systems, programming. **Education:** General. **Health:** Clinical lab technology, EMT paramedic, nursing (RN), physical therapy assistant. **Legal studies:** Prelaw. **Liberal arts:** Arts/sciences. **Math:** General. **Parks/recreation:** Facilities management. **Protective services:** Criminal justice. **Social sciences:** Criminology.

**Computing on campus.** 320 workstations in library, computer center. Online library available.

**Student life. Freshman orientation:** Available. **Housing:** Coed dorms available. $100 deposit. **Activities:** Bands, choral groups, dance, drama, literary magazine, music ensembles, student government, TV station, Florida Turf Grass Association, Florida Student Nurses Association, Phi Theta Kappa, Baptist Student Union, Granger Hall Council, medical lab technology club, physical therapy assistant club, Practical Nurses Association.

**Athletics.** NJCAA. **Intercollegiate:** Baseball M, golf W, softball W. **Intramural:** Basketball, racquetball, softball, table tennis, volleyball. **Team name:** Timberwolves.

**Student services.** Alcohol/substance abuse counseling, career counseling, student employment services, financial aid counseling, personal counseling, veterans' counselor. **Physically disabled:** Services for visually, speech, hearing impaired. **Transfer:** Transfer adviser, college fairs on campus for students transferring to 4-year colleges.

Contact. E-mail: admissions@lakecitycc.edu
Phone: (386) 754-4287 Fax: (386) 754-4787
Vince Rice, Director, Lake City Community College, 149 SE College Place, Lake City, FL 32025-8703

## Lake-Sumter Community College
### Leesburg, Florida
www.lscc.edu                                    CB code: 5376

▶ Public 2-year community college
▶ Commuter campus in small city

**General.** Founded in 1962. Regionally accredited. **Enrollment:** 3,337 degree-seeking undergraduates; 567 non-degree-seeking students. **Degrees:** 489 associate awarded. **Location:** 35 miles from Orlando. **Calendar:** Semester, limited summer session. **Full-time faculty:** 62 total; 21% have terminal degrees, 5% minority, 66% women. **Part-time faculty:** 143 total; 17% have terminal degrees, 12% minority, 55% women. **Class size:** 44% < 20, 55% 20-39, 1% 40-49, less than 1% 50-99. **Special facilities:** Wellness facilities.

**Student profile.** Among degree-seeking undergraduates, 64% enrolled in a transfer program, 24% enrolled in a vocational program, 829 enrolled as first-time, first-year students, 251 transferred in from other institutions.

| | | | |
|---|---|---|---|
| Part-time: | 63% | Asian American: | 2% |
| Out-of-state: | 1% | Hispanic American: | 10% |
| Women: | 66% | International: | 1% |
| African American: | 11% | 25 or older: | 37% |

**Transfer out. Colleges most students transferred to 2007:** University of Central Florida, University of Florida, Florida State University, University of South Florida.

**Basis for selection.** Open admission, but selective for some programs. Special requirements for nursing program. **Homeschooled:** In lieu of a high school diploma or GED, a home-schooled affidavit will be accepted.

**2007-2008 Annual costs.** Tuition/fees: $2,038; $7,581 out-of-state. Books/supplies: $850. Personal expenses: $1,000.

**Financial aid. Need-based:** Need-based aid available for part-time students. Work-study available nights and for part-time students. **Non-need-based:** Scholarships awarded for academics, art, athletics, leadership, minority status, music/drama, state residency.

**Application procedures. Admission:** No deadline. $25 fee. Application must be submitted on paper. Admission notification on a rolling basis. **Financial aid:** Priority date 4/15; no closing date. FAFSA, institutional form required. Applicants notified on a rolling basis starting 7/1.

**Academics. Special study options:** Cooperative education, distance learning, dual enrollment of high school students, independent study, liberal arts/career combination, teacher certification program. Bachelor's degree programs available on campus. License preparation in nursing, real estate. **Credit/placement by examination:** AP, CLEP, institutional tests. 39 credit hours maximum toward associate degree. **Support services:** Learning center, reduced course load, remedial instruction, study skills assistance, tutoring, writing center.

**Majors. Business:** Business admin. **Computer sciences:** Information technology, webmaster. **Education:** Early childhood. **Engineering:** Software. **Health:** EMT paramedic, medical records technology, nursing (RN). **Legal studies:** Paralegal. **Liberal arts:** Arts/sciences. **Parks/recreation:** Sports admin. **Protective services:** Firefighting, law enforcement admin. **Visual/performing arts:** Commercial/advertising art.

**Most popular majors.** Health sciences 15%, liberal arts 75%.

**Computing on campus.** 588 workstations in library, computer center, student center. Commuter students can connect to campus network. Online course registration, online library, wireless network available.

**Student life. Freshman orientation:** Mandatory. Both day and evening sessions are scheduled as well as online orientation. **Activities:** Bands, campus ministries, choral groups, drama, literary magazine, music ensembles, student newspaper, symphony orchestra, TV station, College Democrats, College Republicans, environmental society, Fellowship of Christian Athletes, Health Explorers, Lion's Club.

**Athletics.** NJCAA. **Intercollegiate:** Baseball M, softball W, volleyball W. **Intramural:** Basketball, football (non-tackle), table tennis, tennis, volleyball. **Team name:** Lakers.

**Student services.** Adult student services, career counseling, services for economically disadvantaged, student employment services, financial aid counseling, personal counseling, placement for graduates, veterans' counselor,

women's services. **Physically disabled:** Services for visually, speech, hearing impaired. **Transfer:** Pre-admission transcript evaluation for new students. Transfer adviser, college fairs on campus for students transferring to 4-year colleges.

**Contact.** E-mail: admissinquiry@lscc.edu
Phone: (352) 323-3665 Fax: (352) 365-3553
Mark Swearingen, Director, Admissions/ Registrar, Lake-Sumter Community College, 9501 U.S. Highway 441, Leesburg, FL 34788-8751

## Le Cordon Bleu College of Culinary Arts: Miami
### Hollywood, Florida
www.miamiculinary.com

▶ For-profit 2-year culinary school
▶ Small city

**General.** Accredited by ACCSCT. **Calendar:** Continuous.

**Contact.** Phone: (954) 438-8882
3221 Enterprise Way, Miramar, FL 33025

## Lincoln College of Technology: West Palm Beach
### West Palm Beach, Florida
www.newenglandtech.com                          CB code: 0529

▶ For-profit 2-year technical college
▶ Commuter campus in small city

**General.** Founded in 1982. Accredited by ACICS. **Location:** 75 miles from Miami. **Calendar:** Quarter.

**Annual costs/financial aid.** Tuition and lab fees range from $11,700 to $36,900. Registration fee $125. Books/supplies: $900. Personal expenses: $1,998. Need-based financial aid available for full-time students.

**Contact.** Phone: (561) 842-8324
Admissions Director, 2410 Metrocentre Boulevard, West Palm Beach, FL 33407

## Manatee Community College
### Bradenton, Florida                            CB member
www.mccfl.edu                                    CB code: 5427

▶ Public 2-year community college
▶ Commuter campus in small city

**General.** Founded in 1957. Regionally accredited. **Enrollment:** 8,814 degree-seeking undergraduates; 1,055 non-degree-seeking students. **Degrees:** 1,486 associate awarded. **Location:** 40 miles from Tampa, 20 miles from St. Petersburg. **Calendar:** Semester, extensive summer session. **Full-time faculty:** 169 total; 17% have terminal degrees, 11% minority, 61% women. **Part-time faculty:** 308 total; 6% have terminal degrees, 9% minority, 52% women.

**Student profile.** Among degree-seeking undergraduates, 63% enrolled in a transfer program, 37% enrolled in a vocational program, 1,658 enrolled as first-time, first-year students.

| | | | |
|---|---|---|---|
| Part-time: | 52% | Asian American: | 2% |
| Out-of-state: | 3% | Hispanic American: | 9% |
| Women: | 63% | International: | 2% |
| African American: | 11% | 25 or older: | 37% |

**Basis for selection.** Open admission, but selective for some programs. Limited enrollment in health programs. Interview recommended for nursing, radiologic technology, respiratory therapy, occupational therapy assistant, physical therapist assistant, dental hygiene majors.

**High school preparation.** Recommended units include English 4, mathematics 3, social studies 2, history 1, science 3 and foreign language 2.

**2007-2008 Annual costs.** Tuition/fees: $2,091; $7,908 out-of-state. Books/supplies: $1,202. Personal expenses: $1,910.

**2007-2008 Financial aid. Need-based:** 710 full-time freshmen applied for aid; 510 were judged to have need; 510 of these received aid. Average scholarship/grant was $2,235. Need-based aid available for part-time students. Work-study available nights, weekends and for part-time students.

**Non-need-based:** Awarded to 839 full-time undergraduates, including 254 freshmen. Scholarships awarded for academics, art, athletics, music/drama, state residency.

**Application procedures. Admission:** No deadline. No application fee. Admission notification on a rolling basis. **Financial aid:** Priority date 6/1, closing date 7/28. FAFSA required. Applicants notified on a rolling basis starting 3/15.

**Academics. Special study options:** Accelerated study, cooperative education, distance learning, dual enrollment of high school students, honors, independent study, teacher certification program. License preparation in dental hygiene, nursing, occupational therapy, physical therapy, radiology. **Credit/placement by examination:** AP, CLEP. 30 credit hours maximum toward associate degree. SAT, ACT or CPT (Florida Placement Test) used for placement only. **Support services:** GED preparation, learning center, remedial instruction, study skills assistance, tutoring.

**Majors. Area/ethnic studies:** African, African-American, American, Latin American, women's. **Biology:** General, bacteriology, marine. **Business:** General, accounting, administrative services, business admin. **Communications:** General, advertising, broadcast journalism, digital media, journalism, media studies, public relations, radio/tv. **Communications technology:** Radio/tv. **Computer sciences:** General, information systems, networking, programming, systems analysis. **Education:** General, biology, chemistry, early childhood, elementary, foreign languages, health, kindergarten/preschool, mathematics, music, physics, science, secondary, social studies, trade/industrial. **Engineering:** General, civil, computer, science. **Engineering technology:** Automotive, civil, construction, drafting, electrical. **English:** English lit, speech/rhetoric. **Foreign languages:** French, German, Spanish. **Health:** Clinical lab science, clinical lab technology, community health services, dental hygiene, health care admin, medical radiologic technology/radiation therapy, nuclear medical technology, nursing (RN), occupational therapy assistant, physical therapy assistant, respiratory therapy technology, veterinary technology/assistant. **History:** General. **Legal studies:** General, paralegal, prelaw. **Liberal arts:** Arts/sciences, humanities. **Math:** General. **Parks/recreation:** Sports admin. **Personal/culinary services:** General. **Philosophy/religion:** Philosophy, religion. **Physical sciences:** Atmospheric science, chemistry, physics. **Protective services:** Criminal justice, firefighting. **Psychology:** General. **Public administration:** General, social work. **Social sciences:** General, economics. **Visual/performing arts:** General, art, art history/conservation, commercial/advertising art, dramatic, fashion design, jazz, music theory/composition, studio arts, theater history.

**Most popular majors.** Health sciences 14%, liberal arts 76%.

**Computing on campus.** 2,275 workstations in library, computer center. Online course registration, online library, helpline, repair service, wireless network available.

**Student life. Freshman orientation:** Mandatory. Preregistration for classes offered. **Activities:** Bands, drama, film society, literary magazine, music ensembles, musical theater, opera, student government, student newspaper, symphony orchestra, African-American Student Union, multicultural student club, art club, student Bible club, Manasota Geographic and Anthropological Society, American Chemical Society, student film club, Hispanic-American club.

**Athletics.** NJCAA. **Intercollegiate:** Baseball M, basketball M, softball W, volleyball W. **Intramural:** Basketball, golf, soccer, softball, volleyball, weight lifting. **Team name:** Lancers.

**Student services.** Campus ministries, career counseling, student employment services, financial aid counseling, health services, personal counseling, placement for graduates, veterans' counselor. **Physically disabled:** Services for visually, speech, hearing impaired. **Transfer:** Transfer adviser for students transferring to 4-year colleges.

**Contact.** E-mail: admissions@mccfl.edu
Phone: (941) 752-5031 Fax: (941) 727-6380
Marilynn Lewy, Registrar, Manatee Community College, Box 1849, Bradenton, FL 34206-1849

---

## Miami Dade College

**Miami, Florida**
**www.mdc.edu/home**

**CB member**
**CB code: 5458**

♦ Public 2-year community college
♦ Commuter campus in very large city

**General.** Founded in 1959. Regionally accredited. Multilocation institution consisting of campuses and outreach centers. **Enrollment:** 46,674 degree-seeking undergraduates; 7,420 non-degree-seeking students. **Degrees:** 45 bachelor's, 6,501 associate awarded. **ROTC:** Army, Air Force. **Calendar:** Semester, limited summer session. **Full-time faculty:** 712 total; 25% have terminal degrees, 56% minority, 51% women. **Part-time faculty:** 1,347 total; 14% have terminal degrees, 66% minority, 46% women. **Class size:** 23% < 20, 66% 20-39, 10% 40-49, less than 1% 50-99, less than 1% >100. **Special facilities:** Environmental demonstration center, bilingual center, greenhouse, fire science tower, fire science burn building, emerging technologies center of the Americas, center for the environment, horticulture center, firearms demonstration lab, earth science museum, studio theater, human patient simulator lab, flight simulator lab, child care labs. **Partnerships:** Formal partnerships with Noven Pharmaceuticals, Teva International, Schering-Plough and Kirk Pharmaceuticals, Florida Power and Light (FPL) for the Electrical Power Technology Professional Training Pipeline.

**Student profile.** Among degree-seeking undergraduates, 74% enrolled in a transfer program, 26% enrolled in a vocational program, 1% already have a bachelor's degree or higher, 8,993 enrolled as first-time, first-year students, 1,377 transferred in from other institutions.

| | | | |
|---|---|---|---|
| Part-time: | 61% | Asian American: | 1% |
| Out-of-state: | 6% | Hispanic American: | 67% |
| Women: | 61% | International: | 3% |
| African American: | 19% | 25 or older: | 36% |

**Transfer out.** 79% of students enrolled in the transfer program go on to 4-year colleges. **Colleges most students transferred to 2007:** Florida International University.

**Basis for selection.** Open admission, but selective for some programs. Special requirements for visual and performing arts, honors, allied health, bachelor's in education, bachelor of applied science with major in public safety management, and bachelor's in nursing. Audition required of performing arts majors. Portfolio required of visual arts majors.

**High school preparation.** 24 units recommended. 18 credits with a 3-year high school option or 24 credits with a 4-year high school option.

**2007-2008 Annual costs.** Tuition/fees: $2,068; $6,863 out-of-state.

**2006-2007 Financial aid. Need-based:** 6,007 full-time freshmen applied for aid; 5,342 were judged to have need; 4,983 of these received aid. 77% of total undergraduate aid awarded as scholarships/grants, 23% as loans/jobs. Need-based aid available for part-time students. Work-study available nights, weekends and for part-time students. **Non-need-based:** Scholarships awarded for academics, art, athletics, music/drama, state residency.

**Application procedures. Admission:** No deadline. $20 fee. Application may be submitted online. Admission notification on a rolling basis. **Financial aid:** Priority date 3/15; no closing date. FAFSA required. Applicants notified on a rolling basis starting 5/15.

**Academics. Special study options:** Accelerated study, cooperative education, cross-registration, distance learning, dual enrollment of high school students, ESL, honors, independent study, internships, study abroad, weekend college. Bachelor's degree programs available on campus. License preparation in aviation, dental hygiene, nursing, paramedic, physical therapy, radiology, real estate. **Credit/placement by examination:** AP, CLEP, IB, institutional tests. 45 credit hours maximum toward associate degree, 45 toward bachelor's. **Support services:** GED preparation, learning center, reduced course load, remedial instruction, study skills assistance, tutoring, writing center.

**Majors. Agriculture:** Agribusiness operations, landscaping. **Area/ethnic studies:** American, Asian, Latin American. **Biology:** General. **Business:** Accounting, administrative services, banking/financial services, business admin, management science, office management, office/clerical, real estate, tourism promotion, tourism/travel. **Communications:** Broadcast journalism, journalism. **Communications technology:** General, animation/special effects, graphic/printing, graphics. **Computer sciences:** General, applications programming, information systems, information technology, web page design. **Conservation:** Environmental science, forestry. **Construction:** Maintenance. **Education:** Early childhood, elementary, mathematics, physical, science, secondary, special, technology/industrial arts. **Engineering:** Architectural, civil, electrical. **Engineering technology:** Architectural, civil, electrical, electrical drafting. **English:** American lit, English lit, speech/rhetoric. **Family/consumer sciences:** Child development, food/nutrition. **Foreign languages:** General, sign language interpretation, translation. **Health:** Clinical lab technology, dental hygiene, EMT paramedic, histologic technology, medical assistant, medical radiologic technology/radiation therapy, medical records admin, medical secretary, midwifery, nursing (RN), optician, predental, premedicine, prepharmacy, preveterinary, respiratory therapy technology, veterinary technology/assistant. **History:** General. **Legal studies:** Court reporting, legal secretary, paralegal, prelaw. **Liberal arts:** Arts/sciences. **Math:** General. **Mechanic/repair:** Heating/ac/refrig, industrial. **Parks/recreation:** Exercise sciences. **Personal/culinary services:** Mortuary science. **Philosophy/religion:** Philosophy, religion. **Physical sciences:** Atmospheric science, chemistry, geology, physics. **Protective services:** Criminal justice, fire services admin. **Psychology:** General. **Public administration:** General, human services, social work. **Social sciences:** Anthropology, economics, international relations, political science, sociology. **Transportation:** Aviation, aviation management. **Visual/performing arts:** Cinematography, commercial/advertising art, dance, dramatic, studio arts.

**Most popular majors.** Health sciences 14%, liberal arts 77%.

**Computing on campus.** 8,000 workstations in library, computer center. Commuter students can connect to campus network. Online course registration, online library, helpline, wireless network available.

**Student life. Freshman orientation:** Available. **Activities:** Bands, choral groups, dance, drama, film society, international student organizations, literary magazine, music ensembles, musical theater, radio station, student government, student newspaper, Newman Club.

**Athletics.** NJCAA. **Intercollegiate:** Baseball M, basketball, softball W, volleyball W. **Intramural:** Basketball, soccer, softball, table tennis, tennis. **Team name:** Sharks.

**Student services.** Adult student services, career counseling, services for economically disadvantaged, student employment services, financial aid counseling, personal counseling, placement for graduates, veterans' counselor. **Physically disabled:** Services for visually, speech, hearing impaired. **Transfer:** Transfer center, transfer adviser, college fairs on campus for students transferring to 4-year colleges.

**Contact.** Phone: (305) 237-2222 Fax: (305) 237-2964
Dulce Beltran, College Director, Admissions and Registration Services, Miami Dade College, 11011 SW 104th Street, Miami, FL 33176-3393

## North Florida Community College
**Madison, Florida**
www.nfcc.edu                                    **CB code: 5503**

▶ Public 2-year community college
▶ Commuter campus in rural community

**General.** Founded in 1958. Regionally accredited. **Enrollment:** 820 degree-seeking undergraduates. **Degrees:** 141 associate awarded. **Location:** 56 miles from Tallahassee. **Calendar:** Semester, limited summer session. **Full-time faculty:** 32 total. **Part-time faculty:** 108 total. **Special facilities:** Nature center.

**Student profile.** Among degree-seeking undergraduates, 64% enrolled in a transfer program, 8% enrolled in a vocational program, 410 transferred in from other institutions.

**Transfer out. Colleges most students transferred to 2007:** Florida State University, Florida A&M University, Valdosta State University, University of Florida.

**Basis for selection.** Open admission, but selective for some programs. Limited enrollment for nursing, criminal justice, EMT. Background checks completed by Florida Department of Law Enforcement. Florida College Entry-Level Placement Tests required for all students. Students with satisfactory ACT or SAT scores are exempt from taking FCELPT. **Homeschooled:** Statement describing homeschool structure and mission required. Submit affidavit stating that home education complies with Florida law. **Learning Disabled:** Disabilities must have documentation.

**High school preparation.** 24 units recommended. Recommended units include English 4, mathematics 4, social studies 3, science 2 (laboratory 1) and foreign language 2. Algebra 1 recommended.

**2007-2008 Annual costs.** Tuition/fees: $1,960; $6,826 out-of-state. Books/supplies: $500. Personal expenses: $475.

**2006-2007 Financial aid.** All financial aid based on need. 99% of total undergraduate aid awarded as scholarships/grants, 1% as loans/jobs. Need-based aid available for part-time students. Work-study available nights, weekends and for part-time students.

**Application procedures. Admission:** Priority date 7/1; no deadline. $20 fee, may be waived for applicants with need. Application must be submitted on paper. Admission notification on a rolling basis. **Financial aid:** Priority date 5/15; no closing date. FAFSA required. Applicants notified on a rolling basis starting 6/20; must reply within 2 week(s) of notification.

**Academics. Special study options:** Accelerated study, distance learning, dual enrollment of high school students, independent study, teacher certification program. Bachelor's degree programs available on campus. License preparation in nursing, paramedic, real estate. **Credit/placement by examination:** AP, CLEP, IB, institutional tests. 45 credit hours maximum toward

associate degree. **Support services:** GED preparation and test center, reduced course load, remedial instruction, study skills assistance, tutoring, writing center.

**Majors. Health:** Nursing assistant. **Liberal arts:** Arts/sciences.

**Computing on campus.** 65 workstations in library, computer center, student center. Online course registration, online library, wireless network available.

**Student life. Freshman orientation:** Available. 6-week program of 1-hour sessions 2 or 3 days per week. **Activities:** Jazz band, choral groups, drama, music ensembles, musical theater, student government, student newspaper, environmental awareness group, African-American Association, veterans club, ASL.

**Athletics.** NJCAA. **Intercollegiate:** Baseball M, basketball W, softball W. **Team name:** Sentinels.

**Student services.** Adult student services, career counseling, student employment services, health services, personal counseling, placement for graduates, veterans' counselor. **Physically disabled:** Services for hearing impaired. **Transfer:** Pre-admission transcript evaluation for new students. Transfer adviser, college fairs on campus for students transferring to 4-year colleges.

**Contact.** Phone: (850) 973-1622 Toll-free number: (866) 937-6322 Fax: (850) 973-1697
Mary Wheeler, Dean of Enrollment Services, North Florida Community College, 325 NW Turner Davis Drive, Madison, FL 32340

## North Florida Institute: Orange Park
**Orange Park, Florida**

▶ For-profit 2-year business and health science college
▶ Large city
▶ Interview required

**General.** Accredited by ACICS. **Enrollment:** 348 degree-seeking undergraduates. **Degrees:** 55 associate awarded. **Calendar:** Differs by program.

**Basis for selection.** Interview required to discuss the school's programs in relation to the prospective student's career preferences, training needs, and individual motivation.

**Academics. Credit/placement by examination:** CLEP.

**Majors. Business:** Business admin. **Health:** Management/clinical assistant. **Other:** Surgical technician.

**Contact.** Phone: (904) 269-7086
North Florida Institute: Orange Park, 560 Wells Road, Orange Park, FL 32073

## Orlando Culinary Academy
**Orlando, Florida**
www.orlandoculinary.com

▶ For-profit 2-year culinary school
▶ Very large city

**General.** Accredited by ACICS. **Location:** Downtown. **Calendar:** Continuous.

**Contact.** Phone: (407) 888-4000
8511 Commodity Circle, Suite 100, Orlando, FL 32819

## Palm Beach Community College
**Lake Worth, Florida**                         **CB member**
www.pbcc.edu                                    **CB code: 5531**

▶ Public 2-year community college
▶ Commuter campus in large town

**General.** Founded in 1933. Regionally accredited. Multilocation institution with 4 campuses, numerous other locations throughout service area. **Enrollment:** 14,588 degree-seeking undergraduates; 7,663 non-degree-seeking students. **Degrees:** 1,867 associate awarded. **Location:** 30 miles from Fort Lauderdale. **Calendar:** Semester, limited summer session. **Full-time faculty:** 235 total; 25% minority, 57% women. **Part-time faculty:** 972 total; 21% minority, 41% women. **Special facilities:** Performing arts centers at 3 campuses.

**Student profile.** Among degree-seeking undergraduates, 80% enrolled in a transfer program, 20% enrolled in a vocational program, 2,863 enrolled as first-time, first-year students.

| | | | |
|---|---|---|---|
| Part-time: | 57% | Women: | 58% |
| Out-of-state: | 6% | 25 or older: | 40% |

**Transfer out. Colleges most students transferred to 2007:** Florida Atlantic University, University of Florida, Florida State University, University of South Florida.

**Basis for selection.** Open admission, but selective for some programs. Special requirements for dental, nursing, dietetic, occupational therapy assistant programs. Admission to paramedic, radiography, respiratory care programs based on test scores and GPA. SAT or ACT required for admission to nursing and dental programs. CPT, SAT or ACT used for placement for all incoming freshmen. Interview required for nursing, dental, radiography, respiratory care, paramedic majors. Audition required of music majors. **Homeschooled:** Home education program affidavit required.

**High school preparation.** Special requirements for health program applicants.

**2007-2008 Annual costs.** Tuition/fees: $1,995; $7,110 out-of-state. Books/supplies: $1,000. Personal expenses: $400.

**2007-2008 Financial aid. Need-based:** 78% of total undergraduate aid awarded as scholarships/grants, 22% as loans/jobs. Work-study available nights, weekends and for part-time students. **Non-need-based:** Scholarships awarded for academics, alumni affiliation, athletics, leadership, state residency.

**Application procedures. Admission:** Closing date 8/23. $20 fee. Application may be submitted online. Admission notification on a rolling basis beginning on or about 3/1. **Financial aid:** Priority date 7/1; no closing date. FAFSA, institutional form required. Applicants notified on a rolling basis; must reply within 2 week(s) of notification.

**Academics.** Center for Personalized Instruction offers full assistance in all academic areas for students. **Special study options:** Cooperative education, distance learning, double major, dual enrollment of high school students, ESL, honors, independent study, internships, study abroad, weekend college. License preparation in aviation, dental hygiene, nursing, paramedic, radiology, real estate. **Credit/placement by examination:** AP, CLEP, IB, institutional tests. 45 credit hours maximum toward associate degree. **Support services:** Learning center, pre-admission summer program, reduced course load, remedial instruction, study skills assistance, tutoring, writing center.

**Majors. Agriculture:** Ornamental horticulture. **Architecture:** Interior. **Biology:** General, zoology. **Business:** General, accounting, business admin, finance, hospitality admin, management information systems, marketing, sales/distribution. **Communications:** Broadcast journalism, journalism. **Communications technology:** Graphic/printing. **Computer sciences:** General, applications programming, information systems, programming, systems analysis. **Construction:** Maintenance. **Education:** Art, early childhood, elementary, health, health occupations, music, physical, sales/marketing, science, secondary, social science, voc/tech. **Engineering:** General, electrical. **Engineering technology:** Construction, drafting, electrical, industrial management, surveying. **English:** English lit. **Family/consumer sciences:** General, child care. **Health:** Clinical lab technology, dental hygiene, dietetics, EMT paramedic, health services, massage therapy, medical radiologic technology/radiation therapy, nursing (RN), occupational therapy assistant, premedicine, respiratory therapy technology. **History:** General. **Interdisciplinary:** Biological/physical sciences. **Legal studies:** Paralegal. **Liberal arts:** Arts/sciences. **Math:** General. **Mechanic/repair:** Automotive, marine. **Parks/recreation:** General, health/fitness. **Philosophy/religion:** Philosophy. **Physical sciences:** Chemistry, physics. **Protective services:** Fire services admin, firefighting. **Psychology:** General. **Public administration:** Human services, social work. **Social sciences:** General, anthropology, geography, international relations, political science, sociology. **Transportation:** Aviation. **Visual/performing arts:** General, art history/conservation, cinematography, commercial/advertising art, dance, dramatic, interior design, jazz, photography, studio arts.

**Most popular majors.** Biological/life sciences 10%, health sciences 10%, liberal arts 75%.

**Computing on campus.** 1,500 workstations in library, computer center. Online course registration, online library, helpline, wireless network available.

**Student life. Freshman orientation:** Mandatory. Preregistration for classes offered. **Activities:** Bands, choral groups, dance, drama, literary magazine, music ensembles, musical theater, student government, student newspaper, black student union, Students for International Understanding.

**Athletics.** NJCAA. **Intercollegiate:** Baseball M, basketball, softball W, volleyball W. **Intramural:** Basketball, softball, volleyball. **Team name:** Panthers.

**Student services.** Career counseling, student employment services, personal counseling, placement for graduates, veterans' counselor. **Physically disabled:** Services for visually, speech, hearing impaired. **Transfer:** Transfer adviser, college fairs on campus for students transferring to 4-year colleges.

**Contact.** E-mail: muellere@pbcc.edu
Phone: (561) 868-3300 Fax: (561) 868-3584
Edward Mueller, Admissions Coordinator, Palm Beach Community College, 4200 Congress Avenue, Lake Worth, FL 33461

## Pasco-Hernando Community College
**New Port Richey, Florida**
www.phcc.edu
CB code: 5562

- Public 2-year community college
- Commuter campus in large town

**General.** Founded in 1972. Regionally accredited. District covers counties of Pasco and Hernando; 4 college locations. Distance learning courses are offered for a variety of courses. **Enrollment:** 8,065 degree-seeking undergraduates. **Degrees:** 818 associate awarded. **ROTC:** Army, Naval. **Location:** 35 miles from Tampa. **Calendar:** Semester, limited summer session. **Full-time faculty:** 103 total. **Part-time faculty:** 257 total.

**Student profile.**

| | | | |
|---|---|---|---|
| Out-of-state: | 1% | 25 or older: | 35% |

**Transfer out. Colleges most students transferred to 2007:** University of South Florida, St. Leo University, University of Florida, University of Central Florida, St. Petersburg College.

**Basis for selection.** Open admission, but selective for some programs. Special requirements for nursing, paramedic, dental, radiography. Most placement based on Florida College Entry Level Placement Test (FCELPT), which is administered locally. **Learning Disabled:** Completed no-fee application and appropriate documentation to Office of Disabilities Services required.

**High school preparation.** 24 units recommended. Recommended units include English 4, mathematics 3, social studies 3, science 3 and foreign language 2.

**2007-2008 Annual costs.** Tuition/fees: $1,970; $7,371 out-of-state. Books/supplies: $1,100. Personal expenses: $1,850.

**Financial aid. Need-based:** Need-based aid available for part-time students. Work-study available nights, weekends and for part-time students. **Non-need-based:** Scholarships awarded for academics, athletics, minority status. **Additional information:** Childcare assistance grants available to eligible students.

**Application procedures. Admission:** No deadline. $20 fee. Application may be submitted online. Admission notification on a rolling basis. **Financial aid:** Priority date 4/1; no closing date. FAFSA required. Applicants notified on a rolling basis starting 3/1.

**Academics.** License preparation in radiography. **Special study options:** Accelerated study, combined bachelor's/graduate degree, cross-registration, distance learning, double major, dual enrollment of high school students, ESL, honors, independent study, internships, weekend college. Bachelor's degree programs available on campus. License preparation in dental hygiene, nursing, paramedic, radiology. **Credit/placement by examination:** AP, CLEP, IB, institutional tests. 45 credit hours maximum toward associate degree. **Support services:** GED preparation and test center, learning center, reduced course load, remedial instruction, study skills assistance, tutoring.

**Majors. Business:** Business admin, marketing, office management. **Computer sciences:** Applications programming, information technology, networking, programming, systems analysis, vendor certification. **Health:** Dental hygiene, EMT paramedic, nursing (RN), radiologic technology/medical imaging. **Legal studies:** Paralegal. **Liberal arts:** Arts/sciences. **Protective services:** Law enforcement admin. **Public administration:** Human services.

**Most popular majors.** Computer/information sciences 6%, health sciences 20%, liberal arts 66%.

**Computing on campus.** 1,595 workstations in library, computer center. Online course registration, online library available.

**Student life. Freshman orientation:** Mandatory. 3- to 4-hour program held on variety of days, nights, Saturdays. **Activities:** Choral groups, drama, literary magazine, music ensembles, student government, human services club, drama club, student nursing club, writers' club, Phi Beta Lambda (business), Phi Theta Kappa, Delta Epsilon Chi, Psi Beta (psychology club), STRIKE (Student Tobacco Reform Initiative), computer club.

**Athletics.** NJCAA. **Intercollegiate:** Baseball M, basketball M, softball W, tennis W, volleyball W. **Team name:** Conquistadors.

**Student services.** Career counseling, services for economically disadvantaged, financial aid counseling, minority student services, on-campus daycare, personal counseling, placement for graduates, veterans' counselor. **Physically disabled:** Services for visually, speech, hearing impaired. **Transfer:** College fairs on campus for students transferring to 4-year colleges.

**Contact.** E-mail: bullard@phcc.edu
Phone: (727) 816-3261 Toll-free number: (877) 879-7422
Fax: (727) 816-3389
Debra Bullard, Director of Admissions and Student Records,
Pasco-Hernando Community College, 10230 Ridge Road, New Port
Richey, FL 34654-5199

---

## Pensacola Junior College

**Pensacola, Florida**
www.pjc.edu

**CB member**
**CB code: 5535**

- Public 2-year community college
- Commuter campus in small city

**General.** Founded in 1948. Regionally accredited. Additional campuses: Milton, Warrington, Downtown Center, NAS Center. **Enrollment:** 7,268 degree-seeking undergraduates; 3,460 non-degree-seeking students. **Degrees:** 1,288 associate awarded. **ROTC:** Army. **Location:** 60 miles from Mobile, Alabama. **Calendar:** Semester, extensive summer session. **Full-time faculty:** 222 total; 23% have terminal degrees; 12% minority, 42% women. **Part-time faculty:** 703 total. **Special facilities:** Science and space theater.

**Student profile.** Among degree-seeking undergraduates, 93% enrolled in a transfer program, 6% enrolled in a vocational program, 1% already have a bachelor's degree or higher, 1,255 enrolled as first-time, first-year students.

| | | | |
|---|---|---|---|
| Part-time: | 50% | Women: | 59% |
| Out-of-state: | 2% | 25 or older: | 50% |

**Basis for selection.** Open admission, but selective for some programs. Special requirements for health programs. Florida Entry Level Placement Test must be taken for admission; student may submit SAT or ACT in its place. Scores used for placement only. **Homeschooled:** State high school equivalency certificate required.

**High school preparation.** 24 units recommended. Recommended units include English 4, mathematics 3, social studies 3, science 3, foreign language 2 and academic electives 11. College preparatory program required for associate of arts program: 13 academic units including 4 English, 3 science, 3 mathematics, and 3 social science.

**2007-2008 Annual costs.** Tuition/fees: $1,976; $7,123 out-of-state. Books/supplies: $1,100. Personal expenses: $1,170.

**Financial aid. Non-need-based:** Scholarships awarded for academics, athletics, state residency.

**Application procedures. Admission:** No deadline. $30 fee. Application may be submitted online. Admission notification on a rolling basis. **Financial aid:** Priority date 4/1; no closing date. FAFSA, institutional form required. Applicants notified on a rolling basis starting 7/1; must reply within 2 week(s) of notification.

**Academics. Special study options:** Accelerated study, cooperative education, cross-registration, distance learning, double major, dual enrollment of high school students, ESL, honors, independent study, internships, study abroad, weekend college. License preparation in dental hygiene, nursing, paramedic, radiology. **Credit/placement by examination:** AP, CLEP, IB, institutional tests. 39 credit hours maximum toward associate degree. **Support services:** GED preparation and test center, learning center, reduced course load, remedial instruction, study skills assistance, tutoring, writing center.

**Majors. Agriculture:** General, ornamental horticulture. **Biology:** General, biochemistry, botany, zoology. **Business:** General, accounting, administrative services, banking/financial services, business admin, hospitality/recreation, management information systems, management science, office

management. **Communications:** General, journalism. **Communications technology:** General. **Computer sciences:** General, computer science, information systems, programming. **Conservation:** Forest resources, forestry, management/policy. **Construction:** Maintenance. **Education:** General, art, early childhood, elementary, music, physical, special. **Engineering:** General, civil, computer, electrical. **Engineering technology:** Civil, construction, electrical, hazardous materials, manufacturing. **English:** English lit. **Family/consumer sciences:** Advocacy, child care, food/nutrition, institutional food production. **Health:** Dental hygiene, EMT paramedic, health care admin, medical radiologic technology/radiation therapy, medical records admin, nursing (RN), physical therapy assistant, predental, premedicine, prenursing, prepharmacy, preveterinary, sonography. **History:** General. **Legal studies:** Legal secretary, paralegal, prelaw. **Liberal arts:** Arts/sciences. **Math:** General. **Mechanic/repair:** Automotive. **Personal/culinary services:** Culinary arts. **Philosophy/religion:** Philosophy, religion. **Physical sciences:** Chemistry, geology, physics. **Protective services:** Firefighting, law enforcement admin. **Psychology:** General. **Science technology:** Chemical. **Social sciences:** Sociology. **Visual/performing arts:** Art, commercial/advertising art, dramatic.

**Computing on campus.** 1,500 workstations in library, computer center. Online course registration, wireless network available.

**Student life. Freshman orientation:** Mandatory. **Activities:** Bands, choral groups, dance, drama, international student organizations, literary magazine, music ensembles, musical theater, student government, student newspaper, symphony orchestra, TV station, Baptist campus ministry, Florida African-American Student Association, Wesley Foundation, Phi Theta Kappa, Campus Activities Board, Students for Multi-Cultural Society.

**Athletics.** NJCAA. **Intercollegiate:** Baseball M, basketball, cheerleading, softball W, volleyball W. **Intramural:** Archery, badminton, basketball, bowling, racquetball, skin diving, soccer, softball W, table tennis, tennis, volleyball, water polo, weight lifting. **Team name:** Pirates.

**Student services.** Adult student services, alcohol/substance abuse counseling, campus ministries, career counseling, services for economically disadvantaged, student employment services, financial aid counseling, health services, minority student services, on-campus daycare, personal counseling, placement for graduates, veterans' counselor, women's services. **Physically disabled:** Services for visually, speech, hearing impaired. **Transfer:** Pre-admission transcript evaluation for new students. Transfer adviser, college fairs on campus for students transferring to 4-year colleges.

**Contact.** Phone: (850) 484-1601 Toll-free number: (888) 897-3605
Fax: (850) 484-1829
Martha Caughey, Director Admissions and Registrar, Pensacola Junior
College, 1000 College Boulevard, Pensacola, FL 32504-8998

---

## Polk Community College

**Winter Haven, Florida**
www.polk.edu

**CB member**
**CB code: 5548**

- Public 2-year community college
- Commuter campus in large town

**General.** Founded in 1963. Regionally accredited. Branch campus in Lakeland shared with University of South Florida. **Enrollment:** 6,063 degree-seeking undergraduates; 1,694 non-degree-seeking students. **Degrees:** 857 associate awarded. **ROTC:** Army. **Location:** 60 miles from Tampa, 60 miles from Orlando. **Calendar:** Semester, extensive summer session. **Full-time faculty:** 135 total; 18% have terminal degrees, 16% minority, 52% women. **Part-time faculty:** 402 total; 6% have terminal degrees, 16% minority, 55% women. **Class size:** 36% < 20, 63% 20-39, less than 1% 40-49, less than 1% 50-99, less than 1% >100.

**Student profile.** Among degree-seeking undergraduates, 70% enrolled in a transfer program, 30% enrolled in a vocational program, 1,238 enrolled as first-time, first-year students, 422 transferred in from other institutions.

| | | | |
|---|---|---|---|
| Part-time: | 64% | Asian American: | 3% |
| Out-of-state: | 2% | Hispanic American: | 10% |
| Women: | 65% | International: | 1% |
| African American: | 16% | 25 or older: | 35% |

**Transfer out. Colleges most students transferred to 2007:** University of South Florida, University of Central Florida, University of Florida, Florida State University, Florida Southern College.

**Basis for selection.** Open admission, but selective for some programs. Limited access to nursing, radiology, physical therapy assistant, occupational therapy assistant, repiratory therapy, paramedic programs, cardiovascular tech, medical sonography. Audition recommended for theater, music majors. Portfolio recommended for graphic arts majors. **Homeschooled:**

Adheres to FLDOE policy and Florida state statute: affidavit signed by guardian attesting to home school applicant completion required in place of high school diploma. **Learning Disabled:** Students needing classroom accommodations must provide documentation as required.

**High school preparation.** Recommended units include English 4, mathematics 4, social studies 3, science 3 and foreign language 2.

**2007-2008 Annual costs.** Tuition/fees: $2,006; $7,393 out-of-state. Books/supplies: $1,200. Personal expenses: $1,500.

**Financial aid. Need-based:** Need-based aid available for part-time students. Work-study available nights, weekends and for part-time students. **Non-need-based:** Scholarships awarded for academics, athletics, leadership, state residency.

**Application procedures. Admission:** No deadline. $20 fee, may be waived for applicants with need. Application may be submitted online. Admission notification on a rolling basis. **Financial aid:** Priority date 5/15; no closing date. FAFSA required. Applicants notified on a rolling basis.

**Academics. Special study options:** Accelerated study, cross-registration, distance learning, double major, dual enrollment of high school students, ESL, honors, independent study, internships. License preparation in nursing, occupational therapy, paramedic, physical therapy, radiology. **Credit/placement by examination:** AP, CLEP, IB. 45 credit hours maximum toward associate degree. **Support services:** Learning center, reduced course load, remedial instruction, study skills assistance, tutoring.

**Honors college/program.** High school graduates with 3.5 GPA may apply for honors program and designated courses.

**Majors. Business:** Accounting, administrative services, banking/financial services, business admin, marketing, office management, office/clerical. **Computer sciences:** General, computer graphics, information systems, programming. **Construction:** Power transmission. **Education:** General. **Engineering technology:** Electrical. **English:** English lit. **Family/consumer sciences:** Child care. **Health:** Cardiovascular technology, EMT paramedic, medical records admin, medical records technology, nursing (RN), occupational therapy assistant, physical therapy assistant, respiratory therapy technology, sonography. **Liberal arts:** Arts/sciences. **Mechanic/repair:** Computer. **Protective services:** Criminal justice, firefighting, police science. **Visual/performing arts:** Cinematography.

**Most popular majors.** Health sciences 22%, liberal arts 67%.

**Computing on campus.** 171 workstations in library, computer center, student center. Online course registration available.

**Student life. Freshman orientation:** Available. Preregistration for classes offered. **Activities:** Bands, choral groups, drama, music ensembles, musical theater, student government.

**Athletics.** NJCAA. **Intercollegiate:** Baseball M, basketball M, soccer W, softball W, volleyball W. **Intramural:** Basketball, bowling, football (non-tackle), table tennis, volleyball. **Team name:** Vikings.

**Student services.** Adult student services, career counseling, services for economically disadvantaged, student employment services, financial aid counseling. **Physically disabled:** Services for visually, speech, hearing impaired. **Transfer:** Re-entry adviser for new students. Transfer adviser, college fairs on campus for students transferring to 4-year colleges.

**Contact.** E-mail: StudentServices@polk.edu
Phone: (863) 297-1010 ext. 5225 Fax: (863) 297-1060
Kathy Bucklew, Registrar, Polk Community College, 999 Avenue H NE, Winter Haven, FL 33881-4299

## Professional Golfers Career College: Orlando
### Winter Garden, Florida
### www.golfcollege.edu

- For-profit 2-year branch campus college
- Commuter campus in very large city

**General.** Accredited by ACICS. **Enrollment:** 200 degree-seeking undergraduates. **Degrees:** 69 associate awarded. **Location:** 16 miles from Orlando. **Calendar:** Semester. **Full-time faculty:** 10 total.

**Basis for selection.** Character/personal qualities and level of applicant's interest very important.

**2007-2008 Annual costs.** Tuition/fees: $10,180. Room only: $6,000.

**Application procedures. Admission:** No deadline. $75 fee. Application must be submitted on paper. Admission notification on a rolling basis.

**Academics. Credit/placement by examination:** CLEP, institutional tests.

**Majors. Parks/recreation:** Facilities management.

**Computing on campus.** 12 workstations in computer center. Online library available.

**Student life. Freshman orientation:** Mandatory. **Housing:** Apartments, substance-free housing available. $700 nonrefundable deposit.

**Student services.** Alcohol/substance abuse counseling, career counseling, financial aid counseling, personal counseling, placement for graduates, veterans' counselor.

**Contact.** E-mail: admin@golfcollege.edu
Phone: (407) 905-2200 Toll-free number: (800) 877-4380
Fax: (951) 719-1643
David Wood, Admissions Director, Professional Golfers Career College: Orlando, PO Box 892319, Temecula, CA 92589-2319

## Saint Johns River Community College
### Palatka, Florida
### www.sjrcc.cc.fl.us
**CB member**
**CB code: 5641**

- Public 2-year community college
- Commuter campus in large town

**General.** Founded in 1957. Regionally accredited. **Enrollment:** 4,025 degree-seeking undergraduates. **Degrees:** 579 associate awarded. **Location:** 55 miles from Jacksonville and Daytona Beach. **Calendar:** Trimester, limited summer session. **Full-time faculty:** 106 total. **Part-time faculty:** 153 total.

**Basis for selection.** Open admission, but selective for some programs. Interview, audition, and portfolio required of applicants to Florida School of Arts program.

**High school preparation.** 24 units recommended. Recommended units include English 4, mathematics 3, social studies 3 and science 3.

**2007-2008 Annual costs.** Tuition/fees: $2,091; $7,565 out-of-state. Books/supplies: $752. Personal expenses: $87.

**2006-2007 Financial aid. Need-based:** 70% of total undergraduate aid awarded as scholarships/grants, 30% as loans/jobs. Need-based aid available for part-time students.

**Application procedures. Admission:** Priority date 7/15; no deadline. $30 fee. Admission notification on a rolling basis. **Financial aid:** Priority date 5/15; no closing date. FAFSA required. Applicants notified on a rolling basis.

**Academics. Special study options:** Dual enrollment of high school students. **Credit/placement by examination:** AP, CLEP. 45 credit hours maximum toward associate degree. **Support services:** Remedial instruction, tutoring.

**Majors. Business:** Accounting, accounting technology, administrative services, business admin. **Computer sciences:** Programming, systems analysis. **Engineering technology:** Electrical. **Health:** EMT paramedic. **Liberal arts:** Arts/sciences. **Protective services:** Fire safety technology. **Visual/performing arts:** General.

**Student life. Activities:** Student government, student newspaper, Black Student Union, Circle-K, Compass Club, future educators, Phi Beta Lamba, Mathematical Association of America.

**Athletics.** NJCAA. **Intercollegiate:** Baseball M, basketball M, softball W. **Intramural:** Table tennis.

**Student services.** Career counseling, personal counseling, placement for graduates, veterans' counselor. **Physically disabled:** Services for speech impaired.

**Contact.** Phone: (386) 312-4030 Fax: (386) 312-4048
O'Neal Williams, Admission and Records, Saint Johns River Community College, 5001 St. Johns Avenue, Palatka, FL 32177-3897

## Sanford-Brown Institute: Jacksonville

**Jacksonville, Florida**
**www.sbjacksonville.com**

- For-profit 2-year health science college
- Commuter campus in large city
- Application essay, interview required

**General.** Accredited by ACICS. **Enrollment:** 460 degree-seeking undergraduates. **Calendar:** Continuous. **Full-time faculty:** 7 total. **Part-time faculty:** 30 total.

**Basis for selection. Homeschooled:** Statement describing homeschool structure and mission, transcript of courses and grades, state high school equivalency certificate, interview, letter of recommendation (nonparent) required.

**Application procedures. Admission:** No deadline. $25 fee. Application may be submitted online. Admission notification on a rolling basis.

**Academics. Credit/placement by examination:** CLEP. **Support services:** Learning center, reduced course load, study skills assistance, tutoring.

**Majors. Health:** Cardiovascular technology.

**Computing on campus.** 60 workstations in library, computer center, student center. Commuter students can connect to campus network.

**Student life. Freshman orientation:** Mandatory. Preregistration for classes offered.

**Student services.** Adult student services, career counseling, student employment services, financial aid counseling, health services, personal counseling, placement for graduates. **Physically disabled:** Services for speech, hearing impaired.

**Contact.** Phone: (904) 363-6221
Deborah King, Director of Admissions, Sanford-Brown Institute: Jacksonville, 10255 Fortune Parkway, Suite 501, Jacksonville, FL 32256

## Sanford-Brown Institute: Tampa

**Tampa, Florida**
**www.sbtampa.com**

- For-profit 2-year health science and community college
- Large city

**General.** Accredited by ACICS. **Calendar:** Continuous.

**Contact.** Phone: (813) 621-0072
Director of Admissions, 5701 East Hillsboro Avenue, Tampa, FL 33610

## Santa Fe Community College

**Gainesville, Florida**                    **CB member**
**www.santafe.cc.fl.us**                     **CB code: 5653**

- Public 2-year community college
- Commuter campus in small city

**General.** Founded in 1965. Regionally accredited. Branch campuses located downtown and in Starke. **Enrollment:** 13,544 degree-seeking undergraduates. **Degrees:** 2,108 associate awarded. **ROTC:** Army, Naval, Air Force. **Location:** 80 miles from Jacksonville, 80 miles from Orlando. **Calendar:** Semester, extensive summer session. **Full-time faculty:** 252 total. **Part-time faculty:** 369 total. **Special facilities:** Teaching zoo.

**Student profile.**

| Out-of-state: | 3% | 25 or older: | 28% |
|---|---|---|---|

**Basis for selection.** Open admission, but selective for some programs. Nursing program requires 5 prerequisite courses. Radiologic technology and dental hygiene applicants selected by admissions committee. Radiation therapy students must have X-ray or nuclear medicine license and experience. Computerized Placement Tests may be submitted in place of SAT or ACT.

**High school preparation.** Recommended units include foreign language 2.

**2007-2008 Annual costs.** Tuition/fees: $2,006; $7,577 out-of-state. Books/supplies: $700. Personal expenses: $1,008.

**Financial aid. Need-based:** Need-based aid available for part-time students. **Non-need-based:** Scholarships awarded for academics, art, athletics, leadership, minority status, music/drama, state residency.

**Application procedures. Admission:** No deadline. No application fee. Application may be submitted online. Admission notification on a rolling basis. High school diploma not required of applicants to most vocational programs. **Financial aid:** Priority date 3/15, closing date 6/30. FAFSA required. Applicants notified by 8/1.

**Academics. Special study options:** Cooperative education, cross-registration, distance learning, dual enrollment of high school students, ESL, honors, independent study, weekend college. **Credit/placement by examination:** AP, CLEP, institutional tests. 30 credit hours maximum toward associate degree. **Support services:** GED preparation, learning center, remedial instruction, tutoring.

**Majors. Agriculture:** Ornamental horticulture. **Biology:** Botany. **Business:** Accounting, administrative services, banking/financial services, business admin, fashion, marketing, office technology, office/clerical. **Computer sciences:** Data processing, programming. **Construction:** Maintenance. **Education:** Early childhood. **Engineering technology:** Drafting, electrical. **Family/consumer sciences:** Child care. **Health:** Dental hygiene, EMT paramedic, medical radiologic technology/radiation therapy, medical secretary, nuclear medical technology, nursing (RN), predental, premedicine, prepharmacy, respiratory therapy technology. **Legal studies:** Legal secretary, paralegal. **Liberal arts:** Arts/sciences. **Parks/recreation:** Exercise sciences, facilities management. **Physical sciences:** Astronomy, chemistry. **Protective services:** Fire safety technology, forensics. **Social sciences:** Anthropology. **Visual/performing arts:** Commercial/advertising art, fashion design.

**Most popular majors.** Health sciences 10%, liberal arts 77%.

**Student life. Freshman orientation:** Available. **Activities:** Choral groups, dance, drama, music ensembles, musical theater, radio station, student government, student newspaper, TV station, Black Student Union, Phi Theta Kappa.

**Athletics.** NJCAA. **Intercollegiate:** Baseball M, basketball, softball W. **Intramural:** Basketball, racquetball. **Team name:** Saints.

**Student services.** Career counseling, student employment services, health services, on-campus daycare, personal counseling, placement for graduates, veterans' counselor. **Physically disabled:** Services for visually, speech, hearing impaired. **Transfer:** Transfer adviser for students transferring to 4-year colleges.

**Contact.** E-mail: information@sfcc.edu
Phone: (352) 395-7322 Fax: (352) 395-5581
Lynn Sullivan, Director of Enrollment Services, Santa Fe Community College, 3000 NW 83rd Street, Gainesville, FL 32606

## Seminole Community College

**Sanford, Florida**
**www.scc-fl.edu**                          **CB code: 5662**

- Public 2-year community college
- Commuter campus in large town

**General.** Founded in 1965. Regionally accredited. **Enrollment:** 10,634 degree-seeking undergraduates; 1,723 non-degree-seeking students. **Degrees:** 1,398 associate awarded. **Location:** 21 miles from Orlando. **Calendar:** Semester, limited summer session. **Full-time faculty:** 189 total; 18% have terminal degrees, 15% minority, 62% women. **Part-time faculty:** 671 total; 7% have terminal degrees, 13% minority, 54% women. **Class size:** 30% < 20, 68% 20-39, less than 1% 40-49, less than 1% 50-99, less than 1% >100. **Special facilities:** Planetarium, golf course. **Partnerships:** Formal partnerships with Siemens/Stromberg, local businesses.

**Student profile.** Among degree-seeking undergraduates, 2,157 enrolled as first-time, first-year students.

| Part-time: | 57% | Women: | 60% |
|---|---|---|---|
| Out-of-state: | 3% | 25 or older: | 48% |

**Basis for selection.** Open admission, but selective for some programs. Limited access to associate of science degrees including nursing, physical therapy, and respiratory care. College credit entry students need ACT or SAT scores less than 2 years old for placement, or must take state placement test. Interview recommended for respiratory therapy, nursing, and physical therapy majors. **Homeschooled:** Transcript of courses and grades required. Affidavit of home school completion required.

**High school preparation.** 24 units required. Required units include English 4, mathematics 3, social studies 3, science 3 and academic electives 11.

**2007-2008 Annual costs.** Tuition/fees: $2,081; $7,571 out-of-state. Books/supplies: $1,200. Personal expenses: $900.

**2006-2007 Financial aid. Need-based:** 41% of total undergraduate aid awarded as scholarships/grants, 59% as loans/jobs. Need-based aid available for part-time students. Work-study available for part-time students. **Non-need-based:** Scholarships awarded for academics, art, athletics, leadership, minority status, music/drama, state residency.

**Application procedures. Admission:** Closing date 9/21 (receipt date). No application fee. Application must be submitted on paper. Admission notification on a rolling basis beginning on or about 9/1. **Financial aid:** No deadline. FAFSA required. Applicants notified on a rolling basis starting 4/1.

**Academics. Special study options:** Accelerated study, cooperative education, cross-registration, distance learning, dual enrollment of high school students, ESL, honors, independent study, study abroad, teacher certification program, weekend college. **Credit/placement by examination:** AP, CLEP, IB, institutional tests. 45 credit hours maximum toward associate degree. **Support services:** GED preparation and test center, learning center, reduced course load, remedial instruction, study skills assistance, tutoring.

**Majors. Architecture:** Interior. **Business:** Administrative services, banking/financial services. **Communications:** General. **Communications technology:** General. **Computer sciences:** General, applications programming, computer graphics, computer science, data processing, information systems, networking, programming, systems analysis. **Education:** Kindergarten/preschool. **Engineering:** Electrical, software. **Engineering technology:** Architectural, construction, electrical. **Family/consumer sciences:** Child care. **Health:** EMT paramedic, medical secretary, nursing (RN), physical therapy assistant, respiratory therapy technology. **Legal studies:** Legal secretary, paralegal. **Liberal arts:** Arts/sciences. **Mechanic/repair:** Automotive. **Protective services:** Firefighting, law enforcement admin. **Visual/performing arts:** Interior design.

**Most popular majors.** Health sciences 11%, liberal arts 74%.

**Computing on campus.** 100 workstations in library, computer center. Commuter students can connect to campus network. Online course registration, online library, student web hosting, wireless network available.

**Student life. Freshman orientation:** Mandatory. Preregistration for classes offered. **Activities:** Bands, choral groups, drama, film society, international student organizations, literary magazine, music ensembles, musical theater, student government, student newspaper, symphony orchestra, African American cultural forum, College Republicans, disabled student association, Hispanic student associations, Muslim student association, Unity Organization, Fellowship of Christian Athletes, Latter-day Saint student association.

**Athletics.** NJCAA. **Intercollegiate:** Baseball M, basketball, golf W, softball W. **Team name:** Raider.

**Student services.** Adult student services, alcohol/substance abuse counseling, career counseling, services for economically disadvantaged, student employment services, financial aid counseling, minority student services, personal counseling, placement for graduates, veterans' counselor. **Physically disabled:** Services for visually, speech, hearing impaired. **Transfer:** Transfer adviser for students transferring to 4-year colleges.

**Contact.** E-mail: admissions@scc-fl.edu
Phone: (407) 708-2580 Fax: (407) 708-2395
Pamela Mennechey, Director of Admissions, Seminole Community College, 100 Weldon Boulevard, Sanford, FL 32773-6199

## South Florida Community College

Avon Park, Florida
www.southflorida.edu

CB member
CB code: 5666

- Public 2-year community and technical college
- Commuter campus in small town

**General.** Founded in 1965. Regionally accredited. **Enrollment:** 1,822 degree-seeking undergraduates; 718 non-degree-seeking students. **Degrees:** 254 associate awarded. **ROTC:** Army. **Location:** 90 miles from Orlando. **Calendar:** Semester, limited summer session. **Full-time faculty:** 64 total; 23% have terminal degrees, 6% minority, 53% women. **Part-time faculty:** 137 total; 4% have terminal degrees, 18% minority, 46% women. **Class size:** 57% < 20, 42% 20-39, less than 1% 40-49. **Special facilities:** Museum of florida art and culture, nature walk.

**Student profile.** Among degree-seeking undergraduates, 61% enrolled in a transfer program, 39% enrolled in a vocational program, 459 enrolled as first-time, first-year students, 186 transferred in from other institutions.

| | | | |
|---|---|---|---|
| **Part-time:** | 63% | **Hispanic American:** | 19% |
| **Out-of-state:** | 3% | **Native American:** | 1% |
| **Women:** | 64% | **International:** | 1% |
| **African American:** | 11% | **25 or older:** | 27% |
| **Asian American:** | 2% | **Live on campus:** | 2% |

**Basis for selection.** Open admission, but selective for some programs. Some programs have test and prerequisite requirements. Additional requirements include health screening and financial ability. Interview recommended for selected programs. **Homeschooled:** Students must meet with registrar prior to admission. **Learning Disabled:** Recommend students seek assistance from campus disabilities specialist.

**High school preparation.** 13 units recommended. Recommended units include English 4, mathematics 3, social studies 3 and science 3.

**2007-2008 Annual costs.** Tuition/fees: $2,039; $7,672 out-of-state. Books/supplies: $875. Personal expenses: $1,000.

**2006-2007 Financial aid. Need-based:** 89% of total undergraduate aid awarded as scholarships/grants, 11% as loans/jobs. Need-based aid available for part-time students. Work-study available for part-time students. **Non-need-based:** Scholarships awarded for academics, athletics, leadership, minority status, music/drama, state residency.

**Application procedures. Admission:** No deadline. No application fee. Admission notification on a rolling basis. **Financial aid:** Priority date 3/15; no closing date. FAFSA required. Applicants notified on a rolling basis starting 4/1.

**Academics. Special study options:** Accelerated study, cooperative education, distance learning, double major, dual enrollment of high school students, ESL, external degree, honors, independent study, internships, teacher certification program. Bachelor's degree programs available on campus. License preparation in dental hygiene, nursing, paramedic, radiology. **Credit/placement by examination:** AP, CLEP, IB, institutional tests. 30 credit hours maximum toward associate degree. **Support services:** GED preparation and test center, learning center, reduced course load, remedial instruction, study skills assistance, tutoring, writing center.

**Majors. Agriculture:** General, agribusiness operations, horticultural science, ornamental horticulture. **Business:** Accounting, administrative services, business admin, hospitality admin. **Computer sciences:** LAN/WAN management, programming. **Construction:** General, power transmission. **Education:** Teacher assistance. **Engineering technology:** Biomedical, computer hardware, drafting, electrical. **English:** English lit. **Family/consumer sciences:** Child care. **Health:** Dental hygiene, EMT paramedic, medical secretary, nursing (RN). **Liberal arts:** Arts/sciences. **Protective services:** Firefighting, law enforcement admin.

**Most popular majors.** Health sciences 14%, liberal arts 79%.

**Computing on campus.** 100 workstations in library, computer center, student center. Online course registration, online library, helpline, repair service, wireless network available.

**Student life. Freshman orientation:** Mandatory. Preregistration for classes offered. Online video with review quiz. **Housing:** Coed dorms, substance-free housing available. **Activities:** Campus ministries, international student organizations, music ensembles, student government, student newspaper, Adventist social club, African American association.

**Athletics.** NJCAA. **Intercollegiate:** Baseball M, softball W, volleyball W. **Team name:** Panthers.

**Student services.** Adult student services, career counseling, services for economically disadvantaged, student employment services, financial aid counseling, minority student services, personal counseling, placement for graduates, veterans' counselor, women's services. **Physically disabled:** Services for visually, speech, hearing impaired. **Transfer:** Transfer adviser, college fairs on campus for students transferring to 4-year colleges.

**Contact.** E-mail: Deborah.Fuschetti@southflorida.edu
Phone: (863) 453-6661 ext. 7405 Fax: (863) 453-2365
Deborah Fuschetti, Registrar, South Florida Community College, 600 West College Drive, Avon Park, FL 33825

## Southwest Florida College

Ft. Myers, Florida
www.swfc.edu

CB code: 3445

- Private 2-year junior college
- Commuter campus in small city
- Interview required

**General.** Accredited by ACICS. Additional campus in Tampa. **Enrollment:** 1,489 degree-seeking undergraduates; 10 non-degree-seeking students. **Degrees:** 322 associate awarded. **Location:** 130 miles from Tampa. **Calendar:** Quarter, extensive summer session. **Full-time faculty:** 38 total; 16% have terminal degrees, 8% minority, 55% women. **Part-time faculty:** 69 total; 7% have terminal degrees, 7% minority, 49% women.

**Student profile.** Among degree-seeking undergraduates, 226 enrolled as first-time, first-year students.

| | | | |
|---|---|---|---|
| Part-time: | 15% | 25 or older: | 52% |
| Women: | 72% | | |

**Transfer out. Colleges most students transferred to 2007:** International College.

**Basis for selection.** Open admission, but selective for some programs. Microsoft Network Engineer program requires passing scores in technical and scholastic exam prior to acceptance.

**2008-2009 Annual costs.** Tuition/fees (projected): $9,660. Per-credit charge: $255. Required fees do not include lab or online fees. Books/supplies: $1,725. Personal expenses: $1,551.

**Financial aid. Need-based:** Need-based aid available for part-time students. Work-study available nights and for part-time students.

**Application procedures. Admission:** No deadline. $25 fee. Application must be submitted on paper. Admission notification on a rolling basis. **Financial aid:** Priority date 4/15; no closing date. FAFSA required. Applicants notified on a rolling basis.

**Academics. Special study options:** Cooperative education, distance learning, double major, liberal arts/career combination, weekend college. Bachelor's degree programs available on campus. **Credit/placement by examination:** AP, CLEP, institutional tests. 24 credit hours maximum toward associate degree, 24 toward bachelor's. **Support services:** Learning center, reduced course load, remedial instruction, study skills assistance, tutoring, writing center.

**Majors. Business:** Accounting, business admin, hospitality/recreation. **Computer sciences:** General, computer graphics, security, system admin. **Education:** Early childhood. **Engineering:** Computer. **Engineering technology:** Drafting. **Health:** Medical assistant, medical secretary, medical transcription, pharmacy assistant, surgical technology. **Legal studies:** General, paralegal. **Protective services:** Criminal justice.

**Computing on campus.** 194 workstations in library, computer center, student center. Online library, wireless network available.

**Student life. Freshman orientation:** Mandatory.

**Student services.** Adult student services, career counseling, student employment services, financial aid counseling, placement for graduates. **Physically disabled:** Services for visually, speech, hearing impaired. **Learning disabled:** Comprehensive services available. **Transfer:** Pre-admission transcript evaluation for new students.

**Contact.** E-mail: kreynolds@swfc.edu
Phone: (239) 939-4766 Toll-free number: (866) 793-2669
Fax: (239) 936-4040
Ken Reynolds, Director of Admissions, Southwest Florida College, 1685 Medical Lane, Ft. Myers, FL 33907-1108

## Southwest Florida College: Tampa
**Tampa, Florida**
**www.swfc.edu**

◆ Private 2-year branch campus and junior college
◆ Commuter campus in very large city

**General.** Accredited by ACICS. **Location:** 15 miles from downtown. **Calendar:** Quarter.

**Annual costs/financial aid.** Expenses vary by program.

**Contact.** Phone: (813) 630-4401
Vice President of Admissions, 3910 Riga Boulevard, Tampa, FL 33619

## Stenotype Institute: Jacksonville
**Jacksonville, Florida**
**www.thestenotypeinstitute.com**

◆ For-profit 2-year business and community college
◆ Very large city

**General.** Accredited by ACICS. **Calendar:** Continuous.

**Contact.** Phone: (904) 398-4141
Director Of Admissions, 3986 Boulevard Center Drive, Jacksonville, FL 32207

## Stenotype Institute: Orlando
**Orlando, Florida**

◆ Private 2-year technical college
◆ Very large city

**General.** Accredited by ACICS. **Calendar:** Semester.

**Contact.** Phone: (407) 816-5573
1636 West Oakridge Road, Orlando, FL 32809

## Tallahassee Community College
**Tallahassee, Florida**      **CB member**
**www.tcc.fl.edu**      **CB code: 5794**

◆ Public 2-year community college
◆ Commuter campus in small city

**General.** Founded in 1965. Regionally accredited. **Enrollment:** 12,673 degree-seeking undergraduates. **Degrees:** 1,960 associate awarded. **ROTC:** Army, Naval, Air Force. **Location:** 230 miles from Tampa, 200 miles from Pensacola. **Calendar:** Semester, extensive summer session. **Full-time faculty:** 180 total. **Part-time faculty:** 650 total. **Class size:** 20% < 20, 60% 20-39, 15% 40-49, 6% 50-99.

**Transfer out. Colleges most students transferred to 2007:** Florida State University.

**Basis for selection.** Open admission, but selective for some programs. Special requirements for nursing, dental hygiene, emergency medical technology, radiologic technology and respiratory therapy programs. Each program requires specific course prerequisites or test scores or required GPA in addition to letters of recommendation. SAT/ACT may substitute for Florida CPT for placement. Placement test score required of degree-seeking applicants before enrolling in classes. **Homeschooled:** Present affidavit verifying completion of high school requirements. **Learning Disabled:** If service or accommodations are needed, documentation required.

**2007-2008 Annual costs.** Tuition/fees: $1,875; $6,705 out-of-state. Books/supplies: $800. Personal expenses: $1,800.

**2006-2007 Financial aid. Need-based:** 47% of total undergraduate aid awarded as scholarships/grants, 53% as loans/jobs. Need-based aid available for part-time students. **Non-need-based:** Scholarships awarded for academics, art, athletics, leadership, music/drama, state residency.

**Application procedures. Admission:** Closing date 8/1 (receipt date). No application fee. Application may be submitted online. Admission notification on a rolling basis. Separate application procedure for health programs. **Financial aid:** Priority date 5/1; no closing date. FAFSA, institutional form required. Applicants notified on a rolling basis starting 5/15.

**Academics. Special study options:** Cooperative education, cross-registration, distance learning, double major, dual enrollment of high school students, ESL, honors, independent study, liberal arts/career combination, study abroad. Bachelor's degree programs available on campus. License preparation in dental hygiene, nursing, paramedic, real estate. **Credit/placement by examination:** AP, CLEP, IB, institutional tests. 45 credit hours maximum toward associate degree. **Support services:** GED preparation, learning center, pre-admission summer program, reduced course load, remedial instruction, study skills assistance, tutoring, writing center.

**Majors. Business:** General, accounting, administrative services, banking/financial services, business admin, management information systems, sales/distribution. **Computer sciences:** Computer graphics, networking, programming. **Construction:** Maintenance. **Education:** Early childhood, health. **Engineering:** General, civil, software. **Engineering technology:** Civil, construction, drafting, industrial management. **Health:** Dental hygiene, EMT paramedic, medical radiologic technology/radiation therapy, nursing (RN), respiratory therapy technology. **Legal studies:** Paralegal. **Liberal arts:** Arts/sciences. **Parks/recreation:** Facilities management. **Protective services:** Criminal justice, law enforcement admin. **Public administration:** General. **Social sciences:** General. **Visual/performing arts:** General, commercial/advertising art, film/cinema.

**Most popular majors.** Health sciences 6%, liberal arts 88%.

**Computing on campus.** 1,733 workstations in library, computer center, student center. Commuter students can connect to campus network. Online course registration, online library, helpline, wireless network available.

**Student life. Freshman orientation:** Mandatory. Preregistration for classes offered. All-day event held few days prior to start of term; includes small group meetings and advising. Online orientation also available. **Activities:** Bands, campus ministries, choral groups, dance, drama, international student organizations, literary magazine, music ensembles, musical theater, student government, student newspaper, TV station, Phi Theta Kappa, Black Student Union, Returning Adults Valuing Education, Future Educators of America, students interested in legal careers, College Democrats, BACCHUS, student environmental action coalition.

**Athletics.** NJCAA. **Intercollegiate:** Baseball M, basketball, softball W. **Intramural:** Basketball, golf, soccer, softball, table tennis, tennis. **Team name:** Eagles.

**Student services.** Adult student services, career counseling, services for economically disadvantaged, financial aid counseling, minority student services, on-campus daycare, personal counseling, placement for graduates, veterans' counselor. **Physically disabled:** Services for visually, speech, hearing impaired. **Transfer:** Transfer adviser, college fairs on campus for students transferring to 4-year colleges.

**Contact.** E-mail: enrollment@tcc.fl.edu
Phone: (850) 201-8555 Fax: (850) 201-8474
Katherine Nerona-Balog, Director, Enrollment Services and Testing, Tallahassee Community College, 444 Appleyard Drive, Tallahassee, FL 32304

## Valencia Community College
Orlando, Florida
www.valenciacc.edu

**CB member**
**CB code: 5869**

- Public 2-year community college
- Commuter campus in very large city

**General.** Founded in 1967. Regionally accredited. **Enrollment:** 26,707 degree-seeking undergraduates; 6,163 non-degree-seeking students. **Degrees:** 4,130 associate awarded. **ROTC:** Army. **Location:** 90 miles from Tampa, 145 miles from Jacksonville. **Calendar:** Semester, extensive summer session. **Full-time faculty:** 421 total; 23% have terminal degrees, 22% minority, 57% women. **Part-time faculty:** 915 total; 13% have terminal degrees, 24% minority, 50% women. **Class size:** 20% < 20, 78% 20-39, less than 1% 40-49, less than 1% 50-99, less than 1% >100.

**Student profile.** Among degree-seeking undergraduates, 22% enrolled in a transfer program, 78% enrolled in a vocational program, 6,359 enrolled as first-time, first-year students, 1,205 transferred in from other institutions.

| | | | |
|---|---|---|---|
| Part-time: | 51% | Asian American: | 5% |
| Out-of-state: | 3% | Hispanic American: | 26% |
| Women: | 57% | International: | 3% |
| African American: | 16% | 25 or older: | 25% |

**Transfer out.** 45% of students enrolled in the transfer program go on to 4-year colleges. **Colleges most students transferred to 2007:** University of Central Florida.

**Basis for selection.** Open admission, but selective for some programs. Special requirements for the criminal justice institute programs, A.A. pre-major dance performance, film production technology program, and health sciences programs. **Homeschooled:** Home school diplomas accepted with official Home School Verification Affidavit.

**High school preparation.** Recommended units include English 4, mathematics 3, social studies 3 and science 3.

**2007-2008 Annual costs.** Tuition/fees: $2,091; $7,858 out-of-state. Books/supplies: $1,000. Personal expenses: $4,300.

**Financial aid. Need-based:** Need-based aid available for part-time students. Work-study available nights and for part-time students.

**Application procedures. Admission:** Closing date 8/1 (postmark date). $25 fee. Application may be submitted online. Admission notification on a rolling basis beginning on or about 3/31. **Financial aid:** Closing date 5/15. FAFSA required. Applicants notified on a rolling basis starting 4/2; must reply within 2 week(s) of notification.

**Academics. Special study options:** Cooperative education, distance learning, double major, dual enrollment of high school students, ESL, honors, independent study, internships, student-designed major, study abroad, weekend college. License preparation in dental hygiene, nursing, paramedic, physical therapy, radiology, real estate. **Credit/placement by examination:** AP,

CLEP, IB, institutional tests. 45 credit hours maximum toward associate degree. Less than 75 percent of a program's hours may be met with credit by examination and/or other acceleration mechanisms. **Support services:** Learning center, remedial instruction, study skills assistance, tutoring, writing center.

**Majors. Agriculture:** Horticultural science, landscaping. **Architecture:** Technology. **Biology:** General, marine. **Business:** Accounting, accounting technology, business admin, entrepreneurial studies, finance, hospitality admin, human resources, management information systems, marketing, real estate, restaurant/food services, small business admin. **Communications:** Digital media, journalism, public relations. **Computer sciences:** General, computer science, information technology, programming, systems analysis, webmaster. **Construction:** General. **Education:** General, early childhood. **Engineering:** General. **Engineering technology:** General, CAD/CADD, civil, drafting, electrical. **English:** English lit. **Family/consumer sciences:** Institutional food production. **Foreign languages:** French, Portuguese, Spanish. **Health:** Cardiovascular technology, dental hygiene, EMT paramedic, insurance coding, medical records admin, medical records technology, medical secretary, nursing (RN), radiologic technology/medical imaging, respiratory therapy assistant, respiratory therapy technology, sonography. **History:** General. **Legal studies:** Paralegal. **Liberal arts:** Arts/sciences, humanities. **Math:** General. **Personal/culinary services:** Baking, culinary arts, restaurant/catering. **Philosophy/religion:** Philosophy. **Physical sciences:** Chemistry. **Protective services:** Fire safety technology, law enforcement admin, police science. **Psychology:** General. **Social sciences:** General, economics, political science, sociology. **Visual/performing arts:** Art, dance, graphic design, theater design.

**Most popular majors.** Health sciences 9%, liberal arts 79%.

**Computing on campus.** 2,500 workstations in library, computer center, student center. Commuter students can connect to campus network. Online course registration, online library, helpline, wireless network available.

**Student life. Freshman orientation:** Mandatory. Preregistration for classes offered. 2-hour program. **Activities:** Bands, choral groups, dance, drama, international student organizations, literary magazine, music ensembles, musical theater, student government, student newspaper, symphony orchestra, African American cultural society, Brain Bowl, Latin American student organization, student nurses association, Valencia Volunteers, Phi Beta Lambda, Earth Club, Muslim student organization, Black high achievers club.

**Student services.** Career counseling, student employment services, financial aid counseling, health services, personal counseling, placement for graduates, veterans' counselor. **Physically disabled:** Services for visually, hearing impaired. **Transfer:** College fairs on campus for students transferring to 4-year colleges.

**Contact.** Phone: (407) 582-1507 Fax: (407) 582-1403
Renee Simpson, Director of Admissions and Records, Valencia Community College, PO Box 3028, Orlando, FL 32802-3028

## Virginia College at Pensacola
Pensacola, Florida
www.vc.edu/pensacola

- For-profit 2-year business and health science college
- Commuter campus in small city

**General.** Accredited by ACICS. **Enrollment:** 181 degree-seeking undergraduates. **Degrees:** 81 associate awarded. **Calendar:** Quarter, extensive summer session. **Full-time faculty:** 15 total. **Part-time faculty:** 40 total.

**Basis for selection.** Open admission.

**2007-2008 Annual costs.** Tuition/fees: $11,625. Per-credit charge: $230.

**2006-2007 Financial aid. Need-based:** 85% of total undergraduate aid awarded as scholarships/grants, 15% as loans/jobs.

**Application procedures. Admission:** $100 fee.

**Academics. Credit/placement by examination:** CLEP. **Support services:** Learning center, remedial instruction, tutoring.

**Majors. Business:** Accounting/business management, business admin, fashion, retailing. **Personal/culinary services:** General.

**Computing on campus.** 80 workstations in library, computer center. Online library available.

**Contact.** E-mail: hrobbins@vc.edu
Phone: (850) 436-8444 Toll-free number: (888) 208-6932
Fax: (850) 436-4838
Heather Robbins, Director of Admissions, Virginia College at Pensacola, 19
West Garden Street, Pensacola, FL 32502

# Georgia

## Abraham Baldwin Agricultural College
**Tifton, Georgia**                   **CB member**
www.abac.edu                       **CB code: 5001**

- Public 2-year agricultural and community college
- Commuter campus in large town
- SAT or ACT required

**General.** Founded in 1924. Regionally accredited. Students may pursue programs of study at 3 off-campus sites: Valdosta State College (associate in nursing), Ben-Hill Irwin Technical Institute (associate in applied science), and Moultrie Area Technical Institute. **Enrollment:** 3,665 degree-seeking undergraduates. **Degrees:** 479 associate awarded. **Location:** 100 miles from Macon, 50 miles from Albany. **Calendar:** Semester. **Full-time faculty:** 100 total. **Part-time faculty:** 35 total. **Special facilities:** 200-acre farm.

**Student profile.**

| | | | |
|---|---|---|---|
| Out-of-state: | 7% | Live on campus: | 28% |
| 25 or older: | 12% | | |

**Basis for selection.** 1.8 GPA, 330 SAT verbal and 310 SAT math or 12 ACT English and 14 ACT math necessary to obtain required Freshman Index of 1830. Interview recommended for nursing majors.

**High school preparation.** 16 units required. Required units include English 4, mathematics 3, social studies 3, science 3 and foreign language 2. College-preparatory program not required for students pursuing AAS degree.

**2007-2008 Annual costs.** Tuition/fees: $2,374; $7,990 out-of-state. Per-credit charge: $78 in-state; $312 out-of-state. Room/board: $5,800. Books/supplies: $775. Personal expenses: $1,500.

**Application procedures. Admission:** No deadline. $20 fee. Admission notification on a rolling basis. **Financial aid:** Priority date 5/1; no closing date. FAFSA, institutional form required. Applicants notified on a rolling basis starting 5/15; must reply within 2 week(s) of notification.

**Academics. Special study options:** Dual enrollment of high school students, external degree, honors, independent study, internships, study abroad. **Credit/placement by examination:** AP, CLEP, institutional tests. **Support services:** Learning center, remedial instruction, tutoring.

**Majors. Agriculture:** Animal sciences, business, ornamental horticulture, plant sciences, poultry. **Biology:** General. **Business:** Accounting, business admin, fashion, hospitality admin, office technology, office/clerical. **Communications:** General, journalism. **Computer sciences:** General, applications programming, data processing. **Conservation:** Forestry, wildlife. **Education:** General. **Engineering:** Agricultural. **English:** English lit. **Family/consumer sciences:** General, child care, institutional food production. **Health:** Athletic training, dental hygiene, medical records technology, predental, premedicine, prepharmacy. **History:** General. **Legal studies:** Prelaw. **Liberal arts:** Arts/sciences. **Math:** General. **Parks/recreation:** Facilities management. **Physical sciences:** Chemistry. **Protective services:** Police science. **Psychology:** General. **Social sciences:** General, sociology. **Visual/performing arts:** General, studio arts.

**Computing on campus.** 158 workstations in library, computer center.

**Student life. Housing:** Coed dorms, single-sex dorms available. **Activities:** Bands, choral groups, dance, drama, literary magazine, radio station, student government, student newspaper.

**Athletics.** NJCAA. **Intercollegiate:** Badminton W, baseball M, basketball M, golf M, softball W, tennis, volleyball W. **Intramural:** Softball, volleyball.

**Student services.** Adult student services, career counseling, student employment services, health services, personal counseling, placement for graduates, veterans' counselor. **Transfer:** Transfer adviser, college fairs on campus for students transferring to 4-year colleges.

**Contact.** Phone: (229) 391-5001 Fax: (229) 386-7481
Beth Saxon, Director of Admissions, Abraham Baldwin Agricultural College, ABAC 4, 2802 Moore Highway, Tifton, GA 31793-2601

## Albany Technical College
**Albany, Georgia**
www.albanytech.edu                    **CB code: 3921**

- Public 2-year technical college
- Commuter campus in small city

**General.** Regionally accredited. Hands On Enviroment. **Enrollment:** 2,346 degree-seeking undergraduates; 406 non-degree-seeking students. **Degrees:** 62 associate awarded. **Location:** 225 miles from Atlanta. **Calendar:** Quarter, extensive summer session. **Full-time faculty:** 91 total. **Special facilities:** None.

**Student profile.** Among degree-seeking undergraduates, 436 enrolled as first-time, first-year students.

| | | | |
|---|---|---|---|
| Part-time: | 46% | African American: | 65% |
| Women: | 62% | Hispanic American: | 1% |

**Transfer out. Colleges most students transferred to 2007:** Albany State University.

**Basis for selection.** Open admission. ACT or SAT may be accepted in lieu of COMPASS or ASSET for placement.

**High school preparation.** 22 units recommended. Recommended units include English 4, mathematics 3, social studies 3, science 3, foreign language 1 and academic electives 3. 4 tech prep, 1 science recommended.

**2007-2008 Annual costs.** Tuition/fees: $1,359; $2,475 out-of-state. Per-credit charge: $31 in-state; $62 out-of-state. Books/supplies: $1,260.

**Financial aid. Need-based:** Need-based aid available for part-time students. Work-study available nights and for part-time students. **Non-need-based:** Scholarships awarded for academics, state residency.

**Application procedures. Admission:** Closing date 10/1 (postmark date). $15 fee, may be waived for applicants with need. Application may be submitted online. Admission notification on a rolling basis beginning on or about 8/1. **Financial aid:** No deadline. FAFSA required. Applicants notified on a rolling basis starting 5/1.

**Academics. Special study options:** Distance learning, dual enrollment of high school students. License preparation in nursing, paramedic, radiology. **Credit/placement by examination:** AP, CLEP, institutional tests. **Support services:** GED preparation and test center, remedial instruction, tutoring.

**Majors. Business:** Sales/distribution. **Computer sciences:** Data processing, networking. **Conservation:** Forestry. **Construction:** Carpentry. **Education:** Early childhood. **Engineering technology:** Drafting. **Health:** Pharmacy assistant. **Mechanic/repair:** Electronics/electrical, industrial. **Personal/culinary services:** Chef training. **Protective services:** Criminal justice.

**Most popular majors.** Business/marketing 31%, computer/information sciences 22%, education 24%, health sciences 7%, security/protective services 6%.

**Computing on campus.** Online library available.

**Student life. Freshman orientation:** Available. Preregistration for classes offered. Students contact advisor to register for classes. Advisor registers students via Internet. **Activities:** Choral groups, student government.

**Athletics. Intercollegiate:** Basketball M. **Team name:** Titans.

**Student services.** Adult student services, career counseling, services for economically disadvantaged, student employment services, financial aid counseling, on-campus daycare, personal counseling, placement for graduates, veterans' counselor. **Physically disabled:** Services for visually, speech, hearing impaired. **Transfer:** Pre-admission transcript evaluation for new students.

**Contact.** Phone: (229) 430-3520 Fax: (229) 430-6180
Director of Admissions, Albany Technical College, 1704 South Slappy Boulevard, Albany, GA 31701-3514

## Andrew College
**Cuthbert, Georgia**
www.andrewcollege.edu                  **CB code: 5009**

- Private 2-year junior and liberal arts college affiliated with United Methodist Church
- Residential campus in small town
- SAT or ACT (ACT writing recommended) required

**General.** Founded in 1854. Regionally accredited. **Enrollment:** 271 degree-seeking undergraduates. **Degrees:** 50 associate awarded. **Location:** 60 miles from Columbus, 40 miles from Albany. **Calendar:** Semester, limited summer session. **Full-time faculty:** 23 total. **Part-time faculty:** 2 total. **Class size:** 75% < 20, 25% 20-39.

**Transfer out. Colleges most students transferred to 2007:** Georgia Southwestern State University, Valdosta State University, Georgia Southern University, Columbus State University.

**Basis for selection.** High school academic record, test scores, school and community activities important. Essay recommended. Interview required of the academically weak. Audition required of music majors. Portfolio recommended for art majors. **Homeschooled:** Transcript of courses and grades required.

**High school preparation.** 18 units recommended.

**2007-2008 Annual costs.** Tuition/fees: $10,306. Room/board: $6,474. Books/supplies: $600. Personal expenses: $1,200.

**Financial aid. Need-based:** Need-based aid available for part-time students. **Non-need-based:** Scholarships awarded for academics, art, athletics, leadership, music/drama, religious affiliation, state residency.

**Application procedures. Admission:** Priority date 6/1; deadline 8/1 (receipt date). $20 fee, may be waived for applicants with need. Application may be submitted online. Admission notification on a rolling basis. **Financial aid:** Priority date 4/1, closing date 8/1. FAFSA, institutional form required. Applicants notified on a rolling basis starting 4/15.

**Academics. Special study options:** Double major, dual enrollment of high school students, ESL. **Credit/placement by examination:** AP, CLEP, SAT, ACT, institutional tests. 24 credit hours maximum toward associate degree. **Support services:** Pre-admission summer program, remedial instruction, study skills assistance, tutoring.

**Majors. Agriculture:** General. **Business:** General. **Communications:** General, journalism. **Computer sciences:** Computer science. **Conservation:** Forestry. **Education:** General. **Engineering:** General. **Health:** Athletic training, predental, premedicine, prenursing, prepharmacy, preveterinary. **History:** General. **Legal studies:** Prelaw. **Liberal arts:** Arts/sciences. **Math:** General. **Parks/recreation:** Health/fitness. **Physical sciences:** General. **Psychology:** General. **Social sciences:** General, sociology. **Visual/performing arts:** General, dramatic.

**Most popular majors.** Business/marketing 20%, communications/journalism 6%, education 12%, engineering/engineering technologies 6%, health sciences 14%, legal studies 6%, visual/performing arts 12%.

**Computing on campus.** 100 workstations in dormitories, library, computer center, student center. Dormitories wired for high-speed internet access and linked to campus network. Commuter students can connect to campus network.

**Student life. Freshman orientation:** Mandatory. Preregistration for classes offered. Selected weekends during summer and beginning of fall term, 3-4 days. **Policies:** No alcohol/illegal drugs allowed on campus. **Housing:** Guaranteed on-campus for all undergraduates. Coed dorms, single-sex dorms available. **Activities:** Choral groups, drama, literary magazine, music ensembles, musical theater, student government, student newspaper, Baptist Student Union, Wesley Fellowship, Unity, community service group, interdenominational Christian group.

**Athletics.** NJCAA. **Intercollegiate:** Baseball M, basketball W, cross-country, golf, soccer, softball W. **Intramural:** Archery, badminton, basketball, cheerleading W, cross-country, football (non-tackle) M, golf, racquetball, soccer, softball, swimming, table tennis, tennis, volleyball, weight lifting M. **Team name:** Tigers.

**Student services.** Alcohol/substance abuse counseling, campus ministries, career counseling, services for economically disadvantaged, financial aid counseling, health services, veterans' counselor. **Transfer:** Transfer adviser, college fairs on campus for students transferring to 4-year colleges.

**Contact.** E-mail: admissions@andrewcollege.edu
Phone: (800) 664-9250 Toll-free number: (800) 664-9250
Fax: (229) 732-2176
Bridgett Kurkowski, Director of Admissions and Financial Aid, Andrew College, 413 College Street, Cuthbert, GA 39840-1395

## Athens Technical College
**Athens, Georgia**
www.athenstech.edu                              CB code: 0462

- Public 2-year technical college
- Commuter campus in small city

**General.** Founded in 1959. Regionally accredited. **Enrollment:** 3,436 degree-seeking undergraduates; 605 non-degree-seeking students. **Degrees:** 306 associate awarded. **Location:** 65 miles from Atlanta. **Calendar:** Quarter, extensive summer session. **Full-time faculty:** 81 total. **Part-time faculty:** 208 total. **Class size:** 61% < 20, 36% 20-39, 1% 40-49, 2% 50-99.

**Student profile.** Among degree-seeking undergraduates, 589 enrolled as first-time, first-year students.

| | | | |
|---|---|---|---|
| Part-time: | 58% | Asian American: | 6% |
| Women: | 69% | Hispanic American: | 2% |
| African American: | 24% | | |

**Transfer out. Colleges most students transferred to 2007:** University of Georgia.

**Basis for selection.** Open admission, but selective for some programs. Special requirements for radiology, respiratory therapy, nursing, physical therapy assistant, dental hygiene, surgical technology, veterinary technology dental assisting, medical assisting, practical nursing and diagnostic medical sonography. School record, recommendations, standardized test scores, essay, and interview required or recommended depending on program. COMPASS and ASSET tests required for placement, but under certain conditions ACT or SAT scores may be accepted. Interview required of radiology, respiratory therapy, nursing, physical therapy assistant, dental assisting, and dental hygiene majors. **Homeschooled:** Must provide documentation of designated home study program activities.

**High school preparation.** 22 units recommended. Recommended units include English 4, mathematics 3, social studies 3, science 3, foreign language 1 and academic electives 3. 4 tech prep and 1 health science recommended.

**2007-2008 Annual costs.** Tuition/fees: $1,359; $2,475 out-of-state. Per-credit charge: $31 in-state; $62 out-of-state. Books/supplies: $800. Personal expenses: $1,000.

**Financial aid. Need-based:** Need-based aid available for part-time students. Work-study available for part-time students. **Non-need-based:** Scholarships awarded for academics, leadership.

**Application procedures. Admission:** Priority date 8/1; no deadline. $15 fee. Application may be submitted online. Admission notification on a rolling basis. February 1 deadline for applicants to nursing and dental hygiene programs. March 1 deadline for dental assistance program. April 1 deadline for radiography, surgical technology, diagnostic medical sonography, nursing accelerated, and veterinary technology programs. May 1 deadline for physical therapist assistant, and practical nursing programs. July 1 deadline for respiratory therapy. August 1 deadline for medical assistance program. **Financial aid:** No deadline. FAFSA required. Applicants notified on a rolling basis starting 6/15; must reply within 2 week(s) of notification.

**Academics. Special study options:** Distance learning, dual enrollment of high school students. License preparation in real estate. **Credit/placement by examination:** AP, CLEP, institutional tests. **Support services:** GED preparation and test center, learning center, reduced course load, remedial instruction, study skills assistance, tutoring.

**Majors. Business:** Accounting technology, administrative services, sales/distribution. **Computer sciences:** Applications programming, data processing, networking, programming. **Education:** Early childhood. **Health:** Dental assistant, dental hygiene, nursing (RN), physical therapy assistant, radiologic technology/medical imaging, respiratory therapy technology, sonography, veterinary technology/assistant. **Legal studies:** Paralegal. **Science technology:** Biological.

**Most popular majors.** Business/marketing 24%, computer/information sciences 9%, education 6%, health sciences 41%, legal studies 8%, trade and industry 6%.

**Computing on campus.** 346 workstations in computer center. Commuter students can connect to campus network. Online course registration, online library, wireless network available.

**Student life. Freshman orientation:** Mandatory. Preregistration for classes offered. **Activities:** Student government.

**Student services.** Adult student services, career counseling, student employment services, financial aid counseling, personal counseling, placement for graduates, veterans' counselor. **Physically disabled:** Services for visually, speech, hearing impaired. **Transfer:** Transfer adviser for students transferring to 4-year colleges.

**Contact.** E-mail: admissions@athenstech.edu
Phone: (706) 355-5005 Fax: (706) 369-5756
Daniel Smith, Vice President for Student Development Services, Athens Technical College, 800 US Highway 29 North, Athens, GA 30601-1500

## Atlanta Metropolitan College
**Atlanta, Georgia**
www.atlm.edu

CB member
CB code: 5725

- Public 2-year junior college
- Commuter campus in very large city

**General.** Founded in 1974. Regionally accredited. **Enrollment:** 1,814 degree-seeking undergraduates; 70 non-degree-seeking students. **Degrees:** 182 associate awarded. **Location:** 4 miles from downtown. **Calendar:** Semester, limited summer session. **Full-time faculty:** 47 total; 55% have terminal degrees, 87% minority, 45% women. **Part-time faculty:** 57 total; 9% have terminal degrees, 86% minority, 53% women.

**Student profile.** Among degree-seeking undergraduates, 335 enrolled as first-time, first-year students.

| | | | |
|---|---|---|---|
| Part-time: | 46% | Women: | 65% |

**Basis for selection.** Applicants who have followed college preparatory curriculum must have 2.0 GPA. Applicants who have followed technology/career curriculum must have 2.2 GPA. All applicants must meet immunization requirements. Applicants with 430 SAT verbal or 17 ACT English and completion of college preparatory curriculum in English exempt from taking COMPASS Placement Test in English and Reading. Applicants with 400 SAT math or 17 ACT math and completion of college preparatory curriculum in math exempt from taking COMPASS Placement Test in math. **Homeschooled:** Transcript of courses and grades required.

**High school preparation.** 16 units required. Required units include English 4, mathematics 4, social studies 1, history 2, science 3 (laboratory 2) and foreign language 2.

**2007-2008 Annual costs.** Tuition/fees: $2,040; $7,280 out-of-state. Per-credit charge: $73 in-state; $292 out-of-state. Books/supplies: $1,284. Personal expenses: $2,210.

**2006-2007 Financial aid.** All financial aid based on need. 76% of total undergraduate aid awarded as scholarships/grants, 24% as loans/jobs. Need-based aid available for part-time students. Work-study available nights, weekends and for part-time students.

**Application procedures. Admission:** Priority date 7/15; no deadline. $20 fee. Application may be submitted online. Admission notification on a rolling basis. **Financial aid:** Closing date 6/1. FAFSA required. Applicants notified on a rolling basis; must reply by 6/30.

**Academics.** Academic and technological workshops provided. Tutorial services available in math, physics, chemistry, English, reading, accounting, and general science. **Special study options:** Distance learning, dual enrollment of high school students, independent study, study abroad, weekend college. **Credit/placement by examination:** AP, CLEP. **Support services:** Learning center, remedial instruction, study skills assistance, tutoring, writing center.

**Majors. Area/ethnic studies:** African-American. **Biology:** General. **Business:** Business admin, office management. **Communications:** General. **Computer sciences:** General, computer science. **Education:** Multi-level teacher. **Engineering technology:** General. **English:** English lit, speech/rhetoric. **Foreign languages:** General. **Health:** Medical records admin. **History:** General. **Math:** General. **Parks/recreation:** Health/fitness. **Physical sciences:** Chemistry, physics. **Protective services:** Law enforcement admin. **Psychology:** General. **Public administration:** Social work. **Social sciences:** Political science. **Visual/performing arts:** Art.

**Most popular majors.** Liberal arts 91%.

**Computing on campus.** 580 workstations in library, computer center, student center. Online course registration, online library, helpline, repair service, wireless network available.

**Student life. Freshman orientation:** Mandatory. Preregistration for classes offered. 1 daytime and 1 evening session held each semester. **Activities:** Choral groups, dance, drama, international student organizations, student government, student newspaper.

**Athletics. Team name:** Red-Eyed Panthers.

**Student services.** Services for economically disadvantaged, financial aid counseling, personal counseling, veterans' counselor. **Physically disabled:** Services for visually, speech, hearing impaired. **Transfer:** Pre-admission transcript evaluation for new students. College fairs on campus for students transferring to 4-year colleges.

**Contact.** E-mail: areid@atlm.edu
Phone: (404) 756-4004 Fax: (404) 756-4407
Audrey Reid, Director of Admissions, Atlanta Metropolitan College, 1630 Metropolitan Parkway, SW, Atlanta, GA 30310-4498

## Atlanta Technical College
**Atlanta, Georgia**
www.atlantatech.org

CB code: 5030

- Public 2-year community and technical college
- Commuter campus in very large city

**General.** Regionally accredited. **Enrollment:** 2,937 degree-seeking undergraduates; 390 non-degree-seeking students. **Degrees:** 55 associate awarded. **Location:** 2 miles from downtown. **Calendar:** Quarter. **Full-time faculty:** 86 total. **Part-time faculty:** 102 total.

**Student profile.** Among degree-seeking undergraduates, 2% enrolled in a transfer program, 98% enrolled in a vocational program, 725 enrolled as first-time, first-year students.

| | | | |
|---|---|---|---|
| Part-time: | 48% | Asian American: | 1% |
| Women: | 61% | Hispanic American: | 1% |
| African American: | 93% | 25 or older: | 51% |

**Basis for selection.** Open admission, but selective for some programs. Requirements vary by program for selective admission majors. ACT or SAT may be accepted in lieu of COMPASS or ASSET for placement. **Adult students:** SAT/ACT scores not required. **Homeschooled:** Letter from superintendent's ofice confirming compliance with Georgia/DTAE policies and attendance and final exit exam scores from accredited national testing program required.

**High school preparation.** 22 units recommended. Recommended units include English 4, mathematics 3, social studies 3, science 3, foreign language 1 and academic electives 3. 4 tech prep and 1 health science recommended.

**2007-2008 Annual costs.** Tuition/fees: $1,362; $2,478 out-of-state. Per-credit charge: $31 in-state; $62 out-of-state. Books/supplies: $1,200. Personal expenses: $900.

**Financial aid. Need-based:** Need-based aid available for part-time students. Work-study available nights and for part-time students.

**Application procedures. Admission:** Priority date 9/8; deadline 9/22 (receipt date). $15 fee. Application may be submitted online. Admission notification on a rolling basis. **Financial aid:** Priority date 3/1; no closing date. Applicants notified on a rolling basis starting 4/15.

**Academics. Special study options:** Distance learning, dual enrollment of high school students, ESL. License preparation in aviation, nursing, paramedic, real estate. **Credit/placement by examination:** AP, CLEP, IB, institutional tests. **Support services:** GED test center, learning center, tutoring.

**Majors. Computer sciences:** General. **Legal studies:** Paralegal. **Visual/performing arts:** Music.

**Most popular majors.** Business/marketing 9%, computer/information sciences 20%, education 55%, legal studies 16%.

**Computing on campus.** 55 workstations in library, computer center. Online library, wireless network available.

**Student life. Freshman orientation:** Mandatory. Preregistration for classes offered.

**Student services.** On-campus daycare.

**Contact.** Phone: (404) 225-4447 Fax: (404) 225-4721
Vory Billups, Director of Admissions, Atlanta Technical College, 1560 Metropolitan Parkway, SW, Atlanta, GA 30310-4446

## Augusta Technical College
**Augusta, Georgia**
www.augustatech.edu

CB code: 2620

- Public 2-year technical college
- Commuter campus in large city

**General.** Founded in 1961. Regionally accredited. Additional campuses in Thomson and Waynesboro. **Enrollment:** 4,045 degree-seeking undergraduates; 471 non-degree-seeking students. **Degrees:** 257 associate awarded. **Location:** 145 miles from Atlanta, 75 miles from Columbia, South Carolina. **Calendar:** Quarter, extensive summer session. **Full-time faculty:** 136 total. **Part-time faculty:** 240 total.

**Student profile.** Among degree-seeking undergraduates, 100% enrolled in a vocational program, 760 enrolled as first-time, first-year students.

| | | | |
|---|---|---|---|
| Part-time: | 46% | Asian American: | 2% |
| Women: | 62% | Hispanic American: | 2% |
| African American: | 52% | | |

**Basis for selection.** Open admission, but selective for some programs. Admission to cardiovascular technology, respiratory therapy care, occupational therapy assistant, radiologic technology, and practical nursing competitive. These programs use combination of factors including all or some of the following: required college courses, placement exam scores, interviews, essays, and GPA. ACT or SAT may be accepted in lieu of COMPASS or ASSET for placement.

**High school preparation.** 22 units recommended. Recommended units include English 4, mathematics 3, social studies 3, science 3, foreign language 1 and academic electives 3. Highly recommended that math units include algebra and trigonometry. 4 tech prep and 1 health science recommended.

**2007-2008 Annual costs.** Tuition/fees: $1,371; $2,487 out-of-state. Per-credit charge: $31 in-state; $62 out-of-state. Books/supplies: $450.

**Financial aid. Non-need-based:** Scholarships awarded for state residency.

**Application procedures. Admission:** No deadline. $15 fee, may be waived for applicants with need. Application deadlines exist for competitive healthcare programs and vary by major. **Financial aid:** No deadline. FAFSA, institutional form required. Must reply within 2 week(s) of notification.

**Academics. Special study options:** Distance learning, dual enrollment of high school students. **Credit/placement by examination:** CLEP, institutional tests. **Support services:** GED preparation and test center, learning center, reduced course load, remedial instruction, tutoring.

**Majors. Business:** Accounting, administrative services, sales/distribution. **Computer sciences:** Applications programming. **Engineering technology:** Electrical. **Health:** Cardiovascular technology, clinical lab technology, EMT paramedic, pharmacy assistant, respiratory therapy technology.

**Most popular majors.** Business/marketing 28%, computer/information sciences 13%, education 9%, engineering/engineering technologies 6%, health sciences 21%, security/protective services 15%.

**Computing on campus.** Commuter students can connect to campus network. Online course registration, online library available.

**Student life. Freshman orientation:** Available. Preregistration for classes offered. **Activities:** Student government.

**Student services.** Career counseling, student employment services, financial aid counseling, on-campus daycare, placement for graduates, veterans' counselor. **Physically disabled:** Services for visually, speech, hearing impaired. **Transfer:** Pre-admission transcript evaluation for new students.

**Contact.** Phone: (706) 771-4028 Fax: (706) 771-4034
Brian Roberts, Director of Admissions, Augusta Technical College, 3200 Augusta Tech Drive, Augusta, GA 30906

## Bainbridge College
**Bainbridge, Georgia**
**www.bainbridge.edu**      CB code: 5062

♦ Public 2-year community and technical college
♦ Commuter campus in large town
♦ SAT or ACT required

**General.** Founded in 1973. Regionally accredited. **Enrollment:** 2,654 degree-seeking undergraduates. **Degrees:** 164 associate awarded. **Location:** 43 miles from Tallahassee, Florida. **Calendar:** Semester, limited summer session. **Full-time faculty:** 57 total; 33% have terminal degrees, 7% minority, 49% women. **Part-time faculty:** 69 total; 10% have terminal degrees, 10% minority, 61% women. **Class size:** 60% < 20, 39% 20-39, less than 1% 50-99. **Special facilities:** Nature trail.

**Student profile.** Among degree-seeking undergraduates, 48% enrolled in a transfer program, 52% enrolled in a vocational program, 986 enrolled as first-time, first-year students, 198 transferred in from other institutions.

| | | | |
|---|---|---|---|
| Part-time: | 60% | Women: | 69% |
| Out-of-state: | 1% | 25 or older: | 38% |

**Transfer out.** 65% of students enrolled in the transfer program go on to 4-year colleges. **Colleges most students transferred to 2007:** Valdosta State University, Albany State University.

**Basis for selection.** 330 SAT verbal/13 ACT English, 310 SAT math/14 ACT math, or 1.8 GPA required. College preparatory curriculum required for associate of arts degree-seeking students. Limited number admitted who do not meet admission standards. **Adult students:** SAT/ACT scores not required if out of high school 5 year(s) or more.

**High school preparation.** 16 units required. Required units include English 4, mathematics 4, social studies 3, science 3 and foreign language 2.

**2007-2008 Annual costs.** Tuition/fees: $1,950; $7,190 out-of-state. Per-credit charge: $73 in-state; $292 out-of-state. Books/supplies: $600. Personal expenses: $450.

**Financial aid.** All financial aid based on need. Need-based aid available for part-time students. **Additional information:** 30-day loans available for tuition and fees.

**Application procedures. Admission:** Closing date 8/1. No application fee. Application may be submitted online. Admission notification on a rolling basis. **Financial aid:** Priority date 6/1, closing date 8/1. FAFSA, institutional form required. Applicants notified on a rolling basis starting 6/1; must reply within 2 week(s) of notification.

**Academics. Special study options:** Distance learning, double major, dual enrollment of high school students, honors, independent study, study abroad, weekend college. 2-year registered nursing program. Bachelor's degree programs available on campus. License preparation in nursing, real estate. **Credit/placement by examination:** AP, CLEP, institutional tests. 18 credit hours maximum toward associate degree. **Support services:** GED preparation, learning center, reduced course load, remedial instruction, study skills assistance, tutoring.

**Majors. Business:** General, accounting, administrative services, management information systems, marketing. **Communications:** General. **Computer sciences:** General. **Construction:** Electrician. **Education:** General, early childhood, health, middle, physical, secondary. **Engineering technology:** Drafting, electrical. **English:** English lit. **Foreign languages:** General. **Health:** Nursing (RN). **History:** General. **Math:** General. **Mechanic/repair:** Industrial. **Protective services:** Law enforcement admin. **Psychology:** General. **Social sciences:** Political science.

**Most popular majors.** Business/marketing 29%, liberal arts 61%.

**Computing on campus.** 295 workstations in library, computer center, student center. Wireless network available.

**Student life. Freshman orientation:** Mandatory. Preregistration for classes offered. Held prior to the semester; on-line orientation. **Activities:** Concert band, choral groups, drama, music ensembles, student government, student newspaper, Delta club, service organizations, Phi Theta Kappa, Sigma Kappa Delta.

**Athletics. Intramural:** Basketball M, football (non-tackle), softball, table tennis, tennis, volleyball. **Team name:** Panthers.

**Student services.** Adult student services, career counseling, services for economically disadvantaged, student employment services, financial aid counseling, minority student services, personal counseling, placement for graduates, veterans' counselor. **Physically disabled:** Services for visually, speech, hearing impaired. **Transfer:** Transfer adviser, college fairs on campus for students transferring to 4-year colleges.

**Contact.** E-mail: csnyder@bainbridge.edu
Phone: (229) 248-2504 Fax: (229) 248-2623
Connie Snyder, Director of Admissions and Records, Bainbridge College, 2500 East Shotwell Street, Bainbridge, GA 39818-0990

## Brown Mackie College: Atlanta
**Atlanta, Georgia**

♦ For-profit 2-year business, health science and technical college
♦ Very large city

**General.** Accredited by ACICS. **Enrollment:** 300 degree-seeking undergraduates. **Degrees:** 32 associate awarded. **Calendar:** Quarter. **Full-time faculty:** 7 total. **Part-time faculty:** 7 total.

**Basis for selection.** Open admission.

**2007-2008 Annual costs.** Tuition/fees: $9,303. Full-time cost is based on maximum courseload of 12 hours.

**Academics. Credit/placement by examination:** CLEP.

**Majors. Business:** Accounting, business admin. **Health:** Medical assistant, occupational therapy assistant, surgical technology. **Legal studies:** Paralegal.

**Contact.** E-mail: jthee@brownmackie.edu
Phone: (770) 638-0121 Toll-free number: (888) 301-3670
Jonelle Thee, Enrollment Manager, Brown Mackie College: Atlanta, 6600 Peachtree Dunwoody NE, Atlanta, GA 30328

## Central Georgia Technical College
Macon, Georgia
www.cgtcollege.edu                    CB code: 1709

♦ Public 2-year community and technical college
♦ Commuter campus in small city

**General.** Regionally accredited. **Enrollment:** 4,999 degree-seeking undergraduates; 234 non-degree-seeking students. **Degrees:** 179 associate awarded. **Location:** 80 miles from Atlanta. **Calendar:** Quarter, extensive summer session. **Full-time faculty:** 109 total. **Part-time faculty:** 375 total. **Class size:** 87% < 20, 13% 20-39, less than 1% 40-49. **Partnerships:** Formal partnerships with Cisco and local industries.

**Student profile.** Among degree-seeking undergraduates, 789 enrolled as first-time, first-year students.

| Part-time: | 53% | Asian American: | 1% |
|---|---|---|---|
| Out-of-state: | 1% | Hispanic American: | 1% |
| Women: | 67% | 25 or older: | 35% |
| African American: | 55% | | |

**Basis for selection.** Open admission, but selective for some programs. Requirements vary according to program of study. ACT or SAT may be accepted in lieu of COMPASS or ASSET for placement.

**High school preparation.** 22 units recommended. Recommended units include English 4, mathematics 3, social studies 3, science 3, foreign language 1 and academic electives 3. 4 tech prep and 1 health science recommended.

**2007-2008 Annual costs.** Tuition/fees: $1,359; $2,475 out-of-state. Per-credit charge: $31 in-state; $62 out-of-state. Books/supplies: $750.

**Financial aid. Need-based:** Need-based aid available for part-time students.

**Application procedures. Admission:** $15 fee, may be waived for applicants with need. Admission notification on a rolling basis. Application closing date is one month prior to first day of attendance. **Financial aid:** Closing date 7/14. FAFSA, institutional form required.

**Academics. Special study options:** Distance learning, dual enrollment of high school students, ESL, liberal arts/career combination. License preparation in dental hygiene, nursing, paramedic, radiology, real estate. **Credit/ placement by examination:** CLEP, institutional tests. Dependent on department. **Support services:** GED preparation and test center, reduced course load, remedial instruction, study skills assistance, tutoring.

**Majors. Business:** Accounting technology, administrative services, logistics, operations. **Computer sciences:** Data processing, networking, web page design. **Education:** Early childhood. **Engineering technology:** Drafting. **Health:** Clinical lab technology, dental hygiene, medical assistant. **Protective services:** Criminal justice.

**Most popular majors.** Business/marketing 24%, computer/information sciences 16%, education 11%, health sciences 35%.

**Computing on campus.** 400 workstations in library, computer center. Commuter students can connect to campus network. Online course registration, online library, repair service, wireless network available.

**Student life. Freshman orientation:** Mandatory. Preregistration for classes offered. Held prior to each quarterly registration period. **Activities:** Student government.

**Student services.** Adult student services, career counseling, services for economically disadvantaged, financial aid counseling, on-campus daycare, placement for graduates, veterans' counselor. **Physically disabled:** Services for visually, speech, hearing impaired. **Transfer:** College fairs on campus for students transferring to 4-year colleges.

**Contact.** E-mail: info@cgtcollege.org
Phone: (478) 757-3403 Fax: (478) 757-3454
Tammy Carter, Director of Admissions, Central Georgia Technical College, 3300 Macon Tech Drive, Macon, GA 31206

## Chattahoochee Technical College
Marietta, Georgia
www.chattcollege.com                    CB code: 5441

♦ Public 2-year technical college
♦ Commuter campus in large city

**General.** Founded in 1961. Regionally accredited. **Enrollment:** 4,300 degree-seeking undergraduates; 1,964 non-degree-seeking students. **Degrees:** 278 associate awarded. **Location:** 20 miles from Atlanta. **Calendar:** Quarter, extensive summer session. **Full-time faculty:** 66 total. **Part-time faculty:** 234 total.

**Student profile.** Among degree-seeking undergraduates, 959 enrolled as first-time, first-year students.

| Part-time: | 55% | Asian American: | 2% |
|---|---|---|---|
| Out-of-state: | 5% | Hispanic American: | 4% |
| Women: | 56% | International: | 2% |
| African American: | 40% | 25 or older: | 50% |

**Basis for selection.** Open admission, but selective for some programs. Special requirements for allied health programs. ACT or SAT may be accepted in lieu of COMPASS or ASSET for placement.

**High school preparation.** 22 units recommended. Recommended units include English 4, mathematics 3, social studies 3, science 3, foreign language 1 and academic electives 3. 4 tech prep and 1 health science recommended.

**2007-2008 Annual costs.** Tuition/fees: $1,380; $2,496 out-of-state. Per-credit charge: $31 in-state; $62 out-of-state. Books/supplies: $1,020. Personal expenses: $1,300.

**Financial aid. Need-based:** Need-based aid available for part-time students. Work-study available nights, weekends and for part-time students. **Non-need-based:** Scholarships awarded for state residency.

**Application procedures. Admission:** No deadline. $15 fee. Admission notification on a rolling basis. **Financial aid:** Priority date 7/15; no closing date. FAFSA, institutional form required. Applicants notified on a rolling basis starting 6/15.

**Academics. Special study options:** Distance learning, dual enrollment of high school students. License preparation in nursing. **Credit/placement by examination:** CLEP, institutional tests. 15 credit hours maximum toward associate degree. **Support services:** Learning center, reduced course load, remedial instruction, study skills assistance, tutoring.

**Majors. Business:** General, accounting, administrative services, marketing, office management. **Computer sciences:** General, applications programming. **Engineering technology:** Electrical. **Family/consumer sciences:** Child care. **Mechanic/repair:** Automotive. **Personal/culinary services:** Culinary arts. **Protective services:** Criminal justice.

**Most popular majors.** Business/marketing 53%, communication technologies 8%, computer/information sciences 10%, engineering/engineering technologies 14%.

**Computing on campus.** 857 workstations in library, computer center, student center. Commuter students can connect to campus network. Online course registration, repair service available.

**Student life. Activities:** Student government.

**Student services.** Career counseling, student employment services, personal counseling, placement for graduates, veterans' counselor. **Physically disabled:** Services for visually, hearing impaired. **Transfer:** Pre-admission transcript evaluation for new students. College fairs on campus for students transferring to 4-year colleges.

**Contact.** E-mail: info@chattcollege.com
Phone: (770) 528-4565 Fax: (770) 528-4580
John Parton, Director of Admissions, Chattahoochee Technical College, 980 South Cobb Drive, Marietta, GA 30060-3300

## Coastal Georgia Community College
**Brunswick, Georgia**  **CB member**
www.cgcc.edu  **CB code: 5078**

- Public 2-year community college
- Commuter campus in large town

**General.** Founded in 1961. Regionally accredited. Students may take courses at Camden Center in Kingsland, Georgia. **Enrollment:** 2,943 degree-seeking undergraduates. **Degrees:** 269 associate awarded. **Location:** 70 miles from Savannah, 60 miles from Jacksonville, Florida. **Calendar:** Semester, limited summer session. **Full-time faculty:** 76 total; 13% have terminal degrees, 7% minority, 50% women. **Part-time faculty:** 79 total; 16% have terminal degrees, 11% minority, 53% women. **Class size:** 57% < 20, 43% 20-39, less than 1% 50-99.

**Student profile.** Among degree-seeking undergraduates, 65% enrolled in a transfer program, 35% enrolled in a vocational program, 1% already have a bachelor's degree or higher, 731 enrolled as first-time, first-year students, 53 transferred in from other institutions.

| | | | |
|---|---|---|---|
| Part-time: | 63% | Asian American: | 2% |
| Out-of-state: | 5% | Hispanic American: | 2% |
| Women: | 66% | Native American: | 1% |
| African American: | 27% | International: | 1% |

**Transfer out. Colleges most students transferred to 2007:** Armstrong Atlantic State University, Georgia Southern University.

**Basis for selection.** Open admission, but selective for some programs. Must be graduate of a regionally accredited high school or GED program. Additional requirements for registered nursing and allied health programs. Tests are not required, but will be used to exempt students from placement testing. Interviews required of those applying for registered nursing and allied health programs. **Homeschooled:** Statement describing homeschool structure and mission, transcript of courses and grades, letter of recommendation (nonparent) required. Must take SAT or ACT and score at the average of last year's freshman class. **Learning Disabled:** Students must go through an accreditation process with system agency on learning disabilities to receive accommodations.

**High school preparation.** 16 units recommended. Recommended units include English 4, mathematics 4, social studies 3, science 2 (laboratory 1) and foreign language 2. College-preparatory program recommended only of prebaccalaureate transfer program applicants.

**2007-2008 Annual costs.** Tuition/fees: $1,962; $7,202 out-of-state. Per-credit charge: $73 in-state; $292 out-of-state. Guaranteed tuition plan locks tuition rate for up to 3 years. Cost will vary among students. Books/supplies: $600. Personal expenses: $500.

**Financial aid. Need-based:** Need-based aid available for part-time students. Work-study available nights, weekends and for part-time students. **Non-need-based:** Scholarships awarded for academics, athletics, leadership, state residency.

**Application procedures. Admission:** Priority date 7/15; no deadline. $20 fee, may be waived for applicants with need. Application may be submitted online. Admission notification on a rolling basis. **Financial aid:** Priority date 5/1; no closing date. FAFSA required. Applicants notified on a rolling basis starting 7/1.

**Academics. Special study options:** Accelerated study, cooperative education, distance learning, dual enrollment of high school students, independent study, liberal arts/career combination, study abroad, teacher certification program. Bachelor's degree programs available on campus. License preparation in real estate. **Credit/placement by examination:** AP, CLEP, institutional tests. 24 credit hours maximum toward associate degree. **Support services:** GED preparation and test center, learning center, reduced course load, remedial instruction, study skills assistance, tutoring.

**Majors. Agriculture:** Agribusiness operations. **Biology:** General. **Business:** Accounting, administrative services, management information systems. **Communications:** General. **Computer sciences:** Computer science. **Education:** General, elementary, middle, secondary, special. **Engineering:** General. **Engineering technology:** Drafting. **English:** English lit. **Foreign languages:** General. **Health:** Clinical lab technology, medical radiologic technology/radiation therapy, nursing (RN). **History:** General. **Legal studies:** Prelaw. **Liberal arts:** Arts/sciences. **Math:** General. **Mechanic/repair:** Electronics/electrical. **Parks/recreation:** General. **Physical sciences:** Chemistry, physics. **Production:** Machine tool, welding. **Protective services:** Law enforcement admin. **Psychology:** General. **Social sciences:** Sociology. **Visual/performing arts:** Art.

**Most popular majors.** Health sciences 39%, liberal arts 61%.

**Computing on campus.** 300 workstations in library, computer center, student center. Commuter students can connect to campus network. Online course registration, online library, helpline, wireless network available.

**Student life. Freshman orientation:** Mandatory. Preregistration for classes offered. **Activities:** Literary magazine, student government, student newspaper, minority club, Baptist student union.

**Athletics.** NJCAA. **Intercollegiate:** Basketball M, softball W. **Intramural:** Basketball, bowling, cheerleading W, cross-country, golf, softball, table tennis, tennis, volleyball. **Team name:** Mariners.

**Student services.** Adult student services, career counseling, services for economically disadvantaged, student employment services, financial aid counseling, minority student services, personal counseling, placement for graduates, veterans' counselor. **Physically disabled:** Services for visually, speech, hearing impaired. **Transfer:** College fairs on campus for students transferring to 4-year colleges.

**Contact.** E-mail: admiss@cgcc.edu
Phone: (912) 264-7253 Toll-free number: (800) 675-7235
Fax: (912) 262-3072
Lisa Lesseig, Registrar/Director of Admissions, Coastal Georgia Community College, 3700 Altama Avenue, Brunswick, GA 31520

## Columbus Technical College
**Columbus, Georgia**
www.columbustech.org  **CB code: 7005**

- Public 2-year technical college
- Commuter campus in small city
- Interview required

**General.** Founded in 1961. Regionally accredited. **Enrollment:** 3,467 degree-seeking undergraduates; 137 non-degree-seeking students. **Degrees:** 214 associate awarded. **Location:** 110 miles from Atlanta, 86 miles from Albany. **Calendar:** Quarter, extensive summer session. **Full-time faculty:** 77 total. **Part-time faculty:** 153 total.

**Student profile.** Among degree-seeking undergraduates, 632 enrolled as first-time, first-year students.

| | | | |
|---|---|---|---|
| Part-time: | 58% | Asian American: | 2% |
| Women: | 67% | Hispanic American: | 3% |
| African American: | 45% | Native American: | 1% |

**Basis for selection.** Open admission, but selective for some programs. Special requirements for health programs. SAT required for some programs. ACT or SAT may be accepted in lieu of COMPASS or ASSET for placement.

**High school preparation.** 22 units recommended. Recommended units include English 4, mathematics 3, social studies 3, science 3, foreign language 1 and academic electives 3. 4 tech prep and 1 health science recommended.

**2007-2008 Annual costs.** Tuition/fees: $1,347; $2,463 out-of-state. Per-credit charge: $31 in-state; $62 out-of-state. Books/supplies: $1,600. Personal expenses: $1,100.

**Financial aid. Need-based:** Need-based aid available for part-time students.

**Application procedures. Admission:** Closing date 9/16. $20 fee. Application may be submitted online. Notification before registration date. **Financial aid:** No deadline. FAFSA required. Applicants notified on a rolling basis.

**Academics. Special study options:** Distance learning, dual enrollment of high school students, honors, internships. License preparation in dental hygiene, nursing, paramedic, radiology, real estate. **Credit/placement by examination:** AP, CLEP. **Support services:** Learning center, remedial instruction, study skills assistance, tutoring.

**Majors. Agriculture:** Horticultural science. **Business:** Accounting, administrative services, business admin. **Education:** Early childhood. **Engineering technology:** Electrical. **Health:** Cardiovascular technology, dental hygiene, nursing (RN), surgical technology. **Mechanic/repair:** Automotive, industrial.

**Most popular majors.** Business/marketing 28%, computer/information sciences 21%, engineering/engineering technologies 6%, health sciences 35%.

**Computing on campus.** 40 workstations in library, computer center. Online library available.

**Student life. Freshman orientation:** Mandatory. Preregistration for classes offered. Three-hour orientation held day before start of classes. **Activities:** Student government.

**Student services.** Career counseling, student employment services, financial aid counseling, personal counseling, placement for graduates, veterans' counselor. **Physically disabled:** Services for speech, hearing impaired.

**Contact.** Phone: (706) 649-1800 Fax: (404) 649-1885
Nicole Kennedy, Director of Admissions, Columbus Technical College, 928 Manchester Expressway, Columbus, GA 31904

## Darton College
**Albany, Georgia**     **CB member**
www.darton.edu     **CB code: 5026**

♦ Public 2-year community college
♦ Commuter campus in small city

**General.** Founded in 1963. Regionally accredited. **Enrollment:** 2,102 full-time, degree-seeking students. **Degrees:** 467 associate awarded. **ROTC:** Army. **Location:** 175 miles from Atlanta. **Calendar:** Semester, limited summer session. **Full-time faculty:** 101 total. **Part-time faculty:** 178 total. **Class size:** 52% < 20, 43% 20-39, 3% 40-49, 1% 50-99. **Special facilities:** 50-foot Carolina Tower and climbing wall, nature trail.

**Student profile.**

| | | | |
|---|---|---|---|
| Out-of-state: | 37% | Hispanic American: | 1% |
| African American: | 42% | International: | 1% |
| Asian American: | 1% | 25 or older: | 40% |

**Transfer out. Colleges most students transferred to 2007:** Georgia Southwestern State University, Albany State University, Florida State University, Valdosta State University.

**Basis for selection.** Traditional students must have 2.0 college prep GPA or 2.2 tech prep GPA. 1.8 GPA required for programs of less than 12 credit hours. Interview, portfolios and essays considered when students do not meet minimum admission requirements but show promise. **Adult students:** SAT/ACT scores not required.

**High school preparation.** 16 units required. Required units include English 4, mathematics 4, social studies 3, science 3 and foreign language 2.

**2007-2008 Annual costs.** Tuition/fees: $2,110; $7,350 out-of-state. Per-credit charge: $73 in-state; $292 out-of-state. Books/supplies: $1,100. Personal expenses: $1,200.

**Financial aid. Need-based:** Need-based aid available for part-time students. Work-study available nights, weekends and for part-time students. **Non-need-based:** Scholarships awarded for academics, alumni affiliation, art, athletics, music/drama, state residency. **Additional information:** Auditions, portfolios, essays, extracurricular activities impact scholarship decisions.

**Application procedures. Admission:** Priority date 8/1; no deadline. $20 fee. Application may be submitted online. Admission notification on a rolling basis. Applications must be received 10 days prior to registration. **Financial aid:** No deadline. FAFSA, institutional form required. Applicants notified on a rolling basis; must reply within 3 week(s) of notification.

**Academics.** Career and transfer programs available. Career graduates aggressively recruited. **Special study options:** Cooperative education, cross-registration, distance learning, double major, dual enrollment of high school students, ESL, honors, independent study, liberal arts/career combination, study abroad, weekend college. License preparation in dental hygiene, nursing, occupational therapy, paramedic, physical therapy. **Credit/placement by examination:** AP, CLEP, IB, SAT, ACT, institutional tests. 18-hours residence courses required. **Support services:** Learning center, reduced course load, remedial instruction, study skills assistance, tutoring, writing center.

**Majors. Agriculture:** General, horticulture. **Biology:** General. **Business:** General, accounting, administrative services, business admin, entrepreneurial studies, management information systems, office management. **Communications:** Journalism. **Computer sciences:** General, applications programming, computer science, data processing, information systems, networking, programming. **Conservation:** Environmental studies, forestry. **Education:** General, art, business, foreign languages, kindergarten/preschool, mathematics, middle, multi-level teacher, music, physical, secondary, social science, social studies, speech, teacher assistance, technology/industrial arts, trade/industrial. **Engineering:** General, agricultural. **Engineering technology:** General, drafting, industrial. **English:** English lit, speech/rhetoric. **Family/consumer sciences:** Child care, institutional food production. **Foreign**

**languages:** General. **Health:** Cardiovascular technology, clinical lab science, clinical lab technology, community health services, dental hygiene, EMT paramedic, histologic assistant, licensed practical nurse, medical assistant, medical radiologic technology/radiation therapy, medical records admin, medical records technology, mental health services, nuclear medical technology, nursing (RN), occupational therapy assistant, office admin, ophthalmic lab technology, physical therapy assistant, physician assistant, predental, premedicine, prepharmacy, preveterinary, public health ed, respiratory therapy assistant, respiratory therapy technology, sonography, surgical technology. **History:** General. **Legal studies:** Paralegal. **Liberal arts:** Arts/sciences, humanities. **Math:** General. **Mechanic/repair:** Electronics/electrical, heating/ac/refrig. **Parks/recreation:** General, exercise sciences, health/fitness. **Philosophy/religion:** Philosophy. **Physical sciences:** Chemistry, physics. **Protective services:** Criminal justice, forensics. **Psychology:** General. **Public administration:** General, human services, social work. **Social sciences:** General, anthropology, criminology, economics, geography, political science, sociology. **Visual/performing arts:** General, art, commercial/advertising art, dramatic.

**Computing on campus.** 400 workstations in library, computer center. Commuter students can connect to campus network. Online course registration, online library, helpline, wireless network available.

**Student life. Freshman orientation:** Available. Preregistration for classes offered. Held every semester, required of all students enrolled in learning support classes. **Activities:** Bands, choral groups, dance, drama, literary magazine, music ensembles, musical theater, student government, student newspaper, symphony orchestra, TV station.

**Athletics.** NJCAA. **Intercollegiate:** Baseball M, basketball W, golf, soccer, softball W, swimming. **Intramural:** Basketball, bowling, golf, softball, table tennis, tennis, volleyball. **Team name:** Cavaliers.

**Student services.** Alcohol/substance abuse counseling, career counseling, student employment services, financial aid counseling, minority student services, personal counseling, placement for graduates. **Physically disabled:** Services for visually, speech, hearing impaired. **Transfer:** Preadmission transcript evaluation for new students. Transfer adviser, college fairs on campus for students transferring to 4-year colleges.

**Contact.** E-mail: info@darton.edu
Phone: (229) 430-6740 Toll-free number: (866) 775-1214
Fax: (229) 317-6607
Susan Bowen, Director of Admission, Darton College, 2400 Gillionville Road, Albany, GA 31707-3098

## DeKalb Technical College
**Clarkston, Georgia**
www.dekalbtech.edu     **CB code: 3226**

♦ Public 2-year technical college
♦ Commuter campus in large city

**General.** Founded in 1961. Regionally accredited. Second campus located in Covington. **Enrollment:** 3,691 degree-seeking undergraduates; 128 non-degree-seeking students. **Degrees:** 237 associate awarded. **Location:** 17 miles from Atlanta. **Calendar:** Quarter, extensive summer session. **Full-time faculty:** 96 total. **Part-time faculty:** 363 total. **Class size:** 88% < 20, 12% 20-39. **Partnerships:** Formal partnerships wtih MARTA; Fulton County Government; DeKalb, Rockdale, Newton, Morgan County Schools; Decatur City Schools.

**Student profile.** Among degree-seeking undergraduates, 620 enrolled as first-time, first-year students.

| | | | |
|---|---|---|---|
| Part-time: | 62% | Asian American: | 3% |
| Women: | 61% | Hispanic American: | 2% |
| African American: | 73% | 25 or older: | 40% |

**Transfer out. Colleges most students transferred to 2007:** Georgia State University, Southern Polytechnic State University, DeVry University, Clayton College and State University, Georgia Perimeter College.

**Basis for selection.** Open admission, but selective for some programs. Limited admission to health technologies programs. ACT or SAT may be accepted in lieu of COMPASS or ASSET for placement. Interview recommended.

**High school preparation.** 22 units recommended. Recommended units include English 4, mathematics 3, social studies 3, science 3, foreign language 1 and academic electives 3. 4 tech prep and 1 health science recommended.

**2007-2008 Annual costs.** Tuition/fees: $1,407; $2,523 out-of-state. Per-credit charge: $31 in-state; $62 out-of-state. Truck driving and flight technology are higher cost programs. Books/supplies: $1,200. Personal expenses: $900.

**Financial aid. Need-based:** Need-based aid available for part-time students. Work-study available nights, weekends and for part-time students.

**Application procedures. Admission:** Closing date 8/22 (receipt date). $15 fee. Application must be submitted on paper. Admission notification on a rolling basis. **Financial aid:** Priority date 7/15, closing date 8/20. FAFSA required. Applicants notified on a rolling basis starting 6/1.

**Academics. Special study options:** Distance learning, dual enrollment of high school students. License preparation in nursing, paramedic, real estate. **Credit/placement by examination:** AP, CLEP, institutional tests. 35 credit hours maximum toward associate degree. **Support services:** GED preparation and test center, learning center, reduced course load, remedial instruction, study skills assistance, tutoring.

**Majors. Business:** Accounting, business admin, marketing. **Computer sciences:** General, programming. **Engineering:** Computer, electrical. **Engineering technology:** Electrical, instrumentation. **Health:** Ophthalmic lab technology, optician. **Mechanic/repair:** Automotive.

**Most popular majors.** Business/marketing 45%, computer/information sciences 17%, education 8%, legal studies 10%, security/protective services 8%.

**Computing on campus.** 500 workstations in computer center. Online course registration, online library available.

**Student life. Freshman orientation:** Available. **Activities:** Student government, student newspaper, Delta Epsilon Chi, Collegiate Secretaries International, Noon Net-Working of New Connections, Phi Beta Lambda, Student Optical Society, Licensed Practical Nurses Association, Vocational Industrial Clubs of America, Epsilon Delta Phi Honorary Society, Phi Theta Kappa Honor Society.

**Student services.** Adult student services, career counseling, services for economically disadvantaged, student employment services, financial aid counseling, minority student services, placement for graduates, veterans' counselor, women's services. **Physically disabled:** Services for visually, speech, hearing impaired. **Transfer:** Pre-admission transcript evaluation for new students.

**Contact.** E-mail: admissionsclark@dekalbtech.org
Phone: (404) 297-9522 ext. 1602 Fax: (404) 294-3424
Terry Richardson, Coordinator of Admissions and Special Services, DeKalb Technical College, 495 North Indian Creek Drive, Clarkston, GA 30021-2397

## East Georgia College
Swainsboro, Georgia — CB member
www.ega.edu — CB code: 5200

- Public 2-year community and junior college
- Commuter campus in small town

**General.** Founded in 1973. Regionally accredited. **Enrollment:** 1,987 degree-seeking undergraduates. **Degrees:** 127 associate awarded. **Location:** 85 miles from Savannah and Macon. **Calendar:** Semester, limited summer session. **Full-time faculty:** 42 total; 38% have terminal degrees, 10% minority, 36% women. **Part-time faculty:** 40 total; 12% have terminal degrees, 18% minority, 52% women. **Class size:** 40% < 20, 54% 20-39, 5% 40-49, less than 1% 50-99, less than 1% >100. **Special facilities:** Nature trail, outdoor exercise trail, fitness center.

**Student profile.**

Out-of-state: 1%    25 or older: 20%

**Transfer out. Colleges most students transferred to 2007:** Georgia Southern University.

**Basis for selection.** Graduation from accredited or approved high school or GED, 16 college prep curriculum units, Compass test scores, and 2.0 GPA required. **Homeschooled:** SAT scores equal to or greater than previous year's SAT average for first-time entering freshmen and validation with portfolio of each college prep curriculum area.

**High school preparation.** 16 units recommended. Recommended units include English 4, mathematics 4, social studies 3, science 3 and foreign language 2.

**2007-2008 Annual costs.** Tuition/fees: $1,922; $7,162 out-of-state. Per-credit charge: $73 in-state; $292 out-of-state. Books/supplies: $1,200. Personal expenses: $1,200.

**Financial aid. Need-based:** Need-based aid available for part-time students. **Non-need-based:** Scholarships awarded for academics, leadership, state residency.

**Application procedures. Admission:** No deadline. $20 fee, may be waived for applicants with need. Application may be submitted online. Admission notification on a rolling basis beginning on or about 2/1. **Financial aid:** Priority date 6/15; no closing date. FAFSA, institutional form required. Applicants notified on a rolling basis starting 6/15; must reply within 2 week(s) of notification.

**Academics. Special study options:** Distance learning, double major, dual enrollment of high school students, honors, independent study, study abroad. License preparation in nursing. **Credit/placement by examination:** CLEP, institutional tests. 30 credit hours maximum toward associate degree. **Support services:** Learning center, reduced course load, remedial instruction, study skills assistance, tutoring, writing center.

**Majors. Agriculture:** General. **Biology:** General. **Business:** Business admin. **Computer sciences:** Computer science. **Education:** General, business, multi-level teacher. **English:** English lit. **Family/consumer sciences:** General. **Foreign languages:** Translation. **Health:** Prenursing. **History:** General. **Liberal arts:** Arts/sciences. **Math:** General. **Parks/recreation:** General, exercise sciences, health/fitness. **Physical sciences:** Chemistry, geology. **Protective services:** Criminal justice. **Psychology:** General. **Social sciences:** Anthropology, criminology, political science, sociology. **Visual/performing arts:** Art.

**Computing on campus.** 120 workstations in library, computer center, student center. Commuter students can connect to campus network. Online course registration, online library, wireless network available.

**Student life. Freshman orientation:** Mandatory. Preregistration for classes offered. Combined 1-day orientation/registration event. **Policies:** Substance-free campus. **Activities:** Choral groups, drama, international student organizations, literary magazine, student government, student newspaper, Baptist student union, Afro-American union, earth club, Students in Free Enterprise, Student Professional Association of Georgia Educators, art club, Quiz Bowl, Circle K, non-traditonal club.

**Athletics. Intramural:** Basketball M, football (non-tackle) M, soccer M, softball, table tennis, tennis, volleyball, weight lifting. **Team name:** Bobcats.

**Student services.** Adult student services, career counseling, financial aid counseling, minority student services, personal counseling, veterans' counselor. **Transfer:** Pre-admission transcript evaluation for new students. Transfer adviser, college fairs on campus for students transferring to 4-year colleges.

**Contact.** E-mail: kjones@ega.edu
Phone: (478) 289-2017 Fax: (478) 289-2140
Karen Jones, Director of Admissions, East Georgia College, 131 College Circle, Swainsboro, GA 30401-2699

## Everest Institute
Atlanta, Georgia
www.georgia-med.com

- For-profit 2-year health science college
- Very large city

**General.** Accredited by ACCSCT. **Enrollment:** 407 degree-seeking undergraduates. **Degrees:** 40 associate awarded. **Calendar:** Continuous. **Full-time faculty:** 8 total. **Part-time faculty:** 5 total.

**Basis for selection.** Admission based on secondary school record and institutional testing.

**Academics. Credit/placement by examination:** CLEP.

**Majors. Health:** Respiratory therapy assistant.

**Contact.** Phone: (404) 327-8787
Everest Institute, 1706 Northeast Expressway, Atlanta, GA 30329

## Gainesville State College
Gainesville, Georgia
www.gsc.edu — CB code: 5273

- Public 2-year community and junior college
- Commuter campus in large town

**General.** Founded in 1964. Regionally accredited. **Enrollment:** 7,247 degree-seeking undergraduates. **Degrees:** 570 associate awarded. **Location:** 45 miles from Atlanta, 40 miles from Athens. **Calendar:** Semester, extensive summer session. **Full-time faculty:** 164 total. **Part-time faculty:** 191 total. **Class size:** 22% < 20, 78% 20-39, less than 1% 40-49, less than 1% 50-99.

**Transfer out. Colleges most students transferred to 2007:** North Georgia College and State University, University of Georgia, Brenau University, Georgia State University, Athens Technical College.

**Basis for selection.** 2.0 GPA required for applicants with college prep curriculum diploma; 2.2 GPA required for applicants with technical prep curriculum diploma. SAT or ACT scores may be used for academic advising.

**High school preparation.** 16 units required. Required units include English 4, mathematics 4, social studies 3, science 3 (laboratory 3) and foreign language 2.

**2007-2008 Annual costs.** Tuition/fees: $2,112; $7,728 out-of-state. Per-credit charge: $78 in-state; $312 out-of-state. Books/supplies: $630. Personal expenses: $1,000.

**2006-2007 Financial aid. Need-based:** 71% of total undergraduate aid awarded as scholarships/grants, 29% as loans/jobs. Need-based aid available for part-time students. Work-study available nights, weekends and for part-time students. **Non-need-based:** Scholarships awarded for academics, art, leadership, music/drama.

**Application procedures. Admission:** Closing date 7/1 (postmark date). $25 fee, may be waived for applicants with need. Application may be submitted online. Admission notification on a rolling basis. **Financial aid:** Priority date 6/1; no closing date. FAFSA required. Applicants notified on a rolling basis starting 5/1; must reply within 2 week(s) of notification.

**Academics. Special study options:** Distance learning, dual enrollment of high school students, ESL, honors, study abroad. Bachelor's degree programs available on campus. License preparation in dental hygiene, paramedic. **Credit/placement by examination:** AP, CLEP, institutional tests. 30 credit hours maximum toward associate degree. **Support services:** Learning center, remedial instruction, study skills assistance, tutoring, writing center.

**Majors. Agriculture:** General, business. **Business:** General, accounting, administrative services, business admin. **Communications:** Journalism. **Computer sciences:** General. **Conservation:** Forestry. **Education:** General, art, early childhood, elementary, mathematics, music, physical, science, secondary, social science. **Engineering:** General. **Engineering technology:** Electrical. **English:** English lit. **Family/consumer sciences:** Child care. **Health:** Dental hygiene, EMT paramedic. **History:** General. **Legal studies:** Paralegal. **Liberal arts:** Arts/sciences. **Math:** General. **Physical sciences:** Chemistry, geology, physics. **Protective services:** Criminal justice. **Psychology:** General. **Public administration:** Social work. **Social sciences:** Anthropology, political science, sociology. **Visual/performing arts:** Dramatic, music performance, studio arts.

**Computing on campus.** 840 workstations in library, computer center, student center. Commuter students can connect to campus network. Online course registration, online library, helpline, student web hosting, wireless network available.

**Student life. Freshman orientation:** Mandatory. Preregistration for classes offered. **Activities:** Bands, choral groups, drama, literary magazine, music ensembles, musical theater, student government, student newspaper.

**Athletics. Intramural:** Basketball, bowling, football (non-tackle), golf, softball, tennis, volleyball.

**Student services.** Adult student services, alcohol/substance abuse counseling, career counseling, student employment services, financial aid counseling, minority student services, personal counseling, placement for graduates, veterans' counselor. **Physically disabled:** Services for visually, speech, hearing impaired. **Transfer:** Transfer adviser, college fairs on campus for students transferring to 4-year colleges.

**Contact.** E-mail: admissions@gsc.edu
Phone: (678) 717-3641 Fax: (678) 717-3643
Mack Palmour, Director of Admissions, Gainesville State College, PO Box 1358, Gainesville, GA 30503

---

## Georgia Highlands College
**Rome, Georgia**
www.highlands.edu

**CB member**
**CB code: 5237**

- Public 2-year community and liberal arts college
- Commuter campus in small city

---

**General.** Founded in 1968. Regionally accredited. Classes offered at Cartersville, Acworth, Marietta, Rome. **Enrollment:** 4,346 degree-seeking undergraduates. **Degrees:** 360 associate awarded. **Location:** 75 miles from Atlanta. **Calendar:** Semester, limited summer session. **Full-time faculty:** 85 total. **Part-time faculty:** 110 total. **Special facilities:** Observatory, wetlands preserve.

**Student profile.** Among degree-seeking undergraduates, 1,116 enrolled as first-time, first-year students, 559 transferred in from other institutions.

| | | | |
|---|---|---|---|
| Part-time: | 44% | Asian American: | 2% |
| Women: | 62% | Hispanic American: | 4% |
| African American: | 11% | 25 or older: | 22% |

**Transfer out. Colleges most students transferred to 2007:** Kennesaw State University, State University of West Georgia, Berry College, Shorter College, University of Georgia.

**Basis for selection.** 2.0 college prep or 2.2 technical prep GPA required. SAT or ACT can be used to exempt COMPASS placement examinations. SAT or ACT required for admissions into nursing and dental hygiene programs. **Homeschooled:** Statement describing homeschool structure and mission, transcript of courses and grades, state high school equivalency certificate required. Must submit SAT scores that are equal to or greater than last year's freshman class average and provide completed Home School college prep curriculum evaluation form; portfolio required. **Learning Disabled:** Foreign language college preparatory curriculum may be waived through Georgia Board of Regents Center of Learning Disabilities.

**High school preparation.** 16 units recommended. Recommended units include English 4, mathematics 4, social studies 3, science 3 (laboratory 2) and foreign language 2. College preparatory program required for students planning to transfer to 4-year school.

**2007-2008 Annual costs.** Tuition/fees: $1,948; $7,188 out-of-state. Per-credit charge: $73 in-state; $292 out-of-state. Books/supplies: $750. Personal expenses: $1,550.

**2006-2007 Financial aid. Need-based:** 44% of total undergraduate aid awarded as scholarships/grants, 56% as loans/jobs. Need-based aid available for part-time students. Work-study available nights and for part-time students. **Non-need-based:** Scholarships awarded for academics, art.

**Application procedures. Admission:** Priority date 7/1; no deadline. $20 fee, may be waived for applicants with need. Application may be submitted online. Admission notification on a rolling basis beginning on or about 1/2. **Financial aid:** Closing date 4/1. FAFSA required. Applicants notified on a rolling basis starting 4/1; must reply within 2 week(s) of notification.

**Academics.** All classrooms and many common areas wired for computer usage. **Special study options:** Accelerated study, cooperative education, distance learning, double major, dual enrollment of high school students, independent study, liberal arts/career combination, study abroad. License preparation in dental hygiene, nursing. **Credit/placement by examination:** AP, CLEP, SAT, ACT, institutional tests. **Support services:** Learning center, remedial instruction, study skills assistance, tutoring, writing center.

**Majors. Agriculture:** Horticultural science, landscaping. **Biology:** General. **Business:** General, administrative services, hospitality/recreation. **Communications:** General, journalism. **Computer sciences:** General. **Education:** General, multi-level teacher. **English:** English lit. **Foreign languages:** Sign language interpretation. **Health:** Dental hygiene, EMT paramedic, health services, medical radiologic technology/radiation therapy, medical records admin, nursing (RN), premedicine, prepharmacy, preveterinary, respiratory therapy technology. **Legal studies:** Paralegal. **Liberal arts:** Arts/sciences. **Math:** General. **Mechanic/repair:** Auto body. **Physical sciences:** Chemistry. **Protective services:** Police science. **Psychology:** General. **Social sciences:** General, urban studies.

**Most popular majors.** Business/marketing 17%, education 28%, health sciences 30%, liberal arts 8%.

**Computing on campus.** Commuter students can connect to campus network. Online library, helpline, repair service, wireless network available.

**Student life. Freshman orientation:** Mandatory. **Policies:** Access program tracks all student involvement in school and community activities. Transcripts available for resume use or when transferring to another institution. **Housing:** Housing available through Southern Poly Tech University for Marietta Campus. **Activities:** Literary magazine, student government, student newspaper, TV station, Baptist student union, College Bowl Team, volunteer opportunity center, black student awareness, Insiders, Phi Theta Kappa.

**Athletics. Intramural:** Archery, badminton, basketball, bowling, field hockey W, football (tackle) M, golf, sailing, skiing, soccer, softball, table tennis, tennis, volleyball, wrestling M. **Team name:** Chargers.

**Student services.** Adult student services, alcohol/substance abuse counseling, career counseling, student employment services, financial aid counseling, minority student services, personal counseling, placement for graduates, veterans' counselor. **Physically disabled:** Services for visually, speech, hearing impaired. **Transfer:** Re-entry adviser, pre-admission transcript evaluation for new students. College fairs on campus for students transferring to 4-year colleges.

**Contact.** E-mail: admitme@highlands.edu
Phone: (706) 295-6339 Toll-free number: (800) 332-2406 ext. 6339
Fax: (706) 295-6341
Todd Jones, Director of Admissons, Georgia Highlands College, 3175 Cedartown Highway SE, Rome, GA 30161

## Georgia Military College
**Milledgeville, Georgia**
www.gmc.cc.ga.us                    **CB code: 5249**

▶ Public 2-year community, junior and military college
▶ Commuter campus in large town

**General.** Founded in 1879. Regionally accredited. Multilocation institution. 2-year ROTC commissioning program on main campus. Military base programs and degree programs for civilians. **Enrollment:** 3,186 degree-seeking undergraduates; 92 non-degree-seeking students. **Degrees:** 592 associate awarded. **ROTC:** Army. **Location:** 90 miles from Atlanta, 30 miles from Macon. **Calendar:** Quarter, limited summer session. **Full-time faculty:** 114 total; 100% have terminal degrees, 14% minority, 48% women. **Part-time faculty:** 306 total; 100% have terminal degrees, 59% women. **Class size:** 70% < 20, 30% 20-39.

**Student profile.** Among degree-seeking undergraduates, 1,227 enrolled as first-time, first-year students.

| | | | |
|---|---|---|---|
| Part-time: | 35% | 25 or older: | 35% |
| Out-of-state: | 8% | Live on campus: | 5% |
| Women: | 62% | | |

**Basis for selection.** Open admission, but selective for some programs. ROTC applicants for early commissioning must have 920 SAT (exclusive of Writing) or 19 ACT and 2.0 GPA. Interview recommended for ROTC cadets. **Homeschooled:** Transcript of courses and grades required. List of courses completed and bibliography of textbooks and/or assigned readings required. Must submit writing sample or show successful GED completion.

**2007-2008 Annual costs.** Tuition/fees: $12,050. Per-credit charge: $98 in-district; $98 out-of-district. Quoted full-time tuition and fees are for cadet students. Additional $1,150 for uniforms. Room/board: $4,890. Books/supplies: $1,275. Personal expenses: $600.

**Financial aid. Need-based:** Need-based aid available for part-time students. Work-study available nights and for part-time students. **Non-need-based:** Scholarships awarded for athletics, leadership, ROTC, state residency. **Additional information:** Institutional aid offered to those enrolled in Cadet Corps who reside on campus.

**Application procedures. Admission:** Priority date 8/1; deadline 9/1 (receipt date). $35 fee, may be waived for applicants with need. Application may be submitted online. Admission notification on a rolling basis. August 1 closing date for cadets. Students interested in attending ROTC Basic Camp must apply by May 1. **Financial aid:** No deadline. FAFSA required. Applicants notified on a rolling basis starting 3/1.

**Academics. Special study options:** Cross-registration, double major, external degree, independent study. **Credit/placement by examination:** AP, CLEP, institutional tests. 45 credit hours maximum toward associate degree. **Support services:** Learning center, reduced course load, remedial instruction, study skills assistance, tutoring.

**Majors. Business:** Business admin. **Computer sciences:** General. **Education:** General, early childhood, kindergarten/preschool, secondary. **Engineering technology:** Electrical. **Family/consumer sciences:** Family studies. **Health:** Prenursing. **Mechanic/repair:** Aircraft powerplant. **Protective services:** Criminal justice.

**Most popular majors.** Business/marketing 16%, education 14%, health sciences 11%, legal studies 8%, psychology 6%.

**Computing on campus.** 403 workstations in dormitories, library, computer center, student center. Dormitories wired for high-speed internet access and linked to campus network. Online library available.

**Student life. Freshman orientation:** Available. Preregistration for classes offered. Two summer orientation sessions, college athlete session, early commissioning session, state service scholarship session available. **Policies:** Resident programs only available to members of Corps of Cadets. **Housing:** Single-sex dorms, substance-free housing available. $75 deposit, deadline 9/1. **Activities:** Marching band, choral groups, drama, literary magazine, student government, student newspaper, Circle-K, Phi Theta Kappa, Alpha Phi Omega, Ranger Challenge, drill team, drama club, officer Christians' fellowship, business club, math club, debate/speech organization.

**Athletics.** NJCAA. **Intercollegiate:** Cross-country, football (tackle) M, golf, rifle, soccer, track and field. **Intramural:** Badminton, basketball, bowling, golf, softball, volleyball. **Team name:** Bulldogs.

**Student services.** Alcohol/substance abuse counseling, career counseling, financial aid counseling, health services, personal counseling, veterans' counselor. **Physically disabled:** Services for visually, speech, hearing impaired.

**Contact.** E-mail: Admissionsinfo@gmc.cc.ga.us
Phone: (478) 445-2707 Toll-free number: (800) 342-0413
Fax: (478) 445-2688
Donna Findley, Director of Admissions and Enrollments, Georgia Military College, 201 East Greene Street, Milledgeville, GA 31061

## Georgia Perimeter College
**Clarkston, Georgia**                    **CB member**
www.gpc.edu                    **CB code: 5711**

▶ Public 2-year junior and liberal arts college
▶ Commuter campus in very large city

**General.** Founded in 1964. Regionally accredited. Additional campuses in Alpharetta, Dunwoody, Decatur, Lawrenceville, Newton. **Enrollment:** 19,847 degree-seeking undergraduates; 1,626 non-degree-seeking students. **Degrees:** 1,554 associate awarded. **Calendar:** Semester, extensive summer session. **Full-time faculty:** 391 total; 97% have terminal degrees, 31% minority, 57% women. **Part-time faculty:** 803 total; 82% have terminal degrees, 38% minority. **Class size:** 28% < 20, 69% 20-39, 2% 40-49, less than 1% 50-99, less than 1% >100. **Special facilities:** Botanical gardens.

**Student profile.** Among degree-seeking undergraduates, 91% enrolled in a transfer program, 2% enrolled in a vocational program, 1% already have a bachelor's degree or higher, 3,928 enrolled as first-time, first-year students, 1,268 transferred in from other institutions.

| | | | |
|---|---|---|---|
| Part-time: | 54% | Asian American: | 9% |
| Out-of-state: | 10% | Hispanic American: | 5% |
| Women: | 62% | International: | 5% |
| African American: | 38% | 25 or older: | 31% |

**Transfer out. Colleges most students transferred to 2007:** Georgia State University, University of Georgia.

**Basis for selection.** Admission based on high school GPA. Any college preparatory curriculum deficiencies must be satisfied by placement testing or substituting college coursework. COMPASS used for placement in English, reading, and math. SAT or ACT scores used as supplements to COMPASS results for English and reading. Satisfactory SAT or ACT scores may exempt some students from English and reading placement testing. Interview required of nursing and dental hygiene majors. **Homeschooled:** Transcript of courses and grades required. A detailed portfolio must be submitted.

**High school preparation.** 16 units required. Required units include English 4, mathematics 4, social studies 3, science 3 (laboratory 2) and foreign language 2.

**2007-2008 Annual costs.** Tuition/fees: $2,234; $7,474 out-of-state. Per-credit charge: $73 in-state; $292 out-of-state. Books/supplies: $1,400. Personal expenses: $1,200.

**2006-2007 Financial aid. Need-based:** 64% of total undergraduate aid awarded as scholarships/grants, 36% as loans/jobs. Need-based aid available for part-time students. Work-study available nights, weekends and for part-time students.

**Application procedures. Admission:** Closing date 7/1 (postmark date). $20 fee, may be waived for applicants with need. Application may be submitted online. Admission notification on a rolling basis. **Financial aid:** Closing date 6/1. FAFSA required. Applicants notified on a rolling basis; must reply within 3 week(s) of notification.

**Academics. Special study options:** Accelerated study, distance learning, double major, ESL, honors, liberal arts/career combination, study abroad, weekend college. Bachelor's degree programs available on campus. License preparation in dental hygiene, nursing. **Credit/placement by examination:** AP, CLEP, IB, institutional tests. 21 credit hours maximum toward associate degree. **Support services:** Learning center, remedial instruction, study skills assistance, tutoring, writing center.

**Majors. Biology:** General. **Business:** Business admin. **Communications:** General, journalism. **Computer sciences:** Computer science, information technology. **Education:** General, health, physical. **Engineering:** General. **English:** English lit. **Foreign languages:** General, sign language interpretation. **Health:** Dental hygiene, nursing (RN), predental, premedicine, prepharmacy. **History:** General. **Liberal arts:** Library science. **Math:** General. **Philosophy/religion:** Philosophy. **Physical sciences:** Chemistry, geology, physics. **Protective services:** Fire services admin, law enforcement admin. **Psychology:** General. **Social sciences:** Anthropology, political science, sociology. **Visual/performing arts:** Art, dramatic.

**Most popular majors.** Business/marketing 37%, education 15%, health sciences 12%, liberal arts 9%, psychology 8%, social sciences 6%.

**Computing on campus.** Online course registration, online library, helpline, wireless network available.

**Student life. Freshman orientation:** Mandatory. Preregistration for classes offered. 6 hour program. **Activities:** Bands, choral groups, drama, international student organizations, literary magazine, music ensembles, musical theater, student government, student newspaper, symphony orchestra, international student club, Campus Crusade for Christ, Muslim student association, student government association, math club, drama club, computer club.

**Athletics.** NJCAA. **Intercollegiate:** Baseball M, basketball, soccer, softball W, tennis. **Team name:** Jaguars.

**Student services.** Adult student services, career counseling, services for economically disadvantaged, financial aid counseling, minority student services, personal counseling, veterans' counselor. **Physically disabled:** Services for visually, hearing impaired. **Transfer:** Transfer adviser, college fairs on campus for students transferring to 4-year colleges.

**Contact.** Phone: (678) 891-3250 Toll-free number: (888) 696-2780 Fax: (404) 299-4574
Douglas Ruch, Associate Director for Admissions, Georgia Perimeter College, 555 North Indian Creek Drive, Clarkston, GA 30021-2361

---

## Gordon College
### Barnesville, Georgia
www.gdn.edu

CB member
CB code: 5256

- Public 2-year junior college
- Commuter campus in small town

**General.** Founded in 1852. Regionally accredited. **Enrollment:** 3,629 degree-seeking undergraduates. **Degrees:** 423 associate awarded. **Location:** 57 miles from Atlanta. **Calendar:** Semester, limited summer session. **Full-time faculty:** 98 total. **Part-time faculty:** 79 total. **Class size:** 21% < 20, 77% 20-39, less than 1% 40-49, less than 1% 50-99, less than 1% >100. **Special facilities:** Georgia book collection, performance theater, indoor pool, ropes course, walking trail, ampitheatre.

**Student profile.** Among degree-seeking undergraduates, 1,207 enrolled as first-time, first-year students.

| | | | |
|---|---|---|---|
| Part-time: | 33% | 25 or older: | 31% |
| Out-of-state: | 1% | Live on campus: | 8% |
| Women: | 65% | | |

**Basis for selection.** Test scores, GPA considered in admission decisions. SAT or ACT, SAT Subject Tests recommended. Interview required for nursing program. **Adult students:** Placement test required. **Homeschooled:** Statement describing homeschool structure and mission required.

**High school preparation.** 16 units recommended. Recommended units include English 4, mathematics 4, social studies 3, science 3 and foreign language 2. Foreign language units must be in same language.

**2007-2008 Annual costs.** Tuition/fees: $2,152; $7,768 out-of-state. Per-credit charge: $78 in-state; $312 out-of-state. Room/board: $4,350. Books/supplies: $950. Personal expenses: $903.

**Financial aid. Need-based:** Need-based aid available for part-time students. Work-study available nights, weekends and for part-time students. **Non-need-based:** Scholarships awarded for academics, athletics, music/drama, state residency.

**Application procedures. Admission:** No deadline. $20 fee. Application may be submitted online. Admission notification on a rolling basis. **Financial aid:** Priority date 5/1; no closing date. Institutional form required. Applicants notified on a rolling basis starting 5/1.

**Academics. Special study options:** Distance learning, dual enrollment of high school students, liberal arts/career combination, study abroad. Bachelor's degree programs available on campus. **Credit/placement by examination:** AP, CLEP, SAT, ACT, institutional tests. 45 credit hours maximum toward associate degree. **Support services:** Learning center, remedial instruction, study skills assistance, tutoring, writing center.

**Majors. Agriculture:** Horticultural science. **Biology:** General. **Business:** Administrative services, business admin. **Computer sciences:** Computer science, information systems, information technology, networking. **Conservation:** Forestry. **Education:** General, multi-level teacher. **English:** English lit. **Foreign languages:** General. **Health:** Dental hygiene, medical records admin, nuclear medical technology, nursing (RN), physician assistant, prepharmacy, radiologic technology/medical imaging, respiratory therapy assistant, sonography. **History:** General. **Liberal arts:** Arts/sciences. **Math:** General. **Parks/recreation:** Health/fitness. **Physical sciences:** General, astronomy, chemistry, physics. **Protective services:** Criminal justice. **Psychology:** General. **Public administration:** Social work. **Social sciences:** Political science, sociology. **Visual/performing arts:** Art, dramatic.

**Most popular majors.** Business/marketing 20%, education 16%, health sciences 33%, psychology 7%, social sciences 7%.

**Computing on campus.** 125 workstations in dormitories, library, computer center, student center. Dormitories wired for high-speed internet access and linked to campus network. Commuter students can connect to campus network. Online course registration, online library, helpline, wireless network available.

**Student life. Freshman orientation:** Mandatory. Preregistration for classes offered. Presentation for student and parents, 5-6 hour duration. **Housing:** Coed dorms, single-sex dorms, apartments, substance-free housing available. $250 partly refundable deposit, deadline 7/1. **Activities:** Bands, choral groups, dance, drama, literary magazine, music ensembles, musical theater, student government, student newspaper, Baptist student union, art club, Fellowship of Christian Athletes, minority advising program, Phi Beta Lambda (business), explorers club, Association of Nursing Students, Draftwood, theater club.

**Athletics.** NJCAA. **Intercollegiate:** Baseball M, soccer, softball W, tennis W. **Intramural:** Badminton, basketball, football (non-tackle), handball, racquetball, soccer, softball, table tennis, tennis, volleyball. **Team name:** Highlanders.

**Student services.** Adult student services, alcohol/substance abuse counseling, career counseling, student employment services, financial aid counseling, health services, minority student services, personal counseling, placement for graduates, veterans' counselor. **Physically disabled:** Services for visually impaired. **Transfer:** Pre-admission transcript evaluation for new students. College fairs on campus for students transferring to 4-year colleges.

**Contact.** E-mail: admissions@gdn.edu
Phone: (770) 358-5000 Fax: (770) 358-3031
Lisa Shiveler, Director of Admissions, Gordon College, 419 College Drive, Barnesville, GA 30204

---

## Griffin Technical College
### Griffin, Georgia
www.griffintech.edu

CB code: 5670

- Public 2-year technical college
- Small city

**General.** Regionally accredited. **Enrollment:** 3,635 degree-seeking undergraduates; 397 non-degree-seeking students. **Degrees:** 196 associate awarded. **Calendar:** Quarter. **Full-time faculty:** 68 total. **Part-time faculty:** 172 total.

**Student profile.** Among degree-seeking undergraduates, 800 enrolled as first-time, first-year students.

| | | | |
|---|---|---|---|
| Part-time: | 51% | Asian American: | 2% |
| Women: | 68% | Hispanic American: | 2% |
| African American: | 40% | | |

**Basis for selection.** Open admission, but selective for some programs. Admission criteria vary by program. Must take admissions test if you have not taken the ACT, SAT, CPE, COMPASS or ASSET within the last five years.

**High school preparation.** 22 units recommended. Recommended units include English 4, mathematics 3, social studies 3, science 3, foreign language 1 and academic electives 3. 1 tech prep, 1 science recommended.

**2007-2008 Annual costs.** Tuition/fees: $1,359; $2,475 out-of-state. Per-credit charge: $31 in-state; $62 out-of-state. Books/supplies: $150. Personal expenses: $587.

**Application procedures. Admission:** No deadline. $15 fee. **Financial aid:** FAFSA, institutional form required. Applicants notified on a rolling basis.

**Academics. Special study options:** Distance learning, double major, dual enrollment of high school students. **Credit/placement by examination:** CLEP. **Support services:** GED preparation and test center.

**Majors. Business:** Accounting, administrative services, business admin, management science. **Computer sciences:** General, information systems. **Engineering technology:** Electrical. **Health:** Radiologic technology/medical imaging. **Protective services:** Law enforcement admin.

**Most popular majors.** Business/marketing 30%, computer/information sciences 11%, education 9%, health sciences 23%, security/protective services 13%.

**Contact.** Phone: (770) 228-7348 Fax: (770) 229-3227
Lynn Futral, Vice President of Student Services, Griffin Technical College, 501 Varsity Road, Griffin, GA 30223

## Gupton Jones College of Funeral Service
**Decatur, Georgia**
www.gupton-jones.edu                    **CB code: 6200**

- Private 2-year technical college
- Commuter campus in very large city

**General.** Founded in 1920. Accredited by American Board of Funeral Service Education. **Enrollment:** 175 degree-seeking undergraduates. **Degrees:** 105 associate awarded. **Location:** 18 miles from Atlanta. **Calendar:** Quarter. **Full-time faculty:** 7 total; 14% women. **Part-time faculty:** 1 total; 100% women.

**Student profile.**

| | | | |
|---|---|---|---|
| Out-of-state: | 65% | 25 or older: | 50% |

**Basis for selection.** Open admission.

**2007-2008 Annual costs.** Tuition/fees: $8,400. Personal expenses: $500.

**Financial aid.** All financial aid based on need. Need-based aid available for part-time students.

**Application procedures. Admission:** No deadline. $50 fee. Application may be submitted online. Admission notification on a rolling basis. **Financial aid:** No deadline. FAFSA required. Applicants notified on a rolling basis.

**Academics. Credit/placement by examination:** CLEP.

**Majors. Personal/culinary services:** Mortuary science.

**Computing on campus.** 23 workstations in library, computer center.

**Student life. Freshman orientation:** Mandatory. Preregistration for classes offered.

**Student services.** Career counseling, student employment services, personal counseling, placement for graduates.

**Contact.** E-mail: gjcfs@mindspring.com
Phone: (770) 593-2257 Fax: (770) 593-1891
Patty Hutcheson, President, Gupton Jones College of Funeral Service, 5141 Snapfinger Woods Drive, Decatur, GA 30035

## Gwinnett College
**Lilburn, Georgia**
www.gwinnettcollege.edu

- For-profit 2-year junior and career college
- Commuter campus in large city

**General.** Accredited by ACICS. 3 locations near Atlanta and one in Raleigh, North Carolina. **Enrollment:** 347 degree-seeking undergraduates. **Degrees:** 71 associate awarded. **Location:** 20 miles from Atlanta. **Calendar:** Quarter, extensive summer session. **Full-time faculty:** 7 total. **Part-time faculty:** 35 total.

**Transfer out. Colleges most students transferred to 2007:** DeVry University, American Intercontinental University, University of Phoenix, Colorado Tech Online, Strayer.

**Basis for selection.** Open admission, but selective for some programs. Aptitude testing required for some programs. **Homeschooled:** Transcript of courses and grades required.

**2007-2008 Annual costs.** 2007 tuition $550 per class. Required number of classes varies by program. Massage therapy program charges $179 per credit hour.

**Financial aid. Need-based:** Need-based aid available for part-time students.

**Application procedures. Admission:** No deadline. No application fee. Application must be submitted on paper. **Financial aid:** FAFSA required.

**Academics. Special study options:** Combined bachelor's/graduate degree, double major, internships. **Credit/placement by examination:** CLEP. **Support services:** Reduced course load.

**Majors. Business:** Business admin. **Computer sciences:** Information technology. **Health:** Medical assistant, medical secretary. **Legal studies:** Paralegal.

**Computing on campus.** 100 workstations in library, computer center. Wireless network available.

**Student services.** Adult student services, financial aid counseling, placement for graduates. **Transfer:** Re-entry adviser, pre-admission transcript evaluation for new students.

**Contact.** E-mail: admissions@gwinnettcollege.edu
Phone: (770) 381-7200 Fax: (770) 381-0454
Lee Cates, Director of Admissions, Gwinnett College, 4230 Highway 29, Lilburn, GA 30047

## Gwinnett Technical College
**Lawrenceville, Georgia**                    **CB member**
www.gwinnetttech.edu                          **CB code: 5168**

- Public 2-year technical college
- Commuter campus in large town

**General.** Founded in 1984. Regionally accredited. Internships available with several manufacturers and companies, including Toyota, Nissan, Chrysler, and General Motors. **Enrollment:** 4,579 degree-seeking undergraduates; 210 non-degree-seeking students. **Degrees:** 323 associate awarded. **Location:** 25 miles from Atlanta. **Calendar:** Quarter, extensive summer session. **Full-time faculty:** 71 total. **Part-time faculty:** 135 total. **Class size:** 46% < 20, 51% 20-39, 2% 40-49, less than 1% 50-99. **Special facilities:** Media center, studio, seminar room containing microcomputers and multimedia compilers.

**Student profile.** Among degree-seeking undergraduates, 798 enrolled as first-time, first-year students, 15 transferred in from other institutions.

| | | | |
|---|---|---|---|
| Part-time: | 53% | Asian American: | 7% |
| Women: | 57% | Hispanic American: | 7% |
| African American: | 27% | | |

**Basis for selection.** Open admission, but selective for some programs. Selection criteria vary by program. Competitive screening process for some health science programs. ACT or SAT may be accepted in lieu of COMPASS or ASSET for placement. Interview required of carpentry, automotive, machine tools, drafting majors and health science program applicants.

**High school preparation.** 22 units recommended. Recommended units include English 4, mathematics 3, social studies 3, science 3, foreign language 1 and academic electives 3. 4 tech prep, 1 health science recommended.

**2007-2008 Annual costs.** Tuition/fees: $1,425; $2,541 out-of-state. Per-credit charge: $31 in-state; $62 out-of-state. Books/supplies: $1,600. Personal expenses: $2,800.

**2007-2008 Financial aid. Need-based:** Need-based aid available for part-time students.

**Application procedures. Admission:** Closing date 8/15. $20 fee. Application may be submitted online. Admission notification on a rolling basis. Application closing date for some health sciences programs January 15. **Financial aid:** Closing date 7/1. FAFSA required.

**Academics. Special study options:** Distance learning, dual enrollment of high school students, ESL. License preparation in dental hygiene, nursing, paramedic, physical therapy, radiology, real estate. **Credit/placement by examination:** AP, CLEP, institutional tests. **Support services:** GED preparation and test center, learning center, remedial instruction, study skills assistance, tutoring, writing center.

**Majors. Biology:** Biotechnology. **Business:** Accounting, administrative services, construction management, fashion, human resources, marketing, office management, office technology, restaurant/food services, tourism/travel. **Computer sciences:** Game design, LAN/WAN management, programming, security, web page design. **Construction:** General, site management. **Engineering technology:** Drafting. **Health:** Dental lab technology, EMT paramedic, health services, medical radiologic technology/radiation therapy, radiologic technology/medical imaging, respiratory therapy technology, veterinary technology/assistant. **Mechanic/repair:** Automotive. **Personal/culinary services:** Culinary arts. **Production:** Woodworking. **Protective services:** Firefighting, police science. **Visual/performing arts:** Commercial photography, interior design, photography.

**Most popular majors.** Business/marketing 30%, computer/information sciences 15%, health sciences 22%, trade and industry 9%, visual/performing arts 8%.

**Computing on campus.** 120 workstations in library, computer center, student center. Commuter students can connect to campus network. Online course registration, helpline, repair service, wireless network available.

**Student life. Freshman orientation:** Mandatory. Preregistration for classes offered. One-hour mandatory session, four 30-minute breakout sessions on advisement, financial aid, registration, and online classes. **Activities:** Student government, student newspaper.

**Student services.** Adult student services, career counseling, student employment services, financial aid counseling, placement for graduates, veterans' counselor. **Physically disabled:** Services for visually, speech, hearing impaired.

**Contact.** Phone: (770) 962-7580 ext. 6616 Fax: (770) 685-1267
Florance Halloran, Director of Admissions, Gwinnett Technical College, 5150 Sugarloaf Parkway, Lawrenceville, GA 30243

## High-Tech Institute
**Marietta, Georgia**
**www.high-techinstitute.com**

▶ For-profit 2-year technical college
▶ Commuter campus in very large city

**General.** Accredited by ACCSCT. **Calendar:** Continuous.

**Annual costs/financial aid.** Total costs of associate degree programs including books and supplies range from $21,150 to $31,150.

**Contact.** Phone: (770) 988-9877
Director of Admissions, 1090 Northchase Parkway, Marietta, GA 30067

## ITT Technical Institute: Kennesaw
**Kennesaw, Georgia**

▶ For-profit 2-year business and technical college
▶ Large town

**General.** Accredited by ACICS. **Calendar:** Quarter.

**Contact.** 1000 Cobb Place Boulevard NW, Kennesaw, GA 30144

## Le Cordon Bleu College of Culinary Arts
**Tucker, Georgia**
**www.atlantaculinary.com**

▶ For-profit 2-year branch campus and technical college
▶ Commuter campus in very large city
▶ Interview required

**General.** Accredited by ACCSCT. **Enrollment:** 1,035 degree-seeking undergraduates. **Degrees:** 196 associate awarded. **Location:** 10 miles from Atlanta. **Calendar:** Continuous. **Full-time faculty:** 38 total. **Part-time faculty:** 2 total.

**Basis for selection.** Open admission. Documentation of high school graduation or GED only requirement.

**2007-2008 Annual costs.** Total cost of accelerated 15-month associate degree program including tuition, books, toolkit, uniforms $39,500. Total cost of 12-month certificate program in patisserie and baking $20,425.

**Application procedures. Admission:** No deadline. $50 fee. Application must be submitted on paper. Admission notification on a rolling basis.

**Academics. Credit/placement by examination:** AP, CLEP. **Support services:** Study skills assistance, tutoring.

**Majors. Personal/culinary services:** Culinary arts.

**Computing on campus.** Online library available.

**Student life. Freshman orientation:** Mandatory.

**Student services.** Adult student services, career counseling, student employment services, financial aid counseling, placement for graduates. **Transfer:** Re-entry adviser for new students.

**Contact.** Phone: (770) 938-4711 Toll-free number: (866) 315-2433 Fax: (773) 938-4571
Terri Holte, Vice President of Admissions, Le Cordon Bleu College of Culinary Arts, 1927 Lakeside Parkway, Tucker, GA 30084

## Middle Georgia College
**Cochran, Georgia**
**www.mgc.edu**                                    **CB code: 5411**

▶ Public 2-year junior college
▶ Commuter campus in small town

**General.** Founded in 1884. Regionally accredited. **Enrollment:** 3,086 degree-seeking undergraduates. **Degrees:** 338 associate awarded. **Location:** 39 miles from Macon. **Calendar:** Semester, limited summer session. **Full-time faculty:** 118 total. **Part-time faculty:** 54 total. **Class size:** 38% < 20, 59% 20-39, less than 1% 40-49, 2% 50-99.

**Student profile.**

| | | | |
|---|---|---|---|
| Out-of-state: | 6% | Live on campus: | 30% |
| 25 or older: | 25% | | |

**Transfer out. Colleges most students transferred to 2007:** Georgia College and State University, Macon College, Valdosta State University, Georgia Military College.

**Basis for selection.** Students graduating with college prep diploma must have 2.0 academic core GPA. Students graduating with tech prep/vocational/general diploma must have 2.2 academic core GPA. Students with college preparatory deficiencies may submit SAT Subject Tests scores in the area of deficiencies. Interview and essay required for applicants to Georgia Academy of Mathematics, Engineering, and Science Program. **Homeschooled:** Transcript of courses and grades required. Students must submit home-schooled application and obtain 920 SAT (exclusive of writing) or 19 ACT.

**High school preparation.** 13 units required; 16 recommended. Required and recommended units include English 4, mathematics 3-4, social studies 1, history 2, science 3 (laboratory 2) and foreign language 2.

**2007-2008 Annual costs.** Tuition/fees: $2,246; $7,862 out-of-state. Per-credit charge: $78 in-state; $312 out-of-state. Room/board: $4,770. Books/supplies: $800. Personal expenses: $600.

**Financial aid. Need-based:** Need-based aid available for part-time students. Work-study available nights, weekends and for part-time students. **Non-need-based:** Scholarships awarded for academics, alumni affiliation, art, athletics, job skills, leadership, minority status, music/drama, state residency.

**Application procedures. Admission:** Closing date 7/20 (receipt date). $20 fee, may be waived for applicants with need. Application may be submitted online. Admission notification on a rolling basis. **Financial aid:** Priority date 4/1; no closing date. FAFSA required. Applicants notified on a rolling basis starting 5/1.

**Academics. Special study options:** Accelerated study, cooperative education, distance learning, double major, exchange student, honors, independent study, study abroad, weekend college. Weekend college at Dublin campus only; Georgia Academy of Mathematics, Engineering and Science is 2-year residential joint enrollment program for gifted high school juniors and seniors to pursue associate degree utilizing dual credits. Bachelor's degree programs available on campus. **Credit/placement by examination:** AP, CLEP, institutional tests. 30 credit hours maximum toward associate degree. **Support services:** Learning center, remedial instruction, study skills assistance, tutoring, writing center.

**Majors. Agriculture:** General. **Architecture:** Environmental design. **Biology:** General. **Business:** Accounting, business admin, human resources, merchandising, office technology, sales/distribution. **Communications:** Journalism. **Computer sciences:** General, applications programming, computer science, data entry, information technology, programming. **Conservation:** Forestry. **Education:** Early childhood, elementary, health, middle, secondary, special. **Engineering:** General, civil, computer, electrical. **Engineering technology:** Aerospace, civil, computer, drafting, manufacturing, surveying. **English:** English lit. **Family/consumer sciences:** Family studies. **Foreign languages:** General. **Health:** Dental assistant, dental hygiene, licensed practical nurse, medical assistant, medical radiologic technology/radiation therapy, medical records admin, medical records technology, nursing (RN), occupational therapy assistant, pharmacy assistant, physical therapy assistant, predental, premedicine, prenursing, prepharmacy, preveterinary, respiratory therapy technology, surgical technology. **History:** General. **Legal studies:** Prelaw. **Liberal arts:** Arts/sciences. **Math:** General. **Mechanic/repair:** Aircraft, auto body, automotive, electronics/electrical, heating/ac/refrig, industrial. **Parks/recreation:** General, health/fitness. **Physical sciences:** Chemistry, geology, physics. **Protective services:** Criminal justice, police science. **Psychology:** General. **Public administration:** General, social work. **Social sciences:** Economics, political science, sociology. **Visual/performing arts:** Art, dramatic.

**Most popular majors.** Health sciences 24%, liberal arts 67%.

**Computing on campus.** 464 workstations in dormitories, library. Dormitories wired for high-speed internet access and linked to campus network. Commuter students can connect to campus network. Online course registration, online library, helpline available.

**Student life. Freshman orientation:** Available. Preregistration for classes offered. Spring and summer, 1-day orientation. **Policies:** Alcohol not allowed on campus. Students must live with their immediate families or live in college housing unless given permission to live off-campus. **Housing:** Guaranteed on-campus for all undergraduates. Single-sex dorms, substance-free housing available. $100 deposit, deadline 7/1. **Activities:** Campus ministries, choral groups, dance, drama, literary magazine, music ensembles, musical theater, student government, student newspaper, Baptist student union, Wesley Foundation, minority alliance club, Rotaract, cultural relations club, Young Republicans, Young Democrats, Fellowship of Christian Athletes.

**Athletics.** NJCAA. **Intercollegiate:** Baseball M, basketball, cross-country, soccer, softball W. **Intramural:** Badminton, basketball, football (tackle), golf, handball M, rifle M, softball, tennis, volleyball, weight lifting. **Team name:** Warriors.

**Student services.** Adult student services, alcohol/substance abuse counseling, career counseling, services for economically disadvantaged, student employment services, financial aid counseling, health services, minority student services, personal counseling, veterans' counselor, women's services. **Physically disabled:** Services for visually, hearing impaired. **Learning disabled:** Comprehensive services available. **Transfer:** College fairs on campus for students transferring to 4-year colleges.

**Contact.** E-mail: admissions@mgc.edu
Phone: (478) 934-3103 Fax: (478) 934-3403
Jennifer Brannon, Director of Admissions, Middle Georgia College, 1100 Second Street SE, Cochran, GA 31014

## Middle Georgia Technical College
### Warner Robins, Georgia
### www.middlegatech.edu    CB code: 5035

- Public 2-year technical college
- Commuter campus in small town

**General.** Regionally accredited. **Enrollment:** 2,498 degree-seeking undergraduates; 353 non-degree-seeking students. **Degrees:** 45 associate awarded. **Location:** 105 miles from Atlanta. **Calendar:** Quarter. **Full-time faculty:** 110 total. **Part-time faculty:** 125 total.

**Student profile.** Among degree-seeking undergraduates, 818 enrolled as first-time, first-year students.

| | | | |
|---|---|---|---|
| Part-time: | 40% | Asian American: | 2% |
| Women: | 56% | Hispanic American: | 2% |
| African American: | 33% | | |

**Basis for selection.** Open admission, but selective for some programs. Special requirements for allied health programs. ACT or SAT may be accepted in lieu of COMPASS or ASSET for placement.

**High school preparation.** 22 units recommended. Recommended units include English 4, social studies 3, science 3, foreign language 1 and academic electives 3. 1 tech prep and 1 health science recommended.

**2007-2008 Annual costs.** Tuition/fees: $1,359; $2,475 out-of-state. Per-credit charge: $31 in-state; $62 out-of-state.

**Application procedures. Admission:** No deadline. $15 fee. **Financial aid:** FAFSA required.

**Academics.** Associate of Applied Technology degrees are terminal degrees. Courses cannot be transferred to a higher degree level. **Special study options:** Distance learning, dual enrollment of high school students. License preparation in aviation, dental hygiene, radiology. **Credit/placement by examination:** AP, CLEP. **Support services:** GED preparation and test center, learning center, remedial instruction, tutoring.

**Majors. Business:** Office technology.

**Most popular majors.** Business/marketing 17%, computer/information sciences 13%, education 18%, engineering/engineering technologies 7%, health sciences 36%, trade and industry 7%.

**Student life. Freshman orientation:** Mandatory.

**Student services.** Career counseling, financial aid counseling.

**Contact.** Phone: (478) 988-6850 Toll-free number: (800) 474-1031
Fax: (478) 988-6813
Craig Jackson, Director of Admissions, Middle Georgia Technical College, 80 Cohen Walker Drive, Warner Robins, GA 31088

## North Georgia Technical College
### Clarkesville, Georgia
### www.northgatech.edu

- Public 2-year community and technical college
- Commuter campus in large town

**General.** Regionally accredited. **Enrollment:** 1,940 degree-seeking undergraduates; 24 non-degree-seeking students. **Degrees:** 75 associate awarded. **Calendar:** Quarter, extensive summer session. **Full-time faculty:** 68 total. **Part-time faculty:** 121 total.

**Student profile.** Among degree-seeking undergraduates, 100% enrolled in a vocational program, 5% already have a bachelor's degree or higher, 573 enrolled as first-time, first-year students.

| | | | |
|---|---|---|---|
| Part-time: | 44% | Asian American: | 1% |
| Women: | 59% | Hispanic American: | 2% |
| African American: | 6% | | |

**Basis for selection.** Open admission, but selective for some programs. ACT or SAT may be accepted in lieu of COMPASS or ASSET for placement. **Homeschooled:** Statement describing homeschool structure and mission, transcript of courses and grades required. **Learning Disabled:** Documentation of IEP required.

**High school preparation.** 22 units recommended. Recommended units include English 4, mathematics 3, social studies 3, science 3, foreign language 1 and academic electives 3. 4 tech prep and 1 health science recommended.

**2007-2008 Annual costs.** Tuition varies from $31-$53 per credit hour (excluding Commercial Truck Driving) for Georgia residents, depending on program. Tuition for out-of-state students is twice the rate of Georgia students, and tuition for foreign students is four times the Georgia resident rate. Required fees are $380 a year. Room and board for double occupancy is $3600 annually. Books/supplies: $935.

**Financial aid. Need-based:** Need-based aid available for part-time students. Work-study available nights, weekends and for part-time students.

**Application procedures. Admission:** No deadline. $15 fee ($72 out-of-state). Application may be submitted online.

**Academics. Special study options:** License preparation in nursing, paramedic, real estate. **Credit/placement by examination:** CLEP, institutional tests. 50 credit hours maximum toward associate degree. **Support services:** GED preparation and test center, learning center, remedial instruction, tutoring.

**Majors. Business:** Accounting, office technology. **Computer sciences:** Networking. **Engineering technology:** Environmental. **Mechanic/repair:** Heating/ac/refrig. **Personal/culinary services:** Chef training. **Protective services:** Law enforcement admin.

**Most popular majors.** Business/marketing 39%, computer/information sciences 16%, health sciences 7%, personal/culinary services 13%, security/protective services 15%.

**Computing on campus.** Dormitories wired for high-speed internet access and linked to campus network. Commuter students can connect to campus network. Online course registration, online library, wireless network available.

**Student life. Freshman orientation:** Mandatory.

**Athletics. Intramural:** Basketball, football (tackle), softball. **Team name:** Eagles.

**Contact.** E-mail: amitchell@northgatech.edu
Phone: (706) 754-7724 Fax: (706) 754-7777
Amanda Mitchell, Director of Admissions, North Georgia Technical College, 1500 Highway 197, Clarkesville, GA 30523

---

### North Metro Technical College
**Acworth, Georgia**
**www.northmetrotech.edu**                    **CB code: 5508**

- Public 2-year technical college
- Large town

**General.** Regionally accredited. **Enrollment:** 2,062 degree-seeking undergraduates; 160 non-degree-seeking students. **Degrees:** 21 associate awarded. **Calendar:** Quarter. **Full-time faculty:** 34 total. **Part-time faculty:** 76 total.

**Student profile.** Among degree-seeking undergraduates, 526 enrolled as first-time, first-year students.

| | | | |
|---|---|---|---|
| Part-time: | 57% | Asian American: | 1% |
| Women: | 64% | Hispanic American: | 4% |
| African American: | 19% | | |

**Basis for selection.** Open admission, but selective for some programs. ACT or SAT may be accepted in lieu of COMPASS or ASSET for placement.

**2007-2008 Annual costs.** Tuition/fees: $1,359; $2,475 out-of-state.

**Application procedures. Admission:** No deadline. $15 fee.

**Academics. Special study options:** License preparation in nursing, paramedic, radiology. **Credit/placement by examination:** CLEP. **Support services:** GED preparation and test center.

**Majors. Agriculture:** Horticulture. **Business:** Accounting, management science, marketing. **Computer sciences:** General. **Education:** Early childhood. **Engineering technology:** Electrical. **Health:** Radiologic technology/medical imaging.

**Most popular majors.** Business/marketing 10%, health sciences 48%, personal/culinary services 6%, trade and industry 23%.

**Contact.** E-mail: info@northmetrotech.edu
Phone: (770) 975-4000 Fax: (770) 975-4142
Missy Cusack, Director of Admissions, North Metro Technical College, 5198 Ross Road, Acworth, GA 30102

---

### Northwestern Technical College
**Rock Spring, Georgia**
**www.northwesterntech.edu**                    **CB code: 2860**

- Public 2-year technical college
- Commuter campus in small town

**General.** Regionally accredited. **Enrollment:** 1,537 degree-seeking undergraduates; 738 non-degree-seeking students. **Degrees:** 161 associate awarded. **Calendar:** Quarter. **Full-time faculty:** 49 total. **Part-time faculty:** 61 total.

**Student profile.** Among degree-seeking undergraduates, 387 enrolled as first-time, first-year students.

| | | | |
|---|---|---|---|
| Part-time: | 53% | Hispanic American: | 1% |
| Women: | 60% | Native American: | 1% |
| African American: | 4% | | |

**Basis for selection.** Open admission, but selective for some programs. Special requirements for nursing, emergency medical technician, licensed practical nursing, medical assistant, occupational therapy assistant, and surgical technology programs. ACT or SAT may be accepted in lieu of COMPASS or ASSET for placement.

**High school preparation.** 22 units recommended. Recommended units include English 4, mathematics 3, social studies 3, science 3, foreign language 1 and academic electives 3. 4 tech prep and 1 health science recommended.

**2007-2008 Annual costs.** Tuition/fees: $1,359; $2,475 out-of-state. Per-credit charge: $31 in-state; $62 out-of-state. Truck driving and flight technology are higher cost programs. Books/supplies: $900.

**Financial aid. Need-based:** Need-based aid available for part-time students.

**Application procedures. Admission:** No deadline. $15 fee. Admission notification on a rolling basis. **Financial aid:** No deadline. FAFSA, institutional form required.

**Academics. Special study options:** Distance learning, dual enrollment of high school students, liberal arts/career combination. License preparation in nursing, occupational therapy. **Credit/placement by examination:** CLEP, institutional tests. **Support services:** GED preparation and test center, remedial instruction, study skills assistance, tutoring, writing center.

**Majors. Architecture:** Technology. **Business:** Accounting, business admin, executive assistant, office/clerical. **Communications:** Organizational. **Computer sciences:** General, data entry, data processing, information systems, information technology, LAN/WAN management, networking, programming, web page design, webmaster, word processing. **Education:** Early childhood. **Engineering technology:** Architectural, computer systems, drafting, electrical, industrial, mechanical drafting. **Health:** Cardiovascular technology, medical assistant, nursing (RN), occupational therapy assistant, pharmacy assistant, surgical technology. **Protective services:** Law enforcement admin, police science.

**Most popular majors.** Business/marketing 25%, computer/information sciences 7%, education 12%, health sciences 39%, security/protective services 9%.

**Computing on campus.** 300 workstations in library, computer center.

**Student life. Freshman orientation:** Mandatory. Preregistration for classes offered. **Activities:** Student government.

**Student services.** Adult student services, career counseling, services for economically disadvantaged, student employment services, financial aid counseling, placement for graduates, veterans' counselor, women's services.

**Contact.** E-mail: csolomon@nwtcollege.org
Phone: (706) 764-3514 Toll-free number: (800) 735-5726
Fax: (706) 764-3707
Carolyn Solmon, Director of Admissions and Career Counseling, Northwestern Technical College, 265 Bicentennial Trail, Rock Spring, GA 30739

---

### Oxford College of Emory University
**Oxford, Georgia**                    **CB member**
**www.emory.edu/oxford**                    **CB code: 5186**

- Private 2-year branch campus and liberal arts college affiliated with United Methodist Church
- Residential campus in large town
- SAT or ACT with writing, application essay required

**General.** Founded in 1836. Regionally accredited. One of nine schools within Emory University. Students who successfully complete two years at Oxford automatically continue to Emory College to complete bachelor's degree. Selective continuation to Emory School of Business and Emory

School of Nursing is also available. **Enrollment:** 715 degree-seeking undergraduates. **Degrees:** 237 associate awarded. **Location:** 38 miles from Atlanta. **Calendar:** Semester, extensive summer session. **Full-time faculty:** 53 total; 83% have terminal degrees, 15% minority, 47% women. **Part-time faculty:** 17 total; 29% have terminal degrees, 6% minority, 53% women. **Class size:** 66% < 20, 34% 20-39. **Special facilities:** Center for international studies, two hospitals, regional primate center, Center for Disease Control.

**Student profile.** Among degree-seeking undergraduates, 382 enrolled as first-time, first-year students, 12 transferred in from other institutions.

| | | | |
|---|---|---|---|
| Women: | 59% | Hispanic American: | 4% |
| African American: | 16% | Native American: | 1% |
| Asian American: | 25% | International: | 4% |

**Transfer out.** 100% of students enrolled in the transfer program go on to 4-year colleges.

**Basis for selection.** GED not accepted. High school curriculum and transcript most important, standardized test scores, letters of recommendation, extracurricular activities, and essays also important. **Adult students:** SAT/ACT scores not required if out of high school 1 year(s) or more. **Homeschooled:** Transcript of courses and grades, state high school equivalency certificate required. 3 SAT Subject Tests (one in Math) required.

**High school preparation.** 16 units recommended. Recommended units include English 4, mathematics 4, social studies 3, science 3 (laboratory 3) and foreign language 2. Math units should include geometry and algebra II.

**2008-2009 Annual costs.** Tuition/fees: $30,062. Per-credit charge: $1,233. Room/board: $8,496. Books/supplies: $1,000.

**2006-2007 Financial aid. Need-based:** 79% of total undergraduate aid awarded as scholarships/grants, 21% as loans/jobs. Need-based aid available for part-time students. Work-study available nights and weekends. **Non-need-based:** Scholarships awarded for academics, leadership, religious affiliation, state residency. **Additional information:** Deadline of November 1 to apply for Oxford College Scholars Program.

**Application procedures. Admission:** Priority date 1/15; no deadline. $50 fee, may be waived for applicants with need. Application may be submitted online. Admission notification on a rolling basis beginning on or about 3/15. Must reply by May 1 or within 3 week(s) if notified thereafter. 11/1 deadline for academic scholars program. **Financial aid:** Priority date 2/1, closing date 3/1. FAFSA, CSS PROFILE required. Applicants notified by 4/1; must reply by 5/1 or within 2 week(s) of notification.

**Academics. Special study options:** Cooperative education, cross-registration, distance learning, double major, dual enrollment of high school students, independent study, internships, liberal arts/career combination, study abroad, Washington semester. **Credit/placement by examination:** AP, CLEP, IB, institutional tests. 16 credit hours maximum toward associate degree. **Support services:** Reduced course load, study skills assistance, tutoring, writing center.

**Majors. Liberal arts:** Arts/sciences.

**Computing on campus.** 80 workstations in dormitories, library, computer center, student center. Dormitories wired for high-speed internet access and linked to campus network. Commuter students can connect to campus network. Online course registration, online library, helpline, student web hosting, wireless network available.

**Student life. Freshman orientation:** Mandatory, $100 fee. Six-day program held prior to start of school year; includes registration. **Housing:** Guaranteed on-campus for all undergraduates. Coed dorms, single-sex dorms, special housing for disabled, substance-free housing available. Themed housing for healthy living is available. **Activities:** Campus ministries, choral groups, dance, drama, film society, literary magazine, music ensembles, student government, student newspaper, volunteer club, fellowship club, outdoor club, College Republicans, Circle K, Jewish student union, Catholic student union, Muslim student association, Young Democrats, Hindu student council.

**Athletics.** NJCAA. **Intercollegiate:** Basketball M, soccer W, tennis. **Intramural:** Badminton, basketball, football (non-tackle), soccer, softball, swimming, tennis, volleyball. **Team name:** Eagles.

**Student services.** Alcohol/substance abuse counseling, career counseling, financial aid counseling, health services, minority student services, personal counseling, placement for graduates. **Physically disabled:** Services for visually, speech, hearing impaired.

**Contact.** E-mail: oxadmission@emory.edu
Phone: (770) 784-8328 Toll-free number: (800) 723-8328
Fax: (770) 784-8359
Jennifer Taylor, Dean of Enrollment Services, Oxford College of Emory University, 100 Hamill Street, Oxford, GA 30054-1418

## Savannah River College
### Augusta, Georgia
#### www.savannahrivercollege.edu

- For-profit 2-year junior and technical college
- Small city
- Interview required

**General.** Regionally accredited; also accredited by ACICS. **Enrollment:** 268 degree-seeking undergraduates. **Degrees:** 53 associate awarded. **Calendar:** Quarter. **Full-time faculty:** 7 total; 43% have terminal degrees, 57% minority. **Part-time faculty:** 25 total; 20% have terminal degrees, 72% minority. **Class size:** 96% < 20, 4% 20-39.

**Student profile.** Among degree-seeking undergraduates, 100% enrolled in a vocational program, 32 enrolled as first-time, first-year students, 3 transferred in from other institutions.

| | | | |
|---|---|---|---|
| Part-time: | 4% | Women: | 87% |
| Out-of-state: | 6% | | |

**Basis for selection.** Interview very important. **Homeschooled:** Transcript of courses and grades, state high school equivalency certificate required.

**2007-2008 Annual costs.** Tuition/fees: $8,395.

**2007-2008 Financial aid.** All financial aid based on need. 31 full-time freshmen applied for aid; 26 were judged to have need; 26 of these received aid. Average need met was 100%. Average scholarship/grant was $4,050; average loan $2,625. 43% of total undergraduate aid awarded as scholarships/grants, 57% as loans/jobs. Need-based aid available for part-time students.

**Application procedures. Admission:** No deadline. $50 fee. **Financial aid:** No deadline. FAFSA, institutional form required.

**Academics. Special study options:** Double major, independent study, internships. **Credit/placement by examination:** CLEP. **Support services:** Learning center, reduced course load, study skills assistance, tutoring.

**Majors. Business:** Accounting, administrative services, business admin. **Health:** Insurance specialist, management/clinical assistant, office assistant. **Other:** Microsoft network engineer.

**Most popular majors.** Business/marketing 19%, computer/information sciences 8%, health sciences 74%.

**Computing on campus.** 133 workstations in library. Online library available.

**Student life. Freshman orientation:** Mandatory. **Activities:** Student newspaper.

**Student services. Transfer:** Pre-admission transcript evaluation for new students.

**Contact.** E-mail: info@savannahrivercollege.edu
Phone: (706) 738-5604 Fax: (706) 736-3599
Jeffrey Rainier, Director of Admissions, Savannah River College, 2528 Center West Parkway, Building A, Augusta, GA 30909

## Savannah Technical College
### Savannah, Georgia
#### www.savannahtech.edu — CB code: 3741

- Public 2-year technical college
- Commuter campus in small city

**General.** Regionally accredited. Classes offered at satellite campuses in Liberty and Effingham Counties. **Enrollment:** 3,748 degree-seeking undergraduates; 411 non-degree-seeking students. **Degrees:** 182 associate awarded. **Location:** 250 miles from Atlanta. **Calendar:** Quarter, extensive summer session. **Full-time faculty:** 85 total; 40% minority, 53% women. **Part-time faculty:** 275 total; 52% minority, 62% women. **Class size:** 64% < 20, 36% 20-39.

**Student profile.** Among degree-seeking undergraduates, 913 enrolled as first-time, first-year students.

| | | | |
|---|---|---|---|
| Part-time: | 53% | Asian American: | 2% |
| Out-of-state: | 12% | Hispanic American: | 4% |
| Women: | 68% | International: | 2% |
| African American: | 53% | 25 or older: | 54% |

**Transfer out.** Colleges most students transferred to 2007: Savannah State University.

**Basis for selection.** Open admission, but selective for some programs. Competitive admissions for allied health programs. ACT or SAT may be accepted in lieu of COMPASS or ASSET for placement. **Learning Disabled:** Must meet with disability coordinator.

**High school preparation.** 22 units recommended. Recommended units include English 4, mathematics 3, social studies 3, science 3, foreign language 1 and academic electives 3. 4 tech prep and 1 science recommended.

**2007-2008 Annual costs.** Tuition/fees: $1,359; $2,475 out-of-state. Per-credit charge: $31 in-state; $62 out-of-state. Books/supplies: $1,500.

**2006-2007 Financial aid. Need-based:** Need-based aid available for part-time students. **Non-need-based:** Scholarships awarded for academics, leadership, minority status, state residency.

**Application procedures. Admission:** No deadline. $15 fee. Application must be submitted on paper. Admission notification on a rolling basis. **Financial aid:** No deadline. FAFSA required. Applicants notified on a rolling basis.

**Academics. Special study options:** Distance learning, dual enrollment of high school students. License preparation in nursing, paramedic. **Credit/placement by examination:** AP, CLEP, institutional tests. **Support services:** GED test center, learning center, reduced course load, remedial instruction, study skills assistance, tutoring.

**Majors. Business:** Accounting technology, administrative services, human resources, marketing, operations, sales/distribution. **Computer sciences:** General, data processing, networking, programming. **Construction:** Electrician. **Engineering technology:** Computer, drafting, electrical. **Health:** Dental assistant, EMT paramedic, licensed practical nurse, medical assistant, surgical technology. **Mechanic/repair:** Auto body, automotive, heating/ac/refrig, industrial. **Personal/culinary services:** Chef training, cosmetic. **Production:** Machine shop technology, welding. **Protective services:** Criminal justice, fire safety technology.

**Most popular majors.** Business/marketing 39%, computer/information sciences 17%, education 19%, personal/culinary services 6%, security/protective services 9%.

**Computing on campus.** 100 workstations in library, computer center. Online course registration, online library available.

**Student life. Freshman orientation:** Available. Preregistration for classes offered. **Activities:** Student government.

**Student services.** Career counseling, services for economically disadvantaged, student employment services, financial aid counseling, on-campus daycare, personal counseling, placement for graduates. **Transfer:** Re-entry adviser, pre-admission transcript evaluation for new students.

**Contact.** E-mail: webinfo@savannahtech.edu
Phone: (912) 443-5517 Toll-free number: (800) 769-6362
Fax: (912) 443-5705
Verlene Lampley, Vice President of Student Success, Savannah Technical College, 5717 White Bluff Road, Savannah, GA 31405-5521

## South Georgia College
### Douglas, Georgia
**www.sgc.edu**
CB code: 5619

♦ Public 2-year community and junior college
♦ Commuter campus in large town

**General.** Founded in 1906. Regionally accredited. **Enrollment:** 1,756 degree-seeking undergraduates. **Degrees:** 191 associate awarded. **Location:** 200 miles from Atlanta; 120 miles from Jacksonville, Florida. **Calendar:** Semester, extensive summer session. **Full-time faculty:** 44 total. **Part-time faculty:** 41 total. **Class size:** 39% < 20, 55% 20-39, 6% 40-49, less than 1% 50-99. **Special facilities:** Mobile nursing clinic.

**Transfer out.** Colleges most students transferred to 2007: Valdosta State University, Georgia Southern University, University of Georgia.

**Basis for selection.** Open admission. Students who score below 400 SAT math (16 ACT math) or 430 SAT verbal (18 ACT English) required to take College Placement Exam in English, reading, and/or math. Interview required of nursing majors. **Homeschooled:** Statement describing home-school structure and mission, transcript of courses and grades required.

**High school preparation.** 16 units recommended. Recommended units include English 4, mathematics 4, social studies 3, science 3 (laboratory 3) and foreign language 2.

**2007-2008 Annual costs.** Tuition/fees: $2,076; $7,316 out-of-state. Per-credit charge: $73 in-state; $292 out-of-state. Room/board: $7,060. Books/supplies: $660. Personal expenses: $825.

**Financial aid. Need-based:** Need-based aid available for part-time students. **Non-need-based:** Scholarships awarded for academics.

**Application procedures. Admission:** No deadline. $20 fee, may be waived for applicants with need. Application may be submitted online. Admission notification on a rolling basis. **Financial aid:** Priority date 4/1; no closing date. FAFSA, institutional form required. Applicants notified on a rolling basis starting 7/6; must reply within 2 week(s) of notification.

**Academics.** Students may pursue associate in nursing through South Georgia College/Waycross College campus. **Special study options:** Cooperative education, distance learning, dual enrollment of high school students, independent study, study abroad, teacher certification program. Bachelor's degree programs available on campus. License preparation in nursing. **Credit/placement by examination:** AP, CLEP, IB, institutional tests. 30 credit hours maximum toward associate degree. **Support services:** Learning center, reduced course load, remedial instruction, tutoring.

**Majors. Biology:** General. **Business:** General, accounting, administrative services, banking/financial services, business admin, communications, finance, management information systems, managerial economics, marketing, office management, office technology, office/clerical, operations, statistics. **Communications:** General, journalism. **Computer sciences:** General, applications programming, programming. **Education:** General, business, health, physical. **English:** English lit. **Foreign languages:** General, French, German, Spanish. **Health:** Nursing (RN), predental, premedicine, prepharmacy. **History:** General. **Legal studies:** Prelaw. **Liberal arts:** Arts/sciences. **Math:** General. **Parks/recreation:** General, facilities management, health/fitness, sports admin. **Philosophy/religion:** Philosophy. **Physical sciences:** Chemistry, physics. **Protective services:** Criminal justice, law enforcement admin, police science. **Psychology:** General. **Social sciences:** General, criminology, economics, political science, sociology.

**Most popular majors.** Health sciences 26%, liberal arts 68%.

**Computing on campus.** 80 workstations in dormitories, library, computer center, student center. Dormitories wired for high-speed internet access. Online course registration, helpline available.

**Student life. Freshman orientation:** Mandatory. Preregistration for classes offered. **Housing:** Guaranteed on-campus for all undergraduates. Coed dorms available. $30 deposit. **Activities:** Campus ministries, dance, drama, international student organizations, literary magazine, student government, student newspaper, Baptist student union, Association of Student Nurses, Students for Multicultural Unity, Phi Beta Lambda.

**Athletics.** NJCAA. **Intercollegiate:** Baseball M, softball W, tennis W. **Intramural:** Basketball, softball, swimming, synchronized swimming, table tennis, tennis, volleyball. **Team name:** Tigers.

**Student services.** Student employment services, financial aid counseling, veterans' counselor. **Learning disabled:** Comprehensive services available. **Transfer:** Pre-admission transcript evaluation for new students. College fairs on campus for students transferring to 4-year colleges.

**Contact.** E-mail: admissions@sgc.edu
Phone: (912) 389-4510 Toll-free number: (800) 342-6364
Fax: (912) 389-4388
Wes Brown, Director of Admissions, South Georgia College, 100 West College Park Drive, Douglas, GA 31533-5098

## Southeastern Technical College
### Vidalia, Georgia
**www.southeasterntech.org/**
CB code: 5652

♦ Public 2-year technical college
♦ Large town

**General.** Regionally accredited. **Enrollment:** 911 degree-seeking undergraduates. **Degrees:** 25 associate awarded. **Calendar:** Quarter. **Full-time faculty:** 34 total. **Part-time faculty:** 34 total.

**Basis for selection.** Open admission.

**2007-2008 Annual costs.** Tuition/fees: $1,440; $2,556 out-of-state. Per-credit charge: $31 in-state; $62 out-of-state.

**Financial aid. Need-based:** Need-based aid available for part-time students. Work-study available nights and for part-time students. **Non-need-based:** Scholarships awarded for state residency.

**Application procedures. Admission:** $15 fee. **Financial aid:** No deadline. FAFSA, institutional form required. Applicants notified on a rolling basis starting 4/6.

**Academics. Special study options:** Distance learning. **Credit/placement by examination:** CLEP, institutional tests. **Support services:** GED preparation and test center, tutoring.

**Majors. Business:** Accounting, business admin, marketing. **Computer sciences:** Networking. **Construction:** Electrician. **Education:** Early childhood. **Health:** Clinical lab technology.

**Computing on campus.** Commuter students can connect to campus network. Online library, wireless network available.

**Student life. Freshman orientation:** Mandatory.

**Athletics. Intramural:** Bowling M, volleyball M.

**Student services. Physically disabled:** Services for visually, speech, hearing impaired.

**Contact.** E-mail: brhart@southeasterntech.edu
Phone: (912) 538-3121
Brad Hart, Director of Enrollment Services, Southeastern Technical College, 3001 East First Street, Vidalia, GA 30474

---

## Southwest Georgia Technical College
**Thomasville, Georgia**
**www.southwestgatech.edu**                      CB code: 3627

- Public 2-year technical college
- Commuter campus in large town

**General.** Regionally accredited. **Enrollment:** 1,154 degree-seeking undergraduates; 254 non-degree-seeking students. **Degrees:** 124 associate awarded. **Location:** 35 miles from Tallahassee, Florida. **Calendar:** Quarter, extensive summer session. **Full-time faculty:** 62 total. **Partnerships:** Formal partnership with John Deere.

**Student profile.** Among degree-seeking undergraduates, 228 enrolled as first-time, first-year students.

| | | | |
|---|---|---|---|
| Part-time: | 60% | African American: | 38% |
| Out-of-state: | 3% | Hispanic American: | 2% |
| Women: | 73% | | |

**Basis for selection.** Open admission, but selective for some programs. Most health programs selective due to limited enrollment. Selection process may include required certifications, additional standardized testing, prerequisite courses and physical exam. ACT or SAT may be accepted in lieu of COMPASS or ASSET for placement. **Learning Disabled:** Students seeking accommodations should provide documentation of learning disability.

**High school preparation.** 22 units recommended. Recommended units include English 4, mathematics 3, social studies 3, science 3, foreign language 1 and academic electives 3. 4 tech prep and 1 health science recommended.

**2007-2008 Annual costs.** Tuition/fees: $1,359; $2,475 out-of-state. Per-credit charge: $31 in-state; $62 out-of-state. Truck driving and flight technology are higher cost programs. Books/supplies: $990. Personal expenses: $4,400.

**Financial aid. Need-based:** Need-based aid available for part-time students. Work-study available nights. **Non-need-based:** Scholarships awarded for state residency.

**Application procedures. Admission:** No deadline. $20 fee. Admission notification on a rolling basis. **Financial aid:** No deadline. FAFSA, institutional form required. Applicants notified on a rolling basis starting 7/1.

**Academics. Special study options:** Cooperative education, distance learning, double major, dual enrollment of high school students, internships, liberal arts/career combination. License preparation in nursing, paramedic, physical therapy, radiology, real estate. **Credit/placement by examination:** CLEP,

---

institutional tests. **Support services:** GED preparation and test center, remedial instruction, tutoring.

**Majors. Agriculture:** Equipment technology, power machinery. **Business:** Accounting technology, administrative services, business admin, office/clerical, operations. **Computer sciences:** Data entry, data processing, networking. **Education:** Early childhood. **Health:** Clinical lab technology, medical assistant, medical radiologic technology/radiation therapy, nursing (RN), pharmacy assistant, radiologic technology/medical imaging, respiratory therapy technology, surgical technology. **Mechanic/repair:** Heavy equipment. **Protective services:** Criminal justice, police science.

**Most popular majors.** Business/marketing 17%, computer/information sciences 11%, health sciences 59%.

**Computing on campus.** 42 workstations in library. Online course registration, online library available.

**Student life. Freshman orientation:** Mandatory. Preregistration for classes offered. Held quarterly. **Activities:** Student government, National Vocational honor society, Phi Beta Lambda, SkillsUSA.

**Student services.** Adult student services, career counseling, services for economically disadvantaged, student employment services, financial aid counseling, personal counseling, placement for graduates. **Physically disabled:** Services for visually, hearing impaired. **Transfer:** Pre-admission transcript evaluation for new students.

**Contact.** E-mail: info@southwestgatech.edu
Phone: (229) 225-5060 Fax: (229) 227-2666
Deborah Gray, Registrar, Southwest Georgia Technical College, 15689 US Highway 19N, Thomasville, GA 31792

---

## Waycross College
**Waycross, Georgia**
**www.waycross.edu**                      CB code: 5889

- Public 2-year community and liberal arts college
- Commuter campus in large town
- SAT or ACT required

**General.** Founded in 1976. Regionally accredited. **Enrollment:** 935 degree-seeking undergraduates. **Degrees:** 75 associate awarded. **Location:** 70 miles from Jacksonville, Florida. **Calendar:** Semester, limited summer session. **Full-time faculty:** 20 total. **Part-time faculty:** 27 total. **Special facilities:** Repository of materials about the Okefenokee Swamp.

**Student profile.**

| | | | |
|---|---|---|---|
| Out-of-state: | 10% | 25 or older: | 28% |

**Transfer out. Colleges most students transferred to 2007:** Valdosta State University, Armstrong Atlantic University, Georgia Southern University, University of Georgia.

**Basis for selection.** 330 SAT verbal or 310 SAT math required. Open admissions for all students out of school for over 5 years with high school diploma or GED. Essay required of low-scoring SAT verbal or ACT English applicants and those who have not completed 4 years high school English. **Adult students:** SAT/ACT scores not required if out of high school 5 year(s) or more. COMPASS placement exams required.

**High school preparation.** 16 units required. Required units include English 4, mathematics 4, social studies 3, science 3 and foreign language 2.

**2007-2008 Annual costs.** Tuition/fees: $1,904; $7,144 out-of-state. Per-credit charge: $73 in-state; $292 out-of-state. Books/supplies: $500. Personal expenses: $900.

**Financial aid. Need-based:** Need-based aid available for part-time students. Work-study available nights and for part-time students. **Non-need-based:** Scholarships awarded for academics, alumni affiliation, leadership.

**Application procedures. Admission:** No deadline. $20 fee, may be waived for applicants with need. Application may be submitted online. Admission notification on a rolling basis. **Financial aid:** Priority date 6/1; no closing date. FAFSA, institutional form required. Applicants notified on a rolling basis; must reply within 2 week(s) of notification.

**Academics. Special study options:** Dual enrollment of high school students, independent study, liberal arts/career combination, study abroad. Cooperative nursing programs (RN) with South Georgia College, Valdosta State College. Bachelor's degree programs available on campus. **Credit/placement by examination:** CLEP, institutional tests. 20 credit hours maximum toward associate degree. SAT Subject Tests used to replace courses students did not take in high school. **Support services:** Learning center, reduced course load, remedial instruction, study skills assistance, tutoring, writing center.

**Majors. Biology:** General. **Business:** Accounting, business admin. **Computer sciences:** General, programming. **Conservation:** Environmental science. **Education:** General, physical. **English:** English lit. **Family/ consumer sciences:** Child care. **Health:** Clinical lab technology, dental hygiene, EMT paramedic, medical radiologic technology/radiation therapy, surgical technology. **History:** General. **Math:** General. **Mechanic/repair:** Automotive, electronics/electrical, heating/ac/refrig, industrial. **Parks/recreation:** Health/ fitness. **Personal/culinary services:** Cosmetic. **Physical sciences:** Chemistry. **Psychology:** General. **Social sciences:** Political science, sociology.

**Computing on campus.** 100 workstations in library, computer center, student center. Online course registration available.

**Student life. Freshman orientation:** Mandatory. Preregistration for classes offered. **Activities:** Drama, literary magazine, student government, student newspaper, Baptist student union, multicultural student alliance, Circle-K.

**Athletics. Intramural:** Baseball M, basketball, football (non-tackle), softball. **Team name:** Swamp Fox.

**Student services.** Adult student services, alcohol/substance abuse counseling, career counseling, student employment services, financial aid counseling, minority student services, personal counseling, placement for graduates, veterans' counselor. **Physically disabled:** Services for visually, speech, hearing impaired. **Transfer:** Pre-admission transcript evaluation for new students. Transfer adviser, college fairs on campus for students transferring to 4-year colleges.

**Contact.** E-mail: admiss@waycross.edu
Phone: (912) 285-6133 Fax: (912) 285-6158
Robert Wingfield, Assistant Director of Admissions, Waycross College, 2001 South Georgia Parkway, Waycross, GA 31503

## West Central Technical College
### Waco, Georgia
### www.westcentraltech.edu

- ♦ Public 2-year business and technical college
- ♦ Rural community

**General. Enrollment:** 3,216 degree-seeking undergraduates; 314 non-degree-seeking students. **Degrees:** 154 associate awarded. **Calendar:** Quarter. **Full-time faculty:** 83 total. **Part-time faculty:** 227 total.

**Student profile.** Among degree-seeking undergraduates, 751 enrolled as first-time, first-year students.

| | | | |
|---|---|---|---|
| Part-time: | 67% | Asian American: | 1% |
| Women: | 75% | Hispanic American: | 2% |
| African American: | 25% | | |

**Basis for selection.** Open admission, but selective for some programs. Special requirements for health services programs. ACT or SAT may be accepted in lieu of COMPASS or ASSET for placement.

**High school preparation.** 22 units recommended. Recommended units include English 4, mathematics 3, social studies 3, science 3, foreign language 1 and academic electives 3. 4 tech prep and 1 health science recommended.

**2007-2008 Annual costs.** Tuition/fees: $1,359; $2,475 out-of-state. Per-credit charge: $31 in-state; $62 out-of-state. Truck driving and flight technology are higher cost programs. Books/supplies: $945. Personal expenses: $1,300.

**Application procedures. Admission:** No deadline. $25 fee.

**Academics. Special study options:** Distance learning, dual enrollment of high school students. **Credit/placement by examination:** CLEP.

**Most popular majors.** Business/marketing 27%, computer/information sciences 12%, health sciences 51%.

**Contact.** Phone: (770) 537-5740 Fax: (770) 537-7995
Mary Aderhold, Admissions Director, West Central Technical College, 176 Murphy Campus Boulevard, Waco, GA 30182

## West Georgia Technical College
### LaGrange, Georgia
### www.westgatech.edu
**CB code: 3632**

- ♦ Public 2-year technical college
- ♦ Commuter campus in small city

**General.** Regionally accredited. **Enrollment:** 1,558 degree-seeking undergraduates; 197 non-degree-seeking students. **Degrees:** 65 associate awarded. **Location:** 60 miles from Atlanta. **Calendar:** Quarter, limited summer session. **Full-time faculty:** 46 total. **Part-time faculty:** 96 total. **Class size:** 80% < 20, 20% 20-39.

**Student profile.** Among degree-seeking undergraduates, 409 enrolled as first-time, first-year students.

| | | | |
|---|---|---|---|
| Part-time: | 55% | African American: | 38% |
| Women: | 58% | Hispanic American: | 1% |

**Basis for selection.** Open admission, but selective for some programs. Admission to radiology and nursing programs based on examination, interview and space availability. ACT or SAT may be accepted in lieu of COMPASS or ASSET for placement. **Homeschooled:** Must provide satisfactory documentation indicating the homeschool is approved. Must provide official high school transcript and meet all other admission requirements. **Learning Disabled:** Disabilities must be documented with the on-site coordinator to receive consideration for accommodation.

**High school preparation.** 22 units recommended. Recommended units include English 4, mathematics 3, social studies 3, science 3, foreign language 1 and academic electives 3. 4 tech prep and 1 health science recommended.

**2007-2008 Annual costs.** Tuition/fees: $1,359; $2,475 out-of-state. Per-credit charge: $31 in-state; $62 out-of-state. Tuition reciprocity with bordering states. Commercial truck driving program is $2048 per quarter. Basic welding and EMT programs are $40 per-credit-hour. Books/supplies: $1,283. Personal expenses: $1,300.

**Financial aid. Need-based:** Need-based aid available for part-time students. Work-study available nights and for part-time students. **Non-need-based:** Scholarships awarded for state residency.

**Application procedures. Admission:** No deadline. $15 fee. Application may be submitted online. Admission notification on a rolling basis. **Financial aid:** No deadline. FAFSA, institutional form required. Applicants notified on a rolling basis; must reply within 1 week(s) of notification.

**Academics.** Tutorial program available. **Special study options:** Distance learning, dual enrollment of high school students. License preparation in paramedic, radiology, real estate. **Credit/placement by examination:** AP, CLEP. 15 credit hours maximum toward associate degree. **Support services:** GED preparation and test center, learning center, study skills assistance, tutoring.

**Majors. Business:** Accounting, administrative services, business admin, executive assistant, management science. **Computer sciences:** General, data entry, networking, web page design. **Education:** Early childhood. **Health:** Medical records technology, pharmacy assistant. **Mechanic/repair:** General, electronics/electrical, industrial. **Protective services:** Criminal justice, firefighting.

**Most popular majors.** Business/marketing 28%, computer/information sciences 6%, education 8%, health sciences 28%, security/protective services 28%.

**Computing on campus.** 100 workstations in library, computer center. Online library available.

**Student life. Freshman orientation:** Mandatory. Preregistration for classes offered. **Activities:** Student government, TV station, Phi Beta Lambda.

**Student services.** Adult student services, career counseling, student employment services, financial aid counseling, on-campus daycare, placement for graduates, veterans' counselor, women's services. **Physically disabled:** Services for visually, hearing impaired.

**Contact.** E-mail: lbasham@westgatech.edu
Phone: (706) 845-4244 Fax: (706) 845-4340
Lori Basham, Director of Admission, West Georgia Technical College, 303 Fort Drive, LaGrange, GA 30240

## Young Harris College
**Young Harris, Georgia**
www.yhc.edu                CB code: 5990

- Private 2-year liberal arts college affiliated with United Methodist Church
- Residential campus in rural community
- SAT or ACT with writing required

**General.** Founded in 1886. Regionally accredited. **Enrollment:** 639 degree-seeking undergraduates. **Degrees:** 134 associate awarded. **Location:** 120 miles from Atlanta. **Calendar:** Semester, limited summer session. **Full-time faculty:** 38 total; 63% have terminal degrees, 42% women. **Part-time faculty:** 10 total; 30% women. **Class size:** 65% < 20, 34% 20-39, less than 1% 40-49. **Special facilities:** Planetarium, black box theater, observatory, climbing wall, cross country trail, PDGA certified disc golf course.

**Student profile.** Among degree-seeking undergraduates, 300 enrolled as first-time, first-year students, 13 transferred in from other institutions.

| | | | |
|---|---|---|---|
| Part-time: | 4% | 25 or older: | 1% |
| Out-of-state: | 7% | Live on campus: | 81% |
| Women: | 53% | | |

**Transfer out.** 93% of students enrolled in the transfer program go on to 4-year colleges. **Colleges most students transferred to 2007:** University of Georgia, Georgia College & State University, University of West Georgia, North Georgia College & State University, Kennesaw State University.

**Basis for selection.** Heavy emphasis on academic GPA and SAT or ACT scores. High school record, interview considered. Conditional admission possible. **Adult students:** SAT/ACT scores not required if out of high school 5 year(s) or more. Must be part time, at least 22 years of age, must commute. **Homeschooled:** Transcript of courses and grades required. Possible GED requirement dependent upon SAT and/or ACT scores. **Learning Disabled:** Psycho-educational analysis required.

**High school preparation.** Recommended units include English 4, mathematics 4, social studies 3, science 3 and foreign language 2.

**2008-2009 Annual costs.** Tuition/fees (projected): $16,630. Per-credit charge: $500. Room/board: $5,220. Books/supplies: $800. Personal expenses: $1,050.

**2006-2007 Financial aid.** **Need-based:** 252 full-time freshmen applied for aid; 180 were judged to have need; 180 of these received aid. Average need met was 78%. Average scholarship/grant was $9,750; average loan $2,276. 82% of total undergraduate aid awarded as scholarships/grants, 18% as loans/jobs. Need-based aid available for part-time students. Work-study available nights. **Non-need-based:** Awarded to 329 full-time undergraduates, including 220 freshmen. Scholarships awarded for academics, art, athletics, job skills, music/drama, state residency.

**Application procedures. Admission:** Priority date 1/1; no deadline. $30 fee, may be waived for applicants with need. Application may be submitted online. Admission notification on a rolling basis beginning on or about 9/1. **Financial aid:** Priority date 4/1; no closing date. FAFSA, institutional form required. Applicants notified on a rolling basis starting 3/1; must reply within 2 week(s) of notification.

**Academics. Special study options:** Dual enrollment of high school students, honors, study abroad. **Credit/placement by examination:** AP, CLEP, IB, institutional tests. Student may exempt computer science 101 but receives no credit. **Support services:** Pre-admission summer program, reduced course load, remedial instruction, study skills assistance, tutoring, writing center.

**Majors. Biology:** General. **Business:** General, hospitality admin. **Communications:** General. **Conservation:** Forestry. **Education:** General, art, music. **Engineering:** General. **English:** English lit, speech/rhetoric. **Foreign languages:** General, French, Spanish. **Health:** Predental, premedicine, prenursing, prepharmacy, preveterinary. **History:** General. **Interdisciplinary:** Biological/physical sciences. **Legal studies:** Prelaw. **Liberal arts:** Arts/sciences. **Math:** General. **Parks/recreation:** Health/fitness. **Philosophy/religion:** Religion. **Physical sciences:** Astronomy, chemistry, physics. **Protective services:** Criminal justice. **Psychology:** General. **Social sciences:** General. **Visual/performing arts:** General, art, dramatic, studio arts.

**Most popular majors.** Business/marketing 9%, education 27%, health sciences 7%, liberal arts 22%, physical sciences 21%, visual/performing arts 10%.

**Computing on campus.** 130 workstations in dormitories, library, computer center. Dormitories wired for high-speed internet access and linked to campus network. Commuter students can connect to campus network. On-line library, helpline, wireless network available.

**Student life. Freshman orientation:** Mandatory. Preregistration for classes offered. Two-day,1 night program held during summer prior to fall enrollment. **Policies:** All single freshmen and sophomores under age 22 not living with family must reside in college dormitories. No alcohol allowed on campus. **Housing:** Guaranteed on-campus for all undergraduates. Coed dorms, single-sex dorms, substance-free housing available. $200 deposit. **Activities:** Campus ministries, choral groups, dance, drama, literary magazine, music ensembles, musical theater, student government, student newspaper, Wesley Fellowship, Newman club, honorary service organizations, Pi Sigma Omega (political science), College Republicans, Young Democrats.

**Athletics.** NJCAA. **Intercollegiate:** Baseball M, cross-country, golf, soccer, softball W, tennis W. **Intramural:** Basketball, football (non-tackle), softball, volleyball. **Team name:** Mountain Lions.

**Student services.** Career counseling, financial aid counseling, health services, personal counseling. **Transfer:** Pre-admission transcript evaluation for new students. Transfer center, transfer adviser, college fairs on campus for students transferring to 4-year colleges.

**Contact.** E-mail: admissions@yhc.edu
Phone: (706) 379-3111 Toll-free number: (800) 241-3754
Fax: (706) 379-3108
Clinton Hobbs, Vice President for Enrollment Management, Young Harris College, PO Box 116, Young Harris, GA 30582-0116

# Hawaii

## Hawaii Tokai International College
Honolulu, Hawaii
www.hawaiitokai.edu                    CB code: 2588

- Private 2-year junior and liberal arts college
- Residential campus in large city
- Application essay, interview required

**General.** Regionally accredited. **Enrollment:** 51 degree-seeking undergraduates. **Degrees:** 24 associate awarded. **Calendar:** Quarter, limited summer session. **Full-time faculty:** 7 total; 43% have terminal degrees, 57% women. **Part-time faculty:** 17 total; 12% have terminal degrees, 41% minority, 53% women. **Class size:** 100% < 20.

**Student profile.** Among degree-seeking undergraduates, 100% enrolled in a transfer program, 10 enrolled as first-time, first-year students.

| Women: | 43% | International: | 92% |
|---|---|---|---|
| Asian American: | 8% | Live on campus: | 67% |

**Transfer out.** 98% of students enrolled in the transfer program go on to 4-year colleges. **Colleges most students transferred to 2007:** University of Hawaii at Manoa.

**Basis for selection.** Essay, academic GPA, recommendations, character, interview, and level of interest most important. **Homeschooled:** Transcript of courses and grades, interview, letter of recommendation (nonparent) required.

**2007-2008 Annual costs.** Tuition/fees: $9,150. Room/board: $5,100. Books/supplies: $800. Personal expenses: $1,200.

**Financial aid. Non-need-based:** Scholarships awarded for academics.

**Application procedures. Admission:** Closing date 8/1 (postmark date). $50 fee. Application may be submitted online. Admission notification on a rolling basis. Must reply by May 1 or within 3 week(s) if notified thereafter. **Financial aid:** Institutional form required.

**Academics. Special study options:** ESL, study abroad. **Credit/placement by examination:** CLEP, institutional tests. 12 credit hours maximum toward associate degree. **Support services:** Study skills assistance, tutoring.

**Majors. Liberal arts:** Arts/sciences.

**Computing on campus.** 60 workstations in library, computer center. Dormitories wired for high-speed internet access and linked to campus network. Commuter students can connect to campus network. Online library, wireless network available.

**Student life. Freshman orientation:** Mandatory. Preregistration for classes offered. **Housing:** Guaranteed on-campus for all undergraduates. Coed dorms, substance-free housing available. $20 nonrefundable deposit. **Activities:** Dance, music ensembles, student government, student newspaper.

**Athletics. Intercollegiate:** Judo. **Intramural:** Baseball M, basketball M, soccer M. **Team name:** T-Wave.

**Student services.** Adult student services, alcohol/substance abuse counseling, career counseling, services for economically disadvantaged, student employment services, financial aid counseling, personal counseling. **Physically disabled:** Services for visually impaired. **Transfer:** Re-entry adviser, pre-admission transcript evaluation for new students. Transfer center, transfer adviser, college fairs on campus for students transferring to 4-year colleges.

**Contact.** E-mail: htic@tokai.edu
Phone: (808) 983-4187 Fax: (808) 983-4173
Derrick Kerr, Director, Student Services, Hawaii Tokai International College, 2241 Kapiolani Boulevard, Honolulu, HI 96826

## Heald College: Honolulu
Honolulu, Hawaii
www.heald.edu                    CB code: 4324

- Private 2-year business and technical college
- Commuter campus in very large city

**General.** Founded in 1863. Regionally accredited. **Enrollment:** 995 degree-seeking undergraduates. **Degrees:** 356 associate awarded. **Calendar:** Quarter. **Full-time faculty:** 25 total. **Part-time faculty:** 14 total.

**Basis for selection.** Open admission. Career Program Assessment Test (CPAT) administered prior to application.

**2008-2009 Annual costs.** Tuition/fees: $10,800. Fees vary by program. Books/supplies: $1,500.

**Financial aid.** All financial aid based on need. Need-based aid available for part-time students. Work-study available nights, weekends and for part-time students.

**Application procedures. Admission:** No deadline. $40 fee. Application may be submitted online. Admission notification on a rolling basis. **Financial aid:** No deadline. FAFSA required.

**Academics. Special study options:** Cooperative education, internships. **Credit/placement by examination:** CLEP, institutional tests. **Support services:** Learning center, reduced course load, remedial instruction, tutoring.

**Majors. Business:** Accounting, business admin, hospitality admin, tourism/travel. **Computer sciences:** General, vendor certification. **Engineering technology:** Electrical. **Health:** Medical assistant, medical secretary. **Legal studies:** Legal secretary.

**Computing on campus.** Online library available.

**Student services.** Career counseling, student employment services, financial aid counseling, placement for graduates. **Transfer:** Pre-admission transcript evaluation for new students. Transfer adviser for students transferring to 4-year colleges.

**Contact.** Phone: (808) 955-1500 Toll-free number: (800) 755-3550
Fax: (808) 955-6964
Wendy Nishimura, Director of Admissions, Heald College: Honolulu, 1500 Kapiolani Boulevard, Honolulu, HI 96814-3715

## Remington College: Honolulu
Honolulu, Hawaii
www.remingtoncollege.edu                    CB code: 3507

- For-profit 2-year branch campus college
- Commuter campus in very large city
- Interview required

**General.** Accredited by ACICS. **Enrollment:** 455 degree-seeking undergraduates. **Degrees:** 25 bachelor's, 168 associate awarded. **Calendar:** Quarter. **Full-time faculty:** 35 total. **Part-time faculty:** 20 total.

**Basis for selection.** Interview most important; CPAT assessment test score also important. CPAT entrance examination required.

**2007-2008 Annual costs.** Costs of entire programs leading to certificate, associate degree, bachelor's degree range from $13,000 to $38,880; includes books and supplies. Personal expenses: $1,764.

**Financial aid.** All financial aid based on need.

**Application procedures. Admission:** No deadline. $50 fee. Admission notification on a rolling basis. **Financial aid:** No deadline. FAFSA required. Applicants notified on a rolling basis.

**Academics. Special study options:** Bachelor's degree programs available on campus. **Credit/placement by examination:** CLEP. **Support services:** Tutoring.

**Majors. Business:** International. **Computer sciences:** General, networking. **Health:** Medical assistant. **Protective services:** Criminal justice.

**Computing on campus.** 170 workstations in library, computer center. Online library available.

**Student life. Freshman orientation:** Mandatory. **Activities:** International club.

**Student services.** Student employment services, financial aid counseling, placement for graduates. **Transfer:** Pre-admission transcript evaluation for new students.

**Contact.** E-mail: kheinema@remingtoncollege.edu
Phone: (808) 942-1000 Fax: (808) 533-3064
Kenneth Heinemann, Campus President, Remington College: Honolulu, 1111 Bishop Street, Suite 400, Honolulu, HI 96813-2811

## TransPacific Hawaii College
### Honolulu, Hawaii
www.transpacific.org                    CB code: 4429

- Private 2-year junior and liberal arts college
- Commuter campus in large city
- Application essay required

**General.** Regionally accredited. TransPacific serves as a transitional institution for students from Asia who have the desire to study in America but who lack the language ability and study skills. The college is in session 12 months per year and a student can become fluent in English and gain an Associate of Arts degree in 24 months. **Enrollment:** 176 degree-seeking undergraduates. **Degrees:** 120 associate awarded. **Location:** 6 miles from Honolulu. **Calendar:** Continuous. **Full-time faculty:** 11 total; 36% have terminal degrees, 64% women. **Part-time faculty:** 32 total; 28% have terminal degrees, 53% women. **Class size:** 100% < 20.

**Student profile.** Among degree-seeking undergraduates, 5% already have a bachelor's degree or higher, 176 enrolled as first-time, first-year students, 9 transferred in from other institutions.

| Women: | 63% | International: | 100% |
|---|---|---|---|

**Transfer out.** 100% of students enrolled in the transfer program go on to 4-year colleges. **Colleges most students transferred to 2007:** University of Hawaii, University of Washington, Alliant International University, Ritsumeikan Asia Pacific University, Marymount College.

**Basis for selection.** Secondary school record, essay important.

**High school preparation.** Recommended units include English 4, mathematics 4, social studies 2, history 2, science 2, computer science 1, visual/performing arts 1 and academic electives 5.

**2007-2008 Annual costs.** Tuition/fees: $16,300. Students are responsible for their board with a home stay family, about $750 per month. Books/supplies: $800.

**Application procedures. Admission:** Closing date 8/27 (postmark date). $50 fee. Admission notification on a rolling basis.

**Academics.** Academic program emphasizes crosscultural curriculum. **Special study options:** ESL, independent study, liberal arts/career combination. **Credit/placement by examination:** CLEP, institutional tests. **Support services:** Tutoring.

**Majors. Liberal arts:** Arts/sciences.

**Computing on campus.** 45 workstations in library, computer center. Repair service, wireless network available.

**Student life. Freshman orientation:** Mandatory. Held in Japan during the first week of March. **Housing:** Homestay for majority of students. **Activities:** Student government, student newspaper.

**Student services.** Career counseling, personal counseling. **Transfer:** Transfer center, transfer adviser, college fairs on campus for students transferring to 4-year colleges.

**Contact.** E-mail: akikotyler@transpacific.edu
Phone: (808) 377-5402 Fax: (808) 373-9735
Shungo Kawanishi, Vice President for Global Affairs, TransPacific Hawaii College, 5257 Kalanianaole Highway, Honolulu, HI 96821

## University of Hawaii: Hawaii Community College
### Hilo, Hawaii
www.hawcc.hawaii.edu                    CB code: 1801

- Public 2-year community college
- Small city

**General.** Founded in 1969. Regionally accredited. **Enrollment:** 2,310 degree-seeking undergraduates. **Degrees:** 256 associate awarded. **ROTC:** Naval. **Location:** 200 miles from Honolulu. **Calendar:** Semester, limited summer session. **Full-time faculty:** 96 total. **Part-time faculty:** 33 total.

**Student profile.**

| 25 or older: | 32% | Live on campus: | 35% |
|---|---|---|---|

**Basis for selection.** Open admission.

**2007-2008 Annual costs.** Tuition/fees: $2,024; $7,814 out-of-state. Per-credit charge: $63 in-state; $256 out-of-state. Books/supplies: $672. Personal expenses: $953.

**Financial aid.** All financial aid based on need. Need-based aid available for part-time students. **Additional information:** Hawaii student incentive grants and tuition waivers (merit and need-based) available to Hawaii residents.

**Application procedures. Admission:** Closing date 7/30. No application fee in-state; $25 out-of-state. Admission notification on a rolling basis. **Financial aid:** Priority date 4/1; no closing date. FAFSA required. Applicants notified on a rolling basis starting 5/1; must reply within 2 week(s) of notification.

**Academics. Special study options:** Cooperative education, cross-registration, distance learning, double major, dual enrollment of high school students, ESL, honors, independent study. **Credit/placement by examination:** CLEP. 15 credit hours maximum toward associate degree. **Support services:** Learning center, pre-admission summer program, reduced course load, remedial instruction, tutoring.

**Majors. Agriculture:** General. **Business:** Accounting, administrative services, market research, marketing, operations. **Construction:** Carpentry, power transmission. **Education:** Early childhood. **Engineering technology:** Drafting, electrical. **Family/consumer sciences:** Food/nutrition. **Health:** Nursing (RN). **Liberal arts:** Arts/sciences. **Mechanic/repair:** Auto body, automotive, diesel, electronics/electrical. **Personal/culinary services:** Food service, restaurant/catering. **Protective services:** Criminal justice, law enforcement admin. **Other:** Architectural, engineering and CAD technologies.

**Student life. Freshman orientation:** Available. Preregistration for classes offered. **Housing:** Coed dorms, special housing for disabled, apartments, substance-free housing available. **Activities:** Dance, drama, literary magazine, music ensembles, student government, student newspaper, TV station, Phi Theta Kappa honors society.

**Athletics. Team name:** Hawaii Hawks (i'eo).

**Student services.** Adult student services, career counseling, student employment services, financial aid counseling, health services, on-campus daycare, personal counseling, veterans' counselor. **Physically disabled:** Services for hearing impaired. **Transfer:** Transfer adviser, college fairs on campus for students transferring to 4-year colleges.

**Contact.** E-mail: hawccinf@hawaii.edu
Phone: (808) 974-7661 Fax: (808) 974-7692
David Loeding, Registrar, University of Hawaii: Hawaii Community College, 200 West Kawili Street, Hilo, HI 96720-4091

## University of Hawaii: Honolulu Community College
### Honolulu, Hawaii
honolulu.hawaii.edu                    CB code: 4350

- Public 2-year community and technical college
- Commuter campus in very large city

**General.** Founded in 1920. Regionally accredited. **Enrollment:** 3,326 degree-seeking undergraduates. **Degrees:** 505 associate awarded. **ROTC:** Army, Air Force. **Calendar:** Semester, limited summer session. **Full-time faculty:** 116 total. **Part-time faculty:** 80 total.

**Student profile.** Among degree-seeking undergraduates, 1,304 transferred in from other institutions.

| Out-of-state: | 3% | 25 or older: | 37% |
|---|---|---|---|

**Transfer out. Colleges most students transferred to 2007:** University of Hawaii at Manoa, University of Hawaii at Hilo, Chaminade University, Hawaii Pacific University.

**Basis for selection.** Open admission, but selective for out-of-state students. Out of state and foreign applicants subject to non-resident quota. High school diploma required for cosmetology program.

**2007-2008 Annual costs.** Tuition/fees: $1,920; $7,710 out-of-state. Per-credit charge: $63 in-state; $256 out-of-state. Books/supplies: $773. Personal expenses: $1,166.

**Financial aid. Need-based:** Need-based aid available for part-time students. Work-study available for part-time students. **Non-need-based:** Scholarships awarded for academics, state residency. **Additional information:** Hawaii student incentive grants and tuition waivers (merit and need-based) available to Hawaii residents at participating institutions.

**Application procedures. Admission:** Priority date 7/1; no deadline. No application fee in-state; $25 out-of-state. Admission notification on a rolling basis beginning on or about 3/1. **Financial aid:** Priority date 4/1; no closing date. FAFSA required. Applicants notified on a rolling basis starting 7/1; must reply within 3 week(s) of notification.

**Academics. Special study options:** Cooperative education, cross-registration, distance learning, dual enrollment of high school students, ESL, independent study, internships, student-designed major. License preparation in aviation. **Credit/placement by examination:** AP, CLEP, institutional tests. 30 credit hours maximum toward associate degree. **Support services:** Learning center, remedial instruction, study skills assistance, tutoring.

**Majors. Business:** Fashion. **Communications technology:** Graphic/printing. **Computer sciences:** General, computer graphics, information systems. **Construction:** Carpentry, electrician. **Education:** Early childhood, technology/industrial arts, voc/tech. **Engineering:** Aerospace, architectural, computer, polymer. **Engineering technology:** Drafting, electrical, occupational safety. **Family/consumer sciences:** Child care, institutional food production. **Health:** Occupational health. **Liberal arts:** Arts/sciences. **Mechanic/repair:** General, aircraft, auto body, automotive, diesel, electronics/electrical, heating/ac/refrig, marine. **Personal/culinary services:** Cosmetic. **Protective services:** Criminal justice, fire safety technology, fire services admin, firefighting, law enforcement admin, police science. **Public administration:** Community org/advocacy, human services, social work. **Transportation:** Airline/commercial pilot, aviation management. **Visual/performing arts:** Commercial/advertising art, fashion design.

**Most popular majors.** Engineering/engineering technologies 37%, liberal arts 20%, public administration/social services 8%, security/protective services 11%, trade and industry 16%.

**Computing on campus.** 97 workstations in library, computer center, student center. Commuter students can connect to campus network. Online course registration, wireless network available.

**Student life. Housing:** Dorms and apartments available at University of Hawaii at Manoa campus. **Activities:** Literary magazine, student government, student newspaper, Pacific Islander association, Filipino club.

**Student services.** Career counseling, student employment services, financial aid counseling, health services, on-campus daycare, placement for graduates, veterans' counselor. **Physically disabled:** Services for visually, speech, hearing impaired. **Transfer:** Pre-admission transcript evaluation for new students. Transfer center, transfer adviser, college fairs on campus for students transferring to 4-year colleges.

**Contact.** E-mail: admissions@hcc.hawaii.edu
Phone: (808) 845-9129 Fax: (808) 847-9829
Funai Grace, Admissions Counselor, University of Hawaii: Honolulu Community College, 874 Dillingham Boulevard, Honolulu, HI 96817

## University of Hawaii: Kapiolani Community College
**Honolulu, Hawaii**
**www.kcc.hawaii.edu**
**CB code: 4377**

◗ Public 2-year community college
◗ Commuter campus in very large city

**General.** Founded in 1957. Regionally accredited. **Enrollment:** 4,909 degree-seeking undergraduates. **Degrees:** 709 associate awarded. **Calendar:** Semester, limited summer session. **Full-time faculty:** 245 total. **Part-time faculty:** 150 total. **Class size:** 55% < 20, 45% 20-39, less than 1% 40-49, less than 1% 50-99.

**Student profile.**

| | | | |
|---|---|---|---|
| Out-of-state: | 7% | 25 or older: | 41% |

**Transfer out. Colleges most students transferred to 2007:** University of Hawaii at Manoa.

**Basis for selection.** Open admission, but selective for some programs. Special requirements for health science and nursing programs. High school diploma required for allied health and nursing programs and for students under age 18. Essay recommended. Interview required of allied health, legal assistant, and nursing programs.

**2007-2008 Annual costs.** Tuition/fees: $1,950; $7,740 out-of-state. Per-credit charge: $63 in-state; $256 out-of-state. Books/supplies: $725. Personal expenses: $1,143.

**Financial aid.** All financial aid based on need. Need-based aid available for part-time students. **Additional information:** Hawaii student incentive grants and tuition waivers (merit and need-based) available to Hawaii residents.

**Application procedures. Admission:** Closing date 7/17 (postmark date). $25 fee. Application must be submitted on paper. Admission notification on a rolling basis. Application deadline April 1 for allied health and legal assistant programs; deadline February 1 for registered nursing program. **Financial aid:** Priority date 4/1; no closing date. FAFSA required. Applicants notified on a rolling basis; must reply within 2 week(s) of notification.

**Academics. Special study options:** Cross-registration, distance learning, double major, dual enrollment of high school students, ESL, exchange student, external degree, honors, independent study, internships, study abroad, teacher certification program, weekend college. Service learning. License preparation in nursing, paramedic. **Credit/placement by examination:** CLEP, institutional tests. **Support services:** Learning center, remedial instruction, tutoring.

**Majors. Business:** General, accounting, hospitality/recreation, office technology, sales/distribution. **Computer sciences:** Data processing. **Family/consumer sciences:** Institutional food production. **Health:** Clinical lab technology, dental assistant, dental hygiene, EMT paramedic, licensed practical nurse, medical assistant, medical radiologic technology/radiation therapy, nursing (RN), nursing assistant, occupational therapy assistant, physical therapy assistant, physician assistant, respiratory therapy technology, sonography. **Legal studies:** Legal secretary, paralegal. **Liberal arts:** Arts/sciences. **Personal/culinary services:** Culinary arts.

**Most popular majors.** Business/marketing 30%, computer/information sciences 6%, health sciences 21%, liberal arts 38%.

**Computing on campus.** 150 workstations in library, computer center, student center. Commuter students can connect to campus network. Online course registration, online library, student web hosting, wireless network available.

**Student life. Freshman orientation:** Mandatory. 15 two-hour sessions, any one of which may be attended by a new student. **Housing:** Coed dorms available. Housing available through University of Hawaii system. **Activities:** Choral groups, dance, drama, literary magazine, music ensembles, student government, student newspaper, international students club, marketing association, music club, Phi Theta Kappa, nursing association, Japanese, Chinese and Korean club, Catholic Ministry Association, pre-engineering club.

**Student services.** Career counseling, services for economically disadvantaged, student employment services, financial aid counseling, minority student services, on-campus daycare, personal counseling, placement for graduates, veterans' counselor. **Physically disabled:** Services for visually, speech, hearing impaired.

**Contact.** E-mail: kapinfo@hawaii.edu
Phone: (808) 734-9555 Fax: (808) 734-9896
Sharon Fowler, Coordinator of Enrollment Services, University of Hawaii: Kapiolani Community College, 4303 Diamond Head Road, Honolulu, HI 96816-4421

## University of Hawaii: Kauai Community College
**Lihue, Hawaii**
**www.kauai.hawaii.edu**
**CB code: 4378**

◗ Public 2-year community college
◗ Commuter campus in small city

**General.** Founded in 1928. Regionally accredited. **Enrollment:** 201 degree-seeking undergraduates; 816 non-degree-seeking students. **Degrees:** 90 associate awarded. **Location:** 100 miles from Honolulu. **Calendar:** Semester, limited summer session. **Full-time faculty:** 70 total. **Part-time faculty:** 30 total. **Special facilities:** Botanical facilities.

**Student profile.** Among degree-seeking undergraduates, 201 enrolled as first-time, first-year students.

| Part-time: | 29% | Women: | 56% |
|---|---|---|---|
| Out-of-state: | 2% | | |

**Basis for selection.** Open admission, but selective for out-of-state students. Special requirements for out-of-state residents in nursing, electrical installation and maintenance technology, facilities engineering technology, nurse's aide, electronics technology programs, culinary arts.

**2007-2008 Annual costs.** Tuition/fees: $1,930; $7,720 out-of-state. Per-credit charge: $63 in-state; $256 out-of-state.

**Financial aid. Need-based:** Work-study available nights and for part-time students. **Additional information:** Hawaii student incentive grants and tuition waivers (merit and need-based) available to Hawaii residents.

**Application procedures. Admission:** Priority date 8/1; no deadline. Admission notification on a rolling basis beginning on or about 3/1. Institutional placement test. **Financial aid:** Priority date 4/1, closing date 5/1. FAFSA, institutional form required. Applicants notified on a rolling basis starting 5/1.

**Academics. Special study options:** Cooperative education, cross-registration, distance learning, ESL, internships, study abroad. Bachelor's degree programs available on campus. **Credit/placement by examination:** AP, CLEP, institutional tests. **Support services:** Learning center, tutoring, writing center.

**Majors. Business:** Accounting, hospitality admin, office/clerical. **Construction:** Carpentry, electrician. **Education:** Early childhood. **Engineering technology:** Electrical. **Health:** Nursing (RN). **Liberal arts:** Arts/sciences. **Mechanic/repair:** Auto body, automotive. **Personal/culinary services:** Culinary arts.

**Computing on campus.** 150 workstations in computer center.

**Student life. Freshman orientation:** Available. **Activities:** Concert band, choral groups, music ensembles, student government, international club, Hawaiian club, Pamantasan club, Hawaiian performing arts club, Japanese club, environmental club.

**Athletics. Intramural:** Basketball.

**Student services.** Adult student services, career counseling, student employment services, health services, on-campus daycare, personal counseling, placement for graduates, veterans' counselor. **Physically disabled:** Services for visually, speech, hearing impaired. **Transfer:** Transfer adviser, college fairs on campus for students transferring to 4-year colleges.

**Contact.** E-mail: arkauai@hawaii.edu
Phone: (808) 245-8225 Fax: (808) 245-8297
Leighton Oride, Admissions Officer and Registrar, University of Hawaii: Kauai Community College, 3-1901 Kaumualii Highway, Lihue, HI 96766-9500

## University of Hawaii: Leeward Community College
**Pearl City, Hawaii**
**www.lcc.hawaii.edu**                              CB code: 4410

▶ Public 2-year community college
▶ Commuter campus in large town

**General.** Founded in 1968. Regionally accredited. **Location:** 10 miles from Honolulu. **Calendar:** Semester.

**Annual costs/financial aid.** Tuition/fees (2007-2008): $1,925; $7,715 out-of-state. Books/supplies: $672. Personal expenses: $953. Need-based financial aid available to full-time and part-time students.

**Contact.** Phone: (808) 455-0217
Registrar, 96-045 Ala Ike, Pearl City, HI 96782

## University of Hawaii: Maui Community College
**Kahului, Hawaii**
**www.maui.hawaii.edu**                              CB code: 4510

▶ Public 2-year community college
▶ Commuter campus in small city

**General.** Founded in 1931. Regionally accredited. Branch campuses on Molokai, Lanai and Hana. **Enrollment:** 2,303 degree-seeking undergraduates; 471 non-degree-seeking students. **Degrees:** 240 associate awarded. **Location:** 150 miles from Honolulu. **Calendar:** Semester, limited summer session. **Full-time faculty:** 114 total. **Part-time faculty:** 4 total.

**Student profile.** Among degree-seeking undergraduates, 488 enrolled as first-time, first-year students.

| Part-time: | 56% | Women: | 65% |
|---|---|---|---|
| Out-of-state: | 1% | Live on campus: | 1% |

**Basis for selection.** Open admission, but selective for some programs. Special requirements for nursing program. Interview required of nursing majors.

**2007-2008 Annual costs.** Tuition/fees: $1,940; $9,650 out-of-state. Per-credit charge: $63 in-state; $320 out-of-state.

**2006-2007 Financial aid. Need-based:** 43% of total undergraduate aid awarded as scholarships/grants, 57% as loans/jobs. Need-based aid available for part-time students. Work-study available nights and for part-time students.

**Application procedures. Admission:** Priority date 7/31; no deadline. No application fee in-state; $25 out-of-state. Application may be submitted online. Admission notification on a rolling basis. **Financial aid:** Priority date 4/1; no closing date. FAFSA, institutional form required. Applicants notified on a rolling basis starting 6/1; must reply within 4 week(s) of notification.

**Academics. Special study options:** Cooperative education, distance learning, double major, dual enrollment of high school students, ESL, independent study, liberal arts/career combination, weekend college. **Credit/placement by examination:** CLEP, institutional tests. 30 credit hours maximum toward associate degree. **Support services:** Learning center, pre-admission summer program, reduced course load, remedial instruction, tutoring.

**Majors. Agriculture:** General. **Business:** General, accounting, tourism/travel. **Construction:** Carpentry. **Education:** Early childhood. **Engineering technology:** Drafting. **Family/consumer sciences:** Apparel marketing, food/nutrition. **Liberal arts:** Arts/sciences. **Mechanic/repair:** Auto body, automotive. **Personal/culinary services:** Food service. **Public administration:** Human services.

**Computing on campus.** Dormitories wired for high-speed internet access and linked to campus network. Commuter students can connect to campus network. Online course registration, helpline available.

**Student life. Freshman orientation:** Available. **Housing:** Coed dorms available. $160 deposit, deadline 6/1. **Activities:** Student government, student newspaper, TV station.

**Student services.** Career counseling, student employment services, health services, on-campus daycare, personal counseling, veterans' counselor. **Physically disabled:** Services for visually, speech, hearing impaired. **Transfer:** Transfer adviser for students transferring to 4-year colleges.

**Contact.** Phone: (808) 984-3500 Toll-free number: (800) 479-6692 Fax: (808) 242-9618
Stephen Kameda, Admissions Officer/Registrar, University of Hawaii: Maui Community College, 310 West Kaahumanu Avenue, Kahului, HI 96732-1617

## University of Hawaii: Windward Community College
**Kaneohe, Hawaii**
**www.wcc.hawaii.edu**                              CB code: 4976

▶ Public 2-year community college
▶ Commuter campus in small city

**General.** Founded in 1972. Regionally accredited. **Enrollment:** 1,761 degree-seeking undergraduates. **Degrees:** 123 associate awarded. **ROTC:** Army. **Location:** 10 miles from Honolulu. **Calendar:** Semester, limited summer session. **Full-time faculty:** 40 total. **Part-time faculty:** 32 total. **Special facilities:** Planetarium, greenhouse, observatory.

**Student profile.**

| Out-of-state: | 9% | 25 or older: | 38% |
|---|---|---|---|

**Basis for selection.** Open admission. Students under 18 must have high school diploma. **Adult students:** SAT/ACT scores not required.

Two-Year Colleges

**2007-2008 Annual costs.** Tuition/fees: $1,930; $7,720 out-of-state. Per-credit charge: $63 in-state; $256 out-of-state. Books/supplies: $987. Personal expenses: $1,730.

**Financial aid. Need-based:** Need-based aid available for part-time students. **Additional information:** Hawaii student incentive grants and tuition waivers (merit and need-based) available to Hawaii residents.

**Application procedures. Admission:** Priority date 8/1; no deadline. No application fee in-state; $25 out-of-state. Admission notification on a rolling basis. Out-of-state military dependents not required to pay application fee. **Financial aid:** Priority date 4/1; no closing date. FAFSA required. Applicants notified on a rolling basis starting 3/15; must reply within 2 week(s) of notification.

**Academics. Special study options:** Cooperative education, distance learning, double major, dual enrollment of high school students, independent study, internships, student-designed major. **Credit/placement by examination:** CLEP, institutional tests. **Support services:** Learning center, reduced course load, remedial instruction, study skills assistance, tutoring.

**Majors. Liberal arts:** Arts/sciences.

**Computing on campus.** 30 workstations in library, computer center, student center. Commuter students can connect to campus network. Online course registration, helpline, wireless network available.

**Student life. Freshman orientation:** Mandatory. Preregistration for classes offered. **Activities:** Choral groups, drama, student government, student newspaper.

**Student services.** Adult student services, career counseling, services for economically disadvantaged, student employment services, financial aid counseling, minority student services, personal counseling, placement for graduates, veterans' counselor. **Transfer:** Pre-admission transcript evaluation for new students. Transfer adviser, college fairs on campus for students transferring to 4-year colleges.

**Contact.** E-mail: wccinfo@hawaii.edu
Phone: (808) 235-7432 Fax: (808) 235-9148
Geri Imai, Registrar, University of Hawaii: Windward Community College, 45-720 Kea'ahala Road, Kaneohe, HI 96744

# Idaho

## College of Southern Idaho
### Twin Falls, Idaho
**www.csi.edu**        CB code: 4114

▶ Public 2-year community and junior college
▶ Commuter campus in large town

**General.** Founded in 1964. Regionally accredited. **Enrollment:** 5,227 degree-seeking undergraduates. **Degrees:** 651 associate awarded. **Location:** 130 miles from Boise. **Calendar:** Semester, limited summer session. **Full-time faculty:** 239 total. **Part-time faculty:** 261 total. **Special facilities:** Museum and planetarium including anthropology, archeology, fine arts collections.

**Student profile.**

| | | | |
|---|---|---|---|
| Out-of-state: | 5% | Live on campus: | 5% |
| 25 or older: | 52% | | |

**Transfer out. Colleges most students transferred to 2007:** Boise State University, University of Idaho, Idaho State University, Utah State University, Albertsons College.

**Basis for selection.** Open admission, but selective for some programs. For applicants to registered nursing program, ACT recommended; letters of reference, letter of intent, special tests required. Interview required of registered nursing, technical majors.

**2007-2008 Annual costs.** Tuition/fees: $2,100; $5,900 out-of-state. Per-credit charge: $105 in-state; $295 out-of-state. Room/board: $4,630. Books/supplies: $990. Personal expenses: $1,900.

**Financial aid. Need-based:** Need-based aid available for part-time students. **Additional information:** Out-of-state tuition waivers based on GPA and activities.

**Application procedures. Admission:** No deadline. No application fee. Application may be submitted online. Admission notification on a rolling basis. **Financial aid:** Priority date 3/1; no closing date. FAFSA required. Applicants notified on a rolling basis starting 4/30; must reply within 3 week(s) of notification.

**Academics. Special study options:** Distance learning, dual enrollment of high school students, ESL, honors. License preparation in real estate. **Credit/placement by examination:** AP, CLEP. 21 credit hours maximum toward associate degree. **Support services:** GED preparation and test center, learning center, reduced course load, remedial instruction, study skills assistance, tutoring, writing center.

**Majors. Agriculture:** Aquaculture, business, equestrian studies, horticultural science, range science. **Biology:** General. **Business:** General, accounting, hospitality/recreation, real estate, tourism promotion. **Communications:** General. **Computer sciences:** Computer graphics, computer science, LAN/WAN management. **Conservation:** General, forestry, water/wetlands/marine, wildlife. **Education:** Bilingual, early childhood, elementary, physical, secondary. **Engineering:** Civil, computer, electrical. **Engineering technology:** Computer systems, drafting. **English:** English lit. **Foreign languages:** General, sign language interpretation. **Health:** Dental hygiene, EMT paramedic, nursing (RN), pharmacy assistant, predental, premedicine, prepharmacy, preveterinary, respiratory therapy technology, veterinary technology/assistant. **History:** General. **Interdisciplinary:** Natural sciences. **Legal studies:** Prelaw. **Liberal arts:** Arts/sciences, library science. **Math:** General. **Mechanic/repair:** Auto body, automotive, diesel, heating/ac/refrig. **Parks/recreation:** Health/fitness. **Personal/culinary services:** Culinary arts. **Physical sciences:** Chemistry, geology, physics. **Production:** Welding, woodworking. **Protective services:** Fire safety technology, law enforcement admin. **Psychology:** General. **Public administration:** Human services. **Social sciences:** Anthropology, economics, geography, political science, sociology. **Visual/performing arts:** Art, commercial/advertising art, dramatic, photography.

**Computing on campus.** 350 workstations in dormitories, library, computer center, student center. Dormitories wired for high-speed internet access and linked to campus network. Commuter students can connect to campus network. Online course registration, online library, helpline, student web hosting, wireless network available.

**Student life. Housing:** Coed dorms, apartments, substance-free housing available. $100 fully refundable deposit. **Activities:** Pep band, campus ministries, choral groups, drama, international student organizations, student government, student newspaper, Christian Fellowship, Latter-day Saints student association, Ambassadors, Latinos Unidos, Golden Eagle Native Americans, Chi Alpha, accent club.

**Athletics.** NJCAA. **Intercollegiate:** Baseball M, basketball, equestrian, rodeo, softball, volleyball W. **Intramural:** Basketball, bowling, football (non-tackle), golf, racquetball, soccer, softball, tennis, volleyball. **Team name:** Eagles.

**Student services.** Adult student services, alcohol/substance abuse counseling, career counseling, student employment services, financial aid counseling, health services, minority student services, on-campus daycare, personal counseling, veterans' counselor. **Physically disabled:** Services for visually, hearing impaired. **Transfer:** Re-entry adviser, pre-admission transcript evaluation for new students. College fairs on campus for students transferring to 4-year colleges.

**Contact.** Phone: (208) 732-6792 Fax: (208) 736-3014
Gail Schull, Director of Admissions, College of Southern Idaho, Box 1238, Twin Falls, ID 83303-1238

## Eastern Idaho Technical College
### Idaho Falls, Idaho
**www.eitc.edu**        CB code: 0975

▶ Public 2-year technical college
▶ Commuter campus in small city

**General.** Founded in 1969. Regionally accredited. **Enrollment:** 647 degree-seeking undergraduates; 115 non-degree-seeking students. **Degrees:** 79 associate awarded. **Location:** 280 miles from Boise, 230 miles from Salt Lake City. **Calendar:** Semester, limited summer session. **Full-time faculty:** 43 total; 58% women. **Part-time faculty:** 93 total; 56% women. **Class size:** 78% < 20, 21% 20-39, 2% 40-49. **Partnerships:** Customized work-force training and Tech Prep agreements available. Professional technical high school programs for 7 area high schools taught on campus.

**Student profile.** Among degree-seeking undergraduates, 94 enrolled as first-time, first-year students.

| | | | |
|---|---|---|---|
| Part-time: | 68% | Women: | 68% |

**Transfer out. Colleges most students transferred to 2007:** Idaho State University, Brigham Young University-Idaho, University of Idaho, Boise State University.

**Basis for selection.** Open admission, but selective for some programs. Entrance exam, essay required for nursing. COMPASS required of all applicants. Students who score below acceptable level must take developmental classes before enrolling in degree program.

**High school preparation.** Recommended units include English 8, mathematics 6 and science 6.

**2007-2008 Annual costs.** Tuition/fees: $1,758; $6,112 out-of-state. Per-credit charge: $82 in-state; $164 out-of-state. Fees may vary according to the program of study. Books/supplies: $808. Personal expenses: $1,316.

**Financial aid. Need-based:** Need-based aid available for part-time students. Work-study available for part-time students. **Non-need-based:** Scholarships awarded for academics, job skills, state residency.

**Application procedures. Admission:** Closing date 8/20 (receipt date). $10 fee, may be waived for applicants with need. Application must be submitted on paper. Admission notification on a rolling basis. **Financial aid:** Priority date 6/1; no closing date. FAFSA, institutional form required. Applicants notified on a rolling basis starting 6/6; must reply within 4 week(s) of notification.

**Academics. Special study options:** Distance learning, dual enrollment of high school students, ESL, internships, weekend college. License preparation in nursing, real estate. **Credit/placement by examination:** AP, CLEP. **Support services:** GED preparation and test center, learning center, pre-admission summer program, reduced course load, remedial instruction, study skills assistance, tutoring, writing center.

**Majors. Business:** Accounting, administrative services, marketing. **Computer sciences:** Networking, web page design. **Health:** Medical assistant, nursing (RN), surgical technology. **Legal studies:** Paralegal. **Mechanic/repair:** General, automotive, diesel. **Production:** Welding. **Protective services:** Firefighting.

**Most popular majors.** Business/marketing 20%, computer/information sciences 23%, engineering/engineering technologies 8%, health sciences 35%, trade and industry 11%.

**Computing on campus.** 209 workstations in library, computer center. Online library available.

**Student life. Freshman orientation:** Mandatory. Preregistration for classes offered. **Activities:** Student government.

**Student services.** Adult student services, alcohol/substance abuse counseling, career counseling, student employment services, financial aid counseling, personal counseling, placement for graduates, veterans' counselor, women's services. **Physically disabled:** Services for visually, speech, hearing impaired. **Transfer:** Transfer adviser for students transferring to 4-year colleges.

**Contact.**   E-mail: JMeldrum@eitc.edu
Phone: (208) 524-3000 ext. 3337 Toll-free number: (800) 662-0261
Fax: (208) 525-7026
Jason Meldrum, Director of Admissions and Career Placement, Eastern Idaho Technical College, 1600 South 25th East, Idaho Falls, ID 83404-5788

## North Idaho College
**Coeur d'Alene, Idaho**
www.nic.edu

**CB member**
**CB code: 4539**

- Public 2-year community college
- Commuter campus in large town

**General.** Founded in 1933. Regionally accredited. **Enrollment:** 3,789 degree-seeking undergraduates; 411 non-degree-seeking students. **Degrees:** 447 associate awarded. **Location:** 30 miles from Spokane, Washington. **Calendar:** Semester, limited summer session. **Full-time faculty:** 150 total; 7% have terminal degrees, 3% minority, 53% women. **Part-time faculty:** 169 total; 7% have terminal degrees, 6% minority, 48% women. **Partnerships:** Formal partnerships with local businesses.

**Student profile.** Among degree-seeking undergraduates, 1,032 enrolled as first-time, first-year students.

| | | | |
|---|---|---|---|
| Part-time: | 37% | Asian American: | 1% |
| Women: | 62% | Hispanic American: | 2% |
| African American: | 1% | Native American: | 2% |

**Transfer out. Colleges most students transferred to 2007:** University of Idaho, Lewis-Clark State College, Boise State University, Eastern Washington University, Spokane Community College.

**Basis for selection.** Open admission, but selective for some programs. RN, LPN and other allied health program applicants must submit 3 references and supplemental statement. Professional technical applicants should be interviewed by counselor. ACT, SAT, or COMPASS used for placement; scores must not be more than 2 years old. TOEFL scores used for placement of international students. Interview recommended for professional technical majors. **Homeschooled:** GED highly recommended. **Learning Disabled:** Contact Disability Support Services at time of application.

**High school preparation.** Recommended units include English 4, mathematics 3, social studies 2, science 3 (laboratory 1). Algebra, biology, 2 years chemistry with laboratory, or 1 year chemistry and 1 year physics, with cumulative 2.50 GPA required for registered nursing applicants. Physics, advanced algebra recommended for nursing applicants.

**2007-2008 Annual costs.** Tuition/fees: $2,110; $3,110 out-of-district; $7,478 out-of-state. Per-credit charge: $141 in-district; $204 out-of-district; $426 out-of-state. Room/board: $5,620. Books/supplies: $700. Personal expenses: $926.

**2006-2007 Financial aid. Need-based:** 59% of total undergraduate aid awarded as scholarships/grants, 41% as loans/jobs. Need-based aid available for part-time students. Work-study available weekends and for part-time students. **Non-need-based:** Scholarships awarded for academics, art, athletics, leadership, minority status, music/drama, state residency.

**Application procedures. Admission:** No deadline. $25 fee, may be waived for applicants with need. Application may be submitted online. Admission notification on a rolling basis beginning on or about 1/1. **Financial aid:** Priority date 3/15; no closing date. FAFSA required. Applicants notified on a rolling basis starting 4/1; must reply within 2 week(s) of notification.

**Academics. Special study options:** Cooperative education, distance learning, double major, dual enrollment of high school students, ESL, independent study, internships, liberal arts/career combination, semester at sea. Lewis

Clark State College and University of Idaho upper division and graduate classes on campus. Bachelor's degree programs available on campus. License preparation in nursing. **Credit/placement by examination:** CLEP, SAT, ACT, institutional tests. 24 credit hours maximum toward associate degree. **Support services:** GED preparation and test center, learning center, reduced course load, remedial instruction, study skills assistance, tutoring, writing center.

**Majors. Area/ethnic studies:** Native American. **Biology:** General, botany, zoology. **Business:** Administrative services, business admin. **Communications:** General, journalism, public relations. **Computer sciences:** General, applications programming, programming. **Conservation:** Fisheries, forestry, wildlife. **Construction:** Carpentry. **Education:** General, business, early childhood, elementary, secondary. **Engineering:** General, chemical, civil, electrical. **Engineering technology:** Drafting. **English:** English lit. **Foreign languages:** General. **Health:** Clinical lab assistant, health services, medical assistant, medical secretary, medical transcription, mental health services, nursing (RN), pharmacy assistant, physical therapy assistant, predental, premedicine, prepharmacy, preveterinary. **History:** General. **Legal studies:** Legal secretary, prelaw. **Liberal arts:** Arts/sciences. **Math:** General. **Mechanic/repair:** Auto body, automotive, diesel, heating/ac/refrig, industrial. **Parks/recreation:** Health/fitness. **Philosophy/religion:** Philosophy. **Physical sciences:** Astronomy, chemistry, geology, physics. **Protective services:** Criminal justice, police science. **Psychology:** General. **Public administration:** Human services. **Social sciences:** General, anthropology, political science, sociology. **Visual/performing arts:** Commercial/advertising art, music performance, music theory/composition, studio arts.

**Most popular majors.** Business/marketing 11%, education 7%, health sciences 17%, liberal arts 39%.

**Computing on campus.** 150 workstations in dormitories, library, computer center, student center. Dormitories wired for high-speed internet access and linked to campus network. Commuter students can connect to campus network. Online course registration, helpline, repair service, wireless network available.

**Student life. Freshman orientation:** Available. **Housing:** Coed dorms, special housing for disabled available. $150 deposit, deadline 6/1. Apartment complex adjacent to campus available. **Activities:** Bands, campus ministries, choral groups, dance, drama, international student organizations, literary magazine, music ensembles, musical theater, student government, student newspaper, symphony orchestra, Students for Human Equality, creative writers club, nursing student association, veterans club.

**Athletics.** NJCAA. **Intercollegiate:** Basketball, cheerleading, soccer, softball W, volleyball W, wrestling M. **Intramural:** Basketball, bowling, football (non-tackle), golf, softball, table tennis, tennis, volleyball. **Team name:** Cardinals.

**Student services.** Adult student services, alcohol/substance abuse counseling, career counseling, services for economically disadvantaged, student employment services, financial aid counseling, health services, legal services, minority student services, on-campus daycare, personal counseling, placement for graduates, veterans' counselor, women's services. **Physically disabled:** Services for visually, speech, hearing impaired. **Transfer:** Transfer adviser, college fairs on campus for students transferring to 4-year colleges.

**Contact.**   E-mail: admit@nic.edu
Phone: (208) 769-3311 Toll-free number: (877) 404-4536
Fax: (208) 769-3399
Maxine Gish, Director of Admissions, North Idaho College, 1000 West Garden Avenue, Coeur d'Alene, ID 83814-2199

## Stevens-Henager College: Boise
**Boise, Idaho**
www.stevenshenager.edu/shc/campus/boise.cfm

- For-profit 2-year technical and career college
- Commuter campus in small city
- Application essay, interview required

**General.** Accredited by ACCSCT. **Enrollment:** 318 degree-seeking undergraduates. **Degrees:** 18 bachelor's, 35 associate awarded. **Calendar:** Continuous, extensive summer session. **Full-time faculty:** 8 total; 25% have terminal degrees, 25% women. **Part-time faculty:** 26 total; 38% have terminal degrees, 15% minority, 54% women.

**Student profile.** Among degree-seeking undergraduates, 100% enrolled in a vocational program, 36 transferred in from other institutions.

**Transfer out.** 15% of students enrolled in the transfer program go on to 4-year colleges.

**Basis for selection.** Open admission, but selective for some programs. All applicants must complete a personal interview and submit a personal statement. **Adult students:** SAT/ACT scores not required. **Homeschooled:** Transcript of courses and grades, state high school equivalency certificate, interview required.

**2007-2008 Annual costs.** Tuition/fees: $16,350. Tuition and fees can vary by program.

**Application procedures. Admission:** No deadline. No application fee. Application must be submitted on paper. Admission notification on a rolling basis.

**Academics. Special study options:** Accelerated study, combined bachelor's/graduate degree, distance learning, external degree, liberal arts/career combination, study abroad. Bachelor's degree programs available on campus. **Credit/placement by examination:** CLEP. **Support services:** Study skills assistance, tutoring.

**Majors. Business:** Accounting, business admin. **Health:** Office assistant. **Visual/performing arts:** Graphic design.

**Computing on campus.** 35 workstations in computer center. Commuter students can connect to campus network. Online library, wireless network available.

**Student life. Freshman orientation:** Mandatory.

**Student services.** Adult student services, career counseling, financial aid counseling.

**Contact.** E-mail: jaime.davis@stevenshenager.edu
Phone: (208) 283-5134 Fax: (208) 345-6999
David Breck, Director of Admissions, Stevens-Henager College: Boise, 1444 S Entertainment Avenue, Boise, ID 83709

# Illinois

## Black Hawk College
Moline, Illinois
www.bhc.edu                                    CB code: 1483

▶ Public 2-year community college
▶ Commuter campus in large town

**General.** Founded in 1946. Regionally accredited. **Enrollment:** 4,801 degree-seeking undergraduates; 1,512 non-degree-seeking students. **Degrees:** 607 associate awarded. **Location:** 160 miles from Chicago, 60 miles from Iowa City. **Calendar:** Semester, limited summer session. **Full-time faculty:** 140 total; 16% have terminal degrees, 9% minority, 51% women. **Part-time faculty:** 186 total; 10% have terminal degrees, 6% minority, 54% women. **Class size:** 54% < 20, 44% 20-39, less than 1% 40-49, less than 1% 50-99.

**Student profile.** Among degree-seeking undergraduates, 57% enrolled in a transfer program, 42% enrolled in a vocational program, 4% already have a bachelor's degree or higher, 910 enrolled as first-time, first-year students, 1,949 transferred in from other institutions.

| | | | |
|---|---|---|---|
| Part-time: | 44% | Asian American: | 1% |
| Out-of-state: | 5% | Hispanic American: | 7% |
| Women: | 61% | 25 or older: | 39% |
| African American: | 9% | | |

**Transfer out.** 68% of students enrolled in the transfer program go on to 4-year colleges. **Colleges most students transferred to 2007:** Western Illinois University, Illinois State University, St. Ambrose University, Northern Illinois University, Augustana College.

**Basis for selection.** Open admission, but selective for some programs. Special requirements for health care-related programs, such as nursing and physical therapy assistant. Applicants must submit ACT for course placement.

**High school preparation.** 15 units recommended. Recommended units include English 4, mathematics 3, social studies 3, science 3, foreign language 2 and visual/performing arts 2.

**2007-2008 Annual costs.** Tuition/fees: $2,430; $4,650 out-of-district; $8,220 out-of-state. Per-credit charge: $74 in-district; $148 out-of-district; $267 out-of-state. Agreement with 5 contiguous Iowa counties for special tuition rate of $108 per credit plus required fees of $210. $88 per-credit-hour charge for on-line classes. Books/supplies: $950. Personal expenses: $3,750.

**2006-2007 Financial aid. Need-based:** 638 full-time freshmen applied for aid; 425 were judged to have need; 374 of these received aid. Average need met was 76%. Average scholarship/grant was $2,032; average loan $1,421. 82% of total undergraduate aid awarded as scholarships/grants, 18% as loans/jobs. Need-based aid available for part-time students. Work-study available for part-time students. **Non-need-based:** Awarded to 381 full-time undergraduates, including 171 freshmen. Scholarships awarded for academics, art, athletics, leadership, music/drama, state residency. **Additional information:** 5/15 deadline for scholarships.

**Application procedures. Admission:** No deadline. No application fee. Application may be submitted online. Admission notification on a rolling basis beginning on or about 3/1. **Financial aid:** Priority date 5/15; no closing date. FAFSA required. Applicants notified on a rolling basis starting 5/1.

**Academics. Special study options:** Accelerated study, cooperative education, cross-registration, distance learning, dual enrollment of high school students, ESL, independent study, internships, study abroad, weekend college. License preparation in nursing, physical therapy. **Credit/placement by examination:** AP, CLEP, institutional tests. 30 credit hours maximum toward associate degree. Most CLEP credit awarded to students pursuing associate degree in liberal studies. **Support services:** GED preparation, learning center, reduced course load, remedial instruction, study skills assistance, tutoring.

**Majors. Agriculture:** Animal husbandry, business, crop production, equestrian studies, horticulture, mechanization, production. **Business:** Accounting, accounting technology, administrative services, banking/financial services, business admin, human resources, international, office management,

office technology, retailing, small business admin. **Communications technology:** Radio/tv. **Computer sciences:** Programming. **Construction:** Carpentry. **Education:** Early childhood, mathematics. **Engineering technology:** Civil, electromechanical, environmental, manufacturing, robotics. **English:** Technical writing. **Foreign languages:** Sign language interpretation. **Health:** Electroencephalograph technology, medical radiologic technology/radiation therapy, medical records technology, nursing (RN), physical therapy assistant. **Interdisciplinary:** Biological/physical sciences. **Legal studies:** Legal secretary, paralegal. **Liberal arts:** Arts/sciences. **Mechanic/repair:** Auto body, automotive, diesel, heating/ac/refrig. **Personal/culinary services:** Restaurant/catering. **Protective services:** Fire services admin, police science. **Visual/performing arts:** Design.

**Most popular majors.** Agriculture 7%, health sciences 19%, interdisciplinary studies 14%, liberal arts 48%.

**Computing on campus.** 822 workstations in library, computer center. Commuter students can connect to campus network. Online course registration available.

**Student life. Freshman orientation:** Available. Preregistration for classes offered. Most students required to attend orientation if enrolled in or accumulate 6 credit hours. **Activities:** Jazz band, choral groups, drama, international student organizations, music ensembles, student government, student newspaper, TV station, African-American student union, Alpha Beta Gamma, Association of Latin America, Brotherhood On Campus, College Democrats of America, College Republicans, Sisterhood On Campus, social action connection.

**Athletics.** NJCAA. **Intercollegiate:** Baseball M, basketball, golf M, softball W, volleyball W. **Team name:** Braves.

**Student services.** Career counseling, services for economically disadvantaged, student employment services, financial aid counseling, minority student services, on-campus daycare, personal counseling, placement for graduates, women's services. **Physically disabled:** Services for visually, speech, hearing impaired. **Transfer:** Transfer center, transfer adviser, college fairs on campus for students transferring to 4-year colleges.

**Contact.** Phone: (309) 796-5300 Fax: (309) 792-5976
Richard Vallandingham, Dean of Student Support Services, Black Hawk College, 6600 34th Avenue, Moline, IL 61265-5899

## Black Hawk College: East Campus
Kewanee, Illinois
www.bhc.edu                                    CB code: 0690

▶ Public 2-year community college
▶ Commuter campus in small town

**General.** Founded in 1967. Regionally accredited. **Enrollment:** 800 degree-seeking undergraduates. **Degrees:** 170 associate awarded. **Location:** 45 miles from Peoria. **Calendar:** Semester, extensive summer session. **Full-time faculty:** 24 total. **Part-time faculty:** 40 total.

**Transfer out. Colleges most students transferred to 2007:** Western Illinois University, Illinois State University, University of Illinois.

**Basis for selection.** Open admission, but selective for some programs. Special requirements for physical therapy assistant and nursing programs, limited enrollment in practical nursing and truck driving certificates. SAT or ACT may be used in lieu of placement exam. Interview required of nursing and physical therapy assistant majors.

**2007-2008 Annual costs.** Tuition/fees: $2,430; $4,650 out-of-district; $8,220 out-of-state. Per-credit charge: $74 in-district; $148 out-of-district; $267 out-of-state. Agreement with 5 contiguous Iowa counties for special tuition rate of $100 per credit plus required fees. Online courses are $88 (tuition only) per credit hour. Books/supplies: $600.

**Application procedures. Admission:** No deadline. No application fee. Admission notification on a rolling basis. **Financial aid:** Priority date 5/15; no closing date. FAFSA required. Applicants notified on a rolling basis; must reply within 2 week(s) of notification.

**Academics. Special study options:** Cooperative education, cross-registration, distance learning, double major, dual enrollment of high school students, independent study, internships, study abroad. **Credit/placement by examination:** CLEP, institutional tests. 40 credit hours maximum toward associate degree. **Support services:** GED preparation and test center, learning center, pre-admission summer program, reduced course load, remedial instruction, tutoring.

**Majors. Agriculture:** Business, equestrian studies, horticulture. **Biology:** General. **Business:** General, accounting, administrative services, office technology. **Communications:** Journalism, public relations. **Computer sciences:** General, data processing, programming. **Education:** Elementary, secondary. **English:** English lit. **Health:** Predental, premedicine, prepharmacy. **History:** General. **Interdisciplinary:** Natural sciences. **Legal studies:** Paralegal, prelaw. **Liberal arts:** Arts/sciences. **Math:** General. **Mechanic/repair:** Automotive. **Physical sciences:** Chemistry, planetary. **Psychology:** General. **Social sciences:** Anthropology, economics, political science, sociology. **Visual/performing arts:** Art.

**Computing on campus.** 101 workstations in computer center.

**Student life. Activities:** Student government.

**Athletics.** NJCAA. **Intercollegiate:** Basketball. **Team name:** Warriors/Lady Warriors.

**Student services.** Career counseling, student employment services, personal counseling, placement for graduates, veterans' counselor. **Physically disabled:** Services for visually, speech, hearing impaired. **Transfer:** Transfer adviser, college fairs on campus for students transferring to 4-year colleges.

**Contact.** E-mail: recruiter@bhc.edu
Phone: (309) 852-5671 ext. 6220 Toll-free
number: (800) 233-5671 ext. 6220 Fax: (309) 856-6005
Patricia Varner, Director of Educational Services, Black Hawk College: East Campus, 1501 State Highway 78, Kewanee, IL 61443-8630

## Carl Sandburg College
Galesburg, Illinois
www.sandburg.edu — CB code: 1982

- Public 2-year community college
- Commuter campus in large town

**General.** Founded in 1966. Regionally accredited. Branch center in Carthage, extension center in Bushnell. **Enrollment:** 2,124 degree-seeking undergraduates. **Degrees:** 304 associate awarded. **ROTC:** Army. **Location:** 200 miles from Chicago, 40 miles from Peoria. **Calendar:** Semester, limited summer session. **Full-time faculty:** 61 total. **Part-time faculty:** 129 total. **Special facilities:** Greenhouse, 22-acre agriculture experience plot.

**Student profile.**

| | | | |
|---|---|---|---|
| Out-of-state: | 1% | 25 or older: | 60% |

**Transfer out. Colleges most students transferred to 2007:** Western Illinois University, Illinois State University.

**Basis for selection.** Open admission, but selective for some programs. Special requirements for allied health programs. Interview recommended for radiologic technology, mortuary science, and physical therapy assistant majors.

**High school preparation.** 15 units recommended. Recommended units include English 4, mathematics 3, social studies 2, science 2 (laboratory 2) and academic electives 2.

**2007-2008 Annual costs.** Tuition/fees: $3,285; $4,635 out-of-district; $5,010 out-of-state. Books/supplies: $710. Personal expenses: $880.

**Financial aid. Need-based:** Work-study available for part-time students. **Non-need-based:** Scholarships awarded for academics, art, athletics.

**Application procedures. Admission:** No deadline. No application fee. Admission notification on a rolling basis. **Financial aid:** Priority date 5/1; no closing date. FAFSA, institutional form required. Applicants notified on a rolling basis starting 6/15; must reply within 2 week(s) of notification.

**Academics. Special study options:** Cross-registration, dual enrollment of high school students, ESL, honors, independent study, internships, student-designed major, study abroad. License preparation in dental hygiene, nursing, paramedic, radiology. **Credit/placement by examination:** AP, CLEP, institutional tests. 20 credit hours maximum toward associate degree. **Support services:** GED preparation and test center, learning center, remedial instruction, tutoring.

**Majors. Agriculture:** Business. **Business:** Accounting, administrative services, banking/financial services, business admin, operations. **Computer sciences:** General. **Engineering technology:** Drafting. **Family/consumer sciences:** Child care. **Health:** Nursing (RN). **Mechanic/repair:** Auto body. **Personal/culinary services:** Mortuary science. **Protective services:** Firefighting, law enforcement admin.

**Most popular majors.** Business/marketing 12%, health sciences 26%, liberal arts 45%.

**Computing on campus.** 69 workstations in library, computer center.

**Student life. Activities:** Bands, choral groups, drama, literary magazine, music ensembles, student government.

**Athletics.** NJCAA. **Intercollegiate:** Baseball M, basketball, softball W, volleyball W. **Team name:** Chargers.

**Student services.** Career counseling, student employment services, on-campus daycare, personal counseling, placement for graduates, veterans' counselor. **Physically disabled:** Services for visually, hearing impaired. **Transfer:** Transfer adviser, college fairs on campus for students transferring to 4-year colleges.

**Contact.** Phone: (309) 344-2518 Fax: (309) 344-3526
Carol Kreider, Director of Admissions and Records, Carl Sandburg College, 2400 Tom L. Wilson Boulevard, Galesburg, IL 61401

## City Colleges of Chicago: Harold Washington College
Chicago, Illinois
www.ccc.edu — CB code: 1089

- Public 2-year community college
- Commuter campus in very large city

**General.** Founded in 1962. Regionally accredited. **Enrollment:** 7,623 degree-seeking undergraduates. **Degrees:** 399 associate awarded. **Calendar:** Semester, limited summer session. **Full-time faculty:** 120 total; 53% women. **Part-time faculty:** 273 total; 53% women. **Partnerships:** Formal partnerships with McDonalds, Dominicks, Chicago public schools.

**Transfer out. Colleges most students transferred to 2007:** Chicago State University, Northeastern Illinois University, University of Illinois-Chicago, DePaul University, Roosevelt University.

**Basis for selection.** Open admission, but selective for some programs. Special requirements for physicians assistant and police programs. All incoming freshmen required to take placement tests.

**High school preparation.** 20 units required. Required units include English 4, mathematics 4, social studies 4, science 3 and academic electives 3. 2 additional units in foreign language, art, music, computer science, or other electives required.

**2007-2008 Annual costs.** Tuition/fees: $2,410; $5,949 out-of-district; $9,543 out-of-state. Per-credit charge: $72 in-district; $190 out-of-district; $310 out-of-state. Books/supplies: $600. Personal expenses: $1,761.

**Financial aid.** All financial aid based on need. Need-based aid available for part-time students. Work-study available nights and for part-time students.

**Application procedures. Admission:** No deadline. No application fee. Application may be submitted online. **Financial aid:** Priority date 5/1, closing date 6/30. FAFSA required. Applicants notified on a rolling basis starting 7/1; must reply within 2 week(s) of notification.

**Academics. Special study options:** Cooperative education, cross-registration, distance learning, double major, dual enrollment of high school students, ESL, honors, independent study, internships, liberal arts/career combination. Courses by videocassette at Chicago public libraries; offer license preparation in taxi, limousine, foodservice and sanitation, and substance abuse counseling. **Credit/placement by examination:** AP, CLEP, institutional tests. **Support services:** GED preparation, learning center, reduced course load, remedial instruction, study skills assistance, tutoring.

**Majors. Biology:** General. **Business:** Accounting, administrative services, banking/financial services, business admin, hospitality admin, international, tourism/travel. **Communications:** Journalism. **Computer sciences:** General, data processing, information systems. **Education:** Early childhood, elementary, secondary, teacher assistance. **Engineering:** General. **English:** English lit, speech/rhetoric. **Family/consumer sciences:** Family studies. **Foreign languages:** General, French, German, Japanese, Spanish. **Health:** Predental, premedicine, prepharmacy, substance abuse counseling. **Legal studies:** General, prelaw. **Liberal arts:** Arts/sciences. **Math:** General. **Philosophy/religion:** Philosophy. **Physical sciences:** Chemistry, physics. **Protective services:** Corrections, firefighting, law enforcement admin, police science. **Public administration:** Social work. **Social sciences:** General. **Visual/performing arts:** Art, commercial/advertising art, design, dramatic.

**Most popular majors.** Business/marketing 9%, education 7%, health sciences 6%, liberal arts 66%.

**Computing on campus.** 180 workstations in computer center. Online library available.

**Student life. Freshman orientation:** Mandatory. Preregistration for classes offered. One hour overview. **Activities:** Jazz band, choral groups, drama, literary magazine, music ensembles, student government, student newspaper, black student union, Organization of Latin American Students, Berean Bible club, Circle K.

**Student services.** Adult student services, career counseling, services for economically disadvantaged, student employment services, financial aid counseling, minority student services, personal counseling, placement for graduates, veterans' counselor. **Physically disabled:** Services for visually, speech, hearing impaired. **Learning disabled:** Comprehensive services available. **Transfer:** Transfer adviser, college fairs on campus for students transferring to 4-year colleges.

**Contact.** Phone: (312) 553-6071 Fax: (312) 553-6077
Robert Brown, Registrar, City Colleges of Chicago: Harold Washington College, 30 East Lake Street, Chicago, IL 60601

## City Colleges of Chicago: Harry S. Truman College
### Chicago, Illinois
### www.ccc.edu
### CB code: 1111

- Public 2-year community college
- Commuter campus in very large city

**General.** Founded in 1956. Regionally accredited. **Enrollment:** 4,991 degree-seeking undergraduates. **Degrees:** 243 associate awarded. **Calendar:** Semester, limited summer session. **Full-time faculty:** 89 total; 53% women. **Part-time faculty:** 275 total; 57% women. **Special facilities:** Art gallery for Chicago artists, theater for performing arts. **Partnerships:** Formal partnerships with Chamber of Commerce and aldermanic representative for our ward.

**Transfer out. Colleges most students transferred to 2007:** University of Illinois, Loyola University of Chicago, Roosevelt University, Northeastern Illinois University.

**Basis for selection.** Open admission, but selective for some programs. Test scores, essay considered for nursing and certain allied health programs. Applicants without high school diploma must obtain GED prior to graduation. ACT required of nursing applicants.

**2007-2008 Annual costs.** Tuition/fees: $2,410; $5,949 out-of-district; $9,543 out-of-state. Per-credit charge: $72 in-district; $190 out-of-district; $310 out-of-state. Books/supplies: $800. Personal expenses: $1,530.

**Financial aid.** All financial aid based on need. Need-based aid available for part-time students. Work-study available nights and weekends.

**Application procedures. Admission:** No deadline. No application fee. Application may be submitted online. Admission notification on a rolling basis. **Financial aid:** No deadline. FAFSA required. Applicants notified on a rolling basis starting 7/1; must reply within 3 week(s) of notification.

**Academics. Special study options:** Cooperative education, cross-registration, dual enrollment of high school students, honors, independent study, internships, liberal arts/career combination, weekend college. License preparation in nursing. **Credit/placement by examination:** AP, CLEP, institutional tests. 30 credit hours maximum toward associate degree. **Support services:** GED preparation and test center, learning center, reduced course load, remedial instruction, tutoring.

**Majors. Business:** Business admin. **Computer sciences:** General. **Health:** Nursing (RN).

**Computing on campus.** 86 workstations in library, computer center.

**Student life. Freshman orientation:** Available. **Activities:** Drama, student government, student newspaper, TV station, Latin American center, refugee center, Native American center.

**Athletics.** NJCAA.

**Student services.** Adult student services, career counseling, student employment services, health services, on-campus daycare, personal counseling, placement for graduates, veterans' counselor. **Transfer:** Transfer adviser for students transferring to 4-year colleges.

**Contact.** Phone: (773) 907-6814 Fax: (773) 907-4757
Mylinh Tran, Registrar, City Colleges of Chicago: Harry S. Truman College, 1145 West Wilson Avenue, Chicago, IL 60640

## City Colleges of Chicago: Kennedy-King College
### Chicago, Illinois
### www.ccc.edu
### CB code: 1910

- Public 2-year community college
- Commuter campus in very large city

**General.** Founded in 1935. Regionally accredited. **Enrollment:** 4,245 degree-seeking undergraduates. **Degrees:** 241 associate awarded. **Calendar:** Semester, limited summer session. **Full-time faculty:** 64 total; 50% women. **Part-time faculty:** 124 total; 56% women. **Class size:** 19% < 20, 77% 20-39, 3% 40-49, less than 1% 50-99.

**Student profile.**

| Out-of-state: | 1% | 25 or older: | 65% |
|---|---|---|---|

**Transfer out. Colleges most students transferred to 2007:** University of Illinois at Chicago, Chicago State University.

**Basis for selection.** Open admission. Applicants admitted without high school diploma must pass GED by end of first school year.

**2007-2008 Annual costs.** Tuition/fees: $2,410; $5,949 out-of-district; $9,543 out-of-state. Per-credit charge: $72 in-district; $190 out-of-district; $310 out-of-state. Lab fees for technical and vocational courses. Books/supplies: $1,000. Personal expenses: $2,000.

**Financial aid.** All financial aid based on need. Need-based aid available for part-time students.

**Application procedures. Admission:** No deadline. No application fee. Application may be submitted online. **Financial aid:** Priority date 8/1; no closing date. FAFSA required. Applicants notified on a rolling basis starting 8/15; must reply within 2 week(s) of notification.

**Academics. Special study options:** Cooperative education, cross-registration, distance learning, dual enrollment of high school students, honors, independent study, internships, liberal arts/career combination, weekend college. License preparation in dental hygiene, nursing. **Credit/placement by examination:** AP, CLEP, institutional tests. 15 credit hours maximum toward associate degree. Interview recommended for placement and counseling. **Support services:** GED preparation, learning center, pre-admission summer program, reduced course load, remedial instruction, study skills assistance, tutoring, writing center.

**Majors. Area/ethnic studies:** African-American. **Business:** Accounting, administrative services, business admin. **Communications:** Broadcast journalism, journalism. **Communications technology:** Graphics, printing press operator. **Computer sciences:** General. **Education:** General, early childhood, elementary, middle, voc/tech. **Engineering technology:** Heat/ac/refrig. **English:** English lit. **Family/consumer sciences:** Child development. **Foreign languages:** General. **Health:** Dental hygiene, health services, nursing (RN), predental, premedicine, prepharmacy. **History:** General. **Legal studies:** Prelaw. **Liberal arts:** Arts/sciences. **Math:** General. **Mechanic/repair:** Automotive, heating/ac/refrig. **Physical sciences:** Chemistry, physics. **Psychology:** General. **Public administration:** Social work. **Social sciences:** General. **Visual/performing arts:** General, commercial/advertising art, dramatic, studio arts.

**Computing on campus.** 100 workstations in library, computer center.

**Student life. Freshman orientation:** Available. Preregistration for classes offered. **Activities:** Choral groups, drama, musical theater, radio station, student government, student newspaper, TV station, Phi Theta Kappa, Student Nursing Association, broadcasting club, math club, Future Teachers of Chicago.

**Athletics.** NJCAA. **Intercollegiate:** Basketball. **Intramural:** Basketball M, softball, swimming, volleyball. **Team name:** Statesman, Lady Statesman.

**Student services.** Adult student services, career counseling, student employment services, on-campus daycare, personal counseling, placement for graduates, veterans' counselor. **Physically disabled:** Services for visually, hearing impaired. **Transfer:** Re-entry adviser, pre-admission transcript evaluation for new students. Transfer center, transfer adviser, college fairs on campus for students transferring to 4-year colleges.

**Contact.** E-mail: wmurphy@ccc.edu
Phone: (773) 602-5273 Fax: (773) 602-5247
Marlene Sparrow, Registrar, City Colleges of Chicago: Kennedy-King
College, 6800 South Wentworth Avenue, Chicago, IL 60621

## City Colleges of Chicago: Malcolm X College
**Chicago, Illinois**
www.malcolmx.ccc.edu                CB code: 1144

- Public 2-year community and junior college
- Commuter campus in very large city

**General.** Founded in 1911. Regionally accredited. **Enrollment:** 3,554 degree-seeking undergraduates. **Degrees:** 304 associate awarded. **Location:** 3 miles from downtown. **Calendar:** Semester, limited summer session. **Full-time faculty:** 76 total; 51% women. **Part-time faculty:** 152 total; 50% women. **Class size:** 53% < 20, 47% 20-39. **Partnerships:** Formal partnerships with three middle and six high schools to provide TRIO Talent Search and Upward Bound programs.

**Student profile.**

| | | | |
|---|---|---|---|
| Out-of-state: | 1% | 25 or older: | 58% |

**Transfer out. Colleges most students transferred to 2007:** University of Illinois at Chicago, Chicago State University, Northeastern Illinois University, Robert Morris College, National-Louis University.

**Basis for selection.** Open admission, but selective for some programs. Interview recommended for nursing and allied health applicants. Adults out of high school 5 years or more may be concurrently registered while obtaining GED.

**2007-2008 Annual costs.** Tuition/fees: $2,410; $5,949 out-of-district; $9,543 out-of-state. Per-credit charge: $72 in-district; $190 out-of-district; $310 out-of-state. Some courses require a $20 lab fee. Books/supplies: $800.

**Financial aid.** All financial aid based on need. Need-based aid available for part-time students. Work-study available nights, weekends and for part-time students.

**Application procedures. Admission:** No deadline. No application fee. Admission notification on a rolling basis. **Financial aid:** Priority date 7/1; no closing date. FAFSA, institutional form required. Applicants notified on a rolling basis starting 7/1; must reply within 2 week(s) of notification.

**Academics. Special study options:** Cooperative education, cross-registration, distance learning, dual enrollment of high school students, ESL, internships, liberal arts/career combination, weekend college. License preparation in nursing, paramedic, radiology. **Credit/placement by examination:** AP, CLEP, institutional tests. 30 credit hours maximum toward associate degree. **Support services:** GED preparation, learning center, pre-admission summer program, reduced course load, remedial instruction, study skills assistance, tutoring.

**Majors. Agriculture:** Food science. **Biology:** General. **Business:** General, accounting, administrative services, business admin, office technology. **Education:** Teacher assistance. **Family/consumer sciences:** Child care, institutional food production. **Health:** Clinical lab technology, dialysis technology, EMT paramedic, medical radiologic technology/radiation therapy, nursing (RN), respiratory therapy technology, surgical technology. **Liberal arts:** Arts/sciences. **Personal/culinary services:** Culinary arts, mortuary science.

**Most popular majors.** Biological/life sciences 9%, health sciences 63%, liberal arts 25%.

**Computing on campus.** 275 workstations in library, computer center. Online course registration, online library, repair service, wireless network available.

**Student life. Freshman orientation:** Available. Preregistration for classes offered. **Activities:** Dance, drama, literary magazine, student government, student newspaper.

**Athletics.** NJCAA. **Intercollegiate:** Basketball, cheerleading M, track and field. **Intramural:** Basketball, cheerleading W, table tennis, track and field, volleyball. **Team name:** Hawks.

**Student services.** Adult student services, career counseling, student employment services, financial aid counseling, minority student services, on-campus daycare, personal counseling, placement for graduates, veterans' counselor. **Physically disabled:** Services for visually, speech, hearing impaired. **Learning disabled:** Comprehensive services available. **Transfer:**

Pre-admission transcript evaluation for new students. Transfer center, transfer adviser, college fairs on campus for students transferring to 4-year colleges.

**Contact.** E-mail: mmarsh@ccc.edu
Phone: (312) 850-7126 Fax: (312) 850-7092
Mary Marsh, Registrar, City Colleges of Chicago: Malcolm X College, 1900 West Van Buren Street, Chicago, IL 60612

## City Colleges of Chicago: Olive-Harvey College
**Chicago, Illinois**
www.ccc.edu                CB code: 1584

- Public 2-year community college
- Commuter campus in very large city

**General.** Founded in 1970. Regionally accredited. **Enrollment:** 2,278 degree-seeking undergraduates. **Degrees:** 240 associate awarded. **Location:** 16 miles from downtown. **Calendar:** Semester, limited summer session. **Full-time faculty:** 58 total; 57% women. **Part-time faculty:** 110 total; 48% women. **Special facilities:** Child development, high technology centers.

**Basis for selection.** Open admission, but selective for some programs. Special requirements for nursing, electronics, respiratory care, and local area networking programs.

**High school preparation.** 15 units recommended. Recommended units include English 4, mathematics 3, social studies 3, science 3 and foreign language 2.

**2007-2008 Annual costs.** Tuition/fees: $2,410; $5,949 out-of-district; $9,543 out-of-state. Per-credit charge: $72 in-district; $190 out-of-district; $310 out-of-state. Books/supplies: $600.

**Financial aid. Need-based:** Need-based aid available for part-time students.

**Application procedures. Admission:** No deadline. No application fee. Admission notification on a rolling basis. **Financial aid:** Priority date 8/15; no closing date. FAFSA required. Applicants notified on a rolling basis; must reply within 3 week(s) of notification.

**Academics. Special study options:** Cooperative education, cross-registration, distance learning, dual enrollment of high school students, honors, independent study, internships, student-designed major, study abroad. **Credit/placement by examination:** AP, CLEP, institutional tests. 30 credit hours maximum toward associate degree. **Support services:** Learning center, reduced course load, remedial instruction, tutoring.

**Majors. Area/ethnic studies:** African-American. **Biology:** General. **Business:** General, accounting, administrative services, business admin, management information systems. **Computer sciences:** General, data processing, programming. **Education:** Art. **Engineering:** General, architectural, electrical. **Family/consumer sciences:** Child care, child development. **Foreign languages:** General. **Legal studies:** General. **Liberal arts:** Arts/sciences. **Math:** General. **Philosophy/religion:** Philosophy. **Physical sciences:** Chemistry, physics, planetary. **Social sciences:** General. **Visual/performing arts:** Drawing, painting, photography, studio arts.

**Computing on campus.** 517 workstations in library, computer center.

**Student life. Activities:** Student government, student newspaper, African-American and Latino student groups.

**Athletics.** NJCAA. **Intercollegiate:** Basketball M, volleyball W. **Intramural:** Basketball, volleyball.

**Student services.** Adult student services, career counseling, student employment services, on-campus daycare, placement for graduates, veterans' counselor. **Transfer:** Transfer center, transfer adviser, college fairs on campus for students transferring to 4-year colleges.

**Contact.** Phone: (773) 291-6384 Fax: (773) 291-6185
Valerie Davis, Registrar, City Colleges of Chicago: Olive-Harvey College, 10001 South Woodlawn Avenue, Chicago, IL 60628

## City Colleges of Chicago: Richard J. Daley College
**Chicago, Illinois**
daley.ccc.edu                CB code: 1093

- Public 2-year community college
- Commuter campus in very large city

**General.** Founded in 1960. Regionally accredited. **Enrollment:** 4,015 degree-seeking undergraduates. **Degrees:** 383 associate awarded. **Calendar:** Semester, limited summer session. **Full-time faculty:** 59 total; 44% women. **Part-time faculty:** 221 total; 50% women.

**Basis for selection.** Open admission, but selective for some programs. Special requirements for nursing program.

**High school preparation.** 15 units recommended. Recommended units include English 4, mathematics 3, social studies 3, science 3 and academic electives 2.

**2007-2008 Annual costs.** Tuition/fees: $2,410; $5,949 out-of-district; $9,543 out-of-state. Per-credit charge: $72 in-district; $190 out-of-district; $310 out-of-state. Books/supplies: $800. Personal expenses: $320.

**Application procedures. Admission:** No deadline. No application fee. Admission notification on a rolling basis. **Financial aid:** No deadline. FAFSA required. Applicants notified on a rolling basis.

**Academics.** Cross-registration with other City Colleges of Chicago. **Special study options:** Cooperative education, cross-registration, distance learning, dual enrollment of high school students, honors, independent study, internships, weekend college. **Credit/placement by examination:** AP, CLEP, institutional tests. 30 credit hours maximum toward associate degree. **Support services:** Learning center, reduced course load, remedial instruction, tutoring.

**Majors. Business:** General. **Liberal arts:** Arts/sciences. **Social sciences:** General.

**Computing on campus.** 250 workstations in library, computer center.

**Student life. Activities:** Student government, student newspaper, TV station.

**Athletics.** NJCAA.

**Student services.** Adult student services, career counseling, student employment services, on-campus daycare, personal counseling, placement for graduates, veterans' counselor. **Physically disabled:** Services for visually, speech, hearing impaired. **Transfer:** Transfer adviser, college fairs on campus for students transferring to 4-year colleges.

**Contact.** Phone: (773) 838-7606 Fax: (773) 838-7605
Milton Wright, Registrar, City Colleges of Chicago: Richard J. Daley College, 7500 South Pulaski Road, Chicago, IL 60652

## City Colleges of Chicago: Wright College
**Chicago, Illinois**
www.ccc.edu
CB code: 1925

- Public 2-year community college
- Commuter campus in very large city

**General.** Founded in 1934. Regionally accredited. **Enrollment:** 7,013 degree-seeking undergraduates. **Degrees:** 451 associate awarded. **Location:** 15 miles from downtown. **Calendar:** Semester, limited summer session. **Full-time faculty:** 110 total; 52% women. **Part-time faculty:** 284 total; 52% women. **Class size:** 100% 20-39.

**Transfer out. Colleges most students transferred to 2007:** Northeastern Illinois University, University of Illinois at Chicago, DePaul University.

**Basis for selection.** Open admission.

**2007-2008 Annual costs.** Tuition/fees: $2,410; $5,949 out-of-district; $9,543 out-of-state. Per-credit charge: $72 in-district; $190 out-of-district; $310 out-of-state. Books/supplies: $630. Personal expenses: $1,280.

**Financial aid. Need-based:** Need-based aid available for part-time students. Work-study available nights, weekends and for part-time students.

**Application procedures. Admission:** No deadline. No application fee. Application may be submitted online. Admission notification on a rolling basis. **Financial aid:** Priority date 6/1; no closing date. FAFSA, institutional form required. Applicants notified on a rolling basis starting 7/15.

**Academics. Special study options:** Cross-registration, distance learning, dual enrollment of high school students, ESL, honors, independent study, internships, weekend college. License preparation in nursing, occupational therapy. **Credit/placement by examination:** AP, CLEP, IB, institutional tests. 10 credit hours maximum toward associate degree. **Support services:** GED preparation and test center, learning center, reduced course load, remedial instruction, tutoring.

**Majors. Business:** Accounting, administrative services, business admin, sales/distribution. **Computer sciences:** General, applications programming. **Engineering technology:** Mechanical drafting. **Health:** Licensed practical nurse, medical radiologic technology/radiation therapy, occupational therapy assistant, radiologic technology/medical imaging, sonography. **Interdisciplinary:** Gerontology. **Liberal arts:** Arts/sciences, library assistant. **Mechanic/repair:** Electronics/electrical. **Visual/performing arts:** Design.

**Computing on campus.** 534 workstations in computer center.

**Student life. Freshman orientation:** Available. Preregistration for classes offered. **Activities:** Concert band, choral groups, drama, film society, literary magazine, music ensembles, student government, student newspaper, symphony orchestra, Circle-K, service organization, honor society, various ethnic clubs.

**Athletics.** NJCAA. **Intercollegiate:** Basketball, wrestling M. **Team name:** Rams.

**Student services.** Adult student services, campus ministries, career counseling, student employment services, financial aid counseling, health services, legal services, on-campus daycare, personal counseling, placement for graduates, veterans' counselor. **Physically disabled:** Services for visually, speech, hearing impaired. **Transfer:** Transfer center, transfer adviser, college fairs on campus for students transferring to 4-year colleges.

**Contact.** E-mail: aaiello@ccc.edu
Phone: (773) 481-8259 Fax: (773) 481-8053
Linda Huertas, Registrar, City Colleges of Chicago: Wright College, 4300 North Narragansett Avenue, Chicago, IL 60634-4276

## College of DuPage
**Glen Ellyn, Illinois**
www.cod.edu
CB member
CB code: 1083

- Public 2-year community college
- Commuter campus in large town

**General.** Founded in 1966. Regionally accredited. Continuing Education division offers courses at more than 50 off-campus locations. Selected courses available through the Internet. Adult fast-track program for highly motivated, self-disciplined students 24 years and older. **Enrollment:** 21,988 degree-seeking undergraduates; 3,780 non-degree-seeking students. **Degrees:** 1,877 associate awarded. **Location:** 25 miles from Chicago. **Calendar:** Semester, extensive summer session. **Full-time faculty:** 307 total; 28% have terminal degrees, 12% minority, 54% women. **Part-time faculty:** 1,149 total; 11% have terminal degrees, 12% minority, 58% women. **Class size:** 37% < 20, 60% 20-39, 2% 40-49, less than 1% 50-99, less than 1% >100. **Special facilities:** Older adult institute, prairie-marsh nature preserve, arts center, community recreation center.

**Student profile.** Among degree-seeking undergraduates, 2,742 enrolled as first-time, first-year students.

| | | | |
|---|---|---|---|
| Part-time: | 59% | Asian American: | 11% |
| Women: | 55% | Hispanic American: | 9% |
| African American: | 7% | 25 or older: | 53% |

**Transfer out. Colleges most students transferred to 2007:** Northern Illinois University, Illinois State University, University of Illinois-Chicago, Elmhurst College, North Central College.

**Basis for selection.** Open admission, but selective for some programs. Special requirements for allied health programs.

**2008-2009 Annual costs.** Tuition/fees: $3,240; $8,880 out-of-district; $10,770 out-of-state. Per-credit charge: $88 in-district; $276 out-of-district; $339 out-of-state. Books/supplies: $1,370. Personal expenses: $1,435.

**2006-2007 Financial aid. Need-based:** 713 full-time freshmen applied for aid; 489 were judged to have need; 390 of these received aid. Average need met was 66%. Average scholarship/grant was $3,973; average loan $2,112. 55% of total undergraduate aid awarded as scholarships/grants, 45% as loans/jobs. Need-based aid available for part-time students. Work-study available nights, weekends and for part-time students. **Non-need-based:** Awarded to 105 full-time undergraduates, including 24 freshmen. Scholarships awarded for academics, art, leadership, minority status, music/drama, state residency.

**Application procedures. Admission:** No deadline. $10 fee, may be waived for applicants with need. Application may be submitted online. Admission notification on a rolling basis. **Financial aid:** Priority date 4/30; no closing date. FAFSA required. Applicants notified on a rolling basis starting 6/1; must reply within 2 week(s) of notification.

**Academics. Special study options:** Accelerated study, cooperative education, cross-registration, distance learning, double major, dual enrollment of high school students, ESL, honors, independent study, internships, student-designed major, study abroad, weekend college. License preparation in dental hygiene, nursing, paramedic, real estate. **Credit/placement by examination:** AP, CLEP, institutional tests. 65 credit hours maximum toward associate degree. **Support services:** GED preparation and test center, learning center, pre-admission summer program, reduced course load, remedial instruction, study skills assistance, tutoring, writing center.

**Majors. Agriculture:** Horticulture. **Business:** Accounting, accounting technology, administrative services, business admin, fashion, office management, real estate, sales/distribution, tourism promotion. **Communications technology:** General, graphic/printing. **Computer sciences:** Applications programming. **Construction:** Maintenance. **Engineering:** General. **Engineering technology:** Drafting, electrical, plastics, robotics. **Family/consumer sciences:** Child care. **Health:** Dental hygiene, EMT paramedic, medical radiologic technology/radiation therapy, medical records technology, nursing (RN), occupational therapy assistant, physical therapy assistant, respiratory therapy technology, substance abuse counseling, surgical technology. **Interdisciplinary:** Biological/physical sciences. **Legal studies:** Legal secretary. **Liberal arts:** Arts/sciences, library assistant. **Mechanic/repair:** Automotive, communications systems, electronics/electrical, heating/ac/refrig, industrial electronics. **Personal/culinary services:** Chef training, cosmetic, culinary arts, restaurant/catering. **Protective services:** Fire safety technology, police science. **Public administration:** Social work. **Visual/performing arts:** Art, commercial photography, design.

**Most popular majors.** Business/marketing 9%, health sciences 12%, interdisciplinary studies 7%, liberal arts 53%.

**Computing on campus.** 2,403 workstations in library, computer center. Commuter students can connect to campus network. Online library, helpline, repair service available.

**Student life. Freshman orientation:** Available. Includes campus tour and general session. **Housing:** Housing available in cooperation with nearby private college. **Activities:** Bands, choral groups, dance, drama, literary magazine, music ensembles, Model UN, opera, radio station, student government, student newspaper, symphony orchestra, InterVarsity Christian Fellowship, Endowment for Future Generations, Brothers and Sisters in Christ, black student union, Latino ethnic awareness association, Japanese culture club, La Rencontre Francaise, Muslim student association.

**Athletics.** NJCAA. **Intercollegiate:** Baseball M, basketball, cross-country, diving, football (tackle) M, golf M, soccer, softball W, swimming, tennis, track and field, volleyball W. **Intramural:** Basketball, bowling, diving, football (non-tackle), golf, racquetball, soccer, softball, swimming, tennis, volleyball, weight lifting. **Team name:** Chaparrels.

**Student services.** Adult student services, career counseling, services for economically disadvantaged, student employment services, financial aid counseling, health services, minority student services, on-campus daycare, personal counseling, placement for graduates. **Physically disabled:** Services for visually, speech, hearing impaired. **Transfer:** Transfer center, transfer adviser, college fairs on campus for students transferring to 4-year colleges.

**Contact.** E-mail: admissions@cod.edu
Phone: (630) 942-2482 Fax: (630) 790-2686
Amy Hauenstein, Coordinator of Admission Services; College of DuPage, 425 Fawell Boulevard, Glen Ellyn, IL 60137-6599

---

## College of Lake County
**Grayslake, Illinois**
www.clcillinois.edu

**CB member**
**CB code: 1983**

- Public 2-year community college
- Commuter campus in large town

**General.** Founded in 1967. Regionally accredited. **Enrollment:** 12,192 degree-seeking undergraduates; 3,818 non-degree-seeking students. **Degrees:** 831 associate awarded. **Location:** 40 miles from Chicago, 45 miles from Milwaukee. **Calendar:** Semester, extensive summer session. **Full-time faculty:** 182 total; 20% have terminal degrees, 21% minority, 52% women. **Part-time faculty:** 650 total; 9% have terminal degrees, 12% minority, 53% women. **Class size:** 41% < 20, 59% 20-39, less than 1% 50-99. **Special facilities:** CAD/CAM center, automated industrial center, performing arts center, child care center.

**Student profile.** Among degree-seeking undergraduates, 60% enrolled in a transfer program, 40% enrolled in a vocational program, 9% already have a bachelor's degree or higher, 1,876 enrolled as first-time, first-year students.

| | | | |
|---|---|---|---|
| Part-time: | 64% | Women: | 56% |
| Out-of-state: | 1% | 25 or older: | 47% |

**Transfer out. Colleges most students transferred to 2007:** Northern Illinois University, University of Wisconsin at Parkside, Northeastern Illinois University, Southern Illinois University, DePaul University.

**Basis for selection.** Open admission, but selective for some programs. Open admission for certificate and associate of applied science. College-preparatory high school program required for associate of arts and science. Selective admission for health career programs: academic record, class rank, test scores important; recommendations, interview considered. **Learning Disabled:** Accommodations provided when taking proficiency exams.

**High school preparation.** 15 units recommended. Recommended units include English 4, mathematics 3, social studies 3, (laboratory 3) and academic electives 2. 2 biology and 1 chemistry required for nursing program, mathematics for medical laboratory technician program, chemistry for radiology program. Recommended electives include foreign language, music, vocational education or art.

**2008-2009 Annual costs.** Tuition/fees (projected): $2,700; $6,450 out-of-district; $8,580 out-of-state. Per-credit charge: $76 in-district; $201 out-of-district; $272 out-of-state. Books/supplies: $1,200. Personal expenses: $1,240.

**Financial aid. Need-based:** Need-based aid available for part-time students. Work-study available nights and for part-time students. **Non-need-based:** Scholarships awarded for academics, alumni affiliation, art, athletics, leadership, minority status, music/drama.

**Application procedures. Admission:** No deadline. No application fee. Application may be submitted online. Admission notification on a rolling basis. Application deadlines vary for health career programs. **Financial aid:** Priority date 6/5; no closing date. FAFSA required. Applicants notified on a rolling basis starting 6/15; must reply within 2 week(s) of notification.

**Academics.** High school distribution requirement for associate degree applicants may be fulfilled at college. **Special study options:** Accelerated study, cooperative education, cross-registration, distance learning, dual enrollment of high school students, ESL, honors, independent study, internships, student-designed major, study abroad. License preparation in dental hygiene, nursing, paramedic, radiology, real estate. **Credit/placement by examination:** AP, CLEP, institutional tests. 30 credit hours maximum toward associate degree. **Support services:** GED preparation and test center, learning center, reduced course load, remedial instruction, study skills assistance, tutoring, writing center.

**Majors. Agriculture:** Landscaping, ornamental horticulture, turf management. **Business:** Accounting technology, administrative services, business admin, office technology. **Conservation:** Management/policy. **Construction:** Electrician. **Education:** Music. **Engineering:** General. **Engineering technology:** Civil, construction, electrical, mechanical. **English:** Technical writing. **Health:** Dental hygiene, medical radiologic technology/radiation therapy, nursing (RN), office admin, substance abuse counseling. **Interdisciplinary:** Biological/physical sciences. **Legal studies:** Paralegal. **Liberal arts:** Arts/sciences, library assistant. **Mechanic/repair:** Automotive, computer, heating/ac/refrig, industrial, industrial electronics. **Personal/culinary services:** Restaurant/catering. **Production:** Machine shop technology. **Protective services:** Fire safety technology, police science. **Public administration:** Social work. **Visual/performing arts:** Art.

**Most popular majors.** Biological/life sciences 9%, health sciences 17%, liberal arts 52%.

**Computing on campus.** 800 workstations in library, computer center. Online course registration, wireless network available.

**Student life. Freshman orientation:** Available. **Policies:** Alcohol-free campus, smoking allowed only outside the building. **Activities:** Bands, campus ministries, choral groups, dance, drama, literary magazine, music ensembles, musical theater, radio station, student government, student newspaper, 11 academic organizations, 6 ethnic organizations, 4 religious organizations, 6 health and fitness organizations.

**Athletics.** NJCAA. **Intercollegiate:** Baseball M, basketball, cross-country, golf, soccer, softball W, tennis, volleyball W. **Intramural:** Basketball, golf, soccer, table tennis, tennis, volleyball. **Team name:** Lancers.

**Student services.** Alcohol/substance abuse counseling, career counseling, services for economically disadvantaged, student employment services, financial aid counseling, health services, minority student services, on-campus daycare, personal counseling, placement for graduates, veterans' counselor, women's services. **Physically disabled:** Services for visually, speech, hearing impaired. **Transfer:** Re-entry adviser for new students. Transfer center, transfer adviser, college fairs on campus for students transferring to 4-year colleges.

**Contact.** E-mail: info@clcillinois.edu
Phone: (847) 543-2061 Fax: (847) 543-3061
Karen Hlavin, Director, College of Lake County, 19351 West Washington Street, Grayslake, IL 60030-1198

## College of Office Technology
### Chicago, Illinois
www.cot.edu
CB code: 3527

- For-profit 2-year business college
- Commuter campus in very large city

**General.** Accredited by ACICS. **Enrollment:** 368 degree-seeking undergraduates. **Degrees:** 8 associate awarded. **Calendar:** Continuous, limited summer session. **Full-time faculty:** 16 total; 38% have terminal degrees, 88% minority, 25% women. **Part-time faculty:** 12 total; 92% minority, 33% women.

**Student profile.**

| | | | |
|---|---|---|---|
| African American: | 40% | Hispanic American: | 40% |
| Asian American: | 20% | | |

**Basis for selection.** Open admission.

**2008-2009 Annual costs.** Tuition/fees (projected): $9,925. Personal expenses: $4,574.

**Financial aid.** All financial aid based on need. Need-based aid available for part-time students.

**Application procedures. Admission:** No deadline. $50 fee. Application must be submitted on paper. Admission notification on a rolling basis. **Financial aid:** No deadline. FAFSA required. Applicants notified on a rolling basis.

**Academics. Credit/placement by examination:** AP, CLEP. **Support services:** Tutoring.

**Majors. Computer sciences:** Data entry.

**Computing on campus.** 20 workstations in library.

**Student life. Freshman orientation:** Mandatory.

**Contact.** E-mail: info@cotedu.com
Phone: (773) 278-0042 Toll-free number: (800) 953-6161
Fax: (773) 278-0143
William Bolton, Director of Admissions, College of Office Technology, 1520 West Division Street, Chicago, IL 60622-3312

## Cooking & Hospitality Institute of Chicago
### Chicago, Illinois
www.chic.edu
CB code: 2564

- For-profit 2-year culinary school
- Commuter campus in very large city
- Interview required

**General.** Regionally accredited. Affiliated with Le Cordon Bleu. **Enrollment:** 1,002 degree-seeking undergraduates. **Degrees:** 507 associate awarded. **Location:** Downtown. **Calendar:** Continuous, extensive summer session. **Full-time faculty:** 30 total; 13% minority, 53% women. **Part-time faculty:** 33 total; 12% minority, 42% women. **Special facilities:** Student-run restaurant.

**Student profile.** Among degree-seeking undergraduates, 177 enrolled as first-time, first-year students.

| | | | |
|---|---|---|---|
| Part-time: | 2% | Asian American: | 5% |
| Out-of-state: | 26% | Hispanic American: | 17% |
| Women: | 42% | Native American: | 1% |
| African American: | 20% | 25 or older: | 40% |

**Basis for selection.** Open admission. **Homeschooled:** Portfolio required. **Learning Disabled:** Documentation of learning disability and special accommodations needed must be provided.

**2008-2009 Annual costs.** Tuition for associate of applied science in Le Cordon Bleu Culinary Arts: $39,950; associate of applied science in Le Cordon Bleu Patisserie and Baking: $38,500; certificate in Le Cordon Bleu Culinary Arts: $12,200. Books/supplies: $3,400. Personal expenses: $2,274.

**Financial aid. Need-based:** Need-based aid available for part-time students. Work-study available nights and for part-time students.

**Application procedures. Admission:** No deadline. $100 fee. Application may be submitted online. Admission notification on a rolling basis. **Financial aid:** No deadline. FAFSA, institutional form required. Applicants notified on a rolling basis.

**Academics.** All levels of developmental learning provided. **Special study options:** All programs contain an externship course.. **Credit/placement by examination:** AP, CLEP, SAT, ACT, institutional tests. 12 credit hours maximum toward associate degree. **Support services:** Learning center, remedial instruction, tutoring.

**Majors. Personal/culinary services:** Baking, chef training.

**Computing on campus.** 70 workstations in library, computer center, student center. Commuter students can connect to campus network. Online library, wireless network available.

**Student life. Freshman orientation:** Mandatory. **Activities:** Student newspaper.

**Student services.** Career counseling, student employment services, financial aid counseling, placement for graduates, veterans' counselor.

**Contact.** E-mail: chic@chicnet.org
Phone: (312) 944-0882 Toll-free number: (877) 828-7772
Fax: (312) 944-8557
Matthew Verratti, Vice President of Admissions and Marketing, Cooking & Hospitality Institute of Chicago, 361 West Chestnut, Chicago, IL 60610-3050

## Danville Area Community College
### Danville, Illinois
www.dacc.edu
CB code: 1160

- Public 2-year community college
- Commuter campus in large town

**General.** Founded in 1946. Regionally accredited. **Enrollment:** 2,285 degree-seeking undergraduates. **Degrees:** 204 associate awarded. **Location:** 150 miles from Chicago, 90 miles from Indianapolis. **Calendar:** Semester, limited summer session. **Full-time faculty:** 51 total. **Part-time faculty:** 103 total. **Class size:** 63% < 20, 35% 20-39, less than 1% 40-49, less than 1% 50-99.

**Student profile.**

| | | | |
|---|---|---|---|
| Out-of-state: | 7% | 25 or older: | 50% |

**Transfer out.** 29% of students enrolled in the transfer program go on to 4-year colleges.

**Basis for selection.** Open admission.

**High school preparation.** 15 units recommended. Recommended units include English 4, mathematics 3, social studies 2, science 2 and academic electives 2.

**2007-2008 Annual costs.** Tuition/fees: $2,340; $4,800 out-of-state. Per-credit charge: $68 in-state; $150 out-of-state. Books/supplies: $700. Personal expenses: $1,575.

**2006-2007 Financial aid. Need-based:** Average need met was 67%. Average scholarship/grant was $1,620; average loan $2,625. Need-based aid available for part-time students. Work-study available nights, weekends and for part-time students. **Non-need-based:** Scholarships awarded for academics, athletics, minority status.

**Application procedures. Admission:** No deadline. No application fee. Admission notification on a rolling basis. **Financial aid:** Priority date 7/1; no closing date. FAFSA, institutional form required. Applicants notified on a rolling basis starting 6/1.

**Academics. Special study options:** Distance learning, double major, dual enrollment of high school students, ESL, independent study, internships, liberal arts/career combination. License preparation in nursing, real estate. **Credit/placement by examination:** CLEP, institutional tests. 30 credit hours maximum toward associate degree. **Support services:** GED preparation and test center, learning center, remedial instruction, study skills assistance, tutoring, writing center.

**Majors. Agriculture:** Agribusiness operations, horticultural science. **Biology:** General. **Business:** Accounting, administrative services, finance, management information systems, tourism promotion. **Communications:** General, advertising, journalism. **Computer sciences:** General, information systems, programming. **Education:** General. **Engineering:** General. **Health:** Medical secretary, medical transcription, nursing (RN). **History:** General. **Legal studies:** Prelaw. **Liberal arts:** Arts/sciences. **Math:** General. **Mechanic/repair:** General, diesel, electronics/electrical, industrial. **Personal/culinary services:** Cosmetic. **Physical sciences:** Chemistry. **Protective services:** Law enforcement admin. **Psychology:** General. **Public administration:** Human services. **Social sciences:** Political science, sociology.

**Computing on campus.** 400 workstations in library, computer center, student center. Online course registration, helpline, repair service, wireless network available.

**Student life. Freshman orientation:** Mandatory. Preregistration for classes offered. **Activities:** Choral groups, student government, symphony orchestra, Fellowship of Christian Athletes, Black Student Association, Hispanic Student Association.

**Athletics.** NJCAA. **Intercollegiate:** Baseball M, basketball, cross-country, golf, soccer M, softball W, track and field, volleyball W. **Team name:** Jaguars.

**Student services.** Adult student services, career counseling, student employment services, health services, on-campus daycare, personal counseling, placement for graduates, veterans' counselor. **Physically disabled:** Services for visually, speech, hearing impaired. **Transfer:** Transfer adviser, college fairs on campus for students transferring to 4-year colleges.

**Contact.** Phone: (217) 443-8800 Fax: (217) 443-8560
Stacy Ehmen, Director of Admissions and Records, Danville Area Community College, 2000 East Main Street, Danville, IL 61832

---

## Elgin Community College
**Elgin, Illinois**
www.elgin.edu                                  CB code: 1203

◆  Public 2-year community college
◆  Commuter campus in small city

**General.** Founded in 1949. Regionally accredited. **Enrollment:** 6,589 degree-seeking undergraduates; 3,024 non-degree-seeking students. **Degrees:** 691 associate awarded. **Location:** 35 miles from Chicago. **Calendar:** Semester, extensive summer session. **Full-time faculty:** 119 total; 17% minority, 55% women. **Part-time faculty:** 365 total; 19% minority, 54% women. **Special facilities:** Greenhouse, business conference center, visual and performing arts center, culinary arts program, student-run gourmet restaurant.

**Student profile.** Among degree-seeking undergraduates, 84% enrolled in a transfer program, 16% enrolled in a vocational program, 5% already have a bachelor's degree or higher, 898 enrolled as first-time, first-year students.

| Part-time: | 57% | Asian American: | 8% |
|---|---|---|---|
| Women: | 55% | Hispanic American: | 18% |
| African American: | 5% | 25 or older: | 43% |

**Transfer out.** Colleges most students transferred to 2007: Northern Illinois University, Illinois State University, Southern Illinois University-Carbondale, University of Illinois, University of Illinois at Chicago.

**Basis for selection.** Open admission, but selective for some programs. Additional requirements for nursing and some health professions programs.

**2007-2008 Annual costs.** Tuition/fees: $2,740; $10,789 out-of-district; $13,127 out-of-state. Per-credit charge: $91 in-district; $359 out-of-district; $437 out-of-state. Books/supplies: $1,500. Personal expenses: $3,932.

**Financial aid. Need-based:** Need-based aid available for part-time students. Work-study available nights and weekends. **Non-need-based:** Scholarships awarded for academics, alumni affiliation, art, athletics, job skills, leadership, minority status, music/drama, religious affiliation, ROTC, state residency.

**Application procedures. Admission:** No deadline. No application fee. Application may be submitted online. Admission notification on a rolling basis. **Financial aid:** Priority date 5/15; no closing date. FAFSA, institutional form required. Applicants notified on a rolling basis starting 4/7; must reply within 3 week(s) of notification.

---

**Academics. Special study options:** Accelerated study, cooperative education, distance learning, double major, dual enrollment of high school students, ESL, honors, independent study, internships, study abroad, weekend college. Dual admission with selected 4-year schools. Bachelor's degree programs available on campus. License preparation in aviation, dental hygiene, nursing, paramedic, physical therapy, radiology, real estate. **Credit/placement by examination:** AP, CLEP, institutional tests. 30 credit hours maximum toward associate degree. **Support services:** GED preparation and test center, learning center, reduced course load, remedial instruction, study skills assistance, tutoring, writing center.

**Majors. Business:** Accounting, business admin, entrepreneurial studies, executive assistant, hotel/motel admin, marketing, retailing. **Computer sciences:** Computer graphics, data entry. **Education:** General, physical. **Engineering:** General. **Engineering technology:** CAD/CADD. **Health:** Clinical lab technology, nursing (RN), physical therapy assistant. **Interdisciplinary:** Biological/physical sciences. **Legal studies:** Legal secretary, paralegal. **Liberal arts:** Arts/sciences. **Math:** Applied. **Mechanic/repair:** Automotive, heating/ac/refrig, industrial. **Personal/culinary services:** Baking, chef training, restaurant/catering. **Production:** Machine tool. **Protective services:** Fire services admin, police science. **Public administration:** Social work. **Visual/performing arts:** Art, design, graphic design.

**Most popular majors.** Health sciences 16%, interdisciplinary studies 11%, liberal arts 52%.

**Computing on campus.** 800 workstations in library, computer center, student center. Wireless network available.

**Student life. Freshman orientation:** Mandatory. **Activities:** Bands, choral groups, drama, literary magazine, music ensembles, musical theater, student government, student newspaper, symphony orchestra, Phi Theta Kappa, Alpha Beta Gamma, Latin American organization, United Students of All Cultures, black student association, single parents student group, Advocacy for Disabled and Abled Persons Together, Amnesty International, gay/lesbian/bi-sexual, Earth First.

**Athletics.** NJCAA. **Intercollegiate:** Baseball M, basketball, cross-country, golf M, soccer, softball W, tennis, volleyball W. **Team name:** Spartans.

**Student services.** Adult student services, career counseling, services for economically disadvantaged, student employment services, financial aid counseling, minority student services, on-campus daycare, personal counseling, placement for graduates, veterans' counselor. **Physically disabled:** Services for visually, speech, hearing impaired. **Transfer:** Transfer center, transfer adviser, college fairs on campus for students transferring to 4-year colleges.

**Contact.** E-mail: admissions@elgin.edu
Phone: (847) 214-7385 Fax: (847) 608-5458
Mary Perkins, Associate Dean of Enrollment Management, Elgin Community College, 1700 Spartan Drive, Elgin, IL 60123-7193

---

## Fox College
**Oak Lawn, Illinois**
www.foxcollege.edu                             CB code: 2670

◆  For-profit 2-year junior and technical college
◆  Commuter campus in very large city

**General.** Accredited by ACICS. **Enrollment:** 473 undergraduates. **Degrees:** 68 associate awarded. **Calendar:** Semester. **Full-time faculty:** 10 total. **Part-time faculty:** 10 total.

**Basis for selection.** GED/High school academic record, writing sample, and interview considered.

**2007-2008 Annual costs.** Tuition/fees: $13,720. Additional lab fees for medical assistant and veterinary technician programs.

**Application procedures. Admission:** No deadline. $50 fee. **Financial aid:** No deadline.

**Academics. Credit/placement by examination:** CLEP.

**Majors. Business:** Accounting, administrative services. **Health:** Medical assistant, veterinary technology/assistant.

**Student services.** Career counseling, financial aid counseling, placement for graduates.

**Contact.** E-mail: admissions@foxcollege.edu
Phone: (708) 636-7700 Toll-free number: (708) 636-7700
Fax: (708) 636-8078
Fox College, 4201 West 93rd Street, Oak Lawn, IL 60453

## Harper College
**Palatine, Illinois**
www.harpercollege.edu

CB code: 1932

⬩ Public 2-year community college
⬩ Commuter campus in small city

**General.** Founded in 1965. Regionally accredited. Program for hearing-impaired offered. Bachelor completion program with Indiana University. **Enrollment:** 13,343 degree-seeking undergraduates; 1,813 non-degree-seeking students. **Degrees:** 1,297 associate awarded. **Location:** 30 miles from Chicago. **Calendar:** Semester, extensive summer session. **Full-time faculty:** 191 total; 92% have terminal degrees, 9% minority, 59% women. **Part-time faculty:** 643 total; 70% have terminal degrees, 5% minority, 50% women. **Class size:** 34% < 20, 50% 20-39, 12% 40-49, 3% 50-99, less than 1% >100. **Special facilities:** Observatory.

**Student profile.** Among degree-seeking undergraduates, 52% enrolled in a transfer program, 48% enrolled in a vocational program, 8% already have a bachelor's degree or higher, 2,761 enrolled as first-time, first-year students, 1,063 transferred in from other institutions.

| | | | |
|---|---|---|---|
| Part-time: | 52% | Asian American: | 12% |
| Out-of-state: | 1% | Hispanic American: | 10% |
| Women: | 56% | International: | 1% |
| African American: | 4% | 25 or older: | 37% |

**Transfer out. Colleges most students transferred to 2007:** Northern Illinois University, University of Illinois-Urbana, University of Illinois-Chicago, Illinois State University, Roosevelt University.

**Basis for selection.** Open admission, but selective for some programs. Selective admission to cardiac technology, dental hygiene, emergency medical technician, certified nursing assistant, electrocardiograph technology, emergency medical service paramedic, and diagnostic medical sonography. Prenursing examinations for nursing applicants. Critical thinking test for legal technology applicants. Assessment test battery for full-time students and for placement in English and math for part-time students.

**High school preparation.** 17 units recommended. Recommended units include English 4, mathematics 4, social studies 2 and science 2.

**2008-2009 Annual costs.** Tuition/fees: $3,234; $10,194 out-of-district; $12,504 out-of-state. Per-credit charge: $90 in-district; $322 out-of-district; $399 out-of-state. In-district tuition rates available to employees of in-district companies who reside outside college district. Books/supplies: $1,000. Personal expenses: $1,800.

**2006-2007 Financial aid. Need-based:** 78% of total undergraduate aid awarded as scholarships/grants, 22% as loans/jobs. Need-based aid available for part-time students. Work-study available nights and weekends. **Non-need-based:** Scholarships awarded for academics, art, leadership, minority status, music/drama, state residency.

**Application procedures. Admission:** No deadline. $25 fee, may be waived for applicants with need. Application may be submitted online. Admission notification on a rolling basis. Priority given to applications to nursing program received by December 1. Priority given to applications received by February 1 for all other limited-enrollment programs. **Financial aid:** Priority date 3/1; no closing date. FAFSA, institutional form required. Applicants notified on a rolling basis starting 3/1; must reply within 2 week(s) of notification.

**Academics.** Cooperative career program with in-district high schools. Students begin specialized training in high school and continue in colleges. Team-taught interdisciplinary courses and courseloads offered each semester. **Special study options:** Accelerated study, cooperative education, distance learning, dual enrollment of high school students, ESL, honors, independent study, internships, study abroad, weekend college. Bachelor's degree programs available on campus. License preparation in dental hygiene, nursing, paramedic, radiology, real estate. **Credit/placement by examination:** AP, CLEP, institutional tests. 30 credit hours maximum toward associate degree. Maximum of 50% total hours in any degree program may be earned through credit by examination. **Support services:** GED preparation and test center, learning center, pre-admission summer program, reduced course load, remedial instruction, study skills assistance, tutoring, writing center.

**Majors. Agriculture:** Horticulture, turf management. **Business:** Accounting technology, banking/financial services, business admin, executive assistant, fashion, fashion modeling, hospitality admin, hospitality/recreation, international, sales/distribution, selling, small business admin. **Communications technology:** Graphic/printing. **Computer sciences:** General, applications programming, computer forensics, computer science, data processing, information systems, programming, systems analysis, web page design. **Construction:** Maintenance. **Education:** Teacher assistance. **Engineering:** General. **Engineering technology:** Architectural drafting, electrical. **English:**

English lit. **Family/consumer sciences:** Fashion consultant, home furnishings. **Health:** Cardiovascular technology, dental hygiene, dietetic technician, EMT paramedic, medical secretary, nursing (RN), radiologic technology/medical imaging, sonography. **Legal studies:** Legal secretary, paralegal. **Liberal arts:** Arts/sciences. **Mechanic/repair:** Heating/ac/refrig. **Philosophy/religion:** Philosophy. **Physical sciences:** General. **Protective services:** Emergency management/homeland security, firefighting, police science. **Visual/performing arts:** Studio arts.

**Most popular majors.** Business/marketing 8%, health sciences 14%, liberal arts 64%.

**Computing on campus.** 1,724 workstations in library, computer center, student center. Online course registration, online library, wireless network available.

**Student life. Freshman orientation:** Mandatory. Preregistration for classes offered. Two-day program includes tour, assessment tests, academic advising, registration. Program is optional for part-time students, but still encouraged. **Activities:** Bands, campus ministries, choral groups, dance, drama, international student organizations, literary magazine, music ensembles, musical theater, radio station, student government, student newspaper, service organizations, professional organizations, student ambassadors.

**Athletics.** NJCAA. **Intercollegiate:** Baseball M, basketball, cross-country, football (tackle) M, soccer, softball W, track and field, volleyball W, wrestling M. **Intramural:** Baseball M, basketball M, football (non-tackle) M, racquetball, skiing, softball, table tennis, tennis, volleyball. **Team name:** Hawks.

**Student services.** Adult student services, career counseling, services for economically disadvantaged, student employment services, financial aid counseling, health services, legal services, minority student services, on-campus daycare, personal counseling, veterans' counselor, women's services. **Physically disabled:** Services for visually, speech, hearing impaired. **Transfer:** Transfer adviser, college fairs on campus for students transferring to 4-year colleges.

**Contact.** E-mail: admissions@harpercollege.edu
Phone: (847) 925-6707 Fax: (847) 925-6044
Robert Parzy, Director of Admissions Outreach, Harper College, 1200 West Algonquin Road, Palatine, IL 60067-7398

## Heartland Community College
**Normal, Illinois**
www.heartland.edu

CB code: 1361

⬩ Public 2-year community college
⬩ Commuter campus in small city

**General.** Regionally accredited. Green construction and technology employed in construction projects. **Enrollment:** 4,758 degree-seeking undergraduates; 67 non-degree-seeking students. **Degrees:** 566 associate awarded. **Calendar:** Semester, extensive summer session. **Full-time faculty:** 74 total; 28% have terminal degrees, 11% minority, 55% women. **Part-time faculty:** 197 total; 17% have terminal degrees, 6% minority, 55% women. **Class size:** 46% < 20, 54% 20-39, less than 1% 40-49.

**Student profile.** Among degree-seeking undergraduates, 83% enrolled in a transfer program, 18% enrolled in a vocational program, 4% already have a bachelor's degree or higher, 1,021 enrolled as first-time, first-year students, 643 transferred in from other institutions.

| | | | |
|---|---|---|---|
| Part-time: | 56% | Asian American: | 2% |
| Women: | 55% | Hispanic American: | 3% |
| African American: | 9% | 25 or older: | 32% |

**Transfer out.** 90% of students enrolled in the transfer program go on to 4-year colleges. **Colleges most students transferred to 2007:** Illinois State University.

**Basis for selection.** Open admission, but selective for some programs. Nursing program requires 2.5 GPA; college-level skills attainment in reading, English, biology, and math. Placement testing required to determine readiness in reading, English, and math. Developmental courses may be required before proceeding to college-level courses.

**High school preparation.** Recommended units include English 4, mathematics 3, social studies 2, science 2 and foreign language 2. Social studies units should include history and government.

**2008-2009 Annual costs.** Tuition/fees (projected): $2,310; $4,470 out-of-district; $6,630 out-of-state. Per-credit charge: $72 in-district; $144 out-of-district; $216 out-of-state. Books/supplies: $900. Personal expenses: $902.

**2006-2007 Financial aid. Need-based:** 97% of total undergraduate aid awarded as scholarships/grants, 3% as loans/jobs. Need-based aid available for part-time students. Work-study available nights, weekends and for part-time students. **Non-need-based:** Scholarships awarded for academics, alumni affiliation, athletics, job skills, leadership, minority status, state residency.

**Application procedures. Admission:** Priority date 6/1; no deadline. No application fee. Application may be submitted online. Admission notification on a rolling basis. May defer admission up to one year. Early admission of high school students with recommendation of high school officials. **Financial aid:** Priority date 4/1; no closing date. FAFSA, institutional form required. Applicants notified on a rolling basis starting 5/15; must reply within 2 week(s) of notification.

**Academics. Special study options:** Distance learning, double major, dual enrollment of high school students, ESL, independent study, internships, liberal arts/career combination, study abroad. License preparation in nursing, paramedic, radiology, real estate. **Credit/placement by examination:** AP, CLEP, institutional tests. 15 credit hours maximum toward associate degree. **Support services:** GED preparation and test center, learning center, remedial instruction, study skills assistance, tutoring, writing center.

**Majors. Business:** Insurance. **Computer sciences:** Data entry, information technology, networking. **Construction:** Electrician. **Education:** Mathematics, teacher assistance. **Engineering:** General. **Engineering technology:** CAD/CADD, electrical, manufacturing. **Health:** Nursing (RN), radiologic technology/medical imaging. **Interdisciplinary:** Biological/physical sciences. **Liberal arts:** Arts/sciences. **Mechanic/repair:** Industrial. **Production:** Welding. **Protective services:** Criminal justice. **Visual/performing arts:** Design.

**Most popular majors.** Interdisciplinary studies 13%, liberal arts 75%.

**Computing on campus.** 70 workstations in library, computer center. Commuter students can connect to campus network. Online course registration, online library, helpline, wireless network available.

**Student life. Freshman orientation:** Available. Program includes basic skills assessment, academic advising, and registration assistance. Mandatory half-day sessions for new full-time students. Multiple sessions held; reservations required. Online session required for new part-time students. **Activities:** Jazz band, campus ministries, drama, international student organizations, student government, student newspaper, Alpha Beta Gamma, Christian life club, cine' club, environmental club.

**Athletics. Intercollegiate:** Baseball M, soccer, softball W. **Team name:** Hawks.

**Student services.** Adult student services, alcohol/substance abuse counseling, career counseling, services for economically disadvantaged, student employment services, financial aid counseling, minority student services, on-campus daycare, personal counseling, placement for graduates, veterans' counselor. **Physically disabled:** Services for visually, speech, hearing impaired. **Transfer:** Pre-admission transcript evaluation for new students. Transfer adviser, college fairs on campus for students transferring to 4-year colleges.

**Contact.** E-mail: SOAR@heartland.edu
Phone: (309) 268-8000 Fax: (309) 268-7992
Kathleen Collins, Dean of Student Services, Heartland Community College, 1500 West Raab Road, Normal, IL 61761

## Highland Community College
**Freeport, Illinois**
**www.highland.edu** CB code: 1233

- Public 2-year community college
- Commuter campus in large town

**General.** Founded in 1961. Regionally accredited. **Enrollment:** 1,844 degree-seeking undergraduates; 205 non-degree-seeking students. **Degrees:** 229 associate awarded. **Location:** 100 miles from Chicago, 38 miles from Rockford. **Calendar:** Semester, limited summer session. **Full-time faculty:** 45 total; 11% have terminal degrees, 4% minority, 31% women. **Part-time faculty:** 123 total; 2% have terminal degrees, 4% minority, 65% women. **Class size:** 76% < 20, 21% 20-39, 2% 40-49, less than 1% 50-99. **Special facilities:** Regional arboretum, YMCA on campus.

**Student profile.** Among degree-seeking undergraduates, 55% enrolled in a transfer program, 45% enrolled in a vocational program, 370 enrolled as first-time, first-year students, 98 transferred in from other institutions.

| | | | |
|---|---|---|---|
| Part-time: | 43% | Asian American: | 1% |
| Out-of-state: | 2% | Hispanic American: | 1% |
| Women: | 65% | 25 or older: | 42% |
| African American: | 9% | | |

**Transfer out. Colleges most students transferred to 2007:** Illinois State University, University of Wisconsin-Platteville, Northern Illinois University, Western Illinois University, Columbia College.

**Basis for selection.** Open admission, but selective for some programs. Special criteria for acceptance into nursing program: based on points accumulated by taking prerequisite courses, class rank, test scores considered. **Homeschooled:** Transcript of courses and grades required.

**High school preparation.** 15 units recommended. Recommended units include English 4, mathematics 3, social studies 2, science 2 (laboratory 2) and academic electives 4.

**2007-2008 Annual costs.** Tuition/fees: $2,340; $3,870 out-of-district; $3,870 out-of-state. Per-credit charge: $72 in-district; $123 out-of-district; $123 out-of-state. Books/supplies: $900. Personal expenses: $1,300.

**2006-2007 Financial aid. Need-based:** 79% of total undergraduate aid awarded as scholarships/grants, 21% as loans/jobs. Need-based aid available for part-time students. Work-study available nights and for part-time students. **Non-need-based:** Scholarships awarded for academics, athletics.

**Application procedures. Admission:** No deadline. No application fee. Application may be submitted online. Admission notification on a rolling basis. **Financial aid:** No deadline. FAFSA, institutional form required. Applicants notified on a rolling basis starting 8/1; must reply within 2 week(s) of notification.

**Academics. Special study options:** Distance learning, dual enrollment of high school students, ESL, independent study, internships, student-designed major. Bachelor's degree programs available on campus. **Credit/placement by examination:** AP, CLEP, institutional tests. 21 credit hours maximum toward associate degree. **Support services:** GED preparation and test center, learning center, remedial instruction, tutoring, writing center.

**Majors. Agriculture:** Business. **Business:** Accounting, administrative services, business admin. **Computer sciences:** Information technology. **Education:** Mathematics. **Engineering:** General. **Engineering technology:** Industrial. **Health:** Medical records technology, nursing (RN). **Interdisciplinary:** Biological/physical sciences. **Liberal arts:** Arts/sciences. **Mechanic/repair:** Auto body, automotive. **Visual/performing arts:** Art, graphic design.

**Most popular majors.** Health sciences 14%, interdisciplinary studies 27%, liberal arts 46%.

**Computing on campus.** 366 workstations in library, computer center, student center. Commuter students can connect to campus network. Online course registration, helpline, repair service, wireless network available.

**Student life. Freshman orientation:** Available. **Activities:** Bands, choral groups, dance, drama, literary magazine, music ensembles, musical theater, student government, student newspaper, current issues club, environmental awareness, religious fellowship, international club, People of Color, pride club, student senate.

**Athletics. NJCAA. Intercollegiate:** Baseball M, basketball, golf M, softball W, volleyball W. **Intramural:** Basketball, volleyball. **Team name:** Cougars.

**Student services.** Adult student services, career counseling, veterans' counselor. **Physically disabled:** Services for visually, speech, hearing impaired. **Transfer:** Pre-admission transcript evaluation for new students. Transfer center, transfer adviser, college fairs on campus for students transferring to 4-year colleges.

**Contact.** E-mail: karl.richards@highland.edu
Phone: (815) 235-6121 ext. 3414 Fax: (815) 235-6130
Karl Richards, Dean of Enrollment Services, Highland Community College, 2998 West Pearl City Road, Freeport, IL 61032-9341

## Illinois Central College
**East Peoria, Illinois**
**www.icc.edu** CB code: 1312

- Public 2-year community college
- Commuter campus in large town

**General.** Founded in 1966. Regionally accredited. **Enrollment:** 8,719 degree-seeking undergraduates; 3,085 non-degree-seeking students. **Degrees:** 1,215 associate awarded. **Location:** 150 miles from Chicago, 5 miles from Peoria. **Calendar:** Semester, extensive summer session. **Full-time faculty:** 183 total. **Part-time faculty:** 650 total. **Partnerships:** Formal partnerships with Caterpillar Tractor Company and General Motors.

**Student profile.** Among degree-seeking undergraduates, 46% enrolled in a transfer program, 54% enrolled in a vocational program, 3% already have a bachelor's degree or higher, 1,426 enrolled as first-time, first-year students.

| Part-time: | 51% | African American: | 12% |
|---|---|---|---|
| Out-of-state: | 1% | Asian American: | 2% |
| Women: | 60% | Hispanic American: | 2% |

**Transfer out.** 34% of students enrolled in the transfer program go on to 4-year colleges. **Colleges most students transferred to 2007:** Illinois State University, Bradley University, Western Illinois University, Southern Illinois University: Carbondale, University of Illinois: Urbana-Champaign.

**Basis for selection.** Open admission, but selective for some programs. Special requirements for health occupation programs and diesel mechanics. ACT required for admissions and placement in certain programs. Audition required of music majors.

**High school preparation.** 15 units recommended. Recommended units include English 4, mathematics 3, social studies 2 and science 2.

**2007-2008 Annual costs.** Tuition/fees: $2,250; $4,950 out-of-district; $4,950 out-of-state. Per-credit charge: $75 in-district; $165 out-of-district; $165 out-of-state. Books/supplies: $600. Personal expenses: $2,335.

**Financial aid.** Non-need-based: Scholarships awarded for athletics.

**Application procedures.** Admission: No deadline. No application fee. Application may be submitted online. Admission notification on a rolling basis. **Financial aid:** Priority date 6/15; no closing date. FAFSA, institutional form required. Applicants notified on a rolling basis starting 6/1; must reply within 2 week(s) of notification.

**Academics.** Team-taught, multidisciplinary program available for transfers. **Special study options:** Distance learning, ESL, honors, independent study, internships, weekend college. Bachelor's degree programs available on campus. License preparation in dental hygiene, nursing, occupational therapy, paramedic, physical therapy, radiology, real estate. **Credit/placement by examination:** AP, CLEP, ACT, institutional tests. 30 credit hours maximum toward associate degree. **Support services:** GED preparation and test center, learning center, reduced course load, remedial instruction, study skills assistance, tutoring, writing center.

**Majors. Agriculture:** Business, horticulture. **Architecture:** Interior. **Business:** General, accounting, administrative services, banking/financial services, business admin, international, real estate. **Communications:** Broadcast journalism, journalism. **Computer sciences:** General, applications programming, programming. **Conservation:** General. **Education:** Elementary, physical, secondary, special. **Engineering:** General, agricultural, electrical. **Engineering technology:** Robotics. **English:** English lit, speech/rhetoric. **Family/consumer sciences:** General, child care, food/nutrition. **Foreign languages:** General. **Health:** Clinical lab technology, dental hygiene, health care admin, medical radiologic technology/radiation therapy, medical records technology, occupational therapy assistant, physical therapy assistant, predental, premedicine, prepharmacy, preveterinary, respiratory therapy technology. **Legal studies:** Court reporting, paralegal, prelaw. **Liberal arts:** Arts/sciences, library assistant. **Math:** General. **Physical sciences:** Chemistry, geology, physics, planetary. **Protective services:** Criminal justice, fire safety technology. **Visual/performing arts:** Dance, dramatic, studio arts.

**Computing on campus.** 500 workstations in library, computer center.

**Student life. Activities:** Bands, choral groups, dance, drama, international student organizations, music ensembles, student government, student newspaper, Tomorrow's Black Leaders, College Republicans, College Democrats, Inter-Varsity Christian Fellowship.

**Athletics.** NJCAA. **Intercollegiate:** Baseball M, basketball, golf M, softball W, volleyball W. **Intramural:** Badminton, basketball, golf, table tennis, tennis, volleyball. **Team name:** Cougars.

**Student services.** Adult student services, career counseling, student employment services, health services, on-campus daycare, personal counseling, placement for graduates, veterans' counselor. **Physically disabled:** Services for visually, speech, hearing impaired. **Transfer:** Transfer center, transfer adviser, college fairs on campus for students transferring to 4-year colleges.

**Contact.** E-mail: enroll@icc.edu
Phone: (309) 694-5354 Fax: (309) 694-8461
Guy Goodman, Director of Enrollment Management, Illinois Central College, One College Drive, East Peoria, IL 61635-0001

## Illinois Eastern Community Colleges: Frontier Community College
### Fairfield, Illinois
www.iecc.edu/fcc

CB code: 1894

- ▶ Public 2-year community college
- ▶ Commuter campus in small town

**General.** Founded in 1976. Regionally accredited. **Enrollment:** 1,353 degree-seeking undergraduates. **Degrees:** 75 associate awarded. **Location:** 110 miles from St. Louis. **Calendar:** Semester, extensive summer session. **Full-time faculty:** 5 total. **Part-time faculty:** 230 total.

**Student profile.** Among degree-seeking undergraduates, 43% enrolled in a transfer program, 57% enrolled in a vocational program.

| Out-of-state: | 1% | 25 or older: | 57% |
|---|---|---|---|

**Basis for selection.** Open admission, but selective for some programs. Special requirements for nursing and radiography programs. Preference given to regional residents. Interview recommended for nursing and radiography technology.

**High school preparation.** Recommended units include English 3, mathematics 2 and science 1.

**2007-2008 Annual costs.** Tuition/fees: $1,810; $5,583 out-of-district; $6,905 out-of-state. Per-credit charge: $57 in-district; $183 out-of-district; $227 out-of-state. Students in qualifying Indiana districts pay per-credit-hour rate of $96. Books/supplies: $800. Personal expenses: $1,120.

**Financial aid.** Need-based: Need-based aid available for part-time students. Non-need-based: Scholarships awarded for academics, state residency.

**Application procedures.** Admission: No deadline. $10 fee. Application may be submitted online. Admission notification on a rolling basis beginning on or about 8/1. **Financial aid:** No deadline. FAFSA, institutional form required. Applicants notified on a rolling basis starting 8/1; must reply within 2 week(s) of notification.

**Academics.** Students, with counselors' aid, design own academic programs through nontraditional alternatives to classroom study. **Special study options:** Distance learning, double major, dual enrollment of high school students, ESL, honors, independent study, student-designed major, study abroad, teacher certification program, weekend college. License preparation in nursing. **Credit/placement by examination:** AP, CLEP, institutional tests. 32 credit hours maximum toward associate degree. **Support services:** GED preparation, learning center, remedial instruction, study skills assistance, tutoring.

**Majors. Business:** Administrative services, office technology. **Computer sciences:** General. **Health:** Mental health services. **Liberal arts:** Arts/sciences.

**Most popular majors.** Business/marketing 10%, health sciences 13%, interdisciplinary studies 21%, liberal arts 42%.

**Computing on campus.** 40 workstations in library, computer center. Commuter students can connect to campus network.

**Student life. Freshman orientation:** Available. Preregistration for classes offered. Freshman orientation strongly recommended. **Activities:** Student government, student newspaper.

**Student services.** Adult student services, career counseling, services for economically disadvantaged, student employment services, financial aid counseling, minority student services, personal counseling, placement for graduates, veterans' counselor. **Physically disabled:** Services for visually, speech, hearing impaired. **Transfer:** Pre-admission transcript evaluation for new students. Transfer adviser, college fairs on campus for students transferring to 4-year colleges.

**Contact.** Phone: (618) 842-3711 Toll-free number: (877) 464-3687
Fax: (618) 842-6340
Suzanne Brooks, Coordinator of Admissions and Records, Illinois Eastern Community Colleges: Frontier Community College, 2 Frontier Drive, Fairfield, IL 62837-9801

## Illinois Eastern Community Colleges: Lincoln Trail College

**Robinson, Illinois**
www.iecc.edu/ltc                    CB code: 0758

▶ Public 2-year community college
▶ Commuter campus in small town

**General.** Founded in 1969. Regionally accredited. **Enrollment:** 902 degree-seeking undergraduates; 543 non-degree-seeking students. **Degrees:** 170 associate awarded. **Location:** 200 miles from Indianapolis, 110 miles from St. Louis. **Calendar:** Semester, extensive summer session. **Full-time faculty:** 27 total. **Part-time faculty:** 61 total.

**Student profile.** Among degree-seeking undergraduates, 61% enrolled in a transfer program, 39% enrolled in a vocational program, 134 enrolled as first-time, first-year students.

| | | | |
|---|---|---|---|
| Part-time: | 43% | Women: | 42% |
| Out-of-state: | 1% | 25 or older: | 53% |

**Basis for selection.** Open admission.

**High school preparation.** Recommended units include English 3, mathematics 2 and science 1.

**2007-2008 Annual costs.** Tuition/fees: $1,810; $5,583 out-of-district; $6,905 out-of-state. Per-credit charge: $57 in-district; $183 out-of-district; $227 out-of-state. Students in qualifying Indiana districts pay per-credit-hour rate of $96. Books/supplies: $800. Personal expenses: $1,120.

**Financial aid. Need-based:** Need-based aid available for part-time students. **Non-need-based:** Scholarships awarded for academics, athletics, state residency.

**Application procedures. Admission:** No deadline. $10 fee. Application may be submitted online. Admission notification on a rolling basis beginning on or about 8/1. **Financial aid:** No deadline. FAFSA, institutional form required. Applicants notified on a rolling basis starting 8/1; must reply within 2 week(s) of notification.

**Academics.** Students (with counselors' aid) design academic programs through nontraditional alternatives to classroom study. **Special study options:** Distance learning, double major, dual enrollment of high school students, ESL, honors, independent study, internships, student-designed major, study abroad, weekend college. License preparation in nursing. **Credit/placement by examination:** AP, CLEP, institutional tests. 32 credit hours maximum toward associate degree. **Support services:** GED preparation, learning center, remedial instruction, study skills assistance, tutoring.

**Majors. Agriculture:** Horticulture. **Business:** Administrative services, banking/financial services, office technology. **Computer sciences:** General. **Education:** Music, teacher assistance. **Engineering technology:** Drafting. **Interdisciplinary:** Biological/physical sciences. **Liberal arts:** Arts/sciences. **Mechanic/repair:** Electronics/electrical, heating/ac/refrig.

**Computing on campus.** 91 workstations in library, computer center. Commuter students can connect to campus network.

**Student life. Freshman orientation:** Available. Preregistration for classes offered. **Activities:** Bands, choral groups, drama, music ensembles, musical theater, student government, student newspaper.

**Athletics.** NJCAA. **Intercollegiate:** Baseball M, basketball, softball W. **Intramural:** Basketball, softball. **Team name:** Statesmen.

**Student services.** Career counseling, services for economically disadvantaged, student employment services, financial aid counseling, minority student services, personal counseling, placement for graduates, veterans' counselor. **Physically disabled:** Services for visually, speech, hearing impaired. **Transfer:** Pre-admission transcript evaluation for new students. Transfer adviser, college fairs on campus for students transferring to 4-year colleges.

**Contact.** Phone: (618) 544-8657 Toll-free number: (866) 582-4322 Fax: (618) 544-3957
Becky Mikeworth, Director of Admissions, Illinois Eastern Community Colleges: Lincoln Trail College, 11220 State Highway 1, Robinson, IL 62454-5707

## Illinois Eastern Community Colleges: Olney Central College

**Olney, Illinois**
www.iecc.edu/occ                    CB code: 0827

▶ Public 2-year community college
▶ Commuter campus in small town

**General.** Founded in 1962. Regionally accredited. **Enrollment:** 890 degree-seeking undergraduates; 720 non-degree-seeking students. **Degrees:** 294 associate awarded. **Location:** 200 miles from St. Louis. **Calendar:** Semester, extensive summer session. **Full-time faculty:** 47 total. **Part-time faculty:** 75 total.

**Student profile.** Among degree-seeking undergraduates, 61% enrolled in a transfer program, 39% enrolled in a vocational program, 134 enrolled as first-time, first-year students.

| | | | |
|---|---|---|---|
| Part-time: | 21% | 25 or older: | 40% |
| Women: | 59% | | |

**Basis for selection.** Open admission, but selective for some programs. Special requirements for nursing, radiology programs. Preference given to Illinois Eastern Community College region residents. Interview recommended for nursing, radiology technology majors.

**High school preparation.** Recommended units include English 3, mathematics 2 and science 1.

**2007-2008 Annual costs.** Tuition/fees: $1,810; $5,583 out-of-district; $6,905 out-of-state. Per-credit charge: $57 in-district; $183 out-of-district; $227 out-of-state. Students in qualifying Indiana districts pay per-credit-hour rate of $96. Books/supplies: $800. Personal expenses: $1,120.

**Financial aid. Need-based:** Need-based aid available for part-time students. **Non-need-based:** Scholarships awarded for academics, athletics, state residency.

**Application procedures. Admission:** No deadline. $10 fee. Application may be submitted online. Admission notification on a rolling basis beginning on or about 8/1. **Financial aid:** No deadline. FAFSA, institutional form required. Applicants notified on a rolling basis starting 8/1; must reply within 2 week(s) of notification.

**Academics.** Students design academic programs with aid of counselors through nontraditional alternatives to classroom study. **Special study options:** Distance learning, double major, dual enrollment of high school students, ESL, honors, independent study, internships, student-designed major, study abroad, weekend college. License preparation in nursing, radiology, real estate. **Credit/placement by examination:** AP, CLEP, institutional tests. 32 credit hours maximum toward associate degree. **Support services:** GED preparation, learning center, remedial instruction, study skills assistance, tutoring.

**Majors. Business:** Accounting, administrative services, office technology. **Education:** Music. **Health:** Medical radiologic technology/radiation therapy, medical secretary, nursing (RN). **Liberal arts:** Arts/sciences. **Mechanic/repair:** Auto body, industrial. **Production:** Woodworking. **Protective services:** Police science.

**Computing on campus.** 125 workstations in library, computer center. Commuter students can connect to campus network.

**Student life. Freshman orientation:** Available. Preregistration for classes offered. **Activities:** Bands, choral groups, drama, music ensembles, musical theater, student government, student newspaper.

**Athletics.** NJCAA. **Intercollegiate:** Baseball M, basketball, softball W. **Intramural:** Basketball, softball. **Team name:** Blue Knights.

**Student services.** Career counseling, services for economically disadvantaged, student employment services, financial aid counseling, minority student services, on-campus daycare, personal counseling, placement for graduates, veterans' counselor. **Physically disabled:** Services for visually, speech, hearing impaired. **Transfer:** Pre-admission transcript evaluation for new students. Transfer adviser, college fairs on campus for students transferring to 4-year colleges.

**Contact.** Phone: (618) 395-7777 Toll-free number: (866) 622-4322 Fax: (618) 392-5212
Chris Webber, Assistant Dean of Student Services, Illinois Eastern Community Colleges: Olney Central College, 305 North West Street, Olney, IL 62450

## Illinois Eastern Community Colleges: Wabash Valley College
**Mount Carmel, Illinois**
www.iecc.edu/wvc
**CB code: 1936**

- Public 2-year community college
- Commuter campus in small town

**General.** Founded in 1960. Regionally accredited. **Enrollment:** 841 degree-seeking undergraduates; 3,365 non-degree-seeking students. **Degrees:** 178 associate awarded. **Location:** 40 miles from Evansville, Indiana. **Calendar:** Semester, extensive summer session. **Full-time faculty:** 38 total. **Part-time faculty:** 130 total.

**Student profile.** Among degree-seeking undergraduates, 43% enrolled in a transfer program, 57% enrolled in a vocational program, 123 enrolled as first-time, first-year students.

| | | | |
|---|---|---|---|
| Part-time: | 34% | Women: | 49% |
| Out-of-state: | 1% | 25 or older: | 54% |

**Basis for selection.** Open admission.

**High school preparation.** Recommended units include English 3, mathematics 2 and science 1.

**2007-2008 Annual costs.** Tuition/fees: $1,810; $5,583 out-of-district; $6,905 out-of-state. Per-credit charge: $57 in-district; $183 out-of-district; $227 out-of-state. Students in qualifying Indiana districts pay per-credit-hour rate of $96. Books/supplies: $800. Personal expenses: $1,120.

**Financial aid. Need-based:** Need-based aid available for part-time students. **Non-need-based:** Scholarships awarded for academics, athletics, state residency.

**Application procedures. Admission:** No deadline. $10 fee. Application may be submitted online. Admission notification on a rolling basis beginning on or about 8/1. **Financial aid:** No deadline. FAFSA, institutional form required. Applicants notified on a rolling basis starting 8/1; must reply within 2 week(s) of notification.

**Academics.** Students, with counselor's aid, design own academic programs through nontraditional alternatives to classroom study. **Special study options:** Distance learning, double major, dual enrollment of high school students, ESL, honors, independent study, internships, student-designed major, study abroad, weekend college. License preparation in nursing, real estate. **Credit/placement by examination:** AP, CLEP, institutional tests. 32 credit hours maximum toward associate degree. **Support services:** GED preparation, learning center, remedial instruction, study skills assistance, tutoring.

**Majors. Agriculture:** Business, horticulture, production. **Business:** Accounting technology, administrative services, office technology. **Communications:** Broadcast journalism. **Engineering technology:** Electrical, manufacturing. **Family/consumer sciences:** Child care. **Liberal arts:** Arts/sciences. **Mechanic/repair:** Diesel, industrial. **Production:** Machine shop technology. **Public administration:** Social work.

**Computing on campus.** 100 workstations in library, computer center. Commuter students can connect to campus network.

**Student life. Freshman orientation:** Available. Preregistration for classes offered. **Activities:** Bands, choral groups, drama, music ensembles, musical theater, radio station, student government, student newspaper, TV station.

**Athletics.** NJCAA. **Intercollegiate:** Baseball M, basketball, softball W. **Intramural:** Basketball, softball. **Team name:** Warriors.

**Student services.** Career counseling, services for economically disadvantaged, student employment services, financial aid counseling, minority student services, on-campus daycare, personal counseling, placement for graduates, veterans' counselor. **Physically disabled:** Services for visually, speech, hearing impaired. **Transfer:** Pre-admission transcript evaluation for new students. Transfer adviser, college fairs on campus for students transferring to 4-year colleges.

**Contact.** Phone: (618) 262-8641 Toll-free number: (866) 982-4322 Fax: (618) 262-5347
Diana Spear, Assistant Dean for Student Services, Illinois Eastern Community Colleges: Wabash Valley College, 2200 College Drive, Mount Carmel, IL 62863-2657

## Illinois Valley Community College
**Oglesby, Illinois**
www.ivcc.edu
**CB member**
**CB code: 1397**

- Public 2-year community college
- Commuter campus in small town

**General.** Founded in 1966. Regionally accredited. **Enrollment:** 2,804 degree-seeking undergraduates. **Degrees:** 495 associate awarded. **Location:** 60 miles from Peoria, 95 miles from Chicago. **Calendar:** Semester, extensive summer session. **Full-time faculty:** 89 total; 3% minority, 54% women. **Part-time faculty:** 138 total; 6% minority, 53% women. **Special facilities:** Federal and state nuclear regulatory commission document depositories.

**Transfer out. Colleges most students transferred to 2007:** Illinois State University, Northern Illinois University, Western Illinois University, University of Illinois/Urbana-Champaign, Eastern Illinois University.

**Basis for selection.** Open admission, but selective for some programs. Applicants to nursing programs must have 2.0 GPA for LPN, 2.5 GPA for RN and background in laboratory science; 2.0 GPA required for dental assisting. **Homeschooled:** Transcript of courses and grades required.

**2007-2008 Annual costs.** Tuition/fees: $1,973; $6,639 out-of-district; $7,619 out-of-state. Per-credit charge: $66 in-district; $214 out-of-district; $247 out-of-state. Books/supplies: $900. Personal expenses: $1,170.

**Financial aid. Need-based:** Need-based aid available for part-time students.

**Application procedures. Admission:** No deadline. No application fee. Application may be submitted online. Admission notification on a rolling basis. **Financial aid:** Priority date 5/1; no closing date. FAFSA required. Applicants notified on a rolling basis starting 5/1.

**Academics. Special study options:** Cross-registration, distance learning, dual enrollment of high school students, honors, independent study, internships, study abroad. License preparation in nursing, real estate. **Credit/placement by examination:** AP, CLEP, institutional tests. 16 credit hours maximum toward associate degree. **Support services:** GED preparation and test center, learning center, pre-admission summer program, reduced course load, remedial instruction, study skills assistance, tutoring, writing center.

**Majors. Agriculture:** General. **Biology:** General. **Business:** Management science. **Communications:** General, journalism. **Computer sciences:** General, applications programming, information systems. **Education:** General. **Engineering:** General. **Engineering technology:** Drafting. **English:** American lit, composition, English lit, speech/rhetoric. **Family/consumer sciences:** Child care. **Foreign languages:** General. **Health:** Athletic training, nursing (RN). **History:** General. **Legal studies:** General. **Math:** General, applied. **Parks/recreation:** Health/fitness, sports admin. **Physical sciences:** Chemistry, geology, oceanography, physics, planetary. **Protective services:** Law enforcement admin, police science. **Psychology:** General. **Public administration:** Social work. **Social sciences:** General, political science, sociology. **Visual/performing arts:** General, art, art history/conservation, dramatic, music history, music performance, studio arts.

**Computing on campus.** 200 workstations in library, computer center. Online course registration, online library, helpline, wireless network available.

**Student life. Freshman orientation:** Available. Sessions held in spring and fall. **Activities:** Bands, choral groups, drama, literary magazine, music ensembles, musical theater, student government, student newspaper, Amnesty International, gay/straight alliance, People of the World End Racism (POWER), student nurses association, Young Republicans.

**Athletics.** NJCAA. **Intercollegiate:** Baseball M, basketball, golf M, softball W, tennis, volleyball W. **Intramural:** Basketball, softball, volleyball. **Team name:** Eagles.

**Student services.** Career counseling, student employment services, financial aid counseling, on-campus daycare, personal counseling, placement for graduates, veterans' counselor. **Physically disabled:** Services for visually, hearing impaired. **Transfer:** Transfer adviser for students transferring to 4-year colleges.

**Contact.** E-mail: tracy_morris@ivcc.edu
Phone: (815) 224-0439 Fax: (815) 224-6091
Tracy Morris, Director of Admissions and Records, Illinois Valley Community College, 815 North Orlando Smith Avenue, Oglesby, IL 61348-9693

## John A. Logan College
Carterville, Illinois
www.jalc.edu                                    CB code: 1357

- Public 2-year community college
- Commuter campus in small town

**General.** Founded in 1967. Regionally accredited. **Enrollment:** 2,306 degree-seeking undergraduates; 3,755 non-degree-seeking students. **Degrees:** 554 associate awarded. **ROTC:** Army, Air Force. **Location:** 10 miles from Carbondale. **Calendar:** Semester, limited summer session. **Full-time faculty:** 100 total. **Part-time faculty:** 15 total. **Class size:** 53% < 20, 44% 20-39, less than 1% 40-49, less than 1% 50-99, less than 1% >100.

**Student profile.** Among degree-seeking undergraduates, 58% enrolled in a transfer program, 42% enrolled in a vocational program, 488 enrolled as first-time, first-year students.

| | | | |
|---|---|---|---|
| Part-time: | 25% | Asian American: | 1% |
| Out-of-state: | 1% | Hispanic American: | 2% |
| Women: | 60% | Native American: | 1% |
| African American: | 11% | 25 or older: | 21% |

**Transfer out. Colleges most students transferred to 2007:** Southern Illinois University at Carbondale.

**Basis for selection.** Open admission, but selective for some programs. Admission to allied health programs competitive, unique criteria depending on program. ASSET and/or COMPASS accepted in place of SAT or ACT.

**High school preparation.** College preparatory program required of 2-year transfer degree applicants. Must have 15 high school course units: 4 English, 3 math, 3 laboratory science, 3 social science, 2 electives.

**2007-2008 Annual costs.** Tuition/fees: $2,010. Per-credit charge: $67. Books/supplies: $1,030. Personal expenses: $601.

**Financial aid.** All financial aid based on need. Need-based aid available for part-time students. Work-study available for part-time students.

**Application procedures. Admission:** No deadline. No application fee. Application may be submitted online. Admission notification on a rolling basis. **Financial aid:** Priority date 5/1; no closing date. FAFSA, institutional form required. Applicants notified on a rolling basis starting 5/1.

**Academics. Special study options:** Distance learning, dual enrollment of high school students, liberal arts/career combination. Bachelor's degree programs available on campus. License preparation in dental hygiene, nursing, occupational therapy, paramedic, real estate. **Credit/placement by examination:** CLEP, institutional tests. 30 credit hours maximum toward associate degree. **Support services:** GED preparation and test center, study skills assistance, tutoring, writing center.

**Majors. Agriculture:** Business. **Biology:** General. **Business:** Accounting technology, business admin, executive assistant, office management. **Communications:** Journalism. **Computer sciences:** General. **Construction:** Carpentry. **Education:** Art, early childhood, elementary, history, mathematics, physical, secondary, social studies, special, teacher assistance. **Engineering:** General. **Engineering technology:** Drafting. **English:** English lit. **Health:** Clinical lab technology, dental hygiene, medical records technology, nursing (RN), occupational therapy assistant, prepharmacy, sonography. **Interdisciplinary:** Biological/physical sciences. **Liberal arts:** Arts/sciences. **Math:** General. **Mechanic/repair:** Auto body, automotive, electronics/electrical, industrial. **Personal/culinary services:** Cosmetic. **Physical sciences:** Chemistry, physics. **Production:** Machine shop technology, tool and die, welding. **Protective services:** Corrections, criminal justice. **Psychology:** General. **Public administration:** Social work. **Social sciences:** Economics, international relations, political science, sociology. **Visual/performing arts:** Art, dramatic.

**Computing on campus.** 651 workstations in library, computer center. Online course registration available.

**Student life. Freshman orientation:** Available. **Housing:** Housing at Southern Illinois University - Carbondale. **Activities:** Concert band, choral groups, drama, music ensembles, musical theater, student government, student newspaper.

**Athletics.** NJCAA. **Intercollegiate:** Baseball M, basketball, golf, softball W, volleyball W. **Team name:** Volunteers.

**Student services.** Adult student services, career counseling, student employment services, financial aid counseling, minority student services, on-campus daycare, placement for graduates, veterans' counselor. **Physically**

**disabled:** Services for visually, hearing impaired. **Transfer:** Transfer center, college fairs on campus for students transferring to 4-year colleges.

**Contact.** E-mail: terrycrain@jalc.edu
Phone: (618) 985-3741 ext. 8298 Fax: (618) 985-4433
Terry Crain, Dean of Student Services, John A. Logan College, 700 Logan College Road, Carterville, IL 62918

## John Wood Community College
Quincy, Illinois
www.jwcc.edu                                    CB code: 1374

- Public 2-year community college
- Commuter campus in large town

**General.** Founded in 1974. Regionally accredited. Extension sites in Pittsfiled and Mt. Sterling. **Enrollment:** 1,873 degree-seeking undergraduates; 544 non-degree-seeking students. **Degrees:** 285 associate awarded. **Location:** 140 miles from St. Louis, 100 miles from Springfield. **Calendar:** Semester, extensive summer session. **Full-time faculty:** 52 total. **Part-time faculty:** 157 total. **Class size:** 65% < 20, 34% 20-39, 1% 40-49. **Special facilities:** Truck driver training facility, greenhouse, agricultural center, swine facility.

**Student profile.** Among degree-seeking undergraduates, 544 enrolled as first-time, first-year students.

| | | | |
|---|---|---|---|
| Part-time: | 45% | Asian American: | 1% |
| Out-of-state: | 9% | Hispanic American: | 1% |
| Women: | 62% | 25 or older: | 37% |
| African American: | 3% | | |

**Transfer out. Colleges most students transferred to 2007:** Western Illinois University, Eastern Illinois University, University of Illinois-Springfield, Quincy University.

**Basis for selection.** Open admission, but selective for some programs. Limited enrollment in certificate degree programs in dietary management, practical nursing, nurse assistant and in associate degree program in nursing and truck driver training.

**High school preparation.** Recommended units include English 4, mathematics 3, social studies 3 and science 4.

**2007-2008 Annual costs.** Tuition/fees: $3,120; $6,120 out-of-state. Per-credit charge: $96 in-state; $196 out-of-state. Books/supplies: $1,152. Personal expenses: $720.

**Financial aid. Need-based:** Need-based aid available for part-time students. Work-study available nights and weekends.

**Application procedures. Admission:** No deadline. No application fee. Application may be submitted online. Admission notification on a rolling basis. **Financial aid:** No deadline. FAFSA required. Applicants notified on a rolling basis starting 3/1.

**Academics. Special study options:** Distance learning, dual enrollment of high school students, ESL, independent study, internships, liberal arts/career combination, student-designed major, study abroad. License preparation in nursing, paramedic, real estate. **Credit/placement by examination:** AP, CLEP, institutional tests. 30 credit hours maximum toward associate degree. **Support services:** GED preparation and test center, learning center, reduced course load, remedial instruction, study skills assistance, tutoring, writing center.

**Majors. Agriculture:** General, animal husbandry, animal sciences, business, horticulture. **Biology:** General. **Business:** General, accounting, accounting technology, administrative services, business admin, executive assistant, sales/distribution. **Communications:** General. **Computer sciences:** General, applications programming. **Construction:** Electrician. **Education:** General, early childhood. **Engineering:** General. **Engineering technology:** Mechanical drafting. **Family/consumer sciences:** Child care. **Foreign languages:** Spanish. **Health:** Clinical lab technology, EMT paramedic, medical radiologic technology/radiation therapy, medical secretary, nursing (RN). **History:** General. **Interdisciplinary:** Biological/physical sciences. **Legal studies:** Legal secretary, prelaw. **Liberal arts:** Arts/sciences. **Math:** General. **Mechanic/repair:** Industrial. **Parks/recreation:** Health/fitness. **Personal/culinary services:** Restaurant/catering. **Physical sciences:** General, physics. **Protective services:** Fire safety technology, police science. **Psychology:** General. **Social sciences:** Economics, sociology. **Visual/performing arts:** Art.

**Most popular majors.** Business/marketing 6%, health sciences 16%, interdisciplinary studies 37%, liberal arts 24%, security/protective services 8%.

**Computing on campus.** 350 workstations in library, computer center. Online course registration, helpline available.

**Student life. Freshman orientation:** Mandatory. **Activities:** Jazz band, choral groups, drama, music ensembles, musical theater, student government, service organizations, honor society, Phi Theta Kappa.

**Athletics.** NJCAA. **Intercollegiate:** Baseball M, basketball, golf M, softball W, volleyball W. **Intramural:** Basketball M, bowling, volleyball. **Team name:** Trail Blazers.

**Student services.** Adult student services, career counseling, services for economically disadvantaged, student employment services, financial aid counseling, minority student services, veterans' counselor. **Physically disabled:** Services for visually, speech, hearing impaired. **Transfer:** Transfer adviser, college fairs on campus for students transferring to 4-year colleges.

**Contact.** E-mail: admissions@jwcc.edu
Phone: (217) 641-4338 Fax: (217) 224-4208
Mark McNett, Director of Admissions, John Wood Community College, 1301 South 48th Street, Quincy, IL 62305-8736

---

## Joliet Junior College
### Joliet, Illinois
### www.jjc.edu
**CB code: 1346**

◗ Public 2-year community college
◗ Commuter campus in small city

**General.** Founded in 1901. Regionally accredited. **Enrollment:** 10,722 degree-seeking undergraduates. **Degrees:** 917 associate awarded. **Location:** 45 miles from Chicago. **Calendar:** Semester, extensive summer session. **Full-time faculty:** 206 total. **Part-time faculty:** 473 total. **Class size:** 48% < 20, 51% 20-39, less than 1% 40-49, less than 1% 50-99, less than 1% >100. **Special facilities:** Planetarium, nature trail, arboretum, working farm, fitness center.

**Student profile.**

| | | | |
|---|---|---|---|
| Out-of-state: | 1% | 25 or older: | 42% |

**Transfer out. Colleges most students transferred to 2007:** Northern Illinois University, Illinois State University, University of St. Francis, Lewis University, Governors State University.

**Basis for selection.** Open admission, but selective for some programs and for out-of-state students. Preference given to cooperative programs and in-district applicants. Nursing applicants must have 20 ACT if in top third of high school class or 21 ACT if in top half of class. ACT recommended. Interview recommended for some.

**High school preparation.** 15 units recommended. Recommended units include English 4, mathematics 3, social studies 3, science 3 and academic electives 2.

**2007-2008 Annual costs.** Tuition/fees: $2,280; $7,403 out-of-district; $8,485 out-of-state. Per-credit charge: $62 in-district; $233 out-of-district; $262 out-of-state. Additional course fees range from $3 to $90. Personal expenses: $1,500.

**Financial aid. Need-based:** Need-based aid available for part-time students. Work-study available nights, weekends and for part-time students. **Non-need-based:** Scholarships awarded for academics.

**Application procedures. Admission:** No deadline. No application fee. Application may be submitted online. Admission notification on a rolling basis. **Financial aid:** Priority date 5/1, closing date 6/30. FAFSA, institutional form required. Applicants notified on a rolling basis starting 5/15.

**Academics. Special study options:** Cooperative education, distance learning, dual enrollment of high school students, ESL, honors, independent study, internships, study abroad. License preparation in nursing, paramedic, radiology, real estate. **Credit/placement by examination:** AP, CLEP, institutional tests. 45 credit hours maximum toward associate degree. **Support services:** GED preparation, learning center, pre-admission summer program, reduced course load, remedial instruction, study skills assistance, tutoring, writing center.

**Majors. Agriculture:** General, greenhouse operations, horticulture, landscaping, nursery operations, ornamental horticulture, supplies, turf management. **Biology:** General. **Business:** Accounting, administrative services, business admin, fashion, office management, office technology, office/clerical. **Computer sciences:** General, information systems, programming. **Education:** Early childhood, elementary, secondary, special, teacher assistance.

**Engineering:** Electrical. **Engineering technology:** Architectural, construction, drafting, electrical. **English:** English lit. **Family/consumer sciences:** Clothing/textiles. **Health:** Medical secretary, nursing (RN), veterinary technology/assistant. **History:** General. **Legal studies:** Legal secretary. **Liberal arts:** Arts/sciences. **Math:** General. **Mechanic/repair:** Auto body. **Personal/culinary services:** Culinary arts. **Physical sciences:** Chemistry. **Protective services:** Law enforcement admin. **Psychology:** General. **Social sciences:** Political science, sociology. **Visual/performing arts:** Art, interior design.

**Most popular majors.** Business/marketing 7%, health sciences 15%, liberal arts 49%.

**Computing on campus.** Helpline, repair service available.

**Student life. Freshman orientation:** Available. **Activities:** Bands, choral groups, drama, literary magazine, music ensembles, musical theater, student government, student newspaper, campus ministry, black student organization, Intervarsity Christian Fellowship, Latinos Unidos, Latter Day Saints association, unity club.

**Athletics.** NJCAA. **Intercollegiate:** Baseball M, basketball, cross-country, football (tackle) M, soccer, softball W, tennis, volleyball W. **Team name:** Wolves.

**Student services.** Career counseling, services for economically disadvantaged, student employment services, financial aid counseling, minority student services, on-campus daycare, personal counseling, placement for graduates, veterans' counselor, women's services. **Physically disabled:** Services for visually, speech, hearing impaired. **Transfer:** Transfer center, transfer adviser for students transferring to 4-year colleges.

**Contact.** E-mail: jkloberd@jjc.edu
Phone: (815) 729-9020 Fax: (815) 744-5507
Jennifer Kloberdanz, Director of Admissions and Recruitment, Joliet Junior College, 1215 Houbolt Road, Joliet, IL 60431-8938

---

## Kankakee Community College
### Kankakee, Illinois
### www.kcc.edu
**CB code: 1380**

◗ Public 2-year community college
◗ Commuter campus in large town

**General.** Founded in 1966. Regionally accredited. **Enrollment:** 2,551 degree-seeking undergraduates; 1,040 non-degree-seeking students. **Degrees:** 349 associate awarded. **ROTC:** Army. **Location:** 60 miles from Chicago. **Calendar:** Semester, extensive summer session. **Full-time faculty:** 58 total; 7% have terminal degrees, 9% minority, 53% women. **Part-time faculty:** 116 total; 4% have terminal degrees, 10% minority, 50% women.

**Student profile.** Among degree-seeking undergraduates, 34% enrolled in a transfer program, 66% enrolled in a vocational program, 3% already have a bachelor's degree or higher, 313 enrolled as first-time, first-year students.

| | | | |
|---|---|---|---|
| Part-time: | 55% | Asian American: | 1% |
| Women: | 67% | Hispanic American: | 5% |
| African American: | 15% | | |

**Transfer out. Colleges most students transferred to 2007:** Illinois State University, Governors State University, Olivet Nazarene University, University of Illinois, Eastern Illinois University.

**Basis for selection.** Open admission, but selective for some programs. Criteria for health career programs may include prerequisite coursework, high school record and test scores; separate application and COMPASS required. ASSET required of all students for placement. **Adult students:** COMPASS required.

**High school preparation.** 15 units recommended. Recommended units include English 4, mathematics 3, social studies 2, science 2 (laboratory 1) and academic electives 4.

**2007-2008 Annual costs.** Tuition/fees: $2,070; $5,143 out-of-district; $9,275 out-of-state. Per-credit charge: $69 in-district; $171 out-of-district; $309 out-of-state. Books/supplies: $832. Personal expenses: $1,200.

**Financial aid. Need-based:** Need-based aid available for part-time students. **Non-need-based:** Scholarships awarded for athletics.

**Application procedures. Admission:** No deadline. No application fee. Application must be submitted online. Admission notification on a rolling basis. **Financial aid:** Priority date 6/1; no closing date. FAFSA, institutional form required. Applicants notified on a rolling basis; must reply within 4 week(s) of notification.

**Academics. Special study options:** Cross-registration, distance learning, dual enrollment of high school students, ESL, honors, independent study, internships, study abroad, teacher certification program. License preparation in nursing, paramedic, radiology. **Credit/placement by examination:** AP, CLEP, institutional tests. 16 credit hours maximum toward associate degree. **Support services:** GED preparation and test center, learning center, pre-admission summer program, reduced course load, remedial instruction, study skills assistance, tutoring, writing center.

**Majors. Biology:** General. **Business:** Accounting, administrative services, business admin, construction management. **Communications technology:** Desktop publishing. **Computer sciences:** Information technology. **Education:** General, early childhood, elementary, mathematics, secondary, teacher assistance. **Engineering:** General. **Engineering technology:** Drafting, manufacturing. **Health:** Clinical lab technology, EMT paramedic, medical assistant, nursing (RN), predental, premedicine, prepharmacy, preveterinary, radiologic technology/medical imaging, respiratory therapy technology. **Legal studies:** Paralegal. **Math:** General. **Mechanic/repair:** General, automotive, electronics/electrical, heating/ac/refrig, industrial electronics. **Production:** Welding. **Protective services:** Emergency management/homeland security, police science. **Psychology:** General. **Social sciences:** Political science. **Visual/performing arts:** General, art, studio arts.

**Most popular majors.** Business/marketing 12%, health sciences 33%, liberal arts 31%, security/protective services 6%.

**Computing on campus.** 1,000 workstations in library, computer center, student center. Commuter students can connect to campus network. Online library, helpline, wireless network available.

**Student life. Freshman orientation:** Mandatory. Preregistration for classes offered. Two-hour orientation class held multiple dates and times at beginning of term. **Activities:** Student government.

**Athletics.** NJCAA. **Intercollegiate:** Baseball M, basketball, soccer M, softball W, volleyball W. **Intramural:** Basketball, golf. **Team name:** Cavaliers.

**Student services.** Adult student services, career counseling, student employment services, financial aid counseling, minority student services, on-campus daycare, placement for graduates. **Physically disabled:** Services for visually, speech, hearing impaired. **Transfer:** Pre-admission transcript evaluation for new students. Transfer center, transfer adviser, college fairs on campus for students transferring to 4-year colleges.

**Contact.** Phone: (815) 802-8520 Fax: (815) 802-8101
Michelle Driscoll, Director, Admissions and Registration, Kankakee Community College, 100 College Drive, Kankakee, IL 60901-6505

---

## Kaskaskia College
Centralia, Illinois
www.kaskaskia.edu                    CB code: 1108

- Public 2-year community college
- Commuter campus in large town

**General.** Founded in 1966. Regionally accredited. Child care center available. **Enrollment:** 2,795 degree-seeking undergraduates; 2,246 non-degree-seeking students. **Degrees:** 494 associate awarded. **Location:** 60 miles from St. Louis. **Calendar:** Semester, limited summer session. **Full-time faculty:** 73 total; 7% have terminal degrees, 3% minority, 44% women. **Part-time faculty:** 170 total; 8% have terminal degrees, 4% minority, 55% women. **Class size:** 80% < 20, 18% 20-39, 1% 40-49, less than 1% 50-99, less than 1% >100. **Partnerships:** Formal partnerships with local businesses, hospitals, factories/industries, and correctional institutions that participate in training, apprenticeship, and safety features.

**Student profile.** Among degree-seeking undergraduates, 52% enrolled in a transfer program, 48% enrolled in a vocational program, 513 enrolled as first-time, first-year students, 1,440 transferred in from other institutions.

| | | | |
|---|---|---|---|
| Part-time: | 42% | Hispanic American: | 1% |
| Out-of-state: | 1% | Native American: | 1% |
| Women: | 65% | 25 or older: | 45% |
| African American: | 7% | | |

**Transfer out.** Colleges most students transferred to 2007: Southern Illinois University at Carbondale, Southern Illinois University at Edwardsville, Eastern Illinois University.

**Basis for selection.** Open admission, but selective for some programs. Special requirements for health-related programs. ASSET recommended for practical nursing, cosmetology, dental, radiologic technology, physical therapy assistant program applicants. Nelson-Denny Reading Test recommended and

---

ASSET required for nursing assistant, diagnostic medical sonography, respiratory therapy applicants. Interview required of allied health majors. **Homeschooled:** COMPASS/ACT required.

**High school preparation.** 15 units recommended. Recommended units include English 4, mathematics 3, social studies 3, science 3, foreign language 2 and academic electives 2. Specific requirements for allied health.

**2007-2008 Annual costs.** Tuition/fees: $2,040; $3,720 out-of-district; $8,416 out-of-state. Per-credit charge: $61 in-district; $117 out-of-district; $274 out-of-state.

**2007-2008 Financial aid. Need-based:** 220 full-time freshmen applied for aid; 220 were judged to have need; 220 of these received aid. Average need met was 65%. Average scholarship/grant was $2,261; average loan $1,713. 59% of total undergraduate aid awarded as scholarships/grants, 41% as loans/jobs. Need-based aid available for part-time students. Work-study available for part-time students. **Non-need-based:** Awarded to 600 full-time undergraduates, including 206 freshmen. Scholarships awarded for academics, athletics, state residency.

**Application procedures. Admission:** No deadline. No application fee. Application must be submitted on paper. Admission notification on a rolling basis. Allied health programs have specific closing dates. **Financial aid:** Priority date 5/15; no closing date. FAFSA required. Applicants notified on a rolling basis starting 4/1; must reply within 2 week(s) of notification.

**Academics.** Learning communities available. **Special study options:** Accelerated study, cooperative education, distance learning, double major, dual enrollment of high school students, ESL, honors, independent study, internships, liberal arts/career combination, student-designed major, weekend college. License preparation in nursing, paramedic, physical therapy, radiology. **Credit/placement by examination:** CLEP, institutional tests. 30 credit hours maximum toward associate degree. **Support services:** GED preparation, learning center, reduced course load, remedial instruction, study skills assistance, tutoring.

**Majors. Agriculture:** General. **Business:** General, accounting, executive assistant, office technology. **Computer sciences:** Information systems, system admin. **Construction:** Carpentry. **Education:** Mathematics, teacher assistance. **Engineering technology:** Architectural drafting, electrical. **Health:** EMT paramedic, nursing (RN), physical therapy assistant, radiologic technology/medical imaging, respiratory therapy technology, veterinary technology/assistant. **Interdisciplinary:** Biological/physical sciences. **Liberal arts:** Arts/sciences. **Mechanic/repair:** Auto body, automotive, industrial. **Personal/culinary services:** Chef training. **Protective services:** Juvenile corrections, law enforcement admin.

**Most popular majors.** Business/marketing 6%, health sciences 30%, interdisciplinary studies 6%, liberal arts 40%.

**Computing on campus.** 120 workstations in library, computer center, student center. Commuter students can connect to campus network. Online library, helpline, repair service, wireless network available.

**Student life. Freshman orientation:** Available, $68 fee. Preregistration for classes offered. One-day session on campus held prior to semester; additional online session. **Activities:** Bands, choral groups, drama, film society, music ensembles, student government, student newspaper, Brothers and Sisters in Christ, black student association.

**Athletics.** NJCAA. **Intercollegiate:** Baseball M, basketball, cheerleading, golf, softball W, volleyball W. **Team name:** Blue Devils.

**Student services.** Adult student services, career counseling, services for economically disadvantaged, student employment services, financial aid counseling, minority student services, on-campus daycare, personal counseling, placement for graduates, veterans' counselor. **Physically disabled:** Services for visually, speech, hearing impaired. **Transfer:** Pre-admission transcript evaluation for new students. Transfer center, transfer adviser, college fairs on campus for students transferring to 4-year colleges.

**Contact.** Phone: (618) 545-3040 Fax: (618) 532-1135
Denise Derrick, Director of Admissions and Registration, Kaskaskia College, 27210 College Road, Centralia, IL 62801

---

## Kishwaukee College
Malta, Illinois
www.kishwaukeecollege.edu              CB code: 0511

- Public 2-year community college
- Commuter campus in rural community

**General.** Founded in 1967. Regionally accredited. **Enrollment:** 3,694 degree-seeking undergraduates. **Degrees:** 501 associate awarded. **ROTC:** Army.

**Location:** 7 miles from DeKalb. **Calendar:** Semester, limited summer session. **Full-time faculty:** 83 total. **Part-time faculty:** 174 total.

### Student profile.

Out-of-state: 1%   25 or older: 32%

**Transfer out. Colleges most students transferred to 2007:** Northern Illinois University.

**Basis for selection.** Open admission, but selective for some programs. Special requirements, including interview, for nursing, radiologic technology and therapeutic massage programs. Portfolio recommended for art majors. **Learning Disabled:** Students with learning disabilities should contact disabilities service office at least 30 days before enrollment to assist student with reasonable accommodations.

**High school preparation.** 15 units recommended. Recommended units include English 4, mathematics 3, social studies 3, science 3 and foreign language 2. High school diploma or equivalency required for nursing, radiologic technology, and therapeutic massage applicants.

**2007-2008 Annual costs.** Tuition/fees: $2,310; $8,055 out-of-district; $8,706 out-of-state. Per-credit charge: $68 in-district; $260 out-of-district; $281 out-of-state. Books/supplies: $1,000. Personal expenses: $1,000.

**Financial aid. Need-based:** Need-based aid available for part-time students. Work-study available nights, weekends and for part-time students. **Non-need-based:** Scholarships awarded for academics, athletics, leadership, music/drama, state residency.

**Application procedures. Admission:** No deadline. No application fee. Admission notification on a rolling basis. **Financial aid:** Priority date 5/1; no closing date. FAFSA, institutional form required. Applicants notified on a rolling basis starting 5/1; must reply within 2 week(s) of notification.

**Academics.** Cross-registration with Northern Illinois University and nearby community colleges. Distance Learning Consortium, member Illinois Virtual College (IVC). **Special study options:** Cross-registration, distance learning, double major, dual enrollment of high school students, ESL, independent study, internships, study abroad. License preparation in aviation, nursing, radiology, real estate. **Credit/placement by examination:** AP, CLEP, institutional tests. 48 credit hours maximum toward associate degree. Must complete 15 hours residency prior to posting proficiency credit. **Support services:** GED preparation and test center, learning center, pre-admission summer program, reduced course load, remedial instruction, study skills assistance, tutoring.

**Majors. Agriculture:** Agribusiness operations, animal breeding, business, greenhouse operations, horticultural science, horticulture, landscaping, nursery operations, ornamental horticulture, supplies. **Architecture:** Landscape. **Business:** General, accounting, human resources, management information systems, office management, office/clerical, operations. **Communications:** General, journalism. **Computer sciences:** Applications programming. **Education:** General, early childhood, elementary, physical, secondary, special. **Engineering:** General. **Engineering technology:** Drafting, electrical, manufacturing. **English:** English lit. **Family/consumer sciences:** General, child care. **Foreign languages:** General, French, Spanish. **Health:** Medical radiologic technology/radiation therapy, nursing (RN), predental, premedicine, prenursing, prepharmacy, preveterinary. **History:** General. **Interdisciplinary:** Biological/physical sciences. **Legal studies:** Prelaw. **Liberal arts:** Arts/sciences. **Math:** General. **Mechanic/repair:** Auto body, automotive, diesel. **Parks/recreation:** Health/fitness. **Physical sciences:** Astronomy, chemistry, physics. **Protective services:** Fire safety technology, firefighting, police science. **Psychology:** General. **Public administration:** Social work. **Social sciences:** General, criminology, economics, political science, sociology. **Visual/performing arts:** General, art, dramatic.

**Most popular majors.** Agriculture 7%, health sciences 10%, interdisciplinary studies 51%, liberal arts 29%.

**Computing on campus.** 376 workstations in library, computer center. Online library, helpline available.

**Student life. Freshman orientation:** Available. Preregistration for classes offered. 5 sessions held during summer. **Activities:** Choral groups, drama, literary magazine, music ensembles, musical theater, student government, student newspaper, international student club, Nurses Christian Fellowship, Phi Theta Kappa, Black Student Union, Vocational Industrial Clubs of America, Christian Fellowship, agriculture club, horticulture club, student nurses organization, student radiographers association.

**Athletics.** NJCAA. **Intercollegiate:** Baseball M, basketball, golf, soccer M, softball W, volleyball W. **Intramural:** Badminton, basketball, softball, volleyball. **Team name:** Kougars.

**Student services.** Adult student services, career counseling, services for economically disadvantaged, student employment services, financial aid counseling, health services, minority student services, on-campus daycare, personal counseling, placement for graduates, veterans' counselor, women's services. **Physically disabled:** Services for visually, speech, hearing impaired. **Learning disabled:** Comprehensive services available. **Transfer:** Re-entry adviser, pre-admission transcript evaluation for new students. Transfer center, transfer adviser, college fairs on campus for students transferring to 4-year colleges.

**Contact.** E-mail: arr@kishwaukeecollege.edu
Phone: (815) 825-2086 ext. 218 Fax: (815) 825-2306
Jill Bier, Director of Admissions, Registration and Records, Kishwaukee College, 21193 Malta Road, Malta, IL 60150-9699

## Lake Land College
**Mattoon, Illinois**
**www.lakelandcollege.edu**  CB code: 1424

▶ Public 2-year community college
▶ Commuter campus in large town

**General.** Founded in 1966. Regionally accredited. **Enrollment:** 5,467 degree-seeking undergraduates. **Degrees:** 1,200 associate awarded. **Location:** 45 miles from Decatur, 45 miles from Champaign. **Calendar:** Semester, extensive summer session. **Full-time faculty:** 123 total; 72% have terminal degrees, 6% minority, 45% women. **Part-time faculty:** 329 total; 46% have terminal degrees, 3% minority, 55% women. **Class size:** 55% < 20, 45% 20-39.

**Student profile.** Among degree-seeking undergraduates, 50% enrolled in a transfer program, 50% enrolled in a vocational program, 10% already have a bachelor's degree or higher, 67 transferred in from other institutions.

Out-of-state: 3%   25 or older: 46%

**Transfer out. Colleges most students transferred to 2007:** Eastern Illinois University, Southern Illinois University, University of Illinois.

**Basis for selection.** Open admission, but selective for some programs. Special requirements for dental hygiene, nursing, physical therapist assistant, John Deere agricultural technology, massage therapy, and cosmetology programs. ACT required of dental hygiene applicants for placement only. **Adult students:** Assessment battery test required.

**High school preparation.** Recommended units include English 4, mathematics 3, social studies 3, history 3, science 3 (laboratory 3), foreign language 2 and academic electives 2. Math and biology required for dental hygiene and nursing applicants.

**2007-2008 Annual costs.** Tuition/fees: $2,214; $4,779 out-of-district; $8,769 out-of-state. Per-credit charge: $74 in-district; $144 out-of-district; $277 out-of-state. Books/supplies: $318.

**2006-2007 Financial aid. Need-based:** 78% of total undergraduate aid awarded as scholarships/grants, 22% as loans/jobs. Need-based aid available for part-time students. Work-study available nights, weekends and for part-time students. **Non-need-based:** Scholarships awarded for academics, athletics.

**Application procedures. Admission:** No deadline. No application fee. Application may be submitted online. Admission notification on a rolling basis. **Financial aid:** Priority date 5/1; no closing date. FAFSA required. Applicants notified on a rolling basis starting 6/1.

**Academics. Special study options:** Accelerated study, cooperative education, distance learning, dual enrollment of high school students, ESL, honors, independent study, internships, study abroad, weekend college. License preparation in dental hygiene, nursing, physical therapy. **Credit/placement by examination:** AP, CLEP, institutional tests. 32 credit hours maximum toward associate degree. **Support services:** GED preparation, learning center, reduced course load, remedial instruction, study skills assistance, tutoring.

**Majors. Agriculture:** General. **Business:** General, administrative services, human resources. **Communications:** Broadcast journalism, journalism. **Computer sciences:** LAN/WAN management, networking. **Conservation:** Wildlife. **Education:** General, biology, mathematics, social science. **Engineering:** General, civil. **English:** Speech/rhetoric. **Family/consumer sciences:** General, child care. **Health:** Dental hygiene, nursing (RN), physical therapy assistant, premedicine, prepharmacy, preveterinary. **Legal studies:** Legal secretary, prelaw. **Liberal arts:** Arts/sciences. **Math:** General. **Protective services:** Police science. **Psychology:** General. **Social sciences:** General, economics. **Visual/performing arts:** Studio arts.

**Computing on campus.** 500 workstations in library, computer center. Online course registration available.

**Student life. Freshman orientation:** Available. Preregistration for classes offered. Mandatory for degree-seeking students; approximately 4 hours in length. **Activities:** Choral groups, radio station, student government, student newspaper, Phi Theta Kappa.

**Athletics.** NJCAA. **Intercollegiate:** Baseball M, basketball, softball W, tennis, volleyball W. **Intramural:** Bowling, golf, softball, volleyball. **Team name:** Lakers.

**Student services.** Career counseling, student employment services, health services, on-campus daycare, personal counseling, placement for graduates, veterans' counselor. **Physically disabled:** Services for visually, speech, hearing impaired. **Transfer:** Transfer adviser, college fairs on campus for students transferring to 4-year colleges.

**Contact.** E-mail: admissions@lakeland.cc.il.us
Phone: (217) 234-5434 Fax: (217) 234-5390
Jon VanDyke, Dean of Admission Services, Lake Land College, 5001 Lake Land Boulevard, Mattoon, IL 61938-9366

---

## Lewis and Clark Community College

| | |
|---|---|
| **Godfrey, Illinois** | **CB member** |
| **www.lc.edu** | **CB code: 0623** |

▶ Public 2-year community college
▶ Commuter campus in large town

**General.** Founded in 1970. Regionally accredited. **Enrollment:** 4,393 degree-seeking undergraduates. **Degrees:** 622 associate awarded. **ROTC:** Army. **Location:** 30 miles from St. Louis. **Calendar:** Semester, limited summer session. **Full-time faculty:** 96 total. **Part-time faculty:** 223 total.

**Student profile.** Among degree-seeking undergraduates, 4393% enrolled in a transfer program, 3160% enrolled in a vocational program.

| African American: | 6% | 25 or older: | 44% |
|---|---|---|---|
| Hispanic American: | 1% | | |

**Transfer out. Colleges most students transferred to 2007:** Southern Illinois University: Edwardsville.

**Basis for selection.** Open admission, but selective for some programs. Special requirements for nursing and other allied health programs. Interview required for radio broadcasting, music majors. Audition required for music majors.

**High school preparation.** Recommended units include English 4, mathematics 3 and science 2.

**2007-2008 Annual costs.** Tuition/fees: $2,400; $6,660 out-of-district; $8,790 out-of-state. Per-credit charge: $71 in-district; $213 out-of-district; $284 out-of-state. Out-of-state, out-of-district on-line tuition is $95 per credit including fees. Books/supplies: $435. Personal expenses: $1,100.

**Financial aid. Need-based:** Need-based aid available for part-time students.

**Application procedures. Admission:** No deadline. No application fee. Admission notification on a rolling basis. **Financial aid:** Priority date 6/1; no closing date. FAFSA required. Applicants notified on a rolling basis starting 8/1; must reply within 3 week(s) of notification.

**Academics.** Cross-registration with Blackburn College, cooperative agreements with Southwestern Junior Community College, Illinois Eastern Community College, John Wood College and Lincoln Land Community College. **Special study options:** Cooperative education, cross-registration, distance learning, double major, dual enrollment of high school students, internships, liberal arts/career combination, student-designed major. Bachelor's degree programs available on campus. License preparation in dental hygiene, nursing, occupational therapy, paramedic, real estate. **Credit/placement by examination:** AP, CLEP, institutional tests. 32 credit hours maximum toward associate degree. **Support services:** GED preparation and test center, learning center, remedial instruction, study skills assistance, tutoring, writing center.

**Majors. Business:** General, accounting, banking/financial services, business admin, office/clerical. **Communications:** Radio/tv. **Computer sciences:** General, computer graphics, computer science, data processing, information technology, LAN/WAN management, web page design, webmaster. **Education:** General, early childhood, teacher assistance. **Engineering technology:** Drafting. **Family/consumer sciences:** Child care. **Health:** Dental hygiene, nursing (RN), occupational therapy assistant, predental, premedicine, prenursing, prepharmacy. **Legal studies:** Legal secretary, prelaw. **Liberal arts:** Arts/sciences. **Mechanic/repair:** Automotive. **Protective services:** Criminal justice, firefighting. **Visual/performing arts:** Studio arts.

**Computing on campus.** 300 workstations in library, computer center. Online course registration, online library, wireless network available.

**Student life. Freshman orientation:** Mandatory. Preregistration for classes offered. **Activities:** Bands, choral groups, dance, drama, music ensembles, radio station, student government, student newspaper, TV station, veterans organization, Christian Campus Fellowship, disabled students organization, black student association, political action club.

**Athletics.** NJCAA. **Intercollegiate:** Baseball M, basketball, golf M, soccer, softball W, tennis, volleyball W. **Team name:** Trailblazers.

**Student services.** Adult student services, career counseling, student employment services, health services, on-campus daycare, personal counseling, placement for graduates, veterans' counselor. **Physically disabled:** Services for visually, hearing impaired. **Transfer:** Pre-admission transcript evaluation for new students. Transfer center, transfer adviser, college fairs on campus for students transferring to 4-year colleges.

**Contact.** E-mail: enroll@lc.edu
Phone: (618) 468-2222 Toll-free number: (800) 500-5222
Fax: (618) 468-2310
Peggy Hudson, Director Enrollment Center for Admissions Services, Lewis and Clark Community College, 5800 Godfrey Road, Godfrey, IL 62035-2466

---

## Lincoln College

| | |
|---|---|
| **Lincoln, Illinois** | **CB member** |
| **www.lincolncollege.edu** | **CB code: 1406** |

▶ Private 2-year junior college
▶ Residential campus in large town
▶ SAT or ACT required

**General.** Founded in 1865. Regionally accredited. Liberal arts degree program offered only at main campus. Degree and vocational programs available at extension campus in Normal. **Enrollment:** 800 degree-seeking undergraduates. **Degrees:** 52 bachelor's, 214 associate awarded. **Location:** 185 miles from Chicago, 125 miles from St. Louis. **Calendar:** Semester, limited summer session. **Full-time faculty:** 35 total. **Part-time faculty:** 20 total. **Special facilities:** Museum of the presidents.

**Student profile.**

| Out-of-state: | 9% | Live on campus: | 90% |
|---|---|---|---|
| 25 or older: | 1% | | |

**Transfer out. Colleges most students transferred to 2007:** Illinois State University, Southern Illinois University, Eastern Illinois University, Northern Illinois University, Western Illinois University.

**Basis for selection.** Test scores and high school transcript most important. Interview considered. Normal campus requires 18 ACT score for resident students. Interview recommended for academically weak applicants.

**2007-2008 Annual costs.** Tuition/fees: $18,000. Per-credit charge: $600. Room/board: $6,000. Books/supplies: $240. Personal expenses: $1,000.

**Financial aid. Need-based:** Need-based aid available for part-time students. Work-study available nights and weekends. **Non-need-based:** Scholarships awarded for academics, art, athletics, music/drama. **Additional information:** Auditions recommended for music, speech, theater, broadcasting, and dance scholarship candidates, portfolios recommended for art and technical theater scholarship candidates.

**Application procedures. Admission:** Closing date 8/18 (receipt date). $25 fee. Application may be submitted online. Admission notification on a rolling basis. Freshman enrollment limited. Application process closes early if maximum is reached. **Financial aid:** Priority date 6/1, closing date 7/1. FAFSA required. Applicants notified on a rolling basis starting 6/1; must reply within 3 week(s) of notification.

**Academics. Special study options:** Dual enrollment of high school students, honors, independent study, study abroad. Bachelor's degree programs available on campus. **Credit/placement by examination:** CLEP, institutional tests. 15 credit hours maximum toward associate degree. **Support services:** Learning center, pre-admission summer program, reduced course load, tutoring.

**Majors. Biology:** General. **Business:** General, accounting, business admin, tourism promotion, tourism/travel. **Communications:** General, journalism. **Computer sciences:** Computer science. **Conservation:** General, environmental studies. **Education:** General, art, elementary, multi-level teacher. **English:** American lit, composition, English lit, speech/rhetoric. **History:** General. **Liberal arts:** Arts/sciences. **Math:** General, statistics. **Parks/recreation:** Health/fitness. **Philosophy/religion:** Philosophy, religion. **Physical sciences:** Chemistry, physics. **Protective services:** Law enforcement admin, police science. **Psychology:** General. **Social sciences:** General, economics, geography, sociology. **Visual/performing arts:** General, art, art history/conservation, ceramics, dance, dramatic, drawing, jazz, music history, music performance, music theory/composition, painting, photography, piano/organ, sculpture, studio arts, theater design, voice/opera.

**Computing on campus.** 110 workstations in library, computer center. Dormitories wired for high-speed internet access.

**Student life. Freshman orientation:** Mandatory. Preregistration for classes offered. **Housing:** Guaranteed on-campus for freshmen. Single-sex dorms available. $125 deposit, deadline 8/1. **Activities:** Bands, choral groups, dance, drama, literary magazine, music ensembles, musical theater, student government, Interfaith Committee, Fellowship of Christian Athletes.

**Athletics. NJCAA. Intercollegiate:** Baseball M, basketball, cross-country, diving, golf, soccer, softball W, swimming, volleyball W, wrestling M. **Intramural:** Baseball M, basketball, football (non-tackle), football (tackle), soccer, softball, table tennis, volleyball. **Team name:** Lynx.

**Student services.** Adult student services, career counseling, student employment services, health services, placement for graduates. **Transfer:** Transfer center, transfer adviser, college fairs on campus for students transferring to 4-year colleges.

**Contact.** Phone: (800) 569-0556 Fax: (217) 732-7715
Stacy Rachel, Director of Enrollment Management, Lincoln College, 300 Keokuk Street, Lincoln, IL 62656

## Lincoln Land Community College
### Springfield, Illinois
### www.llcc.edu
**CB code: 1428**

- Public 2-year community and junior college
- Commuter campus in small city

**General.** Founded in 1967. Regionally accredited. **Enrollment:** 5,196 degree-seeking undergraduates; 1,459 non-degree-seeking students. **Degrees:** 643 associate awarded. **ROTC:** Army, Naval, Air Force. **Location:** 180 miles from Chicago, 96 miles from St. Louis. **Calendar:** Semester, extensive summer session. **Full-time faculty:** 125 total; 91% have terminal degrees, 6% minority, 51% women. **Part-time faculty:** 235 total; 3% minority, 46% women. **Class size:** 69% < 20, 31% 20-39, less than 1% 40-49. **Special facilities:** Museum.

**Student profile.** Among degree-seeking undergraduates, 57% enrolled in a transfer program, 30% enrolled in a vocational program, 4% already have a bachelor's degree or higher, 857 enrolled as first-time, first-year students, 69 transferred in from other institutions.

| Part-time: | 56% | Asian American: | 1% |
|---|---|---|---|
| Women: | 60% | Hispanic American: | 2% |
| African American: | 9% | 25 or older: | 40% |

**Transfer out.** 35% of students enrolled in the transfer program go on to 4-year colleges. **Colleges most students transferred to 2007:** University of Illinois: Springfield, Southern Illinois University: Carbondale, Eastern Illinois University, Western Illinois University, Illinois State University.

**Basis for selection.** Open admission, but selective for some programs. Applicants to nursing and allied health programs must rank in top half of high school class and have 20 ACT. ACT required for nursing, respiratory therapy, and radiologic technology applicants. Admissions assessment not required for students with ACT composite score of 22 or above.

**High school preparation.** Recommended units include English 4, mathematics 3, social studies 3, science 3 and foreign language 2.

**2008-2009 Annual costs.** Tuition/fees (projected): $2,760; $4,920 out-of-district; $7,080 out-of-state. Per-credit charge: $82 in-district; $154 out-of-district; $226 out-of-state. Books/supplies: $840. Personal expenses: $1,035.

**Financial aid. Need-based:** Need-based aid available for part-time students. Work-study available nights. **Non-need-based:** Scholarships awarded for academics, athletics, minority status, state residency.

**Application procedures. Admission:** No deadline. No application fee. Application may be submitted online. Admission notification on a rolling basis. **Financial aid:** Priority date 5/1; no closing date. FAFSA, institutional form required. Applicants notified on a rolling basis starting 4/15; must reply within 2 week(s) of notification.

**Academics. Special study options:** Cooperative education, distance learning, double major, dual enrollment of high school students, ESL, honors, independent study, internships, liberal arts/career combination, study abroad, United Nations semester. License preparation in nursing, occupational therapy, paramedic, physical therapy, radiology, real estate. **Credit/placement by examination:** AP, CLEP, institutional tests. 30 credit hours maximum toward associate degree. **Support services:** GED preparation, learning center, reduced course load, remedial instruction, study skills assistance, tutoring, writing center.

**Majors. Agriculture:** Landscaping, production. **Business:** General, accounting, administrative services, hospitality admin, office technology. **Computer sciences:** Applications programming, networking, programming. **Construction:** Maintenance. **Education:** Teacher assistance. **Engineering:** General. **Engineering technology:** Architectural drafting, construction, electrical. **Health:** Nursing (RN), occupational therapy assistant, office assistant, radiologic technology/medical imaging. **Interdisciplinary:** Biological/physical sciences. **Legal studies:** Legal secretary. **Liberal arts:** Arts/sciences. **Mechanic/repair:** Aircraft, auto body, automotive, industrial electronics. **Protective services:** Firefighting, police science. **Transportation:** Aviation management. **Visual/performing arts:** Graphic design, studio arts.

**Most popular majors.** Business/marketing 12%, health sciences 16%, interdisciplinary studies 10%, liberal arts 43%.

**Computing on campus.** 325 workstations in library, computer center, student center. Commuter students can connect to campus network. Online course registration, online library, helpline, wireless network available.

**Student life. Freshman orientation:** Available. Preregistration for classes offered. Half-day program offered at beginning of semester. **Activities:** Bands, choral groups, dance, drama, literary magazine, music ensembles, musical theater, student government, student newspaper.

**Athletics. NJCAA. Intercollegiate:** Baseball M, basketball, soccer M, softball W, volleyball W. **Team name:** Loggers.

**Student services.** Adult student services, career counseling, services for economically disadvantaged, student employment services, financial aid counseling, minority student services, on-campus daycare, personal counseling, placement for graduates, veterans' counselor, women's services. **Physically disabled:** Services for visually, speech, hearing impaired. **Learning disabled:** Comprehensive services available. **Transfer:** Pre-admission transcript evaluation for new students. Transfer adviser, college fairs on campus for students transferring to 4-year colleges.

**Contact.** E-mail: ron.gregoire@llcc.cc.il.us
Phone: (217) 786-2290 Toll-free number: (800) 727-4161
Fax: (217) 786-2492
Ron Gregoire, Director of Admissions and Records, Lincoln Land Community College, 5250 Shepherd Road, Springfield, IL 62794-9256

## MacCormac College
### Chicago, Illinois
### www.maccormac.edu
**CB code: 1520**

- Private 2-year junior college
- Commuter campus in very large city
- Interview required

**General.** Founded in 1904. Regionally accredited. **Enrollment:** 171 degree-seeking undergraduates. **Degrees:** 43 associate awarded. **Calendar:** Semester, extensive summer session. **Full-time faculty:** 5 total. **Part-time faculty:** 21 total.

**Student profile.**

| Out-of-state: | 1% | 25 or older: | 30% |
|---|---|---|---|

**Transfer out. Colleges most students transferred to 2007:** Loyola University, DePaul University, Roosevelt University.

**Basis for selection.** Open admission, but selective for some programs. Minimum typing speed required for court reporting. ACT recommended.

**High school preparation.** 13 units required; 15 recommended. Required and recommended units include English 4, mathematics 2-3, social studies 3-4, history 1, science 2 (laboratory 1).

**2008-2009 Annual costs.** Tuition/fees: $10,060. Per-credit charge: $415. Books/supplies: $1,000.

**Financial aid. Non-need-based:** Scholarships awarded for academics, leadership.

**Application procedures. Admission:** No deadline. $20 fee, may be waived for applicants with need. Application may be submitted online. Admission notification on a rolling basis. **Financial aid:** Closing date 8/15. FAFSA required. Must reply within 2 week(s) of notification.

**Academics. Special study options:** ESL, internships. **Credit/placement by examination:** CLEP, IB, institutional tests. 36 credit hours maximum toward associate degree. **Support services:** Learning center, study skills assistance, tutoring.

**Majors. Business:** General, accounting, administrative services, business admin, hospitality admin, international, international marketing, management information systems, marketing, office management, office technology, office/clerical, tourism promotion, tourism/travel. **Computer sciences:** General, computer science, information systems. **Health:** Medical transcription. **Legal studies:** Court reporting, legal secretary, paralegal.

**Most popular majors.** Business/marketing 80%, legal studies 15%.

**Computing on campus.** 118 workstations in library, computer center.

**Student life. Freshman orientation:** Mandatory. Preregistration for classes offered. **Activities:** Student government, student activities committee, Phi Theta Kappa.

**Student services.** Career counseling, student employment services, financial aid counseling, personal counseling, placement for graduates. **Transfer:** Transfer adviser for students transferring to 4-year colleges.

**Contact.** E-mail: admissions@maccormac.edu
Phone: (312) 922-1884 Fax: (312) 922-3196
David Grassi, Admissions Representative, MacCormac College, 29 East Madison Street, Chicago, IL 60602

---

## McHenry County College
**Crystal Lake, Illinois**
www.mchenry.edu

**CB member**
**CB code: 1525**

- Public 2-year community college
- Commuter campus in large town

**General.** Founded in 1967. Regionally accredited. **Enrollment:** 5,275 degree-seeking undergraduates. **Degrees:** 483 associate awarded. **Location:** 50 miles from Chicago. **Calendar:** Semester, limited summer session. **Full-time faculty:** 92 total; 8% minority, 48% women. **Part-time faculty:** 185 total; 7% minority, 55% women. **Special facilities:** Planetarium, weather cam.

**Transfer out. Colleges most students transferred to 2007:** Northern Illinois University, Illinois State University, University of Illinois at Chicago, Southern Illinois University, Columbia College.

**Basis for selection.** Open admission.

**High school preparation.** 18 units recommended. Recommended units include English 4, mathematics 3, social studies 3, science 3 (laboratory 3) and academic electives 2. 2 units recommended among any of the following: foreign language, music, vocational education, or art.

**2007-2008 Annual costs.** Tuition/fees: $2,474; $8,414 out-of-district; $9,674 out-of-state. Per-credit charge: $73 in-district; $271 out-of-district; $313 out-of-state. Books/supplies: $800. Personal expenses: $1,362.

**Financial aid. Need-based:** Need-based aid available for part-time students. Work-study available nights, weekends and for part-time students. **Non-need-based:** Scholarships awarded for academics, athletics, leadership, music/drama, state residency. **Additional information:** Students can apply throughout the award year for federal and state aid. Students with physical handicaps or learning disabilities may apply for special needs scholarship.

**Application procedures. Admission:** No deadline. $15 fee. Application may be submitted online. Admission notification on a rolling basis. **Financial aid:** Priority date 6/1; no closing date. FAFSA, institutional form required. Applicants notified on a rolling basis starting 5/1.

**Academics. Special study options:** Accelerated study, distance learning, dual enrollment of high school students, ESL, honors, independent study, internships, liberal arts/career combination, study abroad. Cooperative programs (tech prep) with Education for Employment. License preparation in paramedic, real estate. **Credit/placement by examination:** AP, CLEP, institutional tests. 30 credit hours maximum toward associate degree. Local

proficiency exams available for occupational course credit, DANTES exams accepted. **Support services:** GED preparation and test center, learning center, pre-admission summer program, reduced course load, remedial instruction, study skills assistance, tutoring, writing center.

**Majors. Agriculture:** Horticulture. **Business:** Accounting technology, administrative services, business admin, operations, real estate, selling. **Computer sciences:** Applications programming. **Construction:** Building inspection. **Engineering:** General. **Engineering technology:** Electrical, mechanical. **Health:** EMT paramedic. **Interdisciplinary:** Biological/physical sciences. **Liberal arts:** Arts/sciences. **Mechanic/repair:** Automotive. **Protective services:** Firefighting, police science. **Visual/performing arts:** Art.

**Most popular majors.** Business/marketing 6%, interdisciplinary studies 68%, liberal arts 12%.

**Computing on campus.** 153 workstations in library, computer center, student center. Commuter students can connect to campus network. Online course registration, online library available.

**Student life. Freshman orientation:** Available. Preregistration for classes offered. Admitted students from local high schools invited to participate in orientation and preregistration during April and May. **Activities:** Bands, choral groups, drama, literary magazine, music ensembles, student government, student newspaper, Latinos Unidos, Phi Theta Kappa, campus activities board, campus Christian fellowship, Club Concordia, Pride Alliance, black student alliance, Latter-day Saint student association, Special Needs Action Program, student leadership team.

**Athletics.** NJCAA. **Intercollegiate:** Baseball M, basketball, soccer M, softball W, tennis, volleyball W. **Intramural:** Basketball. **Team name:** Fighting Scots.

**Student services.** Adult student services, career counseling, student employment services, financial aid counseling, minority student services, on-campus daycare, personal counseling, placement for graduates, veterans' counselor. **Physically disabled:** Services for visually, speech, hearing impaired. **Transfer:** Pre-admission transcript evaluation for new students. Transfer center, transfer adviser, college fairs on campus for students transferring to 4-year colleges.

**Contact.** E-mail: admissions@mchenry.edu
Phone: (815) 455-8530 Toll-free number: (866) 743-6667
Fax: (815) 455-3766
Marilyn Weniger, Director of Admissions and Advising, McHenry County College, 8900 U.S. Highway 14, Crystal Lake, IL 60012-2761

---

## Moraine Valley Community College
**Palos Hills, Illinois**
www.morainevalley.edu

**CB code: 1524**

- Public 2-year community college
- Commuter campus in large town

**General.** Founded in 1967. Regionally accredited. **Enrollment:** 10,758 degree-seeking undergraduates; 5,101 non-degree-seeking students. **Degrees:** 1,226 associate awarded. **Location:** 25 miles from Chicago. **Calendar:** Semester, extensive summer session. **Full-time faculty:** 171 total; 9% have terminal degrees, 57% women. **Part-time faculty:** 607 total; 8% have terminal degrees, 53% women. **Class size:** 40% < 20, 60% 20-39. **Special facilities:** Nature study area, center for contemporary technology, fine and performing arts center.

**Student profile.** Among degree-seeking undergraduates, 58% enrolled in a transfer program, 32% enrolled in a vocational program, 5% already have a bachelor's degree or higher, 1,830 enrolled as first-time, first-year students, 710 transferred in from other institutions.

| | | | |
|---|---|---|---|
| Part-time: | 47% | Hispanic American: | 12% |
| Women: | 58% | International: | 1% |
| African American: | 9% | 25 or older: | 28% |
| Asian American: | 3% | | |

**Transfer out.** 90% of students enrolled in the transfer program go on to 4-year colleges. **Colleges most students transferred to 2007:** Governors State University, St. Xavier University, University of Illinois-Chicago, Illinois State University, Eastern Illinois University.

**Basis for selection.** Open admission, but selective for some programs. Some health science programs have special admission requirements and limited enrollment. Placement tests may be waived for students with specified ACT scores. COMPASS tests required of all full-time students. **Learning Disabled:** Students should register with Center for Disability Services before May 1.

**High school preparation.** 15 units required. Required units include English 4, mathematics 2, social studies 2, science 2 (laboratory 2) and academic electives 5.

**2008-2009 Annual costs.** Tuition/fees (projected): $2,222; $6,422 out-of-district; $7,712 out-of-state. Per-credit charge: $69 in-district; $209 out-of-district; $252 out-of-state. Books/supplies: $1,760. Personal expenses: $1,632.

**2007-2008 Financial aid. Need-based:** 90% of total undergraduate aid awarded as scholarships/grants, 10% as loans/jobs. Need-based aid available for part-time students. Work-study available nights and for part-time students. **Non-need-based:** Scholarships awarded for academics, athletics, leadership.

**Application procedures. Admission:** No deadline. No application fee. Application may be submitted online. Admission notification on a rolling basis. **Financial aid:** Priority date 5/1; no closing date. FAFSA, institutional form required. Applicants notified on a rolling basis starting 3/1; must reply within 4 week(s) of notification.

**Academics. Special study options:** Accelerated study, cooperative education, distance learning, double major, dual enrollment of high school students, ESL, honors, independent study, internships, liberal arts/career combination, study abroad, weekend college. License preparation in paramedic. **Credit/placement by examination:** AP, CLEP, institutional tests. **Support services:** GED preparation and test center, learning center, reduced course load, remedial instruction, study skills assistance, tutoring, writing center.

**Majors. Business:** General, administrative services, business admin, entrepreneurial studies, hospitality admin, human resources, management information systems, retailing, small business admin, tourism/travel. **Computer sciences:** LAN/WAN management, security, webmaster. **Education:** Mathematics, science, teacher assistance. **Engineering technology:** Instrumentation, mechanical. **Health:** Medical records technology, nursing (RN), radiologic technology/medical imaging, respiratory therapy technology. **Interdisciplinary:** Biological/physical sciences. **Liberal arts:** Arts/sciences. **Mechanic/repair:** Automotive, industrial electronics. **Parks/recreation:** Facilities management. **Personal/culinary services:** Restaurant/catering. **Protective services:** Firefighting, juvenile corrections, police science. **Visual/performing arts:** General, graphic design. **Other:** Recreation therapy.

**Most popular majors.** Health sciences 14%, interdisciplinary studies 42%, liberal arts 30%.

**Computing on campus.** 1,269 workstations in library, computer center, student center. Online course registration, online library, helpline available.

**Student life. Freshman orientation:** Available. Students registering for 12 or more credit hours required to participate in orientation program prior to first registration. **Activities:** Bands, campus ministries, choral groups, dance, drama, international student organizations, literary magazine, music ensembles, musical theater, student government, student newspaper, community service volunteer program, forensics team, inter-club council, peers educating peers, student entertainment board, Muslim student association, Alliance for African-American students, Latin and Arab student groups.

**Athletics.** NJCAA. **Intercollegiate:** Baseball M, basketball, cross-country, golf M, soccer, softball W, tennis, volleyball W. **Intramural:** Badminton, basketball, volleyball W. **Team name:** Cyclones.

**Student services.** Adult student services, career counseling, services for economically disadvantaged, student employment services, financial aid counseling, minority student services, on-campus daycare, personal counseling, placement for graduates, women's services. **Physically disabled:** Services for visually, speech, hearing impaired. **Transfer:** Transfer center, transfer adviser, college fairs on campus for students transferring to 4-year colleges.

**Contact.** E-mail: admissions@morainevalley.edu
Phone: (708) 974-2110 Fax: (708) 974-0974
Wendy Manser, Dean of Enrollment Services, Moraine Valley Community College, 9000 West College Parkway, Palos Hills, IL 60465-0937

## Morrison Institute of Technology
**Morrison, Illinois**
**www.morrison.tec.il.us**
**CB code: 1269**

- Private 2-year junior and technical college
- Residential campus in small town

**General.** Founded in 1973. Accredited by Technology Accreditation Commission of Accreditation Board of Engineering and Technology. **Enrollment:** 144 degree-seeking undergraduates. **Degrees:** 38 associate awarded. **Location:** 100 miles from Chicago, 50 miles from Davenport, Iowa. **Calendar:** Semester, limited summer session. **Full-time faculty:** 10 total; 40%

women. **Part-time faculty:** 1 total; 100% women. **Class size:** 46% < 20, 54% 20-39. **Special facilities:** 4 computer-aided design (CAD) laboratories.

**Student profile.**

| | | | |
|---|---|---|---|
| Out-of-state: | 6% | Live on campus: | 70% |
| 25 or older: | 10% | | |

**Transfer out.** Colleges most students transferred to 2007: Bradley University, University of Wisconsin at Platteville.

**Basis for selection.** Open admission. Interview recommended.

**High school preparation.** Recommended units include mathematics 2 and science 1. Algebra, geometry and drafting recommended.

**2008-2009 Annual costs.** Tuition/fees: $13,360. Per-credit charge: $545. Room only: $2,700. Books/supplies: $850. Personal expenses: $900.

**2007-2008 Financial aid. Need-based:** Need-based aid available for part-time students. Work-study available nights and weekends. **Non-need-based:** Scholarships awarded for academics.

**Application procedures. Admission:** Priority date 8/1; no deadline. $30 fee. Admission notification on a rolling basis. **Financial aid:** No deadline. FAFSA, institutional form required. Applicants notified on a rolling basis; must reply within 2 week(s) of notification.

**Academics. Special study options:** Double major. **Credit/placement by examination:** AP, CLEP, IB, institutional tests. 25 credit hours maximum toward associate degree. SOC approved guidelines. **Support services:** Reduced course load, tutoring.

**Majors. Architecture:** Technology. **Computer sciences:** LAN/WAN management. **Engineering technology:** Architectural, CAD/CADD, civil, construction, manufacturing, surveying.

**Computing on campus.** 80 workstations in library, computer center. Dormitories wired for high-speed internet access and linked to campus network. Wireless network available.

**Student life. Freshman orientation:** Mandatory. Preregistration for classes offered. Five 1-hour presentations during first 5 weeks of semester. **Housing:** Guaranteed on-campus for all undergraduates. Coed dorms, special housing for disabled, substance-free housing available. $100 deposit. **Activities:** Student government, student newspaper, professional societies, student chapters.

**Athletics. Intramural:** Basketball M, bowling, volleyball.

**Student services.** Career counseling, student employment services, personal counseling, placement for graduates. **Transfer:** Transfer adviser, college fairs on campus for students transferring to 4-year colleges.

**Contact.** E-mail: admissions@morrison.tec.il.us
Phone: (815) 772-7218 ext. 11 Fax: (815) 772-7548
Bridgit Schmidt, Director of Admissions, Morrison Institute of Technology, 701 Portland Avenue, Morrison, IL 61270-2959

## Morton College
**Cicero, Illinois**
**www.morton.edu**
**CB code: 1489**

- Public 2-year community college
- Commuter campus in small city

**General.** Founded in 1924. Regionally accredited. **Enrollment:** 2,183 degree-seeking undergraduates; 2,874 non-degree-seeking students. **Degrees:** 315 associate awarded. **Location:** 6 miles from Chicago Loop. **Calendar:** Semester, limited summer session. **Full-time faculty:** 54 total; 13% have terminal degrees, 15% minority, 54% women. **Part-time faculty:** 174 total; 9% have terminal degrees, 17% minority, 55% women. **Class size:** 50% < 20, 49% 20-39, less than 1% 40-49, less than 1% 50-99. **Special facilities:** Planetarium.

**Student profile.** Among degree-seeking undergraduates, 49% enrolled in a transfer program, 46% enrolled in a vocational program, 346 enrolled as first-time, first-year students.

| | | | |
|---|---|---|---|
| Part-time: | 59% | Hispanic American: | 71% |
| Women: | 57% | International: | 3% |
| African American: | 6% | 25 or older: | 33% |
| Asian American: | 2% | | |

**Basis for selection.** Open admission, but selective for some programs and for out-of-state students. Nursing and physical therapist assistant programs have limited space. Preference given to in-district applicants using class rank, mathematics and science course prerequisites, and placement tests as guides.

**High school preparation.** 15 units recommended. Recommended units include English 4, mathematics 3, social studies 3, science 3 and foreign language 2.

**2007-2008 Annual costs.** Tuition/fees: $2,452; $6,292 out-of-district; $8,212 out-of-state. Per-credit charge: $64 in-district; $192 out-of-district; $256 out-of-state.

**Financial aid.** **Need-based:** Need-based aid available for part-time students. Work-study available nights, weekends and for part-time students.

**Application procedures.** **Admission:** No deadline. $10 fee. Application may be submitted online. Admission notification on a rolling basis. **Financial aid:** Priority date 6/1; no closing date. FAFSA, institutional form required. Applicants notified on a rolling basis starting 8/1.

**Academics.** **Special study options:** Distance learning, double major, dual enrollment of high school students, ESL, internships, weekend college. License preparation in nursing, physical therapy. **Credit/placement by examination:** AP, CLEP, IB, institutional tests. 30 credit hours maximum toward associate degree, 30 toward bachelor's. **Support services:** GED preparation, learning center, pre-admission summer program, remedial instruction, tutoring, writing center.

**Majors.** **Business:** Accounting, administrative services, business admin. **Computer sciences:** Information technology. **Engineering technology:** CAD/CADD. **English:** English lit. **Health:** Nursing (RN), physical therapy assistant. **Interdisciplinary:** Biological/physical sciences. **Liberal arts:** Arts/sciences. **Mechanic/repair:** Automotive, heating/ac/refrig. **Protective services:** Police science. **Visual/performing arts:** Studio arts.

**Most popular majors.** Business/marketing 10%, health sciences 20%, interdisciplinary studies 9%, liberal arts 44%, security/protective services 7%.

**Computing on campus.** 314 workstations in library, computer center, student center. Wireless network available.

**Student life.** **Freshman orientation:** Available. Preregistration for classes offered. **Activities:** Jazz band, choral groups, dance, drama, music ensembles, musical theater, student government, student newspaper, art club, nursing students association, Phi Theta Kappa, HALO, College Bowl, film club, Yes We Can!-Si Se Puede!, open options, student success club, automotive club.

**Athletics.** NJCAA. **Intercollegiate:** Baseball M, basketball, cross-country, soccer M, softball W, volleyball W. **Team name:** Panthers.

**Student services.** Career counseling, services for economically disadvantaged, student employment services, financial aid counseling, on-campus daycare, personal counseling, placement for graduates. **Physically disabled:** Services for visually, speech, hearing impaired. **Transfer:** Transfer center, transfer adviser, college fairs on campus for students transferring to 4-year colleges.

**Contact.** E-mail: Enroll@morton.edu
Phone: (708) 656-8000 ext. 346 Fax: (708) 656-9592
Lizette Urbina, Associate Dean Student Development & Records, Morton College, 3801 South Central Avenue, Cicero, IL 60804-4398

## Northwestern Business College
### Chicago, Illinois
www.northwesternbc.edu                     CB code: 2433

- For-profit 2-year technical college
- Commuter campus in very large city

**General.** Founded in 1902. Regionally accredited. Additional campuses in Bridgeview and Naperville. **Enrollment:** 1,987 degree-seeking undergraduates. **Degrees:** 327 associate awarded. **Calendar:** Quarter, extensive summer session. **Full-time faculty:** 40 total; 28% minority, 60% women. **Part-time faculty:** 99 total; 35% minority, 66% women. **Class size:** 78% < 20, 22% 20-39, less than 1% 40-49. **Special facilities:** Health sciences laboratories.

**Student profile.**

| | | | |
|---|---|---|---|
| African American: | 38% | **Hispanic American:** | 37% |
| Asian American: | 2% | **25 or older:** | 31% |

**Basis for selection.** Students must have a 15 ACT, 550 SAT (exclusive of Writing) or pass admissions test administered on campus. COMPASS or ASSET used for placement.

**2008-2009 Annual costs.** Tuition/fees (projected): $18,997. Per-credit charge: $370. Tuition may be higher for some classes. Books/supplies: $1,250. Personal expenses: $1,000.

**2007-2008 Financial aid.** **Need-based:** 50% of total undergraduate aid awarded as scholarships/grants, 50% as loans/jobs. Need-based aid available for part-time students. Work-study available nights and for part-time students. **Non-need-based:** Scholarships awarded for academics. **Additional information:** State grant programs for Illinois residents and alternative loans offered.

**Application procedures.** **Admission:** No deadline. $25 fee. Application may be submitted online. Admission notification on a rolling basis. **Financial aid:** Priority date 6/30; no closing date. FAFSA, institutional form required. Applicants notified on a rolling basis starting 8/15; must reply within 4 week(s) of notification.

**Academics.** Students wishing to graduate early may attend summer quarter. **Special study options:** Double major, internships. License preparation in real estate. **Credit/placement by examination:** AP, CLEP, IB, institutional tests. 50 credit hours maximum toward associate degree. Maximum credit awarded by examination is 25% of major, 50% of program. **Support services:** Learning center, reduced course load, remedial instruction, study skills assistance, tutoring.

**Majors.** **Business:** Accounting, administrative services, business admin, entrepreneurial studies, hospitality admin, tourism/travel. **Computer sciences:** General, applications programming, programming. **Health:** Medical assistant, medical records technology, medical secretary. **Legal studies:** Paralegal.

**Most popular majors.** Business/marketing 30%, computer/information sciences 13%, health sciences 6%, legal studies 26%.

**Computing on campus.** 413 workstations in library, computer center.

**Student life.** **Freshman orientation:** Mandatory. Preregistration for classes offered. Three-hour program offered day and evening. **Activities:** Honor society, clubs related to majors, Junior Achievement.

**Student services.** Alcohol/substance abuse counseling, career counseling, student employment services, financial aid counseling, personal counseling, placement for graduates. **Physically disabled:** Services for visually, speech, hearing impaired. **Transfer:** Pre-admission transcript evaluation for new students. Transfer center, transfer adviser, college fairs on campus for students transferring to 4-year colleges.

**Contact.** Phone: (773) 481-3730 Toll-free number: (800) 396-5613 Fax: (773) 481-3738
Mark Sliz, Director of Admissions, Northwestern Business College, 4839 North Milwaukee Avenue, Chicago, IL 60630

## Oakton Community College
### Des Plaines, Illinois
www.oakton.edu                     CB code: 1573

- Public 2-year community college
- Commuter campus in small city

**General.** Founded in 1969. Regionally accredited. **Enrollment:** 5,066 degree-seeking undergraduates. **Degrees:** 398 associate awarded. **Location:** 15 miles from Chicago. **Calendar:** Semester, limited summer session. **Full-time faculty:** 160 total. **Part-time faculty:** 520 total. **Special facilities:** Campus located within wildlife preserve, visual arts center at Des Plaines campus.

**Student profile.**

| | | | |
|---|---|---|---|
| Out-of-state: | 7% | **25 or older:** | 45% |

**Transfer out.** **Colleges most students transferred to 2007:** University of Illinois-Chicago, Northeastern Illinois University, DePaul University, Loyola University-Chicago.

**Basis for selection.** Open admission, but selective for some programs. Special requirements for health career programs. ACT recommended for placement and counseling; SAT accepted. Scores must be received prior to enrolling in English course. Interview required of health career majors, except for nursing. **Learning Disabled:** Following completion of admission application, students arrange meetings for testing, registration, and provide documentation of disability.

**2007-2008 Annual costs.** Tuition/fees: $2,578; $7,134 out-of-district; $9,016 out-of-state. Per-credit charge: $82 in-district; $234 out-of-district; $297 out-of-state. Books/supplies: $800. Personal expenses: $1,000.

**Financial aid. Need-based:** Need-based aid available for part-time students. Work-study available nights, weekends and for part-time students. **Non-need-based:** Scholarships awarded for academics, art, leadership, minority status, music/drama, state residency. **Additional information:** Foundation Scholarships application available January through mid-March.

**Application procedures. Admission:** No deadline. $25 fee. Application may be submitted online. Admission notification on a rolling basis. **Financial aid:** Priority date 5/1; no closing date. FAFSA, institutional form required. Applicants notified on a rolling basis starting 5/1; must reply within 2 week(s) of notification.

**Academics. Special study options:** Accelerated study, distance learning, dual enrollment of high school students, exchange student, honors, independent study, internships, study abroad, teacher certification program, weekend college. License preparation in nursing, real estate. **Credit/placement by examination:** AP, CLEP, institutional tests. 30 credit hours maximum toward associate degree. **Support services:** GED preparation, learning center, remedial instruction, study skills assistance, tutoring, writing center.

**Majors. Business:** Accounting, business admin, international, office management, real estate. **Computer sciences:** General, data processing. **Construction:** Maintenance. **Education:** Early childhood. **Engineering:** General. **Engineering technology:** Architectural, construction, drafting, electrical, electrical drafting, robotics. **Health:** Clinical lab assistant, medical records technology, nursing (RN), physical therapy assistant. **Liberal arts:** Arts/sciences. **Mechanic/repair:** Automotive. **Production:** Machine shop technology. **Protective services:** Firefighting, police science. **Visual/performing arts:** Commercial/advertising art.

**Computing on campus.** 800 workstations in library, computer center, student center. Commuter students can connect to campus network. Online course registration, online library, helpline, wireless network available.

**Student life. Freshman orientation:** Available. Preregistration for classes offered. **Activities:** Jazz band, choral groups, drama, literary magazine, music ensembles, student government, student newspaper, Christian student association, Indian student association, political science forum, black student union, Hillel, Japanese club, desktop publishing club.

**Athletics.** NJCAA. **Intercollegiate:** Baseball M, basketball, cross-country, golf M, soccer, softball W, tennis, track and field, volleyball W. **Intramural:** Basketball, volleyball. **Team name:** Raiders.

**Student services.** Adult student services, alcohol/substance abuse counseling, career counseling, student employment services, financial aid counseling, health services, minority student services, on-campus daycare, personal counseling, placement for graduates, veterans' counselor. **Transfer:** Transfer center, transfer adviser, college fairs on campus for students transferring to 4-year colleges.

**Contact.** E-mail: admiss@oakton.edu
Phone: (847) 635-1629 Fax: (847) 635-1890
Michele Brown, Director of Admission and Enrollment Management, Oakton Community College, 1600 East Golf Road, Des Plaines, IL 60016

## Parkland College
**Champaign, Illinois**
www.parkland.edu

CB code: 1619

▶ Public 2-year community college
▶ Commuter campus in small city
▶ Interview required

**General.** Founded in 1966. Regionally accredited. Students have access to resources at University of Illinois and within certain guidelines may enroll in University of Illinois classes. **Enrollment:** 9,210 degree-seeking undergraduates; 197 non-degree-seeking students. **Degrees:** 961 associate awarded. **ROTC:** Army, Naval, Air Force. **Location:** 150 miles from Chicago, 120 miles from Indianapolis. **Calendar:** Semester, extensive summer session. **Full-time faculty:** 169 total; 16% have terminal degrees, 12% minority, 49% women. **Part-time faculty:** 350 total; 9% have terminal degrees, 8% minority, 55% women. **Class size:** 64% < 20, 34% 20-39, less than 1% 40-49, less than 1% 50-99, less than 1% >100. **Special facilities:** Planetarium, nature preserve, agricultural technology applications center, land

laboratory. **Partnerships:** Formal partnerships with local businesses including CISCO Systems, Case Corporation, Microsoft, Ford ASSET, LINUX Professional Institute.

**Student profile.** Among degree-seeking undergraduates, 1,957 enrolled as first-time, first-year students, 528 transferred in from other institutions.

| | | | |
|---|---|---|---|
| Part-time: | 53% | Asian American: | 3% |
| Out-of-state: | 65% | Hispanic American: | 4% |
| Women: | 53% | International: | 4% |
| African American: | 12% | 25 or older: | 33% |

**Transfer out. Colleges most students transferred to 2007:** University of Illinois at Urbana-Champaign.

**Basis for selection.** Open admission, but selective for some programs. Limited admissions to health professions and trade union programs. ACT required for health programs. **Homeschooled:** Recommended that students meet with admissions adviser. **Learning Disabled:** Students with learning disabilities encouraged to contact learning disabilities specialist prior to enrolling.

**High school preparation.** 15 units required. Required units include English 4, mathematics 3, social studies 2, science 2, foreign language 2 and academic electives 2.

**2007-2008 Annual costs.** Tuition/fees: $2,550; $6,660 out-of-district; $10,230 out-of-state. Per-credit charge: $82 in-district; $219 out-of-district; $338 out-of-state. For Internet classes, in-district students pay $82; all others pay $122 per credit hour. Books/supplies: $1,200. Personal expenses: $1,500.

**2006-2007 Financial aid. Need-based:** 373 full-time freshmen applied for aid; 313 were judged to have need; 228 of these received aid. Average need met was 65%. Average scholarship/grant was $4,239. 58% of total undergraduate aid awarded as scholarships/grants, 42% as loans/jobs. Work-study available nights. **Non-need-based:** Scholarships awarded for academics, art, athletics, leadership, minority status, music/drama, state residency.

**Application procedures. Admission:** No deadline. No application fee. Admission notification on a rolling basis. **Financial aid:** Priority date 3/1; no closing date. FAFSA, institutional form required. Applicants notified on a rolling basis starting 6/1; must reply within 2 week(s) of notification.

**Academics. Special study options:** Accelerated study, cross-registration, distance learning, double major, dual enrollment of high school students, ESL, honors, independent study, internships, student-designed major, study abroad. Bachelor's degree programs available on campus. License preparation in dental hygiene, nursing, paramedic. **Credit/placement by examination:** AP, CLEP, SAT, ACT, institutional tests. 25 credit hours maximum toward associate degree. Institutionally-prepared proficiency exams are available. **Support services:** GED preparation and test center, learning center, reduced course load, remedial instruction, study skills assistance, tutoring, writing center.

**Majors. Agriculture:** General, animal husbandry, business, landscaping, mechanization. **Business:** General, accounting technology, business admin, executive assistant, hotel/motel admin, marketing, selling. **Communications:** Radio/tv. **Communications technology:** Radio/tv. **Computer sciences:** Applications programming, networking. **Construction:** General, electrician. **Education:** Art, music. **Engineering:** General. **Engineering technology:** Computer systems, industrial, surveying. **Health:** Dental hygiene, nursing (RN), occupational therapy assistant, radiologic technology/medical imaging, respiratory therapy technology, surgical technology, veterinary technology/assistant. **Interdisciplinary:** Biological/physical sciences. **Liberal arts:** Arts/sciences. **Mechanic/repair:** Auto body, automotive, diesel. **Personal/culinary services:** Restaurant/catering. **Protective services:** Fire safety technology, police science. **Public administration:** Social work. **Visual/performing arts:** Art, commercial/advertising art.

**Most popular majors.** Business/marketing 14%, education 7%, health sciences 18%, interdisciplinary studies 20%, liberal arts 14%.

**Computing on campus.** 1,425 workstations in library, computer center. Online course registration available.

**Student life. Freshman orientation:** Mandatory. Preregistration for classes offered. Held at beginning of semester. **Policies:** Students may take part in activities at University of Illinois. **Housing:** Housing available at University of Illinois facilities. **Activities:** Bands, choral groups, dance, drama, international student organizations, literary magazine, music ensembles, musical theater, radio station, student government, student newspaper, TV station, black student association, Phi Theta Kappa, student nurses association, veterinary technology association, Christian Fellowship, Colours, dental assisting association, dental hygienists association.

**Athletics.** NJCAA. **Intercollegiate:** Baseball M, basketball, golf M, soccer, softball W, volleyball W. **Intramural:** Basketball, bowling, softball, tennis, volleyball. **Team name:** Cobras.

**Student services.** Adult student services, career counseling, services for economically disadvantaged, student employment services, financial aid counseling, minority student services, on-campus daycare, personal counseling, placement for graduates, veterans' counselor, women's services. **Physically disabled:** Services for visually, speech, hearing impaired. **Learning disabled:** Comprehensive services available. **Transfer:** Transfer center, transfer adviser, college fairs on campus for students transferring to 4-year colleges.

**Contact.** E-mail: mhenry@parkland.edu
Phone: (217) 351-2208 Toll-free number: (800) 346-8089
Fax: (217) 353-2640
Micheal Henry, Director of Admissions and Records, Parkland College, 2400 West Bradley Avenue, Champaign, IL 61821-1899

## Prairie State College
### Chicago Heights, Illinois
www.prairiestate.edu                    **CB code: 1077**

- Public 2-year community college
- Commuter campus in large town

**General.** Founded in 1957. Regionally accredited. **Enrollment:** 4,642 degree-seeking undergraduates. **Degrees:** 332 associate awarded. **Location:** 30 miles from Chicago. **Calendar:** Semester, limited summer session. **Full-time faculty:** 85 total. **Part-time faculty:** 200 total.

**Transfer out. Colleges most students transferred to 2007:** Governors State University, University of Illinois - Chicago.

**Basis for selection.** Open admission, but selective for some programs. Admission to nursing and dental hygiene programs based on GPA in required courses and test scores.

**High school preparation.** One unit each of chemistry and algebra required for nursing and dental programs, plus 1 unit biology for nursing.

**2007-2008 Annual costs.** Tuition/fees: $2,620; $7,340 out-of-district; $9,980 out-of-state. Per-credit charge: $87 in-district; $244 out-of-district; $332 out-of-state. Books/supplies: $750. Personal expenses: $1,700.

**Financial aid. Need-based:** Need-based aid available for part-time students. Work-study available nights, weekends and for part-time students.

**Application procedures. Admission:** No deadline. $10 fee, may be waived for applicants with need. Admission notification on a rolling basis. **Financial aid:** Priority date 7/1; no closing date. FAFSA, institutional form required. Applicants notified on a rolling basis; must reply within 2 week(s) of notification.

**Academics.** Students completing an Associate in Arts or Science degree are guaranteed their classes will transfer to other Illinois colleges. **Special study options:** Cross-registration, distance learning, dual enrollment of high school students, ESL, honors, independent study, internships, study abroad, weekend college. License preparation in dental hygiene, nursing. **Credit/placement by examination:** CLEP, institutional tests. 45 credit hours maximum toward associate degree. **Support services:** GED preparation and test center, learning center, pre-admission summer program, reduced course load, remedial instruction, study skills assistance, tutoring.

**Majors. Business:** Administrative services, operations. **Computer sciences:** Applications programming, programming. **Construction:** Electrician. **Engineering technology:** Electrical. **Family/consumer sciences:** Child care. **Health:** Dental hygiene, mental health services, nursing (RN), substance abuse counseling. **Interdisciplinary:** Biological/physical sciences. **Liberal arts:** Arts/sciences. **Mechanic/repair:** Automotive. **Protective services:** Fire safety technology, police science. **Visual/performing arts:** Commercial photography, design, interior design, photography.

**Most popular majors.** Business/marketing 12%, education 12%, health sciences 27%, liberal arts 17%, psychology 8%.

**Computing on campus.** 248 workstations in library, computer center, student center. Helpline available.

**Student life. Freshman orientation:** Available. **Activities:** Jazz band, choral groups, dance, drama, musical theater, student government, student newspaper, symphony orchestra, All Latin Alliance, Black Student Union.

**Athletics. Intercollegiate:** Baseball M, basketball M, golf M, soccer M. **Team name:** Pioneers.

**Student services.** Student employment services, financial aid counseling, minority student services, on-campus daycare, personal counseling, placement for graduates. **Physically disabled:** Services for visually, speech, hearing impaired. **Transfer:** Transfer center, transfer adviser, college fairs on campus for students transferring to 4-year colleges.

**Contact.** Phone: (708) 709-3516
Marietta Turner, Coordinator of Admissions and Records, Prairie State College, 202 South Halsted Street, Chicago Heights, IL 60411

## Rend Lake College
### Ina, Illinois
www.rlc.edu                             **CB code: 1673**

- Public 2-year community college
- Commuter campus in rural community

**General.** Founded in 1955. Regionally accredited. Satellite campuses located in Mt. Vernon and Pinckneyville. **Enrollment:** 4,850 degree-seeking undergraduates. **Degrees:** 606 associate awarded. **Location:** 45 miles from Carbondale, 85 miles from St. Louis. **Calendar:** Semester, limited summer session. **Full-time faculty:** 65 total. **Part-time faculty:** 173 total. **Class size:** 68% < 20, 29% 20-39, 2% 40-49, less than 1% 50-99. **Partnerships:** Formal partnerships to provide technical training for employees of General Tire (Mt. Vernon) and Matsushita Universal; mandated federal training provided to Department of Natural Resources-Mines and Minerals; authorized training provided for Cisco curriculum.

**Student profile.**

| | | | |
|---|---|---|---|
| Out-of-state: | 1% | Live on campus: | 1% |
| 25 or older: | 70% | | |

**Transfer out. Colleges most students transferred to 2007:** Southern Illinois University-Carbondale, Southern Illinois University-Edwardsville, Eastern Illinois University, Southeast Missouri State University, Murray State University.

**Basis for selection.** Open admission, but selective for some programs. Special requirements for allied health programs. SAT, ACT, ASSET, or COMPASS scores required for degree-seeking students for placement.

**High school preparation.** 15 units recommended. Recommended units include English 4, mathematics 3, social studies 3, science 3 (laboratory 3) and academic electives 2. Social studies units should include history and government. Electives may include foreign language, vocational education, music, or art. Lowest level math accepted is algebra 1.

**2007-2008 Annual costs.** Tuition/fees: $2,070; $3,060 out-of-district; $4,500 out-of-state. Per-credit charge: $69 in-district; $102 out-of-district; $150 out-of-state. Books/supplies: $900. Personal expenses: $1,636.

**Financial aid. Need-based:** Need-based aid available for part-time students. **Non-need-based:** Scholarships awarded for academics, art, athletics, leadership, music/drama, state residency.

**Application procedures. Admission:** No deadline. No application fee. Application may be submitted online. Admission notification on a rolling basis. **Financial aid:** No deadline. FAFSA required. Applicants notified on a rolling basis starting 3/15; must reply within 4 week(s) of notification.

**Academics. Special study options:** Cooperative education, distance learning, dual enrollment of high school students, ESL, honors, independent study, internships, study abroad. Bachelor's degree programs available on campus. License preparation in nursing, occupational therapy, paramedic, real estate. **Credit/placement by examination:** AP, CLEP, institutional tests. 16 credit hours maximum toward associate degree. Credits awarded for CLEP, proficiency exams and AP scores. **Support services:** GED preparation, learning center, remedial instruction, study skills assistance, tutoring.

**Majors. Agriculture:** Business, horticulture, mechanization, production. **Architecture:** Technology. **Business:** Administrative services, business admin. **Computer sciences:** Applications programming, LAN/WAN management. **Engineering:** General. **Engineering technology:** Manufacturing, surveying. **Family/consumer sciences:** Child development. **Health:** Clinical lab technology, EMT paramedic, medical records technology, nursing (RN), occupational therapy assistant. **Interdisciplinary:** Biological/physical sciences. **Liberal arts:** Arts/sciences. **Mechanic/repair:** Automotive, diesel, heavy equipment, industrial. **Personal/culinary services:** Chef training. **Protective services:** Corrections, fire services admin, police science. **Visual/performing arts:** Art, commercial/advertising art.

**Computing on campus.** 496 workstations in library, computer center. Commuter students can connect to campus network. Online library, wireless network available.

**Student life. Freshman orientation:** Mandatory. **Activities:** Bands, choral groups, dance, drama, music ensembles, musical theater, student government, student newspaper, symphony orchestra, culinary arts club, Active College Christians, practical nursing club, automotive club, horticulture club, art league, criminal justice club.

**Athletics.** NJCAA. **Intercollegiate:** Baseball M, basketball, cheerleading M, cross-country, golf, softball W, tennis W, track and field, volleyball W, wrestling M. **Team name:** Warriors.

**Student services.** Adult student services, career counseling, services for economically disadvantaged, student employment services, financial aid counseling, on-campus daycare, personal counseling, placement for graduates, veterans' counselor. **Physically disabled:** Services for visually, speech, hearing impaired. **Transfer:** Pre-admission transcript evaluation for new students. Transfer adviser, college fairs on campus for students transferring to 4-year colleges.

**Contact.** E-mail: admiss@rlc.edu
Phone: (618) 437-5321 ext. 1230 Fax: (618) 437-5677
Rend Lake College, 468 North Ken Gray Parkway, Ina, IL 62846

## Richland Community College

**Decatur, Illinois** | **CB member**
**www.richland.edu** | **CB code: 0738**

- Public 2-year community college
- Commuter campus in small city

**General.** Founded in 1971. Regionally accredited. **Enrollment:** 2,502 degree-seeking undergraduates; 778 non-degree-seeking students. **Degrees:** 295 associate awarded. **Location:** 180 miles from Chicago, 120 miles from St. Louis. **Calendar:** Semester, limited summer session. **Full-time faculty:** 92 total. **Part-time faculty:** 147 total. **Class size:** 76% < 20, 24% 20-39, less than 1% 40-49. **Special facilities:** Human patient simulator for allied health students.

**Student profile.** Among degree-seeking undergraduates, 45% enrolled in a transfer program, 32% enrolled in a vocational program, 1% already have a bachelor's degree or higher, 472 enrolled as first-time, first-year students.

| | | | |
|---|---|---|---|
| Part-time: | 61% | Hispanic American: | 1% |
| Women: | 62% | Native American: | 1% |
| African American: | 18% | 25 or older: | 50% |
| Asian American: | 1% | | |

**Transfer out. Colleges most students transferred to 2007:** Illinois State University, Millikin University, Southern Illinois University-Carbondale, Eastern Illinois University, University of Illinois-Springfield.

**Basis for selection.** Open admission, but selective for some programs. All allied health programs have a separate admission process.

**High school preparation.** Required units include English 4, mathematics 3, social studies 3, science 3 and foreign language 2.

**2007-2008 Annual costs.** Tuition/fees: $2,070; $10,659 out-of-district; $11,625 out-of-state. Per-credit charge: $65 in-district; $351 out-of-district; $388 out-of-state. Books/supplies: $1,000.

**2006-2007 Financial aid. Need-based:** 153 full-time freshmen applied for aid; 94 were judged to have need; 79 of these received aid. Average need met was 42%. Average scholarship/grant was $3,723; average loan $1,952. 85% of total undergraduate aid awarded as scholarships/grants, 15% as loans/jobs. Need-based aid available for part-time students. Work-study available nights and for part-time students. **Non-need-based:** Awarded to 162 full-time undergraduates, including 47 freshmen. Scholarships awarded for academics.

**Application procedures. Admission:** No deadline. No application fee. Application may be submitted online. Admission notification on a rolling basis. **Financial aid:** Closing date 6/30. FAFSA required. Applicants notified on a rolling basis starting 3/20.

**Academics. Special study options:** Distance learning, dual enrollment of high school students, ESL, honors, independent study, internships, liberal arts/career combination, teacher certification program. License preparation in nursing, paramedic, radiology. **Credit/placement by examination:** AP, CLEP, institutional tests. **Support services:** GED preparation, learning center, reduced course load, remedial instruction, study skills assistance, tutoring, writing center.

**Majors. Agriculture:** Business, horticultural science, horticulture. **Biology:** General. **Business:** General, accounting, hospitality admin, management information systems. **Communications:** Journalism. **Computer sciences:** General, computer graphics, computer science, data entry, programming. **Construction:** Electrician. **Education:** General. **Engineering:** General. **Engineering technology:** Drafting. **English:** American lit, composition, English lit, speech/rhetoric. **Foreign languages:** French, German, Spanish. **Health:** EMT paramedic, nursing (RN), radiologic technology/medical imaging, surgical technology. **History:** General. **Legal studies:** Prelaw. **Liberal arts:** Arts/sciences. **Math:** General. **Mechanic/repair:** General, automotive, electronics/electrical, heating/ac/refrig, industrial. **Philosophy/religion:** Philosophy. **Physical sciences:** Planetary. **Protective services:** Criminal justice, firefighting, police science. **Psychology:** General. **Social sciences:** General, anthropology, archaeology, economics, geography, political science, sociology. **Visual/performing arts:** General, art, art history/conservation, ceramics, drawing, painting, sculpture.

**Most popular majors.** Business/marketing 8%, health sciences 27%, interdisciplinary studies 27%, liberal arts 21%, trade and industry 6%.

**Computing on campus.** 245 workstations in library, computer center. Commuter students can connect to campus network. Online course registration, online library, helpline available.

**Student life. Freshman orientation:** Mandatory. Preregistration for classes offered. 2 hours, includes registering for courses, variety of times available. **Activities:** Drama, student government, student newspaper.

**Athletics. Team name:** Knights.

**Student services.** Adult student services, career counseling, services for economically disadvantaged, student employment services, financial aid counseling, minority student services, on-campus daycare, personal counseling, placement for graduates, veterans' counselor, women's services. **Physically disabled:** Services for visually, speech, hearing impaired. **Transfer:** Pre-admission transcript evaluation for new students. Transfer center, transfer adviser, college fairs on campus for students transferring to 4-year colleges.

**Contact.** Phone: (217) 875-7200 ext. 257 Fax: (217) 875-7783
JoAnn Wirey, Director, Admissions & Records, Richland Community College, One College Park, Decatur, IL 62521

## Rock Valley College

**Rockford, Illinois** | **CB member**
**www.rockvalleycollege.edu** | **CB code: 1674**

- Public 2-year community college
- Commuter campus in small city

**General.** Founded in 1964. Regionally accredited. **Enrollment:** 6,682 degree-seeking undergraduates. **Degrees:** 746 associate awarded. **Location:** 85 miles from Chicago. **Calendar:** Semester, limited summer session. **Full-time faculty:** 138 total; 17% have terminal degrees, 9% minority, 46% women. **Part-time faculty:** 172 total; 9% have terminal degrees, 5% minority, 45% women. **Special facilities:** Outdoor theater. **Partnerships:** Formal partnership with CISCO.

**Transfer out.** 26% of students enrolled in the transfer program go on to 4-year colleges. **Colleges most students transferred to 2007:** Northern Illinois University, Illinois State University, Western Illinois University.

**Basis for selection.** Open admission, but selective for some programs. Special requirements for nursing and respiratory therapy programs. Test scores used for nursing students only. Interview required of respiratory therapy, nursing, aviation maintenance majors. Audition required of music majors.

**High school preparation.** Recommended units include English 4, mathematics 3, social studies 2 and science 2. One chemistry required for nursing applicants, 1 chemistry and 1 algebra for respiratory therapy applicants.

**2007-2008 Annual costs.** Tuition/fees: $2,084; $7,604 out-of-district; $12,284 out-of-state. Per-credit charge: $61 in-district; $245 out-of-district; $401 out-of-state. Costs vary by program. Books/supplies: $900.

**Financial aid. Need-based:** Need-based aid available for part-time students. Work-study available nights and for part-time students. **Non-need-based:** Scholarships awarded for academics, ROTC.

**Application procedures. Admission:** No deadline. No application fee. Application must be submitted on paper. Admission notification on a rolling basis. **Financial aid:** No deadline. FAFSA required. Applicants notified on a rolling basis starting 4/1; must reply within 2 week(s) of notification.

**Academics. Special study options:** Cooperative education, dual enrollment of high school students, ESL, external degree, independent study, internships, liberal arts/career combination, student-designed major, study abroad. License preparation in aviation, dental hygiene, nursing. **Credit/placement by examination:** AP, CLEP, institutional tests. 39 credit hours maximum toward associate degree. **Support services:** GED preparation, learning center, reduced course load, remedial instruction, study skills assistance, tutoring, writing center.

**Majors. Business:** General, accounting, administrative services, business admin, logistics, marketing. **Computer sciences:** General. **Engineering technology:** Construction, electrical, manufacturing. **Family/consumer sciences:** Child care. **Health:** Medical records technology, nursing (RN), respiratory therapy technology. **Legal studies:** Paralegal. **Liberal arts:** Arts/sciences. **Mechanic/repair:** Aircraft, automotive. **Protective services:** Firefighting, law enforcement admin. **Public administration:** Human services.

**Computing on campus.** 130 workstations in library, computer center, student center. Commuter students can connect to campus network. Online course registration, online library, helpline, wireless network available.

**Student life. Freshman orientation:** Available. Preregistration for classes offered. **Activities:** Bands, choral groups, dance, drama, literary magazine, music ensembles, musical theater, student government, student newspaper, 21 student interest groups.

**Athletics.** NJCAA. **Intercollegiate:** Baseball M, basketball, football (tackle) M, golf M, soccer, softball W, squash W, tennis, volleyball W. **Intramural:** Basketball M, skiing. **Team name:** Eagles.

**Student services.** Adult student services, career counseling, student employment services, financial aid counseling, personal counseling, placement for graduates, veterans' counselor. **Physically disabled:** Services for visually, speech, hearing impaired. **Transfer:** Transfer adviser, college fairs on campus for students transferring to 4-year colleges.

**Contact.** Phone: (815) 921-4250 Fax: (815) 921-4269
Lynn Perkins, Rock Valley College, 3301 North Mulford Road, Rockford, IL 61114-5699

## Rockford Business College
**Rockford, Illinois**
**www.rockfordbusinesscollege.edu**          **CB code: 2459**

▶ For-profit 2-year business, technical and career college
▶ Commuter campus in small city
▶ Interview required

**General.** Founded in 1862. Accredited by ACICS. **Enrollment:** 560 degree-seeking undergraduates. **Degrees:** 122 associate awarded. **Location:** 90 miles from Chicago, 75 miles from Madison, Wisconsin. **Calendar:** Quarter, extensive summer session. **Full-time faculty:** 10 total. **Part-time faculty:** 40 total. **Class size:** 88% < 20, 11% 20-39, 1% 40-49.

**Student profile.** Among degree-seeking undergraduates, 1% already have a bachelor's degree or higher, 123 enrolled as first-time, first-year students.

| | | | |
|---|---|---|---|
| Part-time: | 56% | Hispanic American: | 8% |
| Women: | 88% | 25 or older: | 34% |
| African American: | 31% | | |

**Transfer out.** 1% of students enrolled in the transfer program go on to 4-year colleges.

**Basis for selection.** Open admission. **Homeschooled:** State high school equivalency certificate required.

**2008-2009 Annual costs.** Tuition/fees (projected): $9,750. Per-credit charge: $190. Books/supplies: $800. Personal expenses: $2,880.

**Financial aid.** All financial aid based on need. Need-based aid available for part-time students. Work-study available nights.

**Application procedures. Admission:** No deadline. $150 fee. Application must be submitted on paper. Admission notification on a rolling basis. **Financial aid:** No deadline. FAFSA required. Applicants notified on a rolling basis.

**Academics. Special study options:** Independent study, internships. **Credit/placement by examination:** AP, CLEP, IB, institutional tests. 50 credit hours maximum toward associate degree. **Support services:** Study skills assistance, tutoring.

**Majors. Business:** General, accounting, business admin, marketing, office/clerical. **Computer sciences:** General, data processing, information systems. **Health:** Massage therapy, medical assistant, medical secretary, pharmacy assistant, veterinary technology/assistant. **Legal studies:** Legal secretary, paralegal.

**Computing on campus.** 75 workstations in library, computer center.

**Student life. Freshman orientation:** Mandatory. Preregistration for classes offered.

**Student services.** Career counseling, student employment services, financial aid counseling, placement for graduates. **Transfer:** Pre-admission transcript evaluation for new students.

**Contact.** E-mail: info@rbcsuccess.com
Phone: (815) 965-8616 Toll-free number: (866) 722-4632
Fax: (815) 965-0360
David Julius, Director of Enrollment Services, Rockford Business College, 730 North Church Street, Rockford, IL 61103

## Sauk Valley Community College
**Dixon, Illinois**
**www.svcc.edu**          **CB code: 1780**

▶ Public 2-year community college
▶ Commuter campus in large town

**General.** Founded in 1965. Regionally accredited. **Enrollment:** 1,933 degree-seeking undergraduates; 767 non-degree-seeking students. **Degrees:** 276 associate awarded. **Location:** 110 miles from Chicago. **Calendar:** Semester, limited summer session. **Full-time faculty:** 47 total; 17% have terminal degrees, 4% minority, 38% women. **Part-time faculty:** 93 total; 4% have terminal degrees, 11% minority, 57% women. **Class size:** 63% < 20, 33% 20-39, 3% 40-49, less than 1% 50-99. **Special facilities:** Observatory, prairie plots.

**Student profile.** Among degree-seeking undergraduates, 56% enrolled in a transfer program, 44% enrolled in a vocational program, 3% already have a bachelor's degree or higher, 325 enrolled as first-time, first-year students, 1 transferred in from other institutions.

| | | | |
|---|---|---|---|
| Part-time: | 44% | Hispanic American: | 9% |
| Women: | 61% | 25 or older: | 38% |
| African American: | 3% | Live on campus: | 1% |
| Asian American: | 1% | | |

**Transfer out.** 20% of students enrolled in the transfer program go on to 4-year colleges. **Colleges most students transferred to 2007:** Northern Illinois University, Illinois State University, Western Illinois University, University of Illinois, Southern Illinois University.

**Basis for selection.** Open admission, but selective for some programs. Special requirements for allied health programs: academic record, state residency important; class rank, test scores considered. Placement exam required of all students who plan to enroll in English or math courses. **Homeschooled:** Transcript of courses and grades required.

**High school preparation.** 15 units recommended. Recommended units include English 4, mathematics 3, social studies 2, science 2 (laboratory 2) and academic electives 4. Special course requirements for allied health programs.

**2007-2008 Annual costs.** Tuition/fees: $2,460; $7,320 out-of-district; $8,340 out-of-state. Per-credit charge: $82 in-district; $244 out-of-district; $276 out-of-state. Room only: $4,131. Books/supplies: $500.

**2006-2007 Financial aid. Need-based:** 180 full-time freshmen applied for aid; 142 were judged to have need; 123 of these received aid. Average need met was 43%. Average scholarship/grant was $3,669; average loan $1,749. 77% of total undergraduate aid awarded as scholarships/grants, 23% as loans/jobs. Need-based aid available for part-time students. Work-study available nights, weekends and for part-time students. **Non-need-based:** Awarded to 128 full-time undergraduates, including 28 freshmen. Scholarships awarded for academics, art, athletics, leadership, minority status, ROTC, state residency.

**Application procedures. Admission:** No deadline. No application fee. Application may be submitted online. Admission notification on a rolling basis. **Financial aid:** Priority date 3/1; no closing date. FAFSA, institutional form required. Applicants notified on a rolling basis starting 5/1; must reply within 4 week(s) of notification.

**Academics. Special study options:** Cooperative education, distance learning, dual enrollment of high school students, ESL, honors, independent study, internships. License preparation in nursing, paramedic, radiology, real estate. **Credit/placement by examination:** AP, CLEP, institutional tests. 30 credit hours maximum toward associate degree. Both CLEP and DANTES exams are used. **Support services:** GED preparation and test center, learning center, remedial instruction, study skills assistance, tutoring, writing center.

**Majors. Biology:** General. **Business:** General, accounting, administrative services, business admin, management information systems, marketing, office management, office technology, office/clerical. **Communications:** General, journalism, public relations. **Computer sciences:** General, applications programming, data processing, programming. **Education:** General, art, bilingual, biology, chemistry, elementary, English, family/consumer sciences, French, German, gifted/talented, health, history, mathematics, middle, multi-level teacher, music, physical, physically handicapped, physics, sales/marketing, science, secondary, social science, social studies, Spanish, special, speech, technology/industrial arts, voc/tech. **Engineering:** General, civil, electrical, physics. **Engineering technology:** Drafting, manufacturing, solar energy. **English:** Composition, English lit. **Family/consumer sciences:** Child care. **Foreign languages:** General, French, German, Spanish. **Health:** Athletic training, medical radiologic technology/radiation therapy, medical secretary, nursing (RN), predental, premedicine, prenursing, prepharmacy, preveterinary. **History:** General. **Interdisciplinary:** Math/computer science. **Legal studies:** Legal secretary, prelaw. **Liberal arts:** Arts/sciences. **Math:** General. **Mechanic/repair:** Diesel, heating/ac/refrig. **Parks/recreation:** Exercise sciences, sports admin. **Philosophy/religion:** Philosophy. **Physical sciences:** Chemistry, physics. **Protective services:** Criminal justice, law enforcement admin, police science. **Psychology:** General. **Public administration:** Human services, social work. **Social sciences:** General, economics, political science, sociology. **Visual/performing arts:** Art, art history/conservation, commercial/advertising art, dramatic, fashion design, music performance, studio arts, voice/opera.

**Most popular majors.** Business/marketing 17%, health sciences 19%, interdisciplinary studies 28%, liberal arts 25%.

**Computing on campus.** 120 workstations in library, computer center, student center. Dormitories wired for high-speed internet access. Online library, helpline, wireless network available.

**Student life. Freshman orientation:** Mandatory, $82 fee. Preregistration for classes offered. 15 hours held throughout first semester or prior to start of semester. **Housing:** Apartments available. **Activities:** Bands, choral groups, drama, music ensembles, musical theater, student government, student newspaper, symphony orchestra, Association of Latin American Students, Campus Crusade for Christ, Phi Theta Kappa.

**Athletics.** NJCAA. **Intercollegiate:** Baseball M, basketball, cheerleading M, cross-country, golf M, softball W, tennis, volleyball W. **Team name:** Skyhawks.

**Student services.** Adult student services, career counseling, services for economically disadvantaged, student employment services, financial aid counseling, minority student services, on-campus daycare, personal counseling, placement for graduates, veterans' counselor. **Physically disabled:** Services for visually, speech, hearing impaired. **Transfer:** Pre-admission transcript evaluation for new students. Transfer center, transfer adviser, college fairs on campus for students transferring to 4-year colleges.

**Contact.**   Phone: (815) 288-5511 ext. 343 Fax: (815) 288-3190
Pamela Medema, Registrar, Sauk Valley Community College, 173 Illinois Route 2, Dixon, IL 61021-9110

---

## Shawnee Community College
### Ullin, Illinois
www.shawneecc.edu                    CB code: 0882

 Public 2-year community college
 Commuter campus in rural community

**General.** Founded in 1967. Regionally accredited. Extension centers in Anna, Cairo, and Metropolis. **Enrollment:** 1,613 degree-seeking undergraduates. **Degrees:** 254 associate awarded. **ROTC:** Army, Naval, Air Force. **Location:** 40 miles from Paducah, Kentucky. **Calendar:** Semester, extensive summer session. **Full-time faculty:** 42 total. **Part-time faculty:** 170 total.

**Basis for selection.** Open admission, but selective for some programs. Applicants for allied health programs selected on basis of entrance examination score. ACT recommended for placement and counseling. Interview recommended for art, music, speech majors. Audition recommended for speech and music majors. Portfolio recommended for art majors.

**High school preparation.** 15 units recommended. Recommended units include English 4, mathematics 3, social studies 3, science 3 and foreign

language 2. 2 units recommended in foreign language, music, or art. Transfer program applicants must have state mandated high school course requirements or demonstrate proficiency through placement tests.

**2007-2008 Annual costs.** Tuition/fees: $1,950; $3,000 out-of-state. Per-credit charge: $65 in-state; $100 out-of-state. Books/supplies: $500. Personal expenses: $680.

**Financial aid.** All financial aid based on need. Need-based aid available for part-time students.

**Application procedures. Admission:** No deadline. No application fee. Application may be submitted online. Admission notification on a rolling basis beginning on or about 1/15. **Financial aid:** Priority date 9/1; no closing date. FAFSA required. Applicants notified on a rolling basis; must reply within 2 week(s) of notification.

**Academics. Special study options:** Cooperative education, distance learning, dual enrollment of high school students, honors, independent study, internships, liberal arts/career combination. License preparation in nursing, occupational therapy, paramedic, real estate. **Credit/placement by examination:** AP, CLEP, institutional tests. 15 credit hours maximum toward associate degree. **Support services:** GED preparation and test center, learning center, pre-admission summer program, remedial instruction, study skills assistance, tutoring, writing center.

**Majors. Agriculture:** Business, horticulture. **Business:** General, accounting, management science. **Conservation:** Forestry, wildlife. **Engineering technology:** Drafting, electrical. **Family/consumer sciences:** Family/community services, food/nutrition. **Health:** Medical records technology, medical secretary. **Interdisciplinary:** Biological/physical sciences. **Legal studies:** Legal secretary. **Liberal arts:** Arts/sciences.

**Computing on campus.** 120 workstations in library, computer center, student center. Online course registration, online library, helpline, wireless network available.

**Student life. Freshman orientation:** Mandatory. Preregistration for classes offered. **Activities:** Concert band, choral groups, dance, drama, music ensembles, musical theater, student government, student newspaper.

**Athletics.** NJCAA. **Intercollegiate:** Baseball M, basketball, softball W, volleyball W. **Intramural:** Baseball M, basketball, football (non-tackle), table tennis, volleyball. **Team name:** Saints.

**Student services.** Career counseling, services for economically disadvantaged, student employment services, financial aid counseling, on-campus daycare, personal counseling, placement for graduates, veterans' counselor. **Physically disabled:** Services for visually, speech, hearing impaired. **Transfer:** Pre-admission transcript evaluation for new students. Transfer center, transfer adviser, college fairs on campus for students transferring to 4-year colleges.

**Contact.**   E-mail: admissions@shawneecc.edu
Phone: (618) 634-3200 ext. 3247 Fax: (618) 634-3346
Dee Blakely, Director of Admissions and Counseling, Shawnee Community College, 8364 Shawnee College Road, Ullin, IL 62992

---

## South Suburban College of Cook County
### South Holland, Illinois
www.southsuburbancollege.edu                    CB code: 1806

 Public 2-year community college
 Commuter campus in large town

**General.** Founded in 1927. Regionally accredited. **Enrollment:** 5,702 degree-seeking undergraduates. **Degrees:** 443 associate awarded. **Location:** 20 miles from the Chicago Loop. **Calendar:** Semester, limited summer session. **Full-time faculty:** 120 total. **Part-time faculty:** 217 total.

**Student profile.**

| | | | |
|---|---|---|---|
| Out-of-state: | 5.27% | 25 or older: | 48.28% |

**Transfer out. Colleges most students transferred to 2007:** Governors State University, University of Illinois-Chicago, Purdue University-Calumet, Chicago State University.

**Basis for selection.** Open admission, but selective for some programs. Separate requirements for health career programs. Audition recommended for music majors. **Learning Disabled:** Students need to self-declare with counseling center. Accommodations provided as needed.

**High school preparation.** 15 units required. Required units include English 4, mathematics 3, social studies 2, science 2 (laboratory 1) and academic electives 4.

**2007-2008 Annual costs.** Tuition/fees: $3,113; $8,453 out-of-district; $10,103 out-of-state. Per-credit charge: $90 in-district; $268 out-of-district; $323 out-of-state. Some students may qualify for a tuition rate of $105 per credit hour for special programs in other in-state community college districts, in Lake County Illinois and in Chicago. Students need to inquire at the Registration area for additional information. Books/supplies: $500. Personal expenses: $1,000.

**Financial aid. Need-based:** Need-based aid available for part-time students. Work-study available nights and for part-time students. **Non-need-based:** Scholarships awarded for academics, art, athletics, music/drama, state residency.

**Application procedures. Admission:** No deadline. No application fee. Application must be submitted on paper. Admission notification on a rolling basis. **Financial aid:** Priority date 6/1; no closing date. FAFSA required. Applicants notified on a rolling basis starting 7/1.

**Academics. Special study options:** Distance learning, double major, dual enrollment of high school students, ESL, honors, internships, liberal arts/career combination, study abroad. License preparation in nursing, occupational therapy, paramedic, radiology, real estate. **Credit/placement by examination:** AP, CLEP, institutional tests. 15 credit hours maximum toward associate degree. **Support services:** GED preparation and test center, learning center, reduced course load, remedial instruction, study skills assistance, tutoring.

**Majors. Biology:** General, biomedical sciences. **Business:** General, accounting, administrative services, fashion, finance, marketing, office management. **Computer sciences:** General. **Construction:** Maintenance. **Education:** General, early childhood, special, teacher assistance. **Engineering:** General, science. **Engineering technology:** Construction, drafting, electrical. **English:** English lit. **Foreign languages:** Spanish. **Health:** Medical radiologic technology/radiation therapy, nursing (RN), occupational therapy assistant, pharmacy assistant. **History:** General. **Legal studies:** Court reporting, paralegal. **Liberal arts:** Arts/sciences. **Math:** General. **Parks/recreation:** Health/fitness, sports admin. **Philosophy/religion:** Philosophy. **Physical sciences:** Astronomy, chemistry, geology, physics. **Protective services:** Criminal justice. **Psychology:** General. **Public administration:** Human services. **Social sciences:** Anthropology, economics, geography, political science, sociology. **Visual/performing arts:** Dramatic, studio arts.

**Computing on campus.** 622 workstations in library, computer center, student center. Online course registration, online library available.

**Student life. Freshman orientation:** Mandatory. Preregistration for classes offered. Continuous orientation program; specialized high school student success program in summer. **Activities:** Bands, choral groups, drama, literary magazine, music ensembles, opera, student government, business professionals, veterans organization, paralegal association, occupational therapy organization, human service club, Creative Dimensions, nursing club.

**Athletics.** NJCAA. **Intercollegiate:** Baseball M, basketball, soccer M, softball W, volleyball W. **Intramural:** Baseball M, basketball, softball, volleyball. **Team name:** Bulldogs.

**Student services.** Career counseling, student employment services, financial aid counseling, on-campus daycare, personal counseling, veterans' counselor. **Physically disabled:** Services for visually, speech, hearing impaired. **Learning disabled:** Comprehensive services available. **Transfer:** Transfer center, transfer adviser, college fairs on campus for students transferring to 4-year colleges.

**Contact.** E-mail: admissions@southsuburbancollege.edu
Phone: (708) 596-2000 ext. 2329 Fax: (708) 225-5806
Robin Rihacek, Director of Admissions, Registration and Records, South Suburban College of Cook County, 15800 South State Street, South Holland, IL 60473

## Southeastern Illinois College
**Harrisburg, Illinois**
www.sic.edu                                      CB code: 1777

- Public 2-year community college
- Commuter campus in small town

**General.** Founded in 1960. Regionally accredited. **Enrollment:** 1,420 degree-seeking undergraduates. **Degrees:** 221 associate awarded. **Location:** 45 miles from Carbondale; 65 miles from Evansville, Indiana. **Calendar:** Semester, extensive summer session. **Full-time faculty:** 66 total; 39% have terminal degrees, 2% minority, 36% women. **Part-time faculty:** 145 total; 43% have

terminal degrees, 5% minority, 61% women. **Special facilities:** Game preserve management facility, archery range, fire science center. **Partnerships:** Formal partnership with Cummins Corporation for deisel technology.

**Student profile.**

| | | | |
|---|---|---|---|
| African American: | 11% | Hispanic American: | 1% |
| Asian American: | 1% | 25 or older: | 60% |

**Transfer out. Colleges most students transferred to 2007:** Southern Illinois University at Carbondale.

**Basis for selection.** Open admission, but selective for some programs. Special requirements for nursing, medical records, health information technology, surgical nurse, occupational therapy assistant, and conservation game management programs. Admission to health programs based on test scores. Psychological Services Bureau-Health Occupations Examination for medical laboratory technician, ASSET for health information systems. NET test required for Associate degree nursing program and practical nursing program.

**High school preparation.** 15 units required. Required units include English 4, mathematics 3, social studies 3, science 3 and academic electives 2. Applicants to vocational programs exempted from high school requirements.

**2007-2008 Annual costs.** Tuition/fees: $1,980; $2,850 out-of-district; $3,270 out-of-state. Per-credit charge: $64 in-district; $93 out-of-district; $107 out-of-state. Books/supplies: $450. Personal expenses: $1,357.

**Financial aid. Need-based:** Need-based aid available for part-time students. Work-study available for part-time students. **Non-need-based:** Scholarships awarded for academics, alumni affiliation, art, athletics, music/drama.

**Application procedures. Admission:** No deadline. No application fee. Application may be submitted online. Admission notification on a rolling basis beginning on or about 5/1. **Financial aid:** No deadline. FAFSA required. Applicants notified on a rolling basis starting 4/15; must reply within 2 week(s) of notification.

**Academics. Special study options:** Cross-registration, distance learning, double major, dual enrollment of high school students, independent study, internships, student-designed major, study abroad. Bachelor's degree programs available on campus. License preparation in nursing, paramedic, real estate. **Credit/placement by examination:** AP, CLEP, institutional tests. 29 credit hours maximum toward associate degree. **Support services:** GED preparation and test center, learning center, pre-admission summer program, reduced course load, remedial instruction, tutoring.

**Majors. Business:** Administrative services, business admin, office technology. **Computer sciences:** Information systems, LAN/WAN management. **Conservation:** Wildlife. **Education:** General. **Family/consumer sciences:** Child care. **Health:** Clinical lab technology, medical records technology, nursing (RN), occupational therapy assistant, office assistant. **Interdisciplinary:** Behavioral sciences, math/computer science, natural sciences. **Legal studies:** Prelaw. **Liberal arts:** Arts/sciences. **Math:** General. **Mechanic/repair:** Diesel. **Protective services:** Police science. **Public administration:** Human services.

**Computing on campus.** 75 workstations in library, computer center. Wireless network available.

**Student life. Freshman orientation:** Available. Preregistration for classes offered. Individual orientation/advisement/registration appointments held for degree-seeking students. **Activities:** Bands, choral groups, drama, music ensembles, musical theater, student government, student newspaper, art club, math and science club, BASIC, Students in Free Enterprise, Phi Theta Kappa, Phi Beta Lambda, Theta Sigma Phi, Student Association of Family and Consumer Sciences, forensics club.

**Athletics.** NJCAA. **Intercollegiate:** Baseball M, basketball, cheerleading M, softball W. **Intramural:** Basketball, cheerleading W. **Team name:** Falcons.

**Student services.** Career counseling, student employment services, financial aid counseling, on-campus daycare, personal counseling, placement for graduates, veterans' counselor. **Physically disabled:** Services for visually, hearing impaired. **Transfer:** Transfer adviser, college fairs on campus for students transferring to 4-year colleges.

**Contact.** E-mail: registrar@sic.edu
Phone: (618) 252-5400 ext. 2441 Toll-free number: (866) 338-2742
Fax: (618) 252-3062
Kelly Boyd, Director of Enrollment Services, Southeastern Illinois College, 3575 College Road, Harrisburg, IL 62946

## Southwestern Illinois College
### Belleville, Illinois
www.swic.edu                                           CB code: 1057

- Public 2-year community college
- Commuter campus in small city

**General.** Founded in 1946. Regionally accredited. **Location:** 20 miles from St. Louis. **Calendar:** Semester.

**Annual costs/financial aid.** Tuition/fees (2007-2008): $2,040; $5,280 out-of-district; $8,250 out-of-state. Required fees vary by course taken. Those age 60 and over receive a $5 per-credit-hour tuition reduction. Books/supplies: $500. Personal expenses: $1,320. Need-based financial aid available to full-time and part-time students.

**Contact.** Phone: (618) 235-2700 ext. 5526
Director of Admissions, 2500 Carlyle Avenue, Belleville, IL 62221-5899

## Spoon River College
### Canton, Illinois
www.src.edu                                            CB code: 1154

- Public 2-year community college
- Commuter campus in large town

**General.** Founded in 1959. Regionally accredited. **Enrollment:** 1,435 degree-seeking undergraduates. **Degrees:** 269 associate awarded. **ROTC:** Army. **Location:** 35 miles from Peoria. **Calendar:** Semester, limited summer session. **Full-time faculty:** 40 total; 10% have terminal degrees, 2% minority, 50% women. **Part-time faculty:** 89 total; 53% women. **Special facilities:** Natural arboretum, walking trail, and agricultural test plots.

**Transfer out. Colleges most students transferred to 2007:** Western Illinois University.

**Basis for selection.** Open admission, but selective for some programs. Special requirements for nursing program. College-preparatory program recommended for transfer degree programs. Vocational students not required to have specific high school courses. All students must take COMPASS exam for placement; if score indicates, student must be remediated before taking college-level courses.

**High school preparation.** 15 units recommended. Recommended units include English 4, mathematics 3, social studies 3, science 3 (laboratory 3) and academic electives 2.

**2007-2008 Annual costs.** Tuition/fees: $2,370; $4,410 out-of-district; $5,460 out-of-state. Per-credit charge: $69 in-district; $137 out-of-district; $172 out-of-state. Books/supplies: $600.

**2006-2007 Financial aid. Need-based:** 81% of total undergraduate aid awarded as scholarships/grants, 19% as loans/jobs. Need-based aid available for part-time students. Work-study available nights and for part-time students. **Non-need-based:** Scholarships awarded for academics, athletics.

**Application procedures. Admission:** No deadline. No application fee. Admission notification on a rolling basis. **Financial aid:** Closing date 7/2. FAFSA required. Applicants notified on a rolling basis starting 3/15.

**Academics. Special study options:** Distance learning, dual enrollment of high school students, honors, internships. License preparation in nursing. **Credit/placement by examination:** AP, CLEP, IB, institutional tests. 32 credit hours maximum toward associate degree. Maximum of 50% credit hours toward degree may be awarded through CLEP. **Support services:** GED preparation, learning center, reduced course load, remedial instruction, study skills assistance, tutoring, writing center.

**Majors. Agriculture:** Business, equipment technology. **Business:** General, administrative services, managerial economics. **Computer sciences:** Information technology, web page design. **Conservation:** Management/policy. **Education:** Adult/continuing, early childhood, ESL. **English:** English lit. **Health:** Health care admin. **History:** General. **Interdisciplinary:** Biological/physical sciences. **Legal studies:** Prelaw. **Mechanic/repair:** Automotive. **Protective services:** Law enforcement admin. **Visual/performing arts:** Art.

**Computing on campus.** 100 workstations in library, computer center, student center. Online course registration, online library, helpline available.

**Student life. Freshman orientation:** Available. Offered prior to fall semester. **Activities:** Drama, literary magazine, student government, agriculture fraternity, honors fraternity, peer ambassador program, diesel fraternity, Fellowship of Christian Athletes.

**Athletics.** NJCAA. **Intercollegiate:** Baseball M, basketball, softball W. **Team name:** Mudcats.

**Student services.** Adult student services, career counseling, student employment services, financial aid counseling, on-campus daycare, personal counseling, placement for graduates, veterans' counselor. **Physically disabled:** Services for visually, speech, hearing impaired. **Transfer:** Preadmission transcript evaluation for new students. Transfer adviser, college fairs on campus for students transferring to 4-year colleges.

**Contact.** E-mail: admissions@src.edu
Phone: (309) 649-7020 Toll-free number: (800) 334-7337
Fax: (309) 649-6393
Melissa Wilkinson, Director of Admissions and Records, Spoon River College, 23235 North County Road 22, Canton, IL 61520

## Springfield College in Illinois
### Springfield, Illinois
www.sci.edu                                            CB code: 1734

- Private 2-year junior and liberal arts college affiliated with Roman Catholic Church
- Commuter campus in small city
- SAT or ACT (ACT writing optional) required

**General.** Founded in 1929. Regionally accredited. **Enrollment:** 608 degree-seeking undergraduates. **Degrees:** 94 associate awarded. **Location:** 200 miles from Chicago, 100 miles from St. Louis. **Calendar:** 4-1-4, limited summer session. **Full-time faculty:** 25 total. **Part-time faculty:** 44 total.

**Student profile.** Among degree-seeking undergraduates, 153 enrolled as first-time, first-year students, 21 transferred in from other institutions.

| | | | |
|---|---|---|---|
| Part-time: | 53% | African American: | 15% |
| Women: | 70% | | |

**Transfer out. Colleges most students transferred to 2007:** Southern Illinois University-Edwardsville, University of Illinois-Springfield, Illinois State University, Eastern Illinois University, Southern Illinois University-Carbondale.

**Basis for selection.** High school course work, test scores, GPA, class rank required criteria. Interview may be recommended for academically weak applicants. Portfolio recommended for art majors. **Adult students:** SAT/ACT scores not required if applicant over 24. **Homeschooled:** Transcript of courses and grades, state high school equivalency certificate required. GED required to qualify for federal and state financial aid. **Learning Disabled:** Admission requirements for students with learning disabilities handled on case by case basis.

**High school preparation.** Recommended units include English 4, mathematics 3, social studies 2, science 2 and academic electives 2. Mathematics and physical science recommended for all applicants, foreign language for some.

**2007-2008 Annual costs.** Tuition/fees: $7,744. Per-credit charge: $312. Room only: $2,750. Books/supplies: $850. Personal expenses: $1,210.

**Financial aid. Need-based:** Need-based aid available for part-time students. Work-study available nights, weekends and for part-time students. **Non-need-based:** Scholarships awarded for academics, art, athletics, leadership, religious affiliation.

**Application procedures. Admission:** No deadline. $20 fee, may be waived for applicants with need. Application may be submitted online. Admission notification on a rolling basis. **Financial aid:** Priority date 3/1; no closing date. FAFSA, institutional form required. Applicants notified on a rolling basis starting 3/15; must reply within 2 week(s) of notification.

**Academics. Special study options:** Cross-registration, double major, dual enrollment of high school students, honors, independent study, internships, study abroad. **Credit/placement by examination:** AP, CLEP, ACT, institutional tests. 30 credit hours maximum toward associate degree. **Support services:** Learning center, reduced course load, remedial instruction, study skills assistance, tutoring.

**Majors. Business:** General, business admin. **Education:** Elementary, secondary. **Health:** Clinical lab science, predental, premedicine, prenursing, prepharmacy, preveterinary. **Legal studies:** Prelaw. **Liberal arts:** Arts/sciences. **Math:** General. **Philosophy/religion:** Religion. **Public administration:** Social work. **Transportation:** Aviation. **Visual/performing arts:** Art.

**Computing on campus.** 45 workstations in library, computer center. Wireless network available.

**Student life. Freshman orientation:** Mandatory. Preregistration for classes offered. Held Friday before classes begin. **Policies:** Alcohol and other drugs prohibited. **Housing:** Single-sex dorms, substance-free housing available. $300 nonrefundable deposit. **Activities:** Campus ministries, international student organizations, literary magazine, student government, student newspaper, Student Ambassadors, Phi Theta Kappa, arts and cultural events club, Alpha Sigma Lambda.

**Athletics.** NJCAA. **Intercollegiate:** Baseball M, golf M, soccer, softball W, volleyball W. **Team name:** Bulldogs.

**Student services.** Alcohol/substance abuse counseling, campus ministries, career counseling, financial aid counseling, personal counseling, veterans' counselor. **Transfer:** Pre-admission transcript evaluation for new students. Transfer adviser for students transferring to 4-year colleges.

**Contact.** E-mail: admissions@sci.edu
Phone: (217) 525-1420 ext. 287 Toll-free number: (800) 635-7289
Fax: (217) 525-1497
Susan Boehler, Director of Enrollment Services, Springfield College in Illinois, 1500 North Fifth Street, Springfield, IL 62702-2694

---

## Taylor Business Institute
### Chicago, Illinois
**www.tbiil.edu**   **CB code: 2488**

◆ For-profit 2-year business college
◆ Very large city

**General.** Accredited by ACICS. **Calendar:** Continuous.

**Annual costs/financial aid.** Costs vary by program. Tuition for non-degree programs is $16,025-$16,425; associate degree programs are $24,625-$28,025. Fees and book estimates are included in tuition charges. Need-based financial aid available for full-time students.

**Contact.** Phone: (312) 658-5100
Director of Admissions, 318 West Adams Street, #500, Chicago, IL 60007

---

## Triton College
### River Grove, Illinois
**www.triton.edu**   **CB member**
   **CB code: 1821**

◆ Public 2-year community and junior college
◆ Commuter campus in large town

**General.** Founded in 1964. Regionally accredited. **Enrollment:** 10,603 degree-seeking undergraduates; 5,055 non-degree-seeking students. **Degrees:** 825 associate awarded. **Location:** 5 miles from Chicago. **Calendar:** Semester, extensive summer session. **Full-time faculty:** 123 total; 21% have terminal degrees, 20% minority, 55% women. **Part-time faculty:** 644 total; 13% have terminal degrees, 20% minority, 47% women. **Class size:** 37% < 20, 63% 20-39, less than 1% 40-49. **Special facilities:** Earth and space center with planetarium and theater, performing arts center, botanical gardens, educational technology resource center. **Partnerships:** Formal partnerships with Toyota, General Motors, Disney Corporation, over 24 hospitals and health care providers in Chicago area.

**Student profile.** Among degree-seeking undergraduates, 57% enrolled in a transfer program, 43% enrolled in a vocational program, 2,230 enrolled as first-time, first-year students, 434 transferred in from other institutions.

| Part-time: | 67% | Asian American: | 5% |
|---|---|---|---|
| Out-of-state: | 1% | Hispanic American: | 21% |
| Women: | 54% | 25 or older: | 52% |
| African American: | 22% | | |

**Transfer out.** 44% of students enrolled in the transfer program go on to 4-year colleges. **Colleges most students transferred to 2007:** Northern Illinois University, Northeastern Illinois University, University of Illinois at Chicago, DePaul University, Eastern Illinois University.

**Basis for selection.** Open admission, but selective for some programs. Special requirements for most health programs and two manufacturer-related automotive programs. Applicants to allied health program must attend information session. **Learning Disabled:** Students must self identify.

**High school preparation.** Biology, chemistry, or algebra required for most allied health programs. 15 specified units required for university transfer programs.

**2008-2009 Annual costs.** Tuition/fees (projected): $2,170; $5,740 out-of-district; $7,150 out-of-state. Per-credit charge: $64 in-district; $183 out-of-district; $230 out-of-state. Books/supplies: $700. Personal expenses: $1,500.

**2006-2007 Financial aid. Need-based:** 620 full-time freshmen applied for aid; 446 were judged to have need; 446 of these received aid. Average scholarship/grant was $966; average loan $792. 84% of total undergraduate aid awarded as scholarships/grants, 16% as loans/jobs. Need-based aid available for part-time students. Work-study available nights, weekends and for part-time students. **Non-need-based:** Awarded to 392 full-time undergraduates, including 110 freshmen. Scholarships awarded for academics, athletics, leadership.

**Application procedures. Admission:** No deadline. No application fee. Application may be submitted online. Admission notification on a rolling basis. **Financial aid:** Priority date 4/15; no closing date. FAFSA, institutional form required. Applicants notified on a rolling basis starting 4/1; must reply within 2 week(s) of notification.

**Academics. Special study options:** Accelerated study, cooperative education, cross-registration, distance learning, dual enrollment of high school students, ESL, exchange student, honors, independent study, internships, liberal arts/career combination, teacher certification program, weekend college. Bachelor's degree programs available on campus. License preparation in nursing, paramedic, radiology, real estate. **Credit/placement by examination:** AP, CLEP, institutional tests. 30 credit hours maximum toward associate degree. **Support services:** GED preparation, learning center, reduced course load, remedial instruction, study skills assistance, tutoring.

**Honors college/program.** 25 ACT and/or 3.35 GPA required; about 25 admitted each year.

**Majors. Agriculture:** Greenhouse operations, horticulture, landscaping, ornamental horticulture. **Architecture:** Interior. **Area/ethnic studies:** Women's. **Biology:** General. **Business:** Accounting, business admin, construction management, executive assistant, financial planning, hospitality admin, hotel/motel admin, human resources, international, management information systems, marketing, restaurant/food services, sales/distribution, selling. **Communications:** Digital media. **Computer sciences:** General, applications programming, computer graphics, computer science, data processing, information systems, networking. **Education:** General, early childhood, mathematics, science. **Engineering:** General. **Engineering technology:** Architectural drafting, CAD/CADD, computer systems, construction, drafting, electrical, surveying. **English:** English lit, speech/rhetoric. **Family/consumer sciences:** Child care, home furnishings. **Foreign languages:** General, French, Italian, Spanish. **Health:** EMT paramedic, medical radiologic technology/radiation therapy, nuclear medical technology, nursing (RN), ophthalmic lab technology, ophthalmic technology, predental, premedicine, prenursing, prepharmacy, preveterinary, radiologic technology/medical imaging, respiratory therapy technology, sonography, substance abuse counseling. **History:** General. **Interdisciplinary:** Biological/physical sciences, intercultural. **Legal studies:** Prelaw. **Liberal arts:** Arts/sciences. **Math:** General. **Mechanic/repair:** Automotive, avionics, heating/ac/refrig, industrial. **Personal/culinary services:** Chef training, culinary arts. **Philosophy/religion:** Philosophy. **Physical sciences:** Chemistry, geology, physics. **Production:** Welding. **Protective services:** Firefighting, law enforcement admin, police science. **Psychology:** General. **Public administration:** Community org/advocacy, social work. **Social sciences:** Anthropology, economics, geography, political science, sociology. **Visual/performing arts:** Art, commercial/advertising art, design, dramatic, interior design, studio arts.

**Most popular majors.** Biological/life sciences 17%, business/marketing 7%, health sciences 24%, liberal arts 36%.

**Computing on campus.** 700 workstations in library, computer center. Commuter students can connect to campus network. Online course registration, online library, helpline, wireless network available.

**Student life. Freshman orientation:** Available. Sessions held throughout summer months and in December. **Activities:** Jazz band, choral groups, drama, music ensembles, musical theater, radio station, student government, student newspaper, 30 clubs and organizations available.

**Athletics.** NJCAA. **Intercollegiate:** Baseball M, basketball, soccer, softball W, volleyball W, wrestling M. **Team name:** Trojans.

**Student services.** Career counseling, financial aid counseling, health services, minority student services, on-campus daycare, personal counseling, placement for graduates, veterans' counselor. **Physically disabled:** Services for visually, speech, hearing impaired. **Transfer:** Transfer center, transfer adviser, college fairs on campus for students transferring to 4-year colleges.

**Contact.** E-mail: triton@triton.edu
Phone: (708) 456-0300 ext. 3130 Fax: (708) 583-3162
Mary-Rita Moore, Dean, Enrollment Services, Triton College, 2000 North Fifth Avenue, River Grove, IL 60171

## Vatterott College: Quincy
### Quincy, Illinois

◆  For-profit 2-year technical college
◆  Small city

**General.** Accredited by ACCSCT. **Enrollment:** 250 degree-seeking under-graduates. **Degrees:** 14 associate awarded. **Calendar:** Continuous. **Full-time faculty:** 14 total. **Part-time faculty:** 10 total.

**Basis for selection.** Open admission.

**2007-2008 Annual costs.** Program cost ranges: $15,435 to $18,522 (certificate/diploma); $24,696 (associate degree).

**Application procedures. Admission:** No deadline. No application fee.

**Academics. Credit/placement by examination:** CLEP.

**Majors. Computer sciences:** Computer science. **Engineering technology:** CAD/CADD. **Health:** Medical assistant. **Mechanic/repair:** Heating/ac/refrig.

**Contact.**   Phone: (217) 224-0600 Fax: (217) 223-6771
Vatterott College: Quincy, 3609 North Marx Drive, Quincy, IL 62305

## Waubonsee Community College
### Sugar Grove, Illinois
www.waubonsee.edu                      CB code: 1938

◆  Public 2-year community college
◆  Commuter campus in small town

**General.** Founded in 1966. Regionally accredited. Public, comprehensive community college organized in 1966. **Enrollment:** 6,240 degree-seeking undergraduates; 2,491 non-degree-seeking students. **Degrees:** 529 associate awarded. **ROTC:** Army. **Location:** 9 miles from Aurora. **Calendar:** 4-4-1 semester system. Extensive summer session. **Full-time faculty:** 103 total; 13% have terminal degrees, 10% minority, 57% women. **Part-time faculty:** 652 total; 5% have terminal degrees, 13% minority, 62% women. **Special facilities:** Observatory, nature trail.

**Student profile.** Among degree-seeking undergraduates, 54% enrolled in a transfer program, 46% enrolled in a vocational program, 1,512 enrolled as first-time, first-year students.

| | | | |
|---|---|---|---|
| Part-time: | 53% | Hispanic American: | 18% |
| Women: | 56% | Native American: | 1% |
| African American: | 6% | 25 or older: | 45% |
| Asian American: | 3% | | |

**Transfer out. Colleges most students transferred to 2007:** Northern Illinois University, Illinois State University, Aurora University-Illinois, University of Illinois at Urbana-Champaign, University of Illinois at Chicago.

**Basis for selection.** Open admission, but selective for some programs. Admission to limited enrollment programs based on specific assessment testing and/or successful completion of prerequisite coursework.

**High school preparation.** 15 units recommended. Recommended units include English 4, mathematics 3, social studies 3, science 3 and academic electives 2.

**2008-2009 Annual costs.** Tuition/fees (projected): $2,250; $7,337 out-of-district; $8,139 out-of-state. Per-credit charge: $72 in-district; $242 out-of-district; $269 out-of-state. Books/supplies: $1,150. Personal expenses: $1,300.

**2006-2007 Financial aid. Need-based:** 64% of total undergraduate aid awarded as scholarships/grants, 36% as loans/jobs. Need-based aid available for part-time students. Work-study available nights and for part-time students. **Non-need-based:** Scholarships awarded for academics, art, athletics, leadership, minority status, music/drama.

**Application procedures. Admission:** No deadline. No application fee. Application must be submitted on paper. Admission notification on a rolling basis. **Financial aid:** Closing date 12/1. FAFSA required. Applicants notified on a rolling basis.

**Academics. Special study options:** Accelerated study, distance learning, dual enrollment of high school students, ESL, honors, independent study, internships, liberal arts/career combination, study abroad, weekend college.

License preparation in nursing, real estate. **Credit/placement by examination:** AP, CLEP, institutional tests. 30 credit hours maximum toward associate degree. Student must be enrolled before scores can be recorded on transcript. A recording fee may apply. **Support services:** GED preparation, learning center, remedial instruction, study skills assistance, tutoring, writing center.

**Majors. Business:** Accounting technology, administrative services, banking/financial services, business admin, construction management, executive assistant, logistics, office technology, operations, retailing, small business admin. **Communications technology:** Radio/tv. **Computer sciences:** Programming, web page design. **Construction:** Electrician. **Education:** Art, mathematics, multi-level teacher, music, teacher assistance. **Engineering:** General. **Engineering technology:** CAD/CADD, electrical, quality control, robotics. **Foreign languages:** Sign language interpretation, translation. **Health:** Massage therapy, nursing (RN). **Interdisciplinary:** Biological/physical sciences. **Liberal arts:** Arts/sciences. **Mechanic/repair:** Auto body, automotive, heating/ac/refrig, industrial. **Production:** Machine shop technology, machine tool. **Protective services:** Emergency management/homeland security, fire safety technology, police science. **Public administration:** Social work. **Visual/performing arts:** Design, graphic design, studio arts.

**Most popular majors.** Family/consumer sciences 6%, health sciences 16%, interdisciplinary studies 43%, liberal arts 24%.

**Computing on campus.** 140 workstations in computer center, student center. Online course registration, helpline, wireless network available.

**Student life. Freshman orientation:** Available. Optional 1-day program. **Activities:** Bands, choral groups, dance, drama, literary magazine, music ensembles, musical theater, opera, student government, student newspaper, Latino Unidos, Christian fellowship, Amnesty International, African cultural alliance, model Illinois government, Students for a Diverse Society.

**Athletics.** NJCAA. **Intercollegiate:** Baseball M, basketball, cross-country, golf M, soccer, softball W, tennis, volleyball W, wrestling M. **Intramural:** Basketball, bowling, table tennis. **Team name:** Chiefs.

**Student services.** Career counseling, services for economically disadvantaged, student employment services, financial aid counseling, minority student services, on-campus daycare, personal counseling, placement for graduates, veterans' counselor. **Physically disabled:** Services for visually, speech, hearing impaired. **Transfer:** Transfer adviser, college fairs on campus for students transferring to 4-year colleges.

**Contact.**   E-mail: recruitment@waubonsee.edu
Phone: (630) 466-7900 ext. 2370 Fax: (630) 466-4964
Chester Shaw, Recruitment and Retention Manager, Waubonsee Community College, Route 47 at Waubonsee Drive, Sugar Grove, IL 60554-9454

# Indiana

## Ancilla College
### Donaldson, Indiana
www.ancilla.edu                              CB code: 1015

▶ Private 2-year community and liberal arts college affiliated with Roman Catholic Church
▶ Commuter campus in rural community

**General.** Founded in 1937. Regionally accredited. **Enrollment:** 511 degree-seeking undergraduates. **Degrees:** 85 associate awarded. **Location:** 30 miles from South Bend, 7 miles from Plymouth. **Calendar:** Semester, limited summer session. **Full-time faculty:** 25 total. **Part-time faculty:** 33 total. **Class size:** 67% < 20, 33% 20-39.

**Student profile.**

Out-of-state:          1%     25 or older:          40%

**Transfer out. Colleges most students transferred to 2007:** Indiana University South Bend, Purdue North Central, Bethel College.

**Basis for selection.** Open admission, but selective for some programs. Special requirements for nursing program. **Adult students:** SAT/ACT scores not required if out of high school 3 year(s) or more. **Homeschooled:** Transcript of courses and grades required.

**High school preparation.** 21 units recommended. Recommended units include English 4, mathematics 4, social studies 2, history 3, science 3 (laboratory 3) and foreign language 2.

**2008-2009 Annual costs.** Tuition/fees (projected): $12,080. Per-credit charge: $395. Books/supplies: $812. Personal expenses: $612.

**2007-2008 Financial aid. Need-based:** Need-based aid available for part-time students. Work-study available for part-time students. **Non-need-based:** Scholarships awarded for academics, athletics, job skills, leadership.

**Application procedures. Admission:** No deadline. No application fee. Application may be submitted online. Admission notification on a rolling basis. **Financial aid:** Closing date 3/1. FAFSA, institutional form required. Applicants notified on a rolling basis starting 3/1; must reply within 2 week(s) of notification.

**Academics. Special study options:** Accelerated study, cooperative education, double major, dual enrollment of high school students, independent study, liberal arts/career combination. Bachelor's degree programs available on campus. License preparation in real estate. **Credit/placement by examination:** CLEP, institutional tests. 12 credit hours maximum toward associate degree. **Support services:** Learning center, reduced course load, remedial instruction, study skills assistance, tutoring.

**Majors. Biology:** General. **Business:** Business admin. **Communications:** Media studies. **Computer sciences:** General. **Education:** Early childhood, elementary, secondary. **English:** English lit. **Health:** Nursing (RN), prenursing. **History:** General. **Interdisciplinary:** Behavioral sciences. **Liberal arts:** Arts/sciences. **Math:** General. **Physical sciences:** Chemistry. **Protective services:** Criminal justice. **Visual/performing arts:** Graphic design, studio arts.

**Computing on campus.** 53 workstations in library, computer center. Online library available.

**Student life. Freshman orientation:** Mandatory. Preregistration for classes offered. **Activities:** Campus ministries, literary magazine, student government, student newspaper, Student Ambassadors, Phi Theta Kappa.

**Athletics.** NJCAA. **Intercollegiate:** Baseball M, basketball, cheerleading, golf, soccer M, softball W, volleyball W. **Team name:** Chargers.

**Student services.** Campus ministries, career counseling, student employment services, financial aid counseling, personal counseling. **Transfer:** Transfer adviser for students transferring to 4-year colleges.

**Contact.** E-mail: admissions@ancilla.edu
Phone: (574) 936-8898 ext. 330 Fax: (574) 935-1773
Erin Alonzo, Director of Admissions, Ancilla College, 9001 Union Road, Donaldson, IN 46513

## Aviation Institute of Maintenance: Indianapolis
### Indianapolis, Indiana
www.aviationmaintenance.edu/aviation-indianapolis.asp
CB code: 3192

▶ For-profit 2-year technical college
▶ Commuter campus in very large city

**General.** Accredited by ACCSCT. **Location:** 10 miles from downtown. **Calendar:** Continuous.

**Annual costs/financial aid.** Tuition for 18-month associate program $33,120; fees $200. Need-based financial aid available for full-time students.

**Contact.** Phone: (317) 243-4519
Managing Director, 7251 West McCarty Street, Indianapolis, IN 46241-1445

## Brown Mackie College: Fort Wayne
### Fort Wayne, Indiana
www.brownmackie.com                          CB code: 3379

▶ For-profit 2-year branch campus and business college
▶ Large city

**General.** Accredited by ACICS. **Enrollment:** 1,200 full-time, degree-seeking students. **Degrees:** 245 associate awarded. **Calendar:** Quarter. **Full-time faculty:** 32 total. **Part-time faculty:** 75 total.

**Basis for selection.** Open admission.

**2007-2008 Annual costs.** Nursing program tuition $260 per credit hour. Occupational therapy courses $310 per credit hour, with general education courses for occupational therapy $208 per credit hour. $15 per credit hour fee for all courses. All other programs $208 per credit hour. Books/supplies: $1,100.

**Application procedures. Admission:** No deadline. $20 fee.

**Academics. Credit/placement by examination:** CLEP.

**Majors. Business:** Accounting, business admin. **Computer sciences:** General. **Health:** Medical assistant, occupational therapy assistant. **Legal studies:** Paralegal.

**Contact.** E-mail: ktaboh@brownmackie.edu
Phone: (260) 484-4400 Fax: (260) 484-2678
Phil Hooks, Director of Admissions, Brown Mackie College: Fort Wayne, 3000 Coliseum Boulevard, Suite 100, Fort Wayne, IN 46805

## Brown Mackie College: Merrillville
### Merrillville, Indiana
www.brownmackie.edu                          CB code: 7115

▶ For-profit 2-year business college
▶ Small city

**General.** Accredited by ACICS. **Calendar:** Continuous.

**Annual costs/financial aid.** Tuition $250/credit hour; fees $15/credit hour. Books/supplies: $720. Personal expenses: $845.

**Contact.** Phone: (219) 769-3321
Director of Admissions, 1000 East 80th Place, Suite 101N, Merrillville, IN 46410

## Brown Mackie College: Michigan City
### Michigan City, Indiana
www.cbcaec.com                               CB code: 3345

▶ For-profit 2-year branch campus college
▶ Large town

**General.** Accredited by ACICS. **Calendar:** Continuous.

**Annual costs/financial aid.** Tuition/fees (2007-2008): $9,810. Books/supplies: $630. Personal expenses: $2,664.

**Contact.** Phone: (219) 877-3100
Director of Admissions, 325 East US Highway 20, Michigan City, IN
46360-7362

## Brown Mackie College: South Bend
South Bend, Indiana
www.brownmackie.edu
CB code: 3140

- For-profit 2-year community and technical college
- Commuter campus in small city
- Application essay, interview required

**General.** Founded in 1882. Accredited by ACICS. **Enrollment:** 743 degree-seeking undergraduates. **Degrees:** 128 associate awarded. **Location:** 90 miles from Chicago, 150 miles from Indianapolis. **Calendar:** Quarter, extensive summer session. **Full-time faculty:** 17 total. **Part-time faculty:** 26 total. **Class size:** 81% < 20, 19% 20-39.

**Student profile.**

Out-of-state: 7%  25 or older: 45%

**Basis for selection.** Open admission.

**2007-2008 Annual costs.** Tuition/fees: $12,240. Per-credit charge: $260. Books/supplies: $1,200.

**Financial aid.** All financial aid based on need. Need-based aid available for part-time students.

**Application procedures. Admission:** No deadline. No application fee. Must reply by May 1 or within 1 week(s) if notified thereafter. **Financial aid:** No deadline. FAFSA required. Applicants notified on a rolling basis; must reply within 1 week(s) of notification.

**Academics.** 4 day academic week. Friday tutorial sessions (optional). **Special study options:** Accelerated study, double major, independent study, internships. **Credit/placement by examination:** CLEP. 28 credit hours maximum toward associate degree. **Support services:** Remedial instruction, study skills assistance, tutoring.

**Majors. Business:** Accounting, administrative services. **Computer sciences:** General. **Health:** Medical assistant, medical transcription, occupational therapy assistant, physical therapy assistant. **Legal studies:** Legal secretary.

**Most popular majors.** Business/marketing 39%, health sciences 61%.

**Computing on campus.** 60 workstations in computer center.

**Student life. Freshman orientation:** Mandatory. Preregistration for classes offered. Thursday before class starts. Two hours. **Housing:** Students are referred to local apartment complexes.

**Student services.** Career counseling, student employment services, personal counseling, placement for graduates, veterans' counselor. **Transfer:** Transfer adviser for students transferring to 4-year colleges.

**Contact.** E-mail: bmcsbadm@brownmackie.edu
Phone: (574) 237-0774 Toll-free number: (800) 743-2447
Jack Kempt, Director of Admissions, Brown Mackie College: South Bend, 1030 East Jefferson Boulevard, South Bend, IN 46617

## College of Court Reporting
Hobart, Indiana
www.ccr.edu
CB code: 3532

- For-profit 2-year business and technical college
- Small city

**General.** Accredited by ACICS. **Enrollment:** 225 degree-seeking undergraduates. **Degrees:** 16 associate awarded. **Calendar:** Semester. **Part-time faculty:** 20 total.

**Basis for selection.** Open admission.

**2007-2008 Annual costs.** Tuition/fees: $6,600. Per-credit charge: $275.

**Application procedures. Admission:** Closing date 9/30. $50 fee.

**Academics. Credit/placement by examination:** CLEP.

**Majors. Business:** Office technology. **Health:** Medical transcription. **Legal studies:** Court reporting.

**Contact.** E-mail: information@ccr.edu
Phone: (219) 942-1459 Fax: (219) 942-1631
Nicky Rodriguez, Director of Admissions, College of Court Reporting, 111 West 10th Street, Suite 111, Hobart, IN 46342

## Indiana Business College: Anderson
Anderson, Indiana
www.ibcschools.edu
CB code: 3364

- For-profit 2-year business and health science college
- Commuter campus in small city
- Interview required

**General.** Accredited by ACICS. **Enrollment:** 206 degree-seeking undergraduates. **Degrees:** 55 associate awarded. **Location:** 45 miles from Indianapolis. **Calendar:** Quarter, extensive summer session. **Full-time faculty:** 5 total. **Part-time faculty:** 11 total.

**Basis for selection.** Interview and Wonderlic evaluation are main admission criteria. **Adult students:** All students must take and successfully pass the Wonderlic Scholastic Level Exam.

**2007-2008 Annual costs.** Tuition and fees vary by program: $194 to $268 per credit hour.

**Financial aid. Need-based:** Need-based aid available for part-time students. **Additional information:** Work-study programs available.

**Application procedures. Admission:** No deadline. $50 fee. Admission notification on a rolling basis. **Financial aid:** FAFSA required. Applicants notified on a rolling basis.

**Academics. Special study options:** Distance learning, dual enrollment of high school students, internships. **Credit/placement by examination:** CLEP, institutional tests. Free test-out program is available to high school seniors. Test-outs are available to all other students for a $30 fee.

**Majors. Business:** Accounting, administrative services, banking/financial services, business admin, human resources, marketing. **Health:** Insurance coding, medical assistant, medical records technology. **Protective services:** Law enforcement admin.

**Student life. Activities:** Student government.

**Student services.** Career counseling, student employment services, financial aid counseling, placement for graduates.

**Contact.** E-mail: anderson@ibcschools.edu
Phone: (765) 644-7514 Toll-free number: (800) 422-4723
Fax: (765) 644-5724
Matt Stein, Associate Director of Admissions, Indiana Business College: Anderson, 140 East 53rd Street, Anderson, IN 46013

## Indiana Business College: Columbus
Columbus, Indiana
www.ibcschools.edu
CB code: 3349

- For-profit 2-year business and health science college
- Commuter campus in large town
- Interview required

**General.** Accredited by ACICS. **Enrollment:** 270 degree-seeking undergraduates. **Degrees:** 89 associate awarded. **Location:** 50 miles from Indianapolis. **Calendar:** Quarter, extensive summer session. **Full-time faculty:** 5 total. **Part-time faculty:** 4 total.

**Basis for selection.** Interview and Wonderlic evaluation are main admission criteria. **Adult students:** All students must take and successfully pass the Wonderlic Scholastic Level Exam.

**2007-2008 Annual costs.** Tuition and fees vary by program: $194 to $268 per credit hour.

**Financial aid. Need-based:** Need-based aid available for part-time students. **Additional information:** Work-study programs are available.

**Application procedures. Admission:** No deadline. $50 fee. Admission notification on a rolling basis. **Financial aid:** FAFSA required. Applicants notified on a rolling basis.

**Academics.** **Special study options:** Distance learning, dual enrollment of high school students, internships. **Credit/placement by examination:** CLEP, institutional tests. Free test-out program is available to high school seniors. Test-outs are available to other students for a $30 fee.

**Majors.** **Business:** Accounting, administrative services, banking/financial services, business admin, marketing. **Health:** Insurance coding, medical assistant, medical records technology.

**Student services.** Career counseling, student employment services, financial aid counseling, placement for graduates.

**Contact.** E-mail: columbus@ibcschools.edu
Phone: (812) 379-9000 Toll-free number: (800) 422-4723
Fax: (812) 375-0414
Gina Pate, Director of Admissions, Indiana Business College: Columbus, 2222 Poshard Drive, Columbus, IN 47203

## Indiana Business College: Evansville

**Evansville, Indiana**
**www.ibcschools.edu**　　　　　　　**CB code: 3346**

- For-profit 2-year business and health science college
- Commuter campus in small city
- Interview required

**General.** Accredited by ACICS. **Enrollment:** 321 degree-seeking undergraduates. **Degrees:** 84 associate awarded. **Calendar:** Quarter, extensive summer session. **Full-time faculty:** 8 total. **Part-time faculty:** 8 total.

**Basis for selection.** Interview and Wonderlic evaluation are main admission criteria. **Adult students:** All students must take and successfully pass the Wonderlic Scholastic Level Exam.

**2007-2008 Annual costs.** Tuition and fees vary by program: $194 to $268 per credit hour.

**Financial aid.** **Need-based:** Need-based aid available for part-time students. **Additional information:** Work-study programs are available.

**Application procedures.** **Admission:** No deadline. $50 fee. Admission notification on a rolling basis. **Financial aid:** FAFSA required. Applicants notified on a rolling basis.

**Academics.** **Special study options:** Distance learning, dual enrollment of high school students, internships. Bachelor's degree programs available on campus. **Credit/placement by examination:** CLEP, institutional tests. A free test-out program is available to high school seniors. Test-outs are available to all other students for a $30 fee.

**Majors.** **Business:** Accounting, administrative services, banking/financial services, business admin, marketing. **Computer sciences:** Information technology. **Health:** Insurance coding, medical assistant, medical records technology. **Protective services:** Law enforcement admin.

**Student services.** Career counseling, student employment services, financial aid counseling, placement for graduates.

**Contact.** Phone: (812) 476-6000 Toll-free number: (800) 422-4723
Fax: (812) 471-8576
Starlet Gupton, Director of Admissions, Indiana Business College: Evansville, 4601 Theater Drive, Evansville, IN 47715

## Indiana Business College: Fort Wayne

**Fort Wayne, Indiana**
**www.ibcschools.edu**　　　　　　　**CB code: 3867**

- For-profit 2-year business and health science college
- Commuter campus in large city
- Interview required

**General.** Accredited by ACICS. **Enrollment:** 474 degree-seeking undergraduates. **Degrees:** 131 associate awarded. **Calendar:** Quarter, extensive summer session. **Full-time faculty:** 6 total. **Part-time faculty:** 14 total.

**Basis for selection.** Interview and Wonderlic evaluation are main admission criteria. **Adult students:** All students must take and successfully pass the Wonderlic Scholastic Level Exam.

**2007-2008 Annual costs.** Tuition and fees vary by program: $194 to $268 per credit hour.

**Financial aid.** **Need-based:** Need-based aid available for part-time students. **Additional information:** Work-Study programs are available.

**Application procedures.** **Admission:** No deadline. $50 fee. Admission notification on a rolling basis. **Financial aid:** FAFSA required.

**Academics.** **Special study options:** Distance learning, dual enrollment of high school students, internships. Bachelor's degree programs available on campus. **Credit/placement by examination:** CLEP, institutional tests. Free test-out program is available to high school seniors. Test-outs are available to all other students for a $30 fee.

**Majors.** **Business:** Accounting, administrative services, banking/financial services, business admin, marketing. **Computer sciences:** Information technology. **Health:** Medical assistant, medical records technology, surgical technology. **Protective services:** Law enforcement admin.

**Student services.** Career counseling, student employment services, financial aid counseling, placement for graduates.

**Contact.** E-mail: fortwayne@ibcschools.edu
Phone: (260) 471-7667 Toll-free number: (800) 422-4723
Fax: (260) 471-6918
Janet Herman, Executive Director, Indiana Business College: Fort Wayne, 6413 North Clinton Street, Fort Wayne, IN 46825

## Indiana Business College: Indianapolis

**Indianapolis, Indiana**
**www.ibcschools.edu**　　　　　　　**CB code: 2317**

- For-profit 2-year business and health science college
- Commuter campus in very large city

**General.** Founded in 1902. Accredited by ACICS. **Enrollment:** 1,486 degree-seeking undergraduates. **Degrees:** 239 associate awarded. **Calendar:** Quarter, extensive summer session. **Full-time faculty:** 27 total. **Part-time faculty:** 11 total.

**Basis for selection.** Interview and Wonderlic evaluation are main admission criteria. **Adult students:** SAT/ACT scores not required. All students must take and successfully pass the Wonderlic Scholastic Level Exam.

**2007-2008 Annual costs.** Tuition and fees vary by program: $194 to $268 per credit hour.

**Financial aid.** **Need-based:** Need-based aid available for part-time students. **Additional information:** Work-study programs are available.

**Application procedures.** **Admission:** No deadline. $50 fee. Admission notification on a rolling basis. **Financial aid:** FAFSA required. Applicants notified on a rolling basis.

**Academics.** **Special study options:** Distance learning, dual enrollment of high school students, internships. Bachelor's degree programs available on campus. **Credit/placement by examination:** CLEP, institutional tests. Free test-out program is available to high school seniors. Test-outs are available to all other students for a $30 fee per exam.

**Majors.** **Business:** Accounting, administrative services, banking/financial services, business admin, fashion, human resources, marketing. **Computer sciences:** Information technology, networking. **Engineering technology:** Computer systems. **Health:** Medical assistant. **Personal/culinary services:** Culinary arts. **Protective services:** Law enforcement admin.

**Student life.** **Activities:** Student government.

**Student services.** Career counseling, student employment services, financial aid counseling, placement for graduates.

**Contact.** E-mail: indianapolis@ibcschools.edu
Phone: (317) 264-5656 Toll-free number: (800) 422-4723
Fax: (317) 264-5650
Kory Amyx, Director of Admissions, Indiana Business College: Indianapolis, 550 East Washington Street, Indianapolis, IN 46204

## Indiana Business College: Indianapolis Northwest

**Indianapolis, Indiana**
**www.ibcschools.edu**

- For-profit 2-year business and health science college
- Very large city

**General.** Accredited by ACICS. **Enrollment:** 218 degree-seeking undergraduates. **Degrees:** 14 associate awarded. **Calendar:** Quarter. **Full-time faculty:** 8 total. **Part-time faculty:** 5 total.

**Basis for selection. Adult students:** SAT/ACT scores not required.

**2007-2008 Annual costs.** Tuition and fees vary by program: $194 to $268 per credit hour.

**Application procedures. Admission:** $50 fee. Admission notification on a rolling basis. **Financial aid:** FAFSA required.

**Academics. Special study options:** Distance learning, dual enrollment of high school students, internships. **Credit/placement by examination:** CLEP, institutional tests.

**Majors. Business:** Accounting, administrative services, banking/financial services, business admin, marketing. **Health:** Insurance coding, medical assistant, medical records technology, surgical technology, veterinary technology/ assistant.

**Contact.** E-mail: northwest@ibcschools.edu
Phone: (317) 873-6500 Toll-free number: (800) IBC-GRAD
Mark Jones, Director of Admissions, Indiana Business College: Indianapolis Northwest, 6300 Technology Center Drive, Indianapolis, IN 46278

## Indiana Business College: Lafayette
**Lafayette, Indiana**
www.ibcschools.edu                              CB code: 3353

- For-profit 2-year business and health science college
- Commuter campus in small city
- Interview required

**General.** Accredited by ACICS. **Enrollment:** 325 degree-seeking undergraduates. **Degrees:** 65 associate awarded. **Location:** 60 miles from Indianapolis. **Calendar:** Quarter, extensive summer session. **Full-time faculty:** 7 total. **Part-time faculty:** 6 total.

**Basis for selection.** Interview and Wonderlic evaluation are main admission criteria. **Adult students:** All students must take and successfully pass the Wonderlic Scholastic Level Exam.

**2007-2008 Annual costs.** Tuition and fees vary by program: $194 to $268 per credit hour.

**Financial aid. Need-based:** Need-based aid available for part-time students. **Additional information:** Work-Study Programs are available.

**Application procedures. Admission:** No deadline. $50 fee. Admission notification on a rolling basis. **Financial aid:** FAFSA required. Applicants notified on a rolling basis.

**Academics. Special study options:** Distance learning, dual enrollment of high school students, internships. **Credit/placement by examination:** CLEP, institutional tests. Free test-out program is available to high school seniors. Test-outs are available to all other students for a $30 fee.

**Majors. Business:** Accounting, administrative services, banking/financial services, business admin, human resources, marketing. **Health:** Insurance coding, medical assistant, medical records technology.

**Student services.** Career counseling, student employment services, financial aid counseling, placement for graduates.

**Contact.** E-mail: lafayette@ibcschools.edu
Phone: (765) 447-9550 Toll-free number: (800) 422-4723
Fax: (765) 447-0868
Stacy Golleher, Director of Admissions, Indiana Business College: Lafayette, 4705 Meijer Court, Lafayette, IN 47905

## Indiana Business College: Marion
**Marion, Indiana**
www.ibcschools.edu                              CB code: 3360

- For-profit 2-year business and health science college
- Commuter campus in large town
- Interview required

**General.** Accredited by ACICS. **Enrollment:** 137 degree-seeking undergraduates. **Degrees:** 28 associate awarded. **Location:** 70 miles from Indianapolis. **Calendar:** Quarter, extensive summer session. **Full-time faculty:** 3 total. **Part-time faculty:** 8 total.

**Basis for selection.** Interview and Wonderlic evaluation are main admission criteria. **Adult students:** SAT/ACT scores not required. All students must take and successfully pass the Wonderlic Scholastic Level Exam.

**2007-2008 Annual costs.** Tuition and fees vary by program: $194 to $268 per credit hour.

**Financial aid. Need-based:** Need-based aid available for part-time students. **Additional information:** Work-Study Programs are available.

**Application procedures. Admission:** No deadline. $50 fee. Admission notification on a rolling basis. **Financial aid:** FAFSA required. Applicants notified on a rolling basis.

**Academics. Special study options:** Distance learning, dual enrollment of high school students, internships. **Credit/placement by examination:** CLEP, institutional tests. Free test-out program available to high school seniors. Test-outs are available to all other students for a $30 fee per exam.

**Majors. Business:** Accounting, administrative services, banking/financial services, business admin, marketing. **Health:** Insurance coding, medical assistant. **Protective services:** Law enforcement admin.

**Student services.** Career counseling, student employment services, financial aid counseling, placement for graduates.

**Contact.** E-mail: marion@ibcschools.edu
Phone: (765) 662-7497 Toll-free number: (800) 422-4723
Fax: (765) 651-9421
Richard Herman, Executive Director, Indiana Business College: Marion, 830 North Miller Avenue, Marion, IN 46952

## Indiana Business College: Medical
**Indianapolis, Indiana**
www.ibcschools.edu                              CB code: 3370

- For-profit 2-year health science college
- Commuter campus in very large city
- Interview required

**General.** Accredited by ACICS. **Enrollment:** 565 degree-seeking undergraduates. **Degrees:** 200 associate awarded. **Calendar:** Quarter, extensive summer session. **Full-time faculty:** 22 total. **Part-time faculty:** 8 total.

**Basis for selection.** Interview and Wonderlic evaluation are main admission criteria. **Adult students:** SAT/ACT scores not required. Students must take and successfully pass the Wonderlic Scholastic Level Exam.

**2007-2008 Annual costs.** Tuition and fees vary by program: $194 to $268 per credit hour.

**Financial aid. Need-based:** Need-based aid available for part-time students. **Additional information:** Work-study programs are available.

**Application procedures. Admission:** No deadline. $50 fee. Admission notification on a rolling basis. **Financial aid:** FAFSA required. Applicants notified on a rolling basis.

**Academics. Special study options:** Distance learning, dual enrollment of high school students, internships. **Credit/placement by examination:** CLEP, institutional tests. Free test-out program available to high school seniors. Test-outs are available to all other students for a $30 fee per exam. **Support services:** Reduced course load, study skills assistance, tutoring.

**Majors. Business:** Insurance. **Health:** Clinical lab science, insurance coding, massage therapy, medical assistant, medical records technology, nursing (RN), surgical technology.

**Student life. Freshman orientation:** Available. One-hour orientation held quarterly on first day of classes.

**Student services.** Career counseling, student employment services, financial aid counseling, placement for graduates.

**Contact.** E-mail: medical@ibcschools.edu
Phone: (317) 375-8000 Toll-free number: (800) 422-4723
Fax: (317) 351-1871
Alan Bacon, Director of Admissions, Indiana Business College: Medical, 8150 Brookville Road, Indianapolis, IN 46239

## Indiana Business College: Muncie
### Muncie, Indiana
www.ibcschools.edu          CB code: 3347

- For-profit 2-year business and health science college
- Commuter campus in small city
- Interview required

**General.** Accredited by ACICS. **Enrollment:** 323 degree-seeking undergraduates. **Degrees:** 107 associate awarded. **Calendar:** Quarter, extensive summer session. **Full-time faculty:** 4 total. **Part-time faculty:** 13 total.

**Basis for selection.** Interview and Wonderlic evaluation are main admission criteria. **Adult students:** All students must take and successfully pass the Wonderlic Scholastic Level Exam.

**2007-2008 Annual costs.** Tuition and fees vary by program: $194 to $268 per credit hour.

**Financial aid. Need-based:** Need-based aid available for part-time students. **Additional information:** Work-Study Programs are available.

**Application procedures. Admission:** No deadline. $50 fee. Admission notification on a rolling basis. **Financial aid:** FAFSA required. Applicants notified on a rolling basis.

**Academics. Special study options:** Distance learning, dual enrollment of high school students, internships. Bachelor's degree programs available on campus. **Credit/placement by examination:** CLEP, institutional tests. Free test-out program available to high school seniors. Test-outs are available to all other students for a $30 fee per exam. **Support services:** Study skills assistance, tutoring.

**Majors. Business:** Accounting, administrative services, banking/financial services, business admin, human resources, marketing. **Computer sciences:** Information technology. **Engineering technology:** Computer systems. **Health:** Insurance coding, medical assistant. **Protective services:** Law enforcement admin.

**Student life. Freshman orientation:** Mandatory.

**Student services.** Career counseling, student employment services, financial aid counseling, placement for graduates.

**Contact.** E-mail: muncie@ibcschools.edu
Phone: (765) 288-8681 Toll-free number: (800) 422-4723
Fax: (765) 288-8797
Jeremy Linder, Associate Director of Admissions, Indiana Business College: Muncie, 411 West Riggin Road, Muncie, IN 47303

## Indiana Business College: Terre Haute
### Terre Haute, Indiana
www.ibcschools.edu          CB code: 3348

- For-profit 2-year business and health science college
- Commuter campus in small city
- Interview required

**General.** Accredited by ACICS. **Enrollment:** 263 degree-seeking undergraduates. **Degrees:** 75 associate awarded. **Calendar:** Quarter, extensive summer session. **Full-time faculty:** 4 total. **Part-time faculty:** 7 total.

**Basis for selection.** Open admission, but selective for some programs. Interview, Wonderlic evaluation, and a recommendation from the Executive Director are main admission criteria. **Adult students:** All students must take and successfully pass the Wonderlic Scholastic Level Exam.

**2007-2008 Annual costs.** Tuition and fees vary by program: $194 to $268 per credit hour.

**Financial aid. Need-based:** Need-based aid available for part-time students. **Additional information:** Work-study programs are available.

**Application procedures. Admission:** No deadline. $50 fee. Admission notification on a rolling basis. **Financial aid:** FAFSA required. Applicants notified on a rolling basis.

**Academics. Special study options:** Cooperative education, distance learning, dual enrollment of high school students, internships. Bachelor's degree programs available on campus. **Credit/placement by examination:** CLEP, institutional tests. Free test-out program available to high school seniors. Test-outs are available to all other students for a fee of $30 per test. **Support services:** Study skills assistance, tutoring.

**Majors. Business:** Accounting, administrative services, banking/financial services, business admin, human resources, marketing. **Computer sciences:** Information technology, system admin. **Health:** Insurance coding, medical assistant, medical records technology.

**Student services.** Career counseling, student employment services, financial aid counseling, placement for graduates.

**Contact.** E-mail: terrehaute@ibcschools.edu
Phone: (812) 877-2100 Toll-free number: (800) 422-4723
Fax: (812) 877-4440
Pat Mozley, Regional Director, Indiana Business College: Terre Haute, 1378 South State Road 46, Terre Haute, IN 47803

## International Business College: Indianapolis
### Indianapolis, Indiana
www.intlbusinesscollege.com          CB code: 3374

- For-profit 2-year business college
- Commuter campus in very large city

**General.** Accredited by ACICS. **Calendar:** Continuous.

**Annual costs/financial aid.** Tuition/fees (2007-2008): $12,440. Room: $6,300. Books/supplies: $1,400.

**Contact.** Phone: (317) 841-6400
7205 Shadeland Station, Indianapolis, IN 46256

## ITT Technical Institute: Newburgh
### Newburgh, Indiana

- For-profit 2-year business and technical college
- Small town

**General.** Accredited by ACICS. **Calendar:** Quarter.

**Contact.** 10999 Stahl Road, Newburgh, IN 47630

## Ivy Tech Community College: Bloomington
### Bloomington, Indiana
www.ivytech.edu          CB code: 1455

- Public 2-year community college
- Commuter campus in small city

**General. Enrollment:** 4,435 degree-seeking undergraduates; 285 non-degree-seeking students. **Degrees:** 309 associate awarded. **Calendar:** Semester, extensive summer session. **Full-time faculty:** 57 total. **Part-time faculty:** 269 total.

**Student profile.** Among degree-seeking undergraduates, 71% enrolled in a transfer program, 29% enrolled in a vocational program, 1,332 enrolled as first-time, first-year students, 253 transferred in from other institutions.

| | | | |
|---|---|---|---|
| Part-time: | 50% | Asian American: | 1% |
| Out-of-state: | 1% | Hispanic American: | 1% |
| Women: | 60% | International: | 1% |
| African American: | 3% | 25 or older: | 42% |

**Transfer out. Colleges most students transferred to 2007:** Indiana University - Bloomington.

**Basis for selection.** Open admission, but selective for some programs. Special requirements for human services and health technology programs based on test scores and prior academic work. **Adult students:** SAT/ACT scores not required.

**2007-2008 Annual costs.** Tuition/fees: $2,819; $5,653 out-of-state. Per-credit charge: $91 in-state; $186 out-of-state. Out-of-state distance education tuition: $119 per credit hour ($3,584 for academic year). Books/supplies: $988. Personal expenses: $2,224.

**Financial aid. Need-based:** Need-based aid available for part-time students. Work-study available nights and for part-time students.

**Application procedures. Admission:** No deadline. No application fee. Admission notification on a rolling basis. Application closing date for international students at least 60 days prior to start of semester. **Financial aid:**

Priority date 3/1; no closing date. FAFSA required. Applicants notified on a rolling basis starting 7/1.

**Academics. Special study options:** Distance learning, dual enrollment of high school students, internships, liberal arts/career combination, teacher certification program, weekend college. License preparation in nursing. **Credit/placement by examination:** AP, CLEP, institutional tests. 45 credit hours maximum toward associate degree. 15 credits must be earned in residence. **Support services:** Learning center, reduced course load, remedial instruction, tutoring.

**Majors. Biology:** Biotechnology. **Business:** Accounting technology, business admin, executive assistant, hospitality admin. **Computer sciences:** General, information technology. **Construction:** Electrician, maintenance, plumbing. **Education:** General, early childhood. **Engineering technology:** Drafting, electrical. **Health:** EMT paramedic, medical radiologic technology/radiation therapy, medical records technology, mental health services, nursing (RN), respiratory therapy technology. **Legal studies:** Paralegal. **Liberal arts:** Arts/sciences, library assistant. **Mechanic/repair:** General, heating/ac/refrig. **Parks/recreation:** Exercise sciences. **Production:** Cabinetmaking/millwright, machine tool, sheet metal, tool and die. **Protective services:** Criminal justice. **Other:** Manufacturing and industrial technology, Mold and die, Stationary power plant operator.

**Most popular majors.** Business/marketing 26%, computer/information sciences 8%, engineering/engineering technologies 11%, health sciences 16%, liberal arts 20%, security/protective services 11%.

**Computing on campus.** 884 workstations in library, computer center. Online course registration, online library, helpline, repair service, student web hosting available.

**Student life. Freshman orientation:** Available. **Activities:** Student government, Phi Theta Kappa, College Democrats, student leadership academy, Christian Challenge, computer club, cultural awareness.

**Athletics. Intramural:** Basketball, football (non-tackle) M, soccer, softball, volleyball.

**Student services.** Adult student services, career counseling, student employment services, financial aid counseling, minority student services, placement for graduates, veterans' counselor. **Physically disabled:** Services for visually, speech, hearing impaired. **Transfer:** Transfer center, transfer adviser, college fairs on campus for students transferring to 4-year colleges.

**Contact.** E-mail: lhandy1@ivytech.edu
Phone: (812) 330-6023 Toll-free number: (800) 447-0700 ext. 6350
Fax: (812) 330-106
Lori Handy, Director of Enrollment Services, Ivy Tech Community College: Bloomington, 200 Daniels Way, Bloomington, IN 47404-1511

## Ivy Tech Community College: Central Indiana
**Indianapolis, Indiana**
**www.ivytech.edu**                         **CB code: 1311**

- Public 2-year community college
- Commuter campus in very large city

**General.** Founded in 1966. Regionally accredited. Branch location at Lawrence. **Enrollment:** 12,639 degree-seeking undergraduates; 1,815 non-degree-seeking students. **Degrees:** 838 associate awarded. **Location:** 2 miles from downtown. **Calendar:** Semester, extensive summer session. **Full-time faculty:** 149 total. **Part-time faculty:** 594 total.

**Student profile.** Among degree-seeking undergraduates, 57% enrolled in a transfer program, 43% enrolled in a vocational program, 2,395 enrolled as first-time, first-year students, 1,593 transferred in from other institutions.

| | | | |
|---|---|---|---|
| Part-time: | 65% | Hispanic American: | 2% |
| Women: | 58% | International: | 2% |
| African American: | 23% | 25 or older: | 48% |
| Asian American: | 1% | | |

**Transfer out. Colleges most students transferred to 2007:** Indiana University-Purdue University Indianapolis, Vincennes University, Indiana University-Bloomington, Purdue University-West Lafayette, Ball State University.

**Basis for selection.** Open admission, but selective for some programs. Special requirements for human services and health technology programs based on test scores and prior academic work. **Adult students:** SAT/ACT scores not required.

**2007-2008 Annual costs.** Tuition/fees: $2,819; $5,653 out-of-state. Per-credit charge: $91 in-state; $186 out-of-state. Out-of-state distance education tuition: $119 per credit hour ($3,584 for academic year). Books/supplies: $988. Personal expenses: $2,224.

**Financial aid. Need-based:** Need-based aid available for part-time students. Work-study available nights and for part-time students.

**Application procedures. Admission:** No deadline. No application fee. Admission notification on a rolling basis. Application closing date for undergraduate international students at least 60 days prior to start of semester. **Financial aid:** Priority date 3/1; no closing date. FAFSA required. Applicants notified on a rolling basis starting 7/1.

**Academics. Special study options:** Cooperative education, distance learning, dual enrollment of high school students, ESL, internships, liberal arts/career combination, teacher certification program, weekend college. License preparation in nursing, radiology. **Credit/placement by examination:** AP, CLEP, institutional tests. 45 credit hours maximum toward associate degree. 15 credits must be earned in residence. **Support services:** GED preparation and test center, learning center, reduced course load, remedial instruction, tutoring.

**Majors. Biology:** Biotechnology. **Business:** Accounting technology, business admin, executive assistant, hospitality admin, logistics. **Computer sciences:** General, information technology. **Construction:** Carpentry, electrician, glazier, maintenance, masonry, painting, pipefitting, plumbing. **Education:** General, early childhood. **Engineering technology:** Electrical, industrial, occupational safety, telecommunications. **Health:** EMT paramedic, medical assistant, medical radiologic technology/radiation therapy, medical records technology, mental health services, nursing (RN), respiratory therapy technology, surgical technology. **Legal studies:** Paralegal. **Liberal arts:** Arts/sciences, library assistant. **Mechanic/repair:** Automotive, electronics/electrical, heating/ac/refrig, industrial electronics. **Personal/culinary services:** Mortuary science. **Production:** Cabinetmaking/millwright, ironworking, machine shop technology, machine tool, sheet metal, tool and die. **Protective services:** Criminal justice. **Visual/performing arts:** Design. **Other:** Emergency preparedness and management, Floorlayers, Industrial millwright, Manufacturing and industrial technology, Stationary power plant operator.

**Most popular majors.** Business/marketing 19%, computer/information sciences 6%, engineering/engineering technologies 7%, health sciences 28%, trade and industry 24%.

**Computing on campus.** 1,599 workstations in library, computer center. Online course registration, online library, helpline, repair service, student web hosting, wireless network available.

**Student life. Freshman orientation:** Available. **Activities:** Student government, Phi Theta Kappa, accounting association, human service club, radiology technology club, student leadership academy, Black Student Union, Veterans Association.

**Athletics. Intramural:** Basketball, football (non-tackle) M, volleyball.

**Student services.** Adult student services, career counseling, student employment services, financial aid counseling, minority student services, placement for graduates, veterans' counselor. **Physically disabled:** Services for visually, speech, hearing impaired. **Transfer:** Transfer center, transfer adviser, college fairs on campus for students transferring to 4-year colleges.

**Contact.** E-mail: tfunk@ivytech.edu
Phone: (317) 921-4882 Toll-free number: (800) 732-1470
Fax: (317) 921-4753
Tracy Funk, Director of Admissions, Ivy Tech Community College: Central Indiana, 50 West Fall Creek Parkway North Drive, Indianapolis, IN 46208-5752

## Ivy Tech Community College: Columbus
**Columbus, Indiana**
**www.ivytech.edu**                         **CB code: 1286**

- Public 2-year community college
- Commuter campus in large town

**General.** Founded in 1963. Regionally accredited. **Enrollment:** 2,407 degree-seeking undergraduates; 220 non-degree-seeking students. **Degrees:** 208 associate awarded. **Location:** 40 miles from Indianapolis. **Calendar:** Semester, extensive summer session. **Full-time faculty:** 40 total. **Part-time faculty:** 184 total. **Special facilities:** Visual communications gallery.

**Student profile.** Among degree-seeking undergraduates, 45% enrolled in a transfer program, 55% enrolled in a vocational program, 459 enrolled as first-time, first-year students, 197 transferred in from other institutions.

| | | | |
|---|---|---|---|
| Part-time: | 61% | Hispanic American: | 1% |
| Women: | 73% | International: | 1% |
| African American: | 2% | 25 or older: | 52% |

**Transfer out.** Colleges most students transferred to 2007: Indiana University-Purdue University Indianapolis, Indiana University-Bloomington, Purdue University, Vincennes University, Indiana State University.

**Basis for selection.** Open admission, but selective for some programs. Special requirements for human services and health technology programs based on test scores and prior academic work.

**2007-2008 Annual costs.** Tuition/fees: $2,819; $5,653 out-of-state. Per-credit charge: $91 in-state; $186 out-of-state. Out-of-state distance education tuition: $119 per credit hour ($3,584 for academic year). Books/supplies: $988. Personal expenses: $2,224.

**Financial aid. Need-based:** Need-based aid available for part-time students. Work-study available nights and for part-time students.

**Application procedures. Admission:** No deadline. No application fee. Admission notification on a rolling basis. Application closing date for international students at least 60 days prior to start of semester. **Financial aid:** Priority date 3/1; no closing date. FAFSA required. Applicants notified on a rolling basis starting 7/1.

**Academics. Special study options:** Distance learning, dual enrollment of high school students, internships, liberal arts/career combination, teacher certification program, weekend college. License preparation in dental hygiene, nursing, paramedic, radiology. **Credit/placement by examination:** AP, CLEP, institutional tests. 45 credit hours maximum toward associate degree. 15 credits must be earned in residence. **Support services:** Learning center, reduced course load, remedial instruction, tutoring.

**Majors. Agriculture:** General. **Business:** Accounting technology, business admin, executive assistant. **Computer sciences:** General, information technology. **Construction:** Maintenance, masonry. **Education:** General, early childhood. **Engineering technology:** Drafting, electrical. **Health:** EMT paramedic, medical assistant, medical radiologic technology/radiation therapy, mental health services, nursing (RN), ophthalmic technology, surgical technology. **Legal studies:** Paralegal. **Liberal arts:** Arts/sciences, library assistant. **Mechanic/repair:** Automotive, heating/ac/refrig. **Production:** Machine tool, tool and die. **Protective services:** Criminal justice. **Visual/performing arts:** Design, interior design. **Other:** Industrial millwright, Industrial plumber, Manufacturing and industrial technology, Stationary power plant operator.

**Most popular majors.** Business/marketing 14%, computer/information sciences 8%, engineering/engineering technologies 16%, health sciences 51%.

**Computing on campus.** 524 workstations in library, computer center. Online course registration, online library, helpline, repair service, student web hosting available.

**Student life. Freshman orientation:** Available. **Activities:** Student government, student newspaper, Phi Theta Kappa, Student Leadership Academy.

**Student services.** Adult student services, career counseling, student employment services, financial aid counseling, minority student services, placement for graduates, veterans' counselor. **Physically disabled:** Services for visually, speech, hearing impaired. **Transfer:** Transfer adviser, college fairs on campus for students transferring to 4-year colleges.

**Contact.** E-mail: nbagadio@ivytech.edu
Phone: (812) 374-5129 Toll-free number: (800) 922-4838
Fax: (812) 372-0311
Neil Bagadiong, Director of Admissions/Assistant Director of Student Affairs, Ivy Tech Community College: Columbus, 4475 Central Avenue, Columbus, IN 47203-1868

## Ivy Tech Community College: East Central
**Muncie, Indiana**
www.ivytech.edu                                    **CB code: 1279**

▸ Public 2-year community college
▸ Commuter campus in small city

**General.** Founded in 1968. Regionally accredited. Campuses also at Anderson and Marion. **Enrollment:** 5,610 degree-seeking undergraduates; 404 non-degree-seeking students. **Degrees:** 443 associate awarded. **Location:** 50 miles from Indianapolis. **Calendar:** Semester, extensive summer session. **Full-time faculty:** 91 total. **Part-time faculty:** 337 total.

**Student profile.** Among degree-seeking undergraduates, 61% enrolled in a transfer program, 39% enrolled in a vocational program, 1,157 enrolled as first-time, first-year students, 351 transferred in from other institutions.

| | | | |
|---|---|---|---|
| Part-time: | 51% | Hispanic American: | 1% |
| Women: | 69% | 25 or older: | 48% |
| African American: | 7% | | |

**Transfer out.** Colleges most students transferred to 2007: Ball State University, Purdue University-West Lafayette, Indiana University-Kokomo.

**Basis for selection.** Open admission, but selective for some programs. Special requirements for human services and health technology programs based on test scores and prior academic work. **Adult students:** SAT/ACT scores not required.

**2007-2008 Annual costs.** Tuition/fees: $2,819; $5,653 out-of-state. Per-credit charge: $91 in-state; $186 out-of-state. Out-of-state distance education tuition: $119 per credit hour ($3,584 for academic year). Books/supplies: $988. Personal expenses: $2,224.

**Financial aid. Need-based:** Need-based aid available for part-time students. Work-study available nights and for part-time students. **Additional information:** Higher Education Aid (HEA), Child of Disabled/Deceased Veterans (CDV), Ivy Tech Scholarships (IVTC) and grants, vocational rehabilitation and veteran's assistance available. None require repayment.

**Application procedures. Admission:** No deadline. No application fee. Admission notification on a rolling basis. Application closing date for international students at least 60 days prior to start of semester. **Financial aid:** Priority date 3/1; no closing date. FAFSA required. Applicants notified on a rolling basis starting 7/1.

**Academics. Special study options:** Distance learning, dual enrollment of high school students, internships, liberal arts/career combination, teacher certification program, weekend college. License preparation in dental hygiene, nursing, physical therapy, radiology. **Credit/placement by examination:** AP, CLEP, institutional tests. 45 credit hours maximum toward associate degree. 15 credits must be earned in residence. **Support services:** GED preparation and test center, learning center, reduced course load, remedial instruction, tutoring.

**Majors. Agriculture:** General. **Business:** Accounting technology, business admin, executive assistant, hospitality admin. **Computer sciences:** General, information technology. **Construction:** Carpentry, electrician, maintenance, masonry, painting, pipefitting. **Education:** General, early childhood. **Engineering technology:** Drafting, electrical, occupational safety. **Health:** Medical assistant, medical radiologic technology/radiation therapy, mental health services, nursing (RN), physical therapy assistant, respiratory therapy technology, surgical technology. **Legal studies:** Paralegal. **Liberal arts:** Arts/sciences, library assistant. **Mechanic/repair:** Automotive, heating/ac/refrig. **Production:** Machine tool, tool and die. **Protective services:** Criminal justice. **Other:** Industrial millwright, Industrial plumber/pipefitter, Manufacturing and industrial technology, Stationary power plant operator.

**Most popular majors.** Business/marketing 22%, computer/information sciences 7%, engineering/engineering technologies 8%, health sciences 45%.

**Computing on campus.** 1,481 workstations in library, computer center. Online course registration, online library, helpline, repair service, student web hosting available.

**Student life. Freshman orientation:** Available. **Activities:** Student government, Phi Theta Kappa, Skills USA-VICA, early childhood education club, human services club, Student Leadership Academy.

**Student services.** Adult student services, career counseling, student employment services, financial aid counseling, minority student services, placement for graduates, veterans' counselor. **Physically disabled:** Services for visually, speech, hearing impaired. **Transfer:** Transfer center, transfer adviser, college fairs on campus for students transferring to 4-year colleges.

**Contact.** E-mail: csharp@ivytech.edu
Phone: (765) 289-2291 ext. 1479 Toll-free number: (800) 589-8324
Fax: (765) 289-2292 ext. 502
Corey Sharp, Director of Enrollment Management, Ivy Tech Community College: East Central, 4301 South Cowan Road, Muncie, IN 47302-9448

## Ivy Tech Community College: Kokomo
Kokomo, Indiana
www.ivytech.edu

CB code: 1329

◆ Public 2-year community college
◆ Commuter campus in large town

**General.** Founded in 1968. Regionally accredited. Campus also at Logansport. Branch location at Wabash. **Enrollment:** 3,194 degree-seeking undergraduates; 272 non-degree-seeking students. **Degrees:** 223 associate awarded. **Location:** 50 miles from Indianapolis. **Calendar:** Semester, extensive summer session. **Full-time faculty:** 65 total. **Part-time faculty:** 205 total.

**Student profile.** Among degree-seeking undergraduates, 47% enrolled in a transfer program, 53% enrolled in a vocational program, 439 enrolled as first-time, first-year students, 161 transferred in from other institutions.

| | | | |
|---|---|---|---|
| Part-time: | 67% | Hispanic American: | 2% |
| Women: | 69% | Native American: | 1% |
| African American: | 5% | 25 or older: | 58% |

**Transfer out. Colleges most students transferred to 2007:** Indiana University-Kokomo, Purdue University-West Lafayette, Ball State University.

**Basis for selection.** Open admission, but selective for some programs. Special requirements for human services and health technology programs based on test scores and prior academic work. **Adult students:** SAT/ACT scores not required.

**2007-2008 Annual costs.** Tuition/fees: $2,819; $5,653 out-of-state. Per-credit charge: $91 in-state; $186 out-of-state. Out-of-state distance education tuition: $119 per credit hour ($3,584 for academic year). Books/supplies: $988. Personal expenses: $2,224.

**Financial aid. Need-based:** Need-based aid available for part-time students. Work-study available nights and for part-time students.

**Application procedures. Admission:** No deadline. No application fee. Admission notification on a rolling basis. Application closing date for international students at least 60 days prior to start of semester. **Financial aid:** Priority date 3/1; no closing date. FAFSA required. Applicants notified on a rolling basis starting 7/1.

**Academics. Special study options:** Distance learning, dual enrollment of high school students, independent study, internships, liberal arts/career combination, teacher certification program, weekend college. License preparation in nursing, paramedic, physical therapy. **Credit/placement by examination:** AP, CLEP, institutional tests. 45 credit hours maximum toward associate degree. 15 credits must be earned in residence. **Support services:** Learning center, reduced course load, remedial instruction, tutoring.

**Majors. Agriculture:** General. **Business:** Accounting technology, business admin, executive assistant. **Communications:** General. **Computer sciences:** General, information technology. **Construction:** Electrician, maintenance, site management. **Education:** General, early childhood. **Engineering technology:** Drafting, occupational safety. **Health:** EMT paramedic, medical assistant, mental health services, nursing (RN), surgical technology. **Legal studies:** Paralegal. **Liberal arts:** Arts/sciences, library assistant. **Mechanic/repair:** Automotive, heating/ac/refrig. **Production:** Machine tool, tool and die. **Protective services:** Criminal justice. **Visual/performing arts:** Design. **Other;** Industrial millwright, Industrial plumber/pipefitter, Manufacturing and industrial technology, Stationary power plant operator.

**Computing on campus.** 699 workstations in library, computer center. Online course registration, online library, helpline, repair service, student web hosting available.

**Student life. Freshman orientation:** Available. **Activities:** Student government, Phi Theta Kappa, student leadership academy, business administration student organization, professional and trade organization.

**Athletics. Intramural:** Bowling.

**Student services.** Adult student services, career counseling, student employment services, financial aid counseling, minority student services, placement for graduates, veterans' counselor. **Physically disabled:** Services for visually, speech, hearing impaired. **Transfer:** Transfer adviser, college fairs on campus for students transferring to 4-year colleges.

**Contact.** E-mail: sdillman@ivytech.edu
Phone: (765) 459-0561 ext. 318 Toll-free number: (800) 459-0561
Fax: (765) 454-5111
Suzanne Dillman, Director of Admissions, Ivy Tech Community College: Kokomo, 1815 East Morgan Street, Kokomo, IN 46903-1373

## Ivy Tech Community College: Lafayette
Lafayette, Indiana
www.ivytech.edu

CB code: 1282

◆ Public 2-year community college
◆ Commuter campus in large town

**General.** Founded in 1968. Regionally accredited. **Enrollment:** 4,573 degree-seeking undergraduates; 1,524 non-degree-seeking students. **Degrees:** 392 associate awarded. **Location:** 60 miles from Indianapolis. **Calendar:** Semester, extensive summer session. **Full-time faculty:** 80 total. **Part-time faculty:** 264 total. **Special facilities:** Multimedia laboratory.

**Student profile.** Among degree-seeking undergraduates, 44% enrolled in a transfer program, 56% enrolled in a vocational program, 1,004 enrolled as first-time, first-year students, 387 transferred in from other institutions.

| | | | |
|---|---|---|---|
| Part-time: | 45% | Hispanic American: | 4% |
| Women: | 56% | International: | 2% |
| African American: | 3% | 25 or older: | 39% |
| Asian American: | 1% | | |

**Transfer out. Colleges most students transferred to 2007:** Purdue University - West Lafayette, Indiana University - Purdue University Indianapolis.

**Basis for selection.** Open admission, but selective for some programs. Special requirements for human services and health technology programs based on test scores and prior academic work. **Adult students:** SAT/ACT scores not required.

**2007-2008 Annual costs.** Tuition/fees: $2,819; $5,653 out-of-state. Per-credit charge: $91 in-state; $186 out-of-state. Out-of-state distance education tuition: $119 per credit hour ($3,584 for academic year). Books/supplies: $988. Personal expenses: $2,224.

**Financial aid. Need-based:** Need-based aid available for part-time students. Work-study available nights and for part-time students.

**Application procedures. Admission:** No deadline. No application fee. Admission notification on a rolling basis. Application closing date for international students at least 60 days prior to start of semester. **Financial aid:** Priority date 3/1; no closing date. FAFSA required. Applicants notified on a rolling basis starting 7/1.

**Academics. Special study options:** Distance learning, dual enrollment of high school students, internships, liberal arts/career combination, teacher certification program, weekend college. License preparation in dental hygiene, nursing. **Credit/placement by examination:** AP, CLEP, institutional tests. 45 credit hours maximum toward associate degree. 15 credits must be earned in residence. **Support services:** Learning center, reduced course load, remedial instruction, tutoring.

**Majors. Agriculture:** General. **Biology:** Biotechnology. **Business:** Accounting technology, business admin, executive assistant. **Computer sciences:** General, information technology. **Construction:** Carpentry, electrician, lineworker, maintenance, masonry, painting. **Education:** General, early childhood. **Engineering technology:** Drafting, electrical. **Health:** Medical assistant, medical records technology, mental health services, nursing (RN), respiratory therapy technology, surgical technology. **Legal studies:** Paralegal. **Liberal arts:** Arts/sciences, library assistant. **Mechanic/repair:** Automotive, heating/ac/refrig. **Production:** Cabinetmaking/millwright, ironworking, machine tool, sheet metal, tool and die. **Protective services:** Criminal justice. **Other:** Industrial millwright, Industrial plumber, Manufacturing and industrial technology, Stationary power plant operator.

**Most popular majors.** Business/marketing 26%, computer/information sciences 8%, education 6%, engineering/engineering technologies 9%, health sciences 30%, liberal arts 7%, trade and industry 6%.

**Computing on campus.** 1,313 workstations in library, computer center. Online course registration, online library, helpline, repair service, student web hosting available.

**Student life. Freshman orientation:** Available. **Activities:** Student government, Phi Theta Kappa, American Chemical Society, Dental Assistant Society, Respiratory Care Society, student leadership academy, culture club.

**Athletics. Intramural:** Basketball M, volleyball.

**Student services.** Adult student services, career counseling, student employment services, financial aid counseling, minority student services, placement for graduates, veterans' counselor. **Physically disabled:** Services for visually, speech, hearing impaired. **Transfer:** Transfer center, transfer adviser for students transferring to 4-year colleges.

**Contact.** E-mail: jdoppelf@ivytech.edu
Phone: (765) 269-5200 Toll-free number: (800) 669-4882 ext. 5200
Fax: (765) 772-9293
Ivan Hernandez, Director of Admissions, Ivy Tech Community College:
Lafayette, 3101 South Creasy Lane, Lafayette, IN 47905-6299

## Ivy Tech Community College: North Central
**South Bend, Indiana**
**www.ivytech.edu**      **CB code: 1280**

- Public 2-year community college
- Commuter campus in small city

**General.** Founded in 1968. Regionally accredited. Campuses also at War-saw and Elkhart. **Enrollment:** 4,625 degree-seeking undergraduates; 822 non-degree-seeking students. **Degrees:** 345 associate awarded. **Location:** 100 miles from Chicago. **Calendar:** Semester, extensive summer session. **Full-time faculty:** 79 total. **Part-time faculty:** 264 total.

**Student profile.** Among degree-seeking undergraduates, 32% enrolled in a transfer program, 68% enrolled in a vocational program, 901 enrolled as first-time, first-year students, 191 transferred in from other institutions.

| | | | |
|---|---|---|---|
| Part-time: | 68% | Hispanic American: | 5% |
| Women: | 61% | International: | 2% |
| African American: | 16% | 25 or older: | 55% |
| Asian American: | 1% | | |

**Transfer out. Colleges most students transferred to 2007:** Indiana Uni-versity - South Bend, Indiana University - Purdue University Fort Wayne, Purdue University - West Lafayette, Purdue University - North Central.

**Basis for selection.** Open admission, but selective for some programs. Special requirements for human services and health technology programs based on test scores and prior academic work. Comparative Guidance and Placement Program required for admission of allied health applicants. Inter-view required of allied health majors. Portfolio recommended for photo-graphic technology and graphic arts technology majors. **Adult students:** SAT/ACT scores not required.

**High school preparation.** Medical laboratory assistant program re-quires 1 chemistry and 1 algebra.

**2007-2008 Annual costs.** Tuition/fees: $2,819; $5,653 out-of-state. Per-credit charge: $91 in-state; $186 out-of-state. Out-of-state distance educa-tion tuition: $119 per credit hour ($3,584 for academic year). Books/supplies: $988. Personal expenses: $2,224.

**Financial aid. Need-based:** Need-based aid available for part-time stu-dents. Work-study available nights and for part-time students.

**Application procedures. Admission:** No deadline. No application fee. Admission notification on a rolling basis. **Financial aid:** Priority date 3/1; no closing date. FAFSA required. Applicants notified on a rolling basis start-ing 7/1.

**Academics.** Industrial training division offers customized courses and semi-nars to companies and corporations in surrounding community. **Special study options:** Distance learning, dual enrollment of high school students, ESL, internships, liberal arts/career combination, teacher certification program, weekend college. License preparation in nursing. **Credit/placement by ex-amination:** AP, CLEP, institutional tests. 45 credit hours maximum toward associate degree. 15 credits must be earned in residence. **Support services:** Learning center, reduced course load, remedial instruction, tutoring.

**Majors. Agriculture:** General. **Biology:** Biotechnology. **Business:** Account-ing technology, business admin, executive assistant, hospitality admin. **Com-puter sciences:** General, information technology. **Construction:** Carpentry, electrician, maintenance, masonry, painting, pipefitting, plumbing, roofing. **Education:** General, early childhood. **Engineering technology:** Drafting, electrical, occupational safety, telecommunications. **Health:** Clinical lab tech-nology, EMT paramedic, medical assistant, medical radiologic technology/radiation therapy, mental health services, nursing (RN), respiratory therapy technology. **Legal studies:** Paralegal. **Liberal arts:** Arts/sciences, library assistant. **Mechanic/repair:** Automotive, heating/ac/refrig. **Production:** Cabi-netmaking/millwright, ironworking, machine tool, sheet metal, tool and die. **Protective services:** Criminal justice. **Visual/performing arts:** Design, in-terior design. **Other:** Floorlayer, Industrial millwright, Manufacturing and Industrial Technology, Stationary power plant operator.

**Most popular majors.** Business/marketing 20%, computer/information sciences 8%, engineering/engineering technologies 6%, health sciences 32%, trade and industry 15%, visual/performing arts 8%.

**Computing on campus.** 1,178 workstations in library, computer center. Online course registration, online library, helpline, repair service, student web hosting available.

**Student life. Freshman orientation:** Available. **Activities:** Student gov-ernment, Phi Theta Kappa, student leadership academy, student ad club.

**Student services.** Adult student services, career counseling, student em-ployment services, financial aid counseling, minority student services, place-ment for graduates, veterans' counselor. **Physically disabled:** Services for visually, speech, hearing impaired. **Transfer:** Transfer adviser, college fairs on campus for students transferring to 4-year colleges.

**Contact.** E-mail: jaustin@ivytech.edu
Phone: (574) 289-7001 Toll-free number: (888) 489-5463
Fax: (574) 236-7177
Pam Decker, Director of Admissions, Ivy Tech Community College: North Central, 220 Dean Johnson Boulevard, South Bend, IN 46601-3415

## Ivy Tech Community College: Northeast
**Fort Wayne, Indiana**
**www.ivytech.edu**      **CB code: 1278**

- Public 2-year community college
- Commuter campus in small city

**General.** Founded in 1963. Regionally accredited. **Enrollment:** 5,704 degree-seeking undergraduates; 1,420 non-degree-seeking students. **Degrees:** 493 associate awarded. **Location:** 120 miles from Indianapolis. **Calendar:** Se-mester, extensive summer session. **Full-time faculty:** 97 total. **Part-time faculty:** 357 total.

**Student profile.** Among degree-seeking undergraduates, 40% enrolled in a transfer program, 60% enrolled in a vocational program, 874 enrolled as first-time, first-year students, 330 transferred in from other institutions.

| | | | |
|---|---|---|---|
| Part-time: | 58% | Hispanic American: | 3% |
| Out-of-state: | 1% | Native American: | 1% |
| Women: | 64% | International: | 2% |
| African American: | 14% | 25 or older: | 51% |
| Asian American: | 1% | | |

**Transfer out. Colleges most students transferred to 2007:** Indiana Uni-versity, Purdue University-Ft. Wayne, Ball State University.

**Basis for selection.** Open admission, but selective for some programs. Special requirements for human services and health technology programs based on test scores and prior academic work. **Adult students:** SAT/ACT scores not required.

**2007-2008 Annual costs.** Tuition/fees: $2,819; $5,653 out-of-state. Per-credit charge: $91 in-state; $186 out-of-state. Out-of-state distance educa-tion tuition: $119 per credit hour ($3,584 for academic year). Books/supplies: $988. Personal expenses: $2,224.

**Financial aid. Need-based:** Need-based aid available for part-time stu-dents. Work-study available nights and for part-time students.

**Application procedures. Admission:** No deadline. No application fee. Admission notification on a rolling basis. Application closing dates for in-ternational students at least 60 days prior to start of semester. **Financial aid:** Priority date 3/1; no closing date. FAFSA required. Applicants notified on a rolling basis starting 7/1.

**Academics. Special study options:** Distance learning, dual enrollment of high school students, ESL, internships, liberal arts/career combination, teacher certification program, weekend college. License preparation in nursing. **Credit/placement by examination:** AP, CLEP, institutional tests. 45 credit hours maximum toward associate degree. 15 credits must be completed in resi-dence. **Support services:** GED preparation and test center, learning center, reduced course load, remedial instruction, tutoring.

**Majors. Business:** Accounting technology, business admin, executive as-sistant, hospitality admin. **Computer sciences:** General, information tech-nology. **Construction:** Electrician, maintenance, masonry, painting, pipefit-ting, site management. **Education:** General, early childhood. **Engineering technology:** Drafting, occupational safety, telecommunications. **Health:** EMT paramedic, massage therapy, medical assistant, mental health services, nurs-ing (RN), respiratory therapy technology. **Legal studies:** Paralegal. **Liberal arts:** Arts/sciences, library assistant. **Mechanic/repair:** Automotive, heating/ac/refrig. **Production:** Ironworking, machine tool, sheet metal, tool and die. **Protective services:** Criminal justice. **Other:** Construction technology, In-dustrial millwright, Manufacturing and industrial technology, Stationary power plant operator.

**Most popular majors.** Business/marketing 26%, engineering/engineering technologies 10%, health sciences 33%, trade and industry 15%.

**Computing on campus.** 1,511 workstations in library, computer center. Online course registration, online library, helpline, repair service, student web hosting available.

**Student life. Freshman orientation:** Available. **Activities:** Student government, student newspaper, Phi Theta Kappa, multi-cultural organization, Society of Manufacturing Engineers, student leadership academy, Association of Construction Technology Students.

**Student services.** Adult student services, career counseling, student employment services, financial aid counseling, minority student services, placement for graduates, veterans' counselor. **Physically disabled:** Services for visually, speech, hearing impaired. **Transfer:** Transfer center, transfer adviser, college fairs on campus for students transferring to 4-year colleges.

**Contact.** E-mail: sscheer@ivytech.edu
Phone: (260) 480-4221 Toll-free number: (800) 859-4882 ext. 4268
Fax: (260) 480-2053
Steve Scheer, Director of Admissions, Ivy Tech Community College: Northeast, 3800 North Anthony Boulevard, Fort Wayne, IN 46805-1489

## Ivy Tech Community College: Northwest
**Gary, Indiana**
www.ivytech.edu                              CB code: 1281

▶  Public 2-year community college
▶  Commuter campus in small city

**General.** Founded in 1968. Regionally accredited. Campuses also at East Chicago, Valparaiso, and Michigan City. **Enrollment:** 4,540 degree-seeking undergraduates; 783 non-degree-seeking students. **Degrees:** 429 associate awarded. **Location:** 30 miles from Chicago. **Calendar:** Semester, extensive summer session. **Full-time faculty:** 89 total. **Part-time faculty:** 303 total.

**Student profile.** Among degree-seeking undergraduates, 42% enrolled in a transfer program, 58% enrolled in a vocational program, 886 enrolled as first-time, first-year students, 347 transferred in from other institutions.

| | | | |
|---|---|---|---|
| Part-time: | 62% | Asian American: | 1% |
| Women: | 68% | Hispanic American: | 9% |
| African American: | 26% | 25 or older: | 55% |

**Transfer out. Colleges most students transferred to 2007:** Purdue University- Calumet, Indiana University-Northwest, Purdue University-North Central.

**Basis for selection.** Open admission, but selective for some programs. Special requirements for human services and health technology programs based on test scores and prior academic work. **Adult students:** SAT/ACT scores not required.

**2007-2008 Annual costs.** Tuition/fees: $2,819; $5,653 out-of-state. Per-credit charge: $91 in-state; $186 out-of-state. Out-of-state distance education tuition: $119 per credit hour ($3,584 for academic year). Books/supplies: $988. Personal expenses: $2,224.

**Financial aid. Need-based:** Need-based aid available for part-time students. Work-study available nights and for part-time students.

**Application procedures. Admission:** No deadline. No application fee. Admission notification on a rolling basis. Application closing date for international students at least 60 days prior to start of semester. **Financial aid:** Priority date 3/1; no closing date. FAFSA required. Applicants notified on a rolling basis starting 7/1.

**Academics. Special study options:** Distance learning, dual enrollment of high school students, internships, liberal arts/career combination, teacher certification program, weekend college. License preparation in nursing, physical therapy, real estate. **Credit/placement by examination:** AP, CLEP, institutional tests. 45 credit hours maximum toward associate degree. 15 credits must be earned in residence. **Support services:** Learning center, reduced course load, remedial instruction, tutoring.

**Majors. Business:** Accounting technology, administrative services, business admin, executive assistant, hospitality admin. **Computer sciences:** General, information technology. **Construction:** Carpentry, electrician, maintenance, masonry, painting, pipefitting, site management. **Education:** General, early childhood. **Engineering:** General. **Engineering technology:** Drafting, electrical, occupational safety, telecommunications. **Health:** EMT paramedic, medical assistant, medical radiologic technology/radiation therapy, mental health services, nursing (RN), physical therapy assistant, respiratory therapy technology, surgical technology. **Legal studies:** Paralegal. **Liberal**

**arts:** Arts/sciences, library assistant. **Mechanic/repair:** General, automotive, heating/ac/refrig. **Personal/culinary services:** Mortuary science. **Production:** Cabinetmaking/millwright, ironworking, machine tool, sheet metal, tool and die. **Protective services:** Criminal justice. **Other:** Floorlayers, Manufacturing and industrial technology, Stationary power plant operator.

**Most popular majors.** Business/marketing 26%, computer/information sciences 6%, engineering/engineering technologies 6%, health sciences 37%, trade and industry 12%.

**Computing on campus.** 419 workstations in library, computer center. Online course registration, online library, helpline, repair service, student web hosting available.

**Student life. Freshman orientation:** Available. **Activities:** Student government, Phi Theta Kappa, computer club, business club, culinary arts club, medical assistants, mortuary science club, student leadership academy, early childhood development club, nursing club.

**Student services.** Adult student services, career counseling, student employment services, financial aid counseling, minority student services, placement for graduates, veterans' counselor. **Physically disabled:** Services for visually, speech, hearing impaired. **Transfer:** Transfer adviser, college fairs on campus for students transferring to 4-year colleges.

**Contact.** E-mail: tlewis@ivytech.edu
Phone: (219) 981-1111 ext. 2273 Toll-free number: (888) 489-5463
Fax: (219) 981-4415
Twilla Lewis, Associate Dean of Student Affairs, Ivy Tech Community College: Northwest, 1440 East 35th Avenue, Gary, IN 46409-1499

## Ivy Tech Community College: Richmond
**Richmond, Indiana**
www.ivytech.edu                              CB code: 1283

▶  Public 2-year community college
▶  Commuter campus in large town

**General.** Founded in 1968. Regionally accredited. Branch location at Connersville. **Enrollment:** 1,976 degree-seeking undergraduates; 319 non-degree-seeking students. **Degrees:** 134 associate awarded. **Location:** 70 miles from Indianapolis, 45 miles from Dayton, Ohio. **Calendar:** Semester, extensive summer session. **Full-time faculty:** 33 total. **Part-time faculty:** 162 total. **Special facilities:** Student-operated restaurant.

**Student profile.** Among degree-seeking undergraduates, 21% enrolled in a transfer program, 79% enrolled in a vocational program, 333 enrolled as first-time, first-year students, 110 transferred in from other institutions.

| | | | |
|---|---|---|---|
| Part-time: | 64% | African American: | 4% |
| Out-of-state: | 7% | Hispanic American: | 1% |
| Women: | 76% | 25 or older: | 63% |

**Transfer out. Colleges most students transferred to 2007:** Indiana University East, Purdue University-West Lafayette.

**Basis for selection.** Open admission, but selective for some programs. Special requirements for human services and health technology programs based on test scores and prior academic work. **Adult students:** SAT/ACT scores not required.

**2007-2008 Annual costs.** Tuition/fees: $2,819; $5,653 out-of-state. Per-credit charge: $91 in-state; $186 out-of-state. Out-of-state distance education tuition: $119 per credit hour ($3,584 for academic year). Books/supplies: $988. Personal expenses: $2,224.

**Financial aid. Need-based:** Need-based aid available for part-time students. Work-study available nights and for part-time students.

**Application procedures. Admission:** No deadline. No application fee. Admission notification on a rolling basis. Application closing date for international students at least 60 days prior to start of semester. **Financial aid:** Priority date 3/1; no closing date. FAFSA required. Applicants notified on a rolling basis starting 7/1.

**Academics. Special study options:** Distance learning, dual enrollment of high school students, independent study, internships, liberal arts/career combination, teacher certification program, weekend college. License preparation in nursing. **Credit/placement by examination:** AP, CLEP, institutional tests. 45 credit hours maximum toward associate degree. 15 credits must be earned in residence. **Support services:** Learning center, reduced course load, remedial instruction, tutoring.

**Majors. Agriculture:** General. **Business:** Accounting technology, business admin, executive assistant. **Computer sciences:** General, information technology. **Construction:** Maintenance, plumbing. **Education:** General, early childhood. **Engineering technology:** Drafting, electrical. **Health:** EMT paramedic, medical assistant, medical radiologic technology/radiation therapy, mental health services, nursing (RN), respiratory therapy technology. **Legal studies:** Paralegal. **Liberal arts:** Arts/sciences, library assistant. **Mechanic/repair:** Automotive, heating/ac/refrig. **Production:** Machine tool, tool and die. **Protective services:** Criminal justice. **Other:** Industrial millwright, Industrial plumber/pipefitter, Manufacturing and industrial technology, Stationary power plant operator.

**Most popular majors.** Business/marketing 27%, computer/information sciences 7%, education 6%, health sciences 37%, trade and industry 7%.

**Computing on campus.** 857 workstations in library, computer center. Online course registration, online library, helpline, repair service, student web hosting available.

**Student life. Freshman orientation:** Available. **Activities:** Student government, Phi Theta Kappa, Business Professionals of America, student computer association, Student Chapter of the Institute of Management Accounts, Refrigeration service engineers society, student leadership academy, multicultural student organization.

**Student services.** Adult student services, career counseling, student employment services, financial aid counseling, minority student services, placement for graduates, veterans' counselor. **Physically disabled:** Services for visually, speech, hearing impaired. **Transfer:** Transfer adviser for students transferring to 4-year colleges.

**Contact.** E-mail: jplaster@ivytech.edu
Phone: (765) 966-2656 ext. 1212 Toll-free number: (800) 659-4562
Fax: (765) 962-8741
Jeff Plasterer, Director of Admissions, Ivy Tech Community College: Richmond, 2357 Chester Boulevard, Richmond, IN 47374-1298

## Ivy Tech Community College: South Central
### Sellersburg, Indiana
www.ivytech.edu                    CB code: 1273

▶ Public 2-year community college
▶ Commuter campus in small town

**General.** Founded in 1968. Regionally accredited. **Enrollment:** 3,181 degree-seeking undergraduates; 532 non-degree-seeking students. **Degrees:** 330 associate awarded. **Location:** 10 miles from Louisville, Kentucky. **Calendar:** Semester, extensive summer session. **Full-time faculty:** 52 total. **Part-time faculty:** 154 total.

**Student profile.** Among degree-seeking undergraduates, 30% enrolled in a transfer program, 70% enrolled in a vocational program, 774 enrolled as first-time, first-year students, 126 transferred in from other institutions.

| | | | |
|---|---|---|---|
| Part-time: | 62% | African American: | 5% |
| Out-of-state: | 13% | Hispanic American: | 1% |
| Women: | 54% | 25 or older: | 58% |

**Transfer out. Colleges most students transferred to 2007:** Indiana University Southeast.

**Basis for selection.** Open admission, but selective for some programs. Special requirements for human services and health technology programs based on test scores and prior academic work. **Adult students:** SAT/ACT scores not required.

**2007-2008 Annual costs.** Tuition/fees: $2,819; $5,653 out-of-state. Per-credit charge: $91 in-state; $186 out-of-state. Out-of-state distance education tuition: $119 per credit hour ($3,584 for academic year). Books/supplies: $988. Personal expenses: $2,224.

**Financial aid. Need-based:** Need-based aid available for part-time students. Work-study available nights and for part-time students.

**Application procedures. Admission:** No deadline. No application fee. Admission notification on a rolling basis. Application closing date for international students at least 60 days prior to start of semester. **Financial aid:** Priority date 3/1; no closing date. FAFSA required. Applicants notified on a rolling basis starting 7/1.

**Academics. Special study options:** Cooperative education, distance learning, dual enrollment of high school students, internships, liberal arts/career combination, teacher certification program, weekend college. License preparation in nursing, real estate. **Credit/placement by examination:** AP, CLEP, institutional tests. 45 credit hours maximum toward associate degree. 15 credits must be earned in residence. **Support services:** GED preparation and test center, learning center, reduced course load, remedial instruction, tutoring.

**Majors. Business:** Accounting technology, business admin, executive assistant. **Computer sciences:** General, information technology. **Construction:** Electrician, maintenance, masonry, pipefitting. **Education:** General, early childhood. **Engineering technology:** Drafting, electrical, telecommunications. **Health:** Clinical lab technology, medical assistant, medical radiologic technology/radiation therapy, mental health services, nursing (RN), respiratory therapy technology. **Legal studies:** Paralegal. **Liberal arts:** Arts/sciences, library assistant. **Mechanic/repair:** Automotive, heating/ac/refrig. **Production:** Cabinetmaking/millwright, machine tool, sheet metal, tool and die. **Protective services:** Criminal justice. **Visual/performing arts:** Design. **Other:** Floorlayers, Industrial Millwright, Industrial Sheet Metal, Manufacturing and Industrial Technology.

**Most popular majors.** Business/marketing 15%, computer/information sciences 6%, engineering/engineering technologies 10%, health sciences 39%, trade and industry 25%.

**Computing on campus.** 505 workstations in library, computer center. Online course registration, online library, helpline, repair service, student web hosting available.

**Student life. Freshman orientation:** Mandatory. **Activities:** Student government, student newspaper, Phi Theta Kappa, art club, Christian Student Fellowship, C.A.R.E. club, ASN club, Business Professionals of America, human services club, Computer Information Club, Student Leadership Academy.

**Athletics. Intramural:** Baseball M, softball.

**Student services.** Career counseling, student employment services, financial aid counseling, minority student services, placement for graduates, veterans' counselor. **Transfer:** Transfer center, transfer adviser, college fairs on campus for students transferring to 4-year colleges.

**Contact.** E-mail: pfawcett@ivytech.edu
Phone: (812) 246-3301 ext. 4136 Toll-free number: (800) 321-9021
Fax: (812) 246-9905
Pat Fawcett, Director of Enrollment Services, Ivy Tech Community College: South Central, 8204 Highway 311, Sellersburg, IN 47172-1897

## Ivy Tech Community College: Southeast
### Madison, Indiana
www.ivytech.edu                    CB code: 1334

▶ Public 2-year community college
▶ Commuter campus in large town

**General.** Founded in 1968. Regionally accredited. Branch in Lawrenceburg. **Enrollment:** 1,792 degree-seeking undergraduates; 353 non-degree-seeking students. **Degrees:** 111 associate awarded. **Location:** 46 miles from Columbus, Ohio, 88 miles from Indianapolis. **Calendar:** Semester, extensive summer session. **Full-time faculty:** 36 total. **Part-time faculty:** 143 total. **Special facilities:** Gaming training center in Aurora, Indiana.

**Student profile.** Among degree-seeking undergraduates, 45% enrolled in a transfer program, 55% enrolled in a vocational program, 338 enrolled as first-time, first-year students, 70 transferred in from other institutions.

| | | | |
|---|---|---|---|
| Part-time: | 58% | African American: | 1% |
| Out-of-state: | 1% | 25 or older: | 48% |
| Women: | 76% | | |

**Transfer out. Colleges most students transferred to 2007:** Indiana University - Southeast.

**Basis for selection.** Open admission, but selective for some programs. Special requirements for human services and health technology programs based on test scores and prior academic work.

**2007-2008 Annual costs.** Tuition/fees: $2,819; $5,653 out-of-state. Per-credit charge: $91 in-state; $186 out-of-state. Out-of-state distance education tuition: $119 per credit hour ($3,584 for academic year). Books/supplies: $988. Personal expenses: $2,224.

**Financial aid. Need-based:** Need-based aid available for part-time students. Work-study available nights and for part-time students.

**Application procedures. Admission:** No deadline. No application fee. Admission notification on a rolling basis. Application closing date for international students at least 60 days prior to start of semester. **Financial aid:** Priority date 3/1; no closing date. FAFSA required. Applicants notified on a rolling basis starting 7/1.

**Academics. Special study options:** Distance learning, dual enrollment of high school students, internships, liberal arts/career combination, teacher certification program, weekend college. License preparation in nursing. **Credit/placement by examination:** AP, CLEP, institutional tests. 45 credit hours maximum toward associate degree. 15 credit hours must be earned in residence. **Support services:** Learning center, reduced course load, remedial instruction, tutoring.

**Majors. Business:** Accounting technology, business admin, executive assistant. **Computer sciences:** General, information technology. **Education:** General, early childhood. **Engineering technology:** Drafting, electrical. **Health:** Medical assistant, mental health services, nursing (RN). **Legal studies:** Paralegal. **Liberal arts:** Arts/sciences, library assistant. **Protective services:** Criminal justice. **Other:** Manufacturing and industrial technology.

**Most popular majors.** Business/marketing 44%, computer/information sciences 12%, education 8%, engineering/engineering technologies 6%, health sciences 18%, liberal arts 8%.

**Computing on campus.** 710 workstations in library, computer center. Online course registration, online library, helpline, repair service, student web hosting available.

**Student life. Freshman orientation:** Available. **Activities:** Student government, Phi Theta Kappa, student leadership academy, computer club, fitness club.

**Student services.** Career counseling, student employment services, financial aid counseling, minority student services, placement for graduates, veterans' counselor. **Physically disabled:** Services for visually, speech, hearing impaired. **Transfer:** Transfer adviser, college fairs on campus for students transferring to 4-year colleges.

**Contact.** E-mail: chutcher@ivytech.edu
Phone: (812) 265-2580 ext. 4142 Toll-free number: (800) 403-2190
Fax: (812) 265-4028
Cindy Hutcherson, Assistant Director of Admission/Career Services, Ivy Tech Community College: Southeast, 590 Ivy Tech Drive, Madison, IN 47250-1881

## Ivy Tech Community College: Southwest
**Evansville, Indiana**
www.ivytech.edu                               CB code: 1277

- Public 2-year community college
- Commuter campus in small city

**General.** Founded in 1968. Regionally accredited. Branch location at Tell City. **Enrollment:** 4,393 degree-seeking undergraduates; 698 non-degree-seeking students. **Degrees:** 422 associate awarded. **Location:** 180 miles from Indianapolis, 112 miles from Louisville, Kentucky. **Calendar:** Semester, extensive summer session. **Full-time faculty:** 74 total. **Part-time faculty:** 287 total. **Special facilities:** Plastics lab, computer integrated manufacturing lab.

**Student profile.** Among degree-seeking undergraduates, 33% enrolled in a transfer program, 67% enrolled in a vocational program, 715 enrolled as first-time, first-year students, 366 transferred in from other institutions.

| | | | |
|---|---|---|---|
| Part-time: | 58% | Hispanic American: | 1% |
| Out-of-state: | 4% | International: | 1% |
| Women: | 56% | 25 or older: | 49% |
| African American: | 8% | | |

**Transfer out. Colleges most students transferred to 2007:** University of Southern Indiana, Vincennes University, Indiana State University.

**Basis for selection.** Open admission, but selective for some programs. Special requirements for human services and health technology programs based on test scores and prior academic work. **Adult students:** SAT/ACT scores not required.

**2007-2008 Annual costs.** Tuition/fees: $2,819; $5,653 out-of-state. Per-credit charge: $91 in-state; $186 out-of-state. Out-of-state distance education tuition: $119 per credit hour ($3,584 for academic year). Books/supplies: $988. Personal expenses: $2,224.

**Financial aid. Need-based:** Need-based aid available for part-time students. Work-study available nights and for part-time students.

**Application procedures. Admission:** No deadline. No application fee. Admission notification on a rolling basis. Application closing date for international students at least 60 days prior to start of semester. **Financial aid:** Priority date 3/1; no closing date. FAFSA required. Applicants notified on a rolling basis starting 7/1.

**Academics. Special study options:** Cooperative education, distance learning, dual enrollment of high school students, independent study, internships, liberal arts/career combination, teacher certification program, weekend college. License preparation in nursing, paramedic. **Credit/placement by examination:** AP, CLEP, institutional tests. 45 credit hours maximum toward associate degree. 15 credit hours must be earned in residence. **Support services:** Learning center, reduced course load, remedial instruction, tutoring.

**Majors. Agriculture:** General. **Biology:** Biotechnology. **Business:** Accounting technology, business admin, executive assistant, hospitality admin. **Computer sciences:** General, information technology. **Construction:** Carpentry, electrician, maintenance, masonry, painting, pipefitting, site management. **Education:** General, early childhood. **Engineering:** General. **Engineering technology:** Drafting, electrical, occupational safety, telecommunications. **Health:** EMT paramedic, medical assistant, mental health services, nursing (RN), surgical technology. **Legal studies:** Paralegal. **Liberal arts:** Arts/sciences, library assistant. **Mechanic/repair:** Automotive, heating/ac/refrig. **Production:** Boilermaking, cabinetmaking/millwright, ironworking, machine tool, sheet metal, tool and die. **Protective services:** Criminal justice. **Transportation:** Heavy/earthmoving equipment. **Visual/performing arts:** Design, interior design. **Other:** Heat frost and asbestos, Industrial millwight, Manufacturing and industrial technology, Stationary power plant operator.

**Most popular majors.** Business/marketing 25%, engineering/engineering technologies 12%, health sciences 18%, trade and industry 25%, visual/performing arts 7%.

**Computing on campus.** 1,021 workstations in library, computer center. Online course registration, online library, helpline, repair service, student web hosting available.

**Student life. Freshman orientation:** Available. **Housing:** Housing available at University of Southern Indiana. **Activities:** Student government, Phi Theta Kappa, American Institute of Architectural Students, National Association of Industrial Technicians, International Association Of Administrative Professionals, human services club, student leadership academy, art & design club.

**Student services.** Adult student services, career counseling, student employment services, financial aid counseling, minority student services, placement for graduates, veterans' counselor. **Physically disabled:** Services for visually, speech, hearing impaired. **Transfer:** Transfer adviser, college fairs on campus for students transferring to 4-year colleges.

**Contact.** E-mail: ajohnson@ivytech.edu
Phone: (812) 429-1430 Toll-free number: (888) 489-5463
Fax: (812) 429-9878
Denise Johnson-Kincaid, Director of Admissions, Ivy Tech Community College: Southwest, 3501 First Avenue, Evansville, IN 47710-3398

## Ivy Tech Community College: Wabash Valley
**Terre Haute, Indiana**
www.ivytech.edu                               CB code: 1284

- Public 2-year community college
- Commuter campus in small city

**General.** Founded in 1966. Regionally accredited. Branch location at Greencastle. **Enrollment:** 4,647 degree-seeking undergraduates; 859 non-degree-seeking students. **Degrees:** 423 associate awarded. **Location:** 80 miles from Indianapolis. **Calendar:** Semester, extensive summer session. **Full-time faculty:** 85 total. **Part-time faculty:** 247 total. **Special facilities:** Plastics productivity center.

**Student profile.** Among degree-seeking undergraduates, 39% enrolled in a transfer program, 61% enrolled in a vocational program, 794 enrolled as first-time, first-year students, 284 transferred in from other institutions.

| | | | |
|---|---|---|---|
| Part-time: | 54% | Native American: | 1% |
| Out-of-state: | 3% | International: | 1% |
| Women: | 61% | 25 or older: | 52% |
| African American: | 4% | | |

**Transfer out. Colleges most students transferred to 2007:** Indiana State University, Vincennes University, Purdue University - West Lafayette.

**Basis for selection.** Open admission, but selective for some programs. Special requirements for human services and health technology programs based on test scores and prior academic work. **Adult students:** SAT/ACT scores not required.

**2007-2008 Annual costs.** Tuition/fees: $2,819; $5,653 out-of-state. Per-credit charge: $91 in-state; $186 out-of-state. Out-of-state distance education tuition: $119 per credit hour ($3,584 for academic year). Books/supplies: $988. Personal expenses: $2,224.

**Financial aid. Need-based:** Need-based aid available for part-time students. Work-study available nights and for part-time students.

**Application procedures. Admission:** No deadline. No application fee. Admission notification on a rolling basis. Application closing date for international students is at least 60 days prior to start of semester. **Financial aid:** Priority date 3/1; no closing date. FAFSA required. Applicants notified on a rolling basis starting 7/1.

**Academics. Special study options:** Distance learning, dual enrollment of high school students, internships, liberal arts/career combination, teacher certification program, weekend college. License preparation in aviation, nursing, paramedic, radiology. **Credit/placement by examination:** AP, CLEP, institutional tests. 45 credit hours maximum toward associate degree. 15 credits must be earned in residence. **Support services:** Learning center, reduced course load, remedial instruction, tutoring.

**Majors. Agriculture:** General. **Biology:** Biotechnology. **Business:** Accounting technology, business admin, executive assistant. **Computer sciences:** General, information technology. **Construction:** Carpentry, electrician, maintenance, masonry, painting, pipefitting. **Education:** General, early childhood. **Engineering technology:** Drafting, electrical, occupational safety. **Health:** Clinical lab technology, EMT paramedic, medical assistant, medical radiologic technology/radiation therapy, mental health services, nursing (RN), respiratory therapy technology, surgical technology. **Legal studies:** Paralegal. **Liberal arts:** Arts/sciences, library assistant. **Mechanic/repair:** Automotive, heating/ac/refrig. **Production:** Ironworking, machine tool, sheet metal, tool and die. **Protective services:** Criminal justice. **Transportation:** Heavy/earthmoving equipment. **Visual/performing arts:** Design. **Other:** Industrial millwright, Industrial plumber/pipefitter, Manufacturing and industrial technology, Stationary power plant operator. .

**Most popular majors.** Business/marketing 15%, education 7%, engineering/engineering technologies 6%, health sciences 37%, trade and industry 20%.

**Computing on campus.** 1,589 workstations in library, computer center. Online course registration, online library, helpline, repair service, student web hosting, wireless network available.

**Student life. Freshman orientation:** Available. **Activities:** Student government, Phi Theta Kappa, Student Leadership Academy, Practical Nurses Class Organization.

**Athletics. Intramural:** Basketball, volleyball.

**Student services.** Adult student services, career counseling, student employment services, financial aid counseling, minority student services, on-campus daycare, placement for graduates, veterans' counselor. **Physically disabled:** Services for visually, speech, hearing impaired. **Transfer:** Transfer center, transfer adviser, college fairs on campus for students transferring to 4-year colleges.

**Contact.** E-mail: mfisher@ivytech.edu
Phone: (812) 298-2300 Toll-free number: (800) 377-4882
Fax: (812) 299-5723
Michael Fisher, Director of Admissions, Ivy Tech Community College: Wabash Valley, 8000 South Education Drive, Terre Haute, IN 47802-4898

## Kaplan College: Hammond
**Hammond, Indiana**
www.kaplan.com                          CB code: 2461

- For-profit 2-year business and technical college
- Commuter campus in small city
- Interview required

**General.** Founded in 1969. Accredited by ACICS. Branch campus in Merrillville. **Enrollment:** 408 degree-seeking undergraduates. **Degrees:** 178 associate awarded. **Location:** 30 miles from Chicago, 15 miles from Merrillville. **Calendar:** Quarter, extensive summer session. **Full-time faculty:** 13 total. **Part-time faculty:** 14 total.

**Student profile.** Among degree-seeking undergraduates, 100% enrolled in a vocational program, 114 enrolled as first-time, first-year students.

**Basis for selection.** Personal interview with admissions representative and passing score on entrance examination required.

**2007-2008 Annual costs.** Tuition/fees: $9,816. Room/board: $2,805.

**Application procedures. Admission:** No deadline. $20 fee. Admission notification on a rolling basis. **Financial aid:** FAFSA required. Applicants notified on a rolling basis.

**Academics. Special study options:** Internships. **Credit/placement by examination:** CLEP, institutional tests. 24 credit hours maximum toward associate degree. Institutional placement test score must be at least 81%. **Support services:** Remedial instruction, study skills assistance, tutoring.

**Majors. Business:** Accounting, administrative services. **Computer sciences:** General. **Health:** Massage therapy, medical assistant, medical secretary. **Legal studies:** Legal secretary.

**Most popular majors.** Business/marketing 48%, computer/information sciences 52%.

**Computing on campus.** 70 workstations in computer center.

**Student life. Activities:** Student newspaper.

**Student services.** Career counseling, student employment services, personal counseling, placement for graduates. **Transfer:** Pre-admission transcript evaluation for new students.

**Contact.** Phone: (219) 844-0100 Fax: (219) 844-0105
Rodger Schilling, Admissions Director, Kaplan College: Hammond, 7833 Indianapolis Boulevard, Hammond, IN 46324

## Kaplan College: Indianapolis
**Indianapolis, Indiana**
www.kcindy.com                          CB code: 7700

- For-profit 2-year business and health science college
- Commuter campus in very large city
- Application essay, interview required

**General.** Accredited by ACCSCT. **Enrollment:** 10 full-time, degree-seeking students. **Degrees:** 7 associate awarded. **Calendar:** Continuous. **Full-time faculty:** 50 total.

**Basis for selection.** Interview most important. Class rank, school record, recommendations, standardized test scores, and essay also important.

**2007-2008 Annual costs.** Tuition/fees: $11,001. Tuition and fees include uniform cost where applicable. Books/supplies: $500. Personal expenses: $1,472.

**Financial aid.** All financial aid based on need.

**Application procedures. Admission:** No deadline. $20 fee. Admission notification on a rolling basis.

**Academics. Special study options:** Accelerated study, internships. **Credit/placement by examination:** CLEP.

**Majors. Business:** Administrative services, business admin. **Computer sciences:** General, applications programming, data entry, information technology. **Health:** Dental assistant, massage therapy, medical assistant, medical secretary, office admin. **Legal studies:** Legal secretary, paralegal.

**Computing on campus.** 30 workstations in library, computer center.

**Student services.** Financial aid counseling, placement for graduates.

**Contact.** E-mail: jgonzales@kaplan.edu
Phone: (317) 299-6001 Fax: (317) 298-6342
Jeff Gonzales, Director of Admissions, Kaplan College: Indianapolis, 7302 Woodland Drive, Indianapolis, IN 46278-1736

## Kaplan College: Merrillville
**Merrillville, Indiana**
www.sawyercollege.edu                          CB code: 3381

- For-profit 2-year technical college
- Commuter campus in large town
- Interview required

**General.** Accredited by ACICS. **Enrollment:** 347 degree-seeking undergraduates. **Degrees:** 82 associate awarded. **Location:** 35 miles from Chicago. **Calendar:** Quarter. **Full-time faculty:** 11 total.

**Student profile.** Among degree-seeking undergraduates, 66 enrolled as first-time, first-year students.

**Part-time:** 18%   **Women:** 91%

**Basis for selection.** Personal interview with admissions representative and passing score on entrance examination required. **Adult students:** SAT/ACT scores not required. **Homeschooled:** State high school equivalency certificate required.

**2007-2008 Annual costs.** Tuition/fees: $9,813.

**Financial aid. Need-based:** Need-based aid available for part-time students.

**Application procedures. Admission:** No deadline. $20 fee. Admission notification on a rolling basis. **Financial aid:** No deadline. FAFSA required. Applicants notified on a rolling basis.

**Academics. Special study options:** Liberal arts/career combination. **Credit/placement by examination:** CLEP. 50 credit hours maximum toward associate degree. **Support services:** Reduced course load, study skills assistance, tutoring.

**Majors. Health:** Massage therapy, medical assistant, office admin. **Other:** Computer business specialist.

**Computing on campus.** 72 workstations in library, computer center. Online library available.

**Student life. Freshman orientation:** Mandatory. Preregistration for classes offered.

**Student services.** Adult student services, career counseling, student employment services, financial aid counseling, placement for graduates. **Transfer:** Pre-admission transcript evaluation for new students.

**Contact.** Phone: (219) 736-0436 Toll-free number: (800) 964-0218 Fax: (219) 942-3762
Sonya Vance-Brown, Director of Admissions, Kaplan College: Merrillville, 3803 East Lincoln Highway, Merrillville, IN 46410

## Lincoln College of Technology: Indianapolis
### Indianapolis, Indiana
### www.lincolntech.com
**CB code: 3058**

♦ For-profit 2-year technical college
♦ Very large city

**General.** Accredited by ACCSCT. **Calendar:** Continuous.

**Annual costs/financial aid.** Cost for entire AAS diesel & truck service management program $27,705. Other program costs vary. Books/supplies: $1,815.

**Contact.** Phone: (317) 632-5553
7225 Winton Drive, Building 128, Indianapolis, IN 46268

## Mid-America College of Funeral Service
### Jeffersonville, Indiana
### www.mid-america.edu
**CB code: 0644**

♦ Private 2-year school of mortuary science
♦ Commuter campus in large town

**General.** Founded in 1905. **Location:** 5 miles from Louisville, Kentucky. **Calendar:** Quarter.

**Annual costs/financial aid.** Tuition/fees (2007-2008): $8,400. Cost of AAS degree program (including tuition, books, fees) $22,400. Personal expenses: $2,520.

**Contact.** Phone: (812) 288-8878
Director of Admissions, 3111 Hamburg Pike, Jeffersonville, IN 47130

## National College: Indianapolis
### Indianapolis, Indiana

♦ For-profit 2-year branch campus college
♦ Very large city

**General.** Regionally accredited; also accredited by ACICS. **Enrollment:** 290 degree-seeking undergraduates. **Degrees:** 10 associate awarded. **Calendar:** Quarter. **Full-time faculty:** 4 total. **Part-time faculty:** 40 total.

**2008-2009 Annual costs.** Tuition/fees: $9,585. Per-credit charge: $212.

**Application procedures. Admission:** No deadline. $30 fee.

**Academics. Credit/placement by examination:** CLEP.

**Majors. Business:** Accounting/business management, administrative services, business admin. **Engineering technology:** Computer systems. **Health:** Medical assistant, medical records technology, pharmacy assistant, surgical technology.

**Contact.** Phone: (317) 578-7353
Larry Steele, Vice President of Admissions, National College: Indianapolis, 6060 Castleway Drive West, Indianapolis, IN 46250

## Vincennes University
### Vincennes, Indiana
### www.vinu.edu
**CB member**
**CB code: 1877**

♦ Public 2-year junior and technical college
♦ Residential campus in large town

**General.** Founded in 1801. Regionally accredited. **Enrollment:** 8,203 degree-seeking undergraduates; 2,547 non-degree-seeking students. **Degrees:** 26 bachelor's, 1,178 associate awarded. **ROTC:** Army, Air Force. **Location:** 120 miles from Indianapolis, 55 miles from Evansville. **Calendar:** Semester, extensive summer session. **Full-time faculty:** 320 total. **Part-time faculty:** 120 total. **Special facilities:** 2 college-owned airports.

**Student profile.** Among degree-seeking undergraduates, 44% enrolled in a transfer program, 56% enrolled in a vocational program, 2,889 enrolled as first-time, first-year students, 208 transferred in from other institutions.

| | | | |
|---|---|---|---|
| **Part-time:** | 39% | **Hispanic American:** | 2% |
| **Out-of-state:** | 36% | **International:** | 1% |
| **Women:** | 41% | **25 or older:** | 36% |
| **African American:** | 8% | **Live on campus:** | 36% |
| **Asian American:** | 1% | | |

**Transfer out. Colleges most students transferred to 2007:** Indiana University, Indiana State University, Purdue University, University of Southern Indiana, Ball State University.

**Basis for selection.** Open admission, but selective for some programs. Admission to health occupation programs based primarily on school achievement records, test scores, school and community activities, special talents/skills. SAT or ACT (SAT preferred) required for health occupation programs. Audition required of music majors. Portfolio recommended for fine arts, commercial art, design majors. **Homeschooled:** Transcript of courses and grades required. **Learning Disabled:** Students needing special accommodations are required to submit psychometric testing indicating a diagnosis of a specific disability, along with a list of any special services required.

**High school preparation.** Recommended units include English 4, mathematics 3, social studies 2, history 2, science 3 (laboratory 2) and foreign language 2.

**2008-2009 Annual costs.** Tuition/fees (projected): $4,203; $9,932 out-of-state. Per-credit charge: $134 in-state; $327 out-of-state. Students from Crawford, Richland, Lawrence and Wabash counties in Illinois pay tuition of $197.40 per credit hour (including capital improvement and technology fees, not including student activity fee). Room/board: $7,036. Books/supplies: $1,000. Personal expenses: $900.

**Financial aid. Need-based:** Need-based aid available for part-time students. Work-study available nights, weekends and for part-time students. **Non-need-based:** Scholarships awarded for academics, art, athletics, leadership, music/drama, state residency.

**Application procedures. Admission:** No deadline. $20 fee, may be waived for applicants with need. Application may be submitted online. Admission notification on a rolling basis. **Financial aid:** Priority date 3/1, closing date 5/1. FAFSA required. Applicants notified on a rolling basis starting 5/1; must reply by 8/24.

**Academics. Special study options:** Accelerated study, distance learning, dual enrollment of high school students, ESL, external degree, honors, independent study, internships, student-designed major, weekend college. Bachelor's degree programs available on campus. License preparation in aviation, dental hygiene, nursing, paramedic, physical therapy, real estate. **Credit/**

**placement by examination:** AP, CLEP, IB, institutional tests. 18 credit hours maximum toward associate degree. **Support services:** Learning center, pre-admission summer program, reduced course load, remedial instruction, study skills assistance, tutoring, writing center.

**Honors college/program.** 1100 SAT (exclusive of Writing), 25 ACT, leadership qualities, writing sample, 3 references. 20 students admitted for fall.

**Majors. Agriculture:** General, agribusiness operations, business, horticultural science, horticulture, products processing. **Area/ethnic studies:** American. **Biology:** General, botany. **Business:** General, accounting, administrative services, banking/financial services, business admin, fashion, hospitality admin, hospitality/recreation, hotel/motel admin, management information systems, marketing, office management, office technology, office/clerical, restaurant/food services, sales/distribution. **Communications:** General, advertising, digital media, journalism, media studies, photojournalism, public relations, radio/tv. **Communications technology:** Desktop publishing, graphic/printing, graphics, printing press operator, radio/tv. **Computer sciences:** General, applications programming, computer graphics, computer science, computer support specialist, data processing, information systems, LAN/WAN management, networking, programming, security, web page design, webmaster. **Conservation:** General, environmental science, forestry. **Construction:** General, carpentry, maintenance. **Education:** General, art, biology, chemistry, computer, early childhood, elementary, family/consumer sciences, foreign languages, French, health, history, mathematics, middle, multilevel teacher, music, physical, physics, sales/marketing, science, secondary, social science, social studies, Spanish, special, speech, technology/industrial arts, trade/industrial, voc/tech. **Engineering:** General, chemical, civil, construction, electrical, environmental, mechanical, physics, surveying. **Engineering technology:** General, architectural drafting, CAD/CADD, civil, computer, construction, drafting, electrical, manufacturing, mechanical, mining, robotics, surveying. **English:** English lit, speech/rhetoric. **Family/consumer sciences:** General, child care, clothing/textiles, food/nutrition, institutional food production. **Foreign languages:** General, American Sign Language, French, German, sign language interpretation, Spanish. **Health:** Athletic training, dental hygiene, dietician assistant, EMT ambulance attendant, EMT paramedic, licensed practical nurse, massage therapy, medical records admin, medical records technology, medical secretary, medical transcription, nursing (RN), pharmacy assistant, physical therapy assistant, predental, premedicine, prepharmacy, preveterinary, radiologic technology/medical imaging, recreational therapy. **History:** General. **Interdisciplinary:** Gerontology. **Legal studies:** Legal secretary, paralegal, prelaw. **Liberal arts:** Arts/sciences. **Math:** General. **Mechanic/repair:** General, aircraft, auto body, automotive, diesel, electronics/electrical, industrial. **Parks/recreation:** General, exercise sciences, health/fitness, sports admin. **Personal/culinary services:** Cosmetic, culinary arts, food prep, funeral direction, mortuary science, restaurant/catering. **Philosophy/religion:** Philosophy. **Physical sciences:** General, chemistry, geology, physics, planetary. **Protective services:** Corrections, fire safety technology, firefighting, law enforcement admin, police science, security services. **Psychology:** General. **Public administration:** Social work. **Social sciences:** General, anthropology, economics, geography, political science, sociology. **Transportation:** Airline/commercial pilot, aviation management. **Visual/performing arts:** General, art, ceramics, commercial/advertising art, dance, design, directing/producing, dramatic, drawing, fashion design, fiber arts, graphic design, interior design, music performance, music theory/composition, painting, piano/organ, printmaking, sculpture, studio arts, theater design, voice/opera. **Other:** Conservation law enforcement, Drafting and design/CAD, Music/audio recording.

**Computing on campus.** 350 workstations in dormitories, library, computer center, student center. Dormitories wired for high-speed internet access and linked to campus network. Commuter students can connect to campus network. Online library, student web hosting, wireless network available.

**Student life. Freshman orientation:** Mandatory. Preregistration for classes offered. Held the weekend prior to first day of classes; includes study skills, social activities, parent orientation. **Housing:** Guaranteed on-campus for freshmen. Coed dorms, single-sex dorms, special housing for disabled, substance-free housing available. $150 deposit. **Activities:** Bands, campus ministries, choral groups, dance, drama, international student organizations, literary magazine, music ensembles, musical theater, radio station, student government, student newspaper, TV station, Latter Day Saints student association, Black Male Initiative, College Republicans, Christian campus fellowship, Democrat club, Women of Essence and Gospel Choir, social work club.

**Athletics.** NJCAA. **Intercollegiate:** Baseball M, basketball, bowling, cheerleading, cross-country, diving, golf M, swimming, tennis M, track and field, volleyball W. **Intramural:** Baseball M, basketball, bowling, cross-country, golf, gymnastics, handball, racquetball, skiing, softball, swimming, table tennis, tennis, track and field, volleyball, wrestling M. **Team name:** Trailblazers.

**Student services.** Adult student services, alcohol/substance abuse counseling, campus ministries, career counseling, student employment services, financial aid counseling, health services, minority student services, on-campus daycare, personal counseling, placement for graduates, veterans' counselor. **Physically disabled:** Services for visually, hearing impaired. **Learning disabled:** Comprehensive services available. **Transfer:** Transfer adviser for students transferring to 4-year colleges.

**Contact.** E-mail: vuadmit@vinu.edu
Phone: (812) 888-4313 Toll-free number: (800) 742-9198
Fax: (812) 888-5707
Christian Blome, Director of Admissions, Vincennes University, 1002 North First Street, Vincennes, IN 47591

# Iowa

## AIB College of Business
**Des Moines, Iowa**
www.aib.edu
CB code: 7302

- Private 2-year business college
- Residential campus in large city

**General.** Founded in 1921. Regionally accredited. **Enrollment:** 956 degree-seeking undergraduates; 9 non-degree-seeking students. **Degrees:** 256 associate awarded. **Location:** 2 miles from downtown. **Calendar:** Quarter, extensive summer session. **Full-time faculty:** 28 total; 7% have terminal degrees, 68% women. **Part-time faculty:** 42 total; 12% have terminal degrees, 50% women. **Class size:** 75% < 20, 25% 20-39. **Special facilities:** Dictation tape library, video collection, CISCO and Microsoft labs, voice captioning laptops. **Partnerships:** Formal partnerships with IBM and Microsoft.

**Student profile.** Among degree-seeking undergraduates, 163 enrolled as first-time, first-year students, 343 transferred in from other institutions.

| | | | |
|---|---|---|---|
| Part-time: | 40% | Hispanic American: | 3% |
| Out-of-state: | 30% | Native American: | 1% |
| Women: | 71% | 25 or older: | 29% |
| African American: | 2% | Live on campus: | 50% |
| Asian American: | 1% | | |

**Transfer out. Colleges most students transferred to 2007:** Graceland College, Simpson College, Upper Iowa University.

**Basis for selection.** High school record important, test scores considered. All students required to take SAT/ACT or institutional exam. SAT or ACT recommended. Institution's own test administered for students without ACT or for students with less than 18 ACT. **Adult students:** SAT/ACT scores not required if applicant over 24 or out of high school 5 years or more. Testing not required if student has proof of previous college degree. **Homeschooled:** Transcript of courses and grades required.

**2007-2008 Annual costs.** Tuition/fees: $12,231. Per-credit charge: $220. Room only: $2,895. Books/supplies: $924. Personal expenses: $1,095.

**2006-2007 Financial aid. Need-based:** 188 full-time freshmen applied for aid; 171 were judged to have need; 171 of these received aid. Average need met was 66%. Average scholarship/grant was $4,553; average loan $3,062. 56% of total undergraduate aid awarded as scholarships/grants, 44% as loans/jobs. Need-based aid available for part-time students. Work-study available nights, weekends and for part-time students. **Non-need-based:** Awarded to 485 full-time undergraduates, including 182 freshmen. Scholarships awarded for academics, alumni affiliation, leadership.

**Application procedures. Admission:** Closing date 8/1 (receipt date). $25 fee, may be waived for applicants with need. Application may be submitted online. Admission notification on a rolling basis beginning on or about 9/15. **Financial aid:** Priority date 4/1; no closing date. FAFSA, institutional form required. Applicants notified on a rolling basis starting 3/1; must reply within 2 week(s) of notification.

**Academics.** Real-time reporting program approved by National Court Reporters Association. Online bachelor's program available. **Special study options:** Cross-registration, distance learning, double major, dual enrollment of high school students, internships, liberal arts/career combination. Bachelor's degree programs available on campus. **Credit/placement by examination:** AP, CLEP, SAT, ACT, institutional tests. **Support services:** Reduced course load, remedial instruction, study skills assistance, tutoring.

**Majors. Business:** General, accounting, accounting/business management, accounting/finance, administrative services, banking/financial services, business admin, finance, marketing, office management, selling, tourism/travel. **Computer sciences:** Information technology, networking, system admin. **Legal studies:** Court reporting.

**Most popular majors.** Business/marketing 43%, computer/information sciences 6%.

**Computing on campus.** 440 workstations in dormitories, library, student center. Dormitories wired for high-speed internet access and linked to campus network. Commuter students can connect to campus network. Online course registration, online library, helpline, wireless network available.

**Student life. Freshman orientation:** Available. Five 1-day sessions corresponding with student-s major held in late August for students and their families. **Housing:** Coed dorms, special housing for disabled, apartments, fraternity/sorority housing available. $200 fully refundable deposit, deadline 5/1. Housing available for single-parents, married students, families. **Activities:** Student government.

**Athletics.** NJCAA. **Intercollegiate:** Cheerleading M. **Intramural:** Badminton, basketball, bowling, football (non-tackle), golf, softball, table tennis, tennis, volleyball. **Team name:** Eagles.

**Student services.** Adult student services, alcohol/substance abuse counseling, career counseling, student employment services, financial aid counseling, health services, personal counseling, placement for graduates. **Physically disabled:** Services for visually, speech, hearing impaired. **Transfer:** Pre-admission transcript evaluation for new students. Transfer adviser for students transferring to 4-year colleges.

**Contact.** E-mail: admissions@aib.edu
Phone: (515) 246-5358 Toll-free number: (800) 444-1921
Fax: (515) 244-6773
Tim Hauber, Vice President of Enrollment, AIB College of Business, 2500 Fleur Drive, Des Moines, IA 50321-1799

## Clinton Community College
**Clinton, Iowa**
www.eicc.edu
CB code: 6100

- Public 2-year community college
- Commuter campus in large town

**General.** Founded in 1946. Regionally accredited. **Enrollment:** 996 degree-seeking undergraduates; 244 non-degree-seeking students. **Degrees:** 181 associate awarded. **Location:** 40 miles from Davenport. **Calendar:** Semester, limited summer session. **Full-time faculty:** 32 total; 6% minority, 44% women. **Part-time faculty:** 100 total; 2% minority, 58% women. **Class size:** 90% < 20, 9% 20-39, less than 1% 40-49.

**Student profile.** Among degree-seeking undergraduates, 66% enrolled in a transfer program, 34% enrolled in a vocational program, 1% already have a bachelor's degree or higher, 257 enrolled as first-time, first-year students, 10 transferred in from other institutions.

| | | | |
|---|---|---|---|
| Part-time: | 45% | Asian American: | 1% |
| Out-of-state: | 12% | Hispanic American: | 2% |
| Women: | 68% | Native American: | 1% |
| African American: | 5% | 25 or older: | 35% |

**Transfer out. Colleges most students transferred to 2007:** Ashford University, University of Iowa, Iowa State University, University of Northern Iowa, St. Ambrose University.

**Basis for selection.** Open admission, but selective for some programs. Special requirements for nursing program. Interview recommended.

**2007-2008 Annual costs.** Tuition/fees: $3,060; $4,590 out-of-state. Per-credit charge: $102 in-state; $153 out-of-state. Books/supplies: $1,140. Personal expenses: $1,090.

**Application procedures. Admission:** No deadline. No application fee. Application may be submitted online. Admission notification on a rolling basis beginning on or about 9/1. **Financial aid:** Priority date 4/20; no closing date. FAFSA, institutional form required. Applicants notified on a rolling basis starting 5/15; must reply within 2 week(s) of notification.

**Academics. Special study options:** Accelerated study, cooperative education, cross-registration, distance learning, double major, dual enrollment of high school students, ESL, honors, independent study, study abroad, weekend college. License preparation in nursing, paramedic, real estate. **Credit/placement by examination:** AP, CLEP, institutional tests. 30 credit hours maximum toward associate degree. **Support services:** GED preparation and test center, learning center, reduced course load, remedial instruction, study skills assistance, tutoring.

**Majors. Business:** Administrative services. **Communications technology:** Graphic/printing. **Engineering technology:** Drafting, electrical, occupational safety. **Health:** Nursing (RN). **Liberal arts:** Arts/sciences. **Personal/culinary services:** Restaurant/catering.

**Most popular majors.** Health sciences 25%, liberal arts 65%.

Two-Year Colleges

**Computing on campus.** 55 workstations in library, computer center. Commuter students can connect to campus network. Online course registration, helpline, wireless network available.

**Student life. Freshman orientation:** Available. Preregistration for classes offered. **Activities:** Drama, literary magazine, student government, student newspaper, Phi Beta Lambda, Phi Theta Kappa, student senate, Peer Ambassadors, drama/fine arts club, S.N.A.P., drafting club, nursing club, graphic arts/printer club, The Leadership Connection.

**Athletics.** NJCAA. **Intercollegiate:** Basketball M, volleyball W. **Intramural:** Basketball, bowling, softball, table tennis, tennis, volleyball. **Team name:** Cougars.

**Student services.** Career counseling, student employment services, financial aid counseling, personal counseling, placement for graduates, veterans' counselor. **Physically disabled:** Services for visually, speech, hearing impaired. **Transfer:** Transfer adviser, college fairs on campus for students transferring to 4-year colleges.

**Contact.** E-mail: scarmody@eicc.edu
Phone: (888) 336-390 Toll-free number: (888) 336-3907
Fax: (563) 244-7107
Susan Carmody, Admissions Officer, Clinton Community College, 1000 Lincoln Boulevard, Clinton, IA 52732

## Des Moines Area Community College

Ankeny, Iowa — CB member
www.dmacc.edu — CB code: 6177

- Public 2-year community college
- Commuter campus in large town

**General.** Founded in 1966. Regionally accredited. Multilocation institution with campuses at Boone, Des Moines, West Des Moines, Carroll, and Newton. Ankeny campus is primary location and administrative center. **Enrollment:** 18,320 degree-seeking undergraduates. **Degrees:** 1,551 associate awarded. **Location:** 15 miles from downtown Des Moines, 25 miles from Ames. **Calendar:** Semester, extensive summer session. **Full-time faculty:** 282 total. **Part-time faculty:** 599 total. **Special facilities:** Wireless computer technology campus, career academies.

**Student profile.** Among degree-seeking undergraduates, 1% already have a bachelor's degree or higher, 5,183 enrolled as first-time, first-year students.

| | | | |
|---|---|---|---|
| Part-time: | 62% | Hispanic American: | 4% |
| Women: | 55% | International: | 1% |
| African American: | 6% | 25 or older: | 28% |
| Asian American: | 3% | | |

**Transfer out. Colleges most students transferred to 2007:** Iowa State University, Grand View College, University of Northern Iowa.

**Basis for selection.** Open admission, but selective for some programs. Special requirements for dental hygiene, commercial art, nursing, CAP programs. Interview required of dental hygiene, commercial art majors. Portfolio required of commercial art majors.

**High school preparation.** Recommended units include English 4, mathematics 3 and science 3.

**2007-2008 Annual costs.** Tuition/fees: $3,060; $6,120 out-of-state. Per-credit charge: $102 in-state; $204 out-of-state. Books/supplies: $900. Personal expenses: $1,568.

**Financial aid. Need-based:** Need-based aid available for part-time students. Work-study available nights, weekends and for part-time students. **Non-need-based:** Scholarships awarded for academics, athletics, state residency.

**Application procedures. Admission:** No deadline. No application fee. Application may be submitted online. Admission notification on a rolling basis. **Financial aid:** Priority date 4/1; no closing date. FAFSA required. Applicants notified on a rolling basis starting 4/1; must reply within 2 week(s) of notification.

**Academics. Special study options:** Cooperative education, cross-registration, distance learning, dual enrollment of high school students, ESL, honors, independent study, internships, liberal arts/career combination, study abroad, weekend college. Bachelor's degree programs available on campus. License preparation in dental hygiene, nursing, paramedic, real estate. **Credit/placement by examination:** AP, CLEP, institutional tests. 28 credit hours maximum toward associate degree. **Support services:** GED preparation and

test center, learning center, pre-admission summer program, reduced course load, remedial instruction, study skills assistance, tutoring, writing center.

**Majors. Agriculture:** Horticulture, supplies. **Biology:** Biotechnology. **Business:** Accounting, accounting technology, apparel, business admin, hospitality admin, marketing, office management, sales/distribution. **Communications technology:** Desktop publishing. **Computer sciences:** General, applications programming, information technology. **Construction:** Carpentry. **Education:** Early childhood special. **Engineering:** Surveying. **Engineering technology:** Architectural drafting, civil, electrical, mechanical drafting. **Health:** Clinical lab technology, dental hygiene, health care admin, medical secretary, nursing (RN), respiratory therapy technology, veterinary technology/assistant. **Legal studies:** Paralegal. **Liberal arts:** Arts/sciences. **Mechanic/repair:** Auto body, automotive, communications systems, diesel, heating/ac/refrig, industrial, industrial electronics. **Parks/recreation:** Sports admin. **Personal/culinary services:** Chef training. **Production:** Machine tool, tool and die, welding. **Protective services:** Fire safety technology, police science. **Public administration:** Community org/advocacy. **Visual/performing arts:** Commercial/advertising art.

**Computing on campus.** 200 workstations in library, computer center. Commuter students can connect to campus network. Online course registration, online library, helpline, wireless network available.

**Student life. Freshman orientation:** Available. Preregistration for classes offered. Half-day program offered. **Policies:** Student Action Board responsible for many on-campus activities: professional and social. **Activities:** Choral groups, drama, literary magazine, student government, student newspaper.

**Athletics.** NJCAA. **Intercollegiate:** Baseball M, basketball, volleyball W. **Intramural:** Badminton, basketball, bowling, football (non-tackle), golf, softball, table tennis, tennis, volleyball. **Team name:** Bears (Boone campus only).

**Student services.** Adult student services, career counseling, student employment services, financial aid counseling, health services, on-campus daycare, personal counseling, placement for graduates, veterans' counselor. **Physically disabled:** Services for visually, speech, hearing impaired. **Transfer:** Transfer adviser, college fairs on campus for students transferring to 4-year colleges.

**Contact.** E-mail: admissions@dmacc.edu
Phone: (515) 964-6241 Toll-free number: (800) 362-2127 ext. 6241
Fax: (515) 964-6391
Michael Lentsch, Director of Enrollment Management, Des Moines Area Community College, 2006 South Ankeny Boulevard, Ankeny, IA 50023-3993

## Ellsworth Community College

Iowa Falls, Iowa
www.iavalley.cc.ia.us/ecc — CB code: 5528

- Public 2-year community college
- Residential campus in small town

**General.** Founded in 1890. Regionally accredited. **Enrollment:** 1,025 degree-seeking undergraduates. **Degrees:** 163 associate awarded. **Location:** 70 miles from Des Moines. **Calendar:** Semester, limited summer session. **Full-time faculty:** 39 total. **Part-time faculty:** 43 total. **Special facilities:** 80-acre wildlife area.

**Transfer out. Colleges most students transferred to 2007:** University of Northern Iowa, Buena Vista University, Iowa State University, Wartburg College, University of Iowa.

**Basis for selection.** Open admission, but selective for some programs. Special requirements for some nursing programs.

**2007-2008 Annual costs.** Tuition/fees: $4,065; $4,905 out-of-state. Per-credit charge: $112 in-state; $140 out-of-state. Books/supplies: $700. Personal expenses: $1,400.

**2006-2007 Financial aid. Need-based:** 48% of total undergraduate aid awarded as scholarships/grants, 52% as loans/jobs. Need-based aid available for part-time students. Work-study available nights, weekends and for part-time students. **Non-need-based:** Scholarships awarded for academics, art, athletics, leadership, minority status, music/drama.

**Application procedures. Admission:** No deadline. No application fee. Application may be submitted online. Admission notification on a rolling basis. COMPASS required of applicants without SAT or ACT. **Financial aid:** Priority date 4/1; no closing date. FAFSA, institutional form required. Applicants notified on a rolling basis starting 2/15; must reply within 4 week(s) of notification.

**Academics. Special study options:** Cooperative education, cross-registration, distance learning, double major, dual enrollment of high school students, ESL, honors, independent study, internships, liberal arts/career combination. Bachelor's degree programs available on campus. License preparation in nursing. **Credit/placement by examination:** AP, CLEP, institutional tests. 24 credit hours maximum toward associate degree. **Support services:** GED preparation and test center, learning center, remedial instruction, study skills assistance, tutoring, writing center.

**Majors. Agriculture:** Business, equestrian studies, farm/ranch. **Biology:** General, biotechnology. **Business:** General, accounting, administrative services, fashion, insurance, office technology, office/clerical. **Communications:** General. **Computer sciences:** General, computer graphics, computer science, data processing, information systems, LAN/WAN management, programming. **Conservation:** General, wildlife. **Construction:** Carpentry. **Education:** General, agricultural, biology, business, chemistry, elementary, family/consumer sciences, history, mathematics, middle, multi-level teacher, physical, physically handicapped, physics, science, secondary, social science, social studies, teacher assistance. **Engineering:** General. **English:** English lit. **Family/consumer sciences:** General, clothing/textiles, family/community services. **Health:** Athletic training, medical secretary, nursing (RN), predental, premedicine, prepharmacy, preveterinary. **History:** General. **Interdisciplinary:** Behavioral sciences, natural sciences. **Legal studies:** Legal secretary, prelaw. **Liberal arts:** Arts/sciences. **Math:** General. **Parks/recreation:** Health/fitness. **Physical sciences:** Chemistry, physics. **Protective services:** Criminal justice, law enforcement admin. **Psychology:** General. **Public administration:** Human services, social work. **Science technology:** Biological. **Social sciences:** General, criminology, sociology. **Visual/performing arts:** Art, commercial/advertising art, dramatic, studio arts.

**Most popular majors.** Business/marketing 10%, health sciences 10%, liberal arts 59%.

**Computing on campus.** 100 workstations in dormitories, library, computer center, student center. Dormitories wired for high-speed internet access and linked to campus network. Commuter students can connect to campus network. Online library, repair service, wireless network available.

**Student life. Freshman orientation:** Mandatory. Preregistration for classes offered. Six to 8 dates set for orientation, advising, and preregistration. **Housing:** Guaranteed on-campus for freshmen. Single-sex dorms available. $200 deposit. **Activities:** Bands, choral groups, dance, drama, international student organizations, literary magazine, music ensembles, musical theater, student government, student newspaper, Young Democrats, Young Republicans, minority student organization, human services club, agricultural science club, criminal justice club.

**Athletics.** NJCAA. **Intercollegiate:** Baseball M, basketball, cross-country, football (tackle) M, golf, softball W, volleyball W, wrestling M. **Intramural:** Badminton, basketball, bowling, football (non-tackle), handball, racquetball, swimming, tennis, volleyball. **Team name:** Panthers.

**Student services.** Adult student services, alcohol/substance abuse counseling, career counseling, services for economically disadvantaged, student employment services, financial aid counseling, health services, personal counseling, placement for graduates, veterans' counselor. **Transfer:** Preadmission transcript evaluation for new students. Transfer adviser, college fairs on campus for students transferring to 4-year colleges.

**Contact.** Phone: (641) 648-4611 ext. 431 Toll-free number: (800) 322-9253 Fax: (641) 648-3128
Annie Kalous, Director of Admissions, Ellsworth Community College, 1100 College Avenue, Iowa Falls, IA 50126

## Hawkeye Community College
**Waterloo, Iowa**
**www.hawkeyecollege.edu**                    CB code: 6288

- Public 2-year community and technical college
- Commuter campus in small city

**General.** Founded in 1966. Regionally accredited. **Enrollment:** 4,434 degree-seeking undergraduates; 1,016 non-degree-seeking students. **Degrees:** 784 associate awarded. **ROTC:** Army, Naval, Air Force. **Location:** 120 miles from Des Moines; 90 miles from Cedar Rapids, South Dakota. **Calendar:** Semester, limited summer session. **Full-time faculty:** 121 total; 8% have terminal degrees, 4% minority, 45% women. **Part-time faculty:** 210 total; 5% have terminal degrees, 5% minority, 63% women.

**Student profile.** Among degree-seeking undergraduates, 60% enrolled in a transfer program, 40% enrolled in a vocational program, 1,041 enrolled as first-time, first-year students.

| | | | |
|---|---|---|---|
| Part-time: | 48% | Asian American: | 1% |
| Out-of-state: | 1% | Hispanic American: | 2% |
| Women: | 55% | 25 or older: | 24% |
| African American: | 7% | | |

**Transfer out. Colleges most students transferred to 2007:** University of Northern Iowa, University of Iowa, Iowa State University.

**Basis for selection.** Open admission, but selective for some programs. Program requirements and basic skills required for all programs. ACT required for admission to medical laboratory technician and dental hygiene programs only. **Homeschooled:** Transcript of courses and grades required.

**High school preparation.** One year biology required for nursing and medical laboratory technicians. One year chemistry required for respiratory care and nursing. Two semesters of studio art and one computer course required for graphic communications.

**2007-2008 Annual costs.** Tuition/fees: $3,570; $6,810 out-of-state. Per-credit charge: $108 in-state; $216 out-of-state. Books/supplies: $820. Personal expenses: $3,627.

**2007-2008 Financial aid. Need-based:** 42% of total undergraduate aid awarded as scholarships/grants, 58% as loans/jobs. Work-study available nights, weekends and for part-time students. **Non-need-based:** Scholarships awarded for academics, state residency.

**Application procedures. Admission:** No deadline. No application fee. Application may be submitted online. Admission notification on a rolling basis. Accepted students asked to pay first-semester tuition in August to confirm fall enrollment or enter into a tuition payment plan. **Financial aid:** Priority date 3/15; no closing date. FAFSA, institutional form required. Applicants notified on a rolling basis starting 4/25; must reply within 2 week(s) of notification.

**Academics. Special study options:** Cooperative education, distance learning, dual enrollment of high school students, external degree, honors, independent study, internships, liberal arts/career combination, study abroad, weekend college. License preparation in dental hygiene, nursing. **Credit/placement by examination:** AP, CLEP, institutional tests. 30 credit hours maximum toward associate degree. **Support services:** GED preparation and test center, learning center, reduced course load, remedial instruction, study skills assistance, tutoring.

**Majors. Agriculture:** Animal husbandry, horticulture, power machinery, supplies. **Business:** Accounting, executive assistant, sales/distribution. **Communications technology:** Graphics. **Computer sciences:** General, networking, web page design. **Conservation:** Management/policy. **Engineering technology:** Architectural drafting, civil, electrical, manufacturing. **Health:** Clinical lab technology, dental hygiene, medical secretary, nursing (RN), respiratory therapy technology. **Liberal arts:** Arts/sciences. **Mechanic/repair:** Auto body, automotive, diesel. **Production:** Machine tool, tool and die. **Protective services:** Police science. **Visual/performing arts:** Commercial photography, interior design.

**Most popular majors.** Engineering/engineering technologies 6%, health sciences 15%, liberal arts 43%, trade and industry 10%.

**Computing on campus.** 300 workstations in library, computer center. Commuter students can connect to campus network. Online course registration available.

**Student life. Freshman orientation:** Available. Preregistration for classes offered. Held week before classes begin. **Activities:** Student government.

**Athletics. Intramural:** Basketball, bowling, football (non-tackle), softball, volleyball.

**Student services.** Career counseling, student employment services, financial aid counseling, on-campus daycare, personal counseling, placement for graduates, veterans' counselor. **Physically disabled:** Services for visually, hearing impaired. **Transfer:** Pre-admission transcript evaluation for new students. Transfer center, transfer adviser, college fairs on campus for students transferring to 4-year colleges.

**Contact.** E-mail: admission@hawkeyecollege.edu
Phone: (319) 296-4000 Toll-free number: (800) 670-4769 ext. 4000
Fax: (319) 296-4490
David Ball, Director of Admissions & Recruiting, Hawkeye Community College, Box 8015, Waterloo, IA 50704-8015

## Indian Hills Community College
Ottumwa, Iowa
www.indianhills.edu                    CB code: 6312

▶ Public 2-year community college
▶ Commuter campus in large town

**General.** Founded in 1966. Regionally accredited. Main campus located on 126 acres. **Enrollment:** 3,019 degree-seeking undergraduates; 1,154 non-degree-seeking students. **Degrees:** 712 associate awarded. **Location:** 90 miles from Des Moines. **Calendar:** Quarter, extensive summer session. **Full-time faculty:** 127 total. **Part-time faculty:** 25 total. **Class size:** 66% < 20, 27% 20-39, 4% 40-49, 4% 50-99. **Special facilities:** Wildlife sanctuary, outdoor stage, grotto.

**Student profile.** Among degree-seeking undergraduates, 53% enrolled in a transfer program, 44% enrolled in a vocational program, 2% already have a bachelor's degree or higher, 1,049 enrolled as first-time, first-year students, 200 transferred in from other institutions.

| | | | |
|---|---|---|---|
| Part-time: | 22% | Hispanic American: | 2% |
| Out-of-state: | 7% | Native American: | 1% |
| Women: | 57% | International: | 1% |
| African American: | 2% | 25 or older: | 28% |
| Asian American: | 1% | Live on campus: | 15% |

**Basis for selection.** Open admission, but selective for some programs. GPA, any prior college credit, test scores considered for limited enrollment programs. ACT required for technology programs and for counseling. College Qualification Test required for some health occupation program applicants.

**High school preparation.** Recommended units include English 2, mathematics 2, science 2 (laboratory 2).

**2007-2008 Annual costs.** Tuition/fees: $3,405; $5,085 out-of-state. Per-credit charge: $111 in-state; $167 out-of-state. Room/board: $4,875. Books/supplies: $675. Personal expenses: $750.

**Financial aid. Need-based:** Need-based aid available for part-time students. **Non-need-based:** Scholarships awarded for athletics, state residency.

**Application procedures. Admission:** Priority date 7/1; no deadline. No application fee. Application may be submitted online. Admission notification on a rolling basis. **Financial aid:** Priority date 4/1; no closing date. FAFSA, institutional form required. Applicants notified on a rolling basis starting 6/1; must reply within 2 week(s) of notification.

**Academics. Special study options:** Cooperative education, distance learning, dual enrollment of high school students, ESL, honors, independent study, internships, liberal arts/career combination. Bachelor's degree programs available on campus. License preparation in aviation, nursing, paramedic, physical therapy, radiology, real estate. **Credit/placement by examination:** AP, CLEP, institutional tests. 16 credit hours maximum toward associate degree. **Support services:** GED preparation and test center, learning center, reduced course load, remedial instruction, study skills assistance, tutoring.

**Majors. Agriculture:** Production. **Computer sciences:** Applications programming, networking, security. **Construction:** General. **Engineering:** Agricultural. **Engineering technology:** Electrical, laser/optical, mechanical drafting, robotics. **Health:** Clinical lab technology, EMT paramedic, medical records technology, nursing (RN), physical therapy assistant, radiologic technology/medical imaging. **Liberal arts:** Arts/sciences. **Mechanic/repair:** Auto body, automotive, avionics, diesel. **Personal/culinary services:** Chef training. **Production:** Machine tool. **Protective services:** Police science. **Science technology:** Biological. **Transportation:** Airline/commercial pilot.

**Most popular majors.** Computer/information sciences 8%, health sciences 20%, liberal arts 50%, trade and industry 8%.

**Computing on campus.** 742 workstations in dormitories, library, computer center, student center. Commuter students can connect to campus network. Online course registration, online library, helpline, wireless network available.

**Student life. Freshman orientation:** Available. **Housing:** Coed dorms, single-sex dorms available. $50 deposit. **Activities:** Jazz band, campus ministries, choral groups, dance, drama, music ensembles, musical theater, student government.

**Athletics.** NJCAA. **Intercollegiate:** Baseball M, basketball M, golf M, softball W, volleyball W. **Intramural:** Basketball, bowling, fencing, racquetball, softball, tennis, volleyball. **Team name:** Warriors.

**Student services.** Adult student services, career counseling, services for economically disadvantaged, student employment services, financial aid counseling, health services, on-campus daycare, personal counseling, placement for graduates, veterans' counselor. **Physically disabled:** Services for visually, hearing impaired. **Transfer:** Transfer adviser, college fairs on campus for students transferring to 4-year colleges.

**Contact.** E-mail: enrollment_services@ihcc.cc
Phone: (641) 683-5153 Toll-free number: (800) 726-2585 ext. 5153
Fax: (641) 683-5184
Jane Sapp, Admissions Officer, Indian Hills Community College, 623 Indian Hills Drive, Building 12, Ottumwa, IA 52501

## Iowa Central Community College
Fort Dodge, Iowa
www.iowacentral.edu                    CB code: 6217

▶ Public 2-year community college
▶ Commuter campus in large town

**General.** Founded in 1966. Regionally accredited. Courses available at 2 branch campuses: Webster City and Storm Lake. **Enrollment:** 5,731 degree-seeking undergraduates. **Degrees:** 604 associate awarded. **Location:** 90 miles from Des Moines. **Calendar:** Semester, limited summer session. **Full-time faculty:** 77 total. **Part-time faculty:** 351 total. **Special facilities:** Broadcasting suite.

**Student profile.** Among degree-seeking undergraduates, 66% enrolled in a transfer program, 33% enrolled in a vocational program, .5% already have a bachelor's degree or higher.

| | | | |
|---|---|---|---|
| Out-of-state: | 5% | Live on campus: | 25% |

**Transfer out. Colleges most students transferred to 2007:** Buena Vista University, Iowa State University, University of Northern Iowa.

**Basis for selection.** Open admission, but selective for some programs.

**2007-2008 Annual costs.** Tuition/fees: $3,390; $4,920 out-of-state. Per-credit charge: $102 in-state; $153 out-of-state. Room/board: $4,625. Books/supplies: $850. Personal expenses: $1,550.

**Financial aid. Need-based:** Need-based aid available for part-time students. Work-study available nights, weekends and for part-time students. **Non-need-based:** Scholarships awarded for academics, art, athletics, leadership, music/drama.

**Application procedures. Admission:** No deadline. No application fee. Application may be submitted online. Admission notification on a rolling basis. **Financial aid:** Priority date 3/8; no closing date. FAFSA required. Applicants notified on a rolling basis starting 4/15; must reply within 2 week(s) of notification.

**Academics. Special study options:** Accelerated study, cooperative education, cross-registration, distance learning, dual enrollment of high school students, external degree, independent study, internships, study abroad. 2 Plus 2 Agreements with Iowa State University and the University of Iowa, University of Iowa College of Nursing RN-BSN program. Bachelor's degree programs available on campus. License preparation in aviation, dental hygiene, nursing, paramedic, radiology. **Credit/placement by examination:** AP, CLEP. 30 credit hours maximum toward associate degree. ACT may be submitted for placement in lieu of COMPASS or ASSET. **Support services:** GED preparation and test center, learning center, pre-admission summer program, reduced course load, remedial instruction, study skills assistance, tutoring.

**Majors. Agriculture:** Agribusiness operations, turf management. **Business:** Accounting, administrative services, business admin, logistics, operations. **Communications technology:** General, desktop publishing, radio/tv. **Computer sciences:** Web page design, webmaster. **Construction:** General. **Engineering technology:** Electrical, energy systems, manufacturing. **Health:** Clinical lab technology, EMT paramedic, medical assistant, medical radiologic technology/radiation therapy, nursing (RN), occupational therapy assistant, physical therapy assistant, premedicine, prepharmacy, preveterinary, radiologic technology/medical imaging. **Legal studies:** Prelaw. **Liberal arts:** Arts/sciences. **Mechanic/repair:** Auto body, automotive, diesel, industrial electronics. **Personal/culinary services:** Cosmetic, culinary arts. **Production:** Machine tool. **Protective services:** Firefighting, police science. **Public administration:** Social work. **Science technology:** Chemical. **Transportation:** Aviation. **Other:** Industrial business.

**Computing on campus.** 500 workstations in library, computer center, student center. Dormitories wired for high-speed internet access and linked to campus network. Commuter students can connect to campus network. Online course registration, helpline available.

**Student life. Freshman orientation:** Mandatory. Preregistration for classes offered. **Housing:** Coed dorms, single-sex dorms, special housing for disabled, apartments available. $100 nonrefundable deposit. **Activities:** Bands, choral groups, dance, drama, music ensembles, musical theater, radio station, student government, student newspaper, symphony orchestra.

**Athletics.** NJCAA. **Intercollegiate:** Baseball M, basketball, cross-country, football (tackle) M, golf, rodeo, soccer, softball W, swimming, track and field, volleyball W, wrestling M. **Intramural:** Basketball, bowling, golf, volleyball. **Team name:** Tritons.

**Student services.** Career counseling, services for economically disadvantaged, student employment services, financial aid counseling, health services, minority student services, personal counseling, placement for graduates, veterans' counselor. **Physically disabled:** Services for visually, speech, hearing impaired. **Transfer:** Pre-admission transcript evaluation for new students. Transfer adviser, college fairs on campus for students transferring to 4-year colleges.

**Contact.** Phone: (515) 576-7201 ext. 1008 Toll-free number: (800) 362-2793 ext. 1008 Fax: (515) 576-7724
Samantha McClain, Director of Admissions, Iowa Central Community College, 330 Avenue M, Fort Dodge, IA 50501

## Iowa Lakes Community College
**Estherville, Iowa**
**www.iowalakes.edu**                          **CB code: 6196**

- Public 2-year community college
- Commuter campus in small town

**General.** Founded in 1967. Regionally accredited. 3 campuses with dormitories and food service operating in Emmetsburg, Estherville and Spencer. Classes also offered at campuses located in Algona, and Spirit Lake. **Enrollment:** 1,982 degree-seeking undergraduates; 1,013 non-degree-seeking students. **Degrees:** 460 associate awarded. **Location:** 100 miles from Mason City; 100 miles from Sioux Falls, South Dakota. **Calendar:** Semester, limited summer session. **Full-time faculty:** 78 total. **Part-time faculty:** 99 total. **Special facilities:** 360-acre farm, print collection.

**Student profile.** Among degree-seeking undergraduates, 59% enrolled in a transfer program, 41% enrolled in a vocational program, 693 enrolled as first-time, first-year students.

| | | | |
|---|---|---|---|
| Part-time: | 36% | 25 or older: | 21% |
| Out-of-state: | 11% | Live on campus: | 17% |
| Women: | 56% | | |

**Transfer out. Colleges most students transferred to 2007:** University of Northern Iowa, Iowa State University, University of Iowa, Minnesota State University-Mankato, Buena Vista University.

**Basis for selection.** Open admission, but selective for some programs. Special requirements for nursing, aviation/airport management, wind turbine technology, and computer-aided drafting and design programs. ACT required for nursing students. Interview required of career programs. Audition recommended for music majors. Portfolio recommended for advertising design majors.

**2007-2008 Annual costs.** Tuition/fees: $3,822; $3,942 out-of-state. Per-credit charge: $113 in-state; $117 out-of-state. Room/board: $4,350. Books/supplies: $600. Personal expenses: $500.

**Financial aid.** All financial aid based on need. Need-based aid available for part-time students.

**Application procedures. Admission:** No deadline. No application fee. Application may be submitted online. Admission notification on a rolling basis. **Financial aid:** Priority date 4/22; no closing date. FAFSA, institutional form required. Applicants notified on a rolling basis starting 4/15.

**Academics. Special study options:** Cooperative education, cross-registration, distance learning, dual enrollment of high school students, honors, internships, liberal arts/career combination, weekend college. Evening college. License preparation in aviation, nursing, paramedic, real estate. **Credit/placement by examination:** CLEP, institutional tests. 30 credit hours maximum toward associate degree. **Support services:** GED preparation and test center, learning center, reduced course load, remedial instruction, study skills assistance, tutoring.

**Majors. Agriculture:** Landscaping, power machinery, production, supplies. **Business:** Accounting, business admin, hotel/motel admin, office management, restaurant/food services, sales/distribution, tourism promotion. **Communications:** Broadcast journalism, journalism. **Computer sciences:**

Applications programming, networking. **Conservation:** Environmental studies. **Engineering:** Agricultural. **Engineering technology:** Drafting, energy systems, environmental, mechanical drafting. **Health:** EMT paramedic, health care admin, nursing (RN). **Legal studies:** Paralegal. **Liberal arts:** Arts/sciences. **Parks/recreation:** Facilities management. **Protective services:** Police science. **Social sciences:** Cartography. **Transportation:** Aviation. **Visual/performing arts:** Commercial/advertising art, photography. **Other:** Rehabilitation and therapeutic services.

**Computing on campus.** 800 workstations in library, computer center, student center. Dormitories wired for high-speed internet access. Online course registration, online library, helpline, repair service, wireless network available.

**Student life. Freshman orientation:** Mandatory. Preregistration for classes offered. **Housing:** Coed dorms, special housing for disabled, apartments available. **Activities:** Bands, choral groups, drama, international student organizations, literary magazine, music ensembles, musical theater, radio station, student government, student newspaper, TV station.

**Athletics.** NJCAA. **Intercollegiate:** Baseball M, basketball, cross-country, golf, softball W, track and field, volleyball W, wrestling M. **Intramural:** Basketball, bowling, racquetball, skiing, softball, table tennis, volleyball. **Team name:** Lakers.

**Student services.** Adult student services, alcohol/substance abuse counseling, career counseling, services for economically disadvantaged, financial aid counseling, personal counseling, placement for graduates, veterans' counselor, women's services. **Transfer:** Pre-admission transcript evaluation for new students. Transfer adviser, college fairs on campus for students transferring to 4-year colleges.

**Contact.** E-mail: info@iowalakes.edu
Phone: (712) 362-2604 ext. 145 Toll-free number: (800) 521-5054
Fax: (712) 362-3969
Julie Carlson, Dean, Enrollment Management, Iowa Lakes Community College, 300 South 18th Street, Estherville, IA 51334-2725

## Iowa Western Community College
**Council Bluffs, Iowa**
**www.iwcc.edu**                               **CB code: 6302**

- Public 2-year community and technical college
- Commuter campus in small city

**General.** Founded in 1966. Regionally accredited. Branch campus at Clarinda offers liberal arts and vocational programs in practical nursing, secretarial, mechanical technology, and electromechanical technology. Centers in Harlan and Atlantic offer evening programs in liberal arts and business administration. Practical nursing offered at Harlan. **Enrollment:** 5,052 degree-seeking undergraduates. **Degrees:** 708 associate awarded. **ROTC:** Army, Air Force. **Location:** 10 miles from Omaha. **Calendar:** Semester, extensive summer session. **Full-time faculty:** 136 total. **Part-time faculty:** 173 total.

**Student profile.**

| | | | |
|---|---|---|---|
| Out-of-state: | 10% | Live on campus: | 21% |

**Transfer out. Colleges most students transferred to 2007:** University of Iowa, Iowa State University, Northwest Missouri State University, University of Nebraska at Omaha, Buena Vista University.

**Basis for selection.** Open admission, but selective for some programs. Selective admission to some programs, including nursing, dental hygiene, music, automotive technology and veterinary technology. Academic enrichment courses available to help gain proficiency needed for admission to specific programs. COMPASS or ACT/SAT required for placement. Interview required of vocational-technical applicants.

**High school preparation.** Specific subject requirements for some career programs.

**2007-2008 Annual costs.** Tuition/fees: $3,780; $5,280 out-of-state. Per-credit charge: $106 in-state; $159 out-of-state. Room/board: $5,300. Books/supplies: $800. Personal expenses: $1,440.

**2007-2008 Financial aid. Need-based:** 50% of total undergraduate aid awarded as scholarships/grants, 50% as loans/jobs. Need-based aid available for part-time students. **Non-need-based:** Scholarships awarded for athletics, music/drama.

**Application procedures. Admission:** No deadline. No application fee. Application may be submitted online. Admission notification on a rolling basis. Applicants for limited-enrollment programs considered on first applied, first accepted basis. **Financial aid:** Priority date 7/1; no closing date.

FAFSA required. Applicants notified on a rolling basis starting 3/1; must reply within 3 week(s) of notification.

**Academics. Special study options:** Cooperative education, distance learning, dual enrollment of high school students, ESL, independent study, internships, student-designed major. License preparation in aviation, dental hygiene, nursing, paramedic. **Credit/placement by examination:** CLEP, institutional tests. 40 credit hours maximum toward associate degree. **Support services:** GED preparation and test center, learning center, reduced course load, remedial instruction, study skills assistance, tutoring, writing center.

**Majors. Agriculture:** General, agribusiness operations, business. **Biology:** General. **Business:** Administrative services, sales/distribution. **Communications technology:** Graphic/printing. **Computer sciences:** Programming. **Education:** General. **Engineering technology:** Architectural, civil, electrical. **Family/consumer sciences:** Child care, institutional food production. **Foreign languages:** Sign language interpretation. **Health:** Dental hygiene, medical secretary, nursing (RN), substance abuse counseling. **Legal studies:** Legal secretary, paralegal. **Liberal arts:** Arts/sciences. **Math:** General. **Mechanic/repair:** General, aircraft. **Personal/culinary services:** Culinary arts. **Protective services:** Firefighting, forensics. **Psychology:** General. **Public administration:** Human services, social work.

**Computing on campus.** 250 workstations in dormitories, library, computer center, student center. Dormitories wired for high-speed internet access.

**Student life. Freshman orientation:** Mandatory. Preregistration for classes offered. **Housing:** Coed dorms, apartments available. **Activities:** Bands, choral groups, dance, drama, literary magazine, musical theater, radio station, student government, student newspaper, TV station, Christian Fellowship, special interest clubs, Phi Theta Kappa.

**Athletics.** NJCAA. **Intercollegiate:** Baseball M, basketball, softball W, volleyball W. **Intramural:** Basketball, bowling, football (non-tackle), softball, tennis, volleyball. **Team name:** Reivers.

**Student services.** Career counseling, services for economically disadvantaged, student employment services, financial aid counseling, health services, on-campus daycare, placement for graduates, veterans' counselor. **Physically disabled:** Services for visually, speech, hearing impaired. **Transfer:** Pre-admission transcript evaluation for new students. Transfer center, transfer adviser, college fairs on campus for students transferring to 4-year colleges.

**Contact.** E-mail: admissions@iwcc.edu
Phone: (712) 325-3277 Toll-free number: (800) 432-5852
Fax: (712) 325-3720
Chris LaFerla, Director of Admissions, Iowa Western Community College, 2700 College Road, Council Bluffs, IA 51502-3004

---

## Kirkwood Community College
**Cedar Rapids, Iowa**
**www.kirkwood.edu**                          CB code: 6027

- Public 2-year community college
- Commuter campus in small city

**General.** Founded in 1966. Regionally accredited. Off-campus sites in Iowa City, Vinton, Tipton, Williamsburg, Monticello, Washington, Belle Plaine, Marion, Cedar Rapids. **Enrollment:** 15,091 degree-seeking undergraduates. **Degrees:** 1,949 associate awarded. **Location:** 128 miles from Des Moines. **Calendar:** Semester, extensive summer session. **Full-time faculty:** 281 total. **Part-time faculty:** 550 total. **Special facilities:** Telecommunications center, raptor center, equestrian center. **Partnerships:** Formal partnerships with CISCO LAN Management.

**Student profile.**

| | | | |
|---|---|---|---|
| Out-of-state: | 2% | 25 or older: | 27% |

**Transfer out. Colleges most students transferred to 2007:** University of Iowa, University of Northern Iowa, Iowa State University, Mount Mercy College, Coe College.

**Basis for selection.** Open admission, but selective for some programs. Some health science programs require minimum scores on COMPASS exam for admission to program. Interview required of vocational-technical, career option applicants.

**2007-2008 Annual costs.** Tuition/fees: $3,090; $6,180 out-of-state. Per-credit charge: $103 in-state; $206 out-of-state. Books/supplies: $1,410.

**Financial aid. Need-based:** Need-based aid available for part-time students. Work-study available nights, weekends and for part-time students.

**Non-need-based:** Scholarships awarded for art, athletics, leadership, music/drama.

**Application procedures. Admission:** Priority date 3/15; no deadline. No application fee. Application may be submitted online. Admission notification on a rolling basis. **Financial aid:** Priority date 7/1; no closing date. FAFSA required. Applicants notified on a rolling basis starting 4/1.

**Academics. Special study options:** Accelerated study, cooperative education, cross-registration, distance learning, dual enrollment of high school students, ESL, exchange student, external degree, honors, independent study, internships, liberal arts/career combination, student-designed major, study abroad, weekend college. License preparation in dental hygiene, nursing, paramedic, physical therapy, real estate. **Credit/placement by examination:** CLEP, IB, ACT, institutional tests. 21 credit hours maximum toward associate degree. **Support services:** GED preparation and test center, learning center, pre-admission summer program, reduced course load, remedial instruction, study skills assistance, tutoring, writing center.

**Majors. Agriculture:** Equestrian studies, nursery operations, supplies, turf management. **Biology:** Biotechnology. **Business:** Accounting, administrative services, business admin, fashion, finance, office technology, sales/distribution. **Communications technology:** General, graphic/printing. **Computer sciences:** Applications programming. **Conservation:** General. **Construction:** Maintenance, power transmission. **Engineering:** General. **Engineering technology:** Drafting, electrical, surveying. **Family/consumer sciences:** Child care, institutional food production. **Foreign languages:** Sign language interpretation. **Health:** Dental assistant, dental hygiene, dental lab technology, electroencephalograph technology, EMT ambulance attendant, EMT paramedic, medical assistant, medical records technology, medical secretary, nursing (RN), occupational therapy assistant, physical therapy assistant, respiratory therapy technology, surgical technology, veterinary technology/assistant. **Legal studies:** Legal secretary, paralegal. **Liberal arts:** Arts/sciences. **Mechanic/repair:** Automotive, diesel, electronics/electrical. **Personal/culinary services:** Culinary arts. **Protective services:** Fire services admin, firefighting, police science. **Public administration:** Community org/advocacy.

**Computing on campus.** 1,000 workstations in library, computer center, student center. Commuter students can connect to campus network. Online course registration, online library, helpline available.

**Student life. Freshman orientation:** Available. Preregistration for classes offered. Various group sessions held throughout the year. Additional 2-day session held week before fall classes start. **Activities:** Bands, campus ministries, choral groups, drama, film society, literary magazine, music ensembles, musical theater, radio station, student government, student newspaper, symphony orchestra, TV station, over 50 organizations.

**Athletics.** NJCAA. **Intercollegiate:** Baseball M, basketball, golf M, softball W, volleyball W. **Intramural:** Basketball, cheerleading, handball, racquetball, soccer, volleyball. **Team name:** Eagles.

**Student services.** Adult student services, alcohol/substance abuse counseling, career counseling, services for economically disadvantaged, student employment services, financial aid counseling, health services, minority student services, on-campus daycare, personal counseling, placement for graduates, veterans' counselor. **Physically disabled:** Services for visually, speech, hearing impaired. **Learning disabled:** Comprehensive services available. **Transfer:** Pre-admission transcript evaluation for new students. Transfer center, transfer adviser, college fairs on campus for students transferring to 4-year colleges.

**Contact.** E-mail: info@kirkwood.edu
Phone: (319) 398-5517 Toll-free number: (800) 332-2055 ext. 5517
Fax: (319) 398-1244
Doug Bannon, Director of Admissions Services, Kirkwood Community College, 6301 Kirkwood Boulevard SW, Cedar Rapids, IA 52406

---

## Marshalltown Community College
**Marshalltown, Iowa**
**www.marshalltowncommunitycollege.com**   CB code: 6394

- Public 2-year community college
- Residential campus in large town

**General.** Founded in 1927. Regionally accredited. **Enrollment:** 1,078 degree-seeking undergraduates. **Degrees:** 235 associate awarded. **Location:** 50 miles from Des Moines. **Calendar:** Semester, limited summer session. **Full-time faculty:** 44 total. **Part-time faculty:** 79 total. **Special facilities:** Prairie, challenge course.

**Transfer out. Colleges most students transferred to 2007:** Iowa State University, University of Northern Iowa, University of Iowa.

**Basis for selection.** Open admission, but selective for some programs. Special requirements for health career programs. Interview recommended for health careers majors.

**2007-2008 Annual costs.** Tuition/fees: $4,050; $4,890 out-of-district. Per-credit charge: $112 in-state; $140 out-of-state. Room only: $3,750. Books/supplies: $425.

**Application procedures. Admission:** No deadline. No application fee. Admission notification on a rolling basis. **Financial aid:** Priority date 3/1; no closing date. Institutional form required. Applicants notified on a rolling basis starting 6/1; must reply within 2 week(s) of notification.

**Academics. Special study options:** Accelerated study, cooperative education, cross-registration, distance learning, dual enrollment of high school students, ESL, honors, independent study, internships, liberal arts/career combination, study abroad. Bachelor's degree programs available on campus. License preparation in nursing, real estate. **Credit/placement by examination:** AP, CLEP, institutional tests. 30 credit hours maximum toward associate degree. **Support services:** GED preparation and test center, learning center, reduced course load, remedial instruction, study skills assistance, tutoring, writing center.

**Majors. Agriculture:** Business. **Biology:** General, botany. **Business:** General, accounting, administrative services, business admin. **Communications:** Journalism. **Communications technology:** General. **Computer sciences:** General, networking, systems analysis. **Conservation:** Forestry. **Education:** General, elementary, physical, secondary. **Engineering:** General. **Engineering technology:** Drafting. **English:** English lit. **Family/consumer sciences:** General, child care. **Foreign languages:** Spanish. **Health:** Health services, nursing (RN), predental, premedicine, prenursing, prepharmacy, preveterinary, surgical technology. **Legal studies:** Prelaw. **Liberal arts:** Arts/sciences. **Math:** General. **Mechanic/repair:** Heating/ac/refrig, industrial. **Personal/culinary services:** Embalming, mortuary science. **Protective services:** Law enforcement admin, police science. **Psychology:** General. **Public administration:** Community org/advocacy. **Social sciences:** General. **Visual/performing arts:** General, studio arts.

**Most popular majors.** Computer/information sciences 7%, education 8%, health sciences 10%, liberal arts 65%.

**Computing on campus.** 250 workstations in dormitories, library, computer center. Commuter students can connect to campus network. Online library, helpline available.

**Student life. Freshman orientation:** Available. Preregistration for classes offered. **Housing:** Special housing for disabled, apartments available. $300 deposit. **Activities:** Concert band, choral groups, drama, international student organizations, radio station, student government, student newspaper, TV station.

**Athletics.** NJCAA. **Intercollegiate:** Baseball M, basketball, golf, soccer M, softball W. **Intramural:** Basketball, racquetball. **Team name:** Tigers.

**Student services.** Adult student services, career counseling, services for economically disadvantaged, student employment services, financial aid counseling, health services, on-campus daycare, personal counseling, placement for graduates, veterans' counselor. **Physically disabled:** Services for visually, speech, hearing impaired. **Learning disabled:** Comprehensive services available. **Transfer:** College fairs on campus for students transferring to 4-year colleges.

**Contact.** E-mail: dtrawny@iavalley.edu
Phone: (641) 752-7106 ext. 216 Fax: (641) 752-8149
Deana Inman, Director of Admissions, Marshalltown Community College, 3700 South Center Street, Marshalltown, IA 50158

---

a bachelor's degree or higher, 286 enrolled as first-time, first-year students, 30 transferred in from other institutions.

| | | | |
|---|---|---|---|
| Part-time: | 59% | Hispanic American: | 10% |
| Out-of-state: | 5% | Native American: | 2% |
| Women: | 54% | 25 or older: | 31% |
| African American: | 1% | Live on campus: | 3% |
| Asian American: | 1% | | |

**Basis for selection.** Open admission, but selective for some programs. Special requirements for nursing program.

**2007-2008 Annual costs.** Tuition/fees: $3,060; $4,590 out-of-state. Per-credit charge: $102 in-state; $153 out-of-state. Online course tuition: $132 per credit hour. Room only: $3,390. Books/supplies: $900.

**Application procedures. Admission:** No deadline. No application fee. Application may be submitted online. Admission notification on a rolling basis beginning on or about 9/1. **Financial aid:** Priority date 4/20; no closing date. FAFSA required. Applicants notified on a rolling basis starting 5/15; must reply within 2 week(s) of notification.

**Academics. Special study options:** Accelerated study, combined bachelor's/graduate degree, cooperative education, cross-registration, distance learning, double major, dual enrollment of high school students, ESL, honors, independent study, internships, study abroad. Bachelor's degree programs available on campus. License preparation in nursing, real estate. **Credit/placement by examination:** AP, CLEP, institutional tests. 30 credit hours maximum toward associate degree. **Support services:** Learning center, reduced course load, remedial instruction, tutoring.

**Majors. Agriculture:** Supplies. **Business:** Accounting, administrative services, business admin. **Computer sciences:** Applications programming. **Conservation:** General. **Engineering technology:** Computer hardware. **Health:** Nursing (RN). **Liberal arts:** Arts/sciences. **Mechanic/repair:** Heavy equipment, industrial. **Personal/culinary services:** Restaurant/catering.

**Most popular majors.** Agriculture 9%, liberal arts 83%.

**Computing on campus.** 60 workstations in library, computer center. Dormitories wired for high-speed internet access and linked to campus network. Commuter students can connect to campus network. Online course registration, online library, helpline available.

**Student life. Freshman orientation:** Available. Preregistration for classes offered. **Housing:** Apartments, cooperative housing available. **Activities:** Choral groups, drama, film society, music ensembles, student government, student newspaper, TV station, agriculture technology club, All Kinds of People, College Democrats, College Republicans, Delta Epsilon Chi, Business Professionals of America, horticulture club, Phi Theta Kappa, student senate.

**Athletics.** NJCAA. **Intercollegiate:** Baseball M, softball W. **Intramural:** Bowling, football (non-tackle), table tennis. **Team name:** Cardinals.

**Student services.** Adult student services, career counseling, student employment services, financial aid counseling, on-campus daycare, placement for graduates. **Physically disabled:** Services for visually, speech, hearing impaired. **Transfer:** Transfer adviser, college fairs on campus for students transferring to 4-year colleges.

**Contact.** Phone: (563) 288-6000 Toll-free number: (888) 336-3907
Fax: (563) 264-8341
Gary Mohr, Executive Director of External Affairs, Muscatine Community College, 152 Colorado Street, Muscatine, IA 52761-5396

---

## Muscatine Community College
### Muscatine, Iowa
www.eicc.edu
CB code: 6422

- Public 2-year community college
- Commuter campus in large town

**General.** Founded in 1929. Regionally accredited. **Enrollment:** 1,355 degree-seeking undergraduates; 177 non-degree-seeking students. **Degrees:** 188 associate awarded. **Location:** 30 miles from Davenport. **Calendar:** Semester, extensive summer session. **Full-time faculty:** 32 total; 9% minority, 53% women. **Part-time faculty:** 101 total; 8% minority, 57% women. **Class size:** 28% < 20, 4% 20-39, 68% 40-49.

**Student profile.** Among degree-seeking undergraduates, 69% enrolled in a transfer program, 31% enrolled in a vocational program, 1% already have

---

## North Iowa Area Community College
### Mason City, Iowa
www.niacc.edu
CB code: 6400

- Public 2-year community college
- Commuter campus in large town

**General.** Founded in 1918. Regionally accredited. **Enrollment:** 3,100 degree-seeking undergraduates; 172 non-degree-seeking students. **Degrees:** 546 associate awarded. **Location:** 120 miles from Des Moines, 120 miles from Minneapolis-St. Paul. **Calendar:** Semester, limited summer session. **Full-time faculty:** 86 total; 8% have terminal degrees, 2% minority, 37% women. **Part-time faculty:** 77 total; 1% have terminal degrees, 49% women. **Class size:** 65% < 20, 34% 20-39, less than 1% 40-49, less than 1% 50-99. **Special facilities:** Manufacturing technology center, entrepreneurial center, community auditorium, business incubator.

**Student profile.** Among degree-seeking undergraduates, 727 enrolled as first-time, first-year students.

| | | | |
|---|---|---|---|
| Part-time: | 46% | Hispanic American: | 2% |
| Out-of-state: | 6% | International: | 1% |
| Women: | 53% | 25 or older: | 5% |
| African American: | 4% | Live on campus: | 7% |
| Asian American: | 1% | | |

**Transfer out. Colleges most students transferred to 2007:** University of Northern Iowa, Iowa State University, University of Iowa.

**Basis for selection.** Open admission, but selective for some programs. Special admission requirements for nursing and physical therapist assistants.

**2007-2008 Annual costs.** Tuition/fees: $3,363; $4,861 out-of-state. Per-credit charge: $99 in-state; $149 out-of-state. Room/board: $4,280. Books/supplies: $785. Personal expenses: $1,587.

**2006-2007 Financial aid. Need-based:** 602 full-time freshmen applied for aid; 505 were judged to have need; 502 of these received aid. Average need met was 59%. Average scholarship/grant was $2,928; average loan $2,800. 56% of total undergraduate aid awarded as scholarships/grants, 44% as loans/jobs. Need-based aid available for part-time students. Work-study available nights and for part-time students. **Non-need-based:** Scholarships awarded for academics, alumni affiliation, art, athletics, leadership, music/drama.

**Application procedures. Admission:** No deadline. No application fee. Application may be submitted online. Admission notification on a rolling basis. **Financial aid:** Priority date 3/1; no closing date. FAFSA, institutional form required. Applicants notified on a rolling basis starting 4/1; must reply within 2 week(s) of notification.

**Academics. Special study options:** Cooperative education, distance learning, dual enrollment of high school students, honors, independent study, internships, liberal arts/career combination, study abroad. Bachelor's degree programs available on campus. License preparation in real estate. **Credit/placement by examination:** AP, CLEP, institutional tests. 30 credit hours maximum toward associate degree. **Support services:** GED preparation and test center, learning center, remedial instruction, study skills assistance, tutoring, writing center.

**Majors. Agriculture:** General, agribusiness operations, business, farm/ranch, production, supplies. **Business:** Accounting, administrative services, business admin, entrepreneurial studies, hospitality admin. **Computer sciences:** System admin. **Education:** General, early childhood, physical, secondary. **Engineering technology:** Electrical. **Family/consumer sciences:** General. **Health:** Clinical lab technology, EMT paramedic, nursing (RN), physical therapy assistant. **Liberal arts:** Arts/sciences. **Mechanic/repair:** Automotive, heating/ac/refrig, industrial electronics. **Parks/recreation:** Sports admin. **Personal/culinary services:** Mortuary science. **Production:** Machine tool, tool and die. **Protective services:** Fire services admin, police science. **Social sciences:** General, criminology, geography, political science, sociology.

**Computing on campus.** 350 workstations in dormitories, library, computer center. Dormitories wired for high-speed internet access and linked to campus network. Commuter students can connect to campus network. Online library, wireless network available.

**Student life. Freshman orientation:** Mandatory, $25 fee. 5 session online class. **Housing:** Coed dorms, apartments, substance-free housing available. $50 deposit. **Activities:** Bands, choral groups, dance, drama, music ensembles, student government, student newspaper, symphony orchestra, OK House.

**Athletics.** NJCAA. **Intercollegiate:** Baseball M, basketball, cross-country, football (tackle) M, golf, soccer, softball W, track and field, volleyball W, wrestling M. **Intramural:** Basketball, bowling, football (non-tackle), soccer, softball, volleyball. **Team name:** Trojans.

**Student services.** Adult student services, alcohol/substance abuse counseling, career counseling, student employment services, financial aid counseling, health services, personal counseling, placement for graduates, veterans' counselor. **Physically disabled:** Services for visually, speech, hearing impaired. **Transfer:** Transfer adviser, college fairs on campus for students transferring to 4-year colleges.

**Contact.** E-mail: request@niacc.cc.ia.us
Phone: (641) 422-4245 Toll-free number: (888) 466-4222 ext. 4245
Fax: (641) 422-4385
Rachel McGuire, Director of Admissions, North Iowa Area Community College, 500 College Drive, Mason City, IA 50401

---

### Northeast Iowa Community College
Calmar, Iowa     **CB member**
www.nicc.edu     **CB code: 6751**

- Public 2-year community college
- Commuter campus in rural community

**General.** Founded in 1966. Regionally accredited. Branch campus at Peosta, 10 miles from Dubuque. **Enrollment:** 3,028 degree-seeking undergraduates; 1,782 non-degree-seeking students. **Degrees:** 537 associate awarded. **Location:** 60 miles from Waterloo. **Calendar:** Semester, extensive summer session. **Full-time faculty:** 118 total; 6% have terminal degrees, 61% women. **Part-time faculty:** 58 total; 5% have terminal degrees, 72% women.

**Student profile.** Among degree-seeking undergraduates, 37% enrolled in a transfer program, 63% enrolled in a vocational program, 784 enrolled as first-time, first-year students, 323 transferred in from other institutions.

| | | | |
|---|---|---|---|
| Part-time: | 33% | African American: | 2% |
| Out-of-state: | 12% | Hispanic American: | 1% |
| Women: | 64% | 25 or older: | 35% |

**Transfer out. Colleges most students transferred to 2007:** University of Northern Iowa-Cedar Fall, Loras College, Clarke College, University of Dubuque.

**Basis for selection.** Open admission, but selective for some programs. Health students required to meet program specific admission criteria. All degree seeking students required to submit placement test scores and/or prior college coursework.

**2008-2009 Annual costs.** Tuition/fees (projected): $4,050. Per-credit charge: $121. Books/supplies: $1,300. Personal expenses: $1,652.

**Financial aid. Need-based:** Need-based aid available for part-time students. Work-study available nights and for part-time students. **Non-need-based:** Scholarships awarded for academics, leadership.

**Application procedures. Admission:** No deadline. No application fee. Application may be submitted online. Admission notification on a rolling basis. **Financial aid:** Priority date 7/1; no closing date. FAFSA required. Applicants notified on a rolling basis starting 5/1.

**Academics.** Dental assisting certification exam given on-campus. **Special study options:** Cooperative education, distance learning, double major, dual enrollment of high school students, ESL, independent study, internships, student-designed major, study abroad. **Credit/placement by examination:** AP, CLEP. **Support services:** GED preparation and test center, learning center, reduced course load, remedial instruction, study skills assistance, tutoring, writing center.

**Majors. Agriculture:** Agribusiness operations, crop production, dairy husbandry, horticultural science, power machinery, production, products processing, supplies. **Business:** Accounting, administrative services, business admin, office technology, sales/distribution. **Computer sciences:** Applications programming. **Construction:** General, carpentry, electrician, plumbing. **Engineering technology:** Electrical. **Health:** Clinical lab technology, EMT paramedic, massage therapy, medical records technology, nursing (RN), radiologic technology/medical imaging, respiratory therapy technology. **Liberal arts:** Arts/sciences. **Mechanic/repair:** Automotive. **Personal/culinary services:** Cosmetic. **Public administration:** Community org/advocacy, social work.

**Most popular majors.** Agriculture 9%, business/marketing 13%, health sciences 33%, liberal arts 35%.

**Computing on campus.** 800 workstations in library, computer center. Helpline, repair service, wireless network available.

**Student life. Freshman orientation:** Available. One day program with different interest sessions available. **Activities:** Student government, student newspaper.

**Athletics. Intramural:** Basketball, bowling, golf, skiing, softball, volleyball. **Team name:** Cougars.

**Student services.** Adult student services, alcohol/substance abuse counseling, career counseling, services for economically disadvantaged, student employment services, financial aid counseling, health services, on-campus daycare, personal counseling, placement for graduates, veterans' counselor, women's services. **Physically disabled:** Services for visually, speech, hearing impaired. **Transfer:** Pre-admission transcript evaluation for new students. Transfer adviser, college fairs on campus for students transferring to 4-year colleges.

**Contact.** Phone: (563) 562-3263 ext. 234 Toll-free number: (800) 778-2256 ext. 234 Fax: (563) 562-4369 Kristi Strief, Admissions Manager, Northeast Iowa Community College, Box 400, Calmar, IA 52132

## Northwest Iowa Community College
Sheldon, Iowa
www.nwicc.edu

CB code: 1359

- Public 2-year community college
- Commuter campus in small town

**General.** Founded in 1966. Regionally accredited. **Location:** 60 miles from Sioux City, 65 miles from Sioux Falls. **Calendar:** Semester.

**Annual costs/financial aid.** Tuition/fees (2007-2008): $3,900; $5,130 out-of-state. Room/board: $3,200. Books/supplies: $716. Personal expenses: $854. Need-based financial aid available to full-time and part-time students.

**Contact.** Phone: (712) 324-5061 Director of Admissions, 603 West Park Street, Sheldon, IA 51201

## St. Luke's College
Sioux City, Iowa
www.stlukescollege.edu

CB code: 3625

- Private 2-year health science college affiliated with Lutheran and Methodist churches
- Commuter campus in small city
- ACT (writing optional), application essay, interview required

**General.** Regionally accredited. Offers hospital-based health care provider programs. **Enrollment:** 148 degree-seeking undergraduates. **Degrees:** 60 associate awarded. **Location:** 90 miles from Omaha. **Calendar:** Semester, limited summer session. **Full-time faculty:** 17 total. **Part-time faculty:** 9 total. **Class size:** 77% < 20, 23% 20-39.

**Student profile.** Among degree-seeking undergraduates, 24% enrolled in a transfer program, 7% already have a bachelor's degree or higher, 1 enrolled as first-time, first-year students.

| | | | |
|---|---|---|---|
| Part-time: | 47% | Hispanic American: | 5% |
| Women: | 91% | 25 or older: | 29% |
| Asian American: | 1% | | |

**Transfer out.** 72% of students enrolled in the transfer program go on to 4-year colleges. **Colleges most students transferred to 2007:** Morningside College, Briar Cliff College, Western Iowa Tech Community College, Dordt College.

**Basis for selection.** Professional programs require 2.5 GPA or GED and 19 ACT. Pre-professional programs require only one of criteria listed above. ASSET test required of all enrolled students. **Learning Disabled:** Job shadowing recommended.

**High school preparation.** 8 units recommended. Recommended units include English 4, mathematics 2 and science 2. Electives recommended include psychology, computer operations, typing, or keyboarding.

**2008-2009 Annual costs.** Tuition/fees: $13,725. Per-credit charge: $375. Summer general fee: $125. Books/supplies: $1,250. Personal expenses: $1,245.

**2007-2008 Financial aid.** **Need-based:** 1 full-time freshmen applied for aid; 1 were judged to have need; 1 of these received aid. Average scholarship/grant was $1,500; average loan $5,000. 25% of total undergraduate aid awarded as scholarships/grants, 75% as loans/jobs. Need-based aid available for part-time students. Work-study available nights, weekends and for part-time students. **Non-need-based:** Awarded to 32 full-time undergraduates, including 1 freshmen. Scholarships awarded for academics, job skills, leadership.

**Application procedures.** **Admission:** Priority date 11/1; deadline 8/15 (receipt date). $100 fee. Application may be submitted online. **Financial aid:** Priority date 3/1; no closing date. FAFSA required. Applicants notified on a rolling basis starting 4/1; must reply within 2 week(s) of notification.

**Academics.** Students can attend any bachelor's nursing program in Iowa after graduating with associate degree in nursing. Local college offers students access to learning and writing center. **Special study options:** Combined bachelor's/graduate degree, internships. License preparation in nursing, radiology. **Credit/placement by examination:** AP, CLEP. 22 credit hours maximum toward associate degree. **Support services:** Learning center, reduced course load, study skills assistance, tutoring.

**Majors. Health:** Medical radiologic technology/radiation therapy, nursing (RN), respiratory therapy technology.

**Computing on campus.** 18 workstations in library, computer center, student center. Online library, helpline, wireless network available.

**Student life. Freshman orientation:** Mandatory, $20 fee. Preregistration for classes offered. Held week prior to classes. Additional sessions held during first semester for freshmen. **Policies:** Alcohol and drug-free campus. **Activities:** Student government, community service.

**Student services.** Alcohol/substance abuse counseling, campus ministries, student employment services, financial aid counseling, health services, on-campus daycare, personal counseling. **Transfer:** Pre-admission transcript evaluation for new students.

**Contact.** E-mail: mccartsj@stlukes.org Phone: (712) 279-3158 Toll-free number: (800) 352-4660 ext. 3158 Fax: (712) 233-8017 Sherry McCarthy, Enrollment Coordinator, St. Luke's College, 2720 Stone Park Boulevard, Sioux City, IA 51104

## Scott Community College
Bettendorf, Iowa
www.eicc.edu

CB code: 0282

- Public 2-year community college
- Commuter campus in small city

**General.** Founded in 1966. Regionally accredited. **Enrollment:** 3,954 degree-seeking undergraduates; 603 non-degree-seeking students. **Degrees:** 752 associate awarded. **Location:** 3 miles from Davenport. **Calendar:** Semester, extensive summer session. **Full-time faculty:** 80 total; 6% minority, 52% women. **Part-time faculty:** 252 total; 8% minority, 58% women. **Class size:** 80% < 20, 20% 20-39, less than 1% 40-49, less than 1% 50-99.

**Student profile.** Among degree-seeking undergraduates, 53% enrolled in a transfer program, 47% enrolled in a vocational program, 2% already have a bachelor's degree or higher, 823 enrolled as first-time, first-year students, 72 transferred in from other institutions.

| | | | |
|---|---|---|---|
| Part-time: | 52% | Hispanic American: | 5% |
| Out-of-state: | 10% | Native American: | 1% |
| Women: | 62% | International: | 1% |
| African American: | 9% | 25 or older: | 38% |
| Asian American: | 2% | | |

**Transfer out. Colleges most students transferred to 2007:** University of Iowa, Iowa State University, University of Northern Iowa, St. Ambrose University, Western Illinois University.

**Basis for selection.** Open admission, but selective for some programs. Admission to some programs, particularly health occupations, based on academic achievement and previous courses. Interview required for radiologic technology and medical laboratory technician; recommended for nursing, electroneuro diagnostic technology and pharmacy technician.

**2007-2008 Annual costs.** Tuition/fees: $3,060; $4,590 out-of-state. Per-credit charge: $102 in-state; $153 out-of-state. Books/supplies: $1,140. Personal expenses: $1,090.

**Application procedures. Admission:** No deadline. No application fee. Application may be submitted online. Admission notification on a rolling basis beginning on or about 9/1. **Financial aid:** Priority date 4/20; no closing date. FAFSA required. Applicants notified on a rolling basis starting 5/15; must reply within 2 week(s) of notification.

**Academics. Special study options:** Accelerated study, combined bachelor's/graduate degree, cooperative education, cross-registration, distance learning, double major, dual enrollment of high school students, ESL, honors, independent study, internships, liberal arts/career combination, study abroad, weekend college. License preparation in nursing, real estate. **Credit/placement by examination:** AP, CLEP, institutional tests. 30 credit hours maximum toward associate degree. **Support services:** GED preparation and test center, learning center, reduced course load, remedial instruction, tutoring.

**Majors. Business:** Accounting, administrative services. **Communications technology:** General. **Computer sciences:** Applications programming. **Foreign languages:** Sign language interpretation. **Health:** Clinical lab technology, medical radiologic technology/radiation therapy, nursing (RN), pharmacy assistant. **Mechanic/repair:** Auto body, automotive, diesel, heating/ac/refrig. **Personal/culinary services:** Culinary arts, restaurant/catering.

**Most popular majors.** Business/marketing 9%, health sciences 23%, liberal arts 53%, trade and industry 6%.

**Computing on campus.** 125 workstations in library, computer center, student center. Commuter students can connect to campus network. Online course registration, helpline, wireless network available.

**Student life. Freshman orientation:** Available. Preregistration for classes offered. **Activities:** Film society, international student organizations, literary magazine, student government, student newspaper, auto collision repair club, volunteer club, Phi Theta Kappa, nursing club, RadTech club, environmental club, dental assisting club.

**Athletics. Intercollegiate:** Golf, soccer. **Team name:** Eagles.

**Student services.** Career counseling, student employment services, financial aid counseling, on-campus daycare, personal counseling, placement for graduates, veterans' counselor. **Physically disabled:** Services for visually, speech, hearing impaired. **Transfer:** Transfer adviser, college fairs on campus for students transferring to 4-year colleges.

**Contact.** Phone: (563) 441-4004 Toll-free number: (888) 336-3907 Fax: (563) 441-4101
Gary Mohr, Admissions Officer, Scott Community College, 500 Belmont Road, Bettendorf, IA 52722-6804

---

## Southeastern Community College: North Campus

**West Burlington, Iowa**
**www.scciowa.edu**                    CB code: 6048

▸ Public 2-year community and junior college
▸ Commuter campus in large town

**General.** Founded in 1966. Regionally accredited. Campuses in West Burlington, Keokuk, Mt. Pleasant, and Ft. Madison. **Enrollment:** 2,404 degree-seeking undergraduates; 947 non-degree-seeking students. **Degrees:** 462 associate awarded. **Location:** 200 miles from Des Moines, 300 miles from Chicago. **Calendar:** Semester, limited summer session. **Full-time faculty:** 83 total; 8% have terminal degrees, 2% minority, 48% women. **Part-time faculty:** 151 total; 7% minority, 65% women. **Class size:** 67% < 20, 30% 20-39, 2% 40-49, less than 1% 50-99. **Special facilities:** Greenhouse, college operated farm.

**Student profile.** Among degree-seeking undergraduates, 410 enrolled as first-time, first-year students, 16 transferred in from other institutions.

| | | | |
|---|---|---|---|
| Part-time: | 30% | 25 or older: | 34% |
| Out-of-state: | 16% | Live on campus: | 3% |
| Women: | 65% | | |

**Transfer out. Colleges most students transferred to 2007:** University of Iowa, Western Illinois University, Iowa State University, University of Northern Iowa, Iowa Wesleyan College.

**Basis for selection.** Open admission, but selective for some programs. Special requirements for nursing, electronic technology, medical assistant, medical coding and billing, medical transcription, chemical dependency counselor, EMT- Paramedic, and respiratory care.

**2007-2008 Annual costs.** Tuition/fees: $3,210; $3,570 out-of-state. Per-credit charge: $107 in-state; $119 out-of-state.

**2006-2007 Financial aid. Need-based:** 332 full-time freshmen applied for aid; 332 were judged to have need; 321 of these received aid. Average scholarship/grant was $3,633; average loan $2,635. 55% of total undergraduate aid awarded as scholarships/grants, 45% as loans/jobs. Need-based aid available for part-time students. **Non-need-based:** Scholarships awarded for academics, art, athletics, minority status.

**Application procedures. Admission:** No deadline. No application fee. Application may be submitted online. Admission notification on a rolling basis. **Financial aid:** Priority date 7/1; no closing date. FAFSA required. Applicants notified on a rolling basis starting 3/1; must reply within 4 week(s) of notification.

**Academics. Special study options:** Combined bachelor's/graduate degree, cooperative education, cross-registration, distance learning, dual enrollment of high school students, ESL, independent study, internships, weekend college. Bachelor's degree programs available on campus. License preparation in dental hygiene, nursing, occupational therapy, paramedic, physical therapy, radiology, real estate. **Credit/placement by examination:** AP, CLEP, ACT, institutional tests. 30 credit hours maximum toward associate degree. **Support services:** GED preparation and test center, learning center,

pre-admission summer program, reduced course load, remedial instruction, study skills assistance, tutoring.

**Majors. Agriculture:** General, business, supplies. **Business:** General, accounting, administrative services, business admin, construction management, executive assistant, office management, office technology, office/clerical, receptionist. **Communications:** Digital media, journalism. **Communications technology:** Desktop publishing, graphics. **Computer sciences:** Computer graphics, data processing, networking, programming, web page design. **Construction:** Carpentry, maintenance. **Engineering:** Electrical, mechanics. **Engineering technology:** Construction, drafting, electrical, robotics. **Family/consumer sciences:** Child care. **Health:** EMT paramedic, medical assistant, medical radiologic technology/radiation therapy, nursing (RN), substance abuse counseling. **Legal studies:** Legal secretary. **Liberal arts:** Arts/sciences. **Mechanic/repair:** General. **Production:** General, machine tool, tool and die. **Protective services:** Law enforcement admin. **Public administration:** Human services.

**Most popular majors.** Business/marketing 12%, health sciences 19%, liberal arts 51%.

**Computing on campus.** 100 workstations in library, computer center. Dormitories wired for high-speed internet access. Helpline, wireless network available.

**Student life. Freshman orientation:** Mandatory. Preregistration for classes offered. Two-hour session offered both day and evening before term begins. **Housing:** Coed dorms, single-sex dorms, special housing for disabled, apartments, substance-free housing available. $300 fully refundable deposit, deadline 10/26. **Activities:** Jazz band, campus ministries, choral groups, drama, international student organizations, literary magazine, music ensembles, musical theater, student government, student newspaper, symphony orchestra, Campus Crusade for Christ, multicultural club.

**Athletics. NJCAA. Intercollegiate:** Baseball M, basketball, golf, softball W, volleyball W. **Intramural:** Basketball, bowling, cheerleading, football (non-tackle), softball, volleyball. **Team name:** Black Hawks.

**Student services.** Career counseling, services for economically disadvantaged, student employment services, financial aid counseling, minority student services, on-campus daycare, personal counseling, placement for graduates, veterans' counselor. **Physically disabled:** Services for visually, speech, hearing impaired. **Learning disabled:** Comprehensive services available. **Transfer:** Pre-admission transcript evaluation for new students. Transfer adviser, college fairs on campus for students transferring to 4-year colleges.

**Contact.** E-mail: admoff@scciowa.edu
Phone: (319) 752-2731 ext. 5012 Toll-free number: (866) 722-4692 ext. 5012 Fax: (319) 758-6725
Dana Chrisman, Senior Enrollment Officer, Southeastern Community College: North Campus, 1500 West Agency Road, West Burlington, IA 52655-0605

---

## Southeastern Community College: South Campus

**Keokuk, Iowa**
**www.scciowa.edu**                    CB code: 6340

▸ Public 2-year community college
▸ Commuter campus in large town

**General.** Founded in 1966. Regionally accredited. **Location:** 45 miles from Burlington, 45 miles from Quincy, Illinois. **Calendar:** Semester.

**Annual costs/financial aid.** Tuition/fees (2007-2008): $3,210; $3,570 out-of-state. Books/supplies: $600. Need-based financial aid available to full-time and part-time students.

**Contact.** Phone: (319) 524-3221 ext. 8416
Senior Enrollment Officer, Box 6007, Keokuk, IA 52632-6007

---

## Southwestern Community College

**Creston, Iowa**
**www.swcciowa.edu**                    CB code: 6122

▸ Public 2-year community college
▸ Commuter campus in small town

**General.** Founded in 1966. Regionally accredited. **Enrollment:** 1,019 degree-seeking undergraduates. **Degrees:** 187 associate awarded. **Location:** 75 miles from Des Moines; 110 miles from Omaha, Nebraska. **Calendar:** Semester, limited summer session. **Full-time faculty:** 48 total; 4% have terminal degrees, 48% women. **Part-time faculty:** 71 total; 8% have terminal degrees, 1% minority, 51% women. **Class size:** 79% < 20, 18% 20-39, 2% 40-49, 1% 50-99. **Special facilities:** Recording studio.

### Student profile.

| | | | |
|---|---|---|---|
| Out-of-state: | 4% | Live on campus: | 5% |
| 25 or older: | 38% | | |

**Transfer out. Colleges most students transferred to 2007:** Northwest Missouri State University, Buena Vista University, Iowa State University, Graceland College, University of Northern Iowa.

**Basis for selection.** Open admission, but selective for some programs. Special requirements for nursing. LPN criteria includes date nursing application is received and date COMPASS test scores are achieved. ADN requirements are contingent on the application, COMPASS test scores, and a ranking selection process. **Adult students:** Students must take COMPASS test for placement.

**High school preparation.** One chemistry required for health programs.

**2007-2008 Annual costs.** Tuition/fees: $3,920; $4,934 out-of-state. Per-credit charge: $123 in-state; $155 out-of-state. Room/board: $4,500. Books/supplies: $600. Personal expenses: $1,500.

**Financial aid. Need-based:** Need-based aid available for part-time students. Work-study available nights, weekends and for part-time students. **Non-need-based:** Scholarships awarded for academics, athletics, leadership, music/drama, state residency.

**Application procedures. Admission:** Priority date 8/1; no deadline. No application fee. Application may be submitted online. Admission notification on a rolling basis. **Financial aid:** Priority date 7/1; no closing date. FAFSA required. Applicants notified on a rolling basis starting 6/1; must reply within 2 week(s) of notification.

**Academics. Special study options:** Cooperative education, distance learning, double major, dual enrollment of high school students, independent study, internships, liberal arts/career combination. License preparation in nursing. **Credit/placement by examination:** AP, CLEP. 30 credit hours maximum toward associate degree. Arts and science students without ACT composite score of 19 or above required to take ASSET exam. **Support services:** GED preparation and test center, learning center, reduced course load, remedial instruction, study skills assistance, tutoring.

**Majors. Agriculture:** Business, production. **Business:** General, accounting, administrative services, marketing. **Computer sciences:** Applications programming, information systems, webmaster. **Construction:** Carpentry. **Education:** General. **Engineering technology:** Drafting, electrical. **Health:** Medical transcription, nursing (RN). **Liberal arts:** Arts/sciences. **Mechanic/repair:** Auto body, electronics/electrical. **Visual/performing arts:** Music performance.

**Most popular majors.** Business/marketing 10%, computer/information sciences 6%, health sciences 20%, liberal arts 43%, trade and industry 12%.

**Computing on campus.** 140 workstations in dormitories, library, computer center, student center. Dormitories wired for high-speed internet access and linked to campus network. Helpline, repair service, wireless network available.

**Student life. Freshman orientation:** Mandatory. Preregistration for classes offered. **Housing:** Coed dorms, single-sex dorms, substance-free housing available. $100 deposit. **Activities:** Bands, choral groups, music ensembles, student government, student newspaper.

**Athletics.** NJCAA. **Intercollegiate:** Baseball M, basketball, cross-country, golf M, softball W, volleyball W. **Intramural:** Basketball, table tennis, tennis, volleyball. **Team name:** Spartans.

**Student services.** Adult student services, career counseling, services for economically disadvantaged, student employment services, health services, legal services, personal counseling, placement for graduates, veterans' counselor. **Physically disabled:** Services for visually, speech, hearing impaired. **Transfer:** Pre-admission transcript evaluation for new students. Transfer adviser, college fairs on campus for students transferring to 4-year colleges.

**Contact.** E-mail: carstens@swcciowa.edu
Phone: (641) 782-7081 ext. 421 Toll-free number: (800) 247-4023
Fax: (641) 782-3312
Lisa Carstens, Director of Admissions, Southwestern Community College, 1501 West Townline Street, Creston, IA 50801

---

## Vatterott College
### Des Moines, Iowa
### www.vatterott-college.edu
**CB code: 2909**

▸ For-profit 2-year health science and technical college
▸ Commuter campus in large city

**General.** Accredited by ACCSCT. **Calendar:** Continuous.

**Annual costs/financial aid.** Program cost ranges: $9,275 to $21,405 (certificate/diploma); $24,974 to $29,860 (associate degree). Need-based financial aid available for full-time students.

**Contact.** Phone: (515) 309-9000
Director of Admissions, 6100 Thornton, Suite 290, Des Moines, IA 50321

---

## Western Iowa Tech Community College
### Sioux City, Iowa
### www.witcc.com
**CB member**
**CB code: 6950**

▸ Public 2-year community college
▸ Commuter campus in small city

**General.** Founded in 1966. Regionally accredited. Most programs require attendance for at least 4 semester terms. **Enrollment:** 2,444 degree-seeking undergraduates; 2,747 non-degree-seeking students. **Degrees:** 485 associate awarded. **Location:** 200 miles from Des Moines; 90 miles from Omaha, Nebraska. **Calendar:** Semester, extensive summer session. **Full-time faculty:** 83 total; 6% minority, 55% women. **Part-time faculty:** 141 total; 11% minority, 57% women. **Class size:** 81% < 20, 17% 20-39, 1% 40-49, less than 1% 50-99, less than 1% >100.

**Student profile.** Among degree-seeking undergraduates, 35% enrolled in a transfer program, 65% enrolled in a vocational program, 1% already have a bachelor's degree or higher, 408 enrolled as first-time, first-year students.

| | | | |
|---|---|---|---|
| Part-time: | 37% | 25 or older: | 28% |
| Out-of-state: | 10% | Live on campus: | 3% |
| Women: | 64% | | |

**Transfer out. Colleges most students transferred to 2007:** Iowa State University, Briar Cliff College, Morningside College, University of Northern Iowa, Bellevue University.

**Basis for selection.** Open admission, but selective for some programs. Special requirements for nursing, surgical technician, dental assistant, physical therapy assistant, childcare supervision and management, emergency medical technician, police science, and business. LOPE used for placement. Computerized placement test (CPT or ACT) required of all diploma and degree-seeking students and of all students taking English composition and mathematics courses.

**High school preparation.** Recommended units include English 4, mathematics 2, social studies 2, history 2, science 2 and foreign language 1.

**2008-2009 Annual costs.** Tuition/fees (projected): $3,675; $4,455 out-of-state. Per-credit charge: $107 in-state; $133 out-of-state. Room/board: $4,900. Books/supplies: $900. Personal expenses: $1,170.

**2006-2007 Financial aid. Need-based:** 39% of total undergraduate aid awarded as scholarships/grants, 61% as loans/jobs. Need-based aid available for part-time students. Work-study available nights, weekends and for part-time students. **Non-need-based:** Scholarships awarded for academics, leadership, music/drama.

**Application procedures. Admission:** No deadline. $20 fee. Application may be submitted online. Admission notification on a rolling basis. **Financial aid:** No deadline. FAFSA required. Applicants notified on a rolling basis starting 4/1.

**Academics. Special study options:** Accelerated study, distance learning, double major, dual enrollment of high school students, ESL, honors, independent study, internships. License preparation in paramedic. **Credit/placement by examination:** AP, CLEP, institutional tests. **Support services:** GED preparation and test center, learning center, pre-admission summer program, reduced course load, remedial instruction, study skills assistance, tutoring.

**Majors. Agriculture:** Supplies, turf management. **Biology:** Biotechnology. **Business:** Accounting, administrative services, business admin, finance, human resources, office technology, sales/distribution. **Communications technology:** Desktop publishing. **Computer sciences:** A.i./robotics, web page design. **Engineering technology:** Architectural, mechanical drafting, telecommunications. **Health:** Clinical lab technology, dental hygiene, EMT paramedic, medical secretary, nursing (RN), office admin, physical therapy assistant, surgical technology. **Legal studies:** Legal secretary. **Liberal arts:** Arts/sciences. **Mechanic/repair:** Auto body, automotive, industrial, musical instruments. **Protective services:** Juvenile corrections, police science. **Other:** Multiinterdisciplinary technical study.

**Most popular majors.** Business/marketing 14%, engineering/engineering technologies 7%, health sciences 25%, liberal arts 30%, security/protective services 7%.

**Computing on campus.** 1,700 workstations in dormitories, library, computer center, student center. Dormitories wired for high-speed internet access and linked to campus network. Commuter students can connect to campus network. Online course registration, online library, helpline, wireless network available.

**Student life. Freshman orientation:** Available. Preregistration for classes offered. **Housing:** Apartments available. $100 deposit. **Activities:** Choral groups, drama, music ensembles, student government, celebrations, multicultural group, sociology club.

**Athletics. Intramural:** Golf, volleyball.

**Student services.** Adult student services, career counseling, services for economically disadvantaged, student employment services, health services, personal counseling, placement for graduates. **Physically disabled:** Services for visually, speech, hearing impaired. **Transfer:** Transfer center, transfer adviser, college fairs on campus for students transferring to 4-year colleges.

**Contact.** Phone: (712) 274-6403 Toll-free
number: (800) 352-4649 ext. 6403 Fax: (712) 274-6441
Lora VanderZwaag, Director of Admissions, Western Iowa Tech
Community College, Box 5199, Sioux City, IA 51102-5199

# Kansas

## Allen County Community College
### Iola, Kansas
### www.allencc.edu
### CB code: 6305

▶ Public 2-year community college
▶ Commuter campus in small town

**General.** Founded in 1923. Regionally accredited. Two campuses available to serve students in rural or metropolitan area. **Enrollment:** 2,800 degree-seeking undergraduates. **Degrees:** 241 associate awarded. **Location:** 100 miles from Kansas City. **Calendar:** Semester, limited summer session. **Full-time faculty:** 30 total. **Part-time faculty:** 140 total. **Special facilities:** College-operated farm.

### Student profile.

| | | | |
|---|---|---|---|
| Out-of-state: | 3% | Live on campus: | 20% |
| 25 or older: | 31% | | |

**Transfer out. Colleges most students transferred to 2007:** Pittsburg State University, Kansas State University, Emporia State University, University of Kansas, Washburn University.

**Basis for selection.** Open admission. TOEFL score of 520 or higher required for admission of non-English-speaking students. Placement test required. **Homeschooled:** Transcript of courses and grades required. Placement test required (ACT, COMPASS or ASSET). **Learning Disabled:** Copies of a high school IEP are helpful, but not necessary.

**2007-2008 Annual costs.** Tuition/fees: $1,650; $1,740 out-of-district; $1,740 out-of-state. Per-credit charge: $39 in-district; $42 out-of-district; $42 out-of-state. Room/board: $3,800. Books/supplies: $300. Personal expenses: $1,620.

**Financial aid. Need-based:** Need-based aid available for part-time students. Work-study available nights and weekends. **Non-need-based:** Scholarships awarded for academics, art, athletics, music/drama, state residency. **Additional information:** Scholarships for livestock judging, cheerleading, choir, dance, drama, art, academic challenge, and student ambassadors.

**Application procedures. Admission:** No deadline. No application fee. Application may be submitted online. Admission notification on a rolling basis. **Financial aid:** Closing date 8/1. FAFSA required. Applicants notified on a rolling basis starting 6/1; must reply within 2 week(s) of notification.

**Academics. Special study options:** Cooperative education, distance learning, double major, dual enrollment of high school students, independent study, internships, liberal arts/career combination, student-designed major, weekend college. Bachelor's degree programs available on campus. **Credit/placement by examination:** AP, CLEP, institutional tests. 12 credit hours maximum toward associate degree. **Support services:** GED preparation and test center, learning center, reduced course load, remedial instruction, study skills assistance, tutoring, writing center.

**Majors. Agriculture:** Farm/ranch. **Biology:** General. **Business:** Accounting, administrative services, business admin, office management, sales/distribution. **Computer sciences:** General, computer science. **Education:** Mathematics, music, secondary. **Engineering:** Electrical. **Engineering technology:** Drafting. **Health:** EMT paramedic, nursing assistant. **History:** General. **Liberal arts:** Library science. **Math:** General. **Mechanic/repair:** Electronics/electrical. **Physical sciences:** Chemistry, physics. **Production:** Woodworking. **Protective services:** Police science. **Social sciences:** Economics, geography, sociology. **Visual/performing arts:** Art, ceramics, crafts, drawing, painting, studio arts, voice/opera.

**Most popular majors.** Business/marketing 28%, communications/journalism 16%, education 12%, health sciences 12%, liberal arts 13%.

**Computing on campus.** 100 workstations in dormitories, library, computer center, student center. Dormitories wired for high-speed internet access. Online library, repair service, wireless network available.

**Student life. Freshman orientation:** Mandatory. Preregistration for classes offered. **Housing:** Coed dorms, apartments available. $125 fully refundable deposit, deadline 7/7. **Activities:** Bands, choral groups, dance, drama, music ensembles, musical theater, student government, Aggie Club, biology club, Phi Theta Kappa.

**Athletics.** NJCAA. **Intercollegiate:** Baseball M, basketball, cheerleading, cross-country, golf, soccer, softball W, track and field, volleyball W. **Intramural:** Basketball, football (non-tackle), softball, table tennis, tennis, volleyball. **Team name:** Red Devils.

**Student services.** Adult student services, alcohol/substance abuse counseling, career counseling, services for economically disadvantaged, student employment services, financial aid counseling, minority student services, personal counseling, placement for graduates, veterans' counselor, women's services. **Physically disabled:** Services for visually, hearing impaired. **Transfer:** Pre-admission transcript evaluation for new students. Transfer adviser, college fairs on campus for students transferring to 4-year colleges.

**Contact.** E-mail: weber@allencc.edu
Phone: (620) 365-5116 ext. 268 Fax: (620) 365-3284
Randy Weber, Admissions Director, Allen County Community College, 1801 North Cottonwood, Iola, KS 66749

## Barton County Community College
### Great Bend, Kansas
### www.bartonccc.edu
### CB code: 0784

▶ Public 2-year community college
▶ Commuter campus in large town

**General.** Founded in 1965. Regionally accredited. **Enrollment:** 3,057 degree-seeking undergraduates; 843 non-degree-seeking students. **Degrees:** 340 associate awarded. **Location:** 125 miles from Wichita. **Calendar:** Semester, limited summer session. **Full-time faculty:** 72 total; 7% have terminal degrees, 4% minority, 42% women. **Part-time faculty:** 110 total; 2% have terminal degrees, 6% minority, 57% women. **Class size:** 79% < 20, 20% 20-39, 1% 40-49, less than 1% 50-99. **Special facilities:** Natatorium, planetarium.

**Student profile.** Among degree-seeking undergraduates, 1,172 enrolled as first-time, first-year students.

| | | | |
|---|---|---|---|
| Part-time: | 69% | 25 or older: | 46% |
| Out-of-state: | 5% | Live on campus: | 8% |
| Women: | 49% | | |

**Transfer out. Colleges most students transferred to 2007:** Fort Hays State University, Kansas State University, University of Kansas, Wichita State University, Emporia State University.

**Basis for selection.** Open admission, but selective for some programs. Special requirements for medical laboratory technician, nursing, and mobile intensive care technician programs. ACT, SAT, ASSET or ACCUPLACER required for placement in math or English courses. Interview required of nursing majors.

**2007-2008 Annual costs.** Tuition/fees: $2,010; $2,580 out-of-state. Per-credit charge: $49 in-state; $68 out-of-state. Room/board: $3,854. Books/supplies: $830. Personal expenses: $3,042.

**2006-2007 Financial aid. Need-based:** 58% of total undergraduate aid awarded as scholarships/grants, 42% as loans/jobs. Need-based aid available for part-time students. **Non-need-based:** Scholarships awarded for academics, athletics.

**Application procedures. Admission:** No deadline. No application fee. Application must be submitted on paper. Admission notification on a rolling basis. **Financial aid:** Priority date 3/1; no closing date. FAFSA required. Applicants notified on a rolling basis starting 6/1; must reply within 4 week(s) of notification.

**Academics. Special study options:** Accelerated study, cooperative education, distance learning, dual enrollment of high school students, ESL, honors, independent study, internships. License preparation in nursing, paramedic, real estate. **Credit/placement by examination:** AP, CLEP, IB, institutional tests. ACT, SAT, ASSET, or ACCUPLACER is required for enrollment in Math or English coursework. **Support services:** GED preparation and test center, learning center, remedial instruction, tutoring.

**Majors. Agriculture:** General, production. **Biology:** General, wildlife. **Business:** General, accounting, accounting technology, administrative services, human resources, operations. **Communications:** General, journalism. **Computer sciences:** Computer science, data processing, information systems.

**Conservation:** Forestry. **Education:** General. **Engineering:** General. **Engineering technology:** Computer systems, hazardous materials. **English:** English lit. **Family/consumer sciences:** Child care. **Foreign languages:** General. **Health:** Athletic training, clinical lab science, clinical lab technology, dietician assistant, EMT paramedic, health services, medical assistant, medical records admin, nursing (RN), predental, premedicine, prenursing, prepharmacy, preveterinary. **History:** General. **Legal studies:** Prelaw. **Liberal arts:** Arts/sciences. **Math:** General. **Mechanic/repair:** Automotive. **Military:** General. **Parks/recreation:** Exercise sciences, health/fitness, sports admin. **Personal/culinary services:** Mortuary science. **Philosophy/religion:** Philosophy. **Physical sciences:** General, chemistry, physics. **Protective services:** Firefighting, police science, security management. **Psychology:** General. **Public administration:** General, social work. **Social sciences:** Anthropology, economics, political science, sociology. **Visual/performing arts:** Art, dance, dramatic, graphic design.

**Most popular majors.** Business/marketing 11%, health sciences 16%, liberal arts 51%.

**Computing on campus.** 350 workstations in dormitories, library, computer center, student center. Dormitories wired for high-speed internet access and linked to campus network. Commuter students can connect to campus network. Online course registration, online library, helpline available.

**Student life. Freshman orientation:** Mandatory. Preregistration for classes offered. **Housing:** Guaranteed on-campus for freshmen. Coed dorms, substance-free housing available. $100 fully refundable deposit. **Activities:** Bands, choral groups, dance, drama, literary magazine, music ensembles, musical theater, student government, student newspaper, Newman Club, Fellowship of Christian Athletes, Campus Christian Fellowship, Student Ambassadors.

**Athletics.** NJCAA. **Intercollegiate:** Baseball M, basketball, cheerleading, cross-country, golf, soccer, softball W, tennis, track and field, volleyball W. **Intramural:** Baseball M, basketball, football (non-tackle), softball, table tennis, tennis, volleyball. **Team name:** Cougars.

**Student services.** Adult student services, alcohol/substance abuse counseling, career counseling, services for economically disadvantaged, student employment services, financial aid counseling, health services, on-campus daycare, personal counseling, placement for graduates, veterans' counselor. **Physically disabled:** Services for hearing impaired. **Transfer:** Preadmission transcript evaluation for new students. Transfer adviser, college fairs on campus for students transferring to 4-year colleges.

**Contact.** E-mail: admissions@bartonccc.edu
Phone: (620) 792-2701 ext. 286 Toll-free number: (800) 722-6842
Fax: (620) 786-1160
Todd Moore, Director of Marketing, Barton County Community College, 245 North East 30th Road, Great Bend, KS 67530-9283

## Brown Mackie College: Salina
**Salina, Kansas**
**www.brownmackie.edu/Salina/**            CB code: 3366

- For-profit 2-year junior college
- Large town
- Interview required

**General.** Regionally accredited. Branch campus in Kansas City. **Enrollment:** 388 degree-seeking undergraduates. **Degrees:** 65 associate awarded. **Location:** 90 miles from Wichita, 108 miles from Topeka. **Calendar:** Quarter, extensive summer session. **Full-time faculty:** 17 total. **Part-time faculty:** 19 total.

**Transfer out. Colleges most students transferred to 2007:** Kansas Wesleyan University, Kansas State University.

**Basis for selection.** Open admission.

**2007-2008 Annual costs.** Computer networking program $300 per-credit-hour; required fees: $25 per-credit-hour. Nursing program $250 per-credit-hour; required fees: $12 per-credit-hour. Books/supplies: $1,440. Personal expenses: $1,520.

**Application procedures. Admission:** No deadline. No application fee. Application must be submitted on paper. Admission notification on a rolling basis. **Financial aid:** No deadline. Applicants notified on a rolling basis.

**Academics. Special study options:** Internships. **Credit/placement by examination:** CLEP, institutional tests. **Support services:** Remedial instruction, study skills assistance, tutoring.

**Majors. Business:** Accounting, business admin, selling. **Computer sciences:** Information technology, networking. **Engineering technology:** CAD/

CADD. **Health:** Office admin. **Legal studies:** Paralegal. **Protective services:** Law enforcement admin.

**Computing on campus.** 134 workstations in library, computer center.

**Student life. Freshman orientation:** Mandatory. Part-day program held prior to start of classes. **Activities:** Student government, student newspaper.

**Athletics.** NJCAA. **Intercollegiate:** Baseball M, basketball, softball W. **Intramural:** Softball. **Team name:** Lions.

**Student services.** Career counseling, student employment services, placement for graduates.

**Contact.** E-mail: dheath@brownmackie.edu
Phone: (785) 825-5422
Diann Heath, Director of Admissions, Brown Mackie College: Salina, 2106 South Ninth Street, Salina, KS 67401

## Butler County Community College
**El Dorado, Kansas**
**www.butlercc.edu**            CB code: 6191

- Public 2-year community college
- Commuter campus in large town

**General.** Founded in 1927. Regionally accredited. Off-campus sites at Andover, McConnell, Augusta, Flint Hills, Rose Hill and 20 other smaller locations. **Enrollment:** 5,290 degree-seeking undergraduates; 2,806 non-degree-seeking students. **Degrees:** 795 associate awarded. **Location:** 25 miles from Wichita. **Calendar:** Semester, extensive summer session. **Full-time faculty:** 148 total; 17% have terminal degrees, 5% minority, 57% women. **Part-time faculty:** 428 total; 10% minority, 61% women. **Class size:** 70% < 20, 30% 20-39, less than 1% 40-49, less than 1% 50-99.

**Student profile.** Among degree-seeking undergraduates, 1,296 enrolled as first-time, first-year students.

| | | | |
|---|---|---|---|
| Part-time: | 48% | Hispanic American: | 7% |
| Out-of-state: | 1% | Native American: | 1% |
| Women: | 61% | International: | 3% |
| African American: | 11% | 25 or older: | 38% |
| Asian American: | 3% | Live on campus: | 2% |

**Transfer out. Colleges most students transferred to 2007:** Wichita State University, Kansas State University, Emporia State University, University of Kansas, Kansas Newman College.

**Basis for selection.** Open admission, but selective for some programs. Nursing applicants admitted based on GPA in prerequisite courses.

**2007-2008 Annual costs.** Tuition/fees: $1,838; $2,168 out-of-district; $3,548 out-of-state. Per-credit charge: $47 in-district; $58 out-of-district; $104 out-of-state. Room/board: $4,600. Books/supplies: $1,000. Personal expenses: $1,350.

**Financial aid. Need-based:** Need-based aid available for part-time students. Work-study available nights, weekends and for part-time students. **Non-need-based:** Scholarships awarded for academics, art, athletics, music/drama.

**Application procedures. Admission:** No deadline. No application fee. Application may be submitted online. Admission notification on a rolling basis. **Financial aid:** Priority date 4/1; no closing date. FAFSA, institutional form required. Applicants notified on a rolling basis starting 5/1; must reply within 2 week(s) of notification.

**Academics. Special study options:** Accelerated study, cooperative education, distance learning, dual enrollment of high school students, ESL, honors, independent study, internships, liberal arts/career combination, weekend college. License preparation in nursing, paramedic. **Credit/placement by examination:** AP, CLEP, institutional tests. 30 credit hours maximum toward associate degree. **Support services:** GED preparation, learning center, reduced course load, remedial instruction, study skills assistance, tutoring, writing center.

**Majors. Agriculture:** Animal sciences, farm/ranch. **Business:** Accounting, business admin, hospitality admin, hospitality/recreation, office/clerical. **Communications:** Journalism. **Computer sciences:** General, computer science. **Education:** Business, early childhood, elementary, physical, secondary, teacher assistance. **Engineering:** General. **Engineering technology:** Drafting. **English:** Composition, speech/rhetoric. **Family/consumer sciences:** Child care. **Foreign languages:** General, Spanish. **Health:** Licensed practical nurse, nursing (RN), premedicine. **History:** General. **Legal studies:** Prelaw. **Liberal arts:** Arts/sciences. **Math:** General. **Mechanic/**

**repair:** General, auto body, automotive, electronics/electrical. **Physical sciences:** Chemistry, physics. **Protective services:** Criminal justice, firefighting, police science. **Psychology:** General. **Public administration:** Social work. **Social sciences:** Economics, political science. **Visual/performing arts:** Art, dramatic.

**Most popular majors.** Health sciences 15%, liberal arts 75%.

**Computing on campus.** 130 workstations in dormitories, library, computer center, student center. Dormitories wired for high-speed internet access and linked to campus network. Commuter students can connect to campus network. Online course registration, online library, helpline, repair service available.

**Student life. Freshman orientation:** Mandatory. Preregistration for classes offered. **Housing:** Coed dorms, single-sex dorms, special housing for disabled, substance-free housing available. $75 fully refundable deposit. **Activities:** Bands, choral groups, dance, drama, literary magazine, music ensembles, musical theater, radio station, student government, student newspaper, TV station, international student association, Campus Crusade for Christ.

**Athletics.** NJCAA. **Intercollegiate:** Baseball M, basketball, cross-country, football (tackle) M, soccer W, softball W, track and field, volleyball W. **Intramural:** Basketball, bowling, soccer, softball, table tennis, volleyball. **Team name:** Grizzlies.

**Student services.** Adult student services, career counseling, student employment services, financial aid counseling, health services, on-campus daycare, personal counseling, placement for graduates, veterans' counselor. **Physically disabled:** Services for visually, speech, hearing impaired. **Transfer:** Pre-admission transcript evaluation for new students. Transfer adviser, college fairs on campus for students transferring to 4-year colleges.

**Contact.** E-mail: admissions@butlercc.edu
Phone: (316) 322-3255 Fax: (316) 322-3316
Glenn Lygrisse, Director of Enrollment Management, Butler County Community College, 901 South Haverhill Road, El Dorado, KS 67042-3280

## Cloud County Community College
**Concordia, Kansas**
**www.cloud.edu**
CB code: 6137

- Public 2-year community college
- Commuter campus in small town

**General.** Founded in 1965. Regionally accredited. **Enrollment:** 1,009 degree-seeking undergraduates. **Degrees:** 202 associate awarded. **Location:** 200 miles from Kansas City, 140 miles from Topeka. **Calendar:** Semester, limited summer session. **Full-time faculty:** 40 total. **Part-time faculty:** 241 total. **Class size:** 68% < 20, 30% 20-39, 1% 40-49, less than 1% 50-99. **Special facilities:** Theater, observatory, children's center, human cadaver lab. **Partnerships:** Formal partnerships with Tallgrass TechPrep Consortium.

**Student profile.**

| | | | |
|---|---|---|---|
| Out-of-state: | 5% | Live on campus: | 4% |
| 25 or older: | 35% | | |

**Transfer out. Colleges most students transferred to 2007:** Kansas State University, Fort Hays State University, Wichita State University, Kansas Wesleyan University, Kansas University.

**Basis for selection.** Open admission.

**High school preparation.** 18 units recommended. Recommended units include English 4, mathematics 3, social studies 2 and science 4.

**2007-2008 Annual costs.** Tuition/fees: $2,310; $2,970 out-of-state. Per-credit charge: $58 in-state; $99 out-of-state. Room/board: $4,440. Books/supplies: $700. Personal expenses: $1,650.

**Financial aid. Need-based:** Need-based aid available for part-time students. Work-study available nights, weekends and for part-time students.

**Application procedures. Admission:** No deadline. No application fee. Admission notification on a rolling basis. **Financial aid:** Priority date 4/1; no closing date. FAFSA required. Applicants notified on a rolling basis starting 5/1; must reply within 4 week(s) of notification.

**Academics. Special study options:** Cooperative education, distance learning, dual enrollment of high school students, ESL, independent study, internships, teacher certification program. License preparation in nursing. **Credit/**

**placement by examination:** AP, CLEP, institutional tests. 30 credit hours maximum toward associate degree. **Support services:** GED preparation and test center, learning center, remedial instruction, study skills assistance, tutoring, writing center.

**Majors. Agriculture:** Production. **Biology:** General. **Business:** General, business admin, office management, tourism promotion. **Communications:** General. **Computer sciences:** General, networking, programming. **Education:** General. **Engineering:** General. **Engineering technology:** Civil. **English:** English lit. **Family/consumer sciences:** General, child care. **Foreign languages:** General. **Health:** Nursing (RN). **Legal studies:** Paralegal. **Liberal arts:** Arts/sciences. **Math:** General. **Physical sciences:** General. **Protective services:** Firefighting, law enforcement admin, police science. **Psychology:** General. **Social sciences:** General. **Transportation:** Aviation. **Visual/performing arts:** General, commercial/advertising art.

**Most popular majors.** Agriculture 9%, business/marketing 25%, computer/information sciences 6%, education 26%, health sciences 13%, liberal arts 8%.

**Computing on campus.** 100 workstations in dormitories, library, computer center. Dormitories wired for high-speed internet access and linked to campus network. Online library available.

**Student life. Freshman orientation:** Mandatory. Preregistration for classes offered. Held one day prior to registration each Fall semester, from 9am to 3pm. Offers a variety of activities to acquaint students with services available both at the college and in the community. **Housing:** Special housing for disabled, apartments available. $100 deposit. **Activities:** Jazz band, choral groups, dance, drama, music ensembles, radio station, student government, student newspaper, Fellowship of Christian Athletes.

**Athletics.** NJCAA. **Intercollegiate:** Baseball M, basketball, cross-country, soccer, softball W, track and field, volleyball W. **Intramural:** Basketball, football (non-tackle), soccer, softball, volleyball. **Team name:** Thunderbirds.

**Student services.** Alcohol/substance abuse counseling, career counseling, services for economically disadvantaged, student employment services, financial aid counseling, health services, on-campus daycare, personal counseling, placement for graduates, veterans' counselor. **Physically disabled:** Services for visually, speech, hearing impaired.

**Contact.** E-mail: admit@cloud.edu
Phone: (785) 243-1435 ext. 212 Toll-free number: (800) 729-5101
Fax: (785) 243-9380
Kim Reynolds, Director of Admissions, Cloud County Community College, 2221 Campus Drive, Concordia, KS 66901-1002

## Coffeyville Community College
**Coffeyville, Kansas**
**www.coffeyville.edu**
CB code: 6102

- Public 2-year community college
- Commuter campus in large town

**General.** Founded in 1923. Regionally accredited. **Enrollment:** 1,375 degree-seeking undergraduates. **Degrees:** 193 associate awarded. **Location:** 75 miles from Tulsa, Oklahoma, 137 miles from Wichita. **Calendar:** Semester, limited summer session. **Full-time faculty:** 50 total. **Part-time faculty:** 25 total. **Class size:** 64% < 20, 33% 20-39, less than 1% 40-49, 3% 50-99. **Special facilities:** Greenhouse, commercial television station. **Partnerships:** Formal partnership with Wal-Mart.

**Student profile.** Among degree-seeking undergraduates, 70% enrolled in a transfer program, 13% enrolled in a vocational program, 463 enrolled as first-time, first-year students, 35 transferred in from other institutions.

| | | | |
|---|---|---|---|
| Part-time: | 28% | Women: | 47% |
| Out-of-state: | 15% | Live on campus: | 31% |

**Transfer out.** 70% of students enrolled in the transfer program go on to 4-year colleges. **Colleges most students transferred to 2007:** Pittsburg State University, Kansas State University, University of Kansas.

**Basis for selection.** Open admission. **Homeschooled:** ACT or placement test required for placement.

**High school preparation.** 20 units recommended. Recommended units include English 4, mathematics 4, social studies 3, history 2, science 3 (laboratory 2), foreign language 1, computer science 1 and visual/performing arts 1.

**2007-2008 Annual costs.** Tuition/fees: $1,725; $2,925 out-of-state. Per-credit charge: $25 in-state; $65 out-of-state. Oklahoma border county resident tuition: $32.50 per-credit-hour. International students pay $2,835 in required fees. Room/board: $3,825. Books/supplies: $500. Personal expenses: $1,200.

**Financial aid. Need-based:** Need-based aid available for part-time students. Work-study available nights, weekends and for part-time students. **Non-need-based:** Scholarships awarded for academics, alumni affiliation, art, athletics, leadership, music/drama.

**Application procedures. Admission:** No deadline. No application fee. Application may be submitted online. Admission notification on a rolling basis. **Financial aid:** Priority date 8/1; no closing date. FAFSA required. Applicants notified on a rolling basis starting 6/20.

**Academics. Special study options:** Distance learning, double major, dual enrollment of high school students, ESL, honors, independent study, internships, liberal arts/career combination, student-designed major. License preparation in paramedic, real estate. **Credit/placement by examination:** AP, CLEP, institutional tests. **Support services:** GED preparation and test center, learning center, reduced course load, remedial instruction, study skills assistance, tutoring.

**Honors college/program.** Application for Presidential Scholarship, minimum ACT score of 24, minimum 3.5 high school GPA, essay required. Top 12-15 applicants accepted each fall.

**Majors. Agriculture:** General, business, horticulture, supplies. **Biology:** General. **Business:** General, accounting, administrative services, business admin, entrepreneurial studies, management information systems, office management, office/clerical, retailing. **Communications:** General, broadcast journalism, journalism. **Communications technology:** General. **Computer sciences:** General, networking. **Education:** General, early childhood, elementary, multi-level teacher, physical, secondary, speech. **Engineering:** General. **English:** English lit, speech/rhetoric. **Family/consumer sciences:** General, institutional food production. **Foreign languages:** General, Spanish. **Health:** Athletic training, EMT paramedic, predental, premedicine, prenursing, prepharmacy, preveterinary. **History:** General. **Legal studies:** Prelaw. **Liberal arts:** Arts/sciences. **Math:** General. **Parks/recreation:** Health/fitness. **Physical sciences:** Chemistry, physics. **Psychology:** General. **Public administration:** Social work. **Social sciences:** General, economics, political science, sociology. **Visual/performing arts:** General, art, dramatic, studio arts.

**Most popular majors.** Agriculture 6%, business/marketing 17%, education 8%, liberal arts 58%.

**Computing on campus.** 100 workstations in dormitories, library, computer center, student center. Dormitories wired for high-speed internet access. Online course registration available.

**Student life. Freshman orientation:** Mandatory. Preregistration for classes offered. **Housing:** Coed dorms, single-sex dorms available. $100 deposit. **Activities:** Bands, choral groups, dance, drama, film society, music ensembles, musical theater, student government, TV station, international club, Phi Theta Kappa, agriculture club.

**Athletics.** NJCAA. **Intercollegiate:** Baseball M, basketball, cheerleading, cross-country, football (tackle) M, golf, rodeo, soccer, softball W, track and field, volleyball W. **Intramural:** Basketball, bowling, golf, table tennis, volleyball. **Team name:** Red Ravens.

**Student services.** Adult student services, career counseling, student employment services, financial aid counseling, health services, personal counseling, veterans' counselor. **Physically disabled:** Services for visually, speech, hearing impaired. **Learning disabled:** Comprehensive services available. **Transfer:** Transfer adviser, college fairs on campus for students transferring to 4-year colleges.

**Contact.** E-mail: admissions@coffeyville.edu
Phone: (620) 252-7047 Toll-free number: (800) 782-4732
Fax: (316) 252-7399
Kelli Bauer, Admissions Coordinator, Coffeyville Community College, 400 West 11th Street, Coffeyville, KS 67337-5064

## Colby Community College
Colby, Kansas
www.colbycc.edu                           CB code: 6129

▶ Public 2-year community college
▶ Commuter campus in small town
▶ Interview required

**General.** Founded in 1964. Regionally accredited. **Enrollment:** 594 degree-seeking undergraduates; 943 non-degree-seeking students. **Degrees:** 490 associate awarded. **Location:** 100 miles from Hays, 200 miles from Denver. **Calendar:** Semester, limited summer session. **Full-time faculty:** 58 total; 22% have terminal degrees, 5% minority, 59% women. **Part-time faculty:**

95 total; 62% women. **Class size:** 72% < 20, 26% 20-39, less than 1% 40-49, less than 1% 50-99. **Special facilities:** 64-acre farm, cultural arts center, fitness laboratory.

**Student profile.** Among degree-seeking undergraduates, 194 enrolled as first-time, first-year students.

| | | | |
|---|---|---|---|
| Part-time: | 9% | Hispanic American: | 3% |
| Out-of-state: | 30% | Native American: | 1% |
| Women: | 63% | International: | 3% |
| African American: | 4% | 25 or older: | 12% |
| Asian American: | 1% | Live on campus: | 30% |

**Transfer out. Colleges most students transferred to 2007:** Fort Hays State University, Kansas State University, University of Kansas.

**Basis for selection.** Open admission, but selective for some programs. Interview required for physical therapist assistant, veterinary technology, horse production, dental hygiene, and nursing programs. Audition recommended for music majors. Portfolios recommended for art majors. **Adult students:** COMPASS required if 2 or more years since ACT/SAT was taken. **Homeschooled:** Transcript of courses and grades, state high school equivalency certificate required.

**2007-2008 Annual costs.** Tuition/fees: $2,304; $3,474 out-of-state. Per-credit charge: $48 in-state; $87 out-of-state. Nebraska and Colorado border county residents pay $58 per credit hour for tuition, and additional $30 per credit hour for required fees. Room/board: $3,788. Books/supplies: $800. Personal expenses: $700.

**2007-2008 Financial aid. Need-based:** Average scholarship/grant was $3,612; average loan $2,669. 56% of total undergraduate aid awarded as scholarships/grants, 44% as loans/jobs. Need-based aid available for part-time students. Work-study available nights, weekends and for part-time students. **Non-need-based:** Scholarships awarded for academics, athletics, music/drama.

**Application procedures. Admission:** No deadline. No application fee. Application may be submitted online. Admission notification on a rolling basis. **Financial aid:** Priority date 6/1; no closing date. FAFSA required. Applicants notified on a rolling basis starting 5/1.

**Academics. Special study options:** Cooperative education, distance learning, dual enrollment of high school students, honors, independent study, internships, liberal arts/career combination. License preparation in nursing. **Credit/placement by examination:** AP, CLEP, institutional tests. 30 credit hours maximum toward associate degree. **Support services:** GED preparation and test center, learning center, pre-admission summer program, reduced course load, remedial instruction, study skills assistance, tutoring, writing center.

**Majors. Agriculture:** Agribusiness operations, agronomy, animal sciences, equestrian studies, farm/ranch. **Biology:** General. **Business:** General, accounting, office technology. **Communications:** Broadcast journalism, journalism. **Computer sciences:** Data processing. **Conservation:** Forestry, wildlife. **Education:** General, agricultural, art, biology, business, chemistry, elementary, family/consumer sciences, mathematics, music, physical, science, secondary. **Engineering:** General. **English:** English lit. **Family/consumer sciences:** General, child care. **Health:** Dental hygiene, nursing (RN), physical therapy assistant, premedicine, prenursing, prepharmacy, preveterinary, veterinary technology/assistant. **History:** General. **Legal studies:** Prelaw. **Liberal arts:** Arts/sciences. **Math:** General. **Physical sciences:** Chemistry. **Psychology:** General. **Public administration:** Social work. **Social sciences:** Sociology. **Visual/performing arts:** General, dramatic.

**Most popular majors.** Agriculture 7%, health sciences 27%, liberal arts 64%.

**Computing on campus.** 100 workstations in dormitories, library, computer center, student center. Dormitories wired for high-speed internet access. Online course registration, online library, helpline, wireless network available.

**Student life. Freshman orientation:** Mandatory, $15 fee. Preregistration for classes offered. **Housing:** Coed dorms, single-sex dorms, special housing for disabled, substance-free housing available. $100 deposit. **Activities:** Bands, choral groups, drama, literary magazine, music ensembles, musical theater, radio station, student government, student newspaper, TV station.

**Athletics.** NJCAA. **Intercollegiate:** Baseball M, basketball, cross-country, equestrian, golf, rodeo, softball W, track and field, volleyball W, wrestling M. **Intramural:** Basketball, softball, volleyball. **Team name:** Trojans.

**Student services.** Adult student services, alcohol/substance abuse counseling, career counseling, student employment services, financial aid counseling, health services, personal counseling, placement for graduates, veterans' counselor. **Physically disabled:** Services for visually, speech, hearing impaired. **Transfer:** Transfer adviser, college fairs on campus for students transferring to 4-year colleges.

**Contact.** E-mail: bobbi.barton@colbycc.edu
Phone: (785) 460-4690 Toll-free number: (888) 634-9350
Fax: (785) 460-4691
Nikol Nolan, Director of Admissions, Colby Community College, 1255 South Range Avenue, Colby, KS 67701

## Cowley County Community College
**Arkansas City, Kansas**
www.cowley.edu
CB code: 6008

▶ Public 2-year community and technical college
▶ Commuter campus in large town

**General.** Founded in 1922. Regionally accredited. **Enrollment:** 4,280 degree-seeking undergraduates; 189 non-degree-seeking students. **Degrees:** 563 associate awarded. **Location:** 50 miles from Wichita. **Calendar:** Semester, limited summer session. **Full-time faculty:** 41 total; 2% minority, 56% women. **Part-time faculty:** 184 total; 3% minority, 60% women. **Class size:** 66% < 20, 33% 20-39, less than 1% 50-99, less than 1% >100.

**Student profile.** Among degree-seeking undergraduates, 84% enrolled in a transfer program, 16% enrolled in a vocational program, 2% already have a bachelor's degree or higher, 986 enrolled as first-time, first-year students.

| | | | |
|---|---|---|---|
| Part-time: | 49% | Hispanic American: | 4% |
| Out-of-state: | 3% | Native American: | 1% |
| Women: | 60% | International: | 1% |
| African American: | 9% | 25 or older: | 42% |
| Asian American: | 5% | Live on campus: | 7% |

**Basis for selection.** Open admission, but selective for some programs. Special requirements for mobile intensive care and interpreter training programs. **Homeschooled:** Transcript of courses and grades required.

**2007-2008 Annual costs.** Tuition/fees: $1,990; $2,140 out-of-district; $3,700 out-of-state. Per-credit charge: $45 in-district; $50 out-of-district; $102 out-of-state. Oklahoma border county resident tuition: $50 per-credit-hour. Room/board: $3,600. Books/supplies: $600. Personal expenses: $900.

**2007-2008 Financial aid.** **Need-based:** Average scholarship/grant was $1,710; average loan $1,663. 51% of total undergraduate aid awarded as scholarships/grants, 49% as loans/jobs. Need-based aid available for part-time students. **Non-need-based:** Scholarships awarded for academics, art, athletics, leadership, music/drama, state residency.

**Application procedures.** **Admission:** No deadline. No application fee. Application may be submitted online. Admission notification on a rolling basis. **Financial aid:** Priority date 4/15; no closing date. FAFSA required. Applicants notified on a rolling basis starting 1/15; must reply within 2 week(s) of notification.

**Academics.** **Special study options:** Cooperative education, distance learning, double major, dual enrollment of high school students, independent study, internships, teacher certification program. Area vocational-technical school programs available. **Credit/placement by examination:** AP, CLEP. 15 credit hours maximum toward associate degree. Students with ACT scores of 21 on verbal and math not required to take placement test. **Support services:** GED preparation and test center, learning center, reduced course load, remedial instruction, study skills assistance, tutoring.

**Majors.** **Agriculture:** Farm/ranch. **Business:** General, administrative services, business admin, entrepreneurial studies, office/clerical, organizational behavior. **Communications:** General, journalism. **Computer sciences:** Networking. **Education:** General. **Engineering:** General. **English:** English lit. **Family/consumer sciences:** Child care. **Foreign languages:** General, sign language interpretation. **Health:** EMT paramedic, nursing assistant. **Liberal arts:** Arts/sciences. **Math:** General. **Mechanic/repair:** Aircraft, automotive, avionics. **Personal/culinary services:** Cosmetic. **Philosophy/religion:** Philosophy, religion. **Physical sciences:** General, chemistry. **Production:** Machine shop technology, welding. **Protective services:** Corrections, law enforcement admin, police science. **Science technology:** Radiologic. **Social sciences:** General. **Visual/performing arts:** General, art, commercial/advertising art, music.

**Most popular majors.** Business/marketing 15%, education 12%, health sciences 14%, liberal arts 16%.

**Computing on campus.** 130 workstations in dormitories, library, computer center, student center. Dormitories wired for high-speed internet access and linked to campus network. Commuter students can connect to campus network.

**Student life.** **Freshman orientation:** Available. Preregistration for classes offered. **Housing:** Single-sex dorms, substance-free housing available. $100 nonrefundable deposit. **Activities:** Bands, choral groups, drama, music ensembles, student government, student newspaper, student government association, Academic Civic Engagement through Service, Campus Christian Fellowship, Black Student Union, Young Democrats, College Republicans.

**Athletics.** NJCAA. **Intercollegiate:** Baseball M, basketball, cheerleading, cross-country, softball W, tennis, track and field, volleyball W. **Intramural:** Basketball, football (non-tackle), softball, volleyball. **Team name:** Tigers.

**Student services.** Career counseling, student employment services, health services, personal counseling, placement for graduates, veterans' counselor.

**Contact.** Phone: (620) 442-0430 Toll-free number: (800) 593-2222
Fax: (620) 441-5350
Ben Schears, Director of Admissions, Cowley County Community College, PO Box 1147, Arkansas City, KS 67005-1147

## Dodge City Community College
**Dodge City, Kansas**
www.dccc.cc.ks.us
CB code: 6166

▶ Public 2-year community and technical college
▶ Commuter campus in large town

**General.** Founded in 1935. Regionally accredited. **Enrollment:** 1,812 degree-seeking undergraduates. **Degrees:** 41 associate awarded. **Location:** 150 miles from Wichita. **Calendar:** Semester, limited summer session. **Full-time faculty:** 60 total. **Part-time faculty:** 110 total. **Class size:** 25% < 20, 75% 20-39. **Special facilities:** Federal depository of books and documents, horse barn, rodeo practice arena, astronomy center.

**Student profile.**

| | | | |
|---|---|---|---|
| Out-of-state: | 5% | Live on campus: | 33% |
| 25 or older: | 45% | | |

**Transfer out.** **Colleges most students transferred to 2007:** Kansas State University, Fort Hays State University, University of Kansas, Pittsburg State University, Wichita State University.

**Basis for selection.** Open admission, but selective for some programs. Special requirements for nursing program. Students without GED or high school diploma must take test to demonstrate ability to benefit. Michigan test given to ESL students. ASSET used as placement test. Interview recommended for nursing majors. Audition recommended for music majors. Portfolio recommended for art majors.

**High school preparation.** Recommended units include English 4, mathematics 3, social studies 3 and science 3.

**2007-2008 Annual costs.** Tuition/fees: $1,950; $2,850 out-of-state. Per-credit charge: $35 in-state; $45 out-of-state. Room/board: $4,210. Books/supplies: $600. Personal expenses: $1,000.

**Financial aid.** **Need-based:** Need-based aid available for part-time students. Work-study available nights, weekends and for part-time students. **Non-need-based:** Scholarships awarded for academics, athletics, music/drama, state residency.

**Application procedures.** **Admission:** No deadline. No application fee. Admission notification on a rolling basis. **Financial aid:** Priority date 3/15; no closing date. FAFSA, institutional form required. Applicants notified on a rolling basis; must reply within 2 week(s) of notification.

**Academics.** **Special study options:** Cross-registration, distance learning, double major, dual enrollment of high school students, ESL, independent study, internships. Bachelor's degree programs available on campus. License preparation in nursing, paramedic. **Credit/placement by examination:** CLEP. 30 credit hours maximum toward associate degree. ASSET required for placement. **Support services:** GED preparation and test center, learning center, reduced course load, remedial instruction, tutoring, writing center.

**Majors.** **Agriculture:** Agribusiness operations, business, equestrian studies, farm/ranch, horticulture. **Biology:** General. **Business:** General, banking/financial services, management information systems, office management. **Communications:** Broadcast journalism, journalism. **Computer sciences:** General, computer science, data processing. **Education:** General, elementary, secondary. **Engineering:** General. **Family/consumer sciences:** Child care. **Health:** Athletic training, dental assistant, licensed practical nurse, medical records technology, nursing (RN), nursing assistant, premedicine, prepharmacy, preveterinary, substance abuse counseling. **Legal studies:** Legal secretary, prelaw. **Math:** General. **Mechanic/repair:** Electronics/electrical. **Parks/recreation:** Health/fitness. **Physical sciences:** Chemistry. **Protective services:** Firefighting. **Social sciences:** General, economics, sociology. **Visual/performing arts:** Art.

**Computing on campus.** 125 workstations in dormitories, library, computer center, student center. Dormitories wired for high-speed internet access.

**Student life. Freshman orientation:** Mandatory. Held 2 days before classes begins. **Housing:** Guaranteed on-campus for freshmen. Coed dorms, single-sex dorms, substance-free housing available. **Activities:** Bands, choral groups, dance, drama, music ensembles, radio station, student government, student newspaper, TV station, Black student union, Fellowship of Christian Athletes, Hispanic American leadership organization, Newman club.

**Athletics.** NJCAA. **Intercollegiate:** Baseball M, basketball, cross-country, football (tackle) M, golf, softball W, track and field, volleyball W. **Intramural:** Basketball, handball, racquetball, softball W. **Team name:** Conquistadors.

**Student services.** Adult student services, career counseling, student employment services, veterans' counselor. **Physically disabled:** Services for visually, speech, hearing impaired. **Transfer:** Transfer adviser, college fairs on campus for students transferring to 4-year colleges.

**Contact.** Phone: (620) 227-9207 Toll-free number: (800) 367-3222 Fax: (620) 227-9277
Tammy Tabor, Director of Admissions, Dodge City Community College, 2501 North 14th Avenue, Dodge City, KS 67801-2399

## Donnelly College
**Kansas City, Kansas**
**www.donnelly.edu**
**CB code: 6167**

- Private 2-year junior and liberal arts college affiliated with Roman Catholic Church
- Commuter campus in large city

**General.** Founded in 1949. Regionally accredited. **Enrollment:** 565 degree-seeking undergraduates. **Degrees:** 50 associate awarded. **Location:** 5 miles from downtown. **Calendar:** Semester, limited summer session. **Full-time faculty:** 14 total; 7% have terminal degrees, 50% women. **Part-time faculty:** 41 total; 10% have terminal degrees, 42% minority, 66% women. **Class size:** 80% < 20, 12% 20-39.

**Student profile.** Among degree-seeking undergraduates, 90 transferred in from other institutions.

| | | | |
|---|---|---|---|
| Out-of-state: | 9% | **Native American:** | 1% |
| **African American:** | 40% | **International:** | 9% |
| **Asian American:** | 3% | **25 or older:** | 1% |
| **Hispanic American:** | 31% | **Live on campus:** | 3% |

**Transfer out. Colleges most students transferred to 2007:** University of Kansas, University of Missouri-Kansas City, Kansas City Kansas Community College, Kansas State, Johnson County Community College.

**Basis for selection.** Open admission. Michigan Proficiency Test required of foreign applicants. **Homeschooled:** Must take the Ability to Benefit test or have a GED.

**2007-2008 Annual costs.** Tuition/fees: $4,900. Per-credit charge: $175. Books/supplies: $830. Personal expenses: $1,860.

**2006-2007 Financial aid. Need-based:** 23 full-time freshmen applied for aid; 23 were judged to have need; 23 of these received aid. Average need met was 99%. Average scholarship/grant was $2,384; average loan $1,209. 76% of total undergraduate aid awarded as scholarships/grants, 24% as loans/jobs. Need-based aid available for part-time students. Work-study available for part-time students. **Non-need-based:** Scholarships awarded for academics.

**Application procedures. Admission:** No deadline. No application fee. Admission notification on a rolling basis. **Financial aid:** Priority date 4/1; no closing date. FAFSA, institutional form required. Applicants notified on a rolling basis starting 7/1.

**Academics. Special study options:** Distance learning, dual enrollment of high school students, ESL, weekend college. Bachelor's degree programs available on campus. **Credit/placement by examination:** CLEP, institutional tests. 20 credit hours maximum toward associate degree. **Support services:** GED preparation, learning center, reduced course load, remedial instruction, study skills assistance, tutoring.

**Majors. Biology:** General. **Business:** General, accounting, office/clerical. **Computer sciences:** Data processing, programming. **Education:** Early childhood, elementary. **Engineering:** General. **English:** English lit, speech/rhetoric. **Health:** Prenursing. **Math:** General. **Physical sciences:** General. **Psychology:** General. **Social sciences:** General.

**Most popular majors.** Business/marketing 42%, education 18%, English 6%, health sciences 14%, liberal arts 6%.

**Computing on campus.** 116 workstations in library, computer center. Online library available.

**Student life. Freshman orientation:** Available. Preregistration for classes offered. **Activities:** Literary magazine, student newspaper.

**Student services.** Career counseling, services for economically disadvantaged, student employment services, financial aid counseling, personal counseling, placement for graduates, veterans' counselor, women's services. **Physically disabled:** Services for visually, speech, hearing impaired. **Transfer:** Transfer adviser, college fairs on campus for students transferring to 4-year colleges.

**Contact.** E-mail: kevin@donnelly.edu
Phone: (913) 621-8700 Fax: (913) 621-8719
Kevin Kelley, Vice President Marketing, Enrollmentg Management and Community Services, Donnelly College, 608 North 18th Street, Kansas City, KS 66102-4210

## Fort Scott Community College
**Fort Scott, Kansas**
**www.fortscott.edu**
**CB code: 6219**

- Public 2-year community college
- Commuter campus in small town

**General.** Founded in 1919. Regionally accredited. **Enrollment:** 1,696 degree-seeking undergraduates. **Degrees:** 276 associate awarded. **Location:** 25 miles from Pittsburg. **Calendar:** Semester, limited summer session. **Full-time faculty:** 55 total. **Part-time faculty:** 73 total. **Special facilities:** Indoor and outdoor rodeo training facilities.

**Student profile.**

| | | | |
|---|---|---|---|
| Out-of-state: | 14% | **Live on campus:** | 14% |

**Basis for selection.** Open admission.

**2007-2008 Annual costs.** Tuition/fees: $1,922; $3,722 out-of-state. Per-credit charge: $40 in-state; $96 out-of-state. Students from bordering states of Oklahoma, Nebraska, Arkansas, Missouri, and Colorado pay $2,880 annual full-time tuition or $96 per credit hour. Room/board: $3,920. Books/supplies: $550. Personal expenses: $1,020.

**Application procedures. Admission:** No deadline. No application fee. Admission notification on a rolling basis. **Financial aid:** No deadline. Applicants notified on a rolling basis starting 10/1.

**Academics. Special study options:** Cooperative education, distance learning, dual enrollment of high school students, ESL, independent study, internships, study abroad, teacher certification program, weekend college. **Credit/placement by examination:** AP, CLEP. 18 credit hours maximum toward associate degree. **Support services:** Learning center, pre-admission summer program, remedial instruction, tutoring.

**Majors. Agriculture:** Animal sciences, business. **Business:** General, administrative services, business admin, management information systems. **Communications:** General, public relations. **Communications technology:** Graphic/printing. **Computer sciences:** General. **Conservation:** General. **Education:** General. **Health:** Licensed practical nurse. **History:** General. **Liberal arts:** Arts/sciences. **Physical sciences:** Chemistry, physics. **Protective services:** Law enforcement admin. **Psychology:** General. **Social sciences:** General, criminology.

**Student life. Freshman orientation:** Available. Preregistration for classes offered. **Housing:** Coed dorms available. **Activities:** Bands, choral groups, dance, drama, literary magazine, music ensembles, musical theater, student government, student newspaper, symphony orchestra, Christians on Campus.

**Athletics.** NJCAA. **Intercollegiate:** Baseball M, basketball, cheerleading M, cross-country, football (tackle) M, rodeo, softball W, volleyball W. **Intramural:** Basketball, bowling, racquetball. **Team name:** Greyhounds.

**Student services.** Adult student services, services for economically disadvantaged, student employment services, financial aid counseling. **Transfer:** Transfer adviser, college fairs on campus for students transferring to 4-year colleges.

**Contact.** Phone: (620) 223-2700 ext. 353 Fax: (620) 223-6530
Mert Barrows, Director of Admissions, Fort Scott Community College, 2108 South Horton Street, Fort Scott, KS 66701

## Garden City Community College
### Garden City, Kansas
www.gcccks.edu                    CB code: 6246

▶ Public 2-year community college
▶ Commuter campus in large town

**General.** Founded in 1919. Regionally accredited. **Enrollment:** 1,067 degree-seeking undergraduates. **Degrees:** 219 associate awarded. **Location:** 200 miles from Wichita. **Calendar:** Semester, limited summer session. **Full-time faculty:** 70 total. **Part-time faculty:** 90 total. **Class size:** 80% < 20, 19% 20-39, less than 1% 40-49, less than 1% 50-99, less than 1% >100. **Special facilities:** Cadaver lab, art gallery, fire arms training system, fire training tower. **Partnerships:** Formal partnerships with John Deere Company and dealers (John Deere Agricultural technical program,) Centers of excellence in automotive, cosmetology and broadcasting offered in cooperation with area high schools, and Ford Motor Company.

**Student profile.**

| | | | |
|---|---|---|---|
| Out-of-state: | 7% | Live on campus: | 15% |
| 25 or older: | 40% | | |

**Basis for selection.** Open admission, but selective for some programs. Special requirements for nursing program and John Deere agricultural technical program. Michigan English Placement Test required. Compass/ESL Assessment required for placement. Scores valid for one year. Audition recommended for music majors. Portfolio recommended for art and photography majors.

**High school preparation.** Recommended units include English 4, mathematics 2, social studies 2 and science 2.

**2007-2008 Annual costs.** Tuition/fees: $1,860; $2,580 out-of-state. Per-credit charge: $41 in-state; $65 out-of-state. Room/board: $4,250. Books/supplies: $780. Personal expenses: $1,550.

**Financial aid. Need-based:** Need-based aid available for part-time students. Work-study available nights, weekends and for part-time students. **Non-need-based:** Scholarships awarded for academics, art, athletics, leadership, minority status, music/drama, state residency.

**Application procedures. Admission:** No deadline. No application fee. Application must be submitted on paper. Admission notification on a rolling basis. **Financial aid:** Priority date 3/1; no closing date. FAFSA, institutional form required. Applicants notified on a rolling basis starting 4/15; must reply within 2 week(s) of notification.

**Academics. Special study options:** Cooperative education, cross-registration, distance learning, dual enrollment of high school students, ESL, internships, liberal arts/career combination, student-designed major. Bachelor's degree programs available on campus. License preparation in nursing, paramedic, radiology. **Credit/placement by examination:** AP, CLEP, IB, institutional tests. 30 credit hours maximum toward associate degree. **Support services:** GED preparation and test center, learning center, reduced course load, remedial instruction, study skills assistance, tutoring.

**Majors. Agriculture:** General, agronomy, animal sciences, business, economics, farm/ranch. **Biology:** General. **Business:** General. **Communications:** General, journalism. **Computer sciences:** General, computer science, networking. **Conservation:** Forestry, management/policy, wildlife. **Education:** General, art, business, chemistry, early childhood, elementary, health, history, mathematics, middle, music, physical, physics, reading, science, secondary, social science, social studies. **Engineering:** General, science. **Engineering technology:** Drafting. **English:** English lit. **Family/consumer sciences:** General, child care. **Health:** Athletic training, nursing (RN). **Interdisciplinary:** Behavioral sciences, natural sciences. **Legal studies:** Prelaw. **Liberal arts:** Arts/sciences. **Math:** General. **Parks/recreation:** Health/fitness. **Physical sciences:** General, chemistry. **Protective services:** Firefighting, law enforcement admin, police science. **Psychology:** General. **Social sciences:** General. **Visual/performing arts:** General, art, dramatic.

**Most popular majors.** Agriculture 6%, biological/life sciences 8%, business/marketing 14%, education 15%, health sciences 12%, liberal arts 16%.

**Computing on campus.** 150 workstations in dormitories, library, computer center, student center. Dormitories wired for high-speed internet access and linked to campus network.

**Student life. Freshman orientation:** Available. Held prior to start of classes. **Housing:** Coed dorms, apartments, substance-free housing available. $300 deposit, deadline 8/1. **Activities:** Bands, choral groups, dance, drama, literary magazine, music ensembles, musical theater, student government, student newspaper, Newman Club, Hispanic American Leadership Organization, Black Student Union.

**Athletics.** NJCAA. **Intercollegiate:** Baseball M, basketball, cheerleading, cross-country, football (tackle) M, rodeo, soccer, softball W, track and field, volleyball W. **Intramural:** Archery, basketball, bowling, racquetball, rifle, softball, swimming, table tennis, tennis, track and field, volleyball. **Team name:** Broncbusters.

**Student services.** Career counseling, services for economically disadvantaged, student employment services, financial aid counseling, health services, on-campus daycare, personal counseling, veterans' counselor. **Physically disabled:** Services for visually, speech, hearing impaired. **Transfer:** Transfer adviser, college fairs on campus for students transferring to 4-year colleges.

**Contact.** E-mail: nikki.geier@gcccks.edu
Phone: (620) 276-7611 Toll-free number: (800) 658-1696
Fax: (620) 276-9650
Nikki Geier, Director of Admissions, Garden City Community College, 801 Campus Drive, Garden City, KS 67846-6333

## Hesston College
### Hesston, Kansas
www.hesston.edu                    CB code: 6274

▶ Private 2-year junior college affiliated with Mennonite Church
▶ Residential campus in small town

**General.** Founded in 1909. Regionally accredited. **Enrollment:** 420 degree-seeking undergraduates; 12 non-degree-seeking students. **Degrees:** 158 associate awarded. **Location:** 35 miles from Wichita. **Calendar:** Semester, limited summer session. **Full-time faculty:** 24 total; 4% have terminal degrees, 50% women. **Part-time faculty:** 19 total; 10% have terminal degrees, 5% minority, 53% women. **Class size:** 63% < 20, 33% 20-39, 4% 40-49. **Special facilities:** Arboretum, retreat center. **Partnerships:** Formal partnerships with schools in the Mennonite Secondary Education Council.

**Student profile.** Among degree-seeking undergraduates, 60% enrolled in a transfer program, 40% enrolled in a vocational program, 1% already have a bachelor's degree or higher, 174 enrolled as first-time, first-year students, 39 transferred in from other institutions.

| | | | |
|---|---|---|---|
| Part-time: | 9% | Hispanic American: | 3% |
| Out-of-state: | 56% | Native American: | 2% |
| Women: | 61% | International: | 8% |
| African American: | 3% | 25 or older: | 14% |
| Asian American: | 1% | Live on campus: | 71% |

**Transfer out.** 70% of students enrolled in the transfer program go on to 4-year colleges. **Colleges most students transferred to 2007:** Eastern Mennonite College, Goshen College, Wichita State University, Bethel College.

**Basis for selection.** Open admission, but selective for some programs. Special requirements for nursing and pastoral ministries programs. A supplementary application is required for admission to the nursing and pastoral ministries programs. ASSET required for placement if ACT/SAT scores not submitted. **Homeschooled:** Must provide ACT, SAT, ASSET, or COMPASS scores.

**High school preparation.** Recommended units include English 4, mathematics 3, social studies 3 and science 3.

**2007-2008 Annual costs.** Tuition/fees: $17,416. Room/board: $6,180. Books/supplies: $1,500. Personal expenses: $1,500.

**2006-2007 Financial aid. Need-based:** 164 full-time freshmen applied for aid; 148 were judged to have need; 148 of these received aid. Average need met was 80%. Average scholarship/grant was $10,075; average loan $3,600. 61% of total undergraduate aid awarded as scholarships/grants, 39% as loans/jobs. Need-based aid available for part-time students. Work-study available nights, weekends and for part-time students. **Non-need-based:** Awarded to 190 full-time undergraduates, including 106 freshmen. Scholarships awarded for academics, alumni affiliation, athletics, job skills, music/drama.

**Application procedures. Admission:** Priority date 5/1; no deadline. $15 fee. Application may be submitted online. Admission notification on a rolling basis. **Financial aid:** Priority date 4/1; no closing date. FAFSA required. Applicants notified on a rolling basis starting 2/1; must reply within 4 week(s) of notification.

**Academics. Special study options:** Cooperative education, ESL, independent study, internships, liberal arts/career combination. License preparation in aviation, nursing. **Credit/placement by examination:** AP, CLEP, IB, institutional tests. 12 credit hours maximum toward associate degree. **Support services:** Learning center, reduced course load, remedial instruction, study skills assistance, tutoring, writing center.

**Majors. Business:** General. **Computer sciences:** General. **Education:** Early childhood. **Health:** Nursing (RN). **Liberal arts:** Arts/sciences. **Theology:** Theology. **Transportation:** Aviation.

**Most popular majors.** Health sciences 28%, liberal arts 65%.

**Computing on campus.** 78 workstations in library, computer center. Dormitories wired for high-speed internet access and linked to campus network. Wireless network available.

**Student life. Freshman orientation:** Mandatory. Preregistration for classes offered. Held one-day prior to the beginning of classes. All new first-time students are required to enroll during the first semester in either College Orientation/Success or College Learning Strategies. **Policies:** Use of alcohol, drugs, smoking and possession of firearms/fireworks prohibited. Decency in dress and appearance is expected. Chapel attendance is required. Religious observance required. **Housing:** Guaranteed on-campus for all undergraduates. Single-sex dorms, substance-free housing available. $50 deposit. **Activities:** Pep band, choral groups, drama, music ensembles, musical theater, student newspaper, peace and service club, prison ministries, International Christian Fellowship, Students for Responsible Citizenship.

**Athletics.** NJCAA. **Intercollegiate:** Baseball M, basketball, soccer, softball W, tennis, volleyball W. **Intramural:** Basketball, soccer, volleyball. **Team name:** Larks.

**Student services.** Alcohol/substance abuse counseling, campus ministries, career counseling, financial aid counseling, minority student services, personal counseling, veterans' counselor. **Learning disabled:** Comprehensive services available. **Transfer:** Pre-admission transcript evaluation for new students. Transfer adviser, college fairs on campus for students transferring to 4-year colleges.

**Contact.** E-mail: admissions@hesston.edu
Phone: (620) 327-8222 Toll-free number: (800) 995-2757
Fax: (620) 327-8300
Joel Kauffman, Director of Admissions, Hesston College, Box 3000, Hesston, KS 67062-2093

---

## Highland Community College
**Highland, Kansas**
**www.highlandcc.edu**                    CB code: 6276

- Public 2-year community college
- Residential campus in rural community

**General.** Founded in 1857. Regionally accredited. **Enrollment:** 1,329 degree-seeking undergraduates; 1,481 non-degree-seeking students. **Degrees:** 178 associate awarded. **Location:** 26 miles from St. Joseph, Missouri. **Calendar:** Semester, limited summer session. **Full-time faculty:** 34 total. **Part-time faculty:** 185 total. **Special facilities:** Photography studio, sports medicine/athletic trainer facilities, learning skills center, communication technology complex, wellness center.

**Student profile.** Among degree-seeking undergraduates, 574 enrolled as first-time, first-year students.

| | | | |
|---|---|---|---|
| Part-time: | 26% | Asian American: | 1% |
| Women: | 53% | Hispanic American: | 5% |
| African American: | 9% | Native American: | 4% |

**Transfer out. Colleges most students transferred to 2007:** Kansas State University, Emporia State University, University of Kansas, Washburn University, Missouri Western State College.

**Basis for selection.** Open admission, but selective for out-of-state students. Out-of-state applicants must be in top two-thirds of graduating class or have 14 ACT or 660 SAT (exclusive of Writing). Placement tests determine program eligibility. **Adult students:** Full Compass Placement. **Homeschooled:** Transcript of courses and grades required.

**High school preparation.** 11 units recommended. Recommended units include English 3, mathematics 2, social studies 2 and science 4.

**2007-2008 Annual costs.** Tuition/fees: $1,890; $2,280 out-of-district; $3,810 out-of-state. Per-credit charge: $37 in-district; $50 out-of-district; $101 out-of-state. Out-of-state within 150 miles: $63 per-credit-hour. Room/board: $4,550. Books/supplies: $400. Personal expenses: $915.

**2007-2008 Financial aid. Need-based:** 50% of total undergraduate aid awarded as scholarships/grants, 50% as loans/jobs. Need-based aid available for part-time students. Work-study available nights, weekends and for part-time students. **Non-need-based:** Scholarships awarded for academics, alumni affiliation, art, athletics, leadership, minority status, music/drama. **Additional information:** Auditions and portfolios important for certain scholarship candidates.

**Application procedures. Admission:** Priority date 7/1; no deadline. No application fee. Application may be submitted online. Admission notification on a rolling basis beginning on or about 4/1. Application deadline for out-of-state applicants August 1, must reply within 2 weeks. SAT or ACT recommended, ACT preferred. Score report by August 1. **Financial aid:** Priority date 4/1; no closing date. FAFSA, institutional form required. Applicants notified on a rolling basis starting 4/15; must reply within 14 week(s) of notification.

**Academics. Special study options:** Cooperative education, distance learning, double major, dual enrollment of high school students, independent study, student-designed major. 5 non-credit classes given through website. **Credit/placement by examination:** AP, CLEP, institutional tests. 15 credit hours maximum toward associate degree. **Support services:** GED preparation and test center, learning center, pre-admission summer program, reduced course load, remedial instruction, study skills assistance, tutoring.

**Majors. Business:** General. **Education:** General.

**Computing on campus.** 96 workstations in library, computer center. Dormitories linked to campus network. Online course registration available.

**Student life. Freshman orientation:** Mandatory. Preregistration for classes offered. **Housing:** Coed dorms, single-sex dorms, apartments, substance-free housing available. $150 fully refundable deposit. **Activities:** Bands, choral groups, drama, music ensembles, musical theater, student government, student newspaper, campus Christian fellowship, Christian athletes association.

**Athletics.** NJCAA. **Intercollegiate:** Baseball M, basketball, cross-country, football (tackle) M, softball W, track and field, volleyball W. **Intramural:** Badminton, basketball, softball, table tennis, tennis, volleyball. **Team name:** Scotties.

**Student services.** Adult student services, career counseling, student employment services, financial aid counseling, placement for graduates, veterans' counselor. **Physically disabled:** Services for visually, speech, hearing impaired. **Transfer:** Transfer adviser, college fairs on campus for students transferring to 4-year colleges.

**Contact.** Phone: (785) 442-6020 Fax: (785) 442-6106
Cheryl Rasmussen, Vice President for Student Services, Highland Community College, 606 West Main Street, Highland, KS 66035-0068

---

## Hutchinson Community College
**Hutchinson, Kansas**
**www.hutchcc.edu**                    CB code: 6281

- Public 2-year community college
- Commuter campus in large town

**General.** Founded in 1928. Regionally accredited. Additional centers in Newton, McPherson. **Enrollment:** 3,447 degree-seeking undergraduates; 1,152 non-degree-seeking students. **Degrees:** 576 associate awarded. **Location:** 45 miles from Wichita, 200 miles from Kansas City. **Calendar:** Semester, limited summer session. **Full-time faculty:** 113 total; 13% have terminal degrees, 4% minority, 49% women. **Part-time faculty:** 222 total; 3% have terminal degrees, 1% minority, 50% women. **Class size:** 81% <20, 17% 20-39, 1% 40-49, less than 1% 50-99. **Special facilities:** Cosmosphere space center, Kansas state fair, underground salt mine museum.

**Student profile.** Among degree-seeking undergraduates, 58% enrolled in a transfer program, 42% enrolled in a vocational program, 4% already have a bachelor's degree or higher, 968 enrolled as first-time, first-year students.

| | | | |
|---|---|---|---|
| Part-time: | 40% | Hispanic American: | 6% |
| Out-of-state: | 7% | Native American: | 1% |
| Women: | 58% | 25 or older: | 35% |
| African American: | 6% | Live on campus: | 11% |
| Asian American: | 1% | | |

**Transfer out.** 70% of students enrolled in the transfer program go on to 4-year colleges. **Colleges most students transferred to 2007:** Kansas State University, University of Kansas, Wichita State University, Emporia State University, Fort Hays State University.

**Basis for selection.** Open admission, but selective for some programs. Special requirements for associate degree programs in nursing, radiology, emergency medical sciences paramedic, health information technology, and to diploma program in licensed practical nursing and surgical technology. C-NET exam required for nursing program applicants. Interview required for nursing, radiology, paramedic, health information technology, surgical technology programs. **Homeschooled:** Provide home school/high school diploma or GED.

**2007-2008 Annual costs.** Tuition/fees: $2,070; $3,090 out-of-state. Per-credit charge: $54 in-state; $88 out-of-state. Room/board: $4,640. Books/supplies: $1,000. Personal expenses: $1,000.

**Financial aid. Need-based:** Need-based aid available for part-time students. **Non-need-based:** Scholarships awarded for academics, athletics, minority status, state residency.

**Application procedures. Admission:** No deadline. No application fee. Admission notification on a rolling basis. Priority application dates: 1/15 practical nursing, 2/1 nursing, 5/1 paramedic, 6/1 health information. **Financial aid:** Priority date 2/1; no closing date. FAFSA, institutional form required. Applicants notified on a rolling basis starting 4/1; must reply within 2 week(s) of notification.

**Academics. Special study options:** Cooperative education, distance learning, double major, dual enrollment of high school students, ESL, honors, independent study, internships, weekend college. **Credit/placement by examination:** AP, CLEP, institutional tests. 16 credit hours maximum toward associate degree. **Support services:** GED preparation and test center, learning center, remedial instruction, study skills assistance, tutoring, writing center.

**Majors. Agriculture:** General, farm/ranch, power machinery. **Biology:** General. **Business:** General, administrative services, personal/financial services, retailing. **Communications:** General. **Communications technology:** General. **Computer sciences:** General, networking, systems analysis. **Construction:** Carpentry. **Education:** General. **Engineering:** General. **Engineering technology:** Drafting, manufacturing. **English:** English lit. **Family/consumer sciences:** General, child care. **Foreign languages:** General. **Health:** EMT paramedic, medical radiologic technology/radiation therapy, medical records technology, nursing (RN). **Legal studies:** Paralegal. **Liberal arts:** Arts/sciences. **Math:** General. **Mechanic/repair:** Auto body, automotive, electronics/electrical. **Physical sciences:** General. **Production:** Machine tool, welding. **Protective services:** Fire safety technology, police science. **Psychology:** General. **Social sciences:** General. **Visual/performing arts:** General.

**Most popular majors.** Business/marketing 16%, health sciences 20%, liberal arts 22%, security/protective services 9%.

**Computing on campus.** 600 workstations in dormitories, library, computer center, student center. Dormitories wired for high-speed internet access. Helpline, wireless network available.

**Student life. Freshman orientation:** Available. Preregistration for classes offered. **Housing:** Single-sex dorms available. $100 deposit, deadline 7/15. **Activities:** Bands, choral groups, dance, drama, literary magazine, music ensembles, student government, student newspaper, symphony orchestra, Black Cultural Society, Hispanic American leadership organization, Hutchinson Christian Fellowship, Campus Crusade for Christ, Right to Life.

**Athletics.** NJCAA. **Intercollegiate:** Baseball M, basketball, cross-country, football (tackle) M, golf M, soccer W, softball W, tennis, track and field, volleyball W. **Intramural:** Badminton, basketball, bowling, racquetball, soccer, softball, table tennis, tennis, track and field, volleyball. **Team name:** Blue Dragons.

**Student services.** Adult student services, career counseling, student employment services, financial aid counseling, health services, on-campus daycare, personal counseling, placement for graduates, veterans' counselor. **Physically disabled:** Services for visually, speech, hearing impaired. **Transfer:**

Pre-admission transcript evaluation for new students. Transfer adviser, college fairs on campus for students transferring to 4-year colleges.

**Contact.** E-mail: info@hutchcc.edu
Phone: (620) 665-3536 Toll-free number: (800) 289-3501
Fax: (620) 665-3301
Corbin Strobel, Director of Admissions, Hutchinson Community College, 1300 North Plum, Hutchinson, KS 67501

## Independence Community College
**Independence, Kansas**
www.indycc.edu                                   CB code: 6304

◆ Public 2-year community and junior college
◆ Commuter campus in large town

**General.** Founded in 1925. Regionally accredited. **Enrollment:** 676 degree-seeking undergraduates. **Degrees:** 88 associate awarded. **Location:** 110 miles from Tulsa, Oklahoma. **Calendar:** Semester, extensive summer session. **Full-time faculty:** 27 total. **Part-time faculty:** 82 total. **Special facilities:** Collection of original manuscripts, press clippings, personal books and recordings of famous playright William Inge.

**Student profile.**

| | | | |
|---|---|---|---|
| Out-of-state: | 9% | Live on campus: | 10% |
| 25 or older: | 53% | | |

**Transfer out. Colleges most students transferred to 2007:** Pittsburg State University, Emporia State University, Wichita State University, Kansas State University, University of Kansas.

**Basis for selection.** Open admission.

**High school preparation.** 17 units recommended. Recommended units include English 4, mathematics 4, social studies 2, history 2, science 2 (laboratory 1) and foreign language 2.

**2007-2008 Annual costs.** Tuition/fees: $1,650; $1,650 out-of-district; $2,850 out-of-state. Per-credit charge: $25 in-district; $28 out-of-district; $68 out-of-state. Room/board: $4,200. Books/supplies: $500.

**Financial aid. Need-based:** Need-based aid available for part-time students. **Non-need-based:** Scholarships awarded for academics, athletics.

**Application procedures. Admission:** No deadline. No application fee. Application may be submitted online. Admission notification on a rolling basis beginning on or about 5/1. **Financial aid:** Priority date 4/1; no closing date. FAFSA required. Applicants notified on a rolling basis.

**Academics. Special study options:** Distance learning, double major, dual enrollment of high school students, ESL, independent study, internships. Bachelor's degree programs available on campus. **Credit/placement by examination:** CLEP, institutional tests. **Support services:** GED preparation and test center, learning center, reduced course load, remedial instruction, study skills assistance, tutoring, writing center.

**Majors. Agriculture:** Business. **Biology:** General, botany, zoology. **Business:** General, accounting, administrative services, business admin, office technology, office/clerical. **Communications:** General, advertising, broadcast journalism, journalism. **Computer sciences:** General, data processing, information systems, programming, systems analysis. **Education:** General, art, biology, chemistry, computer, early childhood, elementary, English, health, history, mathematics, middle, music, physical, sales/marketing, school counseling, science, social science, social studies, technology/industrial arts, voc/tech. **Engineering:** General, architectural, chemical, civil. **Engineering technology:** Architectural, civil, drafting. **English:** American lit, composition, English lit, technical writing. **Family/consumer sciences:** Child care. **Foreign languages:** General, French, Spanish. **Health:** EMT paramedic, medical secretary, nursing assistant. **History:** General. **Legal studies:** Legal secretary, paralegal, prelaw. **Liberal arts:** Arts/sciences. **Math:** General, applied, statistics. **Physical sciences:** Chemistry. **Psychology:** General. **Public administration:** Human services, social work. **Social sciences:** General, economics, political science, sociology. **Visual/performing arts:** Art, dramatic, studio arts.

**Most popular majors.** Business/marketing 30%, education 10%, liberal arts 52%.

**Computing on campus.** 130 workstations in library, computer center, student center. Online course registration available.

Two-Year Colleges

**Student life. Freshman orientation:** Mandatory, $15 fee. **Housing:** Coed dorms available. $50 deposit. **Activities:** Bands, choral groups, drama, music ensembles, musical theater, radio station, student government, student newspaper.

**Athletics.** NJCAA. **Intercollegiate:** Baseball M, basketball, football (tackle) M, softball W, tennis, track and field, volleyball W. **Intramural:** Basketball. **Team name:** Pirates.

**Student services.** Adult student services, career counseling, student employment services, financial aid counseling, personal counseling, placement for graduates, veterans' counselor. **Transfer:** Pre-admission transcript evaluation for new students. Transfer adviser, college fairs on campus for students transferring to 4-year colleges.

**Contact.** E-mail: admissions@indycc.edu
Phone: (620) 331-4100 Toll-free number: (800) 842-6063 ext. 5400
Fax: (620) 331-0946
Sally Ciufulescu, Director of Admissions, Independence Community College, 1057 West College Avenue, Independence, KS 67301

## Johnson County Community College
**Overland Park, Kansas**
www.jccc.edu
CB code: 6325

- Public 2-year community college
- Commuter campus in very large city

**General.** Founded in 1967. Regionally accredited. **Enrollment:** 7,736 degree-seeking undergraduates. **Degrees:** 1,091 associate awarded. **Location:** 20 miles from downtown Kansas City. **Calendar:** Semester, extensive summer session. **Full-time faculty:** 220 total. **Part-time faculty:** 500 total. **Special facilities:** National academy of railroad sciences.

**Student profile.** Among degree-seeking undergraduates, 43% enrolled in a transfer program, 35% enrolled in a vocational program.

| | | | |
|---|---|---|---|
| Out-of-state: | 6% | 25 or older: | 37% |

**Transfer out. Colleges most students transferred to 2007:** Kansas University, Kansas State University.

**Basis for selection.** Open admission, but selective for some programs. Special requirements for some allied health programs. Test scores cannot be older than two years. SAT critial reading not accepted. ACT required for admission for nursing and dental hygiene applicants. Interview required for nursing, dental hygiene, emergency medical intensive care technician, respiratory therapy, paralegal programs. Portfolio required of art majors. **Adult students:** SAT/ACT scores not required. **Homeschooled:** Transcript of courses and grades required. **Learning Disabled:** Access services office assists students with documented disabilities.

**2007-2008 Annual costs.** Tuition/fees: $1,890; $2,340 out-of-district; $4,320 out-of-state. Per-credit charge: $63 in-district; $78 out-of-district; $144 out-of-state. Books/supplies: $1,000. Personal expenses: $1,500.

**Financial aid. Need-based:** Need-based aid available for part-time students. **Non-need-based:** Scholarships awarded for academics.

**Application procedures. Admission:** No deadline. No application fee. Application may be submitted online. Admission notification on a rolling basis. **Financial aid:** Priority date 4/1; no closing date. FAFSA required. Applicants notified on a rolling basis starting 4/15; must reply within 2 week(s) of notification.

**Academics.** Wide variety of telecourses and courses offered by special arrangement. **Special study options:** Cooperative education, cross-registration, distance learning, double major, dual enrollment of high school students, ESL, exchange student, honors, independent study, internships, study abroad, weekend college. **Credit/placement by examination:** AP, CLEP, institutional tests. 30 credit hours maximum toward associate degree. **Support services:** GED preparation and test center, learning center, reduced course load, remedial instruction, tutoring, writing center.

**Majors. Business:** Accounting, administrative services, business admin, sales/distribution. **Computer sciences:** Applications programming, networking. **Construction:** Power transmission. **Engineering technology:** Civil, drafting, electrical. **Family/consumer sciences:** Child care, institutional food production. **Foreign languages:** Sign language interpretation. **Health:** Dental hygiene, EMT paramedic, medical radiologic technology/radiation therapy, medical records technology, nursing (RN), occupational therapy assistant, physical therapy assistant, respiratory therapy technology, surgical technology, veterinary technology/assistant. **Legal studies:** Paralegal. **Liberal arts:** Arts/sciences. **Mechanic/repair:** Automotive, electronics/electrical. **Protective services:** Firefighting, police science. **Visual/performing arts:** Commercial/advertising art.

**Most popular majors.** Business/marketing 7%, family/consumer sciences 8%, health sciences 12%, liberal arts 60%.

**Computing on campus.** 800 workstations in library, computer center, student center. Online course registration, online library, helpline, wireless network available.

**Student life. Freshman orientation:** Available. **Activities:** Bands, choral groups, drama, student government, student newspaper.

**Athletics.** NJCAA. **Intercollegiate:** Baseball M, basketball, cross-country, golf M, soccer M, softball W, tennis, track and field, volleyball W. **Intramural:** Basketball M, bowling, handball, racquetball, softball M, table tennis M, tennis M, volleyball M. **Team name:** Cavaliers.

**Student services.** Adult student services, career counseling, student employment services, on-campus daycare, personal counseling, placement for graduates, veterans' counselor. **Physically disabled:** Services for visually, hearing impaired. **Transfer:** Transfer adviser, college fairs on campus for students transferring to 4-year colleges.

**Contact.** E-mail: JCCCAdmissions@jccc.edu
Phone: (913) 469-3803 Toll-free number: (866) 896-5893
Fax: (913) 469-2524
Pete Belk, Director of Admission, Johnson County Community College, 12345 College Boulevard, Overland Park, KS 66210-1299

## Kansas City Kansas Community College
**Kansas City, Kansas**
www.kckcc.edu
CB member
CB code: 6333

- Public 2-year community and junior college
- Commuter campus in very large city

**General.** Founded in 1923. Regionally accredited. **Enrollment:** 4,339 degree-seeking undergraduates; 1,462 non-degree-seeking students. **Degrees:** 559 associate awarded. **Calendar:** Semester, extensive summer session. **Full-time faculty:** 118 total; 30% have terminal degrees, 19% minority, 52% women. **Part-time faculty:** 316 total. **Class size:** 74% < 20, 25% 20-39, less than 1% 40-49, less than 1% 50-99.

**Student profile.** Among degree-seeking undergraduates, 80% enrolled in a transfer program, 29% enrolled in a vocational program, 11% already have a bachelor's degree or higher, 918 enrolled as first-time, first-year students.

| | | | |
|---|---|---|---|
| Part-time: | 58% | Hispanic American: | 7% |
| Out-of-state: | 5% | Native American: | 1% |
| Women: | 66% | International: | 2% |
| African American: | 27% | 25 or older: | 48% |
| Asian American: | 2% | | |

**Basis for selection.** Open admission, but selective for some programs. Special requirements for nursing program. **Homeschooled:** Interview required. Admission based on ACT, SAT, or GED scores and interview.

**High school preparation.** 21 units recommended. Recommended units include English 4, mathematics 4, social studies 4, history 4, science 3 and foreign language 2.

**2007-2008 Annual costs.** Tuition/fees: $1,770; $4,710 out-of-state. Per-credit charge: $49 in-state; $147 out-of-state. Fees vary by program. Books/supplies: $850. Personal expenses: $2,250.

**2006-2007 Financial aid. Need-based:** 44% of total undergraduate aid awarded as scholarships/grants, 56% as loans/jobs. Need-based aid available for part-time students. Work-study available nights, weekends and for part-time students. **Non-need-based:** Scholarships awarded for academics, art, athletics, music/drama.

**Application procedures. Admission:** No deadline. No application fee. Application may be submitted online. Admission notification on a rolling basis. **Financial aid:** Priority date 4/15; no closing date. FAFSA required. Applicants notified on a rolling basis starting 5/1; must reply within 4 week(s) of notification.

**Academics.** Extensive online classes. **Special study options:** Cooperative education, distance learning, dual enrollment of high school students, ESL, external degree, honors, internships, liberal arts/career combination, weekend college. PACE (Program for Adult College Education). **Credit/placement by examination:** AP, CLEP, IB, institutional tests. 15 credit hours maximum toward associate degree. **Support services:** GED preparation and test center, learning center, reduced course load, remedial instruction, study skills assistance, tutoring, writing center.

**Majors. Business:** Accounting/business management, administrative services, business admin, marketing. **Communications technology:** Desktop publishing, recording arts. **Computer sciences:** Networking. **Engineering technology:** CAD/CADD, computer, hazardous materials, software. **Family/consumer sciences:** Child care. **Health:** EMT paramedic, nursing (RN), physical therapy assistant, respiratory therapy assistant, respiratory therapy technology, substance abuse counseling. **Legal studies:** Paralegal. **Liberal arts:** Arts/sciences. **Personal/culinary services:** Mortuary science. **Protective services:** Corrections, firefighting, police science. **Other:** Victim/Survivor services.

**Most popular majors.** Health sciences 24%, liberal arts 48%, personal/culinary services 8%, security/protective services 6%.

**Computing on campus.** 900 workstations in library, computer center. Commuter students can connect to campus network. Online course registration, online library, helpline, wireless network available.

**Student life. Freshman orientation:** Mandatory, $59 fee. Preregistration for classes offered. **Activities:** Bands, choral groups, drama, music ensembles, musical theater, student government, student newspaper, TV station, African American Student Union, international student organization, campus forum, Christian Student Union, Phi Theta Kappa, student senate, Out Questioning & Straight Diversity Club, student organization of Latinos, economics club, students in free enterprise.

**Athletics.** NJCAA. **Intercollegiate:** Baseball M, basketball, cross-country, golf M, soccer M, softball W, track and field, volleyball W. **Team name:** Blue Devils.

**Student services.** Adult student services, alcohol/substance abuse counseling, career counseling, services for economically disadvantaged, student employment services, financial aid counseling, health services, on-campus daycare, personal counseling, veterans' counselor, women's services. **Physically disabled:** Services for visually, speech, hearing impaired. **Learning disabled:** Comprehensive services available. **Transfer:** Transfer adviser, college fairs on campus for students transferring to 4-year colleges.

**Contact.** E-mail: admiss@kckcc.edu
Phone: (913) 288-7600 Fax: (913) 288-7648
Denise McDowell, Dean of Enrollment Management and Registrar, Kansas City Kansas Community College, 7250 State Avenue, Kansas City, KS 66112

## Labette Community College
Parsons, Kansas
www.labette.edu                                    CB code: 6576

- Public 2-year community college
- Commuter campus in large town

**General. Founded** in 1923. Regionally accredited. **Enrollment:** 934 degree-seeking undergraduates, 415 non-degree-seeking students. **Degrees:** 188 associate awarded. **Location:** 130 miles from Kansas City, 50 miles from Tulsa, Oklahoma. **Calendar:** Semester, extensive summer session. **Full-time faculty:** 30 total; 23% have terminal degrees, 10% minority, 50% women. **Part-time faculty:** 97 total; 3% have terminal degrees, 65% women. **Class size:** 78% < 20, 22% 20-39, less than 1% 40-49. **Special facilities:** Commercial music program and equipment, health science facilities. **Partnerships:** Formal partnerships with local businesses.

**Student profile.** Among degree-seeking undergraduates, 38% enrolled in a transfer program, 62% enrolled in a vocational program, 1% already have a bachelor's degree or higher, 164 enrolled as first-time, first-year students.

| | | | |
|---|---|---|---|
| Part-time: | 54% | Hispanic American: | 3% |
| Out-of-state: | 5% | Native American: | 4% |
| Women: | 66% | International: | 1% |
| African American: | 5% | 25 or older: | 41% |
| Asian American: | 1% | Live on campus: | 3% |

**Transfer out. Colleges most students transferred to 2007:** Pittsburg State, Emporia State, Wichita State, Kansas University, Kansas State University.

**Basis for selection.** Open admission, but selective for some programs. Special requirements for health and commercial music programs. COMPASS also used to measure language proficiency. ACT, school and College Ability Tests required of nursing applicants. Interview required for nursing, radiology, respiratory therapy programs and commercial music programs. **Homeschooled:** Transcript of courses and grades required. GED and ACT scores may be considered. Placement testing available. **Learning Disabled:** Student must notify campus ADA coordinator at least 30 days prior to first day of classes (earlier in special circumstances).

**2007-2008 Annual costs.** Tuition/fees: $2,130; $2,880 out-of-state. Per-credit charge: $42 in-state; $67 out-of-state. Residents of neighboring states (AR, MO, OK) pay per-credit-hour tuition rate of $63. Books/supplies: $550. Personal expenses: $2,000.

**Financial aid. Need-based:** Need-based aid available for part-time students. Work-study available nights. **Non-need-based:** Scholarships awarded for academics, leadership.

**Application procedures. Admission:** No deadline. No application fee. Admission notification on a rolling basis. **Financial aid:** No deadline. FAFSA required. Applicants notified on a rolling basis starting 4/4; must reply within 2 week(s) of notification.

**Academics.** Extensive PLATO learning system available. Four-year bachelor's program with Emporia State University, Washburn University. **Special study options:** Distance learning, dual enrollment of high school students, liberal arts/career combination. License preparation in nursing, radiology. **Credit/placement by examination:** AP, CLEP, institutional tests. 12 credit hours maximum toward associate degree. **Support services:** GED preparation and test center, learning center, remedial instruction, study skills assistance, tutoring, writing center.

**Majors. Biology:** General. **Business:** Accounting, business admin, office/clerical. **Communications:** Journalism. **Computer sciences:** General, data processing, LAN/WAN management, networking, programming. **Education:** General, business, early childhood, elementary, music, secondary. **English:** English lit. **Health:** Medical secretary, nursing (RN), radiologic technology/medical imaging, respiratory therapy technology. **History:** General. **Legal studies:** Legal secretary, prelaw. **Liberal arts:** Arts/sciences. **Protective services:** Corrections, firefighting, law enforcement admin. **Psychology:** General. **Social sciences:** General, political science. **Visual/performing arts:** Commercial/advertising art, music management, studio arts.

**Most popular majors.** Business/marketing 11%, education 15%, health sciences 53%.

**Computing on campus.** 150 workstations in library, computer center, student center. Commuter students can connect to campus network. Online library, helpline, student web hosting, wireless network available.

**Student life. Freshman orientation:** Mandatory. **Activities:** Bands, choral groups, dance, drama, music ensembles, student government, Christian Club, Phi Beta Lambda, Phi Theta Kappa.

**Athletics.** NJCAA. **Intercollegiate:** Baseball M, basketball, cheerleading, softball W, tennis W, volleyball W, wrestling M. **Team name:** Cardinals.

**Student services.** Adult student services, career counseling, services for economically disadvantaged, student employment services, financial aid counseling, personal counseling, placement for graduates, veterans' counselor. **Physically disabled:** Services for visually, speech, hearing impaired. **Transfer:** Transfer adviser, college fairs on campus for students transferring to 4-year colleges.

**Contact.** Phone: (620) 421-6700 Toll-free number: (888) 522-3883
Fax: (620) 421-0180
Tammy Fuentez, Director of Admissions, Labette Community College, 200 South 14th Street, Parsons, KS 67357

## Manhattan Area Technical College
Manhattan, Kansas
www.matc.net

- Public 2-year technical college
- Commuter campus in large town

**General. Enrollment:** 400 degree-seeking undergraduates. **Degrees:** 99 associate awarded. **Location:** 125 miles from Kansas City. **Calendar:** Semester, limited summer session. **Full-time faculty:** 27 total. **Part-time faculty:** 5 total.

**Basis for selection.** Open admission, but selective for some programs. Practical Nursing applicants must meet testing requirements and be KS licensed Certified Nurse Aide; Associate Degree/Registered Nurse applicants must be KS licensed Practical Nurses; Electric Power & Distribution applicants must be 18 years of age prior to June 1 of their year of enrollment and have or be eligible to receive a Commercial Drivers License by the same date. WorkKeys testing is required for Practical Nursing applicants.

**2007-2008 Annual costs.** Tuition/fees: $2,250. Per-credit charge: $63.

**Financial aid. Need-based:** Need-based aid available for part-time students. **Non-need-based:** Scholarships awarded for academics, leadership.

**Application procedures. Admission:** No deadline. $40 fee. Application must be submitted on paper. Admission notification on a rolling basis. **Financial aid:** No deadline. FAFSA, institutional form required. Applicants notified on a rolling basis.

**Academics. Special study options:** Cooperative education. License preparation in nursing. **Credit/placement by examination:** AP, CLEP, institutional tests. 9 credit hours maximum toward associate degree. **Support services:** Learning center, reduced course load, study skills assistance, tutoring.

**Majors. Business:** Executive assistant. **Computer sciences:** General. **Construction:** Carpentry, power transmission. **Engineering technology:** CAD/CADD, industrial. **Health:** Nursing (RN). **Mechanic/repair:** Auto body, automotive, heating/ac/refrig. **Production:** Welding.

**Most popular majors.** Business/marketing 10%, communication technologies 15%, computer/information sciences 20%, engineering/engineering technologies 20%, health sciences 9%, trade and industry 14%.

**Computing on campus.** 16 workstations in library, student center. Commuter students can connect to campus network. Online library, wireless network available.

**Student life. Freshman orientation:** Mandatory. Preregistration for classes offered. Approximately 6-8 weeks prior to beginning of semester. Half day sessions include pre-enrollment, and pre-testing.

**Student services.** Career counseling, financial aid counseling, personal counseling, placement for graduates. **Transfer:** Pre-admission transcript evaluation for new students.

**Contact.** E-mail: rsmith@matc.net
Phone: (785) 587-2800 ext. 104 Toll-free number: (800) 352-7575 ext. 104
Fax: (785) 587-2804
Rick Smith, Director of Admissions, Manhattan Area Technical College, 3136 Dickens Avenue, Manhattan, KS 66503-2499

---

## Neosho County Community College
Chanute, Kansas
www.neosho.edu                              CB code: 6093

- Public 2-year community college
- Commuter campus in small town

**General.** Founded in 1936. Regionally accredited. **Enrollment:** 1,994 undergraduates. **Degrees:** 183 associate awarded. **Location:** 110 miles from Kansas City, Missouri, 100 miles from Wichita. **Calendar:** Semester, limited summer session. **Full-time faculty:** 50 total. **Part-time faculty:** 130 total. **Class size:** 83% < 20, 15% 20-39, 2% 40-49.

**Student profile.**

| | | | |
|---|---|---|---|
| Out-of-state: | 14% | Live on campus: | 28% |

**Transfer out. Colleges most students transferred to 2007:** Pittsburg State University, Emporia State University, Kansas State University, University of Kansas, Wichita State University.

**Basis for selection.** Open admission, but selective for some programs. Special requirements for nursing program, nursing entrance test (NET) required. Students not submitting ACT scores take college-administered placement exam. **Homeschooled:** Must take GED.

**2007-2008 Annual costs.** Tuition/fees: $1,860; $2,460 out-of-district; $2,910 out-of-state. Per-credit charge: $40. Room/board: $3,940. Books/supplies: $350. Personal expenses: $360.

**Financial aid. Need-based:** Need-based aid available for part-time students. Work-study available nights, weekends and for part-time students. **Non-need-based:** Scholarships awarded for academics, art, athletics, music/drama, state residency.

**Application procedures. Admission:** Priority date 8/15; no deadline. No application fee. Application may be submitted online. Admission notification on a rolling basis. **Financial aid:** Priority date 4/1; no closing date. FAFSA required. Applicants notified on a rolling basis; must reply within 6 week(s) of notification.

**Academics. Special study options:** Cooperative education, distance learning, dual enrollment of high school students, ESL, honors, independent study, liberal arts/career combination, weekend college. License preparation in nursing, real estate. **Credit/placement by examination:** CLEP, institutional tests. 15 credit hours maximum toward associate degree. **Support services:** GED preparation and test center, learning center, reduced course load, remedial instruction, study skills assistance, tutoring, writing center.

**Majors. Biology:** General. **Business:** Accounting, administrative services, banking/financial services, business admin, office management. **Communications:** General. **Computer sciences:** General. **Education:** General, secondary. **Engineering technology:** Computer systems, drafting, industrial. **English:** English lit. **Family/consumer sciences:** General. **Foreign languages:** General. **Health:** Athletic training, health care admin, licensed practical nurse, nursing (RN). **Interdisciplinary:** Natural sciences. **Liberal arts:** Arts/sciences. **Math:** General. **Parks/recreation:** Exercise sciences. **Physical sciences:** Chemistry. **Psychology:** General. **Public administration:** Social work. **Social sciences:** General. **Visual/performing arts:** Art, dramatic, studio arts.

**Most popular majors.** Business/marketing 15%, health sciences 49%, liberal arts 24%.

**Computing on campus.** 120 workstations in dormitories, library, computer center, student center. Dormitories wired for high-speed internet access. Online library, helpline, wireless network available.

**Student life. Freshman orientation:** Mandatory. Preregistration for classes offered. **Housing:** Guaranteed on-campus for freshmen. Coed dorms available. $100 nonrefundable deposit. Home stays with host families for international students. **Activities:** Choral groups, dance, drama, music ensembles, musical theater, student government.

**Athletics.** NJCAA. **Intercollegiate:** Baseball M, basketball, cheerleading, cross-country, soccer, softball W, track and field, volleyball W, wrestling M. **Team name:** Panthers.

**Student services.** Adult student services, career counseling, student employment services, financial aid counseling, personal counseling, placement for graduates, veterans' counselor. **Physically disabled:** Services for visually, speech, hearing impaired. **Transfer:** Pre-admission transcript evaluation for new students. Transfer center, transfer adviser, college fairs on campus for students transferring to 4-year colleges.

**Contact.** E-mail: amkiefer@neosho.edu
Phone: (620) 431-2820 ext. 233 Toll-free number: (800) 729-6222
Fax: (316) 431-6056
Dean of Student Development, Neosho County Community College, 800 West 14th Street, Chanute, KS 66720

---

## North Central Kansas Technical College
Beloit, Kansas
www.ncktc.edu                              CB code: 2616

- Public 2-year technical college
- Small town

**General.** Regionally accredited. Multicampus institution. **Enrollment:** 260 degree-seeking undergraduates. **Degrees:** 170 associate awarded. **Location:** 107 miles from Hays, 175 miles from Topeka. **Calendar:** Semester. **Full-time faculty:** 43 total. **Part-time faculty:** 7 total.

**Student profile.** Among degree-seeking undergraduates, 100% enrolled in a vocational program.

**Basis for selection.** Open admission. **Learning Disabled:** Students must present written documentation from certified professional identifying disability with recommendations for accommodations.

**2007-2008 Annual costs.** Tuition/fees: $3,171. Room/board: $3,950. Books/supplies: $800.

**Financial aid.** All financial aid based on need. Need-based aid available for part-time students. Work-study available nights and for part-time students.

**Application procedures. Admission:** No deadline. $50 fee. Admission notification on a rolling basis. **Financial aid:** No deadline. FAFSA required.

**Academics. Credit/placement by examination:** CLEP.

**Majors. Agriculture:** Equipment technology. **Engineering technology:** Electrical. **Health:** Nursing (RN). **Mechanic/repair:** Automotive, diesel, electronics/electrical.

**Student life. Freshman orientation:** Available. Preregistration for classes offered. **Housing:** Coed dorms available. **Activities:** Student government.

**Athletics. Intramural:** Basketball M, football (non-tackle) M, volleyball, wrestling M.

**Student services.** Career counseling, financial aid counseling, placement for graduates.

**Contact.** Phone: (800) 658-4655 Toll-free number: (800) 658-4655
Fax: (785) 738-2903
David Hughes, Admissions Director, North Central Kansas Technical
College, P.O. Box 507, Beloit, KS 67420

## Pratt Community College
Pratt, Kansas
www.prattcc.edu                                    CB code: 6581

◗ Public 2-year community and technical college
◗ Commuter campus in small town

**General.** Founded in 1938. Regionally accredited. **Enrollment:** 778 degree-seeking undergraduates; 760 non-degree-seeking students. **Degrees:** 179 associate awarded. **Location:** 70 miles from Wichita. **Calendar:** Semester, limited summer session. **Full-time faculty:** 43 total; 7% have terminal degrees, 60% women. **Part-time faculty:** 124 total; 8% have terminal degrees, 8% minority, 52% women. **Class size:** 64% < 20, 33% 20-39, 2% 40-49, less than 1% 50-99. **Special facilities:** Indoor and outdoor rodeo facilities, electrical powerlineman training facility.

**Student profile.** Among degree-seeking undergraduates, 60% enrolled in a transfer program, 40% enrolled in a vocational program, 279 enrolled as first-time, first-year students.

| | | | |
|---|---|---|---|
| Part-time: | 16% | Native American: | 1% |
| Out-of-state: | 16% | International: | 3% |
| Women: | 49% | 25 or older: | 20% |
| African American: | 4% | Live on campus: | 36% |
| Hispanic American: | 4% | | |

**Transfer out. Colleges most students transferred to 2007:** Fort Hays State University, Emporia State University, Kansas State University.

**Basis for selection.** Open admission, but selective for some programs. Special requirements for nursing, agriculture power technology and electrical power distribution programs. ACT scores used if they are high enough for course placement; if not, ASSET administered. Interview required of nursing majors. Audition required of music and drama majors. Portfolio recommended for art majors. **Homeschooled:** Transcript of courses and grades required. **Learning Disabled:** IEP's must be submitted to admissions before initial enrollment and request of services.

**2007-2008 Annual costs.** Tuition/fees: $2,190; $2,190 out-of-state. Per-credit charge: $44 in-state; $44 out-of-state. Out-of-district Kansas residents have additional fee of $100; out-of-state $200, and international students $300 for the year. Technology fee applicable for auto, ag power, and electrical power areas. Room/board: $4,421. Books/supplies: $800. Personal expenses: $1,000.

**2006-2007 Financial aid. Need-based:** 56% of total undergraduate aid awarded as scholarships/grants, 44% as loans/jobs. Need-based aid available for part-time students. Work-study available for part-time students. **Non-need-based:** Scholarships awarded for academics, art, athletics, leadership, minority status, music/drama, state residency.

**Application procedures. Admission:** No deadline. No application fee. Application may be submitted online. Admission notification on a rolling basis beginning on or about 1/1. **Financial aid:** Priority date 5/1, closing date 8/1. FAFSA, institutional form required. Applicants notified on a rolling basis starting 2/1; must reply within 2 week(s) of notification.

**Academics. Special study options:** Combined bachelor's/graduate degree, distance learning, dual enrollment of high school students, honors, independent study, internships, liberal arts/career combination, weekend college. Bachelor's degree programs available on campus. License preparation in nursing. **Credit/placement by examination:** AP, CLEP, IB, institutional tests. 15 credit hours maximum toward associate degree. **Support services:** GED preparation, learning center, remedial instruction, tutoring.

**Majors. Agriculture:** General, animal sciences, business, farm/ranch, range science. **Biology:** General, botany. **Business:** Accounting, business admin, entrepreneurial studies, office management, office technology, office/clerical, operations. **Communications:** General, journalism. **Computer sciences:** General. **Conservation:** Wildlife. **Education:** General, early childhood, elementary, secondary. **Engineering:** General. **English:** English lit, speech/rhetoric. **Health:** Licensed practical nurse, medical secretary, nursing (RN), predental, premedicine, prepharmacy, preveterinary. **History:** General. **Interdisciplinary:** Biological/physical sciences. **Legal studies:** Legal secretary, prelaw. **Liberal arts:** Arts/sciences. **Math:** General. **Mechanic/repair:** Automotive. **Physical sciences:** Chemistry, inorganic chemistry, physics. **Psychology:** General. **Social sciences:** General, political science, sociology. **Visual/performing arts:** General, ceramics, commercial/advertising art, dramatic, drawing, painting, studio arts.

**Most popular majors.** Agriculture 9%, business/marketing 15%, health sciences 28%, liberal arts 21%, trade and industry 16%.

**Computing on campus.** 125 workstations in dormitories, library, computer center. Dormitories wired for high-speed internet access and linked to campus network. Commuter students can connect to campus network. On-line course registration, online library, helpline, wireless network available.

**Student life. Freshman orientation:** Mandatory. Preregistration for classes offered. Held preceding each fall and spring semester. One to 2 days before classes begin. **Policies:** Meningitis inoculations required for dorm students. **Housing:** Coed dorms, single-sex dorms, substance-free housing available. $200 deposit. **Activities:** Bands, choral groups, dance, drama, literary magazine, music ensembles, musical theater, student government, student newspaper, Christian Challenge, Student Senate, Student Ambassadors.

**Athletics.** NJCAA. **Intercollegiate:** Baseball M, basketball, cheerleading, cross-country, golf, rodeo, softball W, track and field, volleyball W, wrestling M. **Intramural:** Basketball, football (non-tackle), rodeo, softball, table tennis, volleyball. **Team name:** Beavers.

**Student services.** Adult student services, career counseling, student employment services, financial aid counseling, health services, on-campus daycare, personal counseling, placement for graduates, veterans' counselor. **Physically disabled:** Services for visually, speech, hearing impaired. **Transfer:** College fairs on campus for students transferring to 4-year colleges.

**Contact.** E-mail: lynnp@prattcc.edu
Phone: (620) 672-5641 ext. 217 Toll-free number: (800) 794-3091 ext. 217
Fax: (620) 672-5288
Lynn Perez, Director of Admissions, Pratt Community College, 348 Northeast State Road 61, Pratt, KS 67124-8317

## Seward County Community College
Liberal, Kansas
www.sccc.edu                                        CB code: 0286

◗ Public 2-year community college
◗ Commuter campus in large town

**General.** Founded in 1967. Regionally accredited. Off-campus classes offered in 7 locations, adult learning center with ESL classes, interactive television classrooms to off-site locations, adult basic education classes, GED testing available. **Enrollment:** 1,387 degree-seeking undergraduates. **Degrees:** 179 associate awarded. **Location:** 210 miles from Wichita, 150 miles from Amarillo, Texas. **Calendar:** Semester, limited summer session. **Full-time faculty:** 46 total. **Part-time faculty:** 98 total. **Class size:** 83% < 20, 16% 20-39, less than 1% 40-49, less than 1% 50-99. **Special facilities:** Wellness center.

**Student profile.**

| | | | |
|---|---|---|---|
| Out-of-state: | 19% | Live on campus: | 15% |
| 25 or older: | 34% | | |

**Transfer out. Colleges most students transferred to 2007:** Kansas State University, Texas Christian University, University of Texas-Arlington, University of Central Oklahoma, Fort Hays State University.

**Basis for selection.** Open admission, but selective for some programs.

**High school preparation.** 20 units recommended. Recommended units include English 4, mathematics 3, social studies 2, science 2 and foreign language 1.

**2007-2008 Annual costs.** Tuition/fees: $1,860; $2,550 out-of-state. Per-credit charge: $40 in-state; $63 out-of-state. Residents of neighboring counties in OK, TX and CO pay per-credit-hour rate of $50. Room/board: $4,100. Books/supplies: $700. Personal expenses: $1,000.

**2006-2007 Financial aid. Need-based:** 42% of total undergraduate aid awarded as scholarships/grants, 58% as loans/jobs. Need-based aid available for part-time students. **Non-need-based:** Scholarships awarded for academics, athletics.

**Application procedures. Admission:** Priority date 4/1; no deadline. No application fee. Admission notification on a rolling basis. **Financial aid:** Priority date 4/1; no closing date. FAFSA, institutional form required. Applicants notified on a rolling basis starting 6/15; must reply within 4 week(s) of notification.

**Academics. Special study options:** Cooperative education, cross-registration, distance learning, double major, dual enrollment of high school students, ESL, external degree, honors, independent study, internships, liberal arts/career combination. Bachelor's degree programs available on campus. License preparation in nursing, paramedic. **Credit/placement by examination:** AP, CLEP, institutional tests. 24 credit hours maximum toward associate degree. **Support services:** GED preparation and test center, learning center, remedial instruction, study skills assistance, tutoring, writing center.

**Majors. Agriculture:** General, animal sciences, business, economics, farm/ranch. **Biology:** General. **Business:** General, accounting, administrative services, business admin, fashion, finance, hospitality admin, office management, office technology, office/clerical, sales/distribution. **Communications:** General, journalism. **Computer sciences:** General, applications programming, computer graphics, computer science, data entry, data processing, information technology, programming. **Conservation:** Forestry, wildlife. **Education:** General, teacher assistance. **Engineering:** General. **English:** English lit. **Health:** Athletic training, clinical lab assistant, clinical lab technology, dental hygiene, medical secretary, nursing (RN), predental, premedicine, prenursing, prepharmacy, preveterinary, respiratory therapy technology. **History:** General. **Interdisciplinary:** Biological/physical sciences, math/computer science, natural sciences. **Legal studies:** Legal secretary, prelaw. **Liberal arts:** Arts/sciences, library assistant. **Math:** General. **Military:** General. **Parks/recreation:** General, exercise sciences, health/fitness. **Personal/culinary services:** Cosmetology. **Philosophy/religion:** Religion. **Physical sciences:** Chemistry, physics. **Protective services:** Law enforcement admin, police science. **Psychology:** General. **Public administration:** Social work. **Social sciences:** General, economics, sociology. **Visual/performing arts:** General, art, ceramics, dramatic, music performance, painting, studio arts, voice/opera.

**Computing on campus.** 450 workstations in dormitories, library, computer center, student center. Dormitories wired for high-speed internet access. Commuter students can connect to campus network. Online course registration, online library, wireless network available.

**Student life. Freshman orientation:** Mandatory. Preregistration for classes offered. **Housing:** Coed dorms available. $100 deposit, deadline 6/30. **Activities:** Bands, choral groups, drama, film society, literary magazine, music ensembles, musical theater, student government, student newspaper, symphony orchestra, TV station.

**Athletics.** NJCAA. **Intercollegiate:** Baseball M, basketball, softball W, tennis, volleyball W. **Intramural:** Basketball, bowling, football (non-tackle), golf, soccer, swimming, table tennis, volleyball. **Team name:** Saints.

**Student services.** Adult student services, career counseling, student employment services, financial aid counseling, personal counseling, veterans' counselor. **Learning disabled:** Comprehensive services available. **Transfer:** Transfer adviser, college fairs on campus for students transferring to 4-year colleges.

**Contact.** E-mail: desiree.maxwell@sccc.edu
Phone: (620) 417-1102 Toll-free number: (800) 373-9951 ext. 1102
Fax: (620) 417-1079
Desiree Maxwell, Director of Admissions, Seward County Community
College, 1801 North Kansas Avenue, Liberal, KS 67905-1137

# Kentucky

## Ashland Community and Technical College
**Ashland, Kentucky**
**www.ashland.kctcs.edu**
**CB code: 0703**

▸ Public 2-year community college
▸ Commuter campus in large town

**General.** Founded in 1957. Regionally accredited. Off-campus classes in surrounding counties. **Enrollment:** 2,422 degree-seeking undergraduates. **Degrees:** 307 associate awarded. **Location:** 120 miles from Lexington; 15 miles from Huntington, West Virginia. **Calendar:** Semester, limited summer session. **Full-time faculty:** 96 total. **Part-time faculty:** 123 total. **Special facilities:** 3 open computer labs, learning assistance center, early intervention program for students at risk.

**Student profile.**

| | | | |
|---|---|---|---|
| Out-of-state: | 26% | 25 or older: | 43% |

**Transfer out. Colleges most students transferred to 2007:** Morehead State University, Marshall University, Shawnee State University.

**Basis for selection.** Open admission, but selective for some programs. Admission to nursing program based on test scores and academic record. COMPASS test used for placement. Interview recommended.

**High school preparation.** 11 units recommended. Recommended units include English 4, mathematics 3, social studies 2, science 2 (laboratory 2).

**2007-2008 Annual costs.** Tuition/fees: $3,450; $10,350 out-of-state. Per-credit charge: $115 in-state; $345 out-of-state. Books/supplies: $450. Personal expenses: $920.

**Financial aid. Non-need-based:** Scholarships awarded for academics, job skills, leadership, minority status, music/drama. **Additional information:** In-state 100% disabled or deceased veterans' children receive tuition waiver from state.

**Application procedures. Admission:** No deadline. No application fee. Application may be submitted online. Admission notification on a rolling basis. Nursing applications due by March 1. **Financial aid:** Priority date 3/15; no closing date. FAFSA, institutional form required. Applicants notified on a rolling basis starting 5/1; must reply within 3 week(s) of notification.

**Academics. Special study options:** Cooperative education, cross-registration, distance learning, dual enrollment of high school students, honors, internships, liberal arts/career combination, weekend college. **Credit/placement by examination:** AP, CLEP, institutional tests. 40 credit hours maximum toward associate degree. **Support services:** GED test center, learning center, pre-admission summer program, reduced course load, remedial instruction, study skills assistance, tutoring.

**Honors college/program.** Participants have option of taking selected honors courses.

**Majors. Business:** Accounting, banking/financial services, business admin, management information systems, office/clerical, real estate. **Computer sciences:** Information systems, vendor certification. **Health:** Medical secretary, nursing (RN), physical therapy assistant, respiratory therapy technology. **Legal studies:** Legal secretary. **Liberal arts:** Arts/sciences. **Protective services:** Police science.

**Most popular majors.** Biological/life sciences 14%, business/marketing 16%, health sciences 49%, liberal arts 16%.

**Computing on campus.** 138 workstations in library, computer center. Commuter students can connect to campus network. Online course registration, helpline available.

**Student life. Freshman orientation:** Mandatory. Preregistration for classes offered. **Activities:** Choral groups, drama, literary magazine, music ensembles, musical theater, student government, student newspaper, Baptist student union/students for Christ, Circle K, drama club, multicultural student affairs, Phi Theta Kappa, students in free enterprise.

**Athletics. Intramural:** Basketball, bowling, fencing, softball, table tennis, tennis, volleyball.

**Student services.** Adult student services, career counseling, student employment services, financial aid counseling, health services, minority student services, on-campus daycare, personal counseling, placement for graduates, veterans' counselor. **Physically disabled:** Services for visually, speech, hearing impaired. **Transfer:** Re-entry adviser for new students. Transfer center, transfer adviser for students transferring to 4-year colleges.

**Contact.** E-mail: willie.mccullough@kctcs.net
Phone: (606) 326-2000 Toll-free number: (800) 370-7191
Fax: (606) 325-8124
Willie McCullough, Dean for Student Affairs, Ashland Community and Technical College, 1400 College Drive, Ashland, KY 41101-3683

## Big Sandy Community and Technical College
**Prestonsburg, Kentucky**
**www.bigsandy.kctcs.edu**
**CB code: 0869**

▸ Public 2-year community and technical college
▸ Commuter campus in small town

**General.** Founded in 1964. Regionally accredited. **Location:** 120 miles from Lexington. **Calendar:** Semester.

**Annual costs/financial aid.** Tuition/fees (2007-2008): $3,450; $10,350 out-of-state. Books/supplies: $450. Personal expenses: $3,000. Need-based financial aid available to full-time and part-time students.

**Contact.** Phone: (606) 886-3863 ext. 67366
Associate Dean of Students, One Bert T. Combs Drive, Prestonsburg, KY 41653

## Bluegrass Community and Technical College
**Lexington, Kentucky**
**www.bluegrass.kctcs.edu**
**CB member**
**CB code: 0645**

▸ Public 2-year community and technical college
▸ Commuter campus in large city

**General.** Founded in 1965. Regionally accredited. Locations include Danville, Georgetown, Lawrenceburg, Lexington, Nicholasville, and Winchester. **Enrollment:** 9,577 degree-seeking undergraduates. **Degrees:** 923 associate awarded. **Location:** 90 miles from Cincinnati, 75 miles from Louisville. **Calendar:** Semester, limited summer session. **Full-time faculty:** 269 total; 8% minority, 50% women. **Part-time faculty:** 405 total; 5% minority, 54% women.

**Student profile.** Among degree-seeking undergraduates, 23% enrolled in a transfer program, 48% enrolled in a vocational program.

| | | | |
|---|---|---|---|
| Out-of-state: | 2% | Live on campus: | 3% |
| 25 or older: | 44% | | |

**Transfer out. Colleges most students transferred to 2007:** University of Kentucky.

**Basis for selection.** Open admission, but selective for some programs. Special requirements for computer information systems, health technologies, nursing, nuclear medicine, radiography, respiratory care, dental hygiene, dental laboratory technology. ACT required for admission to some health programs. NLN preadmission test may be used for nursing rather than ACT. **Homeschooled:** ACT/SAT scores (or COMPASS) and transcript including grading scale required.

**High school preparation.** Students strongly encouraged to follow state pre-college curriculum.

**2007-2008 Annual costs.** Tuition/fees: $3,450; $10,350 out-of-state. Per-credit charge: $115 in-state; $345 out-of-state. Room/board: $5,794. Books/supplies: $800. Personal expenses: $800.

**Financial aid. Need-based:** Need-based aid available for part-time students. Work-study available nights and for part-time students. **Non-need-based:** Scholarships awarded for academics, minority status, state residency.

**Application procedures. Admission:** No deadline. No application fee. Application may be submitted online. Admission notification on a rolling

basis. **Financial aid:** No deadline. FAFSA, institutional form required. Applicants notified on a rolling basis starting 6/5; must reply within 3 week(s) of notification.

**Academics.** Six nationally accredited programs offered in allied health and nursing. **Special study options:** Cooperative education, distance learning, double major, dual enrollment of high school students, ESL, exchange student, internships, study abroad, weekend college. License preparation in dental hygiene, nursing, radiology, real estate. **Credit/placement by examination:** AP, CLEP, institutional tests. **Support services:** GED preparation and test center, learning center, remedial instruction, study skills assistance, tutoring, writing center.

**Majors. Agriculture:** Economics, equestrian studies. **Business:** Administrative services, business admin, executive assistant. **Computer sciences:** General, data processing, information technology. **Conservation:** General, forest sciences, wildlife. **Construction:** Carpentry, electrician. **Education:** Teacher assistance. **Engineering technology:** General, civil, electrical, environmental. **Health:** Clinical lab technology, dental hygiene, dental lab technology, medical assistant, medical radiologic technology/radiation therapy, medical secretary, nuclear medical technology, nursing (RN), respiratory therapy technology, surgical technology. **Liberal arts:** Arts/sciences. **Mechanic/repair:** Automotive, heating/ac/refrig, heavy equipment, industrial electronics. **Production:** Machine shop technology, welding. **Protective services:** Fire safety technology, firefighting. **Public administration:** Social work. **Other:** General occupational technology studies.

**Most popular majors.** Business/marketing 12%, health sciences 20%, interdisciplinary studies 10%, liberal arts 44%, security/protective services 18%.

**Computing on campus.** 400 workstations in library, computer center. Commuter students can connect to campus network. Online course registration, online library, helpline, repair service, wireless network available.

**Student life. Freshman orientation:** Mandatory. Preregistration for classes offered. Four-hour session held periodically throughout summer. **Housing:** Coed dorms, single-sex dorms, apartments available. Students apply for and are assigned housing at University of Kentucky. Applications submitted to Office of Student Housing, University of Kentucky. **Activities:** Choral groups, drama, international student organizations, student government, student newspaper.

**Student services.** Adult student services, alcohol/substance abuse counseling, career counseling, services for economically disadvantaged, student employment services, financial aid counseling, health services, minority student services, personal counseling, placement for graduates, veterans' counselor. **Physically disabled:** Services for visually, speech, hearing impaired. **Transfer:** Pre-admission transcript evaluation for new students. Transfer center, transfer adviser, college fairs on campus for students transferring to 4-year colleges.

**Contact.** E-mail: shelbie.hugle@kctcs.edu
Phone: (859) 246-6210 Toll-free number: (866) 774-4872 ext. 56210
Fax: (859) 246-4666
Shelbie Hugle, Director of Admissions, Bluegrass Community and Technical College, 200 Oswald Building, Cooper Drive, Lexington, KY 40506-0235

## Brown Mackie College: Hopkinsville
### Hopkinsville, Kentucky
www.brownmackie.edu                    CB code: 5375

- For-profit 2-year business and junior college
- Large town

**General.** Accredited by ACICS. **Calendar:** Quarter.

**Annual costs/financial aid.** Tuition/fees (2007-2008): $9,360. Required fees are $45 per class. Books/supplies: $500. Need-based financial aid available for full-time students.

**Contact.** Phone: (270) 886-1302
4001 Fort Campbell Boulevard, Hopkinsville, KY 42240

## Brown Mackie College: Louisville
### Louisville, Kentucky
www.brownmackie.edu                    CB code: 0305

- For-profit 2-year technical college
- Commuter campus in large city
- Interview required

**General.** Founded in 1972. Accredited by ACICS. **Enrollment:** 710 undergraduates. **Degrees:** 93 associate awarded. **Calendar:** Quarter, extensive summer session. **Full-time faculty:** 40 total. **Part-time faculty:** 11 total.

**Student profile.**

| | | | |
|---|---|---|---|
| Out-of-state: | 9% | 25 or older: | 59% |

**Basis for selection.** Open admission.

**2007-2008 Annual costs.** Tuition/fees: $9,360. Per-credit charge: $193. Personal expenses: $896.

**Financial aid.** All financial aid based on need.

**Application procedures. Admission:** No deadline. No application fee. Admission notification on a rolling basis. **Financial aid:** No deadline. FAFSA required. Applicants notified on a rolling basis.

**Academics. Credit/placement by examination:** CLEP. 16 hours of credit by CLEP Engineering Technologies examination may be counted toward associate degree. **Support services:** Tutoring.

**Majors. Computer sciences:** General. **Engineering technology:** Electrical.

**Computing on campus.** 12 workstations in library, computer center.

**Student life. Freshman orientation:** Mandatory. **Activities:** Student government, student newspaper.

**Athletics. Intercollegiate:** Softball M.

**Student services.** Career counseling, student employment services, personal counseling, placement for graduates.

**Contact.** Phone: (502) 968-7191 Toll-free number: (888) 476-1266
Fax: (502) 968-1727
Mark Donahue, Admissions Director, Brown Mackie College: Louisville, 3605 Fern Valley Road, Louisville, KY 40219

## Brown Mackie College: North Kentucky
### Fort Mitchell, Kentucky
www.brownmackie.edu                    CB code: 3419

- For-profit 2-year business and health science college
- Small town

**General.** Accredited by ACICS. **Enrollment:** 474 degree-seeking undergraduates. **Degrees:** 180 associate awarded. **Location:** 8 miles from Cincinnati. **Calendar:** Continuous. **Full-time faculty:** 12 total; 25% have terminal degrees, 67% women. **Part-time faculty:** 24 total; 46% women.

**Student profile.** Among degree-seeking undergraduates, 310 enrolled as first-time, first-year students, 144 transferred in from other institutions.

| | | | |
|---|---|---|---|
| Out-of-state: | 10% | Women: | 65% |

**Basis for selection.** Open admission.

**2007-2008 Annual costs.** Tuition/fees: $8,805. Per-credit charge: $189. Books/supplies: $1,380.

**Application procedures. Admission:** No deadline. No application fee. Admission notification on a rolling basis.

**Academics. Credit/placement by examination:** CLEP. **Support services:** Remedial instruction, tutoring.

**Majors. Business:** Accounting technology, business admin. **Computer sciences:** General. **Health:** Health services.

**Computing on campus.** 16 workstations in library.

**Student life. Freshman orientation:** Mandatory.

**Contact.** Phone: (859) 341-5627 Toll-free number: (800) 888-1445
Terry Fisher, Director of Admissions, Brown Mackie College: North Kentucky, 309 Buttermilk Pike, Fort Mitchell, KY 41017

Two-Year Colleges

## Daymar College: Louisville
**Louisville, Kentucky**
www.daymarcollege.edu                    CB code: 3407

- For-profit 2-year business college
- Large city

**General.** Accredited by ACICS. **Enrollment:** 344 degree-seeking undergraduates. **Degrees:** 67 associate awarded. **Calendar:** Quarter. **Full-time faculty:** 7 total. **Part-time faculty:** 28 total.

**Basis for selection.** Open admission. SAT, ACT, or Wonderlic Scholastic Level Exam required for placement.

**2007-2008 Annual costs.** Diploma program: $16,500-17,500; associate degree program: $25,000-$30,000, inclusive of books and fees. Books/supplies: $950.

**Application procedures. Admission:** No deadline. No application fee.

**Academics. Credit/placement by examination:** AP, CLEP.

**Majors. Business:** Business admin. **Computer sciences:** Networking. **Health:** Medical records technology, office assistant, pharmacy assistant. **Legal studies:** Paralegal.

**Student life. Freshman orientation:** Available.

**Contact.** Phone: (502) 495-1040
Shawn McDaniel, Director of Admissions, Daymar College: Louisville, 4400 Breckinridge Lane, Suite 415, Louisville, KY 40218

## Daymar College: Owensboro
**Owensboro, Kentucky**
www.daymarcollege.edu                    CB code: 0772

- For-profit 2-year business and junior college
- Commuter campus in small city

**General.** Founded in 1963. Accredited by ACICS. **Location:** 120 miles from Louisville, 35 miles from Evansville, Indiana. **Calendar:** Quarter.

**Annual costs/financial aid.** Tuition/fees (2007-2008): $11,370. Books/supplies: $1,400. Need-based financial aid available to full-time and part-time students.

**Contact.** Phone: (270) 926-4040
Director of Admissions, 3361 Buckland Square, Owensboro, KY 42301

## Draughons Junior College
**Bowling Green, Kentucky**
www.draughons.edu                    CB code: 3399

- For-profit 2-year branch campus and junior college
- Commuter campus in large town

**General.** Accredited by ACICS. **Enrollment:** 475 degree-seeking undergraduates. **Degrees:** 186 associate awarded. **Location:** 120 miles from Louisville, 60 miles from Nashville, Tennessee. **Calendar:** Quarter, extensive summer session. **Full-time faculty:** 13 total. **Part-time faculty:** 12 total. **Class size:** 92% < 20, 8% 20-39.

**Transfer out. Colleges most students transferred to 2007:** Western Kentucky University, Lindsey Wilson College, Kentucky Advanced Technology Institute.

**Basis for selection.** Open admission. SAT and ACT scores used for placement and counseling in remedial work.

**2007-2008 Annual costs.** Tuition/fees: $8,415. Per-credit charge: $215. Books/supplies: $2,030.

**Financial aid.** All financial aid based on need. Need-based aid available for part-time students. Work-study available nights.

**Application procedures. Admission:** No deadline. $150 fee. Admission notification on a rolling basis. **Financial aid:** No deadline. FAFSA required.

**Academics. Special study options:** Cooperative education, double major, internships. **Credit/placement by examination:** AP, CLEP, institutional tests. 15 credit hours maximum toward associate degree. **Support services:** Learning center, reduced course load, remedial instruction, tutoring.

**Majors. Business:** Accounting technology, business admin. **Computer sciences:** General, system admin, webmaster. **Health:** Cardiovascular technology, insurance coding, medical assistant, medical secretary, pharmacy assistant. **Legal studies:** Paralegal. **Protective services:** Law enforcement admin.

**Most popular majors.** Business/marketing 12%, computer/information sciences 14%, health sciences 51%, legal studies 14%, security/protective services 9%.

**Computing on campus.** 45 workstations in library, computer center. Online library, wireless network available.

**Student life. Freshman orientation:** Mandatory. Preregistration for classes offered. One-day session held 1 week prior to begining of semester.

**Student services.** Adult student services, career counseling, financial aid counseling, personal counseling, placement for graduates. **Transfer:** Reentry adviser, pre-admission transcript evaluation for new students. Transfer adviser for students transferring to 4-year colleges.

**Contact.** E-mail: thenderson@draughons.edu
Phone: (270) 843-6750 Toll-free number: (800) 541-0296
Fax: (270) 843-6976
Traci Henderson, Admissions, Draughons Junior College, 2421 Fitzgerald Industrial Drive, Bowling Green, KY 42101

## Elizabethtown Community and Technical College
**Elizabethtown, Kentucky**
www.elizabethtown.kctcs.edu                    CB code: 1211

- Public 2-year community and technical college
- Commuter campus in large town

**General.** Founded in 1964. Regionally accredited. **Location:** 40 miles southwest from Louisville. **Calendar:** Semester.

**Annual costs/financial aid.** Tuition/fees (2007-2008): $3,450; $10,350 out-of-state. Books/supplies: $400. Need-based financial aid available to full-time and part-time students.

**Contact.** Phone: (270) 769-1632
Counselor, 600 College Street Road, Elizabethtown, KY 42701

## Hazard Community College
**Hazard, Kentucky**
www.hazard.kctcs.edu                    CB code: 0815

- Public 2-year community and technical college
- Commuter campus in small town

**General.** Founded in 1968. Regionally accredited. **Enrollment:** 4,070 degree-seeking undergraduates. **Degrees:** 330 associate awarded. **Location:** 100 miles from Lexington. **Calendar:** Semester, limited summer session. **Full-time faculty:** 105 total. **Part-time faculty:** 110 total.

**Transfer out. Colleges most students transferred to 2007:** Morehead State University, Eastern Kentucky University, University of Kentucky, Lindsey Wilson College.

**Basis for selection.** Open admission, but selective for some programs. Out-of-state applicants must rank in top half of high school class or have 3.0 GPA.

**High school preparation.** 11 units recommended. Recommended units include English 4, mathematics 3, social studies 1, history 1 and science 2.

**2007-2008 Annual costs.** Tuition/fees: $3,450; $10,350 out-of-state. Per-credit charge: $115 in-state; $345 out-of-state. Books/supplies: $800. Personal expenses: $800.

**Financial aid.** All financial aid based on need. Need-based aid available for part-time students.

**Application procedures. Admission:** Priority date 8/1; no deadline. No application fee. Application may be submitted online. Admission notification on a rolling basis beginning on or about 6/15. **Financial aid:** Priority date 4/1; no closing date. FAFSA required. Applicants notified on a rolling basis starting 6/15; must reply within 2 week(s) of notification.

**Academics. Special study options:** Cooperative education, distance learning, dual enrollment of high school students, honors, independent study, internships, liberal arts/career combination. 2+2 bachelor's degree programs in business administration, elementary education and University Studies with Morehead State University; 2+2 bachelor's degree program in criminal justice, Individualized Studies, nursing and social work with Eastern Kentucky University; 2+2 bachelor's degree in Arts/Human Services and Counseling with Lindsey Wilson and a Master of Education in Mental Health Counseling with Lindsey Wilson. Bachelor's degree programs available on campus. **Credit/placement by examination:** CLEP, institutional tests. **Support services:** GED test center, learning center, remedial instruction, study skills assistance, tutoring, writing center.

**Majors. Business:** Marketing. **Computer sciences:** General. **Education:** Early childhood. **Health:** Medical radiologic technology/radiation therapy, nursing (RN), physical therapy assistant. **Liberal arts:** Arts/sciences. **Mechanic/repair:** Automotive. **Public administration:** Human services.

**Computing on campus.** 494 workstations in library, computer center, student center.

**Student life. Freshman orientation:** Available. **Activities:** Student government.

**Student services. Physically disabled:** Services for visually, speech, hearing impaired. **Transfer:** Pre-admission transcript evaluation for new students. College fairs on campus for students transferring to 4-year colleges.

**Contact.** E-mail: nena.eddington@kctcs.edu
Phone: (606) 436-5721 ext. 73525 Toll-free
number: (800) 246-7521 ext. 73525 Fax: (606) 666-4312
Hallie Bowling, Director of Admission, Hazard Community College, One Community College Drive, Hazard, KY 41701

## Henderson Community College
**Henderson, Kentucky**
www.hencc.kctcs.edu                    CB code: 1307

- Public 2-year community college
- Commuter campus in large town

**General.** Founded in 1960. Regionally accredited. **Enrollment:** 1,539 degree-seeking undergraduates. **Degrees:** 174 associate awarded. **Location:** 10 miles from Evansville, Indiana. **Calendar:** Semester, limited summer session. **Full-time faculty:** 50 total. **Part-time faculty:** 55 total. **Special facilities:** Fine arts center hosting variety of social and cultural activities in visual and performing arts.

**Transfer out. Colleges most students transferred to 2007:** Western Kentucky University, Murray State University, University of Kentucky, University of Southern Indiana, Wesley University.

**Basis for selection.** Open admission, but selective for some programs. Dental hygiene, nursing and clinical lab technician programs selective; test scores and high school GPA important admissions criteria. Though ACT is required, there is no minimum score except in dental hygiene, nursing and clinical technician programs. Interview required for nursing program.

**2007-2008 Annual costs.** Tuition/fees: $3,450; $10,350 out-of-state. Per-credit charge: $115 in-state; $345 out-of-state. Contiguous counties pay $138 per-credit-hour. Books/supplies: $500.

**Application procedures. Admission:** No application fee. Admission notification on a rolling basis beginning on or about 3/1. **Financial aid:** Priority date 4/1; no closing date. FAFSA required. Applicants notified on a rolling basis starting 5/1.

**Academics. Special study options:** Cooperative education, cross-registration, distance learning, double major, dual enrollment of high school students, honors, independent study, liberal arts/career combination, weekend college. License preparation in dental hygiene, nursing. **Credit/placement by examination:** AP, CLEP. **Support services:** GED preparation and test center, learning center, pre-admission summer program, reduced course load, remedial instruction, study skills assistance, tutoring, writing center.

**Majors. Agriculture:** Business technology. **Business:** Administrative services, business admin, management information systems. **Communications:** General. **Computer sciences:** Data processing. **Education:** Early childhood. **Engineering technology:** Electrical. **Health:** Clinical lab technology.

**Liberal arts:** Arts/sciences. **Public administration:** Community org/advocacy, social work.

**Computing on campus.** 99 workstations in library, computer center, student center. Commuter students can connect to campus network. Online course registration, online library, repair service available.

**Student life. Freshman orientation:** Available. Preregistration for classes offered. **Activities:** Choral groups, literary magazine, student government, student newspaper, Baptist Student Union.

**Student services.** Career counseling, financial aid counseling, minority student services, personal counseling, placement for graduates, veterans' counselor. **Transfer:** Re-entry adviser, pre-admission transcript evaluation for new students. Transfer center, transfer adviser, college fairs on campus for students transferring to 4-year colleges.

**Contact.** Phone: (270) 830-5256
Teresa Hamilton, Director of Admissions, Henderson Community College, 2660 South Green Street, Henderson, KY 42420

## Hopkinsville Community College
**Hopkinsville, Kentucky**
www.hopkinsville.kctcs.edu              CB code: 1274

- Public 2-year community college
- Commuter campus in small city

**General.** Founded in 1965. Regionally accredited. **Enrollment:** 2,909 degree-seeking undergraduates; 510 non-degree-seeking students. **Degrees:** 320 associate awarded. **Location:** 70 miles from Nashville, Tennessee, 25 miles from Clarksville, Tennessee. **Calendar:** Semester, limited summer session. **Full-time faculty:** 54 total; 13% have terminal degrees, 9% minority, 41% women. **Part-time faculty:** 76 total; 14% minority, 58% women. **Class size:** 58% < 20, 40% 20-39, 2% 40-49, less than 1% 50-99.

**Student profile.** Among degree-seeking undergraduates, 38% enrolled in a transfer program, 62% enrolled in a vocational program, 581 enrolled as first-time, first-year students, 261 transferred in from other institutions.

| | | | |
|---|---|---|---|
| Part-time: | 55% | Asian American: | 2% |
| Out-of-state: | 26% | Hispanic American: | 4% |
| Women: | 72% | Native American: | 1% |
| African American: | 25% | 25 or older: | 54% |

**Transfer out. Colleges most students transferred to 2007:** Murray State University, Austin Peay State University, Western Kentucky University.

**Basis for selection.** Open admission. ACT scores below 19 require COMPASS for placement.

**2007-2008 Annual costs.** Tuition/fees: $3,450; $10,350 out-of-state. Per-credit charge: $115 in-state; $345 out-of-state. Books/supplies: $800. Personal expenses: $2,260.

**Financial aid. Need-based:** Need-based aid available for part-time students. Work-study available nights. **Non-need-based:** Scholarships awarded for academics, leadership, minority status, state residency. **Additional information:** ACT required for academic scholarships.

**Application procedures. Admission:** No deadline. No application fee. Application may be submitted online. Admission notification on a rolling basis. **Financial aid:** No deadline. FAFSA required. Applicants notified on a rolling basis starting 7/1.

**Academics. Special study options:** Cooperative education, distance learning, dual enrollment of high school students, independent study, internships, weekend college. License preparation in nursing. **Credit/placement by examination:** AP, CLEP. **Support services:** GED preparation and test center, learning center, remedial instruction, study skills assistance, tutoring.

**Majors. Agriculture:** Production. **Business:** Business admin, executive assistant. **Computer sciences:** General. **Education:** Teacher assistance. **Engineering technology:** General, electromechanical. **Health:** Nursing (RN). **Liberal arts:** Arts/sciences. **Protective services:** Law enforcement admin, police science. **Public administration:** Social work. **Other:** General occupational/technical studies.

**Most popular majors.** Business/marketing 7%, health sciences 18%, liberal arts 38%.

**Computing on campus.** Commuter students can connect to campus network. Online course registration, online library, helpline available.

**Student life. Freshman orientation:** Available. Preregistration for classes offered. On-campus orientations held prior to semester; web-based orientation available through a series of video clips. **Activities:** Campus ministries, literary magazine, student government, student newspaper, TV station, College Democrats/Republicans, minority student union, Student Ambassadors.

**Athletics. Intramural:** Football (tackle) M.

**Student services.** Career counseling, services for economically disadvantaged, student employment services, financial aid counseling, minority student services, placement for graduates, veterans' counselor. **Physically disabled:** Services for visually, speech, hearing impaired. **Transfer:** Transfer adviser, college fairs on campus for students transferring to 4-year colleges.

**Contact.** E-mail: hp-admit.record@stu.kctcs.edu
Phone: (270) 707-3810 Fax: (270) 886-0237
Ruth Ann Rettie, Registrar, Hopkinsville Community College, PO Box 2100, Hopkinsville, KY 42241-2100

## Jefferson Community and Technical College
**Louisville, Kentucky**
**www.jefferson.kctcs.edu**               **CB code: 1328**

▶ Public 2-year community and technical college
▶ Commuter campus in large city
▶ Interview required

**General.** Founded in 1968. Regionally accredited. 3 other campuses: southwestern Jefferson County, Shelby County and Carrollton. Courses also offered off-campus and online. **Enrollment:** 11,205 degree-seeking undergraduates; 4,389 non-degree-seeking students. **Degrees:** 870 associate awarded. **ROTC:** Army. **Location:** Downtown. **Calendar:** Semester, extensive summer session. **Full-time faculty:** 321 total. **Part-time faculty:** 307 total. **Class size:** 54% < 20, 40% 20-39, 2% 40-49, 2% 50-99, less than 1% >100. **Special facilities:** Classes taught at local zoo, local pottery, local truck manufacturing plant, multimedia allied health lab, machine shop lab. **Partnerships:** Formal partnerships with United Parcel Service, Ford Motor Company, Norton Hospital, Jewish Hospital, St. Mary's Health Care System and Local Area Technology Centers.

**Student profile.** Among degree-seeking undergraduates, 17% enrolled in a transfer program, 54% enrolled in a vocational program, 1,801 enrolled as first-time, first-year students.

| | | | |
|---|---|---|---|
| Part-time: | 58% | Women: | 59% |
| Out-of-state: | 4% | 25 or older: | 45% |

**Transfer out. Colleges most students transferred to 2007:** University of Louisville, Spalding University, University of Kentucky, Bellarmine University.

**Basis for selection.** Open admission, but selective for some programs. Special requirements for nursing and other allied health programs. Entering freshmen required to take ACT for placement before start of second semester. Interview required for allied health programs: nursing, respiratory therapy, radiology, nuclear medicine, health information technology, occupational therapy, physical therapy, surgical technology, and practical nursing.

**2007-2008 Annual costs.** Tuition/fees: $3,450; $10,350 out-of-state. Per-credit charge: $115 in-state; $345 out-of-state. Books/supplies: $800. Personal expenses: $848.

**Financial aid. Need-based:** Need-based aid available for part-time students. Work-study available for part-time students. **Non-need-based:** Scholarships awarded for academics, art, minority status.

**Application procedures. Admission:** No deadline. No application fee. Application may be submitted online. Admission notification on a rolling basis. **Financial aid:** Priority date 3/15; no closing date. FAFSA, institutional form required. Applicants notified on a rolling basis starting 6/15; must reply within 3 week(s) of notification.

**Academics. Special study options:** Cooperative education, cross-registration, distance learning, dual enrollment of high school students, ESL, honors, independent study, internships, teacher certification program, weekend college. License preparation in aviation, nursing, occupational therapy, physical therapy, radiology, real estate. **Credit/placement by examination:** AP, CLEP, IB, institutional tests. STEP test, challenge exams available. **Support services:** GED preparation and test center, learning center, reduced course load, remedial instruction, study skills assistance, tutoring, writing center.

**Majors. Agriculture:** Horticulture. **Business:** Accounting technology, business admin, executive assistant, real estate. **Communications technology:** General. **Computer sciences:** General, data processing. **Education:** Teacher assistance. **Engineering technology:** General, electromechanical. **Health:** Electrocardiograph technology, medical records technology, nuclear medical technology, nursing (RN), occupational therapy assistant, physical therapy assistant, respiratory therapy technology, sonography. **Liberal arts:** Arts/sciences. **Mechanic/repair:** Automotive. **Personal/culinary services:** Chef training. **Production:** Welding. **Protective services:** Firefighting. **Public administration:** Social work. **Science technology:** Chemical.

**Most popular majors.** Health sciences 30%, interdisciplinary studies 7%, liberal arts 43%.

**Computing on campus.** 1,500 workstations in library, computer center, student center. Commuter students can connect to campus network. Online course registration, online library, helpline available.

**Student life. Freshman orientation:** Mandatory. Preregistration for classes offered. **Activities:** Drama, literary magazine, student government, student newspaper, black student union, Baptist student union, Earth-ecology club, Aspire, international student club, WOW.

**Student services.** Adult student services, career counseling, services for economically disadvantaged, student employment services, financial aid counseling, health services, minority student services, on-campus daycare, personal counseling, placement for graduates, veterans' counselor, women's services. **Physically disabled:** Services for visually, speech, hearing impaired. **Transfer:** Re-entry adviser, pre-admission transcript evaluation for new students. Transfer adviser, college fairs on campus for students transferring to 4-year colleges.

**Contact.** Phone: (502) 213-5333
Denise Gray-Lackey, Dean of Student Affairs, Jefferson Community and Technical College, 109 East Broadway, Louisville, KY 40202

## Louisville Technical Institute
**Louisville, Kentucky**
**www.louisvilletech.edu**               **CB code: 1501**

▶ For-profit 2-year technical college
▶ Commuter campus in very large city
▶ Interview required

**General.** Founded in 1961. Accredited by ACICS. **Enrollment:** 573 degree-seeking undergraduates. **Degrees:** 202 associate awarded. **Location:** 7 miles from downtown. **Calendar:** Quarter, extensive summer session. **Full-time faculty:** 29 total. **Part-time faculty:** 38 total. **Class size:** 94% < 20, 6% 20-39. **Special facilities:** Laboratories for computer-aided graphics, computer-aided drafting; robotics, interior design resource centers, computer networking labs, marine mechanics labs, computer repair labs. **Partnerships:** Formal partnership with a local manufacturer to assist with industrial automation and maintenance education.

**Student profile.** Among degree-seeking undergraduates, 100% enrolled in a vocational program, 2% already have a bachelor's degree or higher, 120 transferred in from other institutions.

| | | | |
|---|---|---|---|
| Out-of-state: | 12% | Live on campus: | 5% |

**Transfer out.** 5% of students enrolled in the transfer program go on to 4-year colleges. **Colleges most students transferred to 2007:** Sullivan University.

**Basis for selection.** Entrance test (CPAt) scores, previous school record and the interview process with an admissions representative are the most important factors in admissions decisions. Equivalent scores from the ACT or SAT can be accepted in place of a CPAt score. CPAt exam used for entrance evaluation. Equivalent scores from the ACT or SAT may be accepted in place of a CPAt score. **Homeschooled:** Statement describing homeschool structure and mission, transcript of courses and grades, state high school equivalency certificate required. **Learning Disabled:** Student must provide documentation from professional analysis indicating the level of disability and recommendation of type of accommodations that may be required.

**2007-2008 Annual costs.** For 2007-08, the cost of associate degree programs range from $28,740 to $33,530. The Computer Graphic Design and Dynamic Web tech fee is $590 per quarter; the tech fee for Computer Network Administration and information Systems Security is $510 per quarter. Books/supplies: $1,500. Personal expenses: $2,259.

**Financial aid. Need-based:** Need-based aid available for part-time students. Work-study available nights. **Non-need-based:** Scholarships awarded for academics, art, job skills.

**Application procedures. Admission:** No deadline. $100 fee, may be waived for applicants with need. Application must be submitted on paper. Admission notification on a rolling basis. **Financial aid:** No deadline. FAFSA required. Applicants notified on a rolling basis; must reply within 2 week(s) of notification.

**Academics. Special study options:** Accelerated study, cooperative education, double major, internships. Bachelor's degree programs available on campus. **Credit/placement by examination:** AP, CLEP, institutional tests. 51 credit hours maximum toward associate degree, 51 toward bachelor's. **Support services:** Learning center, reduced course load, study skills assistance, tutoring.

**Majors. Architecture:** Interior. **Communications technology:** Animation/special effects, desktop publishing, graphics. **Computer sciences:** Computer graphics, information systems, information technology, LAN/WAN management, security, system admin, vendor certification, web page design. **Engineering:** Architectural. **Engineering technology:** Architectural, architectural drafting, CAD/CADD, computer, computer hardware, drafting, electrical, mechanical drafting, robotics. **Mechanic/repair:** Computer. **Visual/performing arts:** Commercial/advertising art, graphic design, illustration, interior design.

**Most popular majors.** Computer/information sciences 32%, engineering/engineering technologies 45%, visual/performing arts 22%.

**Computing on campus.** 250 workstations in library, computer center. Commuter students can connect to campus network. Online library, helpline, repair service available.

**Student life. Freshman orientation:** Mandatory. Preregistration for classes offered. A three-hour orientation session including information sessions, breakout sessions by academic program, a learning style survey and a Q and A session is conducted at the start of each quarter for day and evening students. **Housing:** Coed dorms, apartments, substance-free housing available. $95 nonrefundable deposit. College uses a local apartment complex for student housing. Normally, two to four students may occupy different sized apartments.

**Student services.** Career counseling, student employment services, financial aid counseling, placement for graduates, veterans' counselor. **Transfer:** Re-entry adviser, pre-admission transcript evaluation for new students.

**Contact.** E-mail: kwoods@louisvilletech.edu
Phone: (502) 456-6509 Toll-free number: (800) 844-6528
Fax: (502) 456-2341
Kevin Woods, Director of Admissions, Louisville Technical Institute, 3901 Atkinson Square Drive, Louisville, KY 40218-4524

## Madisonville Community College
**Madisonville, Kentucky**
**www.madisonville.kctcs.edu**　　　　**CB code: 1606**

◗ Public 2-year community college
◗ Commuter campus in large town

**General.** Founded in 1968. Regionally accredited. Campuses include: North Campus, Health Campus, Technology Campus and Muhlenberg County Campus. Classes also offered at area high schools and other off-campus locations, including KET telecourses and online. **Enrollment:** 4,000 undergraduates. **Degrees:** 404 associate awarded. **Location:** 50 miles from Evansville, Indiana. **Calendar:** Semester, extensive summer session. **Full-time faculty:** 94 total. **Part-time faculty:** 74 total. **Special facilities:** Glema Mahr center for the arts.

**Student profile.**

| | | | |
|---|---|---|---|
| Out-of-state: | 1% | **25 or older:** | 41% |

**Transfer out. Colleges most students transferred to 2007:** Murray State University, Western Kentucky University, University of Kentucky.

**Basis for selection.** Open admission. Special requirements for health programs (nursing, physical therapy assistant, radiography, resipiratory, biomedical, occupational therapy assistant, clinical lab technology). ACT or CAPS scores required for placement/counseling. Interview recommended for nursing and physical therapy assistant applicants. **Adult students:** ACT or COMPASS test scores required of all students; scores must be less than 5 years old to be considered. **Homeschooled:** Encouraged to apply for early admissions status prior to completion of high school credential. **Learning Disabled:** Disability resources provided for qualified students.

**High school preparation.** 14 units recommended. Recommended units include English 4, mathematics 3, social studies 2, history 2, science 2 (laboratory 1).

**2007-2008 Annual costs.** Tuition/fees: $3,450; $10,350 out-of-state. Per-credit charge: $115 in-state; $345 out-of-state. Books/supplies: $500. Personal expenses: $1,000.

**Financial aid. Need-based:** Need-based aid available for part-time students. Work-study available nights, weekends and for part-time students. **Non-need-based:** Scholarships awarded for minority status.

**Application procedures. Admission:** Closing date 8/1 (receipt date). No application fee. Application may be submitted online. Admission notification on a rolling basis. **Financial aid:** Priority date 3/15; no closing date. FAFSA, institutional form required. Applicants notified on a rolling basis; must reply within 3 week(s) of notification.

**Academics.** Adult and continuing education programs available both on and off-campus. Tech prep and school-to-work programs available. **Special study options:** Combined bachelor's/graduate degree, cooperative education, distance learning, double major, dual enrollment of high school students, honors, independent study, internships, liberal arts/career combination, weekend college. Bachelor's degree programs available on campus. License preparation in nursing, occupational therapy, physical therapy, radiology, real estate. **Credit/placement by examination:** AP, CLEP, institutional tests. **Support services:** GED preparation and test center, learning center, remedial instruction, study skills assistance, tutoring, writing center.

**Majors. Agriculture:** Production. **Business:** Accounting, administrative services, business admin, finance, management information systems, real estate, sales/distribution. **Computer sciences:** General. **Construction:** Electrician. **Education:** General, early childhood. **Engineering technology:** General, drafting, electromechanical. **Health:** Clinical lab science, clinical lab technology, medical radiologic technology/radiation therapy, medical secretary, nursing (RN), occupational therapy assistant, physical therapy assistant, respiratory therapy technology. **Liberal arts:** Arts/sciences. **Production:** Machine shop technology. **Protective services:** Law enforcement admin.

**Most popular majors.** Business/marketing 14%, health sciences 39%, liberal arts 36%.

**Computing on campus.** 200 workstations in library, computer center, student center. Commuter students can connect to campus network. Online course registration, online library, helpline, wireless network available.

**Student life. Freshman orientation:** Mandatory. Preregistration for classes offered. **Activities:** Choral groups, drama, literary magazine, musical theater, student government, student newspaper, multicultural student organization, Lions Club, Student Ambassadors, Socratic Society, Phi Theta Kappa, student government association, Baptist Student Union.

**Athletics. Intramural:** Basketball.

**Student services.** Adult student services, career counseling, services for economically disadvantaged, student employment services, financial aid counseling, health services, minority student services, placement for graduates, veterans' counselor. **Physically disabled:** Services for visually, speech, hearing impaired. **Transfer:** Pre-admission transcript evaluation for new students. Transfer adviser, college fairs on campus for students transferring to 4-year colleges.

**Contact.** E-mail: aimee.bullock@kctcs.edu
Phone: (270) 821-2250 Toll-free number: (866) 227-4812
Fax: (270) 825-8553
Aimee Bullock, Director of Enrollment Management, Madisonville Community College, 2000 College Drive, Madisonville, KY 42431

## Maysville Community and Technical College
**Maysville, Kentucky**
**www.maysville.kctcs.edu**　　　　**CB code: 0693**

◗ Public 2-year community and technical college
◗ Commuter campus in small town

**General.** Founded in 1968. Regionally accredited. Access to University of Kentucky library through automated system (KYVU). **Enrollment:** 1,852 degree-seeking undergraduates. **Degrees:** 209 associate awarded. **Location:** 60 miles from Lexington, 60 miles from Cincinnati. **Calendar:** Semester, limited summer session. **Full-time faculty:** 87 total; 8% have terminal degrees, 3% minority, 59% women. **Part-time faculty:** 75 total; 4% have terminal degrees, 4% minority, 52% women. **Class size:** 78% < 20, 22% 20-39, less than 1% 50-99.

### Student profile.

Out-of-state: 8%  25 or older: 54%

**Basis for selection.** Open admission, but selective for some programs. High school diploma required and ACT scores considered for nursing program. ACT or COMPASS may be required for placement in degree-seeking programs. Interview required of nursing majors.

**High school preparation.** Recommended units include English 4, mathematics 3, social studies 2, science 2 and foreign language 2.

**2007-2008 Annual costs.** Tuition/fees: $3,450; $10,350 out-of-state. Per-credit charge: $115 in-state; $345 out-of-state. Books/supplies: $1,700. Personal expenses: $1,200.

**2006-2007 Financial aid.** **Need-based:** 57% of total undergraduate aid awarded as scholarships/grants, 43% as loans/jobs. Need-based aid available for part-time students. Work-study available nights. **Non-need-based:** Scholarships awarded for academics.

**Application procedures.** **Admission:** No deadline. $5 fee. Application may be submitted online. Admission notification on a rolling basis. March 1 priority date for nursing applicants. **Financial aid:** Priority date 4/1; no closing date. FAFSA, institutional form required. Applicants notified on a rolling basis starting 3/1; must reply within 3 week(s) of notification.

**Academics.** **Special study options:** Cooperative education, distance learning, double major, dual enrollment of high school students, honors, independent study, internships, teacher certification program. License preparation in nursing, real estate. **Credit/placement by examination:** AP, CLEP, institutional tests. **Support services:** GED preparation and test center, learning center, reduced course load, remedial instruction, study skills assistance, tutoring.

**Majors.** **Agriculture:** Horticultural science. **Business:** General, accounting, business admin, e-commerce, executive assistant, office management. **Computer sciences:** General, computer science, data processing, database management, information systems, programming, security, system admin, web page design. **Conservation:** Environmental studies. **Construction:** Carpentry. **Education:** Early childhood. **Engineering:** Industrial, manufacturing. **Engineering technology:** Electrical, electromechanical, energy systems, industrial, manufacturing. **Health:** Licensed practical nurse, medical secretary, nursing (RN), surgical technology. **Liberal arts:** Arts/sciences. **Mechanic/repair:** General, auto body, automotive, diesel, industrial.

**Computing on campus.** 375 workstations in library, computer center. Commuter students can connect to campus network.

**Student life.** **Freshman orientation:** Mandatory. Preregistration for classes offered. **Activities:** Drama, student government, Phi Theta Kappa, student education association, society of manufacturing student engineers, association of nursing students.

**Athletics.** **Intramural:** Badminton, volleyball.

**Student services.** Adult student services, alcohol/substance abuse counseling, career counseling, services for economically disadvantaged, student employment services, financial aid counseling, personal counseling, placement for graduates, veterans' counselor. **Physically disabled:** Services for hearing impaired. **Transfer:** Transfer adviser, college fairs on campus for students transferring to 4-year colleges.

**Contact.** E-mail: patee.massie@kctcs.edu
Phone: (606) 759-5818 ext. 66186 Fax: (606) 759-5818
Patricia Massie, Registrar/Admissions Officer, Maysville Community and Technical College, 1755 US 68, Maysville, KY 41056

---

## National College: Danville
**Danville, Kentucky**
www.ncbt.edu  CB code: 3413

- For-profit 2-year business college
- Commuter campus in large town

**General.** Accredited by ACICS. **Enrollment:** 279 degree-seeking undergraduates. **Degrees:** 70 associate awarded. **Calendar:** Quarter, extensive summer session. **Full-time faculty:** 4 total. **Part-time faculty:** 22 total.

**Basis for selection.** Open admission. Interviews highly recommended.

**2007-2008 Annual costs.** Tuition/fees: $9,090. Per-credit charge: $202. Books/supplies: $1,200.

---

**Financial aid.** All financial aid based on need. Need-based aid available for part-time students.

**Application procedures.** **Admission:** No deadline. $30 fee, may be waived for applicants with need. Application may be submitted online. Admission notification on a rolling basis. **Financial aid:** No deadline. FAFSA required. Applicants notified on a rolling basis.

**Academics.** **Special study options:** Double major, internships, liberal arts/career combination. **Credit/placement by examination:** CLEP, institutional tests. **Support services:** Learning center, remedial instruction, tutoring.

**Majors.** **Business:** Accounting, administrative services, business admin. **Computer sciences:** Computer science. **Health:** Medical assistant, medical secretary, physician assistant.

**Computing on campus.** 35 workstations in library, computer center.

**Student life.** **Freshman orientation:** Mandatory. Preregistration for classes offered. **Activities:** Student government.

**Student services.** Career counseling, student employment services, financial aid counseling, personal counseling, placement for graduates, veterans' counselor.

**Contact.** E-mail: market@educorp.edu
Phone: (859) 236-6991 Toll-free number: (800) 664-1886
Fax: (859) 236-1063
Larry Steele, Vice President of Admissions, National College: Danville, PO Box 6400, Roanoke, VA 24017

---

## National College: Florence
**Florence, Kentucky**
www.ncbt.edu  CB code: 3408

- For-profit 2-year business college
- Commuter campus in large town

**General.** Accredited by ACICS. **Enrollment:** 156 degree-seeking undergraduates. **Degrees:** 59 associate awarded. **Calendar:** Quarter, limited summer session. **Full-time faculty:** 4 total. **Part-time faculty:** 33 total.

**Basis for selection.** Open admission. Interview highly recommended.

**2007-2008 Annual costs.** Tuition/fees: $9,090. Per-credit charge: $202. Books/supplies: $1,200.

**Financial aid.** All financial aid based on need. Need-based aid available for part-time students.

**Application procedures.** **Admission:** No deadline. $30 fee. Application may be submitted online. Admission notification on a rolling basis. **Financial aid:** No deadline. FAFSA required. Applicants notified on a rolling basis.

**Academics.** **Special study options:** Double major, internships. **Credit/placement by examination:** CLEP, institutional tests. **Support services:** Learning center, remedial instruction, tutoring.

**Majors.** **Business:** Accounting, administrative services, business admin. **Computer sciences:** Computer science. **Health:** Medical assistant, medical secretary.

**Computing on campus.** 35 workstations in library, computer center.

**Student life.** **Freshman orientation:** Mandatory. Preregistration for classes offered. **Activities:** Student government.

**Student services.** Career counseling, student employment services, financial aid counseling, personal counseling, placement for graduates, veterans' counselor.

**Contact.** E-mail: market@educorp.edu
Phone: (606) 525-6510 Fax: (606) 525-8961
Larry Steele, Director of Admissions, National College: Florence, PO Box 6400, Roanoke, VA 24017

---

## National College: Lexington
**Lexington, Kentucky**
www.ncbt.edu  CB code: 0987

- For-profit 2-year business and junior college
- Commuter campus in small city

**General.** Founded in 1941. Accredited by ACICS. **Enrollment:** 503 degree-seeking undergraduates. **Degrees:** 68 associate awarded. **Location:** 100 miles from Cincinnati. **Calendar:** Quarter, limited summer session. **Full-time faculty:** 4 total. **Part-time faculty:** 24 total.

**Basis for selection.** Open admission. Interview recommended.

**2007-2008 Annual costs.** Tuition/fees: $9,090. Per-credit charge: $202. Books/supplies: $1,200.

**Financial aid.** All financial aid based on need. Need-based aid available for part-time students.

**Application procedures. Admission:** No deadline. $30 fee, may be waived for applicants with need. Application may be submitted online. Admission notification on a rolling basis. **Financial aid:** No deadline. FAFSA required. Applicants notified on a rolling basis.

**Academics. Special study options:** Double major, internships. **Credit/placement by examination:** CLEP, institutional tests. **Support services:** Learning center, remedial instruction, tutoring.

**Majors. Business:** Accounting, administrative services, business admin, office management, office/clerical. **Computer sciences:** Computer science. **Health:** Medical assistant, medical secretary, physician assistant. **Legal studies:** Legal secretary.

**Computing on campus.** 35 workstations in library, computer center.

**Student life. Freshman orientation:** Mandatory. Preregistration for classes offered. **Activities:** Student government.

**Student services.** Career counseling, student employment services, personal counseling, placement for graduates, veterans' counselor.

**Contact.** E-mail: market@educorp.edu
Phone: (859) 253-0621 Toll-free number: (800) 664-1886
Fax: (859) 233-3054
Larry Steele, Vice President of Admissions, National College: Lexington, PO Box 6400, Roanoke, VA 24017

## National College: Louisville
**Louisville, Kentucky**
www.ncbt.edu                    CB code: 3415

- For-profit 2-year business college
- Commuter campus in large city

**General.** Accredited by ACICS. **Enrollment:** 819 degree-seeking undergraduates. **Degrees:** 121 associate awarded. **Calendar:** Quarter, limited summer session. **Full-time faculty:** 4 total. **Part-time faculty:** 43 total.

**Basis for selection.** Open admission. Interviews highly recommended.

**2007-2008 Annual costs.** Tuition/fees: $9,090. Per-credit charge: $202. Books/supplies: $1,200.

**Financial aid.** All financial aid based on need. Need-based aid available for part-time students.

**Application procedures. Admission:** No deadline. $30 fee, may be waived for applicants with need. Application may be submitted online. Admission notification on a rolling basis. **Financial aid:** No deadline. FAFSA required. Applicants notified on a rolling basis.

**Academics. Special study options:** Internships. **Credit/placement by examination:** CLEP, institutional tests. **Support services:** Learning center, remedial instruction, tutoring.

**Majors. Business:** Accounting, administrative services, business admin. **Computer sciences:** Computer science. **Health:** Medical assistant, medical secretary. **Legal studies:** Legal secretary.

**Computing on campus.** 35 workstations in library, computer center.

**Student life. Freshman orientation:** Mandatory. Preregistration for classes offered. **Activities:** Student government.

**Student services.** Career counseling, student employment services, personal counseling, placement for graduates, veterans' counselor.

**Contact.** E-mail: market@educorp.edu
Phone: (502) 447-7634 Toll-free number: (800) 664-1886
Fax: (502) 447-7665
Larry Steele, Vice President of Admissions, National College: Louisville, PO Box 6400, Roanoke, VA 24017

## National College: Pikeville
**Pikeville, Kentucky**
www.ncbt.edu                    CB code: 3412

- For-profit 2-year business college
- Commuter campus in large town

**General.** Accredited by ACICS. **Enrollment:** 154 degree-seeking undergraduates. **Degrees:** 35 associate awarded. **Calendar:** Quarter, extensive summer session. **Full-time faculty:** 2 total. **Part-time faculty:** 18 total.

**Basis for selection.** Open admission. Interviews highly recommended.

**2007-2008 Annual costs.** Tuition/fees: $9,090. Per-credit charge: $202. Books/supplies: $1,200.

**Financial aid.** All financial aid based on need. Need-based aid available for part-time students.

**Application procedures. Admission:** No deadline. $30 fee, may be waived for applicants with need. Application may be submitted online. Admission notification on a rolling basis. **Financial aid:** No deadline. FAFSA required.

**Academics. Special study options:** Double major, internships. **Credit/placement by examination:** CLEP, institutional tests. **Support services:** Learning center, remedial instruction, tutoring.

**Majors. Business:** Accounting, administrative services, business admin. **Health:** Medical assistant, medical secretary. **Legal studies:** Legal secretary.

**Computing on campus.** 35 workstations in library, computer center.

**Student life. Freshman orientation:** Mandatory. Preregistration for classes offered. **Activities:** Student government.

**Student services.** Career counseling, student employment services, financial aid counseling, personal counseling, placement for graduates, veterans' counselor.

**Contact.** E-mail: market@educorp.edu
Phone: (606) 432-5477 Toll-free number: (800) 664-1886
Fax: (606) 437-4952
Larry Steele, Vice Presidnet of Admissions, National College: Pikeville, PO Box 6400, Roanoke, VA 24017

## National College: Richmond
**Richmond, Kentucky**
www.ncbt.edu                    CB code: 3414

- For-profit 2-year business college
- Commuter campus in large town

**General.** Accredited by ACICS. **Enrollment:** 287 degree-seeking undergraduates. **Degrees:** 69 associate awarded. **Calendar:** Quarter, limited summer session. **Full-time faculty:** 1 total. **Part-time faculty:** 32 total.

**Basis for selection.** Open admission. Interviews highly recommended.

**2007-2008 Annual costs.** Tuition/fees: $9,090. Per-credit charge: $202. Books/supplies: $1,200.

**Financial aid.** All financial aid based on need. Need-based aid available for part-time students.

**Application procedures. Admission:** No deadline. $30 fee, may be waived for applicants with need. Application may be submitted online. Admission notification on a rolling basis. **Financial aid:** No deadline. FAFSA required. Applicants notified on a rolling basis.

**Academics. Special study options:** Double major, internships. **Credit/placement by examination:** CLEP, institutional tests. **Support services:** Learning center, remedial instruction, tutoring.

**Majors. Business:** Accounting, administrative services, business admin. **Computer sciences:** Computer science. **Health:** Medical assistant, medical secretary.

**Computing on campus.** 35 workstations in library, computer center.

**Student life. Freshman orientation:** Mandatory. Preregistration for classes offered. **Activities:** Student government.

**Student services.** Career counseling, student employment services, financial aid counseling, personal counseling, placement for graduates, veterans' counselor.

**Contact.** E-mail: market@educorp.edu
Phone: (859) 623-8956 Toll-free number: (800) 664-1886
Fax: (859) 624-5544
Larry Steele, Vice President of Admissions, National College: Richmond, PO Box 6400, Roanoke, VA 24017

## Owensboro Community and Technical College
**Owensboro, Kentucky**
**www.octc.kctcs.edu**                           CB code: 0613

- Public 2-year community and technical college
- Commuter campus in small city

**General.** Founded in 1986. Regionally accredited. **Enrollment:** 2,802 degree-seeking undergraduates; 2,637 non-degree-seeking students. **Degrees:** 397 associate awarded. **Location:** 120 miles from Louisville; 40 miles from Evansville, Indiana. **Calendar:** Semester, extensive summer session. **Full-time faculty:** 102 total. **Part-time faculty:** 90 total. **Class size:** 60% < 20, 39% 20-39, 2% 40-49. **Special facilities:** Outdoor classroom/nature area, early Headstart program.

**Student profile.** Among degree-seeking undergraduates, 44% enrolled in a transfer program, 56% enrolled in a vocational program, 587 enrolled as first-time, first-year students.

| | | | |
|---|---|---|---|
| Part-time: | 43% | African American: | 4% |
| Out-of-state: | 5% | Hispanic American: | 1% |
| Women: | 65% | 25 or older: | 32% |

**Transfer out. Colleges most students transferred to 2007:** Western Kentucky University, Kentucky Wesleyan College, Brescia University, University of Southern Indiana, University of Kentucky.

**Basis for selection.** Open admission, but selective for some programs. ACT scores required for nursing, radiography, surgical technology, and early childhood education programs. Placement test required for all new degree-seeking students, although ACT scores may be used in lieu of this requirement. **Homeschooled:** Documentation of courses required.

**High school preparation.** 11 units recommended. Recommended units include English 4, mathematics 3, social studies 1, history 2, science 3 (laboratory 1).

**2007-2008 Annual costs.** Tuition/fees: $3,450; $10,350 out-of-state. Per-credit charge: $115 in-state; $345 out-of-state. Books/supplies: $850. Personal expenses: $1,040.

**Financial aid. Need-based:** Need-based aid available for part-time students. Work-study available for part-time students. **Non-need-based:** Scholarships awarded for academics, state residency.

**Application procedures. Admission:** Priority date 4/1; deadline 8/15 (receipt date). No application fee. Admission notification on a rolling basis beginning on or about 3/1. **Financial aid:** Priority date 3/16; no closing date. FAFSA required. Applicants notified by 6/1; must reply within 2 week(s) of notification.

**Academics. Special study options:** Cooperative education, distance learning, double major, dual enrollment of high school students, independent study, study abroad. License preparation in nursing, paramedic, radiology, real estate. **Credit/placement by examination:** AP, CLEP, IB, institutional tests. **Support services:** Learning center, remedial instruction, study skills assistance, tutoring.

**Majors. Agriculture:** Business. **Biology:** Biotechnology. **Business:** General, accounting, administrative services, business admin, management information systems, office/clerical. **Computer sciences:** Information systems. **Construction:** Carpentry, electrician. **Education:** General, early childhood. **Engineering technology:** Architectural drafting, CAD/CADD, electrical. **Health:** Medical radiologic technology/radiation therapy, medical secretary, medical transcription, nursing (RN), office assistant, sonography. **Liberal arts:** Arts/sciences. **Personal/culinary services:** Chef training. **Production:** Machine tool, welding. **Protective services:** Police science. **Public administration:** Social work.

**Most popular majors.** Business/marketing 8%, health sciences 17%, interdisciplinary studies 14%, liberal arts 45%.

**Computing on campus.** 90 workstations in library, computer center, student center. Commuter students can connect to campus network. Online course registration, online library, helpline, student web hosting, wireless network available.

**Student life. Freshman orientation:** Mandatory. Preregistration for classes offered. Half-day session conducted a month before classes begin. **Activities:** Choral groups, drama, literary magazine, radio station, student government, student newspaper, TV station.

**Athletics. Intramural:** Basketball, softball.

**Student services.** Career counseling, services for economically disadvantaged, student employment services, financial aid counseling, on-campus daycare, personal counseling, placement for graduates, veterans' counselor. **Physically disabled:** Services for visually, speech, hearing impaired. **Transfer:** Pre-admission transcript evaluation for new students. Transfer adviser, college fairs on campus for students transferring to 4-year colleges.

**Contact.** E-mail: octc.admissions@kctcs.edu
Phone: (270) 686-4527 Toll-free number: (877) 734-0694
Fax: (270) 686-4648
Lantana Bray, Dean of Student Affairs, Owensboro Community and Technical College, 4800 New Hartford Road, Owensboro, KY 42303-1899

## Paducah Technical College
**Paducah, Kentucky**
**www.paducahtech.edu**                          CB code: 0669

- For-profit 2-year technical college
- Commuter campus in small city
- Interview required

**General.** Founded in 1964. Accredited by ACCSCT. Associate program completes 3 academic years in 2 calendar years. **Enrollment:** 250 undergraduates. **Degrees:** 36 associate awarded. **Location:** 150 miles from Nashville, Tennessee and St. Louis. **Calendar:** Differs by program, extensive summer session. **Full-time faculty:** 20 total. **Part-time faculty:** 10 total.

**Basis for selection.** Open admission.

**2007-2008 Annual costs.** Cost per academic year approximately $10,320 plus $1,000 in fees. Personal expenses: $2,000.

**Application procedures. Admission:** No deadline. No application fee. Admission notification on a rolling basis. **Financial aid:** No deadline. FAFSA, CSS PROFILE required. Applicants notified on a rolling basis; must reply within 3 week(s) of notification.

**Academics. Credit/placement by examination:** AP, CLEP. **Support services:** Tutoring.

**Majors. Engineering:** Electrical. **Engineering technology:** Electrical. **Health:** Insurance coding, insurance specialist, pharmacy assistant. **Math:** Applied.

**Student life. Freshman orientation:** Mandatory. Preregistration for classes offered.

**Student services.** Alcohol/substance abuse counseling, career counseling, student employment services, financial aid counseling, personal counseling, placement for graduates, veterans' counselor. **Transfer:** Pre-admission transcript evaluation for new students.

**Contact.** Phone: (270) 444-9676 Toll-free number: (800) 995-4438
Fax: (270) 441-7202
Shannon Jones, Director of Admission, Paducah Technical College, 509 South 30th Street, Paducah, KY 42001

## Somerset Community College
**Somerset, Kentucky**
**www.somerset.kctcs.edu**                       CB code: 1779

- Public 2-year community and technical college
- Commuter campus in large town

**General.** Founded in 1965. Regionally accredited. One of 15 community colleges and 12 technical colleges consolidated under one administration. **Enrollment:** 4,848 degree-seeking undergraduates. **Degrees:** 536 associate awarded. **Location:** 70 miles from Lexington. **Calendar:** Semester, limited summer session. **Full-time faculty:** 148 total. **Part-time faculty:** 160 total. **Class size:** 66% < 20, 32% 20-39, less than 1% 40-49, less than 1% 50-99.

**Student profile.**

| | | | |
|---|---|---|---|
| Out-of-state: | 1% | 25 or older: | 47% |

**Transfer out. Colleges most students transferred to 2007:** Morehead State University, University of Kentucky, Western Kentucky University, Eastern Kentucky University.

**Basis for selection.** Open admission, but selective for some programs. Test scores, letters of recommendation, and interview required for limited enrollment programs in allied health. ACT required in admissions process but not ordinarily used as selective criterion.

**High school preparation.** 20 units recommended. Recommended units include English 4, mathematics 3, social studies 2, science 2 and academic electives 9.

**2007-2008 Annual costs.** Tuition/fees: $3,450; $10,350 out-of-state. Per-credit charge: $115 in-state; $345 out-of-state. Books/supplies: $500. Personal expenses: $800.

**2006-2007 Financial aid.** All financial aid based on need. 56% of total undergraduate aid awarded as scholarships/grants, 44% as loans/jobs. Need-based aid available for part-time students. Work-study available for part-time students.

**Application procedures. Admission:** No deadline. No application fee. Application must be submitted on paper. Admission notification on a rolling basis. Admitted students in nursing, clinical laboratory techniques, and physical therapy assisting must reply within 10 days. **Financial aid:** Priority date 3/1; no closing date. FAFSA required. Applicants notified on a rolling basis starting 5/1; must reply within 2 week(s) of notification.

**Academics. Special study options:** Cooperative education, distance learning, dual enrollment of high school students, internships, liberal arts/career combination. Bachelor's degree programs available on campus. License preparation in aviation, dental hygiene, nursing, physical therapy, radiology, real estate. **Credit/placement by examination:** AP, CLEP. 12 credit hours maximum toward associate degree. **Support services:** GED preparation and test center, learning center, reduced course load, remedial instruction, study skills assistance, tutoring, writing center.

**Majors. Business:** Business admin, executive assistant. **Communications technology:** Graphics, printing management. **Computer sciences:** General. **Construction:** Carpentry, electrician, masonry, pipefitting, plumbing. **Education:** General, teacher assistance. **Family/consumer sciences:** Child care. **Health:** Clinical lab assistant, clinical lab technology, licensed practical nurse, medical assistant, medical secretary, nursing (RN), physical therapy assistant. **Liberal arts:** Arts/sciences. **Mechanic/repair:** Aircraft powerplant, auto body, automotive, diesel, industrial, industrial electronics. **Personal/culinary services:** Cosmetology. **Production:** Machine shop technology, welding. **Protective services:** Law enforcement admin, police science.

**Computing on campus.** 947 workstations in library, computer center, student center. Commuter students can connect to campus network. Online course registration, online library, repair service available.

**Student life. Freshman orientation:** Mandatory. Preregistration for classes offered. **Activities:** Choral groups, drama, film society, music ensembles, student government, student newspaper, Baptist Student Union, student government association, Students for Free Enterprise, Phi Beta Lambda, Phi Theta Kappa, criminal justice student organization.

**Athletics. Intramural:** Basketball, football (non-tackle), racquetball, softball, volleyball. **Team name:** Cougars.

**Student services.** Adult student services, career counseling, services for economically disadvantaged, student employment services, financial aid counseling, minority student services, personal counseling, placement for graduates, veterans' counselor. **Physically disabled:** Services for visually, speech, hearing impaired. **Transfer:** Pre-admission transcript evaluation for new students. Transfer adviser, college fairs on campus for students transferring to 4-year colleges.

**Contact.** E-mail: tracy.casada@kctcs.edu
Phone: (606) 451-6630 Toll-free number: (877) 629-9722
Fax: (606) 679-4369
Tracy Casada, Dean of Student Affairs, Somerset Community College, 808 Monticello Street, Somerset, KY 42501

---

## Southeast Kentucky Community and Technical College
**Cumberland, Kentucky**
**www.secc.kctcs.edu**                    CB code: 1770

- Public 2-year community and technical college
- Commuter campus in small town

---

**General.** Founded in 1960. Regionally accredited. Branch campuses at Harlan, Middlesboro, Pineville and Whitesburg. **Enrollment:** 2,061 degree-seeking undergraduates; 2,892 non-degree-seeking students. **Degrees:** 420 associate awarded. **Location:** 150 miles from Lexington. **Calendar:** Semester, limited summer session. **Full-time faculty:** 115 total. **Part-time faculty:** 69 total. **Class size:** 32% < 20, 53% 20-39, 10% 40-49, 4% 50-99. **Special facilities:** Appalachian archives.

**Student profile.** Among degree-seeking undergraduates, 35% enrolled in a transfer program, 65% enrolled in a vocational program, 726 enrolled as first-time, first-year students, 81 transferred in from other institutions.

| | | | |
|---|---|---|---|
| Part-time: | 39% | Women: | 62% |
| Out-of-state: | 4% | 25 or older: | 40% |

**Transfer out.** 26% of students enrolled in the transfer program go on to 4-year colleges. **Colleges most students transferred to 2007:** Lincoln Memorial University, University of Louisville, Eastern Kentucky University.

**Basis for selection.** Open admission, but selective for some programs. ACT required for nursing, radiography, respiratory care and physical therapy programs. **Homeschooled:** Transcript of courses and grades required.

**High school preparation.** 12 units recommended. Recommended units include English 4, mathematics 3, history 2, science 2 (laboratory 1).

**2007-2008 Annual costs.** Tuition/fees: $3,450; $10,350 out-of-state. Per-credit charge: $115 in-state; $345 out-of-state. Books/supplies: $450. Personal expenses: $1,100.

**Financial aid.** All financial aid based on need. Need-based aid available for part-time students. Work-study available for part-time students. **Additional information:** March 15 deadline for state financial aid.

**Application procedures. Admission:** No deadline. No application fee. Application may be submitted online. Admission notification on a rolling basis. **Financial aid:** Priority date 3/15; no closing date. FAFSA required. Applicants notified by 6/15; must reply within 2 week(s) of notification.

**Academics. Special study options:** Cross-registration, distance learning, dual enrollment of high school students, internships, liberal arts/career combination. License preparation in nursing. **Credit/placement by examination:** AP, CLEP, institutional tests. 30 credit hours maximum toward associate degree. **Support services:** GED preparation and test center, learning center, pre-admission summer program, reduced course load, remedial instruction, study skills assistance, tutoring, writing center.

**Majors. Business:** Administrative services, banking/financial services, business admin, finance, management information systems. **Computer sciences:** General, data processing. **Engineering technology:** Computer. **Health:** Clinical lab assistant, medical radiologic technology/radiation therapy, nursing (RN), physical therapy assistant, respiratory therapy technology. **Liberal arts:** Arts/sciences. **Protective services:** Police science.

**Most popular majors.** Business/marketing 15%, education 10%, health sciences 20%, liberal arts 52%.

**Computing on campus.** 46 workstations in library, computer center. Commuter students can connect to campus network. Online course registration, wireless network available.

**Student life. Freshman orientation:** Mandatory. **Activities:** Choral groups, dance, drama, student government, student newspaper, Christian student union, black student union, Professional Business Leaders, wilderness club, nursing club, student government association.

**Athletics. Intramural:** Basketball, golf, table tennis, volleyball.

**Student services.** Adult student services, career counseling, financial aid counseling, personal counseling, placement for graduates, veterans' counselor. **Physically disabled:** Services for visually impaired. **Transfer:** Transfer adviser, college fairs on campus for students transferring to 4-year colleges.

**Contact.** E-mail: cookie.baker@kctcs.edu
Phone: (606) 589-2145 Toll-free number: (888) 274-7332
Fax: (606) 589-5423
Veria Baker, Director of Admissions, Southeast Kentucky Community and Technical College, 700 College Road, Cumberland, KY 40823

---

## Southwestern College: Florence
**Florence, Kentucky**
**www.swcollege.net**                    CB code: 2482

- For-profit 2-year health science and career college
- Residential campus in small city
- Interview required

**General.** Accredited by ACICS. **Enrollment:** 342 undergraduates. **Degrees:** 25 associate awarded. **Location:** 5 miles from Cincinnati. **Calendar:** Quarter, extensive summer session. **Full-time faculty:** 7 total. **Part-time faculty:** 12 total.

**Basis for selection.** Open admission. **Homeschooled:** State high school equivalency certificate required.

**2007-2008 Annual costs.** Tuition/fees: $10,900.

**Application procedures. Admission:** No deadline. $20 fee. Application must be submitted on paper. Admission notification on a rolling basis. **Financial aid:** No deadline. FAFSA required.

**Academics. Special study options:** Liberal arts/career combination. **Credit/placement by examination:** CLEP. **Support services:** GED preparation, study skills assistance, tutoring.

**Majors. Computer sciences:** General. **Health:** Medical assistant.

**Computing on campus.** 50 workstations in library, computer center. Online library available.

**Student life. Freshman orientation:** Mandatory. Preregistration for classes offered. Held on campus before each quarter in mornings and evenings. **Activities:** Student government, student newspaper.

**Student services.** Career counseling, services for economically disadvantaged, student employment services, financial aid counseling, placement for graduates. **Transfer:** Pre-admission transcript evaluation for new students.

**Contact.** E-mail: cbaird@swcollege.net
Phone: (859) 282-9999 Fax: (859) 282-7940
Cathy Baird, Director of Admissions, Southwestern College: Florence, 8095 Connector Drive, Florence, KY 41042

## Spencerian College
**Louisville, Kentucky**
www.spencerian.edu                    CB code: 3422

- For-profit 2-year health science and nursing college
- Commuter campus in large city

**General.** Accredited by ACICS. **Enrollment:** 1,194 degree-seeking undergraduates. **Degrees:** 113 associate awarded. **Location:** 10 miles from Louisville. **Calendar:** Quarter, extensive summer session. **Full-time faculty:** 46 total; 4% have terminal degrees, 83% women. **Part-time faculty:** 56 total; 5% have terminal degrees, 71% women. **Special facilities:** Radiology labs, surgical technology lab, mock operating room, massage therapy lab.

**Student profile.** Among degree-seeking undergraduates, 100% enrolled in a vocational program.

**Basis for selection.** Open admission, but selective for some programs. Requirements vary by program. Interview may be required for nursing, medical laboratory technology, invasive cardiovascular technology, and surgical technology programs. **Homeschooled:** State high school equivalency certificate required.

**2007-2008 Annual costs.** Tuition/fees: $14,010. Room only: $4,320. Personal expenses: $2,619.

**Application procedures. Admission:** No deadline. $100 fee. Application may be submitted online. Admission notification on a rolling basis.

**Academics.** Fridays set aside for catch-up and make-up work for all students whose programs do not require Friday classes or clinicals. **Special study options:** Distance learning, independent study, internships. License preparation in nursing, radiology. **Credit/placement by examination:** CLEP, institutional tests. **Support services:** Learning center, tutoring.

**Majors. Business:** Accounting, business admin. **Health:** Cardiovascular technology, clinical lab technology, insurance specialist, medical radiologic technology/radiation therapy, nursing (RN), office admin.

**Most popular majors.** Health sciences 95%.

**Computing on campus.** 86 workstations in library, computer center. Commuter students can connect to campus network.

**Student life. Freshman orientation:** Mandatory. One day and one evening session held week before classes begin. **Housing:** Apartments available. $95 deposit. **Activities:** Student newspaper.

**Student services.** Career counseling, financial aid counseling, placement for graduates, veterans' counselor. **Transfer:** Re-entry adviser, preadmission transcript evaluation for new students.

**Contact.** Phone: (502) 447-1000 Toll-free number: (800) 264-1799 Fax: (502) 447-4574
Director of Admissions, Spencerian College, 4627 Dixie Highway, Louisville, KY 40216

## Spencerian College: Lexington
**Lexington, Kentucky**
www.spencerian.edu                    CB code: 3424

- For-profit 2-year branch campus and technical college
- Commuter campus in small city

**General.** Accredited by ACICS. **Enrollment:** 646 degree-seeking undergraduates. **Degrees:** 94 associate awarded. **Calendar:** Quarter, limited summer session. **Full-time faculty:** 33 total. **Part-time faculty:** 24 total. **Class size:** 96% < 20, 4% 20-39.

**Student profile.** Among degree-seeking undergraduates, 46% enrolled in a vocational program, 432 enrolled as first-time, first-year students.

| | | | |
|---|---|---|---|
| Part-time: | 31% | African American: | 13% |
| Women: | 57% | Hispanic American: | 2% |

**Transfer out. Colleges most students transferred to 2007:** Lexington Community College, University of Kentucky, Eastern Kentucky University, KCTCS.

**Basis for selection.** Open admission. **Homeschooled:** Transcript of courses and grades, state high school equivalency certificate required.

**2007-2008 Annual costs.** Cost of programs ranges from $8,000 to $40,000; program-specific fees are additional. Cost of housing is $480 per month. Books/supplies: $1,200. Personal expenses: $2,313.

**2007-2008 Financial aid.** All financial aid based on need. 435 full-time freshmen applied for aid; 430 were judged to have need; 430 of these received aid. Average need met was 65%. Average scholarship/grant was $1,500; average loan $4,000. 38% of total undergraduate aid awarded as scholarships/grants, 62% as loans/jobs. Need-based aid available for part-time students.

**Application procedures. Admission:** No deadline. $100 fee. Admission notification on a rolling basis. **Financial aid:** No deadline. FAFSA, institutional form required. Applicants notified on a rolling basis starting 1/1.

**Academics. Special study options:** Cooperative education, double major, independent study, weekend college. License preparation in radiology. **Credit/placement by examination:** CLEP. 23 credit hours maximum toward associate degree. **Support services:** Reduced course load, study skills assistance, tutoring.

**Majors. Computer sciences:** Computer graphics. **Engineering:** Electrical. **Engineering technology:** Drafting, electrical. **Health:** Health services. **Mechanic/repair:** Electronics/electrical. **Visual/performing arts:** Commercial/advertising art.

**Most popular majors.** Architecture 20%, engineering/engineering technologies 28%, visual/performing arts 45%.

**Computing on campus.** 170 workstations in library, computer center. Online library available.

**Student life. Freshman orientation:** Mandatory. Preregistration for classes offered. **Housing:** Single-sex dorms, apartments available. $95 deposit. **Activities:** Student newspaper, Baptist student union, Healing Hands student organization.

**Athletics. Intramural:** Football (non-tackle), softball, volleyball.

**Student services.** Campus ministries, career counseling, student employment services, financial aid counseling, placement for graduates. **Transfer:** Pre-admission transcript evaluation for new students.

**Contact.** Phone: (859) 223-9608 ext. 5460 Toll-free number: (800) 456-3253 ext. 5460 Fax: (859) 224-7744
Buddy Hoskinson, Executive Director, Spencerian College: Lexington, 1575 Winchester Road, Lexington, KY 40505

## West Kentucky Community and Technical College
**Paducah, Kentucky**
www.westkentucky.kctcs.edu          **CB code: 1620**

◗ Public 2-year community and technical college
◗ Commuter campus in large town

**General.** Founded in 1932. Regionally accredited. **Enrollment:** 3,122 degree-seeking undergraduates. **Degrees:** 562 associate awarded. **Location:** 140 miles from Nashville, Tennessee. **Calendar:** Semester, limited summer session. **Full-time faculty:** 341 total. **Part-time faculty:** 208 total.

**Student profile.**

| | | | |
|---|---|---|---|
| Out-of-state: | 4% | 25 or older: | 51% |

**Basis for selection.** Open admission, but selective for some programs. ACT score of 19 required for nursing and physical therapist assistant applicants. CPP placement test required for non-traditional students. ACT required for some applicants and must be received by August 25. Interview required of nursing applicants.

**High school preparation.** 20 units recommended. Recommended units include English 4, mathematics 3, social studies 2 and science 2.

**2007-2008 Annual costs.** Tuition/fees: $3,450; $10,350 out-of-state. Per-credit charge: $115 in-state; $345 out-of-state. Books/supplies: $400. Personal expenses: $425.

**Financial aid. Need-based:** Need-based aid available for part-time students.

**Application procedures. Admission:** No deadline. No application fee. Admission notification on a rolling basis beginning on or about 4/1. **Financial aid:** Priority date 4/1; no closing date. FAFSA required. Applicants notified on a rolling basis starting 7/15; must reply within 4 week(s) of notification.

**Academics. Special study options:** Combined bachelor's/graduate degree, cooperative education, distance learning, dual enrollment of high school students, ESL, honors, weekend college. License preparation in real estate. **Credit/placement by examination:** CLEP. **Support services:** GED test center, learning center, reduced course load, remedial instruction, tutoring.

**Majors. Business:** Accounting, administrative services, banking/financial services, business admin, management information systems, office technology, real estate. **Communications:** General. **Computer sciences:** General, applications programming. **Construction:** Electrician. **Health:** Medical radiologic technology/radiation therapy, nursing (RN), physical therapy assistant, physics/radiologic health, respiratory therapy technology, sonography. **Legal studies:** Court reporting. **Liberal arts:** Arts/sciences. **Mechanic/repair:** Industrial. **Personal/culinary services:** Culinary arts.

**Computing on campus.** 70 workstations in library, computer center.

**Student life. Freshman orientation:** Mandatory. **Activities:** Choral groups, drama, musical theater, radio station, student government, student newspaper, TV station.

**Athletics. Intramural:** Basketball M, golf, volleyball.

**Student services.** Adult student services, career counseling, student employment services, personal counseling, placement for graduates, veterans' counselor. **Physically disabled:** Services for visually, speech, hearing impaired. **Transfer:** Transfer adviser for students transferring to 4-year colleges.

**Contact.** Phone: (270) 534-3462 Fax: (270) 534-6304
Tina White, Director of Admissions, West Kentucky Community and Technical College, 4810 Alben Barkley Drive, Paducah, KY 42002

# Louisiana

## American School of Business
### Shreveport, Louisiana
www.americanschoolofbusiness.com CB code: 3426

- For-profit 1-year business college
- Small city

**General.** Accredited by ACICS. **Calendar:** Continuous.

**Annual costs/financial aid.** Tuition varies by program and ranges from $8,300 to $10,600. Personal expenses: $2,429.

**Contact.** Phone: (318) 798-3333
Admissions Director, 702 Professional Drive North, Shreveport, LA 71105

## Baton Rouge Community College
### Baton Rouge, Louisiana
www.mybrcc.edu CB code: 6023

- Public 2-year community college
- Commuter campus in large city

**General.** Regionally accredited. **Enrollment:** 5,889 degree-seeking undergraduates; 1,142 non-degree-seeking students. **Degrees:** 196 associate awarded. **Calendar:** Semester, extensive summer session. **Full-time faculty:** 100 total; 35% minority, 64% women. **Part-time faculty:** 152 total; 32% minority, 59% women. **Class size:** 24% < 20, 71% 20-39, 5% 40-49.

**Student profile.** Among degree-seeking undergraduates, 12% enrolled in a vocational program, 1,390 enrolled as first-time, first-year students, 949 transferred in from other institutions.

| | | | |
|---|---|---|---|
| Part-time: | 38% | Asian American: | 2% |
| Out-of-state: | 1% | Hispanic American: | 2% |
| Women: | 58% | 25 or older: | 26% |
| African American: | 37% | | |

**Basis for selection.** Open admission, but selective for some programs.

**2007-2008 Annual costs.** Tuition/fees: $1,806; $4,614 out-of-state. Books/supplies: $1,200. Personal expenses: $1,692.

**2006-2007 Financial aid. Need-based:** 95% of total undergraduate aid awarded as scholarships/grants, 5% as loans/jobs.

**Application procedures. Admission:** No deadline. $7 fee. Application may be submitted online. Admission notification on a rolling basis. **Financial aid:** Priority date 4/15; no closing date.

**Academics. Special study options:** Cross-registration, dual enrollment of high school students, ESL, honors, internships. **Credit/placement by examination:** CLEP, institutional tests. **Support services:** Learning center, study skills assistance.

**Majors. Business:** General, office technology. **Health:** Nursing (RN). **Liberal arts:** Arts/sciences.

**Most popular majors.** Business/marketing 20%, liberal arts 50%.

**Computing on campus.** Online course registration, online library, wireless network available.

**Student life. Freshman orientation:** Available. Preregistration for classes offered. **Activities:** Dance, student government, student newspaper.

**Athletics.** NJCAA. **Intercollegiate:** Baseball M. **Team name:** Bears.

**Student services.** Career counseling, financial aid counseling, personal counseling, veterans' counselor. **Physically disabled:** Services for visually, speech, hearing impaired. **Learning disabled:** Comprehensive services available.

**Contact.** E-mail: jacksona@mybrcc.edu
Phone: (225) 216-8700
Alterman Jackson, Executive Director of Enrollment Services, Baton Rouge Community College, 5310 Florida Boulevard, Baton Rouge, LA 70806

## Baton Rouge School of Computers
### Baton Rouge, Louisiana
www.brsc.net CB code: 3197

- For-profit 2-year technical college
- Small city

**General.** Accredited by ACCSCT. **Calendar:** Continuous.

**Annual costs/financial aid.** $10,500 tuition for certificate program, $21,000 for associate degree; $150 registration fee. Additional charge for textbooks. Books/supplies: $500. Personal expenses: $2,400.

**Contact.** Phone: (225) 923-2525
Director of Admissions, 10425 Plaza Americana, Baton Rouge, LA 70816

## Blue Cliff College: Houma
### Houma, Louisiana
www.bluecliffcollege.com

- For-profit 2-year technical college
- Commuter campus in large town

**General.** Accredited by ACCSCT. **Calendar:** Quarter.

**Annual costs/financial aid.** Associate degree program in medical assisting or massage therapy, $19,200 plus $350 in fees; diploma program in medical assisting, $11,600, plus $350 in fees; massage therapy diploma program, $10,600, plus $350 in fees.

**Contact.** Phone: (985) 601-4000
Admissions Representative, 803 Barrow Street, Houma, LA 70360

## Blue Cliff College: Lafayette
### Lafayette, Louisiana
www.bluecliffcollege.com

- For-profit 2-year health science and technical college
- Commuter campus in small city
- Application essay, interview required

**General.** Accredited by ACCSCT. **Enrollment:** 120 degree-seeking undergraduates. **Location:** 60 miles from Baton Rouge. **Calendar:** Quarter, extensive summer session. **Full-time faculty:** 3 total. **Part-time faculty:** 7 total. **Special facilities:** Massage therapy clinics.

**Basis for selection.** Open admission. Wonderlic test given as skills assessment before enrollment. **Homeschooled:** State high school equivalency certificate required.

**High school preparation.** 25 units required. Required units include English 4, mathematics 3, history 3, science 4, foreign language 1 and academic electives 10.

**2007-2008 Annual costs.** Associate degree program in medical assisting or massage therapy, $19,200 plus $350 in fees; diploma program in medical assisting, $11,600, plus $350 in fees; massage therapy diploma program, $10,600, plus $350 in fees.

**Application procedures. Admission:** $25 fee. Application must be submitted on paper.

**Academics. Credit/placement by examination:** CLEP.

**Majors. Health:** Massage therapy. **Protective services:** Criminal justice.

**Athletics. Team name:** Humming Birds.

**Contact.** E-mail: Hildaj@bluecliffcollege.com
Phone: (337) 269-0620 ext. 3209 Toll-free
number: (877) 269-0615 ext. 3204 Fax: (337) 269-0688
Kathy Johnson, Admissions Director, Blue Cliff College: Lafayette, 100 Asma Boulevard, Suite 350, Lafayette, LA 70508

Two-Year Colleges

## Blue Cliff College: Metairie
### Metairie, Louisiana
### www.bluecliffcollege.com

- For-profit 2-year technical college
- Commuter campus in large town

**General.** Accredited by ACCSCT. **Calendar:** Quarter.

**Annual costs/financial aid.** Associate degree program in medical assisting or massage therapy, $19,200 plus $350 in fees; diploma program in medical assisting, $11,600, plus $350 in fees; massage therapy diploma program, $10,600, plus $350 in fees.

**Contact.** Phone: (504) 456-3141
Admissions Officer, 3200 Cleary Avenue, Metairie, LA 70002

## Blue Cliff College: Shreveport
### Shreveport, Louisiana
### www.bluecliffcollege.com

- For-profit 2-year technical college
- Commuter campus in small city

**General.** Accredited by ACCSCT. **Calendar:** Quarter.

**Annual costs/financial aid.** Associate degree program in medical assisting or massage therapy, $19,200 plus $350 in fees; diploma program in medical assisting, $11,600, plus $350 in fees; massage therapy diploma program, $10,600, plus $350 in fees.

**Contact.** Phone: (318) 425-7941
Admissions Representative, 200 North Thomas Drive, Suite A, Shreveport, LA 71107

## Bossier Parish Community College
### Bossier City, Louisiana
### www.bpcc.edu                    CB code: 0787

- Public 2-year community college
- Commuter campus in small city

**General.** Founded in 1966. Regionally accredited. **Enrollment:** 4,227 degree-seeking undergraduates; 759 non-degree-seeking students. **Degrees:** 335 associate awarded. **Location:** 6 miles from downtown Shreveport. **Calendar:** Semester, limited summer session. **Full-time faculty:** 110 total; 8% have terminal degrees, 10% minority, 64% women. **Part-time faculty:** 176 total; 2% have terminal degrees, 12% minority, 54% women. **Class size:** 47% < 20, 52% 20-39, less than 1% 40-49, less than 1% 50-99. **Partnerships:** Formal partnerships with General Motors, Libby Glass.

**Student profile.** Among degree-seeking undergraduates, 8% enrolled in a transfer program, 1,127 enrolled as first-time, first-year students, 297 transferred in from other institutions.

| | | | |
|---|---|---|---|
| Part-time: | 38% | Asian American: | 1% |
| Out-of-state: | 2% | Hispanic American: | 2% |
| Women: | 65% | 25 or older: | 30% |
| African American: | 34% | | |

**Transfer out. Colleges most students transferred to 2007:** Louisiana State University in Shreveport, Northwestern State University of Louisiana, Louisiana Tech University, Southern Arkansas University, Grambling State University.

**Basis for selection.** Open admission, but selective for out-of-state students. ACT scores required for admission for out-of-state students. **Homeschooled:** Students generally expected to complete requirements for GED.

**2007-2008 Annual costs.** Tuition/fees: $1,760; $3,900 out-of-state. Books/supplies: $1,200. Personal expenses: $1,726.

**2006-2007 Financial aid. Need-based:** 732 full-time freshmen applied for aid; 594 were judged to have need; 520 of these received aid. Average need met was 45%. Average scholarship/grant was $3,799; average loan $1,659. 58% of total undergraduate aid awarded as scholarships/grants, 42% as loans/jobs. Need-based aid available for part-time students. Work-study available nights and for part-time students. **Non-need-based:** Awarded to 387 full-time undergraduates, including 294 freshmen. Scholarships awarded for academics, alumni affiliation, athletics, minority status, music/drama.

**Application procedures. Admission:** Closing date 8/8 (receipt date). $15 fee. Admission notification on a rolling basis. **Financial aid:** Closing date 7/1. FAFSA required. Applicants notified on a rolling basis.

**Academics. Special study options:** Accelerated study, distance learning, double major, dual enrollment of high school students, honors, internships. **Credit/placement by examination:** AP, CLEP, institutional tests. 30 credit hours maximum toward associate degree. **Support services:** GED preparation, learning center, remedial instruction, study skills assistance, tutoring.

**Majors. Business:** General. **Communications technology:** Recording arts. **Computer sciences:** Information systems, web page design. **Engineering technology:** CAD/CADD, industrial. **Health:** EMT paramedic, medical assistant, pharmacy assistant, physical therapy assistant, respiratory therapy technology. **Liberal arts:** Arts/sciences. **Mechanic/repair:** Industrial. **Protective services:** Criminal justice. **Visual/performing arts:** Dramatic.

**Most popular majors.** Business/marketing 15%, communications/journalism 8%, computer/information sciences 6%, health sciences 21%, liberal arts 37%, security/protective services 9%.

**Computing on campus.** 120 workstations in library. Online course registration, online library, wireless network available.

**Student life. Freshman orientation:** Available. Preregistration for classes offered. **Activities:** Bands, campus ministries, choral groups, dance, drama, international student organizations, literary magazine, music ensembles, musical theater, radio station, student government, student newspaper, TV station, College Republicans, gospel choir, ADAPTS, Maroon Jackets, NAACP, FCA, SGA.

**Athletics.** NJCAA. **Intercollegiate:** Baseball M, basketball M, cheerleading, soccer W, softball W. **Team name:** Cavaliers.

**Student services.** Career counseling, services for economically disadvantaged, student employment services, financial aid counseling, minority student services, personal counseling, veterans' counselor. **Physically disabled:** Services for visually, speech, hearing impaired. **Transfer:** Preadmission transcript evaluation for new students. College fairs on campus for students transferring to 4-year colleges.

**Contact.** E-mail: Admissions@bpcc.edu
Phone: (318) 678-6004 Fax: (318) 678-6390
Ann Jampole, Admissions Officer, Bossier Parish Community College, 6220 East Texas Street, Bossier City, LA 71111-6922

## Camelot College
### Baton Rouge, Louisiana
### www.camelotcollege.com          CB code: 3427

- For-profit 2-year health science and technical college
- Small city

**General.** Accredited by ACICS. **Calendar:** Continuous.

**Annual costs/financial aid.** Annual tuition $9,340 for computer data processing and medical assistant programs, $10,900 for paralegal and cosmetology programs, $8,141 for cosmetology instructor's training program.

**Contact.** Phone: (225) 928-3005
Admissions Representative, 2618 Wooddale Boulevard, Suite A, Baton Rouge, LA 70805

## Delgado Community College
### New Orleans, Louisiana          CB member
### www.dcc.edu                     CB code: 6176

- Public 2-year community college
- Commuter campus in very large city

**General.** Founded in 1921. Regionally accredited. **Enrollment:** 12,224 degree-seeking undergraduates. **Degrees:** 924 associate awarded. **ROTC:** Army, Air Force. **Calendar:** Semester, extensive summer session. **Full-time faculty:** 389 total; 9% have terminal degrees, 25% minority, 66% women. **Part-time faculty:** 239 total; 26% minority, 51% women. **Class size:** 52% < 20, 45% 20-39, 2% 40-49, less than 1% 50-99. **Special facilities:** Ship simulator, fine arts gallery.

**Student profile.** Among degree-seeking undergraduates, 13% enrolled in a transfer program, 87% enrolled in a vocational program.

| | | | |
|---|---|---|---|
| Out-of-state: | 2% | Native American: | 1% |
| African American: | 39% | International: | 1% |
| Asian American: | 3% | 25 or older: | 48% |
| Hispanic American: | 5% | | |

**Transfer out. Colleges most students transferred to 2007:** University of New Orleans, Southern University at New Orleans, Louisiana State University, Nicholls State University, Southeastern Louisiana University.

**Basis for selection.** Open admission, but selective for some programs. ACT scores may be submitted before or during student's first semester of enrollment. ACT without writing component accepted. **Adult students:** SAT/ACT scores not required if applicant over 25. Adult students without high school diploma or GED required to pass Ability to Benefit Exam. **Home-schooled:** Applicants who have not completed a state or regionally approved program required to have GED or successfully pass Ability to Benefit Exam.

**2007-2008 Annual costs.** Tuition/fees: $1,928; $4,908 out-of-state. Books/supplies: $1,200. Personal expenses: $4,645.

**Financial aid. Need-based:** Need-based aid available for part-time students. Work-study available nights, weekends and for part-time students. **Non-need-based:** Scholarships awarded for academics, athletics, leadership, music/drama, state residency.

**Application procedures. Admission:** No deadline. $25 fee. Application may be submitted online. Admission notification on a rolling basis. **Financial aid:** Priority date 5/1, closing date 7/15. FAFSA, institutional form required. Applicants notified on a rolling basis starting 4/1; must reply within 2 week(s) of notification.

**Academics. Special study options:** Cooperative education, cross-registration, distance learning, double major, dual enrollment of high school students, ESL, honors, independent study, internships, liberal arts/career combination, student-designed major, weekend college. License preparation in nursing, paramedic, physical therapy, real estate. **Credit/placement by examination:** AP, CLEP, institutional tests. 24 credit hours maximum toward associate degree. **Support services:** Learning center, pre-admission summer program, remedial instruction, tutoring.

**Majors. Agriculture:** Horticulture. **Architecture:** Interior. **Business:** Accounting, administrative services, business admin, hospitality admin. **Computer sciences:** Data processing. **Construction:** Maintenance. **Education:** Early childhood. **Engineering technology:** Architectural, biomedical, civil, electrical, occupational safety. **Family/consumer sciences:** Institutional food production. **Foreign languages:** Sign language interpretation. **Health:** Clinical lab technology, dental hygiene, dental lab technology, EMT paramedic, medical radiologic technology/radiation therapy, medical records technology, nursing (RN), occupational therapy assistant, physical therapy assistant, respiratory therapy technology. **Interdisciplinary:** Biological/physical sciences. **Liberal arts:** Arts/sciences. **Mechanic/repair:** Automotive, computer, electronics/electrical. **Personal/culinary services:** Mortuary science. **Production:** Machine shop technology. **Protective services:** Fire safety technology, police science. **Visual/performing arts:** Art, commercial/advertising art, design.

**Most popular majors.** Business/marketing 13%, health sciences 56%.

**Computing on campus.** 555 workstations in library, computer center, student center. Online library, wireless network available.

**Student life. Freshman orientation:** Available. Preregistration for classes offered. **Activities:** Concert band, choral groups, dance, drama, film society, music ensembles, musical theater, student government, student newspaper, TV station, religious organizations available.

**Athletics.** NJCAA. **Intercollegiate:** Baseball M, basketball M, cheerleading. **Intramural:** Archery, badminton, baseball M, basketball, golf, soccer, softball, swimming, table tennis, tennis, volleyball. **Team name:** Dolphins.

**Student services.** Adult student services, career counseling, services for economically disadvantaged, student employment services, financial aid counseling, health services, on-campus daycare, personal counseling, placement for graduates, veterans' counselor. **Physically disabled:** Services for visually, speech, hearing impaired. **Transfer:** Re-entry adviser for new students. Transfer center, transfer adviser, college fairs on campus for students transferring to 4-year colleges.

**Contact.** E-mail: gboutte@dcc.edu
Phone: (504) 671-5099 Fax: (504) 483-1895
Gwen Boutte, Director of Admissions & Enrollment Services, Delgado Community College, 615 City Park Avenue, New Orleans, LA 70119

## Delta College of Arts & Technology
**Baton Rouge, Louisiana**
www.deltacollege.com
CB code: 3131

- For-profit 2-year visual arts and technical college
- Large city

**General.** Accredited by ACCSCT. **Calendar:** Continuous.

**Annual costs/financial aid.** Tuition for full programs ranges from $8,250 to $19,500 and includes books and supplies. Registration fee $100. Books/supplies: $775. Personal expenses: $250.

**Contact.** Phone: (225) 928-7770
Director of Admissions, 7380 Exchange Place, Baton Rouge, LA 70806

## Delta School of Business & Technology
**Lake Charles, Louisiana**
www.deltatech.edu
CB code: 2252

- For-profit 2-year business and technical college
- Small city

**General.** Founded in 1970. Accredited by ACICS. **Enrollment:** 356 degree-seeking undergraduates. **Degrees:** 110 associate awarded. **Location:** 128 miles from Baton Rouge. **Calendar:** Continuous. **Full-time faculty:** 22 total. **Part-time faculty:** 13 total.

**Student profile.**

| | | | |
|---|---|---|---|
| Out-of-state: | 10% | 25 or older: | 40% |

**Basis for selection.** Open admission. Entrance evaluation test used for placement and advising.

**2007-2008 Annual costs.** Cost of associate degree program $9,590 per year, plus books and fees of approximately $2,540; IT program slightly higher at $10,260 per year, plus books and fees of approximately $2,790. One-year diploma programs also available at similar cost. Books/supplies: $800.

**Application procedures. Admission:** No deadline.

**Academics. Special study options:** Accelerated study, distance learning, double major, honors, internships. **Credit/placement by examination:** CLEP. **Support services:** Reduced course load, tutoring.

**Majors. Business:** Accounting, business admin. **Engineering technology:** Drafting. **Health:** Medical assistant. **Mechanic/repair:** Electronics/electrical.

**Computing on campus.** 30 workstations in computer center.

**Student services.** Career counseling, student employment services, placement for graduates.

**Contact.** E-mail: barbara@deltatech.edu
Phone: (337) 439-5765 Toll-free number: (800) 259-5627
Fax: (337) 436-5151
Barbara Holt, Director of Admissions, Delta School of Business & Technology, 517 Broad Street, Lake Charles, LA 70601

## Gretna Career College
**Gretna, Louisiana**
www.gretnacareercollege.edu

- For-profit 2-year technical college
- Commuter campus in large town

**General.** Accredited by ACCSCT. **Calendar:** Semester.

**Annual costs/financial aid.** Tuition varies by program and ranges from $7,340-$12,875 for certificate and diploma programs; $23,700-$24,200 for associate degree programs. Costs include books and supplies.

**Contact.** Phone: (504) 366-5409 ext. 23
Director of Admissions, 1415 Whitney Avenue, Gretna, LA 70053

## ITI Technical College
### Baton Rouge, Louisiana
### www.iticollege.edu

- For-profit 2-year technical college
- Commuter campus in large city
- Interview required

**General.** Accredited by ACCSCT. **Enrollment:** 323 degree-seeking undergraduates; 94 non-degree-seeking students. **Degrees:** 131 associate awarded. **Calendar:** Differs by program. 11 week terms. **Full-time faculty:** 20 total; 25% minority, 20% women. **Part-time faculty:** 30 total; 13% minority, 10% women.

**Student profile.** Among degree-seeking undergraduates, 100% enrolled in a vocational program, 175 enrolled as first-time, first-year students.

| | | | |
|---|---|---|---|
| Out-of-state: | 1% | 25 or older: | 47% |
| Women: | 20% | | |

**Basis for selection.** Open admission. All applicants must pass an entrance examination. Applicant completes application, must interview and tour campus, complete entrance evaluation, settle funding, sign enrollment agreement. **Homeschooled:** Students must have an acceptable certificate or diploma at the time of enrollment. **Learning Disabled:** Students must meet with school director regarding special needs and referral for assistance.

**2007-2008 Annual costs.** Full-time tuition varies by program from $11,400 to $22,900.

**Financial aid.** All financial aid based on need. Need-based aid available for part-time students.

**Application procedures. Admission:** No deadline. No application fee. Admission notification on a rolling basis. **Financial aid:** No deadline. FAFSA required.

**Academics. Credit/placement by examination:** CLEP. **Support services:** Study skills assistance, tutoring.

**Majors. Business:** Administrative services, business admin, executive assistant, office management, office technology. **Communications technology:** General. **Computer sciences:** Data processing, information systems. **Engineering technology:** Drafting, electrical, instrumentation. **Health:** Insurance coding, insurance specialist, medical records admin, medical records technology, medical secretary, medical transcription, office admin, office assistant, office computer specialist, receptionist.

**Computing on campus.** 5 workstations in library.

**Student life. Freshman orientation:** Mandatory.

**Student services.** Career counseling, financial aid counseling, placement for graduates.

**Contact.** E-mail: admissions@iticollege.edu
Phone: (225) 752-4233 Toll-free number: (800) 467-4484
Fax: (225) 756-0903
Joe Martin, Director of Admissions, ITI Technical College, 13944 Airline Highway, Baton Rouge, LA 70817

## Louisiana State University at Eunice
### Eunice, Louisiana
### www.lsue.edu
**CB code: 6386**

- Public 2-year branch campus and community college
- Commuter campus in large town

**General.** Founded in 1964. Regionally accredited. **Enrollment:** 2,864 degree-seeking undergraduates. **Degrees:** 271 associate awarded. **Location:** 40 miles from Lafayette, 90 miles from Baton Rouge. **Calendar:** Semester, limited summer session. **Full-time faculty:** 67 total. **Part-time faculty:** 55 total.

**Student profile.**

| | | | |
|---|---|---|---|
| Out-of-state: | 1% | 25 or older: | 37% |

**Transfer out. Colleges most students transferred to 2007:** Louisiana State University-Baton Rouge, University of Louisiana at Lafayette, McNeese State University, Southern University.

**Basis for selection.** Open admission, but selective for some programs. Test scores, school achievement record, interview considered for admission

to nursing and respiratory care programs. **Homeschooled:** Transcript of courses and grades required. Applicants must be from nationally recognized program from accredited agency and have GED or ACT score equal to or greater than current state average.

**2007-2008 Annual costs.** Tuition/fees: $2,192; $5,192 out-of-state. Per-credit charge: $92. Books/supplies: $1,000.

**2007-2008 Financial aid. Need-based:** 97% of total undergraduate aid awarded as scholarships/grants, 3% as loans/jobs. Need-based aid available for part-time students.

**Application procedures. Admission:** Closing date 8/1. $25 fee. Application may be submitted online. Admission notification on a rolling basis. **Financial aid:** Priority date 6/1; no closing date. FAFSA, institutional form required. Applicants notified on a rolling basis starting 4/1; must reply within 2 week(s) of notification.

**Academics. Special study options:** Distance learning, dual enrollment of high school students, honors, independent study, liberal arts/career combination. Bachelor's degree programs available on campus. License preparation in nursing, physical therapy. **Credit/placement by examination:** AP, CLEP, institutional tests. 30 credit hours maximum toward associate degree. **Support services:** Learning center, remedial instruction, study skills assistance, tutoring.

**Majors. Business:** General, administrative services. **Computer sciences:** General. **Education:** Early childhood. **Health:** Licensed practical nurse, medical radiologic technology/radiation therapy, respiratory therapy technology. **Interdisciplinary:** Natural sciences. **Legal studies:** Paralegal. **Liberal arts:** Arts/sciences. **Protective services:** Criminal justice, fire safety technology.

**Computing on campus.** 150 workstations in library, computer center. Commuter students can connect to campus network. Online course registration, helpline available.

**Student life. Freshman orientation:** Available. Preregistration for classes offered. **Activities:** Drama, student government, student newspaper, Circle-K, Baptist Collegiate Ministry, Newman Club, Rotoract, African American Student Alliance, Students in Free Enterprise, Catholic Student Center.

**Athletics.** NJCAA. **Intercollegiate:** Baseball M, basketball W. **Intramural:** Baseball M, basketball, football (non-tackle) M, softball W, tennis W, volleyball. **Team name:** Bengals.

**Student services.** Adult student services, campus ministries, career counseling, financial aid counseling, health services, personal counseling, placement for graduates, veterans' counselor. **Physically disabled:** Services for visually, hearing impaired. **Transfer:** Transfer adviser, college fairs on campus for students transferring to 4-year colleges.

**Contact.** E-mail: rryder@lsue.edu
Phone: (337) 550-1305 Toll-free number: (888) 367-5783
Fax: (337) 550-1306
Ronald Ryder, Admissions Director, Louisiana State University at Eunice, Box 1129, Eunice, LA 70535

## Nunez Community College
### Chalmette, Louisiana
### www.nunez.edu
**CB code: 0295**

- Public 2-year community and technical college
- Commuter campus in large town

**General.** Founded in 1992. Regionally accredited. **Enrollment:** 847 degree-seeking undergraduates; 824 non-degree-seeking students. **Degrees:** 99 associate awarded. **Location:** 11 miles from New Orleans. **Calendar:** Semester, limited summer session. **Full-time faculty:** 35 total; 6% have terminal degrees, 14% minority, 60% women. **Part-time faculty:** 27 total; 11% have terminal degrees, 15% minority, 67% women. **Class size:** 62% < 20, 37% 20-39, less than 1% 40-49, less than 1% 50-99.

**Student profile.** Among degree-seeking undergraduates, 25% enrolled in a transfer program, 75% enrolled in a vocational program, 142 enrolled as first-time, first-year students.

| | | | |
|---|---|---|---|
| Part-time: | 35% | Hispanic American: | 3% |
| Women: | 62% | Native American: | 2% |
| African American: | 32% | 25 or older: | 30% |
| Asian American: | 2% | | |

**Transfer out. Colleges most students transferred to 2007:** University of New Orleans, Southern University of New Orleans, Louisiana State University-Baton Rouge, Our Lady of Holy Cross College, Loyola University of New Orleans.

**Basis for selection.** Open admission, but selective for some programs. Additional requirements for the Practical Nursing Certificate program and Emergency Medical Technician and Associate of Science in Teaching (Grades 1-5).

**High school preparation.** 12 units recommended. Recommended units include English 4, mathematics 4, social studies 1, history 1, science 2 (laboratory 1).

**2007-2008 Annual costs.** Tuition/fees: $1,770; $4,290 out-of-state. Books/supplies: $1,700.

**Financial aid. Need-based:** Need-based aid available for part-time students. **Additional information:** Pell Grants, Stafford Loans, campus work-study, and tuition waiver scholarships available. Louisiana National Guard tuition exemption, teacher tuition exemption, dependents of injured fire-police tuition waivers.

**Application procedures. Admission:** Priority date 8/1; no deadline. $10 fee. Application must be submitted on paper. Admission notification on a rolling basis. **Financial aid:** Priority date 4/1, closing date 7/1. FAFSA, institutional form required. Applicants notified by 8/1; must reply by 8/15.

**Academics. Special study options:** Cooperative education, cross-registration, distance learning, double major, dual enrollment of high school students, ESL, honors, independent study, internships, student-designed major, weekend college. License preparation in nursing, paramedic. **Credit/placement by examination:** AP, CLEP, institutional tests. 24 credit hours maximum toward associate degree. **Support services:** Learning center, reduced course load, remedial instruction, tutoring.

**Majors. Business:** General. **Computer sciences:** Computer science, information systems. **Education:** General. **Engineering technology:** Industrial. **Health:** Office admin. **Legal studies:** Paralegal. **Mechanic/repair:** Heating/ac/refrig. **Personal/culinary services:** Chef training. **Other:** General Science.

**Most popular majors.** Business/marketing 10%, education 15%, engineering/engineering technologies 8%, liberal arts 53%.

**Computing on campus.** 75 workstations in library, computer center, student center. Online library, helpline available.

**Student life. Freshman orientation:** Mandatory. Preregistration for classes offered. Two-hour orientation offered during registration period. **Activities:** Drama, literary magazine, student government.

**Athletics. Team name:** Pelicans.

**Student services.** Career counseling, financial aid counseling, personal counseling, placement for graduates, veterans' counselor. **Physically disabled:** Services for visually, hearing impaired. **Transfer:** Transfer adviser, college fairs on campus for students transferring to 4-year colleges.

**Contact.** Phone: (504) 278-7467 Fax: (504) 278-7487
Becky Maillet, Director of Admissions and Registration, Nunez Community College, 3710 Paris Road, Chalmette, LA 70043

## Remington College: Baton Rouge
**Baton Rouge, Louisiana**
**www.remingtoncollege.edu/batonrouge/index.html**
**CB code: 3428**

- For-profit 2-year technical college
- Commuter campus in large city
- Interview required

**General.** Accredited by ACICS. **Enrollment:** 410 degree-seeking undergraduates. **Degrees:** 64 associate awarded. **Calendar:** Quarter. **Full-time faculty:** 12 total. **Part-time faculty:** 8 total.

**Basis for selection.** Open admission, but selective for some programs.

**2007-2008 Annual costs.** Costs of entire programs leading to certificate, associate degree, bachelor's degree range from $13,000 to $38,880; includes books and supplies.

**Financial aid.** All financial aid based on need. Work-study available nights.

**Application procedures. Admission:** No deadline. $50 fee. **Financial aid:** No deadline. FAFSA required. Applicants notified on a rolling basis; must reply within 1 week(s) of notification.

**Academics. Special study options:** Liberal arts/career combination. **Credit/placement by examination:** CLEP. **Support services:** Tutoring.

**Majors. Computer sciences:** General, information systems, LAN/WAN management.

**Computing on campus.** PC or laptop required.

**Student life. Freshman orientation:** Mandatory. **Activities:** Student government.

**Student services.** Financial aid counseling, placement for graduates.

**Contact.** Phone: (225) 922-3990 Fax: (225) 922-6569
AcQueena Fuller, Director of Admissions, Remington College: Baton Rouge, 10551 Coursey Boulevard, Baton Rouge, LA 70816

## Remington College: Lafayette
**Lafayette, Louisiana**
**www.remingtoncollege.edu**
**CB code: 7117**

- For-profit 2-year junior college
- Commuter campus in small city
- Interview required

**General.** Founded in 1940. Accredited by ACICS. **Enrollment:** 242 degree-seeking undergraduates. **Degrees:** 72 associate awarded. **Location:** 50 miles from Baton Rouge. **Calendar:** Quarter, extensive summer session. **Full-time faculty:** 8 total; 25% minority, 12% women. **Part-time faculty:** 15 total; 27% minority, 67% women.

**Basis for selection.** Open admission. Wonderlic testing required of all applicants.

**2007-2008 Annual costs.** Costs of entire programs leading to certificate, associate degree, bachelor's degree range from $13,000 to $38,880; includes books and supplies.

**Financial aid.** All financial aid based on need. Work-study available nights.

**Application procedures. Admission:** No deadline. $50 fee. Application must be submitted on paper. Admission notification on a rolling basis. **Financial aid:** No deadline. FAFSA, institutional form required.

**Academics.** Each student is provided with a laptop computer. **Special study options:** Accelerated study, independent study, liberal arts/career combination. **Credit/placement by examination:** CLEP. **Support services:** GED preparation, tutoring.

**Majors. Business:** Business admin. **Computer sciences:** General. **Engineering technology:** Electrical. **Health:** Medical assistant. **Protective services:** Law enforcement admin.

**Computing on campus.** 110 workstations in library, computer center. Online library, helpline, repair service available.

**Student life. Freshman orientation:** Mandatory. Preregistration for classes offered. **Activities:** National Vocational Technical Society (Associate Degree Honors Society), Nightingale Medical Honor Society (Diploma Honors Society).

**Student services.** Student employment services, financial aid counseling, placement for graduates. **Transfer:** Pre-admission transcript evaluation for new students.

**Contact.** Phone: (337) 981-4010 Fax: (337) 983-7130
Sang Nguyen, Director of Recruitment, Remington College: Lafayette, 303 Rue Louis XIV, Lafayette, LA 70508

## River Parishes Community College
**Sorrento, Louisiana**
**www.rpcc.edu**

- Public 2-year community college
- Commuter campus in rural community

**General.** Regionally accredited. **Enrollment:** 1,163 undergraduates. **Degrees:** 65 associate awarded. **Location:** 20 miles from Baton Rouge, 40 miles from New Orleans. **Calendar:** Semester, limited summer session. **Full-time faculty:** 17 total. **Part-time faculty:** 35 total.

**Student profile.**

| Out-of-state: | 1% | 25 or older: | 27% |
|---|---|---|---|

**Basis for selection.** Open admission. **Homeschooled:** Transcript of courses and grades required.

**2007-2008 Annual costs.** Tuition/fees: $1,874; $4,612 out-of-state.

**Application procedures. Admission:** No deadline. $10 fee. Application may be submitted online. Admission notification on a rolling basis. **Financial aid:** Priority date 4/15; no closing date. FAFSA required. Applicants notified on a rolling basis starting 3/1.

**Academics. Credit/placement by examination:** CLEP, SAT, ACT.

**Majors. Liberal arts:** Arts/sciences.

**Computing on campus.** Online library, wireless network available.

**Contact.** Phone: (225) 675-8270 Fax: (225) 675-5478
Jennifer Kleinpeter, Admissions Director, River Parishes Community College, PO Box 310, Sorrento, LA 70778

---

## South Louisiana Community College
### Lafayette, Louisiana
**www.slcc.cc.la.us**       **CB code: 4521**

▸ Public 2-year community college
▸ Small city

**General.** Regionally accredited. **Enrollment:** 1,531 degree-seeking undergraduates. **Degrees:** 66 associate awarded. **Calendar:** Semester. **Full-time faculty:** 27 total. **Part-time faculty:** 84 total.

**Basis for selection.** Open admission, but selective for some programs.

**2007-2008 Annual costs.** Tuition/fees: $1,862; $2,229 out-of-state.

**Application procedures. Admission:** Priority date 7/1; no deadline. $5 fee. **Financial aid:** Priority date 7/1; no closing date.

**Academics. Special study options:** Cross-registration, distance learning, dual enrollment of high school students. **Credit/placement by examination:** CLEP, ACT, institutional tests. **Support services:** Learning center, remedial instruction, study skills assistance, tutoring, writing center.

**Majors. Business:** General. **Education:** Early childhood. **Health:** EMT paramedic. **Liberal arts:** Arts/sciences. **Mechanic/repair:** Industrial. **Protective services:** Criminal justice.

**Computing on campus.** Online library, helpline available.

**Athletics. Team name:** Sabers.

**Contact.** E-mail: admissions@slcc.cc.la.us
Phone: (337) 521-8923 Fax: (337) 262-2101
Arthur Gillis, Director of Admissions, South Louisiana Community College, 320 Devalcourt, Lafayette, LA 70506-4124

---

## Southern University at Shreveport
### Shreveport, Louisiana
**www.susla.edu**       **CB code: 0322**

▸ Public 2-year community college
▸ Commuter campus in small city

**General.** Founded in 1964. Regionally accredited. **Enrollment:** 2,403 degree-seeking undergraduates. **Degrees:** 284 associate awarded. **Calendar:** Semester, limited summer session. **Full-time faculty:** 81 total; 100% have terminal degrees, 69% women. **Part-time faculty:** 81 total; 100% have terminal degrees, 63% women.

**Student profile.** Among degree-seeking undergraduates, 227 enrolled as first-time, first-year students.

| | | | |
|---|---|---|---|
| Part-time: | 46% | **Women:** | 77% |
| Out-of-state: | 16% | | |

**Basis for selection.** Open admission.

**High school preparation.** 15 units recommended. Recommended units include English 3, mathematics 2, social studies 2 and science 5.

**2007-2008 Annual costs.** Tuition/fees: $2,252; $3,382 out-of-state. Books/supplies: $600. Personal expenses: $1,420.

**Application procedures. Admission:** No deadline. $5 fee ($15 out-of-state). Admission notification on a rolling basis. **Financial aid:** No deadline. FAFSA required. Applicants notified on a rolling basis.

**Academics. Special study options:** Cross-registration, internships. License preparation in dental hygiene, nursing, radiology. **Credit/placement by examination:** CLEP, institutional tests. 3 credit hours maximum toward associate degree. **Support services:** GED preparation, remedial instruction, study skills assistance, tutoring, writing center.

**Majors. Biology:** General. **Business:** Accounting, banking/financial services, business admin. **Computer sciences:** General, applications programming, computer science. **Education:** Early childhood. **Engineering technology:** Electrical. **Health:** Clinical lab technology, dental hygiene, health services, medical radiologic technology/radiation therapy, medical records technology, respiratory therapy technology, surgical technology. **Liberal arts:** Arts/sciences. **Physical sciences:** Chemistry. **Protective services:** Law enforcement admin. **Public administration:** Human services. **Social sciences:** General, sociology. **Transportation:** Aviation management.

**Most popular majors.** Business/marketing 20%, education 9%, health sciences 41%, liberal arts 15%.

**Computing on campus.** 50 workstations in library, computer center. Commuter students can connect to campus network. Online course registration, online library available.

**Student life. Freshman orientation:** Mandatory. Preregistration for classes offered. **Activities:** Choral groups, dance, student government, student newspaper, Baptist Student Union, Afro-American Society.

**Athletics.** NJCAA. **Intercollegiate:** Basketball. **Team name:** Jaguars.

**Student services.** Health services, personal counseling, placement for graduates, veterans' counselor.

**Contact.** Phone: (318) 674-3342 Fax: (318) 674-3489
Teresa Jones, Associate Vice Chancellor Enrollment Management, Southern University at Shreveport, 3050 Martin Luther King, Jr. Drive, Shreveport, LA 71107

# Maine

## Andover College
### Portland, Maine
www.andovercollege.edu     CB code: 0688

▶ For-profit 2-year business and junior college
▶ Commuter campus in small city
▶ Interview required

**General.** Founded in 1966. Regionally accredited. **Enrollment:** 501 degree-seeking undergraduates. **Degrees:** 251 associate awarded. **Location:** 115 miles from Boston. **Calendar:** Six 8-week terms. Extensive summer session. **Full-time faculty:** 12 total. **Part-time faculty:** 71 total. **Class size:** 98% < 20, 2% 20-39.

**Student profile.**

| | | | |
|---|---|---|---|
| Out-of-state: | 4% | 25 or older: | 90% |

**Transfer out. Colleges most students transferred to 2007:** University of Southern Maine.

**Basis for selection.** Open admission. **Homeschooled:** Transcript of courses and grades required.

**2007-2008 Annual costs.** Tuition/fees: $8,100. Per-credit charge: $230.

**2006-2007 Financial aid.** All financial aid based on need. 46% of total undergraduate aid awarded as scholarships/grants, 54% as loans/jobs. **Additional information:** Work-study positions available.

**Application procedures. Admission:** No deadline. $20 fee, may be waived for applicants with need. Application must be submitted on paper. Admission notification on a rolling basis. **Financial aid:** No deadline. FAFSA required. Applicants notified on a rolling basis.

**Academics. Special study options:** Accelerated study, cooperative education, double major, dual enrollment of high school students, independent study, internships, liberal arts/career combination, teacher certification program. **Credit/placement by examination:** AP, CLEP, institutional tests. 12 credit hours maximum toward associate degree. **Support services:** Learning center, reduced course load, remedial instruction, study skills assistance, tutoring, writing center.

**Majors. Business:** Accounting, administrative services, business admin, hospitality admin, hospitality/recreation, office management, office technology, office/clerical, tourism promotion, tourism/travel. **Computer sciences:** General, computer science, data processing, programming. **Education:** Early childhood. **Family/consumer sciences:** Child care. **Health:** Medical assistant, medical records admin, medical records technology, medical secretary, medical transcription. **Legal studies:** Legal secretary, paralegal. **Protective services:** Criminal justice, law enforcement admin, police science.

**Most popular majors.** Business/marketing 21%, computer/information sciences 9%, health sciences 17%, legal studies 12%.

**Computing on campus.** 90 workstations in library, computer center, student center. Helpline available.

**Student life. Freshman orientation:** Mandatory. Preregistration for classes offered. **Activities:** Student newspaper, Phi Beta Lambda, C.O.P.S. (criminal justice), APPEAL paralegal professionals, college student advisors.

**Student services.** Adult student services, career counseling, student employment services, financial aid counseling, personal counseling, placement for graduates. **Physically disabled:** Services for hearing impaired.

**Contact.** E-mail: enroll@andovercollege.edu
Phone: (207) 774-6126 Toll-free number: (800) 639-3110
Fax: (207) 774-1715
Wendy Burbank, Director of Admissions, Andover College, 901 Washington Avenue, Portland, ME 04103

## Beal College
### Bangor, Maine
www.bealcollege.edu     CB code: 3114

▶ For-profit 2-year junior and career college
▶ Commuter campus in large town

**General.** Founded in 1891. Accredited by ACICS. **Enrollment:** 453 degree-seeking undergraduates. **Degrees:** 64 associate awarded. **Location:** 250 miles from Boston. **Calendar:** Six 8-week modules per year. Extensive summer session. **Full-time faculty:** 7 total. **Part-time faculty:** 8 total. **Class size:** 59% < 20, 41% 20-39.

**Basis for selection.** Open admission. Interview recommended. **Homeschooled:** Students who earned high school diploma through home school education must provide passing GED scores.

**High school preparation.** Recommended units include English 4, mathematics 4 and science 1.

**2007-2008 Annual costs.** Tuition/fees: $6,270. Per-credit charge: $165. Books/supplies: $1,000. Personal expenses: $700.

**Application procedures. Admission:** No deadline. $25 fee, may be waived for applicants with need. Admission notification on a rolling basis. Mathematics and English pre-admission tests required to determine possible need for remedial coursework. **Financial aid:** No deadline. FAFSA, institutional form required. Applicants notified on a rolling basis starting 6/15; must reply within 2 week(s) of notification.

**Academics.** Students in travel and tourism programs required to complete travel requirements and 80-hour externship. Students in medical assisting program must complete 160-hour practicum. **Special study options:** Accelerated study, double major, independent study. Externships. **Credit/placement by examination:** CLEP, institutional tests. 30 credit hours maximum toward associate degree. **Support services:** Reduced course load, remedial instruction, tutoring.

**Majors. Business:** Accounting, administrative services, business admin, office management, sales/distribution, tourism promotion. **Education:** Early childhood. **Family/consumer sciences:** Family/community services. **Health:** Medical assistant, medical secretary. **Legal studies:** Legal secretary, paralegal. **Protective services:** Police science.

**Computing on campus.** 45 workstations in library, computer center. Wireless network available.

**Student life. Freshman orientation:** Available. **Activities:** Student newspaper.

**Student services.** Adult student services, career counseling, student employment services, placement for graduates, veterans' counselor. **Transfer:** Pre-admission transcript evaluation for new students.

**Contact.** E-mail: admissions@bealcollege.edu
Phone: (207) 947-4591 Fax: (207) 947-0208
Erin Morgan, Admissions Director, Beal College, 99 Farm Road, Bangor, ME 04401

## Central Maine Community College
### Auburn, Maine
www.cmcc.edu     CB member     CB code: 3309

▶ Public 2-year community and technical college
▶ Commuter campus in small city

**General.** Founded in 1964. Regionally accredited. **Enrollment:** 1,881 degree-seeking undergraduates; 440 non-degree-seeking students. **Degrees:** 224 associate awarded. **Location:** One mile from downtown. **Calendar:** Semester, limited summer session. **Full-time faculty:** 53 total. **Part-time faculty:** 82 total. **Partnerships:** Formal partnership with Verizon Telecommunications Technology program.

**Student profile.** Among degree-seeking undergraduates, 899 enrolled as first-time, first-year students.

| | | | |
|---|---|---|---|
| Part-time: | 48% | Women: | 54% |

**Transfer out. Colleges most students transferred to 2007:** University of Maine System.

**Basis for selection.** Open admission, but selective for some programs. Special requirements for nursing and radiologic technology. Many other academic programs have specific academic prerequisites but are not selective in terms of admission to the program. SAT scores or institutional placement test required for all applicants. **Homeschooled:** Transcript of courses and grades required. A copy of the state department of education correspondence granting approval of homeschooling program and the most recent teacher certification recognizing student's grade level and/or appropriate test results required. **Learning Disabled:** Applicants with documented disabilities should contact the college's disability coordinator.

**High school preparation.** Recommended units include English 4, mathematics 2, social studies 1, history 1 and science 2.

**2007-2008 Annual costs.** Tuition/fees: $3,060; $5,490 out-of-state. Per-credit charge: $80 in-state; $161 out-of-state. Room/board: $6,376. Books/supplies: $1,200. Personal expenses: $1,300.

**2007-2008 Financial aid.** All financial aid based on need. 48% of total undergraduate aid awarded as scholarships/grants, 52% as loans/jobs. Need-based aid available for part-time students. Work-study available nights, weekends and for part-time students. **Additional information:** Tuition and/or fee waivers may be available to orphans, Native Americans, fire fighters, police, disabled veterans, dependents or survivors of veterans killed in line of duty.

**Application procedures. Admission:** No deadline. $20 fee, may be waived for applicants with need. Application may be submitted online. Admission notification on a rolling basis beginning on or about 10/1. **Financial aid:** Priority date 5/8; no closing date. FAFSA, institutional form required. Applicants notified on a rolling basis starting 3/15; must reply within 2 week(s) of notification.

**Academics. Special study options:** Distance learning, ESL, independent study, internships, liberal arts/career combination. License preparation in nursing, radiology, real estate. **Credit/placement by examination:** AP, CLEP, IB, institutional tests. Up to 75% of credits may meet curriculum requirements; 25% of credits must be completed in residence. **Support services:** Learning center, reduced course load, remedial instruction, study skills assistance, tutoring, writing center.

**Majors. Business:** Accounting, business admin, hospitality admin, office technology. **Communications technology:** Graphic/printing. **Computer sciences:** Data entry, LAN/WAN management. **Construction:** Maintenance. **Education:** Early childhood, teacher assistance. **Engineering technology:** Civil. **Health:** Medical assistant, medical radiologic technology/radiation therapy, nursing (RN), occupational health. **Liberal arts:** Arts/sciences. **Mechanic/repair:** Automotive, electronics/electrical. **Production:** Machine tool.

**Computing on campus.** 400 workstations in library, computer center. Dormitories wired for high-speed internet access and linked to campus network. Commuter students can connect to campus network. Online library, helpline, wireless network available.

**Student life. Freshman orientation:** Available. Preregistration for classes offered. **Policies:** Student code of conduct observed. **Housing:** Single-sex dorms, apartments available. $50 nonrefundable deposit. **Activities:** Drama, literary magazine, student government.

**Athletics.** USCAA. **Intercollegiate:** Baseball M, basketball. **Intramural:** Basketball, skiing. **Team name:** Mustangs.

**Student services.** Career counseling, services for economically disadvantaged, student employment services, financial aid counseling, personal counseling, placement for graduates, women's services. **Physically disabled:** Services for visually, speech, hearing impaired. **Transfer:** Transfer adviser, college fairs on campus for students transferring to 4-year colleges.

**Contact.** E-mail: enroll@cmcc.edu
Phone: (207) 755-5273 Toll-free number: (800) 891-2002 ext. 273
Fax: (207) 755-5493
Betsy Libby, Director of Admissions, Central Maine Community College, 1250 Turner Street, Auburn, ME 04210

## Central Maine Medical Center College of Nursing and Health Professions

Lewiston, Maine  **CB member**
www.cmmcson.edu  **CB code: 3302**

- Private 2-year nursing college
- Commuter campus in large town
- SAT, application essay required

**General.** Founded in 1891. Regionally accredited. **Enrollment:** 119 degree-seeking undergraduates. **Degrees:** 42 associate awarded. **Location:** 35 miles

from Portland. **Calendar:** Semester, limited summer session. **Full-time faculty:** 15 total; 7% have terminal degrees, 87% women.

**Student profile.** Among degree-seeking undergraduates, 27% already have a bachelor's degree or higher, 2 enrolled as first-time, first-year students.

| | | | |
|---|---|---|---|
| Part-time: | 82% | African American: | 1% |
| Out-of-state: | 3% | Hispanic American: | 1% |
| Women: | 84% | Live on campus: | 5% |

**Basis for selection.** Test scores required. Essay, academic ability very important. SAT may be waived if applicant has completed 12 academic college credits with minimum grade of 2.0. **Homeschooled:** High school diploma or GED required.

**High school preparation.** Required units include science 1. Biology course required.

**2008-2009 Annual costs.** Tuition/fees (projected): $7,188. Per-credit charge: $170. Room only: $1,500. Books/supplies: $2,010. Personal expenses: $2,460.

**2006-2007 Financial aid.** All financial aid based on need. 2 full-time freshmen applied for aid; 2 were judged to have need; 2 of these received aid. Average need met was 26%. Average scholarship/grant was $6,625; average loan $6,625. 36% of total undergraduate aid awarded as scholarships/grants, 64% as loans/jobs. Need-based aid available for part-time students.

**Application procedures. Admission:** Closing date 2/15 (receipt date). $40 fee, may be waived for applicants with need. Admission notification 3/15. Must reply by 5/1. **Financial aid:** Priority date 5/1, closing date 7/1. FAFSA, institutional form required. Applicants notified on a rolling basis starting 4/1; must reply within 2 week(s) of notification.

**Academics. Special study options:** Distance learning, internships. License preparation in nursing. **Credit/placement by examination:** AP, CLEP. 15 credit hours maximum toward associate degree. **Support services:** Learning center, remedial instruction, study skills assistance.

**Majors. Health:** Nursing (RN).

**Computing on campus.** PC or laptop required. 12 workstations in computer center.

**Student life. Freshman orientation:** Mandatory. Preregistration for classes offered. One day program held the first day of the fall semester. **Policies:** Entire campus is smoke-free; zero tolerance for alcohol, drugs, weapons, etc. **Housing:** Coed dorms, substance-free housing available. $50 nonrefundable deposit, deadline 8/15. Single rooms available at extra cost. **Activities:** Student government.

**Student services.** Financial aid counseling, health services, personal counseling, veterans' counselor. **Transfer:** Pre-admission transcript evaluation for new students. College fairs on campus for students transferring to 4-year colleges.

**Contact.** E-mail: jenisod@cmhc.org
Phone: (207) 795-2843 Fax: (207) 795-2849
Peter Miller, Admissions Committee Chairperson, Central Maine Medical Center College of Nursing and Health Professions, 70 Middle Street, Lewiston, ME 04240

## Eastern Maine Community College

Bangor, Maine  **CB member**
www.emcc.edu  **CB code: 3372**

- Public 2-year community and technical college
- Commuter campus in large town
- Application essay required

**General.** Founded in 1966. Regionally accredited. **Enrollment:** 1,577 degree-seeking undergraduates. **Degrees:** 243 associate awarded. **Location:** 250 miles from Boston, 130 miles from Portland. **Calendar:** Semester, limited summer session. **Full-time faculty:** 60 total. **Part-time faculty:** 90 total.

**Student profile.** Among degree-seeking undergraduates, 27% enrolled in a transfer program, 73% enrolled in a vocational program, 2% already have a bachelor's degree or higher, 454 enrolled as first-time, first-year students.

| | | | |
|---|---|---|---|
| Part-time: | 32% | Hispanic American: | 1% |
| Women: | 46% | Native American: | 2% |
| African American: | 1% | Live on campus: | 12% |
| Asian American: | 1% | | |

**Transfer out.** 17% of students enrolled in the transfer program go on to 4-year colleges. **Colleges most students transferred to 2007:** University of Maine-Orono, Husson College.

**Basis for selection.** Open admission, but selective for some programs. School record, recommendations, and essays most important. Entrance requirements vary by program. SAT required for engineering technologies, registered nursing, and medical radiography applicants; score report preferred by April 30. Interview recommended for some majors.

**High school preparation.** Recommended units include English 4, mathematics 3 and science 2. Academic requirements vary by program.

**2007-2008 Annual costs.** Tuition/fees: $3,315; $5,745 out-of-state. Per-credit charge: $80 in-state; $161 out-of-state. Laboratory and technology fees vary with program. Room/board: $6,360. Books/supplies: $800. Personal expenses: $1,500.

**Financial aid.** All financial aid based on need. Need-based aid available for part-time students. Work-study available nights, weekends and for part-time students.

**Application procedures. Admission:** No deadline. $20 fee, may be waived for applicants with need. Application may be submitted online. Admission notification on a rolling basis. Must reply by May 1 or within 4 week(s) if notified thereafter. Deposit refundable up to 60 days before program begins. **Financial aid:** Priority date 5/1; no closing date. FAFSA, institutional form required. Applicants notified on a rolling basis starting 5/1; must reply within 3 week(s) of notification.

**Academics. Special study options:** External degree, internships, student-designed major. **Credit/placement by examination:** CLEP, institutional tests. Maximum of 40% of required credit total in student's field of study may be obtained through credit by examination. **Support services:** Learning center, reduced course load, remedial instruction, study skills assistance, tutoring.

**Majors. Agriculture:** Food science. **Business:** General, administrative services, banking/financial services, business admin, office management. **Construction:** Carpentry, pipefitting, power transmission. **Education:** Early childhood. **Engineering technology:** Construction, electrical. **Health:** Medical radiologic technology/radiation therapy, nursing (RN), preop/surgical nursing. **Liberal arts:** Arts/sciences. **Mechanic/repair:** Automotive, heating/ac/refrig. **Personal/culinary services:** Culinary arts. **Production:** Machine tool, welding. **Protective services:** Firefighting.

**Most popular majors.** Business/marketing 36%, computer/information sciences 17%, health sciences 22%, interdisciplinary studies 11%, personal/culinary services 14%.

**Computing on campus.** 75 workstations in dormitories, library, computer center. Commuter students can connect to campus network. Helpline, wireless network available.

**Student life. Freshman orientation:** Mandatory. Preregistration for classes offered. **Housing:** Guaranteed on-campus for all undergraduates. Coed dorms available. $50 nonrefundable deposit, deadline 7/1. **Activities:** Student government, student newspaper.

**Athletics. Intercollegiate:** Basketball M, golf, soccer. **Intramural:** Badminton, basketball, bowling, ice hockey M, skiing, softball, table tennis, volleyball. **Team name:** Golden Eagles.

**Student services.** Adult student services, career counseling, student employment services, personal counseling, placement for graduates, veterans' counselor.

**Contact.** E-mail: admissions@emcc.edu
Phone: (207) 974-4680 Toll-free number: (800) 286-9357
Fax: (207) 974-4683
Elizabeth Russell, Director of Admissions, Eastern Maine Community College, 354 Hogan Road, Bangor, ME 04401

## Kennebec Valley Community College
**Fairfield, Maine**
www.kvcc.me.edu
**CB code: 3475**

- Public 2-year community and technical college
- Commuter campus in small town

**General.** Founded in 1969. Regionally accredited. **Enrollment:** 1,396 degree-seeking undergraduates. **Degrees:** 246 associate awarded. **Location:** 24 miles from Augusta, 75 miles from Portland. **Calendar:** Semester, limited summer session. **Full-time faculty:** 42 total. **Part-time faculty:** 3 total.

**Basis for selection.** Open admission, but selective for some programs. Special requirements for nursing and allied health programs.

**2007-2008 Annual costs.** Tuition/fees: $2,940; $5,370 out-of-state. Per-credit charge: $80 in-state; $161 out-of-state. Health insurance required if student does not have own insurance. Lab fees vary depending on course. Books/supplies: $737.

**2006-2007 Financial aid. Need-based:** 69% of total undergraduate aid awarded as scholarships/grants, 31% as loans/jobs. Need-based aid available for part-time students.

**Application procedures. Admission:** No deadline. $20 fee. Admission notification on a rolling basis. Only allied health programs have application deadline. **Financial aid:** Priority date 4/1; no closing date. FAFSA, institutional form required. Applicants notified on a rolling basis starting 5/1.

**Academics. Special study options:** Cooperative education, cross-registration, distance learning, internships, liberal arts/career combination. **Credit/placement by examination:** AP, CLEP.

**Majors. Biology:** Biomedical sciences. **Business:** Business admin, office management. **Education:** Teacher assistance. **Engineering:** Electrical. **Engineering technology:** Electrical, manufacturing. **Health:** EMT paramedic, medical assistant, occupational therapy assistant, physical therapy assistant, radiologic technology/medical imaging, respiratory therapy technology. **Liberal arts:** Arts/sciences.

**Student life. Activities:** Student government, student newspaper.

**Athletics. Intercollegiate:** Basketball. **Intramural:** Basketball, volleyball.

**Student services.** Career counseling, student employment services, on-campus daycare, personal counseling, placement for graduates. **Transfer:** Transfer adviser, college fairs on campus for students transferring to 4-year colleges.

**Contact.** E-mail: jbourgoin@kvcc.me.edu
Phone: (207) 453-5131 Toll-free number: (800) 528-5882
Fax: (207) 453-5011
Jim Bourgoin, Director of Admissions, Kennebec Valley Community College, 92 Western Avenue, Fairfield, ME 04937-1367

## Northern Maine Community College
**Presque Isle, Maine**
www.nmcc.edu
**CB code: 3631**

- Public 2-year technical college
- Commuter campus in small town
- Application essay, interview required

**General.** Founded in 1961. Regionally accredited. **Enrollment:** 840 degree-seeking undergraduates. **Degrees:** 133 associate awarded. **Location:** 165 miles from Bangor. **Calendar:** Semester, limited summer session. **Full-time faculty:** 45 total. **Part-time faculty:** 35 total.

**Basis for selection.** School achievement record and test scores important.

**High school preparation.** Required units include English 4 and mathematics 2.

**2007-2008 Annual costs.** Tuition/fees: $2,990; $5,420 out-of-state. Per-credit charge: $80 in-state; $161 out-of-state. Room/board: $5,240. Books/supplies: $1,200. Personal expenses: $1,200.

**Financial aid. Need-based:** Need-based aid available for part-time students.

**Application procedures. Admission:** No deadline. $20 fee, may be waived for applicants with need. Application may be submitted online. Admission notification on a rolling basis. **Financial aid:** Priority date 5/1; no closing date. FAFSA, institutional form required. Applicants notified on a rolling basis starting 4/15; must reply within 2 week(s) of notification.

**Academics. Special study options:** Cross-registration, double major, internships, liberal arts/career combination. **Credit/placement by examination:** CLEP. 15 credit hours maximum toward associate degree. **Support services:** Learning center, pre-admission summer program, reduced course load, remedial instruction, tutoring.

**Majors. Agriculture:** Business. **Business:** Accounting, administrative services, business admin, management information systems, office management, office technology, operations. **Computer sciences:** Applications programming, data processing, programming. **Construction:** Carpentry, electrician, pipefitting, power transmission. **Education:** Early childhood. **Engineering technology:** Drafting, electrical. **Health:** Medical secretary, nursing (RN). **Legal studies:** Legal secretary. **Mechanic/repair:** Auto body, automotive, diesel, electronics/electrical, heating/ac/refrig, industrial. **Production:** Woodworking.

**Computing on campus.** Commuter students can connect to campus network.

**Student life. Freshman orientation:** Mandatory, $60 fee. Preregistration for classes offered. Held both in fall and spring semester. **Housing:** Coed dorms, apartments available. $25 deposit. **Activities:** Student government, student newspaper.

**Athletics. Intercollegiate:** Basketball M, golf, ice hockey, soccer. **Intramural:** Archery, badminton, baseball M, basketball M, racquetball, softball, table tennis, tennis, volleyball.

**Student services.** Adult student services, alcohol/substance abuse counseling, career counseling, student employment services, financial aid counseling, health services, personal counseling, placement for graduates, veterans' counselor. **Transfer:** Transfer adviser for students transferring to 4-year colleges.

**Contact.** E-mail: nbcasava@nmcc.edu
Phone: (207) 768-2700 Fax: (207) 768-2831
William Casavant, Director of Admissions, Northern Maine Community College, 33 Edgemont Drive, Presque Isle, ME 04769

---

## Southern Maine Community College

**South Portland, Maine**
www.smccme.edu

**CB member**
**CB code: 3535**

- Public 2-year community and technical college
- Commuter campus in large town

**General.** Founded in 1946. Regionally accredited. **Enrollment:** 4,947 degree-seeking undergraduates; 166 non-degree-seeking students. **Degrees:** 599 associate awarded. **Location:** 3 miles from Portland, 120 miles from Boston. **Calendar:** Semester, limited summer session. **Full-time faculty:** 90 total. **Part-time faculty:** 170 total.

**Student profile.**

| | | | |
|---|---|---|---|
| Part-time: | 63% | Women: | 52% |

**Basis for selection.** Open admission, but selective for some programs. Special requirements for allied health science programs. Must have prerequisites completed prior to being accepted into the programs. Psychological Services Bureau exam for Allied Health programs. Require ERI/NET exam for nursing applicants.

**High school preparation.** Recommended units include English 4, mathematics 3, science 1 (laboratory 1). Academic subject requirements vary by program.

**2007-2008 Annual costs.** Tuition/fees: $3,335; $5,765 out-of-state. Per-credit charge: $80 in-state; $161 out-of-state. Room and Board charge includes cable, internet services. Room/board: $7,282. Books/supplies: $900. Personal expenses: $1,773.

**Financial aid.** All financial aid based on need. Need-based aid available for part-time students. Work-study available nights, weekends and for part-time students.

**Application procedures. Admission:** Priority date 7/15; no deadline. $20 fee, may be waived for applicants with need. Application may be submitted online. Admission notification on a rolling basis. Must reply by May 1 or within 4 week(s) if notified thereafter. **Financial aid:** Priority date 3/30; no closing date. FAFSA required. Applicants notified on a rolling basis; must reply by 5/1 or within 2 week(s) of notification.

**Academics. Special study options:** Cross-registration, distance learning, double major, dual enrollment of high school students, independent study, internships, liberal arts/career combination. License preparation in nursing, paramedic, radiology. **Credit/placement by examination:** AP, CLEP, institutional tests. **Support services:** Learning center, reduced course load, remedial instruction, study skills assistance, tutoring.

**Majors. Agriculture:** Plant sciences. **Architecture:** Technology. **Biology:** Biotechnology, environmental, marine. **Business:** Business admin, hospitality admin. **Communications:** Media studies. **Computer sciences:** General.

**Construction:** General, masonry. **Education:** Early childhood. **Engineering:** Electrical. **Family/consumer sciences:** Advocacy. **Health:** Cardiovascular technology, dietetic technician, EMT paramedic, medical radiologic technology/radiation therapy, nursing (RN), radiologic technology/medical imaging, respiratory therapy technology, surgical technology. **Liberal arts:** Arts/sciences. **Mechanic/repair:** General, heating/ac/refrig. **Personal/culinary services:** Culinary arts. **Production:** General, machine tool, welding. **Protective services:** Firefighting, law enforcement admin. **Visual/performing arts:** Cinematography.

**Computing on campus.** 300 workstations in library, computer center, student center. Dormitories wired for high-speed internet access and linked to campus network. Commuter students can connect to campus network. Online course registration, helpline, wireless network available.

**Student life. Freshman orientation:** Available. Preregistration for classes offered. **Housing:** Coed dorms available. $50 nonrefundable deposit. **Activities:** Choral groups, student government, student newspaper, Phi Theta Kappa.

**Athletics. Intercollegiate:** Baseball M, basketball, golf, soccer, softball W. **Intramural:** Soccer, volleyball. **Team name:** Seawolves.

**Student services.** Adult student services, alcohol/substance abuse counseling, career counseling, student employment services, financial aid counseling, on-campus daycare, personal counseling, placement for graduates, veterans' counselor. **Physically disabled:** Services for visually, speech, hearing impaired. **Transfer:** Pre-admission transcript evaluation for new students. Transfer adviser, college fairs on campus for students transferring to 4-year colleges.

**Contact.** E-mail: enrollmentservices@smccme.edu
Phone: (207) 741-5800 Toll-free number: (877) 282-2182
Fax: (207) 741-5760
Staci Grasky, Associate Dean for Information and Enrollment Services / Registrar, Southern Maine Community College, 2 Fort Road, South Portland, ME 04106

---

## Washington County Community College

**Calais, Maine**
www.wccc.me.edu

**CB code: 3961**

- Public 2-year community and technical college
- Commuter campus in small town

**General.** Founded in 1969. Regionally accredited. **Enrollment:** 370 degree-seeking undergraduates. **Degrees:** 73 associate awarded. **Location:** 98 miles from Bangor, 75 miles from St. John, Canada. **Calendar:** Semester, limited summer session. **Full-time faculty:** 21 total. **Part-time faculty:** 20 total.

**Student profile.**

| | | | |
|---|---|---|---|
| Part-time: | 28% | 25 or older: | 34% |
| Out-of-state: | 5% | Live on campus: | 25% |
| Women: | 61% | | |

**Transfer out. Colleges most students transferred to 2007:** University of Maine at Machias, University of Maine at Augusta, Husson College.

**Basis for selection.** Open admission, but selective for some programs. Algebra I required for computer support technician program. Algebra I required or placement in the equivalent of MAT106 on accuplacer exam for residential and commercial electricity program. ASSET used for placement. **Homeschooled:** Applicants required to take GED exam or equivalent.

**High school preparation.** 20 units recommended. Recommended units include English 4, mathematics 2, social studies 1, history 2 and science 2. Program-specific requirements apply in some areas.

**2007-2008 Annual costs.** Tuition/fees: $2,990; $5,420 out-of-state. Per-credit charge: $80 in-state; $161 out-of-state. Room only: $2,482. Books/supplies: $1,000. Personal expenses: $1,669.

**Financial aid. Need-based:** Need-based aid available for part-time students. Work-study available for part-time students. **Non-need-based:** Scholarships awarded for academics.

**Application procedures. Admission:** Closing date 8/14. $20 fee, may be waived for applicants with need. Application may be submitted online. Admission notification on a rolling basis. **Financial aid:** Priority date 5/1; no closing date. FAFSA, institutional form required. Applicants notified on a rolling basis starting 6/1; must reply within 2 week(s) of notification.

**Academics. Special study options:** Cooperative education, distance learning, double major, dual enrollment of high school students, independent study, liberal arts/career combination. Offer license preparation program in heating and plumbing. **Credit/placement by examination:** CLEP, IB. **Support services:** GED preparation and test center, learning center, reduced course load, remedial instruction, study skills assistance, tutoring, writing center.

**Majors. Business:** Business admin, office management, small business admin. **Education:** Early childhood. **Family/consumer sciences:** Food/nutrition, institutional food production. **Liberal arts:** Arts/sciences. **Mechanic/repair:** General. **Other:** Adventure Recreation & Tourism.

**Most popular majors.** Business/marketing 19%, computer/information sciences 33%, liberal arts 13%, trade and industry 35%.

**Computing on campus.** 117 workstations in dormitories, library, computer center, student center. Dormitories linked to campus network. Helpline, wireless network available.

**Student life. Freshman orientation:** Mandatory. Preregistration for classes offered. **Housing:** Guaranteed on-campus for all undergraduates. Special housing for disabled, apartments available. $150 deposit. **Activities:** Student government, Gender Equity, Native American club.

**Athletics. Intramural:** Baseball M, basketball, cross-country, golf, skiing, volleyball. **Team name:** Polar Bears.

**Student services.** Adult student services, career counseling, student employment services, on-campus daycare, personal counseling, placement for graduates, veterans' counselor. **Physically disabled:** Services for visually, speech, hearing impaired. **Transfer:** Pre-admission transcript evaluation for new students. College fairs on campus for students transferring to 4-year colleges.

**Contact.** E-mail: admissions@wccc.me.edu
Phone: (207) 454-1049 Toll-free number: (800) 210-6932
Fax: (207) 454-1092
Kent Lyons, Admissions Counselor, Washington County Community College, One College Drive, Calais, ME 04619

## York County Community College
**Wells, Maine**
www.yccc.edu

**CB member**
**CB code: 3990**

- Public 2-year community and technical college
- Commuter campus in small town

**General.** Regionally accredited. **Enrollment:** 889 degree-seeking undergraduates; 102 non-degree-seeking students. **Degrees:** 80 associate awarded. **Location:** 30 miles from Portland. **Calendar:** Semester, extensive summer session. **Full-time faculty:** 13 total; 31% have terminal degrees, 38% women. **Part-time faculty:** 70 total; 13% have terminal degrees, 59% women. **Class size:** 65% < 20, 35% 20-39.

**Student profile.** Among degree-seeking undergraduates, 415 enrolled as first-time, first-year students, 13 transferred in from other institutions.

| | | | |
|---|---|---|---|
| Part-time: | 64% | Asian American: | 1% |
| Out-of-state: | 3% | 25 or older: | 33% |
| Women: | 63% | | |

**Transfer out. Colleges most students transferred to 2007:** University of Southern Maine, University of New England, University of New Hampshire.

**Basis for selection.** Open admission. **Homeschooled:** Transcript of courses and grades, state high school equivalency certificate required.

**2007-2008 Annual costs.** Tuition/fees: $3,050; $5,480 out-of-state. Per-credit charge: $80 in-state; $161 out-of-state. Lecture and lab fees may vary per class. Books/supplies: $1,000. Personal expenses: $1,000.

**2006-2007 Financial aid. Need-based:** 77 full-time freshmen applied for aid; 48 were judged to have need; 46 of these received aid. Average need met was 56%. Average scholarship/grant was $3,472; average loan $1,999. 61% of total undergraduate aid awarded as scholarships/grants, 39% as loans/jobs. Need-based aid available for part-time students. Work-study available nights, weekends and for part-time students. **Non-need-based:** Awarded to 18 full-time undergraduates, including 6 freshmen. Scholarships awarded for academics, art, leadership.

**Application procedures. Admission:** No deadline. $20 fee, may be waived for applicants with need. **Financial aid:** Priority date 5/1; no closing date. FAFSA required. Applicants notified by 3/1; must reply within 2 week(s) of notification.

**Academics. Special study options:** Distance learning, dual enrollment of high school students, honors, liberal arts/career combination. License preparation in nursing, real estate. **Credit/placement by examination:** CLEP, institutional tests. 45 credit hours maximum toward associate degree. **Support services:** Learning center, remedial instruction, study skills assistance, tutoring, writing center.

**Majors. Business:** Accounting, business admin, management information systems. **Engineering technology:** CAD/CADD. **Family/consumer sciences:** General. **Personal/culinary services:** Culinary arts. **Visual/performing arts:** Design. **Other:** Career Studies, Trade Technical Occupations.

**Most popular majors.** Business/marketing 35%, family/consumer sciences 29%, liberal arts 24%.

**Computing on campus.** 160 workstations in library, computer center, student center. Wireless network available.

**Student life. Freshman orientation:** Available. Preregistration for classes offered. **Activities:** Dance, literary magazine, student government, student newspaper.

**Student services.** Career counseling, financial aid counseling. **Transfer:** Transfer adviser, college fairs on campus for students transferring to 4-year colleges.

**Contact.** E-mail: admissions@yccc.edu
Phone: (207) 646-9282 ext. 304
Fred Quistgard, Director of Admissions, York County Community College, 112 College Drive, Wells, ME 04090

# Maryland

---

### Allegany College of Maryland
**Cumberland, Maryland**
www.allegany.edu

CB member
CB code: 5028

▶ Public 2-year community college
▶ Commuter campus in large town

**General.** Founded in 1961. Regionally accredited. **Enrollment:** 2,887 degree-seeking undergraduates; 891 non-degree-seeking students. **Degrees:** 623 associate awarded. **ROTC:** Army. **Location:** 150 miles from Baltimore, 150 miles from Washington, DC. **Calendar:** Semester, limited summer session. **Full-time faculty:** 114 total; 16% have terminal degrees, 54% women. **Part-time faculty:** 118 total; 5% have terminal degrees, 75% women. **Class size:** 74% < 20, 25% 20-39, 1% 40-49, less than 1% >100. **Special facilities:** Greenhouse, arboretum, wetlands, Appalachian Room, labyrinth and serenity garden.

**Student profile.** Among degree-seeking undergraduates, 33% enrolled in a transfer program, 67% enrolled in a vocational program, 2% already have a bachelor's degree or higher, 832 enrolled as first-time, first-year students, 134 transferred in from other institutions.

| | | | |
|---|---|---|---|
| Part-time: | 31% | Asian American: | 1% |
| Out-of-state: | 52% | Hispanic American: | 1% |
| Women: | 67% | 25 or older: | 27% |
| African American: | 9% | Live on campus: | 7% |

**Transfer out.** 70% of students enrolled in the transfer program go on to 4-year colleges. **Colleges most students transferred to 2007:** Frostburg State University, Shippensburg University, University of Pittsburgh at Johnstown.

**Basis for selection.** Open admission, but selective for some programs. Admission to allied health programs based on high school records, test scores. ACT required for allied health applicants.

**2007-2008 Annual costs.** Tuition/fees: $3,130; $5,590 out-of-district; $6,490 out-of-state. Per-credit charge: $96 in-district; $178 out-of-district; $208 out-of-state. Books/supplies: $700. Personal expenses: $1,200.

**2006-2007 Financial aid. Need-based:** 68% of total undergraduate aid awarded as scholarships/grants, 32% as loans/jobs. Need-based aid available for part-time students. Work-study available nights and for part-time students. **Non-need-based:** Scholarships awarded for academics, athletics, leadership, state residency.

**Application procedures. Admission:** No deadline. No application fee. Application may be submitted online. Admission notification on a rolling basis. High school and/or college transcript and placement tests in English, reading, and mathematics required. **Financial aid:** Priority date 3/1; no closing date. FAFSA, institutional form required. Applicants notified on a rolling basis starting 4/15; must reply within 2 week(s) of notification.

**Academics. Special study options:** Accelerated study, distance learning, double major, dual enrollment of high school students, ESL, honors, independent study, internships, liberal arts/career combination. Bachelor's degree programs available on campus. License preparation in dental hygiene, nursing, occupational therapy, physical therapy, radiology, real estate. **Credit/placement by examination:** AP, CLEP, institutional tests. 30 credit hours maximum toward associate degree. **Support services:** Learning center, reduced course load, remedial instruction, study skills assistance, tutoring.

**Majors. Biology:** General. **Business:** General, accounting, accounting technology, administrative services, business admin, hospitality admin, hospitality/recreation, management information systems, managerial economics, marketing. **Communications:** General. **Communications technology:** General. **Computer sciences:** General, computer science, information systems. **Conservation:** Forest management. **Education:** Early childhood, elementary, health, physical, secondary. **Engineering:** General. **English:** English lit. **Foreign languages:** Spanish. **Health:** Clinical lab technology, dental hygiene, health services, massage therapy, medical assistant, medical radiologic technology/radiation therapy, medical secretary, medical transcription, mental health services, nursing (RN), occupational therapy assistant, physical therapy assistant, prepharmacy, respiratory therapy technology. **History:** General. **Liberal arts:** Arts/sciences. **Math:** General. **Mechanic/repair:** Automotive. **Parks/recreation:** Facilities management. **Personal/culinary services:** General, chef training. **Physical sciences:** Chemistry, physics. **Protective services:** Police science. **Psychology:** General. **Public administration:**

Social work. **Social sciences:** General, economics, political science, sociology. **Visual/performing arts:** Art.

**Most popular majors.** Business/marketing 19%, health sciences 46%, liberal arts 20%.

**Computing on campus.** 450 workstations in library, computer center. Online course registration, online library, student web hosting, wireless network available.

**Student life. Freshman orientation:** Available, $4 fee. Preregistration for classes offered. **Housing:** Apartments, substance-free housing available. $300 partly refundable deposit, deadline 8/26. **Activities:** Choral groups, dance, literary magazine, student government, forestry club, Older and Wiser Club, Phi Theta Kappa-Honors Society, Christian Fellowship, chess club, respiratory therapy club, dental hygiene club, medical laboratory technology club.

**Athletics.** NJCAA. **Intercollegiate:** Baseball M, basketball, soccer M, softball W, volleyball W. **Team name:** Trojans.

**Student services.** Career counseling, student employment services, financial aid counseling, on-campus daycare, personal counseling, placement for graduates, veterans' counselor, women's services. **Physically disabled:** Services for visually, speech, hearing impaired. **Transfer:** Pre-admission transcript evaluation for new students. Transfer adviser, college fairs on campus for students transferring to 4-year colleges.

**Contact.** E-mail: cnolan@allegany.edu
Phone: (301) 784-5199 Fax: (301) 784-5027
Cathy Nolan, Director of Admissions and Registration, Allegany College of Maryland, 12401 Willowbrook Road, SE, Cumberland, MD 21502

---

### Anne Arundel Community College
**Arnold, Maryland**
www.aacc.edu

CB member
CB code: 5019

▶ Public 2-year community college
▶ Commuter campus in large town

**General.** Founded in 1964. Regionally accredited. 3 off-campus academic/student services centers: Fort Meade Army Education Center, Glen Burnie Town Center and Arundel Mills. **Enrollment:** 11,973 degree-seeking undergraduates. **Degrees:** 1,219 associate awarded. **Location:** 20 miles from Baltimore, 8 miles from Annapolis. **Calendar:** Semester, limited summer session. **Full-time faculty:** 257 total; 33% have terminal degrees, 12% minority. **Part-time faculty:** 658 total; less than 1% have terminal degrees, 15% minority. **Special facilities:** Off-campus workforce center at Baltimore-Washington International airport, environmental center, astronomy laboratory, center for performing arts, fine arts academic center, allied health/public services center, technology center, architectural, engineering, computer science and cybercrime labs, hospitality, culinary arts and tourism institute, entrepreneurial studies institute.

**Transfer out. Colleges most students transferred to 2007:** University of Maryland-Baltimore County, Towson University, University of Maryland-College Park, Salisbury University, University of Maryland University College.

**Basis for selection.** Open admission, but selective for some programs. Special requirements for certain allied health programs. International students must provide certification of finances. Interview recommended for applicants to nursing, human services, radiologic technology, physician's assistant programs.

**2007-2008 Annual costs.** Tuition/fees: $2,860; $5,230 out-of-district; $9,040 out-of-state. Per-credit charge: $86 in-district; $165 out-of-district; $292 out-of-state. Books/supplies: $900. Personal expenses: $1,300.

**Financial aid. Need-based:** Need-based aid available for part-time students. Work-study available nights, weekends and for part-time students.

**Application procedures. Admission:** No deadline. No application fee. Application may be submitted online. Admission notification on a rolling basis. **Financial aid:** Priority date 5/15; no closing date. FAFSA, institutional form required. Applicants notified on a rolling basis starting 7/1; must reply within 2 week(s) of notification.

**Academics. Special study options:** Combined bachelor's/graduate degree, cooperative education, distance learning, double major, dual enrollment of high school students, ESL, honors, independent study, internships, liberal arts/career combination, student-designed major, weekend college. Bachelor's degree programs available on campus. License preparation in nursing, paramedic, radiology, real estate. **Credit/placement by examination:** AP, CLEP, institutional tests. 15 credit hours maximum toward associate degree. **Support services:** GED preparation, learning center, reduced course load, remedial instruction, study skills assistance, tutoring, writing center.

**Majors. Business:** General, accounting. **Computer sciences:** General. **Education:** General, elementary, secondary. **Engineering:** General. **Engineering technology:** Drafting, electrical. **Family/consumer sciences:** Child care. **Health:** Dental assistant, EMT paramedic, health services, medical assistant, medical radiologic technology/radiation therapy, nursing (RN), pharmacy assistant, physical therapy assistant. **Legal studies:** Paralegal. **Liberal arts:** Arts/sciences. **Math:** General. **Mechanic/repair:** Electronics/electrical. **Parks/recreation:** Health/fitness. **Personal/culinary services:** Baking, chef training, culinary arts, restaurant/catering. **Protective services:** Forensics, law enforcement admin. **Public administration:** Human services. **Visual/performing arts:** Commercial/advertising art, interior design.

**Most popular majors.** Business/marketing 16%, health sciences 13%, liberal arts 56%.

**Computing on campus.** Commuter students can connect to campus network. Online library, helpline, wireless network available.

**Student life. Freshman orientation:** Mandatory. One day orientation program required for all first-time, full-time students. **Activities:** Bands, campus ministries, choral groups, dance, drama, international student organizations, literary magazine, music ensembles, musical theater, opera, student government, student newspaper, symphony orchestra, Black student union, Lambda Pioneers, Fellowship of Christian Athletes.

**Athletics.** NJCAA. **Intercollegiate:** Baseball M, basketball, golf M, lacrosse, soccer, softball W, volleyball W. **Intramural:** Basketball, softball, swimming, table tennis, tennis, volleyball, weight lifting. **Team name:** Pioneers.

**Student services.** Adult student services, alcohol/substance abuse counseling, career counseling, student employment services, financial aid counseling, health services, minority student services, on-campus daycare, personal counseling, placement for graduates, veterans' counselor. **Physically disabled:** Services for visually, speech, hearing impaired. **Transfer:** Transfer center, transfer adviser, college fairs on campus for students transferring to 4-year colleges.

**Contact.** E-mail: admissions@aacc.edu
Phone: (410) 777-2246 Fax: (410) 777-4246
Thomas McGinn, Director of Enrollment Development and Admissions, Anne Arundel Community College, 101 College Parkway, Arnold, MD 21012-1895

---

## Baltimore City Community College
**Baltimore, Maryland**      **CB member**
www.bccc.edu      **CB code: 5051**

▶ Public 2-year community college
▶ Commuter campus in very large city

**General.** Founded in 1947. Regionally accredited. Sites throughout Baltimore. **Enrollment:** 6,814 degree-seeking undergraduates. **Degrees:** 454 associate awarded. **Location:** 50 miles from Washington, DC, 75 miles from Philadelphia. **Calendar:** Semester, extensive summer session. **Full-time faculty:** 133 total. **Part-time faculty:** 424 total. **Special facilities:** Greenhouse, planetarium.

**Student profile.**

| | | | |
|---|---|---|---|
| Out-of-state: | 1% | 25 or older: | 58% |

**Transfer out. Colleges most students transferred to 2007:** Coppin State University, Morgan State University, University of Baltimore, Towson University, University of Maryland Baltimore County.

**Basis for selection.** Open admission, but selective for some programs. Applicants in health sciences must have 2.5 GPA. SAT and ACT scores may be used in place of reading, math, and English proficiency tests required of all first-time students. Interview recommended for applicants to allied health, paralegal, emergency medical services programs. Portfolio recommended for art, fashion design majors.

**2008-2009 Annual costs.** Tuition/fees (projected): $2,722; $5,422 out-of-state. Books/supplies: $500.

**Financial aid.** All financial aid based on need. Need-based aid available for part-time students. Work-study available nights, weekends and for part-time students.

---

**Application procedures. Admission:** No deadline. $10 fee, may be waived for applicants with need. Application may be submitted online. Admission notification on a rolling basis. **Financial aid:** Priority date 6/1; no closing date. FAFSA, institutional form required. Applicants notified on a rolling basis starting 7/1; must reply within 2 week(s) of notification.

**Academics.** Adults without diploma or GED become eligible for degree programs after successfully completing 15 college-level credits. **Special study options:** Cooperative education, distance learning, double major, dual enrollment of high school students, ESL, honors, independent study, internships, liberal arts/career combination, study abroad, teacher certification program, weekend college. License preparation in dental hygiene, nursing, paramedic, physical therapy, real estate. **Credit/placement by examination:** CLEP, IB, institutional tests. 15 credit hours maximum toward associate degree. **Support services:** GED preparation, learning center, preadmission summer program, reduced course load, remedial instruction, study skills assistance, tutoring, writing center.

**Majors. Biology:** Biotechnology. **Business:** General, accounting, administrative services, business admin, fashion, hospitality admin, management information systems, marketing, office management, office technology. **Computer sciences:** General, computer graphics, computer science, information systems, systems analysis. **Education:** General, early childhood, multi-level teacher. **Engineering:** General. **Engineering technology:** Drafting, electrical. **Family/consumer sciences:** Clothing/textiles. **Health:** Dental hygiene, EMT paramedic, health care admin, health services, licensed practical nurse, medical records admin, medical records technology, medical secretary, nursing (RN), physical therapy assistant, respiratory therapy technology. **Interdisciplinary:** Biological/physical sciences. **Legal studies:** Legal secretary, paralegal. **Liberal arts:** Arts/sciences. **Protective services:** Corrections, law enforcement admin, police science. **Public administration:** Social work. **Visual/performing arts:** Art, fashion design.

**Most popular majors.** Business/marketing 14%, computer/information sciences 7%, health sciences 30%, liberal arts 26%, security/protective services 9%.

**Computing on campus.** 200 workstations in library, computer center, student center. Online library available.

**Student life. Freshman orientation:** Mandatory. Preregistration for classes offered. **Activities:** Choral groups, drama, international student organizations, musical theater, radio station, student government, student newspaper, fashion club, human services club, media club, civic organizations, computer club.

**Athletics.** NJCAA. **Intercollegiate:** Baseball M, basketball, volleyball W. **Team name:** Panthers.

**Student services.** Career counseling, student employment services, financial aid counseling, health services, on-campus daycare, personal counseling, placement for graduates, veterans' counselor. **Physically disabled:** Services for visually, speech, hearing impaired. **Learning disabled:** Comprehensive services available. **Transfer:** Pre-admission transcript evaluation for new students. Transfer adviser, college fairs on campus for students transferring to 4-year colleges.

**Contact.** E-mail: admissions@bccc.edu
Phone: (410) 462-8300 Toll-free number: (888) 203-1261
Fax: (410) 462-8345
Deneen Dangerfield, Director of Admissions, Baltimore City Community College, 2901 Liberty Heights Avenue, Baltimore, MD 21215-7893

---

## Carroll Community College
**Westminster, Maryland**
www.carrollcc.edu      **CB code: 5797**

▶ Public 2-year community college
▶ Commuter campus in large town

**General.** Founded in 1993. Regionally accredited. **Enrollment:** 3,413 degree-seeking undergraduates; 28 non-degree-seeking students. **Degrees:** 358 associate awarded. **Location:** 30 miles from Baltimore. **Calendar:** Semester, extensive summer session. **Full-time faculty:** 61 total; 16% have terminal degrees, 8% minority, 59% women. **Part-time faculty:** 162 total; 9% minority, 58% women. **Class size:** 47% < 20, 52% 20-39, less than 1% 40-49. **Special facilities:** Theater, amphitheatre, art gallery.

**Student profile.** Among degree-seeking undergraduates, 876 enrolled as first-time, first-year students, 280 transferred in from other institutions.

| | | | |
|---|---|---|---|
| Part-time: | 53% | Asian American: | 1% |
| Out-of-state: | 2% | Hispanic American: | 2% |
| Women: | 62% | 25 or older: | 26% |
| African American: | 3% | | |

**Transfer out. Colleges most students transferred to 2007:** Towson University, McDaniel College, University of Maryland Baltimore County, Villa Julie College, University of Maryland College Park.

**Basis for selection.** Open admission, but selective for some programs.

**2007-2008 Annual costs.** Tuition/fees: $3,234; $4,476 out-of-district; $6,788 out-of-state. Books/supplies: $1,200. Personal expenses: $1,000.

**2006-2007 Financial aid. Need-based:** 98% of total undergraduate aid awarded as scholarships/grants, 2% as loans/jobs. Need-based aid available for part-time students. Work-study available nights, weekends and for part-time students. **Non-need-based:** Scholarships awarded for academics, art, job skills, leadership, state residency.

**Application procedures. Admission:** No deadline. No application fee. Application must be submitted on paper. Admission notification on a rolling basis. **Financial aid:** Priority date 3/1; no closing date. FAFSA required. Applicants notified by 6/1; must reply within 2 week(s) of notification.

**Academics. Special study options:** Distance learning, dual enrollment of high school students, ESL, honors, independent study, internships, liberal arts/career combination, weekend college. License preparation in nursing. **Credit/placement by examination:** AP, CLEP, institutional tests. 30 credit hours maximum toward associate degree. **Support services:** GED preparation, learning center, remedial instruction, study skills assistance, tutoring, writing center.

**Majors. Business:** General, accounting technology, international, management information systems. **Computer sciences:** Computer graphics. **Education:** General, chemistry, early childhood, elementary, mathematics, Spanish. **Engineering technology:** Architectural drafting. **Family/consumer sciences:** Child care. **Health:** Dental hygiene, nuclear medical technology, nursing (RN), physical therapy assistant, prenursing, radiologic technology/medical imaging, sonography. **Legal studies:** General. **Liberal arts:** Arts/sciences. **Parks/recreation:** Exercise sciences. **Protective services:** Forensics, police science. **Psychology:** General. **Visual/performing arts:** Art, commercial/advertising art, theater design.

**Most popular majors.** Business/marketing 11%, education 6%, health sciences 17%, liberal arts 62%.

**Computing on campus.** 684 workstations in library, computer center, student center. Commuter students can connect to campus network. Online library, helpline, wireless network available.

**Student life. Freshman orientation:** Available. Preregistration for classes offered. 1-day program in late August. **Activities:** Jazz band, choral groups, drama, film society, literary magazine, music ensembles, musical theater, student government, Alliance, Christian club, Leadership Challenge, juggling club, campus activities board, outdoor club, peace club, political awareness club, speech team.

**Student services.** Career counseling, student employment services, financial aid counseling, on-campus daycare, personal counseling. **Physically disabled:** Services for visually, speech, hearing impaired. **Transfer:** Transfer center, transfer adviser, college fairs on campus for students transferring to 4-year colleges.

**Contact.** E-mail: cedwards@carrollcc.edu
Phone: (410) 386-8430 Toll-free number: (888) 221-9748
Fax: (410) 386-8446
Candace Edwards, Coordinator of Admissions, Carroll Community College, 1601 Washington Road, Westminster, MD 21157

## Cecil College
**North East, Maryland**
www.cecil.edu
CB code: 5091

- Public 2-year community college
- Commuter campus in large town

**General.** Founded in 1968. Regionally accredited. **Enrollment:** 1,922 degree-seeking undergraduates; 177 non-degree-seeking students. **Degrees:** 145 associate awarded. **Location:** 50 miles from Baltimore, 50 miles from Philadelphia. **Calendar:** Semester, limited summer session. **Full-time faculty:**

44 total; 18% have terminal degrees, 9% minority, 66% women. **Part-time faculty:** 143 total; 2% have terminal degrees; 9% minority, 52% women. **Class size:** 80% < 20, 18% 20-39, less than 1% 40-49, 1% 50-99, less than 1% >100.

**Student profile.** Among degree-seeking undergraduates, 50% enrolled in a transfer program, 51% enrolled in a vocational program, 565 enrolled as first-time, first-year students, 10 transferred in from other institutions.

| | | | |
|---|---|---|---|
| Part-time: | 66% | Asian American: | 1% |
| Out-of-state: | 10% | Hispanic American: | 2% |
| Women: | 66% | Native American: | 1% |
| African American: | 7% | 25 or older: | 33% |

**Basis for selection.** Open admission, but selective for some programs. Admission to nursing programs based on high school record, test scores, required interview. All students must take Cecil College placement tests.

**2008-2009 Annual costs.** Tuition/fees: $2,912; $5,612 out-of-district; $6,962 out-of-state. Per-credit charge: $85 in-district; $175 out-of-district; $220 out-of-state. Books/supplies: $890. Personal expenses: $1,900.

**2006-2007 Financial aid. Need-based:** 48% of total undergraduate aid awarded as scholarships/grants, 52% as loans/jobs. Work-study available nights, weekends and for part-time students. **Non-need-based:** Scholarships awarded for academics, alumni affiliation, athletics, job skills, state residency.

**Application procedures. Admission:** No deadline. No application fee. Application may be submitted online. Admission notification on a rolling basis. Application deadline for nursing program March 1. **Financial aid:** Priority date 8/1; no closing date. FAFSA required. Applicants notified on a rolling basis; must reply within 2 week(s) of notification.

**Academics. Special study options:** Accelerated study, cooperative education, distance learning, double major, dual enrollment of high school students, ESL, honors, independent study, internships, teacher certification program, weekend college. Bachelor's degree programs available on campus. License preparation in aviation, nursing. **Credit/placement by examination:** AP, CLEP, institutional tests. 45 credit hours maximum toward associate degree. **Support services:** Learning center, reduced course load, remedial instruction, tutoring, writing center.

**Majors. Agriculture:** Equine science. **Biology:** General. **Business:** General, accounting, administrative services, business admin, communications, financial planning, management information systems, office management, transportation. **Computer sciences:** General, applications programming, programming, web page design. **Education:** Elementary, secondary. **Engineering technology:** CAD/CADD, electrical, heat/ac/refrig. **Health:** EMT paramedic, nursing (RN). **Liberal arts:** Arts/sciences. **Math:** General. **Physical sciences:** Chemistry, physics. **Protective services:** Firefighting, police science. **Transportation:** General, air traffic control, aviation. **Visual/performing arts:** Commercial photography, design, drawing, photography, studio arts.

**Most popular majors.** Business/marketing 19%, health sciences 35%, liberal arts 28%, visual/performing arts 11%.

**Computing on campus.** 93 workstations in library, computer center, student center. Commuter students can connect to campus network. Online course registration, online library available.

**Student life. Freshman orientation:** Available. Preregistration for classes offered. **Activities:** Dance, drama, musical theater, student government, student newspaper.

**Athletics.** NJCAA. **Intercollegiate:** Baseball M, basketball, cheerleading M, golf M, soccer M, softball W, tennis, volleyball W. **Team name:** Seahawks.

**Student services.** Adult student services, alcohol/substance abuse counseling, career counseling, student employment services, financial aid counseling, legal services, minority student services, personal counseling, placement for graduates, veterans' counselor. **Transfer:** Transfer adviser, college fairs on campus for students transferring to 4-year colleges.

**Contact.** E-mail: dlane@cecil.edu
Phone: (410) 287-6060 Fax: (410) 287-1026
Diane Lane, Vice President of Student Services, Cecil College, One Seahawk Drive, North East, MD 21901

## Chesapeake College
**Wye Mills, Maryland**
www.chesapeake.edu
CB code: 5143

- Public 2-year community college
- Commuter campus in rural community

**General.** Founded in 1965. Regionally accredited. **Enrollment:** 1,948 degree-seeking undergraduates. **Degrees:** 191 associate awarded. **Location:** 50 miles from Washington, DC, 50 miles from Baltimore. **Calendar:** Semester, limited summer session. **Full-time faculty:** 56 total. **Part-time faculty:** 77 total. **Special facilities:** Performing arts center.

**Student profile.**

| | | | |
|---|---|---|---|
| Out-of-state: | 1% | 25 or older: | 47% |

**Transfer out. Colleges most students transferred to 2007:** Salisbury State College, Towson University, Frostburg State College, University of Maryland.

**Basis for selection.** Open admission, but selective for some programs. Admission to radiological technology, surgical technology, physical therapist assistant and nursing programs based on specific high school courses, cumulative grade point averages, and/or test scores.

**2007-2008 Annual costs.** Tuition/fees: $3,094; $5,154 out-of-district; $7,494 out-of-state. Per-credit charge: $89 in-district; $157 out-of-district; $234 out-of-state. Books/supplies: $1,200. Personal expenses: $1,000.

**Financial aid. Need-based:** Need-based aid available for part-time students. **Non-need-based:** Scholarships awarded for academics, art, athletics, state residency.

**Application procedures. Admission:** No deadline. No application fee. Admission notification on a rolling basis. Early application advised for radiologic technology and nursing programs. **Financial aid:** Priority date 5/1; no closing date. FAFSA, institutional form required. Applicants notified on a rolling basis starting 5/1; must reply within 2 week(s) of notification.

**Academics. Special study options:** Cooperative education, cross-registration, distance learning, dual enrollment of high school students, ESL, honors, independent study, internships, student-designed major, teacher certification program, weekend college. License preparation in nursing, paramedic, physical therapy. **Credit/placement by examination:** CLEP, institutional tests. 32 credit hours maximum toward associate degree. **Support services:** Learning center, reduced course load, remedial instruction, study skills assistance, tutoring, writing center.

**Majors. Business:** General, accounting, administrative services, management information systems, tourism promotion. **Computer sciences:** General. **Education:** General, elementary, secondary. **Engineering technology:** Drafting, manufacturing. **Family/consumer sciences:** Child care. **Health:** Medical radiologic technology/radiation therapy, medical records technology, mental health services, nursing (RN), physical therapy assistant. **Legal studies:** Paralegal. **Liberal arts:** Arts/sciences. **Mechanic/repair:** Aircraft. **Protective services:** Criminal justice, police science. **Psychology:** General. **Social sciences:** General.

**Computing on campus.** Commuter students can connect to campus network. Helpline available.

**Student life. Freshman orientation:** Available. Preregistration for classes offered. **Activities:** Choral groups, drama, student government, TV station, action teams, peer associates, African American student union, Phi Theta Kappa honor society, Best Buddies.

**Athletics.** NJCAA. **Intercollegiate:** Baseball M, basketball, soccer, softball W. **Intramural:** Basketball, soccer. **Team name:** Skipjacks.

**Student services.** Adult student services, career counseling, student employment services, financial aid counseling, minority student services, on-campus daycare, personal counseling, placement for graduates, veterans' counselor. **Physically disabled:** Services for visually, speech, hearing impaired. **Transfer:** Transfer adviser, college fairs on campus for students transferring to 4-year colleges.

**Contact.** E-mail: kpetrichenko@chesapeake.edu
Phone: (410) 822-5400 ext. 287 Fax: (410) 827-5878
Kathy Petrichenko, Dean of Recruitment, Chesapeake College, Box 8, Wye Mills, MD 21679-0008

## College of Southern Maryland
### La Plata, Maryland
www.csmd.edu

CB code: 5144

▶ Public 2-year community college
▶ Commuter campus in large town

**General.** Founded in 1958. Regionally accredited. Additional campuses located in Charles County, Calvert County, and St. Mary's County. **Enrollment:** 5,912 degree-seeking undergraduates; 1,829 non-degree-seeking students. **Degrees:** 724 associate awarded. **Location:** 30 miles from Washington, DC. **Calendar:** Semester, limited summer session. **Full-time faculty:** 125 total; 24% have terminal degrees, 14% minority, 52% women. **Part-time faculty:** 312 total; 9% have terminal degrees, 19% minority, 56% women. **Class size:** 25% < 20, 73% 20-39, 1% 40-49, less than 1% 50-99, less than 1% >100.

**Student profile.** Among degree-seeking undergraduates, 59% enrolled in a transfer program, 41% enrolled in a vocational program, 1,284 enrolled as first-time, first-year students, 233 transferred in from other institutions.

| | | | |
|---|---|---|---|
| Part-time: | 60% | Hispanic American: | 3% |
| Women: | 67% | Native American: | 1% |
| African American: | 20% | 25 or older: | 35% |
| Asian American: | 3% | | |

**Transfer out. Colleges most students transferred to 2007:** University of Maryland: University College, University of Maryland: College Park, Towson University, Salisbury University, St. Mary's College of Maryland.

**Basis for selection.** Open admission, but selective for some programs. Specific requirements for clinical nursing courses include high school diploma or GED, special testing (ACT), minimum 2.0 GPA in high school. Students must take the college skills assessment test unless they have taken the SAT, scored 550 in English and math or the ACT, scored 21 or higher. Interview required of early admission and nursing applicants. **Adult students:** SAT/ACT scores not required.

**2007-2008 Annual costs.** Tuition/fees: $3,384; $5,904 out-of-district; $7,524 out-of-state. Per-credit charge: $94 in-district; $164 out-of-district; $209 out-of-state. Out-of-district fees are an additional $420; out-of-state fees are an additional $690. Books/supplies: $1,000. Personal expenses: $1,000.

**2006-2007 Financial aid. Need-based:** 86% of total undergraduate aid awarded as scholarships/grants, 14% as loans/jobs. Need-based aid available for part-time students. Work-study available nights, weekends and for part-time students. **Non-need-based:** Scholarships awarded for academics, athletics, state residency.

**Application procedures. Admission:** No deadline. No application fee. Application may be submitted online. Admission notification on a rolling basis. **Financial aid:** Priority date 3/1; no closing date. FAFSA required. Applicants notified on a rolling basis starting 5/15; must reply within 2 week(s) of notification.

**Academics. Special study options:** Accelerated study, cooperative education, distance learning, dual enrollment of high school students, honors, independent study, liberal arts/career combination, weekend college. Bachelor's degree programs available on-campus. License preparation in nursing, paramedic, physical therapy, radiology. **Credit/placement by examination:** AP, CLEP, institutional tests. 30 credit hours maximum toward associate degree. **Support services:** Learning center, reduced course load, remedial instruction, study skills assistance, tutoring.

**Majors. Business:** General, accounting technology, business admin. **Computer sciences:** General, information technology, programming. **Construction:** Lineworker. **Education:** General, elementary. **Engineering:** General. **Engineering technology:** Electrical, environmental. **Family/consumer sciences:** Child care. **Health:** Clinical lab technology, EMT paramedic, licensed practical nurse, massage therapy, nursing (RN), physical therapy assistant. **Legal studies:** Paralegal. **Liberal arts:** Arts/sciences. **Parks/recreation:** Health/fitness. **Protective services:** Firefighting, law enforcement admin. **Other:** Mental and Social Health Services and Allied Professions.

**Most popular majors.** Business/marketing 22%, computer/information sciences 7%, education 7%, health sciences 19%, liberal arts 41%.

**Computing on campus.** 639 workstations in library, computer center. Commuter students can connect to campus network. Online course registration, helpline available.

**Student life. Freshman orientation:** Available. Preregistration for classes offered. **Activities:** Jazz band, choral groups, drama, literary magazine, music ensembles, musical theater, student government, student newspaper, BACCHUS Peer Education Network, Black Student Union, Campus Crusade for Christ, El Círculo Cultural Hispánico, Future Teachers Club, The Hawkeye, nursing student association, Phi Theta Kappa, student activities committee, Women on Campus.

**Athletics.** NJCAA. **Intercollegiate:** Baseball M, basketball, cheerleading, golf, lacrosse W, soccer, softball W, tennis, volleyball W. **Team name:** Hawks.

**Student services.** Adult student services, career counseling, student employment services, financial aid counseling, personal counseling, placement

for graduates, veterans' counselor. **Physically disabled:** Services for visually, speech, hearing impaired. **Transfer:** Re-entry adviser for new students. Transfer adviser, college fairs on campus for students transferring to 4-year colleges.

**Contact.** E-mail: info@csmd.edu
Phone: (301) 934-7765 Toll-free number: (800) 933-9177 ext. 7765
Fax: (301) 934-7698
Pat Schroeder, Director of Admissions, College of Southern Maryland, College of Southern Maryland-AOD, La Plata, MD 20646-0910

## Community College of Baltimore County

| Baltimore, Maryland | CB member |
| --- | --- |
| www.ccbcmd.edu | CB code: 5137 |

- Public 2-year community college
- Commuter campus in very large city

**General.** Founded in 1956. Regionally accredited. 3 campuses-Catonsville, Dundalk and Essex; 2 extension centers in Owings Mills and Hunt Valley. **Enrollment:** 16,097 degree-seeking undergraduates; 3,329 non-degree-seeking students. **Degrees:** 1,410 associate awarded. **Location:** 8 miles from Baltimore. **Calendar:** Semester, limited summer session. **Full-time faculty:** 372 total; 22% have terminal degrees, 17% minority, 57% women. **Part-time faculty:** 711 total; 2% have terminal degrees, 20% minority, 55% women. **Special facilities:** Planetarium, occupational training center, performing arts theater, computer integrated manufacturing center. **Partnerships:** Formal partnership with the Baltimore County Public Schools for the Early Assessment and Intervention Project.

**Student profile.** Among degree-seeking undergraduates, 3,457 enrolled as first-time, first-year students.

| Part-time: | 62% | Asian American: | 5% |
| --- | --- | --- | --- |
| Women: | 63% | Hispanic American: | 2% |
| African American: | 34% | 25 or older: | 42% |

**Transfer out. Colleges most students transferred to 2007:** University of Baltimore, University of Maryland Baltimore County, Towson University, Morgan State University.

**Basis for selection.** Open admission, but selective for some programs. Additional requirements for School of Health Professions. In-house placement tests required of applicants not presenting SAT or ACT scores. Score reports preferred by July 1. Interview recommended for applicants under age 16 and early admission applicants.

**High school preparation.** 21 units recommended. Recommended units include English 4, mathematics 3, social studies 4, science 3, foreign language 2 and academic electives 6.

**2007-2008 Annual costs.** Tuition/fees: $3,016; $5,536 out-of-district; $7,396 out-of-state. Per-credit charge: $90 in-district; $174 out-of-district; $236 out-of-state. Books/supplies: $1,000. Personal expenses: $1,200.

**Financial aid. Need-based:** Need-based aid available for part-time students. Work-study available nights, weekends and for part-time students. **Non-need-based:** Scholarships awarded for academics, athletics. **Additional information:** On-campus employment typically available.

**Application procedures. Admission:** No deadline. $15 fee, may be waived for applicants with need. Application may be submitted online. Admission notification on a rolling basis. **Financial aid:** Closing date 3/1. FAFSA required. Applicants notified on a rolling basis starting 5/1; must reply within 2 week(s) of notification.

**Academics. Special study options:** Cooperative education, cross-registration, distance learning, dual enrollment of high school students, ESL, honors, independent study, internships, liberal arts/career combination, study abroad, teacher certification program, weekend college. License preparation in nursing. **Credit/placement by examination:** AP, CLEP, institutional tests. 30 credit hours maximum toward associate degree. **Support services:** GED preparation, learning center, reduced course load, remedial instruction, tutoring.

**Majors. Agriculture:** Horticulture. **Business:** General, accounting technology, administrative services, banking/financial services, business admin, hospitality admin, hotel/motel admin, human resources, labor relations, management information systems, real estate, sales/distribution. **Communications technology:** Radio/tv. **Computer sciences:** General, networking. **Construction:** Building inspection. **Education:** General, chemistry, early childhood, elementary, mathematics, physics, Spanish, special. **Engineering:** General. **Engineering technology:** Architectural drafting, computer systems, drafting, electrical, environmental, hydraulics, industrial, instrumentation, mechanical, occupational safety, quality control, water quality. **English:** English lit. **Family/consumer sciences:** Child care. **Foreign languages:** Sign

language interpretation. **Health:** Dental assistant, EMT paramedic, medical assistant, medical informatics, medical radiologic technology/radiation therapy, medical records technology, medical secretary, mental health services, nuclear medical technology, nursing (RN), physician assistant, preveterinary, respiratory therapy technology, substance abuse counseling, veterinary technology/assistant. **Legal studies:** Paralegal. **Liberal arts:** Arts/sciences. **Mechanic/repair:** Auto body, automotive, diesel, heating/ac/refrig. **Parks/recreation:** General. **Personal/culinary services:** Restaurant/catering. **Social sciences:** Geography. **Transportation:** Aviation. **Visual/performing arts:** General, commercial photography, commercial/advertising art. **Other:** Engineering technology.

**Computing on campus.** 2,359 workstations in library, computer center, student center. Online course registration, online library available.

**Student life. Freshman orientation:** Available. Preregistration for classes offered. One-day program. **Activities:** Choral groups, dance, drama, literary magazine, music ensembles, musical theater, radio station, student government, student newspaper, TV station, black student union, international club, Adventure Society, Christian fellowship.

**Athletics.** NJCAA. **Intercollegiate:** Baseball M, basketball, lacrosse, soccer, softball W, volleyball W.

**Student services.** Career counseling, services for economically disadvantaged, student employment services, financial aid counseling, minority student services, on-campus daycare, personal counseling, placement for graduates, veterans' counselor. **Physically disabled:** Services for visually, speech, hearing impaired. **Transfer:** Pre-admission transcript evaluation for new students. Transfer adviser, college fairs on campus for students transferring to 4-year colleges.

**Contact.** E-mail: essexadmissions@ccbcmd.edu
Phone: (410) 780-6110 Fax: (410) 780-6117
Diane Drake, Director of Admissions, Community College of Baltimore County, 7201 Rossville Boulevard, Baltimore, MD 21237

## Frederick Community College

| Frederick, Maryland | CB member |
| --- | --- |
| www.frederick.edu | CB code: 5230 |

- Public 2-year community college
- Commuter campus in small city

**General.** Founded in 1957. Regionally accredited. **Enrollment:** 4,458 degree-seeking undergraduates; 694 non-degree-seeking students. **Degrees:** 543 associate awarded. **Location:** 40 miles from Washington, DC, 40 miles from Baltimore. **Calendar:** Semester, extensive summer session. **Full-time faculty:** 86 total. **Part-time faculty:** 300 total. **Special facilities:** Culinary Arts Institute.

**Student profile.** Among degree-seeking undergraduates, 1,188 enrolled as first-time, first-year students, 164 transferred in from other institutions.

| Part-time: | 57% | Women: | 60% |
| --- | --- | --- | --- |
| Out-of-state: | 1% | 25 or older: | 50% |

**Transfer out. Colleges most students transferred to 2007:** Hood College, Mount St. Mary's University, Towson University, University of Maryland: College Park, Frostburg University.

**Basis for selection.** Open admission, but selective for some programs. All nursing programs, respiratory therapy, and surgical technology have special requirements. Students must show successful completion of appropriate general education requirements. Score of 550 or higher on either SAT math or verbal will exempt student from appropriate assessment. Interview required of nursing, respiratory therapy applicants. **Learning Disabled:** Meet with Office of Services for Students with Disabilities staff prior to testing/registration.

**2008-2009 Annual costs.** Tuition/fees: $3,128; $6,368 out-of-district; $8,528 out-of-state. Per-credit charge: $92 in-district; $200 out-of-district; $272 out-of-state. Books/supplies: $1,200. Personal expenses: $1,000.

**2006-2007 Financial aid. Need-based:** 82% of total undergraduate aid awarded as scholarships/grants, 18% as loans/jobs. Need-based aid available for part-time students. Work-study available for part-time students. **Non-need-based:** Scholarships awarded for academics, athletics, state residency.

**Application procedures. Admission:** No deadline. No application fee. Application may be submitted online. Admission notification on a rolling basis beginning on or about 1/1. Application deadline for nursing applicants December 15, surgical technology and emergency medical services applicants February 1. **Financial aid:** Priority date 6/15; no closing date. FAFSA, institutional form required. Applicants notified on a rolling basis starting 5/15; must reply within 2 week(s) of notification.

**Academics. Special study options:** Cooperative education, distance learning, dual enrollment of high school students, ESL, honors, independent study, internships, liberal arts/career combination, study abroad, teacher certification program, weekend college. License preparation in nursing, paramedic, real estate. **Credit/placement by examination:** AP, CLEP, institutional tests. 30 credit hours maximum toward associate degree. **Support services:** Learning center, pre-admission summer program, reduced course load, remedial instruction, study skills assistance, tutoring, writing center.

**Majors. Biology:** General. **Business:** Accounting, banking/financial services, business admin, hospitality admin, international. **Communications:** General. **Communications technology:** General. **Computer sciences:** General, applications programming, computer science, information systems, information technology, system admin, systems analysis. **Construction:** General. **Education:** General, early childhood, multi-level teacher, physical, Spanish. **Engineering:** General. **Engineering technology:** Biomedical, CAD/CADD, computer, computer hardware, computer systems, software. **English:** English lit, speech/rhetoric. **Family/consumer sciences:** Child care. **Health:** EMT paramedic, nuclear medical technology, nursing (RN), prenursing, prepharmacy, respiratory therapy technology, surgical technology. **History:** General. **Legal studies:** Legal secretary, paralegal. **Liberal arts:** Arts/sciences. **Math:** General. **Personal/culinary services:** Culinary arts. **Philosophy/religion:** Philosophy. **Physical sciences:** Chemistry. **Protective services:** Criminal justice, emergency management/homeland security, fire services admin, police science. **Psychology:** General. **Public administration:** Human services. **Science technology:** Biological. **Social sciences:** Economics, political science, sociology. **Visual/performing arts:** Art, dramatic.

**Computing on campus.** 150 workstations in library, computer center. Commuter students can connect to campus network. Online course registration, online library, wireless network available.

**Student life. Freshman orientation:** Mandatory. Preregistration for classes offered. Held throughout summer; include advisement and pre-registration. **Activities:** Jazz band, choral groups, dance, drama, film society, literary magazine, music ensembles, student government, student newspaper, multicultural student union, Christian students club, chess club, community service club, environmental awareness club, honors student association, international students club, gay/lesbian/bisexual group, nursing club, young Democrats and Republicans.

**Athletics.** NJCAA. **Intercollegiate:** Baseball M, basketball, golf, soccer, softball W, volleyball W. **Team name:** Cougars.

**Student services.** Adult student services, alcohol/substance abuse counseling, career counseling, student employment services, financial aid counseling, minority student services, on-campus daycare, personal counseling, placement for graduates, veterans' counselor, women's services. **Physically disabled:** Services for visually, speech, hearing impaired. **Transfer:** Transfer center, transfer adviser, college fairs on campus for students transferring to 4-year colleges.

**Contact.** E-mail: kfrawley@frederick.edu
Phone: (301) 846-2431 Fax: (301) 624-2799
Kathy Frawley, Associate Vice President/Registrar, Frederick Community College, 7932 Opossumtown Pike, Frederick, MD 21702

## Garrett College
**McHenry, Maryland**
**www.garrettcollege.edu** CB code: 5279

- Public 2-year community college
- Commuter campus in rural community

**General.** Founded in 1971. Regionally accredited. **Enrollment:** 590 degree-seeking undergraduates. **Degrees:** 69 associate awarded. **Location:** 45 miles from Cumberland, 40 miles from Morgantown, West Virginia. **Calendar:** Semester, limited summer session. **Full-time faculty:** 17 total; 29% have terminal degrees, 6% minority, 29% women. **Part-time faculty:** 76 total; 5% have terminal degrees.

**Student profile.**

| | | | |
|---|---|---|---|
| Out-of-state: | 19% | Live on campus: | 10% |
| 25 or older: | 21% | | |

**Transfer out. Colleges most students transferred to 2007:** Frostburg State University.

**Basis for selection.** Open admission. Applicants without high school diploma must earn diploma or GED before completing 20 credit hours when

enrolling in certificate program, and complete 30 credit hours when enrolling in degree program.

**2007-2008 Annual costs.** Tuition/fees: $2,970; $6,510 out-of-district; $7,590 out-of-state. Per-credit charge: $78 in-district; $196 out-of-district; $232 out-of-state. Room/board: $4,300. Books/supplies: $2,000. Personal expenses: $1,000.

**2007-2008 Financial aid. Need-based:** Need-based aid available for part-time students. **Non-need-based:** Scholarships awarded for academics, athletics, leadership. **Additional information:** Many local scholarships both merit and need based.

**Application procedures. Admission:** No deadline. No application fee. Application may be submitted online. Admission notification on a rolling basis. **Financial aid:** Closing date 3/1. FAFSA required. Applicants notified on a rolling basis starting 5/15; must reply within 2 week(s) of notification.

**Academics. Special study options:** Distance learning, double major, dual enrollment of high school students, honors, independent study. **Credit/placement by examination:** AP, CLEP, institutional tests. 30 credit hours maximum toward associate degree. **Support services:** GED preparation and test center, learning center, pre-admission summer program, reduced course load, remedial instruction, tutoring.

**Majors. Agriculture:** Business. **Business:** General, business admin, office technology. **Conservation:** General, fisheries, wildlife. **Education:** General, elementary, physical, secondary. **Interdisciplinary:** Behavioral sciences. **Liberal arts:** Arts/sciences. **Math:** General. **Parks/recreation:** General. **Psychology:** General. **Visual/performing arts:** General.

**Most popular majors.** Business/marketing 16%, education 23%, liberal arts 39%, parks/recreation 13%, security/protective services 6%.

**Computing on campus.** 80 workstations in library, computer center. Online library, wireless network available.

**Student life. Freshman orientation:** Available. Preregistration for classes offered. **Housing:** Coed dorms, substance-free housing available. $200 non-refundable deposit. **Activities:** Concert band, drama, literary magazine, student government, student newspaper, TV station, art club, adventure sports club, math club, wildlife club, women's athletic club, world view international club.

**Athletics.** NJCAA. **Intercollegiate:** Baseball M, basketball, golf M, skiing M, softball W, volleyball W. **Intramural:** Softball W, volleyball W. **Team name:** Lakers.

**Student services.** Career counseling, student employment services, financial aid counseling. **Physically disabled:** Services for visually, speech, hearing impaired. **Transfer:** Transfer adviser, college fairs on campus for students transferring to 4-year colleges.

**Contact.** E-mail: admissions@garrettcollege.edu
Phone: (301) 387-3044 Toll-free number: (866) 554-2773
Fax: (301) 387-3038
Edward Robinson, Dean of Student Development, Garrett College, 687 Mosser Road, McHenry, MD 21541

## Hagerstown Community College
**Hagerstown, Maryland**
**www.hagerstowncc.edu** CB code: 5290

- Public 2-year community college
- Commuter campus in small city

**General.** Founded in 1946. Regionally accredited. **Enrollment:** 3,010 degree-seeking undergraduates; 709 non-degree-seeking students. **Degrees:** 376 associate awarded. **Location:** 70 miles from Baltimore. **Calendar:** Semester, extensive summer session. **Full-time faculty:** 77 total. **Part-time faculty:** 147 total. **Special facilities:** Technology center, distance learning classrooms, amphitheater, biotechnology/wet labs.

**Student profile.** Among degree-seeking undergraduates, 53% enrolled in a transfer program, 23% enrolled in a vocational program, 825 enrolled as first-time, first-year students, 201 transferred in from other institutions.

| | | | |
|---|---|---|---|
| Part-time: | 56% | Asian American: | 2% |
| Out-of-state: | 23% | Hispanic American: | 3% |
| Women: | 62% | 25 or older: | 34% |
| African American: | 8% | | |

**Transfer out. Colleges most students transferred to 2007:** Frostburg State University, Towson State University, Shepherd University, Shippensburg University, University of Maryland.

**Basis for selection.** Open admission, but selective for some programs. Admission to nursing and radiography programs based on 2.0 GPA, ACT composite score of 21, 1 laboratory chemistry and algebra. SAT/ACT (ACT preferred) and interview required for nursing and radiography program.

**High school preparation.** 16 units recommended. Recommended units include English 4, mathematics 3, social studies 1, history 1, science 3 (laboratory 2) and academic electives 2. One chemistry, 1 biology, 2 algebra required of nursing applicants; 1 physics, 1 chemistry, 2 algebra required of radiologic technologies applicants.

**2007-2008 Annual costs.** Tuition/fees: $3,150; $4,800 out-of-district; $6,210 out-of-state. Per-credit charge: $94 in-district; $149 out-of-district; $196 out-of-state. Books/supplies: $1,000. Personal expenses: $200.

**Financial aid.** All financial aid based on need. Need-based aid available for part-time students. Work-study available nights, weekends and for part-time students.

**Application procedures. Admission:** No deadline. No application fee. Application may be submitted online. Admission notification on a rolling basis. **Financial aid:** Priority date 3/1; no closing date. FAFSA required. Applicants notified on a rolling basis starting 5/1.

**Academics. Special study options:** Accelerated study, cooperative education, cross-registration, distance learning, double major, dual enrollment of high school students, ESL, honors, independent study, internships, liberal arts/career combination. License preparation in nursing, paramedic, radiology, real estate. **Credit/placement by examination:** AP, CLEP, institutional tests. 30 credit hours maximum toward associate degree. **Support services:** GED preparation and test center, learning center, pre-admission summer program, reduced course load, remedial instruction, study skills assistance, tutoring.

**Majors. Business:** General, accounting technology, banking/financial services, business admin, management information systems, transportation. **Communications technology:** Animation/special effects. **Computer sciences:** General, web page design. **Education:** General, early childhood, elementary. **Engineering:** General. **Engineering technology:** Electromechanical, industrial, mechanical. **Family/consumer sciences:** Child care. **Health:** EMT paramedic, medical radiologic technology/radiation therapy, medical secretary, mental health services, nursing (RN). **Liberal arts:** Arts/sciences. **Protective services:** Police science. **Science technology:** Biological. **Visual/performing arts:** Commercial/advertising art.

**Most popular majors.** Business/marketing 18%, education 8%, health sciences 21%, liberal arts 43%.

**Computing on campus.** 500 workstations in library, computer center, student center. Commuter students can connect to campus network. Online course registration, online library, helpline, repair service available.

**Student life. Freshman orientation:** Available. **Activities:** Jazz band, choral groups, drama, international student organizations, literary magazine, musical theater, student government, student newspaper, Intervarsity Christian Fellowship.

**Athletics.** NJCAA. **Intercollegiate:** Baseball M, basketball, cheerleading, cross-country, golf, soccer, softball W, tennis, track and field, volleyball W. **Team name:** Hawks.

**Student services.** Adult student services, career counseling, services for economically disadvantaged, student employment services, financial aid counseling, health services, on-campus daycare, personal counseling, placement for graduates, veterans' counselor. **Physically disabled:** Services for visually, speech, hearing impaired. **Transfer:** Pre-admission transcript evaluation for new students. Transfer adviser, college fairs on campus for students transferring to 4-year colleges.

**Contact.** E-mail: admissions@hagerstowncc.edu
Phone: (301) 790-2800 ext. 238 Fax: (301) 791-9165
Jennifer Fisher, Director of Admissions, Records and Registration, Hagerstown Community College, 11400 Robinwood Drive, Hagerstown, MD 21742

## Harford Community College
**Bel Air, Maryland**
**www.harford.edu**

CB code: 5303

- Public 2-year community college
- Commuter campus in small city

**General.** Founded in 1957. Regionally accredited. **Enrollment:** 4,732 degree-seeking undergraduates. **Degrees:** 533 associate awarded. **Location:** 25 miles from Baltimore. **Calendar:** Semester, limited summer session. **Full-time**

**faculty:** 100 total; 8% minority, 56% women. **Part-time faculty:** 239 total; 9% minority, 51% women. **Special facilities:** Observatory, art galleries, theater.

**Student profile.** Among degree-seeking undergraduates, 321 transferred in from other institutions.

| | | | |
|---|---|---|---|
| Out-of-state: | 1% | Hispanic American: | 3% |
| African American: | 12% | International: | 1% |
| Asian American: | 3% | 25 or older: | 47% |

**Transfer out.** 72% of students enrolled in the transfer program go on to 4-year colleges. **Colleges most students transferred to 2007:** Towson University, University of Maryland at College Park, University of Baltimore, Salisbury University, University of Maryland Baltimore County.

**Basis for selection.** Open admission, but selective for some programs. Some restrictions apply for applicants under 16 years old and international students. Nursing program has specific selection criteria. Students with a SAT score of 550 or higher in the critical reading portion or the math section will be exempt from the corresponding Accuplacer section of the assessment. Students not meeting basic requirements must complete transitional courses. **Adult students:** SAT/ACT scores not required.

**High school preparation.** 12 units recommended. Recommended units include English 4, mathematics 3, social studies 2 and science 3. Several degree programs require additional preparation.

**2008-2009 Annual costs.** Tuition/fees (projected): $2,607; $5,077 out-of-district; $7,347 out-of-state. Per-credit charge: $79 in-district; $158 out-of-district; $237 out-of-state. Required fees based on $79 per credit in-county fee. Books/supplies: $1,300. Personal expenses: $1,000.

**2006-2007 Financial aid. Need-based:** 93% of total undergraduate aid awarded as scholarships/grants, 7% as loans/jobs. Work-study available for part-time students.

**Application procedures. Admission:** No deadline. No application fee. Application may be submitted online. Admission notification on a rolling basis. Application deadline for nursing June 1. Notification within 30 days. **Financial aid:** Priority date 3/15; no closing date. FAFSA, institutional form required. Applicants notified on a rolling basis starting 4/1; must reply within 2 week(s) of notification.

**Academics. Special study options:** Cooperative education, distance learning, double major, dual enrollment of high school students, independent study, internships, liberal arts/career combination, weekend college. License preparation in nursing. **Credit/placement by examination:** AP, CLEP, IB, institutional tests. 30 credit hours maximum toward associate degree. **Support services:** GED preparation and test center, learning center, reduced course load, remedial instruction, study skills assistance, tutoring, writing center.

**Majors. Agriculture:** Business, equestrian studies, horticulture, landscaping, turf management. **Biology:** General. **Business:** General, accounting technology, business admin, golf management, management information systems. **Communications:** Media studies. **Computer sciences:** General, computer science, security. **Conservation:** Environmental science, environmental studies. **Education:** General, chemistry, early childhood, elementary, mathematics, physics, secondary. **Engineering:** General. **Engineering technology:** General, CAD/CADD. **English:** English lit. **Health:** Electroencephalograph technology, massage therapy, medical assistant, nursing (RN). **History:** General. **Interdisciplinary:** Historic preservation. **Legal studies:** General. **Math:** General. **Philosophy/religion:** Philosophy. **Physical sciences:** Chemistry, physics. **Protective services:** Police science. **Psychology:** General. **Public administration:** Social work. **Social sciences:** Anthropology, international relations, political science, sociology. **Visual/performing arts:** General, commercial photography, design, interior design, studio arts, theater design. **Other:** Histotechnology.

**Most popular majors.** Business/marketing 19%, health sciences 16%, liberal arts 40%, personal/culinary services 9%.

**Computing on campus.** 750 workstations in library, computer center, student center. Commuter students can connect to campus network. Online course registration, online library, helpline, student web hosting, wireless network available.

**Student life. Freshman orientation:** Available. Preregistration for classes offered. **Activities:** Bands, choral groups, dance, drama, film society, literary magazine, music ensembles, musical theater, radio station, student government, student newspaper, TV station, Black student union, multinational Hispanic student association, political awareness association, Phi Theta Kappa, Campus Christian Life club, College Democrats, College Republicans, multicultural student association.

**Athletics.** NJCAA. **Intercollegiate:** Baseball M, basketball, golf M, lacrosse, soccer, softball W, tennis, volleyball W. **Intramural:** Badminton, basketball, football (non-tackle), soccer, softball, tennis, volleyball. **Team name:** Fighting Owls.

**Student services.** Career counseling, student employment services, financial aid counseling, on-campus daycare, personal counseling, placement for graduates, veterans' counselor. **Physically disabled:** Services for visually, speech, hearing impaired. **Transfer:** Pre-admission transcript evaluation for new students. Transfer adviser, college fairs on campus for students transferring to 4-year colleges.

**Contact.** E-mail: sendinfo@harford.edu
Phone: (410) 836-4107 Fax: (410) 836-4169
Brian Hammond, Coordinator of Admissions, Harford Community College, 401 Thomas Run Road, Bel Air, MD 21015

## Howard Community College
### Columbia, Maryland
www.howardcc.edu

CB code: 5308

- Public 2-year community college
- Commuter campus in small city

**General.** Founded in 1966. Regionally accredited. **Enrollment:** 6,702 degree-seeking undergraduates; 821 non-degree-seeking students. **Degrees:** 471 associate awarded. **Location:** 20 miles from Baltimore, 30 miles from Washington, DC. **Calendar:** Semester, extensive summer session. **Full-time faculty:** 141 total; 27% have terminal degrees, 22% minority, 64% women. **Part-time faculty:** 552 total; 13% have terminal degrees, 22% minority, 64% women. **Class size:** 54% < 20, 43% 20-39, 1% 40-49, 2% 50-99. **Special facilities:** Practice rooms, recital hall, black box theater, art and dance studios, child care facility, conference center, Center for Entrepreneurial and Business Excellence, wellness center, mediation and conflict resolution center, World Languages Institute. **Partnerships:** Formal partnerships with Novell Education Academic Partner, Microsoft Authorized Academic Training Program, Sylvan/Prometric Authorized Testing/Academic Center, Comp Tia Authorized Education Partner, and Regional Cisco Networking Academy.

**Student profile.** Among degree-seeking undergraduates, 71% enrolled in a transfer program, 29% enrolled in a vocational program, 14% already have a bachelor's degree or higher, 1,439 enrolled as first-time, first-year students.

| | | | |
|---|---|---|---|
| Part-time: | 58% | Hispanic American: | 5% |
| Women: | 57% | Native American: | 1% |
| African American: | 22% | International: | 6% |
| Asian American: | 9% | 25 or older: | 38% |

**Transfer out.** 76% of students enrolled in the transfer program go on to 4-year colleges. **Colleges most students transferred to 2007:** University of Maryland-College Park, University of Maryland-Baltimore County, Towson University, Salisbury University.

**Basis for selection.** Open admission, but selective for some programs. Special requirements for clinical nursing, radiologic technology, emergency medical services, cardiovascular technology applicants. Selective admission to James W. Rouse Scholars and Silas Craft Collegians programs. SAT or ACT required for admission to James W. Rouse Scholars Program. Mandatory assessment policy. Most students must complete placement testing before completing 12 credits. Placement test exemptions allowed based on SAT/ACT scores. Interview and portfolio recommended for some selective admissions programs. **Adult students:** SAT/ACT scores not required.

**High school preparation.** Recommended units include English 4, mathematics 4, social studies 4, history 3, science 3 (laboratory 2) and foreign language 3. Computer related course involving skills such as word-processing, databases and spreadsheets, as well as the Internet.

**2008-2009 Annual costs.** Tuition/fees (projected): $3,993; $6,483 out-of-district; $8,193 out-of-state. Books/supplies: $1,000. Personal expenses: $1,000.

**2006-2007 Financial aid. Need-based:** 76% of total undergraduate aid awarded as scholarships/grants, 24% as loans/jobs. Need-based aid available for part-time students. Work-study available nights, weekends and for part-time students.

**Application procedures. Admission:** No deadline. $25 fee, may be waived for applicants with need. Application may be submitted online. Admission notification on a rolling basis. Specific deadlines apply for applications to James W. Rouse Scholars program and clinical nursing program. **Financial aid:** Priority date 3/1; no closing date. FAFSA required. Applicants notified on a rolling basis starting 4/1.

**Academics.** Pre-admission summer program for disabled students only. **Special study options:** Accelerated study, cooperative education, distance learning, dual enrollment of high school students, ESL, external degree, honors, independent study, internships, liberal arts/career combination, study abroad, teacher certification program, weekend college. License preparation in nursing, paramedic, radiology. **Credit/placement by examination:** AP, CLEP, IB, institutional tests. 30 credit hours maximum toward associate degree. **Support services:** GED preparation, learning center, pre-admission summer program, reduced course load, remedial instruction, study skills assistance, tutoring, writing center.

**Honors college/program.** James W. Rouse Scholar Program: 70-75 HS grads accepted from approx. 135 applicants; Frederick K. Schoenbrodt Honors Program: approx. 30 students accepted (HS grad or current or transfer student) with 3.2 GPA or 1100 SAT (critical reading and Math).

**Majors. Agriculture:** Horticultural science. **Area/ethnic studies:** American, women's. **Biology:** Biomedical sciences. **Business:** Business admin, financial planning, hospitality admin, management information systems, office management, retailing, sales/distribution. **Communications:** Digital media. **Communications technology:** Desktop publishing. **Computer sciences:** Computer graphics, computer science, information technology, networking, security. **Conservation:** General. **Education:** Early childhood, elementary, secondary. **Engineering:** General. **Engineering technology:** Biomedical, CAD/CADD, electrical, laser/optical, telecommunications. **English:** English lit. **Family/consumer sciences:** Child development. **Health:** Athletic training, cardiovascular technology, clinical lab technology, EMT paramedic, health services admin, licensed practical nurse, massage therapy, music therapy, nursing (RN), physical therapy assistant, predental, premedicine, prepharmacy, preveterinary, radiologic technology/medical imaging, respiratory therapy assistant, substance abuse counseling, surgical technology. **History:** General. **Interdisciplinary:** Global studies, intercultural. **Legal studies:** Legal secretary. **Liberal arts:** Arts/sciences. **Math:** General. **Mechanic/repair:** Electronics/electrical. **Parks/recreation:** Exercise sciences, health/fitness. **Philosophy/religion:** Philosophy. **Physical sciences:** General. **Protective services:** Criminal justice. **Psychology:** General. **Social sciences:** General, anthropology, criminology, international economics. **Visual/performing arts:** Art, cinematography, commercial/advertising art, dance, design, dramatic, photography, studio arts, theater design.

**Most popular majors.** Business/marketing 13%, education 6%, health sciences 18%, liberal arts 55%.

**Computing on campus.** 186 workstations in library, computer center, student center. Commuter students can connect to campus network. Online course registration, online library, helpline, repair service, student web hosting, wireless network available.

**Student life. Freshman orientation:** Available. Preregistration for classes offered. 3-4 hour day or evening program the week before start of fall and spring semesters. **Policies:** Drug and alcohol free campus, code of conduct, academic honesty. **Activities:** Jazz band, choral groups, dance, drama, literary magazine, music ensembles, musical theater, student government, student newspaper, TV station, Christian fellowship, Muslim student association, Jewish student union, global student union, African student association, environmental club, nursing club, psychology club, leadership club, hospitality club.

**Athletics.** NJCAA. **Intercollegiate:** Basketball, cross-country, lacrosse, soccer, track and field, volleyball W. **Team name:** Dragons.

**Student services.** Adult student services, career counseling, services for economically disadvantaged, student employment services, financial aid counseling, on-campus daycare, personal counseling, placement for graduates, veterans' counselor, women's services. **Physically disabled:** Services for visually, speech, hearing impaired. **Learning disabled:** Comprehensive services available. **Transfer:** Pre-admission transcript evaluation for new students. Transfer center, transfer adviser, college fairs on campus for students transferring to 4-year colleges.

**Contact.** E-mail: adm-adv@howardcc.edu
Phone: (410) 772-4856 Fax: (410) 772-4589
Christy Thomson, Assistant Director of Admissions, Howard Community College, 10901 Little Patuxent Parkway, Columbia, MD 21044-3197

## Kaplan College: Hagerstown
### Hagerstown, Maryland
www.KC-Hagerstown.com

CB code: 0804

- For-profit 2-year business and junior college
- Commuter campus in large town
- Interview required

**General.** Founded in 1938. Accredited by ACICS. **Enrollment:** 611 degree-seeking undergraduates. **Degrees:** 248 associate awarded. **Location:** 70 miles from Baltimore, 70 miles from Washington, DC. **Calendar:** Quarter, limited summer session. **Full-time faculty:** 55 total. **Part-time faculty:** 25

total. **Special facilities:** Firearms training simulator, forensic recovery and evidence detection lab.

**Student profile.**

| | | | |
|---|---|---|---|
| Out-of-state: | 60% | Live on campus: | 3% |
| 25 or older: | 55% | | |

**Basis for selection.** Open admission, but selective for some programs.

**2007-2008 Annual costs.** Tuition and fees vary from $13,248-$31,229 for entire program. Registration fee $55. Books/supplies: $875. Personal expenses: $960.

**Financial aid. Need-based:** Need-based aid available for part-time students.

**Application procedures. Admission:** No deadline. $20 fee. Admission notification on a rolling basis. **Financial aid:** No deadline. FAFSA, institutional form required. Applicants notified on a rolling basis starting 6/1; must reply within 2 week(s) of notification.

**Academics.** College includes allied health, legal, business, criminal justice, computer forensics and information technology divisions. Several bachelor's programs offered in online courses. **Special study options:** Distance learning, double major, internships. **Credit/placement by examination:** AP, CLEP, institutional tests. 15 credit hours maximum toward associate degree. **Support services:** Reduced course load, remedial instruction, tutoring.

**Majors. Business:** Accounting, administrative services, business admin, office technology. **Computer sciences:** Computer graphics, data processing, LAN/WAN management, system admin, webmaster. **Health:** Medical assistant, medical records technology, medical secretary, medical transcription. **Legal studies:** Paralegal. **Protective services:** Criminal justice, forensics, law enforcement admin.

**Most popular majors.** Business/marketing 22%, computer/information sciences 28%, health sciences 39%, legal studies 11%.

**Computing on campus.** 85 workstations in library, computer center.

**Student life. Freshman orientation:** Mandatory. **Housing:** Coed dorms available. $150 deposit. **Activities:** Student government.

**Student services.** Career counseling, student employment services, financial aid counseling, personal counseling, placement for graduates.

**Contact.** E-mail: info@kc-hagerstown.edu
Phone: (301) 739-2670 Toll-free number: (800) 422-2670
Fax: (301) 791-7661
Jon Filkins, Director of Admissions, Kaplan College: Hagerstown, 18618 Crestwood Drive, Hagerstown, MD 21742

## Montgomery College
**Rockville, Maryland**
www.montgomerycollege.edu

**CB member**
**CB code: 5440**

♦ Public 2-year community college
♦ Commuter campus in very large city

**General.** Founded in 1946. Regionally accredited. Additional campuses in Takoma Park/Silver Spring and Germantown. **Enrollment:** 16,835 degree-seeking undergraduates; 7,032 non-degree-seeking students. **Degrees:** 1,692 associate awarded. **Location:** 5 miles from Washington, DC. **Calendar:** Semester, extensive summer session. **Full-time faculty:** 501 total; 34% have terminal degrees, 28% minority, 55% women. **Part-time faculty:** 867 total; 23% have terminal degrees, 28% minority, 57% women. **Class size:** 36% < 20, 62% 20-39, less than 1% 40-49, 2% 50-99. **Special facilities:** Performing arts center, child care center, planetarium.

**Student profile.** Among degree-seeking undergraduates, 52% enrolled in a transfer program, 19% enrolled in a vocational program, 1% already have a bachelor's degree or higher, 3,475 enrolled as first-time, first-year students, 956 transferred in from other institutions.

| | | | |
|---|---|---|---|
| Part-time: | 57% | Asian American: | 13% |
| Out-of-state: | 4% | Hispanic American: | 13% |
| Women: | 52% | International: | 7% |
| African American: | 26% | 25 or older: | 36% |

**Transfer out.** 63% of students enrolled in the transfer program go on to 4-year colleges. **Colleges most students transferred to 2007:** University of Maryland: College Park, University of Maryland: Baltimore County, Towson State University, University of Maryland: University College, Salisbury University.

**Basis for selection.** Open admission, but selective for some programs. Admission to allied medical health programs considers standardized test scores, secondary school record, geographical residence, and state residence. Montgomery County residents get first priority; GPA rank within residency category is important. Audition required for music majors and School of Art & Design admissions process requires a portfolio review/interview.

**High school preparation.** Recommended units include English 4, mathematics 3 and science 2.

**2007-2008 Annual costs.** Tuition/fees: $3,876; $7,512 out-of-district; $9,996 out-of-state. Per-credit charge: $96 in-district; $197 out-of-district; $266 out-of-state. Books/supplies: $1,200. Personal expenses: $1,380.

**2006-2007 Financial aid. Need-based:** 78% of total undergraduate aid awarded as scholarships/grants, 22% as loans/jobs. Need-based aid available for part-time students. Work-study available nights, weekends and for part-time students. **Non-need-based:** Scholarships awarded for academics, alumni affiliation, art, music/drama, state residency.

**Application procedures. Admission:** No deadline. $25 fee, may be waived for applicants with need. Application may be submitted online. Admission notification on a rolling basis. **Financial aid:** Priority date 5/15; no closing date. FAFSA, institutional form required. Applicants notified on a rolling basis starting 5/30.

**Academics. Special study options:** Accelerated study, cooperative education, distance learning, double major, dual enrollment of high school students, ESL, honors, independent study, internships, student-designed major, study abroad, teacher certification program, weekend college. License preparation in nursing, physical therapy, radiology, real estate. **Credit/placement by examination:** AP, CLEP, IB, institutional tests. 45 credit hours maximum toward associate degree. **Support services:** GED preparation and test center, learning center, pre-admission summer program, remedial instruction, study skills assistance, tutoring, writing center.

**Majors. Agriculture:** General. **Architecture:** Technology. **Biology:** Biochemistry. **Business:** General, accounting technology, business admin, construction management, hospitality admin, hotel/motel admin, international, management information systems. **Communications:** Advertising, broadcast journalism. **Communications technology:** Desktop publishing, graphic/printing, graphics. **Computer sciences:** General, computer graphics, computer science, game design, information systems, programming. **Education:** General, early childhood, science. **Engineering:** General, civil. **Engineering technology:** Architectural, biomedical, civil, drafting, electrical. **Family/consumer sciences:** Child care, institutional food production. **Foreign languages:** American Sign Language. **Health:** Medical radiologic technology/radiation therapy, medical records technology, nursing (RN), physical therapy assistant, predental, premedicine, prepharmacy, sonography, surgical technology. **Interdisciplinary:** Biological/physical sciences. **Legal studies:** Paralegal. **Liberal arts:** Arts/sciences. **Math:** General. **Mechanic/repair:** Automotive. **Parks/recreation:** Exercise sciences. **Physical sciences:** Physics. **Protective services:** Firefighting, law enforcement admin. **Science technology:** Biological. **Visual/performing arts:** General, art history/conservation, commercial photography, commercial/advertising art, dance, interior design, photography, studio arts, theater design. **Other:** Applied Geography.

**Most popular majors.** Business/marketing 18%, engineering/engineering technologies 6%, health sciences 11%, liberal arts 52%.

**Computing on campus.** 400 workstations in library, computer center. Commuter students can connect to campus network. Online course registration, online library, helpline, wireless network available.

**Student life. Freshman orientation:** Available. Preregistration for classes offered. **Activities:** Concert band, choral groups, dance, drama, international student organizations, music ensembles, musical theater, radio station, student government, student newspaper, TV station, Jewish student association, progressive student alliance, Christian fellowship, lesbian student alliance, Students Against Driving Drunk, African-American student organization, Hispanic student organization, Asian student organization.

**Athletics.** NJCAA. **Intercollegiate:** Baseball M, basketball, cross-country, field hockey W, golf M, lacrosse M, soccer, softball W, tennis, track and field, volleyball W, wrestling M. **Intramural:** Basketball.

**Student services.** Adult student services, career counseling, services for economically disadvantaged, student employment services, financial aid counseling, minority student services, on-campus daycare, personal counseling, placement for graduates, veterans' counselor. **Physically disabled:** Services for visually, speech, hearing impaired. **Learning disabled:** Comprehensive services available. **Transfer:** Re-entry adviser, pre-admission transcript evaluation for new students. Transfer center, transfer adviser, college fairs on campus for students transferring to 4-year colleges.

**Contact.** Phone: (240) 567-5034 Fax: (240) 567-5037
Sherman Helberg, Director of Enrollment Management, Montgomery
College, 51 Mannakee Street, Rockville, MD 20850

## Prince George's Community College
Largo, Maryland          CB member
www.pgcc.edu          CB code: 5545

- Public 2-year community college
- Commuter campus in very large city

**General.** Founded in 1958. Regionally accredited. Extension center at Andrews Air Force Base serves both military and civilian personnel. **Enrollment:** 10,512 degree-seeking undergraduates; 1,349 non-degree-seeking students. **Degrees:** 675 associate awarded. **ROTC:** Army, Air Force. **Location:** 10 miles from Washington, DC. **Calendar:** Semester, limited summer session. **Full-time faculty:** 244 total; 29% have terminal degrees, 36% minority, 60% women. **Part-time faculty:** 451 total; 63% minority. **Class size:** 64% < 20, 35% 20-39, less than 1% 40-49, less than 1% 50-99. **Special facilities:** Natatorium, art gallery.

**Student profile.** Among degree-seeking undergraduates, 2,118 enrolled as first-time, first-year students, 943 transferred in from other institutions.

| | | | |
|---|---|---|---|
| Part-time: | 73% | Asian American: | 4% |
| Out-of-state: | 4% | Hispanic American: | 4% |
| Women: | 64% | International: | 5% |
| African American: | 78% | 25 or older: | 47% |

**Transfer out. Colleges most students transferred to 2007:** University of Maryland-College Park, Bowie State University, University of Maryland-University College, Morgan State University.

**Basis for selection.** Open admission, but selective for some programs. Special requirements for health technology programs and for international students. Health technology program requires high school diploma or GED. For some scholarship awards or honors program consideration, SAT combined score of 1050 or above (exclusive of writing) required. SAT or ACT scores may be used in place of college's placement tests.

**High school preparation.** Recommended units include English 4, mathematics 4, social studies 3, history 3, science 3 (laboratory 2) and academic electives 4. One computer literacy recommended.

**2007-2008 Annual costs.** Tuition/fees: $2,900; $5,030 out-of-district; $7,670 out-of-state. Per-credit charge: $94 in-district; $165 out-of-district; $263 out-of-state. Instructional services fees range from $22 to $32 per credit depending on course. Books/supplies: $700.

**2007-2008 Financial aid.** All financial aid based on need. Need-based aid available for part-time students. Work-study available for part-time students.

**Application procedures. Admission:** No deadline. $25 fee. Admission notification on a rolling basis. **Financial aid:** Priority date 6/1; no closing date. FAFSA, institutional form required. Applicants notified on a rolling basis starting 6/1; must reply within 2 week(s) of notification.

**Academics. Special study options:** Cooperative education, distance learning, double major, dual enrollment of high school students, ESL, honors, independent study, liberal arts/career combination, teacher certification program, weekend college. License preparation in nursing, paramedic, real estate. **Credit/placement by examination:** AP, CLEP, institutional tests. 30 credit hours maximum toward associate degree. **Support services:** GED preparation, learning center, reduced course load, remedial instruction, study skills assistance, tutoring, writing center.

**Majors. Area/ethnic studies:** African-American, American, women's. **Biology:** General. **Business:** Accounting, administrative services, business admin, marketing, office management, office technology. **Computer sciences:** General, computer science, information systems, programming, systems analysis. **Education:** Business, early childhood, elementary, health, mathematics, physical, science, secondary. **Engineering:** General, aerospace. **Engineering technology:** Drafting, electrical. **Family/consumer sciences:** Child care. **Health:** EMT paramedic, medical radiologic technology/radiation therapy, medical records admin, medical records technology, medical secretary, nuclear medical technology, nursing (RN), premedicine, prepharmacy, respiratory therapy technology. **Legal studies:** Legal secretary, paralegal. **Liberal arts:** Arts/sciences. **Physical sciences:** Chemistry. **Protective services:** Criminal justice, forensics. **Psychology:** General. **Visual/performing arts:** Commercial/advertising art, studio arts.

**Computing on campus.** 950 workstations in library, computer center, student center. Commuter students can connect to campus network. Helpline, repair service available.

**Student life. Freshman orientation:** Available. Preregistration for classes offered. **Activities:** Choral groups, drama, film society, international student organizations, literary magazine, music ensembles, musical theater, opera, student government, student newspaper, TV station, Union of Black Scholars, Active Seniors (for senior citizens), student program board, Spanish club, French club, Caribbean students club, Muslim society, women's Bible study.

**Athletics.** NJCAA. **Intercollegiate:** Baseball M, basketball, bowling, golf, soccer, softball W, tennis M, volleyball W. **Intramural:** Basketball, bowling, golf, racquetball, soccer, table tennis, volleyball. **Team name:** Owls.

**Student services.** Adult student services, career counseling, services for economically disadvantaged, student employment services, financial aid counseling, health services, minority student services, personal counseling, placement for graduates, veterans' counselor. **Physically disabled:** Services for visually, speech, hearing impaired. **Learning disabled:** Comprehensive services available. **Transfer:** Re-entry adviser for new students. Transfer center, transfer adviser, college fairs on campus for students transferring to 4-year colleges.

**Contact.** E-mail: enrollmentservices@pgcc.edu
Phone: (301) 322-0801 Fax: (301) 322-0119
Vera Bagley, Director of Admissions and Records, Prince George's Community College, 301 Largo Road, Largo, MD 20774

## TESST College of Technology: Baltimore
Baltimore, Maryland
www.tesst.com/tesstPortal

- For-profit 2-year technical college
- Very large city

**General.** Regionally accredited; also accredited by ACCSCT. **Enrollment:** 810 full-time, degree-seeking students. **Degrees:** 21 associate awarded. **Calendar:** Semester. **Full-time faculty:** 60 total. **Part-time faculty:** 40 total.

**Basis for selection.** Open admission, but selective for some programs. Institutional evaluation test may be accepted in lieu of SAT/ACT.

**2007-2008 Annual costs.** Cost for complete program is $11,800-$26=7,800, depending on field of study.

**Application procedures. Admission:** No deadline. $20 fee. Admission notification on a rolling basis. **Financial aid:** No deadline.

**Academics. Credit/placement by examination:** AP, CLEP.

**Majors. Computer sciences:** Information systems. **Engineering technology:** Electrical, telecommunications.

**Contact.** Phone: (410) 644-6400 Fax: (410) 644-6481
William Scott, Director of Admissions, TESST College of Technology: Baltimore, 1520 South Caton Avenue, Baltimore, MD 21227-1063

## TESST College of Technology: Beltsville
Beltsville, Maryland
www.tesst.com

- For-profit 2-year technical college
- Large town

**General.** Accredited by ACCSCT. **Enrollment:** 605 degree-seeking undergraduates. **Degrees:** 91 associate awarded. **Calendar:** Semester. **Full-time faculty:** 10 total.

**Basis for selection.** Open admission.

**2007-2008 Annual costs.** Cost for complete program is $11,800-$27,800 depending on field of study.

**Academics. Credit/placement by examination:** CLEP.

**Majors. Computer sciences:** Data entry, information systems.

**Contact.** E-mail: dedmonds@tesst.com
Phone: (301) 937-8448 Toll-free number: (800) 488-3778
Sandra Ugol, President, TESST College of Technology: Beltsville, 4600 Powder Mill Road, Beltsville, MD 20705

## TESST College of Technology: Towson
Towson, Maryland
www.tesst.com

▶ For-profit 2-year technical college
▶ Small city
▶ Interview required

**General.** Accredited by ACCSCT. **Enrollment:** 500 degree-seeking undergraduates. **Degrees:** 50 associate awarded. **Location:** 15 miles from Baltimore. **Calendar:** Semester. **Full-time faculty:** 15 total. **Part-time faculty:** 20 total.

**Basis for selection.** Open admission, but selective for some programs. **Adult students:** CPAT for all students.

**2007-2008 Annual costs.** 2 year associate degree program, including books, fees and tuition, $24,000 - $28,000; certificate program, $12,000 - $24,000.

**Application procedures. Admission:** No deadline. $20 fee. Admission notification on a rolling basis.

**Academics. Credit/placement by examination:** CLEP. **Support services:** Tutoring.

**Majors. Business:** Management information systems. **Engineering technology:** Electrical. **Protective services:** Law enforcement admin.

**Student life. Freshman orientation:** Mandatory. Preregistration for classes offered.

**Student services.** Career counseling, student employment services, financial aid counseling, placement for graduates, veterans' counselor.

**Contact.** Phone: (410) 296-5350 Fax: (410) 296-5356
Kathleen McDermott, Director of Admissions, TESST College of Technology: Towson, 803 Glen Eagles Court, Towson, MD 21286

## Wor-Wic Community College
Salisbury, Maryland
www.worwic.edu

CB member
CB code: 1613

▶ Public 2-year community college
▶ Commuter campus in large town

**General.** Founded in 1975. Regionally accredited. **Enrollment:** 3,054 degree-seeking undergraduates; 244 non-degree-seeking students. **Degrees:** 228 associate awarded. **Location:** 110 miles from Baltimore, 120 miles from Washington, DC. **Calendar:** Semester, limited summer session. **Full-time faculty:** 62 total; 27% have terminal degrees, 10% minority, 60% women. **Part-time faculty:** 111 total; 8% have terminal degrees, 12% minority, 60% women. **Class size:** 44% < 20, 47% 20-39, 6% 40-49, 3% 50-99. **Partnerships:** Formal partnership with local medical center to provide financial and clinical support to the college's health programs.

**Student profile.** Among degree-seeking undergraduates, 43% enrolled in a transfer program, 57% enrolled in a vocational program, 740 enrolled as first-time, first-year students, 299 transferred in from other institutions.

| | | | |
|---|---|---|---|
| Part-time: | 65% | Asian American: | 2% |
| Out-of-state: | 2% | Hispanic American: | 2% |
| Women: | 66% | 25 or older: | 38% |
| African American: | 24% | | |

**Transfer out.** 73% of students enrolled in the transfer program go on to 4-year colleges. **Colleges most students transferred to 2007:** Salisbury University, University of Maryland Eastern Shore.

**Basis for selection.** Open admission, but selective for some programs. Special requirements for emergency medical services, nursing and radiologic technology programs.

**High school preparation.** Recommended units include English 4 and mathematics 2.

**2007-2008 Annual costs.** Tuition/fees: $2,404; $5,884 out-of-district; $6,844 out-of-state. Per-credit charge: $76 in-district; $192 out-of-district; $224 out-of-state. Books/supplies: $1,400. Personal expenses: $1,000.

**Financial aid. Need-based:** Need-based aid available for part-time students. Work-study available nights, weekends and for part-time students. **Non-need-based:** Scholarships awarded for academics, state residency.

**Application procedures. Admission:** No deadline. No application fee. Application must be submitted on paper. Admission notification on a rolling basis. **Financial aid:** Priority date 6/1; no closing date. FAFSA, institutional form required. Applicants notified on a rolling basis starting 4/1.

**Academics. Special study options:** Distance learning, double major, dual enrollment of high school students, ESL, honors, internships. License preparation in nursing, paramedic, radiology. **Credit/placement by examination:** AP, CLEP, institutional tests. 30 credit hours maximum toward associate degree. **Support services:** Learning center, reduced course load, remedial instruction, tutoring, writing center.

**Majors. Business:** General, accounting technology, administrative services, business admin, hospitality admin. **Computer sciences:** General, systems analysis. **Education:** General, early childhood, elementary. **Engineering technology:** Drafting, electrical. **Family/consumer sciences:** Child care. **Health:** EMT paramedic, medical radiologic technology/radiation therapy, nursing (RN), substance abuse counseling. **Interdisciplinary:** Biological/physical sciences. **Protective services:** Police science.

**Most popular majors.** Business/marketing 24%, education 8%, health sciences 29%, liberal arts 31%.

**Computing on campus.** 613 workstations in library, computer center, student center. Commuter students can connect to campus network. Online library available.

**Student life. Freshman orientation:** Available. Preregistration for classes offered. **Activities:** Choral groups, drama, literary magazine, student government, student newspaper.

**Student services.** Career counseling, student employment services, financial aid counseling, on-campus daycare, personal counseling, placement for graduates, veterans' counselor. **Physically disabled:** Services for visually, speech, hearing impaired. **Transfer:** College fairs on campus for students transferring to 4-year colleges.

**Contact.** E-mail: admissions@worwic.edu
Phone: (410) 334-2895 Fax: (410) 334-2954
Richard Webster, Director of Admissions, Wor-Wic Community College, 32000 Campus Drive, Salisbury, MD 21804

# Massachusetts

## Bay State College
**Boston, Massachusetts**
www.baystate.edu
CB code: 3120

- Private 2-year junior college
- Commuter campus in very large city
- Application essay, interview required

**General.** Founded in 1946. Regionally accredited. **Enrollment:** 810 degree-seeking undergraduates. **Degrees:** 132 associate awarded. **Calendar:** Semester, limited summer session. **Full-time faculty:** 17 total. **Part-time faculty:** 73 total.

**Student profile.**

25 or older: 12%  Live on campus: 19%

**Basis for selection.** Special consideration to students with lower than minimum 2.0 GPA; interview and 2 recommendations from guidance counselors. Writing sample and second interview may be requested.

**High school preparation.** Recommended units include English 4, mathematics 2, social studies 1, history 1, science 2 (laboratory 1).

**2007-2008 Annual costs.** Tuition/fees: $16,850. Per-credit charge: $550. Program specific fees for allied health, $475 and fashion design, $300. Room/board: $10,500. Books/supplies: $900. Personal expenses: $400.

**Financial aid. Need-based:** Need-based aid available for part-time students. Work-study available nights, weekends and for part-time students.

**Application procedures. Admission:** No deadline. $40 fee, may be waived for applicants with need. Application may be submitted online. Admission notification on a rolling basis. **Financial aid:** Closing date 3/15. FAFSA, institutional form required. Applicants notified on a rolling basis starting 3/15; must reply within 3 week(s) of notification.

**Academics. Special study options:** Cooperative education, ESL, honors, independent study, internships. License preparation in occupational therapy, physical therapy. **Credit/placement by examination:** CLEP, IB, institutional tests. 9 credit hours maximum toward associate degree. **Support services:** Learning center, reduced course load, study skills assistance, tutoring.

**Majors. Business:** Accounting, administrative services, business admin, fashion, hospitality/recreation, office management, sales/distribution, tourism promotion. **Computer sciences:** General. **Education:** Early childhood. **Health:** Medical assistant, medical secretary, occupational therapy assistant, physical therapy assistant. **Legal studies:** Legal secretary, paralegal. **Visual/performing arts:** Fashion design.

**Most popular majors.** Business/marketing 73%, health sciences 27%.

**Computing on campus.** 62 workstations in computer center, student center.

**Student life. Freshman orientation:** Mandatory. Preregistration for classes offered. **Housing:** Coed dorms, single-sex dorms available. $200 deposit, deadline 8/1. **Activities:** Literary magazine, clubs associated with majors, student activities club, international club.

**Student services.** Adult student services, career counseling, student employment services, financial aid counseling, health services, personal counseling, placement for graduates, veterans' counselor. **Transfer:** Pre-admission transcript evaluation for new students. Transfer adviser, college fairs on campus for students transferring to 4-year colleges.

**Contact.** E-mail: admissions@baystate.edu
Phone: (617) 236-8000 Toll-free number: (800) 815-3276
Fax: (617) 536-1735
Dominick Miciotta, Vice President fo Enrollment, Bay State College, 122 Commonwealth Avenue, Boston, MA 02116

## Benjamin Franklin Institute of Technology
**Boston, Massachusetts** CB member
www.bfit.edu CB code: 3394

- Private 2-year technical college
- Commuter campus in very large city

**General.** Founded in 1908. Regionally accredited. Founded under provisions of will of Benjamin Franklin and managed by Franklin Foundation. **Enrollment:** 513 undergraduates. **Degrees:** 3 bachelor's, 84 associate awarded. **Calendar:** Semester, limited summer session. **Full-time faculty:** 31 total. **Part-time faculty:** 35 total. **Special facilities:** Extensive labs for automotive, architecture, computer, electronic, electrical, opticianry, pharmacy, and mechanized engineering technologies.

**Student profile.**

Out-of-state: 5%  25 or older: 13%

**Transfer out. Colleges most students transferred to 2007:** Northeastern University, University of Massachusetts at Lowell, Worcester Polytech, Wentworth Institute.

**Basis for selection.** School achievement record, particularly in mathematics and science, most important. SAT or ACT recommended. Interview and essay recommended.

**High school preparation.** 8 units required. Required and recommended units include English 4, mathematics 3-5 and science 1-3. Level of math and science required varies by program.

**2007-2008 Annual costs.** Tuition/fees: $12,750. Per-credit charge: $531. Cost shown is for certificate program. Tuition for associate degree programs is $13,900 per year. Books/supplies: $600.

**Financial aid. Need-based:** Need-based aid available for part-time students. **Non-need-based:** Scholarships awarded for academics.

**Application procedures. Admission:** Priority date 5/1; no deadline. $25 fee, may be waived for applicants with need. Application may be submitted online. Admission notification on a rolling basis. **Financial aid:** Priority date 4/1; no closing date. FAFSA required. Applicants notified on a rolling basis starting 3/1; must reply within 4 week(s) of notification.

**Academics. Special study options:** ESL, liberal arts/career combination. Bachelor's degree programs available on campus. **Credit/placement by examination:** CLEP, IB, institutional tests. **Support services:** Learning center, pre-admission summer program, reduced course load, remedial instruction, study skills assistance, tutoring.

**Majors. Architecture:** Technology. **Biology:** Biomedical sciences. **Computer sciences:** General, programming. **Construction:** Electrician. **Engineering technology:** Architectural, automotive, biomedical, computer, computer hardware, computer systems, electrical, mechanical, mechanical drafting. **Mechanic/repair:** General, automotive.

**Computing on campus.** 120 workstations in library, computer center. Wireless network available.

**Student life. Freshman orientation:** Mandatory. Preregistration for classes offered. Half-day program held in August. **Housing:** Student housing available at Boston University. **Activities:** Student government, student newspaper.

**Athletics.** NJCAA. **Intercollegiate:** Basketball M, soccer M. **Intramural:** Basketball M. **Team name:** Shockers.

**Student services.** Career counseling, student employment services, financial aid counseling, personal counseling, placement for graduates, veterans' counselor. **Transfer:** Pre-admission transcript evaluation for new students. Transfer adviser, college fairs on campus for students transferring to 4-year colleges.

**Contact.** E-mail: admis@bfit.edu
Phone: (617) 423-4630 ext. 121 Fax: (617) 482-3706
Kathleen Lynch, Director of Admissions, Benjamin Franklin Institute of Technology, 41 Berkeley Street, Boston, MA 02116

## Berkshire Community College
**Pittsfield, Massachusetts** CB member
www.berkshirecc.edu CB code: 3102

- Public 2-year community college
- Commuter campus in large town

**General.** Founded in 1960. Regionally accredited. Elderhostel program site, children's circus, site for Berkshire Opera. **Enrollment:** 1,776 degree-seeking undergraduates; 491 non-degree-seeking students. **Degrees:** 245 associate awarded. **Location:** 40 miles from Albany, New York. **Calendar:** Semester, limited summer session. **Full-time faculty:** 54 total; 70% have terminal degrees, 67% women. **Part-time faculty:** 122 total; 50% have terminal degrees, 48% women. **Class size:** 16% < 20, 84% 20-39. **Special facilities:** Global positioning laboratory, nature trail, computer animation, graphics laboratory. **Partnerships:** Formal partnerships with Plastics Network, Applied Technology Council, Berkshire Works, Tech-Prep programs, service learning programs.

**Student profile.** Among degree-seeking undergraduates, 42% enrolled in a transfer program, 58% enrolled in a vocational program, 478 enrolled as first-time, first-year students.

| | | | |
|---|---|---|---|
| Part-time: | 50% | Asian American: | 1% |
| Out-of-state: | 4% | Hispanic American: | 4% |
| Women: | 64% | International: | 2% |
| African American: | 5% | 25 or older: | 41% |

**Transfer out. Colleges most students transferred to 2007:** Massachusetts College of Liberal Arts, Westfield State College, University of Massachusetts-Amherst, Sage Colleges, Smith College.

**Basis for selection.** Open admission, but selective for some programs. Special requirements for nursing and allied health programs. Fall-only admission to nursing and allied health programs.

**High school preparation.** 1 chemistry, 1 biology, 1 algebra, with demonstrated college level English skills required for nursing and health program applicants.

**2007-2008 Annual costs.** Tuition/fees: $3,826; $10,846 out-of-state. Per-credit charge: $26 in-state; $260 out-of-state. $140.50 per credit hour (tuition/fees): New England Regional tuition, New York residents. Books/supplies: $810. Personal expenses: $2,225.

**2006-2007 Financial aid. Need-based:** 69% of total undergraduate aid awarded as scholarships/grants, 31% as loans/jobs. Need-based aid available for part-time students. Work-study available nights, weekends and for part-time students. **Additional information:** Tuition waivers available to Massachusetts residents who fall into one of the following categories: Department of Social Services adopted or foster children, Massachusetts Rehabilitation Commission clients, high-scoring MCAS students, National Guard members, Native Americans, state employees and their dependents, veterans.

**Application procedures. Admission:** No deadline. $10 fee ($35 out-of-state), may be waived for applicants with need. Application must be submitted on paper. Admission notification on a rolling basis. **Financial aid:** Priority date 5/1; no closing date. FAFSA required. Applicants notified on a rolling basis starting 5/10; must reply within 2 week(s) of notification.

**Academics. Special study options:** Combined bachelor's/graduate degree, cooperative education, cross-registration, distance learning, double major, dual enrollment of high school students, ESL, honors, independent study, internships, liberal arts/career combination, student-designed major, study abroad. License preparation in nursing, occupational therapy, physical therapy. **Credit/placement by examination:** AP, CLEP, IB, institutional tests. 30 credit hours maximum toward associate degree. **Support services:** GED test center, learning center, pre-admission summer program, reduced course load, remedial instruction, study skills assistance, tutoring, writing center.

**Majors. Business:** General, business admin, hospitality admin, office technology. **Computer sciences:** General. **Conservation:** Environmental science. **Engineering:** General. **Engineering technology:** Electrical. **Health:** Health services, nursing (RN), physical therapy assistant, respiratory therapy technology. **Liberal arts:** Arts/sciences. **Protective services:** Criminal justice, firefighting. **Public administration:** Community org/advocacy. **Visual/performing arts:** General.

**Most popular majors.** Business/marketing 20%, health sciences 28%, liberal arts 28%, security/protective services 9%.

**Computing on campus.** 478 workstations in library, computer center, student center. Online library, helpline available.

**Student life. Freshman orientation:** Mandatory. Preregistration for classes offered. Variety of options, including 1-day orientation/registration and 2-week summer transition program. **Policies:** Alcohol-free campus. **Activities:** Bands, choral groups, dance, drama, literary magazine, music ensembles, musical theater, student government, TV station, Phi Theta Kappa honor society.

**Student services.** Adult student services, alcohol/substance abuse counseling, career counseling, services for economically disadvantaged, student employment services, financial aid counseling, minority student services,

on-campus daycare, personal counseling, veterans' counselor, women's services. **Physically disabled:** Services for visually, speech, hearing impaired. **Learning disabled:** Comprehensive services available. **Transfer:** Re-entry adviser, pre-admission transcript evaluation for new students. Transfer adviser, college fairs on campus for students transferring to 4-year colleges.

**Contact.** E-mail: admissions@berkshirecc.edu
Phone: (413) 236-1630 Toll-free number: (800) 816-1233 ext. 1630
Fax: (413) 496-9511
Michael Bullock, Dean of Student Affairs and Enrollment Services, Berkshire Community College, 1350 West Street, Pittsfield, MA 01201-5786

## Bristol Community College

**Fall River, Massachusetts**     CB member
www.bristolcc.edu     CB code: 3110

- Public 2-year community college
- Commuter campus in small city

**General.** Founded in 1965. Regionally accredited. **Enrollment:** 5,892 degree-seeking undergraduates. **Degrees:** 735 associate awarded. **Location:** 48 miles from Boston, 17 miles from Providence, Rhode Island. **Calendar:** Semester, extensive summer session. **Full-time faculty:** 100 total. **Part-time faculty:** 330 total. **Special facilities:** Planetarium, greenhouse, robotics laboratory, aquaculture laboratory. **Partnerships:** Formal partnerships with local businesses and non-profit organizations.

**Student profile.**

| | | | |
|---|---|---|---|
| Out-of-state: | 15% | Hispanic American: | 3% |
| African American: | 6% | Native American: | 1% |
| Asian American: | 2% | 25 or older: | 49% |

**Basis for selection.** Open admission, but selective for some programs. Special requirements for health science and culinary arts programs. SAT scores required for allied health programs. **Homeschooled:** Letter of approval from student's school district that authenticates homeschool education required.

**High school preparation.** Specific programs have varying course requirements.

**2007-2008 Annual costs.** Tuition/fees: $3,750; $9,930 out-of-state. Per-credit charge: $24 in-state; $230 out-of-state. Books/supplies: $1,000. Personal expenses: $4,840.

**2006-2007 Financial aid. Need-based:** 82% of total undergraduate aid awarded as scholarships/grants, 18% as loans/jobs. Need-based aid available for part-time students. Work-study available nights, weekends and for part-time students. **Non-need-based:** Scholarships awarded for academics, art, leadership, minority status, music/drama.

**Application procedures. Admission:** Priority date 1/15; no deadline. $10 fee ($35 out-of-state), may be waived for applicants with need. Application may be submitted online. Admission notification on a rolling basis beginning on or about 12/1. Must reply by May 1 or within 2 week(s) if notified thereafter. **Financial aid:** Priority date 5/1; no closing date. FAFSA, institutional form required. Applicants notified on a rolling basis starting 5/1; must reply within 2 week(s) of notification.

**Academics.** Students must complete general education requirement core curriculum prior to graduation. **Special study options:** Cooperative education, cross-registration, distance learning, dual enrollment of high school students, ESL, honors, independent study, internships, student-designed major, weekend college. **Credit/placement by examination:** CLEP, institutional tests. 30 credit hours maximum toward associate degree. **Support services:** GED preparation and test center, learning center, pre-admission summer program, reduced course load, remedial instruction, tutoring, writing center.

**Majors. Business:** Accounting, banking/financial services, business admin. **Communications:** General. **Computer sciences:** General, computer science, data processing, information systems, programming. **Education:** Early childhood, elementary, kindergarten/preschool. **Engineering:** General, environmental, manufacturing, mechanical, science, structural. **Engineering technology:** Environmental, water quality. **Family/consumer sciences:** Child care. **Foreign languages:** American Sign Language. **Health:** Clinical lab technology, dental hygiene, medical records technology, medical secretary, nursing (RN), occupational therapy assistant. **Legal studies:** Paralegal. **Liberal arts:** Arts/sciences. **Protective services:** Criminal justice, firefighting. **Visual/performing arts:** Art, dramatic.

**Most popular majors.** Business/marketing 23%, education 8%, health sciences 12%, liberal arts 31%, security/protective services 9%.

**Computing on campus.** Dormitories linked to campus network. Commuter students can connect to campus network. Online course registration, online library, helpline available.

**Student life. Freshman orientation:** Available. Preregistration for classes offered. **Activities:** Drama, radio station, student government, student newspaper, TV station, Catholic student association, Christian Fellowship, water watch, international club, Portuguese club, Latino club, Cambodian association, human services club, coalition for social justice.

**Athletics. Intercollegiate:** Soccer M.

**Student services.** Adult student services, alcohol/substance abuse counseling, campus ministries, career counseling, student employment services, financial aid counseling, health services, minority student services, on-campus daycare, personal counseling, placement for graduates, veterans' counselor. **Physically disabled:** Services for visually, speech, hearing impaired. **Learning disabled:** Comprehensive services available. **Transfer:** Transfer adviser, college fairs on campus for students transferring to 4-year colleges.

**Contact.** E-mail: admissions@bristolcc.edu
Phone: (508) 678-2811 ext. 2516 Toll-free number: (800) 462-0035
Fax: (508) 730-3265
Rodney Clark, Dean of Admissions, Bristol Community College, 777 Elsbree Street, Fall River, MA 02720-7395

## Bunker Hill Community College

**Boston, Massachusetts**
**www.bhcc.mass.edu**

**CB member**
**CB code: 3123**

- Public 2-year community college
- Commuter campus in very large city

**General.** Founded in 1973. Regionally accredited. **Enrollment:** 6,528 degree-seeking undergraduates. **Degrees:** 652 associate awarded. **Location:** 5 miles from downtown. **Calendar:** Semester, extensive summer session. **Full-time faculty:** 131 total. **Part-time faculty:** 292 total. **Special facilities:** Adaptive computer laboratory.

**Transfer out. Colleges most students transferred to 2007:** University of Massachusetts Boston, Salem State College, Northeastern University, Bentley College, Suffolk University.

**Basis for selection.** Open admission, but selective for some programs. Special requirements for nursing, medical radiography, surgical technology, ultrasound, overhead electrical line worker programs. Allied Health Aptitude Test required for allied health programs; school-administered exam required for nursing and medical imaging programs.

**2007-2008 Annual costs.** Tuition/fees: $3,180; $9,360 out-of-state. Per-credit charge: $24 in-state; $230 out-of-state. New England Regional Tuition: $112 per-credit-hour. Books/supplies: $1,200. Personal expenses: $1,600.

**Financial aid. Need-based:** Need-based aid available for part-time students. Work-study available for part-time students. **Non-need-based:** Scholarships awarded for academics.

**Application procedures. Admission:** Priority date 5/1; deadline 9/2. $10 fee ($35 out-of-state), may be waived for applicants with need. Application must be submitted on paper. Admission notification on a rolling basis. Must reply by May 1 or within 2 week(s) if notified thereafter. **Financial aid:** Priority date 4/15; no closing date. FAFSA required. Applicants notified on a rolling basis starting 6/1; must reply within 2 week(s) of notification.

**Academics.** Some courses taught off-campus in the community. **Special study options:** Cross-registration, distance learning, double major, dual enrollment of high school students, ESL, external degree, honors, independent study, internships, liberal arts/career combination, study abroad, weekend college. License preparation in nursing, paramedic, radiology, real estate. **Credit/placement by examination:** AP, CLEP, institutional tests. 45 credit hours maximum toward associate degree. **Support services:** GED preparation, learning center, pre-admission summer program, reduced course load, remedial instruction, study skills assistance, tutoring, writing center.

**Majors. Biology:** General. **Business:** Accounting, business admin, finance, hospitality admin, international, office/clerical, operations, tourism/travel. **Communications:** General, media studies. **Computer sciences:** Applications programming, computer science, data entry, database management, networking, system admin, web page design. **Education:** General, early childhood. **Engineering technology:** Computer systems, software. **English:** English lit. **Foreign languages:** General. **Health:** Cardiovascular technology, medical radiologic technology/radiation therapy, medical secretary, nursing (RN), sonography. **History:** General. **Math:** General. **Personal/**

culinary services: Chef training. **Physical sciences:** Chemistry, physics. **Protective services:** Corrections, fire safety technology, law enforcement admin, security management. **Psychology:** General. **Public administration:** Human services. **Social sciences:** Sociology. **Visual/performing arts:** Art, design, dramatic.

**Most popular majors.** Business/marketing 29%, computer/information sciences 16%, health sciences 26%, liberal arts 8%.

**Computing on campus.** 640 workstations in library, computer center. Commuter students can connect to campus network. Online course registration, online library, helpline available.

**Student life. Freshman orientation:** Available. Preregistration for classes offered. **Activities:** Jazz band, choral groups, drama, literary magazine, music ensembles, musical theater, radio station, student government, student newspaper, African American cultural society, Alpha Kappa Mu honor society, Amnesty International, Arab students association, Asian students association, Brazilian cultural club, criminal justice society, gay, lesbian, bisexual and transgender student union, multicultural club.

**Athletics.** NJCAA. **Intercollegiate:** Baseball M, basketball, golf, soccer, softball W. **Intramural:** Basketball, table tennis, tennis. **Team name:** Bulldogs.

**Student services.** Adult student services, career counseling, services for economically disadvantaged, student employment services, financial aid counseling, health services, on-campus daycare, personal counseling, placement for graduates, veterans' counselor. **Physically disabled:** Services for visually, speech, hearing impaired. **Transfer:** Re-entry adviser, pre-admission transcript evaluation for new students. Transfer center, transfer adviser, college fairs on campus for students transferring to 4-year colleges.

**Contact.** E-mail: admissions@bhcc.mass.edu
Phone: (617) 228-2422 Fax: (617) 228-2082
Debra Boyer, Registrar/Director of Enrollment Services, Bunker Hill Community College, 250 New Rutherford Avenue, Boston, MA 02129-2925

## Cape Cod Community College

**West Barnstable, Massachusetts**
**www.capecod.edu**

**CB member**
**CB code: 3289**

- Public 2-year community college
- Commuter campus in small town

**General.** Founded in 1961. Regionally accredited. **Enrollment:** 3,339 degree-seeking undergraduates. **Degrees:** 324 associate awarded. **Location:** 79 miles from Boston, 80 miles from Providence, Rhode Island. **Calendar:** Semester, limited summer session. **Full-time faculty:** 64 total. **Part-time faculty:** 214 total. **Special facilities:** Source collection for Cape Cod history, marshland nature preserve, maritime studies collection. **Partnerships:** Formal partnerships with Tech Prep, School-to-Career, Cape Cod Technology Council Apprenticeship Program.

**Transfer out. Colleges most students transferred to 2007:** Bridgewater State College, University of Massachusetts (Amherst, Boston, Dartmouth), Suffolk University.

**Basis for selection.** Open admission, but selective for some programs. Special requirements for dental hygiene and nursing programs; priority given to Massachusetts residents. Interview recommended for dental hygiene and nursing programs.

**High school preparation.** Chemistry with lab and algebra required for dental hygiene and nursing programs. Nursing also requires biology with anatomy and physiology unit labs.

**2007-2008 Annual costs.** Tuition/fees: $3,946; $10,126 out-of-state. Per-credit charge: $24 in-state; $230 out-of-state. Books/supplies: $800. Personal expenses: $1,072.

**Financial aid. Need-based:** Need-based aid available for part-time students. Work-study available for part-time students. **Non-need-based:** Scholarships awarded for academics, art, job skills, leadership, music/drama, state residency.

**Application procedures. Admission:** Priority date 8/10; no deadline. No application fee. Admission notification on a rolling basis. Must reply by May 1 or within 4 week(s) if notified thereafter. January 5 application priority date for nursing, February 1 for dental hygiene. **Financial aid:** Priority date 5/1; no closing date. FAFSA required. Applicants notified on a rolling basis starting 5/1.

**Academics. Special study options:** Accelerated study, cooperative education, cross-registration, distance learning, dual enrollment of high school students, ESL, honors, independent study, internships, study abroad. Bachelor's degree programs available on campus. License preparation in dental hygiene, nursing, paramedic, real estate. **Credit/placement by examination:** AP, CLEP, institutional tests. 30 credit hours maximum toward associate degree. **Support services:** GED preparation and test center, learning center, reduced course load, remedial instruction, study skills assistance, tutoring, writing center.

**Majors. Business:** Accounting, accounting/business management, administrative services, business admin, executive assistant, hotel/motel admin, management science, marketing, office management, office/clerical. **Communications:** General, journalism, media studies, public relations. **Computer sciences:** General, applications programming, computer science, information systems, information technology, LAN/WAN management, networking, web page design, webmaster. **Conservation:** General, environmental science, environmental studies. **Education:** General, early childhood, kindergarten/preschool. **Engineering:** General. **Foreign languages:** General. **Health:** Dental hygiene, EMT paramedic, medical secretary, nursing (RN), predental, premedicine, prenursing, prepharmacy. **Interdisciplinary:** Behavioral sciences, global studies, natural sciences. **Legal studies:** Legal secretary. **Liberal arts:** Arts/sciences. **Math:** General. **Parks/recreation:** General, health/fitness. **Philosophy/religion:** Philosophy. **Physical sciences:** General. **Protective services:** Criminal justice, fire safety technology, firefighting, law enforcement admin. **Psychology:** General. **Public administration:** Human services. **Social sciences:** General, sociology. **Visual/performing arts:** General, commercial/advertising art, dance, dramatic, graphic design.

**Most popular majors.** Business/marketing 13%, health sciences 27%, liberal arts 24%, psychology 6%, security/protective services 10%.

**Computing on campus.** 240 workstations in library, computer center, student center. Commuter students can connect to campus network. Helpline, wireless network available.

**Student life. Freshman orientation:** Mandatory. Preregistration for classes offered. Half-day program includes meeting with assigned adviser. **Activities:** Choral groups, dance, drama, literary magazine, music ensembles, musical theater, radio station, student government, student newspaper, TV station, Phi Theta Kappa, Earth workers club, cultural affairs club, diversity club, learning disability support group, gay-bi-lesbian club.

**Athletics. Intramural:** Badminton, basketball, racquetball, tennis, volleyball. **Team name:** Helmsmen.

**Student services.** Adult student services, alcohol/substance abuse counseling, career counseling, services for economically disadvantaged, student employment services, financial aid counseling, health services, minority student services, on-campus daycare, personal counseling, placement for graduates, veterans' counselor, women's services. **Physically disabled:** Services for visually, speech, hearing impaired. **Transfer:** Re-entry adviser, preadmission transcript evaluation for new students. Transfer adviser, college fairs on campus for students transferring to 4-year colleges.

**Contact.** E-mail: admiss@capecod.mass.edu
Phone: (508) 362-2131 ext. 4311 Toll-free
number: (877) 846-3672 ext. 4311 Fax: (508) 375-4089
Susan Kline-Symington, Director of Admissions, Cape Cod Community College, 2240 Iyanough Road, West Barnstable, MA 02668-1599

---

## Caritas Laboure College
**Boston, Massachusetts**
**www.laboure.edu**      **CB code: 3287**

▶ Private 2-year health science and junior college affiliated with Roman Catholic Church
▶ Commuter campus in very large city
▶ Interview required

**General.** Founded in 1971. Regionally accredited. Affiliated with more than 100 health care agencies in Greater Boston area. **Enrollment:** 533 degree-seeking undergraduates. **Degrees:** 87 associate awarded. **Location:** 5 miles from downtown. **Calendar:** Semester, limited summer session. **Full-time faculty:** 21 total. **Part-time faculty:** 35 total. **Class size:** 87% < 20, 13% 20-39.

**Student profile.**

| | | | |
|---|---|---|---|
| Out-of-state: | 1% | 25 or older: | 70% |

**Basis for selection.** School achievement record, recommendations, interview important, work experience considered.

---

**High school preparation.** 10 units required; 16 recommended. Required and recommended units include English 4, mathematics 3, science 1-2 (laboratory 1).

**2007-2008 Annual costs.** Per-credit charge: $495. Cost of 4-term year is $19,760, inclusive of fees. Professional study courses are $540 per credit. Books/supplies: $800. Personal expenses: $1,000.

**2007-2008 Financial aid. Need-based:** 23% of total undergraduate aid awarded as scholarships/grants, 77% as loans/jobs. Need-based aid available for part-time students. Work-study available nights and for part-time students. **Non-need-based:** Scholarships awarded for academics, alumni affiliation, leadership, religious affiliation. **Additional information:** Allied Health Scholarship: covers cost of general education courses for students enrolled in electroneurodiagnostic technology, health information technology, and nutrition and food management programs; constitutes significant reduction in tuition. Caritas Christi Scholarship: for students who work 16 hours per week at a Caritas Christi healthcare agency; covers 25% of tuition for nursing and radiation therapy courses; also covers 50% of cost of nursing courses for students with LPN credential. Evening LPN Scholarship: discounts tuition 75% for evening nursing majors with LPN credential.

**Application procedures. Admission:** No deadline. $25 fee, may be waived for applicants with need. Admission notification on a rolling basis. **Financial aid:** Priority date 4/1; no closing date. FAFSA, institutional form required. Applicants notified on a rolling basis starting 5/15; must reply within 2 week(s) of notification.

**Academics. Special study options:** Accelerated study, independent study, liberal arts/career combination. License preparation in nursing. **Credit/placement by examination:** CLEP, institutional tests. 23 credit hours maximum toward associate degree. **Support services:** Learning center, preadmission summer program, reduced course load, remedial instruction, tutoring.

**Majors. Health:** Clinical lab science, dietetics, medical radiologic technology/radiation therapy, medical records technology, nuclear medical technology, nursing (RN), radiologic technology/medical imaging.

**Most popular majors.** Family/consumer sciences 8%, health sciences 92%.

**Computing on campus.** 20 workstations in library, computer center.

**Student life. Freshman orientation:** Available, $100 fee. Preregistration for classes offered. One-day information session and tour prior to fall term. **Activities:** Student government.

**Student services.** Campus ministries, career counseling, financial aid counseling, personal counseling.

**Contact.** E-mail: admit@laboure.edu
Phone: (617) 296-8300 ext. 4016 Fax: (617) 296-7947
Gina Morrissette, Director of Admissions, Caritas Laboure College, 2120 Dorchester Avenue, Boston, MA 02124-5698

---

## Dean College
**Franklin, Massachusetts**      **CB member**
**www.dean.edu**      **CB code: 3352**

▶ Private 2-year junior and liberal arts college
▶ Residential campus in large town
▶ SAT or ACT (ACT writing optional), application essay required

**General.** Founded in 1865. Regionally accredited. **Enrollment:** 1,093 degree-seeking undergraduates; 209 non-degree-seeking students. **Degrees:** 35 bachelor's, 248 associate awarded. **Location:** 30 miles from Boston, 30 miles from Providence, Rhode Island. **Calendar:** Semester, limited summer session. **Full-time faculty:** 35 total; 43% have terminal degrees, 6% minority, 54% women. **Part-time faculty:** 68 total; 16% have terminal degrees, 4% minority, 66% women. **Class size:** 63% < 20, 36% 20-39, less than 1% 40-49. **Special facilities:** Telecommunications center, childcare center. **Partnerships:** Formal partnerships with Putnam Investments (students may earn associate's degree while working) and Suffolk University (offers baccalaureate degrees in criminology, business, communications, information technology, and psychology that may be earned entirely in residence).

**Student profile.** Among degree-seeking undergraduates, 544 enrolled as first-time, first-year students, 53 transferred in from other institutions.

| | | | |
|---|---|---|---|
| Part-time: | 8% | Women: | 48% |
| Out-of-state: | 42% | Live on campus: | 87% |

**Transfer out.** 99% of students enrolled in the transfer program go on to 4-year colleges. **Colleges most students transferred to 2007:** Suffolk University, Northeastern University, UMass Amherst, Emerson, Bridgewater State.

**Basis for selection.** School achievement record, recommendations most important. Interview recommended. **Learning Disabled:** Arch program applicants must submit appropriate materials that identify and describe the student's learning abilities and any issues relevant to successful completion of a college program.

**High school preparation.** 8 units required; 14 recommended. Required and recommended units include English 3-4, mathematics 1-2, social studies 1-2, history 1-2, science 1-2 (laboratory 1), foreign language 1 and academic electives 1.

**2007-2008 Annual costs.** Tuition/fees: $25,420. Room/board: $10,960. Books/supplies: $1,000. Personal expenses: $200.

**2006-2007 Financial aid. Need-based:** 396 full-time freshmen applied for aid; 357 were judged to have need; 357 of these received aid. Average scholarship/grant was $9,554; average loan $2,643. 62% of total undergraduate aid awarded as scholarships/grants, 38% as loans/jobs. Need-based aid available for part-time students. Work-study available nights, weekends and for part-time students. **Non-need-based:** Scholarships awarded for academics, athletics, leadership, music/drama, state residency.

**Application procedures. Admission:** No deadline. $35 fee, may be waived for applicants with need. Application may be submitted online. Admission notification on a rolling basis beginning on or about 12/1. Must reply by May 1 or within 2 week(s) if notified thereafter. **Financial aid:** Priority date 3/1; no closing date. FAFSA required. Applicants notified on a rolling basis starting 3/1; must reply by 5/1 or within 3 week(s) of notification.

**Academics. Special study options:** ESL, honors, independent study, student-designed major. Bachelor's degree programs available on campus. **Credit/placement by examination:** AP, CLEP, IB, SAT. **Support services:** Learning center, pre-admission summer program, reduced course load, remedial instruction, study skills assistance, tutoring, writing center.

**Majors. Business:** General, business admin. **Communications:** General. **Computer sciences:** General. **Education:** Early childhood, physical. **Health:** Athletic training, health services. **History:** General. **Liberal arts:** Arts/sciences. **Math:** General. **Parks/recreation:** Health/fitness, sports admin. **Physical sciences:** General. **Protective services:** Criminal justice, law enforcement admin. **Psychology:** General. **Visual/performing arts:** Dance, dramatic.

**Most popular majors.** Business/marketing 25%, communications/journalism 7%, education 6%, health sciences 11%, liberal arts 34%, visual/performing arts 10%.

**Computing on campus.** Wireless network available.

**Student life. Freshman orientation:** Mandatory, $200 fee. Preregistration for classes offered. **Housing:** Guaranteed on-campus for all undergraduates. Coed dorms, single-sex dorms available. $400 deposit, deadline 5/1. **Activities:** Jazz band, choral groups, dance, drama, literary magazine, music ensembles, musical theater, radio station, student government, TV station, Hillel, Christian Fellowship.

**Athletics.** NJCAA. **Intercollegiate:** Baseball M, basketball, football (tackle) M, golf M, lacrosse, soccer, softball W, volleyball W. **Intramural:** Basketball, soccer, softball W, volleyball. **Team name:** Bulldogs.

**Student services.** Adult student services, career counseling, financial aid counseling, health services. **Physically disabled:** Services for visually, speech, hearing impaired. **Learning disabled:** Comprehensive services available. **Transfer:** Transfer center, transfer adviser, college fairs on campus for students transferring to 4-year colleges.

**Contact.** E-mail: admission@dean.edu
Phone: (508) 541-1508 Toll-free number: (877) 879-3326
Fax: (508) 541-8726
Paul Vaccaro, Dean of Admissions, Dean College, 99 Main Street, Franklin, MA 02038-1994

## Fisher College
**Boston, Massachusetts**
**www.fisher.edu**

CB code: 3391

- Private 2-year liberal arts college
- Residential campus in very large city

**General.** Founded in 1903. Regionally accredited. Branch campuses in Boston, North Attleboro and New Bedford. **Enrollment:** 589 degree-seeking undergraduates. **Degrees:** 52 bachelor's, 169 associate awarded. **Location:** Downtown. **Calendar:** Semester, limited summer session. **Full-time faculty:** 21 total; 33% have terminal degrees, 5% minority, 67% women.

**Part-time faculty:** 24 total; 12% minority, 50% women. **Class size:** 53% < 20, 47% 20-39. **Partnerships:** Formal agreements with TechPrep programs in Massachusetts.

**Student profile.**

| | | | |
|---|---|---|---|
| Out-of-state: | 29% | Live on campus: | 51% |
| 25 or older: | 4% | | |

**Basis for selection.** High school GPA, test scores, personal essays and recommendation letters reviewed. Essay recommended. **Homeschooled:** Statement describing homeschool structure and mission required. **Learning Disabled:** Accommodation review available upon request. Students requesting review should submit latest IEP as well as current psychoeducational testing.

**High school preparation.** Recommended units include English 4, mathematics 3, social studies 3 and science 2.

**2008-2009 Annual costs.** Tuition/fees (projected): $23,065. Room/board: $12,125. Books/supplies: $1,200. Personal expenses: $1,200.

**Financial aid. Need-based:** Need-based aid available for part-time students. Work-study available nights, weekends and for part-time students. **Non-need-based:** Scholarships awarded for academics, alumni affiliation, state residency.

**Application procedures. Admission:** No deadline. $50 fee, may be waived for applicants with need. Application may be submitted online. Admission notification on a rolling basis. **Financial aid:** Priority date 3/1; no closing date. FAFSA required. Applicants notified on a rolling basis starting 3/1; must reply within 2 week(s) of notification.

**Academics. Special study options:** Cross-registration, distance learning, double major, ESL, honors, internships, liberal arts/career combination. Bachelor's degree programs available on campus. **Credit/placement by examination:** AP, CLEP, IB, institutional tests. 30 credit hours maximum toward associate degree, 75 toward bachelor's. Institution follows ACE guide for credit by examination. **Support services:** Learning center, reduced course load, remedial instruction, study skills assistance, tutoring, writing center.

**Majors. Business:** Business admin, fashion, hospitality admin, tourism/travel. **Education:** Early childhood. **Family/consumer sciences:** Clothing/textiles. **Liberal arts:** Arts/sciences. **Psychology:** General.

**Most popular majors.** Business/marketing 47%, education 9%, liberal arts 25%, visual/performing arts 7%.

**Computing on campus.** 60 workstations in dormitories, library, computer center, student center. Dormitories wired for high-speed internet access and linked to campus network. Helpline, repair service available.

**Student life. Freshman orientation:** Mandatory. Preregistration for classes offered. Several 1-day preregistration days scheduled throughout summer with full 2-day orientation program prior to start of classes. **Housing:** Coed dorms, single-sex dorms available. $500 fully refundable deposit. **Activities:** Drama, film society, literary magazine, student government.

**Athletics.** NAIA. **Intercollegiate:** Baseball M, basketball, softball W. **Team name:** Falcons.

**Student services.** Adult student services, alcohol/substance abuse counseling, career counseling, student employment services, financial aid counseling, health services, personal counseling, placement for graduates, veterans' counselor. **Transfer:** Re-entry adviser, pre-admission transcript evaluation for new students. Transfer adviser, college fairs on campus for students transferring to 4-year colleges.

**Contact.** E-mail: admissions@fisher.edu
Phone: (617) 236-8818 Toll-free number: (866) 266-6007
Fax: (617) 236-5473
Robert Melaragni, Director of Admissions, Fisher College, 118 Beacon Street, Boston, MA 02116

## Greenfield Community College
**Greenfield, Massachusetts**
**www.gcc.mass.edu**

CB member
CB code: 3420

- Public 2-year community college
- Commuter campus in large town

**General.** Founded in 1962. Regionally accredited. Students may enroll in credit courses taught at Smith College, Veterans Hospital (Northampton),

Massachusetts College of Art, Massachusetts College of Liberal Arts. **Enrollment:** 1,870 degree-seeking undergraduates. **Degrees:** 268 associate awarded. **Location:** 40 miles from Springfield. **Calendar:** Semester, limited summer session. **Full-time faculty:** 60 total. **Part-time faculty:** 140 total. **Class size:** 28% < 20, 70% 20-39, 1% 40-49, less than 1% 50-99.

### Student profile.

| | | | |
|---|---|---|---|
| Out-of-state: | 11% | 25 or older: | 46% |

**Transfer out. Colleges most students transferred to 2007:** University of Massachusetts-Amherst, Elms College, Westfield State College, Smith College, Massachusetts College of Liberal Arts.

**Basis for selection.** Open admission, but selective for some programs. Special entrance requirements for occupational technology, nursing, paramedic, massage therapy, outdoor leadership programs. Students whose native language is not English must take institutional ESOL test.

**High school preparation.** Students from public high schools in the Commonwealth must be MCAS graduates, or demonstrate an ability to benefit.

**2007-2008 Annual costs.** Tuition/fees: $4,488; $12,138 out-of-state. Per-credit charge: $26 in-state; $281 out-of-state. Books/supplies: $850. Personal expenses: $1,560.

**Financial aid.** All financial aid based on need. Need-based aid available for part-time students. Work-study available nights, weekends and for part-time students.

**Application procedures. Admission:** No deadline. $10 fee ($35 out-of-state), may be waived for applicants with need. Admission notification on a rolling basis. Limited space available in nursing and outdoor leadership programs. Application priority date 2/1. **Financial aid:** Priority date 4/15; no closing date. FAFSA, institutional form required. Applicants notified on a rolling basis starting 5/1; must reply within 2 week(s) of notification.

**Academics. Special study options:** Cooperative education, cross-registration, distance learning, dual enrollment of high school students, ESL, independent study, internships, liberal arts/career combination. License preparation in nursing, paramedic, real estate. **Credit/placement by examination:** AP, CLEP, institutional tests. 15 credit hours maximum toward associate degree. **Support services:** GED test center, learning center, reduced course load, remedial instruction, study skills assistance, tutoring.

**Majors. Business:** General, accounting, administrative services, business admin. **Computer sciences:** General. **Education:** Early childhood. **Engineering:** Science. **Health:** Nursing (RN), occupational therapy assistant. **Liberal arts:** Arts/sciences. **Personal/culinary services:** Cosmetic. **Protective services:** Police science. **Visual/performing arts:** Commercial/advertising art.

**Most popular majors.** Business/marketing 17%, health sciences 14%, liberal arts 45%, visual/performing arts 12%.

**Computing on campus.** 212 workstations in library, computer center. Commuter students can connect to campus network. Online library, helpline, repair service, wireless network available.

**Student life. Freshman orientation:** Available. Preregistration for classes offered. **Activities:** Jazz band, choral groups, dance, drama, music ensembles, student government.

**Student services.** Adult student services, career counseling, services for economically disadvantaged, student employment services, financial aid counseling, health services, personal counseling, placement for graduates, veterans' counselor, women's services. **Physically disabled:** Services for visually, speech, hearing impaired. **Transfer:** Re-entry adviser, pre-admission transcript evaluation for new students. Transfer adviser, college fairs on campus for students transferring to 4-year colleges.

**Contact.** E-mail: admissions@gcc.mass.edu
Phone: (413) 775-1809 Fax: (413) 773-5129
Herbert Hentz, Director of Admissions, Greenfield Community College, One College Drive, Greenfield, MA 01301

---

## Holyoke Community College
Holyoke, Massachusetts                    **CB member**
www.hcc.mass.edu                          **CB code: 3437**

◆  Public 2-year community college
◆  Commuter campus in large town

---

**General.** Founded in 1946. Regionally accredited. **Enrollment:** 5,956 degree-seeking undergraduates; 505 non-degree-seeking students. **Degrees:** 702 associate awarded. **ROTC:** Army, Air Force. **Location:** 8 miles from Springfield. **Calendar:** Semester, extensive summer session. **Full-time faculty:** 129 total; 11% minority, 60% women. **Part-time faculty:** 342 total; 10% minority, 54% women. **Class size:** 44% < 20, 56% 20-39, less than 1% 40-49.

### Student profile. Among degree-seeking undergraduates, 1,748 enrolled as first-time, first-year students.

| | | | |
|---|---|---|---|
| Part-time: | 43% | Hispanic American: | 16% |
| Out-of-state: | 1% | Native American: | 1% |
| Women: | 62% | International: | 1% |
| African American: | 6% | 25 or older: | 33% |
| Asian American: | 2% | | |

**Transfer out. Colleges most students transferred to 2007:** University of Massachusetts-Amherst, Western New England College, American International College, Westfield State College, Elms College.

**Basis for selection.** Open admission, but selective for some programs. Special requirements for nursing, radiography, animal sciences, practical nursing programs. Audition required of music majors. Portfolio required of fine arts majors.

**2007-2008 Annual costs.** Tuition/fees: $3,428; $9,608 out-of-state. Per-credit charge: $24 in-state; $230 out-of-state. Books/supplies: $800. Personal expenses: $2,400.

**2006-2007 Financial aid. Need-based:** 79% of total undergraduate aid awarded as scholarships/grants, 21% as loans/jobs. Need-based aid available for part-time students. Work-study available nights and for part-time students. **Non-need-based:** Scholarships awarded for academics, art, leadership, music/drama.

**Application procedures. Admission:** No deadline. $10 fee, may be waived for applicants with need. Admission notification on a rolling basis. **Financial aid:** Priority date 5/1; no closing date. FAFSA required. Applicants notified on a rolling basis starting 5/1; must reply within 2 week(s) of notification.

**Academics. Special study options:** Cooperative education, cross-registration, distance learning, double major, dual enrollment of high school students, ESL, honors, independent study, internships, liberal arts/career combination, student-designed major, study abroad, teacher certification program, weekend college. License preparation in nursing. **Credit/placement by examination:** AP, CLEP, institutional tests. 30 credit hours maximum toward associate degree. **Support services:** GED preparation and test center, learning center, reduced course load, remedial instruction, study skills assistance, tutoring, writing center.

**Majors. Business:** Accounting technology, administrative services, business admin, human resources, restaurant/food services, retailing. **Computer sciences:** Applications programming. **Engineering:** General. **Engineering technology:** Environmental. **Family/consumer sciences:** Child care. **Health:** Medical radiologic technology/radiation therapy, nursing (RN), optician, veterinary technology/assistant. **Liberal arts:** Arts/sciences. **Parks/recreation:** Health/fitness, sports admin. **Protective services:** Criminal justice. **Public administration:** Social work. **Social sciences:** Geography. **Visual/performing arts:** Art.

**Most popular majors.** Business/marketing 21%, health sciences 12%, liberal arts 44%, security/protective services 8%.

**Computing on campus.** 67 workstations in computer center. Commuter students can connect to campus network. Online course registration, online library, helpline, wireless network available.

**Student life. Freshman orientation:** Mandatory. Preregistration for classes offered. **Activities:** Jazz band, choral groups, drama, literary magazine, music ensembles, musical theater, radio station, student government, student newspaper, symphony orchestra, more than 30 clubs and organizations.

**Athletics.** NJCAA. **Intercollegiate:** Baseball M, basketball, cross-country, golf, soccer, softball W, tennis, volleyball W. **Intramural:** Basketball, soccer, softball, tennis, volleyball. **Team name:** Cougars.

**Student services.** Adult student services, alcohol/substance abuse counseling, campus ministries, career counseling, services for economically disadvantaged, student employment services, financial aid counseling, health services, minority student services, on-campus daycare, personal counseling, placement for graduates, veterans' counselor, women's services. **Physically disabled:** Services for visually, speech, hearing impaired. **Transfer:** Transfer adviser, college fairs on campus for students transferring to 4-year colleges.

**Contact.** E-mail: admissions@hcc.mass.edu
Phone: (413) 552-2001 Fax: (413) 552-2045
Marcia Rosbury-Henne, Director of Admissions and Transfer Affairs,
Holyoke Community College, 303 Homestead Avenue, Holyoke, MA
01040

## ITT Technical Institute: Norwood
**Norwood, Massachusetts**
**www.itt-tech.edu**                                                **CB code: 2699**

- For-profit 2-year technical college
- Commuter campus in small city

**General.** Accredited by ACICS. **Calendar:** Quarter.

**Annual costs/financial aid.** Tuition varies by program, $260-$368 per
credit hour.

**Contact.** Phone: (781) 278-7200
Director of Recruitment, 333 Providence Highway, Norwood, MA 02062

## ITT Technical Institute: Woburn
**Woburn, Massachusetts**
**www.itt-tech.edu**

- For-profit 2-year technical college
- Small city

**General.** Accredited by ACICS. **Calendar:** Quarter.

**Annual costs/financial aid.** Tuition varies by program, $260-$368 per
credit hour.

**Contact.** Phone: (781) 937-8324
Director of Recruitment, 10 Forbes Road, Woburn, MA 01801

## Marian Court College
**Swampscott, Massachusetts**                                    **CB member**
**www.mariancourt.edu**                                          **CB code: 9100**

- Private 2-year junior college affiliated with Roman Catholic Church
- Commuter campus in large town
- Application essay, interview required

**General.** Founded in 1964. Regionally accredited. Evening division on
quarter system. **Enrollment:** 220 full-time, degree-seeking students. **Degrees:** 60 associate awarded. **Location:** 5 miles from Lynn, 20 miles from
Boston. **Calendar:** Semester, limited summer session. **Full-time faculty:** 7
total. **Part-time faculty:** 20 total.

**Basis for selection.** High school grades, recommendations, interview
important. Institutional English and math tests used for placement.

**2007-2008 Annual costs.** Tuition/fees: $13,956. Evening program: $675
for 3 credit course. Books/supplies: $600. Personal expenses: $1,957.

**Financial aid. Need-based:** Need-based aid available for part-time students. **Non-need-based:** Scholarships awarded for academics.

**Application procedures. Admission:** Priority date 5/1; no deadline. $25
fee. Admission notification on a rolling basis. Must reply by May 1 or
within 2 week(s) if notified thereafter. **Financial aid:** Priority date 4/1; no
closing date. FAFSA, institutional form required. Applicants notified on a
rolling basis starting 4/15.

**Academics.** Freshman seminar required of all freshmen. Special adult
learner freshman seminars available. Writing lab available evenings for extra assistance. **Special study options:** Cross-registration, double major, honors, independent study, internships, weekend college. Member Northeast
Consortium of Colleges and Universities in Massachusetts. **Credit/
placement by examination:** CLEP, institutional tests. 15 credit hours maximum toward associate degree. **Support services:** Reduced course load, tutoring.

**Majors. Business:** Accounting, administrative services, business admin,
hospitality admin, human resources, management information systems, marketing, tourism/travel. **Computer sciences:** Data entry, web page design.
**Health:** Medical secretary, medical transcription. **Legal studies:** Legal secretary, paralegal. **Liberal arts:** Arts/sciences. **Protective services:** Law enforcement admin, security services.

**Computing on campus.** 53 workstations in library, computer center,
student center.

**Student life. Activities:** Literary magazine, student government, Mercy
Outreach, travel club, student life organization.

**Student services.** Adult student services, career counseling, student employment services, health services, personal counseling, placement for graduates. **Transfer:** Transfer adviser, college fairs on campus for students transferring to 4-year colleges.

**Contact.** E-mail: info@mariancourt.edu
Phone: (781) 595-6768 Fax: (781) 595-3560
Bryan Boppert, Associate Director of Admissions, Marian Court College,
35 Little's Point Road, Swampscott, MA 01907-2896

## Massachusetts Bay Community College
**Wellesley Hills, Massachusetts**                               **CB member**
**www.massbay.edu**                                              **CB code: 3294**

- Public 2-year community college
- Commuter campus in large town

**General.** Founded in 1961. Regionally accredited. **Enrollment:** 4,473 degree-
seeking undergraduates; 545 non-degree-seeking students. **Degrees:** 414 associate awarded. **Location:** 13 miles from Boston. **Calendar:** Semester,
extensive summer session. **Full-time faculty:** 74 total. **Part-time faculty:**
250 total. **Class size:** 40% < 20, 58% 20-39, less than 1% 40-49, 1% 50-99.
**Special facilities:** Advanced technology center (technology and health science laboratories). **Partnerships:** Formal partnerships with Toyota, Chrysler,
General Motors, EMC2.

**Student profile.** Among degree-seeking undergraduates, 1,180 enrolled
as first-time, first-year students.

| | | | |
|---|---|---|---|
| Part-time: | 57% | Asian American: | 4% |
| Out-of-state: | 1% | Hispanic American: | 10% |
| Women: | 59% | International: | 3% |
| African American: | 14% | 25 or older: | 42% |

**Transfer out. Colleges most students transferred to 2007:** Framingham
State College, University of Massachusetts-Boston, Northeastern University, Bentley College.

**Basis for selection.** Open admission, but selective for some programs.
Special requirements for nursing, radiologic technology, paramedic, respiratory therapy programs.

**High school preparation.** Some programs require special academic preparation.

**2007-2008 Annual costs.** Tuition/fees: $3,650; $9,830 out-of-state. Per-
credit charge: $24 in-state; $230 out-of-state. NEBHE tuition rate is 150%
of in-state cost and fees are approximately the same. Books/supplies: $800.
Personal expenses: $2,966.

**2006-2007 Financial aid. Need-based:** 64% of total undergraduate aid
awarded as scholarships/grants, 36% as loans/jobs. Need-based aid available for part-time students.

**Application procedures. Admission:** No deadline. $20 fee, may be
waived for applicants with need. Application may be submitted online. Admission notification on a rolling basis. **Financial aid:** Priority date 8/30; no
closing date. FAFSA, institutional form required. Applicants notified on a
rolling basis starting 4/1.

**Academics. Special study options:** Cooperative education, distance learning, dual enrollment of high school students, honors, internships, liberal
arts/career combination, study abroad. License preparation in nursing, paramedic, physical therapy, radiology. **Credit/placement by examination:** AP,
CLEP, IB, institutional tests. 30 credit hours maximum toward associate
degree. **Support services:** Learning center, reduced course load, remedial
instruction, study skills assistance, tutoring, writing center.

**Majors. Biology:** Marine. **Business:** Accounting, business admin, hospitality admin. **Communications:** General. **Computer sciences:** General, computer science, information systems. **Engineering technology:** Automotive,
computer, electrical, laser/optical. **Family/consumer sciences:** Child care.
**Health:** Medical informatics, medical radiologic technology/radiation therapy,
nursing (RN), occupational therapy assistant, physical therapy assistant, respiratory therapy technology. **Legal studies:** Paralegal. **Liberal arts:** Arts/
sciences. **Protective services:** Forensics, law enforcement admin. **Public
administration:** Human services. **Science technology:** Biological, chemical. **Social sciences:** General. **Visual/performing arts:** Dramatic.

**Computing on campus.** 550 workstations in library, computer center, student center. Commuter students can connect to campus network. Wireless network available.

**Student life. Freshman orientation:** Available. **Activities:** Drama, student government, student newspaper, volunteer service corps, Christian Fellowship, Hillel, New World club, Latino club, sexual orientation support group.

**Athletics.** NJCAA. **Intercollegiate:** Baseball M, basketball, cross-country, golf, soccer M, softball W, tennis. **Intramural:** Ice hockey M, soccer. **Team name:** Buccaneers.

**Student services.** Adult student services, career counseling, student employment services, health services, personal counseling, placement for graduates, veterans' counselor. **Transfer:** Pre-admission transcript evaluation for new students. Transfer adviser, college fairs on campus for students transferring to 4-year colleges.

**Contact.** E-mail: info@massbay.edu
Phone: (781) 239-2500 Fax: (781) 239-1047
Donna Raposa, Director for Admissions, Massachusetts Bay Community College, 50 Oakland Street, Wellesley Hills, MA 02481

## Massasoit Community College
Brockton, Massachusetts — CB member
www.massasoit.mass.edu — CB code: 3549

- Public 2-year community college
- Commuter campus in small city

**General.** Founded in 1966. Regionally accredited. **Location:** 25 miles from Boston. **Calendar:** Semester.

**Annual costs/financial aid.** Tuition/fees (2007-2008): $3,330; $9,510 out-of-state. Books/supplies: $725. Personal expenses: $1,000. Need-based financial aid available for full-time students.

**Contact.** Phone: (508) 588-9100 ext. 1411
Director of Admissions, One Massasoit Boulevard, Brockton, MA 02302-3996

## Middlesex Community College
Bedford, Massachusetts — CB member
www.middlesex.mass.edu — CB code: 3554

- Public 2-year community college
- Commuter campus in small city

**General.** Founded in 1969. Regionally accredited. Second main campus located in Lowell. **Enrollment:** 7,234 degree-seeking undergraduates. **Degrees:** 832 associate awarded. **ROTC:** Air Force. **Location:** 16 miles from Boston. **Calendar:** Semester, limited summer session. **Full-time faculty:** 124 total. **Part-time faculty:** 440 total. **Special facilities:** Dental clinic, law center. **Partnerships:** Formal partnerships with business and industry links.

**Student profile.**

| | | | |
|---|---|---|---|
| Out-of-state: | 1% | 25 or older: | 49% |

**Basis for selection.** Open admission, but selective for some programs. Admission to some health programs based on prerequisite courses in mathematics and science and placement test scores. Some health, counseling, business honors and biotechnology programs require essays, letters of reference and interview.

**High school preparation.** For some health programs, 1 unit each of biology and chemistry required in addition to 2 units of mathematics at the Algebra I level and above.

**2007-2008 Annual costs.** Tuition/fees: $3,860; $13,010 out-of-state. New England resident tuition $135 per credit hour. Books/supplies: $600. Personal expenses: $600.

**Financial aid.** All financial aid based on need. Need-based aid available for part-time students. Work-study available nights, weekends and for part-time students. **Additional information:** Application priority date 5/1 for Massachusetts state funds.

**Application procedures. Admission:** No deadline. No application fee. Application may be submitted online. Admission notification on a rolling basis. Closing date February 1 for dental hygiene, April 1 for diagnostic

medical sonography. Applications received later considered on space-available basis. Applicants must reply within 2 weeks of acceptance. **Financial aid:** Priority date 5/1; no closing date. FAFSA, institutional form required. Applicants notified on a rolling basis starting 6/1; must reply within 2 week(s) of notification.

**Academics. Special study options:** Accelerated study, cooperative education, cross-registration, distance learning, dual enrollment of high school students, ESL, exchange student, honors, independent study, internships, liberal arts/career combination, study abroad, weekend college. **Credit/placement by examination:** AP, CLEP, institutional tests. 45 credit hours maximum toward associate degree. **Support services:** GED preparation, learning center, pre-admission summer program, reduced course load, remedial instruction, study skills assistance, tutoring, writing center.

**Majors. Biology:** Biotechnology. **Business:** Accounting, administrative services, business admin, fashion, hospitality admin, office management, office technology, sales/distribution. **Communications:** General. **Communications technology:** Desktop publishing. **Computer sciences:** Computer science, networking. **Education:** Early childhood. **Engineering:** Science. **Engineering technology:** Drafting. **Health:** Clinical lab technology, dental assistant, dental hygiene, dental lab technology, health services, medical assistant, medical radiologic technology/radiation therapy, nursing (RN), sonography. **Legal studies:** Paralegal. **Liberal arts:** Arts/sciences. **Mechanic/repair:** Aircraft, automotive. **Protective services:** Fire safety technology, law enforcement admin. **Science technology:** Biological. **Visual/performing arts:** General, commercial/advertising art, dramatic, studio arts.

**Most popular majors.** Business/marketing 24%, health sciences 19%, liberal arts 32%, security/protective services 10%, trade and industry 10%.

**Computing on campus.** 350 workstations in library, computer center. Helpline available.

**Student life. Freshman orientation:** Available. **Housing:** Dorm rooms contractable on space-available basis at University of Massachusetts-Lowell. **Activities:** Drama, student government, student newspaper, international club, student activities, mental health club, early childhood education club, art club, MassPIRG.

**Athletics. Intramural:** Table tennis, volleyball.

**Student services.** Adult student services, career counseling, student employment services, health services, on-campus daycare, personal counseling, placement for graduates, veterans' counselor. **Physically disabled:** Services for visually, speech, hearing impaired. **Transfer:** Pre-admission transcript evaluation for new students. Transfer adviser, college fairs on campus for students transferring to 4-year colleges.

**Contact.** E-mail: admissions@middlesex.mass.edu
Phone: (978) 656-3207 Toll-free number: (800) 818-3434
Fax: (978) 656-3322
Laurie Dimitrov, Director of Admissions and Recruitment, Middlesex Community College, 33 Kearney Square, Lowell, MA 01852-1987

## Mount Wachusett Community College
Gardner, Massachusetts — CB member
www.mwcc.edu — CB code: 3545

- Public 2-year community college
- Commuter campus in large town

**General.** Founded in 1963. Regionally accredited. **Enrollment:** 3,604 degree-seeking undergraduates; 543 non-degree-seeking students. **Degrees:** 475 associate awarded. **Location:** 59 miles from Boston. **Calendar:** Semester, extensive summer session. **Full-time faculty:** 71 total; 14% have terminal degrees, 6% minority, 65% women. **Part-time faculty:** 152 total; 5% minority, 64% women. **Class size:** 60% < 20, 35% 20-39, less than 1% 40-49, less than 1% 50-99. **Special facilities:** On-site child-care facility, theater, fitness and wellness center, pool. **Partnerships:** Formal partnership with Tech Prep (high school articulation programs), Nypro, Adams and Associates.

**Student profile.** Among degree-seeking undergraduates, 964 enrolled as first-time, first-year students.

| | | | |
|---|---|---|---|
| Part-time: | 53% | Asian American: | 2% |
| Out-of-state: | 4% | Hispanic American: | 9% |
| Women: | 66% | International: | 1% |
| African American: | 6% | 25 or older: | 45% |

**Transfer out.** 25% of students enrolled in the transfer program go on to 4-year colleges. **Colleges most students transferred to 2007:** Fitchburg State College, University of Massachusetts Amherst, Worcester State College, University of Massachusetts Lowell.

**Basis for selection.** Open admission, but selective for some programs. Special requirements for all health science programs with emphasis on college level academic coursework, life science or other science programs, other academic preparation and work experience. Interview required for early admission of high school students. Portfolio recommended for art programs. **Homeschooled:** Statement describing homeschool structure and mission, transcript of courses and grades, interview required. Applicants must submit copies of curriculum approvals from local secondary school district. **Learning Disabled:** Students advised to meet with coordinator of disabilities services during admissions process.

**High school preparation.** 16 units recommended. Recommended units include English 4, mathematics 3, social studies 1, history 1, science 2 (laboratory 2), foreign language 2 and academic electives 3.

**2007-2008 Annual costs.** Tuition/fees: $4,420; $10,570 out-of-state. Per-credit charge: $25 in-state; $230 out-of-state. New England resident tuition is $1,312. Books/supplies: $1,000. Personal expenses: $1,700.

**2007-2008 Financial aid.** All financial aid based on need. 418 full-time freshmen applied for aid; 316 were judged to have need; 314 of these received aid. Average need met was 67%. Average scholarship/grant was $4,092; average loan $1,423. 69% of total undergraduate aid awarded as scholarships/grants, 31% as loans/jobs. Need-based aid available for part-time students. Work-study available nights and for part-time students.

**Application procedures. Admission:** Priority date 4/1; no deadline. $10 fee, may be waived for applicants with need. Application may be submitted online. Admission notification on a rolling basis beginning on or about 12/1. Nursing, Dental Hygiene must apply by February 1. Clinical Laboratory Science, Physical Therapy Assistant, and Massage Therapy must apply by March 1. **Financial aid:** Priority date 4/15; no closing date. FAFSA, institutional form required. Applicants notified on a rolling basis starting 5/1.

**Academics. Special study options:** Cooperative education, distance learning, double major, dual enrollment of high school students, ESL, honors, independent study, internships, study abroad, weekend college. License preparation in dental hygiene, nursing, physical therapy. **Credit/placement by examination:** AP, CLEP, IB, institutional tests. 30 credit hours maximum toward associate degree. **Support services:** GED preparation and test center, learning center, pre-admission summer program, reduced course load, remedial instruction, study skills assistance, tutoring, writing center.

**Majors. Biology:** Biotechnology. **Business:** Business admin, executive assistant. **Communications technology:** Radio/tv. **Computer sciences:** General, computer graphics, web page design. **Conservation:** Environmental studies. **Engineering technology:** Computer, plastics. **Family/consumer sciences:** Child care, child development. **Health:** Clinical lab technology, dental hygiene, medical assistant, mental health services, nursing (RN), physical therapy assistant. **Legal studies:** Paralegal. **Liberal arts:** Arts/sciences. **Mechanic/repair:** Automotive. **Protective services:** Corrections, criminal justice, fire safety technology, law enforcement admin. **Public administration:** Human services. **Visual/performing arts:** Art.

**Most popular majors.** Business/marketing 16%, health sciences 25%, liberal arts 23%, public administration/social services 6%.

**Computing on campus.** 415 workstations in library, computer center. Commuter students can connect to campus network. Online course registration, online library, helpline, wireless network available.

**Student life. Freshman orientation:** Available. Preregistration for classes offered. One-day session held a week before start of classes. **Housing:** Limited housing available on campus of Fitchburg State College. **Activities:** Drama, international student organizations, literary magazine, musical theater, student government, student newspaper, art club, nursing clubs, student government association, Pride, dental hygiene club, Green Society, Campus Crusade for Christ, Campus Activities Team for Students, MassPIRG, ALANA club.

**Athletics. Intramural:** Badminton, basketball, football (tackle), softball, table tennis, volleyball, water polo. **Team name:** Mountain Lions.

**Student services.** Adult student services, alcohol/substance abuse counseling, campus ministries, career counseling, services for economically disadvantaged, student employment services, financial aid counseling, health services, minority student services, on-campus daycare, personal counseling, placement for graduates, veterans' counselor, women's services. **Physically disabled:** Services for visually, speech, hearing impaired. **Learning disabled:** Comprehensive services available. **Transfer:** Pre-admission transcript evaluation for new students. Transfer adviser, college fairs on campus for students transferring to 4-year colleges.

**Contact.**   E-mail: admissions@mwcc.mass.edu
Phone: (978) 632-6600 ext. 110 Fax: (978) 630-9554
John Walsh, Director of Admissions, Mount Wachusett Community College, 444 Green Street, Gardner, MA 01440-1000

## New England College of Finance
**Boston, Massachusetts**
www.finance.edu                                   CB code: 3376

- For-profit 2-year business college
- Very large city
- Interview required

**General.** Founded in 1909. Regionally accredited. **Enrollment:** 559 degree-seeking undergraduates. **Degrees:** 72 associate awarded. **Calendar:** Continuous, limited summer session. **Part-time faculty:** 180 total. **Partnerships:** Formal partnerships with several financial services companies.

**Basis for selection.** Open admission. Academic background, professional recommendation, demonstrated commitment to program and banking, and interview considered.

**2007-2008 Annual costs.** Cost of 3 credit course is $850 for employees of member companies; cost for non-members is $1025.

**Financial aid. Additional information:** No college-administered financial aid. 90% of students receive tuition reimbursement from employer.

**Application procedures. Admission:** No deadline. $50 fee. Admission notification on a rolling basis. **Financial aid:** No deadline.

**Academics. Special study options:** Accelerated study, dual enrollment of high school students, independent study, student-designed major. **Credit/placement by examination:** CLEP. 9 credit hours maximum toward associate degree. **Support services:** Remedial instruction, tutoring.

**Majors. Business:** General, banking/financial services, business admin.

**Computing on campus.** 24 workstations in computer center.

**Student life. Activities:** Film society, literary magazine.

**Student services.** Personal counseling. **Transfer:** Pre-admission transcript evaluation for new students. Transfer adviser for students transferring to 4-year colleges.

**Contact.**   Phone: (617) 951-2350 Fax: (617) 951-2533
Julie Peterson, Vice President of Admissions, New England College of Finance, 10 High Street, Suite 204, Boston, MA 02110

## North Shore Community College
**Danvers, Massachusetts**                          CB member
www.northshore.edu                                 CB code: 3651

- Public 2-year community college
- Commuter campus in small city

**General.** Founded in 1965. Regionally accredited. Additional campus in Lynn and corporate training center in Beverly. **Enrollment:** 6,331 degree-seeking undergraduates; 776 non-degree-seeking students. **Degrees:** 651 associate awarded. **Location:** 25 miles from Boston. **Calendar:** Semester, limited summer session. **Full-time faculty:** 138 total; 85% have terminal degrees, 12% minority, 64% women. **Part-time faculty:** 287 total; 8% have terminal degrees, 3% minority, 53% women. **Class size:** 49% < 20, 51% 20-39, less than 1% 40-49, less than 1% 50-99. **Special facilities:** Agricultural facility for horticulture, animal science, culinary arts. **Partnerships:** Formal partnership with Verizon, area high schools for Tech Prep, consortium providing distance learning opportunities.

**Student profile.** Among degree-seeking undergraduates, 35% enrolled in a transfer program, 54% enrolled in a vocational program, 1,578 enrolled as first-time, first-year students, 616 transferred in from other institutions.

| | | | |
|---|---|---|---|
| Part-time: | 53% | 25 or older: | 40% |
| Women: | 60% | | |

**Transfer out. Colleges most students transferred to 2007:** Salem State College, University of Massachusetts-Boston, University of Massachusetts-Lowell, Suffolk University, Northeastern University, Lesley College.

**Basis for selection.** Open admission, but selective for some programs. School achievement record considered for health, engineering, computer science programs; some prerequisite course requirements exist. Pre-Nursing Assessment Test required for pre-nursing program; Nurse Entrance Exam required for LPN program. Essay and/or interview may be required in some programs, including health and human services. **Homeschooled:** Home program must be affiliated with accredited agency or local school system. **Learning Disabled:** Students must identify disability, individual test administration available.

**High school preparation.** One algebra, 1 biology, and 1 chemistry required for some health programs and for biotechnology. Trigonometry, physics, chemistry required for engineering. Trigonometry, computer literacy required for computer science.

**2007-2008 Annual costs.** Tuition/fees: $3,630; $10,590 out-of-state. Per-credit charge: $25 in-state; $257 out-of-state. New England regional tuition: $133.50 per credit hour. Books/supplies: $800. Personal expenses: $1,300.

**2006-2007 Financial aid.** All financial aid based on need. Average need met was 29%. Average scholarship/grant was $2,034; average loan $1,559. 75% of total undergraduate aid awarded as scholarships/grants, 25% as loans/jobs. Need-based aid available for part-time students. Work-study available for part-time students.

**Application procedures. Admission:** No deadline. No application fee. Application may be submitted online. Admission notification on a rolling basis. **Financial aid:** Priority date 5/1; no closing date. FAFSA required. Applicants notified on a rolling basis starting 6/1; must reply within 2 week(s) of notification.

**Academics.** Participation in state dual enrollment program which allows high school juniors and seniors to take credit courses contingent upon approval of high school principal. Tuition and fees paid by state. **Special study options:** Accelerated study, cross-registration, distance learning, double major, dual enrollment of high school students, ESL, honors, independent study, internships, student-designed major, study abroad, weekend college. License preparation in aviation, nursing, occupational therapy, physical therapy, radiology, real estate. **Credit/placement by examination:** AP, CLEP, institutional tests. 45 credit hours maximum toward associate degree. DANTES, Excelsior, CLEP tests accepted. CLEP tests in Freshman Composition and Analyzing and Interpreting Literature must be accompanied by essay; lab credit not awarded for Biology and Chemistry tests. **Support services:** GED preparation and test center, learning center, remedial instruction, study skills assistance, tutoring, writing center.

**Majors. Agriculture:** Floriculture, horticulture. **Business:** Accounting technology, business admin, executive assistant, hospitality admin, hotel/motel admin, marketing. **Computer sciences:** General, computer science, programming. **Education:** Early childhood, elementary, kindergarten/preschool, teacher assistance. **Engineering:** General. **Engineering technology:** Telecommunications. **Family/consumer sciences:** Aging. **Health:** Dietetic technician, medical secretary, mental health services, nursing (RN), occupational therapy assistant, physical therapy assistant, radiologic technology/medical imaging, respiratory therapy technology, substance abuse counseling, veterinary technology/assistant. **Legal studies:** Legal secretary, paralegal. **Liberal arts:** Arts/sciences. **Personal/culinary services:** Chef training. **Protective services:** Criminal justice, fire safety technology. **Science technology:** Biological. **Transportation:** Airline/commercial pilot, aviation management. **Visual/performing arts:** Graphic design.

**Most popular majors.** Business/marketing 8%, family/consumer sciences 7%, health sciences 28%, liberal arts 26%, security/protective services 15%.

**Computing on campus.** 300 workstations in library, computer center, student center. Commuter students can connect to campus network. Online course registration, online library, helpline available.

**Student life. Freshman orientation:** Available. Preregistration for classes offered. All day event includes placement testing, adviser assistance. **Activities:** Drama, student government, student newspaper, students against drug abuse, early childhood club, marketing club, engineering club, Harvard Model UN, Women in Transition club, multicultural society, poets and writers club, gerontology club, occupational therapy assistant club.

**Athletics. Team name:** Seahawks.

**Student services.** Career counseling, services for economically disadvantaged, student employment services, financial aid counseling, health services, on-campus daycare, personal counseling, placement for graduates, veterans' counselor, women's services. **Physically disabled:** Services for visually, speech, hearing impaired. **Learning disabled:** Comprehensive services available. **Transfer:** Pre-admission transcript evaluation for new students. Transfer adviser, college fairs on campus for students transferring to 4-year colleges.

**Contact.** E-mail: info@northshore.edu
Phone: (978) 762-4188 Fax: (978) 762-4015
Jennifer Kirk, Director of Recruitment, North Shore Community College, One Ferncroft Road, Danvers, MA 01923-0840

---

## Northern Essex Community College
**Haverhill, Massachusetts**

CB member

www.necc.mass.edu

CB code: 3674

▶ Public 2-year community college
▶ Commuter campus in small city

**General.** Founded in 1960. Regionally accredited. Additional campus in Lawrence. **Enrollment:** 5,618 degree-seeking undergraduates; 908 non-degree-seeking students. **Degrees:** 565 associate awarded. **Location:** 40 miles from Boston. **Calendar:** Semester, extensive summer session. **Full-time faculty:** 99 total; 11% minority, 62% women. **Part-time faculty:** 388 total; 6% minority, 58% women. **Class size:** 38% < 20, 62% 20-39.

**Student profile.** Among degree-seeking undergraduates, 40% enrolled in a transfer program, 60% enrolled in a vocational program, 1,310 enrolled as first-time, first-year students, 2,003 transferred in from other institutions.

| | | | |
|---|---|---|---|
| Part-time: | 59% | Women: | 64% |
| Out-of-state: | 16% | | |

**Basis for selection.** Open admission, but selective for some programs. Special requirements for technology studies (engineering, computer, computer maintenance, electronics) and health and human services. Entrance examination required for schools of practical/vocational nursing. Interview required of health and human services majors.

**High school preparation.** Health and technologies programs have specific math and/or science requirements.

**2007-2008 Annual costs.** Tuition/fees: $3,420; $10,650 out-of-state. Per-credit charge: $25 in-state; $266 out-of-state. New England residents pay $122 per credit hour. Books/supplies: $800. Personal expenses: $850.

**Financial aid. Need-based:** Need-based aid available for part-time students. **Non-need-based:** Scholarships awarded for academics.

**Application procedures. Admission:** Priority date 2/1; no deadline. $25 fee. Admission notification on a rolling basis. **Financial aid:** Priority date 5/1; no closing date. FAFSA required. Applicants notified on a rolling basis starting 3/1; must reply within 2 week(s) of notification.

**Academics. Special study options:** Accelerated study, combined bachelor's/graduate degree, cooperative education, cross-registration, distance learning, double major, dual enrollment of high school students, ESL, exchange student, honors, internships, liberal arts/career combination, study abroad, weekend college. License preparation in dental hygiene, nursing, paramedic, radiology, real estate. **Credit/placement by examination:** AP, CLEP, institutional tests. 36 credit hours maximum toward associate degree. **Support services:** GED preparation and test center, learning center, pre-admission summer program, reduced course load, remedial instruction, study skills assistance, tutoring, writing center.

**Majors. Business:** General, accounting, administrative services, business admin, finance, international, logistics, marketing, office management, office technology, tourism promotion, tourism/travel. **Communications technology:** General. **Computer sciences:** General, computer graphics, computer science, information systems, programming. **Education:** Business, early childhood. **Engineering:** Science. **Engineering technology:** Biomedical, electrical. **Family/consumer sciences:** Child care. **Foreign languages:** Sign language interpretation. **Health:** EMT paramedic, medical records admin, medical secretary, mental health services, nursing (RN), respiratory therapy technology, substance abuse counseling. **Legal studies:** Paralegal. **Liberal arts:** Arts/sciences. **Parks/recreation:** Sports admin. **Protective services:** Criminal justice. **Public administration:** Social work. **Visual/performing arts:** Commercial/advertising art, design. **Other:** Polysomnograry/sleep technology.

**Computing on campus.** 400 workstations in library, computer center, student center. Commuter students can connect to campus network. Online course registration, online library, helpline, wireless network available.

**Student life. Freshman orientation:** Mandatory. Preregistration for classes offered. **Activities:** Choral groups, dance, drama, literary magazine, student government, student newspaper, American Sign Language club, Hispanic cultural club, women's resource network, social club (students with disabilities), Bible club.

**Athletics.** NJCAA. **Intercollegiate:** Baseball M, basketball, golf, soccer M, softball W. **Intramural:** Basketball, cross-country, golf, skiing, softball, table tennis, volleyball. **Team name:** Scarlet Knights.

**Student services.** Adult student services, career counseling, services for economically disadvantaged, student employment services, financial aid counseling, health services, on-campus daycare, personal counseling, placement for graduates, veterans' counselor, women's services. **Physically disabled:** Services for visually, speech, hearing impaired. **Learning disabled:** Comprehensive services available. **Transfer:** Transfer adviser, college fairs on campus for students transferring to 4-year colleges.

**Contact.** E-mail: admissions@necc.mass.edu
Phone: (978) 556-3600
Nora Sheridan, Director of Admissions, Northern Essex Community College, 100 Elliott Street, Haverhill, MA 01830-2399

## Quincy College
**Quincy, Massachusetts**       **CB member**
**www.quincycollege.edu**       **CB code: 3713**

◆ Public 2-year community college
◆ Commuter campus in small city

**General.** Founded in 1956. Regionally accredited. Branch campus in Plymouth. **Enrollment:** 3,800 degree-seeking undergraduates. **Degrees:** 416 associate awarded. **Location:** 10 miles from downtown Boston. **Calendar:** Semester, extensive summer session. **Full-time faculty:** 40 total. **Part-time faculty:** 290 total.

**Student profile.**

| | | | |
|---|---|---|---|
| Out-of-state: | 1% | 25 or older: | 51% |

**Basis for selection.** Open admission, but selective for some programs. Admission to health career programs based on test scores and high school record. College administers MAPS and Michigan exam for placement upon enrollment.

**High school preparation.** College-preparatory program with biology and chemistry required for registered nursing program.

**2007-2008 Annual costs.** Tuition/fees: $4,470. Per-credit charge: $149. Books/supplies: $400. Personal expenses: $400.

**Application procedures. Admission:** No deadline. $30 fee, may be waived for applicants with need. Admission notification on a rolling basis. **Financial aid:** FAFSA required. Applicants notified on a rolling basis starting 5/1; must reply within 2 week(s) of notification.

**Academics. Special study options:** Accelerated study, dual enrollment of high school students, independent study, internships. **Credit/placement by examination:** CLEP, institutional tests. 30 credit hours maximum toward associate degree. **Support services:** Learning center, pre-admission summer program, reduced course load, remedial instruction, tutoring.

**Majors. Business:** General, office technology, tourism/travel. **Computer sciences:** Computer science. **Conservation:** General. **Education:** Early childhood. **Health:** Nursing (RN). **Legal studies:** Paralegal. **Liberal arts:** Arts/sciences. **Protective services:** Criminal justice.

**Computing on campus.** 60 workstations in library, computer center. Wireless network available.

**Student life. Freshman orientation:** Available. **Activities:** Drama.

**Student services.** Adult student services, alcohol/substance abuse counseling, career counseling, student employment services, financial aid counseling, minority student services. **Transfer:** College fairs on campus for students transferring to 4-year colleges.

**Contact.** E-mail: admissions@quincycollege.edu
Phone: (617) 984-1700 Toll-free number: (800) 698-1700
Fax: (617) 984-1669
Lisa Stack, Director of Admissions, Quincy College, 24 Saville Avenue, Quincy, MA 02169

## Quinsigamond Community College
**Worcester, Massachusetts**       **CB member**
**www.qcc.edu**       **CB code: 3714**

◆ Public 2-year community college
◆ Commuter campus in small city

**General.** Founded in 1963. Regionally accredited. **Enrollment:** 5,262 degree-seeking undergraduates; 1,393 non-degree-seeking students. **Degrees:** 575 associate awarded. **ROTC:** Army, Air Force. **Location:** 45 miles from Boston. **Calendar:** Semester, extensive summer session. **Full-time faculty:** 107 total; 66% women. **Part-time faculty:** 304 total. **Special facilities:** Dental hygiene clinic, athletic center. **Partnerships:** Formal partnerships with Intel Corporation, Verizon, National Grid.

**Student profile.** Among degree-seeking undergraduates, 45% enrolled in a transfer program, 34% enrolled in a vocational program, 1,465 enrolled as first-time, first-year students, 524 transferred in from other institutions.

| | | | |
|---|---|---|---|
| Part-time: | 46% | Women: | 59% |
| Out-of-state: | 2% | 25 or older: | 35% |

**Transfer out. Colleges most students transferred to 2007:** Worcester State College, University of Massachusetts-Amherst, Assumption College, Anna Maria College, Framingham State College.

**Basis for selection.** Open admission, but selective for some programs. Special requirements for health programs. **Adult students:** SAT/ACT scores not required.

**High school preparation.** Recommended units include English 4, mathematics 3, social studies 2, history 1, science 3 (laboratory 2), foreign language 2 and computer science 1. English, college math, and laboratory sciences required for health programs. English and math required for business, technology, and early childhood education.

**2007-2008 Annual costs.** Tuition/fees: $3,870; $10,050 out-of-state. Per-credit charge: $24 in-state; $230 out-of-state. Books/supplies: $900. Personal expenses: $1,332.

**Financial aid.** All financial aid based on need. Need-based aid available for part-time students. Work-study available nights, weekends and for part-time students.

**Application procedures. Admission:** No deadline. $20 fee ($50 out-of-state), may be waived for applicants with need. Application may be submitted online. Admission notification on a rolling basis beginning on or about 10/1. Must reply by May 1 or within 2 week(s) if notified thereafter. **Financial aid:** Priority date 4/1; no closing date. FAFSA required. Applicants notified on a rolling basis starting 4/1.

**Academics.** Specialized academic support to those with disabilities. **Special study options:** Accelerated study, cooperative education, cross-registration, distance learning, double major, dual enrollment of high school students, ESL, honors, independent study, internships, liberal arts/career combination, weekend college. Member 13-school Worcester consortium. License preparation in dental hygiene, nursing, occupational therapy, paramedic, radiology. **Credit/placement by examination:** AP, CLEP, IB, institutional tests. **Support services:** GED preparation and test center, learning center, reduced course load, remedial instruction, study skills assistance, tutoring, writing center.

**Majors. Biology:** Biotechnology. **Business:** Administrative services, business admin, hotel/motel admin, office/clerical, restaurant/food services. **Communications technology:** Graphics. **Computer sciences:** General, applications programming, computer forensics, programming. **Education:** Early childhood. **Engineering:** General, computer, computer hardware, electrical, manufacturing. **Engineering technology:** Computer, electrical, electromechanical, manufacturing, telecommunications. **Family/consumer sciences:** Institutional food production. **Health:** Dental hygiene, EMT paramedic, medical assistant, medical radiologic technology/radiation therapy, medical secretary, nursing (RN), occupational therapy assistant, office assistant, respiratory therapy technology. **Liberal arts:** Arts/sciences. **Mechanic/repair:** Automotive, electronics/electrical. **Personal/culinary services:** Food service, restaurant/catering. **Protective services:** Firefighting, law enforcement admin. **Public administration:** Human services.

**Most popular majors.** Business/marketing 13%, health sciences 21%, liberal arts 22%, security/protective services 12%.

**Computing on campus.** 400 workstations in library, computer center. Helpline, wireless network available.

**Student life. Freshman orientation:** Available. Preregistration for classes offered. 1/2 day program; some academic majors hold specialized orientation programs. **Activities:** Campus ministries, choral groups, drama, film society, literary magazine, student government, student newspaper, multicultural club, several occupational groups, academic clubs.

**Athletics.** NJCAA. **Intercollegiate:** Baseball M, basketball, softball W. **Intramural:** Basketball, football (non-tackle), soccer, volleyball. **Team name:** Chiefs.

**Student services.** Campus ministries, career counseling, student employment services, financial aid counseling, health services, minority student services, on-campus daycare, personal counseling, placement for graduates, veterans' counselor. **Physically disabled:** Services for visually, speech, hearing impaired. **Learning disabled:** Comprehensive services available. **Transfer:** Transfer adviser, college fairs on campus for students transferring to 4-year colleges.

**Contact.** E-mail: qccadm@qcc.mass.edu
Phone: (508) 854-4262 Fax: (508) 854-4357
James Fowler, Director of Admissions, Quinsigamond Community College, 670 West Boylston Street, Worcester, MA 01606

## Roxbury Community College
**Roxbury Crossing, Massachusetts**     **CB member**
**www.rcc.mass.edu**     **CB code: 3740**

▶ Public 2-year community college
▶ Commuter campus in very large city

**General.** Founded in 1973. Regionally accredited. **Enrollment:** 2,167 degree-seeking undergraduates; 231 non-degree-seeking students. **Degrees:** 172 associate awarded. **ROTC:** Army. **Calendar:** Semester, extensive summer session. **Full-time faculty:** 50 total; 52% minority, 56% women. **Part-time faculty:** 106 total; 42% women. **Class size:** 73% < 20, 27% 20-39. **Special facilities:** Indoor track and field facilties. **Partnerships:** Formal partnerships with local employers.

**Student profile.** Among degree-seeking undergraduates, 48% enrolled in a transfer program, 52% enrolled in a vocational program, 621 enrolled as first-time, first-year students, 32 transferred in from other institutions.

| | | | |
|---|---|---|---|
| Part-time: | 58% | Hispanic American: | 13% |
| Women: | 69% | International: | 2% |
| African American: | 55% | 25 or older: | 61% |
| Asian American: | 1% | | |

**Transfer out.** 25% of students enrolled in the transfer program go on to 4-year colleges.

**Basis for selection.** Open admission, but selective for some programs. Nursing program has specific admissions criteria.

**2007-2008 Annual costs.** Tuition/fees: $3,660; $10,290 out-of-state. Per-credit charge: $26 in-state; $247 out-of-state. New England Regional per-credit-hour charge $105. Books/supplies: $800. Personal expenses: $1,800.

**Financial aid.** All financial aid based on need. Need-based aid available for part-time students.

**Application procedures. Admission:** No deadline. $10 fee ($35 out-of-state), may be waived for applicants with need. Admission notification on a rolling basis. **Financial aid:** Priority date 5/1; no closing date. FAFSA, institutional form required. Applicants notified on a rolling basis starting 6/15; must reply within 2 week(s) of notification.

**Academics. Special study options:** Cross-registration, double major, dual enrollment of high school students, ESL, honors, independent study, internships, liberal arts/career combination. License preparation in nursing. **Credit/placement by examination:** CLEP, institutional tests. **Support services:** GED preparation and test center, learning center, remedial instruction, tutoring.

**Majors. Architecture:** Technology. **Biology:** General. **Business:** Accounting, administrative services, business admin, hospitality/recreation, management information systems, office management, office technology. **Communications technology:** Radio/tv. **Computer sciences:** General, applications programming. **Conservation:** General. **Education:** Early childhood. **Engineering technology:** CAD/CADD, drafting. **English:** English lit. **Family/consumer sciences:** Child care. **Foreign languages:** French. **Health:** Medical secretary, nursing (RN), prenursing. **Legal studies:** Legal secretary, paralegal. **Liberal arts:** Arts/sciences, humanities. **Math:** General. **Physical sciences:** General. **Protective services:** Law enforcement admin. **Social sciences:** General. **Visual/performing arts:** General.

**Most popular majors.** Business/marketing 27%, health sciences 27%, liberal arts 29%, security/protective services 11%.

**Computing on campus.** 52 workstations in library, computer center.

**Student life. Freshman orientation:** Available. Preregistration for classes offered. **Activities:** Choral groups, dance, drama, student government, student newspaper, Union Estudiantil Latina, international student association, Christian ministry.

**Athletics.** NJCAA. **Intercollegiate:** Basketball, soccer M.

**Student services.** Career counseling, student employment services, financial aid counseling, health services, on-campus daycare, personal counseling, placement for graduates. **Transfer:** Transfer adviser, college fairs on campus for students transferring to 4-year colleges.

---

**Contact.** Phone: (617) 541-5310 Fax: (617) 541-5316
Walter Clark, Director of Admissions, Roxbury Community College, 1234 Columbus Avenue, Roxbury Crossing, MA 02120-3400

## Springfield Technical Community College
**Springfield, Massachusetts**     **CB member**
**www.stcc.edu**     **CB code: 3791**

▶ Public 2-year community and technical college
▶ Commuter campus in small city

**General.** Founded in 1967. Regionally accredited. **Enrollment:** 5,145 degree-seeking undergraduates; 929 non-degree-seeking students. **Degrees:** 704 associate awarded. **Location:** 90 miles from Boston, 30 miles from Hartford, Connecticut. **Calendar:** Semester, limited summer session. **Full-time faculty:** 157 total. **Special facilities:** Armory museum. **Partnerships:** Formal partnerships with Verizon, Microsoft, Novell, A+, Cisco, Ford Asset, IBM.

**Student profile.** Among degree-seeking undergraduates, 1,181 enrolled as first-time, first-year students.

| | | | |
|---|---|---|---|
| Part-time: | 52% | Hispanic American: | 18% |
| Women: | 57% | Native American: | 1% |
| African American: | 14% | International: | 1% |
| Asian American: | 2% | | |

**Transfer out. Colleges most students transferred to 2007:** University of Massachusetts-Amherst, Westfield State College, Elms College, American International College, Springfield College.

**Basis for selection.** Open admission, but selective for some programs. Special requirements for certain health, engineering and science programs. SAT required for selective health and engineering programs. **Homeschooled:** Statement describing homeschool structure and mission required.

**High school preparation.** Math, chemistry, biology and/or physics required for many competitive programs.

**2007-2008 Annual costs.** Tuition/fees: $3,576; $10,086 out-of-state. Per-credit charge: $25 in-state; $242 out-of-state. New England reciprocal rate $232 per credit hour, including fees. Books/supplies: $800. Personal expenses: $2,250.

**2006-2007 Financial aid.** All financial aid based on need. 79% of total undergraduate aid awarded as scholarships/grants, 21% as loans/jobs. Need-based aid available for part-time students. Work-study available for part-time students.

**Application procedures. Admission:** No deadline. $10 fee ($35 out-of-state), may be waived for applicants with need. Application may be submitted online. Admission notification on a rolling basis beginning on or about 3/1. Applicants must reply within 3 weeks of notification of admission. **Financial aid:** Priority date 5/1; no closing date. FAFSA, institutional form required. Applicants notified on a rolling basis starting 7/1.

**Academics. Special study options:** Cooperative education, cross-registration, distance learning, dual enrollment of high school students, ESL, honors, independent study, internships, liberal arts/career combination. License preparation in nursing, radiology. **Credit/placement by examination:** AP, CLEP, institutional tests. 45 credit hours maximum toward associate degree. **Support services:** GED preparation and test center, learning center, reduced course load, remedial instruction, study skills assistance, tutoring, writing center.

**Majors. Agriculture:** Landscaping. **Biology:** General, biotechnology. **Business:** General, accounting, business admin, executive assistant, finance, logistics, marketing, small business admin. **Communications technology:** Animation/special effects, desktop publishing, radio/tv. **Computer sciences:** Applications programming, computer science, data processing, security, system admin, web page design. **Education:** Early childhood, elementary. **Engineering:** General. **Engineering technology:** Automotive, civil, computer, electrical, electromechanical, heat/ac/refrig, laser/optical, mechanical, quality control, telecommunications. **Health:** Clinical lab technology, dental hygiene, insurance coding, massage therapy, medical assistant, medical secretary, nuclear medical technology, nursing (RN), occupational therapy assistant, physical therapy assistant, premedicine, radiologic technology/medical imaging, respiratory therapy technology, sonography, surgical technology. **Liberal arts:** Arts/sciences. **Math:** General. **Parks/recreation:** Sports admin. **Physical sciences:** Chemistry, physics. **Protective services:** Fire safety technology, police science. **Visual/performing arts:** Commercial photography, commercial/advertising art, studio arts.

**Most popular majors.** Business/marketing 14%, engineering/engineering technologies 17%, health sciences 30%, liberal arts 18%, security/protective services 7%.

**Computing on campus.** 1,420 workstations in library, computer center, student center. Commuter students can connect to campus network. Online course registration, online library, helpline, student web hosting, wireless network available.

**Student life. Freshman orientation:** Available. Half-day session three weeks before start of classes. **Policies:** No alcohol permitted. **Activities:** Drama, student government, student newspaper, TV station, business club, gay/lesbian/bisexual alliance, Christian Fellowship, Phi Theta Kappa, Campus Civitan, computer club, gallery players, engineering club, criminal justice club, massage therapy club.

**Athletics.** NJCAA. **Intercollegiate:** Basketball, golf, soccer, tennis, wrestling M. **Team name:** Rams.

**Student services.** Adult student services, alcohol/substance abuse counseling, career counseling, services for economically disadvantaged, student employment services, financial aid counseling, health services, on-campus daycare, personal counseling, placement for graduates, veterans' counselor, women's services. **Physically disabled:** Services for visually, speech, hearing impaired. **Learning disabled:** Comprehensive services available. **Transfer:** Pre-admission transcript evaluation for new students. Transfer center, transfer adviser, college fairs on campus for students transferring to 4-year colleges.

**Contact.** E-mail: admissions@stcc.edu
Phone: (413) 755-4202
Louisa Davis-Freeman, Dean of Admissions, Springfield Technical Community College, One Armory Square, Springfield, MA 01102-9000

## Urban College of Boston
**Boston, Massachusetts**
**www.urbancollege.edu**                    **CB code: 3630**

▶ Private 2-year community college
▶ Commuter campus in very large city

**General.** Regionally accredited. **Enrollment:** 389 degree-seeking undergraduates. **Degrees:** 74 associate awarded. **Calendar:** Semester, limited summer session. **Full-time faculty:** 2 total. **Part-time faculty:** 40 total. **Class size:** 57% < 20, 43% 20-39.

**Transfer out. Colleges most students transferred to 2007:** Lesley College, Springfield College, Cambridge College.

**Basis for selection.** Open admission.

**2007-2008 Annual costs.** Tuition/fees: $4,670. Per-credit charge: $155. Books/supplies: $800. Personal expenses: $2,340.

**Financial aid.** All financial aid based on need. Need-based aid available for part-time students.

**Application procedures. Admission:** No deadline. $10 fee, may be waived for applicants with need. Admission notification on a rolling basis. **Financial aid:** No deadline. FAFSA required. Applicants notified on a rolling basis starting 4/15.

**Academics. Special study options:** Independent study, internships. **Credit/placement by examination:** AP, CLEP, IB. **Support services:** Learning center, study skills assistance, tutoring.

**Majors. Education:** Early childhood. **Liberal arts:** Arts/sciences. **Public administration:** Human services.

**Computing on campus.** 2 workstations in library, computer center.

**Student life. Freshman orientation:** Available. Preregistration for classes offered. **Policies:** Drug and alcohol use prohibited.

**Student services.** Career counseling, services for economically disadvantaged, financial aid counseling, minority student services, personal counseling, placement for graduates. **Transfer:** Transfer adviser for students transferring to 4-year colleges.

**Contact.** Phone: (617) 348-6359 Fax: (617) 423-4758
Henry Johnson, Dean of Enrollment Services, Urban College of Boston, 178 Tremont Street, Seventh Floor, Boston, MA 02111

# Michigan

## Alpena Community College
### Alpena, Michigan
www.alpenacc.edu — CB code: 1011

- Public 2-year community college
- Commuter campus in large town

**General.** Founded in 1952. Regionally accredited. **Enrollment:** 2,056 degree-seeking undergraduates. **Degrees:** 350 associate awarded. **Location:** 240 miles from Detroit. **Calendar:** Semester, limited summer session. **Full-time faculty:** 50 total. **Part-time faculty:** 85 total. **Special facilities:** Museum, planetarium.

**Student profile.**

| | | | |
|---|---|---|---|
| Out-of-state: | 1% | Live on campus: | 3% |
| 25 or older: | 48% | | |

**Transfer out.** Colleges most students transferred to 2007: Lake Superior State University, Central Michigan University, Michigan State University, Ferris State University, Spring Arbor University.

**Basis for selection.** Open admission, but selective for some programs. Special requirements for practical nursing, registered nursing, and utility technician programs. ACT may be used for scholarship consideration or as basis for corroboration of institutional placement exam results. Placement test requirement waived for applicants with ACT composite score of 20 or higher.

**High school preparation.** High school diploma or equivalent required for nursing applicants.

**2008-2009 Annual costs.** Tuition/fees (projected): $3,020; $3,320 out-of-district; $5,720 out-of-state. Per-credit charge: $80 in-district; $120 out-of-district; $160 out-of-state. Books/supplies: $500. Personal expenses: $600.

**2007-2008 Financial aid. Need-based:** 66% of total undergraduate aid awarded as scholarships/grants, 34% as loans/jobs. Need-based aid available for part-time students. Work-study available for part-time students. **Non-need-based:** Scholarships awarded for academics, art, athletics, job skills, leadership, music/drama.

**Application procedures. Admission:** Priority date 6/15; no deadline. No application fee. Application may be submitted online. Admission notification on a rolling basis beginning on or about 2/15. **Financial aid:** Priority date 8/1; no closing date. FAFSA required. Applicants notified on a rolling basis starting 5/15; must reply within 3 week(s) of notification.

**Academics. Special study options:** Distance learning, double major, dual enrollment of high school students, internships, liberal arts/career combination. Bachelor's degree programs available on campus. License preparation in nursing. **Credit/placement by examination:** AP, CLEP, institutional tests. 30 credit hours maximum toward associate degree. **Support services:** Learning center, reduced course load, remedial instruction, study skills assistance, tutoring, writing center.

**Majors. Business:** Accounting, business admin, management information systems. **Communications technology:** Graphic/printing. **Computer sciences:** General, information systems, LAN/WAN management, networking. **Education:** General. **Engineering:** General. **Engineering technology:** Construction, drafting, manufacturing. **Health:** Medical assistant, nursing (RN). **Liberal arts:** Arts/sciences. **Mechanic/repair:** Automotive. **Protective services:** Corrections, law enforcement admin.

**Computing on campus.** 75 workstations in library, computer center. Commuter students can connect to campus network. Online library available.

**Student life. Freshman orientation:** Available. Preregistration for classes offered. One-day program during week prior to start of each semester. **Housing:** Apartments available. $300 deposit, deadline 8/1. **Activities:** Jazz band, dance, drama, musical theater, student government, student newspaper.

**Athletics.** NJCAA. **Intercollegiate:** Basketball, golf M, softball W, volleyball W. **Intramural:** Basketball, bowling, softball, volleyball. **Team name:** Lumberjacks.

**Student services.** Adult student services, alcohol/substance abuse counseling, career counseling, student employment services, financial aid counseling, personal counseling, placement for graduates, veterans' counselor, women's services. **Transfer:** Pre-admission transcript evaluation for new students. Transfer adviser, college fairs on campus for students transferring to 4-year colleges.

**Contact.** E-mail: kollienm@alpenacc.edu
Phone: (989) 358-7339 Toll-free number: (888) 468-6222
Fax: (989) 358-7540
Michael Kollien, Director of Admissions, Alpena Community College, 665 Johnson Street, Alpena, MI 49707

## Bay de Noc Community College
### Escanaba, Michigan
www.baycollege.edu — CB code: 1049

- Public 2-year community college
- Commuter campus in large town

**General.** Founded in 1962. Regionally accredited. **Enrollment:** 1,993 degree-seeking undergraduates; 210 non-degree-seeking students. **Degrees:** 294 associate awarded. **Location:** 110 miles from Green Bay, Wisconsin. **Calendar:** Semester, limited summer session. **Full-time faculty:** 43 total. **Part-time faculty:** 73 total. **Class size:** 61% < 20, 38% 20-39, less than 1% 40-49, less than 1% 50-99. **Special facilities:** Reading, writing, math and computer-assisted instructional laboratories.

**Student profile.** Among degree-seeking undergraduates, 42% enrolled in a transfer program, 48% enrolled in a vocational program, 606 enrolled as first-time, first-year students.

| | | | |
|---|---|---|---|
| Part-time: | 37% | 25 or older: | 34% |
| Out-of-state: | 3% | Live on campus: | 4% |
| Women: | 60% | | |

**Transfer out.** 33% of students enrolled in the transfer program go on to 4-year colleges. **Colleges most students transferred to 2007:** Northern Michigan University, Lake Superior State University, Michigan Technological University.

**Basis for selection.** Open admission, but selective for some programs. Special requirements for nursing program.

**2007-2008 Annual costs.** Tuition/fees: $2,505; $3,795 out-of-district; $4,785 out-of-state. Per-credit charge: $77 in-district; $120 out-of-district; $153 out-of-state. Tuition and instructional fees based on contact hours. Room/board: $2,450. Books/supplies: $1,040. Personal expenses: $500.

**Financial aid. Need-based:** Need-based aid available for part-time students. Work-study available nights, weekends and for part-time students. **Non-need-based:** Scholarships awarded for academics.

**Application procedures. Admission:** Closing date 8/15 (receipt date). $25 fee. Application may be submitted online. Admission notification on a rolling basis. **Financial aid:** Priority date 4/1; no closing date. FAFSA required. Applicants notified on a rolling basis starting 2/1; must reply within 2 week(s) of notification.

**Academics. Special study options:** Cooperative education, distance learning, dual enrollment of high school students, internships, liberal arts/career combination, weekend college. Bachelor's degree programs available on campus. License preparation in nursing. **Credit/placement by examination:** AP, CLEP, institutional tests. 40 credit hours maximum toward associate degree. **Support services:** Pre-admission summer program, reduced course load, remedial instruction, study skills assistance, tutoring, writing center.

**Majors. Architecture:** Landscape. **Business:** Accounting, administrative services, business admin, sales/distribution. **Computer sciences:** Data processing. **Conservation:** Wood science. **Engineering technology:** Drafting, electrical, water quality. **Family/consumer sciences:** Child care. **Health:** Nursing (RN). **Legal studies:** Prelaw. **Liberal arts:** Arts/sciences. **Mechanic/repair:** General, automotive. **Physical sciences:** Astronomy.

**Most popular majors.** Business/marketing 20%, engineering/engineering technologies 8%, health sciences 28%, liberal arts 30%, security/protective services 6%.

**Computing on campus.** 535 workstations in library, computer center. Dormitories wired for high-speed internet access and linked to campus network. Commuter students can connect to campus network. Online course registration, online library, helpline, wireless network available.

**Student life. Freshman orientation:** Mandatory. Students meet with counselors, financial aid officers, student services representatives to determine course of study and expenses. **Housing:** Apartments available. $150 partly refundable deposit, deadline 8/15. **Activities:** Campus ministries, choral groups, drama, literary magazine, student government, student newspaper, student volunteer association, nurses association, student activities board, United Nations club, history club, water tech club, art club.

**Athletics. Intramural:** Basketball, bowling, golf, skiing, softball, swimming, table tennis, volleyball.

**Student services.** Adult student services, career counseling, student employment services, financial aid counseling, on-campus daycare, personal counseling, veterans' counselor. **Physically disabled:** Services for visually, hearing impaired. **Transfer:** Transfer adviser, college fairs on campus for students transferring to 4-year colleges.

**Contact.** E-mail: carterc@baycollege.edu
Phone: (906) 786-5802 ext. 1276 Toll-free
number: (800) 221-2001 ext. 1276 Fax: (906) 786-8515
Cynthia Carter, Director of Admissions, Bay de Noc Community College, 2001 North Lincoln Road, Escanaba, MI 49829-2511

## Bay Mills Community College
### Brimley, Michigan
www.bmcc.edu                                      CB code: 2101

- Public 2-year community college
- Residential campus in rural community

**General.** Regionally accredited. **Enrollment:** 200 full-time, degree-seeking students. **Degrees:** 17 associate awarded. **Location:** 20 miles from Sault Ste. Marie. **Calendar:** Semester. **Full-time faculty:** 10 total; 40% women. **Part-time faculty:** 20 total; 70% women.

**Transfer out. Colleges most students transferred to 2007:** Lake Superior State University.

**Basis for selection.** Open admission. **Homeschooled:** Transcript of courses and grades required.

**2007-2008 Annual costs.** Tuition/fees: $2,910. Per-credit charge: $85. Books/supplies: $200.

**Financial aid. Need-based:** Work-study available nights and for part-time students.

**Application procedures. Admission:** Closing date 8/24 (receipt date). No application fee. Application must be submitted on paper. Admission notification on a rolling basis. **Financial aid:** FAFSA, institutional form required.

**Academics. Special study options:** Combined bachelor's/graduate degree, cooperative education, distance learning, double major, dual enrollment of high school students, independent study, internships. License preparation in paramedic. **Credit/placement by examination:** CLEP, institutional tests. **Support services:** GED preparation and test center, learning center, remedial instruction, study skills assistance, tutoring.

**Majors. Area/ethnic studies:** Native American. **Business:** Business admin. **Computer sciences:** General, computer science. **Construction:** General. **Education:** Early childhood. **Parks/recreation:** Health/fitness.

**Computing on campus.** 30 workstations in library, computer center. Online library, repair service, wireless network available.

**Student life. Freshman orientation:** Available. Preregistration for classes offered. **Activities:** Student government.

**Student services.** Career counseling, financial aid counseling. **Transfer:** Pre-admission transcript evaluation for new students. College fairs on campus for students transferring to 4-year colleges.

**Contact.** E-mail: elehre@bmcc.edu
Phone: (906) 248-3354 ext. 4222 Toll-free number: (800) 844-2622
Fax: (906) 248-3351
Elaine Lehre, Admissions Officer, Bay Mills Community College, 12214 West Lakeshore Drive, Brimley, MI 49715

## Delta College
### University Center, Michigan
www.delta.edu                                      CB code: 1816

- Public 2-year community and junior college
- Commuter campus in small city

**General.** Founded in 1957. Regionally accredited. Classes offered at 21 off-campus sites, including 3 major off-campus facilities. **Enrollment:** 10,422 degree-seeking undergraduates. **Degrees:** 1,304 associate awarded. **Location:** 10 miles from Saginaw, 12 miles from Midland. **Calendar:** Semester, limited summer session. **Full-time faculty:** 211 total. **Part-time faculty:** 285 total. **Class size:** 44% < 20, 55% 20-39, less than 1% 40-49, less than 1% 50-99. **Special facilities:** Planetarium, on-site dental clinic. **Partnerships:** Formal partnership with General Motors (ASEP program for automotive students).

**Student profile.**

| Out-of-state: | 2% | 25 or older: | 43% |
|---|---|---|---|

**Transfer out. Colleges most students transferred to 2007:** Central Michigan University, Saginaw Valley State University, Northwood University, University of Michigan, Michigan State University.

**Basis for selection.** Open admission. ACT, ASSET or COMPASS required of all students for counseling purposes.

**2007-2008 Annual costs.** Tuition/fees: $2,700; $3,810 out-of-district; $5,310 out-of-state. Per-credit charge: $78 in-district; $115 out-of-district; $165 out-of-state. Books/supplies: $767. Personal expenses: $690.

**Financial aid. Need-based:** Need-based aid available for part-time students. Work-study available nights and for part-time students. **Non-need-based:** Scholarships awarded for academics, athletics.

**Application procedures. Admission:** No deadline. $20 fee, may be waived for applicants with need. Application may be submitted online. Admission notification on a rolling basis. **Financial aid:** Priority date 8/1; no closing date. FAFSA required. Applicants notified on a rolling basis; must reply within 2 week(s) of notification.

**Academics. Special study options:** Cooperative education, distance learning, double major, dual enrollment of high school students, honors, independent study, internships, liberal arts/career combination, student-designed major, study abroad, weekend college. Bachelor's in business with Northwood University (3+1 program). License preparation in aviation, dental hygiene, nursing, occupational therapy, physical therapy, radiology, real estate. **Credit/placement by examination:** AP, CLEP, IB, institutional tests. 38 credit hours maximum toward associate degree. **Support services:** GED test center, learning center, reduced course load, remedial instruction, study skills assistance, tutoring.

**Majors. Agriculture:** Business. **Architecture:** Technology. **Biology:** General, biotechnology. **Business:** General, accounting, administrative services, business admin, construction management, international, marketing, merchandising, office management, office technology, small business admin. **Communications:** Journalism. **Communications technology:** General, graphic/printing. **Computer sciences:** General, computer science, information systems, information technology, networking, programming, web page design, webmaster. **Conservation:** General, environmental science, forestry, water/wetlands/marine. **Construction:** General, carpentry, electrician, maintenance, pipefitting, plumbing. **Education:** Art, business, elementary, kindergarten/preschool, music, physical, secondary, special, technology/industrial arts. **Engineering:** General, architectural, mechanical. **Engineering technology:** Drafting, electrical, heat/ac/refrig, industrial, manufacturing. **English:** English lit. **Family/consumer sciences:** Child development. **Foreign languages:** General. **Health:** Clinical lab science, dental assistant, dental hygiene, dietetics, licensed practical nurse, medical assistant, medical radiologic technology/radiation therapy, medical secretary, nursing (RN), office assistant, optometric assistant, pharmacy assistant, physical therapy assistant, physics/radiologic health, predental, premedicine, prenursing, prepharmacy, preveterinary, respiratory therapy assistant, respiratory therapy technology, sonography, surgical technology. **Legal studies:** Legal secretary, paralegal, prelaw. **Liberal arts:** Arts/sciences. **Math:** General. **Mechanic/repair:** Automotive, electronics/electrical, heating/ac/refrig. **Parks/recreation:** Health/fitness. **Personal/culinary services:** Mortuary science. **Physical sciences:** General, chemistry, geology. **Production:** Machine tool, welding. **Protective services:** Corrections, fire safety technology, fire services admin, firefighting, law enforcement admin, police science. **Psychology:** General. **Public administration:** Human services, social work. **Science technology:** Biological, chemical. **Social sciences:** Economics, geography, sociology. **Transportation:** Aviation. **Visual/performing arts:** Art, dramatic, graphic design, interior design, photography.

**Computing on campus.** 350 workstations in library, computer center, student center. Commuter students can connect to campus network. Online course registration, online library, helpline, wireless network available.

**Student life. Freshman orientation:** Mandatory. General campus overview and individual academic counseling/advising assessment required prior to orientation. **Activities:** Drama, radio station, student government, student newspaper, TV station, black student union, Chi Alpha, Delta Collegiate,

Delta Epsilon Chi, health care organizations, InterVarsity Christian Fellowship, Phi Theta Kappa International, Society of Hispanic Leaders, student senate, trilogy club.

**Athletics.** NJCAA. **Intercollegiate:** Basketball, cross-country M, golf, soccer M, softball W, volleyball W. **Team name:** Pioneers.

**Student services.** Adult student services, career counseling, services for economically disadvantaged, student employment services, financial aid counseling, minority student services, placement for graduates, veterans' counselor. **Physically disabled:** Services for visually, speech, hearing impaired. **Transfer:** Transfer adviser, college fairs on campus for students transferring to 4-year colleges.

**Contact.** E-mail: admit@delta.edu
Phone: (989) 686-9093 Toll-free number: (800) 285-1704
Fax: (989) 667-2202
Gary Brasseur, Director of Enrollment Services, Delta College, 1961 Delta Road, University Center, MI 48710

## Glen Oaks Community College
**Centreville, Michigan**
**www.glenoaks.edu**

**CB member**
**CB code: 1261**

- Public 2-year community college
- Commuter campus in rural community

**General.** Founded in 1965. Regionally accredited. **Enrollment:** 925 degree-seeking undergraduates; 472 non-degree-seeking students. **Degrees:** 167 associate awarded. **Location:** 35 miles from Kalamazoo. **Calendar:** Semester, limited summer session. **Full-time faculty:** 27 total. **Part-time faculty:** 80 total. **Special facilities:** Fitness center, nature trails and habitat.

**Student profile.** Among degree-seeking undergraduates, 244 enrolled as first-time, first-year students.

| | | | |
|---|---|---|---|
| Part-time: | 86% | Women: | 68% |
| Out-of-state: | 18% | 25 or older: | 82% |

**Transfer out. Colleges most students transferred to 2007:** Western Michigan University, Grand Valley State University, Kalamazoo Valley Community College, Kellogg Community College, Michigan State University.

**Basis for selection.** Open admission, but selective for some programs. Admission to nursing program based on pre-admission test, high school grades, and health form. ACCUPLACER test requested for certain programs. ACT or SAT may be considered in lieu of ACCUPLACER.

**2007-2008 Annual costs.** Tuition/fees: $2,610. Per-credit charge: $70. In-county residents pay $70 per contact hour. Students from service area counties (Branch and Cass counties in Michigan and LaGrange, Elkheart, Steuben counties in Indiana) pay $109 per contact hour. All others pay $140 per contact hour. Required fees for all students: $510. Books/supplies: $480. Personal expenses: $775.

**Financial aid. Need-based:** Need-based aid available for part-time students. Work-study available nights and for part-time students. **Non-need-based:** Scholarships awarded for academics, art, athletics, leadership, minority status, music/drama.

**Application procedures. Admission:** No deadline. No application fee. Admission notification on a rolling basis. **Financial aid:** No deadline. FAFSA, institutional form required. Applicants notified on a rolling basis.

**Academics. Special study options:** Accelerated study, distance learning, double major, dual enrollment of high school students, independent study, internships, liberal arts/career combination. Bachelor's degree programs available on campus. License preparation in paramedic. **Credit/placement by examination:** AP, CLEP, institutional tests. 47 credit hours maximum toward associate degree. **Support services:** Learning center, remedial instruction, study skills assistance, tutoring.

**Majors. Business:** General. **Education:** Early childhood. **Engineering:** Science. **Family/consumer sciences:** Child care. **Health:** Nursing (RN). **Liberal arts:** Arts/sciences.

**Most popular majors.** Business/marketing 32%, engineering/engineering technologies 7%, health sciences 16%, liberal arts 41%.

**Computing on campus.** 85 workstations in library, computer center. Online library, wireless network available.

**Student life. Freshman orientation:** Available. **Activities:** Choral groups, music ensembles, student government, academic honorary society, Phi Theta Kappa.

**Athletics.** NJCAA. **Intercollegiate:** Baseball M, basketball, golf M, softball W, tennis W, volleyball W. **Intramural:** Table tennis. **Team name:** Vikings.

**Student services.** Career counseling, services for economically disadvantaged, student employment services, financial aid counseling, on-campus daycare, personal counseling, women's services. **Physically disabled:** Services for visually, speech, hearing impaired. **Transfer:** Transfer adviser, college fairs on campus for students transferring to 4-year colleges.

**Contact.** E-mail: jzimmerman@glenoaks.edu
Phone: (269) 467-9945 ext. 320 Toll-free number: (888) 994-7818 ext. 320
Fax: (269) 467-9068
Jean Zimmerman, Director of Admissions, Glen Oaks Community College, 62249 Shimmel Road, Centreville, MI 49032-9719

## Gogebic Community College
**Ironwood, Michigan**
**www.gogebic.edu**

**CB code: 1250**

- Public 2-year community college
- Commuter campus in small town

**General.** Founded in 1932. Regionally accredited. **Enrollment:** 847 degree-seeking undergraduates; 128 non-degree-seeking students. **Degrees:** 110 associate awarded. **Location:** 100 miles from Duluth, Minnesota, 150 miles from Marquette. **Calendar:** Semester, limited summer session. **Full-time faculty:** 29 total. **Part-time faculty:** 60 total. **Class size:** 72% < 20, 27% 20-39, less than 1% 40-49, less than 1% 50-99. **Special facilities:** Arboretum, ski hill, terrain park, tubing park, cross-country ski trails.

**Student profile.** Among degree-seeking undergraduates, 44% enrolled in a transfer program, 57% enrolled in a vocational program, 216 enrolled as first-time, first-year students, 143 transferred in from other institutions.

| | | | |
|---|---|---|---|
| Part-time: | 30% | African American: | 1% |
| Out-of-state: | 20% | Hispanic American: | 1% |
| Women: | 61% | Native American: | 2% |

**Transfer out. Colleges most students transferred to 2007:** Northern Michigan University, University of Wisconsin-Superior, Northland College, Michigan Technological University.

**Basis for selection.** Open admission, but selective for some programs. Students applying to nursing programs required to show competency in biology and chemistry. Admission based on assessment test scores and academic achievement. Interview recommended. **Homeschooled:** Interview required.

**High school preparation.** Nursing applicants must have background in chemistry, math, and biology.

**2007-2008 Annual costs.** Tuition/fees: $2,851; $3,451 out-of-district; $4,231 out-of-state. Per-credit charge: $79 in-district; $99 out-of-district; $125 out-of-state. Room only: $3,570. Books/supplies: $950. Personal expenses: $700.

**Financial aid. Need-based:** Need-based aid available for part-time students. Work-study available nights, weekends and for part-time students. **Non-need-based:** Scholarships awarded for academics, art, athletics, job skills, leadership, music/drama, state residency.

**Application procedures. Admission:** No deadline. $10 fee, may be waived for applicants with need. Application may be submitted online. Admission notification on a rolling basis. **Financial aid:** Priority date 5/1; no closing date. FAFSA required. Applicants notified on a rolling basis starting 3/15; must reply within 2 week(s) of notification.

**Academics. Special study options:** Cooperative education, distance learning, double major, dual enrollment of high school students, honors, independent study, internships, student-designed major. License preparation in nursing, paramedic. **Credit/placement by examination:** AP, CLEP, institutional tests. 12 credit hours maximum toward associate degree. AP exam scores not listed in policy evaluated on individual basis. **Support services:** GED test center, learning center, reduced course load, remedial instruction, study skills assistance, tutoring.

**Majors. Biology:** General. **Business:** General, accounting, administrative services, business admin, entrepreneurial studies, office management, office technology. **Communications technology:** Graphics. **Computer sciences:** General, data processing, programming. **Conservation:** General, forestry. **Construction:** General, carpentry. **Education:** General, early childhood, elementary, secondary, special, teacher assistance. **Engineering:** General. **Engineering technology:** Automotive, CAD/CADD, construction. **Health:** Clinical lab science, EMT paramedic, insurance coding, nursing (RN), predental, premedicine, prenursing, prepharmacy, preveterinary. **History:** General. **Legal studies:** Prelaw. **Liberal arts:** Arts/sciences. **Math:** General. **Mechanic/repair:** Automotive. **Parks/recreation:** Facilities management. **Personal/culinary services:** Mortuary science. **Physical sciences:** General, chemistry, physics. **Protective services:** Law enforcement admin. **Psychology:** General. **Public administration:** Social work. **Social sciences:** General. **Visual/performing arts:** Art, commercial/advertising art.

**Computing on campus.** 240 workstations in dormitories, library, computer center. Dormitories wired for high-speed internet access and linked to campus network. Commuter students can connect to campus network. On-line library, wireless network available.

**Student life. Freshman orientation:** Mandatory. Preregistration for classes offered. Early orientation held in April for accepted students who have completed assessment. Other orientation programs in August and June. **Housing:** Guaranteed on-campus for freshmen. Coed dorms available. **Activities:** Concert band, drama, music ensembles, student government, student newspaper, student senate, student nurses association.

**Athletics.** NJCAA. **Intercollegiate:** Basketball. **Intramural:** Basketball, bowling, cheerleading, football (non-tackle) M, golf, skiing, soccer, softball, tennis, volleyball. **Team name:** Samsons.

**Student services.** Alcohol/substance abuse counseling, career counseling, services for economically disadvantaged, student employment services, financial aid counseling, personal counseling, placement for graduates, veterans' counselor. **Physically disabled:** Services for visually, hearing impaired. **Transfer:** Re-entry adviser for new students. Transfer adviser, college fairs on campus for students transferring to 4-year colleges.

**Contact.** E-mail: debbiej@gogebic.edu
Phone: (906) 932-4231 ext. 207 Toll-free number: (800) 682-5910 ext. 207
Fax: (906) 932-2339
Jeanne Graham, Director of Admissions and Public Information, Gogebic Community College, E4946 Jackson Road, Ironwood, MI 49938

---

## Grand Rapids Community College
**Grand Rapids, Michigan**
www.grcc.edu

CB member
CB code: 1254

- Public 2-year community college
- Commuter campus in small city

**General.** Founded in 1914. Regionally accredited. Evening courses offered at 9 off-campus sites in Western Michigan. **Enrollment:** 13,998 degree-seeking undergraduates; 1,214 non-degree-seeking students. **Degrees:** 1,401 associate awarded. **Location:** 70 miles from Lansing, 180 miles from Chicago. **Calendar:** Semester, extensive summer session. **Full-time faculty:** 213 total; 11% have terminal degrees, 14% minority, 48% women. **Part-time faculty:** 511 total; 6% have terminal degrees, 7% minority, 49% women.

**Student profile.** Among degree-seeking undergraduates, 3,441 enrolled as first-time, first-year students, 557 transferred in from other institutions.

| | | | |
|---|---|---|---|
| Part-time: | 53% | Women: | 52% |
| Out-of-state: | 1% | 25 or older: | 30% |

**Transfer out. Colleges most students transferred to 2007:** Grand Valley State University, Ferris State University, Western Michigan University, Michigan State University, Aquinas College.

**Basis for selection.** Open admission, but selective for some programs. Occupational health program applicants must be high school graduates, have GPAs and completed specific classes with a 2.0 grade or better. **Home-schooled:** Assessment exam required.

**High school preparation.** Recommended units include English 4, mathematics 3, social studies 2 and science 3.

**2008-2009 Annual costs.** Tuition/fees (projected): $2,540; $5,030 out-of-district; $7,280 out-of-state. Per-credit charge: $82 in-district; $165 out-of-district; $240 out-of-state. Books/supplies: $1,524. Personal expenses: $575.

**Financial aid. Need-based:** Need-based aid available for part-time students. Work-study available nights, weekends and for part-time students. **Non-need-based:** Scholarships awarded for academics, alumni affiliation, art, athletics, leadership, minority status, music/drama, state residency. **Additional information:** Tuition reimbursement and/or child-care services for single parents and displaced homemakers who meet Perkins guidelines.

**Application procedures. Admission:** Closing date 8/30 (receipt date). $20 fee, may be waived for applicants with need. Application may be submitted online. Admission notification on a rolling basis. **Financial aid:** Priority date 4/1; no closing date. FAFSA required. Applicants notified on a rolling basis starting 5/1; must reply within 3 week(s) of notification.

**Academics.** Liberal arts and pre-professional curricula along with extensive work-force training and technical seminars offered. **Special study options:** Cooperative education, distance learning, dual enrollment of high school students, ESL, independent study, internships, study abroad, weekend college. License preparation in dental hygiene, nursing, occupational therapy, radiology. **Credit/placement by examination:** AP, CLEP, institutional tests. 30 credit hours maximum toward associate degree. **Support services:** GED test center, learning center, reduced course load, remedial instruction, study skills assistance, tutoring, writing center.

**Majors. Agriculture:** Landscaping. **Architecture:** Technology. **Biology:** General. **Business:** General, accounting technology, business admin, executive assistant, fashion, sales/distribution. **Communications:** Journalism. **Computer sciences:** General, LAN/WAN management, networking, programming, web page design, webmaster. **Conservation:** Fisheries, forestry, management/policy, wildlife. **Education:** Art, business, chemistry, elementary, English, mathematics, multi-level teacher, music, physical, science, teacher assistance, technology/industrial arts. **Engineering:** General. **Engineering technology:** General, architectural drafting, automotive, electrical, heat/ac/refrig, mechanical drafting, plastics, quality control, water quality. **English:** English lit, speech/rhetoric. **Family/consumer sciences:** Aging, child care, child development. **Foreign languages:** General. **Health:** Clinical lab science, dental assistant, dental hygiene, licensed practical nurse, medical radiologic technology/radiation therapy, nursing (RN), occupational therapy assistant, predental, premedicine, prepharmacy, preveterinary, surgical technology. **Legal studies:** Prelaw. **Liberal arts:** Arts/sciences, library science. **Math:** General. **Mechanic/repair:** Electronics/electrical, heating/ac/refrig. **Personal/culinary services:** Chef training, mortuary science, restaurant/catering. **Physical sciences:** Chemistry, geology, oceanography, physics. **Production:** General, machine shop technology, welding. **Protective services:** Corrections, firefighting, law enforcement admin, police science. **Psychology:** General. **Public administration:** Social work. **Science technology:** Chemical. **Social sciences:** Economics, political science, sociology. **Visual/performing arts:** Art, commercial/advertising art, dramatic, interior design, music management, music performance, photography, piano/organ, studio arts, voice/opera. **Other:** Music recording technology, Pre-optometry.

**Most popular majors.** Business/marketing 7%, education 6%, health sciences 19%, liberal arts 31%, personal/culinary services 7%, public administration/social services 7%.

**Computing on campus.** 1,254 workstations in library, computer center. Commuter students can connect to campus network. Online course registration, online library, helpline, wireless network available.

**Student life. Freshman orientation:** Available. Preregistration for classes offered. Provides campus tours and general information about the college. **Activities:** Bands, choral groups, dance, drama, film society, literary magazine, music ensembles, musical theater, student government, student newspaper, symphony orchestra, black student organization, Hispanic student organization, Native American student organization, Vietnamese student organization, Christian Fellowship, content area student organizations, service learning.

**Athletics.** NJCAA. **Intercollegiate:** Baseball M, basketball, cross-country, diving, football (tackle) M, golf M, softball W, swimming, tennis, track and field, volleyball W, wrestling M. **Intramural:** Basketball, racquetball, skiing, soccer M, swimming. **Team name:** Raiders.

**Student services.** Adult student services, career counseling, student employment services, on-campus daycare, personal counseling, placement for graduates. **Physically disabled:** Services for visually, speech, hearing impaired. **Transfer:** Pre-admission transcript evaluation for new students. Transfer adviser, college fairs on campus for students transferring to 4-year colleges.

**Contact.** E-mail: enroll@grcc.edu
Phone: (616) 234-7623 Fax: (616) 234-4107
Diane Patrick, Director of Admissions, Grand Rapids Community College, 143 Bostwick Avenue NE, Grand Rapids, MI 49503-3295

---

## Henry Ford Community College
**Dearborn, Michigan**
www.hfcc.edu

CB code: 1293

- Public 2-year community college
- Commuter campus in small city

**General.** Founded in 1938. Regionally accredited. **Enrollment:** 12,546 degree-seeking undergraduates. **Degrees:** 1,107 associate awarded. **Location:** 8 miles from Detroit. **Calendar:** Semester, limited summer session. **Full-time faculty:** 201 total. **Part-time faculty:** 551 total.

**Student profile.**

Out-of-state: 2%  25 or older: 47%

**Basis for selection.** Open admission, but selective for some programs. Special requirements for specific allied health programs.

**High school preparation.** For allied health programs: 1 year high school biology, chemistry, and algebra.

**2007-2008 Annual costs.** Tuition/fees: $2,112; $3,762 out-of-district; $4,002 out-of-state. Per-credit charge: $57 in-district; $112 out-of-district; $120 out-of-state. Books/supplies: $500. Personal expenses: $585.

**Financial aid. Need-based:** Work-study available nights, weekends and for part-time students.

**Application procedures. Admission:** No deadline. $30 fee, may be waived for applicants with need. Application may be submitted online. Admission notification on a rolling basis. **Financial aid:** Priority date 4/1; no closing date. FAFSA required. Applicants notified on a rolling basis starting 3/1.

**Academics. Special study options:** Cooperative education, distance learning, dual enrollment of high school students, honors, independent study. **Credit/placement by examination:** CLEP. 20 credit hours maximum toward associate degree. **Support services:** Learning center, pre-admission summer program, reduced course load, remedial instruction, tutoring.

**Majors. Area/ethnic studies:** Women's. **Business:** General, accounting, management science, office management, office/clerical, real estate. **Communications:** General, broadcast journalism. **Communications technology:** Graphic/printing. **Computer sciences:** General. **Engineering technology:** Drafting, electrical. **Family/consumer sciences:** Institutional food production. **Health:** EMT paramedic, licensed practical nurse, medical records technology, nursing (RN), physical therapy assistant, respiratory therapy technology. **Legal studies:** Legal secretary, paralegal. **Liberal arts:** Arts/sciences. **Mechanic/repair:** Automotive, heating/ac/refrig. **Parks/recreation:** Exercise sciences, health/fitness. **Personal/culinary services:** Culinary services. **Protective services:** Firefighting, police science, security services. **Transportation:** General. **Visual/performing arts:** Art, ceramics, commercial/advertising art, dramatic, industrial design, interior design.

**Student life. Freshman orientation:** Available. **Activities:** Bands, choral groups, drama, film society, literary magazine, music ensembles, radio station, student government, student newspaper.

**Athletics.** NJCAA. **Intercollegiate:** Baseball M, basketball, golf M, softball W, tennis, volleyball W. **Intramural:** Basketball, bowling, sailing, table tennis.

**Student services.** Adult student services, career counseling, student employment services, on-campus daycare, personal counseling, placement for graduates, veterans' counselor. **Physically disabled:** Services for visually, hearing impaired. **Transfer:** Transfer adviser, college fairs on campus for students transferring to 4-year colleges.

**Contact.** Phone: (313) 845-9613 Toll-free number: (800) 585-4322 Fax: (313) 845-9891
Henry Ford Community College, 5101 Evergreen Road, Dearborn, MI 48128

## ITT Technical Institute: Canton
**Canton, Michigan**

- For-profit 2-year business and technical college
- Commuter campus in small city

**General.** Accredited by ACICS. **Calendar:** Quarter.

**Contact.** 1905 South Haggerty Road, Canton, MI 48188

## ITT Technical Institute: Grand Rapids
**Grand Rapids, Michigan**
www.itt-tech.edu   CB code: 2705

- For-profit 2-year technical college
- Commuter campus in small city

**General.** Accredited by ACICS. **Calendar:** Quarter.

**Annual costs/financial aid.** Tuition varies by program, $260-$368 per credit hour.

**Contact.** Phone: (616) 956-1060
Director of Recruitment, 4020 Sparks Drive Southeast, Grand Rapids, MI 49546

## ITT Technical Institute: Troy
**Troy, Michigan**
www.itt-tech.edu   CB code: 2784

- For-profit 2-year technical college
- Commuter campus in small city

**General.** Accredited by ACICS. **Calendar:** Quarter.

**Annual costs/financial aid.** Tuition varies by program, $260-$368 per credit hour.

**Contact.** Phone: (248) 524-1800
Director of Recruitment, 1522 East Big Beaver Road, Troy, MI 48083-1905

## Jackson Community College
**Jackson, Michigan**   CB member
www.jccmi.edu   CB code: 1340

- Public 2-year community college
- Commuter campus in small city

**General.** Founded in 1928. Regionally accredited. Off-campus locations in Hillsdale County and Lenawee County. **Enrollment:** 6,173 degree-seeking undergraduates. **Degrees:** 540 associate awarded. **Location:** 6 miles from downtown. **Calendar:** Semester, limited summer session. **Full-time faculty:** 90 total. **Part-time faculty:** 302 total. **Class size:** 65% < 20, 34% 20-39, 1% 40-49. **Partnerships:** Formal partnership with Foote Health University to provide education and training for employees.

**Transfer out. Colleges most students transferred to 2007:** Michigan State University, Spring Arbor University, Eastern Michigan University, Siena Heights University, Western Michigan University.

**Basis for selection.** Open admission, but selective for some programs. Special requirements for allied health programs and nursing program. ACT scores used for placement, if submitted. Student not submitting ACT scores must take college-administered placement tests. Second admit programs require interviews and specific academic prerequisites.

**2007-2008 Annual costs.** Tuition/fees: $2,955; $4,035 out-of-district; $5,205 out-of-state. Per-credit charge: $83 in-district; $118 out-of-district; $157 out-of-state. Books/supplies: $672. Personal expenses: $720.

**2007-2008 Financial aid. Need-based:** 85% of total undergraduate aid awarded as scholarships/grants, 15% as loans/jobs. Need-based aid available for part-time students. Work-study available nights, weekends and for part-time students. **Non-need-based:** Scholarships awarded for academics, art, leadership, music/drama, state residency.

**Application procedures. Admission:** No deadline. No application fee. Application may be submitted online. Admission notification on a rolling basis. **Financial aid:** Priority date 6/15; no closing date. FAFSA, institutional form required. Applicants notified on a rolling basis starting 3/1.

**Academics.** Extensive on-line offerings. Students may also complete bachelor's degrees on-campus from partner universities. **Special study options:** Distance learning, dual enrollment of high school students, ESL, independent study, internships, liberal arts/career combination. Bachelor's degree programs available on campus. License preparation in aviation, nursing, paramedic, radiology. **Credit/placement by examination:** AP, CLEP, IB, institutional tests. 30 credit hours maximum toward associate degree. **Support services:** GED preparation and test center, learning center, pre-admission summer program, remedial instruction, study skills assistance, tutoring, writing center.

**Majors. Business:** General, accounting, business admin, finance. **Computer sciences:** Applications programming, computer graphics, data processing, programming, web page design. **Construction:** Electrician. **Education:** Early childhood. **Engineering technology:** Electrical, heat/ac/refrig. **Health:** EMT paramedic, medical assistant, medical transcription, nursing (RN), radiologic technology/medical imaging, sonography. **Liberal arts:** Arts/sciences. **Mechanic/repair:** Automotive, electronics/electrical, heating/

ac/refrig. **Protective services:** Criminal justice. **Visual/performing arts:** Graphic design.

**Most popular majors.** Business/marketing 12%, health sciences 28%, liberal arts 39%, trade and industry 9%.

**Computing on campus.** 356 workstations in library, computer center, student center. Online course registration, helpline available.

**Student life. Freshman orientation:** Available. 2- to 3-hour program prior to each semester. **Activities:** Bands, choral groups, dance, drama, music ensembles, musical theater, student government, student newspaper.

**Athletics. Intramural:** Basketball M, football (non-tackle) M, soccer M. **Team name:** Golden Jets.

**Student services.** Adult student services, career counseling, services for economically disadvantaged, financial aid counseling, minority student services, on-campus daycare. **Physically disabled:** Services for visually, speech, hearing impaired. **Transfer:** Pre-admission transcript evaluation for new students. Transfer center, transfer adviser, college fairs on campus for students transferring to 4-year colleges.

**Contact.** E-mail: admissions@jccmi.edu
Phone: (517) 796-8425 Toll-free number: (888) 522-7344
Fax: (517) 796-8631
Julie Hand, Enrollment Services Team Leader, Jackson Community College, 2111 Emmons Road, Jackson, MI 49201-8399

## Kalamazoo Valley Community College
**Kalamazoo, Michigan**
www.kvcc.edu                                    CB code: 1378

- Public 2-year community college
- Commuter campus in small city

**General.** Founded in 1966. Regionally accredited. Additional campus downtown. **Enrollment:** 10,056 degree-seeking undergraduates. **Degrees:** 738 associate awarded. **Location:** 130 miles from Detroit, 150 miles from Chicago. **Calendar:** Semester, limited summer session. **Full-time faculty:** 140 total. **Part-time faculty:** 374 total. **Class size:** 30% < 20, 59% 20-39, 10% 40-49, less than 1% 50-99.

**Student profile.**

| | | | |
|---|---|---|---|
| Out-of-state: | 1% | 25 or older: | 50% |

**Transfer out. Colleges most students transferred to 2007:** Western Michigan University.

**Basis for selection.** Open admission.

**2007-2008 Annual costs.** Tuition/fees: $1,980; $3,150 out-of-district; $4,230 out-of-state. Per-credit charge: $66 in-district; $105 out-of-district; $141 out-of-state. Books/supplies: $912. Personal expenses: $1,282.

**Financial aid. Need-based:** Need-based aid available for part-time students. Work-study available nights, weekends and for part-time students. **Non-need-based:** Scholarships awarded for academics, athletics.

**Application procedures. Admission:** No deadline. No application fee. Application may be submitted online. Admission notification on a rolling basis. **Financial aid:** Priority date 6/1; no closing date. FAFSA, institutional form required. Applicants notified on a rolling basis starting 5/1; must reply within 2 week(s) of notification.

**Academics. Special study options:** Cooperative education, cross-registration, distance learning, dual enrollment of high school students, ESL, honors, independent study, internships, liberal arts/career combination, weekend college. License preparation in dental hygiene, nursing. **Credit/placement by examination:** CLEP, institutional tests. 32 credit hours maximum toward associate degree. Michigan Language Assessment Battery (MiLAB) may be used for placement. **Support services:** Learning center, reduced course load, remedial instruction, tutoring, writing center.

**Majors. Business:** Accounting, administrative services, business admin, management information systems. **Communications technology:** General. **Computer sciences:** Computer graphics, data processing, programming. **Education:** General. **Engineering:** General. **Engineering technology:** Drafting, electrical. **Family/consumer sciences:** Family studies. **Health:** Dental hygiene, licensed practical nurse, medical assistant, medical secretary, nursing (RN), respiratory therapy technology. **Legal studies:** Legal secretary. **Liberal arts:** Arts/sciences. **Mechanic/repair:** Automotive. **Physical sciences:** General. **Protective services:** Firefighting, law enforcement admin, police science. **Visual/performing arts:** Commercial/advertising art.

**Most popular majors.** Business/marketing 11%, education 11%, engineering/engineering technologies 7%, health sciences 12%, liberal arts 43%.

**Computing on campus.** 1,000 workstations in library, computer center, student center. Online course registration, wireless network available.

**Student life. Freshman orientation:** Available. **Activities:** Choral groups, dance, Fellowship of Christian Athletes, international student club, Student American Dental Hygiene Association, data processing association, African American association, Latino student association, Native American association, deaf student association.

**Athletics.** NJCAA. **Intercollegiate:** Baseball M, basketball, golf M, softball W, tennis, volleyball W. **Intramural:** Basketball M, tennis W, volleyball W. **Team name:** Cougars.

**Student services.** Career counseling, services for economically disadvantaged, student employment services, financial aid counseling, minority student services, on-campus daycare, personal counseling, placement for graduates, women's services. **Physically disabled:** Services for visually, speech, hearing impaired. **Transfer:** Transfer adviser, college fairs on campus for students transferring to 4-year colleges.

**Contact.** E-mail: admissions@kvcc.edu
Phone: (269) 488-4400 Fax: (269) 488-4161
Michael McCall, Director of Admissions, Registration and Records, Kalamazoo Valley Community College, 6767 West O Avenue, Kalamazoo, MI 49003-4070

## Kellogg Community College
**Battle Creek, Michigan**
www.kellogg.edu                                  CB code: 1375

- Public 2-year community college
- Commuter campus in small city

**General.** Founded in 1956. Regionally accredited. Academic centers in Coldwater, Hastings and Albion. Regional manufacturing technical center with open entry/open exit programs in 7 different technical areas. **Enrollment:** 4,368 degree-seeking undergraduates; 1,185 non-degree-seeking students. **Degrees:** 789 associate awarded. **Location:** 20 miles from Kalamazoo, 80 miles from Grand Rapids. **Calendar:** Semester, limited summer session. **Full-time faculty:** 90 total. **Part-time faculty:** 290 total.

**Student profile.** Among degree-seeking undergraduates, 926 enrolled as first-time, first-year students.

| | | | |
|---|---|---|---|
| Part-time: | 62% | Hispanic American: | 3% |
| Women: | 68% | Native American: | 1% |
| African American: | 9% | International: | 1% |
| Asian American: | 1% | 25 or older: | 56% |

**Transfer out. Colleges most students transferred to 2007:** Western Michigan University, Michigan State University, Ferris State University, Grand Valley State University, Central Michigan University.

**Basis for selection.** Open admission, but selective for some programs. Allied health and nursing program applicants must supply high school record and ACT/SAT test scores.

**High school preparation.** Recommended units include English 4, mathematics 4, social studies 1, history 3, science 4 (laboratory 1), foreign language 1 and academic electives 6.

**2007-2008 Annual costs.** Tuition/fees: $2,265; $3,540 out-of-district; $4,980 out-of-state. Books/supplies: $1,300. Personal expenses: $4,190.

**2007-2008 Financial aid. Need-based:** 34% of total undergraduate aid awarded as scholarships/grants, 66% as loans/jobs. Need-based aid available for part-time students. Work-study available nights and for part-time students. **Non-need-based:** Scholarships awarded for academics, alumni affiliation, athletics.

**Application procedures. Admission:** Priority date 8/1; no deadline. No application fee. Application may be submitted online. Admission notification on a rolling basis. **Financial aid:** Priority date 4/1; no closing date. FAFSA, institutional form required. Applicants notified on a rolling basis starting 4/1.

**Academics. Special study options:** Accelerated study, cooperative education, distance learning, double major, dual enrollment of high school students, honors, independent study, internships, liberal arts/career combination, weekend college. Bachelor's degree programs available on campus. License preparation in dental hygiene, nursing, paramedic, physical therapy, radiology. **Credit/placement by examination:** AP, CLEP, IB, institutional tests. Must be 2.0 or above for credit. **Support services:** Learning center, reduced course load, remedial instruction, study skills assistance, tutoring, writing center.

**Majors. Business:** Accounting, administrative services, business admin. **Communications technology:** General. **Computer sciences:** Programming. **Construction:** Electrician, pipefitting. **Engineering technology:** Drafting, electrical. **English:** English lit. **Family/consumer sciences:** Child care. **Health:** Clinical lab technology, dental hygiene, EMT paramedic, health services, medical radiologic technology/radiation therapy, medical secretary, nursing (RN), physical therapy assistant. **Legal studies:** Legal secretary, paralegal. **Liberal arts:** Arts/sciences. **Mechanic/repair:** Heating/ac/refrig, industrial. **Protective services:** Corrections, fire safety technology, police science. **Public administration:** Social work. **Visual/performing arts:** Commercial/advertising art.

**Most popular majors.** Business/marketing 8%, health sciences 21%, liberal arts 58%.

**Computing on campus.** 350 workstations in library, computer center. Commuter students can connect to campus network. Online course registration, online library, helpline, wireless network available.

**Student life. Freshman orientation:** Available. **Activities:** Bands, campus ministries, choral groups, drama, international student organizations, literary magazine, music ensembles, student newspaper, African American cultural enhancement association, human services club, Phi Theta Kappa, literary/photography magazine, art league, crude arts club, tech club.

**Athletics.** NJCAA. **Intercollegiate:** Baseball M, basketball, soccer M, softball W, volleyball W. **Team name:** Bruins.

**Student services.** Student employment services, financial aid counseling, personal counseling, placement for graduates, veterans' counselor. **Physically disabled:** Services for visually, speech, hearing impaired. **Transfer:** Pre-admission transcript evaluation for new students. Transfer adviser, college fairs on campus for students transferring to 4-year colleges.

**Contact.** Phone: (269) 365-4153 Fax: (269) 966-4089
Director of Enrollment Services, Kellogg Community College, 450 North Avenue, Battle Creek, MI 49017-3397

---

### Kirtland Community College
**Roscommon, Michigan**
**www.kirtland.edu**                                **CB code: 1382**

- Public 2-year community college
- Commuter campus in rural community

**General.** Founded in 1966. Regionally accredited. Additional campuses in Roscommon and Gaylord. **Enrollment:** 1,488 degree-seeking undergraduates; 409 non-degree-seeking students. **Degrees:** 124 associate awarded. **Location:** 192 miles from Detroit, 150 miles from Grand Rapids. **Calendar:** Semester, extensive summer session. **Full-time faculty:** 35 total; 11% have terminal degrees, 6% minority, 51% women. **Part-time faculty:** 101 total; 48% women. **Class size:** 86% < 20, 14% 20-39. **Special facilities:** Fitness and nature trail, firing range, Michigan Technical Education Center.

**Student profile.** Among degree-seeking undergraduates, 15% enrolled in a transfer program, 33% enrolled in a vocational program, 297 enrolled as first-time, first-year students, 84 transferred in from other institutions.

| | | | |
|---|---|---|---|
| Part-time: | 57% | 25 or older: | 57% |
| Women: | 61% | Live on campus: | 1% |

**Transfer out. Colleges most students transferred to 2007:** Central Michigan University, Saginaw Valley State University, Mid-Michigan Community College, North Central Michigan College.

**Basis for selection.** Open admission, but selective for some programs. Special requirements for nursing (levels I and II), precorrections, criminal justice administration, criminal justice pre-services, and corrections administration programs. **Homeschooled:** Transcript or record of courses and grades requested.

**High school preparation.** 10 units recommended. Recommended units include English 4, mathematics 2, social studies 2 and science 2.

**2007-2008 Annual costs.** Tuition/fees: $2,753; $4,596 out-of-district; $5,550 out-of-state. Per-credit charge: $74 in-district; $135 out-of-district; $167 out-of-state. Room/board: $4,400. Books/supplies: $900. Personal expenses: $564.

**2007-2008 Financial aid. Need-based:** Average need met was 50%. Average scholarship/grant was $3,675; average loan $913. 60% of total undergraduate aid awarded as scholarships/grants, 40% as loans/jobs. Need-based aid available for part-time students. Work-study available nights, weekends and for part-time students. **Non-need-based:** Scholarships awarded for academics, athletics, minority status. **Additional information:** Federal, state, and institutional work-study programs available.

**Application procedures. Admission:** No deadline. No application fee. Admission notification on a rolling basis. **Financial aid:** Priority date 5/1; no closing date. FAFSA required. Applicants notified on a rolling basis.

**Academics. Special study options:** Accelerated study, cooperative education, distance learning, dual enrollment of high school students, ESL, honors, independent study, internships. **Credit/placement by examination:** AP, CLEP, institutional tests. 45 credit hours maximum toward associate degree. **Support services:** Learning center, reduced course load, remedial instruction, tutoring, writing center.

**Majors. Agriculture:** Landscaping, plant breeding, turf management. **Business:** Administrative services, business admin, management information systems. **Computer sciences:** Systems analysis, webmaster, word processing. **Construction:** Carpentry. **Education:** Multi-level teacher, teacher assistance. **Engineering:** Computer. **Engineering technology:** Drafting, electrical, industrial, manufacturing. **Health:** Cardiovascular technology, EMT paramedic, massage therapy, medical assistant, medical secretary, medical transcription, nursing (RN), predental, premedicine, prepharmacy, preveterinary. **Legal studies:** Legal secretary. **Liberal arts:** Arts/sciences, humanities. **Mechanic/repair:** Automotive, heating/ac/refrig, industrial, small engine. **Personal/culinary services:** Aesthetician, cosmetic, cosmetology, manicurist, salon management. **Production:** Machine tool, welding. **Protective services:** Correctional facilities, corrections, law enforcement admin, police science. **Visual/performing arts:** Graphic design.

**Most popular majors.** Business/marketing 10%, health sciences 30%, liberal arts 40%, security/protective services 11%.

**Computing on campus.** 120 workstations in library, computer center, student center. Dormitories linked to campus network. Online course registration, online library, helpline, wireless network available.

**Student life. Freshman orientation:** Available. Preregistration for classes offered. **Housing:** Single-sex dorms available. $300 partly refundable deposit. **Activities:** Choral groups, drama, literary magazine, student government, student newspaper, student senate, Phi Theta Kappa, Christian Fellowship, criminal justice club.

**Athletics.** NJCAA. **Intercollegiate:** Basketball, cross-country, golf. **Team name:** Firebirds.

**Student services.** Adult student services, career counseling, student employment services, financial aid counseling, on-campus daycare, personal counseling, placement for graduates, veterans' counselor. **Physically disabled:** Services for visually, hearing impaired. **Transfer:** Transfer adviser, college fairs on campus for students transferring to 4-year colleges.

**Contact.** E-mail: admissions@kirtland.edu
Phone: (989) 275-5121 ext. 284 Fax: (989) 275-6727
Susie Allen, Coordinator of Admissions, Kirtland Community College, 10775 North Saint Helen Road, Roscommon, MI 48653

---

### Lake Michigan College
**Benton Harbor, Michigan**
**www.lakemichigancollege.edu**                        **CB code: 1137**

- Public 2-year community college
- Large town

**General.** Founded in 1946. Regionally accredited. Additional campuses located in South Haven and Bertrand Crossing. Michigan Technical Education Center (M-TEC) located in Benton Harbor, which offers programs in drafting and design, electronics, engineering, industrial maintenance, machine tool, and manufacturing. **Enrollment:** 2,916 degree-seeking undergraduates; 824 non-degree-seeking students. **Degrees:** 301 associate awarded. **Location:** 40 miles from South Bend, Indiana, 90 miles from Chicago. **Calendar:** Semester, limited summer session. **Full-time faculty:** 60 total; 33% have terminal degrees, 47% women. **Part-time faculty:** 205 total; 50% women. **Class size:** 71% < 20, 28% 20-39, less than 1% 40-49, less than 1% 50-99. **Special facilities:** Video production facility, nature area.

**Student profile.** Among degree-seeking undergraduates, 44% enrolled in a transfer program, 56% enrolled in a vocational program, 685 enrolled as first-time, first-year students, 116 transferred in from other institutions.

| | | | |
|---|---|---|---|
| Part-time: | 60% | Asian American: | 2% |
| Out-of-state: | 1% | Hispanic American: | 4% |
| Women: | 60% | Native American: | 1% |
| African American: | 18% | 25 or older: | 16% |

**Transfer out.** Colleges most students transferred to 2007: Western Michigan University, Sienna Heights University, Grand Valley State University, Michigan State University, Ferris State University.

**Basis for selection.** Open admission, but selective for some programs. Admission to health sciences programs based on 2.5 high school GPA in academic subjects. Interview required for dental assistant, radiologic technology, nursing majors. **Homeschooled:** State high school equivalency certificate required.

**2007-2008 Annual costs.** Tuition/fees: $3,105; $4,170 out-of-district; $5,190 out-of-state. Per-credit charge: $73 in-district; $108 out-of-district; $142 out-of-state. Books/supplies: $800. Personal expenses: $1,260.

**2006-2007 Financial aid. Need-based:** 91% of total undergraduate aid awarded as scholarships/grants, 9% as loans/jobs.

**Application procedures. Admission:** No deadline. No application fee. Application may be submitted online. Admission notification on a rolling basis. **Financial aid:** Priority date 3/1; no closing date. FAFSA required. Applicants notified on a rolling basis; must reply within 2 week(s) of notification.

**Academics. Special study options:** Cooperative education, cross-registration, distance learning, double major, dual enrollment of high school students, ESL, honors, independent study, internships, liberal arts/career combination, teacher certification program, weekend college. Bachelor's degree programs available on campus. License preparation in nursing, paramedic, radiology. **Credit/placement by examination:** AP, CLEP, institutional tests. 30 credit hours maximum toward associate degree. **Support services:** GED test center, learning center, remedial instruction, tutoring.

**Majors. Biology:** General. **Business:** Accounting, administrative services, business admin, finance, hospitality admin, office/clerical, operations, sales/distribution. **Computer sciences:** Information systems, word processing. **Education:** General, elementary. **Engineering:** General. **Engineering technology:** Drafting, electrical, manufacturing. **English:** English lit. **Foreign languages:** General. **Health:** Dental assistant, medical radiologic technology/radiation therapy, medical secretary, nursing (RN), predental, premedicine, prenursing, prepharmacy, preveterinary. **History:** General. **Interdisciplinary:** Biological/physical sciences. **Legal studies:** Legal secretary. **Liberal arts:** Arts/sciences, humanities. **Math:** General. **Parks/recreation:** Health/fitness. **Philosophy/religion:** Philosophy. **Physical sciences:** General, chemistry, physics. **Production:** Machine tool. **Protective services:** Corrections, police science. **Psychology:** General. **Social sciences:** General, political science, sociology. **Visual/performing arts:** Art, dramatic, graphic design, music performance.

**Most popular majors.** Business/marketing 14%, health sciences 31%, interdisciplinary studies 7%, liberal arts 34%.

**Computing on campus.** 100 workstations in computer center.

**Student life. Freshman orientation:** Mandatory. **Activities:** Bands, choral groups, drama, music ensembles, student government, student newspaper.

**Athletics.** NJCAA. **Intercollegiate:** Baseball M, basketball, golf M, softball W, volleyball W. **Intramural:** Badminton, baseball M, basketball, bowling, softball, table tennis, tennis, volleyball. **Team name:** Indians.

**Student services.** Career counseling, student employment services, health services, personal counseling, placement for graduates, veterans' counselor. **Physically disabled:** Services for visually, hearing impaired. **Transfer:** Re-entry adviser, pre-admission transcript evaluation for new students. College fairs on campus for students transferring to 4-year colleges.

**Contact.** E-mail: dail@lakemichigancollege.edu
Phone: (269) 927-8128 ext. 5035 Toll-free number: (800) 252-1562
Fax: (269) 927-6875
Michael Gantt, Lead Admissions Representative, Lake Michigan College, 2755 East Napier Avenue, Benton Harbor, MI 49022-1899

---

# Lansing Community College
**Lansing, Michigan**
www.lansing.cc.mi.us

**CB member**
**CB code: 1414**

- Public 2-year community college
- Commuter campus in small city

---

**General.** Founded in 1957. Regionally accredited. **Enrollment:** 13,453 degree-seeking undergraduates; 6,012 non-degree-seeking students. **Degrees:** 1,394 associate awarded. **ROTC:** Army, Air Force. **Location:** 90 miles from Detroit. **Calendar:** Semester, extensive summer session. **Full-time faculty:** 237 total; 16% minority, 52% women. **Part-time faculty:** 1,207 total; 11% minority. **Class size:** 65% < 20, 35% 20-39, less than 1% 40-49, less than 1% 50-99, less than 1% >100. **Special facilities:** Planetarium, observatory, science concepts laboratory, computer-integrated manufacturing institute, in-depth photography institute, truck driver training range, technical library.

**Student profile.** Among degree-seeking undergraduates, 30% enrolled in a transfer program, 30% enrolled in a vocational program, 3,636 enrolled as first-time, first-year students.

| | | | |
|---|---|---|---|
| Part-time: | 65% | Hispanic American: | 5% |
| Women: | 55% | Native American: | 1% |
| African American: | 9% | International: | 1% |
| Asian American: | 2% | 25 or older: | 38% |

**Transfer out.** Colleges most students transferred to 2007: Michigan State University, Central Michigan University.

**Basis for selection.** Open admission, but selective for some programs. Special requirements for health, aviation, music, police academy programs, fire academy. MELAB required of foreign students. TOEFL also accepted. Interview required of health program applicants and international applicants. Audition recommended for music, dance, theater majors. Portfolio recommended for art majors.

**2007-2008 Annual costs.** Tuition/fees: $2,100; $3,650 out-of-district; $5,450 out-of-state. Per-credit charge: $67 in-district; $120 out-of-district; $180 out-of-state. Books/supplies: $660. Personal expenses: $1,020.

**Financial aid. Need-based:** Need-based aid available for part-time students. Work-study available nights, weekends and for part-time students. **Non-need-based:** Scholarships awarded for academics, athletics.

**Application procedures. Admission:** No deadline. No application fee. Application may be submitted online. Admission notification on a rolling basis. SAT or ACT recommended for assessment waivers and counseling. **Financial aid:** Priority date 7/5; no closing date. FAFSA required. Applicants notified on a rolling basis starting 4/3.

**Academics.** Several 4-year degree course studies available, students complete 3 years at LCC and 4th year at a 4-year degree institution. **Special study options:** Accelerated study, cooperative education, cross-registration, distance learning, double major, dual enrollment of high school students, exchange student, honors, independent study, internships, study abroad, teacher certification program, weekend college. External bachelor's degree with Northwood Institute, 3+1 degree program, 2+2 degree program. Bachelor's degree programs available on campus. License preparation in aviation, dental hygiene, nursing, paramedic, real estate. **Credit/placement by examination:** AP, CLEP, IB, institutional tests. 40 credit hours maximum toward associate degree. **Support services:** Learning center, pre-admission summer program, reduced course load, remedial instruction, study skills assistance, tutoring, writing center.

**Majors. Architecture:** Interior, landscape. **Area/ethnic studies:** African. **Biology:** General. **Business:** General, accounting, administrative services, business admin, fashion, hospitality/recreation, human resources, insurance, international, management information systems, marketing, office management, office technology, real estate, sales/distribution, tourism promotion, tourism/travel. **Communications:** General, advertising, broadcast journalism, journalism. **Communications technology:** General, graphic/printing. **Computer sciences:** General, applications programming, data processing, networking, programming, systems analysis, vendor certification. **Conservation:** General. **Construction:** Carpentry, maintenance, masonry, pipefitting, power transmission. **Education:** General, art, elementary, mathematics, music, physical, science, secondary, social science, special, speech, trade/industrial. **Engineering:** General. **Engineering technology:** Civil, drafting, electrical, environmental, hydraulics. **English:** American lit, English lit. **Family/consumer sciences:** General, child care, institutional food production. **Foreign languages:** General, French, German, sign language interpretation, Spanish. **Health:** Clinical lab science, dental hygiene, EMT paramedic, health care admin, licensed practical nurse, medical assistant, medical radiologic technology/radiation therapy, medical secretary, nuclear medical technology, physician assistant, predental, respiratory therapy technology, sonography, surgical technology. **History:** General. **Interdisciplinary:** Biological/physical sciences, gerontology. **Legal studies:** Court reporting, legal secretary, paralegal, prelaw. **Liberal arts:** Arts/sciences. **Math:** General, applied. **Mechanic/repair:** General, aircraft, avionics, electronics/electrical, heating/ac/refrig, industrial. **Parks/recreation:** Facilities management. **Personal/culinary services:** Cosmetic, culinary arts. **Philosophy/religion:** Philosophy, religion. **Physical sciences:** Chemistry. **Protective services:** Criminal justice, firefighting, law enforcement admin, police science. **Psychology:** General. **Public administration:** Social work. **Social sciences:** General, anthropology, geography, political science, sociology. **Transportation:** Aviation.

**Visual/performing arts:** General, art, cinematography, commercial/advertising art, dance, dramatic, drawing, music performance, music theory/composition, painting, photography.

**Most popular majors.** Business/marketing 8%, English 48%, health sciences 18%.

**Computing on campus.** 200 workstations in library, computer center. Commuter students can connect to campus network. Online course registration, helpline, wireless network available.

**Student life. Freshman orientation:** Available. Preregistration for classes offered. Occurs first 5 days of open registration. **Activities:** Bands, choral groups, dance, drama, film society, music ensembles, musical theater, radio station, student government, student newspaper, symphony orchestra, TV station, Newman club, black student delegates, Hispanic club, Campus Disciples, Baptist student union, international club, Maranatha Christian Fellowship, student adviser club, substance abuse association.

**Athletics.** NJCAA. **Intercollegiate:** Basketball, cross-country, golf, track and field, volleyball W. **Intramural:** Basketball, bowling, boxing M. **Team name:** Stars.

**Student services.** Adult student services, career counseling, services for economically disadvantaged, student employment services, financial aid counseling, minority student services, personal counseling, placement for graduates, veterans' counselor, women's services. **Physically disabled:** Services for visually, speech, hearing impaired. **Transfer:** Transfer adviser, college fairs on campus for students transferring to 4-year colleges.

**Contact.** Phone: (517) 483-1200 Toll-free number: (800) 644-4522 Fax: (517) 483-9668
Director of Admissions, Lansing Community College, 422 North Washington Square, Lansing, MI 48901

## Macomb Community College
Warren, Michigan
www.macomb.edu

CB member
CB code: 1722

▶ Public 2-year community college
▶ Commuter campus in small city

**General.** Founded in 1954. Regionally accredited. **Enrollment:** 12,902 degree-seeking undergraduates; 9,179 non-degree-seeking students. **Degrees:** 2,190 associate awarded. **Location:** 20 miles from Detroit. **Calendar:** Semester, extensive summer session. **Full-time faculty:** 229 total; 14% have terminal degrees, 4% minority, 44% women. **Part-time faculty:** 803 total; 9% have terminal degrees, 5% minority, 42% women. **Special facilities:** Nature preserves, center for performing arts.

**Student profile.** Among degree-seeking undergraduates, 1,268 enrolled as first-time, first-year students.

| | | | |
|---|---|---|---|
| Part-time: | 63% | Hispanic American: | 1% |
| Women: | 51% | International: | 5% |
| African American: | 6% | 25 or older: | 39% |
| Asian American: | 2% | | |

**Transfer out. Colleges most students transferred to 2007:** Central Michigan University, Oakland University, Walsh College, Wayne State University, Michigan State University.

**Basis for selection.** Open admission, but selective for some programs. Special requirements for nursing, physical therapy assistant, occupational therapy assistant, respiratory therapy assistant, veterinarian technician programs; combination of GPA and test scores considered.

**2007-2008 Annual costs.** Tuition/fees: $2,140; $3,250 out-of-district; $4,210 out-of-state. Per-credit charge: $70 in-district; $107 out-of-district; $139 out-of-state. Books/supplies: $578. Personal expenses: $791.

**2006-2007 Financial aid. Need-based:** Need-based aid available for part-time students. Work-study available nights, weekends and for part-time students. **Non-need-based:** Scholarships awarded for academics, athletics, leadership, music/drama, state residency.

**Application procedures. Admission:** No deadline. No application fee. Admission notification on a rolling basis. January 31 closing date for nursing and physical therapy assistant programs. **Financial aid:** Priority date 4/15; no closing date. FAFSA, institutional form required. Applicants notified on a rolling basis starting 5/15; must reply within 2 week(s) of notification.

**Academics.** Courses toward bachelor's degrees offered on campus by University of Detroit, Walsh College of Accountancy and Business Administration, Wayne State University, Central Michigan University, Oakland University, University of Detroit Mercy, Davenport University, Rochester College. On-line degree program with Franklin University. **Special study options:** Cooperative education, cross-registration, distance learning, dual enrollment of high school students, ESL, independent study, internships, liberal arts/career combination, study abroad, weekend college. **Credit/placement by examination:** AP, CLEP, institutional tests. 47 credit hours maximum toward associate degree. **Support services:** Learning center, reduced course load, remedial instruction, tutoring.

**Majors. Biology:** General. **Business:** General, accounting, administrative services, business admin, marketing, office technology, operations. **Communications:** General, broadcast journalism, public relations. **Communications technology:** Graphic/printing. **Computer sciences:** General, data entry, networking, programming, web page design. **Engineering technology:** Civil, construction, drafting, electrical, manufacturing, surveying. **Family/consumer sciences:** Child care. **Health:** EMT paramedic, health services, medical assistant, medical secretary, nursing (RN), occupational therapy assistant, physical therapy assistant, respiratory therapy technology, surgical technology, veterinary technology/assistant. **Legal studies:** Paralegal. **Liberal arts:** Arts/sciences. **Math:** General. **Mechanic/repair:** Automotive, electronics/electrical, heating/ac/refrig. **Personal/culinary services:** Culinary arts. **Physical sciences:** Chemistry. **Protective services:** Fire safety technology, firefighting, forensics, police science. **Visual/performing arts:** Commercial/advertising art.

**Most popular majors.** Business/marketing 12%, engineering/engineering technologies 6%, health sciences 13%, liberal arts 51%.

**Computing on campus.** 1,800 workstations in library, computer center. Commuter students can connect to campus network.

**Student life. Freshman orientation:** Available. Occurs beginning of semester. **Activities:** Bands, choral groups, dance, drama, music ensembles, musical theater, symphony orchestra, student activities board, College Republicans, service learning and volunteerism, Newman Club, Campus Crusade for Christ, Young Democrats, African American alliance, international culture club, Phi Theta Kappa.

**Athletics.** NJCAA. **Intercollegiate:** Baseball M, basketball, cross-country, soccer M, softball W, volleyball W.

**Student services.** Campus ministries, career counseling, student employment services, financial aid counseling, health services, personal counseling, placement for graduates. **Physically disabled:** Services for visually, speech, hearing impaired. **Transfer:** Transfer adviser, college fairs on campus for students transferring to 4-year colleges.

**Contact.** Phone: (586) 445-7999 Toll-free number: (866) 622-6621 Fax: (586) 445-7157
Ronald Hughes, Director of Enrollment Services, Macomb Community College, 14500 East Twelve Mile Road, Warren, MI 48088-3896

## Mid Michigan Community College
Harrison, Michigan
www.midmich.edu

CB code: 1523

▶ Public 2-year community college
▶ Commuter campus in small town

**General.** Founded in 1965. Regionally accredited. Branch campus in Mt. Pleasant. **Enrollment:** 1,741 full-time, degree-seeking students. **Degrees:** 311 associate awarded. **Location:** 30 miles from Mount Pleasant, 100 miles from Lansing. **Calendar:** Semester, limited summer session. **Full-time faculty:** 40 total. **Part-time faculty:** 150 total. **Class size:** 55% < 20, 42% 20-39, 2% 40-49, less than 1% 50-99.

**Student profile.**

| | | | |
|---|---|---|---|
| Out-of-state: | 5% | 25 or older: | 65% |

**Transfer out. Colleges most students transferred to 2007:** Central Michigan University, Ferris State University, Saginaw Valley State University.

**Basis for selection.** Open admission, but selective for some programs. Admission for health occupations majors based on prerequisite course completion and grades. High school diploma or GED recommended. Interview required of health program applicants. **Learning Disabled:** Students referred to counselor to address special needs.

**High school preparation.** Recommended units include English 4, mathematics 4, social studies 2, history 1, science 3 (laboratory 2) and foreign language 1. One unit chemistry, 1 algebra, 1 biology required for health occupations majors.

**2007-2008 Annual costs.** Tuition/fees: $2,298; $3,698 out-of-district; $7,170 out-of-state. Per-credit charge: $73 in-district; $119 out-of-district; $235 out-of-state. Books/supplies: $766. Personal expenses: $698.

**Financial aid. Need-based:** Need-based aid available for part-time students. Work-study available for part-time students. **Non-need-based:** Scholarships awarded for academics.

**Application procedures. Admission:** No deadline. No application fee. Application may be submitted online. Admission notification on a rolling basis. **Financial aid:** Priority date 5/1; no closing date. FAFSA, institutional form required. Applicants notified on a rolling basis starting 4/1; must reply within 2 week(s) of notification.

**Academics. Special study options:** Cooperative education, distance learning, double major, dual enrollment of high school students, independent study, internships, liberal arts/career combination. License preparation in nursing, paramedic, radiology. **Credit/placement by examination:** AP, CLEP, institutional tests. 15 credit hours maximum toward associate degree. **Support services:** Learning center, reduced course load, remedial instruction, study skills assistance, tutoring, writing center.

**Majors. Biology:** General, biotechnology. **Business:** Accounting, administrative services, banking/financial services, business admin, entrepreneurial studies, marketing. **Communications:** General. **Computer sciences:** General, applications programming, computer science. **Conservation:** General, fisheries. **Education:** Elementary, secondary, teacher assistance. **Engineering:** General. **Engineering technology:** Manufacturing. **English:** Speech/rhetoric. **Family/consumer sciences:** Child care. **Health:** EMT paramedic, medical assistant, medical radiologic technology/radiation therapy, medical secretary, medical transcription, nursing (RN), prepharmacy. **Legal studies:** Legal secretary. **Liberal arts:** Arts/sciences. **Math:** General. **Mechanic/repair:** Heating/ac/refrig. **Physical sciences:** Chemistry. **Protective services:** Firefighting, police science. **Psychology:** General. **Social sciences:** Sociology. **Visual/performing arts:** General, commercial/advertising art, dramatic.

**Computing on campus.** 450 workstations in library, computer center. Commuter students can connect to campus network. Online library, helpline available.

**Student life. Freshman orientation:** Available. Preregistration for classes offered. Scheduled before each semester. **Housing:** Community-wide housing bulletin available on request. **Activities:** Drama, musical theater, student government, Phi Theta Kappa.

**Student services.** Adult student services, alcohol/substance abuse counseling, career counseling, services for economically disadvantaged, student employment services, financial aid counseling, personal counseling, placement for graduates, veterans' counselor. **Physically disabled:** Services for visually, speech, hearing impaired. **Transfer:** Pre-admission transcript evaluation for new students. Transfer adviser, college fairs on campus for students transferring to 4-year colleges.

**Contact.** E-mail: kbarnes@midmich.edu
Phone: (989) 386-6661 Fax: (989) 386-6613
Kim Barnes, Director of Admissions and Placement, Mid Michigan Community College, 1375 South Clare Avenue, Harrison, MI 48625

## Monroe County Community College
Monroe, Michigan
www.monroeccc.edu                                   CB code: 1514

‣ Public 2-year community college
‣ Commuter campus in large town

**General.** Founded in 1964. Regionally accredited. Off-campus site at Whitman Center. **Enrollment:** 4,433 undergraduates. **Degrees:** 448 associate awarded. **Location:** 45 miles from Detroit, 20 miles from Toledo, Ohio. **Calendar:** Semester, limited summer session. **Full-time faculty:** 62 total. **Part-time faculty:** 125 total.

**Student profile.** 49% enrolled in a transfer program, 51% enrolled in a vocational program.

Out-of-state:          1%        25 or older:          40%

**Transfer out. Colleges most students transferred to 2007:** Eastern Michigan University, University of Toledo, Sierra Heights University, Western Michigan University, University of Michigan.

**Basis for selection.** Open admission, but selective for some programs. Admission for nursing, respiratory therapy and medical assistance applicants based on 2.5 high school GPA, 21 ACT preferred. Completion of biological and chemistry courses, and completion of college math required. Culinary skills program also selective. ACT required for nursing and respiratory therapy applicants. Test scores required by March 31. Interview required of respiratory therapy and culinary program applicants.

**High school preparation.** Recommended units include English 4, mathematics 3, social studies 3, history 1 and science 3. Nursing and respiratory therapy applicants must have 1 unit chemistry and 1 biology. Strong science background highly recommended.

**2007-2008 Annual costs.** Tuition/fees: $2,150; $3,530 out-of-district; $3,890 out-of-state. Per-credit charge: $68 in-district; $116 out-of-district; $128 out-of-state. Books/supplies: $700. Personal expenses: $560.

**Financial aid. Need-based:** Need-based aid available for part-time students. Work-study available nights, weekends and for part-time students. **Non-need-based:** Scholarships awarded for academics, alumni affiliation, art, leadership, music/drama, state residency.

**Application procedures. Admission:** Priority date 5/1; no deadline. No application fee. Application may be submitted online. Admission notification on a rolling basis. Closing date for nursing and respiratory therapy applications: 5/10. **Financial aid:** Priority date 4/1; no closing date. FAFSA, institutional form required. Applicants notified on a rolling basis starting 4/1; must reply within 2 week(s) of notification.

**Academics. Special study options:** Accelerated study, combined bachelor's/graduate degree, cooperative education, dual enrollment of high school students, independent study. Bachelor's degree programs available on campus. License preparation in nursing, paramedic, real estate. **Credit/placement by examination:** AP, CLEP, institutional tests. 30 credit hours maximum toward associate degree. **Support services:** Learning center, reduced course load, remedial instruction, tutoring.

**Majors. Business:** Accounting, administrative services, banking/financial services, business admin, office technology, office/clerical. **Computer sciences:** General, applications programming, programming. **Education:** Early childhood. **Engineering:** Electrical. **Engineering technology:** Architectural, drafting, electrical, manufacturing. **Family/consumer sciences:** Child care. **Health:** Medical secretary, nursing (RN), respiratory therapy technology. **Legal studies:** Legal secretary. **Liberal arts:** Arts/sciences. **Personal/culinary services:** Culinary arts. **Visual/performing arts:** Studio arts.

**Computing on campus.** 90 workstations in computer center.

**Student life. Freshman orientation:** Available. **Activities:** Concert band, choral groups, drama, student government, student newspaper, respiratory therapy club, nursing club, Society of Automotive Engineers, campus Bible study.

**Student services.** Career counseling, student employment services, on-campus daycare, personal counseling, placement for graduates. **Physically disabled:** Services for visually, speech, hearing impaired. **Transfer:** Transfer adviser, college fairs on campus for students transferring to 4-year colleges.

**Contact.** E-mail: mhall@monroeccc.edu
Phone: (734) 384-4104 Toll-free number: (877) 937-6222
Fax: (734) 242-9711
Mark Hall, Director of Admissions and Guidance Services, Monroe County Community College, 1555 South Raisinville Road, Monroe, MI 48161-9746

## Montcalm Community College
Sidney, Michigan
www.montcalm.edu                                    CB code: 1522

‣ Public 2-year community and liberal arts college
‣ Commuter campus in rural community

**General.** Founded in 1965. Regionally accredited. Off-campus centers in Ionia, Howard City, Greenville and Alma. **Enrollment:** 2,356 degree-seeking undergraduates; 361 non-degree-seeking students. **Degrees:** 179 associate awarded. **Location:** 50 miles from Grand Rapids, 65 miles from Lansing. **Calendar:** Semester, limited summer session. **Full-time faculty:** 34 total. **Part-time faculty:** 145 total. **Class size:** 55% < 20, 44% 20-39, less than 1% 40-49, less than 1% >100. **Special facilities:** Marked nature preserves and trails, barn theatre.

**Student profile.** Among degree-seeking undergraduates, 350 enrolled as first-time, first-year students.

| | | | |
|---|---|---|---|
| Part-time: | 48% | Hispanic American: | 1% |
| Women: | 70% | Native American: | 1% |

**Transfer out. Colleges most students transferred to 2007:** Central Michigan University, Ferris State University, Grand Valley State University, Davenport University.

**Basis for selection.** Open admission, but selective for some programs. Applicants to nursing program must score 41 on ASSET Reading Skills Test and 41 on Numerical Skills Test, 18 on corresponding ACT subscores, or COMPASS pre-algebra of 44 and reading of 80.

**2007-2008 Annual costs.** Tuition/fees: $2,265; $3,465 out-of-district; $4,425 out-of-state. Per-credit charge: $70 in-district; $111 out-of-district; $149 out-of-state. Personal expenses: $1,739.

**Financial aid. Need-based:** Need-based aid available for part-time students. Work-study available for part-time students. **Non-need-based:** Scholarships awarded for academics, state residency.

**Application procedures. Admission:** No deadline. No application fee. Application may be submitted online. Admission notification on a rolling basis. **Financial aid:** Priority date 2/15; no closing date. FAFSA, institutional form required. Applicants notified on a rolling basis starting 6/15; must reply within 2 week(s) of notification.

**Academics. Special study options:** Cooperative education, distance learning, dual enrollment of high school students, independent study, internships, liberal arts/career combination. License preparation in nursing, paramedic. **Credit/placement by examination:** AP, CLEP, institutional tests. **Support services:** GED test center, learning center, reduced course load, remedial instruction, study skills assistance, tutoring.

**Majors. Business:** Accounting, administrative services, business admin, construction management, entrepreneurial studies, executive assistant, information resources management, management information systems, office technology. **Computer sciences:** General, data processing. **Education:** Teacher assistance. **Engineering technology:** Automotive, drafting, electrical, industrial, manufacturing, surveying. **Family/consumer sciences:** Child care. **Health:** Medical secretary, nursing (RN). **Liberal arts:** Arts/sciences. **Mechanic/repair:** Computer, electronics/electrical. **Personal/culinary services:** Cosmetic. **Protective services:** Criminal justice.

**Most popular majors.** Business/marketing 20%, health sciences 32%, liberal arts 36%.

**Computing on campus.** 450 workstations in library, computer center. Helpline available.

**Student life. Freshman orientation:** Mandatory. **Activities:** Jazz band, choral groups, drama, music ensembles, musical theater, student newspaper, Phi Theta Kappa, future business professionals club, Native American club, nursing club, judo club.

**Athletics. Intramural:** Volleyball.

**Student services.** Career counseling, student employment services, financial aid counseling, placement for graduates. **Physically disabled:** Services for visually, speech, hearing impaired. **Transfer:** Pre-admission transcript evaluation for new students. Transfer adviser, college fairs on campus for students transferring to 4-year colleges.

**Contact.** E-mail: admissions@montcalm.edu
Phone: (989) 328-1250 Toll-free number: (877) 328-2111
Fax: (989) 328-2950
Debra Alexander, Director of Admissions, Montcalm Community College, 2800 College Drive, Sidney, MI 48885

---

# Mott Community College

**Flint, Michigan**      **CB member**
**www.mcc.edu**      **CB code: 1225**

◆ Public 2-year community college
◆ Commuter campus in large city

**General.** Founded in 1923. Regionally accredited. Branch campuses located in Fenton, Lapeer, Livingston, and Clio. **Enrollment:** 7,255 degree-seeking undergraduates; 3,200 non-degree-seeking students. **Degrees:** 1,119 associate awarded. **Location:** 65 miles from Detroit. **Calendar:** Semester, extensive summer session. **Full-time faculty:** 149 total; 19% have terminal degrees, 17% minority, 58% women. **Part-time faculty:** 354 total; 6% have terminal degrees, 16% minority, 56% women. **Special facilities:** Geology

museum, regional technology center, dental clinic, visual arts and design center, greenhouse, student-operated cosmetology/nail technology salon, hospital wing replica, SimMan room, esthetician labs.

**Student profile.** Among degree-seeking undergraduates, 12% enrolled in a transfer program, 75% enrolled in a vocational program, 708 enrolled as first-time, first-year students, 338 transferred in from other institutions.

| | | | |
|---|---|---|---|
| Part-time: | 65% | Hispanic American: | 2% |
| Women: | 64% | Native American: | 1% |
| African American: | 19% | 25 or older: | 48% |
| Asian American: | 1% | | |

**Transfer out. Colleges most students transferred to 2007:** University of Michigan: Flint, Ferris State University, Central Michigan University, Saginaw Valley State University, Eastern Michigan University.

**Basis for selection.** Open admission, but selective for some programs. Special requirements for nursing and allied health programs. Audition recommended for music majors. **Learning Disabled:** Students must request assistance, provide documentation of disabilities, and register with Disability Services before classes begin.

**2007-2008 Annual costs.** Tuition/fees: $2,712; $3,942 out-of-district; $5,172 out-of-state. Per-credit charge: $82 in-district; $123 out-of-district; $164 out-of-state. Books/supplies: $927. Personal expenses: $881.

**2006-2007 Financial aid. Need-based:** 56% of total undergraduate aid awarded as scholarships/grants, 44% as loans/jobs. Need-based aid available for part-time students. Work-study available nights and for part-time students. **Non-need-based:** Scholarships awarded for academics, alumni affiliation, art, athletics, leadership, minority status, music/drama, state residency.

**Application procedures. Admission:** No deadline. No application fee. Application may be submitted online. Admission notification on a rolling basis. **Financial aid:** No deadline. FAFSA required. Applicants notified on a rolling basis starting 5/1.

**Academics.** Distance learning and open entry/open exit modular courses being expanded in Regional Technology Center. **Special study options:** Cooperative education, distance learning, double major, dual enrollment of high school students, ESL, honors, independent study, internships, liberal arts/career combination. Bachelor's degree programs available on campus. License preparation in dental hygiene, nursing, occupational therapy, physical therapy. **Credit/placement by examination:** AP, CLEP, institutional tests. 16 credit hours maximum toward associate degree. **Support services:** Learning center, remedial instruction, study skills assistance, tutoring, writing center.

**Majors. Business:** General, accounting technology, administrative services, business admin, entrepreneurial studies, executive assistant, international, management information systems, marketing, office management, office technology. **Communications technology:** General. **Computer sciences:** Networking. **Education:** Early childhood, teacher assistance. **Engineering technology:** Architectural, drafting, electrical, heat/ac/refrig, manufacturing, mechanical, mechanical drafting, quality control, surveying. **Family/consumer sciences:** Institutional food production. **Foreign languages:** Sign language interpretation. **Health:** Community health services, dental assistant, dental hygiene, EMT paramedic, histologic assistant, medical radiologic technology/radiation therapy, nursing (RN), occupational therapy assistant, physical therapy assistant, respiratory therapy technology. **Liberal arts:** Arts/sciences. **Mechanic/repair:** Auto body, automotive. **Personal/culinary services:** Baking, chef training, salon management. **Protective services:** Fire safety technology, police science. **Visual/performing arts:** Art, graphic design, photography. **Other:** Applied technology, Industrial technology.

**Most popular majors.** Business/marketing 7%, health sciences 19%, liberal arts 54%, security/protective services 7%.

**Computing on campus.** 1,290 workstations in library, computer center, student center. Commuter students can connect to campus network. Online course registration, wireless network available.

**Student life. Freshman orientation:** Mandatory. Three-hour sessions. **Activities:** Bands, choral groups, music ensembles, student government, student newspaper, criminal justice club, connoisseur club, environmental club, Phi Theta Kappa, student nurses association, dental hygiene club, gardening association, social work club, ballroomers/steppers, travel club.

**Athletics.** NJCAA. **Intercollegiate:** Baseball M, basketball, cross-country, golf M, softball W, volleyball W. **Team name:** Bears.

**Student services.** Career counseling, services for economically disadvantaged, student employment services, financial aid counseling, health services, on-campus daycare, personal counseling, placement for graduates.

**Physically disabled:** Services for visually, speech, hearing impaired. **Transfer:** Pre-admission transcript evaluation for new students. Transfer adviser, college fairs on campus for students transferring to 4-year colleges.

**Contact.** E-mail: Inquiry@mcc.edu
Phone: (810) 762-0315 Toll-free number: (800) 852-8614
Fax: (810) 232-9442
Delores Deen, Executive Dean, Student Services, Mott Community College, 1401 East Court Street, Flint, MI 48503-2089

## Muskegon Community College
### Muskegon, Michigan
### www.muskegoncc.edu
**CB code: 1495**

- Public 2-year community college
- Commuter campus in small city

**General.** Founded in 1926. Regionally accredited. Bachelor's and graduate programs offered on-campus with participating 4-year institutions. **Enrollment:** 4,707 degree-seeking undergraduates. **Degrees:** 415 associate awarded. **Location:** 45 miles from Grand Rapids. **Calendar:** Semester, limited summer session. **Full-time faculty:** 110 total. **Part-time faculty:** 150 total. **Special facilities:** Planetarium, nature preserve, herbal garden, observatory.

**Basis for selection.** Open admission, but selective for some programs. Nursing applicants must have math (level 35) and basic college chemistry. High school diploma, GED, 10th-grade reading level on Nelson Denny, or 22 ACT required for select programs and courses. High school diploma, GED or completion of 15 credits with at least a C average required for degree-seeking candidates. **Homeschooled:** Transcript of courses and grades required.

**2007-2008 Annual costs.** Tuition/fees: $2,270; $3,470 out-of-district; $4,610 out-of-state. Per-credit charge: $67 in-district; $107 out-of-district; $145 out-of-state. Students also assessed contact hour fees, which vary according to residency status, and course fees, which vary. Books/supplies: $1,000. Personal expenses: $800.

**Financial aid. Need-based:** Work-study available nights, weekends and for part-time students.

**Application procedures. Admission:** Priority date 5/1; no deadline. No application fee. Application may be submitted online. Admission notification on a rolling basis. **Financial aid:** Priority date 5/1; no closing date. FAFSA, institutional form required. Applicants notified on a rolling basis starting 6/1; must reply within 2 week(s) of notification.

**Academics. Special study options:** Cooperative education, cross-registration, distance learning, double major, dual enrollment of high school students, honors, independent study, internships. License preparation in nursing, real estate. **Credit/placement by examination:** AP, CLEP, institutional tests. 30 credit hours maximum toward associate degree. **Support services:** Learning center, remedial instruction, tutoring, writing center.

**Majors. Business:** Accounting, administrative services, international, marketing. **Communications technology:** Graphic/printing. **Computer sciences:** General, data processing. **Engineering technology:** Drafting, electrical. **Health:** Licensed practical nurse, medical secretary, nursing (RN), respiratory therapy technology. **Legal studies:** Legal secretary. **Mechanic/repair:** General. **Protective services:** Law enforcement admin. **Visual/performing arts:** Commercial/advertising art.

**Computing on campus.** Wireless network available.

**Student life. Freshman orientation:** Available. **Activities:** Bands, choral groups, dance, drama, music ensembles, musical theater, student government, student newspaper, TV station, interdenominational religious group, black student alliance, Students Again Gaining Enlightenment, study opportunities for adults and mature citizens.

**Athletics.** NJCAA. **Intercollegiate:** Baseball M, basketball, golf, softball W, tennis W, volleyball W, wrestling M. **Intramural:** Baseball M, basketball, bowling, golf, softball W, table tennis. **Team name:** Jayhawks.

**Student services.** Career counseling, student employment services, health services, personal counseling, placement for graduates, veterans' counselor. **Physically disabled:** Services for visually, speech, hearing impaired. **Transfer:** College fairs on campus for students transferring to 4-year colleges.

**Contact.** E-mail: darlene.peklar@muskegoncc.edu
Phone: (231) 777-0363 Toll-free number: (866) 711-4622
Fax: (231) 777-0209
Jean Roberts, Director of Records and Registration, Muskegon Community College, 221 South Quarterline Road, Muskegon, MI 49442

## North Central Michigan College
### Petoskey, Michigan
### www.ncmich.edu
**CB code: 1569**

- Public 2-year community college
- Commuter campus in small town

**General.** Founded in 1958. Regionally accredited. **Enrollment:** 2,228 degree-seeking undergraduates. **Degrees:** 255 associate awarded. **Location:** 40 miles from Mackinaw City, 60 miles from Traverse City. **Calendar:** Semester, limited summer session. **Full-time faculty:** 33 total. **Part-time faculty:** 136 total. **Class size:** 100% 20-39. **Special facilities:** Nature preserve.

**Student profile.**

| | | | |
|---|---|---|---|
| Out-of-state: | 5% | Live on campus: | 5% |
| 25 or older: | 57% | | |

**Transfer out. Colleges most students transferred to 2007:** Lake Superior State University, Grand Valley State University, Central Michigan University, Northern Michigan University, Ferris State University.

**Basis for selection.** Open admission, but selective for some programs. Special requirements for nursing program. All degree-seeking students must provide ACT, SAT or COMPASS scores for mandatory placement.

**High school preparation.** Recommended units include English 3, mathematics 3 and science 3. Chemistry recommended for nursing applicants.

**2007-2008 Annual costs.** Tuition/fees: $2,286; $3,549 out-of-district; $4,444 out-of-state. Per-credit charge: $68 in-district; $110 out-of-district; $140 out-of-state. Room only: $2,520. Books/supplies: $750.

**Financial aid. Need-based:** Need-based aid available for part-time students. Work-study available nights, weekends and for part-time students.

**Application procedures. Admission:** No deadline. No application fee. Application must be submitted online. Admission notification on a rolling basis. **Financial aid:** Closing date 4/1. FAFSA, institutional form required. Applicants notified on a rolling basis starting 4/30.

**Academics. Special study options:** Cooperative education, cross-registration, distance learning, dual enrollment of high school students, independent study, internships. Bachelor's degree programs available on campus. **Credit/placement by examination:** AP, CLEP, IB. 15 credit hours maximum toward associate degree. **Support services:** Learning center, remedial instruction, tutoring.

**Majors. Business:** General, accounting, administrative services, business admin, office/clerical. **Computer sciences:** General. **Education:** Early childhood. **Health:** EMT paramedic, nursing (RN). **Legal studies:** Paralegal. **Liberal arts:** Arts/sciences.

**Most popular majors.** Health sciences 21%, liberal arts 71%.

**Computing on campus.** 133 workstations in dormitories, library, computer center, student center. Dormitories wired for high-speed internet access and linked to campus network. Commuter students can connect to campus network. Online course registration available.

**Student life. Freshman orientation:** Available. Preregistration for classes offered. Held in summer before classes begin. **Housing:** Coed dorms available. $50 deposit. **Activities:** Student government, student newspaper, sports clubs, nursing student association, Phi Theta Kappa, Campus Crusade.

**Athletics. Intramural:** Basketball, volleyball.

**Student services.** Career counseling, services for economically disadvantaged, financial aid counseling, personal counseling, veterans' counselor, women's services. **Physically disabled:** Services for visually, speech, hearing impaired. **Learning disabled:** Comprehensive services available. **Transfer:** Transfer adviser, college fairs on campus for students transferring to 4-year colleges.

**Contact.** E-mail: advisor@ncmc.cc.mi.us
Phone: (231) 348-6600 Toll-free number: (888) 298-6605
Fax: (231) 348-6672
Julieanne Tobin, Director Enrollment Management, North Central Michigan College, 1515 Howard Street, Petoskey, MI 49770

## Northwestern Michigan College
**Traverse City, Michigan**
www.nmc.edu                                    CB code: 1564

▸ Public 2-year community and maritime college
▸ Commuter campus in small city

**General.** Founded in 1951. Regionally accredited. **Enrollment:** 4,000 degree-seeking undergraduates. **Degrees:** 441 associate awarded. **Location:** 180 miles from Lansing, 265 miles from Detroit. **Calendar:** Semester, extensive summer session. **Full-time faculty:** 90 total. **Part-time faculty:** 120 total. **Special facilities:** Maritime academy, pilot training center, observatory, culinary arts.

**Student profile.**

| | | | |
|---|---|---|---|
| Out-of-state: | 5% | Live on campus: | 3% |
| 25 or older: | 64% | | |

**Transfer out. Colleges most students transferred to 2007:** Michigan State University, Grand Valley State University, Ferris State University, Central Michigan University.

**Basis for selection.** Open admission, but selective for some programs. Admission for maritime and nursing programs based on school GPA, recommendation and test scores. ACT required for maritime program. **Home-schooled:** Provide transcript of records.

**2007-2008 Annual costs.** Tuition/fees: $2,722; $4,597 out-of-district; $5,621 out-of-state. Per-credit charge: $73 in-district; $132 out-of-district; $164 out-of-state. Room/board: $6,800. Books/supplies: $690. Personal expenses: $690.

**Financial aid. Need-based:** Need-based aid available for part-time students. Work-study available nights, weekends and for part-time students. **Non-need-based:** Scholarships awarded for academics, art, job skills, leadership, minority status, music/drama, ROTC, state residency.

**Application procedures. Admission:** No deadline. $20 fee. Application may be submitted online. Admission notification on a rolling basis. **Financial aid:** Priority date 4/1; no closing date. FAFSA required. Applicants notified on a rolling basis starting 5/1; must reply within 2 week(s) of notification.

**Academics.** Great Lakes Maritime Academy (4-year deck officer and maritime engineer training program) for service in shipping industry on campus. 9 months spent aboard commercial vessels. Bachelor's degree awarded to maritime academy graduates in conjunction with Ferris State University. **Special study options:** Cooperative education, distance learning, dual enrollment of high school students, ESL, honors, independent study, internships, liberal arts/career combination. Bachelor's degree programs available on campus. **Credit/placement by examination:** AP, CLEP, institutional tests. 32 credit hours maximum toward associate degree. **Support services:** Learning center, pre-admission summer program, reduced course load, remedial instruction, study skills assistance, tutoring, writing center.

**Majors. Agriculture:** Crop production, landscaping, nursery operations, turf management. **Biology:** General. **Business:** General, accounting, accounting technology, business admin, management information systems, office technology. **Communications:** General. **Computer sciences:** Information systems. **Education:** General. **Engineering:** General. **Engineering technology:** Drafting, electrical. **English:** English lit. **Health:** Dental assistant, medical assistant, nursing (RN). **Liberal arts:** Arts/sciences. **Math:** General. **Mechanic/repair:** Automotive, electronics/electrical. **Personal/culinary services:** Chef training, culinary arts. **Physical sciences:** General. **Protective services:** Law enforcement admin, police science. **Social sciences:** General. **Transportation:** Airline/commercial pilot, aviation, maritime/Merchant Marine. **Visual/performing arts:** Art, commercial/advertising art, dramatic, piano/organ, studio arts, voice/opera.

**Most popular majors.** Health sciences 19%, liberal arts 52%.

**Computing on campus.** 625 workstations in dormitories, library, computer center, student center. Dormitories wired for high-speed internet access and linked to campus network. Commuter students can connect to campus network. Online course registration, online library, helpline, wireless network available.

**Student life. Freshman orientation:** Mandatory. Multiple one-day sessions prior to the start of each semester. **Housing:** Guaranteed on-campus for freshmen. Coed dorms, special housing for disabled, apartments available. $100 deposit. **Activities:** Bands, choral groups, dance, drama, international student organizations, literary magazine, music ensembles, musical theater, radio station, student government, student newspaper, symphony orchestra, residence hall council, propeller club, Phi Theta Kappa, engineer

club, botany club, law enforcement club, diverse student body group, Native American student group.

**Student services.** Adult student services, career counseling, student employment services, health services, minority student services, personal counseling, placement for graduates, veterans' counselor. **Physically disabled:** Services for visually, speech, hearing impaired. **Transfer:** Re-entry adviser, pre-admission transcript evaluation for new students. Transfer adviser, college fairs on campus for students transferring to 4-year colleges.

**Contact.** E-mail: jbensley@nmc.edu
Phone: (231) 995-1054 Toll-free number: (800) 748-0566
Fax: (231) 995-1339
James Bensley, Coordinator for Admissions, Northwestern Michigan College, 1701 East Front Street, Traverse City, MI 49686

## Oakland Community College
**Bloomfield Hills, Michigan**                      CB member
www.oaklandcc.edu                                   CB code: 1607

▸ Public 2-year community college
▸ Commuter campus in very large city

**General.** Founded in 1964. Regionally accredited. Multicampus institution with locations in Auburn Hills, Farmington Hills, Southfield, Royal Oak, and Waterford. CREST (Combined Regional Emergency Services Training Center) located in Auburn Hills. **Enrollment:** 13,598 degree-seeking undergraduates; 10,934 non-degree-seeking students. **Degrees:** 1,816 associate awarded. **Location:** 30 miles from Detroit. **Calendar:** Semester, limited summer session. **Full-time faculty:** 275 total; 10% minority, 51% women. **Part-time faculty:** 726 total; 8% minority, 51% women. **Class size:** 24% < 20, 76% 20-39.

**Student profile.** Among degree-seeking undergraduates, 18% enrolled in a transfer program, 59% enrolled in a vocational program, 1% already have a bachelor's degree or higher, 1,927 enrolled as first-time, first-year students.

| | | | |
|---|---|---|---|
| Part-time: | 68% | Hispanic American: | 2% |
| Out-of-state: | 1% | Native American: | 1% |
| Women: | 61% | International: | 7% |
| African American: | 18% | 25 or older: | 43% |
| Asian American: | 2% | | |

**Transfer out.** 25% of students enrolled in the transfer program go on to 4-year colleges. **Colleges most students transferred to 2007:** Oakland University, Wayne State University, Walsh College, Eastern Michigan University, University of Michigan-Dearborn.

**Basis for selection.** Open admission. Interview recommended. **Home-schooled:** English and math placement testing mandatory.

**2007-2008 Annual costs.** Tuition/fees: $1,825; $3,040 out-of-district; $4,236 out-of-state. Per-credit charge: $59 in-district; $99 out-of-district; $139 out-of-state. Books/supplies: $930. Personal expenses: $680.

**2007-2008 Financial aid. Need-based:** Average need met was 67%. Average scholarship/grant was $3,800; average loan $2,500. 56% of total undergraduate aid awarded as scholarships/grants, 44% as loans/jobs. Need-based aid available for part-time students. Work-study available for part-time students. **Non-need-based:** Scholarships awarded for academics, athletics.

**Application procedures. Admission:** No deadline. No application fee. Application must be submitted on paper. Admission notification on a rolling basis. **Financial aid:** Priority date 4/15; no closing date. FAFSA required. Applicants notified on a rolling basis starting 4/15.

**Academics. Special study options:** Cooperative education, distance learning, dual enrollment of high school students, ESL, internships, study abroad. Saturday classes offered. License preparation in dental hygiene, nursing, occupational therapy, paramedic, physical therapy, radiology. **Credit/placement by examination:** AP, CLEP, institutional tests. Last 15 credit hours toward degree program must be satisfied with institution's coursework, not credit by exam. **Support services:** Learning center, reduced course load, remedial instruction, study skills assistance, tutoring, writing center.

**Majors. Agriculture:** Landscaping. **Business:** Accounting/business management, business admin, construction management, entrepreneurial studies, hotel/motel admin, international, office technology, operations, restaurant/food services, warehousing. **Communications technology:** Photo/film/video, radio/tv. **Computer sciences:** General, data processing, information technology, programming, security, systems analysis. **Construction:** Carpentry, electrician, pipefitting, site management. **Engineering:** General. **Engineering technology:** Architectural, computer hardware, computer systems, drafting, electrical, electromechanical, heat/ac/refrig, industrial, manufacturing, mechanical drafting, robotics. **Family/consumer sciences:** Child care. **Foreign languages:** Sign language interpretation. **Health:** Community health services, dental hygiene, EMT paramedic, health care admin, histologic technology, massage therapy, medical assistant, medical radiologic technology/radiation therapy, medical transcription, nuclear medical technology, nursing (RN), pharmacy assistant, respiratory therapy technology, sonography, surgical technology. **Legal studies:** Court reporting, paralegal. **Liberal arts:** Arts/sciences, library assistant. **Mechanic/repair:** General, industrial electronics, medium/heavy vehicle. **Parks/recreation:** Exercise sciences. **Personal/culinary services:** Chef training, cosmetic, salon management. **Production:** Machine tool, sheet metal, tool and die, welding. **Protective services:** Corrections, criminalistics, law enforcement admin, police science. **Visual/performing arts:** Art, ceramics, dramatic, graphic design, industrial design, interior design, music performance, music theory/composition, photography, voice/opera. **Other:** Numerical control/vehicle builder, Science.

**Most popular majors.** Business/marketing 15%, health sciences 18%, liberal arts 42%.

**Computing on campus.** 2,501 workstations in library, computer center. Online course registration, online library, helpline available.

**Student life. Freshman orientation:** Available. **Activities:** Bands, choral groups, dance, drama, literary magazine, music ensembles, symphony orchestra, black students association, Students in Free Enterprise, human enrichment center, Students Against Hunger, Phi Theta Kappa, women's center, international club, Jewish student association, optimist club, Student Michigan Education Association.

**Athletics.** NJCAA. **Intercollegiate:** Basketball, cross-country, golf M, softball W, tennis W, volleyball W. **Intramural:** Cross-country, golf M. **Team name:** Raiders.

**Student services.** Career counseling, services for economically disadvantaged, student employment services, financial aid counseling, on-campus daycare, personal counseling, placement for graduates, veterans' counselor, women's services. **Physically disabled:** Services for visually, speech, hearing impaired. **Transfer:** Pre-admission transcript evaluation for new students. Transfer center, transfer adviser, college fairs on campus for students transferring to 4-year colleges.

**Contact.** Phone: (248) 341-2200 Fax: (248) 341-2099
Maurice McCall, Director of Enrollment Services/Registrar, Oakland Community College, 2480 Opdyke Road, Bloomfield Hills, MI 48304-2266

## Saginaw Chippewa Tribal College
**Mount Pleasant, Michigan**
**www.sagchip.org/tribalcollege**

- Public 2-year community college
- Large town

**General. Enrollment:** 45 full-time, degree-seeking students. **Degrees:** 11 associate awarded. **Calendar:** Semester. **Full-time faculty:** 4 total. **Part-time faculty:** 11 total.

**Basis for selection.** Open admission.

**2007-2008 Annual costs.** Tuition/fees: $1,786. Per-credit charge: $55.

**Application procedures. Admission:** No deadline. No application fee. Admission notification on a rolling basis. **Financial aid:** No deadline.

**Academics. Credit/placement by examination:** CLEP.

**Majors. Area/ethnic studies:** Native American. **Business:** Business admin.

**Contact.** Phone: (989) 775-4123
Tracy Reed, Director of Admissions, Saginaw Chippewa Tribal College, 7070 East Broadway, Mount Pleasant, MI 48858

## St. Clair County Community College
**Port Huron, Michigan**
**www.sc4.edu**         CB code: 1628

- Public 2-year community college
- Commuter campus in large town

**General.** Founded in 1923. Regionally accredited. **Enrollment:** 1,860 full-time, degree-seeking students. **Degrees:** 518 associate awarded. **Location:**

55 miles from Detroit. **Calendar:** Semester, limited summer session. **Full-time faculty:** 90 total. **Part-time faculty:** 180 total. **Special facilities:** Fine arts facility, natural history museum.

**Student profile.**

| | | | |
|---|---|---|---|
| Out-of-state: | 2% | 25 or older: | 44% |

**Basis for selection.** Open admission.

**2007-2008 Annual costs.** Tuition/fees: $2,712; $4,767 out-of-district; $6,237 out-of-state. Per-credit charge: $82 in-district; $150 out-of-district; $199 out-of-state. Residents of Lambton County, Canada pay in-state, out-of-district rate for tuition. Lambton County residents pay in-district tuition rate if enrolled in program of study not offered at Lambton College. Books/supplies: $850. Personal expenses: $439.

**Application procedures. Admission:** Closing date 9/1. No application fee. Application may be submitted online. Admission notification on a rolling basis. **Financial aid:** Priority date 6/1; no closing date. FAFSA required. Applicants notified on a rolling basis starting 5/15; must reply within 2 week(s) of notification.

**Academics. Special study options:** Accelerated study, cooperative education, distance learning, double major, dual enrollment of high school students, honors, internships, weekend college. Bachelor's degree programs available on campus. **Credit/placement by examination:** AP, CLEP, institutional tests. 45 credit hours maximum toward associate degree. **Support services:** Learning center, reduced course load, remedial instruction, study skills assistance, tutoring.

**Majors. Agriculture:** Horticultural science, supplies. **Business:** General, accounting, administrative services, business admin, office technology, office/clerical. **Communications:** Broadcast journalism, journalism. **Computer sciences:** Data processing. **Education:** General. **Engineering:** General. **Engineering technology:** Architectural drafting, drafting, electrical, manufacturing. **Family/consumer sciences:** Child care. **Health:** Medical secretary, nursing (RN). **Legal studies:** Legal secretary. **Liberal arts:** Arts/sciences. **Production:** Machine tool, welding. **Protective services:** Law enforcement admin. **Visual/performing arts:** Commercial/advertising art, studio arts. **Other:** Industrial automation.

**Computing on campus.** 229 workstations in library, computer center, student center.

**Student life. Freshman orientation:** Mandatory. Online orientation for all new students. On-campus orientation option available, but limited in dates and times. **Activities:** Concert band, choral groups, drama, music ensembles, radio station, student government, student newspaper, symphony orchestra, TV station, global awareness club.

**Athletics.** NJCAA. **Intercollegiate:** Baseball M, basketball, golf, softball W, volleyball W. **Intramural:** Volleyball M. **Team name:** Skippers.

**Student services.** Career counseling, student employment services, financial aid counseling, on-campus daycare, personal counseling, placement for graduates, veterans' counselor. **Physically disabled:** Services for visually, speech, hearing impaired. **Transfer:** Transfer adviser, college fairs on campus for students transferring to 4-year colleges.

**Contact.** E-mail: enrollment@sc4.edu
Phone: (810) 989-5500 Fax: (810) 984-4730
Pete Lacey, Registrar, St. Clair County Community College, 323 Erie Street, Port Huron, MI 48061-5015

## Schoolcraft College
**Livonia, Michigan**        CB member
**www.schoolcraft.edu**        CB code: 1764

- Public 2-year community college
- Commuter campus in small city

**General.** Founded in 1961. Regionally accredited. **Enrollment:** 9,269 degree-seeking undergraduates; 2,230 non-degree-seeking students. **Degrees:** 1,067 associate awarded. **Location:** 20 miles from Ann Arbor. **Calendar:** Semester, limited summer session. **Full-time faculty:** 94 total; 22% have terminal degrees, 50% women. **Part-time faculty:** 381 total; 49% women.

**Student profile.** Among degree-seeking undergraduates, 33% enrolled in a transfer program, 67% enrolled in a vocational program, 1,851 enrolled as first-time, first-year students.

| | | | |
|---|---|---|---|
| Part-time: | 61% | 25 or older: | 36% |
| Women: | 56% | | |

**Transfer out. Colleges most students transferred to 2007:** Henry Ford Community College, Oakland Community College, Eastern Michigan University, Michigan State University, Wayne State University.

**Basis for selection.** Open admission, but selective for some programs. International students advised to start application process 3 months prior to start date of semester. **Homeschooled:** Interview required.

**2007-2008 Annual costs.** Tuition/fees: $2,290; $3,280 out-of-district; $4,810 out-of-state. Per-credit charge: $70 in-district; $103 out-of-district; $154 out-of-state.

**Financial aid. Need-based:** Need-based aid available for part-time students. Work-study available nights, weekends and for part-time students. **Non-need-based:** Scholarships awarded for academics, athletics, leadership, music/drama, state residency.

**Application procedures. Admission:** No deadline. No application fee. Admission notification on a rolling basis. **Financial aid:** No deadline. FAFSA required. Applicants notified on a rolling basis starting 6/1.

**Academics. Special study options:** Accelerated study, cooperative education, distance learning, double major, dual enrollment of high school students, ESL, external degree, honors, liberal arts/career combination, weekend college. **Credit/placement by examination:** AP, CLEP, institutional tests. 30 credit hours maximum toward associate degree. **Support services:** GED preparation and test center, learning center, remedial instruction, tutoring.

**Honors college/program.** Minimum 3.5 GPA, 25 ACT or 1100 SAT (exclusive of Writing), writing sample, personal interview and 2 letters of recommendation required.

**Majors. Business:** General, accounting technology, administrative services, business admin, entrepreneurial studies, executive assistant, marketing, office technology, small business admin. **Communications technology:** Radio/tv, recording arts. **Computer sciences:** General, applications programming, computer graphics, programming, web page design. **Education:** General. **Engineering:** General. **Engineering technology:** Biomedical, drafting, electrical, environmental, manufacturing, metallurgical, quality control. **Family/consumer sciences:** Child care, child development. **Health:** EMT paramedic, health services, licensed practical nurse, massage therapy, medical records technology, nursing (RN), occupational therapy assistant. **Personal/culinary services:** Chef training. **Protective services:** Corrections, firefighting, police science, security services. **Transportation:** Aviation management.

**Most popular majors.** Business/marketing 18%, education 10%, health sciences 16%, liberal arts 28%, security/protective services 10%.

**Computing on campus.** 930 workstations in library, computer center.

**Student life. Freshman orientation:** Mandatory. **Activities:** Concert band, choral groups, drama, literary magazine, music ensembles, musical theater, student newspaper, music club, beekeepers club, international students club, quilting club, student activities board, Phi Theta Kappa, honors society, gourmet club, occupational therapy club.

**Athletics.** NJCAA. **Intercollegiate:** Basketball, bowling, cross-country W, golf, soccer, volleyball W. **Team name:** Ocelots.

**Student services.** Adult student services, career counseling, services for economically disadvantaged, student employment services, financial aid counseling, health services, legal services, on-campus daycare, personal counseling, placement for graduates, veterans' counselor, women's services. **Physically disabled:** Services for visually, speech, hearing impaired. **Transfer:** College fairs on campus for students transferring to 4-year colleges.

**Contact.** E-mail: admissions@schoolcraft.edu
Phone: (734) 462-4426 Fax: (734) 462-4553
Nicole Wilson-Fennell, Director of Enrollment Management, Schoolcraft College, 18600 Haggerty Road, Livonia, MI 48152-2696

## Southwestern Michigan College
**Dowagiac, Michigan**
**www.swmich.edu**                    CB code: 1783

- Public 2-year community college
- Commuter campus in small town

**General.** Founded in 1964. Regionally accredited. Two traditional semesters (fall and winter) and one optional spring term. Bachelor's degree programs offered in agreement with 4-year colleges and universities including Bethel College, Ferris State University, Western Michigan University. **Enrollment:** 2,032 degree-seeking undergraduates; 461 non-degree-seeking students. **Degrees:** 251 associate awarded. **Location:** 30 miles from South Bend, Indiana. **Calendar:** Semester, extensive summer session. **Full-time faculty:** 49 total; 16% have terminal degrees, 4% minority, 43% women. **Part-time faculty:** 91 total; 3% have terminal degrees, 9% minority, 58% women. **Special facilities:** Museum.

**Student profile.** Among degree-seeking undergraduates, 52% enrolled in a transfer program, 48% enrolled in a vocational program, 505 enrolled as first-time, first-year students, 192 transferred in from other institutions.

| | | | |
|---|---|---|---|
| Part-time: | 50% | Asian American: | 1% |
| Out-of-state: | 8% | Hispanic American: | 4% |
| Women: | 65% | International: | 3% |
| African American: | 8% | 25 or older: | 43% |

**Transfer out. Colleges most students transferred to 2007:** Western Michigan University, Ferris State University, Bethel College, Indiana University of South Bend, Grand Valley State University.

**Basis for selection.** Open admission, but selective for some programs. Special requirements for nursing programs. Assessment tests in reading, writing, and math administered prior to registration for classes. Students may be exempted based upon ACT/SAT scores. Interview required for nursing applicants.

**2007-2008 Annual costs.** Tuition/fees: $2,978; $3,623 out-of-district; $3,863 out-of-state. Per-credit charge: $78 in-district; $100 out-of-district; $108 out-of-state. Books/supplies: $900. Personal expenses: $1,125.

**2006-2007 Financial aid. Need-based:** 87% of total undergraduate aid awarded as scholarships/grants, 13% as loans/jobs. Need-based aid available for part-time students. Work-study available nights, weekends and for part-time students. **Non-need-based:** Scholarships awarded for academics, art, leadership, music/drama.

**Application procedures. Admission:** No deadline. No application fee. Application may be submitted online. Admission notification on a rolling basis. **Financial aid:** Priority date 8/1; no closing date. FAFSA, institutional form required. Applicants notified on a rolling basis starting 4/1; must reply within 2 week(s) of notification.

**Academics. Special study options:** Accelerated study, cooperative education, distance learning, double major, dual enrollment of high school students, ESL, independent study, internships, weekend college. Bachelor's degree programs available on campus. License preparation in nursing, paramedic. **Credit/placement by examination:** AP, CLEP, institutional tests. 13 credit hours maximum toward associate degree. Credit for specific courses may be earned through ACE (Achieved Credit by Examination) testing. **Support services:** Learning center, pre-admission summer program, reduced course load, remedial instruction, study skills assistance, tutoring, writing center.

**Majors. Business:** Accounting technology, administrative services. **Communications technology:** Graphic/printing. **Computer sciences:** General, programming. **Education:** Early childhood, teacher assistance. **Engineering technology:** General, drafting, electrical. **Health:** EMT paramedic, health services, medical assistant, medical records technology, nursing (RN). **Liberal arts:** Arts/sciences. **Mechanic/repair:** General, automotive, industrial. **Production:** Machine tool, tool and die, welding. **Public administration:** Social work.

**Most popular majors.** Business/marketing 6%, engineering/engineering technologies 6%, health sciences 19%, liberal arts 55%.

**Computing on campus.** 76 workstations in library, computer center, student center. Commuter students can connect to campus network. Online course registration, online library, helpline, wireless network available.

**Student life. Freshman orientation:** Available. Preregistration for classes offered. Several half-day sessions available. **Activities:** Bands, choral groups, dance, drama, literary magazine, music ensembles, musical theater, student newspaper, Phi Theta Kappa, business club, Christian bible study, dance club, drama club, international students club, PC gaming club, Spanish club.

**Athletics. Intramural:** Basketball, football (non-tackle), racquetball, soccer, softball, volleyball.

**Student services.** Career counseling, student employment services, financial aid counseling. **Physically disabled:** Services for visually, speech, hearing impaired. **Transfer:** Transfer adviser, college fairs on campus for students transferring to 4-year colleges.

**Contact.** E-mail: enrollment@swmich.edu
Phone: (269) 782-1000 Toll-free number: (800) 456-8675
Fax: (269) 782-1331
Margaret Hay, Dean of Academic Support, Southwestern Michigan College,
58900 Cherry Grove Road, Dowagiac, MI 49047-9793

## Washtenaw Community College
### Ann Arbor, Michigan
### www.wccnet.edu
**CB code: 1935**

- Public 2-year community college
- Commuter campus in small city

**General.** Founded in 1965. Regionally accredited. Classes taught in Brighton, Saline, Chelsea, Ypsilanti and Hartland. **Enrollment:** 3,500 full-time, degree-seeking students. **Degrees:** 994 associate awarded. **ROTC:** Army. **Location:** 40 miles from Detroit. **Calendar:** Trimester, extensive summer session. **Full-time faculty:** 200 total. **Part-time faculty:** 350 total.

**Basis for selection.** Open admission, but selective for some programs. Special requirements for health service technologies programs and some computer technology programs.

**High school preparation.** 15 units recommended. Recommended units include English 4, mathematics 4, social studies 2, science 4 and foreign language 1. Biology, chemistry, and algebra required for health programs. Trigonometry and drafting required for technical programs.

**2007-2008 Annual costs.** Tuition/fees: $2,410; $3,870 out-of-district; $4,860 out-of-state. Per-credit charge: $74 in-district; $122 out-of-district; $155 out-of-state. Books/supplies: $600. Personal expenses: $2,000.

**Financial aid. Non-need-based:** Scholarships awarded for academics.

**Application procedures. Admission:** Priority date 8/12; no deadline. No application fee. Application may be submitted online. Admission notification on a rolling basis beginning on or about 2/20. **Financial aid:** Priority date 6/1, closing date 7/1. FAFSA, institutional form required. Applicants notified on a rolling basis.

**Academics. Special study options:** Cooperative education, cross-registration, distance learning, dual enrollment of high school students, ESL, honors, independent study, internships, liberal arts/career combination, weekend college. Bachelor's degree programs available on campus. **Credit/placement by examination:** AP, CLEP, institutional tests. 45 credit hours maximum toward associate degree. **Support services:** GED preparation and test center, learning center, remedial instruction, study skills assistance, tutoring, writing center.

**Majors. Architecture:** Technology. **Business:** Accounting, administrative services, business admin. **Communications technology:** Graphic/printing. **Computer sciences:** General, applications programming, computer graphics, computer science, data processing, information systems, LAN/WAN management, networking, programming, security, web page design. **Construction:** Maintenance. **Education:** Early childhood, elementary, secondary. **Engineering:** General, mechanics, science. **Engineering technology:** Construction, drafting, electrical. **English:** Technical writing. **Health:** Medical radiologic technology/radiation therapy, medical records admin, nursing (RN), premedicine, respiratory therapy technology, substance abuse counseling. **Liberal arts:** Arts/sciences. **Mechanic/repair:** Auto body, automotive, electronics/electrical, heating/ac/refrig. **Personal/culinary services:** Culinary arts. **Protective services:** Corrections, law enforcement admin, police science. **Social sciences:** General. **Visual/performing arts:** Commercial photography, photography.

**Computing on campus.** 211 workstations in library, computer center, student center. Commuter students can connect to campus network. Online course registration, online library, helpline, repair service, student web hosting available.

**Student life. Freshman orientation:** Mandatory. **Activities:** Jazz band, choral groups, dance, drama, literary magazine, musical theater, student government, student newspaper, African-American student association, Christian Challenge Student Advisory Council, international student association, Phi Theta Kappa, student assembly.

**Student services.** Adult student services, alcohol/substance abuse counseling, career counseling, services for economically disadvantaged, student employment services, financial aid counseling, minority student services, on-campus daycare, personal counseling, placement for graduates, veterans' counselor, women's services. **Physically disabled:** Services for visually, speech, hearing impaired. **Transfer:** Pre-admission transcript evaluation for new students. Transfer center, transfer adviser, college fairs on campus for students transferring to 4-year colleges.

**Contact.** E-mail: studrec@wccnet.org
Phone: (734) 973-3543 Fax: (734) 677-5414
Larry Aeilts, Director of Admissions, Washtenaw Community College,
4800 East Huron River Drive, Ann Arbor, MI 48106-1610

## Wayne County Community College
### Detroit, Michigan
### www.wcccd.edu
**CB code: 1937**

- Public 2-year community and liberal arts college
- Commuter campus in very large city

**General.** Founded in 1967. Regionally accredited. Five campuses and extension site. **Enrollment:** 17,877 degree-seeking undergraduates; 2,627 non-degree-seeking students. **Degrees:** 1,014 associate awarded. **Calendar:** Semester, extensive summer session. **Full-time faculty:** 102 total; 44% minority, 50% women. **Part-time faculty:** 501 total. **Class size:** 36% < 20, 52% 20-39, 10% 40-49, 2% 50-99. **Partnerships:** Formal partnerships with corporations and high schools.

**Student profile.** Among degree-seeking undergraduates, 1% already have a bachelor's degree or higher, 7,970 enrolled as first-time, first-year students.

| | | | |
|---|---|---|---|
| Part-time: | 75% | Asian American: | 1% |
| Women: | 72% | Hispanic American: | 2% |
| African American: | 65% | 25 or older: | 58% |

**Basis for selection.** Open admission. Specific admissions requirements for select programs. **Adult students:** COMPASS placement exam required. **Homeschooled:** Transcript of courses and grades, state high school equivalency certificate required.

**2007-2008 Annual costs.** Tuition/fees: $1,964; $2,462 out-of-district; $3,053 out-of-state. Per-credit charge: $57 in-district; $73 out-of-district; $93 out-of-state. Books/supplies: $1,330.

**2006-2007 Financial aid. Need-based:** 73% of total undergraduate aid awarded as scholarships/grants, 27% as loans/jobs. Need-based aid available for part-time students. Work-study available nights, weekends and for part-time students. **Additional information:** High school diploma, GED, or passing grade on ABT required for financial aid.

**Application procedures. Admission:** No deadline. $10 fee, may be waived for applicants with need. Application may be submitted online. Admission notification on a rolling basis. **Financial aid:** Priority date 5/1; no closing date. FAFSA required. Applicants notified on a rolling basis starting 5/1.

**Academics. Special study options:** Accelerated study, distance learning, double major, dual enrollment of high school students, honors, independent study, internships, liberal arts/career combination, study abroad, weekend college. License preparation in dental hygiene, nursing, occupational therapy, paramedic, real estate. **Credit/placement by examination:** AP, CLEP, institutional tests. 45 credit hours maximum toward associate degree. Recommendation of CAO or program chair. **Support services:** GED preparation, learning center, remedial instruction, study skills assistance, tutoring.

**Majors. Business:** Accounting technology, business admin, labor relations. **Computer sciences:** General, programming. **Education:** General, elementary, secondary. **Engineering:** General. **Engineering technology:** Computer, electrical, electromechanical, telecommunications. **Family/consumer sciences:** Aging, child care, institutional food production. **Health:** Dental hygiene, EMT paramedic, mental health services, nursing (RN), occupational therapy assistant, pharmacy assistant, substance abuse counseling, surgical technology, veterinary technology/assistant. **Legal studies:** Paralegal. **Liberal arts:** Arts/sciences. **Mechanic/repair:** Aircraft, aircraft powerplant, automotive, diesel, heating/ac/refrig. **Philosophy/religion:** Islamic, religion. **Production:** Machine tool, tool and die, welding. **Protective services:** Corrections, fire safety technology, law enforcement admin. **Public administration:** Social work. **Social sciences:** General.

**Most popular majors.** Business/marketing 6%, health sciences 24%, liberal arts 52%.

**Computing on campus.** Commuter students can connect to campus network. Online course registration, helpline, wireless network available.

**Student life. Freshman orientation:** Available. Includes assessment testing. **Policies:** Students must follow the student code of conduct. **Activities:** Choral groups, dance, drama, film society, student government, student newspaper.

**Athletics.** NJCAA. **Intramural:** Basketball, cross-country M, golf M, volleyball W. **Team name:** Wild Cats.

Two-Year Colleges

**Student services.** Adult student services, career counseling, services for economically disadvantaged, student employment services, financial aid counseling, on-campus daycare, personal counseling, placement for graduates, veterans' counselor, women's services. **Physically disabled:** Services for visually, speech, hearing impaired. **Learning disabled:** Comprehensive services available. **Transfer:** Re-entry adviser, pre-admission transcript evaluation for new students. Transfer adviser, college fairs on campus for students transferring to 4-year colleges.

**Contact.** Phone: (313) 496-2600 Fax: (313) 962-1643
Carol Wells, Vice Chancellor Student Services and Enrollment
Management, Wayne County Community College, 801 West Fort Street,
Detroit, MI 48226

## West Shore Community College
### Scottville, Michigan
#### www.westshore.edu                                  CB code: 1941

♦  Public 2-year community college
♦  Commuter campus in rural community

**General.** Founded in 1967. Regionally accredited. **Enrollment:** 517 full-time, degree-seeking students. **Degrees:** 162 associate awarded. **Location:** 54 miles from Muskegon. **Calendar:** Semester, limited summer session. **Full-time faculty:** 26 total. **Part-time faculty:** 69 total.

**Transfer out. Colleges most students transferred to 2007:** Grand Valley State University, Ferris State University, Davenport College, Central Michigan University.

**Basis for selection.** Open admission, but selective for some programs. Applicants to nursing programs must complete prerequisite course work with minimum 2.0 GPA.

**2007-2008 Annual costs.** Tuition/fees: $2,234; $3,584 out-of-district; $4,694 out-of-state. Per-credit charge: $69 in-district; $114 out-of-district; $151 out-of-state. Books/supplies: $700. Personal expenses: $650.

**Financial aid. Need-based:** Need-based aid available for part-time students. Work-study available nights, weekends and for part-time students.

**Application procedures. Admission:** No deadline. $15 fee. Admission notification on a rolling basis. Applicants for associate degree in nursing must apply by January 1, practical nursing applicants by June 1. **Financial aid:** Priority date 3/15; no closing date. FAFSA required. Applicants notified on a rolling basis starting 5/15; must reply within 2 week(s) of notification.

**Academics. Special study options:** Distance learning, dual enrollment of high school students, independent study, internships. Bachelor's degree programs available on campus. License preparation in nursing. **Credit/placement by examination:** AP, CLEP, institutional tests. 10 credit hours maximum toward associate degree. **Support services:** GED test center, learning center, reduced course load, remedial instruction, study skills assistance, tutoring.

**Majors. Business:** General, accounting, administrative services, management information systems, marketing, office technology, office/clerical. **Computer sciences:** Data processing. **Education:** General. **Engineering technology:** CAD/CADD, electrical. **Health:** EMT paramedic, nursing (RN), nursing assistant, prepharmacy. **Legal studies:** Prelaw. **Liberal arts:** Arts/sciences. **Math:** General. **Production:** Welding. **Protective services:** Law enforcement admin.

**Computing on campus.** 300 workstations in library, computer center, student center. Commuter students can connect to campus network. Helpline available.

**Student life. Freshman orientation:** Mandatory. Preregistration for classes offered. Each student meets one-on-one with academic counselor during registration period before classes begin. **Activities:** Choral groups, drama, music ensembles, musical theater, student government, student newspaper, Phi Theta Kappa honor society, law enforcement club, art club, science club, additional special interest clubs.

**Athletics. Intramural:** Basketball, racquetball, softball, volleyball.

**Student services.** Career counseling, student employment services, personal counseling, placement for graduates, veterans' counselor. **Physically disabled:** Services for visually, speech, hearing impaired. **Transfer:** Pre-admission transcript evaluation for new students. Transfer adviser, college fairs on campus for students transferring to 4-year colleges.

**Contact.** E-mail: admissions@westshore.edu
Phone: (231) 845-6211 ext. 3117 Fax: (231) 845-3944
Tom Bell, Director of Admissions, West Shore Community College, 3000
North Stiles Road, Scottville, MI 49454-0277

# Minnesota

## Alexandria Technical College
### Alexandria, Minnesota
www.alextech.edu                                **CB code: 0771**

- Public 2-year technical college
- Commuter campus in large town
- Interview required

**General.** Founded in 1961. Regionally accredited. **Enrollment:** 1,743 degree-seeking undergraduates. **Degrees:** 362 associate awarded. **Location:** 135 miles from Minneapolis-St. Paul. **Calendar:** Semester, limited summer session. **Full-time faculty:** 71 total; 39% women. **Part-time faculty:** 35 total; 3% minority, 60% women.

**Student profile.**

| Out-of-state: | 4% | 25 or older: | 18% |
|---|---|---|---|

**Basis for selection.** Open admission, but selective for some programs. School achievement record, test scores, and interview considered for course placement. Applicants considered in order of applications received. Minnesota Multiphasic Personality Inventory required. ACT recommended and physical agility test required for law enforcement applicants. NET test for practical nursing examination required for practical nursing applicants. Mechanical reasoning tests required for marine and small engine mechanics and diesel mechanics applicants. Portfolio required for communications art and design students.

**2007-2008 Annual costs.** Tuition/fees: $4,329; $4,329 out-of-state. Per-credit charge: $132 in-state; $132 out-of-state. Books/supplies: $1,200. Personal expenses: $1,800.

**Financial aid.** All financial aid based on need. Need-based aid available for part-time students. Work-study available for part-time students.

**Application procedures. Admission:** Priority date 8/1; no deadline. $20 fee. Application may be submitted online. Admission notification on a rolling basis. **Financial aid:** Priority date 5/1; no closing date. FAFSA, institutional form required. Applicants notified on a rolling basis starting 6/30; must reply within 2 week(s) of notification.

**Academics. Special study options:** Distance learning, double major, independent study, internships, student-designed major. Bachelor's degree programs available on campus. License preparation in nursing, real estate. **Credit/placement by examination:** AP, CLEP, institutional tests. No separate limits on CLEP and credit by exam. **Support services:** Reduced course load, remedial instruction, study skills assistance, tutoring, writing center.

**Majors. Business:** Accounting, banking/financial services, business admin, fashion, hospitality admin, marketing, office management, operations. **Computer sciences:** General, networking, programming, web page design. **Engineering technology:** Hydraulics, industrial, manufacturing, mechanical drafting. **Family/consumer sciences:** Child care. **Health:** Clinical lab technology, medical secretary, nursing (RN). **Legal studies:** Legal secretary, paralegal. **Mechanic/repair:** Diesel. **Parks/recreation:** Health/fitness. **Protective services:** Police science. **Public administration:** Human services. **Visual/performing arts:** Commercial/advertising art, interior design.

**Most popular majors.** Business/marketing 20%, computer/information sciences 11%, engineering/engineering technologies 7%, health sciences 6%, security/protective services 30%, visual/performing arts 12%.

**Computing on campus.** 1,100 workstations in library, computer center. Commuter students can connect to campus network. Online course registration, online library, helpline, repair service, wireless network available.

**Student life. Freshman orientation:** Available. Preregistration for classes offered. **Activities:** Campus ministries, student government, Phi Theta Kappa, Business Professionals of America, Delta Epsilon Chi, Skills USA, student senate.

**Athletics. Intramural:** Basketball, softball, volleyball.

**Student services.** Adult student services, alcohol/substance abuse counseling, campus ministries, career counseling, services for economically disadvantaged, student employment services, financial aid counseling, health services, legal services, minority student services, personal counseling, placement for graduates, veterans' counselor, women's services. **Physically disabled:** Services for visually, speech, hearing impaired. **Transfer:** Pre-admission transcript evaluation for new students. Transfer adviser, college fairs on campus for students transferring to 4-year colleges.

**Contact.** E-mail: admissionsrep@alextech.edu
Phone: (320) 762-4520 Toll-free number: (888) 234-1222
Fax: (320) 762-4603
Doug Tatge, Dean of Student Affairs, Alexandria Technical College, 1601 Jefferson Street, Alexandria, MN 56308-3799

## Anoka Technical College
### Anoka, Minnesota
www.anokatech.edu                               **CB code: 6084**

- Public 2-year technical college
- Commuter campus in large town

**General.** Regionally accredited. **Enrollment:** 1,590 degree-seeking undergraduates. **Degrees:** 168 associate awarded. **Location:** 25 miles from Minneapolis-St. Paul. **Calendar:** Semester, limited summer session. **Full-time faculty:** 75 total. **Part-time faculty:** 30 total.

**Student profile.** Among degree-seeking undergraduates, 100% enrolled in a vocational program, 10% already have a bachelor's degree or higher.

| Part-time: | 55% | Women: | 49% |
|---|---|---|---|

**Basis for selection.** Open admission. All new students are required to take the computer-based Accuplacer entrance examination to determine their skill level in mathematics, reading and writing. **Adult students:** SAT/ACT scores not required.

**2007-2008 Annual costs.** Tuition/fees: $4,586; $4,586 out-of-state. Per-credit charge: $139 in-state; $139 out-of-state.

**Financial aid.** All financial aid based on need. Need-based aid available for part-time students. Work-study available nights.

**Application procedures. Admission:** Closing date 8/15 (postmark date). $20 fee, may be waived for applicants with need. Application may be submitted online. Admission notification on a rolling basis. **Financial aid:** No deadline. FAFSA, institutional form required. Applicants notified on a rolling basis starting 5/1.

**Academics. Special study options:** Distance learning, internships, liberal arts/career combination. License preparation in nursing, occupational therapy, paramedic. **Credit/placement by examination:** CLEP, institutional tests. 72 credit hours maximum toward associate degree. **Support services:** GED preparation and test center, learning center, reduced course load, remedial instruction, study skills assistance, tutoring, writing center.

**Majors. Agriculture:** Horticulture, landscaping, nursery operations, turf management. **Computer sciences:** Information systems. **Engineering technology:** Drafting, electrical. **Family/consumer sciences:** Child care. **Health:** Licensed practical nurse, medical secretary, occupational therapy assistant, physical therapy assistant. **Mechanic/repair:** Automotive. **Parks/recreation:** Facilities management. **Transportation:** Air traffic control, aviation, aviation management.

**Computing on campus.** 250 workstations in library, computer center, student center. Online library available.

**Student life. Freshman orientation:** Mandatory. **Activities:** Student government.

**Student services.** Career counseling, student employment services, health services, on-campus daycare, personal counseling, placement for graduates, veterans' counselor. **Physically disabled:** Services for visually, speech, hearing impaired.

**Contact.** E-mail: admissions@anokatech.edu
Phone: (763) 576-4850 Fax: (763) 576-4756
Leo Christenson, Dean of Academic Resources, Anoka Technical College, 1355 West Highway 10, Anoka, MN 55303

## Anoka-Ramsey Community College
### Coon Rapids, Minnesota
www.anokaramsey.edu                             **CB code: 6024**

- Public 2-year community college
- Commuter campus in small city

**General.** Founded in 1965. Regionally accredited. Extension sites at Elk River and Fridley. **Enrollment:** 2,966 full-time, degree-seeking students. **Degrees:** 711 associate awarded. **ROTC:** Army, Naval, Air Force. **Location:** 20 miles from Minneapolis-St. Paul. **Calendar:** Semester, limited summer session. **Full-time faculty:** 110 total. **Part-time faculty:** 173 total. **Special facilities:** Glass-blowing studio, native prairie ground.

**Transfer out. Colleges most students transferred to 2007:** University of Minnesota-Twin Cities, St. Cloud State University.

**Basis for selection.** Open admission, but selective for some programs and for out-of-state students. Special requirements for nursing, biomedical technology, computer networking, and telecommunications programs. National League of Nursing Pre-admissions Test required for nursing applicants.

**High school preparation.** One year laboratory chemistry and 1 year laboratory biology required for nursing applicants out of high school less than 5 years.

**2007-2008 Annual costs.** Tuition/fees: $4,015; $7,540 out-of-state. Per-credit charge: $118 in-state; $235 out-of-state. Various reciprocity agreements with some neighboring states provide tuition reduction to out-of-state students. Books/supplies: $600. Personal expenses: $600.

**Financial aid.** All financial aid based on need. Work-study available nights, weekends and for part-time students.

**Application procedures. Admission:** No deadline. $20 fee, may be waived for applicants with need. Admission notification on a rolling basis. **Financial aid:** Priority date 4/1; no closing date. FAFSA, institutional form required. Applicants notified on a rolling basis; must reply within 2 week(s) of notification.

**Academics. Special study options:** Cross-registration, distance learning, dual enrollment of high school students, independent study, internships, study abroad, weekend college. Joint admission with Colleges of Science and Engineering at Duluth and Mankato State University, University of Minnesota, St. Cloud State University, and University of Minnesota-Twin Cities in agriculture, natural resources, human ecology, and liberal arts. **Credit/placement by examination:** AP, CLEP, institutional tests. 30 credit hours maximum toward associate degree. **Support services:** Learning center, reduced course load, remedial instruction, study skills assistance, tutoring, writing center.

**Majors. Agriculture:** Landscaping, nursery operations, turf management. **Business:** Accounting, administrative services, business admin, marketing. **Computer sciences:** Information systems. **Conservation:** Environmental science. **Engineering:** General. **Engineering technology:** Architectural, electrical. **Family/consumer sciences:** Child care. **Health:** Medical secretary, nursing (RN), occupational therapy assistant, optician, physical therapy assistant. **Legal studies:** Legal secretary. **Liberal arts:** Arts/sciences. **Mechanic/repair:** Automotive. **Parks/recreation:** General.

**Most popular majors.** Business/marketing 11%, health sciences 27%, liberal arts 56%.

**Computing on campus.** 300 workstations in library, computer center.

**Student life. Freshman orientation:** Mandatory. **Activities:** Bands, choral groups, drama, international student organizations, literary magazine, music ensembles, musical theater, student government, student newspaper, symphony orchestra, Phi Theta Kappa, humanities club, Intervarsity Christian Fellowship.

**Athletics.** NJCAA. **Intercollegiate:** Baseball M, basketball, volleyball W. **Intramural:** Archery M, baseball M, basketball, bowling, golf, ice hockey, soccer, softball, volleyball.

**Student services.** Adult student services, career counseling, student employment services, personal counseling, veterans' counselor. **Physically disabled:** Services for visually, speech, hearing impaired. **Transfer:** Transfer adviser, college fairs on campus for students transferring to 4-year colleges.

**Contact.** Phone: (763) 422-3333 Fax: (763) 422-3636
Matthew Crawford, Director of Admissions, Anoka-Ramsey Community College, 11200 Mississippi Boulevard NW, Coon Rapids, MN 55433

---

## Central Lakes College
**Brainerd, Minnesota**
www.clcmn.edu                              **CB code: 6045**

- Public 2-year community and technical college
- Commuter campus in large town

---

**General.** Founded in 1938. Regionally accredited. Access to 1.5 million book titles through participation in online catalog system with 28 other libraries. **Enrollment:** 3,228 degree-seeking undergraduates. **Degrees:** 385 associate awarded. **Location:** 125 miles from Minneapolis-St. Paul. **Calendar:** Semester, limited summer session. **Full-time faculty:** 99 total; 3% minority, 36% women. **Part-time faculty:** 64 total; 2% have terminal degrees, 52% women. **Class size:** 54% < 20, 51% 20-39, 2% 40-49. **Special facilities:** Conservatory, American Indian studies center.

**Student profile.** Among degree-seeking undergraduates, 46% enrolled in a transfer program, 54% enrolled in a vocational program, 191 transferred in from other institutions.

**Basis for selection.** Open admission, but selective for some programs. Applicants to mobility nursing program must have graduate license in practical nursing (LPN). Practical nurse program grades and college grades considered. Instructor and employer references, practical to registered nursing mobility profile, and mathematics test scores also considered.

**2007-2008 Annual costs.** Tuition/fees: $4,419. Per-credit charge: $130. In-state and out-of-state tuition rates same. Books/supplies: $800. Personal expenses: $1,500.

**2006-2007 Financial aid. Need-based:** 44% of total undergraduate aid awarded as scholarships/grants, 56% as loans/jobs. Need-based aid available for part-time students. Work-study available for part-time students.

**Application procedures. Admission:** No deadline. $20 fee. Application may be submitted online. Admission notification on a rolling basis. **Financial aid:** Priority date 6/1; no closing date. FAFSA, institutional form required. Applicants notified on a rolling basis starting 6/10; must reply within 2 week(s) of notification.

**Academics. Special study options:** Combined bachelor's/graduate degree, distance learning, dual enrollment of high school students, independent study, internships, liberal arts/career combination. 2+2 management program with College of St. Scholastica, 2+2 programs with Southwest State in organizational management and teacher education, 2+2 natural resources with University of Minnesota: Crookston. Bachelor's degree programs available on campus. License preparation in nursing. **Credit/placement by examination:** AP, CLEP, IB, institutional tests. **Support services:** Learning center, remedial instruction, study skills assistance, tutoring.

**Majors. Agriculture:** Horticulture. **Business:** Accounting, administrative services, business admin, tourism/travel. **Communications technology:** Photo/film/video. **Computer sciences:** Data processing, networking, programming. **Conservation:** General. **Education:** Teacher assistance. **Engineering:** General. **Engineering technology:** Computer systems, robotics. **Family/consumer sciences:** Child care. **Health:** Medical secretary, nursing (RN). **Liberal arts:** Arts/sciences. **Mechanic/repair:** Automotive, heavy equipment, industrial electronics, marine. **Production:** Welding. **Protective services:** Criminal justice, criminalistics, police science. **Visual/performing arts:** Commercial/advertising art.

**Most popular majors.** Business/marketing 8%, health sciences 11%, liberal arts 57%.

**Computing on campus.** 150 workstations in library, computer center. Commuter students can connect to campus network. Online course registration, online library, repair service, wireless network available.

**Student life. Freshman orientation:** Mandatory. Online orientation required. Orientations also held in-person throughout spring and summer. **Activities:** Bands, choral groups, drama, music ensembles, musical theater, student government, student newspaper, Anishinabe Student Association, campus ambassadors, law enforcement club, mentoring, theater club, Phi Theta Kappa, Spanish club, minority student forum.

**Athletics.** NJCAA. **Intercollegiate:** Baseball M, basketball, football (tackle) M, golf, softball W, volleyball W. **Intramural:** Baseball M, basketball, bowling, golf, softball, volleyball. **Team name:** Raiders.

**Student services.** Adult student services, career counseling, services for economically disadvantaged, financial aid counseling, health services, minority student services, on-campus daycare, personal counseling, placement for graduates, veterans' counselor, women's services. **Physically disabled:** Services for visually, speech, hearing impaired. **Transfer:** Pre-admission transcript evaluation for new students. Transfer adviser, college fairs on campus for students transferring to 4-year colleges.

**Contact.** E-mail: rtretter@clcmn.edu
Phone: (218) 855-8037 Toll-free number: (800) 933-0346
Fax: (218) 855-8230
Charlotte Daniels, Director of Admissions, Central Lakes College, 501 West College Drive, Brainerd, MN 56401

## Century Community and Technical College
### White Bear Lake, Minnesota
www.century.edu

CB code: 6388

- Public 2-year community and technical college
- Commuter campus in large town

**General.** Founded in 1967. Regionally accredited. **Enrollment:** 7,631 degree-seeking undergraduates; 1,197 non-degree-seeking students. **Degrees:** 843 associate awarded. **ROTC:** Air Force. **Location:** 9 miles from Minneapolis-St. Paul. **Calendar:** Semester, limited summer session. **Full-time faculty:** 179 total; 8% minority, 54% women. **Part-time faculty:** 177 total; 9% minority, 51% women. **Class size:** 35% < 20, 55% 20-39, 6% 40-49, 3% 50-99. **Special facilities:** 92-acre nature area, walking trail.

**Student profile.** Among degree-seeking undergraduates, 29% enrolled in a transfer program, 71% enrolled in a vocational program, 2% already have a bachelor's degree or higher, 1,520 enrolled as first-time, first-year students, 799 transferred in from other institutions.

| | | | |
|---|---|---|---|
| Part-time: | 52% | Hispanic American: | 2% |
| Out-of-state: | 6% | Native American: | 1% |
| Women: | 58% | International: | 1% |
| African American: | 9% | 25 or older: | 30% |
| Asian American: | 13% | | |

**Transfer out.** **Colleges most students transferred to 2007:** Metropolitan State University, University of Minnesota, University of Wisconsin-River Falls, Minnesota State University in Mankato, Hamline University.

**Basis for selection.** Open admission, but selective for some programs. Special requirements for nursing, medical imaging orthotics, prosthetics, paramedic, dental assist and dental hygiene programs. LOEP used to determine English proficiency. **Learning Disabled:** Documentation of disability must be provided within the first semester of service.

**2007-2008 Annual costs.** Tuition/fees: $4,409; $4,409 out-of-state. Per-credit charge: $132 in-state; $132 out-of-state. Books/supplies: $1,000.

**2006-2007 Financial aid.** All financial aid based on need. 37% of total undergraduate aid awarded as scholarships/grants, 63% as loans/jobs. Need-based aid available for part-time students. Work-study available for part-time students. **Additional information:** Minnesota resident out of high school or not enrolled in college for 7 years without bachelor's or other higher degree offered cost of tuition and books for 1 course in 1 semester up to maximum of 5 credits.

**Application procedures.** **Admission:** No deadline. $20 fee, may be waived for applicants with need. Application may be submitted online. Admission notification on a rolling basis. **Financial aid:** No deadline. FAFSA required. Applicants notified on a rolling basis starting 5/15.

**Academics.** **Special study options:** Dual enrollment of high school students, ESL, honors, internships, liberal arts/career combination. License preparation in dental hygiene, nursing, paramedic, radiology. **Credit/placement by examination:** AP, CLEP, IB. **Support services:** Learning center, remedial instruction, study skills assistance, tutoring, writing center.

**Majors.** **Agriculture:** Greenhouse operations, horticultural science, landscaping. **Business:** Accounting, administrative services, business admin, marketing. **Communications:** Digital media. **Computer sciences:** General, computer science, networking, security. **Construction:** Maintenance. **Education:** Multi-level teacher, teacher assistance. **Engineering:** General. **Engineering technology:** CAD/CADD, computer systems. **Foreign languages:** Translation. **Health:** Dental assistant, dental hygiene, EMT paramedic, medical secretary, nursing (RN), orthotics/prosthetics, radiologic technology/medical imaging, substance abuse counseling. **Liberal arts:** Arts/sciences. **Mechanic/repair:** Auto body, automotive, heating/ac/refrig. **Parks/recreation:** Sports admin. **Personal/culinary services:** Cosmetic. **Protective services:** Criminal justice, criminalistics, police science. **Public administration:** Human services. **Visual/performing arts:** Interior design. **Other:** Public safety.

**Most popular majors.** Business/marketing 6%, health sciences 29%, liberal arts 44%, security/protective services 9%.

**Computing on campus.** 1,250 workstations in library, computer center. Commuter students can connect to campus network. Online course registration, wireless network available.

**Student life.** **Freshman orientation:** Mandatory. Preregistration for classes offered. 4-hour session preceding semester start. Online orientation also available. **Activities:** Bands, choral groups, drama, literary magazine, music ensembles, student government, symphony orchestra, Alpha & Omega, Asian student association, parliamentary debate, Democrats club, drama club, French club, Phi Theta Kappa, Republicans club, Spanish club, creative arts alliance.

**Athletics.** NJCAA. **Intercollegiate:** Golf. **Intramural:** Badminton, basketball, cross-country, golf, softball, table tennis, tennis, volleyball.

**Student services.** Career counseling, student employment services, financial aid counseling, health services, minority student services, on-campus daycare, personal counseling. **Physically disabled:** Services for visually, speech, hearing impaired. **Transfer:** Transfer adviser, college fairs on campus for students transferring to 4-year colleges.

**Contact.** E-mail: admissions@century.edu
Phone: (651) 779-1700 Toll-free number: (800) 228-1978
Fax: (651) 779-1796
Christine Paulos, Director of Admissions, Century Community and Technical College, 3300 Century Avenue North, White Bear Lake, MN 55110

## Dakota County Technical College
### Rosemount, Minnesota
www.dctc.edu

CB code: 7149

- Public 2-year technical college
- Commuter campus in large town

**General.** Regionally accredited. **Enrollment:** 2,335 degree-seeking undergraduates. **Degrees:** 268 associate awarded. **Location:** 20 miles from Minneapolis-St. Paul. **Calendar:** Semester, limited summer session. **Full-time faculty:** 80 total; 42% women. **Part-time faculty:** 76 total; 7% minority, 43% women. **Class size:** 67% < 20, 32% 20-39, 1% 40-49. **Special facilities:** Greenhouse, truck driving rodeo, skid pad. **Partnerships:** Formal partnership with General Motors for Automotive Service Education Program/Body Service Education Program.

**Basis for selection.** Open admission, but selective for some programs. Minimum test scores required for certain programs. TOEFL required for international students and the CELSA for ESL students. Admissions visit including meeting with the program instructor(s) required. **Homeschooled:** Transcript of courses and grades required.

**2007-2008 Annual costs.** Tuition/fees: $4,749; $8,994 out-of-state. Per-credit charge: $142 in-state; $283 out-of-state. Books/supplies: $1,525. Personal expenses: $1,710.

**Financial aid.** **Need-based:** Need-based aid available for part-time students. Work-study available nights, weekends and for part-time students. **Non-need-based:** Scholarships awarded for academics, leadership.

**Application procedures.** **Admission:** No deadline. $20 fee, may be waived for applicants with need. Application may be submitted online. Admission notification on a rolling basis. **Financial aid:** No deadline. FAFSA required. Applicants notified on a rolling basis starting 3/15.

**Academics.** **Special study options:** Accelerated study, cooperative education, cross-registration, distance learning, double major, ESL, independent study, internships, liberal arts/career combination. Bachelor's degree programs available on campus. License preparation in nursing, real estate. **Credit/placement by examination:** AP, CLEP, institutional tests. **Support services:** Learning center, pre-admission summer program, remedial instruction, study skills assistance, tutoring, writing center.

**Majors.** **Agriculture:** Landscaping. **Business:** Accounting, business admin, executive assistant, marketing, real estate, travel services. **Computer sciences:** Applications programming, database management, networking, programming, web page design, webmaster. **Construction:** Electrician, lineworker, masonry. **Engineering technology:** Architectural drafting, manufacturing, telecommunications. **Health:** Dental assistant, medical assistant, medical secretary. **Legal studies:** Legal secretary. **Mechanic/repair:** Auto body, automotive, communications systems, heavy equipment, medium/heavy vehicle. **Parks/recreation:** Exercise sciences. **Transportation:** Aviation management. **Visual/performing arts:** Commercial/advertising art, graphic design, interior design, photography.

**Most popular majors.** Business/marketing 19%, computer/information sciences 11%, engineering/engineering technologies 10%, health sciences 8%, trade and industry 15%, visual/performing arts 26%.

**Computing on campus.** 200 workstations in library, computer center, student center. Online course registration, online library, wireless network available.

**Student life. Freshman orientation:** Mandatory. Preregistration for classes offered. Sessions available 2-3 months prior to semester. **Activities:** Student government, student newspaper, multicultural club, veterans center.

**Athletics.** NJCAA. **Intercollegiate:** Baseball M, soccer, softball W, wrestling M. **Intramural:** Basketball, ice hockey M, volleyball. **Team name:** Blue Knights.

**Student services.** Career counseling, student employment services, financial aid counseling, health services, minority student services, personal counseling, placement for graduates. **Physically disabled:** Services for visually, hearing impaired. **Learning disabled:** Comprehensive services available. **Transfer:** Re-entry adviser, pre-admission transcript evaluation for new students. Transfer adviser, college fairs on campus for students transferring to 4-year colleges.

**Contact.** E-mail: admissions@dctc.edu
Phone: (651) 423-8301 Toll-free number: (877) 937-3282
Fax: (651) 423-8775
Patrick Lair, Admissions Director, Dakota County Technical College, 1300 145th Street East, Rosemount, MN 55068

## Duluth Business University
**Duluth, Minnesota**
**www.dbumn.edu**                                    **CB code: 3312**

- For-profit 2-year business college
- Small city
- Interview required

**General.** Accredited by ACICS. **Enrollment:** 292 degree-seeking undergraduates. **Degrees:** 46 associate awarded. **Location:** 150 miles from Minneapolis-St. Paul. **Calendar:** Quarter, extensive summer session. **Full-time faculty:** 13 total. **Part-time faculty:** 19 total. **Class size:** 96% < 20, 4% 20-39.

**Basis for selection.** High school diploma or GED and interview required.

**2007-2008 Annual costs.** Tuition/fees: $13,455. Per-credit charge: $299. Vet tech program $320/credit hour.

**Application procedures. Admission:** No deadline. $35 fee. Application must be submitted on paper. Admission notification on a rolling basis.

**Academics. Special study options:** Distance learning, internships. **Credit/placement by examination:** AP, CLEP. **Support services:** Remedial instruction, tutoring.

**Majors. Business:** Business admin. **Legal studies:** Paralegal.

**Most popular majors.** Business/marketing 12%, health sciences 88%.

**Computing on campus.** Helpline, repair service, wireless network available.

**Student life. Freshman orientation:** Mandatory.

**Student services.** Career counseling. **Transfer:** Re-entry adviser, pre-admission transcript evaluation for new students.

**Contact.** E-mail: info@dbumn.edu
Phone: (218) 722-4000 Toll-free number: (800) 777-8406
Fax: (218) 628-2127
David Cook, Educational Recruitment Manager, Duluth Business University, 4727 Mike Colalillo Drive, Duluth, MN 55807

## Dunwoody College of Technology
**Minneapolis, Minnesota**
**www.dunwoody.edu**                                    **CB code: 2265**

- Private 2-year technical college
- Commuter campus in very large city
- Application essay, interview required

**General.** Founded in 1914. Regionally accredited. **Enrollment:** 1,476 degree-seeking undergraduates; 95 non-degree-seeking students. **Degrees:** 355 associate awarded. **Calendar:** Quarter, limited summer session. **Full-time faculty:** 87 total; 6% have terminal degrees, 12% minority, 20% women. **Part-time faculty:** 43 total; 2% have terminal degrees, 14% minority, 21% women. **Class size:** 76% < 20, 23% 20-39, less than 1% 50-99.

**Student profile.** Among degree-seeking undergraduates, 356 enrolled as first-time, first-year students, 248 transferred in from other institutions.

| | | | |
|---|---|---|---|
| Part-time: | 11% | Asian American: | 6% |
| Out-of-state: | 2% | Hispanic American: | 2% |
| Women: | 9% | Native American: | 2% |
| African American: | 10% | 25 or older: | 30% |

**Transfer out. Colleges most students transferred to 2007:** Minneapolis Community and Technical College, Normandale Community College, University of Minnesota-Twin Cities, Inver Hills Community College, Century College.

**Basis for selection.** Institutional entrance test required. Rank in upper-half of high school class preferred. Essay or personal statement required at time of admissions testing. **Homeschooled:** Transcript of courses and grades required. **Learning Disabled:** Students must submit official documentation.

**High school preparation.** 8 units required; 20 recommended. Required and recommended units include English 3-4, mathematics 3-4, social studies 2, history 2, science 1-2 (laboratory 1-2) and academic electives 4.

**2007-2008 Annual costs.** Tuition/fees: $12,633. Per-credit charge: $174. Books/supplies: $883. Personal expenses: $1,035.

**2006-2007 Financial aid. Need-based:** 312 full-time freshmen applied for aid; 213 were judged to have need; 190 of these received aid. Average need met was 41%. Average scholarship/grant was $4,521; average loan $3,447. 39% of total undergraduate aid awarded as scholarships/grants, 61% as loans/jobs. Need-based aid available for part-time students. **Non-need-based:** Awarded to 177 full-time undergraduates, including 88 freshmen. Scholarships awarded for academics.

**Application procedures. Admission:** No deadline. $50 fee, may be waived for applicants with need. Application may be submitted online. Admission notification on a rolling basis. Applicants to architecture, computer and electrical programs should apply at least 6 months prior to beginning of quarter. **Financial aid:** Priority date 6/1; no closing date. FAFSA required. Applicants notified on a rolling basis starting 2/1; must reply within 4 week(s) of notification.

**Academics. Special study options:** Distance learning, double major, ESL, independent study, internships. Bachelor's degree programs available on campus. **Credit/placement by examination:** CLEP, IB, institutional tests. **Support services:** Learning center, pre-admission summer program, reduced course load, remedial instruction, study skills assistance, tutoring, writing center.

**Majors. Agriculture:** Food processing. **Communications technology:** Desktop publishing, printing press operator. **Computer sciences:** Applications programming, networking. **Construction:** Electrician, site management. **Engineering:** Manufacturing. **Engineering technology:** Architectural drafting, electrical, electrical drafting, electromechanical, heat/ac/refrig, robotics, surveying. **Mechanic/repair:** Auto body, automotive, heating/ac/refrig. **Production:** Machine tool. **Visual/performing arts:** Graphic design, interior design.

**Most popular majors.** Computer/information sciences 8%, engineering/engineering technologies 28%, trade and industry 61%.

**Computing on campus.** PC or laptop required. 1,900 workstations in library, computer center. Commuter students can connect to campus network. Helpline, repair service, wireless network available.

**Student life. Freshman orientation:** Mandatory. One-day program, offered multiple times. **Activities:** Student government.

**Student services.** Career counseling, student employment services, financial aid counseling, minority student services, personal counseling, placement for graduates, veterans' counselor, women's services. **Transfer:** Re-entry adviser, pre-admission transcript evaluation for new students. Transfer adviser for students transferring to 4-year colleges.

**Contact.** E-mail: info@dunwoody.edu
Phone: (612) 374-5800 Toll-free number: (800) 292-4625
Fax: (612) 374-4128
Shaun Manning, Director of Admissions, Dunwoody College of Technology, 818 Dunwoody Boulevard, Minneapolis, MN 55403-1192

## Fond du Lac Tribal and Community College
**Cloquet, Minnesota**
**www.fdltcc.edu**                                    **CB code: 7119**

- Public 2-year community college
- Commuter campus in large town

**General.** Founded in 1987. Regionally accredited. **Location:** 16 miles from Duluth. **Calendar:** Semester.

**Annual costs/financial aid.** Tuition/fees (2007-2008): $4,366; $8,278 out-of-state. Cost for double room is $10.18 per day. Books/supplies: $650. Personal expenses: $1,050. Need-based financial aid available to full-time and part-time students.

**Contact.** Phone: (218) 879-0808
Admissions Representative, 2101 14th Street, Cloquet, MN 55720

## Hennepin Technical College
### Brooklyn Park, Minnesota
### www.hennepintech.edu
**CB code: 6290**

♦  Public 2-year technical college
♦  Commuter campus in small city

**General.** Regionally accredited. **Enrollment:** 4,141 full-time, degree-seeking students. **Degrees:** 500 associate awarded. **Location:** 10 miles from Minneapolis-St. Paul. **Calendar:** Semester, limited summer session. **Full-time faculty:** 685 total. **Part-time faculty:** 548 total.

**Student profile.** Among full-time, degree-seeking students, 1,426 transferred in from other institutions.

| | | | |
|---|---|---|---|
| Out-of-state: | 2% | 25 or older: | 64% |

**Basis for selection.** Open admission, but selective for some programs. Special requirements for nursing and dental program. Accuplacer for placement only.

**2007-2008 Annual costs.** Tuition/fees: $4,187; $4,187 out-of-state. Per-credit charge: $131 in-state; $131 out-of-state. Books/supplies: $800.

**Financial aid.** All financial aid based on need.

**Application procedures. Admission:** No deadline. $20 fee, may be waived for applicants with need. Admission notification on a rolling basis. **Financial aid:** No deadline. FAFSA, institutional form required. Applicants notified on a rolling basis starting 3/1.

**Academics. Special study options:** Combined bachelor's/graduate degree, cross-registration, double major, ESL, honors, independent study, internships. License preparation in nursing, paramedic. **Credit/placement by examination:** AP, CLEP. **Support services:** Learning center, pre-admission summer program, reduced course load, remedial instruction, study skills assistance, tutoring.

**Majors. Agriculture:** Floriculture, landscaping, nursery operations. **Business:** Accounting, accounting technology, office technology, office/clerical. **Communications:** Advertising, digital media, publishing. **Communications technology:** General, desktop publishing, graphic/printing, graphics, photo/film/video, printing press operator, recording arts. **Computer sciences:** General, applications programming, computer graphics, data processing, information systems, programming, security, systems analysis, web page design. **Construction:** Carpentry, electrician, maintenance. **Engineering technology:** Architectural drafting, automotive, construction, drafting, electrical, heat/ac/refrig, hydraulics, industrial, manufacturing, mechanical, plastics. **Family/consumer sciences:** Child development. **Health:** Dental assistant, EMT paramedic, licensed practical nurse, medical secretary, office admin, ward clerk. **Mechanic/repair:** General, auto body, automotive, diesel, electronics/electrical, heating/ac/refrig, industrial, marine, medium/heavy vehicle, motorcycle, small engine. **Personal/culinary services:** Chef training, culinary arts, food prep, restaurant/catering. **Production:** Ironworking, machine shop technology, machine tool, sheet metal, tool and die, welding, woodworking.

**Computing on campus.** 75 workstations in library, computer center, student center. Online course registration, online library available.

**Student life. Freshman orientation:** Available. A week before school starts. **Activities:** Student government.

**Athletics.** NAIA.

**Student services.** Career counseling, student employment services, financial aid counseling, personal counseling, placement for graduates, veterans' counselor. **Physically disabled:** Services for visually, speech, hearing impaired. **Transfer:** Pre-admission transcript evaluation for new students. Transfer adviser for students transferring to 4-year colleges.

**Contact.** E-mail: info@hennepintech.edu
Phone: (763) 488-2500 Toll-free number: (800) 345-4655
Fax: (763) 488-2944
Joy Bodin, Director of Admissions, Hennepin Technical College, 9000 Brooklyn Boulevard, Brooklyn Park, MN 55455

## Hibbing Community College
### Hibbing, Minnesota
### www.hibbing.edu
**CB code: 6275**

♦  Public 2-year community and technical college
♦  Commuter campus in large town

**General.** Founded in 1916. Regionally accredited. **Enrollment:** 1,415 degree-seeking undergraduates. **Degrees:** 339 associate awarded. **Location:** 75 miles from Duluth. **Calendar:** Semester, limited summer session. **Full-time faculty:** 65 total. **Part-time faculty:** 45 total. **Special facilities:** Space planetarium.

**Student profile.**

| | | | |
|---|---|---|---|
| Out-of-state: | 13% | Live on campus: | 7% |
| 25 or older: | 40% | | |

**Transfer out. Colleges most students transferred to 2007:** Bemidji State University, University of Minnesota: Duluth, College of St. Scholastica, University of Wisconsin-Superior.

**Basis for selection.** Open admission, but selective for some programs. Special requirements for nursing, dental assistant and law enforcement programs. Academic placement test required. **Homeschooled:** Transcript of courses and grades required.

**2007-2008 Annual costs.** Tuition/fees: $4,344; $5,312 out-of-state. Per-credit charge: $129 in-state; $161 out-of-state. Online students pay an additional $25 per-credit-hour charge. Books/supplies: $800.

**Application procedures. Admission:** Priority date 4/15; no deadline. $20 fee, may be waived for applicants with need. Application may be submitted online. Admission notification on a rolling basis. **Financial aid:** Priority date 7/1; no closing date. Institutional form required. Applicants notified on a rolling basis starting 6/30; must reply within 2 week(s) of notification.

**Academics. Special study options:** Cooperative education, cross-registration, distance learning, dual enrollment of high school students, honors, independent study, internships, liberal arts/career combination, study abroad. Bachelor's degree programs available on campus. License preparation in aviation, nursing, real estate. **Credit/placement by examination:** CLEP, IB, institutional tests. 17 credit hours maximum toward associate degree. **Support services:** Learning center, pre-admission summer program, reduced course load, remedial instruction, study skills assistance, tutoring.

**Majors. Business:** Administrative services, business admin, office/clerical. **Computer sciences:** General, security, web page design. **Health:** Clinical lab technology, dental assistant, medical secretary, nursing (RN). **Legal studies:** Legal secretary. **Liberal arts:** Arts/sciences. **Personal/culinary services:** Culinary arts. **Protective services:** Police science.

**Computing on campus.** 100 workstations in dormitories, library, computer center. Commuter students can connect to campus network. Online course registration, online library available.

**Student life. Freshman orientation:** Available. Preregistration for classes offered. Registration orientation held throughout the summer; all-student orientation held day before classes begin. **Housing:** Coed dorms available. $250 deposit. City-owned housing available to students. **Activities:** Bands, choral groups, drama, music ensembles, musical theater, student government, student newspaper, Phi Theta Kappa.

**Athletics.** NJCAA. **Intercollegiate:** Baseball M, basketball, golf, softball W, volleyball W. **Intramural:** Badminton, baseball M, basketball, bowling, skiing, volleyball. **Team name:** Cardinals.

**Student services.** Adult student services, career counseling, services for economically disadvantaged, student employment services, financial aid counseling, minority student services, personal counseling, placement for graduates, veterans' counselor. **Physically disabled:** Services for visually, speech, hearing impaired. **Transfer:** Pre-admission transcript evaluation for new students. Transfer adviser, college fairs on campus for students transferring to 4-year colleges.

**Contact.** E-mail: admissions@hibbing.edu
Phone: (218) 262-7207 Toll-free number: (800) 224-4422
Fax: (218) 263-2992
Mary Iozzo, Admissions Representative, Hibbing Community College,
1515 East 25th Street, Hibbing, MN 55746

## High-Tech Institute
### St. Louis Park, Minnesota
www.hightechschools.com          CB code: 3042

▶ For-profit 2-year technical college
▶ Small city

**General.** Accredited by ACCSCT. **Calendar:** Continuous.

**Annual costs/financial aid.** Costs for full associate programs range from
$23,850 to $35,350; diploma programs range from $11,550 to $24,950. Fees,
books, uniforms and tools included.

**Contact.** Phone: (952) 417-2200
5100 Gamble Drive, St. Louis Park, MN 55416

## Inver Hills Community College
### Inver Grove Heights, Minnesota
www.inverhills.edu          CB code: 6300

▶ Public 2-year community college
▶ Commuter campus in large town

**General.** Founded in 1967. Regionally accredited. **Enrollment:** 4,574 degree-
seeking undergraduates; 1,156 non-degree-seeking students. **Degrees:** 594
associate awarded. **ROTC:** Air Force. **Location:** 6 miles from Minneapolis-
St. Paul. **Calendar:** Semester, limited summer session. **Full-time faculty:**
91 total; 6% minority, 57% women. **Part-time faculty:** 141 total; 4% minority, 47% women.

**Student profile.** Among degree-seeking undergraduates, 899 enrolled as
first-time, first-year students.

| | | | |
|---|---|---|---|
| Part-time: | 53% | Asian American: | 5% |
| Out-of-state: | 2% | Hispanic American: | 3% |
| Women: | 60% | Native American: | 1% |
| African American: | 7% | 25 or older: | 38% |

**Transfer out. Colleges most students transferred to 2007:** University of
Minnesota, Metro State University, St. Thomas/St. Catherine's University,
University of Wisconsin-River Falls, Minnesota State University-Mankato.

**Basis for selection.** Open admission, but selective for some programs.
Special requirements for nursing and emergency health service programs,
Computer and Networking Technology and international students. **Adult
students:** SAT/ACT scores not required. **Homeschooled:** Transcript of courses
and grades, state high school equivalency certificate required.

**2007-2008 Annual costs.** Tuition/fees: $4,534; $4,534 out-of-state. Per-
credit charge: $137 in-state; $137 out-of-state.

**Financial aid.** All financial aid based on need. Need-based aid available
for part-time students. Work-study available nights, weekends and for part-
time students.

**Application procedures. Admission:** Priority date 8/1; no deadline. $20
fee, may be waived for applicants with need. Application may be submitted
online. Admission notification on a rolling basis. **Financial aid:** No deadline. FAFSA required. Applicants notified on a rolling basis starting 6/1.

**Academics. Special study options:** Accelerated study, distance learning,
dual enrollment of high school students, honors, independent study, internships, liberal arts/career combination, student-designed major, study abroad,
weekend college. License preparation in aviation, nursing, paramedic. **Credit/
placement by examination:** AP, CLEP, IB, institutional tests. 30 credit
hours maximum toward associate degree. **Support services:** GED test center, learning center, pre-admission summer program, reduced course load,
remedial instruction, study skills assistance, tutoring, writing center.

**Majors. Business:** Accounting, business admin, construction management.
**Computer sciences:** Computer science, networking, programming. **Construction:** Building inspection. **Health:** EMT paramedic, nursing (RN). **Legal studies:** Legal secretary, paralegal. **Liberal arts:** Arts/sciences. **Parks/
recreation:** Health/fitness. **Protective services:** Law enforcement admin,
police science. **Public administration:** Social work. **Transportation:** Air
traffic control, airline/commercial pilot, aviation management.

**Most popular majors.** Business/marketing 10%, health sciences 27%,
legal studies 13%, liberal arts 28%, security/protective services 11%.

**Computing on campus.** 141 workstations in library, computer center,
student center. Commuter students can connect to campus network. Online
course registration, online library, helpline, repair service, wireless network
available.

**Student life. Freshman orientation:** Mandatory. Preregistration for classes
offered. Three-hour session before start of semester. Online orientation is
also available. **Activities:** Concert band, choral groups, drama, literary magazine, music ensembles, musical theater, student government, French club,
German club, Spanish club, student senate, Christian Fellowship, international club, Black student union, Progressive Student Alliance, Gay-Straight
Alliance, Somali club.

**Athletics. Intramural:** Basketball, football (non-tackle) M, golf, ice hockey,
soccer M, softball, table tennis, volleyball, weight lifting.

**Student services.** Adult student services, alcohol/substance abuse counseling, career counseling, student employment services, financial aid counseling, health services, minority student services, on-campus daycare, personal counseling, placement for graduates, veterans' counselor. **Physically
disabled:** Services for visually, speech, hearing impaired. **Transfer:** Pre-
admission transcript evaluation for new students. Transfer adviser, college
fairs on campus for students transferring to 4-year colleges.

**Contact.** E-mail: iseekinfo@inverhills.edu
Phone: (651) 450-8503 Fax: (651) 450-8677
Landon Pirius, Director of Enrollment Services, Inver Hills Community
College, 2500 80th Street East, Inver Grove Heights, MN 55076-3224

## Itasca Community College
### Grand Rapids, Minnesota
www.itascacc.edu          CB code: 6309

▶ Public 2-year junior and liberal arts college
▶ Commuter campus in large town

**General.** Founded in 1922. Regionally accredited. **Enrollment:** 984 degree-
seeking undergraduates; 168 non-degree-seeking students. **Degrees:** 216 associate awarded. **Location:** 78 miles from Duluth, 180 miles from Minneapolis-
St. Paul. **Calendar:** Semester, limited summer session. **Full-time faculty:**
41 total; 2% have terminal degrees, 2% minority. **Part-time faculty:** 21
total; 10% have terminal degrees. **Special facilities:** Educational wetland
habitat, University of Minnesota agricultural station, U.S. Forest Service
share campus, 500 acres experimental forest. **Partnerships:** Formal partnerships with local businesses for training, partnership council with area high
schools.

**Student profile.** Among degree-seeking undergraduates, 368 enrolled as
first-time, first-year students.

| | | | |
|---|---|---|---|
| Part-time: | 22% | Hispanic American: | 1% |
| Out-of-state: | 7% | Native American: | 4% |
| Women: | 48% | 25 or older: | 24% |
| African American: | 2% | Live on campus: | 14% |
| Asian American: | 1% | | |

**Transfer out. Colleges most students transferred to 2007:** Bemidji State
University, College of St. Scholastica, University of Minnesota: Duluth, St.
Cloud State University, University of North Dakota.

**Basis for selection.** Open admission. College-level reading and English
testing required for class act teacher education program.

**High school preparation.** 12 units recommended. Recommended units
include English 4, mathematics 2, social studies 2, science 2 and foreign
language 2. Computer skills recommended.

**2007-2008 Annual costs.** Tuition/fees: $4,337; $5,305 out-of-state. Per-
credit charge: $129 in-state; $161 out-of-state. Different reciprocity agreements for Wisconsin, North Dakota, and South Dakota. Books/supplies: $950.
Personal expenses: $1,414.

**2006-2007 Financial aid. Need-based:** 63% of total undergraduate aid
awarded as scholarships/grants, 37% as loans/jobs. Need-based aid available for part-time students. Work-study available nights, weekends and for
part-time students. **Non-need-based:** Scholarships awarded for academics,
leadership, music/drama, state residency.

**Application procedures. Admission:** Priority date 8/1; deadline 8/29
(postmark date). $20 fee, may be waived for applicants with need. Applica-
tion may be submitted online. Admission notification on a rolling basis.

**Financial aid:** Priority date 5/1; no closing date. FAFSA required. Applicants notified on a rolling basis starting 4/1.

**Academics. Special study options:** Cooperative education, dual enrollment of high school students, independent study, internships, liberal arts/career combination, study abroad. License preparation in nursing, real estate. **Credit/placement by examination:** AP, CLEP, IB, institutional tests. 10 credit hours maximum toward associate degree. **Support services:** GED test center, learning center, pre-admission summer program, reduced course load, remedial instruction, study skills assistance, tutoring.

**Majors. Area/ethnic studies:** Native American. **Business:** Accounting, business admin. **Conservation:** General, forestry. **Education:** General, early childhood. **Engineering:** General. **Engineering technology:** General. **Health:** Prenursing. **Liberal arts:** Arts/sciences. **Psychology:** General. **Public administration:** Human services, social work. **Social sciences:** Geography. **Other:** Pulp and paper technician, Wildland firefighting.

**Most popular majors.** Engineering/engineering technologies 16%, liberal arts 64%, natural resources/environmental science 6%.

**Computing on campus.** 275 workstations in dormitories, library, computer center, student center. Dormitories wired for high-speed internet access and linked to campus network. Commuter students can connect to campus network. Online course registration, wireless network available.

**Student life. Freshman orientation:** Available. Preregistration for classes offered. Orientation held before classes begin. **Housing:** Coed dorms available. $200 nonrefundable deposit, deadline 6/30. **Activities:** Literary magazine, student government, Circle-K, business club, Student Ambassadors, Panarama, Global Ed, engineering club, psychology club, STARS.

**Athletics.** NJCAA. **Intercollegiate:** Baseball M, basketball, football (tackle) M, softball W, volleyball W, wrestling M. **Intramural:** Basketball M, bowling, football (non-tackle), softball, table tennis, volleyball. **Team name:** Vikings.

**Student services.** Adult student services, career counseling, student employment services, financial aid counseling, minority student services, personal counseling. **Physically disabled:** Services for visually, speech, hearing impaired. **Learning disabled:** Comprehensive services available. **Transfer:** Transfer adviser for students transferring to 4-year colleges.

**Contact.** E-mail: info@itascacc.edu
Phone: (218) 327-4468 Toll-free number: (800) 996-6422
Fax: (218) 327-4350
Candace Perry, Director of Enrollment Services, Itasca Community College, 1851 Highway 169 East, Grand Rapids, MN 55744

## ITT Technical Institute: Eden Prairie
**Eden Prairie, Minnesota**
**www.itt-tech.edu/campus/school.cfm?lloc_num=27**

- Private 2-year technical college
- Small city

**General.** Accredited by ACICS. **Calendar:** Quarter.

**Contact.** Phone: (952) 914-5300
8911 Columbine Road, Eden Prairie, MN 55347

## Lake Superior College
**Duluth, Minnesota**
**www.lsc.edu**     CB code: 6352

- Public 2-year community and technical college
- Commuter campus in small city

**General.** Regionally accredited. **Enrollment:** 3,406 degree-seeking undergraduates. **Degrees:** 550 associate awarded. **ROTC:** Army, Naval. **Location:** 150 miles from Minneapolis-St. Paul. **Calendar:** Semester, limited summer session. **Full-time faculty:** 98 total. **Part-time faculty:** 151 total. **Class size:** 61% < 20, 38% 20-39, less than 1% 40-49, less than 1% 50-99. **Special facilities:** Emergency response training center, professional pilot programs.

**Student profile.** Among degree-seeking undergraduates, 44% enrolled in a transfer program, 56% enrolled in a vocational program, 431 transferred in from other institutions.

| | | | |
|---|---|---|---|
| **Out-of-state:** | 11% | **Hispanic American:** | 1% |
| **African American:** | 2% | **Native American:** | 3% |
| **Asian American:** | 2% | **25 or older:** | 33% |

**Transfer out. Colleges most students transferred to 2007:** University of Minnesota-Duluth, University of Minnesota-Twin Cities.

**Basis for selection.** Open admission, but selective for some programs. Special requirements for radiology and dental hygiene with minimum 2.6 GPA and nursing with a minimum 2.8 GPA. The Academic Skills Assessment Program Computerized Placement Test required for all students unless transcript shows completion of college level math and English composition.

**2007-2008 Annual costs.** Tuition/fees: $4,157; $7,745 out-of-state. Per-credit charge: $120 in-state; $239 out-of-state. Various reciprocity plans for residents of neighboring states may reduce tuition for out-of-state students. Books/supplies: $800. Personal expenses: $2,162.

**Financial aid. Need-based:** Need-based aid available for part-time students. Work-study available nights, weekends and for part-time students. **Non-need-based:** Scholarships awarded for academics, leadership.

**Application procedures. Admission:** Closing date 8/21 (postmark date). $20 fee, may be waived for applicants with need. Application must be submitted on paper. Admission notification on a rolling basis. **Financial aid:** Priority date 5/1; no closing date. FAFSA required. Applicants notified on a rolling basis starting 5/1.

**Academics. Special study options:** Accelerated study, cooperative education, distance learning, double major, dual enrollment of high school students, ESL, honors, independent study, internships, liberal arts/career combination, study abroad. License preparation in aviation, dental hygiene, nursing, paramedic, physical therapy, radiology, real estate. **Credit/placement by examination:** AP, CLEP, institutional tests. 30 credit hours maximum toward associate degree. **Support services:** Learning center, reduced course load, remedial instruction, study skills assistance, tutoring, writing center.

**Majors. Business:** Accounting, administrative services, business admin, management information systems, marketing, selling. **Computer sciences:** General, database management, networking, programming. **Construction:** Carpentry, electrician. **Engineering technology:** Architectural drafting, CAD/CADD, civil, computer hardware, computer systems, electrical, mechanical drafting, telecommunications. **Health:** Dental hygiene, medical secretary, nursing (RN), occupational therapy assistant, physical therapy assistant, radiologic technology/medical imaging, respiratory therapy technology, surgical technology. **Legal studies:** Legal secretary, paralegal. **Liberal arts:** Arts/sciences. **Mechanic/repair:** Aircraft, automotive. **Production:** Machine tool, welding. **Protective services:** Fire safety technology. **Transportation:** Airline/commercial pilot, aviation management. **Visual/performing arts:** Studio arts.

**Most popular majors.** Business/marketing 9%, engineering/engineering technologies 6%, health sciences 33%, liberal arts 38%.

**Computing on campus.** 500 workstations in library, computer center, student center. Commuter students can connect to campus network. Online course registration, online library, helpline, repair service, student web hosting, wireless network available.

**Student life. Freshman orientation:** Available. Preregistration for classes offered. Half day each semester prior to start of term. **Policies:** Policy describes the student role in the allocation of student activity fees. Students are involved in decision making policies through shared governance. **Activities:** Drama, student government, Intervarsity Christian Fellowship, Phi Theta Kappa, Teachers of Tomorrow, United Multicultural Group, art club, skills, nursing, dental hygiene club, radiology club.

**Athletics. Intramural:** Baseball, basketball, bowling, field hockey, ice hockey, softball, volleyball. **Team name:** Huskies.

**Student services.** Adult student services, alcohol/substance abuse counseling, career counseling, services for economically disadvantaged, student employment services, financial aid counseling, health services, minority student services, on-campus daycare, personal counseling, placement for graduates, veterans' counselor, women's services. **Physically disabled:** Services for visually, speech, hearing impaired. **Transfer:** Pre-admission transcript evaluation for new students. Transfer center, transfer adviser, college fairs on campus for students transferring to 4-year colleges.

**Contact.** E-mail: enroll@lsc.edu
Phone: (218) 733-7601 Toll-free number: (800) 432-2884
Fax: (218) 733-5945
Melissa Leno, Director of Admissions, Lake Superior College, 2101 Trinity Road, Duluth, MN 55811

## Lakeland Academy Division of Herzing College
**Crystal, Minnesota**
www.herzing.edu                          CB code: 3051

- For-profit 2-year health science college
- Large city

**General.** Regionally accredited. **Enrollment:** 273 degree-seeking under-graduates. **Degrees:** 4 bachelor's, 33 associate awarded. **Calendar:** Continuous. **Full-time faculty:** 18 total. **Part-time faculty:** 14 total.

**Basis for selection.** Open admission, but selective for some programs. Qualifications for dental hygiene program include completion of dental hygiene application along with supporting documentation as requested.

**2007-2008 Annual costs.** Cost of full programs ranges from $10,880 to $46,725, including fees and books.

**2006-2007 Financial aid. Need-based:** 39% of total undergraduate aid awarded as scholarships/grants, 61% as loans/jobs.

**Application procedures. Admission:** No deadline. No application fee. Admission notification on a rolling basis. **Financial aid:** FAFSA required.

**Academics. Special study options:** Bachelor's degree programs available on campus. **Credit/placement by examination:** CLEP.

**Majors. Business:** General.

**Contact.** E-mail: info@mpls.herzing.edu
Phone: (763) 535-3000
Shelly Larson, Director of Admissions, Lakeland Academy Division of Herzing College, 5700 West Broadway, Crystal, MN 55428

## Le Cordon Bleu College of Culinary Arts
**Mendota Heights, Minnesota**
www.twincitiesculinary.com

- For-profit 2-year culinary school and technical college
- Commuter campus in very large city
- Interview required

**General.** Accredited by ACCSCT. **Enrollment:** 667 full-time, degree-seeking students. **Degrees:** 425 associate awarded. **Location:** 12 miles from Minneapolis-St. Paul. **Calendar:** Quarter, extensive summer session. **Full-time faculty:** 40 total. **Part-time faculty:** 10 total.

**Basis for selection.** Open admission. **Homeschooled:** Transcript of courses and grades required. **Learning Disabled:** Current IEP.

**High school preparation.** Recommended units include English 3, mathematics 2, social studies 1, history 1 and science 1.

**2007-2008 Annual costs.** Program tuition and fees: $39,500 (culinary), $37,500 (patisserie).

**Financial aid. Non-need-based:** Scholarships awarded for academics, job skills, leadership.

**Application procedures. Admission:** No deadline. $50 fee, may be waived for applicants with need. Application may be submitted online. Admission notification on a rolling basis.

**Academics. Special study options:** Internships. **Credit/placement by examination:** CLEP. **Support services:** Remedial instruction, study skills assistance, tutoring.

**Majors. Personal/culinary services:** General, baking.

**Computing on campus.** 40 workstations in library, computer center. Online library, wireless network available.

**Student life. Freshman orientation:** Mandatory. Several options for orientation including the Saturday prior to beginning classes. **Activities:** Student newspaper.

**Student services.** Financial aid counseling, placement for graduates. **Transfer:** Pre-admission transcript evaluation for new students.

**Contact.** E-mail: info@twinciticsculinary.com
Phone: (651) 675-4700 Toll-free number: (800) 931-6855
Fax: (651) 452-5282
Abby Norbin, Senior Director of Admissions, Le Cordon Bleu College of Culinary Arts, 1315 Mendota Heights Road, Mendota Heights, MN 55120

## Leech Lake Tribal College
**Cass Lake, Minnesota**
www.lltc.edu                          CB code: 3931

- Public 2-year Tribal College grounded in Anishinaabe knowledge and culture.
- Commuter campus in small town

**General.** Regionally accredited. Chartered by the Leech Lake Band of Ojibwe. Grounded in Anishinaabe knowledge and culture. **Enrollment:** 226 degree-seeking undergraduates. **Degrees:** 15 associate awarded. **Location:** 15 miles from Bemidji. **Calendar:** Semester, limited summer session. **Full-time faculty:** 13 total. **Part-time faculty:** 2 total. **Class size:** 100% < 20.

**Basis for selection.** Open admission. **Homeschooled:** Documentation of high school classes required.

**2007-2008 Annual costs.** Tuition/fees: $3,980. Per-credit charge: $125. Books/supplies: $600.

**Financial aid.** All financial aid based on need. Need-based aid available for part-time students.

**Application procedures. Admission:** $15 fee. Application must be submitted on paper. Admission notification on a rolling basis. **Financial aid:** FAFSA required.

**Academics. Special study options:** Cooperative education, double major, independent study, internships, liberal arts/career combination, teacher certification program. **Credit/placement by examination:** CLEP, institutional tests. **Support services:** Reduced course load, remedial instruction, study skills assistance, tutoring.

**Majors. Area/ethnic studies:** Native American. **Business:** Business admin. **Education:** Early childhood. **Health:** Clinical nutrition. **Liberal arts:** Arts/sciences. **Protective services:** Police science.

**Computing on campus.** 31 workstations in library, computer center, student center.

**Student life. Freshman orientation:** Available. Preregistration for classes offered. **Activities:** Choral groups, student government.

**Student services.** Adult student services, financial aid counseling, personal counseling. **Transfer:** Transfer adviser for students transferring to 4-year colleges.

**Contact.** E-mail: liz.jenkins@lltc.edu
Phone: (218) 335-4247 Fax: (218) 335-4209
Christine Fineday, Registrar, Leech Lake Tribal College, PO Box 180, Cass Lake, MN 56633

## Mesabi Range Community and Technical College
**Virginia, Minnesota**
www.mr.mnscu.edu                          CB code: 6432

- Public 2-year community and technical college
- Commuter campus in large town

**General.** Founded in 1918. Regionally accredited. Career/technical programs offered at Eveleth campus. **Enrollment:** 863 full-time, degree-seeking students. **Degrees:** 173 associate awarded. **Location:** 60 miles from Duluth. **Calendar:** Semester, limited summer session. **Full-time faculty:** 48 total; 15% minority. **Part-time faculty:** 31 total.

**Student profile.**

| | | | |
|---|---|---|---|
| Out-of-state: | 9% | Live on campus: | 8% |
| 25 or older: | 26% | | |

**Transfer out. Colleges most students transferred to 2007:** University of Minnesota-Duluth, Bemidji State University, St. Cloud State University, Mankato State University, University of Minnesota-Minneapolis.

**Basis for selection.** Open admission.

**2007-2008 Annual costs.** Tuition/fees: $4,344; $5,312 out-of-state. Per-credit charge: $129 in-state; $161 out-of-state. Books/supplies: $900. Personal expenses: $1,000.

**Financial aid. Need-based:** Need-based aid available for part-time students. Work-study available nights, weekends and for part-time students. **Non-need-based:** Scholarships awarded for state residency.

**Application procedures. Admission:** No deadline. $20 fee, may be waived for applicants with need. Admission notification on a rolling basis beginning on or about 1/1. **Financial aid:** Priority date 4/22; no closing date. FAFSA, institutional form required. Applicants notified on a rolling basis starting 5/1; must reply within 2 week(s) of notification.

**Academics. Special study options:** Dual enrollment of high school students, independent study, internships, liberal arts/career combination, study abroad. Bachelor's degree programs available on campus. License preparation in nursing, paramedic. **Credit/placement by examination:** CLEP, institutional tests. **Support services:** Learning center, reduced course load, remedial instruction, study skills assistance, tutoring.

**Majors. Biology:** General. **Business:** General, administrative services, marketing, office technology. **Communications technology:** Graphic/printing. **Computer sciences:** General, programming, systems analysis. **Construction:** Carpentry. **Education:** General, teacher assistance. **Engineering:** Computer. **Engineering technology:** Robotics. **Health:** Substance abuse counseling. **Liberal arts:** Arts/sciences. **Mechanic/repair:** General, automotive, industrial electronics. **Parks/recreation:** Exercise sciences. **Public administration:** Human services.

**Computing on campus.** Dormitories linked to campus network. Online course registration available.

**Student life. Freshman orientation:** Mandatory. **Housing:** Apartments available. $300 deposit, deadline 9/1. **Activities:** Bands, choral groups, dance, drama, literary magazine, music ensembles, musical theater, student government, student newspaper, symphony orchestra.

**Athletics.** NJCAA. **Intercollegiate:** Baseball M, basketball, football (tackle) M, softball W, volleyball W. **Intramural:** Badminton, basketball, bowling, field hockey W, ice hockey, racquetball, softball, table tennis, volleyball. **Team name:** Norseman.

**Student services.** Career counseling, student employment services, minority student services, on-campus daycare, personal counseling, placement for graduates. **Physically disabled:** Services for visually, hearing impaired. **Transfer:** Pre-admission transcript evaluation for new students.

**Contact.** Phone: (218) 749-0315 Fax: (218) 749-0318
Brenda Kochevar, Director of Enrollment Services, Mesabi Range Community and Technical College, 1001 Chestnut Street West, Virginia, MN 55792-3448

## Minneapolis Business College
### Roseville, Minnesota
### www.mplsbusinesscollege.com
**CB code: 7126**

- For-profit 2-year business and technical college
- Very large city

**General.** Founded in 1874. Accredited by ACICS. **Enrollment:** 284 full-time, degree-seeking students. **Degrees:** 158 associate awarded. **Location:** 10 miles from Minneapolis-St. Paul. **Calendar:** Semester, limited summer session. **Full-time faculty:** 7 total; 57% women. **Part-time faculty:** 8 total; 62% women.

**Student profile.** Among full-time, degree-seeking students, 360 enrolled as first-time, first-year students.

| Out-of-state: | 20% | Live on campus: | 12% |

**Basis for selection.** Open admission. Interview recommended.

**2007-2008 Annual costs.** Tuition/fees: $13,160. Fees for books and supplies vary from $40 to $1,320 per academic year depending on program. Lab fee for medical assistant program $1,160. Room only: $6,600.

**Financial aid. Additional information:** Individual financial planning available for all students to meet the cost of education.

**Application procedures. Admission:** No deadline. $50 fee. Application may be submitted online. Admission notification on a rolling basis beginning on or about 7/1. **Financial aid:** No deadline. Applicants notified on a rolling basis.

**Academics.** Externships related to career available. 14-month associate of applied science degree options. **Credit/placement by examination:** CLEP.

**Majors. Business:** Accounting, administrative services, hospitality admin, management information systems, office management, tourism/travel. **Computer sciences:** Applications programming. **Health:** Medical assistant. **Legal studies:** Legal secretary. **Visual/performing arts:** Commercial/advertising art.

**Student life. Freshman orientation:** Mandatory. **Housing:** Single-sex dorms available. $100 partly refundable deposit. **Activities:** Student government, student newspaper.

**Student services.** Career counseling, placement for graduates.

**Contact.** Phone: (651) 636-7406 Toll-free number: (800) 279-5200 Fax: (651) 636-8185
Lisa Stuart, Admissions Supervisor, Minneapolis Business College, 1711 West County Road B, Roseville, MN 55113

## Minneapolis Community and Technical College
### Minneapolis, Minnesota
### www.minneapolis.edu
**CB member**
**CB code: 6434**

- Public 2-year community and technical college
- Commuter campus in large city

**General.** Founded in 1965. Regionally accredited. **Enrollment:** 9,179 degree-seeking undergraduates. **Degrees:** 635 associate awarded. **Location:** Downtown. **Calendar:** Semester, limited summer session. **Class size:** 53% < 20, 39% 20-39, 6% 40-49, 2% 50-99.

**Student profile.** Among degree-seeking undergraduates, 43% enrolled in a vocational program.

| African American: | 30% | Native American: | 2% |
| Asian American: | 6% | International: | 2% |
| Hispanic American: | 4% | | |

**Transfer out. Colleges most students transferred to 2007:** University of Minnesota, Metro State University.

**Basis for selection.** Open admission, but selective for some programs. The following programs have additional requirements for admission: Nursing, Air Traffic Control, Film, Video, Screenwriting, Sound Arts, Law Enforcement, and Urban Teacher Program.

**2007-2008 Annual costs.** Tuition/fees: $4,442; $4,442 out-of-state. Per-credit charge: $136.

**2006-2007 Financial aid.** All financial aid based on need. 37% of total undergraduate aid awarded as scholarships/grants, 63% as loans/jobs. Need-based aid available for part-time students. Work-study available nights, weekends and for part-time students.

**Application procedures. Admission:** No deadline. $20 fee, may be waived for applicants with need. Application may be submitted online. Admission notification on a rolling basis. **Financial aid:** Priority date 6/1; no closing date. FAFSA required. Applicants notified on a rolling basis starting 7/15; must reply within 2 week(s) of notification.

**Academics. Special study options:** Accelerated study, cross-registration, distance learning, dual enrollment of high school students, ESL, honors, independent study, internships, liberal arts/career combination, weekend college. Bachelor's degree programs available on campus. **Credit/placement by examination:** AP, CLEP, IB, institutional tests. **Support services:** Learning center, remedial instruction, tutoring.

**Majors. Biology:** General, biotechnology. **Business:** Accounting, administrative services, business admin, office technology. **Communications:** Digital media. **Communications technology:** Photo/film/video, recording arts. **Computer sciences:** Networking, programming, security, web page design. **Education:** General. **Family/consumer sciences:** Child care. **Health:** Electroencephalograph technology, nursing (RN), substance abuse counseling. **Liberal arts:** Arts/sciences, library assistant. **Math:** General. **Mechanic/repair:** Aircraft, aircraft powerplant, heating/ac/refrig, watch/jewelry. **Parks/recreation:** General. **Personal/culinary services:** Chef training. **Physical sciences:** Chemistry. **Production:** Cabinetmaking/millwright. **Protective services:** Criminal justice, police science. **Public administration:** General, human services. **Transportation:** Air traffic control. **Visual/performing arts:** Cinematography, commercial photography, design, play/screenwriting, studio arts. **Other:** Polysomnography technology, Women's studies.

**Most popular majors.** Business/marketing 8%, health sciences 27%, liberal arts 28%, security/protective services 7%, visual/performing arts 11%.

**Computing on campus.** 278 workstations in library, computer center. Online course registration, online library, wireless network available.

**Student life. Freshman orientation:** Mandatory. Preregistration for classes offered. **Activities:** Jazz band, choral groups, drama, literary magazine, music ensembles, student government, student newspaper, International Student Association, Phi Theta Kappa Honor Society, Vocational Industrial Clubs of America, Association of Black Collegiates, Student Nurses Association, Business Professionals of America, Chess Club, Education Club, United Nations of Indian Tribes for Education, Out Campus Alliance.

**Athletics.** NJCAA. **Intercollegiate:** Basketball, golf. **Team name:** Mavericks.

**Student services.** Adult student services, career counseling, services for economically disadvantaged, student employment services, financial aid counseling, minority student services, personal counseling, placement for graduates, veterans' counselor. **Physically disabled:** Services for visually, speech, hearing impaired. **Learning disabled:** Comprehensive services available. **Transfer:** Transfer adviser, college fairs on campus for students transferring to 4-year colleges.

**Contact.** E-mail: admissions@minneapolis.edu
Phone: (612) 659-6200 Toll-free number: (800) 247-0911
Fax: (612) 659-6210
Kerri Carlson, Director of Admissions, Minneapolis Community and Technical College, 1501 Hennepin Avenue, Minneapolis, MN 55403-1779

## Minneapolis Drafting School Division of Herzing College
**Minneapolis, Minnesota**
**www.herzing.edu**

- For-profit 2-year technical college
- Large city

**General.** Regionally accredited. **Enrollment:** 254 degree-seeking undergraduates. **Degrees:** 1 bachelor's, 27 associate awarded. **Calendar:** Semester. **Full-time faculty:** 15 total. **Part-time faculty:** 15 total.

**Basis for selection.** Open admission, but selective for some programs. Admissions decisions based on applicant's interest, professional attitude, and performance on standardized tests. Applicants who don't submit SAT or ACT scores must complete an entrance examination for admission.

**2007-2008 Annual costs.** Tuition/fees: $11,605. Per-credit charge: $386. Cost varies; tuition figures shown weighted average of all programs.

**Application procedures. Admission:** No deadline. No application fee. Admission notification on a rolling basis.

**Academics. Credit/placement by examination:** CLEP.

**Majors. Computer sciences:** System admin. **Engineering technology:** Drafting, mechanical drafting.

**Contact.** E-mail: info@mpls.herzing.edu
Phone: (763) 535-3000
Shelly Larson, Director of Admissions, Minneapolis Drafting School Division of Herzing College, 5700 West Broadway, Minneapolis, MN 55428

## Minnesota School of Business: Brooklyn Center
**Brooklyn Center, Minnesota**
**www.msbcollege.edu**      CB code: 3314

- For-profit 2-year business college
- Large town

**General.** Accredited by ACICS. **Calendar:** Continuous.

**Annual costs/financial aid.** Tuition/fees (2007-2008): $17,810. Books/supplies: $1,800. Need-based financial aid available to full-time and part-time students.

**Contact.** Phone: (763) 566-7777
Director of Admissions, 5910 Shingle Creek Parkway, Brooklyn Center, MN 55430

## Minnesota State College - Southeast Technical
**Winona, Minnesota**
**www.southeastmn.edu**      CB code: 7123

- Public 2-year nursing and technical college
- Commuter campus in large town

**General.** Founded in 1949. Regionally accredited. **Enrollment:** 1,863 degree-seeking undergraduates; 139 non-degree-seeking students. **Degrees:** 218 associate awarded. **Location:** 55 miles from Rochester, 32 miles from La Crosse, Wisconsin. **Calendar:** Semester, limited summer session. **Full-time faculty:** 54 total; 48% have terminal degrees, 2% minority, 41% women. **Part-time faculty:** 34 total; 50% have terminal degrees, 3% minority, 74% women. **Class size:** 59% < 20, 35% 20-39, 6% 40-49, less than 1% 50-99. **Partnerships:** Formal partnerships with School-to-Work and Tech Prep programs.

**Student profile.** Among degree-seeking undergraduates, 9% enrolled in a transfer program, 91% enrolled in a vocational program, 748 enrolled as first-time, first-year students, 70 transferred in from other institutions.

| | | | |
|---|---|---|---|
| Part-time: | 38% | Hispanic American: | 1% |
| Out-of-state: | 31% | Native American: | 1% |
| Women: | 62% | International: | 3% |
| African American: | 2% | 25 or older: | 43% |
| Asian American: | 1% | | |

**Basis for selection.** Open admission. **Learning Disabled:** Disability documentation recommended.

**High school preparation.** Recommended units include English 4, mathematics 2 and science 1.

**2007-2008 Annual costs.** Tuition/fees: $4,501; $8,645 out-of-state. Per-credit charge: $138 in-state; $276 out-of-state. Various reciprocity agreements with neighboring states provide tuition reduction to some out-of-state students. Books/supplies: $900. Personal expenses: $3,654.

**Financial aid. Need-based:** Need-based aid available for part-time students. Work-study available for part-time students. **Non-need-based:** Scholarships awarded for academics, leadership.

**Application procedures. Admission:** No deadline. $20 fee, may be waived for applicants with need. Application may be submitted online. Admission notification on a rolling basis. **Financial aid:** Priority date 5/15, closing date 6/30. FAFSA, institutional form required. Applicants notified on a rolling basis; must reply within 3 week(s) of notification.

**Academics. Special study options:** Accelerated study, distance learning, double major, dual enrollment of high school students, internships, liberal arts/career combination. License preparation in nursing. **Credit/placement by examination:** AP, CLEP, IB, institutional tests. **Support services:** GED preparation, learning center, reduced course load, remedial instruction, tutoring.

**Majors. Business:** Accounting, accounting technology, administrative services, business admin, retailing, sales/distribution, selling. **Computer sciences:** Networking, programming, web page design. **Construction:** Carpentry. **Engineering technology:** Computer systems, drafting, electrical, electromechanical. **Family/consumer sciences:** Child care. **Health:** Medical secretary, nursing (RN). **Legal studies:** Legal secretary. **Mechanic/repair:** Auto body, heating/ac/refrig, industrial. **Personal/culinary services:** Cosmetic.

**Most popular majors.** Business/marketing 34%, computer/information sciences 9%, engineering/engineering technologies 8%, health sciences 40%, trade and industry 7%.

**Computing on campus.** 75 workstations in library. Commuter students can connect to campus network. Online course registration, online library, helpline, wireless network available.

**Student life. Freshman orientation:** Mandatory. Preregistration for classes offered. Students are required to participate in an orientation session before classes begin, to meet academic advisors, and purchase photo ID. **Housing:** Cooperative housing available. Privately-owned dormitory near college available for Red Wing campus, cooperative arrangement with Winona State University for Winona campus. **Activities:** Student government, student newspaper.

**Student services.** Career counseling, student employment services, financial aid counseling, minority student services, personal counseling, placement for graduates, veterans' counselor. **Physically disabled:** Services for visually, speech, hearing impaired. **Transfer:** Pre-admission transcript evaluation for new students.

**Contact.** E-mail: enrollmentservices@southeastmn.edu
Phone: (507) 453-2700 Toll-free number: (877) 853-8324
Fax: (507) 453-2715
Al DuCett, Director of Admissions, Minnesota State College - Southeast Technical, 1250 Homer Road, Winona, MN 55987-0409

## Minnesota State Community and Technical College: Fergus Falls
### Fergus Falls, Minnesota
### www.minnesota.edu
**CB code: 2110**

⬥ Public 2-year community and technical college
⬥ Commuter campus in large town

**General.** Founded in 1960. Regionally accredited. Campuses in Detroit Lakes, Fergus Falls, Moorhead, and Wadena. **Enrollment:** 3,318 full-time, degree-seeking students. **Degrees:** 804 associate awarded. **Location:** 180 miles from Minneapolis-St. Paul, 60 miles from Fargo, North Dakota. **Calendar:** Semester, limited summer session. **Full-time faculty:** 188 total. **Part-time faculty:** 152 total. **Partnerships:** Formal partnerships with local high schools; juniors and seniors can enroll in specially designed courses for college credit at their high school.

**Student profile.**

| | | | |
|---|---|---|---|
| Out-of-state: | 10% | Live on campus: | 10% |
| 25 or older: | 28% | | |

**Transfer out.** 80% of students enrolled in the transfer program go on to 4-year colleges. **Colleges most students transferred to 2007:** Minnesota State University: Moorhead, St. Cloud State University, Bemidji State University, Minnesota State University: Mankato, University of Minnesota: Twin Cities.

**Basis for selection.** Open admission. Academic Skills Assessment Program (ASAP) required for English and Math. **Homeschooled:** Statement describing homeschool structure and mission, transcript of courses and grades required. **Learning Disabled:** Special accommodations available for students during placement assessment tests.

**2007-2008 Annual costs.** Tuition/fees: $4,737; $4,737 out-of-state. Per-credit charge: $138 in-state; $138 out-of-state. Room only: $2,450.

**Financial aid. Need-based:** Need-based aid available for part-time students. Work-study available nights and weekends. **Non-need-based:** Scholarships awarded for academics, art, leadership, minority status, music/drama, state residency.

**Application procedures. Admission:** No deadline. $20 fee. Application may be submitted online. Admission notification on a rolling basis. **Financial aid:** Priority date 6/1; no closing date. FAFSA, institutional form required. Applicants notified on a rolling basis starting 7/1.

**Academics. Special study options:** Distance learning, dual enrollment of high school students, ESL, honors, internships, liberal arts/career combination, study abroad, weekend college. Bachelor's degree programs available on campus. License preparation in nursing. **Credit/placement by examination:** AP, CLEP, IB, institutional tests. **Support services:** Learning center, reduced course load, remedial instruction, study skills assistance, tutoring, writing center.

**Majors. Biology:** General. **Business:** Accounting, administrative services, banking/financial services, business admin, fashion, human resources, office technology, sales/distribution, selling. **Computer sciences:** Networking, programming, security, web page design. **Construction:** Carpentry, site management. **Education:** Teacher assistance. **Engineering technology:** Architectural drafting, computer, computer systems, electrical, manufacturing, mechanical drafting, telecommunications. **Health:** Clinical lab technology, dental hygiene, licensed practical nurse, medical records technology, medical secretary, nursing (RN), pharmacy assistant, radiologic technology/medical imaging. **Legal studies:** Legal secretary, paralegal. **Liberal arts:** Arts/sciences. **Mechanic/repair:** Auto body, automotive, diesel, industrial, marine. **Protective services:** Criminal justice. **Visual/performing arts:** Graphic design.

**Most popular majors.** Business/marketing 16%, health sciences 44%, liberal arts 20%.

**Computing on campus.** 200 workstations in library, computer center, student center. Dormitories wired for high-speed internet access and linked to campus network. Online course registration, online library, helpline, wireless network available.

**Student life. Freshman orientation:** Mandatory. Preregistration for classes offered. 5-8 hour session held in summer. **Housing:** Apartments available. Privately owned dormitories within walking distance of the college. **Activities:** Bands, choral groups, drama, music ensembles, musical theater, student government, student newspaper.

**Athletics.** NJCAA. **Intercollegiate:** Baseball M, basketball, football (tackle) M, golf, softball W, volleyball W. **Intramural:** Basketball, bowling, football (non-tackle), football (tackle) M, golf, soccer, softball, volleyball. **Team name:** Spartans.

**Student services.** Adult student services, career counseling, student employment services, financial aid counseling, minority student services, personal counseling, placement for graduates, veterans' counselor. **Physically disabled:** Services for visually, speech, hearing impaired. **Transfer:** Pre-admission transcript evaluation for new students. Transfer adviser, college fairs on campus for students transferring to 4-year colleges.

**Contact.** E-mail: enroll@minnesota.edu
Phone: (218) 736-1525 Toll-free number: (877) 450-3322
Fax: (218) 736-1510
Carrie Brimhall, Director of Enrollment Management, Minnesota State Community and Technical College: Fergus Falls, 1414 College Way, Fergus Falls, MN 56537-1000

## Minnesota West Community and Technical College
### Granite Falls, Minnesota
### www.mnwest.edu
**CB code: 6945**

⬥ Public 2-year community, junior, technical and career college
⬥ Commuter campus in large town

**General.** Founded in 1936. Regionally accredited. In addition to the administrative campus at Granite Falls, there are campuses at Canby, Jackson, Pipestone, and Worthington and three learning sites in Fairmont, Luverne and Marshall, Minnesota. **Enrollment:** 2,859 degree-seeking undergraduates. **Degrees:** 322 associate awarded. **Location:** 200 miles from Minneapolis-St. Paul, 60 miles from Sioux Falls, South Dakota. **Calendar:** Semester, limited summer session. **Full-time faculty:** 86 total. **Part-time faculty:** 136 total.

**Basis for selection.** Open admission. Test scores not required for continuing education students. PSB-Aptitude for Practical Nursing Examination required of nursing applicants. Interview recommended. **Homeschooled:** Transcript of courses and grades required.

**2007-2008 Annual costs.** Tuition/fees: $4,692; $4,692 out-of-state. Per-credit charge: $142. Books/supplies: $600.

**Financial aid. Need-based:** Need-based aid available for part-time students.

**Application procedures. Admission:** No deadline. $20 fee, may be waived for applicants with need. Application may be submitted online. Admission notification on a rolling basis. Priority deadline for practical nursing applicants 02/15. **Financial aid:** Priority date 6/8; no closing date. FAFSA required. Applicants notified on a rolling basis starting 7/8; must reply within 2 week(s) of notification.

**Academics. Special study options:** Cooperative education, cross-registration, distance learning, double major, dual enrollment of high school students, independent study, internships, liberal arts/career combination, student-designed major, study abroad. License preparation in nursing, radiology. **Credit/placement by examination:** AP, CLEP, institutional tests. 60 credit hours maximum toward associate degree. **Support services:** GED preparation and test center, learning center, pre-admission summer program, reduced course load, remedial instruction, study skills assistance, tutoring.

**Majors. Agriculture:** General. **Biology:** General. **Business:** General, accounting, business admin. **Communications:** General, media studies. **Computer sciences:** General. **Education:** General, business, elementary, physical, secondary, special. **English:** English lit. **Health:** Nursing (RN). **History:** General. **Liberal arts:** Arts/sciences. **Math:** General. **Philosophy/religion:** Philosophy. **Physical sciences:** Chemistry, physics. **Psychology:** General. **Social sciences:** Economics, geography, political science, sociology. **Visual/performing arts:** Art, dramatic.

**Most popular majors.** Agriculture 10%, business/marketing 15%, liberal arts 68%.

**Computing on campus.** Online course registration, online library, helpline, wireless network available.

**Student life. Freshman orientation:** Mandatory. **Housing:** Subsidized apartments adjacent to campus. **Activities:** Jazz band, choral groups, drama, music ensembles, musical theater, radio station, student government, student newspaper, TV station, non-traditional student club, student senate, Phi Beta Kappa.

**Athletics.** NJCAA. **Intercollegiate:** Basketball, football (tackle) M, golf, softball W, volleyball W, wrestling M. **Intramural:** Basketball, bowling, golf, skiing, softball, tennis. **Team name:** Blue Jays.

**Student services.** Adult student services, career counseling, student employment services, personal counseling, veterans' counselor. **Physically disabled:** Services for visually, speech, hearing impaired. **Transfer:** Pre-admission transcript evaluation for new students. Transfer adviser, college fairs on campus for students transferring to 4-year colleges.

**Contact.** E-mail: barbara.reinders@mnwest.edu
Phone: (507) 372-3402 Toll-free number: (800) 658-2330
Fax: (507) 372-5803
Barbara Reinders, Director, Student Services, Minnesota West Community and Technical College, 1593 11th Avenue, Granite Falls, MN 56241

---

## Normandale Community College
**Bloomington, Minnesota**
**www.normandale.edu**

**CB member**
**CB code: 6501**

- Public 2-year community college
- Commuter campus in very large city

**General.** Founded in 1968. Regionally accredited. **Enrollment:** 9,239 degree-seeking undergraduates. **Degrees:** 827 associate awarded. **ROTC:** Army, Naval, Air Force. **Location:** 12 miles from Minneapolis-St. Paul. **Calendar:** Semester, extensive summer session. **Full-time faculty:** 185 total. **Part-time faculty:** 136 total. **Class size:** 31% < 20, 52% 20-39, 15% 40-49, 2% 50-99. **Special facilities:** Japanese garden, marshland area, career and academic planning center.

**Student profile.**

| | | | |
|---|---|---|---|
| Out-of-state: | 1% | 25 or older: | 33% |

**Transfer out. Colleges most students transferred to 2007:** University of Minnesota, University of St. Thomas, Minnesota State University: Mankato, St. Cloud State University, Metropolitan State University.

**Basis for selection.** Open admission, but selective for some programs. Admission to health-related programs (dental hygiene, nursing, dietetic technology, radiologic technology) based on high school GPA and completion of specific course requirements. In-house placement tests in English, mathematics, reading administered before registration. **Adult students:** SAT/ACT scores not required.

**2007-2008 Annual costs.** Tuition/fees: $4,512; $4,512 out-of-state. Per-credit charge: $134 in-state; $134 out-of-state. Tuition rates vary in states having reciprocity agreements with Minnesota. Books/supplies: $1,100. Personal expenses: $2,700.

**Financial aid. Need-based:** Need-based aid available for part-time students. Work-study available nights, weekends and for part-time students. **Non-need-based:** Scholarships awarded for academics, leadership, music/drama, state residency.

**Application procedures. Admission:** No deadline. $20 fee, may be waived for applicants with need. Application may be submitted online. Admission notification on a rolling basis. **Financial aid:** Priority date 4/1; no closing date. FAFSA required. Applicants notified on a rolling basis starting 4/15.

**Academics. Special study options:** Accelerated study, cooperative education, distance learning, double major, dual enrollment of high school students, ESL, honors, independent study, internships, liberal arts/career combination, study abroad, teacher certification program, weekend college. Bachelor's degree programs available on campus. License preparation in dental hygiene, nursing, radiology. **Credit/placement by examination:** AP, CLEP, IB, institutional tests. **Support services:** Learning center, reduced course load, remedial instruction, study skills assistance, tutoring, writing center.

**Majors. Business:** Accounting, business admin, hospitality admin, marketing. **Computer sciences:** General, computer science. **Education:** General, elementary, special. **Engineering:** General. **Engineering technology:** Biomedical, computer systems, manufacturing. **Health:** Dental hygiene, dietetics, nursing (RN), radiologic technology/medical imaging. **Liberal arts:**

---

Arts/sciences. **Protective services:** Criminal justice, police science. **Visual/performing arts:** Dramatic, studio arts.

**Most popular majors.** Business/marketing 7%, health sciences 18%, liberal arts 65%, security/protective services 6%.

**Computing on campus.** 575 workstations in library, computer center, student center. Commuter students can connect to campus network. Online course registration, online library, helpline, repair service, wireless network available.

**Student life. Freshman orientation:** Mandatory, $25 fee. **Activities:** Bands, choral groups, drama, literary magazine, music ensembles, musical theater, student government, student newspaper, Christian Fellowship club, Black student alliance, ASIA, single parents, wellness support group, Phi Theta Kappa, Somali student association, Ethiopian student association, Club Latino.

**Athletics. Intramural:** Archery, baseball, basketball, bowling, boxing, cross-country, fencing, field hockey, football (non-tackle), golf, handball, ice hockey, judo, racquetball, skiing, soccer, softball, table tennis, tennis, volleyball, weight lifting. **Team name:** Lions.

**Student services.** Adult student services, career counseling, services for economically disadvantaged, student employment services, financial aid counseling, on-campus daycare, personal counseling, placement for graduates, veterans' counselor. **Physically disabled:** Services for visually, speech, hearing impaired. **Transfer:** Pre-admission transcript evaluation for new students. Transfer adviser, college fairs on campus for students transferring to 4-year colleges.

**Contact.** E-mail: information@normandale.edu
Phone: (952) 487-8201 Toll-free number: (866) 880-8740
Fax: (952) 487-8230
Rick Smith, Director of Admissions, Normandale Community College, 9700 France Avenue South, Bloomington, MN 55431

---

## North Hennepin Community College
**Brooklyn Park, Minnesota**
**www.nhcc.edu**

**CB code: 6498**

- Public 2-year community college
- Commuter campus in small city

**General.** Founded in 1966. Regionally accredited. **Enrollment:** 6,255 degree-seeking undergraduates; 152 non-degree-seeking students. **Degrees:** 710 associate awarded. **Location:** 12 miles from downtown. **Calendar;** Semester, limited summer session. **Full-time faculty:** 99 total; 8% minority, 67% women. **Part-time faculty:** 132 total; 12% minority, 44% women. **Class size:** 33% < 20, 55% 20-39, 7% 40-49, 5% 50-99, less than 1% >100.

**Student profile.** Among degree-seeking undergraduates, 2% already have a bachelor's degree or higher, 1,532 enrolled as first-time, first-year students, 722 transferred in from other institutions.

| | | | |
|---|---|---|---|
| Part-time: | 60% | Hispanic American: | 2% |
| Women: | 58% | Native American: | 1% |
| African American: | 15% | International: | 1% |
| Asian American: | 11% | 25 or older: | 52% |

**Transfer out.** 55% of students enrolled in the transfer program go on to 4-year colleges.

**Basis for selection.** Open admission, but selective for some programs. Competitive admission for medical programs: nursing, non-invasive cardio technology, medical lab technician, histo technician, graphic design. Must show proof of immunization to be enrolled in classes. Assessment test or approved waiver required for registration.

**High school preparation.** 1 unit chemistry and algebra are required for nursing program.

**2007-2008 Annual costs.** Tuition/fees: $4,420; $4,420 out-of-state. Per-credit charge: $137 in-state; $137 out-of-state. Books/supplies: $1,000. Personal expenses: $3,586.

**2006-2007 Financial aid. Need-based:** 39% of total undergraduate aid awarded as scholarships/grants, 61% as loans/jobs. Need-based aid available for part-time students. Work-study available nights, weekends and for part-time students. **Non-need-based:** Scholarships awarded for academics, art, leadership. **Additional information:** Computerized financial aid application.

**Application procedures. Admission:** No deadline. $20 fee. Application must be submitted on paper. Admission notification on a rolling basis.

**Financial aid:** Priority date 4/15; no closing date. FAFSA required. Applicants notified on a rolling basis starting 6/1.

**Academics. Special study options:** Cross-registration, distance learning, dual enrollment of high school students, ESL, honors, independent study, internships, student-designed major, study abroad, weekend college. Bachelor's degree programs available on campus. License preparation in nursing. **Credit/placement by examination:** AP, CLEP, IB, institutional tests. 30 credit hours maximum toward associate degree. **Support services:** Learning center, reduced course load, remedial instruction, study skills assistance, tutoring, writing center.

**Majors. Biology:** General. **Business:** Accounting, accounting technology, business admin, finance, management information systems, marketing, small business admin. **Computer sciences:** Computer science. **Construction:** Building inspection, site management. **Engineering:** General. **Health:** Cardiovascular technology, clinical lab technology, histologic assistant, nursing (RN), radiologic technology/medical imaging. **Legal studies:** Paralegal. **Liberal arts:** Arts/sciences. **Physical sciences:** Chemistry. **Protective services:** Criminal justice, police science. **Visual/performing arts:** Graphic design, studio arts.

**Computing on campus.** 700 workstations in library, computer center, student center. Online course registration, online library, helpline, wireless network available.

**Student life. Freshman orientation:** Mandatory. Preregistration for classes offered. 2 to 3 hour session held prior to the start of each term for all new students. **Activities:** Choral groups, drama, literary magazine, musical theater, student government, student newspaper.

**Athletics. Intramural:** Basketball, bowling, soccer, softball, tennis, volleyball.

**Student services.** Career counseling, student employment services, financial aid counseling, on-campus daycare, personal counseling, placement for graduates. **Physically disabled:** Services for visually, speech, hearing impaired. **Learning disabled:** Comprehensive services available. **Transfer:** Pre-admission transcript evaluation for new students. Transfer adviser, college fairs on campus for students transferring to 4-year colleges.

**Contact.** E-mail: admissions@nhcc.edu
Phone: (763) 424-0719 Toll-free number: (800) 818-0395
Fax: (763) 493-0563
Lori Kirkeby, Registrar, North Hennepin Community College, 7411 85th Avenue North, Minneapolis, MN 55445

## Northland Community & Technical College
**Thief River Falls, Minnesota**
www.northlandcollege.edu                      CB code: 6500

- Public 2-year community and technical college
- Commuter campus in small town

**General.** Founded in 1965. Regionally accredited. Campuses in East Grand Forks and Thief River Falls. **Enrollment:** 1,957 degree-seeking undergraduates. **Degrees:** 475 associate awarded. **Location:** 55 miles from Grand Forks, North Dakota. **Calendar:** Semester, limited summer session. **Full-time faculty:** 203 total; 4% minority, 51% women. **Part-time faculty:** 74 total. **Class size:** 50% < 20, 48% 20-39, 2% 40-49, less than 1% 50-99, less than 1% >100.

**Student profile.** Among degree-seeking undergraduates, 26% enrolled in a transfer program, 64% enrolled in a vocational program, 1% already have a bachelor's degree or higher, 437 transferred in from other institutions.

**Out-of-state:**          35%     **Women:**          55%

**Transfer out. Colleges most students transferred to 2007:** University of North Dakota, North Dakota State University, Bemidji State University, University of Minnesota: Crookston, Moorhead State University, St. Cloud State University.

**Basis for selection.** Open admission. Students are required to go through the ACCUPLACER assessment program to determine level of mathematics, reading and english skills. **Homeschooled:** Transcript of courses and grades required.

**2007-2008 Annual costs.** Tuition/fees: $4,764. Per-credit charge: $145. Tuition is the same for both in-state and out-of-state students. Books/supplies: $600. Personal expenses: $1,350.

**2006-2007 Financial aid. Need-based:** 33% of total undergraduate aid awarded as scholarships/grants, 67% as loans/jobs. Need-based aid available for part-time students. Work-study available nights and for part-time students. **Non-need-based:** Scholarships awarded for academics.

**Application procedures. Admission:** No deadline. $20 fee. Application may be submitted online. Admission notification on a rolling basis. **Financial aid:** Priority date 5/1; no closing date. FAFSA required. Applicants notified on a rolling basis starting 5/15.

**Academics. Special study options:** Combined bachelor's/graduate degree, distance learning, double major, dual enrollment of high school students, external degree, internships, liberal arts/career combination. License preparation in aviation, nursing, occupational therapy, paramedic, physical therapy, radiology. **Credit/placement by examination:** AP, CLEP, institutional tests. 44 credit hours maximum toward associate degree. **Support services:** GED test center, learning center, reduced course load, remedial instruction, study skills assistance, tutoring, writing center.

**Majors. Agriculture:** Business, economics, farm/ranch. **Architecture:** Technology. **Biology:** General. **Business:** Accounting, administrative services, management information systems, marketing, sales/distribution. **Communications:** General, broadcast journalism, journalism, media studies, radio/tv. **Computer sciences:** Networking. **Conservation:** Environmental science, management/policy. **Construction:** General. **Education:** General, early childhood. **Engineering:** General, electrical. **Engineering technology:** Drafting. **English:** English lit. **Foreign languages:** General. **Health:** Athletic training, cardiovascular technology, clinical lab science, clinical lab technology, EMT ambulance attendant, EMT paramedic, health services, insurance coding, medical assistant, medical secretary, medical transcription, nursing (RN), occupational therapy assistant, office assistant, pharmacy assistant, physical therapy assistant, radiologic technology/medical imaging, respiratory therapy assistant, respiratory therapy technology, surgical technology. **Interdisciplinary:** Math/computer science. **Legal studies:** Prelaw. **Liberal arts:** Arts/sciences. **Math:** General. **Mechanic/repair:** Aircraft, auto body, automotive, avionics, electronics/electrical. **Parks/recreation:** General. **Production:** Welding. **Protective services:** Corrections, criminal justice, law enforcement admin, police science. **Psychology:** General. **Public administration:** Human services. **Social sciences:** General. **Visual/performing arts:** General, art, studio arts.

**Computing on campus.** 356 workstations in library, computer center, student center. Online course registration, online library, helpline, repair service, wireless network available.

**Student life. Freshman orientation:** Mandatory. **Activities:** Bands, choral groups, dance, drama, music ensembles, musical theater, radio station, student government, student newspaper, Phi Theta Kappa honor society, multicultural club, SOS club, diversity committee.

**Athletics.** NJCAA. **Intercollegiate:** Baseball M, basketball, football (tackle) M, softball W, volleyball W. **Intramural:** Basketball, bowling, golf, soccer, softball, tennis, volleyball. **Team name:** Pioneers.

**Student services.** Adult student services, career counseling, services for economically disadvantaged, student employment services, financial aid counseling, minority student services, on-campus daycare, personal counseling, placement for graduates, veterans' counselor, women's services. **Physically disabled:** Services for visually, speech, hearing impaired. **Transfer:** Re-entry adviser, pre-admission transcript evaluation for new students. Transfer adviser, college fairs on campus for students transferring to 4-year colleges.

**Contact.** E-mail: admissions@northlandcollege.edu
Phone: (218) 773-3441 Toll-free number: (800) 959-6282
Fax: (218) 681-0774
Eugene Klinke, Enrollment Management Coordinator, Northland Community & Technical College, 1101 Highway One East, Thief River Falls, MN 56701

## Northwest Technical College
**Bemidji, Minnesota**
www.ntcmn.edu                          CB code: 3626

- Public 2-year technical college
- Commuter campus in large town

**General.** Regionally accredited. **Enrollment:** 891 degree-seeking undergraduates; 326 non-degree-seeking students. **Degrees:** 103 associate awarded. **Location:** 229 miles from Minneapolis-St. Paul, 152 miles from Duluth. **Calendar:** Semester, limited summer session. **Full-time faculty:** 29 total; 3% minority, 76% women. **Part-time faculty:** 27 total; 4% minority, 41% women. **Class size:** 66% < 20, 34% 20-39. **Special facilities:** American Indian resource center, lake, 3D hologram technology. **Partnerships:** Advanced Standing agreements with area high schools in several fundamental occupational courses.

**Student profile.** Among degree-seeking undergraduates, 100% enrolled in a vocational program, 3% already have a bachelor's degree or higher,

223 enrolled as first-time, first-year students, 122 transferred in from other institutions.

| | | | |
|---|---|---|---|
| Part-time: | 36% | Asian American: | 1% |
| Out-of-state: | 10% | Native American: | 10% |
| Women: | 68% | 25 or older: | 35% |
| African American: | 1% | Live on campus: | 5% |

**Transfer out. Colleges most students transferred to 2007:** Bemidji State University, Northland Community and Technical College, Minnesota State Community and Technical College.

**Basis for selection.** Open admission. **Learning Disabled:** Procedure: Learners with learning disabilities are encouraged to have an IEP on file with the Learning Services Coordinator and meet with her prior to the start of the semester to develop a Personal Education Plan.

**2007-2008 Annual costs.** Tuition/fees: $4,704; $4,704 out-of-state. Per-credit charge: $147 in-state; $147 out-of-state. Books/supplies: $1,200.

**2007-2008 Financial aid.** All financial aid based on need. 58% of total undergraduate aid awarded as scholarships/grants, 42% as loans/jobs. Need-based aid available for part-time students. Work-study available nights and for part-time students.

**Application procedures. Admission:** No deadline. $20 fee, may be waived for applicants with need. Application may be submitted online. Admission notification on a rolling basis. High school learners can attend the college under the Post-Secondary Enrollment Options program. **Financial aid:** Priority date 7/1; no closing date. FAFSA, institutional form required. Applicants notified on a rolling basis.

**Academics.** NTC learners can take General Education courses from Bemidji State University and/or online from a regional consortium of colleges in fulfillment of general education requirements of degrees at NTC. NTC learners may also enroll in CampusToolkit, an electronic coaching system that provides individual coaching by a college counselor. **Special study options:** Cross-registration, distance learning, double major, dual enrollment of high school students, ESL, independent study, internships, student-designed major. Study abroad options are available through our partnership with Bemidji State University. License preparation in nursing. **Credit/placement by examination:** AP, CLEP, IB, institutional tests. **Support services:** Learning center, pre-admission summer program, reduced course load, remedial instruction, study skills assistance, tutoring.

**Majors. Business:** Accounting, administrative services, business admin, sales/distribution. **Engineering technology:** Industrial, manufacturing. **Family/consumer sciences:** Child care. **Health:** Licensed practical nurse, massage therapy, medical secretary, nursing (RN). **Mechanic/repair:** Engine machinist.

**Most popular majors.** Business/marketing 16%, family/consumer sciences 7%, health sciences 73%.

**Computing on campus.** PC or laptop required. 140 workstations in dormitories, library, computer center, student center. Dormitories wired for high-speed internet access. Commuter students can connect to campus network. Online course registration, online library, helpline, repair service, wireless network available.

**Student life. Freshman orientation:** Mandatory. Preregistration for classes offered. College Success Day held the day before classes start each semester. **Housing:** Coed dorms, apartments, substance-free housing available. $150 partly refundable deposit. NTC learners may reside in Bemidji State University residence halls. **Activities:** Student government, Phi Theta Kappa, Skills USA.

**Student services.** Adult student services, campus ministries, career counseling, services for economically disadvantaged, student employment services, financial aid counseling, health services, minority student services, personal counseling, placement for graduates, veterans' counselor. **Physically disabled:** Services for visually, speech, hearing impaired. **Learning disabled:** Comprehensive services available. **Transfer:** Re-entry adviser, pre-admission transcript evaluation for new students. Transfer adviser, college fairs on campus for students transferring to 4-year colleges.

**Contact.** E-mail: richard.lehmann@ntcmn.edu
Phone: (218) 333-6647 Toll-free number: (800) 942-8324
Fax: (218) 333-6697
Richard Lehmann, Admissions Specialist, Northwest Technical College, 905 Grant Avenue Southeast, Bemidji, MN 56601-4907

## Northwest Technical Institute
**Eagan, Minnesota**
www.nti.edu
**CB code: 1388**

- For-profit 2-year technical college
- Commuter campus in small city
- Application essay, interview required

**General.** Founded in 1957. Accredited by ACCSCT. **Enrollment:** 126 degree-seeking undergraduates. **Degrees:** 72 associate awarded. **Location:** 10 miles from Minneapolis-St. Paul. **Calendar:** Semester, extensive summer session. **Part-time faculty:** 9 total; 22% have terminal degrees, 33% women. **Class size:** 100% < 20.

**Basis for selection.** Open admission.

**High school preparation.** Recommended units include English 2, mathematics 3 and science 2.

**2007-2008 Annual costs.** Tuition/fees: $14,845. Per-credit charge: $463. Books/supplies: $650. Personal expenses: $3,192.

**Financial aid. Need-based:** Need-based aid available for part-time students.

**Application procedures. Admission:** No deadline. $25 fee. Admission notification on a rolling basis. **Financial aid:** No deadline. FAFSA, institutional form required. Applicants notified on a rolling basis; must reply within 2 week(s) of notification.

**Academics. Special study options:** Honors, liberal arts/career combination. **Credit/placement by examination:** AP, CLEP. **Support services:** Tutoring.

**Majors. Architecture:** Technology. **Engineering:** General, mechanical. **Engineering technology:** General, architectural, architectural drafting, drafting, mechanical, mechanical drafting.

**Computing on campus.** 120 workstations in student center.

**Student life. Freshman orientation:** Mandatory.

**Student services.** Career counseling, student employment services, placement for graduates. **Transfer:** Re-entry adviser, pre-admission transcript evaluation for new students.

**Contact.** E-mail: info@nti.edu
Phone: (952) 944-0080 Toll-free number: (800) 443-4223
Fax: (952) 944-9274
John Hartman, Director of Admissions, Northwest Technical Institute, 950 Blue Gentian Road, Eagan, MN 55121

## Pine Technical College
**Pine City, Minnesota**
www.pinetech.edu
**CB code: 7118**

- Public 2-year technical college
- Commuter campus in small town

**General.** Regionally accredited. **Enrollment:** 512 degree-seeking undergraduates. **Degrees:** 24 associate awarded. **Location:** 60 miles from Minneapolis-St. Paul. **Calendar:** Semester, limited summer session. **Full-time faculty:** 10 total; 60% have terminal degrees, 10% minority. **Part-time faculty:** 34 total; 62% have terminal degrees, 3% minority, 76% women. **Class size:** 77% < 20, 18% 20-39, 2% 40-49, 2% 50-99.

**Student profile.**

| | | | |
|---|---|---|---|
| Out-of-state: | 11% | 25 or older: | 35% |

**Transfer out. Colleges most students transferred to 2007:** St. Cloud Technical College, Anoka-Ramsey Community College, Lake Superior Community College, Mesabi Community College, North Hennepin College.

**Basis for selection.** Open admission, but selective for some programs. Additional requirements for some majors. Criminal history check. **Home-schooled:** State high school equivalency certificate required.

**2007-2008 Annual costs.** Tuition/fees: $4,206; $7,986 out-of-state. Per-credit charge: $126 in-state; $252 out-of-state. Various reciprocity agreements with some neighboring states provide tuition reduction to out-of-state students. Books/supplies: $800. Personal expenses: $600.

**Financial aid. Need-based:** Need-based aid available for part-time students. Work-study available for part-time students. **Non-need-based:** Scholarships awarded for academics, state residency.

**Application procedures. Admission:** No deadline. $20 fee, may be waived for applicants with need. Application may be submitted online. Admission notification on a rolling basis. **Financial aid:** Priority date 5/5; no closing date. FAFSA, institutional form required. Applicants notified on a rolling basis starting 6/5.

**Academics. Special study options:** Cross-registration, distance learning, double major, dual enrollment of high school students, honors, independent study, internships, liberal arts/career combination. License preparation in nursing. **Credit/placement by examination:** AP, CLEP, institutional tests. 35 credit hours maximum toward associate degree. **Support services:** Learning center, reduced course load, remedial instruction, study skills assistance, tutoring.

**Majors. Biology:** Biotechnology. **Business:** Accounting, business admin. **Computer sciences:** Data processing, information systems, programming. **Engineering technology:** Manufacturing. **Family/consumer sciences:** Child care. **Health:** Insurance coding. **Mechanic/repair:** Automotive, gunsmithing. **Production:** Machine tool. **Public administration:** Human services.

**Most popular majors.** Business/marketing 62%, family/consumer sciences 31%.

**Computing on campus.** 100 workstations in library, computer center. Commuter students can connect to campus network. Online course registration, online library, helpline, wireless network available.

**Student life. Freshman orientation:** Mandatory. **Activities:** Student government.

**Athletics. Intercollegiate:** Rifle. **Intramural:** Rifle, tennis.

**Student services.** Career counseling, services for economically disadvantaged, student employment services, financial aid counseling, on-campus daycare, personal counseling, placement for graduates. **Physically disabled:** Services for visually, hearing impaired. **Transfer:** Pre-admission transcript evaluation for new students. Transfer adviser, college fairs on campus for students transferring to 4-year colleges.

**Contact.** E-mail: information@pinetech.edu
Phone: (320) 629-5100 Toll-free number: (800) 521-7463
Fax: (320) 629-5101
James Stumne, Admissions Director, Pine Technical College, 900 Fourth Street, SE, Pine City, MN 55063

## Rainy River Community College
**International Falls, Minnesota**
**www.rrcc.mnscu.edu**
CB code: 1637

- Public 2-year community and technical college
- Commuter campus in small town

**General.** Founded in 1967. Regionally accredited. **Enrollment:** 421 degree-seeking undergraduates. **Degrees:** 52 associate awarded. **Location:** 300 miles from Minneapolis-St. Paul, 150 miles from Duluth. **Calendar:** Semester, limited summer session. **Full-time faculty:** 15 total; 7% have terminal degrees, 47% women. **Part-time faculty:** 18 total; 11% minority, 17% women.

**Student profile.**

| | | | |
|---|---|---|---|
| African American: | 21% | Hispanic American: | 2% |
| Asian American: | 1% | Native American: | 5% |

**Transfer out. Colleges most students transferred to 2007:** St. Cloud State University, Bemidji State University, University of Minnesota-Duluth.

**Basis for selection.** Open admission.

**2007-2008 Annual costs.** Tuition/fees: $4,380; $5,348 out-of-state. Per-credit charge: $129 in-state; $161 out-of-state. Books/supplies: $600. Personal expenses: $900.

**Financial aid. Need-based:** Need-based aid available for part-time students. Work-study available nights, weekends and for part-time students. **Non-need-based:** Scholarships awarded for academics, alumni affiliation, minority status, state residency. **Additional information:** Many scholarship and employment opportunities for applicants showing little or no need.

**Application procedures. Admission:** No deadline. $20 fee. Application may be submitted online. Admission notification on a rolling basis. **Financial aid:** Priority date 6/1; no closing date. FAFSA, institutional form required. Applicants notified on a rolling basis starting 5/1; must reply within 3 week(s) of notification.

**Academics. Special study options:** Distance learning, dual enrollment of high school students, honors, independent study, internships, liberal arts/career combination. License preparation in aviation, nursing. **Credit/placement by examination:** AP, CLEP, IB, institutional tests. **Support services:** Learning center, pre-admission summer program, reduced course load, remedial instruction, study skills assistance, tutoring, writing center.

**Majors. Area/ethnic studies:** Native American. **Business:** Office technology. **Computer sciences:** General. **Conservation:** General. **Liberal arts:** Arts/sciences.

**Computing on campus.** 100 workstations in dormitories, library, computer center. Online course registration available.

**Student life. Freshman orientation:** Mandatory. **Housing:** Special housing for disabled, apartments available. $200 deposit. Student apartments equipped with computers. **Activities:** Choral groups, drama, literary magazine, music ensembles, musical theater, student government, Black Student Association club, Native Student club, environment club.

**Athletics.** NJCAA. **Intercollegiate:** Basketball, football (tackle) M, softball W, volleyball W. **Intramural:** Archery, badminton, bowling, cheerleading, cross-country, golf, ice hockey W, racquetball, skiing, softball, table tennis, tennis, volleyball. **Team name:** Voyageurs.

**Student services.** Adult student services, career counseling, services for economically disadvantaged, student employment services, financial aid counseling, minority student services, personal counseling, placement for graduates, veterans' counselor. **Physically disabled:** Services for visually, speech, hearing impaired. **Transfer:** Re-entry adviser, pre-admission transcript evaluation for new students. Transfer adviser, college fairs on campus for students transferring to 4-year colleges.

**Contact.** E-mail: admissions@rrcc.mnscu.edu
Phone: (218) 285-2207 Toll-free number: (800) 456-3996
Fax: (218) 285-2239
Berta Hagen, Registrar, Rainy River Community College, 1501 Highway 71, International Falls, MN 56649

## Rasmussen College: Eden Prairie
**Eden Prairie, Minnesota**
**www.rasmussen.edu**
CB code: 2448

- For-profit 2-year business and junior college
- Commuter campus in very large city

**General.** Regionally accredited. 4 campuses: Eden Prairie, St. Cloud, Eagan, Mankato. **Enrollment:** 506 degree-seeking undergraduates. **Degrees:** 98 associate awarded. **Calendar:** Quarter, extensive summer session. **Full-time faculty:** 7 total. **Part-time faculty:** 25 total.

**Basis for selection.** Open admission.

**2007-2008 Annual costs.** Regular courses: $345/credit; networking classes: $445/credit; child care classes: $255/credit.

**Financial aid. Need-based:** Need-based aid available for part-time students.

**Application procedures. Admission:** No deadline. $60 fee. Admission notification on a rolling basis. **Financial aid:** No deadline. FAFSA, institutional form required. Applicants notified on a rolling basis.

**Academics. Special study options:** Distance learning. **Credit/placement by examination:** CLEP. 12 credit hours maximum toward associate degree. **Support services:** Pre-admission summer program, reduced course load, study skills assistance, tutoring.

**Majors. Business:** Accounting, administrative services, business admin, hospitality admin, international marketing, marketing, office management, office/clerical, operations, tourism/travel. **Health:** Medical assistant, medical records admin, medical records technology, medical secretary. **Legal studies:** Court reporting, legal secretary.

**Computing on campus.** PC or laptop required. Helpline, repair service available.

**Student life. Freshman orientation:** Mandatory.

**Student services.** Career counseling, student employment services, placement for graduates. **Transfer:** Pre-admission transcript evaluation for new students.

**Contact.** Phone: (952) 545-2000
Jeff Lust, Director of Admisson, Rasmussen College: Eden Prairie, 7905 Golden Triangle Drive, Suite 100, Eden Prairie, MN 55344

## Rasmussen College: Mankato
**Mankato, Minnesota**
**www.rasmussen.edu**
CB code: 2453

- For-profit 2-year business college
- Commuter campus in large town
- Interview required

**General.** Founded in 1983. Regionally accredited. **Enrollment:** 610 degree-seeking undergraduates. **Degrees:** 109 associate awarded. **Location:** 60 miles from Minneapolis-St. Paul. **Calendar:** Quarter. **Full-time faculty:** 15 total. **Part-time faculty:** 30 total.

**Basis for selection.** Open admission.

**2007-2008 Annual costs.** Regular courses: $345/credit; networking classes: $445/credit; child care classes: $255/credit. Books/supplies: $450. Personal expenses: $1,575.

**Financial aid. Non-need-based:** Scholarships awarded for academics.

**Application procedures. Admission:** No deadline. $60 fee. Admission notification on a rolling basis. **Financial aid:** No deadline. FAFSA, institutional form required.

**Academics. Special study options:** Cooperative education, internships. **Credit/placement by examination:** CLEP. **Support services:** Tutoring.

**Majors. Business:** General, accounting, business admin, fashion, hospitality admin, sales/distribution, tourism promotion, tourism/travel. **Health:** Licensed practical nurse, massage therapy, medical assistant, medical records technology. **Legal studies:** Court reporting.

**Computing on campus.** PC or laptop required. Helpline, repair service available.

**Student life. Freshman orientation:** Mandatory. **Housing:** Locally owned apartments directly behind college available. **Activities:** Student government, student newspaper.

**Athletics. Intramural:** Volleyball.

**Student services.** Career counseling, student employment services, on-campus daycare, placement for graduates. **Transfer:** Pre-admission transcript evaluation for new students. Transfer adviser, college fairs on campus for students transferring to 4-year colleges.

**Contact.** E-mail: rascoll@ic.mankato.mn.us
Phone: (507) 625-6556 Fax: (507) 625-6557
Kathleen Clifford, Director of Admissions, Rasmussen College: Mankato, 501 Holly Lane, Mankato, MN 56001

## Rasmussen College: St. Cloud
St. Cloud, Minnesota
www.rasmussen.edu                    CB code: 3315

▸ For-profit 2-year community and junior college
▸ Commuter campus in small city

**General.** Regionally accredited. **Location:** 60 miles from Minneapolis-St. Paul. **Calendar:** Quarter.

**Annual costs/financial aid.** Regular courses: $345/credit; networking classes: $445/credit; child care classes: $255/credit. Books/supplies: $1,200. Personal expenses: $1,764. Need-based financial aid available to full-time and part-time students.

**Contact.** Phone: (320) 251-5600
Director of Admissions, 226 Park Avenue South, St. Cloud, MN 56301-3713

## Ridgewater College
Willmar, Minnesota
www.ridgewater.edu                    CB code: 6949

▸ Public 2-year community and technical college
▸ Commuter campus in large town

**General.** Founded in 1961. Regionally accredited. Two campuses: Willmar and Hutchinson. **Enrollment:** 3,676 degree-seeking undergraduates. **Degrees:** 436 associate awarded. **Location:** 100 miles from Minneapolis-St. Paul. **Calendar:** Semester, limited summer session. **Special facilities:** Natural wooded prairie and wetlands areas for biological study, nursing simulation centers.

**Student profile.** Among degree-seeking undergraduates, 49% enrolled in a transfer program, 51% enrolled in a vocational program, 1,576 enrolled as first-time, first-year students.

**Basis for selection.** Open admission, but selective for some programs. Special requirements for practical nursing, registered nursing, radiologic

technology, chemical dependency counseling, veterinary technology, and post-secondary programs. An interview is recommended for the law enforcement, nursing, radiologic technology, and veterinary technology programs.

**High school preparation.** Chemistry and mathematics are recommended for mathematics, science, and health science majors.

**2007-2008 Annual costs.** Tuition/fees: $4,517; $4,517 out-of-state. Per-credit charge: $134 in-state; $134 out-of-state. Some courses may carry higher per credit hour charge. Reciprocity agreements for in-state tuition rates with some neighboring states. Books/supplies: $800. Personal expenses: $1,660.

**2007-2008 Financial aid. Need-based:** 33% of total undergraduate aid awarded as scholarships/grants, 67% as loans/jobs. Need-based aid available for part-time students. Work-study available nights, weekends and for part-time students. **Additional information:** Special funds are available for adult transfer students returning or continuing education after a 7-year absence from academic training. ALLISS grants provide reimbursement for one class, up to five credits for one semester.

**Application procedures. Admission:** Priority date 8/1; no deadline. $20 fee. Application must be submitted on paper. Admission notification on a rolling basis. **Financial aid:** No deadline. FAFSA, institutional form required. Applicants notified on a rolling basis.

**Academics.** Four-year baccalaureate degrees including business administration, psychology, sociology, speech communications taught by state universities available on campus. **Special study options:** Cooperative education, distance learning, dual enrollment of high school students, internships, liberal arts/career combination, student-designed major, study abroad. Bachelor's degree programs available on campus. License preparation in nursing, paramedic, real estate. **Credit/placement by examination:** AP, CLEP, institutional tests. 20 credit hours maximum toward associate degree. **Support services:** GED test center, learning center, pre-admission summer program, reduced course load, remedial instruction, study skills assistance, tutoring.

**Majors. Agriculture:** General, agribusiness operations, agronomy, business, dairy, economics, farm/ranch, production. **Biology:** General, conservation. **Business:** General, accounting, management information systems, marketing, retailing, sales/distribution. **Communications:** General, journalism, media studies, publishing. **Communications technology:** Desktop publishing. **Computer sciences:** General, computer science, networking, web page design, webmaster. **Construction:** Carpentry, electrician. **Education:** General, adult/continuing, art, business, elementary, health, instructional media, mathematics, middle, multi-level teacher, music, physical, science, secondary, special, teacher assistance, voc/tech. **Engineering technology:** General, CAD/CADD, drafting, electrical, instrumentation, metallurgical. **English:** English lit, speech/rhetoric. **Family/consumer sciences:** Family studies. **Health:** Athletic training, health care admin, medical assistant, medical radiologic technology/radiation therapy, medical records technology, medical secretary, nursing (RN), substance abuse counseling, veterinary technology/assistant. **History:** General. **Interdisciplinary:** Math/computer science. **Legal studies:** Legal secretary, prelaw. **Liberal arts:** Arts/sciences. **Math:** General. **Mechanic/repair:** Auto body, automotive. **Parks/recreation:** General, health/fitness. **Personal/culinary services:** Cosmetic. **Physical sciences:** Chemistry, geology. **Production:** Machine tool, tool and die, welding. **Protective services:** Criminal justice, police science. **Psychology:** General. **Public administration:** Social work. **Social sciences:** General, criminology, economics, political science, sociology, urban studies. **Visual/performing arts:** Art, commercial photography, photography, studio arts. **Other:** Activity director, Nondestructive testing technology.

**Computing on campus.** 1,000 workstations in library, computer center. Commuter students can connect to campus network. Online course registration, helpline, repair service, wireless network available.

**Student life. Freshman orientation:** Mandatory. **Housing:** Apartment buildings are adjacent to campus. **Activities:** Choral groups, drama, music ensembles, musical theater, student government, student newspaper, symphony orchestra, Christian Students Together, Connections Club, First Responders, Multicultural Club, Phi Theta Kappa.

**Athletics.** NJCAA. **Intercollegiate:** Baseball M, basketball, football (tackle) M, golf, softball W, volleyball W, wrestling M. **Intramural:** Basketball, football (non-tackle) M, skiing, softball, volleyball, weight lifting. **Team name:** Warriors.

**Student services.** Adult student services, alcohol/substance abuse counseling, campus ministries, career counseling, services for economically disadvantaged, student employment services, financial aid counseling, health services, minority student services, on-campus daycare, personal counseling, placement for graduates. **Physically disabled:** Services for visually, speech, hearing impaired. **Transfer:** Transfer adviser, college fairs on campus for students transferring to 4-year colleges.

**Contact.** E-mail: info@ridgewater.edu
Phone: (320) 222-5976 Toll-free number: (800) 722-1151
Fax: (320) 222-5216
Sally Kerfeld, Director of Admissions, Ridgewater College, 2101 15th
Avenue Northwest, Willmar, MN 56201

## Riverland Community College
### Austin, Minnesota

**CB code: 6017**

- Public 2-year community and technical college
- Commuter campus in large town

**General.** Founded in 1996. Regionally accredited. **Enrollment:** 3,477 degree-seeking undergraduates. **Degrees:** 353 associate awarded. **Location:** 90 miles from Minneapolis-St. Paul. **Calendar:** Semester, limited summer session. **Full-time faculty:** 97 total; 7% have terminal degrees, 3% minority, 41% women. **Part-time faculty:** 125 total; 6% have terminal degrees, 4% minority, 46% women.

**Student profile.** Among degree-seeking undergraduates, 48% enrolled in a transfer program, 52% enrolled in a vocational program, 3% already have a bachelor's degree or higher, 1,333 enrolled as first-time, first-year students.

| | | | |
|---|---|---|---|
| Part-time: | 60% | 25 or older: | 32% |
| Out-of-state: | 2% | Live on campus: | 3% |
| Women: | 53% | | |

**Transfer out. Colleges most students transferred to 2007:** Mankato State University, Winona State University, Southwest Minnesota State University.

**Basis for selection.** Open admission, but selective for some programs. Special requirements for human services, nursing, corrections, networking communications, radiography, and construction electrician. **Homeschooled:** Transcript of courses and grades required.

**High school preparation.** Chemistry required of nursing applicants.

**2007-2008 Annual costs.** Tuition/fees: $4,590; $4,590 out-of-state. Per-credit charge: $136. Some courses carry a higher per-credit-hour charge. Books/supplies: $650. Personal expenses: $1,800.

**2006-2007 Financial aid.** All financial aid based on need. Average scholarship/grant was $2,633; average loan $3,248. 37% of total undergraduate aid awarded as scholarships/grants, 63% as loans/jobs. Need-based aid available for part-time students. Work-study available for part-time students. **Additional information:** One class tuition-free for Minnesota residents over 25 who have not attended college for at least 7 years.

**Application procedures. Admission:** Closing date 8/31. $20 fee, may be waived for applicants with need. Application may be submitted online. Admission notification on a rolling basis. **Financial aid:** Priority date 5/15; no closing date. FAFSA required. Applicants notified on a rolling basis; must reply within 5 week(s) of notification.

**Academics. Special study options:** Cross-registration, distance learning, double major, dual enrollment of high school students, ESL, internships, liberal arts/career combination, New York semester, study abroad, weekend college. Bachelor's degree programs available on campus. License preparation in nursing, radiology, real estate. **Credit/placement by examination:** AP, CLEP, institutional tests. 20 credit hours maximum toward associate degree. **Support services:** Learning center, reduced course load, remedial instruction, study skills assistance, tutoring.

**Majors. Agriculture:** Farm/ranch. **Business:** Accounting, administrative services, management science, marketing. **Computer sciences:** General, LAN/WAN management. **Engineering:** Software. **Health:** Medical radiologic technology/radiation therapy, medical records technology, medical secretary, nursing (RN), occupational therapy assistant, physical therapy assistant. **Legal studies:** Legal secretary. **Liberal arts:** Arts/sciences. **Protective services:** Police science. **Public administration:** Human services.

**Computing on campus.** 250 workstations in library, computer center, student center. Online course registration, helpline available.

**Student life. Freshman orientation:** Mandatory. **Housing:** Coed dorms, substance-free housing available. $350 deposit, deadline 9/1. College foundation-owned student housing. **Activities:** Concert band, choral groups, drama, music ensembles, musical theater, student government, student newspaper.

**Athletics.** NJCAA. **Intercollegiate:** Baseball M, basketball, golf, softball W, volleyball W. **Intramural:** Baseball, basketball, bowling, skiing, softball, volleyball, weight lifting. **Team name:** Blue Devils.

**Student services.** Career counseling, services for economically disadvantaged, student employment services, financial aid counseling, minority student services, on-campus daycare, personal counseling, placement for graduates, veterans' counselor, women's services. **Physically disabled:** Services for visually, speech, hearing impaired. **Transfer:** Transfer adviser, college fairs on campus for students transferring to 4-year colleges.

**Contact.** Phone: (507) 433-0517 Fax: (507) 433-0515
Dani Heiny, Admissions, Riverland Community College, 1900 Eighth Avenue, NW, Austin, MN 55912-1407

## Rochester Community and Technical College
### Rochester, Minnesota
www.roch.edu

**CB code: 6610**

- Public 2-year community and technical college
- Commuter campus in small city

**General.** Founded in 1915. Regionally accredited. University Center offers extension courses from Winona State University, University of Minnesota, Rochester Community and Technical College. **Enrollment:** 3,246 full-time, degree-seeking students. **Degrees:** 782 associate awarded. **Location:** 80 miles from Minneapolis-St. Paul. **Calendar:** Semester, limited summer session. **Full-time faculty:** 155 total. **Part-time faculty:** 182 total. **Class size:** 50% < 20, 47% 20-39, 2% 40-49, less than 1% 50-99. **Special facilities:** Observatory, dental clinic, horticulture technology facility, regional sports center.

**Student profile.**

| | | | |
|---|---|---|---|
| Out-of-state: | 5% | 25 or older: | 40% |

**Transfer out. Colleges most students transferred to 2007:** Winona State University, Minnesota State College: Mankato, University of Minnesota.

**Basis for selection.** Open admission, but selective for some programs. Admission to allied health and technology programs based on course work, class rank, institutional placement test scores.

**High school preparation.** Biology, chemistry, algebra and/or English required for some programs.

**2007-2008 Annual costs.** Tuition/fees: $4,656; $4,656 out-of-state. Per-credit charge: $136 in-state; $136 out-of-state. Personal expenses: $1,860.

**Application procedures. Admission:** Priority date 6/1; deadline 8/14 (postmark date). $20 fee, may be waived for applicants with need. Application may be submitted online. Admission notification on a rolling basis. **Financial aid:** Priority date 4/15; no closing date. FAFSA, institutional form required.

**Academics. Special study options:** Distance learning, dual enrollment of high school students, honors, independent study, internships. Bachelor's degree programs available on campus. License preparation in dental hygiene, nursing, paramedic. **Credit/placement by examination:** AP, CLEP, institutional tests. 16 credit hours maximum toward associate degree. **Support services:** Learning center, reduced course load, remedial instruction, study skills assistance, tutoring, writing center.

**Majors. Agriculture:** Equine science, greenhouse operations, horticultural science, turf management. **Biology:** Biomedical sciences. **Business:** Accounting, administrative services, business admin, customer service, retailing, special products marketing. **Communications:** Digital media, media studies. **Communications technology:** General. **Computer sciences:** General, computer science, system admin, web page design. **Education:** Teacher assistance. **Engineering:** General. **Engineering technology:** CAD/CADD, electrical, manufacturing, mechanical. **Family/consumer sciences:** Child care. **Health:** Cardiovascular technology, clinical lab technology, dental assistant, dental hygiene, electroencephalograph technology, EMT paramedic, health services, medical records technology, medical secretary, mental health services, nursing (RN), premedicine, radiologic technology/medical imaging, surgical technology, veterinary technology/assistant. **Interdisciplinary:** Natural sciences. **Legal studies:** Legal secretary. **Liberal arts:** Arts/sciences. **Parks/recreation:** Sports admin. **Protective services:** Criminal justice, police science. **Visual/performing arts:** Graphic design, music management, music theory/composition.

**Most popular majors.** Business/marketing 8%, health sciences 30%, liberal arts 46%, security/protective services 6%.

**Computing on campus.** 120 workstations in library, computer center. Commuter students can connect to campus network. Online course registration, online library, helpline available.

**Student life. Freshman orientation:** Available. Preregistration for classes offered. **Housing:** Non-college-affiliated student-only housing available near campus. **Activities:** Bands, choral groups, dance, drama, literary magazine, music ensembles, musical theater, student government, student newspaper, International Student Association, Asian club, Intervarsity Christian Fellowship.

**Athletics.** NJCAA. **Intercollegiate:** Baseball M, basketball, football (tackle) M, golf, soccer W, softball W, volleyball W, wrestling M. **Intramural:** Badminton, basketball, football (non-tackle), golf, softball, volleyball. **Team name:** Yellowjackets.

**Student services.** Career counseling, financial aid counseling, health services, on-campus daycare, personal counseling. **Physically disabled:** Services for visually, speech, hearing impaired. **Transfer:** Pre-admission transcript evaluation for new students. Transfer adviser, college fairs on campus for students transferring to 4-year colleges.

**Contact.** Phone: (507) 285-7265 Fax: (507) 280-3529
Holly Bigelow, Registrar, Rochester Community and Technical College, 851 30th Avenue SE, Rochester, MN 55904-4999

## St. Cloud Technical College
### St. Cloud, Minnesota
**www.sctc.edu**  CB code: 1986

♦ Public 2-year technical college
♦ Commuter campus in small city

**General.** Founded in 1948. Regionally accredited. **Enrollment:** 3,333 degree-seeking undergraduates; 510 non-degree-seeking students. **Degrees:** 396 associate awarded. **Location:** 65 miles from Minneapolis-St. Paul. **Calendar:** Semester, limited summer session. **Full-time faculty:** 117 total; 3% have terminal degrees, 2% minority, 43% women. **Part-time faculty:** 67 total; 2% have terminal degrees, 46% women.

**Student profile.** Among degree-seeking undergraduates, 995 enrolled as first-time, first-year students, 457 transferred in from other institutions.

| Part-time: | 28% | Asian American: | 1% |
| Out-of-state: | 2% | Hispanic American: | 1% |
| Women: | 51% | Native American: | 1% |
| African American: | 3% | 25 or older: | 24% |

**Transfer out. Colleges most students transferred to 2007:** St. Cloud State University, Bemidji State University, University of Minnesota.

**Basis for selection.** Open admission, but selective for some programs. Paramedicine applicants must complete EMT basic and emergency cardiac care courses prior to acceptance. Echocardiography, sonography, cardiovascular technician, practical nursing, dental assisting, and dental hygiene all require pre-requisite courses to be completed prior to admission to the major. Programs such as echocardiography, sonography and cardiovascular technician require that students are interviewed as part of the acceptance process. **Homeschooled:** Proof of high school graduation required. **Learning Disabled:** Students with developmental disabilities may take the course placement test with accommodations.

**High school preparation.** Recommended units include English 2, mathematics 2, science 1 (laboratory 1). Mathematics and science classes recommended for technical programs; algebra required for civil engineering; dental hygiene applicants must have all science and nutrition coursework completed; anatomy and physiology, college algebra, and physics required for echocardiography, sonography, and cardiovascular technology.

**2007-2008 Annual costs.** Tuition/fees: $4,424; $4,424 out-of-state. Per-credit charge: $134. Higher per-credit-hour charges may apply to some programs. Various reciprocity agreements with some neighboring states provide tuition reduction to out-of-state students. Tuition for online courses is $144 per credit. Books/supplies: $950. Personal expenses: $1,000.

**2006-2007 Financial aid. Need-based:** 67% of total undergraduate aid awarded as scholarships/grants, 33% as loans/jobs. Need-based aid available for part-time students. Work-study available nights, weekends and for part-time students. **Non-need-based:** Scholarships awarded for academics, leadership, state residency.

**Application procedures. Admission:** Closing date 8/7 (postmark date). $20 fee. Application must be submitted on paper. Admission notification on a rolling basis beginning on or about 10/7. **Financial aid:** No deadline. FAFSA, institutional form required. Applicants notified on a rolling basis starting 6/1.

**Academics. Special study options:** Accelerated study, cooperative education, cross-registration, distance learning, double major, dual enrollment

of high school students, independent study, internships. Bachelor's degree programs available on campus. License preparation in dental hygiene, nursing, paramedic, real estate. **Credit/placement by examination:** AP, CLEP, institutional tests. **Support services:** Learning center, pre-admission summer program, reduced course load, remedial instruction, study skills assistance, tutoring, writing center.

**Majors. Business:** Accounting, banking/financial services, business admin, executive assistant, sales/distribution. **Communications:** Advertising. **Computer sciences:** Networking, programming. **Construction:** Carpentry, electrician, plumbing. **Education:** Teacher assistance. **Engineering technology:** Architectural drafting, CAD/CADD, civil, electrical, instrumentation, mechanical drafting, water quality. **Family/consumer sciences:** Child care. **Health:** Cardiovascular technology, dental assistant, dental hygiene, EMT paramedic, licensed practical nurse, medical records technology, sonography, surgical technology. **Legal studies:** Legal secretary. **Mechanic/repair:** Auto body, automotive, heating/ac/refrig, medium/heavy vehicle. **Production:** Machine tool.

**Most popular majors.** Business/marketing 22%, communications/journalism 6%, computer/information sciences 7%, engineering/engineering technologies 17%, family/consumer sciences 7%, health sciences 35%.

**Computing on campus.** PC or laptop required. 468 workstations in library, computer center, student center. Commuter students can connect to campus network. Online course registration, helpline, repair service, wireless network available.

**Student life. Freshman orientation:** Mandatory. **Housing:** Privately-owned dormitory next to campus. Housing also available at St. Cloud State University. **Activities:** Student government, student newspaper, TV station, Campus Crusade for Christ, Newman Center, Delta Kappa Phi.

**Athletics.** NJCAA. **Intercollegiate:** Baseball M, basketball, softball W, volleyball W. **Intramural:** Basketball, football (non-tackle), football (tackle), golf, ice hockey, racquetball, soccer, softball, tennis, track and field, volleyball. **Team name:** Cyclones.

**Student services.** Adult student services, career counseling, student employment services, financial aid counseling, on-campus daycare, personal counseling, placement for graduates, veterans' counselor. **Physically disabled:** Services for visually, speech, hearing impaired. **Transfer:** Pre-admission transcript evaluation for new students. Transfer adviser for students transferring to 4-year colleges.

**Contact.** E-mail: enroll@sctc.edu
Phone: (320) 308-5089 Toll-free number: (800) 222-1009 ext. 5089
Fax: (320) 308-5981
Jodi Elness, Director of Enrollment Management, St. Cloud Technical College, 1540 Northway Drive, St. Cloud, MN 56303

## St. Paul College
### Saint Paul, Minnesota
**www.saintpaul.edu**  CB code: 0534

♦ Public 2-year community and technical college
♦ Commuter campus in large city

**General.** Founded in 1919. Regionally accredited. **Enrollment:** 4,596 degree-seeking undergraduates; 554 non-degree-seeking students. **Degrees:** 269 associate awarded. **Calendar:** Semester, limited summer session. **Full-time faculty:** 112 total; 8% have terminal degrees, 12% minority, 52% women. **Part-time faculty:** 137 total; 6% minority, 37% women. **Class size:** 53% < 20, 46% 20-39, 1% 40-49.

**Student profile.** Among degree-seeking undergraduates, 10% enrolled in a transfer program, 75% enrolled in a vocational program, 1% already have a bachelor's degree or higher, 756 enrolled as first-time, first-year students.

| Part-time: | 59% | Women: | 51% |
| Out-of-state: | 1% | 25 or older: | 65% |

**Transfer out. Colleges most students transferred to 2007:** Metropoltian State University, Century Community and Technical College, Inver Hills Community College.

**Basis for selection.** Open admission. ACT considered for placement if submitted; scores must be received by July 1. Interview recommended for selected programs. **Homeschooled:** Transcript of courses and grades required.

**High school preparation.** Recommended units include English 3, mathematics 2, social studies 3 and history 3.

**2007-2008 Annual costs.** Tuition/fees: $4,314; $8,304 out-of-state. Per-credit charge: $133 in-state; $266 out-of-state. Various reciprocity agreements with some neighboring states provide tuition reduction to out-of-state students. Books/supplies: $800. Personal expenses: $1,640.

**Financial aid. Need-based:** Need-based aid available for part-time students. Work-study available nights and for part-time students. **Non-need-based:** Scholarships awarded for leadership.

**Application procedures. Admission:** Priority date 7/1; no deadline. $20 fee. Application must be submitted online. Admission notification on a rolling basis. **Financial aid:** No deadline. FAFSA required. Applicants notified on a rolling basis starting 6/1.

**Academics. Special study options:** Distance learning, ESL, internships. License preparation in nursing. **Credit/placement by examination:** AP, CLEP, IB, institutional tests. **Support services:** Learning center, reduced course load, remedial instruction, study skills assistance, tutoring.

**Majors. Business:** General, accounting, administrative services, entrepreneurial studies, human resources, international, international marketing, logistics, management information systems, office management, office technology. **Communications technology:** Animation/special effects. **Computer sciences:** Applications programming, computer science, programming. **Construction:** Site management. **Engineering:** Software. **Engineering technology:** Architectural drafting, drafting, electrical, manufacturing, mechanical drafting, surveying. **Family/consumer sciences:** Child care. **Foreign languages:** Sign language interpretation. **Health:** Athletic training, clinical lab technology, massage therapy, office assistant, respiratory therapy technology. **Liberal arts:** Arts/sciences. **Personal/culinary services:** Aesthetician, chef training, cosmetic. **Science technology:** Chemical.

**Most popular majors.** Business/marketing 26%, engineering/engineering technologies 8%, health sciences 35%, liberal arts 12%, personal/culinary services 10%.

**Computing on campus.** 1,000 workstations in library, computer center. Commuter students can connect to campus network. Online course registration, online library, helpline, wireless network available.

**Student life. Freshman orientation:** Available. Preregistration for classes offered. **Activities:** Student government, Business Professionals of America, Vocational-Industrial Clubs of America, Student Senate, African Heritage student association, Hispanic student association, Asian student association.

**Student services.** Adult student services, alcohol/substance abuse counseling, career counseling, student employment services, financial aid counseling, on-campus daycare, personal counseling, placement for graduates, veterans' counselor. **Physically disabled:** Services for visually, speech, hearing impaired. **Learning disabled:** Comprehensive services available. **Transfer:** Pre-admission transcript evaluation for new students. Transfer center, transfer adviser, college fairs on campus for students transferring to 4-year colleges.

**Contact.** E-mail: admissions@saintpaul.edu
Phone: (651) 846-1555 Toll-free number: (800) 227-6029
Fax: (651) 846-1468
Sarah Carrico, Director of Office of Enrollment Services, St. Paul College, 235 Marshall Avenue, Saint Paul, MN 55102-1800

---

## South Central College
### North Mankato, Minnesota
**www.southcentral.edu**

**CB code: 7124**

- Public 2-year community and technical college
- Commuter campus in large town

**General.** Founded in 1946. Regionally accredited. Campuses in North Mankato and Faribault, MN. **Enrollment:** 2,838 degree-seeking undergraduates; 193 non-degree-seeking students. **Degrees:** 317 associate awarded. **Location:** 80 miles from Minneapolis-St. Paul. **Calendar:** Semester, limited summer session. **Full-time faculty:** 115 total. **Part-time faculty:** 55 total.

**Student profile.** Among degree-seeking undergraduates, 954 enrolled as first-time, first-year students.

| | | | |
|---|---|---|---|
| Part-time: | 47% | Women: | 60% |

**Basis for selection.** Open admission. **Homeschooled:** State high school equivalency certificate required.

**2007-2008 Annual costs.** Tuition/fees: $4,436. Per-credit charge: $133. Books/supplies: $650.

**Financial aid. Need-based:** Need-based aid available for part-time students. Work-study available nights and for part-time students.

**Application procedures. Admission:** $20 fee. Application must be submitted on paper. Admission notification on a rolling basis. **Financial aid:** Priority date 5/1; no closing date. FAFSA, institutional form required. Applicants notified on a rolling basis starting 6/1.

**Academics. Special study options:** Distance learning, dual enrollment of high school students, honors, independent study, internships, liberal arts/career combination. License preparation in nursing, paramedic. **Credit/placement by examination:** AP, CLEP, IB, institutional tests. **Support services:** GED preparation and test center, learning center, reduced course load, remedial instruction, study skills assistance, tutoring, writing center.

**Majors. Agriculture:** General, animal sciences, equipment technology, production. **Business:** Accounting, accounting technology, administrative services, business admin, marketing, restaurant/food services. **Communications technology:** Graphic/printing. **Computer sciences:** Data processing, information technology, LAN/WAN management. **Construction:** General, site management. **Engineering technology:** Civil, drafting, heat/ac/refrig, occupational safety. **Family/consumer sciences:** Child development. **Health:** Clinical lab technology, dental assistant, EMT paramedic, licensed practical nurse, nursing (RN). **Legal studies:** Legal secretary. **Liberal arts:** Arts/sciences. **Mechanic/repair:** Auto body, automotive, heating/ac/refrig. **Personal/culinary services:** Culinary arts, restaurant/catering. **Production:** Cabinetmaking/millwright, machine tool. **Public administration:** Human services. **Visual/performing arts:** Commercial/advertising art, graphic design.

**Computing on campus.** 725 workstations in library, computer center, student center. Commuter students can connect to campus network. Online course registration, online library, helpline, wireless network available.

**Student life. Freshman orientation:** Mandatory. **Activities:** Music ensembles, student government, student newspaper.

**Student services.** Alcohol/substance abuse counseling, career counseling, student employment services, financial aid counseling, on-campus daycare, personal counseling, placement for graduates, veterans' counselor. **Physically disabled:** Services for visually, speech, hearing impaired. **Transfer:** Pre-admission transcript evaluation for new students.

**Contact.** E-mail: admissions@southcentral.edu
Phone: (507) 389-7451 Toll-free number: (800) 722-9359
Fax: (507) 388-9951
Bev Herda, Admissions Director, South Central College, 1920 Lee Boulevard, North Mankato, MN 56003

---

## Vermilion Community College
### Ely, Minnesota
**www.vcc.edu**

**CB code: 6194**

- Public 2-year community and technical college
- Residential campus in small town

**General.** Founded in 1922. Regionally accredited. **Enrollment:** 541 degree-seeking undergraduates; 164 non-degree-seeking students. **Degrees:** 165 associate awarded. **Location:** 100 miles from Duluth. **Calendar:** Semester, limited summer session. **Full-time faculty:** 22 total; 4% minority, 32% women. **Part-time faculty:** 18 total; 6% minority, 39% women. **Special facilities:** 40-acre outdoor learning center near Boundary Waters Canoe Area.

**Student profile.** Among degree-seeking undergraduates, 40% enrolled in a transfer program, 60% enrolled in a vocational program, 5% already have a bachelor's degree or higher, 182 enrolled as first-time, first-year students.

| | | | |
|---|---|---|---|
| Part-time: | 6% | Hispanic American: | 2% |
| Out-of-state: | 5% | Native American: | 1% |
| Women: | 23% | 25 or older: | 18% |
| African American: | 10% | Live on campus: | 40% |
| Asian American: | 1% | | |

**Transfer out.** 85% of students enrolled in the transfer program go on to 4-year colleges.

**Basis for selection.** Open admission. Accuplacer used for placement. Interview required for law enforcement, natural resources, parks and recreation students.

**2007-2008 Annual costs.** Tuition/fees: $4,374; $5,342 out-of-state. Per-credit charge: $129 in-state; $161 out-of-state. Various reciprocity agreements with some neighboring states provide tuition reduction to out-of-state students. Room/board: $4,740. Books/supplies: $600. Personal expenses: $1,500.

**Financial aid. Need-based:** Need-based aid available for part-time students. Work-study available nights and weekends.

**Application procedures. Admission:** No deadline. $20 fee, may be waived for applicants with need. Application may be submitted online. Admission notification on a rolling basis beginning on or about 1/1. **Financial aid:** No deadline. FAFSA, institutional form required. Applicants notified on a rolling basis starting 4/1.

**Academics. Special study options:** Cooperative education, cross-registration, dual enrollment of high school students, honors, independent study, internships, liberal arts/career combination. **Credit/placement by examination:** CLEP. **Support services:** Learning center, pre-admission summer program, reduced course load, remedial instruction, tutoring.

**Majors. Biology:** General. **Business:** General, accounting, business admin. **Communications:** General, journalism. **Conservation:** General, environmental studies, fisheries, forest resources, forestry, management/policy, wildlife. **Education:** General, art, biology, business, chemistry, computer, elementary, geography, health, history, kindergarten/preschool, mathematics, middle, physics, science, secondary, social studies. **Engineering:** Civil. **English:** English lit. **Family/consumer sciences:** General. **Health:** Environmental health, predental, premedicine, preveterinary. **History:** General. **Legal studies:** Prelaw. **Parks/recreation:** General, facilities management. **Physical sciences:** General, astronomy, chemistry, geology, physics. **Protective services:** Criminal justice, law enforcement admin, police science. **Psychology:** General. **Social sciences:** General, criminology, geography, political science. **Transportation:** Aviation, aviation management. **Visual/performing arts:** Dramatic.

**Computing on campus.** Dormitories linked to campus network.

**Student life. Freshman orientation:** Mandatory. 6 different programs from April through start of classes. **Housing:** Coed dorms available. **Activities:** Choral groups, drama, musical theater, student government, student newspaper.

**Athletics.** NJCAA. **Intercollegiate:** Baseball M, basketball, football (tackle) M, softball W, volleyball W. **Intramural:** Basketball, bowling, softball, tennis, volleyball. **Team name:** Ironmen, Ironwomen.

**Student services.** Career counseling, student employment services, personal counseling, placement for graduates, veterans' counselor. **Physically disabled:** Services for visually, speech, hearing impaired. **Transfer:** Transfer adviser, college fairs on campus for students transferring to 4-year colleges.

**Contact.** E-mail: admissions@vcc.edu
Phone: (218) 235-2191 Toll-free number: (800) 657-3608
Fax: (218) 235-2173
Jeff Nelson, Director of Enrollment Services, Vermilion Community College, 1900 East Camp Street, Ely, MN 55731-9989

## White Earth Tribal and Community College
**Mahnomen, Minnesota**
**www.wetcc.org**

- Private 2-year nursing, community, junior, liberal arts and teachers college
- Rural community

**General.** One of three operating Tribal College's in the State of MInnesota; is an Anishinaabe controlled tribal and community college. **Enrollment:** 76 degree-seeking undergraduates. **Degrees:** 3 associate awarded. **Location:** 70 miles east of Fargo/Moorhead and 65 miles west of Bemidji, MN. **Calendar:** Semester, limited summer session. **Full-time faculty:** 8 total. **Part-time faculty:** 5 total. **Class size:** 79% < 20, 21% 20-39. **Special facilities:** The college has an USDA Extension office on campus.

**Student profile.** Among degree-seeking undergraduates, 94% enrolled in a transfer program, 1% enrolled in a vocational program, 3% already have a bachelor's degree or higher.

**Basis for selection.** Open admission. **Learning Disabled:** All non-transfer students are required to take Accuplacer placement exam.

**2007-2008 Annual costs.** Tuition/fees: $3,050. Per-credit charge: $90. Books/supplies: $850. Personal expenses: $1,350.

**Application procedures. Admission:** Closing date 8/21 (receipt date). No application fee. Application must be submitted on paper. Admission notification on a rolling basis.

**Academics. Special study options:** Combined bachelor's/graduate degree, liberal arts/career combination. Nursing Program in cooporation with Northland Community and Technical College; also partnership which enables students to earn a bachelor's in teacher education with licensure. Bachelor's degree programs available on campus. **Credit/placement by examination:** CLEP. **Support services:** GED preparation and test center, remedial instruction, study skills assistance, tutoring.

**Majors. Business:** Business admin. **Computer sciences:** General. **Conservation:** General, environmental studies. **Education:** General, kindergarten/preschool. **Liberal arts:** Humanities.

**Computing on campus.** Online library, wireless network available.

**Student life. Freshman orientation:** Mandatory. Preregistration for classes offered. **Activities:** Student newspaper.

**Contact.** E-mail: molson@wetcc.org
Phone: (218) 936-5731
Debra Bakken, Registrar, White Earth Tribal and Community College, 202 South Main Street, Mahnomen, MN 56557

# Mississippi

## Antonelli College: Hattiesburg
**Hattiesburg, Mississippi**
www.antonellicollege.edu                    CB code: 3195

- For-profit 2-year branch campus and technical college
- Large town
- Interview required

**General.** Accredited by ACCSCT. **Enrollment:** 293 degree-seeking undergraduates. **Degrees:** 95 associate awarded. **Location:** 90 miles from Jacksonville. **Calendar:** Continuous. **Full-time faculty:** 18 total. **Part-time faculty:** 10 total.

**Student profile.** Among degree-seeking undergraduates, 100% enrolled in a vocational program, 165 enrolled as first-time, first-year students.

| | | | |
|---|---|---|---|
| Part-time: | 9% | Asian American: | 1% |
| Women: | 90% | Hispanic American: | 1% |
| African American: | 53% | | |

**Basis for selection.** Open admission. **Homeschooled:** State high school equivalency certificate required.

**2007-2008 Annual costs.** Tuition/fees: $11,370. Books/supplies: $900.

**Application procedures. Admission:** Closing date 9/17 (receipt date). $75 fee, may be waived for applicants with need. Application must be submitted on paper. Admission notification on a rolling basis beginning on or about 8/17.

**Academics. Special study options:** Dual enrollment of high school students, internships. **Credit/placement by examination:** CLEP. **Support services:** GED preparation.

**Majors. Computer sciences:** General.

**Contact.** E-mail: karen.gautreau@antonellicollege.edu
Phone: (601) 583-4100 Fax: (601) 583-0839
Jarita Large, Associate Director, Antonelli College: Hattiesburg, 1500 North 31st Avenue, Hattiesburg, MS 39401

## Antonelli College: Jackson
**Jackson, Mississippi**
www.antonellicollege.edu                    CB code: 3193

- For-profit 2-year technical college
- Commuter campus in small city

**General.** Accredited by ACCSCT. **Enrollment:** 287 degree-seeking undergraduates. **Degrees:** 91 associate awarded. **Calendar:** Quarter. **Full-time faculty:** 18 total. **Part-time faculty:** 20 total.

**Basis for selection.** Open admission.

**2007-2008 Annual costs.** Tuition/fees: $11,370. Books/supplies: $1,200.

**Application procedures. Admission:** No deadline. $75 fee. **Financial aid:** No deadline.

**Academics. Credit/placement by examination:** CLEP, institutional tests. 14 credit hours maximum toward associate degree. **Support services:** Study skills assistance, tutoring.

**Majors. Business:** Accounting, office technology. **Computer sciences:** Computer graphics, data entry, networking, security, web page design, webmaster. **Health:** Insurance coding, massage therapy, medical assistant, medical transcription. **Legal studies:** General. **Visual/performing arts:** Graphic design, interior design.

**Computing on campus.** 100 workstations in library, computer center. Wireless network available.

**Student life. Freshman orientation:** Mandatory. Preregistration for classes offered. Held 2 days prior to start of class. **Activities:** Student newspaper.

**Student services.** Student employment services, financial aid counseling, placement for graduates.

**Contact.** Phone: (601) 362-9991
Adam Grosch, Admissions Director, Antonelli College: Jackson, 2323 Lakeland Drive, Jackson, MS 39232

## Blue Cliff College: Gulfport
**Gulfport, Mississippi**
www.bluecliffcollege.com

- For-profit 2-year technical college
- Small city
- Interview required

**General.** Accredited by ACCSCT. Medical assisting program graduates eligible to sit for the AMA exam. Massage therapy program graduates eligible for provisional license for up to six months until they take national boards. Fees for these exams included in tuition. **Enrollment:** 113 degree-seeking undergraduates. **Calendar:** Quarter, extensive summer session. **Full-time faculty:** 10 total. **Part-time faculty:** 6 total.

**Basis for selection.** Open admission. Wonderlic test required. **Homeschooled:** Transcript of courses and grades required.

**2007-2008 Annual costs.** Tuition/fees: $11,350. Per-credit charge: $200.

**Financial aid.** All financial aid based on need. Need-based aid available for part-time students.

**Application procedures. Admission:** $100 fee. Application must be submitted on paper. **Financial aid:** FAFSA required.

**Academics. Credit/placement by examination:** CLEP. **Support services:** Tutoring.

**Majors. Health:** Massage therapy, office assistant.

**Computing on campus.** 20 workstations in library, computer center, student center. Commuter students can connect to campus network. Online library, helpline, wireless network available.

**Student life. Freshman orientation:** Mandatory.

**Student services.** Career counseling, student employment services, financial aid counseling.

**Contact.** Phone: (288) 896-9727 Fax: (228) 896-8659
Blue Cliff College: Gulfport, 12251 Bernard Parkway, Gulfport, MS 39503

## Coahoma Community College
**Clarksdale, Mississippi**
www.coahomacc.edu                    CB code: 1126

- Public 2-year community college
- Commuter campus in rural community

**General.** Founded in 1949. Regionally accredited. **Enrollment:** 2,216 degree-seeking undergraduates. **Degrees:** 205 associate awarded. **Location:** 65 miles from Memphis, Tennessee. **Calendar:** Semester, limited summer session. **Full-time faculty:** 53 total. **Part-time faculty:** 64 total.

**Transfer out. Colleges most students transferred to 2007:** Alcorn State University, Delta State University, Jackson State University, Mississippi Valley State University, University of Mississippi.

**Basis for selection.** Open admission, but selective for some programs. High school record most important for admission to degree programs. Open admissions to vocational programs. Limited admission to licensed practical nursing and respiratory therapy. ACT/SAT required for nursing. Interview required for nursing students; audition required for music students. **Homeschooled:** Transcript of courses and grades, letter of recommendation (nonparent) required.

**High school preparation.** Recommended units include English 4, mathematics 3, social studies 2, science 3 (laboratory 3) and foreign language 1.

**2007-2008 Annual costs.** Tuition/fees: $1,800; $4,700 out-of-state. Per-credit charge: $90. Room/board: $3,514. Books/supplies: $800. Personal expenses: $700.

Two-Year Colleges

**Financial aid.** All financial aid based on need. Need-based aid available for part-time students.

**Application procedures. Admission:** No deadline. No application fee. Admission notification on a rolling basis. **Financial aid:** Priority date 4/1; no closing date. FAFSA, institutional form required. Applicants notified on a rolling basis starting 7/1.

**Academics. Special study options:** Distance learning, dual enrollment of high school students. License preparation in nursing. **Credit/placement by examination:** CLEP. **Support services:** GED preparation, reduced course load, remedial instruction, tutoring, writing center.

**Majors. Biology:** General. **Business:** General, accounting, hotel/motel admin, office technology. **Communications:** Broadcast journalism, journalism. **Computer sciences:** General, computer science. **Education:** General, art, business, early childhood, elementary, health, mathematics, music, physical, science, social science. **Engineering technology:** Electrical. **Family/consumer sciences:** Child care. **Health:** Clinical lab science, medical records admin, nursing (RN), predental, premedicine, prenursing, prepharmacy, preveterinary, respiratory therapy technology. **Legal studies:** Prelaw. **Math:** General. **Mechanic/repair:** Industrial. **Parks/recreation:** Sports admin. **Physical sciences:** Chemistry. **Protective services:** Criminal justice. **Public administration:** Social work. **Social sciences:** General. **Visual/performing arts:** General.

**Most popular majors.** Business/marketing 16%, education 41%, health sciences 15%, public administration/social services 11%.

**Computing on campus.** Dormitories wired for high-speed internet access and linked to campus network. Online course registration, online library, helpline, wireless network available.

**Student life. Freshman orientation:** Mandatory. Preregistration for classes offered. Semester-long course offered each semester. **Housing:** Single-sex dorms, special housing for disabled, substance-free housing available. $100 deposit, deadline 8/1. **Activities:** Bands, choral groups, music ensembles, student government, student newspaper, Baptist student union, Wesley Foundation, Black literary society.

**Athletics.** NJCAA. **Intercollegiate:** Baseball M, basketball, football (tackle) M, softball W. **Intramural:** Badminton, basketball, bowling, cheerleading W, football (non-tackle) M, football (tackle) M, softball, table tennis, volleyball. **Team name:** Tigers.

**Student services.** Career counseling, services for economically disadvantaged, financial aid counseling, health services, personal counseling. **Physically disabled:** Services for visually, speech, hearing impaired. **Transfer:** Pre-admission transcript evaluation for new students. Transfer adviser, college fairs on campus for students transferring to 4-year colleges.

**Contact.** E-mail: wholmes@coahomacc.edu
Phone: (662) 621-4205 Toll-free number: (800) 844-1222
Fax: (800) 844-1222
Wanda Holmes, Director of Admissions, Coahoma Community College, 3240 Friars Point Road, Clarksdale, MS 38614-9799

## Copiah-Lincoln Community College
**Wesson, Mississippi**
www.colin.edu                                   CB code: 1142

▸ Public 2-year community college
▸ Commuter campus in small town

**General.** Founded in 1928. Regionally accredited. Branch campuses in Natchez and Simpson County. **Enrollment:** 2,149 full-time, degree-seeking students. **Degrees:** 430 associate awarded. **Location:** 45 miles from Jackson. **Calendar:** Semester, limited summer session. **Full-time faculty:** 124 total; 6% have terminal degrees, 10% minority, 58% women. **Part-time faculty:** 94 total; 3% have terminal degrees, 5% minority, 69% women. **Special facilities:** Walking trail, golf course. **Partnerships:** Formal partnerships with over 300 local business and industry, health occupation affiliates, government agencies, and public service groups.

**Student profile.**

| | | | |
|---|---|---|---|
| Out-of-state: | 2% | Live on campus: | 35% |
| 25 or older: | 30% | | |

**Transfer out. Colleges most students transferred to 2007:** University of Southern Mississippi, Alcorn State University, University of Mississippi, Mississippi State University, Jackson State University.

---

**Basis for selection.** Open admission, but selective for some programs. Special requirements for certain technology and health occupation professions programs. ACT required for certain technology and health occupation professions programs. **Homeschooled:** Transcript of courses and grades required. ACT required.

**2007-2008 Annual costs.** Tuition/fees: $1,800; $3,700 out-of-state. Per-credit charge: $105 in-state; $180 out-of-state. Parking Fee: 20.00. Room/board: $3,100. Books/supplies: $600.

**Financial aid. Need-based:** Need-based aid available for part-time students. Work-study available nights, weekends and for part-time students. **Non-need-based:** Scholarships awarded for academics, art, athletics, job skills, leadership, music/drama, state residency.

**Application procedures. Admission:** No deadline. No application fee. Admission notification on a rolling basis. **Financial aid:** Priority date 4/1; no closing date. FAFSA required. Applicants notified on a rolling basis starting 4/1; must reply within 2 week(s) of notification.

**Academics. Special study options:** Distance learning, dual enrollment of high school students, honors. License preparation in nursing, paramedic, radiology. **Credit/placement by examination:** AP, CLEP, institutional tests. 12 credit hours maximum toward associate degree. **Support services:** GED preparation and test center, learning center, remedial instruction, study skills assistance, tutoring.

**Majors. Business:** Accounting, administrative services, business admin, hospitality admin, office technology. **Computer sciences:** Data processing, networking. **Conservation:** Wood science. **Engineering technology:** Drafting, electrical. **Health:** Clinical lab science, clinical lab technology, medical radiologic technology/radiation therapy, nursing (RN), respiratory therapy technology. **Liberal arts:** Arts/sciences. **Mechanic/repair:** Automotive, diesel, electronics/electrical. **Personal/culinary services:** Food service. **Production:** Machine tool. **Other:** Oil/Gas technology.

**Computing on campus.** 1,225 workstations in library, computer center. Dormitories linked to campus network. Online course registration, online library, helpline, student web hosting, wireless network available.

**Student life. Freshman orientation:** Mandatory. Preregistration for classes offered. **Housing:** Guaranteed on-campus for all undergraduates. Single-sex dorms, special housing for disabled, apartments, substance-free housing available. $50 deposit. **Activities:** Bands, campus ministries, choral groups, literary magazine, music ensembles, radio station, student government, student newspaper, Baptist student union, Wesley Foundation, student Christian association, African-American studies club, Co-Lin College Republicans.

**Athletics.** NJCAA. **Intercollegiate:** Baseball M, basketball, cheerleading W, football (tackle) M, golf, soccer, softball W, tennis, track and field M. **Intramural:** Basketball, softball M, volleyball. **Team name:** Wolves.

**Student services.** Career counseling, services for economically disadvantaged, financial aid counseling, health services, on-campus daycare, personal counseling, veterans' counselor. **Physically disabled:** Services for visually, speech, hearing impaired. **Transfer:** Pre-admission transcript evaluation for new students. College fairs on campus for students transferring to 4-year colleges.

**Contact.** E-mail: Phil.Broome@colin.edu
Phone: (601) 643-8307 Fax: (601) 643-8225
Phil Broome, Director of Admissions and Records, Copiah-Lincoln Community College, Box 649, Wesson, MS 39191

## East Central Community College
**Decatur, Mississippi**
www.eccc.edu                                   CB code: 1196

▸ Public 2-year community college
▸ Commuter campus in rural community

**General.** Founded in 1928. Regionally accredited. **Enrollment:** 2,273 degree-seeking undergraduates; 15 non-degree-seeking students. **Degrees:** 405 associate awarded. **Location:** 30 miles from Meridian, 85 miles from Jackson. **Calendar:** Semester, limited summer session. **Full-time faculty:** 73 total. **Part-time faculty:** 64 total.

**Student profile.** Among degree-seeking undergraduates, 664 enrolled as first-time, first-year students.

| | | | |
|---|---|---|---|
| Part-time: | 21% | 25 or older: | 32% |
| Out-of-state: | 2% | Live on campus: | 30% |
| Women: | 61% | | |

**Basis for selection.** Open admission, but selective for some programs. Special requirements for nursing program. All applicants must submit ACT. No minimum score required.

**2007-2008 Annual costs.** Tuition/fees: $1,510; $3,610 out-of-state. Per-credit charge: $75 in-state; $162 out-of-state. Room/board: $2,660. Books/supplies: $800. Personal expenses: $900.

**Financial aid. Non-need-based:** Scholarships awarded for academics, athletics, state residency.

**Application procedures. Admission:** No deadline. No application fee. **Financial aid:** No deadline. FAFSA, institutional form required. Applicants notified on a rolling basis starting 7/31; must reply within 2 week(s) of notification.

**Academics. Special study options:** Distance learning, dual enrollment of high school students, honors. **Credit/placement by examination:** CLEP, institutional tests. 6 credit hours maximum toward associate degree. **Support services:** GED preparation and test center, remedial instruction, study skills assistance, tutoring.

**Majors. Biology:** General. **Business:** General. **Computer sciences:** General, applications programming, data processing, programming. **Education:** General. **Engineering:** General. **Engineering technology:** Drafting, electrical. **English:** Composition. **Health:** Predental, premedicine, prepharmacy, preveterinary. **Interdisciplinary:** Gerontology. **Liberal arts:** Arts/sciences. **Math:** General. **Physical sciences:** Chemistry. **Psychology:** General. **Visual/performing arts:** Studio arts.

**Student life. Housing:** Guaranteed on-campus for freshmen. Single-sex dorms, apartments available. **Activities:** Bands, choral groups, drama, student government, student newspaper.

**Athletics.** NJCAA. **Intercollegiate:** Baseball M, basketball, football (tackle) M, golf, soccer, softball W, tennis. **Intramural:** Basketball, softball, table tennis. **Team name:** Warriors.

**Student services.** Career counseling, health services, on-campus daycare, personal counseling, veterans' counselor. **Transfer:** College fairs on campus for students transferring to 4-year colleges.

**Contact.** Phone: (601) 635-2111 ext. 392 Toll-free number: (877) 462-3222 Fax: (601) 635-4060 Donna Luke, Director of Admissions, East Central Community College, Box 129, Decatur, MS 39327

## East Mississippi Community College
**Scooba, Mississippi**
**www.eastms.edu**                                    **CB code: 1197**

- Public 2-year community college
- Residential campus in rural community

**General.** Founded in 1927. Regionally accredited. **Enrollment:** 4,012 degree-seeking undergraduates. **Degrees:** 474 associate awarded. **ROTC:** Naval. **Location:** 37 miles from Meridian. **Calendar:** Semester, limited summer session. **Full-time faculty:** 103 total. **Part-time faculty:** 108 total.

**Basis for selection.** Open admission, but selective for some programs. Special requirements for practical nursing, cosmetology, and funeral service technology. **Adult students:** SAT/ACT scores not required if applicant over 21.

**2007-2008 Annual costs.** Tuition/fees: $1,820; $3,570 out-of-state. $50 health fee for on-campus residents. Room/board: $2,800. Books/supplies: $900. Personal expenses: $2,200.

**Financial aid. Need-based:** Need-based aid available for part-time students. **Non-need-based:** Scholarships awarded for academics, art, athletics, leadership, music/drama, state residency.

**Application procedures. Admission:** No deadline. No application fee. Admission notification on a rolling basis. **Financial aid:** Priority date 4/1; no closing date. FAFSA, institutional form required. Applicants notified on a rolling basis starting 4/1; must reply within 2 week(s) of notification.

**Academics. Special study options:** Distance learning, dual enrollment of high school students, honors. License preparation in nursing. **Credit/placement by examination:** CLEP, institutional tests. **Support services:** GED preparation and test center, learning center, reduced course load, remedial instruction, tutoring.

**Majors. Business:** Banking/financial services. **Computer sciences:** General, programming. **Engineering technology:** Drafting.

**Computing on campus.** 30 workstations in library, computer center. Dormitories wired for high-speed internet access. Online library, helpline available.

**Student life. Freshman orientation:** Mandatory. Preregistration for classes offered. **Housing:** Single-sex dorms available. $50 deposit. **Activities:** Marching band, choral groups, drama, literary magazine, music ensembles, student government, student newspaper, Gospel Choir, Interdenominational Christian Fellowship Group, Fellowship of Christian Athletes.

**Athletics.** NJCAA. **Intercollegiate:** Baseball M, basketball, football (tackle) M, golf, soccer M, softball W. **Team name:** Lions.

**Student services.** Adult student services, career counseling, services for economically disadvantaged, financial aid counseling, health services, personal counseling, placement for graduates. **Transfer:** Pre-admission transcript evaluation for new students. Transfer adviser, college fairs on campus for students transferring to 4-year colleges.

**Contact.** Phone: (662) 476-8442 Fax: (662) 476-5038 Karen Briggs, Director of Admissions, East Mississippi Community College, Admissions Office, Scooba, MS 39358

## Hinds Community College
**Raymond, Mississippi**
**www.hindscc.edu**                                    **CB code: 1296**

- Public 2-year branch campus and community college
- Commuter campus in small town

**General.** Founded in 1917. Regionally accredited. 6 off-campus credit bearing locations: Raymond, Utica, Rankin, Academic/Technical Center, Nursing/Allied Health Center, Vicksburg Warren County Center. **Enrollment:** 10,013 degree-seeking undergraduates. **Degrees:** 1,065 associate awarded. **ROTC:** Army. **Location:** 10 miles from Jackson. **Calendar:** Semester, extensive summer session. **Full-time faculty:** 390 total. **Part-time faculty:** 530 total. **Class size:** 45% < 20, 48% 20-39, 5% 40-49, less than 1% 50-99, less than 1% >100.

**Student profile.**

| | | | |
|---|---|---|---|
| Out-of-state: | 1% | Live on campus: | 16% |
| 25 or older: | 43% | | |

**Transfer out. Colleges most students transferred to 2007:** Mississippi State University, University of Southern Mississippi, Jackson State, University of Mississippi, Mississippi College.

**Basis for selection.** Open admission, but selective for some programs. Special requirements for allied health, data processing programs. 19 high school units, ACT composite score of 18 may be substituted for diploma. ACT not required for placement in vocational programs. Interview required for allied health, vocational majors.

**High school preparation.** 19 units recommended. Recommended units include English 4, mathematics 2, social studies 2 and science 2.

**2007-2008 Annual costs.** Tuition/fees: $1,740; $3,946 out-of-state. Per-credit charge: $85 in-state; $170 out-of-state. Room/board: $2,530. Books/supplies: $420. Personal expenses: $1,500.

**2006-2007 Financial aid. Need-based:** 98% of total undergraduate aid awarded as scholarships/grants, 2% as loans/jobs. Need-based aid available for part-time students. **Non-need-based:** Scholarships awarded for academics, art, athletics, job skills, leadership, minority status, music/drama, state residency.

**Application procedures. Admission:** No deadline. No application fee. Application may be submitted online. Admission notification on a rolling basis beginning on or about 3/1. **Financial aid:** Priority date 4/1; no closing date. FAFSA required. Applicants notified on a rolling basis starting 5/15; must reply within 2 week(s) of notification.

**Academics. Special study options:** Accelerated study, cooperative education, distance learning, double major, dual enrollment of high school students, honors, independent study, internships, liberal arts/career combination, study abroad. License preparation in nursing. **Credit/placement by examination:** CLEP, institutional tests. 18 credit hours maximum toward associate degree. **Support services:** GED preparation and test center, learning center, remedial instruction, tutoring.

**Majors. Agriculture:** General, agribusiness operations, animal breeding, food science, landscaping. **Biology:** General. **Business:** Administrative services, fashion, finance, management information systems, office management, operations, sales/distribution, tourism promotion. **Communications:**

Two-Year Colleges

Journalism. **Communications technology:** General, graphic/printing. **Computer sciences:** General, data processing. **Education:** Business, elementary, physical, secondary, trade/industrial. **Engineering:** General. **Engineering technology:** Civil, drafting, electrical. **English:** English lit, speech/rhetoric. **Family/consumer sciences:** General, child care, institutional food production. **Foreign languages:** Sign language interpretation. **Health:** Clinical lab assistant, clinical lab technology, dental assistant, EMT paramedic, licensed practical nurse, medical records technology, nursing assistant, respiratory therapy technology, surgical technology, veterinary technology/assistant. **History:** General. **Legal studies:** Legal secretary, paralegal, prelaw. **Liberal arts:** Arts/sciences. **Math:** General. **Mechanic/repair:** Electronics/electrical. **Personal/culinary services:** Culinary arts. **Physical sciences:** Chemistry, geology, physics. **Protective services:** Criminal justice, fire safety technology. **Psychology:** General. **Social sciences:** Political science, sociology. **Visual/performing arts:** Art, commercial/advertising art, dramatic.

**Most popular majors.** Business/marketing 12%, health sciences 28%, liberal arts 45%.

**Computing on campus.** 55 workstations in library, computer center. Online course registration, helpline, repair service available.

**Student life. Freshman orientation:** Available, $65 fee. Preregistration for classes offered. **Housing:** Single-sex dorms available. $50 deposit. **Activities:** Bands, choral groups, dance, drama, music ensembles, musical theater, student government, student newspaper, Baptist Student Union, Afro-American Cultural Society, Catholic Student Organization, College Independents, College Republicans, Fellowship of Christian Athletes, Class/Leadership/Authority and Womanhood, Campus Christian Fellowship.

**Athletics.** NJCAA. **Intercollegiate:** Baseball M, basketball, football (tackle) M, golf M, soccer M, softball W, tennis, track and field M. **Intramural:** Basketball, football (tackle) M, softball M, volleyball. **Team name:** Eagles.

**Student services.** Career counseling, student employment services, personal counseling, placement for graduates. **Physically disabled:** Services for visually, hearing impaired. **Transfer:** Transfer adviser, college fairs on campus for students transferring to 4-year colleges.

**Contact.** E-mail: records@hindscc.edu
Phone: (601) 857-3212 Toll-free number: (800) 446-3722
Fax: (601) 857-3539
Gina Turner, Director of Admissions and Records, Hinds Community College, 505 East Main Street, Raymond, MS 39154-1100

## Holmes Community College
**Goodman, Mississippi**
**www.holmescc.edu**　　　　　　　　　　**CB code: 1299**

▸ Public 2-year community college
▸ Residential campus in rural community

**General.** Founded in 1925. Regionally accredited. Additional campus in Ridgeland and center in Grenada. **Enrollment:** 4,606 degree-seeking undergraduates. **Degrees:** 530 associate awarded. **Calendar:** Semester, extensive summer session. **Full-time faculty:** 128 total. **Part-time faculty:** 80 total. **Special facilities:** Observatory.

**Student profile.**

| | | | |
|---|---|---|---|
| Out-of-state: | 5% | Live on campus: | 25% |
| 25 or older: | 33% | | |

**Transfer out. Colleges most students transferred to 2007:** Mississippi State University, University of Mississippi, Delta State University, University of Southern Mississippi.

**Basis for selection.** Open admission, but selective for some programs. Official high school transcripts must show the date of graduation and be signed by the principal. Applicants for the nursing program are required to have an ACT composite score of 18 or higher, with a score of 17 or higher in math and an 18 or higher in reading. ACT is preferred for placement; however, other tests are available and accepted.

**High school preparation.** 20 units required. Required units include English 4, mathematics 3, social studies 2, science 2 and academic electives 9.

**2007-2008 Annual costs.** Tuition/fees: $1,430; $3,130 out-of-state. Per-credit charge: $65. Room/board: $1,980. Books/supplies: $600. Personal expenses: $1,600.

**Financial aid. Non-need-based:** Scholarships awarded for academics, athletics.

**Application procedures. Admission:** No deadline. No application fee. Application may be submitted online. Admission notification on a rolling basis. **Financial aid:** Priority date 6/1; no closing date. FAFSA, institutional form required. Applicants notified on a rolling basis.

**Academics. Special study options:** Cooperative education, distance learning, dual enrollment of high school students, honors, internships, liberal arts/career combination, weekend college. License preparation in nursing, paramedic. **Credit/placement by examination:** AP, CLEP, SAT, ACT, institutional tests. 30 credit hours maximum toward associate degree. **Support services:** GED test center, learning center, reduced course load, remedial instruction, tutoring.

**Majors. Business:** Administrative services, business admin, fashion. **Computer sciences:** General, computer science, programming. **Conservation:** Forestry. **Education:** Elementary, secondary. **Engineering:** General, architectural, electrical. **Engineering technology:** Drafting. **Health:** Predental, premedicine, prepharmacy, preveterinary. **Liberal arts:** Arts/sciences. **Math:** General. **Mechanic/repair:** Heating/ac/refrig.

**Computing on campus.** 400 workstations in library, computer center. Repair service available.

**Student life. Freshman orientation:** Available. **Housing:** Single-sex dorms available. **Activities:** Bands, choral groups, dance, drama, literary magazine, music ensembles, musical theater, student government, student newspaper, Baptist Student Union, Wesley Foundation, College Republican Club, Fellowship of Christian Athletes.

**Athletics.** NJCAA. **Intercollegiate:** Baseball M, basketball, football (tackle) M, golf M, soccer, softball W, tennis, track and field. **Intramural:** Basketball, football (tackle) M, soccer M, softball, track and field M, volleyball. **Team name:** Bulldogs.

**Student services.** Adult student services, career counseling, personal counseling, veterans' counselor. **Physically disabled:** Services for visually, speech, hearing impaired. **Transfer:** Pre-admission transcript evaluation for new students. Transfer adviser, college fairs on campus for students transferring to 4-year colleges.

**Contact.** Phone: (662) 472-9073 Toll-free number: (800) 465-6374
Fax: (662) 472-9152
Don Burnham, Director of Admissions and Records, Holmes Community College, Box 398, Goodman, MS 39079

## Itawamba Community College
**Fulton, Mississippi**
**www.iccms.edu**　　　　　　　　　　**CB code: 1326**

▸ Public 2-year community and technical college
▸ Commuter campus in small town

**General.** Founded in 1948. Regionally accredited. Addtional campuses in Fulton, Tupelo, and online. **Enrollment:** 5,293 undergraduates. **Degrees:** 460 associate awarded. **Location:** 115 miles from Memphis, Tennessee, 135 miles from Birmingham, Alabama. **Calendar:** Semester, limited summer session. **Full-time faculty:** 123 total; 6% have terminal degrees, 3% minority, 57% women. **Part-time faculty:** 17 total; 6% minority, 41% women. **Class size:** 51% < 20, 43% 20-39, 5% 40-49, 1% 50-99.

**Student profile.** 75% enrolled in a transfer program, 25% enrolled in a vocational program.

| | | | |
|---|---|---|---|
| African American: | 31% | Live on campus: | 18% |
| Hispanic American: | 1% | | |

**Transfer out. Colleges most students transferred to 2007:** Mississippi State University, University of Mississippi.

**Basis for selection.** Open admission, but selective for some programs. Special requirements for health science programs, including minimum test scores on ACT or other discipline-specific tests and grade of at least 2.0 in program prerequisite courses. **Homeschooled:** Must complete GED or appeal to Admissions and Guidance Committee. **Learning Disabled:** Developmental courses recommended. Assistance provided by special needs counselor.

**2007-2008 Annual costs.** Tuition/fees: $1,630; $3,380 out-of-state. Per-credit charge: $85. Room/board: $2,654. Books/supplies: $900. Personal expenses: $180.

**Financial aid. Need-based:** Need-based aid available for part-time students. Work-study available for part-time students. **Non-need-based:** Scholarships awarded for academics, art, athletics, leadership, music/drama, state residency.

**Application procedures. Admission:** No deadline. No application fee. Admission notification on a rolling basis. **Financial aid:** Priority date 4/30; no closing date. FAFSA, institutional form required. Applicants notified on a rolling basis starting 4/15.

**Academics. Special study options:** Accelerated study, cooperative education, distance learning, double major, dual enrollment of high school students, ESL, honors, independent study, internships. License preparation in nursing, paramedic, physical therapy, radiology, real estate. **Credit/ placement by examination:** CLEP, institutional tests. 15 credit hours maximum toward associate degree. **Support services:** GED preparation and test center, learning center, reduced course load, remedial instruction, study skills assistance, tutoring, writing center.

**Majors. Agriculture:** Business. **Business:** General, accounting, administrative services, management information systems, office/clerical. **Communications:** Broadcast journalism, journalism, public relations. **Computer sciences:** General, computer science, data processing, programming. **Conservation:** Forestry. **Construction:** Electrician. **Education:** Art, biology, business, chemistry, elementary, French, health, history, mathematics, music, physical, physics, science, secondary, social studies, Spanish, special, speech. **Engineering:** General, electrical. **Engineering technology:** Electrical. **Family/consumer sciences:** General, child care. **Foreign languages:** French, sign language interpretation, Spanish. **Health:** EMT paramedic, medical radiologic technology/radiation therapy, medical records admin, medical records technology, nursing (RN), occupational health, physical therapy assistant, predental, premedicine, prepharmacy, preveterinary, respiratory therapy technology, sonography, surgical technology. **History:** General. **Legal studies:** Paralegal, prelaw. **Liberal arts:** Arts/sciences, library science. **Math:** General. **Mechanic/repair:** Automotive, diesel, electronics/electrical. **Philosophy/religion:** Philosophy. **Physical sciences:** Chemistry, geology, physics. **Production:** Tool and die. **Protective services:** Criminal justice. **Psychology:** General. **Public administration:** Social work. **Social sciences:** Economics, sociology. **Visual/performing arts:** Art.

**Most popular majors.** Business/marketing 11%, family/consumer sciences 6%, health sciences 36%, liberal arts 42%.

**Computing on campus.** 600 workstations in dormitories, library, computer center. Dormitories wired for high-speed internet access and linked to campus network. Commuter students can connect to campus network. Online course registration, online library, helpline, wireless network available.

**Student life. Freshman orientation:** Available. Preregistration for classes offered. **Housing:** Single-sex dorms, substance-free housing available. $50 deposit. **Activities:** Bands, choral groups, dance, drama, literary magazine, music ensembles, musical theater, student government, student newspaper.

**Athletics.** NJCAA. **Intercollegiate:** Baseball M, basketball, cheerleading, football (tackle) M, golf M, soccer M, softball W. **Intramural:** Basketball. **Team name:** Indians.

**Student services.** Alcohol/substance abuse counseling, campus ministries, career counseling, services for economically disadvantaged, student employment services, financial aid counseling, minority student services, on-campus daycare, placement for graduates, veterans' counselor, women's services. **Physically disabled:** Services for visually, hearing impaired. **Transfer:** Transfer adviser, college fairs on campus for students transferring to 4-year colleges.

**Contact.** E-mail: hgjefcoat@iccms.edu
Phone: (662) 862-8031 Fax: (662) 862-8036
Gregg Jefcoat, Director of Admissions, Itawamba Community College, 602 West Hill Street, Fulton, MS 38843-1099

## Jones County Junior College
### Ellisville, Mississippi
www.jcjc.cc.ms.us                    CB code: 1347

- Public 2-year junior college
- Commuter campus in small town

**General.** Founded in 1927. Regionally accredited. **Location:** 7 miles from Laurel, 20 miles from Hattiesburg. **Calendar:** Semester.

**Annual costs/financial aid.** Tuition/fees (2007-2008): $1,740; $3,640 out-of-state. Room/board: $2,722. Books/supplies: $600. Personal expenses: $1,299. Need-based financial aid available to full-time and part-time students.

**Contact.** Phone: (601) 477-4025
Director of Admissions & Records, 900 South Court Street, Ellisville, MS 39437

## Meridian Community College
### Meridian, Mississippi
www.meridiancc.edu

CB member
CB code: 1461

- Public 2-year community college
- Commuter campus in large town

**General.** Founded in 1937. Regionally accredited. **Enrollment:** 2,582 full-time, degree-seeking students. **Degrees:** 666 associate awarded. **Location:** 90 miles from Jackson, 90 miles from Tuscaloosa, Alabama. **Calendar:** Semester, extensive summer session. **Full-time faculty:** 148 total. **Part-time faculty:** 92 total. **Special facilities:** Fitness center with enclosed swimming pool.

**Student profile.**

| | | | |
|---|---|---|---|
| Out-of-state: | 4% | Live on campus: | 7% |
| 25 or older: | 50% | | |

**Basis for selection.** Open admission, but selective for some programs. Test scores, recommendations considered for health education applicants. Interview recommended for broadcast technology, data processing, graphic communication technology, and health programs majors.

**High school preparation.** Recommended units include English 4, mathematics 3, social studies 3, science 3 and academic electives 2. .5 unit computer applications recommended.

**2007-2008 Annual costs.** Tuition/fees: $1,660; $2,950 out-of-state. Per-credit charge: $80 in-state; $137 out-of-state. Room/board: $3,350. Books/supplies: $1,400. Personal expenses: $1,400.

**Financial aid. Need-based:** Need-based aid available for part-time students. **Non-need-based:** Scholarships awarded for academics, art, athletics, leadership, music/drama, state residency.

**Application procedures. Admission:** Closing date 9/7. No application fee. Admission notification on a rolling basis. **Financial aid:** Priority date 6/1; no closing date. FAFSA, institutional form required. Applicants notified on a rolling basis starting 5/15; must reply within 2 week(s) of notification.

**Academics. Special study options:** Accelerated study, cooperative education, distance learning, dual enrollment of high school students, independent study, internships, weekend college. **Credit/placement by examination:** CLEP. 45 credit hours maximum toward associate degree. **Support services:** GED preparation and test center, learning center, remedial instruction, study skills assistance, tutoring.

**Majors. Agriculture:** Horticulture. **Business:** Administrative services, management information systems. **Communications:** General, broadcast journalism. **Communications technology:** General. **Computer sciences:** General, computer graphics, programming. **Engineering technology:** Drafting. **Family/consumer sciences:** Child care. **Health:** Clinical lab technology, dental hygiene, licensed practical nurse, medical radiologic technology/radiation therapy, medical records technology, medical secretary, physical therapy assistant, respiratory therapy technology. **Legal studies:** Prelaw. **Mechanic/repair:** Electronics/electrical. **Protective services:** Firefighting.

**Computing on campus.** 83 workstations in library, computer center. Dormitories wired for high-speed internet access and linked to campus network. Commuter students can connect to campus network. Online course registration, online library, helpline, repair service available.

**Student life. Freshman orientation:** Mandatory. Orientation sessions specific to certain programs. **Housing:** Coed dorms, single-sex dorms, apartments, substance-free housing available. $100 fully refundable deposit. **Activities:** Bands, choral groups, drama, literary magazine, music ensembles, musical theater, radio station, student government, student newspaper, TV station, Baptist Student Union, T.J. Harris Organization, Wesley Foundation, Fellowship of Christian Athletes, Phi Theta Kappa, multicultural student association.

**Athletics.** NJCAA. **Intercollegiate:** Baseball M, basketball, golf M, soccer M, softball W, tennis. **Intramural:** Basketball, bowling, softball W, swimming, tennis, volleyball. **Team name:** Eagles.

**Student services.** Career counseling, student employment services, personal counseling, placement for graduates, veterans' counselor. **Physically disabled:** Services for visually, speech, hearing impaired. **Transfer:** Pre-admission transcript evaluation for new students. Transfer adviser, college fairs on campus for students transferring to 4-year colleges.

**Contact.** E-mail: dwalton@meridiancc.edu
Phone: (601) 484-8895 Toll-free number: (800) 622-8431
Fax: (601) 484-8838
Dianne Walton, Associate Dean, Enrollment Services, Meridian Community College, 910 Highway 19 North, Meridian, MS 39307-5890

## Mississippi Delta Community College
Moorhead, Mississippi
www.msdelta.edu                     CB code: 1742

- Public 2-year community college
- Commuter campus in rural community

**General.** Founded in 1926. Regionally accredited. **Location:** 20 miles from Greenwood. **Calendar:** Semester.

**Annual costs/financial aid.** Tuition/fees (2007-2008): $1,920; $3,528 out-of-state. Room/board: $4,140. Books/supplies: $450. Personal expenses: $400. Need-based financial aid available for full-time students.

**Contact.** Phone: (662) 246-6306
Chief Admissions Officer, Box 668, Moorhead, MS 38761

## Mississippi Gulf Coast Community College: Jefferson Davis Campus
Perkinston, Mississippi               CB member
www.mgccc.edu                        CB code: 1353

- Public 2-year community college
- Commuter campus in large city

**General.** Founded in 1965. Regionally accredited. Instruction is available at our 3 campuses and 4 centers. **Enrollment:** 8,724 degree-seeking undergraduates; 98 non-degree-seeking students. **Degrees:** 1,249 associate awarded. **Location:** 30 miles from Biloxi, 90 miles from New Orleans. **Calendar:** Semester, limited summer session. **Full-time faculty:** 346 total. **Part-time faculty:** 179 total.

**Student profile.** Among degree-seeking undergraduates, 1,974 enrolled as first-time, first-year students.

| | | | |
|---|---|---|---|
| Part-time: | 36% | 25 or older: | 36% |
| Out-of-state: | 3% | Live on campus: | 8% |
| Women: | 62% | | |

**Transfer out. Colleges most students transferred to 2007:** University of Southern MS; Mississippi State University; University of South Alabama.

**Basis for selection.** Open admission, but selective for some programs. Special requirements for health occupations programs.

**High school preparation.** 19 units recommended. Recommended units include English 3, mathematics 3 and science 3.

**2007-2008 Annual costs.** Tuition/fees: $1,702; $3,548 out-of-state. Per-credit charge: $75 in-state; $152 out-of-state. $25 rental fee required per book. Books/supplies: $520. Personal expenses: $5,268.

**2006-2007 Financial aid.** All financial aid based on need.

**Application procedures. Admission:** No deadline. No application fee. **Financial aid:** Priority date 6/1; no closing date. Institutional form required. Applicants notified on a rolling basis starting 7/1.

**Academics. Special study options:** Accelerated study, cooperative education, distance learning, dual enrollment of high school students, honors, weekend college. License preparation in nursing, paramedic. **Credit/placement by examination:** CLEP. 32 credit hours maximum toward associate degree. **Support services:** GED preparation and test center, learning center, reduced course load, remedial instruction, study skills assistance, tutoring.

**Majors. Agriculture:** General, food science, landscaping, ornamental horticulture, turf management. **Biology:** General, biotechnology. **Business:** General, accounting, administrative services, banking/financial services, business admin, fashion, management information systems, marketing, office technology. **Communications:** General. **Computer sciences:** General. **Conservation:** Fisheries, forestry. **Construction:** Lineworker, pipefitting, power transmission. **Education:** General, art, business, elementary, mathematics, multi-level teacher, science, secondary, trade/industrial. **Engineering:** General. **Engineering technology:** CAD/CADD, drafting. **Health:** Clinical lab science, clinical lab technology, EMT paramedic, medical radiologic technology/

radiation therapy, medical records admin, medical secretary, nursing (RN), optician, orthotics/prosthetics, prepharmacy, respiratory therapy technology, veterinary technology/assistant. **Legal studies:** Court reporting, paralegal, prelaw. **Liberal arts:** Arts/sciences. **Math:** General. **Mechanic/repair:** Electronics/electrical. **Personal/culinary services:** Cosmetic, funeral direction. **Protective services:** Criminal justice, fire safety technology. **Psychology:** General. **Public administration:** Social work. **Visual/performing arts:** Art, commercial/advertising art, interior design, sculpture.

**Most popular majors.** Business/marketing 20%, education 18%, engineering/engineering technologies 6%, health sciences 22%, liberal arts 23%.

**Computing on campus.** 325 workstations in library, computer center, student center. Dormitories wired for high-speed internet access and linked to campus network. Commuter students can connect to campus network. Online course registration available.

**Student life. Freshman orientation:** Mandatory. Preregistration for classes offered. **Housing:** Single-sex dorms, special housing for disabled available. $25 fully refundable deposit. **Activities:** Bands, campus ministries, choral groups, dance, drama, music ensembles, musical theater, student government, student newspaper, Baptist student union, Wesley Foundation, Newman Club, A.D.U.L.T.

**Athletics.** NJCAA. **Intercollegiate:** Baseball M, basketball, cheerleading, football (tackle) M, golf M, softball, tennis. **Intramural:** Baseball, basketball, football (tackle), softball, tennis. **Team name:** Bulldogs.

**Student services.** Adult student services, career counseling, student employment services, financial aid counseling, health services, on-campus daycare, personal counseling, placement for graduates, veterans' counselor. **Physically disabled:** Services for visually, hearing impaired. **Transfer:** Transfer adviser, college fairs on campus for students transferring to 4-year colleges.

**Contact.** E-mail: ladd.taylor@mgccc.edu
Phone: (601) 928-6333 Toll-free number: (866) 735-1122
Fax: (601) 928-6345
Ladd Taylor, Director of Admissions, Mississippi Gulf Coast Community College: Jefferson Davis Campus, PO Box 548, Perkinston, MS 39573

## Northeast Mississippi Community College
Booneville, Mississippi
www.nemcc.edu                        CB code: 1557

- Public 2-year community college
- Commuter campus in small town

**General.** Founded in 1948. Regionally accredited. **Enrollment:** 3,429 degree-seeking undergraduates. **Degrees:** 352 associate awarded. **Location:** 30 miles from Tupelo, 110 miles from Memphis, Tennessee. **Calendar:** Semester, extensive summer session. **Full-time faculty:** 135 total. **Part-time faculty:** 42 total.

**Student profile.** Among degree-seeking undergraduates, 67% enrolled in a transfer program, 32% enrolled in a vocational program, 1,131 enrolled as first-time, first-year students.

| | | | |
|---|---|---|---|
| Part-time: | 12% | Women: | 60% |

**Basis for selection.** Open admission, but selective for some programs. Admission to nursing, dental hygiene, and medical laboratory, medical assistance, practical nursing, radiologic technology, and respiratory technician programs based on test scores. Dental Hygiene Aptitude Test required of dental hygiene applicants. Interview required for dental hygiene, medical laboratory technology, and nursing students. **Adult students:** SAT/ACT scores not required if applicant over 21.

**High school preparation.** 18 units recommended. Recommended units include English 4, mathematics 2, social studies 2 and science 2.

**2008-2009 Annual costs.** Tuition/fees: $1,920; $3,850 out-of-state. Per-credit charge: $105 in-state; $212 out-of-state. Room/board: $2,984. Books/supplies: $840. Personal expenses: $1,989.

**2007-2008 Financial aid. Need-based:** 71% of total undergraduate aid awarded as scholarships/grants, 29% as loans/jobs.

**Application procedures. Admission:** No deadline. No application fee. Application must be submitted on paper. Admission notification on a rolling basis. **Financial aid:** Priority date 4/1, closing date 6/30. FAFSA, institutional form required. Applicants notified on a rolling basis.

**Academics. Special study options:** Distance learning, dual enrollment of high school students, study abroad. **Credit/placement by examination:** AP, CLEP, institutional tests. 18 credit hours maximum toward associate degree.

**Support services:** GED preparation and test center, learning center, pre-admission summer program, reduced course load, remedial instruction, tutoring.

**Majors.** **Health:** Clinical lab assistant, licensed practical nurse, medical assistant, medical radiologic technology/radiation therapy, pharmacy assistant, respiratory therapy technology.

**Computing on campus.** Dormitories wired for high-speed internet access and linked to campus network. Commuter students can connect to campus network. Online library, wireless network available.

**Student life. Freshman orientation:** Available, $25 fee. Preregistration for classes offered. Two one-day orientation/registration sessions are planned for entering freshman and transfer students. New and transfer students will attend Orientation/Registration one of the dates according to their college major. Attendance is highly encouraged. **Housing:** Single-sex dorms available. $100 fully refundable deposit. **Activities:** Bands, choral groups, dance, drama, film society, music ensembles, musical theater, radio station, student government, student newspaper.

**Athletics.** NJCAA. **Intercollegiate:** Baseball M, basketball, football (tackle) M, golf M, softball W, tennis. **Intramural:** Basketball, softball, table tennis, volleyball. **Team name:** Tigers.

**Student services.** Adult student services, career counseling, student employment services, health services, on-campus daycare, personal counseling, placement for graduates. **Physically disabled:** Services for visually, speech, hearing impaired. **Transfer:** Transfer adviser for students transferring to 4-year colleges.

**Contact.** E-mail: admitme@nemcc.edu
Phone: (662) 720-7290 Toll-free number: (800) 555-2154
Fax: (662) 728-1165
Robert Gibson, Director of Enrollment Services/Registrar, Northeast Mississippi Community College, 101 Cunningham Boulevard, Booneville, MS 38829

## Northwest Mississippi Community College
**Senatobia, Mississippi**
**www.northwestms.edu**                          CB code: 1562

♦ Public 2-year community college
♦ Commuter campus in small town

**General.** Founded in 1927. Regionally accredited. **Enrollment:** 6,825 degree-seeking undergraduates. **Degrees:** 638 associate awarded. **ROTC:** Air Force. **Location:** 30 miles from Memphis, Tennessee. **Calendar:** Semester, extensive summer session. **Full-time faculty:** 200 total. **Part-time faculty:** 172 total. **Class size:** 45% < 20, 49% 20-39, 6% 40-49, less than 1% 50-99.

**Student profile.**
Out-of-state:              10%     Live on campus:          40%

**Transfer out. Colleges most students transferred to 2007:** University of Mississipi.

**Basis for selection.** Open admission, but selective for some programs. Special requirements for some technical programs.

**High school preparation.** 17 units recommended. Recommended units include English 4, mathematics 3, social studies 4 and science 2.

**2007-2008 Annual costs.** Tuition/fees: $1,700; $3,700 out-of-state. Per-credit charge: $80 in-state; $155 out-of-state. Lab fees range from $15 to $25 per course. Room/board: $2,994. Books/supplies: $600. Personal expenses: $375.

**2006-2007 Financial aid. Need-based:** 82% of total undergraduate aid awarded as scholarships/grants, 18% as loans/jobs.

**Application procedures. Admission:** No deadline. No application fee. Admission notification on a rolling basis beginning on or about 7/1. **Financial aid:** Priority date 4/1; no closing date. FAFSA required. Applicants notified by 8/16.

**Academics. Special study options:** Accelerated study, independent study, weekend college. Bachelor's degree programs available on campus. **Credit/placement by examination:** CLEP, institutional tests. **Support services:** GED preparation and test center, reduced course load, remedial instruction, tutoring.

**Majors. Agriculture:** Agribusiness operations, animal sciences, dairy, economics, food science, horticulture, plant sciences, poultry. **Business:** Accounting, business admin, fashion, hospitality/recreation, management information systems, office technology. **Communications:** Broadcast journalism, journalism, public relations. **Communications technology:** General, graphic/printing. **Computer sciences:** General, applications programming, data processing, networking, programming. **Education:** General, art, business, elementary, family/consumer sciences, mathematics, music, physical, sales/marketing, science, secondary, social science, social studies, special. **Engineering technology:** Civil, drafting, electrical. **Health:** Medical secretary, respiratory therapy technology. **Legal studies:** Court reporting, legal secretary, paralegal. **Liberal arts:** Arts/sciences. **Mechanic/repair:** Heating/ac/refrig. **Visual/performing arts:** Commercial/advertising art.

**Most popular majors.** Business/marketing 20%, computer/information sciences 15%, education 10%, health sciences 20%.

**Student life. Freshman orientation:** Available. **Housing:** Single-sex dorms, apartments available. **Activities:** Bands, choral groups, drama, music ensembles, musical theater, student government, student newspaper.

**Athletics.** NJCAA. **Intercollegiate:** Baseball M, basketball, cheerleading, football (tackle) M, golf, rodeo, soccer, softball W, tennis, track and field M. **Intramural:** Archery, badminton. **Team name:** Rangers.

**Student services.** Career counseling, health services, personal counseling, veterans' counselor. **Physically disabled:** Services for visually, speech, hearing impaired.

**Contact.** E-mail: jlsimpson@northwestms.edu
Phone: (601) 562-3200 ext. 3219 Fax: (662) 562-3221
Larry Simpson, Registrar, Northwest Mississippi Community College, 4975 Highway 51 North, Senatobia, MS 38668

## Pearl River Community College
**Poplarville, Mississippi**
**www.prcc.edu**                                CB code: 1622

♦ Public 2-year community college
♦ Commuter campus in small town

**General.** Founded in 1921. Regionally accredited. **Enrollment:** 3,791 degree-seeking undergraduates. **Degrees:** 484 associate awarded. **Location:** 35 miles from Hattiesburg, 70 miles from New Orleans. **Calendar:** Semester, limited summer session. **Full-time faculty:** 135 total. **Part-time faculty:** 50 total.

**Student profile.** Among degree-seeking undergraduates, 70% enrolled in a transfer program, 10% enrolled in a vocational program.

Out-of-state:            9%      Live on campus:          25%
25 or older:             23%

**Transfer out.** 49% of students enrolled in the transfer program go on to 4-year colleges.

**Basis for selection.** Open admission, but selective for some programs. Special requirements for health occupation programs. ACT required for placement and counseling. Interview recommended for nursing majors.

**2007-2008 Annual costs.** Tuition/fees: $1,726; $5,511 out-of-state. Per-credit charge: $86 in-state; $244 out-of-state. Room/board: $3,400. Books/supplies: $500.

**Financial aid. Need-based:** Need-based aid available for part-time students. **Non-need-based:** Scholarships awarded for academics, alumni affiliation, athletics, leadership, music/drama, state residency.

**Application procedures. Admission:** No deadline. No application fee. Application may be submitted online. Admission notification on a rolling basis. **Financial aid:** Priority date 4/17; no closing date. FAFSA, institutional form required. Applicants notified on a rolling basis.

**Academics. Special study options:** Cooperative education, dual enrollment of high school students. License preparation in dental hygiene, nursing, occupational therapy, physical therapy, radiology. **Credit/placement by examination:** AP, CLEP, ACT. 30 credit hours maximum toward associate degree. **Support services:** GED preparation and test center, learning center, reduced course load, remedial instruction, tutoring.

**Majors. Business:** Business admin, management information systems, office technology. **Computer sciences:** Applications programming, data processing. **Construction:** Carpentry, masonry, power transmission. **Education:** Multi-level teacher. **Engineering technology:** Drafting, electrical. **Health:** Licensed practical nurse, medical secretary, respiratory therapy technology.

**Legal studies:** Legal secretary. **Liberal arts:** Arts/sciences. **Mechanic/repair:** Auto body, heating/ac/refrig.

**Computing on campus.** 150 workstations in library, computer center. Dormitories wired for high-speed internet access and linked to campus network. Commuter students can connect to campus network. Online course registration, helpline, wireless network available.

**Student life. Freshman orientation:** Available, $25 fee. Preregistration for classes offered. **Housing:** Single-sex dorms, special housing for disabled available. $50 deposit. **Activities:** Bands, choral groups, drama, music ensembles, student government, student newspaper, Black Student Union, Wesley and Newman Clubs, Phi Theta Kappa, Afro-American Club, Baptist Student Union.

**Athletics. NJCAA. Intercollegiate:** Baseball M, basketball, football (tackle) M, golf M, softball W, tennis. **Intramural:** Badminton, basketball, softball, table tennis, tennis, volleyball. **Team name:** Wildcats.

**Student services.** Career counseling, student employment services, health services, personal counseling, placement for graduates, veterans' counselor.

**Contact.** E-mail: dford@prcc.edu
Phone: (601) 403-1214 Fax: (601) 403-1339
Dow Ford, Director of Admissions, Pearl River Community College, 101 Highway 11 North, Poplarville, MS 39470

## Southwest Mississippi Community College
### Summit, Mississippi
www.smcc.edu                              CB code: 1729

- Public 2-year community college
- Commuter campus in rural community

**General.** Founded in 1918. Regionally accredited. Rotary drilling program for oil-well drilling available. **Enrollment:** 1,793 degree-seeking undergraduates; 111 non-degree-seeking students. **Degrees:** 284 associate awarded. **Location:** 76 miles from Jackson, 100 miles from New Orleans. **Calendar:** Semester, limited summer session. **Full-time faculty:** 84 total. **Part-time faculty:** 16 total. **Class size:** 67% < 20, 26% 20-39, 4% 40-49, 2% 50-99, less than 1% >100. **Special facilities:** Observatory.

**Student profile.** Among degree-seeking undergraduates, 63% enrolled in a transfer program, 37% enrolled in a vocational program, 560 enrolled as first-time, first-year students.

| | | | |
|---|---|---|---|
| Part-time: | 13% | African American: | 43% |
| Out-of-state: | 9% | Asian American: | 1% |
| Women: | 65% | Live on campus: | 40% |

**Transfer out. Colleges most students transferred to 2007:** The Univeristy of Southern Mississippi, Southeastern Louisiana University, Mississippi State University, The University of Mississippi, Jackson State University.

**Basis for selection.** Open admission. For ability to benefit from vocational programs, high school graduation or GED preferred. **Homeschooled:** Transcript of courses and grades required.

**2007-2008 Annual costs.** Tuition/fees: $1,800; $4,500 out-of-state. Per-credit charge: $75 in-state; $170 out-of-state. Room/board: $2,180. Books/supplies: $600. Personal expenses: $2,840.

**Financial aid. Need-based:** Need-based aid available for part-time students.

**Application procedures. Admission:** Priority date 8/1; no deadline. No application fee. Application must be submitted on paper. Admission notification on a rolling basis. **Financial aid:** No deadline. Applicants notified on a rolling basis.

**Academics. Special study options:** Distance learning, dual enrollment of high school students. License preparation in nursing. **Credit/placement by examination:** AP, CLEP. 12 credit hours maximum toward associate degree. **Support services:** GED preparation and test center, learning center, reduced course load, remedial instruction, tutoring.

**Majors. Business:** Office/clerical. **Computer sciences:** Data processing. **Liberal arts:** Arts/sciences. **Protective services:** Police science.

**Computing on campus.** 150 workstations in library, computer center. Commuter students can connect to campus network. Wireless network available.

**Student life. Freshman orientation:** Mandatory. Preregistration for classes offered. Orientation sessions are offered during the month of June, and the week before the first day of class. The sessions last approximately 4 hours. **Housing:** Single-sex dorms, apartments available. $30 deposit, deadline 8/1. **Activities:** Bands, choral groups, student government, student newspaper.

**Athletics. NJCAA. Intercollegiate:** Baseball M, basketball, football (tackle) M, golf M, soccer, softball W, tennis, track and field. **Intramural:** Basketball, tennis, volleyball. **Team name:** Bears.

**Student services.** Career counseling, health services, personal counseling, placement for graduates, veterans' counselor. **Transfer:** Transfer adviser, college fairs on campus for students transferring to 4-year colleges.

**Contact.** E-mail: mattc@smcc.edu
Phone: (601) 276-2001 Fax: (601) 276-3888
Matthew Calhoun, Vice President of Admissions, Southwest Mississippi Community College, 1156 College Drive, Summit, MS 39666

## Virginia College
### Jackson, Mississippi
www.vc.edu

- For-profit 2-year community college
- Small city

**General.** Accredited by ACICS. **Calendar:** Quarter.

**Annual costs/financial aid.** Per-credit-hour charge ranges from $285-$385 depending on program and includes fees and books.

**Contact.** Phone: (601) 977-0960
Director, 5360 I-55 North, Jackson, MS 39211

## Virginia College Gulf Coast
### Biloxi, Mississippi
www.vc.edu/gulfcoast/index.cfm

- For-profit 2-year business and health science college
- Small city

**General.** Accredited by ACICS. **Calendar:** Quarter.

**Annual costs/financial aid.** Per-credit-hour charge ranges from $285-$385 depending on program and includes fees and books.

**Contact.** Phone: (228) 392-2994
920 Cedar Lake Road, BIloxi, MS 39532

Two-Year Colleges

# Missouri

## Aviation Institute of Maintenance: Kansas City
**Kansas City, Missouri**
www.aviationmaintenance.edu

- For-profit 2-year technical college
- Large city

**General.** Accredited by ACCSCT. **Calendar:** Continuous.

**Annual costs/financial aid.** Full tuition and fees leading to an associates degree is $34,560.

**Contact.** Phone: (816) 753-9920
4100 Raytown Road, Kansas City, MO 64129-3634

## Bolivar Technical College
**Bolivar, Missouri**
www.bolivarcollege.org

- Private 2-year nursing and technical college
- Small town

**General.** Accredited by ACICS. Additional campus in Houston. **Enrollment:** 98 degree-seeking undergraduates. **Degrees:** 34 associate awarded. **Location:** 120 miles from Kansas City. **Calendar:** Semester. **Full-time faculty:** 5 total; 100% have terminal degrees, 100% women. **Part-time faculty:** 15 total; 100% have terminal degrees, 60% women.

**Basis for selection.** Admission based on composite score of 75% or higher on institutional entrance exams; requires a minimum passing score on each section of the exam.

**2007-2008 Annual costs.** Tuition/fees: $11,620. Per-credit charge: $325. Tuition varies by program, $145-$325 per credit-hour. Books/supplies: $1,000. Personal expenses: $10,083.

**2007-2008 Financial aid. Need-based:** 51% of total undergraduate aid awarded as scholarships/grants, 49% as loans/jobs.

**Application procedures. Admission:** No deadline. $45 fee. **Financial aid:** Priority date 4/1; no closing date.

**Academics. Special study options:** Internships. License preparation in nursing, paramedic. **Credit/placement by examination:** CLEP.

**Majors. Business:** Accounting, administrative services. **Computer sciences:** Data processing. **Health:** EMT paramedic, health services, medical secretary, nursing (RN).

**Contact.** E-mail: info@bolivarcollege.org
Phone: (417) 777-5062 Toll-free number: (800) 440-6135
Fax: (417) 777-8908
Charlotte Gray, Admissions Director, Bolivar Technical College, PO Box 592, Bolivar, MO 65613

## Colorado Technical University: North Kansas City
**North Kansas City, Missouri**
www.ctukansascity.com          CB code: 3322

- For-profit 2-year health science and technical college
- Rural community

**General. Calendar:** Continuous.

**Annual costs/financial aid.** Tuition programs range from $14,000-$32,000. Fees vary depending on program. Books/supplies: $1,620.

**Contact.** Phone: (816) 472-7400
Admissions Director, 520 East 19th Avenue, North Kansas City, MO 64116

## Concorde Career College: Kansas City
**Kansas City, Missouri**
www.concorde.edu/kansas          CB code: 3126

- For-profit 2-year business and health science college
- Large city

**General.** Accredited by ACCSCT. **Calendar:** Continuous.

**Annual costs/financial aid.** Cost of full programs: associate degree programs $21,648; certificates range from $11,200 to $11,700; Practical Nursing program*is $20,500; includes fees, books, uniforms. Books/supplies: $348.

**Contact.** Phone: (816) 531-5223
Campus Director, 3239 Broadway, Kansas City, MO 64111

## Cottey College
**Nevada, Missouri**          **CB member**
www.cottey.edu          **CB code: 6120**

- Private 2-year junior and liberal arts college for women
- Residential campus in small town
- SAT or ACT (ACT writing optional) required

**General.** Founded in 1884. Regionally accredited. Sponsored and supported by P.E.O. Sisterhood, nonsectarian philanthropic educational organization. College owned and supported by women for women. **Enrollment:** 321 degree-seeking undergraduates. **Degrees:** 119 associate awarded. **Location:** 100 miles from Kansas City, 60 miles from Joplin. **Calendar:** Semester. **Full-time faculty:** 35 total. **Part-time faculty:** 4 total. **Special facilities:** 33-acre wooded area with lodge for outings and nature laboratory, women's leadership center.

**Student profile.**

| Out-of-state: | 90% | Live on campus: | 99% |
|---|---|---|---|

**Transfer out. Colleges most students transferred to 2007:** Smith College, Hood College, Truman State University, Boston University, Mount Holyoke College.

**Basis for selection.** High school course of study most important; rank in top half of graduating class, test scores, essay also important. Recommendations and interviews considered when other criteria not met. Interview recommended for all students. Audition recommended for music students; portfolio recommended for art students. Essay requested sometimes. **Homeschooled:** Statement describing homeschool structure and mission, transcript of courses and grades required. Students should take GED examination.

**High school preparation.** 18 units required. Required units include English 4, mathematics 3, social studies 2, science 2 (laboratory 2) and foreign language 2. Mathematics should include algebra I, algebra II, geometry.

**2007-2008 Annual costs.** Tuition/fees: $13,510. Room/board: $5,200. Books/supplies: $800. Personal expenses: $900.

**Financial aid. Need-based:** Need-based aid available for part-time students. Work-study available nights and weekends. **Non-need-based:** Scholarships awarded for academics, alumni affiliation, art, athletics, leadership, music/drama.

**Application procedures. Admission:** Priority date 5/1; no deadline. $40 fee, may be waived for applicants with need. Application may be submitted online. Admission notification on a rolling basis. Must reply by May 1 or within 2 week(s) if notified thereafter. Tuition deposit of $100 required to reserve spot in class and in student housing. **Financial aid:** Priority date 3/1; no closing date. FAFSA required. Applicants notified on a rolling basis starting 3/15; must reply by 5/1 or within 4 week(s) of notification.

**Academics. Special study options:** Cross-registration, dual enrollment of high school students, independent study, internships. **Credit/placement by examination:** AP, CLEP, IB, institutional tests. **Support services:** Study skills assistance, tutoring, writing center.

**Majors. Liberal arts:** Arts/sciences.

**Computing on campus.** 62 workstations in dormitories, library, computer center. Commuter students can connect to campus network. Wireless network available.

**Student life. Freshman orientation:** Mandatory. Held in late August, 5 days prior to the first day of class. **Housing:** Guaranteed on-campus for all undergraduates. Substance-free housing available. **Activities:** Jazz band, choral groups, dance, drama, literary magazine, music ensembles, student government, student newspaper, 35 campus service and social organizations available.

**Athletics.** NJCAA. **Intercollegiate:** Basketball W, volleyball W. **Intramural:** Badminton W, basketball W, cheerleading W, golf W, soccer W, softball W, swimming W, synchronized swimming W, table tennis W, tennis W, volleyball W. **Team name:** Comets.

**Student services.** Campus ministries, career counseling, student employment services, financial aid counseling, health services, personal counseling. **Transfer:** Pre-admission transcript evaluation for new students. Transfer center, transfer adviser, college fairs on campus for students transferring to 4-year colleges.

**Contact.** E-mail: enrollmgt@cottey.edu
Phone: (417) 667-8181 Toll-free number: (888) 526-8839
Fax: (417) 667-1025
Judi Steege, Director of Admission, Cottey College, 1000 West Austin Boulevard, Nevada, MO 64772

---

## Crowder College
### Neosho, Missouri
### www.crowder.edu
**CB code: 6138**

▶ Public 2-year community and liberal arts college
▶ Commuter campus in small town

**General.** Founded in 1963. Regionally accredited. Internationally recognized water resource school and active/passive solar program. **Enrollment:** 2,604 degree-seeking undergraduates; 713 non-degree-seeking students. **Degrees:** 355 associate awarded. **Location:** 70 miles from Springfield, 28 miles from Joplin. **Calendar:** Semester, limited summer session. **Full-time faculty:** 69 total. **Part-time faculty:** 182 total.

**Student profile.** Among degree-seeking undergraduates, 662 enrolled as first-time, first-year students.

| | | | |
|---|---|---|---|
| Part-time: | 41% | Live on campus: | 10% |
| Women: | 66% | | |

**Transfer out. Colleges most students transferred to 2007:** Missouri Southern State College, Pittsburg State University, Southwest Missouri State University.

**Basis for selection.** Open admission, but selective for some programs. For nursing program: interview, 2.75 GPA and minimum 19 ACT score required. **Homeschooled:** Must pass GED.

**High school preparation.** Recommended units include English 4, mathematics 3 and science 3.

**2007-2008 Annual costs.** Tuition/fees: $2,310; $3,090 out-of-district; $3,900 out-of-state. Per-credit charge: $65 in-district; $91 out-of-district; $118 out-of-state. Room/board: $3,870. Books/supplies: $700. Personal expenses: $1,100.

**Financial aid.** All financial aid based on need. Need-based aid available for part-time students. Work-study available nights, weekends and for part-time students.

**Application procedures. Admission:** No deadline. $25 fee, may be waived for applicants with need. Application may be submitted online. Admission notification on a rolling basis. **Financial aid:** Priority date 7/1; no closing date. FAFSA, institutional form required. Applicants notified on a rolling basis starting 5/15.

**Academics. Special study options:** Distance learning, dual enrollment of high school students, ESL, honors, independent study, internships, liberal arts/career combination, study abroad, weekend college. License preparation in nursing. **Credit/placement by examination:** AP, CLEP, institutional tests. 15 credit hours maximum toward associate degree. **Support services:** GED preparation and test center, learning center, reduced course load, remedial instruction, study skills assistance, tutoring.

**Majors. Agriculture:** Agribusiness operations, farm/ranch, poultry production. **Biology:** General. **Business:** General, administrative services, office/clerical. **Communications:** Journalism, public relations. **Computer sciences:** General, system admin. **Education:** Elementary, physical, secondary. **Engineering:** General. **Engineering technology:** Electrical, solar energy. **Foreign languages:** Spanish. **Health:** Environmental health, nursing (RN),

---

office assistant. **History:** General. **Interdisciplinary:** Math/computer science. **Liberal arts:** Arts/sciences. **Math:** General. **Mechanic/repair:** Automotive, diesel, industrial electronics. **Physical sciences:** General, chemistry, physics. **Psychology:** General. **Social sciences:** General. **Visual/performing arts:** Art, theater arts management.

**Most popular majors.** Agriculture 6%, business/marketing 14%, health sciences 18%, liberal arts 48%.

**Computing on campus.** 1,000 workstations in dormitories, library, computer center. Dormitories wired for high-speed internet access. Online library, helpline, wireless network available.

**Student life. Freshman orientation:** Mandatory. Preregistration for classes offered. **Housing:** Guaranteed on-campus for all undergraduates. Single-sex dorms, substance-free housing available. $150 deposit. **Activities:** Bands, choral groups, dance, drama, literary magazine, music ensembles, musical theater, student government, student newspaper, Aggies (agricultural club), art club, Baptist student union, Students in Free Enterprise, Student-Missouri State Teacher's Association, Phi Theta Kappa, Latino union, Habitat for Humanity.

**Athletics.** NJCAA. **Intercollegiate:** Baseball M, basketball W, softball W. **Team name:** Roughriders.

**Student services.** Career counseling, student employment services, financial aid counseling, personal counseling, placement for graduates. **Transfer:** Transfer adviser, college fairs on campus for students transferring to 4-year colleges.

**Contact.** E-mail: admissions@crowder.edu
Phone: (417) 455-5718 Toll-free number: (866) 238-7788
Fax: (417) 455-2439
Jim Riggs, Director of Admission, Crowder College, 601 LaClede Avenue, Neosho, MO 64850

---

## East Central College
### Union, Missouri
### www.eastcentral.edu
**CB code: 0845**

▶ Public 2-year community college
▶ Commuter campus in small town

**General.** Founded in 1968. Regionally accredited. **Enrollment:** 2,305 degree-seeking undergraduates; 1,299 non-degree-seeking students. **Degrees:** 349 associate awarded. **Location:** 45 miles from St. Louis. **Calendar:** Semester, limited summer session. **Full-time faculty:** 63 total; 29% have terminal degrees, 8% minority, 46% women. **Part-time faculty:** 141 total; 8% have terminal degrees, 3% minority, 50% women. **Special facilities:** Learning and assessment center, observatory and natural prairie.

**Student profile.** Among degree-seeking undergraduates, 55% enrolled in a transfer program, 45% enrolled in a vocational program, 695 enrolled as first-time, first-year students.

| | | | |
|---|---|---|---|
| Part-time: | 38% | Asian American: | 1% |
| Women: | 66% | Hispanic American: | 2% |
| African American: | 1% | 25 or older: | 28% |

**Transfer out. Colleges most students transferred to 2007:** Drury University, University of Missouri-Columbia, Missouri State University, St. Louis Community College-Meramec, University of Missouri-St Louis.

**Basis for selection.** Open admission, but selective for some programs. Special requirements for nursing program. ASSET required for placement for degree seeking students but not required for all certificate programs. **Homeschooled:** 21 ACT required without GED.

**2007-2008 Annual costs.** Tuition/fees: $2,130; $2,910 out-of-district; $4,230 out-of-state. Per-credit charge: $61 in-district; $87 out-of-district; $131 out-of-state. Books/supplies: $700. Personal expenses: $662.

**2006-2007 Financial aid. Need-based:** 64% of total undergraduate aid awarded as scholarships/grants, 36% as loans/jobs. Need-based aid available for part-time students. Work-study available nights, weekends and for part-time students. **Non-need-based:** Scholarships awarded for academics, alumni affiliation, art, athletics, music/drama, state residency.

**Application procedures. Admission:** No deadline. No application fee. Application must be submitted on paper. Admission notification on a rolling basis. **Financial aid:** Priority date 3/1; no closing date. FAFSA required. Applicants notified on a rolling basis starting 3/15.

**Academics. Special study options:** Distance learning, dual enrollment of high school students, ESL, honors, independent study, internships, liberal arts/career combination. Central Methodist University classes offered on campus and may count toward 4-year degree. Bachelor's degree programs available on campus. License preparation in nursing, paramedic, radiology. **Credit/placement by examination:** AP, CLEP, institutional tests. **Support services:** GED preparation and test center, learning center, reduced course load, remedial instruction, study skills assistance, tutoring, writing center.

**Majors. Business:** Accounting technology. **Computer sciences:** Networking. **Construction:** General. **Education:** General, teacher assistance. **Engineering:** General. **Engineering technology:** Drafting, manufacturing. **English:** English lit. **Family/consumer sciences:** Child care. **Health:** EMT paramedic, medical radiologic technology/radiation therapy, medical secretary, nursing (RN), respiratory therapy technology. **Legal studies:** Legal secretary. **Mechanic/repair:** Automotive, heating/ac/refrig. **Personal/culinary services:** Chef training. **Production:** Machine tool, welding. **Protective services:** Firefighting, police science. **Visual/performing arts:** Commercial/advertising art. **Other:** Apprenticeship Training - Communication Trades, Apprenticeship Training - Construction Trades, Business Technology - Administrative Assistant, Industrial Engineering Technology, Occupational Education.

**Most popular majors.** Business/marketing 8%, health sciences 16%, liberal arts 60%.

**Computing on campus.** 315 workstations in library, computer center, student center. Online course registration, online library, wireless network available.

**Student life. Freshman orientation:** Mandatory. Preregistration for classes offered. Held prior to start of classes, includes tours, seminars, adviser activities, social activities. **Activities:** Jazz band, choral groups, dance, drama, music ensembles, musical theater, student government, student newspaper, Phi Theta Kappa honor society, student government, variety of religious and social clubs.

**Athletics.** NJCAA. **Intercollegiate:** Soccer M, softball W, volleyball W. **Team name:** Rebels.

**Student services.** Adult student services, career counseling, student employment services, financial aid counseling, personal counseling, placement for graduates, veterans' counselor. **Physically disabled:** Services for visually, hearing impaired. **Transfer:** Pre-admission transcript evaluation for new students. Transfer adviser, college fairs on campus for students transferring to 4-year colleges.

**Contact.** E-mail: wiedaks@eastcentral.edu
Phone: (636) 583-5195 ext. 2221 Fax: (636) 583-1897
Karen Wieda, Registrar, East Central College, 1964 Prairie Dell Road, Union, MO 63084-0529

## Heritage College: Kansas City
**Kansas City, Missouri**
**www.heritage-education.com**

‣ For-profit 2-year health science and technical college
‣ Large city

**General.** Accredited by ACCSCT. **Calendar:** Continuous.

**Contact.** Phone: (816) 942-5474
1200 East 104th Street, Suite 300, Kansas City, MO 64131

## High-Tech Institute
**Kansas City, Missouri**
**www.hightechinstitute.edu**

‣ For-profit 2-year technical college
‣ Very large city

**General.** Accredited by ACCSCT. **Calendar:** Continuous.

**Annual costs/financial aid.** Tuition varies by program length and ranges from $10,150 to $26,850.

**Contact.** Phone: (816) 444-4300
Director of Admissions, 9001 State Line Road, Kansas City, MO 64114

## ITT Technical Institute: Kansas City
**Kansas City, Missouri**

‣ For-profit 2-year business and technical college
‣ Large city

**General.** Accredited by ACICS. **Calendar:** Quarter.

**Contact.** 9150 East 41st Terrace, Kansas City, MO 64133

## Jefferson College
**Hillsboro, Missouri**
**www.jeffco.edu**                                       CB code: 6320

‣ Public 2-year community and technical college
‣ Commuter campus in rural community

**General.** Founded in 1963. Regionally accredited. College also serves as area vocational school, continuing education program, adult basic education center and business and technology customized training center. **Enrollment:** 4,418 degree-seeking undergraduates; 447 non-degree-seeking students. **Degrees:** 536 associate awarded. **Location:** 30 miles from St. Louis. **Calendar:** Semester, limited summer session. **Full-time faculty:** 92 total. **Part-time faculty:** 192 total. **Class size:** 48% < 20, 48% 20-39, 2% 40-49, 2% 50-99, less than 1% >100. **Special facilities:** Outdoor theater, facility for computer-related technologies, graphic design lab, veterinary technology clinic, Law Enforcement Academy.

**Student profile.** Among degree-seeking undergraduates, 58% enrolled in a transfer program, 42% enrolled in a vocational program, 1,207 enrolled as first-time, first-year students.

| | | | |
|---|---|---|---|
| Part-time: | 45% | 25 or older: | 32% |
| Out-of-state: | 2% | Live on campus: | 2% |
| Women: | 60% | | |

**Transfer out. Colleges most students transferred to 2007:** University of Missouri - St. Louis, Missouri Baptist University, Southeast Missouri State University.

**Basis for selection.** Open admission, but selective for some programs. Special requirements for nursing, veterinary technology programs, and law enforcement academy. Interview required for health services technologies students. **Homeschooled:** Transcript of courses and grades required. Minimum placement test scores if high school transcript is not from an approved accrediting body. **Learning Disabled:** Suggested that students with disabilities meet with the campus Assessment Counselor prior to enrollment.

**High school preparation.** Elementary algebra required for electronics; chemistry required for nursing and veterinary technology.

**2008-2009 Annual costs.** Tuition/fees (projected): $2,280; $3,420 out-of-district; $4,560 out-of-state. Per-credit charge: $76 in-district; $114 out-of-district; $152 out-of-state. Room only: $3,170. Books/supplies: $1,000. Personal expenses: $1,000.

**2006-2007 Financial aid. Need-based:** 697 full-time freshmen applied for aid; 450 were judged to have need; 418 of these received aid. Average need met was 42%. Average scholarship/grant was $1,846; average loan $2,102. 57% of total undergraduate aid awarded as scholarships/grants, 43% as loans/jobs. Need-based aid available for part-time students. Work-study available nights and for part-time students. **Non-need-based:** Awarded to 927 full-time undergraduates, including 352 freshmen. Scholarships awarded for academics, art, athletics, leadership, music/drama, state residency.

**Application procedures. Admission:** Priority date 5/3; no deadline. $20 fee, may be waived for applicants with need. Application may be submitted online. Admission notification on a rolling basis. **Financial aid:** Priority date 4/1; no closing date. FAFSA required. Applicants notified on a rolling basis starting 4/15.

**Academics.** Advising and Retention Center available. **Special study options:** Distance learning, double major, dual enrollment of high school students, ESL, honors, independent study, internships, liberal arts/career combination, study abroad. Cooperative agreement with 2 neighboring community colleges. License preparation in nursing, paramedic. **Credit/placement by examination:** AP, CLEP, institutional tests. 30 credit hours maximum toward associate degree. **Support services:** GED preparation and test center, learning center, reduced course load, remedial instruction, study skills assistance, tutoring, writing center.

**Majors. Business:** General, administrative services, office/clerical. **Computer sciences:** General, security. **Education:** Early childhood, secondary. **Engineering:** General. **Engineering technology:** Architectural drafting, drafting, electrical. **Health:** EMT paramedic, medical secretary, nursing (RN), veterinary technology/assistant. **Liberal arts:** Arts/sciences. **Mechanic/repair:** Automotive, heating/ac/refrig, industrial. **Personal/culinary services:** Chef training, culinary arts, food prep, food service, restaurant/catering. **Production:** Machine tool, welding. **Protective services:** Fire safety technology, law enforcement admin, police science. **Science technology:** Biological.

**Most popular majors.** Business/marketing 7%, engineering/engineering technologies 6%, health sciences 13%, liberal arts 62%.

**Computing on campus.** 250 workstations in dormitories, library, computer center, student center. Dormitories wired for high-speed internet access and linked to campus network. Commuter students can connect to campus network. Online course registration, online library, helpline, wireless network available.

**Student life. Freshman orientation:** Mandatory, $76 fee. Preregistration for classes offered. One-credit hour first-year experience course. **Housing:** Apartments, substance-free housing available. $200 partly refundable deposit. **Activities:** Bands, choral groups, drama, literary magazine, music ensembles, musical theater, student government, student newspaper, TV station, Phi Theta Kappa, College Ambassadors, Habitat for Humanity, academic clubs, student senate, cultural club, Missouri Student National Educational Association.

**Athletics.** NJCAA. **Intercollegiate:** Baseball M, basketball W, soccer M, softball W, volleyball W. **Team name:** Vikings.

**Student services.** Adult student services, alcohol/substance abuse counseling, career counseling, services for economically disadvantaged, student employment services, financial aid counseling, on-campus daycare, personal counseling, placement for graduates, veterans' counselor. **Physically disabled:** Services for visually, speech, hearing impaired. **Learning disabled:** Comprehensive services available. **Transfer:** Transfer adviser, college fairs on campus for students transferring to 4-year colleges.

**Contact.** E-mail: admissions@jeffco.edu
Phone: (636) 797-3000 ext. 217 Fax: (636) 789-5103
Julie Fraser, Director of Admissions and Financial Aid, Jefferson College, 1000 Viking Drive, Hillsboro, MO 63050-2441

## L'Ecole Culinaire
St. Louis, Missouri
www.lecoleculinaire.com

- For-profit 2-year culinary school
- Large city

**General.** Accredited by ACCSCT. **Calendar:** Quarter.

**Annual costs/financial aid.** Program costs: $20,350 (certificate/diploma); $31,139 (associate degree).

**Contact.** 9811 South Outer Forty Drive, St. Louis, MO 63124

## Linn State Technical College
Linn, Missouri
www.linnstate.edu

- Public 2-year technical college
- Residential campus in small town

**General. Enrollment:** 861 degree-seeking undergraduates; 12 non-degree-seeking students. **Degrees:** 252 associate awarded. **Calendar:** Semester, limited summer session. **Full-time faculty:** 81 total. **Part-time faculty:** 6 total.

**Student profile.** Among degree-seeking undergraduates, 410 enrolled as first-time, first-year students.

| Part-time: | 9% | Women: | 10% |
|---|---|---|---|

**Basis for selection.** Open admission, but selective for some programs.

**2007-2008 Annual costs.** Tuition/fees: $5,190; $9,390 out-of-state. Per-credit charge: $140 in-state; $280 out-of-state. Room/board: $4,420. Books/supplies: $910. Personal expenses: $1,200.

**Application procedures. Admission:** No application fee. Application may be submitted online. **Financial aid:** Priority date 3/1; no closing date.

**Academics. Credit/placement by examination:** CLEP.

**Majors. Computer sciences:** Networking, programming, systems analysis. **Construction:** Electrician, lineworker, maintenance. **Engineering technology:** Civil, drafting, electrical, laser/optical. **Health:** Physical therapy

assistant. **Mechanic/repair:** Aircraft, aircraft powerplant, auto body, automotive, electronics/electrical, heating/ac/refrig, heavy equipment, medium/heavy vehicle. **Production:** Machine tool. **Science technology:** Radiologic.

**Contact.** E-mail: admissions@linnstate.edu
Phone: (573) 897-5196
Director of Admissions, Linn State Technical College, One Technology Drive, Linn, MO 65051

## Metro Business College
Cape Girardeau, Missouri
www.metrobusinesscollege.edu          CB code: 3316

- For-profit 2-year business college
- Large town

**General.** Accredited by ACICS. **Enrollment:** 125 degree-seeking undergraduates. **Degrees:** 88 associate awarded. **Location:** 125 miles from St. Louis. **Calendar:** Continuous. **Full-time faculty:** 10 total. **Part-time faculty:** 2 total.

**Student profile.** Among degree-seeking undergraduates, 21 transferred in from other institutions.

**Basis for selection.** Open admission, but selective for some programs. **Homeschooled:** State high school equivalency certificate required.

**Academics. Credit/placement by examination:** CLEP. **Support services:** Study skills assistance, tutoring.

**Majors. Business:** Business admin.

**Student life. Freshman orientation:** Mandatory.

**Contact.** E-mail: randy@metrobusinesscollege.edu
Phone: (573) 334-9181 Toll-free number: (800) 467-0785
Fax: (573) 334-0617
Randy Martin, Assistant to the President, Metro Business College, 1732 North Kingshighway, Cape Girardeau, MO 36701

## Metro Business College: Jefferson City
Jefferson City, Missouri
www.metrobusinesscollege.edu          CB code: 3318

- For-profit 2-year business and health science college
- Commuter campus in large town
- Interview required

**General.** Accredited by ACICS. **Enrollment:** 152 degree-seeking undergraduates; 1 non-degree-seeking students. **Degrees:** 37 associate awarded. **Location:** 35 miles from Columbia. **Calendar:** Quarter, extensive summer session. **Full-time faculty:** 8 total; 25% have terminal degrees, 62% women. **Part-time faculty:** 3 total; 67% have terminal degrees, 33% women. **Class size:** 100% 40-49.

**Student profile.** Among degree-seeking undergraduates, 100% enrolled in a vocational program, 3% already have a bachelor's degree or higher, 33 enrolled as first-time, first-year students.

| Part-time: | 12% | Asian American: | 1% |
|---|---|---|---|
| Women: | 89% | Hispanic American: | 3% |
| African American: | 19% | 25 or older: | 32% |

**Transfer out.** 2% of students enrolled in the transfer program go on to 4-year colleges.

**Basis for selection.** Open admission, but selective for some programs. Students must take entrance exam. Required scores vary by program.

**2007-2008 Annual costs.** Tuition/fees: $8,810.

**Financial aid. Need-based:** Need-based aid available for part-time students.

**Application procedures. Admission:** No deadline. $25 fee. Application must be submitted on paper. Admission notification on a rolling basis. **Financial aid:** No deadline. FAFSA, institutional form required. Applicants notified on a rolling basis.

**Academics. Credit/placement by examination:** CLEP. **Support services:** Reduced course load, remedial instruction, study skills assistance, tutoring.

**Majors. Business:** Business admin. **Health:** Office assistant.

**Most popular majors.** Computer/information sciences 58%, health sciences 42%.

**Computing on campus.** 7 workstations in library. Online library, repair service, wireless network available.

**Student life. Freshman orientation:** Mandatory. **Activities:** Student government.

**Student services.** Adult student services, alcohol/substance abuse counseling, services for economically disadvantaged, student employment services, financial aid counseling, personal counseling, placement for graduates. **Transfer:** Pre-admission transcript evaluation for new students.

**Contact.** E-mail: infojeff@metrobusinesscollege.edu
Phone: (573) 635-6600 Toll-free number: (888) 436-3876
Fax: (573) 635-6999
Tanita Jeffries, Admissions Representative, Metro Business College: Jefferson City, 1407 Southwest Boulevard, Jefferson City, MO 65109

## Metro Business College: Rolla
### Rolla, Missouri
www.metrobusinesscollege.edu      CB code: 3317

- For-profit 2-year business college
- Large town

**General.** Accredited by ACICS. **Calendar:** Continuous.

**Contact.** Phone: (573) 364-8464
Director, 1202 East Highway 72, Rolla, MO 65401

## Metropolitan Community College: Blue River
### Independence, Missouri
www.mcckc.edu      CB code: 6060

- Public 2-year community college
- Commuter campus in small city

**General.** Regionally accredited. **Enrollment:** 2,030 degree-seeking undergraduates; 862 non-degree-seeking students. **Degrees:** 262 associate awarded. **Location:** 25 miles from Kansas City. **Calendar:** Semester, limited summer session. **Full-time faculty:** 35 total; 6% minority, 54% women. **Part-time faculty:** 268 total; 6% minority, 38% women. **Class size:** 32% < 20, 67% 20-39, less than 1% 50-99.

**Student profile.** Among degree-seeking undergraduates, 80% enrolled in a transfer program, 20% enrolled in a vocational program, 2% already have a bachelor's degree or higher, 533 enrolled as first-time, first-year students, 71 transferred in from other institutions.

| | | | |
|---|---|---|---|
| Part-time: | 50% | Hispanic American: | 3% |
| Out-of-state: | 1% | Native American: | 1% |
| Women: | 61% | 25 or older: | 32% |
| African American: | 2% | | |

**Basis for selection.** Open admission. **Homeschooled:** Statement describing homeschool structure and mission, transcript of courses and grades, interview required. Provide proof of graduation requirements. Applicants under age 16 must meet with Dean of Student Services and bring student portfolio.

**High school preparation.** 16 units recommended. Recommended units include English 4, mathematics 3, social studies 3, science 3 and foreign language 2. 1 visual/performing arts recommended.

**2007-2008 Annual costs.** Tuition/fees: $2,400; $4,260 out-of-district; $5,700 out-of-state. Per-credit charge: $75 in-district; $137 out-of-district; $185 out-of-state. Books/supplies: $700. Personal expenses: $1,500.

**2006-2007 Financial aid. Need-based:** Average scholarship/grant was $2,488; average loan $2,089. 20% of total undergraduate aid awarded as scholarships/grants, 80% as loans/jobs. Need-based aid available for part-time students. Work-study available nights and for part-time students. **Non-need-based:** Scholarships awarded for academics, athletics, leadership.

**Application procedures. Admission:** No deadline. No application fee. Application may be submitted online. Admission notification on a rolling

basis. **Financial aid:** Priority date 5/30, closing date 8/20. FAFSA, institutional form required. Applicants notified on a rolling basis starting 4/8.

**Academics. Special study options:** Accelerated study, cooperative education, cross-registration, distance learning, dual enrollment of high school students, honors, independent study, internships, weekend college. **Credit/placement by examination:** AP, CLEP, institutional tests. 30 credit hours maximum toward associate degree. **Support services:** GED test center, learning center, remedial instruction, tutoring.

**Majors. Business:** General, business admin. **Computer sciences:** Computer science. **Education:** General. **Engineering:** General. **Engineering technology:** Software. **Liberal arts:** Arts/sciences. **Protective services:** Firefighting, law enforcement admin, police science.

**Most popular majors.** Business/marketing 6%, liberal arts 83%, security/protective services 9%.

**Computing on campus.** 350 workstations in library, computer center. Commuter students can connect to campus network. Online course registration, online library, helpline available.

**Student life. Freshman orientation:** Available. Preregistration for classes offered. **Activities:** Choral groups, student government, student newspaper.

**Athletics. Intercollegiate:** Soccer. **Team name:** Trail Blazers.

**Student services.** Adult student services, career counseling, student employment services, personal counseling, placement for graduates, veterans' counselor. **Physically disabled:** Services for visually, hearing impaired. **Transfer:** Transfer adviser for students transferring to 4-year colleges.

**Contact.** Phone: (816) 220-6577
Basil Lister, Registrar, Metropolitan Community College: Blue River, 3200 Broadway, Kansas City, MO 64111-2429

## Metropolitan Community College: Longview
### Lee's Summit, Missouri
www.mcckc.edu      CB code: 6359

- Public 2-year community college
- Commuter campus in small city

**General.** Founded in 1968. Regionally accredited. **Enrollment:** 3,906 degree-seeking undergraduates; 1,633 non-degree-seeking students. **Degrees:** 455 associate awarded. **Location:** 10 miles from Kansas City. **Calendar:** Semester, extensive summer session. **Full-time faculty:** 84 total; 8% minority, 48% women. **Part-time faculty:** 296 total; 10% minority, 57% women. **Class size:** 38% < 20, 61% 20-39, less than 1% 40-49, less than 1% 50-99.

**Student profile.** Among degree-seeking undergraduates, 82% enrolled in a transfer program, 18% enrolled in a vocational program, 2% already have a bachelor's degree or higher, 1,142 enrolled as first-time, first-year students, 119 transferred in from other institutions.

| | | | |
|---|---|---|---|
| Part-time: | 45% | Asian American: | 1% |
| Out-of-state: | 1% | Hispanic American: | 2% |
| Women: | 60% | 25 or older: | 33% |
| African American: | 11% | | |

**Basis for selection.** Open admission, but selective for some programs. **Homeschooled:** Statement describing homeschool structure and mission, transcript of courses and grades, interview required. Provide proof of graduation requirements. Applicants under the age of 16 must meet with Dean of Student Services and bring student portfolio.

**High school preparation.** 16 units recommended. Recommended units include English 4, mathematics 3, social studies 3, science 3 and foreign language 2. One unit in visual/performing arts recommended.

**2007-2008 Annual costs.** Tuition/fees: $2,400; $4,260 out-of-district; $5,700 out-of-state. Per-credit charge: $75 in-district; $137 out-of-district; $185 out-of-state. Books/supplies: $700. Personal expenses: $1,500.

**2006-2007 Financial aid. Need-based:** Average scholarship/grant was $2,573; average loan $1,850. 29% of total undergraduate aid awarded as scholarships/grants, 71% as loans/jobs. Work-study available nights and for part-time students. **Non-need-based:** Scholarships awarded for academics, athletics, leadership.

**Application procedures. Admission:** No deadline. No application fee. Application may be submitted online. Admission notification on a rolling

basis. **Financial aid:** Priority date 5/30, closing date 8/20. FAFSA, institutional form required. Applicants notified on a rolling basis starting 4/8.

**Academics. Special study options:** Accelerated study, cooperative education, cross-registration, distance learning, dual enrollment of high school students, honors, independent study, internships, weekend college. **Credit/placement by examination:** AP, CLEP, institutional tests. 30 credit hours maximum toward associate degree. **Support services:** GED test center, learning center, remedial instruction, tutoring.

**Majors. Agriculture:** Turf management. **Business:** General, accounting, administrative services, business admin, office management, office technology, sales/distribution. **Computer sciences:** General, applications programming. **Education:** General. **Engineering:** General. **Engineering technology:** Surveying. **Liberal arts:** Arts/sciences. **Mechanic/repair:** Auto body, automotive. **Protective services:** Corrections, criminal justice.

**Most popular majors.** Business/marketing 7%, engineering/engineering technologies 7%, liberal arts 84%.

**Computing on campus.** 627 workstations in library, computer center. Commuter students can connect to campus network. Online course registration, helpline available.

**Student life. Freshman orientation:** Available. Preregistration for classes offered. **Activities:** Choral groups, drama, literary magazine, student government, student newspaper.

**Athletics.** NJCAA. **Intercollegiate:** Baseball M, volleyball W. **Intramural:** Basketball, swimming, volleyball. **Team name:** Lakers.

**Student services.** Adult student services, career counseling, student employment services, on-campus daycare, personal counseling, placement for graduates, veterans' counselor. **Physically disabled:** Services for visually, hearing impaired. **Transfer:** Transfer adviser for students transferring to 4-year colleges.

**Contact.** Phone: (816) 672-2000 Fax: (816) 672-2025
Kathy Hale, Registrar, Metropolitan Community College: Longview, 500 Longview Road, Lee's Summit, MO 64081-2105

## Metropolitan Community College: Maple Woods
### Kansas City, Missouri
www.mcckc.edu · CB code: 6436

- Public 2-year community college
- Commuter campus in large city

**General.** Founded in 1968. Regionally accredited. **Enrollment:** 3,100 degree-seeking undergraduates; 1,382 non-degree-seeking students. **Degrees:** 358 associate awarded. **Location:** 15 miles from downtown. **Calendar:** Semester, limited summer session. **Full-time faculty:** 57 total; 12% minority, 51% women. **Part-time faculty:** 260 total; 5% minority, 56% women. **Class size:** 39% < 20, 60% 20-39, less than 1% 40-49, less than 1% 50-99.

**Student profile.** Among degree-seeking undergraduates, 84% enrolled in a transfer program, 16% enrolled in a vocational program, 2% already have a bachelor's degree or higher, 925 enrolled as first-time, first-year students, 181 transferred in from other institutions.

| | | | |
|---|---|---|---|
| Part-time: | 46% | Asian American: | 2% |
| Women: | 58% | Hispanic American: | 3% |
| African American: | 3% | 25 or older: | 31% |

**Basis for selection.** Open admission, but selective for some programs. Special requirements for animal health technology program. **Home-schooled:** Provide proof of high school graduation. If under 16 years old must meet with Dean of Student Services and bring student portfolio.

**High school preparation.** 16 units recommended. Recommended units include English 4, mathematics 3, social studies 3, science 3 and foreign language 2. One unit in visual/performing arts recommended.

**2007-2008 Annual costs.** Tuition/fees: $2,400; $4,260 out-of-district; $5,700 out-of-state. Per-credit charge: $75 in-district; $137 out-of-district; $185 out-of-state. Books/supplies: $700. Personal expenses: $1,500.

**2006-2007 Financial aid. Need-based:** Average scholarship/grant was $2,634; average loan $1,670. 39% of total undergraduate aid awarded as scholarships/grants, 61% as loans/jobs. Need-based aid available for part-time students. Work-study available nights and for part-time students. **Non-need-based:** Scholarships awarded for academics, athletics, leadership.

**Application procedures. Admission:** No deadline. No application fee. Application may be submitted online. Admission notification on a rolling basis. Separate application required for animal health technology; deadline March 1. **Financial aid:** Priority date 5/30; no closing date. FAFSA, institutional form required. Applicants notified on a rolling basis.

**Academics. Special study options:** Cross-registration, distance learning, dual enrollment of high school students, exchange student, honors, internships. **Credit/placement by examination:** AP, CLEP, institutional tests. 30 credit hours maximum toward associate degree. **Support services:** GED test center, learning center, reduced course load, remedial instruction, tutoring.

**Majors. Business:** General, administrative services, business admin, office technology, sales/distribution. **Computer sciences:** General, applications programming. **Education:** General. **Engineering:** General. **Foreign languages:** Sign language interpretation. **Health:** Nursing (RN), veterinary technology/assistant. **Liberal arts:** Arts/sciences. **Physical sciences:** General. **Protective services:** Criminal justice, law enforcement admin.

**Most popular majors.** Health sciences 7%, liberal arts 83%.

**Computing on campus.** 370 workstations in computer center. Commuter students can connect to campus network. Online course registration, online library, helpline available.

**Student life. Freshman orientation:** Available. Preregistration for classes offered. **Activities:** Choral groups, student government, student newspaper.

**Athletics.** NJCAA. **Intercollegiate:** Baseball M, softball W. **Intramural:** Softball, volleyball W. **Team name:** Centaurs.

**Student services.** Adult student services, career counseling, student employment services, personal counseling, placement for graduates, veterans' counselor. **Physically disabled:** Services for visually, speech, hearing impaired. **Transfer:** Transfer adviser, college fairs on campus for students transferring to 4-year colleges.

**Contact.** Phone: (816) 437-3100 Fax: (816) 437-3049
Dawn Hatterman, Registrar, Metropolitan Community College: Maple Woods, 2601 NE Barry Road, Kansas City, MO 64156-1299

## Metropolitan Community College: Penn Valley
### Kansas City, Missouri
www.mcckc.edu · CB code: 6324

- Public 2-year community college
- Commuter campus in large city

**General.** Regionally accredited. **Enrollment:** 3,509 degree-seeking undergraduates; 1,031 non-degree-seeking students. **Degrees:** 446 associate awarded. **Location:** 2 miles from downtown. **Calendar:** Semester, extensive summer session. **Full-time faculty:** 106 total; 24% minority, 70% women. **Part-time faculty:** 312 total; 31% minority, 67% women. **Class size:** 60% < 20, 39% 20-39, less than 1% 40-49, less than 1% 50-99.

**Student profile.** Among degree-seeking undergraduates, 68% enrolled in a transfer program, 32% enrolled in a vocational program, 5% already have a bachelor's degree or higher, 695 enrolled as first-time, first-year students, 148 transferred in from other institutions.

| | | | |
|---|---|---|---|
| Part-time: | 64% | Asian American: | 3% |
| Out-of-state: | 3% | Hispanic American: | 5% |
| Women: | 73% | 25 or older: | 52% |
| African American: | 30% | | |

**Basis for selection.** Open admission, but selective for some programs. Special requirements for allied health programs. ACT or ASSET required for placement and counseling. **Homeschooled:** Statement describing homeschool structure and mission, transcript of courses and grades, interview required. Students under 16 must bring portfolio to Dean of Student Services.

**High school preparation.** 16 units recommended. Recommended units include English 4, mathematics 3, social studies 3, science 3 and foreign language 2. One unit visual/performing arts recommended.

**2007-2008 Annual costs.** Tuition/fees: $2,400; $4,260 out-of-district; $5,700 out-of-state. Per-credit charge: $75 in-district; $137 out-of-district; $185 out-of-state. Books/supplies: $700. Personal expenses: $1,500.

**2006-2007 Financial aid. Need-based:** Average scholarship/grant was $3,110; average loan $1,748. 13% of total undergraduate aid awarded as scholarships/grants, 87% as loans/jobs. Work-study available nights and for part-time students. **Non-need-based:** Scholarships awarded for academics, athletics, leadership.

**Application procedures. Admission:** No deadline. No application fee. Application may be submitted online. Admission notification on a rolling basis. **Financial aid:** Priority date 5/30; no closing date. FAFSA, institutional form required. Applicants notified on a rolling basis starting 4/8.

**Academics. Special study options:** Cross-registration, distance learning, dual enrollment of high school students, ESL, honors, internships, liberal arts/career combination, weekend college. Cooperative programs in allied health with Johnson County Community College. License preparation in dental hygiene, nursing, occupational therapy, paramedic, physical therapy, radiology. **Credit/placement by examination:** AP, CLEP, institutional tests. 30 credit hours maximum toward associate degree. **Support services:** GED test center, learning center, reduced course load, remedial instruction, tutoring.

**Majors. Business:** General, accounting, administrative services, business admin, fashion, office management, office technology, sales/distribution. **Computer sciences:** General. **Education:** General. **Engineering:** General. **Family/consumer sciences:** Child care. **Health:** Dental assistant, EMT paramedic, medical radiologic technology/radiation therapy, mental health services, nursing (RN), occupational therapy assistant, physical therapy assistant, respiratory therapy technology. **Legal studies:** Paralegal. **Liberal arts:** Arts/sciences. **Mechanic/repair:** Heating/ac/refrig. **Protective services:** Corrections, criminal justice, law enforcement admin. **Visual/performing arts:** Commercial/advertising art, fashion design, graphic design, music.

**Most popular majors.** Business/marketing 6%, family/consumer sciences 9%, health sciences 47%, liberal arts 30%, visual/performing arts 6%.

**Computing on campus.** 1,095 workstations in library, computer center.

**Student life. Freshman orientation:** Available. **Activities:** Jazz band, drama, music ensembles, opera, student government, student newspaper, Black student association, Los Americanos.

**Athletics.** NJCAA. **Intercollegiate:** Basketball M, golf M. **Team name:** Scouts.

**Student services.** Career counseling, student employment services, on-campus daycare, personal counseling, placement for graduates, veterans' counselor. **Physically disabled:** Services for visually, speech, hearing impaired.

**Contact.** Phone: (816) 759-4100 Fax: (816) 759-4161
Carroll O'Neal, Registrar, Metropolitan Community College: Penn Valley, 3201 Southwest Trafficway, Kansas City, MO 64111-2429

## Mineral Area College
**Park Hills, Missouri**
www.mineralarea.edu                    CB code: 6323

- Public 2-year community college
- Commuter campus in small town

**General.** Founded in 1922. Regionally accredited. **Location:** 60 miles from St. Louis. **Calendar:** Semester.

**Annual costs/financial aid.** Tuition/fees (2007-2008): $2,549; $3,293 out-of-district; $3,882 out-of-state. Room/board: $2,700. Books/supplies: $1,400. Need-based financial aid available to full-time and part-time students.

**Contact.** Phone: (573) 518-2206
Admissions Officer, PO Box 1000, Park Hills, MO 63601-1000

## Missouri College
**St. Louis, Missouri**
www.missouricollege.com                 CB code: 3074

- For-profit 2-year technical college
- Commuter campus in large city

**General.** Accredited by ACCSCT. **Calendar:** Continuous.

**Annual costs/financial aid.** Tuition varies by program. Total costs range from $12,019 to $14,450 for diplomas; $24,785 to $25,736 for Associate degrees; $44,703 to $48,525 for Bachelor's degrees. Books/supplies: $1,409. Need-based financial aid available to full-time and part-time students.

**Contact.** Phone: (314) 821-7700
Director of Admissions, 10121 Manchester Road, St. Louis, MO 63122-1583

## Missouri State University: West Plains
**West Plains, Missouri**
www.wp.missouristate.edu                 CB code: 6662

- Public 2-year branch campus college
- Commuter campus in large town

**General.** Regionally accredited. **Enrollment:** 1,340 degree-seeking undergraduates; 417 non-degree-seeking students. **Degrees:** 210 associate awarded. **Location:** 110 miles from Springfield. **Calendar:** Semester, limited summer session. **Full-time faculty:** 30 total; 23% have terminal degrees, 7% minority, 50% women. **Part-time faculty:** 78 total; 13% have terminal degrees, 59% women. **Class size:** 53% < 20, 46% 20-39, less than 1% 40-49.

**Student profile.** Among degree-seeking undergraduates, 74% enrolled in a transfer program, 26% enrolled in a vocational program, 1% already have a bachelor's degree or higher, 423 enrolled as first-time, first-year students, 57 transferred in from other institutions.

| | | | |
|---|---|---|---|
| Part-time: | 28% | Hispanic American: | 1% |
| Out-of-state: | 4% | Native American: | 2% |
| Women: | 62% | 25 or older: | 27% |
| African American: | 2% | Live on campus: | 4% |
| Asian American: | 1% | | |

**Transfer out.** 38% of students enrolled in the transfer program go on to 4-year colleges. **Colleges most students transferred to 2007:** Missouri State University: Springfield.

**Basis for selection.** Open admission, but selective for some programs. Nursing and respiratory therapy programs require separate application and applicants are considered competitively. **Homeschooled:** Transcript of courses and grades required. Must submit ACT score (minimum 18) or official GED transcript.

**2008-2009 Annual costs.** Tuition/fees (projected): $3,304; $6,364 out-of-state. Room/board: $4,632. Books/supplies: $870. Personal expenses: $2,480.

**2006-2007 Financial aid. Need-based:** 65% of total undergraduate aid awarded as scholarships/grants, 35% as loans/jobs. Need-based aid available for part-time students. Work-study available nights, weekends and for part-time students. **Non-need-based:** Scholarships awarded for academics, athletics, state residency.

**Application procedures. Admission:** Closing date 8/21 (postmark date). $15 fee, may be waived for applicants with need. Application may be submitted online. Admission notification on a rolling basis. **Financial aid:** Priority date 3/31; no closing date. FAFSA, institutional form required. Applicants notified on a rolling basis; must reply by 4/15.

**Academics. Special study options:** Distance learning, dual enrollment of high school students, honors, independent study, internships, liberal arts/career combination, student-designed major, study abroad. Bachelor's degree programs available on campus. License preparation in nursing. **Credit/placement by examination:** AP, CLEP, IB, institutional tests. 15 credit hours maximum toward associate degree. **Support services:** GED test center, learning center, remedial instruction, study skills assistance, tutoring, writing center.

**Majors. Agriculture:** Business, food science, horticultural science. **Business:** General, entrepreneurial studies. **Communications technology:** Animation/special effects. **Computer sciences:** General. **Engineering technology:** Industrial, manufacturing. **Family/consumer sciences:** Child care. **Health:** Nursing (RN), respiratory therapy technology. **Liberal arts:** Arts/sciences. **Protective services:** Police science.

**Most popular majors.** Health sciences 27%, liberal arts 64%.

**Computing on campus.** 104 workstations in dormitories, library, computer center, student center. Dormitories wired for high-speed internet access and linked to campus network. Commuter students can connect to campus network. Online course registration, online library, helpline, repair service, wireless network available.

**Student life. Freshman orientation:** Mandatory. Preregistration for classes offered. Half-day sessions held throughout summer. **Housing:** Coed dorms, substance-free housing available. $100 deposit. **Activities:** Pep band, choral groups, drama, student government, Campus Crusade for Christ.

**Athletics.** NJCAA. **Intercollegiate:** Basketball M, cheerleading, volleyball W. **Team name:** Grizzlies.

**Student services.** Career counseling, student employment services, financial aid counseling, health services, minority student services, personal counseling, placement for graduates, veterans' counselor. **Physically disabled:** Services for visually, hearing impaired. **Transfer:** Transfer adviser, college fairs on campus for students transferring to 4-year colleges.

**Contact.** E-mail: wpadmissions@missouristate.edu
Phone: (417) 255-7955 Toll-free number: (888) 466-7897
Fax: (417) 255-7959
Melissa Jett, Coordinator of Admissions, Missouri State University: West Plains, 128 Garfield Avenue, West Plains, MO 65775-2715

## Moberly Area Community College
### Moberly, Missouri
**www.macc.edu**                                    **CB code: 6414**

- Public 2-year community college
- Commuter campus in large town

**General.** Founded in 1927. Regionally accredited. **Enrollment:** 2,984 degree-seeking undergraduates; 1,028 non-degree-seeking students. **Degrees:** 413 associate awarded. **Location:** 35 miles from Columbia. **Calendar:** Semester, extensive summer session. **Full-time faculty:** 66 total. **Part-time faculty:** 191 total. **Special facilities:** Multimedia/instructional television center, graphic arts/fine arts gallery.

**Student profile.** Among degree-seeking undergraduates, 75% enrolled in a transfer program, 25% enrolled in a vocational program, 2% already have a bachelor's degree or higher, 927 enrolled as first-time, first-year students, 187 transferred in from other institutions.

| | | | |
|---|---|---|---|
| Part-time: | 36% | 25 or older: | 24% |
| Out-of-state: | 2% | Live on campus: | 2% |
| Women: | 60% | | |

**Transfer out.** 75% of students enrolled in the transfer program go on to 4-year colleges. **Colleges most students transferred to 2007:** Central Methodist University, Columbia College, University of Missouri.

**Basis for selection.** Open admission, but selective for some programs. Special requirements for allied health and law enforcement programs. ACT scores required for admission to nursing programs. Degree-seeking students, or those taking 14 or more credits, must have ACT or ASSET score for placement purposes; tests also required for students enrolling in English or math courses. **Homeschooled:** Applicants must provide transcript outlining educational process or take GED.

**2007-2008 Annual costs.** Tuition/fees: $2,160; $2,970 out-of-district; $4,380 out-of-state. Per-credit charge: $61 in-district; $88 out-of-district; $135 out-of-state. Room only: $2,200. Books/supplies: $800. Personal expenses: $1,500.

**2007-2008 Financial aid. Need-based:** 575 full-time freshmen applied for aid; 322 were judged to have need; 322 of these received aid. Average need met was 50%. Average scholarship/grant was $2,363; average loan $2,676. 63% of total undergraduate aid awarded as scholarships/grants, 37% as loans/jobs. Need-based aid available for part-time students. Work-study available nights, weekends and for part-time students. **Non-need-based:** Scholarships awarded for academics, alumni affiliation, art, athletics, leadership, music/drama.

**Application procedures. Admission:** No deadline. No application fee. Application may be submitted online. Admission notification on a rolling basis. **Financial aid:** Priority date 4/1; no closing date. FAFSA required. Applicants notified on a rolling basis starting 4/1; must reply by 7/15 or within 2 week(s) of notification.

**Academics. Special study options:** Cooperative education, distance learning, dual enrollment of high school students, honors, internships, study abroad, teacher certification program. License preparation in nursing, paramedic. **Credit/placement by examination:** AP, CLEP, IB, institutional tests. 30 credit hours maximum toward associate degree. **Support services:** GED preparation, learning center, remedial instruction, study skills assistance, tutoring.

**Majors. Business:** Accounting technology, marketing, office/clerical. **Communications:** Journalism. **Communications technology:** Graphic/printing. **Computer sciences:** Programming. **Education:** Voc/tech. **Engineering:** General. **Engineering technology:** Biomedical, drafting, electrical, manufacturing. **Family/consumer sciences:** Child care. **Health:** Nursing (RN). **Liberal arts:** Arts/sciences. **Production:** Welding.

**Most popular majors.** Health sciences 7%, liberal arts 80%.

**Computing on campus.** 750 workstations in dormitories, library, computer center. Dormitories wired for high-speed internet access. Commuter students can connect to campus network. Online library, helpline, repair service, wireless network available.

**Student life. Freshman orientation:** Available. Preregistration for classes offered. Half-day program held during late summer. **Housing:** Single-sex dorms, substance-free housing available. $150 deposit, deadline 8/20. Limited housing available. **Activities:** Choral groups, drama, literary magazine, student government, student newspaper, Phi Theta Kappa, Association for the Education of Young Children, Brothers OX, service organizations, multicultural club.

**Athletics.** NJCAA. **Intercollegiate:** Basketball, cheerleading. **Intramural:** Basketball, volleyball. **Team name:** Greyhounds.

**Student services.** Adult student services, career counseling, services for economically disadvantaged, student employment services, financial aid counseling, placement for graduates. **Physically disabled:** Services for visually, speech, hearing impaired. **Transfer:** Pre-admission transcript evaluation for new students. Transfer adviser, college fairs on campus for students transferring to 4-year colleges.

**Contact.** E-mail: info@macc.edu
Phone: (660) 263-4110 ext. 270 Toll-free number: (800) 622-2070 ext. 270
Fax: (660) 263-2406
James Grant, Dean of Student Services, Moberly Area Community College, 101 College Avenue, Moberly, MO 65270-1304

## North Central Missouri College
### Trenton, Missouri
**www.ncmissouri.edu**                              **CB code: 6830**

- Public 2-year community college
- Commuter campus in small town

**General.** Founded in 1925. Regionally accredited. Evening classes offered at outreach sites in many area communities. **Enrollment:** 1,020 degree-seeking undergraduates. **Degrees:** 208 associate awarded. **Location:** 90 miles from Kansas City. **Calendar:** Semester, limited summer session. **Full-time faculty:** 29 total. **Part-time faculty:** 75 total. **Special facilities:** Academic reinforcement center.

**Student profile.**

| | | | |
|---|---|---|---|
| Out-of-state: | 2% | Live on campus: | 8% |
| 25 or older: | 28% | | |

**Transfer out. Colleges most students transferred to 2007:** Missouri Western State College, Northwest Missouri State University, Southwest Missouri State University, Central Missouri State University.

**Basis for selection.** Open admission, but selective for some programs. Special requirements for associate and certificate programs in nursing. ASSET scores may be substituted for ACT. Interview required for nursing students.

**2007-2008 Annual costs.** Tuition/fees: $2,430; $3,390 out-of-district; $4,470 out-of-state. Per-credit charge: $63 in-district; $95 out-of-district; $131 out-of-state. Room/board: $4,782. Books/supplies: $800. Personal expenses: $1,029.

**Financial aid. Need-based:** Need-based aid available for part-time students. **Non-need-based:** Scholarships awarded for academics, athletics, minority status, music/drama.

**Application procedures. Admission:** No deadline. $15 fee. Application must be submitted on paper. Admission notification on a rolling basis beginning on or about 2/1. **Financial aid:** Priority date 3/15; no closing date. FAFSA, institutional form required. Applicants notified on a rolling basis starting 3/15.

**Academics. Special study options:** Cooperative education, distance learning, double major, dual enrollment of high school students, internships, liberal arts/career combination. Bachelor's degree programs available on campus. License preparation in nursing, paramedic. **Credit/placement by examination:** AP, CLEP, institutional tests. 30 credit hours maximum toward associate degree. **Support services:** GED preparation and test center, learning center, reduced course load, remedial instruction, study skills assistance, tutoring.

**Majors. Agriculture:** Agribusiness operations, farm/ranch. **Business:** Accounting, business admin, office technology, office/clerical. **Computer sciences:** General. **Construction:** Maintenance. **Education:** General. **Health:**

Nursing (RN), office assistant. **Liberal arts:** Arts/sciences. **Mechanic/repair:** General, auto body, electronics/electrical. **Protective services:** Criminal justice. **Public administration:** Human services.

**Most popular majors.** Business/marketing 10%, health sciences 22%, liberal arts 54%.

**Computing on campus.** 163 workstations in dormitories, library, computer center, student center. Dormitories wired for high-speed internet access. Helpline available.

**Student life. Freshman orientation:** Available. **Housing:** Single-sex dorms, substance-free housing available. $100 partly refundable deposit. **Activities:** Drama, student government, Baptist Student Union.

**Athletics.** NJCAA. **Intercollegiate:** Baseball M, basketball, softball W. **Intramural:** Volleyball. **Team name:** Pirates.

**Student services.** Alcohol/substance abuse counseling, career counseling, student employment services, financial aid counseling, personal counseling, placement for graduates. **Physically disabled:** Services for visually, speech, hearing impaired. **Transfer:** Transfer adviser, college fairs on campus for students transferring to 4-year colleges.

**Contact.** E-mail: admissions@mail.ncmissouri.edu
Phone: (660) 359-3948 ext. 401 Toll-free number: (800) 880-6180 ext. 401
Fax: (660) 359-2211
Karla McCollum, Admission Director, North Central Missouri College, 1301 Main Street, Trenton, MO 64683

## Ozarks Technical Community College
### Springfield, Missouri
www.otc.edu                     CB code: 2583

▶ Public 2-year community and technical college
▶ Commuter campus in small city

**General.** Regionally accredited. **Enrollment:** 8,934 degree-seeking undergraduates; 1,315 non-degree-seeking students. **Degrees:** 866 associate awarded. **Location:** 160 miles from Kansas City, 250 miles from St. Louis. **Calendar:** Semester, extensive summer session. **Full-time faculty:** 165 total. **Part-time faculty:** 290 total.

**Student profile.** Among degree-seeking undergraduates, 50% enrolled in a transfer program, 37% enrolled in a vocational program, 1% already have a bachelor's degree or higher, 2,274 enrolled as first-time, first-year students.

| | | | |
|---|---|---|---|
| Part-time: | 44% | Asian American: | 2% |
| Out-of-state: | 1% | Hispanic American: | 2% |
| Women: | 56% | Native American: | 1% |
| African American: | 2% | 25 or older: | 29% |

**Transfer out. Colleges most students transferred to 2007:** Drury University, Evangel University, Southwest Missouri State University.

**Basis for selection.** Open admission, but selective for some programs. Special requirements for some allied health programs.

**2007-2008 Annual costs.** Tuition/fees: $2,850; $3,750 out-of-district; $4,725 out-of-state. Per-credit charge: $78 in-district; $108 out-of-district; $140 out-of-state. Books/supplies: $600. Personal expenses: $1,100.

**Financial aid.** All financial aid based on need. Need-based aid available for part-time students. Work-study available for part-time students.

**Application procedures. Admission:** No deadline. No application fee. Admission notification on a rolling basis. **Financial aid:** Priority date 5/1, closing date 7/1. FAFSA, institutional form required. Applicants notified on a rolling basis starting 5/16.

**Academics. Special study options:** Cooperative education, distance learning, dual enrollment of high school students, ESL, independent study, internships. License preparation in dental hygiene, nursing, paramedic. **Credit/placement by examination:** CLEP, IB, institutional tests. **Support services:** GED preparation and test center, learning center, reduced course load, remedial instruction, study skills assistance, tutoring, writing center.

**Majors. Agriculture:** Turf management. **Business:** Accounting, business admin, hospitality admin, hotel/motel admin, office technology. **Communications:** Digital media. **Communications technology:** Graphic/printing. **Computer sciences:** Information technology, LAN/WAN management, web page design. **Engineering:** Electrical. **Engineering technology:** CAD/CADD, construction, electrical, industrial. **Family/consumer sciences:** Child development. **Health:** Dental hygiene, EMT paramedic, licensed practical nurse,

medical records technology, occupational therapy assistant, physical therapy assistant, respiratory therapy technology. **Liberal arts:** Arts/sciences. **Mechanic/repair:** Auto body, automotive, diesel, heating/ac/refrig, industrial. **Personal/culinary services:** Culinary arts. **Production:** Machine tool, welding. **Protective services:** Fire safety technology. **Visual/performing arts:** Graphic design.

**Most popular majors.** Business/marketing 19%, computer/information sciences 6%, health sciences 7%, liberal arts 50%, trade and industry 8%.

**Computing on campus.** 250 workstations in library, computer center. Commuter students can connect to campus network. Online course registration, online library, helpline, wireless network available.

**Student life. Freshman orientation:** Available. Preregistration for classes offered. **Activities:** Student government, student newspaper, Phi Theta Kappa, National Honor Society, Women in Construction, nursing students groups, Phi Beta Lambda, national business organizations, electronics club, Society of Manufacturing Engineers.

**Athletics. Team name:** Eagles.

**Student services.** Career counseling, student employment services, financial aid counseling, on-campus daycare, personal counseling, placement for graduates. **Physically disabled:** Services for visually, speech, hearing impaired. **Transfer:** Transfer adviser, college fairs on campus for students transferring to 4-year colleges.

**Contact.** Phone: (417) 447-6900 Fax: (417) 447-6906
Peter Sullivan, Director of Admissions, Ozarks Technical Community College, 1001 East Chestnut Expressway, Springfield, MO 65802

## Patricia Stevens College
### St. Louis, Missouri
www.patriciastevenscollege.edu          CB code: 3319

▶ For-profit 2-year junior and liberal arts college
▶ Commuter campus in very large city
▶ Application essay, interview required

**General.** Accredited by ACICS. **Enrollment:** 175 degree-seeking undergraduates. **Degrees:** 95 associate awarded. **Location:** Downtown. **Calendar:** Quarter, extensive summer session. **Full-time faculty:** 5 total. **Part-time faculty:** 18 total. **Class size:** 95% < 20, 5% 20-39.

**Student profile.**

| | | | |
|---|---|---|---|
| Out-of-state: | 26% | 25 or older: | 39% |

**Transfer out. Colleges most students transferred to 2007:** Fontbonne University, Lindenwood University, Maryville University, University of Phoenix, Webster University.

**Basis for selection.** Open admission, but selective for some programs. Every applicant is interviewed by the admissions staff. High school and other college transcripts are analyzed, as are attendance records and college entrance examinations such as SAT and ACT. Other achievements in the community and workplace considered. SAT or ACT scores are only required of students enrolling in a bachelor's degree program with less than 90 quarter hours in transfer credits. SAT or ACT scores are not required for students enrolling in an AAS program. **Homeschooled:** Statement describing homeschool structure and mission, transcript of courses and grades, interview required.

**2007-2008 Annual costs.** Tuition/fees: $10,050. Per-credit charge: $195. Cost of tuition is $210 per credit hour, regardless of the number of hours enrolled per term. Use of textbooks included in tuition.

**Financial aid.** All financial aid based on need. Need-based aid available for part-time students.

**Application procedures. Admission:** No deadline. $15 fee. Application must be submitted on paper. Admission notification on a rolling basis. **Financial aid:** No deadline. FAFSA required. Applicants notified on a rolling basis.

**Academics. Special study options:** Accelerated study, double major, internships. **Credit/placement by examination:** AP, CLEP. **Support services:** Reduced course load, study skills assistance, tutoring.

**Majors. Business:** Business admin, fashion, hospitality admin, retailing, tourism/travel, travel services. **Legal studies:** Paralegal. **Visual/performing arts:** Interior design.

**Most popular majors.** Business/marketing 26%, health sciences 7%, legal studies 24%.

**Computing on campus.** 42 workstations in library, computer center. Wireless network available.

**Student life. Freshman orientation:** Mandatory. Preregistration for classes offered. Held each quarter before start of classes. **Policies:** Dress code and attendance policies enforced.

**Student services.** Adult student services, alcohol/substance abuse counseling, career counseling, student employment services, financial aid counseling, placement for graduates. **Transfer:** Pre-admission transcript evaluation for new students. Transfer adviser, college fairs on campus for students transferring to 4-year colleges.

**Contact.** E-mail: admissions@patriciastevenscollege.edu
Phone: (314) 421-0949 ext. 12 Toll-free number: (800) 871-0949 ext. 12
Fax: (314) 421-0304
John Willmon, Director of Admissions, Patricia Stevens College, 330 North Fourth Street, Suite 306, St. Louis, MO 63102

## Pinnacle Career Institute: Kansas City
### Kansas City, Missouri
www.pcitraining.edu                                   CB code: 2271

- For-profit 2-year technical college
- Large city

**General.** Accredited by ACCSCT. **Enrollment:** 527 full-time, degree-seeking students. **Degrees:** 13 associate awarded. **Calendar:** Quarter, limited summer session. **Full-time faculty:** 5 total. **Part-time faculty:** 18 total.

**Student profile.** Among full-time, degree-seeking students, 100% enrolled in a vocational program. Of all enrolled students, 1% already have a bachelor's degree or higher.

| African American: | 45% | Hispanic American: | 3% |
|---|---|---|---|

**Basis for selection.** Open admission. **Homeschooled:** Transcript of courses and grades, interview required.

**2007-2008 Annual costs.** Books/supplies: $965.

**Application procedures. Admission:** No deadline. $50 fee. Application must be submitted on paper. Admission notification on a rolling basis. **Financial aid:** No deadline.

**Academics. Credit/placement by examination:** CLEP. **Support services:** Study skills assistance, tutoring.

**Majors. Business:** Executive assistant. **Engineering technology:** Electrical. **Health:** Medical assistant.

**Computing on campus.** 30 workstations in computer center.

**Contact.** E-mail: bricks@pcitraining.edu
Phone: (816) 331-5700 Toll-free number: (800) 676-7912
Fax: (816) 331-2026
Maggie Franz, Admissions Coordinator, Pinnacle Career Institute: Kansas City, 1001 East 101st Terrace, Suite 325, Kansas City, MO 64131-3367

## Ranken Technical College
### St. Louis, Missouri
www.ranken.edu                                   CB code: 7028

- Private 2-year technical college
- Commuter campus in very large city
- Interview required

**General.** Founded in 1907. Regionally accredited. **Enrollment:** 1,739 degree-seeking undergraduates. **Degrees:** 11 bachelor's, 316 associate awarded. **Location:** 3 miles from downtown. **Calendar:** Semester, limited summer session. **Full-time faculty:** 58 total; 2% have terminal degrees, 10% minority, 9% women. **Part-time faculty:** 49 total; 2% have terminal degrees, 14% women. **Partnerships:** Formal partnership with the GM-ASEP program.

**Student profile.** Among degree-seeking undergraduates, 100% enrolled in a vocational program, 1% already have a bachelor's degree or higher, 613 enrolled as first-time, first-year students.

| Part-time: | 34% | Asian American: | 1% |
|---|---|---|---|
| Out-of-state: | 43% | Hispanic American: | 1% |
| Women: | 4% | Live on campus: | 3% |
| African American: | 13% | | |

**Basis for selection.** Open admission. Institutional placement test and counseling session required. Admission counseling sessions recommended, but not required. **Homeschooled:** State high school equivalency certificate required. **Learning Disabled:** We have facilities available to students with special accomodations needs with appropriate documentation.

**2007-2008 Annual costs.** Tuition/fees: $11,340. Per-credit charge: $373. Book and tool costs vary by program. Books/supplies: $1,700. Personal expenses: $1,774.

**2006-2007 Financial aid. Need-based:** 17% of total undergraduate aid awarded as scholarships/grants, 83% as loans/jobs. Need-based aid available for part-time students. Work-study available nights.

**Application procedures. Admission:** No deadline. $25 fee, may be waived for applicants with need. Application may be submitted online. Admission notification on a rolling basis. Interview and tour recommended for new applicants. **Financial aid:** No deadline. FAFSA required. Applicants notified on a rolling basis starting 4/1.

**Academics. Special study options:** Combined bachelor's/graduate degree, cooperative education, distance learning, double major, dual enrollment of high school students, internships, study abroad. Bachelor's degree programs available on campus. **Credit/placement by examination:** AP, CLEP, IB, institutional tests. **Support services:** Learning center, pre-admission summer program, reduced course load, remedial instruction, study skills assistance, tutoring, writing center.

**Majors. Architecture:** Environmental design. **Communications technology:** General. **Computer sciences:** General, LAN/WAN management, webmaster. **Construction:** Carpentry. **Engineering technology:** Electrical. **Mechanic/repair:** Auto body, automotive, electronics/electrical, heating/ac/refrig, industrial. **Production:** Machine shop technology.

**Computing on campus.** 60 workstations in library, computer center, student center. Commuter students can connect to campus network. Online library, repair service, wireless network available.

**Student life. Freshman orientation:** Mandatory. Preregistration for classes offered. Four hour session held the week before classes begin. **Housing:** Apartments available. **Activities:** Student government, student newspaper, women's support program, Phi Theta Kappa.

**Student services.** Adult student services, alcohol/substance abuse counseling, career counseling, services for economically disadvantaged, student employment services, financial aid counseling, minority student services, personal counseling, placement for graduates, veterans' counselor, women's services. **Physically disabled:** Services for visually, speech, hearing impaired. **Transfer:** Pre-admission transcript evaluation for new students. Transfer adviser, college fairs on campus for students transferring to 4-year colleges.

**Contact.** E-mail: admissions@ranken.edu
Phone: (314) 371-0236 Toll-free number: (866) 472-6536
Fax: (314) 371-0241
Michael Hawley, Director of Admissions, Ranken Technical College, 4431 Finney Avenue, St. Louis, MO 63113

## St. Charles Community College
### Cottleville, Missouri
www.stchas.edu                                   CB code: 0168

- Public 2-year community college
- Commuter campus in small city

**General.** Founded in 1986. Regionally accredited. **Enrollment:** 6,097 degree-seeking undergraduates; 930 non-degree-seeking students. **Degrees:** 585 associate awarded. **Location:** 35 miles from St. Louis. **Calendar:** Semester, limited summer session. **Full-time faculty:** 90 total; 22% have terminal degrees, 2% minority, 57% women. **Part-time faculty:** 373 total; 5% minority, 59% women.

**Student profile.** Among degree-seeking undergraduates, 83% enrolled in a transfer program, 17% enrolled in a vocational program, 1,528 enrolled as first-time, first-year students.

| | | | |
|---|---|---|---|
| Part-time: | 45% | Hispanic American: | 2% |
| Women: | 61% | International: | 1% |
| African American: | 4% | 25 or older: | 29% |
| Asian American: | 2% | | |

**Transfer out.** 58% of students enrolled in the transfer program go on to 4-year colleges. **Colleges most students transferred to 2007:** University of Missouri: St. Louis, Lindenwood University, University of Missouri: Columbia, Southwest Missouri State University, Maryville University.

**Basis for selection.** Open admission, but selective for some programs. Special requirements for nursing and allied health programs, including ACT. Limited enrollment for nursing program with preference given to in-state applicants. Must submit ACT scores by August 20th for allied health and nursing programs. **Homeschooled:** Transcript of courses and grades required.

**High school preparation.** 16 units recommended. Recommended units include English 4, mathematics 3, social studies 3, science 2, foreign language 2 and academic electives 1. One visual or performing arts recommended.

**2007-2008 Annual costs.** Tuition/fees: $2,400; $3,540 out-of-district; $5,250 out-of-state. Per-credit charge: $80 in-district; $118 out-of-district; $175 out-of-state. Books/supplies: $1,020. Personal expenses: $1,800.

**2006-2007 Financial aid. Need-based:** 60% of total undergraduate aid awarded as scholarships/grants, 40% as loans/jobs. Need-based aid available for part-time students. Work-study available for part-time students. **Non-need-based:** Scholarships awarded for academics, art, athletics, leadership, music/drama.

**Application procedures. Admission:** No deadline. No application fee. Application must be submitted on paper. Admission notification on a rolling basis. **Financial aid:** Priority date 8/1; no closing date. FAFSA, institutional form required. Applicants notified on a rolling basis starting 3/1.

**Academics. Special study options:** Combined bachelor's/graduate degree, distance learning, double major, dual enrollment of high school students, ESL, independent study, internships, liberal arts/career combination, study abroad. License preparation in nursing, occupational therapy, paramedic. **Credit/placement by examination:** AP, CLEP, IB, ACT, institutional tests. 49 credit hours maximum toward associate degree. **Support services:** GED preparation and test center, learning center, pre-admission summer program, remedial instruction, study skills assistance, tutoring, writing center.

**Majors. Biology:** General. **Business:** Accounting technology, marketing, office management. **Computer sciences:** Programming. **Education:** General, teacher assistance. **Engineering:** General, civil, mechanical. **Engineering technology:** Drafting, industrial. **English:** English lit, speech/rhetoric. **Family/consumer sciences:** Child care. **Foreign languages:** General, French, Spanish. **Health:** EMT paramedic, massage therapy, medical records technology, nursing (RN), occupational therapy assistant. **History:** General. **Liberal arts:** Arts/sciences. **Math:** General. **Philosophy/religion:** Philosophy. **Physical sciences:** Chemistry. **Protective services:** Firefighting, police science. **Psychology:** General. **Public administration:** Human services, social work. **Social sciences:** Economics, political science, sociology. **Visual/performing arts:** Commercial/advertising art, dramatic, music history. **Other:** Pre-Chiropractor, Skilled Trades Apprenticeship Training, Teacher Education.

**Most popular majors.** Health sciences 16%, liberal arts 73%.

**Computing on campus.** 131 workstations in library, computer center, student center. Online library, helpline, wireless network available.

**Student life. Freshman orientation:** Available. **Activities:** Choral groups, drama, literary magazine, music ensembles, student government, student newspaper, criminal justice student organization, education of young children club, math club, Phi Theta Kappa, art club, human services student organization, returning learners club, sociology and anthropology club, communications, psychology club.

**Athletics.** NJCAA. **Intercollegiate:** Baseball M, softball W. **Intramural:** Volleyball. **Team name:** Cougars.

**Student services.** Adult student services, career counseling, student employment services, financial aid counseling, on-campus daycare, placement for graduates, veterans' counselor. **Physically disabled:** Services for visually, speech, hearing impaired. **Transfer:** Pre-admission transcript evaluation for new students. Transfer adviser, college fairs on campus for students transferring to 4-year colleges.

**Contact.** E-mail: adm-reg@stchas.edu
Phone: (636) 922-8237 Fax: (636) 922-8236
Kathy Brockgreitens-Gober, Director of Admissions and Financial Assistance, St. Charles Community College, 4601 Mid Rivers Mall Drive, Cottleville, MO 63376

## St. Louis Community College
### St. Louis, Missouri
**www.stlcc.edu**                                     CB code: 6226

- Public 2-year community and junior college
- Commuter campus in large city

**General.** Founded in 1962. Regionally accredited. **Calendar:** Semester.

**Annual costs/financial aid.** Tuition/fees (2007-2008): $2,430; $3,540 out-of-district; $4,440 out-of-state. Books/supplies: $800. Personal expenses: $2,100. Need-based financial aid available to full-time and part-time students.

**Contact.** Phone: (314) 644-9127
Manager, Admissions/Registration, 300 South Broadway, St. Louis, MO 63102-2800

## St. Louis Community College at Florissant Valley
### St. Louis, Missouri
**www.stlcc.edu**                                     CB code: 6225

- Public 2-year branch campus and community college
- Commuter campus in large city

**General.** Founded in 1962. Regionally accredited. **Enrollment:** 6,240 undergraduates. **Degrees:** 454 associate awarded. **ROTC:** Army. **Location:** 17 miles from downtown. **Calendar:** Semester, extensive summer session. **Full-time faculty:** 140 total. **Part-time faculty:** 250 total. **Special facilities:** Observatory, child development center.

**Student profile.**

| | | | |
|---|---|---|---|
| Out-of-state: | 2% | 25 or older: | 48% |

**Basis for selection.** Open admission, but selective for some programs. Nursing program applicants required to pass institutional test.

**2007-2008 Annual costs.** Tuition/fees: $2,430; $3,540 out-of-district; $4,440 out-of-state. Per-credit charge: $81 in-district; $118 out-of-district; $148 out-of-state. Books/supplies: $800. Personal expenses: $2,000.

**Application procedures. Admission:** No deadline. No application fee. Admission notification on a rolling basis. **Financial aid:** Priority date 8/1; no closing date. FAFSA required. Applicants notified on a rolling basis starting 5/1.

**Academics. Special study options:** Cooperative education, cross-registration, distance learning, dual enrollment of high school students, ESL, exchange student, honors, independent study, internships, study abroad, teacher certification program, weekend college. Bachelor's degree programs available on campus. **Credit/placement by examination:** CLEP, institutional tests. 49 credit hours maximum toward associate degree. **Support services:** Learning center, remedial instruction, tutoring.

**Majors. Biology:** General. **Business:** Administrative services, banking/financial services, business admin, fashion, management information systems, office technology. **Communications:** General, advertising, broadcast journalism, journalism, public relations. **Communications technology:** Graphic/printing. **Computer sciences:** General, applications programming, data processing, programming, systems analysis. **Education:** Early childhood, teacher assistance. **Engineering:** General. **Engineering technology:** Civil, computer hardware, drafting, electrical, manufacturing, mechanical. **English:** Speech/rhetoric, technical writing. **Family/consumer sciences:** Child care. **Foreign languages:** Sign language interpretation. **Health:** Predental, premedicine, prepharmacy. **Liberal arts:** Arts/sciences. **Math:** General. **Personal/culinary services:** Culinary arts. **Physical sciences:** Chemistry, physics. **Protective services:** Fire safety technology, police science. **Psychology:** General. **Social sciences:** General. **Visual/performing arts:** General, commercial/advertising art, dramatic, studio arts.

**Student life. Activities:** Concert band, drama, musical theater, radio station, student government, student newspaper, TV station, Black student association.

**Athletics.** NJCAA. **Intercollegiate:** Baseball M, basketball, cross-country, soccer, softball W, track and field, volleyball W.

**Student services.** Career counseling, student employment services, health services, on-campus daycare, personal counseling, placement for graduates. **Physically disabled:** Services for visually, speech, hearing impaired. **Transfer:** Transfer adviser, college fairs on campus for students transferring to 4-year colleges.

**Contact.** Phone: (314) 513-4244 Fax: (314) 513-4724
Brenda Davenport, Manager of Admissions/Registration, St. Louis Community College at Florissant Valley, 3400 Pershall Road, St. Louis, MO 63135

## St. Louis Community College at Meramec
St. Louis, Missouri
www.stlcc.edu                    CB code: 6430

- Public 2-year community college
- Commuter campus in large city

**General.** Founded in 1963. Regionally accredited. Two off-campus sites at South County Education Center and West County Education Center. **Enrollment:** 24,567 undergraduates. **Degrees:** 893 associate awarded. **ROTC:** Army, Air Force. **Location:** 15 miles from St. Louis. **Calendar:** Semester, extensive summer session. **Full-time faculty:** 190 total. **Part-time faculty:** 500 total. **Special facilities:** Center for advanced imaging.

### Student profile.

Out-of-state:           1%        25 or older:        42%

**Basis for selection.** Open admission, but selective for some programs. Nursing, occupational therapy assistant, physical therapist assistant, paramedic technology programs have specific admission requirements. SAT or ACT score used to waive Accuplacer Test. Interview required for some health programs. **Homeschooled:** Transcript of courses and grades, interview required.

**High school preparation.** 22 units recommended. Recommended units include English 4, mathematics 2, social studies 3 and science 2.

**2007-2008 Annual costs.** Tuition/fees: $2,430; $3,540 out-of-district; $4,440 out-of-state. Per-credit charge: $81 in-district; $118 out-of-district; $148 out-of-state. Books/supplies: $800. Personal expenses: $2,100.

**Financial aid. Need-based:** Need-based aid available for part-time students.

**Application procedures. Admission:** Priority date 8/1; no deadline. No application fee. Application may be submitted online. Admission notification on a rolling basis beginning on or about 3/1. **Financial aid:** Closing date 6/30. FAFSA, institutional form required. Applicants notified on a rolling basis starting 2/1.

**Academics. Special study options:** Accelerated study, cross-registration, distance learning, dual enrollment of high school students, ESL, honors, independent study, internships, study abroad. **Credit/placement by examination:** AP, CLEP, institutional tests. 49 credit hours maximum toward associate degree. **Support services:** GED preparation, learning center, pre-admission summer program, reduced course load, remedial instruction, tutoring, writing center.

**Majors. Agriculture:** Horticultural science, ornamental horticulture. **Architecture:** Interior. **Business:** General, accounting, administrative services, banking/financial services, management information systems, office technology, office/clerical, real estate. **Communications:** General. **Computer sciences:** General, applications programming, data processing. **Education:** General, elementary, secondary. **Engineering:** General. **Engineering technology:** Architectural, electrical. **Health:** EMT paramedic, occupational therapy assistant, physical therapy assistant. **Interdisciplinary:** Biological/physical sciences. **Legal studies:** Court reporting, legal secretary, paralegal. **Liberal arts:** Arts/sciences. **Math:** General. **Protective services:** Criminal justice, police science. **Public administration:** Social work. **Social sciences:** General. **Transportation:** Air traffic control. **Visual/performing arts:** Commercial/advertising art, photography, studio arts.

**Computing on campus.** 420 workstations in library, computer center.

**Student life. Freshman orientation:** Mandatory. Preregistration for classes offered. **Activities:** Bands, choral groups, drama, literary magazine, music ensembles, musical theater, student government, student newspaper, symphony orchestra, Phi Theta Kappa, international club, Intervarsity Christian Fellowship, horticulture club, bridge club, engineering club, photo club, scuba club, Student Ambassadors.

**Athletics.** NJCAA. **Intercollegiate:** Baseball M, basketball M, soccer, softball W, volleyball W, wrestling M. **Intramural:** Basketball, volleyball. **Team name:** Magic.

**Student services.** Career counseling, student employment services, financial aid counseling, health services, on-campus daycare, personal counseling, placement for graduates, veterans' counselor. **Physically disabled:** Services for visually, speech, hearing impaired. **Learning disabled:** Comprehensive services available. **Transfer:** Transfer adviser, college fairs on campus for students transferring to 4-year colleges.

**Contact.** Phone: (314) 984-7601 Fax: (314) 984-7051
Mike Cundiff, Director of Admissions, St. Louis Community College at Meramec, 11333 Big Bend Boulevard, Kirkwood, MO 63122-5799

## Sanford-Brown College
Fenton, Missouri
www.sbcfenton.com                    CB code: 3320

- For-profit 2-year business and health science college
- Commuter campus in small town

**General.** Accredited by ACICS. **Calendar:** Continuous.

**Annual costs/financial aid.** Total cost varies by program length. Tuition is $349 per credit hour for full-time students and $300 per credit hour for part-time Bachelor's degree students. Fees vary depending on program. Books/supplies: $1,714. Need-based financial aid available to full-time and part-time students.

**Contact.** Phone: (636) 349-4900
Dean, 1345 Smizer Mill Road, Fenton, MO 63026-1583

## Sanford-Brown College: Hazelwood
Hazelwood, Missouri
www.sanford-brown.edu                    CB code: 3321

- For-profit 2-year business and technical college
- Large town

**General.** Accredited by ACICS. **Enrollment:** 500 degree-seeking undergraduates. **Degrees:** 134 associate awarded. **Calendar:** Continuous. **Full-time faculty:** 8 total. **Part-time faculty:** 37 total.

**Basis for selection.** Open admission.

**2007-2008 Annual costs.** Total cost varies by program length. Tuition is $349 per credit hour for full-time students and $300 per credit hour for part-time Bachelor's degree students. Fees vary depending on program. Books/supplies: $909.

**Application procedures. Admission:** No deadline. $25 fee. **Financial aid:** No deadline.

**Academics. Credit/placement by examination:** CLEP.

**Majors. Business:** Accounting/business management, office technology. **Computer sciences:** General. **Health:** Health services. **Legal studies:** General.

**Contact.** Phone: (314) 731-1101
Phyllis Forney, Director of Admissions, Sanford-Brown College: Hazelwood, 75 Village Square, Hazelwood, MO 63042

## Sanford-Brown College: St. Peters
St. Peters, Missouri
www.sbcstpeters.com                    CB code: 3323

- For-profit 2-year career college
- Small city

**General.** Accredited by ACICS. **Enrollment:** 595 degree-seeking undergraduates. **Degrees:** 311 associate awarded. **Calendar:** Continuous. **Full-time faculty:** 19 total. **Part-time faculty:** 32 total.

**Basis for selection.** Open admission.

**2007-2008 Annual costs.** Total cost varies by program length.

**Academics. Credit/placement by examination:** CLEP.

**Majors. Business:** Business admin. **Computer sciences:** Web page design. **Health:** Massage therapy, medical records technology, nursing (RN). **Legal studies:** Paralegal. **Protective services:** Corrections.

**Contact.** Phone: (636) 696-2300 Toll-free number: (888) 793-2433 Angela Rentfro, Director of Admissions, Sanford-Brown College: St. Peters, 100 Richmond Center Boulevard, St. Peters, MO 63376

## Southeast Missouri Hospital College of Nursing and Health Sciences
### Cape Girardeau, Missouri
www.sehosp.org                          CB code: 4459

♦ Private 2-year health science and nursing college
♦ Large town

**General. Enrollment:** 190 degree-seeking undergraduates. **Degrees:** 43 associate awarded. **Calendar:** Semester. **Full-time faculty:** 33 total.

**Basis for selection.** Open admission, but selective for some programs.

**2008-2009 Annual costs.** Tuition/fees: $10,764. Books/supplies: $500.

**Application procedures. Admission:** No deadline. $40 fee. Admission notification on a rolling basis.

**Academics. Special study options:** License preparation in nursing, radiology. **Credit/placement by examination:** AP, CLEP.

**Majors. Health:** Nursing (RN).

**Contact.** E-mail: dpugh@sehosp.org
Phone: (573) 334-6825 ext. 23 Fax: (573) 339-7805
Don Pugh, Registrar/Enrollment Counselor, Southeast Missouri Hospital College of Nursing and Health Sciences, 2001 William Street, Second Floor, Cape Girardeau, MO 63703

## State Fair Community College
### Sedalia, Missouri
www.sfccmo.edu                          CB code: 6709

♦ Public 2-year community college
♦ Commuter campus in large town

**General. Founded** in 1966. Regionally accredited. **Enrollment:** 2,941 degree-seeking undergraduates; 365 non-degree-seeking students. **Degrees:** 399 associate awarded. **ROTC:** Army. **Location:** 78 miles from Kansas City. **Calendar:** Semester, limited summer session. **Full-time faculty:** 65 total; 100% have terminal degrees, 2% minority, 55% women. **Part-time faculty:** 185 total; 100% have terminal degrees, 5% minority, 60% women.

**Student profile.** Among degree-seeking undergraduates, 63% enrolled in a transfer program, 37% enrolled in a vocational program, 920 enrolled as first-time, first-year students, 156 transferred in from other institutions.

| | | | |
|---|---|---|---|
| Part-time: | 36% | Hispanic American: | 3% |
| Out-of-state: | 2% | Native American: | 1% |
| Women: | 65% | 25 or older: | 38% |
| African American: | 5% | Live on campus: | 4% |
| Asian American: | 1% | | |

**Transfer out. Colleges most students transferred to 2007:** University of Central Missouri, Missouri State University.

**Basis for selection.** Open admission, but selective for some programs. Special requirements for some health programs. ACT, ASSET, or COMPASS score current within the last five years required of full-time students and all degree-seeking students. Mechanical knowledge test required for auto mechanics program. Interview required for radiologic technology program applicants. **Learning Disabled:** Students are encouraged to establish documentation at least two weeks prior to the first day of each semester in order to receive accommodations.

**2007-2008 Annual costs. Tuition/fees:** $2,400; $3,240 out-of-district; $4,920 out-of-state. Per-credit charge: $66 in-district; $94 out-of-district; $150 out-of-state. Books/supplies: $1,100. Personal expenses: $1,400.

**2006-2007 Financial aid.** All financial aid based on need. 40% of total undergraduate aid awarded as scholarships/grants, 60% as loans/jobs. Need-based aid available for part-time students. Work-study available nights and weekends.

**Application procedures. Admission:** No deadline. $25 fee, may be waived for applicants with need. Application may be submitted online. Admission notification on a rolling basis. **Financial aid:** Priority date 7/1; no closing date. FAFSA required. Applicants notified on a rolling basis starting 7/15; must reply within 3 week(s) of notification.

**Academics. Special study options:** Combined bachelor's/graduate degree, cooperative education, cross-registration, distance learning, dual enrollment of high school students, ESL, internships, study abroad. License preparation in dental hygiene, nursing, paramedic, radiology, real estate. **Credit/placement by examination:** AP, CLEP, institutional tests. 30 credit hours maximum toward associate degree. Students may earn a maximum of 30 hours in combination from credit by exam or nontraditional credit toward an AA or AAS degree. **Support services:** GED preparation, learning center, reduced course load, remedial instruction, study skills assistance, tutoring, writing center.

**Majors. Agriculture:** Business, horticulture. **Business:** Accounting, administrative services, business admin, management information systems, special products marketing. **Computer sciences:** Applications programming, networking, programming, web page design. **Construction:** Site management. **Education:** Voc/tech. **Engineering technology:** CAD/CADD. **Family/consumer sciences:** Child care. **Health:** Dental hygiene, insurance coding, medical secretary, medical transcription, nursing (RN), office admin, radiologic technology/medical imaging. **Interdisciplinary:** Accounting/computer science. **Liberal arts:** Arts/sciences. **Mechanic/repair:** Automotive, electronics/electrical, industrial, industrial electronics, marine. **Production:** Machine tool. **Protective services:** Firefighting, police science.

**Most popular majors.** Business/marketing 9%, health sciences 19%, liberal arts 52%.

**Computing on campus.** 360 workstations in dormitories, library, computer center, student center. Dormitories wired for high-speed internet access and linked to campus network. Commuter students can connect to campus network. Online course registration, online library, helpline, wireless network available.

**Student life. Freshman orientation:** Available. Preregistration for classes offered. **Housing:** Coed dorms, substance-free housing available. $100 non-refundable deposit, deadline 7/15. **Activities:** Jazz band, choral groups, dance, drama, music ensembles, student government.

**Athletics.** NJCAA. **Intercollegiate:** Basketball, volleyball W. **Intramural:** Bowling, softball, volleyball. **Team name:** Roadrunners.

**Student services.** Career counseling, services for economically disadvantaged, student employment services, financial aid counseling, minority student services, personal counseling, placement for graduates, veterans' counselor. **Physically disabled:** Services for visually, speech, hearing impaired. **Transfer:** Pre-admission transcript evaluation for new students. Transfer adviser, college fairs on campus for students transferring to 4-year colleges.

**Contact.** E-mail: mcarter@sfccmo.edu
Phone: (660) 530-5833 Toll-free number: (877) 311-7322
Fax: (660) 596-7472
Mark Carter, Director of Admissions, State Fair Community College, 3201 West 16th Street, Sedalia, MO 65301-2199

## Texas County Technical Institute
### Houston, Missouri
www.texascountytech.edu

♦ Private 2-year nursing and technical college
♦ Small town

**General.** Accredited by ACICS. **Calendar:** Semester.

**Annual costs/financial aid. Tuition/fees** (2007-2008): $11,470. Tuition varies by program, $145 to $375 per credit hour. Books/supplies: $1,000. Personal expenses: $1,083.

**Contact.** Phone: (417) 967-5466
Director of Admissions, 6915 South Highway 63, Houston, MO 65483

## Three Rivers Community College
### Poplar Bluff, Missouri
www.trcc.edu                          CB code: 6836

♦ Public 2-year community college
♦ Commuter campus in large town

**General.** Founded in 1966. Regionally accredited. Selected courses offered at area high schools, vocational schools and other off-campus facilities. **Enrollment:** 2,641 degree-seeking undergraduates; 544 non-degree-seeking students. **Degrees:** 364 associate awarded. **Location:** 160 miles from St. Louis. **Calendar:** Semester, limited summer session. **Full-time faculty:** 64 total. **Part-time faculty:** 119 total.

**Student profile.** Among degree-seeking undergraduates, 73% enrolled in a transfer program, 27% enrolled in a vocational program; 691 enrolled as first-time, first-year students.

| | | | |
|---|---|---|---|
| Part-time: | 33% | Hispanic American: | 1% |
| Out-of-state: | 1% | 25 or older: | 36% |
| Women: | 68% | Live on campus: | 6% |
| African American: | 8% | | |

**Transfer out. Colleges most students transferred to 2007:** Southeast Missouri State University, Arkansas State University, Southwest Missouri State University.

**Basis for selection.** Open admission, but selective for some programs. Special requirements for allied health programs and nursing. **Homeschooled:** Statement describing homeschool structure and mission required.

**2007-2008 Annual costs.** Tuition/fees: $2,325; $3,495 out-of-district; $4,245 out-of-state. Per-credit charge: $64 in-district; $103 out-of-district; $128 out-of-state. Book rental $17 per book. Refundable book deposit fee $25 per semester. Lab fees vary per course. Books/supplies: $450. Personal expenses: $1,249.

**2006-2007 Financial aid. Need-based:** 72% of total undergraduate aid awarded as scholarships/grants, 28% as loans/jobs. Need-based aid available for part-time students. Work-study available for part-time students. **Non-need-based:** Scholarships awarded for academics, athletics, state residency.

**Application procedures. Admission:** No deadline. $20 fee. Application must be submitted on paper. Admission notification on a rolling basis. **Financial aid:** Priority date 5/1; no closing date. FAFSA, institutional form required. Applicants notified on a rolling basis starting 6/1; must reply within 2 week(s) of notification.

**Academics. Special study options:** Accelerated study, distance learning, dual enrollment of high school students, independent study, internships, liberal arts/career combination. Bachelor's degree programs available on campus. License preparation in nursing, paramedic. **Credit/placement by examination:** AP, CLEP. 30 credit hours maximum toward associate degree. **Support services:** GED test center, learning center, remedial instruction, study skills assistance, tutoring, writing center.

**Majors. Agriculture:** Business. **Biology:** General. **Business:** Accounting, administrative services, entrepreneurial studies, management information systems, marketing. **Education:** General. **Engineering technology:** Civil, drafting. **English:** English lit, speech/rhetoric. **Foreign languages:** General. **Health:** Clinical lab technology, nursing (RN), premedicine, prepharmacy, preveterinary. **History:** General. **Legal studies:** Prelaw. **Liberal arts:** Arts/sciences, library science. **Math:** General. **Parks/recreation:** Health/fitness. **Philosophy/religion:** Philosophy. **Physical sciences:** Chemistry. **Protective services:** Police science. **Psychology:** General. **Social sciences:** Economics, geography, political science, sociology. **Visual/performing arts:** Studio arts.

**Most popular majors.** Business/marketing 26%, health sciences 12%, liberal arts 49%.

**Computing on campus.** 100 workstations in dormitories, library, computer center, student center. Dormitories wired for high-speed internet access.

**Student life. Freshman orientation:** Available. Preregistration for classes offered. Mini orientation activities are held for incoming freshmen during the registration process. Orientation for new students is offered at the beginning of each semester for students, family and friends. **Housing:** Apartments, substance-free housing available. $200 partly refundable deposit. **Activities:** Concert band, choral groups, drama, music ensembles, student government, Student Senate, Phi Theta Kappa, Marketing Management Association,.

**Athletics. NJCAA. Intercollegiate:** Baseball M, basketball, softball W, volleyball W. **Intramural:** Baseball M, basketball, volleyball W. **Team name:** Raiders.

**Student services.** Career counseling, student employment services, on-campus daycare, placement for graduates, veterans' counselor. **Transfer:** Transfer adviser, college fairs on campus for students transferring to 4-year colleges.

**Contact.** E-mail: mfields@trcc.edu
Phone: (573) 840-9605 ext. 605 Toll-free number: (877) 879-8722 ext. 665
Fax: (573) 840-9058
Marcia Fields, Director of Admissions, Three Rivers Community College, 2080 Three Rivers Boulevard, Poplar Bluff, MO 63901-1308

## Vatterott College
### Berkeley, Missouri
www.vatterott-college.edu      **CB code: 2507**

- For-profit 2-year technical college
- Large city
- Interview required

**General.** Accredited by ACCSCT. **Enrollment:** 700 degree-seeking undergraduates. **Degrees:** 17 bachelor's, 123 associate awarded. **Location:** 20 miles from St. Louis, 310 miles from Chicago. **Calendar:** Continuous. **Full-time faculty:** 15 total. **Part-time faculty:** 5 total.

**Basis for selection.** Open admission. High school achievement, interview, and institutional testing used to determine admission.

**2007-2008 Annual costs.** Program cost ranges: $20,584 to $21,640 (certificate/diploma); $31,498 to $33,115 (associate degree); $64,790 (bachelor's degree).

**Application procedures. Admission:** No deadline. No application fee. Admission notification on a rolling basis. **Financial aid:** No deadline. Institutional form required.

**Academics. Special study options:** Bachelor's degree programs available on campus. **Credit/placement by examination:** CLEP. **Support services:** Remedial instruction, tutoring.

**Majors. Computer sciences:** Programming, system admin. **Construction:** Electrician. **Engineering technology:** Drafting. **Mechanic/repair:** Heating/ac/refrig. **Production:** Welding.

**Student life. Activities:** Literary magazine, TV station.

**Contact.** E-mail: adm@vatterot-college.edu
Phone: (314) 264-1040 Toll-free number: (866) 314-6454
Fax: (314) 522-6174
Shalisa Powell, Director of Admissions, Vatterott College, 8580 Evans Avenue, Berkeley, MO 63134

## Vatterott College: Joplin
### Joplin, Missouri
www.vatterott-college.com

- For-profit 2-year technical college
- Large town

**General.** Accredited by ACCSCT. **Calendar:** Continuous.

**Annual costs/financial aid.** Program cost ranges: $7,700 to $20,582 (certificate/diploma); $28,500 to $31,494 (associate degree).

**Contact.** Phone: (417) 781-5633
809 Illinois Avenue, Joplin, MO 64801

## Vatterott College: Kansas City
### Kansas City, Missouri
www.vatterott-college.edu      **CB code: 2893**

- For-profit 2-year technical college
- Large city

**General.** Accredited by ACCSCT. **Calendar:** Continuous.

**Annual costs/financial aid.** Program cost ranges: $22,000 to $24,000 (certificate/diploma); $35,000 to $36,000 (associate degree).

**Contact.** Phone: (816) 252-3997
Campus Co-Director, 8955 East 38th Terrace, Kansas City, MO 64129

## Vatterott College: O'Fallon
### O'Fallon, Missouri

- Private 2-year branch campus and technical college
- Large city

**General.** Accredited by ACCSCT. **Calendar:** Quarter.

**Annual costs/financial aid.** Program cost ranges: $13,523 to $21,856 (certificate/diploma); $26,069 to $33,444 (associate degree).

**Contact.**  Phone: (636) 978-9488
927 East Terra Lane, O'Fallon, MO 63366

## Vatterott College: St. Joseph
### St. Joseph, Missouri
www.vatterott-college.edu          CB code: 2896

- For-profit 2-year branch campus and technical college
- Commuter campus in small city

**General.** Accredited by ACCSCT. **Enrollment:** 196 degree-seeking undergraduates. **Degrees:** 27 associate awarded. **Location:** 50 miles from Kansas City. **Calendar:** Quarter, extensive summer session. **Full-time faculty:** 18 total. **Part-time faculty:** 3 total.

**Basis for selection.** Open admission.

**2007-2008 Annual costs.** Program cost ranges: $10,483 to $20,966 (certificate/diploma); $24,460 to $30,302 (associate degree). Personal expenses: $1,288.

**Financial aid. Need-based:** Need-based aid available for part-time students.

**Application procedures. Admission:** No deadline. No application fee. Application may be submitted online. **Financial aid:** No deadline. FAFSA required.

**Academics. Credit/placement by examination:** CLEP, institutional tests. 36 credit hours maximum toward associate degree. **Support services:** Tutoring.

**Majors. Computer sciences:** General. **Health:** Medical secretary.

**Student life. Freshman orientation:** Mandatory. Preregistration for classes offered. Held first day of classes. Students are briefed on policies and procedures and are introduced to the directors, career services, instructors and financial aid paperwork.

**Student services.** Career counseling, student employment services, financial aid counseling, placement for graduates, veterans' counselor.

**Contact.**  E-mail: sarah.griffin@vatterott-college.edu
Phone: (816) 364-5399 Toll-free number: (800) 282-5327
Fax: (816) 364-1593
Maggie Franz, Admissions Representative, Vatterott College: St. Joseph, 3131 Frederick Avenue, St. Joseph, MO 64506

## Vatterott College: Springfield
### Springfield, Missouri
www.vatterott-college.edu          CB code: 2895

- For-profit 2-year branch campus and technical college
- Commuter campus in small city

**General.** Accredited by ACCSCT. **Calendar:** Quarter.

**Annual costs/financial aid.** Program cost ranges: $12,979 to $20,208 (certificate/diploma); $27,345 to $30,922 (associate degree). Books/supplies: $2,388. Personal expenses: $2,289.

**Contact.**  Phone: (417) 831-8116
Director of Admissions, 3850 South Campbell, Springfield, MO 65807

## Vatterott College: Sunset Hills
### Sunset Hills, Missouri
www.vatterott-college.com          CB code: 2898

- For-profit 2-year branch campus and technical college
- Very large city

**General.** Accredited by ACCSCT. **Calendar:** Continuous.

**Annual costs/financial aid.** Program cost ranges: $15,290 to $19,616 (certificate/diploma); $23,397 to $30,017 (associate degree); $59,144 (bachelor's degree).

**Contact.**  Phone: (314) 843-4200
Director, 12970 Maurer Industrial Drive, Sunset Hills, MO 63127

## Wentworth Military Junior College
### Lexington, Missouri
wjc.wma.edu          CB code: 6934

- Private 2-year junior and military college
- Commuter campus in small town
- Interview required

**General.** Founded in 1880. Regionally accredited. Adult evening program open to both men and women. **Enrollment:** 565 undergraduates. **Degrees:** 84 associate awarded. **ROTC:** Army. **Location:** 40 miles from Kansas City. **Calendar:** Semester, extensive summer session. **Full-time faculty:** 10 total. **Part-time faculty:** 40 total. **Class size:** 100% < 20. **Special facilities:** Nature trail, military history library, indoor rifle range, athletic facilities.

**Student profile.**

| | | | |
|---|---|---|---|
| Out-of-state: | 55% | Live on campus: | 23% |
| 25 or older: | 30% | | |

**Transfer out. Colleges most students transferred to 2007:** Central Missouri State University, Texas A&M University, Kansas University, Kansas State University, University of Missouri.

**Basis for selection.** Open admission, but selective for some programs. Admittees to senior ROTC programs must meet ROTC admission criteria. ACT/SAT required of applicants to ROTC commissioning program for admission, placement, counseling. Score report by August 1. **Homeschooled:** Transcript of courses and grades, letter of recommendation (nonparent) required.

**High school preparation.** 24 units recommended. Recommended units include English 4, mathematics 3, social studies 3, science 2 (laboratory 2), foreign language 2 and academic electives 8.

**2007-2008 Annual costs.** Uniform: $2,150 for men and women. Books/supplies: $450.

**Financial aid.** All financial aid based on need.

**Application procedures. Admission:** No deadline. $100 fee. Admission notification on a rolling basis. **Financial aid:** Priority date 4/30, closing date 6/30. FAFSA required. Applicants notified on a rolling basis.

**Academics.** Service academy preparatory program. **Special study options:** Accelerated study, combined bachelor's/graduate degree, distance learning, dual enrollment of high school students, ESL, independent study, liberal arts/career combination, teacher certification program. License preparation in aviation, nursing. **Credit/placement by examination:** CLEP, institutional tests. 30 credit hours maximum toward associate degree. **Support services:** Tutoring.

**Majors. Liberal arts:** Arts/sciences.

**Computing on campus.** 50 workstations in library, computer center. Dormitories wired for high-speed internet access and linked to campus network. Commuter students can connect to campus network. Helpline, wireless network available.

**Student life. Policies:** Religious observance required. **Housing:** Single-sex dorms available. $1,500 deposit, deadline 6/30. **Activities:** Bands, choral groups, dance, drama, music ensembles, student government, student newspaper.

**Athletics.** NJCAA. **Intercollegiate:** Cross-country, rifle M, track and field, wrestling M. **Intramural:** Baseball M, basketball M, cheerleading W, football (non-tackle) M, golf, racquetball, rifle, soccer, swimming, tennis, volleyball, weight lifting M. **Team name:** Red Dragons.

**Student services.** Career counseling, financial aid counseling, health services, personal counseling. **Transfer:** Transfer adviser, college fairs on campus for students transferring to 4-year colleges.

**Contact.**  E-mail: admissions@wma.edu
Phone: (660) 259-2221 Toll-free number: (800) 962-7682
Fax: (660) 259-2677
LTC. Mike Herman, Vice President for Enrollment, Wentworth Military Junior College, 1880 Washington Avenue, Lexington, MO 64067-1799

# Montana

## Blackfeet Community College
### Browning, Montana
www.bfcc.org                    CB code: 0379

‣ Public 2-year community college
‣ Commuter campus in small town

**General.** Founded in 1976. Regionally accredited. Tribally controlled college located on Blackfeet Indian reservation. **Enrollment:** 465 degree-seeking undergraduates. **Degrees:** 67 associate awarded. **Location:** 126 miles from Great Falls. **Calendar:** Semester, limited summer session. **Full-time faculty:** 30 total. **Part-time faculty:** 30 total. **Class size:** 77% < 20, 22% 20-39, less than 1% 40-49.

**Basis for selection.** Open admission. **Homeschooled:** State high school equivalency certificate required.

**2007-2008 Annual costs.** Tuition/fees: $2,000. Per-credit charge: $69. Books/supplies: $600. Personal expenses: $1,200.

**Financial aid. Need-based:** Need-based aid available for part-time students.

**Application procedures. Admission:** No deadline. $20 fee. Application must be submitted on paper. Admission notification on a rolling basis. **Financial aid:** No deadline. FAFSA, institutional form required.

**Academics. Special study options:** Distance learning, internships. 2-2 teacher training program with University of Montana. **Credit/placement by examination:** CLEP. **Support services:** GED preparation and test center, pre-admission summer program, remedial instruction, tutoring.

**Majors. Area/ethnic studies:** Native American. **Business:** Business admin, hospitality admin, office management, small business admin. **Computer sciences:** General, networking. **Conservation:** General, environmental science, forestry. **Education:** Early childhood, elementary. **Health:** Health services, prenursing. **Liberal arts:** Arts/sciences. **Psychology:** General. **Public administration:** Human services, social work.

**Most popular majors.** Area/ethnic studies 6%, business/marketing 17%, computer/information sciences 12%, education 12%, health sciences 12%, liberal arts 12%, natural resources/environmental science 12%, psychology 6%, public administration/social services 16%.

**Computing on campus.** 5 workstations in library, computer center, student center.

**Student life. Freshman orientation:** Mandatory. Preregistration for classes offered. **Activities:** Literary magazine, student government, student newspaper.

**Athletics. Intercollegiate:** Basketball, cross-country, rodeo. **Intramural:** Basketball.

**Student services.** Adult student services, career counseling, financial aid counseling, personal counseling. **Transfer:** Transfer adviser for students transferring to 4-year colleges.

**Contact.** Phone: (406) 338-5421 ext. 243 Toll-free number: (800) 549-7457 Fax: (406) 338-3272
Deana McNabb, Registrar/Admissions Officer, Blackfeet Community College, Highway 2 & 89, Browning, MT 59417

## Chief Dull Knife College
### Lame Deer, Montana
www.cdkc.edu                    CB code: 5938

‣ Public 2-year junior college
‣ Rural community

**General.** Regionally accredited. **Enrollment:** 180 degree-seeking undergraduates. **Degrees:** 22 associate awarded. **Location:** 110 miles from Billings. **Calendar:** Semester, limited summer session. **Full-time faculty:** 13 total. **Part-time faculty:** 31 total.

**Basis for selection.** Open admission.

**2007-2008 Annual costs.** Tuition/fees: $300. Per-credit charge: $. Books/supplies: $850. Personal expenses: $800.

**Financial aid. Need-based:** Need-based aid available for part-time students. Work-study available nights and for part-time students.

**Application procedures. Admission:** No deadline. No application fee. Application must be submitted on paper. Admission notification on a rolling basis. **Financial aid:** Priority date 3/1; no closing date. FAFSA, institutional form required. Applicants notified on a rolling basis; must reply within 2 week(s) of notification.

**Academics. Special study options:** Cooperative education, double major, internships. Bachelor's degree programs available on campus. **Credit/placement by examination:** CLEP, institutional tests. 9 credit hours maximum toward associate degree. **Support services:** GED preparation and test center, learning center, remedial instruction, tutoring.

**Computing on campus.** 25 workstations in computer center.

**Student life. Activities:** Student government, student newspaper.

**Athletics. Intramural:** Basketball.

**Student services.** Career counseling, on-campus daycare, personal counseling, veterans' counselor. **Transfer:** Transfer adviser for students transferring to 4-year colleges.

**Contact.** E-mail: zspang@cdkc.edu
Phone: (406) 477-6215 Fax: (406) 477-6219
Zane Spang, Dean of Student Affairs, Chief Dull Knife College, Box 98, Lame Deer, MT 59043

## Dawson Community College
### Glendive, Montana
www.dawson.edu                    CB code: 4280

‣ Public 2-year community college
‣ Commuter campus in small town

**General.** Founded in 1940. Regionally accredited. **Enrollment:** 322 degree-seeking undergraduates; 124 non-degree-seeking students. **Degrees:** 76 associate awarded. **Location:** 220 miles from Billings, 100 miles from Dickinson, North Dakota. **Calendar:** Semester, limited summer session. **Full-time faculty:** 33 total. **Part-time faculty:** 25 total.

**Student profile.** Among degree-seeking undergraduates, 64% enrolled in a transfer program, 36% enrolled in a vocational program, 116 enrolled as first-time, first-year students, 17 transferred in from other institutions.

| | | | |
|---|---|---|---|
| Part-time: | 20% | Hispanic American: | 1% |
| Out-of-state: | 15% | Native American: | 5% |
| Women: | 52% | Live on campus: | 48% |
| African American: | 3% | | |

**Transfer out. Colleges most students transferred to 2007:** Dickinson State University, Montana State University-Bozeman, Montana State University-Billings, University of Montana.

**Basis for selection.** Open admission.

**2007-2008 Annual costs.** Tuition/fees: $2,736; $3,843 out-of-district; $8,499 out-of-state. Per-credit charge: $52 in-district; $89 out-of-district; $244 out-of-state. Western Undergraduate Exchange tuition: $133.80 per credit hour, $3,211 full-time. Books/supplies: $800. Personal expenses: $1,048.

**Financial aid. Need-based:** Work-study available nights, weekends and for part-time students. **Non-need-based:** Scholarships awarded for academics, art, athletics, music/drama.

**Application procedures. Admission:** No deadline. $30 fee. Admission notification on a rolling basis. **Financial aid:** Priority date 3/1; no closing date. FAFSA required. Applicants notified on a rolling basis starting 5/15; must reply within 2 week(s) of notification.

**Academics. Special study options:** Distance learning, double major, dual enrollment of high school students, independent study, internships. **Credit/placement by examination:** CLEP, institutional tests. 15 credit hours maximum toward associate degree. **Support services:** GED preparation and test center, learning center, reduced course load, remedial instruction, study skills assistance, tutoring.

**Majors. Agriculture:** Business, equestrian studies, farm/ranch, power machinery. **Business:** General, administrative services. **Computer sciences:** General, vendor certification. **Education:** Early childhood. **Health:** Medical transcription, substance abuse counseling. **Liberal arts:** Arts/sciences. **Mechanic/repair:** Automotive. **Protective services:** Police science.

**Computing on campus.** 70 workstations in dormitories, library, computer center. Dormitories wired for high-speed internet access and linked to campus network. Wireless network available.

**Student life. Freshman orientation:** Mandatory. Preregistration for classes offered. Held during June and July. **Housing:** Coed dorms available. $150 deposit. Student dormitories include kitchen facilities. **Activities:** Bands, choral groups, drama, music ensembles, musical theater, student government, human services club, law enforcement club, Intervarsity Christian Fellowship.

**Athletics.** NJCAA. **Intercollegiate:** Baseball M, basketball, rodeo, softball W. **Intramural:** Basketball, bowling, golf, racquetball, softball, table tennis, tennis, volleyball. **Team name:** Buccaneers.

**Student services.** Adult student services, career counseling, student employment services, placement for graduates, veterans' counselor. **Physically disabled:** Services for visually, speech, hearing impaired. **Transfer:** Pre-admission transcript evaluation for new students. College fairs on campus for students transferring to 4-year colleges.

**Contact.** E-mail: myers@dawson.edu
Phone: (406) 377-3396 ext. 410 Toll-free number: (800) 821-8320 ext. 410
Fax: (406) 377-8132
Jolene Myers, Director of Admissions, Dawson Community College, 300 College Drive, Glendive, MT 59330

## Flathead Valley Community College
**Kalispell, Montana**
www.fvcc.edu                              **CB code: 4317**

▶ Public 2-year community college
▶ Commuter campus in large town

**General.** Founded in 1967. Regionally accredited. **Enrollment:** 1,291 degree-seeking undergraduates; 620 non-degree-seeking students. **Degrees:** 179 associate awarded. **Location:** 250 miles from Spokane, Washington. **Calendar:** Semester, limited summer session. **Full-time faculty:** 42 total. **Part-time faculty:** 100 total. **Class size:** 86% < 20, 14% 20-39. **Partnerships:** Formal partnerships with Tech Prep and Running Start programs with area high schools.

**Student profile.** Among degree-seeking undergraduates, 277 enrolled as first-time, first-year students.

| | | | |
|---|---|---|---|
| Part-time: | 28% | Women: | 62% |
| Out-of-state: | 3% | | |

**Transfer out. Colleges most students transferred to 2007:** University of Montana, Montana State University - Bozeman.

**Basis for selection.** Radiological technology program requires anatomy and physiology I and II, English composition, intermediate algebra, and medical terminology with a grade of C or better. Practical nursing program requires 8 prerequisite courses with GPA of 3.0. ASSET and COMPASS used for placement purposes. **Homeschooled:** Applicants must have GED or COMPASS test scores.

**2007-2008 Annual costs. Tuition/fees:** $3,080; $4,256 out-of-district; $9,240 out-of-state. Per-credit charge: $110 in-district; $152 out-of-district; $330 out-of-state. Books/supplies: $1,000. Personal expenses: $900.

**Financial aid. Need-based:** Need-based aid available for part-time students. Work-study available for part-time students. **Non-need-based:** Scholarships awarded for academics, athletics.

**Application procedures. Admission:** No deadline. $15 fee. Application must be submitted on paper. Admission notification on a rolling basis. **Financial aid:** Priority date 3/1; no closing date. FAFSA required. Applicants notified by 4/15; must reply within 2 week(s) of notification.

**Academics. Special study options:** Distance learning, dual enrollment of high school students, independent study, internships, liberal arts/career combination. Bachelor's degree programs available on campus. **Credit/placement by examination:** AP, CLEP, IB, institutional tests. 12 AP credits allowed toward associate degree. **Support services:** GED preparation and test center, learning center, reduced course load, remedial instruction, study skills assistance, tutoring, writing center.

**Majors. Business:** General, accounting, management information systems, marketing, office technology. **Conservation:** Management/policy. **Construction:** General. **Engineering:** General. **Engineering technology:** Surveying. **Health:** Health care admin, health services, medical assistant, medical records technology, medical secretary, medical transcription, office admin, office assistant, office computer specialist, receptionist, substance abuse counseling. **Legal studies:** Legal secretary. **Liberal arts:** Arts/sciences, humanities. **Mechanic/repair:** Watch/jewelry. **Protective services:** Law enforcement admin. **Public administration:** Human services.

**Most popular majors.** Business/marketing 6%, health sciences 8%, liberal arts 73%.

**Computing on campus.** 175 workstations in library, computer center. Commuter students can connect to campus network. Online course registration, helpline, wireless network available.

**Student life. Freshman orientation:** Available. Preregistration for classes offered. 4 half-day summer advising and registration programs. **Activities:** Drama, student government, student newspaper, Phi Theta Kappa, veterans organization, forestry club, campus ministry group, Bitta club (Native American), human service club, international student association.

**Athletics.** NJCAA. **Intercollegiate:** Cross-country, soccer M. **Intramural:** Badminton, basketball, football (tackle), golf, skiing, softball, table tennis, tennis, volleyball.

**Student services.** Adult student services, career counseling, services for economically disadvantaged, student employment services, financial aid counseling, health services, personal counseling, placement for graduates, veterans' counselor. **Physically disabled:** Services for visually, hearing impaired. **Transfer:** Pre-admission transcript evaluation for new students. Transfer adviser for students transferring to 4-year colleges.

**Contact.** E-mail: mstoltz@fvcc.edu
Phone: (406) 756-3846 Toll-free number: (800) 313-3822
Fax: (406) 756-3965
Marlene Stoltz, Registrar/Admissions and Records Coordinator, Flathead Valley Community College, 777 Grandview Drive, Kalispell, MT 59901

## Fort Belknap College
**Harlem, Montana**
www.fbcc.edu                              **CB code: 5971**

▶ Public 2-year community college
▶ Commuter campus in rural community

**General.** Regionally accredited. **Enrollment:** 123 degree-seeking undergraduates. **Degrees:** 14 associate awarded. **Location:** On Fort Belknap Reservation. **Calendar:** Semester. **Full-time faculty:** 13 total. **Part-time faculty:** 4 total. **Special facilities:** Native American cultural center.

**Student profile.** Among degree-seeking undergraduates, 8% enrolled in a vocational program, 38 enrolled as first-time, first-year students, 8 transferred in from other institutions.

| | | | |
|---|---|---|---|
| Part-time: | 14% | Hispanic American: | 1% |
| Women: | 55% | Native American: | 89% |

**Transfer out.** 32% of students enrolled in the transfer program go on to 4-year colleges. **Colleges most students transferred to 2007:** University of Missoula.

**Basis for selection.** Open admission. Compass Placement Test required. **Homeschooled:** Transcript of courses and grades, state high school equivalency certificate required.

**2007-2008 Annual costs. Tuition/fees:** $2,410. Per-credit charge: $70. Books/supplies: $910. Personal expenses: $960.

**Application procedures. Admission:** No deadline. $10 fee. Admission notification on a rolling basis. **Financial aid:** No deadline. Applicants notified on a rolling basis.

**Academics. Special study options:** Dual enrollment of high school students. **Credit/placement by examination:** CLEP. **Support services:** GED preparation, learning center, tutoring.

**Majors. Area/ethnic studies:** Native American. **Business:** General. **Computer sciences:** Data processing. **Conservation:** Management/policy. **Education:** Elementary. **Health:** Substance abuse counseling. **Liberal arts:** Arts/sciences. **Public administration:** Human services.

**Most popular majors.** Biological/life sciences 21%, business/marketing 7%, computer/information sciences 29%, education 7%, liberal arts 7%, natural resources/environmental science 21%, psychology 7%.

**Student life. Freshman orientation:** Mandatory. **Activities:** Student government.

**Student services.** Career counseling, financial aid counseling.

**Contact.** Phone: (406) 353-2607 Fax: (406) 353-2898
Dixie Brockie, Registrar/Admissions Officer, Fort Belknap College, Box 159, Harlem, MT 59526-0159

## Fort Peck Community College
**Poplar, Montana**
**www.fpcc.edu**                                    CB code: 5972

▶  Public 2-year community college
▶  Commuter campus in small town

**General.** Regionally accredited. Tribally controlled college. **Enrollment:** 405 degree-seeking undergraduates. **Degrees:** 34 associate awarded. **Location:** 70 miles from Williston, North Dakota; 300 miles from Billings. **Calendar:** Semester, limited summer session. **Full-time faculty:** 25 total. **Part-time faculty:** 14 total. **Special facilities:** Individual student science lab stations.

**Transfer out. Colleges most students transferred to 2007:** Rocky Mountain College.

**Basis for selection.** Open admission. Interview recommended.

**2007-2008 Annual costs.** Tuition/fees: $1,840. Per-credit charge: $60. Books/supplies: $500. Personal expenses: $2,000.

**Financial aid. Need-based:** Need-based aid available for part-time students. Work-study available nights and for part-time students.

**Application procedures. Admission:** Closing date 9/16. $15 fee, may be waived for applicants with need. Admission notification on a rolling basis. **Financial aid:** No deadline. FAFSA, institutional form required. Applicants notified on a rolling basis; must reply within 2 week(s) of notification.

**Academics. Special study options:** Distance learning, double major, dual enrollment of high school students, independent study, internships, teacher certification program. **Credit/placement by examination:** CLEP. **Support services:** GED preparation and test center, learning center, remedial instruction, study skills assistance, tutoring.

**Majors. Area/ethnic studies:** Native American. **Biology:** Biomedical sciences. **Business:** General, administrative services, business admin. **Computer sciences:** Computer graphics, data processing. **Conservation:** General, management/policy. **Education:** General, science. **Health:** Substance abuse counseling. **Mechanic/repair:** Automotive. **Public administration:** Human services. **Visual/performing arts:** Studio arts.

**Computing on campus.** 65 workstations in library, computer center.

**Student life. Freshman orientation:** Available. **Activities:** Student government, student newspaper, American Indian Business Leaders.

**Student services.** Adult student services, career counseling, student employment services, on-campus daycare, personal counseling, placement for graduates, veterans' counselor. **Transfer:** Pre-admission transcript evaluation for new students. Transfer adviser, college fairs on campus for students transferring to 4-year colleges.

**Contact.** Phone: (406) 768-5553 Fax: (406) 768-5552
Leigh Melbourne, Assistant Registrar, Fort Peck Community College, Box 398 605 Indian, Poplar, MT 59255-0398

## Helena College of Technology of the University of Montana
**Helena, Montana**
**www.umhelena.edu**                                CB code: 2022

▶  Public 2-year community and technical college
▶  Commuter campus in large town

**General.** Founded in 1939. Regionally accredited. **Enrollment:** 800 degree-seeking undergraduates. **Degrees:** 161 associate awarded. **Location:** 90 miles from Great Falls. **Calendar:** Semester, limited summer session. **Full-time faculty:** 36 total. **Part-time faculty:** 61 total.

**Student profile.** Among degree-seeking undergraduates, 35% enrolled in a transfer program, 40% enrolled in a vocational program, 82 transferred in

from other institutions. Of all enrolled students, 1% already have a bachelor's degree or higher.

**Basis for selection.** Open admission. Interview recommended.

**High school preparation.** Recommended units include English 3 and mathematics 3.

**2007-2008 Annual costs.** Tuition/fees: $2,978; $7,922 out-of-state. Books/supplies: $600. Personal expenses: $710.

**Financial aid. Need-based:** Need-based aid available for part-time students.

**Application procedures. Admission:** No deadline. $30 fee. Admission notification on a rolling basis beginning on or about 2/15. **Financial aid:** Priority date 3/1; no closing date. FAFSA, institutional form required. Applicants notified on a rolling basis starting 5/1.

**Academics. Special study options:** Dual enrollment of high school students, independent study, internships. License preparation in nursing. **Credit/placement by examination:** AP, CLEP. **Support services:** Learning center, pre-admission summer program, remedial instruction, study skills assistance, tutoring, writing center.

**Majors. Business:** Accounting, administrative services, office technology. **Computer sciences:** Programming. **Construction:** Carpentry. **Health:** Medical secretary. **Legal studies:** Legal secretary, paralegal. **Liberal arts:** Arts/sciences. **Mechanic/repair:** Aircraft, automotive, diesel, electronics/electrical. **Protective services:** Firefighting.

**Computing on campus.** Commuter students can connect to campus network. Online course registration, online library, helpline, wireless network available.

**Student life. Freshman orientation:** Mandatory. Preregistration for classes offered. **Activities:** Student government, student newspaper.

**Athletics. Intramural:** Basketball, volleyball.

**Student services.** Adult student services, career counseling, student employment services, placement for graduates, veterans' counselor. **Physically disabled:** Services for visually, speech, hearing impaired. **Transfer:** Transfer adviser for students transferring to 4-year colleges.

**Contact.** E-mail: info@umh.umt.edu
Phone: (406) 444-6800 Toll-free number: (800) 241-4882
Fax: (406) 444-6892
Michael Brown, Director of Admissions, Helena College of Technology of the University of Montana, 1115 North Roberts Street, Helena, MT 59601-3098

## Little Big Horn College
**Crow Agency, Montana**
**www.lbhc.cc.mt.us**                               CB code: 0536

▶  Private 2-year community college
▶  Commuter campus in rural community

**General.** Founded in 1980. Regionally accredited. **Location:** 60 miles from Billings. **Calendar:** Quarter.

**Annual costs/financial aid.** Tuition/fees (2007-2008): $2,760. Books/supplies: $600. Personal expenses: $600. Need-based financial aid available to full-time and part-time students.

**Contact.** Phone: (406) 638-3116
Admissions Clerk, Box 370, Crow Agency, MT 59022

## Miles Community College
**Miles City, Montana**
**www.milescc.edu**                                 CB code: 4081

▶  Public 2-year community college
▶  Commuter campus in small town

**General.** Founded in 1939. Regionally accredited. **Enrollment:** 420 degree-seeking undergraduates; 47 non-degree-seeking students. **Degrees:** 129 associate awarded. **Location:** 150 miles from Billings. **Calendar:** Semester, limited summer session. **Full-time faculty:** 26 total. **Part-time faculty:** 13 total.

**Student profile.** Among degree-seeking undergraduates, 54% enrolled in a transfer program, 46% enrolled in a vocational program, 135 enrolled as first-time, first-year students, 18 transferred in from other institutions.

| | | | |
|---|---|---|---|
| Part-time: | 15% | 25 or older: | 45% |
| Out-of-state: | 1% | Live on campus: | 25% |
| Women: | 63% | | |

**Transfer out. Colleges most students transferred to 2007:** Montana State University-Billings, Montana State University-Bozeman, Dickinson State University, University of Montana, South Dakota State University.

**Basis for selection.** Open admission, but selective for some programs. Special requirements for nursing program: National League for Nursing Pre-Admission Examination required, Certified Nurse's Aide required. COMPASS required for all students. **Homeschooled:** Minimum COMPASS scores: Writing, 32; Reading, 62; Pre-Algebra/Number Skills, 25; may be used in lieu of high school diploma or GED.

**2007-2008 Annual costs.** Tuition/fees: $3,420; $4,290 out-of-district; $7,080 out-of-state. Per-credit charge: $71 in-district; $100 out-of-district; $193 out-of-state. Room/board: $4,250. Books/supplies: $800. Personal expenses: $630.

**Financial aid. Need-based:** Need-based aid available for part-time students. Work-study available nights, weekends and for part-time students. **Non-need-based:** Scholarships awarded for academics, athletics, leadership.

**Application procedures. Admission:** No deadline. $30 fee. Admission notification on a rolling basis. **Financial aid:** Priority date 3/1; no closing date. FAFSA required. Applicants notified on a rolling basis starting 4/15; must reply within 4 week(s) of notification.

**Academics. Special study options:** Cooperative education, cross-registration, distance learning, dual enrollment of high school students, ESL, independent study, internships. License preparation in nursing. **Credit/placement by examination:** AP, CLEP, IB, institutional tests. 15 credit hours maximum toward associate degree. **Support services:** GED preparation and test center, learning center, pre-admission summer program, reduced course load, remedial instruction, study skills assistance, tutoring, writing center.

**Majors. Agriculture:** Business. **Biology:** General. **Business:** Administrative services, business admin, office management, office/clerical. **Communications:** Journalism. **Computer sciences:** General, computer graphics, data processing. **Conservation:** General, forestry, wildlife. **Construction:** Carpentry, maintenance, power transmission. **Education:** General. **Engineering:** General. **English:** American lit, English lit, speech/rhetoric. **Family/consumer sciences:** General. **Foreign languages:** General. **Health:** Medical secretary, nursing (RN), prenursing. **Liberal arts:** Arts/sciences. **Math:** General. **Parks/recreation:** Health/fitness. **Physical sciences:** General. **Psychology:** General. **Public administration:** General, human services, social work. **Social sciences:** General, economics, political science. **Visual/performing arts:** Art, crafts, dramatic, photography.

**Computing on campus.** 90 workstations in library, computer center. Dormitories wired for high-speed internet access. Commuter students can connect to campus network. Online course registration available.

**Student life. Freshman orientation:** Mandatory. Preregistration for classes offered. **Housing:** Coed dorms available. $200 deposit. **Activities:** Campus ministries, choral groups, dance, drama, international student organizations, student government, Phi Theta Kappa, rodeo club, student senate, student ambassadors.

**Athletics.** NJCAA. **Intercollegiate:** Baseball M, basketball, cheerleading M, golf, rodeo, volleyball W. **Intramural:** Basketball, bowling, fencing, golf, handball, ice hockey, racquetball, soccer, tennis, volleyball, weight lifting. **Team name:** Pioneers.

**Student services.** Adult student services, career counseling, student employment services, financial aid counseling, personal counseling, placement for graduates, veterans' counselor. **Transfer:** Pre-admission transcript evaluation for new students. College fairs on campus for students transferring to 4-year colleges.

**Contact.** E-mail: bluntl@milescc.edu
Phone: (406) 874-6217 Toll-free number: (800) 541-9281
Fax: (406) 874-6283
Darren Pitcher, Dean of Student Services, Miles Community College, 2715 Dickinson Street, Miles City, MT 59301

## Montana State University College of Technology: Great Falls
**Great Falls, Montana**
www.msugf.edu                                CB code: 4482

- Public 2-year community and technical college
- Commuter campus in small city

**General.** Founded in 1969. Regionally accredited. **Enrollment:** 1,273 degree-seeking undergraduates; 798 non-degree-seeking students. **Degrees:** 161 associate awarded. **Location:** 200 miles from Billings, 150 miles from Missoula. **Calendar:** Semester, limited summer session. **Full-time faculty:** 48 total; 12% have terminal degrees, 4% minority, 58% women. **Part-time faculty:** 85 total; 6% minority, 56% women. **Class size:** 66% < 20, 34% 20-39.

**Student profile.** Among degree-seeking undergraduates, 21% enrolled in a transfer program, 41% enrolled in a vocational program, 299 enrolled as first-time, first-year students, 177 transferred in from other institutions.

| | | | |
|---|---|---|---|
| Part-time: | 46% | Asian American: | 1% |
| Out-of-state: | 9% | Hispanic American: | 2% |
| Women: | 74% | Native American: | 5% |
| African American: | 1% | 25 or older: | 36% |

**Transfer out.** 30% of students enrolled in the transfer program go on to 4-year colleges.

**Basis for selection.** Open admission, but selective for some programs. Special requirements for dental hygiene, radiologic technology, practical nursing, dental assistant, surgical technology, and physical therapist assistant programs. **Adult students:** Compass test used to determine placement in courses. All placement tests must have been taken within the past three years. **Homeschooled:** Transcript of courses and grades, letter of recommendation (nonparent) required. Notarized copy of the homeschool curriculum, 2 letters of recommendation from non-family members, parental approval form if under 18 required.

**2007-2008 Annual costs.** Tuition/fees: $2,982; $8,648 out-of-state. Books/supplies: $1,200. Personal expenses: $2,072.

**Financial aid. Need-based:** Need-based aid available for part-time students. Work-study available nights, weekends and for part-time students.

**Application procedures. Admission:** No deadline. $30 fee. Application must be submitted on paper. Admission notification on a rolling basis. **Financial aid:** Priority date 3/1; no closing date. FAFSA, institutional form required. Applicants notified on a rolling basis starting 4/1; must reply within 3 week(s) of notification.

**Academics. Special study options:** Cooperative education, distance learning, double major, dual enrollment of high school students, independent study, internships, liberal arts/career combination. License preparation in aviation, dental hygiene, nursing, paramedic, physical therapy, radiology. **Credit/placement by examination:** AP, CLEP, SAT, ACT, institutional tests. **Support services:** Learning center, remedial instruction, study skills assistance, tutoring.

**Majors. Business:** Accounting, business admin, executive assistant. **Computer sciences:** General, data processing, LAN/WAN management, networking, system admin, webmaster. **Engineering technology:** Drafting. **Health:** Dental hygiene, EMT ambulance attendant, EMT paramedic, licensed practical nurse, medical assistant, medical records technology, medical secretary, office admin, office assistant, physical therapy assistant, radiologic technology/medical imaging, respiratory therapy assistant. **Legal studies:** Legal secretary. **Protective services:** Fire safety technology, firefighting. **Transportation:** Aviation. **Visual/performing arts:** Interior design.

**Most popular majors.** Business/marketing 12%, health sciences 50%, liberal arts 12%, visual/performing arts 8%.

**Computing on campus.** 230 workstations in library, computer center. Online course registration, online library, helpline, wireless network available.

**Student life. Freshman orientation:** Mandatory, $10 fee. Two-hour session in May; day session held week prior to the beginning of fall semester. **Activities:** Drama, literary magazine, student government, student newspaper, Phi Theta Kappa, drama club, literary guild, health occupations student association, Native American student council, interior design students, Chi Alpha, nursing students, dental hygiene students, auto body students.

**Student services.** Career counseling, student employment services, financial aid counseling, placement for graduates. **Physically disabled:** Services for visually, hearing impaired. **Transfer:** Transfer adviser, college fairs on campus for students transferring to 4-year colleges.

**Contact.**  E-mail: information@msugf.edu
Phone: (406) 771-4420 Toll-free number: (800) 446-2698
Fax: (406) 771-4329
Dena Wagner-Fossen, Registrar, Montana State University College of
Technology: Great Falls, 2100 16th Avenue South, Great Falls, MT 59405

## Stone Child College
### Box Elder, Montana
www.stonechild.edu                                    CB code: 7044

◗  Public 2-year community and junior college
◗  Commuter campus in rural community

**General.** Founded in 1984. Regionally accredited. Tribally-controlled college located on the Rocky Boys Indian Reservation. **Enrollment:** 196 degree-
seeking undergraduates. **Degrees:** 26 associate awarded. **Location:** 26 miles
from Havre, 100 miles from Great Falls. **Calendar:** Semester, limited summer session. **Full-time faculty:** 10 total. **Part-time faculty:** 29 total.

**Student profile.**

| Out-of-state: | 2% | 25 or older: | 56% |
|---|---|---|---|

**Transfer out. Colleges most students transferred to 2007:** Montana State
University-Northern, Montana State University-Billings, University of Montana, University of Great Falls.

**Basis for selection.** Open admission.

**High school preparation.** 22 units recommended. Recommended units
include English 4, mathematics 3, social studies 3, history 4, science 3,
foreign language 1 and academic electives 4.

**2007-2008 Annual costs.** Tuition/fees: $670. Per-credit charge: $. Students not members of Federally recognized Native American tribe pay additional $420 in fees/year. Books/supplies: $400.

**Financial aid. Need-based:** Need-based aid available for part-time students. Work-study available for part-time students. **Non-need-based:** Scholarships awarded for academics. **Additional information:** Scholarships available to high school and GED graduates who apply for college admission
during the first term after graduation.

**Application procedures. Admission:** No deadline. $10 fee. Admission
notification on a rolling basis. **Financial aid:** Priority date 3/1, closing date
6/30. FAFSA, institutional form required. Applicants notified on a rolling
basis.

**Academics. Special study options:** Cooperative education, distance learning, double major, dual enrollment of high school students, independent
study, liberal arts/career combination. Hosts distance learning programs from
4-year institutions, bachelors available in computer science, counseling, psychology, criminal justice, health care administration, human services management, marketing, paralegal studies, sociology, theology and religion. **Credit/
placement by examination:** CLEP, institutional tests. 12 credit hours maximum
toward associate degree. **Support services:** GED preparation, learning center, remedial instruction, tutoring.

**Majors. Area/ethnic studies:** Native American. **Business:** General, management information systems, office/clerical. **Computer sciences:** Data processing, information systems. **Education:** Elementary. **Health:** Substance
abuse counseling. **Interdisciplinary:** Biological/physical sciences. **Liberal
arts:** Arts/sciences. **Public administration:** Human services.

**Computing on campus.** 64 workstations in library, computer center,
student center.

**Student life. Freshman orientation:** Mandatory. **Activities:** Student government, student newspaper.

**Athletics. Intercollegiate:** Basketball. **Intramural:** Basketball. **Team name:**
Bear Paws.

**Student services.** Career counseling, on-campus daycare, personal counseling. **Transfer:** Transfer adviser, college fairs on campus for students transferring to 4-year colleges.

**Contact.**  E-mail: tedewhitford@hotmail.com
Phone: (406) 395-4313 ext. 222 Fax: (406) 395-4836
Theodore Whitford, Director of Admissions, Stone Child College, RR1 Box
1082, Box Elder, MT 59521-9796

# Nebraska

## Central Community College
### Grand Island, Nebraska
www.cccneb.edu     CB code: 6136

- Public 2-year community and technical college
- Commuter campus in large town

**General.** Founded in 1966. Regionally accredited. Multilocation institution with campuses at Columbus, Grand Island, and Hastings. Centers located in Holdrege, Kearney, and Lexington. Multiple starting dates for most programs and courses. **Enrollment:** 3,921 degree-seeking undergraduates; 2,309 non-degree-seeking students. **Degrees:** 534 associate awarded. **Location:** 100 miles from Lincoln. **Calendar:** Semester, extensive summer session. **Full-time faculty:** 150 total; 4% have terminal degrees, 3% minority, 49% women. **Part-time faculty:** 108 total; 3% minority, 51% women.

**Student profile.** Among degree-seeking undergraduates, 864 enrolled as first-time, first-year students.

| | | | |
|---|---|---|---|
| Part-time: | 48% | 25 or older: | 63% |
| Out-of-state: | 1% | Live on campus: | 20% |
| Women: | 64% | | |

**Transfer out. Colleges most students transferred to 2007:** University of Nebraska-Kearney, University of Nebraska-Lincoln, University of Nebraska-Omaha, Bellevue University.

**Basis for selection.** Open admission, but selective for some programs and for out-of-state students. Special requirements for dental hygiene, dental assisting, medical assisting, medical laboratory technician, practical nursing, associate degree nursing, health information management services, truck driving programs. ACT or Dental Hygiene Aptitude Test required for dental hygiene program. ACT or ASSET required for nursing programs. Interview recommended for health information management services.

**2007-2008 Annual costs.** Tuition/fees: $2,190; $3,045 out-of-state. Per-credit charge: $73 in-state; $106 out-of-state. Room/board: $4,080. Books/supplies: $1,000. Personal expenses: $1,380.

**Financial aid. Need-based:** Need-based aid available for part-time students. Work-study available nights and for part-time students. **Non-need-based:** Scholarships awarded for academics, art, athletics, job skills, leadership, music/drama.

**Application procedures. Admission:** No deadline. Application may be submitted online. Admission notification on a rolling basis. Score report for dental hygiene applicants due 09/01. Application deadlines: January 15 for dental hygiene, February 15 for associate degree nursing and practical nursing. **Financial aid:** Priority date 6/1; no closing date. FAFSA, institutional form required. Applicants notified on a rolling basis starting 3/1; must reply within 1 week(s) of notification.

**Academics.** Open entry/open exit, self-paced, flexible scheduling for most programs. **Special study options:** Accelerated study, cooperative education, distance learning, double major, dual enrollment of high school students, ESL, honors, independent study, internships, weekend college. License preparation in dental hygiene, nursing, real estate. **Credit/placement by examination:** AP, CLEP, institutional tests. 48 credit hours maximum toward associate degree. **Support services:** GED preparation and test center, learning center, reduced course load, remedial instruction, study skills assistance, tutoring.

**Majors. Agriculture:** Business, horticulture. **Business:** Administrative services, business admin, vehicle parts marketing. **Communications:** Digital media. **Computer sciences:** General. **Construction:** Electrician. **Engineering technology:** Drafting, electrical, quality control. **Family/consumer sciences:** General, child care. **Health:** Clinical lab technology, dental assistant, dental hygiene, licensed practical nurse, medical assistant, medical records technology, nursing (RN). **Legal studies:** Paralegal. **Liberal arts:** Arts/sciences. **Mechanic/repair:** Auto body, automotive, diesel, heating/ac/refrig, industrial. **Personal/culinary services:** Restaurant/catering. **Production:** General, machine tool, welding. **Protective services:** Criminal justice. **Visual/performing arts:** Commercial/advertising art.

**Most popular majors.** Business/marketing 16%, engineering/engineering technologies 8%, family/consumer sciences 6%, health sciences 24%, liberal arts 18%, trade and industry 13%.

**Computing on campus.** Dormitories linked to campus network. Commuter students can connect to campus network. Online course registration, online library, helpline available.

**Student life. Freshman orientation:** Available. Preregistration for classes offered. **Housing:** Coed dorms, single-sex dorms, apartments, substance-free housing available. $150 partly refundable deposit. **Activities:** Jazz band, choral groups, dance, drama, music ensembles, musical theater, radio station, student government, student newspaper.

**Athletics.** NJCAA. **Intercollegiate:** Basketball M, golf M, softball W, volleyball W. **Intramural:** Basketball, bowling, table tennis, volleyball, weight lifting.

**Student services.** Adult student services, career counseling, services for economically disadvantaged, student employment services, financial aid counseling, health services, minority student services, on-campus daycare, personal counseling, placement for graduates, veterans' counselor, women's services. **Physically disabled:** Services for visually, speech, hearing impaired. **Transfer:** Pre-admission transcript evaluation for new students. Transfer adviser, college fairs on campus for students transferring to 4-year colleges.

**Contact.** E-mail: lkohout@cccneb.edu
Phone: (308) 398-7406 Toll-free number: (877) 222-0780
Fax: (308) 398-7398
Liz Kohout, Admissions Director, Central Community College, 3134 West Highway 34, Grand Island, NE 68802-4903

## Kaplan University: Lincoln
### Lincoln, Nebraska
www.hamiltonlincoln.com     CB code: 3385

- For-profit 2-year branch campus college
- Commuter campus in small city

**General.** Founded in 1884. **Enrollment:** 522 degree-seeking undergraduates. **Degrees:** 15 bachelor's, 164 associate awarded. **Calendar:** Continuous, extensive summer session. **Full-time faculty:** 22 total; 4% have terminal degrees, 4% minority, 77% women. **Part-time faculty:** 38 total; 13% have terminal degrees, 8% minority, 63% women. **Class size:** 83% < 20, 17% 20-39.

**Student profile.**

| | | | |
|---|---|---|---|
| Out-of-state: | 2% | Hispanic American: | 3% |
| African American: | 14% | Native American: | 1% |
| Asian American: | 1% | 25 or older: | 54% |

**Transfer out. Colleges most students transferred to 2007:** Southeast Community College.

**Basis for selection.** Students must pass entrance exam. CPAT required of all applicants.

**2008-2009 Annual costs.** Tuition/fees (projected): $23,420. Per-credit charge: $389.58. Full cost of tuition and fees leading to a certificate/diploma: $17,300; associate degree: $34,600; Bachelor's degree: $64,875. Costs listed are inclusive of tuition, fees, books, and supplies.

**2006-2007 Financial aid.** All financial aid based on need. 163 full-time freshmen applied for aid; 163 were judged to have need; 163 of these received aid. Average need met was 6%. Average scholarship/grant was $4,000; average loan $3,500. 33% of total undergraduate aid awarded as scholarships/grants, 67% as loans/jobs. Need-based aid available for part-time students. Work-study available nights, weekends and for part-time students.

**Application procedures. Admission:** No deadline. $25 fee. Admission notification on a rolling basis. **Financial aid:** No deadline. FAFSA, institutional form required. Applicants notified on a rolling basis starting 2/1.

**Academics. Special study options:** Internships. Bachelor's degree programs available on campus. License preparation in nursing. **Credit/placement by examination:** CLEP. **Support services:** Learning center, study skills assistance, tutoring.

**Majors. Business:** Accounting, administrative services, business admin, marketing, tourism promotion, tourism/travel. **Computer sciences:** Applications programming, information systems, programming. **Health:** Medical assistant, medical secretary. **Legal studies:** Legal secretary, paralegal.

**Most popular majors.** Business/marketing 27%, computer/information sciences 6%, health sciences 32%, legal studies 33%.

**Computing on campus.** 70 workstations in library, computer center.

**Student life. Freshman orientation:** Mandatory. Orientation held on first day of classes for all new students. **Housing:** $150 deposit. **Activities:** Tour and travel club, medical club, association of information technology professionals, business club, legal assisting club.

**Athletics.** NJCAA. **Team name:** Aliens.

**Student services.** Career counseling, student employment services, financial aid counseling, placement for graduates, veterans' counselor. **Physically disabled:** Services for visually, hearing impaired. **Transfer:** Pre-admission transcript evaluation for new students.

**Contact.** E-mail: jmathers@kaplan.edu
Phone: (402) 474-5315 Toll-free number: (800) 742-7738
Fax: (402) 474-0896
Jill Mathers, Director of Admissions, Kaplan University: Lincoln, 1821 K Street, Lincoln, NE 68508

## Kaplan University: Omaha
Omaha, Nebraska

CB code: 3326

- For-profit 2-year university and career college
- Commuter campus in large city
- Interview required

**General. Enrollment:** 631 degree-seeking undergraduates. **Degrees:** 5 bachelor's, 106 associate awarded. **Calendar:** Quarter, extensive summer session. **Full-time faculty:** 26 total; 8% minority. **Part-time faculty:** 35 total; 11% minority. **Class size:** 54% < 20, 46% 20-39.

**Basis for selection.** Open admission.

**2008-2009 Annual costs.** Tuition/fees: $4,700. Books/supplies: $100. Personal expenses: $378.

**Financial aid.** All financial aid based on need. Need-based aid available for part-time students.

**Application procedures. Admission:** No deadline. $20 fee. Application must be submitted on paper. Admission notification on a rolling basis. **Financial aid:** No deadline. FAFSA required. Applicants notified on a rolling basis.

**Academics. Special study options:** Accelerated study, double major, internships. License preparation in nursing. **Credit/placement by examination:** CLEP, institutional tests. 32 credit hours maximum toward associate degree. **Support services:** Learning center, reduced course load, study skills assistance, tutoring, writing center.

**Majors. Business:** Accounting, business admin. **Computer sciences:** Networking. **Health:** Medical assistant. **Legal studies:** Paralegal.

**Most popular majors.** Business/marketing 33%, computer/information sciences 28%, health sciences 22%, legal studies 17%.

**Computing on campus.** Commuter students can connect to campus network. Online library available.

**Student life. Freshman orientation:** Mandatory.

**Student services.** Adult student services, career counseling, services for economically disadvantaged, student employment services, financial aid counseling, placement for graduates. **Physically disabled:** Services for visually, speech, hearing impaired. **Transfer:** Pre-admission transcript evaluation for new students.

**Contact.** E-mail: mbaum@kaplan.edu
Phone: (402) 572-8500 Toll-free number: (800) 642-1456
Fax: (402) 573-6482
Mike Baum, Director of Admissions, Kaplan University: Omaha, 3350 North 90th Street, Omaha, NE 68134

## Little Priest Tribal College
Winnebago, Nebraska
www.lptc.bia.edu

CB code: 3616

- Private 2-year community college
- Commuter campus in rural community

**General.** Regionally accredited. **Enrollment:** 108 degree-seeking undergraduates; 12 non-degree-seeking students. **Degrees:** 9 associate awarded. **Location:** 30 miles from Sioux City, Iowa. **Calendar:** Semester, limited summer session. **Full-time faculty:** 4 total; 25% minority, 25% women. **Part-time faculty:** 12 total; 8% minority, 67% women. **Class size:** 82% < 20, 18% 20-39.

**Student profile.** Among degree-seeking undergraduates, 29 enrolled as first-time, first-year students, 10 transferred in from other institutions.

| | | | |
|---|---|---|---|
| Part-time: | 31% | Women: | 65% |
| Out-of-state: | 4% | | |

**Transfer out. Colleges most students transferred to 2007:** Wayne State College, Haskell Indian Nations University.

**Basis for selection.** Open admission.

**High school preparation.** 11 units recommended. Recommended units include English 3, mathematics 3, social studies 3 and science 2.

**2007-2008 Annual costs.** Tuition/fees: $2,985. Per-credit charge: $80. Books/supplies: $700.

**Financial aid. Need-based:** Need-based aid available for part-time students. Work-study available for part-time students.

**Application procedures. Admission:** No deadline. $10 fee. **Financial aid:** No deadline. FAFSA, institutional form required.

**Academics. Special study options:** Dual enrollment of high school students, independent study, liberal arts/career combination. **Credit/placement by examination:** CLEP. **Support services:** GED preparation and test center, learning center, reduced course load, remedial instruction, study skills assistance, tutoring.

**Majors. Area/ethnic studies:** Native American. **Business:** General. **Computer sciences:** General. **Conservation:** General. **Education:** General. **English:** English lit. **Health:** Health services, substance abuse counseling. **Liberal arts:** Arts/sciences. **Math:** General.

**Most popular majors.** Area/ethnic studies 20%, business/marketing 20%, health sciences 20%, liberal arts 40%.

**Computing on campus.** 20 workstations in library, computer center, student center.

**Student life. Freshman orientation:** Available. Preregistration for classes offered. **Activities:** Student government, student newspaper.

**Student services.** Adult student services, financial aid counseling, personal counseling. **Transfer:** Pre-admission transcript evaluation for new students. College fairs on campus for students transferring to 4-year colleges.

**Contact.** Phone: (402) 878-2380 ext. 160 Fax: (402) 878-2355
Darla LaPointe, Dean of Admissions, Little Priest Tribal College, PO Box 270, Winnebago, NE 68071

## Metropolitan Community College
Omaha, Nebraska
www.mccneb.edu

CB member
CB code: 5755

- Public 2-year community and technical college
- Commuter campus in large city

**General.** Founded in 1974. Regionally accredited. Multilocation institution: Fort Omaha, Elkhorn Valley, Fremont, Sarpy Center in La Vista. **Enrollment:** 6,627 degree-seeking undergraduates; 8,177 non-degree-seeking students. **Degrees:** 957 associate awarded. **Location:** 50 miles from Lincoln. **Calendar:** Quarter, extensive summer session. **Full-time faculty:** 206 total; 12% minority, 48% women. **Part-time faculty:** 738 total; 10% minority, 50% women. **Class size:** 72% < 20, 28% 20-39, less than 1% 40-49, less than 1% 50-99. **Special facilities:** CAD/CAM and electronic graphics facilities.

**Student profile.** Among degree-seeking undergraduates, 22% enrolled in a transfer program, 56% enrolled in a vocational program, 1,570 enrolled as first-time, first-year students.

| | | | |
|---|---|---|---|
| Part-time: | 56% | Hispanic American: | 5% |
| Out-of-state: | 3% | Native American: | 1% |
| Women: | 58% | International: | 2% |
| African American: | 14% | 25 or older: | 45% |
| Asian American: | 3% | Live on campus: | 1% |

**Transfer out. Colleges most students transferred to 2007:** University of Nebraska-Omaha, Bellevue University.

**Basis for selection.** Open admission, but selective for some programs. Admission to nursing and allied health programs based on test scores and references. Assessment testing and standardized RN entrance examination required for nursing associate degree programs. Human services programs require a "C" and approval from Human Services Faculty Review Committee. Certain programs may require preparatory work before attending classes. Interview required for nursing and allied health programs.

**High school preparation.** High school diploma or GED required of nursing and allied health applicants.

**2007-2008 Annual costs.** Tuition/fees: $2,070; $2,993 out-of-state. Per-credit charge: $41 in-state; $62 out-of-state. Books/supplies: $1,800. Personal expenses: $1,404.

**Financial aid. Need-based:** Need-based aid available for part-time students. **Non-need-based:** Scholarships awarded for academics.

**Application procedures. Admission:** No deadline. No application fee. Admission notification on a rolling basis. **Financial aid:** Priority date 3/15; no closing date. FAFSA, institutional form required. Applicants notified on a rolling basis starting 4/15.

**Academics.** Individualized, self-paced instruction. Degree through tele-courses available. **Special study options:** Cooperative education, distance learning, double major, dual enrollment of high school students, ESL, honors, independent study, internships, weekend college. License preparation in nursing. **Credit/placement by examination:** AP, CLEP, institutional tests. 81 credit hours maximum toward associate degree. **Support services:** GED preparation and test center, learning center, remedial instruction, tutoring, writing center.

**Majors. Agriculture:** Horticulture, nursery operations. **Architecture:** Interior. **Business:** General, accounting, administrative services, business admin, management information systems. **Communications technology:** Graphic/printing. **Computer sciences:** General, networking. **Construction:** Maintenance, power transmission. **Engineering technology:** Architectural drafting, civil, drafting, electrical, software. **Family/consumer sciences:** Child care, institutional food production. **Foreign languages:** Sign language interpretation. **Health:** Nursing (RN), respiratory therapy technology. **Legal studies:** Paralegal. **Liberal arts:** Arts/sciences. **Mechanic/repair:** Auto body, automotive, heating/ac/refrig, industrial. **Personal/culinary services:** Culinary arts. **Protective services:** Fire services admin, police science. **Public administration:** Social work. **Visual/performing arts:** Commercial photography, commercial/advertising art, studio arts, theater arts management.

**Most popular majors.** Business/marketing 23%, health sciences 9%, liberal arts 27%, security/protective services 6%, trade and industry 8%, visual/performing arts 9%.

**Computing on campus.** 1,550 workstations in library, computer center. Commuter students can connect to campus network. Online course registration, helpline available.

**Student life. Freshman orientation:** Available. Preregistration for classes offered. **Housing:** Coed dorms, single-sex dorms, substance-free housing available. **Activities:** Phi Theta Kappa scholastic honor society.

**Student services.** Adult student services, career counseling, services for economically disadvantaged, student employment services, financial aid counseling, minority student services, personal counseling, placement for graduates, veterans' counselor, women's services. **Physically disabled:** Services for visually, speech, hearing impaired. **Transfer:** Transfer adviser for students transferring to 4-year colleges.

**Contact.** E-mail: bnicks@mccneb.edu
Phone: (402) 457-2422 Toll-free number: (800) 228-9553
Fax: (402) 457-2616
Becky Nicks, Director of Admissions and Records, Metropolitan Community College, Box 3777, Omaha, NE 68103-0777

## Mid-Plains Community College Area
### North Platte, Nebraska
www.mpcc.edu                                   CB code: 6497

- Public 2-year community and technical college
- Commuter campus in large town

**General.** Founded in 1964. Regionally accredited. Two major sites, North Platte and McCook; extended campus sites in Broken Bow, Imperial, Ogallala, and Valentine. **Enrollment:** 1,209 degree-seeking undergraduates. **Degrees:** 276 associate awarded. **Location:** 230 miles from Lincoln, 270 miles from Denver. **Calendar:** Semester, limited summer session. **Full-time faculty:** 65 total. **Part-time faculty:** 219 total. **Partnerships:** Formal partnership with Union Pacific Railroad for apprenticeships, technical training, continuing education.

**Student profile.**

| | | | |
|---|---|---|---|
| Out-of-state: | 5% | Live on campus: | 12% |
| 25 or older: | 75% | | |

**Transfer out. Colleges most students transferred to 2007:** University of Nebraska at Lincoln, University of Nebraska at Kearney, Chadron State College.

**Basis for selection.** Open admission, but selective for some programs. Special requirements for nursing and laboratory technology programs. Psychological Corporation Pre-Nursing Examination required of applicants to nursing program. Minimum ACT score of 17 required for licensed practical nursing and 21 for associate degree nursing. Minimum ASSET score of 40 in all areas required for medical laboratory technology program. Interview required for nursing and medical laboratory technology programs.

**2008-2009 Annual costs.** Tuition/fees: $2,370; $2,970 out-of-state. Per-credit charge: $65 in-state; $85 out-of-state. Room/board: $4,700. Books/supplies: $1,000. Personal expenses: $750.

**2006-2007 Financial aid. Need-based:** 62% of total undergraduate aid awarded as scholarships/grants, 38% as loans/jobs. Need-based aid available for part-time students. Work-study available nights. **Non-need-based:** Scholarships awarded for academics, art, athletics, music/drama.

**Application procedures. Admission:** No deadline. No application fee. Admission notification on a rolling basis. **Financial aid:** Priority date 5/1; no closing date. FAFSA, institutional form required. Applicants notified on a rolling basis starting 5/1; must reply within 3 week(s) of notification.

**Academics. Special study options:** Cooperative education, distance learning, dual enrollment of high school students, exchange student, honors, independent study, internships, liberal arts/career combination. Bachelor's degree programs available on campus. License preparation in dental hygiene, nursing, paramedic, real estate. **Credit/placement by examination:** CLEP. 20 credit hours maximum toward associate degree. **Support services:** GED preparation and test center, remedial instruction, study skills assistance, tutoring.

**Majors. Business:** Business admin, office management. **Computer sciences:** Information technology. **Construction:** Electrician, maintenance. **Engineering technology:** Electrical. **Family/consumer sciences:** Child care. **Health:** Clinical lab technology, dental assistant, nursing (RN). **Liberal arts:** Arts/sciences. **Mechanic/repair:** General, auto body, automotive, diesel, electronics/electrical, heating/ac/refrig. **Production:** Welding. **Protective services:** Firefighting, police science. **Other:** Electro-Mechanical Technology.

**Most popular majors.** Business/marketing 14%, health sciences 16%, liberal arts 58%, trade and industry 8%.

**Computing on campus.** 100 workstations in dormitories, library, computer center, student center. Dormitories wired for high-speed internet access. Commuter students can connect to campus network. Online library, wireless network available.

**Student life. Freshman orientation:** Available. Preregistration for classes offered. **Policies:** Drugs, alcohol, tobacco strictly prohibited. **Housing:** Coed dorms, single-sex dorms, special housing for disabled, apartments available. $200 deposit, deadline 8/15. **Activities:** Bands, choral groups, drama, music ensembles, student government, student newspaper.

**Athletics.** NJCAA. **Intercollegiate:** Baseball M, basketball, golf M, softball W, volleyball W. **Intramural:** Volleyball.

**Student services.** Career counseling, financial aid counseling, on-campus daycare, placement for graduates. **Transfer:** Transfer adviser for students transferring to 4-year colleges.

**Contact.** E-mail: rippenk@mpcc.edu
Phone: (308) 535-3609 Toll-free number: (800) 658-4308 ext. 3609
Fax: (308) 534-5767
Kelly Rippen, Area Admissions Coordinator, Mid-Plains Community College Area, 1101 Halligan Drive, North Platte, NE 69101

## Myotherapy Institute
### Lincoln, Nebraska
### www.myotherapy.edu

- For-profit 2-year health science and community college
- Small city

**General.** Accredited by ACCSCT. **Calendar:** Continuous.

**Contact.** Phone: (402) 421-7410
Director, 6020 South 58th Street, Lincoln, NE 68516

## Nebraska College of Technical Agriculture
### Curtis, Nebraska
### www.ncta.unl.edu                    CB code: 1305

- Public 2-year agricultural college
- Residential campus in rural community

**General.** Founded in 1965. Regionally accredited. **Enrollment:** 262 full-time, degree-seeking students. **Degrees:** 75 associate awarded. **Location:** 40 miles from North Platte. **Calendar:** Semester, limited summer session. **Full-time faculty:** 19 total. **Part-time faculty:** 13 total. **Special facilities:** Farm, community golf course, land lab, cattle working facilities, indoor arena, horticulture greenhouse, vet tech surgery and lab facilities.

**Student profile.**

| | | | |
|---|---|---|---|
| Out-of-state: | 36% | Live on campus: | 58% |
| 25 or older: | 7% | | |

**Basis for selection.** Open admission. ACT scores are criterion in awarding scholarships. **Homeschooled:** State high school equivalency certificate required.

**High school preparation.** 11 units recommended. Recommended units include English 3, mathematics 3, social studies 1 and science 4.

**2007-2008 Annual costs.** Tuition/fees: $3,204; $5,949 out-of-state. Per-credit charge: $92 in-state; $184 out-of-state. Room/board: $4,309. Books/supplies: $800. Personal expenses: $1,375.

**2006-2007 Financial aid.** All financial aid based on need. 49% of total undergraduate aid awarded as scholarships/grants, 51% as loans/jobs. Need-based aid available for part-time students.

**Application procedures. Admission:** Closing date 8/15. $25 fee. Application may be submitted online. Admission notification on a rolling basis. **Financial aid:** Priority date 4/1; no closing date. FAFSA required. Applicants notified on a rolling basis starting 5/1; must reply within 2 week(s) of notification.

**Academics. Special study options:** Distance learning, double major, internships. Bachelor's degree programs available on campus. **Credit/placement by examination:** AP, CLEP, institutional tests. **Support services:** Reduced course load, remedial instruction, study skills assistance, tutoring.

**Majors. Agriculture:** General, agribusiness operations, animal health, business, equestrian studies, greenhouse operations, horticultural science, horticulture, landscaping, nursery operations, ornamental horticulture, turf management. **Conservation:** Management/policy. **Health:** Veterinary technology/assistant.

**Computing on campus.** 75 workstations in dormitories, library, computer center. Dormitories wired for high-speed internet access and linked to campus network. Online course registration, online library, repair service, wireless network available.

**Student life. Freshman orientation:** Mandatory. Preregistration for classes offered. 2-day program. **Housing:** Guaranteed on-campus for freshmen. Single-sex dorms, substance-free housing available. $200 deposit. **Activities:** Dance, drama, student government, student newspaper.

**Athletics. Intercollegiate:** Basketball, equestrian, golf, rodeo, volleyball. **Intramural:** Basketball, football (non-tackle), softball, volleyball. **Team name:** Aggies.

**Student services.** Alcohol/substance abuse counseling, campus ministries, career counseling, student employment services, financial aid counseling, health services, personal counseling, placement for graduates, veterans' counselor. **Transfer:** Pre-admission transcript evaluation for new students. Transfer adviser, college fairs on campus for students transferring to 4-year colleges.

**Contact.** E-mail: sshaner3@unl.edu
Phone: (308) 367-4124 Toll-free number: (800) 328-7847
Fax: (308) 367-5209
Sue Shaner, Admissions/Recruiting, Nebraska College of Technical Agriculture, 404 East 7th Street, Curtis, NE 69025-0069

## Nebraska Indian Community College
### Macy, Nebraska
### www.thenicc.edu                    CB code: 1431

- Public 2-year community college
- Commuter campus in rural community

**General.** Founded in 1979. Regionally accredited. Tribal college. **Enrollment:** 140 degree-seeking undergraduates. **Degrees:** 4 associate awarded. **Location:** 70 miles from Omaha, 30 miles from Sioux City, Iowa. **Calendar:** Semester, limited summer session. **Full-time faculty:** 8 total. **Part-time faculty:** 8 total. **Class size:** 100% < 20.

**Student profile.**

| | | | |
|---|---|---|---|
| Out-of-state: | 20% | 25 or older: | 66% |

**Basis for selection.** Open admission.

**High school preparation.** Strong background in English, mathematics, and science recommended.

**2007-2008 Annual costs.** Tuition/fees: $3,200. Per-credit charge: $80. Books/supplies: $600. Personal expenses: $450.

**Financial aid.** All financial aid based on need. Need-based aid available for part-time students. Work-study available for part-time students.

**Application procedures. Admission:** No deadline. $50 fee, may be waived for applicants with need. Admission notification on a rolling basis. **Financial aid:** Priority date 7/15; no closing date. FAFSA, institutional form required. Applicants notified on a rolling basis starting 8/30; must reply within 2 week(s) of notification.

**Academics. Special study options:** Double major, dual enrollment of high school students, independent study, internships. **Credit/placement by examination:** CLEP, institutional tests. 15 credit hours maximum toward associate degree. **Support services:** GED preparation and test center, remedial instruction, study skills assistance, tutoring.

**Majors. Area/ethnic studies:** Native American. **Business:** Business admin. **Computer sciences:** General, data entry. **Conservation:** General. **Construction:** Carpentry. **Education:** Early childhood. **Liberal arts:** Arts/sciences. **Protective services:** Police science. **Public administration:** Social work.

**Most popular majors.** Business/marketing 36%, computer/information sciences 9%, education 27%, liberal arts 27%.

**Computing on campus.** 40 workstations in library, computer center.

**Student life. Freshman orientation:** Available. Preregistration for classes offered. **Activities:** Student government, student newspaper.

**Student services.** Adult student services, career counseling, financial aid counseling. **Transfer:** Pre-admission transcript evaluation for new students. Transfer adviser, college fairs on campus for students transferring to 4-year colleges.

**Contact.** E-mail: estevens@thenicc.edu
Phone: (402) 344-8428 ext. 14 Toll-free number: (888) 843-6422
Fax: (402) 344-8358
Veda Webster, Director of Admissions, Nebraska Indian Community College, 2451 St. Mary's Avenue, Omaha, NE 68105

## Northeast Community College
### Norfolk, Nebraska
### www.northeastcollege.com                    CB code: 6473

- Public 2-year community college
- Commuter campus in large town

**General.** Founded in 1973. Regionally accredited. **Enrollment:** 2,573 degree-seeking undergraduates; 2,576 non-degree-seeking students. **Degrees:** 716 associate awarded. **Location:** 110 miles from Omaha. **Calendar:** Semester, limited summer session. **Full-time faculty:** 107 total; 4% have terminal degrees, less than 1% minority, 35% women. **Part-time faculty:** 275 total; 4% have terminal degrees, less than 1% minority, 61% women. **Class size:** 78% <20, 22% 20-39, less than 1% 40-49, less than 1% >100. **Special facilities:** College farm.

**Student profile.** Among degree-seeking undergraduates, 844 enrolled as first-time, first-year students.

| | | | |
|---|---|---|---|
| Part-time: | 22% | Hispanic American: | 6% |
| Out-of-state: | 3% | Native American: | 1% |
| Women: | 53% | 25 or older: | 12% |
| African American: | 2% | Live on campus: | 18% |

**Transfer out. Colleges most students transferred to 2007:** Wayne State College, University of Nebraska-Lincoln, University of Nebraska-Omaha, University of Nebraska-Kearney, University of South Dakota.

**Basis for selection.** Open admission, but selective for some programs. Special requirements for nursing programs, physical therapy assistant program, and veterinary technician program. ACT or ASSET scores required for placement for students enrolling in 6 or more credit hours.

**2007-2008 Annual costs.** Tuition/fees: $2,190; $2,910 out-of-state. Per-credit charge: $62 in-state; $86 out-of-state. Room/board: $4,136. Books/supplies: $1,000. Personal expenses: $900.

**Financial aid. Need-based:** Need-based aid available for part-time students. Work-study available nights, weekends and for part-time students. **Non-need-based:** Scholarships awarded for academics, athletics, music/drama.

**Application procedures. Admission:** No deadline. No application fee. Application may be submitted online. Admission notification on a rolling basis. **Financial aid:** No deadline. FAFSA, institutional form required. Applicants notified on a rolling basis; must reply within 2 week(s) of notification.

**Academics.** Off-campus credit classes available. Lifelong Learning Center offers students opportunity to earn advanced degrees on NECC campus. **Special study options:** Accelerated study, cooperative education, cross-registration, distance learning, dual enrollment of high school students, ESL, independent study, internships, liberal arts/career combination. License preparation in nursing, paramedic, real estate. **Credit/placement by examination:** AP, CLEP, institutional tests. **Support services:** GED preparation and test center, learning center, reduced course load, remedial instruction, study skills assistance, tutoring, writing center.

**Majors. Agriculture:** General, agribusiness operations, agronomy, animal sciences, business, equipment technology, farm/ranch, horticultural science, horticulture, livestock, mechanization, production. **Biology:** General. **Business:** Accounting, administrative services, banking/financial services, business admin, entrepreneurial studies, international, marketing, merchandising, office/clerical, real estate. **Communications:** Journalism. **Communications technology:** Radio/tv, recording arts. **Computer sciences:** General, computer science, computer support specialist, programming. **Construction:** Electrician, lineworker. **Education:** Early childhood, elementary, music, secondary. **Engineering:** General. **Engineering technology:** Architectural drafting, electrical, electromechanical, energy systems, heat/ac/refrig. **English:** English lit, speech/rhetoric. **Health:** Dietetics, EMT paramedic, medical radiologic technology/radiation therapy, medical records technology, medical secretary, nursing (RN), physical therapy assistant, predental, premedicine, prenursing, prepharmacy, preveterinary, surgical technology, veterinary technology/assistant. **Legal studies:** Legal secretary, paralegal, prelaw. **Liberal arts:** Arts/sciences, library assistant. **Math:** General. **Mechanic/repair:** Auto body, automotive, diesel, heating/ac/refrig, medium/heavy vehicle. **Parks/recreation:** Health/fitness. **Personal/culinary services:** Chef training. **Physical sciences:** Chemistry, physics. **Protective services:** Corrections. **Psychology:** General. **Social sciences:** General. **Visual/performing arts:** Art, dramatic, music management, music performance. **Other:** Applied horticulture/horticultural business services, Building construction, finishing.

**Most popular majors.** Agriculture 8%, business/marketing 16%, health sciences 18%, liberal arts 12%, trade and industry 22%.

**Computing on campus.** 225 workstations in dormitories, library, computer center, student center. Dormitories linked to campus network. Online course registration, online library, helpline available.

**Student life. Freshman orientation:** Mandatory. **Housing:** Coed dorms, special housing for disabled, apartments, substance-free housing available. $25 deposit. **Activities:** Bands, choral groups, dance, drama, music ensembles, musical theater, radio station, student government, student newspaper, symphony orchestra, TV station, Habitat for Humanity, HOPE, multicultural club, Campus Crusade for Christ, Christian Student Fellowship.

**Athletics.** NJCAA. **Intercollegiate:** Basketball. **Intramural:** Basketball, soccer, softball. **Team name:** Hawks.

**Student services.** Adult student services, career counseling, student employment services, financial aid counseling, health services, minority student services, on-campus daycare, personal counseling, placement for graduates, veterans' counselor. **Physically disabled:** Services for visually, speech, hearing impaired. **Learning disabled:** Comprehensive services available. **Transfer:** Pre-admission transcript evaluation for new students. Transfer adviser for students transferring to 4-year colleges.

**Contact.** E-mail: admission@northeastcollege.com
Phone: (402) 844-7260 Toll-free number: (800) 348-9033
Fax: (402) 844-7400
Sandy Hilliges, Admissions, Northeast Community College, 801 East Benjamin Avenue, Norfolk, NE 68702-0469

## Southeast Community College
Lincoln, Nebraska
www.southeast.edu                    CB code: 1189

▸ Public 2-year community college
▸ Commuter campus in small city

**General.** Founded in 1973. Regionally accredited. Extensive adult and continuing education programs, both credit and noncredit. Additional campuses in Beatrice and Milford. **Enrollment:** 7,520 degree-seeking undergraduates. **Degrees:** 1,363 associate awarded. **Location:** 50 miles from Omaha. **Calendar:** Quarter, extensive summer session. **Full-time faculty:** 195 total. **Part-time faculty:** 225 total. **Special facilities:** Fire service training facility.

**Transfer out. Colleges most students transferred to 2007:** University of Nebraska, Doane-Lincoln, College of St. Mary, Nebraska Wesleyan, University of Nebraska-Kearney.

**Basis for selection.** Open admission.

**2007-2008 Annual costs.** Tuition/fees: $2,070; $2,520 out-of-state. Per-credit charge: $45 in-state; $55 out-of-state. Books/supplies: $1,000. Personal expenses: $1,200.

**Financial aid. Need-based:** Need-based aid available for part-time students. Work-study available nights, weekends and for part-time students. **Non-need-based:** Scholarships awarded for academics.

**Application procedures. Admission:** No deadline. No application fee. Application may be submitted online. Admission notification on a rolling basis. **Financial aid:** No deadline. FAFSA, institutional form required. Applicants notified on a rolling basis; must reply within 2 week(s) of notification.

**Academics.** Academic transfer courses (liberal arts) offered on Saturdays. **Special study options:** Cooperative education, distance learning, dual enrollment of high school students, independent study, internships, liberal arts/career combination, weekend college. License preparation in nursing, paramedic, radiology. **Credit/placement by examination:** CLEP, institutional tests. 33 credit hours maximum toward associate degree. Most applicants required to take COMPASS or ASSET for placement purposes. ACT may be substituted for ASSET. **Support services:** GED preparation and test center, learning center, remedial instruction, study skills assistance, tutoring, writing center.

**Majors. Business:** Accounting, business admin, marketing, office/clerical, purchasing. **Computer sciences:** Information systems. **Engineering technology:** Architectural, drafting, electrical. **Family/consumer sciences:** Child care, institutional food production. **Health:** Clinical lab technology, health services, medical radiologic technology/radiation therapy, nursing (RN), respiratory therapy technology, surgical technology. **Liberal arts:** Arts/sciences. **Personal/culinary services:** Culinary arts. **Production:** Welding. **Protective services:** Fire safety technology.

**Computing on campus.** 300 workstations in library, computer center. Online course registration available.

**Student life. Freshman orientation:** Mandatory. Preregistration for classes offered. **Activities:** Student government, student newspaper, multicultural student organization.

**Athletics. Intercollegiate:** Rowing (crew) W. **Intramural:** Basketball, softball, table tennis, tennis, volleyball.

**Student services.** Career counseling, student employment services, on-campus daycare, personal counseling, placement for graduates, veterans' counselor. **Physically disabled:** Services for visually, speech, hearing impaired. **Transfer:** Transfer adviser, college fairs on campus for students transferring to 4-year colleges.

**Contact.** Phone: (402) 437-2600 Toll-free number: (800) 642-4075 Fax: (402) 437-2402
Robin Moore, Dean of Student Services, Southeast Community College, 8800 O Street, Lincoln, NE 68520

## Vatterott College: Spring Valley
Omaha, Nebraska
www.vatterott-college.com

- For-profit 2-year community and technical college
- Large city

**General.** Accredited by ACCSCT. **Enrollment:** 400 degree-seeking undergraduates. **Degrees:** 132 associate awarded. **Calendar:** Quarter. **Full-time faculty:** 30 total. **Part-time faculty:** 20 total.

**Basis for selection.** Interview most important. High school record also important.

**2007-2008 Annual costs.** Program cost ranges: $18,180 to $23,380 (certificate/diploma); $31,500 to $34,070 (associate degree).

**Application procedures. Admission:** No application fee.

**Academics. Credit/placement by examination:** CLEP.

**Majors. Health:** Medical assistant, medical secretary, pharmacy assistant, substance abuse counseling, veterinary technology/assistant. **Mechanic/repair:** Heating/ac/refrig. **Visual/performing arts:** Graphic design. **Other:** Computer aided drafting technology management, Computer systems and network technology.

**Contact.** Phone: (402) 891-9411 Toll-free number: (888) 886-3856 Fax: (402) 891-9413
Derek Handel, Director of Admissions, Vatterott College: Spring Valley, 11818 I Street, Omaha, NE 68137

## Western Nebraska Community College
Scottsbluff, Nebraska
www.wn.edu                                    CB code: 6648

- Public 2-year community college
- Commuter campus in large town

**General.** Founded in 1926. Regionally accredited. Additional centers at Sidney and Alliance. John N. Harms Advanced Technology Center of Nebraska located in Scottsbluff, Nebraska. **Enrollment:** 1,541 degree-seeking undergraduates; 692 non-degree-seeking students. **Degrees:** 171 associate awarded. **Location:** 100 miles from Cheyenne, Wyoming. **Calendar:** Semester, limited summer session. **Full-time faculty:** 72 total; 7% have terminal degrees, 4% minority, 46% women. **Part-time faculty:** 150 total; 7% have terminal degrees, 2% minority, 59% women. **Class size:** 82% < 20, 17% 20-39, less than 1% 40-49.

**Student profile.** Among degree-seeking undergraduates, 80% enrolled in a transfer program, 20% enrolled in a vocational program, 1% already have a bachelor's degree or higher, 502 enrolled as first-time, first-year students.

| | | | |
|---|---|---|---|
| Part-time: | 39% | Hispanic American: | 13% |
| Out-of-state: | 8% | Native American: | 1% |
| Women: | 65% | International: | 3% |
| African American: | 2% | 25 or older: | 38% |
| Asian American: | 1% | Live on campus: | 7% |

**Transfer out.** 53% of students enrolled in the transfer program go on to 4-year colleges. **Colleges most students transferred to 2007:** Chadron State College, University of Nebraska-Lincoln, University of Wyoming.

**Basis for selection.** Open admission, but selective for some programs. Special requirements for practical nursing, Associate Degree-Nursing, and radiologic technologies programs. ASSET or COMPASS required unless SAT or ACT scores submitted. **Adult students:** ECOMPASS used for proper course placement in writing, mathematics, and classes with a reading prerequisite; ACT, SAT, or ASSET accepted in lieu of eCOMPASS.

**High school preparation.** Recommended units include English 4, mathematics 4, social studies 3, history 3, science 4 (laboratory 2) and foreign language 1.

**2007-2008 Annual costs.** Tuition/fees: $2,220; $2,580 out-of-state. Per-credit charge: $61 in-state; $73 out-of-state. Room/board: $4,100. Books/supplies: $840. Personal expenses: $1,872.

**2007-2008 Financial aid. Need-based:** 297 full-time freshmen applied for aid; 237 were judged to have need; 236 of these received aid. Average need met was 87%. Average scholarship/grant was $3,864; average loan $2,542. 69% of total undergraduate aid awarded as scholarships/grants, 31% as loans/jobs. Need-based aid available for part-time students. Work-study available nights, weekends and for part-time students. **Non-need-based:** Awarded to 493 full-time undergraduates, including 289 freshmen. Scholarships awarded for academics, art, athletics, leadership, music/drama, state residency.

**Application procedures. Admission:** No deadline. No application fee. Application may be submitted online. Admission notification on a rolling basis. **Financial aid:** Priority date 3/1; no closing date. FAFSA required. Applicants notified on a rolling basis starting 4/1.

**Academics. Special study options:** Cooperative education, cross-registration, distance learning, double major, dual enrollment of high school students, ESL, independent study, internships, liberal arts/career combination, student-designed major. Radiological technology program at Regional West Medical Center, respiratory therapy technician and surgical technician in partnership with Southeast Community College. License preparation in aviation, nursing, paramedic, real estate. **Credit/placement by examination:** AP, CLEP, IB, institutional tests. 25 credit hours maximum toward associate degree. **Support services:** GED preparation and test center, learning center, pre-admission summer program, reduced course load, remedial instruction, study skills assistance, tutoring, writing center.

**Majors. Biology:** General, ecology. **Business:** General, accounting, administrative services, business admin, office/clerical. **Communications:** Journalism. **Computer sciences:** General, computer science, programming. **Conservation:** Forestry. **Construction:** Lineworker. **Education:** General, art, early childhood, elementary, music, physical, secondary. **Engineering:** General. **English:** English lit. **Family/consumer sciences:** Food/nutrition. **Foreign languages:** French, German, Spanish. **Health:** Athletic training, medical radiologic technology/radiation therapy, medical records technology, nursing (RN), predental, premedicine, prenursing, prepharmacy, preveterinary. **History:** General. **Legal studies:** Prelaw. **Liberal arts:** Arts/sciences. **Math:** General. **Mechanic/repair:** Aircraft, aircraft powerplant, auto body, automotive. **Parks/recreation:** Health/fitness. **Personal/culinary services:** Cosmetic. **Physical sciences:** Chemistry, physics. **Production:** Welding. **Protective services:** Criminal justice. **Psychology:** General. **Public administration:** Social work. **Social sciences:** Anthropology, economics, geography, political science, sociology. **Visual/performing arts:** Art.

**Most popular majors.** Business/marketing 16%, education 8%, health sciences 23%, liberal arts 24%, trade and industry 10%.

**Computing on campus.** 454 workstations in dormitories, library, computer center. Dormitories wired for high-speed internet access and linked to campus network. Commuter students can connect to campus network. Online course registration, online library, helpline, wireless network available.

**Student life. Freshman orientation:** Available. Preregistration for classes offered. 6 hours held the weekday before classes begin. **Policies:** All buildings are smoke-free. **Housing:** Coed dorms, substance-free housing available. $100 deposit, deadline 8/15. **Activities:** Choral groups, drama, literary magazine, music ensembles, musical theater, student government, student newspaper, Campus Ventures, College Republicans, Student Ambassadors, United Leaders for Cultural Diversity, student senate, student council.

**Athletics.** NJCAA. **Intercollegiate:** Baseball M, basketball, soccer, volleyball W. **Intramural:** Basketball, football (non-tackle), table tennis, volleyball. **Team name:** Cougars.

**Student services.** Adult student services, alcohol/substance abuse counseling, career counseling, student employment services, financial aid counseling, minority student services, on-campus daycare, personal counseling, placement for graduates, veterans' counselor. **Physically disabled:** Services for visually, speech, hearing impaired. **Transfer:** Pre-admission transcript evaluation for new students. Transfer adviser, college fairs on campus for students transferring to 4-year colleges.

**Contact.** E-mail: ali@wncc.net
Phone: (308) 635-6010 Toll-free number: (800) 348-4435 ext. 6010
Fax: (308) 635-6100
Ali Jay, Enrollment Management Director, Western Nebraska Community College, 1601 East 27th Street, Scottsbluff, NE 69361

# Nevada

## Career College of Northern Nevada
### Reno, Nevada
www.ccnn.edu                    CB code: 3202

▸ For-profit 2-year business, health science and technical college
▸ Commuter campus in large city
▸ Interview required

**General.** Accredited by ACCSCT. **Enrollment:** 241 undergraduates. **Degrees:** 56 associate awarded. **Calendar:** Quarter, extensive summer session. **Full-time faculty:** 10 total. **Part-time faculty:** 12 total. **Class size:** 82% < 20, 18% 20-39.

**Basis for selection.** Open admission.

**2007-2008 Annual costs.** Tuition for associate programs ranges from $18,623 to $24,375; diploma programs, $10,822 to $14,820. Fees are $210 to $672; books range from $1,000 to $1,600. Books/supplies: $1,500. Personal expenses: $1,832.

**Financial aid.** All financial aid based on need.

**Application procedures. Admission:** No deadline. $25 fee. Application must be submitted on paper. Admission notification on a rolling basis. **Financial aid:** Closing date 5/30. FAFSA required. Applicants notified on a rolling basis.

**Academics. Special study options:** Accelerated study, cooperative education, internships, liberal arts/career combination. **Credit/placement by examination:** CLEP. **Support services:** Remedial instruction, study skills assistance, tutoring.

**Majors. Business:** Business admin. **Engineering technology:** Electrical. **Health:** Insurance coding, insurance specialist, medical assistant, medical secretary. **Legal studies:** Paralegal.

**Most popular majors.** Business/marketing 13%, computer/information sciences 11%, engineering/engineering technologies 15%, health sciences 50%.

**Computing on campus.** 78 workstations in computer center, student center.

**Student life. Freshman orientation:** Mandatory. Preregistration for classes offered. Held Saturday morning before classes begin.

**Student services.** Adult student services, career counseling, financial aid counseling, placement for graduates.

**Contact.** E-mail: lgoldhammer@ccnn4u.com
Phone: (775) 856-2266
Jim Martin, Director of Admissions, Career College of Northern Nevada, 1195 A Corporate Boulevard, Reno, NV 89502-2331

## College of Southern Nevada
### Las Vegas, Nevada
www.csn.edu                    CB code: 4136

▸ Public 2-year community college
▸ Commuter campus in very large city

**General.** Founded in 1971. Regionally accredited. Branch campuses at Henderson and North Las Vegas. Health science center in West Las Vegas. **Enrollment:** 28,880 degree-seeking undergraduates. **Degrees:** 9 bachelor's, 1,500 associate awarded. **ROTC:** Army. **Location:** 6 miles from downtown. **Calendar:** Semester, limited summer session. **Full-time faculty:** 490 total. **Part-time faculty:** 1,200 total. **Special facilities:** Planetarium, ornamental horticulture demonstration facilities, culinary facilities, telecommunications/multimedia center, automotive technology center, occupational therapy labs.

**Student profile.**
Out-of-state:          2%      25 or older:          54%

**Transfer out. Colleges most students transferred to 2007:** University of Nevada Las Vegas.

**Basis for selection.** Open admission, but selective for some programs. Special requirements for nursing, dental hygiene, and health professions programs. Associate degree and certification required for BS dental hygiene program.

**2007-2008 Annual costs.** Tuition/fees: $1,763; $7,148 out-of-state. Per-credit charge: $55. Reduced tuition for nonresidents within 50 miles of Nevada border. Nonresident additional per-credit-hour charge: $54.75 for 1-6 credits, flat rate assessment of $5,385 for 7 credits and above. Books/supplies: $600. Personal expenses: $1,480.

**Financial aid. Need-based:** Work-study available nights, weekends and for part-time students. **Non-need-based:** Scholarships awarded for state residency.

**Application procedures. Admission:** No deadline. $5 fee, may be waived for applicants with need. Application may be submitted online. Admission notification on a rolling basis. **Financial aid:** Priority date 5/1, closing date 6/30. FAFSA required. Applicants notified on a rolling basis starting 7/15; must reply within 2 week(s) of notification.

**Academics. Special study options:** Cooperative education, cross-registration, distance learning, double major, dual enrollment of high school students, ESL, honors, independent study, internships, liberal arts/career combination, student-designed major, weekend college. Bachelor's degree programs available on campus. License preparation in aviation, dental hygiene, nursing, occupational therapy, paramedic, physical therapy, radiology, real estate. **Credit/placement by examination:** CLEP, institutional tests. 15 credit hours maximum toward associate degree. **Support services:** GED preparation and test center, learning center, remedial instruction, study skills assistance, tutoring, writing center.

**Majors. Agriculture:** Landscaping, ornamental horticulture. **Architecture:** Technology. **Biology:** General, anatomy. **Business:** General, accounting, administrative services, banking/financial services, business admin, hospitality admin, hospitality/recreation, management information systems, office management, real estate, sales/distribution. **Communications:** General. **Communications technology:** Animation/special effects, computer typography, graphic/printing. **Computer sciences:** Computer graphics, data processing, database management, information systems, LAN/WAN management, networking, programming, systems analysis, webmaster. **Education:** Deaf/hearing impaired, early childhood, kindergarten/preschool. **Engineering:** Electrical, software. **Engineering technology:** General, CAD/CADD, drafting, electrical, environmental, mechanical, surveying, water quality. **English:** English lit. **Health:** Acupuncture, clinical lab assistant, clinical lab technology, dental hygiene, EMT paramedic, medical records technology, nursing (RN), optician, orthotics/prosthetics, physical therapy assistant. **Legal studies:** Legal secretary, paralegal. **Liberal arts:** Arts/sciences. **Mechanic/repair:** Automotive, heating/ac/refrig. **Personal/culinary services:** Chef training. **Production:** Welding. **Protective services:** Corrections, criminal justice, fire safety technology, firefighting, police science, security services. **Psychology:** General. **Social sciences:** General. **Visual/performing arts:** Art, commercial photography, commercial/advertising art, studio arts.

**Computing on campus.** 650 workstations in library, computer center. Commuter students can connect to campus network. Online course registration, online library, helpline, wireless network available.

**Student life. Freshman orientation:** Mandatory. Orientation is mandatory for degree-seeking students only. **Activities:** Jazz band, choral groups, dance, drama, literary magazine, music ensembles, musical theater, student government, student newspaper.

**Athletics.** NJCAA. **Intercollegiate:** Baseball M, softball W. **Team name:** Coyotes.

**Student services.** Adult student services, career counseling, student employment services, financial aid counseling, on-campus daycare, personal counseling, placement for graduates, veterans' counselor, women's services. **Physically disabled:** Services for visually, speech, hearing impaired. **Transfer:** Re-entry adviser, pre-admission transcript evaluation for new students. Transfer center, transfer adviser, college fairs on campus for students transferring to 4-year colleges.

**Contact.** E-mail: admrec@ccsn.nevada.edu
Phone: (702) 651-4060 Fax: (702) 651-4811
Patricia Zozaya, Registrar, College of Southern Nevada, 6375 West Charleston Boulevard, Las Vegas, NV 89146-1164

## Heritage College: Las Vegas
**Las Vegas, Nevada**
www.heritagecollege.com
**CB code: 3167**

- For-profit 2-year career college
- Very large city
- Interview required

**General.** Accredited by ACCSCT. **Enrollment:** 325 degree-seeking undergraduates. **Degrees:** 10 associate awarded. **Calendar:** Continuous. **Full-time faculty:** 15 total. **Part-time faculty:** 15 total.

**Basis for selection.** Pharmacy technician program requires clean legal record. Wonderlic SLE exam required for all applicants; cut-off scores vary by program; Ability to Benefit students must also pass the Wonderlic ATB test.

**2007-2008 Annual costs.** Cost of full programs: associate degree programs $26,954, diploma programs $13,654, including fees and books. Personal expenses: $380.

**Application procedures. Admission:** No deadline. No application fee. **Financial aid:** No deadline. FAFSA, institutional form required.

**Academics. Credit/placement by examination:** CLEP. **Support services:** GED preparation, study skills assistance, tutoring.

**Majors. Health:** Insurance coding, office assistant, pharmacy assistant. **Protective services:** Law enforcement admin.

**Computing on campus.** 90 workstations in library, computer center. Online library available.

**Contact.** Phone: (702) 368-2338 Toll-free number: (888) 727-7863 Fax: (702) 368-3853
Queena Fuller, Director of Admissions, Heritage College: Las Vegas, 3315 Spring Mountain Road, Las Vegas, NV 89102

## High-Tech Institute
**Las Vegas, Nevada**
www.hightechinstitute.edu

- For-profit 2-year technical college
- Commuter campus in very large city

**General.** Accredited by ACCSCT. **Calendar:** Semester.

**Annual costs/financial aid.** Associate degree programs: $25,000 - $30,000; diploma programs: $10,000 - $15,000.

**Contact.** Phone: (702) 385-6700
Director of Admissions, 2320 South Rancho Drive, Las Vegas, NV 89102

## Las Vegas College
**Las Vegas, Nevada**
lasvegas-college.com
**CB code: 2149**

- For-profit 2-year business and health science college
- Commuter campus in very large city

**General.** Founded in 1979. Accredited by ACICS. **Calendar:** Quarter.

**Annual costs/financial aid.** Tuition/fees (2007-2008): $13,000. Books/supplies: $300. Personal expenses: $124. Need-based financial aid available to full-time and part-time students.

**Contact.** Phone: (702) 567-1920
Director of Admissions, 170 North Stephanie Street, Las Vegas, NV 89014

## Le Cordon Bleu College of Culinary Arts
**Las Vegas, Nevada**
www.VegasCulinary.com

- For-profit 2-year culinary school
- Commuter campus in very large city

**General.** Accredited by ACCSCT. **Enrollment:** 705 degree-seeking undergraduates. **Degrees:** 413 associate awarded. **Calendar:** Continuous. **Full-time faculty:** 50 total. **Part-time faculty:** 10 total. **Special facilities:** 10 kitchens, student-run restaurant open to general public.

**Basis for selection.** Open admission.

**2007-2008 Annual costs.** Full program cost $41,050.

**Application procedures. Admission:** No deadline. $50 fee. Application may be submitted online. Admission notification on a rolling basis.

**Academics. Special study options:** Accelerated study. **Credit/placement by examination:** CLEP. **Support services:** Learning center, tutoring.

**Majors. Personal/culinary services:** Chef training.

**Student life. Freshman orientation:** Mandatory. **Housing:** Apartments, substance-free housing available. **Activities:** Student newspaper.

**Student services.** Career counseling, student employment services, financial aid counseling. **Transfer:** Re-entry adviser, pre-admission transcript evaluation for new students. Transfer center for students transferring to 4-year colleges.

**Contact.** E-mail: info@vegasculinary.com
Phone: (702) 365-7690 Toll-free number: (866) 450-2433
Fax: (702) 851-5299
John Hayet, Vice President of Admissions, Le Cordon Bleu College of Culinary Arts, 1451 Center Crossing Road, Las Vegas, NV 89144

## Truckee Meadows Community College
**Reno, Nevada**
www.tmcc.edu
**CB code: 1096**

- Public 2-year community and technical college
- Commuter campus in large city

**General.** Founded in 1971. Regionally accredited. Classes offered at over 30 sites in Reno-Sparks area. **Enrollment:** 9,845 degree-seeking undergraduates. **Degrees:** 633 associate awarded. **ROTC:** Army. **Location:** 9 miles from downtown. **Calendar:** Semester, limited summer session. **Full-time faculty:** 183 total. **Part-time faculty:** 494 total. **Class size:** 43% < 20, 54% 20-39, 3% 40-49, less than 1% 50-99.

**Transfer out. Colleges most students transferred to 2007:** University of Nevada-Reno, University of Nevada-Las Vegas.

**Basis for selection.** Open admission, but selective for some programs. High school diploma or GED required if student under 18 years of age. Competitive admission to nursing, dental assistant, and radiological technician programs. **Learning Disabled:** Applicants must contact Disabled Students Office. Accommodations provided according to documentation.

**2007-2008 Annual costs.** Tuition/fees: $1,763; $7,148 out-of-state. Per-credit charge: $55. Good Neighbor tuition: $36.25 per credit hour in addition to registration costs. Nonresident additional per-credit-hour charge: $54.75 for 1-6 credits, flat rate assessment of $5385 per year for 7 credits and above. Books/supplies: $1,092. Personal expenses: $1,298.

**2006-2007 Financial aid. Need-based:** 62% of total undergraduate aid awarded as scholarships/grants, 38% as loans/jobs. Work-study available nights, weekends and for part-time students. **Non-need-based:** Scholarships awarded for academics, art, leadership, minority status, music/drama, state residency. **Additional information:** Institutional grants to state residents, short-term emergency loans available. Work-study applications must reply within 10 days of notification.

**Application procedures. Admission:** No deadline. $10 fee. Application may be submitted online. Admission notification on a rolling basis. Application fee is paid at time of registration for first class. **Financial aid:** Closing date 6/30. FAFSA, institutional form required. Applicants notified by 5/15.

**Academics. Special study options:** Cooperative education, distance learning, dual enrollment of high school students, ESL, honors, internships, liberal arts/career combination, weekend college. License preparation in dental hygiene, nursing, radiology, real estate. **Credit/placement by examination:** CLEP, institutional tests. 15 credit hours maximum toward associate degree. **Support services:** GED preparation and test center, learning center, reduced course load, remedial instruction, study skills assistance, tutoring, writing center.

**Majors. Architecture:** Landscape. **Business:** General, accounting, administrative services, business admin, office management, office technology, real estate. **Computer sciences:** General, data processing, programming. **Conservation:** Environmental studies. **Construction:** Carpentry, maintenance, masonry, pipefitting, power transmission. **Education:** Early childhood, elementary, secondary. **Engineering technology:** Architectural, drafting, solar energy. **Family/consumer sciences:** Child care, institutional food production. **Health:** Dental assistant, dental hygiene, medical radiologic technology/ radiation therapy, medical secretary, nursing (RN), radiologic technology/ medical imaging, substance abuse counseling. **Legal studies:** Legal secretary, paralegal. **Mechanic/repair:** Automotive, diesel, heating/ac/refrig. **Military:** General. **Parks/recreation:** Facilities management. **Protective services:** Corrections, criminal justice, firefighting, juvenile corrections, law enforcement admin, police science. **Social sciences:** Anthropology. **Visual/ performing arts:** Design, dramatic.

**Most popular majors.** Business/marketing 6%, health sciences 15%, liberal arts 54%, physical sciences 7%, security/protective services 7%.

**Computing on campus.** 558 workstations in library, computer center. Helpline, repair service available.

**Student life. Freshman orientation:** Available. Preregistration for classes offered. **Housing:** Housing available 2 miles away at University of Nevada: Reno, for students enrolled for 12 or more credits. **Activities:** Concert band, choral groups, drama, literary magazine, music ensembles, student government, student newspaper, symphony orchestra, social organization for handicapped students.

**Student services.** Adult student services, career counseling, student employment services, financial aid counseling, health services, on-campus daycare, personal counseling, placement for graduates, veterans' counselor. **Physically disabled:** Services for visually, speech, hearing impaired. **Transfer:** Re-entry adviser for new students. Transfer adviser, college fairs on campus for students transferring to 4-year colleges.

**Contact.** E-mail: admissions@tmcc.edu
Phone: (775) 673-7042 Fax: (775) 673-7028
Ty Moore, Assistant Registrar, Truckee Meadows Community College, 7000 Dandini Boulevard, Reno, NV 89512

## Western Nevada College
**Carson City, Nevada**
www.wnc.edu                          CB code: 1141

▶ Public 2-year community college
▶ Commuter campus in small city

**General.** Founded in 1971. Regionally accredited. Three campuses and 6 teaching centers. **Enrollment:** 3,218 degree-seeking undergraduates; 1,603 non-degree-seeking students. **Degrees:** 374 associate awarded. **Location:** 30 miles from Reno. **Calendar:** Semester, limited summer session. **Full-time faculty:** 77 total. **Part-time faculty:** 288 total. **Special facilities:** Observatory, fitness center, baseball field. **Partnerships:** Formal partnerships with selected high schools for dual credit.

**Student profile.** Among degree-seeking undergraduates, 722 enrolled as first-time, first-year students.

| | | | |
|---|---|---|---|
| Part-time: | 72% | Hispanic American: | 9% |
| Women: | 60% | Native American: | 4% |
| African American: | 2% | 25 or older: | 59% |
| Asian American: | 3% | | |

**Transfer out. Colleges most students transferred to 2007:** University of Nevada-Reno.

**Basis for selection.** Open admission, but selective for some programs. Special requirements for nursing and surgical tech programs. SAT and ACT scores accepted, but not required, for math and English placement.

**2007-2008 Annual costs.** Tuition/fees: $1,763; $7,148 out-of-state. Per-credit charge: $55. Good Neighbor tuition: $32.75 additional per-credit-hour charge for student living within 50 miles of Nevada border for 1 year or more, or graduates of specifically designated high schools/community colleges from neighboring states. Nonresident additional per-credit-hour charge: $60.25 for 1-6 credits, flat rate assessment of $5385/yr for 7 credits and above. Books/supplies: $1,100. Personal expenses: $1,200.

**Financial aid. Need-based:** Need-based aid available for part-time students. Work-study available nights and weekends. **Non-need-based:** Scholarships awarded for academics, state residency.

**Application procedures. Admission:** No deadline. $15 fee. Application may be submitted online. No notification sent to applicants except by request. **Financial aid:** Priority date 4/15; no closing date. FAFSA required. Applicants notified on a rolling basis.

**Academics. Special study options:** Accelerated study, cooperative education, distance learning, double major, dual enrollment of high school students, ESL, honors, independent study, internships. Bachelor's degree programs available on campus. License preparation in nursing, paramedic, real estate. **Credit/placement by examination:** AP, CLEP, institutional tests. 30 credit hours maximum toward associate degree. **Support services:** GED preparation and test center, learning center, remedial instruction, study skills assistance, tutoring.

**Majors. Biology:** Biophysics. **Business:** Accounting, business admin, management science, office technology, real estate. **Communications technology:** Graphics. **Computer sciences:** General, LAN/WAN management, webmaster. **Conservation:** General. **Education:** Early childhood. **Engineering:** General. **Engineering technology:** Drafting, electrical. **Health:** Nursing (RN). **Legal studies:** Paralegal. **Liberal arts:** Arts/sciences. **Math:** General. **Mechanic/repair:** Automotive. **Physical sciences:** Chemistry, physics. **Production:** Machine tool, welding. **Protective services:** Corrections, police science.

**Most popular majors.** Business/marketing 12%, health sciences 12%, liberal arts 55%.

**Computing on campus.** 678 workstations in library, computer center, student center. Commuter students can connect to campus network. Online course registration, online library, student web hosting, wireless network available.

**Student life. Freshman orientation:** Available. Preregistration for classes offered. **Activities:** Bands, choral groups, dance, drama, musical theater, student government, student newspaper.

**Athletics.** NJCAA. **Intercollegiate:** Baseball M. **Team name:** Wildcats.

**Student services.** Adult student services, alcohol/substance abuse counseling, career counseling, services for economically disadvantaged, student employment services, financial aid counseling, health services, on-campus daycare, personal counseling, placement for graduates, veterans' counselor, women's services. **Physically disabled:** Services for visually, speech, hearing impaired. **Learning disabled:** Comprehensive services available. **Transfer:** Pre-admission transcript evaluation for new students. Transfer center, transfer adviser for students transferring to 4-year colleges.

**Contact.** E-mail: wncc_aro@wnc.nevada.edu
Phone: (775) 445-3277 Fax: (775) 887-3147
Dianne Hilliard, Director, Admissions and Records, Western Nevada College, 2201 West College Parkway, Carson City, NV 89703-7399

# New Hampshire

---

## Great Bay Community College
### Stratham, New Hampshire
www.stratham.nhctc.edu

**CB member**
**CB code: 3661**

- Public 2-year community and technical college
- Commuter campus in small town

**General.** Founded in 1945. Regionally accredited. **Enrollment:** 1,889 degree-seeking undergraduates. **Degrees:** 149 associate awarded. **Location:** 45 miles from Boston. **Calendar:** Semester, limited summer session. **Full-time faculty:** 38 total. **Part-time faculty:** 87 total. **Special facilities:** Biotechnology lab.

**Student profile.** Among degree-seeking undergraduates, 188 transferred in from other institutions.

**Transfer out. Colleges most students transferred to 2007:** University of New Hampshire, Southern New Hampshire University.

**Basis for selection.** Open admission, but selective for some programs and for out-of-state students. Selective admission to allied health and automotive programs. National League for Nursing Pre-Admission Assessment for Registered Nursing required for applicants to RN program. ACT-PEP Nursing Fundamentals Test required for admission to associate degree nursing program as advanced standing students. Career Guidance Placement Test given to technical majors on selected basis. Interview required for allied health and education applicants. **Adult students:** SAT/ACT scores not required.

**High school preparation.** Recommended units include English 4, mathematics 2, social studies 2 and science 2. High school vocational and college-preparatory courses recommended. For mechanical-technical majors, algebra I and II and geometry recommended. For associate nursing applicants and surgical technology, biology, chemistry, algebra I required. For vet tech, algebra, biology and chemistry are required. For business management, typing or keyboarding skills required.

**2007-2008 Annual costs.** Tuition/fees: $5,400; $12,150 out-of-state. Per-credit charge: $175 in-state; $400 out-of-state. New England Regional tuition: $262 per credit hour. Books/supplies: $600. Personal expenses: $1,000.

**2006-2007 Financial aid.** All financial aid based on need. 83 full-time freshmen applied for aid; 83 were judged to have need; 83 of these received aid. Average need met was 100%. Average scholarship/grant was $3,414; average loan $1,461. 21% of total undergraduate aid awarded as scholarships/grants, 79% as loans/jobs. Need-based aid available for part-time students. Work-study available nights, weekends and for part-time students.

**Application procedures. Admission:** No deadline. $10 fee, may be waived for applicants with need. Application may be submitted online. Admission notification on a rolling basis. Out-of-state students encouraged to apply in early fall of senior year but not before completion of 1 marking period. **Financial aid:** Priority date 3/9; no closing date. FAFSA, institutional form required. Applicants notified on a rolling basis starting 5/9; must reply within 2 week(s) of notification.

**Academics.** Part-time day study available to matriculated and nonmatriculated students. **Special study options:** Accelerated study, distance learning, double major, dual enrollment of high school students, ESL, independent study, internships, liberal arts/career combination. License preparation in nursing. **Credit/placement by examination:** CLEP, institutional tests. **Support services:** GED preparation, learning center, pre-admission summer program, reduced course load, remedial instruction, study skills assistance, tutoring, writing center.

**Majors. Biology:** Biotechnology. **Business:** General, accounting, administrative services, business admin, hospitality admin. **Computer sciences:** Information systems, programming, web page design. **Education:** Social science. **Engineering technology:** Drafting. **Family/consumer sciences:** Child care. **Health:** Nursing (RN), surgical technology, veterinary technology/assistant. **Mechanic/repair:** Automotive. **Protective services:** Law enforcement admin.

**Computing on campus.** 140 workstations in library, computer center. Online library, helpline, wireless network available.

**Student life. Freshman orientation:** Available. **Activities:** Literary magazine, student government, student senate, Phi Theta Kappa.

**Student services.** Career counseling, student employment services, placement for graduates. **Transfer:** Pre-admission transcript evaluation for new students. Transfer adviser, college fairs on campus for students transferring to 4-year colleges.

**Contact.** E-mail: lshennett@ccsnh.edu
Phone: (603) 772-1194 Toll-free number: (800) 522-1194
Fax: (603) 772-1198
Laurilee Shennett, Admissions Coordinator, Great Bay Community College, 277 Portsmouth Avenue, Stratham, NH 03885

---

## Lakes Region Community College
### Laconia, New Hampshire
www.laconia.ccsnh.edu

**CB code: 3850**

- Public 2-year community and technical college
- Commuter campus in large town

**General.** Founded in 1967. Regionally accredited. Numerous satellite programs at various locations. **Enrollment:** 850 degree-seeking undergraduates. **Degrees:** 184 associate awarded. **Location:** 95 miles from Boston, 25 miles from Concord. **Calendar:** Semester, limited summer session. **Full-time faculty:** 40 total. **Part-time faculty:** 20 total. **Special facilities:** Student operated restaurant.

**Student profile.**

| | | | |
|---|---|---|---|
| Out-of-state: | 25% | 25 or older: | 50% |

**Basis for selection.** Open admission, but selective for some programs.

**High school preparation.** Required and recommended units include English 4, mathematics 2-3, social studies 2 and science 4.

**2007-2008 Annual costs.** Tuition/fees: $5,370; $12,120 out-of-state. Per-credit charge: $175 in-state; $400 out-of-state. New England regional tuition per-credit-hour charge: $262.

**2006-2007 Financial aid. Need-based:** 23% of total undergraduate aid awarded as scholarships/grants, 77% as loans/jobs.

**Application procedures. Admission:** No deadline. $10 fee. **Financial aid:** Priority date 5/1; no closing date.

**Academics. Special study options:** Accelerated study, cooperative education, distance learning, double major, honors, independent study, internships, liberal arts/career combination. License preparation in real estate. **Credit/placement by examination:** CLEP, IB, institutional tests. 12 credit hours maximum toward associate degree. **Support services:** GED preparation, learning center, reduced course load, remedial instruction, study skills assistance, tutoring.

**Majors. Business:** Accounting, business admin, hospitality/recreation. **Communications technology:** Graphic/printing. **Computer sciences:** General, data processing, programming. **Construction:** Electrician. **Education:** Early childhood. **Interdisciplinary:** Gerontology. **Liberal arts:** Arts/sciences. **Mechanic/repair:** Automotive, marine. **Personal/culinary services:** Culinary arts. **Protective services:** Fire safety technology, fire services admin, firefighting. **Public administration:** Human services, social work. **Visual/performing arts:** Commercial/advertising art, studio arts.

**Computing on campus.** 100 workstations in library, computer center.

**Student life. Freshman orientation:** Mandatory. Preregistration for classes offered. **Activities:** Literary magazine, student government.

**Athletics.** USCAA. **Intercollegiate:** Baseball M, basketball, soccer, softball W, volleyball W. **Intramural:** Skiing, table tennis. **Team name:** Centurions.

**Student services.** Career counseling, student employment services, financial aid counseling, personal counseling, placement for graduates, veterans' counselor. **Physically disabled:** Services for hearing impaired. **Transfer:** Pre-admission transcript evaluation for new students. Transfer adviser, college fairs on campus for students transferring to 4-year colleges.

**Contact.** E-mail: wfraser@nhctc.edu
Phone: (603) 524-3207 ext. 767 Toll-free number: (800) 357-2992
Fax: (603) 524-8084
Wayne Fraser, Director of Admissions, Lakes Region Community College, 379 Belmont Road, Laconia, NH 03246-9204

## Manchester Community College
**Manchester, New Hampshire**
www.manchester.nhctc.edu

CB member
CB code: 3660

- Public 2-year community and technical college
- Commuter campus in small city

**General.** Founded in 1945. Regionally accredited. Many opportunities for internships and clinicals; strong support for immigrants and first generation college students. **Enrollment:** 2,170 degree-seeking undergraduates. **Degrees:** 155 associate awarded. **Location:** 50 miles from Boston. **Calendar:** Semester, limited summer session. **Full-time faculty:** 70 total. **Part-time faculty:** 125 total. **Partnerships:** Formal partnerships with local businesses.

**Basis for selection.** Open admission, but selective for some programs. Special requirements for nursing program. Ford automotive program students must be sponsored by Ford dealership. NLN pre-admission test required for nursing applicants. ACCUPLACER required for all other applicants. Interview recommended for all, required for human services; portfolio recommended for commercial design and illustration; essay required for exercise science and nursing programs.

**High school preparation.** Recommended units include English 4, mathematics 3 and science 2. Chemistry, algebra, geometry and biology required for some programs.

**2007-2008 Annual costs.** Tuition/fees: $5,430; $12,180 out-of-state. Per-credit charge: $175 in-state; $400 out-of-state. New England Regional tuition: $262 per credit hour. Books/supplies: $550.

**Financial aid.** All financial aid based on need. Work-study available nights, weekends and for part-time students. **Additional information:** 100% of direct educational expenses met for all financial aid applicants.

**Application procedures. Admission:** No deadline. $10 fee, may be waived for applicants with need. Application must be submitted on paper. Admission notification on a rolling basis. **Financial aid:** Priority date 5/1; no closing date. FAFSA, institutional form required. Applicants notified on a rolling basis starting 4/15; must reply within 2 week(s) of notification.

**Academics. Special study options:** Cooperative education, distance learning, double major, ESL, external degree, independent study, internships, liberal arts/career combination, student-designed major. License preparation in nursing, real estate. **Credit/placement by examination:** CLEP, institutional tests. 32 credit hours maximum toward associate degree. **Support services:** Learning center, reduced course load, remedial instruction, study skills assistance, tutoring, writing center.

**Majors. Area/ethnic studies:** American. **Business:** Accounting, administrative services, business admin, management science, marketing, office management. **Communications technology:** Desktop publishing, graphics. **Computer sciences:** General. **Construction:** Maintenance. **Education:** Early childhood. **Engineering technology:** Construction, drafting, electrical. **Health:** Medical assistant, medical records technology, nursing (RN), prenursing. **Liberal arts:** Arts/sciences. **Mechanic/repair:** Automotive, heating/ac/refrig. **Parks/recreation:** Exercise sciences. **Production:** Welding. **Public administration:** Human services. **Visual/performing arts:** Commercial/advertising art, interior design.

**Computing on campus.** 75 workstations in library, computer center. Online library, wireless network available.

**Student life. Freshman orientation:** Available, $25 fee. Preregistration for classes offered. **Activities:** Literary magazine, student government, honor society, community service club, Alternative Spring Break, international club, student senate.

**Athletics. Intercollegiate:** Basketball M, volleyball. **Intramural:** Basketball, skiing, soccer, volleyball.

**Student services.** Career counseling, services for economically disadvantaged, financial aid counseling, minority student services, on-campus daycare. **Physically disabled:** Services for visually, hearing impaired. **Transfer:** Transfer adviser for students transferring to 4-year colleges.

**Contact.** E-mail: jpoirier@ccsnh.edu
Phone: (603) 668-6706 ext. 208 Toll-free number: (800) 924-3445 ext. 208
Fax: (603) 668-5354
Larissa Baia, AVP Enrollment Management, Manchester Community College, 1066 Front Street, Manchester, NH 03102-8518

## Nashua Community College
**Nashua, New Hampshire**
www.nashua.ccsnh.edu

CB member
CB code: 3643

- Public 2-year community and technical college
- Commuter campus in small city
- Interview required

**General.** Founded in 1967. Regionally accredited. Clinical labs and classrooms for nursing students off-campus at Southern New Hampshire Medical Center. **Enrollment:** 1,537 degree-seeking undergraduates. **Degrees:** 201 associate awarded. **Location:** 20 miles from Lowell, Massachusetts. **Calendar:** Semester, limited summer session. **Full-time faculty:** 40 total. **Part-time faculty:** 65 total.

**Transfer out. Colleges most students transferred to 2007:** University of Southern New Hampshire, University of New Hampshire, Keene State College, Plymouth State College.

**Basis for selection.** Open admission, but selective for some programs. Prerequisite courses, references, interview, exam required to apply for Nursing program. Clean driving record to apply for Honda program. Essay and interview with Program Coordinator required for Restaurant Management.

**High school preparation.** One unit algebra required for business and technical programs, 2 for computer/engineering technology.

**2007-2008 Annual costs.** Tuition/fees: $5,730; $12,480 out-of-state. Per-credit charge: $175 in-state; $400 out-of-state. New England regional tuition: $262 per credit hour. Books/supplies: $500. Personal expenses: $500.

**Financial aid.** All financial aid based on need. Need-based aid available for part-time students. Work-study available nights and for part-time students.

**Application procedures. Admission:** No deadline. $10 fee, may be waived for applicants with need. Application must be submitted on paper. Admission notification on a rolling basis. Application priority date of 12/31 for nursing applicants. **Financial aid:** Priority date 5/1; no closing date. FAFSA required. Applicants notified on a rolling basis starting 3/1; must reply within 2 week(s) of notification.

**Academics. Special study options:** Combined bachelor's/graduate degree, distance learning, dual enrollment of high school students, ESL, independent study, internships, student-designed major, weekend college. License preparation in aviation. **Credit/placement by examination:** AP, CLEP, institutional tests. 48 credit hours maximum toward associate degree. **Support services:** Learning center, pre-admission summer program, reduced course load, remedial instruction, study skills assistance, tutoring, writing center.

**Majors. Business:** Accounting, business admin. **Computer sciences:** General, applications programming, computer science, data entry, data processing, information systems, networking, webmaster. **Education:** Early childhood. **Engineering:** Electrical. **Engineering technology:** Drafting, electrical, manufacturing, robotics. **Health:** Nursing (RN). **Legal studies:** Paralegal. **Liberal arts:** Arts/sciences. **Mechanic/repair:** Aircraft, auto body, automotive, electronics/electrical, industrial. **Public administration:** Human services.

**Computing on campus.** 150 workstations in library, computer center. Student web hosting, wireless network available.

**Student life. Freshman orientation:** Mandatory, $30 fee. Preregistration for classes offered. One-day session. **Housing:** Student housing available near campus. **Activities:** Drama, literary magazine, student government, student newspaper, Phi Theta Kappa, Rotoract.

**Athletics. Intramural:** Soccer.

**Student services.** Adult student services, career counseling, services for economically disadvantaged, student employment services, financial aid counseling, personal counseling, placement for graduates, veterans' counselor. **Transfer:** Pre-admission transcript evaluation for new students. Transfer adviser, college fairs on campus for students transferring to 4-year colleges.

**Contact.** E-mail: nashua@ccsnh.edu
Phone: (603) 882-6923 ext. 1461 Fax: (603) 882-8690
Patricia Goodman, Director of Admissions, Nashua Community College, 505 Amherst Street, Nashua, NH 03063-1026

## New Hampshire Technical Institute
Concord, New Hampshire
www.nhti.edu                                    CB code: 3647

- Public 2-year community and technical college
- Commuter campus in large town

**General.** Founded in 1965. Regionally accredited. **Location:** 75 miles from Boston. **Calendar:** Semester.

**Annual costs/financial aid.** Tuition/fees (2007-2008): $5,760; $12,510 out-of-state. New England Regional tuition: $262 per credit hour. Room/board: $7,440. Books/supplies: $600. Personal expenses: $1,600. Need-based financial aid available to full-time and part-time students.

**Contact.**  Phone: (603) 271-7134
Director of Admissions, 31 College Drive, Concord, NH 03301

## River Valley Community College
Claremont, New Hampshire
www.rivervalley.edu
CB code: 3684

- Public 2-year technical college
- Large town

**General.** Founded in 1967. Regionally accredited. Restaurant mangement program includes one year in Switzerland with study at Les Roches. **Enrollment:** 682 degree-seeking undergraduates. **Degrees:** 122 associate awarded. **Location:** 50 miles from Concord. **Calendar:** Semester, limited summer session. **Full-time faculty:** 38 total. **Part-time faculty:** 75 total.

**Basis for selection.** Open admission, but selective for some programs. Special requirements for nursing program. Accuplacer test used for placement.

**High school preparation.** Typing required for medical assistant, chemistry required for nursing and medical laboratory programs. Algebra recommended for all applicants.

**2007-2008 Annual costs.** Tuition/fees: $5,340; $12,090 out-of-state. Per-credit charge: $175 in-state; $400 out-of-state. New England Regional tuition: $262 per credit hour. Books/supplies: $550. Personal expenses: $1,100.

**Financial aid.** All financial aid based on need. Need-based aid available for part-time students.

**Application procedures. Admission:** No deadline. $10 fee. Admission notification on a rolling basis. **Financial aid:** Priority date 4/1, closing date 4/1. FAFSA required. Applicants notified on a rolling basis; must reply within 2 week(s) of notification.

**Academics. Special study options:** Accelerated study, cooperative education, double major, independent study, internships. Joint associate degree program in restaurant management with Les Roches, 2-2 program in teacher education with Keene State College. **Credit/placement by examination:** CLEP, institutional tests. 16 credit hours maximum toward associate degree. **Support services:** Learning center, reduced course load, tutoring.

**Majors. Business:** General, accounting, office technology. **Engineering technology:** Computer systems, manufacturing. **Health:** Clinical lab technology, nursing (RN), occupational therapy assistant, physical therapy assistant, respiratory therapy technology. **Liberal arts:** Arts/sciences. **Parks/recreation:** General. **Public administration:** Human services.

**Most popular majors.** Health sciences 87%.

**Computing on campus.** 45 workstations in library, computer center.

**Student life. Activities:** Student government.

**Student services.** Student employment services, health services, on-campus daycare, personal counseling, placement for graduates, veterans' counselor.

**Contact.**  Phone: (603) 542-7744 Fax: (603) 543-1844
Chuck Kusselow, Director of Admissions, River Valley Community College, One College Drive, Claremont, NH 03743-9707

## White Mountains Community College
Berlin, New Hampshire
www.berlin.ccsnh.edu                              CB code: 3646

- Public 2-year community and technical college
- Commuter campus in large town

**General.** Founded in 1966. Regionally accredited. **Enrollment:** 610 degree-seeking undergraduates. **Degrees:** 110 associate awarded. **Location:** 110 miles from Concord; 100 miles from Portland, Maine. **Calendar:** Semester, limited summer session. **Full-time faculty:** 29 total. **Part-time faculty:** 53 total.

**Basis for selection.** School record, class rank, counselor recommendations, test results, interview considered. NLN PreAdmission Exam-RN required for nursing students. All others participate in ASSET test. Interview recommended.

**2007-2008 Annual costs.** Tuition/fees: $5,370; $12,120 out-of-state. Per-credit charge: $175 in-state; $400 out-of-state. New England Regional tuition: $262 per credit hour. Books/supplies: $500. Personal expenses: $1,500.

**Financial aid.** All financial aid based on need. Need-based aid available for part-time students.

**Application procedures. Admission:** Priority date 5/1; no deadline. $10 fee, may be waived for applicants with need. Admission notification on a rolling basis beginning on or about 12/1. **Financial aid:** Priority date 5/1; no closing date. FAFSA, institutional form required. Applicants notified on a rolling basis starting 5/1; must reply within 2 week(s) of notification.

**Academics. Special study options:** Cooperative education, distance learning, double major, dual enrollment of high school students, independent study, internships, student-designed major. **Credit/placement by examination:** CLEP, institutional tests. 32 credit hours maximum toward associate degree. **Support services:** Learning center, reduced course load, remedial instruction, study skills assistance, tutoring.

**Majors. Business:** Accounting, administrative services, business admin, office technology, office/clerical, restaurant/food services. **Computer sciences:** General. **Conservation:** Environmental studies, forestry, management/policy. **Education:** Early childhood, multi-level teacher. **Engineering technology:** Computer systems, drafting, surveying, water quality. **Health:** Nursing (RN). **Liberal arts:** Arts/sciences. **Mechanic/repair:** Automotive, diesel. **Personal/culinary services:** Chef training, restaurant/catering. **Protective services:** Law enforcement admin. **Public administration:** Human services.

**Computing on campus.** 45 workstations in library, computer center. Online course registration, online library available.

**Student life. Freshman orientation:** Mandatory, $30 fee. **Activities:** Student government.

**Student services.** Adult student services, career counseling, student employment services, financial aid counseling, on-campus daycare, personal counseling, veterans' counselor. **Physically disabled:** Services for visually, hearing impaired. **Transfer:** Transfer adviser for students transferring to 4-year colleges.

**Contact.**  E-mail: berlin4u@ccsnh.edu
Phone: (603) 752-1113 Toll-free number: (800) 445-4525
Fax: (603) 752-6335
Mark Desmarais, Admissions Director, White Mountains Community College, 2020 Riverside Drive, Berlin, NH 03570

Two-Year Colleges

# New Jersey

## Assumption College for Sisters

Mendham, New Jersey
www.acs350.org                                    CB code: 2009

- Private 2-year junior and liberal arts college for women affiliated with Roman Catholic Church
- Residential campus in small town
- Application essay required

**General.** Founded in 1953. Regionally accredited. **Enrollment:** 32 degree-seeking undergraduates; 1 non-degree-seeking students. **Degrees:** 7 associate awarded. **Location:** 35 miles from New York City. **Calendar:** Semester, limited summer session. **Full-time faculty:** 2 total; 100% women. **Part-time faculty:** 11 total; 27% have terminal degrees, 82% women. **Class size:** 100% < 20.

**Student profile.** Among degree-seeking undergraduates, 11 enrolled as first-time, first-year students, 1 transferred in from other institutions.

| | | | |
|---|---|---|---|
| Out-of-state: | 100% | Hispanic American: | 3% |
| Women: | 100% | International: | 94% |

**Basis for selection.** Interview, recommendations, school achievement record, test scores, commitment to obligations of religious vocation as well as acceptance of applicant by a religious community important.

**High school preparation.** 16 units required. Required and recommended units include English 4, mathematics 2-3, history 2, science 2-3, foreign language 2, visual/performing arts 1 and academic electives 4.

**2008-2009 Annual costs.** Tuition/fees (projected): $5,000. Per-credit charge: $150.

**Application procedures. Admission:** No deadline. $50 fee, may be waived for applicants with need. Admission notification on a rolling basis. **Financial aid:** No deadline.

**Academics. Special study options:** ESL. **Credit/placement by examination:** AP, CLEP, SAT. **Support services:** Reduced course load, remedial instruction, study skills assistance, tutoring.

**Majors. Liberal arts:** Arts/sciences.

**Computing on campus.** 21 workstations in library, computer center, student center. Online library, helpline, repair service, wireless network available.

**Student life. Freshman orientation:** Mandatory. **Policies:** Religious observance required. **Housing:** Students reside with their religious congregations or with the Sisters of Christian Charity. **Activities:** Choral groups.

**Student services. Transfer:** Pre-admission transcript evaluation for new students. Transfer adviser for students transferring to 4-year colleges.

**Contact.** E-mail: deanregistrar@acs350.org
Phone: (973) 543-6528 ext. 228 Fax: (973) 543-1738
Sr. Gerardine Tantsits, Academic Dean/Registrar, Assumption College for Sisters, 350 Bernardsville Road, Mendham, NJ 07945-2923

## Atlantic Cape Community College

Mays Landing, New Jersey                          CB member
www.atlantic.edu                                  CB code: 2024

- Public 2-year culinary school and community college
- Commuter campus in small town

**General.** Founded in 1964. Regionally accredited. Instruction and student/academic support services delivered at all 3 campuses (Mays Landing, Atlantic City, Cape May). **Enrollment:** 6,419 degree-seeking undergraduates. **Degrees:** 724 associate awarded. **Location:** 15 miles from Atlantic City, 30 miles from Philadelphia. **Calendar:** Semester, limited summer session. **Full-time faculty:** 98 total. **Part-time faculty:** 256 total. **Special facilities:** Gourmet restaurant run by students enrolled in the Academy of Culinary Arts.

**Transfer out. Colleges most students transferred to 2007:** Richard Stockton State College of New Jersey, Rowan University, Rutgers University.

**Basis for selection.** Open admission, but selective for some programs. Admission to allied health and nursing programs based upon entrance exam scores and GPA. All students must take college basic skills exam after completing 12th credit or when they officially matriculate. Students who score 500 and above on Verbal section, and 470 on Math section of SAT exempt from basic skills testing. **Homeschooled:** Students must be in certified homeschooling program. Letter from certifying school district approving courses required.

**2007-2008 Annual costs.** Tuition/fees: $3,030; $5,520 out-of-district; $10,500 out-of-state. Per-credit charge: $83 in-district; $166 out-of-district; $332 out-of-state. Books/supplies: $1,400.

**Financial aid. Need-based:** Need-based aid available for part-time students. Work-study available for part-time students. **Additional information:** Installment plan available for culinary arts majors. Employees of Atlantic City casinos may attend ACCC at in-county rates regardless of where they live.

**Application procedures. Admission:** Closing date 9/1 (postmark date). $35 fee, may be waived for applicants with need. Application may be submitted online. Admission notification on a rolling basis. Applicants must make arrangements to take the College Basic Skills Placement Test unless SAT scores qualify them for exemption. **Financial aid:** Priority date 5/1; no closing date. FAFSA, institutional form required. Applicants notified on a rolling basis starting 5/1.

**Academics.** 8 associate degrees available through distance education: in liberal arts, history, psychology, business, computer information systems, humanities, general studies, and literature. **Special study options:** Cooperative education, distance learning, double major, dual enrollment of high school students, ESL, independent study, internships, liberal arts/career combination. Bachelor's degree programs available on campus. License preparation in nursing, real estate. **Credit/placement by examination:** CLEP, institutional tests. 32 credit hours maximum toward associate degree. Total of 32 transfer credits may be awarded through combination of: college course transfer, articulation agreements, CLEP, Ponsi/ACE and/or Tech-Prep. **Support services:** GED test center, learning center, pre-admission summer program, reduced course load, remedial instruction, study skills assistance, tutoring, writing center.

**Majors. Biology:** General. **Business:** Accounting, business admin, hospitality admin, management information systems, tourism/travel. **Computer sciences:** General, data processing, programming. **Education:** General. **Family/consumer sciences:** Child care. **Health:** Nursing (RN), occupational therapy assistant, physical therapy assistant, respiratory therapy technology. **History:** General. **Legal studies:** Paralegal. **Math:** General. **Personal/culinary services:** Culinary arts. **Physical sciences:** Chemistry. **Psychology:** General. **Public administration:** Social work. **Social sciences:** General, sociology. **Visual/performing arts:** Studio arts.

**Most popular majors.** Business/marketing 23%, health sciences 11%, interdisciplinary studies 22%, liberal arts 30%.

**Computing on campus.** 430 workstations in library, computer center, student center. Online course registration, online library, helpline available.

**Student life. Freshman orientation:** Available. Preregistration for classes offered. Online orentation. **Housing:** Reserved housing program available. **Activities:** Choral groups, drama, literary magazine, music ensembles, radio station, student government, student newspaper, Human Services club, African American Coalition, international club, Jewish Association of Students, Phi Theta Kappa, Alpha & Omega Christian clubs, Shades of Brown of Atlantic City, special interest clubs.

**Athletics.** NJCAA. **Intercollegiate:** Archery, basketball M, golf, softball W. **Intramural:** Basketball, bowling, soccer, softball, volleyball. **Team name:** Buccaneers.

**Student services.** Adult student services, career counseling, student employment services, health services, on-campus daycare, personal counseling, placement for graduates, veterans' counselor. **Physically disabled:** Services for visually, speech, hearing impaired. **Transfer:** Pre-admission transcript evaluation for new students. Transfer adviser, college fairs on campus for students transferring to 4-year colleges.

**Contact.** E-mail: accadmit@atlantic.edu
Phone: (609) 343-5000 Fax: (609) 343-4921
Regina Skinner, Director, Admission and College Recruitment, Atlantic Cape Community College, 5100 Black Horse Pike, Mays Landing, NJ 08330

## Bergen Community College
**Paramus, New Jersey**
www.bergen.edu

**CB member**
**CB code: 2032**

▶ Public 2-year community college
▶ Commuter campus in large town

**General.** Founded in 1965. Regionally accredited. Center for Deaf Education with counselors and specialized equipment. **Enrollment:** 12,930 degree-seeking undergraduates; 2,128 non-degree-seeking students. **Degrees:** 1,323 associate awarded. **Location:** 12 miles from New York City. **Calendar:** Semester, extensive summer session. **Full-time faculty:** 303 total; 13% minority, 54% women. **Part-time faculty:** 453 total; 15% minority, 51% women.

**Student profile.** Among degree-seeking undergraduates, 76% enrolled in a transfer program, 24% enrolled in a vocational program, 3,097 enrolled as first-time, first-year students.

| | | | |
|---|---|---|---|
| Part-time: | 42% | Hispanic American: | 26% |
| Women: | 53% | International: | 8% |
| African American: | 7% | 25 or older: | 33% |
| Asian American: | 10% | | |

**Transfer out.** Colleges most students transferred to 2007: Montclair State College, William Paterson University, Rutgers University, Ramapo College.

**Basis for selection.** Open admission, but selective for some programs. Admission to allied health programs based on academic record and specific courses taken. Priority given to county residents. High school diploma not required for students over 18 years old. **Learning Disabled:** Students must provide documentation of disability to Office of Specialized Services.

**High school preparation.** Mathematics, biology, and chemistry required for most allied health programs.

**2007-2008 Annual costs.** Tuition/fees: $3,702; $6,840 out-of-district; $7,140 out-of-state. Per-credit charge: $98 in-district; $203 out-of-district; $213 out-of-state.

**2006-2007 Financial aid.** Need-based: 79% of total undergraduate aid awarded as scholarships/grants, 21% as loans/jobs.

**Application procedures. Admission:** No deadline. $25 fee, may be waived for applicants with need. Admission notification on a rolling basis. Application closing date for nursing and dental hygiene March 1. **Financial aid:** No deadline. FAFSA required. Applicants notified on a rolling basis starting 6/1.

**Academics. Special study options:** Cooperative education, distance learning, dual enrollment of high school students, ESL, honors, internships, study abroad. Semester at Disney World for selected students. **Credit/placement by examination:** AP, CLEP, institutional tests. **Support services:** Learning center, pre-admission summer program, reduced course load, remedial instruction, tutoring, writing center.

**Majors. Agriculture:** Horticulture. **Area/ethnic studies:** American. **Business:** Accounting technology, administrative services, banking/financial services, hotel/motel admin, marketing, sales/distribution, special products marketing. **Computer sciences:** Applications programming, information technology. **Education:** Early childhood. **Engineering technology:** General, electrical, manufacturing, mechanical drafting. **Health:** Clinical lab technology, dental hygiene, health services, medical assistant, medical radiologic technology/radiation therapy, nursing (RN), physical therapy assistant, respiratory therapy technology, sonography, veterinary technology/assistant. **Legal studies:** Paralegal. **Liberal arts:** Arts/sciences. **Protective services:** Police science. **Visual/performing arts:** Commercial/advertising art.

**Most popular majors.** Health sciences 21%, liberal arts 62%.

**Student life. Freshman orientation:** Available. Preregistration for classes offered. **Activities:** Choral groups, dance, drama, literary magazine, music ensembles, musical theater, student government, student newspaper.

**Athletics.** NJCAA. **Intercollegiate:** Baseball M, basketball, cross-country, golf M, soccer M, softball W, tennis M, track and field, volleyball W, wrestling M.

**Student services.** Career counseling, student employment services, financial aid counseling, health services, on-campus daycare, personal counseling, placement for graduates, veterans' counselor. **Physically disabled:** Services for visually, speech, hearing impaired. **Transfer:** Transfer adviser, college fairs on campus for students transferring to 4-year colleges.

**Contact.** E-mail: admsoffice@bergen.edu
Phone: (201) 447-7195 Fax: (201) 670-7973
Priscilla Klymenko, Director of Enrollment Services, Bergen Community College, 400 Paramus Road, Paramus, NJ 07652-1595

## Brookdale Community College
**Lincroft, New Jersey**
www.brookdalecc.edu

**CB member**
**CB code: 2181**

▶ Public 2-year community college
▶ Commuter campus in small city

**General.** Founded in 1967. Regionally accredited. **Enrollment:** 12,225 degree-seeking undergraduates. **Degrees:** 1,632 associate awarded. **ROTC:** Army, Air Force. **Location:** 5 miles from Red Bank, 25 miles from New Brunswick. **Calendar:** Semester, extensive summer session. **Full-time faculty:** 225 total. **Part-time faculty:** 626 total.

**Student profile.**

| | | | |
|---|---|---|---|
| Out-of-state: | 1% | 25 or older: | 38% |

**Transfer out.** Colleges most students transferred to 2007: Monmouth University, Rutgers University, Kean University.

**Basis for selection.** Open admission, but selective for some programs. Special requirements for health sciences programs and automative technology programs. Applicants without high school diploma or GED may be admitted. Must take equivalent of GED after specific number of credits in specific distribution. ACCUPLACER used for placement for all degree-seeking students who have reached their 12th credit. Group interview required for nursing, medical laboratory technology, respiratory therapy applicants, radiologic technology.

**High school preparation.** One unit high school or college algebra, 1 chemistry, 1 biology required for allied health programs.

**2007-2008 Annual costs.** Tuition/fees: $3,768; $6,858 out-of-district; $7,428 out-of-state. Per-credit charge: $103 in-district; $206 out-of-district; $225 out-of-state. Books/supplies: $1,000. Personal expenses: $1,195.

**Financial aid. Need-based:** Need-based aid available for part-time students. **Non-need-based:** Scholarships awarded for athletics.

**Application procedures. Admission:** No deadline. $25 fee. Application may be submitted online. Admission notification on a rolling basis. **Financial aid:** Priority date 5/1; no closing date. FAFSA, institutional form required. Applicants notified on a rolling basis starting 5/1; must reply within 2 week(s) of notification.

**Academics. Special study options:** Cooperative education, distance learning, ESL, honors, independent study, internships, study abroad, weekend college. License preparation in dental hygiene, nursing. **Credit/placement by examination:** AP, CLEP, institutional tests. **Support services:** GED preparation and test center, learning center, pre-admission summer program, reduced course load, remedial instruction, tutoring, writing center.

**Majors. Business:** General, accounting, administrative services, business admin, fashion, marketing. **Communications technology:** General, graphic/printing. **Computer sciences:** General. **Education:** General, teacher assistance. **Engineering:** General. **Engineering technology:** Electrical. **Health:** Clinical lab technology, dental hygiene, medical radiologic technology/radiation therapy, nursing (RN), respiratory therapy technology. **Legal studies:** Paralegal. **Liberal arts:** Arts/sciences. **Personal/culinary services:** Culinary arts. **Protective services:** Police science. **Public administration:** Social work. **Social sciences:** General. **Visual/performing arts:** Art, interior design, photography, studio arts.

**Computing on campus.** 1,100 workstations in library, computer center. Commuter students can connect to campus network. Helpline available.

**Student life. Freshman orientation:** Available. Preregistration for classes offered. **Activities:** Dance, drama, film society, literary magazine, musical theater, radio station, student government, student newspaper, TV station.

**Athletics.** NJCAA. **Intercollegiate:** Baseball M, basketball, cross-country, soccer, softball W, tennis. **Intramural:** Basketball, golf M, volleyball. **Team name:** Blues.

**Student services.** Career counseling, student employment services, health services, on-campus daycare, personal counseling, placement for graduates, veterans' counselor. **Physically disabled:** Services for visually, speech, hearing impaired. **Transfer:** Transfer adviser for students transferring to 4-year colleges.

**Contact.** Phone: (732) 224-2375 Fax: (732) 224-2271
Bruce Marich, Director of Admissions, Brookdale Community College, 765
Newman Springs Road, Lincroft, NJ 07738

## Burlington County College
**Pemberton, New Jersey**
www.bcc.edu

**CB member**
**CB code: 2180**

- Public 2-year community college
- Commuter campus in small town

**General.** Founded in 1966. Regionally accredited. Credit courses offered
at the main campus in Pemberton, the Mount Laurel Campus, the Willing-
boro Center, the Mount Holly Center, an educational center at Bordentown
Regional High School; various other county high schools; and on 2 military
bases. **Enrollment:** 7,147 degree-seeking undergraduates; 1,285 non-degree-
seeking students. **Degrees:** 795 associate awarded. **Location:** 30 miles from
Philadelphia, 80 miles from New York City. **Calendar:** Semester, limited
summer session. **Full-time faculty:** 62 total; 16% minority, 45% women.
**Part-time faculty:** 409 total; 15% minority, 56% women. **Class size:** 23%
< 20, 69% 20-39, 2% 40-49, 6% 50-99. **Special facilities:** Sculpture gar-
den, outdoor amphitheatre, small business incubator. **Partnerships:** Formal
partnership with police academy.

**Student profile.** Among degree-seeking undergraduates, 57% enrolled in
a transfer program, 27% enrolled in a vocational program, 1% already have
a bachelor's degree or higher, 1,961 enrolled as first-time, first-year students, 274 transferred in from other institutions.

| | | | |
|---|---|---|---|
| Part-time: | 43% | Asian American: | 4% |
| Out-of-state: | 1% | Hispanic American: | 6% |
| Women: | 59% | 25 or older: | 33% |
| African American: | 21% | | |

**Transfer out. Colleges most students transferred to 2007:** Rutgers University (Camden), Stockton College of NJ, Rowan University, Drexel University, Rider University.

**Basis for selection.** Open admission, but selective for some programs.
Academic high school background required of nursing program applicants.

**2007-2008 Annual costs.** Tuition/fees: $2,685; $3,255 out-of-district;
$5,205 out-of-state. Per-credit charge: $73 in-district; $92 out-of-district;
$157 out-of-state. Books/supplies: $1,200. Personal expenses: $3,438.

**Financial aid.** All financial aid based on need. Need-based aid available
for part-time students. Work-study available nights, weekends and for part-
time students.

**Application procedures. Admission:** No deadline. $20 fee, may be
waived for applicants with need. Admission notification on a rolling basis.
**Financial aid:** No deadline. FAFSA, institutional form required. Applicants
notified on a rolling basis starting 7/1; must reply within 3 week(s) of notification.

**Academics. Special study options:** Cooperative education, distance learning, double major, dual enrollment of high school students, ESL, independent study, study abroad, weekend college. Bachelor's degree programs available on campus. License preparation in dental hygiene, nursing, radiology.
**Credit/placement by examination:** AP, CLEP, institutional tests. 30 credit
hours maximum toward associate degree. **Support services:** GED preparation and test center, learning center, pre-admission summer program, reduced course load, remedial instruction, study skills assistance, tutoring,
writing center.

**Majors. Biology:** Biotechnology. **Business:** General, accounting, accounting technology, business admin, management information systems, restaurant/
food services, sales/distribution. **Communications technology:** Animation/
special effects, photo/film/video, recording arts. **Computer sciences:** Computer
graphics, computer science, data processing, information systems. **Engineering technology:** Automotive, CAD/CADD, civil, construction, electrical.
**Foreign languages:** Sign language interpretation. **Health:** Dental hygiene,
medical radiologic technology/radiation therapy, medical records technology, nursing (RN), sonography. **Legal studies:** Paralegal. **Liberal arts:** Arts/
sciences. **Physical sciences:** General. **Protective services:** Firefighting, police science. **Public administration:** Human services. **Science technology:**
Chemical. **Visual/performing arts:** Fashion design, graphic design, photography. **Other:** Graphical Information Systems, Hearing Instrument Science,
Technical Studies.

**Most popular majors.** Health sciences 17%, liberal arts 67%, security/
protective services 7%.

**Computing on campus.** 1,600 workstations in library, computer center,
student center. Commuter students can connect to campus network. Online
library, helpline, wireless network available.

**Student life. Freshman orientation:** Available. Preregistration for classes
offered. **Activities:** Concert band, choral groups, dance, drama, international student organizations, literary magazine, music ensembles, musical
theater, radio station, student government, minority student union, veterans
club, Phi Theta Kappa, Student Nurses Association, Collegiate Republicans,
Young Democrats, Circle K, Students for Ecological Action, Christian student club.

**Athletics.** NJCAA. **Intercollegiate:** Baseball M, basketball, golf M, soccer, softball W. **Team name:** Barons.

**Student services.** Adult student services, alcohol/substance abuse counseling, career counseling, services for economically disadvantaged, student
employment services, financial aid counseling, health services, minority student services, on-campus daycare, personal counseling, placement for graduates, veterans' counselor. **Physically disabled:** Services for visually, speech,
hearing impaired. **Transfer:** Transfer adviser, college fairs on campus for
students transferring to 4-year colleges.

**Contact.** Phone: (609) 894-9311 ext. 1282 Fax: (609) 894-0764
Elva DeJesus-Lopez, Admissions Coordinator, Burlington County College,
601 Pemberton-Browns Mills Road, Pemberton, NJ 08068-1599

## Camden County College
**Blackwood, New Jersey**
www.camdencc.edu

**CB member**
**CB code: 2121**

- Public 2-year community college
- Commuter campus in large town

**General.** Founded in 1966. Regionally accredited. **Enrollment:** 7,449 degree-
seeking undergraduates. **Degrees:** 1,257 associate awarded. **Location:** 15
miles from Philadelphia, 13 miles from Camden. **Calendar:** Semester, extensive summer session. **Full-time faculty:** 143 total. **Part-time faculty:**
591 total. **Special facilities:** Integrated manufacturing building, laser technology institute for education and research, computer graphics laboratories.

**Student profile.**

| | | | |
|---|---|---|---|
| Out-of-state: | 2% | 25 or older: | 41% |

**Transfer out. Colleges most students transferred to 2007:** Rowan University, Rutgers University-Camden, Temple University, Widener University.

**Basis for selection.** Open admission, but selective for some programs.
Special requirements for allied health, dental, and nursing programs. SAT or
ACT required for admission to certain selective programs. Psychological
Corporation Pre-Nursing examination, entrance examination for School of
Nursing or National League for Nursing, Pre-Nursing and Guidance exami-
nation required of nursing applicants. Mechanical aptitude test required for
General Motors automotive service education program applicants. Dental
Hygiene Aptitude Test required of students entering dental hygiene pro-
gram. Interview recommended for various health and the General Motors
programs.

**2007-2008 Annual costs.** Tuition/fees: $3,000; $3,120 out-of-state. Per-
credit charge: $83 in-state; $87 out-of-state. Books/supplies: $650.

**Financial aid. Need-based:** Need-based aid available for part-time students. Work-study available for part-time students.

**Application procedures. Admission:** No deadline. No application fee.
Application may be submitted online. Admission notification on a rolling
basis beginning on or about 2/3. **Financial aid:** Closing date 7/1. FAFSA,
institutional form required. Applicants notified on a rolling basis starting
7/1.

**Academics.** Strong program in robotics, laser/electro optics technology,
and computer graphics. **Special study options:** Cooperative education, cross-
registration, distance learning, dual enrollment of high school students, ESL,
honors, independent study, internships, liberal arts/career combination, weekend college. General Motors automotive service education program. **Credit/
placement by examination:** CLEP, institutional tests. 30 credit hours maximum toward associate degree. New Jersey College Basic Skills placement
test required. **Support services:** Learning center, pre-admission summer
program, reduced course load, remedial instruction, study skills assistance,
tutoring.

**Majors. Business:** Accounting, banking/financial services, business admin, management information systems, marketing, sales/distribution. **Computer sciences:** General, computer graphics. **Engineering:** Science. **Engineering technology:** Drafting, electrical. **Foreign languages:** Sign language interpretation. **Health:** Clinical lab technology, dental assistant, dental hygiene, nursing (RN), optician, respiratory therapy technology, veterinary technology/assistant. **Liberal arts:** Arts/sciences. **Protective services:** Fire safety technology, police science. **Public administration:** Social work. **Visual/performing arts:** Photography.

**Computing on campus.** 800 workstations in library, computer center.

**Student life. Freshman orientation:** Available. **Activities:** Concert band, choral groups, drama, literary magazine, radio station, student government, student newspaper.

**Athletics.** NJCAA. **Intercollegiate:** Baseball M, basketball, soccer, softball W. **Intramural:** Racquetball W.

**Student services.** Career counseling, student employment services, health services, on-campus daycare, placement for graduates, veterans' counselor. **Physically disabled:** Services for visually, speech, hearing impaired. **Transfer:** Transfer adviser, college fairs on campus for students transferring to 4-year colleges.

**Contact.** Phone: (856) 227-7200 ext. 4200 Toll-free number: (888) 228-2466 Fax: (856) 374-4917
Sharon Wedington, Admissions Director, Camden County College, Box 200, Blackwood, NJ 08012

---

## County College of Morris
**Randolph, New Jersey**
www.ccm.edu

CB member
CB code: 2124

- Public 2-year community college
- Commuter campus in large town

**General.** Founded in 1965. Regionally accredited. Courses available at off-campus sites. **Enrollment:** 6,628 degree-seeking undergraduates. **Degrees:** 1,096 associate awarded. **Location:** 40 miles from New York City. **Calendar:** Semester, extensive summer session. **Full-time faculty:** 148 total. **Part-time faculty:** 357 total. **Special facilities:** Planetarium.

**Student profile.**

| Out-of-state: | 1% | 25 or older: | 25% |

**Transfer out. Colleges most students transferred to 2007:** Montclair State University, William Paterson University of New Jersey, Rutgers University, Kean University, Fairleigh Dickinson University, New Jersey Institute of Technology.

**Basis for selection.** Open admission, but selective for some programs. Restricted admissions to nursing, medical lab technology, radiography, respiratory therapy, and veterinary technology on space-available basis. Applicants who are not native speakers of English required to take LOEP test (Levels of English Proficiency) for placement. SAT required for honors programs. Students who submit SAT scores of 500 (exclusive of Writing) and over exempt from basic skills placement test. Audition required for music programs. **Learning Disabled:** Students may apply to Horizons program if they want accommodations. This is in addition to application for admission.

**High school preparation.** 16 units recommended. Some programs require 2 to 4 units mathematics and 1 to 2 units laboratory science.

**2007-2008 Annual costs.** Tuition/fees: $3,315; $6,195 out-of-district; $8,505 out-of-state. Per-credit charge: $96 in-district; $192 out-of-district; $269 out-of-state. Tuition reciprocity agreements with neighboring counties allow some out-of-county residents to pay in-county rates. Books/supplies: $750. Personal expenses: $1,120.

**Financial aid. Need-based:** Need-based aid available for part-time students. Work-study available for part-time students. **Non-need-based:** Scholarships awarded for athletics.

**Application procedures. Admission:** No deadline. $30 fee. Application may be submitted online. Admission notification on a rolling basis. **Financial aid:** Priority date 3/1; no closing date. FAFSA required. Applicants notified on a rolling basis starting 5/1.

**Academics. Special study options:** Cooperative education, distance learning, double major, dual enrollment of high school students, ESL, exchange student, external degree, honors, independent study, internships, liberal arts/career combination, study abroad, weekend college. Bachelor's degree programs available on campus. License preparation in aviation, nursing. **Credit/**

**placement by examination:** AP, CLEP, institutional tests. **Support services:** GED preparation, learning center, pre-admission summer program, reduced course load, remedial instruction, study skills assistance, tutoring, writing center.

**Majors. Agriculture:** Business. **Business:** Administrative services, business admin, management information systems. **Communications technology:** General. **Education:** Early childhood. **Engineering:** Science. **Engineering technology:** Electrical. **Health:** Clinical lab technology, medical radiologic technology/radiation therapy, nursing (RN), respiratory therapy technology, veterinary technology/assistant. **Liberal arts:** Arts/sciences. **Parks/recreation:** Health/fitness. **Physical sciences:** General. **Protective services:** Police science. **Public administration:** General. **Science technology:** Biological. **Transportation:** Aviation. **Visual/performing arts:** General, commercial/advertising art.

**Computing on campus.** 450 workstations in library, computer center. Commuter students can connect to campus network. Online course registration, online library, helpline available.

**Student life. Freshman orientation:** Available. Preregistration for classes offered. Half-day sessions held 1 week prior to start of academic year. **Activities:** Bands, campus ministries, choral groups, dance, drama, international student organizations, literary magazine, music ensembles, musical theater, radio station, student government, student newspaper, symphony orchestra, Phi Theta Kappa, united Latino organization, student ambassadors, black student union, Asian students association, Jewish students association, campus Christian fellowship, I.E.E.E.

**Athletics.** NJCAA. **Intercollegiate:** Baseball M, basketball, golf, ice hockey M, soccer, softball W, tennis. **Intramural:** Badminton, basketball, bowling, soccer W, softball, tennis, volleyball. **Team name:** Titans.

**Student services.** Adult student services, alcohol/substance abuse counseling, career counseling, services for economically disadvantaged, student employment services, financial aid counseling, health services, minority student services, on-campus daycare, personal counseling, placement for graduates, veterans' counselor, women's services. **Physically disabled:** Services for visually, hearing impaired. **Transfer:** Pre-admission transcript evaluation for new students. Transfer adviser, college fairs on campus for students transferring to 4-year colleges.

**Contact.** E-mail: admis@ccm.edu
Phone: (973) 328-5100 Toll-free number: (888) 226-8001
Fax: (973) 328-5199
Bette Simmons, Director of Admissions, County College of Morris, 214 Center Grove Road, Randolph, NJ 07869-2086

---

## Cumberland County College
**Vineland, New Jersey**
www.cccnj.edu

CB member
CB code: 2118

- Public 2-year community college
- Commuter campus in small city

**General.** Founded in 1963. Regionally accredited. **Enrollment:** 3,527 degree-seeking undergraduates. **Degrees:** 410 associate awarded. **Location:** 35 miles from Philadelphia. **Calendar:** Semester, extensive summer session. **Full-time faculty:** 49 total. **Part-time faculty:** 200 total. **Class size:** 47% < 20, 46% 20-39, 6% 40-49, less than 1% 50-99. **Special facilities:** Fine and performing arts center, conference center.

**Transfer out. Colleges most students transferred to 2007:** Rowan University, Stockton State College, Rutgers University, University of Delaware.

**Basis for selection.** Open admission, but selective for some programs. Special requirements for nursing program. National League for Nursing pre-entrance examination required of nursing applicants.

**2007-2008 Annual costs.** Tuition/fees: $3,330; $5,850 out-of-district; $10,890 out-of-state. Per-credit charge: $84 in-district; $168 out-of-district; $336 out-of-state. Books/supplies: $1,300. Personal expenses: $2,006.

**Financial aid. Need-based:** Need-based aid available for part-time students. Work-study available for part-time students. **Non-need-based:** Scholarships awarded for academics.

**Application procedures. Admission:** No deadline. $25 fee, may be waived for applicants with need. Application may be submitted online. Admission notification on a rolling basis. **Financial aid:** No deadline. FAFSA required. Applicants notified on a rolling basis; must reply within 3 week(s) of notification.

**Academics.** **Special study options:** Accelerated study, distance learning, double major, dual enrollment of high school students, ESL, honors, independent study. Clay College for Ceramics program, regional program for students with learning disabilities. Bachelor's degree programs available on campus. License preparation in nursing, radiology. **Credit/placement by examination:** CLEP, institutional tests. 32 credit hours maximum toward associate degree. **Support services:** GED preparation and test center, learning center, pre-admission summer program, reduced course load, remedial instruction, study skills assistance, tutoring, writing center.

**Majors.** **Agriculture:** General, ornamental horticulture. **Business:** Accounting, administrative services, business admin, hospitality/recreation, management information systems, marketing, office management, operations, tourism/travel. **Communications:** Journalism, radio/tv. **Computer sciences:** Computer science, networking, vendor certification. **Construction:** Site management. **Education:** Art, early childhood, multi-level teacher. **Engineering:** General. **Engineering technology:** Construction, electrical. **Health:** Medical radiologic technology/radiation therapy, nursing (RN), respiratory therapy assistant. **Interdisciplinary:** Biological/physical sciences, math/computer science. **Legal studies:** Paralegal. **Liberal arts:** Arts/sciences. **Math:** General. **Mechanic/repair:** Aircraft, industrial. **Protective services:** Criminal justice, police science. **Public administration:** Social work. **Visual/performing arts:** Art, ceramics, cinematography, commercial/advertising art, dramatic, graphic design, studio arts. **Other:** Philosophy/Religion, Technology Studies.

**Most popular majors.** Business/marketing 9%, health sciences 13%, liberal arts 47%, public administration/social services 12%, social sciences 8%.

**Computing on campus.** 150 workstations in library, computer center, student center. Commuter students can connect to campus network. Online course registration, online library, helpline, wireless network available.

**Student life.** **Freshman orientation:** Mandatory. Preregistration for classes offered. **Policies:** Comprehensive support center for learning disabled students. **Activities:** Choral groups, drama, literary magazine, student government, student newspaper, symphony orchestra, multicultural club, Latin American club, African American club.

**Athletics.** NJCAA. **Intercollegiate:** Baseball M, basketball, cross-country, softball W, track and field. **Intramural:** Cross-country. **Team name:** Dukes, Lady Dukes.

**Student services.** Career counseling, services for economically disadvantaged, student employment services, financial aid counseling, personal counseling, placement for graduates. **Physically disabled:** Services for visually, speech, hearing impaired. **Learning disabled:** Comprehensive services available. **Transfer:** Transfer adviser, college fairs on campus for students transferring to 4-year colleges.

**Contact.** Phone: (609) 691-8600 Fax: (609) 691-6157
Maud Fried-Goodnight, Executive Director of Enrollment and Student Support Services, Cumberland County College, PO Box 1500, Vineland, NJ 08362-9912

## Essex County College

**Newark, New Jersey**
**www.essex.edu**
CB code: 2237

▸ Public 2-year community college
▸ Commuter campus in large city

**General.** Founded in 1966. Regionally accredited. Classes also given at West Caldwell campus and several locations in Essex County and Newark. **Enrollment:** 10,094 degree-seeking undergraduates; 901 non-degree-seeking students. **Degrees:** 865 associate awarded. **Location:** 12 miles from New York City. **Calendar:** Semester, limited summer session. **Full-time faculty:** 160 total; 48% minority, 45% women. **Part-time faculty:** 494 total; 70% minority, 45% women. **Special facilities:** Police academy, Africana Institute.

**Student profile.** Among degree-seeking undergraduates, 75% enrolled in a transfer program, 25% enrolled in a vocational program, 1% already have a bachelor's degree or higher, 2,648 enrolled as first-time, first-year students, 275 transferred in from other institutions.

| | | | |
|---|---|---|---|
| Part-time: | 41% | Asian American: | 3% |
| Out-of-state: | 2% | Hispanic American: | 21% |
| Women: | 62% | International: | 8% |
| African American: | 50% | 25 or older: | 42% |

**Transfer out.** 80% of students enrolled in the transfer program go on to 4-year colleges. **Colleges most students transferred to 2007:** Rutgers University at Newark, Montclair University, Kean University, New Jersey Institute of Technology.

**Basis for selection.** Open admission, but selective for some programs. Special requirements for allied health programs. Priority given to allied health program applications received by April 15. National League for Nursing test required of nursing students. TOEFL recommended for international students. Interview recommended for nursing, ophthalmic science, physical therapy programs. **Adult students:** Companion Placement Test required.

**2007-2008 Annual costs.** Tuition/fees: $3,540; $6,165 out-of-district; $6,165 out-of-state. Per-credit charge: $88 in-district; $175 out-of-district; $175 out-of-state. Books/supplies: $1,000. Personal expenses: $1,061.

**Financial aid.** **Need-based:** Need-based aid available for part-time students.

**Application procedures.** **Admission:** No deadline. $25 fee, may be waived for applicants with need. Admission notification on a rolling basis. **Financial aid:** Priority date 6/30; no closing date. FAFSA, institutional form required. Applicants notified on a rolling basis starting 6/15; must reply within 3 week(s) of notification.

**Academics.** **Special study options:** Cooperative education, cross-registration, double major, dual enrollment of high school students, ESL, honors, independent study, internships, teacher certification program. Cross-registration with other institutions in Council of Higher Education in Newark; civil construction engineering program with New Jersey Institute of Technology; criminal justice program with Rutgers: State University of New Jersey. License preparation in nursing, physical therapy, radiology. **Credit/placement by examination:** AP, CLEP, institutional tests. 30 credit hours maximum toward associate degree. Maximum credits accepted must be 30 credits less than number required for degree at Essex County College; may not include more than half credits required in major field. **Support services:** GED preparation and test center, learning center, reduced course load, remedial instruction, study skills assistance, tutoring, writing center.

**Majors.** **Biology:** General. **Business:** Accounting, accounting technology, administrative services, business admin, hospitality admin, office technology, tourism/travel. **Communications:** Journalism, media studies. **Computer sciences:** General, programming. **Education:** General, elementary, kindergarten/preschool, music, physical, secondary. **Engineering:** General, civil, electrical. **Engineering technology:** Architectural, civil, construction, electrical, manufacturing, surveying. **Health:** Dental hygiene, EMT paramedic, health care admin, health services, medical radiologic technology/radiation therapy, medical secretary, nursing (RN), optician, physical therapy assistant, premedicine, respiratory therapy technology. **Legal studies:** Paralegal. **Liberal arts:** Arts/sciences. **Math:** General. **Physical sciences:** Chemistry. **Protective services:** Criminal justice, firefighting, law enforcement admin, police science. **Public administration:** Human services, social work. **Science technology:** Chemical. **Social sciences:** General. **Visual/performing arts:** Art, commercial/advertising art, dramatic, studio arts, theater design.

**Most popular majors.** Business/marketing 21%, education 14%, health sciences 21%, liberal arts 14%, social sciences 10%.

**Computing on campus.** 825 workstations in library, computer center. Commuter students can connect to campus network. Online course registration available.

**Student life.** **Freshman orientation:** Available. Preregistration for classes offered. **Activities:** Choral groups, drama, music ensembles, musical theater, student government, student newspaper, French club, Islamic student organization, Latin student union, Distributive Education Club of America, criminal justice organization, Black student association, social science club, fashion entertainment board, Phi Theta Kappa.

**Athletics.** NJCAA. **Intercollegiate:** Basketball, soccer M, track and field. **Intramural:** Basketball, table tennis, volleyball. **Team name:** Wolverines.

**Student services.** Alcohol/substance abuse counseling, career counseling, student employment services, financial aid counseling, on-campus daycare, personal counseling, placement for graduates, veterans' counselor, women's services. **Physically disabled:** Services for visually, speech, hearing impaired. **Transfer:** Transfer center, transfer adviser, college fairs on campus for students transferring to 4-year colleges.

**Contact.** Phone: (973) 877-3100 Fax: (973) 623-6449
Marva Mack, Director of Admissions, Essex County College, 303 University Avenue, Newark, NJ 07102

## Gloucester County College
Sewell, New Jersey
www.gccnj.edu

CB member
CB code: 2281

- Public 2-year community college
- Commuter campus in large town

**General.** Founded in 1966. Regionally accredited. **Enrollment:** 3,423 full-time, degree-seeking students. **Degrees:** 598 associate awarded. **Location:** 12 miles from Camden, 16 miles from Philadelphia. **Calendar:** Semester, limited summer session. **Full-time faculty:** 64 total. **Part-time faculty:** 228 total. **Special facilities:** Satellite downlink dish, learning resource center, 60-station computer room for multimedia course delivery and Internet access, interactive television (ITV) distance learning classroom.

**Student profile.**

Out-of-state: 1%      25 or older: 55%

**Transfer out. Colleges most students transferred to 2007:** Rowan University, Rutgers University, Richard Stockton College of New Jersey, Drexel University (PA).

**Basis for selection.** Open admission, but selective for some programs. Special requirements for certain programs including allied health and automotive technology programs. Special-need students, deaf or hearing-impaired evaluated for support college can offer. Institutional placement tests may be used. **Homeschooled:** Eligible, but admission determined on individual basis.

**High school preparation.** Biology and chemistry required for nursing applicants. Algebra also required for respiratory therapy, nuclear medicine, and diagnostic medical sonography applicants.

**2007-2008 Annual costs.** Tuition/fees: $2,880; $2,970 out-of-district; $5,370 out-of-state. Per-credit charge: $77 in-district; $80 out-of-district; $160 out-of-state. Books/supplies: $750.

**Financial aid.** All financial aid based on need. Need-based aid available for part-time students. Work-study available nights and for part-time students.

**Application procedures. Admission:** No deadline. $20 fee, may be waived for applicants with need. Application may be submitted online. Admission notification on a rolling basis beginning on or about 2/28. Application closing dates for selective admission programs vary per program. **Financial aid:** Priority date 5/1; no closing date. FAFSA, institutional form required. Applicants notified on a rolling basis starting 3/20.

**Academics.** Through New Jersey Virtual Community College Consortium, students can take online courses from any New Jersey community college and receive GCC credit at no extra cost. **Special study options:** Cooperative education, distance learning, dual enrollment of high school students, internships. License preparation in nursing. **Credit/placement by examination:** CLEP, institutional tests. 16 credit hours maximum toward associate degree. **Support services:** GED preparation and test center, learning center, pre-admission summer program, reduced course load, study skills assistance, tutoring.

**Majors. Biology:** General. **Business:** General, accounting, administrative services, business admin, finance, hospitality admin, marketing, office management, office technology, office/clerical, sales/distribution. **Communications:** General, journalism. **Computer sciences:** General, computer graphics, computer science, data processing, LAN/WAN management, web page design. **Education:** General, early childhood, multi-level teacher, physical, special. **Engineering:** General, science. **Engineering technology:** Civil, drafting, surveying. **English:** English lit. **Health:** Medical secretary, nuclear medical technology, nursing (RN), respiratory therapy technology, sonography. **History:** General. **Interdisciplinary:** Biological/physical sciences, math/computer science. **Legal studies:** Legal secretary, paralegal. **Liberal arts:** Arts/sciences. **Math:** General. **Mechanic/repair:** Automotive. **Parks/recreation:** Exercise sciences, health/fitness. **Physical sciences:** General, chemistry. **Protective services:** Police science. **Psychology:** General. **Social sciences:** Political science, sociology. **Visual/performing arts:** Art, commercial/advertising art, dramatic.

**Computing on campus.** 750 workstations in library, computer center. Online course registration, online library available.

**Student life. Freshman orientation:** Available. **Activities:** Choral groups, drama, literary magazine, musical theater, radio station, student government, student newspaper, student activities board, student government association, human services club, Equal Opportunity club, Phi Theta Kappa, paralegal club.

**Athletics.** NJCAA. **Intercollegiate:** Baseball M, basketball, cross-country, soccer, softball W, tennis, track and field, wrestling M. **Intramural:** Golf, volleyball.

**Student services.** Career counseling, services for economically disadvantaged, student employment services, financial aid counseling, health services, on-campus daycare, veterans' counselor. **Physically disabled:** Services for visually, speech, hearing impaired. **Transfer:** Pre-admission transcript evaluation for new students. Transfer adviser, college fairs on campus for students transferring to 4-year colleges.

**Contact.** Phone: (856) 415-2209 Fax: (856) 468-8498
Judith Atkinson, Director of Admissions, Gloucester County College, 1400 Tanyard Road, Sewell, NJ 08080

## Hudson County Community College
Jersey City, New Jersey
www.hccc.edu

CB member
CB code: 2291

- Public 2-year community college
- Commuter campus in large city
- Application essay required

**General.** Founded in 1974. Regionally accredited. **Enrollment:** 6,773 degree-seeking undergraduates. **Degrees:** 531 associate awarded. **Location:** 10 miles from New York City. **Calendar:** Semester, limited summer session. **Full-time faculty:** 84 total. **Part-time faculty:** 281 total.

**Student profile.**

Out-of-state: 2%      25 or older: 45%

**Transfer out. Colleges most students transferred to 2007:** New Jersey City University, St. Peter's College.

**Basis for selection.** Open admission. High school diploma required if applicant less than 18 years of age.

**2007-2008 Annual costs.** Tuition/fees: $3,543; $6,123 out-of-district. Per-credit charge: $86 in-district; $172 out-of-district; $258 out-of-state. Books/supplies: $800. Personal expenses: $1,500.

**2006-2007 Financial aid.** All financial aid based on need. 98% of total undergraduate aid awarded as scholarships/grants, 2% as loans/jobs. Need-based aid available for part-time students.

**Application procedures. Admission:** No deadline. $15 fee, may be waived for applicants with need. Admission notification on a rolling basis. **Financial aid:** Priority date 7/15; no closing date. FAFSA required. Applicants notified on a rolling basis starting 6/1; must reply within 1 week(s) of notification.

**Academics.** Students may earn second degree by completing 24 additional credits, including all requirements for second major. **Special study options:** Cross-registration, distance learning, dual enrollment of high school students, ESL, independent study, internships, liberal arts/career combination, weekend college. License preparation in nursing, real estate. **Credit/placement by examination:** CLEP, IB, institutional tests. 12 credit hours maximum toward associate degree. **Support services:** GED preparation and test center, pre-admission summer program, remedial instruction, tutoring, writing center.

**Majors. Business:** Accounting, administrative services, business admin, hospitality admin, management information systems. **Computer sciences:** Computer science, data processing. **Education:** Early childhood. **Engineering:** Science. **Engineering technology:** Computer systems, electrical. **Family/consumer sciences:** Child care. **Health:** Medical assistant, medical records technology, respiratory therapy technology. **History:** General. **Legal studies:** Paralegal. **Liberal arts:** Arts/sciences. **Math:** General. **Personal/culinary services:** Chef training, culinary arts, mortuary science. **Physical sciences:** Chemistry. **Protective services:** Criminal justice. **Social sciences:** Sociology.

**Most popular majors.** Business/marketing 14%, computer/information sciences 6%, health sciences 18%, legal studies 8%, liberal arts 54%.

**Computing on campus.** 645 workstations in library, computer center. Online library available.

**Student life. Freshman orientation:** Mandatory. Preregistration for classes offered. **Activities:** Drama, international student organizations, student government, student newspaper, South Asian society, black history and art society, law club, French club, Hispanos Unidos para el Progreso, women's awareness organization, hospitality club, health information and technology club, medical assisting club.

**Student services.** Adult student services, career counseling, student employment services, personal counseling, placement for graduates, veterans' counselor. **Physically disabled:** Services for visually, speech, hearing impaired. **Transfer:** Pre-admission transcript evaluation for new students. Transfer center, college fairs on campus for students transferring to 4-year colleges.

**Contact.** E-mail: admissions@hccc.edu
Phone: (201) 714-7200 Fax: (201) 714-2136
Peter Vida, Associate Dean of Enrollment Management, Hudson County Community College, 70 Sip Avenue, 1st Floor, Jersey City, NJ 07306

---

### Mercer County Community College
Trenton, New Jersey
www.mccc.edu

**CB member**
**CB code: 2444**

- Public 2-year community college
- Commuter campus in small city

**General.** Founded in 1966. Regionally accredited. Courses also available at downtown Trenton location. External degree program for military service members. **Enrollment:** 7,817 degree-seeking undergraduates; 1,277 non-degree-seeking students. **Degrees:** 748 associate awarded. **Location:** 35 miles from Philadelphia, 60 miles from New York City. **Calendar:** Semester, extensive summer session. **Full-time faculty:** 138 total; 14% minority, 53% women. **Part-time faculty:** 431 total; 18% minority, 46% women. **Class size:** 45% < 20, 53% 20-39, less than 1% 40-49, 1% 50-99. **Special facilities:** CAD laboratory, computer graphics laboratory, greenhouse complex, mortuary science lab.

**Student profile.** Among degree-seeking undergraduates, 60% enrolled in a transfer program, 40% enrolled in a vocational program, 1,993 enrolled as first-time, first-year students, 164 transferred in from other institutions.

| | | | |
|---|---|---|---|
| Part-time: | 57% | Asian American: | 4% |
| Out-of-state: | 2% | Hispanic American: | 10% |
| Women: | 57% | International: | 6% |
| African American: | 27% | 25 or older: | 29% |

**Transfer out. Colleges most students transferred to 2007:** The College of New Jersey, Rider University, Rutgers University, Rowan University, Thomas Edison State College.

**Basis for selection.** Open admission. Applicants without high school diploma or GED must be 18 or older and have completed the New Jersey Basic Skills Placement Examination. Designation of provisional status dependent on skills scores and/or high school units. Interview required for nursing and funeral service programs; recommended for all others.

**2007-2008 Annual costs.** Tuition/fees: $3,060; $4,110 out-of-district; $6,270 out-of-state. Per-credit charge: $102 in-district; $137 out-of-district; $209 out-of-state. Books/supplies: $800. Personal expenses: $2,800.

**Financial aid. Need-based:** Need-based aid available for part-time students. Work-study available nights and for part-time students. **Non-need-based:** Scholarships awarded for academics, athletics, state residency.

**Application procedures. Admission:** No deadline. No application fee. Application may be submitted online. Admission notification on a rolling basis. **Financial aid:** No deadline. FAFSA required. Applicants notified on a rolling basis.

**Academics.** Cross-registration with area hospitals for nursing. **Special study options:** Cooperative education, cross-registration, distance learning, double major, dual enrollment of high school students, ESL, external degree, independent study, internships, liberal arts/career combination, weekend college. License preparation in aviation, nursing, occupational therapy, physical therapy, radiology. **Credit/placement by examination:** AP, CLEP, institutional tests. 45 credit hours maximum toward associate degree. **Support services:** GED preparation and test center, learning center, preadmission summer program, reduced course load, remedial instruction, study skills assistance, tutoring, writing center.

**Majors. Agriculture:** Ornamental horticulture, plant sciences. **Architecture:** Technology. **Biology:** General. **Business:** General, accounting, administrative services, business admin, management information systems. **Communications technology:** General. **Computer sciences:** Networking. **Engineering technology:** Architectural, civil, electrical. **Health:** Clinical lab technology, medical radiologic technology/radiation therapy, nursing (RN), physical therapy assistant, respiratory therapy technology. **Legal studies:** Paralegal. **Liberal arts:** Arts/sciences. **Math:** General. **Mechanic/repair:** Aircraft, automotive. **Personal/culinary services:** Culinary arts, mortuary science. **Protective services:** Fire safety technology, police science. **Public administration:** Human services. **Science technology:** Biological. **Transportation:** Aviation, aviation management, flight attendant. **Visual/performing arts:** General, commercial/advertising art.

**Most popular majors.** Business/marketing 18%, health sciences 20%, liberal arts 21%, security/protective services 6%, visual/performing arts 8%.

**Computing on campus.** 1,100 workstations in library, computer center. Commuter students can connect to campus network. Online course registration, online library, helpline, wireless network available.

**Student life. Freshman orientation:** Available. Preregistration for classes offered. **Activities:** Bands, choral groups, dance, drama, international student organizations, literary magazine, music ensembles, musical theater, radio station, student government, student newspaper, TV station, Christian Fellowship, bilingual club, African-American student organization, Fuerza Latina, ecology club, Educational Opportunity Fund club, gay/straight alliance.

**Athletics.** NJCAA. **Intercollegiate:** Baseball M, basketball, soccer, softball W, tennis, track and field. **Intramural:** Basketball, softball, volleyball. **Team name:** Vikings.

**Student services.** Adult student services, career counseling, services for economically disadvantaged, student employment services, financial aid counseling, minority student services, personal counseling, placement for graduates, veterans' counselor. **Physically disabled:** Services for visually, speech, hearing impaired. **Transfer:** Transfer center, transfer adviser, college fairs on campus for students transferring to 4-year colleges.

**Contact.** E-mail: admiss@mccc.edu
Phone: (609) 570-3207 Fax: (609) 570-3861
Joan Guggenheim, Registrar, Enrollment Services, Mercer County Community College, Box B, Trenton, NJ 08690-1099

---

### Middlesex County College
Edison, New Jersey
www.middlesexcc.edu

**CB member**
**CB code: 2441**

- Public 2-year community college
- Commuter campus in small city

**General.** Founded in 1964. Regionally accredited. **Location:** 5 miles from New Brunswick, 30 miles from New York City. **Calendar:** Semester.

**Annual costs/financial aid.** Tuition/fees (2007-2008): $3,392; $5,955 out-of-district; $5,955 out-of-state. Out-of-county and out-of-state students pay additional $825 in required fees. Books/supplies: $1,162. Personal expenses: $1,643. Need-based financial aid available to full-time and part-time students.

**Contact.** Phone: (732) 906-4243
Director of Admissions and Recruitment, 2600 Woodbridge Avenue, Edison, NJ 08818-3050

---

### Ocean County College
Toms River, New Jersey
www.ocean.edu

**CB code: 2630**

- Public 2-year community college
- Commuter campus in small city

**General.** Founded in 1964. Regionally accredited. Off-campus sites at 13 locations in Ocean County. **Enrollment:** 7,908 degree-seeking undergraduates; 1,443 non-degree-seeking students. **Degrees:** 977 associate awarded. **Location:** 60 miles from Philadelphia, 80 miles from New York City. **Calendar:** Semester, extensive summer session. **Full-time faculty:** 104 total; 9% minority, 59% women. **Part-time faculty:** 347 total; 6% minority, 49% women. **Special facilities:** Planetarium, arboretum, fine arts theater. **Partnerships:** Formal partnerships through Jump Start program that allows high school juniors/seniors to enroll for college credits.

**Student profile.** Among degree-seeking undergraduates, 80% enrolled in a transfer program, 20% enrolled in a vocational program, 1% already have a bachelor's degree or higher, 2,316 enrolled as first-time, first-year students.

| | | | |
|---|---|---|---|
| Part-time: | 38% | 25 or older: | 24% |
| Women: | 57% | | |

**Transfer out.** 85% of students enrolled in the transfer program go on to 4-year colleges. **Colleges most students transferred to 2007:** Georgian Court College, Richard Stockton College of New Jersey, Rutgers University, Rowan University, Kean University.

**Basis for selection.** Open admission, but selective for some programs. Admission to nursing, medical laboratory technology, honors programs based on test scores and academic record. SAT or ACT required of nursing and honors program applicants. Score report by May 30. **Adult students:** SAT/ACT scores not required. **Learning Disabled:** Students invited to share learning disability needs with Disability Resource Center, which then makes appropriate accommodations.

**High school preparation.** Algebra, chemistry, biology required of nursing applicants.

**2007-2008 Annual costs.** Tuition/fees: $3,510; $4,530 out-of-district; $6,900 out-of-state. Per-credit charge: $90 in-district; $124 out-of-district; $203 out-of-state. Books/supplies: $1,000. Personal expenses: $2,500.

**Financial aid.** All financial aid based on need. Need-based aid available for part-time students.

**Application procedures. Admission:** No deadline. No application fee. Application may be submitted online. Admission notification on a rolling basis beginning on or about 11/1. **Financial aid:** Priority date 5/31; no closing date. FAFSA required. Applicants notified on a rolling basis starting 7/15; must reply within 1 week(s) of notification.

**Academics. Special study options:** Combined bachelor's/graduate degree, distance learning, dual enrollment of high school students, ESL, honors, independent study, internships, liberal arts/career combination, study abroad. Bachelor's degree programs available on campus. License preparation in aviation, nursing. **Credit/placement by examination:** AP, CLEP, institutional tests. 30 credit hours maximum toward associate degree. **Support services:** GED test center, learning center, reduced course load, remedial instruction, study skills assistance, tutoring, writing center.

**Honors college/program.** For liberal arts students only; admission based on GPA, test scores, class rank, interview.

**Majors. Agriculture:** Horticulture. **Business:** General, business admin. **Communications:** Broadcast journalism, journalism. **Communications technology:** General, photo/film/video. **Computer sciences:** General, computer science, LAN/WAN management. **Conservation:** Environmental science. **Engineering:** General. **Engineering technology:** Civil, surveying. **Family/consumer sciences:** Child care. **Foreign languages:** Sign language interpretation. **Health:** Clinical lab technology, histologic assistant, medical assistant, nursing (RN). **Interdisciplinary:** Gerontology. **Legal studies:** Paralegal. **Liberal arts:** Arts/sciences. **Protective services:** Fire safety technology, police science. **Psychology:** General. **Public administration:** Human services, social work. **Science technology:** Biological. **Transportation:** Airline/commercial pilot. **Visual/performing arts:** Art, dramatic.

**Most popular majors.** Business/marketing 17%, health sciences 12%, liberal arts 62%, security/protective services 6%.

**Computing on campus.** 500 workstations in library, computer center. Commuter students can connect to campus network. Online library, helpline available.

**Student life. Freshman orientation:** Available. Preregistration for classes offered. **Activities:** Bands, choral groups, dance, drama, literary magazine, musical theater, radio station, student government, student newspaper, TV station, Circle K, Student Life Program Board, Phi Theta Kappa, veterans club, student health organization, disabled students service club, Organization for Black Unity, Women's Network, South Asian American student association.

**Athletics.** NJCAA. **Intercollegiate:** Baseball M, basketball, golf, soccer, softball W, swimming, tennis. **Intramural:** Basketball W, swimming. **Team name:** Vikings.

**Student services.** Alcohol/substance abuse counseling, career counseling, services for economically disadvantaged, student employment services, financial aid counseling, health services, minority student services, personal counseling, placement for graduates, veterans' counselor. **Physically disabled:** Services for visually, speech, hearing impaired. **Learning disabled:** Comprehensive services available. **Transfer:** Re-entry adviser, pre-admission transcript evaluation for new students. Transfer adviser, college fairs on campus for students transferring to 4-year colleges.

**Contact.** E-mail: mfennessy@ocean.edu
Phone: (732) 255-0304 Fax: (732) 255-0444
Mary Fennessy, Director of Admissions and Records, Ocean County College, College Drive, Toms River, NJ 08754-2001

## Passaic County Community College
**Paterson, New Jersey**
www.pccc.edu
CB member
CB code: 2694

- Public 2-year community college
- Commuter campus in small city

**General.** Founded in 1968. Regionally accredited. **Enrollment:** 7,493 degree-seeking undergraduates. **Degrees:** 424 associate awarded. **Location:** 15 miles from New York City. **Calendar:** Semester, limited summer session. **Full-time faculty:** 99 total. **Part-time faculty:** 350 total. **Class size:** 59% < 20, 40% 20-39, less than 1% 40-49. **Special facilities:** 2 art galleries, playhouse, poetry center.

**Transfer out. Colleges most students transferred to 2007:** William Paterson University, Rutgers University, Montclair State University, Bergen County College, Kean University.

**Basis for selection.** Open admission, but selective for some programs. Special requirements for nursing and other allied health programs. Interview recommended.

**2007-2008 Annual costs.** Tuition/fees: $3,126; $5,601 out-of-state. Per-credit charge: $83 in-state; $165 out-of-state. Additional course fees up to maximum of $600 per year. Books/supplies: $839. Personal expenses: $978.

**2006-2007 Financial aid. Need-based:** 99% of total undergraduate aid awarded as scholarships/grants, 1% as loans/jobs. Need-based aid available for part-time students. **Non-need-based:** Scholarships awarded for academics. **Additional information:** Limited scholarship funds available for low income students eligible for federal or state aid.

**Application procedures. Admission:** No deadline. No application fee. Application may be submitted online. Admission notification on a rolling basis. Early admissions available to high school students based on decisions made by high school guidance counselor and college's director of admissions. **Financial aid:** Priority date 8/1; no closing date. FAFSA, CSS PROFILE required. Applicants notified on a rolling basis starting 8/1; must reply within 2 week(s) of notification.

**Academics. Special study options:** Cooperative education, cross-registration, distance learning, double major, dual enrollment of high school students, ESL, honors, independent study, internships, liberal arts/career combination, student-designed major, study abroad, weekend college. License preparation in nursing. **Credit/placement by examination:** AP, CLEP, institutional tests. 12 credit hours maximum toward associate degree. New Jersey Basic Skills test required for placement. **Support services:** Learning center, reduced course load, remedial instruction, study skills assistance, tutoring, writing center.

**Majors. Business:** General, accounting, administrative services, management information systems, marketing, sales/distribution. **Communications:** General. **Computer sciences:** General, applications programming. **Education:** Early childhood. **Engineering:** Science. **Engineering technology:** Electrical. **English:** English lit. **Health:** Medical radiologic technology/radiation therapy, nursing (RN), respiratory therapy technology. **Liberal arts:** Arts/sciences. **Math:** General. **Protective services:** Police science. **Psychology:** General. **Public administration:** Human services. **Social sciences:** Sociology.

**Computing on campus.** 900 workstations in computer center.

**Student life. Freshman orientation:** Mandatory. Preregistration for classes offered. **Activities:** International student organizations, student government, student newspaper, Latin American club, Newman Club, Organization of African Ancestry, earth awareness, fashion awareness, veterans club, Phi Theta Kappa, photography club, Arabic club, poetry club.

**Athletics.** NJCAA. **Intercollegiate:** Basketball, soccer M. **Intramural:** Basketball M, volleyball W. **Team name:** Panthers.

**Student services.** Adult student services, career counseling, services for economically disadvantaged, student employment services, financial aid counseling, minority student services, on-campus daycare, personal counseling, placement for graduates, veterans' counselor, women's services. **Transfer:** Transfer adviser, college fairs on campus for students transferring to 4-year colleges.

**Contact.** Phone: (973) 684-6868 Fax: (973) 684-6778
Patrick Noonan, Director of Admission, Passaic County Community College, One College Boulevard, Paterson, NJ 07505-1179

## Raritan Valley Community College
**Somerville, New Jersey**
www.raritanval.edu
CB member
CB code: 2867

- Public 2-year community college
- Commuter campus in large town

**General.** Founded in 1966. Regionally accredited. **Enrollment:** 5,462 degree-seeking undergraduates; 1,167 non-degree-seeking students. **Degrees:** 544 associate awarded. **ROTC:** Army, Air Force. **Location:** 36 miles from New

York City. **Calendar:** Semester, extensive summer session. **Full-time faculty:** 108 total; 38% have terminal degrees, 11% minority, 56% women. **Special facilities:** Planetarium, professional theater. **Partnerships:** Formal partnership with area high schools for articulated credit program.

**Student profile.** Among degree-seeking undergraduates, 55% enrolled in a transfer program, 42% enrolled in a vocational program, 3% already have a bachelor's degree or higher, 1,275 enrolled as first-time, first-year students, 398 transferred in from other institutions.

| Part-time: | 46% | Asian American: | 6% |
|---|---|---|---|
| Out-of-state: | 1% | Hispanic American: | 11% |
| Women: | 54% | International: | 3% |
| African American: | 8% | 25 or older: | 33% |

**Transfer out.** 21% of students enrolled in the transfer program go on to 4-year colleges. **Colleges most students transferred to 2007:** Rutgers State University, Kean University, Montclair State University, College of NJ, Rider University.

**Basis for selection.** Open admission, but selective for some programs. Special requirements for nursing program; interview recommended. Matriculated students must take New Jersey Basic Skills Placement Test. **Adult students:** SAT/ACT scores not required; however, based on scores, students may be exempt from taking college's placement test. **Homeschooled:** Must provide home school portfolio.

**High school preparation.** 16 units recommended. Recommended units include English 4, mathematics 2 and science 2.

**2007-2008 Annual costs.** Tuition/fees: $3,490. Per-credit charge: $87. Books/supplies: $800. Personal expenses: $1,000.

**2006-2007 Financial aid. Need-based:** 262 full-time freshmen applied for aid; 189 were judged to have need; 189 of these received aid. Average need met was 71%. Average scholarship/grant was $1,765; average loan $1,772. 84% of total undergraduate aid awarded as scholarships/grants, 16% as loans/jobs. Need-based aid available for part-time students. Work-study available for part-time students. **Non-need-based:** Awarded to 151 full-time undergraduates, including 40 freshmen. Scholarships awarded for academics.

**Application procedures. Admission:** No deadline. $25 fee, may be waived for applicants with need. Application may be submitted online. Admission notification on a rolling basis. **Financial aid:** No deadline. FAFSA required. Applicants notified on a rolling basis starting 4/1.

**Academics. Special study options:** Accelerated study, cooperative education, distance learning, double major, dual enrollment of high school students, ESL, external degree, honors, independent study, weekend college. Service learning. Bachelor's degree programs available on campus. License preparation in nursing. **Credit/placement by examination:** AP, CLEP, institutional tests. 45 credit hours maximum toward associate degree. **Support services:** GED test center, learning center, pre-admission summer program, remedial instruction, study skills assistance, tutoring, writing center.

**Majors. Biology:** General, biotechnology. **Business:** General, accounting, accounting technology, banking/financial services, business admin, golf management, international, management information systems, marketing, real estate. **Communications:** General, digital media. **Communications technology:** Animation/special effects. **Computer sciences:** General, applications programming, computer science, data processing, information systems, information technology, networking. **Conservation:** Environmental science. **Education:** General, early childhood, elementary, secondary. **Engineering:** Science. **Engineering technology:** Automotive, construction, electrical, heat/ac/refrig, manufacturing, mechanical. **Health:** Chiropractic assistant, health services, licensed practical nurse, nurse practitioner, nursing (RN), occupational therapy assistant, ophthalmic lab technology, optician, physical therapy assistant, physician assistant, predental, premedicine, prepharmacy, preveterinary, respiratory therapy assistant. **Interdisciplinary:** Global studies. **Legal studies:** Paralegal. **Liberal arts:** Arts/sciences, humanities. **Math:** General. **Mechanic/repair:** Diesel, electronics/electrical, heating/ac/refrig. **Physical sciences:** Chemistry. **Protective services:** Criminal justice, law enforcement admin. **Public administration:** Human services. **Social sciences:** General. **Visual/performing arts:** General, dance, dramatic, graphic design, interior design, studio arts, theater design. **Other:** Fiber Optics.

**Most popular majors.** Business/marketing 21%, education 8%, health sciences 18%, interdisciplinary studies 6%, liberal arts 25%, security/protective services 8%.

**Computing on campus.** 844 workstations in library, computer center, student center. Commuter students can connect to campus network. Online course registration, online library, helpline, wireless network available.

**Student life. Freshman orientation:** Available. Preregistration for classes offered. **Activities:** Dance, drama, international student organizations, student government, student newspaper, Club Black, Latino, Asian, Caucasian

Kollaboration, Students for Environmental Awareness, BLGT Club, Christian Fellowship, Islamic Culture Association, performing artist club, Orgullo Latino/Latin Pride club, social justice club.

**Athletics.** NJCAA. **Intercollegiate:** Baseball M, basketball, golf, soccer M, softball W. **Intramural:** Basketball, softball W, volleyball. **Team name:** Golden Lions.

**Student services.** Adult student services, alcohol/substance abuse counseling, career counseling, student employment services, financial aid counseling, on-campus daycare, personal counseling, placement for graduates, veterans' counselor. **Physically disabled:** Services for visually, hearing impaired. **Transfer:** Re-entry adviser, pre-admission transcript evaluation for new students. Transfer center, transfer adviser, college fairs on campus for students transferring to 4-year colleges.

**Contact.** E-mail: registrar@raritanval.edu
Phone: (908) 526-1200 Fax: (908) 704-3442
Mary O'Malley, Executive Director, Enrollment Services, Raritan Valley Community College, PO Box 3300, Somerville, NJ 08876-1265

## Salem Community College
**Carneys Point, New Jersey**
www.salemcc.edu

CB member
CB code: 2868

▸ Public 2-year community college
▸ Commuter campus in small town

**General.** Founded in 1972. Regionally accredited. **Enrollment:** 980 degree-seeking undergraduates. **Degrees:** 120 associate awarded. **Location:** 25 miles from Philadelphia. **Calendar:** Semester, limited summer session. **Full-time faculty:** 25 total. **Part-time faculty:** 67 total. **Class size:** 63% < 20, 36% 20-39, less than 1% 40-49, less than 1% 50-99. **Special facilities:** Glass art and scientific glass technology laboratories, chemical process technology simulation laboratories, computer graphic arts lab.

**Student profile.**

| Out-of-state: | 22% | 25 or older: | 46% |
|---|---|---|---|

**Transfer out. Colleges most students transferred to 2007:** Rowan University, Wilmington College, Gloucester County College, Rutgers University, Cumberland County College.

**Basis for selection.** Open admission, but selective for some programs. Licensed Practical Nursing applicants must complete 6 prerequisite courses with C+ or higher grade in each course. In addition to 5 of the 6 Licensed Practical Nursing prerequisites, Registered Nursing applicants must complete 4 more prerequisites with C+ or higher grade in each course. Both programs require high school diploma or GED. Interview required for scientific glassblowing and glass art programs. **Learning Disabled:** Students must file release form and documentation of disability to be granted special accommodations.

**2007-2008 Annual costs.** Tuition/fees: $3,395; $3,695 out-of-state. Per-credit charge: $83 in-state; $93 out-of-state. Books/supplies: $1,000. Personal expenses: $600.

**Financial aid.** All financial aid based on need. Need-based aid available for part-time students. Work-study available for part-time students.

**Application procedures. Admission:** No deadline. $25 fee, may be waived for applicants with need. Application must be submitted on paper. Admission notification on a rolling basis. **Financial aid:** Priority date 6/1; no closing date. FAFSA, institutional form required. Applicants notified on a rolling basis starting 4/1; must reply within 2 week(s) of notification.

**Academics. Special study options:** Cooperative education, distance learning, double major, dual enrollment of high school students, ESL, honors, independent study, internships, teacher certification program. License preparation in nursing. **Credit/placement by examination:** AP, CLEP, institutional tests. 30 credit hours maximum toward associate degree. **Support services:** GED preparation and test center, learning center, pre-admission summer program, reduced course load, remedial instruction, study skills assistance, tutoring, writing center.

**Majors. Biology:** General. **Business:** Accounting, business admin, human resources, management information systems, marketing. **Communications:** Journalism. **Computer sciences:** Computer graphics, computer science, webmaster. **Education:** General, early childhood. **English:** English lit. **Health:** Nursing (RN). **History:** General. **Liberal arts:** Arts/sciences, humanities. **Math:** General. **Parks/recreation:** Health/fitness. **Physical sciences:** Chemistry, physics. **Psychology:** General. **Public administration:** Community org/advocacy. **Social sciences:** General, criminology, political science, sociology. **Other:** Glass art, Technical studies.

**Most popular majors.** Business/marketing 15%, health sciences 18%, liberal arts 45%, trade and industry 12%.

**Computing on campus.** 300 workstations in library, computer center. Commuter students can connect to campus network. Online library, helpline available.

**Student life. Freshman orientation:** Available. Preregistration for classes offered. Held at beginning of fall and spring semesters. **Activities:** Choral groups, drama, student government, Chi Alpha Epsilon, Educational Opportunity Fund Students, institutional diversity committee, Phi Theta Kappa, multicultural club.

**Athletics.** NJCAA. **Intercollegiate:** Baseball M, basketball, golf M, soccer W, softball W. **Team name:** Oaks.

**Student services.** Adult student services, career counseling, services for economically disadvantaged, student employment services, financial aid counseling, minority student services, personal counseling, veterans' counselor. **Physically disabled:** Services for visually, speech, hearing impaired. **Transfer:** Re-entry adviser, pre-admission transcript evaluation for new students. Transfer center, transfer adviser, college fairs on campus for students transferring to 4-year colleges.

**Contact.** E-mail: sccinfo@salemcc.edu
Phone: (856) 351-2703 Fax: (856) 299-9193
Scott Hendrickson, Director of Enrollment Services, Salem Community College, 460 Hollywood Avenue, Carneys Point, NJ 08069-2799

---

## Sussex County Community College

Newton, New Jersey
www.sussex.edu

CB member
CB code: 2711

- Public 2-year community college
- Commuter campus in small town

**General.** Founded in 1981. Regionally accredited. Extension sites at Sussex County Technical School, several area high schools, and other locations. **Enrollment:** 2,904 degree-seeking undergraduates. **Degrees:** 348 associate awarded. **Location:** 70 miles from New York City. **Calendar:** Semester, limited summer session. **Full-time faculty:** 45 total. **Part-time faculty:** 240 total. **Class size:** 62% < 20, 38% 20-39, less than 1% 40-49. **Special facilities:** 10 computer laboratories (including graphic design). **Partnerships:** Formal partnerships with Oracle database administration training program, Unix operating system training program, Cisco network training program.

**Student profile.**

| | | | |
|---|---|---|---|
| Out-of-state: | 11% | 25 or older: | 30% |

**Transfer out. Colleges most students transferred to 2007:** Montclair State University, William Paterson University of New Jersey, Rutgers University, Ramapo College of New Jersey, Centenary College.

**Basis for selection.** Open admission, but selective for some programs. Special requirements for the nursing program. Incoming freshmen must pass ACCUPLACER placement test for admission to program of study; those failing any part of test must satisfactorily complete remedial study in appropriate areas before being admitted to program.

**2007-2008 Annual costs.** Tuition/fees: $3,030; $5,490 out-of-state. Per-credit charge: $82 in-district; $164 out-of-district; $164 out-of-state. Residents of Wayne, Monroe and Pike County (PA): $123 per credit hour. Books/supplies: $900. Personal expenses: $1,244.

**Financial aid.** All financial aid based on need. Need-based aid available for part-time students.

**Application procedures. Admission:** No deadline. $15 fee, may be waived for applicants with need. Application must be submitted on paper. Admission notification on a rolling basis. **Financial aid:** Closing date 6/1. FAFSA, institutional form required. Applicants notified on a rolling basis; must reply within 2 week(s) of notification.

**Academics. Special study options:** Distance learning, double major, dual enrollment of high school students, ESL, honors, independent study, internships, teacher certification program. Bachelor's degree programs available on campus. License preparation in nursing, paramedic. **Credit/placement by examination:** CLEP, IB, SAT, institutional tests. 30 credit hours maximum toward associate degree. **Support services:** GED preparation and test center, learning center, reduced course load, remedial instruction, study skills assistance, tutoring, writing center.

**Majors. Biology:** General. **Business:** Accounting, business admin. **Communications:** Journalism. **Computer sciences:** General, applications programming. **Conservation:** Environmental studies. **Education:** Early childhood, elementary, secondary. **Engineering:** General. **Engineering technology:** Automotive. **English:** English lit. **Health:** Clinical lab technology, health services, predental, premedicine, prepharmacy, respiratory therapy technology, veterinary technology/assistant. **Interdisciplinary:** Biological/physical sciences. **Legal studies:** Paralegal. **Liberal arts:** Arts/sciences. **Math:** General. **Mechanic/repair:** Automotive. **Physical sciences:** Chemistry. **Protective services:** Criminal justice, firefighting. **Psychology:** General. **Public administration:** Social work. **Social sciences:** General. **Visual/performing arts:** Art, commercial/advertising art, studio arts.

**Most popular majors.** Business/marketing 16%, liberal arts 53%, security/protective services 11%, visual/performing arts 8%.

**Computing on campus.** 250 workstations in library, computer center, student center. Online library, wireless network available.

**Student life. Freshman orientation:** Mandatory. Preregistration for classes offered. Half-day program held 2 days before regular classes each semester. **Activities:** Choral groups, drama, literary magazine, musical theater, student government, student newspaper, TV station, student ambassadors, humanities club, arts club, broadcasting club, criminal justice club, Law and Justice Society, Phi Theta Kappa, AIDS Brigade, lifestyles and diversity group, psychology club.

**Athletics.** NJCAA. **Intercollegiate:** Baseball M, basketball M, soccer, softball W. **Intramural:** Archery, badminton, basketball, soccer, softball, table tennis, volleyball. **Team name:** Skylanders.

**Student services.** Adult student services, career counseling, student employment services, financial aid counseling, personal counseling, placement for graduates, veterans' counselor, women's services. **Physically disabled:** Services for visually, speech, hearing impaired. **Transfer:** Pre-admission transcript evaluation for new students. Transfer adviser, college fairs on campus for students transferring to 4-year colleges.

**Contact.** E-mail: jdonohue@sussex.edu
Phone: (973) 300-2216 Fax: (973) 579-5226
James Donohue, Director of Admissions, Sussex County Community College, One College Hill Road, Newton, NJ 07860

---

## Union County College

Cranford, New Jersey
www.ucc.edu

CB code: 2921

- Public 2-year community college
- Commuter campus in large town

**General.** Founded in 1933. Regionally accredited. Branch campuses in Elizabeth, Plainfield, and Scotch Plains. **Enrollment:** 9,776 degree-seeking undergraduates; 1,896 non-degree-seeking students. **Degrees:** 705 associate awarded. **ROTC:** Air Force. **Location:** 20 miles from New York City. **Calendar:** Semester, extensive summer session. **Full-time faculty:** 177 total; 30% have terminal degrees, 19% minority, 56% women. **Part-time faculty:** 266 total; 19% have terminal degrees, 25% minority, 47% women. **Special facilities:** Observatory.

**Student profile.** Among degree-seeking undergraduates, 84% enrolled in a transfer program, 16% enrolled in a vocational program, 2,382 enrolled as first-time, first-year students, 611 transferred in from other institutions.

| | | | |
|---|---|---|---|
| Part-time: | 48% | Asian American: | 6% |
| Out-of-state: | 4% | Hispanic American: | 27% |
| Women: | 65% | Native American: | 1% |
| African American: | 24% | International: | 3% |

**Transfer out.** 47% of students enrolled in the transfer program go on to 4-year colleges. **Colleges most students transferred to 2007:** Kean University, Rutgers University, Montclair State University, Jersey City State University.

**Basis for selection.** Open admission, but selective for some programs. Special requirements for allied health and nursing programs. SAT required of dental hygiene program applicants; score report required by April. Essay, interview recommended for nursing, interpreter for the deaf programs.

**High school preparation.** 19 units recommended. Recommended units include English 4, mathematics 3, history 3, science 2 (laboratory 2), foreign language 2 and academic electives 5. Chemistry and biology required of health program applicants. Trigonometry, geometry, algebra, physics and chemistry required of engineering and physical science applicants. Level 3 proficiency in American Sign Language required of interpreter for the deaf program applicants. Algebra and geometry recommended for business majors.

**2007-2008 Annual costs.** Tuition/fees: $3,390; $6,000 out-of-district; $6,000 out-of-state. Per-credit charge: $87 in-district; $174 out-of-district; $174 out-of-state. Books/supplies: $2,100. Personal expenses: $1,500.

**2006-2007 Financial aid.** All financial aid based on need. 78% of total undergraduate aid awarded as scholarships/grants, 22% as loans/jobs. Need-based aid available for part-time students. Work-study available nights, weekends and for part-time students.

**Application procedures. Admission:** No deadline. $35 fee. Application may be submitted online. Admission notification on a rolling basis. **Financial aid:** Priority date 5/1; no closing date. FAFSA, institutional form required. Must reply within 2 week(s) of notification.

**Academics. Special study options:** Accelerated study, combined bachelor's/graduate degree, cross-registration, distance learning, dual enrollment of high school students, ESL, honors, internships, liberal arts/career combination, weekend college. License preparation in dental hygiene, nursing, paramedic, physical therapy, radiology. **Credit/placement by examination:** AP, CLEP, institutional tests. 32 credit hours maximum toward associate degree. **Support services:** GED preparation and test center, learning center, reduced course load, remedial instruction, study skills assistance, tutoring.

**Majors. Biology:** General, biotechnology. **Business:** General, accounting technology, administrative services, business admin, hospitality admin, marketing, restaurant/food services. **Communications:** Media studies. **Communications technology:** Animation/special effects, recording arts. **Computer sciences:** Computer science, game design, information technology. **Engineering:** General. **Engineering technology:** Civil, electromechanical, manufacturing, mechanical. **Foreign languages:** American Sign Language, sign language interpretation, translation. **Health:** Dental hygiene, EMT paramedic, health services, medical radiologic technology/radiation therapy, nuclear medical technology, nursing (RN), physical therapy assistant, radiologic technology/medical imaging, respiratory therapy technology, sonography, vocational rehab counseling. **Interdisciplinary:** Gerontology. **Legal studies:** Paralegal. **Liberal arts:** Arts/sciences. **Parks/recreation:** Sports admin. **Physical sciences:** General, chemistry. **Protective services:** Emergency management/homeland security, fire safety technology, law enforcement admin. **Public administration:** Human services. **Visual/performing arts:** Music. **Other:** Psychosocial Rehabilitation and Treatment.

**Most popular majors.** Business/marketing 19%, health sciences 27%, liberal arts 32%, security/protective services 8%.

**Computing on campus.** 1,021 workstations in library, computer center, student center. Commuter students can connect to campus network. Online library, helpline, repair service available.

**Student life. Freshman orientation:** Available. **Activities:** Drama, international student organizations, literary magazine, radio station, student government, student newspaper, Catholic student organization, UCC Christian Fellowship, student volunteer organization, Phi Theta Kappa, Phi Beta, Union of African Students, gerontology club, French club, Spanish club.

**Athletics.** NJCAA. **Intercollegiate:** Baseball M, basketball, golf, soccer M, volleyball W. **Team name:** Owls; Lady Owls.

**Student services.** Alcohol/substance abuse counseling, campus ministries, career counseling, services for economically disadvantaged, student employment services, financial aid counseling, minority student services, personal counseling, placement for graduates, veterans' counselor. **Physically disabled:** Services for visually, speech, hearing impaired. **Transfer:** Re-entry adviser, pre-admission transcript evaluation for new students. Transfer adviser, college fairs on campus for students transferring to 4-year colleges.

**Contact.** Phone: (908) 709-7500 Fax: (908) 709-7125
JoAnn Davis-Wayne, Registrar, Union County College, 1033 Springfield Avenue, Cranford, NJ 07016-1599

---

## Warren County Community College
### Washington, New Jersey
www.warren.edu                                    CB code: 2722

- Public 2-year community college
- Commuter campus in small town

**General. Founded** in 1981. Regionally accredited. **Enrollment:** 1,743 degree-seeking undergraduates. **Degrees:** 120 associate awarded. **Location:** 10 miles from Phillipsburg. **Calendar:** Semester, extensive summer session. **Full-time faculty:** 23 total; 17% have terminal degrees, 4% minority, 56% women. **Part-time faculty:** 82 total.

---

**Student profile.** Among degree-seeking undergraduates, 75 transferred in from other institutions.

| Out-of-state: | 3% | 25 or older: | 40% |
|---|---|---|---|

**Transfer out. Colleges most students transferred to 2007:** Centenary College, Rutgers-New Brunswick, East Stroudsburg University.

**Basis for selection.** Open admission, but selective for some programs. Interview recommended.

**High school preparation.** High school diploma or GED strongly recommended.

**2007-2008 Annual costs.** Tuition/fees: $3,263; $3,563 out-of-district; $4,163 out-of-state. Per-credit charge: $86 in-district; $96 out-of-district; $116 out-of-state. Books/supplies: $700. Personal expenses: $900.

**Financial aid.** All financial aid based on need. Need-based aid available for part-time students. Work-study available nights, weekends and for part-time students.

**Application procedures. Admission:** No deadline. $25 fee, may be waived for applicants with need. Application must be submitted on paper. Admission notification on a rolling basis. Early admission students ages 16-18 must provide written permission from parent/guardian and high school official. **Financial aid:** Closing date 7/8. FAFSA, institutional form required. Applicants notified on a rolling basis; must reply within 2 week(s) of notification.

**Academics. Special study options:** Cooperative education, cross-registration, distance learning, double major, dual enrollment of high school students, ESL, independent study, internships, liberal arts/career combination, weekend college. Bachelor's degree programs available on campus. License preparation in dental hygiene, nursing, real estate. **Credit/placement by examination:** AP, CLEP, IB, institutional tests. Challenge exams. **Support services:** GED preparation, learning center, pre-admission summer program, reduced course load, remedial instruction, tutoring, writing center.

**Majors. Biology:** General. **Business:** General, accounting, entrepreneurial studies. **Computer sciences:** General. **Conservation:** General, environmental studies. **Education:** General, early childhood. **English:** English lit. **Health:** Health services, nursing (RN). **Interdisciplinary:** Natural sciences. **Legal studies:** General, paralegal, prelaw. **Liberal arts:** Arts/sciences. **Physical sciences:** Chemistry. **Protective services:** Criminal justice. **Social sciences:** General. **Visual/performing arts:** Studio arts.

**Most popular majors.** Business/marketing 10%, education 15%, liberal arts 45%.

**Computing on campus.** 100 workstations in library, computer center. Online library, wireless network available.

**Student life. Freshman orientation:** Mandatory. Preregistration for classes offered. **Activities:** Literary magazine, student government, student newspaper, Phi Theta Kappa Honor Society, criminal justice association.

**Athletics. Team name:** Golden Eagles.

**Student services.** Adult student services, career counseling, student employment services, financial aid counseling, personal counseling, placement for graduates, veterans' counselor. **Physically disabled:** Services for visually, speech, hearing impaired. **Learning disabled:** Comprehensive services available. **Transfer:** Transfer adviser, college fairs on campus for students transferring to 4-year colleges.

**Contact.** Phone: (908) 835-9222 Fax: (908) 689-5824
Shannon Horwath, Associate Director of Admissions, Warren County Community College, Route 57 West, Washington, NJ 07882-4343

# New Mexico

## Central New Mexico Community College

**Albuquerque, New Mexico**      **CB member**
www.cnm.edu      **CB code: 3387**

- Public 2-year community and technical college
- Commuter campus in very large city

**General.** Founded in 1965. Regionally accredited. **Enrollment:** 18,778 degree-seeking undergraduates; 3,981 non-degree-seeking students. **Degrees:** 1,296 associate awarded. **ROTC:** Army, Naval, Air Force. **Calendar:** Trimester, extensive summer session.

**Student profile.** Among degree-seeking undergraduates, 3,130 enrolled as first-time, first-year students, 1,518 transferred in from other institutions.

| | | | |
|---|---|---|---|
| Part-time: | 65% | Hispanic American: | 42% |
| Out-of-state: | 1% | Native American: | 8% |
| Women: | 60% | International: | 1% |
| African American: | 3% | 25 or older: | 51% |
| Asian American: | 2% | | |

**Basis for selection.** Open admission. Submitting test scores for placement is optional.

**2007-2008 Annual costs.** Tuition/fees: $1,074; $1,314 out-of-district; $5,377 out-of-state. Per-credit charge: $41 in-district; $51 out-of-district; $221 out-of-state. In-district students do not pay tuition for technical courses, only arts and sciences courses. Books/supplies: $1,158.

**Financial aid. Need-based:** Need-based aid available for part-time students. Work-study available for part-time students. **Non-need-based:** Scholarships awarded for academics, state residency.

**Application procedures. Admission:** No deadline. No application fee. Application may be submitted online. Admission notification on a rolling basis. **Financial aid:** Priority date 3/1; no closing date. FAFSA required. Applicants notified by 5/1.

**Academics. Special study options:** Cooperative education, distance learning, double major, dual enrollment of high school students, ESL, internships, liberal arts/career combination. Apprenticeships. License preparation in aviation, dental hygiene, nursing, paramedic, radiology, real estate. **Credit/placement by examination:** AP, CLEP, institutional tests. **Support services:** GED preparation and test center, learning center, remedial instruction, study skills assistance, tutoring, writing center.

**Majors. Biology:** Biotechnology. **Business:** Accounting, administrative services, banking/financial services, business admin, hospitality admin. **Computer sciences:** Data processing, information systems, systems analysis. **Education:** Elementary, technology/industrial arts. **Engineering:** General, environmental. **Engineering technology:** Architectural drafting, electrical, electrical drafting, laser/optical, manufacturing, surveying. **Family/consumer sciences:** Child care. **Health:** Clinical lab technology, medical radiologic technology/radiation therapy, medical records admin, nursing (RN), respiratory therapy technology, sonography, veterinary technology/assistant. **Legal studies:** Paralegal. **Liberal arts:** Arts/sciences. **Mechanic/repair:** Aircraft powerplant. **Parks/recreation:** General. **Personal/culinary services:** Chef training, cosmetic. **Protective services:** Criminal justice, fire safety technology. **Transportation:** Airline/commercial pilot.

**Most popular majors.** Business/marketing 19%, engineering/engineering technologies 6%, health sciences 22%, liberal arts 29%.

**Computing on campus.** Commuter students can connect to campus network. Online course registration, online library available.

**Student life. Freshman orientation:** Mandatory. Preregistration for classes offered. **Activities:** Literary magazine, student government, student newspaper.

**Student services.** Adult student services, career counseling, services for economically disadvantaged, student employment services, financial aid counseling, health services, minority student services, placement for graduates. **Physically disabled:** Services for visually, speech, hearing impaired. **Transfer:** Transfer adviser for students transferring to 4-year colleges.

---

**Contact.** Phone: (505) 224-3160 Fax: (505) 224-3237
Jane Campbell, Registrar/Director of Enrollment Services, Central New Mexico Community College, 525 Buena Vista SE, Albuquerque, NM 87106

## Clovis Community College

**Clovis, New Mexico**      **CB member**
www.clovis.edu      **CB code: 4921**

- Public 2-year community and junior college
- Commuter campus in large town

**General.** Founded in 1990. Regionally accredited. **Enrollment:** 1,724 degree-seeking undergraduates; 1,968 non-degree-seeking students. **Degrees:** 199 associate awarded. **Location:** 200 miles from Albuquerque, 100 miles from Lubbock, Texas. **Calendar:** Semester, limited summer session. **Full-time faculty:** 48 total; 6% have terminal degrees, 6% minority, 54% women. **Part-time faculty:** 145 total; 8% have terminal degrees, 12% minority, 64% women. **Class size:** 58% < 20, 41% 20-39, less than 1% 40-49. **Special facilities:** Art collection representing multiple cultures of New Mexico. **Partnerships:** Formal partnerships with 12 high schools for Instructional Television Consortium.

**Student profile.** Among degree-seeking undergraduates, 60% enrolled in a transfer program, 40% enrolled in a vocational program, 179 enrolled as first-time, first-year students, 246 transferred in from other institutions.

| | | | |
|---|---|---|---|
| Part-time: | 52% | Women: | 70% |
| Out-of-state: | 16% | 25 or older: | 47% |

**Transfer out.** Colleges most students transferred to 2007: Eastern New Mexico University, New Mexico State University, University of New Mexico, Texas Tech University, West Texas A&M University.

**Basis for selection.** Open admission, but selective for some programs. Nursing and radiologic technology are selective; criteria include GPA, performance in related science courses. Test of Adult Basic Education (TABE) required for vocational programs, has been replaced with ACCUPLACER for some programs.

**2007-2008 Annual costs.** Tuition/fees: $808; $856 out-of-district; $1,552 out-of-state. Per-credit charge: $49 in-district; $51 out-of-district; $51 out-of-state. Books/supplies: $800. Personal expenses: $1,800.

**2006-2007 Financial aid. Need-based:** 67% of total undergraduate aid awarded as scholarships/grants, 33% as loans/jobs. Need-based aid available for part-time students. Work-study available nights, weekends and for part-time students. **Non-need-based:** Scholarships awarded for academics, state residency.

**Application procedures. Admission:** No deadline. No application fee. Application may be submitted online. Admission notification on a rolling basis. **Financial aid:** Priority date 9/1; no closing date. FAFSA required. Applicants notified on a rolling basis starting 4/15.

**Academics. Special study options:** Cooperative education, distance learning, double major, dual enrollment of high school students, ESL, honors, independent study, internships, teacher certification program, weekend college. License preparation in aviation, nursing, paramedic, radiology. **Credit/placement by examination:** AP, CLEP, institutional tests. 32 credit hours maximum toward associate degree. **Support services:** GED preparation and test center, learning center, remedial instruction, study skills assistance, tutoring, writing center.

**Majors. Business:** General, accounting, administrative services, business admin, management information systems, office management, office technology. **Computer sciences:** General, computer graphics, computer science, information technology, networking, programming, systems analysis. **Education:** General, early childhood, teacher assistance. **Engineering:** Electrical. **Engineering technology:** Drafting. **Health:** Medical radiologic technology/radiation therapy, medical secretary. **Interdisciplinary:** Natural sciences. **Legal studies:** General, legal secretary. **Liberal arts:** Arts/sciences. **Math:** General. **Mechanic/repair:** Automotive, electronics/electrical, heating/ac/refrig, industrial. **Personal/culinary services:** Cosmetic. **Protective services:** Criminal justice. **Psychology:** General. **Transportation:** Aviation. **Visual/performing arts:** Commercial/advertising art, studio arts.

**Most popular majors.** Business/marketing 8%, health sciences 35%, liberal arts 40%.

**Computing on campus.** 240 workstations in library, computer center, student center. Online course registration, helpline, wireless network available.

**Student life. Freshman orientation:** Available. Preregistration for classes offered. 3 hours prior to semester. **Activities:** Choral groups, drama, literary magazine, musical theater, student government, student newspaper, Hispanic advisory council, Phi Theta Kappa, social commmittee, international awareness organization, student ambassadors, black student union, pre-legal society, psychology club.

**Athletics. Intramural:** Basketball, racquetball.

**Student services.** Adult student services, career counseling, services for economically disadvantaged, student employment services, financial aid counseling, minority student services, on-campus daycare, personal counseling, placement for graduates, veterans' counselor. **Physically disabled:** Services for visually, speech, hearing impaired. **Transfer:** Re-entry adviser for new students. Transfer adviser, college fairs on campus for students transferring to 4-year colleges.

**Contact.** E-mail: admissions@clovis.edu
Phone: (575) 769-4025 Fax: (575) 769-4190
Rosie Corrie, Director of Admissions/Registrar, Clovis Community College, 417 Schepps Boulevard, Clovis, NM 88101-8381

---

## Dona Ana Branch Community College of New Mexico State University

**Las Cruces, New Mexico**
www.dacc.nmsu.edu                              CB code: 6296

♦ Public 2-year branch campus and community college
♦ Commuter campus in small city

**General.** Founded in 1973. Regionally accredited. Access to New Mexico State University facilities and activities. **Enrollment:** 7,801 degree-seeking undergraduates. **Degrees:** 544 associate awarded. **ROTC:** Army, Air Force. **Location:** 42 miles from El Paso, Texas. **Calendar:** Semester, limited summer session. **Full-time faculty:** 114 total. **Part-time faculty:** 294 total.

**Student profile.** Among degree-seeking undergraduates, 2,084 enrolled as first-time, first-year students.

Part-time:                    67%    **Women:**                    58%

**Basis for selection.** Open admission, but selective for some programs. Applicants to radiology technology, EMT-paramedic, and respiratory care programs selected on basis of COMPASS scores, Health Occupations Aptitude Test scores, resume, 3 letters of recommendation, clinical observation, and interview. Applicants to nursing program selected on basis of Nursing Entrance Exam scores and completion of requirements. COMPASS required for placement if ACT or SAT not taken.

**2007-2008 Annual costs.** Tuition/fees: $1,152; $1,392 out-of-district; $3,456 out-of-state. Room/board: $5,766. Books/supplies: $664. Personal expenses: $1,215.

**Financial aid. Need-based:** Need-based aid available for part-time students.

**Application procedures. Admission:** No deadline. $15 fee, may be waived for applicants with need. Application may be submitted online. Admission notification on a rolling basis. February 15th application deadline for radiology technology, EMT-paramedic, nursing, and respiratory care programs. **Financial aid:** Priority date 3/1; no closing date. FAFSA required. Applicants notified on a rolling basis starting 5/1.

**Academics. Special study options:** Combined bachelor's/graduate degree, cooperative education, cross-registration, distance learning, double major, dual enrollment of high school students, ESL, independent study, internships. License preparation in dental hygiene, nursing, paramedic, radiology. **Credit/placement by examination:** CLEP, institutional tests. 30 credit hours maximum toward associate degree. **Support services:** GED preparation and test center, learning center, pre-admission summer program, remedial instruction, study skills assistance, tutoring.

**Majors. Agriculture:** Landscaping. **Business:** Administrative services, business admin, fashion, hospitality admin, marketing, office management. **Computer sciences:** Computer graphics, computer science, data processing. **Construction:** Electrician, lineworker, maintenance. **Education:** General, early childhood. **Engineering:** Electrical. **Engineering technology:** Drafting, electrical. **Health:** EMT paramedic, medical radiologic technology/radiation therapy, medical secretary, nursing (RN), respiratory therapy technology. **Legal studies:** Legal secretary, paralegal. **Liberal arts:** Library assistant. **Mechanic/repair:** Automotive, electronics/electrical, heating/ac/refrig. **Protective services:** Firefighting.

**Computing on campus.** 460 workstations in library, computer center. Commuter students can connect to campus network. Online course registration, online library, helpline, repair service, wireless network available.

---

**Student life. Freshman orientation:** Available. **Housing:** Coed dorms, single-sex dorms, special housing for disabled, apartments available. Housing available on adjacent New Mexico State University campus. **Activities:** Student government, student newspaper, Vocational Industrial Clubs of America, Distributive Education Clubs of America, Phi Theta Kappa, fraternities and sororities available through New Mexico State University.

**Student services.** Adult student services, career counseling, student employment services, health services, personal counseling, placement for graduates, veterans' counselor. **Physically disabled:** Services for visually, speech, hearing impaired. **Transfer:** Transfer adviser, college fairs on campus for students transferring to 4-year colleges.

**Contact.** Phone: (575) 527-7710 Fax: (575) 527-7515
Becky Ordunez, Coordinator, Admissions, Dona Ana Branch Community College of New Mexico State University, MSC-3DA, Las Cruces, NM 88003-8001

---

## Eastern New Mexico University: Roswell Campus

**Roswell, New Mexico**                        CB member
www.roswell.enmu.edu                            CB code: 4662

♦ Public 2-year branch campus and community college
♦ Commuter campus in large town

**General.** Founded in 1958. Regionally accredited. **Enrollment:** 2,326 degree-seeking undergraduates. **Degrees:** 476 associate awarded. **Location:** 200 miles from Albuquerque. **Calendar:** Semester, limited summer session. **Full-time faculty:** 77 total. **Part-time faculty:** 183 total. **Class size:** 80% < 20, 18% 20-39, less than 1% 40-49, less than 1% 50-99, less than 1% >100. **Special facilities:** Instructional television, online and on-site classes available from main campus, allowing students to continue upper-division classes without travel.

**Student profile.**

Out-of-state:           12%    Live on campus:           3%
25 or older:            58%

**Transfer out. Colleges most students transferred to 2007:** Eastern New Mexico University-Portales, New Mexico State University, University of New Mexico, New Mexico Highlands University.

**Basis for selection.** Open admission, but selective for some programs. Some Health Services programs require completion of a pre-admission series of courses, have minimum course grades and GPAs. Students must pass university skills placement test to enroll in math or English courses. Remedial reading course required if test not passed. Student may be exempt based on ACT scores. **Adult students:** Some programs require completion of placement testing as prerequisite. **Homeschooled:** ACT score of 15 or more and high school transcript with graduation date required. **Learning Disabled:** Services based on need and disability documentation. Students requiring special services asked to provide information on needs as soon as possible to avoid delays in receiving service.

**2007-2008 Annual costs.** Tuition/fees: $1,124; $1,164 out-of-district; $4,540 out-of-state. Per-credit charge: $41 in-district; $43 out-of-district; $184 out-of-state. Room/board: $4,680. Books/supplies: $731. Personal expenses: $2,177.

**2006-2007 Financial aid. Need-based:** 42% of total undergraduate aid awarded as scholarships/grants, 58% as loans/jobs. Need-based aid available for part-time students. Work-study available nights, weekends and for part-time students.

**Application procedures. Admission:** No deadline. No application fee. Application may be submitted online. Admission notification on a rolling basis. **Financial aid:** Priority date 4/1; no closing date. FAFSA required. Applicants notified on a rolling basis starting 7/1; must reply within 3 week(s) of notification.

**Academics. Special study options:** Distance learning, dual enrollment of high school students, independent study, internships, liberal arts/career combination. License preparation in aviation, nursing, occupational therapy, paramedic. **Credit/placement by examination:** CLEP, IB, institutional tests. 30 credit hours maximum toward associate degree. Credits earned through CLEP and Advanced Placement must be mutually exclusive. **Support services:** GED preparation and test center, learning center, remedial instruction, study skills assistance, tutoring.

**Majors. Business:** General, accounting, administrative services. **Communications technology:** Animation/special effects. **Computer sciences:** General. **Education:** General, teacher assistance. **Engineering technology:** Architectural, drafting. **Family/consumer sciences:** Child care. **Health:** EMT paramedic, medical assistant, medical records technology, occupational therapy assistant, phlebotomy, respiratory therapy assistant. **Legal studies:** Paralegal. **Liberal arts:** Arts/sciences. **Mechanic/repair:** Automotive, avionics, electronics/electrical. **Production:** Welding. **Protective services:** Criminal justice, fire safety technology, police science. **Public administration:** Social work. **Transportation:** Aviation, aviation management.

**Most popular majors.** Business/marketing 12%, health sciences 22%, liberal arts 19%, trade and industry 31%.

**Computing on campus.** 50 workstations in library, computer center. Online course registration, wireless network available.

**Student life. Freshman orientation:** Available. Preregistration for classes offered. One-day program before classes commence. **Housing:** Coed dorms, apartments available. $50 deposit, deadline 8/1. **Activities:** Drama, student government, student newspaper, art club, ski club, computer club, Spanish club, science club, Student Nurses Association, residence hall council, psychology club, electronics club, occupational therapy assistants.

**Athletics. Intramural:** Basketball M, football (non-tackle) M, racquetball, softball W, tennis, volleyball, weight lifting M.

**Student services.** Career counseling, services for economically disadvantaged, student employment services, financial aid counseling, health services, on-campus daycare, personal counseling, placement for graduates, veterans' counselor. **Physically disabled:** Services for visually, speech, hearing impaired. **Transfer:** College fairs on campus for students transferring to 4-year colleges.

**Contact.** E-mail: admissions@roswell.enmu.edu
Phone: (575) 624-7149 Toll-free number: (800) 243-6687 ext. 149
Fax: (575) 624-7144
Ida Stover, Director of Admissions and Records, Eastern New Mexico University: Roswell Campus, Box 6000, Roswell, NM 88202-6000

## Luna Community College
**Las Vegas, New Mexico**
www.luna.edu                    CB code: 2591

♦ Public 2-year community and technical college
♦ Large town

**General.** Regionally accredited. **Calendar:** Semester.

**Annual costs/financial aid.** Tuition/fees (2007-2008): $728; $1,016 out-of-district; $1,952 out-of-state. Books/supplies: $500. Personal expenses: $572.

**Contact.** Phone: (505) 454-2550
Director of Admissions, 366 Luna Drive, Las Vegas, NM 87701

## Mesalands Community College
**Tucumcari, New Mexico**
www.mesalands.edu                    CB code: 3618

♦ Public 2-year community and technical college
♦ Commuter campus in small town

**General.** Regionally accredited. **Enrollment:** 313 degree-seeking undergraduates; 322 non-degree-seeking students. **Degrees:** 43 associate awarded. **Location:** 175 miles from Albuquerque, 110 miles from Amarillo, Texas. **Calendar:** Semester, extensive summer session. **Full-time faculty:** 13 total. **Part-time faculty:** 24 total. **Special facilities:** Museum, foundry.

**Student profile.** Among degree-seeking undergraduates, 134 enrolled as first-time, first-year students.

| Part-time: | 28% | Women: | 45% |
|---|---|---|---|
| Out-of-state: | 10% | | |

**Basis for selection.** Open admission. **Homeschooled:** Ability to Benefit Test or GED required.

**2007-2008 Annual costs.** Tuition/fees: $1,475; $2,387 out-of-state. Per-credit charge: $39 in-state; $69 out-of-state.

**Financial aid. Need-based:** Need-based aid available for part-time students. Work-study available nights and for part-time students. **Non-need-based:** Scholarships awarded for academics, athletics, leadership, minority status, music/drama, state residency.

**Application procedures. Admission:** No deadline. No application fee. Admission notification on a rolling basis. **Financial aid:** Priority date 4/1; no closing date. FAFSA required. Applicants notified on a rolling basis starting 4/1; must reply within 3 week(s) of notification.

**Academics. Special study options:** Distance learning, dual enrollment of high school students, ESL, independent study, internships. Bachelor's degree programs available on campus. **Credit/placement by examination:** AP, CLEP. 18 credit hours maximum toward associate degree. **Support services:** GED preparation and test center, learning center, remedial instruction, study skills assistance, tutoring.

**Majors. Agriculture:** General. **Business:** Business admin. **Computer sciences:** General. **Construction:** General. **Education:** General. **Engineering:** General. **Liberal arts:** Arts/sciences. **Physical sciences:** Geology, paleontology. **Protective services:** Law enforcement admin.

**Computing on campus.** 75 workstations in library, computer center. Online course registration, wireless network available.

**Student life. Freshman orientation:** Available. Preregistration for classes offered. **Activities:** Student government.

**Athletics. Intercollegiate:** Rodeo.

**Student services.** Adult student services, career counseling, financial aid counseling. **Physically disabled:** Services for visually, hearing impaired.

**Contact.** Phone: (575) 461-4413
Mesalands Community College, 911 South Tenth Street, Tucumcari, NM 88401

## Navajo Technical College
**Crownpoint, New Mexico**
www.navajotech.edu

♦ Public 2-year community and technical college
♦ Residential campus in rural community

**General. Enrollment:** 297 full-time, degree-seeking students. **Degrees:** 32 associate awarded. **Calendar:** Semester, limited summer session. **Full-time faculty:** 36 total; 36% women. **Part-time faculty:** 18 total; 44% women. **Special facilities:** Navajo Culture and Visitors Center. **Partnerships:** Formal partnerships with TeraGrid, SC08, Navajo Head Start, University of New Mexico, New Mexico Computing Applications Center, Navajo Rural Systemic Initiative, Navajo Workforce Development, Office of Dine Youth, Lewis and Clark University (Illinois), Southern University (Louisiana), National Museum of the American Indian, UNM Telemedicine Consortium, New Mexico State University's Extension Program, and Sandia National Laboratories.

**Student profile.** Among full-time, degree-seeking students, 79% enrolled in a vocational program.

**Basis for selection.** Open admission. ACCUPLACER required for all students to identify any remedial education requirements. **Adult students:** SAT/ACT scores not required.

**2008-2009 Annual costs.** Tuition/fees: $840. Above figures are quoted for members of federally recognized tribes. Non-members pay $1680 in tuition. Room/board: $4,056. Books/supplies: $800.

**Application procedures. Admission:** No application fee. Application may be submitted online. Admission notification on a rolling basis. **Financial aid:** No deadline.

**Academics. Special study options:** Accelerated study, double major, dual enrollment of high school students, honors, independent study, internships, teacher certification program. License preparation in nursing. **Credit/placement by examination:** CLEP. **Support services:** GED preparation, remedial instruction, study skills assistance, tutoring.

**Majors. Agriculture:** General. **Business:** Accounting. **Computer sciences:** General. **Education:** Early childhood. **Engineering technology:** CAD/CADD, GIS. **Health:** Veterinary technology/assistant. **Legal studies:** Paralegal. **Public administration:** General. **Other:** Professional assistant.

**Most popular majors.** Computer/information sciences 17%, education 10%, engineering/engineering technologies 44%, legal studies 24%.

**Computing on campus.** 40 workstations in library, computer center, student center. Commuter students can connect to campus network. Online course registration, online library, helpline, repair service, wireless network available.

**Student life. Freshman orientation:** Mandatory. Preregistration for classes offered. New Mexico Orientation is an all day event held one week before classes start. **Housing:** Guaranteed on-campus for all undergraduates. Single-sex dorms, apartments, substance-free housing available. **Activities:** Student government, student newspaper, Child Care Services, Behavioral Health Services, Counseling.

**Athletics. Intercollegiate:** Cross-country, rodeo. **Intramural:** Basketball, cross-country, softball, volleyball. **Team name:** Hawks.

**Student services.** Adult student services, alcohol/substance abuse counseling, career counseling, services for economically disadvantaged, student employment services, financial aid counseling, on-campus daycare, personal counseling. **Physically disabled:** Services for visually, speech, hearing impaired. **Learning disabled:** Comprehensive services available.

**Contact.** E-mail: rdamon@navajotech.edu
Phone: (505) 786-4326 Fax: (505) 786-5644
Delores Becenti, Registrar, Navajo Technical College, PO Box 849, Crownpoint, NM 87313

---

## New Mexico Junior College
### Hobbs, New Mexico
www.nmjc.edu                                    CB code: 4553

▸ Public 2-year community and technical college
▸ Commuter campus in large town

**General.** Founded in 1965. Regionally accredited. **Enrollment:** 3,066 degree-seeking undergraduates. **Degrees:** 222 associate awarded. **Location:** 110 miles from Roswell, 100 miles from Lubbock, Texas. **Calendar:** Semester, extensive summer session. **Full-time faculty:** 73 total. **Part-time faculty:** 120 total. **Special facilities:** Western heritage museum, cowboy hall of fame.

**Student profile.** Among degree-seeking undergraduates, 172 transferred in from other institutions.

| | | | |
|---|---|---|---|
| Out-of-state: | 10% | Live on campus: | 8% |
| 25 or older: | 51% | | |

**Transfer out. Colleges most students transferred to 2007:** College of the Southwest, Eastern New Mexico University, Texas Tech University, University of New Mexico, New Mexico State University.

**Basis for selection.** Open admission, but selective for some programs. Special requirements for nursing, law enforcement, and automotive service education programs. Applicants admitted without high school diploma or GED must pass GED before completion of degree program. Interview required for nursing, medical laboratory technician, automotive service education programs.

**High school preparation.** 18 units recommended. Recommended units include English 4, mathematics 3, social studies 4, science 2 and academic electives 5.

**2007-2008 Annual costs.** Tuition/fees: $1,122; $1,554 out-of-district; $1,674 out-of-state. Per-credit charge: $28 in-district; $46 out-of-district; $51 out-of-state. Room/board: $3,750. Books/supplies: $700. Personal expenses: $1,575.

**Financial aid. Need-based:** Need-based aid available for part-time students. Work-study available nights and weekends. **Non-need-based:** Scholarships awarded for academics, art, athletics, leadership, music/drama.

**Application procedures. Admission:** No deadline. No application fee. Application may be submitted online. Admission notification on a rolling basis. **Financial aid:** Priority date 6/1; no closing date. FAFSA required. Applicants notified on a rolling basis; must reply within 2 week(s) of notification.

**Academics. Special study options:** Cooperative education, cross-registration, distance learning, dual enrollment of high school students, ESL, honors, internships, weekend college. License preparation in nursing, radiology, real estate. **Credit/placement by examination:** AP, CLEP, institutional tests. 30 credit hours maximum toward associate degree. **Support services:** GED preparation and test center, learning center, pre-admission summer program, reduced course load, remedial instruction, study skills assistance, tutoring, writing center.

**Majors. Biology:** General. **Business:** General, accounting, administrative services, banking/financial services, business admin, office management, office technology, real estate. **Communications:** General. **Computer sciences:** General, applications programming, computer graphics, programming. **Education:** General, early childhood, elementary, middle, physical,

secondary. **Engineering:** General. **Engineering technology:** Drafting, hazardous materials. **Foreign languages:** Spanish. **Health:** Athletic training, clinical lab assistant, clinical lab technology, EMT paramedic, medical radiologic technology/radiation therapy, predental, premedicine, prepharmacy. **Legal studies:** Legal secretary, paralegal, prelaw. **Liberal arts:** Arts/sciences. **Math:** General. **Mechanic/repair:** Automotive. **Personal/culinary services:** Cosmetic. **Physical sciences:** Chemistry, physics. **Protective services:** Criminal justice, police science. **Psychology:** General. **Social sciences:** General. **Visual/performing arts:** Commercial/advertising art, studio arts.

**Most popular majors.** Agriculture 6%, business/marketing 11%, education 13%, health sciences 24%, liberal arts 10%, mathematics 7%, trade and industry 13%.

**Computing on campus.** 275 workstations in dormitories, library, computer center, student center. Dormitories wired for high-speed internet access. Commuter students can connect to campus network. Helpline available.

**Student life. Freshman orientation:** Mandatory. Preregistration for classes offered. **Housing:** Single-sex dorms, special housing for disabled, substance-free housing available. **Activities:** Bands, choral groups, drama, music ensembles, musical theater, student government, Young Republicans, Young Democrats, student nurses, ambassadors.

**Athletics.** NJCAA. **Intercollegiate:** Baseball M, basketball, golf M. **Intramural:** Badminton, basketball, bowling, golf, handball, racquetball, skiing, soccer, softball, swimming, table tennis, tennis, volleyball. **Team name:** Thunderbirds.

**Student services.** Career counseling, student employment services, financial aid counseling, health services, personal counseling, placement for graduates, veterans' counselor. **Physically disabled:** Services for visually, speech, hearing impaired. **Transfer:** Pre-admission transcript evaluation for new students. Transfer adviser, college fairs on campus for students transferring to 4-year colleges.

**Contact.** Phone: (575) 392-5113 Fax: (575) 392-0322
Michele Clingman, Dean of Enrollment Management, New Mexico Junior College, 5317 Lovington Highway, Hobbs, NM 88240

---

## New Mexico Military Institute
### Roswell, New Mexico                         CB member
www.nmmi.edu                                    CB code: 4534

▸ Public 2-year junior and military college
▸ Residential campus in large town
▸ SAT or ACT (ACT writing optional) required

**General.** Founded in 1891. Regionally accredited. **Enrollment:** 466 degree-seeking undergraduates. **ROTC:** Army. **Location:** 200 miles from Albuquerque; 200 miles from El Paso, Texas. **Calendar:** Semester, limited summer session. **Full-time faculty:** 57 total. **Part-time faculty:** 4 total. **Class size:** 59% < 20, 40% 20-39, 1% 40-49. **Special facilities:** Television production, ropes course.

**Transfer out. Colleges most students transferred to 2007:** University of New Mexico, New Mexico State University, Texas A&M University, University of Colorado.

**Basis for selection.** 2.0 GPA, 19 ACT or 920 SAT (exclusive of writing) for participation in Advanced Army ROTC. 17 ACT or 800 SAT (exclusive of writing) for Basic Army ROTC program. Preference given to in-state applicants. Maximum age of 22 for enrollment. Students cannot be married or have children. Interview recommended for all applicants.

**High school preparation.** 21 units recommended. Recommended units include English 4, mathematics 3, social studies 1, history 2, science 2 (laboratory 2), foreign language 2 and academic electives 5. Computer science 0.5 unit recommended.

**2008-2009 Annual costs.** Tuition/fees (projected): $4,751. Room/board: $3,736. Books/supplies: $700. Personal expenses: $1,000.

**Financial aid. Non-need-based:** Scholarships awarded for academics, alumni affiliation, athletics, ROTC, state residency.

**Application procedures. Admission:** No deadline. $85 fee, may be waived for applicants with need. Admission notification on a rolling basis beginning on or about 9/1. Advanced Army ROTC applicants must pass Army physical examination. **Financial aid:** Priority date 4/1; no closing date. FAFSA required. Applicants notified on a rolling basis starting 5/1; must reply within 3 week(s) of notification.

**Academics. Special study options:** Dual enrollment of high school students. **Credit/placement by examination:** CLEP, institutional tests. 30 credit hours maximum toward associate degree. **Support services:** Learning center, remedial instruction, tutoring.

**Majors. Liberal arts:** Arts/sciences.

**Computing on campus.** 100 workstations in dormitories, library, computer center, student center. Dormitories linked to campus network. Helpline, repair service available.

**Student life. Freshman orientation:** Mandatory. **Housing:** Guaranteed on-campus for all undergraduates. Single-sex dorms available. $100 deposit. All students must live in college housing. **Activities:** Bands, choral groups, film society, music ensembles, student government, student newspaper, symphony orchestra, TV station.

**Athletics.** NJCAA. **Intercollegiate:** Baseball M, basketball M, fencing, football (tackle) M, golf, rifle, tennis, track and field. **Intramural:** Fencing, football (tackle) M, handball, racquetball, skiing, soccer, softball, swimming, tennis, track and field, volleyball. **Team name:** Broncos.

**Student services.** Career counseling, health services, personal counseling. **Transfer:** Pre-admission transcript evaluation for new students.

**Contact.** E-mail: admissions@nmmi.edu
Phone: (505) 624-8050 Toll-free number: (800) 421-5376
Fax: (505) 624-8058
Lt. Col. Jeffrey Savage, Vice President of Enrollment, New Mexico Military Institute, 101 West College Boulevard, Roswell, NM 88201-5173

## New Mexico State University at Alamogordo
**Alamogordo, New Mexico**
alamo.nmsu.edu/                                    CB code: 4012

- Public 2-year branch campus college
- Commuter campus in large town

**General.** Founded in 1958. Regionally accredited. **Enrollment:** 2,017 degree-seeking undergraduates. **Degrees:** 176 associate awarded. **ROTC:** Air Force. **Location:** 65 miles from Las Cruces, 85 miles from El Paso, Texas. **Calendar:** Semester, limited summer session. **Full-time faculty:** 49 total. **Part-time faculty:** 51 total. **Special facilities:** Planetarium.

**Student profile.**

Out-of-state:            6%    25 or older:            55%

**Transfer out. Colleges most students transferred to 2007:** New Mexico State University.

**Basis for selection.** Open admission, but selective for some programs. Special requirements for nursing and medical technologies programs; essay and interview required.

**2007-2008 Annual costs.** Tuition/fees: $1,344; $1,512 out-of-district; $4,008 out-of-state. Per-credit charge: $54 in-district; $61 out-of-district; $165 out-of-state. Books/supplies: $664. Personal expenses: $1,458.

**Financial aid. Need-based:** Need-based aid available for part-time students. **Non-need-based:** Scholarships awarded for academics, state residency.

**Application procedures. Admission:** No deadline. $15 fee. Admission notification on a rolling basis. **Financial aid:** Priority date 3/1; no closing date. FAFSA, institutional form required. Applicants notified by 6/1.

**Academics. Special study options:** Combined bachelor's/graduate degree, cooperative education, cross-registration, distance learning, double major, dual enrollment of high school students, honors, independent study, liberal arts/career combination, weekend college. License preparation in nursing, paramedic. **Credit/placement by examination:** AP, CLEP, institutional tests. 30 credit hours maximum toward associate degree. **Support services:** GED preparation and test center, learning center, reduced course load, remedial instruction, study skills assistance, tutoring, writing center.

**Majors. Business:** General, administrative services, management information systems. **Communications technology:** Photo/film/video. **Computer sciences:** Data processing, information systems, web page design. **Education:** General, early childhood, teacher assistance. **Engineering:** General, computer. **Engineering technology:** Electrical. **Health:** Clinical lab assistant, clinical lab technology. **Legal studies:** Paralegal. **Liberal arts:** Arts/sciences. **Protective services:** Criminal justice, firefighting, forensics. **Public administration:** Social work. **Visual/performing arts:** Art, commercial/advertising art, design.

**Most popular majors.** Business/marketing 17%, education 6%, health sciences 11%, liberal arts 52%.

**Computing on campus.** 203 workstations in library, computer center, student center. Commuter students can connect to campus network. Online course registration, online library, helpline, repair service available.

**Student life. Freshman orientation:** Available. **Activities:** Jazz band, choral groups, drama, music ensembles, student government.

**Athletics. Intramural:** Softball, table tennis, volleyball.

**Student services.** Career counseling, student employment services, financial aid counseling, personal counseling, placement for graduates, veterans' counselor. **Physically disabled:** Services for visually, speech, hearing impaired. **Transfer:** Transfer adviser, college fairs on campus for students transferring to 4-year colleges.

**Contact.** Phone: (505) 439-3700
Kathy Fuller, Admissions Coordinator, New Mexico State University at Alamogordo, 2400 North Scenic Drive, Alamogordo, NM 88310

## New Mexico State University at Carlsbad
**Carlsbad, New Mexico**
cavern.nmsu.edu                                    CB code: 4547

- Public 2-year branch campus and community college
- Commuter campus in large town

**General.** Founded in 1950. Regionally accredited. **Location:** 165 miles from El Paso, Texas. **Calendar:** Semester.

**Annual costs/financial aid.** Tuition/fees (2007-2008): $1,300; $1,420 out-of-district; $2,812 out-of-state. Books/supplies: $580. Personal expenses: $1,300. Need-based financial aid available to full-time and part-time students.

**Contact.** Phone: (505) 234-9223
Director of Admissions, 1500 University Drive, Carlsbad, NM 88220

## New Mexico State University at Grants
**Grants, New Mexico**
www.grants.nmsu.edu                                CB code: 0461

- Public 2-year branch campus and community college
- Commuter campus in small town

**General.** Founded in 1968. Regionally accredited. **Location:** 75 miles from Albuquerque. **Calendar:** Semester.

**Annual costs/financial aid.** Tuition/fees (2007-2008): $1,300; $1,430 out-of-district; $2,784 out-of-state. Books/supplies: $400. Need-based financial aid available to full-time and part-time students.

**Contact.** Phone: (505) 287-7981
Campus Student Services Officer, 1500 North Third Street, Grants, NM 87020

## Northern New Mexico College
**Espanola, New Mexico**
www.nnmc.edu                                       CB code: 0425

- Public 2-year community and teachers college
- Commuter campus in small town

**General.** Founded in 1909. Regionally accredited. Additional center in Tierra Amarilla. **Enrollment:** 692 degree-seeking undergraduates. **Degrees:** 151 associate awarded. **Location:** 24 miles from Santa Fe. **Calendar:** Semester, limited summer session. **Full-time faculty:** 49 total. **Part-time faculty:** 132 total.

**Student profile.**

Out-of-state:    1%    Live on campus:    1%
25 or older:     39%

**Basis for selection.** Open admission, but selective for some programs and for out-of-state students. Nursing, radiography, barbering, and cosmetology programs require separate applications subsequent to admission. 2-year nursing program requires 2.5 GPA and preadmission test. Limited number of out-of-state applicants considered. Four-year programs: applicants must complete 35 credits of general education common core plus 10 additional credits with 2.5 minimum GPA before applying to specific four-year program. No admission tests. Tests administered before or after admission for course placement purposes only, except for those admitted under ability to benefit. **Homeschooled:** Transcript of courses and grades, state high school equivalency certificate required. Applicant must be at least 16.

**2007-2008 Annual costs.** Tuition/fees: $1,030; $2,206 out-of-state. Per-credit charge: $36 in-state; $85 out-of-state. Upper division courses $85 per credit hour for in-state students, $360 per credit hour for out-of-state students. Room/board: $3,028. Books/supplies: $600. Personal expenses: $1,740.

**Financial aid.** All financial aid based on need.

**Application procedures. Admission:** No deadline. No application fee. Application must be submitted on paper. Admission notification on a rolling basis. **Financial aid:** Priority date 3/1; no closing date. FAFSA required. Applicants notified on a rolling basis starting 6/1; must reply within 2 week(s) of notification.

**Academics. Special study options:** Distance learning, dual enrollment of high school students, internships, liberal arts/career combination, teacher certification program. Bachelor's degree programs available on campus. License preparation in nursing, radiology. **Credit/placement by examination:** AP, CLEP, IB, institutional tests. 15 credit hours maximum toward associate degree, 30 toward bachelor's. **Support services:** GED preparation and test center, learning center, remedial instruction, study skills assistance, tutoring, writing center.

**Majors. Area/ethnic studies:** Regional. **Business:** General, accounting, administrative services, business admin, management information systems. **Computer sciences:** General. **Conservation:** General, forestry, management/policy. **Construction:** Electrician, maintenance, pipefitting. **Education:** Early childhood, elementary. **Engineering technology:** Drafting, electrical. **Health:** Medical radiologic technology/radiation therapy, substance abuse counseling. **Interdisciplinary:** Biological/physical sciences. **Liberal arts:** Arts/sciences, library assistant. **Personal/culinary services:** Cosmetic. **Physical sciences:** General. **Production:** Furniture, welding, woodworking. **Protective services:** Criminal justice. **Public administration:** Human services, social work. **Visual/performing arts:** General, art, design, fiber arts, studio arts.

**Computing on campus.** 24 workstations in library, computer center. Commuter students can connect to campus network.

**Student life. Freshman orientation:** Mandatory. Preregistration for classes offered. Three hour sessions held on Tuesdays prior to term. **Housing:** Single-sex dorms, substance-free housing available. **Activities:** Choral groups, drama, music ensembles, student government, Phi Theta Kappa.

**Athletics. Intramural:** Basketball, softball.

**Student services.** Career counseling, student employment services, financial aid counseling, personal counseling, placement for graduates, veterans' counselor. **Physically disabled:** Services for visually, speech, hearing impaired. **Transfer:** Pre-admission transcript evaluation for new students. Transfer adviser, college fairs on campus for students transferring to 4-year colleges.

**Contact.** E-mail: mikec@nnmc.edu
Phone: (505) 747-2112 Fax: (505) 747-5449
Michael Costello, Dean of Student Services, Northern New Mexico College, 921 Paseo de Onate, Espanola, NM 87532

---

## San Juan College
**Farmington, New Mexico**
www.sanjuancollege.edu

**CB member**
**CB code: 4732**

- Public 2-year community college
- Commuter campus in large town

**General.** Founded in 1956. Regionally accredited. **Enrollment:** 4,773 degree-seeking undergraduates; 2,641 non-degree-seeking students. **Degrees:** 414 associate awarded. **Location:** 183 miles from Albuquerque. **Calendar:** Semester, limited summer session. **Full-time faculty:** 116 total; 8% minority, 57% women. **Part-time faculty:** 218 total; 13% minority, 57% women. **Special facilities:** Planetarium, special collection of Southwestern books and materials, geographic information system, art gallery and 800-seat performance hall, fire tower for specialized training, commercial truck driving training range, drilling rig, clean room for instrumentation training, plant operations equipment, jet simulator for pilot training.

**Student profile.** Among degree-seeking undergraduates, 26% enrolled in a transfer program, 27% enrolled in a vocational program, 768 enrolled as first-time, first-year students, 274 transferred in from other institutions.

| | | | |
|---|---|---|---|
| Part-time: | 57% | Asian American: | 1% |
| Women: | 62% | Hispanic American: | 13% |
| African American: | 1% | Native American: | 34% |

**Basis for selection.** Open admission. **Homeschooled:** Transcript of courses and grades required. Minimum score on ACCUPLACER showing ability to benefit required.

**High school preparation.** 13 units recommended. Recommended units include English 4, mathematics 3, social studies 3, science 2 and foreign language 1.

**2007-2008 Annual costs.** Tuition/fees: $720; $960 out-of-state. Per-credit charge: $30 in-state; $40 out-of-state. Books/supplies: $900. Personal expenses: $900.

**2006-2007 Financial aid. Need-based:** 55% of total undergraduate aid awarded as scholarships/grants, 45% as loans/jobs. Need-based aid available for part-time students. Work-study available nights, weekends and for part-time students. **Non-need-based:** Scholarships awarded for academics, state residency.

**Application procedures. Admission:** No deadline. No application fee. Application may be submitted online. Admission notification on a rolling basis. **Financial aid:** No deadline. FAFSA required. Applicants notified on a rolling basis starting 7/1; must reply within 2 week(s) of notification.

**Academics. Special study options:** Combined bachelor's/graduate degree, cooperative education, distance learning, dual enrollment of high school students, ESL, external degree, honors, independent study, internships, liberal arts/career combination, teacher certification program. Bachelor's degree programs available on campus. License preparation in aviation, dental hygiene, nursing, physical therapy, real estate. **Credit/placement by examination:** CLEP, institutional tests. 30 credit hours maximum toward associate degree. **Support services:** GED preparation and test center, learning center, reduced course load, remedial instruction, study skills assistance, tutoring, writing center.

**Majors. Agriculture:** Business, landscaping. **Area/ethnic studies:** Regional. **Biology:** General. **Business:** Accounting technology, administrative services, business admin, office technology, real estate. **Communications:** General. **Computer sciences:** Computer science, data processing, networking. **Conservation:** General. **Construction:** Carpentry, well drilling. **Education:** General, early childhood. **Engineering:** General. **Engineering technology:** Civil drafting, drafting, electrical, industrial, instrumentation, mechanical drafting, solar energy, surveying. **English:** English lit. **Foreign languages:** General. **Health:** Dental hygiene, EMT paramedic, medical records technology, nursing (RN), office admin, physical therapy assistant, premedicine, veterinary technology/assistant. **History:** General. **Legal studies:** Legal secretary. **Liberal arts:** Arts/sciences. **Math:** General. **Mechanic/repair:** Auto body, automotive, diesel, industrial. **Personal/culinary services:** Cosmetic. **Philosophy/religion:** Philosophy. **Physical sciences:** General, chemistry, geology, physics. **Production:** Machine shop technology, welding. **Protective services:** Firefighting, police science. **Psychology:** General. **Public administration:** General, social work. **Social sciences:** Anthropology, archaeology, economics, political science, sociology. **Transportation:** Airline/commercial pilot. **Visual/performing arts:** Art, commercial/advertising art, dramatic, theater design.

**Most popular majors.** Education 8%, engineering/engineering technologies 12%, health sciences 18%, liberal arts 28%, trade and industry 15%.

**Computing on campus.** 952 workstations in library, computer center, student center. Commuter students can connect to campus network. Online course registration, helpline, wireless network available.

**Student life. Freshman orientation:** Mandatory. Preregistration for classes offered. One-day session held prior to beginning of semester. **Activities:** Bands, choral groups, dance, drama, film society, music ensembles, musical theater, radio station, student government, student newspaper, TV station, Native American club, Student Ambassadors, Phi Theta Kappa honor society.

**Athletics. Intramural:** Archery, badminton, baseball M, basketball, bowling, cross-country, golf, handball, racquetball, skiing, softball, table tennis, tennis, volleyball.

**Student services.** Career counseling, student employment services, financial aid counseling, minority student services, on-campus daycare, personal counseling, placement for graduates, veterans' counselor. **Physically disabled:** Services for visually, speech, hearing impaired. **Transfer:** Transfer adviser, college fairs on campus for students transferring to 4-year colleges.

**Contact.** E-mail: florezr@sanjuancollege.edu
Phone: (505) 566-3300 Fax: (505) 566-3500
Jon Betz, Director of Admissions, San Juan College, 4601 College
Boulevard, Farmington, NM 87402-4699

## Santa Fe Community College

Santa Fe, New Mexico
www.sfccnm.edu

CB member
CB code: 4816

- Public 2-year community college
- Commuter campus in small city

**General.** Founded in 1983. Regionally accredited. **Enrollment:** 1,974 degree-seeking undergraduates. **Degrees:** 227 associate awarded. **Location:** 50 miles from Albuquerque. **Calendar:** Semester, limited summer session. **Full-time faculty:** 59 total. **Part-time faculty:** 257 total. **Class size:** 76% < 20, 24% 20-39, less than 1% 40-49. **Special facilities:** Planetarium, art galleries, fine arts studios, fitness center, swimming pools, child development center. **Partnerships:** Formal partnerships with businesses and state agencies.

**Transfer out. Colleges most students transferred to 2007:** University of New Mexico, New Mexico State University, College of Santa Fe.

**Basis for selection.** Open admission. Selective admissions to nursing program. Essay and interview required for international students; interview required for concurrent high school/college students.

**2007-2008 Annual costs.** Tuition/fees: $1,083; $1,404 out-of-district; $2,439 out-of-state. Per-credit charge: $32 in-district; $43 out-of-district; $78 out-of-state. Books/supplies: $600. Personal expenses: $1,500.

**2006-2007 Financial aid. Need-based:** 75% of total undergraduate aid awarded as scholarships/grants, 25% as loans/jobs. Need-based aid available for part-time students. Work-study available nights, weekends and for part-time students. **Non-need-based:** Scholarships awarded for academics, state residency.

**Application procedures. Admission:** No deadline. No application fee. Application may be submitted online. Admission notification on a rolling basis. **Financial aid:** Priority date 5/1; no closing date. FAFSA, institutional form required. Applicants notified on a rolling basis starting 7/15; must reply within 4 week(s) of notification.

**Academics. Special study options:** Accelerated study, cooperative education, cross-registration, distance learning, double major, dual enrollment of high school students, ESL, honors, independent study, internships, liberal arts/career combination, teacher certification program, weekend college. Bachelor's degree programs available on campus. License preparation in dental hygiene, nursing, paramedic, real estate. **Credit/placement by examination:** AP, CLEP, institutional tests. 30 credit hours maximum toward associate degree. Maximum of 9 credit hours can be earned through challenge examinations. **Support services:** GED preparation and test center, reduced course load, remedial instruction, study skills assistance, tutoring, writing center.

**Majors. Area/ethnic studies:** Regional. **Biology:** General. **Business:** General, accounting, banking/financial services, business admin, entrepreneurial studies. **Computer sciences:** General. **Education:** General, kindergarten/preschool. **Engineering:** General. **Engineering technology:** Construction, drafting. **Foreign languages:** Sign language interpretation, Spanish. **Health:** Dental assistant, nursing (RN). **Legal studies:** Paralegal. **Parks/recreation:** Health/fitness. **Personal/culinary services:** Chef training. **Physical sciences:** General. **Protective services:** Criminal justice. **Psychology:** General. **Public administration:** Human services, social work. **Visual/performing arts:** Art, art history/conservation, design, interior design. **Other:** Drafting and engineering technology, Exercise science.

**Most popular majors.** Business/marketing 16%, education 9%, health sciences 22%, legal studies 6%, liberal arts 14%, public administration/social services 8%, security/protective services 6%, visual/performing arts 6%.

**Computing on campus.** 200 workstations in library, computer center, student center. Commuter students can connect to campus network. Online course registration, online library, helpline, wireless network available.

**Student life. Freshman orientation:** Mandatory. Preregistration for classes offered. **Activities:** Choral groups, dance, drama, literary magazine, music ensembles, radio station, student government, TV station, Phi Theta Kappa, Native American student association, student nursing association, student council, Movimiento Estudiantil Chicano de Aztlan, fine arts club, Los Tournants, sign language interpreters club, student ambassadors.

**Student services.** Adult student services, career counseling, services for economically disadvantaged, student employment services, financial aid counseling, on-campus daycare, personal counseling, placement for graduates, veterans' counselor, women's services. **Physically disabled:** Services for visually, speech, hearing impaired. **Transfer:** Transfer adviser, college fairs on campus for students transferring to 4-year colleges.

**Contact.** E-mail: enroll@sfccnm.edu
Phone: (505) 428-1278 Fax: (505) 428-1468
Amy Tilley, Director of Admissions, Santa Fe Community College, 6401 Richards Avenue, Santa Fe, NM 87508-4887

## Southwestern Indian Polytechnic Institute

Albuquerque, New Mexico
www.sipi.bia.edu

CB member
CB code: 7047

- Public 2-year community and technical college
- Residential campus in large city

**General.** Founded in 1971. Regionally accredited. National Indian community college serving American Indians from federally recognized Indian tribes from across the United States. **Enrollment:** 574 degree-seeking undergraduates. **Degrees:** 55 associate awarded. **Calendar:** Trimester, extensive summer session. **Full-time faculty:** 20 total.

**Student profile.** Among degree-seeking undergraduates, 15% enrolled in a transfer program, 44% enrolled in a vocational program, 224 enrolled as first-time, first-year students, 48 transferred in from other institutions.

| Part-time: | 18% | Women: | 55% |

**Transfer out. Colleges most students transferred to 2007:** University of New Mexico, New Mexico State University, New Mexico Highlands University, Fort Lewis College.

**Basis for selection.** Open admission. Applicants must have valid membership in U.S. federally recognized Indian tribe. ACT, COMPASS, and TABE required for placement. **Homeschooled:** Transcript of courses and grades, state high school equivalency certificate required.

**2007-2008 Annual costs.** Required fees: full-time Lodge student $280, full-time commuter $225, part-time $150. Books/supplies: $800. Personal expenses: $1,400.

**Financial aid. Need-based:** Need-based aid available for part-time students. Work-study available nights and weekends. **Non-need-based:** Scholarships awarded for academics, leadership, minority status. **Additional information:** Students with valid membership in recognized Indian tribe attend tuition-free.

**Application procedures. Admission:** Closing date 8/31 (receipt date). No application fee. Admission notification on a rolling basis. **Financial aid:** Closing date 3/1. FAFSA required. Applicants notified on a rolling basis starting 9/30.

**Academics. Special study options:** Cooperative education, distance learning, double major, honors, liberal arts/career combination. **Credit/placement by examination:** AP, CLEP, institutional tests. **Support services:** GED preparation, learning center, remedial instruction, study skills assistance, tutoring.

**Majors. Agriculture:** Agribusiness operations, agronomy, soil science. **Business:** General, accounting technology, business admin, hospitality admin, hospitality/recreation, office technology. **Computer sciences:** General, computer science, LAN/WAN management. **Conservation:** General, environmental science, management/policy. **Education:** Early childhood. **Engineering technology:** Electrical, environmental, manufacturing, surveying. **Family/consumer sciences:** Institutional food production. **Health:** Optician, optometric assistant. **Liberal arts:** Arts/sciences. **Personal/culinary services:** General, culinary arts. **Social sciences:** Cartography.

**Computing on campus.** 15 workstations in dormitories, library, computer center, student center. Dormitories linked to campus network. Wireless network available.

**Student life. Freshman orientation:** Mandatory. Held week prior to start of classes. **Policies:** Zero tolerance policy on alcohol and drugs. **Housing:** Single-sex dorms available. $55 fully refundable deposit. **Activities:** Dance, natural resources club, Native American political action council, Phi Theta Kappa, student senate, dance club, AISES, inter-tribal pow-wow club, music and art club, four winds and golden eagle lodge council.

**Athletics. Intramural:** Basketball, softball, volleyball, weight lifting. **Team name:** Eagles.

**Student services.** Alcohol/substance abuse counseling, campus ministries, career counseling, student employment services, financial aid counseling, health services, personal counseling, placement for graduates. **Transfer:** Transfer adviser, college fairs on campus for students transferring to 4-year colleges.

**Contact.** E-mail: jcarpio@sipi.bia.edu
Phone: (505) 346-2324 Toll-free number: (800) 586-7474
Fax: (505) 346-2373
Joseph Carpio, Registrar, Southwestern Indian Polytechnic Institute, 9169 Coors Road Northwest, Albuquerque, NM 87184

# New York

## Adirondack Community College
**Queensbury, New York**
www.sunyacc.edu                                          CB code: 2017

◆  Public 2-year community college
◆  Commuter campus in large town

**General.** Founded in 1960. Regionally accredited. **Enrollment:** 2,884 degree-seeking undergraduates. **Degrees:** 464 associate awarded. **Location:** 50 miles from Albany, 1 mile from Glens Falls. **Calendar:** Semester, limited summer session. **Full-time faculty:** 92 total. **Part-time faculty:** 145 total. **Special facilities:** Solar botany lab, challenge course, fitness trail, pond preserve, arboretum, weather station, forensic science lab.

**Student profile.**

Out-of-state:                1%        25 or older:                32%

**Transfer out. Colleges most students transferred to 2007:** SUNY Plattsburgh, Siena College, SUNY Albany, College of Saint Rose, SUNY Oneonta.

**Basis for selection.** Open admission, but selective for some programs. Minimum high school average of 80 or minimum GPA of 2.5 for acceptance into nursing program. If submitted, SAT or ACT and SAT Subject Tests used for placement and counseling. Essay and interview recommended. **Homeschooled:** Must take and pass GED or successfuly complete ability to benefit test.

**High school preparation.** 22 units recommended. Recommended units include English 4, mathematics 3, social studies 4, history 2, science 3, foreign language 1 and academic electives 5. Allied health programs require Regents biology, chemistry examinations. Engineering requires Regents biology, chemistry and mathematics through pre-calculus. Computer science, mechanical and electrical technology require mathematics through advanced algebra. Forestry requires Regents biology, chemistry, and mathematics through intermediate algebra.

**2007-2008 Annual costs.** Tuition/fees: $3,357; $6,487 out-of-state. Per-credit charge: $131 in-state; $262 out-of-state. Books/supplies: $1,200. Personal expenses: $990.

**Financial aid.** All financial aid based on need. Need-based aid available for part-time students.

**Application procedures. Admission:** Priority date 3/15; deadline 8/1. $40 fee, may be waived for applicants with need. Application must be submitted on paper. Admission notification on a rolling basis beginning on or about 1/15. **Financial aid:** Priority date 4/15; no closing date. FAFSA, institutional form required. Applicants notified on a rolling basis starting 5/1.

**Academics. Special study options:** Distance learning, double major, dual enrollment of high school students, independent study, internships, liberal arts/career combination, study abroad. Bachelor's degree programs available on campus. License preparation in nursing. **Credit/placement by examination:** AP, CLEP, IB, institutional tests. 34 credit hours maximum toward associate degree. **Support services:** GED preparation, learning center, reduced course load, remedial instruction, study skills assistance, tutoring, writing center.

**Majors. Business:** Accounting, business admin, hospitality/recreation, marketing, tourism promotion. **Communications:** Broadcast journalism, media studies. **Computer sciences:** General, computer science, data processing, information systems, programming. **Engineering:** General. **Engineering technology:** Drafting, electrical. **Health:** Nursing (RN), radiologic technology/medical imaging. **Liberal arts:** Arts/sciences. **Personal/culinary services:** Culinary arts. **Protective services:** Corrections, police science. **Other:** Adventure sports.

**Most popular majors.** Business/marketing 18%, health sciences 18%, liberal arts 46%, security/protective services 6%.

**Computing on campus.** 350 workstations in library, computer center, student center. Online library available.

**Student life. Freshman orientation:** Available. **Activities:** Concert band, choral groups, dance, drama, literary magazine, music ensembles, musical theater, radio station, student government, TV station.

**Athletics.** NJCAA. **Intercollegiate:** Baseball M, basketball, bowling, golf M, soccer, softball W, volleyball W. **Intramural:** Badminton, basketball, football (non-tackle), skiing, softball, volleyball. **Team name:** Timberwolves.

**Student services.** Adult student services, career counseling, student employment services, financial aid counseling, on-campus daycare, personal counseling, placement for graduates, veterans' counselor. **Physically disabled:** Services for visually, speech, hearing impaired. **Transfer:** Transfer adviser, college fairs on campus for students transferring to 4-year colleges.

**Contact.**  E-mail: info@acc.sunyacc.edu
Phone: (518) 743-2264 Fax: (518) 832-7602
Sara Jane Linehan, Director of Enrollment Management, Adirondack Community College, 640 Bay Road, Queensbury, NY 12804

## American Academy McAllister Institute of Funeral Service
**New York, New York**
www.funeraleducation.org                                 CB code: 0774

◆  Private 2-year school of mortuary science
◆  Commuter campus in very large city

**General.** Founded in 1926. **Enrollment:** 178 degree-seeking undergraduates. **Degrees:** 70 associate awarded. **Calendar:** Semester, extensive summer session. **Full-time faculty:** 3 total. **Part-time faculty:** 23 total. **Class size:** 67% 20-39, 33% 40-49.

**Student profile.**

Out-of-state:                26%       25 or older:                39%

**Basis for selection.** Open admission. Interview recommended.

**2007-2008 Annual costs.** Tuition/fees: $11,370. Books/supplies: $709. Personal expenses: $2,635.

**Financial aid.** All financial aid based on need.

**Application procedures. Admission:** Closing date 8/10. $40 fee. Admission notification on a rolling basis. **Financial aid:** FAFSA required. Applicants notified on a rolling basis starting 7/1; must reply by 9/1 or within 3 week(s) of notification.

**Academics. Special study options:** Cross-registration. **Credit/placement by examination:** CLEP. **Support services:** Tutoring.

**Majors. Personal/culinary services:** Mortuary science.

**Computing on campus.** 12 workstations in library.

**Student life. Activities:** Student government.

**Student services.** Personal counseling, placement for graduates. **Transfer:** Transfer adviser for students transferring to 4-year colleges.

**Contact.**  E-mail: info@funeraleducation.org
Phone: (212) 757-1190 Fax: (212) 765-5923
Norman Provost, Director of Admissions/Bursar, American Academy McAllister Institute of Funeral Service, 619 West 54th Street, New York, NY 10019-3602

## American Academy of Dramatic Arts
**New York, New York**
www.aada.org                                             CB code: 2603

◆  Private 2-year junior and performing arts college
◆  Commuter campus in very large city
◆  Application essay, interview required

**General.** Founded in 1884. Regionally accredited. Offers practical conservatory and training. Additional campus in Hollywood, CA. **Enrollment:** 228 degree-seeking undergraduates. **Degrees:** 95 associate awarded. **Location:** Midtown Manhattan. **Calendar:** Semester, limited summer session. **Full-time faculty:** 7 total; 43% have terminal degrees, 57% women. **Part-time faculty:** 19 total; 21% have terminal degrees, 16% minority. **Class size: 89% < 20. **Special facilities:** 3 theaters, dance studio, costume department, property/production areas, audio/visual center, state-of-the-art television studio.

**Student profile.** Among degree-seeking undergraduates, 59 enrolled as first-time, first-year students, 62 transferred in from other institutions.

| Out-of-state: | 87% | 25 or older: | 14% |
|---|---|---|---|

**Basis for selection.** Dramatic ability or potential, academic qualifications, maturity and motivation very important. Audition required; regional audition/interview may be arranged.

**2008-2009 Annual costs.** Tuition/fees: $20,000. Books/supplies: $1,590. Personal expenses: $1,000.

**2006-2007 Financial aid.** All financial aid based on need. 38 full-time freshmen applied for aid; 36 were judged to have need; 31 of these received aid. Average need met was 62%. Average scholarship/grant was $2,000; average loan $2,675. 13% of total undergraduate aid awarded as scholarships/grants, 87% as loans/jobs. **Additional information:** Need-based incentive grants of $200-$500 for first-year students available. Merit awards of $500-$1,500. Scholarships of $500-$3,000 available for second year. Scholarships of $500-$5,000 available for post-degree third year.

**Application procedures. Admission:** No deadline. $50 fee. Application may be submitted online. Admission notification on a rolling basis. **Financial aid:** No deadline. FAFSA, institutional form required. Applicants notified on a rolling basis.

**Academics.** 2-year professional actor training program offered with associate of occupational studies degree. Third year, available by faculty invitation, forms showcase Academy Company. **Special study options:** Students may study 1 year at each of 2 campuses. **Credit/placement by examination:** CLEP. **Support services:** Tutoring.

**Majors. Visual/performing arts:** Acting.

**Most popular majors.** Visual/performing arts 95%.

**Computing on campus.** 6 workstations in library.

**Student life. Freshman orientation:** Mandatory. **Activities:** Drama, student government, student newspaper, various arts-related organizations available.

**Student services.** Career counseling, student employment services, placement for graduates.

**Contact.** E-mail: admissions-ny@aada.org
Phone: (212) 686-9244 Toll-free number: (800) 463-8990
Fax: (212) 685-8093
Karen Higginbotham, Director of Admissions, American Academy of Dramatic Arts, 120 Madison Avenue, New York, NY 10016

## Art Institute of New York City
**New York, New York** — **CB member** — **CB code: 3106**
www.ainyc.artinstitutes.edu

- For-profit 2-year culinary school and technical college
- Commuter campus in very large city
- Application essay, interview required

**General.** Accredited by ACICS. **Enrollment:** 1,590 degree-seeking undergraduates. **Degrees:** 225 associate awarded. **Calendar:** Quarter, extensive summer session. **Full-time faculty:** 75 total. **Part-time faculty:** 22 total.

**Student profile.** Among degree-seeking undergraduates, 100% enrolled in a vocational program, 3% already have a bachelor's degree or higher, 480 enrolled as first-time, first-year students.

| Part-time: | 37% | Asian American: | 6% |
|---|---|---|---|
| Women: | 58% | Hispanic American: | 26% |
| African American: | 24% | Live on campus: | 3% |

**Basis for selection.** Open admission. Accuplacer may be used in placement for certain programs of study. **Homeschooled:** Transcript of courses and grades, state high school equivalency certificate required.

**2007-2008 Annual costs.** Tuition/fees: $24,485. Per-credit charge: $470. Students in nonculinary programs (e.g., graphic design, fashion design, video production, advertising) do not pay $1,925 in additional fees. Fees may vary within culinary programs. Books/supplies: $650.

**Application procedures. Admission:** No deadline. $50 fee. Application may be submitted online. Admission notification on a rolling basis.

**Academics. Special study options:** Internships. **Credit/placement by examination:** AP, CLEP. **Support services:** Learning center, remedial instruction, study skills assistance.

**Majors. Personal/culinary services:** Culinary arts. **Visual/performing arts:** Cinematography, fashion design, graphic design, interior design, multimedia.

**Computing on campus.** 40 workstations in library, computer center. Online library, helpline, repair service available.

**Student life. Freshman orientation:** Mandatory. Preregistration for classes offered. Scheduled prior to class start or in first week. **Activities:** Film society, student newspaper.

**Student services.** Adult student services, career counseling, student employment services, financial aid counseling, personal counseling, placement for graduates. **Transfer:** Re-entry adviser, pre-admission transcript evaluation for new students.

**Contact.** E-mail: mgrillo@aii.edu
Phone: (212) 226-5500 Toll-free number: (800) 654-2433
Fax: (212) 625-6065
Mary Ann Grillo, Senior Director of Admissions, Art Institute of New York City, 75 Varick Street, 16th Floor, New York, NY 10013-1917

## ASA Institute of Business and Computer Technology
**Brooklyn, New York**
www.asa.edu

- For-profit 2-year career college
- Commuter campus in very large city
- ACT with writing, interview required

**General.** Regionally accredited; also accredited by ACICS. **Enrollment:** 2,958 degree-seeking undergraduates; 14 non-degree-seeking students. **Degrees:** 953 associate awarded. **Location:** Located in New York City. **Calendar:** Semester, extensive summer session. **Full-time faculty:** 49 total; 100% have terminal degrees, 45% minority, 49% women. **Part-time faculty:** 174 total; 100% have terminal degrees, 45% minority, 48% women. **Class size:** 68% < 20, 31% 20-39, less than 1% 40-49.

**Student profile.** Among degree-seeking undergraduates, 894 enrolled as first-time, first-year students, 40 transferred in from other institutions.

| Part-time: | 4% | Hispanic American: | 39% |
|---|---|---|---|
| Out-of-state: | 1% | Native American: | 1% |
| Women: | 79% | International: | 5% |
| African American: | 45% | 25 or older: | 58% |
| Asian American: | 4% | | |

**Basis for selection.** Candidates accorded individual consideration through comprehensive evaluation of prior scholastic records and assessment testing results.

**2008-2009 Annual costs.** Tuition/fees (projected): $11,499. Per-credit charge: $470. Books/supplies: $1,000. Personal expenses: $4,838.

**2006-2007 Financial aid. Need-based:** 59% of total undergraduate aid awarded as scholarships/grants, 41% as loans/jobs. Need-based aid available for part-time students. Work-study available nights and weekends. **Non-need-based:** Scholarships awarded for academics, alumni affiliation, leadership, state residency.

**Application procedures. Admission:** No deadline. $25 fee. Application must be submitted on paper. **Financial aid:** No deadline. FAFSA required. Applicants notified on a rolling basis starting 7/6; must reply by 10/6.

**Academics. Special study options:** Accelerated study, distance learning, ESL, internships. **Credit/placement by examination:** AP, CLEP, ACT. **Support services:** GED preparation, learning center, reduced course load, remedial instruction, study skills assistance, tutoring, writing center.

**Majors. Business:** Accounting/business management, business admin. **Computer sciences:** Networking, programming. **Health:** Medical assistant, medical records technology, pharmacy assistant. **Protective services:** Criminal justice.

**Most popular majors.** Business/marketing 17%, computer/information sciences 8%, health sciences 75%.

**Computing on campus.** 700 workstations in library, computer center. Online library, helpline available.

**Student life. Freshman orientation:** Mandatory. **Activities:** Drama, literary magazine, student government.

**Student services.** Adult student services, career counseling, services for economically disadvantaged, student employment services, financial aid counseling, personal counseling, placement for graduates.

**Contact.** E-mail: admissions@asa.edu
Phone: (718) 522-9073 Toll-free number: (877) 867-5327
Fax: (718) 532-1432
Victoria Kostyukov, Vice President of Marketing and Admissions, ASA Institute of Business and Computer Technology, 151 Lawrence Street, Brooklyn, NY 11201

## Bramson ORT College
**Forest Hills, New York**
**www.bramsonort.org**                    CB code: 0944

- Private 2-year junior and technical college affiliated with Jewish faith
- Commuter campus in very large city

**General.** Founded in 1977. Regionally accredited. **Calendar:** Semester.

**Annual costs/financial aid.** Tuition/fees (2007-2008): $9,330.

**Contact.** Phone: (718) 261-5800
Admissions Coordinator, 6930 Austin Street, Forest Hills, NY 11375

## Broome Community College
**Binghamton, New York**                    **CB member**
**www.sunybroome.edu**                    **CB code: 2048**

- Public 2-year community college
- Commuter campus in small city

**General.** Founded in 1946. Regionally accredited. SUNY institution. **Enrollment:** 5,336 degree-seeking undergraduates; 1,222 non-degree-seeking students. **Degrees:** 990 associate awarded. **Location:** 3 miles from downtown. **Calendar:** Semester, extensive summer session. **Full-time faculty:** 168 total. **Part-time faculty:** 238 total. **Class size:** 67% < 20, 31% 20-39, less than 1% 40-49, less than 1% 50-99, less than 1% >100. **Special facilities:** College-operated ice rink.

**Student profile.** Among degree-seeking undergraduates, 47% enrolled in a transfer program, 53% enrolled in a vocational program, 1,433 enrolled as first-time, first-year students.

| | | | |
|---|---|---|---|
| Part-time: | 23% | Asian American: | 2% |
| Out-of-state: | 4% | Hispanic American: | 2% |
| Women: | 54% | International: | 3% |
| African American: | 4% | 25 or older: | 28% |

**Transfer out. Colleges most students transferred to 2007:** Binghamton University, Rochester Institute of Technology, State University of New York Cortland, State University of New York Utica-Rome, Ithaca College.

**Basis for selection.** Open admission, but selective for some programs. Entry into certain health sciences programs (nursing, physical therapy assistant, medical lab technology, medical assistant, radiologic technology, health information technology, dental hygiene) limited on space-available basis. Interview recommended for computer science and health science programs. **Homeschooled:** Provide either 1) letter from superintendent of the school district in which student resides attesting to completion of program meeting requirements of Section 100.10 of the Regulations of the Commissioner of Education or 2) a passing score on GED (and diploma itself when available). Also may be admitted on ability-to-benefit basis.

**2007-2008 Annual costs.** Tuition/fees: $3,363; $6,421 out-of-state. Per-credit charge: $128 in-state; $256 out-of-state. Books/supplies: $1,200. Personal expenses: $938.

**Financial aid. Need-based:** Need-based aid available for part-time students. Work-study available nights.

**Application procedures. Admission:** No deadline. No application fee. Application may be submitted online. Admission notification on a rolling basis. Health Science students should apply and have all transcripts sent by March 15 prior to the fall semester. **Financial aid:** Priority date 3/1; no closing date. FAFSA required. Applicants notified on a rolling basis starting 3/15; must reply within 2 week(s) of notification.

**Academics. Special study options:** Cooperative education, distance learning, dual enrollment of high school students, ESL, exchange student, honors, independent study, internships, student-designed major, study abroad, weekend college. License preparation in dental hygiene, nursing, paramedic, physical therapy, radiology, real estate. **Credit/placement by examination:** AP, CLEP, institutional tests. Contact division dean for assessment of experiential learning or portfolio assessment. **Support services:** Learning center, reduced course load, remedial instruction, study skills assistance, tutoring, writing center.

**Majors. Business:** Accounting technology, business admin, executive assistant, financial planning, hotel/motel admin, international finance. **Communications:** General. **Computer sciences:** General, data processing, information systems. **Engineering:** Science. **Engineering technology:** Civil, computer, electrical, industrial, mechanical, quality control. **Family/consumer sciences:** Child care. **Health:** Clinical lab technology, dental hygiene, EMT paramedic, medical assistant, medical radiologic technology/radiation therapy, medical records technology, nursing (RN), physical therapy assistant, substance abuse counseling. **Legal studies:** Paralegal. **Liberal arts:** Arts/sciences. **Protective services:** Corrections, firefighting, police science.

**Computing on campus.** 500 workstations in library, computer center. Commuter students can connect to campus network. Online course registration, helpline, wireless network available.

**Student life. Freshman orientation:** Available. Preregistration for classes offered. **Activities:** Bands, campus ministries, choral groups, dance, drama, international student organizations, music ensembles, musical theater, student government, student newspaper, black student union, Phi Theta Kappa, Ski Extreme, writing club, chess club, Alpha Beta Gamma, computer club, music association.

**Athletics.** NJCAA. **Intercollegiate:** Baseball M, basketball, cheerleading, cross-country, golf M, ice hockey M, lacrosse M, soccer, tennis M, volleyball W. **Intramural:** Badminton, basketball, bowling, golf, soccer, tennis, volleyball. **Team name:** Hornets.

**Student services.** Adult student services, career counseling, services for economically disadvantaged, student employment services, financial aid counseling, health services, on-campus daycare, personal counseling, placement for graduates, veterans' counselor. **Physically disabled:** Services for visually, speech, hearing impaired. **Transfer:** Transfer adviser, college fairs on campus for students transferring to 4-year colleges.

**Contact.** Phone: (607) 778-5001 Toll-free number: (800) 836-0689
Fax: (607) 778-5310
Anthony Fiorelli, Director of Admissions, Broome Community College, Box 1017, Binghamton, NY 13902

## Bryant & Stratton College: Albany
**Albany, New York**
**www.bryantstratton.edu**                    **CB code: 2018**

- For-profit 2-year business college
- Commuter campus in small city
- Application essay, interview required

**General.** Founded in 1854. Regionally accredited. **Enrollment:** 617 degree-seeking undergraduates; 4 non-degree-seeking students. **Degrees:** 112 associate awarded. **Location:** 2 miles from Albany, 28 miles from Saratoga. **Calendar:** Semester, extensive summer session. **Full-time faculty:** 13 total; 15% have terminal degrees, 8% minority, 31% women. **Part-time faculty:** 47 total; 26% have terminal degrees, 17% minority, 49% women.

**Student profile.** Among degree-seeking undergraduates, 127 enrolled as first-time, first-year students.

| | | | |
|---|---|---|---|
| Part-time: | 32% | 25 or older: | 51% |
| Women: | 78% | | |

**Basis for selection.** High school record, entrance examination score, personal interview and personal essay considered. Portfolio recommended.

**High school preparation.** Business courses recommended. Mathematics concentration preferred.

**2008-2009 Annual costs.** Tuition/fees: $13,740. Tuition may vary depending on program.

**2006-2007 Financial aid.** All financial aid based on need. 45% of total undergraduate aid awarded as scholarships/grants, 55% as loans/jobs. Need-based aid available for part-time students. Work-study available nights, weekends and for part-time students.

**Application procedures. Admission:** No deadline. No application fee. Admission notification on a rolling basis. Must reply by May 1 or within 4 week(s) if notified thereafter. **Financial aid:** No deadline. FAFSA required. Applicants notified on a rolling basis.

**Academics. Special study options:** Distance learning, double major, independent study, internships. **Credit/placement by examination:** CLEP. 31 credit hours maximum toward associate degree. **Support services:** Learning center, reduced course load, remedial instruction, tutoring, writing center.

**Majors. Business:** Accounting, administrative services, business admin, human resources. **Computer sciences:** General. **Health:** Medical assistant. **Legal studies:** Paralegal. **Protective services:** Law enforcement admin.

**Most popular majors.** Business/marketing 46%, computer/information sciences 15%, health sciences 20%, legal studies 18%.

**Computing on campus.** 100 workstations in library, computer center.

**Student life. Freshman orientation:** Mandatory.

**Student services.** Alcohol/substance abuse counseling, career counseling, student employment services, financial aid counseling, personal counseling, placement for graduates, veterans' counselor. **Physically disabled:** Services for visually impaired. **Transfer:** Pre-admission transcript evaluation for new students. Transfer adviser, college fairs on campus for students transferring to 4-year colleges.

**Contact.** Phone: (518) 437-1802 ext. 203 Fax: (518) 437-1049
Robert Ferrell, Director of Admissions, Bryant & Stratton College: Albany, 1259 Central Avenue, Albany, NY 12205

---

## Bryant & Stratton College: Amherst
**Amherst, New York**
www.bryantstratton.edu                    CB code: 3331

- For-profit 2-year business college
- Small town

**General.** Regionally accredited. **Calendar:** Continuous.

**Annual costs/financial aid.** Tuition/fees (2007-2008): $13,185. Books/supplies: $1,200.

**Contact.** Phone: (716) 691-0012
40 Hazelwood Drive, Amherst, NY 14228-2230

---

## Bryant & Stratton College: Buffalo
**Buffalo, New York**
www.bryantstratton.edu                    CB code: 2058

- For-profit 2-year business and career college
- Large city
- Interview required

**General.** Founded in 1854. Regionally accredited. Branch campuses in Amherst and Orchard Park. **Enrollment:** 614 degree-seeking undergraduates. **Degrees:** 92 associate awarded. **Calendar:** Semester, extensive summer session. **Full-time faculty:** 10 total. **Part-time faculty:** 44 total.

**Student profile.** Among degree-seeking undergraduates, 177 enrolled as first-time, first-year students.

| Part-time: | 32% | Hispanic American: | 8% |
|---|---|---|---|
| Women: | 76% | Native American: | 1% |
| African American: | 57% | | |

**Transfer out. Colleges most students transferred to 2007:** Erie Community College.

**Basis for selection.** Open admission. **Learning Disabled:** Students with special needs are invited to discuss their needs with their student services advisor prior to registration. Students requesting accommodations are required to provide current documentation in order to determine reasonable accommodations where appropriate.

**2008-2009 Annual costs.** Tuition/fees: $13,740. Per-credit charge: $458. IT, BBA, medical assisting, medical administrative assistant, paralegal program cost: $14,430 per year, $481 per credit hour. $100 graduation fee in final semester. Books/supplies: $1,200. Personal expenses: $1,350.

---

**2007-2008 Financial aid. Need-based:** 36% of total undergraduate aid awarded as scholarships/grants, 64% as loans/jobs.

**Application procedures. Admission:** No deadline. $25 fee, may be waived for applicants with need. Admission notification on a rolling basis. CPAt entrance exam. **Financial aid:** No deadline. Applicants notified on a rolling basis.

**Academics. Special study options:** Distance learning, internships. Bachelor's degree programs available on campus. **Credit/placement by examination:** AP, CLEP, institutional tests. 45 credit hours maximum toward associate degree. **Support services:** Learning center, remedial instruction, study skills assistance, tutoring, writing center.

**Majors. Business:** General, administrative services. **Computer sciences:** General. **Engineering technology:** Electrical. **Health:** Medical assistant.

**Computing on campus.** 130 workstations in library, computer center. Online library available.

**Student life. Freshman orientation:** Mandatory. Preregistration for classes offered. **Activities:** Radio station, student government, student newspaper, numerous special interest clubs.

**Athletics. Intramural:** Bowling, skiing, softball, swimming.

**Student services.** Career counseling, student employment services, personal counseling, placement for graduates. **Physically disabled:** Services for visually, hearing impaired. **Transfer:** Re-entry adviser, pre-admission transcript evaluation for new students. Transfer adviser, college fairs on campus for students transferring to 4-year colleges.

**Contact.** E-mail: mbrobinson@bryantstratton.edu
Phone: (716) 884-9120 Fax: (716) 884-0091
Philip Struebel, Director of Admissions, Bryant & Stratton College: Buffalo, 465 Main Street, Suite 400, Buffalo, NY 14203

---

## Bryant & Stratton College: Henrietta
**Rochester, New York**
www.bryantstratton.edu

- For-profit 2-year business college
- Commuter campus in small city

**General. Enrollment:** 715 degree-seeking undergraduates. **Degrees:** 189 associate awarded. **Calendar:** Semester. **Full-time faculty:** 23 total. **Part-time faculty:** 78 total.

**Basis for selection.** Interview, entrance evaluation important.

**2007-2008 Annual costs.** Tuition/fees: $13,080. Per-credit charge: $436.

**Application procedures. Admission:** No deadline. No application fee.

**Academics. Credit/placement by examination:** CLEP.

**Majors. Business:** Accounting, administrative services, human resources. **Computer sciences:** Information technology. **Health:** Medical assistant, medical secretary. **Legal studies:** Paralegal. **Protective services:** Law enforcement admin. **Visual/performing arts:** Graphic design.

**Contact.** Phone: (585) 292-5627
Maria Scalise, Admissions Director, Bryant & Stratton College: Henrietta, 1225 Jefferson Road, Rochester, NY 14623

---

## Bryant & Stratton College: Rochester
**Rochester, New York**
www.bryantstratton.edu                    CB code: 7327

- For-profit 2-year business college
- Commuter campus in large city
- Interview required

**General.** Founded in 1973. Regionally accredited. Second campus in Rochester. Degree program runs 4 consecutive semesters. **Enrollment:** 720 degree-seeking undergraduates. **Degrees:** 252 associate awarded. **Calendar:** Continuous, extensive summer session. **Full-time faculty:** 23 total. **Part-time faculty:** 97 total.

**Basis for selection.** Open admission. Character, previous scholastic record, and counselor recommendation important. CPAT required for admission.

**2007-2008 Annual costs.** Tuition/fees: $13,080. Per-credit charge: $436. Books/supplies: $1,000.

**Application procedures. Admission:** No deadline. $25 fee, may be waived for applicants with need. Admission notification on a rolling basis. **Financial aid:** No deadline. FAFSA required. Applicants notified on a rolling basis.

**Academics. Special study options:** Accelerated study, distance learning, double major, internships. **Credit/placement by examination:** CLEP. **Support services:** Learning center, reduced course load, study skills assistance, tutoring.

**Majors. Business:** Accounting, administrative services, business admin, customer service, office technology. **Computer sciences:** Information technology, webmaster. **Health:** Office admin. **Legal studies:** Legal secretary, paralegal. **Visual/performing arts:** Design.

**Computing on campus.** 10 workstations in computer center. Commuter students can connect to campus network.

**Student life. Freshman orientation:** Available. Preregistration for classes offered. **Activities:** Student government, professional interest clubs.

**Athletics. Team name:** Bobcats.

**Student services.** Career counseling, financial aid counseling, personal counseling, placement for graduates. **Transfer:** Pre-admission transcript evaluation for new students. Transfer adviser for students transferring to 4-year colleges.

**Contact.** Phone: (585) 292-5627
Maria Scalise, Director of Admissions, Bryant & Stratton College: Rochester, 1225 Jefferson Road, Rochester, NY 14623

## Bryant & Stratton College: Southtowns
**Orchard Park, New York**
**www.bryantstratton.edu**
**CB code: 3328**

- For-profit 2-year business college
- Commuter campus in large town

**General.** Regionally accredited. **Enrollment:** 315 degree-seeking undergraduates. **Degrees:** 150 associate awarded. **Location:** 11 miles from downtown Buffalo. **Calendar:** Continuous, extensive summer session. **Full-time faculty:** 7 total. **Part-time faculty:** 25 total.

**Basis for selection.** Open admission.

**2007-2008 Annual costs.** Tuition/fees: $13,080. Books/supplies: $1,200.

**Application procedures. Admission:** No deadline. $25 fee. Application may be submitted online.

**Academics. Special study options:** Distance learning, double major. **Credit/placement by examination:** CLEP. **Support services:** Learning center, study skills assistance, tutoring.

**Majors. Business:** Business admin. **Computer sciences:** General.

**Computing on campus.** Online library available.

**Student life. Freshman orientation:** Mandatory. Preregistration for classes offered. **Activities:** Student government, student newspaper.

**Student services.** Career counseling, student employment services, financial aid counseling. **Physically disabled:** Services for visually, hearing impaired. **Transfer:** Pre-admission transcript evaluation for new students.

**Contact.** E-mail: prkehr@bryantstratton.edu
Phone: (716) 677-9500 Fax: (716) 677-9599
Paul Kehr, Director of Admissions, Bryant & Stratton College: Southtowns, 200 Redtail, Orchard Park, NY 14127

## Bryant & Stratton College: Syracuse
**Syracuse, New York**
**www.bryantstratton.edu**
**CB code: 0654**

- For-profit 2-year business college
- Commuter campus in small city

**General.** Founded in 1854. Regionally accredited. **Enrollment:** 809 degree-seeking undergraduates. **Degrees:** 140 associate awarded. **Location:** 75 miles from Rochester. **Calendar:** Trimester, extensive summer session. **Full-time faculty:** 19 total. **Part-time faculty:** 46 total. **Class size:** 54% < 20, 46% 20-39.

**Student profile.**

| Out-of-state: | 2% | Live on campus: | 10% |
| 25 or older: | 45% | | |

**Basis for selection.** Open admission. SAT Subject Tests considered if submitted.

**2007-2008 Annual costs.** Tuition/fees: $13,080. Per-credit charge: $436. Books/supplies: $1,000. Personal expenses: $1,350.

**2007-2008 Financial aid.** All financial aid based on need. Work-study available nights, weekends and for part-time students.

**Application procedures. Admission:** No deadline. No application fee. Application must be submitted on paper. Admission notification on a rolling basis. **Financial aid:** No deadline. FAFSA required. Applicants notified on a rolling basis starting 10/1.

**Academics. Special study options:** Cooperative education, cross-registration, distance learning, double major, honors, internships. **Credit/placement by examination:** AP, CLEP. **Support services:** Learning center, reduced course load, remedial instruction, study skills assistance, tutoring.

**Majors. Business:** Accounting, administrative services, business admin, hotel/motel admin, marketing, office management, sales/distribution, tourism promotion, tourism/travel. **Computer sciences:** General. **Health:** Medical assistant, medical secretary. **Legal studies:** Legal secretary.

**Most popular majors.** Business/marketing 61%, health sciences 35%.

**Computing on campus.** 230 workstations in dormitories, library, computer center, student center. Dormitories wired for high-speed internet access and linked to campus network. Online library available.

**Student life. Freshman orientation:** Mandatory. **Housing:** Single-sex dorms available. $50 deposit. **Activities:** Choral groups, student newspaper.

**Athletics.** NJCAA. **Intercollegiate:** Soccer. **Team name:** Bobcats.

**Student services.** Career counseling, student employment services, financial aid counseling, personal counseling, placement for graduates. **Physically disabled:** Services for visually, speech, hearing impaired. **Transfer:** Re-entry adviser, pre-admission transcript evaluation for new students. Transfer adviser, college fairs on campus for students transferring to 4-year colleges.

**Contact.** Phone: (315) 472-6603 Fax: (315) 474-4383
Andy Cunningham, Director of Admissions, Bryant & Stratton College: Syracuse, 953 James Street, Syracuse, NY 13203

## Bryant & Stratton College: Syracuse North
**Liverpool, New York**
**www.bryantstratton.edu**

- For-profit 2-year business college
- Commuter campus in small town

**General. Enrollment:** 498 degree-seeking undergraduates. **Degrees:** 149 associate awarded. **Location:** 5 miles from Syracuse. **Calendar:** Semester, extensive summer session. **Full-time faculty:** 9 total.

**Basis for selection.** Open admission. ACCUPLACER used for placement/counseling; students with minimum SAT (exclusive of Writing) 956 or 20 ACT not required to take ACCUPLACER.

**2007-2008 Annual costs.** Tuition/fees: $12,450.

**Application procedures. Admission:** No deadline. No application fee.

**Academics. Credit/placement by examination:** AP, CLEP.

**Majors. Business:** General, accounting, administrative services. **Computer sciences:** Information technology. **Legal studies:** Paralegal. **Visual/performing arts:** Graphic design.

**Athletics. Team name:** Bobcats.

**Contact.** Phone: (315) 652-6500
Heather Macknick, Admissions Director, Bryant & Stratton College: Syracuse North, 8687 Carling Road, Liverpool, NY 13090

## Business Informatics Center
**Valley Stream, New York**
www.thecollegeforbusiness.com

- For-profit 2-year business and community college
- Commuter campus in large town
- Interview required

**General.** Accredited by ACCSCT. **Enrollment:** 200 degree-seeking undergraduates. **Degrees:** 52 associate awarded. **Calendar:** Quarter. **Full-time faculty:** 7 total. **Part-time faculty:** 5 total. **Class size:** 92% < 20, 8% 20-39.

**Transfer out. Colleges most students transferred to 2007:** Briarcliff College, Katharine Gibbs.

**Basis for selection.** Open admission.

**2007-2008 Annual costs.** Tuition/fees: $10,950.

**Application procedures. Admission:** No deadline. $50 fee, may be waived for applicants with need. Admission notification on a rolling basis. **Financial aid:** No deadline.

**Academics. Credit/placement by examination:** AP, CLEP, institutional tests. **Support services:** Tutoring.

**Majors. Business:** Office technology. **Legal studies:** Court reporting.

**Most popular majors.** Business/marketing 77%, legal studies 23%.

**Computing on campus.** 50 workstations in library, computer center.

**Student life. Freshman orientation:** Mandatory. **Activities:** Student government.

**Student services.** Financial aid counseling, placement for graduates. **Transfer:** Transfer center for students transferring to 4-year colleges.

**Contact.** Phone: (516) 561-0050
Hank Meaney, Admissions Director, Business Informatics Center, 134 South Central Avenue, Valley Stream, NY 11580-5431

## Cayuga County Community College
**Auburn, New York**
www.cayuga-cc.edu     **CB code: 2010**

- Public 2-year community college
- Commuter campus in large town

**General.** Founded in 1953. Regionally accredited. **Enrollment:** 2,704 degree-seeking undergraduates; 1,346 non-degree-seeking students. **Degrees:** 543 associate awarded. **Location:** 30 miles from Syracuse. **Calendar:** Semester, limited summer session. **Full-time faculty:** 58 total. **Part-time faculty:** 153 total. **Class size:** 53% < 20, 47% 20-39, less than 1% 40-49, less than 1% 50-99. **Special facilities:** Nature trail, multitrack recording studio and video-editing suites, NASA Institute for the Application of Geospatial Technology.

**Student profile.** Among degree-seeking undergraduates, 43% enrolled in a transfer program, 23% enrolled in a vocational program, 537 enrolled as first-time, first-year students, 194 transferred in from other institutions.

| | | | |
|---|---|---|---|
| Part-time: | 24% | Asian American: | 1% |
| Out-of-state: | 1% | Hispanic American: | 2% |
| Women: | 60% | Native American: | 1% |
| African American: | 3% | 25 or older: | 34% |

**Transfer out. Colleges most students transferred to 2007:** SUNY Oswego, SUNY Cortland, SUNY Brockport, Rochester Institute of Technology, SUNY Institute of Technology.

**Basis for selection.** Open admission, but selective for some programs. Special requirements for nursing; interview required. All new students with no prior college credits must take placement test in English and math. **Homeschooled:** Must be able to document completion of high school or equivalent through: 1) official final high school transcript from student's school district indicating graduation or 2) letter on district letterhead from relevant district superintendent certifying that student has documented satisfactory completion of equivalent of 4-year high school program of study or 3) GED achieved by the State Education Department written exam or 4) taking college's placement test; and if Ability to Benefit scores set by college met/exceeded, may matriculate and be considered for financial aid and work

toward satisfying 24-credit option prescribed by New York State Education Department.

**High school preparation.** Recommended units include English 4, mathematics 2, social studies 3 and science 1.

**2007-2008 Annual costs.** Tuition/fees: $3,716; $6,970 out-of-state. Per-credit charge: $120 in-state; $240 out-of-state. Books/supplies: $1,000. Personal expenses: $939.

**2006-2007 Financial aid.** All financial aid based on need. 438 full-time freshmen applied for aid; 413 were judged to have need; 413 of these received aid. 53% of total undergraduate aid awarded as scholarships/grants, 47% as loans/jobs. Need-based aid available for part-time students. Work-study available nights, weekends and for part-time students.

**Application procedures. Admission:** No deadline. No application fee. Application may be submitted online. Admission notification on a rolling basis. **Financial aid:** Closing date 5/1. FAFSA required. Applicants notified on a rolling basis starting 3/15.

**Academics. Special study options:** Accelerated study, distance learning, double major, dual enrollment of high school students, honors, independent study, internships, liberal arts/career combination, study abroad, weekend college. License preparation in nursing. **Credit/placement by examination:** AP, CLEP, institutional tests. 30 credit hours maximum toward associate degree. **Support services:** Learning center, pre-admission summer program, reduced course load, remedial instruction, study skills assistance, tutoring, writing center.

**Majors. Biology:** General. **Business:** Accounting technology, business admin. **Communications:** Broadcast journalism, radio/tv. **Communications technology:** General, photo/film/video, recording arts. **Computer sciences:** General, computer science, web page design. **Education:** Early childhood. **Engineering technology:** Computer hardware, electrical, GIS, mechanical, telecommunications. **Health:** Nursing (RN). **Liberal arts:** Arts/sciences. **Math:** General. **Physical sciences:** Chemistry, geology. **Protective services:** Corrections, police science. **Visual/performing arts:** Art, studio arts.

**Most popular majors.** Business/marketing 14%, health sciences 8%, liberal arts 49%, security/protective services 14%.

**Computing on campus.** 450 workstations in library, computer center. Online library, wireless network available.

**Student life. Freshman orientation:** Available. Held week before classes begin. **Activities:** Choral groups, drama, musical theater, radio station, student government, student newspaper, TV station, honor fraternity, business society, nursing club, multicultural association, criminal justice club, alumni association, diversity club.

**Athletics.** NJCAA. **Intercollegiate:** Basketball, lacrosse, soccer. **Intramural:** Racquetball, skiing, volleyball. **Team name:** Spartans.

**Student services.** Campus ministries, career counseling, student employment services, financial aid counseling, health services, on-campus daycare, personal counseling, placement for graduates, veterans' counselor. **Learning disabled:** Comprehensive services available. **Transfer:** Pre-admission transcript evaluation for new students. Transfer adviser, college fairs on campus for students transferring to 4-year colleges.

**Contact.** E-mail: admissions@cayuga-cc.edu
Phone: (315) 255-1743 ext. 2241 Fax: (315) 255-2117
Bruce Blodgett, Director of Admissions, Cayuga County Community College, 197 Franklin Street, Auburn, NY 13021-3099

## City University of New York: Borough of Manhattan Community College
**New York, New York**     **CB member**
www.bmcc.cuny.edu     **CB code: 2063**

- Public 2-year community college
- Commuter campus in very large city

**General.** Founded in 1963. Regionally accredited. **Enrollment:** 18,462 degree-seeking undergraduates. **Degrees:** 2,213 associate awarded. **Calendar:** Semester, limited summer session. **Full-time faculty:** 397 total. **Part-time faculty:** 724 total. **Special facilities:** 2 theaters, media center, gymnasium with intercollegiate-size swimming pool.

**Student profile.**

| | | | |
|---|---|---|---|
| Out-of-state: | 1% | 25 or older: | 40% |

**Transfer out. Colleges most students transferred to 2007:** Baruch College, Hunter College, City College, Brooklyn College, New York City College of Technology.

**Basis for selection.** Open admission, but selective for some programs. Special requirements for associate degree programs in nursing; admission to clinical sequence of AAS degree programs competitive, based on college GPA. High school academic units recommended for admission must be acquired before graduation.

**High school preparation.** 16 units recommended. Recommended units include English 4, mathematics 3, social studies 4, science 2 (laboratory 2) and foreign language 2. One unit of fine arts recommended.

**2007-2008 Annual costs.** Tuition/fees: $3,068; $5,968 out-of-state. Per-credit charge: $120 in-state; $190 out-of-state. Books/supplies: $938.

**2006-2007 Financial aid.** All financial aid based on need. 82% of total undergraduate aid awarded as scholarships/grants, 18% as loans/jobs. Need-based aid available for part-time students.

**Application procedures. Admission:** Priority date 4/1; no deadline. $65 fee, may be waived for applicants with need. Admission notification on a rolling basis beginning on or about 3/1. **Financial aid:** Priority date 4/15, closing date 5/1. FAFSA, institutional form required. Applicants notified on a rolling basis starting 8/1; must reply within 2 week(s) of notification.

**Academics. Special study options:** Cooperative education, cross-registration, distance learning, dual enrollment of high school students, ESL, exchange student, honors, independent study, internships, study abroad, weekend college. License preparation in nursing. **Credit/placement by examination:** CLEP. 32 credit hours maximum toward associate degree. **Support services:** GED preparation and test center, learning center, pre-admission summer program, remedial instruction, study skills assistance, tutoring, writing center.

**Majors. Business:** Accounting, administrative services, business admin, office management. **Communications technology:** General. **Computer sciences:** Data processing, networking, programming. **Education:** Early childhood. **Engineering:** General, science. **Health:** EMT paramedic, health care admin, nursing (RN), respiratory therapy technology. **Liberal arts:** Arts/sciences. **Math:** General. **Public administration:** Human services. **Visual/performing arts:** Multimedia.

**Computing on campus.** 1,200 workstations in library, computer center, student center. Commuter students can connect to campus network. Online course registration, online library, wireless network available.

**Student life. Freshman orientation:** Mandatory. **Activities:** Jazz band, choral groups, dance, drama, music ensembles, musical theater, student government, student newspaper, numerous organizations.

**Athletics.** NJCAA. **Intercollegiate:** Baseball, basketball, soccer M, volleyball. **Intramural:** Basketball, cricket, football (non-tackle), soccer, table tennis, triathlon, volleyball. **Team name:** Panthers.

**Student services.** Alcohol/substance abuse counseling, career counseling, student employment services, financial aid counseling, health services, on-campus daycare, personal counseling, placement for graduates, veterans' counselor, women's services. **Physically disabled:** Services for visually, speech, hearing impaired. **Transfer:** Pre-admission transcript evaluation for new students. Transfer center, transfer adviser, college fairs on campus for students transferring to 4-year colleges.

**Contact.**   E-mail: ebarrios@bmcc.cuny.edu
Phone: (212) 220-1265 Fax: (212) 220-2366
Eugenio Barrios, Director of Admissions, City University of New York: Borough of Manhattan Community College, 199 Chambers Street, New York, NY 10007-1097

## City University of New York: Bronx Community College

**Bronx, New York**
www.bcc.cuny.edu

**CB member**
**CB code: 2051**

▶  Public 2-year community college
▶  Commuter campus in very large city

**General.** Founded in 1957. Regionally accredited. **Enrollment:** 8,420 degree-seeking undergraduates. **Degrees:** 823 associate awarded. **Calendar:** Semester, limited summer session. **Full-time faculty:** 260 total. **Part-time faculty:** 325 total. **Special facilities:** Hall of Fame for Great Americans.

**Transfer out. Colleges most students transferred to 2007:** Lehman College, City College, Baruch College, Hunter College, John Jay College of Criminal Justice.

**Basis for selection.** Open admission. Units recommended for admission must be acquired before graduation from any CUNY community college.

**High school preparation.** 9 units recommended. Recommended units include English 3, mathematics 2 and science 1.

**2007-2008 Annual costs.** Tuition/fees: $3,104; $6,004 out-of-state. Per-credit charge: $120 in-state; $190 out-of-state. Books/supplies: $759. Personal expenses: $2,100.

**Financial aid. Need-based:** Need-based aid available for part-time students. Work-study available nights and weekends.

**Application procedures. Admission:** Priority date 1/15; deadline 8/15 (postmark date). $60 fee. Application may be submitted online. Admission notification on a rolling basis. **Financial aid:** Closing date 7/15. FAFSA required. Applicants notified on a rolling basis starting 8/1.

**Academics. Special study options:** Cooperative education, cross-registration, distance learning, dual enrollment of high school students, ESL, external degree, honors, independent study, internships, liberal arts/career combination, study abroad, weekend college. License preparation in nursing. **Credit/placement by examination:** AP, CLEP, IB, ACT, institutional tests. 30 credit hours maximum toward associate degree. **Support services:** GED preparation and test center, learning center, pre-admission summer program, reduced course load, remedial instruction, study skills assistance, tutoring, writing center.

**Majors. Agriculture:** Horticultural science. **Business:** General, accounting, administrative services, management information systems, office technology. **Computer sciences:** Computer science, data processing. **Education:** Teacher assistance. **Engineering technology:** Electrical. **Health:** Clinical lab technology, medical assistant, medical radiologic technology/radiation therapy, nuclear medical technology, nursing (RN). **Legal studies:** Paralegal. **Liberal arts:** Arts/sciences. **Visual/performing arts:** Commercial/advertising art.

**Most popular majors.** Business/marketing 21%, computer/information sciences 6%, health sciences 14%, liberal arts 27%, public administration/social services 15%.

**Computing on campus.** 490 workstations in library, computer center. Commuter students can connect to campus network. Online course registration, wireless network available.

**Student life. Freshman orientation:** Available. **Activities:** Choral groups, dance, drama, literary magazine, music ensembles, radio station, student government, student newspaper.

**Athletics. Intercollegiate:** Baseball M, basketball, soccer M, track and field. **Team name:** BCC Broncos.

**Student services.** Career counseling, student employment services, health services, on-campus daycare, personal counseling, placement for graduates, veterans' counselor. **Physically disabled:** Services for visually, speech impaired. **Transfer:** Transfer adviser, college fairs on campus for students transferring to 4-year colleges.

**Contact.**   E-mail: admissions@bcc.cuny.edu
Phone: (718) 289-5895 Fax: (718) 289-6352
Alba Cancetty, Director of Admissions, City University of New York: Bronx Community College, West 181st Street and University Avenue, Bronx, NY 10453

## City University of New York: Hostos Community College

**Bronx, New York**
www.hostos.cuny.edu

**CB member**
**CB code: 2303**

▶  Public 2-year community college
▶  Commuter campus in very large city

**General.** Founded in 1970. Regionally accredited. Bilingual Spanish/English liberal arts program. **Enrollment:** 4,416 degree-seeking undergraduates; 696 non-degree-seeking students. **Degrees:** 420 associate awarded. **Calendar:** Semester, limited summer session. **Full-time faculty:** 174 total; 56% have terminal degrees, 56% minority, 50% women. **Part-time faculty:** 176 total; 28% have terminal degrees, 71% minority, 52% women. **Class size:** 36% < 20, 61% 20-39, 2% 40-49, less than 1% 50-99.

**Student profile.** Among degree-seeking undergraduates, 31% enrolled in a transfer program, 70% enrolled in a vocational program, 2% already have a bachelor's degree or higher, 813 enrolled as first-time, first-year students, 522 transferred in from other institutions.

| | | | |
|---|---|---|---|
| Part-time: | 35% | Asian American: | 3% |
| Out-of-state: | 1% | Hispanic American: | 55% |
| Women: | 71% | International: | 11% |
| African American: | 28% | 25 or older: | 42% |

**Transfer out. Colleges most students transferred to 2007:** CUNY Lehman College, CUNY City College, CUNY John Jay College.

**Basis for selection.** Open admission, but selective for some programs. Admission to allied health programs based on Freshman Skills Assessment and subsequent performance in courses.

**High school preparation.** 16 units recommended. Recommended units include English 4, mathematics 3, social studies 4, science 2 and foreign language 2. 2 fine arts required. High school biology, chemistry, math required of allied health applicants.

**2007-2008 Annual costs.** Tuition/fees: $3,105; $6,005 out-of-state. Per-credit charge: $120 in-state; $190 out-of-state. Books/supplies: $692. Personal expenses: $2,667.

**Financial aid. Need-based:** Need-based aid available for part-time students. Work-study available for part-time students.

**Application procedures. Admission:** Closing date 8/15 (postmark date). $50 fee, may be waived for applicants with need. Application may be submitted online. Admission notification on a rolling basis. **Financial aid:** Priority date 7/1; no closing date. FAFSA, institutional form required. Applicants notified on a rolling basis; must reply within 3 week(s) of notification.

**Academics. Special study options:** Cooperative education, distance learning, dual enrollment of high school students, ESL, honors, independent study, internships, liberal arts/career combination, study abroad, weekend college. Serrano scholars program. License preparation in dental hygiene, nursing, radiology. **Credit/placement by examination:** CLEP, institutional tests. **Support services:** GED preparation and test center, learning center, pre-admission summer program, remedial instruction, study skills assistance, tutoring, writing center.

**Majors. Business:** General, accounting, administrative services, business admin, office technology. **Computer sciences:** Data processing. **Education:** Early childhood. **Engineering:** Chemical, civil, electrical. **Health:** Community health, dental hygiene, medical radiologic technology/radiation therapy, medical secretary, nursing (RN). **Interdisciplinary:** Gerontology. **Legal studies:** Paralegal. **Liberal arts:** Arts/sciences. **Public administration:** General.

**Most popular majors.** Business/marketing 15%, education 9%, health sciences 20%, legal studies 9%, liberal arts 40%.

**Computing on campus.** 1,000 workstations in library, computer center, student center. Commuter students can connect to campus network. Online course registration, online library, helpline, wireless network available.

**Student life. Freshman orientation:** Mandatory. Preregistration for classes offered. Held once a week each semester. **Activities:** Marching band, dance, drama, student government, student newspaper, TV station, Puerto Rican club, Christian club, black student union, Dominican association, South American student union, Ecuadorian student association, dental hygiene club, nursing club, Mexican club, Cuban club.

**Athletics.** NJCAA. **Intercollegiate:** Baseball M, basketball, soccer, volleyball W. **Intramural:** Basketball, volleyball W. **Team name:** Caimans.

**Student services.** Campus ministries, career counseling, services for economically disadvantaged, student employment services, financial aid counseling, health services, on-campus daycare, personal counseling, placement for graduates, veterans' counselor, women's services. **Physically disabled:** Services for visually, speech, hearing impaired. **Transfer:** Re-entry adviser, pre-admission transcript evaluation for new students. Transfer adviser, college fairs on campus for students transferring to 4-year colleges.

**Contact.** E-mail: admissions@hostos.cuny.edu
Phone: (718) 518-4405 Fax: (718) 518-6643
Roland Velez, Director of Admissions/Recruitment, City University of New York: Hostos Community College, 500 Grand Concourse, Bronx, NY 10451

## City University of New York: Kingsborough Community College

**Brooklyn, New York**
www.kbcc.cuny.edu

**CB member**
**CB code: 2358**

- Public 2-year community college
- Commuter campus in very large city

**General.** Founded in 1963. Regionally accredited. **Enrollment:** 10,943 degree-seeking undergraduates; 4,017 non-degree-seeking students. **Degrees:** 1,705 associate awarded. **Location:** 10 miles from midtown. **Calendar:** Semester, extensive summer session. **Full-time faculty:** 291 total; 71% have terminal degrees, 21% minority, 51% women. **Part-time faculty:** 495 total; 19% have terminal degrees, 18% minority, 50% women. **Class size:** 34% < 20, 58% 20-39, 8% 40-49. **Special facilities:** Private beach on campus. **Partnerships:** Formal partnership with College Now program for high school seniors.

**Student profile.** Among degree-seeking undergraduates, 60% enrolled in a transfer program, 40% enrolled in a vocational program, 2,136 enrolled as first-time, first-year students, 1,416 transferred in from other institutions.

| | | | |
|---|---|---|---|
| Part-time: | 27% | Asian American: | 10% |
| Out-of-state: | 1% | Hispanic American: | 14% |
| Women: | 57% | International: | 6% |
| African American: | 33% | 25 or older: | 24% |

**Transfer out. Colleges most students transferred to 2007:** City University of New York: Brooklyn College, Long Island University, Pace University, City University of New York: College of Staten Island, City University of New York: Baruch College.

**Basis for selection.** Open admission. Units recommended for admission must be acquired before graduation from any CUNY community college. Students who achieve high scores on SAT exempted from basic skills remediation.

**High school preparation.** 16 units recommended. Recommended units include English 4, mathematics 3, social studies 4, science 2 and foreign language 2. One unit fine arts.

**2007-2008 Annual costs.** Tuition/fees: $3,100; $6,000 out-of-state. Per-credit charge: $120 in-state; $190 out-of-state. Books/supplies: $879. Personal expenses: $2,710.

**Financial aid.** All financial aid based on need. Need-based aid available for part-time students.

**Application procedures. Admission:** Closing date 8/15. $65 fee, may be waived for applicants with need. Application may be submitted online. Admission notification on a rolling basis beginning on or about 3/31. **Financial aid:** Closing date 4/30. FAFSA required. Applicants notified on a rolling basis; must reply within 2 week(s) of notification.

**Academics. Special study options:** Accelerated study, cross-registration, dual enrollment of high school students, ESL, honors, independent study, internships. My Turn Program for senior citizens, New Start Program for students academically dismissed from 4-year institutions. License preparation in nursing. **Credit/placement by examination:** AP, CLEP, institutional tests. 16 credit hours maximum toward associate degree. **Support services:** GED preparation, learning center, pre-admission summer program, reduced course load, remedial instruction, tutoring, writing center.

**Majors. Biology:** General. **Business:** Accounting, business admin, fashion, office management, tourism promotion, tourism/travel. **Communications:** Broadcast journalism, journalism. **Computer sciences:** Computer science, data processing. **Education:** Early childhood, elementary, teacher assistance. **Engineering:** General. **Health:** Community health services, mental health services, nursing (RN), physical therapy assistant, prenursing, surgical technology. **Legal studies:** Legal secretary. **Liberal arts:** Arts/sciences. **Math:** General. **Parks/recreation:** General, exercise sciences. **Physical sciences:** Chemistry, physics. **Visual/performing arts:** General, commercial/advertising art, studio arts.

**Most popular majors.** Business/marketing 24%, education 8%, health sciences 17%, liberal arts 35%.

**Computing on campus.** 900 workstations in library, computer center. Online course registration available.

**Student life. Freshman orientation:** Available. **Activities:** Bands, choral groups, dance, drama, film society, literary magazine, music ensembles, musical theater, opera, radio station, student government, student newspaper, symphony orchestra, over 60 ethnic, academic, religious, and political groups.

**Athletics.** NJCAA. **Intercollegiate:** Baseball M, basketball, soccer M, softball W, tennis, track and field, volleyball W. **Intramural:** Basketball, bowling, football (non-tackle), racquetball, soccer, softball, swimming, table tennis, tennis, volleyball, weight lifting.

**Student services.** Adult student services, career counseling, student employment services, health services, on-campus daycare, personal counseling, placement for graduates, veterans' counselor. **Physically disabled:** Services for visually, speech, hearing impaired. **Transfer:** Transfer adviser for students transferring to 4-year colleges.

**Contact.** E-mail: info@kbcc.cuny.edu
Phone: (718) 368-4600 Fax: (718) 368-5356
Robert Ingenito, Admissions Information Center Director, City University of New York: Kingsborough Community College, 2001 Oriental Boulevard, Brooklyn, NY 11235

## City University of New York: LaGuardia Community College
### Long Island City, New York
www.lagcc.cuny.edu                    CB code: 2246

- Public 2-year community college
- Commuter campus in very large city

**General.** Founded in 1970. Regionally accredited. **Enrollment:** 12,678 degree-seeking undergraduates; 2,074 non-degree-seeking students. **Degrees:** 1,521 associate awarded. **Calendar:** Semester, limited summer session. **Full-time faculty:** 281 total; 50% have terminal degrees, 39% minority, 56% women. **Part-time faculty:** 740 total; 13% have terminal degrees, 37% minority, 48% women. **Class size:** 28% < 20, 71% 20-39, less than 1% 40-49, less than 1% 50-99. **Special facilities:** LaGuardia and Wagner archives.

**Student profile.** Among degree-seeking undergraduates, 54% enrolled in a transfer program, 42% enrolled in a vocational program, 2,594 enrolled as first-time, first-year students, 1,395 transferred in from other institutions.

| | | | |
|---|---|---|---|
| Part-time: | 38% | Asian American: | 14% |
| Out-of-state: | 1% | Hispanic American: | 34% |
| Women: | 62% | International: | 11% |
| African American: | 17% | 25 or older: | 30% |

**Transfer out.** 52% of students enrolled in the transfer program go on to 4-year colleges. **Colleges most students transferred to 2007:** Baruch College, Hunter College, NYC Technical College, Queens College.

**Basis for selection.** Open admission. Units recommended for admission must be acquired before graduation from any CUNY community college.

**High school preparation.** 13 units recommended. Recommended units include English 4, mathematics 2, social studies 2, science 1 and academic electives 4.

**2007-2008 Annual costs.** Tuition/fees: $3,092; $5,992 out-of-state. Per-credit charge: $120 in-state; $190 out-of-state. Books/supplies: $938. Personal expenses: $1,697.

**2006-2007 Financial aid.** All financial aid based on need. 2,319 full-time freshmen applied for aid; 2,199 were judged to have need; 2,087 of these received aid. Average need met was 54%. Average scholarship/grant was $2,124. 92% of total undergraduate aid awarded as scholarships/grants, 8% as loans/jobs. Need-based aid available for part-time students. Work-study available nights, weekends and for part-time students.

**Application procedures. Admission:** Priority date 1/15; no deadline. $50 fee, may be waived for applicants with need. Application may be submitted online. Admission notification on a rolling basis. **Financial aid:** Priority date 4/15; no closing date. FAFSA, institutional form required. Applicants notified on a rolling basis starting 3/1; must reply within 4 week(s) of notification.

**Academics. Special study options:** Cooperative education, cross-registration, dual enrollment of high school students, independent study, internships, liberal arts/career combination, student-designed major. Summer program with Vassar College. License preparation in nursing, paramedic. **Credit/placement by examination:** AP, CLEP, institutional tests. 10 credit hours maximum toward associate degree. **Support services:** GED preparation and test center, learning center, pre-admission summer program, reduced course load, remedial instruction, tutoring, writing center.

**Majors. Business:** Accounting, administrative services, business admin, tourism promotion. **Computer sciences:** General, computer science, data processing, programming. **Education:** Bilingual. **Engineering:** General, civil, electrical, mechanical. **Family/consumer sciences:** Child care, institutional

food production. **Health:** EMT paramedic, health services, occupational therapy assistant, physical therapy assistant, veterinary technology/assistant. **Interdisciplinary:** Gerontology. **Legal studies:** Legal secretary, paralegal. **Liberal arts:** Arts/sciences. **Personal/culinary services:** Mortuary science. **Visual/performing arts:** Commercial photography, studio arts.

**Most popular majors.** Business/marketing 30%, computer/information sciences 10%, education 6%, health sciences 13%, liberal arts 21%, personal/culinary services 11%.

**Computing on campus.** 909 workstations in library, computer center. Helpline available.

**Student life. Freshman orientation:** Available. Preregistration for classes offered. **Activities:** Bands, choral groups, dance, drama, music ensembles, radio station, student government, student newspaper, TV station.

**Athletics. Intramural:** Basketball, bowling, football (non-tackle) M, football (tackle) M, handball, soccer, softball, swimming, table tennis, volleyball.

**Student services.** Adult student services, career counseling, student employment services, health services, on-campus daycare, personal counseling, placement for graduates, veterans' counselor. **Physically disabled:** Services for visually, speech, hearing impaired. **Transfer:** Transfer adviser, college fairs on campus for students transferring to 4-year colleges.

**Contact.** E-mail: admissions@lagcc.cuny.edu
Phone: (718) 482-7206 Fax: (718) 609-2023
Reine Sarmiento, Senior Director of Admissions, City University of New York: LaGuardia Community College, 31-10 Thomson Avenue, Long Island City, NY 11101

## City University of New York: Queensborough Community College
### Bayside, New York
www.qcc.cuny.edu                    CB code: 2751

- Public 2-year community college
- Commuter campus in very large city

**General.** Founded in 1958. Regionally accredited. **Enrollment:** 11,325 degree-seeking undergraduates. **Degrees:** 1,092 associate awarded. **Location:** 10 miles from midtown Manhattan. **Calendar:** Semester, limited summer session. **Full-time faculty:** 301 total. **Part-time faculty:** 551 total. **Special facilities:** Resource center for Holocaust studies, observatory, art museum. **Partnerships:** Formal partnership with Verizon for Next Step associate degree program in telecommunication technology for Verizon employees.

**Student profile.**

| | | | |
|---|---|---|---|
| Out-of-state: | 1% | 25 or older: | 32% |

**Transfer out. Colleges most students transferred to 2007:** CUNY Queens College, St. John's University.

**Basis for selection.** Open admission. Units recommended for admission must be acquired before graduation from CUNY.

**High school preparation.** 15 units recommended. Recommended units include English 4, mathematics 3, social studies 2, science 2 (laboratory 2) and academic electives 4.

**2007-2008 Annual costs.** Tuition/fees: $3,086; $5,986 out-of-state. Per-credit charge: $120 in-state; $190 out-of-state. Books/supplies: $500. Personal expenses: $2,100.

**Application procedures. Admission:** No deadline. $65 fee, may be waived for applicants with need. Application may be submitted online. Admission notification on a rolling basis. **Financial aid:** No deadline. FAFSA, institutional form required. Applicants notified on a rolling basis starting 7/15.

**Academics. Special study options:** Cooperative education, dual enrollment of high school students, ESL, independent study, internships, liberal arts/career combination. External education for homebound students, honors program for high school seniors. License preparation in nursing. **Credit/placement by examination:** AP, CLEP, institutional tests. **Support services:** Learning center, pre-admission summer program, remedial instruction, tutoring.

**Majors. Biology:** General. **Business:** General, accounting, administrative services, business admin, office management. **Communications technology:** General, recording arts. **Computer sciences:** General, data processing, information systems, programming. **Engineering:** Computer. **Engineering technology:** Drafting, electrical. **Health:** Clinical lab technology, environmental health, nursing (RN). **History:** General. **Liberal arts:** Arts/sciences. **Physical sciences:** Chemistry. **Psychology:** General. **Social sciences:** Political science, sociology. **Visual/performing arts:** General, art, dance, dramatic, music history, photography.

**Computing on campus.** 143 workstations in library, computer center. Online course registration, helpline, wireless network available.

**Student life. Freshman orientation:** Available. Preregistration for classes offered. **Activities:** Bands, choral groups, dance, drama, film society, music ensembles, musical theater, student government, student newspaper, symphony orchestra, architecture club, Asian society, biology club, Chi Alpha Christian, drama society, future teachers society, Hillel club, Muslim student association, Newman club.

**Athletics.** NJCAA. **Intercollegiate:** Baseball M, basketball, cross-country, soccer M, softball W, tennis, track and field, volleyball. **Intramural:** Badminton, basketball, soccer, softball, swimming, table tennis, tennis, track and field, volleyball. **Team name:** Tigers.

**Student services.** Adult student services, career counseling, student employment services, health services, on-campus daycare, personal counseling, placement for graduates, veterans' counselor. **Physically disabled:** Services for visually, speech, hearing impaired. **Transfer:** Transfer adviser, college fairs on campus for students transferring to 4-year colleges.

**Contact.** Phone: (718) 281-5000 Fax: (718) 281-5189 Winston Yarde, Director of Admissions, City University of New York: Queensborough Community College, Springfield Boulevard & 56th Avenue, Bayside, NY 11364-1497

## Clinton Community College
**Plattsburgh, New York**
www.clinton.edu                                         CB code: 2135

- Public 2-year community college
- Commuter campus in large town

**General.** Founded in 1966. Regionally accredited. SUNY institution. **Enrollment:** 1,448 degree-seeking undergraduates. **Degrees:** 271 associate awarded. **Location:** 60 miles from Montreal, Canada, 30 miles from Burlington, Vermont. **Calendar:** Semester, limited summer session. **Full-time faculty:** 54 total. **Part-time faculty:** 93 total. **Class size:** 15% < 20, 83% 20-39, 2% 50-99. **Special facilities:** Science and technology center, special equipment and facilities for clean water research, forensic science. **Partnerships:** Formal partnership with area high schools in collaboration with College Advancement Program (CAP).

**Student profile.** Among degree-seeking undergraduates, 153 transferred in from other institutions.

**Transfer out. Colleges most students transferred to 2007:** SUNY at Plattsburgh.

**Basis for selection.** Open admission, but selective for some programs. Special requirements for nursing, including essay. Test scores may exempt students from taking placement test. **Homeschooled:** State high school equivalency certificate required. Recommend completing GED, must take ability to benefit test.

**High school preparation.** Recommended units include English 4, mathematics 3, social studies 4, history 4, science 2 (laboratory 2) and foreign language 2. Chemistry required for nursing.

**2007-2008 Annual costs.** Tuition/fees: $3,466; $8,296 out-of-state. Per-credit charge: $134 in-state; $335 out-of-state. Books/supplies: $675. Personal expenses: $870.

**Financial aid.** All financial aid based on need. Need-based aid available for part-time students. Work-study available for part-time students.

**Application procedures. Admission:** No deadline. No application fee. Application may be submitted online. Admission notification on a rolling basis. Early application recommended for selective admission programs and financial aid. **Financial aid:** Priority date 6/2; no closing date. FAFSA required. Applicants notified on a rolling basis starting 5/1; must reply within 2 week(s) of notification.

**Academics. Special study options:** Cross-registration, distance learning, dual enrollment of high school students, independent study, internships, liberal arts/career combination, New York semester, student-designed major. Semester in Albany, basic skills program. License preparation in nursing. **Credit/placement by examination:** AP, CLEP, IB, institutional tests. 30

credit hours maximum toward associate degree. **Support services:** GED preparation, reduced course load, remedial instruction, study skills assistance, tutoring, writing center.

**Majors. Business:** Accounting, administrative services, business admin, office management, office technology. **Computer sciences:** General, computer science. **Health:** Clinical lab technology, nursing (RN). **Liberal arts:** Arts/sciences. **Math:** General. **Public administration:** Human services.

**Computing on campus.** 350 workstations in library, computer center. Dormitories wired for high-speed internet access and linked to campus network. Commuter students can connect to campus network. Online library, helpline, wireless network available.

**Student life. Freshman orientation:** Mandatory. Preregistration for classes offered. Held day before classes begin each semester. **Housing:** Guaranteed on-campus for freshmen. Coed dorms, special housing for disabled available. $200 fully refundable deposit. **Activities:** Choral groups, drama, student government, student newspaper, nursing, laboratory technology, art clubs, business club, Native American club, Global Awareness, criminal justice, student activities board, student senate.

**Athletics.** NJCAA. **Intercollegiate:** Baseball M, basketball, soccer, softball W. **Intramural:** Golf, racquetball, tennis. **Team name:** Cougars.

**Student services.** Adult student services, alcohol/substance abuse counseling, career counseling, student employment services, financial aid counseling, health services, on-campus daycare, personal counseling, placement for graduates, veterans' counselor. **Physically disabled:** Services for visually, speech, hearing impaired. **Learning disabled:** Comprehensive services available. **Transfer:** Pre-admission transcript evaluation for new students. Transfer adviser, college fairs on campus for students transferring to 4-year colleges.

**Contact.** E-mail: admissions@clinton.edu Phone: (518) 562-4170 Toll-free number: (800) 552-1160 Fax: (518) 562-4380 Karen Burnam, Director of Admissions/Financial Aid, Clinton Community College, 136 Clinton Point Drive, Plattsburgh, NY 12901-4297

## Cochran School of Nursing-St. John's Riverside Hospital
**Yonkers, New York**
www.cochranschoolofnursing.us                           CB code: 2894

- Private 2-year nursing college
- Commuter campus in small city
- Application essay, interview required

**General.** Founded in 1894. Access to all clinical facilities at St. John's Riverside Hospital. **Enrollment:** 322 degree-seeking undergraduates. **Degrees:** 113 associate awarded. **Location:** 20 miles from New York City. **Calendar:** Semester, limited summer session. **Full-time faculty:** 24 total; 17% minority, 96% women. **Class size:** 20% < 20, 73% 20-39, 7% 40-49.

**Student profile.** Among degree-seeking undergraduates, 99 transferred in from other institutions.

| | | | |
|---|---|---|---|
| Part-time: | 67% | Asian American: | 20% |
| Women: | 82% | Hispanic American: | 12% |
| African American: | 42% | 25 or older: | 80% |

**Transfer out. Colleges most students transferred to 2007:** Mercy College, College of New Rochelle, College of Mount St. Vincent, Adelphi University.

**Basis for selection.** School achievement record, test scores, interview most important. Completion of prerequisite with C+ grade or better. **Learning Disabled:** Must submit necessary documentation of disabilities at time of admission to disability officer.

**High school preparation.** 16 units required. Required and recommended units include English 4, mathematics 4, social studies 2, history 2, science 2 and foreign language 2. Math units should include 1 algebra, science units should include 1 biology and 1 chemistry. 2 units of laboratory recommended.

**2008-2009 Annual costs.** Tuition and fees for full 2-year AAS program $26,683. Books/supplies: $1,800.

**Financial aid.** All financial aid based on need. Need-based aid available for part-time students.

**Application procedures. Admission:** No deadline. $35 fee. Application must be submitted on paper. Admission notification on a rolling basis.

**Financial aid:** No deadline. FAFSA required. Applicants notified on a rolling basis.

**Academics.** Special testing program facilitates career goals of LPNs who want to become RNs. **Special study options:** Accelerated study, combined bachelor's/graduate degree, liberal arts/career combination. License preparation in nursing. **Credit/placement by examination:** AP, CLEP, IB, institutional tests. 27 credit hours maximum toward associate degree. **Support services:** Learning center, tutoring.

**Majors. Health:** Nursing (RN).

**Computing on campus.** 22 workstations in library, computer center, student center. Online library available.

**Student life. Freshman orientation:** Mandatory. **Housing:** Substance-free housing available. **Activities:** Student government, student newspaper.

**Student services.** Adult student services, career counseling, health services, personal counseling. **Transfer:** Pre-admission transcript evaluation for new students. College fairs on campus for students transferring to 4-year colleges.

**Contact.** E-mail: admissions@cochranschoolofnursing.us
Phone: (914) 964-4296 Fax: (914) 964-4796
Kathy Vitola, Admissions Counselor, Cochran School of Nursing-St. John's Riverside Hospital, 967 North Broadway, Yonkers, NY 10701

## College of Westchester
### White Plains, New York
www.cw.edu                    CB code: 1023

- For-profit 2-year business and career college
- Commuter campus in large town
- Application essay, interview required

**General.** Founded in 1915. Candidate for regional accreditation. **Enrollment:** 979 degree-seeking undergraduates; 27 non-degree-seeking students. **Degrees:** 287 associate awarded. **Location:** 30 miles from New York City. **Calendar:** Semester, extensive summer session. **Full-time faculty:** 27 total; 4% have terminal degrees, 26% minority, 52% women. **Part-time faculty:** 59 total; 8% have terminal degrees, 27% minority, 32% women. **Class size:** 67% < 20, 33% 20-39. **Partnerships:** Formal partnerships with local corporations and businesses for internship and co-op work experience programs.

**Student profile.** Among degree-seeking undergraduates, 229 enrolled as first-time, first-year students.

| | | | |
|---|---|---|---|
| Part-time: | 20% | Women: | 56% |
| Out-of-state: | 3% | 25 or older: | 77% |

**Basis for selection.** Interview, prior academic performance, recommendations most important. Activities considered. Test scores considered when available. Institution-administered assessments used for both admissions and academic placement.

**2008-2009 Annual costs.** Tuition/fees (projected): $19,800. Per-credit charge: $630. Books/supplies: $990.

**Financial aid. Need-based:** Need-based aid available for part-time students. Work-study available nights and weekends. **Non-need-based:** Scholarships awarded for academics, alumni affiliation.

**Application procedures. Admission:** No deadline. $40 fee, may be waived for applicants with need. Application may be submitted online. Admission notification on a rolling basis. **Financial aid:** No deadline. FAFSA, institutional form required. Applicants notified on a rolling basis starting 1/7; must reply within 2 week(s) of notification.

**Academics.** 100 credit hours required for graduation in day (quarterly) program, 66 in evening (semester) program. **Special study options:** Accelerated study, cooperative education, distance learning, double major, honors, internships, weekend college. **Credit/placement by examination:** AP, CLEP, institutional tests. **Support services:** GED preparation, learning center, reduced course load, remedial instruction, study skills assistance, tutoring.

**Majors. Business:** Accounting, administrative services, business admin, e-commerce, management information systems, office management, office technology, office/clerical, purchasing. **Computer sciences:** General, applications programming, computer graphics, computer science, data processing, information systems, LAN/WAN management, programming, systems analysis, web page design. **Engineering:** Software. **Health:** Office admin. **Visual/performing arts:** Commercial/advertising art.

**Most popular majors.** Business/marketing 88%, computer/information sciences 12%.

**Computing on campus.** 240 workstations in library, computer center, student center. Commuter students can connect to campus network. Online library, helpline available.

**Student life. Freshman orientation:** Mandatory. **Activities:** Student government, student newspaper, accounting society, management and marketing club, office technology club, computer club, multimedia club, Alpha Beta honor society, women's business issues club, public speaking club.

**Student services.** Adult student services, career counseling, student employment services, financial aid counseling, personal counseling, placement for graduates. **Transfer:** Pre-admission transcript evaluation for new students. Transfer adviser for students transferring to 4-year colleges.

**Contact.** E-mail: admissions@cw.edu
Phone: (914) 948-4442 ext. 318 Toll-free number: (800) 333-4924
Fax: (914) 948-5441
Anthony Peluso, Director of Admissions, College of Westchester, 325 Central Park Avenue, White Plains, NY 10602

## Columbia-Greene Community College
### Hudson, New York
www.sunycgcc.edu                    CB code: 2138

- Public 2-year community college
- Commuter campus in small town

**General.** Founded in 1966. Regionally accredited. SUNY institution. **Enrollment:** 1,438 degree-seeking undergraduates; 385 non-degree-seeking students. **Degrees:** 293 associate awarded. **Location:** 40 miles from Albany. **Calendar:** Semester, limited summer session. **Full-time faculty:** 48 total. **Part-time faculty:** 75 total. **Class size:** 57% < 20, 41% 20-39, 1% 40-49, less than 1% 50-99. **Special facilities:** 4 art galleries, Hudson River biological field station.

**Student profile.** Among degree-seeking undergraduates, 417 enrolled as first-time, first-year students, 120 transferred in from other institutions.

| | | | |
|---|---|---|---|
| Part-time: | 31% | Asian American: | 1% |
| Out-of-state: | 1% | Hispanic American: | 4% |
| Women: | 63% | Native American: | 1% |
| African American: | 4% | 25 or older: | 31% |

**Transfer out.** 45% of students enrolled in the transfer program go on to 4-year colleges.

**Basis for selection.** Open admission, but selective for some programs. Admission to some programs based on school achievement record, test scores, and recommendations. Interview recommended. **Adult students:** SAT/ACT scores not required. **Homeschooled:** Transcript of courses and grades, interview required.

**High school preparation.** Recommended units include English 3, mathematics 3, science 3 and foreign language 3.

**2007-2008 Annual costs.** Tuition/fees: $3,352; $6,394 out-of-state. Per-credit charge: $128 in-state; $256 out-of-state. Books/supplies: $550. Personal expenses: $950.

**Financial aid. Need-based:** Need-based aid available for part-time students. Work-study available nights, weekends and for part-time students. **Non-need-based:** Scholarships awarded for academics, state residency.

**Application procedures. Admission:** No deadline. $30 fee, may be waived for applicants with need. Admission notification on a rolling basis. **Financial aid:** Priority date 5/1; no closing date. FAFSA, institutional form required. Applicants notified on a rolling basis starting 7/1; must reply within 2 week(s) of notification.

**Academics. Special study options:** Combined bachelor's/graduate degree, cooperative education, cross-registration, distance learning, dual enrollment of high school students, honors, independent study, internships, student-designed major, teacher certification program. License preparation in aviation, nursing. **Credit/placement by examination:** AP, CLEP, institutional tests. 30 credit hours maximum toward associate degree. **Support services:** Learning center, pre-admission summer program, remedial instruction, study skills assistance, tutoring, writing center.

**Honors college/program.** Program offers the opportunity to work closely with faculty, conduct research, and participate in seminars and conferences with an interdisciplinary focus.

**Majors. Biology:** General. **Business:** Accounting, administrative services, business admin, office management, office technology. **Computer sciences:** General, applications programming, computer science, LAN/WAN management. **Conservation:** Environmental science. **Education:** Multi-level teacher, physical. **Health:** Massage therapy, nursing (RN). **Liberal arts:** Arts/sciences. **Math:** General. **Mechanic/repair:** Automotive. **Protective services:** Criminal justice, law enforcement admin. **Public administration:** Social work. **Social sciences:** General. **Visual/performing arts:** Studio arts.

**Most popular majors.** Business/marketing 14%, computer/information sciences 6%, health sciences 28%, liberal arts 37%.

**Computing on campus.** 150 workstations in library, computer center. Commuter students can connect to campus network. Online library, wireless network available.

**Student life. Freshman orientation:** Available. Preregistration for classes offered. Held 1 week prior to start of fall classes. **Activities:** Choral groups, dance, drama, music ensembles, musical theater, student government, International Rotary Club, minority alliance group, College Union Board.

**Athletics.** NJCAA. **Intercollegiate:** Baseball M, basketball, bowling, soccer W, softball W. **Intramural:** Basketball, bowling, fencing, table tennis, tennis, volleyball. **Team name:** Twins.

**Student services.** Adult student services, alcohol/substance abuse counseling, career counseling, student employment services, health services, on-campus daycare, personal counseling, placement for graduates, veterans' counselor. **Physically disabled:** Services for visually, hearing impaired. **Transfer:** Transfer adviser, college fairs on campus for students transferring to 4-year colleges.

**Contact.** E-mail: bendel@sunycgcc.edu
Phone: (518) 828-4181 ext. 5513 Fax: (518) 828-8543
Christine Pepitone, Director of Admissions, Columbia-Greene Community College, 4400 Route 23, Hudson, NY 12534

## Corning Community College
**Corning, New York**
www.corning-cc.edu                    **CB code: 2106**

- Public 2-year community college
- Commuter campus in large town

**General.** Founded in 1956. Regionally accredited. SUNY institution. **Enrollment:** 3,203 degree-seeking undergraduates. **Degrees:** 784 associate awarded. **Location:** 70 miles from Binghamton. **Calendar:** Semester, limited summer session. **Full-time faculty:** 102 total. **Part-time faculty:** 116 total. **Class size:** 67% < 20, 31% 20-39, less than 1% 40-49, less than 1% 50-99, less than 1% >100. **Special facilities:** 200-acre nature center, criminal justice complex, observatory with historic working model of Hale telescope, planetarium.

**Student profile.**

| | | | |
|---|---|---|---|
| Out-of-state: | 4% | 25 or older: | 43% |

**Transfer out. Colleges most students transferred to 2007:** Elmira College, Mansfield University, SUNY Cortland, SUNY Binghamton, SUNY Buffalo.

**Basis for selection.** Open admission, but selective for some programs. Applicants without diploma or GED evaluated on individual basis. **Adult students:** SAT/ACT scores not required. **Homeschooled:** Ability to Benefit testing required. **Learning Disabled:** Students should contact disability services to arrange accommodations, including accommodations for placement tests.

**High school preparation.** Recommended units include English 4, mathematics 1, social studies 4, science 1 (laboratory 1). 4 math and 4 science required of engineering science applicants; 1 algebra and 1 biology required of nursing applicants.

**2007-2008 Annual costs.** Tuition/fees: $3,726; $7,076 out-of-state. Per-credit charge: $140 in-state; $280 out-of-state. Books/supplies: $800. Personal expenses: $550.

**Financial aid.** All financial aid based on need. Need-based aid available for part-time students. Work-study available weekends and for part-time students.

**Application procedures. Admission:** No deadline. $25 fee, may be waived for applicants with need. Admission notification on a rolling basis. **Financial aid:** Priority date 4/1; no closing date. FAFSA required. Applicants notified on a rolling basis starting 4/15; must reply within 2 week(s) of notification.

**Academics. Special study options:** Distance learning, double major, dual enrollment of high school students, honors, independent study, internships, study abroad, weekend college. License preparation in nursing, paramedic, real estate. **Credit/placement by examination:** AP, CLEP, institutional tests. 30 credit hours maximum toward associate degree. **Support services:** Learning center, reduced course load, remedial instruction, study skills assistance, tutoring, writing center.

**Majors. Business:** Accounting, administrative services, business admin. **Computer sciences:** General, computer graphics, computer science, programming. **Education:** Early childhood, elementary, health, physical. **Engineering:** Science. **Engineering technology:** Electrical, manufacturing. **Health:** EMT paramedic, nursing (RN), substance abuse counseling. **Interdisciplinary:** Biological/physical sciences. **Legal studies:** Paralegal. **Liberal arts:** Arts/sciences. **Math:** General. **Mechanic/repair:** Automotive, computer. **Parks/recreation:** Health/fitness. **Physical sciences:** General, optics. **Production:** Machine tool. **Protective services:** Corrections, criminal justice, fire safety technology, law enforcement admin. **Public administration:** Human services. **Science technology:** Chemical. **Social sciences:** General.

**Computing on campus.** 360 workstations in library, computer center. Wireless network available.

**Student life. Freshman orientation:** Available, $56 fee. One-day transition course offered in January, end of August. **Activities:** Choral groups, drama, literary magazine, music ensembles, radio station, student government, student newspaper, human services club, law society, Christian club, College Republicans, Phi Theta Kappa, nursing society, multicultural society.

**Athletics.** NJCAA. **Intercollegiate:** Baseball M, basketball, golf, soccer, softball W, volleyball W. **Intramural:** Badminton, basketball, soccer, volleyball. **Team name:** Red Barons.

**Student services.** Adult student services, alcohol/substance abuse counseling, campus ministries, career counseling, services for economically disadvantaged, student employment services, financial aid counseling, health services, personal counseling, placement for graduates. **Physically disabled:** Services for visually, speech, hearing impaired. **Transfer:** Transfer center, transfer adviser, college fairs on campus for students transferring to 4-year colleges.

**Contact.** E-mail: admissions@corning-cc.edu
Phone: (607) 962-9151 Toll-free number: (800) 358-7171 ext. 151
Fax: (607) 962-9582
Karen Brown, Director of Admissions, Corning Community College, One Academic Drive, Corning, NY 14830

## Dutchess Community College
**Poughkeepsie, New York**                    **CB member**
www.sunydutchess.edu                          **CB code: 2198**

- Public 2-year community college
- Commuter campus in large town

**General.** Founded in 1957. Regionally accredited. Extension programs at 6 sites. **Enrollment:** 6,686 degree-seeking undergraduates. **Degrees:** 917 associate awarded. **Location:** 70 miles from New York City. **Calendar:** Semester, limited summer session. **Full-time faculty:** 137 total; 23% have terminal degrees, 11% minority, 55% women. **Part-time faculty:** 292 total; 49% women. **Special facilities:** Biological experimentation site on Hudson River. **Partnerships:** Formal partnership with Verizon.

**Student profile.** Among degree-seeking undergraduates, 64% enrolled in a transfer program, 36% enrolled in a vocational program, 2,147 enrolled as first-time, first-year students, 198 transferred in from other institutions.

| | | | |
|---|---|---|---|
| Out-of-state: | 1% | 25 or older: | 29% |

**Transfer out.** 71% of students enrolled in the transfer program go on to 4-year colleges. **Colleges most students transferred to 2007:** State University of New York at Paltz, Marist College, Mount St. Mary's College, State University of New York at Albany.

**Basis for selection.** Open admission, but selective for some programs. Special requirements for nursing and engineering programs. **Homeschooled:** Students must pass entrance test unless they have local diploma or diploma from accredited school.

**High school preparation.** Recommended units include English 4, mathematics 3, social studies 4, science 3 and foreign language 2.

**2007-2008 Annual costs.** Tuition/fees: $3,217; $6,017 out-of-state. Per-credit charge: $115 in-state; $230 out-of-state. Books/supplies: $1,200. Personal expenses: $1,000.

**2006-2007 Financial aid. Need-based:** 85% of total undergraduate aid awarded as scholarships/grants, 15% as loans/jobs. Need-based aid available for part-time students. Work-study available for part-time students.

**Application procedures. Admission:** No deadline. No application fee. Application may be submitted online. Admission notification on a rolling basis. **Financial aid:** Priority date 5/1; no closing date. FAFSA, institutional form required. Applicants notified on a rolling basis starting 5/15; must reply within 2 week(s) of notification.

**Academics. Special study options:** Cooperative education, cross-registration, distance learning, dual enrollment of high school students, ESL, honors, independent study, internships, liberal arts/career combination, study abroad, weekend college. Combined degree in education with SUNY at New Paltz. License preparation in dental hygiene, nursing, paramedic. **Credit/ placement by examination:** AP, CLEP, institutional tests. 40 credit hours maximum toward associate degree. **Support services:** GED preparation and test center, learning center, pre-admission summer program, reduced course load, remedial instruction, study skills assistance, tutoring, writing center.

**Majors. Business:** Accounting, administrative services, business admin, office technology, sales/distribution, tourism promotion, tourism/travel, travel services. **Communications:** General. **Computer sciences:** General, computer science. **Education:** Biology, chemistry, early childhood, elementary, English, French, German, kindergarten/preschool, mathematics, middle, science, secondary, social studies, Spanish, teacher assistance. **Engineering:** Electrical, science. **Engineering technology:** Architectural, construction, electrical, manufacturing. **Family/consumer sciences:** Child care. **Health:** Clinical lab technology, EMT paramedic, health services, mental health services, nursing (RN), physical therapy assistant. **Legal studies:** Legal secretary, paralegal. **Liberal arts:** Arts/sciences, humanities. **Math:** General. **Parks/ recreation:** General, exercise sciences, facilities management. **Physical sciences:** General. **Protective services:** Criminal justice. **Visual/performing arts:** Commercial/advertising art, dramatic.

**Most popular majors.** Business/marketing 21%, education 10%, health sciences 11%, liberal arts 30%, security/protective services 8%.

**Computing on campus.** 1,000 workstations in library, computer center. Online course registration, online library, helpline, repair service, wireless network available.

**Student life. Freshman orientation:** Available. Preregistration for classes offered. **Activities:** Jazz band, choral groups, dance, drama, film society, literary magazine, music ensembles, musical theater, radio station, student government, student newspaper, TV station, foreign student organization, special interest clubs.

**Athletics.** NJCAA. **Intercollegiate:** Baseball M, basketball M, bowling M, golf M, soccer M, softball W, tennis, volleyball W. **Intramural:** Archery, badminton, basketball, bowling, fencing, racquetball, soccer, softball, tennis, volleyball, weight lifting. **Team name:** Falcons.

**Student services.** Adult student services, career counseling, services for economically disadvantaged, student employment services, financial aid counseling, health services, minority student services, on-campus daycare, personal counseling, placement for graduates, veterans' counselor. **Physically disabled:** Services for visually, speech, hearing impaired. **Transfer:** Pre-admission transcript evaluation for new students. Transfer adviser, college fairs on campus for students transferring to 4-year colleges.

**Contact.** E-mail: admissions@sunydutchess.edu
Phone: (845) 431-8010 Toll-free number: (800) 378-9707
Fax: (845) 431-8605
Rita Banner, Director of Admissions, Dutchess Community College, 53 Pendell Road, Poughkeepsie, NY 12601-1595

## Elmira Business Institute
**Elmira, New York**
**www.ebi-college.com**                          CB code: 3332

- For-profit 2-year business and technical college
- Commuter campus in large town
- Interview required

**General.** Accredited by ACICS. **Enrollment:** 150 degree-seeking undergraduates. **Degrees:** 140 associate awarded. **Calendar:** Trimester. **Full-time faculty:** 5 total. **Part-time faculty:** 27 total.

**Student profile.**

| | | | |
|---|---|---|---|
| Out-of-state: | 30% | 25 or older: | 80% |

**Basis for selection.** Open admission. High school diploma or GED required along with a career planning session. **Homeschooled:** State high school equivalency certificate required.

**2007-2008 Annual costs.** Tuition/fees: $8,450. Per-credit charge: $275.

**Financial aid.** All financial aid based on need. Need-based aid available for part-time students.

**Application procedures. Admission:** No deadline. No application fee. Application may be submitted online. **Financial aid:** Closing date 5/1. FAFSA, institutional form required.

**Academics. Special study options:** Internships, weekend college. **Credit/ placement by examination:** CLEP, institutional tests. **Support services:** Reduced course load, remedial instruction, tutoring.

**Majors. Business:** Accounting. **Health:** Clinical lab assistant, insurance coding, medical assistant, medical records admin, medical records technology, medical secretary, medical transcription. **Legal studies:** Legal secretary, paralegal.

**Computing on campus.** 100 workstations in library, computer center.

**Student life. Freshman orientation:** Mandatory.

**Student services.** Career counseling, financial aid counseling, personal counseling, placement for graduates. **Transfer:** Pre-admission transcript evaluation for new students. College fairs on campus for students transferring to 4-year colleges.

**Contact.** E-mail: lroan@ebi-college.com
Phone: (607) 733-7177 Toll-free number: (800) 843-1812
Fax: (607) 733-7178
Lisa Roan, Director, Elmira Business Institute, 303 North Main Street, Elmira, NY 14901

## Elmira Business Institute: Vestal
**Vestal, New York**

- For-profit 2-year business and technical college
- Commuter campus in small city
- Interview required

**General.** Accredited by ACICS. **Enrollment:** 74 degree-seeking undergraduates. **Degrees:** 78 associate awarded. **Calendar:** Trimester, extensive summer session. **Full-time faculty:** 4 total. **Part-time faculty:** 20 total.

**Student profile.**

| | | | |
|---|---|---|---|
| Part-time: | 31% | Women: | 86% |
| Out-of-state: | 7% | African American: | 1% |

**Transfer out. Colleges most students transferred to 2007:** Broome Community College.

**Basis for selection.** Open admission. Career planning session is required. **Homeschooled:** Statement describing homeschool structure and mission required. Must have a letter from school superintendent or principal.

**2007-2008 Annual costs.** Tuition/fees: $8,450. Per-credit charge: $275.

**Financial aid.** All financial aid based on need. Need-based aid available for part-time students.

**Application procedures. Admission:** No deadline. No application fee. Application may be submitted online. **Financial aid:** No deadline. FAFSA, institutional form required. Applicants notified on a rolling basis.

**Academics. Credit/placement by examination:** CLEP, institutional tests. **Support services:** Reduced course load, remedial instruction, study skills assistance, tutoring.

**Majors. Business:** Accounting technology. **Health:** Clinical lab assistant, insurance coding.

**Computing on campus.** Online library available.

**Student life. Freshman orientation:** Mandatory.

**Student services. Transfer:** Pre-admission transcript evaluation for new students.

**Contact.** Phone: (607) 729-8915
Lisa Roan, Director, Elmira Business Institute: Vestal, 4100 Vestal Road, Vestal, NY 13850

## Erie Community College: City Campus
**Buffalo, New York**  **CB member**
www.ecc.edu  **CB code: 2213**

- Public 2-year community college
- Commuter campus in large city

**General.** Founded in 1971. Regionally accredited. SUNY institution. Main campus located in Buffalo. Additional campuses in Williamsville and Orchard Park. **Enrollment:** 2,656 degree-seeking undergraduates; 372 non-degree-seeking students. **Degrees:** 405 associate awarded. **ROTC:** Army. **Calendar:** Semester, limited summer session. **Full-time faculty:** 84 total; 14% minority, 55% women. **Part-time faculty:** 274 total; 15% minority, 52% women. **Special facilities:** Child care centers, natatorium (City Campus). **Partnerships:** Formal partnerships with Ford Motor Company, Daimler Chrysler, Verizon.

**Student profile.** Among degree-seeking undergraduates, 45% enrolled in a transfer program, 55% enrolled in a vocational program, 1% already have a bachelor's degree or higher, 609 enrolled as first-time, first-year students, 135 transferred in from other institutions.

| | | | |
|---|---|---|---|
| Part-time: | 20% | Asian American: | 2% |
| Out-of-state: | 1% | Hispanic American: | 8% |
| Women: | 63% | Native American: | 1% |
| African American: | 43% | 25 or older: | 43% |

**Transfer out. Colleges most students transferred to 2007:** SUNY College at Buffalo, SUNY College at Fredonia, SUNY College at Brockport, SUNY Buffalo.

**Basis for selection.** Open admission, but selective for some programs. Additional requirements for nursing and radiologic technology programs; interview required. Minimum age is 17 for international students. Students who receive 500 or higher on SAT Critical Reading are waived from the English placement test. A score of 500 or higher on SAT Math will allow the student to be waived from the Math placement test. **Homeschooled:** Applicants follow same criteria as applicants with GED.

**2007-2008 Annual costs.** Tuition/fees: $3,339; $6,326 out-of-district; $6,326 out-of-state. Per-credit charge: $125 in-state; $250 out-of-state. Books/supplies: $900. Personal expenses: $900.

**Financial aid.** All financial aid based on need. Need-based aid available for part-time students. Work-study available weekends and for part-time students.

**Application procedures. Admission:** Priority date 8/1; no deadline. $25 fee. Application may be submitted online. Admission notification on a rolling basis. **Financial aid:** Priority date 6/1; no closing date. FAFSA required. Applicants notified on a rolling basis starting 4/1; must reply within 2 week(s) of notification.

**Academics. Special study options:** Cooperative education, cross-registration, distance learning, double major, dual enrollment of high school students, ESL, exchange student, honors, independent study, internships, liberal arts/career combination, student-designed major, study abroad, teacher certification program, weekend college. Dual admissions with 4-year institutions. License preparation in nursing, paramedic, radiology. **Credit/placement by examination:** AP, CLEP, institutional tests. **Support services:** GED preparation and test center, learning center, pre-admission summer program, reduced course load, remedial instruction, study skills assistance, tutoring, writing center.

**Majors. Business:** Administrative services, business admin, office management. **Computer sciences:** Information systems. **Construction:** Maintenance. **Education:** Physical. **Family/consumer sciences:** Child care. **Health:** Community health services, medical radiologic technology/radiation therapy, nursing (RN), substance abuse counseling. **Legal studies:** Paralegal. **Liberal arts:** Arts/sciences, humanities. **Personal/culinary services:** Chef training. **Protective services:** Law enforcement admin, police science. **Public administration:** General, human services.

**Most popular majors.** Business/marketing 14%, family/consumer sciences 7%, health sciences 18%, legal studies 10%, liberal arts 35%.

**Computing on campus.** 386 workstations in library, computer center. Commuter students can connect to campus network. Online course registration, online library, helpline, repair service, student web hosting, wireless network available.

**Student life. Freshman orientation:** Mandatory, $50 fee. Preregistration for classes offered. **Activities:** Bands, campus ministries, choral groups, dance, drama, literary magazine, music ensembles, musical theater, radio station, student government, student newspaper, Latino student association,

honors association, Habitat for Humanity, Phi Theta Kappa, bilingual club, peer support group, peace & social justice club.

**Athletics.** NJCAA. **Intercollegiate:** Baseball M, basketball, bowling, cheerleading M, cross-country, diving, football (tackle) M, golf, ice hockey M, lacrosse W, soccer, softball W, swimming, track and field, volleyball W. **Team name:** Kats.

**Student services.** Adult student services, campus ministries, career counseling, services for economically disadvantaged, student employment services, financial aid counseling, health services, minority student services, on-campus daycare, personal counseling, placement for graduates, veterans' counselor, women's services. **Physically disabled:** Services for visually, speech, hearing impaired. **Transfer:** Pre-admission transcript evaluation for new students. Transfer adviser, college fairs on campus for students transferring to 4-year colleges.

**Contact.** E-mail: cheatom@ecc.edu
Phone: (716) 851-1155 Fax: (716) 270-2821
Petrina Hill-Cheatom, Director of Admissions, Erie Community College: City Campus, 121 Ellicott Street, Buffalo, NY 14203-2698

## Erie Community College: North Campus
**Williamsville, New York**
www.ecc.edu  **CB code: 2228**

- Public 2-year community college
- Commuter campus in small city

**General.** Founded in 1946. Regionally accredited. SUNY institution. Main campus located in Buffalo. Additional campuses in Williamsville and Orchard Park. **Enrollment:** 5,204 degree-seeking undergraduates; 707 non-degree-seeking students. **Degrees:** 764 associate awarded. **ROTC:** Army. **Location:** 10 miles from Buffalo. **Calendar:** Semester, limited summer session. **Full-time faculty:** 165 total; 8% minority, 53% women. **Part-time faculty:** 395 total; 7% minority, 46% women. **Special facilities:** Child care centers. **Partnerships:** Formal partnerships with Ford Motor Company, Daimler Chrysler, Verizon.

**Student profile.** Among degree-seeking undergraduates, 41% enrolled in a transfer program, 59% enrolled in a vocational program, 1% already have a bachelor's degree or higher, 1,275 enrolled as first-time, first-year students, 361 transferred in from other institutions.

| | | | |
|---|---|---|---|
| Part-time: | 25% | Hispanic American: | 2% |
| Out-of-state: | 1% | Native American: | 1% |
| Women: | 50% | International: | 1% |
| African American: | 13% | 25 or older: | 29% |
| Asian American: | 2% | | |

**Transfer out. Colleges most students transferred to 2007:** SUNY College at Buffalo, SUNY College at Fredonia, SUNY College at Brockport, SUNY Buffalo.

**Basis for selection.** Open admission, but selective for some programs. Additional requirements for nursing and occupational therapy programs; interview required. International students must be at least 17 years of age. Students who receive 500 or higher on SAT Critical Reading are waived from the English placement test. A score of 500 or higher on SAT Math will allow the student to be waived from the Math placement test. **Homeschooled:** Applicants follow same criteria as applicants with GED.

**2007-2008 Annual costs.** Tuition/fees: $3,339; $6,326 out-of-district; $6,326 out-of-state. Per-credit charge: $125 in-state; $250 out-of-state. Books/supplies: $900. Personal expenses: $900.

**Financial aid.** All financial aid based on need. Need-based aid available for part-time students. Work-study available weekends and for part-time students.

**Application procedures. Admission:** Priority date 8/1; no deadline. $25 fee. Application may be submitted online. Admission notification on a rolling basis. **Financial aid:** Priority date 6/1; no closing date. FAFSA required. Applicants notified on a rolling basis starting 4/1; must reply within 2 week(s) of notification.

**Academics. Special study options:** Cooperative education, cross-registration, distance learning, double major, dual enrollment of high school students, ESL, exchange student, honors, independent study, internships, liberal arts/career combination, student-designed major, study abroad, teacher certification program, weekend college. Dual admissions with 4-year institutions. License preparation in dental hygiene, nursing, paramedic. **Credit/placement by examination:** AP, CLEP, institutional tests. **Support services:** GED preparation and test center, learning center, pre-admission summer program, reduced course load, remedial instruction, study skills assistance, tutoring, writing center.

**Majors. Business:** Business admin, construction management, office management. **Computer sciences:** General, information systems. **Education:** Physical. **Engineering:** General. **Engineering technology:** Civil, electrical, industrial, mechanical. **Health:** Clinical lab technology, dental hygiene, dietician assistant, medical records technology, nursing (RN), occupational therapy assistant, office admin, optician, respiratory therapy technology. **Liberal arts:** Arts/sciences, humanities. **Personal/culinary services:** Chef training, restaurant/catering. **Protective services:** Law enforcement admin, police science.

**Most popular majors.** Business/marketing 16%, health sciences 26%, liberal arts 35%, security/protective services 12%.

**Computing on campus.** 436 workstations in library, computer center. Commuter students can connect to campus network. Online course registration, online library, helpline, repair service, student web hosting, wireless network available.

**Student life. Freshman orientation:** Mandatory, $50 fee. Preregistration for classes offered. **Activities:** Bands, campus ministries, choral groups, dance, drama, literary magazine, music ensembles, musical theater, radio station, student government, student newspaper, Latino student association, honors association, Habitat for Humanity, Phi Theta Kappa, bilingual club, peer support group, peace & social justice club.

**Athletics.** NJCAA. **Intercollegiate:** Baseball M, basketball, bowling, cheerleading M, cross-country, diving, football (tackle) M, golf, ice hockey M, lacrosse W, soccer, softball W, swimming, track and field, volleyball W. **Team name:** Kats.

**Student services.** Adult student services, campus ministries, career counseling, services for economically disadvantaged, student employment services, financial aid counseling, health services, minority student services, on-campus daycare, personal counseling, placement for graduates, veterans' counselor, women's services. **Physically disabled:** Services for visually, speech, hearing impaired. **Transfer:** Pre-admission transcript evaluation for new students. Transfer adviser, college fairs on campus for students transferring to 4-year colleges.

**Contact.** E-mail: cheatom@ecc.edu
Phone: (716) 851-1455 Fax: (716) 270-2961
Petrina Hill-Cheatom, Director of Admissions, Erie Community College: North Campus, 6205 Main Street, Williamsville, NY 14221-7095

## Erie Community College: South Campus
**Orchard Park, New York**
www.ecc.edu                                    CB code: 2211

- Public 2-year community college
- Commuter campus in large town

**General.** Founded in 1974. Regionally accredited. SUNY institution. Main campus located in Buffalo. Additional campuses in Williamsville and Orchard Park. **Enrollment:** 3,216 degree-seeking undergraduates; 898 non-degree-seeking students. **Degrees:** 501 associate awarded. **ROTC:** Army. **Location:** 10 miles from Buffalo. **Calendar:** Semester, limited summer session. **Full-time faculty:** 108 total; 6% minority, 41% women. **Part-time faculty:** 365 total; 3% minority, 34% women. **Special facilities:** Child care centers, vehicle training technology center, corporate training facility. **Partnerships:** Formal partnerships with Ford Motor Company, Daimler-Chrysler, Verizon.

**Student profile.** Among degree-seeking undergraduates, 57% enrolled in a transfer program, 43% enrolled in a vocational program, 1% already have a bachelor's degree or higher, 880 enrolled as first-time, first-year students, 145 transferred in from other institutions.

| | | | |
|---|---|---|---|
| Part-time: | 22% | Asian American: | 1% |
| Out-of-state: | 1% | Hispanic American: | 3% |
| Women: | 40% | Native American: | 1% |
| African American: | 6% | 25 or older: | 21% |

**Transfer out. Colleges most students transferred to 2007:** SUNY at Buffalo, SUNY College at Fredonia, SUNY College at Brockport, SUNY College at Buffalo.

**Basis for selection.** Open admission, but selective for some programs. Additional requirements for dental laboratory technician program; interview required. Minimum age is 17 for international students. Students who receive 500 or higher on SAT Critical Reading are waived from the English placement test. A score of 500 or higher on SAT Math will allow the student

to be waived from the Math placement test. **Homeschooled:** Applicants follow same criteria as applicants with GED.

**2007-2008 Annual costs.** Tuition/fees: $3,339; $6,326 out-of-district; $6,326 out-of-state. Per-credit charge: $125 in-state; $250 out-of-state. Books/supplies: $900. Personal expenses: $900.

**Financial aid.** All financial aid based on need. Need-based aid available for part-time students. Work-study available weekends and for part-time students.

**Application procedures. Admission:** Priority date 8/1; no deadline. $25 fee. Application may be submitted online. Admission notification on a rolling basis. **Financial aid:** Priority date 6/1; no closing date. FAFSA required. Applicants notified on a rolling basis starting 4/1; must reply within 2 week(s) of notification.

**Academics. Special study options:** Cooperative education, cross-registration, distance learning, double major, dual enrollment of high school students, ESL, exchange student, honors, independent study, internships, liberal arts/career combination, student-designed major, study abroad, teacher certification program, weekend college. Dual admissions with 4-year institutions. License preparation in paramedic. **Credit/placement by examination:** AP, CLEP, institutional tests. **Support services:** GED preparation and test center, learning center, pre-admission summer program, reduced course load, remedial instruction, study skills assistance, tutoring, writing center.

**Majors. Business:** Business admin, office management. **Communications:** General. **Communications technology:** Graphic/printing. **Computer sciences:** Information systems. **Education:** Physical. **Engineering technology:** Architectural, CAD/CADD, computer systems, industrial, telecommunications. **Health:** Dental lab technology. **Liberal arts:** Arts/sciences, humanities. **Mechanic/repair:** Auto body, automotive, communications systems. **Parks/recreation:** Facilities management. **Protective services:** Fire services admin. **Public administration:** General, human services.

**Most popular majors.** Business/marketing 14%, communications/journalism 10%, engineering/engineering technologies 7%, liberal arts 51%, trade and industry 8%.

**Computing on campus.** 438 workstations in library, computer center. Commuter students can connect to campus network. Online course registration, online library, helpline, repair service, student web hosting, wireless network available.

**Student life. Freshman orientation:** Mandatory, $50 fee. Preregistration for classes offered. **Activities:** Bands, campus ministries, choral groups, dance, drama, literary magazine, music ensembles, musical theater, radio station, student government, student newspaper, Latino student association, honors association, Habitat for Humanity, Phi Theta Kappa, bilingual club, peer support group, peace & social justice club.

**Athletics.** NJCAA. **Intercollegiate:** Baseball M, basketball, bowling, cheerleading M, cross-country, diving, football (tackle) M, golf, ice hockey M, lacrosse W, soccer, softball W, swimming, track and field, volleyball W. **Team name:** Kats.

**Student services.** Adult student services, campus ministries, career counseling, services for economically disadvantaged, student employment services, financial aid counseling, health services, minority student services, on-campus daycare, personal counseling, placement for graduates, veterans' counselor, women's services. **Physically disabled:** Services for visually, speech, hearing impaired. **Transfer:** Pre-admission transcript evaluation for new students. Transfer adviser, college fairs on campus for students transferring to 4-year colleges.

**Contact.** E-mail: cheatom@ecc.edu
Phone: (716) 851-1655 Fax: (716) 851-1687
Petrina Hill-Cheatom, Director of Admissions, Erie Community College: South Campus, 4041 Southwestern Boulevard, Orchard Park, NY 14127-2199

## Finger Lakes Community College
**Canandaigua, New York**
www.flcc.edu                                    CB code: 2134

- Public 2-year community college
- Commuter campus in small town

**General.** Founded in 1965. Regionally accredited. SUNY institution. **Enrollment:** 3,644 degree-seeking undergraduates; 1,707 non-degree-seeking students. **Degrees:** 696 associate awarded. **ROTC:** Army. **Location:** 25 miles from Rochester. **Calendar:** Semester, extensive summer session. **Full-time faculty:** 112 total; 3% minority, 45% women. **Part-time faculty:** 188 total; 58% women. **Class size:** 62% < 20, 38% 20-39, less than 1% 50-99.

**Special facilities:** Outdoor classrooms, nature trails, music recording studio, performing arts center. **Partnerships:** Formal partnerships with local hospitals for nursing clinicals, more informally for cooperative studies and placement of interns.

**Student profile.** Among degree-seeking undergraduates, 66% enrolled in a transfer program, 34% enrolled in a vocational program, 1,302 enrolled as first-time, first-year students, 289 transferred in from other institutions.

| | | | |
|---|---|---|---|
| Part-time: | 22% | Asian American: | 1% |
| Out-of-state: | 1% | Hispanic American: | 2% |
| Women: | 55% | 25 or older: | 29% |
| African American: | 6% | | |

**Transfer out. Colleges most students transferred to 2007:** SUNY at Brockport, SUNY at Geneseo, St. John Fisher College, Nazareth College of Rochester, Rochester Institute of Technology.

**Basis for selection.** Open admission, but selective for some programs. Admission to nursing program based on high school curriculum and GPA. Competitive admission to therapeutic massage/integrated health care program. Interview recommended for all; portfolio recommended for graphic arts program. **Homeschooled:** Student must submit certification of high school equivalent program provided by superintendent of school district in which student resides.

**High school preparation.** 1 each biology, chemistry, and algebra required of nursing applicants. Students without high school diploma or GED must pass federally approved Ability to Benefit test prior to acceptance. 1 biology required for therapeutic massage/integrated health care applicants.

**2007-2008 Annual costs.** Tuition/fees: $3,482; $6,612 out-of-state. Per-credit charge: $120 in-state; $240 out-of-state. Books/supplies: $900. Personal expenses: $978.

**2006-2007 Financial aid.** All financial aid based on need. 68% of total undergraduate aid awarded as scholarships/grants, 32% as loans/jobs. Need-based aid available for part-time students. Work-study available nights, weekends and for part-time students.

**Application procedures. Admission:** No deadline. No application fee. Application may be submitted online. Admission notification on a rolling basis beginning on or about 11/1. Must reply by May 1 or within 4 week(s) if notified thereafter. Application closing date for Nursing and Therapeutic Massage programs is February 1. **Financial aid:** Priority date 4/1; no closing date. FAFSA, institutional form required. Applicants notified on a rolling basis starting 3/1.

**Academics. Special study options:** Cooperative education, cross-registration, distance learning, double major, dual enrollment of high school students, ESL, honors, independent study, internships. Credit-bearing travel opportunities. License preparation in nursing, paramedic. **Credit/placement by examination:** AP, CLEP, IB, institutional tests. 32 credit hours maximum toward associate degree. **Support services:** GED preparation, learning center, pre-admission summer program, reduced course load, remedial instruction, study skills assistance, tutoring, writing center.

**Majors. Agriculture:** Ornamental horticulture. **Biology:** Biotechnology. **Business:** General, accounting, administrative services, banking/financial services, business admin, hospitality/recreation, hotel/motel admin, marketing, sales/distribution, tourism promotion, tourism/travel. **Communications:** General, broadcast journalism. **Communications technology:** Recording arts. **Computer sciences:** General, computer science, information systems, programming. **Conservation:** General, environmental studies, fisheries, management/policy. **Education:** Elementary, physical. **Engineering:** General, science. **Engineering technology:** Architectural, mechanical. **Health:** Athletic training, massage therapy, nursing (RN), substance abuse counseling. **Legal studies:** Paralegal. **Liberal arts:** Arts/sciences. **Parks/recreation:** Sports admin. **Physical sciences:** Chemistry. **Protective services:** Criminal justice. **Public administration:** Human services. **Science technology:** Biological. **Social sciences:** General. **Visual/performing arts:** Commercial/advertising art, dramatic, studio arts.

**Most popular majors.** Business/marketing 16%, health sciences 13%, liberal arts 31%, natural resources/environmental science 11%, visual/performing arts 10%.

**Computing on campus.** 460 workstations in library, computer center, student center. Commuter students can connect to campus network. Online course registration, online library, helpline, student web hosting, wireless network available.

**Student life. Freshman orientation:** Available. Preregistration for classes offered. One-day program with faculty and student leaders. **Policies:** Student code of conduct policy, grievance procedures, procedures for services for students with disabilities. **Activities:** Bands, choral groups, drama, music ensembles, musical theater, radio station, student government, student

newspaper, TV station, Phi Theta Kappa International Honor Society, Sigma Alpha Pi, nursing club, social science/human services club, legal society, College Republicans, College Democrats, Finger Lakes Environmental Action, radio club, Ghost of Ben Franklin (editorial paper).

**Athletics.** NJCAA. **Intercollegiate:** Baseball M, basketball, cross-country, lacrosse, soccer, softball W. **Intramural:** Badminton, basketball, football (non-tackle) M, soccer, softball, tennis, volleyball, weight lifting, wrestling M.

**Student services.** Adult student services, alcohol/substance abuse counseling, career counseling, services for economically disadvantaged, student employment services, financial aid counseling, health services, legal services, on-campus daycare, personal counseling, placement for graduates, veterans' counselor. **Physically disabled:** Services for visually, speech, hearing impaired. **Transfer:** Pre-admission transcript evaluation for new students. Transfer center, transfer adviser, college fairs on campus for students transferring to 4-year colleges.

**Contact.** E-mail: admissions@flcc.edu
Phone: (585) 394-3500 ext. 7278 Fax: (585) 394-5005
Bonnie Ritts, Admissions Office, Finger Lakes Community College, 4355 Lake Shore Drive, Canandaigua, NY 14424-8395

## Fulton-Montgomery Community College
**Johnstown, New York**
**www.fmcc.suny.edu**     **CB code: 2254**

▶ Public 2-year community college
▶ Commuter campus in large town

**General.** Founded in 1963. Regionally accredited. **Enrollment:** 1,722 degree-seeking undergraduates; 513 non-degree-seeking students. **Degrees:** 309 associate awarded. **Location:** 40 miles from Albany, 200 miles from New York City. **Calendar:** Semester, extensive summer session. **Full-time faculty:** 53 total. **Part-time faculty:** 48 total. **Class size:** 46% < 20, 46% 20-39, 7% 40-49, 1% 50-99. **Special facilities:** Regional history study center, BOCES facility co-located on campus.

**Student profile.** Among degree-seeking undergraduates, 45% enrolled in a transfer program, 28% enrolled in a vocational program, 595 enrolled as first-time, first-year students, 73 transferred in from other institutions.

| | | | |
|---|---|---|---|
| Part-time: | 21% | Hispanic American: | 7% |
| Women: | 57% | International: | 5% |
| African American: | 5% | 25 or older: | 25% |
| Asian American: | 1% | | |

**Transfer out. Colleges most students transferred to 2007:** State University of New York at Plattsburgh, College of Saint Rose, SUNY College at Oneonta, University at Albany.

**Basis for selection.** Open admission, but selective for some programs. Admission for nursing and radiologic technology programs based on high school GPA, class rank, and any college experience. Must meet program prerequisites. Focal Skills Test for ESL Placement and COMPASS used for placement. Interview recommended. **Homeschooled:** Applicants applying for financial aid may be required to complete Ability to Benefit Test. Applicants from accredited home school who have received or will receive diploma may not be required to take test.

**2007-2008 Annual costs.** Tuition/fees: $3,468; $6,562 out-of-state. Per-credit charge: $128 in-state; $256 out-of-state. Books/supplies: $500.

**Financial aid. Need-based:** Need-based aid available for part-time students. Work-study available nights, weekends and for part-time students. **Non-need-based:** Scholarships awarded for academics.

**Application procedures. Admission:** No deadline. No application fee. Application may be submitted online. Admission notification on a rolling basis. **Financial aid:** Priority date 6/1; no closing date. FAFSA required. Applicants notified on a rolling basis starting 6/15; must reply within 2 week(s) of notification.

**Academics.** Career-oriented individual studies program offered. Can complete bachelor's degree online through Empire State College (SUNY) or Franklin University (OH); advising for both programs available on campus. **Special study options:** Accelerated study, cooperative education, cross-registration, distance learning, double major, dual enrollment of high school students, ESL, external degree, honors, independent study, internships, student-designed major, study abroad. 1+1 agreements with SUNY Agricultural and Technical Colleges at Canton and Cobleskill; automotive program at Career Education Center, Johnstown; EMT-Paramedic with SUNY Herkimer County

Community College. Bachelor's degree programs available on campus. License preparation in nursing, radiology. **Credit/placement by examination:** AP, CLEP, institutional tests. 30 credit hours maximum toward associate degree. **Support services:** Learning center, reduced course load, remedial instruction, study skills assistance, tutoring, writing center.

**Majors. Business:** General, accounting technology, administrative services, business admin. **Communications:** General, journalism. **Communications technology:** Graphic/printing. **Computer sciences:** General, information systems. **Construction:** General. **Engineering:** General. **Engineering technology:** Computer, electrical. **English:** English lit. **Family/consumer sciences:** Child care. **Health:** Medical radiologic technology/radiation therapy, nursing (RN), office admin. **Liberal arts:** Arts/sciences, humanities. **Mechanic/repair:** Automotive. **Parks/recreation:** Health/fitness. **Personal/culinary services:** Restaurant/catering. **Protective services:** Criminal justice. **Public administration:** Community org/advocacy. **Visual/performing arts:** Art, commercial/advertising art.

**Computing on campus.** 400 workstations in library, computer center, student center. Commuter students can connect to campus network. Helpline available.

**Student life. Freshman orientation:** Available. Preregistration for classes offered. One-day orientation held one or two days before classes begin. **Activities:** Choral groups, drama, musical theater, student government, student newspaper, Phi Theta Kappa, Alpha Omega, international student union, business club, fencing club.

**Athletics.** NJCAA. **Intercollegiate:** Baseball M, basketball, soccer, softball W, volleyball W. **Intramural:** Basketball M, volleyball. **Team name:** Raiders.

**Student services.** Adult student services, student employment services, on-campus daycare, personal counseling, veterans' counselor. **Physically disabled:** Services for visually, speech, hearing impaired. **Transfer:** Preadmission transcript evaluation for new students. Transfer center, college fairs on campus for students transferring to 4-year colleges.

**Contact.** E-mail: geninfo@fmcc.suny.edu
Phone: (518) 736-5300 Fax: (518) 762-4334
Laura LaPorte, Associate Dean of Enrollment Management,
Fulton-Montgomery Community College, 2805 State Highway 67, Johnstown, NY 12095

## Genesee Community College
**Batavia, New York**
www.genesee.edu                              **CB code: 2272**

- Public 2-year community college
- Commuter campus in large town

**General.** Founded in 1966. Regionally accredited. SUNY institution. Mall-type campus, suited to disabled. Off-campus sites in Orleans, Wyoming, and Livingston counties. **Enrollment:** 3,753 degree-seeking undergraduates; 2,719 non-degree-seeking students. **Degrees:** 730 associate awarded. **Location:** 35 miles from Buffalo, 35 miles from Rochester. **Calendar:** Semester, limited summer session. **Full-time faculty:** 76 total. **Part-time faculty:** 240 total. **Special facilities:** Nature preserve, arts center, technology building.

**Student profile.** Among degree-seeking undergraduates, 1,135 enrolled as first-time, first-year students, 351 transferred in from other institutions.

| | | | |
|---|---|---|---|
| Part-time: | 24% | Hispanic American: | 2% |
| Out-of-state: | 1% | Native American: | 1% |
| Women: | 65% | International: | 3% |
| African American: | 6% | 25 or older: | 31% |
| Asian American: | 1% | | |

**Transfer out.** 67% of students enrolled in the transfer program go on to 4-year colleges. **Colleges most students transferred to 2007:** SUNY Brockport, SUNY Buffalo, SUNY Geneseo, Rochester Institute of Technology, St. John Fisher.

**Basis for selection.** Open admission, but selective for some programs. Admission to nursing, physical therapist assistant, paralegal, and respiratory care programs based on academic achievement, test scores, interview, and school and community activities. ACT and COMPASS used for placement. Although SAT not used as placement test, students above 500 on each part are exempted from remedial courses. Portfolio recommended for digital art program.

**High school preparation.** Recommended units include English 4, mathematics 3, social studies 4, science 3 and foreign language 2. Additional units of math and science recommended for students planning to transfer to

4-year programs. 18 units, including biology and chemistry, required for nursing applicants. 18 units, including biology and physics, required for physical therapist assistant applicants.

**2007-2008 Annual costs.** Tuition/fees: $3,590; $4,190 out-of-state. Per-credit charge: $136 in-state; $154 out-of-state. Books/supplies: $900. Personal expenses: $755.

**Financial aid. Need-based:** Need-based aid available for part-time students. Work-study available nights, weekends and for part-time students.

**Application procedures. Admission:** No deadline. No application fee. Application may be submitted online. Admission notification on a rolling basis beginning on or about 11/15. **Financial aid:** Priority date 3/1, closing date 5/1. FAFSA required. Applicants notified on a rolling basis starting 4/15; must reply within 2 week(s) of notification.

**Academics. Special study options:** Cooperative education, cross-registration, distance learning, double major, dual enrollment of high school students, ESL, honors, independent study, internships, liberal arts/career combination. License preparation in nursing, physical therapy. **Credit/placement by examination:** AP, CLEP, IB, institutional tests. 31 credit hours maximum toward associate degree. **Support services:** GED preparation, learning center, reduced course load, remedial instruction, study skills assistance, tutoring, writing center.

**Majors. Biology:** Biotechnology. **Business:** Accounting, accounting technology, administrative services, business admin, fashion, hotel/motel admin, retailing, tourism/travel, travel services. **Communications:** General. **Computer sciences:** Information systems, webmaster. **Education:** Teacher assistance. **Engineering:** Science. **Engineering technology:** Drafting, electrical. **Health:** Medical secretary, nursing (RN), occupational therapy assistant, physical therapy assistant, recreational therapy, respiratory therapy technology, substance abuse counseling. **Legal studies:** Paralegal. **Liberal arts:** Arts/sciences, humanities. **Parks/recreation:** Health/fitness. **Protective services:** Law enforcement admin. **Public administration:** Community org/advocacy. **Visual/performing arts:** Art, dramatic, theater design.

**Most popular majors.** Business/marketing 20%, health sciences 21%, liberal arts 36%, security/protective services 8%.

**Computing on campus.** 350 workstations in dormitories, library, computer center, student center. Dormitories wired for high-speed internet access and linked to campus network. Commuter students can connect to campus network. Online course registration, online library, helpline, wireless network available.

**Student life. Freshman orientation:** Mandatory. Preregistration for classes offered. Day-long orientation before classes begin. **Activities:** Choral groups, drama, film society, international student organizations, literary magazine, musical theater, radio station, student government, student newspaper, Intervarsity Christian Fellowship, Native American student organization, African American interest group, student parents, Enjoying Children Through Recreation and Education, Phi Theta Kappa, Distribution Education Clubs of America, adult student group, Habitat for Humanity.

**Athletics.** NJCAA. **Intercollegiate:** Baseball M, basketball, cross-country, diving, soccer, softball W, swimming, volleyball. **Intramural:** Archery, badminton, baseball M, basketball, golf, skiing, soccer, softball, table tennis, tennis, volleyball. **Team name:** Cougars.

**Student services.** Adult student services, career counseling, student employment services, financial aid counseling, health services, on-campus daycare, personal counseling, placement for graduates, veterans' counselor. **Physically disabled:** Services for visually, speech, hearing impaired. **Transfer:** Re-entry adviser for new students. Transfer center, transfer adviser, college fairs on campus for students transferring to 4-year colleges.

**Contact.** E-mail: tmlanemartin@genesee.suny.edu
Phone: (585) 345-6800 Toll-free number: (866) 225-5422
Fax: (585) 345-6810
Tanya Lane-Martin, Director of Admissions, Genesee Community College, One College Road, Batavia, NY 14020-9704

## Helene Fuld College of Nursing
**New York, New York**
www.helenefuld.edu                            **CB code: 2327**

- Private 2-year nursing and junior college
- Commuter campus in very large city
- Interview required

**General.** Founded in 1945. Regionally accredited. One-year, full-time associate degree program accredited by National League for Nursing Accrediting Commission and Middle States Association of Colleges and Schools.

Career ladder for LPNs. Part-time accredited study also offered. All applicants must be licensed practical nurses. **Enrollment:** 335 degree-seeking undergraduates. **Degrees:** 187 associate awarded. **Location:** Uptown. **Calendar:** Quarter, limited summer session. **Full-time faculty:** 17 total. **Part-time faculty:** 23 total. **Class size:** 6% < 20, 47% 20-39, 29% 40-49, 18% 50-99.

**Basis for selection.** Must be licensed practical nurse with 1 year work experience, PN licensure required. Require satisfactory performance on preentrance exams on practical nursing equivalent, mathematics, and English and completion of a prerequisite chemistry and mathematics course. After all entrance requirements fulfilled, including successful completion of testing, 18 credits granted for practical nursing.

**2007-2008 Annual costs.** Tuition/fees: $14,118. Per-credit charge: $252. Books/supplies: $1,100. Personal expenses: $1,665.

**Financial aid.** All financial aid based on need. Need-based aid available for part-time students.

**Application procedures. Admission:** No deadline. $50 fee. Admission notification on a rolling basis. **Financial aid:** No deadline. FAFSA required. Applicants notified on a rolling basis.

**Academics. Special study options:** Accelerated study, internships, liberal arts/career combination. License preparation in nursing. **Credit/placement by examination:** CLEP, institutional tests. **Support services:** Learning center, reduced course load, study skills assistance, tutoring.

**Majors. Health:** Nursing (RN).

**Computing on campus.** 24 workstations in library, computer center. Commuter students can connect to campus network.

**Student life. Freshman orientation:** Mandatory. Preregistration for classes offered. 2 weeks before term starts. **Activities:** Student government.

**Student services.** Adult student services, career counseling, financial aid counseling, personal counseling. **Transfer:** Pre-admission transcript evaluation for new students. College fairs on campus for students transferring to 4-year colleges.

**Contact.** Phone: (212) 616-7200
Gladys Pineda, Assistant Director of Student Services, Helene Fuld College of Nursing, 24 East 120th Street, New York, NY 10035

## Herkimer County Community College
**Herkimer, New York**
www.herkimer.edu                                    **CB code: 2316**

▶ Public 2-year community college
▶ Commuter campus in small town

**General.** Founded in 1966. Regionally accredited. **Enrollment:** 2,107 full-time, degree-seeking students. **Degrees:** 545 associate awarded. **ROTC:** Army. **Location:** 10 miles from Utica, 55 miles from Syracuse. **Calendar:** Semester, limited summer session. **Full-time faculty:** 115 total. **Part-time faculty:** 25 total. **Class size:** 43% < 20, 55% 20-39, less than 1% 40-49, less than 1% 50-99. **Special facilities:** 500-acre nature center, natural history museum, archeology museum.

**Student profile.**

| | | | |
|---|---|---|---|
| Out-of-state: | 1% | Live on campus: | 25% |
| 25 or older: | 23% | | |

**Transfer out. Colleges most students transferred to 2007:** SUNY Institute of Technology, SUNY Oneonta, SUNY Brockport, SUNY Oswego, SUNY Cortland.

**Basis for selection.** Open admission, but selective for some programs. ASSET scores used to help determine placement into developmental courses. SAT and ACT scores may be used to waive required college placement test. Interview recommended for emergency medical technician, occupational/physical therapy assistant programs. **Homeschooled:** Transcript of courses and grades, letter of recommendation (nonparent) required.

**High school preparation.** Physical/occupational therapist assistant applicants should contact admissions office to review high school course requirements.

**2007-2008 Annual costs.** Tuition/fees: $3,430; $5,430 out-of-state. Per-credit charge: $117 in-state; $208 out-of-state. Apartment-style dorms with a la carte meal service available. Books/supplies: $900. Personal expenses: $670.

**Financial aid. Need-based:** Need-based aid available for part-time students. Work-study available nights, weekends and for part-time students.

**Application procedures. Admission:** Priority date 7/1; no deadline. No application fee. Application may be submitted online. Admission notification on a rolling basis. **Financial aid:** Priority date 5/1; no closing date. FAFSA required. Applicants notified on a rolling basis starting 4/1; must reply within 2 week(s) of notification.

**Academics. Special study options:** Distance learning, dual enrollment of high school students, ESL, honors, independent study, internships, liberal arts/career combination. License preparation in paramedic. **Credit/placement by examination:** AP, CLEP, institutional tests. 32 credit hours maximum toward associate degree. **Support services:** GED preparation, learning center, reduced course load, remedial instruction, study skills assistance, tutoring.

**Honors college/program.** Applicants need high school average of 88. Students must maintain GPA of 3.5.

**Majors. Biology:** General. **Business:** General, accounting, administrative services, business admin, entrepreneurial studies, fashion, human resources, international, logistics, marketing, office management, office technology, office/clerical, tourism/travel. **Communications:** Broadcast journalism, media studies. **Communications technology:** General. **Computer sciences:** Data processing, networking, webmaster. **Education:** Early childhood, physical, teacher assistance. **Engineering technology:** Construction. **Health:** Art therapy, EMT paramedic, health care admin, medical secretary, occupational therapy assistant, physical therapy assistant. **Legal studies:** Legal secretary, paralegal. **Liberal arts:** Arts/sciences. **Math:** General. **Parks/recreation:** Health/fitness. **Protective services:** Criminal justice, forensics, law enforcement admin. **Public administration:** Human services. **Social sciences:** General. **Visual/performing arts:** Art, arts management, photography, studio arts.

**Computing on campus.** 239 workstations in library, computer center. Dormitories linked to campus network. Commuter students can connect to campus network. Online library, helpline available.

**Student life. Freshman orientation:** Mandatory. Preregistration for classes offered. **Housing:** Coed dorms available. $500 deposit. **Activities:** Pep band, dance, drama, literary magazine, musical theater, radio station, student government, student newspaper, TV station, Students for a Better World, social issues club, Students Against Drunk Driving, Campus Christian Fellowship, cultural exchange club, black student union, Phi Theta Kappa.

**Athletics.** NJCAA. **Intercollegiate:** Baseball M, basketball, cross-country, diving, field hockey W, lacrosse, soccer, softball W, swimming, tennis, track and field, volleyball W. **Intramural:** Badminton, baseball M, basketball, bowling, lacrosse, soccer, softball, swimming, tennis, volleyball. **Team name:** Generals.

**Student services.** Adult student services, alcohol/substance abuse counseling, career counseling, student employment services, financial aid counseling, health services, on-campus daycare, personal counseling, placement for graduates, veterans' counselor. **Physically disabled:** Services for visually, hearing impaired. **Transfer:** Re-entry adviser, pre-admission transcript evaluation for new students. Transfer adviser, college fairs on campus for students transferring to 4-year colleges.

**Contact.** E-mail: admissions@herkimer.edu
Phone: (315) 866-0300 ext. 8278 Toll-free
number: (888) 464-4222 ext. 8278 Fax: (315) 866-0062
Herkimer County Community College, 100 Reservoir Road, Herkimer, NY 13350-1598

## Hudson Valley Community College
**Troy, New York**                                    **CB member**
www.hvcc.edu                                          **CB code: 2300**

▶ Public 2-year community college
▶ Commuter campus in small city

**General.** Founded in 1953. Regionally accredited. SUNY institution. **Enrollment:** 6,995 full-time, degree-seeking students. **Degrees:** 1,656 associate awarded. **ROTC:** Army, Air Force. **Location:** 10 miles from Albany. **Calendar:** Semester, limited summer session. **Full-time faculty:** 274 total. **Part-time faculty:** 371 total. **Special facilities:** Language laboratory, computer laboratories.

**Basis for selection.** Open admission, but selective for some programs. Admission to some programs based on school achievement record and test scores. Interview also considered for some programs.

**High school preparation.** Requirements vary for selective programs.

**2007-2008 Annual costs.** Tuition/fees: $3,504; $9,104 out-of-state. Per-credit charge: $116 in-state; $348 out-of-state. Books/supplies: $550. Personal expenses: $800.

**Application procedures. Admission:** No deadline. $30 fee, may be waived for applicants with need. Admission notification on a rolling basis. **Financial aid:** Priority date 5/30; no closing date. FAFSA required. Applicants notified on a rolling basis starting 5/1; must reply within 2 week(s) of notification.

**Academics. Special study options:** Accelerated study, cooperative education, cross-registration, distance learning, double major, internships, student-designed major. License preparation in dental hygiene, nursing, paramedic, radiology. **Credit/placement by examination:** CLEP. 30 credit hours maximum toward associate degree. **Support services:** GED preparation, learning center, pre-admission summer program, reduced course load, remedial instruction, tutoring.

**Majors. Business:** General, accounting, administrative services, business admin, finance, insurance, international, office technology, real estate. **Computer sciences:** Data processing, networking. **Conservation:** Environmental studies. **Construction:** Carpentry, maintenance. **Education:** Physical. **Engineering:** General, science. **Engineering technology:** Civil, drafting, electrical. **Family/consumer sciences:** Child care. **Health:** Clinical lab science, clinical lab technology, dental hygiene, medical radiologic technology/radiation therapy, medical secretary, nursing (RN), physician assistant, respiratory therapy technology, substance abuse counseling. **Mechanic/repair:** Electronics/electrical, heating/ac/refrig. **Personal/culinary services:** Mortuary science. **Physical sciences:** Chemistry. **Protective services:** Forensics. **Public administration:** Community org/advocacy, social work. **Social sciences:** General.

**Computing on campus.** 1,000 workstations in library, computer center.

**Student life. Activities:** Drama, radio station, student government, student newspaper, TV station.

**Athletics.** NJCAA. **Intercollegiate:** Baseball M, basketball, bowling, cross-country, football (tackle) M, golf, ice hockey M, lacrosse M, soccer, softball W, tennis, track and field, volleyball W. **Intramural:** Baseball M, basketball, bowling, cross-country, field hockey W, golf, ice hockey, lacrosse, racquetball, skiing, soccer, softball, table tennis, tennis, track and field, volleyball, wrestling M.

**Student services.** Adult student services, career counseling, student employment services, health services, on-campus daycare, personal counseling, placement for graduates, veterans' counselor. **Physically disabled:** Services for visually, speech, hearing impaired.

**Contact.** E-mail: admissions@hvcc.edu
Phone: (518) 629-7309 Toll-free number: (877) 325-4822
Fax: (518) 629-4576
Mary Bauer, Director of Admissions, Hudson Valley Community College, 80 Vandenburgh Avenue, Troy, NY 12180

## Institute of Design and Construction
**Brooklyn, New York**
www.idc.edu                                       CB code: 0677

- Private 2-year junior and technical college
- Commuter campus in very large city

**General.** Founded in 1947. Regionally accredited. Classes and seminars available for candidates preparing for Architects Registration Exam. **Enrollment:** 120 degree-seeking undergraduates. **Degrees:** 15 associate awarded. **Calendar:** Semester. **Part-time faculty:** 36 total.

**Basis for selection.** Open admission. Interview recommended.

**High school preparation.** Recommended units include English 4, mathematics 3 and science 1. One unit of drafting or architecture recommended.

**2008-2009 Annual costs.** Tuition/fees: $7,800. Per-credit charge: $260. Books/supplies: $800. Personal expenses: $400.

**Application procedures. Admission:** No deadline. $30 fee, may be waived for applicants with need. Admission notification on a rolling basis. **Financial aid:** No deadline. FAFSA, institutional form required. Applicants notified on a rolling basis starting 3/1; must reply within 4 week(s) of notification.

**Academics.** Work and study plan available. Students can spend 2 full-time semesters in accelerated study, then complete degree through part-time

evening study while working during day as junior drafters. Credits transferable to Pratt Institute and New York Institute of Technology. **Special study options:** Double major. Work and study program. **Credit/placement by examination:** CLEP, institutional tests. 12 credit hours maximum toward associate degree. **Support services:** Learning center, reduced course load, remedial instruction, tutoring.

**Majors. Construction:** Maintenance. **Engineering technology:** Architectural, drafting. **Visual/performing arts:** Interior design.

**Computing on campus.** 17 workstations in library, computer center.

**Student services.** Career counseling, student employment services, personal counseling, placement for graduates, veterans' counselor. **Transfer:** Transfer adviser for students transferring to 4-year colleges.

**Contact.** Phone: (718) 855-3661 ext. 16 Fax: (718) 852-5889
Kevin Giannetti, Director of Admissions, Institute of Design and Construction, 141 Willoughby Street, Brooklyn, NY 11201-5380

## Island Drafting and Technical Institute
**Amityville, New York**
www.idti.edu                                      CB code: 3048

- For-profit 2-year technical and career college
- Commuter campus in large town
- Interview required

**General.** Accredited by ACCSCT. **Enrollment:** 123 degree-seeking undergraduates. **Degrees:** 81 associate awarded. **Location:** 25 miles from New York City. **Calendar:** Semester, extensive summer session. **Full-time faculty:** 5 total. **Part-time faculty:** 10 total.

**Student profile.** Among degree-seeking undergraduates, 100% enrolled in a vocational program, 49 enrolled as first-time, first-year students.

| Women: | 18% | 25 or older: | 35% |
|---|---|---|---|

**Basis for selection.** Open admission. School administered test for CADD/Architecture students.

**High school preparation.** Recommended units include English 2 and mathematics 2.

**2007-2008 Annual costs.** Tuition/fees: $12,800. Per-credit charge: $415. Books/supplies: $600.

**Financial aid.** All financial aid based on need.

**Application procedures. Admission:** No deadline. $25 fee, may be waived for applicants with need. Application must be submitted on paper. Admission notification on a rolling basis. **Financial aid:** No deadline. Applicants notified on a rolling basis.

**Academics. Special study options:** Liberal arts/career combination. **Credit/placement by examination:** CLEP. **Support services:** Study skills assistance.

**Majors. Computer sciences:** Computer graphics. **Engineering:** Electrical. **Engineering technology:** Drafting, electrical. **Mechanic/repair:** Electronics/electrical.

**Computing on campus.** 100 workstations in library, computer center.

**Student life. Freshman orientation:** Mandatory.

**Student services.** Alcohol/substance abuse counseling, career counseling, student employment services, financial aid counseling, personal counseling, placement for graduates, veterans' counselor.

**Contact.** E-mail: admissions@idti.edu
Phone: (631) 691-8733 Fax: (631) 691-8738
Steve Rothenberg, Admissions, Island Drafting and Technical Institute, 128 Broadway, Amityville, NY 11701-2704

## ITT Technical Institute: Albany
**Albany, New York**
www.itt-tech.edu                                  CB code: 2689

- For-profit 2-year technical college
- Commuter campus in large city

**General.** Accredited by ACICS. **Calendar:** Quarter.

**Annual costs/financial aid.** Tuition varies by program, $260-$368 per credit hour. Books/supplies: $3,300.

**Contact.** Phone: (518) 452-9300
Director of Recruitment, 13 Airline Drive, Albany, NY 12205

## ITT Technical Institute: Getzville

**Getzville, New York**
www.itt-tech.edu                                    CB code: 2704

- For-profit 2-year technical college
- Commuter campus in rural community

**General.** Accredited by ACICS. **Calendar:** Quarter.

**Annual costs/financial aid.** Tuition varies by program, $260-$368 per credit hour.

**Contact.** Phone: (716) 689-2200
Director of Recruitment, 2295 Millersport Highway, Getzville, NY 14068

## ITT Technical Institute: Liverpool

**Liverpool, New York**
www.itt-tech.edu                                    CB code: 2725

- For-profit 2-year technical college
- Commuter campus in small town

**General.** Accredited by ACICS. **Calendar:** Quarter.

**Annual costs/financial aid.** Tuition varies by program, $260-$368 per credit hour. Books/supplies: $3,300.

**Contact.** Phone: (315) 461-8000
Director of Recruitment, 235 Greenfield Parkway, Liverpool, NY 13088

## Jamestown Business College

**Jamestown, New York**
www.jbcny.org                                    CB code: 2346

- For-profit 2-year business and junior college
- Commuter campus in large town

**General.** Founded in 1886. Regionally accredited. **Enrollment:** 252 degree-seeking undergraduates. **Degrees:** 104 associate awarded. **Location:** 80 miles from Buffalo, 60 miles from Erie, Pennsylvania. **Calendar:** Quarter, limited summer session. **Full-time faculty:** 8 total; 12% have terminal degrees, 12% minority, 75% women. **Part-time faculty:** 8 total; 12% minority, 62% women. **Class size:** 30% < 20, 70% 20-39.

**Student profile.** Among degree-seeking undergraduates, 88 enrolled as first-time, first-year students, 42 transferred in from other institutions.

| | | | |
|---|---|---|---|
| Out-of-state: | 18% | Hispanic American: | 3% |
| Women: | 75% | Native American: | 1% |
| African American: | 2% | 25 or older: | 45% |
| Asian American: | 1% | | |

**Basis for selection.** Class rank and academic record important. School and community activities considered. College uses the Comparative Guidance and Placement program in the admission process. Interview recommended.

**2008-2009 Annual costs.** Tuition/fees (projected): $10,050. Books/supplies: $1,025. Personal expenses: $1,756.

**2006-2007 Financial aid.** **Need-based:** 71% of total undergraduate aid awarded as scholarships/grants, 29% as loans/jobs. Need-based aid available for part-time students. **Non-need-based:** Scholarships awarded for academics.

**Application procedures.** **Admission:** No deadline. $25 fee. Admission notification on a rolling basis. **Financial aid:** No deadline. FAFSA required. Applicants notified on a rolling basis starting 2/15.

**Academics. Credit/placement by examination:** CLEP, institutional tests. **Support services:** Reduced course load, study skills assistance, tutoring.

**Majors. Business:** Accounting, administrative services, business admin, marketing. **Computer sciences:** General, data processing. **Health:** Medical secretary. **Legal studies:** Legal secretary.

**Computing on campus.** 100 workstations in library, computer center. Commuter students can connect to campus network. Online library, wireless network available.

**Student life. Freshman orientation:** Mandatory.

**Athletics. Intramural:** Baseball, basketball, bowling, softball, volleyball.

**Student services.** Adult student services, career counseling, student employment services, personal counseling, placement for graduates, veterans' counselor. **Transfer:** Pre-admission transcript evaluation for new students. Transfer adviser for students transferring to 4-year colleges.

**Contact.** E-mail: admissions@jbcny.org
Phone: (716) 664-5100 Fax: (716) 664-3144
Brenda Salemme, Director of Admissions, Jamestown Business College, 7 Fairmount Avenue, Jamestown, NY 14702-0429

## Jamestown Community College

**Jamestown, New York**
www.sunyjcc.edu                                    CB code: 2335

- Public 2-year community college
- Commuter campus in large town

**General.** Founded in 1950. Regionally accredited. SUNY institution. Branch campus at Olean for Cattaraugus County. Extensions in Dunkirk, Allegany, Warren, PA. Bachelor's degree program through Franklin University. **Enrollment:** 2,983 degree-seeking undergraduates; 382 non-degree-seeking students. **Degrees:** 702 associate awarded. **Location:** 70 miles from Buffalo and Erie, Pennsylvania. **Calendar:** Semester, extensive summer session. **Full-time faculty:** 79 total; 1% minority. **Part-time faculty:** 257 total; 2% minority. **Class size:** 52% < 20, 48% 20-39, less than 1% 50-99. **Special facilities:** Natural history institute.

**Student profile.** Among degree-seeking undergraduates, 71% enrolled in a transfer program, 29% enrolled in a vocational program, 881 enrolled as first-time, first-year students.

| | | | |
|---|---|---|---|
| Part-time: | 23% | Asian American: | 1% |
| Out-of-state: | 8% | Hispanic American: | 3% |
| Women: | 57% | Native American: | 1% |
| African American: | 3% | 25 or older: | 26% |

**Transfer out. Colleges most students transferred to 2007:** SUNY Fredonia, St. Bonaventure University, SUNY College at Buffalo, Houghton College.

**Basis for selection.** Open admission, but selective for some programs. Preference given to area students in highly subscribed programs. Competitive admission to nursing, occupational therapy assistant, with school achievement record very important. ACT and ASSET scores used for placement.

**2007-2008 Annual costs.** Tuition/fees: $3,800; $7,150 out-of-state. Per-credit charge: $140 in-state; $253 out-of-state. Books/supplies: $820. Personal expenses: $600.

**Financial aid. Need-based:** Need-based aid available for part-time students. Work-study available nights, weekends and for part-time students. **Non-need-based:** Scholarships awarded for academics, alumni affiliation, art, athletics, music/drama, state residency. **Additional information:** 100% resident tuition scholarship (less federal and state grants) for students in top 20% of high school graduating class with Regents diploma if residents of Chautauqua, Cattaraugus, or Allegany counties. Guaranteed in-state tuition rate for students in Warren, Potter, McKean and Forest counties in Pennsylvania, in top 20% of graduating class with an academic diploma.

**Application procedures. Admission:** No deadline. $40 fee, may be waived for applicants with need. Application may be submitted online. Admission notification on a rolling basis. Must reply by May 1 or within 2 week(s) if notified thereafter. **Financial aid:** Priority date 3/1; no closing date. FAFSA required. Applicants notified on a rolling basis starting 4/15.

**Academics.** Strong liberal arts tradition, with a balance between transfer and career-oriented programs. **Special study options:** Cross-registration, distance learning, dual enrollment of high school students, honors, independent study, internships, liberal arts/career combination, study abroad, Washington semester, weekend college. License preparation in nursing. **Credit/placement by examination:** AP, CLEP, institutional tests. 36 credit hours maximum toward associate degree. **Support services:** Learning center, pre-admission summer program, reduced course load, remedial instruction, study skills assistance, tutoring.

**Majors. Business:** Accounting technology, banking/financial services, business admin, marketing, office management. **Computer sciences:** Data processing, programming. **Conservation:** Forestry. **Engineering:** General. **Engineering technology:** Electrical, mechanical. **Health:** Clinical lab technology, nursing (RN), occupational therapy assistant. **Liberal arts:** Arts/sciences, humanities. **Mechanic/repair:** Small engine. **Protective services:** Criminal justice, police science. **Public administration:** Human services. **Social sciences:** General. **Transportation:** Airline/commercial pilot. **Visual/performing arts:** Studio arts.

**Most popular majors.** Business/marketing 12%, health sciences 17%, liberal arts 25%, mathematics 7%, security/protective services 9%, social sciences 14%.

**Computing on campus.** 800 workstations in library, computer center, student center. Dormitories wired for high-speed internet access and linked to campus network. Commuter students can connect to campus network. Online course registration, online library, wireless network available.

**Student life. Freshman orientation:** Mandatory. **Housing:** $200 nonrefundable deposit, deadline 3/8. Coed housing available. **Activities:** Bands, choral groups, dance, drama, music ensembles, musical theater, radio station, student government, Earth Awareness, InterVarsity Christian Fellowship, Early Childhood Educators, Political Awareness, nursing club, humanities club, criminal justice club.

**Athletics.** NJCAA. **Intercollegiate:** Baseball M, basketball, cross-country, diving, golf, soccer, softball W, swimming, volleyball W, wrestling M. **Intramural:** Basketball, bowling, softball, table tennis, tennis, volleyball. **Team name:** Jayhawks.

**Student services.** Adult student services, alcohol/substance abuse counseling, career counseling, services for economically disadvantaged, student employment services, financial aid counseling, health services, personal counseling, placement for graduates, veterans' counselor. **Physically disabled:** Services for visually, speech, hearing impaired. **Transfer:** Transfer adviser, college fairs on campus for students transferring to 4-year colleges.

**Contact.** E-mail: admissions@mail.sunyjcc.edu
Phone: (716) 665-5220 ext. 1001 Toll-free number: (800) 388-8557
Fax: (716) 338-1450
Wendy Present, Director, Admissions and Recruitment, Jamestown Community College, 525 Falconer Street, Jamestown, NY 14702-0020

## Jefferson Community College
**Watertown, New York**
www.sunyjefferson.edu **CB code: 2345**

- Public 2-year community college
- Commuter campus in large town

**General.** Founded in 1961. Regionally accredited. **Enrollment:** 2,439 degree-seeking undergraduates; 752 non-degree-seeking students. **Degrees:** 531 associate awarded. **Location:** 70 miles from Syracuse. **Calendar:** Semester, limited summer session. **Full-time faculty:** 74 total. **Part-time faculty:** 90 total.

**Student profile.** Among degree-seeking undergraduates, 839 enrolled as first-time, first-year students.

| | | | |
|---|---|---|---|
| Part-time: | 29% | Women: | 63% |
| Out-of-state: | 1% | 25 or older: | 37% |

**Transfer out. Colleges most students transferred to 2007:** SUNY Empire State College, SUNY Oswego, SUNY Potsdam.

**Basis for selection.** Open admission, but selective for some programs. Admission to some programs based on grades, class rank, test scores, school recommendation, personal interview. Waiting list available for nursing program. Interview recommended for engineering science, nursing programs.

**High school preparation.** Strong background in math and science required for engineering science, computer science, nursing, and science laboratory technologies programs.

**2007-2008 Annual costs.** Tuition/fees: $3,479; $5,989 out-of-state. Per-credit charge: $128 in-state; $233 out-of-state. Books/supplies: $1,150. Personal expenses: $936.

**Financial aid.** All financial aid based on need. Need-based aid available for part-time students. Work-study available for part-time students.

**Application procedures. Admission:** No deadline. No application fee. Admission notification on a rolling basis. **Financial aid:** Priority date 4/1,

closing date 8/15. FAFSA, institutional form required. Applicants notified on a rolling basis starting 4/15; must reply within 2 week(s) of notification.

**Academics.** Students in engineering science, computer science, and computer information systems programs required to purchase or lease microcomputers. **Special study options:** Cooperative education, distance learning, double major, dual enrollment of high school students, honors, independent study, internships, student-designed major, weekend college. Bachelor's degree programs available on campus. **Credit/placement by examination:** AP, CLEP, IB, institutional tests. 30 credit hours maximum toward associate degree. **Support services:** Learning center, reduced course load, remedial instruction, study skills assistance, tutoring.

**Majors. Business:** Accounting, business admin, office management, office technology, sales/distribution, tourism promotion, tourism/travel. **Computer sciences:** General, computer science, information systems. **Education:** Early childhood, elementary. **Engineering:** Science. **Health:** EMT paramedic, nursing (RN). **Legal studies:** Paralegal. **Liberal arts:** Arts/sciences. **Math:** General. **Protective services:** Law enforcement admin. **Public administration:** Human services.

**Most popular majors.** Business/marketing 17%, health sciences 6%, liberal arts 52%, security/protective services 11%.

**Computing on campus.** 354 workstations in library, computer center, student center. Online library available.

**Student life. Freshman orientation:** Available. Half-day program held in August and January. **Housing:** Privately owned apartments available. **Activities:** Bands, choral groups, drama, literary magazine, music ensembles, student government, student newspaper, veterans club, multicultural club, human services club, environmental club, European excursion club, business club, office technology association, political clubs, Brothers and Sisters in Christ.

**Athletics.** NJCAA. **Intercollegiate:** Baseball M, basketball, golf, lacrosse, soccer, softball W, tennis W, volleyball W. **Intramural:** Badminton, basketball, soccer, softball, volleyball. **Team name:** Cannoneers.

**Student services.** Adult student services, campus ministries, career counseling, student employment services, financial aid counseling, health services, on-campus daycare, personal counseling, placement for graduates, veterans' counselor. **Physically disabled:** Services for visually, speech, hearing impaired. **Transfer:** Transfer adviser, college fairs on campus for students transferring to 4-year colleges.

**Contact.** E-mail: admissions@sunyjefferson.edu
Phone: (315) 786-2277 Fax: (315) 786-2459
Rosanne Weir, Director of Admissions, Jefferson Community College, 1220 Coffeen Street, Watertown, NY 13601

## Katharine Gibbs School: Melville
**Melville, New York**
www.gibbslongisland.com **CB code: 1039**

- For-profit 2-year junior college
- Small town

**General.** Founded in 1911. Accredited by ACICS. **Location:** 40 miles from New York City. **Calendar:** Quarter.

**Annual costs/financial aid.** Costs vary by program. Typical associate degree program cost: $26,970. Books/supplies: $700.

**Contact.** Phone: (631) 370-3300
Director of Admissions, 320 South Service Road, Melville, NY 11747

## Long Island Business Institute
**Commack, New York**
www.libi.edu **CB code: 3334**

- For-profit 2-year business college
- Commuter campus in large town
- Application essay, interview required

**General.** Accredited by ACICS. Branch campus located in Flushing, NY. **Enrollment:** 610 degree-seeking undergraduates; 9 non-degree-seeking students. **Degrees:** 180 associate awarded. **Calendar:** Semester, extensive summer session. **Full-time faculty:** 18 total; 6% have terminal degrees, 50% minority, 67% women. **Part-time faculty:** 77 total; 6% have terminal degrees, 44% minority, 61% women. **Class size:** 75% < 20, 25% 20-39.

**Student profile.** Among degree-seeking undergraduates, 100% enrolled in a vocational program, 137 enrolled as first-time, first-year students, 13 transferred in from other institutions.

| | | | |
|---|---|---|---|
| Part-time: | 37% | Hispanic American: | 21% |
| Women: | 79% | International: | 3% |
| African American: | 8% | 25 or older: | 68% |
| Asian American: | 31% | | |

**Transfer out. Colleges most students transferred to 2007:** St. Joseph's College, Mercy College, Briarcliffe College.

**Basis for selection.** Open admission, but selective for some programs. Prospective students should demonstrate an understanding and interest in a program of study through an admissions interview. **Adult students:** SAT/ACT scores not required. **Homeschooled:** State high school equivalency certificate required. **Learning Disabled:** Students must provide to the designated campus professional a recent, appropriate evaluation from a licensed medical professional familiar with the disability, and make a follow-up appointment to discuss accommodations.

**2008-2009 Annual costs.** Tuition/fees (projected): $10,125. Per-credit charge: $325. Tuition varies by program. Books/supplies: $700. Personal expenses: $1,750.

**2007-2008 Financial aid. Need-based:** 98 full-time freshmen applied for aid; 98 were judged to have need; 98 of these received aid. Average need met was 84%. Average scholarship/grant was $3,300; average loan $2,800. 74% of total undergraduate aid awarded as scholarships/grants, 26% as loans/jobs. Need-based aid available for part-time students. Work-study available nights and for part-time students. **Non-need-based:** Scholarships awarded for academics.

**Application procedures. Admission:** No deadline. $50 fee. Admission notification on a rolling basis. **Financial aid:** No deadline. FAFSA required. Must reply within 2 week(s) of notification.

**Academics. Special study options:** ESL, independent study, internships. **Credit/placement by examination:** AP, CLEP, institutional tests. Limited to 50% of specific curriculum total credit hours. **Support services:** Learning center, remedial instruction, tutoring.

**Majors. Business:** Accounting, business admin, office management. **Health:** Medical secretary. **Legal studies:** Court reporting.

**Most popular majors.** Business/marketing 83%, legal studies 16%.

**Computing on campus.** 275 workstations in library, computer center. Online library, wireless network available.

**Student life. Freshman orientation:** Mandatory. Held 2 days prior to each semester start and lasts approximately 4 hours. **Activities:** Student newspaper.

**Student services.** Career counseling, student employment services, financial aid counseling, placement for graduates. **Transfer:** Pre-admission transcript evaluation for new students.

**Contact.** E-mail: admissions@libi.edu
Phone: (631) 499-7100 Fax: (631) 499-7114
Robert Nazar, Director of Admissions, Long Island Business Institute, 6500 Jericho Turnpike, Commack, NY 11725

## Long Island Business Institute: Flushing
**Flushing, New York**
www.libi.edu

- For-profit 2-year business college
- Commuter campus in very large city

**General.** Accredited by ACICS. **Calendar:** Semester.

**Annual costs/financial aid.** Tuition/fees (2007-2008): $10,125. Books/supplies: $400. Need-based financial aid available to full-time and part-time students.

**Contact.** Phone: (718) 939-5100
Director of Admissions, 37-12 Prince Street, Flushing, NY 11354

## Long Island College Hospital School of Nursing
**Brooklyn, New York**
www.futurenurselich.org   CB code: 2377

- Private 2-year nursing college
- Commuter campus in very large city
- Application essay, interview required

**General.** Founded in 1883. Liberal arts courses taken at St. Francis College. **Enrollment:** 172 degree-seeking undergraduates. **Degrees:** 61 associate awarded. **Calendar:** Semester, limited summer session. **Full-time faculty:** 8 total; 100% have terminal degrees, 50% minority, 88% women. **Part-time faculty:** 13 total; 100% have terminal degrees, 38% minority, 100% women. **Class size:** 20% 20-39, 80% 50-99. **Special facilities:** Computer-assisted learning laboratory featuring interactive videodisc technology.

**Student profile.** Among degree-seeking undergraduates, 99% enrolled in a transfer program, 22% already have a bachelor's degree or higher, 1 enrolled as first-time, first-year students, 81 transferred in from other institutions.

| | | | |
|---|---|---|---|
| Part-time: | 59% | Asian American: | 6% |
| Women: | 84% | Hispanic American: | 11% |
| African American: | 56% | | |

**Transfer out.** 95% of students enrolled in the transfer program go on to 4-year colleges.

**Basis for selection.** National League for Nursing RN pre-entrance exam score, high school achievement record, college GPA, 2 references, essay considered together. Selected students interviewed. Final decision made by Academic Standing Committee. **Adult students:** National League for Nursing RN pre-entrance exam. **Homeschooled:** Statement describing homeschool structure and mission, transcript of courses and grades, state high school equivalency certificate, interview, letter of recommendation (nonparent) required. National League for Nursing examination.

**High school preparation.** 19 units recommended. Recommended units include English 4, mathematics 3, social studies 3, history 2, science 2, foreign language 3 and academic electives 2.

**2007-2008 Annual costs.** Tuition/fees: $14,100. Freshmen typically take a combination of nursing courses at $300 per credit hour and liberal arts and sciences courses at $360 per credit hour. Books/supplies: $1,100. Personal expenses: $1,863.

**Application procedures. Admission:** Closing date 4/21 (postmark date). $50 fee. Application must be submitted on paper. Admission notification on a rolling basis beginning on or about 6/1. Must reply by May 1 or within 7 week(s) if notified thereafter. **Financial aid:** Priority date 6/1; no closing date. FAFSA required. Must reply within 2 week(s) of notification.

**Academics. Special study options:** Combined bachelor's/graduate degree, cooperative education, internships. License preparation in nursing. **Credit/placement by examination:** AP, CLEP. **Support services:** Learning center, remedial instruction, tutoring.

**Majors. Health:** Nursing (RN).

**Computing on campus.** 15 workstations in library, computer center, student center.

**Student life. Freshman orientation:** Mandatory. 2 orientations: general orientation and clinical orientation held beginning of first semester. **Housing:** Substance-free housing available. **Activities:** Student government, student newspaper.

**Student services.** Financial aid counseling, health services. **Transfer:** Pre-admission transcript evaluation for new students.

**Contact.** E-mail: mkarpovi@chpnet.org
Phone: (718) 780-1071 Fax: (718) 780-1936
Marina Karpovitch, Manager of Student Services, Long Island College Hospital School of Nursing, 350 Henry Street, 7th Floor, Brooklyn, NY 11201

## Maria College
**Albany, New York**
www.mariacollege.edu   CB member   CB code: 2434

- Private 2-year junior college
- Commuter campus in small city
- SAT or ACT (ACT writing optional), application essay, interview required

**General.** Founded in 1958. Regionally accredited. **Enrollment:** 719 degree-seeking undergraduates; 31 non-degree-seeking students. **Degrees:** 136 associate awarded. **ROTC:** Army, Naval, Air Force. **Location:** 150 miles from New York City and Boston. **Calendar:** Semester, limited summer session. **Full-time faculty:** 31 total; 16% have terminal degrees, 87% women. **Part-time faculty:** 33 total; 15% have terminal degrees, 58% women. **Class size:** 79% < 20, 15% 20-39, less than 1% 40-49, 6% 50-99.

**Student profile.** Among degree-seeking undergraduates, 37% enrolled in a transfer program, 63% enrolled in a vocational program, 8% already have a bachelor's degree or higher, 102 enrolled as first-time, first-year students, 123 transferred in from other institutions.

| | | | |
|---|---|---|---|
| Part-time: | 73% | Asian American: | 3% |
| Out-of-state: | 5% | Hispanic American: | 3% |
| Women: | 88% | Native American: | 2% |
| African American: | 20% | | |

**Transfer out.** 38% of students enrolled in the transfer program go on to 4-year colleges. **Colleges most students transferred to 2007:** College of Saint Rose, State University at Albany, Hudson Valley Community College, The Sage Colleges, Schenectady County Community College.

**Basis for selection.** School achievement record, test scores, interviews, recommendations important. Test required for students with scores on SAT Verbal less than 480, Math less than 490, or ACT Composite less than 19. Dual interview required for Nursing (ADN) and Occupational Therapy Assistant. **Adult students:** SAT/ACT scores not required. Applicants who did not take SAT or ACT may be required to take an admissions test, which may be waived based on prior college credit. **Homeschooled:** Transcript of courses and grades, state high school equivalency certificate, interview, letter of recommendation (nonparent) required. SAT or ACT scores or applicant must take College admissions test for placement purposes. **Learning Disabled:** Must provide documentation regarding specific diagnosis and services/accommodations being requested. Documentation must be within 3 years of acceptance. Must meet with the Dean of Student Services for coordination of support services.

**High school preparation.** 21 units required. Required and recommended units include English 4, mathematics 2-3, social studies 4, science 2-3 (laboratory 3). Requirements vary with program.

**2007-2008 Annual costs.** Tuition/fees: $8,400. Per-credit charge: $295. Books/supplies: $600. Personal expenses: $500.

**2007-2008 Financial aid.** All financial aid based on need. 52 full-time freshmen applied for aid; 49 were judged to have need; 49 of these received aid. Average need met was 89%. Average scholarship/grant was $4,864; average loan $2,425. 43% of total undergraduate aid awarded as scholarships/grants, 57% as loans/jobs. Need-based aid available for part-time students. Work-study available nights, weekends and for part-time students.

**Application procedures. Admission:** Priority date 8/11; deadline 8/24 (receipt date). $35 fee, may be waived for applicants with need. Application must be submitted on paper. Admission notification on a rolling basis. Must reply by May 1 or within 4 week(s) if notified thereafter. Tuition deposit deadline 30 days after acceptance. High school seniors have until May 1. **Financial aid:** No deadline. FAFSA required. Applicants notified on a rolling basis starting 2/1; must reply within 2 week(s) of notification.

**Academics. Special study options:** Accelerated study, cross-registration, distance learning, dual enrollment of high school students, independent study, internships, liberal arts/career combination, weekend college. Advanced placement program in nursing for licensed practical nurse and New York State LPN to ADN Nursing Bridge Course. License preparation in nursing, occupational therapy. **Credit/placement by examination:** AP, CLEP, IB, SAT, ACT, institutional tests. 16 credit hours maximum toward associate degree. **Support services:** Learning center, pre-admission summer program, reduced course load, remedial instruction, study skills assistance, tutoring.

**Majors. Business:** General, accounting, business admin. **Computer sciences:** General. **Education:** Early childhood, teacher assistance. **Health:** Nursing (RN), occupational therapy assistant. **Legal studies:** Paralegal. **Liberal arts:** Arts/sciences. **Science technology:** Biological.

**Most popular majors.** Education 7%, health sciences 76%, liberal arts 11%.

**Computing on campus.** 72 workstations in library, computer center. Commuter students can connect to campus network. Online course registration, online library, wireless network available.

**Student life. Freshman orientation:** Mandatory. Preregistration for classes offered. Held one day prior to the beginning of the semester.

**Student services.** Adult student services, alcohol/substance abuse counseling, campus ministries, career counseling, student employment services, financial aid counseling, personal counseling, placement for graduates. **Physically disabled:** Services for visually impaired. **Transfer:** Re-entry adviser, pre-admission transcript evaluation for new students. Transfer adviser, college fairs on campus for students transferring to 4-year colleges.

**Contact.** E-mail: laurieg@mariacollege.edu
Phone: (518) 438-3111 ext. 217 Fax: (518) 453-1366
Laurie Gilmore, Director of Admissions, Maria College, 700 New Scotland Avenue, Albany, NY 12208

## Mildred Elley
Latham, New York
www.mildred-elley.edu
CB code: 3335

- For-profit 2-year business college
- Commuter campus in very large city

**General.** Accredited by ACICS. **Enrollment:** 409 degree-seeking undergraduates. **Degrees:** 93 associate awarded. **Location:** 10 miles from Albany. **Calendar:** Semester, extensive summer session. **Full-time faculty:** 30 total. **Part-time faculty:** 18 total. **Class size:** 92% < 20, 8% 20-39.

**Basis for selection.** Open admission.

**2007-2008 Annual costs.** Tuition/fees: $9,900. Per-credit charge: $338.

**Financial aid.** All financial aid based on need. Need-based aid available for part-time students. Work-study available nights and for part-time students.

**Application procedures. Admission:** No deadline. $25 fee, may be waived for applicants with need. Admission notification on a rolling basis. **Financial aid:** No deadline. FAFSA required.

**Academics. Special study options:** Cooperative education, double major, independent study, internships. **Credit/placement by examination:** CLEP, institutional tests. **Support services:** GED preparation and test center, learning center, remedial instruction, study skills assistance, tutoring, writing center.

**Majors. Business:** Business admin. **Computer sciences:** General, information systems. **Health:** Massage therapy, medical assistant. **Legal studies:** General, paralegal.

**Most popular majors.** Business/marketing 38%, computer/information sciences 22%, health sciences 21%, legal studies 20%.

**Computing on campus.** Repair service available.

**Student life. Freshman orientation:** Mandatory. Preregistration for classes offered. **Activities:** Drama, student government.

**Student services.** Adult student services, alcohol/substance abuse counseling, career counseling, financial aid counseling, legal services, personal counseling, placement for graduates, veterans' counselor, women's services. **Transfer:** College fairs on campus for students transferring to 4-year colleges.

**Contact.** E-mail: admissions@mildred-elley.edu
Phone: (518) 786-3171 Toll-free number: (800) 622-6327
Fax: (518) 786-0011
George Chakmakas, Admissions Director, Mildred Elley, 800 New Loudon Road, Suite 5120, Latham, NY 12110

## Mohawk Valley Community College
Utica, New York
www.mvcc.edu
CB code: 2414

- Public 2-year community college
- Commuter campus in small city

**General.** Founded in 1946. Regionally accredited. SUNY institution. Branch campus in Rome, New York. **Enrollment:** 4,635 degree-seeking undergraduates; 1,409 non-degree-seeking students. **Degrees:** 727 associate awarded. **ROTC:** Army. **Location:** 55 miles from Syracuse, 95 miles from Albany. **Calendar:** Semester, limited summer session. **Full-time faculty:** 136 total; 7% minority, 38% women. **Part-time faculty:** 236 total; 2% minority, 52% women. **Class size:** 53% < 20, 43% 20-39, 3% 40-49, 1% 50-99. **Special facilities:** Gourmet dining room, human cadaver lab. **Partnerships:** Formal partnership with Verizon for NEXT STEP, a virtual university program for Verizon employees to earn an associate in telecommunications.

**Student profile.** Among degree-seeking undergraduates, 43% enrolled in a transfer program, 57% enrolled in a vocational program, 1,467 enrolled as first-time, first-year students, 213 transferred in from other institutions.

| | | | |
|---|---|---|---|
| Part-time: | 20% | Hispanic American: | 4% |
| Out-of-state: | 1% | Native American: | 1% |
| Women: | 53% | International: | 1% |
| African American: | 6% | 25 or older: | 23% |
| Asian American: | 2% | Live on campus: | 8% |

**Transfer out.** 82% of students enrolled in the transfer program go on to 4-year colleges. **Colleges most students transferred to 2007:** SUNY Institute of Technology (Utica/Rome), Utica College, SUNY College at Oneonta, SUNY College at Oswego, SUNY Albany.

**Basis for selection.** Open admission, but selective for some programs. Applicants' records reviewed for completion of program-specific prerequisites to determine regular or underprepared acceptance to program. Interview recommended for all, required for Airframe & Powerplant Tech applicants. **Homeschooled:** State high school equivalency certificate required. Must pass ability-to-benefit test prior to acceptance. **Learning Disabled:** Learning-disabled applicants should forward copy of IEP to Coordinator of Disabilities Services.

**High school preparation.** Requirements vary for admission to nursing and certain other programs.

**2007-2008 Annual costs.** Tuition/fees: $3,554; $6,704 out-of-state. Per-credit charge: $120 in-state; $240 out-of-state. Room/board: $7,150. Books/supplies: $1,350. Personal expenses: $820.

**Financial aid. Need-based:** Need-based aid available for part-time students. Work-study available nights, weekends and for part-time students.

**Application procedures. Admission:** No deadline. No application fee. Application must be submitted on paper. Admission notification on a rolling basis beginning on or about 12/1. Within 30 days of date of acceptance due to limited housing availability on campus. **Financial aid:** Priority date 4/15; no closing date. FAFSA, institutional form required. Applicants notified on a rolling basis starting 3/1; must reply within 2 week(s) of notification.

**Academics. Special study options:** Cross-registration, distance learning, double major, dual enrollment of high school students, ESL, honors, independent study, internships, student-designed major. Bachelor's degree programs available on campus. License preparation in nursing. **Credit/placement by examination:** AP, CLEP, institutional tests. 45 credit hours maximum toward associate degree. Each department has its own policy. **Support services:** Learning center, reduced course load, remedial instruction, study skills assistance, tutoring, writing center.

**Majors. Business:** Accounting technology, administrative services, banking/financial services, business admin, entrepreneurial studies, hotel/motel admin. **Communications:** Advertising. **Computer sciences:** General, programming, webmaster. **Construction:** Maintenance. **Education:** Elementary, secondary. **Engineering:** General. **Engineering technology:** Civil, drafting, electrical, heat/ac/refrig, mechanical, surveying. **Family/consumer sciences:** Institutional food production. **Health:** EMT paramedic, medical assistant, medical radiologic technology/radiation therapy, medical records technology, nursing (RN), respiratory therapy technology, substance abuse counseling. **Interdisciplinary:** Nutrition sciences. **Liberal arts:** Arts/sciences, humanities. **Mechanic/repair:** Aircraft, communications systems. **Parks/recreation:** Facilities management. **Personal/culinary services:** Restaurant/catering. **Production:** Welding. **Protective services:** Law enforcement admin. **Public administration:** General, community org/advocacy. **Science technology:** Chemical. **Visual/performing arts:** Art, commercial photography, commercial/advertising art, digital art, dramatic. **Other:** Liberal arts and sciences/Psychology, Semiconductor manufacturing technology.

**Most popular majors.** Business/marketing 15%, engineering/engineering technologies 8%, health sciences 13%, liberal arts 34%, security/protective services 8%, visual/performing arts 8%.

**Computing on campus.** 94 workstations in library, computer center. Dormitories wired for high-speed internet access. Commuter students can connect to campus network. Online course registration, online library, helpline, wireless network available.

**Student life. Freshman orientation:** Mandatory, $40 fee. Preregistration for classes offered. Two-hour commuter orientation and 3-day dorm student orientation in January and August. **Housing:** Coed dorms, special housing for disabled, cooperative housing, substance-free housing available. $100 deposit. All halls nonsmoking; 1 residence hall has extended quiet hours. Limited visitation suites available. On-campus housing is on first-come, first-served basis. **Activities:** Bands, drama, film society, international student organizations, music ensembles, musical theater, student government, student newspaper, black student union, international club, Latino student union,

Catch the Spirit Bible Club, student nurses association, Kidz-N-Coaches, women's association, Phi Theta Kappa, returning adult student association.

**Athletics.** NJCAA. **Intercollegiate:** Baseball M, basketball, bowling, cross-country, golf, ice hockey M, lacrosse M, soccer, softball W, tennis, track and field, volleyball W. **Intramural:** Basketball, football (non-tackle), racquetball, softball, tennis, volleyball, weight lifting. **Team name:** Hawks.

**Student services.** Adult student services, alcohol/substance abuse counseling, campus ministries, career counseling, student employment services, financial aid counseling, health services, on-campus daycare, personal counseling, placement for graduates, veterans' counselor. **Physically disabled:** Services for visually, speech, hearing impaired. **Transfer:** Pre-admission transcript evaluation for new students. Transfer center, transfer adviser, college fairs on campus for students transferring to 4-year colleges.

**Contact.** E-mail: admissions@mvcc.edu
Phone: (315) 792-5354 Toll-free number: (800) 733-6822
Fax: (315) 792-5527
Denis Kennelty, Assistant Dean for Enrollment Management, Mohawk Valley Community College, 1101 Sherman Drive, Utica, NY 13501-5394

---

## Monroe Community College
**Rochester, New York**
www.monroecc.edu

**CB member**
**CB code: 2429**

- Public 2-year community college
- Commuter campus in large city

**General.** Founded in 1961. Regionally accredited. SUNY institution. Off-campus extension centers in 2 area high schools, branch campus in downtown Rochester. Applied technology center. **Enrollment:** 15,663 degree-seeking undergraduates. **Degrees:** 2,430 associate awarded. **ROTC:** Army, Naval, Air Force. **Location:** 4 miles from downtown. **Calendar:** Semester, limited summer session. **Full-time faculty:** 308 total. **Part-time faculty:** 547 total. **Class size:** 35% < 20, 59% 20-39, 4% 40-49, 2% 50-99, less than 1% >100. **Special facilities:** Human ecology habitat, human performance laboratory, electronic learning center. **Partnerships:** Design specific programs and offer courses for Xerox, Kodak, Frontier, Wegman's.

**Student profile.**

| | | | |
|---|---|---|---|
| Out-of-state: | 1% | Live on campus: | 2% |
| 25 or older: | 34% | | |

**Basis for selection.** Open admission, but selective for some programs. Admissions to certain programs based on high school records, with preference given to county residents. Applicants to engineering and computer science must have precalculus, chemistry and physics. **Homeschooled:** Must meet Federal Ability to Benefit guidelines on placement exam if not issued a regular high school diploma.

**High school preparation.** Recommended units include English 4, mathematics 4, social studies 4 and science 4. Individual programs have specific math and science requirements.

**2007-2008 Annual costs.** Tuition/fees: $3,190; $5,990 out-of-state. Per-credit charge: $117 in-state; $234 out-of-state. Room only: $5,290. Books/supplies: $450.

**Financial aid.** All financial aid based on need. Need-based aid available for part-time students. Work-study available nights.

**Application procedures. Admission:** Priority date 3/1; no deadline. $20 fee, may be waived for applicants with need. Application may be submitted online. Admission notification on a rolling basis. Application deadline for healthcare programs: 1/31 for fall term, 10/31 for spring term. Applicants to nursing program are encouraged to apply 1 year prior to registration. **Financial aid:** No deadline. FAFSA required. Applicants notified on a rolling basis; must reply within 2 week(s) of notification.

**Academics. Special study options:** Accelerated study, cooperative education, cross-registration, distance learning, dual enrollment of high school students, ESL, exchange student, honors, independent study, internships, liberal arts/career combination, weekend college. License preparation in aviation, dental hygiene, nursing, paramedic, radiology. **Credit/placement by examination:** AP, CLEP, institutional tests. 30 credit hours maximum toward associate degree. **Support services:** Learning center, pre-admission summer program, reduced course load, remedial instruction, study skills assistance, tutoring, writing center.

**Majors. Architecture:** Landscape. **Biology:** General. **Business:** General, accounting, administrative services, international, marketing, sales/distribution, tourism promotion, tourism/travel. **Communications:** General, advertising. **Communications technology:** General. **Computer sciences:** General, computer science. **Construction:** General. **Education:** Music. **Engineering:** Science. **Engineering technology:** Civil, construction, electrical, manufacturing. **Health:** Dental hygiene, medical records technology, nursing (RN), physics/radiologic health. **History:** General. **Liberal arts:** Arts/sciences. **Math:** General. **Mechanic/repair:** Automotive, heating/ac/refrig. **Parks/recreation:** Health/fitness. **Personal/culinary services:** Culinary arts. **Physical sciences:** Chemistry, optics, physics. **Protective services:** Corrections, criminal justice, fire safety technology, police science. **Public administration:** Human services. **Science technology:** Biological. **Social sciences:** General, political science. **Visual/performing arts:** Commercial/advertising art, interior design, music performance, photography, studio arts.

**Computing on campus.** 150 workstations in library, computer center, student center. Dormitories wired for high-speed internet access and linked to campus network. Commuter students can connect to campus network. Helpline available.

**Student life. Freshman orientation:** Mandatory. Orientation held 1 week prior to beginning of semester. **Housing:** Coed dorms available. **Activities:** Bands, choral groups, drama, literary magazine, musical theater, radio station, student government, student newspaper, symphony orchestra, Christian, Jewish, and Christian Science groups; Latin American, Italian-American, black, and international student organizations; veterans and handicapped student clubs; honor society.

**Athletics.** NJCAA. **Intercollegiate:** Baseball M, basketball, diving, golf M, ice hockey M, lacrosse M, soccer, softball W, swimming, tennis, volleyball W. **Intramural:** Archery, basketball, bowling, cheerleading W, cross-country, diving, lacrosse, racquetball, rugby M, skiing, soccer, softball, swimming, tennis, volleyball, water polo M. **Team name:** Tribunes.

**Student services.** Adult student services, career counseling, student employment services, financial aid counseling, health services, on-campus daycare, personal counseling, placement for graduates, veterans' counselor. **Physically disabled:** Services for visually, hearing impaired. **Transfer:** Transfer center, transfer adviser, college fairs on campus for students transferring to 4-year colleges.

**Contact.** Phone: (585) 292-2200 Fax: (585) 292-3680
Andrew Freeman, Director of Admissions, Monroe Community College, Office of Admissions-Monroe Community College, Rochester, NY 14692-8908

---

## Nassau Community College

**Garden City, New York**
**www.ncc.edu**

CB member
CB code: 2563

▶ Public 2-year community college
▶ Commuter campus in large town

**General.** Founded in 1959. Regionally accredited. SUNY institution. Students may attend some courses at off-campus locations. Partnerships with local businesses and industry to provide on-site training to employees. **Enrollment:** 19,872 degree-seeking undergraduates; 1,611 non-degree-seeking students. **Degrees:** 2,722 associate awarded. **ROTC:** Army. **Location:** 25 miles from New York City. **Calendar:** Semester, extensive summer session. **Full-time faculty:** 557 total; 33% have terminal degrees, 14% minority, 57% women. **Part-time faculty:** 901 total; 20% have terminal degrees, 15% minority, 44% women. **Class size:** 100% 20-39.

**Student profile.** Among degree-seeking undergraduates, 5,513 enrolled as first-time, first-year students, 2,212 transferred in from other institutions.

| Part-time: | 29% | Women: | 51% |
|---|---|---|---|

**Transfer out.** 65% of students enrolled in the transfer program go on to 4-year colleges. **Colleges most students transferred to 2007:** Hofstra University, Adelphi University, SUNY Old Westbury, SUNY Stony Brook, Dowling College.

**Basis for selection.** Open admission, but selective for some programs. Class rank and fulfillment of mathematics and science requirements important for admission to accounting, business, engineering, nursing, allied health, mortuary science, civil technology, computer information systems, computer science, electrical technology, paralegal, and telecommunications technology programs. Students without high school diploma or equivalent may apply for GED after successful completion of 24 college credits. SAT scores may result in exemption from placement testing. Interview required for allied health programs; audition required for music program; portfolio review required for fashion apparel design program. **Adult students:** Placement test in reading, English, and math required unless applicant has prior associate's or bachelor's degree or prior college credit for English composition and college-level math. **Homeschooled:** Transcript of courses and grades

required. **Learning Disabled:** Students must submit a copy of their I.E.P. in order to get services through our Center for Students with Disabilities.

**High school preparation.** Recommended units include English 4, mathematics 4, social studies 4, science 4 (laboratory 4), foreign language 3 and academic electives 4.

**2007-2008 Annual costs.** Tuition/fees: $3,574; $6,864 out-of-state. Per-credit charge: $138 in-state; $276 out-of-state. Books/supplies: $1,040. Personal expenses: $1,440.

**2006-2007 Financial aid. Need-based:** 3,683 full-time freshmen applied for aid; 2,765 were judged to have need; 2,425 of these received aid. Average need met was 80%. Average scholarship/grant was $854; average loan $2,294. 82% of total undergraduate aid awarded as scholarships/grants, 18% as loans/jobs. Need-based aid available for part-time students. Work-study available nights, weekends and for part-time students. **Non-need-based:** Awarded to 3,572 full-time undergraduates, including 1,917 freshmen. Scholarships awarded for academics, minority status.

**Application procedures. Admission:** Closing date 8/11 (receipt date). $40 fee. Application may be submitted online. Admission notification on a rolling basis beginning on or about 11/15. **Financial aid:** Priority date 6/7; no closing date. FAFSA required. Applicants notified on a rolling basis; must reply within 1 week(s) of notification.

**Academics. Special study options:** Cooperative education, cross-registration, distance learning, ESL, honors, internships, study abroad, weekend college. Cooperative programs with SUNY College of Technology at Utica-Rome and SUNY at New Paltz, New York State Chiropractic College, Fashion Institute of Technology, Adelphi University; joint admissions with SUNY at Stony Brook and SUNY College at Old Westbury. License preparation in nursing, physical therapy, radiology, real estate. **Credit/placement by examination:** AP, CLEP, IB, institutional tests. 33 credit hours maximum toward associate degree. **Support services:** GED preparation and test center, learning center, reduced course load, remedial instruction, study skills assistance, tutoring, writing center.

**Honors college/program.** Honors applicants must rank in the top 20% of their graduating class and have 3 years of Regents math, English, science and high grades in each.

**Majors. Area/ethnic studies:** African. **Business:** Accounting, administrative services, business admin, fashion, management information systems, sales/distribution. **Communications:** General. **Computer sciences:** General, computer science, programming. **Education:** Early childhood, elementary, middle, secondary. **Engineering:** General. **Engineering technology:** Civil, computer systems, electrical. **Family/consumer sciences:** Food/nutrition. **Health:** Clinical lab science, medical radiologic technology/radiation therapy, medical secretary, nursing (RN), physical therapy assistant, respiratory therapy technology, surgical technology. **Legal studies:** Legal secretary, paralegal. **Liberal arts:** Arts/sciences. **Math:** General. **Personal/culinary services:** Embalming, food service, mortuary science, restaurant/catering. **Protective services:** Law enforcement admin. **Visual/performing arts:** Art, commercial/advertising art, digital art, graphic design, interior design, music performance, photography. **Other:** American Sign Language, Computer Repair Tech, Logistics and Transportation Management.

**Most popular majors.** Business/marketing 11%, family/consumer sciences 6%, health sciences 11%, liberal arts 57%.

**Computing on campus.** 1,300 workstations in library, computer center. Commuter students can connect to campus network. Online library available.

**Student life. Freshman orientation:** Available. Full-day program. **Activities:** Bands, choral groups, dance, drama, literary magazine, music ensembles, musical theater, radio station, student government, student newspaper, symphony orchestra, TV station, Haraya Caribbean students organizations, Asian American society, Irish American club, NYPIRG, women center, Association Catholic Community, Jewish students organization, organization of Latinos, multicultural club, Intervarsity Christian Fellowship.

**Athletics.** NJCAA. **Intercollegiate:** Baseball M, basketball, bowling, cross-country, football (tackle) M, golf, lacrosse, soccer, softball W, tennis, track and field, volleyball W, wrestling M. **Intramural:** Badminton, baseball M, basketball, football (non-tackle) M, handball, judo, racquetball, soccer, softball, swimming, table tennis, tennis, volleyball. **Team name:** Lions.

**Student services.** Adult student services, career counseling, student employment services, financial aid counseling, health services, minority student services, on-campus daycare, personal counseling, placement for graduates, veterans' counselor, women's services. **Physically disabled:** Services for visually, speech, hearing impaired. **Transfer:** Pre-admission transcript evaluation for new students. Transfer center, transfer adviser, college fairs on campus for students transferring to 4-year colleges.

**Contact.** E-mail: admissions@ncc.edu
Phone: (516) 572-7345 Fax: (516) 572-9743
Tika Esler, Associate Dean of Admissions, Nassau Community College,
One Education Drive, Garden City, NY 11530

## New York Career Institute
**New York, New York**
**www.nyci.com**                    CB code: 5324

- For-profit 2-year junior college
- Commuter campus in very large city
- Interview required

**General.** Accredited by New York State Board of Regents. **Enrollment:**
509 degree-seeking undergraduates. **Degrees:** 61 associate awarded. **Calendar:** Trimester, extensive summer session. **Full-time faculty:** 9 total. **Part-time faculty:** 27 total.

**Basis for selection.** CPAT examination performance important. All applicants take English and math placement examinations (CPAT).

**2007-2008 Annual costs.** Full-time tuition and fees for court reporting night program $10,800. Tuition for paralegal program $350 per credit hour. Books/supplies: $800. Personal expenses: $4,000.

**Financial aid. Need-based:** Work-study available nights.

**Application procedures. Admission:** No deadline. $50 fee. Admission notification on a rolling basis. **Financial aid:** No deadline. Applicants notified on a rolling basis.

**Academics. Special study options:** Internships. **Credit/placement by examination:** AP, CLEP, institutional tests. **Support services:** Remedial instruction, study skills assistance.

**Majors. Health:** Medical records admin, medical secretary. **Legal studies:** Court reporting, legal secretary, paralegal.

**Computing on campus.** Repair service available.

**Student life. Freshman orientation:** Mandatory.

**Student services.** Career counseling, student employment services, financial aid counseling, personal counseling, placement for graduates. **Transfer:** Pre-admission transcript evaluation for new students.

**Contact.** E-mail: cmcmahon@nyci.edu
Phone: (212) 962-0002 Fax: (212) 385-7574
Director of Admissions, New York Career Institute, 11 Park Place, New York, NY 10007

## Niagara County Community College
**Sanborn, New York**                    CB member
**www.niagaracc.suny.edu**               CB code: 2568

- Public 2-year community college
- Commuter campus in rural community

**General.** Founded in 1962. Regionally accredited. SUNY institution. **Enrollment:** 4,175 degree-seeking undergraduates; 2,167 non-degree-seeking students. **Degrees:** 817 associate awarded. **ROTC:** Army. **Location:** 10 miles from Niagara Falls. **Calendar:** Semester, limited summer session. **Full-time faculty:** 120 total; 28% have terminal degrees, 7% minority, 51% women. **Part-time faculty:** 251 total; 10% have terminal degrees, 9% minority, 60% women. **Special facilities:** Biofeedback laboratory.

**Student profile.** Among degree-seeking undergraduates, 40% enrolled in a transfer program, 39% enrolled in a vocational program, 1,099 enrolled as first-time, first-year students, 292 transferred in from other institutions.

| | | | |
|---|---|---|---|
| Part-time: | 27% | Hispanic American: | 1% |
| Out-of-state: | 1% | Native American: | 2% |
| Women: | 58% | International: | 1% |
| African American: | 7% | 25 or older: | 27% |
| Asian American: | 1% | | |

**Transfer out. Colleges most students transferred to 2007:** Buffalo State College, Niagara University, SUNY Buffalo, Brockport, Fredonia.

**Basis for selection.** Open admission, but selective for some programs. Admission to nursing, physical therapist assistant, radiologic technology, and surgical technology programs based on school achievement record and

---

test scores. Admission to programs on space-available basis. SAT/ACT reviewed for placement if submitted. Interview recommended.

**High school preparation.** 1 drafting required for drafting applicants, 1 biology or chemistry required for nursing applicants, 3 mathematics for engineering technology, 1 biology, 1 chemistry and 2 mathematics for physical therapist assistant, 1 chemistry, 1 biology, 2 mathematics for radiologic technology, 1 biology for surgical technician, 2 mathematics for business administration.

**2007-2008 Annual costs.** Tuition/fees: $3,506; $5,102 out-of-state. Per-credit charge: $133 in-state; $199 out-of-state. Books/supplies: $700. Personal expenses: $650.

**2006-2007 Financial aid.** All financial aid based on need. 58% of total undergraduate aid awarded as scholarships/grants, 42% as loans/jobs. Need-based aid available for part-time students. Work-study available nights and for part-time students. **Additional information:** Assistance offered placing students in part-time employment. Students can charge books, food coupons, or $100 advance against anticipated financial aid.

**Application procedures. Admission:** Closing date 8/31. No application fee. Application may be submitted online. Admission notification on a rolling basis beginning on or about 8/1. Must reply by May 1 or within 4 week(s) if notified thereafter. **Financial aid:** Priority date 4/1; no closing date. FAFSA required. Applicants notified on a rolling basis starting 5/1; must reply within 2 week(s) of notification.

**Academics.** Orientation program for Distance Learning students. **Special study options:** Cooperative education, cross-registration, distance learning, double major, dual enrollment of high school students, honors, independent study, internships, study abroad. License preparation in nursing. **Credit/placement by examination:** AP, CLEP, IB, institutional tests. 30 credit hours maximum toward associate degree. **Support services:** Learning center, pre-admission summer program, reduced course load, remedial instruction, study skills assistance, tutoring, writing center.

**Majors. Business:** Accounting, administrative services, business admin, hospitality admin, retailing. **Communications:** General, digital media. **Computer sciences:** General, computer science. **Conservation:** Environmental studies. **Education:** Elementary. **Engineering technology:** CAD/CADD, mechanical. **Health:** Medical assistant, medical radiologic technology/radiation therapy, nursing (RN), physical therapy assistant, surgical technology. **Liberal arts:** Arts/sciences, humanities. **Parks/recreation:** Health/fitness. **Personal/culinary services:** Chef training. **Protective services:** Criminalistics, law enforcement admin. **Public administration:** Human services. **Visual/performing arts:** Dramatic, studio arts. **Other:** Science technologies/technicians.

**Most popular majors.** Business/marketing 13%, health sciences 21%, liberal arts 32%, security/protective services 7%, visual/performing arts 7%.

**Computing on campus.** 415 workstations in library, computer center. Online library, helpline available.

**Student life. Freshman orientation:** Available. One day orientation in August. **Activities:** Jazz band, choral groups, dance, drama, music ensembles, musical theater, radio station, student government, student newspaper, disabled student association, comeback club, African American student association, Native American club, nursing club, human services club, international club, women's studies club.

**Athletics.** NJCAA. **Intercollegiate:** Baseball M, basketball, golf, soccer, softball W, volleyball W, wrestling M. **Intramural:** Basketball. **Team name:** Trailblazers.

**Student services.** Adult student services, alcohol/substance abuse counseling, career counseling, student employment services, financial aid counseling, health services, on-campus daycare, personal counseling, placement for graduates, veterans' counselor. **Physically disabled:** Services for visually, speech, hearing impaired. **Transfer:** Pre-admission transcript evaluation for new students. Transfer adviser, college fairs on campus for students transferring to 4-year colleges.

**Contact.** E-mail: admissions@niagaracc.suny.edu
Phone: (716) 614-6200 Fax: (716) 614-6820
Kathy Saunders, Director of Admissions, Niagara County Community College, 3111 Saunders Settlement Road, Sanborn, NY 14132-9460

## North Country Community College
**Saranac Lake, New York**
**www.nccc.edu**                    CB code: 2571

- Public 2-year community college
- Commuter campus in small town

**General.** Founded in 1967. Regionally accredited. SUNY institution. Campuses in Saranac Lake, Malone, and Ticonderoga. **Enrollment:** 1,054 degree-seeking undergraduates; 687 non-degree-seeking students. **Degrees:** 262 associate awarded. **Location:** 150 miles from Albany, 50 miles from Plattsburgh. **Calendar:** Semester, limited summer session. **Full-time faculty:** 43 total; 19% have terminal degrees, 2% minority, 51% women. **Part-time faculty:** 105 total; 6% have terminal degrees, 1% minority, 60% women. **Class size:** 75% < 20, 24% 20-39, 1% 40-49. **Partnerships:** Formal partnerships with local high schools through College Bridge Program.

**Student profile.** Among degree-seeking undergraduates, 47% enrolled in a transfer program, 53% enrolled in a vocational program, 2% already have a bachelor's degree or higher, 331 enrolled as first-time, first-year students, 121 transferred in from other institutions.

| | | | |
|---|---|---|---|
| Part-time: | 13% | Hispanic American: | 1% |
| Out-of-state: | 2% | Native American: | 4% |
| Women: | 65% | International: | 2% |
| African American: | 1% | 25 or older: | 26% |
| Asian American: | 1% | Live on campus: | 6% |

**Transfer out.** 45% of students enrolled in the transfer program go on to 4-year colleges. **Colleges most students transferred to 2007:** SUNY Colleges at Plattsburgh, Potsdam, Cobleskill, Geneseo; SUNY at Buffalo.

**Basis for selection.** Open admission, but selective for some programs. Special requirements for nursing, radiologic technology, and massage therapy. SAT or ACT and placement tests recommended for competitive programs. **Homeschooled:** Must complete and score in appropriate ranges on College Board Descriptive Tests System in math, English, and reading.

**High school preparation.** 16 units recommended. Recommended units include English 4, mathematics 3, social studies 4, science 3 (laboratory 1) and foreign language 3. 5 units of math and science recommended (3 math and 2 science or 2 math and 3 science).

**2007-2008 Annual costs.** Tuition/fees: $4,190; $9,250 out-of-state. Per-credit charge: $160 in-state; $390 out-of-state. Room/board: $8,300. Books/supplies: $800. Personal expenses: $800.

**Financial aid.** All financial aid based on need. Need-based aid available for part-time students. Work-study available nights, weekends and for part-time students.

**Application procedures. Admission:** Priority date 2/1; deadline 9/1 (receipt date). No application fee. Application may be submitted online. Admission notification on a rolling basis. Must reply by May 1 or within 4 week(s) if notified thereafter. **Financial aid:** Priority date 4/1; no closing date. FAFSA required. Applicants notified on a rolling basis starting 4/1; must reply within 3 week(s) of notification.

**Academics.** 23-42 credit hours required in major, 62-70 required for graduation depending on field of study. **Special study options:** Distance learning, double major, dual enrollment of high school students, internships, liberal arts/career combination, student-designed major. License preparation in nursing, radiology. **Credit/placement by examination:** AP, CLEP, institutional tests. 31 credit hours maximum toward associate degree. **Support services:** Learning center, reduced course load, remedial instruction, study skills assistance, tutoring.

**Majors. Business:** General, business admin, office/clerical. **Computer sciences:** Computer graphics. **Health:** Health services, massage therapy, medical radiologic technology/radiation therapy, nursing (RN). **Interdisciplinary:** Biological/physical sciences. **Liberal arts:** Arts/sciences. **Parks/recreation:** Facilities management. **Protective services:** Criminal justice.

**Most popular majors.** Business/marketing 20%, health sciences 25%, liberal arts 28%, security/protective services 12%.

**Computing on campus.** 200 workstations in dormitories, library, computer center, student center. Dormitories linked to campus network. Commuter students can connect to campus network. Online library, helpline, wireless network available.

**Student life. Freshman orientation:** Mandatory. Preregistration for classes offered. Day-long session held 1 day prior to start of classes. **Housing:** Coed dorms, substance-free housing available. $250 nonrefundable deposit. **Activities:** Drama, literary magazine, music ensembles, student government, student newspaper.

**Athletics.** NJCAA. **Intercollegiate:** Basketball M, ice hockey M, soccer, softball W. **Intramural:** Badminton, basketball, bowling, golf, soccer, softball, swimming, volleyball, weight lifting. **Team name:** Saints.

**Student services.** Adult student services, alcohol/substance abuse counseling, career counseling, student employment services, financial aid counseling, personal counseling, placement for graduates. **Physically disabled:** Services for visually, speech, hearing impaired. **Learning disabled:** Comprehensive services available. **Transfer:** Pre-admission transcript evaluation for new students. Transfer adviser, college fairs on campus for students transferring to 4-year colleges.

**Contact.** E-mail: info@nccc.edu
Phone: (518) 891-2915 ext. 233 Toll-free number: (888) 879-6222
Fax: (518) 891-0898
Edwin Trathen, Vice President for Enrollment and Student Services, North Country Community College, 23 Santanoni Avenue, Saranac Lake, NY 12983

## Olean Business Institute
Olean, New York
www.obi.edu                                    CB code: 0630

- For-profit 2-year business college
- Commuter campus in large town

**General.** Founded in 1961. Accredited by ACICS. **Enrollment:** 100 degree-seeking undergraduates. **Degrees:** 24 associate awarded. **Location:** 90 miles from Buffalo, 90 miles from Erie, Pennsylvania. **Calendar:** Semester, limited summer session. **Full-time faculty:** 8 total. **Part-time faculty:** 4 total.

**Student profile.**

| | | | |
|---|---|---|---|
| 25 or older: | 53% | Live on campus: | 2% |

**Basis for selection.** Open admission. School achievement record most important. Interview recommended.

**2008-2009 Annual costs.** Tuition/fees: $10,200. Per-credit charge: $440. Books/supplies: $700.

**Application procedures. Admission:** No deadline. $25 fee, may be waived for applicants with need. Admission notification on a rolling basis. **Financial aid:** Priority date 5/1; no closing date. FAFSA required. Applicants notified on a rolling basis.

**Academics.** Academic offerings intended to provide student with as much work-field knowledge and experience as possible. **Special study options:** Internships. **Credit/placement by examination:** CLEP, institutional tests. **Support services:** Learning center, reduced course load, remedial instruction, tutoring.

**Majors. Business:** General, accounting, accounting/business management, administrative services, business admin, management science, office management, office technology. **Computer sciences:** General, data entry, data processing, information technology, word processing. **Health:** Medical records admin, medical secretary, office admin. **Legal studies:** Paralegal.

**Computing on campus.** 75 workstations in dormitories, library, computer center.

**Student life. Housing:** Single-sex dorms available. Student housing available near campus. **Activities:** Student government.

**Student services.** Adult student services, career counseling, student employment services, personal counseling, placement for graduates. **Transfer:** Transfer adviser for students transferring to 4-year colleges.

**Contact.** E-mail: lkincaid@obi.edu
Phone: (716) 372-7978 Fax: (716) 372-2120
Carl English, Director of Admissions, Olean Business Institute, 301 North Union Street, Olean, NY 14760

## Onondaga Community College
Syracuse, New York                             CB member
www.sunyocc.edu                                CB code: 2627

- Public 2-year community college
- Commuter campus in small city

**General.** Founded in 1962. Regionally accredited. SUNY institution. **Enrollment:** 7,138 degree-seeking undergraduates; 3,499 non-degree-seeking students. **Degrees:** 827 associate awarded. **ROTC:** Army, Air Force. **Location:** 4 miles from downtown Syracuse. **Calendar:** Semester, extensive summer session. **Full-time faculty:** 163 total; 9% minority, 52% women. **Part-time faculty:** 407 total; 6% minority, 51% women. **Special facilities:** Children's learning center, county library branch, applied technology center. **Partnerships:** Formal partnerships with Syracuse City Schools, Manufacturers Association of Central New York.

**Student profile.** Among degree-seeking undergraduates, 66% enrolled in a transfer program, 34% enrolled in a vocational program, 1,655 enrolled as first-time, first-year students, 329 transferred in from other institutions.

| | | | |
|---|---|---|---|
| Part-time: | 25% | Hispanic American: | 2% |
| Out-of-state: | 3% | Native American: | 2% |
| Women: | 51% | International: | 1% |
| African American: | 9% | 25 or older: | 27% |
| Asian American: | 2% | Live on campus: | 6% |

**Transfer out.** 20% of students enrolled in the transfer program go on to 4-year colleges. **Colleges most students transferred to 2007:** SUNY Oswego, SUNY Cortland, Le Moyne College, Syracuse University.

**Basis for selection.** Open admission, but selective for some programs. Admission to some programs based on high school GPA, test scores, and specific program prerequisites. Mandatory developmental skills courses required as condition of acceptance for students lacking adequate academic background. School achievement record, test scores, special talents considered for placement only. Interview, recommendations required for some programs. Interview required for graphic arts, radio-television; recommended for nursing, physical therapist assistant. Audition required for music; portfolio required for art, recommended for photography. **Homeschooled:** Submit diplomas from school districts of record, transcripts if available.

**High school preparation.** 15 units recommended. Recommended units include English 4, mathematics 3, science 3 and foreign language 2. Algebra, biology, chemistry required of respiratory care, surgical technology, nursing applicants. 4 math required for engineering, science, computer science and physical therapy assistant applicants. Language required for humanities.

**2007-2008 Annual costs.** Tuition/fees: $3,641; $6,921 out-of-state. Per-credit charge: $129 in-state; $258 out-of-state. Books/supplies: $1,200. Personal expenses: $650.

**Financial aid.** All financial aid based on need. Need-based aid available for part-time students. Work-study available for part-time students.

**Application procedures. Admission:** Closing date 8/31. $40 fee, may be waived for applicants with need. Application may be submitted online. Admission notification on a rolling basis. **Financial aid:** Priority date 2/15; no closing date. FAFSA required. Applicants notified on a rolling basis starting 4/15; must reply within 4 week(s) of notification.

**Academics. Special study options:** Accelerated study, cooperative education, cross-registration, distance learning, double major, dual enrollment of high school students, ESL, honors, independent study, internships, liberal arts/career combination, New York semester, study abroad. License preparation in nursing. **Credit/placement by examination:** AP, CLEP, institutional tests. 30 credit hours maximum toward associate degree. **Support services:** GED preparation, learning center, pre-admission summer program, reduced course load, remedial instruction, study skills assistance, tutoring, writing center.

**Majors. Architecture:** Interior. **Business:** General, accounting, administrative services, hotel/motel admin, labor relations. **Communications:** Broadcast journalism. **Computer sciences:** General, computer science. **Engineering:** Computer, electrical, science. **Engineering technology:** Construction, electrical. **Health:** Medical records technology, nursing assistant, physical therapy assistant, recreational therapy, respiratory therapy technology. **Interdisciplinary:** Math/computer science. **Liberal arts:** Arts/sciences, humanities. **Mechanic/repair:** Automotive. **Parks/recreation:** Facilities management. **Personal/culinary services:** Culinary arts. **Protective services:** Criminal justice, fire safety technology. **Public administration:** Human services. **Visual/performing arts:** Art, commercial/advertising art, interior design, photography.

**Most popular majors.** Business/marketing 11%, engineering/engineering technologies 6%, health sciences 10%, liberal arts 33%, public administration/social services 8%, security/protective services 11%, visual/performing arts 8%.

**Computing on campus.** PC or laptop required. 1,000 workstations in library, computer center, student center. Dormitories wired for high-speed internet access and linked to campus network. Commuter students can connect to campus network. Online course registration, helpline, repair service, student web hosting, wireless network available.

**Student life. Freshman orientation:** Available. Preregistration for classes offered. Programs held for half day in fall and spring prior to start of classes. **Policies:** Dorms are alcohol free. **Housing:** Coed dorms, substance-free housing available. $300 nonrefundable deposit. Suite-style housing available. **Activities:** Bands, choral groups, drama, film society, international student organizations, music ensembles, musical theater, radio station, student government, student newspaper, international students, minority, veterans, inter-religious, older/returning student clubs.

**Athletics.** NJCAA. **Intercollegiate:** Baseball M, basketball, cross-country, lacrosse M, softball W, tennis, volleyball W. **Intramural:** Basketball, bowling, fencing, golf, lacrosse M, skiing, skin diving, softball W, swimming, tennis, volleyball. **Team name:** Lazers.

**Student services.** Campus ministries, career counseling, services for economically disadvantaged, student employment services, financial aid counseling, health services, minority student services, on-campus daycare, personal counseling, placement for graduates, veterans' counselor. **Physically disabled:** Services for visually, speech, hearing impaired. **Transfer:** Pre-admission transcript evaluation for new students. Transfer adviser, college fairs on campus for students transferring to 4-year colleges.

**Contact.** E-mail: admissions@sunyocc.edu
Phone: (315) 498-2000 Fax: (315) 498-2107
Katherine Perry, Director of Admissions, Onondaga Community College, 4585 West Seneca Turnpike, Syracuse, NY 13215-4585

## Orange County Community College
**Middletown, New York**
orange.cc.ny.us
**CB member**
**CB code: 2625**

- Public 2-year community college
- Commuter campus in large town

**General.** Founded in 1950. Regionally accredited. **Enrollment:** 6,697 degree-seeking undergraduates. **Degrees:** 710 associate awarded. **ROTC:** Army. **Location:** 25 miles from Newburgh, 60 miles from New York City. **Calendar:** Semester, limited summer session. **Full-time faculty:** 142 total. **Part-time faculty:** 265 total.

**Student profile.**

| | | | |
|---|---|---|---|
| Out-of-state: | 2% | 25 or older: | 27% |

**Transfer out. Colleges most students transferred to 2007:** SUNY at New Paltz, Mount St. Mary's College, Marist College, Dominican College of Blauvelt.

**Basis for selection.** Open admission, but selective for some programs. Admission to allied health and nursing programs based on academic record, assessment scores and, to some extent, residency.

**High school preparation.** Regents biology required for physical therapist assistant, occupational therapy assistant, radiologic technologist and dental hygienist. Regents chemistry required for dental hygiene.

**2007-2008 Annual costs.** Tuition/fees: $3,438; $6,538 out-of-state. Per-credit charge: $130 in-state; $260 out-of-state. Books/supplies: $850. Personal expenses: $925.

**Financial aid. Need-based:** Need-based aid available for part-time students.

**Application procedures. Admission:** No deadline. $30 fee, may be waived for applicants with need. Admission notification on a rolling basis. February 1 application closing date for allied health/nursing program. Notification by March 15, must reply within 2 weeks. **Financial aid:** Priority date 5/1; no closing date. FAFSA, institutional form required. Applicants notified on a rolling basis starting 5/1; must reply within 4 week(s) of notification.

**Academics.** Agreement with Franklin University (Ohio) for bachelor's completion program. **Special study options:** Cooperative education, distance learning, dual enrollment of high school students, ESL, honors, independent study, internships, weekend study. License preparation in dental hygiene, nursing, real estate. **Credit/placement by examination:** AP, CLEP, institutional tests. 30 credit hours maximum toward associate degree. **Support services:** GED preparation and test center, learning center, reduced course load, remedial instruction, study skills assistance, tutoring, writing center.

**Majors. Business:** General, accounting, administrative services, business admin, e-commerce, finance, office technology, sales/distribution. **Communications:** General. **Computer sciences:** General, data processing. **Education:** General, elementary. **Engineering:** General. **Engineering technology:** Architectural, electrical. **Family/consumer sciences:** Child care. **Foreign languages:** General, French, Spanish. **Health:** Clinical lab science, clinical lab technology, dental hygiene, health services, medical radiologic technology/radiation therapy, occupational therapy assistant, physical therapy assistant. **Interdisciplinary:** Global studies. **Liberal arts:** Arts/sciences. **Math:** General. **Parks/recreation:** Exercise sciences, facilities management. **Protective services:** Criminal justice, police science. **Public administration:** Human services.

**Computing on campus.** 300 workstations in library, computer center, student center. Online library available.

**Student life. Freshman orientation:** Available. Preregistration for classes offered. **Activities:** Bands, choral groups, dance, drama, music ensembles, musical theater, radio station, student government, student newspaper, black and Latino organization, Helping Hands, social service organization, Habitat for Humanity.

**Athletics.** NJCAA. **Intercollegiate:** Baseball M, basketball, golf, soccer, softball W, swimming, tennis, volleyball W. **Intramural:** Football (non-tackle), racquetball, soccer M, softball, tennis, volleyball. **Team name:** Colts.

**Student services.** Adult student services, alcohol/substance abuse counseling, career counseling, services for economically disadvantaged, student employment services, financial aid counseling, health services, on-campus daycare, personal counseling, placement for graduates, veterans' counselor. **Physically disabled:** Services for visually, speech, hearing impaired. **Transfer:** Transfer adviser, college fairs on campus for students transferring to 4-year colleges.

**Contact.** Phone: (845) 341-4030 Fax: (845) 342-8662
Michael Roe, Director of Admissions, Orange County Community College, 115 South Street, Middletown, NY 10940-0115

## Phillips Beth Israel School of Nursing
### New York, New York
### www.futurenursebi.org
CB code: 2031

- Private 2-year nursing college
- Commuter campus in very large city
- Application essay, interview required

**General.** Founded in 1904. **Enrollment:** 225 degree-seeking undergraduates. **Degrees:** 76 associate awarded. **Calendar:** Semester, limited summer session. **Full-time faculty:** 9 total; 33% have terminal degrees, 44% minority, 89% women. **Part-time faculty:** 20 total; 60% minority, 85% women. **Class size:** 11% < 20, 89% 20-39.

**Student profile.** Among degree-seeking undergraduates, 6 enrolled as first-time, first-year students, 13 transferred in from other institutions.

| | | | |
|---|---|---|---|
| Part-time: | 81% | Asian American: | 22% |
| Out-of-state: | 10% | Hispanic American: | 5% |
| Women: | 78% | International: | 4% |
| African American: | 17% | 25 or older: | 55% |

**Transfer out. Colleges most students transferred to 2007:** Pace University, New York University.

**Basis for selection.** Academic achievement, aptitude test scores, personal interview, recommendations, and prior experience of primary consideration. 55th percentile score on National League for Nursing's Preadmission Examination-RN mandatory (65th percentile score recommended). Standing in top half of high school class recommended. High school GPA of 75 or better, college GPA of 2.5 or better, GED minimum score of 250. **Homeschooled:** Statement describing homeschool structure and mission, transcript of courses and grades, state high school equivalency certificate required.

**High school preparation.** 16 units required. Required units include English 4, mathematics 2, social studies 2, science 2 (laboratory 2). Chemistry and biology required.

**2008-2009 Annual costs.** Tuition/fees: $16,310. Per-credit charge: $340. Books/supplies: $1,400.

**2006-2007 Financial aid. Need-based:** 84% of total undergraduate aid awarded as scholarships/grants, 16% as loans/jobs. Need-based aid available for part-time students.

**Application procedures. Admission:** Closing date 4/1 (postmark date). $50 fee, may be waived for applicants with need. Application must be submitted on paper. Admission notification on a rolling basis beginning on or about 2/1. Must reply within 3 weeks of admission notification. **Financial aid:** Closing date 6/1. FAFSA, institutional form required. Applicants notified by 8/1; must reply within 3 week(s) of notification.

**Academics. Special study options:** Weekend college. License preparation in nursing. **Credit/placement by examination:** AP, CLEP, institutional tests. 23 credit hours maximum toward associate degree. **Support services:** Learning center, pre-admission summer program, reduced course load, remedial instruction, study skills assistance, tutoring.

**Majors. Health:** Nursing (RN).

**Computing on campus.** 15 workstations in library, computer center.

**Student life. Freshman orientation:** Mandatory. 4 full days the week before classes start. **Activities:** Choral groups, student government, student newspaper, National Student Nurses Association Chapter.

**Student services.** Alcohol/substance abuse counseling, career counseling, financial aid counseling, health services, personal counseling. **Physically disabled:** Services for visually, speech, hearing impaired. **Transfer:** Pre-admission transcript evaluation for new students. Transfer adviser, college fairs on campus for students transferring to 4-year colleges.

**Contact.** E-mail: bstern@bethisraelny.org
Phone: (212) 614-6108 Fax: (212) 614-6109
Bernice Pass-Stern, Assistant Dean, Phillips Beth Israel School of Nursing, 776 Sixth Avenue, Fourth Floor, New York, NY 10001

## Plaza College
### Jackson Heights, New York
### www.plazacollege.edu
CB code: 0545

- For-profit 2-year business and junior college
- Commuter campus in very large city
- Application essay, interview required

**General.** Founded in 1916. Regionally accredited. **Enrollment:** 652 degree-seeking undergraduates. **Degrees:** 31 bachelor's, 124 associate awarded. **Calendar:** Semester, extensive summer session. **Full-time faculty:** 11 total. **Part-time faculty:** 30 total.

**Basis for selection.** Essay, interview, and test scores most important. Student must pass entrance examination. CPAT and college-administered writing test required of all students.

**2007-2008 Annual costs.** Tuition/fees: $8,700. 3 semesters required in academic year; costs quoted for 2 of 3 semesters. Books/supplies: $600. Personal expenses: $1,800.

**Application procedures. Admission:** No deadline. $25 fee, may be waived for applicants with need. Application may be submitted online. Admission notification on a rolling basis. **Financial aid:** No deadline. FAFSA, institutional form required. Applicants notified on a rolling basis.

**Academics. Special study options:** Accelerated study, internships. Bachelor's degree programs available on campus. **Credit/placement by examination:** CLEP, institutional tests. 30 credit hours maximum toward associate degree. **Support services:** Learning center, reduced course load, remedial instruction, study skills assistance, tutoring, writing center.

**Majors. Business:** Accounting, business admin. **Computer sciences:** Information systems. **Health:** Medical assistant.

**Computing on campus.** 250 workstations in library, computer center, student center. Wireless network available.

**Student life. Freshman orientation:** Mandatory. Preregistration for classes offered.

**Student services.** Career counseling, financial aid counseling, personal counseling, placement for graduates. **Physically disabled:** Services for visually, speech, hearing impaired. **Transfer:** Transfer adviser for students transferring to 4-year colleges.

**Contact.** E-mail: plazainfo@plazacollege.edu
Phone: (718) 779-1430 Fax: (718) 779-7423
Rose Ann Black, Dean of Admissions, Plaza College, 74-09 37th Avenue, Jackson Heights, NY 11372

## Professional Business College
### New York, New York
### www.pbcny.edu

- Private 2-year business college
- Very large city

**General.** Regionally accredited. **Calendar:** Trimester.

**Contact.** 125 Canal St., New York, NY 10002

## Rockland Community College

**Suffern, New York**
www.sunyrockland.edu

CB member
CB code: 2767

- Public 2-year community college
- Commuter campus in large town

**General.** Founded in 1959. Regionally accredited. SUNY institution. Extension sites/centers located throughout county. **Enrollment:** 5,413 degree-seeking undergraduates. **Degrees:** 757 associate awarded. **Location:** 35 miles from New York City. **Calendar:** Semester, extensive summer session. **Full-time faculty:** 123 total. **Part-time faculty:** 250 total.

**Student profile.**

Out-of-state: 2%  25 or older: 35%

**Transfer out. Colleges most students transferred to 2007:** SUNY New Paltz, Ramapo College, Dominican College.

**Basis for selection.** Open admission. Students required to take assessment examination before enrolling full-time.

**High school preparation.** 18 units recommended. Recommended units include English 4, mathematics 2, social studies 4, history 4, science 2, foreign language 1 and academic electives 4.

**2007-2008 Annual costs.** Tuition/fees: $3,465; $6,665 out-of-state. Per-credit charge: $133 in-state; $266 out-of-state. Books/supplies: $600. Personal expenses: $600.

**2006-2007 Financial aid. Need-based:** 88% of total undergraduate aid awarded as scholarships/grants, 12% as loans/jobs. Need-based aid available for part-time students. Work-study available nights and weekends.

**Application procedures. Admission:** Priority date 8/1; no deadline. $25 fee, may be waived for applicants with need. Application may be submitted online. Admission notification on a rolling basis. **Financial aid:** Priority date 5/31; no closing date. FAFSA, institutional form required. Applicants notified on a rolling basis starting 6/1; must reply within 3 week(s) of notification.

**Academics. Special study options:** Cross-registration, distance learning, double major, dual enrollment of high school students, ESL, honors, independent study, internships, liberal arts/career combination, student-designed major, study abroad, weekend college. **Credit/placement by examination:** AP, CLEP, IB. 45 credit hours maximum toward associate degree. **Support services:** Learning center, remedial instruction, study skills assistance, tutoring, writing center.

**Honors college/program.** Mentor/Talented honors program. Business honors degree requires minimum combined SAT score of 1100 (exclusive of Writing) and at least 90 average; interviews, auditions and portfolios recommended.

**Majors. Business:** General, accounting, accounting technology, administrative services, business admin, hospitality admin, tourism/travel. **Communications:** General. **Computer sciences:** Computer graphics, data processing, programming. **Education:** Elementary. **Engineering technology:** Electrical. **Family/consumer sciences:** Food/nutrition, institutional food production. **Health:** EMT paramedic, medical assistant, medical records technology, nursing (RN), occupational therapy assistant, respiratory therapy technology. **Legal studies:** Paralegal. **Liberal arts:** Arts/sciences. **Mechanic/repair:** Automotive. **Protective services:** Criminal justice, fire safety technology. **Public administration:** Human services. **Social sciences:** General. **Visual/performing arts:** Commercial photography, commercial/advertising art, dramatic, photography, studio arts.

**Most popular majors.** Business/marketing 15%, computer/information sciences 9%, health sciences 18%, liberal arts 48%.

**Computing on campus.** 177 workstations in computer center.

**Student life. Freshman orientation:** Available. Preregistration for classes offered. **Activities:** Jazz band, choral groups, dance, drama, literary magazine, musical theater, radio station, student government, student newspaper, symphony orchestra, TV station, special interest clubs.

**Athletics.** NJCAA. **Intercollegiate:** Baseball M, basketball, bowling, golf M, soccer, softball W, table tennis, tennis, volleyball W. **Intramural:** Basketball, bowling, racquetball, soccer, softball, table tennis, track and field, volleyball. **Team name:** Hawks.

**Student services.** Adult student services, alcohol/substance abuse counseling, campus ministries, career counseling, services for economically disadvantaged, student employment services, financial aid counseling, health services, minority student services, on-campus daycare, personal counseling, placement for graduates, veterans' counselor. **Physically disabled:** Services for visually, speech, hearing impaired. **Transfer:** Pre-admission transcript evaluation for new students. Transfer adviser, college fairs on campus for students transferring to 4-year colleges.

**Contact.** E-mail: info@sunyrockland.edu
Phone: (845) 574-4462 Toll-free number: (800) 722-7666
Fax: (845) 574-4433
Lorraine Glynn, Director of Admissions, Rockland Community College, 145 College Road, Suffern, NY 10901

## St. Elizabeth College of Nursing

**Utica, New York**
www.secon.edu

CB code: 2847

- Private 2-year nursing college affiliated with Roman Catholic Church
- Commuter campus in small city
- SAT or ACT (ACT writing optional), application essay, interview required

**General.** Regionally accredited. **Enrollment:** 184 degree-seeking undergraduates. **Degrees:** 64 associate awarded. **Location:** 40 miles from Albany, 50 miles from Syracuse. **Calendar:** Semester. **Full-time faculty:** 18 total. **Part-time faculty:** 1 total.

**Student profile.**

Out-of-state: 1%  25 or older: 52%

**Basis for selection.** Rigor of secondary record, test scores most important. SAT Subject Tests recommended. **Adult students:** SAT/ACT scores not required. **Homeschooled:** Strong math and science background required, including coursework in chemistry, biology and equivalent of Math Level 1 and 2. **Learning Disabled:** Written documentation of disability required in order to set up special testing.

**High school preparation.** Required and recommended units include English 4, mathematics 2-3, social studies 4, history 4, science 2 (laboratory 2) and foreign language 1.

**2007-2008 Annual costs.** Tuition/fees: $12,350. Per-credit charge: $300. Books/supplies: $2,100. Personal expenses: $1,300.

**Financial aid. Need-based:** Need-based aid available for part-time students.

**Application procedures. Admission:** Priority date 5/30; deadline 6/30 (receipt date). $35 fee, may be waived for applicants with need. Application may be submitted online. Admission notification on a rolling basis. Must reply by May 1 or within 2 week(s) if notified thereafter. Admission application fee $25 if submitted before 2/1. **Financial aid:** No deadline. FAFSA required. Applicants notified on a rolling basis starting 1/1; must reply within 2 week(s) of notification.

**Academics.** One 6-week summer session at end of first year. **Special study options:** Combined bachelor's/graduate degree, distance learning, liberal arts/career combination, weekend college. Articulation agreements with upper division BSN colleges. License preparation in nursing. **Credit/placement by examination:** CLEP, institutional tests. **Support services:** Remedial instruction, study skills assistance, tutoring.

**Majors. Health:** Nursing (RN).

**Computing on campus.** 20 workstations in library, computer center. Commuter students can connect to campus network. Online library, repair service available.

**Student life. Freshman orientation:** Mandatory. Preregistration for classes offered. Held week prior to classes. **Housing:** Option of staying on campus at affiliated college available. **Activities:** Student government, National League of Nursing.

**Student services.** Alcohol/substance abuse counseling, campus ministries, financial aid counseling, health services, on-campus daycare. **Transfer:** Pre-admission transcript evaluation for new students. Transfer adviser for students transferring to 4-year colleges.

**Contact.** E-mail: conadmis@stemc.org
Phone: (315) 798-88189 Fax: (315) 798-8271
Donna Ernst, Recruitment Director, St. Elizabeth College of Nursing, 2215 Genesee Street, Utica, NY 13501

Two-Year Colleges

## St. Joseph's College of Nursing
### Syracuse, New York
### www.sjhsyr.org/nursing
**CB code: 2825**

- Private 2-year nursing college affiliated with Roman Catholic Church
- Commuter campus in small city
- SAT or ACT (ACT writing optional), application essay, interview required

**General.** Founded in 1898. Practice in a variety of settings including medical/surgical, maternity, pediatrics, oncology, psychiatry, ambulatory care clinics, and home care and outpatient experiences. **Enrollment:** 235 degree-seeking undergraduates. **Degrees:** 115 associate awarded. **Calendar:** Semester, limited summer session. **Full-time faculty:** 26 total; 92% women. **Part-time faculty:** 8 total; 12% have terminal degrees, 100% women. **Class size:** 57% 20-39, 29% 40-49, 14% 50-99. **Special facilities:** Cardiovascular lab, electro-physiology lab, home care, outpatient services, 462-bed teaching hospital.

**Student profile.** Among degree-seeking undergraduates, 18 enrolled as first-time, first-year students.

| | | | |
|---|---|---|---|
| Part-time: | 47% | Hispanic American: | 1% |
| Women: | 87% | 25 or older: | 49% |
| African American: | 4% | Live on campus: | 30% |
| Asian American: | 2% | | |

**Transfer out.** Colleges most students transferred to 2007: SUNY Health Science Center, SUNY Utica/Rome.

**Basis for selection.** High school record, SAT/ACT test scores or pre-entrance examination, and personal interview very important. **Adult students:** SAT/ACT scores not required. **Homeschooled:** Transcript of courses and grades, state high school equivalency certificate, letter of recommendation (nonparent) required.

**High school preparation.** 13 units required. Required and recommended units include English 4, mathematics 2-3, social studies 4 and science 3-4. Science units must be in biology and chemistry; advanced biology and/or physics recommended.

**2008-2009 Annual costs.** Tuition/fees (projected): $12,787. Tuition includes liberal arts component of degree taken at other institution. Room only: $3,500. Books/supplies: $1,000. Personal expenses: $1,272.

**2006-2007 Financial aid.** All financial aid based on need. 26% of total undergraduate aid awarded as scholarships/grants, 74% as loans/jobs. Need-based aid available for part-time students.

**Application procedures. Admission:** No deadline. $50 fee, may be waived for applicants with need. Application must be submitted on paper. Admission notification on a rolling basis. **Financial aid:** Priority date 3/1; no closing date. FAFSA required. Applicants notified on a rolling basis starting 6/15.

**Academics.** Weekend program meets every other Friday, Saturday and Sunday year round for 2 years. **Special study options:** Liberal arts/career combination, weekend college. License preparation in nursing. **Credit/placement by examination:** AP, CLEP. **Support services:** Reduced course load, study skills assistance, tutoring.

**Majors. Health:** Nursing (RN).

**Computing on campus.** 31 workstations in dormitories, library, computer center. Dormitories wired for high-speed internet access and linked to campus network. Commuter students can connect to campus network. Online library, helpline, wireless network available.

**Student life. Freshman orientation:** Mandatory. Preregistration for classes offered. 5 days one week prior to opening day. **Housing:** Guaranteed on-campus for all undergraduates. Coed dorms, substance-free housing available. $200 fully refundable deposit. **Activities:** Student government.

**Student services.** Adult student services, alcohol/substance abuse counseling, campus ministries, career counseling, student employment services, financial aid counseling, health services, personal counseling, placement for graduates, veterans' counselor. **Physically disabled:** Services for visually, speech, hearing impaired. **Transfer:** Pre-admission transcript evaluation for new students. Transfer adviser, college fairs on campus for students transferring to 4-year colleges.

**Contact.** E-mail: rhonda.reader@sjhsyr.org
Phone: (315) 448-5040 Fax: (315) 448-5745
Rhonda Reader, Assistant Dean of Admissions, St. Joseph's College of Nursing, 206 Prospect Avenue, Syracuse, NY 13203

## St. Vincent Catholic Medical Centers
### Fresh Meadows, New York
**CB code: 3400**

- Private 2-year nursing college affiliated with Roman Catholic Church
- Commuter campus in very large city
- Application essay, interview required

**General.** Founded in 1969. **Enrollment:** 116 degree-seeking undergraduates. **Degrees:** 50 associate awarded. **Location:** 10 miles from Manhattan. **Calendar:** Semester. **Full-time faculty:** 9 total. **Part-time faculty:** 10 total.

**Basis for selection.** Test scores, high school achievement, interview, and personal essay considered. National League for Nursing test required.

**High school preparation.** 11 units required. Required units include English 4, mathematics 2, social studies 3 and science 2.

**2007-2008 Annual costs.** Tuition/fees: $7,112. Per-credit charge: $310. Books/supplies: $900. Personal expenses: $2,400.

**Application procedures. Admission:** Closing date 4/1. $45 fee. Admission notification on a rolling basis. Must reply by May 1 or within 3 week(s) if notified thereafter. **Financial aid:** No deadline. FAFSA required. Applicants notified on a rolling basis; must reply within 2 week(s) of notification.

**Academics. Special study options:** License preparation in nursing. **Credit/placement by examination:** CLEP.

**Majors. Health:** Nursing (RN).

**Student services.** Health services, personal counseling.

**Contact.** Phone: (718) 357-0500 ext. 131 Fax: (718) 357-4683
Nancy Wolinski, Chairperson, Admissions Committee, St. Vincent Catholic Medical Centers, 175-05 Horace Harding Expressway, Fresh Meadows, NY 11356

## Schenectady County Community College
### Schenectady, New York
### www.sunysccc.edu
**CB code: 2879**

- Public 2-year community college
- Commuter campus in small city

**General.** Founded in 1968. Regionally accredited. SUNY institution. **Enrollment:** 2,933 degree-seeking undergraduates. **Degrees:** 447 associate awarded. **ROTC:** Air Force. **Location:** 150 miles from New York City, 20 miles from Albany. **Calendar:** Semester, limited summer session. **Full-time faculty:** 68 total. **Part-time faculty:** 142 total. **Special facilities:** Child care center.

**Transfer out. Colleges most students transferred to 2007:** SUNY Albany, College of Saint Rose, Siena College, Sage College of Albany.

**Basis for selection.** Open admission, but selective for some programs. Special requirements for music program. Interview recommended for all; audition required for music, music merchandising programs. **Homeschooled:** Letter from school district superintendent where they reside attesting to home school equivalency of public system.

**High school preparation.** Certain programs have specific mathematics and science prerequisites.

**2007-2008 Annual costs.** Tuition/fees: $3,104; $5,994 out-of-state. Per-credit charge: $117 in-state; $234 out-of-state. Books/supplies: $800. Personal expenses: $900.

**Financial aid.** All financial aid based on need. Need-based aid available for part-time students. Work-study available for part-time students.

**Application procedures. Admission:** No deadline. No application fee. Application may be submitted online. Admission notification on a rolling basis. **Financial aid:** Priority date 5/1; no closing date. FAFSA required. Applicants notified on a rolling basis starting 4/15; must reply by 8/31.

**Academics.** 25-32 Credit hours required in major depending on program. 60-66 Credit hours required for graduation depending on program. **Special study options:** Cooperative education, cross-registration, distance learning, dual enrollment of high school students, ESL, honors, independent study, internships, liberal arts/career combination, teacher certification program. License preparation in aviation. **Credit/placement by examination:** AP,

CLEP, institutional tests. 30 credit hours maximum toward associate degree. **Support services:** GED preparation and test center, learning center, reduced course load, remedial instruction, tutoring.

**Majors. Business:** General, tourism promotion, travel services. **Computer sciences:** General, computer science, programming. **Education:** Early childhood, multi-level teacher. **Engineering technology:** Telecommunications. **Interdisciplinary:** Accounting/computer science, math/computer science. **Liberal arts:** Arts/sciences. **Personal/culinary services:** Food service, restaurant/catering. **Physical sciences:** General. **Protective services:** Criminal justice, security services. **Social sciences:** General. **Transportation:** Aviation, aviation management.

**Computing on campus.** 400 workstations in library, computer center, student center.

**Student life. Freshman orientation:** Available. Preregistration for classes offered. **Activities:** Bands, choral groups, drama, literary magazine, music ensembles, student government, Black and Latino student alliance, Christian Fellowship, human services club, disabled student awareness committee, culinary club.

**Athletics.** NJCAA. **Intercollegiate:** Baseball M, basketball, bowling, softball W. **Team name:** The Royals.

**Student services.** Adult student services, alcohol/substance abuse counseling, career counseling, services for economically disadvantaged, student employment services, financial aid counseling, minority student services, on-campus daycare, personal counseling, placement for graduates, veterans' counselor. **Physically disabled:** Services for visually, speech, hearing impaired. **Transfer:** Transfer adviser, college fairs on campus for students transferring to 4-year colleges.

**Contact.** E-mail: sampsondg@gw.sunysccc.edu
Phone: (518) 381-1366 Fax: (518) 346-0379
David Sampson, Director of Admissions, Schenectady County Community College, 78 Washington Avenue, Schenectady, NY 12305

---

## State University of New York College of Agriculture and Technology at Cobleskill
**Cobleskill, New York**
www.cobleskill.edu                                          CB code: 2524

- Public 2-year agricultural and technical college
- Residential campus in small town

**General.** Founded in 1911. Regionally accredited. **Enrollment:** 2,559 degree-seeking undergraduates; 33 non-degree-seeking students. **Degrees:** 190 bachelor's, 318 associate awarded. **Location:** 35 miles from Albany, 39 miles from Oneonta. **Calendar:** Semester, limited summer session. **Full-time faculty:** 110 total; 31% have terminal degrees, 9% minority, 36% women. **Part-time faculty:** 90 total; 4% have terminal degrees, 4% minority, 50% women. **Class size:** 49% < 20, 43% 20-39, 3% 40-49, 4% 50-99, 1% >100. **Special facilities:** Arboretum, 14 greenhouses, livestock pavilion, 350-acre farm, modern chemical and biological technology laboratories, student-operated restaurant, fish hatchery, ski area, equestrian center, child care and development center. **Partnerships:** Formal partnership with John Deere Company for agricultural engineering.

**Student profile.** Among degree-seeking undergraduates, 983 enrolled as first-time, first-year students, 266 transferred in from other institutions.

| | | | |
|---|---|---|---|
| Part-time: | 4% | Hispanic American: | 5% |
| Out-of-state: | 10% | International: | 3% |
| Women: | 47% | 25 or older: | 9% |
| African American: | 8% | Live on campus: | 76% |
| Asian American: | 1% | | |

**Transfer out.** 74% of students enrolled in the transfer program go on to 4-year colleges. **Colleges most students transferred to 2007:** Cornell University, College of St. Rose, SUNY Albany, SUNY Oneonta, SUNY Plattsburgh.

**Basis for selection.** Strength of high school curriculum most important. GPA, SAT/ACT scores considered. Letters of recommendation, interview recommended. SAT or ACT recommended. SAT or ACT optional for associate degree students, depending on degree. SAT required for bachelor degree seeking students. **Homeschooled:** Transcript of courses and grades, letter of recommendation (nonparent) required. Letter of certification from local high school required.

**High school preparation.** 5 units required; 10 recommended. Required and recommended units include English 1, mathematics 2-3, social studies 1, history 1, science 1-3 (laboratory 1), foreign language 1 and computer science 1. Additional recommendations for some programs.

**2007-2008 Annual costs.** Tuition/fees: $5,449; $11,709 out-of-state. Per-credit charge: $181 in-state; $442 out-of-state. Room/board: $8,650. Books/supplies: $1,200. Personal expenses: $1,092.

**2006-2007 Financial aid. Need-based:** 745 full-time freshmen applied for aid; 463 were judged to have need; 395 of these received aid. Average need met was 52%. Average scholarship/grant was $4,195; average loan $2,994. 59% of total undergraduate aid awarded as scholarships/grants, 41% as loans/jobs. Need-based aid available for part-time students. Work-study available nights and weekends. **Non-need-based:** Awarded to 555 full-time undergraduates, including 263 freshmen. Scholarships awarded for academics, alumni affiliation, leadership, state residency. **Additional information:** Application deadline for scholarships March 15. Separate application required, available through admissions office.

**Application procedures. Admission:** Priority date 5/1; no deadline. $40 fee, may be waived for applicants with need. Application may be submitted online. Admission notification on a rolling basis beginning on or about 11/1. Must reply by May 1 or within 2 week(s) if notified thereafter. **Financial aid:** Closing date 2/15. FAFSA required. Applicants notified by 4/15; must reply within 3 week(s) of notification.

**Academics. Special study options:** Cross-registration, distance learning, ESL, honors, independent study, internships, study abroad, weekend college. Bachelor's degree programs available on campus. **Credit/placement by examination:** AP, CLEP, SAT, institutional tests. 33 credit hours maximum toward associate degree, 60 toward bachelor's. **Support services:** Learning center, pre-admission summer program, reduced course load, remedial instruction, study skills assistance, tutoring, writing center.

**Majors. Agriculture:** General, agribusiness operations, agronomy, animal sciences, mechanization, ornamental horticulture, poultry. **Business:** Accounting technology, business admin, hotel/motel admin, travel services. **Communications:** General. **Computer sciences:** General, information systems. **Conservation:** General. **Family/consumer sciences:** Child care, institutional food production. **Mechanic/repair:** Diesel. **Personal/culinary services:** Chef training, restaurant/catering. **Public administration:** Social work. **Science technology:** Biological, chemical. **Visual/performing arts:** Commercial/advertising art. **Other:** Health Science Studies.

**Most popular majors.** Agriculture 22%, business/marketing 17%, family/consumer sciences 7%, liberal arts 21%, natural resources/environmental science 7%, personal/culinary services 7%.

**Computing on campus.** 270 workstations in dormitories, library, computer center, student center. Dormitories wired for high-speed internet access and linked to campus network. Commuter students can connect to campus network. Online course registration, online library, helpline, repair service, student web hosting, wireless network available.

**Student life. Freshman orientation:** Mandatory. Preregistration for classes offered. 2-day academic and social program held first week of classes. **Housing:** Guaranteed on-campus for freshmen. Coed dorms, single-sex dorms, special housing for disabled, substance-free housing available. $55 fully refundable deposit. Designated quiet study, sophomore experience, upperclass experience. **Activities:** Jazz band, campus ministries, drama, international student organizations, student government, student newspaper, Phi Theta Kappa, activities team, community club, Student Christian Fellowship, student medical response team, X-Pressions of Kolor, black and Latino alliance.

**Athletics.** NJCAA. **Intercollegiate:** Baseball M, basketball, cross-country, diving, golf, lacrosse M, soccer, softball W, swimming, tennis, track and field, volleyball W. **Intramural:** Bowling, football (non-tackle), soccer, softball. **Team name:** Tigers.

**Student services.** Adult student services, alcohol/substance abuse counseling, campus ministries, career counseling, student employment services, financial aid counseling, health services, on-campus daycare, personal counseling, placement for graduates, veterans' counselor. **Physically disabled:** Services for visually, speech, hearing impaired. **Learning disabled:** Comprehensive services available. **Transfer:** Pre-admission transcript evaluation for new students. Transfer adviser, college fairs on campus for students transferring to 4-year colleges.

**Contact.** E-mail: admissions@cobleskill.edu
Phone: (518) 255-5525 Toll-free number: (800) 295-8988
Fax: (518) 255-6769
Christopher Tacea, Director of Admissions and Marketing, State University of New York College of Agriculture and Technology at Cobleskill, Knapp Hall, Cobleskill, NY 12043

## State University of New York College of Agriculture and Technology at Morrisville
**Morrisville, New York**
www.morrisville.edu

CB code: 2527

◗ Public 2-year agricultural and technical college
◗ Residential campus in small town

**General.** Founded in 1908. Regionally accredited. Norwich and Oneida evening extension centers offer liberal arts and some technical courses. **Enrollment:** 3,030 degree-seeking undergraduates. **Degrees:** 99 bachelor's, 530 associate awarded. **ROTC:** Army. **Location:** 30 miles from Syracuse and Utica. **Calendar:** Semester, limited summer session. **Full-time faculty:** 138 total. **Part-time faculty:** 105 total. **Class size:** 45% < 20, 48% 20-39, 2% 40-49, 4% 50-99, less than 1% >100. **Special facilities:** Indoor horse riding arena, horse race tracks, dairy farm, aquaculture ponds, observatory, wildlife museum, ice arena, student-operated businesses (flower shop, travel agency, car mechanic shop).

**Student profile.**

| | | | |
|---|---|---|---|
| Out-of-state: | 7% | Live on campus: | 62% |
| 25 or older: | 21% | | |

**Transfer out. Colleges most students transferred to 2007:** Cornell University, Rochester Institute of Technology, Clarkson, State University of New York.

**Basis for selection.** High school record most important. SAT required for bachelor's degree applicants, SAT or ACT required for students seeking academic scholarship. Essays or interviews not required, but students welcome to submit essay or visit for interview. **Homeschooled:** State high school equivalency certificate required. GED required for students without supporting documentation.

**High school preparation.** Recommended units include English 4, mathematics 3, social studies 4 and science 3. Requirements depend on program. Math and science preparation important for technical majors.

**2007-2008 Annual costs.** Tuition/fees: $5,345; $11,605 out-of-state. Per-credit charge: $181 in-state; $442 out-of-state. Out-of-state associate degree students pay $7,210 tuition. Room/board: $7,810. Books/supplies: $800. Personal expenses: $1,150.

**Financial aid. Need-based:** Need-based aid available for part-time students. Work-study available nights, weekends and for part-time students. **Non-need-based:** Scholarships awarded for academics.

**Application procedures. Admission:** No deadline. $40 fee, may be waived for applicants with need. Application may be submitted online. Admission notification on a rolling basis beginning on or about 11/1. Housing deposit refundable only through June 1. **Financial aid:** Priority date 2/1; no closing date. FAFSA required. Applicants notified on a rolling basis starting 3/1; must reply within 3 week(s) of notification.

**Academics.** Think-Pad university in partnership with IBM. **Special study options:** Distance learning, dual enrollment of high school students, ESL, honors, internships, liberal arts/career combination, student-designed major, weekend college. Joint program with SUNY Forest Technology School at Wanakena, 2-2 transfer program with SUNY College of Environmental Science and Forestry. Bachelor's degree programs available on campus. License preparation in nursing. **Credit/placement by examination:** AP, CLEP, institutional tests. 21 credit hours maximum toward associate degree. **Support services:** Learning center, pre-admission summer program, reduced course load, remedial instruction, study skills assistance, tutoring.

**Majors. Agriculture:** General, agribusiness operations, animal husbandry, animal sciences, aquaculture, business, business technology, dairy, dairy husbandry, equestrian studies, equine science, equipment technology, farm/ranch, floriculture, greenhouse operations, horticultural science, horticulture, landscaping, livestock, mechanization, nursery operations, ornamental horticulture, power machinery. **Architecture:** Landscape, technology. **Biology:** General, conservation, marine. **Business:** General, accounting, accounting technology, accounting/business management, accounting/finance, administrative services, business admin, office management, office technology, restaurant/food services, tourism promotion, tourism/travel, travel services. **Communications:** Journalism. **Computer sciences:** General, applications programming, computer science, information technology, programming. **Conservation:** General, environmental science, environmental studies, fisheries, forest management, forest sciences, forest technology, forestry, management/policy, wood science. **Construction:** General, building inspection, carpentry, maintenance. **Engineering:** General, architectural, computer, computer hardware, construction, electrical, mechanics, polymer, science, software. **Engineering technology:** General, architectural, architectural drafting, automotive, CAD/CADD, computer hardware, computer systems, construction, electrical, manufacturing, mechanical, plastics. **English:** English lit, technical writing. **Family/consumer sciences:** Food/nutrition. **Health:** Clinical lab technology, massage therapy, nursing (RN), prenursing. **Interdisciplinary:** Nutrition sciences. **Liberal arts:** Arts/sciences, humanities. **Math:** General. **Mechanic/repair:** Auto body, automotive, diesel, electronics/electrical, heavy equipment. **Parks/recreation:** Exercise sciences, facilities management, health/fitness, sports admin. **Personal/culinary services:** Food service. **Physical sciences:** Chemistry, physics. **Production:** Furniture, woodworking. **Psychology:** General. **Social sciences:** General.

**Most popular majors.** Agriculture 18%, business/marketing 10%, engineering/engineering technologies 7%, health sciences 10%, interdisciplinary studies 11%, liberal arts 16%, natural resources/environmental science 7%, trade and industry 9%.

**Computing on campus.** 140 workstations in dormitories, library, computer center, student center. Dormitories linked to campus network. Commuter students can connect to campus network. Online library, helpline, repair service, wireless network available.

**Student life. Freshman orientation:** Mandatory, $75 fee. **Housing:** Guaranteed on-campus for all undergraduates. Coed dorms, special housing for disabled, substance-free housing available. $50 fully refundable deposit, deadline 5/1. Special interest housing available. **Activities:** Bands, choral groups, dance, drama, literary magazine, music ensembles, musical theater, radio station, student government, student newspaper, Newman Society, Latin American student organization, African student union/black alliance.

**Athletics.** NCAA. **Intercollegiate:** Basketball, diving, equestrian, field hockey W, football (tackle) M, ice hockey M, lacrosse, soccer, softball W, swimming, volleyball W, wrestling M. **Intramural:** Archery, badminton, basketball, diving, equestrian, golf, handball, racquetball, rifle, soccer, swimming, table tennis, tennis, volleyball, wrestling M. **Team name:** Mustangs.

**Student services.** Adult student services, alcohol/substance abuse counseling, campus ministries, career counseling, services for economically disadvantaged, student employment services, financial aid counseling, health services, minority student services, on-campus daycare, personal counseling, placement for graduates, veterans' counselor, women's services. **Physically disabled:** Services for visually, speech, hearing impaired. **Transfer:** Pre-admission transcript evaluation for new students. Transfer center, transfer adviser, college fairs on campus for students transferring to 4-year colleges.

**Contact.** E-mail: admissions@morrisville.edu
Phone: (315) 684-6046 Toll-free number: (800) 258-0111
Fax: (315) 684-6427
Thomas VerDow, Dean of Enrollment Management, State University of New York College of Agriculture and Technology at Morrisville, PO Box 901, Morrisville, NY 13408-0901

## State University of New York College of Technology at Alfred
**Alfred, New York**
www.alfredstate.edu

CB code: 2522

◗ Public 2-year liberal arts and technical college
◗ Residential campus in rural community

**General.** Founded in 1908. Regionally accredited. Vocational campus located in Wellsville. **Enrollment:** 3,027 degree-seeking undergraduates; 77 non-degree-seeking students. **Degrees:** 141 bachelor's, 741 associate awarded. **ROTC:** Army. **Location:** 75 miles from Rochester, 90 miles from Buffalo. **Calendar:** Semester, limited summer session. **Full-time faculty:** 148 total. **Part-time faculty:** 43 total. **Class size:** 42% < 20, 52% 20-39, 4% 40-49, 2% 50-99, less than 1% >100. **Special facilities:** 750-acre dairy farm.

**Student profile.** Among degree-seeking undergraduates, 24% enrolled in a vocational program, 1,303 enrolled as first-time, first-year students, 673 transferred in from other institutions.

| | | | |
|---|---|---|---|
| Part-time: | 6% | 25 or older: | 23% |
| Out-of-state: | 11% | Live on campus: | 80% |
| Women: | 33% | | |

**Basis for selection.** School achievement record most important, test scores, class rank, school and community service considered. Portfolio required for computer art and design program and Digital Media and Animation Programs. Letters of recommendation and personal essay recommended but not required. SAT or ACT recommended. SAT or ACT required for students applying for baccalaureate degree programs. Interview recommended.

**High school preparation.** Recommended units include English 4, mathematics 4, social studies 4 and science 4. Course requirements vary depending on program.

**2007-2008 Annual costs.** Tuition/fees: $5,406; $8,266 out-of-state. Per-credit charge: $181 in-state; $300 out-of-state. Tuition for bachelor's degree: full-time out-of-state tuition $10,610; per-credit-hour $442 out-of-state. Room/board: $8,040. Books/supplies: $1,000. Personal expenses: $700.

**2006-2007 Financial aid. Need-based:** Need-based aid available for part-time students. Work-study available nights, weekends and for part-time students. **Non-need-based:** Scholarships awarded for academics, alumni affiliation, job skills, minority status.

**Application procedures. Admission:** Priority date 11/1; no deadline. $40 fee, may be waived for applicants with need. Application may be submitted online. Admission notification on a rolling basis beginning on or about 11/1. Must reply by May 1 or within 4 week(s) if notified thereafter. Early application recommended for vocational studies. **Financial aid:** Priority date 3/1; no closing date. FAFSA required. Applicants notified on a rolling basis starting 3/1; must reply within 3 week(s) of notification.

**Academics.** Bachelor of science degree offered in several engineering technology and business majors. **Special study options:** Cooperative education, cross-registration, distance learning, honors, independent study, internships, liberal arts/career combination, student-designed major, study abroad. 4-year bachelor programs in business and engineering-related technologies available. Bachelor's degree programs available on campus. License preparation in nursing, real estate. **Credit/placement by examination:** AP, CLEP, IB, institutional tests. 30 credit hours maximum toward associate degree, 60 toward bachelor's. **Support services:** Learning center, reduced course load, remedial instruction, study skills assistance, tutoring, writing center.

**Majors. Agriculture:** Agronomy, animal sciences, business, dairy, landscaping. **Architecture:** Landscape. **Biology:** General. **Business:** Accounting, administrative services, business admin, entrepreneurial studies, finance, financial planning, management information systems, marketing, office technology. **Communications technology:** Graphics. **Computer sciences:** General, computer graphics, computer science, data processing. **Construction:** Carpentry, electrician, maintenance, masonry, pipefitting, site management. **Engineering technology:** Architectural, construction, drafting, electrical, robotics, surveying. **Health:** Clinical lab technology, medical assistant, medical records technology, medical transcription, nursing (RN), veterinary technology/assistant. **Interdisciplinary:** Biological/physical sciences. **Legal studies:** Court reporting. **Liberal arts:** Arts/sciences. **Math:** General. **Mechanic/repair:** General, auto body, automotive, diesel, electronics/electrical, heating/ac/refrig. **Parks/recreation:** Sports admin. **Personal/culinary services:** Culinary arts. **Physical sciences:** Chemistry. **Production:** Welding. **Public administration:** Human services. **Science technology:** Biological. **Social sciences:** General. **Visual/performing arts:** Graphic design, interior design. **Other:** Heavy equipment operations.

**Most popular majors.** Agriculture 7%, biological/life sciences 6%, business/marketing 12%, engineering/engineering technologies 29%, health sciences 9%, social sciences 7%, trade and industry 18%.

**Computing on campus.** 1,600 workstations in dormitories, library, computer center. Dormitories wired for high-speed internet access and linked to campus network. Commuter students can connect to campus network. Online course registration, online library, helpline, repair service, student web hosting, wireless network available.

**Student life. Freshman orientation:** Mandatory, $60 fee. Preregistration for classes offered. Students have option of spending night on campus. Current students assigned as orientation advisers. **Housing:** Guaranteed on-campus for all undergraduates. Coed dorms, fraternity/sorority housing, substance-free housing available. $50 deposit. Smoking, nonsmoking, freshman, computerized, quiet study, wellness, over 21, over 24, single-room options available. **Activities:** Bands, choral groups, drama, literary magazine, music ensembles, musical theater, radio station, student government, student newspaper, symphony orchestra, environmental club, community action group, Alfred/Wellsville activities council, black student union, international club, women in nontraditional studies, rescue and response team, peer education network, outdoor recreation club.

**Athletics.** NJCAA. **Intercollegiate:** Baseball M, basketball, cheerleading, cross-country, football (tackle) M, lacrosse M, soccer, softball W, swimming, track and field, volleyball W, wrestling M. **Intramural:** Baseball M, basketball, bowling, golf, ice hockey M, lacrosse, rifle, soccer, softball, table tennis, tennis, volleyball. **Team name:** Pioneers.

**Student services.** Adult student services, alcohol/substance abuse counseling, campus ministries, career counseling, services for economically disadvantaged, student employment services, financial aid counseling, health services, minority student services, personal counseling, placement for graduates, veterans' counselor. **Physically disabled:** Services for visually, hearing impaired. **Transfer:** Transfer center, transfer adviser, college fairs on campus for students transferring to 4-year colleges.

**Contact.** E-mail: admissions@alfredstate.edu
Phone: (607) 587-4215 Toll-free number: (800) 425-3733
Fax: (607) 587-4299
Deborah Goodrich, Associate Vice President for Enrollment Management, State University of New York College of Technology at Alfred, Huntington Administration Building, Alfred, NY 14802-1196

## State University of New York College of Technology at Delhi
**Delhi, New York**
www.delhi.edu                                      **CB code: 2525**

▶ Public 2-year junior college
▶ Residential campus in rural community

**General.** Founded in 1913. Regionally accredited. **Enrollment:** 2,593 degree-seeking undergraduates. **Degrees:** 75 bachelor's, 498 associate awarded. **Location:** 70 miles from Albany and Binghamton. **Calendar:** Semester, limited summer session. **Full-time faculty:** 118 total. **Part-time faculty:** 59 total. **Class size:** 48% < 20, 44% 20-39, 3% 40-49, 3% 50-99, less than 1% >100. **Special facilities:** Demonstration forest and arboretum, student-operated restaurant, veterinary science laboratories, golf course, CAD laboratory, architecture laboratories.

**Student profile.**

| | | | |
|---|---|---|---|
| Out-of-state: | 2% | Live on campus: | 60% |
| 25 or older: | 16% | | |

**Basis for selection.** Open admission, but selective for some programs. Special requirements for 4-year programs. SAT/ACT required for 4-year program applicants. Interview recommended. **Homeschooled:** Transcript of courses and grades, state high school equivalency certificate required.

**High school preparation.** 18 units recommended. Recommended units include English 4, mathematics 2, social studies 4, science 2 (laboratory 2) and foreign language 2. Requirements vary by program.

**2007-2008 Annual costs.** Tuition/fees: $5,648; $8,508 out-of-state. Out-of-state tuition for bachelor's program: $10,610; per-credit-hour $442. Room/board: $8,490. Books/supplies: $1,200. Personal expenses: $1,410.

**2006-2007 Financial aid. Need-based:** 62% of total undergraduate aid awarded as scholarships/grants, 38% as loans/jobs. Need-based aid available for part-time students.

**Application procedures. Admission:** No deadline. $40 fee, may be waived for applicants with need. Application may be submitted online. Admission notification on a rolling basis beginning on or about 11/1. Must reply by May 1 or within 4 week(s) if notified thereafter. **Financial aid:** Priority date 2/15; no closing date. FAFSA required. Applicants notified on a rolling basis starting 3/1; must reply within 2 week(s) of notification.

**Academics. Special study options:** Bachelor's degree programs available on campus. License preparation in nursing. **Credit/placement by examination:** AP, CLEP, IB, institutional tests. 50 credit hours maximum toward associate degree, 50 toward bachelor's. Maximum of 50 percent of credits required for degree may be earned by combination of transfer, life experience and credit by examination. **Support services:** Learning center, reduced course load, remedial instruction, study skills assistance, tutoring.

**Majors. Agriculture:** Animal sciences, horticultural science, horticulture, landscaping, ornamental horticulture, turf management. **Architecture:** Landscape, technology. **Business:** Accounting, administrative services, business admin, management information systems, tourism promotion, tourism/travel. **Computer sciences:** Data processing. **Construction:** Carpentry, electrician, masonry. **Education:** Physical. **Engineering:** Science. **Engineering technology:** Architectural, construction, drafting. **Family/consumer sciences:** Institutional food production. **Health:** Nursing (RN), veterinary technology/assistant. **Legal studies:** Legal secretary. **Liberal arts:** Arts/sciences. **Mechanic/repair:** Automotive, heating/ac/refrig. **Parks/recreation:** Facilities management. **Social sciences:** General.

**Most popular majors.** Business/marketing 15%, engineering/engineering technologies 7%, health sciences 22%, liberal arts 15%, personal/culinary services 16%, trade and industry 20%.

**Computing on campus.** 230 workstations in library, computer center. Dormitories wired for high-speed internet access and linked to campus network. Commuter students can connect to campus network. Online course registration, helpline, student web hosting, wireless network available.

**Student life. Freshman orientation:** Available, $75 fee. Preregistration for classes offered. **Housing:** Guaranteed on-campus for freshmen. Coed dorms, apartments, substance-free housing available. $100 deposit. **Activities:** Jazz band, dance, drama, literary magazine, musical theater, radio station, student government, student newspaper, TV station, Delhi Interfaith Council, black student union, Latin student association, West Indian coalition.

**Athletics.** NAIA, NJCAA. **Intercollegiate:** Basketball, cross-country, golf, lacrosse M, soccer, softball W, swimming, tennis, track and field, volleyball W. **Intramural:** Basketball, bowling, boxing, football (tackle) M, handball, racquetball, soccer, softball, swimming, table tennis, tennis, volleyball. **Team name:** Broncos.

**Student services.** Adult student services, alcohol/substance abuse counseling, campus ministries, career counseling, services for economically disadvantaged, student employment services, financial aid counseling, health services, minority student services, on-campus daycare, personal counseling, placement for graduates, veterans' counselor, women's services. **Physically disabled:** Services for visually, hearing impaired. **Learning disabled:** Comprehensive services available. **Transfer:** Transfer adviser, college fairs on campus for students transferring to 4-year colleges.

**Contact.** E-mail: enroll@delhi.edu
Phone: (607) 746-4550 Toll-free number: (800) 963-3544
Fax: (607) 746-4104
Robert Mazzei, Director of Admissions, State University of New York College of Technology at Delhi, 2 Main Street, Delhi, NY 13753-1190

## Suffolk County Community College

Selden, New York
www.sunysuffolk.edu
CB member
CB code: 2827

- Public 2-year community college
- Commuter campus in large town

**General.** Founded in 1959. Regionally accredited. 3 campuses in Suffolk County: Brentwood, Selden, Riverhead. Downtown center in Sayville dedicated to nursing, downtown center in Riverhead dedicated to culinary arts. **Enrollment:** 22,664 degree-seeking undergraduates. **Degrees:** 2,659 associate awarded. **Location:** 60 miles from New York City. **Calendar:** Semester, extensive summer session. **Full-time faculty:** 355 total. **Part-time faculty:** 1,113 total. **Special facilities:** Planetarium.

**Student profile.**

| | | | |
|---|---|---|---|
| Out-of-state: | 2% | 25 or older: | 51% |

**Transfer out. Colleges most students transferred to 2007:** SUNY Stony Brook, Hofstra University, St. Joseph's College, C.W. Post, Dowling College.

**Basis for selection.** Open admission, but selective for some programs. Admission to some programs based on high school record. Admission tests may be used for admission or placement in certain programs in conjunction with high school record. Portfolio required for visual arts program; interview recommended for broadcast telecommunications, fine arts, health career, and paralegal assistant programs. Audition recommended for performing arts programs.

**High school preparation.** Special course requirements vary by program.

**2007-2008 Annual costs.** Tuition/fees: $3,574; $6,830 out-of-state. Books/supplies: $900. Personal expenses: $1,048.

**Financial aid. Need-based:** Need-based aid available for part-time students. Work-study available nights, weekends and for part-time students. **Non-need-based:** Scholarships awarded for academics, art, leadership, minority status, music/drama.

**Application procedures. Admission:** No deadline. $35 fee, may be waived for applicants with need. Application may be submitted online. Admission notification on a rolling basis. **Financial aid:** Priority date 4/15, closing date 6/1. FAFSA required. Applicants notified on a rolling basis starting 4/15; must reply within 2 week(s) of notification.

**Academics. Special study options:** Cooperative education, distance learning, dual enrollment of high school students, ESL, honors, independent study, internships, study abroad, weekend college. Joint admissions with other SUNY units and private institutions. License preparation in nursing. **Credit/placement by examination:** AP, CLEP, IB, institutional tests. 30 credit hours maximum toward associate degree. **Support services:** GED preparation and test center, learning center, pre-admission summer program, reduced course load, remedial instruction, study skills assistance, tutoring, writing center.

**Majors. Architecture:** Environmental design, interior. **Area/ethnic studies:** Women's. **Biology:** General. **Business:** General, accounting, administrative services, business admin, finance, human resources, insurance, management science, marketing, office management, office technology, real estate, sales/distribution. **Communications:** General, broadcast journalism. **Communications technology:** General. **Computer sciences:** General, computer graphics, computer science, information systems, information technology, webmaster. **Conservation:** Environmental science, environmental studies. **Education:** Early childhood, secondary. **Engineering:** Electrical, science. **Engineering technology:** Architectural, construction, drafting, electrical, heat/ac/refrig. **Family/consumer sciences:** Food/nutrition. **Foreign languages:** Sign language interpretation. **Health:** Medical assistant, nursing (RN), occupational therapy assistant, optician, physical therapy assistant, substance abuse counseling, veterinary technology/assistant. **History:** General. **Legal studies:** Paralegal. **Liberal arts:** Arts/sciences. **Math:** General. **Mechanic/repair:** Automotive. **Personal/culinary services:** Culinary arts. **Physical sciences:** Astronomy, chemistry, geology, meteorology, physics, planetary. **Protective services:** Firefighting. **Psychology:** General. **Public administration:** Human services. **Social sciences:** General, economics, political science. **Visual/performing arts:** Commercial/advertising art, dramatic, interior design, studio arts, theater design.

**Computing on campus.** 1,785 workstations in library, computer center, student center. Commuter students can connect to campus network. Online course registration, online library, helpline, wireless network available.

**Student life. Freshman orientation:** Available. Preregistration for classes offered. **Activities:** Bands, choral groups, drama, literary magazine, music ensembles, musical theater, radio station, student government, student newspaper, over 60 clubs available.

**Athletics.** NJCAA. **Intercollegiate:** Baseball M, basketball, bowling M, cross-country, golf M, lacrosse M, soccer M, softball, tennis, track and field, triathlon W. **Intramural:** Basketball, bowling, softball.

**Student services.** Adult student services, career counseling, services for economically disadvantaged, student employment services, financial aid counseling, health services, minority student services, on-campus daycare, personal counseling, placement for graduates, veterans' counselor. **Physically disabled:** Services for visually, speech, hearing impaired. **Transfer:** Pre-admission transcript evaluation for new students. Transfer adviser, college fairs on campus for students transferring to 4-year colleges.

**Contact.** E-mail: admissions@sunysuffolk.edu
Phone: (631) 451-4000 Fax: (631) 451-4415
Kate Rowe, College Dean of Enrollment Management, Suffolk County Community College, 533 College Road, Selden, NY 11784

## Sullivan County Community College

Loch Sheldrake, New York
www.sullivan.suny.edu
CB code: 2855

- Public 2-year community college
- Commuter campus in small town

**General.** Founded in 1962. Regionally accredited. **Enrollment:** 1,283 degree-seeking undergraduates. **Degrees:** 250 associate awarded. **Location:** 100 miles from New York City, 90 miles from Binghamton. **Calendar:** 4-1-4, limited summer session. **Full-time faculty:** 49 total; 45% women. **Part-time faculty:** 85 total; 55% women. **Special facilities:** Complete kitchen, dining room for hospitality programs, mini-travel agency for travel and tourism program, color and black and white darkrooms, computer graphics labs, child development center.

**Student profile.**

| | | | |
|---|---|---|---|
| Out-of-state: | 5% | 25 or older: | 43% |

**Basis for selection.** Open admission, but selective for some programs. Special requirements for nursing program and university parallel business administration program. Out-of-county applicants must have 68 or better high school grade point average. SAT or ACT recommended for placement and counseling. Interview recommended.

**High school preparation.** Liberal arts applicants entering science programs should have 3 each in math and science. Computer science applicants, 3 math and 1 chemistry or physics. Nursing applicants, 1 laboratory biology. Engineering science, 3.5 math and 1 chemistry or physics.

**2007-2008 Annual costs.** Tuition/fees: $3,736; $7,096 out-of-state. Per-credit charge: $131 in-state; $168 out-of-state. Books/supplies: $600. Personal expenses: $700.

**Financial aid. Need-based:** Need-based aid available for part-time students. **Additional information:** 60% of students hold part-time jobs locally.

**Application procedures. Admission:** No deadline. No application fee. Admission notification on a rolling basis. Recommended priority application date for nursing department is December 1. **Financial aid:** Priority date 4/15; no closing date. FAFSA required. Applicants notified on a rolling basis starting 5/15; must reply within 2 week(s) of notification.

**Academics.** Practical experience in class laboratory situations emphasized in technical programs. **Special study options:** Dual enrollment of high school students, exchange student, honors, independent study, internships, study abroad. Joint admissions with SUNY New Paltz in elementary education. **Credit/placement by examination:** AP, CLEP, institutional tests. 31 credit hours maximum toward associate degree. **Support services:** Learning center, reduced course load, remedial instruction, tutoring.

**Majors. Business:** General, accounting, business admin, insurance, management information systems, office management, office technology, sales/distribution. **Communications:** General, broadcast journalism. **Computer sciences:** General, data processing. **Conservation:** General, forestry. **Education:** Early childhood, elementary. **Engineering:** General, science. **Engineering technology:** Surveying. **Family/consumer sciences:** Child care, institutional food production. **Health:** Nursing (RN), predental, premedicine, prepharmacy, preveterinary, substance abuse counseling. **History:** General. **Legal studies:** Paralegal, prelaw. **Liberal arts:** Arts/sciences. **Math:** General. **Parks/recreation:** Facilities management. **Personal/culinary services:** Cosmetic. **Philosophy/religion:** Philosophy. **Protective services:** Criminal justice, police science. **Psychology:** General. **Public administration:** Human services. **Social sciences:** General, sociology. **Visual/performing arts:** Commercial photography, commercial/advertising art.

**Computing on campus.** 80 workstations in library, computer center.

**Student life. Policies:** 45 percent of students are county residents. **Housing:** College-approved housing adjacent to campus. **Activities:** Drama, radio station, student government, black student union, Latin student union.

**Athletics.** NJCAA. **Intercollegiate:** Basketball M, golf, softball W, volleyball W. **Intramural:** Archery, badminton, basketball, bowling, equestrian, golf, handball, racquetball, skiing, soccer, softball, swimming, table tennis, tennis, volleyball. **Team name:** Generals.

**Student services.** Adult student services, career counseling, student employment services, health services, on-campus daycare, personal counseling, placement for graduates, veterans' counselor. **Transfer:** Transfer adviser, college fairs on campus for students transferring to 4-year colleges.

**Contact.** Phone: (845) 434-5750 ext. 4287 Toll-free number: (800) 577-5243 Fax: (845) 434-0923 Sari Rosenheck, Director of Admissions and Registration Services, Sullivan County Community College, 112 College Road, Loch Sheldrake, NY 12759-5151

## Swedish Institute
**New York, New York**
**www.swedishinstitute.com**

- For-profit 2-year health science college
- Very large city
- Interview required

**General.** Accredited by ACCSCT. **Enrollment:** 511 degree-seeking undergraduates. **Degrees:** 302 associate awarded; master's offered. **Calendar:** Trimester. **Full-time faculty:** 20 total. **Part-time faculty:** 40 total.

**Basis for selection.** GPA, recommendations considered.

**2007-2008 Annual costs.** Tuition/fees: $8,420. Per-credit charge: $275. Students generally attend 3 semesters/year. Personal expenses: $199.

**Financial aid.** All financial aid based on need. Need-based aid available for part-time students.

**Application procedures. Admission:** No deadline. $45 fee. **Financial aid:** No deadline. FAFSA, institutional form required.

**Academics. Credit/placement by examination:** CLEP, institutional tests. **Support services:** Reduced course load, study skills assistance, tutoring.

**Majors. Health:** Asian bodywork therapy, massage therapy.

**Computing on campus.** 7 workstations in library, computer center.

**Contact.** E-mail: admissions@swedishinstitute.edu Phone: (212) 924-5900 Fax: (212) 924-7600 Swedish Institute, 226 West 26th Street, 5th Floor, New York, NY 10001-6700

## Technical Career Institutes
**New York, New York**
**www.tcicollege.edu**                                    CB code: 2755

- For-profit 2-year junior and technical college
- Commuter campus in very large city
- Interview required

**General.** Founded in 1909. Regionally accredited. **Enrollment:** 3,191 degree-seeking undergraduates. **Degrees:** 609 associate awarded. **Location:** Downtown. **Calendar:** Semester, extensive summer session. **Full-time faculty:** 67 total. **Part-time faculty:** 95 total.

**Basis for selection.** Open admission. Students without GED/high school diploma must pass CPAT to be admitted. **Homeschooled:** Transcript of courses and grades, state high school equivalency certificate required.

**High school preparation.** High school algebra 1 unit, general science 1 required for engineering technology program. Geometry, trigonometry, physics preferred for engineering program.

**2007-2008 Annual costs.** Tuition/fees: $10,165. Per-credit charge: $400. Required fees $250/year for second-year students. Books/supplies: $800. Personal expenses: $1,280.

**Application procedures. Admission:** No deadline. No application fee. Admission notification on a rolling basis beginning on or about 3/1. **Financial aid:** No deadline. FAFSA, institutional form required. Applicants notified on a rolling basis.

**Academics. Special study options:** Cooperative education, distance learning, ESL, honors, independent study, internships. **Credit/placement by examination:** CLEP, institutional tests. **Support services:** Learning center, reduced course load, remedial instruction, tutoring.

**Majors. Business:** Accounting, administrative services, office technology. **Computer sciences:** General, LAN/WAN management. **Engineering technology:** Construction, electrical. **Mechanic/repair:** Electronics/electrical, heating/ac/refrig.

**Computing on campus.** 350 workstations in library, computer center, student center.

**Student life. Activities:** Choral groups, music ensembles, student government, student newspaper, student chapter of Institute of Electrical and Electronics Engineering, Tau Alpha Pi honor fraternity, American Society of Heating, Refrigeration, and Air Conditioning Engineers, chess club, Future Business Leaders, photography club, Society of Women Engineers, Dare to Dream Volunteer Project.

**Athletics.** NJCAA. **Intercollegiate:** Basketball M.

**Student services.** Career counseling, student employment services, personal counseling, placement for graduates, veterans' counselor. **Transfer:** Transfer adviser for students transferring to 4-year colleges.

**Contact.** E-mail: admissions@tcicollege.edu Phone: (212) 594-4001 Toll-free number: (800) 878-8246 Fax: (212) 629-3937 Aldwyn Cook, Director of Admissions, Technical Career Institutes, 320 West 31st Street, New York, NY 10001

## Tompkins-Cortland Community College
**Dryden, New York**
**www.TC3.edu**                                    CB code: 2904

- Public 2-year community college
- Commuter campus in small town

**General.** Founded in 1968. Regionally accredited. SUNY institution. **Enrollment:** 2,842 degree-seeking undergraduates; 371 non-degree-seeking students. **Degrees:** 519 associate awarded. **Location:** 45 miles from Syracuse, 12 miles from Ithaca. **Calendar:** Semester, extensive summer session. **Full-time faculty:** 66 total. **Part-time faculty:** 218 total. **Class size:** 60% < 20, 39% 20-39, less than 1% 40-49, less than 1% 50-99.

**Student profile.** Among degree-seeking undergraduates, 64% enrolled in a transfer program, 36% enrolled in a vocational program, 875 enrolled as first-time, first-year students, 420 transferred in from other institutions.

| | | | |
|---|---|---|---|
| Part-time: | 19% | Hispanic American: | 4% |
| Out-of-state: | 1% | International: | 2% |
| Women: | 55% | 25 or older: | 28% |
| African American: | 7% | Live on campus: | 19% |
| Asian American: | 1% | | |

**Transfer out.** Colleges most students transferred to 2007: SUNY Cortland, Ithaca College, Cornell University, Binghamton University, Oswego State University.

**Basis for selection.** Open admission, but selective for some programs. Special requirements for nursing and aviation science students. Nursing requires high school average of B or better, plus math and science prerequisites. Aviation science requires student to be ready for pre-calculus math. ACT required for nursing program. Interview required for aviation science, recommended for nursing. **Homeschooled:** Completion of an IHIP pursuant to section 100.10 of the Regulations of the Commissions of Education required.

**2007-2008 Annual costs.** Tuition/fees: $3,913; $7,538 out-of-state. Per-credit charge: $128 in-state; $266 out-of-state. Books/supplies: $1,000.

**2006-2007 Financial aid. Need-based:** 49% of total undergraduate aid awarded as scholarships/grants, 51% as loans/jobs. Need-based aid available for part-time students. Work-study available nights, weekends and for part-time students. **Non-need-based:** Scholarships awarded for academics.

**Application procedures. Admission:** No deadline. $15 fee, may be waived for applicants with need. Application may be submitted online. Admission notification on a rolling basis. **Financial aid:** Priority date 4/15; no closing date. FAFSA, institutional form required. Applicants notified on a rolling basis starting 3/15; must reply within 4 week(s) of notification.

**Academics. Special study options:** Cooperative education, cross-registration, distance learning, dual enrollment of high school students, ESL, honors, independent study, internships, liberal arts/career combination, study abroad, weekend college. License preparation in aviation, nursing, real estate. **Credit/placement by examination:** AP, CLEP, IB. 47 credit hours maximum toward associate degree. **Support services:** GED preparation, learning center, reduced course load, remedial instruction, study skills assistance, tutoring, writing center.

**Majors. Biology:** Biotechnology. **Business:** Accounting technology, business admin, hotel/motel admin, international, labor relations, retailing. **Communications:** General, advertising, broadcast journalism. **Communications technology:** Radio/tv. **Computer sciences:** General, computer support specialist, information systems, webmaster. **Conservation:** General. **Construction:** General. **Education:** Early childhood, kindergarten/preschool, secondary. **Engineering:** General. **Engineering technology:** Electrical, mechanical. **Family/consumer sciences:** Child care. **Health:** Nursing (RN), substance abuse counseling. **Legal studies:** Paralegal. **Liberal arts:** Arts/sciences, humanities. **Mechanic/repair:** Avionics. **Parks/recreation:** Facilities management, sports admin. **Protective services:** Forensics, police science. **Public administration:** Community org/advocacy. **Visual/performing arts:** Commercial/advertising art, photography.

**Most popular majors.** Business/marketing 21%, health sciences 13%, liberal arts 33%, security/protective services 8%.

**Computing on campus.** 400 workstations in library, computer center. Dormitories wired for high-speed internet access and linked to campus network. Commuter students can connect to campus network. Online course registration, online library, helpline, wireless network available.

**Student life. Freshman orientation:** Available. Preregistration for classes offered. Held prior to each semester. Multiple sessions offered: new students, international students, and adult students. **Policies:** All campus organizations must apply for recognition, must have staff adviser, and are funded by the activity fee through faculty-student association and student government. **Housing:** Apartments available. $400 fully refundable deposit, deadline 5/15. **Activities:** Choral groups, dance, drama, film society, literary magazine, radio station, student government, student advisory board, Phi Theta Kappa-Alpha Gamma Nu Chapter, political interests coalition, Gay Straight Alliance, Chi Alpha Christian Fellowship, Black Student Union, Asian student association.

**Athletics.** NJCAA. **Intercollegiate:** Baseball M, basketball, golf, lacrosse M, soccer, softball W, volleyball W. **Intramural:** Badminton, basketball, bowling, football (non-tackle), golf, handball, lacrosse, racquetball, skiing, soccer, softball, squash, swimming, table tennis, tennis, volleyball, water polo. **Team name:** Panthers.

**Student services.** Adult student services, career counseling, services for economically disadvantaged, student employment services, financial aid counseling, health services, minority student services, on-campus daycare, personal counseling, placement for graduates, veterans' counselor. **Physically disabled:** Services for visually, speech, hearing impaired. **Transfer:** Re-entry adviser, pre-admission transcript evaluation for new students. Transfer center, transfer adviser, college fairs on campus for students transferring to 4-year colleges.

**Contact.** E-mail: admissions@TC3.edu
Phone: (607) 844-6580 Toll-free number: (888) 567-8211
Fax: (607) 844-6541
Sandy Drumluk, Director of Admissions, Tompkins-Cortland Community College, 170 North Street, Dryden, NY 13053-0139

## Trocaire College
**Buffalo, New York**
**www.trocaire.edu**

**CB code: 2856**

- Private 2-year junior college affiliated with Roman Catholic Church
- Commuter campus in large city

**General.** Founded in 1958. Regionally accredited. Affiliated with Sisters of Mercy, Buffalo Diocese. **Enrollment:** 1,025 degree-seeking undergraduates. **Degrees:** 178 associate awarded. **Calendar:** Semester, limited summer session. **Full-time faculty:** 42 total. **Part-time faculty:** 52 total. **Class size:** 79% < 20, 21% 20-39.

**Basis for selection.** Open admission, but selective for some programs. Special requirements for health-related fields.

**High school preparation.** 16 units required. Laboratory science and mathematics required for some programs.

**2007-2008 Annual costs.** Tuition/fees: $11,054. Per-credit charge: $431. Books/supplies: $1,000. Personal expenses: $700.

**Financial aid. Need-based:** Need-based aid available for part-time students. **Non-need-based:** Scholarships awarded for academics, alumni affiliation.

**Application procedures. Admission:** No deadline. $25 fee, may be waived for applicants with need. Admission notification on a rolling basis. Must reply by May 1 or within 4 week(s) if notified thereafter. **Financial aid:** Priority date 3/31; no closing date. FAFSA required. Applicants notified on a rolling basis starting 3/1; must reply within 2 week(s) of notification.

**Academics. Special study options:** Cross-registration, dual enrollment of high school students, independent study, internships. License preparation in nursing, radiology. **Credit/placement by examination:** CLEP, institutional tests. 30 credit hours maximum toward associate degree. **Support services:** Learning center, reduced course load, remedial instruction, study skills assistance, tutoring.

**Majors. Business:** Administrative services, business admin, office management, sales/distribution. **Education:** Early childhood. **Health:** Massage therapy, medical assistant, medical radiologic technology/radiation therapy, medical records technology, nursing (RN), surgical technology. **Legal studies:** Legal secretary. **Liberal arts:** Arts/sciences.

**Most popular majors.** Business/marketing 16%, education 7%, health sciences 71%.

**Computing on campus.** 114 workstations in library, computer center, student center. Helpline available.

**Student life. Freshman orientation:** Mandatory. **Activities:** Student government.

**Student services.** Adult student services, career counseling, student employment services, health services, personal counseling, placement for graduates, veterans' counselor. **Physically disabled:** Services for visually, hearing impaired. **Transfer:** Pre-admission transcript evaluation for new students. Transfer center, transfer adviser, college fairs on campus for students transferring to 4-year colleges.

**Contact.** E-mail: info@trocaire.edu
Phone: (716) 827-2545 Fax: (716) 828-6107
Claudia Lesinski, Director of Enrollment Management/Admissions, Trocaire College, 360 Choate Avenue, Buffalo, NY 14220

## Ulster County Community College
### Stone Ridge, New York
**www.sunyulster.edu**                    **CB code: 2938**

- Public 2-year community college
- Commuter campus in small town

**General.** Founded in 1963. Regionally accredited. SUNY institution. **Enrollment:** 2,137 degree-seeking undergraduates; 1,160 non-degree-seeking students. **Degrees:** 320 associate awarded. **Location:** 8 miles from Kingston. **Calendar:** Semester, extensive summer session. **Full-time faculty:** 64 total. **Part-time faculty:** 138 total. **Class size:** 54% < 20, 45% 20-39, 1% 40-49. **Special facilities:** Word processing laboratories, computer art graphic laboratory, geological information systems.

**Student profile.** Among degree-seeking undergraduates, 618 enrolled as first-time, first-year students.

| | | | |
|---|---|---|---|
| Part-time: | 31% | Hispanic American: | 6% |
| Women: | 58% | Native American: | 1% |
| African American: | 5% | 25 or older: | 50% |
| Asian American: | 2% | | |

**Basis for selection.** Open admission, but selective for some programs. Special requirements for nursing and honors programs, with school achievement record very important. SAT or ACT recommended for all applicants. Interview required for nursing, honors program, early admissions applicants; recommended for others. Portfolio recommended for graphic arts.

**High school preparation.** 18 units recommended. Recommended units include English 4 and social studies 4. 3 math and 3 science, including chemistry and physics, required of engineering applicants. 4 English, 3 math, 3 language required of honors program applicants.

**2007-2008 Annual costs.** Tuition/fees: $3,831; $7,131 out-of-state. Per-credit charge: $120 in-state; $240 out-of-state. Books/supplies: $1,000. Personal expenses: $800.

**Financial aid. Need-based:** Need-based aid available for part-time students.

**Application procedures. Admission:** No deadline. No application fee. Admission notification on a rolling basis. **Financial aid:** Priority date 6/1; no closing date. FAFSA required. Applicants notified on a rolling basis starting 6/1; must reply within 2 week(s) of notification.

**Academics. Special study options:** Cooperative education, cross-registration, distance learning, double major, dual enrollment of high school students, ESL, honors, independent study, internships, student-designed major. **Credit/placement by examination:** AP, CLEP, institutional tests. 30 credit hours maximum toward associate degree. **Support services:** Learning center, pre-admission summer program, reduced course load, remedial instruction, study skills assistance, tutoring, writing center.

**Majors. Business:** General, accounting, business admin, finance, office technology. **Communications:** General. **Computer sciences:** General. **Education:** Elementary. **Engineering:** General. **Engineering technology:** Drafting. **Health:** Nursing (RN), substance abuse counseling. **Legal studies:** Legal secretary. **Liberal arts:** Arts/sciences. **Math:** General. **Parks/recreation:** General. **Public administration:** Community org/advocacy, social work. **Social sciences:** General. **Visual/performing arts:** Commercial/advertising art.

**Most popular majors.** Business/marketing 9%, education 7%, health sciences 18%, liberal arts 49%.

**Computing on campus.** 243 workstations in computer center.

**Student life. Activities:** Concert band, choral groups, drama, literary magazine, music ensembles, musical theater, radio station, student government, student newspaper, TV station, children's center club, environmental awareness club, international students club, multicultural club, Phi Theta Kappa, earth science/geology club, Brothers and Sisters in Christ.

**Athletics.** NJCAA. **Intercollegiate:** Baseball M, basketball, bowling M, cross-country, golf, skiing, soccer M, softball W, tennis, track and field, volleyball W, wrestling M. **Intramural:** Badminton, basketball M, soccer M, softball, volleyball.

**Student services.** Adult student services, career counseling, student employment services, health services, on-campus daycare, personal counseling, placement for graduates, veterans' counselor. **Transfer:** Transfer adviser, college fairs on campus for students transferring to 4-year colleges.

**Contact.** E-mail: admissions@sunyulster.edu
Phone: (845) 687-5022 Toll-free number: (800) 724-5022
Fax: (845) 687-5090
Susan Weatherly, Director of Admissions, Ulster County Community College, Cottekill Road, Stone Ridge, NY 12484

## Utica School of Commerce
### Utica, New York
**www.uscny.edu**                    **CB code: 0343**

- For-profit 2-year business college
- Commuter campus in small city
- Interview required

**General.** Founded in 1896. Regionally accredited. Branch campuses in Oneonta and Canastota. **Enrollment:** 386 degree-seeking undergraduates. **Degrees:** 76 associate awarded. **Location:** 50 miles from Syracuse. **Calendar:** Semester, extensive summer session. **Full-time faculty:** 47 total. **Part-time faculty:** 64 total. **Special facilities:** Museum of business education.

**Student profile.** Among degree-seeking undergraduates, 81 enrolled as first-time, first-year students.

| | | | |
|---|---|---|---|
| Part-time: | 33% | Women: | 62% |
| Out-of-state: | 1% | 25 or older: | 30% |

**Transfer out. Colleges most students transferred to 2007:** SUNY College of Technology, St. Rose College, SUNY at Oneonta.

**Basis for selection.** Open admission. Admissions interview required. High School diploma or GED required.

**2007-2008 Annual costs.** Tuition/fees: $11,200. Per-credit charge: $450. Books/supplies: $1,185.

**Financial aid.** All financial aid based on need.

**Application procedures. Admission:** No deadline. No application fee. Application may be submitted online. Admission notification on a rolling basis. Must reply by May 1 or within 3 week(s) if notified thereafter. **Financial aid:** No deadline. FAFSA, institutional form required. Applicants notified on a rolling basis.

**Academics. Special study options:** Accelerated study, dual enrollment of high school students, liberal arts/career combination. Joint admissions with SUNY Institute of Technology. **Credit/placement by examination:** CLEP, institutional tests. 30 credit hours maximum toward associate degree. **Support services:** Learning center, reduced course load, remedial instruction, tutoring.

**Majors. Business:** General, accounting, administrative services, business admin, executive assistant, management information systems, nonprofit/public, retailing, sales/distribution. **Computer sciences:** General, data processing, programming, word processing. **Health:** Health care admin, medical records technology, medical secretary. **Legal studies:** Legal secretary.

**Most popular majors.** Business/marketing 81%, computer/information sciences 19%.

**Computing on campus.** 168 workstations in library, computer center.

**Student life. Freshman orientation:** Mandatory. **Activities:** Student government, student newspaper, future secretaries association, accounting association.

**Student services.** Career counseling, student employment services, personal counseling, placement for graduates, veterans' counselor. **Physically disabled:** Services for visually, hearing impaired. **Transfer:** Transfer adviser, college fairs on campus for students transferring to 4-year colleges.

**Contact.** E-mail: admissions@uscny.edu
Phone: (315) 733-2307 Toll-free number: (800) 321-4872
Fax: (315) 733-9281
Director of Admissions, Utica School of Commerce, 201 Bleecker Street, Utica, NY 13501

## Utica School of Commerce: Canastota
### Utica, New York
**www.uscny.edu**                    **CB code: 3340**

- For-profit 2-year business college
- Commuter campus in small town

Two-Year Colleges

**General.** Regionally accredited. **Calendar:** Semester.

**Annual costs/financial aid.** Tuition/fees (2007-2008): $11,200.

**Contact.** Director of Admissions, 201 Bleecker Street, Utica, NY 13501

## Utica School of Commerce: Oneonta
### Oneonta, New York
www.uscny.edu                                      CB code: 3341

- For-profit 2-year branch campus and business college
- Small city

**General.** Regionally accredited. **Location:** 70 miles from Albany. **Calendar:** Quarter.

**Annual costs/financial aid.** Tuition/fees (2007-2008): $11,200.

**Contact.** Phone: (607) 732-7003
17 Elm Street, Oneonta, NY 13820

## Villa Maria College of Buffalo
### Buffalo, New York                    CB member
www.villa.edu                             CB code: 2962

- Private 2-year visual arts and liberal arts college affiliated with Roman Catholic Church
- Commuter campus in large city
- Interview required

**General.** Founded in 1960. Regionally accredited. **Enrollment:** 436 degree-seeking undergraduates; 19 non-degree-seeking students. **Degrees:** 5 bachelor's, 114 associate awarded. **Location:** 2 miles from downtown. **Calendar:** Semester, limited summer session. **Full-time faculty:** 29 total; 28% have terminal degrees, 52% women. **Part-time faculty:** 43 total; 21% have terminal degrees, 2% minority, 44% women. **Class size:** 88% < 20, 12% 20-39. **Special facilities:** Interior design resource center, education resource center, recording studio, digital photography lab.

**Student profile.** Among degree-seeking undergraduates, 81% enrolled in a vocational program, 4% already have a bachelor's degree or higher, 111 enrolled as first-time, first-year students, 59 transferred in from other institutions.

| | | | |
|---|---|---|---|
| Part-time: | 20% | Hispanic American: | 3% |
| Women: | 73% | Native American: | 1% |
| African American: | 25% | 25 or older: | 31% |

**Transfer out.** 54% of students enrolled in the transfer program go on to 4-year colleges. **Colleges most students transferred to 2007:** SUNY at Buffalo, Buffalo State College, Medaille College, D'Youville College, Canisius College.

**Basis for selection.** Open admission, but selective for some programs. Admissions based on academic records, learning experience, and assessment and advisement program results where applicable. Interview, recommendations also considered. Physical therapist assistant program requires 3.5 GPA. Audition required for music programs; portfolio recommended for fine arts, interior design, photography programs. **Homeschooled:** Statement describing homeschool structure and mission, transcript of courses and grades, interview required. Letter verifying completion from school district in which home-schooled individual resides required. **Learning Disabled:** Must submit all documentation to Coordinator for Students with Disabilities prior to admission and must take VMCAPP.

**High school preparation.** Recommended units include English 4, mathematics 3, social studies 4, history 4 and science 3. General physics with lab required for physical therapist assistant applicants.

**2008-2009 Annual costs.** Tuition/fees (projected): $13,990. Per-credit charge: $455. Books/supplies: $2,500. Personal expenses: $700.

**2006-2007 Financial aid. Need-based:** 141 full-time freshmen applied for aid; 122 were judged to have need; 121 of these received aid. Average need met was 83%. Average scholarship/grant was $5,589; average loan $1,864. 46% of total undergraduate aid awarded as scholarships/grants, 54% as loans/jobs. Need-based aid available for part-time students. **Non-need-based:** Awarded to 356 full-time undergraduates, including 125 freshmen. Scholarships awarded for academics, alumni affiliation, art, leadership, minority status, music/drama.

**Application procedures. Admission:** No deadline. No application fee. Application may be submitted online. Admission notification on a rolling basis. **Financial aid:** No deadline. FAFSA required. Applicants notified on a rolling basis starting 2/15; must reply within 2 week(s) of notification.

**Academics.** Implemented Adviser/Advisee Action Plan provides early identification of students encountering difficulty with scheduling, finances, academic skills, personal problems, and employment. **Special study options:** Cooperative education, cross-registration, double major, dual enrollment of high school students, internships, liberal arts/career combination, study abroad. Evening modules for adult students, member Western New York Consortium of Institutions of Higher Education. Bachelor's degree programs available on campus. **Credit/placement by examination:** AP, CLEP, institutional tests. 30 credit hours maximum toward associate degree. **Support services:** Learning center, pre-admission summer program, reduced course load, remedial instruction, study skills assistance, tutoring.

**Majors. Business:** Business admin. **Computer sciences:** General. **Education:** General, early childhood. **Health:** Physical therapy assistant. **Liberal arts:** Arts/sciences, humanities. **Visual/performing arts:** Commercial/advertising art, interior design, jazz, music management, music performance, photography, studio arts.

**Most popular majors.** Business/marketing 19%, education 21%, health sciences 12%, liberal arts 11%, visual/performing arts 36%.

**Computing on campus.** 100 workstations in library, computer center. Commuter students can connect to campus network. Online library available.

**Student life. Freshman orientation:** Mandatory, $50 fee. Preregistration for classes offered. 2 days for students and 1 day for parents/spouses in August. **Activities:** Jazz band, choral groups, literary magazine, music ensembles, student government, student newspaper, Helping Adults' New Dreams Succeed, Students Actively Striving for Success, Students Against Destructive Decision Making, multicultural club.

**Student services.** Adult student services, alcohol/substance abuse counseling, campus ministries, career counseling, services for economically disadvantaged, student employment services, financial aid counseling, health services, minority student services, personal counseling, placement for graduates, veterans' counselor. **Transfer:** Pre-admission transcript evaluation for new students. Transfer center, transfer adviser, college fairs on campus for students transferring to 4-year colleges.

**Contact.** E-mail: admissions@villa.edu
Phone: (716) 896-0700 ext. 1805 Fax: (716) 896-0705
Kevin Donovan, Director of Admissions, Villa Maria College of Buffalo, 240 Pine Ridge Road, Buffalo, NY 14225-3999

## Westchester Community College
### Valhalla, New York                    CB member
www.sunywcc.edu                           CB code: 2972

- Public 2-year community college
- Commuter campus in large town

**General.** Founded in 1946. Regionally accredited. SUNY institution. **Enrollment:** 10,476 degree-seeking undergraduates; 1,597 non-degree-seeking students. **Degrees:** 995 associate awarded. **Location:** 30 miles from New York City, 6 miles from White Plains. **Calendar:** Semester, extensive summer session. **Full-time faculty:** 165 total; 27% have terminal degrees, 10% minority, 52% women. **Part-time faculty:** 321 total; 14% minority, 53% women. **Special facilities:** On-campus child care center.

**Student profile.** Among degree-seeking undergraduates, 2,552 enrolled as first-time, first-year students, 917 transferred in from other institutions.

| | | | |
|---|---|---|---|
| Part-time: | 43% | Women: | 54% |
| Out-of-state: | 1% | 25 or older: | 37% |

**Transfer out. Colleges most students transferred to 2007:** SUNY Purchase, Pace University, Mercy College, Iona College, Manhattanville College.

**Basis for selection.** Open admission, but selective for some programs. Competitive programs in allied health curricula. High school diploma or GED required of applicants 18 years of age or younger. Interview recommended. **Homeschooled:** Statement describing homeschool structure and mission required. Students must submit letter from superintendent of district in which they reside certifying that home instruction program is equivalent of high school program.

**2007-2008 Annual costs.** Tuition/fees: $3,803; $8,979 out-of-state. Per-credit charge: $144 in-state; $360 out-of-state. Books/supplies: $1,200. Personal expenses: $500.

**2006-2007 Financial aid. Need-based:** 90% of total undergraduate aid awarded as scholarships/grants, 10% as loans/jobs. Need-based aid available for part-time students. Work-study available nights, weekends and for part-time students. **Non-need-based:** Scholarships awarded for academics.

**Application procedures. Admission:** No deadline. $25 fee, may be waived for applicants with need. Application must be submitted on paper. Admission notification on a rolling basis beginning on or about 2/1. **Financial aid:** No deadline. FAFSA, institutional form required. Applicants notified on a rolling basis; must reply within 4 week(s) of notification.

**Academics.** Extensive ESL program. **Special study options:** Accelerated study, cooperative education, cross-registration, distance learning, double major, ESL, honors, independent study, internships, liberal arts/career combination, student-designed major, study abroad. Cambridge University summer program; Italian language study program in Italy. License preparation in nursing, paramedic, radiology, real estate. **Credit/placement by examination:** AP, CLEP, IB, institutional tests. 32 credit hours maximum toward associate degree. **Support services:** Learning center, reduced course load, remedial instruction, study skills assistance, tutoring, writing center,

**Majors. Business:** Accounting, administrative services, business admin, international, marketing, merchandising, office/clerical, sales/distribution. **Communications:** General. **Computer sciences:** General, computer science, information systems, LAN/WAN management. **Education:** Early childhood. **Engineering:** General, science. **Engineering technology:** Civil, electrical. **Family/consumer sciences:** Child care, food/nutrition, institutional food production. **Health:** EMT paramedic, medical radiologic technology/radiation therapy, nursing (RN), nursing assistant, respiratory therapy technology, substance abuse counseling. **Legal studies:** Paralegal. **Liberal arts:** Arts/sciences. **Mechanic/repair:** Automotive. **Personal/culinary services:** Culinary arts, restaurant/catering. **Physical sciences:** General. **Protective services:** Corrections, police science. **Public administration:** Social work. **Social sciences:** General. **Visual/performing arts:** General, dramatic, music performance.

**Computing on campus.** 2,245 workstations in library, computer center, student center. Online library, helpline, wireless network available.

**Student life. Freshman orientation:** Available. Held last week in August for fall semester, usually 2-day event. **Activities:** Choral groups, dance, drama, literary magazine, musical theater, radio station, student government, student newspaper, TV station, international friendship club, black student union, Brazilian club, Haitian club, El Club Hispano Americano, Irish society, Jamaican club, Il Club Italiano, French club, Amnesty International.

**Athletics.** NJCAA. **Intercollegiate:** Baseball M, basketball, bowling, golf M, soccer M, softball W, volleyball W. **Intramural:** Basketball M, soccer M, softball, volleyball. **Team name:** Westcos.

**Student services.** Adult student services, alcohol/substance abuse counseling, career counseling, student employment services, financial aid counseling, health services, minority student services, on-campus daycare, personal counseling, placement for graduates, veterans' counselor, women's services. **Physically disabled:** Services for visually, speech, hearing impaired. **Transfer:** Pre-admission transcript evaluation for new students. Transfer center, transfer adviser, college fairs on campus for students transferring to 4-year colleges.

**Contact.** E-mail: admissions@sunywcc.edu
Phone: (914) 606-6735 Fax: (914) 606-6540
Teresita Wisell, Director of Admissions, Westchester Community College, 75 Grasslands Road, Valhalla, NY 10595

---

## Wood Tobe-Coburn School
**New York, New York**
**www.woodtobecoburn.com**          CB code: 2913

- For-profit 2-year career college
- Commuter campus in very large city

**General.** Founded in 1879. Regionally accredited. **Calendar:** Semester.

**Annual costs/financial aid.** Tuition/fees (2007-2008): $14,860. Books/supplies: $1,165. Personal expenses: $2,110.

**Contact.** Phone: (212) 686-9040
Director of Admissions, 8 East 40th Street, New York, NY 10016-0190

# North Carolina

## Alamance Community College
### Graham, North Carolina
### www.alamance.cc.nc.us
**CB code: 5790**

◗ Public 2-year community college
◗ Commuter campus in large town

**General.** Founded in 1958. Regionally accredited. **Enrollment:** 3,569 degree-seeking undergraduates; 848 non-degree-seeking students. **Degrees:** 270 associate awarded. **Location:** 4 miles from Burlington, 30 miles from Greensboro. **Calendar:** Semester, extensive summer session. **Full-time faculty:** 91 total; 9% have terminal degrees, 12% minority, 58% women. **Part-time faculty:** 271 total; 4% have terminal degrees, 8% minority, 36% women. **Class size:** 67% < 20, 32% 20-39, less than 1% 40-49.

**Student profile.** Among degree-seeking undergraduates, 23% enrolled in a transfer program, 77% enrolled in a vocational program, 5% already have a bachelor's degree or higher, 600 enrolled as first-time, first-year students, 3,569 transferred in from other institutions.

| | | | |
|---|---|---|---|
| Part-time: | 55% | Asian American: | 1% |
| Out-of-state: | 1% | Hispanic American: | 3% |
| Women: | 69% | 25 or older: | 54% |
| African American: | 24% | | |

**Transfer out. Colleges most students transferred to 2007:** University of North Carolina System.

**Basis for selection.** Open admission, but selective for some programs. Special requirements for Dental, Phlebotomy and Nursing. SAT or ACT score may waive required testing for placement. Portfolio recommended for advertising design, commercial art majors. **Learning Disabled:** Disabilities must be documented with special needs counselor. Contact Student Development Office.

**High school preparation.** 21 units recommended. Recommended units include English 4, mathematics 3, social studies 2, history 1, science 3 (laboratory 1), foreign language 2 and academic electives 6. Biology, chemistry required for nursing.

**2007-2008 Annual costs.** Tuition/fees: $1,290; $7,029 out-of-state. Per-credit charge: $42 in-state; $233 out-of-state. Books/supplies: $800. Personal expenses: $800.

**2006-2007 Financial aid. Need-based:** 227 full-time freshmen applied for aid; 200 were judged to have need; 185 of these received aid. Average need met was 30%. Average scholarship/grant was $3,000. 95% of total undergraduate aid awarded as scholarships/grants, 5% as loans/jobs. Need-based aid available for part-time students. Work-study available nights, and for part-time students. **Non-need-based:** Awarded to 85 full-time undergraduates, including 100 freshmen. Scholarships awarded for academics, state residency.

**Application procedures. Admission:** No deadline. No application fee. Application may be submitted online. Admission notification on a rolling basis. **Financial aid:** Priority date 5/15; no closing date. FAFSA required. Applicants notified on a rolling basis starting 3/15; must reply within 2 week(s) of notification.

**Academics. Special study options:** Cooperative education, distance learning, double major, dual enrollment of high school students, ESL, independent study, internships, weekend college. License preparation in nursing, real estate. **Credit/placement by examination:** AP, CLEP, IB, institutional tests. 18 credit hours maximum toward associate degree. Maximum 25% of hours for degree by examination. **Support services:** GED preparation and test center, learning center, reduced course load, remedial instruction, study skills assistance, tutoring.

**Majors. Agriculture:** Horticultural science, horticulture. **Biology:** Biotechnology. **Business:** General, accounting, administrative services, banking/financial services, business admin, management science, office management, real estate, sales/distribution. **Computer sciences:** Applications programming, information systems, programming. **Education:** Early childhood. **Engineering:** Electrical. **Engineering technology:** Drafting. **Health:** Clinical lab assistant, clinical lab technology, medical records admin, medical secretary, nursing (RN). **Legal studies:** Legal secretary. **Liberal arts:** Arts/sciences. **Mechanic/repair:** Electronics/electrical, heating/ac/refrig, industrial. **Personal/culinary services:** Culinary arts. **Protective services:** Criminal justice, firefighting, law enforcement admin.

**Most popular majors.** Business/marketing 21%, health sciences 21%, liberal arts 20%.

**Computing on campus.** 152 workstations in library, computer center.

**Student life. Freshman orientation:** Available. Preregistration for classes offered. General orientation available; some programs have additional orientations. **Activities:** Student government, student newspaper, ethnic student association, marketing club, Phi Beta Lambda (service organization), criminal justice club, early childhood education club, Phi Theta Kappa, nursing club, medical assisting club, Sigma Psi, animal care club, biotechnology, college transfer student club.

**Student services.** Career counseling, student employment services, financial aid counseling, health services, on-campus daycare, personal counseling, placement for graduates, veterans' counselor. **Physically disabled:** Services for visually, speech, hearing impaired. **Transfer:** Pre-admission transcript evaluation for new students. Transfer adviser, college fairs on campus for students transferring to 4-year colleges.

**Contact.** E-mail: accadmissions@alamancecc.edu
Phone: (336) 506-4270 Fax: (336) 506-4264
Elizabeth Brehler, Director of Enrollment Management, Alamance Community College, Box 8000, Graham, NC 27253

## Asheville-Buncombe Technical Community College
### Asheville, North Carolina
### www.abtech.edu
**CB member**
**CB code: 5033**

◗ Public 2-year community and technical college
◗ Commuter campus in small city

**General.** Founded in 1959. Regionally accredited. Certain credit courses offered at the Madison Campus during evening hours. **Enrollment:** 4,020 degree-seeking undergraduates. **Degrees:** 609 associate awarded. **Location:** 115 miles from Charlotte. **Calendar:** Semester. **Full-time faculty:** 154 total; 6% have terminal degrees, 1% minority, 58% women. **Part-time faculty:** 482 total; 5% have terminal degrees, 8% minority, 52% women.

**Student profile.**

| | | | |
|---|---|---|---|
| Out-of-state: | 1% | Hispanic American: | 2% |
| African American: | 5% | 25 or older: | 48% |
| Asian American: | 1% | | |

**Basis for selection.** Open admission, but selective for some programs. Admission to allied health programs based on academic record and state residency. Computerized Placement Test (CPT) administered by college. SAT and/or ACT scores may be used in lieu of CPT for English and math placement. For allied health programs, tests used to earn admission through point system. Provisional or unconditional admission to individual programs will be determined by scores on the test requirements. Placement interview required of all entering students; interview required for all medical programs.

**High school preparation.** 8 units recommended. Recommended units include English 4, mathematics 2 and science 2. Algebra I and algebra II or geometry for engineering; algebra I, chemistry and biology for nursing, medical laboratory and dental programs; algebra I for radiologic technology; biology and 1 mathematics for practical nursing.

**2007-2008 Annual costs.** Tuition/fees: $1,304; $7,043 out-of-state. Per-credit charge: $42 in-state; $233 out-of-state. Books/supplies: $550.

**Financial aid. Non-need-based:** Scholarships awarded for academics, leadership.

**Application procedures. Admission:** No deadline. No application fee. Application may be submitted online. **Financial aid:** Priority date 3/15, closing date 3/31. FAFSA required. Applicants notified on a rolling basis starting 5/1; must reply within 2 week(s) of notification.

**Academics. Special study options:** Cooperative education, cross-registration, distance learning, double major, dual enrollment of high school students, independent study, internships, liberal arts/career combination. License preparation in real estate. **Credit/placement by examination:** CLEP, institutional tests. **Support services:** GED preparation and test center, learning center, pre-admission summer program, reduced course load, remedial instruction, tutoring.

**Majors. Business:** Accounting, administrative services, business admin, management information systems, office technology, office/clerical, operations, sales/distribution. **Computer sciences:** Applications programming. **Engineering technology:** Civil, drafting, electrical, surveying. **Family/ consumer sciences:** Child care, institutional food production. **Health:** Clinical lab technology, dental hygiene, EMT paramedic, medical radiologic technology/ radiation therapy, nursing (RN). **Liberal arts:** Arts/sciences. **Mechanic/ repair:** Automotive, heating/ac/refrig. **Protective services:** Police science. **Public administration:** Social work. **Transportation:** Flight attendant.

**Computing on campus.** 300 workstations in library, computer center.

**Student life. Activities:** Drama, literary magazine, student government, student newspaper.

**Student services.** Career counseling, student employment services, on-campus daycare, personal counseling, placement for graduates, veterans' counselor. **Physically disabled:** Services for visually, speech, hearing impaired. **Transfer:** Transfer adviser, college fairs on campus for students transferring to 4-year colleges.

**Contact.** E-mail: admissions@abtech.edu
Phone: (828) 254-1921 ext. 144 Fax: (828) 251-6718
Scott Douglas, Director, Enrollment Management, Asheville-Buncombe Technical Community College, 340 Victoria Road, Asheville, NC 28801-4897

## Beaufort County Community College
### Washington, North Carolina
www.beaufortccc.edu                    CB code: 7307

▸ Public 2-year community college
▸ Commuter campus in small town

**General.** Founded in 1967. Regionally accredited. **Enrollment:** 786 degree-seeking undergraduates. **Degrees:** 152 associate awarded. **Location:** 23 miles from Greenville. **Calendar:** Semester, limited summer session. **Full-time faculty:** 62 total. **Part-time faculty:** 191 total. **Special facilities:** Wachovia Partnership East hub site.

**Transfer out. Colleges most students transferred to 2007:** East Carolina University.

**Basis for selection.** Open admission, but selective for some programs. Special admission requirements for allied health programs and basic law enforcement training. **Homeschooled:** Must provide proof that the home school is registered with the appropriate state agencies.

**High school preparation.** One unit chemistry required for nursing and medical technology applicants.

**2007-2008 Annual costs.** Tuition/fees: $1,324; $7,063 out-of-state. Per-credit charge: $42 in-state; $233 out-of-state. Some programs require insurance and uniforms. Books/supplies: $800.

**Financial aid. Need-based:** Need-based aid available for part-time students. **Non-need-based:** Scholarships awarded for academics.

**Application procedures. Admission:** No deadline. No application fee. Application may be submitted online. **Financial aid:** Priority date 6/1; no closing date. FAFSA required. Applicants notified on a rolling basis starting 5/1; must reply within 2 week(s) of notification.

**Academics. Special study options:** Cooperative education, distance learning, dual enrollment of high school students, ESL, internships, liberal arts/ career combination. Bachelor's degree programs available on campus. License preparation in aviation, nursing, real estate. **Credit/placement by examination:** AP, CLEP, institutional tests. **Support services:** GED preparation and test center, learning center, remedial instruction, study skills assistance, tutoring.

**Majors. Agriculture:** Mechanization. **Business:** Accounting, administrative services, business admin. **Computer sciences:** Applications programming, information systems, networking, programming, vendor certification. **Construction:** Electrician. **Education:** General, early childhood. **Engineering technology:** Drafting, electrical. **Family/consumer sciences:** Child care, child development. **Health:** Clinical lab technology, medical secretary, nursing (RN), office admin. **Liberal arts:** Arts/sciences. **Mechanic/repair:** Automotive, diesel, heavy equipment. **Production:** Welding. **Protective services:** Criminal justice. **Public administration:** Human services. **Science technology:** Biological.

**Computing on campus.** Commuter students can connect to campus network. Online library, wireless network available.

**Student life. Freshman orientation:** Available. Preregistration for classes offered. **Activities:** Student government.

**Student services.** Career counseling, services for economically disadvantaged, student employment services, financial aid counseling, personal counseling, placement for graduates, veterans' counselor. **Transfer:** Pre-admission transcript evaluation for new students. Transfer adviser, college fairs on campus for students transferring to 4-year colleges.

**Contact.** E-mail: garyb@beaufortccc.edu
Phone: (252) 940-6237 Fax: (252) 940-6393
Gary Burbage, Director of Admissions and Recruitment, Beaufort County Community College, Box 1069, Washington, NC 27889

## Bladen Community College
### Dublin, North Carolina
www.bladencc.edu                    CB code: 3082

▸ Public 2-year community college
▸ Commuter campus in rural community

**General.** Founded in 1967. Regionally accredited. **Enrollment:** 1,370 degree-seeking undergraduates. **Degrees:** 110 associate awarded. **Location:** 35 miles from Fayetteville. **Calendar:** Semester, limited summer session. **Full-time faculty:** 50 total; 6% have terminal degrees, 22% minority, 64% women. **Part-time faculty:** 60 total; 7% have terminal degrees, 27% minority, 48% women. **Class size:** 82% < 20, 18% 20-39.

**Student profile.** Among degree-seeking undergraduates, 33% enrolled in a transfer program, 67% enrolled in a vocational program.

**Transfer out. Colleges most students transferred to 2007:** University of North Carolina-Wilmington, University of North Carolina-Pembroke, Fayetteville State University, East Carolina University, North Carolina State University.

**Basis for selection.** Open admission, but selective for some programs. Practical nursing program requires submission of appropriate test results and completion of high school biology and algebra courses with grade of C or better. ADN program requires biology and algebra, plus general chemistry. Biology and chemistry must be within last 5 years for ADN.

**High school preparation.** 26 units recommended. Recommended units include English 4, mathematics 3, social studies 1, history 2, science 3 (laboratory 1), foreign language 2, computer science 1 and academic electives 10.

**2007-2008 Annual costs.** Tuition/fees: $1,326; $7,065 out-of-state. Per-credit charge: $42 in-state; $233 out-of-state. Books/supplies: $800. Personal expenses: $725.

**Financial aid. Need-based:** Need-based aid available for part-time students. Work-study available nights and for part-time students.

**Application procedures. Admission:** Priority date 8/15; no deadline. No application fee. Application may be submitted online. Admission notification on a rolling basis beginning on or about 6/15. **Financial aid:** Priority date 6/1; no closing date. FAFSA required. Applicants notified on a rolling basis starting 8/1; must reply within 2 week(s) of notification.

**Academics. Special study options:** Cooperative education, distance learning, double major, dual enrollment of high school students, ESL, independent study, internships, liberal arts/career combination, weekend college. Bachelor's degree programs available on campus. **Credit/placement by examination:** CLEP, institutional tests. 10 credit hours maximum toward associate degree. **Support services:** GED preparation and test center, learning center, reduced course load, remedial instruction, study skills assistance, tutoring, writing center.

**Majors. Biology:** Biotechnology. **Business:** Business admin, office technology, office/clerical. **Computer sciences:** General, applications programming, programming. **Education:** General. **Engineering technology:** Electrical, industrial. **Health:** Nursing (RN). **Liberal arts:** Arts/sciences. **Mechanic/ repair:** Electronics/electrical. **Personal/culinary services:** Cosmetic. **Production:** Welding. **Protective services:** Law enforcement admin.

**Computing on campus.** 100 workstations in library, computer center, student center. Online course registration, helpline, wireless network available.

**Student life. Freshman orientation:** Mandatory. Preregistration for classes offered. **Activities:** Drama, literary magazine, student government, student newspaper.

**Athletics. Team name:** Eagles.

**Student services.** Adult student services, alcohol/substance abuse counseling, career counseling, services for economically disadvantaged, student employment services, financial aid counseling, minority student services, personal counseling, placement for graduates, veterans' counselor. **Physically disabled:** Services for visually, speech, hearing impaired. **Transfer:** Pre-admission transcript evaluation for new students. Transfer center, transfer adviser, college fairs on campus for students transferring to 4-year colleges.

**Contact.** E-mail: ywilloughby@bladencc.edu
Phone: (910) 879-5593 Fax: (910) 879-5564
Jeffrey Kornegay, Vice President of Student Services, Bladen Community College, Box 266, Dublin, NC 28332-0266

## Blue Ridge Community College
### Flat Rock, North Carolina
### www.blueridge.edu
**CB code: 5644**

- Public 2-year community college
- Commuter campus in small town

**General.** Founded in 1969. Regionally accredited. **Enrollment:** 810 full-time, degree-seeking students. **Degrees:** 145 associate awarded. **Location:** 25 miles from Asheville. **Calendar:** Semester, limited summer session. **Full-time faculty:** 77 total. **Part-time faculty:** 232 total. **Class size:** 81% < 20, 19% 20-39, less than 1% 40-49.

**Student profile.**

| | | | |
|---|---|---|---|
| Out-of-state: | 2% | 25 or older: | 29% |

**Basis for selection.** Open admission, but selective for some programs. Mathematics and science requirements for allied health programs in surgical technology, pharmacy technology, nursing.

**High school preparation.** 3 units of science, one of which must be lab, required for allied health programs only.

**2007-2008 Annual costs.** Tuition/fees: $1,333; $7,072 out-of-state. Per-credit charge: $42 in-state; $233 out-of-state. Books/supplies: $750.

**Financial aid. Need-based:** Need-based aid available for part-time students. Work-study available nights and for part-time students. **Non-need-based:** Scholarships awarded for academics, athletics, leadership, minority status, state residency.

**Application procedures. Admission:** No deadline. No application fee. Application may be submitted online, Admission notification on a rolling basis. **Financial aid:** Priority date 6/30; no closing date. FAFSA, institutional form required. Applicants notified on a rolling basis starting 2/1; must reply within 4 week(s) of notification.

**Academics. Special study options:** Cooperative education, distance learning, double major, dual enrollment of high school students, ESL. Bachelor's degree programs available on campus. License preparation in nursing, paramedic, physical therapy, real estate. **Credit/placement by examination:** CLEP, institutional tests. Maximum of 50% of credit hours by examination may be counted toward degree. **Support services:** GED preparation and test center, learning center, reduced course load, remedial instruction, study skills assistance, tutoring.

**Majors. Agriculture:** Horticulture. **Business:** General, administrative services, sales/distribution, tourism promotion, tourism/travel. **Computer sciences:** Information systems, programming. **Conservation:** General. **Engineering:** Electrical. **Engineering technology:** Drafting, electrical. **Family/consumer sciences:** Child care. **Foreign languages:** Sign language interpretation. **Health:** Nursing (RN), surgical technology. **Liberal arts:** Arts/sciences.

**Most popular majors.** Business/marketing 14%, computer/information sciences 26%, health sciences 12%, liberal arts 23%.

**Computing on campus.** 200 workstations in library, computer center.

**Student life. Freshman orientation:** Mandatory. Preregistration for classes offered. **Activities:** Drama, literary magazine, student government, Circle-K, Rotaract, Phi Theta Kappa, National Vocational-Technical Honor Society.

**Athletics.** NJCAA. **Intercollegiate:** Bowling M, volleyball W.

**Student services.** Adult student services, career counseling, student employment services, financial aid counseling, on-campus daycare, personal

counseling, placement for graduates, veterans' counselor. **Physically disabled:** Services for visually, speech, hearing impaired. **Transfer:** Pre-admission transcript evaluation for new students. Transfer adviser, college fairs on campus for students transferring to 4-year colleges.

**Contact.** E-mail: kirstenb@blueridge.edu
Phone: (828) 694-1800 Fax: (828) 694-1693
Marcia Stoneman, Dean for Student Services, Blue Ridge Community College, 180 West Campus Drive, Flat Rock, NC 28731-9624

## Brunswick Community College
### Supply, North Carolina
### www.brunswickcc.edu
**CB code: 7314**

- Public 2-year community college
- Commuter campus in small town

**General.** Founded in 1979. Regionally accredited. **Enrollment:** 1,136 degree-seeking undergraduates. **Degrees:** 120 associate awarded. **Location:** 25 miles from Wilmington, 30 miles from Myrtle Beach, South Carolina. **Calendar:** Semester, limited summer session. **Full-time faculty:** 42 total. **Part-time faculty:** 151 total. **Class size:** 81% < 20, 18% 20-39, 1% 40-49.

**Student profile.**

| | | | |
|---|---|---|---|
| Out-of-state: | 3% | 25 or older: | 45% |

**Transfer out. Colleges most students transferred to 2007:** University of North Carolina at Wilmington.

**Basis for selection.** Open admission, but selective for some programs. Phlebotomy, basic law enforcement technology, practical nursing, associate degree nursing, and health information technology program applicants must have completed specific course work before they are considered. Limited slots. May also enter based on test scores. SAT accepted in lieu of ASSET Placement Test. Interview is required to review admission procedures and file; does not determine acceptance. **Learning Disabled:** Requests for any accommodations should be made at least 2 weeks prior to beginning of applicant's first semester.

**2007-2008 Annual costs.** Tuition/fees: $1,333; $7,072 out-of-state. Per-credit charge: $42 in-state; $233 out-of-state. Books/supplies: $600. Personal expenses: $800.

**2007-2008 Financial aid. Need-based:** Need-based aid available for part-time students. Work-study available nights, weekends and for part-time students. **Non-need-based:** Scholarships awarded for academics, state residency. **Additional information:** Attendance required at financial aid orientation session for those receiving federal student aid.

**Application procedures. Admission:** No deadline. No application fee. Application may be submitted online. Admission notification on a rolling basis. **Financial aid:** Priority date 6/1, closing date 6/15. FAFSA, institutional form required. Applicants notified on a rolling basis starting 3/1; must reply by 6/15 or within 2 week(s) of notification.

**Academics. Special study options:** Distance learning, dual enrollment of high school students, ESL, internships. License preparation in nursing, paramedic, real estate. **Credit/placement by examination:** AP, CLEP, institutional tests. No limits on credit by examination hours that may be applied toward an associate degree. **Support services:** GED preparation and test center, learning center, reduced course load, remedial instruction, study skills assistance, tutoring.

**Majors. Agriculture:** Aquaculture, horticultural science, turf management. **Business:** Administrative services, business admin. **Computer sciences:** Information systems, programming. **Education:** Early childhood. **Engineering technology:** Electrical. **Health:** Medical records technology, nursing (RN). **Liberal arts:** Arts/sciences. **Mechanic/repair:** Industrial. **Personal/culinary services:** Cosmetic.

**Most popular majors.** Agriculture 11%, business/marketing 11%, computer/information sciences 6%, education 9%, health sciences 8%, liberal arts 46%.

**Computing on campus.** 146 workstations in library, computer center.

**Student life. Freshman orientation:** Available. Preregistration for classes offered. **Policies:** All facilities are nonsmoking. Smoking allowed in designated outdoor areas only. **Activities:** Student government, student newspaper, National Technical Honor Society, Phi Theta Kappa, science club, journalism club.

**Athletics.** NJCAA. **Intercollegiate:** Baseball M, basketball, softball W, volleyball W. **Team name:** Dolphins.

**Student services.** Career counseling, student employment services, financial aid counseling, personal counseling, placement for graduates, veterans' counselor. **Physically disabled:** Services for visually, hearing impaired. **Transfer:** Pre-admission transcript evaluation for new students. Transfer adviser, college fairs on campus for students transferring to 4-year colleges.

**Contact.** E-mail: olsenj@brunswickcc.edu
Phone: (910) 755-7324 Toll-free number: (800) 754-1050 ext. 324
Fax: (910) 754-9609
Christen Cox, Admissions Counselor, Brunswick Community College, Box 30, Supply, NC 28462

## Caldwell Community College and Technical Institute
### Hudson, North Carolina
www.cccti.edu                                    CB code: 5146

♦  Public 2-year community and technical college
♦  Commuter campus in small town

**General.** Founded in 1964. Regionally accredited. **Enrollment:** 3,138 degree-seeking undergraduates. **Degrees:** 340 associate awarded. **Location:** 70 miles from Charlotte. **Calendar:** Semester, limited summer session. **Full-time faculty:** 130 total. **Part-time faculty:** 290 total. **Class size:** 68% < 20, 31% 20-39, 1% 40-49, less than 1% 50-99, less than 1% >100.

**Student profile.**

| | | | |
|---|---|---|---|
| Out-of-state: | 2% | 25 or older: | 43% |

**Basis for selection.** Open admission, but selective for some programs. Limited number of applicants admitted to health science programs, interview required. College-administered examination used for placement.

**2007-2008 Annual costs.** Tuition/fees: $1,292; $7,031 out-of-state. Per-credit charge: $42 in-state; $233 out-of-state. Books/supplies: $925. Personal expenses: $1,350.

**Financial aid.** All financial aid based on need. Need-based aid available for part-time students. Work-study available for part-time students.

**Application procedures. Admission:** No deadline. No application fee. Admission notification on a rolling basis. **Financial aid:** Priority date 6/1; no closing date. FAFSA required. Applicants notified on a rolling basis starting 6/30.

**Academics. Special study options:** Cooperative education, distance learning, dual enrollment of high school students, independent study. License preparation in aviation, nursing, occupational therapy, physical therapy, real estate. **Credit/placement by examination:** CLEP, institutional tests. 16 credit hours maximum toward associate degree. **Support services:** GED preparation and test center, learning center, reduced course load, remedial instruction, tutoring.

**Majors. Business:** Accounting, administrative services, business admin. **Computer sciences:** Applications programming, data processing, programming. **Education:** Early childhood. **Engineering technology:** Drafting, electrical. **Health:** Cardiovascular technology, medical radiologic technology/radiation therapy, medical secretary, nuclear medical technology, nursing (RN), physical therapy assistant, sonography. **Legal studies:** Paralegal. **Liberal arts:** Arts/sciences. **Math:** General. **Mechanic/repair:** Industrial. **Transportation:** Aviation management. **Visual/performing arts:** Art.

**Most popular majors.** Business/marketing 22%, computer/information sciences 12%, health sciences 37%, liberal arts 16%.

**Computing on campus.** 750 workstations in library, computer center.

**Student life. Freshman orientation:** Available. Preregistration for classes offered. 2-day session held prior to beginning of fall semester. **Activities:** Choral groups, drama, student government, TV station, Ebony Kinship, special interest clubs, Phi Theta Kappa, Alpha Omega (non-denominational religious organization).

**Athletics.** NJCAA. **Intercollegiate:** Basketball M, volleyball W. **Intramural:** Basketball, tennis. **Team name:** Cobras.

**Student services.** Career counseling, student employment services, financial aid counseling, personal counseling, placement for graduates, veterans' counselor. **Physically disabled:** Services for visually, hearing impaired. **Transfer:** Transfer adviser, college fairs on campus for students transferring to 4-year colleges.

**Contact.** Phone: (828) 726-2700 Fax: (828) 726-2709
Carolyn Woodard, Director, Enrollment Management Services, Caldwell Community College and Technical Institute, 2855 Hickory Boulevard, Hudson, NC 28638-2672

## Cape Fear Community College
### Wilmington, North Carolina
www.cfcc.edu                                    CB code: 5094

♦  Public 2-year community college
♦  Commuter campus in small city

**General.** Founded in 1959. Regionally accredited. **Location:** 125 miles from Raleigh. **Calendar:** Semester.

**Annual costs/financial aid.** Tuition/fees (2007-2008): $1,328; $7,067 out-of-state. Books/supplies: $900. Personal expenses: $900. Need-based financial aid available to full-time and part-time students.

**Contact.** Phone: (910) 362-7557
Director of Enrollment Management, 411 North Front Street, Wilmington, NC 28401-3910

## Carolinas College of Health Sciences
### Charlotte, North Carolina
www.carolinascollege.edu                         CB code: 6211

♦  Public 2-year health science and junior college
♦  Commuter campus in very large city
♦  SAT or ACT required

**General.** Regionally accredited. Institution supported by public hospital system. **Enrollment:** 467 degree-seeking undergraduates. **Degrees:** 120 associate awarded. **Calendar:** Semester, limited summer session. **Full-time faculty:** 46 total. **Part-time faculty:** 25 total. **Class size:** 40% < 20, 57% 20-39, 3% 40-49.

**Student profile.** Among degree-seeking undergraduates, 100% enrolled in a vocational program. Of all enrolled students, 25% already have a bachelor's degree or higher.

**Transfer out. Colleges most students transferred to 2007:** Queens College, University of North Carolina at Charlotte, Winston-Salem State University, Central Piedmont Community College, Mercy School of Nursing.

**Basis for selection.** Selection based on SAT/ACT test scores and high school GPA. Only students with permanent resident status will be considered for enrollment.

**High school preparation.** 15 units required. Required units include English 4, mathematics 1, social studies 2, history 2, science 2 (laboratory 2) and foreign language 2. Algebra, biology, chemistry required.

**2007-2008 Annual costs.** Tuition/fees: $6,350. Per-credit charge: $205. Tuition varies by program. Books/supplies: $500.

**Financial aid. Need-based:** Need-based aid available for part-time students. Work-study available for part-time students. **Non-need-based:** Scholarships awarded for academics.

**Application procedures. Admission:** Priority date 12/1; deadline 3/1 (receipt date). $50 fee. Application must be submitted on paper. Admission notification on a rolling basis beginning on or about 1/1. Must reply by May 1 or within 4 week(s) if notified thereafter. Application deadlines vary by program. **Financial aid:** Priority date 5/1; no closing date. FAFSA, institutional form required. Applicants notified on a rolling basis starting 5/1.

**Academics.** Post-bachelor's certificate in Medical Technology available. **Special study options:** Distance learning, independent study, liberal arts/career combination. Bachelor's degree programs available on campus. License preparation in nursing. **Credit/placement by examination:** AP, CLEP, IB, institutional tests. 25 credit hours maximum toward associate degree. **Support services:** Learning center, tutoring.

**Majors. Health:** Medical radiologic technology/radiation therapy, nursing (RN).

**Computing on campus.** 30 workstations in computer center. Online library, wireless network available.

**Student life. Freshman orientation:** Mandatory. Preregistration for classes offered. **Housing:** Apartments owned by health care system available. **Activities:** Student government.

**Student services.** Alcohol/substance abuse counseling, campus ministries, career counseling, student employment services, financial aid counseling, health services, personal counseling, placement for graduates, veterans' counselor. **Transfer:** Pre-admission transcript evaluation for new students. College fairs on campus for students transferring to 4-year colleges.

**Contact.** E-mail: cchsinformation@carolinas.org
Phone: (704) 355-5583 Fax: (704) 355-9336
Rhoda Gallo, Admissions Officer, Carolinas College of Health Sciences, PO Box 32861, Charlotte, NC 28232

## Carteret Community College
### Morehead City, North Carolina
### www.carteret.edu
**CB code: 5092**

- Public 2-year community and technical college
- Commuter campus in small town
- Interview required

**General.** Founded in 1963. Regionally accredited. Aquaculture technology and marine technical trades programs. **Enrollment:** 1,175 degree-seeking undergraduates. **Degrees:** 171 associate awarded. **Location:** 150 miles from Raleigh, 87 miles from Wilmington. **Calendar:** Semester, limited summer session. **Full-time faculty:** 59 total. **Part-time faculty:** 82 total. **Special facilities:** Carteret County historical research center, center for marine science and technology.

**Student profile.** Among degree-seeking undergraduates, 65% enrolled in a transfer program, 35% enrolled in a vocational program, 15% already have a bachelor's degree or higher.

| | | | |
|---|---|---|---|
| Part-time: | 38% | Women: | 61% |
| Out-of-state: | 2% | 25 or older: | 48% |

**Transfer out. Colleges most students transferred to 2007:** University of North Carolina at Wilmington, East Carolina University.

**Basis for selection.** Open admission, but selective for some programs. Admission to nursing and allied health programs based upon course work, grades and test scores; interview required. SAT required of radiologic technology and respiratory therapy applicants; score report due by January 1. **Homeschooled:** Transcript of courses and grades required. **Learning Disabled:** Students requesting academic accommodations must present proper documentation.

**High school preparation.** Extensive science and mathematics recommended for allied health programs, particularly respiratory therapy, radiologic technology, and nursing.

**2007-2008 Annual costs.** Tuition/fees: $1,311; $7,050 out-of-state. Per-credit charge: $42 in-state; $233 out-of-state. Books/supplies: $600. Personal expenses: $1,665.

**Financial aid. Need-based:** Need-based aid available for part-time students. **Non-need-based:** Scholarships awarded for academics, leadership, minority status, state residency. **Additional information:** Institutional student loan program administered by college. Student may charge up to $600 for books, supplies and tuition per quarter. Repayment due by 11th week of semester.

**Application procedures. Admission:** No deadline. No application fee. Application may be submitted online. Admission notification on a rolling basis. **Financial aid:** No deadline. FAFSA, institutional form required. Applicants notified on a rolling basis starting 7/1; must reply within 2 week(s) of notification.

**Academics. Special study options:** Cooperative education, cross-registration, distance learning, double major, dual enrollment of high school students, ESL, independent study, internships, liberal arts/career combination, teacher certification program. License preparation in nursing, paramedic, radiology, real estate. **Credit/placement by examination:** AP, CLEP, institutional tests. **Support services:** GED preparation and test center, learning center, pre-admission summer program, reduced course load, remedial instruction, study skills assistance, tutoring, writing center.

**Majors. Agriculture:** Greenhouse operations, horticultural science, horticulture. **Biology:** Biotechnology. **Business:** General, administrative services, e-commerce, hotel/motel admin, office/clerical. **Communications:** Photojournalism. **Communications technology:** Photo/film/video. **Computer sciences:** General, information technology, LAN/WAN management, web page design, webmaster. **Education:** General, teacher assistance. **Family/consumer sciences:** Child development. **Health:** EMT ambulance attendant, massage therapy, medical radiologic technology/radiation therapy, office admin, predental, premedicine, prenursing, prepharmacy, preveterinary, radiologic technology/medical imaging, recreational therapy, respiratory therapy technology. **Legal studies:** Legal secretary, paralegal. **Liberal arts:** Arts/sciences. **Mechanic/repair:** Marine. **Personal/culinary services:** Restaurant/catering. **Protective services:** Criminal justice, police science. **Visual/performing arts:** General, interior design, photography.

**Most popular majors.** Business/marketing 70%, health sciences 25%.

**Computing on campus.** 225 workstations in library, computer center, student center. Online library, helpline, wireless network available.

**Student life. Activities:** Choral groups, drama, literary magazine, student government, student newspaper, Psi Beta (honorary society for psychology majors), Phi Beta Lambda (business organization).

**Student services.** Adult student services, alcohol/substance abuse counseling, career counseling, services for economically disadvantaged, student employment services, financial aid counseling, personal counseling, placement for graduates, veterans' counselor. **Physically disabled:** Services for visually, speech, hearing impaired. **Transfer:** Pre-admission transcript evaluation for new students. Transfer adviser, college fairs on campus for students transferring to 4-year colleges.

**Contact.** E-mail: admissions@carteret.edu
Phone: (252) 222-6154 Fax: (252) 222-6265
Margie Ward, Admissions Officer, Carteret Community College, 3505 Arendell Street, Morehead City, NC 28557-2989

## Catawba Valley Community College
### Hickory, North Carolina
### www.cvcc.edu
**CB code: 5098**

- Public 2-year community college
- Commuter campus in large town

**General.** Founded in 1960. Regionally accredited. **Enrollment:** 3,861 degree-seeking undergraduates; 905 non-degree-seeking students. **Degrees:** 944 associate awarded. **Location:** 50 miles from Charlotte. **Calendar:** Semester, limited summer session. **Full-time faculty:** 144 total; 4% minority, 49% women. **Part-time faculty:** 339 total; 8% minority, 58% women. **Class size:** 59% < 20, 39% 20-39, 2% 40-49.

**Student profile.** Among degree-seeking undergraduates, 44% enrolled in a transfer program, 56% enrolled in a vocational program, 1% already have a bachelor's degree or higher, 921 enrolled as first-time, first-year students, 729 transferred in from other institutions.

| | | | |
|---|---|---|---|
| Part-time: | 60% | 25 or older: | 55% |
| Women: | 62% | | |

**Basis for selection.** Open admission, but selective for some programs. Special requirements for nursing, emergency medical science, surgical technology, respiratory care, health information technology, dental hygiene, speech-language pathology assistant, advertising and graphic design, photography, electroneurodiagnostic technology, polysomnography, radiography. Interview required for health program applicants, advertising and graphic design applicants, and photography applicants; recommended for all others. **Homeschooled:** Transcript of courses and grades, state high school equivalency certificate required.

**2007-2008 Annual costs.** Tuition/fees: $1,284; $7,023 out-of-state. Per-credit charge: $42 in-state; $233 out-of-state. Books/supplies: $700. Personal expenses: $1,386.

**2006-2007 Financial aid. Need-based:** 410 full-time freshmen applied for aid; 321 were judged to have need; 252 of these received aid. 87% of total undergraduate aid awarded as scholarships/grants, 13% as loans/jobs. Need-based aid available for part-time students. **Non-need-based:** Awarded to 19 full-time undergraduates, including 36 freshmen. Scholarships awarded for academics, leadership, music/drama.

**Application procedures. Admission:** No deadline. No application fee. Application may be submitted online. Admission notification on a rolling basis. **Financial aid:** Closing date 3/15. FAFSA required. Applicants notified on a rolling basis starting 5/15.

**Academics. Special study options:** Cooperative education, distance learning, double major, dual enrollment of high school students, ESL, honors, independent study, student-designed major, teacher certification program. License preparation in dental hygiene, nursing, paramedic, real estate. **Credit/placement by examination:** AP, CLEP, IB, institutional tests. Maximum of 65% of total credit hours required for degree may be obtained by examination. **Support services:** GED preparation and test center, learning center, reduced course load, remedial instruction, study skills assistance, tutoring, writing center.

**Majors. Agriculture:** Horticultural science, turf management. **Architecture:** Technology. **Business:** Accounting technology, banking/financial services, business admin, customer service, e-commerce, management information systems, office management, operations, real estate. **Communications technology:** Photo/film/video. **Computer sciences:** Information systems, information technology, LAN/WAN management, programming. **Education:** Early childhood. **Engineering:** Industrial. **Engineering technology:** Architectural, computer, electrical, electromechanical, mechanical. **Health:** Dental hygiene, EMT paramedic, health services, medical radiologic technology/radiation therapy, medical records technology, nursing (RN), office admin, respiratory therapy technology. **Liberal arts:** Arts/sciences. **Mechanic/repair:** Automotive. **Production:** Furniture. **Protective services:** Criminal justice, fire safety technology, forensics. **Visual/performing arts:** Commercial/advertising art. **Other:** Cyber crime technology.

**Most popular majors.** Business/marketing 16%, education 6%, engineering/engineering technologies 8%, health sciences 26%, liberal arts 26%.

**Computing on campus.** 1,360 workstations in library, computer center. Commuter students can connect to campus network. Online course registration, repair service, wireless network available.

**Student life. Freshman orientation:** Available. Available for degree-seeking students. **Activities:** Choral groups, music ensembles, student government, student newspaper, Phi Theta Kappa, Association of Nursing Students, Certifiable Club, Rotaract Club, Student American Dental Hygiene Association, Students in Free Enterprise.

**Athletics.** NJCAA. **Intercollegiate:** Basketball M, volleyball W. **Team name:** Buccaneers.

**Student services.** Career counseling, services for economically disadvantaged, student employment services, financial aid counseling, personal counseling, placement for graduates, veterans' counselor, women's services. **Physically disabled:** Services for visually, hearing impaired. **Transfer:** Pre-admission transcript evaluation for new students. Transfer adviser, college fairs on campus for students transferring to 4-year colleges.

**Contact.** Phone: (828) 327-7000 Fax: (828) 327-7276
Ashley Brown, Director of Enrollment Management, Catawba Valley Community College, 2550 Highway 70 SE, Hickory, NC 28602

---

## Central Carolina Community College
### Sanford, North Carolina
www.cccc.edu                    CB code: 5147

- Public 2-year community college
- Commuter campus in large town

**General.** Founded in 1958. Regionally accredited. **Enrollment:** 4,708 degree-seeking undergraduates. **Degrees:** 329 associate awarded. **Location:** 45 miles from Raleigh. **Calendar:** Semester, limited summer session. **Full-time faculty:** 175 total. **Part-time faculty:** 145 total. **Class size:** 73% < 20, 25% 20-39, less than 1% 40-49, less than 1% 50-99.

**Student profile.**

| | | | |
|---|---|---|---|
| Out-of-state: | 2% | 25 or older: | 49% |

**Transfer out. Colleges most students transferred to 2007:** ECU, NCSU, UNC-G, UNC-W, ASU.

**Basis for selection.** Open-admission, but selective for some programs. Special requirements for veterinary technician, nursing education, radio-television broadcasting, laser electro-optic, electronics and instrumentation technology, cosmetology, medical assisting programs. ACT/SAT scores may exempt student from placement tests. **Homeschooled:** Must be registered with local county Board of Education and NC Non-public Education office; must submit documentation of successful completion of NC Competency Exam, copies of transcript and high school diploma. **Learning Disabled:** Students must sign up with special populations office and request accommodations and services.

**High school preparation.** Strong background in mathematics, biology, and chemistry required for veterinary technician and nursing education option programs.

**2007-2008 Annual costs.** Tuition/fees: $1,328; $7,067 out-of-state. Per-credit charge: $42 in-state; $233 out-of-state. Books/supplies: $666.

**Financial aid. Need-based:** Need-based aid available for part-time students. Work-study available nights and for part-time students. **Non-need-based:** Scholarships awarded for academics.

**Application procedures. Admission:** No deadline. No application fee. Application may be submitted online. Admission notification on a rolling basis. **Financial aid:** Priority date 3/15, closing date 5/1. FAFSA, institutional form required. Applicants notified on a rolling basis starting 7/1; must reply within 2 week(s) of notification.

**Academics. Special study options:** Distance learning, dual enrollment of high school students, honors, independent study, internships, liberal arts/career combination. License preparation in dental hygiene, nursing. **Credit/placement by examination:** CLEP, institutional tests. Placement interview required. **Support services:** GED preparation, learning center, reduced course load, remedial instruction, study skills assistance, tutoring, writing center.

**Majors. Business:** Accounting, administrative services, business admin, office/clerical. **Communications:** Broadcast journalism. **Computer sciences:** Applications programming, information systems, networking, programming. **Education:** General, early childhood. **Engineering:** Civil, computer. **Engineering technology:** Architectural, civil, drafting, electrical, manufacturing, robotics, surveying. **Family/consumer sciences:** Child care. **Health:** Licensed practical nurse, medical assistant, medical secretary, nursing (RN), veterinary technology/assistant. **Legal studies:** Legal secretary, paralegal. **Liberal arts:** Arts/sciences. **Mechanic/repair:** Automotive, industrial. **Personal/culinary services:** Aesthetician, cosmetic, cosmetology. **Protective services:** Criminal justice. **Public administration:** Human services. **Science technology:** Biological.

**Most popular majors.** Business/marketing 35%, health sciences 43%, liberal arts 12%.

**Computing on campus.** Online library, helpline available.

**Student life. Freshman orientation:** Mandatory. **Activities:** Radio station, student government, Student Nurses Association, Student Ambassador Program, Veterinary Medical Technician Student Organization.

**Athletics.** NJCAA. **Intercollegiate:** Basketball M, golf, softball, volleyball. **Intramural:** Basketball M, bowling, golf, softball, tennis M, volleyball.

**Student services.** Career counseling, student employment services, financial aid counseling, personal counseling, placement for graduates, veterans' counselor. **Physically disabled:** Services for visually, speech, hearing impaired. **Transfer:** Transfer adviser for students transferring to 4-year colleges.

**Contact.** E-mail: khoyle@cccc.edu
Phone: (919) 775-5401 Toll-free number: (800) 682-8353
Fax: (919) 718-7379
Ken Hoyle, Dean of Student Support Services, Central Carolina Community College, 1105 Kelly Drive, Sanford, NC 27330

---

## Central Piedmont Community College
### Charlotte, North Carolina                    CB member
www.cpcc.edu                    CB code: 5102

- Public 2-year community college
- Commuter campus in very large city

**General.** Founded in 1963. Regionally accredited. **Enrollment:** 15,569 degree-seeking undergraduates; 2,483 non-degree-seeking students. **Degrees:** 971 associate awarded. **Location:** 247 miles from Atlanta. **Calendar:** Semester, extensive summer session. **Full-time faculty:** 318 total. **Part-time faculty:** 1,410 total.

**Student profile.** Among degree-seeking undergraduates, 56% enrolled in a transfer program, 44% enrolled in a vocational program, 5% already have a bachelor's degree or higher, 2,833 enrolled as first-time, first-year students.

| | | | |
|---|---|---|---|
| Part-time: | 63% | Women: | 59% |
| Out-of-state: | 2% | 25 or older: | 45% |

**Basis for selection.** Open admission, but selective for some programs. Placement test scores used for admission to some programs with specific requirements.

**High school preparation.** Recommended units include English 4, mathematics 3, social studies 3 and science 3.

**2007-2008 Annual costs.** Tuition/fees: $1,440; $7,179 out-of-state. Per-credit charge: $42 in-state; $233 out-of-state. Books/supplies: $1,100. Personal expenses: $596.

**Financial aid. Need-based:** Need-based aid available for part-time students. **Non-need-based:** Scholarships awarded for academics, minority status.

**Application procedures. Admission:** No deadline. No application fee. Application may be submitted online. Admission notification on a rolling basis. **Financial aid:** Priority date 4/1, closing date 6/1. FAFSA required. Applicants notified on a rolling basis.

**Academics. Special study options:** Cooperative education, cross-registration, distance learning, double major, dual enrollment of high school students, ESL, honors, independent study, internships, study abroad, weekend college. **Credit/placement by examination:** AP, CLEP, institutional tests. **Support services:** GED preparation and test center, learning center, reduced course load, remedial instruction, study skills assistance, tutoring, writing center.

**Majors. Agriculture:** Horticulture, turf management. **Business:** Accounting technology, administrative services, business admin, hospitality admin, international, management information systems, real estate, retailing, tourism/travel. **Communications technology:** Graphic/printing. **Computer sciences:** Database management, information technology, LAN/WAN management, programming, webmaster. **Construction:** Electrician. **Education:** Early childhood. **Engineering technology:** Architectural, civil, electrical, industrial management, mechanical, occupational safety, surveying. **Family/consumer sciences:** Child care. **Foreign languages:** Sign language interpretation. **Health:** Cardiovascular technology, clinical lab assistant, cytotechnology, dental hygiene, medical assistant, medical records technology, mental health services, nursing (RN), physical therapy assistant, respiratory therapy technology, substance abuse counseling. **Legal studies:** Legal secretary, paralegal. **Liberal arts:** Arts/sciences. **Mechanic/repair:** Automotive, diesel, heating/ac/refrig. **Parks/recreation:** Facilities management. **Personal/culinary services:** Chef training. **Production:** Machine shop technology, welding. **Protective services:** Corrections, fire safety technology. **Visual/performing arts:** Commercial/advertising art, interior design.

**Most popular majors.** Business/marketing 10%, health sciences 18%, liberal arts 41%.

**Computing on campus.** 2,591 workstations in library, computer center, student center. Commuter students can connect to campus network. Online course registration, helpline, wireless network available.

**Student life. Freshman orientation:** Available. **Activities:** Bands, choral groups, dance, drama, film society, international student organizations, literary magazine, music ensembles, musical theater, opera, radio station, student government, student newspaper, symphony orchestra, TV station, Afro-American cultural club, Baptist Student Union, chess club, Phi Theta Kappa.

**Athletics.** NJCAA. **Intramural:** Soccer.

**Student services.** Adult student services, campus ministries, career counseling, student employment services, financial aid counseling, personal counseling, placement for graduates, veterans' counselor, women's services. **Physically disabled:** Services for visually, speech, hearing impaired. **Transfer:** Re-entry adviser, pre-admission transcript evaluation for new students. Transfer adviser, college fairs on campus for students transferring to 4-year colleges.

**Contact.** Phone: (704) 330-2722 Fax: (704) 330-6007
Linda McComb, Associate Dean of Admissions/Registration/Records, Central Piedmont Community College, Box 35009, Charlotte, NC 28235-5009

## Cleveland Community College
**Shelby, North Carolina**
www.clevelandcommunitycollege.edu
**CB member**
**CB code: 5140**

♦ Public 2-year community college
♦ Commuter campus in large town

**General.** Founded in 1965. Regionally accredited. **Enrollment:** 3,104 degree-seeking undergraduates. **Degrees:** 166 associate awarded. **Location:** 45 miles from Charlotte. **Calendar:** Semester, limited summer session. **Full-time faculty:** 84 total. **Part-time faculty:** 265 total. **Class size:** 71% < 20, 28% 20-39, less than 1% 40-49. **Special facilities:** Nature trail. **Partnerships:** Tech Prep, Huskins Classes.

**Student profile.**

| | | | |
|---|---|---|---|
| Out-of-state: | 1% | 25 or older: | 68% |

**Transfer out. Colleges most students transferred to 2007:** Gardner-Webb University, University of North Carolina-Charlotte, Appalachian State University, Western Carolina University, North Carolina State University.

**Basis for selection.** Open admission, but selective for some programs. Special requirements for allied health programs. Satisfactory SAT or ACT scores may be used in lieu of academic placement testing for all programs

except allied health. Interview required for nursing, radiography, and phlebotomy programs. **Learning Disabled:** Contact Director of Admissions for assistance.

**2007-2008 Annual costs.** Tuition/fees: $1,298; $7,037 out-of-state. Per-credit charge: $42 in-state; $233 out-of-state. Books/supplies: $800.

**Financial aid. Need-based:** Need-based aid available for part-time students. Work-study available nights and for part-time students.

**Application procedures. Admission:** No deadline. No application fee. Application may be submitted online. Applicants notified immediately except for allied health applicants. **Financial aid:** Priority date 7/1; no closing date. FAFSA required. Applicants notified on a rolling basis.

**Academics. Special study options:** Accelerated study, cooperative education, cross-registration, distance learning, double major, dual enrollment of high school students, ESL, honors, independent study, internships, liberal arts/career combination. Bachelor's degree programs available on campus. License preparation in nursing, paramedic, real estate. **Credit/placement by examination:** AP, CLEP, IB, institutional tests. 28 credit hours maximum toward associate degree. Credit determined on individual basis. **Support services:** GED preparation and test center, learning center, reduced course load, remedial instruction, study skills assistance, tutoring.

**Majors. Business:** Accounting, administrative services, business admin, e-commerce, operations. **Communications technology:** General. **Computer sciences:** Applications programming, information systems, networking, programming. **Engineering:** General. **Engineering technology:** General, electrical. **Family/consumer sciences:** Child care. **Health:** Medical radiologic technology/radiation therapy, medical secretary, nursing (RN). **Legal studies:** Legal secretary. **Liberal arts:** Arts/sciences. **Protective services:** Criminal justice, fire safety technology.

**Computing on campus.** 372 workstations in library, computer center. Online library available.

**Student life. Freshman orientation:** Available. Preregistration for classes offered. **Activities:** Choral groups, drama, musical theater, student government, student newspaper, TV station, black awareness club, communications club, criminal justice club, radiologic technology club, nursing club, Students in Free Enterprise, Mu Epsilon Delta, Baptist Union.

**Athletics. Intramural:** Basketball, golf, softball, tennis.

**Student services.** Adult student services, career counseling, student employment services, financial aid counseling, personal counseling, placement for graduates, veterans' counselor. **Physically disabled:** Services for visually, speech, hearing impaired. **Transfer:** Pre-admission transcript evaluation for new students. Transfer adviser, college fairs on campus for students transferring to 4-year colleges.

**Contact.** E-mail: maddox@cleveland.cc.nc.us
Phone: (704) 484-4103 Fax: (704) 484-5305
Andy Gardner, Dean of Enrollment Management, Cleveland Community College, 137 South Post Road, Shelby, NC 28152

## Coastal Carolina Community College
**Jacksonville, North Carolina**
www.coastal.cc.nc.us
**CB code: 5134**

♦ Public 2-year community college
♦ Commuter campus in large town

**General.** Founded in 1964. Regionally accredited. Off-campus classes available at Camp Lejeune Marine Corps Base and New River Marine Corps Air Station. **Enrollment:** 4,055 degree-seeking undergraduates; 201 non-degree-seeking students. **Degrees:** 417 associate awarded. **Location:** 100 miles from Raleigh. **Calendar:** Semester, limited summer session. **Full-time faculty:** 127 total; 13% have terminal degrees, 9% minority, 56% women. **Part-time faculty:** 158 total; 11% have terminal degrees, 10% minority, 63% women. **Class size:** 67% < 20, 33% 20-39.

**Student profile.** Among degree-seeking undergraduates, 71% enrolled in a transfer program, 29% enrolled in a vocational program, 2% already have a bachelor's degree or higher, 971 enrolled as first-time, first-year students, 654 transferred in from other institutions.

| | | | |
|---|---|---|---|
| Part-time: | 53% | Hispanic American: | 9% |
| Out-of-state: | 31% | Native American: | 1% |
| Women: | 65% | International: | 1% |
| African American: | 18% | 25 or older: | 44% |
| Asian American: | 4% | | |

**Transfer out. Colleges most students transferred to 2007:** University of North Carolina - Wilmington, East Carolina University, North Carolina State University.

**Basis for selection.** Open admission, but selective for some programs. Admission to limited enrollment programs based on examination. **Adult students:** SAT/ACT scores not required. **Homeschooled:** Transcript of courses and grades required.

**High school preparation.** 20 units recommended. Recommended units include English 4, mathematics 3, social studies 2, history 1, science 3 (laboratory 1) and academic electives 6. Recommended units may vary by college.

**2007-2008 Annual costs.** Tuition/fees: $1,290; $7,029 out-of-state. Per-credit charge: $42 in-state; $233 out-of-state. Books/supplies: $1,000. Personal expenses: $1,934.

**2006-2007 Financial aid. Need-based:** 292 full-time freshmen applied for aid; 265 were judged to have need; 260 of these received aid. Average need met was 28%. Average scholarship/grant was $2,640. Need-based aid available for part-time students. Work-study available nights, weekends and for part-time students. **Non-need-based:** Scholarships awarded for academics, state residency.

**Application procedures. Admission:** No deadline. No application fee. Application may be submitted online. Admission notification on a rolling basis beginning on or about 2/15. **Financial aid:** Priority date 5/15; no closing date. FAFSA, institutional form required. Applicants notified on a rolling basis starting 5/15; must reply within 2 week(s) of notification.

**Academics. Special study options:** Cooperative education, distance learning, dual enrollment of high school students, independent study, internships, liberal arts/career combination. License preparation in dental hygiene, nursing, paramedic. **Credit/placement by examination:** AP, CLEP, IB, institutional tests. 30 credit hours maximum toward associate degree. **Support services:** GED preparation and test center, learning center, reduced course load, remedial instruction, tutoring.

**Majors. Business:** Accounting technology, administrative services, business admin, information resources management. **Computer sciences:** Information systems. **Education:** Early childhood. **Engineering technology:** Architectural. **Health:** Clinical lab technology, dental hygiene, EMT paramedic, nursing (RN). **Legal studies:** Paralegal. **Liberal arts:** Arts/sciences. **Mechanic/repair:** Electronics/electrical, heating/ac/refrig. **Protective services:** Fire safety technology, police science.

**Most popular majors.** Business/marketing 6%, health sciences 17%, liberal arts 57%.

**Computing on campus.** 720 workstations in library, computer center, student center. Commuter students can connect to campus network. Online library, helpline available.

**Student life. Freshman orientation:** Available. Preregistration for classes offered. Orientation sessions available throughout the month prior to start of each term. **Activities:** Concert band, choral groups, drama, music ensembles, student government, Phi Theta Kappa, Star of Life, Association of Nursing Students, social science club, Practical Nursing Students, fine arts society, Extreme Science, SGA, Fellowship of Christian Athletes.

**Athletics. Intercollegiate:** Soccer W.

**Student services.** Adult student services, alcohol/substance abuse counseling, career counseling, services for economically disadvantaged, student employment services, financial aid counseling, minority student services, personal counseling, placement for graduates, veterans' counselor. **Physically disabled:** Services for visually, speech, hearing impaired. **Transfer:** Transfer adviser, college fairs on campus for students transferring to 4-year colleges.

**Contact.** E-mail: herringd@coastal.cc.nc.us
Phone: (910) 938-6332 Fax: (910) 455-2767
Don Herring, Division Chair for Admissions, Coastal Carolina Community College, 444 Western Boulevard, Jacksonville, NC 28546-6877

## College of the Albemarle
**Elizabeth City, North Carolina**
www.albemarle.cc.nc.us        CB code: 5133

- Public 2-year branch campus and community college
- Commuter campus in large town

**General.** Founded in 1960. Regionally accredited. Multi-campus institution with campuses in: Elizabeth City, Dare County, and Edenton-Chowan.

**Enrollment:** 1,653 degree-seeking undergraduates; 464 non-degree-seeking students. **Degrees:** 199 associate awarded. **ROTC:** Army. **Location:** 45 miles from Norfolk, Virginia. **Calendar:** Semester, limited summer session. **Full-time faculty:** 92 total; 5% have terminal degrees, 9% minority, 58% women. **Part-time faculty:** 196 total; 5% have terminal degrees, 12% minority, 45% women. **Special facilities:** Community theater, civic auditorium.

**Student profile.** Among degree-seeking undergraduates, 58% enrolled in a transfer program, 42% enrolled in a vocational program, 356 enrolled as first-time, first-year students.

| | | | |
|---|---|---|---|
| Part-time: | 57% | Asian American: | 1% |
| Out-of-state: | 1% | Hispanic American: | 2% |
| Women: | 73% | Native American: | 1% |
| African American: | 25% | 25 or older: | 43% |

**Transfer out. Colleges most students transferred to 2007:** Elizabeth City State University, East Carolina University, North Carolina State University, UNC-Chapel Hill, UNC-Wilmington.

**Basis for selection.** Open admission, but selective for some programs. Limited enrollment programs have additional admissions criteria. Admission limited to fall semester for associate degree in nursing, practical nursing, associate degree nursing, electrical/electronics technology, AC/HR, machining technology, surgical technology, medical assisting, and Phlebotomy. New students admitted to cosmetology program as spaces become available. All degree-seeking students required to take placement test. Students may waive placement test if scores for SAT or ACT are acceptable. Interview required for allied health programs.

**High school preparation.** Recommended units include English 4, mathematics 3, social studies 3, history 3, science 3 and academic electives 6.

**2007-2008 Annual costs.** Tuition/fees: $1,414; $7,535 out-of-state. Per-credit charge: $42 in-state; $233 out-of-state. Books/supplies: $1,000.

**Financial aid. Need-based:** Need-based aid available for part-time students. **Non-need-based:** Scholarships awarded for academics, art, leadership, minority status, music/drama, state residency. **Additional information:** Separate application must be submitted for COA Private Scholarships.

**Application procedures. Admission:** No deadline. No application fee. Application must be submitted on paper. Admission notification on a rolling basis. Application deadline for allied health January 15 prior to fall semester. **Financial aid:** Priority date 3/15; no closing date. FAFSA required. Applicants notified on a rolling basis starting 5/1; must reply within 2 week(s) of notification.

**Academics. Special study options:** Cooperative education, distance learning, double major, dual enrollment of high school students, ESL, honors, independent study, internships, liberal arts/career combination. Agreement with Elizabeth City State University to offer the first 2 years of Elementary Education. License preparation in nursing, real estate. **Credit/placement by examination:** AP, CLEP, institutional tests. 30 credit hours maximum toward associate degree. Credit by examination not granted until examinee has enrolled at COA and passed 12 credit hours with 2.0 or better grade point average. **Support services:** GED preparation and test center, learning center, reduced course load, remedial instruction, study skills assistance, tutoring, writing center.

**Majors. Architecture:** Technology. **Business:** Administrative services, business admin, office/clerical. **Computer sciences:** General, applications programming, information systems, networking, programming. **Conservation:** Fisheries. **Education:** General, early childhood. **Engineering:** Computer. **Engineering technology:** Electrical, heat/ac/refrig. **Health:** Clinical lab science, medical assistant, medical secretary, nursing (RN), office admin. **Legal studies:** Prelaw. **Liberal arts:** Arts/sciences. **Production:** Machine shop technology. **Protective services:** Law enforcement admin. **Visual/performing arts:** Art, dramatic.

**Computing on campus.** 475 workstations in library, computer center. Commuter students can connect to campus network. Online library, wireless network available.

**Student life. Freshman orientation:** Available. Preregistration for classes offered. Monthly information sessions held for all COA programs. **Activities:** Bands, drama, literary magazine, musical theater, student government, student newspaper, Phi Theta Kappa, Environmental club, Literacy Round Table, Nursing club, SADD.

**Athletics. Intramural:** Archery, badminton, baseball, basketball, bowling, football (non-tackle), golf, racquetball, sailing, soccer, softball, swimming, tennis, volleyball.

**Student services.** Adult student services, career counseling, services for economically disadvantaged, student employment services, financial aid counseling, personal counseling, placement for graduates, veterans' counselor.

**Physically disabled:** Services for visually, speech, hearing impaired. **Transfer:** Pre-admission transcript evaluation for new students. College fairs on campus for students transferring to 4-year colleges.

**Contact.** Phone: (252) 335-0821 ext. 2290 Fax: (252) 335-2011
Kenneth Krentz, Assistant Dean for Admissions and Testing, College of the Albemarle, 1208 North Road Street, Elizabeth City, NC 27906-2327

## Craven Community College
### New Bern, North Carolina
www.cravencc.edu                                    CB code: 5148

- Public 2-year community college
- Commuter campus in large town
- Interview required

**General.** Founded in 1965. Regionally accredited. Campuses in New Bern and Havelock. **Enrollment:** 2,533 degree-seeking undergraduates. **Degrees:** 365 associate awarded. **Location:** 100 miles from Raleigh, 45 miles from Greenville. **Calendar:** Semester, limited summer session. **Full-time faculty:** 81 total. **Part-time faculty:** 253 total. **Class size:** 69% < 20, 31% 20-39, less than 1% 40-49.

**Student profile.**

Out-of-state:              17%     **25 or older:**              50%

**Transfer out. Colleges most students transferred to 2007:** East Carolina University, University of North Carolina at Wilmington, North Carolina State University, Mount Olive College.

**Basis for selection.** Open admission, but selective for some programs. Admission to nursing program based on school achievement record and test scores. Tests in math, English and reading required for placement for degree-seeking students.

**High school preparation.** 20 units recommended. Recommended units include English 4, mathematics 3, social studies 1, history 1, science 3 (laboratory 1), foreign language 2 and academic electives 6.

**2007-2008 Annual costs.** Tuition/fees: $1,330; $7,069 out-of-state. Per-credit charge: $42 in-state; $233 out-of-state. Books/supplies: $700. Personal expenses: $1,056.

**2006-2007 Financial aid.** All financial aid based on need. 94% of total undergraduate aid awarded as scholarships/grants, 6% as loans/jobs.

**Application procedures. Admission:** No deadline. No application fee. Application may be submitted online. Admission notification on a rolling basis. **Financial aid:** Priority date 3/31; no closing date. FAFSA required. Applicants notified on a rolling basis starting 6/1.

**Academics.** Level 2 CRLA tutoring center. **Special study options:** Accelerated study, cooperative education, distance learning, double major, dual enrollment of high school students, independent study, internships, liberal arts/career combination, student-designed major, study abroad. Bachelor's degree programs available on campus. License preparation in aviation, nursing. **Credit/placement by examination:** AP, CLEP, institutional tests. 20 credit hours maximum toward associate degree. **Support services:** GED preparation and test center, learning center, reduced course load, remedial instruction, study skills assistance, tutoring, writing center.

**Majors. Business:** Accounting, business admin, management information systems, sales/distribution. **Computer sciences:** Applications programming, networking. **Education:** Teacher assistance. **Engineering technology:** Electrical, manufacturing. **Family/consumer sciences:** Child care. **Health:** Medical assistant, medical secretary, nursing (RN), office admin. **Legal studies:** Legal secretary. **Liberal arts:** Arts/sciences. **Mechanic/repair:** Automotive, heating/ac/refrig, industrial. **Protective services:** Law enforcement admin.

**Computing on campus.** 500 workstations in library, computer center.

**Student life. Freshman orientation:** Available. Preregistration for classes offered. **Activities:** Concert band, choral groups, drama, film society, literary magazine, music ensembles, student government, student newspaper, Phi Beta Lambda (business), cosmetology club, nursing club, accounting club, banking and marketing club, Spanish club, Bible club, criminal justice club, electronics club, learning community club.

**Athletics. Intramural:** Baseball M, basketball, bowling, football (non-tackle) M, golf, soccer, tennis, volleyball. **Team name:** Panthers.

**Student services.** Career counseling, student employment services, financial aid counseling, personal counseling, placement for graduates, veterans' counselor. **Physically disabled:** Services for visually, speech, hearing

impaired. **Transfer:** Pre-admission transcript evaluation for new students. Transfer center, transfer adviser, college fairs on campus for students transferring to 4-year colleges.

**Contact.** Phone: (252) 638-7227 Fax: (252) 638-4649
Wanda Thomas, Director of Admissions and Counseling Services, Craven Community College, 800 College Court, New Bern, NC 28562

## Davidson County Community College
### Lexington, North Carolina
www.davidson.cc.nc.us                               CB code: 5170

- Public 2-year community college
- Commuter campus in large town

**General.** Founded in 1958. Regionally accredited. Davie Campus in Mocksville has 3 buildings and an emergency services training facility on 45 acres. **Enrollment:** 2,931 degree-seeking undergraduates. **Degrees:** 318 associate awarded. **Location:** 30 miles from Greensboro. **Calendar:** Semester, limited summer session. **Full-time faculty:** 97 total. **Part-time faculty:** 120 total. **Class size:** 59% < 20, 39% 20-39, less than 1% 40-49, less than 1% 50-99.

**Student profile.**

Out-of-state:              1%     **25 or older:**              46%

**Transfer out. Colleges most students transferred to 2007:** University of North Carolina-Greensboro, University of North Carolina-Charlotte, High Point University, Winston-Salem State University, Catawba College.

**Basis for selection.** Open admission, but selective for some programs. Admissions to nursing program under points system; based on test scores and grades. ASSET required unless acceptable test scores submitted.

**High school preparation.** Recommended units include English 4, mathematics 3, social studies 2, history 2, science 3 and foreign language 2.

**2007-2008 Annual costs.** Tuition/fees: $1,333; $7,072 out-of-state. Per-credit charge: $42 in-state; $233 out-of-state. Books/supplies: $1,000. Personal expenses: $600.

**2006-2007 Financial aid. Need-based:** 98% of total undergraduate aid awarded as scholarships/grants, 2% as loans/jobs. Need-based aid available for part-time students. **Non-need-based:** Scholarships awarded for academics, leadership.

**Application procedures. Admission:** No deadline. No application fee. Application may be submitted online. Admission notification on a rolling basis. Nursing program deadline 1/31, Allied Health program deadlines 3/15 to 5/15. **Financial aid:** Priority date 3/31, closing date 6/1. FAFSA, institutional form required. Applicants notified on a rolling basis starting 7/1; must reply within 2 week(s) of notification.

**Academics. Special study options:** Distance learning, dual enrollment of high school students, ESL, independent study. License preparation in nursing, paramedic, real estate. **Credit/placement by examination:** AP, CLEP, institutional tests. Students must complete 25% of hours required for graduation in residence. **Support services:** GED preparation and test center, learning center, pre-admission summer program, reduced course load, remedial instruction, study skills assistance, tutoring, writing center.

**Majors. Biology:** Zoology. **Business:** Accounting, business admin, human resources. **Computer sciences:** Information technology, networking, programming. **Education:** Early childhood. **Engineering technology:** Electrical. **Health:** Clinical lab technology, EMT paramedic, medical assistant, medical records technology, nursing (RN). **Legal studies:** Paralegal. **Liberal arts:** Arts/sciences. **Mechanic/repair:** Automotive. **Protective services:** Criminal justice, fire safety technology. **Other:** Community Spanish Interpreter.

**Computing on campus.** 450 workstations in library, computer center. Commuter students can connect to campus network. Helpline available.

**Student life. Freshman orientation:** Available. Preregistration for classes offered. **Activities:** Literary magazine, student government, criminal justice club, association of nursing students, Phi Theta Kappa, Rotaract, spanish club, cosmetology club, Christian organization, computer system technology association, future educators club.

**Athletics. Intramural:** Basketball, golf.

**Student services.** Career counseling, student employment services, financial aid counseling, on-campus daycare, personal counseling, placement for graduates, veterans' counselor. **Physically disabled:** Services for visually, speech, hearing impaired. **Transfer:** Pre-admission transcript evaluation for new students. Transfer adviser, college fairs on campus for students transferring to 4-year colleges.

**Contact.** E-mail: admissions@davidsonccc.edu
Phone: (336) 249-8186 ext. 6731 Fax: (336) 224-0240
Lori Blevins, Director of Admissions, Davidson County Community College, PO Box 1287, Lexington, NC 27293-1287

## Durham Technical Community College
### Durham, North Carolina
**www.durhamtech.edu**                                   **CB code: 5172**

- Public 2-year community and technical college
- Commuter campus in small city

**General.** Founded in 1958. Regionally accredited. Most programs are structured to begin in fall and continue for 5 or 6 consecutive semesters. Satellite sites in northern Durham and Orange Counties. **Enrollment:** 3,000 degree-seeking undergraduates. **Degrees:** 356 associate awarded. **Location:** 25 miles from Raleigh, 50 miles from Greensboro. **Calendar:** Semester, limited summer session. **Full-time faculty:** 150 total. **Part-time faculty:** 390 total.

**Transfer out. Colleges most students transferred to 2007:** University of North Carolina - Chapel Hill, North Carolina Central University, North Carolina State University.

**Basis for selection.** Open admission, but selective for some programs. Admission to some allied health programs based on placement test and completion of prerequisite courses. Placement testing required. ASSET and COMPASS used. **Homeschooled:** Documentation of state recognition of home school required.

**High school preparation.** Algebra, chemistry, and biology required for allied health programs. Algebra and science courses recommended for most associate degree programs.

**2007-2008 Annual costs.** Tuition/fees: $1,330; $7,069 out-of-state. Per-credit charge: $42 in-state; $233 out-of-state. Personal expenses: $562.

**Financial aid. Need-based:** Need-based aid available for part-time students. Work-study available nights and for part-time students. **Non-need-based:** Scholarships awarded for academics, minority status, state residency. **Additional information:** Special funds available to single parents for tuition, fees, books, supplies and child care expenses.

**Application procedures. Admission:** Closing date 8/8 (receipt date). No application fee. Application may be submitted online. Admission notification on a rolling basis. **Financial aid:** FAFSA required. Applicants notified on a rolling basis starting 1/31; must reply within 3 week(s) of notification.

**Academics. Special study options:** Distance learning, dual enrollment of high school students, ESL, weekend college. License preparation in nursing, occupational therapy, paramedic, real estate. **Credit/placement by examination:** AP, CLEP, institutional tests. Maximum of 10% of total curriculum hours of credit by examination may be counted toward degree. **Support services:** GED preparation and test center, learning center, remedial instruction, study skills assistance, tutoring.

**Majors. Architecture:** Technology. **Biology:** Biotechnology. **Business:** Accounting, administrative services, business admin, operations. **Computer sciences:** Applications programming, data processing, information technology, networking, programming, security, systems analysis. **Education:** Early childhood, teacher assistance. **Engineering:** Electrical. **Engineering technology:** Architectural, drafting, electrical. **Health:** Dental lab technology, environmental health, medical records admin, medical secretary, nursing (RN), occupational health, occupational therapy assistant, office admin, optician, respiratory therapy assistant, respiratory therapy technology. **Legal studies:** Paralegal. **Liberal arts:** Arts/sciences. **Mechanic/repair:** Automotive, electronics/electrical.

**Student life. Freshman orientation:** Available. Preregistration for classes offered. **Activities:** Drama, literary magazine, student government.

**Student services.** Career counseling, services for economically disadvantaged, financial aid counseling, minority student services, personal counseling, veterans' counselor. **Physically disabled:** Services for visually, speech, hearing impaired. **Transfer:** College fairs on campus for students transferring to 4-year colleges.

**Contact.** E-mail: admissions@durhamtech.edu
Phone: (919) 686-3333 Fax: (919) 686-3669
Penny Augustine, Director of Admissions & Student Records, Durham Technical Community College, 1637 Lawson Street, Durham, NC 27703

## Edgecombe Community College
### Tarboro, North Carolina                              **CB member**
**www.edgecombe.edu**                                    **CB code: 5199**

- Public 2-year community college
- Commuter campus in large town

**General.** Founded in 1967. Regionally accredited. Branch campus in Rocky Mount. **Enrollment:** 2,510 degree-seeking undergraduates. **Degrees:** 184 associate awarded. **Location:** 75 miles from Raleigh. **Calendar:** Semester, limited summer session. **Full-time faculty:** 78 total; 12% have terminal degrees, 49% minority. **Part-time faculty:** 112 total; 7% have terminal degrees, 35% minority. **Class size:** 77% < 20, 20% 20-39, 2% 40-49, less than 1% 50-99. **Special facilities:** Wildlife preserve.

**Student profile.**

| | | | |
|---|---|---|---|
| Out-of-state: | 1% | 25 or older: | 46% |

**Transfer out. Colleges most students transferred to 2007:** East Carolina University, Pitt Community College, NC Wesleyan College, North Carolina Agricultural and Technical State University.

**Basis for selection.** Open admission, but selective for some programs. Special requirements for allied health programs and networking technology. Criteria include admission tests and rankings. TEAS Nursing Test required for nursing applicants.

**2007-2008 Annual costs.** Tuition/fees: $1,284; $7,023 out-of-state. Per-credit charge: $42 in-state; $220 out-of-state. Books/supplies: $750. Personal expenses: $1,800.

**Financial aid.** All financial aid based on need. Need-based aid available for part-time students.

**Application procedures. Admission:** No deadline. No application fee. Application may be submitted online. Admission notification on a rolling basis. **Financial aid:** Closing date 6/30. FAFSA, institutional form required. Applicants notified on a rolling basis starting 8/15; must reply within 3 week(s) of notification.

**Academics. Special study options:** Combined bachelor's/graduate degree, cooperative education, distance learning, double major, dual enrollment of high school students, ESL, independent study. License preparation in nursing, radiology. **Credit/placement by examination:** AP, CLEP, institutional tests. 24 credit hours maximum toward associate degree. **Support services:** GED preparation and test center, learning center, reduced course load, remedial instruction, study skills assistance, tutoring.

**Majors. Business:** Accounting, administrative services, business admin. **Computer sciences:** General, information systems, networking. **Education:** Early childhood, teacher assistance. **Engineering:** Manufacturing. **Engineering technology:** Electrical, manufacturing, plastics. **Family/consumer sciences:** Child care. **Health:** Medical assistant, medical radiologic technology/radiation therapy, medical records technology, nursing (RN), respiratory therapy technology. **Liberal arts:** Arts/sciences. **Personal/culinary services:** Mortuary science. **Protective services:** Criminal justice.

**Most popular majors.** Business/marketing 13%, education 14%, health sciences 48%, liberal arts 13%.

**Computing on campus.** 120 workstations in library, computer center. Online library, helpline available.

**Student life. Activities:** Drama, student government.

**Athletics. Team name:** Eagles.

**Student services.** Alcohol/substance abuse counseling, career counseling, student employment services, financial aid counseling, minority student services, personal counseling, placement for graduates, veterans' counselor. **Physically disabled:** Services for visually, hearing impaired. **Transfer:** Pre-admission transcript evaluation for new students. Transfer adviser, college fairs on campus for students transferring to 4-year colleges.

**Contact.** Phone: (252) 823-5166 ext. 254 Fax: (252) 823-6817
Ginny McLendon, Dean of Enrollment Management, Edgecombe Community College, 2009 West Wilson Street, Tarboro, NC 27886

## Fayetteville Technical Community College
### Fayetteville, North Carolina
**www.faytechcc.edu**                                    **CB code: 5208**

- Public 2-year community and technical college
- Commuter campus in large city

**General.** Founded in 1961. Regionally accredited. Offers only funeral services curriculum in North Carolina community college system. **Enrollment:** 8,471 degree-seeking undergraduates; 1,661 non-degree-seeking students. **Degrees:** 938 associate awarded. **Location:** 60 miles from Raleigh. **Calendar:** Semester, limited summer session. **Full-time faculty:** 304 total; 26% minority, 56% women. **Part-time faculty:** 518 total; 35% minority, 58% women. **Class size:** 67% < 20, 32% 20-39, less than 1% 40-49, less than 1% 50-99. **Special facilities:** Center for applied technology; virtual college center; horticulture educational center. **Partnerships:** Formal partnerships with Cumberland County High School system, and EArmyU.

**Student profile.** Among degree-seeking undergraduates, 15% enrolled in a transfer program, 85% enrolled in a vocational program, .2% already have a bachelor's degree or higher, 7,447 enrolled as first-time, first-year students, 654 transferred in from other institutions.

| Part-time: | 67% | Women: | 71% |
|---|---|---|---|
| Out-of-state: | 11% | 25 or older: | 87% |

**Transfer out. Colleges most students transferred to 2007:** Forsyth Technical Community College, Central Piedmont Community College, Wilson Technical Community College, Pitt Community College, Catawba Community College.

**Basis for selection.** Open admission, but selective for some programs. Admission of health applicants based on transcripts, academic average, interview, and institutional assessment of reading, writing, and math. Group interview required for health and paralegal programs. **Learning Disabled:** Documentation of disability required if applicant desires any academic accommodations.

**High school preparation.** Engineering and College Transfer programs require 2 algebra. Health programs require up to 2 algebra, 1 biology, and 1 chemistry.

**2007-2008 Annual costs.** Tuition/fees: $1,320; $7,059 out-of-state. Per-credit charge: $42 in-state; $233 out-of-state. Books/supplies: $1,750. Personal expenses: $3,800.

**2006-2007 Financial aid. Need-based:** 54% of total undergraduate aid awarded as scholarships/grants, 46% as loans/jobs. Need-based aid available for part-time students. Work-study available for part-time students.

**Application procedures. Admission:** No deadline. No application fee. Application may be submitted online. Admission notification on a rolling basis. Deadline for health program applicants is January 30. Applicants admitted to these programs must reply immediately upon notification. **Financial aid:** Priority date 6/1, closing date 7/15. FAFSA required. Applicants notified on a rolling basis starting 2/1.

**Academics. Special study options:** Cooperative education, distance learning, dual enrollment of high school students, ESL, liberal arts/career combination, weekend college. License preparation in dental hygiene, nursing, paramedic, physical therapy, radiology, real estate. **Credit/placement by examination:** AP, CLEP, institutional tests. **Support services:** GED preparation and test center, learning center, pre-admission summer program, reduced course load, remedial instruction, study skills assistance, tutoring.

**Majors. Agriculture:** Horticulture. **Architecture:** Technology. **Business:** Accounting, banking/financial services, business admin, e-commerce, hotel/motel admin, human resources, marketing, office management, operations. **Computer sciences:** Information systems, information technology, networking, programming, security, web page design. **Construction:** General, electrician. **Education:** General, early childhood, elementary, special. **Engineering technology:** Architectural, civil, electrical, surveying. **Foreign languages:** Translation. **Health:** Dental hygiene, EMT paramedic, management/clinical assistant, medical radiologic technology/radiation therapy, medical records technology, nuclear medical technology, nursing (RN), office admin, physical therapy assistant, radiologic technology/medical imaging, respiratory therapy technology, surgical technology. **Legal studies:** Paralegal. **Liberal arts:** Arts/sciences. **Mechanic/repair:** Automotive, heating/ac/refrig. **Personal/culinary services:** Chef training, mortuary science. **Production:** Machine shop technology. **Protective services:** Criminal justice, fire safety technology, forensics. **Public administration:** General. **Science technology:** Biological. **Visual/performing arts:** Commercial/advertising art. **Other:** Emergency preparedness technology, Occupational technology, Postal service technology.

**Most popular majors.** Business/marketing 13%, education 22%, health sciences 20%, liberal arts 16%.

**Computing on campus.** 200 workstations in library, computer center. Online library available.

**Student life. Freshman orientation:** Mandatory. Preregistration for classes offered. Two hours, held the first day of new student registration. **Activities:** Drama, international student organizations, student government, student newspaper, TV station, African-American heritage club, Democratic club, Latino cultural organization, Parents for Higher Education, Students Against Destructive Decisions, Republican Club.

**Athletics. Intramural:** Basketball, bowling, football (non-tackle), golf, softball, tennis, volleyball.

**Student services.** Alcohol/substance abuse counseling, career counseling, student employment services, financial aid counseling, health services, on-campus daycare, personal counseling, placement for graduates, veterans' counselor. **Physically disabled:** Services for visually, speech, hearing impaired. **Transfer:** Transfer adviser, college fairs on campus for students transferring to 4-year colleges.

**Contact.** E-mail: kelleyj@faytechcc.edu
Phone: (910) 678-8274 Fax: (910) 678-8407
James Kelley, Director of Admissions, Fayetteville Technical Community College, PO Box 35236, Fayetteville, NC 28303-0236

---

## Forsyth Technical Community College
**Winston-Salem, North Carolina**      **CB member**
www.forsythtech.edu      **CB code: 5234**

- Public 2-year community and technical college
- Commuter campus in small city

**General.** Founded in 1964. Regionally accredited. **Enrollment:** 6,140 degree-seeking undergraduates; 1,063 non-degree-seeking students. **Degrees:** 632 associate awarded. **Location:** 32 miles from Greensboro, 85 miles from Charlotte. **Calendar:** Semester, extensive summer session. **Full-time faculty:** 115 total; 12% have terminal degrees, 85% women. **Part-time faculty:** 311 total; 8% have terminal degrees.

**Student profile.** Among degree-seeking undergraduates, 1,202 enrolled as first-time, first-year students.

| Part-time: | 55% | African American: | 27% |
|---|---|---|---|
| Out-of-state: | 1% | Asian American: | 1% |
| Women: | 64% | Hispanic American: | 4% |

**Transfer out. Colleges most students transferred to 2007:** Winston-Salem State University, Gardner-Webb University, High Point University, Appalachian State University, North Carolina A&T State University.

**Basis for selection.** Open admission, but selective for some programs. Admission to health program based on school record and test scores. Health information session attendance required. SAT or ACT used for admission to health and developmental programs and for placement in other programs. **Homeschooled:** NCDPI registration information or similar information from the respective state's department of education authorizing the home school to provide instruction.

**High school preparation.** Algebra I required for allied health and engineering programs. Biology and chemistry required for allied health programs.

**2007-2008 Annual costs.** Tuition/fees: $1,322; $7,061 out-of-state. Per-credit charge: $42 in-state; $233 out-of-state. Books/supplies: $650. Personal expenses: $750.

**Financial aid. Need-based:** Need-based aid available for part-time students. Work-study available nights and for part-time students. **Non-need-based:** Scholarships awarded for academics, state residency. **Additional information:** Apply for aid as close to January 1 as possible for best consideration.

**Application procedures. Admission:** Priority date 5/1; no deadline. No application fee. Application may be submitted online. Admission notification on a rolling basis. **Financial aid:** Priority date 6/1; no closing date. FAFSA, institutional form required. Applicants notified on a rolling basis starting 7/1; must reply within 2 week(s) of notification.

**Academics. Special study options:** Cooperative education, cross-registration, distance learning, double major, dual enrollment of high school students, ESL, exchange student, external degree, honors, independent study, internships, liberal arts/career combination, student-designed major. License preparation in dental hygiene, nursing, radiology, real estate. **Credit/placement by examination:** AP, CLEP, institutional tests. **Support services:** GED preparation and test center, learning center, pre-admission summer program, reduced course load, remedial instruction, study skills assistance, tutoring, writing center.

**Majors. Agriculture:** Horticulture. **Business:** Accounting, business admin, finance, office/clerical. **Computer sciences:** Applications programming, data entry. **Education:** Early childhood, science. **Engineering technology:** Architectural, drafting, electrical, robotics. **Health:** Licensed practical nurse, medical assistant, medical radiologic technology/radiation therapy, nuclear medical technology, nursing (RN), respiratory therapy technology, sonography. **Legal studies:** Paralegal. **Liberal arts:** Arts/sciences. **Protective services:** Law enforcement admin.

**Computing on campus.** 400 workstations in library, computer center.

**Student life. Freshman orientation:** Mandatory. Preregistration for classes offered. **Activities:** Literary magazine, student government, student newspaper, Circle-K, Afro-American Society, minority male mentoring program, women's center.

**Athletics.** NJCAA. **Intercollegiate:** Basketball M, softball. **Intramural:** Basketball, bowling, golf, softball, volleyball. **Team name:** Tech Tigers.

**Student services.** Adult student services, alcohol/substance abuse counseling, career counseling, services for economically disadvantaged, student employment services, financial aid counseling, health services, minority student services, personal counseling, placement for graduates, veterans' counselor, women's services. **Physically disabled:** Services for visually, speech, hearing impaired. **Transfer:** Transfer adviser, college fairs on campus for students transferring to 4-year colleges.

**Contact.** Phone: (336) 734-7253 Fax: (336) 734-7291
Patrice Mitchell, Dean of Enrollment Management, Forsyth Technical Community College, 2100 Silas Creek Parkway, Winston-Salem, NC 27103

## Gaston College
### Dallas, North Carolina
www.gaston.cc.nc.us                 CB code: 5262

- Public 2-year community college
- Commuter campus in small town

**General.** Founded in 1963. Regionally accredited. Branch campus at Lincolnton. **Enrollment:** 4,522 degree-seeking undergraduates. **Degrees:** 627 associate awarded. **Location:** 25 miles from Charlotte. **Calendar:** Semester, limited summer session. **Full-time faculty:** 121 total. **Part-time faculty:** 432 total.

**Student profile.**

| | | | |
|---|---|---|---|
| Out-of-state: | 1% | 25 or older: | 54% |

**Basis for selection.** Open admission, but selective for some programs. Admission to health services programs, including nursing, based on ACT scores and interview. Basic literacy must be demonstrated, after admission, in order to take certain courses. ACT required for health services programs. Interview recommended for emergency medical technician, medical assistant, nursing programs; audition recommended for music programs; portfolio recommended for art programs.

**2007-2008 Annual costs.** Tuition/fees: $1,300; $7,039 out-of-state. Per-credit charge: $42 in-state; $233 out-of-state. Books/supplies: $1,000. Personal expenses: $1,000.

**Financial aid. Need-based:** Work-study available for part-time students. **Non-need-based:** Scholarships awarded for academics, state residency. **Additional information:** Grants/scholarships available for women pursuing nontraditional roles.

**Application procedures. Admission:** No deadline. No application fee. Application may be submitted online. Admission notification on a rolling basis. **Financial aid:** Priority date 3/15; no closing date. FAFSA, institutional form required. Applicants notified on a rolling basis.

**Academics. Special study options:** Cooperative education, cross-registration, distance learning, double major, dual enrollment of high school students, ESL, independent study, internships, weekend college. **Credit/placement by examination:** CLEP, institutional tests. 18 credit hours maximum toward associate degree. **Support services:** GED preparation and test center, learning center, reduced course load, remedial instruction, study skills assistance, tutoring, writing center.

**Majors. Architecture:** Technology. **Business:** Accounting, administrative services, business admin. **Communications:** Broadcast journalism. **Computer sciences:** Applications programming, information technology, programming. **Education:** Early childhood. **Engineering technology:** Architectural, biomedical, civil, computer, electrical, industrial. **Health:** Dietetic technician, EMT paramedic, massage therapy, medical assistant, medical

secretary, nursing (RN), office admin, veterinary technology/assistant. **Legal studies:** Legal secretary, paralegal. **Liberal arts:** Arts/sciences. **Protective services:** Fire safety technology. **Public administration:** Social work.

**Computing on campus.** 233 workstations in library, computer center.

**Student life. Freshman orientation:** Available. **Activities:** Literary magazine, music ensembles, radio station, student government.

**Student services.** Adult student services, career counseling, student employment services, financial aid counseling, on-campus daycare, placement for graduates, veterans' counselor. **Physically disabled:** Services for visually, speech, hearing impaired. **Transfer:** Transfer adviser, college fairs on campus for students transferring to 4-year colleges.

**Contact.** E-mail: wray.michelle@gaston.edu
Phone: (704) 922-6214 Fax: (704) 922-2344
Michelle Wray, Director of Admissions/Enrollment Management, Gaston College, 201 Highway 321 South, Dallas, NC 28034-1499

## Guilford Technical Community College
### Jamestown, North Carolina
www.gtcc.edu                 CB code: 5275

- Public 2-year community college
- Commuter campus in large city

**General.** Founded in 1958. Regionally accredited. Campuses in Greensboro and High Point. **Enrollment:** 9,730 degree-seeking undergraduates. **Degrees:** 687 associate awarded. **ROTC:** Army, Naval, Air Force. **Location:** 2 miles from Greensboro, 5 miles from High Point. **Calendar:** Semester, limited summer session. **Full-time faculty:** 248 total. **Part-time faculty:** 269 total. **Special facilities:** Observatory.

**Student profile.**

| | | | |
|---|---|---|---|
| Out-of-state: | 2% | 25 or older: | 43% |

**Transfer out. Colleges most students transferred to 2007:** University of North Carolina-Greensboro, University of North Carolina-Charlotte, North Carolina A&T, University of North Carolina-Chapel Hill, North Carolina State University.

**Basis for selection.** Open admission, but selective for some programs. Admission to allied health programs is highly competitive. Each program has specific requirements that must be met to be considered for admission. Some programs require students to take standardized test administered by college. **Learning Disabled:** Contact Disability Access Services office.

**High school preparation.** Allied health programs have specific course requirements that vary according to program.

**2007-2008 Annual costs.** Tuition/fees: $1,392; $7,131 out-of-state. Per-credit charge: $42 in-state; $233 out-of-state. Books/supplies: $900. Personal expenses: $1,151.

**Financial aid. Need-based:** Need-based aid available for part-time students. Work-study available for part-time students.

**Application procedures. Admission:** No deadline. No application fee. Application may be submitted online. Admission notification on a rolling basis. Applicants for limited enrollment programs (nursing, aviation maintenance/mechanic, dental hygiene, dental assistant, medical assistant, surgical technology cosmetology, emergency medical science) advised to apply before December 31. **Financial aid:** Priority date 3/15; no closing date. FAFSA required. Applicants notified on a rolling basis starting 7/1; must reply within 2 week(s) of notification.

**Academics. Special study options:** Cooperative education, cross-registration, distance learning, dual enrollment of high school students, ESL, independent study, internships. License preparation in aviation, dental hygiene, nursing, paramedic, physical therapy, real estate. **Credit/placement by examination:** AP, CLEP, IB, institutional tests. 60 credit hours maximum toward associate degree. **Support services:** GED preparation and test center, learning center, reduced course load, remedial instruction, study skills assistance, tutoring, writing center.

**Majors. Agriculture:** Turf management. **Business:** Accounting technology, business admin, executive assistant, human resources, management information systems. **Communications technology:** Recording arts. **Computer sciences:** Information systems. **Construction:** Electrician, maintenance. **Education:** General, early childhood. **Engineering technology:** Architectural, civil, electrical, mechanical, plastics, surveying. **Health:** Dental hygiene, EMT, medical assistant, mental health services, nursing

(RN), physical therapy assistant, substance abuse counseling, surgical technology. **Legal studies:** Paralegal. **Liberal arts:** Arts/sciences. **Mechanic/repair:** Automotive, avionics, heating/ac/refrig. **Personal/culinary services:** Cosmetic. **Production:** Machine shop technology. **Protective services:** Criminal justice, fire safety technology. **Science technology:** Chemical. **Transportation:** Airline/commercial pilot. **Visual/performing arts:** Commercial/advertising art, music management.

**Computing on campus.** 130 workstations in library, computer center. Online library, helpline, repair service, wireless network available.

**Student life. Freshman orientation:** Available. **Activities:** Drama, student government, student newspaper, American Muslim student association, Ambassadors for Christ, international student association, market place of ideas (political), Nurses Christian Fellowship, veterans and students organization, Black student union, single parent club, students in free enterprise.

**Athletics.** NJCAA. **Intercollegiate:** Basketball M, volleyball W. **Team name:** Titans.

**Student services.** Career counseling, student employment services, financial aid counseling, on-campus daycare, personal counseling, placement for graduates, veterans' counselor. **Physically disabled:** Services for visually, speech, hearing impaired. **Transfer:** Transfer adviser, college fairs on campus for students transferring to 4-year colleges.

**Contact.** E-mail: jmgroome@gtcc.edu
Phone: (336) 334-4822 ext. 5350 Fax: (336) 819-2022
Bernard Washington, Director of Admissions, Guilford Technical Community College, PO Box 309, Jamestown, NC 27282

## Halifax Community College
### Weldon, North Carolina
### www.hcc.cc.nc.us                          CB code: 0621

- Public 2-year community college
- Small town

**General.** Founded in 1967. Regionally accredited. **Enrollment:** 1,326 degree-seeking undergraduates. **Degrees:** 128 associate awarded. **Location:** 83 miles from Raleigh. **Calendar:** Semester, limited summer session. **Full-time faculty:** 65 total. **Part-time faculty:** 99 total. **Special facilities:** Performing arts auditorium.

**Basis for selection.** Open admission, but selective for some programs. Special requirements for nursing and allied health programs.

**High school preparation.** High school chemistry or equivalent and developmental mathematics required for nursing applicants.

**2007-2008 Annual costs.** Tuition/fees: $1,356; $7,095 out-of-state. Per-credit charge: $42 in-state; $233 out-of-state. Books/supplies: $500. Personal expenses: $896.

**2006-2007 Financial aid. Need-based:** 94% of total undergraduate aid awarded as scholarships/grants, 6% as loans/jobs.

**Application procedures. Admission:** No deadline. No application fee. Admission notification on a rolling basis. **Financial aid:** Priority date 6/1; no closing date. Applicants notified on a rolling basis starting 8/1; must reply within 2 week(s) of notification.

**Academics. Special study options:** Dual enrollment of high school students, independent study, internships. **Credit/placement by examination:** CLEP, institutional tests. **Support services:** Learning center, reduced course load, remedial instruction, tutoring.

**Majors. Business:** Accounting, business admin, office management, office technology, office/clerical. **Communications:** Advertising. **Computer sciences:** General. **Conservation:** Wood science. **Education:** Early childhood, multi-level teacher, teacher assistance. **Engineering technology:** Electrical. **Health:** Clinical lab technology, medical secretary, nursing (RN), phlebotomy. **Liberal arts:** Arts/sciences. **Mechanic/repair:** Industrial. **Production:** Welding. **Public administration:** Human services, social work. **Visual/performing arts:** Commercial/advertising art, interior design.

**Most popular majors.** Business/marketing 11%, engineering/engineering technologies 18%, health sciences 29%, liberal arts 15%, security/protective services 14%, visual/performing arts 8%.

**Computing on campus.** 100 workstations in computer center.

**Student life. Freshman orientation:** Available. Preregistration for classes offered. **Activities:** Student government, student newspaper.

**Student services.** Career counseling, student employment services, personal counseling, placement for graduates, veterans' counselor. **Transfer:** Transfer adviser, college fairs on campus for students transferring to 4-year colleges.

**Contact.** E-mail: vassorc@halifax.hcc.cc.nc.us
Phone: (252) 536-7220 Fax: (252) 538-4311
Cathy Vassor, Director of Admissions, Halifax Community College, Drawer 809, Weldon, NC 27890

## Haywood Community College
### Clyde, North Carolina                    CB member
### www.haywood.edu                          CB code: 5289

- Public 2-year community and technical college
- Commuter campus in rural community

**General.** Founded in 1965. Regionally accredited. **Enrollment:** 1,520 degree-seeking undergraduates. **Degrees:** 270 associate awarded. **Location:** 25 miles from Asheville. **Calendar:** Semester, extensive summer session. **Full-time faculty:** 70 total. **Part-time faculty:** 135 total. **Class size:** 85% < 20, 14% 20-39, less than 1% 40-49.

**Student profile.**

| | | | |
|---|---|---|---|
| Out-of-state: | 14% | 25 or older: | 39% |

**Transfer out. Colleges most students transferred to 2007:** Western Carolina University, Appalachian State University, University of North Carolina - Asheville.

**Basis for selection.** Open admission, but selective for some programs. Admission to nursing program based on admission test score, high school record, GPA, prerequisite courses, and health occupations aptitude examination. Completion of Accuplacer, SAT score of 500 or higher on each section, ACT composite score of 21 or higher, or official transcript with "C" or better in college-level English and algebra required. Informational interview required for electrical engineering technology, manufacturing engineering technology, cosmetology, and professional crafts programs. **Learning Disabled:** Accommodations made upon request.

**High school preparation.** Algebra, biology and chemistry required for nursing. Algebra recommended for electrical and manufacturing engineering, microcomputer systems and college transfer.

**2008-2009 Annual costs.** Tuition/fees (projected): $1,332. Per-credit charge: $42. Books/supplies: $1,000. Personal expenses: $1,656.

**2006-2007 Financial aid. Need-based:** 98% of total undergraduate aid awarded as scholarships/grants, 2% as loans/jobs. Need-based aid available for part-time students. Work-study available for part-time students. **Non-need-based:** Scholarships awarded for academics. **Additional information:** Complete FAFSA by priority filing date for consideration for institutional scholarships.

**Application procedures. Admission:** No deadline. No application fee. Application may be submitted online. Admission notification on a rolling basis. **Financial aid:** Priority date 4/1; no closing date. FAFSA, institutional form required. Applicants notified on a rolling basis starting 4/15; must reply within 2 week(s) of notification.

**Academics. Special study options:** Cooperative education, distance learning, dual enrollment of high school students, independent study, internships. **Credit/placement by examination:** CLEP, institutional tests. 18 credit hours maximum toward associate degree. **Support services:** GED preparation and test center, learning center, reduced course load, remedial instruction, tutoring.

**Majors. Agriculture:** Horticulture. **Business:** Accounting, administrative services, business admin. **Computer sciences:** Applications programming, networking. **Conservation:** Fisheries, forest resources, forestry, wildlife, wood science. **Construction:** Electrician, maintenance. **Engineering:** Computer. **Engineering technology:** Electrical, industrial management. **Family/consumer sciences:** Child care. **Health:** Medical assistant, nursing (RN). **Liberal arts:** Arts/sciences. **Mechanic/repair:** Automotive. **Personal/culinary services:** Cosmetic. **Production:** Woodworking. **Protective services:** Criminal justice. **Visual/performing arts:** Ceramics, fiber arts, metal/jewelry.

**Most popular majors.** Agriculture 6%, business/marketing 10%, engineering/engineering technologies 7%, family/consumer sciences 6%, health sciences 10%, liberal arts 15%, natural resources/environmental science 19%, trade and industry 8%, visual/performing arts 8%.

**Computing on campus.** 10 workstations in library.

**Student life. Freshman orientation:** Available. Preregistration for classes offered. **Activities:** Student government, Phi Theta Kappa, Phi Beta Lambda.

**Athletics. Intramural:** Basketball, bowling, football (non-tackle), softball, volleyball.

**Student services.** Career counseling, student employment services, financial aid counseling, on-campus daycare, personal counseling, placement for graduates, veterans' counselor. **Physically disabled:** Services for visually, speech, hearing impaired. **Transfer:** Transfer adviser for students transferring to 4-year colleges.

**Contact.** E-mail: drowland@haywood.cc.nc.us
Phone: (828) 627-4505 Toll-free number: (866) 468-6422
Fax: (828) 627-4513
Jennifer Herrera, Director of Enrollment Management, Haywood Community College, 185 Freelander Drive, Clyde, NC 28721-9454

## Isothermal Community College
### Spindale, North Carolina
www.isothermal.edu                          CB code: 5319

◆ Public 2-year community college
◆ Commuter campus in small town

**General.** Founded in 1964. Regionally accredited. **Enrollment:** 1,590 degree-seeking undergraduates; 541 non-degree-seeking students. **Degrees:** 191 associate awarded. **Location:** 65 miles from Charlotte, 48 miles from Asheville. **Calendar:** Semester, extensive summer session. **Full-time faculty:** 69 total. **Part-time faculty:** 72 total. **Class size:** 79% < 20, 21% 20-39, less than 1% 40-49.

**Student profile.** Among degree-seeking undergraduates, 32% enrolled in a transfer program, 68% enrolled in a vocational program, 241 enrolled as first-time, first-year students.

| | | | |
|---|---|---|---|
| Part-time: | 45% | Hispanic American: | 2% |
| Women: | 64% | 25 or older: | 51% |
| African American: | 16% | | |

**Basis for selection.** Open admission.

**2007-2008 Annual costs.** Tuition/fees: $1,298; $7,037 out-of-state. Per-credit charge: $42 in-state; $233 out-of-state. Books/supplies: $500. Personal expenses: $760.

**Financial aid. Need-based:** Need-based aid available for part-time students. Work-study available nights and for part-time students. **Non-need-based:** Scholarships awarded for academics, job skills, leadership, minority status, music/drama, state residency.

**Application procedures. Admission:** No deadline. No application fee. Application may be submitted online. Admission notification on a rolling basis. **Financial aid:** Priority date 5/31; no closing date. FAFSA, institutional form required. Applicants notified on a rolling basis starting 4/30; must reply within 4 week(s) of notification.

**Academics. Special study options:** Cooperative education, distance learning, dual enrollment of high school students, ESL, honors, independent study. Bachelor's degree programs available on campus. License preparation in nursing, real estate. **Credit/placement by examination:** CLEP, institutional tests. 12 credit hours maximum toward associate degree. **Support services:** GED preparation and test center, learning center, pre-admission summer program, reduced course load, remedial instruction, tutoring.

**Majors. Business:** Banking/financial services, business admin, e-commerce, marketing, office management, operations. **Communications technology:** Radio/tv. **Computer sciences:** Applications programming, information systems, information technology, networking, security. **Construction:** Electrician. **Education:** General, early childhood, elementary. **Engineering technology:** Computer, electrical, mechanical, mechanical drafting, plastics. **Health:** Nursing (RN), office admin. **Legal studies:** Paralegal. **Liberal arts:** Arts/sciences. **Mechanic/repair:** Auto body. **Personal/culinary services:** Cosmetic. **Production:** Machine shop technology, welding. **Protective services:** Criminal justice. **Visual/performing arts:** Commercial/advertising art.

**Most popular majors.** Business/marketing 8%, education 7%, health sciences 11%, liberal arts 13%.

**Computing on campus.** 44 workstations in library, computer center. Wireless network available.

**Student life. Freshman orientation:** Available. Preregistration for classes offered. **Activities:** Choral groups, drama, literary magazine, radio station,

---

student government, student newspaper, TV station, Afro-American club, Phi Theta Kappa, Phi Beta Lambda.

**Athletics. Intramural:** Basketball, football (non-tackle), volleyball.

**Student services.** Career counseling, health services, placement for graduates, veterans' counselor. **Transfer:** College fairs on campus for students transferring to 4-year colleges.

**Contact.** Phone: (828) 286-3636 ext. 288 Fax: (828) 286-8109
Maggie Killoran, Director, Enrollment Management, Isothermal Community College, PO Box 804, Spindale, NC 28160

## James Sprunt Community College
### Kenansville, North Carolina
www.jamessprunt.edu                          CB code: 6256

◆ Public 2-year community college
◆ Commuter campus in rural community

**General.** Founded in 1964. Regionally accredited. **Enrollment:** 956 degree-seeking undergraduates; 229 non-degree-seeking students. **Degrees:** 199 associate awarded. **Location:** 75 miles from Raleigh, 45 miles from Wilmington. **Calendar:** Semester, limited summer session. **Full-time faculty:** 60 total; 3% have terminal degrees, 13% minority, 57% women. **Part-time faculty:** 66 total; 3% have terminal degrees, 27% minority, 56% women. **Class size:** 77% < 20, 22% 20-39, 2% 40-49.

**Student profile.** Among degree-seeking undergraduates, 25% enrolled in a transfer program, 52% enrolled in a vocational program, 1% already have a bachelor's degree or higher, 174 enrolled as first-time, first-year students, 255 transferred in from other institutions.

| | | | |
|---|---|---|---|
| Part-time: | 48% | Women: | 71% |
| Out-of-state: | 1% | 25 or older: | 54% |

**Transfer out.** 85% of students enrolled in the transfer program go on to 4-year colleges. **Colleges most students transferred to 2007:** University of North Carolina at Wilmington, East Carolina University, Mount Olive College, North Carolina State University, Fayetteville State University.

**Basis for selection.** Open admission, but selective for some programs. Admission to nursing programs based on test scores and high school courses. 2.0 GPA in biology, chemistry, and algebra required. SAT or ACT accepted in lieu of academic placement tests. Nursing Entrance Test (NET) required for nursing applicants. Credit may be awarded for graphic arts classes based on portfolio. **Homeschooled:** Letter from State Board of Education giving approval for home school. **Learning Disabled:** Submit letter from professional stating disabilities.

**2007-2008 Annual costs.** Tuition/fees: $1,330; $7,069 out-of-state. Per-credit charge: $42 in-state; $233 out-of-state. Books/supplies: $1,400. Personal expenses: $900.

**2007-2008 Financial aid.** All financial aid based on need. 75 full-time freshmen applied for aid; 75 were judged to have need; 75 of these received aid. Average need met was 60%. Average scholarship/grant was $600; average loan $3,000. 81% of total undergraduate aid awarded as scholarships/grants, 19% as loans/jobs. Need-based aid available for part-time students. Work-study available nights and for part-time students.

**Application procedures. Admission:** No deadline. No application fee. Application may be submitted online. Admission notification on a rolling basis. **Financial aid:** Priority date 6/1; no closing date. FAFSA, institutional form required. Applicants notified on a rolling basis starting 7/15; must reply within 2 week(s) of notification.

**Academics. Special study options:** Cooperative education, distance learning, double major, dual enrollment of high school students, ESL, internships, liberal arts/career combination. License preparation in nursing. **Credit/placement by examination:** AP, CLEP, institutional tests. 16 credit hours maximum toward associate degree. **Support services:** GED preparation and test center, learning center, pre-admission summer program, reduced course load, remedial instruction, study skills assistance, tutoring.

**Majors. Agriculture:** Animal husbandry, animal sciences, business, poultry. **Business:** Accounting, administrative services, business admin. **Computer sciences:** Applications programming. **Education:** General, elementary, secondary. **Family/consumer sciences:** Child care. **Health:** Medical assistant, nursing (RN). **Liberal arts:** Arts/sciences. **Personal/culinary services:** Cosmetic. **Protective services:** Police science. **Visual/performing arts:** Commercial/advertising art.

**Most popular majors.** Business/marketing 11%, education 15%, health sciences 28%, liberal arts 36%.

**Computing on campus.** 261 workstations in library, computer center.

**Student life. Freshman orientation:** Available. Preregistration for classes offered. **Activities:** Student government, student newspaper, Phi Theta Kappa, student nurses association, National Vocational-Technical Honor Society, ambassador program, criminal justice club.

**Athletics. Intercollegiate:** Softball, tennis, volleyball.

**Student services.** Career counseling, services for economically disadvantaged, student employment services, financial aid counseling, personal counseling, placement for graduates, veterans' counselor. **Physically disabled:** Services for visually, hearing impaired. **Transfer:** Pre-admission transcript evaluation for new students. Transfer adviser, college fairs on campus for students transferring to 4-year colleges.

**Contact.** E-mail: lgrady@jamessprunt.edu
Phone: (910) 296-2500 Fax: (910) 296-1222
Lea Grady, Admissions Specialist, James Sprunt Community College, PO Box 398, Kenansville, NC 28349-0398

## Johnston Community College
**Smithfield, North Carolina**
www.johnstoncc.edu

**CB member**
**CB code: 0727**

- Public 2-year community and technical college
- Commuter campus in large town

**General.** Founded in 1969. Regionally accredited. **Enrollment:** 4,174 degree-seeking undergraduates. **Degrees:** 322 associate awarded. **Location:** 30 miles from Raleigh. **Calendar:** Semester, limited summer session. **Full-time faculty:** 130 total. **Part-time faculty:** 239 total. **Class size:** 66% < 20, 33% 20-39, less than 1% 40-49, less than 1% 50-99, less than 1% >100.

**Student profile.** Among degree-seeking undergraduates, 55% enrolled in a transfer program, 45% enrolled in a vocational program.

| | | | |
|---|---|---|---|
| Out-of-state: | 1% | Hispanic American: | 5% |
| African American: | 20% | Native American: | 1% |
| Asian American: | 1% | | |

**Transfer out.** Colleges most students transferred to 2007: East Carolina University, University of North Carolina at Wilmington, North Carolina State University.

**Basis for selection.** Open admission, but selective for some programs. Admission to health programs based on test scores, high school record and related completed courses. PSB required for admission to nursing and radiologic technology programs. Placement interview required for all applicants; interview required for health programs.

**2007-2008 Annual costs.** Tuition/fees: $1,330; $7,069 out-of-state. Per-credit charge: $42 in-state; $233 out-of-state. Books/supplies: $1,012. Personal expenses: $1,137.

**Financial aid.** All financial aid based on need. Need-based aid available for part-time students. Work-study available for part-time students.

**Application procedures. Admission:** Priority date 8/1; no deadline. No application fee. Application may be submitted online. Admission notification on a rolling basis. **Financial aid:** Priority date 5/31; no closing date. FAFSA, institutional form required. Applicants notified on a rolling basis starting 6/1; must reply within 2 week(s) of notification.

**Academics. Special study options:** Cross-registration, distance learning, double major, dual enrollment of high school students, internships. **Credit/placement by examination:** AP, CLEP, institutional tests. **Support services:** GED preparation and test center, learning center, pre-admission summer program, reduced course load, remedial instruction, tutoring.

**Majors. Business:** Accounting, administrative services, business admin, office/clerical, operations. **Computer sciences:** Programming. **Engineering:** Civil. **Family/consumer sciences:** Child care. **Health:** Cardiopulmonary technology, medical assistant, medical radiologic technology/radiation therapy, medical secretary, radiologic technology/medical imaging. **Legal studies:** Paralegal. **Liberal arts:** Arts/sciences. **Mechanic/repair:** Diesel, heating/ac/refrig. **Protective services:** Law enforcement admin, police science. **Visual/performing arts:** Commercial/advertising art.

**Most popular majors.** Business/marketing 16%, computer/information sciences 9%, education 8%, health sciences 21%, liberal arts 26%, visual/performing arts 8%.

**Computing on campus.** 29 workstations in library, computer center. Commuter students can connect to campus network.

**Student life. Freshman orientation:** Mandatory, $40 fee. Preregistration for classes offered. **Activities:** Jazz band, choral groups, student government.

**Athletics.** NJCAA. **Intercollegiate:** Basketball M, golf M. **Team name:** Jaguars.

**Student services.** Campus ministries, career counseling, student employment services, financial aid counseling, minority student services, on-campus daycare, personal counseling, placement for graduates, veterans' counselor. **Physically disabled:** Services for visually, speech, hearing impaired. **Transfer:** Pre-admission transcript evaluation for new students. College fairs on campus for students transferring to 4-year colleges.

**Contact.** Phone: (919) 209-2128 Fax: (919) 989-7862
Joan McLendon, Director of Admissions and Counseling, Johnston Community College, Box 2350, Smithfield, NC 27577

## King's College
**Charlotte, North Carolina**
www.kingscollegecharlotte.edu

**CB code: 5361**

- For-profit 2-year college
- Large city
- Interview required

**General.** Accredited by ACICS. **Enrollment:** 545 degree-seeking undergraduates. **Degrees:** 158 associate awarded. **Calendar:** Semester. **Full-time faculty:** 16 total. **Part-time faculty:** 9 total.

**Basis for selection.** Interview required, class rank and standardized test scores important.

**2007-2008 Annual costs.** Tuition/fees: $12,440. Room/board: $6,080.

**Application procedures. Admission:** No deadline. $50 fee. Admission notification on a rolling basis.

**Academics. Credit/placement by examination:** CLEP.

**Majors. Business:** Accounting, administrative services, tourism/travel. **Computer sciences:** Applications programming. **Health:** Medical secretary. **Legal studies:** Legal secretary, paralegal. **Visual/performing arts:** Commercial/advertising art.

**Student life. Freshman orientation:** Mandatory. Held on the day prior to the start of classes. **Policies:** Dress code observed; no alcoholic beverages or drugs on campus. **Housing:** Single-sex dorms available. **Activities:** Student government, Sigma Chi Kappa, Lambda Epsilon Chi.

**Student services.** Career counseling, financial aid counseling, placement for graduates.

**Contact.** Phone: (704) 372-0266 Toll-free number: (800) 768-2255 Fax: (704) 348-2029
Diane Ryon, Director, King's College , 322 Lamar Avenue, Charlotte, NC 28204

## Lenoir Community College
**Kinston, North Carolina**
www.lenoir.cc.nc.us

**CB code: 5378**

- Public 2-year community college
- Commuter campus in large town

**General.** Founded in 1958. Regionally accredited. Extension campuses in Jones and Greene Counties. **Enrollment:** 2,172 degree-seeking undergraduates. **Degrees:** 274 associate awarded. **Location:** 75 miles from Raleigh, 25 miles from Greenville. **Calendar:** Semester, extensive summer session. **Full-time faculty:** 105 total. **Part-time faculty:** 240 total. **Class size:** 73% < 20, 26% 20-39, 1% 40-49, less than 1% 50-99. **Special facilities:** Facility for local history, genealogy collection.

**Transfer out.** Colleges most students transferred to 2007: East Carolina University.

**Basis for selection.** Open admission, but selective for some programs. Special requirements for allied health programs. Interview required for surgical technology program.

**High school preparation.** Recommended units include English 4, mathematics 2, social studies 2, history 1, science 2 (laboratory 1). One biology, 1 chemistry required for registered nursing program.

**2007-2008 Annual costs.** Tuition/fees: $1,336; $7,075 out-of-state. Per-credit charge: $42 in-state; $233 out-of-state. Books/supplies: $800. Personal expenses: $540.

**Financial aid. Need-based:** Need-based aid available for part-time students. Work-study available nights and for part-time students. **Non-need-based:** Scholarships awarded for academics, athletics, leadership, state residency.

**Application procedures. Admission:** No deadline. No application fee. Application may be submitted online. Admission notification on a rolling basis. Separate application required for allied health programs. January 31 deadline for nursing and April 30 for surgical technology. **Financial aid:** Priority date 7/1, closing date 8/15. Institutional form required. Applicants notified on a rolling basis starting 8/1; must reply within 2 week(s) of notification.

**Academics. Special study options:** Cooperative education, distance learning, dual enrollment of high school students, honors, liberal arts/career combination, study abroad, weekend college. License preparation in aviation, nursing, paramedic, real estate. **Credit/placement by examination:** CLEP, IB, institutional tests. **Support services:** GED preparation and test center, learning center, pre-admission summer program, reduced course load, remedial instruction, tutoring.

**Majors. Agriculture:** Horticulture. **Business:** Accounting, administrative services, business admin, e-commerce, executive assistant, management information systems. **Computer sciences:** Data processing, programming. **Conservation:** Water/wetlands/marine. **Education:** General, art, biology, chemistry, early childhood, elementary, health, history, physical, social science, teacher assistance. **Engineering:** General. **Engineering technology:** Electrical, mechanical. **Family/consumer sciences:** Child care. **Health:** Massage therapy, medical assistant, medical secretary, nursing (RN), radiologic technology/medical imaging. **Legal studies:** Court reporting. **Liberal arts:** Arts/sciences. **Math:** General. **Mechanic/repair:** Automotive, electronics/electrical. **Personal/culinary services:** Culinary arts. **Production:** Machine shop technology, welding. **Psychology:** General. **Public administration:** Social work. **Transportation:** Airline/commercial pilot, aviation management. **Visual/performing arts:** Commercial/advertising art, studio arts.

**Computing on campus.** 100 workstations in library, computer center, student center. Commuter students can connect to campus network. Online course registration available.

**Student life. Freshman orientation:** Available. Preregistration for classes offered. **Activities:** Choral groups, radio station, student government, student newspaper, Phi Theta Kappa, various clubs related to major fields of study.

**Athletics.** NJCAA. **Intercollegiate:** Baseball M, basketball M, volleyball W. **Intramural:** Basketball M. **Team name:** Lancers.

**Student services.** Adult student services, career counseling, student employment services, financial aid counseling, health services, personal counseling, placement for graduates, veterans' counselor. **Transfer:** Pre-admission transcript evaluation for new students. Transfer adviser, college fairs on campus for students transferring to 4-year colleges.

**Contact.** Phone: (252) 527-6223 Fax: (252) 527-6223 ext. 323
Myra Poole, Director of Enrollment Management, Lenoir Community College, Box 188, Kinston, NC 28502-0188

## Louisburg College
**Louisburg, North Carolina**
www.louisburg.edu
**CB member**
**CB code: 5369**

- Private 2-year junior college affiliated with United Methodist Church
- Residential campus in small town
- SAT or ACT (ACT writing optional) required

**General.** Founded in 1787. Regionally accredited. **Enrollment:** 730 degree-seeking undergraduates. **Degrees:** 90 associate awarded. **Location:** 30 miles from Raleigh. **Calendar:** Semester, limited summer session. **Full-time faculty:** 35 total. **Part-time faculty:** 20 total.

**Student profile.**

| | | | |
|---|---|---|---|
| Out-of-state: | 20% | Live on campus: | 80% |
| 25 or older: | 3% | | |

**Transfer out.** Colleges most students transferred to 2007: North Carolina State University, East Carolina University, Appalachian State University, University of North Carolina at Wilmington, University of North Carolina at Greensboro, University of North Carolina at Chapel Hill.

**Basis for selection.** School achievement most important, followed by test scores and recommendations. Interview recommended for some applicants. Students more than one year out of high school not required to submit test scores. **Learning Disabled:** Comprehensive tutorial program available for learning-disabled students.

**High school preparation.** 20 units recommended. Recommended units include English 4, mathematics 3, social studies 3, science 2 and foreign language 2.

**2007-2008 Annual costs.** Tuition/fees: $12,425. Room/board: $7,775. Books/supplies: $900. Personal expenses: $1,125.

**Financial aid. Need-based:** Work-study available nights and weekends. **Additional information:** Job location and development program helps students obtain work in the community.

**Application procedures. Admission:** No deadline. $25 fee, may be waived for applicants with need. Admission notification on a rolling basis. Must reply by May 1 or within 2 week(s) if notified thereafter. **Financial aid:** Priority date 3/1; no closing date. FAFSA, institutional form required. Applicants notified on a rolling basis starting 3/15.

**Academics. Special study options:** Cooperative education, dual enrollment of high school students, independent study. Louisburg Learning Partners for Students with Learning Differences. **Credit/placement by examination:** AP, CLEP, IB, institutional tests. 30 credit hours maximum toward associate degree. **Support services:** Learning center, pre-admission summer program, reduced course load, remedial instruction, study skills assistance, tutoring, writing center.

**Majors. Biology:** General. **Business:** General, business admin. **Communications:** General. **Computer sciences:** General. **Education:** General, biology, chemistry, early childhood, elementary, history, mathematics, physical, science, secondary. **Engineering:** General. **English:** English lit. **Health:** Athletic training, premedicine, prepharmacy. **History:** General. **Liberal arts:** Arts/sciences. **Math:** General. **Parks/recreation:** General, exercise sciences, facilities management. **Physical sciences:** Chemistry. **Psychology:** General. **Public administration:** Social work. **Social sciences:** General, sociology. **Visual/performing arts:** Art, dance, dramatic.

**Most popular majors.** Liberal arts 92%.

**Computing on campus.** 75 workstations in library, computer center. Dormitories linked to campus network. Online library available.

**Student life. Freshman orientation:** Mandatory. Preregistration for classes offered. **Policies:** Non-resident undergraduates under 21 must live at home. **Housing:** Guaranteed on-campus for all undergraduates. Single-sex dorms available. $200 deposit. **Activities:** Choral groups, dance, drama, literary magazine, music ensembles, musical theater, radio station, student government, student newspaper, Christian Life Council, Young Democrats, Young Republicans, Spanish club, Workers Actively Volunteering Energetic Services, peace group, French club, Phi Theta Kappa, Appalachian Trail White Water Club, ecological concerns club.

**Athletics.** NJCAA. **Intercollegiate:** Baseball M, basketball, cheerleading, golf, soccer, softball W, volleyball W. **Intramural:** Basketball, football (tackle), soccer, softball, table tennis, tennis, volleyball. **Team name:** Hurricanes.

**Student services.** Adult student services, alcohol/substance abuse counseling, campus ministries, career counseling, student employment services, financial aid counseling, health services, personal counseling, veterans' counselor. **Learning disabled:** Comprehensive services available. **Transfer:** Transfer adviser, college fairs on campus for students transferring to 4-year colleges.

**Contact.** E-mail: admissions@louisburg.edu
Phone: (919) 497-3222 Toll-free number: (800) 775-0208
Fax: (919) 496-1788
Tracey Sala, Vice President of Enrollment Management, Louisburg College, 501 North Main Street, Louisburg, NC 27549

## Martin Community College
**Williamston, North Carolina**
www.martincc.edu
**CB member**
**CB code: 5445**

- Public 2-year community and technical college
- Commuter campus in small town

**General.** Founded in 1967. Regionally accredited. **Enrollment:** 612 degree-seeking undergraduates. **Degrees:** 92 associate awarded. **Location:** 30 miles from Greenville, 100 miles from Raleigh. **Calendar:** Semester, limited summer session. **Full-time faculty:** 30 total. **Part-time faculty:** 60 total. **Special facilities:** Equine arena, bull riding, rodeos.

**Student profile.** Among degree-seeking undergraduates, 79 transferred in from other institutions.

Out-of-state: 1%   25 or older: 58%

**Transfer out. Colleges most students transferred to 2007:** East Carolina University.

**Basis for selection.** Open admission, but selective for some programs. Limited enrollment in physical therapy assistant program. Selection based on high school record, placement test results, completion of required courses and interview. Selection of Dental Assisting applications includes high school record, completion of required courses, and an interview. COMPASS required of some students. Interview required for physical therapist assistant applicants and dental assisting applicants. **Homeschooled:** Statement describing homeschool structure and mission, transcript of courses and grades required.

**High school preparation.** 22 units recommended. Recommended units include English 4, mathematics 3, social studies 2, history 1, science 3 (laboratory 1) and academic electives 9.

**2007-2008 Annual costs.** Tuition/fees: $1,298; $7,037 out-of-state. Per-credit charge: $42 in-state; $233 out-of-state. Books/supplies: $600. Personal expenses: $400.

**Financial aid. Need-based:** Need-based aid available for part-time students. Work-study available nights and for part-time students. **Non-need-based:** Scholarships awarded for academics.

**Application procedures. Admission:** No deadline. No application fee. Application may be submitted online. Admission notification on a rolling basis. Closing date for physical therapist assistant program applicants May 15. **Financial aid:** Priority date 5/1; no closing date. FAFSA required. Applicants notified on a rolling basis starting 5/1.

**Academics. Special study options:** Cooperative education, distance learning, double major, dual enrollment of high school students, ESL, independent study, internships, liberal arts/career combination. License preparation in real estate. **Credit/placement by examination:** AP, CLEP, institutional tests. No more than half of credits required in program of study may be earned through credit by exam (including CLEP). **Support services:** GED preparation and test center, learning center, reduced course load, remedial instruction, study skills assistance, tutoring.

**Majors. Agriculture:** Equestrian studies. **Business:** Accounting technology, business admin, executive assistant, management information systems. **Computer sciences:** Information systems. **Construction:** Electrician. **Education:** General, early childhood, elementary, secondary. **Health:** Medical assistant, medical secretary, physical therapy assistant. **Liberal arts:** Arts/sciences. **Mechanic/repair:** Automotive, heating/ac/refrig. **Personal/culinary services:** Cosmetic.

**Most popular majors.** Agriculture 6%, business/marketing 43%, education 15%, health sciences 27%.

**Computing on campus.** 31 workstations in library, computer center. Commuter students can connect to campus network.

**Student life. Freshman orientation:** Available. Offered on registration day. **Activities:** Student government, physical therapist assistant club, Phi Theta Kappa, equine club, medical assisting club, Alpha Beta Gamma.

**Athletics. Team name:** Screaming Eagles.

**Student services.** Career counseling, services for economically disadvantaged, student employment services, financial aid counseling, on-campus daycare, personal counseling, placement for graduates, veterans' counselor. **Transfer:** Pre-admission transcript evaluation for new students. Transfer adviser, college fairs on campus for students transferring to 4-year colleges.

**Contact.** E-mail: jbussell@martincc.edu
Phone: (252) 792-1521 ext. 268 Fax: (252) 792-0826
Jim Bussell, Admissions Officer, Martin Community College, 1161 Kehukee Park Road, Williamston, NC 27892-9988

## Mayland Community College
**Spruce Pine, North Carolina**
www.mayland.edu
**CB member**
**CB code: 0795**

- Public 2-year community college
- Commuter campus in rural community

**General.** Founded in 1971. Regionally accredited. **Enrollment:** 1,800 degree-seeking undergraduates. **Degrees:** 125 associate awarded. **Location:** 50 miles from Asheville. **Calendar:** Semester, limited summer session. **Full-time faculty:** 47 total. **Part-time faculty:** 50 total. **Class size:** 71% < 20, 29% 20-39. **Special facilities:** Child development center, interactive TV facility.

**Transfer out. Colleges most students transferred to 2007:** Appalachian State University, University of North Carolina-Asheville, Western Carolina University, Mars Hill College, East Tennessee State University.

**Basis for selection.** Open admission, but selective for some programs. Admission to associate degree nursing program and practical nursing program based on competitive ranking system. Medical assisting admissions based on completion of requirements and timely application. Placement assessment required of all degree-seeking students. **Homeschooled:** Transcript of courses and grades required.

**2007-2008 Annual costs.** Tuition/fees: $1,332; $7,071 out-of-state. Per-credit charge: $42 in-state; $233 out-of-state. Books/supplies: $750. Personal expenses: $1,087.

**Financial aid. Need-based:** Need-based aid available for part-time students.

**Application procedures. Admission:** No deadline. No application fee. Application may be submitted online. Admission notification on a rolling basis beginning on or about 3/1. Application by February 28 required for nursing program. **Financial aid:** Priority date 3/15; no closing date. FAFSA, institutional form required. Applicants notified on a rolling basis starting 6/15.

**Academics. Special study options:** Cooperative education, cross-registration, distance learning, double major, dual enrollment of high school students, independent study, internships, liberal arts/career combination. Bachelor's degree programs available on campus. License preparation in nursing, real estate. **Credit/placement by examination:** AP, CLEP, institutional tests. Maximum 25% of program hours can be earned via credit by examination. **Support services:** GED preparation and test center, learning center, pre-admission summer program, reduced course load, remedial instruction, study skills assistance, tutoring, writing center.

**Majors. Agriculture:** Horticulture. **Business:** Accounting, administrative services, business admin. **Computer sciences:** Systems analysis. **Education:** General, early childhood. **Engineering:** Electrical. **Health:** Medical secretary, nursing (RN). **Liberal arts:** Arts/sciences. **Personal/culinary services:** Cosmetic.

**Most popular majors.** Business/marketing 28%, education 7%, engineering/engineering technologies 7%, health sciences 31%, liberal arts 19%.

**Computing on campus.** 150 workstations in library, computer center. Commuter students can connect to campus network. Online course registration, online library, helpline, student web hosting available.

**Student life. Freshman orientation:** Mandatory. Preregistration for classes offered. One-hour class each semester. **Activities:** Literary magazine, student government, Phi Theta Kappa, National Nursing Association, early childhood students' association.

**Student services.** Career counseling, services for economically disadvantaged, student employment services, financial aid counseling, on-campus daycare, personal counseling, placement for graduates, veterans' counselor. **Physically disabled:** Services for visually, speech, hearing impaired. **Transfer:** Pre-admission transcript evaluation for new students. Transfer adviser, college fairs on campus for students transferring to 4-year colleges.

**Contact.** Phone: (828) 765-7351 Toll-free number: (800) 462-9526
Fax: (828) 765-0728
Cathy Morrison, Director of Enrollment Management, Mayland Community College, Box 547, Spruce Pine, NC 28777

## McDowell Technical Community College
**Marion, North Carolina**
www.mcdowelltech.edu
**CB code: 0789**

- Public 2-year community and technical college
- Commuter campus in small town

**General.** Founded in 1964. Regionally accredited. **Enrollment:** 930 degree-seeking undergraduates. **Degrees:** 126 associate awarded. **Location:** 35 miles from Asheville. **Calendar:** Semester, limited summer session. **Full-time faculty:** 35 total; 57% women. **Part-time faculty:** 72 total; 3% minority, 49% women. **Special facilities:** Color and black/white photography laboratories.

**Student profile.**

Out-of-state:          2%          **25 or older:**          58%

**Basis for selection.** Open admission, but selective for some programs. Special requirements for allied health programs. Interview required for some allied health programs. **Adult students:** Must take required placement tests. **Homeschooled:** Transcript of courses and grades required.

**2007-2008 Annual costs.** Tuition/fees: $1,316; $7,055 out-of-state. Per-credit charge: $42 in-state; $233 out-of-state. Books/supplies: $900. Personal expenses: $1,714.

**2006-2007 Financial aid.** All financial aid based on need. 99% of total undergraduate aid awarded as scholarships/grants, 1% as loans/jobs. Need-based aid available for part-time students. Work-study available nights and for part-time students.

**Application procedures. Admission:** No deadline. No application fee. Application must be submitted on paper. Admission notification on a rolling basis. **Financial aid:** Priority date 3/15; no closing date. FAFSA, institutional form required. Applicants notified on a rolling basis starting 7/1.

**Academics. Special study options:** Cooperative education, distance learning, double major, dual enrollment of high school students, independent study, internships, liberal arts/career combination. Bachelor's degree programs available on campus. License preparation in nursing. **Credit/placement by examination:** CLEP, institutional tests. 20 credit hours maximum toward associate degree. **Support services:** GED preparation and test center, learning center, reduced course load, remedial instruction, tutoring.

**Majors. Business:** General, accounting, office/clerical. **Communications technology:** Graphic/printing. **Computer sciences:** Applications programming, programming. **Education:** General. **Health:** Nursing (RN). **Liberal arts:** Arts/sciences. **Mechanic/repair:** Electronics/electrical, industrial. **Visual/performing arts:** Commercial photography, commercial/advertising art.

**Most popular majors.** Business/marketing 13%, computer/information sciences 6%, education 16%, health sciences 25%, liberal arts 14%, trade and industry 20%.

**Computing on campus.** 80 workstations in library, computer center.

**Student life. Freshman orientation:** Available. Preregistration for classes offered. Two-hour orientation held one day prior to registration day. **Activities:** Student government.

**Student services.** Adult student services, career counseling, student employment services, on-campus daycare, personal counseling, placement for graduates, veterans' counselor. **Physically disabled:** Services for visually, speech, hearing impaired. **Transfer:** Transfer adviser for students transferring to 4-year colleges.

**Contact.** E-mail: rickw@mcdowelltech.edu
Phone: (828) 652-0632 Fax: (828) 652-1014
Rick Wilson, Director of Admissions, McDowell Technical Community College, 54 College Drive, Marion, NC 28752

---

## Miller-Motte Technical College: Cary
**Cary, North Carolina**
**www.mmccary.net**

⬧ For-profit 2-year technical college
⬧ Small city

**General.** Regionally accredited; also accredited by ACICS. **Enrollment:** 459 degree-seeking undergraduates. **Degrees:** 36 associate awarded. **Location:** 10 miles from downtown Raleigh. **Calendar:** Quarter. **Full-time faculty:** 14 total. **Part-time faculty:** 16 total.

**2008-2009 Annual costs.** Tuition/fees: $10,440. Per-credit charge: $232.

**Application procedures. Admission:** No deadline. $35 fee. **Financial aid:** No deadline.

**Academics. Credit/placement by examination:** CLEP.

**Majors. Health:** Massage therapy, medical assistant, surgical technology.

**Contact.** Alison Mecca, Admissions Director, Miller-Motte Technical College: Cary, 2205 Walnut Street, Cary, NC 27518

---

## Mitchell Community College
**Statesville, North Carolina**          **CB member**
**www.mitchellcc.edu**          **CB code: 5412**

⬧ Public 2-year community college
⬧ Commuter campus in large town

**General.** Founded in 1852. Regionally accredited. **Enrollment:** 2,687 degree-seeking undergraduates. **Degrees:** 202 associate awarded. **Location:** 40 miles from Charlotte, 40 miles from Winston-Salem. **Calendar:** Semester, limited summer session. **Full-time faculty:** 66 total. **Part-time faculty:** 80 total.

**Student profile.**

Out-of-state:          70%          **25 or older:**          49%

**Transfer out. Colleges most students transferred to 2007:** University of North Carolina-Charlotte, Appalachian State University, Gardner-Webb University, Lenoir-Rhyne University.

**Basis for selection.** Open admission, but selective for some programs. Nursing program applicants must meet minimum admissions requirements; interview and essay required. All applicants must take college placement tests to determine readiness for college-level studies.

**2007-2008 Annual costs.** Tuition/fees: $1,328; $7,067 out-of-state. Per-credit charge: $42 in-state; $233 out-of-state. Books/supplies: $900. Personal expenses: $1,448.

**Financial aid. Need-based:** Need-based aid available for part-time students. Work-study available for part-time students.

**Application procedures. Admission:** No deadline. No application fee. Admission notification on a rolling basis. **Financial aid:** No deadline. FAFSA, institutional form required. Applicants notified on a rolling basis starting 3/1; must reply within 2 week(s) of notification.

**Academics. Special study options:** Cooperative education, distance learning, dual enrollment of high school students, independent study. License preparation in nursing, paramedic, real estate. **Credit/placement by examination:** AP, CLEP, institutional tests. 20 credit hours maximum toward associate degree. **Support services:** GED preparation and test center, learning center, reduced course load, remedial instruction, tutoring.

**Majors. Business:** Accounting, administrative services, business admin, operations. **Computer sciences:** Information systems, programming. **Education:** Early childhood, teacher assistance. **Engineering:** Electrical. **Engineering technology:** Construction, drafting, electrical, industrial management, manufacturing. **Health:** Nursing (RN), predental, premedicine, prepharmacy, preveterinary. **Legal studies:** Prelaw. **Liberal arts:** Arts/sciences. **Mechanic/repair:** Industrial. **Production:** Machine shop technology. **Protective services:** Police science. **Public administration:** Human services. **Visual/performing arts:** Studio arts.

**Most popular majors.** Business/marketing 15%, computer/information sciences 13%, engineering/engineering technologies 6%, health sciences 26%, liberal arts 18%, personal/culinary services 8%.

**Computing on campus.** 45 workstations in library, computer center.

**Student life. Freshman orientation:** Available. Usually held immediately prior to fall semester for approximately 2.5 hours. **Activities:** Concert band, choral groups, literary magazine, student government, Circle-K, Christian Student Fellowship, Ebony Kinship.

**Student services.** Campus ministries, career counseling, student employment services, financial aid counseling, personal counseling, placement for graduates, veterans' counselor. **Physically disabled:** Services for visually, hearing impaired. **Transfer:** College fairs on campus for students transferring to 4-year colleges.

**Contact.** E-mail: gstanley@mitchell.cc.nc.us
Phone: (704) 878-3243 Fax: (704) 878-0872
Brenda Sawyer, Director of Admissions and Records, Mitchell Community College, 500 West Broad Street, Statesville, NC 28677

---

## Montgomery Community College
**Troy, North Carolina**
**www.montgomery.edu**          **CB code: 0785**

⬧ Public 2-year community college
⬧ Commuter campus in small town

**General.** Founded in 1967. Regionally accredited. **Enrollment:** 991 degree-seeking undergraduates. **Degrees:** 98 associate awarded. **Location:** 50 miles from Greensboro, 62 miles from Charlotte. **Calendar:** Semester, limited summer session. **Full-time faculty:** 40 total. **Part-time faculty:** 32 total. **Class size:** 91% < 20, 7% 20-39, 2% 40-49, less than 1% 50-99. **Special facilities:** Rifle/pistol firing range.

**Student profile.** Among degree-seeking undergraduates, 187 transferred in from other institutions.

**Out-of-state:** 1% **25 or older:** 55%

**Transfer out. Colleges most students transferred to 2007:** Pfeiffer University, Gardner-Webb University, University of North Carolina at Greensboro.

**Basis for selection.** Open admission, but selective for some programs. Special requirements for nursing program. Secondary school record and test scores considered. **Homeschooled:** Home school must provide copy of "Notification of intent to operate" card from NC Department of Non-Public Education.

**High school preparation.** 28 units recommended. Recommended units include English 4, mathematics 3, social studies 3, science 3 (laboratory 1) and academic electives 15.

**2007-2008 Annual costs.** Tuition/fees: $1,320; $7,059 out-of-state. Per-credit charge: $42 in-state; $233 out-of-state. Books/supplies: $1,050.

**Financial aid. Need-based:** Need-based aid available for part-time students. Work-study available nights and for part-time students. **Non-need-based:** Scholarships awarded for academics, minority status, state residency.

**Application procedures. Admission:** No deadline. No application fee. Application may be submitted online. Admission notification on a rolling basis. Practical Nursing Program applicants must apply by October 15 for following fall program. **Financial aid:** Priority date 7/15; no closing date. FAFSA, institutional form required. Applicants notified on a rolling basis starting 6/1.

**Academics. Special study options:** Distance learning, double major, dual enrollment of high school students. License preparation in nursing. **Credit/placement by examination:** AP, CLEP, institutional tests. 16 credit hours maximum toward associate degree. **Support services:** GED preparation and test center, learning center, reduced course load, remedial instruction, tutoring.

**Majors. Business:** Accounting, business admin, office management. **Computer sciences:** Information systems, information technology. **Conservation:** Forest technology. **Construction:** Electrician. **Education:** Early childhood. **Health:** Medical assistant. **Liberal arts:** Arts/sciences. **Mechanic/repair:** Gunsmithing. **Protective services:** Criminal justice. **Visual/performing arts:** Crafts.

**Most popular majors.** Business/marketing 19%, education 10%, health sciences 18%, liberal arts 20%, natural resources/environmental science 17%, trade and industry 8%.

**Computing on campus.** 90 workstations in library, computer center. Commuter students can connect to campus network.

**Student life. Freshman orientation:** Available. **Activities:** Student government, gunsmithing society, forestry club, business technologies club, practical nursing club, medical assisting club.

**Student services.** Career counseling, student employment services, financial aid counseling, on-campus daycare, personal counseling, veterans' counselor. **Physically disabled:** Services for visually, speech, hearing impaired. **Transfer:** Transfer adviser, college fairs on campus for students transferring to 4-year colleges.

**Contact.** E-mail: fryek@montgomery.edu
Phone: (910) 576-6222 ext. 240 Toll-free number: (800) 839-6222
Fax: (910) 576-2176
Karen Frye, Admissions Officer, Montgomery Community College, 1011 Page Street, Troy, NC 27371-0787

## Nash Community College
**Rocky Mount, North Carolina**
www.nash.cc.nc.us

CB member
CB code: 5881

- Public 2-year community college
- Commuter campus in small city

**General.** Founded in 1967. Regionally accredited. **Enrollment:** 2,000 degree-seeking undergraduates. **Degrees:** 153 associate awarded. **Location:** 55 miles from Raleigh. **Calendar:** Semester, limited summer session. **Full-time faculty:** 75 total. **Part-time faculty:** 150 total. **Class size:** 54% < 20, 46% 20-39. **Partnerships:** Formal partnership with high schools to provide students opportunity to earn college credit.

**Student profile.**

**Out-of-state:** 1% **25 or older:** 52%

**Transfer out. Colleges most students transferred to 2007:** University of North Carolina system universities.

**Basis for selection.** Open admission, but selective for some programs. Special requirements for nursing, physical therapy assistant, phlebotomy, cosmetology programs. Students may use ACT or SAT scores for placement, or take ASSET or COMPASS. **Adult students:** College recommends ASSET or COMPASS placement test if student does not have SAT scores.

**High school preparation.** Appropriate biology courses required for nursing and physical therapist assistant programs.

**2007-2008 Annual costs.** Tuition/fees: $1,350; $7,089 out-of-state. Per-credit charge: $42 in-state; $233 out-of-state. Books/supplies: $900. Personal expenses: $2,000.

**Financial aid. Need-based:** Need-based aid available for part-time students. **Non-need-based:** Scholarships awarded for academics.

**Application procedures. Admission:** No deadline. No application fee. Admission notification on a rolling basis. **Financial aid:** Priority date 6/30; no closing date. FAFSA, institutional form required. Applicants notified on a rolling basis starting 7/15.

**Academics. Special study options:** Accelerated study, distance learning, dual enrollment of high school students, ESL, liberal arts/career combination. License preparation in nursing, paramedic, physical therapy, real estate. **Credit/placement by examination:** CLEP, IB, institutional tests. **Support services:** GED preparation and test center, learning center, reduced course load, remedial instruction, study skills assistance, tutoring.

**Majors. Architecture:** Technology. **Business:** Accounting, administrative services, business admin, hotel/motel admin, management information systems. **Computer sciences:** Information systems. **Construction:** Lineworker. **Education:** General, early childhood, teacher assistance. **Engineering:** Electrical. **Engineering technology:** Architectural, computer, electrical, industrial safety. **Family/consumer sciences:** Child care. **Health:** Licensed practical nurse, medical secretary, nursing (RN). **Legal studies:** Legal secretary. **Liberal arts:** Arts/sciences. **Personal/culinary services:** Culinary arts. **Protective services:** Police science.

**Most popular majors.** Business/marketing 18%, computer/information sciences 8%, engineering/engineering technologies 16%, health sciences 21%, liberal arts 21%, social sciences 7%.

**Computing on campus.** 110 workstations in library, computer center. Online library available.

**Student life. Freshman orientation:** Available. Preregistration for classes offered. **Activities:** Student government.

**Student services.** Career counseling, services for economically disadvantaged, student employment services, financial aid counseling, placement for graduates, veterans' counselor. **Physically disabled:** Services for visually, speech, hearing impaired. **Transfer:** Pre-admission transcript evaluation for new students. Transfer adviser, college fairs on campus for students transferring to 4-year colleges.

**Contact.** Phone: (252) 443-4011 ext. 300 Fax: (252) 443-0828
Dot Gardner, Admissions Officer, Nash Community College, Box 7488, Rocky Mount, NC 27804-0488

## Pamlico Community College
**Grantsboro, North Carolina**
www.pamlicocc.edu

CB code: 0864

- Public 2-year community college
- Commuter campus in rural community

**General.** Founded in 1962. Regionally accredited. **Enrollment:** 393 degree-seeking undergraduates. **Degrees:** 28 associate awarded. **Location:** 20 miles from New Bern. **Calendar:** Semester, limited summer session. **Full-time faculty:** 20 total. **Part-time faculty:** 10 total.

**Basis for selection.** Open admission.

**2007-2008 Annual costs.** Tuition/fees: $1,295; $7,034 out-of-state. Per-credit charge: $42 in-state; $233 out-of-state. Books/supplies: $380. Personal expenses: $1,630.

**Financial aid. Additional information:** Jobs Training Partner Act and Displaced Homemaker Programs cover tuition, books, fees.

**Application procedures. Admission:** No deadline. No application fee. Admission notification on a rolling basis. **Financial aid:** Priority date 3/15; no closing date. FAFSA required. Applicants notified on a rolling basis.

**Academics. Special study options:** Dual enrollment of high school students, independent study, internships. **Credit/placement by examination:** CLEP, institutional tests. **Support services:** Learning center, reduced course load, remedial instruction, tutoring.

**Majors. Business:** Accounting, business admin, office/clerical. **Conservation:** General. **Education:** General, early childhood. **Engineering:** Electrical. **Engineering technology:** Electrical.

**Computing on campus.** 40 workstations in library.

**Student life. Freshman orientation:** Available. **Activities:** Student government, student newspaper.

**Athletics. Intramural:** Basketball, softball, table tennis, tennis, volleyball.

**Student services.** Career counseling, student employment services, health services, personal counseling, placement for graduates, veterans' counselor.

**Contact.** E-mail: jgibbs@pamlicocc.edu
Phone: (252) 249-1851 Fax: (252) 249-2377
Jamie Gibbs, Dean of Student Enrollment Services, Pamlico Community College, PO Box 185, Grantsboro, NC 28529

---

## Piedmont Community College
**Roxboro, North Carolina**
www.piedmontcc.edu                    CB code: 5518

- Public 2-year community college
- Small town

**General.** Founded in 1970. Regionally accredited. Branch campus in Caswell County. Correctional education offered at Hillsborough, Yanceyville, and Roxboro. **Enrollment:** 2,610 degree-seeking undergraduates. **Degrees:** 173 associate awarded. **Location:** 30 miles from Durham, 45 miles from Chapel Hill. **Calendar:** Semester, limited summer session. **Full-time faculty:** 75 total. **Part-time faculty:** 70 total. **Special facilities:** 4-mile nature trail.

**Student profile.**

Out-of-state:            5%    **25 or older:**            51%

**Basis for selection.** Open admission, but selective for some programs. Admission for nursing based on test scores, interview and recommendations. Nursing applicants must provide health data.

**2007-2008 Annual costs.** Tuition/fees: $1,290; $7,029 out-of-state. Per-credit charge: $42 in-state; $233 out-of-state. Books/supplies: $800. Personal expenses: $750.

**Application procedures. Admission:** No deadline. No application fee. Admission notification on a rolling basis. Certain certificate programs do not require high school diploma. **Financial aid:** Priority date 4/15; no closing date. FAFSA required. Applicants notified on a rolling basis; must reply within 2 week(s) of notification.

**Academics. Special study options:** Cooperative education, cross-registration, distance learning, double major, dual enrollment of high school students, independent study, internships, weekend college. License preparation in nursing. **Credit/placement by examination:** CLEP, institutional tests. Maximum of 50% of coursework may be completed through credit by examination. **Support services:** GED preparation and test center, learning center, reduced course load, remedial instruction, study skills assistance, tutoring.

**Majors. Business:** General, accounting, administrative services, business admin, office technology. **Computer sciences:** Applications programming, programming. **Health:** Medical secretary, nursing (RN). **Legal studies:** Legal secretary. **Liberal arts:** Arts/sciences. **Mechanic/repair:** Electronics/electrical, gunsmithing. **Personal/culinary services:** General, cosmetic. **Protective services:** Criminal justice. **Public administration:** Social work.

**Computing on campus.** 140 workstations in library, computer center.

**Student life. Freshman orientation:** Available. **Activities:** Student government, student newspaper, Phi Theta Kappa, Student Nursing Association, gunsmithing club, taxidermy club, cosmetology club, criminal justice club, CARE.

**Athletics. Team name:** Pacers.

**Student services.** Career counseling, services for economically disadvantaged, student employment services, financial aid counseling, on-campus daycare, personal counseling, placement for graduates, veterans' counselor. **Physically disabled:** Services for visually, hearing impaired. **Transfer:** Transfer adviser for students transferring to 4-year colleges.

**Contact.** Phone: (336) 599-1181 Fax: (336) 597-3817
Shelia Williamson, Coordinator of Admissions, Piedmont Community College, 1715 College Drive, Roxboro, NC 27573-1197

---

## Pitt Community College
**Greenville, North Carolina**                    **CB member**
www.pittcc.edu                                    **CB code: 5556**

- Public 2-year community and technical college
- Commuter campus in small city

**General.** Founded in 1961. Regionally accredited. **Enrollment:** 5,302 degree-seeking undergraduates. **Degrees:** 681 associate awarded. **ROTC:** Army. **Location:** 85 miles from Raleigh. **Calendar:** Semester, limited summer session. **Full-time faculty:** 176 total. **Part-time faculty:** 342 total. **Class size:** 66% < 20, 34% 20-39, less than 1% 40-49, less than 1% 50-99.

**Student profile.**

Out-of-state:            2%    **25 or older:**            39%

**Transfer out. Colleges most students transferred to 2007:** East Carolina University, University of North Carolina at Wilmington, Barton College.

**Basis for selection.** Open admission, but selective for some programs. Special admission requirements for some allied health programs. SAT and/or ACT may be used in lieu of the college's placement test for placement into English and math courses.

**2007-2008 Annual costs.** Tuition/fees: $1,330; $7,069 out-of-state. Per-credit charge: $42 in-state; $233 out-of-state. Books/supplies: $600.

**Financial aid. Need-based:** Need-based aid available for part-time students. Work-study available nights and for part-time students. **Non-need-based:** Scholarships awarded for academics, athletics, ROTC.

**Application procedures. Admission:** No deadline. No application fee. Application may be submitted online. Admission notification on a rolling basis. **Financial aid:** Priority date 3/15; no closing date. FAFSA required. Applicants notified on a rolling basis starting 2/1.

**Academics. Special study options:** Cooperative education, distance learning, double major, dual enrollment of high school students, ESL, internships. License preparation in nursing, occupational therapy, paramedic, radiology, real estate. **Credit/placement by examination:** CLEP, institutional tests. 40 credit hours maximum toward associate degree. Credit by examination can not be included in the 25% residency requirement. **Support services:** GED preparation and test center, learning center, remedial instruction, tutoring.

**Majors. Business:** Accounting, business admin, e-commerce, human resources, marketing, office management, operations, sales/distribution, training/development. **Computer sciences:** Applications programming, information systems, vendor certification. **Construction:** Electrician. **Education:** Early childhood. **Engineering technology:** Architectural, electrical, industrial management, manufacturing. **Health:** Health services, medical assistant, medical radiologic technology/radiation therapy, medical records technology, medical secretary, mental health services, nuclear medical technology, nursing (RN), occupational therapy assistant, office admin, respiratory therapy assistant, respiratory therapy technology, sonography. **Legal studies:** Paralegal. **Liberal arts:** Arts/sciences. **Mechanic/repair:** Automotive, electronics/electrical, heating/ac/refrig. **Personal/culinary services:** Cosmetic, mortuary science. **Production:** Machine shop technology, welding. **Protective services:** Criminal justice, police science. **Science technology:** Biological. **Visual/performing arts:** Commercial/advertising art.

**Most popular majors.** Business/marketing 10%, computer/information sciences 10%, engineering/engineering technologies 10%, health sciences 33%, liberal arts 20%, trade and industry 15%.

**Computing on campus.** 50 workstations in library, computer center. Helpline available.

**Student life. Freshman orientation:** Available. Preregistration for classes offered. **Activities:** Student government, Gamma Beta Phi, student government association, Southern Organization of Human Services Organization, Society of Advancement of Management, Delta Epsilon Chi, multicultural/international Club, Students Monitoring Students.

**Athletics.** NJCAA. **Intercollegiate:** Baseball M, golf M, softball W, volleyball W. **Intramural:** Basketball, football (non-tackle), volleyball. **Team name:** Bulldogs.

**Student services.** Adult student services, alcohol/substance abuse counseling, career counseling, services for economically disadvantaged, student employment services, financial aid counseling, on-campus daycare, personal counseling, veterans' counselor. **Physically disabled:** Services for visually, speech, hearing impaired. **Transfer:** Transfer adviser, college fairs on campus for students transferring to 4-year colleges.

**Contact.** E-mail: pittadm@pcc.pitt.cc.nc.us
Phone: (252) 321-4245 Fax: (252) 321-4612
Joanne Ceres, Director of Admissions, Pitt Community College, PO Drawer 7007, Greenville, NC 27835-7007

## Randolph Community College
**Asheboro, North Carolina**
www.randolph.edu
**CB code: 5585**

- Public 2-year community and technical college
- Commuter campus in large town

**General.** Founded in 1962. Regionally accredited. **Enrollment:** 4,549 degree-seeking undergraduates. **Degrees:** 275 associate awarded. **Location:** 65 miles from Charlotte, 26 miles from Greensboro. **Calendar:** Semester, limited summer session. **Full-time faculty:** 50 total. **Part-time faculty:** 151 total.

**Transfer out. Colleges most students transferred to 2007:** University of North Carolina-Greensboro, High Point University, Guilford College, University of North Carolina-Charlotte.

**Basis for selection.** Open admission, but selective for some programs. Admission to nursing and radiography program based primarily on competitive admission. ASSET/COMPASS used for placement for all associate-level admission. Appropriate test scores are prerequisites for certain English and math courses.

**2007-2008 Annual costs.** Tuition/fees: $1,320; $7,059 out-of-state. Per-credit charge: $42 in-state; $233 out-of-state. Books/supplies: $950. Personal expenses: $1,040.

**2006-2007 Financial aid. Need-based:** 98% of total undergraduate aid awarded as scholarships/grants, 2% as loans/jobs. Work-study available nights and for part-time students. **Non-need-based:** Scholarships awarded for academics, leadership, minority status, state residency.

**Application procedures. Admission:** No deadline. No application fee. Admission notification on a rolling basis. **Financial aid:** No deadline. FAFSA required. Applicants notified on a rolling basis.

**Academics. Special study options:** Cooperative education, distance learning, double major, dual enrollment of high school students, ESL, internships, liberal arts/career combination, weekend college. **Credit/placement by examination:** CLEP, IB, institutional tests. 16 credit hours maximum toward associate degree. **Support services:** GED preparation and test center, learning center, remedial instruction, tutoring.

**Majors. Business:** Accounting, administrative services, business admin, management information systems. **Communications technology:** Photo/film/video. **Computer sciences:** Networking. **Construction:** Electrician. **Engineering technology:** Electrical, manufacturing. **Family/consumer sciences:** Child care. **Foreign languages:** Sign language interpretation. **Health:** EMT paramedic, nursing (RN). **Interdisciplinary:** Historic preservation. **Liberal arts:** Arts/sciences. **Mechanic/repair:** Automotive. **Protective services:** Police science. **Visual/performing arts:** Commercial photography, commercial/advertising art, interior design, photography, studio arts.

**Most popular majors.** Business/marketing 44%, health sciences 11%, liberal arts 12%, security/protective services 6%, visual/performing arts 22%.

**Computing on campus.** Online library, wireless network available.

**Student life. Freshman orientation:** Mandatory. 30 minute overview of policies and procedures. **Activities:** Student government, student newspaper.

**Athletics. Team name:** Armadillos.

**Student services.** Adult student services, career counseling, student employment services, financial aid counseling, personal counseling, placement for graduates, veterans' counselor. **Physically disabled:** Services for visually, speech, hearing impaired. **Transfer:** Pre-admission transcript evaluation for new students. Transfer adviser, college fairs on campus for students transferring to 4-year colleges.

**Contact.** E-mail: masmith@randolph.edu
Phone: (336) 633-0239 Fax: (336) 629-9547
Brandi Hagerman, Director of Admissions/Registrar, Randolph Community College, PO Box 1009, Asheboro, NC 27204-1009

## Richmond Community College
**Hamlet, North Carolina**
www.richmondcc.edu
**CB member**
**CB code: 5588**

- Public 2-year community college
- Commuter campus in small town

**General.** Founded in 1964. Regionally accredited. **Enrollment:** 1,800 degree-seeking undergraduates. **Degrees:** 200 associate awarded. **Location:** 75 miles from Charlotte. **Calendar:** Semester, limited summer session. **Full-time faculty:** 60 total. **Part-time faculty:** 140 total. **Special facilities:** Health science building with exam rooms and simulation areas.

**Student profile.**

| | | | |
|---|---|---|---|
| **Out-of-state:** | 2% | **25 or older:** | 45% |

**Transfer out. Colleges most students transferred to 2007:** UNC-Pembroke, Gardner-Webb University, UNC-Charlotte, Fayetteville State.

**Basis for selection.** Open admission, but selective for some programs. Admission to nursing program based on academic record and completion of admission requirements, interview required. **Homeschooled:** Transcript of courses and grades required.

**2007-2008 Annual costs.** Tuition/fees: $1,298; $7,037 out-of-state. Per-credit charge: $42 in-state; $233 out-of-state. Books/supplies: $600. Personal expenses: $900.

**Financial aid. Need-based:** Need-based aid available for part-time students. Work-study available nights and for part-time students. **Non-need-based:** Scholarships awarded for academics, leadership.

**Application procedures. Admission:** No deadline. No application fee. Application may be submitted online. Admission notification on a rolling basis. **Financial aid:** No deadline. FAFSA, institutional form required. Applicants notified on a rolling basis starting 7/8; must reply within 2 week(s) of notification.

**Academics. Special study options:** Cooperative education, cross-registration, distance learning, double major, dual enrollment of high school students, ESL, independent study, internships, student-designed major, teacher certification program. License preparation in nursing. **Credit/placement by examination:** AP, CLEP, institutional tests. 15 credit hours maximum toward associate degree. Interview required for placement and counseling. **Support services:** GED preparation and test center, learning center, reduced course load, remedial instruction, study skills assistance, tutoring.

**Majors. Business:** Accounting, administrative services, business admin, management information systems. **Computer sciences:** Information systems, networking. **Engineering:** Electrical. **Engineering technology:** Electrical, manufacturing. **Family/consumer sciences:** Child care. **Health:** Medical assistant, mental health services, nursing (RN). **Liberal arts:** Arts/sciences. **Public administration:** Social work.

**Computing on campus.** 250 workstations in library, computer center.

**Student life. Freshman orientation:** Mandatory. **Activities:** Student government, student newspaper.

**Student services.** Career counseling, student employment services, financial aid counseling, health services, personal counseling, placement for graduates, veterans' counselor. **Physically disabled:** Services for visually, hearing impaired. **Transfer:** Transfer adviser, college fairs on campus for students transferring to 4-year colleges.

**Contact.** Phone: (910) 410-1736 Fax: (910) 582-7102
Wanda Watts, Director of Admissions and Registrar, Richmond Community College, Box 1189, Hamlet, NC 28345

## Roanoke-Chowan Community College
**Ahoskie, North Carolina**
www.roanokechowan.edu          CB code: 5564

▶ Public 2-year community college
▶ Commuter campus in small town

**General.** Founded in 1967. Regionally accredited. **Enrollment:** 955 degree-seeking undergraduates. **Degrees:** 63 associate awarded. **Location:** 60 miles from Greenville, 65 miles from Norfolk, Virginia. **Calendar:** Semester, limited summer session. **Full-time faculty:** 37 total. **Part-time faculty:** 52 total. **Class size:** 70% < 20, 29% 20-39, 2% 40-49. **Special facilities:** Arboretum/environmental science outdoor laboratory.

**Basis for selection.** Open admission, but selective for some programs. Admission to nursing program based on interview and test scores.

**2007-2008 Annual costs.** Tuition/fees: $1,394; $7,133 out-of-state. Per-credit charge: $42 in-state; $233 out-of-state. Books/supplies: $680. Personal expenses: $1,555.

**Financial aid. Need-based:** Need-based aid available for part-time students. **Non-need-based:** Scholarships awarded for academics.

**Application procedures. Admission:** No deadline. No application fee. Admission notification on a rolling basis. **Financial aid:** Priority date 3/15; no closing date. FAFSA required. Applicants notified on a rolling basis starting 7/1.

**Academics. Special study options:** Cooperative education, distance learning, dual enrollment of high school students, independent study, internships, liberal arts/career combination. License preparation in nursing, real estate. **Credit/placement by examination:** CLEP, institutional tests. **Support services:** GED preparation and test center, learning center, reduced course load, remedial instruction, study skills assistance, tutoring.

**Majors. Architecture:** Technology. **Business:** Administrative services, business admin, management information systems. **Computer sciences:** Information systems. **Conservation:** Environmental science. **Education:** Early childhood, teacher assistance. **Engineering technology:** Industrial. **Family/consumer sciences:** Child care. **Health:** Mental health services, nursing (RN), substance abuse counseling. **Interdisciplinary:** Global studies. **Liberal arts:** Arts/sciences. **Protective services:** Criminal justice.

**Most popular majors.** Business/marketing 56%, education 8%, health sciences 22%, liberal arts 6%, security/protective services 6%.

**Computing on campus.** 200 workstations in library, computer center. Online library available.

**Student life. Freshman orientation:** Available. Preregistration for classes offered. Held week before fall semester registration. **Activities:** Student government.

**Athletics. Intercollegiate:** Basketball M. **Intramural:** Basketball, softball, volleyball.

**Student services.** Career counseling, services for economically disadvantaged, student employment services, financial aid counseling, personal counseling, placement for graduates, veterans' counselor. **Physically disabled:** Services for visually, speech, hearing impaired. **Transfer:** Transfer adviser for students transferring to 4-year colleges.

**Contact.** Phone: (252) 862-1200 Fax: (252) 862-1355
Sandra Copeland, Director of Admissions/Counseling, Roanoke-Chowan Community College, 109 Community College Road, Ahoskie, NC 27910-9522

## Robeson Community College
**Lumberton, North Carolina**
www.robeson.edu          CB code: 5594

▶ Public 2-year community and technical college
▶ Commuter campus in large town

**General.** Founded in 1965. Regionally accredited. **Enrollment:** 2,099 degree-seeking undergraduates. **Degrees:** 140 associate awarded. **Location:** 30 miles from Fayetteville. **Calendar:** Semester, limited summer session. **Full-time faculty:** 70 total. **Part-time faculty:** 76 total.

**Basis for selection.** Open admission, but selective for some programs. Special requirements for allied health programs. Interview recommended.

**2007-2008 Annual costs.** Tuition/fees: $1,320; $7,059 out-of-state. Per-credit charge: $42 in-state; $233 out-of-state. Books/supplies: $600. Personal expenses: $75.

**Financial aid. Need-based:** Need-based aid available for part-time students.

**Application procedures. Admission:** Closing date 7/1. No application fee. Admission notification on a rolling basis. **Financial aid:** Priority date 5/15; no closing date. FAFSA required. Applicants notified on a rolling basis starting 7/31.

**Academics. Special study options:** Distance learning, double major, dual enrollment of high school students. **Credit/placement by examination:** CLEP, institutional tests. 40 credit hours maximum toward associate degree. **Support services:** Learning center, reduced course load, remedial instruction, tutoring.

**Majors. Business:** Business admin. **Computer sciences:** Information technology. **Engineering technology:** Electrical. **Health:** EMT paramedic, nursing (RN), radiologic technology/medical imaging, respiratory therapy technology, surgical technology. **Personal/culinary services:** Culinary arts. **Protective services:** Criminal justice.

**Student life. Activities:** Choral groups, literary magazine, student government, student newspaper.

**Student services.** Adult student services, career counseling, student employment services, health services, personal counseling, placement for graduates, veterans' counselor. **Physically disabled:** Services for hearing impaired. **Transfer:** Transfer adviser, college fairs on campus for students transferring to 4-year colleges.

**Contact.** E-mail: jrevels@robeson.cc.nc.us
Phone: (910) 272-3700 ext. 3347 Fax: (910) 618-5686
Judith Revels, Director of Admissions, Robeson Community College, PO Box 1420, Lumberton, NC 28359

## Rockingham Community College
**Wentworth, North Carolina**
www.rockinghamcc.edu          CB code: 5582

▶ Public 2-year community college
▶ Commuter campus in rural community

**General.** Founded in 1963. Regionally accredited. **Enrollment:** 1,777 degree-seeking undergraduates; 236 non-degree-seeking students. **Degrees:** 202 associate awarded. **Location:** 26 miles from Greensboro. **Calendar:** Semester, extensive summer session. **Full-time faculty:** 65 total. **Part-time faculty:** 45 total.

**Student profile.** Among degree-seeking undergraduates, 441 enrolled as first-time, first-year students.

| | | | |
|---|---|---|---|
| Part-time: | 52% | African American: | 19% |
| Out-of-state: | 1% | Asian American: | 1% |
| Women: | 66% | Hispanic American: | 1% |

**Transfer out. Colleges most students transferred to 2007:** University of North Carolina at Greensboro, North Carolina A&T University.

**Basis for selection.** Open admission, but selective for some programs. All allied health programs and some other programs require all or some of the following: qualifying high school and college GPA, placement testing, specific high school courses, professional certification, other exams. Interview required for nursing and occupational therapy assistant programs. **Homeschooled:** Need complete record of all courses taken in grades 9-12.

**High school preparation.** Recommended units include English 4, mathematics 3, social studies 2, history 1, science 3 (laboratory 1) and foreign language 2.

**2007-2008 Annual costs.** Tuition/fees: $1,413; $7,534 out-of-state. Per-credit charge: $42 in-state; $233 out-of-state. Books/supplies: $450. Personal expenses: $1,000.

**Financial aid. Need-based:** Need-based aid available for part-time students. **Non-need-based:** Scholarships awarded for academics, art, job skills, leadership, minority status, state residency.

**Application procedures. Admission:** No deadline. No application fee. Admission notification on a rolling basis. **Financial aid:** Priority date 3/15; no closing date. FAFSA, institutional form required. Applicants notified on a rolling basis starting 5/30; must reply within 2 week(s) of notification.

**Academics. Special study options:** Cooperative education, distance learning, dual enrollment of high school students, independent study, student-designed major. Preengineering program leading to transfer to North Carolina State University, North Carolina Agricultural and Technical State University, or University of North Carolina at Charlotte. License preparation in nursing. **Credit/placement by examination:** AP, CLEP, institutional tests. **Support services:** GED preparation and test center, learning center, reduced course load, remedial instruction, study skills assistance, tutoring.

**Majors. Agriculture:** Horticultural science. **Business:** Accounting, business admin, office technology, office/clerical. **Computer sciences:** Information systems. **Education:** Early childhood. **Engineering:** Electrical. **Health:** Medical secretary, nursing (RN), respiratory therapy technology. **Liberal arts:** Arts/sciences. **Mechanic/repair:** Electronics/electrical. **Production:** Furniture. **Protective services:** Law enforcement admin. **Visual/performing arts:** Studio arts.

**Most popular majors.** Business/marketing 14%, education 8%, engineering/engineering technologies 7%, health sciences 42%, liberal arts 19%, security/protective services 6%.

**Computing on campus.** 200 workstations in library, computer center.

**Student life. Freshman orientation:** Mandatory. **Activities:** Student government, student newspaper, Phi Theta Kappa, nature study club, astronomy club, science fiction club, trips and outings clubs, cultural diversity awareness club.

**Athletics.** NJCAA. **Intercollegiate:** Baseball M, basketball M, cheerleading M, golf M, softball W, volleyball W. **Intramural:** Basketball, table tennis, tennis, volleyball. **Team name:** Eagles.

**Student services.** Career counseling, student employment services, on-campus daycare, personal counseling, placement for graduates. **Physically disabled:** Services for visually, hearing impaired. **Transfer:** Transfer adviser, college fairs on campus for students transferring to 4-year colleges.

**Contact.** E-mail: dunnm@rockinghamcc.edu
Phone: (336) 342-4261 ext. 2114 Fax: (336) 342-1809
Leigh Hawkins, Admissions Director, Rockingham Community College, Box 38, Wentworth, NC 27375-0038

## Rowan-Cabarrus Community College
**Salisbury, North Carolina**
www.rowancabarrus.edu              CB code: 5589

- Public 2-year community and technical college
- Commuter campus in large town

**General.** Founded in 1961. Regionally accredited. **Enrollment:** 5,275 degree-seeking undergraduates. **Degrees:** 490 associate awarded. **Location:** 40 miles from Charlotte. **Calendar:** Semester, extensive summer session. **Full-time faculty:** 153 total. **Part-time faculty:** 190 total. **Class size:** 58% < 20, 39% 20-39, 2% 40-49, less than 1% 50-99.

**Transfer out. Colleges most students transferred to 2007:** University of North Carolina-Charlotte, Pfeiffer University, Catawba College.

**Basis for selection.** Open admission, but selective for some programs. Interview required for allied health programs. Placement test required for all allied health applicants and candidates for diplomas, AAS degrees, or AA degrees.

**2007-2008 Annual costs.** Tuition/fees: $1,324; $7,063 out-of-state. Per-credit charge: $42 in-state; $230 out-of-state.

**Financial aid. Need-based:** Need-based aid available for part-time students. Work-study available nights and for part-time students. **Non-need-based:** Scholarships awarded for academics, job skills, state residency.

**Application procedures. Admission:** No deadline. No application fee. Admission notification on a rolling basis. **Financial aid:** Priority date 3/15, closing date 8/1. FAFSA required. Applicants notified on a rolling basis starting 5/1; must reply within 3 week(s) of notification.

**Academics. Special study options:** Cooperative education, distance learning, dual enrollment of high school students, ESL, liberal arts/career combination, teacher certification program. License preparation in nursing, radiology, real estate. **Credit/placement by examination:** CLEP, institutional tests. 75 credit hours maximum toward associate degree. Student must complete 25% of credits required for graduation in resident classes. **Support services:** GED preparation and test center, learning center, reduced course load, remedial instruction, tutoring, writing center.

**Majors. Business:** Accounting, business admin, office technology. **Computer sciences:** Information systems, programming. **Education:** Early childhood. **Engineering technology:** Biomedical, drafting, electrical, industrial. **Health:** Nursing (RN), radiologic technology/medical imaging. **Legal studies:** Paralegal. **Mechanic/repair:** Industrial. **Protective services:** Criminal justice, fire safety technology.

**Student life. Freshman orientation:** Available. Fall and spring orientation. **Activities:** Student government.

**Student services.** Career counseling, student employment services, on-campus daycare, personal counseling, placement for graduates, veterans' counselor. **Physically disabled:** Services for visually, speech, hearing impaired. **Learning disabled:** Comprehensive services available. **Transfer:** Pre-admission transcript evaluation for new students. College fairs on campus for students transferring to 4-year colleges.

**Contact.** Phone: (704) 637-0760 Fax: (704) 633-6804
Gail Cummins, Director, Admissions and Recruitment, Rowan-Cabarrus Community College, Box 1595, Salisbury, NC 28145

## Sampson Community College
**Clinton, North Carolina**
www.sampsoncc.edu              CB code: 0505

- Public 2-year community college
- Commuter campus in small town

**General.** Founded in 1965. Regionally accredited. **Enrollment:** 1,550 degree-seeking undergraduates. **Degrees:** 117 associate awarded. **Location:** 30 miles from Fayetteville. **Calendar:** Semester, limited summer session. **Full-time faculty:** 55 total. **Part-time faculty:** 57 total.

**Student profile.** Among degree-seeking undergraduates, 639 enrolled as first-time, first-year students.

| Part-time: | 59% | Women: | 73% |
| Out-of-state: | 1% | 25 or older: | 47% |

**Transfer out. Colleges most students transferred to 2007:** Fayetteville State University, UNC-Wilmington, Campbell University, Mt. Olive College.

**Basis for selection.** Open admission, but selective for some programs. Special requirements for nursing and practical nursing; secondary school record and test scores important. Interview required for nursing programs.

**High school preparation.** 15 units recommended. Recommended units include English 4, mathematics 3, social studies 3, science 4 and foreign language 2. Algebra, chemistry and biology required for nursing programs.

**2007-2008 Annual costs.** Tuition/fees: $1,316; $7,055 out-of-state. Per-credit charge: $42 in-state; $233 out-of-state. Books/supplies: $600. Personal expenses: $900.

**Financial aid. Need-based:** Need-based aid available for part-time students. **Non-need-based:** Scholarships awarded for academics, state residency. **Additional information:** Short-term loans available to students waiting for federal aid to be approved. Covers tuition, fees and books only.

**Application procedures. Admission:** No deadline. No application fee. Admission notification on a rolling basis. **Financial aid:** Priority date 7/1; no closing date. FAFSA required. Applicants notified on a rolling basis starting 7/15; must reply within 2 week(s) of notification.

**Academics. Special study options:** Cooperative education, distance learning, dual enrollment of high school students, independent study, internships, liberal arts/career combination, weekend college. License preparation in nursing, real estate. **Credit/placement by examination:** AP, CLEP, institutional tests. 15 credit hours maximum toward associate degree. **Support services:** GED preparation and test center, learning center, pre-admission summer program, reduced course load, remedial instruction, study skills assistance, tutoring.

**Majors. Agriculture:** Horticulture, ornamental horticulture. **Business:** Accounting, administrative services, business admin, office/clerical. **Computer sciences:** General, applications programming, information systems. **Construction:** Carpentry. **Education:** General, early childhood. **Health:** Licensed practical nurse, nursing (RN). **Mechanic/repair:** Industrial. **Personal/culinary services:** Cosmetic.

**Computing on campus.** 110 workstations in library, computer center.

**Student life. Freshman orientation:** Mandatory. Preregistration for classes offered. **Activities:** Student government, student newspaper.

**Athletics. Intercollegiate:** Golf M. **Intramural:** Basketball M. **Team name:** Vikings.

**Student services.** Adult student services, career counseling, student employment services, financial aid counseling, personal counseling, placement for graduates, veterans' counselor. **Physically disabled:** Services for visually, speech, hearing impaired. **Transfer:** Pre-admission transcript evaluation for new students. Transfer adviser, college fairs on campus for students transferring to 4-year colleges.

**Contact.** Phone: (910) 592-8084 Fax: (910) 592-8048
William Jordan, Director of Admissions, Sampson Community College, PO Box 318, Clinton, NC 28329

## Sandhills Community College
**Pinehurst, North Carolina**
**www.sandhills.edu**                    **CB code: 5649**

- Public 2-year community college
- Commuter campus in large town

**General.** Founded in 1963. Regionally accredited. **Enrollment:** 3,580 degree-seeking undergraduates. **Degrees:** 326 associate awarded. **Location:** 41 miles from Fayetteville, 71 miles from Raleigh. **Calendar:** Semester, limited summer session. **Full-time faculty:** 125 total. **Part-time faculty:** 135 total. **Class size:** 51% < 20, 46% 20-39, 1% 40-49, 2% 50-99. **Special facilities:** Student maintained 30-acre garden, culinary arts lab.

**Student profile.**

| | | | |
|---|---|---|---|
| Out-of-state: | 1% | 25 or older: | 39% |

**Transfer out. Colleges most students transferred to 2007:** University of North Carolina-Chapel Hill, University of North Carolina-Charlotte, University of North Carolina-Pembroke, North Carolina State University, Appalachian State University.

**Basis for selection.** Open admission, but selective for some programs. Specific scores on Accuplacer required for admission to landscape gardening, golf course turf management and health sciences programs. Students not achieving minimum scores may enroll in general college, take developmental courses and reapply for programs later. Chemistry, algebra, and NA registry required for entrance into associate nursing program. Students with minimum SAT score of 500 verbal and 500 math or ACT scores of 21 English, 21 math, and 21 reading may be placed in college-level English and math without taking ASSET or COMPASS. All students applying to restricted enrollment programs must have taken ASSET or COMPASS within past 5 years. Nursing program accepts SAT and ACT scores for exemption, however the HOBET must be taken. **Homeschooled:** Transcript of courses and grades required. Copy of state registration required. **Learning Disabled:** Students with learning disabilities recommended to take classes in Continuing Education Program first.

**2007-2008 Annual costs.** Tuition/fees: $1,330; $7,069 out-of-state. Per-credit charge: $42 in-state; $233 out-of-state. Books/supplies: $547. Personal expenses: $1,080.

**Financial aid. Need-based:** Need-based aid available for part-time students. **Non-need-based:** Scholarships awarded for academics. **Additional information:** Scholarships available, limited loan capability.

**Application procedures. Admission:** No deadline. No application fee. Application may be submitted online. Admission notification on a rolling basis. **Financial aid:** Priority date 6/1; no closing date. FAFSA required. Applicants notified on a rolling basis starting 2/1; must reply by 8/1 or within 4 week(s) of notification.

**Academics.** Weekend support services held at satellite campus. **Special study options:** Combined bachelor's/graduate degree, cooperative education, distance learning, double major, dual enrollment of high school students, ESL, honors, independent study, internships, liberal arts/career combination, teacher certification program. Third and fourth year courses offered on campus evenings by St. Andrews Presbyterian College and UNC Pembroke, distance learning classes through Franklin University. License preparation in nursing, paramedic, radiology, real estate. **Credit/placement by examination:** AP, CLEP, institutional tests. **Support services:** GED preparation and test center, learning center, reduced course load, remedial instruction, study skills assistance, tutoring.

**Majors. Agriculture:** Landscaping, turf management. **Architecture:** Technology. **Biology:** General. **Business:** Accounting, administrative services, business admin, e-commerce, hotel/motel admin, restaurant/food services. **Computer sciences:** General, applications programming, computer science,

information systems, programming, webmaster. **Education:** Biology, chemistry, early childhood, elementary, history, science, secondary, social science, social studies, teacher assistance. **Engineering technology:** Architectural, civil, computer, drafting, surveying. **Family/consumer sciences:** Child care. **Health:** Clinical lab technology, EMT ambulance attendant, EMT paramedic, massage therapy, medical radiologic technology/radiation therapy, medical records admin, nursing (RN), predental, premedicine, prenursing, prepharmacy, preveterinary, respiratory therapy technology, substance abuse counseling, surgical technology. **Legal studies:** Prelaw. **Liberal arts:** Arts/sciences. **Math:** General. **Mechanic/repair:** Automotive. **Personal/culinary services:** Cosmetic, culinary arts. **Protective services:** Criminal justice. **Psychology:** General. **Public administration:** Social work. **Social sciences:** General. **Visual/performing arts:** Art.

**Most popular majors.** Business/marketing 8%, computer/information sciences 6%, health sciences 42%, liberal arts 11%, trade and industry 11%.

**Computing on campus.** 400 workstations in library, computer center. Commuter students can connect to campus network.

**Student life. Freshman orientation:** Mandatory. Preregistration for classes offered. 2-hour information session, course planning, and registration. **Activities:** Bands, choral groups, music ensembles, student government, student newspaper, symphony orchestra, Minority Students for Academic and Cultural Enrichment, Circle-K, Young Democrats, Young Republicans, Phi Theta Kappa, Student Government Association.

**Student services.** Alcohol/substance abuse counseling, career counseling, student employment services, financial aid counseling, personal counseling, placement for graduates, veterans' counselor. **Physically disabled:** Services for visually, hearing impaired. **Transfer:** Pre-admission transcript evaluation for new students. Transfer adviser, college fairs on campus for students transferring to 4-year colleges.

**Contact.** E-mail: mcallisterr@sandhills.edu
Phone: (910) 692-6185 Toll-free number: (800) 338-3944
Fax: (910) 695-3981
Rosa McAllister-McRae, Admissions Coordinator, Sandhills Community College, 3395 Airport Road, Pinehurst, NC 28374

## South College
**Asheville, North Carolina**
**www.southcollegenc.com**                **CB code: 0508**

- For-profit 2-year health science and technical college
- Commuter campus in small city
- Interview required

**General.** Founded in 1905. Candidate for regional accreditation; also accredited by ACICS. **Enrollment:** 135 degree-seeking undergraduates. **Degrees:** 16 associate awarded. **Location:** 4 miles from downtown. **Calendar:** Quarter, extensive summer session. **Full-time faculty:** 12 total. **Part-time faculty:** 18 total. **Class size:** 91% < 20, 9% 20-39.

**Transfer out. Colleges most students transferred to 2007:** Asheville-Buncombe Technical Community College, Blue Ridge Community College, Mars Hill College, Montreat College.

**Basis for selection.** Open admission, but selective for some programs. College-administered exam required of all applicants. Scores used for admission and program placement. **Homeschooled:** Copy of homeschool diploma required.

**2007-2008 Annual costs.** Tuition/fees: $12,000. Books/supplies: $1,050. Personal expenses: $1,080.

**Financial aid. Need-based:** Need-based aid available for part-time students. Work-study available for part-time students.

**Application procedures. Admission:** No deadline. $40 fee, may be waived for applicants with need. Admission notification on a rolling basis. **Financial aid:** No deadline. FAFSA required. Applicants notified on a rolling basis.

**Academics. Special study options:** Accelerated study, cooperative education, double major, internships, liberal arts/career combination. Bachelor's degree programs available on campus. License preparation in physical therapy, radiology. **Credit/placement by examination:** CLEP, institutional tests. Varies with program, but no more than 60% of any program. **Support services:** Reduced course load, study skills assistance, tutoring.

**Majors. Business:** Accounting, administrative services, business admin, office technology. **Computer sciences:** General. **Health:** Medical assistant. **Legal studies:** Paralegal. **Protective services:** Law enforcement admin.

**Computing on campus.** 28 workstations in library, computer center.

**Student life. Freshman orientation:** Mandatory. Orientation is held prior to each quarter.

**Student services.** Career counseling, student employment services, financial aid counseling, personal counseling, placement for graduates, veterans' counselor. **Transfer:** Pre-admission transcript evaluation for new students.

**Contact.** Phone: (828) 277-5521 Fax: (828) 252-8558
Duff Moore, Director of Admissions, South College, 29 Turtle Creek Drive, Asheville, NC 28803

## South Piedmont Community College
Polkton, North Carolina
www.spcc.edu                                    CB code: 0457

♦ Public 2-year community college
♦ Commuter campus in small city

**General.** Founded in 1962. Regionally accredited. Multiple campus locations near Charlotte. **Enrollment:** 2,258 degree-seeking undergraduates. **Degrees:** 119 associate awarded. **Location:** 60 miles from Charlotte. **Calendar:** Semester, limited summer session. **Full-time faculty:** 75 total. **Part-time faculty:** 200 total. **Partnerships:** Formal partnership with local high schools.

**Student profile.**

Out-of-state:              1%        25 or older:         57%

**Basis for selection.** Open admission, but selective for some programs. Special requirements for health technology programs. **Homeschooled:** Students should have state certification number, successful completion of competency exam, registered with local board of education, copy of transcript and diploma.

**2007-2008 Annual costs.** Tuition/fees: $1,332; $7,071 out-of-state. Per-credit charge: $42 in-state; $233 out-of-state. Books/supplies: $650. Personal expenses: $900.

**2007-2008 Financial aid. Need-based:** 98% of total undergraduate aid awarded as scholarships/grants, 2% as loans/jobs. Need-based aid available for part-time students. Work-study available nights and weekends. **Additional information:** Small amount of nonfederal scholarship aid available.

**Application procedures. Admission:** No deadline. No application fee. Application may be submitted online. Admission notification on a rolling basis. **Financial aid:** No deadline. FAFSA required. Applicants notified on a rolling basis.

**Academics. Special study options:** Cooperative education, cross-registration, distance learning, dual enrollment of high school students, independent study, internships. **Credit/placement by examination:** CLEP, institutional tests. **Support services:** GED preparation and test center, learning center, reduced course load, remedial instruction, study skills assistance, tutoring.

**Majors. Business:** Accounting, administrative services, business admin, logistics, office/clerical. **Computer sciences:** General, applications programming, information systems, networking, programming. **Education:** General. **Engineering technology:** Drafting, electrical, manufacturing. **Family/consumer sciences:** Child care. **Health:** Health services, medical assistant, medical records technology, medical secretary. **Legal studies:** Legal secretary, paralegal. **Liberal arts:** Arts/sciences. **Mechanic/repair:** Heating/ac/refrig. **Protective services:** Criminal justice. **Public administration:** Human services. **Visual/performing arts:** Commercial/advertising art.

**Computing on campus.** 200 workstations in library, computer center.

**Student life. Freshman orientation:** Available. Preregistration for classes offered. **Activities:** Student government, student newspaper, Phi Beta Lambda business organization, criminal justice student association, social services club, Phi Theta Kappa.

**Athletics. Team name:** Patriots.

**Student services.** Alcohol/substance abuse counseling, career counseling, student employment services, financial aid counseling, personal counseling, placement for graduates, veterans' counselor. **Physically disabled:** Services for visually, hearing impaired. **Transfer:** Transfer adviser for students transferring to 4-year colleges.

**Contact.** E-mail: jcurtis@spcc.edu
Phone: (704) 272-5324 Toll-free number: (800) 766-0319
Fax: (704) 272-5303
John Curtis, Director, Admissions/ Enrollment, South Piedmont Community College, PO Box 126, Polkton, NC 28135

## Southeastern Community College
Whiteville, North Carolina
www.sccnc.edu                                   CB code: 5651

♦ Public 2-year community college
♦ Commuter campus in small town

**General.** Founded in 1964. Regionally accredited. **Enrollment:** 1,750 degree-seeking undergraduates. **Degrees:** 137 associate awarded. **Location:** 45 miles from Wilmington. **Calendar:** Semester, limited summer session. **Full-time faculty:** 81 total; 2% have terminal degrees, 11% minority, 58% women. **Part-time faculty:** 130 total; 4% have terminal degrees, 18% minority, 52% women. **Class size:** 64% < 20, 33% 20-39, 2% 40-49, less than 1% 50-99. **Special facilities:** Outdoor natural resources lab of 23 acres of hardwood and pine forest, signed nature trail, butterfly garden. **Partnerships:** Formal partnership with Columbus County School System.

**Student profile.** Among degree-seeking undergraduates, 12% enrolled in a transfer program, 37% enrolled in a vocational program, 2% already have a bachelor's degree or higher.

Out-of-state:              1%        25 or older:         45%

**Transfer out. Colleges most students transferred to 2007:** University of North Carolina at Wilmington, University of North Carolina at Pembroke, Fayetteville State University, East Carolina University.

**Basis for selection.** Open admission, but selective for some programs. Basic law Enforcement Training: Age 21 and Reading test requirements. Allied Health: Reading, Math, CNA 1 certification, points requirements. SAT may be substituted for placement test. **Homeschooled:** Transcript of courses and grades required. Documentation from state showing authorization. **Learning Disabled:** Applicant must provide proof of disability from specialist, and list of required accommodations from specialist, and list of requested accomodations from student.

**High school preparation.** Recommended units include English 6, mathematics 6, social studies 6 and science 6.

**2007-2008 Annual costs.** Tuition/fees: $1,329; $7,068 out-of-state. Per-credit charge: $42 in-state; $233 out-of-state. Books/supplies: $910. Personal expenses: $972.

**2006-2007 Financial aid. Need-based:** 89% of total undergraduate aid awarded as scholarships/grants, 11% as loans/jobs. Need-based aid available for part-time students. Work-study available for part-time students. **Non-need-based:** Scholarships awarded for academics, athletics, leadership, music/drama, state residency.

**Application procedures. Admission:** No deadline. No application fee. Application may be submitted online. Admission notification on a rolling basis. **Financial aid:** Priority date 4/1; no closing date. FAFSA required. Applicants notified on a rolling basis starting 6/1; must reply within 2 week(s) of notification.

**Academics. Special study options:** Cooperative education, distance learning, double major, dual enrollment of high school students, honors, independent study, internships, liberal arts/career combination. License preparation in nursing, real estate. **Credit/placement by examination:** AP, CLEP, institutional tests. **Support services:** GED preparation and test center, learning center, reduced course load, remedial instruction, study skills assistance, tutoring, writing center.

**Majors. Biology:** Biotechnology. **Business:** General, accounting technology, accounting/finance, banking/financial services, business admin, finance, marketing, office technology, office/clerical. **Communications:** General. **Communications technology:** Radio/tv. **Computer sciences:** General, information technology, networking, web page design, word processing. **Conservation:** Environmental science, forest technology. **Education:** Early childhood, elementary, secondary. **Engineering technology:** Electrical. **Family/consumer sciences:** Child care. **Health:** Clinical lab technology, nursing (RN). **Interdisciplinary:** Biological/physical sciences. **Liberal arts:** Arts/sciences. **Mechanic/repair:** Industrial. **Parks/recreation:** Facilities management. **Personal/culinary services:** Cosmetic. **Visual/performing arts:** Art.

**Most popular majors.** Business/marketing 8%, education 6%, health sciences 42%, visual/performing arts 16%.

**Computing on campus.** 115 workstations in library, computer center.

**Student life. Freshman orientation:** Mandatory, $42 fee. Preregistration for classes offered. College Student Success is a required one credit class with 16 contact hours, 4 of which are online. Topics covered are college life, college skills, and personal awareness. **Activities:** Concert band, choral groups, drama, literary magazine, student government, student newspaper, Student Ambassadors.

**Athletics.** NJCAA. **Intercollegiate:** Baseball M, volleyball W. **Team name:** Rams.

**Student services.** Adult student services, career counseling, services for economically disadvantaged, student employment services, financial aid counseling, on-campus daycare, personal counseling, placement for graduates, veterans' counselor. **Physically disabled:** Services for visually, speech, hearing impaired. **Transfer:** Pre-admission transcript evaluation for new students. Transfer adviser, college fairs on campus for students transferring to 4-year colleges.

**Contact.** E-mail: start@sccnc.edu
Phone: (910) 642-7141 ext. 249 Fax: (910) 642-1267
Sylvia Tart, Director of Student Records/Registrar, Southeastern Community College, 4564 Chadbourn Highway, Whiteville, NC 28472-0151

## Southwestern Community College
### Sylva, North Carolina
### www.southwestern008.edu
**CB code: 5667**

- Public 2-year community college
- Commuter campus in rural community

**General.** Founded in 1964. Regionally accredited. Five off-campus sites serve two adjoining counties. **Enrollment:** 809 full-time, degree-seeking students. **Degrees:** 222 associate awarded. **Location:** 48 miles from Asheville. **Calendar:** Semester, limited summer session. **Full-time faculty:** 73 total. **Part-time faculty:** 121 total. **Class size:** 80% < 20, 20% 20-39.

**Student profile.**

| | | | |
|---|---|---|---|
| Out-of-state: | 1% | 25 or older: | 46% |

**Transfer out. Colleges most students transferred to 2007:** Western Carolina University.

**Basis for selection.** Open admission, but selective for some programs. Admission to allied health programs based on test scores, academic record, interview, and recommendations. Interview required for allied health applicants; recommended for all others.

**High school preparation.** Algebra, biology, and chemistry required for allied health program applicants.

**2007-2008 Annual costs.** Tuition/fees: $1,321; $7,060 out-of-state. Per-credit charge: $42 in-state; $233 out-of-state. Books/supplies: $750. Personal expenses: $1,238.

**Financial aid. Need-based:** Need-based aid available for part-time students. Work-study available for part-time students.

**Application procedures. Admission:** No deadline. No application fee. Admission notification on a rolling basis. **Financial aid:** Priority date 4/30; no closing date. FAFSA required. Applicants notified on a rolling basis starting 5/1; must reply within 2 week(s) of notification.

**Academics. Special study options:** Cooperative education, double major, dual enrollment of high school students, ESL, independent study, internships, liberal arts/career combination. License preparation in nursing, paramedic, physical therapy, radiology, real estate. **Credit/placement by examination:** CLEP, institutional tests. **Support services:** GED preparation and test center, learning center, reduced course load, remedial instruction, tutoring.

**Majors. Business:** Accounting, administrative services, business admin, marketing. **Computer sciences:** General, networking, programming. **Education:** General, early childhood, trade/industrial. **Engineering:** Computer, electrical, surveying. **Engineering technology:** Electrical. **Family/consumer sciences:** Child care. **Health:** Clinical lab science, clinical lab technology, EMT paramedic, medical radiologic technology/radiation therapy, medical records technology, mental health services, nursing (RN), physical therapy assistant, respiratory therapy assistant, respiratory therapy technology, sonography, substance abuse counseling. **Legal studies:** Paralegal. **Liberal arts:** Arts/sciences. **Mechanic/repair:** Automotive. **Parks/recreation:** General. **Personal/culinary services:** Cosmetic, culinary arts. **Protective services:** Criminal justice. **Visual/performing arts:** Commercial/advertising art.

**Most popular majors.** Business/marketing 7%, health sciences 35%, liberal arts 22%, security/protective services 10%.

**Computing on campus.** 200 workstations in computer center. Commuter students can connect to campus network.

**Student life. Freshman orientation:** Mandatory. Preregistration for classes offered. One-day live orientation held on Jackson Campus at beginning of Fall Semester for all students enrolling for first time. New students enrolling in Spring or Summer semesters take on-line orientation program. **Activities:** Literary magazine, student government, Phi Theta Kappa, Native American Society, Spanish Club.

**Student services.** Career counseling, services for economically disadvantaged, student employment services, financial aid counseling, on-campus daycare, personal counseling, placement for graduates, veterans' counselor. **Physically disabled:** Services for visually, speech, hearing impaired. **Transfer:** Pre-admission transcript evaluation for new students. Transfer adviser for students transferring to 4-year colleges.

**Contact.** Phone: (828) 586-4091 ext. 352 Toll-free number: (800) 447-4091 Fax: (828) 586-3129
Phil Weast, Dean of Student Services, Southwestern Community College, 447 College Drive, Sylva, NC 28779.

## Stanly Community College
### Albemarle, North Carolina
### www.stanly.edu
**CB code: 0496**

- Public 2-year community college
- Commuter campus in large town

**General.** Founded in 1971. Regionally accredited. **Enrollment:** 1,600 degree-seeking undergraduates. **Degrees:** 268 associate awarded. **Location:** 30 miles from Charlotte. **Calendar:** Semester, limited summer session. **Full-time faculty:** 88 total. **Part-time faculty:** 167 total.

**Transfer out. Colleges most students transferred to 2007:** University of North Carolina at Charlotte, Pfeiffer University.

**Basis for selection.** Open admission, but selective for some programs. Special requirements for nursing, radiography, respiratory therapy, and medical lab assistant majors. **Learning Disabled:** Written verification of disability, no more than five years old, required at least 60 days prior to enrollment.

**2007-2008 Annual costs.** Tuition/fees: $1,354; $7,093 out-of-state. Per-credit charge: $42 in-state; $233 out-of-state. Books/supplies: $900. Personal expenses: $1,050.

**Financial aid.** All financial aid based on need. Need-based aid available for part-time students. Work-study available for part-time students.

**Application procedures. Admission:** No deadline. No application fee. Application may be submitted online. Admission notification on a rolling basis. **Financial aid:** Closing date 4/15. FAFSA, institutional form required. Applicants notified on a rolling basis starting 6/1; must reply within 2 week(s) of notification.

**Academics. Special study options:** Distance learning, dual enrollment of high school students, ESL, weekend college. **Credit/placement by examination:** AP, CLEP, institutional tests. **Support services:** GED preparation and test center, remedial instruction, study skills assistance, tutoring.

**Majors. Business:** Accounting, business admin, human resources. **Computer sciences:** Computer graphics, game design, information systems, information technology, LAN/WAN management, networking, security. **Education:** Early childhood, elementary, special. **Engineering technology:** Biomedical, computer, electrical. **Health:** Clinical lab assistant, EMT paramedic, medical assistant, nursing (RN), radiologic technology/medical imaging, respiratory therapy technology. **Liberal arts:** Arts/sciences. **Personal/culinary services:** Cosmetic. **Protective services:** Criminal justice.

**Most popular majors.** Business/marketing 13%, computer/information sciences 11%, education 13%, engineering/engineering technologies 9%, health sciences 21%, liberal arts 12%, security/protective services 13%, social sciences 7%.

**Computing on campus.** 100 workstations in library, computer center, student center. Commuter students can connect to campus network. Online library, helpline, wireless network available.

**Student life. Freshman orientation:** Available. Preregistration for classes offered. **Activities:** Student government.

**Athletics.** NJCAA. **Intercollegiate:** Softball W, volleyball W. **Team name:** Eagles.

**Student services.** Adult student services, alcohol/substance abuse counseling, career counseling, services for economically disadvantaged, student employment services, financial aid counseling, minority student services, personal counseling, placement for graduates, veterans' counselor, women's services. **Transfer:** Pre-admission transcript evaluation for new students. Transfer adviser, college fairs on campus for students transferring to 4-year colleges.

**Contact.** E-mail: SCCAdmissions@stanly.edu
Phone: (704) 991-0226 Fax: (704) 991-0255
Ronnie Hinson, Dean of Students, Stanly Community College, 141 College Drive, Albemarle, NC 28001

## Surry Community College
**Dobson, North Carolina**
www.surry.edu
CB code: 5656

▶ Public 2-year community college
▶ Commuter campus in rural community

**General.** Founded in 1964. Regionally accredited. **Enrollment:** 1,578 full-time, degree-seeking students. **Degrees:** 298 associate awarded. **Location:** 40 miles from Winston-Salem. **Calendar:** Semester, extensive summer session. **Full-time faculty:** 100 total. **Part-time faculty:** 220 total. **Special facilities:** Working vineyard and wine-making facilities.

**Student profile.**

| | | | |
|---|---|---|---|
| Out-of-state: | 3% | 25 or older: | 44% |

**Transfer out. Colleges most students transferred to 2007:** Appalachian State University, Gardner-Webb University, Lees-McRae University, University of North Carolina-Greensboro, Winston-Salem State University.

**Basis for selection.** Open admission, but selective for some programs. Competitive admission to associate degree nursing program (RN) and practical nursing program (LPN) based primarily on academic standing; test scores considered. Portfolio required for admission to advertising and graphic design programs.

**2007-2008 Annual costs.** Tuition/fees: $1,331; $7,070 out-of-state. Per-credit charge: $42 in-state; $233 out-of-state. Books/supplies: $800. Personal expenses: $900.

**Financial aid. Need-based:** Need-based aid available for part-time students. Work-study available nights and for part-time students. **Non-need-based:** Scholarships awarded for academics.

**Application procedures. Admission:** No deadline. No application fee. Application may be submitted online. Admission notification on a rolling basis. **Financial aid:** Priority date 5/1; no closing date. FAFSA, institutional form required. Applicants notified on a rolling basis starting 6/1; must reply within 2 week(s) of notification.

**Academics. Special study options:** Accelerated study, cooperative education, distance learning, double major, dual enrollment of high school students, ESL, independent study, internships, weekend college. Bachelor's degree programs available on campus. License preparation in nursing, paramedic, physical therapy, real estate. **Credit/placement by examination:** AP, CLEP, institutional tests. **Support services:** GED preparation and test center, learning center, reduced course load, remedial instruction, study skills assistance, tutoring.

**Majors. Agriculture:** Horticulture. **Business:** Accounting, business admin, office/clerical. **Computer sciences:** Game design, information systems. **Construction:** Carpentry, site management. **Education:** Early childhood, early childhood special. **Engineering:** Computer, electrical. **Engineering technology:** Drafting. **Foreign languages:** Translation. **Health:** Medical assistant, nursing (RN), office admin. **Legal studies:** Paralegal. **Liberal arts:** Arts/sciences. **Mechanic/repair:** Automotive, heating/ac/refrig, industrial, industrial electronics. **Personal/culinary services:** Cosmetic. **Protective services:** Law enforcement admin. **Visual/performing arts:** Commercial/advertising art.

**Computing on campus.** 500 workstations in library, computer center. Online library, helpline, wireless network available.

**Student life. Freshman orientation:** Mandatory. Preregistration for classes offered. **Activities:** Choral groups, literary magazine, radio station, student government, student newspaper.

**Athletics.** NJCAA. **Intercollegiate:** Baseball M, basketball M, volleyball W. **Team name:** Knights.

**Student services.** Adult student services, career counseling, services for economically disadvantaged, student employment services, financial aid counseling, personal counseling, placement for graduates, veterans' counselor. **Physically disabled:** Services for visually, hearing impaired. **Transfer:** Transfer adviser, college fairs on campus for students transferring to 4-year colleges.

**Contact.** E-mail: childressj@surry.edu
Phone: (336) 386-3392 Fax: (336) 386-8951
Jamie Childress, Associate Vice President for Student Services, Surry Community College, 630 South Main Street, Dobson, NC 27017

## Tri-County Community College
**Murphy, North Carolina**
www.tricountycc.edu
CB code: 5785

▶ Public 2-year community college
▶ Commuter campus in rural community
▶ Interview required

**General.** Founded in 1964. Regionally accredited. **Enrollment:** 785 degree-seeking undergraduates. **Degrees:** 118 associate awarded. **Location:** 110 miles from Asheville, 96 miles from Chattanooga, Tennessee. **Calendar:** Semester, extensive summer session. **Full-time faculty:** 37 total. **Part-time faculty:** 42 total. **Class size:** 22% < 20, 57% 20-39, 20% 40-49, 1% 50-99.

**Student profile.**

| | | | |
|---|---|---|---|
| Out-of-state: | 9% | 25 or older: | 54% |

**Transfer out. Colleges most students transferred to 2007:** Western Carolina University, South Western Community College.

**Basis for selection.** Open admission. Interview required for placement and counseling. **Learning Disabled:** Tutoring is available.

**2007-2008 Annual costs.** Tuition/fees: $1,319; $7,058 out-of-state. Per-credit charge: $42 in-state; $233 out-of-state. Books/supplies: $300. Personal expenses: $450.

**Financial aid.** All financial aid based on need. Need-based aid available for part-time students.

**Application procedures. Admission:** No deadline. No application fee. Admission notification on a rolling basis. **Financial aid:** Priority date 6/30; no closing date. FAFSA required. Applicants notified on a rolling basis starting 6/1; must reply within 4 week(s) of notification.

**Academics. Special study options:** Double major, dual enrollment of high school students, independent study, internships. License preparation in real estate. **Credit/placement by examination:** CLEP, institutional tests. 6 credit hours maximum toward associate degree. **Support services:** GED preparation and test center, learning center, reduced course load, remedial instruction, study skills assistance, tutoring.

**Majors. Business:** Accounting, administrative services, business admin. **Computer sciences:** Information systems. **Construction:** Electrician. **Engineering technology:** Surveying. **Health:** EMT paramedic, medical assistant, nursing (RN). **Liberal arts:** Arts/sciences. **Mechanic/repair:** Automotive, electronics/electrical.

**Most popular majors.** Business/marketing 24%, liberal arts 43%, trade and industry 35%.

**Computing on campus.** 42 workstations in library, computer center. Online library available.

**Student life. Freshman orientation:** Mandatory. Preregistration for classes offered. **Activities:** Student government, student newspaper, honor society.

**Student services.** Career counseling, services for economically disadvantaged, student employment services, financial aid counseling, on-campus daycare, personal counseling, placement for graduates, veterans' counselor. **Physically disabled:** Services for visually, hearing impaired. **Transfer:** Pre-admission transcript evaluation for new students. College fairs on campus for students transferring to 4-year colleges.

**Contact.** E-mail: jchambers@tricountycc.edu
Phone: (828) 837-6810 Toll-free number: (828) 835-4225
Fax: (828) 837-3266
Jason Chambers, Director of Admissions, Tri-County Community College, 4600 Highway 64 East, Murphy, NC 28906

## Vance-Granville Community College

Henderson, North Carolina

**CB member**

www.vgcc.edu

**CB code: 0617**

- Public 2-year community college
- Commuter campus in large town

**General.** Founded in 1969. Regionally accredited. 4 rural counties served with satellite campuses in Warrenton, Butner and Louisburg. **Enrollment:** 3,343 degree-seeking undergraduates. **Degrees:** 362 associate awarded. **Location:** 42 miles from Raleigh. **Calendar:** Semester, limited summer session. **Full-time faculty:** 185 total. **Part-time faculty:** 435 total.

**Basis for selection.** Open admission, but selective for some programs. Admission to nursing, radiologic technology, and medical assisting is based on academic record, health education aptitude test, and other criteria. Test scores neither required nor recommended. Used for placement if available. Interview recommended for nursing, radiologic technology programs.

**2007-2008 Annual costs.** Tuition/fees: $1,298; $7,037 out-of-state. Per-credit charge: $42 in-state; $233 out-of-state. Books/supplies: $800. Personal expenses: $400.

**2006-2007 Financial aid. Need-based:** Need-based aid available for part-time students. **Non-need-based:** Scholarships awarded for academics.

**Application procedures. Admission:** No deadline. No application fee. Admission notification on a rolling basis. Application deadlines apply and may vary for Allied Health programs. College placement examinations required of all students, unless acceptable scores on SAT/ACT or special students. **Financial aid:** Closing date 3/15. FAFSA required. Applicants notified on a rolling basis starting 5/1; must reply within 2 week(s) of notification.

**Academics. Special study options:** Cooperative education, distance learning, double major, dual enrollment of high school students, ESL, independent study, internships. License preparation in nursing, radiology, real estate. **Credit/placement by examination:** CLEP, institutional tests. **Support services:** GED preparation and test center, learning center, pre-admission summer program, reduced course load, remedial instruction, study skills assistance, tutoring.

**Majors. Business:** Accounting, administrative services, business admin, office technology. **Computer sciences:** Information technology, networking, security, web page design. **Education:** General, early childhood, teacher assistance. **Engineering:** Electrical. **Engineering technology:** Electrical. **Family/consumer sciences:** Child care. **Health:** Medical assistant, medical radiologic technology/radiation therapy, nursing (RN), recreational therapy. **Liberal arts:** Arts/sciences. **Mechanic/repair:** Electronics/electrical. **Parks/recreation:** General. **Personal/culinary services:** Culinary arts. **Protective services:** Law enforcement admin. **Public administration:** Human services. **Science technology:** Biological.

**Most popular majors.** Business/marketing 17%, computer/information sciences 9%, education 14%, health sciences 21%, liberal arts 8%, security/protective services 7%.

**Computing on campus.** 48 workstations in library, computer center.

**Student life. Freshman orientation:** Available. **Activities:** Drama, student government, departmental clubs.

**Student services.** Adult student services, career counseling, student employment services, financial aid counseling, on-campus daycare, personal counseling, placement for graduates, veterans' counselor. **Physically disabled:** Services for visually, hearing impaired. **Transfer:** Transfer adviser for students transferring to 4-year colleges.

**Contact.** Phone: (252) 492-2061 Fax: (252) 430-0460
Kathy Ktul, Registrar/Director of Admissions, Vance-Granville Community College, Box 917, Henderson, NC 27536

## Wake Technical Community College

Raleigh, North Carolina

www.waketech.edu

**CB code: 5928**

- Public 2-year community and technical college
- Commuter campus in small city

**General.** Founded in 1958. Regionally accredited. **Enrollment:** 11,997 degree-seeking undergraduates. **Degrees:** 977 associate awarded. **Location:** 10 miles from Raleigh. **Calendar:** Semester, extensive summer session. **Full-time faculty:** 310 total. **Part-time faculty:** 630 total.

**Student profile.** Among degree-seeking undergraduates, 40% enrolled in a transfer program, 60% enrolled in a vocational program, 9% already have a bachelor's degree or higher.

**Transfer out. Colleges most students transferred to 2007:** North Carolina State University, University of North Carolina at Chapel Hill, East Carolina University, University of North Carolina at Greensboro, Appalachian State University.

**Basis for selection.** Open admission, but selective for some programs. Admission to health programs based on standardized test scores, postsecondary coursework. Placement tests required of all degree and diploma students with SAT scores below 480 verbal or math, or below ACT math 20, reading 19, and writing 19. Interview recommended. **Homeschooled:** Must include transcript and test scores.

**High school preparation.** Recommended units include English 4 and mathematics 4. 1 chemistry required for health sciences associate degree programs.

**2007-2008 Annual costs.** Tuition/fees: $1,320; $7,059 out-of-state. Per-credit charge: $42 in-state; $233 out-of-state. Books/supplies: $1,000. Personal expenses: $1,350.

**Financial aid. Need-based:** Need-based aid available for part-time students. Work-study available for part-time students. **Non-need-based:** Scholarships awarded for academics, job skills, leadership, state residency.

**Application procedures. Admission:** No deadline. No application fee. Application may be submitted online. Admission notification on a rolling basis. **Financial aid:** Priority date 3/15; no closing date. FAFSA, institutional form required. Applicants notified on a rolling basis starting 4/1; must reply within 2 week(s) of notification.

**Academics. Special study options:** Cooperative education, distance learning, double major, dual enrollment of high school students, ESL, honors, liberal arts/career combination. License preparation in dental hygiene, nursing, paramedic, radiology, real estate. **Credit/placement by examination:** AP, CLEP, IB, institutional tests. 25% of degree requirement must be taken in residence. **Support services:** GED preparation and test center, learning center, pre-admission summer program, reduced course load, remedial instruction, tutoring.

**Majors. Architecture:** Landscape. **Business:** General, accounting, administrative services, hospitality/recreation. **Computer sciences:** General, applications programming, computer graphics, programming. **Conservation:** General. **Construction:** Power transmission. **Education:** Early childhood. **Engineering technology:** Architectural, civil, drafting, electrical, manufacturing, robotics, surveying. **Health:** Clinical lab technology, dental hygiene, EMT paramedic, medical assistant, medical radiologic technology/radiation therapy, medical records technology, medical secretary, nursing (RN), surgical technology. **Interdisciplinary:** Global studies. **Legal studies:** Legal secretary. **Liberal arts:** Arts/sciences. **Mechanic/repair:** Electronics/electrical, industrial. **Personal/culinary services:** Culinary arts. **Protective services:** Police science. **Public administration:** Human services.

**Most popular majors.** Business/marketing 22%, computer/information sciences 15%, engineering/engineering technologies 17%, health sciences 15%, liberal arts 25%.

**Computing on campus.** 62 workstations in library, computer center, student center. Online course registration, helpline, wireless network available.

**Student life. Freshman orientation:** Available. Held on first day of class. **Activities:** Choral groups, drama, radio station, student government, student newspaper.

**Student services.** Career counseling, student employment services, health services, on-campus daycare, personal counseling, placement for graduates, veterans' counselor. **Physically disabled:** Services for visually, speech, hearing impaired. **Transfer:** Transfer adviser, college fairs on campus for students transferring to 4-year colleges.

**Contact.** Phone: (919) 866-5500 Fax: (919) 661-0117
Susan Bloomfield, Director of Admissions, Wake Technical Community College, 9101 Fayetteville Road, Raleigh, NC 27603

## Wayne Community College

Goldsboro, North Carolina

www.waynecc.edu

**CB code: 5926**

- Public 2-year community college
- Commuter campus in large town
- Interview required

**General.** Founded in 1957. Regionally accredited. **Enrollment:** 2,950 degree-seeking undergraduates. **Degrees:** 330 associate awarded. **Location:** 55 miles from Raleigh. **Calendar:** Semester, limited summer session. **Full-time faculty:** 121 total. **Part-time faculty:** 154 total.

**Student profile.**

| | | | |
|---|---|---|---|
| Out-of-state: | 16% | 25 or older: | 45% |

**Transfer out. Colleges most students transferred to 2007:** East Carolina University, Mount Olive College, Bonton College, Campbell University, North Carolina State.

**Basis for selection.** Open admission, but selective for some programs. Admission to allied health programs based on placement test, academic record, interview.

**High school preparation.** 14 units recommended. Recommended units include English 4, mathematics 3, social studies 1, history 1, science 3 (laboratory 1) and foreign language 2.

**2007-2008 Annual costs.** Tuition/fees: $1,316; $7,055 out-of-state. Per-credit charge: $42 in-state; $233 out-of-state. Books/supplies: $800. Personal expenses: $400.

**2006-2007 Financial aid. Need-based:** 89% of total undergraduate aid awarded as scholarships/grants, 11% as loans/jobs. Need-based aid available for part-time students. Work-study available nights and for part-time students. **Non-need-based:** Scholarships awarded for academics, job skills.

**Application procedures. Admission:** No deadline. No application fee. Application may be submitted online. Admission notification on a rolling basis. **Financial aid:** Priority date 3/15; no closing date. FAFSA, institutional form required. Applicants notified on a rolling basis starting 6/1; must reply within 2 week(s) of notification.

**Academics. Special study options:** Accelerated study, cooperative education, distance learning, double major, dual enrollment of high school students, internships, weekend college. License preparation in aviation, dental hygiene, nursing, occupational therapy, paramedic, real estate. **Credit/placement by examination:** AP, CLEP, institutional tests. **Support services:** GED preparation and test center, learning center, reduced course load, remedial instruction, study skills assistance, tutoring, writing center.

**Majors. Agriculture:** Agribusiness operations, poultry, turf management. **Business:** General, accounting, administrative services, business admin, sales/distribution. **Conservation:** Forest resources. **Family/consumer sciences:** Child care. **Health:** Dental hygiene, licensed practical nurse, medical assistant, medical secretary, mental health services, nursing (RN). **Interdisciplinary:** Biological/physical sciences. **Legal studies:** Legal secretary. **Liberal arts:** Arts/sciences. **Mechanic/repair:** Aircraft. **Parks/recreation:** Facilities management. **Protective services:** Police science. **Public administration:** Human services.

**Computing on campus.** 400 workstations in library, computer center. Online course registration available.

**Student life. Freshman orientation:** Mandatory. Preregistration for classes offered. **Policies:** Student government organizes sports program. **Activities:** Concert band, choral groups, student government, student newspaper.

**Athletics. Intramural:** Basketball, bowling, golf, softball, table tennis, tennis, volleyball. **Team name:** Bisons.

**Student services.** Adult student services, career counseling, student employment services, financial aid counseling, health services, minority student services, on-campus daycare, personal counseling, placement for graduates, veterans' counselor, women's services. **Physically disabled:** Services for visually, speech, hearing impaired. **Transfer:** Transfer center, transfer adviser, college fairs on campus for students transferring to 4-year colleges.

**Contact.** E-mail: msm@waynecc.edu
Phone: (919) 735-5151 ext. 238 Fax: (919) 736-9425
Susan Sasser, Director of Admissions and Records, Wayne Community College, PO Box 8002, Goldsboro, NC 27533-8002

## Western Piedmont Community College
**Morganton, North Carolina**
www.wpcc.edu
CB code: 5922

- Public 2-year community college
- Commuter campus in large town

**General.** Founded in 1964. Regionally accredited. **Enrollment:** 2,026 degree-seeking undergraduates; 619 non-degree-seeking students. **Degrees:** 351 associate awarded. **Location:** 60 miles from Charlotte. **Calendar:** Semester, extensive summer session. **Full-time faculty:** 74 total; 7% have terminal degrees, 5% minority, 57% women. **Part-time faculty:** 306 total; 1% have terminal degrees, 6% minority, 55% women. **Special facilities:** Greenhouses, fitness and nature trails, alpine climbing tower, Senator Sam J. Ervin Jr. library and museum.

**Student profile.** Among degree-seeking undergraduates, 36% enrolled in a transfer program, 63% enrolled in a vocational program, 428 enrolled as first-time, first-year students.

| | | | |
|---|---|---|---|
| Part-time: | 45% | Women: | 61% |
| Out-of-state: | 20% | 25 or older: | 51% |

**Transfer out. Colleges most students transferred to 2007:** Appalachian State University, Gardner-Webb University, Western Carolina University, Lenoir-Rhyne College, Lees McRae.

**Basis for selection.** Open admission, but selective for some programs. Special requirements for health programs.

**2007-2008 Annual costs.** Tuition/fees: $1,287; $7,026 out-of-state. Per-credit charge: $42 in-state; $233 out-of-state. Books/supplies: $1,168. Personal expenses: $2,482.

**2006-2007 Financial aid. Need-based:** 196 full-time freshmen applied for aid; 163 were judged to have need; 143 of these received aid. Average need met was 65%. Average scholarship/grant was $2,401; average loan $2,900. 88% of total undergraduate aid awarded as scholarships/grants, 12% as loans/jobs. Need-based aid available for part-time students. Work-study available for part-time students. **Non-need-based:** Awarded to 48 full-time undergraduates, including 21 freshmen. Scholarships awarded for academics.

**Application procedures. Admission:** No deadline. No application fee. Application may be submitted online. Admission notification on a rolling basis. Application closing date for nursing, medical laboratory applicants is January 1 for fall admission. **Financial aid:** Priority date 6/1; no closing date. FAFSA required. Applicants notified on a rolling basis starting 6/15; must reply within 2 week(s) of notification.

**Academics. Special study options:** Cooperative education, distance learning, dual enrollment of high school students. License preparation in nursing. **Credit/placement by examination:** AP, CLEP, IB, institutional tests. 15 credit hours maximum toward associate degree. **Support services:** GED preparation and test center, learning center, reduced course load, remedial instruction, tutoring.

**Majors. Agriculture:** Horticulture. **Business:** Accounting, administrative services, business admin, office technology, office/clerical, operations, sales/distribution. **Computer sciences:** Computer science, data processing, information systems, systems analysis. **Conservation:** General. **Construction:** Maintenance. **Education:** Early childhood. **Engineering:** General, civil, electrical, mechanical. **Engineering technology:** Construction. **Family/consumer sciences:** Child care. **Health:** Clinical lab assistant, medical assistant, nursing (RN), office admin, recreational therapy. **Interdisciplinary:** Natural sciences. **Legal studies:** Paralegal. **Liberal arts:** Arts/sciences. **Protective services:** Criminal justice. **Visual/performing arts:** Interior design, studio arts.

**Most popular majors.** Business/marketing 21%, health sciences 24%, liberal arts 26%, security/protective services 9%.

**Computing on campus.** 280 workstations in library, computer center. Commuter students can connect to campus network. Online library, wireless network available.

**Student life. Freshman orientation:** Available. Preregistration for classes offered. **Activities:** Drama, student government, Phi Beta Lambda, Phi Theta Kappa, African American Students Association, Students for Christ.

**Athletics. Team name:** Pioneers.

**Student services.** Adult student services, career counseling, services for economically disadvantaged, student employment services, financial aid counseling, personal counseling, placement for graduates, veterans' counselor. **Physically disabled:** Services for visually, speech, hearing impaired. **Transfer:** Transfer adviser, college fairs on campus for students transferring to 4-year colleges.

**Contact.** E-mail: swilliams@wpcc.edu
Phone: (828) 438-6051 Fax: (828) 438-6065
Susan Williams, Director of Admissions, Western Piedmont Community College, 1001 Burkemont Avenue, Morganton, NC 28655-4504

# Wilkes Community College
## Wilkesboro, North Carolina
www.wilkescc.edu      CB code: 5921

♦ Public 2-year community college
♦ Commuter campus in small town

**General.** Founded in 1965. Regionally accredited. **Enrollment:** 2,536 degree-seeking undergraduates. **Degrees:** 318 associate awarded. **Location:** 50 miles from Winston-Salem. **Calendar:** Semester, limited summer session. **Full-time faculty:** 77 total. **Part-time faculty:** 256 total. **Class size:** 80% < 20, 19% 20-39, 1% 40-49, less than 1% 50-99. **Special facilities:** Community center.

**Student profile.**

Out-of-state:     1%     25 or older:     39%

**Transfer out. Colleges most students transferred to 2007:** Appalachian State University, Gardner-Webb University, Winston-Salem State University.

**Basis for selection.** Open admission, but selective for some programs. Special requirements for nursing program.

**High school preparation.** 20 units recommended. Recommended units include English 4, mathematics 4, social studies 3, history 2, science 3 (laboratory 1), foreign language 2 and academic electives 2.

**2007-2008 Annual costs.** Tuition/fees: $1,340; $7,079 out-of-state. Per-credit charge: $42 in-state; $233 out-of-state. Books/supplies: $1,000. Personal expenses: $500.

**Financial aid. Need-based:** Need-based aid available for part-time students. Work-study available nights and for part-time students. **Non-need-based:** Scholarships awarded for academics, art, job skills, leadership, minority status, music/drama, state residency.

**Application procedures. Admission:** No deadline. No application fee. Application may be submitted online. Admission notification on a rolling basis. **Financial aid:** Priority date 5/1, closing date 6/1. FAFSA required. Applicants notified on a rolling basis starting 4/1; must reply by 8/1.

**Academics. Special study options:** Cooperative education, distance learning, double major, dual enrollment of high school students, ESL, independent study, internships. Bachelor's degree programs available on campus. License preparation in nursing, paramedic, real estate. **Credit/placement by examination:** AP, CLEP, IB, institutional tests. 16 credit hours maximum toward associate degree. **Support services:** GED preparation and test center, learning center, pre-admission summer program, reduced course load, remedial instruction, study skills assistance, tutoring, writing center.

**Majors. Agriculture:** Horticulture. **Business:** Accounting, business admin, marketing, office management. **Communications technology:** Radio/tv. **Computer sciences:** Computer graphics, information systems, information technology, LAN/WAN management, programming. **Construction:** General, electrician. **Education:** Early childhood, elementary. **Engineering technology:** Architectural, computer, electrical, industrial. **Health:** Health services, medical assistant, nursing (RN). **Liberal arts:** Arts/sciences. **Mechanic/repair:** Automotive, diesel. **Personal/culinary services:** Baking, chef training. **Protective services:** Criminal justice.

**Most popular majors.** Business/marketing 18%, education 7%, engineering/engineering technologies 11%, health sciences 16%, liberal arts 26%, trade and industry 9%.

**Computing on campus.** 150 workstations in library, computer center, student center.

**Student life. Freshman orientation:** Mandatory. Preregistration for classes offered. **Activities:** Choral groups, drama, literary magazine, music ensembles, musical theater, radio station, student government, student newspaper, Baptist student union, Ye Hosts food service club, camera club, Phi Theta Kappa, Association of Information Technology Professionals, Rotaract, human services club, medical assisting club, student government association, Student Ambassadors.

**Athletics.** NJCAA. **Intercollegiate:** Baseball M, basketball, volleyball W. **Intramural:** Basketball, table tennis, tennis, volleyball. **Team name:** Cougars.

**Student services.** Adult student services, career counseling, services for economically disadvantaged, student employment services, financial aid counseling, minority student services, personal counseling, placement for graduates, veterans' counselor. **Physically disabled:** Services for visually, speech,

hearing impaired. **Transfer:** Pre-admission transcript evaluation for new students. Transfer adviser, college fairs on campus for students transferring to 4-year colleges.

**Contact.** E-mail: mac.warren@wilkescc.edu
Phone: (336) 838-6135 Fax: (336) 838-6547
C Warren, Director of Admissions, Wilkes Community College, 1328 South Collegiate Drive, Wilkesboro, NC 28697-0120

# Wilson Community College
## Wilson, North Carolina
www.wilsoncc.edu      CB code: 5930

♦ Public 2-year community college
♦ Commuter campus in large town

**General.** Founded in 1958. Regionally accredited. **Enrollment:** 1,510 degree-seeking undergraduates. **Degrees:** 204 associate awarded. **Location:** 50 miles from Raleigh. **Calendar:** Semester, limited summer session. **Full-time faculty:** 57 total. **Part-time faculty:** 52 total. **Class size:** 64% < 20, 33% 20-39, 2% 40-49, less than 1% 50-99.

**Student profile.**

Out-of-state:     1%     25 or older:     57%

**Basis for selection.** Open admission, but selective for some programs. Admission for nursing based on test scores, high school record, skills, and experience. Health requirement for emergency medical technology. Interview recommended.

**High school preparation.** High school diploma not required for certificate programs.

**2007-2008 Annual costs.** Tuition/fees: $1,301; $7,040 out-of-state. Per-credit charge: $42 in-state; $233 out-of-state. Books/supplies: $800. Personal expenses: $4,200.

**Financial aid. Need-based:** Need-based aid available for part-time students. **Non-need-based:** Scholarships awarded for academics.

**Application procedures. Admission:** No deadline. No application fee. Admission notification on a rolling basis beginning on or about 1/1. Applicants accepted to nursing program must reply by May 1. **Financial aid:** Priority date 3/15; no closing date. FAFSA, institutional form required. Applicants notified on a rolling basis.

**Academics.** Special program assistance for hearing-impaired students. **Special study options:** Cooperative education, distance learning, double major, dual enrollment of high school students, ESL, liberal arts/career combination. License preparation in nursing. **Credit/placement by examination:** AP, CLEP, institutional tests. 50 credit hours maximum toward associate degree. **Support services:** GED preparation and test center, learning center, pre-admission summer program, reduced course load, remedial instruction, tutoring.

**Majors. Business:** Accounting, business admin, executive assistant, operations. **Computer sciences:** General, applications programming, programming, systems analysis. **Conservation:** General. **Education:** Early childhood. **Engineering:** Polymer. **Engineering technology:** Drafting, electrical. **Family/consumer sciences:** Child care. **Foreign languages:** Sign language interpretation, translation. **Health:** Licensed practical nurse, nursing (RN). **Legal studies:** Paralegal. **Liberal arts:** Arts/sciences. **Mechanic/repair:** Electronics/electrical. **Protective services:** Criminal justice, fire safety technology.

**Most popular majors.** Business/marketing 13%, education 27%, health sciences 15%, legal studies 8%, liberal arts 11%, security/protective services 14%.

**Computing on campus.** 33 workstations in library, computer center.

**Student life. Freshman orientation:** Available. Preregistration for classes offered. **Activities:** Choral groups, student government.

**Student services.** Career counseling, services for economically disadvantaged, student employment services, placement for graduates, veterans' counselor. **Physically disabled:** Services for hearing impaired. **Transfer:** Transfer adviser, college fairs on campus for students transferring to 4-year colleges.

**Contact.** E-mail: lmansfield@email.wilsoncc.edu
Phone: (252) 246-1285 Fax: (252) 246-1384
Leonard Mansfield, Director of Admissions and Records, Wilson Community College, Box 4305, Wilson, NC 27893-0305

# North Dakota

## Bismarck State College
### Bismarck, North Dakota
### www.bismarckstate.edu
**CB code: 6041**

- Public 2-year community college
- Commuter campus in small city

**General.** Founded in 1939. Regionally accredited. **Enrollment:** 3,591 degree-seeking undergraduates. **Degrees:** 603 associate awarded. **Location:** 200 miles from Fargo. **Calendar:** Semester, limited summer session. **Full-time faculty:** 110 total. **Part-time faculty:** 160 total.

**Student profile.** Among degree-seeking undergraduates, 50% enrolled in a transfer program, 37% enrolled in a vocational program, 827 enrolled as first-time, first-year students, 235 transferred in from other institutions.

| | | | |
|---|---|---|---|
| Part-time: | 35% | 25 or older: | 30% |
| Out-of-state: | 11% | Live on campus: | 11% |
| Women: | 47% | | |

**Basis for selection.** Open admission, but selective for some programs. Test scores required for selective admission programs in air conditioning, heating and refrigeration, automotive technology, automotive collision technology, carpentry, electronics technology, line worker (electrical), power plant technology, process plant technology, welding, hotel restaurant management, commercial art. Interview recommended for some programs; portfolio recommended for graphic arts program. **Adult students:** Students aged 25 or older must submit COMPASS assessment scores in the areas of English, math, and reading.

**High school preparation.** Recommended units include English 4, mathematics 3, social studies 3, science 3 and foreign language 2.

**2007-2008 Annual costs.** Tuition/fees: $3,773; $9,124 out-of-state. Per-credit charge: $107 in-state; $285 out-of-state. Full-time annual tuition for residents of Minnesota: $4,063. Full-time annual tuition for residents of South Dakota, Montana, Manitoba, Saskatchewan: $4,005. Room/board: $4,004. Books/supplies: $750. Personal expenses: $1,900.

**Financial aid.** All financial aid based on need. Need-based aid available for part-time students. Work-study available nights, weekends and for part-time students.

**Application procedures. Admission:** No deadline. $35 fee. Application may be submitted online. Admission notification on a rolling basis beginning on or about 1/1. **Financial aid:** Priority date 3/15; no closing date. FAFSA required. Applicants notified on a rolling basis starting 6/1; must reply within 3 week(s) of notification.

**Academics.** Academic advising focus over the summer with 20+ sessions offered to students who are enrolling for the following fall session. Online academic support services available. **Special study options:** Cooperative education, distance learning, dual enrollment of high school students, internships, liberal arts/career combination. Bachelor's degree programs available on campus. License preparation in nursing, paramedic. **Credit/placement by examination:** AP, CLEP, institutional tests. 30 credit hours maximum toward associate degree. **Support services:** Learning center, remedial instruction, study skills assistance, tutoring, writing center.

**Majors. Agriculture:** Business, farm/ranch. **Business:** General, administrative services, hospitality admin, office technology, transportation. **Communications:** Public relations. **Computer sciences:** Networking, web page design. **Construction:** Carpentry, lineworker. **Education:** Teacher assistance. **Engineering technology:** General, electrical, GIS, industrial, nuclear. **Health:** Clinical lab technology, EMT paramedic, licensed practical nurse, medical secretary, nursing (RN), surgical technology. **Legal studies:** Legal secretary. **Liberal arts:** Arts/sciences. **Mechanic/repair:** Auto body, automotive, heating/ac/refrig, industrial. **Production:** Welding. **Protective services:** Criminal justice. **Public administration:** Human services. **Visual/performing arts:** Commercial/advertising art.

**Most popular majors.** Business/marketing 6%, engineering/engineering technologies 22%, health sciences 9%, liberal arts 49%.

**Computing on campus.** 450 workstations in library, computer center, student center. Dormitories wired for high-speed internet access. Commuter students can connect to campus network. Online course registration, online library, helpline, wireless network available.

**Student life. Freshman orientation:** Available. Preregistration for classes offered. **Housing:** Single-sex dorms, substance-free housing available. $100 deposit. **Activities:** Bands, choral groups, dance, drama, literary magazine, music ensembles, musical theater, student government, student newspaper.

**Athletics.** NJCAA. **Intercollegiate:** Baseball M, basketball, golf, tennis, volleyball W. **Intramural:** Basketball, bowling, golf, soccer, softball, table tennis, volleyball. **Team name:** Mystics.

**Student services.** Career counseling, student employment services, financial aid counseling, personal counseling, placement for graduates, veterans' counselor. **Physically disabled:** Services for visually, speech, hearing impaired. **Transfer:** Pre-admission transcript evaluation for new students. Transfer adviser, college fairs on campus for students transferring to 4-year colleges.

**Contact.** E-mail: karla.gabriel@bsc.nodak.edu
Phone: (701) 224-5429 Toll-free number: (800) 445-5073
Fax: (701) 224-5643
Karla Gabriel, Dean of Admissions and Enrollment Services, Bismarck State College, PO Box 5587, Bismarck, ND 58506-5587

## Cankdeska Cikana Community College
### Fort Totten, North Dakota
### www.littlehoop.edu
**CB code: 1306**

- Public 2-year community college
- Residential campus in rural community

**General.** Founded in 1974. Regionally accredited. **Location:** 13 miles from Devils Lake. **Calendar:** Semester.

**Annual costs/financial aid.** Books/supplies: $600. Personal expenses: $1,000. Need-based financial aid available to full-time and part-time students.

**Contact.** Phone: (701) 766-1342
Registrar, Box 269, Fort Totten, ND 58335

## Fort Berthold Community College
### New Town, North Dakota
### www.fbcc.bia.edu
**CB code: 7304**

- Public 2-year community college
- Small town

**General.** Founded in 1973. Regionally accredited. Affiliated with American Indian Higher Education Consortium. **Enrollment:** 201 degree-seeking undergraduates. **Degrees:** 16 associate awarded. **Location:** 80 miles from Minot, 150 miles from Bismarck. **Calendar:** Semester, limited summer session. **Full-time faculty:** 20 total. **Part-time faculty:** 40 total.

**Student profile.** Among degree-seeking undergraduates, 41 enrolled as first-time, first-year students, 201 transferred in from other institutions.

| | | | |
|---|---|---|---|
| Part-time: | 37% | Women: | 68% |

**Transfer out.** 20% of students enrolled in the transfer program go on to 4-year colleges.

**Basis for selection.** Open admission.

**2007-2008 Annual costs.** Tuition/fees: $3,340. Per-credit charge: $110. Books/supplies: $400. Personal expenses: $800.

**Application procedures. Admission:** No deadline. No application fee.

**Academics. Special study options:** Double major, independent study. **Credit/placement by examination:** CLEP. **Support services:** Remedial instruction, tutoring.

**Majors. Business:** Business admin. **Construction:** General. **Health:** Medical secretary.

**Student life. Activities:** Drama, student government.

**Athletics. Intercollegiate:** Basketball, cross-country.

**Student services.** Adult student services, personal counseling, veterans' counselor. **Transfer:** Transfer adviser for students transferring to 4-year colleges.

Two-Year Colleges

**Contact.** Phone: (701) 627-4738 ext. 286 Fax: (701) 627-4790
Twila Aulaumea, Registrar/Admissions Director, Fort Berthold Community
College, Box 490, New Town, ND 58763

## Lake Region State College
### Devils Lake, North Dakota
**www.lrsc.nodak.edu**                    **CB code: 6163**

- Public 2-year community and technical college
- Commuter campus in small town

**General.** Founded in 1941. Regionally accredited. Satellite center at Grand
Forks Air Force Base. **Enrollment:** 645 degree-seeking undergraduates. **Degrees:** 164 associate awarded. **Location:** 90 miles from Grand Forks, 400
miles from Minneapolis-St. Paul. **Calendar:** Semester, limited summer session. **Full-time faculty:** 30 total. **Part-time faculty:** 80 total. **Partnerships:** Formal partnership with CISCO.

**Student profile.**

| | | | |
|---|---|---|---|
| Out-of-state: | 10% | Live on campus: | 20% |
| 25 or older: | 28% | | |

**Transfer out. Colleges most students transferred to 2007:** Mayville State
University, Minot State University, University of North Dakota, North Dakota State University, Valley City State University.

**Basis for selection.** Open admission, but selective for some programs.
Special requirements for peace officer training program, nursing, sign language and interpretive studies.

**High school preparation.** Recommended units include English 4, mathematics 3, social studies 3, science 3 (laboratory 2) and foreign language 2.

**2007-2008 Annual costs.** Tuition/fees: $3,762; $3,762 out-of-state. Per-credit charge: $122 in-state; $122 out-of-state. Room/board: $4,537.

**2006-2007 Financial aid. Need-based:** 77% of total undergraduate aid
awarded as scholarships/grants, 23% as loans/jobs. Need-based aid available for part-time students. Work-study available nights, weekends and for
part-time students. **Non-need-based:** Scholarships awarded for academics,
athletics, leadership, minority status, music/drama.

**Application procedures. Admission:** No deadline. $35 fee. Application may be submitted online. Admission notification on a rolling basis.
**Financial aid:** Priority date 3/15; no closing date. FAFSA required. Applicants notified on a rolling basis starting 5/15; must reply within 2 week(s)
of notification.

**Academics. Special study options:** Combined bachelor's/graduate degree, cooperative education, distance learning, dual enrollment of high school
students, ESL, internships, liberal arts/career combination. License preparation in nursing. **Credit/placement by examination:** AP, CLEP, institutional
tests. **Support services:** GED preparation and test center, learning center,
reduced course load, remedial instruction, study skills assistance, tutoring,
writing center.

**Majors. Business:** Accounting, accounting technology, administrative services, business admin, executive assistant, fashion, management information systems, market research, office management, office/clerical, sales/
distribution, small business admin. **Computer sciences:** General, computer
science, data processing, networking, vendor certification. **Education:** Voc/
tech. **Engineering:** Electrical. **Family/consumer sciences:** Child care. **Health:**
Licensed practical nurse, medical secretary. **Legal studies:** Legal secretary,
paralegal. **Liberal arts:** Arts/sciences. **Mechanic/repair:** Automotive, avionics, diesel, electronics/electrical. **Protective services:** Police science. **Transportation:** General.

**Most popular majors.** Business/marketing 27%, health sciences 9%, liberal arts 46%, security/protective services 6%.

**Computing on campus.** 305 workstations in dormitories, library, computer center, student center. Dormitories wired for high-speed internet access and linked to campus network. Commuter students can connect to campus network. Online course registration, online library, helpline available.

**Student life. Freshman orientation:** Mandatory, $10 fee. Preregistration
for classes offered. Summer orientation available. Mandatory session the
day before classes start. **Policies:** Alcohol not allowed on campus. **Housing:** Single-sex dorms, special housing for disabled, apartments, substance-free housing available. $50 nonrefundable deposit, deadline 9/1. **Activities:**
Drama, international student organizations, literary magazine, musical theater, student government, symphony orchestra, Distributive Education Clubs
of America, Vocational Industrial Clubs of America, Students Other than

Average, business club, legal assistant club, simulator maintenance technician club, Campus Crusade for Christ, agriculture club.

**Athletics.** NJCAA. **Intercollegiate:** Basketball. **Intramural:** Basketball,
bowling, football (non-tackle), golf, ice hockey, softball, table tennis, volleyball. **Team name:** Royals.

**Student services.** Adult student services, career counseling, services for
economically disadvantaged, student employment services, financial aid counseling, on-campus daycare, personal counseling, placement for graduates,
veterans' counselor, women's services. **Physically disabled:** Services for
speech, hearing impaired. **Learning disabled:** Comprehensive services available. **Transfer:** Transfer adviser, college fairs on campus for students transferring to 4-year colleges.

**Contact.** E-mail: lrsc.admissions@lrsc.nodak.edu
Phone: (701) 662-1514 Toll-free number: (800) 443-1313
Fax: (701) 662-1581
Laurel Goulding, Vice President of Student Services, Lake Region State
College, 1801 College Drive North, Devils Lake, ND 58301-1598

## Minot State University: Bottineau Campus
### Bottineau, North Dakota
**www.misu-b.nodak.edu**                    **CB code: 1540**

- Public 2-year branch campus and junior college
- Residential campus in small town

**General.** Founded in 1907. Regionally accredited. **Enrollment:** 637 degree-seeking undergraduates. **Degrees:** 96 associate awarded. **Location:** 80 miles
from Minot. **Calendar:** Semester, limited summer session. **Full-time faculty:** 27 total; 7% have terminal degrees, 22% women. **Part-time faculty:**
38 total; 3% have terminal degrees, 71% women. **Special facilities:** Headquarters for North Dakota Forest Service, outdoor laboratories on state and
federally owned refuges, forests, and parklands. **Partnerships:** Formal partnerships with high schools where students have taken CISCO and A+ modules for certification to transfer into information technology - network engineering program.

**Student profile.** Among degree-seeking undergraduates, 50% enrolled in
a transfer program, 50% enrolled in a vocational program, 461 enrolled as
first-time, first-year students.

| | | | |
|---|---|---|---|
| Part-time: | 52% | Native American: | 8% |
| Out-of-state: | 7% | International: | 4% |
| Women: | 54% | 25 or older: | 39% |
| African American: | 2% | Live on campus: | 22% |
| Hispanic American: | 2% | | |

**Basis for selection.** Open admission. ACT examination offered on campus first weekend. **Adult students:** SAT/ACT scores not required if applicant over 25.

**2007-2008 Annual costs.** Tuition/fees: $3,634; $5,120 out-of-state. Per-credit charge: $124 in-state; $310 out-of-state. Room/board: $3,980. Books/
supplies: $900. Personal expenses: $1,900.

**Financial aid. Need-based:** Need-based aid available for part-time students. Work-study available nights, weekends and for part-time students.
**Non-need-based:** Scholarships awarded for academics, alumni affiliation,
athletics, music/drama.

**Application procedures. Admission:** No deadline. $35 fee. Application may be submitted online. Admission notification on a rolling basis.
**Financial aid:** Priority date 4/15; no closing date. FAFSA required. Applicants notified on a rolling basis starting 6/1; must reply within 2 week(s) of
notification.

**Academics. Special study options:** Cooperative education, distance learning, double major, dual enrollment of high school students, independent
study, internships, liberal arts/career combination. License preparation in
nursing. **Credit/placement by examination:** CLEP, institutional tests. **Support services:** Learning center, reduced course load, remedial instruction,
study skills assistance, tutoring.

**Majors. Agriculture:** Greenhouse operations, landscaping, turf management. **Biology:** General. **Business:** Accounting technology, administrative
services. **Communications:** Advertising. **Computer sciences:** Webmaster.
**Conservation:** General, urban forestry, wildlife. **Education:** Teacher assistance. **Engineering technology:** Environmental, water quality. **English:** English lit. **Health:** Medical assistant, medical secretary, nursing (RN). **History:** General. **Liberal arts:** Arts/sciences.

**Most popular majors.** Agriculture 18%, health sciences 23%, liberal
arts 56%.

**Computing on campus.** 80 workstations in library, computer center, student center. Dormitories wired for high-speed internet access. Online course registration, online library, repair service, wireless network available.

**Student life. Freshman orientation:** Mandatory. Preregistration for classes offered. Two sessions offered. **Housing:** Guaranteed on-campus for all undergraduates. Single-sex dorms, substance-free housing available. $75 nonrefundable deposit. **Activities:** Jazz band, campus ministries, drama, music ensembles, student government, student newspaper.

**Athletics.** NJCAA. **Intercollegiate:** Baseball M, basketball, football (tackle) M, ice hockey M, softball W, volleyball W. **Intramural:** Badminton, basketball, bowling, football (non-tackle), racquetball, skiing, soccer, softball, volleyball. **Team name:** Lumberjacks and Ladyjacks.

**Student services.** Adult student services, alcohol/substance abuse counseling, career counseling, student employment services, financial aid counseling, health services, personal counseling, veterans' counselor. **Learning disabled:** Comprehensive services available. **Transfer:** Transfer adviser, college fairs on campus for students transferring to 4-year colleges.

**Contact.** E-mail: jessica.migler@misu.nodak.edu
Phone: (701) 228-5426 Toll-free number: (800) 542-6866
Fax: (701) 228-5499
Paula Berg, Associate Dean, Minot State University: Bottineau Campus, 105 Simrall Boulevard, Bottineau, ND 58318-1198

## North Dakota State College of Science
### Wahpeton, North Dakota
### www.ndscs.nodak.edu
**CB code: 6476**

- Public 2-year junior and technical college
- Residential campus in small town

**General.** Founded in 1903. Regionally accredited. **Enrollment:** 3,190 undergraduates. **Degrees:** 577 associate awarded. **Location:** 50 miles from Fargo, 200 miles from Sioux Falls, South Dakota. **Calendar:** Semester, limited summer session. **Full-time faculty:** 123 total; 4% have terminal degrees. **Part-time faculty:** 93 total. **Class size:** 57% < 20, 36% 20-39, 5% 40-49, 2% 50-99. **Partnerships:** Formal partnerships with Caterpillar Corporation and John Deere.

**Student profile.** 1,482 transferred in from other institutions.

| | | | |
|---|---|---|---|
| Out-of-state: | 28% | Live on campus: | 52% |
| 25 or older: | 20% | | |

**Transfer out.** Colleges most students transferred to 2007: Minnesota State University Moorhead, North Dakota State University, University of North Dakota, Northwest Technical College-Moorhead.

**Basis for selection.** Open admission, but selective for some programs. Special requirements for allied health programs. **Adult students:** SAT/ACT scores not required if applicant over 25.

**High school preparation.** Chemistry, English and anatomy & physiology required for dental hygiene.

**2007-2008 Annual costs.** Tuition/fees: $3,695; $9,051 out-of-state. Per-credit charge: $107 in-state; $285 out-of-state. Full-time tuition for Minnesota residents: $4,932. Full-time tuition for South Dakota, Montana, Saskatchewan, Manitoba residents: $4,776. Room/board: $4,258. Books/supplies: $700. Personal expenses: $1,850.

**Financial aid. Need-based:** Need-based aid available for part-time students. Work-study available nights, weekends and for part-time students. **Non-need-based:** Scholarships awarded for academics, athletics, job skills, music/drama, state residency.

**Application procedures. Admission:** No deadline. $35 fee, may be waived for applicants with need. Application may be submitted online. Admission notification on a rolling basis. **Financial aid:** Priority date 4/15; no closing date. FAFSA, institutional form required. Applicants notified on a rolling basis starting 6/1; must reply within 2 week(s) of notification.

**Academics. Special study options:** Cooperative education, distance learning, dual enrollment of high school students, ESL, internships, liberal arts/career combination, student-designed major. License preparation in dental hygiene, nursing, occupational therapy. **Credit/placement by examination:** CLEP, institutional tests. **Support services:** Learning center, preadmission summer program, reduced course load, remedial instruction, study skills assistance, tutoring, writing center.

**Majors. Agriculture:** Agribusiness operations, business, power machinery, supplies. **Architecture:** Technology. **Business:** General, administrative

services, banking/financial services, business admin, executive assistant, finance, office management, office/clerical, restaurant/food services. **Computer sciences:** Applications programming, data entry, information systems, LAN/WAN management, web page design. **Construction:** General, electrician. **Engineering technology:** Architectural, architectural drafting, automotive, civil, civil drafting, computer hardware, construction, electrical, heat/ac/refrig, software. **Family/consumer sciences:** Institutional food production. **Health:** Dental hygiene, insurance coding, licensed practical nurse, medical records technology, medical transcription, mental health services, occupational therapy assistant, office admin, office assistant, pharmacy assistant. **Liberal arts:** Arts/sciences. **Mechanic/repair:** Auto body, automotive, diesel, electronics/electrical, heating/ac/refrig, small engine. **Personal/culinary services:** Baking, culinary arts, restaurant/catering. **Production:** Machine tool, welding.

**Most popular majors.** Architecture 6%, health sciences 25%, liberal arts 22%, trade and industry 28%.

**Computing on campus.** 550 workstations in dormitories, library, computer center, student center. Dormitories linked to campus network. Online course registration, helpline, wireless network available.

**Student life. Freshman orientation:** Mandatory, $25 fee. Preregistration for classes offered. Orientation held the day before classes start. **Housing:** Guaranteed on-campus for freshmen. Coed dorms, single-sex dorms, special housing for disabled, apartments available. $40 deposit. **Activities:** Bands, choral groups, drama, music ensembles, student government, Intervarsity Christian Fellowship.

**Athletics.** NJCAA. **Intercollegiate:** Basketball, football (tackle) M, volleyball W. **Intramural:** Basketball, racquetball, softball, volleyball. **Team name:** Wildcats.

**Student services.** Alcohol/substance abuse counseling, career counseling, student employment services, financial aid counseling, health services, on-campus daycare, personal counseling, placement for graduates, veterans' counselor. **Physically disabled:** Services for visually, hearing impaired. **Transfer:** Pre-admission transcript evaluation for new students. Transfer adviser, college fairs on campus for students transferring to 4-year colleges.

**Contact.** E-mail: ndscs.admissions@ndscs.edu
Phone: (701) 671-2202 Toll-free number: (800) 342-4325 ext. 32202
Fax: (701) 671-2201
Karen Reilly, Director of Enrollment Services and Records, North Dakota State College of Science, 800 North 6th Street, Wahpeton, ND 58076

## Rasmussen College: Bismarck
### Bismarck, North Dakota
### www.rasmussen.edu

- For-profit 2-year branch campus and career college
- Commuter campus in small city

**General.** Accredited by ACICS. **Enrollment:** 380 undergraduates. **Degrees:** 68 associate awarded. **Calendar:** Quarter.

**Basis for selection.** Open admission.

**2007-2008 Annual costs.** Tuition/fees: $11,700. Per course tuition ranges from $845 to $1025 depending on course level.

**Academics. Credit/placement by examination:** CLEP.

**Contact.** Phone: (701) 530-9600 Toll-free number: (877) 530-9600
Fax: (701) 530-9604
Mike Heitkamp, Director of Admissions, Rasmussen College: Bismarck, 1701 E. century Avenue, Bismarck, ND 58503

## Sitting Bull College
### Fort Yates, North Dakota
### www.sittingbull.edu
**CB code: 0310**

- Public 2-year community college
- Residential campus in small town

**General.** Founded in 1971. Regionally accredited. **Enrollment:** 310 degree-seeking undergraduates. **Degrees:** 5 associate awarded. **Location:** 75 miles from Bismarck; 60 miles from Mobridge, South Dakota. **Calendar:** Semester, limited summer session. **Full-time faculty:** 20 total. **Part-time faculty:** 25 total.

**Transfer out. Colleges most students transferred to 2007:** Northern State College, Black Hills State College, Minot State University, United Tribes Technical College.

**Basis for selection.** Open admission. High school students may enroll with approval of Vice President of academic affairs and parents. Letters of recommendation from high school counselor or principal required. TABE (Test of Adult Basic Education) required of students without 2-year college degree. **Adult students:** Compass Test required for placement in Math and English.

**2007-2008 Annual costs.** Tuition/fees: $3,140. Per-credit charge: $100. Books/supplies: $800. Personal expenses: $1,170.

**Financial aid. Need-based:** Need-based aid available for part-time students.

**Application procedures. Admission:** No deadline. $10 fee. Admission notification on a rolling basis. **Financial aid:** Priority date 5/1; no closing date. FAFSA, institutional form required. Applicants notified on a rolling basis starting 7/15; must reply within 6 week(s) of notification.

**Academics. Special study options:** Cooperative education, dual enrollment of high school students, independent study. Bachelor's degree programs available on campus. **Credit/placement by examination:** CLEP. **Support services:** GED preparation and test center, learning center, remedial instruction, study skills assistance, tutoring.

**Majors. Agriculture:** Agribusiness operations. **Area/ethnic studies:** Native American. **Business:** Business admin, entrepreneurial studies, office technology, small business admin. **Computer sciences:** Applications programming. **Conservation:** Environmental science, wildlife. **Construction:** Carpentry. **Education:** Early childhood, elementary, multi-level teacher. **Health:** Licensed practical nurse. **Public administration:** Human services.

**Computing on campus.** Online course registration, wireless network available.

**Student life. Housing:** Very limited housing available for single parents or married students. **Activities:** Student government, cultural club, Phi Beta Lambda, rodeo club.

**Athletics. Team name:** Suns.

**Student services.** Career counseling, student employment services, personal counseling, placement for graduates, veterans' counselor. **Transfer:** Transfer adviser for students transferring to 4-year colleges.

**Contact.** E-mail: melodya@sbci.edu
Phone: (701) 854-8000 ext. 8020 Fax: (701) 854-3403
Melody Azure, Director of Admissions/Registrar, Sitting Bull College, 1341 92nd Street, Fort Yates, ND 58538

## Turtle Mountain Community College
**Belcourt, North Dakota**
www.tm.edu  CB code: 0352

- Public 2-year community college
- Commuter campus in rural community

**General.** Regionally accredited. **Enrollment:** 956 undergraduates. **Degrees:** 46 associate awarded. **Calendar:** Semester. **Full-time faculty:** 40 total. **Part-time faculty:** 20 total.

**Basis for selection.** Open admission, but selective for some programs. Special requirements for Bachelor of Science Elementary Education program.

**2007-2008 Annual costs.** Tuition/fees: $2,000. Room/board: $3,664. Books/supplies: $400.

**Application procedures. Admission:** No deadline. No application fee. Admission notification on a rolling basis. **Financial aid:** Priority date 4/15, closing date 5/1. FAFSA required.

**Academics. Special study options:** Bachelor's degree programs available on campus. **Credit/placement by examination:** CLEP.

**Majors. Business:** Business admin. **Computer sciences:** Computer science. **Construction:** General. **Education:** Early childhood. **Health:** Insurance coding.

**Student life. Activities:** Student government.

**Contact.** E-mail: jlafontaine@tm.edu
Phone: (701) 477-7862 Fax: (701) 477-7892
Joni LaFontaine, Admissions/Records Officer, Turtle Mountain Community College, PO Box 340, Belcourt, ND 58316

## United Tribes Technical College
**Bismarck, North Dakota**
www.uttc.edu  CB code: 4915

- Private 2-year technical college
- Residential campus in small city

**General.** Regionally accredited. Native American college. **Enrollment:** 588 degree-seeking undergraduates. **Degrees:** 102 associate awarded. **Location:** One mile from Bismarck. **Calendar:** Semester, limited summer session. **Full-time faculty:** 50 total. **Part-time faculty:** 10 total. **Special facilities:** Elementary school on campus.

**Basis for selection.** Open admission, but selective for some programs. Some programs have limited enrollment and/or more stringent academic, medical, and legal requirements. Admittance priority given to those who are members of recognized tribe. **Homeschooled:** Statement describing home-school structure and mission, transcript of courses and grades, state high school equivalency certificate required.

**2007-2008 Annual costs.** Books/supplies: $600. Personal expenses: $1,880.

**Financial aid. Need-based:** Need-based aid available for part-time students. Work-study available nights and weekends.

**Application procedures. Admission:** Closing date 8/17. No application fee. Application must be submitted on paper. Admission notification on a rolling basis. **Financial aid:** Priority date 5/29; no closing date. FAFSA required. Applicants notified on a rolling basis starting 5/29; must reply within 2 week(s) of notification.

**Academics. Special study options:** Accelerated study, distance learning. **Credit/placement by examination:** CLEP. **Support services:** Learning center, remedial instruction, study skills assistance, tutoring.

**Majors. Business:** Administrative services, business admin. **Education:** General. **Health:** Licensed practical nurse. **Protective services:** Law enforcement admin.

**Computing on campus.** 40 workstations in computer center. Commuter students can connect to campus network. Online course registration, repair service available.

**Student life. Freshman orientation:** Mandatory. Preregistration for classes offered. **Housing:** Coed dorms, single-sex dorms, substance-free housing available. **Activities:** Student newspaper.

**Athletics.** NJCAA. **Intercollegiate:** Basketball, cross-country. **Team name:** Thunderbirds.

**Student services.** Adult student services, alcohol/substance abuse counseling, campus ministries, career counseling, financial aid counseling, health services, on-campus daycare, personal counseling, placement for graduates, women's services. **Transfer:** Pre-admission transcript evaluation for new students.

**Contact.** E-mail: vgillette@uttc.edu
Phone: (701) 255-3285 ext. 1334 Toll-free number: (800) 643-8882
Fax: (701) 530-0640
Vivian Gillette, Director of Admissions, United Tribes Technical College, 3315 University Drive, Bismarck, ND 58504

## Williston State College
**Williston, North Dakota**
www.wsc.nodak.edu  CB code: 6905

- Public 2-year community college
- Commuter campus in large town

**General.** Founded in 1957. Regionally accredited. Baccalaureate, post-baccalaureate programs from other campuses available on-campus, all via interactive video network. **Enrollment:** 582 degree-seeking undergraduates. **Degrees:** 216 associate awarded. **Location:** 250 miles from Bismarck, 130 miles from Minot. **Calendar:** Semester, limited summer session. **Full-time faculty:** 26 total. **Part-time faculty:** 65 total. **Class size:** 100% < 20.

## Student profile.

**Out-of-state:** 12%   **Live on campus:** 20%
**25 or older:** 28%

**Transfer out.** 46% of students enrolled in the transfer program go on to 4-year colleges. **Colleges most students transferred to 2007:** University of North Dakota, Minot State University, Dickinson State University, North Dakota State University, Montana State University.

**Basis for selection.** Open admission, but selective for some programs. Special requirements for practical nursing and physical therapist assistant programs. Immunization records required for applicants born after 1956.

**High school preparation.** 15 units recommended. Recommended units include English 4, mathematics 3, social studies 3, science 3 (laboratory 1) and foreign language 1.

**2007-2008 Annual costs.** Tuition/fees: $3,219; $4,466 out-of-state. Per-credit charge: $96 in-state; $144 out-of-state. Tuition for Minnesota residents: $3,521. Tuition for South Dakota, Montana, and Canadian residents: $2,493. Room/board: $3,044. Books/supplies: $600. Personal expenses: $500.

**Financial aid. Need-based:** Need-based aid available for part-time students. Work-study available nights, weekends and for part-time students. **Non-need-based:** Scholarships awarded for academics, athletics.

**Application procedures. Admission:** No deadline. $35 fee. Application may be submitted online. Admission notification on a rolling basis. **Financial aid:** Priority date 3/15; no closing date. FAFSA required. Applicants notified on a rolling basis starting 5/15.

**Academics. Special study options:** Cooperative education, cross-registration, distance learning, double major, dual enrollment of high school students, internships, liberal arts/career combination, student-designed major. Bachelor's degree programs available on campus. License preparation in aviation, nursing, physical therapy. **Credit/placement by examination:** AP, CLEP, institutional tests. 15 credit hours maximum toward associate degree. **Support services:** GED preparation and test center, learning center, reduced course load, remedial instruction, study skills assistance, tutoring, writing center.

**Majors. Business:** Accounting technology, administrative services, entrepreneurial studies, marketing. **Computer sciences:** Data processing, system admin, systems analysis, vendor certification, web page design. **Education:** Teacher assistance. **Health:** Massage therapy, medical records technology, medical transcription, nursing (RN), physical therapy assistant. **Liberal arts:** Arts/sciences. **Mechanic/repair:** Automotive, diesel. **Transportation:** Airline/commercial pilot.

**Most popular majors.** Health sciences 37%, liberal arts 51%.

**Computing on campus.** 70 workstations in library, computer center. Dormitories linked to campus network. Online course registration, online library, wireless network available.

**Student life. Freshman orientation:** Available. Preregistration for classes offered. Activities take place on the day prior to first day of fall semester. **Housing:** Coed dorms, single-sex dorms, apartments, substance-free housing available. $100 fully refundable deposit. Separate housing for athletes. **Activities:** Choral groups, drama, literary magazine, music ensembles, student government, Campus Crusade.

**Athletics.** NJCAA. **Intercollegiate:** Baseball M, basketball, volleyball W. **Intramural:** Basketball, softball, volleyball. **Team name:** Tetons.

**Student services.** Alcohol/substance abuse counseling, career counseling, student employment services, financial aid counseling, minority student services, personal counseling, placement for graduates, veterans' counselor. **Physically disabled:** Services for visually, speech, hearing impaired. **Transfer:** Pre-admission transcript evaluation for new students. Transfer adviser, college fairs on campus for students transferring to 4-year colleges.

**Contact.** E-mail: wsc.admission@wsc.nodak.edu
Phone: (701) 774-4210 Toll-free number: (888) 863-9455
Fax: (701) 774-4211
Keith Dawson, Director for Admission & Records, Williston State College, 1410 University Avenue, Williston, ND 58802-1326

# Ohio

## Academy of Court Reporting: Akron
### Akron, Ohio
**CB code: 3250**

- For-profit 2-year college of court reporting
- Commuter campus in small city

**General.** Accredited by ACICS. **Location:** 30 miles from Cleveland. **Calendar:** Continuous.

**Annual costs/financial aid.** Books/supplies: $1,500. Personal expenses: $1,000.

**Contact.** Phone: (330) 867-4030
Director of Admissions, 2930 West Market Street, Akron, OH 44333

## Academy of Court Reporting: Cincinnati
### Cincinnati, Ohio

- For-profit 2-year business college
- Large city

**General.** Accredited by ACICS. **Calendar:** Quarter.

**Contact.** Phone: (513) 723-0520
830 Main Street, Suite 1000, Cincinnati, OH 45202

## Academy of Court Reporting: Cleveland
### Cleveland, Ohio
**CB code: 2173**

- For-profit 2-year technical college
- Commuter campus in very large city

**General.** Accredited by ACICS. **Calendar:** Quarter.

**Annual costs/financial aid.** Books/supplies: $1,500. Need-based financial aid available to full-time and part-time students.

**Contact.** Phone: (216) 861-3222
Director of Admissions, 614 Superior Avenue NW, Cleveland, OH 44113

## Academy of Court Reporting: Columbus
### Columbus, Ohio
**CB code: 3344**

- For-profit 2-year junior college
- Commuter campus in very large city

**General.** Accredited by ACICS. **Calendar:** Continuous.

**Annual costs/financial aid.** Books/supplies: $1,500.

**Contact.** Phone: (614) 221-7770
Director of Admissions, 150 East Gay Street, 15th Floor, Columbus, OH 43215

## Akron Institute
### Akron, Ohio
### www.akroninstitute.com

- For-profit 2-year technical college
- Commuter campus in small city

**General.** Accredited by ACCSCT. **Location:** 3 miles from downtown. **Calendar:** Semester.

**Annual costs/financial aid.** Tuition/fees (2007-2008): $13,525.

**Contact.** Phone: (330) 724-1600
Director of Admissions, 1600 South Arlington Street, Suite 100, Akron, OH 44306-3958

## Antonelli College
### Cincinnati, Ohio
### www.antonellic.com
**CB code: 0611**

- For-profit 2-year visual arts and technical college
- Commuter campus in large city

**General.** Founded in 1947. Accredited by ACCSCT. **Location:** 55 miles from Dayton, 90 miles from Lexington, Kentucky. **Calendar:** Quarter.

**Annual costs/financial aid.** Tuition and fees vary by program. Quoted tuition is an average.

**Contact.** Phone: (513) 241-4338
Registrar, 124 East Seventh Street, Cincinnati, OH 45202

## Art Institute of Cincinnati
### Cincinnati, Ohio
### www.theartinstituteofcincinnati.com
**CB code: 3181**

- For-profit 2-year visual arts college
- Commuter campus in large city
- Application essay, interview required

**General.** Accredited by ACCSCT. **Enrollment:** 75 degree-seeking undergraduates. **Degrees:** 32 associate awarded. **Location:** 12 miles from downtown. **Calendar:** Quarter. **Full-time faculty:** 8 total. **Part-time faculty:** 5 total.

**Basis for selection.** Admission determined by applicant's artistic ability. Portfolio, letter of recommendation from art teacher required. **Home-schooled:** Portfolio presentation of at least 10 pieces of art with variety of media and subject matter.

**High school preparation.** Required and recommended units include English 2-3, mathematics 1, social studies 1, history 1, science 1 and foreign language 1.

**2007-2008 Annual costs.** Tuition/fees: $13,147. Books/supplies: $1,515.

**Financial aid. Non-need-based:** Scholarships awarded for academics, art.

**Application procedures. Admission:** Closing date 8/30 (receipt date). $100 fee. Application must be submitted on paper. Admission notification on a rolling basis. **Financial aid:** No deadline. FAFSA required. Applicants notified on a rolling basis starting 9/1; must reply within 1 week(s) of notification.

**Academics. Credit/placement by examination:** CLEP. **Support services:** Study skills assistance.

**Majors. Computer sciences:** Computer graphics. **Visual/performing arts:** Design.

**Computing on campus.** Online library, student web hosting available.

**Student life. Freshman orientation:** Mandatory.

**Student services.** Financial aid counseling, personal counseling, placement for graduates. **Transfer:** Pre-admission transcript evaluation for new students.

**Contact.** E-mail: aic@theartinstituteofcincinnati.com
Phone: (513) 751-1206 Fax: (513) 751-1209
Cyndi Mendell, Vice President, Admissions, Art Institute of Cincinnati, 1171 East Kemper Road, Cincinnati, OH 45246

## Art Institute of Ohio: Cincinnati
### Cincinnati, Ohio
### www.artinstitutes.edu/cincinnati/

- For-profit 2-year culinary school, branch campus, visual arts and technical college
- Very large city
- Application essay, interview required

**General.** Regionally accredited; also accredited by ACICS. **Enrollment:** 569 degree-seeking undergraduates. **Degrees:** 82 associate awarded. **Calendar:** Quarter, extensive summer session. **Full-time faculty:** 7 total; 14% have terminal degrees, 29% women. **Part-time faculty:** 58 total; 7% minority, 53% women. **Class size:** 62% < 20, 38% 20-39, less than 1% 40-49.

**Student profile.** Among degree-seeking undergraduates, 100% enrolled in a vocational program, 6% already have a bachelor's degree or higher, 161 enrolled as first-time, first-year students.

| | | | |
|---|---|---|---|
| Part-time: | 31% | Asian American: | 3% |
| Women: | 65% | Hispanic American: | 2% |
| African American: | 24% | Native American: | 1% |

**Basis for selection.** Open admission. Application essay required. Application essay required. **Homeschooled:** Transcript of courses and grades required.

**2007-2008 Annual costs.** Books/supplies: $2,353. Personal expenses: $7,453.

**Application procedures. Admission:** No deadline. $50 fee, may be waived for applicants with need. Application must be submitted on paper. Admission notification on a rolling basis.

**Academics. Special study options:** Distance learning. **Credit/placement by examination:** CLEP, SAT, ACT, institutional tests. 8 credit hours maximum toward associate degree. **Support services:** Reduced course load, remedial instruction, tutoring.

**Majors. Business:** Fashion. **Personal/culinary services:** Chef training. **Visual/performing arts:** Cinematography, graphic design, interior design, multimedia.

**Most popular majors.** Visual/performing arts 96%.

**Student life. Freshman orientation:** Available. **Housing:** $200 partly refundable deposit, deadline 9/7.

**Contact.** E-mail: dichardson@aii.edu
Don Richardson, Director of Admissions, Art Institute of Ohio: Cincinnati, 8845 Governor's Hill Drive, Suite 100, Cincinnati, OH 45249-3317

## ATS Institute of Technology
### Highland Heights, Ohio
### www.atsinstitute.com

- For-profit 2-year nursing and technical college
- Very large city

**General.** Accredited by ACICS. **Calendar:** Quarter.

**Annual costs/financial aid.** Tuition and fees vary by program. Practical nursing program: $9,570 per year; $224 testing fee; $20 malpractice insurance fee; $60 computer lab fee; $150 clinical fee; additional fees for uniforms, books and supplies. Books/supplies: $900.

**Contact.** Phone: (440) 449-1700
Academic Director, 325 Alpha Park, Highland Heights, OH 44143

## Aultman College of Nursing and Health Sciences
### Canton, Ohio
### www.aultmancollege.org

- Private 2-year health science and nursing college
- Small city
- SAT or ACT required

**General.** Candidate for regional accreditation. **Enrollment:** 220 degree-seeking undergraduates. **Degrees:** 25 associate awarded. **Calendar:** Semester, limited summer session. **Full-time faculty:** 12 total. **Part-time faculty:** 1 total.

**Basis for selection.** Academic GPA and test scores very important.

**2007-2008 Annual costs.** Tuition/fees: $11,925.

**2006-2007 Financial aid. Need-based:** 72% of total undergraduate aid awarded as scholarships/grants, 28% as loans/jobs.

**Application procedures. Admission:** Closing date 8/1. $30 fee. **Financial aid:** Priority date 5/1, closing date 10/1.

**Academics. Credit/placement by examination:** CLEP.

**Majors. Health:** Nursing (RN).

**Student life. Activities:** Student newspaper.

**Contact.** E-mail: mspeedy@aultman.com
Phone: (330) 363-5075
Michelle Speedy, Admissions Director, Aultman College of Nursing and Health Sciences, 2600 Sixth St. SW, Canton, OH 44710

## Belmont Technical College
### St. Clairsville, Ohio
### www.btc.edu
### CB code: 1072

- Public 2-year community and technical college
- Commuter campus in small town
- Interview required

**General.** Founded in 1969. Regionally accredited. **Enrollment:** 975 degree-seeking undergraduates. **Degrees:** 221 associate awarded. **Location:** 15 miles from Wheeling, West Virginia. **Calendar:** Quarter, limited summer session. **Full-time faculty:** 45 total. **Part-time faculty:** 120 total. **Class size:** 79% < 20, 20% 20-39, less than 1% 40-49, less than 1% 50-99.

**Student profile.**

| | | | |
|---|---|---|---|
| Out-of-state: | 15% | 25 or older: | 45% |

**Transfer out. Colleges most students transferred to 2007:** Wheeling Jesuit University, Ohio University Eastern Campus, West Liberty State College.

**Basis for selection.** Open admission, but selective for some programs. Admission to registered nursing and LPN programs predicated on completion of remediation with grade of C or better and completion of selected general courses with C or better, based on ACCUPLACER placement test scores. Applicants for paramedic program must take admissions test on campus. ACT scores accepted for placement if provided. Interview required for nursing and paramedic applicants after admission to program, recommended for all others. **Homeschooled:** State high school equivalency certificate required.

**2007-2008 Annual costs.** Tuition/fees: $3,784; $6,585 out-of-state. Per-credit charge: $61 in-state; $123 out-of-state. Books/supplies: $600.

**Financial aid. Need-based:** Need-based aid available for part-time students. **Non-need-based:** Scholarships awarded for state residency.

**Application procedures. Admission:** No deadline. No application fee. Application may be submitted online. Admission notification on a rolling basis. **Financial aid:** No deadline. FAFSA required. Applicants notified on a rolling basis starting 6/1; must reply within 2 week(s) of notification.

**Academics. Special study options:** Cross-registration, distance learning, double major, dual enrollment of high school students, internships, student-designed major, weekend college. **Credit/placement by examination:** CLEP, institutional tests. **Support services:** GED test center, learning center, reduced course load, remedial instruction, tutoring.

**Majors. Business:** General, accounting, office/clerical. **Computer sciences:** General, computer graphics, programming. **Education:** Early childhood. **Engineering:** Civil, electrical. **Health:** EMT paramedic, health services, medical assistant, nursing (RN). **Interdisciplinary:** Historic preservation. **Mechanic/repair:** Heating/ac/refrig.

**Most popular majors.** Business/marketing 15%, computer/information sciences 11%, engineering/engineering technologies 18%, health sciences 10%, security/protective services 6%, social sciences 7%.

**Computing on campus.** 250 workstations in library, computer center, student center. Wireless network available.

**Student life. Freshman orientation:** Available. Preregistration for classes offered. **Activities:** Phi Theta Kappa.

**Athletics. Intercollegiate:** Football (non-tackle).

**Student services.** Adult student services, career counseling, student employment services, financial aid counseling, on-campus daycare, personal counseling, placement for graduates, veterans' counselor. **Physically disabled:** Services for visually impaired, hearing impaired. **Transfer:** Pre-admission transcript evaluation for new students. Transfer adviser, college fairs on campus for students transferring to 4-year colleges.

**Contact.** E-mail: info@btc.edu
Phone: (740) 695-9500 ext. 1158 Fax: (740) 699-3049
Timothy Houston, Dean of Student Services, Belmont Technical College,
120 Fox Shannon Place, St. Clairsville, OH 43950

## Bohecker College
Ravenna, Ohio
www.boheckers.com          CB code: 2195

- For-profit 2-year business college
- Large town

**General.** Accredited by ACICS. **Calendar:** Five 10-week sessions per calendar year.

**Annual costs/financial aid.** Tuition/fees (2007-2008): $8,472. Need-based financial aid available to full-time and part-time students.

**Contact.** Phone: (330) 297-7319
Director of Admissions, 326 East Main Street, Ravenna, OH 44266

## Bowling Green State University: Firelands College
Huron, Ohio
www.firelands.bgsu.edu          CB code: 0749

- Public 2-year branch campus college
- Commuter campus in small town

**General.** Founded in 1967. Regionally accredited. **Enrollment:** 1,837 degree-seeking undergraduates. **Degrees:** 155 associate awarded. **Location:** 50 miles from Cleveland, 60 miles from Toledo. **Calendar:** Semester, limited summer session. **Full-time faculty:** 43 total; 56% have terminal degrees, 12% minority, 51% women. **Part-time faculty:** 65 total; 15% have terminal degrees, 3% minority, 54% women. **Class size:** 54% < 20, 45% 20-39, less than 1% 40-49. **Special facilities:** Arboretum.

**Basis for selection.** Open admission. ACT or SAT scores recommended of students who graduated from high school within last 3 years. However, no minimum score required. If ACT or SAT not available, COMPASS test administered to determine placement. **Homeschooled:** Home school program must be accredited.

**High school preparation.** 16 units recommended. Recommended units include English 4, mathematics 3, social studies 3, science 3 (laboratory 2) and foreign language 2. One visual or performing arts recommended.

**2007-2008 Annual costs.** Tuition/fees: $4,228; $11,536 out-of-state. Books/supplies: $1,140. Personal expenses: $2,600.

**2006-2007 Financial aid.** All financial aid based on need. 242 full-time freshmen applied for aid; 209 were judged to have need; 201 of these received aid. Average need met was 59%. Average scholarship/grant was $4,484; average loan $3,782. 36% of total undergraduate aid awarded as scholarships/grants, 64% as loans/jobs. Need-based aid available for part-time students. Work-study available for part-time students. **Additional information:** Scholarship application deadline May 1. Technology computer loan program available. Based on need, students may receive computer on semester by semester loan basis.

**Application procedures. Admission:** Priority date 2/1; deadline 7/15 (receipt date). $40 fee, may be waived for applicants with need. Application may be submitted online. Admission notification on a rolling basis. **Financial aid:** Priority date 3/1; no closing date. FAFSA required. Applicants notified on a rolling basis starting 4/15; must reply within 2 week(s) of notification.

**Academics.** Upper-division program in nursing available for registered nurses who hold associate degree or have completed 3-year diploma program. Satellite associate degree registered nursing program from Lorain County Community College. Upper division programs available in liberal studies, general studies in business, applied health science, early childhood studies, criminal justice, manufacturing technology, visual communication technology. **Special study options:** Cross-registration, distance learning, dual enrollment of high school students, independent study, internships, liberal arts/career combination, student-designed major, teacher certification program. Satellite associate degree registered nurse program from Lorain County Community College. Bachelor's degree programs available on campus. License preparation in nursing. **Credit/placement by examination:** AP, CLEP, institutional tests. 15 credit hours maximum toward associate degree. **Support services:** Learning center, reduced course load, remedial instruction, tutoring.

**Majors. Business:** General, accounting, administrative services, business admin, operations. **Communications technology:** General. **Computer sciences:** Programming. **Engineering:** Electrical. **Engineering technology:** General, computer, electrical, manufacturing. **Health:** Medical radiologic technology/radiation therapy, medical records technology, nursing (RN), respiratory therapy technology. **Interdisciplinary:** Biological/physical sciences. **Liberal arts:** Arts/sciences. **Protective services:** Criminal justice. **Public administration:** Human services. **Social sciences:** General.

**Most popular majors.** Business/marketing 10%, health sciences 25%, liberal arts 21%.

**Computing on campus.** 300 workstations in library, computer center. Commuter students can connect to campus network. Online library, helpline, wireless network available.

**Student life. Freshman orientation:** Available. **Activities:** Drama, student government, student newspaper, allied health club, Campus Fellowship, theater group, writing center, Model United Nations, Peace and Justice club, virtual communication technology organization, women's resource group.

**Athletics. Intramural:** Basketball, football (non-tackle) M, table tennis, volleyball.

**Student services.** Adult student services, career counseling, student employment services, financial aid counseling, personal counseling, placement for graduates. **Physically disabled:** Services for visually, hearing impaired. **Transfer:** Transfer adviser, college fairs on campus for students transferring to 4-year colleges.

**Contact.** E-mail: fireadm@bgsu.edu
Phone: (419) 433-5560 ext. 20607 Fax: (419) 372-0604
Debralee Divers, Director of Admissions and Financial Aid, Bowling Green State University: Firelands College, One University Drive, Huron, OH 44839

## Bradford School
Columbus, Ohio
www.bradfordschoolcolumbus.edu          CB code: 3952

- For-profit 2-year business and technical college
- Commuter campus in very large city

**General.** Founded in 1911. Accredited by ACICS. **Enrollment:** 473 degree-seeking undergraduates. **Degrees:** 87 associate awarded. **Calendar:** Semester, extensive summer session. **Full-time faculty:** 16 total. **Part-time faculty:** 11 total.

**Basis for selection.** Interview required to ensure interest in business or health care education.

**2007-2008 Annual costs.** Tuition/fees: $12,640. Room only: $5,800.

**Application procedures. Admission:** No deadline. $50 fee. Application may be submitted online. Admission notification on a rolling basis.

**Academics. Credit/placement by examination:** CLEP.

**Majors. Business:** Accounting, office management. **Computer sciences:** LAN/WAN management, programming. **Health:** Veterinary technology/assistant. **Legal studies:** Legal secretary, paralegal.

**Student life. Housing:** Single-sex dorms available.

**Student services.** Career counseling, financial aid counseling, placement for graduates.

**Contact.** E-mail: bradfordcols@bradfordschoolcolumbus.edu
Phone: (614) 416-6200 Toll-free number: (800) 678-7981
Fax: (614) 416-6210
Director of Admissions, Bradford School, 2469 Stelzer Road, Columbus, OH 43219

## Brown Mackie College: Akron
Akron, Ohio
www.brownmackie.edu          CB code: 3266

- For-profit 2-year business college
- Commuter campus in small city

**General.** Accredited by ACICS. **Calendar:** Quarter.

**Annual costs/financial aid.** Books/supplies: $1,000. Personal expenses: $2,664.

**Contact.** Phone: (330) 733-8766
Director of Admissions, 2791 Mogadore Road, Akron, OH 44312

## Brown Mackie College: Cincinnati
Cincinnati, Ohio
www.brownmackie.edu                                   CB code: 0297

▶ For-profit 2-year business and nursing college
▶ Commuter campus in large city

**General.** Founded in 1927. Accredited by ACICS. 4 branch campuses in Akron, Cincinnati, Findlay, and Ft. Mitchell, Kentucky. **Enrollment:** 1,496 degree-seeking undergraduates. **Degrees:** 257 associate awarded. **Location:** 10 miles from downtown. **Calendar:** Quarter, extensive summer session. **Full-time faculty:** 25 total. **Part-time faculty:** 30 total. **Class size:** 45% < 20, 55% 20-39.

**Basis for selection.** Open admission, but selective for some programs. Must have high school diploma or GED. Computer networking program admission based on previous college and/or work history. Students entering Computer Networking (MCSE) program who do not have associate degree required to have 21 ACT composite score or 1000 SAT composite score (exclusive of Writing). Interview required for some students.

**2007-2008 Annual costs.** Books/supplies: $675.

**Financial aid.** All financial aid based on need. Need-based aid available for part-time students.

**Application procedures. Admission:** No deadline. No application fee. Admission notification on a rolling basis. **Financial aid:** Priority date 3/15; no closing date. FAFSA, institutional form required. Applicants notified on a rolling basis.

**Academics. Special study options:** Cooperative education, independent study. Externship. **Credit/placement by examination:** CLEP, institutional tests. 24 credit hours maximum toward associate degree. **Support services:** Learning center, remedial instruction, tutoring.

**Majors. Business:** Accounting, management science. **Computer sciences:** Computer science. **Engineering technology:** Drafting. **Health:** Health care admin, medical assistant, optician, pharmacy assistant, surgical technology.

**Most popular majors.** Business/marketing 39%, computer/information sciences 21%, health sciences 16%.

**Computing on campus.** 142 workstations in library, computer center.

**Student life. Freshman orientation:** Mandatory.

**Student services.** Career counseling, student employment services, financial aid counseling, personal counseling, placement for graduates, veterans' counselor. **Transfer:** Pre-admission transcript evaluation for new students. Transfer adviser for students transferring to 4-year colleges.

**Contact.** Phone: (513) 771-2424 Toll-free number: (800) 888-1445
Fax: (513) 771-3413
Jodi Marlow, Director of Admissions, Brown Mackie College: Cincinnati, 1011 Glendale-Milford Road, Cincinnati, OH 45215

## Brown Mackie College: Findlay
Findlay, Ohio
www.brownmackie.edu

▶ For-profit 2-year business and junior college
▶ Commuter campus in small city
▶ Interview required

**General.** Accredited by ACICS. **Enrollment:** 202 degree-seeking undergraduates; 521 non-degree-seeking students. **Degrees:** 53 associate awarded. **Location:** 20 miles Bowling Green, 48 miles from Toledo. **Calendar:** Quarter, extensive summer session. **Full-time faculty:** 13 total; 85% women. **Part-time faculty:** 69 total; 3% have terminal degrees, 4% minority, 71% women. **Class size:** 74% < 20, 26% 20-39.

**Student profile.** Among degree-seeking undergraduates, 1% already have a bachelor's degree or higher, 74 enrolled as first-time, first-year students.

| | | | |
|---|---|---|---|
| Part-time: | 50% | Asian American: | 3% |
| Out-of-state: | 31% | Hispanic American: | 7% |
| Women: | 96% | Native American: | 1% |
| African American: | 37% | 25 or older: | 72% |

**Basis for selection.** Open admission. **Homeschooled:** State high school equivalency certificate required.

**2008-2009 Annual costs.** Tuition/fees (projected): $12,880. Per-credit charge: $260. Books/supplies: $1,850. Personal expenses: $2,700.

**2006-2007 Financial aid. Need-based:** 73 full-time freshmen applied for aid; 71 were judged to have need; 71 of these received aid. Average need met was 50%. Average loan was $1,167. 56% of total undergraduate aid awarded as scholarships/grants, 44% as loans/jobs. Need-based aid available for part-time students. Work-study available nights, weekends and for part-time students. **Non-need-based:** Awarded to 464 full-time undergraduates, including 71 freshmen. Scholarships awarded for academics, state residency.

**Application procedures. Admission:** No deadline. No application fee. Admission notification on a rolling basis. **Financial aid:** No deadline. FAFSA required.

**Academics. Special study options:** License preparation in nursing. **Credit/placement by examination:** CLEP, institutional tests. **Support services:** Learning center, remedial instruction, study skills assistance, tutoring.

**Majors. Business:** Accounting technology, business admin, office technology. **Health:** Health care admin, medical assistant, pharmacy assistant, surgical technology. **Legal studies:** Paralegal. **Protective services:** Law enforcement admin.

**Most popular majors.** Business/marketing 23%, health sciences 58%, legal studies 11%, security/protective services 8%.

**Computing on campus.** 10 workstations in library. Commuter students can connect to campus network.

**Student life. Freshman orientation:** Mandatory. **Activities:** Student newspaper.

**Student services.** Career counseling, student employment services, financial aid counseling, placement for graduates. **Physically disabled:** Services for visually impaired.

**Contact.** Phone: (419) 423-2211 Toll-free number: (800) 842-3687
Fax: (419) 423-0725
Thomas Smith, Admissions Director, Brown Mackie College: Findlay, 1700 Fostoria Avenue, Suite 100, Findlay, OH 45840

## Brown Mackie College: North Canton
Canton, Ohio

▶ For-profit 2-year career college
▶ Commuter campus in small city
▶ Interview required

**General.** Accredited by ACICS. **Enrollment:** 1,090 degree-seeking undergraduates. **Degrees:** 230 associate awarded. **Calendar:** Continuous. **Full-time faculty:** 14 total. **Part-time faculty:** 59 total.

**Basis for selection.** Open admission. **Adult students:** SAT/ACT scores not required. **Homeschooled:** Transcript of courses and grades required.

**2007-2008 Annual costs.** Tuition $208 per credit hour; fees $15 per credit hour.

**Financial aid. Need-based:** Work-study available nights.

**Application procedures. Admission:** No deadline. No application fee. Admission notification on a rolling basis. **Financial aid:** FAFSA required.

**Academics. Special study options:** License preparation in nursing. **Credit/placement by examination:** CLEP. **Support services:** Remedial instruction, tutoring.

**Majors. Business:** Accounting, business admin. **Computer sciences:** Networking. **Health:** Health care admin, office assistant, pharmacy assistant, surgical technology. **Legal studies:** Paralegal. **Protective services:** Criminal justice.

**Most popular majors.** Business/marketing 18%, computer/information sciences 18%, health sciences 40%, legal studies 18%.

**Computing on campus.** 25 workstations in library.

**Student life. Freshman orientation:** Mandatory.

**Contact.** Phone: (330) 494-1214 Fax: (330) 494-8112 Jack Kempt, Director of Admissions, Brown Mackie College: North Canton, 4300 Munson Street Northwest, Canton, OH 44718-3674

## Bryant & Stratton College: Cleveland
### Cleveland, Ohio
www.bryantstratton.edu                    CB code: 0814

- For-profit 2-year technical college
- Commuter campus in very large city
- Interview required

**General.** Founded in 1929. Regionally accredited. **Enrollment:** 248 full-time, degree-seeking students. **Degrees:** 4 bachelor's, 40 associate awarded. **Location:** Downtown. **Calendar:** Trimester, extensive summer session. **Full-time faculty:** 15 total. **Part-time faculty:** 30 total. **Class size:** 79% < 20, 21% 20-39.

**Transfer out. Colleges most students transferred to 2007:** ITT Technical Institute, Cuyahoga Community College, Myer University, Cleveland State University.

**Basis for selection.** Institutional test scores and interview most important. Passing scores on entrance exams required. CPAT entrance exam required. If ACT or SAT scores high enough, may be submitted in lieu of CPAT.

**2007-2008 Annual costs.** Tuition/fees: $13,080. Per-credit charge: $436. Books/supplies: $1,800. Personal expenses: $1,530.

**Financial aid. Need-based:** Need-based aid available for part-time students. Work-study available nights. **Non-need-based:** Scholarships awarded for academics.

**Application procedures. Admission:** No deadline. $25 fee. Application may be submitted online. Admission notification on a rolling basis. **Financial aid:** No deadline. FAFSA, institutional form required. Applicants notified on a rolling basis starting 5/1; must reply within 2 week(s) of notification.

**Academics. Special study options:** Distance learning, double major, independent study, internships, liberal arts/career combination. Bachelor's degree programs available on campus. **Credit/placement by examination:** AP, CLEP, institutional tests. 26 credit hours maximum toward associate degree. **Support services:** Learning center, reduced course load, remedial instruction, study skills assistance, tutoring, writing center.

**Majors. Business:** General, administrative services. **Computer sciences:** Information technology. **Engineering technology:** CAD/CADD, electrical.

**Most popular majors.** Architecture 38%, computer/information sciences 38%, engineering/engineering technologies 25%.

**Computing on campus.** 106 workstations in library, computer center. Online library available.

**Student life. Freshman orientation:** Available. Preregistration for classes offered. 3-hour session 1 week prior to start of semester. **Activities:** Literary magazine, student government, student newspaper.

**Athletics. Intramural:** Softball. **Team name:** Bobcats.

**Student services.** Adult student services, alcohol/substance abuse counseling, career counseling, student employment services, financial aid counseling, personal counseling, placement for graduates. **Transfer:** Pre-admission transcript evaluation for new students. Transfer adviser, college fairs on campus for students transferring to 4-year colleges.

**Contact.** E-mail: stkampa@bryantstratton.edu Phone: (216) 771-1700 Fax: (216) 771-7787 Shawn Kampa, Director of Admissions, Bryant & Stratton College: Cleveland, 1700 East 13th Street, Cleveland, OH 44114-3203

## Central Ohio Technical College
### Newark, Ohio
www.cotc.edu                    CB code: 7331

- Public 2-year technical college
- Commuter campus in large town

**General.** Founded in 1971. Regionally accredited. Campus shared with Ohio State University: Newark campus. Off-campus evening classes are taught in Mount Vernon and Coshocton. Students can take classes at Ohio State Newark. **Enrollment:** 3,105 undergraduates. **Degrees:** 383 associate awarded. **Location:** 45 miles from Columbus. **Calendar:** Quarter, limited summer session. **Full-time faculty:** 64 total. **Part-time faculty:** 206 total. **Class size:** 73% < 20, 26% 20-39, less than 1% 40-49.

**Student profile.**

| | | | |
|---|---|---|---|
| Out-of-state: | 1% | Live on campus: | 1% |
| 25 or older: | 52% | | |

**Transfer out. Colleges most students transferred to 2007:** Franklin University, Mount Vernon Nazarene, Ohio State University.

**Basis for selection.** Open admission, but selective for some programs. High ACT scores may replace COMPASS placement tests. **Homeschooled:** Degree-seeking applicants must be 18 years or older and meet minimum scores on the COTC COMPASS test or ACT or meet COTC waiver eligibility of all 3 COMPASS tests due to applicant transferring from another college. COMPASS scores must be at least 32 on writing, 62 on reading and 25 on pre-algebra test. ACT of at least 14 in English and 15 in Math.

**High school preparation.** 1 chemistry, 1 algebra and 1 biology required for medical sonography, nursing and surgical technology; 1 chemistry, 1 algebra, 1 math beyond algebra I, 1 biology required for radiographic.

**2007-2008 Annual costs.** Tuition/fees: $3,600; $6,300 out-of-state. Per-credit charge: $100 in-state; $175 out-of-state. Books/supplies: $1,251. Personal expenses: $2,178.

**Financial aid. Need-based:** Need-based aid available for part-time students. Work-study available nights, weekends and for part-time students. **Non-need-based:** Scholarships awarded for academics.

**Application procedures. Admission:** Priority date 6/15; no deadline. $20 fee, may be waived for applicants with need. Application may be submitted online. Admission notification on a rolling basis. **Financial aid:** Priority date 3/1; no closing date. FAFSA required. Applicants notified on a rolling basis starting 5/1; must reply within 3 week(s) of notification.

**Academics. Special study options:** Cooperative education, double major, dual enrollment of high school students, ESL, internships, weekend college. License preparation in nursing, paramedic, radiology. **Credit/placement by examination:** CLEP, IB, institutional tests. 55 credit hours maximum toward associate degree. **Support services:** Learning center, reduced course load, remedial instruction, study skills assistance, tutoring.

**Majors. Business:** Accounting, administrative services, business admin, human resources. **Communications technology:** Desktop publishing. **Computer sciences:** Applications programming, data entry, web page design. **Education:** Early childhood. **Engineering technology:** Architectural drafting, CAD/CADD, civil drafting, electrical, electromechanical. **Health:** Medical radiologic technology/radiation therapy, nursing (RN), sonography, surgical technology. **Protective services:** Criminal justice, forensics, law enforcement admin. **Public administration:** Human services, social work.

**Most popular majors.** Business/marketing 9%, health sciences 63%, public administration/social services 6%, security/protective services 7%.

**Computing on campus.** 40 workstations in library, computer center. Commuter students can connect to campus network. Online course registration, helpline, wireless network available.

**Student life. Freshman orientation:** Mandatory. Preregistration for classes offered. 3-hour program. **Housing:** Apartments available. **Activities:** Choral groups, drama, music ensembles, student government, student newspaper, Phi Theta Kappa, theatre arts association, student nurses organization, criminal justice club, rad tech club, Habitat for Humanity College Chapter, ski club, students in free enterpise.

**Athletics.** NJCAA. **Intercollegiate:** Baseball M, basketball, cross-country, golf, soccer M, softball W, volleyball. **Intramural:** Badminton, basketball, bowling, football (non-tackle), softball, table tennis, tennis, volleyball.

**Student services.** Career counseling, student employment services, financial aid counseling, minority student services, on-campus daycare, personal counseling, placement for graduates, veterans' counselor. **Physically disabled:** Services for visually, speech, hearing impaired. **Transfer:** Transfer adviser, college fairs on campus for students transferring to 4-year colleges.

**Contact.** E-mail: kquick@cotc.tec.oh.us
Phone: (740) 366-9222 Fax: (740) 366-5047
John Merrin, Coordinator of Admissions, Central Ohio Technical College, 1179 University Drive, Newark, OH 43055

## Chatfield College
### St. Martin, Ohio
www.chatfield.edu                    CB code: 1143

◆ Private 2-year community and liberal arts college affiliated with Roman Catholic Church
◆ Commuter campus in rural community

**General.** Founded in 1970. Regionally accredited. **Enrollment:** 218 degree-seeking undergraduates. **Degrees:** 36 associate awarded. **Location:** 40 miles from Cincinnati. **Calendar:** Semester, limited summer session. **Full-time faculty:** 1 total. **Part-time faculty:** 61 total. **Class size:** 95% < 20, 5% 20-39.

**Transfer out.** Colleges most students transferred to 2007: Wilmington College, Xavier University, Mount St. Joseph, Northern Kentucky University.

**Basis for selection.** Open admission. Interview recommended. **Homeschooled:** Official documentation of home school program required.

**High school preparation.** 16 units recommended. Recommended units include English 4, mathematics 3, social studies 3, science 3 and foreign language 2. Computer science recommended.

**2007-2008 Annual costs.** Tuition/fees: $9,190. Per-credit charge: $295. Books/supplies: $650. Personal expenses: $1,922.

**Financial aid. Need-based:** Need-based aid available for part-time students. Work-study available for part-time students. **Non-need-based:** Scholarships awarded for academics, leadership. **Additional information:** Institutional grants/scholarships given primarily to first-year students to reduce debt load during initial year.

**Application procedures. Admission:** No deadline. $10 fee. Application may be submitted online. Admission notification on a rolling basis. **Financial aid:** Priority date 4/25, closing date 8/3. FAFSA, institutional form required. Applicants notified on a rolling basis starting 4/1; must reply within 2 week(s) of notification.

**Academics. Special study options:** Cooperative education, cross-registration, dual enrollment of high school students, independent study, internships, liberal arts/career combination. Cooperative programs leading to bachelor's in business and liberal studies with 2 local institutions. Third-year option: student can complete junior year at school through arrangements with several regional 4-year colleges. **Credit/placement by examination:** CLEP, institutional tests. **Support services:** Learning center, remedial instruction, study skills assistance, tutoring, writing center.

**Majors. Business:** Business admin. **Education:** Early childhood. **Liberal arts:** Arts/sciences. **Public administration:** Human services.

**Computing on campus.** 26 workstations in library, computer center.

**Student life. Freshman orientation:** Available. **Activities:** Student newspaper.

**Student services.** Adult student services, career counseling, financial aid counseling, personal counseling. **Transfer:** Transfer adviser, college fairs on campus for students transferring to 4-year colleges.

**Contact.** E-mail: admissions@chatfield.edu
Phone: (513) 875-3344 Fax: (513) 875-3912
Anna Jones, Director of Advancement, Chatfield College, 20918 State Route 251, St. Martin, OH 45118

## Cincinnati State Technical and Community College
### Cincinnati, Ohio
www.cincinnatistate.edu                    CB code: 1984

◆ Public 2-year community and technical college
◆ Commuter campus in large city

**General.** Founded in 1966. Regionally accredited. **Enrollment:** 7,487 degree-seeking undergraduates; 1,020 non-degree-seeking students. **Degrees:** 1,001 associate awarded. **ROTC:** Army. **Location:** 5 miles from downtown. **Calendar:** Five 10-week terms. Extensive summer session. **Full-time faculty:** 175 total; 11% have terminal degrees, 15% minority, 56% women. **Part-time faculty:** 444 total. **Class size:** 63% < 20, 36% 20-39, less than 1% 40-49. **Special facilities:** Aviation maintenance facility, culinary facility, television studio.

**Student profile.** Among degree-seeking undergraduates, 16% enrolled in a transfer program, 84% enrolled in a vocational program, 5% already have a bachelor's degree or higher, 1,967 enrolled as first-time, first-year students.

| | | | |
|---|---|---|---|
| Part-time: | 56% | Asian American: | 1% |
| Out-of-state: | 11% | Hispanic American: | 1% |
| Women: | 54% | International: | 2% |
| African American: | 25% | 25 or older: | 45% |

**Transfer out.** 65% of students enrolled in the transfer program go on to 4-year colleges. **Colleges most students transferred to 2007:** University of Cincinnati, Northern Kentucky University, Wilmington College, College of Mount St. Joseph, Xavier University.

**Basis for selection.** Open admission, but selective for some programs. Health technology programs require biology and chemistry courses to have been taken in last 7 years. COMPASS test required for placement. **Homeschooled:** Statement describing homeschool structure and mission, transcript of courses and grades required.

**High school preparation.** Specific course prerequisites for some programs.

**2007-2008 Annual costs.** Tuition/fees: $3,867; $7,476 out-of-state. Per-credit charge: $80 in-state; $160 out-of-state. Books/supplies: $1,700. Personal expenses: $1,260.

**2006-2007 Financial aid. Need-based:** 81% of total undergraduate aid awarded as scholarships/grants, 19% as loans/jobs. Need-based aid available for part-time students. Work-study available nights, weekends and for part-time students. **Non-need-based:** Scholarships awarded for academics, athletics, state residency.

**Application procedures. Admission:** No deadline. No application fee. Application may be submitted online. Admission notification on a rolling basis. **Financial aid:** Priority date 2/15; no closing date. FAFSA required. Applicants notified on a rolling basis starting 3/15; must reply within 4 week(s) of notification.

**Academics. Special study options:** Cooperative education, cross-registration, distance learning, double major, dual enrollment of high school students, ESL, honors, independent study, internships, student-designed major. Bachelor's degree programs available on campus. License preparation in aviation, nursing, occupational therapy, paramedic, real estate. **Credit/placement by examination:** AP, CLEP, IB, institutional tests. 55 credit hours maximum toward associate degree. **Support services:** GED preparation and test center, reduced course load, remedial instruction, study skills assistance, tutoring, writing center.

**Majors. Agriculture:** Landscaping, turf management. **Business:** Accounting, accounting technology, business admin, executive assistant, finance, hotel/motel admin, international, marketing, office management, office/clerical, purchasing, real estate, restaurant/food services. **Communications technology:** Desktop publishing. **Computer sciences:** General, applications programming, networking. **Education:** Deaf/hearing impaired, early childhood. **Engineering technology:** Aerospace, architectural, automotive, biomedical, civil, computer, computer systems, construction, electrical, electromechanical, environmental, industrial, laser/optical, manufacturing, mechanical, occupational safety, plastics, surveying. **English:** Technical writing. **Family/consumer sciences:** Child care, institutional food production. **Foreign languages:** Sign language interpretation. **Health:** Clinical lab assistant, clinical lab technology, dietetic technician, EMT paramedic, massage therapy, medical records technology, nursing (RN), occupational therapy assistant, respiratory therapy technology, sonography, surgical technology, ward clerk. **Legal studies:** Legal secretary. **Liberal arts:** Arts/sciences. **Mechanic/repair:** Aircraft, automotive, computer. **Personal/culinary services:** Chef training, restaurant/catering. **Production:** Machine tool. **Protective services:** Firefighting. **Visual/performing arts:** Cinematography, commercial/advertising art.

**Most popular majors.** Business/marketing 19%, engineering/engineering technologies 19%, family/consumer sciences 6%, health sciences 21%, liberal arts 17%.

**Computing on campus.** 175 workstations in library, computer center, student center. Commuter students can connect to campus network. Online course registration, online library, helpline, wireless network available.

**Student life. Freshman orientation:** Available. Preregistration for classes offered. 3-4 hour programs held during the day and in the evening before start of classes. **Activities:** Drama, student government, TV station, United African American Association, international students, Phi Theta Kappa, adult learners on campus, environmental club, students in free enterprise.

**Athletics.** NJCAA. **Intercollegiate:** Basketball, golf, soccer. **Team name:** Surge.

**Student services.** Adult student services, alcohol/substance abuse counseling, career counseling, services for economically disadvantaged, student employment services, financial aid counseling, on-campus daycare, personal counseling, veterans' counselor. **Physically disabled:** Services for visually, speech, hearing impaired. **Transfer:** College fairs on campus for students transferring to 4-year colleges.

**Contact.** E-mail: adm@cincinnatistate.edu
Phone: (513) 861-7700 Fax: (513) 569-1562
Gabriele Boeckermann, Director of Admission, Cincinnati State Technical and Community College, 3520 Central Parkway, Cincinnati, OH 45223-2690

## Clark State Community College
### Springfield, Ohio
**www.clarkstate.edu**  CB code: 0777

- Public 2-year community college
- Commuter campus in small city

**General.** Founded in 1966. Regionally accredited. **Enrollment:** 1,249 full-time, degree-seeking students. **Degrees:** 337 associate awarded. **Location:** 30 miles from Dayton, 45 miles from Columbus. **Calendar:** Quarter, limited summer session. **Full-time faculty:** 65 total. **Part-time faculty:** 440 total. **Special facilities:** Performing arts center.

**Student profile.** Among full-time, degree-seeking students, 864 transferred in from other institutions.

| | | | |
|---|---|---|---|
| Out-of-state: | 1% | Hispanic American: | 1% |
| African American: | 11% | 25 or older: | 45% |
| Asian American: | 1% | | |

**Transfer out. Colleges most students transferred to 2007:** Wright State University.

**Basis for selection.** Open admission, but selective for some programs. Nursing and allied health applicants must have high school chemistry; allied health must also have algebra or equivalent with grade of 2.0 or better. Mathematics placement test with score of 12 or better required for nursing.

**High school preparation.** 15 units recommended. Recommended units include English 4, mathematics 3, social studies 3, science 3 and foreign language 2. Chemistry required for nursing and medical technology. Algebra required for medical technology. 2 units mathematics required for engineering programs.

**2007-2008 Annual costs.** Tuition/fees: $3,684; $6,828 out-of-state. Per-credit charge: $78 in-state; $143 out-of-state. Books/supplies: $800. Personal expenses: $550.

**Financial aid. Need-based:** Work-study available nights, weekends and for part-time students.

**Application procedures. Admission:** No deadline. $15 fee. Application may be submitted online. Admission notification on a rolling basis. Early admission open to high school juniors and seniors. Placement test and high school approval required. High school GPA must be 3.0 or higher. **Financial aid:** Priority date 6/15; no closing date. FAFSA required. Applicants notified on a rolling basis.

**Academics. Special study options:** Accelerated study, cooperative education, cross-registration, distance learning, double major, dual enrollment of high school students, honors, independent study, internships, liberal arts/career combination, student-designed major, study abroad, weekend college. Bachelor's degree programs available on campus. License preparation in nursing, paramedic, physical therapy, real estate. **Credit/placement by examination:** AP, CLEP, institutional tests. 24 credit hours maximum toward associate degree. **Support services:** Learning center, pre-admission summer program, reduced course load, remedial instruction, tutoring, writing center.

**Majors. Agriculture:** Business, horticulture. **Business:** Accounting technology, business admin, human resources, logistics, marketing. **Computer**

**sciences:** Applications programming, networking. **Education:** Early childhood, kindergarten/preschool. **Engineering:** Agricultural. **Engineering technology:** Drafting, industrial, mechanical. **Health:** Clinical lab technology, EMT paramedic, medical assistant, medical secretary, nursing (RN), physical therapy assistant. **Legal studies:** Court reporting, legal secretary. **Liberal arts:** Arts/sciences. **Protective services:** Corrections, law enforcement admin. **Public administration:** Social work. **Visual/performing arts:** Commercial/advertising art.

**Most popular majors.** Business/marketing 18%, health sciences 30%, liberal arts 24%, public administration/social services 8%, security/protective services 7%.

**Computing on campus.** Commuter students can connect to campus network. Online course registration, online library, helpline, wireless network available.

**Student life. Freshman orientation:** Available. Preregistration for classes offered. **Activities:** Campus ministries, choral groups, dance, drama, student government, student newspaper, professional and technological fraternities and sororities, minority student forum, Phi Theta Kappa, social work club.

**Athletics.** NJCAA. **Intercollegiate:** Baseball M, basketball, softball W, volleyball W. **Intramural:** Basketball, volleyball. **Team name:** Eagles.

**Student services.** Campus ministries, career counseling, services for economically disadvantaged, student employment services, financial aid counseling, health services, minority student services, on-campus daycare, personal counseling, placement for graduates, veterans' counselor. **Physically disabled:** Services for visually, speech, hearing impaired. **Transfer:** Transfer adviser, college fairs on campus for students transferring to 4-year colleges.

**Contact.** Phone: (937) 328-6028 Fax: (937) 328-3853
Corey Holliday, Director of Admissions, Clark State Community College, Box 570, Springfield, OH 45501-0570

## Cleveland Institute of Electronics
### Cleveland, Ohio
**www.cie-wc.edu**  CB code: 0802

- For-profit 2-year technical college
- Very large city

**General.** Founded in 1934. Accredited by DETC. Curriculum completed entirely through distance learning with no classroom attendance. **Enrollment:** 2,002 undergraduates. **Degrees:** 69 associate awarded. **Calendar:** Continuous. **Full-time faculty:** 5 total. **Part-time faculty:** 75 total.

**Basis for selection.** Open admission.

**2008-2009 Annual costs.** Tuition/fees (projected): $3,540. The associate degree tuition is $1770 per 6 month term. Books/supplies: $675.

**Application procedures. Admission:** No deadline. No application fee. Application may be submitted online. Admission notification on a rolling basis. High school students permitted to enroll with signed approval of parents and guidance counselors (if students are minors). **Financial aid:** No deadline.

**Academics. Special study options:** Accelerated study, distance learning, independent study. **Credit/placement by examination:** CLEP.

**Majors. Engineering technology:** Electrical. **Mechanic/repair:** Electronics/electrical.

**Computing on campus.** Online course registration available.

**Student life. Activities:** Student newspaper.

**Student services.** Student employment services, veterans' counselor.

**Contact.** E-mail: instruct@cie-wc.edu
Phone: (216) 781-9400 Toll-free number: (800) 243-6446
Fax: (216) 781-0331
Keith Conn, Admissions Director, Cleveland Institute of Electronics, 1776 East 17th Street, Cleveland, OH 44114-3679

## Columbus State Community College
### Columbus, Ohio
**www.cscc.edu**  CB code: 1148

- Public 2-year community and technical college
- Commuter campus in very large city

**General.** Founded in 1967. Regionally accredited. Courses offered at 10 off-campus centers. **Enrollment:** 13,051 degree-seeking undergraduates. **Degrees:** 1,428 associate awarded. **ROTC:** Army, Air Force. **Location:** 2 miles from downtown. **Calendar:** Quarter, extensive summer session. **Full-time faculty:** 278 total. **Part-time faculty:** 1,170 total. **Special facilities:** College-owned building for aviation maintenance program at Bolton Field Airport.

**Basis for selection.** Open admission, but selective for some programs. Select applicant populations such as underage, international, felon, and dismissed transfer students may be required to submit documentation to determine admission status. Some technology programs have special admission requirements. English as a Second Language applicants required to complete ESL placement test. Placement testing required for all students who plan to take courses that have an English, math, and/or reading prerequisite. COMPASS required for placement. Interview required for chef apprenticeship and some health and human service techology programs. **Home-schooled:** Some academic programs may require completion of GED. Recommend completing COMPASS Ability to Benefit Placement Test if applying for financial aid. **Learning Disabled:** Students must provide documentation and register with Disability Services to receive services.

**High school preparation.** Algebra required for transfer programs and engineering, health, and business technology programs. Chemistry and biology required for health programs.

**2007-2008 Annual costs.** Tuition/fees: $3,555; $7,875 out-of-state. Per-credit charge: $79 in-state; $175 out-of-state. Books/supplies: $1,050. Personal expenses: $168.

**Financial aid. Need-based:** Need-based aid available for part-time students. Work-study available nights, weekends and for part-time students. **Non-need-based:** Scholarships awarded for athletics, state residency.

**Application procedures. Admission:** No deadline. No application fee. Application must be submitted online. Admission notification on a rolling basis. Many health programs admit qualified students on space-available basis; students advised to apply early. **Financial aid:** Priority date 7/24; no closing date. FAFSA required. Applicants notified on a rolling basis starting 4/1.

**Academics. Special study options:** Cooperative education, cross-registration, distance learning, double major, dual enrollment of high school students, ESL, honors, independent study, internships, liberal arts/career combination, student-designed major, study abroad, teacher certification program, weekend college. License preparation in dental hygiene, nursing, paramedic, real estate. **Credit/placement by examination:** AP, CLEP, IB, institutional tests. **Support services:** GED preparation and test center, learning center, reduced course load, remedial instruction, study skills assistance, tutoring, writing center.

**Majors. Architecture:** Landscape. **Business:** Accounting, administrative services, business admin, hospitality admin, hospitality/recreation, human resources, logistics, office management, office technology, office/clerical, purchasing, real estate, sales/distribution, tourism promotion, tourism/travel. **Communications technology:** General, graphic/printing. **Computer sciences:** Computer graphics, information systems, programming. **Conservation:** Environmental studies. **Construction:** Maintenance. **Education:** Early childhood. **Engineering technology:** Architectural, civil, construction, electrical. **Foreign languages:** Sign language interpretation. **Health:** Clinical lab assistant, clinical lab technology, dental hygiene, dental lab technology, EMT paramedic, health services, medical radiologic technology/radiation therapy, medical records technology, medical secretary, mental health services, nursing (RN), respiratory therapy technology, substance abuse counseling, surgical technology, veterinary technology/assistant. **Legal studies:** Legal secretary, paralegal. **Liberal arts:** Arts/sciences. **Mechanic/repair:** Aircraft, automotive, electronics/electrical, heating/ac/refrig. **Parks/recreation:** Facilities management, sports admin. **Personal/culinary services:** Culinary arts. **Protective services:** Corrections, firefighting, law enforcement admin, police science. **Transportation:** General.

**Computing on campus.** Commuter students can connect to campus network. Online course registration, online library, helpline, wireless network available.

**Student life. Freshman orientation:** Available. **Housing:** Students may live in residence halls of other local colleges if space is available. **Activities:** Concert band, choral groups, dance, drama, international student organizations, literary magazine, music ensembles, musical theater, student government, student newspaper.

**Athletics.** NJCAA. **Intercollegiate:** Basketball, cross-country, golf M, volleyball W. **Intramural:** Basketball, bowling, football (non-tackle), volleyball. **Team name:** Cougars.

**Student services.** Adult student services, alcohol/substance abuse counseling, career counseling, services for economically disadvantaged, student employment services, financial aid counseling, minority student services,

on-campus daycare, personal counseling, placement for graduates, veterans' counselor. **Physically disabled:** Services for visually, speech, hearing impaired. **Learning disabled:** Comprehensive services available. **Transfer:** Transfer adviser, college fairs on campus for students transferring to 4-year colleges.

**Contact.** Phone: (614) 287-2669 Toll-free number: (800) 621-6407 ext. 2669 Fax: (614) 287-6019 Tari Blaney, Director of Admissions, Columbus State Community College, 550 East Spring Street, Columbus, OH 43216-1609

## Cuyahoga Community College: Eastern Campus
**Highland Hills, Ohio**
www.tri-c.cc.oh.us                                    **CB code: 1978**

- Public 2-year branch campus and community college
- Commuter campus in large city

**General.** Founded in 1971. Regionally accredited. **Location:** 3 miles from Cleveland. **Calendar:** Semester.

**Annual costs/financial aid.** Tuition/fees (2007-2008): $2,416; $3,194 out-of-district; $6,541 out-of-state. Books/supplies: $900. Personal expenses: $1,504. Need-based financial aid available to full-time and part-time students.

**Contact.** Phone: (216) 987-2024
Director of Admissions, 4250 Richmond Road, Highland Hills, OH 44122

## Cuyahoga Community College: Metropolitan Campus
**Cleveland, Ohio**                                    **CB member**
www.tri-c.edu                                          **CB code: 1159**

- Public 2-year community college
- Commuter campus in very large city

**General.** Founded in 1963. Regionally accredited. Additional campuses in Highland Hills, Westlake and Parma. **Enrollment:** 11,073 degree-seeking undergraduates; 14,085 non-degree-seeking students. **Degrees:** 1,644 associate awarded. **ROTC:** Naval, Air Force. **Location:** Downtown. **Calendar:** Semester, limited summer session. **Full-time faculty:** 354 total; 23% have terminal degrees, 20% minority, 57% women. **Part-time faculty:** 1,089 total; 9% have terminal degrees, 16% minority, 52% women. **Class size:** 59% < 20, 38% 20-39, 2% 40-49, 1% 50-99, less than 1% >100. **Special facilities:** Technology center.

**Student profile.** Among degree-seeking undergraduates, 37% enrolled in a transfer program, 63% enrolled in a vocational program, 2,004 enrolled as first-time, first-year students, 717 transferred in from other institutions.

| | | | |
|---|---|---|---|
| Part-time: | 54% | Hispanic American: | 4% |
| Women: | 59% | International: | 2% |
| African American: | 31% | 25 or older: | 49% |
| Asian American: | 2% | | |

**Transfer out.** 62% of students enrolled in the transfer program go on to 4-year colleges. **Colleges most students transferred to 2007:** Cleveland State University, Baldwin-Wallace College, Kent State University, University of Akron.

**Basis for selection.** Open admission, but selective for some programs. Special requirements for some health technology programs (SAT or ACT required). English placement test required.

**2007-2008 Annual costs.** Tuition/fees: $2,416; $3,194 out-of-district; $6,541 out-of-state. Per-credit charge: $81 in-district; $106 out-of-district; $218 out-of-state. Books/supplies: $1,400. Personal expenses: $1,320.

**2007-2008 Financial aid. Need-based:** Average need met was 100%. Average scholarship/grant was $5,517; average loan $1,943. 87% of total undergraduate aid awarded as scholarships/grants, 13% as loans/jobs. Need-based aid available for part-time students. Work-study available nights, weekends and for part-time students. **Non-need-based:** Scholarships awarded for academics, art, athletics, leadership, minority status, music/drama.

**Application procedures. Admission:** No deadline. No application fee. Application may be submitted online. Admission notification on a rolling basis. **Financial aid:** No deadline. FAFSA, institutional form required. Applicants notified on a rolling basis starting 5/8.

**Academics.** **Special study options:** Cooperative education, cross-registration, distance learning, dual enrollment of high school students, ESL, honors, independent study. **Credit/placement by examination:** AP, CLEP, institutional tests. 30 credit hours maximum toward associate degree. **Support services:** GED preparation and test center, learning center, reduced course load, remedial instruction, study skills assistance, tutoring, writing center.

**Majors.** **Agriculture:** Horticulture. **Business:** General, accounting, administrative services, business admin, entrepreneurial studies, hospitality admin, management information systems, real estate. **Communications technology:** General. **Computer sciences:** General. **Education:** Early childhood. **Engineering technology:** Architectural, drafting, electrical. **Family/consumer sciences:** Child care. **Foreign languages:** Sign language interpretation. **Health:** Clinical lab technology, dental assistant, dental hygiene, dental lab technology, EMT paramedic, health services, medical assistant, medical records admin, medical records technology, nursing (RN), occupational therapy assistant, optician, pharmacy assistant, physical therapy assistant, surgical technology. **Legal studies:** Court reporting, paralegal. **Liberal arts:** Arts/sciences. **Mechanic/repair:** Automotive. **Personal/culinary services:** Culinary arts. **Protective services:** Corrections, fire safety technology, police science. **Visual/performing arts:** Commercial/advertising art, photography.

**Most popular majors.** Business/marketing 11%, health sciences 35%, liberal arts 37%.

**Computing on campus.** 1,000 workstations in library, computer center, student center. Online course registration, online library, helpline available.

**Student life.** **Freshman orientation:** Mandatory. Preregistration for classes offered. **Activities:** Bands, choral groups, dance, drama, musical theater, student government, student newspaper, Hillel, Afro-American Society, veterans service fraternity, Young Socialist Alliance, Student Coalition Against Racism, National Education Association, Hispanic club, Phi Theta Kappa.

**Athletics.** NJCAA. **Intercollegiate:** Baseball M, basketball, cross-country, soccer, softball W, track and field, volleyball W, wrestling M. **Intramural:** Baseball M, basketball, bowling, gymnastics, handball, racquetball, softball, tennis, volleyball, weight lifting. **Team name:** Challengers.

**Student services.** Adult student services, alcohol/substance abuse counseling, career counseling, student employment services, financial aid counseling, health services, minority student services, on-campus daycare, personal counseling, placement for graduates, veterans' counselor, women's services. **Physically disabled:** Services for visually, speech, hearing impaired. **Learning disabled:** Comprehensive services available. **Transfer:** Transfer adviser, college fairs on campus for students transferring to 4-year colleges.

**Contact.** E-mail: customerservice@tri-c.edu
Phone: (216) 987-4200 Fax: (216) 696-2567
Rena Mason, Director of Admissions, Cuyahoga Community College: Metropolitan Campus, 2900 Community College Avenue, Cleveland, OH 44115-2878

## Cuyahoga Community College: Western Campus
### Parma, Ohio
### www.tri-c.edu
**CB code: 1985**

◆ Public 2-year community college
◆ Commuter campus in small city

**General.** Founded in 1966. Regionally accredited. **Location:** 15 miles from Cleveland. **Calendar:** Semester.

**Annual costs/financial aid.** Tuition/fees (2007-2008): $2,416; $3,194 out-of-district; $6,541 out-of-state. Books/supplies: $900. Personal expenses: $1,504. Need-based financial aid available to full-time and part-time students.

**Contact.** Phone: (216) 987-5150
Director of Admissions and Records, 11000 Pleasant Valley Road, Parma, OH 44130

## Davis College
### Toledo, Ohio
### www.daviscollege.edu
**CB code: 2155**

◆ For-profit 2-year junior college
◆ Commuter campus in large city
◆ Interview required

**General.** Founded in 1858. Regionally accredited. **Enrollment:** 479 degree-seeking undergraduates; 5 non-degree-seeking students. **Degrees:** 79 associate awarded. **Location:** 6 miles from downtown, 45 miles from Detroit. **Calendar:** Quarter, limited summer session. **Full-time faculty:** 15 total; 80% women. **Part-time faculty:** 12 total; 42% women. **Class size:** 74% < 20, 26% 20-39.

**Student profile.** Among degree-seeking undergraduates, 48 enrolled as first-time, first-year students, 128 transferred in from other institutions.

| | | | |
|---|---|---|---|
| Part-time: | 56% | African American: | 31% |
| Out-of-state: | 3% | Hispanic American: | 1% |
| Women: | 84% | 25 or older: | 58% |

**Transfer out.** Colleges most students transferred to 2007: Lourdes College, Spring Arbor University, University of Toledo, Owens Community College, Monroe Community College.

**Basis for selection.** Character and personal qualities very important; CPAT test score, interview, talent and ability important. School and College Ability Tests (CPAT) required. Portfolio required for some graphic design degree programs. **Homeschooled:** State high school equivalency certificate required.

**2007-2008 Annual costs.** Tuition/fees: $10,965. Per-credit charge: $233. Books/supplies: $1,275. Personal expenses: $2,019.

**Financial aid.** All financial aid based on need. Need-based aid available for part-time students. Work-study available nights and weekends.

**Application procedures.** **Admission:** Closing date 9/1 (receipt date). $30 fee. Application may be submitted online. Admission notification on a rolling basis. **Financial aid:** No deadline. FAFSA required. Applicants notified on a rolling basis.

**Academics.** **Special study options:** Distance learning, internships, liberal arts/career combination. **Credit/placement by examination:** CLEP, institutional tests. 16 credit hours maximum toward associate degree. **Support services:** Reduced course load, remedial instruction, tutoring.

**Majors.** **Business:** General, accounting, accounting technology, administrative services, business admin, fashion, human resources, marketing. **Computer sciences:** Networking, webmaster. **Education:** Early childhood. **Health:** Insurance coding, medical assistant, medical secretary, medical transcription. **Legal studies:** Legal secretary. **Visual/performing arts:** Graphic design, interior design. **Other:** Sports and recreation marketing.

**Most popular majors.** Business/marketing 38%, computer/information sciences 6%, health sciences 42%, visual/performing arts 14%.

**Computing on campus.** 78 workstations in library, computer center. Wireless network available.

**Student life.** **Freshman orientation:** Mandatory. **Activities:** Student newspaper.

**Student services.** Career counseling, student employment services, financial aid counseling, personal counseling, placement for graduates, veterans' counselor. **Transfer:** Pre-admission transcript evaluation for new students.

**Contact.** E-mail: dstern@daviscollege.edu
Phone: (419) 473-2700 Toll-free number: (800) 477-7021
Fax: (419) 473-2472
Dana Stern, Senior Career Coordinator, Davis College, 4747 Monroe Street, Toledo, OH 43623

## Edison State Community College
### Piqua, Ohio
### www.edisonohio.edu
**CB code: 1191**

◆ Public 2-year community college
◆ Commuter campus in large town

**General.** Founded in 1973. Regionally accredited. **Enrollment:** 866 full-time, degree-seeking students. **Degrees:** 302 associate awarded. **Location:** 30 miles from Dayton. **Calendar:** Semester, extensive summer session. **Full-time faculty:** 47 total; 23% have terminal degrees, 2% minority, 43% women. **Part-time faculty:** 174 total; 3% have terminal degrees, 5% minority, 48% women. **Class size:** 82% < 20, 18% 20-39, less than 1% 40-49, less than 1% 50-99. **Partnerships:** Formal partnership with Tech Prep.

**Student profile.** Among full-time, degree-seeking students, 41% enrolled in a transfer program, 59% enrolled in a vocational program, 1% already have a bachelor's degree or higher, 119 transferred in from other institutions.

| | | | |
|---|---|---|---|
| Out-of-state: | 1% | **Hispanic American:** | 1% |
| **African American:** | 2% | **25 or older:** | 42% |
| **Asian American:** | 1% | | |

**Transfer out. Colleges most students transferred to 2007:** Ohio State, Sinclair Community College, Bowling Green, Miami, Ohio University.

**Basis for selection.** Open admission, but selective for some programs. Special admissions requirements for nursing, early childhood education, human services programs. Degree-seeking students without recent ACT or SAT scores must complete COMPASS or ASSET for placement. **Adult students:** SAT/ACT scores not required.

**High school preparation.** Recommended units include English 4, mathematics 3, social studies 3, science 3 and foreign language 2. 1 fine arts.

**2007-2008 Annual costs.** Tuition/fees: $3,450; $6,420 out-of-state. Per-credit charge: $99 in-state; $198 out-of-state. Books/supplies: $1,300. Personal expenses: $756.

**Financial aid. Need-based:** Need-based aid available for part-time students. Work-study available nights and weekends. **Non-need-based:** Scholarships awarded for academics, athletics.

**Application procedures. Admission:** No deadline. $20 fee, may be waived for applicants with need. Application may be submitted online. Admission notification on a rolling basis. **Financial aid:** Priority date 5/2; no closing date. FAFSA, institutional form required. Applicants notified on a rolling basis starting 5/15.

**Academics. Special study options:** Combined bachelor's/graduate degree, cross-registration, distance learning, double major, dual enrollment of high school students, independent study, internships, student-designed major, weekend college. License preparation in nursing, real estate. **Credit/placement by examination:** AP, CLEP, institutional tests. 30 credit hours maximum toward associate degree. DANTE, DSST and professional exams recommended by American Council on Education accepted. **Support services:** Learning center, pre-admission summer program, reduced course load, remedial instruction, study skills assistance, tutoring, writing center.

**Majors. Business:** General, accounting, administrative services, business admin, communications, executive assistant, finance, human resources, labor relations, logistics, marketing, office management, operations, real estate, sales/distribution. **Computer sciences:** General, computer graphics, game design, information technology, LAN/WAN management, networking, programming, security, system admin, web page design, webmaster. **Education:** General, early childhood. **Engineering:** General, electrical. **Engineering technology:** Computer, electrical, industrial, manufacturing, mechanical, mechanical drafting, plastics, quality control. **English:** Technical writing. **Family/consumer sciences:** Child care, child development. **Health:** Medical assistant, medical secretary, medical transcription, nursing (RN), office admin, prenursing, receptionist. **Legal studies:** Legal secretary, paralegal. **Liberal arts:** Arts/sciences. **Mechanic/repair:** Electronics/electrical. **Production:** Welding. **Protective services:** Police science. **Public administration:** Human services. **Visual/performing arts:** Art, commercial/advertising art, design, dramatic.

**Most popular majors.** Business/marketing 18%, computer/information sciences 7%, engineering/engineering technologies 11%, health sciences 18%, liberal arts 28%, public administration/social services 7%.

**Computing on campus.** 67 workstations in library, student center. Commuter students can connect to campus network. Online course registration, online library, helpline, wireless network available.

**Student life. Freshman orientation:** Available. **Activities:** Drama, student government, Phi Theta Kappa, photo society, writers club, student ambassadors, theater group, international club, digital media club, arts league, society of human resource management, Campus Crusade for Christ.

**Athletics.** NJCAA. **Intercollegiate:** Basketball, golf, volleyball W. **Team name:** Chargers.

**Student services.** Adult student services, career counseling, student employment services, financial aid counseling, health services, on-campus daycare, personal counseling, placement for graduates, veterans' counselor. **Physically disabled:** Services for visually, speech, hearing impaired. **Transfer:** Pre-admission transcript evaluation for new students. Transfer adviser, college fairs on campus for students transferring to 4-year colleges.

**Contact.** E-mail: info@edisonohio.edu
Phone: (937) 778-7868 Toll-free number: (800) 922-3722 ext. 7868
Fax: (937) 778-1920
Velina Bogart, Coordinator of Admissions, Edison State Community College, 1973 Edison Drive, Piqua, OH 45356-9253

## ETI Technical College of Niles
### Niles, Ohio
www.eticollege.edu     **CB code: 3149**

- For-profit 2-year technical college
- Commuter campus in large city
- Interview required

**General.** Accredited by ACCSCT. **Enrollment:** 296 degree-seeking undergraduates. **Degrees:** 101 associate awarded. **Location:** 50 miles from Cleveland and Pittsburgh. **Calendar:** Semester. **Full-time faculty:** 9 total. **Part-time faculty:** 16 total.

**Basis for selection.** Open admission, but selective for some programs.

**2008-2009 Annual costs.** Tuition/fees (projected): $7,317. Per-credit charge: $227. Full-time tuition varies by program: $6,560-$7,056. Books/supplies: $1,300. Personal expenses: $2,140.

**Application procedures. Admission:** No deadline. $50 fee. Admission notification on a rolling basis.

**Academics. Special study options:** Internships. License preparation in real estate. **Credit/placement by examination:** CLEP. **Support services:** GED preparation, tutoring.

**Majors. Business:** Accounting, administrative services. **Computer sciences:** Information technology, web page design. **Engineering technology:** Electrical. **Health:** Insurance coding, medical assistant, medical secretary, medical transcription. **Legal studies:** Legal secretary, paralegal.

**Most popular majors.** Business/marketing 24%, engineering/engineering technologies 16%, health sciences 50%, legal studies 11%.

**Student life. Freshman orientation:** Available. **Activities:** Student government.

**Student services.** Career counseling, financial aid counseling, placement for graduates.

**Contact.** E-mail: etiadmissionsdir@hotmail.com
Phone: (330) 652-9919 Fax: (330) 652-4399
Diane Marsteller, Director of Admissions, ETI Technical College of Niles, 2076 Youngstown Warren Road, Niles, OH 44446-4398

## Gallipolis Career College
### Gallipolis, Ohio
www.gallipoliscareercollege.com     **CB code: 2469**

- For-profit 2-year business and technical college
- Commuter campus in small town
- Interview required

**General.** Accredited by ACICS. **Enrollment:** 138 degree-seeking undergraduates; 4 non-degree-seeking students. **Degrees:** 35 associate awarded. **Location:** 45 miles from Huntington, West Virginia. **Calendar:** Quarter, extensive summer session. **Full-time faculty:** 2 total; 50% women. **Part-time faculty:** 14 total; 64% women. **Class size:** 89% < 20, 11% 20-39.

**Student profile.** Among degree-seeking undergraduates, 39 enrolled as first-time, first-year students.

| | | | |
|---|---|---|---|
| Part-time: | 7% | **Women:** | 85% |
| **Out-of-state:** | 3% | **25 or older:** | 60% |

**Transfer out. Colleges most students transferred to 2007:** University of Rio Grande.

**Basis for selection.** Open admission. Testing for counseling/placement purposes only.

**2007-2008 Annual costs.** Tuition/fees: $9,170. Per-credit charge: $190. Books/supplies: $1,400. Personal expenses: $4,000.

**Financial aid.** All financial aid based on need. Need-based aid available for part-time students.

**Application procedures. Admission:** No deadline. $50 fee. Application must be submitted on paper. Admission notification on a rolling basis. **Financial aid:** No deadline. FAFSA, institutional form required.

**Academics. Special study options:** Double major, independent study, internships. License preparation in real estate. **Credit/placement by examination:** CLEP. 16 credit hours maximum toward associate degree. **Support services:** Remedial instruction, tutoring.

**Majors. Business:** Accounting, administrative services, business admin. **Computer sciences:** General. **Health:** Medical secretary.

**Most popular majors.** Business/marketing 23%, computer/information sciences 27%.

**Computing on campus.** 36 workstations in library, computer center.

**Student life. Freshman orientation:** Available. Preregistration for classes offered. Held quarterly at 6:00 pm on Monday preceding quarter start, lasts approximately 1 hour. **Activities:** Student newspaper.

**Student services.** Career counseling, student employment services, financial aid counseling, placement for graduates. **Transfer:** Pre-admission transcript evaluation for new students.

**Contact.** Phone: (740) 446-4367 ext. 12 Toll-free number: (800) 214-0452 Fax: (740) 446-4124
Jack Henson, Director of Admissions, Gallipolis Career College, 1176 Jackson Pike, Suite 312, Gallipolis, OH 45631

## Good Samaritan College of Nursing and Health Science
Cincinnati, Ohio
www.gscollege.edu                    CB code: 1259

- Private 2-year nursing college
- Very large city
- SAT or ACT (ACT writing optional) required

**General. Enrollment:** 304 degree-seeking undergraduates. **Degrees:** 101 associate awarded. **Calendar:** Semester, limited summer session. **Full-time faculty:** 22 total. **Part-time faculty:** 9 total.

**Student profile.** Among degree-seeking undergraduates, 7% already have a bachelor's degree or higher, 18 enrolled as first-time, first-year students.

| Part-time: | 64% | Women: | 93% |
|---|---|---|---|

**Basis for selection.** Test scores very important. COMPASS and ATI-critical thinking used for advising only. **Adult students:** SAT/ACT scores not required if out of high school 5 year(s) or more.

**High school preparation.** 14 units required. Required and recommended units include English 4, mathematics 4, social studies 3, history 2, science 3, foreign language 2 and computer science 1.

**2007-2008 Annual costs.** Tuition/fees: $15,938. Per-credit charge: $368. Books/supplies: $1,254. Personal expenses: $7,700.

**Application procedures. Admission:** No deadline. $40 fee. Admission notification on a rolling basis.

**Academics. Credit/placement by examination:** CLEP. **Support services:** Learning center, study skills assistance, tutoring.

**Majors. Health:** Nursing (RN).

**Contact.** E-mail: joan_dornette@trihealth.com
Phone: (513) 872-2743
Mose Cartier, Admissions Director, Good Samaritan College of Nursing and Health Science, 375 Dixmyth Avenue, Cincinnati, OH 45220

## Hocking College
Nelsonville, Ohio
www.hocking.edu                    CB code: 1822

- Public 2-year technical college
- Commuter campus in small town

**General.** Founded in 1968. Regionally accredited. Courses available at Perry Campus, New Lexington High School, Logan Hocking High School, Miller High School, Sauber Center, 5 prisons (classes available for inmates and employees). Courses also available online. Great Oaks Career Center,

Tri County Career Center. Co-ops with several trade associations. **Enrollment:** 3,792 degree-seeking undergraduates; 1,583 non-degree-seeking students. **Degrees:** 752 associate awarded. **ROTC:** Army, Air Force. **Location:** 15 miles from Athens, 55 miles from Columbus. **Calendar:** Quarter, limited summer session. **Full-time faculty:** 180 total; 8% have terminal degrees, 1% minority, 48% women. **Part-time faculty:** 269 total; less than 1% have terminal degrees, 3% minority, 41% women. **Class size:** 59% < 20, 35% 20-39, 4% 40-49, 2% 50-99, less than 1% >100. **Special facilities:** Nature center, living history village, college-operated inn, land lab, firing range, burn building, college operated travel agency, early learning center, fish hatchery. **Partnerships:** Formal partnerships with local career centers.

**Student profile.** Among degree-seeking undergraduates, 2% already have a bachelor's degree or higher, 1,165 enrolled as first-time, first-year students.

| Part-time: | 29% | 25 or older: | 23% |
|---|---|---|---|
| Out-of-state: | 2% | Live on campus: | 8% |
| Women: | 52% | | |

**Transfer out.** 14% of students enrolled in the transfer program go on to 4-year colleges. **Colleges most students transferred to 2007:** Ohio University, Rio Grande University, Franklin University.

**Basis for selection.** Open admission, but selective for some programs. Special admissions requirements to nursing program (based on test scores), physical therapist assistant program (based on grades), and radiologic and surgical/operating room technology (based on test scores and grades). Some programs have additional admission requirements. Interview recommended. **Homeschooled:** Applicants to health and public safety technology must have GED before classes begin. **Learning Disabled:** Documentation required for services in the Access Center - Office of Disability Services.

**High school preparation.** Recommended units include English 4, mathematics 3 and science 3. 1 algebra, 1 biology highly recommended for recreation/wildlife and forestry applicants.

**2007-2008 Annual costs.** Tuition/fees: $3,546; $7,092 out-of-state. Per-credit charge: $99 in-state; $197 out-of-state. Books/supplies: $1,200. Personal expenses: $550.

**2006-2007 Financial aid. Need-based:** 2,232 full-time freshmen applied for aid; 1,786 were judged to have need; 1,786 of these received aid. 60% of total undergraduate aid awarded as scholarships/grants, 40% as loans/jobs. Need-based aid available for part-time students. Work-study available nights, weekends and for part-time students. **Non-need-based:** Awarded to 1,411 full-time undergraduates, including 937 freshmen. Scholarships awarded for academics, minority status, state residency.

**Application procedures. Admission:** No deadline. $15 fee. Application may be submitted online. Admission notification on a rolling basis. **Financial aid:** Priority date 2/28; no closing date. FAFSA, institutional form required. Applicants notified on a rolling basis starting 4/15.

**Academics.** Self paced online courses available. Enrollment possible any day college is in session. **Special study options:** Accelerated study, combined bachelor's/graduate degree, cooperative education, cross-registration, distance learning, double major, dual enrollment of high school students, ESL, independent study, internships, student-designed major, study abroad. Bachelor's degree programs available on campus. License preparation in nursing, paramedic, physical therapy, radiology, real estate. **Credit/placement by examination:** AP, CLEP, institutional tests. 60 credit hours maximum toward associate degree. **Support services:** GED test center, learning center, pre-admission summer program, reduced course load, remedial instruction, study skills assistance, tutoring, writing center.

**Majors. Agriculture:** Equestrian studies. **Architecture:** Landscape. **Biology:** Biomedical sciences. **Business:** General, accounting technology, administrative services, hotel/motel admin. **Communications technology:** Radio/tv. **Computer sciences:** Networking, programming. **Conservation:** General, fisheries, forest management, management/policy, wildlife. **Construction:** Carpentry, electrician. **Education:** Teacher assistance. **Engineering:** Materials science. **Engineering technology:** Construction, drafting, electrical, energy systems. **Health:** EMT paramedic, massage therapy, medical assistant, medical records technology, nursing (RN), optician, physical therapy assistant. **Parks/recreation:** Sports admin. **Personal/culinary services:** Chef training. **Protective services:** Corrections, firefighting, police science. **Public administration:** Human services. **Visual/performing arts:** Art, theater design.

**Most popular majors.** Agriculture 6%, business/marketing 12%, health sciences 25%, natural resources/environmental science 19%, security/protective services 16%.

**Computing on campus.** 863 workstations in dormitories, library, computer center, student center. Dormitories wired for high-speed internet access and linked to campus network. Commuter students can connect to campus network. Online course registration, online library, helpline, repair service, wireless network available.

**Student life. Freshman orientation:** Mandatory, $20 fee. Preregistration for classes offered. **Policies:** All students have full use of student center. Clubs must be sanctioned by college. **Housing:** Coed dorms, substance-free housing available. $100 partly refundable deposit. **Activities:** Campus ministries, dance, drama, literary magazine, radio station, student government, student newspaper, Phi Theta Kappa, Kappa Beta Delta, SIFE, Unity Board, technology based clubs, Hocking Heights hall council.

**Athletics. Intramural:** Basketball, football (non-tackle), golf, soccer, softball, swimming, table tennis, tennis, volleyball, weight lifting, wrestling.

**Student services.** Adult student services, alcohol/substance abuse counseling, campus ministries, career counseling, student employment services, financial aid counseling, health services, legal services, on-campus daycare, personal counseling, placement for graduates, veterans' counselor, women's services. **Physically disabled:** Services for visually, speech, hearing impaired. **Transfer:** Pre-admission transcript evaluation for new students. Transfer center, transfer adviser, college fairs on campus for students transferring to 4-year colleges.

**Contact.** E-mail: admissions@hocking.edu
Phone: (740) 753-7049 Toll-free number: (800) 282-4163
Fax: (740) 753-7065
Lynn Hull, Dean of Enrollment Services, Hocking College, 3301 Hocking Parkway, Nelsonville, OH 45764-9704

## Hondros College
**Westerville, Ohio**
www.hondros.edu                                  CB code: 3255

- For-profit 2-year business, nursing and technical college
- Commuter campus in very large city
- Interview required

**General.** Accredited by ACICS. **Enrollment:** 45 degree-seeking undergraduates. **Degrees:** 44 associate awarded. **Location:** 10 miles from Columbus. **Calendar:** Quarter, extensive summer session. **Part-time faculty:** 150 total.

**Transfer out. Colleges most students transferred to 2007:** University of Phoenix.

**Basis for selection.** Open admission. **Adult students:** SAT/ACT scores not required.

**2007-2008 Annual costs.** Tuition/fees: $6,850. Per-credit charge: $150. Per-credit-hour charges vary by program.

**Application procedures. Admission:** No deadline. $100 fee. Application must be submitted on paper. Admission notification on a rolling basis.

**Academics. Special study options:** Accelerated study, combined bachelor's/graduate degree, distance learning, liberal arts/career combination. License preparation in real estate. **Credit/placement by examination:** CLEP.

**Majors. Business:** Real estate, selling. **Health:** Nursing (RN). **Visual/performing arts:** Music.

**Most popular majors.** Business/marketing 66%, health sciences 33%.

**Computing on campus.** 10 workstations in library, computer center. Online library, helpline available.

**Student life. Freshman orientation:** Mandatory.

**Student services.** Student employment services.

**Contact.** E-mail: degreeadmissions@hondros.edu
Phone: (614) 508-6252 Toll-free number: (800) 783-0095 ext. 6252
Fax: (614) 508-6269
Sarah Williams, Manager, Degree Admissions & Advising, Hondros College, 4140 Executive Parkway, Westerville, OH 43081-3855

## International College of Broadcasting
**Dayton, Ohio**
www.icbcollege.com                                CB code: 3047

- For-profit 2-year technical college
- Commuter campus in small city

**General.** Accredited by ACCSCT. **Enrollment:** 104 degree-seeking undergraduates. **Degrees:** 53 associate awarded. **Location:** 50 miles from Cincinnati, 70 miles from Columbus. **Calendar:** Semester, limited summer session. **Full-time faculty:** 10 total. **Part-time faculty:** 4 total.

**Student profile.**

| | | | |
|---|---|---|---|
| Out-of-state: | 3% | 25 or older: | 20% |

**Basis for selection.** Open admission. Tour of the campus and interview required before admission.

**2007-2008 Annual costs.** Tuition/fees: $8,715. Personal expenses: $2,862.

**Financial aid. Need-based:** Need-based aid available for part-time students.

**Application procedures. Admission:** No deadline. $100 fee. **Financial aid:** No deadline. FAFSA required. Applicants notified on a rolling basis starting 11/1.

**Academics. Credit/placement by examination:** CLEP. **Support services:** Reduced course load.

**Majors. Communications:** General. **Visual/performing arts:** General.

**Computing on campus.** Wireless network available.

**Contact.** E-mail: zenaicb@aol.com
Phone: (937) 258-8251 ext. 202 Fax: (937) 258-8714
Aan McIntosh, Director of Admissions, International College of Broadcasting, 6 South Smithville Road, Dayton, OH 45431

## ITT Technical Institute: Dayton
**Dayton, Ohio**
www.itt-tech.edu                                  CB code: 7312

- For-profit 2-year technical college
- Commuter campus in small city

**General.** Founded in 1935. Accredited by ACICS. **Location:** 5 miles from downtown. **Calendar:** Quarter.

**Annual costs/financial aid.** Tuition varies by program, $260-$368 per credit hour.

**Contact.** Phone: (937) 454-2267
Director of Recruitment, 3325 Stop Eight Road, Dayton, OH 45414

## ITT Technical Institute: Hilliard
**Hilliard, Ohio**

- For-profit 2-year business and technical college
- Large town

**General.** Accredited by ACICS. **Calendar:** Quarter.

**Contact.** 3781 Park Mill Run Drive, Suite 1, Hilliard, OH 43026

## ITT Technical Institute: Norwood
**Norwood, Ohio**
www.itt-tech.edu                                  CB code: 2739

- For-profit 2-year technical college
- Commuter campus in large town

**General.** Accredited by ACICS. **Calendar:** Quarter.

**Annual costs/financial aid.** Tuition varies by program, $260-$368 per credit hour.

**Contact.** Phone: (513) 531-8300
Director of Recruitment, 4750 Wesley Avenue, Norwood, OH 45212

## ITT Technical Institute: Strongsville
**Strongsville, Ohio**
www.itt-tech.edu                                  CB code: 2773

- For-profit 2-year technical college
- Commuter campus in large town

Two-Year Colleges

**General.** Accredited by ACICS. **Calendar:** Quarter.

**Annual costs/financial aid.** Tuition varies by program, $260-$368 per credit hour.

**Contact.** Phone: (440) 234-9091
Director of Recruitment, 14955 Sprague Road, Strongsville, OH 44136

## ITT Technical Institute: Youngstown
Youngstown, Ohio
www.itt-tech.edu                              CB code: 0418

- For-profit 2-year technical college
- Commuter campus in small city

**General.** Founded in 1967. Accredited by ACICS. **Location:** 60 miles from Cleveland, 60 miles from Pittsburgh. **Calendar:** Quarter.

**Annual costs/financial aid.** Tuition varies by program, $260-$368 per credit hour.

**Contact.** Phone: (330) 270-1600
Director of Recruitment, 1030 North Meridian Road, Youngstown, OH 44509

## James A. Rhodes State College
Lima, Ohio
www.rhodesstate.edu                           CB code: 0754

- Public 2-year technical college
- Commuter campus in large town

**General.** Founded in 1971. Regionally accredited. **Enrollment:** 3,386 degree-seeking undergraduates. **Degrees:** 437 associate awarded. **Location:** 75 miles from Dayton, 75 miles from Toledo. **Calendar:** Quarter, limited summer session. **Full-time faculty:** 66 total. **Part-time faculty:** 9 total. **Class size:** 66% < 20, 29% 20-39, 4% 40-49, 1% 50-99. **Special facilities:** Ford training center, child care center. **Partnerships:** Formal partnerships with Tech Prep/PSEOP, Ford Training Center, Lima City High School, Allen County Health Partners, Agile Manufacturing, and West Ohio Manufacturing Consortium.

**Transfer out. Colleges most students transferred to 2007:** Bowling Green State University, University of Toledo, Ohio State University, Wright State University, University of Miami.

**Basis for selection.** Open admission, but selective for some programs. Special requirements for health programs (ACT required); interview recommended. **Adult students:** SAT/ACT scores not required. **Homeschooled:** Transcript of courses and grades required. **Learning Disabled:** Students must self-disclose; accommodations are available.

**High school preparation.** Recommended units include English 4, mathematics 3, social studies 3 and science 3.

**2007-2008 Annual costs.** Tuition/fees: $4,229; $8,382 out-of-state. Per-credit charge: $92 in-state; $185 out-of-state. Books/supplies: $945. Personal expenses: $473.

**Financial aid. Need-based:** Need-based aid available for part-time students. Work-study available nights, weekends and for part-time students. **Non-need-based:** Scholarships awarded for academics.

**Application procedures. Admission:** No deadline. $25 fee ($25 out-of-state). Application may be submitted online. Admission notification on a rolling basis. **Financial aid:** Priority date 2/15; no closing date. FAFSA required. Applicants notified on a rolling basis starting 5/1; must reply within 2 week(s) of notification.

**Academics.** Associate of technical studies degree program offered, integrating technology and business. **Special study options:** Cooperative education, cross-registration, distance learning, double major, dual enrollment of high school students, independent study, internships, liberal arts/career combination, student-designed major. License preparation in dental hygiene, nursing, occupational therapy, paramedic, physical therapy, radiology, real estate. **Credit/placement by examination:** AP, CLEP, institutional tests. 15 credit hours maximum toward associate degree. ASSET required for placement for all new students. Maximum 45 credit hours, 15 each from life experiences (non-academic learning); knowledge (by exam) and work training/experience. **Support services:** Learning center, pre-admission summer program, reduced course load, remedial instruction, study skills assistance, tutoring.

**Majors. Business:** General, accounting, administrative services, business admin, finance, management information systems, marketing, office management. **Computer sciences:** General, LAN/WAN management, networking, programming, security, web page design. **Education:** Early childhood. **Engineering technology:** General, civil, electrical, environmental, GIS, industrial, industrial safety, manufacturing, mechanical, quality control. **Family/consumer sciences:** Family/community services. **Health:** Dental assistant, EMT paramedic, medical assistant, medical radiologic technology/radiation therapy, medical secretary, nursing (RN), occupational therapy assistant, office assistant, phlebotomy, physical therapy assistant, radiologic technology/medical imaging, respiratory therapy assistant. **Legal studies:** Legal secretary, paralegal. **Protective services:** Corrections, law enforcement admin, police science. **Public administration:** Human services.

**Most popular majors.** Business/marketing 19%, computer/information sciences 15%, engineering/engineering technologies 12%, health sciences 30%, public administration/social services 7%, security/protective services 7%.

**Computing on campus.** 332 workstations in library, computer center. Commuter students can connect to campus network. Online course registration, helpline, repair service, student web hosting available.

**Student life. Freshman orientation:** Mandatory. Preregistration for classes offered. Orientation programs are held before each quarter begins; specific dates and times are mailed after application is made. **Activities:** Campus ministries, choral groups, drama, music ensembles, student government, academic area organizations, political party clubs, special interest clubs, fellowship and bible study.

**Athletics. Intercollegiate:** Golf M. **Intramural:** Baseball M, basketball, bowling, football (non-tackle), softball, volleyball. **Team name:** Barons.

**Student services.** Career counseling, student employment services, financial aid counseling, on-campus daycare, placement for graduates, veterans' counselor. **Physically disabled:** Services for visually, speech, hearing impaired. **Transfer:** Pre-admission transcript evaluation for new students. College fairs on campus for students transferring to 4-year colleges.

**Contact.** E-mail: admissions@rhodesstate.edu
Phone: (419) 995-8320 Fax: (419) 995-8098
Traci Cox, Director of Admissions, Student Advising and Development, James A. Rhodes State College, 4240 Campus Drive, PS 148, Lima, OH 45804-3597

## Jefferson Community College
Steubenville, Ohio
www.jcc.edu                                   CB code: 2264

- Public 2-year community and technical college
- Commuter campus in large town

**General.** Founded in 1966. Regionally accredited. **Enrollment:** 1,727 degree-seeking undergraduates. **Degrees:** 176 associate awarded. **Location:** 30 miles from Pittsburgh. **Calendar:** Semester, limited summer session. **Full-time faculty:** 32 total. **Part-time faculty:** 145 total. **Class size:** 75% < 20, 25% 20-39, less than 1% 40-49.

**Student profile.** Among degree-seeking undergraduates, 32% enrolled in a transfer program, 68% enrolled in a vocational program, 634 enrolled as first-time, first-year students.

| | | | |
|---|---|---|---|
| Part-time: | 47% | African American: | 5% |
| Out-of-state: | 18% | Asian American: | 1% |
| Women: | 62% | Hispanic American: | 1% |

**Transfer out. Colleges most students transferred to 2007:** Franciscan University of Steubenville, Franklin University, West Liberty State College, Kent State University.

**Basis for selection.** Open admission, but selective for some programs. Special requirements for all allied health technologies programs. ACT required for admission to radiology, medical laboratory, medical assisting, and dental assisting technologies. **Homeschooled:** Final transcript showing successful home school completion signed and dated by home school principal required.

**2007-2008 Annual costs.** Tuition/fees: $2,700; $2,880 out-of-district; $3,690 out-of-state. Per-credit charge: $90 in-district; $96 out-of-district; $123 out-of-state. Residents of 5 neighboring West Virginia counties eligible for in-state, out-of-district tuition rates. Books/supplies: $700. Personal expenses: $400.

**Financial aid.** All financial aid based on need. Need-based aid available for part-time students. Work-study available nights, weekends and for part-time students.

**Application procedures. Admission:** No deadline. $20 fee. Admission notification on a rolling basis. **Financial aid:** Priority date 7/1; no closing date. FAFSA, institutional form required. Applicants notified on a rolling basis starting 6/15.

**Academics. Special study options:** Distance learning, double major, dual enrollment of high school students, external degree, honors, independent study, internships, weekend college. License preparation in paramedic, radiology, real estate. **Credit/placement by examination:** AP, CLEP, institutional tests. 42 credit hours maximum toward associate degree. **Support services:** GED preparation and test center, learning center, pre-admission summer program, remedial instruction, study skills assistance, tutoring, writing center.

**Majors. Biology:** General. **Business:** General, accounting, administrative services, banking/financial services, business admin, e-commerce, management information systems, office management. **Computer sciences:** General, applications programming, computer science, data processing, information systems, systems analysis. **Construction:** Maintenance, power transmission. **Education:** Early childhood. **Engineering:** General, science, systems. **Engineering technology:** Construction, drafting, electrical, manufacturing, robotics. **English:** English lit. **Family/consumer sciences:** Child care. **Health:** Clinical lab assistant, clinical lab technology, dental assistant, EMT paramedic, medical assistant, medical radiologic technology/radiation therapy, medical secretary, respiratory therapy technology, ward clerk. **Interdisciplinary:** Biological/physical sciences, math/computer science. **Legal studies:** Legal secretary. **Liberal arts:** Arts/sciences. **Mechanic/repair:** Electronics/electrical, industrial. **Physical sciences:** Chemistry, physics. **Protective services:** Police science. **Psychology:** General.

**Most popular majors.** Business/marketing 16%, engineering/engineering technologies 16%, family/consumer sciences 10%, health sciences 32%, liberal arts 21%.

**Computing on campus.** 225 workstations in library, computer center. Online library, wireless network available.

**Student life. Freshman orientation:** Mandatory. **Housing:** Students may live in dormitory of local university on space-available basis. **Activities:** Drama, student government, student newspaper.

**Athletics. Intramural:** Baseball M, basketball, bowling, football (non-tackle), softball, table tennis, tennis, volleyball.

**Student services.** Adult student services, career counseling, student employment services, financial aid counseling, health services, on-campus daycare, personal counseling, placement for graduates, veterans' counselor. **Physically disabled:** Services for visually, hearing impaired. **Transfer:** Re-entry adviser, pre-admission transcript evaluation for new students. Transfer center, transfer adviser, college fairs on campus for students transferring to 4-year colleges.

**Contact.** E-mail: cmascellino@jcc.edu
Phone: (740) 264-5591 ext. 106 Toll-free number: (800) 682-6553 ext. 106
Fax: (740) 266-2944
Chuck Mascellino, Director of Admissions, Jefferson Community College, 4000 Sunset Boulevard, Steubenville, OH 43952

---

## Kent State University: Ashtabula
**Ashtabula, Ohio**
**www.ashtabula.kent.edu**                    **CB code: 1485**

◆  Public 2-year branch campus college
◆  Commuter campus in large town

**General.** Founded in 1958. Regionally accredited. Off-site courses available. **Enrollment:** 1,376 degree-seeking undergraduates; 193 non-degree-seeking students. **Degrees:** 133 associate awarded. **ROTC:** Army, Air Force. **Location:** 50 miles from Cleveland. **Calendar:** Semester, limited summer session. **Full-time faculty:** 48 total; 8% minority, 56% women. **Part-time faculty:** 59 total; 3% minority, 52% women. **Class size:** 65% < 20, 30% 20-39, 3% 40-49, 1% 50-99, less than 1% >100. **Special facilities:** Interactive television link with all county high schools.

**Student profile.** Among degree-seeking undergraduates, 2% already have a bachelor's degree or higher, 255 enrolled as first-time, first-year students, 112 transferred in from other institutions.

| | | | |
|---|---|---|---|
| Part-time: | 54% | Asian American: | 1% |
| Out-of-state: | 1% | Hispanic American: | 2% |
| Women: | 69% | 25 or older: | 51% |
| African American: | 5% | | |

**Transfer out. Colleges most students transferred to 2007:** Lakeland Community College, Mount Union College, University of Akron.

**Basis for selection.** Open admission, but selective for some programs. Special requirements for nursing, human services, physical therapy assisting progams.

**High school preparation.** 16 units recommended. Recommended units include English 4, mathematics 3, social studies 3, science 3 (laboratory 2) and foreign language 2. One art unit recommended.

**2007-2008 Annual costs.** Tuition/fees: $4,770; $12,202 out-of-state. Per-credit charge: $217 in-state; $555 out-of-state. Books/supplies: $990. Personal expenses: $1,900.

**2007-2008 Financial aid. Need-based:** 175 full-time freshmen applied for aid; 159 were judged to have need; 159 of these received aid. Average need met was 58%. Average scholarship/grant was $5,487; average loan $3,362. 40% of total undergraduate aid awarded as scholarships/grants, 60% as loans/jobs. Need-based aid available for part-time students. **Non-need-based:** Scholarships awarded for academics, alumni affiliation, art, athletics, job skills, leadership, minority status, music/drama, ROTC, state residency.

**Application procedures. Admission:** No deadline. $30 fee, may be waived for applicants with need. Application may be submitted online. Admission notification on a rolling basis beginning on or about 10/1. **Financial aid:** Priority date 3/1; no closing date. FAFSA required. Applicants notified on a rolling basis starting 3/15; must reply within 2 week(s) of notification.

**Academics. Special study options:** Accelerated study, distance learning, double major, dual enrollment of high school students, independent study, internships, liberal arts/career combination, student-designed major. Bachelor's degree programs available on campus. License preparation in nursing. **Credit/placement by examination:** AP, CLEP, institutional tests. 12 credit hours maximum toward associate degree. **Support services:** Learning center, remedial instruction, tutoring.

**Majors. Business:** General, accounting technology, administrative services. **Computer sciences:** Applications programming. **Education:** Early childhood. **Engineering technology:** Electrical, mechanical. **Health:** Health care admin, nursing (RN), physical therapy assistant, preop/surgical nursing. **Liberal arts:** Arts/sciences. **Protective services:** Criminal justice.

**Most popular majors.** Business/marketing 11%, health sciences 62%, liberal arts 14%.

**Computing on campus.** 82 workstations in library, computer center. Online course registration, online library, helpline, student web hosting available.

**Student life. Freshman orientation:** Available. Preregistration for classes offered. **Activities:** Dance, drama, radio station, student government, student newspaper, world affairs club, social issues club.

**Athletics. Intramural:** Basketball, football (non-tackle), softball W, volleyball, weight lifting. **Team name:** Golden Flashes.

**Student services.** Adult student services, career counseling, student employment services, on-campus daycare, personal counseling, placement for graduates, veterans' counselor. **Physically disabled:** Services for visually impaired. **Transfer:** Transfer adviser for students transferring to 4-year colleges.

**Contact.** E-mail: sanford@ashtabula.kent.edu
Phone: (440) 964-4217 Fax: (440) 964-4217
Kelly Sanford, Admissions Counselor, Kent State University: Ashtabula, 3325 West 13th Street, Ashtabula, OH 44004

---

## Kent State University: East Liverpool
**East Liverpool, Ohio**
**www.kenteliv.kent.edu**                    **CB code: 0328**

◆  Public 2-year branch campus college
◆  Commuter campus in large town

**General.** Founded in 1965. Regionally accredited. **Enrollment:** 803 degree-seeking undergraduates; 98 non-degree-seeking students. **Degrees:** 130 associate awarded. **ROTC:** Army, Air Force. **Location:** 45 miles from Youngstown, 40 miles from Pittsburgh. **Calendar:** Semester, extensive summer session. **Full-time faculty:** 26 total; 15% minority, 50% women. **Part-time faculty:** 35 total; 57% women. **Class size:** 69% < 20, 29% 20-39, 2% 40-49, less than 1% 50-99.

**Student profile.** Among degree-seeking undergraduates, 1% already have a bachelor's degree or higher, 144 enrolled as first-time, first-year students, 77 transferred in from other institutions.

| | | | |
|---|---|---|---|
| Part-time: | 59% | African American: | 4% |
| Out-of-state: | 3% | Hispanic American: | 1% |
| Women: | 74% | 25 or older: | 42% |

**Transfer out. Colleges most students transferred to 2007:** Youngstown State University, Jefferson Community College, West Virginia Northern Community College, Hannah Mullins School of Nursing.

**Basis for selection.** Open admission, but selective for some programs. Special requirements for nursing, occupational therapy, and physical therapy applicants. ACT recommended for students under 21. Interview recommended. **Adult students:** SAT/ACT scores not required if applicant over 21.

**High school preparation.** 16 units recommended. Recommended units include English 4, mathematics 3, social studies 3, science 3 (laboratory 2) and foreign language 2. One unit algebra, 1 unit chemistry, 1 unit biology required for nursing applicants. One unit algebra, 1 unit biology required for physical therapy and occupational therapy. One art unit recommended for all.

**2007-2008 Annual costs.** Tuition/fees: $4,770; $12,202 out-of-state. Per-credit charge: $217 in-state; $555 out-of-state. Books/supplies: $550. Personal expenses: $1,315.

**2007-2008 Financial aid. Need-based:** 109 full-time freshmen applied for aid; 99 were judged to have need; 99 of these received aid. Average need met was 52%. Average scholarship/grant was $5,189; average loan $3,468. 42% of total undergraduate aid awarded as scholarships/grants, 58% as loans/jobs. Need-based aid available for part-time students. Work-study available for part-time students. **Non-need-based:** Scholarships awarded for academics, alumni affiliation, art, athletics, leadership, minority status, music/drama, ROTC, state residency.

**Application procedures. Admission:** Priority date 8/1; no deadline. $30 fee, may be waived for applicants with need. Application may be submitted online. Admission notification on a rolling basis beginning on or about 10/1. All new applicants must complete basic skills assessment tests. **Financial aid:** Priority date 3/1; no closing date. FAFSA required. Applicants notified on a rolling basis starting 3/15; must reply within 2 week(s) of notification.

**Academics. Special study options:** Accelerated study, distance learning, double major, dual enrollment of high school students, independent study, internships, student-designed major. Bachelor's degree programs available on campus. License preparation in nursing. **Credit/placement by examination:** AP, CLEP, institutional tests. 14 credit hours maximum toward associate degree. **Support services:** Learning center, pre-admission summer program, reduced course load, remedial instruction, study skills assistance, tutoring, writing center.

**Honors college/program.** 3.5 GPA, 24 ACT, recommendation, interview, placement exam required. Various course offerings plus Freshman Year Colloquium to replace university composition requirement.

**Majors. Business:** General, accounting technology. **Computer sciences:** Applications programming. **Health:** Nursing (RN), occupational therapy assistant, physical therapy assistant. **Legal studies:** Paralegal. **Liberal arts:** Arts/sciences. **Protective services:** Criminal justice.

**Most popular majors.** Health sciences 82%.

**Computing on campus.** 114 workstations in library, computer center. Online course registration, online library, helpline, student web hosting available.

**Student life. Freshman orientation:** Available. Preregistration for classes offered. **Activities:** Literary magazine, student government, student newspaper.

**Athletics. Team name:** Golden Flashes.

**Student services.** Career counseling, student employment services, placement for graduates, veterans' counselor. **Learning disabled:** Comprehensive services available. **Transfer:** Transfer adviser, college fairs on campus for students transferring to 4-year colleges.

**Contact.** E-mail: admissions@eliv.kent.edu
Phone: (330) 385-3805 Fax: (330) 382-7562
Nancy Dellavecchia, Director, Kent State University: East Liverpool, 400 East Fourth Street, East Liverpool, OH 43920

## Kent State University: Geauga
**Burton, Ohio**
**www.geauga.kent.edu**

- Public 2-year branch campus college
- Rural community

**General.** Regionally accredited. **Enrollment:** 1,191 degree-seeking undergraduates; 56 non-degree-seeking students. **Degrees:** 49 associate awarded. **Calendar:** Semester. **Full-time faculty:** 21 total; 19% minority, 71% women. **Part-time faculty:** 57 total; 9% minority, 53% women. **Class size:** 78% < 20, 22% 20-39.

**Student profile.** Among degree-seeking undergraduates, 2% already have a bachelor's degree or higher, 143 enrolled as first-time, first-year students, 73 transferred in from other institutions.

| | | | |
|---|---|---|---|
| Part-time: | 68% | Asian American: | 1% |
| Out-of-state: | 1% | Hispanic American: | 1% |
| Women: | 61% | Native American: | 1% |
| African American: | 9% | 25 or older: | 38% |

**Basis for selection.** Open admission. **Adult students:** SAT/ACT scores not required if applicant over 21. **Homeschooled:** Transcript of courses and grades required.

**High school preparation.** 16 units recommended. Recommended units include English 4, mathematics 3, social studies 3, science 3 (laboratory 2) and foreign language 2.

**2007-2008 Annual costs.** Tuition/fees: $4,770; $12,202 out-of-state. Per-credit charge: $217 in-state; $555 out-of-state.

**2007-2008 Financial aid. Need-based:** Average need met was 53%. Average scholarship/grant was $4,139; average loan $3,408. 32% of total undergraduate aid awarded as scholarships/grants, 68% as loans/jobs. Need-based aid available for part-time students. **Non-need-based:** Scholarships awarded for academics, alumni affiliation, art, athletics, leadership, minority status, music/drama, ROTC, state residency.

**Application procedures. Admission:** No deadline. $30 fee, may be waived for applicants with need. Application may be submitted online. Admission notification on a rolling basis beginning on or about 10/1. **Financial aid:** Priority date 3/1; no closing date. FAFSA required. Applicants notified by 3/15; must reply within 2 week(s) of notification.

**Academics. Special study options:** Accelerated study, distance learning, double major, dual enrollment of high school students, independent study, internships, student-designed major. **Credit/placement by examination:** AP, CLEP, institutional tests. **Support services:** Learning center, pre-admission summer program, reduced course load, remedial instruction, study skills assistance, tutoring, writing center.

**Honors college/program.** 3.5 GPA, 24 ACT, recommendation, interview, placement exam required. Various course offerings, freshman year colloquium to replace university composition requirement.

**Majors. Agriculture:** Horticultural science. **Engineering technology:** Computer systems, industrial. **Health:** EMT paramedic. **Liberal arts:** Arts/sciences.

**Most popular majors.** Computer/information sciences 29%, liberal arts 65%.

**Computing on campus.** Online course registration, online library, helpline, student web hosting available.

**Student life. Freshman orientation:** Available. Preregistration for classes offered.

**Athletics. Team name:** Golden Flashes.

**Student services. Transfer:** Transfer adviser, college fairs on campus for students transferring to 4-year colleges.

**Contact.** E-mail: info@geauga.kent.edu
Phone: (440) 834-4187
Nancy Dellavecchia, Director, Admissions, Kent State University: Geauga, Office of Admissions, Burton, OH 44021

## Kent State University: Salem
Salem, Ohio
www.salem.kent.edu

CB code: 0683

◗ Public 2-year branch campus college
◗ Commuter campus in large town

**General.** Founded in 1962. Regionally accredited. **Enrollment:** 1,203 degree-seeking undergraduates; 48 non-degree-seeking students. **Degrees:** 23 bachelor's, 100 associate awarded. **ROTC:** Army, Air Force. **Location:** 25 miles from Youngstown, 40 miles from Canton. **Calendar:** Semester, limited summer session. **Full-time faculty:** 42 total; 12% minority, 64% women. **Part-time faculty:** 55 total; 2% minority, 71% women. **Class size:** 69% < 20, 30% 20-39, less than 1% 40-49, less than 1% 50-99. **Special facilities:** Writers' workshop, science and mathematics lab, academic center.

**Student profile.** Among degree-seeking undergraduates, 2% already have a bachelor's degree or higher, 196 enrolled as first-time, first-year students, 83 transferred in from other institutions.

| | | | |
|---|---|---|---|
| Part-time: | 49% | African American: | 2% |
| Out-of-state: | 1% | Asian American: | 1% |
| Women: | 72% | 25 or older: | 40% |

**Transfer out. Colleges most students transferred to 2007:** Youngstown State University, Stark State College of Technology, University of Akron, Ohio State University, ITT Technical Institute.

**Basis for selection.** Open admission, but selective for some programs. Radiologic technology program requires 2.5 minimum GPA, completion of certain courses. Nursing program requires 2.5 minimum GPA. SAT or ACT required for admission to nursing, radiologic technology programs.

**High school preparation.** College-preparatory program recommended. 16 units recommended. Recommended units include English 4, mathematics 3, social studies 3, science 3 (laboratory 2) and foreign language 2. One visual or performing arts may be substituted for 1 foreign language.

**2007-2008 Annual costs.** Tuition/fees: $4,770; $12,202 out-of-state. Per-credit charge: $217 in-state; $555 out-of-state. Books/supplies: $700. Personal expenses: $1,500.

**2007-2008 Financial aid. Need-based:** 136 full-time freshmen applied for aid; 123 were judged to have need; 123 of these received aid. Average need met was 60%. Average scholarship/grant was $4,810; average loan $3,482. 43% of total undergraduate aid awarded as scholarships/grants, 57% as loans/jobs. Need-based aid available for part-time students. **Non-need-based:** Scholarships awarded for academics, alumni affiliation, art, athletics, leadership, minority status, music/drama, ROTC.

**Application procedures. Admission:** Priority date 8/1; no deadline. $30 fee, may be waived for applicants with need. Application may be submitted online. Admission notification on a rolling basis beginning on or about 10/1. **Financial aid:** Priority date 3/1; no closing date. FAFSA required. Applicants notified on a rolling basis starting 3/15; must reply within 2 week(s) of notification.

**Academics. Special study options:** Accelerated study, distance learning, double major, dual enrollment of high school students, independent study, internships, liberal arts/career combination, student-designed major. Bachelor's degree programs available on campus. **Credit/placement by examination:** AP, CLEP, institutional tests. 24 credit hours maximum toward associate degree. **Support services:** Learning center, remedial instruction, study skills assistance, tutoring, writing center.

**Honors college/program.** 17 students admitted each year. Minimum 3.3 GPA and 23 ACT score required. Full tuition scholarships awarded renewable for 1 additional year.

**Majors. Agriculture:** Horticulture. **Business:** General, administrative services. **Computer sciences:** Applications programming. **Education:** Elementary. **Engineering technology:** Industrial. **Health:** Health care admin, medical radiologic technology/radiation therapy, nuclear medical technology. **Liberal arts:** Arts/sciences. **Protective services:** Criminal justice.

**Most popular majors.** Agriculture 6%, business/marketing 12%, computer/information sciences 6%, education 21%, health sciences 42%, liberal arts 8%.

**Computing on campus.** 118 workstations in library, computer center. Commuter students can connect to campus network. Online course registration, student web hosting available.

**Student life. Freshman orientation:** Available. Preregistration for classes offered. **Activities:** Choral groups, drama, music ensembles, student government, student newspaper, professional business and engineering clubs, art

club, nontraditional student club, ski club, Women of Wonder, horticulture, criminal justice club, psychology club.

**Athletics. Intramural:** Basketball, racquetball, skiing, table tennis, tennis, volleyball. **Team name:** Golden Flashes.

**Student services.** Adult student services, career counseling, financial aid counseling, personal counseling, placement for graduates, veterans' counselor. **Physically disabled:** Services for visually, hearing impaired. **Learning disabled:** Comprehensive services available. **Transfer:** Transfer adviser for students transferring to 4-year colleges.

**Contact.** E-mail: ask-us@salem.kent.edu
Phone: (330) 332-0361 Fax: (330) 332-9256
Michelle Schuster, Director, Enrollment Management and Student Services, Kent State University: Salem, 2491 State Route 45 South, Salem, OH 44460

## Kent State University: Stark
Canton, Ohio
www.stark.kent.edu

CB code: 0585

◗ Public 2-year branch campus college
◗ Commuter campus in small city

**General.** Founded in 1946. Regionally accredited. **Enrollment:** 3,499 degree-seeking undergraduates; 299 non-degree-seeking students. **Degrees:** 83 associate awarded. **ROTC:** Army, Air Force. **Location:** 14 miles from Akron, 60 miles from Cleveland. **Calendar:** Semester, limited summer session. **Full-time faculty:** 100 total; 11% minority, 51% women. **Part-time faculty:** 107 total; 4% minority, 41% women. **Class size:** 44% < 20, 45% 20-39, 7% 40-49, 4% 50-99.

**Student profile.** Among degree-seeking undergraduates, 2% already have a bachelor's degree or higher, 692 enrolled as first-time, first-year students, 331 transferred in from other institutions.

| | | | |
|---|---|---|---|
| Part-time: | 42% | Asian American: | 1% |
| Women: | 61% | Hispanic American: | 1% |
| African American: | 7% | 25 or older: | 30% |

**Basis for selection.** Open admission, but selective for some programs. Special requirements for honors college, art, music, education, nursing, business. COMPASS test required for placement. Essay required for honors college, early admission; audition required for music programs; portfolio required for art programs.

**High school preparation.** 16 units recommended. Recommended units include English 4, mathematics 3, social studies 3, science 3 (laboratory 2) and foreign language 2. One unit of fine arts may be substituted for 1 unit of foreign language; math units should be in algebra I & II and geometry.

**2007-2008 Annual costs.** Tuition/fees: $4,770; $12,202 out-of-state. Per-credit charge: $217 in-state; $555 out-of-state. Books/supplies: $900. Personal expenses: $1,826.

**2007-2008 Financial aid. Need-based:** 445 full-time freshmen applied for aid; 378 were judged to have need; 378 of these received aid. Average need met was 62%. Average scholarship/grant was $4,281; average loan $3,359. 38% of total undergraduate aid awarded as scholarships/grants, 62% as loans/jobs. Need-based aid available for part-time students. Work-study available for part-time students. **Non-need-based:** Scholarships awarded for academics, alumni affiliation, art, athletics, leadership, minority status, music/drama, ROTC, state residency.

**Application procedures. Admission:** No deadline. $30 fee, may be waived for applicants with need. Application may be submitted online. Admission notification on a rolling basis beginning on or about 10/1. Early admission available to high school juniors or seniors in top 15 percent of class with ACT of 24 or above and GPA of 3.4 or higher through Ohio PSEO Program. **Financial aid:** Priority date 3/1; no closing date. FAFSA required. Applicants notified on a rolling basis starting 3/15; must reply within 2 week(s) of notification.

**Academics. Special study options:** Accelerated study, distance learning, double major, dual enrollment of high school students, honors, independent study, internships, student-designed major. Access program for senior citizens, video conference advising. Bachelor's degree programs available on campus. **Credit/placement by examination:** AP, CLEP, institutional tests. 24 credit hours maximum toward associate degree. **Support services:** Learning center, reduced course load, remedial instruction, study skills assistance, tutoring, writing center.

**Honors college/program.** 3.2 cumulative high school GPA, essay, ACT Composite score of 24 required.

**Majors. Liberal arts:** Arts/sciences. **Protective services:** Criminal justice.

**Most popular majors.** Liberal arts 93%, security/protective services 7%.

**Computing on campus.** 145 workstations in library, computer center, student center. Commuter students can connect to campus network. Online course registration, online library, helpline, student web hosting available.

**Student life. Freshman orientation:** Mandatory. **Activities:** Bands, campus ministries, choral groups, dance, drama, literary magazine, music ensembles, musical theater, student government, political science forum, Academy of Life Sciences, student education association, Pan African Student Alliance.

**Athletics. Team name:** Golden Flashes.

**Student services.** Campus ministries, career counseling, student employment services, financial aid counseling, personal counseling, veterans' counselor. **Physically disabled:** Services for visually, speech, hearing impaired. **Transfer:** Transfer adviser for students transferring to 4-year colleges.

**Contact.** E-mail: admit@stark.kent.edu
Phone: (330) 499-9600 Fax: (330) 494-0301
Deborah Speck, Director of Admissions, Kent State University: Stark, 6000 Frank Avenue NW, Canton, OH 44720-7599

## Kent State University: Trumbull
### Warren, Ohio
### www.trumbull.kent.edu                    CB code: 0593

▶ Public 2-year branch campus college
▶ Commuter campus in small city

**General.** Founded in 1954. Regionally accredited. **Enrollment:** 1,972 degree-seeking undergraduates; 132 non-degree-seeking students. **Degrees:** 87 associate awarded. **ROTC:** Army, Air Force. **Location:** 2 miles from downtown. **Calendar:** Semester, limited summer session. **Full-time faculty:** 58 total; 16% minority, 34% women. **Part-time faculty:** 59 total; 3% minority, 44% women. **Class size:** 54% < 20, 44% 20-39, 2% 40-49.

**Student profile.** Among degree-seeking undergraduates, 1% already have a bachelor's degree or higher, 360 enrolled as first-time, first-year students, 112 transferred in from other institutions.

| | | | |
|---|---|---|---|
| Part-time: | 50% | Asian American: | 1% |
| Women: | 64% | Hispanic American: | 1% |
| African American: | 11% | 25 or older: | 45% |

**Basis for selection.** Open admission. Current high school students eligible for part-time early admission with a 3.5 GPA, 26 ACT, and letter of recommendation. COMPASS may be used for placement only. Interview recommended.

**High school preparation.** 16 units recommended. Recommended units include English 4, mathematics 3, social studies 3, science 3 (laboratory 2) and foreign language 2. 1 art recommended.

**2007-2008 Annual costs.** Tuition/fees: $4,770; $12,202 out-of-state. Per-credit charge: $217 in-state; $555 out-of-state. Books/supplies: $990. Personal expenses: $1,900.

**2007-2008 Financial aid. Need-based:** 232 full-time freshmen applied for aid; 206 were judged to have need; 206 of these received aid. Average need met was 61%. Average scholarship/grant was $4,782; average loan $3,351. 40% of total undergraduate aid awarded as scholarships/grants, 60% as loans/jobs. Need-based aid available for part-time students. **Non-need-based:** Scholarships awarded for academics, alumni affiliation, art, athletics, leadership, minority status, music/drama, ROTC, state residency.

**Application procedures. Admission:** No deadline. $30 fee, may be waived for applicants with need. Application may be submitted online. Admission notification on a rolling basis beginning on or about 10/1. International students must apply through main campus at Kent. **Financial aid:** Priority date 3/1; no closing date. FAFSA required. Applicants notified on a rolling basis starting 3/15; must reply within 2 week(s) of notification.

**Academics. Special study options:** Accelerated study, distance learning, double major, dual enrollment of high school students, honors, independent study, internships, student-designed major, weekend college. **Credit/placement by examination:** AP, CLEP, IB, institutional tests. 6 credit hours maximum toward associate degree. **Support services:** Learning center, preadmission summer program, reduced course load, remedial instruction, tutoring.

**Majors. Biology:** General. **Business:** General, accounting technology, administrative services, office technology, office/clerical. **Computer sciences:**

Applications programming. **Engineering technology:** Electrical, industrial, mechanical, plastics. **Legal studies:** Paralegal. **Liberal arts:** Arts/sciences. **Protective services:** Criminal justice.

**Most popular majors.** Business/marketing 26%, computer/information sciences 28%, liberal arts 25%, security/protective services 6%.

**Computing on campus.** 265 workstations in library, computer center. Online course registration, online library, helpline, student web hosting available.

**Student life. Freshman orientation:** Available. Preregistration for classes offered. **Activities:** Drama, student government, student newspaper, nontraditional student and minority student organizations, independent black/minority coalition, Christian Fellowship, environmental council, alcohol, drugs and AIDS awareness programs.

**Athletics.** NJCAA. **Team name:** Golden Flashes.

**Student services.** Adult student services, career counseling, student employment services, health services, personal counseling, placement for graduates, veterans' counselor. **Physically disabled:** Services for visually, speech, hearing impaired. **Transfer:** Transfer adviser, college fairs on campus for students transferring to 4-year colleges.

**Contact.** E-mail: info@trumbull.kent.edu
Phone: (330) 847-0571 Fax: (330) 847-6571
Randi Schneider, Director of Enrollment Management, Kent State University: Trumbull, 4314 Mahoning Avenue, NW, Warren, OH 44483-1998

## Kent State University: Tuscarawas
### New Philadelphia, Ohio
### www.tusc.kent.edu                    CB code: 1434

▶ Public 2-year branch campus college
▶ Commuter campus in large town

**General.** Founded in 1962. Regionally accredited. **Enrollment:** 1,757 degree-seeking undergraduates; 240 non-degree-seeking students. **Degrees:** 243 associate awarded. **ROTC:** Army, Air Force. **Location:** 80 miles from Cleveland. **Calendar:** Semester, limited summer session. **Full-time faculty:** 48 total; 17% minority, 50% women. **Part-time faculty:** 55 total; 53% women. **Class size:** 50% < 20, 42% 20-39, 4% 40-49, 4% 50-99. **Partnerships:** Formal partnership with Buckeye Career Center engaged in Tech Prep program.

**Student profile.** Among degree-seeking undergraduates, 1% already have a bachelor's degree or higher, 368 enrolled as first-time, first-year students, 102 transferred in from other institutions.

| | | | |
|---|---|---|---|
| Part-time: | 46% | African American: | 1% |
| Out-of-state: | 1% | Asian American: | 1% |
| Women: | 60% | 25 or older: | 36% |

**Basis for selection.** Open admission, but selective for some programs and for out-of-state students. Special requirements for nursing program. **Adult students:** Test scores not required for placement if applicant is over 21 years of age.

**High school preparation.** 16 units recommended. Recommended units include English 4, mathematics 3, social studies 3, science 3 (laboratory 2) and foreign language 2. One arts unit recommended.

**2007-2008 Annual costs.** Tuition/fees: $4,770; $12,202 out-of-state. Per-credit charge: $217 in-state; $555 out-of-state.

**2007-2008 Financial aid. Need-based:** 257 full-time freshmen applied for aid; 227 were judged to have need; 227 of these received aid. Average need met was 61%. Average scholarship/grant was $4,904; average loan $3,480. 40% of total undergraduate aid awarded as scholarships/grants, 60% as loans/jobs. Need-based aid available for part-time students. Work-study available nights, weekends and for part-time students. **Non-need-based:** Scholarships awarded for academics, alumni affiliation, art, athletics, leadership, minority status, music/drama, ROTC.

**Application procedures. Admission:** No deadline. $30 fee, may be waived for applicants with need. Application may be submitted online. Admission notification on a rolling basis. **Financial aid:** Closing date 3/1. FAFSA required. Applicants notified on a rolling basis starting 3/15; must reply within 2 week(s) of notification.

**Academics. Special study options:** Accelerated study, distance learning, double major, dual enrollment of high school students, honors, independent study, internships, student-designed major. License preparation in nursing.

**Credit/placement by examination:** AP, CLEP, institutional tests. 15 credit hours maximum toward associate degree. **Support services:** Learning center, reduced course load, remedial instruction, study skills assistance, tutoring, writing center.

**Majors. Business:** General, accounting technology, administrative services. **Computer sciences:** Applications programming. **Education:** Early childhood. **Engineering technology:** Industrial, mechanical, plastics. **Health:** Nursing (RN). **Liberal arts:** Arts/sciences. **Protective services:** Criminal justice.

**Most popular majors.** Business/marketing 8%, computer/information sciences 9%, engineering/engineering technologies 16%, health sciences 29%, liberal arts 31%.

**Computing on campus.** 300 workstations in library, computer center. Online course registration, online library, helpline, student web hosting available.

**Student life. Freshman orientation:** Mandatory. Preregistration for classes offered. **Activities:** Choral groups.

**Athletics. Intramural:** Basketball M, volleyball. **Team name:** Golden Flashes.

**Student services.** Career counseling, student employment services, on-campus daycare. **Physically disabled:** Services for visually, hearing impaired. **Transfer:** Transfer adviser for students transferring to 4-year colleges.

**Contact.** E-mail: info@tusc.kent.edu
Phone: (330) 339-3391 ext. 47425 Fax: (330) 339-3321
Denise Testa, Director of Enrollment Management, Kent State University: Tuscarawas, 330 University Drive Northeast, New Philadelphia, OH 44663-9403

## Lakeland Community College
**Kirtland, Ohio**
www.lakelandcc.edu
**CB member**
**CB code: 1422**

- Public 2-year community college
- Commuter campus in large town

**General.** Founded in 1967. Regionally accredited. **Enrollment:** 8,780 degree-seeking undergraduates. **Degrees:** 744 associate awarded. **Location:** 15 miles from Cleveland. **Calendar:** Semester, extensive summer session. **Full-time faculty:** 125 total. **Part-time faculty:** 500 total. **Special facilities:** Planetarium, observatory, licensed preschool program laboratory.

**Student profile.**

Out-of-state: 1%    25 or older: 46%

**Transfer out. Colleges most students transferred to 2007:** Cleveland State University, University of Akron, Kent State University, Ohio State University, John Carroll University.

**Basis for selection.** Open admission, but selective for some programs. Admissions to health technology programs based on test scores and school achievement record.

**High school preparation.** Recommended units include English 4, mathematics 3, social studies 3, science 3 and foreign language 2. Health technology programs require algebra, biology, chemistry.

**2007-2008 Annual costs.** Tuition/fees: $2,698; $3,306 out-of-district; $7,067 out-of-state. Per-credit charge: $79 in-district; $99 out-of-district; $225 out-of-state. Books/supplies: $775. Personal expenses: $1,350.

**Financial aid. Need-based:** Need-based aid available for part-time students. Work-study available nights, weekends and for part-time students. **Non-need-based:** Scholarships awarded for academics, art, athletics, job skills, leadership, minority status, music/drama, state residency. **Additional information:** Loans available for tuition and books.

**Application procedures. Admission:** No deadline. $15 fee, may be waived for applicants with need. Application may be submitted online. Admission notification on a rolling basis beginning on or about 12/1. **Financial aid:** Priority date 3/1; no closing date. FAFSA, institutional form required. Applicants notified on a rolling basis starting 5/1.

**Academics. Special study options:** Cooperative education, cross-registration, distance learning, dual enrollment of high school students, independent study, liberal arts/career combination, weekend college. Bachelor's degree programs available on campus. License preparation in nursing,

real estate. **Credit/placement by examination:** AP, CLEP, institutional tests. 44 credit hours maximum toward associate degree. **Support services:** Learning center, reduced course load, remedial instruction, study skills assistance, tutoring.

**Majors. Biology:** Biotechnology. **Business:** Accounting, administrative services, business admin, e-commerce, hospitality admin, management information systems, small business admin, tourism promotion, tourism/travel. **Computer sciences:** Information systems, LAN/WAN management, programming, web page design. **Education:** Early childhood. **Engineering technology:** Civil, electrical, electrical drafting, manufacturing, mechanical, nuclear. **Family/consumer sciences:** Child care. **Health:** Clinical lab technology, dental hygiene, histologic technology, medical radiologic technology/radiation therapy, nursing (RN), ophthalmic lab technology, optician, respiratory therapy technology, surgical technology. **Legal studies:** Paralegal. **Liberal arts:** Arts/sciences. **Protective services:** Corrections, firefighting, police science, security services. **Public administration:** Human services. **Science technology:** Biological, nuclear power. **Visual/performing arts:** Commercial/advertising art.

**Computing on campus.** 500 workstations in library, computer center, student center. Online course registration available.

**Student life. Freshman orientation:** Available. **Activities:** Bands, choral groups, drama, music ensembles, radio station, student government, student newspaper, TV station, Access Unlimited, Minority Student Union, Newman Catholic Student Association, La Tertulia.

**Athletics.** NJCAA. **Intercollegiate:** Baseball M, basketball, golf, soccer M, softball W, volleyball W. **Intramural:** Basketball, racquetball, skiing, softball, tennis, volleyball. **Team name:** Lakers.

**Student services.** Adult student services, career counseling, student employment services, financial aid counseling, health services, on-campus daycare, personal counseling, placement for graduates, veterans' counselor, women's services. **Physically disabled:** Services for visually, speech, hearing impaired. **Transfer:** Transfer center, transfer adviser, college fairs on campus for students transferring to 4-year colleges.

**Contact.** E-mail: tcooper@lakelandcc.edu
Phone: (440) 953-7100 Toll-free number: (800) 589-8520
Fax: (440) 975-4330
Tracey Cooper, Director of Admissions/Registrar, Lakeland Community College, 7700 Clocktower Drive, Kirtland, OH 44094

## Lorain County Community College
**Elyria, Ohio**
www.lorainccc.edu
**CB code: 1417**

- Public 2-year community college
- Commuter campus in small city

**General.** Founded in 1963. Regionally accredited. Unique programs serving high school through master's degrees available. Entrepreneurial incubator located on campus. **Enrollment:** 10,894 degree-seeking undergraduates. **Degrees:** 968 associate awarded. **Location:** 26 miles south of Cleveland. **Calendar:** Semester, extensive summer session. **Full-time faculty:** 132 total. **Part-time faculty:** 491 total. **Special facilities:** Performing arts center, advanced technologies center, technology park, conference center.

**Student profile.**

Out-of-state: 1%    25 or older: 44%

**Basis for selection.** Open admission. **Homeschooled:** GED required.

**2007-2008 Annual costs.** Tuition/fees: $2,400; $2,890 out-of-district; $5,838 out-of-state. Per-credit charge: $88 in-district; $106 out-of-district; $220 out-of-state. Books/supplies: $955.

**Financial aid. Need-based:** Need-based aid available for part-time students. Work-study available nights, weekends and for part-time students. **Non-need-based:** Scholarships awarded for academics.

**Application procedures. Admission:** No deadline. No application fee. Application may be submitted online. Admission notification on a rolling basis beginning on or about 4/15. **Financial aid:** Priority date 8/15; no closing date. FAFSA required. Applicants notified on a rolling basis starting 7/1; must reply within 3 week(s) of notification.

**Academics. Special study options:** Cooperative education, cross-registration, distance learning, dual enrollment of high school students, ESL, independent study, liberal arts/career combination, study abroad, teacher certification program, weekend college. Bachelor's degree programs available on campus. License preparation in dental hygiene, nursing, paramedic, physical therapy, radiology. **Credit/placement by examination:** AP, CLEP, institutional tests. 30 credit hours maximum toward associate degree. **Support services:** GED preparation and test center, learning center, pre-admission summer program, reduced course load, remedial instruction, study skills assistance, tutoring.

**Majors. Biology:** General. **Business:** General, accounting, administrative services, banking/financial services, business admin, entrepreneurial studies, hotel/motel admin, human resources, tourism/travel. **Computer sciences:** General, information technology, networking, web page design. **Education:** Early childhood, multi-level teacher. **Engineering:** General, electrical, industrial. **Engineering technology:** General, electrical, manufacturing. **Health:** Athletic training, clinical lab technology, dental hygiene, medical assistant, medical radiologic technology/radiation therapy, medical secretary, nuclear medical technology, nursing (RN), physical therapy assistant, sonography, surgical technology. **Interdisciplinary:** Global studies. **Liberal arts:** Arts/sciences. **Math:** General. **Parks/recreation:** Sports admin. **Personal/culinary services:** Electrolysis. **Production:** Welding. **Protective services:** Corrections, firefighting, police science. **Public administration:** General, social work. **Social sciences:** General.

**Most popular majors.** Business/marketing 13%, engineering/engineering technologies 6%, health sciences 29%, liberal arts 39%.

**Computing on campus.** 250 workstations in library, computer center. Online course registration, online library, helpline, wireless network available.

**Student life. Freshman orientation:** Mandatory. All students enrolled in 12 or fewer credits must take College Experience course. **Activities:** Bands, choral groups, drama, film society, music ensembles, musical theater, radio station, student government, student newspaper, symphony orchestra, TV station, Black Progressives, Los Unidos, student nurses association, Phi Theta Kappa, campus Baptist ministries, Campus Crusades for Christ, student dental hygienist club, early childhood education club.

**Athletics. Intramural:** Archery, badminton, basketball, bowling, cross-country, golf, racquetball, rifle, soccer, softball, tennis, volleyball. **Team name:** Commodores.

**Student services.** Adult student services, alcohol/substance abuse counseling, campus ministries, career counseling, services for economically disadvantaged, student employment services, financial aid counseling, health services, on-campus daycare, personal counseling, placement for graduates, veterans' counselor, women's services. **Physically disabled:** Services for visually, hearing impaired. **Transfer:** Transfer center, transfer adviser, college fairs on campus for students transferring to 4-year colleges.

**Contact.** Phone: (440) 366-4032 Toll-free number: (800) 995-5222 Fax: (440) 366-4167
Thalia Fountain, Director of Enrollment Services, Lorain County Community College, 1005 Abbe Road North, Elyria, OH 44035-1691

## Marion Technical College
**Marion, Ohio**
**www.mtc.edu**                                    CB code: 0699

- Public 2-year technical college
- Commuter campus in large town

**General.** Founded in 1971. Regionally accredited. Common campus and some shared facilities with Ohio State University: Marion. **Enrollment:** 1,410 degree-seeking undergraduates. **Degrees:** 239 associate awarded. **Location:** 45 miles from Columbus. **Calendar:** Quarter, limited summer session. **Full-time faculty:** 41 total. **Part-time faculty:** 3 total.

**Student profile.**

| | | | |
|---|---|---|---|
| Out-of-state: | 1% | 25 or older: | 52% |

**Basis for selection.** Open admission, but selective for some programs. Selective programs include medical assisting, phlebotomy, human and social services, medical administrative assistant, medical lab technician, nursing, PTA, radiology. Application to program additional to application to college. Programs accept on rolling basis once minimum criteria are met. ACT scores required of nursing, human and social services applicants and recommended for PTA and med lab technician applicants for admissions; placement and counseling; recommended for other applicants for counseling. Interview required for health technologies, human and social services, law enforcement academy. **Adult students:** ACT may be required for limited enrollment programs. **Homeschooled:** Transcript of courses and grades, interview required. Appropriate standardized test or other documentation as defined by policy. **Learning Disabled:** Students must meet with Student Resource Center for assessment of special accommodations.

**High school preparation.** Recommended units include English 4, mathematics 2, social studies 1, science 2 and foreign language 2. Algebra, biology, and chemistry required for health technology applicants. Algebra and physics recommended for engineering applicants.

**2007-2008 Annual costs.** Tuition/fees: $3,860; $5,768 out-of-state. Per-credit charge: $101 in-state; $154 out-of-state. Books/supplies: $800. Personal expenses: $900.

**2007-2008 Financial aid. Need-based:** 68% of total undergraduate aid awarded as scholarships/grants, 32% as loans/jobs. Need-based aid available for part-time students. Work-study available for part-time students. **Non-need-based:** Scholarships awarded for academics, leadership, minority status.

**Application procedures. Admission:** Priority date 6/1; no deadline. $20 fee, may be waived for applicants with need. Application may be submitted online. Admission notification on a rolling basis. **Financial aid:** Closing date 6/1. FAFSA, institutional form required. Applicants notified on a rolling basis.

**Academics. Special study options:** Cooperative education, cross-registration, distance learning, double major, dual enrollment of high school students, independent study, internships, liberal arts/career combination, student-designed major. License preparation in nursing, physical therapy, radiology, real estate. **Credit/placement by examination:** AP, CLEP, institutional tests. Maximum of 48 quarter hours of credit may be earned through exam, life experience or combination. **Support services:** Learning center, reduced course load, remedial instruction, tutoring.

**Majors. Business:** General, accounting, accounting technology, administrative services, business admin, e-commerce, executive assistant, human resources, marketing, office management, office technology, real estate. **Computer sciences:** General, applications programming, data entry, information technology, LAN/WAN management, networking, programming, vendor certification, web page design, webmaster, word processing. **Engineering technology:** Electrical, electromechanical, manufacturing, mechanical, quality control, telecommunications. **Health:** Clinical lab technology, medical radiologic technology/radiation therapy, medical secretary, nursing (RN), physical therapy assistant. **Legal studies:** Paralegal. **Protective services:** Law enforcement admin. **Public administration:** Human services. **Other:** Industrial Mechanical Maintenance.

**Computing on campus.** 229 workstations in computer center.

**Student life. Freshman orientation:** Available. Held week or two before classes begin. **Activities:** Campus ministries, choral groups, drama, literary magazine, student government, joint activities committee, Campus Christian Fellowship, program of outdoor pursuits club, cultural arts program, student organized clubs/organizations, indoor rock climbing, wellness and conditioning, aerobics center, Beta Nu Pi honorary society (Phi Theta Kappa local chapter).

**Athletics. Intercollegiate:** Basketball, cheerleading M, golf, soccer, volleyball W. **Intramural:** Badminton, basketball, cross-country, football (non-tackle), racquetball, skiing, softball, table tennis, tennis, volleyball.

**Student services.** Adult student services, career counseling, student employment services, financial aid counseling, personal counseling, placement for graduates, veterans' counselor. **Physically disabled:** Services for visually, speech, hearing impaired. **Transfer:** College fairs on campus for students transferring to 4-year colleges.

**Contact.** E-mail: enroll@mtc.edu
Phone: (740) 389-4636 ext. 260 Fax: (740) 389-6136
Joel Liles, Director of Admission and Career Services, Marion Technical College, 1467 Mount Vernon Avenue, Marion, OH 43302-5694

## Miami University: Hamilton Campus
**Hamilton, Ohio**
**www.ham.muohio.edu**                          CB code: 1526

- Public 2-year branch campus college
- Commuter campus in small city

**General.** Founded in 1968. Regionally accredited. Degrees earned on Hamilton campus conferred by main (Oxford) campus. **Enrollment:** 3,247 degree-seeking undergraduates; 102 non-degree-seeking students. **Degrees:** 28 bachelor's, 116 associate awarded. **ROTC:** Naval, Air Force. **Location:** 25 miles from Cincinnati. **Calendar:** Semester, limited summer session. **Full-time faculty:** 81 total. **Part-time faculty:** 140 total. **Class size:** 51% < 20, 41% 20-39, 5% 40-49, 2% 50-99. **Special facilities:** Botanical conservatory.

**Student profile.** Among degree-seeking undergraduates, 659 enrolled as first-time, first-year students.

| | | | |
|---|---|---|---|
| Part-time: | 24% | 25 or older: | 24% |
| Women: | 55% | | |

**Basis for selection.** Open admission, but selective for some programs. Open admission policy with additional application required for competitive nursing program. Test scores required for consideration in nursing and teacher education programs. **Adult students:** SAT/ACT scores not required if out of high school 2 year(s) or more. **Homeschooled:** Applicants must present GED scores or credentials that demonstrate equivalent levels of academic achievement, ability and performance to that of state-chartered diploma at least 8 weeks before classes begin.

**High school preparation.** 16 units recommended. Recommended units include English 4, mathematics 3, social studies 2, history 1, science 3, foreign language 2 and visual/performing arts 1.

**2007-2008 Annual costs.** Tuition/fees: $4,320; $16,452 out-of-state. Per-credit charge: $180 in-state; $708 out-of-state. Books/supplies: $580. Personal expenses: $1,732.

**Financial aid. Need-based:** Need-based aid available for part-time students. Work-study available nights, weekends and for part-time students. **Non-need-based:** Scholarships awarded for academics, athletics, leadership, minority status, state residency. **Additional information:** Special gift funds for needy, multicultural students who enter with appropriate academic record. Separate application required for scholarships; closing date January 31.

**Application procedures. Admission:** No deadline. $35 fee, may be waived for applicants with need. Application may be submitted online. Admission notification on a rolling basis. Nursing application deadline for Fall admission 2/01. **Financial aid:** Priority date 2/15; no closing date. FAFSA required. Applicants notified on a rolling basis starting 4/1.

**Academics.** Some upper division and graduate coursework available. **Special study options:** Cooperative education, cross-registration, distance learning, double major, dual enrollment of high school students, ESL, honors, independent study, internships, liberal arts/career combination, student-designed major, study abroad, teacher certification program. Bachelor's degree programs available on campus. License preparation in nursing, real estate. **Credit/placement by examination:** AP, CLEP, IB, institutional tests. 32 credit hours maximum toward associate degree, 32 toward bachelor's. **Support services:** Learning center, reduced course load, remedial instruction, study skills assistance, tutoring, writing center.

**Majors. Business:** Accounting, business admin, management information systems, marketing, office management, office/clerical, real estate. **Computer sciences:** General. **Education:** Kindergarten/preschool. **Engineering technology:** Computer systems, electrical, industrial management, mechanical. **Health:** Nursing (RN).

**Computing on campus.** 300 workstations in library, computer center, student center. Commuter students can connect to campus network. Online course registration, helpline, wireless network available.

**Student life. Freshman orientation:** Available. **Activities:** Choral groups, drama, musical theater, student government, campus activities committee, ski club, student nursing association, minority action committee, Campus Crusade for Christ, athletic club, Organization for Wiser and Worldwide Learners, fitness and weightlifting club, soccer club.

**Athletics. Intramural:** Basketball, bowling, skiing, soccer, softball, table tennis, tennis, volleyball, weight lifting. **Team name:** Harriers.

**Student services.** Career counseling, student employment services, financial aid counseling, minority student services, on-campus daycare, personal counseling, placement for graduates, veterans' counselor. **Physically disabled:** Services for visually, speech, hearing impaired. **Transfer:** Pre-admission transcript evaluation for new students.

**Contact.** Phone: (513) 785-3111 Fax: (513) 785-1807
Archie Nelson, Director of Admission and Financial Aid, Miami University: Hamilton Campus, 1601 University Boulevard, Hamilton, OH 45011-3399

**General.** Founded in 1963. Regionally accredited. Degrees earned on Middletown campus conferred by main (Oxford) campus. **Enrollment:** 2,398 degree-seeking undergraduates. **ROTC:** Naval, Air Force. **Location:** 30 miles from Cincinnati, 20 miles from Dayton. **Calendar:** Semester, extensive summer session. **Full-time faculty:** 80 total. **Part-time faculty:** 150 total. **Special facilities:** Nature trail.

**Student profile.**

| | | | |
|---|---|---|---|
| Out-of-state: | 1% | 25 or older: | 28% |

**Basis for selection.** Open admission, but selective for some programs. Special requirements for allied health programs. SAT or ACT scores required but do not affect admissions decision. Interview recommended for nursing program. **Homeschooled:** Submit curriculum and description of resources used during last 4 years.

**High school preparation.** 16 units recommended. Recommended units include English 4, mathematics 3, social studies 3, science 3, foreign language 2 and academic electives 1. One fine arts also recommended.

**2007-2008 Annual costs.** Tuition/fees: $4,350; $17,210 out-of-state. Per-credit charge: $180 in-state; $716 out-of-state. Students paying by the credit hour pay $15 general fee per credit hour. Books/supplies: $600. Personal expenses: $1,912.

**Financial aid.** All financial aid based on need. Need-based aid available for part-time students. Work-study available for part-time students.

**Application procedures. Admission:** Priority date 8/1; no deadline. $35 fee, may be waived for applicants with need. Application may be submitted online. Admission notification on a rolling basis beginning on or about 3/1. **Financial aid:** Priority date 2/15; no closing date. FAFSA required. Applicants notified on a rolling basis.

**Academics. Special study options:** Cooperative education, cross-registration, distance learning, double major, dual enrollment of high school students, independent study, internships, liberal arts/career combination, student-designed major, study abroad, teacher certification program. License preparation in nursing. **Credit/placement by examination:** AP, CLEP, IB, institutional tests. 30 credit hours maximum toward bachelor's degree. **Support services:** Learning center, pre-admission summer program, reduced course load, remedial instruction, study skills assistance, tutoring, writing center.

**Majors. Biology:** Molecular, zoology. **Business:** General, accounting, administrative services, business admin, finance, office management, office/clerical. **Communications:** General. **Computer sciences:** General, applications programming, systems analysis. **Engineering technology:** Computer systems, electrical. **English:** English lit. **Foreign languages:** Spanish. **Health:** Nursing (RN). **History:** General. **Liberal arts:** Arts/sciences, humanities. **Math:** General. **Philosophy/religion:** Philosophy. **Physical sciences:** Chemistry, physics. **Psychology:** General. **Social sciences:** Anthropology, geography, political science, sociology.

**Computing on campus.** 170 workstations in library, computer center. Commuter students can connect to campus network. Online course registration, online library, helpline, student web hosting available.

**Student life. Freshman orientation:** Mandatory. Full-day program, choice of 5 days ranging from June 4 through August 11. **Activities:** Drama, literary magazine, student government, student newspaper.

**Athletics. Intercollegiate:** Baseball M, basketball, golf, tennis, volleyball W. **Intramural:** Basketball, golf, racquetball, soccer, softball, table tennis, tennis, volleyball. **Team name:** Thunder Hawks.

**Student services.** Adult student services, career counseling, student employment services, financial aid counseling, minority student services, on-campus daycare, personal counseling, placement for graduates, veterans' counselor. **Physically disabled:** Services for visually, speech, hearing impaired. **Transfer:** College fairs on campus for students transferring to 4-year colleges.

**Contact.** E-mail: mlflynn@muohio.edu
Phone: (513) 727-3216 Fax: (513) 727-3223
Stacey Adams, Admissions Director, Miami University: Middletown Campus, 4200 East University Boulevard, Middletown, OH 45042

## Miami University: Middletown Campus
**Middletown, Ohio**
www.mid.muohio.edu                    **CB code: 1509**

▸ Public 2-year branch campus and community college
▸ Commuter campus in large town

## Miami-Jacobs Career College
**Dayton, Ohio**
www.miamijacobs.edu                    **CB code: 1528**

▸ For-profit 2-year junior college
▸ Commuter campus in small city

**General.** Founded in 1860. Accredited by ACICS. **Location:** Downtown. **Calendar:** Quarter.

**Annual costs/financial aid.** Tuition/fees (2007-2008): $10,440. Personal expenses: $2,500. Need-based financial aid available to full-time and part-time students.

**Contact.** Phone: (937) 222-7337
Director of Admissions, 110 North Patterson Boulevard, Dayton, OH 45402

## National College: Cincinnati
Cincinnati, Ohio

- For-profit 2-year branch campus college
- Large city

**General.** Regionally accredited; also accredited by ACICS. **Enrollment:** 389 degree-seeking undergraduates. **Degrees:** 55 associate awarded. **Calendar:** Quarter. **Full-time faculty:** 3 total. **Part-time faculty:** 44 total.

**2008-2009 Annual costs.** Tuition/fees: $9,585. Per-credit charge: $212.

**Application procedures. Admission:** No deadline. $30 fee.

**Academics. Credit/placement by examination:** CLEP.

**Majors. Business:** Accounting/business management, administrative services, business admin. **Engineering technology:** Computer systems. **Health:** Pharmacy assistant, surgical technology. **Other:** Information systems engineering.

**Contact.** Phone: (513) 761-1291
Larry Steele, Vice President of Admissions, National College: Cincinnati, 6871 Steger Drive, Cincinnati, OH 45237

## National College: Dayton
Kettering, Ohio

- For-profit 2-year business and technical college
- Large city

**General.** Accredited by ACICS. **Enrollment:** 391 degree-seeking undergraduates. **Degrees:** 84 associate awarded. **Calendar:** Quarter. **Full-time faculty:** 3 total. **Part-time faculty:** 39 total.

**Basis for selection.** Open admission.

**2007-2008 Annual costs.** Tuition/fees: $9,090. Per-credit charge: $202.

**Application procedures. Admission:** No deadline. $30 fee. **Financial aid:** No deadline.

**Academics. Credit/placement by examination:** CLEP.

**Contact.** Phone: (937) 299-9450
Larry Steele, Director of Admissions, National College: Dayton, 1837 Woodman Center Drive, Kettering, OH 45420

## National College: Stow
Stow, Ohio

- For-profit 2-year branch campus college
- Large town

**General.** Regionally accredited; also accredited by ACICS. **Enrollment:** 38 degree-seeking undergraduates. **Calendar:** Quarter. **Part-time faculty:** 5 total.

**2008-2009 Annual costs.** Tuition/fees: $9,585. Per-credit charge: $212.

**Application procedures. Admission:** No deadline. $30 fee.

**Academics. Credit/placement by examination:** CLEP.

**Majors. Business:** Accounting/business management, administrative services, business admin. **Engineering technology:** Computer systems. **Health:** Medical assistant, medical records technology, pharmacy assistant. **Other:** Information systems engineering.

**Contact.** Larry Steele, Vice President of Admissions, National College: Stow, 3855 Fishercreek Road, Stow, OH 44224

## National College: Youngstown
Youngstown, Ohio

- For-profit 2-year branch campus college
- Small city

**General.** Regionally accredited; also accredited by ACICS. **Enrollment:** 42 degree-seeking undergraduates. **Calendar:** Quarter. **Part-time faculty:** 5 total.

**2008-2009 Annual costs.** Tuition/fees: $9,585. Per-credit charge: $212.

**Application procedures. Admission:** No deadline. $30 fee. **Financial aid:** No deadline.

**Academics. Credit/placement by examination:** CLEP.

**Majors. Business:** Business admin. **Engineering technology:** Computer systems. **Health:** Medical records technology, office assistant, physical therapy assistant. **Other:** Information systems engineering.

**Contact.** Larry Steele, Vice President of Admissions, National College: Youngstown, 3487 Belmont Avenue, Youngstown, OH 44505

## National Institute of Technology
Cuyahoga Falls, Ohio
www.nationalinstituteoftechnology.edu

- For-profit 2-year health science and technical college
- Commuter campus in small city

**General.** Accredited by ACCSCT. **Calendar:** Continuous.

**Annual costs/financial aid.** Program cost for associate degree in medical assisting $20,862; associate in dental assisting, $20,400; associate in registered nursing, $21,500; associate in criminal justice, $21,224; associate in business administration, $21,480; associate in electronics $21,480; associate in computer information systems, $21,480; diploma in medical billing and coding, $12,960. Fees for books, labs not included.

**Contact.** Phone: (330) 923-9959 ext. 14
Director of Admissions, 2545 Bailey Road, Cuyahoga Falls, OH 44221

## North Central State College
Mansfield, Ohio
www.ncstatecollege.edu     CB code: 0721

- Public 2-year technical college
- Commuter campus in small city

**General.** Founded in 1961. Regionally accredited. **Enrollment:** 2,681 degree-seeking undergraduates. **Degrees:** 392 associate awarded. **Location:** 70 miles from Cleveland and Columbus. **Calendar:** Quarter, limited summer session. **Full-time faculty:** 72 total. **Part-time faculty:** 124 total. **Special facilities:** Wooded hiking trails.

**Student profile.**

| | | | |
|---|---|---|---|
| Out-of-state: | 1% | 25 or older: | 53% |

**Transfer out. Colleges most students transferred to 2007:** Ashland University, Mount Vernon Nazarene College, University of Cincinnati, Franklin University.

**Basis for selection.** Open admission, but selective for some programs. ACT scores used for admission to physical therapist assistant and radiology programs; score report by September 15. Interview recommended for all health and public service programs.

**High school preparation.** One algebra and 1 chemistry required for nursing, physical therapist assistant, respiratory therapy, radiologic technology and pharmacy technology programs.

**2007-2008 Annual costs.** Tuition/fees: $2,907; $5,804 out-of-state. Per-credit charge: $81 in-state; $162 out-of-state. Books/supplies: $705. Personal expenses: $726.

**Financial aid.** All financial aid based on need. Need-based aid available for part-time students.

**Application procedures. Admission:** No deadline. No application fee. Application may be submitted online. Admission notification on a rolling

basis. **Financial aid:** Priority date 4/1; no closing date. FAFSA required. Applicants notified on a rolling basis starting 5/30; must reply within 1 week(s) of notification.

**Academics. Special study options:** Distance learning, dual enrollment of high school students, independent study, internships, student-designed major, weekend college. **Credit/placement by examination:** CLEP, institutional tests. **Support services:** GED preparation, learning center, reduced course load, remedial instruction, study skills assistance, tutoring, writing center.

**Majors. Business:** General, accounting, administrative services, business admin, operations. **Communications:** Digital media. **Communications technology:** Animation/special effects, radio/tv. **Computer sciences:** General, applications programming, programming. **Education:** Early childhood, teacher assistance. **Engineering technology:** Computer, drafting, electrical, heat/ac/refrig, mechanical. **Health:** Health services, medical radiologic technology/radiation therapy, mental health services, nursing (RN), physical therapy assistant, radiologic technology/medical imaging, respiratory therapy technology. **Legal studies:** Legal secretary, paralegal. **Mechanic/repair:** Electronics/electrical, heating/ac/refrig. **Production:** Tool and die. **Protective services:** Criminal justice, law enforcement admin, police science.

**Computing on campus.** 144 workstations in library, computer center.

**Student life. Freshman orientation:** Available. 2-3 hour evening program held prior to beginning of each quarter. **Activities:** Choral groups, student government, student newspaper.

**Athletics. Intramural:** Basketball, bowling, football (non-tackle), golf, softball, table tennis, tennis, volleyball. **Team name:** Mavericks.

**Student services.** Career counseling, student employment services, financial aid counseling, on-campus daycare, personal counseling, placement for graduates, veterans' counselor. **Physically disabled:** Services for visually, speech, hearing impaired. **Transfer:** College fairs on campus for students transferring to 4-year colleges.

**Contact.** E-mail: admissions@ncstatecollege.edu
Phone: (419) 755-4888 Toll-free number: (888) 755-4899
Fax: (419) 755-4757
Nikia Fletcher, Director of Student Development/Admissions, North Central State College, Box 698, Mansfield, OH 44901

## Northwest State Community College
### Archbold, Ohio
### www.northweststate.edu
**CB code: 1235**

- Public 2-year community and technical college
- Commuter campus in small town

**General.** Founded in 1968. Regionally accredited. **Enrollment:** 1,830 degree-seeking undergraduates. **Degrees:** 402 associate awarded. **Location:** 45 miles from Toledo. **Calendar:** Semester, limited summer session. **Full-time faculty:** 50 total. **Part-time faculty:** 194 total. **Class size:** 68% < 20, 32% 20-39, less than 1% 40-49. **Special facilities:** Childcare center. **Partnerships:** Tech Prep courses taught at local high school.

**Student profile.**

| | | | |
|---|---|---|---|
| Out-of-state: | 2% | 25 or older: | 46% |

**Basis for selection.** Open admission, but selective for some programs. Special requirements for nursing program; interview required. COMPASS test required for all new students for placement in mathematics, English, reading.

**High school preparation.** Recommended units include English 4, mathematics 3, social studies 3 and science 3. College-preparatory program preferred.

**2007-2008 Annual costs.** Tuition/fees: $4,080; $8,160 out-of-state. Per-credit charge: $136 in-state; $272 out-of-state. Personal expenses: $750.

**Financial aid. Need-based:** Need-based aid available for part-time students. **Non-need-based:** Scholarships awarded for academics.

**Application procedures. Admission:** No deadline. $20 fee. Application may be submitted online. Admission notification on a rolling basis. **Financial aid:** Priority date 6/1; no closing date. FAFSA, institutional form required. Applicants notified on a rolling basis starting 4/1.

**Academics. Special study options:** Cooperative education, distance learning, dual enrollment of high school students, independent study, internships,

student-designed major, weekend college. Bachelor's degree programs available on campus. License preparation in nursing, real estate. **Credit/placement by examination:** CLEP, institutional tests. 40 credit hours maximum toward associate degree. **Support services:** Learning center, remedial instruction, tutoring.

**Majors. Business:** General, accounting, administrative services, business admin, finance, marketing, office technology. **Computer sciences:** LAN/WAN management, programming. **Education:** General. **Engineering technology:** Drafting, electrical, industrial management, mechanical, plastics, quality control. **Family/consumer sciences:** Child development, family studies. **Health:** Medical secretary, nursing (RN). **Legal studies:** Legal secretary, paralegal. **Liberal arts:** Arts/sciences. **Production:** Machine tool, sheet metal, tool and die. **Protective services:** Corrections, criminal justice, law enforcement admin, police science. **Public administration:** Social work. **Visual/performing arts:** Design.

**Computing on campus.** 400 workstations in library, computer center. Online library, wireless network available.

**Student life. Freshman orientation:** Available. Preregistration for classes offered. **Activities:** Student government, Student Nurses Association, Phi Theta Kappa, Campus Crusade for Christ, student body organization.

**Athletics. Intramural:** Basketball, bowling, football (non-tackle), softball, table tennis, volleyball. **Team name:** Pacers.

**Student services.** Adult student services, career counseling, student employment services, financial aid counseling, on-campus daycare, personal counseling, placement for graduates, veterans' counselor. **Physically disabled:** Services for visually, hearing impaired. **Transfer:** Transfer adviser, college fairs on campus for students transferring to 4-year colleges.

**Contact.** E-mail: admissions@northweststate.edu
Phone: (419) 267-5511 ext. 320 Fax: (419) 267-5604
Kathy Thompson, Director of Admissions, Northwest State Community College, 22600 State Route 34, Archbold, OH 43502

## Ohio Business College
### Lorain, Ohio
### www.ohiobusinesscollege.edu
**CB code: 2470**

- For-profit 2-year branch campus and business college
- Commuter campus in small city

**General.** Founded in 1903. Accredited by ACICS. **Enrollment:** 177 degree-seeking undergraduates. **Degrees:** 40 associate awarded. **Location:** 35 miles from Cleveland. **Calendar:** Quarter, extensive summer session. **Full-time faculty:** 4 total. **Part-time faculty:** 15 total.

**Basis for selection.** Open admission. Entrance examinations required of all applicants for placement purposes.

**2008-2009 Annual costs.** Tuition/fees: $9,705. Per-credit charge: $205. Books/supplies: $1,080.

**Financial aid. Need-based:** Need-based aid available for part-time students.

**Application procedures. Admission:** No deadline. $25 fee. Admission notification on a rolling basis. **Financial aid:** No deadline. FAFSA required. Applicants notified on a rolling basis.

**Academics.** All students exposed to extensive computer usage regardless of major. **Special study options:** Double major, independent study, internships. **Credit/placement by examination:** CLEP, institutional tests. 80 credit hours maximum toward associate degree. **Support services:** Remedial instruction, tutoring.

**Majors. Business:** Accounting, administrative services, business admin, office technology. **Health:** Medical secretary.

**Computing on campus.** 55 workstations in computer center.

**Student life. Freshman orientation:** Available. **Activities:** Student government, student newspaper, Business Professionals of America.

**Student services.** Adult student services, career counseling, student employment services, placement for graduates, veterans' counselor. **Physically disabled:** Services for visually, hearing impaired. **Transfer:** Transfer adviser for students transferring to 4-year colleges.

**Contact.** E-mail: lorain@ohiobusinesscollege.edu
Phone: (440) 277-0021 Toll-free number: (888) 514-3126
Fax: (440) 277-7989
John Tobin, Admissions Manager, Ohio Business College, 1907 North
Ridge Road, Lorain, OH 44055

## Ohio Business College: Sandusky
### Sandusky, Ohio
### www.ohiobusinesscollege.edu
### CB code: 3260

- For-profit 2-year business college
- Commuter campus in small city
- Interview required

**General.** Accredited by ACICS. **Enrollment:** 270 degree-seeking undergraduates. **Degrees:** 50 associate awarded. **Location:** 60 miles from Cleveland and Toledo. **Calendar:** Quarter, limited summer session. **Full-time
faculty:** 5 total. **Part-time faculty:** 15 total.

**Transfer out. Colleges most students transferred to 2007:** Ashland University.

**Basis for selection.** Open admission. CPAT required for placement.

**2008-2009 Annual costs.** Tuition/fees (projected): $9,585. Per-credit
charge: $205. Books/supplies: $1,200.

**Financial aid. Need-based:** Need-based aid available for part-time students.

**Application procedures. Admission:** No deadline. $25 fee. Applica-
tion must be submitted on paper. Admission notification on a rolling basis.
**Financial aid:** No deadline. FAFSA required.

**Academics. Special study options:** Double major, independent study,
liberal arts/career combination. Externships. License preparation in real estate. **Credit/placement by examination:** CLEP. **Support services:** Tutoring.

**Majors. Business:** Accounting, administrative services, banking/financial
services, business admin, human resources. **Computer sciences:** Data entry, programming, web page design. **Engineering:** Software. **Health:** Medical records admin, medical secretary. **Legal studies:** Legal secretary.

**Most popular majors.** Business/marketing 55%, computer/information
sciences 12%, health sciences 25%, legal studies 8%.

**Student life. Freshman orientation:** Available.

**Contact.** E-mail: sandusky@ohiobusinesscollege.edu
Phone: (419) 627-8345 Toll-free number: (888) 627-8345
Fax: (419) 627-1958
Cecilia Blevins, Director of Admissions, Ohio Business College: Sandusky,
5202 Timber Commons Drive, Sandusky, OH 44870

## Ohio College of Massotherapy
### Akron, Ohio
### www.ocm.edu
### CB code: 2985

- For-profit 2-year health science college
- Commuter campus in very large city

**General.** Accredited by ACCSCT. **Enrollment:** 264 degree-seeking undergraduates. **Degrees:** 43 associate awarded. **Calendar:** Continuous. **Part-
time faculty:** 19 total. **Special facilities:** Massage and spa clinic.

**Basis for selection.** Open admission. **Homeschooled:** State high school
equivalency certificate required.

**Application procedures. Admission:** No deadline. $25 fee. **Financial
aid:** Priority date 10/1; no closing date.

**Academics. Special study options:** Distance learning. **Credit/placement
by examination:** CLEP. **Support services:** Reduced course load, tutoring.

**Majors. Health:** Massage therapy.

**Computing on campus.** 4 workstations in computer center.

**Student life. Freshman orientation:** Mandatory.

**Contact.** E-mail: admissions@ocm.edu
Phone: (330) 665-1084 Fax: (330) 665-5021
Jeff Morrow, Admissions/Marketing Manager, Ohio College of
Massotherapy, 225 Heritage Woods Drive, Akron, OH 44321

## Ohio Institute of Health Careers: Columbus
### Columbus, Ohio
### www.ohioinstituteofhealthcareers.edu

- For-profit 2-year health science college
- Very large city

**General.** Accredited by ACCSCT. **Enrollment:** 240 degree-seeking undergraduates. **Calendar:** Continuous. **Full-time faculty:** 15 total. **Part-time
faculty:** 15 total.

**Basis for selection.** Open admission.

**Application procedures. Admission:** No deadline. $40 fee.

**Academics. Credit/placement by examination:** CLEP.

**Majors. Health:** Massage therapy, medical assistant.

**Contact.** Phone: (614) 891-5030 Toll-free number: (800) 954-4274
Duane Landrum, Admissions Director, Ohio Institute of Health Careers:
Columbus, 1880 East Dublin-Granville Road, Suite 100, Columbus, OH
43229

## Ohio Institute of Health Careers: Elyria
### Sheffield Village, Ohio
### www.ohioinstituteofhealthcareers.edu

- For-profit 2-year health science college
- Small city

**General.** Accredited by ACCSCT. **Enrollment:** 140 degree-seeking undergraduates. **Degrees:** 6 associate awarded. **Calendar:** Quarter. **Full-time faculty:** 9 total. **Part-time faculty:** 10 total.

**Basis for selection.** Open admission.

**Application procedures. Admission:** No deadline. $35 fee.

**Academics. Credit/placement by examination:** CLEP.

**Majors. Health:** Medical assistant, office assistant.

**Contact.** Phone: (866) 636-47347 Toll-free number: (440) 934-3101
Fax: (440) 934-3105
John Tobin, Admissions Director, Ohio Institute of Health Careers: Elyria,
5095 Waterford Drive, Sheffield Village, OH 44035-0701

## Ohio Institute of Photography and Technology
### Dayton, Ohio
### www.oipt.com
### CB code: 3380

- For-profit 2-year technical college
- Commuter campus in very large city
- Interview required

**General.** Founded in 1971. Accredited by ACCSCT. **Enrollment:** 566 degree-
seeking undergraduates. **Degrees:** 210 associate awarded. **Location:** 55 miles
from Cincinnati, 80 miles from Columbus. **Calendar:** Quarter, extensive
summer session. **Full-time faculty:** 19 total; 10% have terminal degrees,
10% minority, 58% women. **Part-time faculty:** 25 total; 4% have terminal
degrees, 12% minority, 52% women. **Special facilities:** Photographic laboratories and computer laboratory for digital imaging.

**Student profile.** Among degree-seeking undergraduates, 100% enrolled
in a vocational program.

| Out-of-state: | 19% | 25 or older: | 33% |
|---|---|---|---|

**Basis for selection.** Open admission, but selective for some programs.
CPAT test and interview required. Minimum CPAT score of 150 required
for pharmacy technician students. Essay and portfolio recommended.

**2007-2008 Annual costs.** Tuition/fees: $19,833. Per-credit charge: $333. Tuition listed reflects the Photographic Technology program. Tuition varies by program. Books/supplies: $1,350. Personal expenses: $1,701.

**Financial aid. Need-based:** Need-based aid available for part-time students.

**Application procedures. Admission:** No deadline. No application fee. Application may be submitted online. Admission notification on a rolling basis. **Financial aid:** No deadline. FAFSA, institutional form required. Applicants notified on a rolling basis starting 3/1.

**Academics.** Training directed toward technical and professional aspects of photography. **Special study options:** Double major, independent study, internships. **Credit/placement by examination:** AP, CLEP. **Support services:** GED preparation, reduced course load, tutoring.

**Majors. Health:** Office admin. **Protective services:** Law enforcement admin. **Visual/performing arts:** Commercial photography, graphic design, photography.

**Computing on campus.** 36 workstations in library.

**Student life. Freshman orientation:** Available. Preregistration for classes offered. 3 hours, prior to first day of classes.

**Student services.** Adult student services, career counseling, student employment services, financial aid counseling, placement for graduates. **Transfer:** Pre-admission transcript evaluation for new students. Transfer adviser for students transferring to 4-year colleges.

**Contact.**   E-mail: info@oipt.com
Phone: (937) 294-6155 Toll-free number: (800) 932-9698
Fax: (937) 294-2259
Todd Harlow, Director of Admissions, Ohio Institute of Photography and Technology, 2029 Edgefield Road, Dayton, OH 45439

## Ohio State University Agricultural Technical Institute
### Wooster, Ohio
### www.ati.osu.edu                                CB code: 1009

▶ Public 2-year agricultural college
▶ Residential campus in large town

**General.** Founded in 1971. Regionally accredited. **Enrollment:** 723 degree-seeking undergraduates; 25 non-degree-seeking students. **Degrees:** 186 associate awarded. **Location:** 30 miles from Akron, 60 miles from Cleveland. **Calendar:** Quarter, limited summer session. **Full-time faculty:** 34 total; 97% have terminal degrees, 6% minority, 29% women. **Part-time faculty:** 29 total; 7% minority, 31% women. **Class size:** 56% < 20, 39% 20-39, 2% 40-49, 3% 50-99. **Special facilities:** 18 hole public golf course, 1800-acre farm operation/enterprise laboratory, horticulture complex including greenhouses, conservatory and display gardens.

**Student profile.** Among degree-seeking undergraduates, 307 enrolled as first-time, first-year students, 34 transferred in from other institutions.

| Part-time: | 12% | Hispanic American: | 1% |
|---|---|---|---|
| Out-of-state: | 3% | 25 or older: | 9% |
| Women: | 37% | Live on campus: | 51% |
| African American: | 1% | | |

**Basis for selection.** Open admission, but selective for out-of-state students. Out-of-state applicants evaluated on basis of GPA, class rank, curriculum, principal/counselor recommendations, and SAT or ACT scores. **Adult students:** SAT/ACT scores not required if applicant over 21. **Home-schooled:** Interview required. SAT or ACT required.

**High school preparation.** Required and recommended units include English 4, mathematics 3-4, social studies 2-3, science 2-3 (laboratory 2-3), foreign language 2-3 and academic electives 1. Science units should include biology and chemistry. Physics recommended for engineering technology majors. One unit of visual or performing arts recommended.

**2007-2008 Annual costs.** Tuition/fees: $5,859; $18,468 out-of-state. Books/supplies: $1,317. Personal expenses: $3,426.

**2007-2008 Financial aid.** All financial aid based on need. 253 full-time freshmen applied for aid; 207 were judged to have need; 204 of these received aid. Average need met was 60%. Average scholarship/grant was $4,496; average loan $4,081. 35% of total undergraduate aid awarded as scholarships/grants, 65% as loans/jobs. Need-based aid available for part-time students. Work-study available nights, weekends and for part-time students.

**Application procedures. Admission:** Closing date 8/6 (postmark date). $40 fee, may be waived for applicants with need. Application may be submitted online. Admission notification on a rolling basis beginning on or about 10/1. Must reply by May 1 or within 4 week(s) if notified thereafter. **Financial aid:** Priority date 3/1; no closing date. FAFSA required. Applicants notified on a rolling basis starting 5/1; must reply within 4 week(s) of notification.

**Academics.** One-quarter of occupational internship required. **Special study options:** Cross-registration, double major, dual enrollment of high school students, independent study, internships, student-designed major, study abroad. **Credit/placement by examination:** AP, CLEP, SAT, ACT, institutional tests. 45 credit hours maximum toward associate degree. **Support services:** Learning center, reduced course load, remedial instruction, study skills assistance, tutoring, writing center.

**Majors. Agriculture:** General, agronomy, animal husbandry, business, communications, crop production, dairy, equine science, equipment technology, floriculture, greenhouse operations, horticultural science, horticulture, landscaping, nursery operations, ornamental horticulture, plant sciences, power machinery, soil science, turf management. **Business:** Business admin, restaurant/food services. **Conservation:** General, environmental studies. **Construction:** Power transmission. **Education:** Agricultural. **Engineering technology:** Construction, hydraulics. **Personal/culinary services:** Restaurant/catering.

**Most popular majors.** Agriculture 85%, education 6%.

**Computing on campus.** 85 workstations in dormitories, library, computer center. Dormitories wired for high-speed internet access. Commuter students can connect to campus network. Online course registration, online library, helpline, repair service, wireless network available.

**Student life. Freshman orientation:** Mandatory, $75 fee. **Policies:** Resident freshmen under 21 required to live on campus. **Housing:** Apartments, substance-free housing available. $100 nonrefundable deposit. **Activities:** Campus ministries, student government, Phi Theta Kappa.

**Athletics. Intramural:** Basketball, football (tackle), racquetball, softball, volleyball.

**Student services.** Adult student services, career counseling, student employment services, health services, minority student services, personal counseling, placement for graduates. **Physically disabled:** Services for visually, speech, hearing impaired.

**Contact.**   E-mail: ati@osu.edu
Phone: (330) 264-3911 ext. 1327 Toll-free number: (800) 647-8283
Fax: (330) 287-1333
Jill Byers, Coordinator of Admissions, Ohio State University Agricultural Technical Institute, 1328 Dover Road, Wooster, OH 44691

## Ohio Technical College
### Cleveland, Ohio
### www.ohiotechnicalcollege.com            CB code: 2999

▶ For-profit 2-year technical college
▶ Very large city

**General.** Accredited by ACCSCT. **Calendar:** Continuous.

**Annual costs/financial aid.** Tuition for full associate program $22,300 or $22,800 depending on program; full diploma programs range from $16,900 to $26,900; full certificate programs range from $1,974 to $4,927. Fees are $100. Books/supplies: $850. Personal expenses: $1,837.

**Contact.**   Phone: (216) 881-1700
President, 1374 East 51st Street, Cleveland, OH 44103-1269

## Ohio Valley College of Technology
### East Liverpool, Ohio
### www.ovct.edu                                    CB code: 5852

▶ For-profit 2-year business and technical college
▶ Commuter campus in large town
▶ Interview required

**General.** Founded in 1886. Accredited by ACICS. **Enrollment:** 128 degree-seeking undergraduates. **Degrees:** 72 associate awarded. **Location:** 30 miles from Youngstown, 35 miles from Pittsburgh. **Calendar:** Semester, extensive summer session. **Full-time faculty:** 4 total. **Part-time faculty:** 7 total.

**Student profile.**

| | | | |
|---|---|---|---|
| Out-of-state: | 13% | **25 or older:** | 75% |

**Basis for selection.** CPAT scores most important.

**2007-2008 Annual costs.** Tuition/fees: $8,180.

**Financial aid.** All financial aid based on need. Need-based aid available for part-time students.

**Application procedures. Admission:** No deadline. $95 fee. Admission notification on a rolling basis. **Financial aid:** Priority date 10/1; no closing date. FAFSA required. Applicants notified on a rolling basis; must reply within 6 week(s) of notification.

**Academics. Special study options:** Double major, internships, liberal arts/career combination. **Credit/placement by examination:** CLEP, institutional tests. **Support services:** Reduced course load, remedial instruction.

**Majors. Business:** General, accounting, administrative services, office/clerical. **Computer sciences:** General, data processing. **Health:** Dental assistant, medical assistant, medical secretary.

**Computing on campus.** 20 workstations in computer center.

**Student life. Activities:** Student government.

**Student services.** Student employment services, personal counseling, placement for graduates. **Transfer:** Transfer adviser for students transferring to 4-year colleges.

**Contact.** E-mail: info@ovct.edu
Phone: (330) 385-1070 Fax: (330) 385-4606
Scott Rogers, Director of Admissions, Ohio Valley College of Technology, 16808 St. Clair Avenue, PO Box 7000, East Liverpool, OH 43920

## Owens Community College: Toledo
**Toledo, Ohio**
**www.owens.edu**                          CB code: 1643

♦ Public 2-year community college
♦ Commuter campus in large city

**General.** Founded in 1966. Regionally accredited. Branch campus in Findlay 45 miles from Toledo campus. **Enrollment:** 9,191 degree-seeking undergraduates; 11,218 non-degree-seeking students. **Degrees:** 1,087 associate awarded. **ROTC:** Army, Air Force. **Location:** 6 miles from downtown. **Calendar:** Semester, limited summer session. **Full-time faculty:** 193 total; 17% have terminal degrees, 5% minority, 51% women. **Part-time faculty:** 1,466 total; 8% have terminal degrees, 7% minority, 53% women. **Class size:** 78% < 20, 20% 20-39, 1% 40-49, less than 1% 50-99.

**Student profile.** Among degree-seeking undergraduates, 2,054 enrolled as first-time, first-year students, 141 transferred in from other institutions.

| | | | |
|---|---|---|---|
| Part-time: | 54% | **Asian American:** | 1% |
| Out-of-state: | 3% | **Hispanic American:** | 4% |
| Women: | 62% | **International:** | 4% |
| African American: | 12% | **25 or older:** | 46% |

**Transfer out. Colleges most students transferred to 2007:** Bowling Green State University, Lourdes College, University of Findlay, University of Toledo.

**Basis for selection.** Open admission, but selective for some programs. Admission to health technologies, Peace Officer Academy, and early childhood education requires high school transcripts and test scores. ACT required for select health technology programs.

**High school preparation.** 19 units recommended. Recommended units include English 4, science 3 (laboratory 3).

**2007-2008 Annual costs.** Tuition/fees: $3,352; $5,932 out-of-state. Per-credit charge: $123 in-state; $231 out-of-state. Books/supplies: $750.

**2007-2008 Financial aid. Need-based:** Average need met was 2%. Average scholarship/grant was $5,064; average loan $3,201. Need-based aid available for part-time students. Work-study available nights, weekends and for part-time students. **Non-need-based:** Scholarships awarded for academics, alumni affiliation, athletics, leadership, state residency. **Additional information:** Other types of financial aid available: federal family education loan program, private foundation loan (SCHELL).

**Application procedures. Admission:** No deadline. No application fee. Application must be submitted on paper. Admission notification on a rolling

basis. February 1 application deadline for dental hygiene and physical therapist assistant programs. **Financial aid:** Priority date 3/31; no closing date. FAFSA required. Applicants notified by 2/7.

**Academics. Special study options:** Cooperative education, distance learning, double major, dual enrollment of high school students, ESL, honors, independent study, internships, student-designed major, weekend college. License preparation in dental hygiene, nursing, paramedic, radiology, real estate. **Credit/placement by examination:** AP, CLEP, institutional tests. No limit placed upon number of credit hours student may obtain via proficiency exams as long as student has met graduation residency requirement. **Support services:** GED preparation, learning center, pre-admission summer program, reduced course load, remedial instruction, study skills assistance, tutoring, writing center.

**Majors. Agriculture:** Business, landscaping, mechanization. **Area/ethnic studies:** African-American, Canadian, women's. **Biology:** General, biotechnology. **Business:** General, accounting technology, business admin, executive assistant, office management, operations, restaurant/food services. **Communications:** General. **Communications technology:** General. **Computer sciences:** Applications programming, information technology. **Education:** General, early childhood, multi-level teacher. **Engineering:** General. **Engineering technology:** Architectural, architectural drafting, automotive, biomedical, computer, construction, electrical, electromechanical, environmental, hydraulics, industrial, manufacturing, mechanical, quality control, surveying. **English:** Creative writing, English lit. **Foreign languages:** General. **Health:** Dental hygiene, dietetics, health care admin, management/clinical assistant, medical radiologic technology/radiation therapy, medical records technology, medical secretary, nuclear medical technology, nursing (RN), occupational therapy assistant, physical therapy assistant, sonography, surgical technology. **History:** General. **Math:** General. **Military:** General. **Physical sciences:** Chemistry. **Production:** Tool and die, welding. **Protective services:** Corrections, fire safety technology, firefighting, law enforcement admin, police science, security services. **Psychology:** General. **Public administration:** General, social work. **Social sciences:** Sociology. **Visual/performing arts:** Arts management, commercial photography, commercial/advertising art, dance, dramatic, interior design, music history, music management, music performance, theater design. **Other:** Gender studies.

**Computing on campus.** 1,345 workstations in library, computer center. Commuter students can connect to campus network. Online course registration, online library, helpline, wireless network available.

**Student life. Freshman orientation:** Available. **Activities:** Jazz band, choral groups, dance, drama, international student organizations, literary magazine, student government, student newspaper, Bible study club, College Republicans, environmental club, Japanese club, ski club, students in free enterprise.

**Athletics.** NJCAA. **Intercollegiate:** Baseball M, basketball, soccer, softball W, volleyball W. **Intramural:** Basketball, bowling, football (non-tackle), golf, skiing, softball, table tennis, tennis, volleyball, weight lifting. **Team name:** Express.

**Student services.** Adult student services, career counseling, services for economically disadvantaged, student employment services, financial aid counseling, health services, on-campus daycare, personal counseling, placement for graduates, veterans' counselor. **Physically disabled:** Services for visually, hearing impaired. **Transfer:** Pre-admission transcript evaluation for new students. Transfer adviser, college fairs on campus for students transferring to 4-year colleges.

**Contact.** Phone: (567) 661-7225 Toll-free
number: (800) 466-9367 ext. 7777 Fax: (567) 661-7734
Donna Gruber, Director Enrollment Services, Owens Community College: Toledo, PO Box 10000, Toledo, OH 43699-1947

## Remington College: Cleveland
**Cleveland, Ohio**
**www.remingtoncollege.edu**              CB code: 3154

♦ For-profit 2-year technical and career college
♦ Very large city
♦ Interview required

**General.** Accredited by ACCSCT. **Enrollment:** 600 degree-seeking undergraduates. **Degrees:** 109 associate awarded. **Location:** 8 miles from Cleveland. **Calendar:** Continuous. **Full-time faculty:** 40 total. **Part-time faculty:** 10 total.

**Basis for selection.** The Wonderlic SLE exam will be used as the sole acceptable entrance exam for all applicants seeking admission. The required passing score for the Wonderlic exam will be 17 or higher for the Computer and Network Administration associate degree program, 13 or higher for all other associate degrees, and 12 or higher for all diploma programs. Applicants will be allowed to take the entrance exam a maximum of three times.

**2007-2008 Annual costs.** Tuition includes textbooks and supplies.

**Application procedures. Admission:** No deadline. $50 fee.

**Academics. Special study options:** Independent study. Externships. **Credit/placement by examination:** CLEP. **Support services:** Learning center.

**Majors. Business:** Business admin. **Computer sciences:** Networking.

**Computing on campus.** Online library available.

**Student services.** Career counseling, financial aid counseling, placement for graduates.

**Contact.** E-mail: jeri.prochaska@remingtoncollege.edu
Phone: (216) 475-7520 Fax: (216) 475-6055
Jeri Prochaska, Director of Recruitment, Remington College: Cleveland, 14445 Broadway Avenue, Cleveland, OH 44125

## Remington College: Cleveland West
### North Olmsted, Ohio
www.remingtoncollege.edu/clevelandwest/   CB code: 4200

◗ Private 2-year technical college
◗ Large town

**General.** Accredited by ACCSCT. **Enrollment:** 580 undergraduates. **Degrees:** 61 associate awarded. **Calendar:** Quarter. **Full-time faculty:** 15 total. **Part-time faculty:** 15 total.

**Basis for selection.** Selective admissions to allied health programs.

**2007-2008 Annual costs.** Tuition/fees: $13,910.

**Application procedures. Admission:** No deadline.

**Academics. Special study options:** Internships. **Credit/placement by examination:** CLEP. **Support services:** GED test center.

**Majors. Business:** Business admin. **Computer sciences:** Networking. **Protective services:** Criminal justice, law enforcement admin, police science.

**Contact.** Phone: (440) 777-2560
James Malley, Director of Recruitment, Remington College: Cleveland West, 26350 Brookpark Road, North Olmsted, OH 44070

## RETS Tech Center
### Centerville, Ohio
www.retstechcenter.com          CB code: 1610

◗ For-profit 2-year junior and technical college
◗ Commuter campus in large town

**General.** Founded in 1953. Accredited by ACCSCT. **Location:** 15 miles from Dayton. **Calendar:** Semester.

**Annual costs/financial aid.** Costs are charged per entire associate degree or diploma program and vary with specific program. Associate programs range from $17,015 to $24,785. Diploma programs range from $8,400 to $17,085. Books/supplies: $950. Personal expenses: $945. Need-based financial aid available to full-time and part-time students.

**Contact.** Phone: (937) 433-3410
Director, 555 East Alex Bell Road, Centerville, OH 45459-9627

## Rosedale Bible College
### Irwin, Ohio
www.rosedale.edu          CB code: 3936

◗ Private 2-year Bible and junior college affiliated with Mennonite Church
◗ Residential campus in rural community

**General.** Accredited by ABHE. **Enrollment:** 81 degree-seeking undergraduates. **Degrees:** 16 associate awarded. **Location:** 20 miles from Columbus. **Calendar:** Semester. **Part-time faculty:** 14 total. **Class size:** 57% < 20, 43% 20-39.

**Basis for selection.** Loyal devotion tó Christ most important. **Adult students:** SAT/ACT scores not required.

**2007-2008 Annual costs.** Tuition/fees: $6,405. Per-credit charge: $206. Room/board: $4,675.

**Application procedures. Admission:** No deadline. $50 fee. Application may be submitted online. Admission notification on a rolling basis. **Financial aid:** FAFSA, institutional form required. Applicants notified on a rolling basis.

**Academics. Special study options:** Dual enrollment of high school students. **Credit/placement by examination:** CLEP. **Support services:** Reduced course load.

**Majors. Theology:** Bible.

**Computing on campus.** 12 workstations in library, computer center. Wireless network available.

**Student life. Freshman orientation:** Mandatory. Preregistration for classes offered. **Policies:** Religious observance required. **Housing:** Guaranteed on-campus for all undergraduates. Single-sex dorms, apartments, substance-free housing available. **Activities:** Choral groups, drama, student government, student newspaper.

**Athletics. Intramural:** Basketball, soccer, table tennis, volleyball.

**Student services.** Campus ministries, financial aid counseling, health services. **Transfer:** Pre-admission transcript evaluation for new students.

**Contact.** E-mail: admissions@rosedale.edu
Phone: (740) 857-1311 Fax: (877) 857-1312
Brittany Tull, Enrollment Services Coordinator, Rosedale Bible College, 2270 Rosedale Road, Irwin, OH 43029

## Samuel Stephen College
### Chillicothe, Ohio
www.samuelstephencollege.edu          CB code: 2468

◗ For-profit 2-year business college
◗ Commuter campus in large town
◗ Interview required

**General.** Founded in 1962. Accredited by ACICS. **Enrollment:** 62 degree-seeking undergraduates. **Degrees:** 25 associate awarded. **Location:** 45 miles from Columbus, 90 miles from Cincinnati. **Calendar:** Quarter, limited summer session. **Full-time faculty:** 1 total. **Part-time faculty:** 14 total.

**Basis for selection.** Open admission. Placement tests in English and math required.

**2007-2008 Annual costs.** Tuition/fees: $7,035. Per-credit charge: $185.

**Financial aid.** All financial aid based on need. Need-based aid available for part-time students.

**Application procedures. Admission:** $50 fee. Admission notification on a rolling basis. **Financial aid:** No deadline. FAFSA, institutional form required.

**Academics. Credit/placement by examination:** CLEP. **Support services:** Remedial instruction, tutoring.

**Majors. Business:** Accounting, administrative services, business admin. **Computer sciences:** System admin. **Health:** Medical secretary.

**Computing on campus.** 28 workstations in computer center.

**Student life. Freshman orientation:** Mandatory.

**Student services.** Career counseling, financial aid counseling, placement for graduates.

**Contact.** E-mail: admissions@samuelstephencollege.edu
Phone: (740) 774-6300 Fax: (740) 774-6317
Admissions Representative, Samuel Stephen College, 1410 Industrial Drive, Chillicothe, OH 45601

## School of Advertising Art
### Kettering, Ohio
### www.saacollege.com

- For-profit 2-year visual arts and technical college
- Commuter campus in small city
- Interview required

**General.** Accredited by ACCSCT. **Enrollment:** 150 degree-seeking undergraduates. **Degrees:** 54 associate awarded. **Location:** 5 miles from downtown. **Calendar:** Quarter. **Full-time faculty:** 10 total. **Part-time faculty:** 5 total. **Class size:** 100% < 20.

### Student profile.

Out-of-state: 6%    25 or older: 3%

**Transfer out. Colleges most students transferred to 2007:** Art Institute of Pittsburgh, Art Institute of Atlanta, Columbus College of Art and Design, American Inter-Continental University of London, England.

**Basis for selection.** Portfolio and creative potential most important. Portfolio of 8 to 12 pieces of own artwork required. Depending on GPA and attendance, personal essay and 2 letters of recommendation may be required. **Homeschooled:** Proof of completion of high school requirements required.

**High school preparation.** Recommended units include English 4. 3 art units recommended.

**2007-2008 Annual costs.** Tuition/fees: $20,540. First year tuition for diploma program $16,200, required fees $2,150. Books/supplies: $2,210. Personal expenses: $500.

**Financial aid.** All financial aid based on need.

**Application procedures. Admission:** No deadline. No application fee. Application may be submitted online. Admission notification on a rolling basis. Conditional acceptance notification given at time of portfolio review and remains pending until final high school transcripts received. **Financial aid:** No deadline. FAFSA, institutional form required. Applicants notified by 7/1; must reply by 7/1 or within 1 week(s) of notification.

**Academics. Special study options:** Internships. **Credit/placement by examination:** CLEP, institutional tests. **Support services:** Remedial instruction, study skills assistance, tutoring.

**Majors. Communications:** Advertising. **Computer sciences:** Computer graphics, webmaster. **Visual/performing arts:** Commercial/advertising art.

**Computing on campus.** PC or laptop required. 16 workstations in computer center. Student web hosting, wireless network available.

**Student life. Freshman orientation:** Mandatory. Four-hour session held on a Saturday in the spring. **Activities:** Student government.

**Student services.** Career counseling, financial aid counseling, personal counseling, placement for graduates. **Transfer:** Re-entry adviser, pre-admission transcript evaluation for new students. Transfer adviser for students transferring to 4-year colleges.

**Contact.** E-mail: jessica@saacollege.com
Phone: (937) 294-0592 ext. 102 Toll-free number: (877) 300-9326 ext. 102
Fax: (937) 294-5869
Jessica Kantner, Director of Admissions, School of Advertising Art, 1725 East David Road, Kettering, OH 45440-1612

## Sinclair Community College
### Dayton, Ohio
### www.sinclair.edu
**CB member**
**CB code: 1720**

- Public 2-year community college
- Commuter campus in small city

**General.** Founded in 1887. Regionally accredited. Member of the League for Innovation. College offers both transfer and technical academic programs. **Enrollment:** 6,920 full-time, degree-seeking students. **Degrees:** 1,399 associate awarded. **ROTC:** Army, Air Force. **Location:** 50 miles from Cincinnati, 80 miles from Columbus. **Calendar:** Quarter, extensive summer session. **Full-time faculty:** 480 total. **Part-time faculty:** 690 total. **Class size:** 54% < 20, 45% 20-39, less than 1% 40-49, less than 1% 50-99, less than 1% >100. **Special facilities:** Art galleries, theater, center for corporate

and community events. **Partnerships:** Formal partnerships with eight area high schools.

### Student profile.

Out-of-state: 2%    25 or older: 47%

**Transfer out. Colleges most students transferred to 2007:** Wright State University, University of Cincinnati, University of Dayton, Capital University, Park College, Ohio State University.

**Basis for selection.** Open admission, but selective for some programs. Admission to allied health programs, paralegal program, tool and machining program, early childhood education all based on placement test scores and/or high school grades and specific program criteria. Allied Health Aptitude Test required for some selective programs. PAX required for nursing program. Interview required for some allied health programs.

**2007-2008 Annual costs.** Tuition/fees: $2,025; $3,307 out-of-district; $6,525 out-of-state. Per-credit charge: $45 in-district; $74 out-of-district; $145 out-of-state. Books/supplies: $810. Personal expenses: $2,000.

**Financial aid. Need-based:** Need-based aid available for part-time students. Work-study available nights, weekends and for part-time students. **Non-need-based:** Scholarships awarded for academics, athletics, state residency.

**Application procedures. Admission:** No deadline. $20 fee. Application may be submitted online. Admission notification on a rolling basis. Closing dates for allied health programs vary by program. **Financial aid:** Priority date 5/1, closing date 8/1. FAFSA, institutional form required. Applicants notified on a rolling basis.

**Academics. Special study options:** Cooperative education, cross-registration, distance learning, dual enrollment of high school students, ESL, honors, independent study, internships, liberal arts/career combination, student-designed major. License preparation in aviation, dental hygiene, nursing, occupational therapy, paramedic, physical therapy, radiology, real estate. **Credit/placement by examination:** AP, CLEP, IB, institutional tests. 45 credit hours maximum toward associate degree. **Support services:** Learning center, pre-admission summer program, reduced course load, remedial instruction, study skills assistance, tutoring, writing center.

**Majors. Architecture:** Technology. **Area/ethnic studies:** African-American. **Biology:** General, biotechnology. **Business:** General, accounting, administrative services, banking/financial services, business admin, hospitality admin, labor relations, labor studies, logistics, purchasing, real estate, retailing, sales/distribution, tourism promotion, tourism/travel. **Communications:** General. **Computer sciences:** General, applications programming, webmaster. **Education:** Elementary, multiple handicapped, music, physical, secondary, special. **Engineering:** General. **Engineering technology:** Architectural, automotive, CAD/CADD, civil, drafting, electrical, electromechanical, environmental, manufacturing, mechanical, plastics, robotics, surveying. **English:** English lit. **Family/consumer sciences:** Child care, food/nutrition, institutional food production. **Foreign languages:** Sign language interpretation. **Health:** Dental hygiene, dietetic technician, EMT paramedic, health services, licensed practical nurse, massage therapy, medical radiologic technology/radiation therapy, medical records technology, mental health services, occupational therapy assistant, physical therapy assistant, radiologic technology/medical imaging, respiratory therapy assistant, respiratory therapy technology, surgical technology. **History:** General. **Legal studies:** Legal secretary, paralegal. **Liberal arts:** Arts/sciences. **Math:** General. **Mechanic/repair:** Automotive, heating/ac/refrig. **Parks/recreation:** Health/fitness. **Personal/culinary services:** Culinary arts. **Physical sciences:** Chemistry, geology, physics. **Production:** Tool and die. **Protective services:** Corrections, criminal justice, fire safety technology, police science. **Psychology:** General. **Public administration:** General, human services, social work. **Social sciences:** Geography, sociology, urban studies. **Transportation:** Aviation management. **Visual/performing arts:** General, commercial/advertising art, dance, dramatic, interior design, music history, music performance, studio arts, theater design.

**Most popular majors.** Business/marketing 17%, computer/information sciences 6%, engineering/engineering technologies 10%, health sciences 27%, liberal arts 12%, visual/performing arts 6%.

**Computing on campus.** 1,000 workstations in library, computer center, student center. Commuter students can connect to campus network. Online course registration, helpline available.

**Student life. Freshman orientation:** Mandatory. Required for degree and certificate-seeking students. **Activities:** Bands, choral groups, dance, drama, music ensembles, musical theater, opera, student government, student newspaper, African American cultural club, Native American cultural club, Latinos Unidos en Sinclair club, Phi Theta Kappa honorary club, Rowdy Tartan pep club, social issues club, Appalachian club, College Republican's club, international students' club, think tank.

**Athletics.** NJCAA. **Intercollegiate:** Baseball M, basketball, golf, tennis, volleyball W. **Team name:** Tartans.

**Student services.** Adult student services, alcohol/substance abuse counseling, campus ministries, career counseling, services for economically disadvantaged, student employment services, financial aid counseling, personal counseling, placement for graduates, veterans' counselor, women's services. **Physically disabled:** Services for visually, speech, hearing impaired. **Transfer:** Pre-admission transcript evaluation for new students. Transfer adviser for students transferring to 4-year colleges.

**Contact.** E-mail: admit@sinclair.edu
Phone: (937) 512-3000 Toll-free number: (800) 315-3000
Fax: (937) 512-2393
Greg Potts, Director and Systems Manager for Outreach Services, Sinclair Community College, 444 West Third Street, Dayton, OH 45402-1460

## Southeastern Business College: Jackson
### Jackson, Ohio
www.southeasternbusinesscollege.com          CB code: 3264

- For-profit 2-year business college
- Commuter campus in large town

**General.** Accredited by ACICS. **Calendar:** Quarter.

**Annual costs/financial aid.** Books/supplies: $1,200. Need-based financial aid available to full-time and part-time students.

**Contact.** Phone: (740) 286-1554
Director/Registrar, 504 McCarty Lane, Jackson, OH 45640

## Southeastern Business College: Lancaster
### Lancaster, Ohio
www.careersohio.com          CB code: 3263

- For-profit 2-year business and technical college
- Residential campus in large town

**General.** Accredited by ACICS. **Location:** 25 miles from Columbus. **Calendar:** Quarter.

**Annual costs/financial aid.** Books/supplies: $1,380. Personal expenses: $2,460. Need-based financial aid available to full-time and part-time students.

**Contact.** Phone: (740) 687-6126
Admissions, 1522 Sheridan Drive, Lancaster, OH 43130-1303

## Southeastern Business College: New Boston
### New Boston, Ohio
www.southeasternbusinesscollege.com

- For-profit 2-year branch campus and business college
- Commuter campus in rural community

**General.** Accredited by ACICS. **Enrollment:** 50 undergraduates. **Degrees:** 16 associate awarded. **Calendar:** Quarter. **Full-time faculty:** 1 total. **Part-time faculty:** 13 total.

**Basis for selection.** Open admission.

**Financial aid. Need-based:** Need-based aid available for part-time students.

**Application procedures. Admission:** No deadline. $50 fee. Application must be submitted on paper. **Financial aid:** No deadline. FAFSA required.

**Academics. Special study options:** Cooperative education. **Credit/placement by examination:** AP, CLEP. 16 credit hours maximum toward associate degree. **Support services:** Tutoring.

**Majors. Business:** Accounting, administrative services, business admin. **Computer sciences:** General. **Health:** Office admin.

**Computing on campus.** 30 workstations in library, computer center.

**Student life. Freshman orientation:** Mandatory.

**Student services.** Career counseling, financial aid counseling.

**Contact.** E-mail: admit_nb@yahoo.com
Phone: (740) 456-4124 Fax: (740) 456-5163
Rebecca Mowery, Admissions Representative, Southeastern Business College: New Boston, 3879 Rhodes Avenue, New Boston, OH 45662

## Southern State Community College
### Hillsboro, Ohio
www.sscc.edu          CB code: 1752

- Public 2-year community college
- Commuter campus in small town

**General.** Founded in 1975. Regionally accredited. **Enrollment:** 2,419 degree-seeking undergraduates. **Degrees:** 318 associate awarded. **Location:** 60 miles from Cincinnati, 55 miles from Columbus. **Calendar:** Quarter, limited summer session. **Full-time faculty:** 47 total; 17% have terminal degrees, 49% women. **Part-time faculty:** 96 total; 3% have terminal degrees, 52% women. **Class size:** 61% < 20, 37% 20-39, less than 1% 40-49, less than 1% 50-99.

**Student profile.** Among degree-seeking undergraduates, 51% enrolled in a transfer program, 49% enrolled in a vocational program, 756 enrolled as first-time, first-year students, 93 transferred in from other institutions.

| | | | |
|---|---|---|---|
| Part-time: | 45% | Hispanic American: | 1% |
| Women: | 72% | Native American: | 1% |
| African American: | 2% | 25 or older: | 58% |
| Asian American: | 1% | | |

**Basis for selection.** Open admission, but selective for some programs. Special requirements for nursing, respiratory therapy, EMT programs. Interview required for nursing program. **Learning Disabled:** If modifications requested, appointment with Disabilities Service Coordinator required.

**2007-2008 Annual costs.** Tuition/fees: $3,390; $6,528 out-of-state. Per-credit charge: $87 in-state; $168 out-of-state. Books/supplies: $1,500.

**2006-2007 Financial aid. Need-based:** 54% of total undergraduate aid awarded as scholarships/grants, 46% as loans/jobs. Need-based aid available for part-time students. Work-study available for part-time students. **Non-need-based:** Scholarships awarded for academics, art, athletics, music/drama.

**Application procedures. Admission:** No deadline. No application fee. Application must be submitted on paper. Admission notification on a rolling basis. **Financial aid:** Priority date 7/1, closing date 9/1. FAFSA, institutional form required. Applicants notified by 4/15; must reply within 2 week(s) of notification.

**Academics. Special study options:** Cross-registration, distance learning, dual enrollment of high school students, liberal arts/career combination, student-designed major. License preparation in nursing, paramedic, real estate. **Credit/placement by examination:** AP, CLEP, institutional tests. 45 credit hours maximum toward associate degree. **Support services:** GED preparation and test center, learning center, remedial instruction, tutoring.

**Majors. Agriculture:** General. **Business:** General, accounting technology, administrative services, business admin, real estate. **Computer sciences:** Applications programming, programming, systems analysis. **Education:** Early childhood, teacher assistance. **Engineering technology:** CAD/CADD, computer systems, drafting, electrical. **Health:** EMT paramedic, medical assistant, nursing (RN), respiratory therapy technology, substance abuse counseling. **Liberal arts:** Arts/sciences. **Protective services:** Corrections, police science. **Public administration:** Human services.

**Most popular majors.** Business/marketing 15%, computer/information sciences 7%, health sciences 35%, liberal arts 32%.

**Computing on campus.** 300 workstations in library, computer center. Commuter students can connect to campus network. Online library, help-line, wireless network available.

**Student life. Freshman orientation:** Mandatory. Preregistration for classes offered. **Activities:** Bands, choral groups, drama.

**Athletics. Intercollegiate:** Basketball, soccer M, softball W, volleyball W. **Team name:** Patriots.

**Student services.** Career counseling, student employment services, financial aid counseling, on-campus daycare, placement for graduates. **Physically disabled:** Services for visually, speech, hearing impaired. **Transfer:** Transfer adviser, college fairs on campus for students transferring to 4-year colleges.

**Contact.** E-mail: info@sscc.edu
Phone: (937) 393-3431 ext. 2607 Fax: (937) 393-6682
Wendy Johnson, Director of Admissions, Southern State Community
College, 100 Hobart Drive, Hillsboro, OH 45133

## Southwestern College: Dayton
Dayton, Ohio
www.swcollege.net                    CB code: 2483

- For-profit 2-year business college
- Commuter campus in small city

**General.** Accredited by ACICS. **Calendar:** Quarter.

**Annual costs/financial aid.** Books/supplies: $600. Need-based finan-
cial aid available to full-time and part-time students.

**Contact.** Phone: (937) 224-0061
Director, 111 West 1st Street, Dayton, OH 45402

## Southwestern College: Franklin
Franklin, Ohio
www.swcollege.net                    CB code: 3268

- For-profit 2-year technical and career college
- Large town

**General.** Accredited by ACICS. **Calendar:** Quarter.

**Annual costs/financial aid.** Tuition/fees (2007-2008): $10,150.

**Contact.** Phone: (937) 746-6633 ext. 45103
Director of Admissions, 201 East Second Street, Franklin, OH 45005

## Southwestern College: Tri-County
Cincinnati, Ohio
www.swcollege.net                    CB code: 2478

- For-profit 2-year career college
- Small city
- Interview required

**General.** Accredited by ACICS. **Enrollment:** 725 degree-seeking undergraduates. **Degrees:** 20 associate awarded. **Calendar:** Quarter, extensive
summer session. **Full-time faculty:** 10 total. **Part-time faculty:** 20 total.

**Basis for selection.** Open admission. **Homeschooled:** High school diploma or GED is required but will accept non-high school graduates if they
pass the Ability-to-Benefit examination and must obtain their GED prior to
graduation from college.

**2007-2008 Annual costs.** Tuition/fees: $10,050.

**Financial aid.** All financial aid based on need.

**Application procedures.** **Admission:** No deadline. $100 fee. Applica-
tion must be submitted on paper. Admission notification on a rolling basis.
**Financial aid:** No deadline. FAFSA required.

**Academics.** **Credit/placement by examination:** CLEP. **Support services:** GED preparation, tutoring.

**Majors.** **Business:** Accounting, business admin. **Health:** Medical assistant. **Protective services:** Law enforcement admin.

**Computing on campus.** Online library available.

**Student life.** **Freshman orientation:** Available.

**Contact.** E-mail: rkimble@swcollege.net
Phone: (513) 874-0432
Roy Kimble, Director of Admissions, Southwestern College; Tri-County,
149 Northland Boulevard, Cincinnati, OH 45246

## Southwestern College: Vine Street Campus
Cincinnati, Ohio
www.swcollege.net                    CB code: 3267

- For-profit 2-year business and health science college
- Large city
- Interview required

**General.** Accredited by ACICS. **Enrollment:** 416 degree-seeking undergraduates; 416 non-degree-seeking students. **Degrees:** 43 associate awarded.
**Location:** Downtown. **Calendar:** Quarter, extensive summer session. **Full-
time faculty:** 5 total; 60% minority, 60% women. **Part-time faculty:** 12
total; 67% minority, 58% women.

**Student profile.**

| | | | |
|---|---|---|---|
| African American: | 83% | 25 or older: | 65% |

**Transfer out.** 1% of students enrolled in the transfer program go on to
4-year colleges. **Colleges most students transferred to 2007:** Southwestern College: Tri-County Campus.

**Basis for selection.** Open admission. **Homeschooled:** Interview required. Applicants without high school diploma or GED must pass an ATB
exam. **Learning Disabled:** Recommend applicants with high school IEP to
inform Education department, but not required.

**2007-2008 Annual costs.** Personal expenses: $2,500.

**Financial aid.** All financial aid based on need. Need-based aid available
for part-time students.

**Application procedures.** **Admission:** No deadline. $20 fee. Applica-
tion may be submitted online. **Financial aid:** FAFSA required.

**Academics.** **Credit/placement by examination:** CLEP. **Support services:** GED preparation and test center, remedial instruction, study skills
assistance, tutoring.

**Majors.** **Business:** General.

**Computing on campus.** 65 workstations in library, computer center.
Online library available.

**Student life.** **Freshman orientation:** Mandatory.

**Contact.** Phone: (513) 421-3212 Fax: (513) 421-8325
Roy Kimble, Director of Admission, Southwestern College: Vine Street
Campus, 632 Vine Street, Cincinnati, OH 45202

## Stark State College of Technology
North Canton, Ohio
www.starkstate.edu                    CB code: 1688

- Public 2-year technical college
- Commuter campus in small city

**General.** Founded in 1970. Regionally accredited. **Enrollment:** 7,165 degree-
seeking undergraduates. **Degrees:** 753 associate awarded. **Location:** 50 miles
from Cleveland. **Calendar:** Semester, limited summer session. **Full-time
faculty:** 145 total. **Part-time faculty:** 460 total.

**Student profile.**

| | | | |
|---|---|---|---|
| Out-of-state: | 1% | 25 or older: | 50% |

**Basis for selection.** Open admission, but selective for some programs.
Special requirements for allied health programs. **Adult students:** SAT/ACT
scores not required if out of high school 5 year(s) or more. **Learning Disabled:** All students should meet with disability services coordinator.

**High school preparation.** Recommended units include English 4, mathematics 4, social studies 3, science 3 and foreign language 1.

**2007-2008 Annual costs.** Tuition/fees: $3,810; $5,610 out-of-state. Per-
credit charge: $103 in-state; $163 out-of-state. Books/supplies: $900.

**Financial aid.** All financial aid based on need. Need-based aid available
for part-time students. Work-study available nights, weekends and for part-
time students.

**Application procedures. Admission:** Priority date 6/1; no deadline. $65 fee. Application may be submitted online. Admission notification on a rolling basis. **Financial aid:** Priority date 5/1; no closing date. FAFSA, institutional form required. Applicants notified on a rolling basis starting 4/1; must reply within 4 week(s) of notification.

**Academics. Special study options:** Accelerated study, cooperative education, cross-registration, distance learning, double major, dual enrollment of high school students, independent study, internships, liberal arts/career combination, student-designed major, weekend college. License preparation in dental hygiene, nursing, paramedic. **Credit/placement by examination:** CLEP, institutional tests. 12 credit hours maximum toward associate degree. **Support services:** Learning center, pre-admission summer program, reduced course load, remedial instruction, study skills assistance, tutoring, writing center.

**Majors. Architecture:** Environmental design, urban/community planning. **Business:** General, accounting, accounting technology, accounting/business management, accounting/finance, administrative services, business admin, communications, construction management, e-commerce, executive assistant, hospitality admin, international, logistics, management information systems, market research, marketing, office management, office technology, operations, sales/distribution, taxation. **Computer sciences:** General, applications programming, computer graphics, computer science, data entry, data processing, database management, information systems, information technology, networking, programming, security, systems analysis, web page design, webmaster, word processing. **Conservation:** Environmental studies. **Education:** Early childhood. **Engineering:** Architectural, civil, electrical, environmental, software. **Engineering technology:** Architectural, civil, construction, electrical, manufacturing, surveying. **Family/consumer sciences:** Aging. **Health:** Clinical lab assistant, clinical lab technology, dental hygiene, massage therapy, medical assistant, medical records technology, nursing (RN), occupational therapy assistant, office assistant, physical therapy assistant, respiratory therapy assistant, respiratory therapy technology. **Legal studies:** Court reporting, legal secretary. **Liberal arts:** Arts/sciences. **Math:** General. **Mechanic/repair:** Automotive, electronics/electrical, heating/ac/refrig, industrial. **Protective services:** Firefighting. **Public administration:** Human services. **Social sciences:** General.

**Computing on campus.** 500 workstations in computer center, student center. Commuter students can connect to campus network. Online course registration, helpline, wireless network available.

**Student life. Freshman orientation:** Available. Preregistration for classes offered. Half-day prior to all semesters. Evening sessions are 2 hours. **Activities:** Literary magazine, student newspaper, Bible study group, Minority Awareness Association, Phi Theta Kappa.

**Athletics. Team name:** Spartans.

**Student services.** Adult student services, campus ministries, career counseling, services for economically disadvantaged, student employment services, financial aid counseling, minority student services, on-campus daycare, personal counseling, placement for graduates, veterans' counselor. **Physically disabled:** Services for visually, speech, hearing impaired. **Learning disabled:** Comprehensive services available. **Transfer:** Pre-admission transcript evaluation for new students. Transfer adviser, college fairs on campus for students transferring to 4-year colleges.

**Contact.** E-mail: info@starkstate.edu
Phone: (330) 494-6170 ext. 4228 Toll-free number: (800) 797-8275
Fax: (330) 497-6313
Wallace Hoffer, Dean of Student Services, Stark State College of Technology, 6200 Frank Avenue NW, North Canton, OH 44720

## Stautzenberger College
Maumee, Ohio
www.sctoday.edu                    CB code: 2487

- For-profit 2-year business and technical college
- Commuter campus in large city
- Interview required

**General.** Founded in 1928. Accredited by ACICS. **Enrollment:** 759 degree-seeking undergraduates. **Degrees:** 162 associate awarded. **Location:** 50 miles from Detroit, 120 miles from Cleveland. **Calendar:** Quarter, extensive summer session. **Full-time faculty:** 10 total. **Part-time faculty:** 40 total. **Class size:** 85% < 20, 15% 20-39. **Special facilities:** Veterinary technician labs, medical assisting labs, massage therapy clinic. **Partnerships:** Formal partnerships with Microsoft IT Academy, Novell Training Partner.

**Basis for selection.** Open admission. Campus visit and completion of Program Questionaire required. **Learning Disabled:** Any special accommodations must be requested in writing with appropriate documentation. Approval needed before acceptance.

**2008-2009 Annual costs.** Tuition ranges from $195 to $360 per credit hour; required fees, $270. Books/supplies: $1,050. Personal expenses: $2,619.

**Financial aid.** All financial aid based on need. Need-based aid available for part-time students.

**Application procedures. Admission:** No deadline. $25 fee. Application must be submitted on paper. Admission notification on a rolling basis. **Financial aid:** No deadline. FAFSA required. Applicants notified on a rolling basis.

**Academics. Special study options:** License preparation in real estate. **Credit/placement by examination:** CLEP. **Support services:** Learning center, study skills assistance, tutoring.

**Majors. Business:** Accounting technology, entrepreneurial studies, office technology. **Computer sciences:** Data entry, LAN/WAN management, web page design. **Health:** Insurance coding, massage therapy, medical assistant, medical secretary, medical transcription, receptionist, veterinary technology/assistant. **Legal studies:** Court reporting, paralegal. **Other:** Personal Fitness Trainer.

**Computing on campus.** 200 workstations in library, computer center.

**Student life. Freshman orientation:** Available.

**Student services.** Financial aid counseling, placement for graduates, veterans' counselor. **Transfer:** Pre-admission transcript evaluation for new students.

**Contact.** E-mail: admissions@stautzenberger.com
Phone: (419) 866-0261 Toll-free number: (800) 552-5099
Fax: (419) 867-9821
Karen Fitzgerald, Director of Admission, Stautzenberger College, 1796 Indian Wood Circle, Maumee, OH 43537

## Stautzenberger College: Strongsville
Strongsville, Ohio
www.sctoday.edu/strongsville

- For-profit 2-year career college
- Large town
- Interview required

**General.** Accredited by ACICS. **Enrollment:** 299 degree-seeking undergraduates. **Degrees:** 14 associate awarded. **Calendar:** Quarter, extensive summer session. **Full-time faculty:** 8 total; 88% have terminal degrees, 75% women. **Part-time faculty:** 25 total; 44% have terminal degrees, 56% women. **Class size:** 77% < 20, 23% 20-39.

**Student profile.** Among degree-seeking undergraduates, 100% enrolled in a vocational program, 4% already have a bachelor's degree or higher, 129 enrolled as first-time, first-year students.

| | | | |
|---|---|---|---|
| Part-time: | 66% | Hispanic American: | 3% |
| Women: | 93% | 25 or older: | 35% |
| African American: | 3% | | |

**Transfer out. Colleges most students transferred to 2007:** Cuyahoga Community College, Stautzenberger College Toledo, Lorain County Community College.

**Basis for selection.** Open admission. **Homeschooled:** Interview required.

**2007-2008 Annual costs.** Tuition/fees: $9,045. Per-credit charge: $195.

**Financial aid.** All financial aid based on need. Need-based aid available for part-time students.

**Application procedures. Admission:** No deadline. $25 fee. Application may be submitted online. Admission notification on a rolling basis. **Financial aid:** No deadline. FAFSA required. Applicants notified on a rolling basis.

**Academics. Special study options:** Internships. **Credit/placement by examination:** CLEP. **Support services:** Reduced course load, study skills assistance, tutoring.

**Majors. Health:** Veterinary technology/assistant. **Legal studies:** Paralegal.

**Computing on campus.** Online library, wireless network available.

**Student life. Freshman orientation:** Mandatory.

**Student services. Transfer:** Pre-admission transcript evaluation for new students.

**Contact.** E-mail: rsgreen@stautzenberger.com
Phone: (440) 846-1999
Rober Green, Director of Admissions, Stautzenberger College: Strongsville, 12925 Pearl Road, Strongsville, OH 44136

## Technology Education College
**Columbus, Ohio**
**www.teccollege.com**                   **CB code: 3035**

- For-profit 2-year business, health science, technical and career college
- Commuter campus in very large city
- Application essay, interview required

**General.** Accredited by ACCSCT. **Enrollment:** 244 degree-seeking undergraduates. **Degrees:** 146 associate awarded. **Calendar:** Quarter, extensive summer session. **Full-time faculty:** 25 total. **Part-time faculty:** 10 total.

**Basis for selection.** Open admission. Applicants with ACT score of 18 or SAT score of 840 (exclusive of Writing) not required to take entrance examination.

**2007-2008 Annual costs.** Tuition varies per program, but averages $11,300 per academic year. Books/supplies: $700.

**Financial aid.** All financial aid based on need. Need-based aid available for part-time students. Work-study available nights.

**Application procedures. Admission:** No deadline. $20 fee. Admission notification on a rolling basis. **Financial aid:** No deadline. FAFSA required. Applicants notified on a rolling basis.

**Academics. Credit/placement by examination:** CLEP. **Support services:** Learning center, study skills assistance, tutoring.

**Majors. Engineering technology:** CAD/CADD. **Health:** Medical assistant. **Protective services:** Police science.

**Computing on campus.** 100 workstations in library, computer center, student center. Helpline available.

**Student life. Freshman orientation:** Mandatory. **Housing:** Single-sex dorms available.

**Student services.** Career counseling, student employment services, financial aid counseling, personal counseling, placement for graduates.

**Contact.** Phone: (614) 456-4600 Toll-free number: (800) 838-3233
Fax: (614) 456-4640
Sarah Bode, Director of Admissions, Technology Education College, 2745 Winchester Pike, Columbus, OH 43232

## Terra State Community College
**Fremont, Ohio**
**www.terra.edu**                   **CB code: 0365**

- Public 2-year community and technical college
- Commuter campus in large town

**General.** Founded in 1968. Regionally accredited. **Enrollment:** 2,260 degree-seeking undergraduates. **Degrees:** 190 associate awarded. **Location:** 33 miles from Toledo, 86 miles from Columbus. **Calendar:** Semester, limited summer session. **Full-time faculty:** 50 total. **Part-time faculty:** 150 total.

**Transfer out. Colleges most students transferred to 2007:** Bowling Green State University, University of Toledo, Owens Community College, Ohio State University, Tiffin University.

**Basis for selection.** Open admission.

**High school preparation.** Recommended units include English 4, mathematics 3, social studies 3 and science 3. Algebra recommended for engineering and computer programming applicants.

**2007-2008 Annual costs.** Tuition/fees: $3,406; $5,656 out-of-state. Per-credit charge: $108 in-state; $176 out-of-state. Books/supplies: $1,350. Personal expenses: $890.

**Financial aid. Need-based:** Need-based aid available for part-time students. Work-study available for part-time students. **Non-need-based:** Scholarships awarded for academics.

**Application procedures. Admission:** No deadline. No application fee. Application may be submitted online. Admission notification on a rolling basis. **Financial aid:** Priority date 5/1; no closing date. FAFSA, institutional form required. Applicants notified on a rolling basis starting 5/15.

**Academics. Special study options:** Accelerated study, cooperative education, distance learning, double major, dual enrollment of high school students, honors, independent study, internships, student-designed major, study abroad, weekend college. Bachelor's degree programs available on campus. License preparation in real estate. **Credit/placement by examination:** AP, CLEP, institutional tests. **Support services:** GED test center, learning center, reduced course load, remedial instruction, study skills assistance, tutoring, writing center.

**Majors. Biology:** General. **Business:** General, accounting, administrative services, business admin, finance, marketing, office management, office/clerical, real estate. **Communications:** General. **Computer sciences:** General, computer graphics, information systems, programming. **Education:** General, early childhood. **Engineering:** Mechanical, polymer. **Engineering technology:** Architectural, construction, drafting, electrical, manufacturing, plastics, robotics, surveying. **English:** English lit, technical writing. **Foreign languages:** Comparative lit, sign language interpretation. **Health:** Medical secretary. **Interdisciplinary:** Natural sciences. **Liberal arts:** Arts/sciences. **Mechanic/repair:** Automotive, heating/ac/refrig. **Physical sciences:** Chemistry, physics. **Production:** Machine tool, welding. **Protective services:** Police science. **Visual/performing arts:** Commercial/advertising art.

**Computing on campus.** 299 workstations in library, computer center. Online course registration, online library available.

**Student life. Freshman orientation:** Mandatory, $16 fee. **Activities:** Jazz band, choral groups, music ensembles, student government, Phi Theta Kappa, Koinonia, Society of Plastic Engineers.

**Athletics.** NJCAA. **Intramural:** Basketball, bowling, football (non-tackle) M, softball, table tennis, tennis, volleyball. **Team name:** Thunder-Cats.

**Student services.** Career counseling, student employment services, on-campus daycare, placement for graduates, veterans' counselor. **Physically disabled:** Services for visually, speech, hearing impaired. **Transfer:** Re-entry adviser, pre-admission transcript evaluation for new students. Transfer center, transfer adviser, college fairs on campus for students transferring to 4-year colleges.

**Contact.** E-mail: admissions@terra.edu
Phone: (419) 559-2349 Toll-free number: (866) 288-3772 ext. 2349
Fax: (419) 334-9035
Cory Stine, Assistant Dean of Student Support Services, Terra State Community College, 2830 Napoleon Road, Fremont, OH 43420-9600

## Trumbull Business College
**Warren, Ohio**
**www.tbc-trumbullbusiness.com**                   **CB code: 3270**

- For-profit 2-year business college
- Commuter campus in large town

**General.** Accredited by ACICS. **Enrollment:** 325 degree-seeking undergraduates. **Degrees:** 97 associate awarded. **Calendar:** Quarter. **Full-time faculty:** 15 total. **Part-time faculty:** 10 total.

**Basis for selection.** Open admission.

**2007-2008 Annual costs.** Tuition/fees: $11,055. Per-credit charge: $244.

**Financial aid. Need-based:** Need-based aid available for part-time students.

**Application procedures. Admission:** No deadline. $75 fee. Admission notification on a rolling basis. **Financial aid:** FAFSA required.

**Academics. Credit/placement by examination:** AP, CLEP.

**Majors. Business:** Accounting, business admin, office technology. **Computer sciences:** General, applications programming. **Health:** Medical secretary. **Legal studies:** Legal secretary.

**Computing on campus.** 100 workstations in library, computer center.

**Student life. Freshman orientation:** Available.

**Student services.** Career counseling, financial aid counseling, placement for graduates.

**Contact.** E-mail: admissions@tbc-trumbullbusiness.com
Phone: (330) 369-3200 ext. 26
Shirlee Rohrbaugh, Director of Admissions, Trumbull Business College,
3200 Ridge Road, Warren, OH 44484

## University of Akron: Wayne College
### Orrville, Ohio
**www.wayne.uakron.edu**                    CB code: 1892

- Public 2-year branch campus and junior college
- Commuter campus in small town

**General.** Founded in 1972. Regionally accredited. **Enrollment:** 1,559 degree-seeking undergraduates. **Degrees:** 100 associate awarded. **ROTC:** Army, Air Force. **Location:** 35 miles from Akron. **Calendar:** Semester, limited summer session. **Full-time faculty:** 26 total. **Part-time faculty:** 126 total. **Class size:** 65% < 20, 31% 20-39, 3% 40-49, less than 1% 50-99. **Special facilities:** Nature trail, arboretum, wetlands, mock hazardous spill facility, distance learning room.

**Transfer out. Colleges most students transferred to 2007:** Ashland University, Kent State, Cleveland State, Ohio State, Ohio University.

**Basis for selection.** Open admission. **Adult students:** SAT/ACT scores not required if applicant over 21. **Homeschooled:** Recommend completion of GED.

**High school preparation.** Recommended units include English 4, mathematics 3, social studies 3, science 3 and foreign language 2.

**2007-2008 Annual costs.** Tuition/fees: $5,485; $12,854 out-of-state. Books/supplies: $600. Personal expenses: $1,465.

**Financial aid. Need-based:** Need-based aid available for part-time students. Work-study available nights and weekends. **Non-need-based:** Scholarships awarded for academics, art, athletics, leadership, minority status, music/drama, state residency. **Additional information:** All financial aid processed through University of Akron.

**Application procedures. Admission:** No deadline. $30 fee, may be waived for applicants with need. Application may be submitted online. Admission notification on a rolling basis. **Financial aid:** Closing date 3/15. FAFSA, institutional form required. Applicants notified on a rolling basis starting 4/15.

**Academics.** First 2 years of general bachelor's degree classes available for students who plan to continue at University of Akron or other colleges and universities. Paraprofessional and technical programs (associates and certificates) available in business, industry, public services occupation areas. **Special study options:** Cooperative education, cross-registration, distance learning, dual enrollment of high school students, honors, independent study, internships, liberal arts/career combination, student-designed major, weekend college. **Credit/placement by examination:** AP, CLEP, institutional tests. **Support services:** Learning center, remedial instruction, study skills assistance, tutoring, writing center.

**Majors. Business:** General, accounting, administrative services, business admin, management information systems, marketing, office management, office technology. **Computer sciences:** Applications programming, data processing, networking. **Health:** Environmental health, health care admin, medical assistant, medical radiologic technology/radiation therapy, medical secretary, respiratory therapy technology, surgical technology. **Legal studies:** Legal secretary. **Liberal arts:** Arts/sciences. **Public administration:** Social work.

**Most popular majors.** Business/marketing 57%, health sciences 6%, liberal arts 20%, security/protective services 13%.

**Computing on campus.** 140 workstations in library, computer center, student center. Commuter students can connect to campus network. Online course registration, helpline available.

**Student life. Freshman orientation:** Mandatory. **Activities:** Literary magazine, student government, student newspaper.

**Athletics.** NJCAA. **Intercollegiate:** Basketball, cheerleading M, golf M, volleyball W. **Intramural:** Basketball, racquetball, volleyball W. **Team name:** Warriors.

**Student services.** Adult student services, career counseling, student employment services, financial aid counseling, personal counseling, placement for graduates, veterans' counselor. **Physically disabled:** Services for visually, speech, hearing impaired. **Learning disabled:** Comprehensive services available. **Transfer:** Pre-admission transcript evaluation for new students. Transfer adviser, college fairs on campus for students transferring to 4-year colleges.

**Contact.** E-mail: wayneadmissions@uakron.edu
Phone: (330) 683-2010 Toll-free number: (800) 221-8308 ext. 8900
Fax: (330) 684-8989
Alicia Broadus, Enrollment Specialist, University of Akron: Wayne College, 1901 Smucker Road, Orrville, OH 44667-9758

## University of Cincinnati: Clermont College
### Batavia, Ohio
**www.ucclermont.edu**                    CB code: 3073

- Public 2-year branch campus college
- Commuter campus in small town

**General.** Founded in 1972. Regionally accredited. College serves Clermont, Brown, and eastern Hamilton counties. One of 2 open-access regional campuses of the University of Cincinnati. **Enrollment:** 2,506 degree-seeking undergraduates; 436 non-degree-seeking students. **Degrees:** 320 associate awarded. **ROTC:** Army. **Location:** 17 miles from Cincinnati. **Calendar:** Quarter, limited summer session. **Full-time faculty:** 55 total; 40% have terminal degrees, 11% minority, 47% women. **Part-time faculty:** 2 total; 50% women. **Partnerships:** Formal partnerships with Barnes Aerospace and the Tech Prep Consortium.

**Student profile.** Among degree-seeking undergraduates, 632 enrolled as first-time, first-year students, 144 transferred in from other institutions.

| | | | |
|---|---|---|---|
| Part-time: | 33% | Asian American: | 1% |
| Out-of-state: | 1% | Hispanic American: | 1% |
| Women: | 60% | Native American: | 1% |
| African American: | 2% | 25 or older: | 36% |

**Transfer out. Colleges most students transferred to 2007:** Northern Kentucky University, University of Cincinnati, Wilmington College.

**Basis for selection.** Open admission, but selective for some programs. Admissions to surgical technology and respiratory programs requires satisfactory completion of biology and chemistry within past 5 years. **Homeschooled:** All existing school records and formal documentation of high school curriculum required. Course content descriptions, copy of superintendent release form, notarized statement from parent, and precollege curriculum form completed and signed by parent may also be required. Appointment involving student, teacher, and admissions representative may be encouraged.

**High school preparation.** 16 units recommended. Recommended units include English 4, mathematics 3, social studies 2, science 2, foreign language 2 and academic electives 2. 1 fine arts recommended.

**2007-2008 Annual costs.** Tuition/fees: $4,542; $11,394 out-of-state. Per-credit charge: $127 in-state; $317 out-of-state.

**Financial aid. Need-based:** Need-based aid available for part-time students. Work-study available nights, weekends and for part-time students. **Non-need-based:** Scholarships awarded for academics, state residency. **Additional information:** All financial aid applications and awards administered through Uptown campus except in-house loans and scholarships.

**Application procedures. Admission:** No deadline. $35 fee, may be waived for applicants with need. Application may be submitted online. Admission notification on a rolling basis. **Financial aid:** No deadline. FAFSA required. Applicants notified on a rolling basis.

**Academics. Special study options:** Cooperative education, cross-registration, distance learning, double major, dual enrollment of high school students, honors, independent study, internships, student-designed major, study abroad, weekend college. Bachelor's degree programs available on campus. License preparation in aviation, nursing, paramedic, real estate. **Credit/placement by examination:** AP, CLEP, IB, institutional tests. 50% of hours needed for degree may be earned by examination. **Support services:** GED test center, learning center, reduced course load, remedial instruction, study skills assistance, tutoring.

**Majors. Architecture:** Urban/community planning. **Biology:** General. **Business:** General, accounting technology, administrative services, business admin, office management, office technology. **Communications:** Digital media. **Computer sciences:** General, applications programming, computer graphics, data entry, data processing, information technology, networking, programming, vendor certification, web page design. **Education:** Early childhood, elementary, kindergarten/preschool, middle, secondary. **Engineering**

**technology:** CAD/CADD, computer systems. **Health:** EMT ambulance attendant, EMT paramedic, nursing (RN), predental, premedicine, prenursing, prepharmacy, preveterinary, respiratory therapy technology, surgical technology. **Legal studies:** Legal secretary, paralegal, prelaw. **Liberal arts:** Arts/sciences. **Physical sciences:** Chemistry. **Protective services:** Corrections, criminal justice, forensics, law enforcement admin, security services. **Psychology:** General. **Public administration:** Social work. **Social sciences:** Urban studies. **Transportation:** Aviation, flight instructor.

**Computing on campus.** 77 workstations in library, computer center, student center. Commuter students can connect to campus network. Online course registration, online library, helpline, wireless network available.

**Student life. Freshman orientation:** Mandatory. Preregistration for classes offered. Programs held each quarter for 2-3 hours. **Activities:** Campus ministries, dance, student government, student newspaper, student tribunal, Christian Fellowship, foreign language club, Young Democrats, Circle K Club (Kiwanis).

**Athletics.** USCAA. **Intercollegiate:** Basketball, cheerleading M, golf M, softball W, tennis, volleyball W. **Intramural:** Volleyball. **Team name:** Cougars.

**Student services.** Alcohol/substance abuse counseling, campus ministries, career counseling, services for economically disadvantaged, student employment services, financial aid counseling, personal counseling, placement for graduates, veterans' counselor, women's services. **Physically disabled:** Services for visually, speech, hearing impaired. **Transfer:** Transfer adviser, college fairs on campus for students transferring to 4-year colleges.

**Contact.** E-mail: clc.admissions@uc.edu
Phone: (513) 732-5202 Toll-free number: (866) 446-2822
Fax: (513) 732-5303
Blaine Kelley, Senior Enrollment Advisor, University of Cincinnati: Clermont College, 4200 Clermont College Drive, Batavia, OH 45103

## University of Cincinnati: Raymond Walters College
Cincinnati, Ohio
www.rwc.uc.edu                                            CB code: 0354

- Public 2-year branch campus college
- Commuter campus in large city

**General.** Founded in 1967. Regionally accredited. **Location:** 15 miles from downtown. **Calendar:** Quarter.

**Annual costs/financial aid.** Tuition/fees (2007-2008): $5,232; $13,566 out-of-state. Books/supplies: $700. Need-based financial aid available to full-time and part-time students.

**Contact.** Phone: (513) 745-5700
Director, Enrollment Services, 9555 Plainfield Road, Cincinnati, OH 45236-1096

## University of Northwestern Ohio
Lima, Ohio
www.unoh.edu                                              CB code: 0816

- Private 2-year business and technical college
- Residential campus in large town

**General.** Founded in 1920. Regionally accredited. **Enrollment:** 2,935 degree-seeking undergraduates. **Degrees:** 83 bachelor's, 598 associate awarded. **Location:** 75 miles from Toledo, 90 miles from Columbus. **Calendar:** Differs by program. Quarter and 6-week session. Extensive summer session. **Full-time faculty:** 90 total. **Part-time faculty:** 42 total.

**Student profile.**

| | | | |
|---|---|---|---|
| Out-of-state: | 21% | Live on campus: | 65% |
| 25 or older: | 18% | | |

**Transfer out.** Colleges most students transferred to 2007: Lima Technical College, Ohio State University, Wright State University, Bowling Green State University.

**Basis for selection.** Students with high school GPA of 1.5 or lower admitted conditionally. **Homeschooled:** Statement describing homeschool structure and mission required. **Learning Disabled:** Students must self-disclose personal needs and provide IEP.

**2007-2008 Annual costs.** Tuition/fees: $8,820. Per-credit charge: $190. $245 per credit hour charge for virtual classes. Room only: $2,640. Books/supplies: $1,798. Personal expenses: $1,818.

**2006-2007 Financial aid. Need-based:** 37% of total undergraduate aid awarded as scholarships/grants, 63% as loans/jobs. Need-based aid available for part-time students. Work-study available nights and for part-time students. **Non-need-based:** Scholarships awarded for academics, job skills, minority status.

**Application procedures. Admission:** No deadline. $50 fee. Application may be submitted online. Admission notification on a rolling basis. **Financial aid:** Priority date 4/1; no closing date. FAFSA required. Applicants notified on a rolling basis starting 4/30; must reply within 2 week(s) of notification.

**Academics.** Students wanting credit for life experience must register for 1-hour course in portfolio development. **Special study options:** Accelerated study, cooperative education, distance learning, double major, weekend college. Bachelor's degree programs available on campus. **Credit/placement by examination:** AP, CLEP, institutional tests. 25 credit hours maximum toward associate degree. **Support services:** Learning center, remedial instruction, tutoring.

**Majors. Agriculture:** Business. **Business:** Accounting, administrative services, business admin, marketing, office technology, tourism/travel. **Computer sciences:** General, applications programming. **Health:** Medical assistant, medical secretary, pharmacy assistant. **Legal studies:** Legal secretary, paralegal. **Mechanic/repair:** Automotive, diesel, heating/ac/refrig.

**Most popular majors.** Business/marketing 6%, trade and industry 73%.

**Computing on campus.** 212 workstations in library, computer center, student center. Commuter students can connect to campus network. Online course registration available.

**Student life. Freshman orientation:** Available. Held 4 to 6 weeks before quarter or session begins. **Housing:** Guaranteed on-campus for all undergraduates. Single-sex dorms, special housing for disabled, apartments, substance-free housing available. $100 deposit. **Activities:** Student government, student newspaper, TV station.

**Athletics. Intramural:** Bowling, volleyball.

**Student services.** Adult student services, career counseling, student employment services, financial aid counseling, minority student services, personal counseling, placement for graduates, veterans' counselor. **Physically disabled:** Services for visually, hearing impaired. **Transfer:** Pre-admission transcript evaluation for new students.

**Contact.** E-mail: info@unoh.edu
Phone: (419) 998-3120 Fax: (419) 229-6926
Rick Morrison, Director of Admissions, University of Northwestern Ohio, 1441 North Cable Road, Lima, OH 45805

## Vatterott College: Cleveland
Broadview Heights, Ohio
www.vatterott-college.edu

- For-profit 2-year technical college
- Commuter campus in large town

**General.** Accredited by ACCSCT. **Calendar:** Semester.

**Annual costs/financial aid.** Program cost ranges: $19,500 to $21,500 (certificate/diploma); $30,900 to $32,000 (associate degree).

**Contact.** Phone: (440) 526-1660
Director of Admissions, 5025 East Royalton Road, Broadview Heights, OH 44147

## Virginia Marti College of Art and Design
Lakewood, Ohio
www.vmcad.edu                                             CB code: 0396

- For-profit 2-year visual arts and business college
- Commuter campus in small city
- Application essay, interview required

**General.** Founded in 1966. Accredited by ACCSCT. **Enrollment:** 178 degree-seeking undergraduates. **Degrees:** 96 associate awarded. **Location:** 7 miles from Cleveland. **Calendar:** Continuous, extensive summer session. **Full-time faculty:** 10 total. **Part-time faculty:** 52 total.

**Basis for selection.** School achievement record, admission test scores and interview considered. Portfolio review required for commercial art and interior design majors; in lieu of portfolio, preliminary art courses required in first quarter. Essay questions and letter of recommendation reviewed. Career Ability Placement Survey (CAPS) required for admission. Portfolio required for graphic design, fashion design, interior design programs. **Learning Disabled:** Provide high school IEP for review of special needs.

**2007-2008 Annual costs.** Tuition/fees: $15,075. Per-credit charge: $325. Books/supplies: $1,200. Personal expenses: $1,746.

**Financial aid.** All financial aid based on need.

**Application procedures. Admission:** No deadline. $50 fee. Application may be submitted online. Admission notification on a rolling basis. **Financial aid:** No deadline. FAFSA required. Applicants notified on a rolling basis.

**Academics. Special study options:** Dual enrollment of high school students, independent study, internships, study abroad. **Credit/placement by examination:** CLEP, institutional tests. **Support services:** Remedial instruction, study skills assistance, tutoring.

**Majors. Business:** Fashion. **Computer sciences:** Computer science. **Visual/performing arts:** Art, art history/conservation, commercial/advertising art, design, fashion design, illustration, interior design, photography.

**Computing on campus.** 14 workstations in library, computer center. Commuter students can connect to campus network. Online course registration, wireless network available.

**Student life. Freshman orientation:** Mandatory. All-day program approximately 1 week prior to start of classes. **Policies:** Students participate in yearly fashion shows, competitions, trips to New York, France, and Italy. **Activities:** Student government, student newspaper, Student chapters of American Institute of Graphic Artists, Fashion Group International, American Society of Interior Designers.

**Student services.** Career counseling, student employment services, personal counseling, placement for graduates, veterans' counselor. **Transfer:** Pre-admission transcript evaluation for new students. Transfer adviser for students transferring to 4-year colleges.

**Contact.** E-mail: dmarti@vmcad.edu
Phone: (216) 221-8584 Toll-free number: (800) 473-4350
Quinn Marti, Director of Admissions, Virginia Marti College of Art and Design, 11724 Detroit Avenue, Lakewood, OH 44107

## Washington State Community College
### Marietta, Ohio
### www.wscc.edu
CB code: 0381

- Public 2-year community college
- Commuter campus in large town

**General.** Founded in 1971. Regionally accredited. **Enrollment:** 2,209 undergraduates. **Degrees:** 361 associate awarded. **Location:** 112 miles from Columbus. **Calendar:** Quarter, limited summer session. **Full-time faculty:** 60 total. **Part-time faculty:** 111 total.

**Student profile.**

| | | | |
|---|---|---|---|
| Out-of-state: | 12% | 25 or older: | 46% |

**Basis for selection.** Open admission, but selective for some programs. Special requirements for medical laboratory technology, nursing, physical therapist assistant, radiology, respiratory therapy programs. ACT required for nursing, radiologic technology programs. 3/28 scores submission deadline for nursing program. Interview required for programs with selective admission.

**2007-2008 Annual costs.** Tuition/fees: $3,555; $6,975 out-of-state. Per-credit charge: $76 in-state; $152 out-of-state. Books/supplies: $705. Personal expenses: $4,145.

**Application procedures. Admission:** No deadline. No application fee. Application may be submitted online. Admission notification on a rolling basis. **Financial aid:** No deadline. FAFSA, institutional form required. Applicants notified on a rolling basis starting 5/15; must reply within 2 week(s) of notification.

**Academics. Special study options:** Distance learning, double major, dual enrollment of high school students, independent study, internships, student-designed major. License preparation in nursing, radiology. **Credit/**

**placement by examination:** CLEP, institutional tests. 60 credit hours maximum toward associate degree. **Support services:** Learning center, pre-admission summer program, reduced course load, remedial instruction, tutoring.

**Majors. Business:** General, accounting, business admin, e-commerce, marketing. **Communications:** Broadcast journalism, media studies. **Communications technology:** Animation/special effects. **Computer sciences:** Computer graphics, data processing, programming. **Education:** General, elementary, multi-level teacher, secondary. **Engineering:** General, electrical. **Engineering technology:** Drafting, electrical. **Health:** Clinical lab assistant, medical radiologic technology/radiation therapy, medical transcription, nursing (RN), physical therapy assistant, respiratory therapy technology. **Interdisciplinary:** Natural sciences. **Liberal arts:** Arts/sciences. **Math:** General. **Mechanic/repair:** Automotive, diesel, heating/ac/refrig. **Protective services:** Corrections, law enforcement admin. **Public administration:** Human services. **Science technology:** Biological.

**Student life. Freshman orientation:** Available. Preregistration for classes offered. **Activities:** Choral groups, music ensembles, student government, student newspaper, veterans club, Phi Theta Kappa honor fraternity.

**Student services.** Adult student services, career counseling, student employment services, financial aid counseling, personal counseling, placement for graduates, veterans' counselor. **Physically disabled:** Services for visually, hearing impaired. **Transfer:** Transfer adviser, college fairs on campus for students transferring to 4-year colleges.

**Contact.** E-mail: admissions@wscc.edu
Phone: (740) 568-1900 Fax: (740) 373-7496
Rebecca Peroni, Director of Admissions, Washington State Community College, 710 Colegate Drive, Marietta, OH 45750

## Wright State University: Lake Campus
### Celina, Ohio
### www.wright.edu/lake
CB code: 1947

- Public 2-year branch campus college
- Commuter campus in small town

**General.** Founded in 1969. Regionally accredited. **Enrollment:** 588 degree-seeking undergraduates; 128 non-degree-seeking students. **Degrees:** 69 associate awarded; master's offered. **Location:** 70 miles from Dayton. **Calendar:** Quarter, limited summer session. **Full-time faculty:** 20 total. **Part-time faculty:** 50 total. **Class size:** 80% < 20, 20% 20-39.

**Student profile.** Among degree-seeking undergraduates, 6% enrolled in a transfer program, 2% already have a bachelor's degree or higher, 139 enrolled as first-time, first-year students, 47 transferred in from other institutions.

| | | | |
|---|---|---|---|
| Part-time: | 22% | Hispanic American: | 1% |
| Women: | 65% | Native American: | 1% |
| African American: | 1% | 25 or older: | 17% |
| Asian American: | 1% | | |

**Basis for selection.** Open admission, but selective for some programs. Special requirements for engineering and education programs. SAT/ACT required for all students but only used for placement in selective programs.

**High school preparation.** 16 units recommended. Recommended units include English 4, mathematics 3, social studies 3, science 3 (laboratory 3) and foreign language 2. One unit of art recommended.

**2007-2008 Annual costs.** Tuition/fees: $4,893; $11,619 out-of-state. Per-credit charge: $148 in-state; $354 out-of-state.

**Financial aid. Need-based:** Need-based aid available for part-time students. **Non-need-based:** Scholarships awarded for academics, athletics, state residency. **Additional information:** Academic scholarship application deadline February 1. All financial aid applications and awards administered by Dayton campus.

**Application procedures. Admission:** No deadline. $30 fee. Application may be submitted online. Admission notification on a rolling basis. **Financial aid:** Priority date 2/15; no closing date. FAFSA, institutional form required. Applicants notified on a rolling basis; must reply within 2 week(s) of notification.

**Academics.** Bachelor's degrees awarded through main campus. **Special study options:** Cooperative education, cross-registration, distance learning, double major, dual enrollment of high school students, honors, independent study, internships, student-designed major. Bachelor's degree programs available on campus. **Credit/placement by examination:** CLEP, IB, institutional tests. **Support services:** Learning center, pre-admission summer program, reduced course load, remedial instruction, tutoring.

**Majors. Biology:** General. **Business:** General, business admin, management information systems. **Communications:** General. **Computer sciences:** Information systems. **Engineering technology:** General, drafting, manufacturing. **English:** English lit. **History:** General. **Liberal arts:** Arts/sciences. **Physical sciences:** Chemistry. **Psychology:** General. **Public administration:** Social work. **Social sciences:** Sociology.

**Most popular majors.** Business/marketing 48%, communications/journalism 7%, computer/information sciences 11%, engineering/engineering technologies 22%.

**Computing on campus.** 105 workstations in computer center. Commuter students can connect to campus network. Online library available.

**Student life. Freshman orientation:** Available. **Activities:** Drama, student government, student newspaper, Business Professionals of America, Student Manufacturing Engineers.

**Athletics.** NCAA. **Intercollegiate:** Basketball, golf M, volleyball W. **Team name:** Raiders.

**Student services.** Adult student services, career counseling, financial aid counseling, on-campus daycare, personal counseling, placement for graduates, veterans' counselor. **Physically disabled:** Services for visually, hearing impaired.

**Contact.** Phone: (419) 586-0324 Toll-free number: (800) 237-1477 Fax: (419) 586-0358
BJ Hobbler, Student Services Officer, Wright State University: Lake Campus, 7600 State Route 703, Celina, OH 45822-2952

## Youngstown College of Massotherapy
### Struthers, Ohio
### www.ycm.edu

- For-profit 2-year health science and technical college
- Commuter campus in small city

**General.** Accredited by ACCSCT. **Calendar:** Semester.

**Contact.** Phone: (330) 755-1406
Admissions Director, 14 Highland Avenue, Struthers, OH 44471

## Zane State College
### Zanesville, Ohio
### www.zanestate.edu                    CB code: 1535

- Public 2-year technical college
- Commuter campus in large town

**General.** Founded in 1969. Regionally accredited. **Enrollment:** 1,751 degree-seeking undergraduates; 298 non-degree-seeking students. **Degrees:** 343 associate awarded. **Location:** 60 miles from Columbus. **Calendar:** Quarter, limited summer session. **Full-time faculty:** 46 total. **Part-time faculty:** 101 total. **Special facilities:** Natural resource center.

**Student profile.** Among degree-seeking undergraduates, 5% enrolled in a transfer program, 401 enrolled as first-time, first-year students.

| | | |
|---|---|---|
| **Part-time:** | 43% | **African American:** 4% |
| **Women:** | 64% | |

**Transfer out. Colleges most students transferred to 2007:** Ohio University, Ohio State University, Muskingum College, Franklin University.

**Basis for selection.** Open admission, but selective for some programs. Special requirements for allied health programs.

**High school preparation.** 15 units recommended. Recommended units include English 4, mathematics 3, social studies 4 and science 4.

**2007-2008 Annual costs.** Tuition/fees: $3,825; $7,650 out-of-state. Per-credit charge: $85 in-state; $170 out-of-state. Books/supplies: $1,500.

**Financial aid. Need-based:** Need-based aid available for part-time students.

**Application procedures. Admission:** No deadline. $20 fee. Application must be submitted on paper. Admission notification on a rolling basis. **Financial aid:** Priority date 5/1, closing date 7/15. FAFSA required. Must reply by 9/1.

**Academics. Special study options:** Cross-registration, distance learning, dual enrollment of high school students, internships, student-designed major. **Credit/placement by examination:** AP, CLEP, institutional tests. All new freshmen must take assessment tests for English and mathematics. **Support services:** Learning center, reduced course load, remedial instruction, study skills assistance, tutoring, writing center.

**Majors. Business:** Accounting, administrative services, business admin, marketing, sales/distribution. **Computer sciences:** General, computer science, information systems. **Conservation:** Management/policy. **Engineering technology:** Drafting, electrical. **Family/consumer sciences:** Child care. **Health:** Clinical lab technology, health services, medical assistant, medical radiologic technology/radiation therapy, occupational therapy assistant, physical therapy assistant. **Legal studies:** Paralegal. **Mechanic/repair:** Automotive. **Personal/culinary services:** Culinary arts. **Production:** Tool and die. **Public administration:** Social work.

**Most popular majors.** Business/marketing 40%, computer/information sciences 19%, engineering/engineering technologies 9%, health sciences 29%, parks/recreation 7%.

**Computing on campus.** Online library, wireless network available.

**Student life. Freshman orientation:** Available. **Activities:** Student government.

**Athletics. Intramural:** Golf M.

**Student services.** Adult student services, career counseling, student employment services, financial aid counseling, personal counseling, placement for graduates, veterans' counselor. **Transfer:** Pre-admission transcript evaluation for new students. Transfer adviser for students transferring to 4-year colleges.

**Contact.** E-mail: pyoung@zanestate.edu
Phone: (740) 454-2501 ext. 1225 Toll-free number: (800) 686-8324 ext. 1226 Fax: (740) 454-0035
Paul Young, Director of Admissions, Zane State College, 1555 Newark Road, Zanesville, OH 43701-2626

# Oklahoma

## Carl Albert State College
Poteau, Oklahoma
www.carlalbert.edu
CB code: 1474

- Public 2-year community and junior college
- Commuter campus in large town

**General.** Founded in 1932. Regionally accredited. **Enrollment:** 2,575 degree-seeking undergraduates. **Degrees:** 432 associate awarded. **Location:** 35 miles from Fort Smith, Arkansas. **Calendar:** Semester, limited summer session. **Full-time faculty:** 40 total. **Part-time faculty:** 8 total.

**Transfer out. Colleges most students transferred to 2007:** Northeastern State University, University of Arkansas, Southeastern State University, University of Central Oklahoma.

**Basis for selection.** Open admission, but selective for some programs. Nursing, radiographic technology, and physical therapy assistant programs employ selective enrollment. ACT required for all students under 21 and all international students. SAT considered if submitted. **Adult students:** SAT/ACT scores not required if applicant over 21. Admissions testing is required, but adult students may test with COMPASS in lieu of ACT.

**High school preparation.** 15 units recommended. Recommended units include English 4, mathematics 3, social studies 1, history 2, science 2 (laboratory 2) and academic electives 1. One social science unit should be in American history.

**2007-2008 Annual costs.** Tuition/fees: $2,145; $5,115 out-of-state. Per-credit charge: $48 in-state; $147 out-of-state. Room/board: $3,124. Books/supplies: $750. Personal expenses: $1,678.

**Financial aid.** All financial aid based on need. Need-based aid available for part-time students. Work-study available nights and for part-time students.

**Application procedures. Admission:** No deadline. No application fee. Admission notification on a rolling basis. **Financial aid:** No deadline. FAFSA, institutional form required. Applicants notified on a rolling basis.

**Academics. Special study options:** Distance learning, dual enrollment of high school students, honors, independent study, liberal arts/career combination. Bachelor's degree programs available on campus. License preparation in nursing, physical therapy, radiology. **Credit/placement by examination:** AP, CLEP, institutional tests. 18 credit hours maximum toward associate degree. **Support services:** GED test center, learning center, remedial instruction, study skills assistance, tutoring.

**Majors. Biology:** General, zoology. **Business:** General, accounting, administrative services, business admin. **Communications:** Journalism. **Computer sciences:** Computer science. **Education:** Elementary, secondary. **English:** English lit, speech/rhetoric. **Health:** Nursing (RN), physical therapy assistant, premedicine, prepharmacy, preveterinary. **Legal studies:** Prelaw. **Math:** General. **Parks/recreation:** Health/fitness. **Protective services:** Criminal justice. **Psychology:** General. **Social sciences:** General, sociology. **Visual/performing arts:** Art, dramatic.

**Most popular majors.** Business/marketing 17%, education 19%, family/consumer sciences 8%, health sciences 23%, social sciences 13%.

**Computing on campus.** 50 workstations in library, computer center. Dormitories wired for high-speed internet access. Commuter students can connect to campus network. Online library available.

**Student life. Freshman orientation:** Mandatory. Preregistration for classes offered. 1 day session held at beginning of semester offered as online course. **Housing:** Single-sex dorms available. Scholar's housing available. **Activities:** Choral groups, dance, drama, music ensembles, musical theater, radio station, student government, student newspaper, African-American Awareness, American Indian Student Association, Young Democrats, Young Republicans.

**Athletics.** NJCAA. **Intercollegiate:** Baseball M, basketball M, cheerleading M. **Team name:** Vikings.

**Student services.** Campus ministries, career counseling, services for economically disadvantaged, financial aid counseling, on-campus daycare, veterans' counselor. **Physically disabled:** Services for hearing impaired. **Transfer:** Pre-admission transcript evaluation for new students. Transfer adviser, college fairs on campus for students transferring to 4-year colleges.

**Contact.** E-mail: ddickerson@carlalbert.edu
Phone: (918) 647-1300 Fax: (918) 647-1306
Dee Ann Dickerson, Registrar, Carl Albert State College, 1507 South McKenna, Poteau, OK 74953-5208

## Connors State College
Warner, Oklahoma
www.connorsstate.edu
CB code: 6117

- Public 2-year community and junior college
- Commuter campus in rural community

**General.** Founded in 1908. Regionally accredited. Main campus in Warner. Branch campus in Muskogee. **Enrollment:** 1,690 degree-seeking undergraduates; 563 non-degree-seeking students. **Degrees:** 391 associate awarded. **Location:** 20 miles from Muskogee, 65 miles from Tulsa. **Calendar:** Semester, extensive summer session. **Full-time faculty:** 50 total. **Part-time faculty:** 60 total. **Class size:** 64% < 20, 32% 20-39, 3% 40-49, 1% 50-99. **Special facilities:** 1300 acre wetlands and nature preserve.

**Student profile.** Among degree-seeking undergraduates, 628 enrolled as first-time, first-year students.

| | | | |
|---|---|---|---|
| Part-time: | 30% | Hispanic American: | 2% |
| Out-of-state: | 4% | Native American: | 27% |
| Women: | 71% | 25 or older: | 42% |
| African American: | 11% | Live on campus: | 10% |
| Asian American: | 1% | | |

**Transfer out. Colleges most students transferred to 2007:** Northeastern State University, Oklahoma State University.

**Basis for selection.** Open admission, but selective for some programs. Special requirements for nursing and equine programs; interview required. **Adult students:** SAT/ACT scores not required if applicant over 21. Must complete secondary assessment. **Homeschooled:** The student's equivalent public high school class must have graduated; must take ACT; proficiency in subject area curricula required. **Learning Disabled:** Students with documented disabilities must complete designated paperwork in the office of the VP for Student Services.

**High school preparation.** Required and recommended units include English 4, mathematics 3-4, history 3, science 2-3 (laboratory 2-3), visual/performing arts 2 and academic electives 3.

**2007-2008 Annual costs.** Tuition/fees: $2,379; $5,694 out-of-state. Per-credit charge: $60 in-state; $171 out-of-state. Room/board: $6,161. Books/supplies: $1,200.

**Financial aid. Need-based:** Need-based aid available for part-time students. **Non-need-based:** Scholarships awarded for academics, alumni affiliation, athletics, leadership, state residency.

**Application procedures. Admission:** No deadline. No application fee. Admission notification on a rolling basis. Admission available to all students 18 years or over or younger than 18 years with a high school diploma. **Financial aid:** Priority date 2/28, closing date 5/1. FAFSA, institutional form required. Applicants notified on a rolling basis starting 4/1; must reply within 2 week(s) of notification.

**Academics. Special study options:** Distance learning, dual enrollment of high school students, internships, liberal arts/career combination. License preparation in nursing. **Credit/placement by examination:** AP, CLEP, institutional tests. 18 credit hours maximum toward associate degree. **Support services:** Learning center, remedial instruction, tutoring.

**Majors. Agriculture:** Equestrian studies. **Biology:** General. **Business:** General, accounting, business admin. **Communications:** General, journalism. **Computer sciences:** General, data processing. **Education:** General, early childhood, elementary, physical, secondary. **Engineering:** General. **English:** English lit, speech/rhetoric. **Family/consumer sciences:** General, business, child care. **Health:** Nursing (RN), predental, premedicine, prepharmacy, preveterinary. **History:** General. **Interdisciplinary:** Math/computer science. **Legal studies:** Prelaw. **Liberal arts:** Arts/sciences. **Math:** General. **Physical sciences:** Chemistry, physics. **Protective services:** Police science. **Psychology:** General. **Public administration:** Social work. **Social sciences:** General, sociology. **Visual/performing arts:** Art, music history.

**Two-Year Colleges**

**Computing on campus.** 217 workstations in dormitories, library, computer center. Dormitories wired for high-speed internet access and linked to campus network. Online library, wireless network available.

**Student life. Freshman orientation:** Available. Preregistration for classes offered. **Housing:** Single-sex dorms, apartments, substance-free housing available. $55 deposit. **Activities:** Drama, student government, student newspaper, Phi Theta Kappa, Mu Alpha Theta, Aggie Club, Black Student Society, Indian club, business club, English club, psychology club.

**Athletics.** NJCAA. **Intercollegiate:** Baseball M, basketball, rodeo, softball W. **Intramural:** Basketball, softball, tennis. **Team name:** Cowboys.

**Student services.** Career counseling, health services, on-campus daycare, personal counseling, veterans' counselor. **Transfer:** Pre-admission transcript evaluation for new students. College fairs on campus for students transferring to 4-year colleges.

**Contact.** Phone: (918) 463-2931 Toll-free number: (918) 463-2931 ext. 6300 Fax: (918) 463-6336
Ronald Ramming, Dean of Enrollment Services, Connors State College, RR 1, Box 1000, Warner, OK 74469-9700

## Eastern Oklahoma State College
### Wilburton, Oklahoma
### www.eosc.edu
**CB code: 6189**

- Public 2-year community college
- Commuter campus in small town

**General.** Founded in 1908. Regionally accredited. **Location:** 90 miles from Tulsa. **Calendar:** Semester.

**Annual costs/financial aid.** Tuition/fees (2007-2008): $2,580; $6,197 out-of-state. Room/board: $3,796. Books/supplies: $578. Personal expenses: $500. Need-based financial aid available to full-time and part-time students.

**Contact.** Phone: (918) 465-2361
Director of Enrollment Management, 1301 West Main Street, Wilburton, OK 74578-4999

## Heritage College: Oklahoma City
### Oklahoma City, Oklahoma
### www.heritage-education.com

- For-profit 2-year community college
- Very large city

**General.** Accredited by ACCSCT. **Calendar:** Continuous.

**Annual costs/financial aid.** Costs vary by program from $8,031 to $19,850 including tuition, fees, books, and supplies.

**Contact.** Phone: (405) 631-3399
Director of Admissions, 7100 I-35 Services Road, Suite 7118, Oklahoma City, OK 73149

## Murray State College
### Tishomingo, Oklahoma
### www.mscok.edu
**CB code: 6421**

- Public 2-year junior college
- Commuter campus in small town

**General.** Founded in 1908. Regionally accredited. **Enrollment:** 1,855 degree-seeking undergraduates; 303 non-degree-seeking students. **Degrees:** 345 associate awarded. **Location:** 32 miles from Ardmore. **Calendar:** Semester, limited summer session. **Full-time faculty:** 40 total. **Part-time faculty:** 45 total.

**Student profile.** Among degree-seeking undergraduates, 61% enrolled in a transfer program, 39% enrolled in a vocational program.

| Part-time: | 40% | Asian American: | 1% |
|---|---|---|---|
| Out-of-state: | 3% | Hispanic American: | 4% |
| Women: | 68% | Native American: | 19% |
| African American: | 7% | Live on campus: | 6% |

**Basis for selection.** Open admission, but selective for some programs. Special requirements for nursing and vet tech programs.

**High school preparation.** 15 units recommended. Recommended units include English 4, mathematics 3, social studies 1, history 2, science 2 (laboratory 2) and academic electives 3. Recommend 1 unit in citizenship.

**2007-2008 Annual costs.** Tuition/fees: $2,615; $6,095 out-of-state. Per-credit charge: $74 in-state; $190 out-of-state. Room/board: $5,380. Books/supplies: $600. Personal expenses: $1,984.

**Application procedures. Admission:** No deadline. No application fee. Admission notification on a rolling basis beginning on or about 4/15. **Financial aid:** Priority date 4/15; no closing date. Applicants notified on a rolling basis starting 5/1.

**Academics. Special study options:** Honors. License preparation in nursing. **Credit/placement by examination:** CLEP. **Support services:** Learning center, remedial instruction, tutoring.

**Majors. Business:** Administrative services, business admin. **Computer sciences:** General, computer science. **Education:** Elementary. **English:** English lit. **Family/consumer sciences:** Child care. **Health:** Preveterinary. **History:** General. **Interdisciplinary:** Behavioral sciences. **Liberal arts:** Arts/sciences. **Math:** General. **Visual/performing arts:** General.

**Most popular majors.** Business/marketing 18%, health sciences 30%, liberal arts 39%.

**Computing on campus.** Commuter students can connect to campus network. Helpline available.

**Student life. Freshman orientation:** Mandatory. **Housing:** Coed dorms available. $50 deposit. **Activities:** Drama, music ensembles, student government.

**Athletics.** NJCAA. **Intercollegiate:** Baseball M, basketball. **Intramural:** Baseball M, basketball.

**Student services.** Career counseling, veterans' counselor. **Transfer:** College fairs on campus for students transferring to 4-year colleges.

**Contact.** Phone: (580) 371-2371 ext. 108 Fax: (580) 371-9844
Ann Beck, Registrar and Director of Admissions, Murray State College, One Murray Campus, Tishomingo, OK 73460

## Northeastern Oklahoma Agricultural and Mechanical College
### Miami, Oklahoma
### www.neo.edu
**CB member**
**CB code: 6484**

- Public 2-year community and junior college
- Commuter campus in large town

**General.** Founded in 1919. Regionally accredited. Extension courses offered in neighboring towns and on the Internet. **Enrollment:** 1,767 degree-seeking undergraduates; 132 non-degree-seeking students. **Degrees:** 295 associate awarded. **ROTC:** Air Force. **Location:** 76 miles from Tulsa. **Calendar:** Semester, limited summer session. **Full-time faculty:** 77 total. **Part-time faculty:** 33 total. **Class size:** 58% < 20, 42% 20-39, less than 1% 40-49, less than 1% 50-99. **Special facilities:** College farm, equine center.

**Student profile.** Among degree-seeking undergraduates, 71% enrolled in a transfer program, 29% enrolled in a vocational program, 1% already have a bachelor's degree or higher, 642 enrolled as first-time, first-year students, 159 transferred in from other institutions.

| Part-time: | 21% | Asian American: | 1% |
|---|---|---|---|
| Out-of-state: | 16% | Hispanic American: | 2% |
| Women: | 57% | Native American: | 22% |
| African American: | 8% | International: | 1% |

**Transfer out. Colleges most students transferred to 2007:** Oklahoma State University, Missouri Southern State College, Pittsburg State University, Northeastern State University, Rogers State University.

**Basis for selection.** Open admission. **Adult students:** SAT/ACT scores not required if applicant over 21. Students over the age of 21 must complete placement testing (CPT) before enrolling in classes. **Homeschooled:** Transcript of courses and grades required.

**High school preparation.** 15 units recommended. Recommended units include English 4, mathematics 3, history 3, science 2 (laboratory 2) and academic electives 3. History and citizenship skills, including 1 unit of U.S. history and 2 additional units from the subjects of history, economics, geography, government, or non-Western culture.

**2007-2008 Annual costs.** Tuition/fees: $2,286; $5,761 out-of-state. Per-credit charge: $53 in-state; $169 out-of-state. Room/board: $3,664. Books/supplies: $800. Personal expenses: $1,000.

**2006-2007 Financial aid. Need-based:** 609 full-time freshmen applied for aid; 440 were judged to have need; 439 of these received aid. Average need met was 70%. Average scholarship/grant was $4,548; average loan $2,241. 68% of total undergraduate aid awarded as scholarships/grants, 32% as loans/jobs. Need-based aid available for part-time students. Work-study available nights, weekends and for part-time students. **Non-need-based:** Awarded to 688 full-time undergraduates, including 364 freshmen. Scholarships awarded for academics, art, athletics, leadership, music/drama, state residency.

**Application procedures. Admission:** No deadline. No application fee. Application may be submitted online. Admission notification on a rolling basis. **Financial aid:** Priority date 4/1; no closing date. FAFSA required. Applicants notified on a rolling basis starting 4/1; must reply by 8/30 or within 2 week(s) of notification.

**Academics. Special study options:** Distance learning, double major, dual enrollment of high school students, independent study, internships. Bachelor's degree programs available on campus. License preparation in nursing, physical therapy. **Credit/placement by examination:** AP, CLEP, institutional tests. 36 credit hours maximum toward associate degree. **Support services:** GED preparation and test center, learning center, reduced course load, remedial instruction, study skills assistance, tutoring, writing center.

**Majors. Agriculture:** General, equestrian studies, farm/ranch. **Area/ethnic studies:** Native American. **Biology:** General. **Business:** Accounting, administrative services, business admin, marketing. **Communications:** Radio/tv. **Computer sciences:** General, programming. **Conservation:** Forestry. **Education:** Early childhood. **Engineering technology:** CAD/CADD. **English:** English lit. **Health:** Athletic training, clinical lab technology, medical secretary, nursing (RN), physical therapy assistant, predental, premedicine, prenursing, prepharmacy, preveterinary. **Legal studies:** Legal secretary. **Math:** General. **Parks/recreation:** Health/fitness. **Physical sciences:** General. **Protective services:** Criminal justice. **Psychology:** General. **Social sciences:** General. **Visual/performing arts:** Art, dramatic.

**Most popular majors.** Agriculture 8%, business/marketing 10%, education 17%, health sciences 21%, liberal arts 25%.

**Computing on campus.** 85 workstations in dormitories, library, computer center. Dormitories linked to campus network. Commuter students can connect to campus network. Online library, helpline, wireless network available.

**Student life. Freshman orientation:** Mandatory, $69 fee. Preregistration for classes offered. One day, on Saturday before the beginning of fall classes. **Policies:** Single students under the age of 21 who reside more than 50 miles from campus are required to live on campus. **Housing:** Guaranteed on-campus for all undergraduates. Single-sex dorms, special housing for disabled, apartments, substance-free housing available. $75 deposit. **Activities:** Bands, choral groups, drama, music ensembles, musical theater, student government, student newspaper, TV station, Ministerial Alliance, Baptist student union, Aggie Society, Collegiates for Christ, Young Democrats, Young Republicans, Phi Theta Kappa, Afro-American Society, Native American student association, Masquers.

**Athletics.** NJCAA. **Intercollegiate:** Baseball M, basketball, football (tackle) M, rodeo, softball W, volleyball W. **Intramural:** Baseball, basketball, bowling, football (tackle) M, soccer, softball, swimming, volleyball, weight lifting. **Team name:** Norsemen.

**Student services.** Alcohol/substance abuse counseling, career counseling, services for economically disadvantaged, financial aid counseling, health services, personal counseling, veterans' counselor. **Physically disabled:** Services for visually, hearing impaired. **Transfer:** Transfer adviser, college fairs on campus for students transferring to 4-year colleges.

**Contact.** E-mail: neoadmission@neo.edu
Phone: (918) 540-6210 Toll-free number: (888) 464-6636
Fax: (918) 540-6946
Amy Ishmael, Vice President of Enrollment Management and Student Records, Northeastern Oklahoma Agricultural and Mechanical College, 200 I Street Northeast, Miami, OK 74354-6497

## Northern Oklahoma College
Tonkawa, Oklahoma
www.north-ok.edu
**CB member**
**CB code: 6486**

- Public 2-year community college
- Commuter campus in small town

**General.** Founded in 1901. Regionally accredited. **Location:** 90 miles from Oklahoma City, 70 miles from Wichita, Kansas. **Calendar:** Semester.

**Annual costs/financial aid.** Tuition/fees (2007-2008): $2,102; $5,366 out-of-state. Room/board: $3,440. Books/supplies: $600. Personal expenses: $1,200. Need-based financial aid available to full-time and part-time students.

**Contact.** Phone: (580) 628-6221
Associate Vice President, Box 310, Tonkawa, OK 74653-0310

## Oklahoma City Community College
Oklahoma City, Oklahoma
www.occc.edu
**CB member**
**CB code: 0270**

- Public 2-year community college
- Commuter campus in large city

**General.** Founded in 1969. Regionally accredited. **Enrollment:** 10,151 degree-seeking undergraduates; 1,800 non-degree-seeking students. **Degrees:** 1,068 associate awarded. **Calendar:** Semester, extensive summer session. **Full-time faculty:** 148 total. **Part-time faculty:** 411 total. **Class size:** 33% < 20, 59% 20-39, 7% 40-49, less than 1% 50-99. **Special facilities:** Olympic size swimming pool, diving well.

**Student profile.** Among degree-seeking undergraduates, 55% enrolled in a transfer program, 45% enrolled in a vocational program, 3% already have a bachelor's degree or higher, 2,295 enrolled as first-time, first-year students.

| | | | |
|---|---|---|---|
| Part-time: | 61% | Hispanic American: | 6% |
| Out-of-state: | 1% | Native American: | 6% |
| Women: | 57% | International: | 5% |
| African American: | 9% | 25 or older: | 39% |
| Asian American: | 4% | | |

**Transfer out. Colleges most students transferred to 2007:** University of Central Oklahoma, University of Oklahoma-OU Health Science Center, Oklahoma State University, University of Oklahoma, Oklahoma City University.

**Basis for selection.** Open admission, but selective for some programs. Special requirements for nursing, occupational therapy and physical therapy programs; reading test required. **Homeschooled:** Transcript of courses and grades required. If under the age of 21, student must have official high school transcript and official ACT scores.

**High school preparation.** 15 units recommended. Required and recommended units include English 4, mathematics 3, history 3, science 2 (laboratory 2), foreign language 3 and academic electives 1. History requirement includes 1 unit of American history and 2 units of citizenship skills or other history.

**2007-2008 Annual costs.** Tuition/fees: $2,340; $6,240 out-of-state. Per-credit charge: $55 in-state; $185 out-of-state. Books/supplies: $1,500. Personal expenses: $700.

**2006-2007 Financial aid. Need-based:** 53% of total undergraduate aid awarded as scholarships/grants, 47% as loans/jobs. Need-based aid available for part-time students. Work-study available nights, weekends and for part-time students. **Non-need-based:** Scholarships awarded for academics, state residency.

**Application procedures. Admission:** No deadline. $25 fee, may be waived for applicants with need. Application must be submitted on paper. Admission notification on a rolling basis. **Financial aid:** Priority date 7/1; no closing date. FAFSA required. Applicants notified on a rolling basis starting 2/1.

**Academics. Special study options:** Accelerated study, distance learning, double major, dual enrollment of high school students, ESL, honors, independent study, internships, liberal arts/career combination, student-designed major, weekend college. License preparation in nursing, occupational therapy, paramedic, physical therapy, real estate. **Credit/placement by examination:** AP, CLEP, IB, institutional tests. 45 credit hours maximum toward associate degree. Credit will not be transcripted until 12 resident hours have been completed. **Support services:** GED preparation and test center, learning center, reduced course load, remedial instruction, study skills assistance, tutoring, writing center.

**Majors. Biology:** General, bioinformatics, biotechnology. **Business:** General, finance, office/clerical, real estate, tourism promotion, tourism/travel. **Communications:** Broadcast journalism, journalism. **Communications technology:** Desktop publishing, graphics, photo/film/video. **Computer sciences:** General, computer science, data processing, programming, security, systems analysis, web page design. **Education:** General, multi-level teacher, secondary. **Engineering:** General. **Engineering technology:** Drafting, electrical, manufacturing. **Family/consumer sciences:** Child care. **Foreign languages:** French, Spanish, translation. **Health:** EMT paramedic, nursing (RN), occupational therapy assistant, physical therapy assistant. **History:** General. **Legal studies:** Legal secretary, prelaw. **Liberal arts:** Arts/sciences. **Math:** General. **Mechanic/repair:** General. **Physical sciences:** Chemistry, physics. **Psychology:** General. **Social sciences:** Sociology. **Transportation:** Aviation. **Visual/performing arts:** Commercial/advertising art, studio arts, theater design.

**Computing on campus.** 2,000 workstations in library, computer center, student center. Commuter students can connect to campus network. Online course registration, online library, helpline, wireless network available.

**Student life. Freshman orientation:** Available. Preregistration for classes offered. Held the week prior to classes for 3 hours on days, evenings and weekends. **Activities:** Campus ministries, choral groups, drama, literary magazine, music ensembles, student government, student newspaper, Phi Theta Kappa, Chi Alpha, Christians on Campus, African-American Student Association, Asian Cultural Exchange, Native American Cultural Awareness Organization, Young Democrats, Deaf Student Association.

**Athletics. Intramural:** Baseball M, basketball, golf, soccer, softball, volleyball.

**Student services.** Career counseling, student employment services, financial aid counseling, on-campus daycare, personal counseling, placement for graduates, veterans' counselor. **Physically disabled:** Services for visually, speech, hearing impaired. **Transfer:** Transfer adviser, college fairs on campus for students transferring to 4-year colleges.

**Contact.** E-mail: psst@occc.edu
Phone: (405) 682-6222 Fax: (405) 682-7817
Director of Admissions, Oklahoma City Community College, 7777 South May Avenue, Oklahoma City, OK 73159

## Oklahoma State University: Oklahoma City
**Oklahoma City, Oklahoma**  **CB member**
**www.osuokc.edu**  **CB code: 1436**

- Public 2-year branch campus and technical college
- Commuter campus in very large city

**General.** Founded in 1961. Regionally accredited. **Enrollment:** 5,474 degree-seeking undergraduates. **Degrees:** 515 associate awarded. **Location:** 5 miles from downtown. **Calendar:** Semester, extensive summer session. **Full-time faculty:** 71 total. **Part-time faculty:** 226 total. **Special facilities:** Horticulture center, precision driving training center, child development center, golf maintenance training facility, learning resource center, power transmission distribution pole yard.

**Transfer out. Colleges most students transferred to 2007:** University of Central Oklahoma, Oklahoma State University - Stillwater, University of Oklahoma.

**Basis for selection.** Open admission, but selective for some programs. Special requirements for nursing program and emergency responder bachelor program. All students required to take COMPASS Test. Veterinarian Tech students required to take ACT test. Interviews required for nursing program. **Adult students:** ACT/SAT not required for placement if applicant is over 21 years of age.

**High school preparation.** 15 units recommended. Recommended units include English 4, mathematics 3, social studies 1, history 2, (laboratory 2) and academic electives 3. Other: from any of the subjects listed above or selected from the following: Computer Science, Foreign Language.

**2007-2008 Annual costs.** Tuition/fees: $2,705; $7,175 out-of-state. Per-credit charge: $71 in-state; $220 out-of-state. Books/supplies: $1,080.

**Financial aid.** All financial aid based on need. Need-based aid available for part-time students.

**Application procedures. Admission:** No deadline. No application fee in-state; $15 out-of-state. Application may be submitted online. Admission notification on a rolling basis. **Financial aid:** Priority date 7/15; no closing date. FAFSA required. Applicants notified on a rolling basis starting 8/1; must reply within 2 week(s) of notification.

**Academics. Special study options:** Cooperative education, distance learning, double major, dual enrollment of high school students, honors, independent study, liberal arts/career combination, weekend college. Fire/police/EMS training available. Bachelor's degree programs available on campus. License preparation in nursing, paramedic, radiology. **Credit/placement by examination:** CLEP, institutional tests. 30 credit hours maximum toward associate degree. Credit for: Fundamentals of Nursing (6 hrs.), Adult Nursing (8 hrs.). **Support services:** GED preparation and test center, learning center, remedial instruction, study skills assistance, tutoring, writing center.

**Majors. Agriculture:** Horticulture, turf management. **Business:** Accounting technology, accounting/finance, business admin, construction management, management science, office technology. **Computer sciences:** Applications programming, computer graphics. **Education:** Bilingual. **Engineering technology:** General, architectural drafting, civil, construction, electrical. **Family/consumer sciences:** Child care. **Foreign languages:** Sign language interpretation, sign language linguistics. **Health:** Cardiovascular technology, EMT paramedic, environmental health, health care admin, health services, nursing (RN), radiologic technology/medical imaging, sonography, substance abuse counseling, veterinary technology/assistant. **Protective services:** Firefighting, police science. **Visual/performing arts:** Commercial/advertising art. **Other:** Emergency management, Power transmission distribution technology, Public service.

**Computing on campus.** 372 workstations in library, computer center, student center. Commuter students can connect to campus network. Online course registration, repair service, wireless network available.

**Student life. Freshman orientation:** Mandatory. Preregistration for classes offered. **Activities:** Student government, student newspaper, Students Offering Support, Phi Theta Kappa, Project Second Chance, Native American Students, student government association, Hispanic student association, College Republicans, Young Democrats, Deaf/Hearing student association, student nursing association.

**Student services.** Adult student services, career counseling, student employment services, financial aid counseling, on-campus daycare, personal counseling, placement for graduates, veterans' counselor. **Physically disabled:** Services for visually, speech, hearing impaired. **Transfer:** Transfer center, transfer adviser, college fairs on campus for students transferring to 4-year colleges.

**Contact.** E-mail: jkubier@osuokc.edu
Phone: (405) 945-3224 Toll-free number: (800) 560-4099
Fax: (405) 945-3277
Jeanne Kubier, Director of Admissions, Oklahoma State University: Oklahoma City, 900 North Portland, Oklahoma City, OK 73107-6195

## Oklahoma State University: Okmulgee
**Okmulgee, Oklahoma**  **CB member**
**www.osu-okmulgee.edu**  **CB code: 3382**

- Public 2-year branch campus and technical college
- Commuter campus in large town

**General.** Founded in 1946. Regionally accredited. **Enrollment:** 2,034 degree-seeking undergraduates. **Degrees:** 43 bachelor's, 552 associate awarded. **Location:** 35 miles from Tulsa. **Calendar:** Trimester, extensive summer session. **Full-time faculty:** 130 total. **Part-time faculty:** 25 total.

**Student profile.**

| | | | |
|---|---|---|---|
| Out-of-state: | 9% | Live on campus: | 35% |
| 25 or older: | 33% | | |

**Basis for selection.** Open admission, but selective for some programs. Special requirements for multimedia and engineering technologies programs.

**High school preparation.** Recommended units include English 4, mathematics 3, social studies 2, science 2, foreign language 3 and academic electives 1.

**2007-2008 Annual costs.** Tuition/fees: $3,480; $8,370 out-of-state. Per-credit charge: $85 in-state; $248 out-of-state. Room/board: $5,652. Books/supplies: $1,050.

**2006-2007 Financial aid. Need-based:** 38% of total undergraduate aid awarded as scholarships/grants, 62% as loans/jobs. Need-based aid available for part-time students. Work-study available nights, weekends and for part-time students.

**Application procedures. Admission:** No deadline. $15 fee. Application may be submitted online. Admission notification on a rolling basis. **Financial aid:** Priority date 4/1; no closing date. FAFSA, institutional form required. Applicants notified on a rolling basis.

**Academics. Special study options:** Cooperative education, distance learning, double major, dual enrollment of high school students, internships, liberal arts/career combination. Bachelor's degree programs available on campus. License preparation in nursing. **Credit/placement by examination:** AP, CLEP, institutional tests. **Support services:** Learning center, remedial instruction, tutoring.

**Majors. Agriculture:** Business. **Business:** General, accounting, administrative services, business admin, hospitality/recreation, management information systems. **Communications technology:** Graphic/printing. **Computer sciences:** General, applications programming, computer graphics, networking, programming. **Construction:** Electrician, maintenance, pipefitting, power transmission. **Education:** General. **Engineering:** Civil, electrical. **Engineering technology:** Biomedical, civil, construction, drafting, electrical, manufacturing. **Health:** Medical secretary, medical transcription, orthotics/prosthetics. **Legal studies:** Legal secretary. **Mechanic/repair:** Auto body, automotive, diesel, heating/ac/refrig, watch/jewelry. **Personal/culinary services:** Culinary arts. **Visual/performing arts:** Commercial/advertising art, photography.

**Computing on campus.** 50 workstations in dormitories, library, computer center. Dormitories wired for high-speed internet access and linked to campus network. Online library, helpline, repair service, wireless network available.

**Student life. Freshman orientation:** Available. **Housing:** Guaranteed on-campus for all undergraduates. Coed dorms, single-sex dorms, apartments available. $100 deposit. Housing for parents with dependent children available. **Activities:** Film society, student government, student newspaper, Baptist Student Union, Black Student Society, Native American student association, Junior Ambassadors.

**Athletics.** NAIA. **Intercollegiate:** Rodeo. **Intramural:** Basketball, bowling, football (non-tackle), handball, racquetball, soccer, softball, table tennis, volleyball. **Team name:** Cowboys.

**Student services.** Alcohol/substance abuse counseling, career counseling, student employment services, financial aid counseling, health services, on-campus daycare, personal counseling, placement for graduates, veterans' counselor. **Physically disabled:** Services for visually, speech, hearing impaired. **Transfer:** Pre-admission transcript evaluation for new students. College fairs on campus for students transferring to 4-year colleges.

**Contact.** E-mail: admissions@okstate.edu
Phone: (918) 293-4680 Toll-free number: (800) 722-4471 ext. 4680
Fax: (918) 293-4643
Mary Graves, Director of Retention & Career Services, Oklahoma State University: Okmulgee, 1801 East Fourth Street, Okmulgee, OK 74447-3901

## Platt College: Oklahoma City Central
### Oklahoma City, Oklahoma

- For-profit 1-year branch campus and health science college
- Small city
- Interview required

**General.** Accredited by ACCSCT. **Enrollment:** 325 undergraduates. **Degrees:** 69 associate awarded. **Calendar:** Continuous. **Full-time faculty:** 40 total. **Part-time faculty:** 2 total.

**Basis for selection.** Open admission, but selective for some programs. Students admitted based on interview, High School Diploma, GED or ATB. Entrance exam required for Practical Nursing and Surgical Technologist Programs.

**2007-2008 Annual costs.** Tuition varies by program. Full-time tuition ranges from $8,945 to $19,945. Required fees $150.

**Application procedures. Admission:** No deadline. $100 fee. Admission notification on a rolling basis. **Financial aid:** FAFSA required.

**Academics. Credit/placement by examination:** CLEP.

**Majors. Health:** Licensed practical nurse.

**Student life. Freshman orientation:** Mandatory.

**Student services.** Adult student services, alcohol/substance abuse counseling, career counseling, financial aid counseling, personal counseling, placement for graduates.

**Contact.** E-mail: angiem@plattcollege.org
Phone: (405) 946-7799 Fax: (405) 943-2150
R. Jackson, Director of Admissions, Platt College: Oklahoma City Central, 309 South Ann Arbor, Oklahoma City, OK 73128

## Platt College: Tulsa
### Tulsa, Oklahoma
www.plattcollege.org

- For-profit 2-year health science college
- Commuter campus in large city
- Interview required

**General.** Accredited by ACCSCT. **Enrollment:** 74 degree-seeking undergraduates. **Degrees:** 110 associate awarded. **Calendar:** Continuous. **Full-time faculty:** 35 total. **Part-time faculty:** 20 total. **Class size:** 100% < 20.

**Student profile.** Among degree-seeking undergraduates, 35% enrolled in a transfer program, 65% enrolled in a vocational program, 21 transferred in from other institutions.

**Basis for selection.** Open admission, but selective for some programs. High school diploma or GED are required for some programs. Others require successful completion of entrance exams. Nursing programs required an additional interview with the Director of Nursing. **Homeschooled:** State high school equivalency certificate required.

**2007-2008 Annual costs.** Tuition varies by program.

**Financial aid.** All financial aid based on need. Need-based aid available for part-time students.

**Application procedures. Admission:** No deadline. $100 fee. **Financial aid:** No deadline. FAFSA required.

**Academics. Special study options:** Liberal arts/career combination. Bachelor's degree programs available on campus. License preparation in nursing. **Credit/placement by examination:** CLEP. **Support services:** Remedial instruction, tutoring.

**Majors. Health:** Licensed practical nurse, nursing (RN).

**Computing on campus.** 35 workstations in library, computer center. Online library, wireless network available.

**Student life. Freshman orientation:** Mandatory. Preregistration for classes offered. Held for 5 hours on the first day of classes.

**Student services.** Student employment services, financial aid counseling, placement for graduates. **Transfer:** Pre-admission transcript evaluation for new students.

**Contact.** E-mail: stephanieh@plattcollege.org
Phone: (918) 663-9000 Fax: (918) 622-1240
Stephanie Holderman, Admission Director, Platt College: Tulsa, 3801 South Sheridan, Tulsa, OK 74145-1132

## Redlands Community College
### El Reno, Oklahoma
www.redlandscc.edu

CB code: 7324

- Public 2-year community college
- Commuter campus in large town

**General.** Founded in 1938. Regionally accredited. **Enrollment:** 2,215 degree-seeking undergraduates. **Degrees:** 246 associate awarded. **Location:** 25 miles from Oklahoma City. **Calendar:** Semester, limited summer session. **Full-time faculty:** 35 total. **Part-time faculty:** 76 total. **Class size:** 67% < 20, 31% 20-39, 1% 40-49, less than 1% 50-99, less than 1% >100. **Special facilities:** Applied agricultural research center, ranch, working farm and equine centers.

**Student profile.** Among degree-seeking undergraduates, 43% enrolled in a transfer program, 34% enrolled in a vocational program, 1% already have a bachelor's degree or higher, 381 enrolled as first-time, first-year students.

| | | | |
|---|---|---|---|
| Part-time: | 60% | Hispanic American: | 4% |
| Out-of-state: | 3% | Native American: | 8% |
| Women: | 68% | 25 or older: | 39% |
| African American: | 6% | Live on campus: | 4% |
| Asian American: | 3% | | |

**Transfer out. Colleges most students transferred to 2007:** University of Central Oklahoma, Southwestern Oklahoma State University, Oklahoma State University, University of Oklahoma.

**Basis for selection.** Open admission, but selective for some programs. Nursing, EMT and Honors programs are competitive. Assessment test administered for students not submitting ACT scores. Interviews are required for nursing program admission. **Adult students:** Students without ACT scores or ACT scores below 19 are required to take the COMPASS placement test offered on campus.

**High school preparation.** Recommended units include English 4, mathematics 3, social studies 2, science 2 and foreign language 1.

**2007-2008 Annual costs.** Tuition/fees: $2,640; $4,890 out-of-state. Per-credit charge: $88 in-state; $163 out-of-state. Books/supplies: $960. Personal expenses: $1,500.

**Financial aid. Need-based:** Need-based aid available for part-time students. Work-study available nights, weekends and for part-time students. **Non-need-based:** Scholarships awarded for academics, athletics, leadership.

**Application procedures. Admission:** No deadline. $25 fee, may be waived for applicants with need. Application may be submitted online. Admission notification on a rolling basis. **Financial aid:** Priority date 3/30; no closing date. FAFSA required. Applicants notified on a rolling basis starting 6/1; must reply within 2 week(s) of notification.

**Academics. Special study options:** Accelerated study, combined bachelor's/graduate degree, cooperative education, cross-registration, distance learning, dual enrollment of high school students, honors, independent study, internships, liberal arts/career combination. License preparation in nursing, paramedic. **Credit/placement by examination:** AP, CLEP, institutional tests. 32 credit hours maximum toward associate degree. **Support services:** Learning center, pre-admission summer program, reduced course load, remedial instruction, study skills assistance, tutoring.

**Majors. Agriculture:** General, agronomy, equestrian studies. **Business:** Business admin. **Computer sciences:** General. **Education:** General. **English:** English lit, speech/rhetoric. **Family/consumer sciences:** Child care, child development. **Health:** EMT paramedic, health services, nursing (RN), veterinary technology/assistant. **Math:** General. **Parks/recreation:** Exercise sciences, health/fitness. **Physical sciences:** General. **Protective services:** Police science. **Psychology:** General. **Social sciences:** General. **Visual/performing arts:** Art. **Other:** Applied technology.

**Most popular majors.** Agriculture 7%, business/marketing 10%, family/consumer sciences 6%, health sciences 27%, liberal arts 31%, security/protective services 11%.

**Computing on campus.** 180 workstations in dormitories, library, computer center. Commuter students can connect to campus network. Online library, helpline, wireless network available.

**Student life. Freshman orientation:** Available. Preregistration for classes offered. Class held the Thursday and Friday prior to start of Fall semester. **Housing:** Apartments, substance-free housing available. $200 partly refundable deposit. Limited housing for agriculture students at working ranch available. **Activities:** Choral groups, Model UN, student government, nursing student association, Aggie Club, Phi Theta Kappa, Young Democrats, College Republicans, art club, Students in Free Enterprise, fencing club, photography club.

**Athletics.** NJCAA. **Intercollegiate:** Baseball M, basketball, golf W, volleyball W. **Intramural:** Cheerleading. **Team name:** Cougars.

**Student services.** Adult student services, career counseling, services for economically disadvantaged, student employment services, financial aid counseling, placement for graduates, veterans' counselor. **Transfer:** Transfer adviser, college fairs on campus for students transferring to 4-year colleges.

**Contact.** E-mail: studentservices@redlandscc.edu
Phone: (405) 262-2552 ext. 1417 Toll-free number: (866) 415-6367
Fax: (405) 422-1239
Tricia Hobson, Director of Enrollment Management, Redlands Community College, 1300 South Country Club Road, El Reno, OK 73036

## Rose State College
**Midwest City, Oklahoma**
www.rose.edu                                    CB code: 1462

- Public 2-year community college
- Commuter campus in small city

**General.** Founded in 1968. Regionally accredited. **Enrollment:** 7,107 degree-seeking undergraduates; 1,350 non-degree-seeking students. **Degrees:** 754 associate awarded. **ROTC:** Army, Air Force. **Location:** 5 miles from Oklahoma City. **Calendar:** Semester, extensive summer session. **Full-time faculty:** 124 total; 14% have terminal degrees, 8% minority, 61% women. **Part-time faculty:** 263 total. **Special facilities:** Regional history center, 1400-seat performing arts theater, wetlands project.

**Student profile.** Among degree-seeking undergraduates, 77% enrolled in a transfer program, 23% enrolled in a vocational program, 1,129 enrolled as first-time, first-year students, 895 transferred in from other institutions.

| | | | |
|---|---|---|---|
| Part-time: | 61% | Asian American: | 3% |
| Out-of-state: | 1% | Hispanic American: | 4% |
| Women: | 61% | Native American: | 10% |
| African American: | 17% | 25 or older: | 47% |

**Transfer out. Colleges most students transferred to 2007:** Oklahoma State University, Southwestern Oklahoma State University, University of Oklahoma, University of Central Oklahoma.

**Basis for selection.** Interview required for health science programs. **Adult students:** COMPASS Placement test required. **Homeschooled:** Peer class must have graduated. **Learning Disabled:** If student indicates that he or she has a disability, they are referred to the disability counselor.

**High school preparation.** 15 units required. Required units include English 4, mathematics 3, social studies 1, history 2, science 2 (laboratory 2) and academic electives 3. May include English, laboratory science, mathematics, history/citizenship skills, computer science or foreign language.

**2007-2008 Annual costs.** Tuition/fees: $2,340; $6,798 out-of-state. Per-credit charge: $60 in-state; $209 out-of-state. Books/supplies: $1,250.

**2006-2007 Financial aid. Need-based:** 50% of total undergraduate aid awarded as scholarships/grants, 50% as loans/jobs. Need-based aid available for part-time students. Work-study available nights, weekends and for part-time students. **Non-need-based:** Scholarships awarded for academics, athletics.

**Application procedures. Admission:** Closing date 8/20 (receipt date). No application fee. Application must be submitted on paper. Admission notification on a rolling basis. International students must meet immigration requirements as defined by Dept. of Homeland Security and students with English as a second language must pass the necessary test or transfer in coursework for admission. **Financial aid:** Priority date 6/1; no closing date. FAFSA required. Applicants notified on a rolling basis starting 3/1; must reply within 4 week(s) of notification.

**Academics. Special study options:** Accelerated study, cooperative education, cross-registration, distance learning, double major, dual enrollment of high school students, honors, independent study, internships, liberal arts/career combination, weekend college. Bachelor's degree programs available on campus. License preparation in dental hygiene, nursing, radiology. **Credit/placement by examination:** AP, CLEP, IB, institutional tests. 50 credit hours maximum toward associate degree. **Support services:** GED preparation and test center, learning center, reduced course load, remedial instruction, study skills assistance, tutoring, writing center.

**Majors. Biology:** General. **Business:** General, accounting technology, business admin, e-commerce, human resources, small business admin. **Communications:** Broadcast journalism, digital media, journalism. **Computer sciences:** General, LAN/WAN management, networking, web page design, webmaster. **Conservation:** Environmental science. **Construction:** Carpentry, masonry, plumbing. **Education:** Multi-level teacher. **Engineering:** General. **Engineering technology:** Drafting, electrical, heat/ac/refrig, telecommunications, water quality. **English:** English lit. **Family/consumer sciences:** General, child care, child development. **Foreign languages:** General. **Health:** Athletic training, clinical lab assistant, clinical lab technology, dental assistant, dental hygiene, EMT paramedic, medical records technology, nursing (RN), predental, premedicine, prenursing, prepharmacy, radiologic technology/medical imaging, respiratory therapy assistant, respiratory therapy technology. **History:** General. **Legal studies:** Court reporting, paralegal. **Liberal arts:** Arts/sciences, library assistant. **Math:** General. **Mechanic/repair:** Auto body, automotive, heating/ac/refrig. **Parks/recreation:** Health/fitness. **Physical sciences:** Chemistry, geology, physics. **Protective services:** Police science. **Psychology:** General. **Public administration:** Social work. **Social sciences:** General, political science, sociology. **Transportation:** Aviation. **Visual/performing arts:** Art, dramatic.

**Computing on campus.** 150 workstations in library, computer center, student center. Commuter students can connect to campus network. Online course registration, online library, helpline, student web hosting, wireless network available.

**Student life. Freshman orientation:** Mandatory. Preregistration for classes offered. **Activities:** Jazz band, choral groups, dance, drama, music ensembles, student government, student newspaper, Phi Theta Kappa, Future

Criminal Justice Club, Black Student Association, broadcasting club, drama club, Oklahoma Intercollegiate Legislature, American Indian Association.

**Athletics.** NJCAA. **Intercollegiate:** Baseball M, softball W. **Intramural:** Bowling, soccer, swimming, table tennis, tennis, volleyball. **Team name:** Raiders.

**Student services.** Adult student services, alcohol/substance abuse counseling, career counseling, student employment services, financial aid counseling, on-campus daycare, personal counseling, placement for graduates, veterans' counselor. **Physically disabled:** Services for visually, speech, hearing impaired. **Learning disabled:** Comprehensive services available. **Transfer:** Pre-admission transcript evaluation for new students. Transfer center, transfer adviser, college fairs on campus for students transferring to 4-year colleges.

**Contact.** Phone: (405) 733-7312 Toll-free number: (866) 621-0987 Fax: (405) 736-0309
Mechelle Aitson-Roessler, Registrar/Director of Admissions, Rose State College, 6420 SE 15th Street, Midwest City, OK 73110

## Seminole State College
Seminole, Oklahoma
www.ssc.cc.ok.us
CB code: 0316

- Public 2-year community and junior college
- Commuter campus in small town

**General.** Founded in 1931. Regionally accredited. **Enrollment:** 1,820 degree-seeking undergraduates. **Degrees:** 281 associate awarded. **Location:** 55 miles from Oklahoma City. **Calendar:** Semester, extensive summer session. **Full-time faculty:** 43 total. **Part-time faculty:** 60 total.

**Student profile.** Among degree-seeking undergraduates, 120 transferred in from other institutions.

| | | | |
|---|---|---|---|
| Out-of-state: | 3% | Live on campus: | 3% |

**Basis for selection.** Open admission, but selective for some programs. Additional requirements for admission to A.D. Nursing Program and MLT Program include minimum ACT composite score of 19 and minimum score of 15 on Nelson Denny Reading Test.

**High school preparation.** 15 units recommended. Recommended units include English 4, mathematics 3, social studies 2, history 2, science 2 and academic electives 2.

**2007-2008 Annual costs.** Tuition/fees: $2,594; $6,078 out-of-state. Per-credit charge: $53 in-state; $169 out-of-state. Room/board: $5,420. Books/supplies: $350. Personal expenses: $920.

**Financial aid. Non-need-based:** Scholarships awarded for academics, athletics, state residency.

**Application procedures. Admission:** No deadline. $15 fee. Admission notification on a rolling basis. **Financial aid:** Priority date 4/1; no closing date. FAFSA, institutional form required. Applicants notified on a rolling basis starting 3/1; must reply within 4 week(s) of notification.

**Academics. Special study options:** Dual enrollment of high school students, honors. Bachelor's degree programs available on campus. **Credit/placement by examination:** CLEP, institutional tests. 30 credit hours maximum toward associate degree. **Support services:** Learning center, remedial instruction, tutoring, writing center.

**Majors. Business:** Business admin, office management, office/clerical. **Computer sciences:** Computer science. **Education:** General, elementary. **Health:** Clinical lab technology, nursing (RN). **Interdisciplinary:** Behavioral sciences. **Liberal arts:** Arts/sciences. **Math:** General. **Parks/recreation:** Health/fitness. **Social sciences:** General. **Visual/performing arts:** Art.

**Most popular majors.** Business/marketing 20%, computer/information sciences 10%, health sciences 10%, liberal arts 60%.

**Computing on campus.** 310 workstations in dormitories, library, computer center, student center. Dormitories wired for high-speed internet access and linked to campus network. Commuter students can connect to campus network. Helpline, repair service available.

**Student life. Freshman orientation:** Mandatory. Preregistration for classes offered. **Housing:** Coed dorms, single-sex dorms available. $50 deposit. **Activities:** Concert band, student government, student newspaper, student government, Native American student association, Baptist student union.

**Athletics.** NJCAA. **Intercollegiate:** Baseball M, basketball, golf, softball W, tennis, volleyball. **Intramural:** Baseball M, basketball. **Team name:** Trojans.

**Student services.** Career counseling, services for economically disadvantaged, financial aid counseling, personal counseling, veterans' counselor. **Physically disabled:** Services for visually, speech, hearing impaired. **Transfer:** Transfer adviser, college fairs on campus for students transferring to 4-year colleges.

**Contact.** E-mail: c.lindley@sscok.edu
Phone: (405) 382-9950 ext. 230 Fax: (405) 382-9524
Chris Lindley, Director of Enrollment Management, Seminole State College, 2701 Boren Boulevard, Seminole, OK 74868

## Tulsa Community College
Tulsa, Oklahoma
www.tulsacc.edu
CB member
CB code: 6839

- Public 2-year community college
- Commuter campus in large city

**General.** Founded in 1968. Regionally accredited. 4 branch campuses located in Tulsa. **Enrollment:** 11,512 degree-seeking undergraduates; 5,466 non-degree-seeking students. **Degrees:** 1,959 associate awarded. **Calendar:** Semester, extensive summer session. **Full-time faculty:** 291 total. **Part-time faculty:** 710 total. **Class size:** 60% < 20, 19% 20-39, 5% 40-49, 7% 50-99, 9% >100.

**Student profile.** Among degree-seeking undergraduates, 74% enrolled in a transfer program, 26% enrolled in a vocational program, 3% already have a bachelor's degree or higher, 2,934 enrolled as first-time, first-year students.

| | | | |
|---|---|---|---|
| Part-time: | 59% | Asian American: | 2% |
| Out-of-state: | 2% | Hispanic American: | 4% |
| Women: | 65% | Native American: | 9% |
| African American: | 10% | 25 or older: | 59% |

**Transfer out. Colleges most students transferred to 2007:** University of Oklahoma, Oklahoma State University, Northeastern Oklahoma State University, Tulsa University, University of Central Oklahoma.

**Basis for selection.** Open admission, but selective for some programs. Special requirements for health-related, legal assistant, and management programs. Interview required for health, legal assistant, and nursing programs. **Adult students:** SAT/ACT scores not required. If no ACT score, students must take Accuplacer CPT.

**High school preparation.** 15 units recommended. Recommended units include English 4, mathematics 3, social studies 1, history 2, science 2 (laboratory 2) and academic electives 3.

**2007-2008 Annual costs.** Tuition/fees: $2,568; $6,880 out-of-state. Per-credit charge: $58 in-state; $201 out-of-state. Books/supplies: $600. Personal expenses: $900.

**Financial aid. Need-based:** 1,258 full-time freshmen applied for aid; 830 were judged to have need; 830 of these received aid. Need-based aid available for part-time students. Work-study available nights, weekends and for part-time students. **Non-need-based:** Scholarships awarded for academics, art, leadership, music/drama, state residency.

**Application procedures. Admission:** No deadline. $20 fee. Admission notification on a rolling basis. **Financial aid:** Priority date 8/1; no closing date. FAFSA, institutional form required. Applicants notified on a rolling basis starting 4/1; must reply within 2 week(s) of notification.

**Academics.** Many short-period intensive courses within conventional semesters. **Special study options:** Cross-registration, distance learning, dual enrollment of high school students, ESL, honors, independent study, internships, weekend college. **Credit/placement by examination:** CLEP, institutional tests. 30 credit hours maximum toward associate degree. **Support services:** Learning center, remedial instruction, study skills assistance, tutoring, writing center.

**Majors. Agriculture:** Horticultural science. **Business:** General, accounting, administrative services, business admin, fashion, finance, hospitality admin, hospitality/recreation, human resources, insurance, management information systems, managerial economics, office technology, real estate, tourism/travel. **Communications:** Journalism. **Communications technology:** General. **Computer sciences:** General, applications programming, programming. **Education:** General, physical. **Engineering:** General. **Engineering technology:** Civil, drafting, electrical. **English:** English lit, speech/rhetoric. **Family/**

consumer sciences: Child care. **Foreign languages:** French, German, Italian, Japanese, Russian, sign language interpretation, Spanish. **Health:** Clinical lab assistant, clinical lab technology, dental hygiene, medical assistant, medical radiologic technology/radiation therapy, medical secretary, occupational therapy assistant, physical therapy assistant, respiratory therapy technology. **History:** General. **Legal studies:** Legal secretary, paralegal. **Liberal arts:** Library science. **Math:** General. **Mechanic/repair:** Avionics, electronics/electrical, heating/ac/refrig. **Philosophy/religion:** Philosophy. **Physical sciences:** Astronomy, chemistry, geology, physics. **Protective services:** Criminal justice, fire safety technology, police science. **Psychology:** General. **Social sciences:** General, economics, geography, political science, sociology. **Transportation:** Aviation management. **Visual/performing arts:** Dramatic, interior design.

**Computing on campus.** 2,306 workstations in library, computer center. Online course registration, online library available.

**Student life. Freshman orientation:** Available. **Activities:** Bands, choral groups, drama, music ensembles, student government, student newspaper.

**Athletics. Intramural:** Basketball, soccer, softball, table tennis, tennis, volleyball.

**Student services.** Career counseling, student employment services, health services, on-campus daycare, personal counseling, placement for graduates, veterans' counselor. **Physically disabled:** Services for visually, hearing impaired. **Transfer:** College fairs on campus for students transferring to 4-year colleges.

**Contact.** E-mail: lbrewer@tulsacc.edu
Phone: (918) 595-7811 Fax: (918) 595-7987
Leanne Brewer, Director of Admissions and Records, Tulsa Community College, 6111 East Skelly Drive, Tulsa, OK 74135

## Tulsa Welding School
**Tulsa, Oklahoma**
www.weldingschool.com                    **CB code: 2958**

- For-profit 2-year technical college
- Commuter campus in very large city
- Interview required

**General.** Accredited by ACCSCT. **Enrollment:** 736 degree-seeking undergraduates. **Degrees:** 25 associate awarded. **Calendar:** Continuous. **Full-time faculty:** 16 total. **Part-time faculty:** 1 total.

**Student profile.**

| Out-of-state: | 41% | 25 or older: | 36% |
|---|---|---|---|

**Basis for selection.** Open admission. Must have high school diploma or GED or pass the ATB test. **Homeschooled:** Applicants must pass ATB test.

**2007-2008 Annual costs.** Tuition and fees vary by program from $7,910 to $13,900.

**Financial aid.** All financial aid based on need.

**Application procedures. Admission:** No deadline. No application fee. Admission notification on a rolling basis. **Financial aid:** FAFSA required.

**Academics. Credit/placement by examination:** CLEP.

**Majors. Production:** Welding.

**Computing on campus.** 3 workstations in library.

**Student life. Freshman orientation:** Mandatory. Preregistration for classes offered.

**Student services.** Career counseling, student employment services, financial aid counseling, personal counseling, placement for graduates. **Physically disabled:** Services for hearing impaired.

**Contact.** E-mail: tws@ionet.net
Phone: (918) 587-6789 ext. 240 Toll-free number: (800) 331-2934 ext. 221
Fax: (918) 587-8170
Mike Thurber, Director of Admissions, Tulsa Welding School, 2545 East 11th Street, Tulsa, OK 74104-3909

## Vatterott College: Tulsa
**Tulsa, Oklahoma**
www.vatterott-college.edu                 **CB code: 3637**

- For-profit 2-year branch campus and technical college
- Commuter campus in large city

**General.** Accredited by ACCSCT. **Calendar:** Continuous.

**Annual costs/financial aid.** Program cost ranges: $17,646 to $21,414 (certificate/diploma); $27,136 to $32,930 (associate degree).

**Contact.** Phone: (918) 835-8288
Director of Admissions, 4343 South 118th East Avenue, Tulsa, OK 74146

## Western Oklahoma State College
**Altus, Oklahoma**                                      **CB member**
www.wosc.edu                                             **CB code: 6020**

- Public 2-year community college
- Commuter campus in large town

**General.** Founded in 1926. Regionally accredited. **Enrollment:** 580 full-time, degree-seeking students. **Degrees:** 259 associate awarded. **Location:** 60 miles from Lawton, 140 miles from Oklahoma City. **Calendar:** Semester, limited summer session. **Full-time faculty:** 46 total; 4% have terminal degrees. **Part-time faculty:** 56 total. **Class size:** 78% < 20, 20% 20-39, less than 1% 40-49, 1% 50-99.

**Transfer out.** 60% of students enrolled in the transfer program go on to 4-year colleges. **Colleges most students transferred to 2007:** Southwestern Oklahoma State University, Cameron University, Oklahoma State University, University of Central Oklahoma, University of Oklahoma.

**Basis for selection.** Open admission. SAT or ACT required for applicants under 21 for placement; no minimum score required. **Adult students:** ACT required for adults who don't have high school diploma or GED. Must demonstrate proficiency in English, math, science, and reading through COMPASS or ACT subtest scores. **Homeschooled:** Transcript of courses and grades, letter of recommendation (nonparent) required. Must have ACT or SAT. High school class must have graduated and must satisfy curricular requirements.

**High school preparation.** 15 units recommended. Recommended units include English 4, mathematics 3, history 3, science 2 and academic electives 3. 2 fine arts recommended.

**2007-2008 Annual costs.** Tuition/fees: $2,471; $5,771 out-of-state. Per-credit charge: $52 in-state; $162 out-of-state. Room/board: $3,750. Books/supplies: $1,000. Personal expenses: $1,200.

**2006-2007 Financial aid. Need-based:** 65% of total undergraduate aid awarded as scholarships/grants, 35% as loans/jobs. Need-based aid available for part-time students. Work-study available nights, weekends and for part-time students. **Non-need-based:** Scholarships awarded for academics, alumni affiliation, art, athletics, leadership, music/drama, state residency.

**Application procedures. Admission:** No deadline. $15 fee. Application may be submitted online. Admission notification on a rolling basis. **Financial aid:** Priority date 3/1; no closing date. FAFSA, institutional form required. Applicants notified on a rolling basis; must reply within 3 week(s) of notification.

**Academics. Special study options:** Distance learning, dual enrollment of high school students, honors, liberal arts/career combination. Cooperative agreements with local technology centers. Students may co-enroll and earn college credits for votech courses. License preparation in aviation, nursing, radiology. **Credit/placement by examination:** AP, CLEP, institutional tests. 30 credit hours maximum toward associate degree. **Support services:** Learning center, remedial instruction, study skills assistance, tutoring.

**Majors. Biology:** General. **Business:** General, administrative services, business admin, management science, office technology, office/clerical. **Computer sciences:** General, computer science, information systems, programming. **Conservation:** Wildlife. **Education:** General, physical, social studies. **Engineering:** General. **Engineering technology:** Construction, drafting, manufacturing. **English:** English lit. **Family/consumer sciences:** Child care. **Foreign languages:** Spanish. **Health:** EMT paramedic, medical radiologic technology/radiation therapy, medical records admin, medical secretary, nursing (RN). **History:** General. **Liberal arts:** Arts/sciences. **Math:** General. **Mechanic/repair:** Auto body, automotive, diesel, electronics/electrical. **Parks/recreation:** Health/fitness. **Protective services:** Corrections, firefighting, police science. **Psychology:** General. **Social sciences:** General, political science, sociology. **Transportation:** Aviation, aviation management. **Visual/performing arts:** Art.

**Most popular majors.** Health sciences 16%, liberal arts 11%.

**Computing on campus.** 50 workstations in library. Dormitories wired for high-speed internet access and linked to campus network. Commuter students can connect to campus network. Online course registration, online library, helpline, wireless network available.

**Student life. Freshman orientation:** Mandatory. Preregistration for classes offered. **Housing:** Coed dorms, substance-free housing available. $50 deposit. **Activities:** Bands, choral groups, drama, music ensembles, musical theater, radio station, student government, student newspaper, Baptist Student Union, Wesley Foundation, tutoring club, College Democrats, College Republicans, Fellowship of Christians.

**Athletics.** NJCAA. **Intercollegiate:** Baseball M, basketball, softball W. **Intramural:** Basketball, volleyball. **Team name:** Pioneers.

**Student services.** Career counseling, financial aid counseling, health services, personal counseling, veterans' counselor. **Transfer:** Transfer adviser, college fairs on campus for students transferring to 4-year colleges.

**Contact.** E-mail: tanya.wingate@wosc.edu
Phone: (580) 477-2000 Fax: (580) 477-7723
Larry Paxton, Director of Academic Services, Western Oklahoma State
College, 2801 North Main Street, Altus, OK 73521

# Oregon

transfer adviser, college fairs on campus for students transferring to 4-year colleges.

**Contact.** E-mail: getinfo@bluecc.edu
Phone: (541) 278-5759 Fax: (541) 278-5871
Theresa Bosworth, Director of Admissions, Records & Testing/Registrar, Blue Mountain Community College, 2411 Northwest Carden Avenue, Pendleton, OR 97801

---

## Blue Mountain Community College
Pendleton, Oregon
www.bluecc.edu     **CB code: 4025**

▶ Public 2-year community college
▶ Commuter campus in large town

**General.** Founded in 1962. Regionally accredited. Located in agricultural area. **Enrollment:** 1,400 degree-seeking undergraduates. **Degrees:** 159 associate awarded. **Location:** 200 miles from Portland. **Calendar:** Quarter, limited summer session. **Full-time faculty:** 45 total. **Part-time faculty:** 155 total. **Class size:** 74% < 20, 25% 20-39, less than 1% 40-49, less than 1% 50-99.

**Student profile.**

| | | | |
|---|---|---|---|
| Out-of-state: | 6% | 25 or older: | 55% |

**Transfer out. Colleges most students transferred to 2007:** Eastern Oregon University, Oregon State University, University of Oregon.

**Basis for selection.** Open admission, but selective for some programs. Admission to nursing program based on prerequisite course work, GPA, security check, point system. Dental Assisting students admitted based on prerequisites and GPA.

**2007-2008 Annual costs.** Tuition/fees: $2,989; $8,704 out-of-state. Per-credit charge: $64 in-state; $191 out-of-state. Washington, Idaho, Nevada, Montana, and California state residents pay in-state tuition. Books/supplies: $1,000. Personal expenses: $390.

**Financial aid. Need-based:** Need-based aid available for part-time students. Work-study available nights, weekends and for part-time students. **Non-need-based:** Scholarships awarded for athletics, music/drama.

**Application procedures. Admission:** No deadline. No application fee. Application may be submitted online. Admission notification on a rolling basis. **Financial aid:** Priority date 3/30; no closing date. FAFSA required. Applicants notified on a rolling basis starting 4/1; must reply within 2 week(s) of notification.

**Academics.** Learning disabilities diagnostician available. **Special study options:** Cooperative education, cross-registration, distance learning, double major, dual enrollment of high school students, ESL, liberal arts/career combination. Bachelor's degree programs available on campus. License preparation in nursing. **Credit/placement by examination:** AP, CLEP, institutional tests. 15 credit hours maximum toward associate degree. **Support services:** GED preparation and test center, learning center, reduced course load, remedial instruction, study skills assistance, tutoring.

**Majors. Agriculture:** Animal husbandry, business, crop production, farm/ranch, production. **Business:** Accounting technology, administrative services, business admin, marketing. **Education:** Early childhood, teacher assistance. **Engineering technology:** Civil, drafting, electrical. **Family/consumer sciences:** Family/community services. **Health:** Medical secretary, nursing (RN). **Liberal arts:** Arts/sciences. **Mechanic/repair:** Industrial. **Parks/recreation:** Health/fitness. **Public administration:** Human services.

**Computing on campus.** 200 workstations in library, computer center. Commuter students can connect to campus network. Online course registration, online library, wireless network available.

**Student life. Freshman orientation:** Available, $10 fee. Preregistration for classes offered. 1/2 day session in fall prior to classes. **Activities:** Jazz band, choral groups, drama, music ensembles, musical theater, student government, multicultural club, MECHA, Native American club.

**Athletics. Intercollegiate:** Baseball M, basketball, rodeo, softball W, volleyball W. **Team name:** Timberwolves.

**Student services.** Alcohol/substance abuse counseling, career counseling, services for economically disadvantaged, student employment services, financial aid counseling, personal counseling, placement for graduates, veterans' counselor. **Physically disabled:** Services for visually, speech, hearing impaired. **Learning disabled:** Comprehensive services available. **Transfer:** Pre-admission transcript evaluation for new students. Transfer center,

---

## Central Oregon Community College
Bend, Oregon
www.cocc.edu     **CB code: 4090**

▶ Public 2-year community college
▶ Commuter campus in small city

**General.** Founded in 1949. Regionally accredited. **Enrollment:** 3,643 degree-seeking undergraduates; 797 non-degree-seeking students. **Degrees:** 335 associate awarded. **ROTC:** Army. **Location:** 150 miles from Portland, 120 miles from Salem. **Calendar:** Quarter, limited summer session. **Full-time faculty:** 89 total; 39% have terminal degrees, 4% minority, 53% women. **Part-time faculty:** 117 total; 4% minority, 56% women. **Class size:** 40% < 20, 57% 20-39, 2% 40-49, 1% 50-99. **Special facilities:** Exercise physiology laboratory, dental clinic.

**Student profile.** Among degree-seeking undergraduates, 67% enrolled in a transfer program, 32% enrolled in a vocational program, 10% already have a bachelor's degree or higher, 785 enrolled as first-time, first-year students, 529 transferred in from other institutions.

| | | | |
|---|---|---|---|
| Part-time: | 56% | Hispanic American: | 5% |
| Out-of-state: | 5% | Native American: | 3% |
| Women: | 58% | 25 or older: | 35% |
| African American: | 1% | Live on campus: | 3% |
| Asian American: | 2% | | |

**Transfer out. Colleges most students transferred to 2007:** Oregon State University, University of Oregon, Southern Oregon University, Portland State University.

**Basis for selection.** Open admission, but selective for some programs. Special requirements for nursing, emergency medical services. Limited enrollment (first-come first-served basis, with fall term only start date) for medical assistant, dental assistant, and massage therapy. **Homeschooled:** High school diploma or GED is not required if student is 18 or older.

**2007-2008 Annual costs.** Tuition/fees: $2,958; $3,993 out-of-district; $8,088 out-of-state. Per-credit charge: $63 in-district; $86 out-of-district; $176 out-of-state. Residents of WA, ID, NV and CA pay the in-state, out-of-district tuition. Emergency Medical Services, Aviation, Nursing, Culinary and Massage Therapy programs carry additional fees. Room/board: $7,084. Books/supplies: $1,050. Personal expenses: $1,100.

**2007-2008 Financial aid. Need-based:** 269 full-time freshmen applied for aid; 202 were judged to have need; 188 of these received aid. Average need met was 78%. Average scholarship/grant was $4,770; average loan $3,197. 40% of total undergraduate aid awarded as scholarships/grants, 60% as loans/jobs. Need-based aid available for part-time students. Work-study available for part-time students. **Non-need-based:** Awarded to 53 full-time undergraduates, including 21 freshmen. Scholarships awarded for academics, state residency. **Additional information:** Institution-sponsored short-term loans. Extensive part-time student employment.

**Application procedures. Admission:** Priority date 6/15; no deadline. $25 fee, may be waived for applicants with need. Application may be submitted online. Admission notification on a rolling basis. **Financial aid:** No deadline. FAFSA required. Applicants notified on a rolling basis starting 3/30; must reply within 4 week(s) of notification.

**Academics. Special study options:** Cooperative education, distance learning, double major, dual enrollment of high school students, ESL, independent study, internships, student-designed major, study abroad. Bachelor's degree programs available on campus. License preparation in aviation, nursing, paramedic, physical therapy. **Credit/placement by examination:** AP, CLEP, IB, institutional tests. Credit for prior training or certification varies by program. **Support services:** GED preparation, learning center, pre-admission summer program, reduced course load, remedial instruction, study skills assistance, tutoring, writing center.

**Majors. Agriculture:** General, horticultural science. **Architecture:** Landscape. **Biology:** General. **Business:** Accounting, administrative services, business admin, customer service, hospitality/recreation, management information systems, marketing. **Communications:** General. **Computer sciences:**

General, computer science, computer support specialist, networking. **Conservation:** General, forest technology, forestry. **Education:** General. **Engineering:** General. **Engineering technology:** CAD/CADD, drafting, GIS, industrial, manufacturing. **English:** English lit. **Foreign languages:** General. **Health:** EMT paramedic, massage therapy, medical records technology, nursing (RN), premedicine, prepharmacy, radiologic technology/medical imaging. **History:** General. **Legal studies:** Prelaw. **Liberal arts:** Arts/sciences, humanities. **Math:** General. **Parks/recreation:** General, health/fitness. **Physical sciences:** General, chemistry, geology, physics. **Protective services:** Criminal justice, firefighting. **Psychology:** General. **Social sciences:** General, anthropology, criminology, economics, political science, sociology. **Transportation:** Airline/commercial pilot. **Visual/performing arts:** General, studio arts.

**Most popular majors.** Health sciences 17%, liberal arts 63%, security/protective services 8%.

**Computing on campus.** 350 workstations in dormitories, library, computer center. Dormitories wired for high-speed internet access and linked to campus network. Commuter students can connect to campus network. Online course registration, online library, helpline, wireless network available.

**Student life. Freshman orientation:** Available, $25 fee. Preregistration for classes offered. **Housing:** Coed dorms available. $350 partly refundable deposit, deadline 8/15. **Activities:** Bands, campus ministries, choral groups, drama, music ensembles, student government, student newspaper, symphony orchestra.

**Athletics. Intramural:** Basketball, cross-country, football (non-tackle), golf, soccer, softball, table tennis, track and field, volleyball, weight lifting. **Team name:** Bobcats.

**Student services.** Adult student services, alcohol/substance abuse counseling, career counseling, services for economically disadvantaged, student employment services, financial aid counseling, health services, minority student services, personal counseling, placement for graduates, veterans' counselor, women's services. **Physically disabled:** Services for visually, speech, hearing impaired. **Transfer:** Pre-admission transcript evaluation for new students. Transfer adviser, college fairs on campus for students transferring to 4-year colleges.

**Contact.** E-mail: welcome@cocc.edu
Phone: (541) 383-7500 Fax: (541) 383-7506
Aimee Metcalf, Director, Admissions and Records, Central Oregon Community College, 2600 Northwest College Way, Bend, OR 97701-5998

## Chemeketa Community College
Salem, Oregon
www.chemeketa.edu
CB code: 4745

- Public 2-year community and junior college
- Commuter campus in small city

**General.** Founded in 1962. Regionally accredited. **Enrollment:** 6,350 degree-seeking undergraduates; 905 non-degree-seeking students. **Degrees:** 392 associate awarded. **Location:** 45 miles from Portland. **Calendar:** Quarter, extensive summer session. **Full-time faculty:** 221 total; 81% have terminal degrees, 13% minority, 53% women. **Part-time faculty:** 485 total; 7% minority, 59% women. **Class size:** 43% < 20, 52% 20-39, 4% 40-49, less than 1% 50-99, less than 1% >100. **Special facilities:** Planetarium, vineyard and winemaking facility. **Partnerships:** Formal partnerships with local high schools.

**Student profile.** Among degree-seeking undergraduates, 860 enrolled as first-time, first-year students.

| | | | |
|---|---|---|---|
| Part-time: | 57% | Women: | 55% |
| Out-of-state: | 5% | 25 or older: | 60% |

**Transfer out. Colleges most students transferred to 2007:** University of Oregon, Oregon State University, Western Oregon University, Eastern Oregon University, Portland State University.

**Basis for selection.** Open admission, but selective for some programs. Interview required for limited enrollment programs; preparatory courses may be required. Placement tests required for degree-seeking students, available to all students.

**2007-2008 Annual costs.** Tuition/fees: $2,790; $9,135 out-of-state. Per-credit charge: $58 in-state; $199 out-of-state. International students have additional required fees. Individual courses may have extra fees. Books/supplies: $1,200. Personal expenses: $300.

**Financial aid.** All financial aid based on need. Need-based aid available for part-time students. Work-study available nights, weekends and for part-time students.

**Application procedures. Admission:** No deadline. No application fee. Application may be submitted online. Admission notification on a rolling basis. **Financial aid:** Priority date 4/1; no closing date. FAFSA required. Applicants notified on a rolling basis starting 6/30; must reply within 2 week(s) of notification.

**Academics. Special study options:** Accelerated study, combined bachelor's/graduate degree, cooperative education, distance learning, double major, dual enrollment of high school students, ESL, independent study, internships, study abroad, teacher certification program, weekend college. License preparation in dental hygiene, nursing, paramedic. **Credit/placement by examination:** AP, CLEP, IB, institutional tests. 12 credit hours maximum toward associate degree. **Support services:** GED preparation and test center, learning center, pre-admission summer program, remedial instruction, study skills assistance, tutoring, writing center.

**Majors. Agriculture:** Agribusiness operations, horticultural science. **Biology:** General, anatomy, botany, pharmacology, zoology. **Business:** Accounting, administrative services, business admin, hospitality admin, management information systems, management science, office management, office technology, operations, real estate, tourism/travel. **Communications:** Journalism. **Communications technology:** Graphic/printing. **Computer sciences:** General, applications programming, programming. **Conservation:** Forest management, forest sciences, forestry. **Construction:** Building inspection, maintenance. **Education:** Bilingual, early childhood, elementary, health, physical, secondary, teacher assistance, technology/industrial arts. **Engineering:** General, electrical. **Engineering technology:** Civil, construction, drafting, electrical. **English:** English lit, speech/rhetoric. **Family/consumer sciences:** General, child care, family studies. **Foreign languages:** Sign language interpretation. **Health:** Dental assistant, dental hygiene, EMT ambulance attendant, EMT paramedic, health care admin, health services, medical records admin, medical records technology, medical secretary, medical transcription, nursing (RN), office admin, office assistant, office computer specialist, predental, premedicine, prenursing, prepharmacy, substance abuse counseling. **History:** General, American. **Interdisciplinary:** Gerontology. **Legal studies:** Legal secretary, prelaw. **Liberal arts:** Arts/sciences. **Math:** General, algebra, computational, geometry, probability, statistics. **Mechanic/repair:** Automotive, industrial. **Parks/recreation:** General. **Philosophy/religion:** Philosophy. **Physical sciences:** Chemistry, geology, physics. **Protective services:** Criminal justice, fire safety technology, firefighting, law enforcement admin, police science. **Psychology:** General. **Public administration:** Community org/advocacy, human services, social work. **Social sciences:** Anthropology, economics, geography, political science, sociology. **Visual/performing arts:** Art, design, theater design.

**Computing on campus.** 1,000 workstations in library, computer center. Commuter students can connect to campus network. Online course registration, online library, helpline, wireless network available.

**Student life. Freshman orientation:** Available. Preregistration for classes offered. **Activities:** Choral groups, dance, literary magazine, student government, student newspaper, TV station, Triangle Society (sexual minority students), Christian Student Organization, LDS Club, College Republicans, Democratic Students, Phi Theta Kappa, Latino Development Network.

**Athletics. NJCAA. Intercollegiate:** Baseball M, basketball, softball W, volleyball W. **Intramural:** Softball W, tennis. **Team name:** The Storm.

**Student services.** Adult student services, alcohol/substance abuse counseling, career counseling, student employment services, financial aid counseling, minority student services, on-campus daycare, placement for graduates. **Physically disabled:** Services for visually, speech, hearing impaired. **Learning disabled:** Comprehensive services available. **Transfer:** Pre-admission transcript evaluation for new students. Transfer adviser, college fairs on campus for students transferring to 4-year colleges.

**Contact.** E-mail: admissions@chemeketa.edu
Phone: (503) 399-5006 Fax: (503) 399-3918
Melissa Frey, Enrollment Services Coordinator, Chemeketa Community College, Admissions Office, Salem, OR 97305-1453

## Clackamas Community College
Oregon City, Oregon
www.clackamas.edu
CB code: 4111

- Public 2-year community college
- Commuter campus in small city

**General.** Founded in 1966. Regionally accredited. **Enrollment:** 1,960 full-time, degree-seeking students. **Degrees:** 579 associate awarded. **ROTC:** Air Force. **Location:** 15 miles from Portland. **Calendar:** Quarter, limited summer session. **Full-time faculty:** 157 total; 8% have terminal degrees, 8% minority, 46% women. **Part-time faculty:** 429 total; 9% minority, 51% women. **Class size:** 67% < 20, 32% 20-39, 1% 40-49. **Special facilities:**

Environmental learning center, observatory. **Partnerships:** Formal partnerships with Intel Microelectronics and Portland General Electric/Pacificorps.

**Student profile.**

Out-of-state: 2%     25 or older: 47%

**Transfer out. Colleges most students transferred to 2007:** Portland State University, Oregon State University, University of Oregon.

**Basis for selection.** Open admission, but selective for some programs. Special prerequisite requirements for nursing, dental assistant, medical technician and water quality programs. Special admission process for accelerated degree and CCC/PSU co-admittance programs.

**2007-2008 Annual costs.** Tuition/fees: $2,790; $9,135 out-of-state. Per-credit charge: $57 in-state; $198 out-of-state. In-state tuition applies to residents of Oregon, Washington, Idaho, Nevada and California. Books/supplies: $1,200. Personal expenses: $900.

**Financial aid. Need-based:** Need-based aid available for part-time students. Work-study available nights, weekends and for part-time students. **Non-need-based:** Scholarships awarded for academics, art, athletics, leadership, music/drama. **Additional information:** Institutional tuition rebate guarantee. Frozen tuition rates for new fall students who graduate within 3 years. Any tuition increase levied by college during those 3 years will be refunded to student upon graduation.

**Application procedures. Admission:** No deadline. No application fee. Application may be submitted online. Admission notification on a rolling basis. **Financial aid:** Priority date 4/10; no closing date. FAFSA, institutional form required. Applicants notified on a rolling basis starting 3/15; must reply within 3 week(s) of notification.

**Academics.** Some occupational technologies offered as self-paced programs. **Special study options:** Accelerated study, combined bachelor's/graduate degree, cooperative education, cross-registration, distance learning, double major, dual enrollment of high school students, ESL, honors, independent study, internships, liberal arts/career combination, study abroad. License preparation in nursing, paramedic. **Credit/placement by examination:** AP, CLEP, institutional tests. 12 credit hours maximum toward associate degree. **Support services:** GED preparation and test center, learning center, reduced course load, remedial instruction, study skills assistance, tutoring.

**Majors. Agriculture:** Horticulture, landscaping, ornamental horticulture. **Business:** Accounting, administrative services, business admin, e-commerce, marketing, office management, operations, sales/distribution. **Communications technology:** General. **Computer sciences:** Applications programming, networking, web page design, webmaster. **Construction:** General. **Education:** Early childhood. **Engineering:** Industrial. **Engineering technology:** Architectural drafting, CAD/CADD, construction, drafting, electrical, electrical drafting, GIS, industrial, manufacturing, water quality. **Family/consumer sciences:** Child care. **Health:** Nursing (RN). **Liberal arts:** Arts/sciences. **Mechanic/repair:** Auto body, automotive, electronics/electrical. **Production:** Machine shop technology, welding. **Protective services:** Corrections, firefighting, police science. **Public administration:** Community org/advocacy, social work. **Other:** Music technology.

**Computing on campus.** 500 workstations in library, computer center. Commuter students can connect to campus network. Online course registration, helpline available.

**Student life. Freshman orientation:** Available. One-day program during week before classes begin. **Activities:** Jazz band, choral groups, drama, literary magazine, music ensembles, student government, student newspaper, environmental group, Baptist student ministries, foreign language clubs, Campus Crusade for Christ, nursing organization, Chatino club, service club, computer club, rainbow club, speech/forensics club.

**Athletics.** NJCAA. **Intercollegiate:** Baseball M, basketball, cross-country, soccer W, softball W, track and field, volleyball W, wrestling M. **Intramural:** Basketball, racquetball, soccer W, tennis, volleyball W. **Team name:** Cougars.

**Student services.** Adult student services, alcohol/substance abuse counseling, career counseling, student employment services, financial aid counseling, minority student services, on-campus daycare, personal counseling, placement for graduates, veterans' counselor, women's services. **Physically disabled:** Services for visually, speech, hearing impaired. **Transfer:** Transfer adviser, college fairs on campus for students transferring to 4-year colleges.

**Contact.** E-mail: pattyw@clackamas.edu
Phone: (503) 657-6958 ext. 2263 Fax: (503) 722-5864
Tara Sprehe, Registrar, Clackamas Community College, 19600 Molalla Avenue, Oregon City, OR 97045

## Clatsop Community College
Astoria, Oregon
www.clatsopcollege.com     CB code: 4089

- Public 2-year community college
- Commuter campus in large town

**General.** Founded in 1958. Regionally accredited. Vessel fire fighting training program available. **Enrollment:** 567 degree-seeking undergraduates. **Degrees:** 71 associate awarded. **Location:** 100 miles from Portland. **Calendar:** Quarter, limited summer session. **Full-time faculty:** 45 total. **Part-time faculty:** 80 total. **Class size:** 83% < 20, 15% 20-39, less than 1% 40-49, 1% 50-99, less than 1% >100. **Special facilities:** 51-foot commercial fishing vessel.

**Student profile.**

Out-of-state: 13%     25 or older: 42%

**Basis for selection.** Open admission, but selective for some programs. Special admissions requirements for nursing program applicants and international students.

**2007-2008 Annual costs.** Tuition/fees: $3,105; $5,940 out-of-state. Per-credit charge: $63 in-state; $126 out-of-state. Books/supplies: $1,200. Personal expenses: $648.

**2006-2007 Financial aid. Need-based:** 66% of total undergraduate aid awarded as scholarships/grants, 34% as loans/jobs. Need-based aid available for part-time students. Work-study available for part-time students. **Non-need-based:** Scholarships awarded for academics.

**Application procedures. Admission:** No deadline. $15 fee. Admission notification on a rolling basis. **Financial aid:** Priority date 5/1; no closing date. FAFSA, institutional form required. Applicants notified on a rolling basis starting 2/1.

**Academics. Special study options:** Cooperative education, distance learning, double major, dual enrollment of high school students, student-designed major, teacher certification program. License preparation in nursing. **Credit/placement by examination:** CLEP, institutional tests. 24 credit hours maximum toward associate degree. **Support services:** GED preparation and test center, learning center, reduced course load, remedial instruction, study skills assistance, tutoring, writing center.

**Majors. Business:** Accounting, business admin, management information systems, office management, office technology. **Computer sciences:** Applications programming, networking. **Health:** Medical assistant, medical secretary, nursing (RN). **Legal studies:** Legal secretary. **Liberal arts:** Arts/sciences. **Protective services:** Criminal justice, firefighting.

**Most popular majors.** Business/marketing 7%, health sciences 23%, liberal arts 64%.

**Computing on campus.** 80 workstations in library, computer center, student center.

**Student life. Freshman orientation:** Mandatory. Preregistration for classes offered. **Activities:** Concert band, dance, drama, student government.

**Athletics. Intramural:** Volleyball M.

**Student services.** Career counseling, services for economically disadvantaged, student employment services, financial aid counseling, personal counseling, veterans' counselor. **Physically disabled:** Services for visually, speech, hearing impaired. **Transfer:** Pre-admission transcript evaluation for new students. Transfer center, transfer adviser, college fairs on campus for students transferring to 4-year colleges.

**Contact.** Phone: (503) 338-2411 Toll-free number: (866) 252-8768
Fax: (503) 325-5738
Kristen Lee, Coordinator of Admissions, Clatsop Community College, 1653 Jerome Avenue, Astoria, OR 97103

## Heald College: Portland
Portland, Oregon
www.heald.edu

- Private 2-year business and technical college
- Very large city

**General. Enrollment:** 180 degree-seeking undergraduates. **Degrees:** 72 associate awarded. **Calendar:** Quarter. **Full-time faculty:** 6 total. **Part-time faculty:** 12 total.

**Basis for selection.** Open admission.

**2007-2008 Annual costs.** Tuition/fees: $11,000. Books/supplies: $1,500.

**Application procedures. Admission:** No deadline. No application fee. Admission notification on a rolling basis.

**Academics. Credit/placement by examination:** CLEP.

**Majors. Business:** Business admin. **Computer sciences:** General. **Health:** Medical assistant, medical secretary.

**Student life. Freshman orientation:** Available.

**Contact.** Phone: (503) 229-0492
Heald College: Portland, 625 SW Broadway, Portland, OR 97205

## Klamath Community College
**Klamath Falls, Oregon**
www.kcc.cc.or.us
**CB code: 4127**

- Public 2-year community college
- Small city

**General.** Regionally accredited. **Enrollment:** 858 degree-seeking undergraduates. **Degrees:** 68 associate awarded. **Calendar:** Quarter. **Full-time faculty:** 20 total. **Part-time faculty:** 60 total.

**Basis for selection.** Open admission. COMPASS used for placement only.

**2007-2008 Annual costs.** Tuition/fees: $2,940; $6,450 out-of-state. Per-credit charge: $63 in-state; $141 out-of-state.

**Application procedures. Admission:** No deadline. No application fee. **Financial aid:** No deadline. FAFSA required.

**Academics. Credit/placement by examination:** CLEP.

**Majors. Computer sciences:** LAN/WAN management.

**Contact.** Phone: (541) 882-3521
Mary Beard, Student Services Offices, Klamath Community College, 7390 South 6th Street, Klamath Falls, OR 97603

## Lane Community College
**Eugene, Oregon**
www.lanecc.edu
**CB member**
**CB code: 4407**

- Public 2-year community college
- Commuter campus in small city

**General.** Founded in 1964. Regionally accredited. Outreach centers in downtown Eugene, Cottage Grove and Florence. **Enrollment:** 5,500 degree-seeking undergraduates. **Degrees:** 678 associate awarded. **Location:** 110 miles from Portland. **Calendar:** Quarter, extensive summer session. **Full-time faculty:** 250 total. **Part-time faculty:** 300 total. **Partnerships:** Formal partnerships with professional technical advisory groups.

**Student profile.**

| Out-of-state: | 2% | 25 or older: | 40% |

**Transfer out. Colleges most students transferred to 2007:** University of Oregon, Oregon State University.

**Basis for selection.** Open admission, but selective for some programs. Special requirements for allied health and flight technology programs. Sequential Tests of Educational Progress required for dental applicants, School and College Ability Tests for nursing applicants, Nelson-Denny Reading Test for dental and medical assistant applicants.

**2007-2008 Annual costs.** Tuition/fees: $3,615; $11,625 out-of-state. Per-credit charge: $73 in-state; $251 out-of-state. Books/supplies: $1,086. Personal expenses: $1,035.

**Financial aid. Need-based:** Need-based aid available for part-time students. Work-study available nights and weekends. **Non-need-based:** Scholarships awarded for art, athletics, minority status, music/drama.

**Application procedures. Admission:** No deadline. No application fee. Admission notification on a rolling basis. **Financial aid:** Priority date 2/15; no closing date. FAFSA required. Applicants notified on a rolling basis starting 6/1; must reply within 2 week(s) of notification.

**Academics. Special study options:** Accelerated study, cooperative education, cross-registration, distance learning, double major, dual enrollment of high school students, ESL, independent study, internships, liberal arts/career combination, study abroad, weekend college. License preparation in aviation, nursing. **Credit/placement by examination:** CLEP, institutional tests. **Support services:** GED preparation and test center, learning center, pre-admission summer program, reduced course load, remedial instruction, study skills assistance, tutoring, writing center.

**Majors. Business:** Accounting, administrative services, office management, real estate. **Communications:** Broadcast journalism, journalism. **Communications technology:** General. **Computer sciences:** Data processing, programming, systems analysis, web page design. **Construction:** Electrician, maintenance. **Engineering technology:** Construction, drafting, electrical. **Family/consumer sciences:** Child care. **Health:** Dental hygiene, EMT paramedic, nursing (RN), respiratory therapy technology, substance abuse counseling. **Legal studies:** Legal secretary. **Liberal arts:** Arts/sciences. **Mechanic/repair:** Aircraft, auto body, automotive, diesel, electronics/electrical, heating/ac/refrig. **Parks/recreation:** Health/fitness. **Personal/culinary services:** Culinary arts. **Production:** Machine tool. **Protective services:** Criminal justice. **Public administration:** Community org/advocacy. **Transportation:** Aviation. **Visual/performing arts:** Commercial/advertising art.

**Most popular majors.** Business/marketing 7%, computer/information sciences 7%, health sciences 17%, liberal arts 51%, trade and industry 9%.

**Computing on campus.** 800 workstations in library, computer center. Commuter students can connect to campus network. Helpline available.

**Student life. Freshman orientation:** Available. Preregistration for classes offered. Each field of study has its own orientation program. Program also available for undecided majors. **Activities:** Bands, choral groups, dance, drama, literary magazine, music ensembles, musical theater, radio station, student government, student newspaper, OSPIRG, campus ministry, women's center, associate student group.

**Athletics. Intercollegiate:** Baseball M, basketball, cross-country, track and field, volleyball W. **Intramural:** Badminton, basketball, golf, skiing, soccer, volleyball.

**Student services.** Adult student services, campus ministries, career counseling, student employment services, financial aid counseling, health services, minority student services, on-campus daycare, personal counseling, placement for graduates, veterans' counselor, women's services. **Physically disabled:** Services for visually, speech, hearing impaired. **Transfer:** Pre-admission transcript evaluation for new students. Transfer adviser, college fairs on campus for students transferring to 4-year colleges.

**Contact.** E-mail: garretth@lanecc.edu
Phone: (541) 463-3100 Fax: (541) 463-3995
Helen Garrett, Director of Admissions, Lane Community College, 4000 East 30th Avenue, Eugene, OR 97405

## Linn-Benton Community College
**Albany, Oregon**
www.linnbenton.edu
**CB member**
**CB code: 4413**

- Public 2-year community college
- Commuter campus in large town

**General.** Founded in 1966. Regionally accredited. Courses available at off-campus centers in Corvallis, Lebanon, and Sweet Home. **Enrollment:** 4,986 degree-seeking undergraduates; 152 non-degree-seeking students. **Degrees:** 500 associate awarded. **ROTC:** Army, Air Force. **Location:** 70 miles from Portland, 45 miles from Eugene. **Calendar:** Quarter, limited summer session. **Full-time faculty:** 159 total; 6% minority, 58% women. **Part-time faculty:** 328 total; 6% minority, 66% women. **Class size:** 61% < 20, 38% 20-39, less than 1% 40-49, less than 1% 50-99. **Special facilities:** Stables, riding arena.

**Student profile.** Among degree-seeking undergraduates, 1,189 enrolled as first-time, first-year students, 422 transferred in from other institutions.

| Part-time: | 48% | Women: | 53% |

**Transfer out. Colleges most students transferred to 2007:** Oregon State University, Western Oregon University, University of Oregon, Portland State University, Southern Oregon University.

**Basis for selection.** Open admission, but selective for some programs. Special requirements for nursing, dental assistant, veterinary technology, pharmacy technology, phlebotomy, public safety dispatcher and radiologic technology programs. High school diploma or GED required of applicants under 18.

**2007-2008 Annual costs.** Tuition/fees: $3,112; $7,657 out-of-state. Per-credit charge: $65 in-state; $166 out-of-state. Books/supplies: $1,260. Personal expenses: $4,551.

**2006-2007 Financial aid. Need-based:** 62% of total undergraduate aid awarded as scholarships/grants, 38% as loans/jobs. Need-based aid available for part-time students. Work-study available nights, weekends and for part-time students. **Non-need-based:** Scholarships awarded for academics, art, job skills, leadership, music/drama, state residency.

**Application procedures. Admission:** Priority date 7/14; deadline 10/4 (receipt date). $25 fee. Admission notification on a rolling basis beginning on or about 7/1. **Financial aid:** Priority date 4/1; no closing date. FAFSA required. Applicants notified on a rolling basis starting 4/15; must reply within 2 week(s) of notification.

**Academics. Special study options:** Cooperative education, cross-registration, distance learning, dual enrollment of high school students, ESL, independent study, internships, student-designed major, study abroad. Evening degree program. License preparation in nursing, paramedic, radiology, real estate. **Credit/placement by examination:** AP, CLEP, institutional tests. 24 credit hours maximum toward associate degree. **Support services:** GED preparation and test center, learning center, remedial instruction, study skills assistance, tutoring, writing center.

**Majors. Agriculture:** General, animal sciences, business, dairy, equestrian studies, equine science, horticultural science. **Biology:** General. **Business:** Accounting technology, administrative services, business admin, office management. **Communications:** Journalism. **Computer sciences:** General, applications programming, system admin. **Construction:** Carpentry, electrician, painting, pipefitting. **Education:** General, elementary, physical, secondary, teacher assistance. **Engineering:** General. **Engineering technology:** Drafting, electrical, water quality. **English:** English lit, speech/rhetoric, technical writing. **Family/consumer sciences:** General, child care. **Foreign languages:** Spanish. **Health:** Medical assistant, medical records admin, medical secretary, nursing (RN), office assistant, predental, premedicine, prenursing, prepharmacy, preveterinary. **History:** General. **Interdisciplinary:** Biological/physical sciences. **Legal studies:** Legal secretary, paralegal, pre-law. **Liberal arts:** Arts/sciences. **Math:** General. **Mechanic/repair:** General, automotive, diesel, electronics/electrical, heavy equipment, industrial. **Personal/culinary services:** Chef training, restaurant/catering. **Physical sciences:** Chemistry, physics. **Protective services:** Criminal justice, police science. **Psychology:** General. **Social sciences:** General, anthropology, economics, geography, political science, sociology. **Visual/performing arts:** Art, commercial/advertising art, dramatic, photography.

**Computing on campus.** 500 workstations in library, computer center, student center. Commuter students can connect to campus network. Online course registration, online library, helpline, wireless network available.

**Student life. Freshman orientation:** Mandatory. 2-hour program. Orientation also available on-line. **Activities:** Concert band, choral groups, dance, drama, student government, student newspaper, Pacific party, Campus Crusade for Christ, Baha'i, Christians on Campus, Chi Alpha Radical Reality, Phi Theta Kappa, campus family co-op, student ambassadors, livestock judging.

**Athletics. Intercollegiate:** Baseball M, basketball, equestrian, volleyball W. **Intramural:** Basketball, bowling, tennis. **Team name:** Roadrunners.

**Student services.** Adult student services, career counseling, services for economically disadvantaged, student employment services, financial aid counseling, minority student services, on-campus daycare, personal counseling, placement for graduates, veterans' counselor. **Physically disabled:** Services for visually, speech, hearing impaired. **Transfer:** Transfer center, transfer adviser, college fairs on campus for students transferring to 4-year colleges.

**Contact.** E-mail: admissions@linnbenton.edu
Phone: (541) 917-4811 Fax: (541) 917-4868
Christine Baker, Admissions Outreach Coordinator, Linn-Benton Community College, 6500 SW Pacific Boulevard, Albany, OR 97321-3779

## Mt. Hood Community College
**Gresham, Oregon**
**www.mhcc.cc.or.us**    CB code: 4508

▶ Public 2-year community college
▶ Commuter campus in small city

**General.** Founded in 1965. Regionally accredited. **Enrollment:** 6,964 degree-seeking undergraduates; 624 non-degree-seeking students. **Degrees:** 816 associate awarded. **Location:** 12 miles from Portland. **Calendar:** Quarter, limited summer session. **Full-time faculty:** 157 total; 100% have terminal degrees, 6% minority, 54% women. **Part-time faculty:** 404 total; 7% minority, 58% women. **Special facilities:** Planetarium, solar observatory.

**Student profile.** Among degree-seeking undergraduates, 32% enrolled in a transfer program, 32% enrolled in a vocational program, 6% already have a bachelor's degree or higher, 1,908 enrolled as first-time, first-year students.

| | | | |
|---|---|---|---|
| Part-time: | 58% | Asian American: | 7% |
| Out-of-state: | 1% | Hispanic American: | 7% |
| Women: | 59% | Native American: | 1% |
| African American: | 4% | 25 or older: | 45% |

**Transfer out.** 18% of students enrolled in the transfer program go on to 4-year colleges. **Colleges most students transferred to 2007:** Portland State University, Oregon State University, Eastern Oregon University, Concordia University, University of Phoenix.

**Basis for selection.** Open admission, but selective for some programs. Special requirements for nursing and graphic design programs. Allied health programs require minimum 2.5 GPA. SAT scores may be used in place of in-house placement test. Interview required for cosmetology and most health services.

**High school preparation.** Requirements for health programs include 1 algebra, 1 biology, and 1 chemistry.

**2007-2008 Annual costs.** Tuition/fees: $3,240; $9,675 out-of-state. Per-credit charge: $66 in-state; $209 out-of-state. Books/supplies: $1,011. Personal expenses: $1,971.

**2006-2007 Financial aid. Need-based:** 585 full-time freshmen applied for aid; 386 were judged to have need; 369 of these received aid. Average need met was 69%. Average scholarship/grant was $3,452; average loan $1,848. 65% of total undergraduate aid awarded as scholarships/grants, 35% as loans/jobs. Need-based aid available for part-time students. **Non-need-based:** Awarded to 433 full-time undergraduates, including 168 freshmen. Scholarships awarded for academics.

**Application procedures. Admission:** No deadline. $25 fee. Application must be submitted on paper. Admission notification on a rolling basis. Most health services majors must apply between November 1 and March 30 for fall admission. Application fee for these programs $15. Application deadlines and priority dates vary by program. **Financial aid:** No deadline. FAFSA, institutional form required. Applicants notified on a rolling basis starting 2/15; must reply within 4 week(s) of notification.

**Academics. Special study options:** Accelerated study, cooperative education, distance learning, double major, dual enrollment of high school students, ESL, exchange student, external degree, honors, independent study, internships, study abroad, weekend college. Bachelor's degree programs available on campus. License preparation in dental hygiene, nursing, paramedic, physical therapy. **Credit/placement by examination:** CLEP, institutional tests. 45 credit hours maximum toward associate degree. College placement test required for chemistry, math, writing, or reading courses. **Support services:** GED preparation and test center, learning center, pre-admission summer program, reduced course load, remedial instruction, tutoring.

**Majors. Agriculture:** Horticulture. **Business:** General, accounting, administrative services, hospitality admin, tourism/travel. **Communications:** Broadcast journalism, journalism. **Communications technology:** Graphic/printing. **Computer sciences:** General. **Conservation:** Fisheries, forestry, management/policy. **Education:** Early childhood. **Engineering technology:** Architectural, civil. **Health:** Dental hygiene, health services, medical assistant, medical records admin, occupational therapy assistant, physical therapy assistant, respiratory therapy technology, surgical technology. **Legal studies:** Legal secretary. **Mechanic/repair:** Automotive, electronics/electrical. **Personal/culinary services:** Cosmetic, mortuary science. **Protective services:** Firefighting. **Transportation:** Aviation. **Visual/performing arts:** Commercial/advertising art, dramatic.

**Most popular majors.** Business/marketing 7%, health sciences 20%, liberal arts 55%, personal/culinary services 6%.

**Student life. Freshman orientation:** Available. Preregistration for classes offered. **Activities:** Bands, choral groups, dance, drama, music ensembles, musical theater, radio station, student government, student newspaper, symphony orchestra, TV station, Asian cultures appreciation, Campus Agnostics of America, Campus Ambassadors, Chako-Kumtux club, human services student support club, Latino club, Latter-Day Saint student association, radio interest group, science club, writers club.

**Athletics.** NCAA. **Intercollegiate:** Baseball M, basketball, cross-country, golf M, tennis, track and field, volleyball W. **Intramural:** Archery, badminton M, basketball, bowling, cross-country, golf, racquetball, skiing, soccer, softball, swimming, tennis, track and field, volleyball, wrestling M. **Team name:** Saints.

**Student services.** Career counseling, student employment services, financial aid counseling, health services, minority student services, on-campus daycare, personal counseling, placement for graduates, veterans' counselor. **Physically disabled:** Services for visually, speech, hearing impaired. **Transfer:** Transfer adviser, college fairs on campus for students transferring to 4-year colleges.

**Contact.** Phone: (503) 491-7391 Fax: (503) 491-6006
Patricia Martin, Associate Dean, Enrollment Services, Mt. Hood Community College, 26000 Southeast Stark Street, Gresham, OR 97030

## Pioneer Pacific College: Springfield
### Springfield, Oregon
### www.pioneerpacific.edu

♦ For-profit 2-year branch campus and technical college
♦ Commuter campus in small city
♦ Interview required

**General.** Accredited by ACICS. Multi-campus institution with main campus in Wilsonville, Health Career Institute in Wilsonville, Learning Site in Clackamas, Branch Campus in Springfield, and Oregon Culinary Institute in Portland. **Enrollment:** 166 degree-seeking undergraduates; 112 non-degree-seeking students. **Degrees:** 81 associate awarded. **Location:** 10 miles from Eugene. **Calendar:** Continuous, extensive summer session. **Full-time faculty:** 12 total; 33% have terminal degrees, 17% minority, 50% women. **Part-time faculty:** 25 total; 20% have terminal degrees, 28% minority, 60% women. **Class size:** 79% < 20, 21% 20-39.

**Student profile.** Among degree-seeking undergraduates, 42 enrolled as first-time, first-year students.

| | | | |
|---|---|---|---|
| Part-time: | 22% | 25 or older: | 67% |
| Women: | 68% | | |

**Transfer out. Colleges most students transferred to 2007:** Clackamas Community College, Chemeketa Community College, University of Phoenix.

**Basis for selection.** Open admission, but selective for some programs.

**2008-2009 Annual costs.** Tuition/fees (projected): $10,677. Per-credit charge: $411. Costs vary by program from $7,250 to $25,045. Certain programs have additional lab fees. Personal expenses: $3,262.

**Application procedures. Admission:** No deadline. $50 fee. Application must be submitted on paper. Admission notification on a rolling basis. **Financial aid:** No deadline. FAFSA required. Applicants notified on a rolling basis starting 3/15.

**Academics. Special study options:** Accelerated study, honors, liberal arts/career combination, weekend college. **Credit/placement by examination:** CLEP. **Support services:** Study skills assistance, tutoring.

**Majors. Business:** Accounting, business admin, marketing. **Computer sciences:** Information systems. **Health:** Health care admin, medical assistant. **Protective services:** Criminal justice.

**Most popular majors.** Business/marketing 32%, computer/information sciences 19%, health sciences 36%, security/protective services 13%.

**Computing on campus.** 90 workstations in computer center. Online library available.

**Student life. Freshman orientation:** Mandatory.

**Student services.** Career counseling, student employment services, financial aid counseling, placement for graduates.

**Contact.** E-mail: inquiries@pioneerpacific.edu
Phone: (541) 684-4644 Toll-free number: (800) 772-4636
Fax: (541) 684-0665
Vickie Church, Director of Admissions, Pioneer Pacific College: Springfield, 3800 Sports Way, Springfield, OR 97477

## Portland Community College
### Portland, Oregon — CB member
### www.pcc.edu — CB code: 4617

♦ Public 2-year community college
♦ Commuter campus in very large city

**General.** Founded in 1961. Regionally accredited. 3 comprehensive campuses; classes offered at several centers throughout district. **Enrollment:** 24,363 degree-seeking undergraduates. **Degrees:** 1,736 associate awarded. **Location:** 5 miles from downtown. **Calendar:** Quarter, extensive summer session. **Full-time faculty:** 387 total; 10% minority, 52% women. **Part-time faculty:** 837 total; 10% minority, 57% women.

**Student profile.** Among degree-seeking undergraduates, 58% enrolled in a transfer program, 42% enrolled in a vocational program.

| | | | |
|---|---|---|---|
| Out-of-state: | 4% | 25 or older: | 52% |

**Transfer out. Colleges most students transferred to 2007:** Portland State University, University of Oregon, Oregon State University.

**Basis for selection.** Open admission, but selective for some programs. Enrollment in certain programs or courses may require prerequisite course work or permission by a department representative.

**High school preparation.** High school diploma required for some allied health programs.

**2007-2008 Annual costs.** Tuition/fees: $3,330; $9,045 out-of-state. Per-credit charge: $68 in-state; $195 out-of-state. Books/supplies: $1,320. Personal expenses: $1,140.

**2007-2008 Financial aid.** All financial aid based on need. 38% of total undergraduate aid awarded as scholarships/grants, 62% as loans/jobs. Need-based aid available for part-time students. Work-study available nights, weekends and for part-time students.

**Application procedures. Admission:** No deadline. $25 fee. Application may be submitted online. **Financial aid:** Priority date 3/1; no closing date. FAFSA required. Applicants notified on a rolling basis starting 6/1; must reply within 3 week(s) of notification.

**Academics. Special study options:** Cooperative education, distance learning, double major, dual enrollment of high school students, ESL, internships, study abroad, weekend college. License preparation in aviation, dental hygiene, nursing, paramedic, radiology, real estate. **Credit/placement by examination:** AP, CLEP, institutional tests. 45 credit hours maximum toward associate degree. **Support services:** GED preparation and test center, learning center, reduced course load, remedial instruction, study skills assistance, tutoring, writing center.

**Majors. Agriculture:** Landscaping. **Business:** General, accounting, administrative services, business admin, office management, office technology, real estate. **Construction:** Building inspection. **Education:** Early childhood. **Engineering technology:** Civil, computer systems, construction, drafting, electrical, manufacturing. **Family/consumer sciences:** Child care. **Foreign languages:** Sign language interpretation. **Health:** Clinical lab technology, dental hygiene, dental lab technology, EMT paramedic, medical radiologic technology/radiation therapy, medical records admin, substance abuse counseling, veterinary technology/assistant. **Interdisciplinary:** Gerontology. **Legal studies:** Legal secretary, paralegal. **Liberal arts:** Arts/sciences. **Mechanic/repair:** Aircraft, aircraft powerplant, auto body, automotive, diesel, heating/ac/refrig. **Parks/recreation:** Health/fitness. **Protective services:** Criminal justice, fire safety technology. **Visual/performing arts:** Commercial/advertising art, interior design, music performance.

**Most popular majors.** Business/marketing 8%, health sciences 16%, liberal arts 58%, trade and industry 7%.

**Computing on campus.** 3,100 workstations in library, computer center, student center. Commuter students can connect to campus network. Online course registration, online library, helpline, wireless network available.

**Student life. Freshman orientation:** Mandatory. Online orientation available. **Activities:** Bands, choral groups, dance, drama, international student organizations, literary magazine, music ensembles, musical theater, student government, student newspaper.

**Athletics.** NJCAA. **Intercollegiate:** Basketball. **Intramural:** Basketball, bowling, cross-country, golf, racquetball, soccer, softball, swimming, tennis, volleyball. **Team name:** Panthers.

**Student services.** Career counseling, services for economically disadvantaged, student employment services, financial aid counseling, minority student services, on-campus daycare, personal counseling, placement for graduates, veterans' counselor, women's services. **Physically disabled:** Services for visually, speech, hearing impaired. **Learning disabled:** Comprehensive services available. **Transfer:** Pre-admission transcript evaluation for new students. Transfer adviser, college fairs on campus for students transferring to 4-year colleges.

**Contact.** Phone: (503) 977-4519 Fax: (503) 977-4740
Veronica Garcia, Dean of Enrollment Services, Portland Community College, Box 19000, Portland, OR 97280-0990

## Rogue Community College
**Grants Pass, Oregon**
www.roguecc.edu                                    CB code: 4653

- Public 2-year community college
- Commuter campus in large town

**General.** Founded in 1970. Regionally accredited. Branch campuses in Medford and White City, learning centers in Medford and Cave Junction. **Enrollment:** 2,731 degree-seeking undergraduates; 1,660 non-degree-seeking students. **Degrees:** 292 associate awarded. **Location:** 30 miles from Medford, 240 miles from Portland. **Calendar:** Quarter, limited summer session. **Full-time faculty:** 91 total; 1% minority, 57% women. **Part-time faculty:** 257 total; 3% minority, 49% women. **Class size:** 62% < 20, 36% 20-39, 1% 40-49, less than 1% 50-99. **Special facilities:** Outdoor concert bowl.

**Student profile.** Among degree-seeking undergraduates, 78% enrolled in a transfer program, 22% enrolled in a vocational program, 5% already have a bachelor's degree or higher, 608 enrolled as first-time, first-year students.

| | | | |
|---|---|---|---|
| Part-time: | 60% | Hispanic American: | 7% |
| Women: | 61% | Native American: | 2% |
| African American: | 1% | 25 or older: | 50% |
| Asian American: | 2% | | |

**Transfer out.** 17% of students enrolled in the transfer program go on to 4-year colleges.

**Basis for selection.** Open admission, but selective for some programs. Special requirements for nursing, respiratory therapy, emergency medical technology, human services, mental health technician. Interview recommended for allied health, nursing programs. **Adult students:** SAT/ACT scores not required. Satisfactory scores on the COMPASS or ASSET placement test.

**2007-2008 Annual costs.** Tuition/fees: $3,300; $3,930 out-of-state. Per-credit charge: $66 in-state; $80 out-of-state. Washington, Idaho, Nevada, and California residents pay in-state tuition. Books/supplies: $1,200. Personal expenses: $1,200.

**2006-2007 Financial aid. Need-based:** 119 full-time freshmen applied for aid; 96 were judged to have need; 89 of these received aid. Average need met was 59%. Average scholarship/grant was $833; average loan $835. 69% of total undergraduate aid awarded as scholarships/grants, 31% as loans/jobs. Need-based aid available for part-time students. **Non-need-based:** Awarded to 491 full-time undergraduates, including 76 freshmen.

**Application procedures. Admission:** No deadline. No application fee. Admission notification on a rolling basis. **Financial aid:** Priority date 5/1; no closing date. FAFSA, institutional form required. Applicants notified on a rolling basis; must reply within 2 week(s) of notification.

**Academics. Special study options:** Cooperative education, distance learning, double major, dual enrollment of high school students, ESL, independent study, study abroad. License preparation in nursing, paramedic. **Credit/placement by examination:** AP, CLEP, institutional tests. Students required to take ASSET or COMPASS test prior to registration. **Support services:** GED preparation and test center, learning center, remedial instruction, study skills assistance, tutoring, writing center.

**Majors. Business:** General, business admin. **Construction:** General. **Engineering technology:** Construction, electrical, manufacturing. **Family/consumer sciences:** Child care. **Health:** EMT paramedic, nursing (RN), substance abuse counseling. **Liberal arts:** Arts/sciences. **Mechanic/repair:** Automotive. **Production:** Welding. **Protective services:** Fire safety technology, police science. **Public administration:** Social work.

**Most popular majors.** Business/marketing 8%, health sciences 14%, liberal arts 59%, trade and industry 6%.

**Computing on campus.** 115 workstations in library, computer center. Commuter students can connect to campus network. Online course registration available.

**Student life. Freshman orientation:** Available. Preregistration for classes offered. **Activities:** Concert band, choral groups, drama, literary magazine, musical theater, student government, student newspaper, Club Latino.

**Athletics. Intramural:** Basketball, volleyball.

**Student services.** Career counseling, services for economically disadvantaged, student employment services, financial aid counseling, on-campus daycare, personal counseling, placement for graduates, veterans' counselor. **Physically disabled:** Services for visually, speech, hearing impaired. **Transfer:** Pre-admission transcript evaluation for new students. Transfer adviser, college fairs on campus for students transferring to 4-year colleges.

**Contact.** E-mail: Csullivan@roguecc.edu
Phone: (541) 956-7427
Claudia Sullivan, Director of Enrollment Services, Rogue Community College, 3345 Redwood Highway, Grants Pass, OR 97527

## Southwestern Oregon Community College
**Coos Bay, Oregon**
www.socc.edu                                    CB code: 4729

- Public 2-year culinary school and community college
- Commuter campus in large town

**General.** Founded in 1961. Regionally accredited. **Enrollment:** 1,573 degree-seeking undergraduates. **Degrees:** 210 associate awarded. **Location:** 125 miles from Eugene, 225 miles from Portland. **Calendar:** Quarter, limited summer session. **Full-time faculty:** 80 total. **Part-time faculty:** 195 total. **Special facilities:** Culinary institute, small business development center, university center.

**Student profile.**

| | | | |
|---|---|---|---|
| Out-of-state: | 17% | Live on campus: | 17% |
| 25 or older: | 34% | | |

**Transfer out. Colleges most students transferred to 2007:** Oregon State University, Southern Oregon University, University of Oregon, Linfield College, Eastern Oregon University.

**Basis for selection.** Open admission, but selective for some programs. Separate application process for nursing students. Background check required for emergency response and EMTs.

**2007-2008 Annual costs.** Tuition/fees: $3,660. Per-credit charge: $62. Room/board: $6,160. Books/supplies: $1,200. Personal expenses: $540.

**Financial aid. Need-based:** Need-based aid available for part-time students.

**Application procedures. Admission:** No deadline. $30 fee, may be waived for applicants with need. Application may be submitted online. Admission notification on a rolling basis. **Financial aid:** Priority date 2/28, closing date 6/30. FAFSA required. Applicants notified on a rolling basis starting 5/1; must reply within 3 week(s) of notification.

**Academics. Special study options:** Combined bachelor's/graduate degree, cooperative education, distance learning, double major, dual enrollment of high school students, ESL, honors, independent study, internships, liberal arts/career combination. Bachelor's degree programs available on campus. License preparation in nursing. **Credit/placement by examination:** AP, CLEP, institutional tests. **Support services:** GED preparation and test center, learning center, reduced course load, remedial instruction, study skills assistance, tutoring, writing center.

**Majors. Agriculture:** Turf management. **Business:** Accounting technology, administrative services, banking/financial services, business admin, entrepreneurial studies, management information systems, office management, sales/distribution. **Computer sciences:** Applications programming, computer science, information systems, webmaster. **Conservation:** Environmental studies. **Education:** Teacher assistance. **Engineering:** General. **Family/consumer sciences:** Child care, family studies. **Health:** Licensed practical nurse, medical assistant, substance abuse counseling. **Interdisciplinary:** Biological/physical sciences. **Liberal arts:** Arts/sciences. **Math:** General. **Personal/culinary services:** Culinary arts. **Production:** Welding. **Protective services:** Corrections, criminal justice, firefighting, police science. **Public administration:** Social work.

**Most popular majors.** Business/marketing 10%, health sciences 8%, liberal arts 58%, security/protective services 8%.

**Computing on campus.** 338 workstations in dormitories, library, computer center. Dormitories wired for high-speed internet access. Online course registration, online library, helpline, wireless network available.

**Student life. Freshman orientation:** Available. Preregistration for classes offered. **Housing:** Guaranteed on-campus for freshmen. Single-sex dorms, special housing for disabled, apartments, substance-free housing available. $250 partly refundable deposit. **Activities:** Bands, choral groups, drama, literary magazine, music ensembles, student government, student newspaper, Rotaract, Phi Theta Kappa.

**Athletics.** NJCAA. **Intercollegiate:** Baseball M, basketball, cross-country, golf, soccer, softball W, track and field, volleyball W, wrestling M. **Intramural:** Basketball. **Team name:** Lakers.

**Student services.** Adult student services, alcohol/substance abuse counseling, career counseling, services for economically disadvantaged, student employment services, financial aid counseling, health services, on-campus daycare, personal counseling, placement for graduates, veterans' counselor. **Physically disabled:** Services for visually, speech, hearing impaired. **Learning disabled:** Comprehensive services available. **Transfer:** Transfer center, college fairs on campus for students transferring to 4-year colleges.

**Contact.** E-mail: admissions@socc.edu
Phone: (541) 888-7636 Toll-free number: (800) 962-2838 ext. 7636
Fax: (541) 888-7247
Tom Nicholls, Director of Enrollment Management, Southwestern Oregon Community College, 1988 Newmark Avenue, Coos Bay, OR 97420-2956

## Treasure Valley Community College
Ontario, Oregon
www.tvcc.cc
**CB code: 4825**

◆ Public 2-year community college
◆ Commuter campus in small town

**General.** Founded in 1961. Regionally accredited. **Enrollment:** 1,820 degree-seeking undergraduates; 190 non-degree-seeking students. **Degrees:** 196 associate awarded. **Location:** 60 miles from Boise, Idaho. **Calendar:** Quarter, limited summer session. **Full-time faculty:** 45 total. **Part-time faculty:** 30 total. **Class size:** 67% < 20, 31% 20-39, 2% 40-49, less than 1% 50-99.

**Student profile.** Among degree-seeking undergraduates, 652 enrolled as first-time, first-year students, 127 transferred in from other institutions.

| | | | |
|---|---|---|---|
| Part-time: | 46% | Hispanic American: | 17% |
| Out-of-state: | 64% | Native American: | 2% |
| Women: | 63% | 25 or older: | 39% |
| African American: | 1% | Live on campus: | 6% |
| Asian American: | 2% | | |

**Basis for selection.** Open admission, but selective for some programs. Special requirements for nursing program.

**2008-2009 Annual costs.** Tuition/fees (projected): $3,420; $3,870 out-of-state. Per-credit charge: $66 in-state; $76 out-of-state. Room/board: $6,390. Books/supplies: $1,050. Personal expenses: $1,500.

**2007-2008 Financial aid. Need-based:** Average need met was 37%. Average scholarship/grant was $3,757; average loan $2,856. 54% of total undergraduate aid awarded as scholarships/grants, 46% as loans/jobs. Need-based aid available for part-time students. Work-study available for part-time students. **Non-need-based:** Scholarships awarded for academics, athletics, leadership, music/drama, state residency.

**Application procedures. Admission:** No deadline. No application fee. Application may be submitted online. Admission notification on a rolling basis. **Financial aid:** Priority date 4/1; no closing date. FAFSA required. Applicants notified on a rolling basis starting 5/1.

**Academics. Special study options:** Cooperative education, distance learning, double major, dual enrollment of high school students, ESL, independent study, internships. Elementary education program with Eastern Oregon State College and satellite program with Boise State University. License preparation in nursing. **Credit/placement by examination:** AP, CLEP, institutional tests. 45 credit hours maximum toward associate degree. **Support services:** GED preparation and test center, learning center, pre-admission summer program, reduced course load, remedial instruction, tutoring, writing center.

**Majors. Agriculture:** Agronomy, animal sciences, business, economics, farm/ranch. **Biology:** General. **Business:** General, business admin, management information systems, office management, office/clerical. **Communications:** General. **Computer sciences:** General, computer science. **Conservation:** Management/policy, wildlife. **Education:** Bilingual, elementary, secondary.

**Engineering:** General. **Engineering technology:** Computer, drafting. **Foreign languages:** General. **Health:** Athletic training, medical secretary, medical transcription, nursing (RN), predental, premedicine, preveterinary. **History:** General. **Legal studies:** Legal secretary, paralegal, prelaw. **Liberal arts:** Arts/sciences. **Math:** General. **Physical sciences:** Chemistry, geology, physics. **Production:** Welding. **Protective services:** Criminal justice, fire safety technology, firefighting, law enforcement admin, police science. **Psychology:** General. **Public administration:** Social work. **Social sciences:** General, political science. **Visual/performing arts:** General, art.

**Computing on campus.** 250 workstations in library, computer center. Dormitories wired for high-speed internet access and linked to campus network. Online course registration, online library, helpline, repair service, wireless network available.

**Student life. Freshman orientation:** Available. Preregistration for classes offered. Online orientation available. **Housing:** Single-sex dorms, substance-free housing available. $200 partly refundable deposit. **Activities:** Bands, choral groups, drama, music ensembles, musical theater, student government.

**Athletics. Intercollegiate:** Baseball M, basketball, cross-country, golf, rodeo, soccer, tennis, track and field, volleyball. **Intramural:** Basketball, softball, volleyball. **Team name:** Chukars.

**Student services.** Career counseling, student employment services, health services, on-campus daycare, personal counseling, placement for graduates, veterans' counselor, women's services. **Physically disabled:** Services for visually impaired. **Transfer:** Pre-admission transcript evaluation for new students. College fairs on campus for students transferring to 4-year colleges.

**Contact.** E-mail: admissions@tvcc.cc
Phone: (541) 881-8822 ext. 339 Fax: (541) 881-2721
Stephanie Oester, Director of Admissions, Treasure Valley Community College, 650 College Boulevard, Ontario, OR 97914

## Umpqua Community College
Roseburg, Oregon
www.umpqua.edu
**CB code: 4862**

◆ Public 2-year community college
◆ Commuter campus in large town

**General.** Founded in 1964. Regionally accredited. **Enrollment:** 994 degree-seeking undergraduates; 1,348 non-degree-seeking students. **Degrees:** 239 associate awarded. **Location:** 60 miles from Eugene. **Calendar:** Quarter, limited summer session. **Full-time faculty:** 62 total; 5% minority, 48% women. **Part-time faculty:** 161 total; 2% minority, 50% women. **Class size:** 70% < 20, 27% 20-39, 2% 40-49, 1% 50-99.

**Student profile.** Among degree-seeking undergraduates, 3% already have a bachelor's degree or higher, 288 enrolled as first-time, first-year students.

| | | | |
|---|---|---|---|
| Part-time: | 40% | Asian American: | 1% |
| Out-of-state: | 25% | Hispanic American: | 3% |
| Women: | 60% | Native American: | 2% |
| African American: | 1% | 25 or older: | 42% |

**Transfer out. Colleges most students transferred to 2007:** Oregon State University, University of Oregon, Northwest Christian College, Western Oregon University, Southern Oregon University.

**Basis for selection.** Open admission, but selective for some programs. Special requirements for nursing program. COMPASS placement test and/or ACT ASSET test used for placement only. **Homeschooled:** High school release required.

**2007-2008 Annual costs.** Tuition/fees: $3,195; $8,775 out-of-state. Per-credit charge: $62 in-state; $186 out-of-state. Books/supplies: $1,200. Personal expenses: $1,200.

**2006-2007 Financial aid.** All financial aid based on need. 129 full-time freshmen applied for aid; 120 were judged to have need; 117 of these received aid. 56% of total undergraduate aid awarded as scholarships/grants, 44% as loans/jobs. Need-based aid available for part-time students.

**Application procedures. Admission:** No deadline. $25 fee. Application must be submitted on paper. Admission notification on a rolling basis. **Financial aid:** Priority date 3/1; no closing date. FAFSA required. Applicants notified on a rolling basis starting 5/1; must reply within 2 week(s) of notification.

**Academics. Special study options:** Cooperative education, distance learning, double major, ESL, independent study, internships, student-designed major. Bachelor's degree programs available on campus. License preparation in aviation, nursing, paramedic. **Credit/placement by examination:** AP, CLEP, SAT, institutional tests. 45 credit hours maximum toward associate degree. 24 hours of credit by exam may be counted toward 1-year certificate program. **Support services:** GED preparation and test center, learning center, remedial instruction, study skills assistance, tutoring.

**Majors. Business:** General, accounting, administrative services. **Computer sciences:** Information systems. **Education:** General, early childhood. **Engineering technology:** Civil. **Health:** EMT paramedic, medical secretary, nursing (RN). **Legal studies:** Legal secretary. **Liberal arts:** Arts/sciences. **Mechanic/repair:** Automotive, electronics/electrical. **Personal/culinary services:** Cosmetic. **Protective services:** Firefighting.

**Most popular majors.** Business/marketing 9%, health sciences 29%.

**Computing on campus.** 200 workstations in library, computer center, student center. Commuter students can connect to campus network. Online course registration, helpline, wireless network available.

**Student life. Freshman orientation:** Mandatory. Preregistration for classes offered. Orientation held the Thursday or Friday prior to the beginning of term. **Activities:** Bands, choral groups, drama, music ensembles, musical theater, student government, student newspaper.

**Athletics. Intercollegiate:** Basketball. **Team name:** Riverhawks.

**Student services.** Career counseling, student employment services, on-campus daycare, personal counseling, placement for graduates, veterans' counselor. **Physically disabled:** Services for visually, hearing impaired. **Transfer:** Pre-admission transcript evaluation for new students. Transfer center, transfer adviser, college fairs on campus for students transferring to 4-year colleges.

**Contact.** E-mail: LaVera.Nordling@umpqua.edu
Phone: (541) 440-7743 Toll-free number: (800) 820-5161
Fax: (541) 440-4612
David Farrington, Director of Enrollment Services, Umpqua Community College, 1140 College Road, Roseburg, OR 97470-0226

## Western Culinary Institute
### Portland, Oregon
### www.wci.edu

◗ For-profit 2-year college
◗ Commuter campus in very large city

**General.** Accredited by ACCSCT. **Calendar:** Semester. 8 start dates per year.

**Annual costs/financial aid.** Full programs range from $17,500 to $42,000.

**Contact.** Phone: (503) 223-2245
Vice President of Marketing & Admissions, 921 SW Morrison Street, Suite 400, Portland, OR 97205

# Pennsylvania

## Allied Medical and Technical Institute
**Forty Fort, Pennsylvania**
**www.alliedteched.edu**                    CB code: 3190

- For-profit 2-year technical college
- Small town

**General.** Accredited by ACCSCT. **Calendar:** Continuous.

**Annual costs/financial aid.** Cost of full programs ranges from $9,474 to $19,470 depending on program.

**Contact.** Phone: (570) 288-8400
Admissions Director, 166 Slocum Avenue, Forty Fort, PA 18704-2936

## Antonelli Institute of Art and Photography
**Erdenheim, Pennsylvania**
**www.antonelli.edu**                    CB code: 0971

- For-profit 2-year visual arts and junior college
- Commuter campus in large town
- Interview required

**General.** Founded in 1938. Accredited by ACCSCT. **Enrollment:** 235 degree-seeking undergraduates; 4 non-degree-seeking students. **Degrees:** 72 associate awarded. **Location:** One mile from Philadelphia. **Calendar:** Semester, limited summer session. **Full-time faculty:** 13 total; 8% women. **Part-time faculty:** 3 total. **Class size:** 100% < 20. **Special facilities:** Black and white darkroom, computer graphics labs, digital photo darkrooms.

**Student profile.** Among degree-seeking undergraduates, 100% enrolled in a vocational program, 3% already have a bachelor's degree or higher, 136 enrolled as first-time, first-year students, 2 transferred in from other institutions.

| | | | |
|---|---|---|---|
| Part-time: | 1% | Asian American: | 1% |
| Out-of-state: | 20% | Hispanic American: | 5% |
| Women: | 63% | 25 or older: | 6% |
| African American: | 3% | Live on campus: | 51% |

**Transfer out. Colleges most students transferred to 2007:** Brooks Institute, University of the Arts, Arcadia University, Point Park College.

**Basis for selection.** Emphasis placed on interview, recommendations, and samples of art and photography or portfolio. Although not required, student portfolios will be evaluated. **Homeschooled:** Documentation of high school graduation/equivalency from local school district, state department of education or recognized home school organization required. If these items are not available, a GED will be required.

**2008-2009 Annual costs.** Tuition/fees (projected): $19,325. Per-credit charge: $640. Annual tuition for graphic design/commercial art students is $17,200; for photography students $19,200. Room only: $7,400. Books/supplies: $3,400. Personal expenses: $3,240.

**2006-2007 Financial aid.** All financial aid based on need. 104 full-time freshmen applied for aid; 97 were judged to have need; 97 of these received aid. Average need met was 22%. Average scholarship/grant was $5,800; average loan $2,625. 27% of total undergraduate aid awarded as scholarships/grants, 73% as loans/jobs. Need-based aid available for part-time students. Work-study available nights.

**Application procedures. Admission:** No deadline. $25 fee, may be waived for applicants with need. Application may be submitted online. Admission notification on a rolling basis. **Financial aid:** No deadline. FAFSA required. Applicants notified on a rolling basis; must reply within 2 week(s) of notification.

**Academics. Credit/placement by examination:** CLEP.

**Majors. Visual/performing arts:** Commercial photography, commercial/advertising art, design, photography.

**Computing on campus.** 60 workstations in library, computer center. Online library available.

**Student life. Freshman orientation:** Mandatory. Preregistration for classes offered. **Housing:** Coed dorms, apartments, substance-free housing available. $375 fully refundable deposit. Dormitory facilities available from local apartments.

**Athletics. Intramural:** Volleyball.

**Student services.** Career counseling, student employment services, financial aid counseling, personal counseling, placement for graduates. **Transfer:** Pre-admission transcript evaluation for new students. Transfer adviser for students transferring to 4-year colleges.

**Contact.** E-mail: admissions@antonelli.edu
Phone: (800) 722-7871 Toll-free number: (800) 722-7871
Fax: (215) 836-2794
Anthony DeTore, Director of Admissions, Antonelli Institute of Art and Photography, 300 Montgomery Avenue, Erdenheim, PA 19038-8242

## Art Institute of York
**York, Pennsylvania**
**www.aiba.artinstitutes.edu**                    CB code: 1548

- For-profit 2-year visual arts and technical college
- Commuter campus in large town
- Application essay, interview required

**General.** Founded in 1952. Accredited by ACCSCT. **Enrollment:** 417 full-time, degree-seeking students. **Degrees:** 379 associate awarded. **Location:** 20 miles from Harrisburg, 90 miles from Philadelphia. **Calendar:** Quarter, extensive summer session. **Full-time faculty:** 21 total. **Part-time faculty:** 34 total. **Class size:** 86% < 20, 14% 20-39.

**Basis for selection.** High school record, recommendations, and admissions interview most important. SAT or ACT recommended. Portfolio required for animation program. **Homeschooled:** Transcript of courses and grades, state high school equivalency certificate, interview required.

**2007-2008 Annual costs.** Tuition/fees: $16,740. Books/supplies: $1,250. Personal expenses: $2,610.

**Financial aid.** All financial aid based on need.

**Application procedures. Admission:** No deadline. $50 fee. Application may be submitted online. Admission notification on a rolling basis. Admitted applicants must reply within 10 days of personal interview. **Financial aid:** Priority date 8/1; no closing date. FAFSA required. Applicants notified on a rolling basis starting 6/1.

**Academics.** All students in degree programs (except Fashion Marketing) required to own laptop computer. Laptop specifications for each program available through Information Technology Department. **Special study options:** Internships. **Credit/placement by examination:** CLEP, SAT, ACT, institutional tests. **Support services:** Learning center, pre-admission summer program, reduced course load, remedial instruction, study skills assistance, tutoring, writing center.

**Majors. Business:** Fashion. **Communications technology:** Animation/special effects. **Computer sciences:** Web page design. **Visual/performing arts:** Commercial/advertising art, interior design.

**Most popular majors.** Business/marketing 15%, visual/performing arts 85%.

**Computing on campus.** PC or laptop required. 175 workstations in library, computer center, student center. Repair service, wireless network available.

**Student life. Freshman orientation:** Mandatory. Half-day program, 3-6 days before school starts. **Activities:** Student government, student newspaper.

**Student services.** Career counseling, student employment services, financial aid counseling, personal counseling, placement for graduates. **Transfer:** Pre-admission transcript evaluation for new students.

**Contact.** E-mail: info@bradlyacademy.edu
Phone: (800) 864-7725 Fax: (717) 840-1951
Diane Merino, Director of Admissions, Art Institute of York, 1409 Williams Road, York, PA 17402

## Berean Institute

**Philadelphia, Pennsylvania**
www.bereaninstitute.org                    CB code: 1045

- Private 2-year business and technical college
- Very large city

**General.** Founded in 1899. Accredited by ACCSCT. **Enrollment:** 240 degree-seeking undergraduates. **Degrees:** 5 associate awarded. **Location:** Downtown. **Calendar:** Trimester, limited summer session. **Full-time faculty:** 15 total.

**Basis for selection.** Open admission. Admissions based on high school record and Wonderlic exam.

**2007-2008 Annual costs.** Tuition ranges from $4,500 to $9,000, depending on program. Books/supplies: $400. Personal expenses: $500.

**Application procedures. Admission:** Closing date 5/1. $50 fee, may be waived for applicants with need. Application may be submitted online. Admission notification on a rolling basis. Interview required.

**Academics. Special study options:** Independent study, internships, liberal arts/career combination. **Credit/placement by examination:** CLEP, institutional tests. 30 credit hours maximum toward associate degree. **Support services:** Learning center, pre-admission summer program, tutoring.

**Majors. Business:** Accounting, business admin. **Computer sciences:** General. **Engineering technology:** Electrical.

**Student life. Activities:** Drama, student government, student newspaper.

**Athletics. Intercollegiate:** Basketball M. **Intramural:** Basketball M.

**Student services.** Adult student services, career counseling, personal counseling, placement for graduates, veterans' counselor.

**Contact.** Phone: (215) 763-4833 Fax: (215) 236-6011
Nannette Lomax, Coordinator of Admission, Berean Institute, 1901 West Girard Avenue, Philadelphia, PA 19130

## Berks Technical Institute

**Wyomissing, Pennsylvania**
www.berks.edu                    CB code: 3198

- For-profit 2-year business and technical college
- Commuter campus in small city

**General.** Accredited by ACCSCT. **Location:** 64 miles from Philadelphia. **Calendar:** Quarter.

**Annual costs/financial aid.** Approximate cost for diploma program, $9,600 to $17,000; for degree program, $21,000 to $30,000. Books/supplies: $992. Need-based financial aid available to full-time and part-time students.

**Contact.** Phone: (610) 372-1722
Registrar, 2205 Ridgewood Road, Wyomissing, PA 19610

## Bidwell Training Center

**Pittsburgh, Pennsylvania**
www.bidwell-training.org                    CB code: 3199

- For-profit 1-year business and health science college
- Commuter campus in large city

**General.** Accredited by ACCSCT. **Calendar:** Continuous.

**Annual costs/financial aid.** Tuition per year ranges from $6,000 to $10,000, including all fees. Programs offered at no cost to Pennsylvania residents. Need-based financial aid available for full-time students.

**Contact.** Phone: (412) 323-4000 ext. 156
Director of Student Services, 1815 Metropolitan Street, Pittsburgh, PA 15233

## Bradford School: Pittsburgh

**Pittsburgh, Pennsylvania**
www.bradfordpittsburgh.edu                    CB code: 2206

- For-profit 2-year junior college
- Commuter campus in very large city
- Interview required

**General.** Accredited by ACICS. **Enrollment:** 425 full-time, degree-seeking students. **Degrees:** 179 associate awarded. **Calendar:** Semester.

**Basis for selection.** High school record, class rank, recommendations, interview most important.

**Application procedures. Admission:** Closing date 8/15. $50 fee. Admission notification on a rolling basis. Must reply by 7/15. **Financial aid:** FAFSA required.

**Academics. Credit/placement by examination:** CLEP.

**Majors. Business:** Accounting, administrative services, hospitality admin, sales/distribution, tourism/travel. **Computer sciences:** Programming. **Health:** Medical assistant. **Legal studies:** Paralegal. **Visual/performing arts:** Commercial/advertising art.

**Computing on campus.** 150 workstations in library.

**Student life. Housing:** Coed dorms available.

**Student services.** Financial aid counseling, placement for graduates.

**Contact.** Phone: (412) 391-6710 Toll-free number: (800) 391-6810 Fax: (412) 471-6714
Lucille McLaughlin, Director of Admissions, Bradford School: Pittsburgh, 125 West Station Square Drive, Pittsburgh, PA 15219

## Bucks County Community College

**Newtown, Pennsylvania**                    CB member
www.bucks.edu                    CB code: 2066

- Public 2-year community college
- Commuter campus in large town

**General.** Founded in 1964. Regionally accredited. Credit courses available at several off-campus locations. **Enrollment:** 9,649 degree-seeking undergraduates. **Degrees:** 773 associate awarded. **Location:** 35 miles from Philadelphia. **Calendar:** Semester, limited summer session. **Full-time faculty:** 152 total; 24% have terminal degrees, 7% minority, 52% women. **Part-time faculty:** 416 total; 6% minority, 51% women. **Class size:** 99% < 20, less than 1% 50-99. **Partnerships:** Formal partnerships with Bucks County Technical High School, Eastern Center for Arts & Technology, Middle Bucks Institute of Technology, Northern Montgomery County Technical Career Center, Upper Bucks County Area Vocational Technical High School, Western Center for Technical Studies.

**Student profile.** Among degree-seeking undergraduates, 74% enrolled in a transfer program, 23% enrolled in a vocational program, 3,033 enrolled as first-time, first-year students, 195 transferred in from other institutions.

| | | | |
|---|---|---|---|
| Part-time: | 57% | Asian American: | 2% |
| Out-of-state: | 1% | Hispanic American: | 1% |
| Women: | 58% | International: | 6% |
| African American: | 3% | 25 or older: | 36% |

**Transfer out.** 57% of students enrolled in the transfer program go on to 4-year colleges. **Colleges most students transferred to 2007:** Temple University, Holy Family University, Pennsylvania State University, Drexel University.

**Basis for selection.** Open admission, but selective for some programs. Admissions to nursing, fine arts, chef apprenticeship and fine woodworking programs based on GPA and satisfaction of prerequisites. Admission to music program based on above, plus audition. Admission to art program based on above, plus portfolio. College's own test administered for placement purposes, after admission. Interview required for chef apprentice, fine arts, fine woodworking, and nursing programs. Audition required for music program; portfolio required for art, fine woodworking programs; essay required for chef apprentice program. **Adult students:** Students over 65 exempt from placement tests. **Homeschooled:** Final official transcript certified by state required. **Learning Disabled:** Special testing accommodations can be provided for the entrance assessment test for students with learning disabilities.

**2007-2008 Annual costs.** Tuition/fees: $3,434; $6,524 out-of-district; $9,614 out-of-state. Per-credit charge: $93 in-district; $186 out-of-district; $279 out-of-state. Books/supplies: $1,350. Personal expenses: $1,350.

**2006-2007 Financial aid.** Need-based: 70% of total undergraduate aid awarded as scholarships/grants, 30% as loans/jobs. Need-based aid available for part-time students. Work-study available nights, weekends and for part-time students. **Non-need-based:** Scholarships awarded for academics.

**Application procedures. Admission:** Closing date 5/1 (postmark date). $30 fee. Application must be submitted on paper. Admission notification on a rolling basis. **Financial aid:** Closing date 5/1. FAFSA required. Applicants notified on a rolling basis starting 6/1; must reply within 2 week(s) of notification.

**Academics. Special study options:** Cooperative education, distance learning, dual enrollment of high school students, ESL, external degree, honors, independent study, internships, student-designed major, weekend college. Bachelor's degree programs available on campus. License preparation in nursing, occupational therapy, physical therapy, radiology, real estate. **Credit/placement by examination:** AP, CLEP, institutional tests. 30 credit hours maximum toward associate degree. **Support services:** GED preparation and test center, learning center, reduced course load, remedial instruction, study skills assistance, tutoring, writing center.

**Majors. Area/ethnic studies:** American. **Biology:** General. **Business:** General, accounting, administrative services, business admin, hospitality admin, hotel/motel admin, marketing, office management, office/clerical, operations, restaurant/food services, retailing, small business admin, tourism/travel. **Communications:** General, digital media, journalism. **Communications technology:** Animation/special effects, graphic/printing. **Computer sciences:** General, computer graphics, computer science, data processing, information systems, information technology, networking, programming. **Conservation:** Environmental science. **Education:** General, biology, chemistry, early childhood, health, mathematics, physical, teacher assistance. **Engineering:** General. **Family/consumer sciences:** Institutional food production. **Health:** Health services, management/clinical assistant, medical assistant, nursing (RN), office assistant. **Legal studies:** Legal secretary, paralegal. **Liberal arts:** Arts/sciences, humanities. **Math:** General. **Parks/recreation:** Health/fitness, sports admin. **Personal/culinary services:** Baking, chef training, culinary arts, restaurant/catering. **Physical sciences:** Chemistry. **Production:** Woodworking. **Protective services:** Correctional facilities, corrections, criminal justice, firefighting, police science. **Psychology:** General. **Public administration:** Social work. **Social sciences:** General. **Visual/performing arts:** General, cinematography, commercial/advertising art, dramatic, graphic design, studio arts.

**Most popular majors.** Business/marketing 19%, education 14%, health sciences 14%, liberal arts 13%, visual/performing arts 6%.

**Computing on campus.** 450 workstations in library, computer center. Commuter students can connect to campus network. Online course registration, online library, helpline, wireless network available.

**Student life. Freshman orientation:** Available. **Activities:** Bands, choral groups, dance, drama, film society, literary magazine, music ensembles, student government, student newspaper, TV station, wide variety of service, social, and recreational programs.

**Athletics.** NJCAA. **Intercollegiate:** Baseball M, basketball M, equestrian, golf, soccer, tennis, volleyball W. **Intramural:** Baseball M, basketball M, bowling W, equestrian, skiing, softball, volleyball. **Team name:** Centurions.

**Student services.** Adult student services, alcohol/substance abuse counseling, career counseling, services for economically disadvantaged, student employment services, financial aid counseling, minority student services, on-campus daycare, personal counseling, veterans' counselor, women's services. **Physically disabled:** Services for visually, speech, hearing impaired. **Learning disabled:** Comprehensive services available. **Transfer:** Pre-admission transcript evaluation for new students. Transfer center, transfer adviser, college fairs on campus for students transferring to 4-year colleges.

**Contact.** E-mail: admissions@bucks.edu
Phone: (215) 968-8100 Fax: (215) 968-8110
Amy Wilson-Laible, Director of Admissions, Bucks County Community College, 275 Swamp Road, Newtown, PA 18940

## Business Institute of Pennsylvania
**Sharon, Pennsylvania**
www.biop.edu
CB code: 2466

- For-profit 2-year business and technical college
- Commuter campus in large town
- Interview required

**General.** Accredited by ACICS. Branch campus located in Meadville. **Enrollment:** 140 degree-seeking undergraduates. **Degrees:** 61 associate awarded. **Location:** 50 miles from Pittsburgh; 15 miles from Youngstown, Ohio. **Calendar:** Quarter, extensive summer session. **Full-time faculty:** 3 total. **Part-time faculty:** 6 total. **Class size:** 76% < 20, 24% 20-39.

**Student profile.**

| | | | |
|---|---|---|---|
| Out-of-state: | 7% | 25 or older: | 45% |

**Basis for selection.** All applicants must take CPAt for skill assessment and placement. If SAT or ACT submitted, CPAt requirement may be waived.

**High school preparation.** Recommended units include English 3, mathematics 3 and science 2. Accounting, business, computer and English preferred.

**2007-2008 Annual costs.** Tuition/fees: $9,240. Per-credit charge: $240. Books/supplies: $1,500.

**Financial aid. Non-need-based:** Scholarships awarded for academics.

**Application procedures. Admission:** No deadline. $50 fee. Admission notification on a rolling basis. **Financial aid:** Closing date 7/31. Institutional form required.

**Academics. Special study options:** Internships. **Credit/placement by examination:** CLEP, institutional tests. 15 credit hours maximum toward associate degree. **Support services:** Study skills assistance.

**Majors. Business:** Accounting, accounting technology, accounting/business management, administrative services, business admin, executive assistant, marketing, office technology. **Computer sciences:** General, data entry, data processing, information technology, word processing. **Health:** Insurance coding, insurance specialist, medical records admin, medical records technology, medical secretary, office admin, office assistant, office computer specialist, receptionist. **Legal studies:** Legal secretary.

**Most popular majors.** Business/marketing 15%, computer/information sciences 15%.

**Computing on campus.** 35 workstations in computer center.

**Student life. Freshman orientation:** Mandatory. Orientation takes place the first day of each quarter. **Activities:** Student government, student newspaper.

**Student services.** Career counseling, financial aid counseling, placement for graduates. **Transfer:** Pre-admission transcript evaluation for new students.

**Contact.** Phone: (724) 983-0700 Fax: (724) 983-8355
Irene Lewis, Admissions Officer, Business Institute of Pennsylvania, 335 Boyd Drive, Sharon, PA 16146

## Butler County Community College
**Butler, Pennsylvania**
www.bc3.edu
CB code: 2069

- Public 2-year community college
- Commuter campus in large town

**General.** Founded in 1965. Regionally accredited. Classes offered in Cranberry township, Mercer, and Lawrence counties. **Enrollment:** 3,656 degree-seeking undergraduates. **Degrees:** 373 associate awarded. **Location:** 35 miles from Pittsburgh. **Calendar:** Semester, limited summer session. **Full-time faculty:** 63 total; 16% have terminal degrees, 52% women. **Part-time faculty:** 233 total; 1% have terminal degrees, 43% women. **Special facilities:** Environmental education center, cultural center/theater, meteorology lab, computer forensics lab. **Partnerships:** Formal partnerships with American Management Association, Workforce & Economic Development Network of PA, Backflow Management, Inc., Carnegie Mellon University, 13 regional fire schools, 12 local high schools.

**Student profile.** Among degree-seeking undergraduates, 66% enrolled in a transfer program, 34% enrolled in a vocational program.

| | | | |
|---|---|---|---|
| Part-time: | 46% | Women: | 61% |
| Out-of-state: | 1% | 25 or older: | 37% |

**Transfer out.** 75% of students enrolled in the transfer program go on to 4-year colleges. **Colleges most students transferred to 2007:** Slippery Rock University of Pennsylvania, Clarion University of Pennsylvania, Indiana University of Pennsylvania.

**Basis for selection.** Open admission, but selective for some programs. Admission to nursing, medical assistant, physical therapist assistant, massage therapy, and metrology programs based on high school record.

**2007-2008 Annual costs.** Tuition/fees: $2,790; $4,980 out-of-district; $7,170 out-of-state. Per-credit charge: $73 in-district; $146 out-of-district; $219 out-of-state. Books/supplies: $850. Personal expenses: $1,000.

**2006-2007 Financial aid. Need-based:** 50% of total undergraduate aid awarded as scholarships/grants, 50% as loans/jobs. Need-based aid available for part-time students. Work-study available for part-time students. **Non-need-based:** Scholarships awarded for academics, state residency.

**Application procedures. Admission:** No deadline. $25 fee, may be waived for applicants with need. Application must be submitted on paper. Admission notification on a rolling basis. **Financial aid:** Priority date 4/15; no closing date. FAFSA required. Applicants notified on a rolling basis starting 5/1; must reply within 2 week(s) of notification.

**Academics. Special study options:** Cooperative education, distance learning, independent study, internships. License preparation in nursing, physical therapy. **Credit/placement by examination:** AP, CLEP, institutional tests. 45 credit hours maximum toward associate degree. **Support services:** GED preparation, learning center, pre-admission summer program, reduced course load, remedial instruction, study skills assistance, tutoring, writing center.

**Majors. Biology:** General. **Business:** Accounting technology, administrative services, business admin, human resources, marketing, tourism promotion. **Communications:** Organizational. **Computer sciences:** Programming, security, web page design. **Education:** Elementary, kindergarten/preschool, secondary. **Engineering:** General. **Engineering technology:** Architectural drafting, civil, computer systems, electrical, industrial management, instrumentation, manufacturing, mechanical drafting. **English:** English lit. **Family/consumer sciences:** Institutional food production. **Health:** Health care admin, medical assistant, nursing (RN), physical therapy assistant. **Legal studies:** Legal secretary. **Math:** General. **Parks/recreation:** General, sports admin. **Physical sciences:** General. **Production:** Machine shop technology. **Protective services:** Law enforcement admin, police science. **Psychology:** General. **Visual/performing arts:** Graphic design.

**Most popular majors.** Business/marketing 17%, education 12%, engineering/engineering technologies 11%, health sciences 21%, liberal arts 9%, security/protective services 7%, visual/performing arts 6%.

**Computing on campus.** 108 workstations in library, computer center. Online course registration available.

**Student life. Freshman orientation:** Available. **Activities:** Drama, literary magazine, student government, student newspaper, Christian outreach organization.

**Athletics.** NJCAA. **Intercollegiate:** Baseball M, basketball, cheerleading, golf M, softball W, volleyball W. **Intramural:** Basketball, golf, table tennis, volleyball, weight lifting. **Team name:** Pioneers.

**Student services.** Adult student services, career counseling, services for economically disadvantaged, student employment services, financial aid counseling, on-campus daycare, personal counseling, placement for graduates, veterans' counselor. **Physically disabled:** Services for visually, hearing impaired. **Transfer:** Pre-admission transcript evaluation for new students. Transfer adviser, college fairs on campus for students transferring to 4-year colleges.

**Contact.** E-mail: pattie.bajuszik@bc3.edu
Phone: (724) 287-8711 ext. 8346 Toll-free number: (888) 826-2829
Fax: (724) 287-3460
Pattie Bajuszik, Director of Admissions, Butler County Community College, PO Box 1203, Butler, PA 16003-1203

## Cambria-Rowe Business College
**Johnstown, Pennsylvania**
www.crbc.net                    CB code: 2210

- For-profit 2-year business college
- Commuter campus in small city

**General.** Founded in 1891. Accredited by ACICS. **Enrollment:** 185 degree-seeking undergraduates. **Degrees:** 93 associate awarded. **Location:** 60 miles from Pittsburgh. **Calendar:** Quarter, extensive summer session. **Full-time faculty:** 10 total.

**Student profile.** Among degree-seeking undergraduates, 82 transferred in from other institutions.

**Transfer out. Colleges most students transferred to 2007:** Saint Francis University, Mount Aloysius College.

**Basis for selection.** Students must pass entrance exam. High school transcript, GED scores reviewed. Interview recommended. **Homeschooled:** Transcript of courses and grades required.

**2007-2008 Annual costs.** Tuition/fees: $9,075. Depending on choice of laptop, fees could be as much as $1,140. Books/supplies: $1,000.

**Financial aid. Need-based:** Need-based aid available for part-time students. **Non-need-based:** Scholarships awarded for academics, leadership.

**Application procedures. Admission:** No deadline. $15 fee. Application may be submitted online. Students notified within 2 weeks of receipt of application. **Financial aid:** Closing date 8/1. FAFSA required. Applicants notified on a rolling basis.

**Academics. Special study options:** Accelerated study, liberal arts/career combination. **Credit/placement by examination:** CLEP, institutional tests. **Support services:** Pre-admission summer program, reduced course load, tutoring.

**Majors. Business:** General, accounting, administrative services, business admin. **Health:** Medical secretary, medical transcription. **Legal studies:** Legal secretary.

**Computing on campus.** PC or laptop required. Online library, repair service, wireless network available.

**Student life. Freshman orientation:** Mandatory. Preregistration for classes offered. Usually held 3 weeks prior to start date.

**Student services.** Adult student services, career counseling, student employment services, financial aid counseling, personal counseling, placement for graduates. **Transfer:** Transfer adviser for students transferring to 4-year colleges.

**Contact.** E-mail: admissions@crbc.net
Phone: (814) 536-5168 Fax: (814) 536-5160
Amanda Artim, Director of Admissions, Cambria-Rowe Business College, 221 Central Avenue, Johnstown, PA 15902

## Cambria-Rowe Business College: Indiana
**Indiana, Pennsylvania**
www.crbc.net                    CB code: 3274

- For-profit 2-year business and technical college
- Commuter campus in small town
- Interview required

**General.** Accredited by ACICS. **Enrollment:** 195 degree-seeking undergraduates. **Degrees:** 51 associate awarded. **Calendar:** Quarter. **Full-time faculty:** 8 total; 100% women.

**Student profile.** Among degree-seeking undergraduates, 54 enrolled as first-time, first-year students.

| Part-time: | 7% | Women: | 88% |
|---|---|---|---|

**Basis for selection.** Open admission. **Homeschooled:** Transcript of courses and grades, interview required.

**2008-2009 Annual costs.** Tuition/fees (projected): $9,440. Per-credit charge: $250. Depending on choice of laptop, fees could be as much as $1125.

**Financial aid. Need-based:** Need-based aid available for part-time students.

**Application procedures. Admission:** No deadline. $15 fee. Admission notification on a rolling basis. **Financial aid:** No deadline. FAFSA required. Applicants notified on a rolling basis.

**Academics. Special study options:** Double major. **Credit/placement by examination:** AP, CLEP, institutional tests. **Support services:** Tutoring.

**Majors. Business:** Accounting, administrative services, business admin, management information systems. **Computer sciences:** Computer support specialist. **Health:** Medical secretary.

**Computing on campus.** PC or laptop required. Online library, repair service, wireless network available.

**Student life. Freshman orientation:** Mandatory.

**Student services. Transfer:** Pre-admission transcript evaluation for new students.

**Contact.** E-mail: rhavener@crbc.net
Phone: (724) 463-0222 Toll-free number: (800) 639-2273
Rachel Havener, Admissions Representative, Cambria-Rowe Business College: Indiana, 422 South 13th Street, Indiana, PA 15701

## Career Training Academy
**New Kensington, Pennsylvania**
**www.careerta.com**                              CB code: 3205

- For-profit 2-year career college
- Commuter campus in small town
- Application essay required

**General.** Accredited by ACCSCT. **Enrollment:** 85 degree-seeking undergraduates. **Degrees:** 17 associate awarded. **Location:** 18 miles from Pittsburgh. **Calendar:** Quarter, extensive summer session. **Full-time faculty:** 15 total. **Part-time faculty:** 3 total. **Special facilities:** Day care center. **Partnerships:** Formal partnership with Children's Community Pediatrics for the Medical Assistant Comprehensive and Advanced Medical Coder/Biller programs.

**Basis for selection.** Open admission, but selective for some programs. Health programs require interview, essay, 1.5+ GPA or 235+ GED, and health form. Paralegal program requires 45 collegiate credits.

**2007-2008 Annual costs.** Total cost of 15-month associate degree program in massage therapy: $22,378 (includes tuition, books, portable massage table, uniforms, lab fees, insurance, graduation fees). Total cost of 15-month associate degree program in medical assistance: $18,812 (includes tuition, books, uniforms, lab fees, insurance, graduation fees). Other diploma programs will vary in cost and required length of study.

**Financial aid.** All financial aid based on need. **Additional information:** Work study available after class day.

**Application procedures. Admission:** No deadline. $30 fee. Application must be submitted on paper. Admission notification on a rolling basis. **Financial aid:** No deadline. FAFSA, institutional form required.

**Academics.** Mentor program available to all students. **Special study options:** Internships. Externships. **Credit/placement by examination:** CLEP, IB.

**Majors. Health:** Massage therapy, medical assistant, medical secretary.

**Student life. Freshman orientation:** Mandatory. Preregistration for classes offered.

**Student services.** Adult student services, alcohol/substance abuse counseling, career counseling, services for economically disadvantaged, student employment services, financial aid counseling, on-campus daycare, personal counseling, placement for graduates, veterans' counselor, women's services. **Transfer:** Pre-admission transcript evaluation for new students.

**Contact.** Phone: (724) 337-1000 Fax: (724) 335-7140
Tyna Putignano, Director of Admissions, Career Training Academy, 950 Fifth Avenue, New Kensington, PA 15068

## Career Training Academy: Monroeville
**Monroeville, Pennsylvania**
**www.careerta.edu**                              CB code: 3207

- For-profit 2-year branch campus college
- Commuter campus in small city
- Application essay required

**General.** Accredited by ACCSCT. **Enrollment:** 45 degree-seeking undergraduates. **Degrees:** 20 associate awarded. **Location:** 10 miles from Pittsburgh. **Calendar:** Continuous. **Full-time faculty:** 10 total. **Part-time faculty:** 5 total.

**Basis for selection.** Open admission, but selective for some programs.

**2007-2008 Annual costs.** Tuition ranges from $3,700 to $17,900 depending on program; required fees range from $210 to $3,100 depending on program. Books/supplies: $750. Personal expenses: $2,889.

**Financial aid.** All financial aid based on need. Need-based aid available for part-time students.

**Application procedures. Admission:** No deadline. $30 fee. **Financial aid:** FAFSA, institutional form required.

**Academics. Special study options:** Internships. **Credit/placement by examination:** CLEP. **Support services:** Remedial instruction, study skills assistance, tutoring.

**Majors. Health:** Medical assistant, ward clerk.

**Student life. Freshman orientation:** Mandatory.

**Student services.** Career counseling, student employment services, financial aid counseling, placement for graduates.

**Contact.** E-mail: Admissions2@careerta.edu
Phone: (412) 372-3900
Tyna Putignano, Director of Admissions, Career Training Academy: Monroeville, 4314 Old William Penn Highway #103, Monroeville, PA 15146

## Career Training Academy: Pittsburgh
**Pittsburgh, Pennsylvania**
**www.careerta.edu**

- For-profit 2-year branch campus college
- Small city

**General.** Regionally accredited; also accredited by ACCSCT. **Enrollment:** 45 degree-seeking undergraduates. **Degrees:** 18 associate awarded. **Calendar:** Continuous. **Full-time faculty:** 8 total. **Part-time faculty:** 4 total.

**Basis for selection.** Open admission, but selective for some programs.

**2007-2008 Annual costs.** Cost of entire 18 month associate degree programs: $18,000; 12 month diploma programs: $12,000.

**Application procedures. Admission:** No deadline.

**Academics. Credit/placement by examination:** CLEP.

**Majors. Health:** Insurance specialist, massage therapy, medical assistant.

**Contact.** E-mail: admissions3@careerta.edu
Phone: (412) 367-4000
Career Training Academy: Pittsburgh, 1500 Shoppes at Northway, Pittsburgh, PA 15237

## CHI Institute: Broomall
**Broomall, Pennsylvania**
**www.chitraining.com**                              CB code: 3398

- For-profit 2-year technical and career college
- Large town
- Application essay, interview required

**General.** Accredited by ACCSCT. **Enrollment:** 1,015 degree-seeking undergraduates. **Degrees:** 85 associate awarded. **Location:** 7 miles from Philadelphia. **Calendar:** Quarter, extensive summer session. **Full-time faculty:** 40 total. **Part-time faculty:** 10 total.

**Basis for selection.** Open admission.

**2007-2008 Annual costs.** Tuition ranges from $13,251- $20,154 per 18-month program associate degree program, inclusive of books and fees.

**Financial aid. Need-based:** Need-based aid available for part-time students.

**Application procedures. Admission:** No deadline. $20 fee. Admission notification on a rolling basis. **Financial aid:** No deadline. FAFSA required. Applicants notified on a rolling basis.

**Academics. Credit/placement by examination:** CLEP. **Support services:** Remedial instruction, tutoring.

**Majors. Engineering technology:** Electrical.

**Student life. Freshman orientation:** Available.

**Student services.** Adult student services, career counseling, student employment services, personal counseling, placement for graduates, veterans' counselor.

**Contact.** Phone: (610) 355-3300
Timothy Parsons, Director of Admissions, CHI Institute: Broomall, 1991
Sproul Road, Suite 42, Broomall, PA 19008

## CHI Institute: Franklin Mills
**Philadelphia, Pennsylvania**
www.chitraining.com                    CB code: 3386

- For-profit 2-year technical college
- Commuter campus in large town
- Interview required

**General.** Founded in 1981. Accredited by ACCSCT. **Enrollment:** 700 undergraduates. **Degrees:** 100 associate awarded. **Location:** 5 miles from Philadelphia. **Calendar:** Continuous, extensive summer session. **Full-time faculty:** 30 total. **Part-time faculty:** 15 total.

**Basis for selection.** Open admission.

**2007-2008 Annual costs.** Costs vary by program. Books/supplies: $765.

**Financial aid. Additional information:** Scholarships for graduating seniors. Awards based on institutional scholarship aptitude test and interview with independent committee. Parental income not considered.

**Application procedures. Admission:** No deadline. No application fee. Admission notification on a rolling basis. **Financial aid:** Closing date 9/20. Applicants notified on a rolling basis.

**Academics. Special study options:** Internships. **Credit/placement by examination:** CLEP.

**Majors. Computer sciences:** Computer graphics, computer science, programming, systems analysis. **Engineering technology:** Electrical. **Protective services:** Criminal justice.

**Student services.** Career counseling, student employment services, placement for graduates.

**Contact.** Phone: (215) 357-5100
Eric Heller, Admissions Director, CHI Institute: Franklin Mills, 125
Franklin Mills Boulevard, Philadelphia, PA 19154

## Commonwealth Technical Institute
**Johnstown, Pennsylvania**
www.hgac.org                    CB code: 3125

- Private 2-year technical college
- Residential campus in small city

**General.** Accredited by ACCSCT. Specially geared toward students with disabilities. **Enrollment:** 94 degree-seeking undergraduates; 154 non-degree-seeking students. **Degrees:** 60 associate awarded. **Calendar:** Semester. **Full-time faculty:** 35 total; 3% have terminal degrees, 34% women.

**Student profile.** Among degree-seeking undergraduates, 94 enrolled as first-time, first-year students.

**Transfer out. Colleges most students transferred to 2007:** Cambria County Area Community College.

**Basis for selection.** Open admission.

**2007-2008 Annual costs.** Tuition/fees: $11,224. Room/board: $9,516.

**Financial aid.** All financial aid based on need. Need-based aid available for part-time students. Work-study available nights and weekends.

**Application procedures. Admission:** No deadline. No application fee. Admission notification on a rolling basis. **Financial aid:** Closing date 5/1. FAFSA required. Applicants notified on a rolling basis.

**Academics. Credit/placement by examination:** CLEP. **Support services:** Remedial instruction, tutoring.

**Majors. Business:** Accounting. **Engineering technology:** Architectural drafting, computer systems, mechanical drafting. **Health:** Dental lab technology, medical secretary. **Personal/culinary services:** Chef training.

**Computing on campus.** Dormitories wired for high-speed internet access.

**Student life. Housing:** Single-sex dorms, special housing for disabled, substance-free housing available. **Activities:** Choral groups, student government.

**Athletics. Intramural:** Basketball, volleyball.

**Student services.** Alcohol/substance abuse counseling, financial aid counseling, health services, personal counseling, veterans' counselor. **Physically disabled:** Services for visually, speech, hearing impaired.

**Contact.** Phone: (814) 255-8237
Rebecca Halza, Director of Admissions, Commonwealth Technical
Institute, 727 Goucher Street, Johnstown, PA 15905-3902

## Community College of Allegheny County
**Pittsburgh, Pennsylvania**            CB member
www.ccac.edu                    CB code: 2122

- Public 2-year community college
- Commuter campus in very large city

**General.** Founded in 1966. Regionally accredited. Campuses located in and around Pittsburgh. **Enrollment:** 16,907 degree-seeking undergraduates; 1,614 non-degree-seeking students. **Degrees:** 1,896 associate awarded. **Calendar:** Semester, extensive summer session. **Full-time faculty:** 203 total; 17% have terminal degrees, 11% minority, 53% women. **Part-time faculty:** 898 total; 5% have terminal degrees, 9% minority, 48% women. **Class size:** 56% < 20, 43% 20-39, less than 1% 40-49, less than 1% 50-99, less than 1% >100.

**Student profile.** Among degree-seeking undergraduates, 4,345 enrolled as first-time, first-year students, 912 transferred in from other institutions.

| | | | |
|---|---|---|---|
| Part-time: | 57% | Asian American: | 1% |
| Out-of-state: | 1% | Hispanic American: | 1% |
| Women: | 56% | Native American: | 1% |
| African American: | 15% | 25 or older: | 52% |

**Transfer out. Colleges most students transferred to 2007:** University of Pittsburgh, Robert Morris University, Duquesne University, Point Park University, Carlow College.

**Basis for selection.** Open admission, but selective for some programs. Special requirements for some health-related, culinary arts, and automotive programs. COMPASS used for placement. Audition recommended for music program.

**2007-2008 Annual costs.** Tuition/fees: $2,669; $5,069 out-of-district; $7,469 out-of-state. Per-credit charge: $80 in-district; $160 out-of-district; $240 out-of-state. If county does not have community college, tuition is $2820 per year. Nursing and allied health courses subject to additional fees. Books/supplies: $700. Personal expenses: $3,737.

**Financial aid. Need-based:** Need-based aid available for part-time students. Work-study available nights, weekends and for part-time students. **Non-need-based:** Scholarships awarded for academics, minority status.

**Application procedures. Admission:** No deadline. No application fee. Admission notification on a rolling basis. **Financial aid:** Priority date 5/1; no closing date. FAFSA required. Applicants notified on a rolling basis starting 5/1.

**Academics. Special study options:** Cross-registration, distance learning, dual enrollment of high school students, ESL, external degree, honors, independent study, liberal arts/career combination, study abroad. License preparation in nursing. **Credit/placement by examination:** AP, CLEP, institutional tests. 30 credit hours maximum toward associate degree. **Support services:** GED preparation and test center, learning center, reduced course load, remedial instruction, study skills assistance, tutoring, writing center.

**Majors. Agriculture:** Horticulture, landscaping, turf management. **Biology:** General. **Business:** Accounting technology, administrative services, banking/financial services, business admin, entrepreneurial studies, human resources, management information systems, marketing. **Communications:** Journalism. **Construction:** General, electrician, maintenance, painting, power transmission. **Education:** Elementary, teacher assistance. **Engineering technology:** Automotive, civil, electrical, environmental, hydraulics, robotics. **Family/consumer sciences:** Child development. **Foreign languages:** General. **Health:** Cardiovascular technology, clinical lab technology, medical assistant, medical radiologic technology/radiation therapy, medical records technology, mental health services, nuclear medical technology, nursing (RN), occupational therapy assistant, pharmacy assistant, physical therapy assistant, respiratory therapy technology, sonography, surgical technology. **Liberal arts:** Arts/sciences, humanities. **Math:** General. **Mechanic/repair:** Business machine, heating/ac/refrig. **Parks/recreation:** Health/fitness. **Personal/**

culinary services: Chef training, restaurant/catering. **Physical sciences:** Chemistry, physics. **Production:** Welding. **Protective services:** Corrections, fire safety technology, police science. **Psychology:** General. **Public administration:** Social work. **Science technology:** Chemical. **Social sciences:** General, sociology. **Transportation:** Airline/commercial pilot, aviation management. **Visual/performing arts:** Art, commercial/advertising art.

**Most popular majors.** Business/marketing 12%, health sciences 36%, liberal arts 26%, trade and industry 7%.

**Computing on campus.** 3,700 workstations in library, computer center. Commuter students can connect to campus network. Helpline available.

**Student life. Freshman orientation:** Available. **Activities:** Jazz band, choral groups, drama, music ensembles, student government, student newspaper.

**Athletics.** NJCAA. **Intercollegiate:** Baseball M, basketball, bowling, golf, ice hockey M, softball W, tennis, volleyball W.

**Student services.** Adult student services, career counseling, student employment services, health services, on-campus daycare, personal counseling, placement for graduates, veterans' counselor. **Physically disabled:** Services for visually, speech, hearing impaired. **Transfer:** Transfer adviser for students transferring to 4-year colleges.

**Contact.**   Phone: (412) 323-2323
Community College of Allegheny County, 800 Allegheny Avenue, Pittsburgh, PA 15233

## Community College of Beaver County
**Monaca, Pennsylvania**                    **CB member**
**www.ccbc.edu**                            **CB code: 2126**

♦  Public 2-year community college
♦  Commuter campus in small town

**General.** Founded in 1966. Regionally accredited. **Enrollment:** 1,865 degree-seeking undergraduates; 769 non-degree-seeking students. **Degrees:** 436 associate awarded. **Location:** 30 miles from Pittsburgh. **Calendar:** Semester, limited summer session. **Full-time faculty:** 46 total; 4% minority, 63% women. **Part-time faculty:** 121 total; 2% minority, 46% women. **Class size:** 58% < 20, 41% 20-39, less than 1% 40-49. **Special facilities:** Student-monitored control tower for aviation, computerized mannequins/patient simulators for nursing.

**Student profile.** Among degree-seeking undergraduates, 29% enrolled in a transfer program, 71% enrolled in a vocational program, 528 enrolled as first-time, first-year students.

| Part-time: | 39% | African American: | 8% |
|---|---|---|---|
| Out-of-state: | 5% | Hispanic American: | 1% |
| Women: | 55% | 25 or older: | 31% |

**Transfer out. Colleges most students transferred to 2007:** Slippery Rock State University, Geneva College, Robert Morris College, Edinboro State University.

**Basis for selection.** Open admission, but selective for some programs. NLN Pre-Admission PN test given for admission into nursing program. Interview recommended.

**2007-2008 Annual costs.** Tuition/fees: $3,180; $5,880 out-of-district; $8,880 out-of-state. Per-credit charge: $85 in-district; $170 out-of-district; $255 out-of-state. Books/supplies: $1,000. Personal expenses: $1,200.

**2006-2007 Financial aid. Need-based:** Average scholarship/grant was $1,862; average loan $1,567. 48% of total undergraduate aid awarded as scholarships/grants, 52% as loans/jobs. Need-based aid available for part-time students. Work-study available nights, weekends and for part-time students. **Non-need-based:** Scholarships awarded for academics, athletics, state residency.

**Application procedures. Admission:** Priority date 6/1; no deadline. No application fee. Application must be submitted on paper. Admission notification on a rolling basis. Application deadline January 20 for nursing, must reply within 3 weeks of notification. **Financial aid:** Priority date 5/1, closing date 7/1. FAFSA, institutional form required. Applicants notified on a rolling basis starting 8/5; must reply within 2 week(s) of notification.

**Academics. Special study options:** Cross-registration, distance learning, double major, dual enrollment of high school students, independent study, internships, liberal arts/career combination. License preparation in aviation, nursing, radiology. **Credit/placement by examination:** AP, CLEP, institutional tests. 45 credit hours maximum toward associate degree. **Support**

services: GED preparation and test center, learning center, reduced course load, remedial instruction, study skills assistance, tutoring, writing center.

**Majors. Agriculture:** Landscaping. **Business:** Accounting technology, business admin, human resources, management information systems, marketing. **Communications:** Digital media. **Communications technology:** General. **Computer sciences:** Applications programming, networking. **Education:** Teacher assistance. **Engineering:** Materials. **Engineering technology:** Aerospace, heat/ac/refrig. **Health:** Health aide, medical secretary, nursing (RN). **Interdisciplinary:** Biological/physical sciences. **Liberal arts:** Arts/sciences, humanities. **Personal/culinary services:** Chef training. **Production:** Machine tool, welding. **Protective services:** Police science. **Social sciences:** General. **Transportation:** Air traffic control, aviation management. **Visual/performing arts:** Studio arts.

**Most popular majors.** Business/marketing 13%, health sciences 19%, liberal arts 10%, security/protective services 17%, trade and industry 28%.

**Computing on campus.** 220 workstations in library, computer center, student center. Online library available.

**Student life. Freshman orientation:** Available. Preregistration for classes offered. **Activities:** Drama, literary magazine, student government, student newspaper.

**Athletics.** NJCAA. **Intercollegiate:** Basketball M, softball W, volleyball W. **Intramural:** Basketball M, golf, softball, table tennis, volleyball. **Team name:** Titans.

**Student services.** Adult student services, career counseling, services for economically disadvantaged, financial aid counseling, on-campus daycare, personal counseling, veterans' counselor. **Physically disabled:** Services for visually, speech, hearing impaired. **Transfer:** Transfer adviser, college fairs on campus for students transferring to 4-year colleges.

**Contact.**   E-mail: dan.slater@ccbc.edu
Phone: (724) 775-8561 ext. 330 Toll-free number: (800) 335-0222 ext. 330 Fax: (724) 728-7599
Daniel Slater, Registrar, Community College of Beaver County, One Campus Drive, Monaca, PA 15061-2588

## Community College of Philadelphia
**Philadelphia, Pennsylvania**              **CB member**
**www.ccp.edu**                             **CB code: 2682**

♦  Public 2-year community college
♦  Commuter campus in very large city

**General.** Founded in 1965. Regionally accredited. Regional centers located in northeast, northwest, and west Philadelphia. Many additional temporary facilities located throughout city. **Enrollment:** 17,339 degree-seeking undergraduates. **Degrees:** 1,517 associate awarded. **ROTC:** Army. **Calendar:** Semester, extensive summer session. **Full-time faculty:** 407 total; 25% minority, 49% women. **Part-time faculty:** 646 total; 32% minority, 47% women. **Class size:** 36% < 20, 64% 20-39, less than 1% 40-49.

**Student profile.** Among degree-seeking undergraduates, 78% enrolled in a transfer program, 22% enrolled in a vocational program, 3,963 enrolled as first-time, first-year students, 559 transferred in from other institutions.

| Part-time: | 67% | Asian American: | 8% |
|---|---|---|---|
| Out-of-state: | 1% | Hispanic American: | 6% |
| Women: | 67% | 25 or older: | 50% |
| African American: | 47% | | |

**Transfer out. Colleges most students transferred to 2007:** Temple University, Drexel University, St. Joseph's University, Holy Family College, Chestnut Hill College.

**Basis for selection.** Open admission, but selective for some programs. Special requirements for health, music, art and some technical programs. Audition required for music program; portfolio required for art program.

**High school preparation.** One chemistry, 2 math required of health program applicants.

**2007-2008 Annual costs.** Tuition/fees: $4,410; $8,160 out-of-district; $11,910 out-of-state. Per-credit charge: $115 in-district; $230 out-of-district; $345 out-of-state. Books/supplies: $545. Personal expenses: $856.

**2007-2008 Financial aid.** All financial aid based on need. 57% of total undergraduate aid awarded as scholarships/grants, 43% as loans/jobs. Need-based aid available for part-time students. Work-study available nights, weekends and for part-time students.

**Application procedures. Admission:** No deadline. $20 fee. Application may be submitted online. Admission notification on a rolling basis. **Financial aid:** Closing date 5/1. FAFSA, institutional form required. Applicants notified on a rolling basis.

**Academics. Special study options:** Accelerated study, distance learning, dual enrollment of high school students, ESL, honors, internships, study abroad, weekend college. License preparation in dental hygiene, nursing, radiology, real estate. **Credit/placement by examination:** AP, CLEP, institutional tests. 30 credit hours maximum toward associate degree. **Support services:** GED preparation and test center, learning center, pre-admission summer program, reduced course load, remedial instruction, tutoring.

**Majors. Area/ethnic studies:** Women's. **Business:** General, accounting, administrative services, business admin, fashion, international marketing, office/clerical, operations, real estate, sales/distribution. **Communications technology:** Recording arts. **Computer sciences:** General, applications programming, networking, programming, security, system admin, webmaster. **Education:** General, business, secondary. **Engineering:** General. **Engineering technology:** Architectural, biomedical, CAD/CADD, computer, computer systems, construction, electrical, environmental. **English:** Speech/rhetoric. **Family/consumer sciences:** Child care, institutional food production. **Foreign languages:** Sign language interpretation. **Health:** Clinical lab technology, dental hygiene, medical assistant, medical radiologic technology/radiation therapy, medical records technology, mental health services, nursing (RN), respiratory therapy technology. **Legal studies:** Paralegal. **Liberal arts:** Arts/sciences. **Math:** General. **Personal/culinary services:** Chef training, restaurant/catering. **Physical sciences:** General. **Protective services:** Fire safety technology, forensics, police science. **Public administration:** Human services. **Science technology:** Chemical. **Social sciences:** Geography. **Visual/performing arts:** Art, commercial photography, commercial/advertising art, dramatic, music performance.

**Most popular majors.** Business/marketing 16%, health sciences 15%, liberal arts 33%, public administration/social services 7%.

**Computing on campus.** 994 workstations in library, student center. Commuter students can connect to campus network. Helpline available.

**Student life. Freshman orientation:** Available. Preregistration for classes offered. **Activities:** Jazz band, choral groups, dance, drama, music ensembles, radio station, student government, student newspaper, TV station, Christian Coalition, Newman club, Black Student Congress, Latin American student organization, Phi Theta Kappa, Muslim student association, Vietnamese student organization, Asian-American association.

**Athletics. Intercollegiate:** Baseball M, basketball, cross-country, soccer M, softball W, volleyball W. **Intramural:** Basketball, soccer, softball, tennis, track and field, volleyball. **Team name:** Colonials.

**Student services.** Adult student services, career counseling, student employment services, financial aid counseling, health services, on-campus daycare, personal counseling, placement for graduates, women's services. **Physically disabled:** Services for visually, speech, hearing impaired. **Transfer:** Transfer adviser, college fairs on campus for students transferring to 4-year colleges.

**Contact.** E-mail: admissions@ccp.edu
Phone: (215) 751-8010
Luke Kasim, Director of Recruitment and Admissions, Community College of Philadelphia, 1700 Spring Garden Street, Philadelphia, PA 19130-3991

## Consolidated School of Business: Lancaster

**Lancaster, Pennsylvania**
www.csb.edu                                          **CB code: 2240**

- For-profit 2-year business college
- Commuter campus in small city
- Interview required

**General.** Founded in 1986. Accredited by ACICS. Additional campus in York. **Enrollment:** 166 degree-seeking undergraduates. **Degrees:** 66 associate awarded. **Location:** 85 miles from Philadelphia, 35 miles from Harrisburg. **Calendar:** Continuous. **Full-time faculty:** 15 total. **Part-time faculty:** 5 total.

**Basis for selection.** Open admission.

**High school preparation.** Recommended computer application coursework for accelerated or advanced placement.

**2007-2008 Annual costs.** Tuition/fees: $11,500. Books/supplies: $1,500.

**Financial aid. Need-based:** Need-based aid available for part-time students.

**Application procedures. Admission:** No deadline. $25 fee. Admission notification on a rolling basis. **Financial aid:** No deadline. FAFSA required. Applicants notified on a rolling basis.

**Academics.** Programs consist of 3 core elements: business English, computer applications and approximately 34 credit hours of specialty courses. Curriculum developed with area employer's input to maximize job placement. **Special study options:** Accelerated study, internships. **Credit/placement by examination:** CLEP. **Support services:** Study skills assistance, tutoring.

**Majors. Business:** Accounting, accounting technology, administrative services, business admin, executive assistant, office technology. **Computer sciences:** Data entry, data processing, web page design, webmaster, word processing. **Health:** Insurance coding, insurance specialist, management/clinical assistant, medical records admin, medical secretary, medical transcription, office admin, office assistant, office computer specialist, receptionist, ward clerk. **Legal studies:** Legal secretary.

**Computing on campus.** 125 workstations in library.

**Student life. Freshman orientation:** Mandatory.

**Student services.** Adult student services, career counseling, student employment services, financial aid counseling, placement for graduates. **Physically disabled:** Services for speech, hearing impaired. **Transfer:** Pre-admission transcript evaluation for new students.

**Contact.** E-mail: admissions@csb.edu
Phone: (717) 394-6211 Toll-free number: (800) 541-8298
Fax: (717) 394-6213
Consolidated School of Business: Lancaster, 2124 Ambassador Circle, Lancaster, PA 17603

## Consolidated School of Business: York

**York, Pennsylvania**
www.csb.edu                                          **CB code: 2242**

- For-profit 2-year business college
- Commuter campus in small city
- Interview required

**General.** Founded in 1986. Accredited by ACICS. Additional campus in Lancaster. **Enrollment:** 140 degree-seeking undergraduates. **Degrees:** 86 associate awarded. **Location:** 28 miles from Harrisburg, 33 miles from Baltimore. **Calendar:** Continuous. **Full-time faculty:** 26 total; 8% have terminal degrees, 4% minority, 81% women. **Part-time faculty:** 6 total; 17% have terminal degrees, 83% women.

**Basis for selection.** Open admission. Interview and tour must be completed before acceptance issued. All financial aid matters must be satisfied before classes begin.

**2007-2008 Annual costs.** Tuition/fees: $11,850. Pre-evaluation/placement testing fee $50. Books/supplies: $900.

**Financial aid. Need-based:** Need-based aid available for part-time students.

**Application procedures. Admission:** No deadline. $25 fee. Admission notification on a rolling basis. **Financial aid:** No deadline. FAFSA required. Applicants notified on a rolling basis.

**Academics.** Programs consist of 3 core elements: business English, computer applications and approximately 34 credit hours of specialty courses. Curriculum developed with area employers' input to maximize job placement. **Special study options:** Accelerated study, internships. **Credit/placement by examination:** CLEP. **Support services:** Study skills assistance, tutoring.

**Majors. Business:** Accounting, accounting technology, administrative services, business admin, executive assistant, office technology, tourism promotion, tourism/travel, travel services. **Computer sciences:** Data processing, LAN/WAN management, web page design, webmaster, word processing. **Health:** Insurance coding, insurance specialist, management/clinical assistant, medical secretary, medical transcription, office computer specialist, receptionist, ward clerk. **Legal studies:** Legal secretary, paralegal.

**Student life. Freshman orientation:** Mandatory.

**Student services.** Adult student services, career counseling, student employment services, placement for graduates. **Transfer:** Pre-admission transcript evaluation for new students.

**Contact.** E-mail: admissions@csb.edu
Phone: (717) 764-9550 Toll-free number: (800) 520-0691
Robert Safran, Vice President of Administration, Director of Admissions, Consolidated School of Business: York, York City Business and Industry Park, York, PA 17404

## Dean Institute of Technology
### Pittsburgh, Pennsylvania
### www.deantech.edu
**CB code: 2199**

- For-profit 2-year technical college
- Commuter campus in large city
- Interview required

**General.** Founded in 1948. Accredited by ACCSCT. **Enrollment:** 207 degree-seeking undergraduates. **Degrees:** 51 associate awarded. **Location:** 2 miles from downtown. **Calendar:** Quarter, extensive summer session. **Full-time faculty:** 10 total. **Part-time faculty:** 10 total.

**Student profile.** Among degree-seeking undergraduates, 66 enrolled as first-time, first-year students.

| | | | |
|---|---|---|---|
| Part-time: | 33% | Women: | 3% |
| Out-of-state: | 2% | | |

**Transfer out.** 91% of students enrolled in the transfer program go on to 4-year colleges. **Colleges most students transferred to 2007:** Point Park College.

**Basis for selection.** Open admission.

**2008-2009 Annual costs.** Tuition/fees (projected): $18,550. Per-credit charge: $215. Books/supplies: $709. Personal expenses: $1,440.

**Financial aid. Need-based:** Need-based aid available for part-time students.

**Application procedures. Admission:** No deadline. $50 fee. Admission notification on a rolling basis. Must reply by May 1 or within 3 week(s) if notified thereafter. **Financial aid:** Closing date 8/1. FAFSA required. Applicants notified on a rolling basis; must reply within 8 week(s) of notification.

**Academics. Special study options:** Cooperative education. **Credit/placement by examination:** CLEP, institutional tests. 12 credit hours maximum toward associate degree. **Support services:** Tutoring.

**Majors. Construction:** Power transmission. **Mechanic/repair:** Heating/ac/refrig.

**Computing on campus.** 30 workstations in computer center.

**Student services.** Career counseling, personal counseling, placement for graduates, veterans' counselor. **Transfer:** Transfer adviser for students transferring to 4-year colleges.

**Contact.** E-mail: info@deantech.edu
Phone: (412) 531-4433 Fax: (412) 531-4435
Richard Ali, Admissions Director, Dean Institute of Technology, 1501 West Liberty Avenue, Pittsburgh, PA 15226

## Douglas Education Center
### Monessen, Pennsylvania
### www.douglas-school.com
**CB code: 3288**

- For-profit 2-year visual arts and business college
- Small town
- Interview required

**General.** Accredited by ACICS. **Enrollment:** 140 degree-seeking undergraduates. **Degrees:** 144 associate awarded. **Location:** 25 miles from Pittsburgh. **Calendar:** Semester, extensive summer session. **Full-time faculty:** 12 total. **Part-time faculty:** 8 total.

**Basis for selection.** Open admission. Portfolios recommended.

**2007-2008 Annual costs.** All-inclusive associate, certificate and diploma programs in art, business, cosmetology and medical fields available from $3,235 to $35,750. Books/supplies: $2,000.

**Financial aid.** All financial aid based on need. Need-based aid available for part-time students. Work-study available nights, weekends and for part-time students.

**Application procedures. Admission:** $50 fee. Application may be submitted online. Admission notification on a rolling basis. **Financial aid:** No deadline. Applicants notified on a rolling basis.

**Academics. Special study options:** Accelerated study, double major, internships, liberal arts/career combination. **Credit/placement by examination:** CLEP. **Support services:** GED preparation, learning center, reduced course load, remedial instruction, study skills assistance, tutoring.

**Majors. Business:** Business admin, executive assistant. **Communications technology:** Animation/special effects. **Computer sciences:** Computer graphics, webmaster. **Health:** Medical assistant, medical secretary, office admin, office assistant. **Visual/performing arts:** General, commercial/advertising art.

**Student life. Freshman orientation:** Available.

**Student services.** Adult student services, alcohol/substance abuse counseling, career counseling, services for economically disadvantaged, student employment services, financial aid counseling, placement for graduates. **Transfer:** Pre-admission transcript evaluation for new students. Transfer center for students transferring to 4-year colleges.

**Contact.** E-mail: dec@douglas-school.com
Phone: (724) 684-3684 ext. 100 Toll-free number: (800) 416-6013 ext. 100
Sherry Walters, Admissions Director, Douglas Education Center, 130 Seventh Street, Monessen, PA 15062

## DuBois Business College
### DuBois, Pennsylvania
### www.dbcollege.com
**CB code: 3886**

- For-profit 2-year business and technical college
- Commuter campus in large town
- Interview required

**General.** Founded in 1885. Accredited by ACICS. **Enrollment:** 265 degree-seeking undergraduates. **Degrees:** 125 associate awarded. **Location:** 100 miles from Pittsburgh. **Calendar:** Quarter, extensive summer session. **Full-time faculty:** 15 total. **Part-time faculty:** 2 total. **Partnerships:** Formal partnerships with 32 Tech Prep high schools.

**Student profile.**

| | | | |
|---|---|---|---|
| Out-of-state: | 1% | Live on campus: | 40% |
| 25 or older: | 40% | | |

**Basis for selection.** Open admission.

**High school preparation.** Courses in shorthand, accounting, computer, typing, law, psychology, and speech recommended.

**2007-2008 Annual costs.** Tuition/fees: $9,000. Per-credit charge: $190. Books/supplies: $1,000.

**Application procedures. Admission:** No deadline. $25 fee, may be waived for applicants with need. Application may be submitted online. Admission notification on a rolling basis. Must reply by May 1 or within 5 week(s) if notified thereafter. **Financial aid:** Closing date 8/1. FAFSA required. Applicants notified on a rolling basis.

**Academics. Special study options:** Cooperative education, double major, internships, liberal arts/career combination, study abroad. **Credit/placement by examination:** AP, CLEP, institutional tests. **Support services:** Reduced course load, remedial instruction, tutoring.

**Majors. Business:** General, accounting, administrative services, business admin. **Health:** Medical secretary. **Legal studies:** Legal secretary.

**Computing on campus.** 100 workstations in library, computer center.

**Student life. Freshman orientation:** Mandatory. **Housing:** Single-sex dorms available. $225 deposit. **Activities:** Student government, student newspaper, student association.

**Athletics. Intercollegiate:** Volleyball. **Intramural:** Volleyball.

**Student services.** Adult student services, career counseling, student employment services, financial aid counseling, personal counseling, placement

for graduates, veterans' counselor. **Physically disabled:** Services for visually, speech, hearing impaired. **Transfer:** Transfer adviser for students transferring to 4-year colleges.

**Contact.** E-mail: admissions@dbcollege.com
Phone: (814) 371-6920 Toll-free number: (800) 692-6213
Fax: (814) 371-3974
Director of Admissions, DuBois Business College, One Beaver Drive, DuBois, PA 15801

## DuBois Business College: Huntingdon
### Huntingdon, Pennsylvania
www.dbcollege.com        **CB code: 3290**

▶ For-profit 2-year business college
▶ Small town

**General.** Accredited by ACICS. **Enrollment:** 70 degree-seeking undergraduates. **Degrees:** 15 associate awarded. **Calendar:** Continuous. **Full-time faculty:** 5 total. **Part-time faculty:** 2 total.

**Basis for selection.** Open admission.

**2007-2008 Annual costs.** Tuition/fees: $9,000. Per-credit charge: $190.

**Application procedures. Admission:** No deadline. $25 fee. Admission notification on a rolling basis. **Financial aid:** Closing date 8/1.

**Academics. Credit/placement by examination:** CLEP.

**Majors. Business:** General, accounting. **Health:** Medical secretary. **Legal studies:** Legal secretary.

**Contact.** Phone: (814) 371-6920
Lisa Doty, Admissions Director, DuBois Business College: Huntingdon, 1001 Moore Street, Huntingdon, PA 16652

## DuBois Business College: Oil City
### Oil City, Pennsylvania
www.dbcollege.com        **CB code: 3292**

▶ For-profit 2-year branch campus and business college
▶ Large town

**General.** Accredited by ACICS. **Enrollment:** 85 degree-seeking undergraduates. **Degrees:** 45 associate awarded. **Location:** 90 miles from Pittsburgh. **Calendar:** Quarter. **Full-time faculty:** 5 total. **Part-time faculty:** 2 total.

**Basis for selection.** Open admission.

**2007-2008 Annual costs.** Tuition/fees: $9,000. Per-credit charge: $190. Books/supplies: $2,500.

**Application procedures. Admission:** No deadline. $25 fee. Admission notification on a rolling basis. **Financial aid:** FAFSA required.

**Academics. Credit/placement by examination:** CLEP.

**Majors. Business:** Accounting, administrative services. **Computer sciences:** Information systems. **Health:** Medical secretary. **Legal studies:** Legal secretary.

**Contact.** Phone: (814) 677-1322
Lisa Doty, Director of Admissions, DuBois Business College: Oil City, 701 East Third Street, Oil City, PA 16301

## Erie Business Center
### Erie, Pennsylvania
www.eriebc.edu        **CB code: 2215**

▶ For-profit 2-year business college
▶ Commuter campus in small city

**General.** Founded in 1884. Accredited by ACICS. **Enrollment:** 325 degree-seeking undergraduates. **Degrees:** 100 associate awarded. **Location:** 95 miles from Cleveland. **Calendar:** Trimester, extensive summer session. **Full-time faculty:** 17 total. **Part-time faculty:** 13 total.

**Basis for selection.** Open admission.

**2007-2008 Annual costs.** Tuition/fees: $10,800. Per-credit charge: $328. Books/supplies: $800.

**Financial aid. Need-based:** Need-based aid available for part-time students.

**Application procedures. Admission:** No deadline. $25 fee, may be waived for applicants with need. Application may be submitted online. Admission notification on a rolling basis. **Financial aid:** No deadline. FAFSA required.

**Academics. Credit/placement by examination:** CLEP. **Support services:** Reduced course load, study skills assistance, tutoring.

**Majors. Business:** Accounting, administrative services, marketing, tourism/travel. **Computer sciences:** Computer graphics, networking, programming. **Health:** Medical assistant, medical secretary, medical transcription. **Legal studies:** Legal secretary, paralegal.

**Computing on campus.** Online library available.

**Student life. Freshman orientation:** Mandatory, $25 fee. Preregistration for classes offered. **Activities:** Drama, musical theater.

**Student services.** Student employment services, financial aid counseling, placement for graduates.

**Contact.** E-mail: admissions@eriebc.edu
Phone: (814) 456-7504 ext. 102 Toll-free number: (800) 352-3743 ext. 102
Fax: (814) 459-3701
Denise Potter, Admissions Administrator, Erie Business Center, 246 West Ninth Street, Erie, PA 16501

## Erie Business Center South
### New Castle, Pennsylvania
www.eriebc.edu/newcastle        **CB code: 2577**

▶ For-profit 2-year branch campus and business college
▶ Commuter campus in small city
▶ Application essay, interview required

**General.** Accredited by ACICS. **Enrollment:** 67 degree-seeking undergraduates; 8 non-degree-seeking students. **Degrees:** 30 associate awarded. **Location:** 60 miles from Pittsburgh. **Calendar:** Trimester. **Full-time faculty:** 2 total; 100% have terminal degrees. **Part-time faculty:** 2 total; 50% have terminal degrees, 50% women. **Partnerships:** Formal partnerships with Laurel HIgh School, Lincoln High School, Neshannock High School, West Middlesex High School, Beaver Falls High School, Union High School, Seneca Valley High School.

**Student profile.** Among degree-seeking undergraduates, 22 enrolled as first-time, first-year students, 30 transferred in from other institutions.

**Transfer out.** Colleges most students transferred to 2007: Thiel College, Slippery Rock University, Edinboro University.

**Basis for selection.** Open admission. **Homeschooled:** Transcript of courses and grades, state high school equivalency certificate, interview required.

**2007-2008 Annual costs.** $12,525 tuition for full two-year associate degree program. Books/supplies: $900. Personal expenses: $1,107.

**Application procedures. Admission:** No deadline. $25 fee. Application may be submitted online.

**Academics. Special study options:** Internships. **Credit/placement by examination:** CLEP. **Support services:** Reduced course load, tutoring.

**Majors. Business:** Accounting, business admin, marketing, tourism/travel. **Computer sciences:** General. **Health:** Medical records admin, medical transcription. **Legal studies:** Legal secretary.

**Computing on campus.** Online library available.

**Student life. Freshman orientation:** Mandatory. Preregistration for classes offered. **Activities:** Student government, student newspaper.

**Student services.** Career counseling, student employment services, financial aid counseling, placement for graduates. **Transfer:** Pre-admission transcript evaluation for new students. Transfer adviser for students transferring to 4-year colleges.

**Contact.** E-mail: hallr@eriebcs.com
Phone: (724) 658-9066 Toll-free number: (800) 722-6227
Fax: (724) 658-3083
Rose Hall, Admissions Coordinator, Erie Business Center South, 170 Cascade Galleria, New Castle, PA 16101

## Erie Institute of Technology
**Erie, Pennsylvania**
**www.erieit.org**                           **CB code: 2284**

- For-profit 2-year technical college
- Small city

**General.** Accredited by ACCSCT. **Enrollment:** 190 degree-seeking undergraduates. **Degrees:** 47 associate awarded. **Calendar:** Semester. **Full-time faculty:** 20 total. **Part-time faculty:** 4 total.

**Basis for selection.** Open admission, but selective for some programs. Math requirement for some programs.

**2007-2008 Annual costs.** Tuition/fees: $9,920.

**Application procedures. Admission:** No deadline. $25 fee. Admission notification on a rolling basis.

**Academics. Credit/placement by examination:** CLEP.

**Majors. Computer sciences:** General. **Engineering technology:** Electrical.

**Contact.** Phone: (814) 868-9900 Toll-free number: (866) 868-3743 Fax: (814) 868-9977
Brian Boyce, Director of Admissions, Erie Institute of Technology, 940 Millcreek Mall, Erie, PA 16565

## Harcum College
**Bryn Mawr, Pennsylvania**                 **CB member**
**www.harcum.edu**                          **CB code: 2287**

- Private 2-year junior college
- Commuter campus in large town
- Application essay required

**General.** Founded in 1915. Regionally accredited. **Enrollment:** 832 degree-seeking undergraduates. **Degrees:** 218 associate awarded. **Location:** 10 miles from Philadelphia. **Calendar:** Semester, limited summer session. **Full-time faculty:** 36 total. **Part-time faculty:** 92 total. **Class size:** 87% < 20, 12% 20-39, less than 1% 40-49. **Special facilities:** Veterinary services building, physical therapist assistant lab, dental clinic, nursing lab, radiology lab.

**Student profile.**

| | | | |
|---|---|---|---|
| Out-of-state: | 10% | Live on campus: | 17% |
| 25 or older: | 40% | | |

**Transfer out. Colleges most students transferred to 2007:** Cabrini College, West Chester University, Temple University, Rosemont College, Widener University.

**Basis for selection.** School record of primary importance. Writing sample required. 750 SAT (exclusive of Writing) and/or 2.0 GPA required. Nursing, dental hygiene, physical therapy assistant, veterinary technology require 900 SAT (exclusive of Writing) and 2.5 GPA. SAT or ACT recommended. Interview required of dental hygiene, radiology technician, nursing and neurodiagnostic technician programs; recommended for all others. **Adult students:** SAT/ACT scores not required if out of high school 3 year(s) or more. **Learning Disabled:** Must provide documentation of disability to ensure proper accommodations are made.

**High school preparation.** Recommended units include English 4, mathematics 2, social studies 2, history 2, science 2 and academic electives 2. Required units for veterinary technnology, dental hygiene, and physical therapy assistant programs include 2 algebra, geometry, biology, chemistry. 1 unit biology and algebra required for dental assisting program. 2 algebra, biology, and chemistry required for medical laboratory technology.

**2007-2008 Annual costs.** Tuition/fees: $16,200. Per-credit charge: $533. Room/board: $7,480. Books/supplies: $1,200. Personal expenses: $2,792.

**2007-2008 Financial aid. Need-based:** 97% of total undergraduate aid awarded as scholarships/grants, 3% as loans/jobs. Need-based aid available for part-time students. Work-study available nights, weekends and for part-time students. **Non-need-based:** Scholarships awarded for academics, leadership.

**Application procedures. Admission:** Priority date 5/1; no deadline. $25 fee, may be waived for applicants with need. Application may be submitted online. Admission notification on a rolling basis. **Financial aid:** Priority date 4/15; no closing date. FAFSA, institutional form required. Applicants notified on a rolling basis starting 3/1; must reply within 3 week(s) of notification.

**Academics.** 86% of academic programs offered have internship/practicum component. **Special study options:** Accelerated study, cooperative education, distance learning, double major, dual enrollment of high school students, ESL, independent study, internships, liberal arts/career combination, study abroad. License preparation in dental hygiene, nursing, physical therapy, radiology. **Credit/placement by examination:** AP, CLEP, institutional tests. 20 credit hours maximum toward associate degree. Maximum of 30 credits total for transfer credits, life experience, challenge examination, and CLEP. **Support services:** Learning center, pre-admission summer program, reduced course load, remedial instruction, study skills assistance, tutoring.

**Majors. Agriculture:** Animal sciences. **Business:** General, business admin, fashion, sales/distribution. **Education:** Early childhood. **Health:** Clinical lab technology, dental assistant, dental hygiene, health services, physical therapy assistant, radiologic technology/medical imaging, veterinary technology/assistant. **Liberal arts:** Arts/sciences. **Protective services:** Law enforcement admin. **Psychology:** General. **Visual/performing arts:** Fashion design, interior design.

**Most popular majors.** Business/marketing 8%, education 9%, health sciences 63%, visual/performing arts 14%.

**Computing on campus.** 86 workstations in dormitories, library, computer center, student center. Commuter students can connect to campus network. Online course registration, online library, helpline available.

**Student life. Freshman orientation:** Available. Preregistration for classes offered. One-day introduction to campus services, separate evening orientation for Lifelong Learners. **Housing:** Guaranteed on-campus for all undergraduates. Coed dorms, special housing for disabled available. $200 deposit. **Activities:** International student organizations, literary magazine, student government, student newspaper, ebony club, Campus Ambassadors, animal technician student organization, Phi Theta Kappa, peer mentors, community service club, dental assisting club, Association for the Education of Young Children, physical therapy assistant club.

**Athletics.** NJCAA. **Intercollegiate:** Basketball, volleyball W. **Team name:** Bears.

**Student services.** Adult student services, alcohol/substance abuse counseling, career counseling, services for economically disadvantaged, student employment services, financial aid counseling, health services, minority student services, on-campus daycare, personal counseling, placement for graduates, veterans' counselor, women's services. **Physically disabled:** Services for visually, speech, hearing impaired. **Transfer:** Re-entry adviser, pre-admission transcript evaluation for new students. Transfer center, transfer adviser, college fairs on campus for students transferring to 4-year colleges.

**Contact.** E-mail: journey@harcum.edu
Phone: (610) 526-6050 Toll-free number: (800) 345-2600
Fax: (610) 526-6147
Nicola DiFronzo-Heitzer, Dean of Admissions, Harcum College, 750 Montgomery Avenue, Bryn Mawr, PA 19010-3476

## Harrisburg Area Community College
**Harrisburg, Pennsylvania**                 **CB member**
**www.hacc.edu**                             **CB code: 2309**

- Public 2-year community college
- Commuter campus in small city

**General.** Founded in 1964. Regionally accredited. County high schools utilized for credit-course offerings. Availability varies by semester. **Enrollment:** 11,180 degree-seeking undergraduates; 7,660 non-degree-seeking students. **Degrees:** 1,518 associate awarded. **ROTC:** Army. **Location:** 90 miles from Philadelphia, 180 miles from New York City. **Calendar:** Semester, limited summer session. **Full-time faculty:** 302 total; 16% have terminal degrees, 13% minority, 61% women. **Part-time faculty:** 867 total; less than 1% have terminal degrees, 7% minority, 57% women. **Class size:** 50% < 20, 48% 20-39, 1% 40-49, less than 1% 50-99.

**Student profile.** Among degree-seeking undergraduates, 27% enrolled in a transfer program, 73% enrolled in a vocational program, 1,929 enrolled as first-time, first-year students, 1,535 transferred in from other institutions.

| | | | |
|---|---|---|---|
| Part-time: | 67% | Asian American: | 3% |
| Out-of-state: | 1% | Hispanic American: | 6% |
| Women: | 71% | International: | 1% |
| African American: | 10% | 25 or older: | 42% |

**Transfer out.** 67% of students enrolled in the transfer program go on to 4-year colleges. **Colleges most students transferred to 2007:** Penn State University, Shippensburg University, Millersville University, Elizabethtown College, York College.

**Basis for selection.** Open admission, but selective for some programs. Special requirements for allied health programs and chef's apprenticeship. ACT required for allied health programs, score report by February 1. Interview required for allied health, and chef apprenticeship programs; essay required for chef apprenticeship program. **Homeschooled:** Statement describing homeschool structure and mission, transcript of courses and grades, letter of recommendation (nonparent) required.

**2007-2008 Annual costs.** Tuition/fees: $3,000; $5,640 out-of-district; $8,280 out-of-state. Per-credit charge: $83 in-district; $166 out-of-district; $249 out-of-state. Books/supplies: $1,560. Personal expenses: $1,600.

**2006-2007 Financial aid.** **Need-based:** 1,438 full-time freshmen applied for aid; 960 were judged to have need; 863 of these received aid. Average need met was 89%. Average scholarship/grant was $1,621; average loan $2,588. 29% of total undergraduate aid awarded as scholarships/grants, 71% as loans/jobs. Need-based aid available for part-time students. Work-study available for part-time students. **Non-need-based:** Awarded to 86 full-time undergraduates, including 8 freshmen. Scholarships awarded for academics. **Additional information:** Federal work study community service positions available.

**Application procedures.** **Admission:** No deadline. $35 fee, may be waived for applicants with need. Application may be submitted online. Admission notification on a rolling basis. Must reply by May 1 or within 5 week(s) if notified thereafter. **Financial aid:** Priority date 3/15; no closing date. FAFSA, institutional form required. Applicants notified on a rolling basis starting 6/1.

**Academics.** **Special study options:** Distance learning, double major, dual enrollment of high school students, ESL, honors, independent study, internships, student-designed major, study abroad, weekend college. Dual admissions with 6 United Negro College Fund institutions, with Penn State Harrisburg Capital College, and with Cheney University of Pennsylvania. License preparation in dental hygiene, nursing, paramedic, radiology, real estate. **Credit/placement by examination:** AP, CLEP, IB, institutional tests. 30 credit hours maximum toward associate degree. **Support services:** GED preparation and test center, learning center, pre-admission summer program, reduced course load, remedial instruction, study skills assistance, tutoring, writing center.

**Majors. Agriculture:** Agribusiness operations. **Biology:** General. **Business:** General, accounting technology, accounting/business management, administrative services, banking/financial services, business admin, hospitality admin, hotel/motel admin, real estate, restaurant/food services, retailing, sales/distribution, small business admin, tourism/travel. **Communications:** Media studies. **Computer sciences:** General, computer science, information technology, networking, web page design. **Conservation:** Environmental science, environmental studies. **Construction:** General, building inspection, electrician, lineworker. **Education:** Early childhood, elementary, secondary. **Engineering:** General. **Engineering technology:** Architectural, civil, construction, electrical, mechanical. **Family/consumer sciences:** Institutional food production. **Health:** Cardiovascular technology, clinical lab technology, dental hygiene, dietetics, EMT paramedic, health care admin, health services admin, medical assistant, medical records admin, nuclear medical technology, nursing (RN), radiologic technology/medical imaging, respiratory therapy technology, sonography, surgical technology. **Legal studies:** Paralegal. **Math:** General. **Mechanic/repair:** Automotive, computer, heating/ac/refrig, industrial. **Personal/culinary services:** Chef training. **Physical sciences:** General, chemistry. **Protective services:** Criminalistics, firefighting, law enforcement admin, police science. **Psychology:** General. **Public administration:** Human services, social work. **Social sciences:** General, international relations. **Visual/performing arts:** General, art, crafts, design, dramatic, graphic design, music management, photography.

**Most popular majors.** Business/marketing 26%, education 10%, health sciences 18%, liberal arts 9%, security/protective services 7%, visual/performing arts 7%.

**Computing on campus.** 280 workstations in library, computer center, student center. Commuter students can connect to campus network. Online course registration, online library, helpline, wireless network available.

**Student life.** **Freshman orientation:** Mandatory. Preregistration for classes offered. **Activities:** Jazz band, choral groups, drama, music ensembles, musical theater, student government, student newspaper, Allies, African American student association, Christian student fellowship, international awareness, Student Environmental Action Coalition, Students for a Free Tibet, Phi Beta Lambda.

**Athletics. Intercollegiate:** Basketball, soccer M, tennis, volleyball W. **Intramural:** Basketball, soccer, swimming, tennis, volleyball.

**Student services.** Career counseling, student employment services, financial aid counseling, minority student services, on-campus daycare, personal counseling, placement for graduates, veterans' counselor. **Physically disabled:** Services for visually, hearing impaired. **Transfer:** Transfer adviser, college fairs on campus for students transferring to 4-year colleges.

**Contact.** E-mail: admit@hacc.edu
Phone: (717) 780-2400 Toll-free number: (800) 222-4222
Fax: (717) 236-7674
Jennifer Bucher, Director of Admissions, Harrisburg Area Community College, One HACC Drive, Cooper 206, Harrisburg, PA 17110-2999

## Hussian School of Art
### Philadelphia, Pennsylvania
www.hussianart.edu                     CB code: 7309

- For-profit 2-year visual arts and technical college
- Commuter campus in very large city
- Interview required

**General.** Founded in 1946. Accredited by ACCSCT. Associates degree is a 4-year, full-time program. **Enrollment:** 142 degree-seeking undergraduates. **Degrees:** 22 associate awarded. **Calendar:** Semester. **Full-time faculty:** 3 total; 33% women. **Part-time faculty:** 23 total; 13% have terminal degrees, 4% minority, 22% women. **Class size:** 31% < 20, 69% 20-39. **Special facilities:** Air-brush and computer graphics facilities.

**Student profile.** Among degree-seeking undergraduates, 100% enrolled in a vocational program, 48 enrolled as first-time, first-year students, 1 transferred in from other institutions.

| | | | |
|---|---|---|---|
| Out-of-state: | 10% | 25 or older: | 2% |
| Women: | 30% | | |

**Basis for selection.** Interview, portfolio, and talent/ability most important. Portfolio required.

**High school preparation.** High school art or other art training recommended.

**2008-2009 Annual costs.** Tuition/fees (projected): $11,550. Supply costs for freshmen are additional; estimated at $375. Books/supplies: $725. Personal expenses: $2,196.

**Application procedures.** **Admission:** No deadline. $25 fee, may be waived for applicants with need. Admission notification on a rolling basis. **Financial aid:** No deadline. FAFSA, institutional form required. Applicants notified on a rolling basis starting 2/15; must reply within 3 week(s) of notification.

**Academics.** Second-semester freshmen must earn GPA of 2.0 or above to continue in good standing. Associate's degree is a 4-year, full-time program. **Special study options:** Internships. **Credit/placement by examination:** CLEP. **Support services:** Pre-admission summer program, tutoring.

**Majors. Visual/performing arts:** Commercial/advertising art, graphic design.

**Computing on campus.** PC or laptop required. 60 workstations in computer center. Wireless network available.

**Student life.** **Freshman orientation:** Available. Preregistration for classes offered. Morning program held 2 weeks prior to official start of classes.

**Student services.** Career counseling, financial aid counseling, placement for graduates. **Transfer:** Pre-admission transcript evaluation for new students.

**Contact.** E-mail: info@hussianart.edu
Phone: (215) 981-0900 Fax: (215) 864-9115
Lynne Wartman, Admissions Director, Hussian School of Art, 1118 Market Street, Philadelphia, PA 19107

## ITT Technical Institute: Bensalem
### Bensalem, Pennsylvania
www.itt-tech.edu

- For-profit 2-year technical college
- Small city

**General.** Accredited by ACICS. **Calendar:** Quarter.

**Annual costs/financial aid.** Tuition varies by program, $260-$368 per credit hour.

**Contact.** Phone: (215) 244-8871
Director of Recruitment, 3330 Tillman Drive, Bensalem, PA 19020

## ITT Technical Institute: King of Prussia
### King of Prussia, Pennsylvania

- For-profit 2-year visual arts and technical college
- Large town

**General.** Accredited by ACICS. **Calendar:** Quarter.

**Contact.** 760 Moore Road, Suite 150, King of Prussia, PA 19406-1212

## ITT Technical Institute: Mechanicsburg
### Mechanicsburg, Pennsylvania
www.itt-tech.edu          CB code: 2730

- For-profit 2-year technical college
- Commuter campus in small town

**General.** Accredited by ACICS. **Calendar:** Quarter.

**Annual costs/financial aid.** Tuition varies by program, $260-$368 per credit hour.

**Contact.** Phone: (717) 691-9263
Director of Recruitment, 5020 Louise Drive, Mechanicsburg, PA 17055

## ITT Technical Institute: Monroeville
### Monroeville, Pennsylvania
www.itt-tech.edu          CB code: 2735

- For-profit 2-year technical college
- Commuter campus in large town

**General.** Accredited by ACICS. **Calendar:** Quarter.

**Annual costs/financial aid.** Tuition varies by program, $260-$368 per credit hour.

**Contact.** Phone: (412) 856-5920
Director of Recruitment, 105 Mall Boulevard, Suite 200E, Monroeville, PA 15146

## ITT Technical Institute: Pittsburgh
### Pittsburgh, Pennsylvania
www.itt-tech.edu          CB code: 2745

- For-profit 2-year technical college
- Commuter campus in large city

**General.** Accredited by ACICS. **Calendar:** Quarter.

**Annual costs/financial aid.** Tuition varies by program, $260-$368 per credit hour.

**Contact.** Phone: (412) 937-9150
Director of Recruitment, 10 Parkway Center, Pittsburgh, PA 15220

## JNA Institute of Culinary Arts
### Philadelphia, Pennsylvania
www.culinaryarts.com          CB code: 3049

- For-profit 2-year technical college
- Commuter campus in very large city

**General.** Accredited by ACCSCT. **Enrollment:** 75 degree-seeking undergraduates. **Degrees:** 20 associate awarded. **Calendar:** Quarter, extensive summer session. **Full-time faculty:** 5 total; 20% minority, 20% women. **Part-time faculty:** 7 total; 14% minority, 57% women. **Special facilities:** Student operated restaurant and catering services.

**Student profile.**

| | | | |
|---|---|---|---|
| Out-of-state: | 12% | 25 or older: | 38% |

**Basis for selection.** Open admission.

**2008-2009 Annual costs.** Tuition for 15-month associate program, $17,000; 6-month professional cooking diploma program, $8,500. Required fees $75 for both programs. Books and supplies are $225 for the diploma program and $1,050 for the associate program.

**Application procedures. Admission:** No deadline. No application fee. **Financial aid:** FAFSA required.

**Academics. Special study options:** Internships. **Credit/placement by examination:** AP, CLEP.

**Majors. Personal/culinary services:** Culinary arts.

**Student life. Freshman orientation:** Mandatory.

**Student services.** Alcohol/substance abuse counseling, career counseling, student employment services, financial aid counseling, legal services, placement for graduates.

**Contact.** E-mail: admissions@culinaryarts.edu
Phone: (215) 468-8800 Toll-free number: (877) 872-3197
Darrance Dubose, Director of Admissions, JNA Institute of Culinary Arts, 1212 South Broad Street, Philadelphia, PA 19146

## Johnson College
### Scranton, Pennsylvania
www.johnson.edu          CB member
CB code: 1542

- Private 2-year technical college
- Commuter campus in small city
- Application essay required

**General.** Founded in 1912. Accredited by ACCSCT. **Enrollment:** 376 degree-seeking undergraduates. **Degrees:** 135 associate awarded. **Location:** 117 miles from Philadelphia, 125 miles from New York City. **Calendar:** Semester, limited summer session. **Full-time faculty:** 25 total. **Part-time faculty:** 5 total. **Class size:** 44% < 20, 56% 20-39. **Special facilities:** Materials test laboratory, veterinary hospital. **Partnerships:** Formal partnerships with tech prep programs.

**Student profile.** Among degree-seeking undergraduates, 100% enrolled in a vocational program, 1% already have a bachelor's degree or higher, 156 enrolled as first-time, first-year students.

| | | | |
|---|---|---|---|
| Part-time: | 3% | 25 or older: | 13% |
| Out-of-state: | 2% | Live on campus: | 10% |
| Women: | 28% | | |

**Transfer out. Colleges most students transferred to 2007:** State University of New York Utica/Rome.

**Basis for selection.** Open admission, but selective for some programs. Limited admissions to veterinary technology and radiologic technology programs.

**High school preparation.** 3 units required. Required units include English 2 and mathematics 1. One year chemistry and biology with C or higher required for veterinary science technology majors. One year chemistry or biology and one year algebra II or geometry with C or higher required for radiologic technology.

**2007-2008 Annual costs.** Tuition/fees: $13,858. Per-credit charge: $350. Room only: $3,400. Books/supplies: $1,500. Personal expenses: $4,500.

**Financial aid. Need-based:** Need-based aid available for part-time students. Work-study available nights, weekends and for part-time students. **Non-need-based:** Scholarships awarded for academics.

**Application procedures. Admission:** Closing date 8/1 (receipt date). $30 fee, may be waived for applicants with need. Application may be submitted online. Admission notification on a rolling basis. Must reply within 30 days. **Financial aid:** Priority date 4/28; no closing date. FAFSA, institutional form required. Applicants notified on a rolling basis starting 4/15; must reply within 2 week(s) of notification.

**Academics.** Extensive shop and laboratory facilities. **Special study options:** Internships. License preparation in radiology. **Credit/placement by examination:** AP, CLEP, institutional tests. 9 credit hours maximum toward associate degree. **Support services:** Learning center, pre-admission summer program, reduced course load, remedial instruction, study skills assistance, tutoring.

**Majors. Business:** Logistics. **Computer sciences:** Networking. **Construction:** Carpentry. **Engineering technology:** Architectural drafting, biomedical, electrical. **Health:** Radiologic technology/medical imaging, veterinary technology/assistant. **Mechanic/repair:** General, automotive, diesel, electronics/electrical, industrial. **Production:** Machine tool.

**Most popular majors.** Computer/information sciences 11%, engineering/engineering technologies 22%, health sciences 27%, trade and industry 40%.

**Computing on campus.** 52 workstations in library, computer center. Repair service available.

**Student life. Freshman orientation:** Mandatory, $125 fee. **Housing:** Apartments available. $300 fully refundable deposit, deadline 6/1. **Activities:** Student government, Social Force.

**Athletics. Intercollegiate:** Basketball, bowling, cross-country, golf. **Intramural:** Basketball, football (non-tackle) M, skiing, soccer, softball, table tennis, volleyball. **Team name:** Jaguars.

**Student services.** Career counseling, student employment services, financial aid counseling, personal counseling, placement for graduates, veterans' counselor. **Physically disabled:** Services for visually, hearing impaired. **Transfer:** Pre-admission transcript evaluation for new students. Transfer adviser, college fairs on campus for students transferring to 4-year colleges.

**Contact.** E-mail: admit@johnson.edu
Phone: (570) 702-8911 Toll-free number: (800) 293-9675
Fax: (570) 348-2181
Melissa Ide, Director of Admissions, Johnson College, 3427 North Main Avenue, Scranton, PA 18508

## Kaplan Career Institute: Harrisburg
**Harrisburg, Pennsylvania**
**www.kci-harrisburg.com**                          CB code: 3212

- For-profit 2-year health science and technical college
- Commuter campus in small city
- Application essay, interview required

**General.** Accredited by ACICS. Formerly known as Thompson Institute. **Enrollment:** 515 degree-seeking undergraduates. **Degrees:** 100 associate awarded. **Calendar:** Differs by program, extensive summer session. **Full-time faculty:** 18 total. **Part-time faculty:** 14 total.

**Basis for selection.** Open admission, but selective for some programs. Students entering the Criminal Justice curriculum must achieve a passing score on assessment exam. **Homeschooled:** State high school equivalency certificate, interview required. **Learning Disabled:** Student must request assistance and provide documentation of learning disabilities.

**2007-2008 Annual costs.** Tuition/fees: $12,231. Figures provided represent average costs of tuition and fees based on three quarters. Books/supplies: $2,040. Personal expenses: $2,862.

**Application procedures. Admission:** No deadline. No application fee. Admission notification on a rolling basis.

**Academics. Credit/placement by examination:** CLEP, institutional tests. Credits in any combination (CLEP, experiential, examination, transfer) may not exceed 50% of the program. **Support services:** Reduced course load, study skills assistance, tutoring.

**Majors. Business:** Business admin. **Computer sciences:** LAN/WAN management, networking, web page design, webmaster. **Health:** Medical assistant. **Protective services:** Corrections, criminal justice, law enforcement admin.

**Computing on campus.** 12 workstations in library. Online library, student web hosting available.

**Student life. Freshman orientation:** Mandatory.

**Student services.** Adult student services, career counseling, services for economically disadvantaged, student employment services, financial aid counseling, placement for graduates.

**Contact.** E-mail: nsnyder@kaplan.edu
Phone: (717) 564-4112 Toll-free number: (888) 532-7645
Fax: (717) 564-3779
Mark Hale, Director of Admissions, Kaplan Career Institute: Harrisburg, 5650 Derry Street, Harrisburg, PA 17111-4112

## Kaplan Career Institute: Pittsburgh
**Pittsburgh, Pennsylvania**
**www.icmschool.com**                          CB code: 3823

- For-profit 2-year business and health science college
- Commuter campus in large city
- Application essay, interview required

**General.** Accredited by ACICS. **Enrollment:** 827 degree-seeking undergraduates. **Degrees:** 247 associate awarded. **Calendar:** Quarter, extensive summer session. **Full-time faculty:** 24 total; 33% have terminal degrees, 8% minority, 58% women. **Part-time faculty:** 32 total; 41% have terminal degrees, 6% minority, 38% women. **Special facilities:** Firearms training simulator.

**Student profile.** Among degree-seeking undergraduates, 100% enrolled in a vocational program.

**Basis for selection.** Wonderlic required.

**2008-2009 Annual costs.** Tuition/fees (projected): $17,080. Tuition costs include books and supplies. Books/supplies: $305.

**Financial aid.** All financial aid based on need. Need-based aid available for part-time students. Work-study available nights and for part-time students.

**Application procedures. Admission:** No deadline. $20 fee, may be waived for applicants with need. Admission notification on a rolling basis. **Financial aid:** Closing date 4/30. FAFSA, institutional form required. Applicants notified on a rolling basis.

**Academics. Special study options:** Double major, internships. License preparation in occupational therapy. **Credit/placement by examination:** CLEP. 11 credit hours maximum toward associate degree. **Support services:** Reduced course load, study skills assistance, tutoring.

**Majors. Business:** Accounting, administrative services, business admin, fashion. **Computer sciences:** General, applications programming, information technology, LAN/WAN management, programming, security, systems analysis, webmaster. **Engineering:** Computer. **Health:** Medical assistant, medical secretary, occupational therapy assistant. **Legal studies:** Legal secretary. **Protective services:** Corrections, criminal justice, law enforcement admin, police science, security services.

**Computing on campus.** 225 workstations in library, computer center. Online library, helpline, repair service available.

**Student life. Freshman orientation:** Mandatory. Preregistration for classes offered.

**Student services.** Career counseling, student employment services, financial aid counseling, personal counseling, placement for graduates.

**Contact.** E-mail: rsabo@kaplan.edu
Phone: (412) 261-2647 Toll-free number: (800) 441-5222
Fax: (412) 261-0998
Rebekah Sabo, Director of Admissions, Kaplan Career Institute: Pittsburgh, 10 Wood Street, Pittsburgh, PA 15222

## Keystone Technical Institute
**Harrisburg, Pennsylvania**
**www.kti.edu**                          CB code: 3188

- For-profit 2-year health science and technical college
- Commuter campus in small city
- Interview required

**General.** Accredited by ACCSCT. **Enrollment:** 282 degree-seeking undergraduates. **Degrees:** 59 associate awarded. **Location:** 206 miles from Philadelphia, 200 miles from Washington, DC. **Calendar:** Continuous. **Full-time faculty:** 8 total; 12% have terminal degrees, 75% women. **Part-time faculty:** 7 total; 29% have terminal degrees, 86% women.

**Student profile.**

| African American: | 21% | Hispanic American: | 2% |
|---|---|---|---|
| Asian American: | 1% | | |

**Basis for selection.** All applicants must tour campus. **Homeschooled:** For state grants, applicants must submit either accredited diploma or certification from local superintendent of compliance with Home Education Act. **Learning Disabled:** Provide copy of independent educational program.

**2007-2008 Annual costs.** Tuition/fees: $13,006. Books/supplies: $1,430. Personal expenses: $1,000.

**Financial aid.** All financial aid based on need. Need-based aid available for part-time students. Work-study available nights.

**Application procedures. Admission:** No deadline. $20 fee. Admission notification on a rolling basis. **Financial aid:** No deadline. FAFSA required. Applicants notified on a rolling basis.

**Academics. Special study options:** Dual enrollment of high school students, honors, internships. License preparation in radiology. **Credit/placement by examination:** AP, CLEP. **Support services:** Study skills assistance, tutoring.

**Majors. Computer sciences:** Data entry, data processing. **Family/consumer sciences:** Child care. **Health:** Asian bodywork therapy, Chinese medicine/herbology, dental assistant, massage therapy, medical assistant, medical records admin, medical records technology, medical secretary, medical transcription, movement therapy. **Legal studies:** Paralegal. **Personal/culinary services:** Chef training, culinary arts.

**Most popular majors.** Health sciences 76%, legal studies 15%.

**Computing on campus.** 65 workstations in library. Online library, helpline, repair service available.

**Student life. Freshman orientation:** Mandatory. Preregistration for classes offered. Held first day of class for all new students.

**Student services.** Adult student services, alcohol/substance abuse counseling, career counseling, services for economically disadvantaged, student employment services, financial aid counseling, on-campus daycare, placement for graduates. **Transfer:** Re-entry adviser, pre-admission transcript evaluation for new students. Transfer adviser, college fairs on campus for students transferring to 4-year colleges.

**Contact.** E-mail: info@kti.edu
Phone: (717) 545-4747
Tom Bogush, Admissions Director, Keystone Technical Institute, 2301 Academy Drive, Harrisburg, PA 17112-1012

## Lackawanna College
### Scranton, Pennsylvania
### www.lackawanna.edu
**CB code: 2373**

- Private 2-year junior college
- Commuter campus in small city
- Interview required

**General.** Founded in 1894. Regionally accredited. **Enrollment:** 1,274 degree-seeking undergraduates; 227 non-degree-seeking students. **Degrees:** 226 associate awarded. **ROTC:** Army, Air Force. **Location:** 150 miles from New York City, 120 miles from Philadelphia. **Calendar:** Semester, limited summer session. **Full-time faculty:** 24 total; 12% have terminal degrees, 33% women. **Part-time faculty:** 141 total; 6% have terminal degrees, 49% women. **Class size:** 75% < 20, 25% 20-39. **Partnerships:** Formal partnerships with Tobyhanna Army Depot and Cinram Corporation; IT Security Pipeline Program and Misericordia University.

**Student profile.** Among degree-seeking undergraduates, 401 enrolled as first-time, first-year students.

| Part-time: | 27% | 25 or older: | 27% |
|---|---|---|---|
| Out-of-state: | 9% | Live on campus: | 18% |
| Women: | 55% | | |

**Transfer out. Colleges most students transferred to 2007:** Marywood University, Keystone College, Misericordia University, East Stroudsburg University, Bloomsburg University.

**Basis for selection.** Open admission. College-administered tests or SAT/ACT required for placement. **Homeschooled:** Transcript of courses and grades, state high school equivalency certificate, interview required. **Learning Disabled:** Submit current documentation of disability for arrangement of accommodations.

**High school preparation.** 11 units recommended. Recommended units include English 4, mathematics 3, social studies 1 and science 3.

**2007-2008 Annual costs.** Tuition/fees: $10,150. Per-credit charge: $335. Room/board: $6,600. Books/supplies: $1,200. Personal expenses: $1,290.

**2007-2008 Financial aid. Need-based:** Average need met was 61%. Average scholarship/grant was $6,050; average loan $3,376. 48% of total undergraduate aid awarded as scholarships/grants, 52% as loans/jobs. Need-based aid available for part-time students. Work-study available nights, weekends and for part-time students. **Non-need-based:** Scholarships awarded for academics, athletics, leadership.

**Application procedures. Admission:** Priority date 8/15; no deadline. $30 fee, may be waived for applicants with need. Application may be submitted online. Admission notification on a rolling basis. **Financial aid:** Priority date 5/1; no closing date. FAFSA, institutional form required. Applicants notified on a rolling basis starting 5/1.

**Academics. Special study options:** Cooperative education, double major, dual enrollment of high school students, ESL, honors, independent study, internships. Bachelor's degree programs available on campus. License preparation in nursing, paramedic. **Credit/placement by examination:** AP, CLEP, IB, institutional tests. 31 credit hours maximum toward associate degree. **Support services:** GED preparation and test center, learning center, pre-admission summer program, reduced course load, remedial instruction, study skills assistance, tutoring, writing center.

**Majors. Biology:** Biotechnology. **Business:** General, accounting, administrative services, banking/financial services, business admin. **Communications:** Media studies. **Computer sciences:** General. **Conservation:** Environmental studies. **Education:** General, early childhood. **Engineering technology:** Industrial. **Health:** Cardiovascular technology, EMT paramedic, medical secretary. **Legal studies:** Paralegal. **Liberal arts:** Arts/sciences, humanities. **Mechanic/repair:** Industrial electronics. **Protective services:** Criminal justice, police science. **Public administration:** Human services.

**Most popular majors.** Business/marketing 36%, education 10%, health sciences 23%, liberal arts 11%, security/protective services 17%.

**Computing on campus.** 300 workstations in dormitories, library, computer center. Dormitories wired for high-speed internet access. Online library, helpline available.

**Student life. Freshman orientation:** Mandatory. One-day program. **Housing:** Single-sex dorms, substance-free housing available. $250 fully refundable deposit, deadline 8/15. **Activities:** Choral groups, drama, literary magazine, student government, student newspaper, diversity club and social justice center.

**Athletics.** NJCAA. **Intercollegiate:** Baseball M, basketball, cheerleading M, cross-country, football (tackle) M, golf, soccer W, softball W, volleyball W. **Team name:** FIghting Falcons.

**Student services.** Adult student services, career counseling, services for economically disadvantaged, student employment services, financial aid counseling, minority student services, personal counseling, placement for graduates, veterans' counselor. **Transfer:** Pre-admission transcript evaluation for new students. Transfer adviser, college fairs on campus for students transferring to 4-year colleges.

**Contact.** E-mail: adminfo@lackawanna.edu
Phone: (570) 961-7814 Toll-free number: (877) 346-3552
Fax: (570) 961-7843
Brian Costanzo, Director of Admissions, Lackawanna College, 501 Vine Street, Scranton, PA 18509

## Lansdale School of Business
### North Wales, Pennsylvania
### www.lsb.edu
**CB code: 5853**

- For-profit 2-year career college
- Commuter campus in small town
- Interview required

**General.** Accredited by ACICS. **Enrollment:** 163 full-time, degree-seeking students. **Degrees:** 92 associate awarded. **Location:** 25 miles from Philadelphia. **Calendar:** Semester, extensive summer session. **Full-time faculty:** 12 total. **Part-time faculty:** 30 total.

**Transfer out. Colleges most students transferred to 2007:** Eastern College, Delaware Valley College.

**Basis for selection.** Open admission.

**2007-2008 Annual costs.** 17-month associate degree program: $17,360 tuition; $75 required fees; $285 per-credit-hour charge for day, $248 for evening; $2,050 books and supplies estimate. Computer lab fees vary by program.

**Application procedures. Admission:** No deadline. $30 fee. Admission notification on a rolling basis. **Financial aid:** Priority date 7/1, closing date 8/16. FAFSA required.

**Academics. Special study options:** Double major, internships. Bachelor's degree programs available on campus. **Credit/placement by examination:** CLEP, institutional tests. 30 credit hours maximum toward associate degree. **Support services:** Reduced course load.

**Majors. Business:** Accounting, office management. **Health:** Medical assistant.

**Most popular majors.** Business/marketing 40%, computer/information sciences 40%, health sciences 20%.

**Computing on campus.** 64 workstations in library, computer center.

**Student life. Freshman orientation:** Mandatory. Preregistration for classes offered. **Activities:** Student government.

**Contact.** E-mail: mjohnson@lsb.edu
Phone: (215) 699-5700 Fax: (215) 699-8770
Marianne Johnson, Director of Admissions, Lansdale School of Business, 201 Church Road, North Wales, PA 19454

## Laurel Business Institute
Uniontown, Pennsylvania
www.laurel.edu                    CB code: 2329

▶ For-profit 2-year technical college
▶ Commuter campus in large town
▶ Application essay, interview required

**General.** Founded in 1985. Accredited by ACICS. **Enrollment:** 310 degree-seeking undergraduates. **Degrees:** 103 associate awarded. **Location:** 50 miles from Pittsburgh. **Calendar:** Trimester, extensive summer session. **Full-time faculty:** 23 total. **Part-time faculty:** 17 total. **Class size:** 95% < 20, 5% 20-39. **Special facilities:** Microsoft testing center, Prometric testing site. **Partnerships:** Formal partnership with Nemacolin Woodlands resort.

**Student profile.** Among degree-seeking undergraduates, 100% enrolled in a vocational program, 1% already have a bachelor's degree or higher, 182 enrolled as first-time, first-year students.

| | | | |
|---|---|---|---|
| Out-of-state: | 1% | 25 or older: | 85% |
| Women: | 76% | | |

**Transfer out.** 2% of students enrolled in the transfer program go on to 4-year colleges. **Colleges most students transferred to 2007:** Robert Morris University, Point Park College, California University of PA, Carlow University, University of Phoenix.

**Basis for selection.** Test scores, high school grades or GED, and personal interview most important.

**2007-2008 Annual costs.** Cost of 18-month associate program ranges from $17,005 to $25,000. Fees vary by program. Books/supplies: $750.

**Financial aid.** All financial aid based on need. Need-based aid available for part-time students. Work-study available for part-time students.

**Application procedures. Admission:** No deadline. $55 fee. Admission notification on a rolling basis. **Financial aid:** Closing date 8/1. FAFSA, institutional form required. Applicants notified on a rolling basis; must reply within 4 week(s) of notification.

**Academics. Special study options:** Accelerated study, double major, dual enrollment of high school students, honors, internships. **Credit/placement**

**by examination:** AP, CLEP, institutional tests. 24 credit hours maximum toward associate degree. **Support services:** Reduced course load, tutoring.

**Majors. Business:** Accounting, administrative services, business admin. **Computer sciences:** Computer science, networking. **Family/consumer sciences:** Child care. **Health:** Insurance coding, massage therapy, medical assistant, medical transcription, nursing assistant, office assistant, pharmacy assistant, respiratory therapy technology. **Legal studies:** Legal secretary. **Personal/culinary services:** Cosmetic.

**Most popular majors.** Business/marketing 23%, computer/information sciences 14%, education 12%, family/consumer sciences 6%, health sciences 28%, personal/culinary services 19%.

**Computing on campus.** 50 workstations in library, computer center. Online library available.

**Student life. Freshman orientation:** Mandatory. **Policies:** Attendance required in all classes. Excessive absences will result in points being deducted from final grade. **Activities:** Student newspaper, Phi Beta Lambda.

**Student services.** Student employment services, placement for graduates. **Physically disabled:** Services for visually, speech impaired. **Transfer:** Pre-admission transcript evaluation for new students.

**Contact.** E-mail: ddecker@laurel.edu
Phone: (724) 439-4900 Fax: (724) 439-3607
Douglas Decker, Admissions Director, Laurel Business Institute, 11 East Penn Street, Uniontown, PA 15401

## Lehigh Carbon Community College
Schnecksville, Pennsylvania
www.lccc.edu                    CB code: 2381

▶ Public 2-year community college
▶ Commuter campus in small town

**General.** Founded in 1966. Regionally accredited. 3 campuses enable students from northern rural areas as well as city dwellers residing south of main campus to take classes close to home. **Enrollment:** 6,116 degree-seeking undergraduates; 1,068 non-degree-seeking students. **Degrees:** 617 associate awarded. **ROTC:** Army. **Location:** 8 miles from Allentown, 50 miles from Philadelphia. **Calendar:** Semester, limited summer session. **Full-time faculty:** 106 total; 12% have terminal degrees, 5% minority, 66% women. **Part-time faculty:** 390 total; 7% minority, 47% women. **Class size:** 56% < 20, 44% 20-39.

**Student profile.** Among degree-seeking undergraduates, 64% enrolled in a transfer program, 36% enrolled in a vocational program, 1,829 enrolled as first-time, first-year students, 279 transferred in from other institutions.

| | | | |
|---|---|---|---|
| Part-time: | 56% | Women: | 62% |
| Out-of-state: | 1% | 25 or older: | 34% |

**Transfer out.** 70% of students enrolled in the transfer program go on to 4-year colleges. **Colleges most students transferred to 2007:** Kutztown University, DeSales University, Cedar Crest College, Albright College, Penn State University.

**Basis for selection.** Open admission, but selective for some programs. Special requirements for aviation, allied health, nursing and veterinary technician programs. High school diploma or GED required of applicants to allied health and professional pilot programs, and applicants under the age of 18. COMPASS used for course placement. Interview required for allied health, aviation, medical assistant, veterinary technician programs. **Home-schooled:** Personal interview encouraged.

**High school preparation.** Special requirements for allied health programs and nursing.

**2007-2008 Annual costs.** Tuition/fees: $2,850; $5,520 out-of-district; $8,190 out-of-state. Per-credit charge: $80 in-district; $169 out-of-district; $243 out-of-state. Books/supplies: $1,200. Personal expenses: $1,000.

**2006-2007 Financial aid. Need-based:** 720 full-time freshmen applied for aid; 380 were judged to have need; 352 of these received aid. Average scholarship/grant was $1,858; average loan $1,877. 77% of total undergraduate aid awarded as scholarships/grants, 23% as loans/jobs. Need-based aid available for part-time students. Work-study available nights and for part-time students. **Non-need-based:** Awarded to 262 full-time undergraduates, including 320 freshmen. Scholarships awarded for academics, state residency.

**Application procedures. Admission:** No deadline. $30 fee. Application may be submitted online. Admission notification on a rolling basis.

**Financial aid:** No deadline. FAFSA required. Applicants notified on a rolling basis starting 5/5; must reply within 2 week(s) of notification.

**Academics. Special study options:** Cooperative education, cross-registration, distance learning, dual enrollment of high school students, ESL, external degree, honors, independent study, internships, study abroad. Bachelor's degree programs available on campus. License preparation in aviation, nursing, occupational therapy, physical therapy, real estate. **Credit/ placement by examination:** AP, CLEP, institutional tests. 18 credit hours maximum toward associate degree. **Support services:** GED preparation and test center, learning center, pre-admission summer program, reduced course load, remedial instruction, study skills assistance, tutoring, writing center.

**Honors college/program.** Top 10% of sponsoring school district, with 1200 SAT, skills assessment score of 90 or above in reading and writing, and 70 or above in algebra required.

**Majors. Agriculture:** Horticultural science. **Biology:** General, biotechnology. **Business:** Accounting technology, administrative services, business admin, construction management, executive assistant, hotel/motel admin, human resources, logistics, operations, resort management, restaurant/food services, tourism/travel. **Communications:** General, radio/tv. **Communications technology:** Animation/special effects, recording arts. **Computer sciences:** Information systems, networking, programming, security, systems analysis, web page design. **Construction:** Lineworker. **Education:** General, early childhood, Montessori teacher, special, teacher assistance. **Engineering:** General, mechanical. **Engineering technology:** Biomedical, computer, construction, drafting, electrical, manufacturing. **Health:** Medical assistant, medical records technology, nursing (RN), occupational therapy assistant, physical therapy assistant, veterinary technology/assistant. **Legal studies:** Legal secretary, paralegal. **Liberal arts:** Arts/sciences, humanities. **Math:** General. **Mechanic/repair:** Avionics, heating/ac/refrig, industrial electronics. **Parks/ recreation:** Sports admin. **Personal/culinary services:** Culinary arts. **Physical sciences:** General. **Protective services:** Criminal justice, law enforcement admin. **Psychology:** General. **Public administration:** Human services. **Science technology:** Chemical. **Social sciences:** General. **Transportation:** Airline/commercial pilot, aviation, aviation management. **Visual/ performing arts:** Art, commercial/advertising art, fashion design, interior design. **Other:** Computer Specialist-custom, Mechanical Technology.

**Most popular majors.** Business/marketing 17%, education 17%, health sciences 17%, liberal arts 15%, security/protective services 8%.

**Computing on campus.** 830 workstations in library, computer center. Commuter students can connect to campus network. Online course registration, online library, wireless network available.

**Student life. Freshman orientation:** Available. Morning or afternoon sessions at 3 separate campuses 1 week before classes. Lasts about 2 hours. **Policies:** Must follow student bill of rights and responsibilities. **Activities:** Choral groups, drama, literary magazine, radio station, student government, Campus Christian Fellowship, multicultural student association, political society, justice society, returning adult program, entertainment club.

**Athletics. Intercollegiate:** Baseball, basketball, cheerleading, golf, soccer M, softball W, volleyball W. **Intramural:** Baseball, basketball, bowling, field hockey W, football (non-tackle), golf, racquetball, soccer, softball, table tennis, tennis, track and field M, volleyball, weight lifting. **Team name:** Cougars.

**Student services.** Adult student services, career counseling, services for economically disadvantaged, student employment services, financial aid counseling, minority student services, on-campus daycare, personal counseling, placement for graduates, veterans' counselor. **Physically disabled:** Services for visually, speech, hearing impaired. **Transfer:** Pre-admission transcript evaluation for new students. Transfer adviser, college fairs on campus for students transferring to 4-year colleges.

**Contact.** E-mail: tellme@lccc.edu
Phone: (610) 799-1575 Toll-free number: (800) 414-3975
Fax: (610) 799-1629
Rafael Limon, Associate Dean of Admissions, Lehigh Carbon Community College, 4525 Education Park Drive, Schnecksville, PA 18078

## Lincoln Technical Institute: Allentown
**Allentown, Pennsylvania**
**www.lincolntech.com**
CB code: 2741

- For-profit 2-year technical college
- Commuter campus in small city
- Interview required

**General.** Founded in 1946. Accredited by ACCSCT. **Enrollment:** 455 degree-seeking undergraduates. **Degrees:** 111 associate awarded. **Location:** 60 miles from Philadelphia. **Calendar:** Continuous.

**Basis for selection.** Open admission, but selective for some programs.

**2007-2008 Annual costs.** Total program costs range from $11,515 to $28,393. Cost of books is included in tuition.

**Application procedures. Admission:** No deadline. $25 fee, may be waived for applicants with need. **Financial aid:** No deadline.

**Academics. Credit/placement by examination:** AP, CLEP.

**Majors. Engineering technology:** Drafting, electrical.

**Student life. Freshman orientation:** Mandatory. **Housing:** Substance-free housing available. **Activities:** TV station.

**Contact.** Phone: (610) 398-5300 Fax: (610) 395-2706
Mark Garner, Director of Admissions, Lincoln Technical Institute: Allentown, 5151 Tilghman Street, Allentown, PA 18104

## Lincoln Technical Institute: Northeast Philadelphia
**Philadelphia, Pennsylvania**
**www.lincolntech.com**

- For-profit 2-year technical college
- Very large city

**General.** Accredited by ACICS. **Enrollment:** 204 degree-seeking undergraduates. **Degrees:** 10 associate awarded. **Calendar:** Continuous. **Full-time faculty:** 16 total; 12% minority, 81% women. **Part-time faculty:** 8 total; 38% minority, 50% women.

**Student profile.** Among degree-seeking undergraduates, 100% enrolled in a vocational program, 5% already have a bachelor's degree or higher, 204 enrolled as first-time, first-year students.

| | | | |
|---|---|---|---|
| Part-time: | 32% | Asian American: | 2% |
| Women: | 80% | Hispanic American: | 20% |
| African American: | 30% | | |

**Basis for selection.** Open admission.

**2007-2008 Annual costs.** Cost of diploma programs ranges from $11,735. $14,755; associate degree programs, $22,180 to $26,265. Program cost includes books, uniforms, and fees.

**Application procedures. Admission:** No deadline. No application fee.

**Academics. Credit/placement by examination:** CLEP. **Support services:** Tutoring.

**Majors. Computer sciences:** System admin. **Health:** Office assistant.

**Computing on campus.** Online library available.

**Student life. Freshman orientation:** Mandatory.

**Contact.** Phone: (215) 969-0869 Fax: (215) 969-3457
Janie Muschlitz, Regional Director of Admissions, Lincoln Technical Institute: Northeast Philadelphia, 2180 Hornig Road, Philadelphia, PA 19116

## Lincoln Technical Institute: Philadelphia
**Philadelphia, Pennsylvania**
**www.lincolntech.com**
CB code: 9010

- For-profit 2-year technical college
- Very large city

**General.** Accredited by ACCSCT. **Enrollment:** 455 full-time, degree-seeking students. **Degrees:** 244 associate awarded. **Calendar:** Quarter. **Full-time faculty:** 20 total.

**Basis for selection.** Open admission.

**2007-2008 Annual costs.** Cost of diploma programs ranges from $11,600 to $13,840; associate degree programs, $23,090 to $27,290. Cost of books and tools included in tuition.

**Application procedures. Admission:** No deadline. $25 fee. Admission notification on a rolling basis.

**Academics. Credit/placement by examination:** CLEP.

**Majors. Mechanic/repair:** General, automotive, diesel.

**Contact.** E-mail: dcunningham@lincolntech.com
Phone: (215) 335-0800
Pat Fittipaldi, Director of Admissions, Lincoln Technical Institute:
Philadelphia, 9191 Torresdale Avenue, Philadelphia, PA 19136

## Lincoln Technical Institute: Plymouth Meeting
### Plymouth Meeting, Pennsylvania
www.lincolntech.com

- For-profit 2-year technical college
- Small town

**General.** Accredited by ACICS. **Calendar:** Continuous.

**Annual costs/financial aid.** Tuition and fees for diploma programs:
$11,880 to $16,185; associate degree programs: $23,090.

**Contact.** Phone: (610) 941-0319
Director of Admissions, One Plymouth Meeting Mall, #300, Plymouth
Meeting, PA 19462

## Luzerne County Community College
### Nanticoke, Pennsylvania
www.luzerne.edu                    CB code: 2382

- Public 2-year community college
- Commuter campus in large town

**General.** Founded in 1966. Regionally accredited. **Enrollment:** 6,007 degree-seeking undergraduates; 316 non-degree-seeking students. **Degrees:** 831 associate awarded. **ROTC:** Air Force. **Location:** 8 miles from Wilkes-Barre. **Calendar:** Semester, extensive summer session. **Full-time faculty:** 142 total. **Part-time faculty:** 416 total.

**Student profile.** Among degree-seeking undergraduates, 52% enrolled in a transfer program, 48% enrolled in a vocational program, 1,533 enrolled as first-time, first-year students.

| | | | |
|---|---|---|---|
| Part-time: | 47% | Asian American: | 1% |
| Women: | 59% | Hispanic American: | 3% |
| African American: | 2% | 25 or older: | 35% |

**Transfer out. Colleges most students transferred to 2007:** Bloomsburg University, Wilkes University, King's College, College Misericordia.

**Basis for selection.** Open admission, but selective for some programs. High school record, interview, and test scores considered for admission to health sciences programs. Nurse Entrance Test required of nursing applicants. Interview recommended for health sciences program. **Learning Disabled:** Comprehensive services for special needs students at no cost providing the students present the required documentation.

**High school preparation.** One algebra, 1 chemistry, 1 biology required of nursing, respiratory therapy, and dental hygiene applicants.

**2007-2008 Annual costs.** Tuition/fees: $2,880; $5,580 out-of-district; $8,280 out-of-state. Per-credit charge: $80 in-district; $160 out-of-district; $240 out-of-state. Books/supplies: $800.

**Financial aid. Need-based:** Need-based aid available for part-time students.

**Application procedures. Admission:** No deadline. $40 fee. Admission notification on a rolling basis. **Financial aid:** Priority date 4/15; no closing date. FAFSA, institutional form required. Applicants notified on a rolling basis starting 7/1.

**Academics. Special study options:** Cooperative education, distance learning, dual enrollment of high school students, ESL, external degree, honors, independent study, internships, liberal arts/career combination, weekend college. **Credit/placement by examination:** AP, CLEP, institutional tests. 30 credit hours maximum toward associate degree. **Support services:** GED preparation and test center, learning center, pre-admission summer program, reduced course load, remedial instruction, study skills assistance, tutoring, writing center.

**Majors. Agriculture:** Landscaping. **Business:** General, accounting, accounting technology, administrative services, banking/financial services, business

admin, international, management information systems, real estate, tourism/travel. **Communications:** Advertising, journalism. **Communications technology:** Recording arts. **Computer sciences:** General, applications programming, computer graphics, security, web page design. **Construction:** Electrician, maintenance. **Education:** General, teacher assistance. **Engineering technology:** Architectural drafting, CAD/CADD, computer systems, electrical, nuclear, robotics. **Family/consumer sciences:** Institutional food production. **Health:** Dental hygiene, EMT paramedic, insurance specialist, nursing (RN), office admin, prepharmacy, respiratory therapy technology, surgical technology. **Interdisciplinary:** Biological/physical sciences. **Legal studies:** Court reporting, paralegal. **Liberal arts:** Arts/sciences, humanities. **Math:** General. **Mechanic/repair:** Automotive, heating/ac/refrig. **Parks/recreation:** Health/fitness. **Personal/culinary services:** Mortuary science. **Protective services:** Criminal justice, fire safety technology. **Public administration:** Human services. **Science technology:** Biological. **Social sciences:** General. **Transportation:** Airline/commercial pilot, aviation management. **Visual/performing arts:** Graphic design, illustration, photography.

**Most popular majors.** Business/marketing 14%, education 8%, health sciences 27%, liberal arts 9%, security/protective services 6%, trade and industry 8%, visual/performing arts 6%.

**Computing on campus.** 150 workstations in library, computer center, student center. Commuter students can connect to campus network. Online course registration, online library, helpline, wireless network available.

**Student life. Freshman orientation:** Mandatory. Preregistration for classes offered. **Activities:** Drama, literary magazine, radio station, student government, student newspaper, TV station, Circle K, Brothers and Sisters in Christ.

**Athletics.** NJCAA. **Intercollegiate:** Baseball M, basketball, cross-country, golf, soccer W, softball W, volleyball W. **Intramural:** Badminton, basketball, bowling, football (non-tackle), softball, tennis, volleyball. **Team name:** Trailblazers.

**Student services.** Adult student services, career counseling, student employment services, health services, personal counseling, placement for graduates, veterans' counselor. **Transfer:** Transfer adviser, college fairs on campus for students transferring to 4-year colleges.

**Contact.** E-mail: admissions@luzerne.edu
Phone: (570) 740-0337 Fax: (570) 740-0238
Francis Curry, Director of Admissions, Luzerne County Community College, 1333 South Prospect Street, Nanticoke, PA 18634-9804

## Manor College
### Jenkintown, Pennsylvania
www.manor.edu                    CB code: 2260

- Private 2-year junior college affiliated with Ukrainian Catholic Church
- Commuter campus in small town
- SAT or ACT (ACT writing optional), interview required

**General.** Founded in 1947. Regionally accredited. **Enrollment:** 768 degree-seeking undergraduates; 214 non-degree-seeking students. **Degrees:** 175 associate awarded. **Location:** 15 miles from Philadelphia. **Calendar:** Semester, limited summer session. **Full-time faculty:** 24 total; 25% have terminal degrees, 79% women. **Part-time faculty:** 102 total; 38% have terminal degrees, 9% minority, 55% women. **Class size:** 76% < 20, 24% 20-39. **Special facilities:** Ukrainian heritage studies center and museum, dental health center, law library, veterinary technology radiology lab, surgical suite, Civil War library.

**Student profile.** Among degree-seeking undergraduates, 69% enrolled in a transfer program, 31% enrolled in a vocational program, 3% already have a bachelor's degree or higher, 193 enrolled as first-time, first-year students, 128 transferred in from other institutions.

| | | | |
|---|---|---|---|
| Part-time: | 41% | Asian American: | 3% |
| Out-of-state: | 9% | Hispanic American: | 4% |
| Women: | 80% | International: | 1% |
| African American: | 19% | Live on campus: | 11% |

**Transfer out.** 96% of students enrolled in the transfer program go on to 4-year colleges. **Colleges most students transferred to 2007:** Holy Family University, LaSalle University, Temple University, Drexel University, Thomas Jefferson University.

**Basis for selection.** Class rank, GPA, course selection, recommendation of counselor or teacher, SAT/ACT scores, interview with admissions counselor most important. Institutional entrance test required of all applicants except those holding bachelor's degree. **Adult students:** SAT/ACT scores not required if applicant over 21. **Homeschooled:** State high school equivalency certificate, interview required. GED. **Learning Disabled:** IEP required of all with diagnosed disability.

**High school preparation.** 16 units required. Required and recommended units include English 4, mathematics 2, social studies 2, science 1-2 (laboratory 1-2) and academic electives 6. Biology with laboratory, chemistry with laboratory, 3 math courses required of all allied health science applicants.

**2007-2008 Annual costs.** Tuition/fees: $11,754. Per-credit charge: $245. Tuition for allied health program: $11,854; $335 per credit hour. Room/board: $5,510. Books/supplies: $960. Personal expenses: $2,315.

**2007-2008 Financial aid. Need-based:** 151 full-time freshmen applied for aid; 147 were judged to have need; 147 of these received aid. Average need met was 32%. Average scholarship/grant was $4,850; average loan $3,025. 54% of total undergraduate aid awarded as scholarships/grants, 46% as loans/jobs. Need-based aid available for part-time students. Work-study available nights, weekends and for part-time students. **Non-need-based:** Awarded to 191 full-time undergraduates, including 92 freshmen. Scholarships awarded for academics, alumni affiliation, art.

**Application procedures. Admission:** Closing date 9/1 (postmark date). $25 fee, may be waived for applicants with need. Application may be submitted online. Admission notification on a rolling basis beginning on or about 10/15. Must reply by May 1 or within 2 week(s) if notified thereafter. **Financial aid:** Priority date 4/1; no closing date. FAFSA required. Applicants notified on a rolling basis starting 3/1; must reply within 2 week(s) of notification.

**Academics. Special study options:** Accelerated study, distance learning, double major, dual enrollment of high school students, ESL, honors, independent study, internships. License preparation in real estate. **Credit/placement by examination:** AP, CLEP, institutional tests. 30 credit hours maximum toward associate degree. **Support services:** Learning center, pre-admission summer program, reduced course load, remedial instruction, study skills assistance, tutoring, writing center.

**Majors. Business:** General, accounting, business admin, human resources, international, marketing. **Communications:** General. **Computer sciences:** Applications programming. **Education:** Early childhood, elementary. **Health:** Dental assistant, dental hygiene, health services, prenursing, preveterinary, veterinary technology/assistant. **Legal studies:** Paralegal. **Liberal arts:** Arts/sciences. **Psychology:** General. **Theology:** Religious ed.

**Computing on campus.** 111 workstations in dormitories, library, computer center. Dormitories wired for high-speed internet access and linked to campus network. Commuter students can connect to campus network. Online library, helpline, wireless network available.

**Student life. Freshman orientation:** Mandatory, $25 fee. Four 1-day orientations held annually in January, June, and August; includes testing. **Policies:** Alcohol and drug policy reinforced. **Housing:** Guaranteed on-campus for all undergraduates. Coed dorms, substance-free housing available. $100 partly refundable deposit. **Activities:** Campus ministries, dance, drama, international student organizations, literary magazine, music ensembles, student government, students united for nature, black cultural awareness club, community outreach program, Rotaract, music ministry, student senate, admissions ambassadors.

**Athletics. Intercollegiate:** Basketball, soccer. **Team name:** Blue Jays.

**Student services.** Adult student services, alcohol/substance abuse counseling, campus ministries, career counseling, student employment services, financial aid counseling, health services, personal counseling, placement for graduates, women's services. **Transfer:** Pre-admission transcript evaluation for new students. Transfer center, transfer adviser, college fairs on campus for students transferring to 4-year colleges.

**Contact.** E-mail: ftadmiss@manor.edu
Phone: (215) 884-2216 Fax: (215) 576-6564
I. Jerry Czenstuch, Vice President for Enrollment Management, Manor College, 700 Fox Chase Road, Jenkintown, PA 19046-3319

## McCann School of Business and Technology: Hazleton
### Hazleton, Pennsylvania
### www.mccannschool.com
**CB code: 3887**

- For-profit 2-year business college
- Commuter campus in small town

**General.** Founded in 1897. Accredited by ACICS. **Location:** 20 miles from Hazleton. **Calendar:** Quarter.

**Annual costs/financial aid.** Costs vary by program of study. Cost of entire associate degree program: $18,816 - $20, 384; diploma program: $2,744 - $12,544. Books/supplies: $900. Personal expenses: $1,600.

**Contact.** Phone: (570) 454-6172
Director of Admissions, 14 Maplewood Drive, Hazleton, PA 18202

## McCann School of Business and Technology: Pottsville
### Pottsville, Pennsylvania
### www.mccannschool.edu
**CB code: 3296**

- For-profit 2-year branch campus and technical college
- Small town

**General.** Accredited by ACICS. **Calendar:** Quarter.

**Annual costs/financial aid.** Costs vary by program of study. Cost of entire associate degree program: $18,816 - $20, 384; diploma program: $2,744 - $12,544.

**Contact.** Phone: (570) 622-7622
Director, 2650 Woodglen Road, Pottsville, PA 17901

## McCann School of Business and Technology: Scranton
### Scranton, Pennsylvania
### www.mccannschool.com/student

- For-profit 2-year business and technical college
- Commuter campus in small city

**General.** Accredited by ACICS. **Calendar:** Quarter.

**Annual costs/financial aid.** Costs vary by program of study. Cost of entire associate degree program: $18,816 - $20, 384; diploma program: $2,744 - $12,544.

**Contact.** Phone: (570) 969-4330
Admissions Representative, 201 Lackawanna Avenue, Scranton, PA 18503

## McCann School of Business and Technology: Sunbury
### Sunbury, Pennsylvania
### www.mccannschool.com
**CB code: 3298**

- For-profit 2-year branch campus and technical college
- Small town

**General.** Accredited by ACICS. **Calendar:** Quarter.

**Annual costs/financial aid.** Costs vary by program of study. Cost of entire associate degree program: $18,816 - $20, 384; diploma program: $2,744 - $12,544.

**Contact.** Phone: (570) 286-3058
Lead Admissions Representative, 1147 North 4th Street, Sunbury, PA 17801

## Metropolitan Career Center Computer Technology Institute
### Philadelphia, Pennsylvania
### www.mccweb-gt.org

- Private 2-year technical college
- Very large city

**General.** Accredited by ACCSCT. **Calendar:** Continuous.

**Annual costs/financial aid.** Full program cost is $18,050, and includes all fees and supplies. Additional charge for books.

**Contact.** Phone: (215) 568-9215
Admissions Director, 100 South Broad Street, Suite 830, Philadelphia, PA 19110

## Montgomery County Community College

Blue Bell, Pennsylvania      **CB member**
www.mc3.edu      **CB code: 2445**

- Public 2-year community college
- Commuter campus in large town

**General.** Founded in 1964. Regionally accredited. Campus in Pottstown serves students in western part of the county. Several off-campus sites: Lansdale, Willow Grove Naval Air Station. **Enrollment:** 11,592 degree-seeking undergraduates. **Degrees:** 950 associate awarded. **Location:** 20 miles from Philadelphia. **Calendar:** Semester, extensive summer session. **Full-time faculty:** 169 total; 7% minority, 53% women. **Part-time faculty:** 517 total; 7% minority, 54% women. **Class size:** 58% < 20, 42% 20-39. **Special facilities:** Dental hygiene clinic.

**Student profile.** Among degree-seeking undergraduates, 62% enrolled in a transfer program, 38% enrolled in a vocational program, 4,153 enrolled as first-time, first-year students, 403 transferred in from other institutions.

| | | | |
|---|---|---|---|
| Part-time: | 56% | Asian American: | 6% |
| Out-of-state: | 1% | Hispanic American: | 3% |
| Women: | 58% | International: | 1% |
| African American: | 11% | 25 or older: | 37% |

**Transfer out.** 74% of students enrolled in the transfer program go on to 4-year colleges. **Colleges most students transferred to 2007:** Temple University, Gwynedd Mercy College, West Chester University, Penn State, Kutztown University.

**Basis for selection.** Open admission, but selective for some programs. Special requirements for allied health and automotive technology programs. County residents given priority. High school transcript required for students less than 5 years out of high school. ACT or SAT required for allied health applicants; report score by August 1. **Homeschooled:** Transcript of courses and grades required. Must provide approved curriculum and portfolio. **Learning Disabled:** Recommend meeting with Director of Services for Students with Disabilities. Require current documentation from students of accommodations needed.

**High school preparation.** Biology, chemistry, and algebra required of nursing and medical laboratory technician applicants, chemistry of dental hygiene applicants.

**2008-2009 Annual costs.** Tuition/fees (projected): $3,090; $6,030 out-of-district; $8,970 out-of-state. Per-credit charge: $88 in-district; $176 out-of-district; $264 out-of-state. In-state, out-of-district tuition and out-of-state tuition both include additional fees per credit hour. Books/supplies: $1,200. Personal expenses: $1,640.

**2006-2007 Financial aid.** Need-based: 879 full-time freshmen applied for aid; 685 were judged to have need; 612 of these received aid. Average need met was 15%. Average scholarship/grant was $1,941; average loan $1,656. 68% of total undergraduate aid awarded as scholarships/grants, 32% as loans/jobs. Need-based aid available for part-time students. Work-study available nights, weekends and for part-time students. **Non-need-based:** Awarded to 713 full-time undergraduates, including 274 freshmen. Scholarships awarded for academics.

**Application procedures.** **Admission:** No deadline. $25 fee, may be waived for applicants with need. Application may be submitted online. Admission notification on a rolling basis. **Financial aid:** Priority date 5/1; no closing date. FAFSA required. Applicants notified on a rolling basis starting 2/1.

**Academics.** **Special study options:** Accelerated study, cooperative education, distance learning, dual enrollment of high school students, ESL, honors, independent study, internships, student-designed major, study abroad, teacher certification program, weekend college. Bachelor's degree programs available on campus. License preparation in dental hygiene, nursing, radiology, real estate. **Credit/placement by examination:** AP, CLEP, institutional tests. 30 credit hours maximum toward associate degree. **Support services:** GED preparation, learning center, reduced course load, remedial instruction, study skills assistance, tutoring.

**Majors.** **Biology:** General, biotechnology. **Business:** General, accounting, accounting technology, administrative services, business admin, communications, hospitality/recreation, management information systems, real estate, sales/distribution, travel services. **Communications:** General. **Computer sciences:** General, information systems, programming. **Education:** Elementary, physical, secondary, teacher assistance. **Engineering:** Science. **Engineering technology:** General, automotive, drafting. **Family/consumer sciences:** Child care. **Health:** Clinical lab technology, dental hygiene, medical radiologic technology/radiation therapy, mental health services, nursing (RN), surgical technology. **Liberal arts:** Arts/sciences, humanities. **Math:**

General. **Personal/culinary services:** Baking, chef training. **Physical sciences:** General. **Protective services:** Fire safety technology, police science, security services. **Social sciences:** General. **Visual/performing arts:** Art, commercial/advertising art.

**Most popular majors.** Business/marketing 15%, education 6%, health sciences 19%, liberal arts 39%.

**Computing on campus.** 1,228 workstations in library, student center. Commuter students can connect to campus network. Online course registration, online library, helpline, wireless network available.

**Student life.** **Freshman orientation:** Available. Preregistration for classes offered. One day, week before semester starts. **Housing:** Housing for up to 8 foreign students (F1 visas) available. **Activities:** Jazz band, choral groups, dance, drama, film society, literary magazine, music ensembles, radio station, student government, student newspaper, TV station, African-American club, Asian club, environmental club, writers' club, Meridian club, animal rights club, Christian fellowship club, diversity club, Hola club, S-Flag, Muslim club.

**Athletics.** **Intramural:** Badminton, baseball M, basketball, bowling, cross-country, football (non-tackle) M, judo, racquetball, soccer, softball, table tennis, tennis, volleyball, weight lifting. **Team name:** Mustangs.

**Student services.** Career counseling, student employment services, financial aid counseling, health services, minority student services, on-campus daycare, personal counseling, placement for graduates, veterans' counselor. **Physically disabled:** Services for visually, speech, hearing impaired. **Transfer:** Pre-admission transcript evaluation for new students. Transfer center, transfer adviser, college fairs on campus for students transferring to 4-year colleges.

**Contact.** E-mail: admissionsregistration@mc3.edu
Phone: (215) 641-6551 Fax: (215) 641-6681
Penny Sawyer, Director of Admissions, Montgomery County Community College, 340 DeKalb Pike, Blue Bell, PA 19422

## New Castle School of Trades

Pulaski, Pennsylvania
www.ncstrades.com      **CB code: 2404**

- For-profit 2-year technical college
- Commuter campus in rural community
- Interview required

**General.** Accredited by ACCSCT. **Enrollment:** 380 degree-seeking undergraduates. **Degrees:** 197 associate awarded. **Location:** 10 miles from Youngstown, Ohio. **Calendar:** Differs by program. **Full-time faculty:** 20 total. **Part-time faculty:** 15 total.

**Basis for selection.** Secondary school record and Wonderlic test scores most important. Wonderlic exam used for admission.

**2007-2008 Annual costs.** Tuition varies by program from $4,838 to $16,950. Costs include fees. Books and tool expenses additional, up to $2,672. Books/supplies: $1,000.

**Financial aid.** **Need-based:** Need-based aid available for part-time students.

**Application procedures.** **Admission:** No deadline. $25 fee. Admission notification on a rolling basis.

**Academics.** **Credit/placement by examination:** CLEP. **Support services:** Study skills assistance, tutoring.

**Majors.** **Engineering technology:** Construction, electrical. **Mechanic/repair:** Automotive.

**Student life.** **Freshman orientation:** Available. Preregistration for classes offered.

**Student services.** Career counseling, financial aid counseling, personal counseling, placement for graduates.

**Contact.** E-mail: ncstrades@aol.com
Phone: (724) 964-8811 Toll-free number: (800) 837-8299
Fax: (724) 964-8177
Jim Catheline, Director of Admissions, New Castle School of Trades, 4164 US 422, Pulaski, PA 16143-9721

## Newport Business Institute: Lower Burrell
### Lower Burrell, Pennsylvania
### www.newportbusiness.com
**CB code: 2413**

- For-profit 2-year business college
- Commuter campus in small town
- Interview required

**General.** Accredited by ACICS. **Enrollment:** 85 undergraduates. **Degrees:** 56 associate awarded. **Location:** 15 miles from Pittsburgh. **Calendar:** Quarter. **Full-time faculty:** 8 total. **Special facilities:** All students receive a laptop to use while enrolled. **Partnerships:** Formal partnerships with Microsoft Testing Center, Prometrics Testing Center.

**Basis for selection.** Open admission.

**2007-2008 Annual costs.** Tuition/fees: $9,525. Books/supplies: $1,125.

**Financial aid. Need-based:** Need-based aid available for part-time students. **Non-need-based:** Scholarships awarded for academics, leadership.

**Application procedures. Admission:** No deadline. $25 fee, may be waived for applicants with need. Application may be submitted online. Admission notification on a rolling basis. **Financial aid:** Closing date 5/1. FAFSA required. Applicants notified on a rolling basis starting 5/1.

**Academics. Special study options:** Liberal arts/career combination. Bachelor's degree programs available on campus. **Credit/placement by examination:** CLEP. **Support services:** Tutoring.

**Majors. Business:** Accounting, accounting technology, accounting/business management, administrative services, business admin, customer service, executive assistant, hospitality admin, hospitality/recreation, hotel/motel admin, office technology, office/clerical, receptionist, resort management, retailing, small business admin, tourism/travel, travel services. **Computer sciences:** Data entry, data processing, database management, web page design, word processing. **Health:** Insurance coding, insurance specialist, medical records admin, medical secretary, medical transcription, office admin, office assistant, office computer specialist, receptionist. **Visual/performing arts:** Music.

**Most popular majors.** Business/marketing 60%, computer/information sciences 34%, health sciences 16%.

**Computing on campus.** PC or laptop required. 2 workstations in computer center. Helpline, repair service, wireless network available.

**Student life. Freshman orientation:** Mandatory. Preregistration for classes offered. **Activities:** Student newspaper.

**Student services.** Adult student services, career counseling, student employment services, financial aid counseling, placement for graduates. **Transfer:** Pre-admission transcript evaluation for new students.

**Contact.** E-mail: admissions1@newportbusiness.com
Phone: (724) 339-7542 Toll-free number: (800) 752-7695
Fax: (724) 339-2950
Melissa Beck, Assistant Director of Admissions, Newport Business Institute: Lower Burrell, 945 Greensburg Road, Lower Burrell, PA 15068

## Newport Business Institute: Williamsport
### Williamsport, Pennsylvania
### www.newportbusiness.com
**CB code: 2551**

- For-profit 2-year business and career college
- Commuter campus in small city
- Interview required

**General.** Accredited by ACICS. **Enrollment:** 77 degree-seeking undergraduates. **Degrees:** 43 associate awarded. **Calendar:** Quarter. **Full-time faculty:** 6 total; 67% women.

**Student profile.** Among degree-seeking undergraduates, 100% enrolled in a vocational program, 16 enrolled as first-time, first-year students, 10 transferred in from other institutions.

| Women: | 95% | African American: | 6% |
|---|---|---|---|

**Basis for selection.** Open admission.

**2007-2008 Annual costs.** Tuition/fees: $9,750. Per-credit charge: $258. Books/supplies: $900.

**Application procedures. Admission:** No deadline. $25 fee. Application may be submitted online. Admission notification on a rolling basis. **Financial aid:** No deadline. FAFSA required.

**Academics. Special study options:** Internships. **Credit/placement by examination:** CLEP.

**Majors. Business:** Business admin, executive assistant. **Health:** Medical secretary. **Legal studies:** Legal secretary.

**Most popular majors.** Business/marketing 40%, health sciences 44%, legal studies 16%.

**Student life. Freshman orientation:** Mandatory.

**Student services.** Financial aid counseling, personal counseling, placement for graduates. **Transfer:** Pre-admission transcript evaluation for new students.

**Contact.** E-mail: admissions1_nbi@comcast.net
Phone: (570) 326-2869 Fax: (570) 326-2136
Mary Weaver, Director, Newport Business Institute: Williamsport, 941 West Third Street, Williamsport, PA 17701

## Northampton Community College
### Bethlehem, Pennsylvania
### www.northampton.edu
**CB member**
**CB code: 2573**

- Public 2-year community college
- Commuter campus in small city

**General.** Founded in 1966. Regionally accredited. Branch campus at Monroe County. Off-campus sites in southside Bethlehem, Lehigh Valley Industrial Park IV and in Pike County. Individualized transfer study program. **Enrollment:** 9,319 degree-seeking undergraduates; 328 non-degree-seeking students. **Degrees:** 875 associate awarded. **Location:** 60 miles from Philadelphia, 90 miles from New York City. **Calendar:** Semester, limited summer session. **Full-time faculty:** 119 total; 44% have terminal degrees, 18% minority, 59% women. **Part-time faculty:** 462 total; 17% have terminal degrees, 5% minority, 54% women. **Special facilities:** Electrotechnology applications center. **Partnerships:** Formal partnerships with General Motors, Daimler Chrysler.

**Student profile.** Among degree-seeking undergraduates, 60% enrolled in a transfer program, 40% enrolled in a vocational program, 3% already have a bachelor's degree or higher, 2,857 enrolled as first-time, first-year students, 856 transferred in from other institutions.

| Part-time: | 55% | Hispanic American: | 10% |
|---|---|---|---|
| Out-of-state: | 2% | International: | 1% |
| Women: | 62% | 25 or older: | 37% |
| African American: | 8% | Live on campus: | 3% |
| Asian American: | 2% | | |

**Transfer out.** 72% of students enrolled in the transfer program go on to 4-year colleges. **Colleges most students transferred to 2007:** East Stroudsburg University, Kutztown University, Temple University, DeSales University, Moravian College.

**Basis for selection.** Open admission, but selective for some programs. Special requirements for allied health, veterinary technician, and culinary arts programs. Interview required for radiography, veterinary technology, and diagnostic medical sonography programs; portfolio required for communication design, fine arts programs; audition required for theater program.

**High school preparation.** Biology, chemistry, and algebra requirements for allied health, veterinary technician, and culinary arts programs.

**2007-2008 Annual costs.** Tuition/fees: $3,000; $5,190 out-of-district; $7,380 out-of-state. Per-credit charge: $73 in-district; $146 out-of-district; $219 out-of-state. Room/board: $6,352. Books/supplies: $1,300. Personal expenses: $2,455.

**2007-2008 Financial aid. Need-based:** 72% of total undergraduate aid awarded as scholarships/grants, 28% as loans/jobs. Need-based aid available for part-time students. Work-study available nights, weekends and for part-time students. **Non-need-based:** Scholarships awarded for academics, alumni affiliation, art, leadership, minority status, music/drama.

**Application procedures. Admission:** No deadline. $25 fee, may be waived for applicants with need. Application may be submitted online. Admission notification on a rolling basis. **Financial aid:** Priority date 3/31; no closing date. FAFSA, institutional form required. Applicants notified on a rolling basis starting 6/1; must reply within 2 week(s) of notification.

**Academics. Special study options:** Accelerated study, combined bachelor's/graduate degree, cooperative education, distance learning, double major, dual enrollment of high school students, ESL, honors, internships, student-designed major, study abroad, teacher certification program. Bachelor's degree programs available on campus. License preparation in dental hygiene, nursing, radiology, real estate. **Credit/placement by examination:** AP, CLEP, institutional tests. 30 credit hours maximum toward associate degree. **Support services:** GED preparation, learning center, reduced course load, remedial instruction, study skills assistance, tutoring, writing center.

**Majors. Biology:** General, biotechnology. **Business:** General, accounting technology, administrative services, business admin, hotel/motel admin, marketing, restaurant/food services. **Communications:** General, journalism. **Communications technology:** Radio/tv. **Computer sciences:** Computer science, networking, programming, security. **Construction:** Electrician. **Education:** General, teacher assistance. **Engineering:** General. **Engineering technology:** Architectural, CAD/CADD, electrical, electromechanical, quality control. **Health:** Dental hygiene, medical secretary, nursing (RN), radiologic technology/medical imaging, sonography, surgical technology, veterinary technology/assistant. **Legal studies:** Legal secretary, paralegal. **Liberal arts:** Arts/sciences. **Math:** General. **Mechanic/repair:** Automotive, computer, heating/ac/refrig, industrial electronics. **Parks/recreation:** Sports admin. **Personal/culinary services:** Chef training, mortuary science. **Physical sciences:** Chemistry, physics. **Protective services:** Criminal justice, fire services admin. **Public administration:** Social work. **Science technology:** Chemical. **Visual/performing arts:** Acting, graphic design, interior design, studio arts.

**Most popular majors.** Business/marketing 15%, education 7%, health sciences 21%, liberal arts 12%, security/protective services 6%.

**Computing on campus.** 1,600 workstations in dormitories, library, computer center, student center. Dormitories wired for high-speed internet access and linked to campus network. Commuter students can connect to campus network. Online course registration, online library, helpline, student web hosting, wireless network available.

**Student life. Freshman orientation:** Available. Preregistration for classes offered. 1/2 day program offered over 2 weeks in summer. **Housing:** Coed dorms, apartments available. $150 deposit. **Activities:** Choral groups, drama, film society, radio station, student government, student newspaper.

**Athletics. Intercollegiate:** Baseball M, basketball, bowling, golf, ice hockey, soccer, softball W, tennis, volleyball. **Intramural:** Basketball, bowling, football (non-tackle), golf, racquetball, soccer, volleyball. **Team name:** Spartans.

**Student services.** Adult student services, alcohol/substance abuse counseling, career counseling, services for economically disadvantaged, financial aid counseling, health services, minority student services, on-campus daycare, personal counseling, placement for graduates. **Physically disabled:** Services for visually, speech, hearing impaired. **Learning disabled:** Comprehensive services available. **Transfer:** Pre-admission transcript evaluation for new students. Transfer center, transfer adviser, college fairs on campus for students transferring to 4-year colleges.

**Contact.** E-mail: adminfo@northampton.edu
Phone: (610) 861-5500 Fax: (610) 861-4560
James McCarthy, Director of Admissions, Northampton Community College, 3835 Green Pond Road, Bethlehem, PA 18020

## Oakbridge Academy of Arts
**Lower Burrell, Pennsylvania**
**www.oaa.edu**          **CB code: 2984**

- For-profit 2-year visual arts college
- Commuter campus in large town
- Interview required

**General.** Accredited by ACCSCT. **Enrollment:** 55 degree-seeking undergraduates. **Degrees:** 26 associate awarded. **Location:** 21 miles from Pittsburgh. **Calendar:** Quarter, extensive summer session. **Full-time faculty:** 2 total. **Part-time faculty:** 5 total; 40% women. **Class size:** 100% < 20.

**Basis for selection.** Good attendance record required for admission. Portfolio review required for commercial arts program and recommended for photography program.

**2008-2009 Annual costs.** Tuition/fees (projected): $9,750. Books/supplies: $1,000. Personal expenses: $4,123.

**Financial aid.** All financial aid based on need. Need-based aid available for part-time students.

**Application procedures. Admission:** No deadline. $25 fee. Application may be submitted online. Admission notification on a rolling basis. **Financial aid:** Closing date 5/1. FAFSA required. Applicants notified on a rolling basis.

**Academics. Special study options:** Internships. **Credit/placement by examination:** CLEP.

**Majors. Communications:** Advertising. **Visual/performing arts:** General, commercial photography, commercial/advertising art, design, drawing, graphic design, painting, photography.

**Computing on campus.** 40 workstations in computer center.

**Student life. Freshman orientation:** Mandatory. Preregistration for classes offered. **Activities:** Student government.

**Student services.** Placement for graduates.

**Contact.** E-mail: admissions@oakbridgeacademy.com
Phone: (724) 335-5336 Toll-free number: (800) 734-5601
Fax: (724) 339-2950
Melissa Beck, Assistant Director of Admissions, Oakbridge Academy of Arts, 1250 Greensburg Road, Lower Burrell, PA 15068

## Orleans Technical Institute - Center City Campus
**Philadelphia, Pennsylvania**
**www.orleanstech.edu**          **CB code: 3127**

- Private 2-year technical college
- Commuter campus in very large city
- Interview required

**General.** Accredited by ACCSCT. **Enrollment:** 365 full-time, degree-seeking students. **Degrees:** 14 associate awarded. **Calendar:** Continuous, extensive summer session. **Full-time faculty:** 6 total. **Part-time faculty:** 15 total.

**Transfer out. Colleges most students transferred to 2007:** Community College of Philadelphia.

**Basis for selection.** Open admission.

**2007-2008 Annual costs.** Tuition for full associate program (3 years, including internship) is $32,000. Books/supplies: $2,000.

**Financial aid. Need-based:** Need-based aid available for part-time students.

**Application procedures. Admission:** No deadline. $125 fee. Admission notification on a rolling basis. **Financial aid:** No deadline. FAFSA, institutional form required. Applicants notified on a rolling basis.

**Academics. Credit/placement by examination:** CLEP, institutional tests. **Support services:** Tutoring.

**Majors. Business:** Business admin.

**Student life. Freshman orientation:** Mandatory.

**Student services.** Adult student services, career counseling, financial aid counseling, personal counseling, placement for graduates. **Physically disabled:** Services for visually impaired. **Transfer:** Re-entry adviser, pre-admission transcript evaluation for new students.

**Contact.** E-mail: bellod@jevs.org
Phone: (215) 728-4426 Fax: (215) 745-1689
Debbie Bello, Director, Orleans Technical Institute - Center City Campus, 2770 Red Lion Road, Philadelphia, PA 19114

## Pace Institute
**Reading, Pennsylvania**
**www.paceinstitute.com**          **CB code: 2438**

- For-profit 2-year junior college
- Large city

**General.** Accredited by ACICS. **Enrollment:** 170 degree-seeking undergraduates. **Degrees:** 43 associate awarded. **Calendar:** Continuous. **Full-time faculty:** 5 total. **Part-time faculty:** 15 total.

**Basis for selection.** Open admission.

**2007-2008 Annual costs.** Tuition varies by program from $7,310 to $22,006 annually.

**Application procedures. Admission:** No deadline. $10 fee, may be waived for applicants with need.

**Academics. Credit/placement by examination:** CLEP.

**Majors. Business:** Accounting, administrative services, business admin, fashion, tourism/travel. **Computer sciences:** Programming. **Engineering:** Electrical. **Health:** Medical secretary. **Legal studies:** Paralegal.

**Contact.** E-mail: pace4u2@aol.com
Phone: (610) 375-1212
Amy Hafer, Admissions Representative, Pace Institute, 606 Court Street, Reading, PA 19601

## Penn Commercial Business and Technical School
**Washington, Pennsylvania**
www.penncommercial.edu
CB code: 3300

♦ For-profit 2-year business and technical college
♦ Small city

**General.** Accredited by ACICS. **Enrollment:** 375 degree-seeking undergraduates. **Degrees:** 103 associate awarded. **Calendar:** Continuous. **Full-time faculty:** 12 total. **Part-time faculty:** 35 total.

**Basis for selection.** Open admission, but selective for some programs.

**2007-2008 Annual costs.** Tuition and fees range from $8,810 to $9,610 per academic year depending on program. Books/supplies: $945. Personal expenses: $2,438.

**Application procedures. Admission:** No deadline. $25 fee. Admission notification on a rolling basis. **Financial aid:** No deadline.

**Academics. Credit/placement by examination:** CLEP.

**Majors. Business:** General, administrative services, business admin. **Computer sciences:** Information technology, networking. **Engineering technology:** Computer systems, drafting, heat/ac/refrig. **Health:** Medical secretary, office assistant. **Legal studies:** Legal secretary. **Mechanic/repair:** General.

**Contact.** E-mail: pcadmissions@penncommercial.edu
Phone: (724) 222-5330 ext. 1 Fax: (724) 225-3561
Stephanie Franks, Admissions Director, Penn Commercial Business and Technical School, 242 Oak Spring Road, Washington, PA 15301

## Pennco Tech
**Bristol, Pennsylvania**
www.penncotech.com
CB code: 0380

♦ For-profit 2-year technical college
♦ Large town
♦ Interview required

**General.** Founded in 1973. Accredited by ACCSCT. Branch campus in Blackwood, New Jersey. **Enrollment:** 360 full-time, degree-seeking students. **Degrees:** 63 associate awarded. **Location:** 18 miles from Philadelphia. **Calendar:** Modular, year-round calendar. Limited summer session. **Full-time faculty:** 70 total. **Part-time faculty:** 10 total.

**Basis for selection.** Institution's entrance examination and campus interview most important.

**2007-2008 Annual costs.** Tuition ranges from $6,000 to $28,000 depending on program. Books/supplies: $850.

**Application procedures. Admission:** No deadline. $100 fee. Admission notification on a rolling basis. **Financial aid:** No deadline. Applicants notified on a rolling basis.

**Academics. Credit/placement by examination:** CLEP, institutional tests. 30 credit hours maximum toward associate degree. **Support services:** Tutoring.

**Majors. Business:** Hospitality admin. **Computer sciences:** Programming. **Engineering:** Electrical. **Mechanic/repair:** Auto body, automotive.

**Student life. Housing:** Single-sex dorms available. **Activities:** Choral groups, TV station.

**Student services.** Career counseling, student employment services, on-campus daycare, personal counseling, placement for graduates.

**Contact.** E-mail: admissions@penncotech.com
Phone: (215) 824-3200 Toll-free number: (800) 575-9399
Glenn Slater, Director of Admissions, Pennco Tech, 3815 Otter Street, Bristol, PA 19007

## Pennsylvania Culinary Institute
**Pittsburgh, Pennsylvania**
www.paculinary.com
CB code: 2440

♦ For-profit 2-year culinary school and technical college
♦ Residential campus in large city
♦ Interview required

**General.** Founded in 1986. Accredited by ACCSCT. **Enrollment:** 1,100 full-time, degree-seeking students. **Degrees:** 594 associate awarded. **Location:** 300 miles from Philadelphia. **Calendar:** Semester, extensive summer session. **Full-time faculty:** 40 total.

**Student profile.**

| | | | |
|---|---|---|---|
| Out-of-state: | 49% | Live on campus: | 25% |
| 25 or older: | 21% | | |

**Basis for selection.** Interview, high school diploma or GED, Wonderlic reading assessment important. SAT or ACT recommended. Wonderlic assessment required of all students who do not provide qualified SAT or ACT scores. **Homeschooled:** State high school equivalency certificate required.

**2007-2008 Annual costs.** Total costs vary by program: Culinary Arts $41,870; Patisserie & Baking $36,470; Hospitality & Restaurant Management $35,503. Books/supplies: $1,671.

**Financial aid.** All financial aid based on need.

**Application procedures. Admission:** No deadline. $50 fee. Application may be submitted online. Admission notification on a rolling basis. **Financial aid:** No deadline. FAFSA, institutional form required. Applicants notified on a rolling basis.

**Academics. Special study options:** Internships. **Credit/placement by examination:** AP, CLEP, institutional tests. **Support services:** Learning center, remedial instruction, study skills assistance, tutoring.

**Majors. Personal/culinary services:** Culinary arts.

**Computing on campus.** 80 workstations in library, computer center. Online library available.

**Student life. Freshman orientation:** Mandatory. Approximately 2 hours, held day before classes start. **Housing:** Guaranteed on-campus for all undergraduates. Coed dorms available. $200 deposit. **Activities:** Student government, student newspaper.

**Student services.** Alcohol/substance abuse counseling, career counseling, student employment services, financial aid counseling, personal counseling, placement for graduates. **Transfer:** Pre-admission transcript evaluation for new students.

**Contact.** E-mail: info@paculinary.com
Phone: (412) 566-2433 Toll-free number: (800) 432-2433
Fax: (412) 566-2434
Ted Wiechman, Vice President of Admissions and Marketing, Pennsylvania Culinary Institute, 717 Liberty Avenue, Pittsburgh, PA 15222

## Pennsylvania Highlands Community College
**Johnstown, Pennsylvania**
www.pennhighlands.edu
CB code: 2484

♦ Public 2-year community college
♦ Commuter campus in large town

**General.** Regionally accredited. **Enrollment:** 1,064 degree-seeking undergraduates; 294 non-degree-seeking students. **Degrees:** 141 associate awarded. **Location:** 70 miles from Pittsburgh. **Calendar:** Semester, extensive summer session.

**Student profile.** Among degree-seeking undergraduates, 24% enrolled in a transfer program, 76% enrolled in a vocational program, 330 enrolled as first-time, first-year students.

| | | | |
|---|---|---|---|
| Part-time: | 46% | Asian American: | 1% |
| Women: | 55% | Hispanic American: | 2% |
| African American: | 7% | | |

**Transfer out. Colleges most students transferred to 2007:** University of Pittsburgh at Johnstown, Indiana University of Pennsylvania, Mount Aloysius College, Penn State University, Saint Francis University.

**Basis for selection.** Open admission.

**2007-2008 Annual costs.** Tuition/fees: $3,180; $5,730 out-of-district; $8,280 out-of-state. Per-credit charge: $85 in-district; $170 out-of-district; $255 out-of-state. Students in Windber and Conemaugh Twp pay rate of $110 per credit hour. Students outside Cambria County pay additional fee of $5 per credit. Books/supplies: $900.

**Financial aid. Need-based:** Need-based aid available for part-time students. Work-study available nights and for part-time students. **Non-need-based:** Scholarships awarded for academics, state residency.

**Application procedures. Admission:** No deadline. $20 fee, may be waived for applicants with need. Application must be submitted on paper. Admission notification on a rolling basis. **Financial aid:** Closing date 4/1. FAFSA required. Applicants notified on a rolling basis; must reply by 8/1.

**Academics. Special study options:** Cooperative education, distance learning, dual enrollment of high school students, honors, independent study, internships. **Credit/placement by examination:** CLEP, institutional tests. **Support services:** Learning center, reduced course load, remedial instruction, study skills assistance, tutoring.

**Majors. Biology:** Biotechnology. **Business:** Accounting technology, administrative services, business admin, restaurant/food services. **Communications:** General. **Computer sciences:** Database management, networking, security, web page design. **Construction:** Lineworker. **Education:** General, teacher assistance. **Engineering technology:** Architectural, electrical, environmental, manufacturing. **Family/consumer sciences:** Aging. **Health:** Medical transcription. **Legal studies:** Court reporting. **Liberal arts:** Arts/sciences. **Protective services:** Corrections, law enforcement admin. **Public administration:** Human services. **Other:** Health and medical administrative services.

**Most popular majors.** Business/marketing 29%, computer/information sciences 12%, education 8%, engineering/engineering technologies 7%, health sciences 18%, liberal arts 10%, public administration/social services 9%.

**Computing on campus.** 250 workstations in library, computer center, student center.

**Student life. Freshman orientation:** Available. Preregistration for classes offered. **Activities:** Literary magazine.

**Student services.** Career counseling, services for economically disadvantaged, student employment services, financial aid counseling, placement for graduates. **Transfer:** Pre-admission transcript evaluation for new students. College fairs on campus for students transferring to 4-year colleges.

**Contact.** E-mail: jmaul@pennhighlands.edu
Phone: (814) 262-6446 Toll-free number: (888) 385-7325
Fax: (814) 262-6420
Jeff Maul, Director of Admissions, Pennsylvania Highlands Community College, PO Box 68, Johnstown, PA 15907-0068

## Pennsylvania Institute of Technology
**Media, Pennsylvania**
**www.pit.edu**                                        CB code: 2675

▶ Private 2-year technical college
▶ Commuter campus in small town
▶ Application essay, interview required

**General.** Founded in 1953. Regionally accredited. **Enrollment:** 668 degree-seeking undergraduates; 11 non-degree-seeking students. **Degrees:** 37 associate awarded. **Location:** 13 miles from Philadelphia, 15 miles from Wilmington, Delaware. **Calendar:** Semester, extensive summer session. **Full-time faculty:** 21 total. **Part-time faculty:** 26 total. **Class size:** 99% < 20,

less than 1% 20-39. **Partnerships:** Formal partnerships with Tech Prep in high schools.

**Student profile.** Among degree-seeking undergraduates, 415 enrolled as first-time, first-year students.

| | | | |
|---|---|---|---|
| Part-time: | 19% | 25 or older: | 42% |
| Women: | 64% | | |

**Basis for selection.** Open admission. Selective admissions to Practical Nursing program. Interview and essay used for placement purposes only.

**2007-2008 Annual costs.** Tuition/fees: $9,000. All students pay a technology fee of $11 per credit hour. Books/supplies: $900.

**Financial aid. Need-based:** Need-based aid available for part-time students. Work-study available nights, weekends and for part-time students. **Non-need-based:** Scholarships awarded for academics, leadership.

**Application procedures. Admission:** No deadline. $25 fee, may be waived for applicants with need. Application may be submitted online. Admission notification on a rolling basis. **Financial aid:** Closing date 8/1. FAFSA, institutional form required. Applicants notified on a rolling basis starting 7/1.

**Academics.** Curricula designed to prepare students for positions in industry through combination of general education and job specific courses. **Special study options:** Accelerated study, cooperative education, double major, dual enrollment of high school students, independent study, internships. **Credit/placement by examination:** AP, CLEP, institutional tests. 60 credit hours maximum toward associate degree. **Support services:** Learning center, reduced course load, remedial instruction, tutoring.

**Majors. Business:** Administrative services, business admin. **Computer sciences:** Computer science, networking. **Engineering technology:** Architectural, civil, electrical. **Health:** Medical secretary.

**Most popular majors.** Business/marketing 18%, computer/information sciences 56%, engineering/engineering technologies 26%.

**Computing on campus.** 80 workstations in library, computer center, student center. Commuter students can connect to campus network. Online library available.

**Student life. Freshman orientation:** Mandatory. Orientation lasts several days, held 1 week before start of classes. **Activities:** Radio station, student government, student newspaper, amateur radio club.

**Athletics. Intramural:** Basketball M, softball M, volleyball.

**Student services.** Adult student services, career counseling, student employment services, personal counseling, placement for graduates, veterans' counselor. **Physically disabled:** Services for speech, hearing impaired. **Transfer:** Transfer adviser, college fairs on campus for students transferring to 4-year colleges.

**Contact.** E-mail: info@pit.edu
Phone: (610) 565-7900 Fax: (610) 892-1510
Angela Cassetta, Director of Admissions, Pennsylvania Institute of Technology, 800 Manchester Avenue, Media, PA 19063-4098

## Pennsylvania School of Business
**Allentown, Pennsylvania**
**www.pennschoolofbusiness.edu-search.com**
                                                   CB code: 3044

▶ For-profit 2-year business and technical college
▶ Small city

**General.** Accredited by ACCSCT. **Calendar:** Continuous.

**Annual costs/financial aid.** Tuition for associate-degree program (15 months): $25,250. Books/supplies: $800. Need-based financial aid available to full-time and part-time students.

**Contact.** Phone: (610) 841-3333
Director of Admissions, 406 West Hamilton Street, Allentown, PA 18101

## Pittsburgh Institute of Aeronautics
**Pittsburgh, Pennsylvania**
**www.pia.edu**                                      CB code: 0652

▶ Private 2-year technical college
▶ Commuter campus in large city

**General.** Founded in 1929. Accredited by ACCSCT. Located in active county airport. **Enrollment:** 400 degree-seeking undergraduates. **Degrees:** 69 associate awarded. **Location:** 8 miles from Pittsburgh. **Calendar:** Quarter, extensive summer session. **Full-time faculty:** 25 total. **Part-time faculty:** 1 total. **Special facilities:** Modern aviation maintenance, aviation electronics, and electronic systems laboratories.

## Student profile.

| | | | |
|---|---|---|---|
| Out-of-state: | 35% | 25 or older: | 25% |

**Basis for selection.** Open admission.

**2007-2008 Annual costs.** Tuition/fees: $11,352. Books/supplies: $900. Personal expenses: $400.

**Application procedures. Admission:** No deadline. $150 fee. Admission notification on a rolling basis. **Financial aid:** Priority date 5/1; no closing date. FAFSA required. Applicants notified on a rolling basis.

**Academics. Special study options:** License preparation in aviation. **Credit/placement by examination:** CLEP, institutional tests. **Support services:** Remedial instruction, tutoring.

**Majors. Education:** Technology/industrial arts, voc/tech. **Engineering:** General, electrical. **Engineering technology:** Electrical. **Mechanic/repair:** Aircraft, electronics/electrical.

**Computing on campus.** 30 workstations in computer center. Commuter students can connect to campus network.

**Student life. Housing:** Referral housing available. **Activities:** Student government.

**Student services.** Adult student services, career counseling, student employment services, personal counseling, placement for graduates, veterans' counselor. **Transfer:** Pre-admission transcript evaluation for new students.

**Contact.** E-mail: admissions@pia.edu
Phone: (412) 346-2100 Toll-free number: (800) 444-1440
Fax: (412) 466-0513
Vincent Mezza, Director of Admissions, Pittsburgh Institute of Aeronautics, Box 10897, Pittsburgh, PA 15236-0897

## Pittsburgh Institute of Mortuary Science
**Pittsburgh, Pennsylvania**
www.pims.edu                                    CB code: 7030

- Private 2-year technical college
- Commuter campus in large city

**General.** Founded in 1939. Accredited by American Board of Funeral Services Education, Inc. **Enrollment:** 85 full-time, degree-seeking students. **Degrees:** 43 associate awarded. **Calendar:** Trimester, extensive summer session. **Full-time faculty:** 4 total; 25% women. **Part-time faculty:** 21 total; 14% have terminal degrees, 5% minority, 24% women. **Special facilities:** Preparation center, specialized library.

**Transfer out. Colleges most students transferred to 2007:** Point Park College.

**Basis for selection.** Open admission. **Homeschooled:** Transcript of courses and grades, state high school equivalency certificate required. **Learning Disabled:** Diagnosis documentation within 3 years of enrollment required.

**2007-2008 Annual costs.** Tuition/fees: $14,587. Books/supplies: $700.

**Financial aid. Need-based:** Need-based aid available for part-time students.

**Application procedures. Admission:** Priority date 9/1; no deadline. $40 fee. Application may be submitted online. Admission notification on a rolling basis. **Financial aid:** No deadline. FAFSA required. Applicants notified on a rolling basis.

**Academics.** Four-pronged approach to funeral service management via natural sciences, social sciences, mortuary sciences, and business studies. Students with previous associate degrees will earn diploma or another associate degree in embalming and funeral directing. **Special study options:** Distance learning. **Credit/placement by examination:** CLEP, institutional tests. 48 credit hours maximum toward associate degree. All transfer credit via challenge examination. **Support services:** Reduced course load, tutoring.

**Majors. Personal/culinary services:** Mortuary science.

**Computing on campus.** 10 workstations in library, computer center.

**Student life. Freshman orientation:** Mandatory. Generally held week before start of classes. **Housing:** Housing available at local funeral homes. **Activities:** Student government.

**Student services.** Career counseling, student employment services, financial aid counseling, personal counseling, placement for graduates, veterans' counselor. **Transfer:** Pre-admission transcript evaluation for new students. Transfer adviser for students transferring to 4-year colleges.

**Contact.** E-mail: pims5808@aol.com
Phone: (412) 362-8500 Toll-free number: (800) 933-5808
Fax: (412) 362-1684
Karen Rocco, Registrar, Pittsburgh Institute of Mortuary Science, 5808 Baum Boulevard, Pittsburgh, PA 15206-3706

## Pittsburgh Technical Institute
**Oakdale, Pennsylvania**
www.pti.edu                                    CB code: 0382

- For-profit 2-year technical and career college
- Commuter campus in large town
- Interview required

**General.** Founded in 1946. Locations in Oakdale and at the Regional Learning Alliance. Evening certificate and on-line/on-site degrees for adult students ages 22+ through PTI Center for Certification and Adult Learning. **Enrollment:** 2,065 degree-seeking undergraduates; 3 non-degree-seeking students. **Degrees:** 580 associate awarded. **Location:** 12 miles from Pittsburgh. **Calendar:** Quarter, extensive summer session. **Full-time faculty:** 70 total; 27% women. **Part-time faculty:** 35 total; 51% women. **Class size:** 51% < 20, 49% 20-39. **Special facilities:** MILO Range Pro training system; A/V Suite with 2 video shooting studios, control room and 4 recording booths; fully integrated 2-room house complete with functioning home theater, security, surveillance and lighting systems; Forensic Recovery of Evidence Device (FRED) for computer security analysis; 3D modeling equipment; laproscopic camera with light source and monitor; anatomical model for simulating surgery; functional anesthesia machine; hospitality lab; therapeutic massage lab.

**Student profile.** Among degree-seeking undergraduates, 1,035 enrolled as first-time, first-year students, 1,098 transferred in from other institutions.

| | | | |
|---|---|---|---|
| Out-of-state: | 20% | 25 or older: | 18% |
| Women: | 32% | | |

**Transfer out. Colleges most students transferred to 2007:** Robert Morris University, Point Park University, University of Phoenix.

**Basis for selection.** Open admission, but selective for some programs. Upper 50% of class or passing score on CPAT required for Computer Programming. Criminal background check required for Safety and Security Administration. Upper 80% of class or passing score on CPAT and portfolio review required for Graphic Design and Multimedia Technologies. Criminal background check and dexterity test required for Surgical Technology. International students must complete application in English, show official certification of fund sources and amounts, and submit letter certifying sponsorship. **Learning Disabled:** Students disclosing a learning disability and requesting accommodations must provide documentation confirming the disability.

**2007-2008 Annual costs.** Tuition and supply costs vary by program and student use. Tuition does not increase if student maintains continuous and consistent enrollment.

**2006-2007 Financial aid. Need-based:** 56% of total undergraduate aid awarded as scholarships/grants, 44% as loans/jobs. Need-based aid available for part-time students.

**Application procedures. Admission:** No deadline. No application fee. Application may be submitted online. Admission notification on a rolling basis. **Financial aid:** No deadline. FAFSA, institutional form required. Applicants notified on a rolling basis.

**Academics.** All associate degree programs and selected certificate programs include industry-based internship. **Special study options:** Distance learning, double major, internships. PTI Plus Program provides students the opportunity to take cross-curricular courses in addition to their required course load if they maintain a 3.0 GPA and 90% attendance. No tuition fee is assessed for PTI Plus courses. **Credit/placement by examination:** CLEP, institutional tests. **Support services:** Learning center, remedial instruction, study skills assistance, tutoring, writing center.

**Majors. Business:** Accounting, business admin, hotel/motel admin, retailing, sales/distribution, tourism promotion. **Computer sciences:** Programming, web page design. **Engineering technology:** Computer systems, drafting, electrical. **Health:** Management/clinical assistant, office assistant, surgical technology. **Protective services:** Criminal justice. **Visual/performing arts:** Commercial/advertising art, graphic design.

**Most popular majors.** Business/marketing 17%, computer/information sciences 28%, engineering/engineering technologies 24%, health sciences 6%, security/protective services 6%, visual/performing arts 19%.

**Computing on campus.** 841 workstations in library, computer center, student center. Commuter students can connect to campus network. Online library, helpline, student web hosting, wireless network available.

**Student life. Freshman orientation:** Mandatory. Held every June and September. **Housing:** Apartments available. $350 fully refundable deposit. **Activities:** Drama, student newspaper, Christian Connection.

**Athletics. Intramural:** Basketball, softball, volleyball.

**Student services.** Adult student services, alcohol/substance abuse counseling, career counseling, student employment services, financial aid counseling, personal counseling, placement for graduates. **Transfer:** Pre-admission transcript evaluation for new students. Transfer adviser, college fairs on campus for students transferring to 4-year colleges.

**Contact.** E-mail: james@pti.edu
Phone: (412) 809-5100 Toll-free number: (800) 784-9675
Fax: (412) 809-5388
Marylu Zuk, Vice President of Enrollment, Pittsburgh Technical Institute, 1111 McKee Road, Oakdale, PA 15071-3205

## PJA School
**Upper Darby, Pennsylvania**
**www.pjaschool.com**                    **CB code: 2887**

▶ For-profit 2-year business and career college
▶ Commuter campus in very large city
▶ Application essay, interview required

**General.** Accredited by ACCSCT. **Enrollment:** 160 degree-seeking undergraduates. **Degrees:** 77 associate awarded. **Location:** 4 miles from Philadelphia. **Calendar:** Semester, extensive summer session. **Full-time faculty:** 5 total. **Part-time faculty:** 15 total. **Class size:** 43% < 20, 57% 20-39. **Special facilities:** Law library.

**Student profile.**

| | | | |
|---|---|---|---|
| Out-of-state: | 6% | 25 or older: | 58% |

**Basis for selection.** Test scores, essay, interview, talents, and character most important. Student must pass institutional exam for admission. **Adult students:** SAT/ACT scores not required. Applicant must pass institutional test for admission.

**2007-2008 Annual costs.** Tuition/fees: $10,630. Books and materials included in cost of tuition. Personal expenses: $2,067.

**Financial aid.** All financial aid based on need. Need-based aid available for part-time students. **Additional information:** Interest-free payment plan available.

**Application procedures. Admission:** No deadline. No application fee. Admission notification on a rolling basis. **Financial aid:** No deadline. FAFSA, institutional form required. Applicants notified on a rolling basis.

**Academics. Special study options:** Accelerated study, double major, independent study, internships, liberal arts/career combination, weekend college. Bachelor's degree programs available on campus. **Credit/placement by examination:** AP, CLEP, institutional tests. No more than 20% of credits required for degree may be awarded for prior work or life experience. **Support services:** Learning center, reduced course load, remedial instruction, study skills assistance, tutoring.

**Majors. Business:** General, accounting. **Legal studies:** Paralegal.

**Most popular majors.** Business/marketing 20%, interdisciplinary studies 20%, legal studies 61%.

**Computing on campus.** 120 workstations in library, computer center, student center.

**Student life. Freshman orientation:** Mandatory. Preregistration for classes offered.

**Student services.** Adult student services, career counseling, student employment services, financial aid counseling, personal counseling, placement for graduates, veterans' counselor.

**Contact.** E-mail: dgentile@pjaschool.com
Phone: (610) 789-6700 Toll-free number: (800) 746-4752
Fax: (610) 789-5208
Dina Gentile, Director of Admissions, PJA School, 7900 West Chester Pike, Upper Darby, PA 19082

## Reading Area Community College
**Reading, Pennsylvania**
**www.racc.edu**                    **CB code: 2743**

▶ Public 2-year community college
▶ Commuter campus in small city

**General.** Founded in 1971. Regionally accredited. **Enrollment:** 3,917 degree-seeking undergraduates; 765 non-degree-seeking students. **Degrees:** 370 associate awarded. **Location:** 55 miles from Philadelphia. **Calendar:** Semester, limited summer session. **Full-time faculty:** 75 total. **Part-time faculty:** 176 total. **Class size:** 43% < 20, 55% 20-39, less than 1% 40-49, less than 1% 50-99. **Special facilities:** Arts center, training and technology center.

**Student profile.** Among degree-seeking undergraduates, 41% enrolled in a transfer program, 51% enrolled in a vocational program, 810 enrolled as first-time, first-year students.

| | | | |
|---|---|---|---|
| Part-time: | 53% | Asian American: | 2% |
| Out-of-state: | 1% | Hispanic American: | 19% |
| Women: | 68% | Native American: | 1% |
| African American: | 12% | 25 or older: | 40% |

**Transfer out. Colleges most students transferred to 2007:** Albright College, Kutztown University, Alvernia College, West Chester University, Penn State-Berks.

**Basis for selection.** Open admission, but selective for some programs. Special requirements for nursing, radiology, respiratory therapy and clinical portion of medical laboratory technician program. Interview, science background considered. Interview recommended.

**High school preparation.** 16 units required for nursing program, including 4 English, 3 social studies, 2 math (1 must be algebra), and 2 science with related laboratory or equivalent.

**2007-2008 Annual costs.** Tuition/fees: $3,180; $5,310 out-of-district; $7,380 out-of-state. Per-credit charge: $69 in-district; $138 out-of-district; $207 out-of-state. Books/supplies: $500. Personal expenses: $1,200.

**Application procedures. Admission:** Closing date 8/15 (receipt date). No application fee. Admission notification on a rolling basis. **Financial aid:** Priority date 7/1; no closing date. FAFSA, institutional form required. Applicants notified on a rolling basis starting 4/15; must reply within 2 week(s) of notification.

**Academics. Special study options:** Cooperative education, cross-registration, distance learning, dual enrollment of high school students, ESL, honors, independent study, internships, student-designed major. License preparation in nursing. **Credit/placement by examination:** AP, CLEP, institutional tests. 45 credit hours maximum toward associate degree. **Support services:** GED preparation and test center, learning center, pre-admission summer program, reduced course load, remedial instruction, tutoring.

**Majors. Biology:** General. **Business:** General, accounting, administrative services, banking/financial services, business admin, entrepreneurial studies, human resources, management information systems, office management, office technology, office/clerical, operations, tourism promotion. **Computer sciences:** Data processing, networking, programming. **Education:** General, business, early childhood, elementary, middle, secondary. **Engineering:** General, electrical. **Engineering technology:** Electrical. **Family/consumer sciences:** Child care. **Health:** Clinical lab science, health services, licensed practical nurse, medical radiologic technology/radiation therapy, medical secretary, nursing (RN), predental, premedicine, prepharmacy, respiratory therapy technology. **Interdisciplinary:** Gerontology. **Legal studies:** Legal secretary, prelaw. **Liberal arts:** Arts/sciences. **Mechanic/repair:** Industrial. **Personal/culinary services:** Culinary arts. **Physical sciences:** Chemistry. **Protective services:** Law enforcement admin, police science. **Psychology:** General. **Public administration:** General, social work. **Social sciences:** General, criminology.

**Most popular majors.** Business/marketing 18%, education 7%, health sciences 23%, liberal arts 16%, psychology 10%, security/protective services 7%.

**Computing on campus.** 90 workstations in library, computer center. Online course registration available.

**Student life. Freshman orientation:** Mandatory. Preregistration for classes offered. **Activities:** Choral groups, international student organizations, radio station, student government, student newspaper, TV station.

**Athletics. Intercollegiate:** Basketball M, cross-country, soccer M, volleyball W. **Intramural:** Basketball M. **Team name:** Ravens.

**Student services.** Career counseling, student employment services, on-campus daycare, personal counseling, placement for graduates, veterans' counselor. **Physically disabled:** Services for visually, hearing impaired. **Transfer:** Transfer adviser, college fairs on campus for students transferring to 4-year colleges.

**Contact.** E-mail: admissions@racc.edu
Phone: (610) 607-6224 Toll-free number: (800) 626-1665
Fax: (610) 607-6238
Maria Mitchell, Associate Vice-President, Enrollment Management/Student Services, Reading Area Community College, 10 South Second Street, Reading, PA 19603-1706

## Rosedale Technical Institute
**Pittsburgh, Pennsylvania**
**www.rosedaletech.org**    CB code: 3025

- Private 2-year technical college
- Large city

**General.** Accredited by ACCSCT. **Calendar:** Continuous.

**Annual costs/financial aid.** Tuition/fees (2007-2008): $11,610. Need-based financial aid available for full-time students.

**Contact.** Phone: (412) 521-6200
Director of Admissions, 215 Beecham Drive, Pittsburgh, PA 15205-9791

## South Hills School of Business & Technology
**State College, Pennsylvania**
**www.southhills.edu**    CB code: 2467

- For-profit 2-year business and technical college
- Commuter campus in large town
- Interview required

**General.** Founded in 1970. Regionally accredited; also accredited by ACICS. Free brush-up classes and career services for graduates. Branch campuses in Altoona, Lewistown, and Philipsburg. **Enrollment:** 637 degree-seeking undergraduates; 3 non-degree-seeking students. **Degrees:** 201 associate awarded. **Location:** 125 miles from Pittsburgh, 200 miles from Philadelphia. **Calendar:** Quarter, limited summer session. **Full-time faculty:** 37 total; 3% have terminal degrees, 73% women. **Part-time faculty:** 23 total; 4% have terminal degrees, 52% women.

**Student profile.** Among degree-seeking undergraduates, 100% enrolled in a vocational program, 2% already have a bachelor's degree or higher, 310 enrolled as first-time, first-year students.

| | | | |
|---|---|---|---|
| Part-time: | 10% | Women: | 68% |
| Out-of-state: | 1% | 25 or older: | 30% |

**Transfer out. Colleges most students transferred to 2007:** St. Francis University, Lock Haven University, Mount Aloysius, Pennsylvania State University.

**Basis for selection.** Open admission, but selective for some programs. **Homeschooled:** Transcript of courses and grades required.

**High school preparation.** Recommended units include English 4, mathematics 3, social studies 4 and science 3.

**2007-2008 Annual costs.** Tuition/fees: $12,319. Per-credit charge: $339. Books/supplies: $1,500.

**2007-2008 Financial aid.** All financial aid based on need. Average need met was 10%. Average scholarship/grant was $1,896; average loan $3,500. 38% of total undergraduate aid awarded as scholarships/grants, 62% as loans/jobs. Need-based aid available for part-time students.

**Application procedures. Admission:** No deadline. $25 fee. Application may be submitted online. Admission notification on a rolling basis.

**Financial aid:** Closing date 6/30. FAFSA required. Applicants notified on a rolling basis starting 7/5.

**Academics. Special study options:** Double major, internships. Technical preparatory program. **Credit/placement by examination:** AP, CLEP. 51 credit hours maximum toward associate degree. **Support services:** Preadmission summer program, study skills assistance, tutoring.

**Majors. Business:** Accounting, marketing. **Computer sciences:** Computer science. **Engineering technology:** Industrial. **Health:** Medical records technology, medical secretary, sonography. **Legal studies:** Legal secretary. **Protective services:** Criminal justice. **Visual/performing arts:** Graphic design.

**Most popular majors.** Business/marketing 30%, computer/information sciences 38%, health sciences 24%.

**Computing on campus.** 383 workstations in library, computer center, student center. Commuter students can connect to campus network. Online library, wireless network available.

**Student life. Freshman orientation:** Mandatory. One-day program. **Activities:** Choral groups, student government, student newspaper.

**Student services.** Career counseling, student employment services, financial aid counseling, placement for graduates. **Transfer:** Pre-admission transcript evaluation for new students. Transfer adviser, college fairs on campus for students transferring to 4-year colleges.

**Contact.** E-mail: admissions@southhills.edu
Phone: (814) 234-7755 Toll-free number: (888) 282-7427
Fax: (814) 234-0926
Whitney Merinar, Director of Admissions, South Hills School of Business & Technology, 480 Waupelani Drive, State College, PA 16801-4516

## South Hills School of Business & Technology
**Altoona, Pennsylvania**
**www.southhills.edu**    CB code: 2176

- For-profit 2-year business and technical college
- Commuter campus in small city
- Interview required

**General.** Accredited by ACICS. Free brush-up classes and career services assistance for graduates. Campuses in State College, Lewistown, and Philipsburg. **Enrollment:** 150 degree-seeking undergraduates. **Degrees:** 150 associate awarded. **Calendar:** Quarter, limited summer session. **Full-time faculty:** 9 total; 56% women. **Part-time faculty:** 5 total; 60% women.

**Basis for selection.** Open admission, but selective for some programs. **Homeschooled:** Transcript of courses and grades required. **Learning Disabled:** Documentation of disability required for student file.

**High school preparation.** Recommended units include English 4, mathematics 3, social studies 4 and science 3.

**2008-2009 Annual costs.** Tuition/fees (projected): $12,981. Per-credit charge: $356. Books/supplies: $1,500.

**Financial aid.** All financial aid based on need. Need-based aid available for part-time students.

**Application procedures. Admission:** No deadline. $25 fee. Admission notification on a rolling basis. **Financial aid:** Closing date 6/30. FAFSA required. Applicants notified on a rolling basis starting 7/1.

**Academics. Credit/placement by examination:** CLEP.

**Majors. Business:** Accounting, accounting technology, administrative services, business admin, management information systems, marketing, office management, office/clerical, retailing. **Computer sciences:** Computer science. **Engineering technology:** General. **Health:** Medical records technology, medical secretary, office computer specialist. **Legal studies:** Legal secretary.

**Most popular majors.** Business/marketing 55%, computer/information sciences 29%, health sciences 16%.

**Computing on campus.** 100 workstations in library. Commuter students can connect to campus network. Online library, repair service, wireless network available.

**Student life. Freshman orientation:** Mandatory. One-day orientation program. **Housing:** Off-campus housing information available upon request. **Activities:** Student government.

**Student services.** Career counseling, student employment services, financial aid counseling, placement for graduates.

**Contact.** E-mail: admisssions@southhills.edu
Phone: (814) 944-6134 Toll-free number: (888) 282-7427
Fax: (814) 944-4684
Holly Emerick, Director of Admissions, South Hills School of Business & Technology, 508 58th Street, Altoona, PA 16602

---

## Thaddeus Stevens College of Technology
**Lancaster, Pennsylvania**
**www.stevenscollege.edu**          CB code: 0560

- Public 2-year technical college
- Residential campus in small city

**General.** Founded in 1905. Regionally accredited. **Enrollment:** 767 degree-seeking undergraduates. **Degrees:** 188 associate awarded. **Location:** 60 miles from Philadelphia, 30 miles from Harrisburg. **Calendar:** Semester, limited summer session. **Full-time faculty:** 40 total. **Part-time faculty:** 10 total.

**Student profile.**

| | | | |
|---|---|---|---|
| 25 or older: | 8% | Live on campus: | 50% |

**Basis for selection.** Priority given to orphans and financially needy students. Admission based on school achievement record and institutional placement examination (COMPASS). Interview recommended for associate of specialized technology program. **Homeschooled:** Transcript of courses and grades required.

**High school preparation.** 14 units required. Required and recommended units include English 4, mathematics 2-4 and science 2-6. Algebra required for entry to some associate degree programs.

**2007-2008 Annual costs.** Tuition/fees: $5,670. Per-credit charge: $135. Room/board: $5,592. Books/supplies: $275. Personal expenses: $300.

**Financial aid. Additional information:** Tuition and room and board costs waived for students with adjusted family income of $18,500 or less. Tuition and other costs also waived for orphans.

**Application procedures. Admission:** Priority date 1/1; deadline 7/30. $25 fee, may be waived for applicants with need. Application may be submitted online. Admission notification on a rolling basis beginning on or about 10/15. Applicant must reply within 30 days of receiving notification of decision. **Financial aid:** Priority date 3/15; no closing date. Applicants notified on a rolling basis starting 7/15.

**Academics. Credit/placement by examination:** CLEP, institutional tests. **Support services:** Learning center, pre-admission summer program, reduced course load, remedial instruction, tutoring.

**Majors. Business:** Office/clerical. **Communications technology:** Graphic/printing. **Construction:** Power transmission. **Engineering technology:** Drafting. **Mechanic/repair:** Electronics/electrical, heating/ac/refrig.

**Computing on campus.** 32 workstations in library, computer center. Dormitories linked to campus network.

**Student life. Freshman orientation:** Mandatory. **Housing:** Single-sex dorms available. **Activities:** Student government, student newspaper, Bible study group, dormitory council, outdoor club.

**Athletics.** NJCAA. **Intercollegiate:** Basketball M, cross-country, football (tackle) M, track and field M, wrestling M. **Intramural:** Archery, badminton, basketball, bowling, fencing, golf, soccer, softball, table tennis, tennis, track and field, volleyball, wrestling M. **Team name:** Bulldogs.

**Student services.** Adult student services, career counseling, student employment services, health services, personal counseling, placement for graduates. **Transfer:** Transfer adviser for students transferring to 4-year colleges.

**Contact.** Phone: (717) 299-7701 Toll-free number: (800) 842-3832
Fax: (717) 391-6929
Erin Nelsen, Director of Enrollment Services, Thaddeus Stevens College of Technology, 750 East King Street, Lancaster, PA 17602

---

## Tri-State Business Institute
**Erie, Pennsylvania**
**www.tsbi.edu**          CB code: 2502

- For-profit 2-year business college
- Small city

**General.** Accredited by ACICS. **Enrollment:** 210 degree-seeking undergraduates. **Degrees:** 196 associate awarded. **Calendar:** Quarter, extensive summer session. **Full-time faculty:** 15 total. **Part-time faculty:** 20 total. **Class size:** 100% < 20.

**Basis for selection.** Open admission, but selective for some programs. Special requirements for nursing program.

**2007-2008 Annual costs.** Tuition ranges from $7,400 to $12,950; required fees, including books, from $1,180 to $1,920 per academic year, depending on program.

**Application procedures. Admission:** No deadline. $50 fee. Admission notification on a rolling basis.

**Academics. Special study options:** Internships, liberal arts/career combination. **Credit/placement by examination:** CLEP.

**Majors. Business:** Accounting, business admin. **Computer sciences:** General, computer science, information systems, programming. **Health:** Medical records technology, medical transcription. **Legal studies:** Paralegal.

**Most popular majors.** Business/marketing 17%, computer/information sciences 60%, health sciences 14%, legal studies 9%.

**Student life. Freshman orientation:** Mandatory.

**Student services.** Career counseling, student employment services, personal counseling, placement for graduates, veterans' counselor. **Transfer:** Transfer adviser for students transferring to 4-year colleges.

**Contact.** E-mail: webadmissions@tsbi.edu
Phone: (814) 838-7673 Fax: (814) 838-8642
Karen LaPaglia, Enrollment Coordinator, Tri-State Business Institute, 5757 West Twenty-Sixth Street, Erie, PA 16506

---

## Triangle Tech: Bethlehem
**Bethlehem, Pennsylvania**
**www.triangle-tech.edu**

- For-profit 2-year branch campus and technical college
- Commuter campus in small city
- Interview required

**General.** Regionally accredited; also accredited by ACCSCT. **Enrollment:** 114 degree-seeking undergraduates. **Degrees:** 19 associate awarded. **Calendar:** Semester, extensive summer session. **Full-time faculty:** 9 total. **Part-time faculty:** 3 total; 33% women.

**Student profile.** Among degree-seeking undergraduates, 100% enrolled in a vocational program, 40 enrolled as first-time, first-year students, 1 transferred in from other institutions.

| | | | |
|---|---|---|---|
| Out-of-state: | 3% | Hispanic American: | 11% |
| Women: | 4% | 25 or older: | 34% |
| African American: | 4% | | |

**Transfer out.** 5% of students enrolled in the transfer program go on to 4-year colleges.

**Basis for selection.** Admission by high school diploma or equivalent. Students take TABE skills test to determine reading and math competencies prior to start of class. School tour required. **Homeschooled:** State high school equivalency certificate required.

**High school preparation.** Recommended units include mathematics 3.

**2007-2008 Annual costs.** Tuition/fees: $12,919. Per-credit charge: $349.

**2007-2008 Financial aid. Need-based:** 117 full-time freshmen applied for aid; 117 were judged to have need; 117 of these received aid. Average need met was 31%. Average scholarship/grant was $4,000; average loan $3,721. 42% of total undergraduate aid awarded as scholarships/grants, 58% as loans/jobs. Need-based aid available for part-time students. Work-study available nights.

**Application procedures. Admission:** No deadline. No application fee. Admission notification on a rolling basis. **Financial aid:** No deadline. FAFSA required. Applicants notified on a rolling basis.

**Academics. Credit/placement by examination:** CLEP, institutional tests. **Support services:** Learning center, remedial instruction, study skills assistance, tutoring.

**Majors. Construction:** General, carpentry, electrician.

**Computing on campus.** 42 workstations in library, computer center.

**Student life. Freshman orientation:** Mandatory. Preregistration for classes offered.

**Student services. Transfer:** Re-entry adviser, pre-admission transcript evaluation for new students. Transfer center, transfer adviser, college fairs on campus for students transferring to 4-year colleges.

**Contact.** Phone: (610) 691-1300 Fax: (610) 691-7525
Jason Vallozzi, Director of Admissions, Triangle Tech: Bethlehem, 31 South Commerce Way, LVIP IV, Bethlehem, PA 18017

## Triangle Tech: DuBois
**DuBois, Pennsylvania**
**www.triangle-tech.edu**
**CB code: 7133**

- For-profit 2-year technical college
- Commuter campus in large town
- Interview required

**General.** Accredited by ACCSCT. **Enrollment:** 271 degree-seeking undergraduates. **Degrees:** 170 associate awarded. **Location:** 145 miles from Pittsburgh. **Calendar:** Semester, extensive summer session. **Full-time faculty:** 19 total; 26% women. **Class size:** 89% < 20, 11% 20-39.

**Student profile.** Among degree-seeking undergraduates, 100% enrolled in a vocational program, 183 enrolled as first-time, first-year students.

| | | | |
|---|---|---|---|
| Women: | 7% | African American: | 1% |

**Transfer out.** 1% of students enrolled in the transfer program go on to 4-year colleges.

**Basis for selection.** Open admission. **Homeschooled:** State high school equivalency certificate required.

**High school preparation.** Recommended units include English 4 and mathematics 4.

**2008-2009 Annual costs.** Tuition/fees (projected): $12,977. Per-credit charge: $349. Books/supplies: $1,072. Personal expenses: $1,608.

**2006-2007 Financial aid.** All financial aid based on need. 180 full-time freshmen applied for aid; 180 were judged to have need; 180 of these received aid. Average need met was 100%. Average scholarship/grant was $3,375; average loan $2,825. 53% of total undergraduate aid awarded as scholarships/grants, 47% as loans/jobs. Need-based aid available for part-time students.

**Application procedures. Admission:** No deadline. No application fee. Admission notification on a rolling basis. **Financial aid:** No deadline. FAFSA, institutional form required. Applicants notified on a rolling basis.

**Academics. Special study options:** Cooperative education, dual enrollment of high school students. **Credit/placement by examination:** CLEP. **Support services:** Learning center, remedial instruction, study skills assistance, tutoring.

**Majors. Construction:** Carpentry, electrician. **Engineering technology:** Architectural drafting, mechanical drafting. **Production:** Welding.

**Most popular majors.** Engineering/engineering technologies 17%, trade and industry 83%.

**Computing on campus.** 53 workstations in library, computer center.

**Student life. Freshman orientation:** Mandatory. Orientation held Thursday before classes begin, approximately 1-1/2 hours in length. **Activities:** Student government.

**Student services.** Alcohol/substance abuse counseling, career counseling, student employment services, financial aid counseling, legal services, personal counseling, placement for graduates. **Transfer:** Pre-admission transcript evaluation for new students.

**Contact.** Phone: (814) 371-2090 Toll-free number: (800) 874-8324 Fax: (814) 371-9227
Jason Vallozzi, Director of Admissions, Triangle Tech: DuBois, PO Box 551, DuBois, PA 15801-0551

## Triangle Tech: Erie
**Erie, Pennsylvania**
**www.triangle-tech.edu**
**CB code: 1572**

- For-profit 2-year technical college
- Commuter campus in small city
- Interview required

**General.** Founded in 1976. Accredited by ACCSCT. **Enrollment:** 176 degree-seeking undergraduates. **Degrees:** 79 associate awarded. **Location:** 100 miles from Pittsburgh and Cleveland. **Calendar:** Semester, extensive summer session. **Full-time faculty:** 14 total; 14% women. **Part-time faculty:** 1 total.

**Student profile.** Among degree-seeking undergraduates, 100% enrolled in a vocational program, 1% already have a bachelor's degree or higher, 72 enrolled as first-time, first-year students.

| | | | |
|---|---|---|---|
| Part-time: | 3% | Women: | 5% |
| Out-of-state: | 12% | 25 or older: | 41% |

**Basis for selection.** Open admission.

**2007-2008 Annual costs.** Tuition/fees: $12,869. Per-credit charge: $349. Books/supplies: $873. Personal expenses: $1,608.

**2006-2007 Financial aid. Need-based:** 49% of total undergraduate aid awarded as scholarships/grants, 51% as loans/jobs. Need-based aid available for part-time students.

**Application procedures. Admission:** No deadline. $75 fee. Admission notification on a rolling basis. **Financial aid:** FAFSA required. Applicants notified on a rolling basis.

**Academics. Credit/placement by examination:** AP, CLEP, institutional tests. **Support services:** Remedial instruction, study skills assistance, tutoring.

**Majors. Construction:** Carpentry, electrician. **Engineering technology:** Architectural drafting, mechanical drafting.

**Computing on campus.** 50 workstations in computer center.

**Student life. Freshman orientation:** Mandatory. Preregistration for classes offered. **Activities:** Student government, student newspaper.

**Student services.** Career counseling, student employment services, financial aid counseling, personal counseling, placement for graduates. **Transfer:** Re-entry adviser, pre-admission transcript evaluation for new students. Transfer center, transfer adviser for students transferring to 4-year colleges.

**Contact.** Phone: (814) 453-6016 Fax: (814) 454-2818
Jason Vallozzi, Director of Admissions, Triangle Tech: Erie, 2000 Liberty Street, Erie, PA 16502-2594

## Triangle Tech: Greensburg
**Greensburg, Pennsylvania**
**www.triangle-tech.edu**
**CB code: 0658**

- For-profit 2-year technical college
- Commuter campus in large town
- Interview required

**General.** Founded in 1944. Accredited by ACCSCT. **Enrollment:** 266 degree-seeking undergraduates; 16 non-degree-seeking students. **Degrees:** 136 associate awarded. **Location:** 40 miles from Pittsburgh. **Calendar:** Semester, extensive summer session. **Full-time faculty:** 20 total; 5% have terminal degrees, 15% women. **Part-time faculty:** 4 total. **Class size:** 68% < 20, 32% 20-39.

**Student profile.** Among degree-seeking undergraduates, 100% enrolled in a vocational program, 1% already have a bachelor's degree or higher, 122 enrolled as first-time, first-year students.

| | | | |
|---|---|---|---|
| Out-of-state: | 1% | Native American: | 1% |
| Women: | 3% | 25 or older: | 42% |
| African American: | 2% | | |

**Transfer out.** 2% of students enrolled in the transfer program go on to 4-year colleges.

**Basis for selection.** Open admission.

**2007-2008 Annual costs.** Tuition/fees: $12,850. Per-credit charge: $349. Books/supplies: $1,176. Personal expenses: $1,608.

**2006-2007 Financial aid. Need-based:** 229 full-time freshmen applied for aid; 229 were judged to have need; 229 of these received aid. Average need met was 80%. Average scholarship/grant was $8,962; average loan $2,625. 44% of total undergraduate aid awarded as scholarships/grants, 56% as loans/jobs. Need-based aid available for part-time students. **Non-need-based:** Awarded to 46 full-time undergraduates, including 46 freshmen.

**Application procedures. Admission:** No deadline. No application fee. Admission notification on a rolling basis. **Financial aid:** No deadline. FAFSA required. Applicants notified on a rolling basis.

**Academics. Credit/placement by examination:** AP, CLEP, institutional tests. **Support services:** Learning center, remedial instruction, study skills assistance, tutoring.

**Majors. Construction:** Carpentry, electrician. **Engineering technology:** Architectural drafting, heat/ac/refrig, mechanical drafting.

**Most popular majors.** Engineering/engineering technologies 39%, trade and industry 61%.

**Computing on campus.** 52 workstations in library, computer center.

**Student life. Freshman orientation:** Mandatory. Preregistration for classes offered. **Activities:** Student government, student newspaper.

**Student services.** Career counseling, student employment services, personal counseling, placement for graduates, veterans' counselor. **Transfer:** Re-entry adviser, pre-admission transcript evaluation for new students. Transfer adviser for students transferring to 4-year colleges.

**Contact.** Phone: (724) 832-1050 Toll-free number: (800) 874-8324
Fax: (724) 834-0325
Jason Vallozzi, Director of Admissions, Triangle Tech: Greensburg, 222 East Pittsburgh Street, Suite A, Greensburg, PA 15601-3304

### Triangle Tech: Pittsburgh
**Pittsburgh, Pennsylvania**
**www.triangle-tech.edu**                    CB code: 0734

- For-profit 2-year technical college
- Commuter campus in large city

**General.** Founded in 1944. Accredited by ACCSCT. **Enrollment:** 277 degree-seeking undergraduates; 19 non-degree-seeking students. **Degrees:** 119 associate awarded. **Location:** 5 miles from downtown. **Calendar:** Semester, extensive summer session. **Full-time faculty:** 25 total. **Part-time faculty:** 5 total.

**Student profile.** Among degree-seeking undergraduates, 91 enrolled as first-time, first-year students.

| | | | |
|---|---|---|---|
| Out-of-state: | 15% | African American: | 20% |
| Women: | 4% | 25 or older: | 46% |

**Transfer out. Colleges most students transferred to 2007:** Point Park College, Robert Morris College, Edinboro University, Slippery Rock University, University of PIttsburg.

**Basis for selection.** Open admission. Must have high school diploma or GED. Applicants must take TABE test for placement. **Homeschooled:** Transcript of courses and grades, state high school equivalency certificate required.

**2007-2008 Annual costs.** Tuition/fees: $12,930. Per-credit charge: $349. Books/supplies: $1,010. Personal expenses: $1,608.

**2006-2007 Financial aid.** All financial aid based on need. 286 full-time freshmen applied for aid; 286 were judged to have need; 286 of these received aid. Average need met was 57%. Average scholarship/grant was $2,267; average loan $5,868. 48% of total undergraduate aid awarded as scholarships/grants, 52% as loans/jobs. Work-study available nights.

**Application procedures. Admission:** No deadline. $75 fee. Admission notification on a rolling basis. **Financial aid:** No deadline. Institutional form required. Applicants notified on a rolling basis.

**Academics. Credit/placement by examination:** CLEP. 36 credit hours maximum toward associate degree. **Support services:** Learning center, tutoring.

**Majors. Construction:** Carpentry, electrician, power transmission. **Engineering technology:** Drafting. **Mechanic/repair:** Heating/ac/refrig.

**Computing on campus.** 46 workstations in library, computer center. Online library available.

**Student life. Freshman orientation:** Mandatory. Held approximately 5 days prior to start; approximately 2-and-one-half hours long.

**Student services.** Career counseling, student employment services, financial aid counseling, personal counseling, placement for graduates. **Transfer:** Pre-admission transcript evaluation for new students. College fairs on campus for students transferring to 4-year colleges.

**Contact.** E-mail: info@triangle-tech.edu
Phone: (412) 359-1000 Toll-free number: (800) 874-8324
Fax: (412) 359-1012
John Mazzarese, Vice President of Admissions, Triangle Tech: Pittsburgh, 1940 Perrysville Avenue, Pittsburgh, PA 15214-3897

### Triangle Tech: Sunbury
**Sunbury, Pennsylvania**
**www.triangle-tech.edu**

- For-profit 2-year technical college
- Commuter campus in large town
- Interview required

**General.** Accredited by ACCSCT. **Enrollment:** 76 degree-seeking undergraduates. **Degrees:** 60 associate awarded. **Calendar:** Semester. **Full-time faculty:** 10 total; 10% women. **Part-time faculty:** 1 total. **Class size:** 100% < 20.

**Student profile.** Among degree-seeking undergraduates, 100% enrolled in a vocational program, 46 enrolled as first-time, first-year students.

**Basis for selection.** High school GPA important. Test scores and recommendations considered.

**2007-2008 Annual costs.** Tuition/fees: $13,042. Per-credit charge: $349. Books/supplies: $1,034. Personal expenses: $1,608.

**2007-2008 Financial aid. Need-based:** Average need met was 94%. Average scholarship/grant was $3,561; average loan $4,786. 49% of total undergraduate aid awarded as scholarships/grants, 51% as loans/jobs. Work-study available nights.

**Application procedures. Admission:** No deadline. No application fee. Admission notification on a rolling basis. **Financial aid:** No deadline. FAFSA, institutional form required.

**Academics. Credit/placement by examination:** AP, CLEP, institutional tests. **Support services:** Tutoring.

**Majors. Construction:** General, carpentry. **Engineering technology:** Electrical.

**Computing on campus.** 27 workstations in library, computer center.

**Student life. Freshman orientation:** Mandatory.

**Student services.** Adult student services, student employment services, financial aid counseling, placement for graduates.

**Contact.** E-mail: jdrumm@triangle-tech.edu
Phone: (570) 988-0700 Toll-free number: (800) 874-8324
Fax: (570) 988-4641
John Mazzarese, Vice President of Admissions, Triangle Tech: Sunbury, RR 1 Box 51, Sunbury, PA 17801

### University of Pittsburgh at Titusville
**Titusville, Pennsylvania**
**www.upt.pitt.edu**                    CB code: 2937

- Public 2-year branch campus and liberal arts college
- Residential campus in small town
- SAT or ACT (ACT writing optional) required

**General.** Founded in 1963. Regionally accredited. **Enrollment:** 557 degree-seeking undergraduates; 16 non-degree-seeking students. **Degrees:** 50 associate awarded. **Location:** 100 miles from Pittsburgh, 50 miles from Erie. **Calendar:** Semester, limited summer session. **Full-time faculty:** 20 total. **Part-time faculty:** 40 total. **Class size:** 62% < 20, 37% 20-39, less than 1% 40-49, less than 1% 50-99.

**Student profile.** Among degree-seeking undergraduates, 86% enrolled in a transfer program, 224 enrolled as first-time, first-year students, 37 transferred in from other institutions.

| | | | |
|---|---|---|---|
| Part-time: | 19% | Hispanic American: | 2% |
| Women: | 61% | Native American: | 1% |
| African American: | 18% | 25 or older: | 13% |
| Asian American: | 3% | Live on campus: | 50% |

**Transfer out.** 52% of students enrolled in the transfer program go on to 4-year colleges. **Colleges most students transferred to 2007:** Clarion University, Edinboro University, Indiana University of Pennsylvania, Penn State University, Mercyhurst College.

**Basis for selection.** Decisions based on academic performance. Applicants deserving additional consideration referred to Admissions Committee. Essay, interview recommended. **Homeschooled:** Math/English placement tests required. **Learning Disabled:** Students with disabilities asked to provide comprehensive documentation to Disability Resources and Services representative to establish eligibility for accommodations.

**High school preparation.** 15 units required. Required and recommended units include English 4, mathematics 2, science 1 (laboratory 1), foreign language 3 and academic electives 7. One unit lab science required.

**2007-2008 Annual costs.** Tuition/fees: $10,058; $18,692 out-of-state. Per-credit charge: $388 in-state; $748 out-of-state. Room/board: $7,594. Books/supplies: $800. Personal expenses: $1,600.

**2007-2008 Financial aid. Need-based:** Average need met was 85%. Average scholarship/grant was $7,235; average loan $3,224. 52% of total undergraduate aid awarded as scholarships/grants, 48% as loans/jobs. Need-based aid available for part-time students. Work-study available nights and weekends. **Non-need-based:** Scholarships awarded for academics, athletics, state residency.

**Application procedures. Admission:** No deadline. $45 fee, may be waived for applicants with need. Application may be submitted online. Admission notification on a rolling basis beginning on or about 11/1. **Financial aid:** Priority date 3/1; no closing date. FAFSA required. Applicants notified on a rolling basis; must reply within 2 week(s) of notification.

**Academics. Special study options:** Combined bachelor's/graduate degree, cross-registration, dual enrollment of high school students, internships, study abroad. Bachelor's degree programs available on campus. License preparation in real estate. **Credit/placement by examination:** AP, CLEP, SAT, ACT, institutional tests. 6 credit hours maximum toward associate degree. **Support services:** Learning center, reduced course load, remedial instruction, study skills assistance, tutoring.

**Majors. Business:** General, accounting, management information systems. **Family/consumer sciences:** General. **Health:** Nursing (RN), physical therapy assistant. **Interdisciplinary:** Natural sciences. **Liberal arts:** Arts/sciences.

**Most popular majors.** Biological/life sciences 16%, business/marketing 24%, health sciences 44%, liberal arts 12%.

**Computing on campus.** 62 workstations in dormitories, library, computer center, student center. Dormitories wired for high-speed internet access and linked to campus network. Commuter students can connect to campus network. Online library, helpline, student web hosting, wireless network available.

**Student life. Freshman orientation:** Mandatory, $60 fee. Preregistration for classes offered. **Policies:** Organizations must complete 1 community service and fundraising activity per year to receive student activity funding. **Housing:** Guaranteed on-campus for all undergraduates. Coed dorms, special housing for disabled, substance-free housing available. $100 fully refundable deposit. Townhouse apartments without cooking facilities available. **Activities:** Choral groups, dance, drama, student government, diversity club, Students in Free Enterprise, commuter student association, Alpha Omega Christian fellowship, Phi Theta Kappa, student activities board, chemistry club, travel club, student physical therapy association.

**Athletics.** NJCAA. **Intercollegiate:** Basketball, golf M, volleyball W. **Intramural:** Basketball, bowling, football (non-tackle), racquetball, skiing, soccer, softball, swimming, table tennis, tennis, volleyball. **Team name:** Panthers.

**Student services.** Adult student services, alcohol/substance abuse counseling, campus ministries, career counseling, student employment services, financial aid counseling, health services, minority student services, personal counseling, placement for graduates. **Physically disabled:** Services for visually impaired. **Transfer:** Transfer adviser, college fairs on campus for students transferring to 4-year colleges.

**Contact.** E-mail: uptadm@pitt.edu
Phone: (814) 827-4427 Toll-free number: (888) 878-0462
Fax: (814) 827-4519
John Mumford, Executive Director of Enrollment Management, University of Pittsburgh at Titusville, UPT Admissions Office, Titusville, PA 16354-0287

## Valley Forge Military College
Wayne, Pennsylvania
www.vfmac.edu

CB member
CB code: 2955

- Private 2-year junior and military college
- Residential campus in small city
- SAT or ACT (ACT writing optional) required

**General.** Founded in 1928. Regionally accredited. One of only 5 military junior colleges in nation offering Army ROTC early commissioning program leading to commission as second lieutenant in U.S. Army Reserve at end of second year. Regimental marching band, drum and bugle corps, regimental choir. **Enrollment:** 216 degree-seeking undergraduates. **Degrees:** 59 associate awarded. **ROTC:** Army, Air Force. **Location:** 15 miles from Philadelphia. **Calendar:** Semester. **Full-time faculty:** 13 total. **Part-time faculty:** 20 total. **Special facilities:** Motorized artillery unit, mounted cavalry troop, aviation training.

**Student profile.** Among degree-seeking undergraduates, 124 transferred in from other institutions.

| | | | |
|---|---|---|---|
| Out-of-state: | 78% | Live on campus: | 100% |

**Transfer out. Colleges most students transferred to 2007:** Lehigh University, Villanova University, Drexel University, The Citadel, George Mason University.

**Basis for selection.** School achievement record, test scores, and personal character most important. TOEFL score accepted in lieu of SAT or ACT scores for international students. Interview recommended. **Homeschooled:** Statement describing homeschool structure and mission, transcript of courses and grades, interview, letter of recommendation (nonparent) required.

**High school preparation.** Required and recommended units include English 4, mathematics 3, science 3 and foreign language 2.

**2007-2008 Annual costs.** Tuition/fees: $25,766. Room/board: $8,035. Books/supplies: $1,000.

**Financial aid. Need-based:** Work-study available nights, weekends and for part-time students. **Non-need-based:** Scholarships awarded for academics, alumni affiliation, athletics, music/drama, ROTC, state residency. **Additional information:** Students enrolled in advanced military science program can receive up to $5,000 from the Army. In addition, competitively awarded ROTC scholarships pay average of another $14,100 per school year for direct educational expenses.

**Application procedures. Admission:** Closing date 8/1 (receipt date). $25 fee, may be waived for applicants with need. Application may be submitted online. Admission notification on a rolling basis. Must reply by May 1 or within 2 week(s) if notified thereafter. **Financial aid:** Closing date 5/1. FAFSA, institutional form required. Applicants notified on a rolling basis starting 5/15; must reply within 2 week(s) of notification.

**Academics. Special study options:** Double major, dual enrollment of high school students, ESL, honors, study abroad. **Credit/placement by examination:** AP, CLEP, SAT, ACT, institutional tests. 30 credit hours maximum toward associate degree. **Support services:** Reduced course load, remedial instruction, tutoring, writing center.

**Majors. Business:** General. **Engineering:** General, science. **Liberal arts:** Arts/sciences. **Protective services:** Criminal justice.

**Computing on campus.** PC or laptop required. 44 workstations in library, computer center. Dormitories wired for high-speed internet access and linked to campus network. Helpline, repair service, wireless network available.

**Student life. Freshman orientation:** Mandatory. Preregistration for classes offered. 3-day orientation with placement testing. **Policies:** Religious observance required. **Housing:** Guaranteed on-campus for all undergraduates.

Single-sex dorms, substance-free housing available. $1,000 partly refundable deposit, deadline 5/1. **Activities:** Bands, choral groups, drama, music ensembles, radio station, student government, student newspaper, Catholic Fellowship, Jewish Fellowship, Christian Fellowship, Muslim Fellowship, Young Republicans.

**Athletics. Intercollegiate:** Basketball M, cross-country M, equestrian M, football (tackle) M, lacrosse M, rifle M, soccer M, tennis M, wrestling M. **Intramural:** Baseball M, basketball M, fencing M, football (tackle) M, golf M, judo M, rugby M, soccer M, softball M, volleyball M, water polo M, weight lifting M. **Team name:** Trojans.

**Student services.** Career counseling, health services, personal counseling, placement for graduates. **Transfer:** Pre-admission transcript evaluation for new students. Transfer adviser for students transferring to 4-year colleges.

**Contact.** E-mail: admission@vfmac.edu
Phone: (610) 989-1300 Toll-free number: (800) 234-8362
Fax: (610) 688-1545
Greg Potts, Director of Enrollment Managment, Valley Forge Military College, 1001 Eagle Road, Wayne, PA 19087

## Vet Tech Institute
### Pittsburgh, Pennsylvania
www.vettechinstitute.com          CB code: 7134

♦ For-profit 2-year health science and technical college
♦ Commuter campus in large city

**General.** Accredited by ACCSCT. Veterinary technician AVMA accredited. **Enrollment:** 325 degree-seeking undergraduates. **Degrees:** 158 associate awarded. **Calendar:** Semester. **Full-time faculty:** 9 total. **Part-time faculty:** 2 total. **Special facilities:** Animal tech rooms, on-site kennel.

**Transfer out. Colleges most students transferred to 2007:** Point Park College.

**Basis for selection.** Satisfactory performance on school admission test required. Essay, interview recommended.

**2008-2009 Annual costs.** Tuition/fees (projected): $28,620.

**Financial aid. Need-based:** Work-study available nights. **Non-need-based:** Scholarships awarded for academics.

**Application procedures. Admission:** No deadline. $50 fee. Application may be submitted online. Admission notification on a rolling basis. **Financial aid:** No deadline. FAFSA required. Applicants notified on a rolling basis.

**Academics. Special study options:** Internships. **Credit/placement by examination:** AP, CLEP. **Support services:** Tutoring.

**Majors. Health:** Veterinary technology/assistant.

**Computing on campus.** 38 workstations in library, computer center.

**Student life. Freshman orientation:** Mandatory.

**Student services.** Career counseling, placement for graduates.

**Contact.** E-mail: admissions@vettechinstitute.edu
Phone: (412) 391-7021 Toll-free number: (800) 570-0693
Fax: (412) 232-4348
Terry Taylor, Senior Admissions Coordinator, Vet Tech Institute, 125 Seventh Street, Pittsburgh, PA 15222-3400

## West Virginia Career Institute
### Mount Braddock, Pennsylvania
www.wvci.edu          CB code: 3214

♦ For-profit 2-year business college
♦ Small town
♦ Interview required

**General.** Accredited by ACICS. **Enrollment:** 175 degree-seeking undergraduates. **Degrees:** 74 associate awarded. **Calendar:** Continuous. **Full-time faculty:** 5 total. **Part-time faculty:** 4 total.

**Basis for selection.** Open admission.

**2007-2008 Annual costs.** Cost of entire associate degree program: $18,000; diploma program: $12,000.

**Application procedures. Admission:** No deadline. $25 fee.

**Academics. Credit/placement by examination:** CLEP.

**Majors. Business:** General, administrative services. **Health:** Medical secretary.

**Contact.** Phone: (724) 437-4600 Fax: (724) 437-6053
Mary Jo Barnhart, Director of Student Services, West Virginia Career Institute, Route 119 North and Mount Braddock Road, Mount Braddock, PA 15465

## Western School of Health and Business Careers
### Pittsburgh, Pennsylvania
www.westernschoolpitt.com          CB code: 2933

♦ For-profit 2-year technical college
♦ Very large city

**General.** Accredited by ACCSCT. **Location:** Downtown. **Calendar:** Continuous.

**Annual costs/financial aid.** Tuition ranges from $10,030 to $38,760 and includes books, registration and lab fees. Need-based financial aid available for full-time students.

**Contact.** Phone: (800) 333-6607
Director of Admissions, 421 Seventh Avenue, Pittsburgh, PA 15219

## Western School of Health and Business Careers: Monroeville
### Monroeville, Pennsylvania
www.wshb-monroeville.com          CB code: 2939

♦ For-profit 2-year business and health science college
♦ Large town

**General.** Accredited by ACCSCT. **Calendar:** Courses begin every 3 months.

**Annual costs/financial aid.** Tuition ranges from $13,950 to $38,610 and includes books, registration and lab fees. Need-based financial aid available to full-time and part-time students.

**Contact.** Phone: (412) 373-6400
Director of Admission, One Monroeville Center, Suite 125, Monroeville, PA 15146

## Westmoreland County Community College
### Youngwood, Pennsylvania
www.wccc.edu          CB code: 2968

♦ Public 2-year community college
♦ Commuter campus in small town

**General.** Founded in 1970. Regionally accredited. **Enrollment:** 5,381 degree-seeking undergraduates; 878 non-degree-seeking students. **Degrees:** 514 associate awarded. **Location:** 30 miles from Pittsburgh. **Calendar:** Semester, limited summer session. **Full-time faculty:** 85 total; 5% minority, 52% women. **Part-time faculty:** 357 total; 2% minority, 52% women. **Class size:** 67% < 20, 33% 20-39. **Special facilities:** Culinary arts kitchens, greenhouse, student lounges, theater.

**Student profile.** Among degree-seeking undergraduates, 26% enrolled in a transfer program, 74% enrolled in a vocational program, 1,768 enrolled as first-time, first-year students.

| | | | |
|---|---|---|---|
| Part-time: | 48% | Hispanic American: | 1% |
| Women: | 60% | 25 or older: | 43% |
| African American: | 3% | | |

**Transfer out. Colleges most students transferred to 2007:** University of Pittsburgh, Indiana University of Pennsylvania, California University of Pennsylvania, Seton Hill University, St. Vincent College.

**Basis for selection.** Open admission, but selective for some programs. Allied Health program applicants required to take Comparative Guidance and Placement test, submit application by November 30 of the year prior to enrollment, and satisfactory results from pre-entrance physicals. Interview recommended.

**2008-2009 Annual costs.** Tuition/fees (projected): $2,820; $5,340 out-of-district; $7,680 out-of-state. Per-credit charge: $78 in-district; $156 out-of-district; $234 out-of-state. Books/supplies: $750.

**Financial aid. Need-based:** Need-based aid available for part-time students. Work-study available nights and for part-time students. **Non-need-based:** Scholarships awarded for academics.

**Application procedures. Admission:** No deadline. $10 fee, may be waived for applicants with need. Application may be submitted online. Admission notification on a rolling basis. **Financial aid:** No deadline. FAFSA, institutional form required. Applicants notified on a rolling basis starting 5/1.

**Academics. Special study options:** Cooperative education, cross-registration, distance learning, double major, honors, independent study, internships, student-designed major, study abroad. Bachelor's degree programs available on campus. License preparation in dental hygiene, nursing, radiology, real estate. **Credit/placement by examination:** AP, CLEP, institutional tests. 30 credit hours maximum toward associate degree. **Support services:** GED preparation and test center, learning center, remedial instruction, study skills assistance, tutoring.

**Majors. Agriculture:** Floriculture, horticultural science, horticulture, turf management. **Business:** Accounting technology, administrative services, banking/financial services, business admin, executive assistant, hotel/motel admin, human resources, marketing, real estate, retailing, tourism/travel. **Communications technology:** Photo/film/video. **Computer sciences:** Computer science, database management, networking, programming, security, web page design. **Engineering technology:** Architectural drafting, computer, computer hardware, electrical, environmental, manufacturing, mechanical, mechanical drafting. **Health:** Dental hygiene, dietetic technician, medical secretary, mental health services, nursing (RN), optician. **Legal studies:** Paralegal. **Liberal arts:** Arts/sciences. **Mechanic/repair:** Heating/ac/refrig, industrial. **Personal/culinary services:** Baking, chef training, restaurant/catering. **Production:** Machine shop technology, machine tool, welding. **Protective services:** Criminal justice, fire safety technology. **Public administration:** Human services. **Science technology:** Biological. **Visual/performing arts:** Commercial/advertising art, photography.

**Most popular majors.** Business/marketing 24%, health sciences 28%, liberal arts 12%, security/protective services 10%.

**Computing on campus.** 600 workstations in library, computer center. Commuter students can connect to campus network. Online course registration, online library, helpline, student web hosting, wireless network available.

**Student life. Freshman orientation:** Available. **Policies:** All clubs required to complete 10 hours of community service per semester. **Activities:** Choral groups, drama, literary magazine, musical theater, student government, student newspaper, cultural awareness coalition, Reach Out club, Republican club.

**Athletics.** NJCAA. **Intercollegiate:** Baseball M, basketball, bowling, golf, softball W, volleyball W. **Intramural:** Baseball M, basketball, bowling, golf, skiing, soccer, softball, table tennis, volleyball. **Team name:** Wolfpack.

**Student services.** Career counseling, services for economically disadvantaged, student employment services, financial aid counseling, on-campus daycare, personal counseling, placement for graduates, veterans' counselor. **Physically disabled:** Services for visually, speech, hearing impaired. **Transfer:** Pre-admission transcript evaluation for new students. Transfer adviser, college fairs on campus for students transferring to 4-year colleges.

**Contact.** E-mail: tatarj@wccc.edu
Phone: (724) 925-4077 Toll-free number: (800) 262-2103 ext. 4077
Fax: (724) 925-5802
Janice Grabowski, Director of Admissions, Westmoreland County Community College, 145 Pavilion Lane, Youngwood, PA 15697-1895

## Yorktowne Business Institute
**York, Pennsylvania**
**www.ybi.edu**                                        CB code: 2553

◆ For-profit 2-year business and health science college
◆ Commuter campus in small city

**General.** Founded in 1976. Accredited by ACICS. **Location:** 100 miles from Philadelphia, 50 miles from Baltimore. **Calendar:** Trimester.

**Annual costs/financial aid.** Tuition $18,750 for business and medical programs, $28,470 for culinary program. Fees vary and are charged on a per term basis. Books/supplies: $2,900. Personal expenses: $1,128. Need-based financial aid available to full-time and part-time students.

**Contact.** Phone: (717) 846-5000
Director of Admissions, West 7th Avenue, York, PA 17404-2034

## YTI Career Institute: Lancaster
**Lancaster, Pennsylvania**
**www.yti.edu**

◆ For-profit 2-year business and technical college
◆ Small city

**General.** Accredited by ACCSCT. **Enrollment:** 585 degree-seeking undergraduates. **Degrees:** 150 associate awarded. **Calendar:** Quarter. **Full-time faculty:** 45 total. **Part-time faculty:** 10 total.

**Basis for selection.** Open admission.

**2007-2008 Annual costs.** Diploma programs: $15,000 to $20,000; associate degree programs: $25,000 to $40,000. Additional supply costs of $1,000 to $2,000 may apply, depending on program.

**Application procedures. Admission:** No deadline. $100 fee.

**Academics. Special study options:** Internships. License preparation in radiology. **Credit/placement by examination:** CLEP.

**Majors. Health:** Medical assistant. **Personal/culinary services:** Restaurant/catering. **Protective services:** Law enforcement admin.

**Contact.** E-mail: amy.daveler@yti.edu
Phone: (717) 295-1100 Toll-free number: (866) 984-5262
Fax: (717) 295-1135
Amy Daveler, Director of Admissions, YTI Career Institute: Lancaster, 3050 Hempland Road, Lancaster, PA 17601

## YTI Career Institute: York
**York, Pennsylvania**
**www.yti.edu**                                        CB code: 2943

◆ For-profit 2-year career college
◆ Commuter campus in small city

**General.** Candidate for regional accreditation; also accredited by ACCSCT. **Enrollment:** 850 degree-seeking undergraduates. **Degrees:** 507 associate awarded. **Calendar:** Quarter, extensive summer session. **Full-time faculty:** 60 total. **Part-time faculty:** 20 total.

**Student profile.**

| | | | |
|---|---|---|---|
| Out-of-state: | 8% | 25 or older: | 15% |

**Basis for selection.** Open admission, but selective for some programs. Medical Office Assistant and Medical Assistant programs require criminal background check and health information form completed by certified physician to include documentation for Hepatitis B and TB immunizations. Dental Assisting Program requires verification of Hepatitis B vaccination. Criminal Justice and First Response program requires background/record check, valid driver-s license, and applicants must be at least 18 years of age at time of matriculation. COMPASS used for placement.

**2007-2008 Annual costs.** Depending on program, cost of full diploma and associate programs ranges from $15,000 - $39,970; Books and supplies, $685 - $2,310 additional charge. Books/supplies: $1,500.

**Application procedures. Admission:** No deadline. $100 fee, may be waived for applicants with need. Application may be submitted online. Admission notification on a rolling basis.

**Academics. Special study options:** Cooperative education, internships. **Credit/placement by examination:** CLEP, institutional tests. **Support services:** Remedial instruction, study skills assistance, tutoring.

**Majors. Business:** Accounting, business admin, golf management, hospitality admin, marketing. **Computer sciences:** Security, systems analysis. **Engineering technology:** CAD/CADD, electrical. **Health:** Medical assistant. **Personal/culinary services:** Culinary arts. **Protective services:** Law enforcement admin, police science, security services.

**Computing on campus.** 250 workstations in library, computer center. Commuter students can connect to campus network. Helpline, repair service, wireless network available.

**Student life. Freshman orientation:** Mandatory. Preregistration for classes offered. **Housing:** Apartments available.

**Student services.** Adult student services, career counseling, student employment services, financial aid counseling, placement for graduates. **Transfer:** Re-entry adviser, pre-admission transcript evaluation for new students. Transfer adviser for students transferring to 4-year colleges.

**Contact.** Phone: (717) 757-1100 Toll-free number: (800) 227-9675 Fax: (717) 757-4964
Director of Admissions, YTI Career Institute: York, 1405 Williams Road, York, PA 17402

# Puerto Rico

## Centro de Estudios Multidisciplinarios
### San Juan, Puerto Rico
### www.cempr.edu

- Private 2-year health science college
- Large city

**General.** Accredited by ACCSCT. **Calendar:** Quarter.

**Contact.** Phone: (787) 765-4210
Director of Admissions, PO Box 191317, San Juan, PR 00926-1931

## Colegio de las Ciencias Artes y Television
### Bayamon, Puerto Rico
### www.ccat.edu

- Private 2-year liberal arts and technical college
- Small city

**General.** Accredited by ACCSCT. **Calendar:** Semester.

**Contact.** Phone: (787) 779-2500
P.O. Box 10774, San Juan, PR 00922

## Columbia Centro Universitario: Yauco
### Yauco, Puerto Rico
### www.columbiaco.edu          CB code: 3215

- For-profit 2-year business and nursing college
- Large town
- Interview required

**General.** Regionally accredited; also accredited by ACICS. **Enrollment:** 440 undergraduates. **Degrees:** 14 bachelor's, 54 associate awarded. **Calendar:** Continuous. **Full-time faculty:** 15 total. **Part-time faculty:** 25 total.

**Student profile.** 33% enrolled in a transfer program, 1% enrolled in a vocational program, 35% already have a bachelor's degree or higher, 539 transferred in from other institutions.

**Transfer out.** 1% of students enrolled in the transfer program go on to 4-year colleges.

**Basis for selection.** Open admission, but selective for some programs. **Homeschooled:** Transcript of courses and grades, state high school equivalency certificate, interview required.

**2007-2008 Annual costs.** Tuition/fees: $3,850. Per-credit charge: $145.

**Financial aid.** All financial aid based on need. Need-based aid available for part-time students. Work-study available nights and for part-time students.

**Application procedures. Admission:** $50 fee. **Financial aid:** FAFSA, institutional form required.

**Academics. Special study options:** Combined bachelor's/graduate degree. Bachelor's degree programs available on campus. License preparation in nursing. **Credit/placement by examination:** CLEP. **Support services:** Learning center, study skills assistance, tutoring.

**Majors. Business:** Business admin., office technology. **Computer sciences:** Programming. **Health:** Nursing (RN).

**Student services. Transfer:** Pre-admission transcript evaluation for new students.

**Contact.** E-mail: rpadilla@columbiaco.edu
Phone: (787) 743-4041 Toll-free number: (800) 981-4877
Fax: (787) 744-7031
Rosario Padilla, Director, Columbia Centro Universitario: Yauco, Box 3062, Yauco, PR 00698-3062

## EDIC College
### Caguas, Puerto Rico
### www.ediccollege.com

- For-profit 2-year health science and technical college
- Large city

**General.** Regionally accredited. **Calendar:** Semester.

**Annual costs/financial aid.** Tuition/fees (2007-2008): $4,910.

**Contact.** Phone: (787) 744-8519 ext. 229
Box 9120, Caguas, PR 00726-9120

## Huertas Junior College
### Caguas, Puerto Rico
### www.huertas.edu

**CB member**
**CB code: 3406**

- For-profit 2-year junior and technical college
- Commuter campus in small city

**General.** Founded in 1945. Accredited by ACICS. **Enrollment:** 1,665 degree-seeking undergraduates. **Degrees:** 283 associate awarded. **Location:** 25 miles from San Juan, 32 miles from Navanjito. **Calendar:** Semester, extensive summer session. **Full-time faculty:** 24 total; 4% have terminal degrees, 100% minority, 58% women. **Part-time faculty:** 85 total; 8% have terminal degrees, 100% minority, 61% women. **Class size:** 69% < 20, 31% 20-39, less than 1% 40-49.

**Student profile.** Among degree-seeking undergraduates, 427 enrolled as first-time, first-year students.

| | | | |
|---|---|---|---|
| Part-time: | 16% | Women: | 52% |

**Basis for selection.** Open admission, but selective for some programs.

**2007-2008 Annual costs.** Tuition/fees: $4,960. Books/supplies: $700.

**2007-2008 Financial aid.** All financial aid based on need. Need-based aid available for part-time students.

**Application procedures. Admission:** No deadline. $25 fee. Application must be submitted on paper. Admission notification on a rolling basis. **Financial aid:** No deadline. FAFSA, institutional form required. Applicants notified on a rolling basis.

**Academics. Special study options:** Cooperative education, dual enrollment of high school students, ESL, independent study, internships. **Credit/placement by examination:** CLEP. **Support services:** GED preparation, remedial instruction, tutoring.

**Majors. Business:** General, accounting, administrative services, business admin. **Computer sciences:** Computer science, programming. **Health:** Dental assistant, medical records admin, medical records technology, pharmacy assistant, respiratory therapy technology. **Mechanic/repair:** Electronics/electrical, heating/ac/refrig.

**Computing on campus.** 50 workstations in computer center.

**Student life. Freshman orientation:** Mandatory. Program held in first 2 weeks of classes. **Activities:** Choral groups, literary magazine, student government.

**Student services.** Career counseling, student employment services, health services, personal counseling, placement for graduates, veterans' counselor. **Physically disabled:** Services for hearing impaired. **Transfer:** Transfer adviser for students transferring to 4-year colleges.

**Contact.** E-mail: admisiones@huertas.edu
Phone: (787) 743-1242 Fax: (787) 743-0203
Barbara Hassim, Director of Admissions, Huertas Junior College, P.O. Box 8429, Caguas, PR 00726

## Humacao Community College
### Humacao, Puerto Rico
### CB code: 2313

- Private 2-year business and community college
- Commuter campus in small city
- Interview required

**General.** Founded in 1956. Accredited by ACICS. **Enrollment:** 750 degree-seeking undergraduates. **Degrees:** 98 associate awarded. **Location:** 42 miles from San Juan. **Calendar:** Trimester. **Full-time faculty:** 10 total; 100% minority. **Part-time faculty:** 19 total; 100% minority.

**Student profile.** Among degree-seeking undergraduates, 1% already have a bachelor's degree or higher, 251 enrolled as first-time, first-year students.

| | | | |
|---|---|---|---|
| Part-time: | 19% | 25 or older: | 38% |
| Women: | 62% | | |

**Transfer out. Colleges most students transferred to 2007:** Turabo University, University of Puerto Rico (all campuses), Inter American University of Puerto Rico (all campuses), Huertas Junior College.

**Basis for selection.** Open admission.

**High school preparation.** 15 units recommended. Recommended units include English 3, mathematics 3, social studies 3, science 3 and academic electives 3.

**2007-2008 Annual costs.** Books/supplies: $937. Personal expenses: $1,530.

**2006-2007 Financial aid.** All financial aid based on need. 235 full-time freshmen applied for aid; 235 were judged to have need; 235 of these received aid. 98% of total undergraduate aid awarded as scholarships/grants, 2% as loans/jobs. Need-based aid available for part-time students. Work-study available nights and for part-time students.

**Application procedures. Admission:** No deadline. $17 fee. Application must be submitted on paper. Admission notification on a rolling basis. **Financial aid:** Priority date 1/1, closing date 6/30. FAFSA, institutional form required. Applicants notified on a rolling basis starting 3/4.

**Academics. Special study options:** Internships. **Credit/placement by examination:** AP, CLEP. 9 credit hours maximum toward associate degree. **Support services:** Learning center, remedial instruction, tutoring.

**Majors. Business:** Administrative services, business admin. **Computer sciences:** Information systems. **Engineering technology:** Electrical, heat/ac/refrig. **Health:** Medical secretary, pharmacy assistant.

**Most popular majors.** Business/marketing 27%, computer/information sciences 26%, health sciences 39%.

**Computing on campus.** 104 workstations in library, computer center, student center. Online library available.

**Student life. Freshman orientation:** Mandatory. Preregistration for classes offered. Counseling and Orientation Department holds group meetings (75 participants per session) for all freshmen. Usually held during the first four weeks of each term, these meetings have a duration of approximately 90 minutes. **Activities:** Student government.

**Student services.** Adult student services, alcohol/substance abuse counseling, career counseling, student employment services, financial aid counseling, personal counseling, placement for graduates. **Transfer:** Pre-admission transcript evaluation for new students. Transfer adviser for students transferring to 4-year colleges.

**Contact.** Phone: (787) 852-1430 ext. 31 Fax: (787) 850-1577 Ursula Marchese, Admissions Director, Humacao Community College, PO Box 9139, Humacao, PR 00792-9139

## ICPR Junior College
San Juan, Puerto Rico
www.icprjc.edu

CB member
CB code: 7315

- For-profit 2-year business and junior college
- Commuter campus in large city

**General.** Founded in 1946. Regionally accredited. Multicampus institution with main campus in Hato Rey and branch campuses in Arecibo and Mayaguez. **Enrollment:** 1,426 undergraduates. **Degrees:** 280 associate awarded. **Calendar:** Trimester. **Full-time faculty:** 29 total. **Part-time faculty:** 59 total.

**Basis for selection.** Open admission. Interview required for tourism; hotel management; and bilingual clerk programs.

**2007-2008 Annual costs.** Books/supplies: $954. Personal expenses: $2,556.

**Financial aid. Non-need-based:** Scholarships awarded for state residency.

**Application procedures. Admission:** Closing date 8/15. $25 fee. Admission notification on a rolling basis. **Financial aid:** Closing date 4/15. FAFSA, institutional form required. Applicants notified on a rolling basis starting 11/15.

**Academics.** Word and data processing included in all business programs. **Credit/placement by examination:** CLEP. **Support services:** Tutoring.

**Majors. Business:** Accounting, administrative services, business admin, hotel/motel admin, management information systems, marketing, office technology, tourism/travel. **Computer sciences:** General, applications programming. **Health:** Medical secretary.

**Computing on campus.** 208 workstations in library, computer center.

**Student services.** Career counseling, student employment services, personal counseling, placement for graduates, veterans' counselor. **Physically disabled:** Services for hearing impaired.

**Contact.** E-mail: mvelez@icprjc.edu
Phone: (787) 763-1010 Fax: (787) 763-7249
Maria Velez, Director of Admissions, ICPR Junior College, PO Box 190304, San Juan, PR 00919-0304

## International Junior College of Business and Technology
San Juan, Puerto Rico

CB code: 3220

- For-profit 2-year business and technical college
- Commuter campus in large city

**General.** Accredited by ACICS. **Calendar:** Semester.

**Contact.** Phone: (787) 722-2293
Admissions Director, P.O. Box 19828, San Juan, PR 00910-1828

## National College of Business and Technology: Arecibo
Arecibo, Puerto Rico
www.nationalcollegepr.edu

CB code: 3222

- For-profit 2-year business and technical college
- Commuter campus in small city

**General.** Accredited by ACICS. **Enrollment:** 1,617 degree-seeking undergraduates. **Degrees:** 70 bachelor's, 142 associate awarded. **Calendar:** Trimester. **Full-time faculty:** 28 total; 75% women. **Part-time faculty:** 57 total; 70% women. **Class size:** 44% < 20, 56% 20-39.

**Student profile.**

| | | | |
|---|---|---|---|
| Hispanic American: | 100% | 25 or older: | 2% |

**Basis for selection.** Open admission, but selective for some programs. Admissions based on high school record and test scores. College Entrance Examination Board test or institutional tests required for admissions. **Home-schooled:** State high school equivalency certificate required.

**High school preparation.** 18 units required. Required units include English 3, mathematics 3, history 3, science 3, foreign language 3 and academic electives 3.

**2007-2008 Annual costs.** Tuition/fees: $6,295. Per-credit charge: $135.

**Financial aid. Need-based:** Need-based aid available for part-time students. Work-study available nights, weekends and for part-time students.

**Application procedures. Admission:** No deadline. $25 fee. Application must be submitted on paper. Admission notification on a rolling basis. **Financial aid:** Priority date 12/31, closing date 4/29. Applicants notified on a rolling basis starting 5/2; must reply by 5/15 or within 2 week(s) of notification.

**Academics. Special study options:** ESL, independent study, internships, teacher certification program. **Credit/placement by examination:** AP, CLEP. **Support services:** Tutoring.

**Majors. Business:** Administrative services, business admin, office/clerical, tourism/travel. **Computer sciences:** General. **Engineering technology:** Electrical. **Health:** Dental assistant, medical secretary, nursing (RN), pharmacy assistant. **Legal studies:** Legal secretary.

**Computing on campus.** Online library, helpline, student web hosting available.

**Student life. Freshman orientation:** Available. Preregistration for classes offered. **Activities:** Student newspaper.

**Athletics. Intramural:** Basketball, softball, table tennis, volleyball.

**Student services.** Career counseling, financial aid counseling, personal counseling, placement for graduates, veterans' counselor. **Transfer:** Re-entry adviser for new students. Transfer adviser for students transferring to 4-year colleges.

**Contact.** E-mail: aaviles@nationalcollegepr.edu
Phone: (787) 879-5044 ext. 2504 Toll-free number: (800) 780-5134
Fax: (787) 879-5047
Mercedes Pagán, Admissions Director, National College of Business and Technology: Arecibo, PO Box 4035, MSC 452, Arecibo, PR 00614

## National College of Business and Technology: Bayamon
Bayamón, Puerto Rico                                   CB member
www.nationalcollegepr.edu                              CB code: 7135

♦ For-profit 2-year business and technical college
♦ Commuter campus in small city

**General.** Accredited by ACICS. **Enrollment:** 2,408 degree-seeking undergraduates. **Degrees:** 52 bachelor's, 296 associate awarded. **Location:** 25 miles from San Juan. **Calendar:** Trimester. **Full-time faculty:** 39 total; 62% women. **Part-time faculty:** 70 total; 73% women. **Class size:** 38% < 20, 58% 20-39, 4% 40-49.

**Student profile.** Of all enrolled students, 5% already have a bachelor's degree or higher.

| Hispanic American: | 100% | 25 or older: | 70% |
|---|---|---|---|

**Transfer out. Colleges most students transferred to 2007:** Inter-American University, UCB-Central University of Bayamon, Caribbean University.

**Basis for selection.** Open admission, but selective for some programs. **Homeschooled:** State high school equivalency certificate required.

**High school preparation.** 18 units required. Required units include English 3, mathematics 3, history 3, science 3, foreign language 3 and academic electives 3.

**2007-2008 Annual costs.** Tuition/fees: $6,295. Per-credit charge: $135.

**Financial aid.** All financial aid based on need. Need-based aid available for part-time students. Work-study available nights, weekends and for part-time students.

**Application procedures. Admission:** No deadline. $25 fee. Application must be submitted on paper. Admission notification on a rolling basis. **Financial aid:** Priority date 12/31, closing date 4/29. FAFSA required. Applicants notified on a rolling basis starting 5/2; must reply by 5/15 or within 2 week(s) of notification.

**Academics. Special study options:** ESL, independent study, internships, teacher certification program. Bachelor's degree programs available on campus. **Credit/placement by examination:** AP, CLEP. **Support services:** Tutoring.

**Majors. Business:** Accounting, administrative services, entrepreneurial studies, office technology, tourism/travel. **Computer sciences:** Information systems, programming. **Engineering technology:** Electrical. **Health:** Dental assistant, nursing (RN), pharmacy assistant. **Legal studies:** Legal secretary.

**Computing on campus.** Online library, student web hosting available.

**Student life. Freshman orientation:** Available. Preregistration for classes offered. **Housing:** Substance-free housing available. **Activities:** Student newspaper.

**Athletics. Intramural:** Basketball M, softball M, table tennis, volleyball W.

**Student services.** Career counseling, financial aid counseling, personal counseling, placement for graduates, veterans' counselor. **Transfer:** Re-entry adviser for new students. Transfer adviser for students transferring to 4-year colleges.

**Contact.** E-mail: mepagan@nationalcollegepr.edu
Phone: (787) 780-5134 ext. 4000 Toll-free number: (800) 780-5134
Fax: (787) 740-7360
Mercedes Pagán, Admissions and Marketing Director, National College of Business and Technology: Bayamon, PO Box 2036, Bayamón, PR 00960

## National College of Business and Technology: Rio Grande
Río Grande, Puerto Rico
www.nationalcollegepr.edu

♦ For-profit 2-year business and technical college
♦ Commuter campus in small town

**General.** Accredited by ACICS. **Enrollment:** 1,221 degree-seeking undergraduates. **Degrees:** 2 bachelor's, 168 associate awarded. **Calendar:** Trimester. **Full-time faculty:** 19 total; 63% women. **Part-time faculty:** 58 total; 69% women. **Class size:** 59% < 20, 37% 20-39, 4% 40-49.

**Basis for selection.** Open admission, but selective for some programs. **Homeschooled:** State high school equivalency certificate required.

**High school preparation.** 18 units required. Required units include English 3, mathematics 3, history 3, science 3, foreign language 3 and academic electives 3.

**2007-2008 Annual costs.** Tuition/fees: $6,295. Per-credit charge: $135.

**Financial aid.** All financial aid based on need. Need-based aid available for part-time students. Work-study available nights, weekends and for part-time students.

**Application procedures. Admission:** No deadline. $25 fee. Application must be submitted on paper. Admission notification on a rolling basis. **Financial aid:** FAFSA required. Applicants notified by 12/31; must reply by 5/15 or within 2 week(s) of notification.

**Academics. Special study options:** ESL, independent study, internships, teacher certification program. **Credit/placement by examination:** CLEP. **Support services:** GED preparation, tutoring.

**Majors. Business:** Accounting, business admin, entrepreneurial studies, tourism/travel. **Computer sciences:** Data processing, information technology. **Health:** Dental assistant, medical secretary, nursing (RN), pharmacy assistant. **Legal studies:** Legal secretary.

**Most popular majors.** Business/marketing 29%, computer/information sciences 9%, health sciences 62%.

**Student life. Freshman orientation:** Available. Preregistration for classes offered. **Housing:** Substance-free housing available. **Activities:** Choral groups.

**Athletics. Intramural:** Table tennis, volleyball.

**Student services.** Career counseling, financial aid counseling, personal counseling. **Transfer:** Re-entry adviser for new students. Transfer adviser for students transferring to 4-year colleges.

**Contact.** E-mail: lalvira@nationalcollegepr.edu
Phone: (800) 981-0812
Lourdes Balseiro-Astor, Executive Director, National College of Business and Technology: Rio Grande, PO Box 3064, Río Grande, PR 00745

## Ponce Paramedical College
Ponce, Puerto Rico
www.popac.edu

♦ For-profit 2-year health science and junior college
♦ Small city

**General.** Accredited by ACCSCT. **Enrollment:** 2,693 degree-seeking undergraduates. **Degrees:** 87 associate awarded. **Calendar:** Differs by program, extensive summer session. **Full-time faculty:** 55 total; 6% have terminal degrees, 74% women. **Part-time faculty:** 182 total; 11% have terminal degrees, 52% women.

**Student profile.** Among degree-seeking undergraduates, 1,184 enrolled as first-time, first-year students.

| Part-time: | 15% | Women: | 67% |
|---|---|---|---|

**Basis for selection.** Open admission. **Homeschooled:** Transcript of courses and grades, state high school equivalency certificate, interview required.

**Application procedures. Admission:** No deadline. $25 fee. Admission notification on a rolling basis.

**Academics. Credit/placement by examination:** CLEP. **Support services:** Tutoring.

**Majors. Health:** Nursing (RN), respiratory therapy technology.

**Computing on campus.** Online library available.

**Student life. Activities:** Student newspaper.

**Contact.** E-mail: admisiones@popac-pr.com
Phone: (787) 848-1589 ext. 413 Toll-free number: (800) 981-7184
Ruth Negron, Director of Admissions, Ponce Paramedical College, Calle Acacia L-1213, Urb. Villa Flores, Ponce, PR 00731

## Puerto Rico Tech Junior College
### Hato Rey, Puerto Rico
www.puertoricotechjuniorcollege.com          CB code: 3022

- For-profit 2-year technical college
- Large city

**General.** Accredited by ACCSCT. **Calendar:** Continuous.

**Annual costs/financial aid.** Tuition $8,175 for 20 month associate's program.

**Contact.** Phone: (787) 751-0628
Director of Admissions, Avenue Ponce de Leon #703, Esq. Calle Ponce, Hato Rey, PR 00917

## Ramirez College of Business and Technology
### San Juan, Puerto Rico
www.ramirezcollege.com          CB code: 0386

- For-profit 2-year business and technical college
- Large city

**General.** Accredited by ACICS. **Enrollment:** 512 undergraduates. **Degrees:** 55 associate awarded. **Calendar:** Quarter. **Full-time faculty:** 26 total. **Part-time faculty:** 26 total.

**Basis for selection.** Applicants should have a 2.0 grade, interview also considered.

**2007-2008 Annual costs.** Books/supplies: $325. Personal expenses: $1,300.

**Financial aid.** All financial aid based on need. Need-based aid available for part-time students.

**Application procedures. Admission:** No deadline. $25 fee. **Financial aid:** Priority date 5/1, closing date 6/30. Applicants notified on a rolling basis starting 9/30; must reply within 2 week(s) of notification.

**Academics. Special study options:** License preparation in dental hygiene, nursing. **Credit/placement by examination:** CLEP. **Support services:** GED preparation.

**Majors. Business:** General, accounting, administrative services, office/clerical. **Computer sciences:** Programming. **Health:** Dental assistant, licensed practical nurse. **Visual/performing arts:** General, commercial/advertising art, industrial design.

**Student life. Freshman orientation:** Mandatory. Preregistration for classes offered. Beginning of each trimester.

**Athletics. Intercollegiate:** Cross-country, softball, table tennis, track and field, volleyball M. **Intramural:** Track and field.

**Contact.** E-mail: ramirezcollege@prtc.net
Phone: (787) 763-3120 Fax: (787) 728-7023
Arnaldo Melendez, Admissions Director, Ramirez College of Business and Technology, PO Box 21360, San Juan, PR 00928-1360

## Universal Technology College of Puerto Rico
### Aguadilla, Puerto Rico
www.unitecpr.edu/

- Private 2-year health science and career college
- Commuter campus in small city

**General.** Accredited by ACCSCT. **Enrollment:** 1,206 degree-seeking undergraduates. **Degrees:** 71 associate awarded. **Calendar:** Semester, limited summer session. **Full-time faculty:** 76 total; 8% have terminal degrees, 100% minority, 59% women. **Part-time faculty:** 39 total. **Class size:** 10% < 20, 90% 20-39. **Special facilities:** Art gallery, peace gallery (commemorating winners of Nobel Prize).

**Student profile.** Among degree-seeking undergraduates, 6% enrolled in a vocational program, .41% already have a bachelor's degree or higher, 600 enrolled as first-time, first-year students, 80 transferred in from other institutions.

| | | | |
|---|---|---|---|
| Part-time: | 1% | 25 or older: | 28% |
| Women: | 59% | | |

**Basis for selection.** Open admission. **Homeschooled:** State high school equivalency certificate required.

**High school preparation.** 21 units required. Required units include English 3, mathematics 1, history 1, science 1, computer science 1, visual/performing arts 1 and academic electives 12. 3 Spanish units required.

**2007-2008 Annual costs.** Books/supplies: $450. Personal expenses: $250.

**2006-2007 Financial aid.** All financial aid based on need. 594 full-time freshmen applied for aid; 582 were judged to have need; 580 of these received aid. Average need met was 98%. Average scholarship/grant was $115. 98% of total undergraduate aid awarded as scholarships/grants, 2% as loans/jobs. Need-based aid available for part-time students. Work-study available nights, weekends and for part-time students.

**Application procedures. Admission:** No deadline. $20 fee. Application must be submitted on paper. Admission notification on a rolling basis. **Financial aid:** Priority date 4/30, closing date 6/30. FAFSA, institutional form required. Applicants notified on a rolling basis starting 2/1; must reply by 6/30.

**Academics. Special study options:** Weekend college. License preparation in nursing, paramedic. **Credit/placement by examination:** CLEP. **Support services:** Reduced course load, study skills assistance, tutoring.

**Majors. Business:** Administrative services. **Computer sciences:** Programming. **Health:** Nursing (RN).

**Most popular majors.** Business/marketing 30%, health sciences 70%.

**Student life. Freshman orientation:** Mandatory. **Activities:** Student newspaper.

**Athletics. Team name:** Delfines.

**Student services.** Financial aid counseling, on-campus daycare, placement for graduates, veterans' counselor. **Transfer:** Re-entry adviser, preadmission transcript evaluation for new students.

**Contact.** E-mail: admisiones@unitecpr.net
Phone: (787) 882-2065 ext. 308 Toll-free number: (188) 864-8322 ext. 308
Fax: (787) 891-2370
Teresita Rivera, Admissions Coordinator, Universal Technology College of Puerto Rico, Apartado 1955, Victoria Station, Aguadilla, PR 00605

# Rhode Island

## Community College of Rhode Island
**Warwick, Rhode Island**
www.ccri.edu

CB member
CB code: 3733

▶ Public 2-year community college
▶ Commuter campus in small city

**General.** Founded in 1964. Regionally accredited. Additional campuses in Lincoln, Providence and Newport. **Enrollment:** 15,081 degree-seeking undergraduates; 1,730 non-degree-seeking students. **Degrees:** 1,145 associate awarded. **ROTC:** Army. **Location:** 10 miles from Providence. **Calendar:** Semester, extensive summer session. **Full-time faculty:** 295 total; 61% women. **Part-time faculty:** 418 total; 48% women. **Special facilities:** Observatory.

**Student profile.** Among degree-seeking undergraduates, 3,737 enrolled as first-time, first-year students, 397 transferred in from other institutions.

| | | | |
|---|---|---|---|
| Part-time: | 59% | Asian American: | 3% |
| Out-of-state: | 6% | Hispanic American: | 12% |
| Women: | 63% | Native American: | 1% |
| African American: | 7% | 25 or older: | 40% |

**Transfer out. Colleges most students transferred to 2007:** Rhode Island College, University of Rhode Island, New England Institute of Technology, Johnson and Wales University, Roger Williams University.

**Basis for selection.** Open admission, but selective for some programs. Placement testing in mathematics and English is required and chemistry may be required for programs with limited enrollment.

**High school preparation.** Some programs may require mathematics and science background. Special considerations for nursing and allied health applicants.

**2007-2008 Annual costs.** Tuition/fees: $2,846; $7,766 out-of-state. Per-credit charge: $117 in-state; $356 out-of-state. Books/supplies: $935. Personal expenses: $1,251.

**Financial aid. Need-based:** Need-based aid available for part-time students. Work-study available nights, weekends and for part-time students. **Non-need-based:** Scholarships awarded for athletics.

**Application procedures. Admission:** No deadline. $20 fee, may be waived for applicants with need. Application must be submitted on paper. Admission notification on a rolling basis beginning on or about 1/1. Application closing date and admitted student reply deadline is the first week of fall semester in September and first week of spring semester in January. After the first week of each semester, applicants are processed for the following semester. **Financial aid:** Priority date 3/1; no closing date. FAFSA, institutional form required. Applicants notified on a rolling basis starting 5/1; must reply within 2 week(s) of notification.

**Academics. Special study options:** Cooperative education, cross-registration, distance learning, double major, dual enrollment of high school students, ESL, honors, internships, study abroad, weekend college. License preparation in dental hygiene, nursing, occupational therapy, physical therapy, radiology, real estate. **Credit/placement by examination:** AP, CLEP. 30 credit hours maximum toward associate degree. **Support services:** GED preparation and test center, learning center, reduced course load, remedial instruction, study skills assistance, tutoring, writing center.

**Majors. Biology:** Biotechnology. **Business:** General, accounting, administrative services, banking/financial services, business admin, customer service, marketing. **Computer sciences:** General, applications programming, networking, webmaster. **Education:** Kindergarten/preschool, special. **Engineering:** General, surveying. **Engineering technology:** Computer, computer hardware, electrical, mechanical, telecommunications. **Family/consumer sciences:** Aging. **Health:** Clinical lab technology, dental hygiene, histologic assistant, massage therapy, medical secretary, nursing (RN), occupational therapy assistant, physical therapy assistant, radiologic technology/medical imaging, respiratory therapy technology, sonography, substance abuse counseling. **Interdisciplinary:** Biological/physical sciences. **Legal studies:** Legal secretary, paralegal. **Liberal arts:** Arts/sciences. **Protective services:** Firefighting, police science. **Public administration:** Social work. **Science technology:** Chemical. **Visual/performing arts:** Art, dramatic, jazz, theater design.

**Most popular majors.** Business/marketing 11%, education 6%, health sciences 32%, liberal arts 30%, security/protective services 8%.

**Computing on campus.** 1,200 workstations in library, computer center, student center. Commuter students can connect to campus network. Online course registration, online library, helpline available.

**Student life. Freshman orientation:** Mandatory. Preregistration for classes offered. **Activities:** Bands, choral groups, dance, drama, music ensembles, student government, student newspaper, Black American student association, Latin American student organization, Spanish club, German club, Portuguese club, French club, South East Asian club, organization for students with disabilities, minority mentoring program, Distributive Education Club of America.

**Athletics.** NJCAA. **Intercollegiate:** Baseball M, basketball, cross-country, golf, soccer, softball W, tennis, track and field, volleyball W. **Intramural:** Basketball, cross-country, volleyball, water polo. **Team name:** Knights.

**Student services.** Adult student services, alcohol/substance abuse counseling, campus ministries, career counseling, services for economically disadvantaged, student employment services, financial aid counseling, health services, minority student services, on-campus daycare, personal counseling, placement for graduates, veterans' counselor, women's services. **Physically disabled:** Services for visually, speech, hearing impaired. **Transfer:** Re-entry adviser, pre-admission transcript evaluation for new students. Transfer adviser, college fairs on campus for students transferring to 4-year colleges.

**Contact.** Phone: (401) 825-2003 Fax: (401) 825-2394
Nick Figueroa, Assistant Dean of Enrollment Services, Community College of Rhode Island, 400 East Avenue, Warwick, RI 02886-1807

# South Carolina

Two-Year Colleges

## Aiken Technical College
Aiken, South Carolina
www.atc.edu                              CB code: 5037

◆ Public 2-year community and technical college
◆ Commuter campus in small city

**General.** Founded in 1972. Regionally accredited. **Enrollment:** 2,529 degree-seeking undergraduates. **Degrees:** 202 associate awarded. **Location:** 8 miles from Aiken, 10 miles from Augusta, Georgia. **Calendar:** Semester, extensive summer session. **Full-time faculty:** 57 total. **Part-time faculty:** 76 total. **Class size:** 67% < 20, 33% 20-39.

**Student profile.**

| | | | |
|---|---|---|---|
| Out-of-state: | 13% | 25 or older: | 40% |

**Transfer out. Colleges most students transferred to 2007:** Augusta State University, Lander University, University of South Carolina.

**Basis for selection.** Open admission, but selective for some programs. Special requirements for nursing, dental assisting, predental hygiene, pre-physical therapy, and prepharmacy technician. Test scores considered if submitted. Interview recommended. **Adult students:** SAT/ACT scores not required.

**High school preparation.** 18 units recommended. Recommended units include English 4, mathematics 4, social studies 2, history 2, science 2, foreign language 2 and academic electives 2.

**2007-2008 Annual costs.** Tuition/fees: $3,298; $3,658 out-of-district; $8,982 out-of-state. Books/supplies: $450. Personal expenses: $900.

**Financial aid. Need-based:** Need-based aid available for part-time students. Work-study available nights, weekends and for part-time students. **Non-need-based:** Scholarships awarded for academics, athletics, leadership, minority status, state residency.

**Application procedures. Admission:** Priority date 7/1; no deadline. No application fee. Application may be submitted online. Admission notification on a rolling basis. **Financial aid:** Priority date 5/1, closing date 6/30. FAFSA required. Applicants notified on a rolling basis starting 4/1; must reply within 2 week(s) of notification.

**Academics. Special study options:** Combined bachelor's/graduate degree, cooperative education, cross-registration, distance learning, double major, dual enrollment of high school students, ESL, independent study, internships, liberal arts/career combination. License preparation in aviation, nursing, real estate. **Credit/placement by examination:** AP, CLEP, institutional tests. **Support services:** Learning center, reduced course load, remedial instruction, study skills assistance, tutoring, writing center.

**Majors. Business:** Accounting, administrative services, business admin, sales/distribution. **Computer sciences:** Data processing. **Education:** Voc/tech. **Engineering:** Computer, electrical. **Engineering technology:** Computer, electrical, electromechanical, mechanical drafting. **Health:** Medical radiologic technology/radiation therapy, nursing (RN). **Liberal arts:** Arts/sciences. **Mechanic/repair:** Industrial. **Production:** Machine tool. **Protective services:** Criminal justice. **Public administration:** Human services, social work. **Science technology:** Nuclear power.

**Most popular majors.** Business/marketing 20%, computer/information sciences 6%, engineering/engineering technologies 6%, family/consumer sciences 11%, interdisciplinary studies 21%, liberal arts 17%, public administration/social services 7%.

**Computing on campus.** 1,005 workstations in library, computer center, student center. Online library, helpline, repair service available.

**Student life. Freshman orientation:** Available. Preregistration for classes offered. **Activities:** Drama, student government, student newspaper, Phi Theta Kappa Honor Society.

**Athletics.** NJCAA. **Intercollegiate:** Basketball M, golf M, softball W. **Intramural:** Basketball, softball, volleyball. **Team name:** Knights.

**Student services.** Adult student services, career counseling, services for economically disadvantaged, student employment services, financial aid counseling, minority student services, on-campus daycare, personal counseling, placement for graduates, veterans' counselor. **Physically disabled:** Services for visually, speech, hearing impaired. **Transfer:** Pre-admission transcript evaluation for new students. Transfer adviser, college fairs on campus for students transferring to 4-year colleges.

**Contact.** E-mail: admiss2@atc.edu
Phone: (803) 593-9954 ext. 1223 Fax: (803) 593-6526
Dawn Butts, Director of Admissions and Records, Aiken Technical College, PO Drawer 696, Aiken, SC 29802

## Central Carolina Technical College
Sumter, South Carolina
www.cctech.edu                           CB code: 5665

◆ Public 2-year community and technical college
◆ Commuter campus in large town

**General.** Founded in 1963. Regionally accredited. Branch campuses in Clarendon, Kershaw, and Lee Counties. Additional facility located at Shaw Air Force Base. **Enrollment:** 3,283 degree-seeking undergraduates. **Degrees:** 217 associate awarded. **Location:** 45 miles from Columbia. **Calendar:** Semester, limited summer session. **Full-time faculty:** 81 total. **Part-time faculty:** 154 total. **Special facilities:** South Carolina Environmental Training Center.

**Transfer out. Colleges most students transferred to 2007:** Unversity of South Carolina, Clemson University, Coker College, Lander University, St Leo University.

**Basis for selection.** Open admission, but selective for some programs. Minimum SAT Verbal 510 and Math 510 or minimum ACT 22 composite required of nursing applicants. Test scores required for placement. Interview required for nursing program.

**2007-2008 Annual costs.** Tuition/fees: $2,925; $3,425 out-of-district; $5,181 out-of-state. Books/supplies: $900.

**2006-2007 Financial aid.** All financial aid based on need. 84% of total undergraduate aid awarded as scholarships/grants, 16% as loans/jobs. Need-based aid available for part-time students. Work-study available nights and for part-time students.

**Application procedures. Admission:** No deadline. $25 fee. Application may be submitted online. Admission notification on a rolling basis. **Financial aid:** Priority date 6/15; no closing date. FAFSA required. Applicants notified on a rolling basis; must reply within 2 week(s) of notification.

**Academics. Special study options:** Cooperative education, distance learning, dual enrollment of high school students, independent study, internships. License preparation in nursing. **Credit/placement by examination:** AP, CLEP, institutional tests. 15 credit hours maximum toward associate degree. **Support services:** GED preparation and test center, learning center, reduced course load, remedial instruction, study skills assistance, tutoring.

**Majors. Business:** Accounting, administrative services, management science, marketing. **Computer sciences:** Programming. **Conservation:** Management/policy. **Engineering technology:** Civil, drafting. **Health:** Nursing (RN), surgical technology. **Legal studies:** Paralegal. **Liberal arts:** Arts/sciences.

**Computing on campus.** 125 workstations in library, computer center. Commuter students can connect to campus network. Online library, helpline available.

**Student life. Freshman orientation:** Available. Preregistration for classes offered. **Activities:** Phi Theta Kappa, Earth club, computer club.

**Student services.** Career counseling, student employment services, financial aid counseling, personal counseling, placement for graduates, veterans' counselor, women's services. **Physically disabled:** Services for visually, speech, hearing impaired. **Transfer:** Pre-admission transcript evaluation for new students. Transfer adviser, college fairs on campus for students transferring to 4-year colleges.

**Contact.** E-mail: admissions@sumtec.sc.us
Phone: (803) 778-6605 Toll-free number: (800) 221-8711 ext. 205
Fax: (803) 778-6696
Lisa Bracken, Director of Admissions and Student Services, Central Carolina Technical College, 506 North Guignard Drive, Sumter, SC 29150-2499

## Denmark Technical College
**Denmark, South Carolina**
www.denmarktech.edu

CB code: 5744

- Public 2-year technical college
- Residential campus in small town

**General.** Founded in 1948. Regionally accredited. **Enrollment:** 1,348 degree-seeking undergraduates; 223 non-degree-seeking students. **Degrees:** 107 associate awarded. **ROTC:** Army. **Location:** 55 miles from Columbia. **Calendar:** Semester, extensive summer session. **Full-time faculty:** 41 total; 100% have terminal degrees, 51% women. **Part-time faculty:** 9 total; 100% have terminal degrees, 11% women.

**Student profile.** Among degree-seeking undergraduates, 709 enrolled as first-time, first-year students.

| | | | |
|---|---|---|---|
| Part-time: | 32% | Women: | 59% |
| Out-of-state: | 3% | Live on campus: | 50% |

**Basis for selection.** Open admission. Interview recommended.

**High school preparation.** Recommended units include English 4, mathematics 4, social studies 2, science 2 and foreign language 2. College preparatory program required for AA and AS transfer college programs.

**2007-2008 Annual costs.** Tuition/fees: $2,378; $4,466 out-of-state. Room/board: $3,310. Books/supplies: $1,100. Personal expenses: $2,000.

**Financial aid. Need-based:** Need-based aid available for part-time students.

**Application procedures. Admission:** No deadline. $10 fee, may be waived for applicants with need. Admission notification on a rolling basis. **Financial aid:** No deadline. FAFSA required. Applicants notified on a rolling basis starting 6/1; must reply within 2 week(s) of notification.

**Academics. Special study options:** Cooperative education, cross-registration, independent study, internships. License preparation in nursing. **Credit/placement by examination:** AP, CLEP, institutional tests. **Support services:** GED preparation, learning center, reduced course load, remedial instruction, tutoring.

**Majors. Business:** General. **Health:** Licensed practical nurse. **Liberal arts:** Arts/sciences. **Mechanic/repair:** Electronics/electrical. **Public administration:** Human services.

**Computing on campus.** 85 workstations in library. Dormitories wired for high-speed internet access and linked to campus network. Commuter students can connect to campus network. Wireless network available.

**Student life. Freshman orientation:** Mandatory. Preregistration for classes offered. **Housing:** Single-sex dorms available. **Activities:** Choral groups, student government, student newspaper, Student Christian Association.

**Athletics. Intercollegiate:** Basketball. **Intramural:** Basketball. **Team name:** Panthers and Lady Panthers.

**Student services.** Career counseling, student employment services, health services, personal counseling, placement for graduates, veterans' counselor. **Learning disabled:** Comprehensive services available. **Transfer:** College fairs on campus for students transferring to 4-year colleges.

**Contact.** Phone: (803) 793-5176 Fax: (803) 793-5942
Tonya Thomas, Dean of Enrollment Management, Denmark Technical College, Solomon Blatt Boulevard, Denmark, SC 29042

## Florence-Darlington Technical College
**Florence, South Carolina**
www.fdtc.edu

CB member
CB code: 5207

- Public 2-year community and technical college
- Commuter campus in small city

**General.** Founded in 1964. Regionally accredited. **Enrollment:** 2,192 full-time, degree-seeking students. **Degrees:** 395 associate awarded. **Location:** 80 miles from Columbia, 50 miles from Myrtle Beach. **Calendar:** Semester, limited summer session. **Full-time faculty:** 105 total. **Part-time faculty:** 115 total. **Partnerships:** Formal partnerships with local, regional, and national corporations which enhance student opportunities for training.

**Transfer out.** Colleges most students transferred to 2007: Francis Marion University, Clemson University, University of South Carolina.

**Basis for selection.** Open admission, but selective for some programs. Special requirements for allied health and nursing programs. Computerized Placement Test administered as alternative to SAT or ACT for placement for most programs. RSAT, NLN, HOAE or HOBET required for some allied health programs. Interview required for allied health, nursing programs. **Homeschooled:** GED may be required.

**High school preparation.** Recommended units include English 4, mathematics 3, social studies 2, history 1, science 2 (laboratory 2), foreign language 2 and academic electives 2. Algebra I, algebra II, biology, and chemistry required for most health programs.

**2007-2008 Annual costs.** Tuition/fees: $3,190; $3,452 out-of-district; $5,286 out-of-state. Books/supplies: $900. Personal expenses: $2,338.

**Financial aid. Need-based:** Need-based aid available for part-time students. Work-study available for part-time students. **Non-need-based:** Scholarships awarded for academics.

**Application procedures. Admission:** Priority date 7/15; deadline 8/10. No application fee. Application may be submitted online. Admission notification on a rolling basis beginning on or about 1/1. **Financial aid:** Priority date 5/1; no closing date. FAFSA required. Applicants notified on a rolling basis starting 7/1; must reply within 2 week(s) of notification.

**Academics. Special study options:** Cooperative education, cross-registration, distance learning, dual enrollment of high school students, independent study, internships, liberal arts/career combination. Cooperative program with Greenville Technical College for physical therapy, Fayetteville Technical College for funeral services. License preparation in dental hygiene, nursing, physical therapy. **Credit/placement by examination:** AP, CLEP, IB, institutional tests. Student may receive credit for up to 50% of the course work required by his or her major. **Support services:** GED preparation, learning center, reduced course load, remedial instruction, tutoring.

**Majors. Business:** Accounting, administrative services, entrepreneurial studies, sales/distribution. **Computer sciences:** Data processing. **Education:** Voc/tech. **Engineering technology:** Civil, drafting, electrical. **Health:** Clinical lab technology, dental hygiene, medical radiologic technology/radiation therapy, medical records technology, nursing (RN), physical therapy assistant, respiratory therapy technology. **Legal studies:** Paralegal. **Liberal arts:** Arts/sciences. **Mechanic/repair:** Automotive, heating/ac/refrig. **Personal/culinary services:** Mortuary science. **Physical sciences:** General. **Protective services:** Criminal justice. **Public administration:** Social work.

**Computing on campus.** 128 workstations in library, computer center. Commuter students can connect to campus network.

**Student life. Freshman orientation:** Mandatory. Preregistration for classes offered. **Activities:** Music ensembles, student government, student newspaper.

**Athletics.** NJCAA. **Intercollegiate:** Baseball M, softball W. **Team name:** Stingers.

**Student services.** Career counseling, services for economically disadvantaged, student employment services, financial aid counseling, on-campus daycare, personal counseling, placement for graduates, veterans' counselor. **Physically disabled:** Services for hearing impaired. **Transfer:** Transfer adviser for students transferring to 4-year colleges.

**Contact.** E-mail: admissions@fdtc.edu
Phone: (843) 661-8324 Toll-free number: (800) 228-5745
Fax: (843) 661-8041
Vivian Gallman, Director of Admissions, Florence-Darlington Technical College, PO Box 100548, Florence, SC 29501-0548

## Forrest Junior College
**Anderson, South Carolina**
www.forrestcollege.edu

CB code: 7138

- For-profit 2-year community and junior college
- Commuter campus in large town
- Application essay, interview required

**General.** Accredited by ACICS. Majority of students are working adults with children. Free child care provided. **Enrollment:** 106 degree-seeking undergraduates. **Degrees:** 21 associate awarded. **Location:** 30 miles from Greenville. **Calendar:** Quarter, extensive summer session. **Full-time faculty:** 3 total; 33% have terminal degrees, 100% women. **Part-time faculty:** 20 total; 75% have terminal degrees, 35% minority, 75% women.

Two-Year Colleges

**Student profile.** Among degree-seeking undergraduates, 86 enrolled as first-time, first-year students.

| | | | |
|---|---|---|---|
| Part-time: | 6% | 25 or older: | 60% |
| Women: | 92% | | |

**Transfer out.** 15% of students enrolled in the transfer program go on to 4-year colleges. **Colleges most students transferred to 2007:** Greenville Technical College, Piedmont Technical College, Lander University, Strayer University, Webster University.

**Basis for selection.** Open admission, but selective for some programs. Audition, portfolio recommended.

**2007-2008 Annual costs.** Tuition/fees: $7,160. Per-credit charge: $148.

**Financial aid.** All financial aid based on need. Need-based aid available for part-time students. Work-study available nights, weekends and for part-time students.

**Application procedures. Admission:** No deadline. $50 fee. Admission notification on a rolling basis. **Financial aid:** No deadline. FAFSA required. Applicants notified on a rolling basis starting 4/30; must reply by 5/31 or within 4 week(s) of notification.

**Academics. Special study options:** Cooperative education, double major, ESL, independent study, internships, liberal arts/career combination, weekend college. **Credit/placement by examination:** AP, CLEP, institutional tests. **Support services:** Reduced course load, tutoring.

**Majors. Business:** General, accounting, administrative services, business admin, communications, human resources, managerial economics, marketing, office management, office technology, office/clerical. **Computer sciences:** General, information systems. **Education:** Early childhood, sales/marketing, teacher assistance. **Family/consumer sciences:** Child care. **Health:** Clinical lab assistant, clinical lab technology, medical assistant, medical records admin, medical records technology, medical secretary, medical transcription. **Legal studies:** Legal secretary, paralegal. **Personal/culinary services:** General.

**Computing on campus.** 52 workstations in library, computer center. Online library, repair service available.

**Student life. Freshman orientation:** Mandatory. Preregistration for classes offered. **Activities:** Literary magazine, student government, student newspaper.

**Student services.** Adult student services, career counseling, student employment services, financial aid counseling, on-campus daycare, placement for graduates. **Transfer:** Pre-admission transcript evaluation for new students.

**Contact.** E-mail: janieturmon@forrestcollege.edu
Phone: (864) 225-7653 ext. 210 Fax: (864) 261-7471
Janie Turmon, Admissions Officer, Forrest Junior College, 601 East River Street, Anderson, SC 29624

## Golf Academy of the Carolinas
**Myrtle Beach, South Carolina**
**www.sdgagolf.com**          CB code: 3223

- For-profit 2-year golf academy
- Large town

**General.** Accredited by ACICS. **Calendar:** Continuous.

**Annual costs/financial aid.** Books/supplies: $700. Personal expenses: $1,552.

**Contact.** Phone: (480) 905-9288
Admissions Director, 7373 North Scottsdale Road, Suite B-100, Scottsdale, AZ 82253

## Greenville Technical College
**Greenville, South Carolina**
**www.gvltec.edu**          CB code: 5278

- Public 2-year community and technical college
- Commuter campus in large city

**General.** Founded in 1962. Regionally accredited. Classes and some programs offered at satellite campuses in Greenville County. **Enrollment:** 12,899

degree-seeking undergraduates; 1,401 non-degree-seeking students. **Degrees:** 974 associate awarded. **Calendar:** Semester, extensive summer session. **Full-time faculty:** 335 total; 9% have terminal degrees, 12% minority, 59% women. **Part-time faculty:** 431 total; 15% have terminal degrees, 12% minority, 63% women.

**Student profile.** Among degree-seeking undergraduates, 29% enrolled in a transfer program, 71% enrolled in a vocational program, 3,018 enrolled as first-time, first-year students.

| | | | |
|---|---|---|---|
| Part-time: | 54% | Asian American: | 2% |
| Out-of-state: | 1% | Hispanic American: | 3% |
| Women: | 62% | Live on campus: | 3% |
| African American: | 24% | | |

**Transfer out.** 92% of students enrolled in the transfer program go on to 4-year colleges.

**Basis for selection.** Open admission, but selective for some programs. Weighted admissions requirements for registered nursing, licensed practical nursing, certain allied health programs. ASSET/COMPASS scores may be submitted for placement in place of SAT or ACT scores. Minimum SAT, ACT, or ASSET scores required for allied health and nursing applicants. Interview required for allied health sciences, nursing, photography, and aircraft mechanic applicants and recommended for all others. Portfolio required for visual arts program. **Learning Disabled:** Contact Student Disability Services early in admission process for appropriate accommodations. Self-identification and documentation required.

**High school preparation.** Algebra, biology, and chemistry are required for most health care program applicants.

**2007-2008 Annual costs.** Tuition/fees: $3,290; $3,566 out-of-district; $6,698 out-of-state. Books/supplies: $976. Personal expenses: $656.

**Financial aid. Need-based:** Need-based aid available for part-time students. Work-study available nights and for part-time students. **Non-need-based:** Scholarships awarded for academics, state residency.

**Application procedures. Admission:** No deadline. $35 fee. Application may be submitted online. Admission notification on a rolling basis. **Financial aid:** Priority date 5/1; no closing date. FAFSA required. Applicants notified on a rolling basis starting 6/15; must reply within 2 week(s) of notification.

**Academics. Special study options:** Accelerated study, cooperative education, distance learning, dual enrollment of high school students, ESL, honors, independent study, internships, liberal arts/career combination, teacher certification program, weekend college. License preparation in aviation, dental hygiene, nursing, occupational therapy, paramedic, physical therapy, radiology, real estate. **Credit/placement by examination:** AP, CLEP, IB, institutional tests. Credits for work experience evaluated and awarded by program department head. Courses requiring research cannot be completed by exam. **Support services:** GED preparation, learning center, reduced course load, remedial instruction, study skills assistance, tutoring, writing center.

**Honors college/program.** Require 3.5 GPA and interview with head of department.

**Majors. Biology:** General. **Business:** Accounting, administrative services, business admin, purchasing, sales/distribution. **Computer sciences:** Data processing. **Engineering technology:** Architectural, construction, electrical, mechanical, mechanical drafting. **Family/consumer sciences:** Child care. **Health:** Clinical lab technology, dental hygiene, EMT paramedic, medical radiologic technology/radiation therapy, medical records technology, nursing (RN), occupational therapy assistant, physical therapy assistant, respiratory therapy technology, sonography. **Legal studies:** Paralegal. **Liberal arts:** Arts/sciences. **Mechanic/repair:** Automotive, industrial. **Personal/culinary services:** Institutional food service. **Production:** Machine tool. **Protective services:** Criminal justice. **Public administration:** Social work. **Social sciences:** Cartography.

**Most popular majors.** Business/marketing 13%, health sciences 38%, liberal arts 19%, trade and industry 6%.

**Computing on campus.** 1,068 workstations in library, computer center. Dormitories wired for high-speed internet access. Commuter students can connect to campus network. Online library, wireless network available.

**Student life. Freshman orientation:** Mandatory. Preregistration for classes offered. **Housing:** $150 nonrefundable deposit. College-affiliated housing available on Barton campus. **Activities:** Campus ministries, drama, international student organizations, student government, American Criminal Justice Association, Campus Crusade for Christ, human services organization, Spanish club, national technical honor society, Phi Theta Kappa, critics choice club.

**Student services.** Adult student services, alcohol/substance abuse counseling, campus ministries, career counseling, services for economically disadvantaged, student employment services, financial aid counseling, on-campus daycare, personal counseling, placement for graduates, veterans' counselor. **Physically disabled:** Services for visually, speech, hearing impaired. **Transfer:** Pre-admission transcript evaluation for new students. Transfer adviser for students transferring to 4-year colleges.

**Contact.** E-mail: carolyn.watkins@gvltec.edu
Phone: (864) 250-8109 Toll-free number: (800) 922-1183
Fax: (864) 250-8534
Carolyn Watkins, Dean of Admissions, Greenville Technical College, PO Box 5616, Greenville, SC 29606-5616

## Horry-Georgetown Technical College
### Conway, South Carolina
www.hgtc.edu
CB code: 5305

- Public 2-year community and technical college
- Commuter campus in large town

**General.** Founded in 1965. Regionally accredited. **Enrollment:** 5,249 degree-seeking undergraduates; 551 non-degree-seeking students. **Degrees:** 565 associate awarded. **Location:** 4 miles from Conway, 8 miles from Myrtle Beach. **Calendar:** Semester, extensive summer session. **Full-time faculty:** 134 total. **Part-time faculty:** 165 total. **Special facilities:** Art gallery, golf course.

**Student profile.** Among degree-seeking undergraduates, 1,158 enrolled as first-time, first-year students.

| | | | |
|---|---|---|---|
| Part-time: | 56% | Asian American: | 1% |
| Out-of-state: | 10% | Hispanic American: | 2% |
| Women: | 67% | Native American: | 1% |
| African American: | 24% | International: | 2% |

**Transfer out.** Colleges most students transferred to 2007: Coastal Carolina University.

**Basis for selection.** Open admission, but selective for some programs. Special requirements for engineering, technology, allied health, science programs.

**2007-2008 Annual costs.** Tuition/fees: $3,114; $3,882 out-of-district; $4,914 out-of-state. Books/supplies: $1,000. Personal expenses: $1,615.

**Financial aid. Need-based:** Need-based aid available for part-time students. **Non-need-based:** Scholarships awarded for academics, state residency. **Additional information:** Participates in South Carolina lottery tuition assistance program. Full-time technical college students who are state residents receive assistance for tuition not covered by federal or need-based grants.

**Application procedures. Admission:** No deadline. $25 fee, may be waived for applicants with need. Application may be submitted online. Admission notification on a rolling basis. **Financial aid:** Priority date 4/1, closing date 6/30. FAFSA required. Applicants notified on a rolling basis starting 4/1.

**Academics. Special study options:** Distance learning, double major, dual enrollment of high school students, exchange student, independent study, internships. License preparation in dental hygiene, nursing, radiology, real estate. **Credit/placement by examination:** CLEP, institutional tests. **Support services:** Learning center, reduced course load, remedial instruction, study skills assistance, tutoring.

**Majors. Agriculture:** Horticulture, turf management. **Business:** General, accounting, administrative services, hotel/motel admin. **Computer sciences:** Data processing. **Conservation:** Forest technology. **Education:** Voc/tech. **Engineering:** Electrical. **Engineering technology:** Civil, construction, electrical. **Family/consumer sciences:** Child care. **Health:** Dental hygiene, EMT paramedic, medical radiologic technology/radiation therapy, nursing (RN), pharmacy assistant. **Legal studies:** Paralegal. **Liberal arts:** Arts/sciences. **Mechanic/repair:** Heating/ac/refrig, industrial electronics. **Personal/culinary services:** Chef training. **Production:** Machine tool. **Protective services:** Criminal justice. **Public administration:** Social work. **Visual/performing arts:** Design.

**Most popular majors.** Business/marketing 16%, engineering/engineering technologies 6%, family/consumer sciences 11%, health sciences 26%, liberal arts 17%, security/protective services 6%.

**Computing on campus.** 900 workstations in library, computer center, student center. Commuter students can connect to campus network. Online course registration, online library, helpline, wireless network available.

**Student life. Freshman orientation:** Available. Preregistration for classes offered. **Activities:** Choral groups.

**Student services.** Career counseling, financial aid counseling, on-campus daycare, personal counseling, placement for graduates, veterans' counselor.

**Contact.** E-mail: Admissions@hgtc.edu
Phone: (843) 349-5277 Fax: (843) 349-7501
George Swindoll, Assistant Vice President for Enrollment Development and Registration, Horry-Georgetown Technical College, PO Box 261966, Conway, SC 29528

## Midlands Technical College
### Columbia, South Carolina
www.midlandstech.edu
CB member
CB code: 5584

- Public 2-year technical college
- Commuter campus in large city

**General.** Founded in 1974. Regionally accredited. Additional campuses include Airport Campus, Beltline Campus, Batesburg-Leesville Center, Enterprise Campus/Center and Harbison Center. **Enrollment:** 10,406 degree-seeking undergraduates; 300 non-degree-seeking students. **Degrees:** 824 associate awarded. **ROTC:** Army, Naval, Air Force. **Location:** 10 miles from Columbia. **Calendar:** Semester, limited summer session. **Full-time faculty:** 247 total; 17% have terminal degrees, 16% minority, 59% women. **Part-time faculty:** 416 total; 10% have terminal degrees, 20% minority, 52% women. **Class size:** 58% < 20, 42% 20-39. **Partnerships:** Formal partnerships with middle schools.

**Student profile.** Among degree-seeking undergraduates, 37% enrolled in a transfer program, 63% enrolled in a vocational program, 2,265 enrolled as first-time, first-year students.

| | | | |
|---|---|---|---|
| Part-time: | 53% | Women: | 61% |
| Out-of-state: | 2% | 25 or older: | 38% |

**Transfer out.** 35% of students enrolled in the transfer program go on to 4-year colleges. **Colleges most students transferred to 2007:** University of South Carolina.

**Basis for selection.** Open admission, but selective for some programs. High school record, SAT/ACT or college placement test scores, and interviews considered for nursing/health science applicants. Admission cut-off scores established for full admission into each program. Students falling below cut-off scores may enter in developmental studies. National League for Nursing Test required of nursing applicants in place of SAT or ACT. Interview, orientation required for health science and nursing programs. **Homeschooled:** Must be an approved Home School Association in South Carolina. If home schooler is applying for concurrent admission they must have a letter of permission from the home school association and a letter of permission from their parent/guardian.

**2007-2008 Annual costs.** Tuition/fees: $3,244; $4,036 out-of-district; $9,532 out-of-state. Books/supplies: $1,240. Personal expenses: $1,200.

**2006-2007 Financial aid. Need-based:** Average need met was 66%. Average scholarship/grant was $3,516; average loan $2,957. 56% of total undergraduate aid awarded as scholarships/grants, 44% as loans/jobs. Need-based aid available for part-time students.

**Application procedures. Admission:** Priority date 7/20; no deadline. No application fee. Application may be submitted online. Admission notification on a rolling basis. **Financial aid:** Priority date 4/15; no closing date. FAFSA required. Applicants notified on a rolling basis; must reply within 2 week(s) of notification.

**Academics. Special study options:** Combined bachelor's/graduate degree, cooperative education, distance learning, dual enrollment of high school students, ESL, liberal arts/career combination. License preparation in nursing, physical therapy, radiology. **Credit/placement by examination:** AP, CLEP, institutional tests. **Support services:** GED preparation, learning center, remedial instruction, study skills assistance, tutoring, writing center.

**Majors. Business:** Accounting, administrative services, business admin. **Computer sciences:** Computer science, data processing, information systems. **Engineering technology:** Architectural, civil, electrical, mechanical drafting. **Health:** Clinical lab technology, dental assistant, dental hygiene, medical radiologic technology/radiation therapy, medical records technology, nuclear medical technology, nursing (RN), pharmacy assistant, physical therapy assistant, respiratory therapy technology. **Legal studies:** Court reporting, paralegal. **Liberal arts:** Arts/sciences. **Mechanic/repair:** Automotive, heating/ac/refrig. **Protective services:** Criminal justice. **Public administration:** Social work. **Visual/performing arts:** Commercial/advertising art.

**Most popular majors.** Business/marketing 10%, computer/information sciences 7%, engineering/engineering technologies 7%, family/consumer sciences 8%, interdisciplinary studies 11%, legal studies 8%, liberal arts 11%, public administration/social services 11%, security/protective services 11%, visual/performing arts 11%.

**Computing on campus.** 46 workstations in library, computer center, student center. Commuter students can connect to campus network. Online course registration, online library, helpline, wireless network available.

**Student life. Freshman orientation:** Available. Preregistration for classes offered. **Activities:** Campus ministries, drama, international student organizations, literary magazine, student government, student newspaper, Campus Crusade for Christ, student human services organization, African American student organization.

**Athletics. Intramural:** Baseball, bowling, equestrian, football (non-tackle), softball, volleyball.

**Student services.** Adult student services, career counseling, services for economically disadvantaged, student employment services, financial aid counseling, placement for graduates, veterans' counselor. **Physically disabled:** Services for visually, speech, hearing impaired. **Learning disabled:** Comprehensive services available. **Transfer:** Re-entry adviser, pre-admission transcript evaluation for new students. Transfer adviser, college fairs on campus for students transferring to 4-year colleges.

**Contact.** E-mail: mtcinfo@midlandstech.edu
Phone: (803) 738-8324 Toll-free number: (800) 922-8038
Fax: (803) 738-7784
Sylvia Littlejohn, Director of Enrollment Services, Midlands Technical College, PO Box 2408, Columbia, SC 29202

---

## Miller-Motte Technical College
### North Charleston, South Carolina
### www.miller-motte.net

- For-profit 2-year branch campus and technical college
- Small city

**General.** Accredited by ACICS. **Enrollment:** 650 degree-seeking undergraduates. **Degrees:** 261 associate awarded. **Calendar:** Quarter. **Full-time faculty:** 40 total. **Part-time faculty:** 50 total.

**2007-2008 Annual costs.** Tuition/fees: $9,225. Per-credit charge: $205. Fees vary according to programs from $6-$20 per credit hour.

**Application procedures. Admission:** No deadline. $35 fee. **Financial aid:** FAFSA, institutional form required. Applicants notified on a rolling basis.

**Academics. Credit/placement by examination:** CLEP.

**Majors. Business:** Accounting/business management, business admin. **Health:** Massage therapy, medical assistant, surgical technology. **Legal studies:** Paralegal.

**Contact.** Phone: (843) 574-0101 Toll-free number: (877) 617-4740
Fax: (843) 266-3424
David Sessoms, Director of Education, Miller-Motte Technical College, 8085 Rivers Avenue, Suite E, North Charleston, SC 29406

---

## Northeastern Technical College
### Cheraw, South Carolina
### www.netc.edu
**CB code: 5095**

- Public 2-year community and technical college
- Commuter campus in small town

**General.** Founded in 1969. Regionally accredited. High percentage of non-traditional students. **Enrollment:** 924 degree-seeking undergraduates; 52 non-degree-seeking students. **Degrees:** 140 associate awarded. **Location:** 89 miles from Columbia. **Calendar:** Semester, extensive summer session. **Full-time faculty:** 30 total; 3% have terminal degrees, 3% minority, 57% women. **Part-time faculty:** 100 total; 3% have terminal degrees, 20% minority, 53% women.

**Student profile.** Among degree-seeking undergraduates, 249 enrolled as first-time, first-year students, 32 transferred in from other institutions.

| | | | |
|---|---|---|---|
| Part-time: | 52% | Women: | 73% |
| Out-of-state: | 1% | 25 or older: | 87% |

---

**Transfer out. Colleges most students transferred to 2007:** Francis Marion University, Clemson University, Coastal Carolina University, Florence-Darlington Technical College, University of South Carolina.

**Basis for selection.** Open admission, but selective for some programs. Special requirements for nursing program, including high school math and science courses and SAT (exclusive of Writing) combined score of 960. Interview recommended. **Homeschooled:** Must be under auspices of school district or an approved homeschool agency.

**High school preparation.** Algebra I and II, chemistry with laboratory required for nursing applicants.

**2007-2008 Annual costs.** Tuition/fees: $2,982; $3,174 out-of-district; $5,454 out-of-state. Books/supplies: $1,200. Personal expenses: $1,800.

**Application procedures. Admission:** Closing date 8/14. $25 fee, may be waived for applicants with need. Admission notification on a rolling basis. **Financial aid:** No deadline. FAFSA required. Applicants notified on a rolling basis; must reply within 8 week(s) of notification.

**Academics. Special study options:** Cross-registration, distance learning, dual enrollment of high school students, independent study, liberal arts/career combination. **Credit/placement by examination:** AP, CLEP, institutional tests. Credit by examination limited to 50% of semester hours required for degree. ASSET and English language proficiency required for placement. **Support services:** Remedial instruction, tutoring.

**Majors. Business:** Accounting, administrative services, business admin, office technology, office/clerical. **Computer sciences:** Data processing. **Education:** General. **Engineering technology:** Electrical. **Health:** Licensed practical nurse. **Liberal arts:** Arts/sciences.

**Computing on campus.** 125 workstations in library, computer center. Online library available.

**Student life. Freshman orientation:** Available. Preregistration for classes offered. Four early orientations held in the summer. **Activities:** Student government, service-leadership organization.

**Student services.** Career counseling, student employment services, personal counseling, placement for graduates, veterans' counselor. **Transfer:** Transfer adviser for students transferring to 4-year colleges.

**Contact.** E-mail: mnewton@netc.edu
Phone: (843) 921-6900 Fax: (843) 921-1476
Mary Newton, Dean of Students, Northeastern Technical College, Drawer 1007, Cheraw, SC 29520

---

## Orangeburg-Calhoun Technical College
### Orangeburg, South Carolina
### www.octech.edu
**CB code: 5527**

- Public 2-year community and technical college
- Commuter campus in large town

**General.** Founded in 1968. Regionally accredited. **Enrollment:** 2,188 degree-seeking undergraduates; 211 non-degree-seeking students. **Degrees:** 459 associate awarded. **ROTC:** Army. **Location:** 75 miles from Charleston, 45 miles from Columbia. **Calendar:** Semester, extensive summer session. **Full-time faculty:** 84 total. **Part-time faculty:** 69 total.

**Student profile.** Among degree-seeking undergraduates, 514 enrolled as first-year, first-year students.

| | | | |
|---|---|---|---|
| Part-time: | 45% | Native American: | 1% |
| Women: | 74% | 25 or older: | 41% |
| African American: | 61% | | |

**Basis for selection.** Open admission, but selective for some programs. Admission to nursing and allied health programs based on school achievement record and test scores. ASSET used for placement. SAT or ACT may be submitted in place of ASSET.

**High school preparation.** 24 units recommended. Recommended units include English 4, mathematics 3, social studies 3, history 2, science 2, foreign language 3 and academic electives 7.

**2007-2008 Annual costs.** Tuition/fees: $2,832; $3,528 out-of-district; $4,464 out-of-state. Books/supplies: $400. Personal expenses: $500.

**Financial aid.** All financial aid based on need. Need-based aid available for part-time students.

**Application procedures. Admission:** No deadline. $15 fee, may be waived for applicants with need. Application may be submitted online. Admission notification on a rolling basis beginning on or about 1/1. $15 application processing fee due upon notification of acceptance. **Financial aid:** Priority date 6/4; no closing date. FAFSA, institutional form required. Applicants notified on a rolling basis starting 5/1; must reply within 2 week(s) of notification.

**Academics. Special study options:** Cooperative education, cross-registration, distance learning, double major, dual enrollment of high school students, independent study, liberal arts/career combination. License preparation in nursing, radiology, real estate. **Credit/placement by examination:** CLEP, institutional tests. 60% of hours needed for degree may be earned by examination. **Support services:** GED preparation and test center, learning center, pre-admission summer program, reduced course load, remedial instruction, study skills assistance, tutoring, writing center.

**Majors. Business:** General, accounting, administrative services. **Computer sciences:** Data processing, programming. **Conservation:** Forest resources. **Engineering technology:** Drafting, electrical. **Health:** Clinical lab assistant, clinical lab technology, medical radiologic technology/radiation therapy, nursing (RN). **Legal studies:** Paralegal. **Liberal arts:** Arts/sciences. **Mechanic/repair:** Automotive, electronics/electrical. **Protective services:** Criminal justice.

**Computing on campus.** 100 workstations in library, computer center, student center. Commuter students can connect to campus network. Online course registration, online library, helpline, repair service, wireless network available.

**Student life. Freshman orientation:** Available. Preregistration for classes offered. **Activities:** Student government, honor fraternities, curriculum clubs.

**Athletics. Intramural:** Basketball, volleyball.

**Student services.** Adult student services, career counseling, services for economically disadvantaged, student employment services, financial aid counseling, minority student services, personal counseling, placement for graduates, veterans' counselor. **Physically disabled:** Services for visually, speech, hearing impaired. **Transfer:** Pre-admission transcript evaluation for new students. Transfer adviser, college fairs on campus for students transferring to 4-year colleges.

**Contact.** E-mail: felderb@octech.edu
Phone: (803) 535-1218 Fax: (803) 535-1388
Bobbie Felder, Dean of Students, Orangeburg-Calhoun Technical College, 3250 St. Matthews Road, Orangeburg, SC 29118-8222

## Piedmont Technical College
**Greenwood, South Carolina**
**www.ptc.edu**
CB code: 5550

- Public 2-year community and technical college
- Commuter campus in small city

**General.** Founded in 1966. Regionally accredited. Serves 7-county region of the state (satellite campus in each county offering Internet classes, traditional classes and interactive televised classes with main campus). **Enrollment:** 3,948 degree-seeking undergraduates. **Degrees:** 485 associate awarded. **Location:** 75 miles from Columbia, 50 miles from Greenville. **Calendar:** Semester, extensive summer session. **Full-time faculty:** 100 total. **Part-time faculty:** 145 total. **Class size:** 72% < 20, 28% 20-39, less than 1% 40-49, less than 1% 50-99. **Special facilities:** Engineering lab, South Carolina Center for Funeral Service Education, technologically advanced nursing labs equipped with SIMS man Bruce.

**Student profile.**

| | | |
|---|---|---|
| Out-of-state: | 1% | 25 or older: | 45% |

**Transfer out. Colleges most students transferred to 2007:** Lander University, Clemson University, University of South Carolina, South Carolina State University.

**Basis for selection.** Open admission, but selective for some programs. Students with SAT Verbal of at least 480 and SAT Math of at least 440 or ACT Composite of at least 20 do not need to take institutional placement tests.

**2007-2008 Annual costs.** Tuition/fees: $3,126; $3,534 out-of-district; $4,734 out-of-state. In Service Area, not fully supporting tuition, $3,288. Books/supplies: $850. Personal expenses: $200.

**Financial aid.** All financial aid based on need. Need-based aid available for part-time students. Work-study available nights, weekends and for part-time students.

**Application procedures. Admission:** No deadline. No application fee. Application may be submitted online. Admission notification on a rolling basis. **Financial aid:** Priority date 5/1; no closing date. FAFSA required. Applicants notified on a rolling basis starting 6/1; must reply within 2 week(s) of notification.

**Academics. Special study options:** Cooperative education, distance learning, double major, dual enrollment of high school students, independent study, internships, liberal arts/career combination, weekend college. Bachelor's degree programs available on campus. License preparation in nursing, real estate. **Credit/placement by examination:** CLEP, IB, institutional tests. 24 credit hours maximum toward associate degree. **Support services:** GED preparation, learning center, pre-admission summer program, reduced course load, remedial instruction, study skills assistance, tutoring, writing center.

**Majors. Business:** General, administrative services. **Computer sciences:** Data processing. **Education:** Voc/tech. **Engineering technology:** Construction, drafting, electrical, surveying. **Health:** Medical radiologic technology/radiation therapy, nursing (RN), respiratory therapy technology. **Interdisciplinary:** Global studies. **Liberal arts:** Arts/sciences. **Mechanic/repair:** Automotive, electronics/electrical, heating/ac/refrig, industrial electronics. **Personal/culinary services:** Mortuary science. **Production:** Machine tool, welding. **Protective services:** Criminal justice. **Public administration:** Social work.

**Most popular majors.** Business/marketing 25%, engineering/engineering technologies 9%, health sciences 13%, liberal arts 13%, security/protective services 10%, trade and industry 26%.

**Computing on campus.** 250 workstations in computer center, student center. Commuter students can connect to campus network. Online library, helpline, repair service available.

**Student life. Freshman orientation:** Available. Preregistration for classes offered. **Activities:** Alpha Delta Omega, Christian sudent union, computer club, horticulture club, Kappa Beta Delta, Lambda Chi Nu, Phi Theta Kappa, psychology club, rad tech club, student nurses association.

**Student services.** Adult student services, career counseling, services for economically disadvantaged, student employment services, financial aid counseling, minority student services, personal counseling, placement for graduates, veterans' counselor. **Transfer:** Pre-admission transcript evaluation for new students. Transfer adviser, college fairs on campus for students transferring to 4-year colleges.

**Contact.** E-mail: king.m@ptc.edu
Phone: (864) 941-8369 Toll-free number: (800) 868-5528
Fax: (864) 941-8555
Zeolean Kinard, Dean of Enrollment Management, Piedmont Technical College, PO Box 1467, Greenwood, SC 29648

## Spartanburg Community College
**Spartanburg, South Carolina**
**www.sccsc.edu**
CB member
CB code: 5668

- Public 2-year community and technical college
- Commuter campus in small city
- Interview required

**General.** Founded in 1961. Regionally accredited. Satellite campuses located in Greer and Gaffney. **Enrollment:** 2,419 full-time, degree-seeking students. **Degrees:** 345 associate awarded. **Location:** 4 miles from downtown. **Calendar:** Semester, limited summer session. **Full-time faculty:** 110 total. **Part-time faculty:** 170 total. **Special facilities:** Horticultural arboretum. **Partnerships:** Formal partnership with Ford Asset Program (mechanic training program).

**Student profile.** Among full-time, degree-seeking students, 45% enrolled in a transfer program, 55% enrolled in a vocational program, 10% already have a bachelor's degree or higher.

| | | |
|---|---|---|
| Out-of-state: | 2% | 25 or older: | 38% |

**Transfer out.** 82% of students enrolled in the transfer program go on to 4-year colleges. **Colleges most students transferred to 2007:** Clemson University, University of South Carolina Upstate, University of South Carolina at Columbia, Wofford College, Spartanburg Methodist College.

**Basis for selection.** Open admission, but selective for some programs. Admission to some health science programs usually based on size of class. Test of Adult Basic Education required for admissions. Programmer's Aptitude Test required for computer programming and data processing. Essay recommended.

**High school preparation.** 21 units required. Required units include English 4, mathematics 2, social studies 2, history 2, science 2 (laboratory 2), foreign language 1 and academic electives 6. One biology and/or chemistry and 1 algebra required for most health programs. Algebra required for all engineering and computer programs.

**2007-2008 Annual costs.** Tuition/fees: $3,194; $3,980 out-of-district; $6,088 out-of-state. Books/supplies: $900. Personal expenses: $2,484.

**2006-2007 Financial aid. Need-based:** 98% of total undergraduate aid awarded as scholarships/grants, 2% as loans/jobs. Need-based aid available for part-time students. Work-study available for part-time students. **Additional information:** Participates in South Carolina lottery tuition assistance program. Full-time technical college students who are state residents receive assistance for tuition not covered by federal or need-based grants.

**Application procedures. Admission:** No deadline. No application fee. Application may be submitted online. Admission notification on a rolling basis. **Financial aid:** Priority date 2/28, closing date 5/1. FAFSA required. Applicants notified on a rolling basis starting 5/1.

**Academics. Special study options:** Cooperative education, distance learning, double major, dual enrollment of high school students, ESL, independent study, weekend college. License preparation in dental hygiene, nursing, occupational therapy, physical therapy, radiology. **Credit/placement by examination:** AP, CLEP, institutional tests. **Support services:** GED preparation and test center, learning center, remedial instruction, tutoring, writing center.

**Majors. Agriculture:** Horticulture. **Business:** Accounting, administrative services, business admin, hospitality admin, hotel/motel admin, marketing, restaurant/food services. **Computer sciences:** General. **Education:** Voc/tech. **Engineering technology:** General, civil, electrical, mechanical. **Health:** Clinical lab technology, medical radiologic technology/radiation therapy, nursing (RN), predental, respiratory therapy technology. **Liberal arts:** Arts/sciences. **Mechanic/repair:** Automotive, industrial electronics. **Production:** Machine tool.

**Computing on campus.** 750 workstations in library, computer center, student center. Commuter students can connect to campus network. Online course registration, helpline, repair service, wireless network available.

**Student life. Freshman orientation:** Available. Preregistration for classes offered. **Activities:** Drama, student government, student newspaper.

**Student services.** Adult student services, career counseling, student employment services, financial aid counseling, personal counseling, placement for graduates, veterans' counselor, women's services. **Physically disabled:** Services for visually, speech, hearing impaired. **Transfer:** Transfer adviser, college fairs on campus for students transferring to 4-year colleges.

**Contact.** Phone: (864) 592-4800 Toll-free number: (866) 592-4700 Fax: (864) 592-4642
Kathy McKinzie, Director of Enrollment Services, Spartanburg Community College, Box 4386, Spartanburg, SC 29305-4386

## Spartanburg Methodist College
**Spartanburg, South Carolina**
www.smcsc.edu

**CB member**
**CB code: 5627**

- Private 2-year junior and liberal arts college affiliated with United Methodist Church
- Residential campus in small city
- SAT or ACT with writing required

**General.** Founded in 1911. Regionally accredited. **Enrollment:** 770 degree-seeking undergraduates; 27 non-degree-seeking students. **Degrees:** 153 associate awarded. **ROTC:** Army. **Location:** 30 miles from Greenville, 60 miles from Charlotte, North Carolina. **Calendar:** Semester, limited summer session. **Full-time faculty:** 23 total; 26% have terminal degrees, 9% minority, 56% women. **Part-time faculty:** 19 total; 26% have terminal degrees, 16% minority, 53% women. **Class size:** 33% < 20, 63% 20-39, 3% 40-49, less than 1% >100.

**Student profile.** Among degree-seeking undergraduates, 100% enrolled in a transfer program, 441 enrolled as first-time, first-year students, 7 transferred in from other institutions.

| | | | |
|---|---|---|---|
| Part-time: | 2% | Women: | 48% |
| Out-of-state: | 5% | Live on campus: | 74% |

**Transfer out. Colleges most students transferred to 2007:** University of South Carolina Upstate, Clemson University, University of South Carolina, Lander University, College of Charleston.

**Basis for selection.** High school GPA, SAT/ACT scores, and class rank very important. Audition, essay, interview recommended. **Adult students:** SAT/ACT scores not required if applicant over 21. **Homeschooled:** Applicants need complete high school academic transcript. Recommend students be supervised through accredited home school association to provide curriculum and academic oversight throughout high school program.

**High school preparation.** Recommended units include English 4, mathematics 4, social studies 2, history 1, science 3, foreign language 1 and academic electives 7. One computer science recommended.

**2007-2008 Annual costs.** Tuition/fees: $11,000. Per-credit charge: $293. $150 enrollment fee for first-time enrollees. Room/board: $6,420.

**Financial aid. Need-based:** Need-based aid available for part-time students. Work-study available nights, weekends and for part-time students. **Non-need-based:** Scholarships awarded for academics, athletics, job skills, leadership, music/drama, religious affiliation, state residency.

**Application procedures. Admission:** No deadline. $20 fee, may be waived for applicants with need. Application may be submitted online. Admission notification on a rolling basis beginning on or about 9/1. Housing deposit refundable until June 1. Applicant notified of decision within a week. **Financial aid:** Priority date 6/30, closing date 8/22. FAFSA required. Applicants notified on a rolling basis starting 3/1; must reply within 2 week(s) of notification.

**Academics. Special study options:** Dual enrollment of high school students, ESL, honors, independent study, liberal arts/career combination, study abroad. **Credit/placement by examination:** AP, CLEP, SAT, ACT, institutional tests. 15 credit hours maximum toward associate degree. **Support services:** Learning center, pre-admission summer program, reduced course load, remedial instruction, study skills assistance, tutoring, writing center.

**Majors. Liberal arts:** Arts/sciences. **Protective services:** Law enforcement admin.

**Most popular majors.** Liberal arts 93%, security/protective services 7%.

**Computing on campus.** 45 workstations in dormitories, library, computer center, student center. Dormitories wired for high-speed internet access and linked to campus network. Commuter students can connect to campus network. Online library, helpline available.

**Student life. Freshman orientation:** Mandatory, $25 fee. Preregistration for classes offered. 3 sessions in mid-July and late August; 1 session during move-in weekend. **Policies:** No alcohol, drugs, or firearms allowed on campus. All campus buildings smoke free. **Housing:** Guaranteed on-campus for all undergraduates. Coed dorms, single-sex dorms, special housing for disabled, substance-free housing available. $100 fully refundable deposit, deadline 11/30. **Activities:** Jazz band, campus ministries, choral groups, dance, drama, literary magazine, music ensembles, student government, student newspaper, computer programming club, Psi Omega Theatre Fraternity, People Organizing People Successfully, Presbyterian Student Association, Wesly Fellowship, Campus Crusade for Christ, Sigma Kappa Delta, Phi Theta Kappa, Psi Beta.

**Athletics.** NJCAA. **Intercollegiate:** Baseball M, basketball, cheerleading, cross-country, golf, soccer, softball W, tennis, volleyball W, wrestling M. **Intramural:** Basketball, football (non-tackle) M, softball, table tennis, tennis, volleyball. **Team name:** Pioneers.

**Student services.** Adult student services, alcohol/substance abuse counseling, campus ministries, career counseling, services for economically disadvantaged, student employment services, financial aid counseling, health services, personal counseling, placement for graduates, veterans' counselor. **Physically disabled:** Services for visually, speech, hearing impaired. **Transfer:** Pre-admission transcript evaluation for new students. Transfer center, transfer adviser, college fairs on campus for students transferring to 4-year colleges.

**Contact.** E-mail: admiss@smcsc.edu
Phone: (864) 587-4213 Toll-free number: (800) 772-7286
Fax: (864) 587-4355
Daniel Philbeck, Vice President for Enrollment Management, Spartanburg Methodist College, 1000 Powell Mill Road, Spartanburg, SC 29301-5899

## Technical College of the Lowcountry
**Beaufort, South Carolina**
www.tcl.edu

**CB code: 5047**

- Public 2-year community and technical college
- Commuter campus in small town

**General.** Founded in 1972. Regionally accredited. Several off-campus extension locations, including Hampton, Parris Island, Marine Corps Air Station. **Enrollment:** 1,893 degree-seeking undergraduates. **Degrees:** 122 associate awarded. **Location:** 45 miles from Hilton Head, 45 miles from Savannah, Georgia. **Calendar:** Semester, extensive summer session. **Full-time faculty:** 53 total. **Part-time faculty:** 60 total.

**Student profile.**

Out-of-state: 3%  25 or older: 95%

**Basis for selection.** Open admission, but selective for some programs. Nursing students are encouraged to have a personal interview and must submit NET test results. SAT or ACT required for placement and counseling. Interview recommended for nursing program. **Adult students:** After admission all students take either COMPASS or ASSET for placement.

**2007-2008 Annual costs.** Tuition/fees: $3,150; $6,912 out-of-state. Books/supplies: $425. Personal expenses: $1,600.

**Financial aid.** All financial aid based on need. Need-based aid available for part-time students. **Additional information:** State lottery aid may be available to South Carolina residents who take 6 credit hours or more.

**Application procedures. Admission:** No deadline. $25 fee. Admission notification on a rolling basis beginning on or about 5/1. **Financial aid:** No deadline. FAFSA required. Applicants notified on a rolling basis starting 7/1.

**Academics. Special study options:** Cooperative education, cross-registration, distance learning, double major, dual enrollment of high school students, ESL, independent study, internships. License preparation in nursing, radiology, real estate. **Credit/placement by examination:** AP, CLEP, institutional tests. **Support services:** GED preparation and test center, learning center, pre-admission summer program, reduced course load, remedial instruction, study skills assistance, tutoring.

**Majors. Agriculture:** Horticulture. **Business:** General, accounting, administrative services, hospitality/recreation, office management. **Computer sciences:** General, data processing, programming. **Engineering:** Electrical. **Engineering technology:** Construction. **Family/consumer sciences:** Child care. **Health:** Nursing (RN). **Liberal arts:** Arts/sciences. **Mechanic/repair:** Heating/ac/refrig. **Personal/culinary services:** Cosmetic. **Protective services:** Criminal justice, law enforcement admin.

**Most popular majors.** Business/marketing 6%, health sciences 35%, legal studies 14%, trade and industry 38%.

**Computing on campus.** 400 workstations in library, computer center, student center. Online library, helpline available.

**Student life. Freshman orientation:** Available. Preregistration for classes offered. 1-day on-campus orientation at start of fall semester. **Activities:** Student government, Phi Theta Kappa, Rotaract Club, professional societies.

**Student services.** Career counseling, student employment services, personal counseling, placement for graduates, veterans' counselor. **Transfer:** Transfer adviser for students transferring to 4-year colleges.

**Contact.** E-mail: mgallion@tcl.edu
Phone: (843) 525-8208 Toll-free number: (800) 768-8252
Fax: (843) 525-8285
Melanie Gallion, Director of Admissions, Technical College of the Lowcountry, 921 South Ribaut Road, Beaufort, SC 29901-1288

## Tri-County Technical College
**Pendleton, South Carolina**
www.tctc.edu
CB code: 5789

- Public 2-year community and technical college
- Commuter campus in small town

**General.** Founded in 1962. Regionally accredited. **Enrollment:** 4,100 degree-seeking undergraduates. **Degrees:** 490 associate awarded. **ROTC:** Army, Air Force. **Location:** 5 miles from Clemson. **Calendar:** Semester, limited summer session. **Full-time faculty:** 115 total. **Part-time faculty:** 160 total. **Special facilities:** Amphitheater. **Partnerships:** Formal partnerships with 7 area school districts, local businesses and industries, National Drop-out Prevention Center at Clemson, the Anderson and Oconee County Business and Education Partnerships, the Career Center and Technology Center, and Tri-County Tech in a Partnership for Academic and Career Education (business and education consortium to initiate Tech Prep/School-to-Work programs).

**Student profile.**

Out-of-state: 2%  25 or older: 85%

**Transfer out. Colleges most students transferred to 2007:** Clemson University.

**Basis for selection.** Open admission, but selective for some programs. SAT used only for admission to nursing: 450 verbal and 420 math score required.

**High school preparation.** High school unit or college course in chemistry, biology, and algebra taken within past 5 years required for nursing, medical laboratory, practical nursing, surgical technology, dental assisting, and veterinary technology.

**2007-2008 Annual costs.** Tuition/fees: $2,976; $3,294 out-of-district; $6,594 out-of-state. Books/supplies: $650.

**Financial aid. Need-based:** Need-based aid available for part-time students. Work-study available nights and for part-time students. **Non-need-based:** Scholarships awarded for academics, state residency. **Additional information:** Deadline for application to institutional scholarships April 2.

**Application procedures. Admission:** No deadline. $20 fee. Application must be submitted on paper. Admission notification on a rolling basis. **Financial aid:** Priority date 6/30; no closing date. FAFSA required. Applicants notified on a rolling basis starting 6/15; must reply within 2 week(s) of notification.

**Academics.** Electronic engineering majors may transfer to any 4-year college accredited by the Technology Accreditation Commission of the Accreditation Board for Engineering and Technology. **Special study options:** Cooperative education, distance learning, dual enrollment of high school students, ESL, internships, liberal arts/career combination, student-designed major. License preparation in dental hygiene, nursing, real estate. **Credit/placement by examination:** AP, CLEP, institutional tests. Credit available from documented work experience, course waiver, noncollective organization training programs, technical advanced placement. **Support services:** GED preparation, learning center, reduced course load, remedial instruction, study skills assistance, tutoring, writing center.

**Majors. Business:** Accounting, administrative services, business admin. **Communications:** Broadcast journalism. **Computer sciences:** General, data processing, programming. **Engineering technology:** Drafting, electrical. **Family/consumer sciences:** Clothing/textiles. **Health:** Clinical lab technology, nursing (RN), veterinary technology/assistant. **Liberal arts:** Arts/sciences. **Mechanic/repair:** Heating/ac/refrig, industrial.

**Computing on campus.** 700 workstations in library, computer center. Online course registration, online library, helpline available.

**Student life. Freshman orientation:** Available. Preregistration for classes offered. **Activities:** International student organizations, student government, student newspaper, minority student association, criminal justice club, gospel choir, North American Veterinary Technician Association, student nurses association, forensics team, South Carolina Society of Clinical Laboratory Science.

**Athletics.** NJCAA. **Intercollegiate:** Golf M, soccer M. **Team name:** Lynx.

**Student services.** Alcohol/substance abuse counseling, career counseling, services for economically disadvantaged, student employment services, financial aid counseling, minority student services, placement for graduates, veterans' counselor. **Transfer:** Transfer adviser, college fairs on campus for students transferring to 4-year colleges.

**Contact.** E-mail: infocent@tctc.edu
Phone: (864) 646-1550 Fax: (864) 646-1890
Renae Frazier, Director of Admissions, Tri-County Technical College, Box 587, Pendleton, SC 29670

## Trident Technical College
**Charleston, South Carolina**
www.tridenttech.edu
CB code: 5049

- Public 2-year community and technical college
- Commuter campus in large city

**General.** Founded in 1964. Regionally accredited. 3 campuses: Palmer Campus in downtown Charleston, Main Campus in North Charleston and Berkeley Campus in Moncks Corner. **Enrollment:** 10,700 degree-seeking undergraduates; 1,376 non-degree-seeking students. **Degrees:** 998 associate awarded. **Location:** 15 miles from downtown. **Calendar:** Semester, extensive summer session. **Full-time faculty:** 299 total; 11% minority, 54% women.

**Part-time faculty:** 329 total; 15% minority, 61% women. **Class size:** 63% < 20, 32% 20-39, 2% 40-49, 2% 50-99, less than 1% >100.

**Student profile.** Among degree-seeking undergraduates, 2,222 enrolled as first-time, first-year students, 824 transferred in from other institutions.

| | | | |
|---|---|---|---|
| Part-time: | 52% | Asian American: | 2% |
| Out-of-state: | 4% | Hispanic American: | 2% |
| Women: | 64% | 25 or older: | 42% |
| African American: | 28% | | |

**Basis for selection.** Open admission, but selective for some programs. Selective admisssion for nursing students. **Learning Disabled:** Student should provide current medical, psychological, and/or psychiatric documentation providing a diagnosis and describing how his/her disability affects his/her ability to function in a collegiate, adult learning environment. Documentation indicating what accommodations the student received in high school and/or at another college may also be helpful.

**2007-2008 Annual costs.** Tuition/fees: $3,220; $3,574 out-of-district; $6,200 out-of-state. Books/supplies: $1,150. Personal expenses: $1,183.

**Financial aid. Need-based:** Need-based aid available for part-time students. Work-study available nights, weekends and for part-time students.

**Application procedures. Admission:** Closing date 8/4 (postmark date). $25 fee. Application may be submitted online. Admission notification on a rolling basis. Applicants to early admissions program must rank in upper half of high school class and must have combined SAT score (exclusive of Writing) of 800 or ACT composite score of 17. **Financial aid:** No deadline. FAFSA required. Applicants notified on a rolling basis; must reply within 6 week(s) of notification.

**Academics. Special study options:** Accelerated study, cooperative education, cross-registration, distance learning, double major, dual enrollment of high school students, ESL, independent study, internships. **Credit/placement by examination:** AP, CLEP, IB, institutional tests. **Support services:** Learning center, reduced course load, remedial instruction, study skills assistance, tutoring, writing center.

**Majors. Agriculture:** Horticultural science, horticulture. **Business:** General, accounting, administrative services, business admin, customer service, e-commerce, entrepreneurial studies, hospitality admin, hotel/motel admin, logistics, marketing, office management, restaurant/food services, tourism/travel, transportation. **Communications:** Broadcast journalism. **Communications technology:** General. **Computer sciences:** Data processing, information systems, programming. **Construction:** Electrician. **Education:** Voc/tech. **Engineering technology:** Architectural, civil, electrical, manufacturing, robotics. **Family/consumer sciences:** Child care. **Health:** Clinical lab technology, dental hygiene, medical radiologic technology/radiation therapy, nursing (RN), occupational therapy assistant, physical therapy assistant, respiratory therapy technology. **Legal studies:** Paralegal. **Liberal arts:** Arts/sciences. **Mechanic/repair:** General, aircraft, aircraft powerplant, automotive, industrial. **Personal/culinary services:** Culinary arts. **Physical sciences:** General. **Protective services:** Fire services admin, law enforcement admin. **Public administration:** Human services. **Transportation:** General, aviation. **Visual/performing arts:** Commercial/advertising art, graphic design.

**Most popular majors.** Business/marketing 12%, health sciences 27%, liberal arts 33%.

**Computing on campus.** 3,000 workstations in library, computer center, student center. Online library, wireless network available.

**Student life. Freshman orientation:** Available. Preregistration for classes offered. 45-minute ongoing service. **Activities:** Student government, student newspaper, Phi Theta Kappa international honor society, Alpha Mu Gamma, Asian Studies, Black Student Association, Campus Crusade for Christ, La Sociedad Hispanoamericana, International Club, Society of Student Leaders.

**Student services.** Adult student services, alcohol/substance abuse counseling, career counseling, services for economically disadvantaged, student employment services, financial aid counseling, personal counseling, placement for graduates, veterans' counselor. **Physically disabled:** Services for visually, hearing impaired. **Transfer:** Pre-admission transcript evaluation for new students. Transfer adviser, college fairs on campus for students transferring to 4-year colleges.

**Contact.** E-mail: admissions@tridenttech.edu
Phone: (843) 574-6125 Toll-free number: (877) 349-7184
Fax: (843) 574-6483
Clara Martin, Director of Admissions, Trident Technical College, Box 118067, AM-M, Charleston, SC 29423-8067

## University of South Carolina at Lancaster
**Lancaster, South Carolina**
usclancaster.sc.edu                    CB code: 5849

- Public 2-year branch campus and junior college
- Commuter campus in large town

**General.** Founded in 1959. Regionally accredited. **Enrollment:** 1,047 degree-seeking undergraduates; 455 non-degree-seeking students. **Degrees:** 153 associate awarded. **ROTC:** Army. **Location:** 50 miles from Columbia, 40 miles from Charlotte, North Carolina. **Calendar:** Semester, limited summer session. **Full-time faculty:** 34 total. **Part-time faculty:** 23 total. **Special facilities:** Health sciences facilities, diabetic education center.

**Student profile.** Among degree-seeking undergraduates, 360 enrolled as first-time, first-year students, 360 transferred in from other institutions.

| | | | |
|---|---|---|---|
| Part-time: | 31% | Women: | 67% |
| Out-of-state: | 1% | 25 or older: | 17% |

**Transfer out.** 90% of students enrolled in the transfer program go on to 4-year colleges. **Colleges most students transferred to 2007:** University of South Carolina-Columbia, Winthrop University, Clemson University, York Technical College.

**Basis for selection.** Open admission. SAT or ACT required in admissions process but applicants with scores below required levels will be admitted provisionally. **Adult students:** SAT/ACT scores not required if applicant over 25.

**High school preparation.** 20 units recommended. Recommended units include English 4, mathematics 3, social studies 3, science 3 (laboratory 3), foreign language 2 and academic electives 4. One unit physical education/ROTC required.

**2007-2008 Annual costs.** Tuition/fees: $4,888; $11,500 out-of-state. Per-credit charge: $192 in-state; $480 out-of-state. Books/supplies: $500. Personal expenses: $938.

**Application procedures. Admission:** Priority date 8/30; no deadline. $40 fee, may be waived for applicants with need. Application may be submitted online. Admission notification on a rolling basis. **Financial aid:** Priority date 4/15; no closing date. FAFSA required. Applicants notified on a rolling basis starting 6/1; must reply within 2 week(s) of notification.

**Academics. Special study options:** Accelerated study, combined bachelor's/graduate degree, cross-registration, distance learning, dual enrollment of high school students, honors, independent study, internships, liberal arts/career combination. Bachelor's degree programs available on campus. License preparation in nursing. **Credit/placement by examination:** AP, CLEP, IB, institutional tests. 30 credit hours maximum toward associate degree. **Support services:** Learning center, study skills assistance, tutoring, writing center.

**Majors. Business:** Administrative services, business admin. **Health:** Nursing (RN). **Liberal arts:** Arts/sciences. **Protective services:** Criminal justice. **Visual/performing arts:** Art.

**Computing on campus.** 110 workstations in library, computer center. Commuter students can connect to campus network. Online course registration, repair service, wireless network available.

**Student life. Freshman orientation:** Mandatory, $35 fee. Preregistration for classes offered. 2-day program. **Activities:** Campus ministries, drama, literary magazine, student government, student newspaper, Black awareness group, adult group for education, Campus Crusade for Christ.

**Athletics. Intramural:** Basketball, table tennis, volleyball. **Team name:** Lancers.

**Student services.** Adult student services, career counseling, student employment services, financial aid counseling, health services, personal counseling, veterans' counselor. **Transfer:** Pre-admission transcript evaluation for new students.

**Contact.** Phone: (803) 313-7073 Fax: (803) 313-7116
Karen Faile, Director of Enrollment Management, University of South Carolina at Lancaster, Box 889, Lancaster, SC 29721

## University of South Carolina at Sumter
**Sumter, South Carolina**
www.uscsumter.edu                    CB code: 5821

- Public 2-year branch campus college
- Commuter campus in small city
- SAT or ACT (ACT writing optional) required

**General.** Founded in 1966. Regionally accredited. **Enrollment:** 949 degree-seeking undergraduates. **Degrees:** 54 associate awarded. **ROTC:** Army. **Location:** 40 miles from Columbia, 98 miles from Charleston. **Calendar:** Semester, limited summer session. **Full-time faculty:** 44 total. **Part-time faculty:** 39 total. **Class size:** 68% < 20, 30% 20-39, 2% 40-49. **Partnerships:** Formal partnerships with high schools (college-level courses for eligible high school students.).

**Student profile.**

| Out-of-state: | 1% | 25 or older: | 28% |
|---|---|---|---|

**Transfer out. Colleges most students transferred to 2007:** Central Carolina Technical College, College of Charleston, Midlands Technical College.

**Basis for selection.** Entering freshmen must have 2.25 GPA. Class rank and test scores also important. All freshmen required to take foreign language tests. Placement in mathematics may require additional testing. Interview required for academically marginal. **Adult students:** SAT/ACT scores not required if applicant over 23. **Homeschooled:** Official transcripts, SAT/ACT and a GPR converted to the South Carolina Uniform grading scale if home schooled in South Carolina. **Learning Disabled:** Must submit recent documentation.

**High school preparation.** 20 units required. Required and recommended units include English 4, mathematics 3-4, social studies 3, history 2, science 3 (laboratory 3), foreign language 2-3 and academic electives 4. 1 physical education required, 1 computer science recommended.

**2007-2008 Annual costs.** Tuition/fees: $4,888; $11,800 out-of-state. Per-credit charge: $192 in-state; $480 out-of-state. Books/supplies: $932. Personal expenses: $2,053.

**Financial aid.** All financial aid based on need. Need-based aid available for part-time students. Work-study available nights, weekends and for part-time students.

**Application procedures. Admission:** Priority date 8/1; no deadline. $40 fee, may be waived for applicants with need. Application may be submitted online. Admission notification on a rolling basis. **Financial aid:** Priority date 4/15; no closing date. FAFSA required. Applicants notified on a rolling basis starting 4/16; must reply within 2 week(s) of notification.

**Academics. Special study options:** Combined bachelor's/graduate degree, cross-registration, distance learning, dual enrollment of high school students, independent study, liberal arts/career combination, student-designed major, teacher certification program. Bachelor's degree programs available on campus. **Credit/placement by examination:** AP, CLEP, institutional tests. 30 credit hours maximum toward associate degree. **Support services:** Learning center, remedial instruction, study skills assistance, tutoring, writing center.

**Majors. Liberal arts:** Arts/sciences.

**Computing on campus.** 195 workstations in library, computer center, student center. Commuter students can connect to campus network. Online course registration, online library, student web hosting, wireless network available.

**Student life. Freshman orientation:** Mandatory. Preregistration for classes offered. **Activities:** Choral groups, drama, literary magazine, music ensembles, student government, student newspaper, African-American club, Baptist Student clubs, campus activities board, Circle K, student art guild, student education association, student nursing organization, environmental club.

**Athletics. NJCAA. Intercollegiate:** Baseball M. **Intramural:** Baseball M, basketball, bowling, football (non-tackle), golf, handball, racquetball, soccer M, softball, table tennis, tennis, volleyball, weight lifting.

**Student services.** Adult student services, campus ministries, career counseling, services for economically disadvantaged, student employment services, financial aid counseling, personal counseling, veterans' counselor. **Physically disabled:** Services for visually, speech, hearing impaired.

**Contact.** E-mail: kbritton@uscsumter.edu
Phone: (803) 938-3762 Fax: (803) 938-3901
Keith Britton, Director of Admissions, University of South Carolina at Sumter, 200 Miller Road, Sumter, SC 29150-2498

---

## University of South Carolina at Union
### Union, South Carolina
uscunion.sc.edu

**CB code: 5846**

- Public 2-year branch campus college
- Commuter campus in small town
- SAT or ACT required

---

**General.** Founded in 1965. Regionally accredited. Off-campus site at Laurens offers full range of courses. **Enrollment:** 277 degree-seeking undergraduates. **Degrees:** 68 associate awarded. **Location:** 30 miles from Spartanburg, 60 miles from Columbia. **Calendar:** Semester, limited summer session. **Full-time faculty:** 8 total. **Part-time faculty:** 15 total.

**Student profile.**

| Out-of-state: | 1% | Native American: | 1% |
|---|---|---|---|
| African American: | 25% | 25 or older: | 40% |

**Transfer out.** 60% of students enrolled in the transfer program go on to 4-year colleges.

**Basis for selection.** Secondary school record most important. Standardized test scores and class rank also important. Students with high school diploma or GED but without required high school curriculum units may be admitted into Opportunity Program based on school achievement record and SAT or ACT scores. Institutional placement tests in mathematics and writing required of all freshmen. **Adult students:** SAT/ACT scores not required.

**High school preparation.** 20 units required. Required units include English 4, mathematics 3, social studies 3, science 3 (laboratory 3), foreign language 2 and academic electives 4.

**2007-2008 Annual costs.** Tuition/fees: $4,888; $11,800 out-of-state. Per-credit charge: $192 in-state; $480 out-of-state. Books/supplies: $744. Personal expenses: $1,307.

**Financial aid.** All financial aid based on need. Work-study available nights, weekends and for part-time students.

**Application procedures. Admission:** No deadline. $40 fee, may be waived for applicants with need. Admission notification on a rolling basis beginning on or about 6/1. **Financial aid:** Priority date 4/15; no closing date. FAFSA required. Applicants notified on a rolling basis starting 7/15; must reply within 2 week(s) of notification.

**Academics.** Upper division courses leading to bachelor's degree in interdisciplinary studies available. Degree awarded by Columbia campus. **Special study options:** Cross-registration, distance learning, dual enrollment of high school students, independent study, internships, student-designed major. Bachelor's degree programs available on campus. **Credit/placement by examination:** AP, CLEP, institutional tests. **Support services:** Pre-admission summer program, reduced course load, remedial instruction, tutoring.

**Majors. Liberal arts:** Arts/sciences.

**Student life. Freshman orientation:** Mandatory. Preregistration for classes offered. **Activities:** Drama, literary magazine, student government, student newspaper, Afro-American and political groups, student media association, computer club, history club, art club, travel club, music club, biology club.

**Athletics. Intercollegiate:** Basketball M, softball W. **Intramural:** Baseball M, basketball, bowling, gymnastics, racquetball, skiing, softball, table tennis, tennis, volleyball.

**Student services.** Adult student services, career counseling, student employment services, on-campus daycare, personal counseling. **Transfer:** College fairs on campus for students transferring to 4-year colleges.

**Contact.** Phone: (864) 429-8728 Fax: (864) 427-3682
Terry Young, Director of Enrollment Services, University of South Carolina at Union, PO Drawer 729, Union, SC 29379

---

## University of South Carolina: Salkehatchie Regional Campus
### Allendale, South Carolina
uscsalkehatchie.sc.edu

**CB code: 5847**

- Public 2-year branch campus college
- Commuter campus in small town
- SAT or ACT required

**General.** Founded in 1965. Regionally accredited. **Enrollment:** 702 degree-seeking undergraduates. **Degrees:** 62 associate awarded. **ROTC:** Army, Naval, Air Force. **Location:** 75 miles from Columbia, 75 miles from Charleston. **Calendar:** Semester, limited summer session. **Full-time faculty:** 25 total. **Part-time faculty:** 40 total. **Special facilities:** Civic arts center.

**Student profile.**

| Out-of-state: | 1% | 25 or older: | 26% |
|---|---|---|---|

**Transfer out. Colleges most students transferred to 2007:** University of South Carolina-Columbia, University of South Carolina-Aiken.

**Basis for selection.** Secondary school record and class rank most important. Standardized test scores also important. **Adult students:** SAT/ACT scores not required if applicant over 25.

**High school preparation.** Required units include English 4, mathematics 3, social studies 3, history 1, science 2 (laboratory 2), foreign language 2 and academic electives 2.

**2007-2008 Annual costs.** Tuition/fees: $4,888; $11,800 out-of-state. Per-credit charge: $192 in-state; $480 out-of-state. Books/supplies: $744. Personal expenses: $1,159.

**Financial aid. Need-based:** Need-based aid available for part-time students. Work-study available nights, weekends and for part-time students. **Non-need-based:** Scholarships awarded for academics.

**Application procedures. Admission:** Priority date 8/19; no deadline. $40 fee, may be waived for applicants with need. Admission notification on a rolling basis. **Financial aid:** Priority date 4/30; no closing date. FAFSA required. Applicants notified on a rolling basis starting 6/1.

**Academics. Special study options:** Cross-registration, dual enrollment of high school students, independent study, student-designed major, study abroad. **Credit/placement by examination:** CLEP, IB, institutional tests. 15 credit hours maximum toward associate degree. **Support services:** Learning center, pre-admission summer program, reduced course load, remedial instruction, tutoring.

**Majors. Liberal arts:** Arts/sciences.

**Computing on campus.** 102 workstations in library, computer center.

**Student life. Freshman orientation:** Mandatory. **Activities:** Choral groups, drama, student government, student newspaper, minority student organization.

**Athletics.** NJCAA. **Intercollegiate:** Baseball M. **Intramural:** Basketball, soccer, softball W, table tennis, tennis, volleyball.

**Student services.** Career counseling, personal counseling, veterans' counselor. **Physically disabled:** Services for visually, hearing impaired.

**Contact.** Phone: (803) 584-3446 Toll-free number: (800) 922-5500
Fax: (803) 584-5038
Jane Brewer, Dean for Student Services, University of South Carolina: Salkehatchie Regional Campus, PO Box 617, Allendale, SC 29810

## Williamsburg Technical College
**Kingstree, South Carolina**
www.wiltech.edu
CB code: 5892

- Public 2-year community and technical college
- Commuter campus in small town

**General.** Founded in 1969. Regionally accredited. **Enrollment:** 563 degree-seeking undergraduates; 38 non-degree-seeking students. **Degrees:** 52 associate awarded. **Location:** 75 miles from Charleston, 40 miles from Florence. **Calendar:** Semester, extensive summer session. **Full-time faculty:** 19 total. **Part-time faculty:** 25 total. **Class size:** 90% < 20, 10% 20-39. **Partnerships:** Formal partnerships with Tupperware, Firestone and Williamsburg County school district.

**Student profile.** Among degree-seeking undergraduates, 45% enrolled in a transfer program, 55% enrolled in a vocational program, 226 enrolled as first-time, first-year students.

| Part-time: | 65% | 25 or older: | 52% |
|---|---|---|---|
| Women: | 65% | | |

**Transfer out. Colleges most students transferred to 2007:** Francis Marion University, Coker College, Limestone College, University of South Carolina, Coastal Carolina University.

**Basis for selection.** Open admission. Academically weak students must enroll in Applied Studies Program.

**High school preparation.** 25 units recommended. Recommended units include English 4, mathematics 4, social studies 3, history 1, science 3,

foreign language 1 and academic electives 7. Recommend one unit physical education/JROTC. 1 unit computer technology, 6 or more units in occupational area will substitute for one science.

**2007-2008 Annual costs.** Tuition/fees: $2,830; $2,950 out-of-district; $5,292 out-of-state.

**Financial aid. Need-based:** Need-based aid available for part-time students. Work-study available nights, weekends and for part-time students. **Non-need-based:** Scholarships awarded for academics, leadership, minority status, state residency. **Additional information:** Tuition waivers for children of war veterans.

**Application procedures. Admission:** No deadline. $10 fee, may be waived for applicants with need. Admission notification on a rolling basis. **Financial aid:** Priority date 4/15; no closing date. FAFSA required. Applicants notified on a rolling basis starting 7/1; must reply within 4 week(s) of notification.

**Academics. Special study options:** Distance learning, double major, dual enrollment of high school students, honors, independent study, internships, liberal arts/career combination, student-designed major. License preparation in nursing. **Credit/placement by examination:** CLEP, institutional tests. 18 credit hours maximum toward associate degree. **Support services:** Learning center, pre-admission summer program, remedial instruction, study skills assistance, tutoring.

**Majors. Business:** General, administrative services, information resources management, office management. **Computer sciences:** General. **Education:** Early childhood, teacher assistance. **Engineering:** Electrical. **Engineering technology:** Drafting. **Liberal arts:** Arts/sciences. **Mechanic/repair:** General, heating/ac/refrig. **Production:** Machine tool.

**Computing on campus.** 60 workstations in library, computer center. Online library, wireless network available.

**Student life. Freshman orientation:** Available. **Activities:** Student government.

**Student services.** Career counseling, services for economically disadvantaged, financial aid counseling, personal counseling, placement for graduates, veterans' counselor. **Physically disabled:** Services for hearing impaired. **Transfer:** Pre-admission transcript evaluation for new students. College fairs on campus for students transferring to 4-year colleges.

**Contact.** E-mail: wrighta@wiltech.edu
Phone: (843) 355-4162 Toll-free number: (800) 768-2021 ext. 4162
Fax: (843) 355-4289
Alexis Wright, Admissions Director, Williamsburg Technical College, 601 Martin Luther King Jr. Avenue, Kingstree, SC 29556-4197

## York Technical College
**Rock Hill, South Carolina**
www.yorktech.com
CB code: 5989

- Public 2-year technical college
- Commuter campus in large town

**General.** Founded in 1962. Regionally accredited. Member of Charlotte Area Consortium of Colleges and Universities. **Enrollment:** 4,011 degree-seeking undergraduates; 720 non-degree-seeking students. **Degrees:** 394 associate awarded. **Location:** 70 miles from Columbia, 14 miles from Charlotte, North Carolina. **Calendar:** Semester, extensive summer session. **Full-time faculty:** 128 total. **Part-time faculty:** 139 total.

**Student profile.** Among degree-seeking undergraduates, 24% enrolled in a transfer program, 76% enrolled in a vocational program, 10% already have a bachelor's degree or higher, 1,105 enrolled as first-time, first-year students.

| Part-time: | 44% | Women: | 64% |
|---|---|---|---|
| Out-of-state: | 5% | 25 or older: | 65% |

**Transfer out. Colleges most students transferred to 2007:** Winthrop University, Clemson University, University of South Carolina.

**Basis for selection.** Open admission, but selective for some programs. Open admission policy for applicants meeting minimum reading skills. Additional specific qualification criteria required for admission to limited enrollment Health Science programs. All students whose goal is a Health Science degree program are encouraged to prepare for college level coursework and take the SAT or ACT. COMPASS, SAT, or ACT scores may be used for placement. **Homeschooled:** Applicants must have graduated from approved South Carolina Homeschool Association or a homeschool recognized by the Department of Education in its home state. **Learning Disabled:** Students with disabilities who wish to receive special testing accommodations should contact Special Resources Office in Student Services.

**High school preparation.** College prep chemistry required for dental hygiene and nursing programs.

**2007-2008 Annual costs.** Tuition/fees: $3,124; $3,448 out-of-district; $7,000 out-of-state. Books/supplies: $900.

**2006-2007 Financial aid. Need-based:** 96% of total undergraduate aid awarded as scholarships/grants, 4% as loans/jobs. Need-based aid available for part-time students. Work-study available nights and for part-time students. **Non-need-based:** Scholarships awarded for academics, leadership, state residency.

**Application procedures. Admission:** Closing date 8/22. No application fee. Application may be submitted online. Admission notification on a rolling basis. **Financial aid:** Priority date 6/1; no closing date. FAFSA required. Applicants notified on a rolling basis starting 3/1.

**Academics. Special study options:** Cooperative education, distance learning, dual enrollment of high school students, ESL, liberal arts/career combination. License preparation in dental hygiene, nursing, paramedic, radiology, real estate. **Credit/placement by examination:** AP, CLEP, institutional tests. At least 25% of semester credit hours required for program completion must be earned through instruction at York Technical College. **Support services:** Learning center, pre-admission summer program, reduced course load, remedial instruction, study skills assistance, tutoring, writing center.

**Majors. Business:** General, accounting, administrative services, business admin, human resources, logistics. **Computer sciences:** Applications programming, LAN/WAN management, programming. **Construction:** General. **Education:** Early childhood. **Engineering technology:** Computer, computer systems, drafting, electrical, heat/ac/refrig, mechanical, mechanical drafting. **Health:** Clinical lab technology, dental hygiene, medical radiologic technology/radiation therapy, nursing (RN), radiologic technology/medical imaging. **Legal studies:** Paralegal. **Liberal arts:** Arts/sciences. **Mechanic/repair:** General, automotive, electronics/electrical, heating/ac/refrig, industrial. **Production:** Machine tool, tool and die, welding. **Protective services:** Fire services admin, police science. **Other:** Logistics management.

**Most popular majors.** Business/marketing 34%, engineering/engineering technologies 10%, family/consumer sciences 9%, health sciences 16%, liberal arts 15%.

**Computing on campus.** 180 workstations in library, computer center. Commuter students can connect to campus network. Online course registration, online library, wireless network available.

**Student life. Freshman orientation:** Mandatory. Preregistration for classes offered. START Center provides first-time freshmen students with orientation and first-semester advising and registration. **Activities:** Student government, student newspaper, Jacobin Society, Phi Theta Kappa, Christian Fellowship, Students With Vision.

**Student services.** Career counseling, student employment services, financial aid counseling, on-campus daycare, personal counseling, placement for graduates, veterans' counselor, women's services. **Physically disabled:** Services for visually, hearing impaired. **Transfer:** Transfer adviser, college fairs on campus for students transferring to 4-year colleges.

**Contact.** E-mail: admissionsoffice@yorktech.com
Phone: (803) 327-8008 Toll-free number: (800) 922-8324
Fax: (803) 327-7237
Kenny Aldridge, Admissions Department Manager, York Technical College, 452 South Anderson Road, Rock Hill, SC 29730

# South Dakota

## Kilian Community College
**Sioux Falls, South Dakota**
www.kilian.edu                    CB code: 6149

▸ Private 2-year community college
▸ Commuter campus in small city

**General.** Founded in 1976. Regionally accredited. **Enrollment:** 391 degree-seeking undergraduates; 11 non-degree-seeking students. **Degrees:** 60 associate awarded. **Location:** 180 miles from Omaha, Nebraska, 240 miles from Minneapolis-St. Paul. **Calendar:** Trimester, limited summer session. **Full-time faculty:** 7 total; 14% have terminal degrees, 86% women. **Part-time faculty:** 48 total; 10% have terminal degrees, 10% minority, 52% women. **Class size:** 89% < 20, 11% 20-39.

**Student profile.** Among degree-seeking undergraduates, 54% enrolled in a transfer program, 46% enrolled in a vocational program, 1% already have a bachelor's degree or higher, 57 enrolled as first-time, first-year students, 48 transferred in from other institutions.

| | | | |
|---|---|---|---|
| Part-time: | 80% | Asian American: | 1% |
| Out-of-state: | 4% | Hispanic American: | 3% |
| Women: | 77% | Native American: | 10% |
| African American: | 9% | 25 or older: | 61% |

**Transfer out. Colleges most students transferred to 2007:** University of Sioux Falls, Colorado Technical University, University of South Dakota, South Dakota State University.

**Basis for selection.** Open admission. Non-native speaking applicants, must take a COMPASS-ESL assessment and receive at least a level 3. Students graduating from non-US high schools must have a 12-year, translated high school diploma and a minimum score of 3 on the Compass ESL assessment. **Adult students:** SAT/ACT scores not required. **Learning Disabled:** Must provide documentation to the Director of the Student Success Center prior to enrolling in classes.

**2007-2008 Annual costs.** Tuition/fees: $6,675. Per-credit charge: $215. Books/supplies: $1,020. Personal expenses: $725.

**2006-2007 Financial aid. Need-based:** 32 full-time freshmen applied for aid; 32 were judged to have need; 32 of these received aid. Average scholarship/grant was $1,453; average loan $1,166. 41% of total undergraduate aid awarded as scholarships/grants, 59% as loans/jobs. Need-based aid available for part-time students. Work-study available nights and for part-time students. **Non-need-based:** Scholarships awarded for academics, leadership, minority status.

**Application procedures. Admission:** No deadline. $25 fee. Application must be submitted on paper. Admission notification on a rolling basis. **Financial aid:** No deadline. FAFSA, institutional form required. Applicants notified on a rolling basis starting 7/1; must reply within 2 week(s) of notification.

**Academics. Special study options:** Cross-registration, double major, dual enrollment of high school students, ESL, internships. Bachelor's degree programs available on campus. **Credit/placement by examination:** AP, CLEP, institutional tests. 18 credit hours maximum toward associate degree. **Support services:** GED test center, learning center, remedial instruction, study skills assistance, tutoring, writing center.

**Majors. Business:** Accounting, business admin, entrepreneurial studies, executive assistant. **Computer sciences:** Information systems, LAN/WAN management, vendor certification. **Education:** General. **English:** English lit. **Health:** Health aide, medical secretary, substance abuse counseling. **History:** General. **Liberal arts:** Arts/sciences. **Protective services:** Law enforcement admin. **Psychology:** General. **Public administration:** Social work. **Visual/performing arts:** Music.

**Most popular majors.** Business/marketing 24%, health sciences 15%, liberal arts 27%, public administration/social services 21%, security/protective services 8%.

**Computing on campus.** 48 workstations in computer center, student center. Online library available.

**Student life. Freshman orientation:** Available. 2-3 hour program held the week before classes begin. **Activities:** Student newspaper.

**Student services.** Adult student services, career counseling, financial aid counseling, personal counseling, veterans' counselor. **Transfer:** Pre-admission transcript evaluation for new students. Transfer adviser, college fairs on campus for students transferring to 4-year colleges.

**Contact.** E-mail: amodrell@kilian.edu
Phone: (605) 221-3100 Toll-free number: (800) 888-1147
Fax: (605) 336-2606
Amy Modrell, Director of Admissions, Kilian Community College, 300 East 6th Street, Sioux Falls, SD 57103-7020

## Lake Area Technical Institute
**Watertown, South Dakota**
www.lakeareatech.edu              CB code: 0717

▸ Public 2-year technical college
▸ Commuter campus in large town

**General.** Founded in 1965. Regionally accredited. **Enrollment:** 1,250 degree-seeking undergraduates. **Degrees:** 327 associate awarded. **Location:** 90 miles from Sioux Falls. **Calendar:** Semester, limited summer session. **Full-time faculty:** 85 total. **Part-time faculty:** 10 total.

**Basis for selection.** Test scores most important; school record important. ACT recommended. Testing requirements vary by program. Interview required for medical laboratory technician, physical therapy assistant, practical nursing, occupational therapy assistant programs.

**High school preparation.** 3 units mathematics/science required. 1 Latin and typing recommended.

**2007-2008 Annual costs.** Tuition/fees: $4,000. Per-credit charge: $74. Fees vary by program. Books/supplies: $550. Personal expenses: $750.

**Financial aid.** All financial aid based on need. Need-based aid available for part-time students.

**Application procedures. Admission:** No deadline. $20 fee. Application may be submitted online. Admission notification on a rolling basis. **Financial aid:** Priority date 4/15; no closing date. FAFSA required. Applicants notified on a rolling basis starting 5/1.

**Academics. Special study options:** Internships. **Credit/placement by examination:** CLEP, institutional tests. **Support services:** Learning center, pre-admission summer program, reduced course load, tutoring.

**Majors. Agriculture:** General, agribusiness operations. **Business:** Accounting, banking/financial services, business admin, finance. **Computer sciences:** General, data processing, programming. **Engineering:** Civil, mechanical. **Engineering technology:** Drafting. **Health:** Clinical lab technology, nursing (RN), occupational therapy assistant, physical therapy assistant. **Mechanic/repair:** General, aircraft, aircraft powerplant, automotive, diesel, electronics/electrical. **Production:** Tool and die, welding.

**Most popular majors.** Agriculture 27%, business/marketing 43%, computer/information sciences 25%.

**Computing on campus.** 70 workstations in library, computer center.

**Student life. Activities:** Student government, student newspaper.

**Athletics. Intercollegiate:** Rodeo. **Intramural:** Basketball, bowling, softball, volleyball.

**Student services.** Career counseling, student employment services, health services, on-campus daycare, personal counseling, placement for graduates, veterans' counselor. **Transfer:** Transfer adviser for students transferring to 4-year colleges.

**Contact.** Phone: (605) 882-5284 Toll-free number: (800) 657-4344
Fax: (605) 882-6299
Kim Bellum, Dean of Curriculum Coordinator, Lake Area Technical Institute, PO Box 730, Watertown, SD 57201

## Mitchell Technical Institute
**Mitchell, South Dakota**
www.mitchelltech.com              CB code: 7038

▸ Public 2-year culinary school and technical college
▸ Residential campus in large town

**General.** Founded in 1968. Regionally accredited. **Enrollment:** 568 degree-seeking undergraduates; 161 non-degree-seeking students. **Degrees:** 185 associate awarded. **Location:** 70 miles from Sioux Falls. **Calendar:** Semester, limited summer session. **Full-time faculty:** 47 total. **Part-time faculty:** 5 total. **Special facilities:** Satellite communications earth station, day care center.

**Student profile.** Among degree-seeking undergraduates, 346 enrolled as first-time, first-year students, 16 transferred in from other institutions.

| | | | |
|---|---|---|---|
| Part-time: | 10% | **Women:** | 31% |
| Out-of-state: | 7% | | |

**Basis for selection.** Open admission, but selective for some programs. Admission decisions based on high school GPA and ACT score. TABE test used for placement. Interview recommended.

**High school preparation.** 16 units recommended. Recommended units include English 4, mathematics 2, social studies 2 and science 2.

**2008-2009 Annual costs.** Tuition/fees: $4,370. Books/supplies: $700. Personal expenses: $750.

**2006-2007 Financial aid. Need-based:** 31% of total undergraduate aid awarded as scholarships/grants, 69% as loans/jobs. Need-based aid available for part-time students.

**Application procedures. Admission:** No deadline. $35 fee. Application may be submitted online. Admission notification on a rolling basis. **Financial aid:** No deadline. FAFSA required. Applicants notified on a rolling basis; must reply within 3 week(s) of notification.

**Academics. Special study options:** Cooperative education, distance learning, dual enrollment of high school students, independent study, internships. **Credit/placement by examination:** AP, CLEP, institutional tests. **Support services:** Learning center, pre-admission summer program, reduced course load, remedial instruction, study skills assistance, tutoring.

**Majors. Architecture:** Technology. **Computer sciences:** General. **Health:** Clinical lab technology, medical radiologic technology/radiation therapy, medical transcription, office assistant. **Mechanic/repair:** Electronics/electrical, heating/ac/refrig.

**Computing on campus.** 40 workstations in library, computer center. Commuter students can connect to campus network. Repair service, wireless network available.

**Student life. Freshman orientation:** Mandatory. Preregistration for classes offered. **Activities:** Student government, student newspaper.

**Athletics. Intercollegiate:** Rodeo. **Intramural:** Basketball, bowling, volleyball. **Team name:** Mavericks.

**Student services.** Adult student services, career counseling, services for economically disadvantaged, student employment services, financial aid counseling, on-campus daycare, personal counseling, placement for graduates, veterans' counselor, women's services. **Physically disabled:** Services for visually, speech, hearing impaired.

**Contact.** E-mail: questions@mitchelltech.edu
Phone: (605) 995-3025 Toll-free number: (800) 684-1969
Fax: (605) 996-3299
Tim Edwards, Director of Student Services, Mitchell Technical Institute, 821 North Capital Street, Mitchell, SD 57301

## Sisseton Wahpeton College
Sisseton, South Dakota
www.swc.tc
CB code: 3403

- Public 2-year community and technical college
- Commuter campus in rural community

**General.** Founded in 1979. Regionally accredited. Member of American Indian Higher Education Consortium. Dakota language and culture resource. **Enrollment:** 240 degree-seeking undergraduates; 5 non-degree-seeking students. **Degrees:** 23 associate awarded. **Location:** 48 miles from Watertown, 85 miles from Fargo, North Dakota. **Calendar:** Semester, limited summer session. **Full-time faculty:** 26 total; 27% minority, 58% women. **Part-time faculty:** 7 total; 57% minority, 43% women. **Special facilities:** Indians in North America book collection, Song to the Great Spirit building, institute for excellence in Dakota language.

**Student profile.** Among degree-seeking undergraduates, 20% enrolled in a transfer program, 76% enrolled in a vocational program, 46 enrolled as first-time, first-year students.

| | | | |
|---|---|---|---|
| Part-time: | 25% | **Women:** | 74% |
| Out-of-state: | 3% | **25 or older:** | 45% |

**Transfer out.** 10% of students enrolled in the transfer program go on to 4-year colleges. **Colleges most students transferred to 2007:** University of Minnesota, North Dakota State University, University of North Dakota, South Dakota State University, University of South Dakota.

**Basis for selection.** Open admission. If student is member of recognized Native American tribe, must submit certification of tribal membership. **Adult students:** COMPASS test is given to all new/returning students. **Homeschooled:** State high school equivalency certificate required.

**High school preparation.** 16 units recommended. Recommended units include English 4, mathematics 4 and science 8.

**2008-2009 Annual costs.** Tuition/fees (projected): $3,790. Books/supplies: $440. Personal expenses: $1,680.

**Application procedures. Admission:** Closing date 7/1. No application fee. Admission notification on a rolling basis beginning on or about 7/1. **Financial aid:** No deadline. FAFSA required. Applicants notified on a rolling basis.

**Academics. Special study options:** Distance learning, double major, dual enrollment of high school students, independent study, internships, liberal arts/career combination. Bachelor's degree programs available on campus. **Credit/placement by examination:** CLEP, institutional tests. **Support services:** GED preparation and test center, learning center, remedial instruction, tutoring.

**Majors. Area/ethnic studies:** Native American. **Business:** Accounting, business admin, hospitality admin. **Computer sciences:** General. **Education:** Early childhood. **Family/consumer sciences:** Food/nutrition. **Health:** Nursing (RN), substance abuse counseling. **Interdisciplinary:** Natural sciences. **Liberal arts:** Arts/sciences. **Physical sciences:** Planetary.

**Computing on campus.** 136 workstations in library, computer center, student center. Wireless network available.

**Student life. Freshman orientation:** Mandatory. Preregistration for classes offered. 2-day program. **Activities:** Student government.

**Student services.** Career counseling, personal counseling. **Transfer:** Transfer adviser for students transferring to 4-year colleges.

**Contact.** E-mail: dredday@swc.tc
Phone: (605) 698-3966 Fax: (605) 698-3132
Darlene Redday, Admissions Officer/Registrar, Sisseton Wahpeton College, BIA 700, Box 689, Agency Village, SD 57262-0689

## Southeast Technical Institute
Sioux Falls, South Dakota
www.southeasttech.edu
CB code: 7054

- Public 2-year technical college
- Commuter campus in small city

**General.** Founded in 1969. Regionally accredited. **Enrollment:** 2,151 degree-seeking undergraduates; 50 non-degree-seeking students. **Degrees:** 600 associate awarded. **Location:** 220 miles from Minneapolis-St. Paul, 200 miles from Omaha, Nebraska. **Calendar:** Semester, limited summer session. **Full-time faculty:** 81 total; 4% have terminal degrees. **Part-time faculty:** 46 total; 9% have terminal degrees.

**Student profile.** Among degree-seeking undergraduates, 100% enrolled in a vocational program, 5% already have a bachelor's degree or higher, 642 enrolled as first-time, first-year students, 1,155 transferred in from other institutions.

| | | | |
|---|---|---|---|
| Part-time: | 20% | **Asian American:** | 1% |
| Out-of-state: | 9% | **Native American:** | 1% |
| Women: | 44% | **25 or older:** | 16% |
| African American: | 1% | **Live on campus:** | 1% |

**Basis for selection.** Open admission, but selective for some programs. Additional testing and background checks required for all health and criminal justice programs. ACT recommended for those programs that are not open admissions. **Homeschooled:** Statement describing homeschool structure and mission, transcript of courses and grades, interview required. ACT and institutional entrance exam required.

**High school preparation.** 18 units recommended. Recommended units include English 4, mathematics 2, social studies 2, science 2 and academic electives 8.

**2007-2008 Annual costs.** Tuition/fees: $3,577. Per-credit charge: $74. $450 per semester laptop fee required for some students. Students able to keep laptop after paying for 4 semesters of the lease. Books/supplies: $900. Personal expenses: $1,350.

**Financial aid.** All financial aid based on need. Need-based aid available for part-time students.

**Application procedures. Admission:** No deadline. No application fee. Application may be submitted online. Admission notification on a rolling basis. Must reply by May 1 or within 4 week(s) if notified thereafter. **Financial aid:** Priority date 5/1; no closing date. FAFSA required. Applicants notified on a rolling basis starting 5/1; must reply within 3 week(s) of notification.

**Academics. Special study options:** Accelerated study, double major. Bachelor's degree programs available on campus. License preparation in nursing, real estate. **Credit/placement by examination:** AP, CLEP, IB, institutional tests. 30 credit hours maximum toward associate degree. **Support services:** GED preparation and test center, learning center, reduced course load, remedial instruction, study skills assistance, tutoring.

**Majors. Agriculture:** Greenhouse operations, horticulture, landscaping, nursery operations, turf management. **Biology:** Biomedical sciences. **Business:** Accounting, banking/financial services, business admin, marketing. **Communications:** Advertising. **Communications technology:** Graphic/printing. **Computer sciences:** General, applications programming, LAN/WAN management, networking, programming. **Engineering technology:** Architectural, biomedical, civil, computer hardware, construction, drafting, electrical, heat/ac/refrig, mechanical, mechanical drafting, surveying. **Health:** Cardiovascular technology, electroencephalograph technology, medical transcription, nuclear medical technology, sonography. **Mechanic/repair:** General, auto body, automotive, diesel, electronics/electrical, heating/ac/refrig. **Production:** Machine shop technology, machine tool. **Protective services:** Law enforcement admin. **Visual/performing arts:** Commercial/advertising art. **Other:** Animation.

**Most popular majors.** Business/marketing 40%, health sciences 25%, trade and industry 23%.

**Computing on campus.** PC or laptop required. 88 workstations in library, computer center. Commuter students can connect to campus network. Online library, helpline, repair service, student web hosting, wireless network available.

**Student life. Freshman orientation:** Available. Preregistration for classes offered. **Housing:** Apartments available. $100 fully refundable deposit, deadline 7/1. **Activities:** Student government.

**Athletics. Intramural:** Basketball, bowling, football (non-tackle), volleyball.

**Student services.** Career counseling, student employment services, financial aid counseling, on-campus daycare, personal counseling, placement for graduates. **Physically disabled:** Services for visually, speech, hearing impaired. **Transfer:** Pre-admission transcript evaluation for new students. College fairs on campus for students transferring to 4-year colleges.

**Contact.** E-mail: jim.rokusek@southeasttech.edu
Phone: (605) 367-7624 Toll-free number: (800) 247-0789
Fax: (605) 367-4372
Jim Rokusek, Director of Student Services, Southeast Technical Institute, 2320 North Career Avenue, Sioux Falls, SD 57107

## Western Dakota Technical Institute
**Rapid City, South Dakota**
**www.wdt.edu**                    CB code: 6393

- Public 2-year technical college
- Commuter campus in small city

**General.** Founded in 1978. Regionally accredited. **Enrollment:** 1,026 degree-seeking undergraduates. **Degrees:** 201 associate awarded. **Location:** 3 miles from downtown. **Calendar:** Semester, limited summer session. **Full-time faculty:** 60 total. **Part-time faculty:** 20 total. **Special facilities:** 500-acre operating ranch for agricultural production students.

**Student profile.**

| Out-of-state: | 8% | 25 or older: | 41% |
|---|---|---|---|

**Transfer out. Colleges most students transferred to 2007:** Black Hills State University.

**Basis for selection.** Open admission, but selective for some programs. Special requirements for nursing, law enforcement, surgical technology, phlebotomy and paralegal programs. Applicants may be placed on waiting lists for programs reaching capacity. Institution requires Test of Adult Basic Education or equivalent unless other recent test results indicate ability to benefit from instruction. Interview, recommendations required for law enforcement, practical nursing, surgical technology and phlebotomy programs.

**High school preparation.** Recommended units include English 4 and mathematics 2.

**2007-2008 Annual costs.** Tuition/fees: $3,720. Per-credit charge: $74. Total program cost ranges from $4,850- $13,150 depending on course of study. Books/supplies: $816. Personal expenses: $1,353.

**Financial aid. Need-based:** Need-based aid available for part-time students. Work-study available nights, weekends and for part-time students.

**Application procedures. Admission:** Closing date 8/1 (postmark date). $20 fee. Application may be submitted online. Admission notification on a rolling basis. **Financial aid:** Priority date 4/20; no closing date. FAFSA required. Applicants notified on a rolling basis starting 6/30; must reply within 2 week(s) of notification.

**Academics. Special study options:** Distance learning, dual enrollment of high school students, internships. License preparation in nursing. **Credit/placement by examination:** CLEP, institutional tests. 35 credit hours maximum toward associate degree. **Support services:** Learning center, pre-admission summer program, reduced course load, remedial instruction, study skills assistance, tutoring.

**Majors. Agriculture:** General, agribusiness operations, business, farm/ranch. **Business:** Accounting, marketing. **Construction:** Electrician, power transmission. **Engineering:** Geotechnical. **Engineering technology:** Drafting. **Health:** Medical transcription. **Legal studies:** Paralegal. **Mechanic/repair:** Automotive, electronics/electrical, industrial. **Protective services:** Police science.

**Computing on campus.** 210 workstations in library, computer center. Commuter students can connect to campus network. Online course registration, helpline, repair service, wireless network available.

**Student life. Freshman orientation:** Mandatory. Preregistration for classes offered. 1-day session held prior to start of classes. **Policies:** Regular attendance required. Must make commitment to attend classes/labs 5 days a week from 8 a.m. to 3 p.m. **Activities:** Student government, student newspaper, minority club, single-parent club.

**Student services.** Adult student services, alcohol/substance abuse counseling, career counseling, services for economically disadvantaged, student employment services, financial aid counseling, minority student services, on-campus daycare, personal counseling, placement for graduates, veterans' counselor, women's services. **Physically disabled:** Services for visually, speech, hearing impaired. **Transfer:** Pre-admission transcript evaluation for new students. Transfer adviser for students transferring to 4-year colleges.

**Contact.** E-mail: admissions@wdt.edu
Phone: (605) 718-2411 Toll-free number: (800) 544-8765
Fax: (605) 394-2204
Jill Elder, Admissions Coordinator, Western Dakota Technical Institute, 800 Mickelson Drive, Rapid City, SD 57703

# Tennessee

## Chattanooga State Technical Community College
### Chattanooga, Tennessee
www.chattanoogastate.edu

**CB code: 1084**

♦ Public 2-year community and technical college
♦ Commuter campus in small city

**General.** Founded in 1963. Regionally accredited. Credit-bearing courses offered at various off-campus locations. **Enrollment:** 6,437 degree-seeking undergraduates. **Degrees:** 693 associate awarded. **Location:** 129 miles from Nashville. **Calendar:** Semester, limited summer session. **Full-time faculty:** 209 total.

**Student profile.** Among degree-seeking undergraduates, 34% enrolled in a transfer program, 47% enrolled in a vocational program.

**Transfer out. Colleges most students transferred to 2007:** Austin Peay State University, East Tennessee State University, Middle Tennessee State University, Tennessee Tech University, University of Tennessee at Chattanooga.

**Basis for selection.** Open admission, but selective for some programs. Special requirements for allied health program. National standardized dental assisting and dental hygiene tests required of applicants to these programs. Interview required for allied health, nursing programs. **Adult students:** SAT/ACT scores not required if applicant over 21. Placement Test. **Homeschooled:** Transcript of courses and grades required. Students are required to register with their local department/board of education or present affiliation with accredited home school agency.

**High school preparation.** 19 units recommended. Recommended units include English 4, mathematics 3, social studies 1, history 1, science 2 (laboratory 1), foreign language 2 and visual/performing arts 1. College preparatory program required for students choosing transfer majors.

**2007-2008 Annual costs.** Tuition/fees: $2,641; $9,717 out-of-state. Per-credit charge: $101 in-state; $407 out-of-state.

**Financial aid. Need-based:** Need-based aid available for part-time students. Work-study available nights, weekends and for part-time students. **Non-need-based:** Scholarships awarded for state residency.

**Application procedures. Admission:** Priority date 8/15; no deadline. $15 fee. Application may be submitted online. Admission notification on a rolling basis. **Financial aid:** Priority date 4/1; no closing date. FAFSA required. Applicants notified on a rolling basis starting 4/1; must reply within 2 week(s) of notification.

**Academics. Special study options:** Accelerated study, cooperative education, cross-registration, distance learning, double major, dual enrollment of high school students, honors, independent study, internships, student-designed major, weekend college. Bachelor's degree programs available on campus. License preparation in dental hygiene, nursing, paramedic, radiology, real estate. **Credit/placement by examination:** AP, CLEP, IB, institutional tests. Final 20 hours must be taken in residency; maximun of 40 hours may be awarded by combination of credit by exam and credit for experience. **Support services:** GED preparation and test center, learning center, pre-admission summer program, reduced course load, remedial instruction, study skills assistance, tutoring, writing center.

**Honors college/program.** ACT Composite score 25 or higher; SAT score 1130-1160; HS GPA of 3.5 or higher; College GPA of 3.5 or higher based on min. of 12 hours of college-level courses. Designated Honors courses restricted to eligible students.

**Majors. Business:** Accounting, management science, office/clerical. **Communications:** Advertising. **Computer sciences:** Information systems, programming. **Education:** Early childhood. **Engineering:** Civil, mechanical. **English:** Technical writing. **Health:** Dental hygiene, medical radiologic technology/radiation therapy, medical records admin, physical therapy assistant, respiratory therapy technology. **Legal studies:** Court reporting, paralegal. **Liberal arts:** Arts/sciences. **Visual/performing arts:** Commercial/advertising art.

**Computing on campus.** 1,200 workstations in library, computer center, student center. Commuter students can connect to campus network. Online course registration, online library, helpline, wireless network available.

**Student life. Freshman orientation:** Mandatory, $10 fee. Preregistration for classes offered. 5-hour sessions begin in July and end in August for the fall term. **Activities:** Jazz band, choral groups, drama, music ensembles, radio station, student government, student newspaper, TV station, Baptist student union.

**Athletics.** NJCAA. **Intercollegiate:** Baseball M, basketball. **Intramural:** Racquetball, soccer, softball, table tennis, tennis. **Team name:** Tigers.

**Student services.** Adult student services, alcohol/substance abuse counseling, career counseling, services for economically disadvantaged, student employment services, financial aid counseling, minority student services, on-campus daycare, personal counseling, placement for graduates, veterans' counselor. **Physically disabled:** Services for visually, speech, hearing impaired. **Learning disabled:** Comprehensive services available. **Transfer:** Transfer adviser, college fairs on campus for students transferring to 4-year colleges.

**Contact.** E-mail: admissions@chattanoogastate.edu
Phone: (423) 697-4401 Fax: (423) 697-4709
Diane Norris, Director, Chattanooga State Technical Community College, 4501 Amnicola Highway, Chattanooga, TN 37406

## Cleveland State Community College
### Cleveland, Tennessee
www.clevelandstatecc.edu

**CB code: 2848**

♦ Public 2-year community college
♦ Commuter campus in small city

**General.** Founded in 1967. Regionally accredited. **Enrollment:** 2,295 degree-seeking undergraduates; 704 non-degree-seeking students. **Degrees:** 252 associate awarded. **Location:** 30 miles from Chattanooga, 80 miles from Knoxville. **Calendar:** Semester, limited summer session. **Full-time faculty:** 70 total; 14% have terminal degrees, 9% minority, 50% women. **Part-time faculty:** 109 total; 11% have terminal degrees, 2% minority, 53% women. **Class size:** 56% < 20, 41% 20-39, less than 1% 40-49, 2% 50-99, less than 1% >100. **Special facilities:** Observatory.

**Student profile.** Among degree-seeking undergraduates, 38% enrolled in a transfer program, 45% enrolled in a vocational program, 548 enrolled as first-time, first-year students, 182 transferred in from other institutions.

| Part-time: | 39% | Women: | 63% |
|---|---|---|---|
| Out-of-state: | 3% | 25 or older: | 41% |

**Transfer out. Colleges most students transferred to 2007:** University of Tennessee-Chattanooga, University of Tennessee-Knoxville, Tennessee Technological University, Lee University.

**Basis for selection.** Open admission, but selective for some programs. Program admission required for nursing and medical office assistant. **Adult students:** SAT/ACT scores not required if applicant over 21. California Critical Thinking and Skills Test (CCTST). **Homeschooled:** Transcript of courses and grades required.

**High school preparation.** 14 units required. Required units include English 4, mathematics 3, social studies 1, history 1, science 2 (laboratory 1), foreign language 2 and academic electives 1. College-preparatory program required for transfer programs: 14 total academic units, 4 English, 2 foreign language, 3 mathematics, 1 social science, 2 science, 1 US history, 1 visual or performing arts. Same units recommended for career/technical programs.

**2007-2008 Annual costs.** Tuition/fees: $2,627; $9,703 out-of-state. Per-credit charge: $101 in-state; $407 out-of-state. Books/supplies: $1,000. Personal expenses: $900.

**2007-2008 Financial aid. Need-based:** 448 full-time freshmen applied for aid; 280 were judged to have need; 269 of these received aid. Average need met was 77%. Average scholarship/grant was $4,247; average loan $2,679. 71% of total undergraduate aid awarded as scholarships/grants, 29% as loans/jobs. Need-based aid available for part-time students. **Non-need-based:** Awarded to 405 full-time undergraduates, including 242 freshmen. Scholarships awarded for athletics, minority status.

**Application procedures. Admission:** No deadline. $10 fee. Application must be submitted on paper. Admission notification on a rolling basis. **Financial aid:** Priority date 6/15; no closing date. FAFSA, institutional form required. Applicants notified on a rolling basis starting 7/1; must reply within 2 week(s) of notification.

**Academics. Special study options:** Cooperative education, cross-registration, distance learning, double major, dual enrollment of high school students, honors, independent study, internships, study abroad. License preparation in nursing. **Credit/placement by examination:** AP, CLEP, institutional tests. 15 credit hours maximum toward associate degree. Students scoring above 32 on the English portion of the enhanced ACT receive 6 credits of English composition. AP credit awarded is determined on an individual basis by the relevant department for grades of 3 or higher. **Support services:** GED test center, learning center, reduced course load, remedial instruction, study skills assistance, tutoring.

**Majors. Business:** Administrative services, business admin. **Education:** General. **Engineering technology:** Industrial. **Family/consumer sciences:** Child development. **Health:** Nursing (RN). **Liberal arts:** Arts/sciences. **Other:** General Technology, Public and Govt Services.

**Most popular majors.** Business/marketing 15%, engineering/engineering technologies 7%, family/consumer sciences 6%, health sciences 17%, liberal arts 50%, science technologies 6%.

**Computing on campus.** 550 workstations in library, computer center, student center. Commuter students can connect to campus network. Online course registration, online library, helpline, wireless network available.

**Student life. Freshman orientation:** Available. Preregistration for classes offered. Half-day program includes campus tour, career and academic counseling, placement assessment, and registration. **Activities:** Campus ministries, choral groups, literary magazine, student government, student newspaper, Baptist Student Union, Circle-K, Phi Theta Kappa, Professional Secretaries International, Adult Student League.

**Athletics.** NJCAA. **Intercollegiate:** Baseball M, basketball, cheerleading, softball W. **Intramural:** Badminton, golf, table tennis, tennis, volleyball. **Team name:** Cougars.

**Student services.** Adult student services, career counseling, student employment services, financial aid counseling, minority student services, personal counseling, placement for graduates, veterans' counselor. **Physically disabled:** Services for visually, speech, hearing impaired. **Transfer:** Reentry adviser, pre-admission transcript evaluation for new students. Transfer adviser, college fairs on campus for students transferring to 4-year colleges.

**Contact.** E-mail: mburnette@clevelandstatecc.edu
Phone: (423) 478-6212 Toll-free number: (800) 604-2722
Fax: (423) 478-6255
Midge Burnette, Director of Admissions and Records, Cleveland State Community College, 3535 Adkisson Drive, Cleveland, TN 37320-3570

## Columbia State Community College
**Columbia, Tennessee**
**www.columbiastate.edu**                CB code: 1081

- Public 2-year community college
- Commuter campus in large town

**General.** Founded in 1966. Regionally accredited. **Enrollment:** 4,633 degree-seeking undergraduates. **Degrees:** 497 associate awarded. **Location:** 40 miles from Nashville. **Calendar:** Semester, limited summer session. **Full-time faculty:** 106 total. **Part-time faculty:** 140 total. **Class size:** 34% < 20, 21% 20-39, 9% 40-49, 16% 50-99, 20% >100.

**Basis for selection.** Open admission, but selective for some programs. Special requirements for allied health sciences.

**High school preparation.** Recommended units include English 4, mathematics 3, social studies 1, history 1, science 2 (laboratory 1) and foreign language 2. One visual and performing arts recommended.

**2007-2008 Annual costs.** Tuition/fees: $2,605; $9,681 out-of-state. Per-credit charge: $101 in-state; $407 out-of-state. Personal expenses: $625.

**Financial aid. Need-based:** Need-based aid available for part-time students. **Non-need-based:** Scholarships awarded for academics, athletics, state residency.

**Application procedures. Admission:** Closing date 8/22. $10 fee. Admission notification on a rolling basis. **Financial aid:** Closing date 3/15. FAFSA, institutional form required. Applicants notified on a rolling basis starting 5/15; must reply within 2 week(s) of notification.

**Academics. Special study options:** Cooperative education, distance learning, dual enrollment of high school students. **Credit/placement by examination:** AP, CLEP. 30 credit hours maximum toward associate degree. **Support services:** Learning center, remedial instruction, study skills assistance, tutoring.

**Majors. Agriculture:** Business. **Biology:** General. **Business:** General, accounting, administrative services. **Communications:** Journalism. **Computer sciences:** General. **Education:** Early childhood, elementary. **Engineering:** General. **Engineering technology:** Electrical. **Health:** Clinical lab technology, dental hygiene, medical radiologic technology/radiation therapy, predental, premedicine, prepharmacy, respiratory therapy technology, veterinary technology/assistant. **History:** General. **Legal studies:** Prelaw. **Liberal arts:** Arts/sciences. **Math:** General. **Parks/recreation:** Health/fitness. **Physical sciences:** Chemistry, physics. **Psychology:** General. **Social sciences:** Economics, geography, sociology. **Visual/performing arts:** Art.

**Most popular majors.** Business/marketing 6%, health sciences 29%, liberal arts 58%.

**Computing on campus.** 60 workstations in library, computer center.

**Student life. Activities:** Choral groups, drama, student government, Baptist Student Union, Students in Free Enterprise, Circle K Club, Collegiate Secretaries International, computer club, Geste, Gamma Beta Phi, returning adults organization.

**Athletics.** NJCAA. **Intercollegiate:** Baseball M, basketball, softball W. **Intramural:** Basketball, softball M, table tennis, volleyball. **Team name:** Chargers, Lady Chargers.

**Student services.** Career counseling, health services, personal counseling, placement for graduates, veterans' counselor. **Physically disabled:** Services for visually, hearing impaired. **Transfer:** College fairs on campus for students transferring to 4-year colleges.

**Contact.** E-mail: scruggs@columbiastate.edu
Phone: (931) 540-2545 Fax: (931) 540-2535
Pauletta Burns, Director of Admissions/Registrar, Columbia State Community College, 1665 Hampshire Pike, Columbia, TN 38401

## Draughons Junior College: Clarksville
**Clarksville, Tennessee**
**www.draughons.edu**                CB code: 3225

- For-profit 2-year business and career college
- Small city

**General.** Accredited by ACICS. **Enrollment:** 690 undergraduates. **Degrees:** 138 associate awarded. **Calendar:** Continuous. **Full-time faculty:** 14 total. **Part-time faculty:** 23 total.

**Basis for selection.** Open admission.

**2007-2008 Annual costs.** Books/supplies: $700.

**Application procedures. Admission:** No deadline. $20 fee.

**Academics. Credit/placement by examination:** CLEP.

**Majors. Business:** Accounting, administrative services, business admin. **Computer sciences:** General. **Health:** Medical assistant, medical records technology. **Legal studies:** General.

**Contact.** E-mail: chays@draughons.edu
Phone: (931) 552-7600 Toll-free number: (877) 258-7796
Amy Melton, Campus Director, Draughons Junior College: Clarksville, 1860 Wilma Rudolph Boulevard, Clarksville, TN 37040

## Draughons Junior College: Murfreesboro
**Murfreesboro, Tennessee**
**www.draughons.edu**

- For-profit 2-year junior college
- Commuter campus in very large city

**General.** Accredited by ACICS. **Enrollment:** 540 degree-seeking undergraduates. **Degrees:** 121 associate awarded. **Location:** 25 miles from Nashville. **Calendar:** Quarter, extensive summer session. **Full-time faculty:** 20 total. **Part-time faculty:** 30 total.

**Basis for selection.** Open admission.

**2007-2008 Annual costs.** Tuition/fees: $10,669. Per-credit charge: $215. Books/supplies: $2,250.

**Application procedures. Admission:** No deadline. No application fee. **Financial aid:** No deadline.

**Academics. Credit/placement by examination:** CLEP.

**Majors. Business:** Accounting, accounting/business management. **Computer sciences:** General. **Health:** Medical assistant, pharmacy assistant. **Legal studies:** Paralegal. **Protective services:** Corrections.

**Student life. Activities:** Student newspaper.

**Athletics. Team name:** N/A.

**Contact.** E-mail: bday@draughons.edu
Phone: (615) 217-9347 Toll-free number: (877) 258-7796
Stacey Sharkey, Director of Admissions, Draughons Junior College: Murfreesboro, 415 Golden Bear Court, Murfreesboro, TN 37128

## Draughons Junior College: Nashville
### Nashville, Tennessee
www.draughons.edu                                     CB code: 7325

- For-profit 2-year business, junior and career college
- Commuter campus in very large city
- Interview required

**General.** Founded in 1884. Accredited by ACICS. Branch campuses in Clarksville, Murfreesboro, Bowling Green, Kentucky. **Enrollment:** 332 degree-seeking undergraduates; 1 non-degree-seeking students. **Degrees:** 146 associate awarded. **Location:** 2 miles from downtown. **Calendar:** Quarter, limited summer session. **Full-time faculty:** 20 total. **Part-time faculty:** 40 total. **Class size:** 30% < 20, 15% 20-39, 21% 40-49, 34% 50-99, less than 1% >100.

**Student profile.** Among degree-seeking undergraduates, 100% enrolled in a vocational program, 196 enrolled as first-time, first-year students.

| | | | |
|---|---|---|---|
| Part-time: | 35% | Asian American: | 1% |
| Out-of-state: | 5% | Hispanic American: | 3% |
| Women: | 82% | 25 or older: | 75% |
| African American: | 55% | | |

**Transfer out. Colleges most students transferred to 2007:** Middle Tennessee State University, Tennessee State University, Western Kentucky University, David Lipscomb University, Fisk University.

**Basis for selection.** Open admission. Institutional assessment requirement waived for applicants who submit ACT composite score of 18 or higher, or who have transfer credits in English and math.

**Financial aid.** All financial aid based on need. Need-based aid available for part-time students. Work-study available nights. **Additional information:** Financial aid form for in-state applicants must be filed before 5/1.

**Application procedures. Admission:** No deadline. No application fee. Application may be submitted online. Admission notification on a rolling basis. **Financial aid:** No deadline. FAFSA required. Applicants notified on a rolling basis.

**Academics. Special study options:** Distance learning, ESL, independent study, internships, liberal arts/career combination, weekend college. **Credit/placement by examination:** CLEP, institutional tests. 15 credit hours maximum toward associate degree. Students with GED must take Math, English, Reading Assessment test (MAPS) and take courses for any deficiencies found. ACT composite score of 18 exempts students with GED from MAPS. College Board AP examinations required for placement. **Support services:** GED preparation, learning center, reduced course load, remedial instruction, study skills assistance, tutoring, writing center.

**Majors. Business:** Accounting, business admin. **Computer sciences:** General, information technology, web page design. **Health:** Medical assistant, medical records admin, pharmacy assistant. **Legal studies:** Paralegal.

**Most popular majors.** Business/marketing 21%, computer/information sciences 17%, health sciences 37%, legal studies 25%.

**Computing on campus.** 75 workstations in library, computer center. Online library available.

**Student life. Freshman orientation:** Mandatory. Preregistration for classes offered. **Activities:** Student government, student newspaper.

**Student services.** Adult student services, career counseling, student employment services, financial aid counseling, personal counseling, placement for graduates. **Transfer:** Pre-admission transcript evaluation for new students.

**Contact.** E-mail: ecollier@draughons.edu
Phone: (615) 361-7555 Toll-free number: (877) 258-7796
Elizabeth Collier, Director of Admissions, Draughons Junior College: Nashville, 340 Plus Park at Pavilion Boulevard, Nashville, TN 37217

## Dyersburg State Community College
### Dyersburg, Tennessee
www.dscc.edu                                          CB code: 7323

- Public 2-year community college
- Commuter campus in large town

**General.** Founded in 1967. Regionally accredited. **Enrollment:** 2,078 degree-seeking undergraduates; 490 non-degree-seeking students. **Degrees:** 214 associate awarded. **Location:** 78 miles from Memphis. **Calendar:** Semester, limited summer session. **Full-time faculty:** 52 total; 27% have terminal degrees, 14% minority, 62% women. **Part-time faculty:** 120 total. **Class size:** 46% < 20, 52% 20-39, 1% 40-49, less than 1% 50-99.

**Student profile.** Among degree-seeking undergraduates, 585 enrolled as first-time, first-year students.

| | | | |
|---|---|---|---|
| Part-time: | 39% | Asian American: | 1% |
| Out-of-state: | 1% | Hispanic American: | 1% |
| Women: | 73% | Native American: | 1% |
| African American: | 20% | 25 or older: | 39% |

**Transfer out. Colleges most students transferred to 2007:** University of Tennessee-Martin, University of Memphis, Middle Tennessee State University.

**Basis for selection.** Open admission, but selective for some programs. Acceptance into nursing program is based on point system, taking into consideration National League of Nursing test score, GPA, science courses completed with grade of C or above, and required courses that have been successfully completed. High school students who meet specific admission requirements may enroll as first time freshmen. **Learning Disabled:** Students are encouraged to self-identify with the college's ADA coordinator.

**High school preparation.** 14 units recommended. Recommended units include English 4, mathematics 3, social studies 2, history 1, science 2 and foreign language 2.

**2007-2008 Annual costs.** Tuition/fees: $2,635; $9,711 out-of-state. Per-credit charge: $101 in-state; $407 out-of-state. Books/supplies: $1,000. Personal expenses: $990.

**Financial aid. Need-based:** Need-based aid available for part-time students. Work-study available nights and for part-time students. **Non-need-based:** Scholarships awarded for academics, alumni affiliation, athletics, job skills, leadership, minority status, music/drama, state residency.

**Application procedures. Admission:** Priority date 8/1; no deadline. $10 fee. Admission notification on a rolling basis. **Financial aid:** Priority date 3/1; no closing date. FAFSA required. Applicants notified on a rolling basis starting 3/1; must reply within 2 week(s) of notification.

**Academics. Special study options:** Cooperative education, distance learning, dual enrollment of high school students, honors, independent study, internships, liberal arts/career combination. **Credit/placement by examination:** AP, CLEP, institutional tests. 24 credit hours maximum toward associate degree. **Support services:** GED preparation and test center, learning center, reduced course load, remedial instruction, study skills assistance, tutoring.

**Majors. Biology:** General. **Business:** Business admin. **Computer sciences:** Information systems. **Education:** General. **Engineering technology:** Electrical. **Family/consumer sciences:** Child development. **Health:** Medical records technology, nursing (RN). **Liberal arts:** Arts/sciences. **Math:** General. **Protective services:** Police science. **Psychology:** General. **Social sciences:** General.

**Most popular majors.** Business/marketing 19%, communication technologies 6%, education 19%, health sciences 38%.

**Computing on campus.** 542 workstations in library, computer center, student center. Commuter students can connect to campus network. Online course registration, online library, helpline available.

**Student life. Freshman orientation:** Available. Preregistration for classes offered. Half-day programs with pre-registration. **Activities:** Campus ministries, choral groups, drama, music ensembles, student government, student newspaper, American Chemical Society Affiliates, business and office systems association, student nurses association, Minority Association for Successful Students, astronomy club, advanced technology association, music club, Phi Theta Kappa, psychology club.

**Athletics.** NJCAA. **Intercollegiate:** Baseball M, basketball, softball W. **Intramural:** Basketball, volleyball. **Team name:** Eagles.

**Student services.** Adult student services, alcohol/substance abuse counseling, career counseling, services for economically disadvantaged, student employment services, financial aid counseling, minority student services, personal counseling, placement for graduates, veterans' counselor, women's services. **Physically disabled:** Services for visually, speech, hearing impaired. **Transfer:** Pre-admission transcript evaluation for new students. Transfer adviser, college fairs on campus for students transferring to 4-year colleges.

**Contact.** E-mail: enroll@dscc.edu
Phone: (731) 286-3330 Fax: (731) 286-3325
J Gullett, Assistant Vice President for Academic Affairs, Dyersburg State Community College, 1510 Lake Road, Dyersburg, TN 38024

## Electronic Computer Programming College
Chattanooga, Tennessee
www.ecpconline.com                    CB code: 2267

- For-profit 2-year technical college
- Large city

**General.** Accredited by ACCSCT. **Calendar:** Quarter.

**Contact.** Phone: (423) 624-0077
Director of Admissions, 3805 Brainerd Road, Chattanooga, TN 37411

## Fountainhead College of Technology
Knoxville, Tennessee
www.fountainheadcollege.edu           CB code: 0446

- For-profit 2-year technical and career college
- Commuter campus in small city
- Interview required

**General.** Founded in 1947. Accredited by ACCSCT. **Enrollment:** 114 degree-seeking undergraduates. **Degrees:** 61 bachelor's, 105 associate awarded. **Location:** 200 miles from Nashville, 200 miles from Atlanta. **Calendar:** Semester, extensive summer session. **Full-time faculty:** 30 total.

**Student profile.** Among degree-seeking undergraduates, 100% enrolled in a vocational program, 1% already have a bachelor's degree or higher.

**Transfer out.** 30% of students enrolled in the transfer program go on to 4-year colleges.

**Basis for selection.** Open admission, but selective for some programs. Test scores, interview important. Institutional aptitude test required for admissions.

**2007-2008 Annual costs.** Books/supplies: $1,250. Personal expenses: $1,200.

**Financial aid.** All financial aid based on need.

**Application procedures. Admission:** No deadline. $100 fee. Admission notification on a rolling basis. **Financial aid:** No deadline. FAFSA required. Applicants notified on a rolling basis.

**Academics. Special study options:** Bachelor's degree programs available on campus. **Credit/placement by examination:** CLEP, institutional tests. 27 credit hours maximum toward associate degree. **Support services:** Tutoring.

**Majors. Engineering technology:** Electrical.

**Computing on campus.** PC or laptop required. 200 workstations in computer center. Online library, wireless network available.

**Student life. Freshman orientation:** Mandatory. Preregistration for classes offered.

**Student services.** Career counseling, student employment services, personal counseling, placement for graduates.

**Contact.** E-mail: info@fountainheadcollege.com
Phone: (865) 688-9422 Toll-free number: (888) 218-7335
Fax: (865) 688-2419
Christopher Hill, Director of Administration, Fountainhead College of Technology, 3203 Tazewell Pike, Knoxville, TN 37918

## High-Tech Institute
Nashville, Tennessee
www.hightechinstitute.edu

- For-profit 2-year technical and career college
- Very large city

**General.** Accredited by ACCSCT. **Calendar:** Continuous.

**Contact.** Phone: (615) 232-3700
Director of Admissions, 560 Royal Parkway, Nashville, TN 37214

## Hiwassee College
Madisonville, Tennessee
www.hiwassee.edu                      CB code: 1298

- Private 2-year junior and liberal arts college affiliated with United Methodist Church
- Residential campus in small town
- SAT or ACT (ACT writing optional) required

**General.** Founded in 1849. Regionally accredited. Christian principles emphasized; involvement in total campus life encouraged. **Enrollment:** 341 degree-seeking undergraduates; 77 non-degree-seeking students. **Degrees:** 42 associate awarded. **Location:** 50 miles from Knoxville, 75 miles from Chattanooga. **Calendar:** Semester, limited summer session. **Full-time faculty:** 17 total; 47% have terminal degrees, 6% minority, 41% women. **Part-time faculty:** 10 total; 50% have terminal degrees, 30% women. **Class size:** 58% < 20, 40% 20-39, less than 1% 50-99, less than 1% >100. **Special facilities:** Nature preserve, equestrian facilities, natatorium.

**Student profile.** Among degree-seeking undergraduates, 99% enrolled in a transfer program, 1% enrolled in a vocational program, 181 enrolled as first-time, first-year students, 30 transferred in from other institutions.

| | | | |
|---|---|---|---|
| Part-time: | 12% | Hispanic American: | 1% |
| Out-of-state: | 7% | Native American: | 1% |
| Women: | 55% | International: | 6% |
| African American: | 11% | 25 or older: | 7% |
| Asian American: | 1% | Live on campus: | 45% |

**Transfer out.** 97% of students enrolled in the transfer program go on to 4-year colleges. **Colleges most students transferred to 2007:** University of Tennessee- Knoxville, University of Tennessee- Chattanooga, Tennessee Weleyan College, Tennessee Technological University, Lincoln Memorial University.

**Basis for selection.** Minimum high school GPA of 2.5, class rank in top two-thirds, and test scores important. Students admitted conditionally or provisionally required to take ACT COMPASS placement exam in reading, writing, and mathematics. An additional timed writing sample is also necessary for proper placement. Interview recommended for academically weak. **Adult students:** ACT/COMPASS test required. **Homeschooled:** Statement describing homeschool structure and mission, transcript of courses and grades, state high school equivalency certificate required. **Learning Disabled:** Accommodation requests must be made known to the Admissions Staff, Academic Dean, and appropriate faculty members.

**High school preparation.** Required and recommended units include English 4, mathematics 3, social studies 3, history 1, science 3 (laboratory 2), foreign language 2 and academic electives 4.

**2007-2008 Annual costs.** Tuition/fees: $11,130. Per-credit charge: $445. Room/board: $6,370. Books/supplies: $800. Personal expenses: $1,300.

**Financial aid. Need-based:** Need-based aid available for part-time students. Work-study available nights, weekends and for part-time students. **Non-need-based:** Scholarships awarded for academics, alumni affiliation, athletics, job skills, leadership, music/drama, religious affiliation, state residency.

**Application procedures. Admission:** Priority date 5/1; no deadline. No application fee. Application may be submitted online. Admission notification on a rolling basis beginning on or about 10/1. **Financial aid:** Priority date 5/1; no closing date. FAFSA, institutional form required. Applicants notified on a rolling basis starting 4/1; must reply within 2 week(s) of notification.

**Academics. Special study options:** Distance learning, dual enrollment of high school students, ESL, honors, independent study, internships, study abroad. License preparation in nursing. **Credit/placement by examination:** AP, CLEP, institutional tests. 33 credit hours maximum toward associate degree. **Support services:** Learning center, pre-admission summer program, reduced course load, remedial instruction, study skills assistance, tutoring.

**Majors. Agriculture:** Animal sciences, business, economics, food science, horticultural science, plant sciences, soil science. **Biology:** General. **Business:** General, accounting, business admin, finance, hospitality admin, hospitality/recreation, managerial economics. **Communications:** General. **Computer sciences:** General. **Conservation:** Forest resources, forestry. **Education:** General, college student counseling, early childhood, elementary, music, physical, secondary. **English:** English lit. **Family/consumer sciences:** General, clothing/textiles, food/nutrition. **Foreign languages:** French, Spanish. **Health:** Predental, premedicine, prenursing, prepharmacy, preveterinary. **History:** General. **Legal studies:** Prelaw. **Liberal arts:** Arts/sciences. **Math:** General. **Parks/recreation:** Health/fitness. **Philosophy/religion:** Religion. **Physical sciences:** Chemistry, physics. **Protective services:** Criminal justice. **Psychology:** General. **Public administration:** Human services. **Social sciences:** General, criminology, economics, sociology. **Theology:** Bible, preministerial. **Visual/performing arts:** Dramatic, music performance, piano/organ, voice/opera.

**Most popular majors.** Agriculture 8%, business/marketing 10%, education 14%, health sciences 37%, natural resources/environmental science 6%, visual/performing arts 6%.

**Computing on campus.** 61 workstations in library, computer center, student center. Dormitories wired for high-speed internet access and linked to campus network. Commuter students can connect to campus network. Online library, helpline, repair service, wireless network available.

**Student life. Freshman orientation:** Mandatory. Preregistration for classes offered. **Policies:** Religious observance required. **Housing:** Guaranteed on-campus for all undergraduates. Single-sex dorms, substance-free housing available. $50 fully refundable deposit, deadline 8/1. **Activities:** Campus ministries, choral groups, dance, drama, literary magazine, music ensembles, musical theater, student government, student newspaper, Christian Student Movement, Circle K.

**Athletics.** NJCAA. **Intercollegiate:** Baseball M, basketball, cheerleading, cross-country, golf, soccer, softball W, volleyball W. **Intramural:** Basketball, football (non-tackle), softball, swimming, table tennis, tennis, volleyball. **Team name:** Tigers.

**Student services.** Adult student services, alcohol/substance abuse counseling, campus ministries, career counseling, services for economically disadvantaged, financial aid counseling, health services, personal counseling, veterans' counselor. **Transfer:** Pre-admission transcript evaluation for new students. Transfer adviser, college fairs on campus for students transferring to 4-year colleges.

**Contact.** E-mail: enroll@hiwassee.edu
Phone: (423) 420-1212 Toll-free number: (800) 356-2187
Fax: (423) 442-3520
Jodie Moser, Director of Admissions, Hiwassee College, 225 Hiwassee College Drive, Madisonville, TN 37354-6099

## Huntington College of Health Sciences
**Knoxville, Tennessee**
**www.hchs.edu**
**CB code: 3945**

▶ For-profit 2-year health science college
▶ Very large city

**General.** Accredited by DETC. **Enrollment:** 78 degree-seeking undergraduates. **Degrees:** 7 associate awarded. **Calendar:** Continuous, limited summer session. **Part-time faculty:** 21 total.

**Basis for selection.** Open admission, but selective for some programs.

**2007-2008 Annual costs.** Tuition/fees: $5,150. Per-credit charge: $165. Books/supplies: $1,350.

**Application procedures. Admission:** No deadline. No application fee. **Financial aid:** No deadline.

**Academics. Credit/placement by examination:** CLEP.

**Majors. Health:** Clinical nutrition.

**Student life. Activities:** Student newspaper.

**Contact.** E-mail: studentservices@hchs.edu
Phone: (865) 524-8079 Toll-free number: (800) 290-4226
Fax: (865) 524-8339
Cheryl Freeman, Registrar, Director of Student Services, Huntington College of Health Sciences, 1204D Kenesaw, Knoxville, TN 37919-7736

## Jackson State Community College
**Jackson, Tennessee**
**www.jscc.edu**
**CB code: 2266**

▶ Public 2-year community college
▶ Commuter campus in small city

**General.** Founded in 1965. Regionally accredited. **Enrollment:** 4,387 degree-seeking undergraduates; 8 non-degree-seeking students. **Degrees:** 420 associate awarded. **ROTC:** Army. **Location:** 80 miles from Memphis, 130 miles from Nashville. **Calendar:** Semester, limited summer session. **Full-time faculty:** 110 total. **Part-time faculty:** 190 total. **Class size:** 45% < 20, 52% 20-39, 2% 40-49, 1% 50-99, less than 1% >100.

**Student profile.** Among degree-seeking undergraduates, 39% enrolled in a transfer program, 61% enrolled in a vocational program, 1% already have a bachelor's degree or higher, 920 enrolled as first-time, first-year students.

| | | | |
|---|---|---|---|
| Part-time: | 45% | Asian American: | 1% |
| Out-of-state: | 1% | Hispanic American: | 1% |
| Women: | 66% | 25 or older: | 38% |
| African American: | 17% | | |

**Transfer out. Colleges most students transferred to 2007:** Union University, University of Memphis, University of Tennessee at Martin, Middle Tennessee State University, Lambuth University.

**Basis for selection.** Open admission, but selective for some programs. Special requirements for nursing, medical laboratory technology, radiology, respiratory care, physical therapy assistant, and emergency medical technician programs. ACT for placement must be received by registration for fall-term admission. Interview required for allied health, nursing programs. **Adult students:** SAT/ACT scores not required if applicant over 21. Compass test if degree-seeking first-time adult students. **Homeschooled:** Transcript of courses and grades required.

**High school preparation.** 14 units recommended. Recommended units include English 4, mathematics 3, social studies 1, history 1, science 2 (laboratory 1), foreign language 2 and visual/performing arts 1. One visual and performing arts credit recommended. College preparatory program required by state for transfer associate degree programs; not required for other programs.

**2007-2008 Annual costs.** Tuition/fees: $2,617; $9,693 out-of-state. Per-credit charge: $101 in-state; $407 out-of-state. Books/supplies: $1,000. Personal expenses: $884.

**2006-2007 Financial aid. Need-based:** 578 full-time freshmen applied for aid; 465 were judged to have need; 452 of these received aid. Average need met was 84%. Average scholarship/grant was $3,294; average loan $3,150. 98% of total undergraduate aid awarded as scholarships/grants, 2% as loans/jobs. Need-based aid available for part-time students. Work-study available nights, weekends and for part-time students. **Non-need-based:** Awarded to 452 full-time undergraduates, including 177 freshmen. Scholarships awarded for academics, art, athletics, job skills, leadership, minority status, music/drama.

**Application procedures. Admission:** Priority date 7/1; no deadline. $10 fee. Application may be submitted online. Closing date for applications to Allied Health and Nursing programs April 15th. **Financial aid:** Priority date 3/15; no closing date. FAFSA, institutional form required. Applicants notified on a rolling basis starting 6/1; must reply within 2 week(s) of notification.

**Academics. Special study options:** Combined bachelor's/graduate degree, cooperative education, distance learning, dual enrollment of high school students, honors, internships, liberal arts/career combination, weekend college. License preparation in nursing, paramedic, physical therapy, radiology, real estate. **Credit/placement by examination:** AP, CLEP, institutional tests. 21 credit hours maximum toward associate degree. Must complete additional 15 college credit hours before credit by examination is awarded. **Support services:** GED preparation and test center, learning center, reduced course load, remedial instruction, study skills assistance, tutoring, writing center.

**Majors. Agriculture:** Business. **Biology:** General. **Business:** Accounting, business admin. **Communications:** General. **Computer sciences:** General. **Education:** General, early childhood. **Engineering:** General. **Engineering**

technology: Industrial. **English:** English lit. **Health:** Clinical lab technology, medical radiologic technology/radiation therapy, nursing (RN), physical therapy assistant, premedicine, prenursing, respiratory therapy technology. **History:** General. **Legal studies:** Prelaw. **Liberal arts:** Arts/sciences. **Math:** General. **Parks/recreation:** Health/fitness. **Philosophy/religion:** Philosophy. **Physical sciences:** General, chemistry. **Protective services:** Police science. **Psychology:** General. **Public administration:** General, social work. **Social sciences:** Political science, sociology. **Visual/performing arts:** Art, commercial/advertising art.

**Most popular majors.** Business/marketing 10%, health sciences 44%, liberal arts 41%.

**Computing on campus.** 871 workstations in library, student center. Commuter students can connect to campus network. Online course registration, online library, wireless network available.

**Student life. Freshman orientation:** Available. **Activities:** Choral groups, drama, music ensembles, student government.

**Athletics.** NJCAA. **Intercollegiate:** Baseball M, basketball, softball W. **Team name:** Generals.

**Student services.** Career counseling, student employment services, financial aid counseling, health services, personal counseling, placement for graduates, veterans' counselor. **Physically disabled:** Services for visually, speech, hearing impaired. **Transfer:** College fairs on campus for students transferring to 4-year colleges.

**Contact.** E-mail: mray@jscc.edu
Phone: (731) 425-8844 Fax: (731) 425-9559
Monica Ray, Director of Admissions/Records, Jackson State Community College, 2046 North Parkway, Jackson, TN 38301-3797

## John A. Gupton College
### Nashville, Tennessee
### www.guptoncollege.com
### CB code: 0539

- Private 2-year school of mortuary science
- Commuter campus in large city

**General.** Founded in 1946. Regionally accredited. **Enrollment:** 111 degree-seeking undergraduates. **Degrees:** 32 associate awarded. **Calendar:** Semester, limited summer session. **Full-time faculty:** 6 total. **Part-time faculty:** 9 total. **Class size:** 8% < 20, 33% 20-39, 58% 50-99.

**Student profile.** Among degree-seeking undergraduates, 48 enrolled as first-time, first-year students, 48 transferred in from other institutions.

| | | | |
|---|---|---|---|
| Part-time: | 6% | 25 or older: | 55% |
| Out-of-state: | 27% | Live on campus: | 12% |
| Women: | 54% | | |

**Transfer out. Colleges most students transferred to 2007:** Middle Tennessee State University, Western Kentucky University, Jackson State Community College.

**Basis for selection.** 2 letters of recommendation are needed, plus completed health form as required by the Tennessee State Board of Health. SAT or ACT required for files and not used in admissions decisions. Interview recommended. **Homeschooled:** Transcript of courses and grades, state high school equivalency certificate, letter of recommendation (nonparent) required.

**High school preparation.** 10 units recommended. Recommended units include English 4, mathematics 3 and science 3.

**2007-2008 Annual costs.** Tuition/fees: $6,960. Per-credit charge: $232. Room only: $3,600. Books/supplies: $850.

**Financial aid.** All financial aid based on need. Need-based aid available for part-time students.

**Application procedures. Admission:** No deadline. $20 fee. Application must be submitted on paper. Admission notification on a rolling basis. **Financial aid:** No deadline. FAFSA required. Applicants notified on a rolling basis.

**Academics. Credit/placement by examination:** AP, CLEP.

**Majors. Personal/culinary services:** Funeral direction, mortuary science.

**Computing on campus.** 8 workstations in library, computer center. Helpline available.

**Student life. Freshman orientation:** Mandatory. Preregistration for classes offered. **Housing:** Apartments, substance-free housing available. $450 deposit. **Activities:** Student government.

**Student services.** Career counseling. **Transfer:** Pre-admission transcript evaluation for new students.

**Contact.** E-mail: bolin@guptoncollege.edu
Phone: (615) 327-3927 Fax: (615) 321-4518
Lisa Bolin, Registrar, John A. Gupton College, 1616 Church Street, Nashville, TN 37203-2920

## Miller-Motte Technical College: Chattanooga
### Chattanooga, Tennessee
### www.miller-motte.com/chattanoogawelcome.html

- For-profit 2-year technical college
- Commuter campus in large city

**General.** Accredited by ACICS. **Calendar:** Quarter.

**Contact.** Phone: (423) 510-9675
Director of Admissions, 6020 Shallowford Road, Suite 100, Chattanooga, TN 37421

## Miller-Motte Technical College: Clarksville
### Clarksville, Tennessee
### www.miller-motte.com
### CB code: 3228

- For-profit 2-year business and health science college
- Commuter campus in small city
- Interview required

**General.** Accredited by ACICS. **Enrollment:** 550 degree-seeking undergraduates. **Degrees:** 87 associate awarded. **Location:** 45 miles from Nashville. **Calendar:** Quarter, extensive summer session. **Full-time faculty:** 20 total. **Part-time faculty:** 40 total. **Special facilities:** Simulated operating rooms, medical laboratories, simulated doctor's exam room.

**Student profile.**

| | | | |
|---|---|---|---|
| Out-of-state: | 50% | 25 or older: | 60% |

**Transfer out. Colleges most students transferred to 2007:** Austin Peay University, Hopkinsville Community College.

**Basis for selection.** Open admission, but selective for some programs. 2 years experience or 2-year/4-year degree and interview with department head required for entrance into network administration certificate program. **Learning Disabled:** Letter of request for any accommodation required.

**2007-2008 Annual costs.** Tuition/fees: $9,900. Per-credit charge: $220. Required fees vary by program. Books/supplies: $900. Personal expenses: $1,350.

**Financial aid.** All financial aid based on need. Need-based aid available for part-time students. Work-study available nights, weekends and for part-time students.

**Application procedures. Admission:** No deadline. No application fee. Application must be submitted on paper. Admission notification on a rolling basis. **Financial aid:** No deadline. FAFSA, institutional form required. Applicants notified on a rolling basis.

**Academics. Special study options:** Weekend college. **Credit/placement by examination:** CLEP, institutional tests. 40 credit hours maximum toward associate degree. No more than 50% of required credit hours in a major and/or entire program. **Support services:** Reduced course load, remedial instruction, study skills assistance, tutoring.

**Majors. Business:** Accounting, business admin. **Computer sciences:** General. **Health:** Massage therapy, medical assistant, phlebotomy, surgical technology. **Legal studies:** Paralegal.

**Most popular majors.** Business/marketing 7%, computer/information sciences 22%, engineering/engineering technologies 6%, health sciences 46%, legal studies 15%.

**Computing on campus.** 75 workstations in library, computer center. Online library available.

**Student life. Freshman orientation:** Mandatory. Preregistration for classes offered. **Activities:** Student government.

**Student services.** Adult student services, career counseling, student employment services, financial aid counseling, placement for graduates, veterans' counselor. **Transfer:** Re-entry adviser, pre-admission transcript evaluation for new students.

**Contact.**  E-mail: gcastleberry@miller-motte.com
Phone: (931) 553-0071 Toll-free number: (800) 558-0071
Ginny Malmsten, Admissions Director, Miller-Motte Technical College: Clarksville, 1820 Business Park Drive, Clarksville, TN 37040

## Motlow State Community College
### Lynchburg, Tennessee
www.mscc.cc.tn.us                          CB code: 1543

- Public 2-year community college
- Commuter campus in rural community.

**General.** Founded in 1969. Regionally accredited. **Enrollment:** 3,436 degree-seeking undergraduates; 677 non-degree-seeking students. **Degrees:** 40 associate awarded. **Location:** 65 miles from Nashville. **Calendar:** Semester, limited summer session. **Full-time faculty:** 76 total; 67% women. **Part-time faculty:** 144 total. **Class size:** 38% < 20, 57% 20-39, 3% 40-49, 2% >100.

**Student profile.** Among degree-seeking undergraduates, 60% enrolled in a transfer program, 49% enrolled in a vocational program, 1% already have a bachelor's degree or higher, 1,079 enrolled as first-time, first-year students, 331 transferred in from other institutions.

| | | | |
|---|---|---|---|
| Part-time: | 36% | Women: | 63% |
| Out-of-state: | 1% | 25 or older: | 29% |

**Transfer out.** 55% of students enrolled in the transfer program go on to 4-year colleges. **Colleges most students transferred to 2007:** Middle Tennessee State University, Tennessee Technological University.

**Basis for selection.** Open admission, but selective for some programs. Students entering into the college's Nursing Program have different admissions criteria. Interview required for nursing program. **Adult students:** SAT/ACT scores not required if applicant over 21. **Homeschooled:** Transcript of courses and grades required.

**High school preparation.** 16 units recommended. Recommended units include English 4, mathematics 3, social studies 2, history 1, science 2 (laboratory 1) and foreign language 2.

**2007-2008 Annual costs.** Tuition/fees: $2,623; $9,699 out-of-state. Per-credit charge: $101 in-state; $407 out-of-state. Books/supplies: $1,200. Personal expenses: $1,000.

**2006-2007 Financial aid. Need-based:** 73% of total undergraduate aid awarded as scholarships/grants, 27% as loans/jobs. Need-based aid available for part-time students. Work-study available for part-time students. **Non-need-based:** Scholarships awarded for academics, alumni affiliation, art, athletics, leadership, state residency.

**Application procedures. Admission:** $10 fee. Application may be submitted online. Admission notification on a rolling basis. **Financial aid:** No deadline. FAFSA required. Applicants notified on a rolling basis starting 3/15.

**Academics. Special study options:** Accelerated study, cooperative education, distance learning, double major, dual enrollment of high school students, honors, independent study, internships, weekend college. License preparation in nursing. **Credit/placement by examination:** AP, CLEP, institutional tests. Maximum number of credits by examination that may be earned is limited to 25% of total number of credits needed for graduation. **Support services:** Learning center, reduced course load, remedial instruction, study skills assistance, tutoring, writing center.

**Majors. Business:** Business admin. **Education:** General, elementary, secondary. **Health:** Nursing (RN). **Liberal arts:** Arts/sciences.

**Most popular majors.** Business/marketing 6%, health sciences 13%, liberal arts 78%.

**Computing on campus.** 250 workstations in library, computer center. Commuter students can connect to campus network. Online course registration, online library, helpline, repair service, wireless network available.

**Student life. Freshman orientation:** Mandatory. Preregistration for classes offered. **Activities:** Choral groups, drama, literary magazine, music ensembles, student government, student newspaper, Baptist Student Union,

African American Student Association, outing club, communications club, law and government club, literary club, Phi Theta Kappa, psychology club, Tennessee Association of Student Nurses.

**Athletics.** NJCAA. **Intercollegiate:** Baseball M, basketball, softball W. **Intramural:** Baseball M, basketball, bowling, softball. **Team name:** Bucks.

**Student services.** Adult student services, alcohol/substance abuse counseling, career counseling, student employment services, financial aid counseling, health services, personal counseling, placement for graduates, veterans' counselor. **Physically disabled:** Services for visually impaired. **Transfer:** Pre-admission transcript evaluation for new students. College fairs on campus for students transferring to 4-year colleges.

**Contact.**  E-mail: galsup@mscc.edu
Phone: (931) 393-1529 Toll-free number: (800) 654-4877
Fax: (931) 393-1971
Greer Alsup, Director of Admissions and Records, Motlow State Community College, Box 8500, Lynchburg, TN 37352-8500

## Nashville Auto-Diesel College
### Nashville, Tennessee
www.nadcedu.com                          CB code: 3098

- For-profit 1-year technical college
- Commuter campus in large city
- Interview required

**General.** Accredited by ACCSCT. **Enrollment:** 2,700 degree-seeking undergraduates. **Degrees:** 106 associate awarded. **Calendar:** Continuous, extensive summer session. **Full-time faculty:** 75 total. **Class size:** 100% 20-39.

**Student profile.**

| | | | |
|---|---|---|---|
| Out-of-state: | 90% | Live on campus: | 30% |
| 25 or older: | 1% | | |

**Basis for selection.** Secondary school record, interview, test scores most important. State proficiency tests used in admission decisions.

**2007-2008 Annual costs.** Tuition/fees: $14,195. Full program costs range from $21,400 to $32,600 for diploma programs; $27,400 to $34,900 for associate programs. Room/board: $5,502. Books/supplies: $987.

**Financial aid.** All financial aid based on need. Work-study available nights and weekends.

**Application procedures. Admission:** No deadline. $100 fee. Admission notification on a rolling basis. **Financial aid:** No deadline. FAFSA required. Applicants notified on a rolling basis.

**Academics. Credit/placement by examination:** AP, CLEP, institutional tests. **Support services:** Study skills assistance, tutoring.

**Majors. Mechanic/repair:** General, auto body, automotive, diesel, heavy equipment.

**Computing on campus.** 46 workstations in library, computer center. Dormitories wired for high-speed internet access. Online library available.

**Student life. Freshman orientation:** Mandatory. **Housing:** Single-sex dorms available. $200 deposit.

**Student services.** Career counseling, student employment services, financial aid counseling, placement for graduates, veterans' counselor. **Physically disabled:** Services for visually impaired.

**Contact.**  E-mail: admissions@nadcedu.com
Phone: (615) 226-3990 Toll-free number: (800) 228-6232
Fax: (615) 262-8466
Bill Ormsby, Vice President, Nashville Auto-Diesel College, 1524 Gallatin Road, Nashville, TN 37206

## Nashville State Community College
### Nashville, Tennessee
www.nscc.edu                          CB code: 0850

- Public 2-year community and technical college
- Commuter campus in large city

**General.** Founded in 1969. Regionally accredited. **Enrollment:** 7,077 degree-seeking undergraduates. **Degrees:** 583 associate awarded. **Location:** 6 miles from Nashville, 200 miles from Memphis. **Calendar:** Semester, limited summer session. **Full-time faculty:** 136 total. **Part-time faculty:** 267 total. **Special facilities:** Television production studio.

**Student profile.**

| | | | |
|---|---|---|---|
| Out-of-state: | 6% | 25 or older: | 54% |

**Transfer out. Colleges most students transferred to 2007:** Middle Tennessee University, Tennessee State University, Tennessee Technical University.

**Basis for selection.** Open admission, but selective for some programs. Students may have to take AAPT for placement. Interview required for automotive services technology, occupational therapy assistant, surgical technology programs.

**High school preparation.** Recommended units include English 4, mathematics 3, social studies 2, science 2 and foreign language 2. One visual/performing art recommended. Business technologies majors: 1 unit bookkeeping or accounting recommended. Engineering technologies majors: additional math and science recommended.

**2007-2008 Annual costs.** Tuition/fees: $2,589; $9,665 out-of-state. Per-credit charge: $101 in-state; $407 out-of-state. Books/supplies: $1,000. Personal expenses: $544.

**2007-2008 Financial aid. Need-based:** 63% of total undergraduate aid awarded as scholarships/grants, 37% as loans/jobs. Need-based aid available for part-time students. Work-study available nights, weekends and for part-time students. **Non-need-based:** Scholarships awarded for academics, minority status.

**Application procedures. Admission:** No deadline. $5 fee. Application may be submitted online. Admission notification on a rolling basis. Automotive services technology applicants must have automobile dealer sponsorship prior to acceptance. **Financial aid:** Priority date 3/1; no closing date. FAFSA, institutional form required. Applicants notified on a rolling basis starting 6/1; must reply within 2 week(s) of notification.

**Academics. Special study options:** Cooperative education, distance learning, double major, dual enrollment of high school students, ESL, honors, internships, student-designed major. **Credit/placement by examination:** CLEP, institutional tests. 20 credit hours maximum toward associate degree. **Support services:** GED preparation, learning center, reduced course load, remedial instruction, study skills assistance, tutoring, writing center.

**Majors. Business:** Accounting, business admin. **Communications technology:** General. **Computer sciences:** General. **Education:** Early childhood. **Engineering technology:** Architectural, civil, construction, electrical. **Foreign languages:** Sign language interpretation. **Health:** Medical secretary. **Legal studies:** Legal secretary. **Mechanic/repair:** Automotive. **Personal/culinary services:** Culinary arts. **Protective services:** Police science. **Visual/performing arts:** Commercial/advertising art, photography.

**Computing on campus.** 518 workstations in library, computer center. Commuter students can connect to campus network. Online course registration, helpline available.

**Student life. Freshman orientation:** Available. **Activities:** International student organizations, literary magazine, student government, student newspaper, Black student organization.

**Athletics. Intramural:** Softball, table tennis, volleyball.

**Student services.** Adult student services, career counseling, student employment services, personal counseling, placement for graduates, veterans' counselor. **Physically disabled:** Services for visually, hearing impaired. **Transfer:** Pre-admission transcript evaluation for new students. College fairs on campus for students transferring to 4-year colleges.

**Contact.** Phone: (615) 353-3333 Toll-free number: (800) 272-7363 Fax: (615) 353-3243
Laura Potter, Director of Admissions, Nashville State Community College, 120 White Bridge Road, Nashville, TN 37209-4515

## National College: Bartlett
**Bartlett, Tennessee**

- For-profit 2-year branch campus college
- Large town

**General.** Regionally accredited; also accredited by ACICS. **Enrollment:** 78 degree-seeking undergraduates. **Calendar:** Quarter. **Part-time faculty:** 5 total.

**2008-2009 Annual costs.** Tuition/fees: $9,585. Per-credit charge: $212.

**Application procedures. Admission:** No deadline. $30 fee.

**Academics. Credit/placement by examination:** CLEP.

**Majors. Business:** Accounting/business management, administrative services, business admin. **Engineering technology:** Computer systems. **Health:** Medical assistant, medical records technology, pharmacy assistant.

**Contact.** Phone: (901) 213-1681
Larry Steele, Vice President of Admissions, National College: Bartlett, 5760 Stage Road, Bartlett, TN 38134

## National College: Bristol
**Bristol, Tennessee**
**www.ncbt.edu**

**CB code: 3247**

- For-profit 2-year business college
- Commuter campus in large town

**General.** Accredited by ACICS. Eight campuses in Virginia. **Enrollment:** 277 degree-seeking undergraduates. **Degrees:** 44 associate awarded. **Calendar:** Quarter, limited summer session. **Full-time faculty:** 1 total. **Part-time faculty:** 32 total.

**Basis for selection.** Open admission. Interview recommended.

**2007-2008 Annual costs.** Tuition/fees: $9,135. Per-credit charge: $202. Books/supplies: $1,200.

**Financial aid.** All financial aid based on need. Need-based aid available for part-time students.

**Application procedures. Admission:** No deadline. $30 fee, may be waived for applicants with need. Application may be submitted online. Admission notification on a rolling basis. **Financial aid:** No deadline. FAFSA required. Applicants notified on a rolling basis starting 9/1.

**Academics. Special study options:** Double major, internships. **Credit/placement by examination:** CLEP, institutional tests. **Support services:** Tutoring.

**Majors. Business:** Accounting, administrative services, business admin, office management. **Computer sciences:** Computer science. **Health:** Medical assistant.

**Computing on campus.** 35 workstations in library, computer center.

**Student life. Freshman orientation:** Mandatory.

**Student services.** Career counseling, personal counseling.

**Contact.** E-mail: market@educorp.edu
Phone: (423) 878-4440
Larry Steele, Director of Admissions, National College: Bristol, 1328 Highway 11W, Bristol, TN 37620

## National College: Knoxville
**Knoxville, Tennessee**
**www.ncbt.edu**

- For-profit 2-year business and technical college
- Large city

**General.** Accredited by ACICS. **Enrollment:** 441 degree-seeking undergraduates. **Degrees:** 62 associate awarded. **Calendar:** Quarter. **Full-time faculty:** 4 total. **Part-time faculty:** 36 total.

**Basis for selection.** Open admission. Interview recommended.

**2007-2008 Annual costs.** Tuition/fees: $9,090. Per-credit charge: $202.

**Application procedures. Admission:** No deadline. $30 fee. **Financial aid:** No deadline.

**Academics. Credit/placement by examination:** CLEP.

**Majors. Business:** Accounting, administrative services, business admin. **Health:** Medical assistant, medical records admin, pharmacy assistant, surgical technology.

**Contact.** Phone: (865) 539-2011
Larry Steele, Director of Admissions, National College: Knoxville, 8415 Kingston Pike, Knoxville, TN 37919

## National College: Madison
### Madison, Tennessee

◗ For-profit 2-year branch campus college
◗ Large town

**General.** Regionally accredited; also accredited by ACICS. **Enrollment:** 136 degree-seeking undergraduates. **Calendar:** Quarter. **Part-time faculty:** 22 total.

**2008-2009 Annual costs.** Tuition/fees: $9,585. Per-credit charge: $212.

**Application procedures. Admission:** No deadline. $30 fee. **Financial aid:** No deadline.

**Academics. Credit/placement by examination:** CLEP.

**Majors. Business:** Accounting/business management, administrative services, business admin, hospitality admin, tourism/travel. **Engineering technology:** Computer systems. **Health:** Medical assistant, medical records technology, pharmacy assistant.

**Contact.** Phone: (615) 612-3015
Larry Steele, Vice President of Admissions, National College: Madison, 900 Madison Square, Madison, TN 37115

## National College: Memphis
### Memphis, Tennessee

◗ For-profit 2-year branch campus college
◗ Very large city

**General.** Regionally accredited; also accredited by ACICS. **Enrollment:** 233 degree-seeking undergraduates. **Calendar:** Quarter. **Full-time faculty:** 2 total. **Part-time faculty:** 10 total.

**2008-2009 Annual costs.** Tuition/fees: $9,585. Per-credit charge: $212.

**Application procedures. Admission:** No deadline. $30 fee. **Financial aid:** No deadline.

**Academics. Credit/placement by examination:** CLEP.

**Majors. Business:** Accounting/business management, administrative services, business admin. **Engineering technology:** Computer systems. **Health:** Medical assistant, medical records technology, pharmacy assistant, surgical technology.

**Contact.** Phone: (901) 363-9046
Larry Steel, Vice President of Admissions, National College: Memphis, 3545 Lamar Avenue, Suite 1, Memphis, TN 38118

## National College: Nashville
### Nashville, Tennessee
### www.ncbt.edu                                CB code: 3227

◗ For-profit 2-year business and technical college
◗ Commuter campus in large city

**General.** Accredited by ACICS. **Enrollment:** 327 degree-seeking undergraduates. **Degrees:** 81 associate awarded. **Calendar:** Quarter. **Full-time faculty:** 8 total. **Part-time faculty:** 21 total.

**Basis for selection.** Open admission. Interview recommended.

**2007-2008 Annual costs.** Tuition/fees: $9,090. Per-credit charge: $202. Books/supplies: $900. Personal expenses: $3,259.

**Financial aid.** All financial aid based on need. Need-based aid available for part-time students.

**Application procedures. Admission:** No deadline. $30 fee. **Financial aid:** No deadline. FAFSA required.

**Academics. Special study options:** Liberal arts/career combination. **Credit/placement by examination:** CLEP.

**Majors. Business:** Accounting, administrative services, business admin. **Computer sciences:** General. **Health:** Medical assistant, medical secretary.

**Student life. Freshman orientation:** Mandatory. Preregistration for classes offered.

**Contact.** E-mail: market@educorp.edu
Phone: (615) 333-3344
Larry Steele, Director of Admission, National College: Nashville, PO Box 6400, Roanoke, VA 24017

## Northeast State Technical Community College
### Blountville, Tennessee
### www.NortheastState.edu                      CB code: 0453

◗ Public 2-year community and technical college
◗ Commuter campus in small city

**General.** Founded in 1965. Regionally accredited. **Enrollment:** 5,237 degree-seeking undergraduates. **Degrees:** 556 associate awarded. **Location:** 12 miles from Johnson City, 10 miles from Kingsport. **Calendar:** Semester, limited summer session. **Full-time faculty:** 106 total. **Part-time faculty:** 159 total.

**Transfer out. Colleges most students transferred to 2007:** East Tennessee State University, Milligan College, Tennessee Tech, University of Tennessee.

**Basis for selection.** Open admission, but selective for some programs. Special requirements for health related professions division. **Adult students:** COMPASS test required for applicants 21 and older without math or English transfer credit.

**High school preparation.** Required units include English 4, mathematics 3, social studies 1, history 1, science 2 and foreign language 2. Visual/performing arts 1 indicated.

**2007-2008 Annual costs.** Tuition/fees: $2,625; $9,701 out-of-state. Per-credit charge: $101 in-state; $407 out-of-state.

**Financial aid. Need-based:** Need-based aid available for part-time students. Work-study available nights and for part-time students. **Non-need-based:** Scholarships awarded for academics, alumni affiliation, art, job skills, leadership, minority status, music/drama, religious affiliation.

**Application procedures. Admission:** No deadline. $10 fee. Application may be submitted online. Admission notification on a rolling basis beginning on or about 6/1. **Financial aid:** Priority date 3/31; no closing date. FAFSA required. Applicants notified on a rolling basis starting 3/1; must reply within 3 week(s) of notification.

**Academics. Special study options:** Accelerated study, cooperative education, distance learning, double major, dual enrollment of high school students, honors, weekend college. License preparation in paramedic. **Credit/placement by examination:** AP, CLEP, institutional tests. 15 credit hours maximum toward associate degree. **Support services:** GED test center, reduced course load, remedial instruction, tutoring.

**Majors. Business:** Administrative services, business admin. **Computer sciences:** General, webmaster. **Construction:** Electrician, power transmission. **Engineering technology:** Drafting, electrical, mechanical drafting. **Family/consumer sciences:** Child development, family studies. **Health:** Cardiovascular technology, clinical lab assistant, dental lab technology, medical assistant. **Liberal arts:** Arts/sciences. **Mechanic/repair:** General, automotive, industrial. **Social sciences:** General.

**Most popular majors.** Business/marketing 13%, computer/information sciences 9%, education 11%, health sciences 16%, trade and industry 45%.

**Computing on campus.** 900 workstations in library, computer center. Commuter students can connect to campus network. Online library available.

**Student life. Freshman orientation:** Mandatory. Preregistration for classes offered. Orientation is online and takes place prior to registration for classes. **Activities:** Drama, literary magazine, student government, Campus Christian Fellowship.

**Athletics. Intramural:** Golf.

**Student services.** Career counseling, services for economically disadvantaged, student employment services, financial aid counseling, health services, minority student services, personal counseling, placement for graduates, veterans' counselor. **Physically disabled:** Services for visually, speech, hearing impaired. **Transfer:** Transfer adviser, college fairs on campus for students transferring to 4-year colleges.

**Contact.** E-mail: jgstarling@NortheastState.edu
Phone: (423) 323-0253 Toll-free number: (800) 836-7822
Fax: (423) 323-0215
Jennifer Starling, Northeast State Technical Community College, Box 246, Blountville, TN 37617-0246

## Nossi College of Art
### Goodlettsville, Tennessee
**www.nossi.com**      **CB code: 3118**

- Private 2-year visual arts and technical college
- Commuter campus in large town
- Interview required

**General.** Accredited by ACCSCT. **Enrollment:** 400 degree-seeking undergraduates. **Degrees:** 8 bachelor's, 70 associate awarded. **Location:** 20 miles from Nashville. **Calendar:** Semester, extensive summer session. **Part-time faculty:** 20 total.

**Basis for selection.** Interview and talent most important. Portfolio required for commercial art program. **Adult students:** SAT/ACT scores not required.

**2007-2008 Annual costs.** Tuition for first year (3 semesters) $10,500; required fees $240. Books/supplies: $1,800.

**Financial aid. Need-based:** Need-based aid available for part-time students.

**Application procedures. Admission:** No deadline. $100 fee.

**Academics. Credit/placement by examination:** CLEP.

**Majors. Visual/performing arts:** General, commercial photography, commercial/advertising art.

**Computing on campus.** 40 workstations in library, computer center.

**Student life. Freshman orientation:** Mandatory.

**Student services.** Alcohol/substance abuse counseling, career counseling, student employment services, financial aid counseling, personal counseling, placement for graduates.

**Contact.** E-mail: admissions@nossi.com
Phone: (615) 851-1088 ext. 17 Toll-free number: (887) 860-1601
Fax: (615) 851-1087
Mary Alexander, Director of Admissions, Nossi College of Art, 907 Rivergate Parkway, Building E-6, Goodlettsville, TN 37072

## Pellissippi State Technical Community College
### Knoxville, Tennessee
**www.pstcc.edu**      **CB code: 0319**

- Public 2-year community and technical college
- Commuter campus in small city

**General.** Founded in 1974. Regionally accredited. **Enrollment:** 8,608 degree-seeking undergraduates. **Degrees:** 652 associate awarded. **ROTC:** Army. **Location:** 178 miles from Nashville, 388 miles from Memphis. **Calendar:** Semester, extensive summer session. **Full-time faculty:** 185 total. **Part-time faculty:** 287 total. **Class size:** 46% < 20, 52% 20-39, 2% 40-49, less than 1% 50-99, less than 1% >100.

**Student profile.**

| | | | |
|---|---|---|---|
| Out-of-state: | 1% | 25 or older: | 40% |

**Transfer out. Colleges most students transferred to 2007:** University of Tennessee in Knoxville, East Tennessee State University, Tennessee Technological University, Maryville College, Middle Tennessee State University.

**Basis for selection.** Open admission. Credit may be awarded for coursework taken at international colleges or universities. ACT/SAT scores for placement purposes. **Adult students:** SAT/ACT scores not required if applicant over 21. Institutional placement test required of students 21 and older who have not had college-level math or English. **Learning Disabled:** Accommodations for testing/programs are provided on a case-by-case basis with supporting documentation.

**High school preparation.** 14 units recommended. Recommended units include English 4, mathematics 3, social studies 1, history 1, science 1 (laboratory 1) and foreign language 2. 1 U.S. history and one visual and performing arts required.

**2007-2008 Annual costs.** Tuition/fees: $2,657; $9,733 out-of-state. Per-credit charge: $101 in-state; $407 out-of-state. Books/supplies: $800. Personal expenses: $1,500.

**Financial aid. Need-based:** Need-based aid available for part-time students. Work-study available nights, weekends and for part-time students. **Non-need-based:** Scholarships awarded for academics, art, minority status, music/drama.

**Application procedures. Admission:** Closing date 8/15 (postmark date). $100 fee, may be waived for applicants with need. Application may be submitted online. Admission notification on a rolling basis beginning on or about 9/1. **Financial aid:** Priority date 5/1; no closing date. FAFSA required. Applicants notified on a rolling basis starting 7/15; must reply within 2 week(s) of notification.

**Academics. Special study options:** Cooperative education, distance learning, double major, dual enrollment of high school students, ESL, honors, independent study, internships, liberal arts/career combination, weekend college. **Credit/placement by examination:** AP, CLEP, IB, institutional tests. 36 credit hours maximum toward associate degree. **Support services:** GED preparation and test center, learning center, pre-admission summer program, reduced course load, remedial instruction, study skills assistance, tutoring, writing center.

**Majors. Business:** Accounting technology, administrative services, business admin, e-commerce. **Computer sciences:** Computer science, information systems, web page design. **Engineering technology:** CAD/CADD, civil, electrical, mechanical. **Family/consumer sciences:** Child development. **Legal studies:** Paralegal. **Liberal arts:** Arts/sciences. **Public administration:** Community org/advocacy. **Social sciences:** Cartography. **Visual/performing arts:** Cinematography, commercial/advertising art, interior design.

**Most popular majors.** Business/marketing 9%, liberal arts 59%, visual/performing arts 9%.

**Computing on campus.** 1,290 workstations in library, computer center, student center. Commuter students can connect to campus network. Online course registration, online library, helpline, repair service, wireless network available.

**Student life. Freshman orientation:** Available. Preregistration for classes offered. **Activities:** Jazz band, campus ministries, choral groups, drama, international student organizations, literary magazine, music ensembles, musical theater, student government, student newspaper, Association of Information Technology Professionals, Institute of Electrical and Electronics Engineers, paralegal association, Active Black Students Association, Students In Free Enterprise, Phi Theta Kappa.

**Athletics. Intramural:** Archery, basketball, football (non-tackle), golf, soccer, softball, tennis, volleyball.

**Student services.** Career counseling, student employment services, personal counseling, placement for graduates, veterans' counselor. **Physically disabled:** Services for visually, speech, hearing impaired. **Transfer:** Transfer adviser, college fairs on campus for students transferring to 4-year colleges.

**Contact.** E-mail: latouzeau@pstcc.edu
Phone: (865) 694-6570 Fax: (865) 539-7217
Leigh Ann Touzeau, Director of Admissions, Pellissippi State Technical Community College, Box 22990, Knoxville, TN 37933-0990

## Remington College: Memphis
### Memphis, Tennessee
**www.remingtoncollege.edu**      **CB code: 3159**

- For-profit 2-year business and technical college
- Commuter campus in very large city
- Interview required

**General.** Accredited by ACCSCT. **Enrollment:** 400 degree-seeking undergraduates. **Degrees:** 136 bachelor's, 2 associate awarded. **Calendar:** Quarter, extensive summer session. **Full-time faculty:** 55 total. **Part-time faculty:** 15 total. **Class size:** 81% < 20, 19% 20-39.

**Basis for selection.** All applicants must pass college administered entrance exam prior to acceptance.

**2007-2008 Annual costs.** Costs of entire programs leading to certificate, associate degree, bachelor's degree range from $13,000 to $36,960; includes books and supplies.

**Financial aid.** All financial aid based on need. Need-based aid available for part-time students.

**Application procedures. Admission:** No deadline. $50 fee. Admission notification on a rolling basis. **Financial aid:** No deadline. FAFSA, institutional form required. Applicants notified on a rolling basis; must reply within 2 week(s) of notification.

**Academics. Special study options:** Cooperative education, independent study, liberal arts/career combination. Bachelor's degree programs available on campus. **Credit/placement by examination:** CLEP, institutional tests. 48 credit hours maximum toward associate degree, 96 toward bachelor's. **Support services:** Tutoring.

**Majors. Business:** Office technology. **Computer sciences:** LAN/WAN management. **Engineering technology:** Electrical. **Protective services:** Criminal justice.

**Computing on campus.** Commuter students can connect to campus network. Helpline, repair service, wireless network available.

**Student life. Freshman orientation:** Mandatory. 3-hour session held Saturday two weeks before quarter begins. **Activities:** Student newspaper.

**Student services.** Adult student services, career counseling, student employment services, financial aid counseling, placement for graduates. **Transfer:** Pre-admission transcript evaluation for new students.

**Contact.** Phone: (901) 345-1000 Fax: (901) 396-8310
Kevin Wilkinson, Director of Admissions, Remington College: Memphis, 2710 Nonconnah Boulevard, Memphis, TN 38132

## Remington College: Nashville
Nashville, Tennessee
www.remingtoncollege.edu

♦ For-profit 2-year health science and technical college
♦ Small city

**General.** Accredited by ACCSCT. **Calendar:** Quarter.

**Annual costs/financial aid.** Costs of entire programs leading to certificate, associate degree, bachelor's degree range from $13,000 to $38,880; includes books and supplies.

**Contact.** 441 Donelson Pike, Suite 150, Nashville, TN 37214

## Roane State Community College
Harriman, Tennessee
www.roanestate.edu          CB code: 1656

♦ Public 2-year community and junior college
♦ Commuter campus in small town

**General.** Founded in 1971. Regionally accredited. **Enrollment:** 4,427 degree-seeking undergraduates; 977 non-degree-seeking students. **Degrees:** 672 associate awarded. **ROTC:** Army, Air Force. **Location:** 40 miles from Knoxville. **Calendar:** Semester, limited summer session. **Full-time faculty:** 136 total; 11% minority, 52% women. **Part-time faculty:** 197 total; 4% minority, 55% women. **Class size:** 48% < 20, 49% 20-39, 2% 40-49, less than 1% 50-99. **Special facilities:** Observatory.

**Student profile.** Among degree-seeking undergraduates, 50% enrolled in a transfer program, 50% enrolled in a vocational program, 1,071 enrolled as first-time, first-year students.

| | | | |
|---|---|---|---|
| Part-time: | 34% | Asian American: | 1% |
| Out-of-state: | 1% | Hispanic American: | 1% |
| Women: | 68% | 25 or older: | 37% |
| African American: | 3% | | |

**Transfer out. Colleges most students transferred to 2007:** University of Tennessee-Knoxville, Tennessee Technological University, Middle Tennessee State University, East Tennessee State University.

**Basis for selection.** Open admission, but selective for some programs. All health science A.A.S. programs require minimum ACT score of 20 and 2.5 GPA for 8 hours general course work. Additional requirements for nursing program: minimum 2.75 GPA for 12 hours general course work and pre-admissions test. Interview required for some health programs; audition required for some music programs. **Adult students:** SAT/ACT scores not required if applicant over 21. Those who do not submit SAT/ACT scores must undergo placement assessment. **Homeschooled:** State high school equivalency certificate required.

**High school preparation.** 20 units recommended. Recommended units include English 4, mathematics 3, social studies 1, history 1, science 2 and foreign language 2.

**2007-2008 Annual costs.** Tuition/fees: $2,645; $9,721 out-of-state. Per-credit charge: $101 in-state; $407 out-of-state. Books/supplies: $1,000. Personal expenses: $2,555.

**Financial aid. Need-based:** Need-based aid available for part-time students. Work-study available nights, weekends and for part-time students. **Non-need-based:** Scholarships awarded for academics, art, athletics, leadership, music/drama, state residency.

**Application procedures. Admission:** No deadline. $10 fee. Application may be submitted online. Admission notification on a rolling basis. **Financial aid:** Priority date 4/1; no closing date. FAFSA, institutional form required. Applicants notified on a rolling basis starting 5/1.

**Academics. Special study options:** Accelerated study, cooperative education, distance learning, double major, dual enrollment of high school students, honors, independent study, internships, liberal arts/career combination, study abroad, teacher certification program, weekend college. License preparation in dental hygiene, nursing, occupational therapy, paramedic, physical therapy, radiology. **Credit/placement by examination:** AP, CLEP, institutional tests. 18 credit hours maximum toward associate degree. **Support services:** GED test center, learning center, remedial instruction, study skills assistance, tutoring, writing center.

**Majors. Biology:** General. **Business:** Business admin, management science. **Education:** General. **English:** English lit. **Family/consumer sciences:** Child development. **Health:** Dental hygiene, environmental health, medical radiologic technology/radiation therapy, medical records technology, nursing (RN), occupational therapy assistant, optician, physical therapy assistant, respiratory therapy technology. **Legal studies:** Paralegal. **Math:** General. **Protective services:** Police science. **Social sciences:** Cartography. **Other:** General Technology.

**Most popular majors.** Business/marketing 9%, health sciences 35%, liberal arts 39%, science technologies 9%.

**Computing on campus.** 600 workstations in library, computer center, student center. Commuter students can connect to campus network. Online course registration, helpline available.

**Student life. Freshman orientation:** Mandatory. Preregistration for classes offered. One half-day orientation. **Activities:** Jazz band, campus ministries, choral groups, dance, drama, international student organizations, music ensembles, musical theater, student government, student newspaper, Coffee House Writers Workshop, College Republican Club, Life Enablers, Oak Ridge Institute for Contined Learning, Phi Theta Kappa, Playmakers, SADD, Students in Free Enterprise, Tao Astronomical Society, Southwest Field Trip.

**Athletics.** NJCAA. **Intercollegiate:** Baseball M, basketball, softball W. **Intramural:** Basketball, cheerleading W, football (non-tackle) M, softball. **Team name:** Raiders.

**Student services.** Career counseling, student employment services, financial aid counseling, health services, minority student services, personal counseling, placement for graduates, veterans' counselor. **Physically disabled:** Services for visually, speech, hearing impaired. **Transfer:** Transfer adviser, college fairs on campus for students transferring to 4-year colleges.

**Contact.** E-mail: marinegl@roanestate.edu
Phone: (865) 882-4523 Toll-free number: (866) 462-7722 ext. 4523
Fax: (865) 882-4562
Maria Gonzales, Director of Admissions, Roane State Community College, 276 Patton Lane, Harriman, TN 37748

## Southwest Tennessee Community College
### Memphis, Tennessee
www.southwest.tn.edu                    CB code: 0274

- Public 2-year community and technical college
- Commuter campus in very large city

**General.** Founded in 1970. Regionally accredited. **Enrollment:** 9,486 degree-seeking undergraduates. **Degrees:** 748 associate awarded. **ROTC:** Army, Air Force. **Calendar:** Semester, extensive summer session. **Full-time faculty:** 240 total. **Part-time faculty:** 387 total.

**Student profile.**

| | | | |
|---|---|---|---|
| Out-of-state: | 3% | 25 or older: | 50% |

**Transfer out. Colleges most students transferred to 2007:** University of Memphis, Christian Brothers University.

**Basis for selection.** Open admission, but selective for some programs. Special requirements for admission to nursing, dietetic technician, laboratory phlebotomy, medical assistant, medical laboratory technician, physical therapist assistant, radiologic technology, paramedic programs. **Adult students:** SAT/ACT scores not required if applicant over 21. ACT COMPASS exam required. **Learning Disabled:** Require documentation of disability to be shown to disability counselor.

**High school preparation.** 14 units recommended. Recommended units include English 4, mathematics 3, social studies 1, history 1, science 2 (laboratory 1), foreign language 2 and academic electives 1.

**2007-2008 Annual costs.** Tuition/fees: $2,649; $9,725 out-of-state. Per-credit charge: $101 in-state; $407 out-of-state. Personal expenses: $1,400.

**Financial aid.** All financial aid based on need. Need-based aid available for part-time students. Work-study available nights, weekends and for part-time students. **Additional information:** State grants available to eligible students who apply by 4/1.

**Application procedures. Admission:** No deadline. $10 fee. Application must be submitted on paper. Admission notification on a rolling basis. **Financial aid:** Priority date 3/15; no closing date. FAFSA required. Applicants notified on a rolling basis starting 6/1; must reply within 4 week(s) of notification.

**Academics. Special study options:** Cooperative education, distance learning, double major, dual enrollment of high school students, ESL, honors, independent study, internships, liberal arts/career combination, student-designed major, weekend college. On-site extension courses at business, industry and government installations. License preparation in nursing, paramedic, physical therapy, radiology, real estate. **Credit/placement by examination:** AP, CLEP, institutional tests. **Support services:** GED preparation and test center, learning center, pre-admission summer program, reduced course load, remedial instruction, study skills assistance, tutoring.

**Majors. Agriculture:** Horticulture. **Business:** General, accounting, administrative services, business admin, finance, management information systems, office technology. **Computer sciences:** General, computer science. **Construction:** Maintenance. **Education:** General, early childhood. **Engineering technology:** Architectural, civil, electrical. **Family/consumer sciences:** Child care, family studies, food/nutrition, institutional food production. **Health:** Clinical lab technology, EMT paramedic, medical radiologic technology/radiation therapy, medical transcription, nursing (RN), physical therapy assistant. **Legal studies:** Court reporting, paralegal. **Liberal arts:** Arts/sciences. **Mechanic/repair:** General, automotive, electronics/electrical, industrial. **Physical sciences:** General. **Protective services:** Firefighting, police science. **Social sciences:** Geography. **Visual/performing arts:** Commercial/advertising art.

**Most popular majors.** Business/marketing 21%, engineering/engineering technologies 9%, health sciences 22%, liberal arts 34%.

**Computing on campus.** 350 workstations in library, computer center. Commuter students can connect to campus network. Online course registration, online library, helpline, wireless network available.

**Student life. Freshman orientation:** Available. Preregistration for classes offered. **Activities:** Bands, choral groups, drama, music ensembles, student government, student newspaper, NAACP, Baptist Student Union, Human

Key Society, National Student Support Council for Africa, Black Student Association, Phi Theta Kappa Honor Society, Police Science Association, science club, Radiologic Technology Student Association, Collegiate Secretaries.

**Athletics.** NJCAA. **Intercollegiate:** Baseball M, basketball, softball W. **Team name:** Saluqis.

**Student services.** Adult student services, campus ministries, career counseling, services for economically disadvantaged, student employment services, financial aid counseling, on-campus daycare, personal counseling, placement for graduates, veterans' counselor. **Physically disabled:** Services for visually, speech, hearing impaired. **Transfer:** Pre-admission transcript evaluation for new students. Transfer center, transfer adviser, college fairs on campus for students transferring to 4-year colleges.

**Contact.** Phone: (901) 333-5924 Toll-free number: (877) 717-7822 Fax: (901) 333-4473
Thalia Wilson, Director Enrollment Operation, Southwest Tennessee Community College, PO Box 780, Memphis, TN 38101-0780

## Vatterott College: Memphis
### Memphis, Tennessee
www.vatterott-college.edu

- For-profit 2-year technical college
- Commuter campus in large city

**General.** Accredited by ACCSCT. **Enrollment:** 468 degree-seeking undergraduates. **Degrees:** 35 associate awarded. **Calendar:** Continuous. **Full-time faculty:** 20 total. **Part-time faculty:** 15 total.

**Basis for selection.** Open admission.

**2007-2008 Annual costs.** Program cost ranges: $12,500 to $19,677 (certificate/diploma); $24,977 to $30,109 (associate degree).

**Application procedures. Admission:** No deadline. No application fee.

**Academics. Credit/placement by examination:** CLEP, institutional tests. **Support services:** Learning center.

**Majors. Computer sciences:** System admin. **Engineering technology:** CAD/CADD, heat/ac/refrig.

**Computing on campus.** 20 workstations in library.

**Contact.** E-mail: paulette.thomas@vatterott-college.edu
Phone: (901) 761-5730 Fax: (901) 763-2897
Paulette Thomas, Director of Admissions, Vatterott College: Memphis, 2655 Dividend Drive, Memphis, TN 38132

## Volunteer State Community College
### Gallatin, Tennessee
www.volstate.edu                    CB code: 1881

- Public 2-year community and junior college
- Commuter campus in small city

**General.** Founded in 1970. Regionally accredited. **Enrollment:** 5,446 degree-seeking undergraduates; 1,619 non-degree-seeking students. **Degrees:** 663 associate awarded. **Location:** 25 miles from Nashville. **Calendar:** Semester, limited summer session. **Full-time faculty:** 143 total; 16% have terminal degrees, 15% minority, 50% women. **Part-time faculty:** 231 total; 9% minority, 58% women. **Class size:** 58% < 20, 41% 20-39, 1% 40-49, less than 1% 50-99. **Partnerships:** Formal partnerships with GAP Inc., Peterbilt Motors, Bosch Braking Systems.

**Student profile.** Among degree-seeking undergraduates, 58% enrolled in a transfer program, 42% enrolled in a vocational program, 1,251 enrolled as first-time, first-year students, 609 transferred in from other institutions.

| | | | |
|---|---|---|---|
| Part-time: | 41% | Asian American: | 1% |
| Out-of-state: | 1% | Hispanic American: | 2% |
| Women: | 64% | International: | 1% |
| African American: | 9% | 25 or older: | 34% |

**Transfer out. Colleges most students transferred to 2007:** Middle Tennessee State University, Austin Peay State University, Tennessee State University, Tennessee Technical University.

**Basis for selection.** Open admission, but selective for some programs. Allied health students screened into programs after completing designated amount of college coursework. Screening based on GPA and interview. Test scores where required in selective programs must be received by August 30. Interview required for allied health program. **Adult students:** SAT/ACT scores not required if applicant over 21. Unless exempt by ACT scores, must take COMPASS or ASSET Placement test. **Homeschooled:** Transcript must be an official copy from an affiliated organization as defined by state law or be accompanied by a certification of registration with the superintendent of the local education agency, which the student would otherwise attend.

**High school preparation.** 14 units recommended. Recommended units include English 4, mathematics 3, social studies 1, history 1, science 2 (laboratory 1) and foreign language 2. 1 visual and/or performing arts also required.

**2007-2008 Annual costs.** Tuition/fees: $2,625; $9,701 out-of-state. Per-credit charge: $101 in-state; $407 out-of-state.

**Financial aid. Need-based:** Need-based aid available for part-time students. Work-study available for part-time students. **Non-need-based:** Scholarships awarded for academics, art, athletics, leadership, minority status, music/drama, religious affiliation, state residency.

**Application procedures. Admission:** Priority date 7/31; deadline 8/28 (receipt date). $10 fee. Application may be submitted online. Admission notification on a rolling basis. **Financial aid:** Priority date 4/15; no closing date. FAFSA, institutional form required. Applicants notified on a rolling basis; must reply within 2 week(s) of notification.

**Academics. Special study options:** Cooperative education, distance learning, double major, dual enrollment of high school students, ESL, honors, independent study. Bachelor's degree programs available on campus. License preparation in dental hygiene, paramedic, physical therapy, radiology, real estate. **Credit/placement by examination:** AP, CLEP, institutional tests. 36 credit hours maximum toward associate degree. Maximum 12 hours of credit by examination in specific allied health programs. **Support services:** GED test center, learning center, pre-admission summer program, reduced course load, remedial instruction, study skills assistance, tutoring, writing center.

**Majors. Business:** Business admin. **Family/consumer sciences:** Child development. **Health:** Clinical lab technology, medical radiologic technology/radiation therapy, medical records technology, ophthalmic technology, physical therapy assistant, respiratory therapy technology. **Legal studies:** Paralegal. **Liberal arts:** Arts/sciences. **Protective services:** Firefighting. **Public administration:** Community org/advocacy.

**Most popular majors.** Business/marketing 11%, health sciences 25%, liberal arts 58%.

**Computing on campus.** 800 workstations in library, computer center. Commuter students can connect to campus network. Online course registration, online library, helpline, wireless network available.

**Student life. Freshman orientation:** Mandatory. Preregistration for classes offered. One-day program held multiple times prior to registration both on campus and online. **Activities:** Campus ministries, choral groups, drama, literary magazine, radio station, student government, student newspaper, African-American Student Union, returning women's organization, College Democrats, College Republicans.

**Athletics.** NJCAA. **Intercollegiate:** Baseball M, basketball, softball W. **Team name:** Pioneers.

**Student services.** Career counseling, services for economically disadvantaged, financial aid counseling, health services, personal counseling, placement for graduates, veterans' counselor. **Physically disabled:** Services for visually, speech, hearing impaired. **Transfer:** Pre-admission transcript evaluation for new students. Transfer adviser, college fairs on campus for students transferring to 4-year colleges.

**Contact.** E-mail: admissions@volstate.edu
Phone: (615) 452-8600 ext. 3688 Toll-free
number: (888) 335-8722 ext. 3688 Fax: (615) 230-4875
Tim Amyx, Director of Admissions, Volunteer State Community College, 1480 Nashville Pike, Gallatin, TN 37066

## Walters State Community College
**Morristown, Tennessee**
www.ws.edu

CB member
CB code: 1893

- Public 2-year culinary school and community college
- Commuter campus in small city

**General.** Founded in 1970. Regionally accredited. Degree programs and a variety of courses at sites throughout 10-county service delivery area with facilities located in Greeneville, Sevierville, and Tazewell. Instructional alternatives include interactive television, web-based, videostreaming, and telecourses. **Enrollment:** 4,607 degree-seeking undergraduates; 1,131 non-degree-seeking students. **Degrees:** 597 associate awarded. **ROTC:** Army. **Location:** 45 miles from Knoxville. **Calendar:** Semester, limited summer session. **Full-time faculty:** 140 total; 23% have terminal degrees, 7% minority, 53% women. **Part-time faculty:** 189 total; 15% have terminal degrees, 2% minority, 57% women. **Special facilities:** Observatory, training restaurant, exposition center, industrial technology manufacturing laboratory with complete computer integrated manufacturing (CIM), work center and coordinate measuring machine (MM), public safety law enforcement training center, greenhouse, production horticulture lab, arboretum, center for workforce education.

**Student profile.** Among degree-seeking undergraduates, 53% enrolled in a transfer program, 47% enrolled in a vocational program, 1% already have a bachelor's degree or higher, 1,233 enrolled as first-time, first-year students, 257 transferred in from other institutions.

| | | | |
|---|---|---|---|
| Part-time: | 36% | Asian American: | 1% |
| Women: | 64% | Hispanic American: | 1% |
| African American: | 3% | 25 or older: | 35% |

**Transfer out. Colleges most students transferred to 2007:** University of Tennessee-Knoxville, East Tennessee State University, Carson Newman College.

**Basis for selection.** Open admission, but selective for some programs. Special requirements for education programs, allied health, public safety. International students must submit application 60 days prior to start of term. Placement test required for applicants with ACT scores below 18. **Adult students:** SAT/ACT scores not required if applicant over 21. Required to take placement assessment prior to enrollment.

**High school preparation.** 14 units required. Required units include English 4, mathematics 3, social studies 1, history 1, science 2 (laboratory 1), foreign language 2 and academic electives 1. College-preparatory program required for 2-year transfer program: 1 unit biological science, 4 English, 2 foreign language, 3 mathematics, 1 physical science, 2 social science, 1 visual or performing arts. Same preparation recommended for all students.

**2007-2008 Annual costs.** Tuition/fees: $2,637; $10,043 out-of-state. Per-credit charge: $101 in-state; $407 out-of-state. Books/supplies: $1,000. Personal expenses: $1,030.

**2006-2007 Financial aid. Need-based:** 818 full-time freshmen applied for aid; 570 were judged to have need; 540 of these received aid. Average need met was 75%. Average scholarship/grant was $3,618; average loan $1,916. 80% of total undergraduate aid awarded as scholarships/grants, 20% as loans/jobs. Need-based aid available for part-time students. **Non-need-based:** Awarded to 1,014 full-time undergraduates, including 497 freshmen. Scholarships awarded for academics, athletics, music/drama, state residency.

**Application procedures. Admission:** No deadline. $10 fee. Application must be submitted on paper. Admission notification on a rolling basis. **Financial aid:** No deadline. FAFSA required. Applicants notified on a rolling basis.

**Academics. Special study options:** Distance learning, dual enrollment of high school students, ESL, honors, liberal arts/career combination, weekend college. Bachelor's degree programs available on campus. License preparation in nursing, paramedic, physical therapy. **Credit/placement by examination:** AP, CLEP, institutional tests. 40 credit hours maximum toward associate degree. **Support services:** GED test center, learning center, reduced course load, remedial instruction, study skills assistance, tutoring, writing center.

**Majors. Agriculture:** Ornamental horticulture. **Business:** Administrative services, business admin, management information systems. **Education:** General. **Engineering technology:** Industrial. **English:** English lit. **Family/consumer sciences:** Child development. **Health:** EMT paramedic, medical records technology, nursing (RN), physical therapy assistant, respiratory therapy technology. **Liberal arts:** Arts/sciences. **Protective services:** Police science.

**Most popular majors.** Business/marketing 15%, health sciences 31%, liberal arts 47%.

**Computing on campus.** 900 workstations in library, computer center, student center. Commuter students can connect to campus network. Online course registration, online library, helpline, wireless network available.

**Student life. Freshman orientation:** Mandatory. Preregistration for classes offered. **Activities:** Bands, choral groups, dance, drama, literary magazine, music ensembles, student government, student newspaper.

**Athletics.** NJCAA. **Intercollegiate:** Baseball M, basketball, golf, softball W. **Intramural:** Basketball, soccer, softball. **Team name:** Senators.

**Student services.** Adult student services, alcohol/substance abuse counseling, campus ministries, career counseling, student employment services, financial aid counseling, health services, minority student services, personal counseling, placement for graduates, veterans' counselor. **Physically disabled:** Services for visually, speech, hearing impaired. **Transfer:** Re-entry adviser for new students. Transfer center, transfer adviser, college fairs on campus for students transferring to 4-year colleges.

**Contact.** E-mail: kim.gunnin@ws.edu
Phone: (423) 585-2685 Toll-free number: (800) 225-4770
Fax: (423) 585-6786
Mike Campbell, Assistant Vice President for Student Affairs, Walters State Community College, 500 South Davy Crockett Parkway, Morristown, TN 37813-6899

## West Tennessee Business College
### Jackson, Tennessee
www.wtbc.com

▶ For-profit 2-year business and health science college
▶ Commuter campus in small city

**General.** Accredited by ACICS. **Location:** 90 miles from Memphis. **Calendar:** Quarter.

**Annual costs/financial aid.** Program costs vary by program. Total cost of medical/clinical assistant program: 11,150.

**Contact.** Phone: (731) 668-7240
Admissions Director, 1186 Highway 45 Bypass, Jackson, TN 38301

# Texas

## Alvin Community College
**Alvin, Texas**
www.alvincollege.edu                                    CB code: 6005

- Public 2-year community and liberal arts college
- Residential campus in large town

**General.** Founded in 1948. Regionally accredited. **Enrollment:** 2,604 degree-seeking undergraduates. **Degrees:** 421 associate awarded. **Location:** 32 miles from Houston. **Calendar:** Semester, extensive summer session. **Full-time faculty:** 100 total. **Part-time faculty:** 160 total. **Special facilities:** Radio station, recording studio, indoor firing range for law enforcement program, Nolan Ryan exhibit.

**Transfer out. Colleges most students transferred to 2007:** University of Houston-Clear Lake, University of Houston, Texas A&M, Sam Houston State University, Southwest Texas State University.

**Basis for selection.** Open admission, but selective for some programs. Special requirements for nursing, respiratory therapy, criminal justice, court reporting, musical theater, EMT, diagnostic cardiovascular sonography programs. Texas Academic Skills Program test required by Texas law. Interview required for court reporting, medical laboratory technology, nursing, respiratory therapy programs; audition required for music, musical theater programs.

**High school preparation.** 25 units recommended. Recommended units include English 4, mathematics 4, social studies 4, science 3, foreign language 3 and academic electives 7.

**2007-2008 Annual costs.** Tuition/fees: $1,250; $2,090 out-of-district; $3,650 out-of-state. Per-credit charge: $30 in-district; $58 out-of-district; $110 out-of-state. Books/supplies: $1,447. Personal expenses: $1,608.

**Financial aid.** All financial aid based on need. Need-based aid available for part-time students. Work-study available nights, weekends and for part-time students.

**Application procedures. Admission:** No deadline. No application fee. Admission notification on a rolling basis. **Financial aid:** Priority date 6/30; no closing date. FAFSA required. Applicants notified on a rolling basis; must reply within 2 week(s) of notification.

**Academics. Special study options:** Cooperative education, cross-registration, distance learning, dual enrollment of high school students, ESL, honors, internships, liberal arts/career combination, study abroad. License preparation in nursing, paramedic. **Credit/placement by examination:** CLEP, institutional tests. **Support services:** GED preparation and test center, learning center, reduced course load, remedial instruction, study skills assistance, tutoring, writing center.

**Majors. Biology:** General. **Business:** General, business admin, executive assistant. **Communications:** Radio/tv. **Computer sciences:** Programming. **Education:** Early childhood, physical. **Engineering technology:** Electrical. **Family/consumer sciences:** Child development. **Health:** Cardiovascular technology, EMT paramedic, mental health services, nursing (RN), respiratory therapy technology. **Legal studies:** Paralegal. **Liberal arts:** Arts/sciences. **Math:** General. **Parks/recreation:** Health/fitness. **Physical sciences:** General. **Protective services:** Corrections, criminal justice. **Science technology:** Chemical. **Visual/performing arts:** Art, dramatic, music performance.

**Most popular majors.** Business/marketing 10%, health sciences 23%, liberal arts 37%, science technologies 7%.

**Computing on campus.** 600 workstations in library, computer center. Online course registration, online library available.

**Student life. Freshman orientation:** Mandatory. Preregistration for classes offered. **Housing:** Housing provided for scholarship athletes. **Activities:** Bands, choral groups, drama, literary magazine, music ensembles, musical theater, radio station, student government, student newspaper, TV station, Newman Association, Phi Theta Kappa, Pan American College Forum, Baptist student union.

**Athletics.** NJCAA. **Intercollegiate:** Baseball M, softball W, volleyball W. **Team name:** Dolphins.

**Student services.** Career counseling, student employment services, financial aid counseling, on-campus daycare, personal counseling, placement for graduates, veterans' counselor. **Physically disabled:** Services for visually, speech, hearing impaired. **Transfer:** Transfer adviser, college fairs on campus for students transferring to 4-year colleges.

**Contact.** E-mail: admiss@alvincollege.edu
Phone: (281) 756-3531 Fax: (281) 756-3843
Stephanie Stockstill, Director of Admissions/Academic Advising, Alvin Community College, 3110 Mustang Road, Alvin, TX 77511-4898

## Amarillo College
**Amarillo, Texas**
www.actx.edu                                            CB code: 6006

- Public 2-year community college
- Commuter campus in small city

**General.** Founded in 1929. Regionally accredited. **Location:** 300 miles from Dallas, 300 miles from Denver. **Calendar:** Semester.

**Annual costs/financial aid.** Tuition/fees (2007-2008): $1,614; $2,094 out-of-district; $3,114 out-of-state. Room: $2,000. Books/supplies: $996. Personal expenses: $1,302.

**Contact.** Phone: (806) 371-5030
Registrar and Director of Admissions, Box 447, Amarillo, TX 79178

## Angelina College
**Lufkin, Texas**
www.angelina.edu                                        CB code: 6025

- Public 2-year community college
- Commuter campus in large town

**General.** Founded in 1966. Regionally accredited. Teaching centers located in 5 contiguous counties. Branch campus located in Jasper. **Enrollment:** 4,680 degree-seeking undergraduates. **Degrees:** 329 associate awarded. **ROTC:** Army. **Location:** 125 miles from Houston. **Calendar:** Semester, extensive summer session. **Full-time faculty:** 97 total; 10% have terminal degrees, 8% minority, 60% women. **Part-time faculty:** 212 total; 7% have terminal degrees, 8% minority, 60% women. **Class size:** 71% < 20, 29% 20-39, less than 1% 40-49. **Special facilities:** Computer-aided design laboratory, environmental trail, performing arts center.

**Student profile.** Among degree-seeking undergraduates, 1,392 enrolled as first-time, first-year students, 369 transferred in from other institutions.

| | | | |
|---|---|---|---|
| **Part-time:** | 65% | **Asian American:** | 1% |
| **Out-of-state:** | 1% | **Hispanic American:** | 9% |
| **Women:** | 63% | **25 or older:** | 27% |
| **African American:** | 9% | **Live on campus:** | 2% |

**Transfer out. Colleges most students transferred to 2007:** Stephen F. Austin State University, Sam Houston State University.

**Basis for selection.** Open admission, but selective for some programs. Special requirements for nursing, respiratory care, EMS, pharmacy, and radiologic technology programs; interview required. General Aptitude Test Battery required of nursing applicants. All students must take Texas Higher Education Assessment Test or ACCUPLACER before enrolling. **Adult students:** Physical education requirements waived for veterans, adults 25 and over, and some part-time students. **Homeschooled:** Transcript of courses and grades required. **Learning Disabled:** May have to take different test based on disability.

**2008-2009 Annual costs.** Tuition/fees: $1,200; $1,800 out-of-district; $2,550 out-of-state. Per-credit charge: $33 in-district; $53 out-of-district; $78 out-of-state. Students taking 1-3 credits pay higher per-credit-hour charge. Room/board: $5,550. Books/supplies: $1,280. Personal expenses: $1,920.

**2006-2007 Financial aid.** All financial aid based on need. 99% of total undergraduate aid awarded as scholarships/grants, 1% as loans/jobs. Need-based aid available for part-time students. Work-study available nights and for part-time students.

**Application procedures. Admission:** No deadline. No application fee. Application may be submitted online. Admission notification on a rolling basis. **Financial aid:** Priority date 7/15; no closing date. FAFSA, institutional form required. Applicants notified on a rolling basis starting 7/15.

**Academics. Special study options:** Accelerated study, cooperative education, distance learning, dual enrollment of high school students, internships, liberal arts/career combination. License preparation in nursing, paramedic, radiology, real estate. **Credit/placement by examination:** AP, CLEP, institutional tests. 15 credit hours maximum toward associate degree. **Support services:** Learning center, reduced course load, remedial instruction, study skills assistance, tutoring.

**Majors. Biology:** General. **Business:** General, accounting, administrative services, business admin. **Communications:** General. **Computer sciences:** General, data processing. **Education:** General, elementary, health. **Engineering:** General. **Engineering technology:** Drafting, electrical, electromechanical, environmental. **Family/consumer sciences:** Child development. **Health:** Clinical lab technology, EMT paramedic, nursing (RN), predental, premedicine, prepharmacy, preveterinary, radiologic technology/medical imaging, respiratory therapy technology, substance abuse counseling. **Interdisciplinary:** Science/society. **Legal studies:** Paralegal, prelaw. **Math:** General. **Physical sciences:** Physics. **Production:** Machine tool, welding. **Protective services:** Criminal justice. **Public administration:** Human services, social work. **Visual/performing arts:** Art, design, dramatic, music management, piano/organ, voice/opera. **Other:** Pre-physical therapy/pre-occupational therapy.

**Computing on campus.** 200 workstations in library, computer center, student center. Online course registration, online library available.

**Student life. Freshman orientation:** Mandatory. Preregistration for classes offered. **Housing:** Coed dorms, substance-free housing available. $100 fully refundable deposit, deadline 7/15. Apartments for single mothers. **Activities:** Concert band, choral groups, dance, drama, music ensembles, musical theater, student government, student newspaper, Baptist student union.

**Athletics.** NJCAA. **Intercollegiate:** Baseball M, basketball, cheerleading M. **Intramural:** Golf, volleyball. **Team name:** Roadrunners.

**Student services.** Adult student services, career counseling, services for economically disadvantaged, student employment services, financial aid counseling, health services, personal counseling, placement for graduates, veterans' counselor. **Physically disabled:** Services for visually, speech, hearing impaired. **Transfer:** Pre-admission transcript evaluation for new students. Transfer adviser, college fairs on campus for students transferring to 4-year colleges.

**Contact.** E-mail: registrar@angelina.edu
Phone: (936) 639-5212 Fax: (936) 633-5455
James Twohig, Dean of Students, Angelina College, PO Box 1768, Lufkin, TX 75902-1768

---

## ATI Career Training Center: Dallas
**Dallas, Texas**
www.aticareertraining.edu

- For-profit 2-year technical college
- Very large city

**General.** Accredited by ACCSCT. **Calendar:** Semester.

**Annual costs/financial aid.** One-time comprehensive rate per program ranging from $3,715 for 12-month massage therapy program to $31,243 for 2-year respiratory therapy technician program. Need-based financial aid available for full-time students.

**Contact.** Phone: (214) 902-8191
Director of Admissions, 10003 Technology Boulevard, West, Dallas, TX 75220

---

## Austin Business College
**Austin, Texas**
www.abctx.edu                                        CB code: 3230

- For-profit 2-year business and technical college
- Very large city

**General.** Accredited by ACICS. **Calendar:** Continuous.

**Annual costs/financial aid.** Tuition for certificate programs range from $8,015 - $11,476. Tuition for associate degree programs range from $21,008 - $23,292. Books/supplies: $913.

**Contact.** Phone: (512) 447-9415
Director of Admissions, 2101 IH 35 South, Third Floor, Austin, TX 78741

---

## Austin Community College
**Austin, Texas**                                      CB member
www.austincc.edu                                       CB code: 6759

- Public 2-year community college
- Commuter campus in very large city

**General.** Founded in 1972. Regionally accredited. 8 campuses serving greater Austin, 9 instructional centers in surrounding towns. **Enrollment:** 33,508 degree-seeking undergraduates. **Degrees:** 1,021 associate awarded. **ROTC:** Army, Air Force. **Location:** 85 miles from San Antonio. **Calendar:** Semester, extensive summer session. **Full-time faculty:** 498 total; 24% minority, 46% women. **Part-time faculty:** 1,224 total; 20% minority, 45% women. **Class size:** 45% < 20, 54% 20-39, less than 1% 40-49. **Special facilities:** Water-quality monitoring well. **Partnerships:** Formal partnerships with Sustainability Project, Semiconductor Manufacturing Program, Seton Health.

**Student profile.** Among degree-seeking undergraduates, 84% enrolled in a transfer program, 16% enrolled in a vocational program, 5% already have a bachelor's degree or higher.

| Part-time: | 72% | Women: | 57% |
| Out-of-state: | 2% | 25 or older: | 38% |

**Transfer out. Colleges most students transferred to 2007:** University of Texas at Austin, Texas State University.

**Basis for selection.** Open admission, but selective for some programs. Special requirements for health sciences programs. Students may submit SAT or ACT test scores for exemption from Texas Academic Skills Program (TASP) requirements. **Adult students:** SAT/ACT scores not required. Texas Success Initiative test may be required.

**2007-2008 Annual costs.** Tuition/fees: $1,608; $3,978 out-of-district; $8,208 out-of-state. Per-credit charge: $39 in-district; $118 out-of-district; $259 out-of-state. Books/supplies: $800. Personal expenses: $1,310.

**2006-2007 Financial aid. Need-based:** 684 full-time freshmen applied for aid; 679 were judged to have need; 679 of these received aid. 35% of total undergraduate aid awarded as scholarships/grants, 65% as loans/jobs. Need-based aid available for part-time students.

**Application procedures. Admission:** No deadline. No application fee. Application may be submitted online. No notification. Applications accepted at all times for any future semester enrollment. **Financial aid:** Closing date 4/1. FAFSA, institutional form required. Applicants notified on a rolling basis starting 6/1; must reply within 2 week(s) of notification.

**Academics. Special study options:** Accelerated study, distance learning, dual enrollment of high school students, ESL, honors, independent study, internships, study abroad, teacher certification program, weekend college. License preparation in dental hygiene, nursing, occupational therapy, paramedic, physical therapy, radiology, real estate. **Credit/placement by examination:** AP, CLEP, institutional tests. 30 credit hours maximum toward associate degree. **Support services:** GED preparation and test center, learning center, reduced course load, remedial instruction, study skills assistance, tutoring.

**Majors. Biology:** General. **Business:** General, accounting technology, administrative services, banking/financial services, business admin, hospitality admin, international, marketing, real estate. **Communications:** Radio/tv. **Computer sciences:** General, networking, programming. **Construction:** Carpentry. **Education:** Health, middle. **Engineering:** General. **Engineering technology:** Drafting, electrical, environmental, heat/ac/refrig, quality control, surveying. **English:** Composition, English lit, speech/rhetoric, technical writing. **Family/consumer sciences:** Child development. **Foreign languages:** General, French, German, Japanese, Latin, Russian, sign language interpretation, Spanish. **Health:** Clinical lab technology, dental hygiene, EMT paramedic, nursing (RN), occupational therapy assistant, physical therapy assistant, predental, premedicine, prepharmacy, preveterinary, radiologic technology/medical imaging, recreational therapy, sonography, substance abuse counseling, surgical technology. **History:** General. **Legal studies:** Paralegal. **Liberal arts:** Arts/sciences. **Math:** General. **Mechanic/repair:** Automotive, watch/jewelry. **Parks/recreation:** Health/fitness. **Personal/culinary services:** Chef training. **Philosophy/religion:** Philosophy. **Physical sciences:** General, chemistry, geology, physics. **Production:** Welding. **Protective services:** Corrections, fire safety technology, police science. **Psychology:** General. **Public administration:** Human services, social work. **Science technology:** Biological. **Social sciences:** Anthropology, economics, geography, political science, sociology. **Visual/performing arts:** Art, commercial photography, commercial/advertising art, dance, dramatic, music management.

**Most popular majors.** Business/marketing 15%, engineering/engineering technologies 8%, health sciences 33%, security/protective services 6%, visual/performing arts 8%.

**Computing on campus.** 307 workstations in library, computer center. Commuter students can connect to campus network. Online course registration, online library, helpline available.

**Student life. Freshman orientation:** Mandatory. Preregistration for classes offered. **Policies:** No alcohol, no drugs, no hazing. **Activities:** Jazz band, dance, drama, literary magazine, music ensembles, student government, student newspaper, Phi Theta Kappa, Hispanic student association, Biomass, Peer Players, Austin Society for Semi-Conductor Electronics Technicians, Campus Crusade for Christ, Toastmasters, American Drafting Design Association, associate degree student nursing association, black student alliance.

**Student services.** Alcohol/substance abuse counseling, career counseling, services for economically disadvantaged, student employment services, financial aid counseling, minority student services, on-campus daycare, placement for graduates, veterans' counselor. **Physically disabled:** Services for visually, speech, hearing impaired. **Transfer:** Transfer center, transfer adviser, college fairs on campus for students transferring to 4-year colleges.

**Contact.** E-mail: admission@austincc.edu
Phone: (512) 223-7503 Fax: (512) 223-7665
Linda Kluck, Director of Admissions and Records, Austin Community College, 5930 Middle Fiskville Road, Austin, TX 78752-4390

---

## Blinn College
### Brenham, Texas
### www.blinn.edu
**CB code: 6043**

- Public 2-year junior college
- Commuter campus in large town

**General.** Founded in 1883. Regionally accredited. **Enrollment:** 14,710 degree-seeking undergraduates. **Degrees:** 751 associate awarded. **Location:** 79 miles from Houston, 90 miles from Austin. **Calendar:** Semester, limited summer session. **Full-time faculty:** 222 total. **Part-time faculty:** 348 total. **Special facilities:** College-operated museum, ice cream factory.

**Student profile.** Among degree-seeking undergraduates, 57% enrolled in a transfer program, 43% enrolled in a vocational program, 1% already have a bachelor's degree or higher, 9,000 transferred in from other institutions.

| | | | |
|---|---|---|---|
| Out-of-state: | 1% | Live on campus: | 10% |
| 25 or older: | 14% | | |

**Transfer out. Colleges most students transferred to 2007:** Texas A&M-College Station, Sam Houston State University, Texas State University, University of Texas at Austin, University of Houston.

**Basis for selection.** Open admission, but selective for some programs. Special requirements for registered nursing program, dental hygiene, physical therapy, various other allied health and some technology-based programs. TASP test required for all as per Texas state law. **Homeschooled:** Transcript of courses and grades required.

**2007-2008 Annual costs.** Tuition/fees: $1,890; $2,760 out-of-district; $5,040 out-of-state. Per-credit charge: $35 in-district; $64 out-of-district; $140 out-of-state. Room/board: $4,425. Books/supplies: $1,018. Personal expenses: $1,350.

**2007-2008 Financial aid. Need-based:** 47% of total undergraduate aid awarded as scholarships/grants, 53% as loans/jobs. Need-based aid available for part-time students.

**Application procedures. Admission:** No deadline. No application fee. Application may be submitted online. Admission notification on a rolling basis. **Financial aid:** Priority date 6/1; no closing date. FAFSA, institutional form required. Applicants notified on a rolling basis starting 7/1.

**Academics. Special study options:** Cross-registration, distance learning, dual enrollment of high school students, ESL, liberal arts/career combination, teacher certification program. License preparation in dental hygiene, nursing, paramedic, physical therapy, radiology, real estate. **Credit/placement by examination:** AP, CLEP, IB, institutional tests. 12 credit hours maximum toward associate degree. THEA (Texas Higher Education Assessment) test used for placement; students submitting sufficient score on TAKS, SAT or ACT exempt (Education students must take THEA). **Support services:** GED preparation and test center, learning center, preadmission summer program, reduced course load, remedial instruction, study skills assistance, tutoring, writing center.

**Majors. Biology:** General. **Business:** General, accounting, office/clerical. **Communications:** General. **Computer sciences:** General. **English:** English lit, speech/rhetoric. **Family/consumer sciences:** Child care. **Foreign languages:** General, French, German, sign language interpretation, Spanish. **Health:** Dental hygiene, medical radiologic technology/radiation therapy, mental health services, nursing (RN). **History:** General. **Legal studies:** Paralegal. **Liberal arts:** Arts/sciences. **Math:** General. **Parks/recreation:** Exercise sciences. **Philosophy/religion:** Philosophy. **Physical sciences:** Chemistry, physics. **Protective services:** Criminal justice, firefighting. **Psychology:** General.

**Most popular majors.** Biological/life sciences 10%, business/marketing 20%, English 7%, health sciences 15%, liberal arts 7%, security/protective services 7%.

**Computing on campus.** 500 workstations in library; computer center. Dormitories wired for high-speed internet access and linked to campus network. Commuter students can connect to campus network. Online course registration, online library, helpline, wireless network available.

**Student life. Freshman orientation:** Available. Held 3-4 times during summer, parents welcome. **Housing:** Single-sex dorms, special housing for disabled, apartments, substance-free housing available. $200 fully refundable deposit. **Activities:** Bands, campus ministries, choral groups, dance, drama, international student organizations, music ensembles, musical theater, student government, Circle K International, Phi Theta Kappa, Fellowship of Christian Athletes, College Republicans, Young Democrats.

**Athletics.** NJCAA. **Intercollegiate:** Baseball M, basketball, football (tackle) M, softball W, volleyball W. **Intramural:** Basketball, softball, volleyball. **Team name:** Buccaneer.

**Student services.** Career counseling, financial aid counseling, personal counseling, veterans' counselor. **Physically disabled:** Services for visually, speech, hearing impaired. **Transfer:** Transfer adviser, college fairs on campus for students transferring to 4-year colleges.

**Contact.** E-mail: recruit@blinn.edu
Phone: (979) 830-4140 Fax: (979) 830-4009
Dennis Crowson, Dean of Admissions/Registrar, Blinn College, 902 College Avenue, Brenham, TX 77833

---

## Bradford School of Business
### Houston, Texas
### www.bradfordschoolhouston.edu

- For-profit 2-year technical college
- Very large city
- Interview required

**General.** Regionally accredited; also accredited by ACICS. **Enrollment:** 53 degree-seeking undergraduates. **Degrees:** 3 associate awarded. **Calendar:** Semester. **Full-time faculty:** 7 total. **Part-time faculty:** 7 total.

**Basis for selection.** Interviews required.

**2008-2009 Annual costs.** Tuition/fees (projected): $12,760. Lab fees vary depending upon program selected.

**Application procedures. Admission:** No deadline. $50 fee.

**Academics. Credit/placement by examination:** CLEP. **Support services:** Learning center, tutoring.

**Majors. Business:** Accounting. **Health:** Veterinary technology/assistant. **Legal studies:** Legal secretary.

**Contact.** E-mail: mortiz@bradfordschoolhouston.edu
Phone: (713) 629-1500
Philip Heine, Director of Admissions, Bradford School of Business, 4669 Southwest Freeway, Houston, TX 77027

---

## Brazosport College
### Lake Jackson, Texas
### www.brazosport.edu
**CB code: 6054**

- Public 2-year community college
- Commuter campus in large town

**General.** Founded in 1948. Regionally accredited. **Location:** 50 miles from Houston. **Calendar:** Semester.

**Annual costs/financial aid.** Tuition/fees (2007-2008): $1,290; $1,920 out-of-district; $3,330 out-of-state. Books/supplies: $910. Personal expenses: $2,504. Need-based financial aid available to full-time and part-time students.

**Contact.** Phone: (979) 230-3216
Director of Admissions and Registrar, 500 College Drive, Lake Jackson, TX 77566

## Brookhaven College
### Farmers Branch, Texas
www.brookhavencollege.edu          CB code: 6070

◆ Public 2-year community college
◆ Commuter campus in large town

**General.** Founded in 1965. Regionally accredited. **Enrollment:** 8,480 degree-seeking undergraduates; 2,579 non-degree-seeking students. **Degrees:** 456 associate awarded. **Location:** 12 miles from downtown Dallas. **Calendar:** Semester, limited summer session. **Full-time faculty:** 128 total. **Part-time faculty:** 588 total.

**Student profile.** Among degree-seeking undergraduates, 976 enrolled as first-time, first-year students.

| | | | |
|---|---|---|---|
| Part-time: | 77% | Asian American: | 13% |
| Women: | 59% | Hispanic American: | 25% |
| African American: | 15% | International: | 1% |

**Basis for selection.** Open admission. Observes TASP guidelines.

**2007-2008 Annual costs.** Tuition/fees: $1,170; $2,160 out-of-district; $3,450 out-of-state. Per-credit charge: $39 in-district; $72 out-of-district; $115 out-of-state. Books/supplies: $1,200. Personal expenses: $920.

**Financial aid. Additional information:** Some tuition waivers available based upon state residency.

**Application procedures. Admission:** No deadline. No application fee. Application may be submitted online. Admission notification on a rolling basis. **Financial aid:** Priority date 6/1; no closing date. FAFSA required. Applicants notified on a rolling basis.

**Academics. Special study options:** Cooperative education, distance learning, dual enrollment of high school students, ESL, honors, internships, study abroad, weekend college. License preparation in nursing, paramedic, radiology, real estate. **Credit/placement by examination:** CLEP, IB. At least 25% of credit hours required for graduation must be taken by instruction and not by credit-by-exam. **Support services:** GED preparation, remedial instruction, study skills assistance, tutoring, writing center.

**Majors. Business:** General, accounting, apparel, business admin, e-commerce, entrepreneurial studies, executive assistant, fashion, management information systems, marketing, office management, office technology. **Computer sciences:** Information systems, programming. **Education:** Early childhood. **Engineering technology:** Electrical. **Family/consumer sciences:** Child care. **Health:** Nursing (RN), radiologic technology/medical imaging. **Legal studies:** Legal secretary. **Mechanic/repair:** Automotive. **Transportation:** General. **Visual/performing arts:** Commercial/advertising art, design.

**Most popular majors.** Business/marketing 12%, health sciences 17%, liberal arts 55%, trade and industry 7%.

**Computing on campus.** Commuter students can connect to campus network. Helpline, wireless network available.

**Student life. Freshman orientation:** Mandatory. **Activities:** Choral groups, drama, film society, music ensembles, musical theater, student newspaper.

**Athletics.** NJCAA. **Intercollegiate:** Baseball M, golf M, soccer M, tennis. **Intramural:** Soccer. **Team name:** Bears.

**Student services.** Adult student services, career counseling, student employment services, health services, personal counseling, placement for graduates, veterans' counselor. **Physically disabled:** Services for visually, speech impaired. **Transfer:** College fairs on campus for students transferring to 4-year colleges.

**Contact.** E-mail: bhcAdmissions@dcccd.edu
Phone: (972) 860-4883 Fax: (972) 860-4886
Thoa Vo, Director of Admissions, Brookhaven College, 3939 Valley View Lane, Farmers Branch, TX 75244-4997

## Cedar Valley College
### Lancaster, Texas
www.cedarvalleycollege.edu          CB code: 6148

◆ Public 2-year community college
◆ Commuter campus in large town

**General.** Founded in 1974. Regionally accredited. One of seven colleges in the Dallas County Community College District. **Enrollment:** 4,200 degree-seeking undergraduates. **Degrees:** 256 associate awarded. **Location:** 10 miles from Dallas. **Calendar:** Semester, limited summer session. **Full-time faculty:** 66 total. **Part-time faculty:** 140 total. **Special facilities:** Veterinary technology facilities, commercial music facilities including recording studios. **Partnerships:** Formal partnerships with Vartec, Owens Corning, University of North Texas, Upward Bound.

**Student profile.** Among degree-seeking undergraduates, 68% enrolled in a transfer program, 32% enrolled in a vocational program.

**Transfer out. Colleges most students transferred to 2007:** University of Texas at Arlington, Texas A&M at Commerce, University of North Texas.

**Basis for selection.** Open admission. Student must be graduate of accredited high school, or at least 18 years of age, or be admitted by individual approval. **Homeschooled:** Interview required.

**2007-2008 Annual costs.** Tuition/fees: $1,170; $2,160 out-of-district; $3,450 out-of-state. Per-credit charge: $39 in-district; $72 out-of-district; $115 out-of-state. Books/supplies: $800. Personal expenses: $1,045.

**Application procedures. Admission:** No deadline. No application fee. Application must be submitted on paper. Admission notification on a rolling basis. **Financial aid:** Priority date 5/1; no closing date. FAFSA required. Applicants notified on a rolling basis.

**Academics. Special study options:** Cooperative education, distance learning, dual enrollment of high school students, liberal arts/career combination, student-designed major, study abroad, weekend college. License preparation in real estate. **Credit/placement by examination:** CLEP, institutional tests. 45 credit hours maximum toward associate degree. **Support services:** GED preparation, learning center, reduced course load, remedial instruction, study skills assistance, tutoring, writing center.

**Majors. Business:** Accounting/business management, administrative services, business admin, management information systems, marketing, office management, office technology, real estate. **Communications technology:** Recording arts. **Computer sciences:** Data processing, networking, programming. **Health:** Veterinary technology/assistant. **Mechanic/repair:** Heating/ac/refrig. **Protective services:** Law enforcement admin. **Visual/performing arts:** Design, music performance.

**Computing on campus.** 400 workstations in library, computer center, student center. Commuter students can connect to campus network. Online course registration, helpline, repair service, wireless network available.

**Student life. Freshman orientation:** Mandatory. 1-day program includes assessment testing. **Activities:** Jazz band, choral groups, drama, music ensembles, musical theater, student government, student newspaper, student government, Sierra club, Christian student union, Latin American student organization, Phi Theta Kappa, student ambassadors, preprofessional club, art club, veterinary technology club.

**Athletics.** NJCAA. **Intercollegiate:** Baseball M, basketball M. **Intramural:** Cheerleading W, football (non-tackle) M, golf, soccer W, volleyball W. **Team name:** Suns.

**Student services.** Career counseling, services for economically disadvantaged, student employment services, financial aid counseling, health services, personal counseling, placement for graduates, veterans' counselor. **Physically disabled:** Services for visually, speech, hearing impaired. **Transfer:** Pre-admission transcript evaluation for new students. College fairs on campus for students transferring to 4-year colleges.

**Contact.** E-mail: cdw3310@dcccd.edu
Phone: (972) 860-8201 Fax: (972) 860-8001
Carolyn Boswell-Ward, Director of Admissions and Registrar, Cedar Valley College, 3030 North Dallas Avenue, Lancaster, TX 75134

## Central Texas College
### Killeen, Texas
www.ctcd.edu          CB code: 6130

◆ Public 2-year community and technical college
◆ Commuter campus in small city

**General.** Founded in 1965. Regionally accredited. **Enrollment:** 17,996 degree-seeking undergraduates; 276 non-degree-seeking students. **Degrees:** 2,437 associate awarded. **ROTC:** Army. **Location:** 5 miles from Killeen, 60 miles from Austin. **Calendar:** Semester, extensive summer session. **Full-time faculty:** 155 total. **Part-time faculty:** 235 total. **Special facilities:** Planetarium, space theater. **Partnerships:** Formal partnerships with Killeen and Copperas Cove ISDs (school to career facilitator program).

**Student profile.** Among degree-seeking undergraduates, 19% enrolled in a transfer program, 81% enrolled in a vocational program, 7,538 enrolled as first-time, first-year students, 4,297 transferred in from other institutions.

| | | | |
|---|---|---|---|
| Part-time: | 85% | Hispanic American: | 16% |
| Out-of-state: | 3% | Native American: | 1% |
| Women: | 48% | International: | 1% |
| African American: | 29% | 25 or older: | 60% |
| Asian American: | 4% | Live on campus: | 2% |

**Transfer out. Colleges most students transferred to 2007:** University of Mary Hardin-Baylor, Tarleton State University, Texas State University, University of North Texas, Texas Tech.

**Basis for selection.** Open admission, but selective for some programs. Special requirements for registered nursing, paramedic, EMT, aviation science programs. Observes TASP requirements. Interview required for medical laboratory technician, nursing programs; audition recommended for music; portfolio recommended for art. **Homeschooled:** Transcript of courses and grades required.

**High school preparation.** 22 units recommended. Recommended units include English 4, mathematics 3, social studies 1.5, history 1, science 2 (laboratory 1) and academic electives 1. 0.5 economics, 0.5 speech, 1 technology applications, 1 physical education, 0.5 foundations of personal fitness, 0.5 health, 5.5 electives recommended.

**2007-2008 Annual costs.** Tuition/fees: $1,470; $1,770 out-of-district; $4,290 out-of-state. Per-credit charge: $36 in-district; $46 out-of-district; $130 out-of-state. Room/board: $3,300. Books/supplies: $1,140. Personal expenses: $1,200.

**Financial aid.** All financial aid based on need. Need-based aid available for part-time students. Work-study available nights, weekends and for part-time students.

**Application procedures. Admission:** No deadline. No application fee. Application must be submitted on paper. Admission notification on a rolling basis. **Financial aid:** Closing date 7/1. FAFSA, institutional form required. Applicants notified on a rolling basis starting 3/1; must reply within 4 week(s) of notification.

**Academics. Special study options:** Cross-registration, distance learning, dual enrollment of high school students, ESL, independent study, internships, liberal arts/career combination. License preparation in aviation, nursing, paramedic, real estate. **Credit/placement by examination:** AP, CLEP, IB, institutional tests. 48 credit hours maximum toward associate degree. **Support services:** GED preparation and test center, learning center, reduced course load, remedial instruction, study skills assistance, tutoring.

**Majors. Agriculture:** Farm/ranch. **Biology:** General. **Business:** General, administrative services, business admin, hospitality admin, office management, real estate, tourism promotion. **Communications:** Broadcast journalism. **Communications technology:** Graphic/printing. **Computer sciences:** General, computer science, data processing, information systems, networking, programming. **Education:** General. **Engineering:** General. **Engineering technology:** Drafting. **Family/consumer sciences:** Child care. **Foreign languages:** General. **Health:** Clinical lab assistant, clinical lab technology, nursing (RN), premedicine, substance abuse counseling. **Interdisciplinary:** Biological/physical sciences. **Legal studies:** General, paralegal, prelaw. **Liberal arts:** Arts/sciences. **Math:** General. **Mechanic/repair:** General, auto body, automotive, diesel, electronics/electrical, heating/ac/refrig. **Personal/culinary services:** Culinary arts. **Physical sciences:** Chemistry, geology, physics. **Protective services:** Law enforcement admin. **Social sciences:** General. **Visual/performing arts:** Art.

**Most popular majors.** Interdisciplinary studies 70%, military 9%.

**Computing on campus.** 600 workstations in library, computer center. Online course registration, online library, helpline available.

**Student life. Freshman orientation:** Available. Preregistration for classes offered. **Housing:** Coed dorms, apartments available. $100 nonrefundable deposit, deadline 8/1. **Activities:** Choral groups, drama, radio station, student government, student newspaper, TV station.

**Student services.** Adult student services, alcohol/substance abuse counseling, career counseling, services for economically disadvantaged, student employment services, financial aid counseling, on-campus daycare, placement for graduates, veterans' counselor. **Physically disabled:** Services for visually, speech, hearing impaired. **Transfer:** Pre-admission transcript evaluation for new students. Transfer center, transfer adviser, college fairs on campus for students transferring to 4-year colleges.

**Contact.** E-mail: admissions@ctcd.edu
Phone: (254) 526-1696 Toll-free number: (800) 792-3348 ext. 1696
Fax: (254) 526-1481
Dottie Kyle, Director, Admissions and Recruitment, Central Texas College, Box 1800, Killeen, TX 76540

## Cisco Junior College
### Cisco, Texas
www.cisco.cc.tx.us                    CB code: 6096

▶ Public 2-year junior college
▶ Commuter campus in small town

**General.** Founded in 1940. Regionally accredited. **Enrollment:** 3,364 degree-seeking undergraduates. **Degrees:** 198 associate awarded. **Location:** 100 miles from Fort Worth. **Calendar:** Semester, limited summer session. **Full-time faculty:** 73 total. **Part-time faculty:** 93 total.

**Student profile.**

| | | | |
|---|---|---|---|
| Out-of-state: | 8% | Live on campus: | 28% |
| 25 or older: | 90% | | |

**Basis for selection.** Open admission.

**2007-2008 Annual costs.** Tuition/fees: $2,010; $2,340 out-of-district; $2,646 out-of-state. Room/board: $3,100. Books/supplies: $800. Personal expenses: $1,986.

**Application procedures. Admission:** No deadline. No application fee. Admission notification on a rolling basis. **Financial aid:** Priority date 8/15; no closing date. FAFSA required. Applicants notified on a rolling basis starting 8/15.

**Academics. Special study options:** Dual enrollment of high school students. **Credit/placement by examination:** CLEP. 22 credit hours maximum toward associate degree. **Support services:** GED test center, remedial instruction, tutoring.

**Majors. Agriculture:** Animal sciences, business. **Biology:** General. **Business:** General, accounting. **Communications:** General. **Computer sciences:** General. **Education:** General. **Engineering:** General. **Engineering technology:** Drafting. **Foreign languages:** French, Spanish. **Health:** Medical records technology. **History:** General. **Legal studies:** Prelaw. **Math:** General. **Mechanic/repair:** General. **Physical sciences:** Chemistry. **Psychology:** General. **Public administration:** Social work. **Social sciences:** General, economics, sociology. **Visual/performing arts:** Art, dramatic.

**Student life. Housing:** Single-sex dorms available. **Activities:** Bands, choral groups, drama, music ensembles, student government, student newspaper.

**Athletics. Intercollegiate:** Baseball W, basketball, football (tackle) M, golf, rodeo, soccer W, volleyball W. **Intramural:** Basketball, track and field. **Team name:** Wranglers.

**Student services.** Health services, personal counseling.

**Contact.** Phone: (254) 442-2567 Fax: (254) 442-2546
Olin Odom, Dean of Enrollment Management, Cisco Junior College, 101 College Heights, Cisco, TX 76437

## Clarendon College
### Clarendon, Texas
www.clarendoncollege.edu              CB code: 6097

▶ Public 2-year community college
▶ Residential campus in rural community

**General.** Founded in 1898. Regionally accredited. **Enrollment:** 1,029 degree-seeking undergraduates; 97 non-degree-seeking students. **Degrees:** 97 associate awarded. **Location:** 60 miles from Amarillo. **Calendar:** Semester, limited summer session. **Full-time faculty:** 32 total; 3% have terminal degrees, 44% women. **Part-time faculty:** 45 total; 7% have terminal degrees, 64% women. **Class size:** 69% < 20, 30% 20-39, 1% 50-99. **Partnerships:** Formal partnership with Tech Prep.

**Student profile.** Among degree-seeking undergraduates, 11% enrolled in a vocational program, 506 enrolled as first-time, first-year students, 88 transferred in from other institutions.

| | | | |
|---|---|---|---|
| Part-time: | 52% | **Hispanic American:** | 18% |
| Out-of-state: | 9% | **Native American:** | 1% |
| Women: | 45% | **International:** | 1% |
| African American: | 10% | **Live on campus:** | 25% |
| Asian American: | 1% | | |

**Transfer out. Colleges most students transferred to 2007:** West Texas A&M University, Texas Tech University, Texas A&M University, Tarleton State University, Midwestern State University.

**Basis for selection.** Open admission, but selective for some programs. Special requirements for certain technical programs and vocational nursing. SAT/ACT used for counseling; ACT preferred. Institution observes all TASP requirements. Pre-entrance examination required for vocational nursing applicants. Interview before May 1 required for ranch and feedlot operations program. 3 personal references, interview required for vocational nursing program. **Homeschooled:** Transcript of courses and grades required. A request for admission by Individual Approval should be submitted to the Admissions Office.

**High school preparation.** 24 units recommended. Recommended units include English 4, mathematics 4, social studies 2, history 2, science 4, foreign language 2, academic electives 3.5. 0.5 health, 0.5 economics, 1 computer, 0.5 speech recommended.

**2007-2008 Annual costs.** Tuition/fees: $2,280; $2,850 out-of-district; $3,420 out-of-state. Room/board: $3,350. Books/supplies: $800. Personal expenses: $2,075.

**Financial aid. Need-based:** Need-based aid available for part-time students. Work-study available nights, weekends and for part-time students. **Non-need-based:** Scholarships awarded for academics, art, athletics, leadership, music/drama, state residency.

**Application procedures. Admission:** Priority date 8/15; no deadline. No application fee. Admission notification on a rolling basis. **Financial aid:** Priority date 7/1, closing date 9/1. FAFSA, institutional form required. Applicants notified on a rolling basis starting 8/1; must reply by 8/15 or within 2 week(s) of notification.

**Academics. Special study options:** Cross-registration, distance learning, dual enrollment of high school students, internships, liberal arts/career combination, student-designed major. License preparation in nursing. **Credit/placement by examination:** AP, CLEP. 30 credit hours maximum toward associate degree. **Support services:** GED test center, remedial instruction, tutoring.

**Majors. Agriculture:** General, agronomy, animal sciences, business, economics, equestrian studies, farm/ranch. **Biology:** General. **Business:** General, accounting, finance, management science, marketing, office technology. **Communications:** General. **Computer sciences:** General. **Conservation:** Environmental science. **Education:** General, elementary, secondary. **Engineering:** General. **Engineering technology:** Computer systems. **English:** English lit, speech/rhetoric. **Foreign languages:** General. **Health:** EMT paramedic, health services, nursing (RN), predental, premedicine, prepharmacy, preveterinary. **History:** General. **Legal studies:** Prelaw. **Liberal arts:** Arts/sciences. **Math:** General. **Parks/recreation:** General, exercise sciences, health/fitness. **Philosophy/religion:** Religion. **Physical sciences:** Chemistry, geology, physics. **Protective services:** Criminal justice. **Psychology:** General. **Public administration:** Social work. **Social sciences:** Economics, political science, sociology. **Visual/performing arts:** Art, commercial/advertising art, dramatic.

**Most popular majors.** Agriculture 20%, business/marketing 13%, education 11%, health sciences 15%, liberal arts 22%.

**Computing on campus.** 221 workstations in library, computer center. Dormitories wired for high-speed internet access. Commuter students can connect to campus network. Online course registration, online library, wireless network available.

**Student life. Freshman orientation:** Mandatory, $79 fee. Preregistration for classes offered. Two-week face-to-face lecture, twice a week, followed by a 6-week Internet course. **Housing:** Coed dorms, single-sex dorms, special housing for disabled, apartments, substance-free housing available. $100 partly refundable deposit. **Activities:** Jazz band, choral groups, drama, music ensembles, student government, multicultural club, student ambassadors, Block & Bridle, rodeo club.

**Athletics. NJCAA. Intercollegiate:** Baseball M, basketball, cheerleading, rodeo, softball W, volleyball W. **Intramural:** Basketball, football (non-tackle), golf, rodeo, table tennis, volleyball. **Team name:** Bulldogs.

**Student services.** Career counseling, financial aid counseling. **Physically disabled:** Services for visually, speech, hearing impaired. **Transfer:** College fairs on campus for students transferring to 4-year colleges.

**Contact.** E-mail: admissions@clarendoncollege.edu
Phone: (806) 874-3571 Toll-free number: (800) 687-9737
Fax: (806) 874-3201
Sharon Hannon, Director of Admissions and Registrar, Clarendon College, PO Box 968, Clarendon, TX 79226

## Coastal Bend College
**Beeville, Texas**
www.coastalbend.edu                    **CB code: 6055**

- Public 2-year community and junior college
- Commuter campus in large town

**General.** Founded in 1965. Regionally accredited. In addition to main campus in Beeville, there are campuses in Alice, Kingsville, and Pleasanton. **Enrollment:** 3,142 degree-seeking undergraduates. **Degrees:** 229 associate awarded. **Location:** 60 miles from Corpus Christi, 90 miles from San Antonio. **Calendar:** Semester, limited summer session. **Full-time faculty:** 75 total. **Part-time faculty:** 83 total. **Partnerships:** Formal partnerships with national corporations to provide truck driver training, with local businesses to provide training for employees, and with high schools and tech prep programs.

**Student profile.**

| | | | |
|---|---|---|---|
| Out-of-state: | 1% | **Hispanic American:** | 64% |
| African American: | 4% | **25 or older:** | 60% |
| Asian American: | 1% | **Live on campus:** | 5% |

**Transfer out. Colleges most students transferred to 2007:** Texas A&M-Corpus Christi, Texas A&M-Kingsville, Southwest Texas State University, Texas A&M-College Station, University of Texas.

**Basis for selection.** Open admission, but selective for some programs. Special requirements for dental hygiene and vocational nursing programs. Texas requires that all students satisfy Texas THEA test requirements before being enrolled in college-level courses in public college or university. Scores not used in admission decisions. **Homeschooled:** Transcript of courses and grades required. Transcript must be notarized.

**2007-2008 Annual costs.** Tuition/fees: $1,730; $3,500 out-of-district; $3,950 out-of-state. Meal ticket (a la carte) food service available. Room only: $1,560. Books/supplies: $600. Personal expenses: $1,500.

**2006-2007 Financial aid. Need-based:** 67% of total undergraduate aid awarded as scholarships/grants, 33% as loans/jobs. Need-based aid available for part-time students. **Non-need-based:** Scholarships awarded for academics, leadership.

**Application procedures. Admission:** No deadline. No application fee. Application may be submitted online. Admission notification on a rolling basis. **Financial aid:** Priority date 4/1; no closing date. FAFSA, institutional form required. Applicants notified on a rolling basis starting 5/1; must reply within 2 week(s) of notification.

**Academics. Special study options:** Cooperative education, cross-registration, distance learning, dual enrollment of high school students, independent study, internships, liberal arts/career combination. License preparation in dental hygiene, nursing. **Credit/placement by examination:** CLEP, institutional tests. 30 credit hours maximum toward associate degree. ACCUPLACER, ASSET, COMPASS, MAPS tests may be used instead of THEA. **Support services:** GED test center, learning center, remedial instruction, study skills assistance, tutoring.

**Majors. Biology:** General. **Business:** General, accounting, administrative services, business admin, office technology, office/clerical. **Communications:** General. **Computer sciences:** General, computer science, data processing, programming. **Conservation:** General. **Education:** General, elementary, secondary. **Engineering:** General. **Engineering technology:** Drafting. **English:** English lit, speech/rhetoric. **Family/consumer sciences:** General, child care. **Foreign languages:** Spanish. **Health:** Dental hygiene, medical records technology, medical secretary, nursing (RN), predental, premedicine, prepharmacy, preveterinary. **History:** General. **Legal studies:** Prelaw. **Liberal arts:** Arts/sciences. **Math:** General. **Physical sciences:** Chemistry, geology, physics. **Protective services:** Corrections, criminal justice, police science. **Psychology:** General. **Social sciences:** Political science, sociology. **Visual/performing arts:** General, commercial/advertising art, studio arts.

**Computing on campus.** 700 workstations in library, computer center. Dormitories wired for high-speed internet access and linked to campus network. Commuter students can connect to campus network. Online course registration, online library, helpline, wireless network available.

**Student life. Freshman orientation:** Mandatory. Preregistration for classes offered. Half-day program, parents welcome. **Housing:** Single-sex dorms, apartments available. $100 partly refundable deposit, deadline 8/15. **Activities:** Student government, Baptist Student Union, Newman Club.

**Athletics. Intercollegiate:** Basketball, volleyball W. **Intramural:** Archery, badminton, basketball, bowling, cross-country, golf, soccer, softball, swimming, table tennis, tennis, track and field, volleyball, weight lifting. **Team name:** Cougars.

**Student services.** Career counseling, services for economically disadvantaged, student employment services, financial aid counseling, on-campus daycare, personal counseling, placement for graduates, veterans' counselor. **Physically disabled:** Services for visually, speech, hearing impaired. **Transfer:** Pre-admission transcript evaluation for new students. Transfer adviser, college fairs on campus for students transferring to 4-year colleges.

**Contact.**  E-mail: register@coastalbend.edu
Phone: (361) 354-2254 Toll-free number: (800) 722-2838 ext. 2254
Fax: (361) 354-2554
Alicia Ulloa, Registrar and Director Admissions, Coastal Bend College, 3800 Charco Road, Beeville, TX 78102

---

## College of the Mainland
**Texas City, Texas**
www.com.edu                                              CB code: 6133

- Public 2-year community and technical college
- Commuter campus in large town

**General.** Founded in 1966. Regionally accredited. **Enrollment:** 1,059 full-time, degree-seeking students. **Degrees:** 200 associate awarded. **Location:** 25 miles from Houston. **Calendar:** Semester, extensive summer session. **Full-time faculty:** 94 total; 97% have terminal degrees, 55% minority. **Part-time faculty:** 138 total.

**Student profile.**

| | | | |
|---|---|---|---|
| Out-of-state: | 1% | 25 or older: | 44% |

**Transfer out. Colleges most students transferred to 2007:** University of Houston-Clear Lake.

**Basis for selection.** Open admission, but selective for some programs. Special requirements for nursing program.

**2007-2008 Annual costs.** Tuition/fees: $1,282; $2,302 out-of-district; $3,262 out-of-state. Books/supplies: $800. Personal expenses: $1,087.

**Financial aid.** All financial aid based on need. Need-based aid available for part-time students. Work-study available nights, weekends and for part-time students.

**Application procedures. Admission:** No deadline. No application fee. Application may be submitted online. Admission notification on a rolling basis. **Financial aid:** No deadline. FAFSA, institutional form required. Applicants notified on a rolling basis.

**Academics. Special study options:** Cooperative education, cross-registration, distance learning, double major, dual enrollment of high school students, independent study, internships, weekend college. License preparation in nursing, paramedic, real estate. **Credit/placement by examination:** CLEP, institutional tests. 24 credit hours maximum toward associate degree. **Support services:** GED preparation and test center, learning center, remedial instruction, tutoring, writing center.

**Majors. Biology:** General. **Business:** General, accounting, administrative services, banking/financial services, business admin, labor relations, marketing, office management, office technology, office/clerical, real estate. **Communications:** Journalism. **Computer sciences:** General, programming. **Education:** Elementary, secondary. **Engineering:** General. **Engineering technology:** Drafting, electrical. **Family/consumer sciences:** Child care. **Health:** Licensed practical nurse. **History:** General. **Interdisciplinary:** Biological/physical sciences. **Liberal arts:** Arts/sciences. **Math:** General. **Mechanic/repair:** Diesel, heating/ac/refrig. **Physical sciences:** Chemistry, planetary. **Protective services:** Fire safety technology, police science. **Psychology:** General. **Public administration:** General, social work. **Social sciences:** General, economics, political science, sociology. **Visual/performing arts:** General, dramatic, studio arts.

**Computing on campus.** 100 workstations in library, computer center. Online course registration, wireless network available.

**Student life. Freshman orientation:** Mandatory. Preregistration for classes offered. **Activities:** Bands, choral groups, drama, literary magazine, music

---

ensembles, musical theater, student government, Phi Beta Kappa, Students for Christ, COM Amigos, Organization of African-American Culture, biology club.

**Athletics. Intramural:** Basketball, football (non-tackle) M, racquetball, soccer, softball, tennis, volleyball. **Team name:** Ducks.

**Student services.** Career counseling, student employment services, financial aid counseling, on-campus daycare, personal counseling, placement for graduates, veterans' counselor. **Physically disabled:** Services for visually, speech, hearing impaired. **Transfer:** Transfer adviser, college fairs on campus for students transferring to 4-year colleges.

**Contact.**  Phone: (409) 938-1211 ext. 264 Fax: (409) 938-3126
Kelly Musick, Director of Admissions and Records, College of the Mainland, 1200 Amburn Road, Texas City, TX 77591

---

## Collin County Community College District
**Plano, Texas**                                         CB member
www.ccccd.edu                                            CB code: 1951

- Public 2-year community college
- Commuter campus in large city

**General.** Founded in 1985. Regionally accredited. **Enrollment:** 19,754 degree-seeking undergraduates; 389 non-degree-seeking students. **Degrees:** 1,110 associate awarded. **ROTC:** Army. **Location:** 25 miles from Dallas. **Calendar:** Semester, extensive summer session. **Full-time faculty:** 274 total; 12% minority, 57% women. **Part-time faculty:** 859 total; 19% minority, 56% women. **Class size:** 31% < 20, 66% 20-39, 2% 40-49, less than 1% 50-99. **Special facilities:** Regional fire training facility. **Partnerships:** Formal partnership with Cisco to provide Certified Network Professional Certification.

**Student profile.** Among degree-seeking undergraduates, 4,160 enrolled as first-time, first-year students, 2,659 transferred in from other institutions.

| | | | |
|---|---|---|---|
| Part-time: | 59% | Hispanic American: | 12% |
| Out-of-state: | 4% | Native American: | 1% |
| Women: | 56% | International: | 2% |
| African American: | 9% | 25 or older: | 4% |
| Asian American: | 9% | | |

**Transfer out. Colleges most students transferred to 2007:** University of Texas at Dallas, University of North Texas, Texas A&M University, University of Texas at Austin, Texas Tech University.

**Basis for selection.** Open admission, but selective for some programs. Special requirements for programs in nursing, dental hygiene, emergency medical services, firefighter, respiratory care, interpreter prep, honors institute, center for advanced study in mathematics and natural sciences. For placement only, institution administers local assessments in reading, writing, math to new students. TASP guidelines observed, though TASP testing waived if acceptable scores on ACT, SAT or other accepted substitute tests presented. **Homeschooled:** If under 18 years must provide written parental/guardian permission.

**High school preparation.** 17 units recommended. Recommended units include English 4, mathematics 3, social studies 2, history 2, science 2 (laboratory 2) and foreign language 2.

**2007-2008 Annual costs.** Books/supplies: $638.

**2006-2007 Financial aid. Need-based:** 846 full-time freshmen applied for aid; 641 were judged to have need; 537 of these received aid. Average need met was 29%. Average scholarship/grant was $3,283; average loan $1,983. 62% of total undergraduate aid awarded as scholarships/grants, 38% as loans/jobs. Need-based aid available for part-time students. Work-study available nights, weekends and for part-time students. **Non-need-based:** Awarded to 569 full-time undergraduates, including 227 freshmen. Scholarships awarded for academics, art, athletics, music/drama.

**Application procedures. Admission:** No deadline. No application fee. Application may be submitted online. Admission notification on a rolling basis. **Financial aid:** Priority date 6/1, closing date 6/30. FAFSA, institutional form required. Applicants notified on a rolling basis starting 5/1; must reply within 2 week(s) of notification.

**Academics. Special study options:** Cooperative education, distance learning, dual enrollment of high school students, ESL, honors, internships, teacher certification program, weekend college. Learning communities; service learning opportunities; dual admissions agreements with University of North Texas, University of Texas at Dallas, Southern Methodist University, Texas Women-s

University, Texas Tech University, Texas A&M University-Commerce, Baylor University, Texas A&M. License preparation in dental hygiene, nursing. **Credit/placement by examination:** CLEP, institutional tests. 18 credit hours maximum toward associate degree. 6 hours traditional credit must be completed in residence before examination credit awarded. **Support services:** Learning center, remedial instruction, study skills assistance, tutoring, writing center.

**Honors college/program.** Students with GPA of 3.5 or over admitted to Honors Institute.

**Majors. Business:** Business admin, hospitality admin, office technology, real estate, sales/distribution. **Communications technology:** Animation/special effects. **Computer sciences:** General, networking, programming, web page design. **Engineering technology:** Drafting, electrical, electrical drafting, telecommunications. **Family/consumer sciences:** Child development. **Foreign languages:** Sign language interpretation. **Health:** Dental hygiene, EMT paramedic, nursing (RN), respiratory therapy technology. **Legal studies:** Paralegal. **Mechanic/repair:** Electronics/electrical. **Protective services:** Fire safety technology. **Science technology:** Biological. **Visual/performing arts:** Commercial/advertising art, interior design, music management.

**Computing on campus.** 1,980 workstations in library, computer center. Online course registration, helpline, repair service, wireless network available.

**Student life. Freshman orientation:** Available. One-day program; online section available for distance learning students. **Housing:** Apartments available. **Activities:** Jazz band, campus ministries, choral groups, dance, drama, international student organizations, literary magazine, music ensembles, Model UN, musical theater, student government, American Sign Language club, black student association, nursing student association, hospitality and culinary arts student society, Latter-day Saints student association, Muslim student association, College Republicans.

**Athletics.** NJCAA. **Intercollegiate:** Basketball, tennis. **Team name:** Cougars.

**Student services.** Adult student services, alcohol/substance abuse counseling, career counseling, student employment services, financial aid counseling, on-campus daycare, personal counseling, placement for graduates. **Physically disabled:** Services for visually, speech, hearing impaired. **Transfer:** Transfer adviser, college fairs on campus for students transferring to 4-year colleges.

**Contact.** E-mail: smeinhardt@ccccd.edu
Phone: (972) 881-5710 Fax: (972) 881-5175
Stephanie Meinhardt, Registrar/ Director of Admissions, Collin County Community College District, 2800 East Spring Creek Parkway, Plano, TX 75074

## Commonwealth Institute of Funeral Service
Houston, Texas
www.commonwealthinst.org          CB code: 7031

- Private 2-year school of mortuary science
- Commuter campus in very large city

**General.** Founded in 1988. Accredited by American Board of Funeral Service Education, Inc. **Enrollment:** 115 degree-seeking undergraduates. **Degrees:** 62 associate awarded. **Location:** 15 miles from downtown. **Calendar:** Quarter. **Full-time faculty:** 6 total. **Part-time faculty:** 8 total. **Class size:** 50% < 20, 50% 50-99.

**Student profile.**

Out-of-state:          20%    **25 or older:**          49%

**Basis for selection.** Class rank and standardized test scores most important. SAT or ACT recommended. TASP required.

**2008-2009 Annual costs.** Tuition/fees: $6,290. Per-credit charge: $143. Books/supplies: $1,183. Personal expenses: $1,102.

**Financial aid.** All financial aid based on need. Need-based aid available for part-time students.

**Application procedures. Admission:** $50 fee. Admission notification on a rolling basis beginning on or about 8/28. Application deadline is 3 days after enrollment date. **Financial aid:** Priority date 7/20; no closing date. FAFSA required. Applicants notified on a rolling basis starting 7/12.

**Academics. Credit/placement by examination:** CLEP. **Support services:** Tutoring.

**Majors. Personal/culinary services:** Mortuary science.

**Computing on campus.** 15 workstations in library, computer center.

**Student life. Housing:** Some local funeral homes provide student employees accommodations while attending college. **Activities:** Student government.

**Student services.** Career counseling, student employment services, financial aid counseling, personal counseling, placement for graduates, veterans' counselor. **Transfer:** Re-entry adviser, pre-admission transcript evaluation for new students. Transfer adviser for students transferring to 4-year colleges.

**Contact.** Phone: (281) 873-0262 Fax: (281) 873-5232
Patricia Moreno, Registrar, Commonwealth Institute of Funeral Service, 415 Barren Springs Drive, Houston, TX 77090-5913

## Court Reporting Institute of Dallas
Dallas, Texas
www.crid.com          CB code: 3231

- For-profit 2-year technical college
- Very large city

**General.** Accredited by ACICS. **Calendar:** Quarter.

**Annual costs/financial aid.** Program cost ranges: $32,600 to $41,400 (associate degree). Books/supplies: $700.

**Contact.** Phone: (214) 350-9722
Director of Admissions, 1341 West Mockingbird Lane, Suite 200E, Dallas, TX 75247

## Court Reporting Institute of Houston
Houston, Texas
www.crid.com

- For-profit 2-year technical college
- Commuter campus in very large city
- Application essay, interview required

**General.** Accredited by ACICS. **Enrollment:** 340 degree-seeking undergraduates. **Calendar:** Quarter.

**Basis for selection.** Open admission. **Homeschooled:** Transcript of courses and grades required.

**2007-2008 Annual costs.** Program cost ranges: $32,600 to $41,400 (associate degree).

**Application procedures. Admission:** No deadline. $100 fee, may be waived for applicants with need.

**Academics. Credit/placement by examination:** CLEP.

**Student life. Freshman orientation:** Mandatory. Preregistration for classes offered. One week before classes start; 2 hours long. **Activities:** Student newspaper.

**Contact.** E-mail: ssanders@crid.com
Phone: (713) 996-8300 Toll-free number: (866) 996-8300
Fax: (713) 996-8360
Sonya Sanders, Director of Admissions, Court Reporting Institute of Houston, 13101 Northwest Freeway, Suite 100, Houston, TX 77040

## Dallas Institute of Funeral Service
Dallas, Texas
www.dallasinstitute.edu          CB code: 7032

- Private 2-year school of mortuary science
- Commuter campus in very large city

**General.** Regionally accredited. 15-month AAS in funeral service program and 6-month funeral director's program (Texas, Louisiana, and Missouri students only). **Enrollment:** 126 degree-seeking undergraduates. **Degrees:** 76 associate awarded. **Calendar:** Quarter, limited summer session. **Full-time faculty:** 5 total. **Part-time faculty:** 4 total. **Special facilities:** On-campus embalming facilities.

**Basis for selection.** Open admission.

**2007-2008 Annual costs.** Tuition/fees: $8,400. Per-credit charge: $200. Tuition $14,000 for 15-month associate program; $5,600 for 6-month funeral director program. Personal expenses: $1,190.

**Application procedures. Admission:** $50 fee. Application may be submitted online. Admission notification on a rolling basis. Application deadline is 30 days prior to enrollment. **Financial aid:** No deadline. Applicants notified on a rolling basis.

**Academics. Special study options:** Distance learning. **Credit/placement by examination:** AP, CLEP, IB. **Support services:** Study skills assistance, tutoring.

**Majors. Personal/culinary services:** Mortuary science.

**Computing on campus.** 26 workstations in library, computer center.

**Student services. Physically disabled:** Services for visually, hearing impaired.

**Contact.** Phone: (214) 388-5466 Fax: (214) 388-0316
Terry Parrish, Director of Admissions, Dallas Institute of Funeral Service, 3909 South Buckner Boulevard, Dallas, TX 75227-4314

## Del Mar College
**Corpus Christi, Texas**
www.delmar.edu
CB code: 6160

- Public 2-year community college
- Commuter campus in large city

**General.** Founded in 1935. Regionally accredited. Courses taught at 7 off-campus sites in the Coastal Bend Region. Center for Early Learning provides day-care on campus. **Enrollment:** 11,168 degree-seeking undergraduates. **Degrees:** 918 associate awarded. **ROTC:** Army. **Location:** 155 miles from San Antonio. **Calendar:** Semester, extensive summer session. **Full-time faculty:** 329 total; 19% have terminal degrees, 29% minority, 50% women. **Part-time faculty:** 268 total. **Partnerships:** Formal partnerships with Corpus Christi Army Depot, University of the Incarnate Word.

**Student profile.** Among degree-seeking undergraduates, 48% enrolled in a transfer program, 46% enrolled in a vocational program, 2% already have a bachelor's degree or higher, 1,211 enrolled as first-time, first-year students.

| | | | |
|---|---|---|---|
| Part-time: | 72% | Asian American: | 2% |
| Out-of-state: | 1% | Hispanic American: | 57% |
| Women: | 60% | 25 or older: | 38% |
| African American: | 3% | | |

**Transfer out. Colleges most students transferred to 2007:** Texas A&M University (College Station, Corpus Christi, Kingsville); University of Texas (Austin, San Antonio).

**Basis for selection.** Open admission, but selective for some programs. Admissions criteria for health science programs vary by program. Interview required for health science programs. **Homeschooled:** Students admitted under individual approval plan. Must provide notarized transcript with date of graduation. **Learning Disabled:** Designated registration time for students with disabilities.

**High school preparation.** 24 units recommended. Recommended units include English 4, mathematics 3, social studies 1, history 2, science 2, foreign language 2 and academic electives 10.

**2007-2008 Annual costs.** Tuition/fees: $1,914; $4,914 out-of-district; $6,024 out-of-state. Per-credit charge: $35 in-district; $135 out-of-district; $172 out-of-state. Books/supplies: $1,000. Personal expenses: $1,000.

**2006-2007 Financial aid.** All financial aid based on need. 75% of total undergraduate aid awarded as scholarships/grants, 25% as loans/jobs. Need-based aid available for part-time students. Work-study available nights, weekends and for part-time students.

**Application procedures. Admission:** No deadline. No application fee. Application must be submitted on paper. Admission notification on a rolling basis. **Financial aid:** Priority date 5/1; no closing date. FAFSA required. Applicants notified on a rolling basis starting 7/1; must reply within 2 week(s) of notification.

**Academics.** Short semester courses, accelerated associate degree program. **Special study options:** Accelerated study, combined bachelor's/graduate degree, cooperative education, distance learning, dual enrollment of high school students, ESL, honors, independent study, internships, teacher certification program, weekend college. License preparation in aviation, dental hygiene, nursing, occupational therapy, paramedic, physical therapy, radiology, real estate. **Credit/placement by examination:** AP, CLEP, IB, institutional tests. 30 credit hours maximum toward associate degree. Credit may not be earned by examination for most performance-oriented courses. **Support services:** GED preparation and test center, learning center, remedial instruction, study skills assistance, tutoring, writing center.

**Majors. Biology:** General. **Business:** General, accounting technology, administrative services, business admin, finance, management information systems. **Communications:** Advertising, journalism, radio/tv. **Communications technology:** Photo/film/video. **Construction:** Maintenance. **Education:** Art, bilingual, elementary, English, history, mathematics, middle, social studies, special. **Engineering technology:** Architectural, drafting, electrical, occupational safety. **English:** English lit, speech/rhetoric. **Family/consumer sciences:** Child care, child development. **Foreign languages:** General, sign language interpretation. **Health:** Clinical lab technology, dental assistant, dental hygiene, EMT paramedic, medical records technology, medical secretary, nursing (RN), occupational therapy assistant, physical therapy assistant, radiologic technology/medical imaging, respiratory therapy assistant, respiratory therapy technology, sonography, substance abuse counseling, surgical technology. **History:** General. **Legal studies:** Court reporting, paralegal. **Liberal arts:** Arts/sciences. **Math:** General. **Mechanic/repair:** Aircraft, aircraft powerplant, automotive, diesel, heating/ac/refrig. **Parks/recreation:** Health/fitness. **Personal/culinary services:** Chef training, food service, restaurant/catering. **Physical sciences:** Chemistry. **Production:** Machine tool, welding. **Protective services:** Criminal justice, fire safety technology, police science. **Psychology:** General. **Public administration:** Social work. **Science technology:** Chemical. **Social sciences:** Political science, sociology. **Visual/performing arts:** Art, dramatic, music performance, music theory/composition.

**Most popular majors.** Business/marketing 17%, education 6%, health sciences 32%, liberal arts 10%.

**Computing on campus.** 2,570 workstations in library, computer center, student center. Commuter students can connect to campus network. Online course registration, online library, helpline, wireless network available.

**Student life. Freshman orientation:** Available. Preregistration for classes offered. 2-hour session held 6 weeks prior to scheduled registration. **Activities:** Bands, campus ministries, choral groups, dance, drama, international student organizations, literary magazine, music ensembles, opera, student government, student newspaper, Newman Club, Latter-day Saints, Baptist student union, InterCambio club, students with disabilities.

**Athletics. Intramural:** Badminton, basketball, bowling, cross-country, golf, racquetball, sailing, softball, swimming, table tennis, tennis, track and field, volleyball. **Team name:** Vikings.

**Student services.** Adult student services, career counseling, student employment services, financial aid counseling, on-campus daycare, personal counseling, placement for graduates, veterans' counselor. **Physically disabled:** Services for visually, speech, hearing impaired. **Transfer:** College fairs on campus for students transferring to 4-year colleges.

**Contact.** E-mail: reginfo@delmar.edu
Phone: (361) 698-1255 Toll-free number: (800) 652-3357
Fax: (361) 698-1595
Frances Jordan, Assistant Dean of Enrollment Services and Registrar, Del Mar College, 101 Baldwin Boulevard, Corpus Christi, TX 78404-3897

## Eastfield College
**Mesquite, Texas**
www.efc.dcccd.edu
CB code: 6201

- Public 2-year community and liberal arts college
- Commuter campus in small city

**General.** Founded in 1970. Regionally accredited. **Enrollment:** 5,427 degree-seeking undergraduates; 4,369 non-degree-seeking students. **Degrees:** 401 associate awarded. **Location:** One mile from Dallas. **Calendar:** Semester, limited summer session. **Full-time faculty:** 117 total; 30% minority, 39% women. **Part-time faculty:** 458 total; 23% minority, 50% women. **Class size:** 75% < 20, 23% 20-39, 1% 40-49, less than 1% 50-99, less than 1% >100. **Special facilities:** Automotive diagnostic center.

**Student profile.** Among degree-seeking undergraduates, 546 enrolled as first-time, first-year students, 78 transferred in from other institutions.

| | | | |
|---|---|---|---|
| Part-time: | 77% | Women: | 64% |
| Out-of-state: | 1% | 25 or older: | 45% |

**Transfer out. Colleges most students transferred to 2007:** University of Texas-Arlington, University of Texas-Dallas, University of North Texas, Texas A&M-Commerce, Southern Methodist University.

**Basis for selection.** Open admission. Interview recommended for international students.

**High school preparation.** 22 units recommended. Recommended units include English 4, mathematics 3, social studies 1, history 1, science 2, academic electives 5.5. 0.5 health education; 0.5 speech; 1 history, geography or science; 1 technical applications; 1 history or geography recommended.

**2007-2008 Annual costs.** Tuition/fees: $1,170; $2,160 out-of-district; $3,450 out-of-state. Per-credit charge: $39 in-district; $72 out-of-district; $115 out-of-state. Books/supplies: $400. Personal expenses: $935.

**Financial aid. Need-based:** Need-based aid available for part-time students. Work-study available nights, weekends and for part-time students.

**Application procedures. Admission:** No deadline. No application fee. Admission notification on a rolling basis. **Financial aid:** Priority date 5/1; no closing date. FAFSA, institutional form required. Applicants notified on a rolling basis starting 4/15.

**Academics. Special study options:** Cooperative education, distance learning, dual enrollment of high school students, ESL, honors, independent study, weekend college. **Credit/placement by examination:** CLEP, IB, institutional tests. 15 credit hours maximum toward associate degree. **Support services:** GED preparation, learning center, pre-admission summer program, remedial instruction, tutoring.

**Majors. Business:** General, accounting, administrative services, business admin, management information systems, office management, office technology. **Communications technology:** Graphic/printing. **Computer sciences:** General, applications programming, computer science, data processing, networking, programming. **Engineering technology:** CAD/CADD, electrical. **Family/consumer sciences:** Child development. **Foreign languages:** Sign language interpretation. **Health:** Mental health services, substance abuse counseling. **Liberal arts:** Arts/sciences. **Mechanic/repair:** Auto body, automotive, diesel, heating/ac/refrig. **Protective services:** Criminal justice. **Public administration:** Social work.

**Most popular majors.** Business/marketing 8%, engineering/engineering technologies 7%, liberal arts 62%, trade and industry 7%.

**Computing on campus.** 152 workstations in library, computer center. Online library available.

**Student life. Freshman orientation:** Available. Online and on-campus orientations offered. **Policies:** Student code of conduct in effect. **Activities:** Bands, choral groups, dance, drama, music ensembles, musical theater, student government, student newspaper, Fellowship of Christian Athletes, Latter-day Saint student association, multicultural club, Vital Signers, piano club, poetry club, automotive club, jazz dance club.

**Athletics.** NJCAA. **Intercollegiate:** Baseball M, basketball M, golf M, soccer W, volleyball W. **Intramural:** Archery, basketball M, bowling, golf M, gymnastics, tennis, volleyball. **Team name:** Harvesters.

**Student services.** Career counseling, student employment services, health services, personal counseling, placement for graduates, veterans' counselor. **Physically disabled:** Services for visually, speech, hearing impaired. **Transfer:** College fairs on campus for students transferring to 4-year colleges.

**Contact.** E-mail: efc@dcccd.edu
Phone: (972) 860-7100 Fax: (972) 860-8306
Linda Richardson, Dean of Admissions and Testing, Eastfield College, 3737 Motley Drive, Mesquite, TX 75150

---

## El Centro College
**Dallas, Texas**
www.elcentrocollege.edu | CB code: 6199

▶ Public 2-year community college
▶ Commuter campus in very large city

**General.** Founded in 1966. Regionally accredited. **Enrollment:** 5,527 degree-seeking undergraduates; 1,025 non-degree-seeking students. **Degrees:** 532 associate awarded. **ROTC:** Army. **Location:** Downtown. **Calendar:** Semester, limited summer session. **Full-time faculty:** 112 total; 36% minority, 66% women. **Part-time faculty:** 296 total; 40% minority, 55% women. **Class size:** 70% < 20, 27% 20-39, 1% 40-49, 1% 50-99. **Special facilities:**

Outdoor amphitheater, art studios, interior design and fashion design studios, allied health laboratories. **Partnerships:** Formal partnerships with regional CISCO training center, many local businesses, and area high schools.

**Student profile.** Among degree-seeking undergraduates, 43% enrolled in a transfer program, 57% enrolled in a vocational program, 4% already have a bachelor's degree or higher, 1,158 enrolled as first-time, first-year students, 633 transferred in from other institutions.

| | | | |
|---|---|---|---|
| Part-time: | 77% | Hispanic American: | 29% |
| Out-of-state: | 2% | Native American: | 1% |
| Women: | 69% | International: | 3% |
| African American: | 33% | 25 or older: | 52% |
| Asian American: | 4% | | |

**Transfer out. Colleges most students transferred to 2007:** University of Texas at Arlington, University of North Texas, University of Texas at Dallas, Southern Methodist University.

**Basis for selection.** Open admission, but selective for some programs. Specific application requirements for nursing, some allied health, and food and hospitality programs. Interview recommended for international students.

**2007-2008 Annual costs.** Tuition/fees: $1,170; $2,160 out-of-district; $3,450 out-of-state. Per-credit charge: $39 in-district; $72 out-of-district; $115 out-of-state. Books/supplies: $600. Personal expenses: $600.

**Financial aid. Need-based:** Need-based aid available for part-time students. **Additional information:** Interview required for financial aid applicants.

**Application procedures. Admission:** No deadline. No application fee. Application may be submitted online. Admission notification on a rolling basis beginning on or about 6/1. **Financial aid:** Priority date 5/1; no closing date. FAFSA required. Applicants notified on a rolling basis; must reply within 2 week(s) of notification.

**Academics. Special study options:** Accelerated study, combined bachelor's/graduate degree, cooperative education, cross-registration, distance learning, double major, dual enrollment of high school students, ESL, external degree, honors, internships, liberal arts/career combination, teacher certification program. License preparation in nursing, paramedic, radiology. **Credit/placement by examination:** AP, CLEP, IB, institutional tests. 45 credit hours maximum toward associate degree. **Support services:** GED preparation, learning center, reduced course load, remedial instruction, study skills assistance, tutoring.

**Majors. Business:** Accounting, business admin, executive assistant, management information systems. **Computer sciences:** Data processing, information systems, programming. **Education:** Teacher assistance. **Health:** Cardiovascular technology, clinical lab technology, medical radiologic technology/radiation therapy, medical records admin, medical records technology, nursing (RN), respiratory therapy technology, sonography. **Legal studies:** Paralegal. **Liberal arts:** Arts/sciences. **Personal/culinary services:** Baking, chef training. **Science technology:** Biological. **Visual/performing arts:** Fashion design, interior design.

**Most popular majors.** Health sciences 54%, legal studies 12%, liberal arts 17%, personal/culinary services 6%.

**Computing on campus.** 832 workstations in library, computer center, student center. Commuter students can connect to campus network. Online course registration, online library, helpline available.

**Student life. Freshman orientation:** Mandatory. Preregistration for classes offered. **Activities:** Choral groups, drama, music ensembles, musical theater, student government, Phi Theta Kappa, organization of Latin American students, El Centro computer society, international college association, Disabled and Realizing Excellence, teacher education preparatory program, Circle-K, association of black college students.

**Athletics. Intramural:** Basketball, volleyball, weight lifting.

**Student services.** Adult student services, career counseling, services for economically disadvantaged, student employment services, financial aid counseling, health services, minority student services, personal counseling, placement for graduates, veterans' counselor. **Physically disabled:** Services for visually, hearing impaired. **Transfer:** Transfer adviser, college fairs on campus for students transferring to 4-year colleges.

**Contact.** E-mail: rgarza@dcccd.edu
Phone: (214) 860-2311 Fax: (214) 860-2233
Rebecca Garza, Director of Admissions/Registrar, El Centro College, 801 Main Street, Dallas, TX 75202

## El Paso Community College

**El Paso, Texas**
www.epcc.edu

CB member
CB code: 6203

- ◆ Public 2-year community college
- ◆ Commuter campus in very large city

**General.** Founded in 1969. Regionally accredited. Comprised of five campuses in greater El Paso. **Enrollment:** 23,509 degree-seeking undergraduates. **Degrees:** 1,838 associate awarded. **ROTC:** Army. **Location:** 240 miles from Albuquerque, New Mexico. **Calendar:** Semester, extensive summer session. **Full-time faculty:** 391 total; 54% minority, 52% women. **Part-time faculty:** 1,017 total; 64% minority, 48% women. **Special facilities:** Advanced technology center. **Partnerships:** Formal partnerships with local high schools for Tech Prep programs and with hospitals for health programs.

**Student profile.** Among degree-seeking undergraduates, 4,221 enrolled as first-time, first-year students.

| | | | |
|---|---|---|---|
| Out-of-state: | 6% | 25 or older: | 37% |

**Transfer out. Colleges most students transferred to 2007:** University of Texas at El Paso, New Mexico State University.

**Basis for selection.** Open admission, but selective for some programs. Certain reading level requirements and GPA for some health occupations programs with selective admission. Nelson-Denny Reading Test and institutional math test required for admission to health programs. Observes TASP requirements.

**2007-2008 Annual costs.** Tuition/fees: $1,700; $2,442 out-of-state. Per-credit charge: $47 in-state; $71 out-of-state. Per-credit-hour costs listed are for each additional credit-hour beyond one credit-hour for in-state students, and beyond six credit-hours for out-of-state students. Books/supplies: $545. Personal expenses: $1,223.

**Financial aid. Need-based:** Work-study available nights, weekends and for part-time students. **Non-need-based:** Scholarships awarded for academics, athletics.

**Application procedures. Admission:** No deadline. $15 fee. Admission notification on a rolling basis. **Financial aid:** Priority date 5/1; no closing date. FAFSA, institutional form required. Applicants notified on a rolling basis starting 7/1; must reply within 2 week(s) of notification.

**Academics. Special study options:** Cooperative education, cross-registration, distance learning, double major, dual enrollment of high school students, ESL, honors, independent study, internships, teacher certification program, weekend college. License preparation in dental hygiene, nursing, physical therapy, radiology. **Credit/placement by examination:** AP, CLEP, IB, institutional tests. 45 credit hours maximum toward associate degree. **Support services:** GED preparation and test center, learning center, remedial instruction, study skills assistance, tutoring, writing center.

**Majors. Area/ethnic studies:** Women's. **Biology:** General. **Business:** General, accounting, administrative services, business admin, fashion, finance, hospitality/recreation, international, management science, office/clerical, operations, real estate, tourism promotion, tourism/travel. **Communications:** General, journalism. **Communications technology:** General. **Computer sciences:** General, computer science, information systems, programming, systems analysis. **Education:** Elementary, physical, secondary, special, technology/industrial arts. **Engineering:** General. **Engineering technology:** Drafting, electrical. **English:** English lit, speech/rhetoric. **Family/consumer sciences:** Child care, family studies, institutional food production. **Foreign languages:** General, sign language interpretation. **Health:** Clinical lab technology, dental assistant, dental hygiene, dietetics, medical assistant, medical radiologic technology/radiation therapy, medical records technology, mental health services, nursing (RN), optician, physical therapy assistant, predental, premedicine, prepharmacy, preveterinary, respiratory therapy technology, substance abuse counseling, surgical technology. **History:** General. **Legal studies:** Court reporting, paralegal. **Liberal arts:** Arts/sciences. **Math:** General. **Mechanic/repair:** Electronics/electrical, heating/ac/refrig. **Parks/recreation:** Health/fitness. **Personal/culinary services:** Culinary arts. **Physical sciences:** Chemistry, geology, physics. **Protective services:** Corrections, criminal justice, fire safety technology. **Psychology:** General. **Social sciences:** General, political science, sociology. **Visual/performing arts:** Art, cinematography, commercial photography, commercial/advertising art, dramatic, fashion design, interior design, photography.

**Computing on campus.** 2,000 workstations in library, computer center. Wireless network available.

**Student life. Freshman orientation:** Mandatory. **Activities:** Jazz band, choral groups, dance, drama, film society, literary magazine, music ensembles, radio station, student government, student newspaper, TV station,

Phi Theta Kappa, African-American coalition, art student society, architecture club, social science club.

**Athletics.** NJCAA. **Intercollegiate:** Baseball M, softball W. **Intramural:** Basketball, bowling, cross-country, soccer, softball, table tennis, tennis, track and field, volleyball, weight lifting. **Team name:** Tejanos/Tejanas.

**Student services.** Career counseling, student employment services, health services, personal counseling, placement for graduates, veterans' counselor, women's services. **Physically disabled:** Services for visually, speech, hearing impaired. **Transfer:** Transfer adviser, college fairs on campus for students transferring to 4-year colleges.

**Contact.** Phone: (915) 831-2580 Fax: (915) 831-2161
Daryle Hendry, Director of Admissions, El Paso Community College, Box 20500, El Paso, TX 79998

## Everest College: Arlington

**Arlington, Texas**
www.everest-college.com

- ◆ For-profit 2-year business and technical college
- ◆ Commuter campus in large city

**General.** Accredited by ACICS. **Enrollment:** 244 degree-seeking undergraduates. **Degrees:** 182 associate awarded. **Location:** 10 miles from Dallas. **Calendar:** Differs by program. **Full-time faculty:** 6 total. **Part-time faculty:** 32 total.

**Basis for selection.** Open admission, but selective for some programs. High school record important.

**2007-2008 Annual costs.** Tuition/fees: $15,360. Per-credit charge: $268. Books/supplies: $680.

**Application procedures. Admission:** No deadline. $25 fee. Application may be submitted online.

**Academics. Credit/placement by examination:** CLEP.

**Majors. Business:** Business admin. **Protective services:** Security management.

**Student life. Freshman orientation:** Mandatory.

**Student services.** Adult student services, career counseling, financial aid counseling, placement for graduates.

**Contact.** E-mail: tevans@cci.edu
Phone: (817) 652-7790 Toll-free number: (888) 741-4270
Fax: (817) 649-6033
Terri Evans, Director of Admissions, Everest College: Arlington, 2801 East Division Street, Suite 250, Arlington, TX 76011

## Frank Phillips College

**Borger, Texas**
www.fpctx.edu

CB code: 6222

- ◆ Public 2-year community and junior college
- ◆ Commuter campus in large town

**General.** Founded in 1948. Regionally accredited. Guaranteed transfer program. Contract training provided on site or at on-campus location for Occupational Safety and Health Administration mandated certification. **Enrollment:** 721 degree-seeking undergraduates; 493 non-degree-seeking students. **Degrees:** 60 associate awarded. **Location:** 60 miles from Amarillo. **Calendar:** Semester, extensive summer session. **Full-time faculty:** 100 total; 2% have terminal degrees. **Part-time faculty:** 100 total; 1% have terminal degrees. **Class size:** 31% < 20, 68% 20-39, 1% 40-49.

**Student profile.** Among degree-seeking undergraduates, 69% enrolled in a transfer program, 31% enrolled in a vocational program, 1% already have a bachelor's degree or higher, 251 enrolled as first-time, first-year students, 30 transferred in from other institutions.

| | | | |
|---|---|---|---|
| Part-time: | 46% | Native American: | 1% |
| Out-of-state: | 4% | International: | 3% |
| Women: | 55% | 25 or older: | 32% |
| African American: | 4% | Live on campus: | 20% |
| Hispanic American: | 21% | | |

**Transfer out. Colleges most students transferred to 2007:** West Texas A&M University, Texas A&M University.

**Basis for selection.** Open admission. SAT/ACT, COMPASS, ASSET, TAKS, or ACCUPLACER may be used in lieu of THEA. Veterans receive preferential admission. Texas Success Initiative guidelines followed. **Home-schooled:** Transcript of courses and grades required.

**2007-2008 Annual costs.** Tuition/fees: $2,296; $2,926 out-of-district; $3,136 out-of-state. Per-credit charge: $64 in-district; $106 out-of-district; $120 out-of-state. Room/board: $3,820. Books/supplies: $605. Personal expenses: $985.

**Financial aid. Need-based:** Need-based aid available for part-time students. Work-study available nights, weekends and for part-time students. **Non-need-based:** Scholarships awarded for academics, athletics, music/drama, state residency. **Additional information:** Some Texas fire department and police department personnel, active duty military personnel, children of military missing in action may qualify for reduced or waived tuition. Out-of-state tuition waived for students living in Oklahoma counties adjacent to Texas.

**Application procedures. Admission:** No deadline. No application fee. Application may be submitted online. Admission notification on a rolling basis. **Financial aid:** FAFSA, institutional form required. Applicants notified on a rolling basis; must reply within 2 week(s) of notification.

**Academics. Special study options:** Cooperative education, distance learning, dual enrollment of high school students, internships, liberal arts/career combination. License preparation in nursing. **Credit/placement by examination:** AP, CLEP, IB, institutional tests. 24 credit hours maximum toward associate degree. **Support services:** GED preparation and test center, learning center, pre-admission summer program, reduced course load, remedial instruction, study skills assistance, tutoring, writing center.

**Majors. Agriculture:** Equestrian studies, farm/ranch, range science. **Biology:** General. **Business:** General, accounting, administrative services, business admin. **Computer sciences:** General. **Construction:** Pipefitting, power transmission. **Education:** General, elementary, secondary. **Engineering technology:** Manufacturing. **English:** English lit. **Health:** Medical secretary. **History:** General. **Legal studies:** Legal secretary. **Liberal arts:** Arts/sciences. **Math:** General. **Philosophy/religion:** Philosophy. **Physical sciences:** Chemistry, physics. **Psychology:** General. **Social sciences:** General, political science, sociology.

**Computing on campus.** 59 workstations in dormitories, library, student center. Dormitories wired for high-speed internet access.

**Student life. Freshman orientation:** Mandatory. Preregistration for classes offered. Session available at start of and during semester. **Housing:** Single-sex dorms, apartments, substance-free housing available. $135 fully refundable deposit, deadline 8/1. **Activities:** Choral groups, drama, music ensembles, student government, rodeo club, agriculture club, Phi Theta Kappa, cosmetology club, licensed vocational nursing club, Circle K, business club, art club, computer club, Future Educators Association.

**Athletics.** NJCAA. **Intercollegiate:** Baseball M, basketball, softball W, volleyball W. **Intramural:** Basketball, bowling, cheerleading, racquetball, softball, table tennis, tennis, volleyball. **Team name:** Plainsmen.

**Student services.** Adult student services, alcohol/substance abuse counseling, career counseling, services for economically disadvantaged, student employment services, financial aid counseling, personal counseling, placement for graduates, veterans' counselor. **Transfer:** Re-entry adviser, pre-admission transcript evaluation for new students. Transfer adviser, college fairs on campus for students transferring to 4-year colleges.

**Contact.** E-mail: admissions@fpctx.edu
Phone: (806) 457-4200 ext. 740 Fax: (806) 457-4225
Beth Raper, Director of Enrollment Management, Frank Phillips College, Box 5118, Borger, TX 79008-5118

---

## Galveston College
### Galveston, Texas
www.gc.edu                                    CB code: 6255

- Public 2-year community college
- Commuter campus in small city

**General.** Founded in 1967. Regionally accredited. **Enrollment:** 2,044 degree-seeking undergraduates. **Degrees:** 195 associate awarded. **Location:** 50 miles from Houston. **Calendar:** Semester, limited summer session. **Full-time faculty:** 37 total; 22% have terminal degrees, 22% minority, 43% women. **Part-time faculty:** 96 total; 2% have terminal degrees, 24% minority, 53% women. **Class size:** 76% < 20, 24% 20-39, less than 1% >100. **Special facilities:** Center for health related technology. **Partnerships:** Formal partnerships with UTMB in health career profession.

**Student profile.** Among degree-seeking undergraduates, 60% enrolled in a transfer program, 40% enrolled in a vocational program, 285 enrolled as first-time, first-year students, 317 transferred in from other institutions.

| | | | |
|---|---|---|---|
| Part-time: | 70% | Asian American: | 3% |
| Out-of-state: | 4% | Hispanic American: | 25% |
| Women: | 65% | International: | 2% |
| African American: | 20% | 25 or older: | 44% |

**Transfer out. Colleges most students transferred to 2007:** University of Houston-Clear Lake.

**Basis for selection.** Open admission, but selective for some programs. Health occupations majors have special admission requirements.

**2007-2008 Annual costs.** Tuition/fees: $1,414; $2,314 out-of-state. Per-credit charge: $30 in-state; $60 out-of-state. Books/supplies: $876. Personal expenses: $1,380.

**2006-2007 Financial aid.** All financial aid based on need. 77% of total undergraduate aid awarded as scholarships/grants, 23% as loans/jobs. Need-based aid available for part-time students. Work-study available for part-time students.

**Application procedures. Admission:** No deadline. No application fee. Application must be submitted on paper. Admission notification on a rolling basis. **Financial aid:** Priority date 6/9; no closing date. FAFSA required. Applicants notified on a rolling basis starting 6/1.

**Academics. Special study options:** Cooperative education, distance learning, dual enrollment of high school students, independent study, internships, weekend college. License preparation in dental hygiene, nursing, paramedic, radiology, real estate. **Credit/placement by examination:** CLEP. 24 credit hours maximum toward associate degree. **Support services:** GED test center, learning center, remedial instruction, tutoring.

**Majors. Biology:** General, marine. **Business:** Accounting, administrative services, business admin, entrepreneurial studies, marketing, office/clerical. **Computer sciences:** General, computer science, information systems, programming. **Education:** Elementary, physical. **Engineering:** General. **English:** English lit, speech/rhetoric. **Family/consumer sciences:** Family studies. **Foreign languages:** Spanish. **Health:** EMT paramedic, health care admin, medical radiologic technology/radiation therapy, medical records technology, medical secretary, nuclear medical technology, nursing (RN), predental, premedicine, preveterinary. **History:** General. **Interdisciplinary:** Biological/physical sciences. **Legal studies:** Prelaw. **Liberal arts:** Arts/sciences. **Math:** General. **Personal/culinary services:** Culinary arts. **Physical sciences:** Chemistry, geology, physics. **Protective services:** Criminal justice, fire safety technology. **Psychology:** General. **Public administration:** Social work. **Social sciences:** Anthropology, economics, geography, political science, sociology. **Visual/performing arts:** Art, dramatic.

**Computing on campus.** 170 workstations in library, computer center, student center. Commuter students can connect to campus network. Online library, helpline, wireless network available.

**Student life. Freshman orientation:** Mandatory. Preregistration for classes offered. **Housing:** Special housing for scholarship athletes. **Activities:** Choral groups, drama, music ensembles, student government, student newspaper, student activities council, journalism club, African American club, Campus Crusade for Christ, Hispanic student organization, single parents organization, environmental awareness club, Phi Theta Kappa, nuclear medicine club, student nurses association.

**Athletics.** NJCAA. **Intercollegiate:** Baseball M, softball W, volleyball W. **Intramural:** Bowling, golf, tennis. **Team name:** Whitecaps.

**Student services.** Career counseling, student employment services, on-campus daycare, personal counseling, placement for graduates, veterans' counselor. **Physically disabled:** Services for visually, speech, hearing impaired. **Transfer:** Transfer adviser, college fairs on campus for students transferring to 4-year colleges.

**Contact.** E-mail: blowery@gc.edu
Phone: (409) 944-1230 Fax: (409) 944-1501
Brian Lowery, Director of Admissions/Registrar, Galveston College, 4015 Avenue Q, Galveston, TX 77550-7447

---

## Grayson County College
### Denison, Texas
www.grayson.edu                              CB code: 6254

- Public 2-year community and technical college
- Commuter campus in large town

**General.** Founded in 1963. Regionally accredited. **Enrollment:** 3,786 degree-seeking undergraduates. **Degrees:** 375 associate awarded. **Location:** 7 miles from Sherman, 75 miles from Dallas. **Calendar:** Semester, limited summer session. **Full-time faculty:** 44 total. **Part-time faculty:** 131 total. **Special facilities:** Vineyard.

**Student profile.**

Out-of-state: 2%    Live on campus: 6%

**Basis for selection.** Open admission, but selective for some programs. Special requirements for nursing, radiology, medical lab tech, vocational nursing certificate, EMT/paramedic programs. Observes TASP requirements. **Homeschooled:** Transcript of courses and grades required.

**2008-2009 Annual costs.** Tuition/fees (projected): $1,344. Per-credit charge: $43. Room/board: $3,556. Books/supplies: $594. Personal expenses: $1,412.

**Financial aid. Need-based:** Need-based aid available for part-time students. **Additional information:** Short term loans available.

**Application procedures. Admission:** No deadline. No application fee. Application must be submitted online. Admission notification on a rolling basis. Priority date for receipt of applications vary. Dates are published in the schedule of classes. **Financial aid:** Priority date 6/1; no closing date. FAFSA required. Applicants notified on a rolling basis; must reply within 5 week(s) of notification.

**Academics. Special study options:** Combined bachelor's/graduate degree, distance learning, dual enrollment of high school students, ESL, honors. Bachelor's degree programs available on campus. License preparation in nursing, paramedic, radiology, real estate. **Credit/placement by examination:** AP, CLEP, institutional tests. 31 credit hours maximum toward associate degree. **Support services:** GED preparation and test center, learning center, reduced course load, remedial instruction, study skills assistance, tutoring.

**Majors. Biology:** General. **Business:** General, accounting, administrative services, office management, office technology, office/clerical. **Computer sciences:** General, programming. **Education:** General, elementary, secondary. **Engineering:** General. **Engineering technology:** Drafting, electrical. **English:** Speech/rhetoric. **Health:** Clinical lab science, EMT paramedic, nursing (RN), substance abuse counseling. **Liberal arts:** Arts/sciences. **Math:** General. **Mechanic/repair:** Auto body, electronics/electrical, heating/ac/refrig. **Physical sciences:** Chemistry, geology, physics. **Protective services:** Law enforcement admin, police science. **Psychology:** General. **Social sciences:** Sociology. **Visual/performing arts:** Art, commercial/advertising art, dramatic.

**Computing on campus.** 150 workstations in library, computer center. Dormitories wired for high-speed internet access and linked to campus network. Online course registration, online library, wireless network available.

**Student life. Freshman orientation:** Available. Preregistration for classes offered. Web-based program. Dates vary. **Housing:** Coed dorms, special housing for disabled, substance-free housing available. $175 fully refundable deposit. **Activities:** Jazz band, choral groups, drama, music ensembles, student government, student newspaper.

**Athletics.** NJCAA. **Intercollegiate:** Baseball M, basketball, softball W. **Intramural:** Baseball M, basketball, softball W. **Team name:** Vikings.

**Student services.** Adult student services, career counseling, services for economically disadvantaged, financial aid counseling, personal counseling, veterans' counselor. **Physically disabled:** Services for visually, speech, hearing impaired. **Transfer:** College fairs on campus for students transferring to 4-year colleges.

**Contact.** Phone: (903) 465-8604 Fax: (903) 463-8758
Kim Faris, Director of Admissions and Records, Grayson County College, 6101 Grayson Drive, Denison, TX 75020

## Hallmark College of Aeronautics
**San Antonio, Texas**
**www.hallmarkcollege.edu**
CB code: 3166

- For-profit 2-year technical college
- Commuter campus in very large city
- Interview required

**General.** Accredited by ACCSCT. Located at San Antonio International Airport. **Enrollment:** 196 degree-seeking undergraduates. **Degrees:** 90 associate awarded. **Calendar:** Continuous, extensive summer session. **Full-time faculty:** 8 total. **Part-time faculty:** 8 total.

**Student profile.**

Out-of-state: 3%    25 or older: 49%

**Transfer out. Colleges most students transferred to 2007:** Texas State Technical College, Palo Alto College.

**Basis for selection.** Aviation entrance test and interview required. **Homeschooled:** Transcript of courses and grades required.

**2007-2008 Annual costs.** Tuition for combined associate program in airframe technology or powerplant technology: $21,915. Tuition for diploma programs ranges from $12,181 to $17,384. Costs include books, equipment and supplies. Required fees: $200. Registration fee: $100. Course fees vary. International students pay additional 8%.

**Application procedures. Admission:** No deadline. $110 fee. Admission notification on a rolling basis. **Financial aid:** No deadline. FAFSA required. Applicants notified on a rolling basis.

**Academics. Special study options:** Accelerated study, honors, liberal arts/career combination. License preparation in aviation. **Credit/placement by examination:** AP, CLEP. 49 credit hours maximum toward associate degree. **Support services:** Tutoring.

**Majors. Mechanic/repair:** Aircraft, aircraft powerplant, avionics.

**Computing on campus.** Online library available.

**Student life. Freshman orientation:** Mandatory.

**Student services.** Career counseling, student employment services, financial aid counseling, placement for graduates. **Transfer:** Pre-admission transcript evaluation for new students.

**Contact.** E-mail: slava.ross@hallmarkcollege.edu
Phone: (210) 826-1000 Toll-free number: (888) 656-9300
Fax: (210) 826-3707
Slava Ross, Director of Admissions, Hallmark College of Aeronautics, 8901 Wetmore Road, San Antonio, TX 78230

## Hallmark College of Technology
**San Antonio, Texas**
**www.hallmarkcollege.com**
CB code: 2307

- For-profit 2-year business and technical college
- Commuter campus in very large city
- Interview required

**General.** Founded in 1969. Accredited by ACCSCT. Additional campus focusing on aeronautics (known as Hallmark Institute of Aeronautics) located on property of San Antonio Airport. **Enrollment:** 484 degree-seeking undergraduates. **Degrees:** 258 associate awarded. **Location:** 5 miles from San Antonio, 80 miles from Austin. **Calendar:** Continuous, extensive summer session. **Full-time faculty:** 15 total. **Part-time faculty:** 26 total.

**Student profile.** Among degree-seeking undergraduates, 100% enrolled in a vocational program, 7% already have a bachelor's degree or higher.

**Basis for selection.** Standardized test scores, interview important. High school diploma or GED required. **Homeschooled:** Transcript of courses and grades required.

**2008-2009 Annual costs.** Costs for associate programs range from $17,500 to $26,985; additional registration fee $110 for all programs.

**Application procedures. Admission:** No deadline. $110 fee. Admission notification on a rolling basis. **Financial aid:** No deadline. FAFSA required. Applicants notified on a rolling basis.

**Academics. Special study options:** Accelerated study. License preparation in aviation. **Credit/placement by examination:** AP, CLEP. 36 credit hours maximum toward associate degree. **Support services:** Tutoring.

**Majors. Business:** Office technology. **Computer sciences:** Networking. **Engineering technology:** Electrical. **Health:** Medical assistant.

**Most popular majors.** Business/marketing 29%, computer/information sciences 25%, engineering/engineering technologies 28%, health sciences 17%.

**Computing on campus.** 193 workstations in library, computer center. Online library, wireless network available.

**Student life. Freshman orientation:** Mandatory. **Activities:** Student newspaper.

**Student services.** Career counseling, student employment services, financial aid counseling, placement for graduates. **Transfer:** Pre-admission transcript evaluation for new students.

**Contact.** E-mail: sross@hallmarkcollege.com
Phone: (210) 690-9000 Toll-free number: (800) 880-6600
Fax: (210) 697-8225
Sonia Ross, Director of Admissions, Hallmark College of Technology, 10401 IH 10 West, San Antonio, TX 78230-1737

## Hill College
### Hillsboro, Texas
www.hillcollege.edu CB code: 6285

- Public 2-year community and junior college
- Commuter campus in small town

**General.** Founded in 1923. Regionally accredited. **Enrollment:** 3,544 degree-seeking undergraduates. **Degrees:** 225 associate awarded. **Location:** 64 miles from Dallas. **Calendar:** Semester, limited summer session. **Full-time faculty:** 73 total. **Part-time faculty:** 134 total. **Special facilities:** History complex including gun museum and Civil War research center.

### Student profile.

Out-of-state: 1% Live on campus: 14%

**Transfer out. Colleges most students transferred to 2007:** Tarleton State University, Tarrant County Junior College, University of Texas at Arlington.

**Basis for selection.** Open admission, but selective for some programs. Special requirements for nursing program. Observes TASP guidelines. THEA Test or Approved State Alternative Test required for academic students unless exempted by state. **Homeschooled:** Transcript of courses and grades required.

**2007-2008 Annual costs.** Tuition/fees: $1,560; $1,950 out-of-district; $2,350 out-of-state. Room/board: $2,800. Books/supplies: $2,000. Personal expenses: $1,440.

**2007-2008 Financial aid. Need-based:** 98% of total undergraduate aid awarded as scholarships/grants, 2% as loans/jobs. Need-based aid available for part-time students. Work-study available for part-time students. **Non-need-based:** Scholarships awarded for academics, athletics, music/drama.

**Application procedures. Admission:** No deadline. No application fee. Application must be submitted on paper. Admission notification on a rolling basis. **Financial aid:** Priority date 7/1; no closing date. FAFSA, institutional form required. Applicants notified on a rolling basis.

**Academics. Special study options:** Combined bachelor's/graduate degree, cooperative education, distance learning, dual enrollment of high school students, honors, independent study, internships, liberal arts/career combination. Bachelor's degree programs available on campus. **Credit/placement by examination:** AP, CLEP. 24 credit hours maximum toward associate degree. **Support services:** GED test center, learning center, reduced course load, remedial instruction, study skills assistance, tutoring.

**Majors. Agriculture:** Business. **Biology:** General, botany. **Business:** Administrative services, business admin, office management, office technology, office/clerical, real estate. **Communications:** General, journalism. **Computer sciences:** General, applications programming, computer science, data processing, programming. **Education:** General. **Engineering:** General. **Engineering technology:** Drafting, electrical, robotics. **English:** English lit. **Family/consumer sciences:** Institutional food production. **Foreign languages:** General. **Health:** Licensed practical nurse. **Interdisciplinary:** Biological/physical sciences. **Legal studies:** Prelaw. **Liberal arts:** Arts/sciences. **Math:** General. **Mechanic/repair:** Auto body, heating/ac/refrig. **Parks/recreation:** Health/fitness. **Physical sciences:** Chemistry, geology, physics. **Protective services:** Criminal justice, fire services admin, law enforcement admin, police science, security services. **Psychology:** General. **Visual/performing arts:** General, art, commercial/advertising art.

**Most popular majors.** Business/marketing 11%, education 14%, engineering/engineering technologies 6%, liberal arts 43%.

**Computing on campus.** 65 workstations in library, computer center. Online library, helpline available.

**Student life. Freshman orientation:** Mandatory. Preregistration for classes offered. **Housing:** Single-sex dorms, substance-free housing available. $50 deposit. International students must live in dormitories. **Activities:** Bands,

choral groups, drama, film society, music ensembles, student government, Circle K, Young Democrats, Young Republicans, Baptist Student Union, student council.

**Athletics.** NJCAA. **Intercollegiate:** Baseball M, basketball, soccer W, softball W, volleyball W. **Intramural:** Volleyball.

**Student services.** Adult student services, career counseling, services for economically disadvantaged, student employment services, financial aid counseling, personal counseling, placement for graduates, veterans' counselor. **Physically disabled:** Services for visually, speech, hearing impaired. **Transfer:** Transfer adviser, college fairs on campus for students transferring to 4-year colleges.

**Contact.** Phone: (254) 582-2555 Fax: (254) 582-7591
Pat Davis, Director of Admissions, Hill College, Box 619, Hillsboro, TX 76645

## Houston Community College System
### Houston, Texas
www.hccs.edu CB code: 0929

- Public 2-year community college
- Commuter campus in very large city

**General.** Founded in 1971. Regionally accredited. Multicampus system. Students may attend campus of choice. College system manages cable television channel with production facilities. **Enrollment:** 29,537 degree-seeking undergraduates. **Degrees:** 2,190 associate awarded. **ROTC:** Army, Air Force. **Calendar:** Semester, extensive summer session. **Full-time faculty:** 821 total; 42% minority, 51% women. **Part-time faculty:** 2,499 total; 55% minority, 50% women. **Partnerships:** Formal partnerships with local high schools for tech-prep and school-to-work programs; contract training agreements with industry.

**Transfer out. Colleges most students transferred to 2007:** University of Houston-Central, University of Texas-Austin, Texas A&M College Station, University of Houston-Downtown.

**Basis for selection.** Open admission, but selective for some programs. High school transcript, assessment, personal interview required for admission to some health programs. According to Texas state law, students must take TASP (Texas Academic Skills Program) test or TASP alternative. Some students may qualify for TASP exemptions. International students must demonstrate English proficiency by taking TASP (or accepted alternative) and CELSA. Interview required for health careers.

**2007-2008 Annual costs.** Tuition/fees: $1,636; $3,256 out-of-district; $3,856 out-of-state.

**2006-2007 Financial aid. Need-based:** Need-based aid available for part-time students. Work-study available nights and weekends.

**Application procedures. Admission:** No deadline. No application fee. Application may be submitted online. **Financial aid:** No deadline. Applicants notified on a rolling basis starting 6/1; must reply within 2 week(s) of notification.

**Academics. Special study options:** Cooperative education, distance learning, dual enrollment of high school students, ESL, honors, independent study, internships, study abroad, weekend college. Alternative teacher certification program. License preparation in aviation, dental hygiene, nursing, occupational therapy, paramedic, physical therapy, radiology, real estate. **Credit/placement by examination:** AP, CLEP, institutional tests. 15 credit hours maximum toward associate degree. **Support services:** GED preparation and test center, learning center, remedial instruction, tutoring.

**Majors. Agriculture:** Horticulture. **Business:** Accounting, administrative services, banking/financial services, business admin, communications, fashion, hotel/motel admin, international, logistics, marketing, operations, real estate, tourism/travel. **Communications technology:** Graphic/printing, radio/tv. **Computer sciences:** General, programming. **Engineering technology:** Computer, construction, drafting, electrical, industrial, water quality. **Family/consumer sciences:** Child care. **Foreign languages:** Sign language interpretation. **Health:** Clinical lab technology, EMT paramedic, histologic assistant, medical radiologic technology/radiation therapy, medical records technology, medical secretary, mental health services, nuclear medical technology, nursing (RN), occupational therapy assistant, physical therapy assistant, respiratory therapy technology. **Legal studies:** Court reporting, paralegal. **Mechanic/repair:** Automotive. **Parks/recreation:** Health/fitness. **Personal/culinary services:** Cosmetic. **Protective services:** Fire safety technology, police science. **Science technology:** Biological, chemical. **Social sciences:** Cartography. **Visual/performing arts:** Commercial photography, commercial/advertising art, fashion design, interior design, music management, music performance, music theory/composition.

**Most popular majors.** Business/marketing 8%, health sciences 14%, liberal arts 63%.

**Computing on campus.** 4,121 workstations in library, computer center. Online course registration, helpline available.

**Student life. Freshman orientation:** Mandatory. Various locations. **Activities:** Drama, international student organizations, literary magazine, student government, student newspaper, TV station, international student association, Vietnamese student association, United Student Council, Black Student Union, Association of Latin American Students, Phi Theta Kappa.

**Athletics. Intramural:** Football (tackle) M.

**Student services.** Alcohol/substance abuse counseling, career counseling, services for economically disadvantaged, student employment services, financial aid counseling, minority student services, on-campus daycare, personal counseling, placement for graduates, veterans' counselor, women's services. **Physically disabled:** Services for visually, speech, hearing impaired. **Transfer:** College fairs on campus for students transferring to 4-year colleges.

**Contact.** Phone: (713) 718-8500 Fax: (713) 718-2111
Mary Lemburg, Registrar, Houston Community College System, 3100 Main, Houston, TX 77266-7517

## Howard College
**Big Spring, Texas**
www.howardcollege.edu   **CB code: 6277**

- Public 2-year community college
- Commuter campus in large town

**General.** Founded in 1945. Regionally accredited. **Enrollment:** 3,192 degree-seeking undergraduates; 137 non-degree-seeking students. **Degrees:** 227 associate awarded. **Location:** 105 miles from Lubbock, 40 miles from Midland. **Calendar:** Semester, limited summer session. **Full-time faculty:** 132 total; 5% have terminal degrees, 12% minority, 54% women. **Part-time faculty:** 109 total; 14% minority, 57% women. **Special facilities:** Rodeo arena, arts center, coliseum.

**Student profile.** Among degree-seeking undergraduates, 30% enrolled in a transfer program, 70% enrolled in a vocational program, 1% already have a bachelor's degree or higher, 343 enrolled as first-time, first-year students, 250 transferred in from other institutions.

| Part-time: | 65% | 25 or older: | 28% |
|---|---|---|---|
| Out-of-state: | 2% | Live on campus: | 8% |
| Women: | 63% | | |

**Transfer out. Colleges most students transferred to 2007:** Texas Tech University, Angelo State University, Tarleton State University, University of Texas-Permian Basin, Texas A&M University.

**Basis for selection.** Open admission, but selective for some programs. Special requirements for health, cosmetology programs. Interview required for dental hygiene, degree and licensed vocational nursing, cosmetology programs.

**2007-2008 Annual costs.** Tuition/fees: $1,664; $2,084 out-of-district; $2,784 out-of-state. Room/board: $3,400. Books/supplies: $800. Personal expenses: $3,220.

**Financial aid. Need-based:** Need-based aid available for part-time students. Work-study available for part-time students. **Non-need-based:** Scholarships awarded for academics, art, athletics, leadership, music/drama.

**Application procedures. Admission:** No deadline. No application fee. Admission notification on a rolling basis. **Financial aid:** Priority date 4/1; no closing date. FAFSA, institutional form required. Applicants notified on a rolling basis starting 7/15; must reply within 2 week(s) of notification.

**Academics. Special study options:** Cooperative education, cross-registration, distance learning, dual enrollment of high school students, ESL, liberal arts/career combination, weekend college. License preparation in dental hygiene, nursing, occupational therapy, paramedic, physical therapy, radiology, real estate. **Credit/placement by examination:** CLEP, institutional tests. 18 credit hours maximum toward associate degree. **Support services:** GED preparation and test center, learning center, pre-admission summer program, reduced course load, remedial instruction, study skills assistance, tutoring, writing center.

**Majors. Agriculture:** General, business. **Biology:** General. **Business:** General, accounting, office/clerical. **Communications:** Journalism. **Computer**

**sciences:** General. **Education:** General. **English:** English lit. **Family/consumer sciences:** Child care. **Foreign languages:** General, sign language interpretation. **Health:** Athletic training, dental hygiene, dental lab technology, EMT ambulance attendant, medical assistant, medical records admin, medical records technology, nursing (RN), physical therapy assistant, predental, premedicine, respiratory therapy technology, substance abuse counseling. **Legal studies:** Paralegal. **Liberal arts:** Arts/sciences. **Math:** General. **Parks/recreation:** Health/fitness. **Physical sciences:** Chemistry, physics. **Protective services:** Corrections, forensics, law enforcement admin. **Psychology:** General. **Social sciences:** General. **Visual/performing arts:** General, art, dramatic.

**Most popular majors.** Business/marketing 11%, computer/information sciences 6%, health sciences 16%, liberal arts 59%.

**Computing on campus.** 100 workstations in dormitories, library, computer center. Dormitories wired for high-speed internet access and linked to campus network. Commuter students can connect to campus network. Online course registration, online library, helpline, wireless network available.

**Student life. Freshman orientation:** Available. Preregistration for classes offered. **Housing:** Single-sex dorms, substance-free housing available. **Activities:** Bands, choral groups, dance, drama, music ensembles, musical theater, student government.

**Athletics. NJCAA. Intercollegiate:** Baseball M, basketball, cheerleading, rodeo, softball W. **Intramural:** Basketball, bowling, golf, handball, racquetball, softball, table tennis, tennis, volleyball. **Team name:** Hawks.

**Student services.** Adult student services, career counseling, services for economically disadvantaged, student employment services, financial aid counseling, health services, on-campus daycare, personal counseling, placement for graduates, veterans' counselor. **Physically disabled:** Services for hearing impaired. **Transfer:** Transfer adviser, college fairs on campus for students transferring to 4-year colleges.

**Contact.** E-mail: dmerrick@howardcollege.edu
Phone: (432) 264-5000 Fax: (432) 264-5604
Donna Merrick, Registrar, Howard College, 1001 Birdwell Lane, Big Spring, TX 79720

## ITT Technical Institute: Arlington
**Arlington, Texas**
www.itt-tech.edu   **CB code: 3572**

- For-profit 2-year technical college
- Commuter campus in large city

**General.** Founded in 1982. Accredited by ACICS. **Location:** 11 miles from Fort Worth, 18 miles from Dallas. **Calendar:** Quarter.

**Annual costs/financial aid.** Tuition varies by program, $260-$368 per credit hour.

**Contact.** Phone: (817) 794-5100
Director of Recruitment, 551 Ryan Plaza Drive, Arlington, TX 76011

## ITT Technical Institute: Austin
**Austin, Texas**
www.itt-tech.edu   **CB code: 2692**

- For-profit 2-year technical college
- Commuter campus in large city

**General.** Accredited by ACICS. **Calendar:** Quarter.

**Annual costs/financial aid.** Tuition varies by program, $260-$368 per credit hour.

**Contact.** Phone: (512) 467-6800
Director of Recruitment, 6330 Highway 290 East, Austin, TX 78723

## ITT Technical Institute: Houston
**Houston, Texas**
www.itt-tech.edu   **CB code: 3573**

- For-profit 2-year technical college
- Commuter campus in very large city

**General.** Founded in 1983. Accredited by ACICS. **Calendar:** Quarter.

**Annual costs/financial aid.** Tuition varies by program, $260-$368 per credit hour.

**Contact.** Phone: (713) 952-2294
Director of Recruitment, 2950 South Gessner, Houston, TX 77063-3751

## ITT Technical Institute: Houston North
Houston, Texas
www.itt-tech.edu                        CB code: 2712

- For-profit 2-year technical college
- Commuter campus in very large city

**General.** Accredited by ACICS. **Calendar:** Quarter.

**Annual costs/financial aid.** Tuition varies by program, $260-$368 per credit hour.

**Contact.** Phone: (281) 873-0512
Director of Recruitment, 15621 Blue Ash Drive, Houston, TX 77090-5818

## ITT Technical Institute: Houston South
Webster, Texas
www.itt-tech.edu                        CB code: 2715

- For-profit 2-year technical college
- Commuter campus in very large city

**General.** Accredited by ACICS. **Calendar:** Quarter.

**Annual costs/financial aid.** Tuition varies by program, $260-$368 per credit hour.

**Contact.** Director of Recruitment, 1001 Magnolia Avenue, Webster, TX 77598

## ITT Technical Institute: Richardson
Richardson, Texas
www.itt-tech.edu                        CB code: 2747

- For-profit 2-year technical college
- Commuter campus in small city

**General.** Accredited by ACICS. **Location:** 12 miles from Dallas. **Calendar:** Quarter.

**Annual costs/financial aid.** Tuition varies by program, $260-$368 per credit hour.

**Contact.** Phone: (972) 690-9100
Director of Recruitment, 2101 Waterview Parkway, Richardson, TX 75080

## ITT Technical Institute: San Antonio
San Antonio, Texas
www.itt-tech.edu                        CB code: 2328

- For-profit 2-year technical college
- Commuter campus in very large city

**General.** Founded in 1988. Accredited by ACICS. **Location:** 200 miles from Houston, 75 miles from Austin. **Calendar:** Quarter.

**Annual costs/financial aid.** Tuition varies by program, $260-$368 per credit hour.

**Contact.** Phone: (210) 694-4612
Director of Recruitment, 5700 Northwest Parkway, San Antonio, TX 78249

## Jacksonville College
Jacksonville, Texas
www.jacksonville-college.edu             CB code: 6317

- Private 2-year junior and liberal arts college affiliated with Baptist faith
- Commuter campus in large town

**General.** Founded in 1899. Regionally accredited. Owned and operated by the Baptist Missionary Association of Texas and affiliated with the Southern Baptists of Texas Convention. **Enrollment:** 230 degree-seeking undergraduates. **Degrees:** 31 associate awarded. **Location:** 120 miles from Dallas, 25 miles from Tyler. **Calendar:** Semester, limited summer session. **Full-time faculty:** 13 total. **Part-time faculty:** 15 total. **Class size:** 67% < 20, 32% 20-39, 1% >100.

**Student profile.** Among degree-seeking undergraduates, 100% enrolled in a transfer program.

Out-of-state:               6%       Live on campus:              32%

**Transfer out. Colleges most students transferred to 2007:** University of Texas at Tyler, Stephen F. Austin State University, Dallas Baptist University, East Texas Baptist University.

**Basis for selection.** Open admission. Interview recommended. **Home-schooled:** Must take ACT, SAT, or THEA.

**2007-2008 Annual costs.** Tuition/fees: $6,146. Per-credit charge: $185. Room/board: $2,746. Books/supplies: $910. Personal expenses: $1,310.

**Financial aid. Need-based:** Need-based aid available for part-time students. **Non-need-based:** Scholarships awarded for academics, athletics, leadership, music/drama, religious affiliation, state residency.

**Application procedures. Admission:** Priority date 8/15; no deadline. $15 fee. Application may be submitted online. Admission notification on a rolling basis beginning on or about 1/15. **Financial aid:** Priority date 8/1; no closing date. FAFSA, institutional form required. Applicants notified on a rolling basis.

**Academics. Special study options:** Dual enrollment of high school students. **Credit/placement by examination:** AP, CLEP, institutional tests. **Support services:** Reduced course load, remedial instruction, tutoring.

**Majors. Liberal arts:** Arts/sciences.

**Computing on campus.** 45 workstations in dormitories, library, computer center. Dormitories wired for high-speed internet access and linked to campus network. Commuter students can connect to campus network. Wireless network available.

**Student life. Freshman orientation:** Available. Preregistration for classes offered. **Housing:** Single-sex dorms, apartments available. $80 deposit. **Activities:** Concert band, choral groups, drama, music ensembles, student government, student newspaper, ministerial alliance, mission band.

**Athletics.** NJCAA. **Intercollegiate:** Basketball. **Intramural:** Basketball, football (non-tackle), softball, table tennis, tennis, volleyball. **Team name:** Jaguars.

**Student services.** Campus ministries, career counseling, financial aid counseling, health services, personal counseling. **Transfer:** Transfer adviser, college fairs on campus for students transferring to 4-year colleges.

**Contact.** E-mail: admissions@jacksonville-college.edu
Phone: (903) 586-2518 Toll-free number: (800) 256-8522
Fax: (903) 586-0743
Melissa Walles, Director of Admissions, Jacksonville College, 105 B.J. Albritton Drive, Jacksonville, TX 75766-4759

## Kilgore College
Kilgore, Texas
www.kilgore.edu                          CB code: 6341

- Public 2-year community college
- Commuter campus in large town

**General.** Founded in 1935. Regionally accredited. **Enrollment:** 5,150 degree-seeking undergraduates. **Degrees:** 500 associate awarded. **Location:** 120 miles from Dallas, 60 miles from Shreveport, Louisiana. **Calendar:** Semester, extensive summer session. **Full-time faculty:** 135 total. **Part-time faculty:** 127 total. **Class size:** 39% < 20, 59% 20-39, 2% 40-49, less than 1% 50-99. **Special facilities:** Experimental farm, oil museum.

**Student profile.** Among degree-seeking undergraduates, 55% enrolled in a transfer program, 45% enrolled in a vocational program, 2% already have a bachelor's degree or higher, 1,188 enrolled as first-time, first-year students.

Part-time:         48%     25 or older:        31%
Out-of-state:       4%     Live on campus:     10%
Women:             63%

**Transfer out. Colleges most students transferred to 2007:** University of Texas at Tyler, University of North Texas, Stephen F. Austin State University, Texas A&M University, University of Texas at Austin.

**Basis for selection.** Open admission, but selective for some programs. For health occupation programs and some public service programs, standardized test scores, secondary school record, essay used as admissions criteria.

**2007-2008 Annual costs.** Tuition/fees: $1,290; $2,700 out-of-district; $3,660 out-of-state. Per-credit charge: $21 in-district; $68 out-of-district; $100 out-of-state. Room/board: $3,630. Books/supplies: $1,000. Personal expenses: $1,200.

**Financial aid. Need-based:** Need-based aid available for part-time students. Work-study available for part-time students. **Non-need-based:** Scholarships awarded for academics, alumni affiliation, art, athletics, job skills, leadership, music/drama, state residency. **Additional information:** State of Texas grants and loans available for honor graduates with unmet needs and for non-traditional students.

**Application procedures. Admission:** Priority date 8/15; no deadline. No application fee. Application may be submitted online. Admission notification on a rolling basis. **Financial aid:** Priority date 6/1, closing date 7/15. FAFSA, institutional form required. Applicants notified on a rolling basis starting 3/1; must reply within 2 week(s) of notification.

**Academics. Special study options:** Cooperative education, distance learning, dual enrollment of high school students, ESL, internships. License preparation in nursing. **Credit/placement by examination:** AP, CLEP, institutional tests. 14 credit hours maximum toward associate degree. **Support services:** GED preparation and test center, learning center, pre-admission summer program, reduced course load, remedial instruction, study skills assistance, tutoring, writing center.

**Majors. Agriculture:** General. **Biology:** General. **Business:** General, accounting, business admin, e-commerce, executive assistant, management information systems, operations, real estate. **Communications:** General, journalism. **Computer sciences:** General, programming, systems analysis. **Education:** General, art, biology, chemistry, health, health occupations, history, social science. **Engineering:** General, chemical, civil. **Engineering technology:** Civil, drafting, electrical, metallurgical, occupational safety. **English:** English lit. **Family/consumer sciences:** Child care. **Foreign languages:** French, German, Spanish. **Health:** Clinical lab technology, EMT paramedic, medical assistant, medical radiologic technology/radiation therapy, nursing (RN), physical therapy assistant, surgical technology. **History:** General. **Legal studies:** Court reporting, legal secretary, paralegal, prelaw. **Liberal arts:** Arts/sciences. **Math:** General. **Mechanic/repair:** Auto body, automotive, diesel, electronics/electrical. **Parks/recreation:** Health/fitness. **Physical sciences:** Chemistry, physics. **Production:** Machine tool. **Protective services:** Criminal justice, law enforcement admin, police science. **Psychology:** General. **Social sciences:** Sociology. **Visual/performing arts:** Art, commercial photography, commercial/advertising art, dance, dramatic.

**Computing on campus.** 350 workstations in library, computer center, student center. Online course registration available.

**Student life. Freshman orientation:** Mandatory. Preregistration for classes offered. **Housing:** Single-sex dorms available. $100 deposit, deadline 8/15. **Activities:** Bands, choral groups, dance, drama, music ensembles, musical theater, radio station, student government, student newspaper, TV station, church organizations, rodeo club, physical therapy club.

**Athletics.** NJCAA. **Intercollegiate:** Basketball, football (tackle) M. **Intramural:** Badminton, bowling, handball, racquetball, softball, swimming, tennis, volleyball. **Team name:** Rangers.

**Student services.** Career counseling, student employment services, health services, on-campus daycare, personal counseling, placement for graduates, veterans' counselor. **Physically disabled:** Services for visually, speech, hearing impaired. **Transfer:** Pre-admission transcript evaluation for new students. College fairs on campus for students transferring to 4-year colleges.

**Contact.** Phone: (903) 983-8209 Fax: (903) 983-8607
Eloise Ashley, Director of Admissions, Kilgore College, 1100 Broadway, Kilgore, TX 75662-3299

## Lamar Institute of Technology
**Beaumont, Texas**
**www.lit.edu**

- Public 2-year technical college
- Commuter campus in small city

**General.** LIT students have access to Lamar University dormitories, recreational sports center, and library as part of intercomponent service agreement. **Enrollment:** 2,491 degree-seeking undergraduates. **Degrees:** 413 associate awarded. **Location:** 80 miles from Houston. **Calendar:** Semester, limited summer session. **Full-time faculty:** 74 total. **Part-time faculty:** 76 total. **Class size:** 63% < 20, 35% 20-39, 1% 40-49, less than 1% 50-99.

**Student profile.**

| | | | |
|---|---|---|---|
| Out-of-state: | 2% | Live on campus: | 3% |
| 25 or older: | 35% | | |

**Basis for selection.** Open admission, but selective for some programs. Special requirements for various Allied Health programs (Dental Hygiene, Sonography, Health Information Technology, Radiology, Respiratory Care).

**2008-2009 Annual costs.** Tuition/fees: $3,810; $12,090 out-of-state. Per-credit charge: $86 in-state; $362 out-of-state.

**Application procedures. Admission:** No deadline. No application fee. Admission notification on a rolling basis. **Financial aid:** Priority date 4/1; no closing date.

**Academics. Credit/placement by examination:** CLEP, IB, SAT, ACT, institutional tests.

**Majors. Business:** Accounting technology, administrative services, business admin, real estate. **Computer sciences:** General. **Engineering technology:** Computer systems, drafting, GIS, heat/ac/refrig, instrumentation, occupational safety. **Health:** Dental hygiene, EMT paramedic, medical radiologic technology/radiation therapy, medical records technology, respiratory therapy technology, sonography. **Mechanic/repair:** Diesel, industrial. **Personal/culinary services:** Institutional food service. **Production:** Machine tool, welding. **Protective services:** Fire safety technology, forensics. **Public administration:** General. **Science technology:** Chemical.

**Most popular majors.** Business/marketing 17%, computer/information sciences 6%, engineering/engineering technologies 26%, health sciences 26%, science technologies 13%.

**Computing on campus.** 150 workstations in library, computer center. Dormitories wired for high-speed internet access and linked to campus network. Online course registration, online library, wireless network available.

**Student life. Freshman orientation:** Available. Preregistration for classes offered. **Housing:** Single-sex dorms, substance-free housing available. Access to dormitories located on Lamar University campus.

**Student services.** Alcohol/substance abuse counseling, career counseling, services for economically disadvantaged, student employment services, financial aid counseling, health services, placement for graduates, veterans' counselor. **Physically disabled:** Services for visually, hearing impaired.

**Contact.** Phone: (409) 880-8321 Toll-free number: (800) 950-6989 Fax: (409) 880-1711
Vivian Jefferson, Director of Admissions, Lamar Institute of Technology, PO Box 10043, Beaumont, TX 77705

## Lamar State College at Orange
**Orange, Texas**
**www.lsco.edu**
**CB code: 1694**

- Public 2-year junior and liberal arts college
- Commuter campus in small city

**General.** Regionally accredited. **Enrollment:** 1,756 degree-seeking undergraduates; 249 non-degree-seeking students. **Degrees:** 121 associate awarded. **Location:** 92 miles from Houston. **Calendar:** Semester, limited summer session. **Full-time faculty:** 50 total; 12% have terminal degrees, 8% minority, 72% women. **Part-time faculty:** 46 total; 11% have terminal degrees, 9% minority, 72% women. **Partnerships:** Formal partnership with CISCO.

**Student profile.** Among degree-seeking undergraduates, 396 enrolled as first-time, first-year students, 136 transferred in from other institutions.

| | | | |
|---|---|---|---|
| Part-time: | 47% | Women: | 74% |
| Out-of-state: | 9% | 25 or older: | 35% |

**Transfer out. Colleges most students transferred to 2007:** Lamar University, Texas A&M-College Station, Sam Houston State University, Lamar State College-Port Arthur.

**Basis for selection.** Open admission, but selective for some programs. Nursing program competitive; high school record and test scores may be evaluated for admission. Interview required for students without high school diploma or GED, to determine if applicant can benefit from available educational programs.

**High school preparation.** 12 units recommended. Recommended units include English 4, mathematics 3, history 2 and science 3.

**2007-2008 Annual costs.** Tuition/fees: $3,340; $11,680 out-of-state. Per-credit charge: $82 in-state; $360 out-of-state. Books/supplies: $560. Personal expenses: $1,562.

**Financial aid.** All financial aid based on need. Need-based aid available for part-time students. Work-study available for part-time students.

**Application procedures. Admission:** No deadline. No application fee. Admission notification on a rolling basis. **Financial aid:** Priority date 4/1; no closing date. FAFSA, institutional form required. Applicants notified on a rolling basis starting 5/15; must reply within 2 week(s) of notification.

**Academics. Special study options:** Distance learning, dual enrollment of high school students, internships, liberal arts/career combination, teacher certification program. License preparation in nursing, paramedic. **Credit/placement by examination:** CLEP. 15 credit hours maximum toward associate degree. **Support services:** GED test center, learning center, remedial instruction, study skills assistance, tutoring.

**Majors. Biology:** General. **Business:** Accounting technology, administrative services, business admin. **Computer sciences:** General. **Education:** General. **Engineering technology:** Environmental. **Health:** Clinical lab technology, EMT paramedic, medical secretary, nursing (RN). **Liberal arts:** Arts/sciences. **Social sciences:** Sociology.

**Most popular majors.** Business/marketing 23%, health sciences 29%, liberal arts 22%.

**Computing on campus.** 150 workstations in library, computer center, student center. Commuter students can connect to campus network. Online library, helpline, wireless network available.

**Student life. Freshman orientation:** Available. Preregistration for classes offered. **Activities:** Student government.

**Athletics. Intramural:** Basketball, racquetball, volleyball.

**Student services.** Career counseling, financial aid counseling, placement for graduates, veterans' counselor. **Physically disabled:** Services for visually, hearing impaired.

**Contact.** Phone: (409) 882-3364 Fax: (409) 882-3055
Kerry Olson, Director of Admissions and Financial Aid, Lamar State College at Orange, 410 Front Street, Orange, TX 77630

## Lamar State College at Port Arthur
**Port Arthur, Texas**
www.lamarpa.edu                    CB code: 6589

▶ Public 2-year community and technical college
▶ Commuter campus in small city

**General.** Regionally accredited. **Enrollment:** 2,279 degree-seeking undergraduates. **Degrees:** 200 associate awarded. **Location:** 90 miles from Houston. **Calendar:** Semester, limited summer session. **Full-time faculty:** 75 total. **Part-time faculty:** 46 total. **Partnerships:** Formal partnerships with Microsoft and Novell (authorized training center).

**Student profile.**

| | | | |
|---|---|---|---|
| Out-of-state: | 1% | 25 or older: | 39% |

**Transfer out. Colleges most students transferred to 2007:** Lamar University.

**Basis for selection.** Open admission, but selective for some programs. Special requirements for nursing programs only.

**2007-2008 Annual costs.** Tuition/fees: $3,448; $11,788 out-of-state. Books/supplies: $950. Personal expenses: $1,723.

**Financial aid.** All financial aid based on need. Need-based aid available for part-time students. Work-study available nights, weekends and for part-time students.

**Application procedures. Admission:** No deadline. No application fee. Application may be submitted online. Admission notification on a rolling

basis. **Financial aid:** Priority date 4/1; no closing date. FAFSA, institutional form required. Applicants notified on a rolling basis starting 4/15; must reply within 2 week(s) of notification,

**Academics. Special study options:** Cooperative education, cross-registration, distance learning, double major, dual enrollment of high school students, ESL, external degree, honors, independent study, internships, liberal arts/career combination, weekend college. License preparation in nursing. **Credit/placement by examination:** CLEP, institutional tests. SAT used for math placement if submitted. **Support services:** Learning center, pre-admission summer program, reduced course load, remedial instruction, study skills assistance, tutoring.

**Majors. Business:** Accounting, administrative services, business admin. **Computer sciences:** General. **Engineering technology:** Electrical, instrumentation. **Family/consumer sciences:** General, child care. **Health:** Medical secretary, nursing (RN), substance abuse counseling, surgical technology. **Legal studies:** Legal secretary. **Mechanic/repair:** Automotive, heating/ac/refrig. **Personal/culinary services:** Cosmetic. **Protective services:** Criminal justice.

**Computing on campus.** 50 workstations in library, student center. Online course registration, online library available.

**Student life. Freshman orientation:** Available. Preregistration for classes offered. Held 1 day in July and 1 in August. **Activities:** Campus ministries, choral groups, drama, musical theater, student government, association of family and consumer sciences, criminal justice association, Epsilon Delta Phi, legal assistant student school organization, historical society, Phi Theta Kappa.

**Athletics.** NJCAA. **Intercollegiate:** Basketball M, softball W. **Team name:** Seahawks.

**Student services.** Adult student services, career counseling, services for economically disadvantaged, student employment services, financial aid counseling, on-campus daycare, personal counseling, placement for graduates, veterans' counselor. **Physically disabled:** Services for visually, speech, hearing impaired. **Transfer:** Pre-admission transcript evaluation for new students. College fairs on campus for students transferring to 4-year colleges.

**Contact.** E-mail: Connie.Nicholas@lamarpa.edu
Phone: (409) 984-6168 Toll-free number: (800) 477-5872 ext. 6168
Fax: (409) 984-6025
Connie Nicholas, Registrar, Lamar State College at Port Arthur, Box 310, Port Arthur, TX 77641-0310

## Laredo Community College
**Laredo, Texas**
www.laredo.edu          CB member
          CB code: 6362

▶ Public 2-year community college
▶ Commuter campus in large city

**General.** Founded in 1946. Regionally accredited. Two-campus institution. **Enrollment:** 6,914 degree-seeking undergraduates; 917 non-degree-seeking students. **Degrees:** 605 associate awarded. **ROTC:** Army. **Location:** 150 miles from San Antonio, 140 miles from Corpus Christi. **Calendar:** Semester, extensive summer session. **Full-time faculty:** 192 total; 12% have terminal degrees, 72% minority, 40% women. **Part-time faculty:** 108 total; 7% have terminal degrees, 82% minority, 41% women. **Special facilities:** Environmental science center, special collections relating to regional history.

**Student profile.** Among degree-seeking undergraduates, 57% enrolled in a transfer program, 43% enrolled in a vocational program, 1% already have a bachelor's degree or higher, 1,087 enrolled as first-time, first-year students, 142 transferred in from other institutions.

| | | | |
|---|---|---|---|
| Part-time: | 61% | 25 or older: | 32% |
| Out-of-state: | 4% | Live on campus: | 2% |
| Women: | 59% | | |

**Transfer out. Colleges most students transferred to 2007:** Texas A&M International University, University of Texas at San Antonio.

**Basis for selection.** Open admission, but selective for some programs. Special admissions requirements for nursing and allied health programs.

**2007-2008 Annual costs.** Tuition/fees: $1,716; $2,766 out-of-district; $3,816 out-of-state. Per-credit charge: $35 in-district; $70 out-of-district; $105 out-of-state. Room/board: $4,374. Books/supplies: $1,250. Personal expenses: $1,354.

**2006-2007 Financial aid. Need-based:** 90% of total undergraduate aid awarded as scholarships/grants, 10% as loans/jobs.

**Application procedures. Admission:** No deadline. No application fee. Admission notification on a rolling basis. **Financial aid:** Priority date 5/1; no closing date. FAFSA, institutional form required. Applicants notified on a rolling basis.

**Academics.** Mandatory assessment program provides effective educational services for students. **Special study options:** Accelerated study, cooperative education, cross-registration, distance learning, dual enrollment of high school students, ESL, exchange student, honors, liberal arts/career combination, teacher certification program, weekend college. License preparation in nursing, occupational therapy, paramedic, physical therapy, radiology, real estate. **Credit/placement by examination:** AP, CLEP, institutional tests. 30 credit hours maximum toward associate degree. **Support services:** GED preparation and test center, learning center, remedial instruction, tutoring.

**Majors. Agriculture:** General. **Biology:** General, bacteriology, botany, marine. **Business:** General, accounting, administrative services, fashion, finance, marketing, office management, office technology, office/clerical, real estate, sales/distribution. **Communications:** General, broadcast journalism. **Computer sciences:** General, computer science, information systems, programming. **Construction:** Power transmission. **Education:** General, agricultural, art, bilingual, biology, business, chemistry, computer, early childhood, elementary, English, family/consumer sciences, foreign languages, health, history, mathematics, music, physical, physics, reading, Spanish, special, speech. **Engineering:** General, aerospace, agricultural, architectural, electrical, petroleum. **Engineering technology:** Civil. **English:** English lit. **Family/consumer sciences:** General, child care. **Foreign languages:** General, Spanish. **Health:** Clinical lab technology, EMT paramedic, medical assistant, medical radiologic technology/radiation therapy, medical secretary, mental health services, nursing (RN), occupational health, occupational therapy assistant, physical therapy assistant, predental, premedicine, prepharmacy, preveterinary. **History:** General. **Interdisciplinary:** Math/computer science. **Liberal arts:** Arts/sciences. **Math:** General. **Mechanic/repair:** Electronics/electrical. **Philosophy/religion:** Philosophy. **Physical sciences:** Chemistry, geology, physics. **Protective services:** Criminal justice, fire safety technology. **Psychology:** General. **Public administration:** Human services, social work. **Social sciences:** General, economics, political science, sociology. **Visual/performing arts:** Art, dramatic.

**Most popular majors.** Business/marketing 14%, education 16%, health sciences 8%, liberal arts 31%.

**Computing on campus.** 514 workstations in library, computer center. Online course registration, online library, repair service available.

**Student life. Freshman orientation:** Available. Preregistration for classes offered. **Housing:** Coed dorms available. $100 fully refundable deposit. **Activities:** Bands, choral groups, dance, drama, literary magazine, music ensembles, musical theater, opera, student government, student newspaper, symphony orchestra, TV station.

**Athletics.** NJCAA. **Intercollegiate:** Baseball M, tennis, volleyball W. **Intramural:** Baseball M, basketball, bowling, football (tackle) M, golf, handball, racquetball, softball, tennis, volleyball. **Team name:** Palominos.

**Student services.** Alcohol/substance abuse counseling, campus ministries, career counseling, services for economically disadvantaged, student employment services, financial aid counseling, health services, on-campus daycare, personal counseling, placement for graduates, veterans' counselor. **Physically disabled:** Services for visually, speech, hearing impaired. **Transfer:** Transfer adviser, college fairs on campus for students transferring to 4-year colleges.

**Contact.** E-mail: admissions@laredo.edu
Phone: (956) 721-5117 Fax: (956) 721-5493
Felix Gamez, Director of Admissions and Records, Laredo Community College, West End Washington Street, Laredo, TX 78040-4395

---

## Lee College
**Baytown, Texas**
www.lee.edu

CB member
CB code: 6363

◗ Public 2-year community college
◗ Commuter campus in small city

**General.** Founded in 1934. Regionally accredited. **Enrollment:** 5,754 degree-seeking undergraduates. **Degrees:** 538 associate awarded. **Location:** 25 miles from Houston. **Calendar:** Semester, limited summer session. **Full-time faculty:** 160 total. **Part-time faculty:** 200 total.

**Basis for selection.** Open admission, but selective for some programs. Special requirements for allied health programs. TASP guidelines.

**2007-2008 Annual costs.** Tuition/fees: $1,302; $2,052 out-of-district; $3,102 out-of-state. Per-credit charge: $25 in-district; $50 out-of-district; $85 out-of-state. Books/supplies: $600. Personal expenses: $1,248.

**Financial aid. Need-based:** Need-based aid available for part-time students. Work-study available for part-time students. **Non-need-based:** Scholarships awarded for academics, art, athletics, job skills, music/drama.

**Application procedures. Admission:** No deadline. No application fee. Admission notification on a rolling basis. **Financial aid:** Priority date 4/1; no closing date. FAFSA required. Applicants notified on a rolling basis starting 6/1.

**Academics. Special study options:** Cooperative education, distance learning, dual enrollment of high school students, ESL, honors, independent study, internships, weekend college. **Credit/placement by examination:** CLEP, institutional tests. 30 credit hours maximum toward associate degree. **Support services:** GED preparation and test center, learning center, remedial instruction, tutoring.

**Majors. Business:** Accounting, administrative services, business admin, office/clerical. **Communications technology:** Graphic/printing. **Computer sciences:** General, data processing, information systems, programming. **Construction:** Pipefitting. **Engineering technology:** Drafting, electrical. **English:** English lit, technical writing. **Foreign languages:** General. **Health:** EMT paramedic, medical records technology, substance abuse counseling. **Interdisciplinary:** Natural sciences. **Legal studies:** Paralegal. **Liberal arts:** Arts/sciences. **Math:** General. **Mechanic/repair:** Electronics/electrical, heating/ac/refrig. **Parks/recreation:** Health/fitness. **Physical sciences:** General. **Protective services:** Police science. **Visual/performing arts:** Dramatic.

**Computing on campus.** 500 workstations in library, computer center, student center. Online course registration, online library, helpline, wireless network available.

**Student life. Freshman orientation:** Available. Preregistration for classes offered. **Activities:** Bands, choral groups, drama, literary magazine, music ensembles, student government, Baptist student union, awareness club, Phi Theta Kappa, nursing students association, environmental science club, cosmetology club, digital information society, student honors council.

**Athletics.** NJCAA. **Intercollegiate:** Basketball M, tennis W, volleyball W. **Intramural:** Basketball, bowling, football (non-tackle), softball, table tennis, volleyball. **Team name:** Rebels.

**Student services.** Adult student services, career counseling, student employment services, financial aid counseling, personal counseling, placement for graduates, veterans' counselor. **Physically disabled:** Services for hearing impaired. **Transfer:** Transfer adviser for students transferring to 4-year colleges.

**Contact.** E-mail: admissions@lee.edu
Phone: (281) 425-6393 Fax: (281) 425-6831
Becki Griffith, Registrar, Lee College, Box 818, Baytown, TX 77522

---

## Lon Morris College
**Jacksonville, Texas**
www.lonmorris.edu

CB code: 6369

◗ Private 2-year junior and liberal arts college affiliated with United Methodist Church
◗ Residential campus in large town
◗ SAT or ACT (ACT writing optional) required

**General.** Founded in 1873. Regionally accredited. **Enrollment:** 395 degree-seeking undergraduates. **Degrees:** 63 associate awarded. **ROTC:** Army, Naval, Air Force. **Location:** 100 miles from Dallas, 25 miles from Tyler. **Calendar:** Semester, limited summer session. **Full-time faculty:** 27 total; 15% have terminal degrees, 7% minority, 59% women. **Part-time faculty:** 20 total; 45% have terminal degrees, 5% minority, 50% women. **Class size:** 39% < 20, 58% 20-39, 3% 40-49.

**Student profile.** Among degree-seeking undergraduates, 100% enrolled in a transfer program, 209 enrolled as first-time, first-year students, 27 transferred in from other institutions.

| | | | |
|---|---|---|---|
| Part-time: | 14% | Women: | 50% |
| Out-of-state: | 7% | Live on campus: | 76% |

**Transfer out.** 96% of students enrolled in the transfer program go on to 4-year colleges. **Colleges most students transferred to 2007:** Stephen F.

Austin State University, University of Texas at Tyler, Schreiner University, Southwestern University.

**Basis for selection.** School achievement record, minimum GPA of 2.0, recommendation, ACT/SAT scores important. Audition required for choral, drama; interview recommended for academically weak; portfolio recommended for art. **Homeschooled:** Transcript of courses and grades required. **Learning Disabled:** Students with learning disabilities SAT/ACT exempt.

**High school preparation.** 9 units recommended. Recommended units include English 4, social studies 2, science 2 and foreign language 1.

**2007-2008 Annual costs.** Tuition/fees: $10,950. Room/board: $6,000. Books/supplies: $617. Personal expenses: $2,295.

**Financial aid.** All financial aid based on need. Need-based aid available for part-time students. Work-study available nights, weekends and for part-time students.

**Application procedures. Admission:** No deadline. $35 fee, may be waived for applicants with need. Application may be submitted online. Admission notification on a rolling basis. **Financial aid:** Priority date 5/1; no closing date. FAFSA, institutional form required. Applicants notified on a rolling basis starting 2/15; must reply within 2 week(s) of notification.

**Academics. Special study options:** Distance learning, dual enrollment of high school students, ESL, independent study, study abroad. **Credit/placement by examination:** AP, CLEP, IB, SAT, ACT, institutional tests. 30 credit hours maximum toward associate degree. **Support services:** Learning center, pre-admission summer program, reduced course load, remedial instruction, study skills assistance, tutoring, writing center.

**Majors. Biology:** General. **Business:** General, accounting. **Computer sciences:** Computer science. **Education:** General. **English:** English lit, speech/rhetoric. **Foreign languages:** Spanish. **Health:** Predental, premedicine, prenursing, prepharmacy, preveterinary. **History;** General. **Legal studies:** Prelaw. **Liberal arts:** Arts/sciences. **Math:** General. **Philosophy/religion:** Philosophy, religion. **Physical sciences:** Astronomy, chemistry, physics. **Protective services:** Criminal justice. **Psychology:** General. **Social sciences:** General, economics, political science, sociology. **Visual/performing arts:** General, art, art history/conservation, dramatic, music history, music performance, music theory/composition, piano/organ, studio arts, theater design, voice/opera.

**Most popular majors.** Liberal arts 81%, visual/performing arts 19%.

**Computing on campus.** 50 workstations in library, computer center. Dormitories wired for high-speed internet access and linked to campus network. Commuter students can connect to campus network. Online course registration, online library available.

**Student life. Freshman orientation:** Mandatory. Preregistration for classes offered. Held the week before classes begin. Students have opportunity to pay bills and move into dorms. **Housing:** Single-sex dorms, substance-free housing available. $100 deposit. **Activities:** Bands, choral groups, dance, drama, literary magazine, music ensembles, musical theater, ecology club, poetry and literary group, midnight club, Christian service organization, Disciples on Campus, Christian worship group, international club, student senate, LMC Chamber, student activity association.

**Athletics.** NJCAA. **Intercollegiate:** Baseball M, basketball, cheerleading, golf, soccer, softball W. **Intramural:** Baseball M, basketball, football (non-tackle), soccer, softball, swimming, table tennis, tennis, volleyball. **Team name:** Bearcats.

**Student services.** Campus ministries, career counseling, student employment services, financial aid counseling, health services, personal counseling. **Physically disabled:** Services for visually, speech, hearing impaired. **Learning disabled:** Comprehensive services available. **Transfer:** Pre-admission transcript evaluation for new students. Transfer adviser, college fairs on campus for students transferring to 4-year colleges.

**Contact.** E-mail: phorton@lonmorris.edu
Phone: (903) 589-4005 Toll-free number: (800) 259-5753
Fax: (903) 589-4006
Pam Horton, Director of Admissions, Lon Morris College, 800 College Avenue, Jacksonville, TX 75766

## McLennan Community College

Waco, Texas
www.mclennan.edu

CB member
CB code: 6429

- Public 2-year community and junior college
- Commuter campus in small city

**General.** Founded in 1965. Regionally accredited. **Enrollment:** 8,079 degree-seeking undergraduates. **Degrees:** 539 associate awarded. **ROTC:** Air Force. **Location:** 100 miles from Dallas and Austin. **Calendar:** Semester, extensive summer session. **Full-time faculty:** 194 total. **Part-time faculty:** 181 total.

**Basis for selection.** Open admission, but selective for some programs. Admission to health careers programs is competitive. Institution observes TASP guidelines in testing for placement.

**2007-2008 Annual costs.** Tuition/fees: $1,950; $2,310 out-of-district; $3,750 out-of-state. Per-credit charge: $56 in-district; $68 out-of-district; $116 out-of-state. Books/supplies: $725. Personal expenses: $1,596.

**2006-2007 Financial aid. Need-based:** 61% of total undergraduate aid awarded as scholarships/grants, 39% as loans/jobs. **Non-need-based:** Scholarships awarded for athletics.

**Application procedures. Admission:** No deadline. No application fee. Admission notification on a rolling basis. **Financial aid:** Priority date 6/1; no closing date. FAFSA required. Applicants notified on a rolling basis starting 5/1.

**Academics. Special study options:** Distance learning, dual enrollment of high school students, honors, internships, study abroad. **Credit/placement by examination:** CLEP, institutional tests. 24 credit hours maximum toward associate degree. **Support services:** Learning center, reduced course load, remedial instruction, tutoring.

**Majors. Business:** General, accounting, office technology, real estate. **Communications:** General. **Computer sciences:** General, data processing, programming. **Family/consumer sciences:** Child care. **Foreign languages:** Sign language interpretation. **Health:** Clinical lab technology, EMT paramedic, medical radiologic technology/radiation therapy, medical records technology, medical secretary, mental health services, respiratory therapy technology, substance abuse counseling. **Interdisciplinary:** Gerontology. **Legal studies:** Legal secretary, paralegal. **Protective services:** Law enforcement admin.

**Computing on campus.** 425 workstations in library, computer center, student center.

**Student life. Freshman orientation:** Available. **Activities:** Bands, choral groups, dance, drama, music ensembles, musical theater, student government, student newspaper.

**Athletics.** NJCAA. **Intercollegiate:** Baseball M, basketball, golf M, tennis W. **Intramural:** Baseball M, basketball, gymnastics M, softball W, track and field.

**Student services.** Adult student services, career counseling, student employment services, health services, on-campus daycare, personal counseling, placement for graduates, veterans' counselor. **Physically disabled:** Services for visually, hearing impaired. **Transfer:** Transfer adviser, college fairs on campus for students transferring to 4-year colleges.

**Contact.** Phone: (254) 299-8628 Fax: (254) 299-8694
Karen Clark, Director of Admissions, McLennan Community College, 1400 College Drive, Waco, TX 76708

## Midland College

Midland, Texas
www.midland.edu

CB code: 6459

- Public 2-year community college
- Commuter campus in small city
- Interview required

**General.** Founded in 1969. Regionally accredited. **Enrollment:** 3,485 degree-seeking undergraduates; 2,235 non-degree-seeking students. **Degrees:** 8 bachelor's, 390 associate awarded. **Location:** 300 miles from El Paso, 300 miles from Dallas. **Calendar:** Semester, extensive summer session. **Full-time faculty:** 134 total; 14% have terminal degrees, 9% minority, 54% women. **Part-time faculty:** 158 total; 4% have terminal degrees, 10% minority, 55% women. **Class size:** 29% < 20, 71% 20-39.

**Student profile.** Among degree-seeking undergraduates, 41% enrolled in a transfer program, 59% enrolled in a vocational program, 741 enrolled as first-time, first-year students, 469 transferred in from other institutions.

| | | | |
|---|---|---|---|
| Part-time: | 68% | 25 or older: | 60% |
| Out-of-state: | 1% | Live on campus: | 2% |
| Women: | 55% | | |

**Transfer out.** 40% of students enrolled in the transfer program go on to 4-year colleges. **Colleges most students transferred to 2007:** University of Texas of the Permian Basin, Texas A&M University, Angelo State University, West Texas A&M University, Texas Tech University.

**Basis for selection.** Open admission, but selective for some programs. Special requirements for allied health science programs. Observes TASP requirements.

**2007-2008 Annual costs.** Tuition/fees: $1,590; $1,950 out-of-district; $2,820 out-of-state. Per-credit charge: $43 in-district; $55 out-of-district; $94 out-of-state. Additional $48 charge per credit hour for baccalaureate program. Room/board: $3,420. Books/supplies: $666. Personal expenses: $1,450.

**Financial aid.** **Need-based:** Need-based aid available for part-time students. Work-study available for part-time students. **Non-need-based:** Scholarships awarded for academics, athletics, minority status, music/drama, state residency.

**Application procedures.** **Admission:** Priority date 9/1; no deadline. No application fee. Application may be submitted online. Admission notification on a rolling basis. **Financial aid:** Priority date 4/2, closing date 6/1. FAFSA required. Applicants notified on a rolling basis starting 5/15; must reply within 2 week(s) of notification.

**Academics.** **Special study options:** Cooperative education, cross-registration, distance learning, dual enrollment of high school students, ESL, honors, internships, liberal arts/career combination, Washington semester. Bachelor's degree programs available on campus. License preparation in aviation, nursing, paramedic, radiology, real estate. **Credit/placement by examination:** AP, CLEP, IB, institutional tests. 12 credit hours maximum toward associate degree. **Support services:** GED preparation and test center, learning center, reduced course load, remedial instruction, study skills assistance, tutoring, writing center.

**Majors.** **Biology:** General. **Business:** General, accounting, administrative services, business admin, entrepreneurial studies, management information systems, management science, managerial economics, office technology, office/clerical. **Communications:** General, broadcast journalism, journalism. **Communications technology:** Graphic/printing. **Computer sciences:** General, computer graphics, data processing, information systems, programming. **Conservation:** Environmental science. **Education:** Physical, teacher assistance. **Engineering:** Petroleum. **Engineering technology:** Drafting, electrical. **English:** English lit, speech/rhetoric. **Family/consumer sciences:** Child care. **Foreign languages:** General, French, Spanish. **Health:** EMT ambulance attendant, EMT paramedic, medical radiologic technology/radiation therapy, medical records technology, nursing (RN), predental, premedicine, prepharmacy, respiratory therapy technology, substance abuse counseling, veterinary technology/assistant. **History:** General. **Legal studies:** Legal secretary, paralegal, prelaw. **Math:** General. **Mechanic/repair:** Automotive, electronics/electrical, heating/ac/refrig. **Parks/recreation:** Exercise sciences. **Physical sciences:** Chemistry, geology, physics. **Production:** Welding. **Protective services:** Fire safety technology, firefighting, law enforcement admin, police science. **Psychology:** General. **Public administration:** Social work. **Social sciences:** General, economics, political science, sociology. **Transportation:** Airline/commercial pilot. **Visual/performing arts:** Art, dramatic, music performance.

**Computing on campus.** 274 workstations in library, computer center, student center. Dormitories wired for high-speed internet access and linked to campus network. Online course registration, repair service, wireless network available.

**Student life.** **Freshman orientation:** Available. Preregistration for classes offered. 3-hour session held 5 times throughout year. **Housing:** Coed dorms, single-sex dorms, apartments available. $100 deposit, deadline 7/1. **Activities:** Bands, choral groups, drama, literary magazine, music ensembles, student government, student newspaper, several religious groups, ethnic and service clubs, clubs related to majors.

**Athletics.** NJCAA. **Intercollegiate:** Basketball, golf M, softball W. **Intramural:** Basketball, bowling, football (non-tackle), soccer M, table tennis, tennis, volleyball. **Team name:** Chaparrals.

**Student services.** Career counseling, student employment services, on-campus daycare, personal counseling, placement for graduates, veterans' counselor. **Physically disabled:** Services for visually, speech, hearing impaired. **Transfer:** Transfer center, transfer adviser, college fairs on campus for students transferring to 4-year colleges.

**Contact.** E-mail: rhaines@midland.edu
Phone: (432) 685-4502 Fax: (432) 685-4623
Ryan Gibbs, Admissions Director, Midland College, 3600 North Garfield, Midland, TX 79705

## Mountain View College
### Dallas, Texas
www.mvc.dcccd.edu
**CB code: 6438**

♦ Public 2-year community college
♦ Commuter campus in very large city

**General.** Founded in 1970. Regionally accredited. College campus designated as Urban Wildlife Sanctuary by the Humane Society of the United States. **Enrollment:** 6,827 degree-seeking undergraduates. **Degrees:** 322 associate awarded. **ROTC:** Army. **Location:** 8 miles from downtown. **Calendar:** Semester, extensive summer session. **Full-time faculty:** 75 total. **Part-time faculty:** 120 total. **Partnerships:** Formal partnerships with many local businesses and local offices of national/international corporations.

**Student profile.**

| | | | |
|---|---|---|---|
| Out-of-state: | 1% | 25 or older: | 38% |

**Transfer out.** **Colleges most students transferred to 2007:** University of Texas at Arlington, University of North Texas, Texas A&M University.

**Basis for selection.** Open admission. High school students accepted if principal recommends enrollment. Observes TASP guidelines. **Home-schooled:** Transcript of courses and grades required.

**2007-2008 Annual costs.** Tuition/fees: $1,170; $2,160 out-of-district; $3,450 out-of-state. Per-credit charge: $39 in-district; $72 out-of-district; $115 out-of-state. Books/supplies: $1,200. Personal expenses: $1,664.

**Financial aid.** **Need-based:** Need-based aid available for part-time students. Work-study available nights and weekends. **Non-need-based:** Scholarships awarded for academics.

**Application procedures.** **Admission:** No deadline. No application fee. Application may be submitted online. Admission notification on a rolling basis. **Financial aid:** Priority date 5/1; no closing date. FAFSA, institutional form required. Applicants notified on a rolling basis starting 6/1.

**Academics.** **Special study options:** Accelerated study, combined bachelor's/graduate degree, cooperative education, distance learning, double major, dual enrollment of high school students, ESL, honors, independent study, liberal arts/career combination, study abroad, teacher certification program, weekend college. License preparation in aviation, nursing. **Credit/placement by examination:** AP, CLEP, IB, institutional tests. 45 credit hours maximum toward associate degree. Test scores or local assessment must show ability to enroll in college level classes. **Support services:** GED preparation and test center, learning center, reduced course load, remedial instruction, study skills assistance, tutoring, writing center.

**Majors.** **Business:** General, accounting, business admin, e-commerce, executive assistant. **Computer sciences:** Computer science, data processing, LAN/WAN management, networking, programming, web page design. **Education:** Early childhood, kindergarten/preschool, middle. **Engineering technology:** Computer, drafting, electrical. **Health:** Medical records technology. **Interdisciplinary:** Natural sciences. **Liberal arts:** Arts/sciences. **Math:** General. **Production:** Welding. **Protective services:** Criminal justice. **Science technology:** Biological. **Transportation:** Air traffic control, airline/commercial pilot, aviation management. **Visual/performing arts:** Studio arts.

**Computing on campus.** 700 workstations in library, computer center, student center. Commuter students can connect to campus network. Online course registration, online library, helpline, wireless network available.

**Student life.** **Freshman orientation:** Available. Preregistration for classes offered. **Activities:** Concert band, choral groups, dance, drama, international student organizations, music ensembles, musical theater, student government, LULAC, black student club.

**Athletics.** NJCAA. **Intercollegiate:** Baseball M, basketball, soccer, softball W, volleyball W. **Intramural:** Basketball, soccer, tennis, volleyball. **Team name:** Lions.

**Student services.** Adult student services, career counseling, services for economically disadvantaged, student employment services, financial aid counseling, health services, minority student services, personal counseling, placement for graduates, veterans' counselor, women's services. **Physically disabled:** Services for visually, speech, hearing impaired. **Transfer:** Transfer center, transfer adviser, college fairs on campus for students transferring to 4-year colleges.

**Contact.** E-mail: GMH9782@dcccd.edu
Phone: (214) 860-8600 Fax: (214) 860-8570
Linda Osagie, Director of Admissions, Mountain View College, 4849 West Illinois Avenue, Dallas, TX 75211-6599

# Navarro College
## Corsicana, Texas
www.navarrocollege.edu

CB code: 6465

▶ Public 2-year community and junior college
▶ Commuter campus in large town

**General.** Founded in 1946. Regionally accredited. **Enrollment:** 7,560 degree-seeking undergraduates. **Degrees:** 555 associate awarded. **Location:** 50 miles from Dallas. **Calendar:** Semester, extensive summer session. **Full-time faculty:** 137 total. **Part-time faculty:** 351 total. **Special facilities:** Arts, science and technology center; IMAX theater.

**Student profile.** Among degree-seeking undergraduates, 65% enrolled in a transfer program, 35% enrolled in a vocational program, 1,627 enrolled as first-time, first-year students.

| | | | |
|---|---|---|---|
| Part-time: | 55% | Hispanic American: | 13% |
| Out-of-state: | 1% | Native American: | 1% |
| Women: | 63% | International: | 2% |
| African American: | 19% | Live on campus: | 11% |
| Asian American: | 1% | | |

**Basis for selection.** Open admission, but selective for some programs. Special requirements for health professions programs. Portfolio required for art.

**2008-2009 Annual costs.** Tuition/fees (projected): $2,156; $2,906 out-of-district; $3,756 out-of-state. Room/board: $4,265. Books/supplies: $1,268. Personal expenses: $2,193.

**Application procedures. Admission:** No deadline. No application fee. Admission notification on a rolling basis. **Financial aid:** Priority date 6/1; no closing date. FAFSA required. Applicants notified on a rolling basis starting 7/1; must reply within 2 week(s) of notification.

**Academics. Special study options:** Distance learning, dual enrollment of high school students, ESL, honors, independent study, internships, liberal arts/career combination. Bachelor's degree programs available on campus. License preparation in paramedic. **Credit/placement by examination:** CLEP, institutional tests. 30 credit hours maximum toward associate degree. CLEP credit awarded only after successful completion of 12 credit hours in residence. **Support services:** GED preparation and test center, learning center, reduced course load, remedial instruction, tutoring.

**Majors. Agriculture:** Business, farm/ranch. **Biology:** General. **Business:** General, accounting, administrative services, business admin, management information systems, office technology, real estate, taxation. **Communications:** General, broadcast journalism, journalism. **Communications technology:** Graphic/printing. **Computer sciences:** General. **Education:** General, elementary, physical, secondary. **Engineering:** General. **Engineering technology:** Drafting. **English:** English lit, speech/rhetoric. **Family/consumer sciences:** Child care, clothing/textiles. **Foreign languages:** Linguistics. **Health:** EMT paramedic, licensed practical nurse, medical radiologic technology/radiation therapy, predental, premedicine, prepharmacy, preveterinary. **Interdisciplinary:** Biological/physical sciences. **Liberal arts:** Arts/sciences. **Math:** General. **Physical sciences:** Chemistry, physics. **Protective services:** Criminal justice, fire safety technology, police science. **Psychology:** General. **Social sciences:** General. **Transportation:** Aviation. **Visual/performing arts:** Art, commercial/advertising art, dramatic, music performance, voice/opera.

**Computing on campus.** Dormitories wired for high-speed internet access and linked to campus network. Online course registration, wireless network available.

**Student life. Freshman orientation:** Available. Preregistration for classes offered. **Housing:** Single-sex dorms available. $200 deposit. **Activities:** Bands, choral groups, drama, music ensembles, student government, religious organizations, honorary and special interest clubs.

**Athletics.** NJCAA. **Intercollegiate:** Baseball M, basketball M, cheerleading, football (tackle) M, soccer W, softball W, tennis, volleyball W. **Intramural:** Softball. **Team name:** Bulldogs.

**Student services.** Career counseling, student employment services, personal counseling, placement for graduates, veterans' counselor. **Transfer:** Pre-admission transcript evaluation for new students. Transfer adviser, college fairs on campus for students transferring to 4-year colleges.

**Contact.** E-mail: keely.tucker@navarrocollege.edu
Phone: (903) 874-6501 Toll-free number: (800) 628-2776
Fax: (903) 875-7353
David Edwards, Registrar, Navarro College, 3200 West Seventh Avenue, Corsicana, TX 75110

# North Central Texas College
## Gainesville, Texas
www.nctc.edu

CB code: 6245

▶ Public 2-year community college
▶ Commuter campus in large town

**General.** Founded in 1924. Regionally accredited. **Enrollment:** 7,444 degree-seeking undergraduates. **Degrees:** 351 associate awarded. **ROTC:** Air Force. **Location:** 70 miles from Dallas. **Calendar:** Semester, extensive summer session. **Full-time faculty:** 111 total. **Part-time faculty:** 231 total. **Special facilities:** Planetarium, experimental farm, cattle center, horse arena.

**Student profile.**

| | | | |
|---|---|---|---|
| Out-of-state: | 9% | Live on campus: | 3% |
| 25 or older: | 40% | | |

**Basis for selection.** Open admission, but selective for some programs. Special requirements for some health professions programs. Observes TASP guidelines.

**High school preparation.** 16 units recommended. Recommended units include English 4, mathematics 2, social studies 2 and science 2.

**2007-2008 Annual costs.** Tuition/fees: $1,290; $2,160 out-of-district; $3,210 out-of-state. Per-credit charge: $34 in-district; $63 out-of-district; $98 out-of-state. Room/board: $3,390. Books/supplies: $1,050. Personal expenses: $1,300.

**Financial aid.** All financial aid based on need. Need-based aid available for part-time students. Work-study available nights and for part-time students.

**Application procedures. Admission:** No deadline. No application fee. Admission notification on a rolling basis. High school transcript, proof of state residency, pre-TASP placement required for certain courses of study. **Financial aid:** Priority date 5/1; no closing date. FAFSA required. Applicants notified on a rolling basis starting 6/1; must reply within 4 week(s) of notification.

**Academics. Special study options:** Cross-registration, distance learning, dual enrollment of high school students. **Credit/placement by examination:** AP, CLEP, institutional tests. 18 credit hours maximum toward associate degree. **Support services:** Learning center, remedial instruction, tutoring.

**Majors. Agriculture:** Equestrian studies, farm/ranch. **Business:** General, administrative services, office technology, office/clerical. **Computer sciences:** General, data processing. **Engineering technology:** Drafting, electrical. **Health:** EMT paramedic, nursing (RN), occupational health, occupational therapy assistant. **Interdisciplinary:** Biological/physical sciences. **Legal studies:** Legal secretary, paralegal. **Mechanic/repair:** Diesel. **Protective services:** Criminal justice, police science. **Social sciences:** Criminology. **Visual/performing arts:** Commercial photography.

**Computing on campus.** 60 workstations in dormitories, library, computer center, student center. Dormitories linked to campus network. Commuter students can connect to campus network. Online course registration, online library, helpline available.

**Student life. Freshman orientation:** Mandatory. One-day program throughout summer and when classes commence. **Housing:** Coed dorms, special housing for disabled, substance-free housing available. $150 deposit. **Activities:** Choral groups, drama, literary magazine, music ensembles, student government, Baptist student union, Future Farmers of America, honor society, Young Republicans, nursing student association, criminal justice club, Methodist student organization, computer club.

**Athletics.** NJCAA. **Intercollegiate:** Baseball M, rodeo, tennis W, volleyball W. **Intramural:** Badminton, basketball, bowling, equestrian, golf, racquetball, softball, table tennis, tennis, track and field, volleyball. **Team name:** Lions.

**Student services.** Adult student services, career counseling, student employment services, personal counseling, veterans' counselor, women's services. **Transfer:** Transfer adviser for students transferring to 4-year colleges.

**Contact.** E-mail: admissions@nctc.edu
Phone: (940) 668-4222 ext. 222 Fax: (940) 668-6049
Melinda Carroll, Director of Admissions, North Central Texas College, 1525 West California Street, Gainesville, TX 76240

Two-Year Colleges

## North Harris Montgomery Community College
### The Woodlands, Texas
www.nhmccd.edu

CB member
CB code: 6508

- Public 2-year community college
- Commuter campus in very large city

**General.** Founded in 1972. Regionally accredited. Includes 5 colleges: Cy-Fair College, Kingwood College, North Harris College, Montgomery College, Tomball College. **Enrollment:** 35,850 degree-seeking undergraduates; 6,426 non-degree-seeking students. **Degrees:** 2,214 associate awarded. **Location:** 40 miles from Houston. **Calendar:** Semester, extensive summer session. **Full-time faculty:** 670 total; 31% have terminal degrees, 19% minority, 58% women. **Part-time faculty:** 1,698 total; 16% have terminal degrees, 28% minority, 54% women. **Class size:** 47% < 20, 53% 20-39, less than 1% 40-49, less than 1% 50-99, less than 1% >100.

**Student profile.** Among degree-seeking undergraduates, 74% enrolled in a transfer program, 26% enrolled in a vocational program, 3% already have a bachelor's degree or higher, 5,331 enrolled as first-time, first-year students.

| | | | |
|---|---|---|---|
| Part-time: | 74% | Asian American: | 6% |
| Out-of-state: | 1% | Hispanic American: | 24% |
| Women: | 61% | International: | 3% |
| African American: | 12% | 25 or older: | 30% |

**Transfer out. Colleges most students transferred to 2007:** University of Houston, Sam Houston State University, Texas A&M-College Station, University of Texas-Austin.

**Basis for selection.** Open admission, but selective for some programs. Special requirements for nursing, respiratory therapy, occupational therapy, physical therapist assistant program, veterinary technician, diagnostic medical imagery, cosmetology. Placement testing required in reading, writing, and math.

**2008-2009 Annual costs.** Tuition/fees: $1,360; $2,860 out-of-district; $3,310 out-of-state. Per-credit charge: $36 in-district; $86 out-of-district; $101 out-of-state. Books/supplies: $600. Personal expenses: $1,600.

**2006-2007 Financial aid. Need-based:** 81% of total undergraduate aid awarded as scholarships/grants, 19% as loans/jobs. Need-based aid available for part-time students. Work-study available nights and weekends. **Non-need-based:** Scholarships awarded for academics.

**Application procedures. Admission:** No deadline. No application fee. Application may be submitted online. Admission notification on a rolling basis. **Financial aid:** Priority date 4/1; no closing date. FAFSA, institutional form required. Applicants notified on a rolling basis starting 4/1.

**Academics. Special study options:** Cooperative education, distance learning, double major, dual enrollment of high school students, ESL, honors, independent study, internships, study abroad, teacher certification program, weekend college. Bachelor's degree programs available on campus. License preparation in dental hygiene, nursing, occupational therapy, paramedic, physical therapy, radiology, real estate. **Credit/placement by examination:** AP, CLEP, IB, institutional tests. 42 credit hours maximum toward associate degree. **Support services:** GED preparation and test center, learning center, pre-admission summer program, reduced course load, remedial instruction, study skills assistance, tutoring, writing center.

**Majors. Architecture:** Technology. **Business:** Accounting, administrative services, business admin, hospitality admin. **Computer sciences:** General. **Education:** Early childhood, instructional media, kindergarten/preschool, middle. **Engineering technology:** Industrial, telecommunications. **Family/consumer sciences:** Child care. **Foreign languages:** Sign language interpretation. **Health:** Dental hygiene, EMT paramedic, medical radiologic technology/radiation therapy, medical records technology, medical secretary, nursing (RN), occupational therapy assistant, pharmacy assistant, physical therapy assistant, respiratory therapy technology, sonography, substance abuse counseling, veterinary technology/assistant. **Legal studies:** Paralegal. **Liberal arts:** Arts/sciences. **Mechanic/repair:** Automotive, heating/ac/refrig. **Personal/culinary services:** Cosmetic. **Production:** Welding. **Protective services:** Firefighting. **Science technology:** Biological. **Social sciences:** Cartography. **Visual/performing arts:** Interior design.

**Most popular majors.** Health sciences 21%, liberal arts 66%.

**Computing on campus.** 500 workstations in library, computer center, student center. Commuter students can connect to campus network. Online course registration, online library, helpline, wireless network available.

**Student life. Freshman orientation:** Available. Preregistration for classes offered. Available on campus and online. **Activities:** Bands, choral groups, dance, drama, international student organizations, literary magazine, music ensembles, musical theater, radio station, student government, student newspaper, symphony orchestra, TV station, Phi Theta Kappa, honors student association, student nurses association, African American society, Latin American student association, Asian student association, Campus Crusade for Christ, Muslim student organization, Show of Hands (deaf students).

**Athletics. Intercollegiate:** Baseball M. **Intramural:** Badminton, basketball, bowling, football (non-tackle), golf, racquetball, soccer, softball, table tennis, tennis, volleyball.

**Student services.** Adult student services, career counseling, services for economically disadvantaged, student employment services, financial aid counseling, minority student services, on-campus daycare, personal counseling, placement for graduates, veterans' counselor. **Physically disabled:** Services for visually, speech, hearing impaired. **Transfer:** Transfer adviser, college fairs on campus for students transferring to 4-year colleges.

**Contact.** Phone: (832) 813-6500
Glen Wood, Director of Records and Reporting, North Harris Montgomery Community College, 5000 Research Forest Drive, The Woodlands, TX 77381-4356

## North Lake College
### Irving, Texas
www.northlakecollege.edu

CB member
CB code: 6519

- Public 2-year community and liberal arts college
- Commuter campus in small city

**General.** Founded in 1977. Regionally accredited. **Enrollment:** 8,067 degree-seeking undergraduates. **Degrees:** 350 associate awarded. **Location:** 15 miles from Dallas. **Calendar:** Semester, limited summer session. **Full-time faculty:** 90 total; 23% have terminal degrees, 31% minority, 46% women. **Part-time faculty:** 439 total; 1% have terminal degrees, 22% minority, 44% women. **Class size:** 59% < 20, 36% 20-39, 3% 40-49, less than 1% 50-99, less than 1% >100. **Special facilities:** Natatorium, pool.

**Student profile.** Among degree-seeking undergraduates, 50% enrolled in a transfer program.

| | | | |
|---|---|---|---|
| Out-of-state: | 3% | 25 or older: | 40% |

**Transfer out. Colleges most students transferred to 2007:** University of Texas at Arlington, University of North Texas, University of Texas at Dallas.

**Basis for selection.** Open admission. **Homeschooled:** Interview required. Must take placement test.

**2007-2008 Annual costs.** Tuition/fees: $1,170; $2,160 out-of-district; $3,450 out-of-state. Per-credit charge: $39 in-district; $72 out-of-district; $115 out-of-state. Books/supplies: $600.

**Financial aid. Need-based:** Need-based aid available for part-time students. **Non-need-based:** Scholarships awarded for academics, minority status, state residency.

**Application procedures. Admission:** No deadline. No application fee. Application may be submitted online. Admission notification on a rolling basis. **Financial aid:** Priority date 3/1, closing date 5/1. FAFSA required. Applicants notified on a rolling basis starting 7/1.

**Academics. Special study options:** Accelerated study, cooperative education, cross-registration, distance learning, double major, dual enrollment of high school students, ESL, honors, independent study, internships, liberal arts/career combination, study abroad, teacher certification program. License preparation in nursing, real estate. **Credit/placement by examination:** AP, CLEP. 15 credit hours maximum toward associate degree. **Support services:** GED preparation and test center, learning center, remedial instruction, study skills assistance, tutoring, writing center.

**Majors. Architecture:** Technology. **Business:** Accounting, administrative services, business admin, management science, office management, office technology, real estate. **Communications:** General. **Computer sciences:** General, information technology, programming, web page design. **Construction:** Carpentry, power transmission. **Education:** Adult literacy, elementary, ESL, kindergarten/preschool, music, teacher assistance. **Engineering technology:** Electrical. **Liberal arts:** Arts/sciences. **Math:** General, applied, computational, statistics. **Psychology:** General. **Visual/performing arts:** Cinematography.

**Most popular majors.** Computer/information sciences 8%.

**Computing on campus.** 1,100 workstations in library, computer center, student center. Online course registration, online library, wireless network available.

**Student life. Freshman orientation:** Mandatory. Preregistration for classes offered. **Activities:** Jazz band, choral groups, dance, drama, film society, international student organizations, literary magazine, music ensembles, musical theater, opera, student government, student newspaper, association of black collegians, environmental club, Christians on Campus, Phi Theta Kappa, single parents association, Estamos Unidos, South Asian student organization, student ambassadors, anime club.

**Athletics.** NJCAA. **Intercollegiate:** Baseball, basketball, cheerleading M, gymnastics, swimming, volleyball, weight lifting. **Intramural:** Baseball, basketball, cheerleading W, soccer, swimming. **Team name:** Blazers.

**Student services.** Alcohol/substance abuse counseling, career counseling, services for economically disadvantaged, student employment services, financial aid counseling, health services, minority student services, personal counseling, placement for graduates, veterans' counselor. **Physically disabled:** Services for visually, hearing impaired. **Transfer:** Pre-admission transcript evaluation for new students. Transfer center, transfer adviser, college fairs on campus for students transferring to 4-year colleges.

**Contact.** Phone: (972) 273-3183 Fax: (972) 273-3112
Stephen Twenge, Director of Admissions and Registration, North Lake College, 5001 North MacArthur Boulevard, Irving, TX 75038-3899

## Northeast Texas Community College
**Mount Pleasant, Texas**
www.ntcc.edu                                CB code: 6531

- Public 2-year community college
- Commuter campus in large town

**General.** Founded in 1984. Regionally accredited. **Enrollment:** 2,458 degree-seeking undergraduates. **Degrees:** 547 associate awarded. **Location:** 60 miles from Texarkana, 118 miles from Dallas. **Calendar:** Semester, extensive summer session. **Full-time faculty:** 57 total. **Part-time faculty:** 102 total. **Class size:** 68% < 20, 32% 20-39, less than 1% 40-49.

**Student profile.**

| | | | |
|---|---|---|---|
| Out-of-state: | 1% | Live on campus: | 4% |
| 25 or older: | 33% | | |

**Basis for selection.** Open admission, but selective for some programs. Special requirements for health science programs, cosmetology, some criminal justice programs.

**High school preparation.** 19 units recommended. Recommended units include English 4, mathematics 2, social studies 4, science 2 and foreign language 3. 0.5 fine arts recommended.

**2007-2008 Annual costs.** Tuition/fees: $1,800; $2,640 out-of-district; $3,956 out-of-state. Per-credit charge: $28 in-district; $56 out-of-district; $96 out-of-state. Room/board: $3,660. Books/supplies: $600. Personal expenses: $1,477.

**2006-2007 Financial aid. Need-based:** 97% of total undergraduate aid awarded as scholarships/grants, 3% as loans/jobs. Need-based aid available for part-time students. **Non-need-based:** Scholarships awarded for academics, art, athletics, job skills, music/drama, state residency.

**Application procedures. Admission:** No deadline. No application fee. Admission notification on a rolling basis. **Financial aid:** Priority date 6/1; no closing date. FAFSA, institutional form required. Applicants notified on a rolling basis starting 6/1.

**Academics. Special study options:** Cooperative education, distance learning, dual enrollment of high school students, ESL, liberal arts/career combination. Bachelor's degree programs available on campus. License preparation in dental hygiene, nursing, paramedic, real estate. **Credit/placement by examination:** CLEP. 15 credit hours maximum toward associate degree. **Support services:** GED preparation and test center, learning center, remedial instruction, study skills assistance, tutoring, writing center.

**Majors. Agriculture:** Business. **Biology:** General. **Business:** Banking/financial services, business admin, office technology, real estate. **Computer sciences:** Programming. **Education:** Teacher assistance. **Engineering:** Physics. **English:** English lit, speech/rhetoric. **Foreign languages:** Spanish. **Health:** Clinical lab technology, dental hygiene, EMT paramedic, medical assistant, medical radiologic technology/radiation therapy, medical secretary, nursing (RN), physical therapy assistant. **History:** General. **Liberal arts:** Arts/

sciences. **Math:** General. **Mechanic/repair:** Auto body, automotive, diesel. **Parks/recreation:** Health/fitness. **Personal/culinary services:** Cosmetic. **Physical sciences:** Chemistry. **Protective services:** Police science. **Psychology:** General. **Social sciences:** Political science, sociology. **Visual/performing arts:** Art, dramatic.

**Computing on campus.** 150 workstations in dormitories, library, computer center. Dormitories wired for high-speed internet access. Commuter students can connect to campus network. Online course registration, online library, wireless network available.

**Student life. Freshman orientation:** Mandatory. Preregistration for classes offered. Online program. **Housing:** Single-sex dorms available. **Activities:** Jazz band, choral groups, drama, literary magazine, music ensembles, musical theater, student government, student newspaper, student coordinating board, Baptist student union, student nurses, Phi Theta Kappa, computer club, career opportunities in protective services.

**Athletics.** NJCAA. **Intercollegiate:** Baseball M, softball W. **Intramural:** Basketball M, softball, tennis, volleyball. **Team name:** Eagles.

**Student services.** Career counseling, services for economically disadvantaged, student employment services, financial aid counseling, personal counseling, placement for graduates, veterans' counselor. **Transfer:** Pre-admission transcript evaluation for new students. Transfer center, college fairs on campus for students transferring to 4-year colleges.

**Contact.** E-mail: AdmRec@ntcc.edu
Phone: (903) 572-1911 ext. 263 Toll-free number: (800) 870-0142 ext. 263
Fax: (903) 572-6712
Director of Admissions, Northeast Texas Community College, Box 1307, Mount Pleasant, TX 75456-1307

## Northwest Vista College
**San Antonio, Texas**
www.accd.edu/nvc                             CB code: 6517

- Public 2-year community college
- Commuter campus in very large city

**General.** Regionally accredited. **Enrollment:** 10,672 degree-seeking undergraduates. **Degrees:** 548 associate awarded. **Location:** 16 miles from downtown. **Calendar:** Semester, extensive summer session. **Full-time faculty:** 110 total. **Part-time faculty:** 450 total.

**Student profile.**

| | | | |
|---|---|---|---|
| Out-of-state: | 1% | 25 or older: | 22% |

**Transfer out. Colleges most students transferred to 2007:** University of Texas at San Antonio, Texas State University, Palo Alto College, San Antonio College, St. Philip's College.

**Basis for selection.** Open admission. All students required to comply with Texas Academic Skills Program, which includes assessment, placement, remediation if necessary. **Homeschooled:** Transcript of courses and grades required.

**High school preparation.** 22 units recommended. Recommended units include English 4, mathematics 3, social studies 5, history 1, science 3, foreign language 2 and academic electives 3.

**2007-2008 Annual costs.** Tuition/fees: $1,790; $3,110 out-of-district; $5,750 out-of-state.

**Financial aid. Need-based:** Need-based aid available for part-time students. Work-study available nights, weekends and for part-time students. **Non-need-based:** Scholarships awarded for academics, leadership.

**Application procedures. Admission:** Priority date 4/23; deadline 8/19. No application fee. Application may be submitted online. **Financial aid:** Priority date 4/1; no closing date. FAFSA required. Applicants notified on a rolling basis starting 5/15; must reply within 2 week(s) of notification.

**Academics. Special study options:** Cross-registration, distance learning, dual enrollment of high school students, ESL, liberal arts/career combination, weekend college. **Credit/placement by examination:** CLEP, institutional tests. 32 credit hours maximum toward associate degree. **Support services:** Learning center, remedial instruction, study skills assistance, tutoring.

**Majors. Biology:** General. **Business:** Business admin. **Communications:** General, journalism, media studies. **Communications technology:** General. **Computer sciences:** General, computer science, networking, programming. **Education:** General. **English:** English lit, speech/rhetoric. **Foreign languages: General. **Health:** Health services. **History:** General. **Interdisciplinary:** Behavioral sciences. **Legal studies:** Prelaw. **Liberal arts:** Arts/sciences. **Math:** General. **Parks/recreation:** Exercise sciences, health/fitness. **Physical sciences:** Chemistry. **Psychology:** General. **Public administration:** Social work. **Science technology:** Biological. **Social sciences:** General, economics, political science, sociology.

**Computing on campus.** 600 workstations in library, computer center, student center. Commuter students can connect to campus network. Online course registration, online library, helpline available.

**Student life. Freshman orientation:** Mandatory. Preregistration for classes offered. **Activities:** Dance, film society, student government, student newspaper.

**Athletics. Team name:** Wildcats.

**Student services.** Career counseling, student employment services, financial aid counseling, personal counseling, placement for graduates, veterans' counselor. **Physically disabled:** Services for visually, speech, hearing impaired. **Learning disabled:** Comprehensive services available. **Transfer:** Pre-admission transcript evaluation for new students. Transfer center, transfer adviser, college fairs on campus for students transferring to 4-year colleges.

**Contact.** E-mail: nvcinfo@accd.edu
Phone: (210) 348-2020 Fax: (210) 348-2024
Elaine Lang, Director of Admissions, Northwest Vista College, 3535 North Ellison Drive, San Antonio, TX 78251-4217

---

## Odessa College
**Odessa, Texas**
**www.odessa.edu**                              CB code: 6540

- Public 2-year community college
- Commuter campus in small city

**General.** Founded in 1946. Regionally accredited. Extension centers in Pecos, Monahans, Andrews, Crane, Kermit, McCamey, Seminole. **Enrollment:** 3,806 degree-seeking undergraduates; 783 non-degree-seeking students. **Degrees:** 280 associate awarded. **Location:** 140 miles from Lubbock, 290 miles from El Paso. **Calendar:** Semester, extensive summer session. **Full-time faculty:** 117 total. **Part-time faculty:** 146 total. **Special facilities:** College-owned and operated NPR radio station.

**Student profile.** Among degree-seeking undergraduates, 714 enrolled as first-time, first-year students.

| | | | |
|---|---|---|---|
| Part-time: | 64% | Hispanic American: | 51% |
| Out-of-state: | 1% | Native American: | 1% |
| Women: | 64% | 25 or older: | 33% |
| African American: | 4% | Live on campus: | 5% |
| Asian American: | 1% | | |

**Basis for selection.** Open admission, but selective for some programs. Allied health programs require successful completion of placement exams, supporting applications, and interviews. Requirements for other selective programs vary. **Homeschooled:** Transcript of courses and grades required.

**2007-2008 Annual costs.** Tuition/fees: $1,590; $2,040 out-of-district; $2,790 out-of-state. Room/board: $5,570. Books/supplies: $1,000. Personal expenses: $1,071.

**Financial aid. Need-based:** Need-based aid available for part-time students. Work-study available nights and for part-time students. **Non-need-based:** Scholarships awarded for academics, athletics, music/drama.

**Application procedures. Admission:** No deadline. No application fee. Application may be submitted online. Admission notification on a rolling basis. **Financial aid:** Priority date 5/1; no closing date. FAFSA required. Applicants notified on a rolling basis starting 6/15.

**Academics. Special study options:** Cooperative education, cross-registration, distance learning, dual enrollment of high school students, independent study, internships, liberal arts/career combination. License preparation in nursing, paramedic, physical therapy, radiology. **Credit/placement by examination:** AP, CLEP, institutional tests. 15 credit hours maximum toward associate degree. **Support services:** GED preparation and test center, learning center, reduced course load, remedial instruction, study skills assistance, tutoring, writing center.

**Majors. Biology:** General. **Business:** General, administrative services, business admin. **Communications:** Radio/tv. **Computer sciences:** Computer

science, information systems, programming. **Construction:** Carpentry, maintenance. **Education:** General, teacher assistance. **Engineering technology:** Drafting, occupational safety, petroleum. **Family/consumer sciences:** Child care. **Foreign languages:** General. **Health:** Clinical lab science, EMT paramedic, medical radiologic technology/radiation therapy, medical secretary, nursing (RN), physical therapy assistant, respiratory therapy technology, substance abuse counseling, surgical technology. **Legal studies:** Legal secretary, paralegal. **Liberal arts:** Arts/sciences. **Math:** General. **Mechanic/repair:** Automotive, diesel, electronics/electrical, heating/ac/refrig. **Personal/culinary services:** Chef training, cosmetic. **Physical sciences:** Chemistry, geology. **Production:** Machine tool, welding. **Protective services:** Fire safety technology, firefighting, police science. **Psychology:** General. **Social sciences:** General. **Visual/performing arts:** Art, commercial photography.

**Computing on campus.** 775 workstations in dormitories, library, computer center, student center. Dormitories wired for high-speed internet access and linked to campus network. Commuter students can connect to campus network. Online course registration, online library, student web hosting, wireless network available.

**Student life. Freshman orientation:** Available. Preregistration for classes offered. **Housing:** Apartments available. $200 partly refundable deposit. **Activities:** Bands, choral groups, music ensembles, radio station, student government, Baptist student union, black organization of successful students, student alliance of Latinos succeeding academically, changing attitudes helping others overcome the situation.

**Athletics.** NJCAA. **Intercollegiate:** Baseball M, basketball, golf M, rodeo, softball W. **Intramural:** Racquetball, softball, table tennis, tennis, volleyball. **Team name:** Wranglers.

**Student services.** Campus ministries, career counseling, student employment services, financial aid counseling, on-campus daycare, personal counseling, placement for graduates, veterans' counselor. **Physically disabled:** Services for visually, hearing impaired. **Transfer:** Pre-admission transcript evaluation for new students. Transfer adviser, college fairs on campus for students transferring to 4-year colleges.

**Contact.** E-mail: ngarcia@odessa.edu
Phone: (432) 335-6432 Fax: (432) 335-6824
Tracy Hilliard, Assistant Director of Admissions, Odessa College, 201 West University, Odessa, TX 79764-7127

---

## Palo Alto College
**San Antonio, Texas**                          CB member
**www.accd.edu**                                CB code: 3730

- Public 2-year community college
- Commuter campus in very large city

**General.** Founded in 1987. Regionally accredited. **Enrollment:** 8,021 degree-seeking undergraduates. **Degrees:** 619 associate awarded. **Calendar:** Semester, limited summer session. **Full-time faculty:** 142 total. **Part-time faculty:** 258 total. **Special facilities:** FAA aviation education resource center. **Partnerships:** Formal partnership with a car/truck manufacturing company for occupational training.

**Student profile.** Among degree-seeking undergraduates, 1,173 transferred in from other institutions.

| | | | |
|---|---|---|---|
| Out-of-state: | 1% | 25 or older: | 33% |

**Transfer out. Colleges most students transferred to 2007:** University of Texas at San Antonio, St. Mary's University, Our Lady of the Lake University, University of the Incarnate Word.

**Basis for selection.** Open admission. SLEP used for placement of non-native speakers.

**2007-2008 Annual costs.** Tuition/fees: $1,652; $2,972 out-of-district; $5,384 out-of-state. Books/supplies: $500.

**2006-2007 Financial aid.** All financial aid based on need. 86% of total undergraduate aid awarded as scholarships/grants, 14% as loans/jobs. Need-based aid available for part-time students.

**Application procedures. Admission:** No deadline. No application fee. Application may be submitted online. Admission notification on a rolling basis. **Financial aid:** Priority date 4/1, closing date 6/1. FAFSA required. Applicants notified on a rolling basis starting 5/31.

**Academics. Special study options:** Cooperative education, distance learning, dual enrollment of high school students, ESL, honors, internships, liberal arts/career combination, weekend college. Bachelor's degree programs available on campus. License preparation in aviation. **Credit/placement by**

examination: CLEP, institutional tests. 32 credit hours maximum toward associate degree. **Support services:** GED preparation, learning center, remedial instruction, study skills assistance, tutoring, writing center.

**Majors. Agriculture:** Agribusiness operations, animal sciences, horticultural science, landscaping, ornamental horticulture, turf management. **Area/ethnic studies:** Hispanic-American/Latino/Chicano, Latin American. **Biology:** General. **Business:** Accounting, administrative services, banking/financial services, business admin, entrepreneurial studies, fashion, logistics, office management, office technology. **Communications:** General, advertising, journalism. **Computer sciences:** General, computer science, information systems, programming. **Conservation:** Environmental science. **Education:** General. **Engineering:** General, environmental. **Engineering technology:** Environmental. **English:** English lit. **Family/consumer sciences:** Food/nutrition. **Foreign languages:** General. **Health:** Health services, nursing assistant. **History:** General. **Interdisciplinary:** Biological/physical sciences. **Liberal arts:** Arts/sciences. **Math:** General. **Parks/recreation:** Exercise sciences. **Philosophy/religion:** Philosophy. **Physical sciences:** General, chemistry, physics. **Protective services:** Law enforcement admin. **Psychology:** General. **Public administration:** Social work. **Social sciences:** Anthropology, economics, political science, sociology. **Transportation:** Aviation. **Visual/performing arts:** Art, studio arts.

**Computing on campus.** Commuter students can connect to campus network. Online course registration, online library, wireless network available.

**Student life. Freshman orientation:** Mandatory. Preregistration for classes offered. **Activities:** Jazz band, campus ministries, choral groups, dance, drama, music ensembles, student government, student newspaper, international club, veterinary technician association, Phi Theta Kappa.

**Athletics.** NJCAA. **Intercollegiate:** Cross-country, diving, swimming. **Intramural:** Weight lifting. **Team name:** Palominos.

**Student services.** Adult student services, career counseling, services for economically disadvantaged, student employment services, financial aid counseling, health services, on-campus daycare, personal counseling, veterans' counselor. **Physically disabled:** Services for visually, speech, hearing impaired. **Learning disabled:** Comprehensive services available. **Transfer:** Transfer center, transfer adviser, college fairs on campus for students transferring to 4-year colleges.

**Contact.** Phone: (210) 921-5270 Fax: (210) 921-5310
Rachel Montejano, Director of Enrollment Management, Palo Alto College, 1400 West Villaret Boulevard, San Antonio, TX 78224-2499

## Panola College
### Carthage, Texas
www.panola.edu

CB code: 6572

- Public 2-year community and junior college
- Commuter campus in small town

**General.** Founded in 1947. Regionally accredited. Additional campuses in Marshall and Center. Wide variety of online and interactive television classes offered in Marshall and Center as well as area high schools. **Enrollment:** 1,879 degree-seeking undergraduates; 12 non-degree-seeking students. **Degrees:** 185 associate awarded. **Location:** 40 miles from Shreveport, Louisiana, 160 miles from Dallas. **Calendar:** Semester, limited summer session. **Full-time faculty:** 60 total; 10% have terminal degrees, 10% minority, 55% women. **Part-time faculty:** 54 total; 4% have terminal degrees, 2% minority, 48% women. **Class size:** 64% < 20, 32% 20-39, 4% 40-49, less than 1% 50-99.

**Student profile.** Among degree-seeking undergraduates, 14% enrolled in a transfer program, 86% enrolled in a vocational program, 23% already have a bachelor's degree or higher, 349 enrolled as first-time, first-year students, 187 transferred in from other institutions.

| Part-time: | 54% | Native American: | .1% |
|---|---|---|---|
| Women: | 67% | International: | 1% |
| African American: | 16% | 25 or older: | 27% |
| Asian American: | 1% | Live on campus: | 9% |
| Hispanic American: | 5% | | |

**Transfer out.** 21% of students enrolled in the transfer program go on to 4-year colleges. **Colleges most students transferred to 2007:** Stephen F. Austin State University, University of Texas at Tyler, Texas A&M Commerce, East Texas Baptist University.

**Basis for selection.** Open admission, but selective for some programs. Institution observes Texas Success Initiative guidelines. Departmental admission required prior to registration for some occupational/vocational programs of study. Early admissions for dual credit, tech prep. Interview required for some health program applicants. Auditions required for some fine arts scholarships.

**High school preparation.** Recommended units include English 4, mathematics 3, social studies 4, science 3, foreign language 2, academic electives 5.5.

**2007-2008 Annual costs.** Tuition/fees: $1,560; $2,670 out-of-district; $3,330 out-of-state. Room/board: $4,042. Books/supplies: $1,400. Personal expenses: $2,870.

**Financial aid. Need-based:** Need-based aid available for part-time students. Work-study available nights, weekends and for part-time students. **Non-need-based:** Scholarships awarded for academics, alumni affiliation, art, athletics, leadership, music/drama.

**Application procedures. Admission:** No deadline. No application fee. Application may be submitted online. **Financial aid:** Priority date 6/1; no closing date. FAFSA, institutional form required. Applicants notified on a rolling basis starting 6/1.

**Academics. Special study options:** Distance learning, dual enrollment of high school students, liberal arts/career combination. License preparation in nursing, occupational therapy. **Credit/placement by examination:** AP, CLEP. 12 credit hours maximum toward associate degree. **Support services:** GED preparation and test center, learning center, remedial instruction, study skills assistance, tutoring.

**Majors. Business:** General, administrative services, management information systems. **Computer sciences:** General. **Education:** General. **Engineering technology:** Industrial. **English:** English lit. **Health:** Medical records technology, nursing (RN), occupational therapy assistant. **Liberal arts:** Arts/sciences.

**Most popular majors.** Health sciences 38%, liberal arts 57%.

**Computing on campus.** 376 workstations in dormitories, library, computer center, student center. Dormitories wired for high-speed internet access and linked to campus network. Commuter students can connect to campus network. Online course registration, online library, helpline, wireless network available.

**Student life. Freshman orientation:** Available. Preregistration for classes offered. **Housing:** Coed dorms, single-sex dorms, apartments, substance-free housing available. $150 partly refundable deposit, deadline 7/15. **Activities:** Bands, campus ministries, choral groups, drama, literary magazine, music ensembles, musical theater, student government, student newspaper, Young Republicans, Excel club, forensics club, chemistry club, Phi Theta Kappa, computer club, nursing club, biology club, Circle K.

**Athletics.** NJCAA. **Intercollegiate:** Baseball M, basketball, rodeo, volleyball W. **Intramural:** Basketball, football (non-tackle), racquetball, softball, volleyball. **Team name:** Ponies and Fillies.

**Student services.** Alcohol/substance abuse counseling, career counseling, services for economically disadvantaged, financial aid counseling, personal counseling, veterans' counselor. **Physically disabled:** Services for visually, speech, hearing impaired. **Transfer:** College fairs on campus for students transferring to 4-year colleges.

**Contact.** E-mail: bsimpson@panola.edu
Phone: (903) 693-2038 Fax: (903) 693-2031
Barbara Simpson, Registrar/Director of Admissions, Panola College, 1109 West Panola Street, Carthage, TX 75633

## Paris Junior College
### Paris, Texas
www.parisjc.edu

CB member
CB code: 6573

- Public 2-year community and junior college
- Commuter campus in large town

**General.** Founded in 1924. Regionally accredited. **Enrollment:** 1,819 full-time, degree-seeking students. **Degrees:** 287 associate awarded. **Location:** 110 miles from Dallas. **Calendar:** Semester, limited summer session. **Full-time faculty:** 108 total. **Part-time faculty:** 98 total. **Special facilities:** Regional archives, collection of historical documents and artifacts of region, biological field laboratory with nature trails.

**Student profile.**

| Out-of-state: | 13% | Live on campus: | 12% |
|---|---|---|---|
| 25 or older: | 40% | | |

**Basis for selection.** Open admission, but selective for some programs. Special admission to nursing program; interview required.

**2007-2008 Annual costs.** Tuition/fees: $1,290; $2,190 out-of-district; $3,390 out-of-state. Room/board: $3,896. Books/supplies: $500.

**2006-2007 Financial aid. Need-based:** Need-based aid available for part-time students. **Non-need-based:** Scholarships awarded for athletics, music/drama.

**Application procedures. Admission:** No deadline. No application fee. Admission notification on a rolling basis. **Financial aid:** No deadline. FAFSA required. Applicants notified on a rolling basis starting 6/1.

**Academics. Special study options:** Accelerated study, cross-registration, dual enrollment of high school students. **Credit/placement by examination:** CLEP, institutional tests. **Support services:** GED preparation and test center, learning center, reduced course load, remedial instruction, tutoring.

**Majors. Biology:** General. **Business:** General, accounting, administrative services, business admin, office management, office technology, real estate. **Communications:** Journalism. **Computer sciences:** Data processing. **Construction:** Carpentry. **Education:** General. **Engineering technology:** Drafting, electrical. **English:** English lit. **Foreign languages:** General, French, German, Spanish. **Health:** Licensed practical nurse, medical records technology, predental, premedicine, prepharmacy, preveterinary. **History:** General. **Legal studies:** Prelaw. **Liberal arts:** Arts/sciences. **Math:** General. **Mechanic/repair:** Heating/ac/refrig, watch/jewelry. **Physical sciences:** Chemistry, physics. **Production:** Welding. **Psychology:** General. **Social sciences:** Political science, sociology. **Visual/performing arts:** Dramatic, metal/jewelry, studio arts.

**Computing on campus.** Dormitories wired for high-speed internet access and linked to campus network.

**Student life. Freshman orientation:** Available. Preregistration for classes offered. **Housing:** Single-sex dorms, apartments available. **Activities:** Campus ministries, choral groups, drama, music ensembles, student government, student newspaper, Baptist student union, Afro-American club, honorary business fraternity, honorary scholastic fraternity.

**Athletics.** NJCAA. **Intercollegiate:** Baseball M, basketball, golf M, softball W, volleyball W. **Team name:** Dragons.

**Student services.** Career counseling, services for economically disadvantaged, student employment services, financial aid counseling, health services, personal counseling, placement for graduates, veterans' counselor.

**Contact.** Phone: (903) 785-7661 Fax: (903) 784-9370
Shelia Reese, Director of Admissions, Paris Junior College, 2400 Clarksville Street, Paris, TX 75460

## Ranger College
**Ranger, Texas**
www.rangercollege.edu
CB code: 6608

- Public 2-year junior college
- Rural community

**General.** Founded in 1926. Regionally accredited. **Enrollment:** 788 degree-seeking undergraduates. **Degrees:** 30 associate awarded. **Location:** 85 miles from Fort Worth, 65 miles from Abilene. **Calendar:** Semester, limited summer session. **Full-time faculty:** 24 total; 21% have terminal degrees. **Part-time faculty:** 25 total; 16% have terminal degrees.

**Basis for selection.** Open admission, but selective for some programs. Observe all TSI guidelines. Special requirements for vocational nursing program candidates include additional applications and testing.

**2007-2008 Annual costs.** Tuition/fees: $2,194; $2,294 out-of-state. Per-credit charge: $43 in-state; $49 out-of-state. Room/board: $3,372. Books/supplies: $1,000.

**Financial aid.** All financial aid based on need. Need-based aid available for part-time students.

**Application procedures. Admission:** No deadline. No application fee. Application must be submitted on paper. Candidates accepted into the vocational nursing program will receive notification and must reply by the date indicated. **Financial aid:** Priority date 6/1, closing date 7/24. FAFSA required. Applicants notified on a rolling basis; must reply within 2 week(s) of notification.

**Academics. Special study options:** Distance learning, dual enrollment of high school students, honors. 2-2 programs in education, business administration, computer systems, and information sciences with Tarleton State University. License preparation in nursing. **Credit/placement by examination:** CLEP, institutional tests. 12 credit hours maximum toward associate degree.

**Support services:** GED test center, learning center, reduced course load, remedial instruction.

**Majors. Business:** Administrative services. **Computer sciences:** General. **Liberal arts:** Arts/sciences. **Production:** Welding.

**Computing on campus.** 30 workstations in library, computer center.

**Student life. Freshman orientation:** Mandatory. **Housing:** Single-sex dorms available. **Activities:** Bands, dance, music ensembles, student government, student newspaper.

**Athletics.** NJCAA. **Intercollegiate:** Baseball M, basketball, cheerleading, golf, rodeo, soccer, softball W, volleyball W. **Team name:** Rangers.

**Student services.** Career counseling, student employment services, health services, personal counseling, placement for graduates, veterans' counselor. **Transfer:** Transfer adviser for students transferring to 4-year colleges.

**Contact.** Phone: (254) 647-3234 ext. 215 Fax: (254) 647-3739
Roseatta Stephens, Registrar, Ranger College, 1100 College Circle, Ranger, TX 76470

## Remington College: Dallas
**Garland, Texas**
www.educationamerica.com
CB code: 3232

- For-profit 2-year junior and technical college
- Small city

**General.** Accredited by ACICS. **Calendar:** Continuous.

**Annual costs/financial aid.** Costs of entire programs leading to certificate, associate degree, bachelor's degree range from $13,000 to $38,880; includes books and supplies. Personal expenses: $3,360.

**Contact.** Phone: (972) 686-7878
1800 Eastgate Drive, Garland, TX 75041

## Remington College: Fort Worth
**Fort Worth, Texas**
www.remingtoncollege.edu
CB code: 3151

- For-profit 2-year technical and career college
- Large city
- Interview required

**General.** Accredited by ACCSCT. **Enrollment:** 409 degree-seeking undergraduates. **Degrees:** 102 associate awarded. **Location:** 7 miles from downtown. **Calendar:** Continuous. **Full-time faculty:** 17 total. **Part-time faculty:** 6 total.

**Basis for selection.** Programs offered on a monthly basis. **Home-schooled:** Transcript of courses and grades required.

**2007-2008 Annual costs.** Tuition includes books and supplies.

**Application procedures. Admission:** No deadline. $50 fee.

**Academics. Credit/placement by examination:** CLEP.

**Majors. Business:** Business admin. **Computer sciences:** Computer graphics, networking. **Protective services:** Criminal justice.

**Student services.** Career counseling, financial aid counseling, placement for graduates.

**Contact.** E-mail: marcia.kline@remingtoncollege.edu
Phone: (817) 451-0017 Fax: (817) 496-1257
Marcia Kline, Director of Recruitment, Remington College: Fort Worth, 300 East Loop 820, Fort Worth, TX 76112

## Remington College: Houston
**Houston, Texas**
www.remingtoncollege.edu
CB code: 3152

- For-profit 2-year technical college
- Commuter campus in very large city

**General.** Accredited by ACCSCT. **Enrollment:** 213 degree-seeking undergraduates. **Degrees:** 85 associate awarded. **Calendar:** Quarter. **Full-time faculty:** 25 total. **Part-time faculty:** 6 total.

**Basis for selection.** Open admission. ASSET used as admissions exams for degree programs.

**2007-2008 Annual costs.** Costs of entire programs leading to certificate, associate degree, bachelor's degree range from $13,000 to $38,880; includes books and supplies. Personal expenses: $1,764.

**Financial aid. Need-based:** Need-based aid available for part-time students. Work-study available nights. **Non-need-based:** Scholarships awarded for state residency.

**Application procedures. Admission:** No deadline. $50 fee. Application must be submitted on paper. Admission notification on a rolling basis. **Financial aid:** No deadline. FAFSA, institutional form required. Applicants notified on a rolling basis.

**Academics. Special study options:** Internships. **Credit/placement by examination:** CLEP. **Support services:** Tutoring.

**Majors. Computer sciences:** General, applications programming, networking, programming, systems analysis. **Engineering:** Electrical, software.

**Computing on campus.** 200 workstations in library, computer center. Online library, helpline, repair service available.

**Student services.** Adult student services, career counseling, student employment services, financial aid counseling. **Transfer:** Pre-admission transcript evaluation for new students.

**Contact.** Phone: (281) 899-1240 Fax: (281) 597-8466
Kevin Wilkinson, Director of Recruitment, Remington College: Houston, 3110 Hayes Road, Suite 380, Houston, TX 77082

## Remington College: North Houston
Houston, Texas
www.remingtoncollege.edu

- For-profit 2-year health science and technical college
- Very large city

**General.** Accredited by ACCSCT. **Calendar:** Quarter.

**Annual costs/financial aid.** Costs of entire programs leading to certificate, associate degree, bachelor's degree range from $13,000 to $38,880; includes books and supplies.

**Contact.** Phone: (281) 885-4450
11310 Greens Crossing, Suite 200, Houston, TX 77067

## Richland College
Dallas, Texas
www.rlc.dcccd.edu

CB member
CB code: 6607

- Public 2-year community college
- Commuter campus in very large city

**General.** Founded in 1972. Regionally accredited. **Enrollment:** 11,702 degree-seeking undergraduates. **Degrees:** 782 associate awarded. **Location:** 15 miles from downtown. **Calendar:** Semester, extensive summer session. **Full-time faculty:** 140 total. **Part-time faculty:** 643 total. **Special facilities:** Planetarium, laser light theater, horticulture demonstration garden, meditation labyrinth.

**Student profile.**

| Out-of-state: | 2% | 25 or older: | 39% |
|---|---|---|---|

**Basis for selection.** Open admission. Students required by legislative mandate to take TASP test or alternative assessment before enrolling in college-level courses. **Homeschooled:** Require completed application, concurrent enrollment permission form, student information profile sheet, student health history form, authorization to release test scores, official home school transcripts.

**2007-2008 Annual costs.** Tuition/fees: $1,170; $2,160 out-of-district; $3,450 out-of-state. Per-credit charge: $39 in-district; $72 out-of-district; $115 out-of-state. Books/supplies: $350. Personal expenses: $935.

**2006-2007 Financial aid. Need-based:** 31% of total undergraduate aid awarded as scholarships/grants, 69% as loans/jobs. Need-based aid available for part-time students. Work-study available nights and for part-time students. **Non-need-based:** Scholarships awarded for art, leadership, music/drama.

**Application procedures. Admission:** No deadline. No application fee. Application may be submitted online. Admission notification on a rolling basis. **Financial aid:** Priority date 5/2, closing date 7/30. FAFSA required. Applicants notified on a rolling basis starting 6/1; must reply within 2 week(s) of notification.

**Academics. Special study options:** Cooperative education, cross-registration, distance learning, dual enrollment of high school students, ESL, honors, independent study, internships, study abroad, teacher certification program, weekend college. License preparation in real estate. **Credit/placement by examination:** AP, CLEP, institutional tests. 45 credit hours maximum toward associate degree. **Support services:** Learning center, remedial instruction, study skills assistance, tutoring.

**Majors. Agriculture:** Horticultural science, horticulture. **Business:** Accounting, administrative services, business admin, entrepreneurial studies, management information systems, real estate, tourism/travel. **Communications technology:** General. **Computer sciences:** General, applications programming. **Education:** Bilingual, teacher assistance. **Engineering technology:** Electrical, manufacturing. **Health:** Insurance coding, medical informatics, medical records technology. **Liberal arts:** Arts/sciences.

**Computing on campus.** 210 workstations in library, computer center. Commuter students can connect to campus network. Online course registration, online library, wireless network available.

**Student life. Freshman orientation:** Mandatory. Sessions held online. **Activities:** Bands, campus ministries, choral groups, dance, drama, music ensembles, musical theater, student government, student newspaper, TV station, Spanish heritage association, arts club, Educators of America, Sierra Student Coalition, German film club.

**Athletics.** NJCAA. **Intercollegiate:** Baseball M, basketball M, soccer, volleyball W. **Intramural:** Basketball, bowling, cross-country, football (non-tackle), golf, soccer, softball, tennis, volleyball. **Team name:** Thunder Ducks.

**Student services.** Adult student services, career counseling, services for economically disadvantaged, student employment services, financial aid counseling, health services, personal counseling, placement for graduates, veterans' counselor, women's services. **Physically disabled:** Services for visually, speech, hearing impaired. **Transfer:** Transfer adviser, college fairs on campus for students transferring to 4-year colleges.

**Contact.** Phone: (972) 238-6106 Fax: (972) 238-6346
Oscar Lopez, Registrar and Director of Admissions, Richland College, 12800 Abrams Road, Dallas, TX 75243-2199

## St. Philip's College
San Antonio, Texas
www.accd.edu/spc

CB member
CB code: 6642

- Public 2-year community college
- Commuter campus in very large city

**General.** Founded in 1898. Regionally accredited. Some courses held at off-campus sites throughout San Antonio. **Enrollment:** 9,256 degree-seeking undergraduates. **Degrees:** 773 associate awarded. **ROTC:** Army. **Location:** 1 mile from downtown. **Calendar:** Semester, extensive summer session. **Full-time faculty:** 205 total; 10% have terminal degrees, 44% minority, 42% women. **Part-time faculty:** 362 total; 6% have terminal degrees, 48% minority, 40% women. **Class size:** 64% < 20, 35% 20-39, less than 1% 40-49, less than 1% 50-99. **Special facilities:** Restaurant on campus run by hospitality students, human patient simulator for nursing and allied health students. **Partnerships:** Formal partnerships with Boeing and Dee Howard for aircraft technology training.

**Student profile.** Among degree-seeking undergraduates, 52% enrolled in a transfer program, 48% enrolled in a vocational program, 1,554 enrolled as first-time, first-year students.

| Part-time: | 58% | Asian American: | 2% |
|---|---|---|---|
| Out-of-state: | 1% | Hispanic American: | 46% |
| Women: | 57% | 25 or older: | 49% |
| African American: | 16% | | |

**Transfer out.** Colleges most students transferred to 2007: University of Texas at San Antonio, Texas State University.

**Two-Year Colleges**

**Basis for selection.** Open admission. Selective admissions to certain programs (e.g. Nursing and certain Allied Health programs). PTASP or AC-CUPLACER may be taken at entry in lieu of TASP, SAT, or ACT scores for placement. **Adult students:** Students age 65 and older do not have to test if they are auditing classes. **Homeschooled:** Transcript of courses and grades required.

**2007-2008 Annual costs.** Tuition/fees: $1,652; $2,972 out-of-district; $5,612 out-of-state. Per-credit charge: $44 in-district; $88 out-of-district; $176 out-of-state. Books/supplies: $900. Personal expenses: $2,185.

**2006-2007 Financial aid.** All financial aid based on need. 69% of total undergraduate aid awarded as scholarships/grants, 31% as loans/jobs. Need-based aid available for part-time students. Work-study available nights, weekends and for part-time students.

**Application procedures. Admission:** No deadline. No application fee. Application may be submitted online. **Financial aid:** Priority date 3/1; no closing date. FAFSA required. Applicants notified on a rolling basis starting 7/15.

**Academics. Special study options:** Accelerated study, cooperative education, cross-registration, distance learning, double major, dual enrollment of high school students, ESL, honors, internships, teacher certification program, weekend college. License preparation in aviation, nursing, occupational therapy, physical therapy, radiology. **Credit/placement by examination:** AP, CLEP, institutional tests. 32 credit hours maximum toward associate degree. **Support services:** GED preparation and test center, learning center, pre-admission summer program, reduced course load, remedial instruction, study skills assistance, tutoring, writing center.

**Majors. Architecture:** Interior. **Biology:** General, biomedical sciences. **Business:** Accounting, accounting technology, administrative services, business admin, construction management, hospitality admin, tourism/travel. **Communications technology:** General. **Computer sciences:** Data entry, data processing, information systems, LAN/WAN management, programming, webmaster. **Construction:** Carpentry, electrician, maintenance. **Education:** General, teacher assistance. **Engineering:** General. **Engineering technology:** Biomedical, computer hardware, construction, drafting, electrical, heat/ac/refrig, instrumentation. **English:** Composition, speech/rhetoric. **Family/consumer sciences:** Child care, institutional food production. **Foreign languages:** General, Spanish. **Health:** Clinical lab technology, medical radiologic technology/radiation therapy, medical records admin, medical records technology, medical secretary, nursing (RN), occupational therapy assistant, physical therapy assistant, predental, premedicine, prenursing, respiratory therapy technology. **History:** General. **Legal studies:** Legal secretary, paralegal, prelaw. **Liberal arts:** Arts/sciences. **Math:** General. **Mechanic/repair:** Aircraft, aircraft powerplant, auto body, automotive, communications systems, diesel, electronics/electrical, heating/ac/refrig. **Parks/recreation:** Health/fitness. **Personal/culinary services:** Chef training, culinary arts, restaurant/catering. **Philosophy/religion:** Philosophy. **Physical sciences:** Chemistry, geology. **Production:** Machine tool, welding. **Protective services:** Law enforcement admin. **Psychology:** General. **Public administration:** Social work. **Social sciences:** Economics, political science, sociology, urban studies. **Visual/performing arts:** Art, dramatic, studio arts. **Other:** Railroad operation mechanic.

**Most popular majors.** Business/marketing 11%, health sciences 39%, liberal arts 11%, personal/culinary services 6%, trade and industry 13%.

**Computing on campus.** 1,000 workstations in library, computer center. Commuter students can connect to campus network. Online course registration, online library, helpline, repair service available.

**Student life. Freshman orientation:** Mandatory. Preregistration for classes offered. **Activities:** Jazz band, campus ministries, choral groups, dance, drama, literary magazine, music ensembles, musical theater, student government, student newspaper, Phi Theta Kappa, Black Educational Network, Los Unidos, MECHA, Native American club.

**Athletics. Intramural:** Basketball, swimming, table tennis, tennis, volleyball, weight lifting. **Team name:** Tigers.

**Student services.** Adult student services, campus ministries, career counseling, services for economically disadvantaged, student employment services, financial aid counseling, health services, on-campus daycare, personal counseling, placement for graduates, veterans' counselor, women's services. **Physically disabled:** Services for visually, hearing impaired. **Transfer:** Transfer center, transfer adviser, college fairs on campus for students transferring to 4-year colleges.

**Contact.** E-mail: angarza2@mail.accd.edu
Phone: (210) 531-4831 Fax: (210) 531-4836
Burton Crow, Dean of Enrollment Management, St. Philip's College, 1801 Martin Luther King Drive, San Antonio, TX 78203

## San Antonio College
San Antonio, Texas

**CB member**
**CB code: 6645**

www.accd.edu/sac

- Public 2-year community college
- Commuter campus in very large city

**General.** Founded in 1925. Regionally accredited. **Enrollment:** 21,479 degree-seeking undergraduates. **Degrees:** 923 associate awarded. **ROTC:** Army, Air Force. **Location:** Downtown. **Calendar:** Semester, extensive summer session. **Full-time faculty:** 400 total. **Part-time faculty:** 627 total. **Special facilities:** Planetarium.

**Transfer out. Colleges most students transferred to 2007:** University of Texas at San Antonio.

**Basis for selection.** Open admission, but selective for some programs. Nursing requires 2.5 GPA, satisfactory completion of human anatomy/physiology and ethics. Mortuary science program requires admissions interview, proof of complete hepatitis B vaccination series (or submit a waiver/declination form), and counseling card. Dental assisting requires complete dental assisting technology program application, proof of advisement, formal admission to college, and counseling card. **Adult students:** Texas Higher Education Assessment required.

**2007-2008 Annual costs.** Tuition/fees: $1,576; $2,836 out-of-district; $5,356 out-of-state. Per-credit charge: $42 in-district; $84 out-of-district; $168 out-of-state. Books/supplies: $1,200. Personal expenses: $2,571.

**Financial aid.** All financial aid based on need. Need-based aid available for part-time students. Work-study available nights, weekends and for part-time students. **Additional information:** Leveraging Educational Assistance Partnership (LEAP), public student incentive grant, towards excellence access and success grants (Texas and Texas II grants) available.

**Application procedures. Admission:** Closing date 8/25. No application fee. Application must be submitted online. Admission notification on a rolling basis. Nursing applicants must apply by January 15. **Financial aid:** Priority date 3/1; no closing date. FAFSA required. Applicants notified by 7/1.

**Academics. Special study options:** Cooperative education, cross-registration, distance learning, double major, dual enrollment of high school students, ESL, honors, internships, liberal arts/career combination, study abroad, weekend college. Internet courses, premedical/predental program, alternative teacher certification program, basic skills enrichment program, distance education through Virtual College of Texas, teaching academy program. License preparation in dental hygiene, nursing, paramedic, real estate. **Credit/placement by examination:** AP, CLEP, IB, institutional tests. 32 credit hours maximum toward associate degree. Student must earn 6 credits at college before credit by examination may be posted on transcript. No credit by examination may be earned for course already completed in classroom. **Support services:** GED preparation and test center, learning center, reduced course load, remedial instruction, study skills assistance, tutoring.

**Majors. Business:** Accounting technology, business admin. **Communications:** Journalism, radio/tv. **Computer sciences:** Programming, security. **Education:** Teacher assistance. **Engineering:** General. **Engineering technology:** Architectural, civil, electrical, occupational safety, telecommunications. **Family/consumer sciences:** Child development. **Foreign languages:** Sign language interpretation. **Health:** Medical assistant, nursing (RN), substance abuse counseling. **Interdisciplinary:** Global studies. **Legal studies:** Paralegal. **Math:** General. **Personal/culinary services:** Mortuary science. **Protective services:** Corrections, criminal justice, fire safety technology, police science, security management. **Psychology:** General. **Public administration:** General. **Visual/performing arts:** Graphic design.

**Computing on campus.** 325 workstations in library, computer center, student center. Online course registration, online library, helpline, wireless network available.

**Student life. Freshman orientation:** Mandatory. **Housing:** Special program places students in homes of elderly residents who have spare rooms and need assistance. **Activities:** Bands, choral groups, dance, drama, film society, literary magazine, music ensembles, musical theater, radio station, student government, student newspaper, symphony orchestra, TV station, Baptist student center, Catholic student center, Methodist student center, Church of Christ student center, black student alliance, United Mexican-American Students, College Republicans, Young Democrats, Young Socialist Alliance.

**Athletics. Intramural:** Basketball, bowling, cheerleading, cross-country, fencing, golf, racquetball, soccer, softball, swimming, table tennis, tennis, triathlon, volleyball, water polo. **Team name:** Rangers.

Student services. Adult student services, alcohol/substance abuse counseling, campus ministries, career counseling, services for economically disadvantaged, student employment services, financial aid counseling, health services, on-campus daycare, personal counseling, placement for graduates, veterans' counselor, women's services. **Physically disabled:** Services for visually, speech, hearing impaired. **Transfer:** Pre-admission transcript evaluation for new students. Transfer center, transfer adviser, college fairs on campus for students transferring to 4-year colleges.

**Contact.** E-mail: sacar@accd.edu
Phone: (210) 733-2583 Toll-free number: (800) 944-7575
Fax: (210) 733-2579
J. Martin Ortega, Director of Admissions and Records, San Antonio College, 1300 San Pedro Avenue, San Antonio, TX 78212-4299

## San Jacinto College
### Pasadena, Texas
www.sanjac.edu                                    CB code: 6694

- Public 2-year community and technical college
- Commuter campus in very large city

**General.** Founded in 1960. Regionally accredited. Campuses in Houston and Pasadena and multiple extension centers. Aerospace and Biotechnology Academy (NASA-Johnson Space Center), pilot program, and truck driving program. **Enrollment:** 23,805 degree-seeking undergraduates. **Degrees:** 1,742 associate awarded. **Location:** 20 miles from Houston. **Calendar:** Semester, limited summer session. **Full-time faculty:** 439 total; 20% have terminal degrees, 18% minority, 52% women. **Part-time faculty:** 550 total; 11% have terminal degrees, 27% minority, 56% women. **Class size:** 46% < 20, 51% 20-39, 2% 40-49, 1% 50-99, less than 1% >100. **Special facilities:** Nature preserve. **Partnerships:** Formal partnerships with NASA Space Center Houston, Partnership for Innovation in Biotechnology and Life Sciences, Boeing for Reduced Gravity Student Flight Program, University of Houston-College of Engineering for Aerospace Workforce Innovation Network.

**Student profile.** Among degree-seeking undergraduates, 75% enrolled in a transfer program, 25% enrolled in a vocational program, 5,468 enrolled as first-time, first-year students, 2,419 transferred in from other institutions.

| | | | |
|---|---|---|---|
| Part-time: | 60% | Women: | 57% |
| Out-of-state: | 1% | 25 or older: | 37% |

**Basis for selection.** Open admission, but selective for some programs. Special requirements for health science program. Psychological Services Bureau test and interview required of nursing applicants. In some selective programs, specific courses taken successfully within San Jacinto district may obviate need for qualifying SAT/ACT scores. SAT or ACT score used for nursing, medical laboratory technology, radiography, and respiratory programs. Interview recommended for nursing program, and EMT programs. **Learning Disabled:** Students should meet with Special Populations counselor after registering for classes.

**2007-2008 Annual costs.** Tuition/fees: $1,250; $2,000 out-of-district; $3,500 out-of-state. Per-credit charge: $33 in-district; $58 out-of-district; $108 out-of-state.

**2006-2007 Financial aid.** All financial aid based on need. 68% of total undergraduate aid awarded as scholarships/grants, 32% as loans/jobs. Need-based aid available for part-time students. Work-study available nights, weekends and for part-time students.

**Application procedures. Admission:** No deadline. No application fee. Application must be submitted online. Admission notification on a rolling basis. **Financial aid:** Priority date 7/1; no closing date. FAFSA, institutional form required. Applicants notified on a rolling basis starting 4/1; must reply within 4 week(s) of notification.

**Academics. Special study options:** Accelerated study, combined bachelor's/graduate degree, cooperative education, cross-registration, distance learning, double major, dual enrollment of high school students, ESL, honors, internships, teacher certification program, weekend college. License preparation in aviation, nursing, paramedic, radiology, real estate. **Credit/placement by examination:** AP, CLEP, institutional tests. Freshman College Composition CLEP subject examination must be accompanied by essay. **Support services:** GED preparation and test center, learning center, pre-admission summer program, remedial instruction, study skills assistance, tutoring, writing center.

**Majors. Business:** General, administrative services, fashion, hospitality/recreation, management information systems, office technology, real estate. **Communications technology:** Graphic/printing. **Engineering technology:** Drafting. **English:** English lit. **Family/consumer sciences:** Institutional food

production. **Health:** Clinical lab science, medical assistant, medical radiologic technology/radiation therapy, nursing (RN), respiratory therapy technology. **Parks/recreation:** Health/fitness. **Protective services:** Fire safety technology, police science. **Theology:** Bible. **Transportation:** Airline/commercial pilot. **Visual/performing arts:** Commercial/advertising art.

**Most popular majors.** Business/marketing 15%, English 12%, health sciences 22%, library sciences 8%, social sciences 11%.

**Computing on campus.** 200 workstations in library, computer center. Online course registration, helpline, repair service, wireless network available.

**Student life. Freshman orientation:** Available. 4-hour sessions scheduled several times prior to beginning of semester. **Policies:** Student conduct code. **Activities:** Jazz band, choral groups, dance, drama, literary magazine, music ensembles, musical theater, student government, student newspaper, Phi Theta Kappa honor society, Latin American student organization, College Republicans, College Democrats, Phi Beta Lambda business, Texas student education association, student government association.

**Athletics.** NJCAA. **Intercollegiate:** Baseball M, basketball, volleyball W. **Intramural:** Badminton, basketball, racquetball, softball, swimming, tennis, volleyball, weight lifting. **Team name:** Ravens / Gators / Coyotes.

**Student services.** Alcohol/substance abuse counseling, career counseling, student employment services, financial aid counseling, on-campus daycare, personal counseling, placement for graduates. **Transfer:** Transfer adviser, college fairs on campus for students transferring to 4-year colleges.

**Contact.** E-mail: information@sjcd.edu
Phone: (281) 998-6150 Fax: (281) 478-2720
Wanda Simpson, Director of Enrollment Services, San Jacinto College, 8060 Spencer Highway, Pasadena, TX 77505-5999

## South Plains College
### Levelland, Texas
www.southplainscollege.edu                        CB code: 6695

- Public 2-year community and junior college
- Commuter campus in large town

**General.** Founded in 1957. Regionally accredited. Continuing education and workforce development programs available. **Enrollment:** 9,197 degree-seeking undergraduates. **Degrees:** 760 associate awarded. **Location:** 30 miles from Lubbock. **Calendar:** Semester, extensive summer session. **Full-time faculty:** 275 total. **Part-time faculty:** 173 total. **Special facilities:** Audio/video recording studio.

**Student profile.** Among degree-seeking undergraduates, 42% enrolled in a transfer program, 26% enrolled in a vocational program, 1% already have a bachelor's degree or higher, 3,456 enrolled as first-time, first-year students.

| | | | |
|---|---|---|---|
| Part-time: | 56% | Hispanic American: | 28% |
| Out-of-state: | 3% | Native American: | 1% |
| Women: | 52% | International: | 1% |
| African American: | 5% | 25 or older: | 21% |
| Asian American: | 1% | Live on campus: | 10% |

**Transfer out.** 43.1% of students enrolled in the transfer program go on to 4-year colleges. **Colleges most students transferred to 2007:** Texas Tech University, San Angelo State University, West Texas A&M University, Eastern New Mexico State University.

**Basis for selection.** Open admission, but selective for some programs. Special requirements for allied health, cosmetology, law enforcement academy programs. State law requires TASP exam before student may enroll in college-level course work. Interview required for health care.

**2007-2008 Annual costs.** Tuition/fees: $1,892; $2,552 out-of-district; $3,032 out-of-state. Room/board: $3,200. Books/supplies: $580. Personal expenses: $1,100.

**Financial aid. Need-based:** Need-based aid available for part-time students. **Non-need-based:** Scholarships awarded for academics, athletics.

**Application procedures. Admission:** No deadline. No application fee. Admission notification on a rolling basis. **Financial aid:** Priority date 6/1; no closing date. FAFSA required. Applicants notified on a rolling basis starting 6/30; must reply within 2 week(s) of notification.

**Academics. Special study options:** Distance learning, dual enrollment of high school students, internships. License preparation in nursing, occupational therapy, paramedic, physical therapy, radiology, real estate. **Credit/**

**placement by examination:** AP, CLEP, institutional tests. 15 credit hours maximum toward associate degree. **Support services:** GED preparation, learning center, remedial instruction, study skills assistance, tutoring.

**Majors. Agriculture:** Business. **Biology:** General. **Business:** Accounting, administrative services, business admin, fashion, office management, real estate. **Communications:** General, broadcast journalism, journalism. **Communications technology:** Graphic/printing. **Computer sciences:** General, computer science, data processing. **Construction:** Power transmission. **Education:** General. **Engineering:** General. **Engineering technology:** Drafting. **English:** English lit. **Family/consumer sciences:** General, child care. **Foreign languages:** French, Spanish. **Health:** Athletic training, EMT paramedic, health services, medical radiologic technology/radiation therapy, medical records technology, medical secretary, nursing (RN), predental, premedicine, prenursing, preop/surgical nursing, prepharmacy, preveterinary, respiratory therapy technology. **History:** General. **Interdisciplinary:** Behavioral sciences. **Legal studies:** Legal secretary, paralegal. **Liberal arts:** Arts/sciences. **Math:** General. **Mechanic/repair:** Auto body, automotive, diesel, electronics/electrical, heating/ac/refrig. **Parks/recreation:** Health/fitness. **Physical sciences:** Chemistry, geology, physics. **Protective services:** Fire safety technology, firefighting, law enforcement admin. **Psychology:** General. **Public administration:** Human services. **Social sciences:** Criminology, political science, sociology. **Visual/performing arts:** Cinematography, commercial/advertising art, design, dramatic.

**Computing on campus.** 2,000 workstations in library, computer center, student center. Dormitories linked to campus network. Commuter students can connect to campus network. Online course registration, online library, wireless network available.

**Student life. Freshman orientation:** Mandatory. Preregistration for classes offered. **Housing:** Single-sex dorms, special housing for disabled, apartments available. $100 deposit. **Activities:** Bands, choral groups, dance, drama, literary magazine, music ensembles, musical theater, radio station, student government, student newspaper, TV station.

**Athletics.** NJCAA. **Intercollegiate:** Basketball, cheerleading, cross-country, rodeo, track and field. **Intramural:** Basketball, racquetball, softball, table tennis, volleyball. **Team name:** Texans/Lady Texans.

**Student services.** Career counseling, student employment services, financial aid counseling, health services, minority student services, personal counseling, placement for graduates, veterans' counselor. **Physically disabled:** Services for visually, hearing impaired. **Transfer:** Transfer adviser, college fairs on campus for students transferring to 4-year colleges.

**Contact.** E-mail: arangel@southplainscollege.edu
Phone: (806) 894-9611 ext. 2373 Fax: (806) 897-3167
Andrea Rangel, Dean of Admissions and Records, South Plains College, 1401 South College Avenue, Levelland, TX 79336

## South Texas College
McAllen, Texas
www.southtexascollege.edu
CB code: 6654

- Public 2-year community and technical college
- Commuter campus in small city

**General.** Regionally accredited. **Enrollment:** 19,973 degree-seeking undergraduates. **Degrees:** 1,314 associate awarded. **Calendar:** Semester, extensive summer session. **Full-time faculty:** 435 total. **Part-time faculty:** 124 total.

**Basis for selection.** Open admission, but selective for some programs. Special requirements for nursing program. **Homeschooled:** Transcript of courses and grades required.

**2007-2008 Annual costs.** Tuition/fees: $2,207; $2,720 out-of-district; $6,497 out-of-state. Books/supplies: $1,000. Personal expenses: $1,200.

**2007-2008 Financial aid.** All financial aid based on need. 99% of total undergraduate aid awarded as scholarships/grants, 1% as loans/jobs. Need-based aid available for part-time students. Work-study available nights, weekends and for part-time students.

**Application procedures. Admission:** No deadline. No application fee. Application must be submitted on paper. **Financial aid:** Priority date 3/1; no closing date. FAFSA required. Applicants notified on a rolling basis starting 4/15.

**Academics. Special study options:** Cooperative education, distance learning, dual enrollment of high school students, ESL, weekend college. Bachelor's degree programs available on campus. **Credit/placement by examination:** CLEP, institutional tests. **Support services:** Learning center, remedial instruction, study skills assistance, tutoring, writing center.

**Majors. Architecture:** Technology. **Biology:** General. **Business:** Accounting, banking/financial services, business admin, marketing, office management. **Computer sciences:** General, applications programming, computer science, computer support specialist, database management, networking, security, web page design, webmaster. **Conservation:** Environmental studies. **Education:** Early childhood, elementary, middle, secondary. **Engineering:** General. **Engineering technology:** Drafting. **English:** English lit. **Family/consumer sciences:** Child development. **Health:** EMT paramedic, medical records technology, nursing assistant, occupational therapy assistant, office assistant, pharmacy assistant, physical therapy assistant, radiologic technology/medical imaging. **History:** General. **Interdisciplinary:** Intercultural. **Legal studies:** Legal secretary, paralegal. **Liberal arts:** Arts/sciences. **Math:** General. **Mechanic/repair:** Automotive, diesel, heating/ac/refrig. **Personal/culinary services:** General, restaurant/catering. **Philosophy/religion:** Philosophy. **Physical sciences:** Chemistry, physics. **Production:** General. **Protective services:** Law enforcement admin. **Public administration:** Human services. **Social sciences:** General, political science. **Visual/performing arts:** General, studio arts.

**Computing on campus.** Online course registration available.

**Student life. Freshman orientation:** Mandatory. Preregistration for classes offered. **Activities:** Drama, student government.

**Athletics. Intramural:** Basketball, football (non-tackle), football (tackle), softball, volleyball. **Team name:** Jaguars.

**Student services.** Career counseling, student employment services, financial aid counseling, personal counseling, placement for graduates, veterans' counselor. **Physically disabled:** Services for visually, speech, hearing impaired. **Learning disabled:** Comprehensive services available. **Transfer:** Transfer center, transfer adviser, college fairs on campus for students transferring to 4-year colleges.

**Contact.** Phone: (956) 618-8311
Matthew Hebbard, Director of Admissions and Registrar, South Texas College, 3201 West Pecan Boulevard, McAllen, TX 78502

## Southwest Institute of Technology
Austin, Texas
www.switaustin.com
CB code: 2471

- For-profit 2-year technical college
- Commuter campus in large city

**General.** Accredited by ACCSCT. **Enrollment:** 35 degree-seeking undergraduates. **Degrees:** 28 associate awarded. **Calendar:** Quarter. **Full-time faculty:** 4 total. **Part-time faculty:** 3 total. **Class size:** 100% < 20.

**Basis for selection.** Open admission. Interview recommended.

**2008-2009 Annual costs.** Tuition/fees: $19,419. Per-credit charge: $325. Books/supplies: $1,526.

**2007-2008 Financial aid.** All financial aid based on need. 55% of total undergraduate aid awarded as scholarships/grants, 45% as loans/jobs. Work-study available nights and weekends.

**Application procedures. Admission:** No deadline. $100 fee, may be waived for applicants with need. **Financial aid:** No deadline. FAFSA, institutional form required.

**Academics. Special study options:** Cooperative education. **Credit/placement by examination:** CLEP. **Support services:** Learning center, tutoring.

**Majors. Engineering:** Electrical.

**Computing on campus.** Repair service available.

**Student life. Freshman orientation:** Mandatory.

**Student services.** Career counseling, student employment services, financial aid counseling, placement for graduates, veterans' counselor.

**Contact.** Phone: (512) 892-2640
Dick Roose, Director of Admissions, Southwest Institute of Technology, 5424 Highway 290 West, Suite 200, Austin, TX 78735

## Southwest Texas Junior College
Uvalde, Texas
www.swtjc.cc.tx.us
CB code: 6666

- Public 2-year community and junior college
- Commuter campus in large town

**General.** Founded in 1946. Regionally accredited. **Location:** 80 miles from San Antonio, 70 miles from Del Rio. **Calendar:** Semester.

**Annual costs/financial aid.** Tuition/fees (2007-2008): $1,931; $2,816 out-of-district; $3,341 out-of-state. Additional fees for off-campus classes may apply. Room/board: $3,100. Books/supplies: $900. Personal expenses: $745. Need-based financial aid available to full-time and part-time students.

**Contact.** Phone: (830) 278-4401
Dean of Admissions/Student Services, Garner Field Road, Uvalde, TX 78801

## Tarrant County College
### Fort Worth, Texas
www.tccd.edu                CB code: 6834

▶ Public 2-year community and liberal arts college
▶ Commuter campus in very large city

**General.** Founded in 1965. Regionally accredited. **Enrollment:** 37,951 undergraduates. **Degrees:** 2,178 associate awarded. **ROTC:** Army, Air Force. **Calendar:** Semester, extensive summer session. **Full-time faculty:** 574 total; 18% have terminal degrees, 23% minority, 55% women. **Part-time faculty:** 965 total; 12% have terminal degrees, 19% minority, 49% women.

**Student profile.**

| | | | |
|---|---|---|---|
| Out-of-state: | 1% | 25 or older: | 45% |

**Transfer out. Colleges most students transferred to 2007:** University of Texas at Arlington, University of North Texas, Texas Woman's University, Texas Tech University, Texas State University.

**Basis for selection.** Open admission, but selective for some programs. Special requirements for nursing and allied health programs, honors program, and certain automotive programs; must submit separate application and meet highly selective admission criteria. Placement testing required of all first-time college students and for those entering certain English, math, and reading-based courses. Interview and essay may be required for selective admission programs. **Homeschooled:** Transcript of courses and grades required.

**2007-2008 Annual costs.** Tuition/fees: $1,500; $1,890 out-of-district; $4,500 out-of-state. Per-credit charge: $50 in-district; $63 out-of-district; $150 out-of-state. Books/supplies: $1,310. Personal expenses: $1,693.

**2006-2007 Financial aid. Need-based:** 74% of total undergraduate aid awarded as scholarships/grants, 26% as loans/jobs. Need-based aid available for part-time students. **Non-need-based:** Scholarships awarded for academics.

**Application procedures. Admission:** No deadline. No application fee. Application may be submitted online. Admission notification on a rolling basis. There is a deadline for International applicants. Applicants 18 years of age or older without high school diploma may be admitted on individual basis. **Financial aid:** Priority date 5/1; no closing date. FAFSA, institutional form required. Applicants notified on a rolling basis starting 5/1; must reply within 2 week(s) of notification.

**Academics.** Core curriculum guaranteed to transfer to any Texas public university. **Special study options:** Distance learning, double major, dual enrollment of high school students, ESL, honors, liberal arts/career combination. Limited Saturday classes available. License preparation in aviation, dental hygiene, nursing, paramedic, physical therapy, radiology, real estate. **Credit/placement by examination:** AP, CLEP, institutional tests. 18 credit hours maximum toward associate degree. **Support services:** GED preparation and test center, learning center, reduced course load, remedial instruction, study skills assistance, tutoring, writing center.

**Majors. Agriculture:** Horticulture. **Business:** General, accounting, administrative services, business admin, entrepreneurial studies, fashion, hospitality admin, operations, real estate, sales/distribution, tourism/travel. **Communications technology:** General, graphic/printing. **Computer sciences:** General, programming. **Engineering technology:** Architectural, drafting, electrical. **Family/consumer sciences:** Child care, institutional food production. **Foreign languages:** Sign language interpretation. **Health:** Dental hygiene, EMT paramedic, medical radiologic technology/radiation therapy, medical records technology, mental health services, nursing (RN), physical therapy assistant, respiratory therapy technology. **Legal studies:** Paralegal. **Mechanic/repair:** Aircraft, auto body, automotive, electronics/electrical, heating/ac/refrig. **Protective services:** Criminal justice, fire safety technology, firefighting, police science. **Public administration:** General.

**Computing on campus.** 3,000 workstations in library, computer center, student center. Commuter students can connect to campus network. Online course registration, online library available.

**Student life. Freshman orientation:** Available. Preregistration for classes offered. 1-2 hours, held intermittently. **Activities:** Bands, choral groups, dance, drama, literary magazine, music ensembles, student government, student newspaper.

**Athletics. Intramural:** Basketball M, table tennis.

**Student services.** Adult student services, career counseling, services for economically disadvantaged, student employment services, financial aid counseling, health services, personal counseling, placement for graduates. **Physically disabled:** Services for visually, speech, hearing impaired. **Transfer:** College fairs on campus for students transferring to 4-year colleges.

**Contact.** E-mail: suzanne.carter@tccd.edu
Phone: (817) 515-8223 Fax: (817) 515-5283
Suzanne Carter, Director of Admissions Services, Tarrant County College, 1500 Houston Street, Fort Worth, TX 76102-6599

## Temple College
### Temple, Texas
www.templejc.edu                CB code: 6818

▶ Public 2-year community college
▶ Commuter campus in small city

**General.** Founded in 1926. Regionally accredited. **Enrollment:** 4,624 degree-seeking undergraduates; 163 non-degree-seeking students. **Degrees:** 289 associate awarded. **Location:** 65 miles from Austin. **Calendar:** Semester, limited summer session. **Full-time faculty:** 107 total; 17% have terminal degrees, 11% minority, 58% women. **Part-time faculty:** 138 total; 10% have terminal degrees, 9% minority, 54% women. **Special facilities:** Health sciences simulation center. **Partnerships:** Formal partnerships with area high schools for tech prep programs.

**Student profile.** Among degree-seeking undergraduates, 69% enrolled in a transfer program, 22% enrolled in a vocational program, 1% already have a bachelor's degree or higher, 780 enrolled as first-time, first-year students, 239 transferred in from other institutions.

| | | | |
|---|---|---|---|
| Part-time: | 61% | Asian American: | 2% |
| Out-of-state: | 1% | Hispanic American: | 16% |
| Women: | 66% | Native American: | 1% |
| African American: | 17% | 25 or older: | 32% |

**Transfer out.** 64% of students enrolled in the transfer program go on to 4-year colleges. **Colleges most students transferred to 2007:** Texas A&M University, Tarleton State University, Texas State University, University of Texas at Austin, University of Mary Hardin-Baylor.

**Basis for selection.** Open admission, but selective for some programs. Limited enrollment in allied health programs; interview required. **Homeschooled:** Transcript of courses and grades required.

**High school preparation.** 23 units recommended. Recommended units include English 4, mathematics 3, social studies 2, history 2, science 3, foreign language 2 and academic electives 7.

**2007-2008 Annual costs.** Tuition/fees: $2,100; $3,300 out-of-district; $5,280 out-of-state. Per-credit charge: $70 in-district; $110 out-of-district; $176 out-of-state. Books/supplies: $1,200. Personal expenses: $1,407.

**Financial aid.** All financial aid based on need. Need-based aid available for part-time students. Work-study available nights and for part-time students.

**Application procedures. Admission:** No deadline. No application fee. Application must be submitted on paper. Admission notification on a rolling basis. **Financial aid:** Priority date 6/1; no closing date. FAFSA required. Applicants notified on a rolling basis starting 5/1; must reply within 4 week(s) of notification.

**Academics. Special study options:** Accelerated study, cooperative education, distance learning, dual enrollment of high school students, ESL, honors, internships. License preparation in dental hygiene, nursing, paramedic. **Credit/placement by examination:** AP, CLEP, IB, institutional tests. 32 credit hours maximum toward associate degree. Last 16 hours or total 32 hours earned in residence may not be earned by credit by examination. **Support services:** GED preparation, learning center, remedial instruction, study skills assistance, tutoring, writing center.

**Majors. Biology:** General. **Business:** General, office management. **Computer sciences:** General, data entry, LAN/WAN management, programming, system admin, webmaster. **Education:** Elementary, teacher assistance. **Engineering:** General. **Engineering technology:** Drafting. **Family/consumer sciences:** Child development. **Health:** Dental hygiene, EMT paramedic, nursing (RN), respiratory therapy technology, sonography. **Liberal arts:** Arts/sciences. **Math:** General. **Mechanic/repair:** Computer, electronics/electrical. **Protective services:** Criminal justice. **Public administration:** Social work. **Science technology:** Biological. **Social sciences:** Cartography. **Visual/performing arts:** Art.

**Most popular majors.** Business/marketing 15%, health sciences 32%, liberal arts 36%, security/protective services 6%.

**Computing on campus.** 150 workstations in dormitories, library, computer center, student center. Dormitories wired for high-speed internet access and linked to campus network. Commuter students can connect to campus network. Online library, repair service available.

**Student life. Freshman orientation:** Available. Preregistration for classes offered. Held prior to fall semester; 4 hours over 2 days. **Housing:** Apartments available. Privately run student apartments on campus. **Activities:** Bands, campus ministries, choral groups, dance, drama, literary magazine, music ensembles, musical theater, student government, symphony orchestra, black American cultural club, society of Latin American cultures, College Republicans, Young Democrats, literary club.

**Athletics.** NJCAA. **Intercollegiate:** Baseball M, basketball, softball W, tennis, volleyball W. **Intramural:** Basketball, bowling, football (nontackle), golf, racquetball, soccer, softball, swimming, table tennis, tennis, volleyball. **Team name:** Leopards.

**Student services.** Adult student services, career counseling, services for economically disadvantaged, student employment services, financial aid counseling, personal counseling, placement for graduates, veterans' counselor. **Physically disabled:** Services for visually, hearing impaired. **Learning disabled:** Comprehensive services available. **Transfer:** Pre-admission transcript evaluation for new students. Transfer adviser for students transferring to 4-year colleges.

**Contact.** E-mail: toni.borras@templejc.edu
Phone: (254) 298-8300 Toll-free number: (800) 460-4636
Fax: (254) 298-8288
Toni Borras, Director of Admission and Records, Temple College, 2600 South First Street, Temple, TX 76504-7435

## Texarkana College
Texarkana, Texas
www.texarkanacollege.edu
CB code: 6819

- Public 2-year community college
- Commuter campus in small city

**General.** Founded in 1927. Regionally accredited. **Enrollment:** 4,299 degree-seeking undergraduates. **Degrees:** 273 associate awarded. **Location:** 80 miles from Shreveport, Louisiana, 180 miles from Dallas. **Calendar:** Semester, limited summer session. **Full-time faculty:** 95 total. **Part-time faculty:** 118 total. **Special facilities:** 365-acre farm.

**Student profile.**

| | | | |
|---|---|---|---|
| Out-of-state: | 30% | Live on campus: | 3% |
| 25 or older: | 38% | | |

**Transfer out. Colleges most students transferred to 2007:** Texas A&M at Texarkana, Southern Arkansas University.

**Basis for selection.** Open admission. Interview recommended for nursing program.

**2008-2009 Annual costs.** Tuition/fees (projected): $1,080. Per-credit charge: $33. Arkansas and Oklahoma residents pay out-of-district rates. Books/supplies: $750. Personal expenses: $1,200.

**Financial aid. Need-based:** Need-based aid available for part-time students. Work-study available nights, weekends and for part-time students. **Non-need-based:** Scholarships awarded for academics, athletics.

**Application procedures. Admission:** No deadline. No application fee. Application may be submitted online. Admission notification on a rolling basis. **Financial aid:** Priority date 6/1; no closing date. FAFSA, institutional form required. Applicants notified on a rolling basis starting 3/1.

**Academics. Special study options:** Cooperative education, cross-registration, distance learning, dual enrollment of high school students, internships, liberal arts/career combination. License preparation in nursing, paramedic, real estate. **Credit/placement by examination:** AP, CLEP. 14 credit hours maximum toward associate degree. **Support services:** GED test center, learning center, remedial instruction, tutoring.

**Majors. Agriculture:** General. **Biology:** General. **Business:** General, administrative services, business admin, marketing. **Communications:** Journalism. **Computer sciences:** General. **Engineering:** General. **Engineering technology:** Drafting, electrical. **Family/consumer sciences:** Child development. **Foreign languages:** General. **Health:** EMT paramedic, nursing (RN), substance abuse counseling. **History:** General. **Liberal arts:** Humanities. **Math:** General. **Physical sciences:** Chemistry, physics. **Protective services:** Criminal justice, law enforcement admin. **Social sciences:** General, political science. **Visual/performing arts:** Art, dramatic.

**Most popular majors.** Business/marketing 11%, health sciences 32%, liberal arts 31%.

**Computing on campus.** 500 workstations in library, computer center. Dormitories wired for high-speed internet access.

**Student life. Freshman orientation:** Available. Preregistration for classes offered. **Housing:** Coed dorms available. **Activities:** Concert band, choral groups, drama, literary magazine, musical theater, radio station, student government, student newspaper.

**Athletics.** NJCAA. **Intercollegiate:** Baseball M, softball W. **Intramural:** Archery, badminton, basketball, bowling, handball, racquetball, sailing, skin diving, swimming, tennis, volleyball. **Team name:** Bulldogs.

**Student services.** Career counseling, student employment services, personal counseling, veterans' counselor.

**Contact.** E-mail: admissions@texarkanacollege.edu
Phone: (903) 832-5565 ext. 3358 Fax: (903) 832-5030
Van Miller, Director of Admissions and Registrar, Texarkana College, 2500 North Robison Road, Texarkana, TX 75599

## Texas Culinary Academy
Austin, Texas
www.tca.edu

- For-profit 2-year technical college
- Very large city

**General.** Accredited by ACICS. **Enrollment:** 917 degree-seeking undergraduates. **Degrees:** 427 associate awarded. **Calendar:** Semester. **Full-time faculty:** 41 total. **Part-time faculty:** 8 total.

**2007-2008 Annual costs.** Tuition/fees: $38,850. Books/supplies: $3,355.

**Application procedures. Admission:** No deadline.

**Academics. Credit/placement by examination:** CLEP.

**Majors. Personal/culinary services:** Chef training.

**Contact.** E-mail: info@txca.com
Phone: (512) 837-2665
Texas Culinary Academy, 11400 Burnet Road, Suite 2100, Austin, TX 78758

## Texas Southmost College
Brownsville, Texas
www.utb.edu
CB code: 6825

- Public 2-year community college
- Commuter campus in small city

**General.** Founded in 1926. Regionally accredited. **Enrollment:** 10,539 degree-seeking undergraduates. **Degrees:** 902 associate awarded. **Location:** 160 miles from Corpus Christi. **Calendar:** Semester, extensive summer session. **Full-time faculty:** 371 total. **Part-time faculty:** 346 total.

**Basis for selection.** Open admission, but selective for some programs. For some allied health programs, entrance examination may be required.

**2007-2008 Annual costs.** Books/supplies: $578. Personal expenses: $1,348.

**Application procedures. Admission:** No deadline. No application fee. Admission notification on a rolling basis. **Financial aid:** Priority date 4/1, closing date 6/1. FAFSA required. Applicants notified on a rolling basis starting 7/1; must reply by 8/1.

**Academics. Special study options:** Cooperative education, cross-registration, dual enrollment of high school students, honors. **Credit/placement by examination:** AP, CLEP, institutional tests. 38 credit hours maximum toward associate degree. **Support services:** Remedial instruction, tutoring.

**Majors. Business:** General, accounting, business admin, hospitality admin, office management, office technology, sales/distribution. **Computer sciences:** General. **Engineering technology:** Drafting, electrical. **Family/consumer sciences:** Child care. **Health:** Clinical lab science, EMT paramedic, medical radiologic technology/radiation therapy, nursing (RN), respiratory therapy technology, substance abuse counseling. **Legal studies:** Legal secretary. **Liberal arts:** Arts/sciences. **Protective services:** Corrections, law enforcement admin, police science.

**Student life. Freshman orientation:** Mandatory, $15 fee. **Activities:** Bands, choral groups, dance, drama, music ensembles, student government, student newspaper, symphony orchestra.

**Athletics.** NJCAA. **Intercollegiate:** Badminton, baseball M, volleyball W. **Intramural:** Archery, basketball, bowling, golf, gymnastics, handball, sailing, soccer M, softball, table tennis, tennis, volleyball.

**Student services.** Career counseling, student employment services, health services, on-campus daycare, personal counseling, placement for graduates, veterans' counselor.

**Contact.** Phone: (956) 882-8254 Fax: (956) 882-8832
Rene Villarreal, Director of Enrollment, Registrar, Texas Southmost College, 80 Fort Brown, Brownsville, TX 78520

---

## Texas State Technical College: Harlingen
### Harlingen, Texas
www.harlingen.tstc.edu                    CB code: 6843

- Public 2-year technical college
- Commuter campus in small city

**General.** Founded in 1969. Regionally accredited. **Enrollment:** 1,703 degree-seeking undergraduates. **Degrees:** 267 associate awarded. **Location:** 25 miles from Brownsville, 30 miles from South Padre Island. **Calendar:** Semester, extensive summer session. **Full-time faculty:** 149 total; 7% have terminal degrees, 60% minority, 38% women. **Part-time faculty:** 24 total; 8% have terminal degrees, 38% minority, 50% women. **Class size:** 46% < 20, 48% 20-39, 3% 40-49, 2% 50-99. **Special facilities:** Computer labs with digital imaging technology, semi-conductor technology training center.

### Student profile.

| | | | |
|---|---|---|---|
| Out-of-state: | 1% | International: | 1% |
| Asian American: | 1% | 25 or older: | 35% |
| Hispanic American: | 90% | Live on campus: | 12% |

**Transfer out. Colleges most students transferred to 2007:** University of Texas at Brownsville, University of Texas-Pan American, University of Texas-San Antonio, South Texas College, Texas Southmost College.

**Basis for selection.** Open admission, but selective for some programs. Competitive admissions for dental assisting, surgical technology, dental hygiene, and health information technology programs. Associate degree candidates required to take state-mandated Texas Academic Skills Program. Results used only for placement. SAT/ACT scores may be substituted. **Homeschooled:** Statement describing homeschool structure and mission required.

**2007-2008 Annual costs.** Tuition/fees: $2,690; $6,200 out-of-state. Per-credit charge: $65 in-state; $182 out-of-state. Room/board: $3,650. Books/supplies: $900. Personal expenses: $1,380.

**2007-2008 Financial aid. Need-based:** 72% of total undergraduate aid awarded as scholarships/grants, 28% as loans/jobs. Need-based aid available for part-time students.

**Application procedures. Admission:** No deadline. No application fee. Application may be submitted online. Admission notification on a rolling basis. **Financial aid:** Closing date 4/30. FAFSA, institutional form required. Applicants notified on a rolling basis starting 6/30; must reply within 2 week(s) of notification.

**Academics. Special study options:** Combined bachelor's/graduate degree, cooperative education, distance learning, dual enrollment of high school students, ESL, independent study, internships, liberal arts/career combination, teacher certification program, weekend college. License preparation in aviation, dental hygiene, paramedic. **Credit/placement by examination:** AP, CLEP, institutional tests. **Support services:** GED preparation and test center, learning center, remedial instruction, study skills assistance, tutoring.

**Majors. Agriculture:** Business technology. **Business:** Administrative services. **Computer sciences:** Networking, programming. **Education:** Teacher assistance. **Engineering technology:** Biomedical, computer systems, construction, drafting, electrical, electromechanical, telecommunications. **Health:** Dental hygiene, dental lab technology, EMT paramedic, medical assistant, medical records technology, surgical technology. **Legal studies:** Legal secretary. **Mechanic/repair:** Aircraft, auto body, heating/ac/refrig. **Personal/culinary services:** Institutional food service. **Production:** Tool and die. **Science technology:** Chemical.

**Computing on campus.** 1,750 workstations in library, computer center. Online library, helpline available.

**Student life. Freshman orientation:** Available. Preregistration for classes offered. **Housing:** Guaranteed on-campus for all undergraduates. Coed dorms, special housing for disabled, apartments, substance-free housing available. $100 deposit. **Activities:** Dance, literary magazine, student government, student newspaper, Baptist student union, Hispanic club.

**Athletics. Intramural:** Baseball, basketball, football (tackle), racquetball, soccer, softball, table tennis, tennis, track and field, volleyball, weight lifting.

**Student services.** Alcohol/substance abuse counseling, career counseling, student employment services, financial aid counseling, health services, on-campus daycare, personal counseling, placement for graduates, veterans' counselor, women's services. **Physically disabled:** Services for visually, speech, hearing impaired. **Transfer:** Transfer adviser, college fairs on campus for students transferring to 4-year colleges.

**Contact.** E-mail: blanca.guerra@harlingen.tstc.edu
Phone: (956) 364-4320 Toll-free number: (800) 852-8784
Fax: (956) 364-5117
Blanca Guerra, Director of Admissions and Records, Texas State Technical College: Harlingen, 1902 North Loop 499, Harlingen, TX 78550-3697

---

## Texas State Technical College: Marshall
### Marshall, Texas
www.marshall.tstc.edu

- Public 2-year technical college
- Large town

**General.** Regionally accredited. **Enrollment:** 424 degree-seeking undergraduates. **Degrees:** 103 associate awarded. **Location:** 150 miles from Dallas, 230 miles from Houston. **Calendar:** Semester, extensive summer session. **Full-time faculty:** 31 total. **Part-time faculty:** 18 total.

**Basis for selection.** Open admission. Admission tests used only for placement.

**2007-2008 Annual costs.** Tuition/fees: $2,710; $6,220 out-of-state. Per-credit charge: $65 in-state; $182 out-of-state. Room only: $2,390.

**Application procedures. Admission:** No deadline. No application fee. Admission notification on a rolling basis. **Financial aid:** Priority date 6/1; no closing date. FAFSA required.

**Academics. Credit/placement by examination:** CLEP.

**Majors. Business:** E-commerce. **Communications technology:** General. **Computer sciences:** A.i./robotics, LAN/WAN management, networking. **Engineering technology:** Industrial, telecommunications. **Health:** Environmental health.

**Student life. Freshman orientation:** Mandatory. **Activities:** Student newspaper.

**Contact.** Phone: (903) 935-1010
Susan Carter, Director of Admissions, Texas State Technical College: Marshall, 2400 East End Boulevard South, Marshall, TX 75672

---

## Texas State Technical College: Sweetwater
### Sweetwater, Texas
www.westtexas.tstc.edu                    CB code: 3137

- Public 2-year technical college
- Commuter campus in large town

**General.** Founded in 1970. Regionally accredited. **Enrollment:** 1,498 degree-seeking undergraduates; 189 non-degree-seeking students. **Degrees:** 158 associate awarded. **Location:** 50 miles from Abilene. **Calendar:** Semester, limited summer session. **Full-time faculty:** 147 total; 16% minority, 53%

women. **Part-time faculty:** 40 total; 5% minority, 35% women. **Special facilities:** Robotics lab, Cisco Academy, Microsoft Academy. **Partnerships:** Formal partnership with Florida Power & Light Energy for development of TSTC West Texas' Wind Energy Technology Program.

**Student profile.** Among degree-seeking undergraduates, 274 enrolled as first-time, first-year students, 250 transferred in from other institutions.

| | | | |
|---|---|---|---|
| Part-time: | 84% | 25 or older: | 44% |
| Out-of-state: | 1% | Live on campus: | 16% |
| Women: | 48% | | |

**Basis for selection.** Open admission, but selective for some programs. Base score on placement test considered for nursing program. Standardized test scores, if submitted, may be used in placement and counseling. SAT and ACT scores, if high enough, may exempt an applicant from THEA testing requirements.

**2007-2008 Annual costs.** Tuition/fees: $2,710; $6,220 out-of-state. Per-credit charge: $65 in-state; $182 out-of-state. Room/board: $3,850. Books/supplies: $1,100. Personal expenses: $650.

**2006-2007 Financial aid. Need-based:** 20% of total undergraduate aid awarded as scholarships/grants, 80% as loans/jobs. Need-based aid available for part-time students. Work-study available nights, weekends and for part-time students. **Non-need-based:** Scholarships awarded for academics, leadership.

**Application procedures. Admission:** Priority date 8/1; no deadline. No application fee. Application may be submitted online. Admission notification on a rolling basis. **Financial aid:** Priority date 5/1; no closing date. FAFSA, institutional form required. Applicants notified on a rolling basis starting 7/1.

**Academics. Special study options:** Cooperative education, cross-registration, distance learning, dual enrollment of high school students, internships, liberal arts/career combination. 1-1 and 1-1-2 electronics technology programs with numerous area institutions. License preparation in aviation, nursing, paramedic. **Credit/placement by examination:** AP, CLEP, institutional tests. Varies per program and individual student. **Support services:** GED test center, learning center, reduced course load, remedial instruction, study skills assistance, tutoring.

**Majors. Business:** Management information systems. **Communications technology:** General. **Computer sciences:** Networking, programming, web page design. **Conservation:** Environmental science. **Engineering technology:** Construction, drafting, electrical, robotics. **Health:** EMT paramedic, licensed practical nurse, medical records technology, substance abuse counseling. **Mechanic/repair:** Aircraft, automotive, diesel. **Personal/culinary services:** Chef training. **Production:** Machine tool. **Visual/performing arts:** Design.

**Computing on campus.** 50 workstations in library, student center. Dormitories wired for high-speed internet access. Commuter students can connect to campus network. Online library, helpline, wireless network available.

**Student life. Freshman orientation:** Mandatory, $15 fee. Preregistration for classes offered. Held day before start of classes. **Housing:** Coed dorms, special housing for disabled, apartments, substance-free housing available. $150 deposit. Pets allowed in dorm rooms. **Activities:** Student government, student newspaper, Mexican American club, Baptist student union, technical students association, data processing management association, Business Professionals of America, society of manufacturing engineers, Vocational Industrial Clubs of America.

**Athletics. Intramural:** Basketball, bowling, golf, softball, swimming, table tennis, tennis, volleyball W.

**Student services.** Career counseling, services for economically disadvantaged, student employment services, financial aid counseling, health services, personal counseling, placement for graduates, veterans' counselor, women's services. **Physically disabled:** Services for hearing impaired. **Transfer:** Transfer adviser, college fairs on campus for students transferring to 4-year colleges.

**Contact.** E-mail: Maria.Aguirre@tstc.edu
Phone: (325) 235-7300 Toll-free number: (800) 592-8784
Fax: (325) 235-7416
Maria Aguirre-Acuna, Director of Admissions & Records, Texas State Technical College: Sweetwater, 300 Homer K Taylor Drive, Sweetwater, TX 79556

## Texas State Technical College: Waco
Waco, Texas
www.waco.tstc.edu
CB code: 6328

- Public 2-year technical college
- Residential campus in small city

**General.** Founded in 1965. Regionally accredited. **Enrollment:** 4,210 degree-seeking undergraduates. **Degrees:** 649 associate awarded. **Location:** 90 miles from Dallas, 99 miles from Austin. **Calendar:** Semester, extensive summer session. **Full-time faculty:** 243 total. **Part-time faculty:** 20 total. **Special facilities:** Advanced manufacturing center, 8,600-foot runway at TSTC-Waco airport, institutionally owned and operated 18-hole golf course.

**Basis for selection.** Open admission. Accuplacer or THEA test required prior to enrollment; used for placement purposes only. Interview recommended for students without high school diploma or GED. **Homeschooled:** Transcript of courses and grades required.

**2007-2008 Annual costs.** Tuition/fees: $2,714; $6,224 out-of-state. Per-credit charge: $85 in-state; $182 out-of-state. Room/board: $4,050. Books/supplies: $751. Personal expenses: $1,899.

**2006-2007 Financial aid.** All financial aid based on need. 54% of total undergraduate aid awarded as scholarships/grants, 46% as loans/jobs. Need-based aid available for part-time students. Work-study available for part-time students.

**Application procedures. Admission:** No deadline. No application fee. Application may be submitted online. Admission notification on a rolling basis. **Financial aid:** Priority date 6/1; no closing date. FAFSA required. Applicants notified on a rolling basis starting 5/15.

**Academics. Special study options:** Cooperative education, distance learning, double major, dual enrollment of high school students. License preparation in aviation. **Credit/placement by examination:** AP, CLEP, IB, institutional tests. 24 credit hours maximum toward associate degree. **Support services:** GED test center, learning center, remedial instruction, study skills assistance, tutoring.

**Majors. Agriculture:** Turf management. **Business:** Operations. **Communications technology:** General, graphic/printing. **Computer sciences:** General, computer science, data processing, information systems, programming. **Construction:** Maintenance, power transmission. **Engineering technology:** Drafting, electrical. **Family/consumer sciences:** Institutional food production. **Health:** Clinical lab science. **Mechanic/repair:** General, aircraft, auto body, automotive, avionics, diesel, electronics/electrical, heating/ac/refrig, industrial. **Physical sciences:** General. **Transportation:** Aviation. **Visual/performing arts:** Cinematography, commercial/advertising art.

**Computing on campus.** 1,000 workstations in library, computer center, student center. Dormitories wired for high-speed internet access and linked to campus network. Commuter students can connect to campus network. Helpline, student web hosting, wireless network available.

**Student life. Freshman orientation:** Mandatory, $10 fee. Preregistration for classes offered. Held prior to semester. **Housing:** Coed dorms, single-sex dorms, special housing for disabled, apartments, substance-free housing available. $150 fully refundable deposit. Duplexes and houses available to married students or students with families. **Activities:** Student government, student newspaper.

**Athletics. Intramural:** Basketball, football (non-tackle), golf, racquetball, softball, volleyball. **Team name:** Tornadoes.

**Student services.** Adult student services, career counseling, student employment services, financial aid counseling, health services, on-campus daycare, personal counseling, placement for graduates, veterans' counselor, women's services. **Physically disabled:** Services for visually, speech, hearing impaired. **Transfer:** Pre-admission transcript evaluation for new students. Transfer adviser for students transferring to 4-year colleges.

**Contact.** Phone: (254) 867-2361 Toll-free number: (800) 792-8784 ext. 2361 Fax: (254) 867-2250
Dawn Khoury, Director of Admissions and Records, Texas State Technical College: Waco, 3801 Campus Drive, Waco, TX 76705

## Trinity Valley Community College
Athens, Texas
www.tvcc.edu
CB code: 6271

- Public 2-year community college
- Commuter campus in large town

**General.** Founded in 1946. Regionally accredited. 3 extension centers in state. **Enrollment:** 5,615 degree-seeking undergraduates. **Degrees:** 678 associate awarded. **Location:** 70 miles from Dallas. **Calendar:** Semester, limited summer session. **Full-time faculty:** 125 total. **Part-time faculty:** 82 total. **Special facilities:** 2 operating ranches with more than 500 acres.

**Student profile.**

Out-of-state:                    3%       Live on campus:                    10%

**Basis for selection.** Open admission, but selective for some programs. Special requirements for nursing program. Institution observes all TASP requirements.

**2007-2008 Annual costs.** Tuition/fees: $1,050; $1,650 out-of-district; $2,400 out-of-state. Per-credit charge: $20 in-district; $40 out-of-district; $65 out-of-state. Room/board: $3,400. Books/supplies: $435. Personal expenses: $980.

**Financial aid. Need-based:** Need-based aid available for part-time students. Work-study available nights and weekends. **Non-need-based:** Scholarships awarded for academics, athletics.

**Application procedures. Admission:** No deadline. No application fee. Admission notification on a rolling basis. **Financial aid:** Priority date 7/1; no closing date. FAFSA, institutional form required. Applicants notified on a rolling basis starting 7/1; must reply within 2 week(s) of notification.

**Academics. Special study options:** Distance learning, dual enrollment of high school students, honors, internships, liberal arts/career combination, weekend college. **Credit/placement by examination:** CLEP. 18 credit hours maximum toward associate degree. **Support services:** GED preparation and test center, learning center, remedial instruction, tutoring.

**Majors. Agriculture:** Business, farm/ranch, horticulture. **Biology:** General. **Business:** Accounting, administrative services, business admin, office technology. **Communications:** General, journalism. **Computer sciences:** General, computer graphics, data processing, programming. **Education:** General, early childhood, elementary, middle. **Engineering:** General, polymer. **Engineering technology:** Drafting. **English:** English lit, speech/rhetoric. **Family/consumer sciences:** Child care. **Foreign languages:** Spanish. **Health:** Nursing (RN), predental, premedicine, prenursing, prepharmacy, preveterinary. **Legal studies:** Legal secretary, paralegal, prelaw. **Liberal arts:** Arts/sciences. **Math:** General. **Parks/recreation:** Health/fitness. **Physical sciences:** Chemistry, physics. **Protective services:** Firefighting, law enforcement admin. **Psychology:** General. **Social sciences:** General, sociology. **Visual/performing arts:** General, art, dramatic.

**Student life. Freshman orientation:** Available, $20 fee. **Housing:** Single-sex dorms available. **Activities:** Bands, campus ministries, choral groups, dance, drama, international student organizations, music ensembles, student government, student newspaper, Baptist student union, nontraditional student organization, Phi Beta Kappa, criminal justice fraternity.

**Athletics.** NJCAA. **Intercollegiate:** Basketball, football (tackle) M. **Intramural:** Basketball, bowling, handball M, racquetball, soccer M, softball, table tennis, tennis, volleyball. **Team name:** Cardinals.

**Student services.** Career counseling, student employment services, personal counseling, placement for graduates, veterans' counselor. **Physically disabled:** Services for speech impaired. **Transfer:** Pre-admission transcript evaluation for new students. Transfer adviser, college fairs on campus for students transferring to 4-year colleges.

**Contact.** Phone: (903) 675-6357 Fax: (903) 675-6209
Audrey Hawkins, Director of School Relations, Trinity Valley Community College, 100 Cardinal Drive, Athens, TX 75751

## Tyler Junior College
Tyler, Texas
www.tjc.edu                                    CB code: 6833

♦ Public 2-year junior college
♦ Commuter campus in small city

**General.** Founded in 1926. Regionally accredited. **Enrollment:** 8,217 degree-seeking undergraduates; 2 non-degree-seeking students. **Degrees:** 1,707 associate awarded. **Location:** 85 miles from Dallas, 85 miles from Shreveport, Louisiana. **Calendar:** Semester, extensive summer session. **Full-time faculty:** 255 total. **Part-time faculty:** 258 total. **Class size:** 48% < 20, 46% 20-39, 4% 40-49, 1% 50-99, less than 1% >100. **Special facilities:** Planetarium, conservatory.

**Student profile.** Among degree-seeking undergraduates, 65% enrolled in a transfer program, 35% enrolled in a vocational program, 1% already have a bachelor's degree or higher, 2,119 enrolled as first-time, first-year students.

| | | | |
|---|---|---|---|
| Part-time: | 40% | Hispanic American: | 11% |
| Out-of-state: | 2% | Native American: | 1% |
| Women: | 58% | International: | 1% |
| African American: | 21% | 25 or older: | 28% |
| Asian American: | 1% | Live on campus: | 1% |

**Transfer out. Colleges most students transferred to 2007:** Stephen F. Austin State University, Texas A&M University, University of Texas at Tyler.

**Basis for selection.** Open admission, but selective for some programs. Admission to allied health programs based on test scores. High school units mandated by state law may vary by program. Texas Higher Education Assessment (THEA) required by Texas law for all incoming students. Interview required for some allied health programs, recommended for others. **Homeschooled:** Must complete equivalent of accepted high school diploma.

**2007-2008 Annual costs.** Tuition/fees: $1,592; $2,552 out-of-district; $3,392 out-of-state. Per-credit charge: $48 in-district; $80 out-of-district; $108 out-of-state. Room/board: $4,000. Books/supplies: $1,000. Personal expenses: $1,866.

**Financial aid. Need-based:** Need-based aid available for part-time students. Work-study available for part-time students. **Non-need-based:** Scholarships awarded for academics, alumni affiliation, art, athletics, leadership, music/drama.

**Application procedures. Admission:** No deadline. No application fee. Admission notification on a rolling basis. **Financial aid:** Priority date 6/1; no closing date. FAFSA, institutional form required. Applicants notified on a rolling basis starting 3/1; must reply within 2 week(s) of notification.

**Academics. Special study options:** Accelerated study, cooperative education, cross-registration, distance learning, dual enrollment of high school students, ESL, honors, internships, liberal arts/career combination, weekend college. License preparation in dental hygiene, nursing, paramedic, radiology, real estate. **Credit/placement by examination:** AP, CLEP, IB, institutional tests. **Support services:** GED preparation and test center, learning center, remedial instruction, study skills assistance, tutoring.

**Honors college/program.** SAT 1070 (exclusive of Writing), minimum 500 Math and Verbal; ACT 23, minimum 19 in each area.

**Majors. Agriculture:** General, farm/ranch. **Biology:** General. **Business:** General, accounting technology, administrative services, business admin, managerial economics, marketing, office management. **Communications:** Journalism. **Communications technology:** Graphic/printing. **Computer sciences:** General, applications programming, information systems, web page design. **Construction:** Electrician, maintenance. **Education:** General. **Engineering:** General. **Engineering technology:** Civil drafting, drafting, electrical, surveying. **English:** English lit, speech/rhetoric. **Family/consumer sciences:** General, child care. **Foreign languages:** General, French, sign language interpretation, Spanish. **Health:** Clinical lab assistant, dental hygiene, EMT ambulance attendant, EMT paramedic, medical radiologic technology/radiation therapy, medical records technology, medical secretary, nursing (RN), office admin, ophthalmic lab technology, predental, premedicine, prenursing, prepharmacy, preveterinary, radiologic technology/medical imaging, respiratory therapy technology, sonography, substance abuse counseling, surgical technology. **History:** General. **Interdisciplinary:** Natural sciences. **Legal studies:** Legal secretary, paralegal, prelaw. **Liberal arts:** Arts/sciences. **Math:** General. **Mechanic/repair:** Automotive, heating/ac/refrig. **Parks/recreation:** Exercise sciences, health/fitness. **Physical sciences:** Chemistry, geology, physics. **Protective services:** Criminal justice, fire safety technology, police science. **Psychology:** General. **Public administration:** Human services. **Social sciences:** General, sociology. **Visual/performing arts:** General, art, commercial/advertising art, dance, dramatic, interior design, music performance, studio arts.

**Computing on campus.** 95 workstations in library, computer center, student center. Dormitories wired for high-speed internet access. Commuter students can connect to campus network. Online course registration, online library, helpline, repair service, student web hosting, wireless network available.

**Student life. Freshman orientation:** Mandatory, $50 fee. Preregistration for classes offered. 2-day orientation program in summer. **Housing:** Single-sex dorms available. $200 partly refundable deposit. **Activities:** Bands, campus ministries, choral groups, dance, drama, international student organizations, literary magazine, music ensembles, musical theater, student government, student newspaper, symphony orchestra, TV station, Wesleyan Ministries, Phi Theta Kappa, Hispanic student organization.

**Athletics.** NAIA, NJCAA. **Intercollegiate:** Baseball M, basketball, cheerleading, football (tackle) M, golf, soccer M, tennis, volleyball W. **Intramural:** Badminton, basketball, football (tackle) M, handball, racquetball, softball, table tennis, tennis, volleyball M. **Team name:** Apaches.

**Student services.** Adult student services, alcohol/substance abuse counseling, campus ministries, career counseling, services for economically disadvantaged, student employment services, financial aid counseling, health services, personal counseling, placement for graduates, veterans' counselor, women's services. **Physically disabled:** Services for visually, speech, hearing impaired. **Transfer:** College fairs on campus for students transferring to 4-year colleges.

**Contact.** E-mail: admissions@tjc.edu
Phone: (903) 510-2523 Toll-free number: (800) 687-5680 ext. 2523
Fax: (903) 510-2161
Craig Turnage, Director of Enrollment Management, Tyler Junior College, Box 9020, Tyler, TX 75711-9020

## Vernon College
### Vernon, Texas
### www.vernoncollege.edu
**CB code: 6913**

- Public 2-year community and junior college
- Commuter campus in large town

**General.** Founded in 1970. Regionally accredited. **Enrollment:** 2,813 degree-seeking undergraduates. **Degrees:** 211 associate awarded. **Location:** 50 miles from Wichita Falls. **Calendar:** Semester, extensive summer session. **Full-time faculty:** 70 total. **Part-time faculty:** 80 total.

**Student profile.**

| | | | |
|---|---|---|---|
| Out-of-state: | 5% | Live on campus: | 6% |
| 25 or older: | 49% | | |

**Basis for selection.** Open admission, but selective for some programs. Additional requirements for nursing and cosmetology applicants.

**2008-2009 Annual costs.** Tuition/fees (projected): $1,875. Per-credit charge: $55. Room/board: $3,125. Books/supplies: $1,000. Personal expenses: $1,238.

**2007-2008 Financial aid.** All financial aid based on need. 82% of total undergraduate aid awarded as scholarships/grants, 18% as loans/jobs. Need-based aid available for part-time students. Work-study available nights, weekends and for part-time students.

**Application procedures. Admission:** No deadline. $10 fee. Application may be submitted online. Admission notification on a rolling basis. **Financial aid:** Priority date 7/1; no closing date. FAFSA required. Applicants notified on a rolling basis starting 4/1.

**Academics. Special study options:** Cooperative education, distance learning, dual enrollment of high school students, internships. License preparation in aviation, nursing, paramedic, real estate. **Credit/placement by examination:** AP, CLEP, IB, institutional tests. **Support services:** GED test center, learning center, reduced course load, remedial instruction, study skills assistance, tutoring, writing center.

**Majors. Agriculture:** Farm/ranch. **Business:** General, accounting, administrative services, human resources, marketing, office technology. **Computer sciences:** Data processing. **Engineering technology:** Drafting. **Health:** Nursing (RN). **Legal studies:** Paralegal. **Liberal arts:** Arts/sciences. **Mechanic/repair:** Electronics/electrical. **Protective services:** Criminal justice.

**Computing on campus.** 60 workstations in library, computer center. Dormitories wired for high-speed internet access. Online course registration available.

**Student life. Freshman orientation:** Available. **Housing:** Single-sex dorms available. **Activities:** Choral groups, drama, music ensembles, musical theater, student government.

**Athletics.** NJCAA. **Intercollegiate:** Baseball M, rodeo, softball W, volleyball W. **Intramural:** Archery, badminton, baseball M, basketball, football (non-tackle), golf, handball, racquetball, softball, swimming, table tennis, tennis, track and field, volleyball. **Team name:** Chaparral.

**Student services.** Adult student services, career counseling, services for economically disadvantaged, student employment services, financial aid counseling, health services, personal counseling, placement for graduates, veterans' counselor. **Physically disabled:** Services for visually, speech, hearing impaired. **Transfer:** Transfer adviser for students transferring to 4-year colleges.

**Contact.** E-mail: sdavenport@vernoncollege.edu
Phone: (940) 552-6291 Fax: (940) 553-1753
Joe Hite, Dean of Admissions and Financial Aid/Registrar, Vernon College, 4400 College Drive, Vernon, TX 76384-4092

## Victoria College
### Victoria, Texas
### www.victoriacollege.edu
**CB code: 6915**

- Public 2-year community college
- Commuter campus in small city

**General.** Founded in 1925. Regionally accredited. **Enrollment:** 3,988 degree-seeking undergraduates. **Degrees:** 295 associate awarded. **Location:** 110 miles from San Antonio, 125 miles from Austin. **Calendar:** Semester, limited summer session. **Full-time faculty:** 80 total. **Part-time faculty:** 40 total.

**Student profile.** Among degree-seeking undergraduates, 64% enrolled in a transfer program, 36% enrolled in a vocational program, 2% already have a bachelor's degree or higher, 681 enrolled as first-time, first-year students, 241 transferred in from other institutions.

| | | | |
|---|---|---|---|
| Part-time: | 67% | Asian American: | 1% |
| Women: | 67% | Hispanic American: | 33% |
| African American: | 5% | | |

**Basis for selection.** Open admission, but selective for some programs. Special requirements for allied health programs; interview required. THEA required.

**High school preparation.** 24 units recommended. Recommended units include English 4, mathematics 3, social studies 2.5, history 1, science 3, foreign language 2, academic electives 3.5. 0.5 economics, 1 fine arts, 0.5 speech, 1 technical applications recommended.

**2007-2008 Annual costs.** Tuition/fees: $1,470; $2,130 out-of-district; $2,310 out-of-state. Books/supplies: $1,400. Personal expenses: $2,442.

**Financial aid. Need-based:** Work-study available for part-time students. **Non-need-based:** Scholarships awarded for academics, art, minority status, music/drama.

**Application procedures. Admission:** No deadline. No application fee. Application may be submitted online. Admission notification on a rolling basis beginning on or about 7/1. **Financial aid:** Priority date 4/15; no closing date. FAFSA, institutional form required. Applicants notified on a rolling basis.

**Academics. Special study options:** Distance learning, dual enrollment of high school students. 2+2 plans with University of Texas-San Antonio, University of Houston-Victoria, Texas A&M-Corpus Christi, University of Texas-Brownsville. Bachelor's degree programs available on campus. **Credit/placement by examination:** AP, CLEP, IB, institutional tests. **Support services:** GED preparation and test center, learning center, remedial instruction, tutoring.

**Majors. Business:** Administrative services, business admin. **Computer sciences:** General, information systems, networking, programming, system admin, web page design, webmaster. **Engineering technology:** Electrical, instrumentation. **Health:** Clinical lab technology, EMT paramedic, nursing (RN), respiratory therapy technology. **Legal studies:** Paralegal. **Liberal arts:** Arts/sciences.

**Computing on campus.** 500 workstations in library, computer center, student center. Commuter students can connect to campus network. Online course registration, online library, helpline, wireless network available.

**Student life. Freshman orientation:** Mandatory, $20 fee. Summer 1-day orientation sessions; online orientation also available. **Activities:** Bands, campus ministries, choral groups, drama, literary magazine, music ensembles, student government, student newspaper.

**Athletics. Intramural:** Baseball, basketball, bowling, golf, swimming, tennis, volleyball, weight lifting. **Team name:** Pirates.

**Student services.** Career counseling, services for economically disadvantaged, student employment services, financial aid counseling, personal counseling, veterans' counselor. **Physically disabled:** Services for visually impaired. **Transfer:** College fairs on campus for students transferring to 4-year colleges.

**Contact.** E-mail: registrar@victoriacollege.edu
Phone: (361) 572-6408 Fax: (361) 582-2525
LaVern Dentler, Registrar, Victoria College, 2200 East Red River, Victoria, TX 77901

## Virginia College at Austin
### Austin, Texas
www.vc.edu/austin

- For-profit 2-year business and technical college
- Commuter campus in very large city

**General.** Accredited by ACICS. **Calendar:** Continuous.

**Contact.** Phone: (512) 371-3500
Director of Admissions, 6301 East Highway 290, Austin, TX 78723

## Wade College
### Dallas, Texas
www.wadecollege.com                    CB code: 1537

- For-profit 2-year junior college
- Residential campus in very large city

**General.** Founded in 1965. Regionally accredited. **Location:** 2 miles from downtown. **Calendar:** Trimester.

**Annual costs/financial aid.** Need-based financial aid available to full-time and part-time students.

**Contact.** Phone: (800) 624-4850
Director of Admissions, Dallas Market Center, PO Box 421149, Dallas, TX 75342

## Weatherford College
### Weatherford, Texas
www.wc.edu                    CB code: 6931

- Public 2-year community college
- Commuter campus in large town

**General.** Founded in 1869. Regionally accredited. Off-campus courses held in Mineral Wells, Decatur, Aledo, Bridgeport, Granbury, Jacksboro, Spring-town, Azle. **Enrollment:** 4,092 degree-seeking undergraduates; 421 non-degree-seeking students. **Degrees:** 430 associate awarded. **ROTC:** Air Force. **Location:** 25 miles from Fort Worth. **Calendar:** Semester, extensive summer session. **Full-time faculty:** 90 total. **Part-time faculty:** 105 total. **Special facilities:** 300-acre college farm. **Partnerships:** Formal partnerships with tech prep program and dual credit articulation agreements.

**Student profile.** Among degree-seeking undergraduates, 892 enrolled as first-time, first-year students.

| | | | |
|---|---|---|---|
| Part-time: | 49% | Hispanic American: | 10% |
| Out-of-state: | 3% | Native American: | 1% |
| Women: | 62% | International: | 1% |
| African American: | 2% | 25 or older: | 50% |
| Asian American: | 1% | Live on campus: | 5% |

**Transfer out. Colleges most students transferred to 2007:** Tarleton State University, University of North Texas, University of Texas at Arlington, Texas Tech University.

**Basis for selection.** Open admission, but selective for some programs. Nursing school, fire science requires entrance examination. Peace officer requires physical, drug testing, background check. Texas Academic Skills Program (TASP) required of all students unless TASP-exempt.

**2007-2008 Annual costs.** Tuition/fees: $1,680; $2,430 out-of-district; $3,750 out-of-state. Per-credit charge: $56 in-district; $81 out-of-district; $125 out-of-state. Room/board: $7,080. Books/supplies: $580. Personal expenses: $1,116.

**Financial aid.** All financial aid based on need. Work-study available nights, weekends and for part-time students.

**Application procedures. Admission:** No deadline. No application fee. Application may be submitted online. Admission notification on a rolling basis. **Financial aid:** Priority date 7/3; no closing date. FAFSA required. Applicants notified on a rolling basis; must reply within 2 week(s) of notification.

**Academics. Special study options:** Cooperative education, distance learning, dual enrollment of high school students, ESL, honors, internships, liberal arts/career combination, teacher certification program, weekend college. License preparation in nursing, paramedic, radiology, real estate. **Credit/placement by examination:** AP, CLEP, institutional tests. 30 credit hours maximum toward associate degree. Credit earned by examination does not reduce resident requirement of 15 semester hours of class completed at college. **Support services:** GED preparation and test center, learning center, remedial instruction, study skills assistance, tutoring.

**Majors. Agriculture:** Business, equestrian studies, farm/ranch. **Business:** General, accounting, administrative services, human resources, marketing, office/clerical, operations. **Communications:** General. **Computer sciences:** General, data processing, programming. **Engineering technology:** Electrical. **English:** Speech/rhetoric. **Family/consumer sciences:** Child care. **Health:** EMT paramedic, licensed practical nurse, phlebotomy, predental, premedicine, prenursing, prepharmacy, respiratory therapy assistant, respiratory therapy technology. **Liberal arts:** Arts/sciences. **Personal/culinary services:** Cosmetic. **Protective services:** Corrections, police science. **Social sciences:** Sociology.

**Computing on campus.** 300 workstations in library, computer center. Dormitories linked to campus network. Commuter students can connect to campus network. Online course registration available.

**Student life. Freshman orientation:** Mandatory. Half-day sessions held before registration. **Housing:** Special housing for disabled, apartments, substance-free housing available. $100 deposit, deadline 8/15. **Activities:** Jazz band, choral groups, dance, drama, music ensembles, musical theater, student government, black awareness student organization, Hispanic student organization, Baptist student union, international student organization, Wesleyan foundation, Baptist student ministries, A Better Life Through Education, disabled club.

**Athletics.** NJCAA. **Intercollegiate:** Baseball M, basketball, cheerleading, rodeo, tennis W. **Intramural:** Badminton, basketball, golf, softball, tennis, volleyball. **Team name:** Coyotes.

**Student services.** Adult student services, career counseling, services for economically disadvantaged, student employment services, financial aid counseling, personal counseling, placement for graduates, veterans' counselor. **Physically disabled:** Services for visually, speech, hearing impaired. **Transfer:** Pre-admission transcript evaluation for new students. Transfer adviser, college fairs on campus for students transferring to 4-year colleges.

**Contact.** Phone: (817) 598-6241 Toll-free number: (800) 287-5471 Fax: (817) 598-6205
Ralph Willingham, Director, Weatherford College, 225 College Park Drive, Weatherford, TX 76086

## Western Technical College
### El Paso, Texas
www.wtc-ep.edu                    CB code: 2941

- For-profit 2-year technical college
- Commuter campus in very large city

**General.** Accredited by ACCSCT. Two campuses: main campus downtown, branch campus in NE section. **Enrollment:** 500 degree-seeking undergraduates. **Degrees:** 550 associate awarded. **Calendar:** Continuous. **Full-time faculty:** 97 total. **Part-time faculty:** 34 total.

**Student profile.** Among degree-seeking undergraduates, 100% enrolled in a vocational program.

| | | | |
|---|---|---|---|
| Part-time: | 20% | Women: | 28% |

**Transfer out.** 10% of students enrolled in the transfer program go on to 4-year colleges.

**Basis for selection.** Open admission, but selective for some programs. Some programs require CPAT or other entrance requirements.

**2007-2008 Annual costs.** Tuition varies by program. Automotive: $20,595; refrigeration: $20,595; welding: $14,040; computer: $24,714; medical assisting: $9,828; massage therapy: $6,300; health information: $14,150. Registration fee $100.

**Financial aid.** All financial aid based on need. Need-based aid available for part-time students.

**Application procedures. Admission:** No deadline. No application fee. **Financial aid:** No deadline. FAFSA required. Applicants notified on a rolling basis.

**Academics. Credit/placement by examination:** CLEP. **Support services:** GED preparation, remedial instruction, tutoring.

**Majors. Mechanic/repair:** General.

**Computing on campus.** 200 workstations in library, computer center, student center. Online library, wireless network available.

**Contact.** Phone: (915) 532-3737
Jerry Martin, Director of Admissions, Western Technical College, 9624 Plaza Circle, El Paso, TX 79927

## Western Technical College: Diana Drive
### El Paso, Texas
### www.wtc-ep.edu

◆ For-profit 2-year technical college
◆ Very large city

**General.** Accredited by ACCSCT. **Calendar:** Continuous.

**Annual costs/financial aid.** Tuition varies by program. Automotive: $19,800.00; refrigeration: $19,80.00; welding: $13,500.00; computer: $23,760.00; electronics: $23,760.00; medical assisting: $9,450.00; health information: $13,600.00.

**Contact.** Phone: (915) 566-9621
Director of Admissions, 9451 Diana Drive, El Paso, TX 79924

## Western Texas College
### Snyder, Texas
### www.wtc.edu
**CB code: 6951**

◆ Public 2-year community and junior college
◆ Commuter campus in large town

**General.** Founded in 1969. Regionally accredited. **Enrollment:** 1,977 degree-seeking undergraduates. **Degrees:** 123 associate awarded. **Location:** 80 miles from Lubbock. **Calendar:** Semester, extensive summer session. **Full-time faculty:** 29 total; 14% have terminal degrees, 17% minority, 48% women. **Part-time faculty:** 59 total; 3% have terminal degrees, 44% women. **Class size:** 83% < 20, 16% 20-39, less than 1% 40-49, less than 1% 50-99.

**Student profile.** Among degree-seeking undergraduates, 75% enrolled in a transfer program, 25% enrolled in a vocational program, 1% already have a bachelor's degree or higher, 495 enrolled as first-time, first-year students, 125 transferred in from other institutions.

| | | | |
|---|---|---|---|
| Part-time: | 66% | 25 or older: | 32% |
| Out-of-state: | 3% | Live on campus: | 15% |
| Women: | 44% | | |

**Transfer out. Colleges most students transferred to 2007:** Texas Tech University, Angelo State University, University of Texas, Texas A&M University.

**Basis for selection.** Open admission, but selective for some programs. Special requirements for nursing program. Institutional placement tests may be submitted in place of SAT/ACT. Interview recommended.

**2007-2008 Annual costs.** Tuition/fees: $1,740; $1,950 out-of-district; $2,340 out-of-state. Per-credit charge: $39 in-district; $46 out-of-district; $59 out-of-state. Room/board: $4,100. Books/supplies: $500. Personal expenses: $900.

**2007-2008 Financial aid. Need-based:** 191 full-time freshmen applied for aid; 140 were judged to have need; 90 of these received aid. Average need met was 50%. Average scholarship/grant was $1,000; average loan $3,000. 81% of total undergraduate aid awarded as scholarships/grants, 19% as loans/jobs. Need-based aid available for part-time students. Work-study available nights and weekends. **Non-need-based:** Awarded to 94 full-time undergraduates, including 129 freshmen. Scholarships awarded for academics, art, athletics, leadership, music/drama, state residency.

**Application procedures. Admission:** No deadline. No application fee. Application must be submitted on paper. Admission notification on a rolling basis beginning on or about 11/5. **Financial aid:** Priority date 7/1; no closing date. FAFSA, institutional form required. Applicants notified on a rolling basis starting 5/1; must reply within 2 week(s) of notification.

**Academics. Special study options:** Distance learning, dual enrollment of high school students, honors, independent study, internships. License preparation in nursing, paramedic. **Credit/placement by examination:** AP, CLEP, institutional tests. 12 credit hours maximum toward associate degree. **Support services:** GED preparation and test center, learning center, pre-admission summer program, reduced course load, remedial instruction, tutoring.

**Majors. Agriculture:** Animal sciences, greenhouse operations, horticulture, landscaping, nursery operations. **Biology:** General. **Business:** General, accounting, administrative services, business admin. **Communications:** Journalism. **Computer sciences:** General, computer science, data processing, LAN/WAN management, programming. **Education:** General, early childhood. **Engineering:** General. **English:** English lit. **Foreign languages:** General. **Health:** EMT paramedic, predental, premedicine, prenursing, prepharmacy, preveterinary. **History:** General. **Legal studies:** Prelaw. **Liberal arts:** Arts/sciences. **Math:** General. **Parks/recreation:** Facilities management, health/fitness. **Philosophy/religion:** Philosophy. **Physical sciences:** Chemistry, geology, physics. **Production:** Welding. **Protective services:** Corrections, law enforcement admin, police science. **Psychology:** General. **Social sciences:** General, economics, geography, international relations, political science, sociology. **Visual/performing arts:** Art, ceramics, dramatic, drawing, metal/jewelry, painting, photography, sculpture.

**Computing on campus.** 70 workstations in dormitories, library, computer center, student center. Dormitories wired for high-speed internet access and linked to campus network. Online library available.

**Student life. Freshman orientation:** Available. Preregistration for classes offered. **Housing:** Guaranteed on-campus for all undergraduates. Single-sex dorms, apartments available. $50 deposit. **Activities:** Drama, literary magazine, musical theater, student government, TV station, Baptist student union, Phi Theta Kappa.

**Athletics.** NJCAA. **Intercollegiate:** Baseball M, cheerleading M, cross-country, rodeo, softball W, volleyball W. **Intramural:** Basketball, bowling, diving, golf, handball, racquetball, softball, swimming, volleyball, weight lifting. **Team name:** Westerners.

**Student services.** Adult student services, alcohol/substance abuse counseling, career counseling, services for economically disadvantaged, student employment services, financial aid counseling, personal counseling, placement for graduates, veterans' counselor. **Transfer:** Pre-admission transcript evaluation for new students. Transfer adviser, college fairs on campus for students transferring to 4-year colleges.

**Contact.** E-mail: cmadrid@wtc.edu
Phone: (325) 573-8511 ext. 372 Toll-free number: (888) 468-6982
Fax: (325) 573-9321
Ralph Ramon, Dean of Student Services, Western Texas College, 6200 College Avenue, Snyder, TX 79549

## Westwood College: Dallas
### Dallas, Texas
### www.westwoodcollege.com

◆ For-profit 2-year technical college
◆ Commuter campus in very large city

**General.** Accredited by ACICS. **Calendar:** Continuous.

**Contact.** Phone: (214) 570-0100
Director of Admissions, 8390 LBJ Freeway, Dallas, TX 75243

## Westwood College: Fort Worth
### Fort Worth, Texas
### www.westwood.edu/location/texas/fort-worth.asp

◆ For-profit 2-year health science and technical college
◆ Commuter campus in very large city

**General.** Accredited by ACICS. **Calendar:** Continuous.

**Contact.** Phone: (817) 547-9600
Director of Admissions, 4232 North Freeway, Fort Worth, TX 76137

## Westwood College: Houston South
### Houston, Texas
### www.westwood.edu/

◆ For-profit 2-year technical college
◆ Commuter campus in very large city
◆ Application essay, interview required

**General.** Accredited by ACCSCT. **Enrollment:** 300 degree-seeking undergraduates. **Degrees:** 61 associate awarded. **Calendar:** Continuous. **Full-time faculty:** 8 total; 100% minority. **Part-time faculty:** 25 total; 96% minority.

**Student profile.** Among degree-seeking undergraduates, 100% enrolled in a vocational program, 1% already have a bachelor's degree or higher.

**Basis for selection.** Interview and documentation of prior education important; must demonstrate proficiency in basic college-level skills. SAT or ACT recommended. SAT/ACT test scores accepted. If student has not taken either we will administer ACCUPLACER (for Degree Programs) and Wonderlic (SLE) assessments for entry. **Homeschooled:** State high school equivalency certificate required. Provide copy of applicant's certificate of a home school program if applicant's home state recognizes the home school. Documentation of the state's recognition must be evident in applicant's records. **Learning Disabled:** All reasonable accommodations will be made for documented disabilities.

**2007-2008 Annual costs.** Tool Kits Range; $198 - $617 (one time charge). Books/supplies: $660. Personal expenses: $19,752.

**Financial aid. Need-based:** Need-based aid available for part-time students.

**Application procedures. Admission:** Closing date 8/6 (receipt date). $25 fee, may be waived for applicants with need. Application may be submitted online. **Financial aid:** No deadline. FAFSA, institutional form required.

**Academics. Special study options:** Accelerated study, distance learning, independent study, internships. **Credit/placement by examination:** AP, CLEP, institutional tests. **Support services:** Learning center, reduced course load, remedial instruction, study skills assistance, tutoring.

**Majors. Engineering:** Computer. **Engineering technology:** CAD/CADD. **Visual/performing arts:** Graphic design, multimedia.

**Computing on campus.** Online library, wireless network available.

**Student life. Freshman orientation:** Mandatory. **Activities:** Student newspaper.

**Student services.** Adult student services, alcohol/substance abuse counseling, career counseling, services for economically disadvantaged, student employment services, financial aid counseling, legal services, minority student services, placement for graduates, veterans' counselor. **Transfer:** Reentry adviser, pre-admission transcript evaluation for new students.

**Contact.** E-mail: tlevinthal@westwood.edu
Phone: (866) 340-3677 Toll-free number: (866) 340-3677
Fax: (713) 219-2088
Tara Levinthal, Director of Admissions, Westwood College: Houston South, 7322 Southwest Freeway, Houston, TX 77074

## Wharton County Junior College
### Wharton, Texas
www.wcjc.edu                                   CB code: 6939

- Public 2-year junior college
- Commuter campus in small town

**General.** Founded in 1946. Regionally accredited. **Enrollment:** 5,892 degree-seeking undergraduates. **Degrees:** 368 associate awarded. **Location:** 60 miles from Houston. **Calendar:** Semester, limited summer session. **Full-time faculty:** 138 total; 80% have terminal degrees, 18% minority, 62% women. **Part-time faculty:** 128 total; 80% have terminal degrees, 25% minority, 60% women.

**Student profile.** Among degree-seeking undergraduates, 72% enrolled in a transfer program, 28% enrolled in a vocational program, 1% already have a bachelor's degree or higher, 1,299 enrolled as first-time, first-year students, 424 transferred in from other institutions.

| | | | |
|---|---|---|---|
| Part-time: | 56% | Hispanic American: | 26% |
| Out-of-state: | 2% | International: | 3% |
| Women: | 58% | 25 or older: | 18% |
| African American: | 9% | Live on campus: | 3% |
| Asian American: | 5% | | |

**Transfer out.** 18% of students enrolled in the transfer program go on to 4-year colleges. **Colleges most students transferred to 2007:** Texas A&M University, University of Houston, Sam Houston State University, Texas State University, University of Texas.

**Basis for selection.** Open admission, but selective for some programs. Test scores and school achievement record important factors for admission into nursing, dental hygiene, physical therapy, and radiology programs. Audition required for music scholarship applicants.

**High school preparation.** Recommended units include English 4, mathematics 3, science 3 and foreign language 2.

**2008-2009 Annual costs.** Tuition/fees (projected): $1,620; $2,580 out-of-state. Per-credit charge: $32 in-state; $64 out-of-state. Room/board: $2,700. Books/supplies: $825. Personal expenses: $1,500.

**Financial aid. Need-based:** Need-based aid available for part-time students. **Non-need-based:** Scholarships awarded for academics, athletics, music/drama.

**Application procedures. Admission:** Priority date 7/1; no deadline. No application fee. Application must be submitted on paper. Admission notification on a rolling basis beginning on or about 2/1. **Financial aid:** Closing date 6/1. FAFSA required. Applicants notified on a rolling basis starting 8/1; must reply by 8/15.

**Academics. Special study options:** Cooperative education, cross-registration, distance learning, dual enrollment of high school students, internships, teacher certification program. License preparation in dental hygiene, nursing, paramedic, physical therapy, radiology. **Credit/placement by examination:** AP, CLEP, institutional tests. 16 credit hours maximum toward associate degree. **Support services:** GED preparation and test center, learning center, remedial instruction, tutoring.

**Majors. Agriculture:** Business technology. **Biology:** General. **Business:** Administrative services, business admin. **Communications technology:** Graphics. **Computer sciences:** General, networking. **Education:** Early childhood, elementary. **Engineering technology:** Drafting, electrical. **English:** English lit. **Family/consumer sciences:** Child development. **Health:** Clinical lab technology, dental hygiene, EMT paramedic, medical records technology, mental health services, nursing (RN), physical therapy assistant, radiologic technology/medical imaging. **History:** General. **Legal studies:** Paralegal. **Liberal arts:** Arts/sciences. **Math:** General. **Mechanic/repair:** Automotive. **Physical sciences:** Chemistry, physics. **Protective services:** Police science. **Psychology:** General. **Science technology:** Chemical. **Social sciences:** Criminology, sociology. **Visual/performing arts:** Art, dramatic.

**Computing on campus.** 500 workstations in library, computer center, student center. Online course registration, online library available.

**Student life. Freshman orientation:** Available. Preregistration for classes offered. **Housing:** Single-sex dorms available. $100 deposit, deadline 7/1. **Activities:** Bands, choral groups, dance, drama, music ensembles, musical theater, student government.

**Athletics.** NJCAA. **Intercollegiate:** Baseball M, rodeo, volleyball W. **Team name:** Pioneers.

**Student services.** Career counseling, personal counseling, placement for graduates. **Physically disabled:** Services for visually, speech, hearing impaired. **Transfer:** Transfer adviser, college fairs on campus for students transferring to 4-year colleges.

**Contact.** E-mail: registrar@wcjc.edu
Phone: (979) 532-4560 ext. 6303 Toll-free number: (800) 561-9252
Fax: (979) 532-6494
Karen Preisler, Director of Admissions/Registrar, Wharton County Junior College, 911 Boling Highway, Wharton, TX 77488-0080

# Utah

## Careers Unlimited
Orem, Utah
www.ucdh.edu/

- For-profit 2-year health science college
- Commuter campus in large city

**General.** Accredited by ACCSCT. 3 year bachelor's degree program offered. **Enrollment:** 104 degree-seeking undergraduates. **Degrees:** 50 associate awarded. **Calendar:** Semester. **Full-time faculty:** 7 total; 14% have terminal degrees, 14% minority, 71% women. **Part-time faculty:** 16 total; 94% women. **Special facilities:** 53 dental operatories, 10 xray/operative rooms.

**Basis for selection.** Open admission.

**Academics. Special study options:** Bachelor's degree programs available on campus. **Credit/placement by examination:** CLEP.

**Majors. Health:** Dental hygiene.

**Contact.** E-mail: admissions@ucdh.edu
Phone: (801) 226-1081
Careers Unlimited, 1176 South 1480 West, Orem, UT 84058

## College of Eastern Utah
Price, Utah
www.ceu.edu                    CB code: 4040

- Public 2-year community college
- Commuter campus in small town

**General.** Founded in 1938. Regionally accredited. **Enrollment:** 1,414 degree-seeking undergraduates. **Degrees:** 373 associate awarded. **Location:** 65 miles from Provo, 125 miles from Salt Lake City. **Calendar:** Semester, limited summer session. **Full-time faculty:** 74 total. **Part-time faculty:** 101 total. **Class size:** 80% < 20, 17% 20-39, 2% 40-49, less than 1% 50-99, less than 1% >100. **Special facilities:** Observatory, prehistoric museum.

**Student profile.**

| | | | |
|---|---|---|---|
| Out-of-state: | 6% | Live on campus: | 15% |
| 25 or older: | 26% | | |

**Basis for selection.** Open admission, but selective for some programs. Admission to nursing program based on test scores and prerequisites.

**2007-2008 Annual costs.** Tuition/fees: $2,161; $7,964 out-of-state. Room/board: $4,118. Books/supplies: $750. Personal expenses: $1,179.

**Financial aid. Need-based:** Need-based aid available for part-time students. Work-study available nights and weekends. **Non-need-based:** Scholarships awarded for academics, art, athletics, leadership, minority status, music/drama, religious affiliation, state residency.

**Application procedures. Admission:** Priority date 3/1; no deadline. $25 fee. Admission notification on a rolling basis. **Financial aid:** Priority date 2/1; no closing date. FAFSA, institutional form required. Applicants notified on a rolling basis starting 3/15; must reply within 2 week(s) of notification.

**Academics. Special study options:** Cooperative education, distance learning, double major, dual enrollment of high school students, ESL. **Credit/placement by examination:** AP, CLEP, institutional tests. 32 credit hours maximum toward associate degree. **Support services:** GED preparation and test center, learning center, remedial instruction, study skills assistance, tutoring, writing center.

**Majors. Business:** Administrative services, business admin. **Computer sciences:** Computer graphics, systems analysis. **Construction:** Carpentry. **Education:** Early childhood. **Family/consumer sciences:** Child care. **Liberal arts:** Arts/sciences. **Mechanic/repair:** Diesel. **Personal/culinary services:** Cosmetic.

**Computing on campus.** 150 workstations in dormitories, library, computer center, student center. Dormitories linked to campus network. Commuter students can connect to campus network. Online course registration, online library, helpline available.

**Student life. Freshman orientation:** Mandatory, $10 fee. Preregistration for classes offered. **Housing:** Coed dorms, single-sex dorms available. $100 deposit. **Activities:** Bands, choral groups, dance, drama, literary magazine, music ensembles, musical theater, radio station, student government, student newspaper, religious clubs, Catholic Newman Club, theater club, Native American club, recreation club, leadership club, PBL (business) club.

**Athletics.** NJCAA. **Intercollegiate:** Baseball M, basketball, golf M, volleyball W. **Intramural:** Basketball M, racquetball, tennis. **Team name:** Eagles.

**Student services.** Adult student services, alcohol/substance abuse counseling, career counseling, services for economically disadvantaged, student employment services, financial aid counseling, health services, personal counseling, placement for graduates, veterans' counselor, women's services. **Physically disabled:** Services for visually, speech, hearing impaired. **Transfer:** Transfer adviser for students transferring to 4-year colleges.

**Contact.** E-mail: jan.young@ceu.edu
Phone: (435) 613-5226 Fax: (435) 613-5814
Todd Olsen, Director of Admissions and Scholarships, College of Eastern Utah, 451 East 400 North, Price, UT 84501

## Eagle Gate College: Layton
Layton, Utah
www.eaglegatecollege.edu

- For-profit 2-year business and technical college
- Small city

**General.** Accredited by ACICS. **Calendar:** Five ten-week terms.

**Contact.** Phone: (801) 546-7500
915 North 400 West Layton, Layton, UT 84041

## Eagle Gate College: Murray
Murray, Utah
www.eaglegatecollege.edu

- For-profit 2-year business and technical college
- Large town

**General.** Accredited by ACICS. **Calendar:** Five ten-week terms.

**Contact.** Phone: (801) 281-7700
5588 South Green Street, Murray, UT 84123

## Eagle Gate College: Salt Lake City
Salt Lake City, Utah
www.eaglegatecollege.edu

- For-profit 2-year business and technical college
- Small city

**General.** Accredited by ACICS. **Calendar:** Five ten-week terms.

**Contact.** Phone: (801) 287-9640
405 South Main Street, Suite 130, Salt Lake City, UT 84111

## LDS Business College
Salt Lake City, Utah
www.ldsbc.edu                    CB code: 4412

- Private 2-year business and junior college affiliated with Church of Jesus Christ of Latter-day Saints
- Commuter campus in small city
- Interview required

**General.** Founded in 1886. Regionally accredited. **Enrollment:** 1,350 degree-seeking undergraduates. **Degrees:** 341 associate awarded. **ROTC:** Army, Air Force. **Calendar:** Semester, limited summer session. **Full-time faculty:** 18 total; 17% have terminal degrees, 28% women. **Part-time faculty:** 87 total; 1% have terminal degrees, 49% women. **Class size:** 37% < 20, 53% 20-39, 8% 40-49, 3% 50-99.

**Student profile.** Among degree-seeking undergraduates, 474 transferred in from other institutions.

| | | | |
|---|---|---|---|
| Out-of-state: | 50% | Live on campus: | 12% |
| 25 or older: | 23% | | |

**Transfer out. Colleges most students transferred to 2007:** Brigham Young University, University of Utah, Utah State University.

**Basis for selection.** Open admission. Color board required for placement in interior design program. SAT/ACT recommended for counseling, used as pre-test and placement in English or math. **Adult students:** Students who have not taken ACT or SAT must take COMPASS for placement in English and math. **Homeschooled:** Students must submit transcript or GED if not from accredited program. Students qualify for admission after reaching age 17. **Learning Disabled:** Must submit documentation under ADA.

**2007-2008 Annual costs.** Tuition/fees: $2,600. Per-credit charge: $108. Students who are not members of The Church of Jesus Christ of Latter-day Saints pay tuition of $5,200 per academic year, $1216 per-credit-hour. Room/board: $4,580. Books/supplies: $950. Personal expenses: $1,500.

**Financial aid. Need-based:** Need-based aid available for part-time students. **Non-need-based:** Scholarships awarded for academics, leadership.

**Application procedures. Admission:** No deadline. $30 fee. Application may be submitted online. Admission notification on a rolling basis. **Financial aid:** Priority date 7/1; no closing date. FAFSA required. Applicants notified on a rolling basis starting 3/1; must reply within 3 week(s) of notification.

**Academics. Special study options:** Cooperative education, dual enrollment of high school students, internships. **Credit/placement by examination:** AP, CLEP, IB, institutional tests. 30 credit hours maximum toward associate degree. **Support services:** Reduced course load, study skills assistance, tutoring.

**Majors. Business:** General, accounting, administrative services, business admin, executive assistant, office management. **Computer sciences:** Information technology. **Health:** Medical records admin, medical secretary, office admin, office assistant. **Legal studies:** Legal secretary. **Visual/performing arts:** Interior design.

**Most popular majors.** Business/marketing 9%, liberal arts 32%.

**Computing on campus.** 350 workstations in dormitories, library, computer center. Dormitories linked to campus network. Helpline available.

**Student life. Freshman orientation:** Available. Preregistration for classes offered. Full-day session held Friday before start of classes. **Policies:** Religious observance required. **Housing:** Single-sex dorms, substance-free housing available. $100 fully refundable deposit. **Activities:** Choral groups, student government, Latter-Day Saint student association, men's association, women's association, service-learning council.

**Student services.** Career counseling, student employment services, financial aid counseling, health services, personal counseling, placement for graduates. **Transfer:** Transfer adviser, college fairs on campus for students transferring to 4-year colleges.

**Contact.** E-mail: admissions@ldsbc.edu
Phone: (801) 524-8145 Toll-free number: (800) 999-5767
Fax: (801) 524-1900
Renae Richards, Director of Enrollment Management, LDS Business College, 95 North 300 West, Salt Lake City, UT 84101-3500

## Provo College
**Provo, Utah**
**www.provocollege.edu**                          **CB code: 3021**

- For-profit 2-year junior college
- Small city

**General.** Accredited by ACCSCT. **Calendar:** Quarter.

**Annual costs/financial aid.** Books/supplies: $600. Personal expenses: $2,088.

**Contact.** Phone: (801) 375-1861
Director of Admissions, 1450 West 820 North, Provo, UT 84601

## Salt Lake Community College
**Salt Lake City, Utah**                          **CB member**
**www.slcc.edu**                                  **CB code: 4864**

- Public 2-year community and technical college
- Commuter campus in very large city

**General.** Founded in 1948. Regionally accredited. 5 campus locations, 9 teaching centers. **Enrollment:** 23,375 degree-seeking undergraduates; 899 non-degree-seeking students. **Degrees:** 2,692 associate awarded. **ROTC:** Army, Air Force. **Location:** 5 miles from downtown Salt Lake City. **Calendar:** Semester, extensive summer session. **Full-time faculty:** 350 total; 10% minority, 49% women. **Part-time faculty:** 1,059 total; 3% minority, 40% women. **Class size:** 55% < 20, 44% 20-39, 1% 40-49, less than 1% 50-99.

**Student profile.** Among degree-seeking undergraduates, 3,540 enrolled as first-time, first-year students, 1,288 transferred in from other institutions.

| | | | |
|---|---|---|---|
| Part-time: | 68% | Hispanic American: | 9% |
| Out-of-state: | 6% | Native American: | 1% |
| Women: | 49% | International: | 1% |
| African American: | 2% | 25 or older: | 40% |
| Asian American: | 4% | | |

**Transfer out. Colleges most students transferred to 2007:** University of Utah, Utah State University, Weber State University, Westminster College.

**Basis for selection.** Open admission, but selective for some programs. Admission for flight technology programs based on testing, and for health sciences based on school records, testing and prerequisite courses.

**High school preparation.** 27 units recommended. Recommended units include English 4, mathematics 2, social studies 3, science 2 and academic electives 11. Biological science recommended for health science programs. Algebra recommended for preengineering and electronics.

**2007-2008 Annual costs.** Tuition/fees: $2,536; $7,958 out-of-state. Books/supplies: $1,580. Personal expenses: $1,510.

**Financial aid. Need-based:** Need-based aid available for part-time students. Work-study available nights, weekends and for part-time students. **Non-need-based:** Scholarships awarded for academics, alumni affiliation, art, athletics, leadership, minority status, music/drama.

**Application procedures. Admission:** No deadline. $35 fee. Application may be submitted online. Admission notification on a rolling basis. **Financial aid:** Priority date 5/1; no closing date. FAFSA, institutional form required. Applicants notified on a rolling basis starting 5/1; must reply within 4 week(s) of notification.

**Academics. Special study options:** Cooperative education, distance learning, dual enrollment of high school students, ESL, exchange student, study abroad. Bachelor's degree programs available on campus. License preparation in aviation, dental hygiene, nursing. **Credit/placement by examination:** AP, CLEP, IB, SAT, ACT, institutional tests. 50 credit hours maximum toward associate degree. **Support services:** GED preparation and test center, learning center, pre-admission summer program, reduced course load, remedial instruction, study skills assistance, tutoring, writing center.

**Majors. Agriculture:** Landscaping. **Biology:** General. **Business:** General, accounting technology, business admin, entrepreneurial studies, finance, logistics, marketing, restaurant/food services. **Communications:** General, digital media. **Communications technology:** Animation/special effects, photo/film/video, radio/tv. **Computer sciences:** General, computer science. **Construction:** Carpentry, concrete, electrician, maintenance, pipefitting, plumbing, site management. **Education:** Early childhood special. **Engineering:** Electrical, manufacturing, materials, mechanical. **Engineering technology:** Architectural drafting, civil drafting, computer, computer systems, drafting, environmental, instrumentation, manufacturing, mechanical, surveying, telecommunications. **English:** English lit. **Family/consumer sciences:** Family studies. **Foreign languages:** Sign language interpretation. **Health:** Clinical lab technology, dental hygiene, medical radiologic technology/radiation therapy, nursing (RN), occupational therapy assistant, physical therapy assistant, surgical technology. **History:** General. **Interdisciplinary:** Global studies. **Legal studies:** Paralegal. **Liberal arts:** Humanities. **Mechanic/repair:** Auto body, automotive, avionics, diesel, electronics/electrical, heating/ac/refrig, heavy equipment, industrial. **Parks/recreation:** Sports admin. **Personal/culinary services:** Chef training, cosmetic. **Physical sciences:** Chemistry, geology, physics. **Production:** Cabinetmaking/millwright, ironworking, machine tool, sheet metal, welding. **Protective services:** Criminal justice. **Psychology:** General. **Public administration:** Social work. **Science technology:** Biological, chemical, radiologic. **Social sciences:** Economics, geography, political science, sociology. **Transportation:** Airline/commercial pilot. **Visual/performing arts:** Design, photography, theater design.

**Most popular majors.** Business/marketing 9%, health sciences 15%, liberal arts 50%.

**Computing on campus.** 2,400 workstations in library, computer center, student center. Commuter students can connect to campus network. Online course registration, helpline, wireless network available.

**Student life. Freshman orientation:** Available, $3 fee. Preregistration for classes offered. One-day program. **Activities:** Bands, choral groups, dance, drama, literary magazine, radio station, student government, student newspaper, TV station, Circle-K, Latter-Day Saints student association, Hispanos Unidos, African-American student association, American Indian club, Asian club, Polynesian club, American Sign Language club, professional societies.

**Athletics.** NJCAA. **Intercollegiate:** Baseball M, basketball, softball W, volleyball W. **Team name:** Bruins.

**Student services.** Alcohol/substance abuse counseling, career counseling, services for economically disadvantaged, student employment services, financial aid counseling, health services, minority student services, on-campus daycare, personal counseling, placement for graduates, veterans' counselor. **Physically disabled:** Services for visually, speech, hearing impaired. **Transfer:** Transfer center, transfer adviser, college fairs on campus for students transferring to 4-year colleges.

**Contact.** E-mail: futurestudents@slcc.edu
Phone: (801) 957-4298 Fax: (801) 957-4961
Eric Weber, Dean of Student Enrollment Services, Salt Lake Community College, 4600 South Redwood Road, Salt Lake City, UT 84130-0808

---

## Snow College
**Ephraim, Utah**
**www.snow.edu**                          CB code: 4727

▶ Public 2-year community and junior college
▶ Residential campus in small town

**General.** Founded in 1888. Regionally accredited. Collaborative program with Julliard in music and theatre arts. **Enrollment:** 3,745 degree-seeking undergraduates. **Degrees:** 676 associate awarded. **Location:** 120 miles from Salt Lake City, 70 miles from Provo. **Calendar:** Semester, limited summer session. **Full-time faculty:** 118 total; 3% minority, 25% women. **Part-time faculty:** 127 total. **Class size:** 72% < 20, 26% 20-39, 2% 40-49, less than 1% 50-99, less than 1% >100.

**Student profile.** Among degree-seeking undergraduates, 8% enrolled in a vocational program, 1,196 enrolled as first-time, first-year students.

| | | | |
|---|---|---|---|
| Part-time: | 44% | 25 or older: | 14% |
| Out-of-state: | 2% | Live on campus: | 10% |
| Women: | 52% | | |

**Transfer out.** 70% of students enrolled in the transfer program go on to 4-year colleges. **Colleges most students transferred to 2007:** Utah State University, Salt Lake Community College, Utah Valley State College, Southern Utah University.

**Basis for selection.** Open admission. Auditions recommended for fine arts. **Homeschooled:** State high school equivalency certificate required.

**High school preparation.** 15 units recommended. Recommended units include English 4, mathematics 2, social studies 3, science 3 (laboratory 3).

**2007-2008 Annual costs.** Tuition/fees: $2,262; $7,889 out-of-state. Room/board: $2,750. Books/supplies: $530. Personal expenses: $900.

**Financial aid. Need-based:** Work-study available for part-time students. **Non-need-based:** Scholarships awarded for academics, alumni affiliation, athletics, leadership, music/drama, state residency.

**Application procedures. Admission:** Priority date 6/1; no deadline. $30 fee. Application must be submitted on paper. Admission notification on a rolling basis beginning on or about 12/1. Applications received after May 15 will be on a space-available basis. **Financial aid:** Priority date 3/1, closing date 7/15. FAFSA, institutional form required. Applicants notified on a rolling basis starting 8/1; must reply within 1 week(s) of notification.

**Academics. Special study options:** Cooperative education, distance learning, dual enrollment of high school students, ESL, honors, independent study. **Credit/placement by examination:** AP, CLEP, institutional tests. 45 credit hours maximum toward associate degree. **Support services:** GED test center, learning center, reduced course load, remedial instruction, study skills assistance, tutoring, writing center.

**Majors. Agriculture:** Agribusiness operations, animal sciences, business, farm/ranch. **Biology:** General, bacteriology, botany, pharmacology, physiology, zoology. **Business:** General, accounting, business admin, managerial economics. **Communications:** Journalism. **Computer sciences:** General, computer science, information systems. **Conservation:** General, forestry, management/policy, wildlife. **Construction:** General. **Education:** General, business, early childhood, elementary, ESL, family/consumer sciences, health, physical, secondary, special. **Engineering:** General. **Engineering technology:** Drafting. **English:** Composition, English lit. **Family/consumer sciences:** General, child care, clothing/textiles, family/community services, food/nutrition. **Foreign languages:** General, French, Japanese, Spanish. **Health:** Clinical lab science, EMT paramedic, licensed practical nurse, predental, premedicine, prenursing, prepharmacy, preveterinary, veterinary technology/assistant. **History:** General. **Interdisciplinary:** Biological/physical sciences, natural sciences. **Legal studies:** Prelaw. **Math:** General, statistics. **Mechanic/repair:** General. **Parks/recreation:** General, health/fitness. **Personal/culinary services:** Barbering, chef training, cosmetic, cosmetology, culinary arts. **Philosophy/religion:** Philosophy. **Physical sciences:** Astronomy, chemistry, geochemistry, geology, geophysics, physics. **Protective services:** Law enforcement admin. **Psychology:** General. **Public administration:** Social work. **Social sciences:** General, anthropology, economics, geography, political science, sociology. **Visual/performing arts:** General, art, dance.

**Computing on campus.** 450 workstations in library, computer center, student center. Dormitories wired for high-speed internet access. Online course registration, helpline, wireless network available.

**Student life. Freshman orientation:** Available. Graded one credit course held two days prior to fall semester and also three times during the semester. Comprised of 30 or fewer students, led by faculty section leader and two sophomore mentors. **Housing:** Coed dorms, single-sex dorms, apartments available. $200 partly refundable deposit, deadline 6/1. **Activities:** Bands, choral groups, dance, drama, literary magazine, music ensembles, musical theater, radio station, student government, student newspaper, symphony orchestra, Latter-Day Saints Student Association, Associated Women Students, Associated Men Students, Badgers Against Alcohol & Drugs, Polynesian Club, ski club, Spanish Club, international club.

**Athletics.** NJCAA. **Intercollegiate:** Basketball, football (tackle) M, softball W, volleyball W. **Intramural:** Basketball, football (non-tackle) M, golf, racquetball, soccer, softball, tennis, volleyball. **Team name:** Badgers.

**Student services.** Adult student services, alcohol/substance abuse counseling, career counseling, services for economically disadvantaged, financial aid counseling, health services, on-campus daycare, personal counseling, veterans' counselor. **Physically disabled:** Services for visually, hearing impaired. **Learning disabled:** Comprehensive services available. **Transfer:** Pre-admission transcript evaluation for new students. Transfer adviser, college fairs on campus for students transferring to 4-year colleges.

**Contact.** E-mail: hsrelations@snow.edu
Phone: (435) 283-7150 Toll-free number: (800) 848-3399
Fax: (435) 283-6879
Tim Dolan, Director of Admissiosn, Snow College, 150 East College Avenue, Ephraim, UT 84627

# Vermont

## Community College of Vermont
**Waterbury, Vermont**
www.ccv.edu

CB member
CB code: 3286

▶ Public 2-year community college
▶ Commuter campus in small town

**General.** Founded in 1970. Regionally accredited. Courses offered in 12 locations statewide and online. **Enrollment:** 3,869 degree-seeking undergraduates. **Degrees:** 457 associate awarded. **Calendar:** Semester, limited summer session. **Part-time faculty:** 600 total.

**Transfer out. Colleges most students transferred to 2007:** University of Vermont, Johnson State College.

**Basis for selection.** Open admission. Skill assessments administered by college required for placement purposes. International students must provide TOEFL score. Recommendation required if applicant has neither high school diploma nor GED.

**2007-2008 Annual costs.** Tuition/fees: $5,500; $10,900 out-of-state. Per-credit charge: $180 in-state; $360 out-of-state. New England Board of Higher Education rate for students from other New England states: 150% of Vermont resident tuition. Available to degree candidates in academic areas not offered by educational institutions in their home states. Books/supplies: $600.

**Financial aid.** All financial aid based on need. Need-based aid available for part-time students. Work-study available nights.

**Application procedures. Admission:** No deadline. No application fee. Application may be submitted online. Admission notification on a rolling basis. **Financial aid:** No deadline. FAFSA, institutional form required. Applicants notified on a rolling basis starting 9/1; must reply within 3 week(s) of notification.

**Academics. Special study options:** Cooperative education, cross-registration, distance learning, double major, dual enrollment of high school students, ESL, external degree, independent study, internships, liberal arts/career combination, student-designed major, study abroad, weekend college. **Credit/placement by examination:** AP, CLEP, institutional tests. 50 credit hours maximum toward associate degree. **Support services:** Learning center, reduced course load, remedial instruction, study skills assistance, tutoring, writing center.

**Majors. Business:** General. **Education:** General. **Health:** Health services. **Liberal arts:** Arts/sciences. **Mechanic/repair:** General.

**Most popular majors.** Business/marketing 22%, education 6%, liberal arts 58%, public administration/social services 7%.

**Computing on campus.** 300 workstations in library, computer center. Online course registration, online library, wireless network available.

**Student life. Freshman orientation:** Available. Preregistration for classes offered. **Activities:** Choral groups, student government.

**Student services.** Adult student services, career counseling, student employment services, financial aid counseling, placement for graduates, veterans' counselor. **Physically disabled:** Services for visually, speech, hearing impaired. **Transfer:** Transfer adviser for students transferring to 4-year colleges.

**Contact.** Phone: (802) 241-3535 Toll-free number: (800) 228-6686 Fax: (802) 254-3473
Susan Henry, Admissions Director, Community College of Vermont, PO BOX 120, Waterbury, VT 05676-0120

## Landmark College
**Putney, Vermont**
www.landmark.edu

CB code: 0081

▶ Private 2-year liberal arts college
▶ Residential campus in small town
▶ Application essay, interview required

**General.** Founded in 1983. Regionally accredited. College exclusively for bright students with dyslexia, attention disorders, or specific learning disabilities. We also offer professional development workshops and consultancies. **Enrollment:** 462 degree-seeking undergraduates; 17 non-degree-seeking students. **Degrees:** 67 associate awarded. **Location:** 8 miles from Brattleboro, 23 miles from Keene, New Hampshire. **Calendar:** Semester, limited summer session. **Full-time faculty:** 96 total; 9% have terminal degrees, 2% minority, 60% women. **Part-time faculty:** 33 total; 3% minority, 94% women. **Class size:** 100% < 20, less than 1% 20-39. **Special facilities:** Fine arts building, ropes course.

**Student profile.** Among degree-seeking undergraduates, 100% enrolled in a transfer program, 125 enrolled as first-time, first-year students, 91 transferred in from other institutions.

| | | | |
|---|---|---|---|
| Part-time: | 38% | Hispanic American: | 3% |
| Out-of-state: | 96% | International: | 4% |
| Women: | 22% | 25 or older: | 3% |
| African American: | 4% | Live on campus: | 95% |
| Asian American: | 2% | | |

**Transfer out.** 76% of students enrolled in the transfer program go on to 4-year colleges.

**Basis for selection.** Successful applicants are highly motivated, have average-to-superior intellectual ability and diagnosis of dyslexia, attentional disorder (ADHD), or specific learning disability. WAIS III or Woodcock Johnson Cognitive assessment required. Nelson-Denny reading scores required. **Learning Disabled:** Students must have a diagnosed learning disability and must submit the results of cognitive and achievement testing.

**High school preparation.** Recommended units include English 4, mathematics 3, social studies 3, history 3, science 3, foreign language 1, visual/performing arts 1 and academic electives 1.

**2008-2009 Annual costs.** Tuition/fees: $43,575. Notebook computer and software required. Approximate cost through school $2,500. Room/board: $7,800. Books/supplies: $1,200. Personal expenses: $500.

**2007-2008 Financial aid. Need-based:** 71% of total undergraduate aid awarded as scholarships/grants, 29% as loans/jobs. Need-based aid available for part-time students. Work-study available nights, weekends and for part-time students. **Non-need-based:** Scholarships awarded for academics, art, athletics, leadership, minority status, music/drama. **Additional information:** Students encouraged to apply to their state departments of vocational rehabilitation for additional financial assistance.

**Application procedures. Admission:** Priority date 5/15; no deadline. $75 fee, may be waived for applicants with need. Application must be submitted on paper. Admission notification on a rolling basis beginning on or about 12/1. **Financial aid:** Priority date 3/15; no closing date. FAFSA required. Applicants notified on a rolling basis starting 4/15; must reply within 2 week(s) of notification.

**Academics. Special study options:** Internships, study abroad. **Credit/placement by examination:** AP, CLEP, SAT, ACT, institutional tests. **Support services:** Learning center, pre-admission summer program, reduced course load, remedial instruction, study skills assistance, writing center.

**Majors. Business:** Business admin. **Liberal arts:** Arts/sciences.

**Most popular majors.** Liberal arts 97%.

**Computing on campus.** PC or laptop required. 50 workstations in dormitories, library, student center. Dormitories wired for high-speed internet access and linked to campus network. Online library, helpline, repair service, wireless network available.

**Student life. Freshman orientation:** Mandatory. **Policies:** Alcohol not permitted on campus. **Housing:** Guaranteed on-campus for all undergraduates. Coed dorms, special housing for disabled, substance-free housing available. All new students must live on campus. Others may petition to live off-campus. **Activities:** Jazz band, choral groups, dance, drama, literary magazine, music ensembles, student government, Phi Theta Kappa honor society, Society for Social Justice.

**Athletics. Intercollegiate:** Baseball, basketball, cross-country, soccer, softball W. **Intramural:** Basketball, volleyball. **Team name:** Landsharks.

**Student services.** Adult student services, alcohol/substance abuse counseling, career counseling, financial aid counseling, health services, personal counseling, placement for graduates, women's services. **Learning disabled:** Comprehensive services available. **Transfer:** Transfer center, transfer adviser, college fairs on campus for students transferring to 4-year colleges.

**Contact.** E-mail: admissions@landmark.edu
Phone: (802) 387-6718 Fax: (802) 387-6868
Dale Herold, Vice President for Enrollment Management, Landmark
College, River Road South, Putney, VT 05346

## New England Culinary Institute
### Montpelier, Vermont
www.neci.edu                                    CB code: 3405

- For-profit 2-year culinary school
- Residential campus in small town
- Application essay required

**General.** Founded in 1980. Accredited by ACCSCT. Branch campus located in Essex, VT. **Enrollment:** 637 degree-seeking undergraduates. **Degrees:** 13 bachelor's, 161 associate awarded. **Location:** 39 miles from Burlington. **Calendar:** Differs by program, extensive summer session. **Full-time faculty:** 70 total. **Part-time faculty:** 15 total. **Special facilities:** Gourmet restaurant, bakeshop, cafeteria, catering business, American cuisine restaurant. **Partnerships:** Formal partnership with the Council of Independent Restaurants of America.

**Student profile.** Among degree-seeking undergraduates, 20% already have a bachelor's degree or higher, 127 enrolled as first-time, first-year students.

**Basis for selection.** High school achievement record, essay or personal statement demonstrating understanding of and passion for the industry. Advanced placement standing available to students through school testing. Interview may be required and a tour is always recommended. **Home-schooled:** Personal interview may be required. **Learning Disabled:** Recommend a shadow experience if there is question regarding ability to succeed in the program.

**High school preparation.** Transcript must demonstrate proficiency in English and mathematics. Foreign language and culinary arts training highly desirable.

**2007-2008 Annual costs.** Tuition/fees: $25,652. Costs vary with program. Required fees include books, knife kit, and library and room deposit. Room/board: $6,828. Books/supplies: $664.

**Financial aid. Need-based:** Work-study available nights and weekends. **Non-need-based:** Scholarships awarded for academics, alumni affiliation, job skills.

**Application procedures. Admission:** No deadline. No application fee. Application may be submitted online. Admission notification on a rolling basis. **Financial aid:** No deadline. FAFSA required. Applicants notified on a rolling basis.

**Academics. Special study options:** Accelerated study, distance learning, dual enrollment of high school students, internships. Bachelor's degree programs available on campus. **Credit/placement by examination:** AP, CLEP, IB. **Support services:** Learning center, study skills assistance, tutoring.

**Majors. Business:** Hospitality admin, restaurant/food services. **Personal/culinary services:** Baking, chef training, culinary arts, food prep, food service, restaurant/catering.

**Computing on campus.** PC or laptop required. 40 workstations in library, computer center. Dormitories wired for high-speed internet access. Commuter students can connect to campus network.

**Student life. Freshman orientation:** Mandatory. Orientation and registration held 2-3 days prior to first day of classes. **Housing:** Coed dorms, single-sex dorms, apartments, substance-free housing available. Students have own bedroom and share kitchen, living room and bathroom space in apartment-style housing units. **Activities:** Student government, student newspaper.

**Student services.** Career counseling, student employment services, financial aid counseling, placement for graduates, veterans' counselor.

**Contact.** E-mail: admissions@neci.edu
Phone: (802) 223-6324 Toll-free number: (877) 223-6324
Fax: (802) 225-3280
Jan Knutsen, Director of Admissions/Marketing, New England Culinary Institute, 56 College Street, Montpelier, VT 05602

## New England Culinary Institute: Essex Junction
### Essex Junction, Vermont
www.neci.edu                                    CB code: 3100

- For-profit 2-year culinary school and business college
- Small city

**General.** Accredited by ACCSCT. **Location:** 8 miles from Burlington. **Calendar:** Quarter.

**Annual costs/financial aid.** Tuition/fees (2007-2008): $25,652. Costs will vary by program. Required fees include books, knife kit and library and room deposit. Room/board: $6,828. Books/supplies: $1,000. Need-based financial aid available for full-time students.

**Contact.** Phone: (802) 872-3400
Admissions Director, 5 Franklin Street, Essex Junction, VT 05452

# Virginia

## Advanced Technology Institute
### Virginia Beach, Virginia
www.auto.edu

▶ For-profit 2-year technical college
▶ Commuter campus in large city

**General.** Accredited by ACCSCT. **Calendar:** Continuous.

**Annual costs/financial aid.** Total program cost varies by program: $15,200 - $29,900.

**Contact.** Phone: (757) 490-1241
Director of Admissions, 5700 Southern Boulevard, Virginia Beach, VA 23462

## Aviation Institute of Maintenance: Virginia Beach
### Chesapeake, Virginia
www.aviationmaintenance.edu

▶ For-profit 2-year technical college
▶ Large city

**General.** Accredited by ACCSCT. **Enrollment:** 65 degree-seeking undergraduates. **Degrees:** 65 associate awarded. **Calendar:** Differs by program. **Full-time faculty:** 30 total.

**2008-2009 Annual costs.** Tuition/fees: $17,097.

**Academics. Credit/placement by examination:** CLEP.

**Majors. Mechanic/repair:** Avionics. **Transportation:** Aviation.

**Contact.** Phone: (757) 363-2121
Mel Rudd, Director of Admissions, Aviation Institute of Maintenance: Virginia Beach, 2211 South Military Highway, Chesapeake, VA 23320

## Beta Tech: Richmond South
### Richmond, Virginia
www.betatech.edu

▶ For-profit 2-year business and health science college
▶ Commuter campus in small city

**General.** Accredited by ACCSCT. **Enrollment:** 100 degree-seeking undergraduates. **Degrees:** 100 associate awarded. **Calendar:** Continuous. **Full-time faculty:** 30 total.

**Basis for selection.** Open admission.

**2007-2008 Annual costs.** Tuition/fees: $11,060. Annual tuition and fees will vary by program.

**Application procedures. Admission:** No deadline.

**Academics. Credit/placement by examination:** CLEP.

**Majors. Computer sciences:** LAN/WAN management. **Health:** Massage therapy, medical assistant. **Legal studies:** Paralegal.

**Contact.** E-mail: admdirbtr@betatech.edu
Phone: (804) 330-0111
Beta Tech: Richmond South, 7914 Midlothian Turnpike, Richmond, VA 23608

## Beta Tech: Richmond West
### Richmond, Virginia
www.betatech.edu

▶ For-profit 2-year business and health science college
▶ Commuter campus in small city

**General.** Accredited by ACCSCT. **Enrollment:** 55 degree-seeking undergraduates. **Degrees:** 30 associate awarded. **Calendar:** Continuous. **Full-time faculty:** 20 total.

**Basis for selection.** Open admission.

**2007-2008 Annual costs.** Tuition/fees: $11,060. Annual tuition and fees vary by program.

**Application procedures. Admission:** No deadline. $25 fee.

**Academics. Credit/placement by examination:** CLEP.

**Majors. Business:** Business admin. **Computer sciences:** General. **Health:** Medical assistant.

**Contact.** E-mail: admdirbtw@betatech.edu
Phone: (804) 672-2300
Tammy Hammerick, Director of Admissions, Beta Tech: Richmond West, 7001 West Broad Street, Richmond, VA 23294

## Blue Ridge Community College
### Weyers Cave, Virginia
www.brcc.edu          CB code: 5083

▶ Public 2-year community college
▶ Commuter campus in rural community

**General.** Founded in 1965. Regionally accredited. **Enrollment:** 4,084 degree-seeking undergraduates. **Degrees:** 496 associate awarded. **Location:** 12 miles from Harrisonburg, 15 miles from Staunton. **Calendar:** Semester, limited summer session. **Full-time faculty:** 74 total; 12% have terminal degrees, 46% women. **Part-time faculty:** 125 total; 55% women. **Special facilities:** Arboretum. **Partnerships:** Tech Prep Consortium.

**Student profile.** Among degree-seeking undergraduates, 39% enrolled in a transfer program, 61% enrolled in a vocational program, 1% already have a bachelor's degree or higher, 369 transferred in from other institutions.

| | | | |
|---|---|---|---|
| Part-time: | 59% | Asian American: | 2% |
| Out-of-state: | 3% | Hispanic American: | 3% |
| Women: | 58% | 25 or older: | 34% |
| African American: | 5% | | |

**Transfer out.** 56% of students enrolled in the transfer program go on to 4-year colleges. **Colleges most students transferred to 2007:** James Madison University, Mary Baldwin College, Old Dominion University, Eastern Mennonite University, Bridgewater College.

**Basis for selection.** Open admission, but selective for some programs. Special requirements for veterinary assistant technology and nursing programs; interview required.

**High school preparation.** 8 units recommended. Recommended units include English 4, mathematics 2, social studies 1 and science 1.

**2007-2008 Annual costs.** Tuition/fees: $2,470; $7,634 out-of-state. Per-credit charge: $77 in-state; $249 out-of-state. Out of state students pay an additional $90 capital outlay fee. Books/supplies: $600. Personal expenses: $900.

**2006-2007 Financial aid. Need-based:** Need-based aid available for part-time students. **Non-need-based:** Scholarships awarded for academics, job skills, leadership, minority status.

**Application procedures. Admission:** No deadline. No application fee. Application may be submitted online. Admission notification on a rolling basis. Closing date for veterinary assistant technology is January 1. Nursing clinical component application deadline is January 31. **Financial aid:** Priority date 5/1; no closing date. FAFSA, institutional form required. Applicants notified on a rolling basis starting 5/30; must reply within 2 week(s) of notification.

**Academics. Special study options:** Accelerated study, cross-registration, distance learning, double major, dual enrollment of high school students,

ESL, honors, independent study, internships, study abroad. Bachelor's degree programs available on campus. License preparation in nursing. **Credit/placement by examination:** AP, CLEP, institutional tests. Credit cannot duplicate earned course credits, nor courses audited or failed. **Support services:** Learning center, remedial instruction, tutoring.

**Majors. Agriculture:** Animal sciences. **Business:** Accounting, administrative services, business admin. **Computer sciences:** General, information systems, programming, systems analysis. **Engineering technology:** Electrical. **Health:** Health services, nursing (RN), veterinary technology/assistant. **Liberal arts:** Arts/sciences. **Public administration:** Human services.

**Computing on campus.** 285 workstations in library, computer center, student center. Online course registration, online library, wireless network available.

**Student life. Freshman orientation:** Mandatory. Preregistration for classes offered. **Activities:** Student government, Phi Theta Kappa, Christian Fellowship, special interest groups.

**Athletics. Intramural:** Basketball M.

**Student services.** Career counseling, student employment services, financial aid counseling, minority student services, personal counseling, placement for graduates, veterans' counselor, women's services. **Physically disabled:** Services for visually, speech, hearing impaired. **Transfer:** Transfer adviser, college fairs on campus for students transferring to 4-year colleges.

**Contact.** Phone: (540) 234-9261 ext. 2287 Toll-free number: (888) 750-2722 ext. 2287 Fax: (540) 453-2437 Mary Wayland, Dean of Academic Support Services, Blue Ridge Community College, Box 80, Weyers Cave, VA 24486-9989

## Bryant & Stratton College: Richmond
**Richmond, Virginia**
**www.bryantstratton.edu**
**CB code: 4762**

- For-profit 2-year career college
- Commuter campus in small city

**General. Enrollment:** 516 degree-seeking undergraduates. **Degrees:** 12 bachelor's, 90 associate awarded. **Calendar:** Semester, extensive summer session. **Full-time faculty:** 55 total. **Part-time faculty:** 48 total. **Class size:** 84% < 20, 16% 20-39.

**Student profile.** Among degree-seeking undergraduates, 183 enrolled as first-time, first-year students.

| | | | |
|---|---|---|---|
| Part-time: | 51% | Asian American: | 1% |
| Women: | 83% | Hispanic American: | 3% |
| African American: | 80% | | |

**Basis for selection.** Open admission, but selective for some programs.

**2007-2008 Annual costs.** Tuition/fees: $13,185. Per-credit charge: $415. Annual tuition for bachelor's degree may vary by program. Books/supplies: $738. Personal expenses: $1,384.

**2006-2007 Financial aid.** All financial aid based on need. 31% of total undergraduate aid awarded as scholarships/grants, 69% as loans/jobs. Need-based aid available for part-time students.

**Application procedures. Admission:** No deadline. **Financial aid:** No deadline. FAFSA required.

**Academics. Special study options:** Distance learning, double major, independent study, internships. **Credit/placement by examination:** CLEP, institutional tests. Up to 75% of the total credit hours required for graduation, including 75% of the total required hours in major study areas may be earned through a combination of transfer credits and proficiency evaluations. **Support services:** Study skills assistance, tutoring.

**Majors. Business:** Accounting, administrative services, business admin, human resources. **Computer sciences:** Information technology. **Health:** Medical assistant, medical secretary. **Legal studies:** Paralegal. **Protective services:** Criminal justice.

**Computing on campus.** 100 workstations in library, computer center. Online course registration, online library, wireless network available.

**Student life. Freshman orientation:** Mandatory. Preregistration for classes offered. Day and evening orientation is conducted the Monday before classes begin.

**Contact.** Phone: (804) 745-2444 Fax: (804) 745-6884 David Mayle, Director of Admissions, Bryant & Stratton College: Richmond, 8141 Hull Street Road, Richmond, VA 23235

## Bryant & Stratton College: Virginia Beach
**Virginia Beach, Virginia**
**www.bryantstratton.edu**
**CB code: 4761**

- For-profit 2-year business and junior college
- Commuter campus in large city
- Interview required

**General.** Founded in 1952. Regionally accredited. **Enrollment:** 477 degree-seeking undergraduates. **Degrees:** 22 bachelor's, 97 associate awarded. **Location:** 10 miles from Norfolk. **Calendar:** Semester, extensive summer session. **Full-time faculty:** 13 total; 54% have terminal degrees, 38% minority, 31% women. **Part-time faculty:** 32 total; 31% have terminal degrees, 56% minority, 50% women. **Class size:** 89% < 20, 11% 20-39.

**Student profile.** Among degree-seeking undergraduates, 175 enrolled as first-time, first-year students.

| | | | |
|---|---|---|---|
| Part-time: | 57% | 25 or older: | 59% |
| Women: | 82% | | |

**Transfer out. Colleges most students transferred to 2007:** Tidewater Community College, Strayer University, University of Phoenix.

**Basis for selection.** Open admission. Personal interview most important. TOEFL used for non-native English speakers.

**High school preparation.** Recommended units include English 4, mathematics 2, social studies 3, science 2, foreign language 2 and academic electives 1.

**2008-2009 Annual costs.** Tuition/fees (projected): $13,205. Per-credit charge: $436. Books/supplies: $1,300. Personal expenses: $1,600.

**Financial aid. Need-based:** Need-based aid available for part-time students. Work-study available nights and for part-time students.

**Application procedures. Admission:** No deadline. $25 fee, may be waived for applicants with need. Application may be submitted online. Admission notification on a rolling basis. **Financial aid:** No deadline. FAFSA required. Applicants notified on a rolling basis.

**Academics.** Free tutoring and extensive academic advising available. Portfolio projects in all classes. **Special study options:** Cooperative education, double major, independent study, internships, liberal arts/career combination, weekend college. Bachelor's degree programs available on campus. **Credit/placement by examination:** AP, CLEP, institutional tests. 45 credit hours maximum toward associate degree, 90 toward bachelor's. **Support services:** Learning center, reduced course load, remedial instruction, study skills assistance, tutoring.

**Majors. Business:** Accounting, administrative services, business admin, human resources. **Computer sciences:** General. **Health:** Medical assistant, office assistant. **Legal studies:** General. **Protective services:** Law enforcement admin.

**Most popular majors.** Business/marketing 38%, computer/information sciences 6%, health sciences 23%, legal studies 28%.

**Computing on campus.** 100 workstations in library, computer center.

**Student life. Freshman orientation:** Mandatory. Preregistration for classes offered. Held week classes start, 2 to 3 hours. **Activities:** Student government, student newspaper, Alpha Beta Gamma, Phi Beta Lambda, law society, medical club, computer club, Society for the Advancement of Management.

**Student services.** Adult student services, career counseling, student employment services, on-campus daycare, personal counseling, placement for graduates, veterans' counselor. **Transfer:** Pre-admission transcript evaluation for new students.

**Contact.** E-mail: dmsoutherland@bryantstratton.edu Phone: (757) 499-7900 Fax: (757) 499-9977 Deana Southerland, Director of Admissions, Bryant & Stratton College: Virginia Beach, 301 Centre Pointe Drive, Virginia Beach, VA 23462-4417

## Central Virginia Community College
**Lynchburg, Virginia**
www.cv.cc.va.us

CB member
CB code: 5141

- Public 2-year community college
- Commuter campus in small city

**General.** Founded in 1966. Regionally accredited. **Enrollment:** 2,968 degree-seeking undergraduates. **Degrees:** 276 associate awarded. **Location:** 120 miles from Richmond. **Calendar:** Semester, limited summer session. **Full-time faculty:** 62 total. **Part-time faculty:** 183 total.

**Transfer out. Colleges most students transferred to 2007:** Lynchburg College, Virginia Polytechnic Institute and State University, Longwood College, Old Dominion University.

**Basis for selection.** Open admission, but selective for some programs. Allied health program applicants must have 2 interviews with program head and meet specific criteria. Only 15 applicants accepted into each program each year. Interview required for health program.

**2007-2008 Annual costs.** Tuition/fees: $2,450; $7,614 out-of-state. Per-credit charge: $77 in-state; $249 out-of-state. Out of state students pay an additional $90 capital outlay fee. Books/supplies: $600. Personal expenses: $1,550.

**Financial aid. Need-based:** Work-study available for part-time students. **Non-need-based:** Scholarships awarded for academics, alumni affiliation. **Additional information:** Payment plan available.

**Application procedures. Admission:** Priority date 9/5; no deadline. No application fee. Admission notification on a rolling basis. **Financial aid:** Priority date 3/15; no closing date. FAFSA required. Applicants notified on a rolling basis starting 5/1; must reply within 2 week(s) of notification.

**Academics.** GPA of 2.0 required to graduate. System-wide core curriculum to ensure ease of transfer. **Special study options:** Cooperative education, distance learning, dual enrollment of high school students, independent study, internships. Bachelor's degree programs available on campus. **Credit/placement by examination:** AP, CLEP, IB, institutional tests. 45 credit hours maximum toward associate degree. **Support services:** Learning center, reduced course load, remedial instruction, study skills assistance, tutoring.

**Majors. Business:** General, accounting, administrative services, business admin, finance, management information systems. **Computer sciences:** Information systems. **Education:** General. **Engineering technology:** Architectural, civil, electrical. **Health:** Clinical lab technology, physics/radiologic health. **Liberal arts:** Arts/sciences. **Protective services:** Law enforcement admin. **Visual/performing arts:** Commercial/advertising art.

**Computing on campus.** 230 workstations in library, computer center. Commuter students can connect to campus network. Online library available.

**Student life. Freshman orientation:** Mandatory, $65 fee. **Activities:** Drama, literary magazine, student government, student newspaper, Black Student Union, art club, honor society, Students Together For Environmental Protection, data processing management association, Spanish club, medical lab club, respiratory club, radiology club.

**Athletics. Intramural:** Softball, volleyball.

**Student services.** Career counseling, student employment services, financial aid counseling, personal counseling, placement for graduates, veterans' counselor. **Physically disabled:** Services for visually, speech, hearing impaired. **Transfer:** Transfer adviser, college fairs on campus for students transferring to 4-year colleges.

**Contact.** Phone: (434) 832-7633 Toll-free number: (800) 562-3060 Fax: (434) 832-7793
Geoffrey Hicks, Chief Academic Officer, Central Virginia Community College, 3506 Wards Road, Lynchburg, VA 24502-2498

## Dabney S. Lancaster Community College
**Clifton Forge, Virginia**
www.dslcc.edu

CB code: 5139

- Public 2-year community college
- Commuter campus in small town

**General.** Founded in 1967. Regionally accredited. **Enrollment:** 527 degree-seeking undergraduates. **Degrees:** 103 associate awarded. **Location:** 55 miles

from Roanoke. **Calendar:** Semester, extensive summer session. **Full-time faculty:** 20 total. **Part-time faculty:** 90 total. **Class size:** 88% < 20, 11% 20-39, less than 1% 40-49. **Special facilities:** Modern sawmill.

**Basis for selection.** Open admission, but selective for some programs. Special requirements for nursing program. High school diploma or GED required of applicants under 18. Interview required for nursing program.

**High school preparation.** Course recommendations vary according to planned curriculum.

**2007-2008 Annual costs.** Tuition/fees: $2,441; $7,605 out-of-state. Per-credit charge: $77 in-state; $249 out-of-state. Out of state students pay an additional $90 capital outlay fee. Books/supplies: $580. Personal expenses: $1,680.

**Financial aid.** All financial aid based on need. Need-based aid available for part-time students.

**Application procedures. Admission:** No deadline. No application fee. Application may be submitted online. Admission notification on a rolling basis beginning on or about 2/1. **Financial aid:** Priority date 3/15; no closing date. FAFSA, institutional form required. Applicants notified on a rolling basis starting 4/15; must reply within 2 week(s) of notification.

**Academics. Special study options:** Cooperative education, distance learning, double major, dual enrollment of high school students, independent study, internships. Bachelor's degree programs available on campus. **Credit/placement by examination:** CLEP, institutional tests. **Support services:** Learning center, pre-admission summer program, reduced course load, remedial instruction, study skills assistance, tutoring, writing center.

**Majors. Business:** Administrative services, business admin, communications, office management, office/clerical. **Communications technology:** Graphic/printing. **Computer sciences:** General. **Conservation:** Forestry. **Engineering technology:** Electrical. **Liberal arts:** Arts/sciences. **Personal/culinary services:** Food prep. **Protective services:** Criminal justice, police science.

**Most popular majors.** Education 9%, health sciences 36%, liberal arts 12%, natural resources/environmental science 15%, security/protective services 6%.

**Computing on campus.** 60 workstations in library, computer center. Helpline, wireless network available.

**Student life. Freshman orientation:** Mandatory. Preregistration for classes offered. **Activities:** Choral groups, drama, literary magazine, student government, student newspaper, various social, religious and service clubs available.

**Athletics. Intramural:** Basketball, softball, volleyball.

**Student services.** Career counseling, student employment services, personal counseling, placement for graduates, veterans' counselor. **Physically disabled:** Services for visually, speech, hearing impaired. **Transfer:** Transfer adviser, college fairs on campus for students transferring to 4-year colleges.

**Contact.** Phone: (540) 863-2815 Fax: (540) 863-2915
Mary Wilson, Director of Student Services, Dabney S. Lancaster Community College, Box 1000, Clifton Forge, VA 24422

## Danville Community College
**Danville, Virginia**
www.dcc.vccs.edu

CB code: 5163

- Public 2-year community college
- Commuter campus in small city

**General.** Founded in 1967. Regionally accredited. **Enrollment:** 2,168 degree-seeking undergraduates. **Degrees:** 235 associate awarded. **Location:** 45 miles from Greensboro, North Carolina. **Calendar:** Semester, limited summer session. **Full-time faculty:** 150 total. **Part-time faculty:** 200 total. **Class size:** 71% < 20, 28% 20-39, 1% 50-99.

**Student profile.**

| | | | |
|---|---|---|---|
| Out-of-state: | 2% | 25 or older: | 52% |

**Transfer out. Colleges most students transferred to 2007:** Averett University, Virginia Polytechnic Institute, Radford University.

**Basis for selection.** Open admission, but selective for some programs. Special requirements for nursing program.

**High school preparation.** Recommended units include English 4 and mathematics 1.

**2007-2008 Annual costs.** Tuition/fees: $2,437; $7,601 out-of-state. Per-credit charge: $77 in-state; $249 out-of-state. Out of state students pay an additional $90 capital outlay fee. Books/supplies: $700. Personal expenses: $1,328.

**Financial aid.** All financial aid based on need. Need-based aid available for part-time students. Work-study available for part-time students.

**Application procedures. Admission:** Priority date 8/20; no deadline. No application fee. Admission notification on a rolling basis beginning on or about 1/15. **Financial aid:** Priority date 6/1; no closing date. FAFSA required. Applicants notified on a rolling basis starting 5/1; must reply within 2 week(s) of notification.

**Academics.** System-wide core curriculum to ensure ease of transfer. **Special study options:** Accelerated study, cooperative education, distance learning, double major, dual enrollment of high school students, honors, independent study, internships. Bachelor's degree programs available on campus. License preparation in dental hygiene, nursing, real estate. **Credit/placement by examination:** AP, CLEP, institutional tests. **Support services:** GED preparation and test center, learning center, pre-admission summer program, reduced course load, remedial instruction, study skills assistance, tutoring.

**Majors. Business:** General, accounting, administrative services, business admin, executive assistant, receptionist. **Communications technology:** Graphic/printing. **Computer sciences:** General, computer science, programming. **Engineering:** General. **Engineering technology:** Drafting, manufacturing. **Family/consumer sciences:** Child development. **Health:** Dental hygiene, medical secretary, office assistant, respiratory therapy assistant. **Interdisciplinary:** Biological/physical sciences, science/society. **Liberal arts:** Arts/sciences, humanities. **Mechanic/repair:** Heating/ac/refrig. **Protective services:** Law enforcement admin.

**Most popular majors.** Business/marketing 40%, education 15%, liberal arts 33%, security/protective services 11%.

**Computing on campus.** 425 workstations in library, computer center. Online course registration, online library available.

**Student life. Freshman orientation:** Mandatory. Preregistration for classes offered. Two 1-day summer sessions to choose from. **Activities:** Choral groups, student government, African-American culture club, Christian Students Fellowship, graphics club, International Association of Administrative Professionals, Phi Theta Kappa, National Vocational-Technical Honor Society, gospel club, Lambda Alpha Epsilon (criminal justice).

**Athletics. Team name:** Knights.

**Student services.** Adult student services, campus ministries, career counseling, student employment services, financial aid counseling, on-campus daycare, personal counseling, placement for graduates, veterans' counselor, women's services. **Physically disabled:** Services for visually, speech, hearing impaired. **Transfer:** College fairs on campus for students transferring to 4-year colleges.

**Contact.** E-mail: ethornton@dcc.vccs.edu
Phone: (434) 797-8467 Toll-free number: (800) 560-4291
Fax: (434) 797-8451
Peter Castiglione, Director of Student Development & Enrollment Management, Danville Community College, 1008 South Main Street, Danville, VA 24541

## Eastern Shore Community College
### Melfa, Virginia
### www.es.vccs.edu
**CB code: 5844**

- Public 2-year community college
- Commuter campus in rural community

**General.** Founded in 1971. Regionally accredited. **Enrollment:** 571 degree-seeking undergraduates. **Degrees:** 45 associate awarded. **Location:** 70 miles from Norfolk. **Calendar:** Semester, limited summer session. **Full-time faculty:** 20 total. **Part-time faculty:** 55 total.

**Student profile.** Among degree-seeking undergraduates, 48% enrolled in a transfer program, 52% enrolled in a vocational program.

**Basis for selection.** Open admission. **Learning Disabled:** ESCC honors all reasonable, documented requests for accommodations. In order to obtain special accommodations, a student must meet with a counselor prior to classes.

**High school preparation.** 18 units recommended. Recommended units include English 4, mathematics 3, social studies 2 and science 2.

**2007-2008 Annual costs.** Tuition/fees: $2,465; $7,629 out-of-state. Per-credit charge: $77 in-state; $249 out-of-state. Out of state students pay an additional $90 capital outlay fee. Books/supplies: $500. Personal expenses: $1,196.

**Financial aid.** All financial aid based on need. Need-based aid available for part-time students. **Additional information:** ESCC is a member of the Servicemembers Opportunity Colleges (SOC) program. This is a world-wide network of colleges and universities working with the Armed Forces dedicated to helping service people and their families get college degrees.

**Application procedures. Admission:** No deadline. No application fee. Application may be submitted online. Admission notification on a rolling basis. **Financial aid:** Priority date 5/1; no closing date. FAFSA required. Applicants notified on a rolling basis starting 6/1; must reply within 2 week(s) of notification.

**Academics. Special study options:** Cross-registration, distance learning, dual enrollment of high school students, ESL. Bachelor's degree programs available on campus. License preparation in real estate. **Credit/placement by examination:** AP, CLEP, institutional tests. 30 credit hours maximum toward associate degree. Students who do not achieve minimum scores on institutional placement tests must enroll in developmental courses. **Support services:** GED preparation and test center, learning center, reduced course load, remedial instruction, study skills assistance, tutoring.

**Majors. Business:** Business admin, office/clerical. **Computer sciences:** General. **Education:** General, science. **Engineering:** Electrical. **Liberal arts:** Arts/sciences. **Mechanic/repair:** Electronics/electrical.

**Computing on campus.** 53 workstations in library, computer center. Online course registration, online library, helpline, wireless network available.

**Student life. Freshman orientation:** Available. Preregistration for classes offered. **Activities:** Student government, Phi Theta Kappa, Phi Beta Lambda.

**Student services.** Career counseling, student employment services, financial aid counseling, health services, personal counseling, placement for graduates, veterans' counselor. **Physically disabled:** Services for visually, hearing impaired. **Transfer:** Transfer adviser for students transferring to 4-year colleges.

**Contact.** E-mail: fwilson@es.vccs.edu
Phone: (757) 789-1731 Fax: (757) 789-1737
P. Smith, Dean of Student Services, Eastern Shore Community College, 29300 Lankford Highway, Melfa, VA 23410-9755

## ECPI Technical College: Richmond
### Richmond, Virginia
### www.ecpi.edu
**CB code: 3145**

- For-profit 2-year technical college
- Small city

**General.** Accredited by ACCSCT. **Enrollment:** 343 degree-seeking undergraduates. **Degrees:** 47 bachelor's, 172 associate awarded. **Calendar:** Continuous. **Full-time faculty:** 12 total. **Part-time faculty:** 8 total.

**Basis for selection.** Program-specific admission test required.

**2007-2008 Annual costs.** Tuition/fees: $10,150. Personal expenses: $2,072.

**Application procedures. Admission:** No deadline. $50 fee. Admission notification on a rolling basis. **Financial aid:** No deadline.

**Academics. Credit/placement by examination:** CLEP.

**Majors. Computer sciences:** General.

**Contact.** Phone: (804) 359-3535 Toll-free number: (800) 290-7177
Ronald Tracey, Director of Admissions, ECPI Technical College: Richmond, 800 Moorefield Park Drive, Richmond, VA 23236

## ECPI Technical College: Roanoke
### Roanoke, Virginia
### www.ecpitech.edu
**CB code: 3147**

- For-profit 2-year technical college
- Commuter campus in small city
- Interview required

**General.** Accredited by ACCSCT. **Enrollment:** 295 degree-seeking undergraduates. **Degrees:** 75 associate awarded. **Calendar:** Continuous, extensive summer session. **Full-time faculty:** 16 total. **Part-time faculty:** 14 total.

**Student profile.**

| | | | |
|---|---|---|---|
| Out-of-state: | 5% | 25 or older: | 40% |

**Basis for selection.** Interview important; program-specific admissions tests required. No special considerations given.

**2007-2008 Annual costs.** Tuition/fees: $10,150. Personal expenses: $2,072.

**Financial aid. Need-based:** Need-based aid available for part-time students.

**Application procedures. Admission:** No deadline. $50 fee. Application may be submitted online. Admission notification on a rolling basis. **Financial aid:** No deadline. FAFSA required. Applicants notified on a rolling basis.

**Academics. Special study options:** Accelerated study, distance learning. Bachelor's degree programs available on campus. **Credit/placement by examination:** AP, CLEP. 15 credit hours maximum toward associate degree, 30 toward bachelor's. **Support services:** Remedial instruction, tutoring.

**Majors. Business:** Accounting, administrative services, office technology, office/clerical, taxation. **Communications technology:** General. **Computer sciences:** General, applications programming, computer science, data entry, data processing, information systems, information technology, LAN/WAN management, networking, programming, security, system admin, systems analysis, web page design, webmaster, word processing. **Engineering:** Electrical. **Engineering technology:** Computer hardware, computer systems, electrical, telecommunications. **Health:** Health care admin, medical assistant, medical records admin, medical records technology, medical secretary, medical transcription. **Mechanic/repair:** Communications systems, computer, electronics/electrical, industrial electronics.

**Computing on campus.** 180 workstations in library, computer center. Online library available.

**Student services.** Career counseling, student employment services, financial aid counseling, placement for graduates, veterans' counselor.

**Contact.** Phone: (540) 563-8080
Carol Rouch, Director, ECPI Technical College: Roanoke, 5234 Airport Road, Roanoke, VA 24012

---

## Germanna Community College
**Locust Grove, Virginia**
www.germanna.edu                                  CB code: 5276

- Public 2-year community college
- Commuter campus in rural community

**General.** Founded in 1969. Regionally accredited. Off-campus sites in high schools; dual enrollment courses offered at area high schools. **Enrollment:** 3,092 degree-seeking undergraduates; 2,363 non-degree-seeking students. **Degrees:** 425 associate awarded. **Location:** 15 miles from Culpeper, 18 miles from Fredericksburg. **Calendar:** Semester, limited summer session. **Full-time faculty:** 55 total; 64% women. **Part-time faculty:** 293 total; 56% women. **Class size:** 39% < 20, 61% 20-39, less than 1% 50-99. **Special facilities:** Art exhibits, local history collection.

**Student profile.** Among degree-seeking undergraduates, 64% enrolled in a transfer program, 36% enrolled in a vocational program.

| | | | |
|---|---|---|---|
| Part-time: | 68% | Women: | 62% |
| Out-of-state: | 1% | 25 or older: | 29% |

**Transfer out.** 65% of students enrolled in the transfer program go on to 4-year colleges. **Colleges most students transferred to 2007:** University of Mary Washington, Old Dominion University, Radford University, Virginia Commonwealth University, James Madison University.

**Basis for selection.** Open admission, but selective for some programs. Special requirements for nursing program with local applicants given preference. **Adult students:** SAT scores, GCC placement tests, or proof of college transcripts required. **Homeschooled:** Transcript of courses and grades required. Provide current copy of signed home school agreement between appropriate school system and authorizing parent or guardian. Provide written recommendation from home school teacher or tutor.

**2007-2008 Annual costs.** Tuition/fees: $2,458; $7,622 out-of-state. Per-credit charge: $77 in-state; $249 out-of-state. An indirect cost fee of $31 per

---

credit hour is charged to all out-of-state distance learning students. Books/supplies: $800. Personal expenses: $2,770.

**2006-2007 Financial aid. Need-based:** 98% of total undergraduate aid awarded as scholarships/grants, 2% as loans/jobs. Need-based aid available for part-time students. Work-study available for part-time students. **Non-need-based:** Scholarships awarded for academics.

**Application procedures. Admission:** No deadline. No application fee. Application may be submitted online. Admission notification on a rolling basis. Nursing program applications must be completed by February 1. **Financial aid:** Priority date 4/1; no closing date. FAFSA required. Applicants notified on a rolling basis starting 5/15; must reply within 2 week(s) of notification.

**Academics.** Systemwide core curriculum to ensure ease of transfer. **Special study options:** Accelerated study, distance learning, double major, dual enrollment of high school students, ESL, independent study, internships, liberal arts/career combination. Bachelor's degree programs available on campus. License preparation in dental hygiene, nursing. **Credit/placement by examination:** AP, CLEP, institutional tests. 8 credit hours maximum toward associate degree. **Support services:** GED test center, pre-admission summer program, reduced course load, remedial instruction, study skills assistance, tutoring.

**Majors. Biology:** General. **Business:** General, business admin. **Computer sciences:** Information technology. **Education:** General, elementary. **Health:** Dental hygiene, nursing (RN). **Liberal arts:** Arts/sciences. **Protective services:** Police science.

**Most popular majors.** Business/marketing 18%, computer/information sciences 6%, education 8%, health sciences 16%, liberal arts 44%.

**Computing on campus.** 90 workstations in library, computer center. Online course registration, online library, wireless network available.

**Student life. Freshman orientation:** Mandatory. Preregistration for classes offered. **Activities:** Student government, Black studies, student Christian associations.

**Athletics. Team name:** Grizzly Bears.

**Student services.** Career counseling, student employment services, financial aid counseling, personal counseling, placement for graduates, veterans' counselor. **Physically disabled:** Services for visually, hearing impaired. **Transfer:** Transfer adviser, college fairs on campus for students transferring to 4-year colleges.

**Contact.** Phone: (540) 423-9122 Fax: (540) 423-9158
Rita Dunston, Registrar, Germanna Community College, 2130 Germanna Highway, Locust Grove, VA 22508-2102

---

## Heritage Institute: Manassas
**Manassas, Virginia**
www.heritage-education.com

- For-profit 2-year health science and technical college affiliated with None
- Large town

**General.** Accredited by ACCSCT. **Calendar:** Continuous.

**Contact.** Phone: (703) 361-7775
8255 Shopper's Square, Manassas, VA 20111

---

## J. Sargeant Reynolds Community College
**Richmond, Virginia**
www.reynolds.edu                                  CB code: 5676

- Public 2-year community college
- Commuter campus in very large city

**General.** Founded in 1972. Regionally accredited. **Enrollment:** 8,048 degree-seeking undergraduates. **Degrees:** 766 associate awarded. **ROTC:** Army. **Location:** Downtown. **Calendar:** Semester, extensive summer session. **Full-time faculty:** 137 total. **Part-time faculty:** 469 total. **Special facilities:** Hospitality development center, distance education center. **Partnerships:** Formal partnerships with local medical facilities, Microsoft, IBM, Heilig Meyers, Richmond-Times Dispatch, Henrico Industrial Authority, Henrico County.

**Student profile.**

Out-of-state: 1%   25 or older: 39%

**Transfer out. Colleges most students transferred to 2007:** Virginia Commonwealth University, Old Dominion University.

**Basis for selection.** Open admission, but selective for some programs. Special requirements for nursing, health technology, engineering, legal assisting programs; interview recommended.

**High school preparation.** College preparatory units recommended for applicants to college transfer programs. Recommended units vary per program of study and include up to 4 English, 4 mathematics, 2 lab science, 2 foreign language, 2 social studies.

**2007-2008 Annual costs.** Tuition/fees: $2,597; $7,761 out-of-state. Per-credit charge: $77 in-state; $249 out-of-state. Out of state students pay an additional $90 capital outlay fee. Books/supplies: $1,000. Personal expenses: $900.

**Financial aid. Need-based:** Need-based aid available for part-time students. Work-study available nights, weekends and for part-time students. **Non-need-based:** Scholarships awarded for academics.

**Application procedures. Admission:** No deadline. No application fee. Application may be submitted online. Admission notification on a rolling basis beginning on or about 1/15. **Financial aid:** Priority date 6/30; no closing date. FAFSA required. Applicants notified on a rolling basis starting 7/15; must reply within 2 week(s) of notification.

**Academics. Special study options:** Cooperative education, distance learning, double major, dual enrollment of high school students, ESL, independent study, internships, weekend college. License preparation in dental hygiene, nursing, paramedic, real estate. **Credit/placement by examination:** AP, CLEP, IB, institutional tests. 53 credit hours maximum toward associate degree. Essay required for composition and literature subject exams (CLEP). **Support services:** Learning center, pre-admission summer program, reduced course load, remedial instruction, study skills assistance, tutoring, writing center.

**Majors. Agriculture:** Horticulture, landscaping, ornamental horticulture, turf management. **Architecture:** Technology. **Business:** General, accounting, administrative services, business admin, fashion, hospitality admin, marketing. **Computer sciences:** General, computer science, data processing, information systems, programming. **Education:** Early childhood, teacher assistance. **Engineering:** General. **Engineering technology:** Architectural, civil, electrical. **Family/consumer sciences:** Child care, institutional food production. **Health:** Clinical lab technology, dental lab technology, nursing (RN), occupational therapy assistant, optician, respiratory therapy technology. **Interdisciplinary:** Biological/physical sciences, math/computer science, natural sciences. **Legal studies:** Paralegal. **Liberal arts:** Arts/sciences. **Math:** General. **Mechanic/repair:** Auto body, automotive. **Personal/culinary services:** Baking, chef training, culinary arts, restaurant/catering. **Protective services:** Criminal justice, firefighting. **Public administration:** Community org/advocacy. **Social sciences:** General. **Other:** Social Sciences studies.

**Computing on campus.** 1,100 workstations in library, computer center, student center. Commuter students can connect to campus network. Online course registration, helpline, repair service, wireless network available.

**Student life. Freshman orientation:** Available. Preregistration for classes offered. **Activities:** Music ensembles, student government, TV station, culinary arts, horticultural club, music club, PAVE club, Phi Beta Lambda, Phi Theta Kappa, photography club, sign language club, Student Virginia Education Association, sustainable agriculture club.

**Student services.** Career counseling, student employment services, financial aid counseling, veterans' counselor. **Physically disabled:** Services for visually, speech, hearing impaired. **Transfer:** Transfer adviser, college fairs on campus for students transferring to 4-year colleges.

**Contact.** E-mail: kpettis-walden@reynolds.edu
Phone: (804) 523-5029 Fax: (804) 371-3650
Karen Pettis-Walden, Director of Admissions and Records, J. Sargeant Reynolds Community College, Box 85622, Richmond, VA 23285-5622

**General.** Founded in 1965. Regionally accredited. **Enrollment:** 4,578 degree-seeking undergraduates; 3,504 non-degree-seeking students. **Degrees:** 499 associate awarded. **ROTC:** Army. **Location:** 16 miles from Richmond. **Calendar:** Semester, extensive summer session. **Full-time faculty:** 74 total. **Part-time faculty:** 253 total. **Partnerships:** Formal partnership with Virginia Power.

**Student profile.** Among degree-seeking undergraduates, 35% enrolled in a transfer program, 30% enrolled in a vocational program, 1,018 enrolled as first-time, first-year students.

| | | | |
|---|---|---|---|
| Part-time: | 60% | Women: | 67% |
| Out-of-state: | 2% | 25 or older: | 43% |

**Basis for selection.** Open admission, but selective for some programs. Special requirements for nursing, funeral services and police science programs.

**High school preparation.** Required units include English 4 and mathematics 4. Biology and/or chemistry required for allied health programs.

**2007-2008 Annual costs.** Tuition/fees: $2,455; $7,619 out-of-state. Per-credit charge: $77 in-state; $249 out-of-state. Out of state students pay an additional $90 capital outlay fee.

**Financial aid. Need-based:** Need-based aid available for part-time students. Work-study available nights, weekends and for part-time students. **Non-need-based:** Scholarships awarded for academics, state residency.

**Application procedures. Admission:** Priority date 8/1; no deadline. No application fee. Admission notification on a rolling basis. High school students may attend with written approval of school principal. **Financial aid:** Priority date 5/15, closing date 7/15. FAFSA required. Applicants notified on a rolling basis starting 6/15.

**Academics.** Students seeking associate degree must complete 25 percent of core courses at college. **Special study options:** Cooperative education, distance learning, dual enrollment of high school students, internships, weekend college. 2-2 transfer programs in various engineering technology disciplines and business education; 1-3 transfer certificate in art. License preparation in nursing. **Credit/placement by examination:** AP, CLEP, IB, institutional tests. **Support services:** Learning center, remedial instruction, study skills assistance, tutoring.

**Majors. Business:** General, administrative services. **Computer sciences:** General, programming, systems analysis. **Education:** Teacher assistance. **Engineering:** Architectural, civil, electrical, environmental, mechanical. **Engineering technology:** Architectural, electrical, manufacturing, mechanical. **Family/consumer sciences:** Child care. **Health:** Nursing (RN). **Liberal arts:** Arts/sciences. **Personal/culinary services:** Mortuary science. **Public administration:** Human services. **Visual/performing arts:** Studio arts.

**Most popular majors.** Business/marketing 11%, education 6%, engineering/engineering technologies 15%, health sciences 22%, liberal arts 34%, personal/culinary services 8%.

**Computing on campus.** 165 workstations in library, student center. Commuter students can connect to campus network. Online course registration, online library available.

**Student life. Freshman orientation:** Mandatory. Preregistration for classes offered. **Activities:** Drama, literary magazine, student government, student newspaper, student nurses association, data processing club, human services organization, business honor society, funeral services student organization, biology club, art club.

**Student services.** Adult student services, alcohol/substance abuse counseling, career counseling, financial aid counseling, personal counseling, veterans' counselor. **Physically disabled:** Services for visually, speech, hearing impaired. **Transfer:** Transfer adviser, college fairs on campus for students transferring to 4-year colleges.

**Contact.** E-mail: AdmissionsandRecords@jtcc.edu
Phone: (804) 706-5220 Toll-free number: (800) 552-3490
Fax: (804) 796-4362
Joy James, Coordinator of Admission, John Tyler Community College, 13101 Jefferson Davis Highway, Chester, VA 23831-5316

## John Tyler Community College
**Chester, Virginia**
www.jtcc.edu

**CB member**
**CB code: 5342**

♦ Public 2-year community college
♦ Commuter campus in small city

## Lord Fairfax Community College
**Middletown, Virginia**
www.lfcc.edu

**CB member**
**CB code: 5381**

♦ Public 2-year community college
♦ Commuter campus in rural community

**General.** Founded in 1969. Regionally accredited. **Enrollment:** 3,425 degree-seeking undergraduates. **Degrees:** 429 associate awarded. **Calendar:** Semester, limited summer session. **Full-time faculty:** 61 total. **Part-time faculty:** 225 total.

**Student profile.** Among degree-seeking undergraduates, 37% enrolled in a transfer program, 21% enrolled in a vocational program.

**Transfer out. Colleges most students transferred to 2007:** Shenandoah University, Old Dominion University.

**Basis for selection.** Open admission.

**2007-2008 Annual costs.** Tuition/fees: $2,467; $7,631 out-of-state. Per-credit charge: $77 in-state; $249 out-of-state. Out-of-state students pay an additional $90 capital outlay fee. Books/supplies: $800.

**Financial aid.** All financial aid based on need. Need-based aid available for part-time students.

**Application procedures. Admission:** No deadline. No application fee. Application may be submitted online. Admission notification on a rolling basis. **Financial aid:** Priority date 5/1; no closing date. FAFSA required. Applicants notified on a rolling basis starting 6/1.

**Academics.** System-wide core curriculum to ensure ease of transfer. **Special study options:** Cooperative education, distance learning, double major, dual enrollment of high school students, ESL, honors, independent study. Bachelor's degree programs available on campus. License preparation in dental hygiene, nursing. **Credit/placement by examination:** AP, CLEP, institutional tests. **Support services:** Learning center, reduced course load, remedial instruction, tutoring.

**Majors. Business:** Accounting, administrative services, business admin, management information systems, marketing, office management. **Communications:** General. **Computer sciences:** General, database management, networking, webmaster. **Education:** General. **Engineering:** General, civil, electrical, mechanical. **Engineering technology:** Electrical. **Health:** Dental hygiene, nursing (RN). **Interdisciplinary:** Biological/physical sciences. **Liberal arts:** Arts/sciences. **Philosophy/religion:** Philosophy, religion.

**Computing on campus.** 650 workstations in library, computer center, student center. Online course registration, online library available.

**Student life. Freshman orientation:** Available. Preregistration for classes offered. **Activities:** Drama, musical theater, student government, special interest and program-related organizations, ambassadors club, honor society, business fraternity.

**Athletics. Intercollegiate:** Soccer. **Team name:** Cannons.

**Student services.** Adult student services, career counseling, services for economically disadvantaged, student employment services, financial aid counseling, personal counseling, placement for graduates, veterans' counselor, women's services. **Physically disabled:** Services for visually, speech, hearing impaired. **Transfer:** Transfer center, transfer adviser, college fairs on campus for students transferring to 4-year colleges.

**Contact.** E-mail: admissions@lfcc.edu
Phone: (540) 868-7105 Toll-free number: (800) 906-5322 ext. 7105
Fax: (540) 868-7005
Aaron Whitacre, Registrar, Lord Fairfax Community College, 173 Skirmisher Lane, Middletown, VA 22645

## Miller-Motte Technical College: Lynchburg
**Lynchburg, Virginia**
**www.miller-motte.com**

- For-profit 2-year technical college
- Commuter campus in small city
- Interview required

**General.** Accredited by ACICS. **Enrollment:** 295 degree-seeking undergraduates. **Degrees:** 60 associate awarded. **Location:** 60 miles from Charlottesville, 180 miles from Richmond. **Calendar:** Quarter. **Full-time faculty:** 6 total; 17% minority, 67% women. **Part-time faculty:** 31 total; 6% have terminal degrees, 3% minority, 84% women. **Special facilities:** College-operated massage therapy clinic, aesthetics clinic.

**Student profile.** Among degree-seeking undergraduates, 66 transferred in from other institutions.

**Basis for selection.** Open admission. **Homeschooled:** Statement describing homeschool structure and mission required.

**2007-2008 Annual costs.** Tuition/fees: $6,450. Per-credit charge: $215.

**Financial aid.** All financial aid based on need. Need-based aid available for part-time students. Work-study available nights and for part-time students.

**Application procedures. Admission:** No deadline. $35 fee. Application must be submitted on paper. Admission notification on a rolling basis. **Financial aid:** No deadline. FAFSA required. Applicants notified on a rolling basis.

**Academics. Special study options:** Cooperative education, dual enrollment of high school students. **Credit/placement by examination:** AP, CLEP, institutional tests. Students are encouraged to test out of introductory classes if they feel they have the necessary experience. There is a $100 non-refundable examination fee. Students are not encouraged to test out of advanced classes leading to the associate degree. **Support services:** Learning center, tutoring.

**Majors. Business:** Management science. **Computer sciences:** General. **Health:** Massage therapy, medical assistant, office assistant, pharmacy assistant, surgical technology.

**Computing on campus.** 75 workstations in library, computer center.

**Student life. Freshman orientation:** Available. Preregistration for classes offered.

**Student services.** Student employment services, financial aid counseling.

**Contact.** Phone: (434) 239-5222 Toll-free number: (877) 333-6622
Fax: (434) 239-1069
Miller-Motte Technical College: Lynchburg, 1011 Creekside Lane, Lynchburg, VA 24502

## Mountain Empire Community College
**Big Stone Gap, Virginia**
**www.mecc.edu**                                    **CB code: 5451**

- Public 2-year community college
- Commuter campus in small town

**General.** Founded in 1970. Regionally accredited. **Enrollment:** 1,930 degree-seeking undergraduates. **Degrees:** 184 associate awarded. **Location:** 40 miles from Bristol. **Calendar:** Semester, limited summer session. **Full-time faculty:** 47 total. **Part-time faculty:** 113 total.

**Student profile.**

| Out-of-state: | 4% | 25 or older: | 40% |
|---|---|---|---|

**Transfer out. Colleges most students transferred to 2007:** University of Virginia's College at Wise, Radford University, Virginia Polytechnic Institute and State University, East Tennessee State University.

**Basis for selection.** Open admission, but selective for some programs. Nursing students must meet admission test score, plus biology, chemistry and algebra I required. Respiratory therapy students must meet admission test score, plus algebra I and biology required. High school diploma or GED required for practical nursing, nursing and respiratory care programs.

**High school preparation.** Recommended units include English 4, mathematics 1 and social studies 2. 1 algebra, 1 biology, 1 chemistry required for nursing program; 1 algebra, 1 biology required for respiratory care program.

**2007-2008 Annual costs.** Tuition/fees: $2,495; $7,659 out-of-state. Per-credit charge: $77 in-state; $249 out-of-state. Out of state students pay an additional $90 capital outlay fee. Books/supplies: $860.

**2006-2007 Financial aid. Need-based:** Need-based aid available for part-time students. Work-study available for part-time students. **Non-need-based:** Scholarships awarded for academics, state residency. **Additional information:** The college does not participate in loan programs. All financial aid is in form of grants, scholarships, or work study.

**Application procedures. Admission:** No deadline. No application fee. Application may be submitted online. Admission notification on a rolling basis beginning on or about 1/1. **Financial aid:** Priority date 5/1; no closing date. FAFSA required. Applicants notified on a rolling basis starting 1/1.

**Academics.** System-wide core curriculum to ensure ease of transfer. **Special study options:** Accelerated study, distance learning, double major, dual enrollment of high school students, independent study, internships, liberal arts/career combination, student-designed major. Bachelor's degree programs available on campus. **Credit/placement by examination:** AP, CLEP, IB, institutional tests. 16 credit hours maximum toward associate degree. Maximum 25% of credits awarded for work and/or life experience. **Support services:** Learning center, pre-admission summer program, reduced course load, remedial instruction, tutoring.

**Majors. Agriculture:** Soil science. **Biology:** General. **Business:** General, accounting, business admin, office management, office/clerical. **Computer sciences:** General, information systems, information technology, networking, word processing. **Conservation:** General, environmental science, forestry. **Education:** General. **Engineering:** Electrical, manufacturing. **Engineering technology:** CAD/CADD, computer hardware, electrical, manufacturing. **Health:** EMT paramedic, medical secretary, medical transcription, nursing (RN), predental, premedicine, prepharmacy, preveterinary, respiratory therapy technology. **Legal studies:** Legal secretary, paralegal, prelaw. **Liberal arts:** Arts/sciences. **Math:** General. **Mechanic/repair:** Electronics/electrical. **Protective services:** Corrections, criminal justice, law enforcement admin. **Public administration:** Social work.

**Most popular majors.** Business/marketing 17%, computer/information sciences 16%, education 12%, health sciences 10%, legal studies 6%, liberal arts 26%.

**Computing on campus.** 400 workstations in library, computer center.

**Student life. Freshman orientation:** Mandatory. Preregistration for classes offered. **Activities:** Drama, student government, student newspaper, service, business, nursing organizations available.

**Athletics. Intramural:** Archery, badminton, basketball, bowling, softball, table tennis, tennis, volleyball. **Team name:** Red Fox Fliers.

**Student services.** Career counseling, student employment services, financial aid counseling, health services, personal counseling, placement for graduates, veterans' counselor. **Transfer:** Pre-admission transcript evaluation for new students. Transfer adviser for students transferring to 4-year colleges.

**Contact.** E-mail: khall@me.vccs.edu
Phone: (276) 523-2400 Fax: (276) 523-8297
Kristy Hall, Director of Enrollment Services, Mountain Empire Community College, 3441 Mountain Empire Road, Big Stone Gap, VA 24219

## National College: Bluefield
**Bluefield, Virginia**
www.ncbt.edu
CB code: 3246

- For-profit 2-year business college
- Commuter campus in small city

**General.** Accredited by ACICS. **Enrollment:** 190 degree-seeking undergraduates. **Degrees:** 28 associate awarded. **Calendar:** Quarter. **Full-time faculty:** 3 total. **Part-time faculty:** 10 total.

**Basis for selection.** Open admission. Interview recommended.

**2008-2009 Annual costs.** Tuition/fees: $9,585. Per-credit charge: $212. Books/supplies: $1,200.

**Financial aid.** All financial aid based on need. Need-based aid available for part-time students.

**Application procedures. Admission:** No deadline. $30 fee, may be waived for applicants with need. Application may be submitted online. Admission notification on a rolling basis. **Financial aid:** No deadline. FAFSA required. Applicants notified on a rolling basis starting 9/1.

**Academics.** Special study options: Double major, internships, liberal arts/career combination. **Credit/placement by examination:** CLEP, institutional tests. **Support services:** Tutoring.

**Majors. Business:** Accounting, administrative services, business admin, office management. **Computer sciences:** Computer science. **Health:** Medical assistant.

**Computing on campus.** 35 workstations in computer center.

**Student life. Freshman orientation:** Mandatory. Preregistration for classes offered.

**Student services.** Career counseling, personal counseling.

---

**Contact.** E-mail: tharris@national-college.edu
Phone: (540) 326-3621 Fax: (276) 650-2516
Larry Steele, Vice President of Admissions, National College: Bluefield, 100 Logan Street, Bluefield, VA 24605

## National College: Charlottesville
**Charlottesville, Virginia**
www.ncbt.edu
CB code: 3248

- For-profit 2-year business college
- Commuter campus in small city
- Interview required

**General.** Accredited by ACICS. **Enrollment:** 174 degree-seeking undergraduates. **Degrees:** 24 associate awarded. **Calendar:** Quarter, limited summer session. **Full-time faculty:** 1 total. **Part-time faculty:** 24 total.

**Basis for selection.** Open admission.

**2008-2009 Annual costs.** Tuition/fees: $9,585. Per-credit charge: $212. Books/supplies: $1,200.

**Financial aid.** All financial aid based on need. Need-based aid available for part-time students.

**Application procedures. Admission:** No deadline. $30 fee, may be waived for applicants with need. Application may be submitted online. Admission notification on a rolling basis. **Financial aid:** No deadline. FAFSA required. Applicants notified on a rolling basis.

**Academics.** Special study options: Double major, internships, liberal arts/career combination. **Credit/placement by examination:** CLEP, institutional tests. **Support services:** Tutoring.

**Majors. Business:** Accounting, administrative services, business admin. **Computer sciences:** Computer science. **Health:** Medical assistant.

**Computing on campus.** 35 workstations in library, computer center.

**Student life. Freshman orientation:** Mandatory. Preregistration for classes offered.

**Contact.** Phone: (804) 295-0136 Toll-free number: (800) 664-1886
Fax: (804) 979-8061
Larry Steele, Vice President of Admissions, National College: Charlottesville, 1819 Emmet Street, Charlottesville, VA 22901

## National College: Danville
**Danville, Virginia**
www.ncbt.edu
CB code: 3249

- For-profit 2-year branch campus and business college
- Commuter campus in small city

**General.** Accredited by ACICS. **Enrollment:** 312 degree-seeking undergraduates. **Degrees:** 51 associate awarded. **Calendar:** Quarter, limited summer session. **Full-time faculty:** 4 total. **Part-time faculty:** 40 total.

**Basis for selection.** Open admission. Interview recommended.

**2008-2009 Annual costs.** Tuition/fees: $9,585. Per-credit charge: $212. Books/supplies: $1,200.

**Financial aid.** All financial aid based on need. Need-based aid available for part-time students.

**Application procedures. Admission:** No deadline. $30 fee, may be waived for applicants with need. Application may be submitted online. Admission notification on a rolling basis. **Financial aid:** No deadline. FAFSA required. Applicants notified on a rolling basis starting 9/1.

**Academics.** Special study options: Double major, internships. **Credit/placement by examination:** CLEP, institutional tests. **Support services:** Tutoring.

**Majors. Business:** Accounting, administrative services, business admin. **Computer sciences:** Computer science. **Health:** Medical assistant.

**Computing on campus.** 35 workstations in library, computer center.

**Student life. Freshman orientation:** Mandatory. Preregistration for classes offered.

**Student services.** Career counseling, student employment services, personal counseling, placement for graduates.

**Contact.** E-mail: market@educorp.edu
Phone: (804) 793-6822
Larry Steele, Director of Admissions, National College: Danville, PO Box 6400, Roanoke, VA 24017

## National College: Harrisonburg
**Harrisonburg, Virginia**
www.national-college.edu                    CB code: 3173

◆ For-profit 2-year business college
◆ Commuter campus in large town

**General.** Accredited by ACICS. **Enrollment:** 282 degree-seeking undergraduates. **Degrees:** 56 associate awarded. **Calendar:** Quarter, limited summer session. **Full-time faculty:** 1 total. **Part-time faculty:** 24 total.

**Basis for selection.** Open admission. Interview recommended.

**2008-2009 Annual costs.** Tuition/fees: $9,585. Per-credit charge: $212. Books/supplies: $1,200.

**Financial aid.** All financial aid based on need. Need-based aid available for part-time students.

**Application procedures. Admission:** No deadline. $30 fee, may be waived for applicants with need. Application may be submitted online. Admission notification on a rolling basis. **Financial aid:** No deadline. FAFSA required. Applicants notified on a rolling basis starting 9/1.

**Academics. Special study options:** Double major, internships. **Credit/placement by examination:** CLEP, institutional tests. **Support services:** Tutoring.

**Majors. Business:** Accounting, administrative services, business admin, office management. **Computer sciences:** Computer science. **Health:** Medical assistant.

**Computing on campus.** 35 workstations in library, computer center.

**Student life. Freshman orientation:** Mandatory.

**Student services.** Career counseling, personal counseling.

**Contact.** E-mail: market@national-college.edu
Phone: (540) 432-0943 Fax: (540) 432-1133
Larry Steele, Director of Admissions, National College: Harrisonburg, PO Box 6400, Roanoke, VA 24017

## National College: Lynchburg
**Lynchburg, Virginia**
www.national-college.edu                    CB code: 3172

◆ For-profit 2-year business college
◆ Commuter campus in small city

**General.** Accredited by ACICS. **Enrollment:** 260 degree-seeking undergraduates. **Degrees:** 63 associate awarded. **Calendar:** Quarter, limited summer session. **Full-time faculty:** 1 total. **Part-time faculty:** 24 total.

**Basis for selection.** Open admission. Interview recommended.

**2008-2009 Annual costs.** Tuition/fees: $9,585. Per-credit charge: $212. Books/supplies: $1,200.

**Financial aid.** All financial aid based on need. Need-based aid available for part-time students.

**Application procedures. Admission:** No deadline. $30 fee, may be waived for applicants with need. Application may be submitted online. Admission notification on a rolling basis. **Financial aid:** No deadline. FAFSA required. Applicants notified on a rolling basis starting 9/1.

**Academics. Special study options:** Double major, internships. **Credit/placement by examination:** CLEP, institutional tests. **Support services:** Tutoring.

**Majors. Business:** Accounting, administrative services, business admin. **Computer sciences:** General, computer science. **Health:** Medical assistant.

**Computing on campus.** 35 workstations in library, computer center.

**Student life. Freshman orientation:** Mandatory. Preregistration for classes offered.

**Student services.** Career counseling, student employment services, financial aid counseling, personal counseling, placement for graduates, veterans' counselor.

**Contact.** E-mail: market@national-college.edu
Phone: (804) 239-3500 Toll-free number: (800) 664-1886
Larry Steele, Vice President of Admissions, National College: Lynchburg, PO Box 6400, Roanoke, VA 24017

## National College: Martinsville
**Martinsville, Virginia**
www.national-college.edu                    CB code: 3171

◆ Private 2-year business and junior college
◆ Commuter campus in small city

**General.** Accredited by ACICS. **Enrollment:** 267 degree-seeking undergraduates. **Degrees:** 44 associate awarded. **Calendar:** Quarter, limited summer session. **Full-time faculty:** 4 total. **Part-time faculty:** 22 total.

**Basis for selection.** Open admission.

**2008-2009 Annual costs.** Tuition/fees: $9,585. Per-credit charge: $212. Books/supplies: $1,200.

**Financial aid.** All financial aid based on need. Need-based aid available for part-time students.

**Application procedures. Admission:** No deadline. $30 fee, may be waived for applicants with need. Application may be submitted online. Admission notification on a rolling basis. **Financial aid:** No deadline. FAFSA required. Applicants notified on a rolling basis.

**Academics. Special study options:** Double major, internships. **Credit/placement by examination:** CLEP, institutional tests. **Support services:** Tutoring.

**Majors. Business:** Accounting, administrative services, business admin. **Computer sciences:** Computer science.

**Computing on campus.** 35 workstations in library, computer center.

**Student life. Freshman orientation:** Mandatory. Preregistration for classes offered.

**Student services.** Career counseling, student employment services, personal counseling.

**Contact.** Phone: (540) 632-5621
Larry Steele, Admissions Vice President, National College: Martinsville, PO Box 6400, Roanoke, VA 24017

## New River Community College
**Dublin, Virginia**
www.nr.edu                    CB code: 5513

◆ Public 2-year community college
◆ Commuter campus in rural community

**General.** Founded in 1966. Regionally accredited. **Enrollment:** 2,865 degree-seeking undergraduates. **Degrees:** 391 associate awarded. **ROTC:** Naval. **Location:** 50 miles from Roanoke. **Calendar:** Semester, limited summer session. **Full-time faculty:** 55 total. **Part-time faculty:** 136 total. **Class size:** 57% < 20, 36% 20-39, 5% 40-49, 1% 50-99, less than 1% >100.

**Transfer out. Colleges most students transferred to 2007:** Radford University, Virginia Tech, Old Dominion University.

**Basis for selection.** Open admission. Interview required for nursing program. **Adult students:** SAT/ACT scores not required.

**2007-2008 Annual costs.** Tuition/fees: $2,467; $7,631 out-of-state. Per-credit charge: $77 in-state; $249 out-of-state. Out of state students pay an additional $90 capital outlay fee. Books/supplies: $700. Personal expenses: $1,200.

**Financial aid. Need-based:** Need-based aid available for part-time students.

**Application procedures. Admission:** No deadline. No application fee. Admission notification on a rolling basis. **Financial aid:** Priority date 4/15; no closing date. FAFSA, institutional form required. Applicants notified on a rolling basis starting 6/1.

**Academics. Special study options:** Cooperative education, distance learning, dual enrollment of high school students, teacher certification program. License preparation in real estate. **Credit/placement by examination:** AP, CLEP, IB, institutional tests. **Support services:** GED preparation and test center, learning center, remedial instruction, study skills assistance, tutoring, writing center.

**Majors. Business:** Accounting, administrative services, business admin, logistics, office technology. **Computer sciences:** Computer graphics, game design, information technology, programming. **Education:** General, early childhood. **Engineering:** General, computer. **Engineering technology:** Architectural, drafting, electrical, instrumentation. **Health:** Medical secretary. **Interdisciplinary:** Biological/physical sciences, gerontology. **Legal studies:** Legal secretary, paralegal. **Liberal arts:** Arts/sciences. **Mechanic/repair:** Automotive. **Production:** Machine shop technology. **Protective services:** Forensics, law enforcement admin. **Public administration:** Human services.

**Computing on campus.** Commuter students can connect to campus network. Online course registration, online library, repair service, wireless network available.

**Student life. Freshman orientation:** Available. Preregistration for classes offered. **Activities:** Concert band, choral groups, literary magazine, music ensembles, TV station, Black Awareness Association, Phi Beta Lambda, Phi Theta Kappa.

**Athletics. Intramural:** Baseball M, basketball, cheerleading, soccer, softball, table tennis, tennis, volleyball. **Team name:** Knights.

**Student services.** Career counseling, student employment services, financial aid counseling, on-campus daycare, personal counseling, placement for graduates, veterans' counselor. **Physically disabled:** Services for visually, speech, hearing impaired. **Learning disabled:** Comprehensive services available. **Transfer:** Transfer adviser, college fairs on campus for students transferring to 4-year colleges.

**Contact.** E-mail: nrtaylm@nr.edu
Phone: (540) 674-3603 Toll-free number: (866) 462-6722
Fax: (540) 674-3644
Margaret Taylor, Coordinator of Admissions and Records, New River Community College, Drawer 1127, Dublin, VA 24084

---

## Northern Virginia Community College
**Annandale, Virginia**
www.nvcc.edu
CB member
CB code: 5515

- Public 2-year community college
- Commuter campus in small city

**General.** Founded in 1965. Regionally accredited. 6 campuses in Alexandria, Annandale, Loudoun County, Manassas, Springfield (medical education), Woodbridge. **Enrollment:** 14,971 full-time, degree-seeking students. **Degrees:** 2,815 associate awarded. **Location:** 12 miles from Washington, DC. **Calendar:** Semester, limited summer session. **Full-time faculty:** 566 total. **Part-time faculty:** 1,117 total.

**Transfer out. Colleges most students transferred to 2007:** George Mason University.

**Basis for selection.** Open admission, but selective for some programs. Admission to health and veterinary technology programs based on academic prerequisites, placement tests, and space availability. Interview recommended for allied health, animal science, dental hygiene, nursing programs.

**2007-2008 Annual costs.** Tuition/fees: $2,715; $7,959 out-of-state. Per-credit charge: $83 in-state; $257 out-of-state. Out of state students pay an additional $90 capital outlay fee. Books/supplies: $850. Personal expenses: $2,159.

**Financial aid. Non-need-based:** Scholarships awarded for academics, athletics, state residency.

**Application procedures. Admission:** No deadline. No application fee. Admission notification on a rolling basis. **Financial aid:** Priority date 3/1; no closing date. FAFSA, institutional form required. Applicants notified on a rolling basis starting 5/15; must reply within 2 week(s) of notification.

**Academics.** Systemwide core curriculum to ensure ease of transfer. **Special study options:** Cooperative education, distance learning, double major, dual enrollment of high school students, ESL, honors, independent study, internships, liberal arts/career combination, student-designed major, study abroad, weekend college. Old Dominion University Teletechnet degree programs. **Credit/placement by examination:** AP, CLEP, IB, institutional tests. Maximum of 75% of credit hours required for program may be awarded through CLEP. 25% of requirements must be completed at institution. **Support services:** Learning center, reduced course load, remedial instruction, tutoring, writing center.

**Majors. Agriculture:** Horticultural science. **Business:** Accounting, business admin, international, management information systems, office management, purchasing, real estate, tourism/travel. **Communications:** General. **Computer sciences:** General, computer science, programming. **Education:** Art, early childhood. **Engineering:** Civil. **Engineering technology:** Architectural, civil, drafting, electrical. **Family/consumer sciences:** Institutional food production. **Health:** Clinical lab assistant, clinical lab technology, dental hygiene, EMT paramedic, medical radiologic technology/radiation therapy, medical records technology, physical therapy assistant, respiratory therapy technology, substance abuse counseling, veterinary technology/assistant. **Interdisciplinary:** Biological/physical sciences, biopsychology, gerontology. **Legal studies:** Paralegal. **Liberal arts:** Arts/sciences. **Math:** General. **Mechanic/repair:** Aircraft, automotive, electronics/electrical, heating/ac/refrig. **Parks/recreation:** Facilities management. **Protective services:** Fire safety technology, fire services admin, law enforcement admin, security services. **Psychology:** General. **Public administration:** Human services. **Transportation:** Aviation. **Visual/performing arts:** Commercial photography, commercial/advertising art, interior design, photography, studio arts.

**Computing on campus.** 2,000 workstations in library, computer center.

**Student life. Activities:** Bands, choral groups, dance, drama, international student organizations, music ensembles, musical theater, student government, student newspaper, symphony orchestra, TV station, honor societies, African American student organizations, religious groups, Korean and Vietnamese student organizations, data processing management club, art association, physical therapist assistants club, Omega Engineering Students.

**Athletics. Intramural:** Basketball, football (tackle), soccer, volleyball.

**Student services.** Career counseling, veterans' counselor. **Physically disabled:** Services for visually, hearing impaired. **Transfer:** Transfer adviser, college fairs on campus for students transferring to 4-year colleges.

**Contact.** Phone: (703) 323-3000
Northern Virginia Community College, 4001 Wakefield Chapel Road, Annandale, VA 22003-3796

---

## Patrick Henry Community College
**Martinsville, Virginia**
www.ph.vccs.edu
CB code: 5549

- Public 2-year community college
- Commuter campus in large town

**General.** Founded in 1962. Regionally accredited. **Enrollment:** 2,888 degree-seeking undergraduates. **Degrees:** 202 associate awarded. **Location:** 50 miles from Roanoke, 50 miles from Greensboro, North Carolina. **Calendar:** Semester, limited summer session. **Full-time faculty:** 50 total. **Part-time faculty:** 113 total. **Special facilities:** Southern history collection, Virginia literature collection, fine arts theater.

**Student profile.**

| | | | |
|---|---|---|---|
| Out-of-state: | 1% | 25 or older: | 50% |

**Basis for selection.** Open admission. High school diploma or GED required for some programs.

**2007-2008 Annual costs.** Tuition/fees: $2,445; $7,605 out-of-state. Per-credit charge: $77 in-state; $249 out-of-state. Out of state students pay an additional $90 capital outlay fee. Books/supplies: $500. Personal expenses: $840.

**Financial aid. Need-based:** Need-based aid available for part-time students.

**Application procedures. Admission:** Priority date 8/1; no deadline. No application fee. Admission notification on a rolling basis beginning on or about 2/1. Deadline for nursing applicants March 1. **Financial aid:** Priority date 6/1; no closing date. FAFSA required. Applicants notified on a rolling basis starting 6/15.

**Academics.** System-wide core curriculum to ensure ease of transfer. **Special study options:** Cooperative education, distance learning, double major, dual enrollment of high school students, independent study, internships, teacher certification program, weekend college. Bachelor's degree programs available on campus. License preparation in nursing. **Credit/placement by examination:** CLEP, institutional tests. 12 credit hours maximum toward associate degree. **Support services:** Learning center, pre-admission summer program, reduced course load, remedial instruction, study skills assistance, tutoring, writing center.

**Majors. Business:** Accounting, business admin. **Computer sciences:** General, programming. **Engineering technology:** Drafting. **Legal studies:** Paralegal. **Liberal arts:** Arts/sciences.

**Computing on campus.** 500 workstations in library, computer center. Commuter students can connect to campus network. Online library, helpline, repair service available.

**Student life. Activities:** Choral groups, drama, musical theater, student government, student newspaper, TV station, Black student association, Phi Theta Kappa, campus awareness network, nurses association.

**Athletics. Intercollegiate:** Baseball M, basketball M, soccer M, softball M. **Intramural:** Basketball, football (tackle) M, soccer, softball, table tennis, tennis, volleyball. **Team name:** Patriots.

**Student services.** Adult student services, career counseling, student employment services, personal counseling, placement for graduates, veterans' counselor. **Physically disabled:** Services for visually, speech, hearing impaired. **Transfer:** Transfer adviser, college fairs on campus for students transferring to 4-year colleges.

**Contact.** E-mail: ttisdale@ph.vccs.edu
Phone: (276) 656-0325 Toll-free number: (800) 232-7997
Fax: (276) 656-0352
Graham Valentine, Admissions Counselor, Patrick Henry Community College, Box 5311, Martinsville, VA 24115-5311

---

## Paul D. Camp Community College
**Franklin, Virginia**
www.pc.vccs.edu                                    CB code: 5557

- Public 2-year community college
- Commuter campus in small town

**General.** Founded in 1970. Regionally accredited. Campuses in Franklin and Suffolk, site in Smithfield. **Enrollment:** 756 degree-seeking undergraduates. **Degrees:** 125 associate awarded. **Location:** 50 miles from Norfolk. **Calendar:** Semester, limited summer session. **Full-time faculty:** 23 total. **Part-time faculty:** 60 total. **Class size:** 87% < 20, 11% 20-39, 2% 40-49.

**Transfer out. Colleges most students transferred to 2007:** Old Dominion University, Christopher Newport University, Norfolk State University.

**Basis for selection.** Open admission, but selective for some programs. Limited enrollment to nursing programs. **Homeschooled:** Student must provide Admissions and Records Office current copy of signed home school agreement between appropriate school system and authorizing parent or guardian.

**High school preparation.** Recommended units include English 4, mathematics 2, social studies 2, history 2, science 2 (laboratory 2) and foreign language 1.

**2007-2008 Annual costs.** Tuition/fees: $2,405; $7,569 out-of-state. Per-credit charge: $77 in-state; $249 out-of-state. Out of state students pay an additional $90 capital outlay fee. Books/supplies: $500. Personal expenses: $900.

**Financial aid. Need-based:** Need-based aid available for part-time students. Work-study available nights and for part-time students.

**Application procedures. Admission:** Priority date 8/1; no deadline. No application fee. Application may be submitted online. Admission notification on a rolling basis. **Financial aid:** Priority date 6/1; no closing date. FAFSA required. Applicants notified on a rolling basis starting 8/1; must reply within 2 week(s) of notification.

**Academics. Special study options:** Cross-registration, distance learning, dual enrollment of high school students, honors, independent study, internships. License preparation in nursing, real estate. **Credit/placement by examination:** AP, CLEP, institutional tests. 52 credit hours maximum toward associate degree. **Support services:** Learning center, pre-admission summer program, reduced course load, remedial instruction, study skills assistance, tutoring.

---

**Majors. Business:** Administrative services, business admin, office management. **Computer sciences:** General. **Education:** General. **Engineering technology:** Drafting, electrical. **Health:** Nursing (RN). **Interdisciplinary:** Biological/physical sciences. **Mechanic/repair:** Electronics/electrical. **Protective services:** Police science.

**Most popular majors.** Business/marketing 22%, computer/information sciences 13%, interdisciplinary studies 6%, liberal arts 37%, security/protective services 18%.

**Computing on campus.** 100 workstations in library, computer center. Online course registration, online library available.

**Student life. Freshman orientation:** Mandatory. Preregistration for classes offered. **Activities:** Student government, student newspaper, honor societies, Circle K.

**Athletics. Intramural:** Volleyball.

**Student services.** Career counseling, student employment services, personal counseling, placement for graduates, veterans' counselor. **Transfer:** Pre-admission transcript evaluation for new students. College fairs on campus for students transferring to 4-year colleges.

**Contact.** Phone: (757) 569-6700 Fax: (757) 569-6795
Monette Williams, Director of Student Development Services, Paul D. Camp Community College, 100 North College Drive, Franklin, VA 23851-0737

---

## Piedmont Virginia Community College
**Charlottesville, Virginia**                      CB member
www.pvcc.edu                                        CB code: 5561

- Public 2-year community college
- Commuter campus in large town

**General.** Founded in 1969. Regionally accredited. **Enrollment:** 2,953 degree-seeking undergraduates; 1,722 non-degree-seeking students. **Degrees:** 308 associate awarded. **ROTC:** Army, Air Force. **Location:** 70 miles from Richmond. **Calendar:** Semester, limited summer session. **Full-time faculty:** 67 total; 40% have terminal degrees, 10% minority, 51% women. **Part-time faculty:** 155 total; 46% women. **Class size:** 54% < 20, 45% 20-39, 1% 40-49. **Partnerships:** Formal partnerships with local businesses, including nursing/retirement home and hospitals.

**Student profile.** Among degree-seeking undergraduates, 48% enrolled in a transfer program, 15% enrolled in a vocational program, 6% already have a bachelor's degree or higher, 519 enrolled as first-time, first-year students, 177 transferred in from other institutions.

| Part-time: | 68% | Women: | 60% |
| Out-of-state: | 5% | 25 or older: | 35% |

**Transfer out.** 75% of students enrolled in the transfer program go on to 4-year colleges. **Colleges most students transferred to 2007:** University of Virginia, James Madison University, Virginia Commonwealth University, Virginia Polytech and State University, Old Dominion University.

**Basis for selection.** Open admission, but selective for some programs. Special requirements for nursing program; interview recommended. **Homeschooled:** Students must meet with Dean of Student Services prior to enrolling.

**2007-2008 Annual costs.** Tuition/fees: $2,470; $7,634 out-of-state. Per-credit charge: $77 in-state; $249 out-of-state. Out of state students pay an additional $90 capital outlay fee. Books/supplies: $950. Personal expenses: $1,908.

**2006-2007 Financial aid. Need-based:** 66% of total undergraduate aid awarded as scholarships/grants, 34% as loans/jobs. Need-based aid available for part-time students. Work-study available nights, weekends and for part-time students. **Non-need-based:** Scholarships awarded for academics.

**Application procedures. Admission:** No deadline. No application fee. Application must be submitted online. Admission notification on a rolling basis. Accepted applicants to nursing program must reply within 10 days. **Financial aid:** No deadline. FAFSA required. Applicants notified on a rolling basis starting 4/1.

**Academics.** System-wide core curriculum to ensure ease of transfer. **Special study options:** Accelerated study, cooperative education, distance learning, dual enrollment of high school students, ESL, honors, independent study, internships, weekend college. License preparation in aviation, nursing, paramedic, real estate. **Credit/placement by examination:** AP, CLEP, institutional tests. Must obtain 25% of degree requirement credits at PVCC. **Support services:** Learning center, reduced course load, remedial instruction, study skills assistance, tutoring, writing center.

**Majors. Business:** General, business admin. **Computer sciences:** General. **Construction:** Carpentry, electrician, lineworker, masonry, plumbing. **Education:** General. **Engineering:** General. **Engineering technology:** Electrical, industrial, mechanical. **Health:** EMT paramedic, nursing (RN). **Interdisciplinary:** Biological/physical sciences. **Liberal arts:** Arts/sciences. **Protective services:** Police science. **Science technology:** Biological. **Visual/performing arts:** General.

**Most popular majors.** Business/marketing 21%, education 8%, engineering/engineering technologies 7%, health sciences 28%, liberal arts 28%.

**Computing on campus.** 124 workstations in library, computer center. Online course registration, online library, helpline, wireless network available.

**Student life. Freshman orientation:** Mandatory. Preregistration for classes offered. Six-week student development program for first-time students in their first semester. **Activities:** Choral groups, dance, drama, international student organizations, music ensembles, student government, student newspaper, Black student alliance, Phi Theta Kappa, Christian Fellowship Organization, Ambassadors club, engineering club, Masquers club, chemistry club.

**Athletics. Intramural:** Golf, soccer, tennis.

**Student services.** Adult student services, career counseling, services for economically disadvantaged, student employment services, financial aid counseling, personal counseling, placement for graduates, veterans' counselor. **Physically disabled:** Services for visually, speech, hearing impaired. **Transfer:** Transfer adviser, college fairs on campus for students transferring to 4-year colleges.

**Contact.** E-mail: admissions@pvcc.edu
Phone: (434) 961-6551 Fax: (434) 961-5425
Erica Spangler, Registrar, Piedmont Virginia Community College, 501 College Drive, Charlottesville, VA 22902-7589

## Rappahannock Community College
**Glenns, Virginia**
www.rappahannock.edu
CB code: 5590

- Public 2-year community college
- Commuter campus in rural community

**General.** Founded in 1970. Regionally accredited. **Enrollment:** 1,448 degree-seeking undergraduates. **Degrees:** 172 associate awarded. **Location:** 60 miles from Richmond. **Calendar:** Semester, limited summer session. **Full-time faculty:** 30 total. **Part-time faculty:** 100 total.

**Student profile.** Among degree-seeking undergraduates, 55% enrolled in a transfer program, 45% enrolled in a vocational program.

**Transfer out. Colleges most students transferred to 2007:** Old Dominion University.

**Basis for selection.** Open admission. In-house test used for assessment purposes.

**2007-2008 Annual costs.** Tuition/fees: $2,534; $7,599 out-of-state. Per-credit charge: $77 in-state; $249 out-of-state. Out of state students pay an additional $90 capital outlay fee. Books/supplies: $690. Personal expenses: $1,500.

**Financial aid. Need-based:** Need-based aid available for part-time students.

**Application procedures. Admission:** No deadline. No application fee. Application may be submitted online. Admission notification on a rolling basis. **Financial aid:** Priority date 5/15; no closing date. FAFSA, institutional form required. Applicants notified on a rolling basis starting 6/30.

**Academics. Special study options:** Cooperative education, cross-registration, distance learning, double major, dual enrollment of high school students, independent study, internships, liberal arts/career combination. Bachelor's degree programs available on campus. License preparation in nursing. **Credit/placement by examination:** AP, CLEP, institutional tests. **Support services:** Learning center, reduced course load, remedial instruction, study skills assistance, tutoring.

**Majors. Business:** Accounting, accounting/business management, business admin. **Computer sciences:** Information systems. **Education:** General. **Engineering technology:** General, electrical, electromechanical. **Health:** Nursing (RN). **Liberal arts:** Arts/sciences. **Protective services:** Criminal justice.

**Computing on campus.** 48 workstations in library, computer center. Online course registration, online library available.

**Student life. Freshman orientation:** Mandatory. Preregistration for classes offered. **Activities:** Student government, Phi Theta Kappa Honors Society.

**Athletics. Intramural:** Baseball M, basketball M, bowling, softball W, table tennis, tennis, volleyball.

**Student services.** Adult student services, career counseling, services for economically disadvantaged, student employment services, financial aid counseling, personal counseling, placement for graduates, veterans' counselor. **Physically disabled:** Services for visually, speech, hearing impaired. **Transfer:** Transfer adviser, college fairs on campus for students transferring to 4-year colleges.

**Contact.** Phone: (804) 758-6700 Fax: (804) 758-3852
Wilnet Willis, Admissions and Student Records Officer, Rappahannock Community College, 12745 College Drive, Glenns, VA 23149-2616

## Richard Bland College
**Petersburg, Virginia**
www.rbc.edu
CB member
CB code: 5574

- Public 2-year junior and liberal arts college
- Commuter campus in small city
- Application essay required

**General.** Founded in 1960. Regionally accredited. General education program prepares students to transfer with junior status to a wide variety of public and private institutions located in Virginia. Affiliated with The College of William and Mary. College will accept residential students in Fall 2008. **Enrollment:** 1,060 degree-seeking undergraduates; 342 non-degree-seeking students. **Degrees:** 210 associate awarded. **ROTC:** Army. **Location:** 25 from Richmond. **Calendar:** Semester, limited summer session. **Full-time faculty:** 34 total; 44% have terminal degrees, 12% minority, 56% women. **Part-time faculty:** 32 total; 25% have terminal degrees, 9% minority, 53% women. **Class size:** 50% < 20, 42% 20-39, 7% 40-49, less than 1% 50-99. **Special facilities:** Nature trail, Civil War sites.

**Student profile.** Among degree-seeking undergraduates, 415 enrolled as first-time, first-year students.

| | | | |
|---|---|---|---|
| Part-time: | 26% | Women: | 62% |
| Out-of-state: | 2% | 25 or older: | 15% |

**Transfer out.** 66% of students enrolled in the transfer program go on to 4-year colleges. **Colleges most students transferred to 2007:** Virginia Commonwealth University, College of William and Mary, James Madison University, Longwood University, Virginia Tech University, Virginia State University.

**Basis for selection.** Academic record most important; test scores, essay also important; recommendations, extracurricular activities, interview considered. SAT or ACT recommended. All incoming students who have not completed college-level course work in English and/or mathematics must take the COMPASS placement tests. Interview recommended depending on GPA. **Homeschooled:** Transcript of courses and grades required. GED or SAT required. SAT scores must be equal to or greater than the mean score for current RBC students. **Learning Disabled:** Students eligible for ADA should contact the Division of Student Affairs one month prior to the start of classes to request services.

**High school preparation.** 13 units required. Required units include English 4, mathematics 3, history 2, science 2 and foreign language 2.

**2007-2008 Annual costs.** Tuition/fees: $2,644; $10,802 out-of-state. Per-credit charge: $103 in-state; $451 out-of-state. Books/supplies: $850. Personal expenses: $1,876.

**Financial aid. Need-based:** Need-based aid available for part-time students. **Non-need-based:** Scholarships awarded for academics.

**Application procedures. Admission:** Priority date 5/15; deadline 8/15 (receipt date). $20 fee, may be waived for applicants with need. Admission notification on a rolling basis beginning on or about 2/1. **Financial aid:** Priority date 5/1; no closing date. FAFSA, institutional form required. Applicants notified by 6/1; must reply within 2 week(s) of notification.

**Academics. Special study options:** Dual enrollment of high school students. Educational trips abroad during spring break and summer session for academic credit. **Credit/placement by examination:** AP, CLEP, institutional tests. 30 credit hours maximum toward associate degree. **Support services:** Reduced course load, remedial instruction, study skills assistance, tutoring, writing center.

**Majors. Liberal arts:** Arts/sciences.

**Computing on campus.** 75 workstations in library, computer center, student center. Commuter students can connect to campus network. Online course registration, online library available.

**Student life. Freshman orientation:** Available. Preregistration for classes offered. One-day program. **Policies:** Campus-wide honor code observed. **Housing:** Single-sex dorms available. **Activities:** Campus ministries, choral groups, dance, drama, international student organizations, literary magazine, student government, student newspaper, Spanish club, Gay Lesbian Bisexual Transgender Alliance, Student Ambassadors, wellness club.

**Athletics. Intramural:** Basketball, cheerleading W, softball, tennis, volleyball.

**Student services.** Financial aid counseling. **Physically disabled:** Services for visually, speech, hearing impaired. **Transfer:** Pre-admission transcript evaluation for new students. Transfer adviser, college fairs on campus for students transferring to 4-year colleges.

**Contact.** E-mail: admit@rbc.edu
Phone: (804) 862-6249 Fax: (804) 862-6490
Randy Dean, Assistant Provost for Student Activities, Richard Bland College, 11301 Johnson Road, Petersburg, VA 23805

## Southside Virginia Community College
Alberta, Virginia
www.sv.vccs.edu                    CB code: 5660

▶ Public 2-year community college
▶ Commuter campus in rural community
▶ Interview required

**General.** Founded in 1970. Regionally accredited. Additional campuses at John H. Daniel Campus, Keysville, VA; Campus Without Walls, Emporia, VA. **Enrollment:** 2,484 degree-seeking undergraduates. **Degrees:** 328 associate awarded. **ROTC:** Army. **Location:** 70 miles from Richmond. **Calendar:** Semester, limited summer session. **Full-time faculty:** 84 total. **Part-time faculty:** 222 total. **Special facilities:** Nature trail, fitness trail.

**Student profile.**

| | | | |
|---|---|---|---|
| Out-of-state: | 1% | 25 or older: | 36% |

**Transfer out. Colleges most students transferred to 2007:** Longwood University, Old Dominion University, Saint Paul's College, Virginia Commonwealth University.

**Basis for selection.** Open admission, but selective for some programs. National League for Nursing Pre-Admissions Examination required for nursing applicants. Psychological Services Bureau Revised Aptitude for Practical Nursing Examination required for practical nursing applicants. **Home-schooled:** If not enrolled in program leading to completion credential, student should obtain GED.

**2007-2008 Annual costs.** Tuition/fees: $2,465; $7,629 out-of-state. Per-credit charge: $77 in-state; $249 out-of-state. Out of state students pay an additional $90 capital outlay fee. Books/supplies: $1,040. Personal expenses: $2,340.

**2007-2008 Financial aid. Need-based:** 97% of total undergraduate aid awarded as scholarships/grants, 3% as loans/jobs. Need-based aid available for part-time students. Work-study available nights and for part-time students. **Non-need-based:** Scholarships awarded for academics.

**Application procedures. Admission:** No deadline. No application fee. Application may be submitted online. Admission notification on a rolling basis. **Financial aid:** Priority date 6/1, closing date 8/1. FAFSA required. Applicants notified on a rolling basis starting 6/15.

**Academics.** System-wide core curriculum to ensure ease of transfer. **Special study options:** Cross-registration, distance learning, dual enrollment of high school students, honors, internships, study abroad. Cooperative programs in respiratory therapy with J. Sargeant Reynolds Community College, medical laboratory program with Central Virginia Community College. Bachelor's degree programs available on campus. License preparation in nursing. **Credit/placement by examination:** AP, CLEP, institutional tests.

45 credit hours maximum toward associate degree. **Support services:** GED preparation and test center, reduced course load, remedial instruction, study skills assistance, tutoring.

**Majors. Business:** Administrative services, business admin, management science. **Computer sciences:** General. **Education:** General. **Engineering technology:** Drafting, electrical. **Health:** Clinical lab technology, nursing (RN), respiratory therapy technology. **Interdisciplinary:** Biological/physical sciences. **Liberal arts:** Arts/sciences. **Protective services:** Police science. **Public administration:** Human services.

**Most popular majors.** Business/marketing 18%, health sciences 22%, liberal arts 47%, security/protective services 10%.

**Computing on campus.** 200 workstations in library, computer center.

**Student life. Freshman orientation:** Mandatory, $78 fee. Preregistration for classes offered. **Activities:** Choral groups, drama, music ensembles, student government, Phi Theta Kappa, Criminal Justice Organization, Phi Beta Lambda, Lambda Alpha Epsilon, Alpha Delta Omega.

**Athletics. Intramural:** Basketball, softball, table tennis, tennis, volleyball.

**Student services.** Career counseling, financial aid counseling, personal counseling, veterans' counselor. **Transfer:** Pre-admission transcript evaluation for new students. College fairs on campus for students transferring to 4-year colleges.

**Contact.** E-mail: Rhina.Jones@sv.vccs.edu
Phone: (434) 949-1000 Fax: (434) 949-7863
Brent Richey, Dean of Admissions, Records and Institutional Research, Southside Virginia Community College, 109 Campus Drive, Alberta, VA 23821

## Southwest Virginia Community College
Richlands, Virginia
www.sw.edu                    CB code: 5659

▶ Public 2-year community college
▶ Commuter campus in small town

**General.** Founded in 1967. Regionally accredited. **Enrollment:** 2,481 degree-seeking undergraduates; 1,099 non-degree-seeking students. **Degrees:** 300 associate awarded. **Location:** 45 miles from Bluefield and Bristol. **Calendar:** Semester, extensive summer session. **Full-time faculty:** 73 total. **Part-time faculty:** 220 total. **Class size:** 89% < 20, 7% 20-39, 2% 40-49, 2% 50-99. **Special facilities:** Community center, art gallery.

**Student profile.** Among degree-seeking undergraduates, 39% enrolled in a transfer program, 61% enrolled in a vocational program, 1% already have a bachelor's degree or higher, 541 enrolled as first-time, first-year students, 102 transferred in from other institutions.

| | | | |
|---|---|---|---|
| Part-time: | 48% | Women: | 60% |
| Out-of-state: | 2% | 25 or older: | 55% |

**Transfer out.** 50% of students enrolled in the transfer program go on to 4-year colleges. **Colleges most students transferred to 2007:** Virginia Tech, Radford University, University of Virginia at Wise, East Tennessee State University.

**Basis for selection.** Open admission, but selective for some programs. Special requirements for engineering and health programs. Students are required to take COMPASS, ASSET or some other placement test with the scores used to determine if students will need to take developmental English, mathematics or reading. Interview required for full-time.

**High school preparation.** Subject and unit requirements vary with degree programs.

**2007-2008 Annual costs.** Tuition/fees: $2,450; $7,614 out-of-state. Per-credit charge: $77 in-state; $249 out-of-state. Out of state students pay an additional $90 capital outlay fee. Books/supplies: $1,000. Personal expenses: $1,150.

**Financial aid.** All financial aid based on need. Need-based aid available for part-time students. Work-study available for part-time students.

**Application procedures. Admission:** No deadline. No application fee. Admission notification on a rolling basis. Applicants for nursing and allied health programs must apply by January 15 and reply within 2 weeks of acceptance. No deferred admission for these programs. **Financial aid:** Priority date 5/30; no closing date. FAFSA, institutional form required. Applicants notified on a rolling basis starting 7/1.

**Academics. Special study options:** Accelerated study, cooperative education, distance learning, double major, dual enrollment of high school students, honors, independent study, internships. Bachelor's degree programs available on campus. **Credit/placement by examination:** AP, CLEP. **Support services:** Learning center, pre-admission summer program, reduced course load, remedial instruction, study skills assistance, tutoring, writing center.

**Majors. Business:** General, accounting, administrative services, business admin, managerial economics. **Computer sciences:** General. **Conservation:** Environmental studies. **Education:** General, early childhood. **Engineering:** General, electrical. **Health:** EMT paramedic, health services, medical radiologic technology/radiation therapy, medical secretary, nursing (RN), radiologic technology/medical imaging, respiratory therapy assistant. **Liberal arts:** Arts/sciences. **Protective services:** Corrections, police science. **Public administration:** Human services.

**Most popular majors.** Business/marketing 9%, education 10%, engineering/engineering technologies 9%, health sciences 35%, liberal arts 28%.

**Computing on campus.** 150 workstations in library, computer center. Commuter students can connect to campus network. Online course registration, online library available.

**Student life. Freshman orientation:** Mandatory, $81 fee. Preregistration for classes offered. **Activities:** Jazz band, choral groups, international student organizations, literary magazine, student government, student newspaper, Intervoice Club, Black Student Union, Phi Theta Kappa, Lion's Club, Phi Beta Lambda, Lambda Alpha Epsilon, Helping Minds, Campus Crusade for Christ.

**Athletics. Intercollegiate:** Baseball M, basketball M, cheerleading M. **Intramural:** Baseball M, basketball M, racquetball. **Team name:** Eagles.

**Student services.** Career counseling, services for economically disadvantaged, student employment services, financial aid counseling, health services, minority student services, personal counseling, placement for graduates, veterans' counselor. **Physically disabled:** Services for visually, speech, hearing impaired. **Transfer:** Transfer adviser, college fairs on campus for students transferring to 4-year colleges.

**Contact.** E-mail: admissions@sw.edu
Phone: (276) 964-2555 Toll-free number: (800) 822-7822
Fax: (276) 964-7716
Jim Farris, Director of Admissions and Counseling, Southwest Virginia Community College, PO Box SVCC, Richlands, VA 24641

---

## TESST College of Technology: Alexandria
**Alexandria, Virginia**
www.tesst.com

- For-profit 2-year technical college
- Small city

**General.** Accredited by ACCSCT. **Calendar:** Semester.

**Annual costs/financial aid.** Tuition and fees $12,000 per year: Medical, IT, and Criminal Justice programs leading to an associate degree.

**Contact.** Phone: (703) 354-1005
Executive Director, 6315 Bren Mar Drive, Alexandria, VA 22312

---

## Thomas Nelson Community College
**Hampton, Virginia**
www.tncc.edu                    CB code: 5793

- Public 2-year community college
- Commuter campus in small city

**General.** Founded in 1967. Regionally accredited. **Enrollment:** 7,001 degree-seeking undergraduates. **Degrees:** 335 associate awarded. **ROTC:** Army. **Location:** 20 miles from Norfolk, 35 miles from Virginia Beach. **Calendar:** Semester, extensive summer session. **Full-time faculty:** 109 total. **Part-time faculty:** 335 total.

**Transfer out. Colleges most students transferred to 2007:** Christopher Newport University, Old Dominion University, Norfolk State University, Hampton University.

**Basis for selection.** Open admission, but selective for some programs. Special requirements for nursing program. **Homeschooled:** Must be 18 or have GED.

**High school preparation.** Nursing program requires specific high school units.

**2007-2008 Annual costs.** Tuition/fees: $2,446; $7,610 out-of-state. Per-credit charge: $77 in-state; $249 out-of-state. Out of state students pay an additional $90 capital outlay fee. Books/supplies: $800. Personal expenses: $1,600.

**2007-2008 Financial aid. Need-based:** 78% of total undergraduate aid awarded as scholarships/grants, 22% as loans/jobs. Need-based aid available for part-time students. Work-study available nights and for part-time students.

**Application procedures. Admission:** No deadline. No application fee. Application may be submitted online. Admission notification on a rolling basis. **Financial aid:** Priority date 5/1; no closing date. FAFSA, institutional form required. Applicants notified on a rolling basis starting 6/1; must reply within 2 week(s) of notification.

**Academics.** System-wide core curriculum to ensure ease of transfer, 2-2 program available. **Special study options:** Accelerated study, cooperative education, cross-registration, distance learning, dual enrollment of high school students, ESL, honors, independent study, internships, weekend college. License preparation in nursing. **Credit/placement by examination:** AP, CLEP, institutional tests. SAT Critical Reading or ACT English tests may be substituted for institutional placement examinations if scores high enough. **Support services:** Learning center, remedial instruction, study skills assistance, tutoring, writing center.

**Majors. Business:** Accounting, business admin, management science, office management. **Computer sciences:** General, computer graphics, computer science, information systems, networking, programming. **Education:** Early childhood. **Engineering:** General, electrical. **Engineering technology:** CAD/CADD, electrical. **Health:** Optician. **Interdisciplinary:** Natural sciences. **Liberal arts:** Arts/sciences. **Mechanic/repair:** Automotive. **Protective services:** Fire services admin, law enforcement admin. **Public administration:** General, human services, social work. **Social sciences:** General. **Visual/performing arts:** Commercial/advertising art, photography, studio arts.

**Computing on campus.** Online library available.

**Student life. Freshman orientation:** Available. **Activities:** Choral groups, dance, drama, literary magazine, student government, student newspaper, Digital Arts Society, international club, philosophy and religion club, science club, Phi Theta Kappa.

**Athletics. Intramural:** Basketball. **Team name:** Gators.

**Student services.** Career counseling, student employment services, financial aid counseling, personal counseling, placement for graduates, veterans' counselor. **Physically disabled:** Services for visually, speech, hearing impaired. **Transfer:** Transfer center, transfer adviser, college fairs on campus for students transferring to 4-year colleges.

**Contact.** E-mail: Admissions@tncc.edu
Phone: (757) 825-2800 Fax: (757) 825-2763
Vicki Richmond, Associate Vice President for Enrollment Services, Thomas Nelson Community College, Box 9407, Hampton, VA 23670

---

## Tidewater Community College
**Norfolk, Virginia**                    CB member
www.tcc.vccs.edu                    CB code: 5226

- Public 2-year community college
- Commuter campus in large city

**General.** Founded in 1968. Regionally accredited. Multi-location institution with campuses at Portsmouth, Virginia Beach, Chesapeake, and Norfolk. **Enrollment:** 21,649 degree-seeking undergraduates. **Degrees:** 1,957 associate awarded. **Calendar:** Semester, extensive summer session. **Full-time faculty:** 350 total; 15% minority, 45% women. **Part-time faculty:** 853 total. **Class size:** 49% < 20, 51% 20-39, less than 1% 40-49, less than 1% 50-99. **Special facilities:** Visual arts center, observatory.

**Student profile.** Among degree-seeking undergraduates, 2,186 transferred in from other institutions.

| Out-of-state: | 10% | 25 or older: | 53% |
|---|---|---|---|

**Transfer out. Colleges most students transferred to 2007:** Old Dominion University, Norfolk State University, Virginia Wesleyan College, Christopher Newport University.

**Basis for selection.** Open admission, but selective for some programs. Special requirements for health science programs. ACT required for placement for students enrolling in English or mathematics courses. Interview required for medical technologies and other limited enrollment programs. **Homeschooled:** Transcript of courses and grades, letter of recommendation (nonparent) required.

**2007-2008 Annual costs.** Tuition/fees: $2,566; $7,730 out-of-state. Per-credit charge: $77 in-state; $249 out-of-state. Out of state students pay an additional $90 capital outlay fee. Books/supplies: $1,200. Personal expenses: $710.

**2006-2007 Financial aid.** All financial aid based on need. Need-based aid available for part-time students.

**Application procedures. Admission:** No deadline. No application fee. Application may be submitted online. Admission notification on a rolling basis. **Financial aid:** Priority date 4/1; no closing date. FAFSA required. Applicants notified on a rolling basis starting 4/1.

**Academics.** System-wide core curriculum to ensure ease of transfer. **Special study options:** Cooperative education, cross-registration, distance learning, double major, dual enrollment of high school students, ESL, honors, independent study, internships, study abroad, weekend college. Member Virginia Tidewater Consortium of Higher Education. License preparation in real estate. **Credit/placement by examination:** AP, CLEP, institutional tests. **Support services:** GED preparation and test center, learning center, reduced course load, remedial instruction, study skills assistance, tutoring, writing center.

**Majors. Agriculture:** Business technology, horticulture. **Business:** Accounting, administrative services, banking/financial services, business admin, hospitality admin, real estate, sales/distribution. **Computer sciences:** General, networking, systems analysis. **Conservation:** Environmental studies. **Education:** General, early childhood, teacher assistance. **Engineering:** General, industrial. **Engineering technology:** CAD/CADD, civil, drafting, electro-mechanical, occupational safety, quality control. **Foreign languages:** American Sign Language. **Health:** EMT paramedic, medical radiologic technology/radiation therapy, medical records technology, nursing (RN), occupational therapy assistant, physical therapy assistant, respiratory therapy technology. **Interdisciplinary:** Biological/physical sciences. **Legal studies:** Paralegal. **Liberal arts:** Arts/sciences. **Mechanic/repair:** Automotive, industrial. **Parks/recreation:** General, facilities management. **Personal/culinary services:** Culinary arts. **Production:** Welding. **Protective services:** Firefighting. **Public administration:** General. **Social sciences:** General. **Transportation:** Truck/bus/commercial vehicle. **Visual/performing arts:** Commercial/advertising art, graphic design, interior design, multimedia, photography, studio arts.

**Most popular majors.** Biological/life sciences 8%, business/marketing 21%, engineering/engineering technologies 8%, health sciences 11%, liberal arts 22%, social sciences 14%.

**Computing on campus.** Commuter students can connect to campus network. Online course registration, online library, wireless network available.

**Student life. Freshman orientation:** Available. Preregistration for classes offered. 3 hour sessions. **Activities:** Choral groups, drama, music ensembles, student government, student newspaper, honorary societies, Black Student Alliance, Inter-Varsity Christian Fellowship, student nurses association.

**Athletics. Intramural:** Basketball. **Team name:** Storm.

**Student services.** Adult student services, career counseling, student employment services, financial aid counseling, personal counseling, placement for graduates, veterans' counselor, women's services. **Physically disabled:** Services for visually, speech, hearing impaired. **Transfer:** Transfer adviser, college fairs on campus for students transferring to 4-year colleges.

**Contact.** E-mail: tcc@tcc.vccs.edu
Phone: (757) 822-1100 Fax: (757) 822-1247
Michael Summers, Vice President for Academic and Student Affairs, Tidewater Community College, 7000 College Drive/Portsmouth Campus, Portsmouth, VA 23703

## Tidewater Tech: Chesapeake
**Chesapeake, Virginia**
**www.tidewatertech.edu**

- For-profit 2-year business and health science college
- Commuter campus in large city

**General.** Accredited by ACCSCT. **Enrollment:** 184 degree-seeking undergraduates. **Degrees:** 184 associate awarded. **Calendar:** Continuous. **Full-time faculty:** 30 total. **Part-time faculty:** 10 total.

**Basis for selection.** Open admission.

**2007-2008 Annual costs.** Tuition/fees: $11,060. Annual tuition and fees vary by program.

**Application procedures. Admission:** No deadline.

**Academics. Special study options:** Accelerated study. **Credit/placement by examination:** CLEP.

**Majors. Business:** Business admin, office technology. **Computer sciences:** LAN/WAN management. **Health:** Medical assistant, medical secretary. **Legal studies:** Paralegal.

**Contact.** E-mail: admdirttc@tidewatertech.edu
Fax: (757) 548-1196
Monica Lamb, Director of Admission, Tidewater Tech: Chesapeake, 932 Ventures Way, Chesapeake, VA 23320-2882

## Tidewater Tech: Newport News
**Newport News, Virginia**
**www.tidewatertech.edu**

- For-profit 2-year business and technical college
- Commuter campus in small city

**General.** Accredited by ACCSCT. **Enrollment:** 227 degree-seeking undergraduates. **Degrees:** 199 associate awarded. **Calendar:** Continuous. **Full-time faculty:** 30 total.

**Basis for selection.** Open admission.

**2008-2009 Annual costs.** Tuition/fees: $15,075. Annual tuition and fees vary by program.

**Application procedures. Admission:** No deadline. $25 fee, may be waived for applicants with need.

**Academics. Credit/placement by examination:** CLEP.

**Majors. Business:** Business admin. **Computer sciences:** Networking. **Health:** Massage therapy, medical assistant.

**Contact.** E-mail: admdirttp@tidewatertech.edu
Phone: (757) 874-2121 Fax: (757) 874-3857
Pam Brown, Director of Admissions, Tidewater Tech: Newport News, 616 Denbigh Boulevard, Newport News, VA 23608

## Tidewater Tech: Norfolk
**Norfolk, Virginia**
**www.tidewatertech.edu/tidewater-tech-norfolk.asp**

- For-profit 2-year branch campus and career college
- Commuter campus in large city

**General.** Accredited by ACCSCT. **Enrollment:** 375 full-time, degree-seeking students. **Degrees:** 23 associate awarded. **Calendar:** Continuous. **Full-time faculty:** 30 total.

**Basis for selection.** Open admission. **Homeschooled:** State high school equivalency certificate required.

**2007-2008 Annual costs.** Tuition/fees: $11,060. Annual tuition and fees reported are representative and will vary depending on program.

**Application procedures. Admission:** No deadline. $25 fee, may be waived for applicants with need.

**Academics. Special study options:** Bachelor's degree programs available on campus. License preparation in dental hygiene, nursing, radiology. **Credit/placement by examination:** CLEP. **Support services:** Tutoring.

**Majors. Health:** Medical assistant, office assistant.

**Student life. Freshman orientation:** Available. **Activities:** Student newspaper.

**Contact.** E-mail: admdirttn@tidetech.com
Phone: (757) 853-2121 Toll-free number: (877) 604-2121
Fax: (757) 852-9017
Laura Silva, Admissions Director, Tidewater Tech: Norfolk, 7020 North Military Highway, Norfolk, VA 23518-4202

## Tidewater Tech: Virginia Beach
### Virginia Beach, Virginia
### www.tidewatertech.edu

♦ For-profit 2-year technical college
♦ Commuter campus in small city

**General.** Accredited by ACCSCT. **Enrollment:** 184 degree-seeking undergraduates. **Degrees:** 176 associate awarded. **Calendar:** Modules begin every 5 weeks. **Full-time faculty:** 10 total. **Part-time faculty:** 20 total.

**Basis for selection.** Open admission, but selective for some programs.

**2008-2009 Annual costs.** Tuition/fees: $15,075. Annual tuition and fees reported are representative and will vary depending on program.

**Application procedures. Admission:** No deadline. $25 fee.

**Academics. Special study options:** Accelerated study, distance learning. **Credit/placement by examination:** CLEP.

**Majors. Business:** General. **Computer sciences:** Networking. **Health:** Management/clinical assistant, massage therapy, office assistant. **Legal studies:** Paralegal. **Protective services:** Law enforcement admin.

**Contact.** E-mail: directorttv@tidetech.com
Phone: (757) 340-2121 Fax: (757) 340-9704
Nida Rogers, Director of Admissions, Tidewater Tech: Virginia Beach, 2697 Dean Drive, Suite 100, Virginia Beach, VA 23452

## Virginia Highlands Community College
### Abingdon, Virginia
### www.vhcc.edu          CB code: 5927

♦ Public 2-year community college
♦ Commuter campus in small town

**General.** Founded in 1967. Regionally accredited. **Enrollment:** 1,002 full-time, degree-seeking students. **Degrees:** 203 associate awarded. **Location:** 120 miles from Roanoke. **Calendar:** Semester, extensive summer session. **Full-time faculty:** 48 total; 10% have terminal degrees, 4% minority, 58% women. **Part-time faculty:** 116 total; 8% have terminal degrees, less than 1% minority, 46% women. **Special facilities:** Greenhouse.

**Student profile.**

| Out-of-state: | 11% | 25 or older: | 36% |
|---|---|---|---|

**Transfer out. Colleges most students transferred to 2007:** East Tennessee State University, Virginia Tech, Radford University, Old Dominion University, University of Virginia at Wise.

**Basis for selection.** Open admission, but selective for some programs. Paramedic, nursing, radiography, physical therapy, dental hygiene, and medical laboratory technology programs have special requirements. COMPASS required for placement. **Learning Disabled:** Developmental courses are to be taken by students who test below set standards on COMPASS and/or ASSET test.

**High school preparation.** 12 units recommended. Recommended units include English 4, mathematics 2, social studies 4, science 1 (laboratory 1).

**2007-2008 Annual costs.** Tuition/fees: $2,435; $7,599 out-of-state. Per-credit charge: $77 in-state; $249 out-of-state. Out of state students pay an additional $90 capital outlay fee. Books/supplies: $750. Personal expenses: $1,272.

**Financial aid. Need-based:** Work-study available for part-time students.

**Application procedures. Admission:** No deadline. No application fee. Application may be submitted online. Admission notification on a rolling basis. **Financial aid:** No deadline. FAFSA, institutional form required. Applicants notified on a rolling basis starting 5/1.

**Academics. Special study options:** Cooperative education, distance learning, double major, dual enrollment of high school students, independent study, internships, liberal arts/career combination. License preparation in nursing, paramedic, real estate. **Credit/placement by examination:** AP, CLEP, institutional tests. 45 credit hours maximum toward associate degree. **Support services:** Learning center, pre-admission summer program, reduced course load, remedial instruction, tutoring.

**Majors. Agriculture:** Farm/ranch. **Business:** Accounting, administrative services, business admin, office management. **Computer sciences:** General,

data processing. **Education:** General, drama/dance. **Engineering technology:** Drafting, electrical. **Health:** Clinical lab assistant, dental hygiene, medical radiologic technology/radiation therapy, nursing (RN), physical therapy assistant. **Interdisciplinary:** Biological/physical sciences. **Legal studies:** Legal secretary. **Liberal arts:** Arts/sciences. **Protective services:** Police science. **Public administration:** Social work.

**Computing on campus.** 230 workstations in library, computer center, student center. Online course registration, wireless network available.

**Student life. Freshman orientation:** Mandatory, $68 fee. Preregistration for classes offered. **Activities:** Choral groups, drama, music ensembles, musical theater, student government, student newspaper, IMPACT club, law enforcement club, Roteract club, College Republicans, College Democrats, anglers' club, VATNP (nursing) club, National Honors Society, Christian club.

**Athletics. Intramural:** Basketball.

**Student services.** Career counseling, services for economically disadvantaged, student employment services, financial aid counseling, personal counseling, placement for graduates, veterans' counselor. **Physically disabled:** Services for visually, speech, hearing impaired. **Transfer:** Transfer adviser, college fairs on campus for students transferring to 4-year colleges.

**Contact.** E-mail: dbarrett@vhcc.edu
Phone: (276) 739-2460 Fax: (276) 739-2591
David Matlock, Director of Admissions, Records and Financial Aid, Virginia Highlands Community College, PO Box 828, Abingdon, VA 24212-0828

## Virginia Western Community College
### Roanoke, Virginia
### www.virginiawestern.edu          CB code: 5868

♦ Public 2-year community college
♦ Commuter campus in small city

**General.** Founded in 1966. Regionally accredited. **Enrollment:** 4,665 degree-seeking undergraduates. **Degrees:** 496 associate awarded. **Location:** 3 miles from downtown. **Calendar:** Semester, extensive summer session. **Full-time faculty:** 89 total. **Part-time faculty:** 279 total. **Special facilities:** Arboretum.

**Student profile.** Among degree-seeking undergraduates, 30% enrolled in a transfer program, 28% enrolled in a vocational program.

**Transfer out. Colleges most students transferred to 2007:** Virginia Tech, Radford University, Old Dominion University, Roanoke College, Hollins University.

**Basis for selection.** Open admission, but selective for some programs. Special requirements for health programs and communication design program. Interview required for health technologies. **Adult students:** SAT/ACT scores not required. **Learning Disabled:** Student Support Services/REACH program to provide accommodations for students with learning disabilities.

**2007-2008 Annual costs.** Tuition/fees: $2,453; $7,617 out-of-state. Per-credit charge: $77 in-state; $249 out-of-state. Out of state students pay an additional $90 capital outlay fee. Books/supplies: $550. Personal expenses: $1,200.

**Financial aid. Need-based:** Need-based aid available for part-time students. **Non-need-based:** Scholarships awarded for academics, state residency.

**Application procedures. Admission:** No deadline. No application fee. Admission notification on a rolling basis. **Financial aid:** No deadline. FAFSA required. Applicants notified on a rolling basis starting 4/1.

**Academics. Special study options:** Combined bachelor's/graduate degree, distance learning, dual enrollment of high school students, external degree, honors, independent study, internships, liberal arts/career combination, study abroad, weekend college. License preparation in dental hygiene, nursing, radiology, real estate. **Credit/placement by examination:** AP, CLEP, IB, institutional tests. **Support services:** Learning center, reduced course load, remedial instruction, study skills assistance, tutoring, writing center.

**Majors. Agriculture:** Horticultural science, horticulture, landscaping. **Business:** General, accounting, administrative services, banking/financial services, business admin, management information systems, office technology, real estate. **Communications technology:** General. **Computer sciences:** General, computer science. **Education:** General, early childhood, social science. **Engineering:** General. **Engineering technology:** Architectural, civil, electrical. **Family/consumer sciences:** Child care. **Health:** Dental hygiene, health services, medical radiologic technology/radiation therapy, medical secretary, mental health services, nursing (RN). **Interdisciplinary:** Biological/physical sciences, natural sciences. **Legal studies:** Legal secretary, paralegal. **Liberal arts:** Arts/sciences. **Math:** General. **Mechanic/repair:** General, heating/ac/refrig. **Personal/culinary services:** General. **Protective services:** Criminal justice, police science. **Public administration:** Human services. **Social sciences:** General. **Visual/performing arts:** Commercial/advertising art, studio arts.

**Computing on campus.** 100 workstations in library, computer center. Online course registration, helpline, wireless network available.

**Student life. Freshman orientation:** Mandatory. Preregistration for classes offered. **Activities:** Choral groups, drama, student government, student newspaper, minority student alliance, Christian Fellowship.

**Athletics. Intramural:** Basketball, cheerleading W.

**Student services.** Adult student services, alcohol/substance abuse counseling, career counseling, services for economically disadvantaged, student employment services, financial aid counseling, minority student services, personal counseling, placement for graduates, veterans' counselor. **Physically disabled:** Services for visually, speech, hearing impaired. **Learning disabled:** Comprehensive services available. **Transfer:** Transfer center, transfer adviser, college fairs on campus for students transferring to 4-year colleges.

**Contact.** E-mail: mpatterson@vw.vccs.edu
Phone: (540) 857-7231 Fax: (540) 857-6102
Meg Patterson, Admissions and Records Coordinator/Registrar, Virginia Western Community College, Box 14007, Roanoke, VA 24038

## Wytheville Community College
**Wytheville, Virginia**
**www.wcc.vccs.edu**                    CB code: 5917

- Public 2-year community college
- Commuter campus in small town

**General.** Founded in 1962. Regionally accredited. **Enrollment:** 1,668 degree-seeking undergraduates. **Degrees:** 266 associate awarded. **Location:** 74 miles from Roanoke. **Calendar:** Semester, limited summer session. **Full-time faculty:** 38 total; 3% minority, 68% women. **Part-time faculty:** 93 total; 59% women.

**Student profile.** Among degree-seeking undergraduates, 30 transferred in from other institutions.

| | | | |
|---|---|---|---|
| Out-of-state: | 4% | 25 or older: | 44% |

**Basis for selection.** Open admission, but selective for some programs. Limited admissions to allied health programs. High school transcripts required of all allied health applicants. Interview required for allied health, police science. **Homeschooled:** Statement describing homeschool structure and mission required.

**2007-2008 Annual costs.** Tuition/fees: $2,435; $7,599 out-of-state. Per-credit charge: $77 in-state; $249 out-of-state. Out of state students pay an additional $90 capital outlay fee. Books/supplies: $840. Personal expenses: $250.

**2006-2007 Financial aid.** All financial aid based on need. 94% of total undergraduate aid awarded as scholarships/grants, 6% as loans/jobs. Need-based aid available for part-time students.

**Application procedures. Admission:** No deadline. No application fee. Admission notification on a rolling basis. **Financial aid:** Priority date 4/1; no closing date. FAFSA, institutional form required. Applicants notified on a rolling basis starting 5/1; must reply within 4 week(s) of notification.

**Academics. Special study options:** Distance learning, dual enrollment of high school students, honors, independent study, internships. License preparation in dental hygiene, nursing, physical therapy. **Credit/placement by examination:** AP, CLEP, institutional tests. **Support services:** Remedial instruction, tutoring.

**Majors. Business:** Accounting, administrative services, business admin, managerial economics. **Computer sciences:** Information systems. **Construction:** Electrician, plumbing. **Education:** General. **Engineering:** Computer. **Engineering technology:** Drafting, electrical. **Family/consumer sciences:** Child care. **Health:** Clinical lab technology, dental hygiene, nursing (RN), physical therapy assistant, radiologic technology/medical imaging, respiratory therapy technology. **Interdisciplinary:** Biological/physical sciences. **Liberal arts:** Arts/sciences. **Protective services:** Police science.

**Most popular majors.** Education 9%, health sciences 44%, liberal arts 6%, security/protective services 8%.

**Computing on campus.** 133 workstations in library, computer center, student center.

**Student life. Activities:** Concert band, drama, student government, student newspaper.

**Athletics. Intramural:** Basketball, softball, table tennis, tennis, volleyball.

**Student services.** Career counseling, student employment services, personal counseling, placement for graduates, veterans' counselor. **Physically disabled:** Services for visually, hearing impaired. **Transfer:** College fairs on campus for students transferring to 4-year colleges.

**Contact.** E-mail: wcdixxs@wcc.vccs.edu
Phone: (276) 223-4700 Toll-free number: (800) 468-1195
Fax: (276) 223-4860
Sherry Dix, Registrar, Wytheville Community College, 1000 East Main Street, Wytheville, VA 24382

# Washington

## Bates Technical College
Tacoma, Washington
www.bates.ctc.edu

CB code: 4152

- Public 2-year technical college
- Small city

**General. Enrollment:** 1,210 degree-seeking undergraduates. **Degrees:** 126 associate awarded. **Calendar:** Quarter, extensive summer session. **Full-time faculty:** 143 total.

**Basis for selection.** Open admission. COMPASS required for admission. **Adult students:** SAT/ACT scores not required.

**2007-2008 Annual costs.** Programs range in costs from $3,841 to $5,055; cost includes tuition and some fees.

**Financial aid.** All financial aid based on need. Need-based aid available for part-time students. Work-study available nights and for part-time students.

**Application procedures. Admission:** No deadline. $56 fee. Application must be submitted on paper. **Financial aid:** No deadline. FAFSA, institutional form required. Applicants notified on a rolling basis starting 9/7.

**Academics. Special study options:** Distance learning, dual enrollment of high school students, ESL, internships. License preparation in dental hygiene, nursing. **Credit/placement by examination:** CLEP, IB. **Support services:** GED preparation and test center, learning center, reduced course load, remedial instruction, study skills assistance, tutoring.

**Majors. Architecture:** Technology. **Biology:** Biotechnology. **Business:** Accounting technology, administrative services, marketing, retailing. **Communications technology:** General, radio/tv. **Computer sciences:** Computer support specialist, database management, information technology, networking, programming, web page design, webmaster. **Construction:** General, carpentry, electrician, maintenance, metal building assembly. **Education:** Early childhood, kindergarten/preschool. **Engineering:** Architectural, civil, electrical, mechanical, surveying, textile. **Engineering technology:** General, architectural drafting, biomedical, civil drafting, computer, electrical, electrical drafting, electromechanical, industrial safety, mechanical, surveying. **Family/consumer sciences:** Institutional food production. **Health:** Dental assistant, dental lab technology, licensed practical nurse, medical secretary. **Legal studies:** Legal secretary. **Mechanic/repair:** General, auto body, automotive, communications systems, diesel, electronics/electrical, heating/ac/refrig, heavy equipment, industrial electronics, small engine. **Personal/culinary services:** General, cosmetic, culinary arts. **Production:** Cabinetmaking/millwright, machine tool, sheet metal, welding. **Protective services:** Fire safety technology, fire services admin, firefighting. **Science technology:** Biological. **Visual/performing arts:** Fashion design. **Other:** Boat building.

**Computing on campus.** Commuter students can connect to campus network. Online library available.

**Student life. Freshman orientation:** Available. Preregistration for classes offered.

**Contact.** E-mail: registration@bates.ctc.edu
Phone: (253) 680-7002
Steve Ashpole, Admissions Director, Bates Technical College, 1101 South Yakima Avenue, Tacoma, WA 98405

## Bellevue Community College
Bellevue, Washington
www.bcc.ctc.edu

CB code: 4029

- Public 2-year community college
- Commuter campus in small city

**General.** Founded in 1965. Regionally accredited. **Enrollment:** 5,000 degree-seeking undergraduates. **Degrees:** 1,500 associate awarded. **Location:** 12 miles from Seattle. **Calendar:** Quarter, limited summer session. **Full-time**

**faculty:** 162 total. **Part-time faculty:** 543 total. **Special facilities:** Planetarium, National Workforce Center for Emerging Technologies, greenhouses, observatory, scanning electron microscope.

**Transfer out. Colleges most students transferred to 2007:** University of Washington, Washington State University, Central Washington University, Seattle University, Western Washington University.

**Basis for selection.** Open admission, but selective for some programs. Interview, essay, 2 letters of recommendation, transcripts required of applicants to allied health programs, including radiologic technology, diagnostic ultrasound, radiation therapy. **Homeschooled:** Must be at least 18 years old. **Learning Disabled:** Through Disability Support Services Office, student may request reasonable classroom accommodations. Student must provide documentation from appropriate professional.

**High school preparation.** Allied health programs have special requirements.

**2007-2008 Annual costs.** Tuition/fees: $3,096; $8,304 out-of-state. Per-credit charge: $81 in-state; $253 out-of-state. Books/supplies: $750. Personal expenses: $1,968.

**2006-2007 Financial aid. Need-based:** 77% of total undergraduate aid awarded as scholarships/grants, 23% as loans/jobs. Need-based aid available for part-time students. Work-study available nights, weekends and for part-time students. **Non-need-based:** Scholarships awarded for academics, athletics.

**Application procedures. Admission:** No deadline. $28 fee. Application may be submitted online. Admission notification on a rolling basis. **Financial aid:** Priority date 4/16; no closing date. FAFSA, institutional form required. Applicants notified on a rolling basis starting 8/1.

**Academics. Special study options:** Distance learning, dual enrollment of high school students, ESL, honors, independent study, internships, study abroad. Bachelor's degree programs available on campus. **Credit/placement by examination:** AP, CLEP, institutional tests. 15 credit hours maximum toward associate degree. **Support services:** GED preparation and test center, learning center, remedial instruction, tutoring, writing center.

**Majors. Business:** Accounting, accounting technology, administrative services, business admin, marketing, office management, real estate. **Computer sciences:** General, computer graphics, database management, networking, programming, security, web page design. **Education:** Early childhood. **Health:** Medical radiologic technology/radiation therapy, nuclear medical technology, nursing (RN), sonography. **Liberal arts:** Arts/sciences. **Parks/recreation:** General. **Protective services:** Fire safety technology, fire services admin, firefighting, law enforcement admin. **Visual/performing arts:** Interior design.

**Most popular majors.** Business/marketing 12%, computer/information sciences 8%, health sciences 8%, liberal arts 64%.

**Computing on campus.** 244 workstations in library, computer center. Commuter students can connect to campus network. Online course registration, online library, helpline, student web hosting, wireless network available.

**Student life. Freshman orientation:** Available. Quarterly, prior to start of term. **Activities:** Jazz band, choral groups, dance, drama, literary magazine, music ensembles, musical theater, radio station, student government, student newspaper, TV station.

**Athletics.** NAIA, NJCAA. **Intercollegiate:** Baseball M, basketball, cross-country, golf M, soccer, softball W, tennis, track and field, volleyball W. **Intramural:** Badminton, basketball, racquetball, soccer W, softball W, table tennis, tennis, volleyball. **Team name:** Bulldogs.

**Student services.** Career counseling, services for economically disadvantaged, student employment services, financial aid counseling, health services, minority student services, on-campus daycare, personal counseling, placement for graduates, veterans' counselor, women's services. **Physically disabled:** Services for visually, speech, hearing impaired. **Transfer:** Transfer center, transfer adviser, college fairs on campus for students transferring to 4-year colleges.

**Contact.** E-mail: admissions@bcc.ctc.edu
Phone: (425) 564-2222 Fax: (425) 564-4065
Robin Young, Director of Admissions, Bellevue Community College, 3000 Landerholm Circle SE, Bellevue, WA 98007-6484

## Bellingham Technical College
Bellingham, Washington
www.btc.ctc.edu

CB member
CB code: 3499

- Public 2-year technical college
- Commuter campus in small city

**General.** Regionally accredited. **Enrollment:** 2,084 degree-seeking undergraduates. **Degrees:** 257 associate awarded. **Location:** 90 miles from Seattle. **Calendar:** Quarter, limited summer session. **Full-time faculty:** 66 total; 6% minority, 50% women. **Part-time faculty:** 116 total. **Class size:** 84% < 20, 15% 20-39, less than 1% 40-49, less than 1% 50-99.

**Student profile.** Among degree-seeking undergraduates, 89% enrolled in a vocational program, 10% already have a bachelor's degree or higher.

| | | | |
|---|---|---|---|
| Out-of-state: | 1% | **25 or older:** | 52% |

**Basis for selection.** Open admission. **Adult students:** SAT/ACT scores not required.

**2007-2008 Annual costs.** Tuition/fees: $3,345. Books/supplies: $2,029. Personal expenses: $1,623.

**Financial aid.** All financial aid based on need. Need-based aid available for part-time students. Work-study available for part-time students.

**Application procedures. Admission:** No deadline. $35 fee. Application must be submitted on paper. Admission notification on a rolling basis. **Financial aid:** Priority date 4/30; no closing date. FAFSA required. Applicants notified on a rolling basis starting 7/1; must reply within 2 week(s) of notification.

**Academics. Special study options:** Distance learning, ESL, internships. License preparation in nursing, paramedic, real estate. **Credit/placement by examination:** CLEP, institutional tests. **Support services:** GED preparation and test center, learning center, remedial instruction, study skills assistance, tutoring.

**Majors. Business:** Accounting technology, executive assistant, human resources, marketing, operations. **Computer sciences:** Data entry, networking. **Conservation:** Fisheries. **Construction:** Electrician, maintenance. **Education:** Voc/tech. **Engineering technology:** Biomedical, civil, computer systems, instrumentation, manufacturing, mechanical, surveying. **Health:** Dental hygiene, EMT paramedic, insurance coding, medical radiologic technology/radiation therapy, nursing (RN), radiologic technology/medical imaging. **Legal studies:** Legal secretary. **Mechanic/repair:** Appliance, auto body, automotive, communications systems, diesel, heating/ac/refrig, industrial. **Personal/culinary services:** Chef training. **Production:** Machine tool, welding. **Other:** Process technology.

**Computing on campus.** 14 workstations in library. Commuter students can connect to campus network. Online course registration, online library, wireless network available.

**Student life. Freshman orientation:** Available. Orientation is held quarterly for new students within the month prior to students' start date. **Activities:** Student government.

**Student services.** Adult student services, career counseling, services for economically disadvantaged, financial aid counseling, minority student services, veterans' counselor. **Physically disabled:** Services for visually, speech, hearing impaired. **Transfer:** Pre-admission transcript evaluation for new students.

**Contact.** E-mail: admissions@btc.ctc.edu
Phone: (360) 785-8345 Fax: (360) 676-2798
Erin Runestrand, Director of Admissions, Bellingham Technical College, 3028 Lindbergh Avenue, Bellingham, WA 98225

---

## Big Bend Community College
**Moses Lake, Washington**
www.bigbend.edu
CB code: 4024

- Public 2-year community college
- Commuter campus in large town

**General.** Founded in 1962. Regionally accredited. **Enrollment:** 1,154 degree-seeking undergraduates; 714 non-degree-seeking students. **Degrees:** 339 associate awarded. **Location:** 107 miles from Spokane, 170 miles from Seattle. **Calendar:** Quarter, limited summer session. **Full-time faculty:** 55 total; 9% have terminal degrees, 7% minority, 34% women. **Part-time faculty:** 91 total; 2% have terminal degrees, 26% minority, 53% women. **Partnerships:** Formal partnership with high schools for Tech Prep programs.

**Student profile.** Among degree-seeking undergraduates, 60% enrolled in a transfer program, 40% enrolled in a vocational program, 1% already have

a bachelor's degree or higher, 286 enrolled as first-time, first-year students, 77 transferred in from other institutions.

| | | | |
|---|---|---|---|
| Part-time: | 25% | Hispanic American: | 23% |
| Out-of-state: | 5% | Native American: | 1% |
| Women: | 58% | 25 or older: | 47% |
| African American: | 1% | Live on campus: | 5% |
| Asian American: | 2% | | |

**Transfer out. Colleges most students transferred to 2007:** Central Washington University, Eastern Washington University, Washington State University.

**Basis for selection.** Open admission, but selective for some programs. Special admission criteria for aviation and nursing programs.

**2007-2008 Annual costs.** Tuition/fees: $2,766; $3,156 out-of-state. Per-credit charge: $74 in-state; $88 out-of-state. Room only: $2,790. Books/supplies: $984. Personal expenses: $1,560.

**2006-2007 Financial aid.** All financial aid based on need. 79% of total undergraduate aid awarded as scholarships/grants, 21% as loans/jobs. Need-based aid available for part-time students. Work-study available nights, weekends and for part-time students.

**Application procedures. Admission:** No deadline. $30 fee. Application may be submitted online. Admission notification on a rolling basis. **Financial aid:** Priority date 4/15; no closing date. FAFSA, institutional form required. Applicants notified on a rolling basis starting 5/15; must reply within 2 week(s) of notification.

**Academics. Special study options:** Cooperative education, distance learning, dual enrollment of high school students, liberal arts/career combination. Bachelor's degree programs available on campus. License preparation in aviation, nursing. **Credit/placement by examination:** AP, CLEP, institutional tests. 45 credit hours maximum toward associate degree. **Support services:** GED preparation and test center, learning center, reduced course load, remedial instruction, study skills assistance, tutoring, writing center.

**Majors. Agriculture:** Production. **Business:** Accounting technology, office management. **Computer sciences:** General, programming. **Construction:** Electrician. **Education:** Teacher assistance. **Engineering technology:** Civil. **Health:** Medical assistant, nursing (RN), office admin. **Liberal arts:** Arts/sciences. **Mechanic/repair:** Aircraft, automotive, industrial. **Physical sciences:** General. **Production:** Welding. **Transportation:** Airline/commercial pilot.

**Most popular majors.** Health sciences 8%, liberal arts 76%, trade and industry 9%.

**Computing on campus.** 432 workstations in dormitories, library, computer center, student center. Dormitories wired for high-speed internet access and linked to campus network. Online course registration, student web hosting, wireless network available.

**Student life. Freshman orientation:** Available. Preregistration for classes offered. Half-day fall student advising and registration sessions held throughout the summer. Full-day student orientation held in September. **Housing:** Coed dorms, substance-free housing available. $200 partly refundable deposit. **Activities:** Choral groups, music ensembles, student government.

**Athletics. Intercollegiate:** Baseball M, basketball, softball W, volleyball W. **Team name:** Vikings.

**Student services.** Career counseling, student employment services, financial aid counseling, minority student services, on-campus daycare, personal counseling, placement for graduates, veterans' counselor. **Physically disabled:** Services for visually, hearing impaired. **Transfer:** Transfer adviser, college fairs on campus for students transferring to 4-year colleges.

**Contact.** E-mail: admissions@bigbend.edu
Phone: (509) 793-2061 Toll-free number: (877) 745-1212
Fax: (509) 762-6243
Candy Lacher, Dean of Enrollment Services, Big Bend Community College, 7662 Chanute Street, Moses Lake, WA 98837-3299

---

## Cascadia Community College
**Bothell, Washington**
www.cascadia.edu
CB code: 2859

- Public 2-year community college
- Commuter campus in large town

Two-Year Colleges

**General.** Commitment to themes of global perspective and sustainability infused into most courses. **Enrollment:** 1,367 degree-seeking undergraduates. **Degrees:** 263 associate awarded. **Location:** 15 miles from Seattle. **Calendar:** Quarter, extensive summer session.

**Student profile.** Among degree-seeking undergraduates, 77% enrolled in a transfer program, 6% enrolled in a vocational program.

**Basis for selection.** Open admission. The college requires all students who take credit classes to assess their current skill levels in English and Math with the COMPASS placement test.

**2007-2008 Annual costs.** Tuition/fees: $2,796; $8,004 out-of-state.

**Financial aid.** **Need-based:** Work-study available nights, weekends and for part-time students.

**Application procedures.** **Admission:** No deadline. No application fee. Application may be submitted online. **Financial aid:** Priority date 4/16; no closing date. FAFSA, institutional form required.

**Academics.** **Special study options:** Distance learning, dual enrollment of high school students, ESL, independent study, internships, study abroad. **Credit/placement by examination:** AP, CLEP. **Support services:** GED preparation, learning center, study skills assistance, tutoring, writing center.

**Majors.** **Biology:** General. **Computer sciences:** General. **Conservation:** Environmental science. **Physical sciences:** Atmospheric physics, chemistry, geology, physics.

**Computing on campus.** Online library, helpline, wireless network available.

**Student life.** **Activities:** Film society, literary magazine, student government, student newspaper.

**Athletics.** **Team name:** Kodiaks.

**Contact.** E-mail: admissions@cascadia.edu
Phone: (425) 352-8860
Cascadia Community College, 18345 Campus Way, NE, Bothell, WA 98011

## Centralia College
**Centralia, Washington**
**www.centralia.edu**

**CB code: 4045**

- Public 2-year community college
- Commuter campus in large town

**General.** Founded in 1925. Regionally accredited. **Enrollment:** 3,566 degree-seeking undergraduates. **Degrees:** 334 associate awarded. **Location:** 90 miles from Seattle, 90 miles from Portland, Oregon. **Calendar:** Quarter, extensive summer session. **Full-time faculty:** 58 total; 19% have terminal degrees, 5% minority, 52% women. **Part-time faculty:** 176 total; 2% have terminal degrees, 2% minority, 43% women. **Class size:** 50% < 20, 43% 20-39, 5% 40-49, 2% 50-99.

**Student profile.** Among degree-seeking undergraduates, 40% enrolled in a transfer program, 35% enrolled in a vocational program, 1% already have a bachelor's degree or higher, 106 transferred in from other institutions.

| | | | |
|---|---|---|---|
| Out-of-state: | 1% | Native American: | 2% |
| African American: | 1% | International: | 2% |
| Asian American: | 2% | 25 or older: | 53% |
| Hispanic American: | 11% | | |

**Transfer out.** 50% of students enrolled in the transfer program go on to 4-year colleges. **Colleges most students transferred to 2007:** Western Washington University, Washington State University, The Evergreen State College, Saint Martin's College, Central Washington University.

**Basis for selection.** Open admission, but selective for some programs. Special requirements for nursing program, includes prerequisites and grade point average criteria. **Homeschooled:** Transcript of courses and grades required.

**High school preparation.** 16 units recommended. Recommended units include English 4, mathematics 3, social studies 2, history 1, science 2 (laboratory 1), foreign language 2 and academic electives 1.

**2007-2008 Annual costs.** Tuition/fees: $2,946; $3,335 out-of-state. Per-credit charge: $74 in-state; $88 out-of-state. Books/supplies: $924. Personal expenses: $1,524.

**Financial aid.** **Need-based:** Need-based aid available for part-time students. Work-study available for part-time students. **Non-need-based:** Scholarships awarded for academics, alumni affiliation, art, athletics, leadership, minority status, music/drama.

**Application procedures.** **Admission:** Priority date 9/1; no deadline. No application fee. Application may be submitted online. Admission notification on a rolling basis beginning on or about 12/1. **Financial aid:** Priority date 5/1, closing date 9/1. FAFSA, institutional form required. Applicants notified on a rolling basis starting 7/10; must reply within 2 week(s) of notification.

**Academics.** **Special study options:** Cooperative education, cross-registration, distance learning, double major, dual enrollment of high school students, ESL, honors, independent study, internships, liberal arts/career combination, student-designed major, study abroad, weekend college. Bachelor's degree programs available on campus. License preparation in nursing, paramedic, real estate. **Credit/placement by examination:** AP, CLEP, IB, institutional tests. 45 credit hours maximum toward associate degree. **Support services:** GED preparation and test center, learning center, reduced course load, remedial instruction, study skills assistance, tutoring, writing center.

**Honors college/program.** Selective application process after completion of 30 college credits. Space limited to 20 students per year.

**Majors.** **Biology:** General, botany. **Business:** General, accounting, business admin, marketing, office technology, office/clerical, receptionist, sales/distribution. **Communications:** Broadcast journalism, journalism, radio/tv. **Communications technology:** Graphics, radio/tv. **Computer sciences:** General, computer science, data processing, information systems, LAN/WAN management, networking, programming. **Conservation:** Environmental studies, forestry. **Education:** General, early childhood. **Engineering:** General. **Engineering technology:** Civil, civil drafting, drafting, electrical, surveying. **English:** English lit. **Family/consumer sciences:** Child care. **Foreign languages:** General, French, German, Spanish. **Health:** Athletic training, medical records technology, medical secretary, nursing (RN), office assistant, predental, premedicine, prenursing, prepharmacy, preveterinary, receptionist. **History:** General. **Interdisciplinary:** Biological/physical sciences. **Legal studies:** Legal secretary, prelaw. **Liberal arts:** Arts/sciences. **Math:** General. **Mechanic/repair:** Diesel, electronics/electrical. **Parks/recreation:** Exercise sciences, health/fitness. **Physical sciences:** General, chemistry, geology, physics, planetary. **Production:** Welding. **Protective services:** Criminal justice, law enforcement admin, police science. **Psychology:** General. **Social sciences:** General, anthropology, economics, sociology. **Visual/performing arts:** General, art, commercial/advertising art, dramatic, graphic design, music theory/composition, studio arts.

**Most popular majors.** Health sciences 7%, liberal arts 68%.

**Computing on campus.** 150 workstations in library, computer center, student center. Online course registration, online library, helpline, wireless network available.

**Student life.** **Freshman orientation:** Available, $20 fee. Preregistration for classes offered. Held 2 days prior to fall quarter. **Activities:** Bands, choral groups, drama, literary magazine, music ensembles, musical theater, radio station, student government, student newspaper, symphony orchestra, TV station, honors club, international student club, Rotaract.

**Athletics.** **Intercollegiate:** Baseball M, basketball, golf W, softball W, volleyball W. **Team name:** Trailblazers.

**Student services.** Adult student services, career counseling, services for economically disadvantaged, student employment services, financial aid counseling, minority student services, on-campus daycare, personal counseling, placement for graduates, veterans' counselor. **Physically disabled:** Services for visually, speech, hearing impaired. **Transfer:** Re-entry adviser, preadmission transcript evaluation for new students. Transfer center, transfer adviser, college fairs on campus for students transferring to 4-year colleges.

**Contact.** E-mail: admissions@centralia.edu
Phone: (360) 736-9391 ext. 221 Fax: (360) 330-7503
Scott Copeland, Director of Enrollment Services and College Registrar, Centralia College, 600 Centralia College Boulevard, Centralia, WA 98531

## Clark College
**Vancouver, Washington**
**www.clark.edu**

**CB code: 4055**

- Public 2-year community college
- Commuter campus in small city

**General.** Founded in 1933. Regionally accredited. **Enrollment:** 5,237 degree-seeking undergraduates. **Degrees:** 1,019 associate awarded. **ROTC:** Army,

**Air Force. Location:** 8 miles from Portland, Oregon. **Calendar:** Quarter, extensive summer session. **Full-time faculty:** 179 total; 15% have terminal degrees. **Part-time faculty:** 391 total; 8% have terminal degrees. **Class size:** 38% < 20, 55% 20-39, 7% 40-49, less than 1% 50-99, less than 1% >100. **Special facilities:** Environmental education center, arboretum. **Partnerships:** Formal partnerships with Toyota T-10 and Cisco; industry partnerships to train students in specific equipment use.

**Student profile.**

Out-of-state:     4%     **25 or older:**     35%

**Transfer out. Colleges most students transferred to 2007:** Washington State University-Vancouver, Portland State University, Washington State University-Pullman, Western Washington University, University of Washington.

**Basis for selection.** Open admission, but selective for some programs. ASSET required for placement in math and English. Interview required for dental hygiene, nursing, and pharmacy technician applicants.

**2007-2008 Annual costs.** Tuition/fees: $2,912; $8,048 out-of-state. Per-credit charge: $80 in-state; $252 out-of-state. Books/supplies: $924. Personal expenses: $1,884.

**2006-2007 Financial aid. Need-based:** 71% of total undergraduate aid awarded as scholarships/grants, 29% as loans/jobs. Need-based aid available for part-time students. Work-study available nights, weekends and for part-time students. **Non-need-based:** Scholarships awarded for academics, alumni affiliation, art, athletics, job skills, leadership, minority status, music/drama, religious affiliation, ROTC, state residency.

**Application procedures. Admission:** Priority date 8/4; no deadline. No application fee. Application may be submitted online. Admission notification on a rolling basis. **Financial aid:** Priority date 5/1; no closing date. FAFSA, institutional form required. Applicants notified on a rolling basis starting 5/1; must reply within 2 week(s) of notification.

**Academics. Special study options:** Combined bachelor's/graduate degree, cooperative education, cross-registration, distance learning, dual enrollment of high school students, ESL, honors, independent study, internships, liberal arts/career combination, study abroad. Bachelor's degree programs available on campus. License preparation in dental hygiene, nursing, radiology. **Credit/placement by examination:** AP, CLEP, IB, institutional tests. 30 credit hours maximum toward associate degree. **Support services:** GED preparation and test center, learning center, reduced course load, remedial instruction, study skills assistance, tutoring, writing center.

**Majors. Agriculture:** Horticulture, landscaping. **Business:** Accounting technology, business admin, executive assistant, human resources, office technology, retailing, selling. **Communications technology:** Graphics. **Computer sciences:** Data entry, networking, programming, webmaster. **Education:** Early childhood. **Engineering technology:** Construction, electrical, manufacturing, telecommunications. **Health:** Dental hygiene, EMT paramedic, medical assistant, medical secretary, nursing (RN), radiologic technology/medical imaging, substance abuse counseling. **Legal studies:** Legal secretary, paralegal. **Liberal arts:** Arts/sciences. **Mechanic/repair:** Automotive, diesel. **Parks/recreation:** Sports admin. **Personal/culinary services:** Baking, chef training. **Production:** Machine tool, welding.

**Most popular majors.** Business/marketing 13%, health sciences 16%, liberal arts 55%.

**Computing on campus.** 760 workstations in library, computer center, student center. Online course registration, online library, helpline, wireless network available.

**Student life. Freshman orientation:** Available. Preregistration for classes offered. Sessions held during quarterly registration period. Online orientation option available. **Activities:** Bands, choral groups, dance, drama, international student organizations, literary magazine, music ensembles, musical theater, student government, student newspaper, symphony orchestra, anime & Japanese cultural club, Latter-day Saints student association, Alpha Sigma Phi, Addiction Counseling Education Students, Northwest Collegiate Ministries, Young Democrats, Club for Social Action, Queer Penguins & Allies, NAACP college chapter.

**Athletics. Intercollegiate:** Basketball, cross-country, soccer, track and field, volleyball W. **Intramural:** Basketball, fencing, football (non-tackle), soccer, softball, table tennis, volleyball. **Team name:** Penguins.

**Student services.** Adult student services, alcohol/substance abuse counseling, career counseling, services for economically disadvantaged, student employment services, financial aid counseling, health services, legal services, minority student services, on-campus daycare, personal counseling, placement for graduates, veterans' counselor, women's services. **Physically**

**disabled:** Services for visually, speech, hearing impaired. **Transfer:** Transfer adviser, college fairs on campus for students transferring to 4-year colleges.

**Contact.** E-mail: admissionrequest@clark.edu
Phone: (360) 992-2107 Fax: (360) 992-2867
Sheryl Anderson, Director of Admissions, Clark College, 1933 Fort Vancouver Way, Vancouver, WA 98663

## Clover Park Technical College
### Lakewood, Washington
### www.cptc.edu      CB code: 3971

♦ Public 2-year technical college
♦ Commuter campus in small city

**General.** Regionally accredited. **Enrollment:** 2,290 degree-seeking undergraduates. **Degrees:** 325 associate awarded. **Location:** 10 miles from Tacoma, 40 miles from Seattle. **Calendar:** Quarter, extensive summer session. **Full-time faculty:** 91 total. **Part-time faculty:** 134 total. **Class size:** 70% < 20, 27% 20-39, 2% 40-49, 1% 50-99.

**Basis for selection.** Open admission, but selective for some programs. Some programs have test score minimums and/or course prerequisite requirements.

**2007-2008 Annual costs.** Tuition/fees: $3,070; $3,070 out-of-state. Books/supplies: $900. Personal expenses: $1,440.

**Financial aid.** All financial aid based on need. Need-based aid available for part-time students. Work-study available nights and weekends.

**Application procedures. Admission:** No deadline. $41 fee. Application may be submitted online. Admission notification on a rolling basis. **Financial aid:** Priority date 6/15, closing date 8/25. FAFSA, institutional form required. Applicants notified on a rolling basis.

**Academics. Special study options:** Cooperative education, distance learning, dual enrollment of high school students, ESL, internships. License preparation in aviation, nursing. **Credit/placement by examination:** CLEP, institutional tests. 15 credit hours maximum toward associate degree. 25 percent of total approved hours may be awarded for prior work and/or life experience. **Support services:** GED preparation and test center, tutoring.

**Majors. Agriculture:** Landscaping. **Business:** Accounting technology, marketing, office management. **Communications technology:** Graphic/printing, radio/tv. **Computer sciences:** LAN/WAN management, networking, programming, security, web page design. **Education:** Early childhood, teacher assistance. **Engineering technology:** Architectural, environmental, mechanical. **Health:** Clinical lab assistant, dental assistant, health services, licensed practical nurse, massage therapy, pharmacy assistant, surgical technology. **Legal studies:** Legal secretary. **Mechanic/repair:** Aircraft powerplant, automotive, avionics, business machine, heating/ac/refrig, heavy equipment. **Personal/culinary services:** Aesthetician. **Production:** Machine tool. **Transportation:** Airline/commercial pilot. **Visual/performing arts:** Interior design.

**Most popular majors.** Computer/information sciences 14%, education 8%, health sciences 34%, trade and industry 15%.

**Computing on campus.** 94 workstations in library. Online library available.

**Student life. Freshman orientation:** Available. **Activities:** Student government.

**Student services.** Adult student services, career counseling, services for economically disadvantaged, student employment services, financial aid counseling, minority student services, on-campus daycare, veterans' counselor. **Physically disabled:** Services for visually, speech, hearing impaired.

**Contact.** Phone: (253) 589-5678 Fax: (253) 589-5852
Judy MacDougall, Registrar, Clover Park Technical College, 4500 Steilacoom Boulevard, SW, Lakewood, WA 98499-4098

## Columbia Basin College
### Pasco, Washington
### www.columbiabasin.edu      CB code: 4077

♦ Public 2-year community college
♦ Commuter campus in small city

**General.** Founded in 1955. Regionally accredited. **Enrollment:** 7,140 degree-seeking undergraduates. **Degrees:** 746 associate awarded. **Location:** 130 miles from Spokane, 200 miles from Seattle. **Calendar:** Quarter, limited summer session. **Full-time faculty:** 119 total. **Part-time faculty:** 227 total. **Special facilities:** Performing arts theatre, health science building, observatory, math & science working atrium, regional medical library, tutor & writing center.

**Student profile.** Among degree-seeking undergraduates, 61% enrolled in a transfer program, 36% enrolled in a vocational program. Of all enrolled students, 3% already have a bachelor's degree or higher.

| | | | |
|---|---|---|---|
| Out-of-state: | 1% | Hispanic American: | 18% |
| African American: | 2% | Native American: | 1% |
| Asian American: | 2% | 25 or older: | 58% |

**Transfer out. Colleges most students transferred to 2007:** Washington State University.

**Basis for selection.** Open admission, but selective for some programs. Special requirements for Nursing, Dental Hygiene, Radiologic Technology, Paramedic and Medical Assistant programs. Applicants who are not graduates of regionally accredited high school or have a GED must submit Washington Pre-College Test, SAT, or ACT scores.

**High school preparation.** 11 units recommended. Recommended units include English 3, mathematics 2, social studies 3, science 2 and foreign language 1.

**2007-2008 Annual costs.** Tuition/fees: $2,866; $3,864 out-of-state. Books/supplies: $924. Personal expenses: $1,524.

**Financial aid. Need-based:** Need-based aid available for part-time students. Work-study available nights, weekends and for part-time students. **Non-need-based:** Scholarships awarded for academics, athletics, state residency.

**Application procedures. Admission:** No deadline. $28 fee, may be waived for applicants with need. Application must be submitted on paper. Admission notification on a rolling basis. **Financial aid:** Priority date 4/10; no closing date. FAFSA, institutional form required. Applicants notified on a rolling basis starting 6/15; must reply within 2 week(s) of notification.

**Academics. Special study options:** Cross-registration, distance learning, dual enrollment of high school students, ESL, internships, liberal arts/career combination, weekend college. Bachelor's degree programs available on campus. License preparation in dental hygiene, nursing, paramedic, radiology. **Credit/placement by examination:** CLEP, IB, institutional tests. 30 credit hours maximum toward associate degree. **Support services:** GED preparation and test center, learning center, reduced course load, remedial instruction, study skills assistance, tutoring, writing center.

**Majors. Agriculture:** Agribusiness operations, business. **Business:** Accounting, administrative services, management information systems, office management, purchasing, sales/distribution. **Computer sciences:** General, computer science, data processing, programming. **Construction:** Carpentry. **Education:** General, early childhood. **Engineering technology:** Electrical. **Family/consumer sciences:** Child care. **Health:** Clinical lab technology, dental hygiene, EMT paramedic, licensed practical nurse, medical records admin, medical transcription. **Interdisciplinary:** Biological/physical sciences, math/computer science. **Legal studies:** Paralegal. **Liberal arts:** Arts/sciences. **Mechanic/repair:** Auto body, automotive, diesel. **Physical sciences:** General. **Protective services:** Firefighting, law enforcement admin, police science. **Public administration:** Human services. **Visual/performing arts:** General, commercial/advertising art.

**Most popular majors.** Health sciences 7%, liberal arts 77%.

**Computing on campus.** 680 workstations in library, computer center. Online course registration, online library, wireless network available.

**Student life. Freshman orientation:** Mandatory. **Activities:** Bands, choral groups, drama, music ensembles, musical theater, student government, student newspaper.

**Athletics.** NJCAA. **Intercollegiate:** Baseball M, basketball, golf, soccer, softball W, volleyball W. **Intramural:** Basketball, bowling, soccer M, softball, volleyball. **Team name:** Hawks.

**Student services.** Adult student services, career counseling, student employment services, minority student services, personal counseling, placement for graduates, veterans' counselor, women's services. **Physically disabled:** Services for visually, speech, hearing impaired. **Learning disabled:** Comprehensive services available. **Transfer:** Transfer adviser, college fairs on campus for students transferring to 4-year colleges.

**Contact.** E-mail: dkorstad@cbc2.org
Phone: (509) 547-0511 Fax: (509) 546-0401
Patricia Campbell, Director of Admissions and Registration, Columbia Basin College, 2600 North 20th Avenue, Pasco, WA 99301

## Edmonds Community College
Lynnwood, Washington
www.edcc.edu
**CB member**
**CB code: 4307**

- Public 2-year community college
- Commuter campus in small city

**General.** Founded in 1967. Regionally accredited. **Enrollment:** 7,761 degree-seeking undergraduates. **Degrees:** 766 associate awarded. **Location:** 15 miles from Seattle. **Calendar:** Quarter, extensive summer session. **Full-time faculty:** 138 total. **Part-time faculty:** 306 total. **Special facilities:** Center for Business and Employment Development, golf course.

**Student profile.** Among degree-seeking undergraduates, 40% enrolled in a transfer program, 30% enrolled in a vocational program.

**Transfer out. Colleges most students transferred to 2007:** University of Washington, Central Washington University, Western Washington University, Washington State University.

**Basis for selection.** Open admission. ASSET required for all students for placement. Interview recommended for international studies, travel tourism majors; audition required for music performance majors. **Learning Disabled:** SSD is available to provide appropriate accommodation.

**2007-2008 Annual costs.** Tuition/fees: $3,167; $8,375 out-of-state. Books/supplies: $900. Personal expenses: $1,824.

**Financial aid. Need-based:** Need-based aid available for part-time students. Work-study available nights and for part-time students. **Non-need-based:** Scholarships awarded for athletics.

**Application procedures. Admission:** No deadline. $18 fee, may be waived for applicants with need. Application may be submitted online. Admission notification on a rolling basis. TOEFL optional for students whose first language is not English. **Financial aid:** Priority date 5/1; no closing date. FAFSA, institutional form required. Applicants notified on a rolling basis starting 6/1; must reply within 4 week(s) of notification.

**Academics. Special study options:** Cooperative education, cross-registration, distance learning, dual enrollment of high school students, ESL, exchange student, honors, independent study, internships, study abroad, weekend college. **Credit/placement by examination:** CLEP, institutional tests. 15 credit hours maximum toward associate degree. **Support services:** GED preparation and test center, learning center, remedial instruction, tutoring, writing center.

**Majors. Agriculture:** Business technology, landscaping, nursery operations. **Business:** Accounting technology, business admin, construction management, hospitality admin, human resources, international, office management, office/clerical, travel services. **Computer sciences:** Computer graphics, data processing, database management, networking, security, web page design, webmaster. **Education:** Early childhood, elementary. **Engineering:** Chemical, electrical, mechanical. **Engineering technology:** General, electrical, occupational safety. **Health:** Community health services, medical radiologic technology/radiation therapy, medical records technology, mental health services, nursing (RN), substance abuse counseling, vocational rehab counseling. **Legal studies:** Legal secretary, paralegal. **Liberal arts:** Arts/sciences. **Personal/culinary services:** Chef training. **Protective services:** Fire services admin. **Science technology:** Chemical. **Visual/performing arts:** Commercial photography.

**Computing on campus.** 1,129 workstations in library, computer center. Commuter students can connect to campus network. Online course registration available.

**Student life. Freshman orientation:** Available. Students receive brief orientation prior to placement test. **Housing:** Host families available for international students. **Activities:** Jazz band, choral groups, dance, drama, international student organizations, literary magazine, music ensembles, student government, student newspaper, Phi Theta Kappa, Design and Invention Club, I-Hope Club, DESI Club, Baptist Collegiate Ministry, Black Student Association, American Indian Student Association, Gay and Lesbian Alliance, Digital Production Club.

**Athletics. Intercollegiate:** Baseball M, basketball, golf, soccer, softball W, volleyball W. **Intramural:** Basketball M, bowling, golf, table tennis, volleyball. **Team name:** Tritons.

**Student services.** Adult student services, career counseling, student employment services, financial aid counseling, minority student services, on-campus daycare, personal counseling, placement for graduates, women's services. **Physically disabled:** Services for visually, speech, hearing impaired. **Transfer:** Transfer center, transfer adviser, college fairs on campus for students transferring to 4-year colleges.

**Contact.** E-mail: admiss@edcc.edu
Phone: (425) 640-1459 Fax: (425) 640-1159
Nanci Froemming, Office Manager, Enrollment Services, Edmonds Community College, 20000 68th Avenue West, Lynnwood, WA 98036-5912

---

## Everett Community College
### Everett, Washington
**www.everettcc.edu**                 CB code: 4303

- Public 2-year community college
- Commuter campus in small city

**General.** Founded in 1941. Regionally accredited. **Enrollment:** 3,435 degree-seeking undergraduates; 2,713 non-degree-seeking students. **Degrees:** 814 associate awarded. **Location:** 30 miles from Seattle. **Calendar:** Quarter, limited summer session. **Full-time faculty:** 129 total; 31% have terminal degrees, 16% minority, 58% women. **Part-time faculty:** 209 total. **Class size:** 53% < 20, 42% 20-39, 4% 40-49, 1% 50-99. **Partnerships:** Formal partnership with Boeing.

**Student profile.** Among degree-seeking undergraduates, 55% enrolled in a transfer program, 45% enrolled in a vocational program, 3% already have a bachelor's degree or higher, 538 enrolled as first-time, first-year students, 124 transferred in from other institutions.

| | | | |
|---|---|---|---|
| Part-time: | 44% | Hispanic American: | 4% |
| Out-of-state: | 3% | Native American: | 2% |
| Women: | 62% | International: | 1% |
| African American: | 3% | 25 or older: | 35% |
| Asian American: | 6% | | |

**Transfer out.** 56% of students enrolled in the transfer program go on to 4-year colleges. **Colleges most students transferred to 2007:** Western Washington University, University of Washington, Central Washington University, Washington State University.

**Basis for selection.** Open admission, but selective for some programs. Special requirements for nursing, fire science, and criminal justice. Interview recommended for nursing.

**High school preparation.** 16 units recommended. Recommended units include English 4, mathematics 3, social studies 3, history 2, science 2 and foreign language 2.

**2007-2008 Annual costs.** Tuition/fees: $2,781; $7,989 out-of-state. Per-credit charge: $74 in-state; $246 out-of-state. Books/supplies: $900. Personal expenses: $1,548.

**2006-2007 Financial aid.** All financial aid based on need. 186 full-time freshmen applied for aid; 148 were judged to have need; 130 of these received aid. Average need met was 27%. Average scholarship/grant was $4,980; average loan $2,146. 77% of total undergraduate aid awarded as scholarships/grants, 23% as loans/jobs. Need-based aid available for part-time students. Work-study available nights, weekends and for part-time students.

**Application procedures. Admission:** No deadline. No application fee. Application may be submitted online. Admission notification on a rolling basis. **Financial aid:** Priority date 5/5; no closing date. FAFSA, institutional form required. Applicants notified on a rolling basis starting 4/15; must reply within 4 week(s) of notification.

**Academics.** Offers direct-transfer associate degrees that assure full transfer to most Washington and Oregon universities. Transfer degrees for specific majors at designated universities can be designed by the student and faculty advisor. **Special study options:** Cooperative education, distance learning, dual enrollment of high school students, ESL, independent study, internships, study abroad. Bachelor's degree programs available on campus. License preparation in aviation, nursing, paramedic. **Credit/placement by examination:** AP, CLEP, IB, institutional tests. 45 credit hours maximum toward associate degree. **Support services:** GED preparation and test center, learning center, reduced course load, remedial instruction, study skills assistance, tutoring, writing center.

**Majors. Agriculture:** Animal sciences. **Area/ethnic studies:** Asian. **Biology:** General. **Business:** General, accounting, administrative services, business admin, management information systems, office/clerical. **Communications:** General, advertising, journalism. **Computer sciences:** General, computer graphics, computer science, information systems, networking, programming, webmaster. **Conservation:** General, environmental science. **Education:** General, early childhood. **Engineering:** General. **Engineering technology:** General, CAD/CADD, manufacturing. **English:** American lit, composition, creative writing, English lit, speech/rhetoric, technical writing. **Foreign languages:** General, comparative lit, French, German, Japanese, Russian, Spanish. **Health:** Dental hygiene, medical assistant, nursing (RN), predental, premedicine, prepharmacy, preveterinary. **History:** General. **Interdisciplinary:** Natural sciences. **Legal studies:** Prelaw. **Liberal arts:** Arts/sciences. **Math:** General. **Mechanic/repair:** Aircraft powerplant. **Personal/culinary services:** Cosmetology. **Philosophy/religion:** Philosophy. **Physical sciences:** Astronomy, atmospheric science, chemistry, geology, oceanography, physics. **Protective services:** Corrections, firefighting, law enforcement admin. **Psychology:** General. **Public administration:** Human services. **Social sciences:** General, anthropology, economics, geography, political science, sociology. **Visual/performing arts:** General, art, commercial/advertising art, dramatic, music performance, photography, studio arts.

**Most popular majors.** Business/marketing 8%, health sciences 13%, liberal arts 68%.

**Computing on campus.** 900 workstations in library, computer center, student center. Online course registration, wireless network available.

**Student life. Freshman orientation:** Mandatory. Preregistration for classes offered. One day program of placement testing, orientation and advising sessions. **Housing:** Housing in private homes available for foreign students. **Activities:** Choral groups, drama, literary magazine, music ensembles, musical theater, student government, student newspaper, 25 student clubs.

**Athletics. Intercollegiate:** Baseball M, basketball, cross-country, soccer, softball W, volleyball W. **Intramural:** Basketball, bowling, golf, soccer, softball, tennis, volleyball, weight lifting. **Team name:** Trojans.

**Student services.** Adult student services, career counseling, services for economically disadvantaged, student employment services, financial aid counseling, minority student services, on-campus daycare, personal counseling, placement for graduates, veterans' counselor, women's services. **Physically disabled:** Services for visually, speech, hearing impaired. **Transfer:** Transfer adviser, college fairs on campus for students transferring to 4-year colleges.

**Contact.** E-mail: admissions@everettcc.edu
Phone: (425) 388-9219 Fax: (425) 388-9173
Linda Baca, Admissions Manager, Everett Community College, 2000 Tower Street, Everett, WA 98201-1352

---

## Grays Harbor College
### Aberdeen, Washington
**www.ghc.ctc.edu**                 CB code: 4332

- Public 2-year community college
- Commuter campus in large town

**General.** Founded in 1930. Regionally accredited. **Enrollment:** 578 degree-seeking undergraduates; 1,595 non-degree-seeking students. **Degrees:** 207 associate awarded. **Location:** 100 miles from Seattle. **Calendar:** Quarter, limited summer session. **Full-time faculty:** 62 total; 3% minority, 37% women. **Part-time faculty:** 88 total; 3% minority, 65% women. **Class size:** 77% < 20, 22% 20-39, less than 1% 40-49, less than 1% 50-99. **Special facilities:** 4-acre lake linked to Grays Harbor estuary and fish hatcheries, 440 seat theater. **Partnerships:** Formal partnerships with local businesses for internships and short-term training.

**Student profile.** Among degree-seeking undergraduates, 39% enrolled in a transfer program, 61% enrolled in a vocational program, 2% already have a bachelor's degree or higher, 132 enrolled as first-time, first-year students, 21 transferred in from other institutions.

| | | | |
|---|---|---|---|
| Part-time: | 63% | Women: | 63% |
| Out-of-state: | 1% | 25 or older: | 51% |

**Transfer out. Colleges most students transferred to 2007:** Washington State University, Evergreen State College, Western Washington University, Central Washington University, Eastern Washington University.

**Basis for selection.** Open admission, but selective for some programs. High School diploma or GED required of applicants under 18 years of age. Limited admission to nursing program.

**2007-2008 Annual costs.** Tuition/fees: $3,113; $8,321 out-of-state. Books/supplies: $750. Personal expenses: $2,178.

**2006-2007 Financial aid. Need-based:** 82% of total undergraduate aid awarded as scholarships/grants, 18% as loans/jobs. Need-based aid available for part-time students. Work-study available nights and for part-time students. **Non-need-based:** Scholarships awarded for academics, art, athletics, music/drama.

**Application procedures. Admission:** Priority date 9/1; no deadline. No application fee. Application may be submitted online. Admission notification on a rolling basis. **Financial aid:** Priority date 5/1; no closing date. FAFSA, institutional form required. Applicants notified on a rolling basis starting 5/15.

**Academics. Special study options:** Accelerated study, cooperative education, distance learning, double major, dual enrollment of high school students, ESL, independent study, internships, teacher certification program. Bachelor's degree programs available on campus. License preparation in nursing. **Credit/placement by examination:** AP, CLEP, institutional tests. 45 credit hours maximum toward associate degree. **Support services:** GED preparation and test center, learning center, reduced course load, remedial instruction, study skills assistance, tutoring, writing center.

**Majors. Business:** Accounting technology, business admin, office management. **Computer sciences:** Data processing. **Conservation:** General, wildlife. **Construction:** Carpentry. **Education:** Teacher assistance. **Health:** Nursing (RN). **Liberal arts:** Arts/sciences. **Mechanic/repair:** Automotive, diesel. **Production:** Welding. **Protective services:** Police science. **Public administration:** Human services.

**Most popular majors.** Health sciences 22%, liberal arts 67%.

**Computing on campus.** 382 workstations in library, computer center, student center. Online course registration, online library, student web hosting, wireless network available.

**Student life. Freshman orientation:** Mandatory. Preregistration for classes offered. Offered online or face to face. **Activities:** Bands, choral groups, drama, music ensembles, musical theater, student government, student newspaper, symphony orchestra, Native American Student Association, the Tyee Honorary Service Club, Human Services Student Association, AGAPE Christian ministry, Foreign Language and Culture, Student Nurses Association.

**Athletics. Intercollegiate:** Baseball M, basketball, golf, softball W, volleyball W. **Team name:** Chokers.

**Student services.** Career counseling, services for economically disadvantaged, student employment services, financial aid counseling, minority student services, on-campus daycare, personal counseling, placement for graduates, veterans' counselor. **Physically disabled:** Services for visually, speech, hearing impaired. **Transfer:** Pre-admission transcript evaluation for new students. Transfer adviser, college fairs on campus for students transferring to 4-year colleges.

**Contact.** E-mail: bdell@ghc.edu
Phone: (360) 538-4026 Toll-free number: (800) 562-4830
Fax: (360) 538-4293
Nancy DeVerse, Associate Dean for Student Services/Registrar, Grays Harbor College, 1620 Edward P Smith Drive, Aberdeen, WA 98520

## Green River Community College
Auburn, Washington
www.greenriver.edu
CB code: 4337

- Public 2-year community college
- Commuter campus in large town

**General.** Founded in 1965. Regionally accredited. **Enrollment:** 819 degree-seeking undergraduates. **Degrees:** 944 associate awarded. **Location:** 35 miles from Seattle. **Calendar:** Quarter, limited summer session. **Full-time faculty:** 137 total. **Part-time faculty:** 217 total.

**Basis for selection.** Open admission, but selective for some programs. Special requirements for health occupation programs. Interview required for occupational therapy.

**2007-2008 Annual costs.** Tuition/fees: $3,045; $3,468 out-of-state. Per-credit charge: $74 in-state; $246 out-of-state. Books/supplies: $939. Personal expenses: $1,170.

**Financial aid.** All financial aid based on need. Need-based aid available for part-time students.

**Application procedures. Admission:** No deadline. No application fee. Application may be submitted online. Admission notification on a rolling basis. **Financial aid:** Priority date 4/15; no closing date. FAFSA, institutional form required. Applicants notified on a rolling basis starting 6/30; must reply within 2 week(s) of notification.

**Academics. Special study options:** Cooperative education, cross-registration, distance learning, dual enrollment of high school students, ESL, independent study, internships, study abroad. **Credit/placement by examination:** AP, CLEP, institutional tests. **Support services:** GED preparation and test center, learning center, reduced course load, remedial instruction, tutoring, writing center.

**Majors. Business:** Accounting, marketing, office technology, office/clerical, real estate. **Computer sciences:** Information systems. **Conservation:** Forest resources. **Construction:** Carpentry. **Education:** Early childhood. **Engineering technology:** Drafting, electrical, hazardous materials. **Health:** Medical secretary, occupational therapy assistant, physical therapy assistant. **Legal studies:** Court reporting, legal secretary. **Liberal arts:** Arts/sciences. **Mechanic/repair:** Auto body. **Protective services:** Police science. **Transportation:** General, aviation. **Visual/performing arts:** General.

**Computing on campus.** 210 workstations in library, computer center.

**Student life. Freshman orientation:** Available. **Housing:** Apartments available. **Activities:** Jazz band, choral groups, dance, drama, music ensembles, radio station, student government, student newspaper, Asian Student Union, Black Student Union, Native American Student Association, Los Latinos Unidos, Phi Theta Kappa, Teachers of Tomorrow, Skills USA, forestry club, court reporting club, American Society of Mechanical Engineers.

**Athletics. NJCAA. Intercollegiate:** Baseball M, basketball, golf, soccer, softball W, tennis, volleyball W. **Intramural:** Badminton, baseball M, basketball, soccer, softball, tennis, volleyball. **Team name:** Gators.

**Student services.** Career counseling, services for economically disadvantaged, student employment services, financial aid counseling, health services, minority student services, on-campus daycare, personal counseling, placement for graduates, veterans' counselor, women's services. **Physically disabled:** Services for visually, hearing impaired. **Transfer:** Transfer center, transfer adviser, college fairs on campus for students transferring to 4-year colleges.

**Contact.** Phone: (253) 833-9111 ext. 2500 Fax: (253) 288-3454
Denise Bennatts, Registrar, Green River Community College, 12401 SE 320th Street, Auburn, WA 98092

## Highline Community College
Des Moines, Washington
www.highline.edu
CB code: 4348

- Public 2-year community college
- Commuter campus in small city

**General.** Founded in 1961. Regionally accredited. **Enrollment:** 2,828 full-time, degree-seeking students. **Degrees:** 976 associate awarded. **ROTC:** Army, Air Force. **Location:** 18 miles from Seattle. **Calendar:** Quarter, limited summer session. **Full-time faculty:** 150 total. **Part-time faculty:** 185 total.

**Student profile.** Among full-time, degree-seeking students, 57% enrolled in a transfer program, 32% enrolled in a vocational program. Of all enrolled students, 1% already have a bachelor's degree or higher.

**Basis for selection.** Open admission, but selective for some programs. School achievement record considered for health programs. College and work experience also considered for nursing.

**High school preparation.** Health occupation programs require chemistry and algebra.

**2007-2008 Annual costs.** Tuition/fees: $2,751; $3,140 out-of-state. Per-credit charge: $74 in-state; $88 out-of-state. Books/supplies: $618. Personal expenses: $1,644.

**Financial aid. Need-based:** Need-based aid available for part-time students.

**Application procedures. Admission:** No deadline. $23 fee. Admission notification on a rolling basis. **Financial aid:** Priority date 5/31; no closing date. FAFSA required. Applicants notified on a rolling basis starting 6/1.

**Academics. Special study options:** Accelerated study, cooperative education, cross-registration, distance learning, double major, dual enrollment of high school students, ESL, honors, independent study, internships, student-designed major. **Credit/placement by examination:** CLEP, institutional tests. **Support services:** GED preparation and test center, learning center, pre-admission summer program, reduced course load, remedial instruction, tutoring.

**Majors. Business:** General, accounting, administrative services, business admin, fashion, hospitality/recreation, international, office/clerical, sales/distribution, tourism/travel. **Communications:** General, journalism. **Computer sciences:** General. **Education:** General, teacher assistance. **Engineering:** General. **Engineering technology:** Drafting, manufacturing. **English:** English lit. **Family/consumer sciences:** General, child care, food/nutrition. **Foreign languages:** General, French, German, linguistics. **Health:** Dental assistant, health care admin, medical assistant, medical transcription, nursing (RN), respiratory therapy technology. **History:** General. **Legal studies:** General, paralegal, prelaw. **Liberal arts:** Arts/sciences, library assistant. **Math:** General. **Parks/recreation:** Health/fitness. **Physical sciences:** Astronomy, geology. **Psychology:** General. **Public administration:** Human services. **Social sciences:** General, anthropology, economics, geography, sociology. **Transportation:** General, aviation. **Visual/performing arts:** General, art, commercial/advertising art, dramatic, multimedia.

**Most popular majors.** Business/marketing 6%, computer/information sciences 6%, health sciences 9%, liberal arts 66%.

**Computing on campus.** 100 workstations in library, computer center, student center.

**Student life. Activities:** Bands, choral groups, drama, literary magazine, music ensembles, student government, student newspaper, TV station, Indian and international student clubs, political forum, paralegal and arts societies, respiratory care club, academic honor society, campus crusade for Christ.

**Athletics.** NJCAA. **Intercollegiate:** Basketball, cross-country, soccer, softball W, track and field, volleyball W, wrestling M. **Team name:** Thunderbirds.

**Student services.** Adult student services, career counseling, student employment services, health services, minority student services, on-campus daycare, personal counseling, placement for graduates, veterans' counselor, women's services. **Physically disabled:** Services for visually, speech, hearing impaired. **Transfer:** Transfer adviser, college fairs on campus for students transferring to 4-year colleges.

**Contact.** E-mail: lwestergard@highline.edu
Phone: (206) 878-3710 ext. 3559 Fax: (206) 870-3782
Laura Westergard, Assistant Registrar, Highline Community College, 2400 South 240th Street, Des Moines, WA 98198-9800

## Lake Washington Technical College
**Kirkland, Washington**
www.lwtc.ctc.edu
CB code: 1453

♦ Public 2-year technical college
♦ Commuter campus in large town

**General.** Founded in 1949. Regionally accredited. **Enrollment:** 4,811 degree-seeking undergraduates. **Degrees:** 341 associate awarded. **Location:** 10 miles from Seattle. **Calendar:** Quarter, extensive summer session. **Full-time faculty:** 196 total. **Part-time faculty:** 179 total. **Class size:** 3% < 20, 97% 20-39. **Partnerships:** High Tech Center at local high school.

**Basis for selection.** Open admission, but selective for some programs. Limited admissions for dental hygiene; special requirements for other allied health programs and hospitality programs.

**2007-2008 Annual costs.** $75 per credit hour (1-5 credits); $37 per credit hour (more than 5 credits). Books/supplies: $1,152. Personal expenses: $1,548.

**2006-2007 Financial aid. Need-based:** 64% of total undergraduate aid awarded as scholarships/grants, 36% as loans/jobs. Need-based aid available for part-time students. Work-study available for part-time students.

**Application procedures. Admission:** No application fee. Application may be submitted online. Admission notification on a rolling basis. **Financial aid:** Priority date 4/15; no closing date. FAFSA, institutional form required. Applicants notified on a rolling basis.

**Academics. Special study options:** Cooperative education, distance learning, dual enrollment of high school students, ESL, internships, liberal arts/career combination, weekend college. License preparation in dental hygiene, nursing, real estate. **Credit/placement by examination:** CLEP. 15 credit hours maximum toward associate degree. **Support services:** GED preparation and test center, learning center, reduced course load, remedial instruction, study skills assistance, tutoring, writing center.

**Majors. Agriculture:** Horticulture. **Business:** Accounting, administrative services, hospitality/recreation. **Computer sciences:** Data processing. **Engineering technology:** Architectural, drafting, electrical. **Family/consumer**

**sciences:** Child care. **Health:** Dental assistant, dental hygiene, licensed practical nurse, medical assistant. **Legal studies:** Legal secretary, paralegal. **Mechanic/repair:** Auto body, automotive, diesel. **Personal/culinary services:** Culinary arts.

**Computing on campus.** 1,200 workstations in library, computer center.

**Student life. Freshman orientation:** Available. **Activities:** Student government, John 3:16 Club, Chinese club, single parent program/displaced homemakers, Welfare-to-Work, wellness group.

**Student services.** Adult student services, career counseling, student employment services, on-campus daycare, placement for graduates. **Physically disabled:** Services for visually, speech, hearing impaired. **Transfer:** Pre-admission transcript evaluation for new students. Transfer adviser for students transferring to 4-year colleges.

**Contact.** E-mail: admissions@lwtc.edu
Phone: (425) 739-8104 Fax: (425) 739-8110
James West, Director of Admissions, Lake Washington Technical College, 11605 132nd Avenue, NE, Kirkland, WA 98034

## Lower Columbia College
**Longview, Washington**
www.lowercolumbia.edu
CB code: 4402

♦ Public 2-year community college
♦ Commuter campus in small city

**General.** Founded in 1934. Regionally accredited. **Enrollment:** 1,408 degree-seeking undergraduates; 1,860 non-degree-seeking students. **Degrees:** 386 associate awarded. **Location:** 50 miles from Portland, Oregon, 120 miles from Seattle. **Calendar:** Quarter, limited summer session. **Full-time faculty:** 76 total; 5% minority, 37% women. **Part-time faculty:** 104 total; 3% minority, 62% women. **Class size:** 74% < 20, 24% 20-39, less than 1% 40-49, less than 1% 50-99, less than 1% >100. **Special facilities:** Fine and performing arts center.

**Student profile.** Among degree-seeking undergraduates, 23% enrolled in a transfer program, 42% enrolled in a vocational program, 3% already have a bachelor's degree or higher, 278 enrolled as first-time, first-year students.

| | | | |
|---|---|---|---|
| Part-time: | 33% | Asian American: | 2% |
| Out-of-state: | 1% | Hispanic American: | 4% |
| Women: | 63% | Native American: | 1% |
| African American: | 1% | 25 or older: | 56% |

**Transfer out.** 19% of students enrolled in the transfer program go on to 4-year colleges. **Colleges most students transferred to 2007:** Washington State University-Vancouver, Washington State University-Pullman, Central Washington University, Eastern Washington University, Western Washington University.

**Basis for selection.** Open admission, but selective for some programs. Special requirements for nursing program and medical assistant program.

**2007-2008 Annual costs.** Tuition/fees: $2,874; $3,586 out-of-state. Per-credit charge: $74 in-state; $96 out-of-state. Full-time "border county" tuition for students in Oregon's Clatsop, Multnomah, Washington, and Columbia counties: $2,881. Books/supplies: $1,110. Personal expenses: $1,800.

**2006-2007 Financial aid. Need-based:** 59% of total undergraduate aid awarded as scholarships/grants, 41% as loans/jobs. Need-based aid available for part-time students. Work-study available for part-time students.

**Application procedures. Admission:** No deadline. $14 fee. Application may be submitted online. Admission notification on a rolling basis. **Financial aid:** Priority date 5/1; no closing date. Institutional form, CSS PROFILE required. Applicants notified on a rolling basis starting 4/21; must reply within 2 week(s) of notification.

**Academics. Special study options:** Cooperative education, cross-registration, distance learning, dual enrollment of high school students, ESL, honors, independent study, liberal arts/career combination, student-designed major, teacher certification program. Bachelor's degree programs available on campus. License preparation in nursing. **Credit/placement by examination:** AP, CLEP, institutional tests. **Support services:** GED preparation and test center, learning center, remedial instruction, study skills assistance, tutoring.

**Majors. Business:** Accounting, accounting technology, administrative services, business admin, office technology, office/clerical. **Computer sciences:** General, computer science, data entry, data processing, networking, programming. **Education:** Elementary, teacher assistance. **Engineering:** General. **Engineering technology:** Electrical. **English:** English lit. **Family/**

consumer sciences: Child development. **Health:** Licensed practical nurse, medical assistant, medical secretary, nursing (RN), nursing assistant, substance abuse counseling. **Legal studies:** Legal secretary, paralegal. **Liberal arts:** Arts/sciences. **Mechanic/repair:** Auto body, automotive, diesel, heavy equipment, industrial, industrial electronics. **Production:** Welding. **Protective services:** Law enforcement admin. **Other:** Contemporary musicianship and audio production.

**Most popular majors.** Business/marketing 6%, health sciences 29%, liberal arts 51%.

**Computing on campus.** 450 workstations in library, computer center, student center. Online course registration, online library, helpline, wireless network available.

**Student life. Freshman orientation:** Available. **Housing:** Apartments normally available in local community. **Activities:** Bands, choral groups, drama, international student organizations, literary magazine, music ensembles, musical theater, student government, student newspaper, theater club, student nurses organization, services and relations club, campus entertainment, diesel mechanics club, Phi Theta Kappa.

**Athletics.** NJCAA. **Intercollegiate:** Baseball M, basketball, soccer W, softball W, volleyball W. **Team name:** Red Devils.

**Student services.** Adult student services, career counseling, services for economically disadvantaged, student employment services, financial aid counseling, on-campus daycare, personal counseling, placement for graduates, veterans' counselor. **Physically disabled:** Services for visually, hearing impaired. **Transfer:** Transfer center, transfer adviser, college fairs on campus for students transferring to 4-year colleges.

**Contact.** E-mail: entry@lowercolumbia.edu
Phone: (360) 442-2311 Toll-free number: (866) 900-2311
Fax: (360) 442-2379
Lynn Lawrence, Registrar, Lower Columbia College, 1600 Maple Street, Longview, WA 98632-0310

---

## North Seattle Community College
### Seattle, Washington
### www.northseattle.edu
**CB code: 4554**

- Public 2-year community college
- Commuter campus in very large city

**General.** Founded in 1970. Regionally accredited. Associate degree programs available via distance learning. College's Watchmaking Institute one of only 3 certified programs in country. **Enrollment:** 2,056 degree-seeking undergraduates; 4,228 non-degree-seeking students. **Degrees:** 443 associate awarded. **Location:** 8 miles from downtown. **Calendar:** Quarter, limited summer session. **Full-time faculty:** 98 total; 6% have terminal degrees, 26% minority, 53% women. **Part-time faculty:** 172 total; 1% have terminal degrees, 9% minority, 62% women. **Class size:** 38% < 20, 60% 20-39, 1% 40-49, less than 1% 50-99. **Special facilities:** Wetlands, wellness center, observatory.

**Student profile.** Among degree-seeking undergraduates, 45% enrolled in a transfer program, 41% enrolled in a vocational program, 20% already have a bachelor's degree or higher, 746 enrolled as first-time, first-year students.

| | | | |
|---|---|---|---|
| Part-time: | 54% | Asian American: | 15% |
| Out-of-state: | 4% | Hispanic American: | 6% |
| Women: | 54% | Native American: | 2% |
| African American: | 8% | 25 or older: | 54% |

**Transfer out. Colleges most students transferred to 2007:** University of Washington.

**Basis for selection.** Open admission. Applicants with deficient English or Math skills are required to take remedial courses to qualify for college level work. Test scores required in English and mathematics for placement only.

**2007-2008 Annual costs.** Tuition/fees: $2,935; $8,143 out-of-state. Per-credit charge: $74 in-state; $246 out-of-state. Books/supplies: $924. Personal expenses: $1,590.

**Financial aid. Need-based:** Need-based aid available for part-time students. Work-study available nights, weekends and for part-time students.

**Application procedures. Admission:** No deadline. No application fee. Admission notification on a rolling basis. **Financial aid:** Priority date 4/30, closing date 8/31. FAFSA, institutional form required. Applicants notified on a rolling basis starting 8/1; must reply within 2 week(s) of notification.

**Academics. Special study options:** Cooperative education, cross-registration, distance learning, dual enrollment of high school students, ESL, independent study, internships, liberal arts/career combination, study abroad. License preparation in nursing, radiology, real estate. **Credit/placement by examination:** AP, CLEP, IB, institutional tests. 45 credit hours maximum toward associate degree. **Support services:** GED preparation and test center, learning center, reduced course load, remedial instruction, study skills assistance, tutoring, writing center.

**Majors. Business:** General, accounting technology, administrative services, office management, office technology, office/clerical, real estate. **Communications technology:** General. **Computer sciences:** Networking. **Education:** General, early childhood. **Engineering technology:** Biomedical, civil drafting, electrical. **Health:** Licensed practical nurse, medical assistant, nursing (RN), office assistant, pharmacy assistant, radiologic technology/medical imaging. **Mechanic/repair:** Heating/ac/refrig, industrial electronics, watch/jewelry. **Visual/performing arts:** General, art, dramatic, studio arts. **Other:** Nanotechnology.

**Most popular majors.** Business/marketing 19%, health sciences 10%, liberal arts 58%.

**Computing on campus.** 2,000 workstations in library, computer center, student center. Commuter students can connect to campus network. Online course registration, online library, helpline, repair service, student web hosting, wireless network available.

**Student life. Freshman orientation:** Available. Preregistration for classes offered. Students can select from in-person or on-line orientations. **Activities:** Bands, choral groups, drama, international student organizations, literary magazine, music ensembles, student government, student newspaper, TV station, Phi Theta Kappa, Black student union, Indonesian community club, Vietnamese student association, art group, student leadership, Muslim student association, biomed club, golf club.

**Athletics. Intercollegiate:** Basketball. **Intramural:** Basketball. **Team name:** Storm.

**Student services.** Adult student services, career counseling, services for economically disadvantaged, student employment services, financial aid counseling, minority student services, on-campus daycare, personal counseling, placement for graduates, veterans' counselor, women's services. **Physically disabled:** Services for visually, speech, hearing impaired. **Transfer:** Transfer adviser, college fairs on campus for students transferring to 4-year colleges.

**Contact.** E-mail: NSCCRegistration@sccd.ctc.edu
Phone: (206) 527-3663 Fax: (206) 527-3671
Betsy Abts, Registrar / Director of Amdissions, North Seattle Community College, 9600 College Way North, Seattle, WA 98103

---

## Northwest Aviation College
### Auburn, Washington
### www.afsnac.com
**CB code: 3115**

- Private 2-year technical college
- Large town

**General.** Accredited by ACCSCT. **Location:** 7 miles from Seattle. **Calendar:** Quarter.

**Annual costs/financial aid.** Program costs for Associate program in Aviation Flight Technology: $49,906; Certificate programs for Professional Pilot 1: $39,380; Professional Pilot 2: $43,606; Professional Pilot 3: $54,303. All costs include tuition, books, materials, aircraft rental.

**Contact.** Phone: (253) 854-4960
Assistant Director of Education, 506 23rd Street, NE, Auburn, WA 98002

---

## Northwest Indian College
### Bellingham, Washington
### www.nwic.edu
**CB code: 3973**

- Public 2-year community college
- Commuter campus in small town

**General.** Regionally accredited. **Enrollment:** 465 degree-seeking undergraduates. **Degrees:** 44 associate awarded. **Calendar:** Quarter, limited summer session. **Full-time faculty:** 22 total. **Part-time faculty:** 45 total.

**2007-2008 Annual costs.** Tuition/fees: $2,796; $7,332 out-of-state. Per-credit charge: $74 in-state; $200 out-of-state. Eligibility to pay in-district costs based on tribal enrollment verification.

**Academics. Special study options:** Bachelor's degree programs available on campus. **Credit/placement by examination:** CLEP.

**Majors. Area/ethnic studies:** Native American. **Business:** General. **Computer sciences:** Networking. **Visual/performing arts:** Art.

**Computing on campus.** 90 workstations in library, computer center, student center. Dormitories wired for high-speed internet access and linked to campus network. Helpline, repair service, wireless network available.

**Student life. Freshman orientation:** Available. **Housing:** Coed dorms available. **Activities:** Drama, student government, student newspaper.

**Athletics. Team name:** Eagles.

**Student services.** Adult student services, alcohol/substance abuse counseling, career counseling, services for economically disadvantaged, student employment services, financial aid counseling, minority student services.

**Contact.** Phone: (360) 676-2772 ext. 4269 Toll-free number: (866) 676-2772 ext. 4269 Fax: (360) 392-4333 Crystal Bagby, Director of Admissions, Northwest Indian College, 2522 Kwina Road, Bellingham, WA 98226-9217

## Northwest School of Wooden Boatbuilding
**Port Hadlock, Washington**
www.nwboatschool.org                    CB code: 3116

◗ Private 1-year technical and maritime college
◗ Commuter campus in large town

**General.** Accredited by ACCSCT. **Location:** 60 miles from Seattle. **Calendar:** Quarter.

**Annual costs/financial aid.** Twelve month programs offered at a cost of $14,800. Estimated cost of tools $1,075. Nine month diploma program $11,625, six month diploma program $7,850. Books/supplies: $1,000.

**Contact.** Phone: (360) 385-4948
42 North Water Street, Port Hadlock, WA 98339

## Olympic College
**Bremerton, Washington**                    **CB member**
www.olympic.edu                    **CB code: 4583**

◗ Public 2-year community and liberal arts college
◗ Commuter campus in large town

**General.** Founded in 1946. Regionally accredited. Campuses at Shelton and Poulsbo. Classes also offered off-campus at Naval Base Kitsap, Bremerton and Bangor, and some local high schools. **Enrollment:** 6,675 degree-seeking undergraduates. **Degrees:** 988 associate awarded. **Location:** 30 miles from Seattle, 35 miles from Tacoma. **Calendar:** Quarter, extensive summer session. **Full-time faculty:** 115 total. **Part-time faculty:** 375 total. **Partnerships:** Formal partnerships with Puget Sound Naval Shipyard, Running Start (high schools), West Sound Technical (cosmetology), US Navy, Service Corps of Retired Executives, the NW Women's Business Center, and Kitsap Regional Library.

**Student profile.**

| | | | |
|---|---|---|---|
| Out-of-state: | 1% | Hispanic American: | 4% |
| African American: | 3% | Native American: | 2% |
| Asian American: | 9% | 25 or older: | 48% |

**Transfer out. Colleges most students transferred to 2007:** University of Washington, Central Washington University, Washington State University, Western Washington University.

**Basis for selection.** Open admission, but selective for some programs. Admissions to registered nursing, licensed practical nursing, and medical office assistant program based several requirements including prerequisites, academic GPA, and test scores. English and math placement assessment is administered to degree/certificate-seeking applicants or for those who wish to enroll in English or math classes. Nursing and health occupation programs require students to attend a pre-application orientation. **Adult students:** SAT/ACT scores not required. **Homeschooled:** Transcript of courses and grades required.

**2007-2008 Annual costs.** Tuition/fees: $2,881; $4,168 out-of-state. Per-credit charge: $74 in-state; $117 out-of-state. Books/supplies: $924. Personal expenses: $1,524.

**2007-2008 Financial aid. Need-based:** 76% of total undergraduate aid awarded as scholarships/grants, 24% as loans/jobs. Need-based aid available for part-time students. Work-study available nights and for part-time students. **Non-need-based:** Scholarships awarded for academics, state residency.

**Application procedures. Admission:** No deadline. No application fee. Application may be submitted online. Admission notification on a rolling basis. **Financial aid:** Priority date 3/1; no closing date. FAFSA, institutional form required. Applicants notified on a rolling basis starting 6/1; must reply within 2 week(s) of notification.

**Academics. Special study options:** Combined bachelor's/graduate degree, cooperative education, cross-registration, distance learning, dual enrollment of high school students, ESL, independent study, internships, liberal arts/career combination, study abroad. 2-2 program with Old Dominion University permits completion of bachelor degree on premises at Olympic College, programs with Western Washington University and St. Martin's College. Running Start Program available for high school juniors/seniors with 2.5 GPA. Special articulation for professional/technical programs to transfer to Evergreen State College, Old Dominion, University of Washington-Tacoma in Business Management. Bachelor of Science in Nursing through UWT. Bachelor's degree programs available on campus. License preparation in nursing, physical therapy. **Credit/placement by examination:** AP, CLEP, IB, institutional tests. Credit awarded for credit by exam, experiential credit, or CLEP varies by degree program. **Support services:** GED preparation and test center, learning center, remedial instruction, study skills assistance, tutoring, writing center.

**Majors. Business:** General, accounting technology, administrative services, business admin. **Communications:** General. **Communications technology:** Animation/special effects. **Computer sciences:** Computer science, networking, programming, security. **Construction:** Electrician, plumbing. **Education:** General, early childhood. **Engineering:** General. **Engineering technology:** Drafting, electrical, industrial. **Health:** Licensed practical nurse, medical assistant, nursing (RN). **Legal studies:** Legal secretary. **Liberal arts:** Arts/sciences. **Mechanic/repair:** Automotive, marine. **Personal/culinary services:** Barbering, chef training, cosmetic. **Physical sciences:** Chemistry, geology, physics. **Production:** Welding. **Protective services:** Fire services admin, firefighting, police science. **Social sciences:** Anthropology, political science, sociology. **Visual/performing arts:** General, art.

**Computing on campus.** 670 workstations in library, computer center, student center. Commuter students can connect to campus network. Online course registration, online library, helpline, student web hosting, wireless network available.

**Student life. Freshman orientation:** Available. Preregistration for classes offered. In person or online. In person orientation takes place before advising. **Policies:** Student code of conduct. **Housing:** Apartments available for out-of-region students. **Activities:** Bands, choral groups, drama, music ensembles, musical theater, opera, student government, student newspaper, symphony orchestra, Phi Theta Kappa.

**Athletics.** NJCAA. **Intercollegiate:** Baseball M, basketball, golf, soccer, softball W, volleyball W, weight lifting. **Intramural:** Golf, soccer, weight lifting. **Team name:** Rangers.

**Student services.** Adult student services, career counseling, services for economically disadvantaged, student employment services, financial aid counseling, minority student services, on-campus daycare, personal counseling, placement for graduates, veterans' counselor, women's services. **Physically disabled:** Services for visually, speech, hearing impaired. **Transfer:** Re-entry adviser for new students. Transfer adviser, college fairs on campus for students transferring to 4-year colleges.

**Contact.** E-mail: prospect@olympic.edu
Phone: (360) 475-7479 Toll-free number: (800) 259-6718 ext. 7479
Fax: (360) 475-7202
Becky Harris, Director of Admissions, Olympic College, 1600 Chester Avenue, Bremerton, WA 98337-1699

## Peninsula College
**Port Angeles, Washington**
www.pc.ctc.edu                    CB code: 4615

◗ Public 2-year community college
◗ Commuter campus in large town

**General.** Founded in 1961. Regionally accredited. **Enrollment:** 980 degree-seeking undergraduates; 3,677 non-degree-seeking students. **Degrees:** 224 associate awarded. **Location:** 75 miles from Seattle. **Calendar:** Quarter, limited summer session. **Full-time faculty:** 60 total; 32% have terminal degrees, 13% minority, 40% women. **Part-time faculty:** 119 total; 6% minority, 63% women. **Class size:** 82% < 20, 17% 20-39, less than 1% 40-49, less than 1% 50-99. **Special facilities:** Marine laboratory, dam removal project.

**Student profile.** Among degree-seeking undergraduates, 286 enrolled as first-time, first-year students.

| | | | |
|---|---|---|---|
| Part-time: | 38% | Hispanic American: | 4% |
| Out-of-state: | 1% | Native American: | 3% |
| Women: | 63% | International: | 7% |
| African American: | 1% | 25 or older: | 41% |
| Asian American: | 3% | | |

**Basis for selection.** Open admission, but selective for some programs. Special requirements for nursing program. Admission to college does not guarantee admission to all courses or vocational education programs. Additional applications may be necessary. ASSET required for full-time applicants for placement only.

**2007-2008 Annual costs.** Tuition/fees: $2,763; $3,152 out-of-state. Per-credit charge: $77 in-state; $90 out-of-state. Books/supplies: $900. Personal expenses: $1,548.

**Financial aid. Need-based:** Need-based aid available for part-time students. **Non-need-based:** Scholarships awarded for academics, athletics, job skills.

**Application procedures. Admission:** No deadline. No application fee. Application may be submitted online. Admission notification on a rolling basis. **Financial aid:** Priority date 4/1; no closing date. FAFSA, institutional form required. Applicants notified on a rolling basis starting 6/1; must reply within 2 week(s) of notification.

**Academics. Special study options:** Distance learning, double major, dual enrollment of high school students, ESL, honors, internships, liberal arts/career combination, study abroad. License preparation in dental hygiene, nursing. **Credit/placement by examination:** AP, CLEP, institutional tests. 10 credit hours maximum toward associate degree. Must complete minimum 30 quarter hours of credit in residency with 2.75 GPA. **Support services:** Learning center, reduced course load, remedial instruction, study skills assistance, tutoring, writing center.

**Majors. Business:** Accounting, accounting technology, administrative services, business admin, marketing, office management. **Communications:** Journalism. **Computer sciences:** General, applications programming, data processing, networking, vendor certification, web page design. **Conservation:** Fisheries. **Education:** Early childhood. **Engineering technology:** Surveying. **Family/consumer sciences:** Child care. **Health:** Home attendant, medical assistant, medical secretary, nursing (RN), substance abuse counseling. **Liberal arts:** Arts/sciences. **Mechanic/repair:** Automotive, diesel, electronics/electrical. **Production:** Welding. **Protective services:** Corrections, law enforcement admin.

**Computing on campus.** 38 workstations in library, computer center, student center. Online course registration, online library, wireless network available.

**Student life. Activities:** Jazz band, choral groups, dance, drama, literary magazine, music ensembles, student government, student newspaper, symphony orchestra, Christian Collegiate Fellowship, Communications Careers Club, Native American Nations, Phi Theta Kappa, Phi Beta Lambda, IT club, Basketball Club, German Club.

**Athletics. Intercollegiate:** Basketball, soccer M, softball W. **Intramural:** Basketball, bowling, football (non-tackle) M, golf, soccer, softball, tennis, volleyball. **Team name:** Pirates.

**Student services.** Adult student services, career counseling, services for economically disadvantaged, student employment services, financial aid counseling, on-campus daycare, personal counseling, placement for graduates, veterans' counselor. **Physically disabled:** Services for visually, hearing impaired. **Transfer:** Pre-admission transcript evaluation for new students. Transfer adviser, college fairs on campus for students transferring to 4-year colleges.

**Contact.** E-mail: admissions@pcadmin.ctc.edu
Phone: (360) 452-9277 Toll-free number: (877) 452-9277
Fax: (360) 417-6581
Cindy Lauderback, Enrollment Service Manager, Peninsula College, 1502 East Lauridsen Boulevard, Port Angeles, WA 98362

## Pierce College
### Lakewood, Washington
### www.pierce.ctc.edu
**CB code: 4103**

- Public 2-year community college
- Commuter campus in small city

**General.** Founded in 1967. Regionally accredited. **Location:** 10 miles from downtown. **Calendar:** Quarter.

**Annual costs/financial aid.** Tuition/fees (2007-2008): $2,931; $3,384 out-of-state. Books/supplies: $894. Personal expenses: $1,476. Need-based financial aid available to full-time and part-time students.

**Contact.** Phone: (253) 964-6501
Registrar, 9401 Farwest Drive SW, Lakewood, WA 98498-1999

## Renton Technical College
### Renton, Washington
### www.RTC.edu
**CB code: 0790**

- Public 2-year technical college
- Commuter campus in large town

**General.** Founded in 1942. Regionally accredited. **Enrollment:** 1,047 degree-seeking undergraduates. **Degrees:** 128 associate awarded. **Location:** 10 miles from Seattle. **Calendar:** Quarter, extensive summer session. **Full-time faculty:** 87 total. **Part-time faculty:** 147 total. **Special facilities:** Technology resource center.

**Basis for selection.** Open admission. ACT, ASSET and SLEP scores required for all applicants for placement purposes. Interview recommended. **Adult students:** Students must complete on-campus assessment.

**2007-2008 Annual costs.** Tuition/fees: $3,618; $3,618 out-of-state. Books/supplies: $690.

**2006-2007 Financial aid.** All financial aid based on need. 84% of total undergraduate aid awarded as scholarships/grants, 16% as loans/jobs. Need-based aid available for part-time students.

**Application procedures. Admission:** No deadline. $25 fee, may be waived for applicants with need. Application must be submitted on paper. Admission notification on a rolling basis. **Financial aid:** Priority date 5/1; no closing date. FAFSA, institutional form required. Applicants notified on a rolling basis.

**Academics.** Many programs have co-op component. **Special study options:** Cooperative education, distance learning, dual enrollment of high school students, ESL, external degree, internships, liberal arts/career combination, student-designed major. License preparation in nursing, real estate. **Credit/placement by examination:** CLEP. 30 credit hours maximum toward associate degree. **Support services:** GED preparation and test center, learning center, remedial instruction, study skills assistance, tutoring.

**Majors. Business:** Accounting, administrative services, office management, office/clerical. **Computer sciences:** Applications programming, computer science, networking, programming. **Construction:** Carpentry. **Education:** Business, early childhood, teacher assistance, voc/tech. **Engineering:** Electrical. **Engineering technology:** CAD/CADD, drafting, surveying. **Family/consumer sciences:** Child care. **Health:** Dental assistant, insurance coding, licensed practical nurse, massage therapy, medical assistant, medical records admin, medical secretary, pharmacy assistant, surgical technology. **Legal studies:** Legal secretary. **Mechanic/repair:** Auto body, automotive, electronics/electrical, heating/ac/refrig, industrial, musical instruments. **Personal/culinary services:** Culinary arts. **Production:** Machine shop technology.

**Computing on campus.** 150 workstations in library, computer center, student center. Online library available.

**Student life. Freshman orientation:** Available. **Activities:** Student newspaper.

**Student services.** Career counseling, student employment services, financial aid counseling, on-campus daycare, personal counseling, placement for graduates. **Physically disabled:** Services for visually, speech, hearing impaired. **Transfer:** Pre-admission transcript evaluation for new students. Transfer adviser for students transferring to 4-year colleges.

**Contact.** E-mail: briverman@rtc.edu
Phone: (425) 235-5840 Fax: (425) 235-7832
Jon Pozega, Vice President Student Services, Renton Technical College, 3000 NE Fourth Street, Renton, WA 98056-4195

## Seattle Central Community College
### Seattle, Washington
### www.seattlecentral.org
**CB code: 4741**

- Public 2-year community college
- Commuter campus in very large city

**General.** Founded in 1966. Regionally accredited. **Calendar:** Quarter.

**Annual costs/financial aid.** Tuition/fees (2007-2008): $2,842; $8,050 out-of-state. Books/supplies: $720. Personal expenses: $1,896. Need-based financial aid available to full-time and part-time students.

**Contact.** Phone: (206) 587-5450
Admissions Director, 1701 Broadway, Seattle, WA 98122

## Shoreline Community College
Shoreline, Washington
www.shoreline.edu                     CB code: 4738

♦  Public 2-year community college
♦  Commuter campus in small city

**General.** Founded in 1964. Regionally accredited. **Location:** 10 miles from Seattle. **Calendar:** Quarter.

**Annual costs/financial aid.** Tuition/fees (2007-2008): $2,833; $5,229 out-of-state. Books/supplies: $924. Personal expenses: $3,516.

**Contact.** Phone: (206) 546-4621
Registrar, 16101 Greenwood Avenue North, Seattle, WA 98133

## Skagit Valley College
Mount Vernon, Washington
www.skagit.edu                     CB code: 4699

♦  Public 2-year community college
♦  Commuter campus in large town

**General.** Founded in 1926. Regionally accredited. **Location:** 60 miles from Seattle, 90 miles from Vancouver, British Columbia. **Calendar:** Quarter.

**Annual costs/financial aid.** Tuition/fees (2007-2008): $2,801; $3,190 out-of-state. Room: $3,300. Books/supplies: $645. Need-based financial aid available to full-time and part-time students.

**Contact.** Phone: (360) 416-7697
Recruitment and Admissions, 2405 East College Way, Mount Vernon, WA 98273

## South Puget Sound Community College
Olympia, Washington
www.spscc.ctc.edu                     CB code: 4578

♦  Public 2-year community college
♦  Commuter campus in small city

**General.** Founded in 1962. Regionally accredited. **Enrollment:** 2,749 degree-seeking undergraduates; 2,170 non-degree-seeking students. **Degrees:** 649 associate awarded. **ROTC:** Air Force. **Location:** 60 miles from Seattle. **Calendar:** Quarter, limited summer session. **Full-time faculty:** 94 total; 49% women. **Part-time faculty:** 246 total; 61% women.

**Student profile.** Among degree-seeking undergraduates, 369 enrolled as first-time, first-year students.

| | | | |
|---|---|---|---|
| Part-time: | 44% | Women: | 61% |
| Out-of-state: | 5% | 25 or older: | 45% |

**Transfer out. Colleges most students transferred to 2007:** Evergreen State College, University of Washington, Washington State University, Western Washington State University.

**Basis for selection.** Open admission, but selective for some programs. Special requirements for nursing, dental assisting, fire protection. **Adult students:** CASAS required for Adult Basic Education.

**2007-2008 Annual costs.** Tuition/fees: $2,774; $3,164 out-of-state. Per-credit charge: $74 in-state; $87 out-of-state. Books/supplies: $900. Personal expenses: $1,896.

**Financial aid. Need-based:** Need-based aid available for part-time students. **Non-need-based:** Scholarships awarded for academics, athletics.

**Application procedures. Admission:** Priority date 5/19; no deadline. No application fee. Admission notification on a rolling basis beginning on or about 12/1. Early applicants register in mid-July for fall quarter. **Financial aid:** Priority date 5/1; no closing date. FAFSA, institutional form required. Applicants notified on a rolling basis starting 7/10; must reply within 2 week(s) of notification.

**Academics. Special study options:** Cooperative education, cross-registration, distance learning, dual enrollment of high school students, ESL, honors, independent study, internships, study abroad, weekend college. License preparation in nursing. **Credit/placement by examination:** AP, CLEP, IB, institutional tests. 45 credit hours maximum toward associate degree. **Support services:** GED preparation and test center, learning center, remedial instruction, study skills assistance, tutoring, writing center.

**Majors. Agriculture:** Horticulture, ornamental horticulture. **Business:** General, accounting, administrative services, hospitality admin, office/clerical. **Computer sciences:** Applications programming, data processing, information systems. **Education:** Early childhood. **Engineering technology:** Drafting, electrical. **Health:** Dental assistant, medical assistant, medical secretary, nursing assistant. **Legal studies:** Legal secretary, paralegal. **Liberal arts:** Arts/sciences. **Personal/culinary services:** Culinary arts. **Protective services:** Firefighting.

**Computing on campus.** 100 workstations in library, computer center, student center. Commuter students can connect to campus network. Online course registration, wireless network available.

**Student life. Freshman orientation:** Available. **Activities:** Jazz band, choral groups, drama, international student organizations, literary magazine, music ensembles, musical theater, student government, student newspaper.

**Athletics.** NJCAA. **Intercollegiate:** Basketball, soccer M, softball W. **Team name:** Clippers.

**Student services.** Adult student services, career counseling, services for economically disadvantaged, student employment services, financial aid counseling, minority student services, on-campus daycare, personal counseling, placement for graduates, veterans' counselor. **Physically disabled:** Services for visually, speech, hearing impaired. **Transfer:** Transfer adviser, college fairs on campus for students transferring to 4-year colleges.

**Contact.** E-mail: enrollmentservices@spscc.ctc.edu
Phone: (360) 754-7711 ext. 5241 Fax: (360) 596-5907
Kathy Lundeen, Dean of Enrollment Services, South Puget Sound Community College, 2011 Mottman Road, SW, Olympia, WA 98512-6218

## Spokane Community College
Spokane, Washington
www.scc.spokane.edu                     CB code: 4739

♦  Public 2-year community college
♦  Commuter campus in small city

**General.** Founded in 1963. Regionally accredited. **Enrollment:** 6,027 degree-seeking undergraduates; 633 non-degree-seeking students. **Degrees:** 1,005 associate awarded. **ROTC:** Army, Naval, Air Force. **Location:** 2 miles from downtown. **Calendar:** Quarter, limited summer session. **Full-time faculty:** 196 total. **Part-time faculty:** 213 total. **Special facilities:** Nursery, floral shop, automotive repair service center, cosmetology center.

**Student profile.** Among degree-seeking undergraduates, 27% enrolled in a transfer program, 54% enrolled in a vocational program, 3% already have a bachelor's degree or higher, 2,107 enrolled as first-time, first-year students.

| | | | |
|---|---|---|---|
| Part-time: | 28% | Women: | 60% |
| Out-of-state: | 4% | 25 or older: | 54% |

**Transfer out. Colleges most students transferred to 2007:** Eastern Washington University, Washington State University.

**Basis for selection.** Open admission, but selective for some programs. Some programs require prerequisites or have special selection procedures. Admission to college does not guarantee acceptance in every program. ASSET used for placement. **Homeschooled:** If under 18, must be deemed able to benefit from curricular offerings of college. Required to take ASSET or COMPASS tests and must place at college level.

**2007-2008 Annual costs.** Tuition/fees: $2,849; $3,373 out-of-state. Per-credit charge: $74 in-state; $100 out-of-state. Books/supplies: $780. Personal expenses: $3,012.

**Financial aid. Non-need-based:** Scholarships awarded for athletics.

**Application procedures. Admission:** No deadline. $15 fee, may be waived for applicants with need. Admission notification on a rolling basis beginning on or about 1/1. **Financial aid:** No deadline. FAFSA, institutional form required. Applicants notified on a rolling basis; must reply within 2 week(s) of notification.

**Academics. Special study options:** Cooperative education, cross-registration, distance learning, dual enrollment of high school students, ESL, independent study, internships, student-designed major, study abroad. License preparation in nursing, paramedic. **Credit/placement by examination:** AP, CLEP, institutional tests. 60 credit hours maximum toward associate degree. **Support services:** Learning center, reduced course load, remedial instruction, study skills assistance, tutoring, writing center.

**Majors. Agriculture:** Business, greenhouse operations, horticulture, nursery operations, soil science, turf management. **Business:** General, accounting, administrative services, banking/financial services, business admin, management information systems, marketing, office management, office technology, office/clerical, selling, vehicle parts marketing. **Computer sciences:** Applications programming, data processing, information systems. **Conservation:** Forest resources, forestry, water/wetlands/marine, wildlife. **Construction:** Carpentry, power transmission. **Engineering technology:** Architectural, civil, construction, electrical, hydraulics, robotics. **Health:** Cardiovascular technology, clinical lab technology, dental assistant, EMT paramedic, medical secretary, optician, pharmacy assistant, recreational therapy, respiratory therapy technology, surgical technology, ward clerk. **Legal studies:** Legal secretary, paralegal, prelaw. **Liberal arts:** Arts/sciences. **Mechanic/repair:** Aircraft, auto body, diesel, electronics/electrical, heating/ac/refrig, industrial. **Parks/recreation:** Facilities management. **Personal/culinary services:** Cosmetic, culinary arts. **Protective services:** Corrections, fire services admin, law enforcement admin, police science, security services.

**Computing on campus.** 913 workstations in library, computer center, student center. Online course registration available.

**Student life. Freshman orientation:** Available. Preregistration for classes offered. **Activities:** Drama, literary magazine, student government, student newspaper.

**Athletics. Intercollegiate:** Baseball M, basketball, cross-country, golf, soccer, softball W, tennis, track and field, volleyball W. **Team name:** Big Foot.

**Student services.** Adult student services, career counseling, services for economically disadvantaged, student employment services, financial aid counseling, minority student services, on-campus daycare, personal counseling, placement for graduates, veterans' counselor. **Physically disabled:** Services for visually, speech, hearing impaired. **Transfer:** College fairs on campus for students transferring to 4-year colleges.

**Contact.** Phone: (509) 533-8860 Toll-free number: (800) 248-5644 Fax: (509) 533-8860
Doug Jones, Dean of Student Services for Enrollment Services, Spokane Community College, 1810 North Greene Street, Spokane, WA 99217-5399

## Spokane Falls Community College
Spokane, Washington
www.spokanefalls.edu
CB code: 4752

- Public 2-year community college
- Commuter campus in small city
- Interview required

**General.** Founded in 1967. Regionally accredited. **Enrollment:** 5,392 degree-seeking undergraduates; 263 non-degree-seeking students. **Degrees:** 880 associate awarded. **ROTC:** Army. **Location:** 4 miles from downtown. **Calendar:** Quarter, limited summer session. **Full-time faculty:** 161 total; 11% minority, 58% women. **Part-time faculty:** 412 total; 3% minority, 46% women. **Special facilities:** Theater, performing arts center, art gallery, 60-foot Foucault pendulum.

**Student profile.** Among degree-seeking undergraduates, 3% already have a bachelor's degree or higher, 1,772 enrolled as first-time, first-year students.

| | | | |
|---|---|---|---|
| Part-time: | 28% | 25 or older: | 30% |
| Women: | 57% | | |

**Transfer out. Colleges most students transferred to 2007:** Spokane Community Colleges, Big Bend Community College.

**Basis for selection.** Open admission, but selective for some programs. Certain programs require prerequisites or have special selection procedures. Admission to college does not guarantee acceptance to every program. ASSET test required for placement.

**2007-2008 Annual costs.** Tuition/fees: $2,807; $3,331 out-of-state. Per-credit charge: $74 in-state; $100 out-of-state. Books/supplies: $924. Personal expenses: $3,110.

**Financial aid.** All financial aid based on need. Need-based aid available for part-time students.

**Application procedures. Admission:** No deadline. $15 fee. Application may be submitted online. Admission notification on a rolling basis. **Financial aid:** Priority date 4/1; no closing date. FAFSA, institutional form required. Applicants notified on a rolling basis starting 5/15; must reply within 2 week(s) of notification.

**Academics. Special study options:** Cooperative education, cross-registration, distance learning, dual enrollment of high school students, ESL, honors, independent study, internships, study abroad, weekend college. License preparation in aviation, physical therapy. **Credit/placement by examination:** AP, CLEP, institutional tests. 60 credit hours maximum toward associate degree. **Support services:** GED preparation and test center, learning center, remedial instruction, study skills assistance, tutoring, writing center.

**Majors. Architecture:** Interior. **Business:** General, accounting, administrative services, banking/financial services, business admin, fashion, international, management information systems, marketing, office management, office/clerical, tourism/travel. **Communications:** Journalism. **Communications technology:** General. **Computer sciences:** General, computer graphics, computer science, information systems, web page design. **Education:** General, early childhood, special, teacher assistance. **Engineering:** General. **Engineering technology:** Architectural, drafting, electrical. **English:** English lit. **Foreign languages:** General, sign language interpretation. **Health:** Athletic training, clinical lab technology, health services, medical assistant, medical records technology, nursing (RN), occupational therapy assistant, orthotics/prosthetics, physical therapy assistant, prenursing, substance abuse counseling, vocational rehab counseling. **Legal studies:** Paralegal. **Liberal arts:** Arts/sciences. **Math:** General. **Mechanic/repair:** Automotive. **Parks/recreation:** Sports admin. **Protective services:** Firefighting, law enforcement admin. **Transportation:** General. **Visual/performing arts:** Commercial photography, commercial/advertising art, interior design.

**Most popular majors.** Health sciences 6%, liberal arts 74%.

**Computing on campus.** 400 workstations in library, computer center.

**Student life. Freshman orientation:** Mandatory. Preregistration for classes offered. **Policies:** Student conduct code. **Activities:** Bands, choral groups, drama, literary magazine, music ensembles, opera, student government, student newspaper, symphony orchestra.

**Athletics. Intercollegiate:** Baseball M, basketball, cross-country, golf, soccer, softball W, tennis, track and field. **Intramural:** Basketball, soccer, table tennis, tennis, volleyball.

**Student services.** Adult student services, career counseling, services for economically disadvantaged, student employment services, financial aid counseling, health services, minority student services, on-campus daycare, personal counseling, placement for graduates, veterans' counselor, women's services. **Physically disabled:** Services for visually, hearing impaired. **Transfer:** Transfer adviser, college fairs on campus for students transferring to 4-year colleges.

**Contact.** Phone: (509) 533-3305 Toll-free number: (888) 509-7944 Fax: (509) 533-3237
Vice President of Student Services, Spokane Falls Community College, 3410 West Fort George Wright Drive, Spokane, WA 99224

## Tacoma Community College
Tacoma, Washington
www.tacomacc.edu
CB member
CB code: 4826

- Public 2-year community college
- Commuter campus in small city

**General.** Founded in 1965. Regionally accredited. Programs offered at Tacoma Campus, Tacoma Mall, and Gig Harbor Center. **Enrollment:** 5,142 degree-seeking undergraduates. **Degrees:** 800 associate awarded. **Location:** 30 miles from Seattle, 30 miles from Olympia. **Calendar:** Quarter, limited summer session. **Full-time faculty:** 132 total. **Part-time faculty:** 255 total.

**Student profile.**

| | | | |
|---|---|---|---|
| Part-time: | 40% | Women: | 63% |
| Out-of-state: | 1% | 25 or older: | 49% |

**Transfer out. Colleges most students transferred to 2007:** University of Washington.

**Basis for selection.** Open admission. **Learning Disabled:** Students who wish to receive accommodations need to present documentation to the college.

**2007-2008 Annual costs.** Tuition/fees: $2,909; $3,298 out-of-state. Books/supplies: $800.

**Financial aid.** All financial aid based on need. Need-based aid available for part-time students. Work-study available nights, weekends and for part-time students.

**Application procedures. Admission:** No deadline. No application fee. Application may be submitted online. Admission notification on a rolling basis. **Financial aid:** Priority date 3/26; no closing date. FAFSA, institutional form required. Applicants notified on a rolling basis starting 7/20; must reply within 4 week(s) of notification.

**Academics. Special study options:** Combined bachelor's/graduate degree, distance learning, dual enrollment of high school students, ESL, internships, study abroad. Concurrent enrollment with nearby community colleges. Bachelor's degree programs available on campus. License preparation in nursing, paramedic, radiology. **Credit/placement by examination:** AP, CLEP, IB, institutional tests. 45 credit hours maximum toward associate degree. **Support services:** GED preparation and test center, learning center, reduced course load, remedial instruction, study skills assistance, tutoring, writing center.

**Majors. Computer sciences:** General. **Education:** Teacher assistance. **Health:** EMT paramedic. **Liberal arts:** Arts/sciences. **Protective services:** Corrections.

**Computing on campus.** 185 workstations in library, computer center, student center. Online course registration, online library, wireless network available.

**Student life. Freshman orientation:** Mandatory. Preregistration for classes offered. **Housing:** Homestay Program available for international students. **Activities:** Jazz band, choral groups, drama, literary magazine, music ensembles, student government, student newspaper.

**Athletics. Intercollegiate:** Baseball M, basketball, golf, soccer, volleyball W. **Team name:** Titans.

**Student services.** Adult student services, career counseling, student employment services, financial aid counseling, minority student services, on-campus daycare, personal counseling, veterans' counselor. **Physically disabled:** Services for visually, speech, hearing impaired. **Transfer:** Pre-admission transcript evaluation for new students. Transfer adviser, college fairs on campus for students transferring to 4-year colleges.

**Contact.** Phone: (253) 566-5001 Fax: (253) 566-6011
Mary McCabe, Registrar, Tacoma Community College, 6501 South 19th Street, Tacoma, WA 98466-9971

---

## Walla Walla Community College
**Walla Walla, Washington**
**www.wwcc.edu**                                    CB code: 4963

▸ Public 2-year community and technical college
▸ Commuter campus in large town

**General.** Founded in 1967. Regionally accredited. Academic and vocational courses offered at educational center at Clarkston, Washington and Department of Corrections at the Washington State Penitentiary. **Enrollment:** 2,183 degree-seeking undergraduates; 3,733 non-degree-seeking students. **Degrees:** 563 associate awarded. **Location:** 158 miles from Spokane, 262 miles from Seattle. **Calendar:** Quarter, limited summer session. **Full-time faculty:** 122 total; 8% minority, 42% women. **Part-time faculty:** 170 total; 12% minority, 65% women. **Class size:** 78% < 20, 19% 20-39, less than 1% 40-49, 2% 50-99. **Special facilities:** Enology (winemaking), viticulture, culinary and John Deere facilities. **Partnerships:** Formal partnerships with John Deere & Company training center, Cisco Corporation.

**Student profile.** Among degree-seeking undergraduates, 35% enrolled in a transfer program, 65% enrolled in a vocational program, 5% already have a bachelor's degree or higher, 551 enrolled as first-time, first-year students.

| | | | |
|---|---|---|---|
| Part-time: | 30% | Asian American: | 2% |
| Out-of-state: | 20% | Hispanic American: | 16% |
| Women: | 54% | Native American: | 2% |
| African American: | 3% | 25 or older: | 45% |

**Transfer out.** Colleges most students transferred to 2007: Washington State University, Lewis & Clark College, Walla Walla University, Eastern Washington University, University of Idaho.

---

**Basis for selection.** Open admission, but selective for some programs. Special requirements for health science and vocational programs. TOEFL score of 500 or higher needed to demonstrate English proficiency. COMPASS or ASSET placement tests used for English, reading, math. **Learning Disabled:** Flexible procedures; early registration.

**High school preparation.** Recommended units include English 4, mathematics 4 and science 3.

**2007-2008 Annual costs.** Tuition/fees: $2,916; $4,009 out-of-state. Per-credit charge: $82 in-state; $96 out-of-state. Books/supplies: $924. Personal expenses: $1,800.

**2006-2007 Financial aid. Need-based:** 62% of total undergraduate aid awarded as scholarships/grants, 38% as loans/jobs. Need-based aid available for part-time students. Work-study available nights and for part-time students. **Non-need-based:** Scholarships awarded for academics, athletics, leadership, music/drama.

**Application procedures. Admission:** No deadline. No application fee. Application may be submitted online. Admission notification on a rolling basis. **Financial aid:** Priority date 3/1; no closing date. FAFSA, institutional form required. Applicants notified on a rolling basis starting 6/1; must reply within 2 week(s) of notification.

**Academics. Special study options:** Combined bachelor's/graduate degree, cooperative education, distance learning, dual enrollment of high school students, ESL, external degree, honors, independent study, internships, liberal arts/career combination. License preparation in nursing, paramedic. **Credit/placement by examination:** AP, CLEP, institutional tests. 23 credit hours maximum toward associate degree. **Support services:** GED preparation and test center, learning center, pre-admission summer program, reduced course load, remedial instruction, study skills assistance, tutoring, writing center.

**Majors. Agriculture:** Business, equipment technology, mechanization, production, turf management. **Business:** Accounting technology, banking/financial services, business admin, executive assistant, office management, retailing. **Communications technology:** Desktop publishing. **Computer sciences:** Data entry, data processing, information systems, networking, web page design, webmaster. **Construction:** Carpentry. **Education:** Early childhood, teacher assistance. **Engineering technology:** Civil. **Health:** Medical secretary, nursing (RN). **Legal studies:** Legal secretary. **Liberal arts:** Arts/sciences. **Mechanic/repair:** General, auto body, automotive, computer, heating/ac/refrig. **Parks/recreation:** Facilities management. **Personal/culinary services:** Chef training, cosmetic, cosmetology. **Production:** Machine tool, welding. **Protective services:** Corrections, criminal justice, firefighting.

**Most popular majors.** Agriculture 10%, business/marketing 6%, health sciences 22%, liberal arts 39%, trade and industry 10%.

**Computing on campus.** 716 workstations in library, computer center, student center. Commuter students can connect to campus network. Online course registration, online library, helpline, repair service, student web hosting, wireless network available.

**Student life. Freshman orientation:** Mandatory. **Activities:** Jazz band, choral groups, dance, drama, international student organizations, music ensembles, musical theater, student government, student newspaper, Warriors for Christ, ecology club.

**Athletics.** NJCAA. **Intercollegiate:** Baseball M, basketball, cheerleading W, golf, rodeo, soccer, softball W, volleyball W. **Intramural:** Basketball, softball, volleyball. **Team name:** Warriors.

**Student services.** Adult student services, career counseling, services for economically disadvantaged, student employment services, financial aid counseling, minority student services, on-campus daycare, personal counseling, placement for graduates, veterans' counselor, women's services. **Physically disabled:** Services for visually, speech, hearing impaired. **Transfer:** Re-entry adviser, pre-admission transcript evaluation for new students. Transfer center, transfer adviser, college fairs on campus for students transferring to 4-year colleges.

**Contact.** E-mail: admissions@wwcc.edu
Phone: (509) 527-4283 Toll-free number: (877) 992-9922
Fax: (509) 527-3661
Sally Wagoner, Director of Admissions and Registrar, Walla Walla Community College, 500 Tausick Way, Walla Walla, WA 99362-9972

---

## Wenatchee Valley College
**Wenatchee, Washington**
**www.wvc.edu**                                    CB code: 4942

▸ Public 2-year community college
▸ Commuter campus in small city

**General.** Founded in 1939. Regionally accredited. Washington State University and Central Washington University have branch facilities on campus. **Enrollment:** 2,878 degree-seeking undergraduates; 337 non-degree-seeking students. **Degrees:** 529 associate awarded. **Location:** 145 miles from Seattle, 170 miles from Spokane. **Calendar:** Quarter, limited summer session. **Full-time faculty:** 75 total; 76% have terminal degrees, 9% minority, 47% women. **Part-time faculty:** 184 total; 48% have terminal degrees, 8% minority, 56% women. **Class size:** 55% < 20, 43% 20-39, 1% 40-49, less than 1% 50-99, less than 1% >100.

**Student profile.** Among degree-seeking undergraduates, 4% already have a bachelor's degree or higher, 573 enrolled as first-time, first-year students, 519 transferred in from other institutions.

| | | | |
|---|---|---|---|
| Part-time: | 19% | Women: | 64% |
| Out-of-state: | 2% | 25 or older: | 51% |

**Transfer out. Colleges most students transferred to 2007:** Central Washington University, Washington State University, Eastern Washington University, University of Washington, Western Washington University.

**Basis for selection.** Open admission, but selective for some programs. Allied health applicants must submit supplemental application form that details work completed in specific program prerequisites. **Homeschooled:** Statement describing homeschool structure and mission, transcript of courses and grades, interview required. Applicants must be affiliated with their local school district. **Learning Disabled:** Students are encouraged to meet with our Special Populations Coordinator at 509-682-6854.

**2007-2008 Annual costs.** Tuition/fees: $2,772; $3,161 out-of-state. Per-credit charge: $74 in-state; $88 out-of-state. Books/supplies: $900. Personal expenses: $1,548.

**Financial aid. Need-based:** Need-based aid available for part-time students. Work-study available for part-time students. **Non-need-based:** Scholarships awarded for academics, athletics, leadership.

**Application procedures. Admission:** No deadline. No application fee. Application may be submitted online. Admission notification on a rolling basis. **Financial aid:** Closing date 3/1. FAFSA required. Applicants notified by 7/2; must reply within 3 week(s) of notification.

**Academics. Special study options:** Accelerated study, cooperative education, cross-registration, distance learning, double major, dual enrollment of high school students, ESL, independent study, internships, liberal arts/career combination, student-designed major. Bachelor's degree programs available on campus. License preparation in nursing, paramedic, radiology. **Credit/placement by examination:** AP, CLEP, institutional tests. 15 credit hours maximum toward associate degree. At least 15 credits must be completed in residence before credits earned by examination will be applied. **Support services:** GED preparation and test center, remedial instruction, study skills assistance, tutoring, writing center.

**Majors. Agriculture:** Production, products processing. **Business:** Accounting technology, business admin, office management. **Computer sciences:** Networking, programming. **Conservation:** General. **Education:** Early childhood. **Foreign languages:** Sign language interpretation. **Health:** Clinical lab assistant, nursing (RN), radiologic technology/medical imaging, sonography, substance abuse counseling. **Liberal arts:** Arts/sciences. **Mechanic/repair:** Automotive, heating/ac/refrig, industrial electronics. **Protective services:** Firefighting.

**Most popular majors.** Health sciences 19%, liberal arts 69%.

**Computing on campus.** 75 workstations in library, computer center, student center. Online course registration, online library, helpline, student web hosting, wireless network available.

**Student life. Freshman orientation:** Available. **Activities:** Jazz band, choral groups, dance, drama, music ensembles, student government, student newspaper, professional associations, Inter-Varsity Fellowship.

**Athletics.** NJCAA. **Intercollegiate:** Baseball M, basketball, soccer, softball W, volleyball W. **Intramural:** Basketball. **Team name:** Knights.

**Student services.** Adult student services, career counseling, services for economically disadvantaged, student employment services, financial aid counseling, minority student services, on-campus daycare, personal counseling, veterans' counselor. **Physically disabled:** Services for visually, speech, hearing impaired. **Learning disabled:** Comprehensive services available. **Transfer:** Re-entry adviser, pre-admission transcript evaluation for new students. Transfer adviser, college fairs on campus for students transferring to 4-year colleges.

**Contact.** Phone: (509) 682-6806 Toll-free number: (877) 982-4698 Fax: (509) 682-6801
William Maxwell, Director of Enrollment Services, Wenatchee Valley College, 1300 Fifth Street, Wenatchee, WA 98801-1799

## Whatcom Community College
Bellingham, Washington
www.whatcom.ctc.edu

CB member
CB code: 1275

- Public 2-year community college
- Commuter campus in small city

**General.** Founded in 1970. Regionally accredited. **Enrollment:** 2,796 degree-seeking undergraduates. **Degrees:** 678 associate awarded. **Location:** 90 miles from Seattle, 60 miles from Vancouver, Canada. **Calendar:** Quarter, limited summer session. **Full-time faculty:** 75 total. **Part-time faculty:** 150 total. **Class size:** 18% < 20, 77% 20-39, less than 1% 40-49, 4% 50-99.

**Transfer out. Colleges most students transferred to 2007:** Western Washington University, University of Washington, Washington State University, Central Washington University, Eastern Washington University.

**Basis for selection.** Open admission.

**High school preparation.** Recommended units include English 4, mathematics 4, social studies 3, science 2 (laboratory 1), foreign language 3 and academic electives 1. One Fine Arts.

**2007-2008 Annual costs.** Tuition/fees: $2,745; $7,953 out-of-state. Per-credit charge: $77 in-state; $248 out-of-state. Books/supplies: $924. Personal expenses: $1,692.

**Financial aid. Need-based:** Need-based aid available for part-time students. Work-study available nights and for part-time students. **Non-need-based:** Scholarships awarded for academics, athletics, state residency.

**Application procedures. Admission:** Priority date 6/23; no deadline. No application fee. Application may be submitted online. Admission notification on a rolling basis. **Financial aid:** No deadline. FAFSA, institutional form required. Applicants notified on a rolling basis starting 7/1; must reply within 3 week(s) of notification.

**Academics. Special study options:** Cooperative education, cross-registration, distance learning, dual enrollment of high school students, ESL, honors, independent study, internships, student-designed major, study abroad. License preparation in nursing. **Credit/placement by examination:** AP, CLEP, institutional tests. 15 credit hours maximum toward associate degree. **Support services:** GED preparation and test center, learning center, reduced course load, remedial instruction, study skills assistance, tutoring, writing center.

**Majors. Business:** General, accounting. **Computer sciences:** Computer science, data processing, systems analysis. **Education:** General, early childhood, teacher assistance. **Health:** Massage therapy, medical assistant, medical secretary, nursing (RN), physical therapy assistant. **Legal studies:** Paralegal. **Liberal arts:** Arts/sciences. **Protective services:** Police science. **Visual/performing arts:** Commercial/advertising art.

**Most popular majors.** Liberal arts 87%.

**Computing on campus.** 294 workstations in library, computer center, student center. Online course registration, online library available.

**Student life. Freshman orientation:** Available. **Activities:** Jazz band, choral groups, drama, film society, student government, student newspaper, Phi Theta Kappa, Anime Anonymous, Deaf Students Fellowship, health & wellness club, international friendship club, snow club, Gay/Straight Alliance (GSA), multicultural club.

**Athletics. Intercollegiate:** Basketball, soccer M, volleyball W. **Intramural:** Badminton, basketball, soccer, tennis, volleyball. **Team name:** Orcas.

**Student services.** Adult student services, alcohol/substance abuse counseling, career counseling, student employment services, financial aid counseling, on-campus daycare, personal counseling, veterans' counselor. **Physically disabled:** Services for visually, speech, hearing impaired. **Learning disabled:** Comprehensive services available. **Transfer:** Re-entry adviser for new students. Transfer center, transfer adviser, college fairs on campus for students transferring to 4-year colleges.

**Contact.** E-mail: admit@whatcom.ctc.edu
Phone: (360) 676-2170 ext. 3214 Fax: (360) 676-2171
Janelle Miner, Registrar, Whatcom Community College, 237 West Kellogg Road, Bellingham, WA 98226

## Yakima Valley Community College
Yakima, Washington
www.yvcc.edu

CB code: 4993

- Public 2-year community college
- Commuter campus in small city

**General.** Founded in 1928. Regionally accredited. Additional campus in Grandview. **Enrollment:** 2,829 degree-seeking undergraduates; 1,479 non-degree-seeking students. **Degrees:** 664 associate awarded. **Location:** 150 miles from Seattle. **Calendar:** Quarter, extensive summer session. **Full-time faculty:** 116 total; 11% have terminal degrees, 10% minority, 57% women. **Part-time faculty:** 212 total; 12% have terminal degrees, 14% minority, 54% women.

**Student profile.** Among degree-seeking undergraduates, 33% enrolled in a transfer program, 33% enrolled in a vocational program, 494 enrolled as first-time, first-year students.

| | | | |
|---|---|---|---|
| Part-time: | 28% | Hispanic American: | 31% |
| Out-of-state: | 10% | Native American: | 3% |
| Women: | 67% | 25 or older: | 49% |
| African American: | 2% | Live on campus: | 2% |
| Asian American: | 2% | | |

**Transfer out. Colleges most students transferred to 2007:** Central Washington University, Washington State University.

**Basis for selection.** Open admission, but selective for some programs. Special requirements for allied health programs. ACT/ASSET required for placement and advising of degree seeking students and for math/English placement. Previous college/university transcripts showing successful completion of English and math courses may replace ASSET. Essay required for radiologic technology.

**2007-2008 Annual costs.** Tuition/fees: $2,766; $3,162 out-of-state. Per-credit charge: $74 in-state; $88 out-of-state. Books/supplies: $720. Personal expenses: $1,575.

**2006-2007 Financial aid. Need-based:** 68% of total undergraduate aid awarded as scholarships/grants, 32% as loans/jobs. Need-based aid available for part-time students. Work-study available nights, weekends and for part-time students. **Non-need-based:** Scholarships awarded for academics, athletics.

**Application procedures. Admission:** Priority date 5/26; no deadline. $20 fee. Application may be submitted online. Admission notification on a rolling basis. **Financial aid:** Priority date 5/1; no closing date. FAFSA required. Applicants notified on a rolling basis starting 8/1; must reply within 2 week(s) of notification.

**Academics. Special study options:** Cooperative education, distance learning, dual enrollment of high school students, ESL, internships, liberal arts/career combination, weekend college. Bachelor's degree programs available on campus. License preparation in dental hygiene, nursing, radiology. **Credit/placement by examination:** AP, CLEP, IB, institutional tests. 45 credit hours maximum toward associate degree. **Support services:** GED preparation and test center, learning center, remedial instruction, study skills assistance, tutoring, writing center.

**Majors. Agriculture:** General, business, food processing, products processing, supplies. **Business:** General, accounting, accounting technology, administrative services, business admin, e-commerce, entrepreneurial studies, marketing, office management. **Communications technology:** Graphic/printing. **Computer sciences:** General, information systems, web page design. **Construction:** Electrician. **Education:** General, early childhood. **Engineering:** General. **Engineering technology:** Drafting, instrumentation. **Family/consumer sciences:** Child care. **Health:** Dental hygiene, insurance coding, licensed practical nurse, medical assistant, medical radiologic technology/radiation therapy, medical secretary, nursing (RN), pharmacy assistant, substance abuse counseling, surgical technology, veterinary technology/assistant. **Liberal arts:** Arts/sciences. **Mechanic/repair:** Automotive. **Protective services:** Criminal justice, fire services admin, firefighting, law enforcement admin. **Visual/performing arts:** Design.

**Most popular majors.** Business/marketing 12%, computer/information sciences 6%, health sciences 14%, liberal arts 59%.

**Computing on campus.** 300 workstations in dormitories, library, computer center, student center. Dormitories wired for high-speed internet access. Online course registration, wireless network available.

**Student life. Freshman orientation:** Available. Preregistration for classes offered. **Housing:** Single-sex dorms, substance-free housing available. $200 deposit. **Activities:** Jazz band, choral groups, drama, music ensembles, musical theater, student government, student newspaper, Mecha, Veterans, Tiin Ma, International Club, Phi Theta Kappa, Action, Auto, allied health clubs.

**Athletics.** NJCAA. **Intercollegiate:** Baseball M, basketball, soccer W, softball W, volleyball W, wrestling M. **Intramural:** Basketball. **Team name:** Yaks.

**Student services.** Career counseling, services for economically disadvantaged, financial aid counseling, health services, minority student services, on-campus daycare, personal counseling, veterans' counselor, women's services. **Physically disabled:** Services for visually, speech, hearing impaired. **Transfer:** Transfer adviser, college fairs on campus for students transferring to 4-year colleges.

**Contact.** E-mail: admis@yvcc.edu
Phone: (509) 574-4712 Fax: (509) 574-4649
Denise Anderson, Registrar and Director for Enrollment Services, Yakima Valley Community College, PO Box 22520, Yakima, WA 98907-2520

Two-Year Colleges

# West Virginia

## Blue Ridge Community and Technical College
**Martinsburg, West Virginia**
www.blueridgectc.edu

- Public 2-year community and technical college
- Commuter campus in small city

**General.** Regionally accredited. **Enrollment:** 1,018 degree-seeking undergraduates; 1,174 non-degree-seeking students. **Degrees:** 167 associate awarded. **Location:** Downtown. **Calendar:** Semester, limited summer session. **Full-time faculty:** 21 total; 10% have terminal degrees, 5% minority, 67% women. **Part-time faculty:** 74 total; 12% have terminal degrees, 1% minority, 61% women. **Class size:** 76% < 20, 18% 20-39, 4% 40-49, 1% 50-99, less than 1% >100.

**Student profile.** Among degree-seeking undergraduates, 18% enrolled in a transfer program, 82% enrolled in a vocational program, 1% already have a bachelor's degree or higher, 303 enrolled as first-time, first-year students.

| | | | |
|---|---|---|---|
| Part-time: | 44% | Asian American: | 1% |
| Out-of-state: | 4% | Hispanic American: | 2% |
| Women: | 63% | 25 or older: | 40% |
| African American: | 12% | | |

**Basis for selection.** Open admission. **Adult students:** Students without ACT/SAT may take the Accuplacer inhouse. **Homeschooled:** Transcript of courses and grades required.

**High school preparation.** Recommended units include English 4, mathematics 4, social studies 2, history 1, science 3 (laboratory 3), foreign language 2 and visual/performing arts 1.

**2007-2008 Annual costs.** Tuition/fees: $2,944; $8,518 out-of-state. Per-credit charge: $123 in-state; $355 out-of-state. Books/supplies: $500.

**Application procedures. Admission:** No deadline. $25 fee, may be waived for applicants with need. Application must be submitted on paper. Admission notification on a rolling basis.

**Academics. Special study options:** Dual enrollment of high school students, ESL, independent study, liberal arts/career combination. License preparation in dental hygiene, nursing, paramedic, real estate. **Credit/placement by examination:** AP, CLEP, SAT, ACT, institutional tests. **Support services:** GED test center, learning center, reduced course load, remedial instruction, tutoring, writing center.

**Majors. Business:** General. **Computer sciences:** Information systems. **Engineering technology:** Automotive, electromechanical. **Health:** EMT paramedic, nursing (RN). **Legal studies:** Paralegal. **Mechanic/repair:** Automotive, heating/ac/refrig. **Personal/culinary services:** Chef training. **Protective services:** Firefighting, law enforcement admin. **Other:** Occupational development, Technical studies.

**Most popular majors.** Business/marketing 14%, engineering/ engineering technologies 7%, health sciences 22%, liberal arts 40%, security/ protective services 7%.

**Computing on campus.** 70 workstations in computer center, student center. Online course registration, online library, helpline, student web hosting, wireless network available.

**Student life. Freshman orientation:** Mandatory, $25 fee. Preregistration for classes offered. **Activities:** Student government.

**Athletics. Team name:** Bruins.

**Student services.** Adult student services, career counseling, student employment services, financial aid counseling, placement for graduates, veterans' counselor. **Physically disabled:** Services for visually, speech, hearing impaired. **Learning disabled:** Comprehensive services available. **Transfer:** Pre-admission transcript evaluation for new students. College fairs on campus for students transferring to 4-year colleges.

**Contact.** E-mail: ewoolast@blueridgectc.edu
Phone: (304) 260-4380 ext. 2103 Fax: (304) 260-4376
Blue Ridge Community and Technical College, 400 West Stephen Street, Martinsburg, WV 25401

## Eastern West Virginia Community and Technical College
**Moorefield, West Virginia**
www.eastern.wvnet.edu
CB code: 3837

- Public 2-year community and technical college
- Commuter campus in rural community

**General.** Regionally accredited. **Enrollment:** 199 degree-seeking undergraduates; 436 non-degree-seeking students. **Degrees:** 22 associate awarded. **Location:** 55 miles from Winchester, Virginia. **Calendar:** Semester, limited summer session. **Part-time faculty:** 36 total. **Partnerships:** Formal partnership with all schools in the district for a program called EDGE (Earn a Degree Graduate Early).

**Student profile.** Among degree-seeking undergraduates, 39% enrolled in a transfer program, 61% enrolled in a vocational program, 59 enrolled as first-time, first-year students.

| | | | |
|---|---|---|---|
| Part-time: | 71% | 25 or older: | 27% |
| Women: | 81% | | |

**Transfer out. Colleges most students transferred to 2007:** Shepherd College, West Virginia University, Potomac State College.

**Basis for selection.** Open admission. Degree-seeking students required to take ACCUPLACER. **Homeschooled:** Applicants advised to take GED.

**2007-2008 Annual costs.** Tuition/fees: $1,776; $6,822 out-of-state. Per-credit charge: $74 in-state; $284 out-of-state. Books/supplies: $1,200. Personal expenses: $1,000.

**Financial aid. Need-based:** Need-based aid available for part-time students.

**Application procedures. Admission:** No deadline. No application fee. Admission notification on a rolling basis. **Financial aid:** Priority date 6/1; no closing date. FAFSA, institutional form required. Applicants notified on a rolling basis; must reply within 2 week(s) of notification.

**Academics. Special study options:** Distance learning, dual enrollment of high school students, external degree, internships, student-designed major. License preparation in nursing. **Credit/placement by examination:** AP, CLEP, institutional tests. **Support services:** GED preparation, reduced course load, remedial instruction, study skills assistance, tutoring.

**Majors. Business:** Administrative services, business admin. **Computer sciences:** Information systems. **Liberal arts:** Arts/sciences. **Mechanic/repair:** Industrial.

**Computing on campus.** Online library available.

**Student life. Freshman orientation:** Available. Preregistration for classes offered. General orientation program is 3 hours long. Second program required for students taking online courses.

**Student services.** Adult student services, career counseling, services for economically disadvantaged, financial aid counseling, veterans' counselor. **Physically disabled:** Services for visually, hearing impaired. **Transfer:** College fairs on campus for students transferring to 4-year colleges.

**Contact.** E-mail: askeast@eastern.wvnet.edu
Phone: (304) 434-8000 Toll-free number: (877) 982-2322
Fax: (304) 434-7000
Robert Eagle, Dean of Learner Support Services, Eastern West Virginia Community and Technical College, 1929 State Road 55, Moorefield, WV 26836

## Huntington Junior College
**Huntington, West Virginia**
www.huntingtonjuniorcollege.edu
CB code: 7310

- For-profit 2-year junior college
- Commuter campus in small city

**General.** Founded in 1936. Regionally accredited. **Location:** 45 miles from Charleston. **Calendar:** Quarter.

**Two-Year Colleges**

**Annual costs/financial aid.** Tuition/fees (2007-2008): $6,900. Tuition includes books.

**Contact.** Phone: (304) 697-7550
Director of Marketing and Education Services, 900 Fifth Avenue, Huntington, WV 25701

## Mountain State College
### Parkersburg, West Virginia
### www.mountainstate.org
CB code: 2389

▸ For-profit 2-year business and technical college
▸ Commuter campus in large town

**General.** Founded in 1888. Accredited by ACICS. **Location:** 81 miles from Charleston. **Calendar:** Quarter.

**Annual costs/financial aid.** Tuition/fees (2007-2008): $7,165. Books/supplies: $600.

**Contact.** Phone: (304) 485-5487
Director of Student Services, Spring at 16th Street, Parkersburg, WV 26101-3993

## New River Community and Technical College
### Beckley, West Virginia
### www.newriver.edu

▸ Public 2-year community and technical college
▸ Commuter campus in large town

**General.** Regionally accredited. **Enrollment:** 2,156 degree-seeking undergraduates. **Degrees:** 156 associate awarded. **Calendar:** Semester, limited summer session. **Full-time faculty:** 32 total. **Part-time faculty:** 125 total.

**Basis for selection.** Open admission.

**2007-2008 Annual costs.** Tuition/fees: $2,748; $6,150 out-of-state. Per-credit charge: $115 in-state; $256 out-of-state.

**Application procedures. Admission:** No deadline. No application fee. Application may be submitted online.

**Academics. Credit/placement by examination:** CLEP, SAT, ACT, institutional tests.

**Majors. Agriculture:** Aquaculture. **Business:** General, accounting, banking/financial services, hospitality admin, marketing, tourism/travel. **Communications technology:** General. **Computer sciences:** General, information technology, LAN/WAN management. **Conservation:** Environmental science. **Education:** General, teacher assistance. **Health:** Medical assistant. **Legal studies:** Legal secretary. **Protective services:** Corrections, law enforcement admin. **Science technology:** Biological.

**Student life. Freshman orientation:** Available. **Activities:** Student government, student newspaper.

**Student services.** Career counseling, financial aid counseling.

**Contact.** Phone: (304) 255-5812 Fax: (304) 255-5889
Michael Palm, Dean of Student Services, New River Community and Technical College, 167 Dye Drive, Beckley, WV 25801

## Potomac State College of West Virginia University
### Keyser, West Virginia
### www.potomacstatecollege.edu
CB code: 5539

▸ Public 2-year branch campus and junior college
▸ Commuter campus in small town

**General.** Founded in 1901. Regionally accredited. **Enrollment:** 1,198 degree-seeking undergraduates. **Degrees:** 2 bachelor's, 172 associate awarded. **Location:** 80 miles from Morgantown, 150 miles from Baltimore. **Calendar:** Semester, limited summer session. **Full-time faculty:** 37 total; 35% have terminal degrees, 46% women. **Part-time faculty:** 78 total. **Special facilities:** 2 fully operational farms.

**Transfer out. Colleges most students transferred to 2007:** West Virginia University, Fairmont State College, Frostburg State University.

**Basis for selection.** Open admission. English ACT score used in conjunction with high school GPA to place students in either college-level or remedial composition courses. Scores also used for math placement. Audition recommended for music applicants and for scholarship consideration. **Adult students:** SAT/ACT scores not required if out of high school 5 year(s) or more.

**2007-2008 Annual costs.** Tuition/fees: $2,596; $8,360 out-of-state. Per-credit charge: $108 in-state; $348 out-of-state. Students residing in selected counties in bordering states receive reduced out-of-state tuition rates. Room/board: $6,494. Books/supplies: $750.

**Financial aid. Need-based:** Need-based aid available for part-time students. Work-study available nights and weekends. **Non-need-based:** Scholarships awarded for academics, athletics, leadership.

**Application procedures. Admission:** No deadline. No application fee. Application may be submitted online. Admission notification on a rolling basis beginning on or about 9/15. **Financial aid:** Priority date 3/1; no closing date. FAFSA required. Applicants notified on a rolling basis starting 4/1; must reply within 2 week(s) of notification.

**Academics. Special study options:** Distance learning, double major, dual enrollment of high school students, honors, internships, study abroad. Bachelor's degree programs available on campus. **Credit/placement by examination:** AP, CLEP, institutional tests. 30 credit hours maximum toward associate degree. **Support services:** Learning center, reduced course load, remedial instruction, tutoring.

**Majors. Agriculture:** General, agronomy, animal sciences, horticultural science. **Biology:** General. **Business:** General, accounting, administrative services, business admin, entrepreneurial studies, management information systems, managerial economics. **Communications:** Journalism. **Computer sciences:** General, applications programming, data processing, information technology, programming. **Conservation:** General, forest management, forest resources, forest technology, forestry, wildlife, wood science. **Education:** General, elementary, physical, secondary. **Engineering:** General, civil, electrical, mechanical. **English:** English lit. **Foreign languages:** Spanish. **Health:** Predental, premedicine, prepharmacy, preveterinary. **History:** General. **Legal studies:** Prelaw. **Liberal arts:** Arts/sciences. **Math:** General. **Parks/recreation:** Facilities management. **Personal/culinary services:** General. **Physical sciences:** Chemistry, geology, physics. **Protective services:** Correctional facilities, criminal justice, law enforcement admin. **Psychology:** General. **Public administration:** Social work. **Social sciences:** Economics, political science, sociology.

**Most popular majors.** Business/marketing 27%, education 14%, liberal arts 24%.

**Computing on campus.** 100 workstations in library, computer center, student center. Dormitories wired for high-speed internet access. Helpline, repair service available.

**Student life. Freshman orientation:** Mandatory. Preregistration for classes offered. **Housing:** Coed dorms, single-sex dorms available. $150 deposit, deadline 8/15. **Activities:** Bands, campus ministries, choral groups, drama, music ensembles, student government, student newspaper, agriculture and forestry club, Circle K, equestrian club, criminal justice club, engineering club, PAWS (Peer Advocates), life sciences club.

**Athletics.** NJCAA. **Intercollegiate:** Baseball M, basketball, golf, soccer, softball W, volleyball W. **Intramural:** Basketball. **Team name:** Catamounts.

**Student services.** Adult student services, career counseling, services for economically disadvantaged, student employment services, financial aid counseling, health services, minority student services, on-campus daycare, personal counseling, placement for graduates, veterans' counselor, women's services. **Physically disabled:** Services for visually, hearing impaired. **Transfer:** Pre-admission transcript evaluation for new students. Transfer adviser, college fairs on campus for students transferring to 4-year colleges.

**Contact.** E-mail: go2psc@mail.wvu.edu
Phone: (304) 788-6820 Toll-free number: (800) 262-7332
Fax: (304) 788-6939
Beth Little, Director of Enrollment Services, Potomac State College of West Virginia University, One Grand Central Park, Suite 2090, Keyser, WV 26726

## Southern West Virginia Community and Technical College
**Mount Gay, West Virginia**
www.southernwv.edu

CB member
CB code: 0770

◗ Public 2-year community college
◗ Commuter campus in small town

**General.** Founded in 1971. Regionally accredited. Additional campuses in Williamson, Saulsville and Madison. **Enrollment:** 2,516 degree-seeking undergraduates. **Degrees:** 344 associate awarded. **Location:** 60 miles from Charleston. **Calendar:** Semester, limited summer session. **Full-time faculty:** 52 total. **Part-time faculty:** 116 total. **Special facilities:** Allied health and technology building.

**Student profile.** Among degree-seeking undergraduates, 52 transferred in from other institutions.

| | | | |
|---|---|---|---|
| Out-of-state: | 5% | African American: | 2% |

**Transfer out. Colleges most students transferred to 2007:** Marshall University, West Virginia University, West Virginia State University, Mountain State University, Concord University.

**Basis for selection.** Open admission, but selective for some programs. Limited admissions to salon management/cosmetology, nursing, medical laboratory, radiologic technology, dental hygiene, paramedic science, respiratory technology, and surgical technology programs. Nursing and medical laboratory program applicants require minimum ACT score of 21. Interview recommended. **Adult students:** Adult students may also take AC-CUPLACER to determine placement in English and math. **Homeschooled:** Transcript of courses and grades required. **Learning Disabled:** Recommend meeting with disability counselor.

**2007-2008 Annual costs.** Tuition/fees: $1,776; $6,624 out-of-state. Per-credit charge: $74 in-state; $276 out-of-state. Books/supplies: $450. Personal expenses: $900.

**Financial aid. Need-based:** Need-based aid available for part-time students.

**Application procedures. Admission:** No deadline. No application fee. Application may be submitted online. Admission notification on a rolling basis. Application for limited admissions programs must be submitted by January 31. **Financial aid:** No deadline. FAFSA required. Applicants notified on a rolling basis.

**Academics. Special study options:** Distance learning, dual enrollment of high school students, independent study, internships, teacher certification program. Fast Track courses. Bachelor's degree programs available on campus. License preparation in dental hygiene, nursing, paramedic, radiology. **Credit/placement by examination:** AP, CLEP, institutional tests. **Support services:** GED preparation, learning center, reduced course load, remedial instruction, tutoring.

**Majors. Business:** General, accounting, administrative services, business admin, entrepreneurial studies, hospitality admin, marketing, small business admin. **Communications technology:** General. **Computer sciences:** General, information technology. **Engineering technology:** Drafting, electrical, environmental. **Health:** Clinical lab technology, health services, medical radiologic technology/radiation therapy, nursing (RN). **Liberal arts:** Arts/sciences. **Protective services:** Forensics.

**Most popular majors.** Business/marketing 15%, computer/information sciences 10%, health sciences 40%, liberal arts 35%.

**Computing on campus.** 7 workstations in library. Online course registration, online library, helpline available.

**Student life. Freshman orientation:** Available. Orientation courses offered to first time freshman, or students with less than 30 credit hours. **Activities:** Drama, musical theater, student government, special interest clubs.

**Student services.** Career counseling, student employment services, on-campus daycare, personal counseling, placement for graduates, veterans' counselor. **Physically disabled:** Services for visually, speech, hearing impaired. **Transfer:** Transfer adviser, college fairs on campus for students transferring to 4-year colleges.

**Contact.** Phone: (304) 896-7443 Toll-free number: (304) 896-7348 Fax: (304) 792-7056
Teri Wells, Student Records Assistant, Southern West Virginia Community and Technical College, PO Box 2900, Mount Gay, WV 25637

## Valley College of Technology
**Martinsburg, West Virginia**
www.vct.edu

CB code: 3176

◗ For-profit 2-year business and career college
◗ Commuter campus in small city
◗ Interview required

**General.** Accredited by ACICS. **Enrollment:** 43 degree-seeking undergraduates. **Degrees:** 8 associate awarded. **Location:** 20 miles from Winchester, Virginia. **Calendar:** Semester, extensive summer session. **Full-time faculty:** 4 total; 25% minority, 50% women. **Part-time faculty:** 1 total. **Class size:** 100% < 20.

**Student profile.** Among degree-seeking undergraduates, 10 enrolled as first-time, first-year students.

| | | | |
|---|---|---|---|
| Women: | 79% | Hispanic American: | 5% |
| African American: | 16% | 25 or older: | 53% |

**Transfer out. Colleges most students transferred to 2007:** Mountain State University, Shepherd University.

**Basis for selection.** Admission based primarily on high school record, standardized test scores, and interview. If no SAT or ACT scores available, institutional test administered. **Homeschooled:** State high school equivalency certificate required.

**2008-2009 Annual costs.** Tuition/fees (projected): $7,300. Per-credit charge: $225. Tuition varies according to program. Books/supplies: $1,185. Personal expenses: $7,653.

**2006-2007 Financial aid. Need-based:** 59% of total undergraduate aid awarded as scholarships/grants, 41% as loans/jobs. Need-based aid available for part-time students.

**Application procedures. Admission:** No deadline. No application fee. Application must be submitted on paper. Admission notification on a rolling basis. **Financial aid:** No deadline. FAFSA, institutional form required. Applicants notified on a rolling basis.

**Academics. Credit/placement by examination:** CLEP. 29 credit hours maximum toward associate degree. **Support services:** Remedial instruction, study skills assistance.

**Majors. Business:** General, business admin, small business admin.

**Computing on campus.** 42 workstations in computer center.

**Student life. Freshman orientation:** Mandatory. Orientation held during first week of classes.

**Student services.** Career counseling, student employment services, financial aid counseling, placement for graduates. **Transfer:** Pre-admission transcript evaluation for new students.

**Contact.** E-mail: martinsburg@vct.edu
Phone: (304) 263-0979 Fax: (304) 263-2413
Gail Kennedy, Admissions Director, Valley College of Technology, 287 Aikens Center, Martinsburg, WV 25404

## West Virginia Business College
**Wheeling, West Virginia**
www.wvbc.edu

CB code: 2546

◗ For-profit 2-year business college
◗ Commuter campus in small city
◗ Interview required

**General.** Accredited by ACICS. **Enrollment:** 64 degree-seeking undergraduates. **Degrees:** 30 associate awarded. **Calendar:** Quarter. **Part-time faculty:** 13 total; 15% have terminal degrees, 62% women.

**Transfer out. Colleges most students transferred to 2007:** West Virginia Northern Community College, Belmont Technical College.

**Basis for selection.** Open admission, but selective for some programs. Acceptance based on interview by an admissions representative; acceptance by college director; completion of college entrance evaluation. Score of a least 20 required for acceptance directly into associate degree programs. Office administration/medical assistant associate degree programs require score of 25. Acceptance into any degree program is guaranteed after completion of diploma program at WVBC.

**2007-2008 Annual costs.** Diploma program is $9,000. Associate degree program costs $17,000 for entire 2-year program. Books/supplies: $2,124.

**Application procedures. Admission:** No deadline. $75 fee. Application must be submitted on paper.

**Academics. Credit/placement by examination:** CLEP. **Support services:** Reduced course load, tutoring.

**Majors. Business:** Accounting, administrative services, business admin. **Health:** Medical secretary. **Legal studies:** Legal secretary, paralegal.

**Most popular majors.** Business/marketing 11%, health sciences 11%, legal studies 78%.

**Computing on campus.** 16 workstations in library, computer center.

**Student life. Freshman orientation:** Mandatory, $125 fee. **Activities:** Student government.

**Student services.** Financial aid counseling, personal counseling, placement for graduates.

**Contact.** E-mail: kcarpenter@wvbc.edu
Phone: (304) 232-0361 Fax: (304) 232-0363
Karen Shaw, Director, West Virginia Business College, 1052 Main Street, Wheeling, WV 26003

## West Virginia Business College
**Wheeling, West Virginia**
**www.wvbc.edu**

- For-profit 2-year business, junior, technical and career college
- Commuter campus in small city
- Interview required

**General.** Accredited by ACICS. **Enrollment:** 60 degree-seeking undergraduates. **Degrees:** 28 associate awarded. **Location:** 35 miles from Morgantown, 50 miles from Pittsburgh. **Calendar:** Quarter, extensive summer session. **Part-time faculty:** 8 total.

**Basis for selection.** Open admission. **Homeschooled:** State high school equivalency certificate required.

**2007-2008 Annual costs.** Diploma program is $9,000. Associate degree program costs $17,000 for entire 2-year program. Books/supplies: $475.

**Application procedures. Admission:** No deadline. $75 fee. Application must be submitted on paper.

**Academics. Credit/placement by examination:** CLEP.

**Majors. Business:** Administrative services, business admin. **Legal studies:** Paralegal.

**Student life. Activities:** Student newspaper.

**Student services.** Career counseling, financial aid counseling, placement for graduates.

**Contact.** E-mail: info@wvbc.edu
Phone: (304) 624-7695 Toll-free number: (304) 232-0361
Fax: (304) 232-0363
Gary Gorby, General Manager, West Virginia Business College, 1052 Main Street, Wheeling, WV 26003

## West Virginia Junior College
**Morgantown, West Virginia**
**www.wvjc.edu**
CB code: 3179

- For-profit 2-year junior college
- Large town

**General.** Accredited by ACICS. **Calendar:** Quarter.

**Annual costs/financial aid.** Tuition/fees (2007-2008): $9,450. Cost of books/supplies included in tuition/fees. Personal expenses: $2,529. Need-based financial aid available to full-time and part-time students.

**Contact.** Phone: (304) 296-8282
148 Willey Street, Morgantown, WV 26505

## West Virginia Junior College: Bridgeport
**Bridgeport, West Virginia**
**www.wvjcinfo.net**

- For-profit 2-year business and health science college
- Large town

**General.** Accredited by ACICS. **Enrollment:** 203 degree-seeking undergraduates. **Degrees:** 103 associate awarded. **Location:** 120 miles from Charleston. **Calendar:** Quarter. **Full-time faculty:** 19 total.

**Basis for selection.** Open admission.

**Academics. Credit/placement by examination:** CLEP.

**Majors. Business:** Business admin. **Computer sciences:** Information technology. **Health:** Dental assistant, medical assistant.

**Contact.** Phone: (304) 842-4007
West Virginia Junior College: Bridgeport, 176 Thompson Drive, Bridgeport, WV 26330

## West Virginia Junior College: Charleston
**Charleston, West Virginia**
**www.wvjc.com**
CB code: 3180

- For-profit 2-year junior and technical college
- Commuter campus in small city

**General.** Accredited by ACICS. **Calendar:** Quarter.

**Annual costs/financial aid.** Need-based financial aid available to full-time and part-time students.

**Contact.** Phone: (304) 345-2820
Associate Director, 1000 Virginia Street East, Charleston, WV 25301

## West Virginia Northern Community College
**Wheeling, West Virginia**
**www.northern.wvnet.edu**
CB code: 0674

- Public 2-year community college
- Commuter campus in large town

**General.** Founded in 1972. Regionally accredited. **Location:** 50 miles from Pittsburgh. **Calendar:** Semester.

**Annual costs/financial aid.** Tuition/fees (2007-2008): $1,896; $4,224 out-of-district; $6,096 out-of-state. Books/supplies: $600. Personal expenses: $1,153. Need-based financial aid available to full-time and part-time students.

**Contact.** Phone: (304) 233-5900 ext. 4247
Dean of Enrollment Management, 1704 Market Street, Wheeling, WV 26003

## West Virginia State Community and Technical College
**Institute, West Virginia**
**www.wvsctc.edu**

- Public 2-year community and technical college
- Small town

**General.** Regionally accredited. Located on West Virginia State University campus. **Enrollment:** 1,639 degree-seeking undergraduates. **Degrees:** 251 associate awarded. **Location:** 8 miles from Charleston. **Calendar:** Semester, limited summer session. **Full-time faculty:** 41 total; 10% have terminal degrees, 12% minority, 66% women. **Part-time faculty:** 41 total; 2% have terminal degrees, 5% minority, 56% women. **Partnerships:** Formal partnerships with with Charleston Area Medical Center, American Electric Power .

**Student profile.** Among degree-seeking undergraduates, 60% enrolled in a transfer program, 40% enrolled in a vocational program, 337 enrolled as first-time, first-year students, 140 transferred in from other institutions.

| | | | |
|---|---|---|---|
| **Part-time:** | 37% | **Asian American:** | 1% |
| **Women:** | 67% | **Hispanic American:** | 1% |
| **African American:** | 17% | | |

**Transfer out.** 43% of students enrolled in the transfer program go on to 4-year colleges.

**Basis for selection.** Open admission, but selective for some programs. Selective admission for nursing and nuclear medicine technology programs. Nursing requirements include 3.0 GPA and minimum ACT composite of 21 or SAT score of 1000, exclusive of Writing. Nuclear medicine technology requires interview with the program director or clinical coordinator and submission of SAT or ACT scores. Immunization records required for born after January 1, 1957. Statement of activities is requested for students out of high school six months or longer. **Homeschooled:** Statement describing homeschool structure and mission, transcript of courses and grades required. Must provide detailed description of home school curriculum.

**High school preparation.** Recommended units include English 4, mathematics 4, social studies 4, science 3 (laboratory 2) and foreign language 2.

**2007-2008 Annual costs.** Tuition/fees: $2,766; $7,718 out-of-state. Books/supplies: $1,009. Personal expenses: $3,141.

**Financial aid. Need-based:** Work-study available nights, weekends and for part-time students. **Non-need-based:** Scholarships awarded for academics, state residency. **Additional information:** All students, part-time or full-time may apply for tuition waivers.

**Application procedures. Admission:** No deadline. No application fee. Application may be submitted online. Admission notification on a rolling basis. **Financial aid:** Closing date 6/15.

**Academics. Special study options:** Double major, dual enrollment of high school students, honors, internships, study abroad. Bachelor's degree programs available on campus. License preparation in aviation, dental hygiene, nursing, occupational therapy, paramedic, real estate. **Credit/placement by examination:** CLEP, SAT, ACT, institutional tests. **Support services:** GED preparation and test center, remedial instruction, study skills assistance, tutoring, writing center.

**Majors. Business:** Accounting, accounting technology, administrative services, banking/financial services, business admin, finance, sales/distribution. **Communications:** General. **Computer sciences:** Computer science, information systems. **Engineering technology:** Architectural drafting, drafting, electrical, manufacturing. **Health:** EMT paramedic, mental health services, nuclear medical technology, nursing (RN). **Interdisciplinary:** Gerontology, science/society. **Liberal arts:** Arts/sciences. **Physical sciences:** Meteorology. **Protective services:** Police science. **Other:** Allied health & human technology, Occupational development, Technical studies.

**Most popular majors.** Business/marketing 18%, engineering/engineering technologies 15%, health sciences 22%, interdisciplinary studies 9%, liberal arts 29%.

**Computing on campus.** Dormitories wired for high-speed internet access and linked to campus network. Commuter students can connect to campus network. Online course registration, online library, helpline, wireless network available.

**Student life. Housing:** $125 nonrefundable deposit. **Activities:** Student newspaper.

**Athletics. Team name:** Yellow Jackets.

**Student services. Transfer:** College fairs on campus for students transferring to 4-year colleges.

**Contact.** E-mail: admissions@wvsctc.edu
Phone: (304) 766-3221 Toll-free number: (800) 987-2112
Fax: (304) 766-4104
Tryreno Sowell, Director, West Virginia State Community and Technical College, PO Box 1000, Institute, WV 25112-1000

# Wisconsin

## Blackhawk Technical College
Janesville, Wisconsin
www.blackhawk.edu                    CB code: 7319

- Public 2-year technical college
- Commuter campus in small city

**General.** Founded in 1912. Regionally accredited. **Enrollment:** 2,294 degree-seeking undergraduates. **Degrees:** 241 associate awarded. **Location:** 75 miles from Milwaukee and Chicago. **Calendar:** Semester, limited summer session. **Full-time faculty:** 102 total; 2% have terminal degrees, 6% minority, 55% women. **Part-time faculty:** 261 total; 6% minority, 48% women. **Class size:** 81% < 20, 18% 20-39, less than 1% 40-49, less than 1% 50-99.

**Student profile.** Among degree-seeking undergraduates, 100% enrolled in a vocational program, 3% already have a bachelor's degree or higher, 543 enrolled as first-time, first-year students.

| | | | |
|---|---|---|---|
| Part-time: | 56% | Asian American: | 1% |
| Out-of-state: | 1% | Hispanic American: | 4% |
| Women: | 62% | Native American: | 1% |
| African American: | 7% | | |

**Basis for selection.** Open admission, but selective for some programs. Applicants to nursing, dental hygiene, radiography, sonography, and physical therapist assistant programs must meet additional testing and course requirements. National League for Nursing, Pre-Nursing and Guidance examination required for nursing applicants.

**2007-2008 Annual costs.** Tuition/fees: $2,958; $17,313 out-of-state. Per-credit charge: $92 in-state; $571 out-of-state. Material fees vary by program; minimum $4 per course. $10 per credit fee for online courses. Books/supplies: $1,050. Personal expenses: $1,175.

**2006-2007 Financial aid. Need-based:** 54% of total undergraduate aid awarded as scholarships/grants, 46% as loans/jobs. Need-based aid available for part-time students.

**Application procedures. Admission:** Priority date 9/1; no deadline. $30 fee. Application may be submitted online. Admission notification on a rolling basis beginning on or about 10/1. **Financial aid:** Priority date 4/30; no closing date. Applicants notified on a rolling basis starting 3/15; must reply within 2 week(s) of notification.

**Academics. Special study options:** Accelerated study, distance learning, dual enrollment of high school students, ESL, external degree, independent study, internships, student-designed major. Bachelor's degree programs available on campus. License preparation in aviation, nursing, physical therapy, radiology. **Credit/placement by examination:** CLEP. 30 credit hours maximum toward associate degree. **Support services:** GED preparation and test center, learning center, pre-admission summer program, reduced course load, remedial instruction, study skills assistance, tutoring.

**Majors. Business:** Accounting, administrative services, marketing, office management, operations. **Computer sciences:** LAN/WAN management, security, web page design. **Engineering:** Electrical. **Engineering technology:** Drafting, robotics. **Family/consumer sciences:** Institutional food production. **Health:** Medical radiologic technology/radiation therapy, medical secretary, nursing (RN), physical therapy assistant, sonography. **Legal studies:** Legal secretary. **Mechanic/repair:** Diesel. **Personal/culinary services:** Culinary arts. **Protective services:** Fire safety technology, police science.

**Most popular majors.** Business/marketing 16%, computer/information sciences 8%, education 11%, engineering/engineering technologies 7%, health sciences 31%, security/protective services 18%.

**Computing on campus.** 58 workstations in library, computer center. Online course registration, helpline, wireless network available.

**Student life. Freshman orientation:** Available. **Activities:** Student government, student newspaper.

**Student services.** Alcohol/substance abuse counseling, career counseling, services for economically disadvantaged, student employment services, financial aid counseling, minority student services, on-campus daycare, personal counseling, placement for graduates, veterans' counselor. **Physically disabled:** Services for visually, speech, hearing impaired.

**Contact.** Phone: (608) 757-7665 Fax: (608) 743-4407
Barbara Erlandson, Student Services Manager, Blackhawk Technical College, Box 5009, Janesville, WI 53547-5009

## Bryant & Stratton College: Milwaukee
Milwaukee, Wisconsin
www.bryantstratton.edu               CB code: 3617

- For-profit 2-year business and junior college
- Commuter campus in very large city

**General.** Founded in 1854. Regionally accredited. **Location:** 75 miles from Chicago. **Calendar:** Trimester.

**Annual costs/financial aid.** Tuition/fees (2007-2008): $13,185. Tuition and fees provided are for Associate degrees only. Bachelor's program tuition and fees may vary. Books/supplies: $750.

**Contact.** Phone: (414) 276-5200
Director of Admissions, 310 West Wisconsin Avenue, Suite 500, Milwaukee, WI 53203

## Chippewa Valley Technical College
Eau Claire, Wisconsin
www.cvtc.edu                         CB code: 0786

- Public 2-year technical college
- Commuter campus in small city

**General.** Founded in 1912. Regionally accredited. **Enrollment:** 5,529 degree-seeking undergraduates. **Degrees:** 695 associate awarded. **Location:** 90 miles from Minneapolis-St. Paul. **Calendar:** Semester, limited summer session. **Full-time faculty:** 241 total; 12% have terminal degrees, 2% minority, 54% women. **Part-time faculty:** 353 total; 1% minority, 39% women. **Special facilities:** Health Education Center with state-of the art equipment and lab facilites, NanoRite Facility.

**Transfer out. Colleges most students transferred to 2007:** University of Wisconsin-Stout.

**Basis for selection.** Open admission, but selective for some programs. Additional testing and course requirements for applicants to nursing, dental hygiene, radiography, surgical technologist, medical assistant and physical therapist assistant programs. Entrance examination required for dental hygienist and nursing applicants. Interview required for alcohol abuse prevention and other drug abuse prevention associate programs, and fire protective service technician program.

**High school preparation.** Algebra and science requirements for some degree programs.

**2007-2008 Annual costs.** Tuition/fees: $2,936; $17,291 out-of-state. Per-credit charge: $92 in-state; $571 out-of-state. Material fees vary by program; minimum $4 per course. $10 per credit fee for online courses. Books/supplies: $853. Personal expenses: $1,370.

**Financial aid. Need-based:** Need-based aid available for part-time students. Work-study available nights, weekends and for part-time students.

**Application procedures. Admission:** Priority date 8/15; no deadline. $30 fee, may be waived for applicants with need. Application may be submitted online. Admission notification on a rolling basis. **Financial aid:** Priority date 3/15; no closing date. FAFSA required. Applicants notified on a rolling basis starting 6/1; must reply within 2 week(s) of notification.

**Academics. Special study options:** Distance learning, double major, dual enrollment of high school students, ESL, external degree, independent study, internships, liberal arts/career combination, student-designed major, weekend college. License preparation in dental hygiene, nursing, paramedic, real estate. **Credit/placement by examination:** CLEP, institutional tests. 34 credit hours maximum toward associate degree. 50% of semester hours needed for degree may be earned as credit by examination. **Support services:** GED preparation and test center, learning center, reduced course load, remedial instruction, study skills assistance, tutoring.

**Majors. Agriculture:** General, agronomy, animal sciences. **Business:** General, accounting, administrative services, hospitality/recreation, logistics, office technology, operations. **Computer sciences:** General, applications programming, programming. **Engineering:** Civil. **Engineering technology:** Civil, drafting, electrical, robotics. **Health:** Clinical lab assistant, clinical lab technology, dental hygiene, medical radiologic technology/radiation therapy, medical records technology, nursing (RN), sonography, substance abuse counseling. **Legal studies:** Paralegal. **Mechanic/repair:** Electronics/electrical, heating/ac/refrig, industrial. **Protective services:** Firefighting, police science.

**Most popular majors.** Business/marketing 30%, computer/information sciences 13%, health sciences 8%, security/protective services 19%, trade and industry 19%.

**Computing on campus.** 500 workstations in library, computer center.

**Student life. Freshman orientation:** Mandatory. **Activities:** Student government, student newspaper.

**Athletics. Intramural:** Basketball, skiing, softball, table tennis, tennis, volleyball.

**Student services.** Career counseling, student employment services, on-campus daycare, personal counseling, placement for graduates, veterans' counselor. **Physically disabled:** Services for visually, speech, hearing impaired. **Transfer:** Pre-admission transcript evaluation for new students. College fairs on campus for students transferring to 4-year colleges.

**Contact.** E-mail: tshepardson@cvtc.edu
Phone: (715) 833-6246 Toll-free number: (800) 547-2882
Fax: (715) 833-6470
Tim Shepardson, Admissions Manager, Chippewa Valley Technical College, 620 West Clairemont Avenue, Eau Claire, WI 54701-6162

## College of Menominee Nation
Keshena, Wisconsin
www.menominee.edu
CB code: 3974

- Private 2-year community college
- Commuter campus in rural community

**General.** Regionally accredited. **Enrollment:** 505 degree-seeking undergraduates. **Degrees:** 56 associate awarded. **Location:** 150 miles from Madison, 35 miles from Green Bay. **Calendar:** Semester, limited summer session. **Full-time faculty:** 15 total. **Part-time faculty:** 20 total. **Class size:** 77% < 20, 23% 20-39.

**Student profile.** Among degree-seeking undergraduates, 82 enrolled as first-time, first-year students.

| Part-time: | 54% | Women: | 70% |
|---|---|---|---|

**Transfer out. Colleges most students transferred to 2007:** UW-Green Bay, UW-Oshkosh, Silver Lake College.

**Basis for selection.** Open admission, but selective for some programs. ACCUPLACER required of all students for placement. **Adult students:** SAT/ACT scores not required. **Homeschooled:** Must present state certification of completion of requirements. **Learning Disabled:** Students are requested to meet with disability advisor upon registration.

**2007-2008 Annual costs.** Tuition/fees: $6,100. Per-credit charge: $200. Books/supplies: $1,140.

**Financial aid.** All financial aid based on need. Need-based aid available for part-time students. Work-study available nights and for part-time students.

**Application procedures. Admission:** Closing date 8/30 (receipt date). No application fee. Admission notification on a rolling basis. Students notified of acceptance as early as possible. **Financial aid:** FAFSA required. Applicants notified on a rolling basis.

**Academics.** Some courses are offered off-site via broadcasting. **Special study options:** Double major, independent study, internships, liberal arts/career combination. **Credit/placement by examination:** CLEP, institutional tests. **Support services:** Reduced course load, remedial instruction, study skills assistance, tutoring.

**Majors. Biology:** General. **Business:** Accounting, administrative services, business admin. **Computer sciences:** General. **Conservation:** General. **Education:** Early childhood, kindergarten/preschool. **Family/consumer sciences:** Food/nutrition. **Health:** Prenursing. **Legal studies:** Paralegal. **Liberal arts:** Arts/sciences. **Math:** General. **Public administration:** Human services. **Social sciences:** General. **Other:** Sustainable development.

**Computing on campus.** 65 workstations in library, computer center. Commuter students can connect to campus network. Online library, wireless network available.

**Student life. Freshman orientation:** Mandatory. Preregistration for classes offered. Held for 3 hours approximately 1 week prior to classes. **Activities:** Student government, Circle K, Young Democrats.

**Student services.** Adult student services, alcohol/substance abuse counseling, career counseling, services for economically disadvantaged, financial aid counseling, minority student services, personal counseling, veterans' counselor. **Physically disabled:** Services for visually, speech, hearing impaired. **Transfer:** Pre-admission transcript evaluation for new students. College fairs on campus for students transferring to 4-year colleges.

**Contact.** E-mail: cynthia@menominee.edu
Phone: (715) 799-5600 ext. 3053 Toll-free
number: (800) 567-2344 ext. 3053 Fax: (715) 799-4392
Cynthia Norton, Admissions Representative, College of Menominee Nation, N 172 State Highway 47/55, Keshena, WI 54135

## Fox Valley Technical College
Appleton, Wisconsin
www.fvtc.edu
CB member
CB code: 0747

- Public 2-year technical college
- Commuter campus in small city

**General.** Founded in 1967. Regionally accredited. **Enrollment:** 5,694 degree-seeking undergraduates; 1,936 non-degree-seeking students. **Degrees:** 816 associate awarded. **Location:** 100 miles from Milwaukee. **Calendar:** Semester, limited summer session. **Full-time faculty:** 302 total. **Part-time faculty:** 30 total.

**Student profile.** Among degree-seeking undergraduates, 942 enrolled as first-time, first-year students.

| Part-time: | 57% | Women: | 51% |
|---|---|---|---|
| Out-of-state: | 1% | 25 or older: | 25% |

**Basis for selection.** Open admission, but selective for some programs. Special requirements for nursing and criminal justice programs. ACT, ACCUPLACER, COMPASS required for placement.

**2007-2008 Annual costs.** Tuition/fees: $3,185; $17,540 out-of-state. Per-credit charge: $92 in-state; $571 out-of-state. Material fees vary by program; minimum $4 per course. $10 per credit fee for online courses. Books/supplies: $910. Personal expenses: $1,461.

**2006-2007 Financial aid. Need-based:** 44% of total undergraduate aid awarded as scholarships/grants, 56% as loans/jobs.

**Application procedures. Admission:** No deadline. $30 fee, may be waived for applicants with need. Application may be submitted online. Admission notification on a rolling basis. **Financial aid:** Priority date 3/1; no closing date. FAFSA required. Applicants notified on a rolling basis.

**Academics. Special study options:** Accelerated study, distance learning, double major, dual enrollment of high school students, ESL, internships, student-designed major. License preparation in aviation, dental hygiene, nursing, occupational therapy, paramedic, physical therapy. **Credit/placement by examination:** AP, CLEP, institutional tests. 45 credit hours maximum toward associate degree. **Support services:** GED preparation and test center, reduced course load, remedial instruction, tutoring.

**Majors. Agriculture:** Agribusiness operations, business, horticulture, supplies. **Business:** General, accounting, administrative services, banking/financial services, hospitality admin, hospitality/recreation, human resources, office technology, restaurant/food services, tourism promotion, training/development. **Communications technology:** Graphic/printing. **Computer sciences:** Applications programming, data processing, information systems. **Conservation:** General. **Construction:** General. **Engineering technology:** Drafting, electrical, mechanical drafting. **Family/consumer sciences:** Child care, institutional food production. **Health:** Dental hygiene, nursing (RN), occupational therapy assistant, substance abuse counseling. **Legal studies:** Legal secretary, paralegal. **Mechanic/repair:** Aircraft, aircraft powerplant, auto body, automotive, avionics. **Parks/recreation:** Facilities management. **Personal/culinary services:** Baking, chef training, culinary arts. **Protective services:** Criminal justice, fire safety technology, police science. **Public administration:** Human services. **Transportation:** Airline/commercial pilot. **Visual/performing arts:** Interior design.

**Computing on campus.** 260 workstations in library, computer center, student center. Online library, helpline, repair service, wireless network available.

**Student life. Freshman orientation:** Mandatory. Held on various dates 2 months prior to beginning of semester. **Activities:** Student government, student newspaper, 28 curriculum-related clubs.

**Athletics.** NJCAA. **Intercollegiate:** Basketball M. **Intramural:** Basketball, bowling, football (non-tackle), golf, soccer, softball, table tennis, volleyball. **Team name:** Fighting Foxes.

**Student services.** Adult student services, alcohol/substance abuse counseling, career counseling, services for economically disadvantaged, student employment services, financial aid counseling, health services, minority student services, on-campus daycare, personal counseling, placement for graduates, veterans' counselor, women's services. **Physically disabled:** Services for visually, speech, hearing impaired.

**Contact.** Phone: (920) 735-5645 Toll-free number: (800) 735-3882 Fax: (920) 735-2484
Melissa Kohlbeck, Associate Director, Enrollment Services, Fox Valley Technical College, 1825 North Bluemound Drive, Appleton, WI 54912-2277

---

## Gateway Technical College
### Kenosha, Wisconsin
### www.gtc.edu
CB member
CB code: 0761

♦ Public 2-year technical college
♦ Commuter campus in small city

**General.** Founded in 1911. Regionally accredited. Campuses at Burlington, Elkhorn, Kenosha and Racine. **Enrollment:** 5,442 degree-seeking undergraduates. **Degrees:** 331 associate awarded. **Location:** 30 miles from Milwaukee, 60 miles from Chicago. **Calendar:** Semester, limited summer session. **Full-time faculty:** 300 total. **Part-time faculty:** 100 total.

**Student profile.**

| | | | |
|---|---|---|---|
| Out-of-state: | 3% | 25 or older: | 60% |

**Basis for selection.** Open admission, but selective for some programs. GED or high school diploma required for some programs.

**High school preparation.** Chemistry and biology required for nursing program applicants.

**2007-2008 Annual costs.** Tuition/fees: $3,280; $17,635 out-of-state. Per-credit charge: $92 in-state; $571 out-of-state. Materials fees vary by program; minimum $4 per course. Books/supplies: $910. Personal expenses: $1,461.

**Financial aid. Need-based:** Need-based aid available for part-time students. Work-study available for part-time students. **Non-need-based:** Scholarships awarded for state residency.

**Application procedures. Admission:** No deadline. $30 fee. Application may be submitted online. Admission notification on a rolling basis. **Financial aid:** Priority date 7/1; no closing date. FAFSA, institutional form required. Applicants notified on a rolling basis starting 5/1; must reply within 2 week(s) of notification.

**Academics. Special study options:** Cross-registration, distance learning, dual enrollment of high school students, ESL, independent study, internships. License preparation in aviation, nursing, paramedic, physical therapy, radiology. **Credit/placement by examination:** CLEP, institutional tests. 48 credit hours maximum toward associate degree. Institutional biology and chemistry test required for nursing applicants. **Support services:** GED preparation and test center, learning center, remedial instruction, tutoring.

**Majors. Agriculture:** Horticulture. **Business:** Accounting, administrative services, hotel/motel admin, marketing, operations. **Communications technology:** Radio/tv. **Computer sciences:** Computer support specialist, networking, programming, webmaster. **Education:** Early childhood, teacher assistance. **Engineering technology:** Civil, electrical, electromechanical, heat/ac/refrig, manufacturing, mechanical, quality control, robotics. **English:** Technical writing. **Family/consumer sciences:** Child care. **Foreign languages:** Sign language interpretation. **Health:** Clinical lab technology, dental hygiene, medical radiologic technology/radiation therapy, medical records technology, nursing (RN), occupational therapy assistant, physical therapy assistant, respiratory therapy assistant, surgical technology. **Legal studies:** Court reporting. **Mechanic/repair:** Automotive, industrial. **Personal/culinary services:** Restaurant/catering. **Protective services:** Firefighting, police science. **Public administration:** Human services. **Science technology:** Biological. **Transportation:** Airline/commercial pilot. **Visual/performing arts:** Graphic design, interior design.

**Computing on campus.** 270 workstations in library, computer center. Wireless network available.

**Student life. Freshman orientation:** Available. Preregistration for classes offered. **Activities:** Radio station, student government, student newspaper,

wide variety of occupationally-oriented and community-related organizations available.

**Student services.** Adult student services, alcohol/substance abuse counseling, career counseling, student employment services, financial aid counseling, health services, minority student services, on-campus daycare, personal counseling, placement for graduates, veterans' counselor. **Physically disabled:** Services for visually, speech, hearing impaired. **Transfer:** Transfer adviser, college fairs on campus for students transferring to 4-year colleges.

**Contact.** E-mail: admissions@gtc.edu
Phone: (262) 564-2912 Toll-free number: (800) 353-3151 ext. 2912
Fax: (262) 564-2127
Susan Roberts, Director of Admissions, Gateway Technical College, 3520 30th Avenue, Kenosha, WI 53144-1690

---

## Lac Courte Oreilles Ojibwa Community College
### Hayward, Wisconsin
### www.lco.edu
CB code: 7351

♦ Public 2-year community college
♦ Commuter campus in small town

**General.** Regionally accredited. **Enrollment:** 576 degree-seeking undergraduates. **Degrees:** 78 associate awarded. **Calendar:** Semester, limited summer session. **Full-time faculty:** 20 total. **Part-time faculty:** 50 total.

**Student profile.** Among degree-seeking undergraduates, 147 enrolled as first-time, first-year students.

| | | | |
|---|---|---|---|
| Part-time: | 41% | Women: | 72% |

**Basis for selection.** Open admission. **Homeschooled:** State high school equivalency certificate required.

**2008-2009 Annual costs.** Tuition/fees: $4,075; $4,075 out-of-state. Per-credit charge: $135.

**Application procedures. Admission:** No deadline. $10 fee, may be waived for applicants with need. Application must be submitted on paper. Admission notification on a rolling basis. **Financial aid:** No deadline. FAFSA required. Applicants notified on a rolling basis.

**Academics. Special study options:** Cooperative education, distance learning, double major, independent study, liberal arts/career combination. **Credit/placement by examination:** AP, CLEP. **Support services:** GED test center, remedial instruction, study skills assistance, tutoring.

**Majors. Area/ethnic studies:** Native American. **Business:** Business admin, logistics, office management. **Computer sciences:** Systems analysis. **Health:** Medical assistant. **Liberal arts:** Arts/sciences. **Public administration:** Human services.

**Student life. Freshman orientation:** Available. Preregistration for classes offered.

**Student services.** Career counseling, financial aid counseling. **Transfer:** Transfer center, college fairs on campus for students transferring to 4-year colleges.

**Contact.** Phone: (715) 634-4790 ext. 104 Fax: (715) 634-5049
Lac Courte Oreilles Ojibwa Community College, 13466 West Trepania Road, Hayward, WI 54843

---

## Lakeshore Technical College
### Cleveland, Wisconsin
### www.gotoltc.edu
CB member
CB code: 0618

♦ Public 2-year technical college
♦ Commuter campus in rural community

**General.** Founded in 1912. Regionally accredited. **Enrollment:** 2,121 degree-seeking undergraduates; 606 non-degree-seeking students. **Degrees:** 309 associate awarded. **Location:** 15 miles from Sheboygan, 65 miles from Milwaukee. **Calendar:** Semester, limited summer session. **Full-time faculty:** 100 total. **Part-time faculty:** 300 total. **Special facilities:** Wind turbine, photovoltaic panels (solar), emergency operations center. **Partnerships:** Formal partnerships with Tech Prep with all public schools and employers in Manitowoc and Sheboygan counties.

**Student profile.** Among degree-seeking undergraduates, 3% already have a bachelor's degree or higher, 299 enrolled as first-time, first-year students.

| | | | |
|---|---|---|---|
| Part-time: | 67% | Hispanic American: | 2% |
| Out-of-state: | 1% | Native American: | 1% |
| Women: | 59% | 25 or older: | 55% |
| Asian American: | 3% | | |

**Transfer out. Colleges most students transferred to 2007:** Silver Lake College, Lakeland College.

**Basis for selection.** Open admission. All health-related, public safety and child care programs require background checks and physical examinations. International students whose first language is not English must have minimum 550 TOEFL. ASSET, COMPASS, ACCUPLACER are preferred placement exams, but will accept ACT/SAT. **Homeschooled:** State high school equivalency certificate required.

**2007-2008 Annual costs.** Tuition/fees: $2,895; $17,250 out-of-state. Per-credit charge: $92 in-state; $571 out-of-state. Materials fees vary by program; minimum $4 per course. $10 per credit fee for online courses. Books/supplies: $1,050. Personal expenses: $1,625.

**Financial aid.** All financial aid based on need. Need-based aid available for part-time students. Work-study available nights and for part-time students.

**Application procedures. Admission:** No deadline. $30 fee, may be waived for applicants with need. Application may be submitted online. Admission notification on a rolling basis. **Financial aid:** Priority date 6/1; no closing date. FAFSA, institutional form required. Applicants notified on a rolling basis starting 6/1; must reply within 3 week(s) of notification.

**Academics. Special study options:** Accelerated study, combined bachelor's/graduate degree, cross-registration, distance learning, double major, dual enrollment of high school students, ESL, honors, independent study, internships, student-designed major. License preparation in nursing, paramedic, real estate. **Credit/placement by examination:** AP, CLEP, institutional tests. **Support services:** GED preparation and test center, learning center, pre-admission summer program, reduced course load, remedial instruction, study skills assistance, tutoring.

**Majors. Business:** Accounting, administrative services, business admin, hospitality admin, logistics, marketing, office technology, operations, training/development, warehousing. **Communications technology:** Desktop publishing. **Computer sciences:** Networking, webmaster. **Education:** Early childhood. **Engineering technology:** Drafting, electromechanical, hazardous materials, mechanical drafting, quality control. **Health:** Clinical lab technology, EMT paramedic, medical radiologic technology/radiation therapy, medical secretary, nursing (RN). **Legal studies:** Court reporting, paralegal. **Protective services:** Police science. **Science technology:** Nuclear power. **Other:** Broadcast captioning, Computer support specialist, Wind energy technology.

**Most popular majors.** Business/marketing 33%, computer/information sciences 6%, education 7%, engineering/engineering technologies 9%, health sciences 20%, interdisciplinary studies 9%, legal studies 7%, security/protective services 6%.

**Computing on campus.** 950 workstations in library, computer center, student center. Online course registration, online library, helpline, wireless network available.

**Student life. Freshman orientation:** Available. Preregistration for classes offered. **Activities:** Student government, student newspaper.

**Athletics. Intramural:** Basketball, football (non-tackle), volleyball.

**Student services.** Adult student services, alcohol/substance abuse counseling, career counseling, services for economically disadvantaged, student employment services, financial aid counseling, health services, minority student services, on-campus daycare, personal counseling, placement for graduates. **Physically disabled:** Services for visually, speech, hearing impaired. **Transfer:** Re-entry adviser, pre-admission transcript evaluation for new students. Transfer adviser, college fairs on campus for students transferring to 4-year colleges.

**Contact.** E-mail: enroll@gotoltc.edu
Phone: (920) 693-1000 Toll-free number: (888) 468-6582
Fax: (920) 693-3561
Scott Lieburn, Manager Student Services, Lakeshore Technical College, 1290 North Avenue, Cleveland, WI 53015-9761

---

# Madison Area Technical College
## Madison, Wisconsin
### www.madison.tec.wi.us
CB code: 1536

- Public 2-year community and technical college
- Commuter campus in small city

**General.** Founded in 1912. Regionally accredited. Campuses in Fort Atkinson, Portage, Reedsburg, and Watertown. **Enrollment:** 14,647 degree-seeking undergraduates. **Degrees:** 1,280 associate awarded. **Calendar:** Semester, limited summer session. **Full-time faculty:** 400 total. **Part-time faculty:** 1,100 total. **Special facilities:** Satellite downlink.

**Student profile.**

| | | | |
|---|---|---|---|
| Out-of-state: | 2% | 25 or older: | 10% |

**Basis for selection.** Open admission, but selective for some programs. School achievement record, class rank, test scores considered for all health occupation programs. SAT or ACT (ACT preferred) required of health occupation applicants only.

**High school preparation.** High school academic subject requirements for health and technical programs.

**2007-2008 Annual costs.** Tuition/fees: $2,921; $17,366 out-of-state. Per-credit charge: $92 in-state; $571 out-of-state. Material fees vary by program; minimum $4 per course. $10 per credit fee for online courses. Books/supplies: $760. Personal expenses: $1,340.

**2006-2007 Financial aid. Need-based:** 55% of total undergraduate aid awarded as scholarships/grants, 45% as loans/jobs.

**Application procedures. Admission:** Priority date 11/20; no deadline. $30 fee, may be waived for applicants with need. Admission notification on a rolling basis. Early application recommended for programs with limited enrollment. **Financial aid:** Priority date 4/15; no closing date. FAFSA required. Applicants notified on a rolling basis starting 4/15.

**Academics.** Technical College offering a college transfer program, advanced technical certificates, apprenticeships, English as a second language, adult continuing education and basic skills education. **Special study options:** Accelerated study, cross-registration, distance learning, dual enrollment of high school students, ESL, external degree, internships. Bachelor's degree programs available on campus. License preparation in nursing. **Credit/placement by examination:** CLEP, institutional tests. 32 credit hours maximum toward associate degree. **Support services:** GED preparation, learning center, reduced course load, remedial instruction, study skills assistance, tutoring.

**Majors. Agriculture:** General, animal sciences, horticulture. **Business:** Accounting, administrative services, business admin, communications, fashion, finance, hospitality admin, hospitality/recreation, insurance, office management, real estate, tourism/travel. **Communications technology:** Graphic/printing. **Computer sciences:** General, programming. **Engineering technology:** Architectural, civil. **Family/consumer sciences:** Child care, food/nutrition. **Health:** Clinical lab technology, dental hygiene, EMT paramedic, medical assistant, medical radiologic technology/radiation therapy, medical records admin, medical secretary, mental health services, nursing (RN), occupational therapy assistant, respiratory therapy technology, veterinary technology/assistant. **Interdisciplinary:** Biological/physical sciences. **Legal studies:** Court reporting. **Liberal arts:** Arts/sciences. **Mechanic/repair:** Electronics/electrical. **Personal/culinary services:** Cosmetic, culinary arts. **Protective services:** Police science. **Science technology:** Biological. **Visual/performing arts:** Commercial photography, commercial/advertising art, design, interior design.

**Most popular majors.** Business/marketing 28%, computer/information sciences 7%, family/consumer sciences 6%, health sciences 19%, trade and industry 12%, visual/performing arts 7%.

**Computing on campus.** 470 workstations in library, computer center.

**Student life. Freshman orientation:** Available. **Policies:** Student life department promotes a variety of cultural diversity and activities and plays an active role in student government activities. **Activities:** Jazz band, choral groups, drama, music ensembles, student government, student newspaper.

**Athletics.** NJCAA. **Intercollegiate:** Baseball M, basketball, bowling, cross-country M, golf M, softball W, volleyball W, wrestling M. **Intramural:** Basketball, racquetball, soccer, swimming, table tennis, tennis, volleyball. **Team name:** Wolf Pack.

**Student services.** Career counseling, student employment services, health services, on-campus daycare, personal counseling, placement for graduates, veterans' counselor. **Physically disabled:** Services for visually, speech, hearing impaired. **Transfer:** Transfer adviser for students transferring to 4-year colleges.

**Contact.** Phone: (608) 246-6205 Fax: (608) 258-2329
Jennifer Hoege, Admissions Administrator, Madison Area Technical College, 3350 Anderson Street, Madison, WI 53704-2599

## Madison Media Institute
**Madison, Wisconsin**
**www.madisonmedia.edu**

- For-profit 2-year visual arts and music college
- Large city
- Application essay, interview required

**General.** Accredited by ACCSCT. **Enrollment:** 355 degree-seeking undergraduates. **Degrees:** 136 associate awarded. **Calendar:** Trimester, extensive summer session. **Full-time faculty:** 15 total. **Part-time faculty:** 10 total.

**Basis for selection.** Open admission.

**Application procedures. Admission:** No deadline. $30 fee. Application may be submitted online. Admission notification on a rolling basis. **Financial aid:** No deadline.

**Academics. Special study options:** Accelerated study, internships. **Credit/placement by examination:** CLEP. **Support services:** Tutoring.

**Majors. Communications:** Digital media. **Communications technology:** Animation/special effects, recording arts.

**Computing on campus.** 150 workstations in computer center.

**Student life. Freshman orientation:** Available. Preregistration for classes offered.

**Student services. Transfer:** Re-entry adviser, pre-admission transcript evaluation for new students. Transfer adviser for students transferring to 4-year colleges.

**Contact.** E-mail: mmi@madisonmedia.com
Phone: (800) 236-4997 Toll-free number: (800) 236-4997
Steve Hutchings, Director of Admissions, Madison Media Institute, 2702 Agriculture Drive, Madison, WI 53718

## Mid-State Technical College
**Wisconsin Rapids, Wisconsin**    **CB member**
**www.mstc.edu**    **CB code: 0635**

- Public 2-year technical college
- Commuter campus in large town

**General.** Founded in 1967. Regionally accredited. Branch campuses in Marshfield and Stevens Point, outreach center in Adams. **Enrollment:** 2,960 undergraduates. **Degrees:** 350 associate awarded. **Location:** 20 miles from Stevens Point, 115 miles from Madison. **Calendar:** Semester, limited summer session. **Full-time faculty:** 95 total.

**Student profile.**

| | | | |
|---|---|---|---|
| Out-of-state: | 1% | 25 or older: | 15% |

**Basis for selection.** Open admission, but selective for some programs. Students must take Accuplacer entrance exam. Certain programs have additional admission requirements. Accuplacer required for placement. ACT, SAT, ASSET scores accepted for placement if submitted. **Homeschooled:** Proof of completion of 12th grade is required.

**High school preparation.** Biology, anatomy, physiology, chemistry, medical terminology recommended for health programs. Information processing, general business, business law, economics, accounting recommended for business programs. Geometry, drafting, chemistry, advanced math recommended for technical and industrial programs.

**2007-2008 Annual costs.** Tuition/fees: $3,056; $17,411 out-of-state. Per-credit charge: $92 in-state; $571 out-of-state. Material fees vary by program; minimum $4 per course. Books/supplies: $986. Personal expenses: $1,500.

**Financial aid. Need-based:** Need-based aid available for part-time students. Work-study available nights, weekends and for part-time students. **Non-need-based:** Scholarships awarded for academics, leadership.

**Application procedures. Admission:** No deadline. $30 fee, may be waived for applicants with need. Application may be submitted online. Admission notification on a rolling basis. **Financial aid:** No deadline. FAFSA required. Applicants notified on a rolling basis starting 5/30; must reply within 2 week(s) of notification.

**Academics. Special study options:** Accelerated study, cooperative education, distance learning, double major, dual enrollment of high school students, ESL, independent study, internships. License preparation in nursing, paramedic. **Credit/placement by examination:** AP, CLEP, institutional tests. 32 credit hours maximum toward associate degree. **Support services:** GED preparation and test center, learning center, reduced course load, remedial instruction, study skills assistance, tutoring.

**Majors. Business:** Accounting, administrative services, business admin, human resources, marketing, office management, office/clerical. **Computer sciences:** LAN/WAN management, networking, programming, web page design. **Conservation:** Urban forestry. **Education:** Early childhood. **Engineering technology:** Civil, computer systems, electrical, industrial, instrumentation, manufacturing. **Health:** EMT paramedic, nursing (RN), respiratory therapy assistant, respiratory therapy technology. **Mechanic/repair:** Electronics/electrical. **Protective services:** Corrections, firefighting, police science. **Other:** Paper & Chemical Technology.

**Computing on campus.** 600 workstations in library, computer center, student center. Online course registration, online library, helpline available.

**Student life. Freshman orientation:** Available. **Activities:** Student government, student newspaper, animation/video game club, Association for Information Technology Professionals, Campus Crusade for Christ, civil technology club, criminal justice-corrections club, cosmetology & barbering club, electronics club, Law Enforcement Organization, Student Nurses' association, student senate, Student Society of Arborists.

**Athletics.** NJCAA. **Intercollegiate:** Basketball, volleyball W. **Team name:** Cougars.

**Student services.** Adult student services, alcohol/substance abuse counseling, career counseling, services for economically disadvantaged, student employment services, financial aid counseling, minority student services, personal counseling, placement for graduates, veterans' counselor, women's services. **Physically disabled:** Services for visually, speech, hearing impaired. **Learning disabled:** Comprehensive services available. **Transfer:** Pre-admission transcript evaluation for new students. Transfer adviser, college fairs on campus for students transferring to 4-year colleges.

**Contact.** Phone: (715) 422-5444 Toll-free number: (888) 575-6782
Fax: (715) 422-5440
Jim Barrett, Director of Admissions, Mid-State Technical College, 500 32nd Street North, Wisconsin Rapids, WI 54494

## Milwaukee Area Technical College
**Milwaukee, Wisconsin**    **CB member**
**www.matc.edu**    **CB code: 1475**

- Public 2-year junior and technical college
- Commuter campus in very large city

**General.** Founded in 1912. Regionally accredited. Campuses in Milwaukee, Oak Creek, Mequon, and West Allis. **Enrollment:** 14,482 degree-seeking undergraduates; 2,711 non-degree-seeking students. **Degrees:** 1,272 associate awarded. **Location:** 85 miles from Chicago. **Calendar:** Semester, limited summer session. **Full-time faculty:** 588 total; 9% have terminal degrees, 27% minority, 49% women. **Part-time faculty:** 768 total; 4% have terminal degrees, 19% minority, 51% women. **Class size:** 81% < 20, 19% 20-39.

**Student profile.** Among degree-seeking undergraduates, 14% enrolled in a transfer program, 86% enrolled in a vocational program, 10% already have a bachelor's degree or higher, 1,771 enrolled as first-time, first-year students, 310 transferred in from other institutions.

| | | | |
|---|---|---|---|
| Part-time: | 65% | Asian American: | 4% |
| Out-of-state: | 1% | Hispanic American: | 9% |
| Women: | 59% | Native American: | 1% |
| African American: | 25% | 25 or older: | 54% |

**Transfer out.** 25% of students enrolled in the transfer program go on to 4-year colleges. **Colleges most students transferred to 2007:** University of Wisconsin-Milwaukee, Waukesha County Technical College, Cardinal Stritch University, Gateway Technical College, Alverno College.

**Basis for selection.** Open admission, but selective for some programs and for out-of-state students. Special requirements for health programs. ACCUPLACER required for placement. Institutionally administered reading, math, and English examinations required for all applicants if SAT or ACT not taken. **Homeschooled:** Must complete ACCUPLACER testing.

**High school preparation.** Specific subject requirements for some programs.

**2007-2008 Annual costs.** Tuition/fees: $2,954; $17,399 out-of-state. Per-credit charge: $92 in-state; $571 out-of-state. Material fees vary by program; minimum $4 per course. $10 per credit fee for online courses. Books/supplies: $1,000.

**Financial aid. Need-based:** Need-based aid available for part-time students. Work-study available for part-time students. **Non-need-based:** Scholarships awarded for academics.

**Application procedures. Admission:** Closing date 8/19 (postmark date). $30 fee. Application may be submitted online. Admission notification on a rolling basis. **Financial aid:** Priority date 3/15; no closing date. FAFSA required. Applicants notified on a rolling basis starting 4/15.

**Academics. Special study options:** Accelerated study, cooperative education, distance learning, double major, dual enrollment of high school students, ESL, honors, independent study, internships, liberal arts/career combination, weekend college. Teacher education program with guaranteed admission to University of Wisconsin-Milwaukee. License preparation in aviation, dental hygiene, nursing. **Credit/placement by examination:** AP, CLEP, institutional tests. **Support services:** GED preparation and test center, learning center, reduced course load, remedial instruction, study skills assistance, tutoring, writing center.

**Majors. Agriculture:** Landscaping. **Business:** Accounting, administrative services, apparel, banking/financial services, business admin, e-commerce, hotel/motel admin, international marketing, logistics, marketing, operations, real estate, tourism/travel. **Communications technology:** Graphic/printing, graphics, radio/tv. **Computer sciences:** Computer graphics, networking, programming, security, systems analysis. **Engineering:** Materials. **Engineering technology:** Architectural, biomedical, civil, computer systems, electrical, heat/ac/refrig, industrial, mechanical drafting, plastics, water quality. **Foreign languages:** Sign language interpretation. **Health:** Anesthesiologist assistant, cardiovascular technology, clinical lab technology, dental hygiene, dietetic technician, electroencephalograph technology, medical radiologic technology/radiation therapy, medical records technology, medical secretary, nursing (RN), occupational therapy assistant, physical therapy assistant, respiratory therapy technology, surgical technology. **Legal studies:** Legal secretary, paralegal. **Liberal arts:** Arts/sciences. **Mechanic/repair:** Automotive. **Personal/culinary services:** Mortuary science, restaurant/catering. **Production:** Welding. **Protective services:** Firefighting, police science. **Science technology:** Chemical. **Visual/performing arts:** Commercial photography, graphic design, interior design, music performance. **Other:** Computer support specialist.

**Most popular majors.** Business/marketing 17%, computer/information sciences 7%, engineering/engineering technologies 6%, health sciences 32%, liberal arts 7%, security/protective services 8%.

**Computing on campus.** 275 workstations in library, computer center, student center. Online course registration, online library, helpline, wireless network available.

**Student life. Freshman orientation:** Mandatory. **Housing:** Certified housing available at nearby colleges and other facilities. **Activities:** Literary magazine, student government, student newspaper, TV station, student senate, student life committee, African American student club, American Culinary Federation, architectural technology club, Association of Information Technology Professionals, campus bible fellowship, criminal justice student organization, environmental club, Phi Theta Kappa Honor Society, paralegal association.

**Athletics.** NJCAA. **Intercollegiate:** Baseball M, basketball M, golf, soccer M, softball W, volleyball W. **Intramural:** Basketball, table tennis, volleyball. **Team name:** Lakestormers.

**Student services.** Alcohol/substance abuse counseling, career counseling, services for economically disadvantaged, student employment services, financial aid counseling, health services, legal services, minority student services, on-campus daycare, personal counseling, placement for graduates, veterans' counselor, women's services. **Physically disabled:** Services for visually, speech, hearing impaired. **Learning disabled:** Comprehensive services available. **Transfer:** Transfer center, transfer adviser, college fairs on campus for students transferring to 4-year colleges.

**Contact.** E-mail: bullockr@matc.edu
Phone: (414) 297-6370 Fax: (414) 297-7800
Robert Bullock, Director, Admissions and Testing, Milwaukee Area Technical College, 700 West State Street, Milwaukee, WI 53233-1443

## Moraine Park Technical College
Fond du Lac, Wisconsin
www.morainepark.edu
CB code: 0667

- Public 2-year technical college
- Commuter campus in large town
- Interview required

**General.** Founded in 1967. Regionally accredited. Campus locations in Beaver Dam and West Bend. **Enrollment:** 4,000 degree-seeking undergraduates. **Degrees:** 443 associate awarded. **Location:** 60 miles from Milwaukee. **Calendar:** Semester, limited summer session. **Full-time faculty:** 145 total. **Part-time faculty:** 200 total.

**Student profile.** Among degree-seeking undergraduates, 100% enrolled in a vocational program.

**Basis for selection.** Open admission, but selective for some programs. Students without high school diploma may be admitted to certain job-entry preparation programs. ACT required of associate-degree-seeking nursing applicants.

**High school preparation.** 16 units recommended. Recommended units include English 3, mathematics 2, social studies 2 and science 2.

**2007-2008 Annual costs.** Tuition/fees: $2,803; $17,248 out-of-state. Per-credit charge: $92 in-state; $571 out-of-state. Material fees vary by program; minimum $4 per course. $10 per credit fee for online courses. Books/supplies: $900.

**Financial aid. Need-based:** Need-based aid available for part-time students. Work-study available nights and for part-time students. **Non-need-based:** Scholarships awarded for academics, job skills, leadership, minority status, state residency.

**Application procedures. Admission:** No deadline. $30 fee, may be waived for applicants with need. Application may be submitted online. Admission notification on a rolling basis. Some programs may have application windows. Please check with admissions department or on the admissions Web page. Limited enrollment health care programs have varying application deadlines. **Financial aid:** Priority date 5/1; no closing date. FAFSA, institutional form required. Applicants notified on a rolling basis starting 6/15; must reply within 2 week(s) of notification.

**Academics. Special study options:** Accelerated study, distance learning, double major, dual enrollment of high school students, ESL, independent study, internships, weekend college. **Credit/placement by examination:** CLEP, institutional tests. 30 credit hours maximum toward associate degree. **Support services:** GED preparation and test center, learning center, preadmission summer program, reduced course load, remedial instruction, tutoring.

**Majors. Business:** Accounting, administrative services, marketing, office management, office technology, sales/distribution. **Communications technology:** Graphic/printing. **Computer sciences:** Applications programming, data processing. **Engineering technology:** Civil, drafting. **Family/consumer sciences:** Child care, family studies. **Health:** EMT paramedic, health services, medical records technology, medical secretary, nursing (RN), substance abuse counseling. **Legal studies:** Legal secretary. **Mechanic/repair:** Electronics/electrical, heating/ac/refrig. **Personal/culinary services:** Culinary arts. **Protective services:** Corrections, fire safety technology, police science.

**Most popular majors.** Business/marketing 24%, computer/information sciences 9%, engineering/engineering technologies 12%, health sciences 26%, trade and industry 9%.

**Student life. Freshman orientation:** Mandatory. **Activities:** Student government.

**Student services.** Career counseling, student employment services, health services, on-campus daycare, personal counseling, placement for graduates, veterans' counselor. **Physically disabled:** Services for visually, hearing impaired. **Transfer:** College fairs on campus for students transferring to 4-year colleges.

**Contact.** Phone: (920) 924-3408 Toll-free number: (800) 472-4554
Fax: (920) 924-3421
Richard Barnhouse, Admissions Director, Moraine Park Technical College, 235 North National Avenue, Fond du Lac, WI 54935-1940

## Nicolet Area Technical College
### Rhinelander, Wisconsin
www.nicoletcollege.edu     CB code: 0713

- Public 2-year community and technical college
- Commuter campus in small town
- Interview required

**General.** Founded in 1967. Regionally accredited. Lakeland branch campus in Minocqua. **Enrollment:** 1,100 degree-seeking undergraduates. **Degrees:** 158 associate awarded. **Location:** 225 miles from Milwaukee, 200 miles from Madison. **Calendar:** Semester, limited summer session. **Full-time faculty:** 59 total. **Part-time faculty:** 134 total. **Class size:** 74% < 20, 26% 20-39. **Special facilities:** Theater, sustainable energy initiative including wind turbine, solar powered day care center, alternative energy demonstration sites; walking trail; canoe/kayak rental.

**Student profile.**

| | | | |
|---|---|---|---|
| Out-of-state: | 1% | 25 or older: | 52% |

**Transfer out. Colleges most students transferred to 2007:** UW Stevens Point, UW Eau Claire, UW Madison, UW Wisconsin-Oshkosh.

**Basis for selection.** Open admission, but selective for some programs. ACCUPLACER scores determine admission to programs at associate degree and transfer levels. ACT and high school grades used in some cases. Conditional admission to degree programs for students who receive lower ACCUPLACER scores than required by programs. Refresher course must be taken. ACCUPLACER and ACT test scores used for admission into degree programs, not the college. **Homeschooled:** Federal ability to benefit criteria is used for non-high school grads.

**High school preparation.** Recommended units include English 4, mathematics 3, social studies 3 and science 3.

**2007-2008 Annual costs.** Tuition/fees: $2,873; $17,228 out-of-state. Per-credit charge: $92 in-state; $571 out-of-state. Material fees vary by program; minimum $4 per course. $10 per credit fee for online courses. Books/supplies: $760. Personal expenses: $1,249.

**Financial aid. Need-based:** Work-study available nights, weekends and for part-time students.

**Application procedures. Admission:** $30 fee, may be waived for applicants with need. Application may be submitted online. Admission notification on a rolling basis beginning on or about 9/1. **Financial aid:** Priority date 4/15; no closing date. FAFSA, institutional form required. Applicants notified on a rolling basis starting 6/1; must reply within 2 week(s) of notification.

**Academics. Special study options:** Accelerated study, distance learning, double major, dual enrollment of high school students, ESL, independent study, internships, liberal arts/career combination, student-designed major. Bachelor's degree programs available on campus. License preparation in nursing, radiology, real estate. **Credit/placement by examination:** AP, CLEP, ACT, institutional tests. 44 credit hours maximum toward associate degree. **Support services:** GED preparation and test center, learning center, reduced course load, remedial instruction, study skills assistance, tutoring.

**Majors. Business:** Accounting, administrative services, business admin. **Communications technology:** Graphics. **Computer sciences:** General, computer graphics, computer science, data processing, information technology, LAN/WAN management, networking, programming, web page design, webmaster. **Education:** Early childhood. **Engineering technology:** Surveying. **Family/consumer sciences:** Child care. **Health:** Nursing (RN), radiologic technology/medical imaging, surgical technology. **Liberal arts:** Arts/sciences. **Personal/culinary services:** Culinary arts. **Protective services:** Police science. **Visual/performing arts:** Graphic design.

**Most popular majors.** Business/marketing 28%, computer/information sciences 15%, education 8%, engineering/engineering technologies 7%, health sciences 14%, liberal arts 12%, security/protective services 9%.

**Computing on campus.** 80 workstations in library, computer center. Commuter students can connect to campus network. Online course registration, online library, helpline, wireless network available.

**Student life. Freshman orientation:** Mandatory. Held 2 days before start of classes for a half day. Optional evening session. **Activities:** Drama, musical theater, student government, Business Professionals of America, Phi Theta Kappa, Peace Coalition, Campus Crusade for Christ, Junior Chapter of American Culinary Federation, SAGED.

**Student services.** Adult student services, alcohol/substance abuse counseling, career counseling, services for economically disadvantaged, student employment services, financial aid counseling, minority student services, on-campus daycare, personal counseling, placement for graduates, veterans' counselor, women's services. **Physically disabled:** Services for visually, speech, hearing impaired. **Learning disabled:** Comprehensive services available. **Transfer:** Pre-admission transcript evaluation for new students. Transfer center, transfer adviser, college fairs on campus for students transferring to 4-year colleges.

**Contact.** E-mail: inquire@nicoletcollege.edu
Phone: (715) 365-4451 Toll-free number: (800) 544-3039
Fax: (715) 365-4901
Susan Kordula, Director of Enrollment Management, Nicolet Area Technical College, Box 518, Rhinelander, WI 54501

## Northcentral Technical College
### Wausau, Wisconsin
www.ntc.edu     CB code: 0735

- Public 2-year community and technical college
- Commuter campus in small city

**General.** Founded in 1911. Regionally accredited. Regional campuses located in Antigo, Medford, Phillips, Wittenberg and Spencer. Public safety training center in Merrill. **Enrollment:** 2,634 degree-seeking undergraduates; 1,095 non-degree-seeking students. **Degrees:** 446 associate awarded. **Location:** 200 miles from Milwaukee and Minneapolis-St. Paul, 150 miles from Madison. **Calendar:** Semester, limited summer session. **Full-time faculty:** 151 total. **Part-time faculty:** 8 total.

**Student profile.** Among degree-seeking undergraduates, 100% enrolled in a vocational program, 699 enrolled as first-time, first-year students.

| | | | |
|---|---|---|---|
| Part-time: | 55% | Asian American: | 4% |
| Women: | 59% | Hispanic American: | 1% |
| African American: | 1% | Native American: | 1% |

**Basis for selection.** Open admission, but selective for some programs. Special requirements for health programs including application portfolio. Accuplacer or ACT required for placement. **Homeschooled:** Transcript of courses and grades required.

**High school preparation.** 3 units each of math and science required for the following programs: radiography, nursing, dental hygiene. Math emphasis for technical programs, chemistry for nursing.

**2007-2008 Annual costs.** Tuition/fees: $2,912; $17,267 out-of-state. Per-credit charge: $92 in-state; $571 out-of-state. Materials fees vary by program; minimum $4 per course.

**Financial aid. Need-based:** Need-based aid available for part-time students. Work-study available nights and for part-time students.

**Application procedures. Admission:** No deadline. $30 fee, may be waived for applicants with need. Application may be submitted online. Admission notification on a rolling basis. **Financial aid:** No deadline. FAFSA required. Applicants notified on a rolling basis.

**Academics. Special study options:** Accelerated study, distance learning, double major, dual enrollment of high school students, ESL, internships, student-designed major, weekend college. Bachelor's degree programs available on campus. License preparation in dental hygiene, nursing, paramedic, radiology. **Credit/placement by examination:** AP, CLEP, IB, institutional tests. 24 credit hours maximum toward associate degree. **Support services:** GED preparation and test center, learning center, pre-admission summer program, reduced course load, remedial instruction, study skills assistance, tutoring, writing center.

**Majors. Architecture:** Technology. **Business:** Accounting, administrative services, business admin, entrepreneurial studies, office technology, operations. **Communications technology:** Graphic/printing. **Computer sciences:** Computer support specialist, programming, systems analysis. **Construction:** General. **Engineering:** Electrical, mechanics. **Engineering technology:** Drafting, electrical. **Foreign languages:** Sign language interpretation. **Health:** Clinical lab assistant, clinical lab technology, dental hygiene, medical radiologic technology/radiation therapy, medical records technology, medical secretary, nursing (RN), radiologic technology/medical imaging, sonography, surgical technology. **Legal studies:** Legal secretary. **Mechanic/repair:** Auto body, automotive. **Production:** Machine tool, welding. **Protective services:** Police science.

**Computing on campus.** 1,200 workstations in library, computer center, student center. Commuter students can connect to campus network. Online course registration, online library, helpline, repair service, wireless network available.

**Student life. Freshman orientation:** Available. Preregistration for classes offered. **Housing:** Coed dorms available. **Activities:** Radio station, student government, student newspaper, Campus Crusade for Christ, international student club, multicultural student club.

**Athletics. Intramural:** Basketball, football (non-tackle), softball, volleyball. **Team name:** Timberwolves.

**Student services.** Adult student services, career counseling, services for economically disadvantaged, student employment services, financial aid counseling, health services, minority student services, on-campus daycare, personal counseling, placement for graduates. **Physically disabled:** Services for visually, speech, hearing impaired. **Transfer:** Pre-admission transcript evaluation for new students. Transfer adviser, college fairs on campus for students transferring to 4-year colleges.

**Contact.** E-mail: admissions@ntc.edu
Phone: (715) 675-3331 ext. 4482 Toll-free number: (888) 682-7144
Fax: (715) 675-0629
Erin McNally, Director of Admissions, Northcentral Technical College, 1000 West Campus Drive, Wausau, WI 54401

## Northeast Wisconsin Technical College
**Green Bay, Wisconsin**
**www.nwtc.edu**                    **CB code: 4190**

- Public 2-year community and technical college
- Commuter campus in small city

**General.** Founded in 1913. Regionally accredited. **Enrollment:** 5,853 degree-seeking undergraduates; 5,630 non-degree-seeking students. **Degrees:** 770 associate awarded. **Location:** 129 miles from Milwaukee, 150 miles from Madison. **Calendar:** Semester, limited summer session. **Full-time faculty:** 240 total. **Part-time faculty:** 700 total.

**Student profile.** Among degree-seeking undergraduates, 1,478 enrolled as first-time, first-year students.

| | | | |
|---|---|---|---|
| Part-time: | 57% | Hispanic American: | 2% |
| Women: | 62% | Native American: | 3% |
| African American: | 1% | 25 or older: | 15% |
| Asian American: | 2% | | |

**Transfer out. Colleges most students transferred to 2007:** University of Wisconsin-Green Bay, University of Wisconsin-Oshkosh.

**Basis for selection.** Open admission, but selective for some programs. Special requirements for health programs. ACCUPLACER required unless applicant has minimum ACT, SAT, ASSET, or COMPASS score or previously earned bachelor's or associate degree from Wisconsin technical college. **Homeschooled:** State high school equivalency certificate required.

**2007-2008 Annual costs.** Tuition/fees: $2,962; $17,407 out-of-state. Per-credit charge: $92 in-state; $571 out-of-state. Material fees vary by program; minimum $4 per course. Books/supplies: $1,020. Personal expenses: $1,758.

**2006-2007 Financial aid. Need-based:** 57% of total undergraduate aid awarded as scholarships/grants, 43% as loans/jobs. Need-based aid available for part-time students. Work-study available nights and for part-time students.

**Application procedures. Admission:** Closing date 8/31 (receipt date). $30 fee, may be waived for applicants with need. Application may be submitted online. Admission notification on a rolling basis beginning on or about 9/4. **Financial aid:** Priority date 4/1; no closing date. FAFSA required. Applicants notified on a rolling basis starting 5/1; must reply within 2 week(s) of notification.

**Academics. Special study options:** Accelerated study, distance learning, double major, ESL, honors, independent study, internships, liberal arts/career combination. License preparation in dental hygiene, nursing, paramedic, physical therapy, radiology, real estate. **Credit/placement by examination:** AP, CLEP, institutional tests. 48 credit hours maximum toward associate degree. **Support services:** GED preparation and test center, learning center, reduced course load, remedial instruction, study skills assistance, tutoring.

**Majors. Agriculture:** Business, farm/ranch, food science. **Business:** General, accounting, administrative services, business admin, hospitality/recreation, logistics, office management, office technology, sales/distribution, tourism/travel. **Computer sciences:** General, data processing, networking, programming. **Engineering:** Civil. **Engineering technology:** Architectural, civil, drafting, electrical, industrial management. **Health:** Dental hygiene, health care admin, medical records admin, medical secretary,

nursing (RN), physical therapy assistant, respiratory therapy technology. **Legal studies:** Paralegal. **Mechanic/repair:** Heating/ac/refrig, industrial. **Protective services:** Fire safety technology, police science. **Transportation:** General.

**Most popular majors.** Business/marketing 27%, computer/information sciences 7%, engineering/engineering technologies 14%, health sciences 27%, trade and industry 7%.

**Computing on campus.** Online course registration, online library, helpline, wireless network available.

**Student life. Freshman orientation:** Available. Preregistration for classes offered. 2-hour program in conjunction with registration. **Activities:** Student government, Asian American student association, African American student association, Native American student association, Hispanic student association, Students Taking Responsibility in Drug Education, Phi Theta Kappa International Honor Society.

**Athletics. Intramural:** Basketball, football (non-tackle), volleyball.

**Student services.** Adult student services, alcohol/substance abuse counseling, career counseling, services for economically disadvantaged, student employment services, health services, minority student services, personal counseling, placement for graduates, veterans' counselor. **Physically disabled:** Services for visually, speech, hearing impaired. **Transfer:** Re-entry adviser for new students.

**Contact.** Phone: (920) 498-5444 Toll-free number: (800) 422-6982 ext. 5444 Fax: (920) 498-6882
Christine Lemerande, Program Enrollment Supervisor, Northeast Wisconsin Technical College, 2740 West Mason Street, Green Bay, WI 54307-9042

## Southwest Wisconsin Technical College
**Fennimore, Wisconsin**
**www.swtc.edu**                    **CB code: 0900**

- Public 2-year technical college
- Commuter campus in rural community
- Interview required

**General.** Founded in 1967. Regionally accredited. **Enrollment:** 1,457 degree-seeking undergraduates. **Degrees:** 212 associate awarded. **Location:** 75 miles from Madison, 38 miles from Dubuque, Iowa. **Calendar:** Semester, limited summer session. **Full-time faculty:** 90 total. **Part-time faculty:** 18 total.

**Student profile.**

| | | | |
|---|---|---|---|
| Out-of-state: | 1% | Live on campus: | 1% |
| 25 or older: | 71% | | |

**Basis for selection.** Interview and Test of Adult Basic Education required for admission. Secondary school record not considered. Students may have admissions requirements based on admission test scores. Psychological Services Bureau Test required for nursing RN applicants, C-NET test required for LPN applicants.

**2007-2008 Annual costs.** Tuition/fees: $2,872; $17,227 out-of-state. Per-credit charge: $92 in-state; $571 out-of-state. Materials fees vary by program; minimum $4 per course. $10 per credit fee for online courses. Books/supplies: $760. Personal expenses: $1,248.

**Financial aid. Need-based:** Work-study available nights and for part-time students.

**Application procedures. Admission:** No deadline. $30 fee. Admission notification on a rolling basis beginning on or about 9/1. Students notified of admission before July 1 must pay tuition deposit of $100 by July 1; students applying after that date must pay deposit as part of application process. **Financial aid:** Priority date 4/15; no closing date. FAFSA, institutional form required. Applicants notified on a rolling basis starting 5/15; must reply within 4 week(s) of notification.

**Academics. Special study options:** Accelerated study, distance learning, double major, dual enrollment of high school students, ESL, internships, student-designed major. License preparation in nursing, real estate. **Credit/placement by examination:** CLEP, institutional tests. **Support services:** GED preparation and test center, learning center, pre-admission summer program, reduced course load, remedial instruction, study skills assistance, tutoring, writing center.

**Majors. Agriculture:** Agribusiness operations, business. **Business:** Accounting, administrative services. **Computer sciences:** Networking, programming, systems analysis. **Education:** Teacher assistance. **Engineering**

Two-Year Colleges

technology: Drafting, electrical. **Family/consumer sciences:** Child care, institutional food production. **Health:** Nursing (RN). **Legal studies:** Legal secretary. **Mechanic/repair:** Electronics/electrical. **Personal/culinary services:** Culinary arts. **Public administration:** Human services.

**Computing on campus.** 250 workstations in library, computer center. Dormitories wired for high-speed internet access. Online library, helpline, wireless network available.

**Student life. Freshman orientation:** Mandatory. Preregistration for classes offered. One-half day session held one day prior to beginning of classes. **Housing:** Special housing for disabled, apartments available. $200 deposit, deadline 5/1. **Activities:** Student government, student newspaper, marketing and management association, Business Professionals of America, Vocational and Industrial Clubs of America, professional food preparers, Health Occupations Students of America, National Student Nursing Association, post-secondary agricultural students, cross-cultural communications club.

**Athletics. Intramural:** Basketball, softball, volleyball.

**Student services.** Alcohol/substance abuse counseling, career counseling, services for economically disadvantaged, student employment services, financial aid counseling, health services, minority student services, on-campus daycare, personal counseling, placement for graduates, women's services. **Physically disabled:** Services for visually, hearing impaired. **Transfer:** Transfer adviser for students transferring to 4-year colleges.

**Contact.** E-mail: studentservices@swtc.edu
Phone: (608) 822-3262 ext. 2354 Toll-free
number: (800) 362-3322 ext. 2354 Fax: (608) 822-6019
Lisa Schaefer, Director of Student Services, Southwest Wisconsin Technical College, 1800 Bronson Boulevard, Fennimore, WI 53809

## University of Wisconsin-Baraboo/Sauk County
**Baraboo, Wisconsin**
**www.baraboo.uwc.edu**                 **CB code: 1996**

▶ Public 2-year branch campus and liberal arts college
▶ Commuter campus in large town
▶ SAT or ACT (ACT writing optional) required

**General.** Founded in 1968. Regionally accredited. **Enrollment:** 520 degree-seeking undergraduates. **Degrees:** 75 associate awarded. **Location:** 40 miles from Madison. **Calendar:** Semester, limited summer session. **Full-time faculty:** 21 total; 81% have terminal degrees, 19% minority, 43% women. **Part-time faculty:** 29 total; 14% have terminal degrees, 7% minority, 48% women. **Class size:** 57% < 20, 42% 20-39, less than 1% 40-49.

**Student profile.**

| | | | |
|---|---|---|---|
| Out-of-state: | 1% | 25 or older: | 17% |

**Transfer out. Colleges most students transferred to 2007:** University of Wisconsin-Madison, University of Wisconsin-LaCrosse, University of Wisconsin-Stevens Point, University of Wisconsin-Whitewater, University of Wisconsin-Platteville.

**Basis for selection.** High school courses, rank in upper 75% of class, ACT or SAT test scores most important. Students in bottom 25% may be admitted based on individual record and circumstances. Students not admitted may be deferred and admitted following semester. Special attention given to returning adult, homeschooled, learning disabled, and minority students. ACT or SAT scores must be submitted but are used for advisory purposes only for most students. Interview required for those with borderline academic records and class rank and recommended for others with special circumstances. **Adult students:** SAT/ACT scores not required if applicant over 21. University of Wisconsin Placement Test required of all students not having had college credit English and/or math courses. **Homeschooled:** Transcript of courses and grades, interview required. Interview, portfolio of curriculum, method of assessment, work samples and experiences recommended. **Learning Disabled:** Interview recommended, recent professional testing required to create program accommodations for special needs.

**High school preparation.** 17 units required. Required and recommended units include English 4, mathematics 3-4, social studies 3, science 3-4 (laboratory 3-4), foreign language 2 and academic electives 4. Math must be college preparatory.

**2007-2008 Annual costs.** Tuition/fees: $4,710; $11,694 out-of-state. Per-credit charge: $178 in-state; $469 out-of-state. Minnesota reciprocity tuition: $164 per credit hour. Books/supplies: $680. Personal expenses: $2,660.

**Financial aid.** All financial aid based on need. Need-based aid available for part-time students. Work-study available nights and for part-time students.

**Application procedures. Admission:** Priority date 6/1; deadline 8/31 (receipt date). $35 fee, may be waived for applicants with need. Application may be submitted online. Admission notification on a rolling basis beginning on or about 9/15. **Financial aid:** Priority date 4/15; no closing date. FAFSA, institutional form required. Applicants notified on a rolling basis starting 4/15; must reply within 3 week(s) of notification.

**Academics.** Required courses for associate degree available evenings over 4-year period. Bachelor's degree available on campus through University of Wisconsin Milwaukee. **Special study options:** Cross-registration, distance learning, dual enrollment of high school students, external degree, honors, independent study, internships, liberal arts/career combination, study abroad. Bachelor's degree programs available on campus. **Credit/placement by examination:** AP, CLEP, IB, institutional tests. **Support services:** Learning center, reduced course load, remedial instruction, study skills assistance, tutoring, writing center.

**Majors. Liberal arts:** Arts/sciences.

**Computing on campus.** 60 workstations in library, computer center, student center. Commuter students can connect to campus network. Online course registration, online library, wireless network available.

**Student life. Freshman orientation:** Mandatory, $200 fee. Preregistration for classes offered. Orientation in 3 parts over summer. **Policies:** Students participate actively in campus governance and committee work with faculty and staff. **Housing:** Privately owned apartments adjacent to campus. **Activities:** Bands, choral groups, drama, literary magazine, music ensembles, student government, student newspaper, Campus Crusade for Christ, Phi Theta Kappa, Wellness Alliance, business club, Native American club, cine club, UWB Ambassadors, green club, art club, Future Educators.

**Athletics. NJCAA. Intercollegiate:** Basketball M, soccer, tennis, volleyball W. **Intramural:** Basketball, cross-country, racquetball, softball, volleyball. **Team name:** Fighting Spirits.

**Student services.** Adult student services, alcohol/substance abuse counseling, career counseling, financial aid counseling, minority student services, personal counseling, veterans' counselor. **Physically disabled:** Services for visually, speech, hearing impaired. **Transfer:** Pre-admission transcript evaluation for new students. Transfer adviser, college fairs on campus for students transferring to 4-year colleges.

**Contact.** E-mail: apply@wisconsin.edu
Phone: (608) 355-5230 Fax: (608) 355-5289
Ruth Joyce, Assistant Dean for Student Services, University of Wisconsin-Baraboo/Sauk County, 1006 Connie Road, Baraboo, WI 53913-1098

## University of Wisconsin-Barron County
**Rice Lake, Wisconsin**
**www.barron.uwc.edu**                 **CB code: 1772**

▶ Public 2-year branch campus and junior college
▶ Commuter campus in small town

**General.** Founded in 1966. Regionally accredited. **Location:** 80 miles from Minneapolis-St. Paul, 50 miles from Eau Claire. **Calendar:** Semester.

**Annual costs/financial aid.** Tuition/fees (2007-2008): $4,652; $11,636 out-of-state. Minnesota reciprocity tuition: $164 per credit hour. Books/supplies: $150. Need-based financial aid available to full-time and part-time students.

**Contact.** Phone: (715) 234-8024
Director of Student Services, 1800 College Drive, Rice Lake, WI 54868

## University of Wisconsin-Fond du Lac
**Fond du Lac, Wisconsin**
**www.fdl.uwc.edu**                 **CB code: 1942**

▶ Public 2-year junior college
▶ Commuter campus in large town
▶ SAT or ACT (ACT writing optional) required

**General.** Founded in 1968. Regionally accredited. **Enrollment:** 714 degree-seeking undergraduates; 41 non-degree-seeking students. **Degrees:** 125 associate awarded. **Location:** 70 miles from Milwaukee. **Calendar:** Semester, limited summer session. **Full-time faculty:** 22 total. **Part-time faculty:** 18 total. **Special facilities:** Nature preserve, arboretum.

**Student profile.** Among degree-seeking undergraduates, 274 enrolled as first-time, first-year students, 67 transferred in from other institutions.

| | | | |
|---|---|---|---|
| Part-time: | 34% | Women: | 52% |
| Out-of-state: | 1% | 25 or older: | 30% |

**Transfer out.** Colleges most students transferred to 2007: UW Oshkosh, UW Milwaukee, UW Madison, UW Stevens Point, UW Green Bay.

**Basis for selection.** Rank in upper 75% of class ensures admission. Students in bottom 25% will be considered. Students with Wisconsin GED score of 250 or higher ensured admission. Applicants admitted who rank in bottom 25% of class may have course credit restrictions during first semester or required to participate in summer school classes as condition of continued enrollment. ACT preferred. Interview required for students in bottom 25% of high school. **Adult students:** SAT/ACT scores not required if applicant over 21. **Homeschooled:** Transcript of courses and grades required.

**High school preparation.** 17 units required. Required units include English 4, mathematics 3, social studies 3, science 3 and academic electives 4.

**2007-2008 Annual costs.** Tuition/fees: $4,543; $11,527 out-of-state. Per-credit charge: $178 in-state; $469 out-of-state. Minnesota reciprocity tuition: $164 per credit hour. Books/supplies: $810. Personal expenses: $1,620.

**2006-2007 Financial aid. Need-based:** 57% of total undergraduate aid awarded as scholarships/grants, 43% as loans/jobs. Need-based aid available for part-time students. Work-study available for part-time students. **Non-need-based:** Scholarships awarded for academics, leadership, music/drama.

**Application procedures. Admission:** Priority date 6/30; no deadline. $35 fee. Application may be submitted online. Admission notification on a rolling basis. **Financial aid:** Priority date 4/15; no closing date. FAFSA required. Applicants notified on a rolling basis starting 6/1; must reply within 2 week(s) of notification.

**Academics. Special study options:** Accelerated study, cross-registration, distance learning, dual enrollment of high school students, independent study, liberal arts/career combination, study abroad, teacher certification program. Bachelor's degree programs available on campus. **Credit/placement by examination:** AP, CLEP, IB, institutional tests. 18 credit hours maximum toward associate degree. **Support services:** Learning center, pre-admission summer program, reduced course load, remedial instruction, study skills assistance, tutoring.

**Majors. Liberal arts:** Arts/sciences.

**Computing on campus.** 60 workstations in library, computer center. Commuter students can connect to campus network. Online course registration, online library, wireless network available.

**Student life. Freshman orientation:** Mandatory, $65 fee. **Housing:** Student housing available at nearby Marian College. **Activities:** Bands, choral groups, drama, literary magazine, music ensembles, musical theater, student government, student newspaper, symphony orchestra.

**Athletics.** NJCAA. **Intercollegiate:** Baseball M, basketball, golf, soccer, tennis, volleyball W. **Intramural:** Basketball M, bowling, football (non-tackle), volleyball. **Team name:** Falcons.

**Student services.** Career counseling, financial aid counseling, personal counseling, veterans' counselor. **Physically disabled:** Services for visually, speech, hearing impaired. **Transfer:** Transfer adviser for students transferring to 4-year colleges.

**Contact.** Phone: (920) 929-3606 Fax: (920) 929-3626
Tom Martin, Assistant Campus Dean for Student Services, University of Wisconsin-Fond du Lac, 400 University Drive, Fond du Lac, WI 54935-2998

## University of Wisconsin-Fox Valley
Menasha, Wisconsin
www.uwfoxvalley.uwc.edu               CB code: 1889

- Public 2-year liberal arts college
- Commuter campus in small city
- SAT or ACT (ACT writing optional) required

**General.** Founded in 1933. Regionally accredited. **Enrollment:** 1,747 degree-seeking undergraduates. **Degrees:** 150 associate awarded. **Location:** 90 miles from Milwaukee. **Calendar:** Semester, limited summer session. **Full-time faculty:** 50 total. **Part-time faculty:** 32 total. **Class size:** 100% < 20. **Special facilities:** Observatory, planetarium, earth science museum.

**Basis for selection.** Rank in upper 75% of class ensures admission. Students in bottom 25% may be placed on waiting list. Course unit requirements must be met. Wisconsin state law requires submission of ACT or SAT before registration. Scores not normally considered by college for admission, but may be required for students in bottom 25% of graduating class. Interview required for those in bottom 25% of class and those submitting GED scores. **Adult students:** SAT/ACT scores not required if applicant over 21. **Homeschooled:** Transcript of courses and grades required.

**High school preparation.** 17 units required. Required and recommended units include English 4, mathematics 3, social studies 3, science 3, foreign language 2 and academic electives 4. Math units must be in algebra, geometry, or higher level.

**2007-2008 Annual costs.** Tuition/fees: $4,492; $11,476 out-of-state. Per-credit charge: $178 in-state; $469 out-of-state. Minnesota reciprocity tuition: $164 per credit hour. Books/supplies: $455. Personal expenses: $810.

**Financial aid. Need-based:** Need-based aid available for part-time students. Work-study available nights, weekends and for part-time students.

**Application procedures. Admission:** Priority date 5/1; no deadline. $35 fee, may be waived for applicants with need. Admission notification on a rolling basis. **Financial aid:** Priority date 4/15; no closing date. FAFSA required. Applicants notified on a rolling basis starting 6/1; must reply within 3 week(s) of notification.

**Academics.** Enrollment includes admissions to all University of Wisconsin campuses. **Special study options:** Accelerated study, distance learning, dual enrollment of high school students, honors, independent study, study abroad. **Credit/placement by examination:** AP, CLEP, institutional tests. **Support services:** Learning center, reduced course load, remedial instruction, study skills assistance, tutoring, writing center.

**Majors. Liberal arts:** Arts/sciences.

**Computing on campus.** Online course registration, online library, student web hosting, wireless network available.

**Student life. Freshman orientation:** Mandatory, $135 fee. Day-long program. **Activities:** Bands, choral groups, dance, drama, film society, music ensembles, musical theater, radio station, student government, student newspaper, symphony orchestra, TV station.

**Athletics.** NJCAA. **Intercollegiate:** Basketball, golf, soccer, tennis, volleyball. **Team name:** Cyclones.

**Student services.** Adult student services, career counseling, on-campus daycare, veterans' counselor. **Physically disabled:** Services for visually, speech, hearing impaired. **Transfer:** Transfer adviser, college fairs on campus for students transferring to 4-year colleges.

**Contact.** Phone: (920) 832-2620 Fax: (920) 832-2850
Carla Rabe, Assistant Campus Dean for Student Services, University of Wisconsin-Fox Valley, 1478 Midway Road, Menasha, WI 54952-2850

## University of Wisconsin-Manitowoc
Manitowoc, Wisconsin
www.manitowoc.uwc.edu               CB code: 1890

- Public 2-year branch campus and liberal arts college
- Commuter campus in large town
- SAT or ACT (ACT writing optional) required

**General.** Founded in 1933. Regionally accredited. Collaborative bachelor's degree program with UW Milwaukee and ADN - BSN completion program from UW Oshkosh. **Enrollment:** 530 degree-seeking undergraduates; 66 non-degree-seeking students. **Degrees:** 134 associate awarded. **Location:** 45 miles from Green Bay. **Calendar:** Semester, limited summer session. **Full-time faculty:** 20 total. **Part-time faculty:** 20 total. **Class size:** 26% < 20, 67% 20-39, 2% 40-49, 5% 50-99.

**Student profile.** Among degree-seeking undergraduates, 192 enrolled as first-time, first-year students, 29 transferred in from other institutions.

| | | | |
|---|---|---|---|
| Part-time: | 26% | Women: | 50% |
| Out-of-state: | 1% | 25 or older: | 27% |

Two-Year Colleges

**Transfer out. Colleges most students transferred to 2007:** UW Green Bay, UW Oshkosh, UW Madison, UW Milwaukee, UW Stevens Point.

**Basis for selection.** Rank in top 75% of high school class ensures admission. Students in bottom 25% will be considered but may require campus interview. Students not admitted for specific semester applied for will be admitted at later date. Interview required for applicants in bottom quarter of class. **Adult students:** SAT/ACT scores not required if applicant over 21. **Homeschooled:** Transcript of courses and grades required. 19 ACT required. **Learning Disabled:** Students must meet with campus coordinator for students with disabilities for information about support programs.

**High school preparation.** 17 units required. Required units include English 4, mathematics 3, social studies 3, science 3 and academic electives 4.

**2007-2008 Annual costs.** Tuition/fees: $4,899; $11,882 out-of-state. Books/supplies: $515. Personal expenses: $990.

**Financial aid.** All financial aid based on need. Need-based aid available for part-time students. Work-study available nights and for part-time students.

**Application procedures. Admission:** Priority date 7/1; no deadline. $44 fee, may be waived for applicants with need. Application may be submitted online. Admission notification on a rolling basis beginning on or about 9/15. **Financial aid:** Priority date 3/1; no closing date. FAFSA, institutional form required. Applicants notified on a rolling basis starting 5/1; must reply within 2 week(s) of notification.

**Academics. Special study options:** Cross-registration, dual enrollment of high school students, independent study. Bachelor's degree programs available on campus. **Credit/placement by examination:** AP, CLEP, IB, institutional tests. 18 credit hours maximum toward associate degree. **Support services:** Learning center, reduced course load, remedial instruction, tutoring, writing center.

**Majors. Liberal arts:** Arts/sciences.

**Computing on campus.** 60 workstations in library, computer center. Commuter students can connect to campus network. Online course registration, online library, helpline, wireless network available.

**Student life. Freshman orientation:** Mandatory, $50 fee. Preregistration for classes offered. One day program. **Activities:** Bands, choral groups, drama, literary magazine, music ensembles, student government, student newspaper, symphony orchestra, College Democrats.

**Athletics.** NAIA, NJCAA. **Intercollegiate:** Basketball, golf, tennis, volleyball W. **Intramural:** Badminton, football (non-tackle). **Team name:** Blue Devils.

**Student services.** Adult student services, career counseling, financial aid counseling, on-campus daycare, personal counseling, veterans' counselor. **Physically disabled:** Services for visually, speech, hearing impaired. **Transfer:** Re-entry adviser for new students. Transfer adviser for students transferring to 4-year colleges.

**Contact.** E-mail: manadmit@uwc.edu
Phone: (920) 683-4707 Fax: (920) 683-4776
Christopher Lewis, Assistant Dean for Student Services, University of Wisconsin-Manitowoc, 705 Viebahn Street, Manitowoc, WI 54220-6699

---

## University of Wisconsin-Marathon County
**Wausau, Wisconsin**
**www.uwmc.uwc.edu**      **CB code: 1995**

◆ Public 2-year college
◆ Commuter campus in small city
◆ SAT or ACT (ACT writing optional) required

**General.** Founded in 1933. Regionally accredited. Guaranteed transfer program to University of Wisconsin 4-year schools. **Enrollment:** 1,380 degree-seeking undergraduates. **Degrees:** 102 associate awarded. **Location:** 180 miles from Milwaukee, 180 miles from Minneapolis-St. Paul. **Calendar:** Semester, limited summer session. **Full-time faculty:** 48 total. **Part-time faculty:** 28 total. **Special facilities:** Planetarium, hiking and cross-country ski trails, indoor skating and curling rinks.

**Student profile.** Among degree-seeking undergraduates, 5% enrolled in a transfer program. Of all enrolled students, 1% already have a bachelor's degree or higher.

| | | | |
|---|---|---|---|
| Out-of-state: | 3% | Live on campus: | 12% |
| 25 or older: | 28% | | |

**Transfer out.** 75% of students enrolled in the transfer program go on to 4-year colleges.

**Basis for selection.** Rank in upper 75% of class ensures admission. Students in bottom 25% and those with GED admitted on basis of interview. **Adult students:** SAT/ACT scores not required if applicant over 21. **Learning Disabled:** Must provide official documentation for review of accommodations 90 days in advance.

**High school preparation.** 17 units required. Required and recommended units include English 4, mathematics 3-4, social studies 3-4, science 3-4 and foreign language 4. Math units must be algebra, geometry or other courses leading to calculus.

**2007-2008 Annual costs.** Tuition/fees: $4,507; $11,491 out-of-state. Per-credit charge: $178 in-state; $469 out-of-state. Minnesota reciprocity tuition: $164 per credit hour. Books/supplies: $700. Personal expenses: $810.

**2006-2007 Financial aid.** All financial aid based on need. Need-based aid available for part-time students. Work-study available nights and for part-time students.

**Application procedures. Admission:** Priority date 8/1; no deadline. $35 fee, may be waived for applicants with need. Application may be submitted online. Admission notification on a rolling basis. **Financial aid:** Priority date 4/15; no closing date. FAFSA, institutional form required. Applicants notified on a rolling basis starting 6/1; must reply within 3 week(s) of notification.

**Academics. Special study options:** Cross-registration, dual enrollment of high school students, honors, independent study, internships, liberal arts/career combination, study abroad. Bachelor's degree programs available on campus. **Credit/placement by examination:** AP, CLEP, IB, institutional tests. 18 credit hours maximum toward associate degree. **Support services:** Learning center, pre-admission summer program, reduced course load, remedial instruction, study skills assistance, tutoring, writing center.

**Majors. Liberal arts:** Arts/sciences.

**Computing on campus.** 92 workstations in dormitories, library, computer center. Dormitories wired for high-speed internet access and linked to campus network. Online library, helpline available.

**Student life. Freshman orientation:** Available, $15 fee. Preregistration for classes offered. 1-day program held week before start of fall classes. **Policies:** Zero tolerance alcohol and drug policy in residence hall. **Housing:** Coed dorms available. $100 deposit. **Activities:** Bands, choral groups, drama, literary magazine, music ensembles, musical theater, student government, student newspaper, symphony orchestra, Christian Fellowship, business club, computer club, drama club, international relations club, biology club, gay lesbian bisexual student association.

**Athletics.** NJCAA. **Intercollegiate:** Basketball, golf, soccer, tennis, volleyball W. **Intramural:** Archery, badminton, basketball, bowling, fencing, golf, handball, racquetball, skiing, skin diving, softball, swimming, table tennis, tennis, volleyball. **Team name:** Huskies.

**Student services.** Adult student services, career counseling, student employment services, personal counseling, veterans' counselor. **Physically disabled:** Services for visually, hearing impaired. **Transfer:** Transfer adviser, college fairs on campus for students transferring to 4-year colleges.

**Contact.** E-mail: uwmc@uwe.edu
Phone: (715) 261-6241 Toll-free number: (888) 367-8962
Fax: (715) 261-6331
Nolan "Whiz" Beck, Director of Student Services, University of Wisconsin-Marathon County, 518 South Seventh Avenue, Wausau, WI 54401-5396

---

## University of Wisconsin-Marinette
**Marinette, Wisconsin**
**www.marinette.uwc.edu**      **CB code: 1891**

◆ Public 2-year branch campus and liberal arts college
◆ Commuter campus in large town
◆ SAT or ACT (ACT writing optional), application essay required

**General.** Founded in 1946. Regionally accredited. **Enrollment:** 327 degree-seeking undergraduates. **Degrees:** 67 associate awarded. **Location:** 50 miles from Green Bay, 170 miles from Milwaukee. **Calendar:** Semester, limited summer session. **Full-time faculty:** 17 total; 94% have terminal degrees, 6% minority, 41% women. **Part-time faculty:** 16 total; 19% have terminal degrees, 56% women.

**Student profile.**

Out-of-state:          23%     25 or older:          26%

**Transfer out. Colleges most students transferred to 2007:** UW-Green Bay, UW-Oshkosh, UW-Stevens Point, UW-Madison, Northern Michigan University.

**Basis for selection.** Class rank, GPA, courses, ACT scores, and involvement important. Applicants not meeting minimum standards may be accepted but required to take reduced course load and/or noncredit courses to remedy deficiencies. **Adult students:** SAT/ACT scores not required if applicant over 21.

**High school preparation.** 17 units required. Required units include English 4, mathematics 3, social studies 3 and science 3. 4 electives of computer science, business, foreign language and/or fine arts required.

**2007-2008 Annual costs.** Tuition/fees: $4,490; $11,474 out-of-state. Per-credit charge: $178 in-state; $469 out-of-state. Minnesota reciprocity tuition: $163.75 per credit hour. Books/supplies: $600.

**Financial aid.** All financial aid based on need. Need-based aid available for part-time students. Work-study available nights and for part-time students.

**Application procedures. Admission:** Priority date 7/1; no deadline. $35 fee, may be waived for applicants with need. Application may be submitted online. Admission notification on a rolling basis. Students may be conditionally admitted prior to receipt of ACT scores, but may not register for classes until scores are received. **Financial aid:** Priority date 4/15; no closing date. FAFSA required. Applicants notified on a rolling basis.

**Academics. Special study options:** Cross-registration, distance learning, dual enrollment of high school students, ESL, independent study, study abroad. Bachelor's degree programs available on campus. **Credit/placement by examination:** AP, CLEP, institutional tests. **Support services:** Reduced course load, remedial instruction, study skills assistance, tutoring, writing center.

**Majors. Area/ethnic studies:** Women's. **Liberal arts:** Arts/sciences.

**Computing on campus.** 80 workstations in library, computer center, student center. Online course registration, online library, wireless network available.

**Student life. Freshman orientation:** Mandatory, $50 fee. **Activities:** Bands, choral groups, drama, literary magazine, music ensembles, musical theater, student government, student newspaper, Phi Theta Kappa.

**Athletics.** NJCAA. **Intercollegiate:** Basketball, volleyball W. **Intramural:** Basketball, bowling, football (non-tackle), skiing, table tennis, volleyball. **Team name:** Buccaneers.

**Student services.** Adult student services, career counseling, services for economically disadvantaged, student employment services, financial aid counseling, minority student services, personal counseling, veterans' counselor. **Physically disabled:** Services for visually, speech, hearing impaired. **Transfer:** Transfer adviser, college fairs on campus for students transferring to 4-year colleges.

**Contact.**  E-mail: ssinfo@uwc.edu
Phone: (715) 735-4301 Fax: (715) 735-4304
Cynthia Bailey, Assistant Campus Dean for Student Services, University of Wisconsin-Marinette, 750 West Bay Shore Street, Marinette, WI 54143

## University of Wisconsin-Marshfield/Wood County
Marshfield, Wisconsin
www.marshfield.uwc.edu                    CB code: 1997

▶  Public 2-year branch campus college
▶  Commuter campus in large town

**General.** Founded in 1964. Regionally accredited. **Location:** 138 miles from Madison. **Calendar:** Semester.

**Annual costs/financial aid.** Tuition/fees (2007-2008): $4,525; $11,509 out-of-state. Minnesota reciprocity tuition: $164 per credit hour. Books/

supplies: $500. Personal expenses: $1,022. Need-based financial aid available to full-time and part-time students.

**Contact.**  Phone: (715) 389-6500
Director of Student Services, 2000 West Fifth Street, Marshfield, WI 54449

## University of Wisconsin-Richland
Richland Center, Wisconsin
www.richland.uwc.edu                    CB code: 1662

▶  Public 2-year liberal arts college
▶  Commuter campus in small town
▶  SAT or ACT (ACT writing optional) required

**General.** Founded in 1967. Regionally accredited. **Enrollment:** 452 degree-seeking undergraduates. **Degrees:** 78 associate awarded. **Location:** 60 miles from Madison, 60 miles from LaCrosse. **Calendar:** Semester, limited summer session. **Full-time faculty:** 17 total. **Part-time faculty:** 13 total. **Class size:** 57% < 20, 43% 20-39.

**Student profile.** Among degree-seeking undergraduates, 100% enrolled in a transfer program.

Out-of-state:          1%     **Live on campus:**          40%
25 or older:          22%

**Transfer out.** 95% of students enrolled in the transfer program go on to 4-year colleges. **Colleges most students transferred to 2007:** University of Wisconsin-LaCrosse, University of Wisconsin-Stevens Point, University of Wisconsin-Platteville, University of Wisconsin-Madison, University of Wisconsin-Eau Claire, University of Wisconsin-Whitewater.

**Basis for selection.** Rank in upper 75% of class ensures admission. Students in bottom 25% may be admitted on a discretionary category basis. Students not admitted for specific semester applied for will be admitted at later date. Test scores for matriculating students must be received prior to enrollment. Interview required for applicants in bottom 25% of class; recommended for all others. **Adult students:** SAT/ACT scores not required if applicant over 21. **Homeschooled:** 19 ACT required.

**High school preparation.** 17 units required. Required units include English 4, mathematics 3, social studies 3, science 3 and academic electives 4. 4 of the required units may be in foreign language, fine arts, computer science or other academic areas.

**2007-2008 Annual costs.** Tuition/fees: $4,690; $11,674 out-of-state. Per-credit charge: $178 in-state; $469 out-of-state. Minnesota reciprocity tuition: $164 per credit hour. Books/supplies: $515. Personal expenses: $990.

**2006-2007 Financial aid.** All financial aid based on need. 47% of total undergraduate aid awarded as scholarships/grants, 53% as loans/jobs. Need-based aid available for part-time students. Work-study available nights, weekends and for part-time students.

**Application procedures. Admission:** $35 fee, may be waived for applicants with need. Application may be submitted online. Admission notification on a rolling basis. **Financial aid:** Priority date 4/15; no closing date. FAFSA required. Applicants notified on a rolling basis starting 5/15; must reply within 3 week(s) of notification.

**Academics.** Associate of arts and science degree accepted throughout University of Wisconsin System as transfer tool; satisfies general education requirements of any system campus. Online writing lab available to students at all times. **Special study options:** Cross-registration, distance learning, dual enrollment of high school students, independent study, study abroad, teacher certification program. Bachelor's degree programs available on campus. **Credit/placement by examination:** AP, CLEP, IB, institutional tests. **Support services:** Reduced course load, remedial instruction, study skills assistance, tutoring, writing center.

**Majors. Liberal arts:** Arts/sciences.

**Computing on campus.** 60 workstations in dormitories, library, computer center. Dormitories wired for high-speed internet access and linked to campus network. Commuter students can connect to campus network. Online library, wireless network available.

**Student life. Freshman orientation:** Mandatory, $35 fee. Preregistration for classes offered. Orientation held during the first week of fall classes. **Housing:** Coed dorms, apartments available. $200 deposit. **Activities:** Concert band, choral groups, drama, literary magazine, music ensembles, musical theater, student government, student newspaper, Educators of the Future, Student Wisconsin Education Association, international club, student senate.

**Athletics. Intercollegiate:** Basketball, volleyball W. **Intramural:** Basketball, football (non-tackle), racquetball, softball, swimming, tennis, volleyball. **Team name:** Roadrunners.

**Student services.** Adult student services, alcohol/substance abuse counseling, career counseling, student employment services, financial aid counseling, personal counseling. **Transfer:** Transfer adviser, college fairs on campus for students transferring to 4-year colleges.

**Contact.** E-mail: rlninfo@uwc.edu
Phone: (608) 647-6186 ext. 3 Fax: (608) 647-2275
John Poole, Director of Student Services, University of
Wisconsin-Richland, 1200 Highway 14 West, Richland Center, WI 53581

## University of Wisconsin-Rock County
**Janesville, Wisconsin**
**www.rock.uwc.edu**                     **CB code: 1998**

- Public 2-year branch campus and liberal arts college
- Commuter campus in small city
- SAT or ACT (ACT writing optional) required

**General.** Founded in 1966. Regionally accredited. **Enrollment:** 848 degree-seeking undergraduates. **Degrees:** 102 associate awarded. **Location:** 40 miles from Madison. **Calendar:** Semester, limited summer session. **Full-time faculty:** 33 total. **Part-time faculty:** 17 total. **Class size:** 51% < 20, 46% 20-39, 2% 40-49, less than 1% 50-99.

**Student profile.** Among degree-seeking undergraduates, 109 transferred in from other institutions.

Out-of-state:          1%      25 or older:          25%

**Transfer out. Colleges most students transferred to 2007:** University of Wisconsin-Whitewater, University of Wisconsin-Madison.

**Basis for selection.** Rank in upper 75% of class ensures admission. Students in bottom 25% and those with GED admitted under special conditions. SAT or ACT scores used for students with GED or in bottom 25% of class. Essays considered. **Adult students:** SAT/ACT scores not required if applicant over 21. **Homeschooled:** Transcript of courses and grades required.

**High school preparation.** 17 units recommended. Recommended units include English 4, mathematics 3, social studies 3, science 3 and academic electives 4.

**2007-2008 Annual costs.** Tuition/fees: $4,543; $11,527 out-of-state. Per-credit charge: $178 in-state; $468 out-of-state. Books/supplies: $500. Personal expenses: $810.

**Financial aid.** All financial aid based on need. Need-based aid available for part-time students. Work-study available nights, weekends and for part-time students.

**Application procedures. Admission:** No deadline. $35 fee. Application may be submitted online. Admission notification on a rolling basis. **Financial aid:** Priority date 4/15; no closing date. FAFSA, institutional form required. Applicants notified on a rolling basis starting 6/1; must reply within 3 week(s) of notification.

**Academics. Special study options:** Cross-registration, distance learning, dual enrollment of high school students, independent study, study abroad. Bachelor's degree programs available on campus. **Credit/placement by examination:** AP, CLEP, institutional tests. **Support services:** Learning center, reduced course load, remedial instruction, study skills assistance, tutoring, writing center.

**Majors. Liberal arts:** Arts/sciences.

**Computing on campus.** 50 workstations in library, computer center. Commuter students can connect to campus network.

**Student life. Freshman orientation:** Mandatory, $30 fee. Three-hour sessions held in May, June, July, and August. **Activities:** Bands, choral groups, dance, drama, literary magazine, music ensembles, student government, student newspaper, symphony orchestra, SGA, MSU, GLBSA, Future Educators, adult student organization.

**Athletics.** NJCAA. **Intercollegiate:** Soccer, tennis, volleyball W. **Intramural:** Badminton, basketball, soccer, softball, tennis, volleyball. **Team name:** Rattlers.

**Student services.** Adult student services, alcohol/substance abuse counseling, career counseling, services for economically disadvantaged, student

employment services, financial aid counseling, minority student services, personal counseling, veterans' counselor. **Physically disabled:** Services for visually, hearing impaired. **Transfer:** Re-entry adviser for new students. Transfer adviser, college fairs on campus for students transferring to 4-year colleges.

**Contact.** E-mail: rckinfo@uwc.edu
Phone: (608) 758-6523 Fax: (608) 758-6579
Steve Ullrick, Assistant Campus Dean for Student Services, University of Wisconsin-Rock County, 2909 Kellogg Avenue, Janesville, WI 53546-5699

## University of Wisconsin-Sheboygan
**Sheboygan, Wisconsin**
**www.sheboygan.uwc.edu**               **CB code: 1994**

- Public 2-year community and junior college
- Commuter campus in small city
- SAT or ACT (ACT writing optional) required

**General.** Founded in 1933. Regionally accredited. Several collaborative degrees with 4-year institutions so students can earn bachelor's degree. **Enrollment:** 728 degree-seeking undergraduates. **Degrees:** 92 associate awarded. **Location:** 60 miles from Milwaukee, 50 miles from Green Bay. **Calendar:** Semester, limited summer session. **Full-time faculty:** 22 total. **Part-time faculty:** 25 total.

**Student profile.**

Out-of-state:          1%      25 or older:          24%

**Transfer out. Colleges most students transferred to 2007:** University of Wisconsin-Milwaukee, University of Wisconsin-Green Bay, University of Wisconsin-Whitewater, University of Wisconsin-Madison, University of Wisconsin-Oshkosh.

**Basis for selection.** Admissions based on secondary school record and class rank. Standardized test scores also important. ACT preferred. Interview recommended. **Adult students:** SAT/ACT scores not required if applicant over 21.

**High school preparation.** 17 units required. Required units include English 4, mathematics 3, social studies 3 and science 3. Additional 4 units required from English, social science, math, natural science, foreign language, fine arts, or computer science.

**2007-2008 Annual costs.** Tuition/fees: $4,535; $11,519 out-of-state. Per-credit charge: $178 in-state; $469 out-of-state. Books/supplies: $470. Personal expenses: $900.

**2007-2008 Financial aid. Need-based:** 66% of total undergraduate aid awarded as scholarships/grants, 34% as loans/jobs. Need-based aid available for part-time students. **Non-need-based:** Scholarships awarded for academics, leadership, music/drama. **Additional information:** Scholarship deadline 2/28.

**Application procedures. Admission:** Priority date 6/30; no deadline. $35 fee, may be waived for applicants with need. Admission notification on a rolling basis. **Financial aid:** Priority date 4/15; no closing date. FAFSA, institutional form required. Applicants notified on a rolling basis starting 6/1; must reply within 2 week(s) of notification.

**Academics. Special study options:** Distance learning, dual enrollment of high school students, exchange student, honors, independent study, study abroad. Bachelor's degree programs available on campus. **Credit/placement by examination:** AP, CLEP, IB, institutional tests. **Support services:** GED test center, learning center, reduced course load, remedial instruction, study skills assistance, tutoring, writing center.

**Majors. Liberal arts:** Arts/sciences.

**Computing on campus.** 80 workstations in library, computer center. Commuter students can connect to campus network. Helpline available.

**Student life. Freshman orientation:** Mandatory, $75 fee. **Activities:** Bands, choral groups, drama, film society, literary magazine, musical theater, student government, student newspaper, TV station, Intervarsity Christian Fellowship, Circle K, 10% Society, Zoomers Club.

**Athletics.** NJCAA. **Intercollegiate:** Basketball, golf, tennis, volleyball W. **Intramural:** Badminton, basketball, football (tackle) M, soccer, softball, volleyball. **Team name:** Wombats.

**Student services.** Adult student services, career counseling, financial aid counseling, personal counseling, veterans' counselor. **Physically disabled:** Services for visually, speech, hearing impaired. **Transfer:** Pre-admission transcript evaluation for new students. Transfer center, transfer adviser, college fairs on campus for students transferring to 4-year colleges.

**Contact.** E-mail: braffael@uwc.edu
Phone: (920) 459-6633 Fax: (920) 459-6662
Steve Ullrick, Assistant Campus Dean for Student Services, University of Wisconsin-Sheboygan, One University Drive, Sheboygan, WI 53081

## University of Wisconsin-Washington County
**West Bend, Wisconsin**
washington.uwc.edu                          CB code: 1993

- Public 2-year branch campus and liberal arts college
- Commuter campus in large town
- SAT or ACT (ACT writing optional) required

**General.** Founded in 1968. Regionally accredited. **Enrollment:** 917 degree-seeking undergraduates; 101 non-degree-seeking students. **Degrees:** 97 associate awarded. **Location:** 70 miles from Madison, 35 miles from Milwaukee. **Calendar:** Semester, limited summer session. **Full-time faculty:** 32 total. **Part-time faculty:** 20 total. **Special facilities:** Observatory.

**Student profile.** Among degree-seeking undergraduates, 100% enrolled in a transfer program, 5% already have a bachelor's degree or higher, 73 transferred in from other institutions.

| Part-time: | 30% | Women: | 53% |
|---|---|---|---|
| Out-of-state: | 2% | 25 or older: | 17% |

**Transfer out.** 98% of students enrolled in the transfer program go on to 4-year colleges. **Colleges most students transferred to 2007:** University of Wisconsin-Milwaukee, University of Wisconsin-Oshkosh, University of Wisconsin-Whitewater, University of Wisconsin-Madison.

**Basis for selection.** Open admission. Rank in top 75% of class ensures admission. Students in bottom 25% placed in discretionary category. Qualified students not admitted for specific semester applied for will be admitted at later date. ACT preferred. Interview required for applicants with GED or those ranking in bottom 25% of high school class. **Adult students:** SAT/ACT scores not required if applicant over 21. **Homeschooled:** Transcript of courses and grades required.

**High school preparation.** 17 units required. Required units include English 4, mathematics 3, social studies 3, science 3 and academic electives 4.

**2007-2008 Annual costs.** Tuition/fees: $4,528; $11,512 out-of-state. Per-credit charge: $178 in-state; $469 out-of-state. Books/supplies: $552. Personal expenses: $930.

**Financial aid. Need-based:** Need-based aid available for part-time students. Work-study available weekends and for part-time students. **Non-need-based:** Scholarships awarded for academics.

**Application procedures. Admission:** Priority date 8/1; no deadline. $35 fee, may be waived for applicants with need. Application may be submitted online. Admission notification on a rolling basis beginning on or about 11/1. **Financial aid:** Priority date 4/15; no closing date. FAFSA required. Applicants notified on a rolling basis starting 4/30; must reply within 3 week(s) of notification.

**Academics. Special study options:** Cross-registration, distance learning, dual enrollment of high school students, honors, independent study, internships, study abroad. Collaborative B.A. degree programs in organizational administration, information resources, communications, BSN in nursing, all in cooperation with University of Wisconsin-Milwaukee. Bachelor's degree programs available on campus. **Credit/placement by examination:** AP, CLEP, IB, institutional tests. **Support services:** Learning center, pre-admission summer program, reduced course load, remedial instruction, study skills assistance, tutoring, writing center.

**Majors. Liberal arts:** Arts/sciences.

**Computing on campus.** 78 workstations in library, computer center. Commuter students can connect to campus network. Wireless network available.

**Student life. Freshman orientation:** Mandatory, $50 fee. Preregistration for classes offered. **Activities:** Bands, choral groups, dance, drama, literary magazine, music ensembles, musical theater, student government, student newspaper, symphony orchestra, Phi Theta Kappa honorary society, Literary Guild, business club, Student Impact.

**Athletics.** NAIA. **Intercollegiate:** Basketball, golf, soccer, tennis, volleyball W. **Intramural:** Basketball, softball, volleyball. **Team name:** Wildcats.

**Student services.** Adult student services, career counseling, financial aid counseling, personal counseling, veterans' counselor. **Physically disabled:** Services for hearing impaired. **Transfer:** Pre-admission transcript evaluation for new students. Transfer center, transfer adviser, college fairs on campus for students transferring to 4-year colleges.

**Contact.** Phone: (262) 335-5201 Fax: (262) 335-5274
Martha Nelson, Assistant Campus Dean for Student Services, University of Wisconsin-Washington County, 400 University Drive, West Bend, WI 53095

## University of Wisconsin-Waukesha
**Waukesha, Wisconsin**
www.waukesha.uwc.edu                          CB code: 1999

- Public 2-year branch campus and junior college
- Commuter campus in small city
- SAT or ACT (ACT writing optional) required

**General.** Founded in 1966. Regionally accredited. **Enrollment:** 1,777 degree-seeking undergraduates; 263 non-degree-seeking students. **Degrees:** 143 associate awarded. **Location:** 17 miles from Milwaukee. **Calendar:** Semester, limited summer session. **Full-time faculty:** 60 total. **Part-time faculty:** 28 total. **Special facilities:** 98-acre environmental studies field station.

**Student profile.** Among degree-seeking undergraduates, 10% enrolled in a transfer program, 1,311 enrolled as first-time, first-year students.

| Part-time: | 35% | Women: | 48% |
|---|---|---|---|
| Out-of-state: | 5% | 25 or older: | 29% |

**Transfer out. Colleges most students transferred to 2007:** University of Wisconsin-Milwaukee, University of Wisconsin-Whitewater, University of Wisconsin-Madison.

**Basis for selection.** Rank in top 75% of class ensures admission. Students in bottom 25% and those with GED considered for admission based on interview; if ACT score 19 or higher admission granted. Interview recommended for applicants in bottom 25% of class. **Adult students:** SAT/ACT scores not required if applicant over 21.

**High school preparation.** 17 units required. Required and recommended units include English 4, mathematics 3, social studies 3, science 3, foreign language 2 and academic electives 4.

**2007-2008 Annual costs.** Tuition/fees: $4,507; $11,491 out-of-state. Per-credit charge: $178 in-state; $469 out-of-state. Minnesota reciprocity tuition: $175 per credit hour. Books/supplies: $500. Personal expenses: $1,000.

**Financial aid. Need-based:** Need-based aid available for part-time students. Work-study available nights, weekends and for part-time students. **Non-need-based:** Scholarships awarded for academics, art, leadership, minority status, music/drama.

**Application procedures. Admission:** Priority date 4/1; no deadline. $35 fee, may be waived for applicants with need. Application may be submitted online. Admission notification on a rolling basis beginning on or about 8/1. **Financial aid:** Priority date 4/15; no closing date. FAFSA required. Applicants notified on a rolling basis starting 5/15; must reply within 3 week(s) of notification.

**Academics. Special study options:** Cross-registration, distance learning, dual enrollment of high school students, honors, independent study, study abroad. Bachelor's degree programs available on campus. **Credit/placement by examination:** AP, CLEP, institutional tests. CLEP general exams must be taken before 16 degree credits completed. **Support services:** Learning center, pre-admission summer program, reduced course load, remedial instruction, study skills assistance, tutoring, writing center.

**Majors. Liberal arts:** Arts/sciences.

**Computing on campus.** 90 workstations in library, computer center, student center. Commuter students can connect to campus network. Online course registration, wireless network available.

**Student life. Freshman orientation:** Mandatory, $100 fee. Held periodically throughout the summer and fall semester. **Activities:** Bands, choral groups, drama, literary magazine, music ensembles, musical theater, radio station, student government, student newspaper, multicultural student alliance, ecology club, philosophy club, Phi Theta Kappa honor society.

**Athletics.** NJCAA. **Intercollegiate:** Basketball, golf, soccer, tennis, volleyball W. **Team name:** Cougars.

**Student services.** Adult student services, career counseling, financial aid counseling, on-campus daycare, personal counseling, veterans' counselor. **Physically disabled:** Services for visually, speech, hearing impaired. **Transfer:** Transfer adviser, college fairs on campus for students transferring to 4-year colleges.

**Contact.** E-mail: becky.gill@uwc.edu
Phone: (262) 521-5040 Toll-free number: (888) 289-9285
Fax: (262) 521-5530
Becky Gill, Admissions, University of Wisconsin-Waukesha, 1500 University Drive, Waukesha, WI 53188

## Waukesha County Technical College
### Pewaukee, Wisconsin
**www.wctc.edu**      **CB code: 0724**

▶ Public 2-year technical college
▶ Commuter campus in large town

**General.** Founded in 1923. Regionally accredited. **Enrollment:** 5,047 degree-seeking undergraduates; 2,380 non-degree-seeking students. **Degrees:** 529 associate awarded. **Location:** 15 miles from Milwaukee. **Calendar:** Semester, limited summer session. **Full-time faculty:** 176 total. **Part-time faculty:** 661 total.

**Student profile.** Among degree-seeking undergraduates, 22% enrolled in a vocational program, 5% already have a bachelor's degree or higher, 852 enrolled as first-time, first-year students.

| | | | |
|---|---|---|---|
| Part-time: | 63% | **Hispanic American:** | 4% |
| Women: | 53% | **Native American:** | 1% |
| African American: | 4% | **25 or older:** | 46% |
| Asian American: | 2% | | |

**Basis for selection.** Open admission, but selective for some programs. Individual programs may have additional requirements or prerequisites, and some programs may have wait lists. Some health occupations programs may require interviews and a general college preparatory background of prerequisites. **Homeschooled:** Transcript of courses and grades required.

**2007-2008 Annual costs.** Tuition/fees: $3,047; $17,402 out-of-state. Per-credit charge: $92 in-state; $571 out-of-state. Materials fees vary by program; minimum $4 per course. $10 per credit fee for online courses. Books/supplies: $927. Personal expenses: $2,820.

**Financial aid. Need-based:** Work-study available nights. **Non-need-based:** Scholarships awarded for academics.

**Application procedures. Admission:** No deadline. $30 fee, may be waived for applicants with need. Application may be submitted online. Admission notification on a rolling basis. **Financial aid:** Priority date 3/31; no closing date. FAFSA, institutional form required. Applicants notified on a rolling basis.

**Academics. Special study options:** Accelerated study, cooperative education, distance learning, double major, dual enrollment of high school students, ESL, independent study, internships, student-designed major, study abroad. License preparation in dental hygiene, nursing, real estate. **Credit/placement by examination:** CLEP, institutional tests. **Support services:** GED preparation and test center, learning center, reduced course load, remedial instruction, study skills assistance, tutoring, writing center.

**Majors. Business:** Accounting, administrative services, financial planning, hospitality admin, international marketing, marketing, operations, real estate, retailing. **Communications technology:** Graphics. **Computer sciences:** Networking, programming, systems analysis. **Education:** Early childhood, teacher assistance. **Engineering:** Mechanical, mechanics. **Engineering technology:** Architectural drafting, electrical, mechanical drafting, telecommunications. **Family/consumer sciences:** Child care. **Health:** Dental hygiene, nursing (RN), surgical technology. **Mechanic/repair:** Automotive, computer. **Personal/culinary services:** Restaurant/catering. **Protective services:** Police science. **Public administration:** Human services. **Visual/performing arts:** Graphic design, interior design.

**Most popular majors.** Business/marketing 24%, computer/information sciences 10%, engineering/engineering technologies 9%, health sciences 19%, security/protective services 10%, visual/performing arts 11%.

**Computing on campus.** Online course registration, online library, wireless network available.

---

**Student life. Freshman orientation:** Available. Preregistration for classes offered. **Activities:** Student government.

**Student services.** Adult student services, alcohol/substance abuse counseling, career counseling, services for economically disadvantaged, student employment services, financial aid counseling, health services, minority student services, on-campus daycare, personal counseling, placement for graduates. **Physically disabled:** Services for visually, speech, hearing impaired. **Transfer:** Pre-admission transcript evaluation for new students. College fairs on campus for students transferring to 4-year colleges.

**Contact.** Phone: (262) 691-5275 Fax: (262) 691-5593
Kathleen Kazda, Manager, Admissions & Assessment, Waukesha County Technical College, 800 Main Street, Pewaukee, WI 53072

## Western Technical College
### La Crosse, Wisconsin
**www.westerntc.edu**      **CB code: 1087**

▶ Public 2-year community and technical college
▶ Residential campus in small city

**General.** Founded in 1912. Regionally accredited. **Enrollment:** 4,564 degree-seeking undergraduates. **Degrees:** 490 associate awarded. **Location:** 200 miles from Milwaukee, 150 miles from Minneapolis-St. Paul. **Calendar:** Semester, limited summer session. **Full-time faculty:** 204 total. **Class size:** 100% < 20.

**Student profile.** Among degree-seeking undergraduates, 66 transferred in from other institutions.

**Basis for selection.** Open admission, but selective for some programs. Standardized test scores required for admission into selected health programs. COMPASS required for placement if ACT scores not available. Interviews recommended for placement, portfolios recommended for commercial art applicants for placement.

**High school preparation.** Recommended units include English 3, mathematics 2, social studies 3 and science 2.

**2007-2008 Annual costs.** Tuition/fees: $2,998; $17,353 out-of-state. Per-credit charge: $92 in-state; $571 out-of-state. Materials fees vary by program; minimum $4 per course. Room/board: $3,820. Books/supplies: $910. Personal expenses: $1,461.

**Financial aid. Need-based:** Need-based aid available for part-time students. Work-study available nights, weekends and for part-time students.

**Application procedures. Admission:** No deadline. $30 fee, may be waived for applicants with need. Application may be submitted online. Admission notification on a rolling basis. **Financial aid:** Priority date 3/1; no closing date. FAFSA, institutional form required. Applicants notified on a rolling basis starting 4/1.

**Academics. Special study options:** Accelerated study, cooperative education, distance learning, double major, ESL, independent study, internships, liberal arts/career combination, student-designed major, weekend college. License preparation in dental hygiene, nursing, occupational therapy, paramedic, physical therapy, radiology, real estate. **Credit/placement by examination:** AP, CLEP, institutional tests. 45 credit hours maximum toward associate degree. **Support services:** GED preparation and test center, learning center, reduced course load, remedial instruction, study skills assistance, tutoring, writing center.

**Majors. Agriculture:** Business technology. **Architecture:** Technology. **Business:** Accounting, administrative services, business admin, finance, human resources, operations, sales/distribution. **Communications:** Media studies. **Communications technology:** General, desktop publishing. **Computer sciences:** Applications programming, data entry, data processing, LAN/WAN management, networking. **Education:** Teacher assistance. **Engineering technology:** Biomedical, computer, electrical, electromechanical, heat/ac/refrig, mechanical, mechanical drafting. **Family/consumer sciences:** Child care. **Health:** Clinical lab technology, dental hygiene, electroencephalograph technology, medical radiologic technology/radiation therapy, medical records technology, nursing (RN), occupational therapy assistant, physical therapy assistant, respiratory therapy technology. **Legal studies:** Paralegal. **Mechanic/repair:** Automotive, diesel. **Personal/culinary services:** Restaurant/catering. **Production:** Machine shop technology, tool and die. **Protective services:** Fire safety technology, police science. **Public administration:** Community org/advocacy. **Visual/performing arts:** Design, graphic design, interior design, music.

**Most popular majors.** Business/marketing 28%, computer/information sciences 9%, family/consumer sciences 7%, health sciences 22%, trade and industry 12%, visual/performing arts 9%.

**Computing on campus.** 145 workstations in dormitories, library, computer center. Dormitories wired for high-speed internet access and linked to campus network. Commuter students can connect to campus network. Online course registration, online library, helpline, repair service available.

**Student life. Freshman orientation:** Available. Preregistration for classes offered. General school orientation held in August. **Housing:** Coed dorms available. **Activities:** Student government, student newspaper, TV station, multicultural club, Campus Crusade for Christ.

**Athletics.** NJCAA. **Intercollegiate:** Baseball M, basketball, volleyball W. **Intramural:** Basketball, volleyball. **Team name:** Cavaliers.

**Student services.** Adult student services, alcohol/substance abuse counseling, career counseling, services for economically disadvantaged, student employment services, financial aid counseling, health services, minority student services, on-campus daycare, personal counseling, placement for graduates, veterans' counselor, women's services. **Physically disabled:** Services for visually, speech, hearing impaired. **Transfer:** Pre-admission transcript evaluation for new students.

**Contact.** E-mail: wellsj@westerntc.edu
Phone: (608) 785-9158 Toll-free number: (800) 322-9982
Fax: (608) 785-9148
Jayne Wells, Admissions, Registration and Records, Western Technical College, PO Box 908, La Crosse, WI 54602-0908

## Wisconsin Indianhead Technical College
### Shell Lake, Wisconsin
www.witc.edu                                    CB code: 1580

- Public 2-year technical college
- Commuter campus in rural community
- Interview required

**General.** Founded in 1972. Regionally accredited. 4 campuses covering 11 county area. **Enrollment:** 3,106 degree-seeking undergraduates; 572 non-degree-seeking students. **Degrees:** 368 associate awarded. **Calendar:** Semester, limited summer session. **Full-time faculty:** 140 total. **Part-time faculty:** 1,281 total.

**Student profile.** Among degree-seeking undergraduates, 99% enrolled in a vocational program, 1% already have a bachelor's degree or higher, 802 enrolled as first-time, first-year students.

| Part-time: | 51% | Asian American: | 1% |
|---|---|---|---|
| Out-of-state: | 5% | Hispanic American: | 1% |
| Women: | 62% | Native American: | 3% |
| African American: | 1% | 25 or older: | 26% |

**Transfer out. Colleges most students transferred to 2007:** University of Wisconsin.

**Basis for selection.** Open admission, but selective for some programs. Required ASSET scores: 44 for nursing program, 39 for other associate degree programs, 36 for technical diplomas. SAT or ACT can be used in lieu of ASSET assessment. **Homeschooled:** Must pass ability to benefit assessment.

**2007-2008 Annual costs.** Tuition/fees: $3,037; $17,392 out-of-state. Per-credit charge: $92 in-state; $571 out-of-state. Materials fees vary by program; minimum $4 per course. $10 per credit fee for online courses. Books/supplies: $808. Personal expenses: $1,128.

**2006-2007 Financial aid.** All financial aid based on need, 49% of total undergraduate aid awarded as scholarships/grants, 51% as loans/jobs. Need-based aid available for part-time students. Work-study available nights, weekends and for part-time students.

**Application procedures. Admission:** No deadline. $30 fee. Admission notification on a rolling basis. **Financial aid:** Priority date 4/1; no closing date. FAFSA required. Applicants notified on a rolling basis starting 5/9; must reply by 9/1 or within 4 week(s) of notification.

**Academics. Special study options:** Accelerated study, distance learning, double major, internships. **Credit/placement by examination:** AP, CLEP, institutional tests. **Support services:** GED preparation and test center, learning center, pre-admission summer program, reduced course load, remedial instruction, tutoring.

**Majors. Business:** Accounting, administrative services, business admin, finance, marketing, operations, retailing. **Computer sciences:** General, networking, programming, web page design. **Education:** Early childhood, teacher assistance. **Engineering technology:** Architectural, computer systems, heat/ac/refrig, manufacturing, mechanical drafting. **Health:** Medical secretary,

nursing (RN), occupational therapy assistant. **Mechanic/repair:** Communications systems, computer. **Protective services:** Corrections, police science. **Other:** Individual Technical Studies.

**Most popular majors.** Business/marketing 39%, computer/information sciences 7%, education 8%, engineering/engineering technologies 10%, health sciences 30%.

**Computing on campus.** PC or laptop required. 1,900 workstations in library, computer center, student center. Online course registration, online library, helpline, wireless network available.

**Student life. Freshman orientation:** Available. Preregistration for classes offered: **Activities:** Student government, student newspaper, technical student organizations, vocational student organizations.

**Student services.** Adult student services, career counseling, services for economically disadvantaged, student employment services, financial aid counseling, health services, minority student services, on-campus daycare, personal counseling, placement for graduates, veterans' counselor, women's services. **Physically disabled:** Services for hearing impaired. **Transfer:** College fairs on campus for students transferring to 4-year colleges.

**Contact.** Phone: (715) 468-2815 Toll-free number: (800) 243-9482
Fax: (715) 468-2819
Miriam Crandall, Registrar, Wisconsin Indianhead Technical College, 505 Pine Ridge Drive, Shell Lake, WI 54871

# Wyoming

---

## Casper College
**Casper, Wyoming**
**www.caspercollege.edu**          CB code: 4043

◗ Public 2-year community college
◗ Commuter campus in small city

**General.** Founded in 1945. Regionally accredited. **Enrollment:** 2,875 degree-seeking undergraduates; 1,460 non-degree-seeking students. **Degrees:** 535 associate awarded. **Location:** 280 miles from Denver. **Calendar:** Semester, limited summer session. **Full-time faculty:** 161 total; 27% have terminal degrees, 5% minority, 45% women. **Part-time faculty:** 113 total; 11% have terminal degrees, 4% minority, 45% women. **Class size:** 74% < 20, 23% 20-39, 2% 40-49, 2% 50-99. **Special facilities:** Wildlife museum, geological museum, family resource center, fitness center.

**Student profile.** Among degree-seeking undergraduates, 64% enrolled in a transfer program, 36% enrolled in a vocational program, 679 enrolled as first-time, first-year students, 221 transferred in from other institutions.

| | | | |
|---|---|---|---|
| Part-time: | 36% | Hispanic American: | 4% |
| Out-of-state: | 7% | Native American: | 1% |
| Women: | 61% | International: | 1% |
| African American: | 1% | 25 or older: | 39% |
| Asian American: | 1% | Live on campus: | 14% |

**Transfer out.** 40% of students enrolled in the transfer program go on to 4-year colleges. **Colleges most students transferred to 2007:** University of Wyoming, University of North Dakota, Colorado State University, Montana State University, Black Hills State University.

**Basis for selection.** Open admission, but selective for some programs and for out-of-state students. 2.0 GPA required for out-of-state applicants. Selective admission for nursing, respiratory therapy, radiology; requirements vary by program. Audition recommended for music, theater, athletics and forensics; portfolio recommended for art. **Homeschooled:** Program must be accredited and recognized by state department of education as being equivalent to high school diploma.

**2007-2008 Annual costs.** Tuition/fees: $1,668; $4,644 out-of-state. Per-credit charge: $63 in-state; $187 out-of-state. Western Undergraduate Exchange students pay $93.50 per credit-hour and $2244 per year for full-time students. Room/board: $3,830. Books/supplies: $888. Personal expenses: $2,250.

**Financial aid. Need-based:** Need-based aid available for part-time students. Work-study available nights, weekends and for part-time students. **Non-need-based:** Scholarships awarded for academics, art, athletics, leadership, music/drama, state residency.

**Application procedures. Admission:** Priority date 8/1; deadline 8/15 (postmark date). No application fee. Application may be submitted online. Admission notification on a rolling basis beginning on or about 2/1. **Financial aid:** Priority date 3/15; no closing date. FAFSA required. Applicants notified on a rolling basis starting 4/1.

**Academics. Special study options:** Cooperative education, cross-registration, distance learning, dual enrollment of high school students, honors, independent study, internships. Bachelor's degree programs available on campus. License preparation in nursing, radiology. **Credit/placement by examination:** AP, CLEP, IB, institutional tests. 30 credit hours maximum toward associate degree. **Support services:** GED preparation and test center, learning center, remedial instruction, study skills assistance, tutoring, writing center.

**Majors. Agriculture:** General, animal husbandry, business, range science. **Area/ethnic studies:** Women's. **Biology:** General. **Business:** Accounting, accounting technology, administrative services, business admin, construction management, hospitality admin, management information systems, marketing, office technology, retailing. **Communications:** General. **Computer sciences:** Applications programming, information technology, networking, programming, vendor certification, web page design. **Conservation:** Environmental science, wildlife. **Construction:** General. **Education:** Art, kindergarten/preschool, music, physical, social studies, teacher assistance, technology/industrial arts. **Engineering:** General. **Engineering technology:** Drafting, electrical, GIS, manufacturing, mining, robotics, water quality. **English:** English lit. **Foreign languages:** General. **Health:** Athletic training, clinical lab technology, health services, medical transcription, nursing (RN), occupational therapy assistant, pharmacy assistant, predental, premedicine, prepharmacy, preveterinary, radiologic technology/medical imaging, respiratory therapy technology, substance abuse counseling. **History:** General. **Interdisciplinary:** Museum, nutrition sciences. **Legal studies:** Paralegal, prelaw. **Liberal arts:** Arts/sciences. **Math:** General. **Mechanic/repair:** Auto body, automotive, diesel, industrial. **Physical sciences:** Chemistry, geology, physics. **Production:** Machine tool, welding. **Protective services:** Criminal justice, firefighting, forensics. **Psychology:** General. **Public administration:** Social work. **Social sciences:** Anthropology, economics, international relations, political science, sociology. **Transportation:** Airline/commercial pilot. **Visual/performing arts:** Acting, art, dance, dramatic, graphic design, music performance, musical theater, photography, studio arts, theater design. **Other:** Applied statistics.

**Most popular majors.** Business/marketing 6%, education 14%, health sciences 23%, liberal arts 11%, security/protective services 6%.

**Computing on campus.** 120 workstations in library, computer center. Dormitories wired for high-speed internet access and linked to campus network. Commuter students can connect to campus network. Helpline, wireless network available.

**Student life. Freshman orientation:** Mandatory. Preregistration for classes offered. One-day program, held 4 times in summer. **Housing:** Coed dorms, apartments, substance-free housing available. $200 fully refundable deposit. **Activities:** Bands, choral groups, dance, drama, literary magazine, music ensembles, musical theater, student government, student newspaper, united campus ministry, Latter-day Saints student association, Baptist student union, Phi Theta Kappa, Phi Rho Pi, student nurses association, Students in Free Enterprise, AG club, student activities board, Bakkai.

**Athletics.** NJCAA. **Intercollegiate:** Basketball, cheerleading, rodeo, volleyball W. **Intramural:** Basketball, bowling, football (non-tackle), racquetball, soccer, softball, tennis, volleyball. **Team name:** Thunderbirds.

**Student services.** Adult student services, alcohol/substance abuse counseling, career counseling, student employment services, financial aid counseling, health services, on-campus daycare, personal counseling, placement for graduates, veterans' counselor. **Physically disabled:** Services for visually, speech, hearing impaired. **Transfer:** Transfer adviser, college fairs on campus for students transferring to 4-year colleges.

**Contact.** E-mail: kfoltz@caspercollege.edu
Phone: (307) 268-2458 Toll-free number: (800) 442-2963
Fax: (307) 268-2611
Kyla Foltz, Admissions Coordinator, Casper College, 125 College Drive, Casper, WY 82601

---

## Central Wyoming College
**Riverton, Wyoming**
**www.cwc.edu**          CB code: 4115

◗ Public 2-year community college
◗ Commuter campus in large town

**General.** Founded in 1966. Regionally accredited. **Enrollment:** 1,155 degree-seeking undergraduates; 878 non-degree-seeking students. **Degrees:** 117 associate awarded. **Location:** 120 miles from Casper, 240 miles from Billings, MT. **Calendar:** Semester, limited summer session. **Full-time faculty:** 43 total; 72% have terminal degrees, 12% minority, 54% women. **Part-time faculty:** 54 total; 20% have terminal degrees, 30% minority, 46% women. **Class size:** 86% < 20, 13% 20-39, less than 1% 40-49. **Special facilities:** Rodeo arena, fine arts center, Microsoft training laboratory, Cisco training laboratory, Native American artifacts, canyon center, Wyoming PBS station. **Partnerships:** Formal partnerships with Microsoft, Cisco (training labs, software), National Outdoor Leadership School (NOLS).

**Student profile.** Among degree-seeking undergraduates, 56% enrolled in a transfer program, 44% enrolled in a vocational program, 1% already have a bachelor's degree or higher, 335 enrolled as first-time, first-year students, 136 transferred in from other institutions.

| | | | |
|---|---|---|---|
| Part-time: | 43% | Hispanic American: | 5% |
| Out-of-state: | 11% | Native American: | 16% |
| Women: | 65% | International: | 1% |
| African American: | 1% | 25 or older: | 43% |
| Asian American: | 1% | Live on campus: | 9% |

**Transfer out.** **Colleges most students transferred to 2007:** University of Wyoming, Colorado State University, Montana State University, University of Utah, Chadron.

**Basis for selection.** Open admission, but selective for some programs. Special admission to nursing program; minimum GPA and test scores required. COMPASS placement tests required for all first-time students who have not taken ACT or SAT. Certain music courses require audition.

**2007-2008 Annual costs.** Tuition/fees: $1,992; $4,968 out-of-state. Per-credit charge: $62 in-state; $186 out-of-state. Western Undergraduate Exchange students pay $2,232 or $93 per credit hour. Room/board: $3,100. Books/supplies: $900. Personal expenses: $1,500.

**2007-2008 Financial aid. Need-based:** 133 full-time freshmen applied for aid; 101 were judged to have need; 101 of these received aid. 70% of total undergraduate aid awarded as scholarships/grants, 30% as loans/jobs. Need-based aid available for part-time students. Work-study available nights, weekends and for part-time students. **Non-need-based:** Awarded to 263 full-time undergraduates, including 82 freshmen. Scholarships awarded for academics, alumni affiliation, art, athletics, leadership, minority status, music/drama, state residency.

**Application procedures. Admission:** No deadline. No application fee. Application may be submitted online. Admission notification on a rolling basis beginning on or about 1/1. **Financial aid:** Priority date 4/15; no closing date. FAFSA, institutional form required. Applicants notified on a rolling basis starting 5/1; must reply within 2 week(s) of notification.

**Academics. Special study options:** Cooperative education, cross-registration, distance learning, double major, dual enrollment of high school students, ESL, external degree, honors, independent study, student-designed major, teacher certification program. Bachelor's degree programs available on campus. License preparation in dental hygiene, nursing, paramedic. **Credit/placement by examination:** AP, CLEP, institutional tests. 32 credit hours maximum toward associate degree. Some DANTES and APE exams accepted. **Support services:** GED preparation and test center, learning center, reduced course load, remedial instruction, study skills assistance, tutoring, writing center.

**Majors. Agriculture:** Business, equestrian studies, range science. **Area/ethnic studies:** Native American. **Biology:** General. **Business:** Accounting, accounting technology, administrative services, business admin, management information systems, office technology. **Communications:** Radio/tv. **Communications technology:** Radio/tv. **Computer sciences:** Computer graphics, computer science, web page design. **Conservation:** Environmental science. **Construction:** Carpentry. **Education:** Early childhood, elementary, secondary, teacher assistance. **Engineering:** General. **Engineering technology:** Computer systems. **English:** English lit. **Family/consumer sciences:** Child care. **Health:** Health services, medical transcription, nursing (RN). **Legal studies:** Prelaw. **Math:** General. **Mechanic/repair:** Automotive. **Parks/recreation:** General, facilities management. **Personal/culinary services:** Chef training. **Physical sciences:** General, geology. **Production:** Welding. **Protective services:** Emergency management/homeland security, firefighting, law enforcement admin. **Psychology:** General. **Public administration:** Human services. **Social sciences:** General. **Visual/performing arts:** Acting, art, dramatic, theater design. **Other:** Business Office systems, Western American studies.

**Most popular majors.** Business/marketing 10%, education 10%, health sciences 15%, liberal arts 28%, security/protective services 8%.

**Computing on campus.** 300 workstations in dormitories, library, computer center, student center. Dormitories wired for high-speed internet access and linked to campus network. Commuter students can connect to campus network. Online course registration, online library, wireless network available.

**Student life. Freshman orientation:** Mandatory. Preregistration for classes offered. **Housing:** Coed dorms, apartments available. $225 partly refundable deposit, deadline 5/1. **Activities:** Bands, choral groups, dance, drama, music ensembles, musical theater, radio station, student government, student newspaper, TV station, American Indian club, multicultural club, social science club, veterans club, Hispanic club, law and justice club, science club, Phi Theta Kappa, American Indian science and engineering society.

**Athletics.** NJCAA. **Intercollegiate:** Basketball, rodeo, volleyball W. **Intramural:** Badminton, basketball, skiing, soccer, softball, swimming, table tennis, tennis, volleyball, weight lifting. **Team name:** Rustlers.

**Student services.** Adult student services, alcohol/substance abuse counseling, career counseling, services for economically disadvantaged, student employment services, financial aid counseling, personal counseling, placement for graduates, veterans' counselor. **Physically disabled:** Services for visually, hearing impaired. **Transfer:** College fairs on campus for students transferring to 4-year colleges.

**Contact.** E-mail: admit@cwc.edu
Phone: (307) 855-2119 Toll-free number: (800) 865-0193
Fax: (307) 855-2093
Brenda Barlow, Admissions Office Assistant, Central Wyoming College, 2660 Peck Avenue, Riverton, WY 82501

---

# Eastern Wyoming College
## Torrington, Wyoming
ewc.wy.edu                                    CB code: 4700

◆ Public 2-year community college
◆ Commuter campus in small town

**General.** Founded in 1948. Regionally accredited. **Enrollment:** 618 degree-seeking undergraduates; 887 non-degree-seeking students. **Degrees:** 107 associate awarded. **Location:** 190 miles from Denver. **Calendar:** Semester, limited summer session. **Full-time faculty:** 49 total; 16% have terminal degrees. **Part-time faculty:** 67 total.

**Student profile.** Among degree-seeking undergraduates, 24% enrolled in a transfer program, 16% enrolled in a vocational program, 215 enrolled as first-time, first-year students.

| | | | |
|---|---|---|---|
| Part-time: | 30% | Hispanic American: | 6% |
| Out-of-state: | 27% | Native American: | 1% |
| Women: | 64% | International: | 1% |
| African American: | 2% | 25 or older: | 31% |

**Transfer out. Colleges most students transferred to 2007:** University of Wyoming, Chadron State College.

**Basis for selection.** Open admission. **Homeschooled:** Transcript of courses and grades required. ACT recommended but not required. Signed statement that student was homeschooled required for financial aid.

**2007-2008 Annual costs.** Tuition/fees: $1,968; $4,944 out-of-state. Per-credit charge: $62 in-state; $186 out-of-state. Students from Western Undergraduate Exchange pay $2,232 tuition plus fees per year; $93 per credit hour. Room/board: $3,594. Books/supplies: $950. Personal expenses: $1,370.

**Financial aid. Need-based:** Need-based aid available for part-time students. Work-study available nights, weekends and for part-time students. **Non-need-based:** Scholarships awarded for academics, alumni affiliation, art, athletics, leadership, music/drama. **Additional information:** Installment payment plan on room and board contracts offered.

**Application procedures. Admission:** No deadline. No application fee. Application may be submitted online. Admission notification on a rolling basis. **Financial aid:** Priority date 3/15; no closing date. FAFSA, institutional form required. Applicants notified on a rolling basis starting 1/1.

**Academics. Special study options:** Cross-registration, distance learning, dual enrollment of high school students, ESL, independent study, internships. License preparation on campus for welding and joining, veterinary technology, and cosmetology. Bachelor's degree programs available on campus. **Credit/placement by examination:** AP, CLEP, IB, institutional tests. 16 credit hours maximum toward associate degree. **Support services:** GED preparation and test center, learning center, reduced course load, remedial instruction, study skills assistance, tutoring.

**Majors. Agriculture:** General, agribusiness operations, animal sciences, economics, farm/ranch, range science. **Biology:** General, environmental. **Business:** Accounting, administrative services, business admin, management information systems, office management. **Communications:** General. **Conservation:** Wildlife. **Education:** Agricultural, business, elementary, mathematics, music, physical, secondary. **English:** English lit. **Foreign languages:** General. **Health:** Predental, premedicine, prepharmacy, preveterinary, veterinary technology/assistant. **History:** General. **Liberal arts:** Arts/sciences. **Math:** General, statistics. **Personal/culinary services:** Cosmetic. **Production:** Welding. **Protective services:** Criminal justice, police science. **Psychology:** General. **Social sciences:** Economics, political science, sociology. **Visual/performing arts:** Art.

**Most popular majors.** Business/marketing 14%, education 19%, health sciences 14%, liberal arts 25%, personal/culinary services 8%, security/protective services 6%, trade and industry 7%.

**Computing on campus.** 120 workstations in dormitories, library, student center. Dormitories wired for high-speed internet access. Online course registration available.

**Student life. Freshman orientation:** Available. Preregistration for classes offered. Held in fall 1 day prior to first day of classes. **Housing:** Coed dorms, substance-free housing available. $100 fully refundable deposit. **Activities:** Campus ministries, choral groups, musical theater, student government, student newspaper.

**Athletics.** NJCAA. **Intercollegiate:** Basketball M, golf M, rodeo, volleyball W. **Intramural:** Basketball, bowling, handball, racquetball, rodeo, softball, tennis, volleyball, weight lifting. **Team name:** Lancers.

**Student services.** Adult student services, alcohol/substance abuse counseling, campus ministries, career counseling, student employment services, financial aid counseling, health services, personal counseling, placement for graduates, veterans' counselor. **Physically disabled:** Services for visually, speech, hearing impaired. **Transfer:** Re-entry adviser, pre-admission transcript evaluation for new students. Transfer adviser, college fairs on campus for students transferring to 4-year colleges.

**Contact.** E-mail: marilyn.cotant@ewc.wy.edu
Phone: (307) 532-8230 Toll-free number: (800) 658-3195
Fax: (307) 532-8222
Marilyn Cotant, Dean of Students, Eastern Wyoming College, 3200 West C Street, Torrington, WY 82240

---

## Institute of Business & Medical Careers
### Cheyenne, Wyoming
### www.ibmcedu.com

- For-profit 2-year business and health science college
- Small city

**General.** Accredited by ACICS. **Calendar:** Continuous.

**Contact.** Phone: (307) 433-8363
3425 Dell Range Boulevard, Cheyenne, WY 82009

---

## Laramie County Community College
### Cheyenne, Wyoming
### www.lccc.wy.edu          CB code: 0360

- Public 2-year community college
- Commuter campus in small city

**General.** Founded in 1968. Regionally accredited. Additional campus in Laramie, outreach center in Pine Bluffs. **Enrollment:** 2,931 degree-seeking undergraduates; 1,865 non-degree-seeking students. **Degrees:** 406 associate awarded. **ROTC:** Air Force. **Location:** 4 miles from downtown, 100 miles from Denver. **Calendar:** Semester, limited summer session. **Full-time faculty:** 92 total; 8% have terminal degrees, 3% minority, 60% women. **Part-time faculty:** 190 total; 6% minority, 53% women. **Class size:** 79% < 20, 19% 20-39, less than 1% 40-49, 1% 50-99. **Special facilities:** Bureau of Land Management Park, indoor arena, networking laboratory.

**Student profile.** Among degree-seeking undergraduates, 35% enrolled in a transfer program, 23% enrolled in a vocational program, 1% already have a bachelor's degree or higher, 351 enrolled as first-time, first-year students, 782 transferred in from other institutions.

| | | | |
|---|---|---|---|
| Part-time: | 42% | Hispanic American: | 8% |
| Out-of-state: | 12% | Native American: | 1% |
| Women: | 64% | International: | 1% |
| African American: | 2% | 25 or older: | 50% |
| Asian American: | 2% | Live on campus: | 2% |

**Transfer out.** 55% of students enrolled in the transfer program go on to 4-year colleges.

**Basis for selection.** Open admission, but selective for some programs. Special requirements for nursing, radiography, equine studies, dental hygiene programs. Interview required for equine studies. **Homeschooled:** Students must complete institutional home schooler form and attach to transcript. **Learning Disabled:** Interview with Disability Resource Center coordinator to arrange accomodations.

**2007-2008 Annual costs.** Tuition/fees: $2,088; $5,064 out-of-state. Per-credit charge: $62 in-state; $186 out-of-state. Students from Western Undergraduate Exchange schools and Nebraska residents pay $2,832 in tuition and fees per year; $118 per credit hour. Room/board: $5,472. Books/supplies: $850.

**2007-2008 Financial aid.** **Need-based:** Need-based aid available for part-time students. **Non-need-based:** Scholarships awarded for academics, art, athletics, music/drama.

**Application procedures.** **Admission:** No deadline. $20 fee. Application may be submitted online. Admission notification on a rolling basis. Nursing, radiology, and dental hygiene applications must be received by February 1. **Financial aid:** Priority date 4/1; no closing date. FAFSA, institutional form required. Applicants notified on a rolling basis starting 6/1; must reply within 2 week(s) of notification.

**Academics. Special study options:** Cooperative education, distance learning, dual enrollment of high school students, internships. License preparation in dental hygiene, nursing, radiology. **Credit/placement by examination:** AP, CLEP, IB, institutional tests. 15 credit hours maximum toward associate degree. **Support services:** GED preparation and test center, learning center, remedial instruction, study skills assistance, tutoring.

**Majors. Agriculture:** General, agribusiness operations, business technology, equestrian studies, production. **Biology:** General. **Business:** General, accounting, business admin, entrepreneurial studies, management science. **Communications:** General, digital media, media studies. **Computer sciences:** General, computer science, information technology, programming, systems analysis, web page design. **Conservation:** Wildlife. **Construction:** General. **Education:** General, early childhood, physical, special. **Engineering:** General. **Engineering technology:** Civil. **English:** English lit. **Foreign languages:** Spanish. **Health:** Dental hygiene, medical radiologic technology/radiation therapy, nursing (RN), physical therapy assistant, predental, premedicine, prepharmacy, preveterinary, radiologic technology/medical imaging, sonography, surgical technology. **History:** General. **Interdisciplinary:** Biological/physical sciences. **Legal studies:** Paralegal, prelaw. **Liberal arts:** Humanities. **Math:** General. **Mechanic/repair:** Auto body, automotive, diesel. **Philosophy/religion:** Philosophy, religion. **Physical sciences:** Chemistry. **Protective services:** Corrections, emergency management/homeland security, law enforcement admin. **Psychology:** General. **Public administration:** General, human services. **Social sciences:** General, anthropology, economics, political science, sociology. **Visual/performing arts:** General, dramatic.

**Most popular majors.** Business/marketing 9%, education 12%, health sciences 25%, interdisciplinary studies 19%.

**Computing on campus.** Dormitories wired for high-speed internet access. Online course registration, helpline, wireless network available.

**Student life. Freshman orientation:** Available. Preregistration for classes offered. **Housing:** Coed dorms, substance-free housing available. $100 deposit. **Activities:** Bands, choral groups, drama, literary magazine, music ensembles, musical theater, student government, student newspaper, TV station.

**Athletics.** NJCAA. **Intercollegiate:** Basketball M, equestrian, rodeo, soccer, volleyball W. **Intramural:** Soccer. **Team name:** Golden Eagles.

**Student services.** Adult student services, alcohol/substance abuse counseling, career counseling, services for economically disadvantaged, student employment services, financial aid counseling, on-campus daycare, personal counseling, placement for graduates, veterans' counselor. **Physically disabled:** Services for visually, speech, hearing impaired. **Transfer:** College fairs on campus for students transferring to 4-year colleges.

**Contact.** E-mail: LearnMore@lccc.wy.edu
Phone: (307) 778-1357 Toll-free number: (800) 522-2993 ext. 1357
Fax: (307) 778-1350
Holly Allison, Director of Admissions, Laramie County Community College, 1400 East College Drive, Cheyenne, WY 82007-3299

---

## Northwest College
### Powell, Wyoming
### www.northwestcollege.edu          CB code: 4542

- Public 2-year community college
- Residential campus in small town

**General.** Founded in 1946. Regionally accredited. **Enrollment:** 1,765 degree-seeking undergraduates. **Degrees:** 336 associate awarded. **Location:** 90 miles from Billings, Montana. **Calendar:** Semester, limited summer session. **Full-time faculty:** 85 total. **Part-time faculty:** 65 total. **Class size:** 85% < 20, 15% 20-39, less than 1% 40-49.

**Student profile.**

| | | | |
|---|---|---|---|
| Out-of-state: | 26% | Live on campus: | 40% |
| 25 or older: | 24% | | |

**Transfer out.** **Colleges most students transferred to 2007:** University of Wyoming, Montana State University-Bozeman, Montana State University-Billings.

**Basis for selection.** Open admission, but selective for some programs and for out-of-state students. Admissions for out-of-state applicants based on high school GPA and test scores. Nursing, photography, and equestrian training programs require extra applications and qualifications. Placement tests in math and English required for all first-time freshmen. SAT or ACT required of out-of-state students. **Learning Disabled:** Individuals must identify needs in order to to procure services.

**High school preparation.** Recommended units include English 4, mathematics 2, social studies 2 and science 1.

**2007-2008 Annual costs.** Tuition/fees: $2,022; $4,998 out-of-state. Per-credit charge: $62 in-state; $186 out-of-state. Students from Western Undergraduate Exchange schools pay $2,232 tuition; $93 per credit hour. Room/board: $3,488. Books/supplies: $700. Personal expenses: $1,285.

**Financial aid. Need-based:** Work-study available nights and for part-time students. **Non-need-based:** Scholarships awarded for academics, athletics. **Additional information:** Interview, essay recommended for scholarships.

**Application procedures. Admission:** No deadline. No application fee. Admission notification on a rolling basis. **Financial aid:** Priority date 5/1; no closing date. FAFSA, institutional form required. Applicants notified on a rolling basis starting 5/1; must reply within 2 week(s) of notification.

**Academics. Special study options:** Accelerated study, cooperative education, distance learning, double major, dual enrollment of high school students, honors, independent study, internships, liberal arts/career combination, study abroad, teacher certification program. Bachelor's degree programs available on campus. License preparation in nursing. **Credit/placement by examination:** CLEP, institutional tests. 16 credit hours maximum toward associate degree. **Support services:** GED preparation and test center, learning center, reduced course load, remedial instruction, study skills assistance, tutoring. ·

**Majors. Agriculture:** General, animal sciences, business, equestrian studies, range science, soil science. **Biology:** General. **Business:** General, administrative services, business admin, management information systems, managerial economics, office management, tourism promotion. **Communications:** General, journalism. **Communications technology:** Graphic/printing. **Computer sciences:** General, information systems. **Conservation:** Forestry, management/policy, wildlife. **Education:** General, agricultural, early childhood, elementary, secondary, special. **Engineering:** General. **Engineering technology:** Drafting. **English:** English lit. **Foreign languages:** General. **Health:** Predental, premedicine, prepharmacy, preveterinary. **History:** General. **Interdisciplinary:** Biological/physical sciences. **Legal studies:** Prelaw. **Liberal arts:** Arts/sciences. **Math:** General. **Parks/recreation:** Facilities management. **Physical sciences:** Chemistry, physics. **Psychology:** General. **Social sciences:** General, political science, sociology. **Visual/performing arts:** Commercial photography, commercial/advertising art, design, photography.

**Computing on campus.** 134 workstations in dormitories, library, computer center, student center. Commuter students can connect to campus network.

**Student life. Freshman orientation:** Available, $35 fee. Preregistration for classes offered. Held once in June, July, and August. **Housing:** Coed dorms, single-sex dorms, apartments available. $100 deposit. Theme houses available. **Activities:** Bands, choral groups, dance, drama, literary magazine, music ensembles, musical theater, student government, student newspaper, symphony orchestra, Northwest Trail Blazers, civic service organization.

**Athletics.** NJCAA. **Intercollegiate:** Basketball, volleyball W, wrestling M. **Intramural:** Archery, badminton, baseball M, basketball, cross-country, field hockey W, golf, handball, racquetball, rifle M, sailing, skiing, soccer, softball, squash, swimming, table tennis, tennis, volleyball, wrestling M. **Team name:** Trappers.

**Student services.** Adult student services, alcohol/substance abuse counseling, campus ministries, career counseling, student employment services, financial aid counseling, health services, minority student services, on-campus daycare, personal counseling, placement for graduates, veterans' counselor. **Physically disabled:** Services for visually, speech, hearing impaired. **Transfer:** Pre-admission transcript evaluation for new students. Transfer adviser, college fairs on-campus for students transferring to 4-year colleges.

**Contact.** E-mail: admissions@northwestcollege.edu
Phone: (307) 754-6101 Toll-free number: (800) 560-4692
Fax: (307) 754-6249
Brad Hammond, Registrar, Northwest College, 231 West 6th Street, Powell, WY 82435

## Sheridan College
**Sheridan, Wyoming**
**www.sheridan.edu**

CB code: 4536

♦ Public 2-year community college
♦ Commuter campus in large town

**General.** Founded in 1948. Regionally accredited. **Enrollment:** 1,518 degree-seeking undergraduates; 1,229 non-degree-seeking students. **Degrees:** 222 associate awarded. **Location:** 130 miles from Casper; 130 miles from Billings, Montana. **Calendar:** Semester, limited summer session. **Full-time faculty:** 83 total; 19% have terminal degrees, 4% minority, 59% women. **Part-time faculty:** 81 total; 4% have terminal degrees, 2% minority, 62% women. **Class size:** 75% < 20, 24% 20-39, 1% 40-49. **Special facilities:** Geological museum, federal depository for government publications, observatory.

**Student profile.** Among degree-seeking undergraduates, 29% enrolled in a transfer program, 26% enrolled in a vocational program, 349 enrolled as first-time, first-year students, 130 transferred in from other institutions.

| | | | |
|---|---|---|---|
| Part-time: | 35% | Hispanic American: | 3% |
| Out-of-state: | 15% | Native American: | 2% |
| Women: | 64% | International: | 1% |
| African American: | 1% | 25 or older: | 37% |
| Asian American: | 1% | Live on campus: | 9% |

**Transfer out. Colleges most students transferred to 2007:** University of Wyoming, Chadron State College, Black Hills State University, Montana State University.

**Basis for selection.** Open admission, but selective for some programs. Special admissions for nursing, dental hygiene, massage therapy; requirements vary by program.

**High school preparation.** One chemistry required of dental hygiene applicants.

**2007-2008 Annual costs.** Tuition/fees: $2,016; $4,992 out-of-state. Per-credit charge: $62 in-state; $186 out-of-state. Room/board: $3,920. Books/supplies: $900. Personal expenses: $1,800.

**2006-2007 Financial aid. Need-based:** 64% of total undergraduate aid awarded as scholarships/grants, 36% as loans/jobs. Need-based aid available for part-time students. Work-study available nights, weekends and for part-time students. **Non-need-based:** Scholarships awarded for academics, art, athletics, leadership, music/drama, state residency.

**Application procedures. Admission:** No deadline. No application fee. Application may be submitted online. Admission notification on a rolling basis. **Financial aid:** Priority date 3/1; no closing date. FAFSA, institutional form required. Applicants notified on a rolling basis; must reply within 3 week(s) of notification.

**Academics. Special study options:** Cooperative education, distance learning, double major, dual enrollment of high school students, ESL, independent study, internships, liberal arts/career combination. Bachelor's degree programs available on campus. License preparation in dental hygiene, nursing. **Credit/placement by examination:** AP, CLEP, institutional tests. 18 credit hours maximum toward associate degree. **Support services:** GED preparation and test center, learning center, reduced course load, remedial instruction, study skills assistance, tutoring, writing center.

**Majors. Agriculture:** General, animal sciences, business, food science, horticultural science, range science. **Biology:** General, microbiology. **Business:** General, administrative services, hospitality admin. **Communications:** General. **Computer sciences:** General, information systems, webmaster. **Education:** Elementary, secondary, teacher assistance. **Engineering:** General. **Engineering technology:** CAD/CADD, surveying. **English:** English lit. **Foreign languages:** General, Spanish. **Health:** Dental hygiene, massage therapy, nursing (RN). **History:** General. **Interdisciplinary:** Biological/physical sciences. **Legal studies:** Legal secretary. **Liberal arts:** Arts/sciences, humanities. **Math:** General. **Mechanic/repair:** Diesel. **Parks/recreation:** Health/fitness. **Personal/culinary services:** Chef training. **Physical sciences:** General, chemistry. **Production:** Machine tool, welding. **Protective services:** Criminal justice, police science. **Psychology:** General. **Public administration:** Social work. **Social sciences:** General, political science, sociology. **Visual/performing arts:** Art, dramatic.

**Most popular majors.** Business/marketing 12%, health sciences 26%, interdisciplinary studies 9%, liberal arts 18%, trade and industry 10%.

**Computing on campus.** 500 workstations in dormitories, library, student center. Dormitories wired for high-speed internet access and linked to campus network. Commuter students can connect to campus network. Online library, helpline, student web hosting, wireless network available.

**Student life. Freshman orientation:** Mandatory. Preregistration for classes offered. Online orientation. **Housing:** Coed dorms, single-sex dorms, special housing for disabled, apartments available. $60 fully refundable deposit. Apartments available for single parents. **Activities:** Bands, choral groups, drama, music ensembles, student government, student newspaper, art club, nursing clubs, dental auxiliary, multidiversity club.

**Athletics.** NJCAA. **Intercollegiate:** Basketball, rodeo, volleyball W. **Intramural:** Basketball, bowling, soccer, softball, tennis, volleyball. **Team name:** Generals.

**Student services.** Adult student services, career counseling, student employment services, financial aid counseling, health services, personal counseling, placement for graduates. **Physically disabled:** Services for visually, speech, hearing impaired. **Transfer:** Pre-admission transcript evaluation for new students. Transfer adviser, college fairs on campus for students transferring to 4-year colleges.

**Contact.** E-mail: admissions@sheridan.edu
Phone: (307) 674-6446 ext. 2002 Toll-free number: (800) 913-9139
Fax: (307) 674-3373
Zane Garstad, Director of Admissions, Sheridan College, PO Box 1500, Sheridan, WY 82801-1500

## Western Wyoming Community College
### Rock Springs, Wyoming
www.wwcc.wy.edu                    CB code: 4957

- Public 2-year community college
- Commuter campus in large town

**General.** Founded in 1959. Regionally accredited. **Enrollment:** 2,139 degree-seeking undergraduates; 1,231 non-degree-seeking students. **Degrees:** 321 associate awarded. **Location:** 180 miles from Salt Lake City. **Calendar:** Semester, limited summer session. **Full-time faculty:** 70 total; 21% have terminal degrees, 6% minority, 56% women. **Part-time faculty:** 149 total. **Class size:** 82% < 20, 18% 20-39. **Special facilities:** Dinosaur museum, natural history museum, wildlife exhibit.

**Student profile.** Among degree-seeking undergraduates, 58% enrolled in a transfer program, 21% enrolled in a vocational program, 1% already have a bachelor's degree or higher, 555 enrolled as first-time, first-year students.

| | | | |
|---|---|---|---|
| Part-time: | 54% | Native American: | 1% |
| Out-of-state: | 14% | International: | 4% |
| Women: | 61% | 25 or older: | 48% |
| Asian American: | 1% | Live on campus: | 30% |
| Hispanic American: | 7% | | |

**Transfer out.** 66% of students enrolled in the transfer program go on to 4-year colleges. **Colleges most students transferred to 2007:** University of Wyoming, Utah State University, Idaho State University.

**Basis for selection.** Open admission, but selective for some programs. Admissions to nursing program based on academic performance, pre-entrance exam and prerequisite course completion. **Homeschooled:** If home school is not through an accredited institution, student needs to obtain GED.

**High school preparation.** Recommended units include English 4, mathematics 3, social studies 2, science 3 (laboratory 1) and foreign language 2.

**2007-2008 Annual costs.** Tuition/fees: $1,828; $4,804 out-of-state. Per-credit charge: $59 in-state; $178 out-of-state. Room/board: $3,610. Books/supplies: $700.

**2007-2008 Financial aid.** **Need-based:** Average scholarship/grant was $1,331; average loan $1,088. 56% of total undergraduate aid awarded as scholarships/grants, 44% as loans/jobs. Need-based aid available for part-time students. Work-study available for part-time students. **Non-need-based:** Scholarships awarded for academics, art, athletics, music/drama, state residency.

**Application procedures.** **Admission:** No deadline. No application fee. Application may be submitted online. Admission notification on a rolling basis. **Financial aid:** Priority date 4/1; no closing date. FAFSA required. Applicants notified on a rolling basis starting 3/15; must reply within 2 week(s) of notification.

**Academics.** Provide online turtoring through Smart Thinking at no charge to students. **Special study options:** Cooperative education, distance learning, dual enrollment of high school students, ESL, external degree, honors, independent study, internships. Bachelor's degree programs available on campus. License preparation in nursing. **Credit/placement by examination:** AP, CLEP, IB, institutional tests. 40 credit hours maximum toward associate degree. **Support services:** GED preparation and test center, learning center, remedial instruction, study skills assistance, tutoring.

**Honors college/program.** Competitive program, open to 20 students a year. Students participate in challenging courses and travel to cultural and educational events at the expense of the institution.

**Majors. Biology:** General, ecology, wildlife. **Business:** Accounting, administrative services, business admin, marketing, office technology. **Communications:** General, journalism. **Computer sciences:** General, computer science, data processing, information systems. **Conservation:** General, environmental studies, water/wetlands/marine, wildlife. **Education:** General, elementary, multi-level teacher, secondary. **Engineering:** General. **Engineering technology:** Instrumentation, mining. **English:** English lit. **Family/consumer sciences:** General. **Foreign languages:** Spanish. **Health:** Licensed practical nurse, medical assistant, medical secretary, predental, premedicine, prenursing, prepharmacy, preveterinary. **History:** General. **Legal studies:** Prelaw. **Math:** General. **Mechanic/repair:** Automotive, diesel, electronics/electrical, heavy equipment, industrial, industrial electronics. **Parks/recreation:** Exercise sciences. **Physical sciences:** Chemistry, geology. **Production:** Welding. **Protective services:** Law enforcement admin. **Psychology:** General. **Public administration:** Social work. **Social sciences:** General, anthropology, archaeology, criminology, economics, international relations, political science, sociology. **Visual/performing arts:** General, art, ceramics, dance, dramatic, studio arts, theater design.

**Most popular majors.** Business/marketing 9%, education 7%, engineering/engineering technologies 9%, health sciences 20%, liberal arts 21%, trade and industry 10%.

**Computing on campus.** 210 workstations in dormitories, library, computer center, student center. Dormitories wired for high-speed internet access and linked to campus network. Commuter students can connect to campus network. Online course registration, online library, helpline, wireless network available.

**Student life.** **Freshman orientation:** Mandatory. Preregistration for classes offered. Program for students and parents. **Housing:** Coed dorms, special housing for disabled, apartments available. $150 partly refundable deposit. **Activities:** Bands, choral groups, dance, drama, music ensembles, musical theater, student government, student newspaper, Phi Theta Kappa, outdoor club, ambassadors, Students Without Borders.

**Athletics.** NJCAA. **Intercollegiate:** Basketball, cheerleading, soccer, volleyball W, wrestling M. **Intramural:** Basketball, football (non-tackle), softball, table tennis, tennis, volleyball. **Team name:** Mustangs.

**Student services.** Adult student services, alcohol/substance abuse counseling, career counseling, student employment services, financial aid counseling, on-campus daycare, personal counseling, placement for graduates, veterans' counselor. **Physically disabled:** Services for visually, hearing impaired. **Transfer:** Pre-admission transcript evaluation for new students. Transfer adviser, college fairs on campus for students transferring to 4-year colleges.

**Contact.** E-mail: admissions@wwcc.wy.edu
Phone: (307) 382-1648 Toll-free number: (800) 226-1181
Fax: (307) 382-1636
Joe Mueller, Director of Admissions, Western Wyoming Community College, Box 428, Rock Springs, WY 82902-0428

## WyoTech: Laramie
### Laramie, Wyoming
www.wyotech.com                    CB code: 7141

- For-profit 2-year technical college
- Large town
- Interview required

**General.** Founded in 1966. Accredited by ACCSCT. **Enrollment:** 1,391 degree-seeking undergraduates. **Degrees:** 2,547 associate awarded. **Location:** 50 miles from Cheyenne, 70 miles from Ft. Collins, Colorado. **Calendar:** Differs by program. **Full-time faculty:** 79 total.

**Basis for selection.** Open admission.

**2007-2008 Annual costs.** Tuition ranges from $23,700 to $32,400 depending on program. Books and tools loaned at no additional charge except for $100 refundable tool deposit. Room rent in institutional housing $250-$400 per month.

**Financial aid.** All financial aid based on need.

**Application procedures.** **Admission:** No deadline. No application fee. Admission notification on a rolling basis. **Financial aid:** No deadline. FAFSA required. Applicants notified on a rolling basis.

**Academics.** **Special study options:** Double major. **Credit/placement by examination:** CLEP. **Support services:** Tutoring.

**Majors. Mechanic/repair:** Auto body, automotive, diesel.

**Computing on campus.** 2 workstations in library.

**Student life. Freshman orientation:** Mandatory. **Housing:** Guaranteed on-campus for all undergraduates. Coed dorms, special housing for disabled, apartments available. $100 fully refundable deposit.

**Athletics. Intramural:** Basketball, bowling, football (non-tackle), softball M, volleyball, weight lifting.

**Student services.** Career counseling, student employment services, personal counseling, placement for graduates. **Physically disabled:** Services for visually, hearing impaired.

**Contact.** E-mail: admissions@wyotech.com
Phone: (307) 742-3776 Toll-free number: (800) 521-7158
Fax: (307) 742-4852
Glenn Halsey, Director of Admissions, WyoTech: Laramie, 4373 North Third Street, Laramie, WY 82072

# American Samoa

# Guam

## American Samoa Community College
Pago Pago, American Samoa
www.amsamoa.edu                    CB code: 0020

- Public 2-year community college
- Commuter campus in large town

**General.** Founded in 1970. Regionally accredited. Only institution of higher education in American Samoa and only land grant institution in the South Pacific. Students seeking 4-year degrees often transfer to colleges in Hawaii or mainland United States. **Enrollment:** 1,684 degree-seeking undergraduates. **Degrees:** 217 associate awarded. **ROTC:** Army. **Location:** 9 miles from downtown. **Calendar:** Semester, limited summer session. **Full-time faculty:** 55 total; 13% have terminal degrees, 100% minority, 44% women. **Part-time faculty:** 33 total; 100% minority, 39% women.

**Basis for selection.** Open admission. Institutional placement exam may be required for applicants without SAT/ACT scores.

**2007-2008 Annual costs.** Tuition/fees: $1,410; $1,860 out-of-state. Per-credit charge: $45 in-state; $60 out-of-state. Books/supplies: $800. Personal expenses: $900.

**Application procedures. Admission:** No deadline. No application fee. Admission notification on a rolling basis. **Financial aid:** No deadline. FAFSA required. Applicants notified on a rolling basis; must reply within 3 week(s) of notification.

**Academics. Special study options:** Distance learning, independent study, teacher certification program. Bachelor's degree programs available on campus. License preparation in nursing. **Credit/placement by examination:** CLEP, institutional tests. Credit by examination for course credit may be taken only once. "E" grades for credit by examination will not be counted toward overall grade point average and cumulative grade point average. Credits earned by examination are not covered under federal financial aid. **Support services:** GED preparation, learning center, reduced course load, remedial instruction, study skills assistance, tutoring.

**Majors. Agriculture:** Business. **Business:** Accounting, business admin, office management. **Conservation:** Management/policy. **Construction:** Maintenance. **Education:** General, multi-level teacher. **Engineering technology:** Architectural drafting, civil. **Legal studies:** Prelaw. **Liberal arts:** Arts/sciences. **Mechanic/repair:** Auto body, automotive, electronics/electrical. **Production:** Welding. **Protective services:** Forensics. **Public administration:** Human services. **Transportation:** Maritime/Merchant Marine. **Visual/performing arts:** Art.

**Computing on campus.** 104 workstations in library, computer center. Helpline, repair service available.

**Student life. Freshman orientation:** Available. Preregistration for classes offered. **Activities:** Bands, choral groups, dance, drama, music ensembles, musical theater, student government, student newspaper, Phi Theta Kappa, Polynesian club, Christian club, You Are Not Alone Coalition (emotional support for young people).

**Athletics. Intramural:** Basketball, golf, tennis, volleyball, weight lifting. **Team name:** Chiefs.

**Student services.** Career counseling, health services, personal counseling, veterans' counselor. **Transfer:** Transfer adviser for students transferring to 4-year colleges.

**Contact.** E-mail: admissions@amsamoa.edu
Phone: (684) 699-9155 ext. 411 Fax: (684) 699-1083
James Sutherland, Admissions Officer, American Samoa Community College, PO Box 2609, Pago Pago, AS 96799-2609

## Guam Community College
Barrigada, Guam                    CB member
www.guamcc.edu                     CB code: 2302

- Public 2-year community and technical college
- Commuter campus in small city

**General.** Founded in 1977. Regionally accredited. Multicultural U.S. territory with island setting. **Enrollment:** 977 degree-seeking undergraduates. **Degrees:** 67 associate awarded. **ROTC:** Army. **Location:** 1,500 miles from Manila, Philippines; 3,600 miles from Honolulu. **Calendar:** Semester, limited summer session. **Full-time faculty:** 53 total. **Part-time faculty:** 74 total. **Special facilities:** Rare book collection of more than 400 volumes devoted to history of Guam, Micronesia, and the Pacific.

**Transfer out. Colleges most students transferred to 2007:** University of Guam.

**Basis for selection.** Open admission. **Homeschooled:** Official high school transcript required.

**High school preparation.** Recommended units include English 4, mathematics 3, social studies 3, science 2 and academic electives 9.

**2007-2008 Annual costs.** Tuition/fees: $2,966; $3,716 out-of-state. Per-credit charge: $90 in-state; $115 out-of-state. Books/supplies: $800. Personal expenses: $2,250.

**Financial aid. Additional information:** Tuition assistance available for students in nontraditional courses.

**Application procedures. Admission:** No deadline. No application fee. Application must be submitted on paper. Admission notification on a rolling basis. **Financial aid:** Priority date 5/1; no closing date. FAFSA, institutional form required. Applicants notified on a rolling basis starting 8/28; must reply within 2 week(s) of notification.

**Academics. Special study options:** Cooperative education, cross-registration, double major, dual enrollment of high school students, independent study, internships. **Credit/placement by examination:** AP, CLEP, institutional tests. 48 credit hours maximum toward associate degree. **Support services:** GED preparation and test center, learning center, remedial instruction, study skills assistance, tutoring.

**Majors. Business:** Accounting, office management, office technology, sales/distribution, tourism/travel. **Computer sciences:** Computer science. **Education:** Early childhood, teacher assistance. **Family/consumer sciences:** Institutional food production. **Health:** Medical assistant. **Liberal arts:** Arts/sciences. **Mechanic/repair:** Automotive. **Personal/culinary services:** Chef training. **Protective services:** Law enforcement admin. **Visual/performing arts:** Graphic design.

**Computing on campus.** 79 workstations in library, computer center, student center. Online library, repair service available.

**Student life. Freshman orientation:** Available. Held 1 week before start of semester. **Activities:** Student government, Habitat for Humanity, Health Occupational Students of America, Phi Theta Kappa, Postsecondary Tourism Association.

**Student services.** Adult student services, alcohol/substance abuse counseling, career counseling, services for economically disadvantaged, student employment services, financial aid counseling, health services, personal counseling, placement for graduates, veterans' counselor. **Physically disabled:** Services for visually, speech, hearing impaired. **Transfer:** Re-entry adviser for new students.

**Contact.** E-mail: pclymer@guamcc.edu
Phone: (671) 735-5531 Fax: (671) 734-5238
Patrick Clymer, Coordinator of Admissions and Registration, Guam Community College, PO Box 23069 GMF, Barrigada, GU 96921

# Northern Mariana Islands

---

### Northern Marianas College
Saipan, Northern Mariana Islands
www.nmcnet.edu

CB code: 0781

- Public 2-year community and liberal arts college
- Commuter campus in large town

**General.** Founded in 1981. Regionally accredited. **Location:** 150 miles from Guam, 3,000 miles from Hawaii. **Calendar:** Semester.

**Annual costs/financial aid.** Personal expenses: $775.

**Contact.** Phone: (670) 234-3690 ext. 1528, 1539
Registrar, PO Box 501250, Saipan, MP 96950

---

# Marshall Islands

---

### College of the Marshall Islands
Majuro, Marshall Islands
www.cmiedu.net

CB code: 7142

- Public 2-year community and junior college
- Commuter campus in large town

**General.** Regionally accredited. **Location:** 2,280 miles from Honolulu. **Calendar:** Semester.

**Annual costs/financial aid.** Books/supplies: $600.

**Contact.** Phone: (692) 625-6895
Director of Admissions and Records, Box 1258, Majuro, MH 96960

---

# Micronesia

---

### College of Micronesia-FSM
Kolonia, Micronesia
www.comfsm.fm

CB code: 0115

- Public 2-year community college
- Commuter campus in small city

**General.** Founded in 1963. Regionally accredited. **Enrollment:** 2,349 degree-seeking undergraduates. **Degrees:** 233 associate awarded. **Calendar:** Semester, limited summer session. **Full-time faculty:** 110 total.

**Student profile.**

| | | | |
|---|---|---|---|
| Out-of-state: | 7% | Live on campus: | 20% |
| 25 or older: | 16% | | |

**Transfer out. Colleges most students transferred to 2007:** University of Hawaii at Hilo, University of Guam, Southwestern Adventist University, Chaminade University, Durham Community College.

**Basis for selection.** Minimum 2.0 high school GPA and institutional test scores required. **Homeschooled:** Transcript of courses and grades, letter of recommendation (nonparent) required. First-time students should pass the College of Micronesia-FSM Entrance Test in order to be eligible for admission into degree or certificate programs.

**2007-2008 Annual costs.** Tuition/fees: $3,050. Per-credit charge: $95. Room/board: $3,086. Books/supplies: $530.

**Financial aid.** All financial aid based on need. Work-study available nights and weekends.

**Application procedures. Admission:** Closing date 6/15. $10 fee. Admission notification on a rolling basis. **Financial aid:** No deadline. FAFSA, institutional form required. Applicants notified on a rolling basis.

**Academics. Special study options:** Cooperative education, distance learning, independent study, internships, liberal arts/career combination, teacher certification program. Bachelor's degree programs available on campus. **Credit/placement by examination:** CLEP. **Support services:** Learning center, remedial instruction, study skills assistance, tutoring.

**Majors. Agriculture:** General. **Biology:** Marine. **Business:** General, accounting. **Computer sciences:** General, computer science. **Education:** Elementary, multi-level teacher, special. **Liberal arts:** Arts/sciences.

**Computing on campus.** 6 workstations in dormitories, library, computer center, student center. Dormitories linked to campus network. Online library, repair service available.

**Student life. Freshman orientation:** Mandatory. Preregistration for classes offered. Week-long orientation held beginning of fall semester. **Housing:** Single-sex dorms available. $50 nonrefundable deposit, deadline 6/15. On-campus housing for all undergraduates on space available basis. **Activities:** Choral groups, dance, drama, radio station, student government.

**Athletics. Intercollegiate:** Basketball, softball, track and field, volleyball. **Intramural:** Basketball, softball, volleyball. **Team name:** Sharks.

**Student services.** Alcohol/substance abuse counseling, career counseling, financial aid counseling, health services, personal counseling. **Transfer:** Pre-admission transcript evaluation for new students. Transfer center, transfer adviser for students transferring to 4-year colleges.

**Contact.** E-mail: oar@comfsm.fm
Phone: (691) 320-2480 ext. 150 Fax: (691) 320-2479
Arlene Dumantay, Coordinator, College of Micronesia-FSM, PO Box 159, Kolonia, FM 96941

---

# Palau

---

### Palau Community College
Koror, Palau
www.palau.edu

CB code: 7329

- Public 2-year community and technical college
- Commuter campus in small city

**General.** Founded in 1969. Regionally accredited. **Enrollment:** 626 degree-seeking undergraduates. **Degrees:** 53 associate awarded. **Location:** 800 miles from Guam, 600 miles from Manila. **Calendar:** Semester, limited summer session. **Full-time faculty:** 28 total. **Part-time faculty:** 14 total.

**Basis for selection.** Open admission, but selective for some programs. To enter the associate of applied science degree program, a student must be a high school graduate with cumulative grade point average of 2.0 or possess a GED certificate; associate of science and associate of arts degree programs require a TOEFL score of 500 or better in addition to the above requirements; exceptions are degree programs in education and liberal arts, which require 2.5 cumulatve GPA.

**2007-2008 Annual costs.** Tuition/fees: $2,560. Per-credit charge: $70. Room/board: $2,352. Books/supplies: $1,000.

**Financial aid. Need-based:** Work-study available nights, weekends and for part-time students.

**Application procedures. Admission:** Closing date 8/29 (receipt date). $10 fee. Application must be submitted on paper. Admission notification on a rolling basis beginning on or about 4/30. **Financial aid:** Priority date 4/1; no closing date. FAFSA required. Applicants notified on a rolling basis starting 5/1.

**Academics. Special study options:** Double major, dual enrollment of high school students, internships. **Credit/placement by examination:** CLEP, institutional tests. **Support services:** Learning center, remedial instruction, study skills assistance, tutoring.

**Majors. Agriculture:** Plant breeding. **Business:** Administrative services, hospitality admin. **Conservation:** Environmental studies. **Construction:** Electrician. **Education:** Early childhood, elementary, special. **Engineering:** Electrical, mechanics. **Engineering technology:** Construction, electrical. **Liberal arts:** Arts/sciences, library science. **Mechanic/repair:** General, electronics/electrical, heating/ac/refrig. **Protective services:** Police science.

**Computing on campus.** 60 workstations in library, computer center, student center. Online library available.

**Student life. Freshman orientation:** Mandatory. Week-long program held prior to first week of classes each term designed to familiarize students with facility, programs, and services; includes administration of placement tests, academic advising, and registration. **Policies:** Possession, consumption, and storage of alcoholic beverages and illegal drugs are prohibited. **Housing:** Coed dorms, single-sex dorms available. **Activities:** Student government, Yapese, Chuukese, Kosrean, Pohnpeians, Palauans, and Marshallese ethnic clubs, Pacific writers club, agriculture science majors club.

**Athletics. Intramural:** Basketball M, softball, swimming, table tennis, volleyball, weight lifting M, wrestling M.

**Student services.** Alcohol/substance abuse counseling, career counseling, student employment services, financial aid counseling, health services, on-campus daycare, personal counseling, placement for graduates. **Physically disabled:** Services for visually impaired. **Transfer:** Pre-admission transcript evaluation for new students.

**Contact.** E-mail: dahliapcc@palaunet.com
Phone: (680) 488-2470 Fax: (680) 488-4468
Dahlia Katosang, Director of Admissions & Financial Aid, Palau Community College, PO Box 9, Koror, PW 96940

# Bermuda

<table>
<tr><td colspan="2">Bermuda College<br>Paget, Bermuda<br>www.bercol.bm</td><td>CB code: 2581</td></tr>
</table>

◗ Public 2-year community college
◗ Commuter campus in small city

**General. Enrollment:** 939 degree-seeking undergraduates. **Degrees:** 78 associate awarded. **Calendar:** Semester, limited summer session. **Full-time faculty:** 70 total.

**Basis for selection.** Open admission, but selective for out-of-state students. Overseas students must receive permission from Immigration Department to attend.

**2007-2008 Annual costs.** Tuition and fees are 3,280 BMD per year. Additional required fees for international students. Books/supplies: $400.

**Application procedures. Admission:** Priority date 2/1; deadline 5/1 (receipt date). $25 fee. Application must be submitted on paper. Admission notification on a rolling basis.

**Academics. Special study options:** Bachelor's degree programs available on campus. **Credit/placement by examination:** AP, CLEP, institutional tests. **Support services:** Study skills assistance, tutoring.

**Majors. Business:** Business admin, hospitality admin, office management. **Computer sciences:** General. **Construction:** Carpentry, plumbing. **Education:** General. **Engineering technology:** Automotive, electrical, heat/ac/

refrig, telecommunications. **Personal/culinary services:** Culinary arts. **Public administration:** Human services.

**Computing on campus.** 70 workstations in library, computer center. Wireless network available.

**Student life. Freshman orientation:** Available. Preregistration for classes offered. **Activities:** Dance, drama, literary magazine, music ensembles, student government.

**Student services.** Career counseling. **Transfer:** College fairs on campus for students transferring to 4-year colleges.

**Contact.** E-mail: admissions@college.bm
Phone: (441) 236-9000 ext. 4343 Fax: (441) 239-4051
Bermuda College, PO Box PG 297, Paget, BM

# Early decision and early action table

The following table lists early decision and early action policies at 446 colleges, which are listed alphabetically by state or country. Colleges were asked to supply the deadline for student applications and the date by which the college will notify the applicant of a decision to admit, deny admission, or defer the application to the regular admission cycle. If a college offers two early decision cycles, both sets of dates are listed.

Some colleges support both a binding early decision plan and a nonbinding early action plan and report dates for both. Colleges with binding early decision plans were asked to give the number of students who applied for early decision and the number of those applicants admitted to the fall 2007 freshman class.

| Institution | Early Applicants | | Early Decision | | Early Action | |
|---|---|---|---|---|---|---|
| | Number applied | Number admitted | Apply by | Notified by | Apply by | Notified by |
| **Alabama** | | | | | | |
| University of Mobile | | | | | 11/1 | 11/15 |
| **Arizona** | | | | | | |
| Prescott College | 27 | 27 | 12/1 | 12/15 | | |
| **Arkansas** | | | | | | |
| Philander Smith College | | | 11/1 | 11/15 | | |
| University of Arkansas | | | | | 11/15 | 12/15 |
| **California** | | | | | | |
| American Jewish University | 2 | 2 | 12/31 | 1/31 | | |
| Azusa Pacific University | | | | | 12/1 | 1/15 |
| Biola University | | | | | 12/1 | 1/15 |
| California Baptist University | | | | | 12/1 | 12/20 |
| California Design College | | | | | | |
| California Institute of Technology | 683 | 183 | | | 11/1 | 12/15 |
| California Lutheran University | 878 | 519 | | | 11/15 | 1/15 |
| California Polytechnic State University: San Luis Obispo | | | 10/31 | 12/15 | | |
| California State University: Sacramento | | | | | 11/30 | 11/1 |
| California State University: Stanislaus | | | | | 11/30 | 3/1 |
| Chapman University | 1990 | 1124 | | | 11/15 | 1/15 |
| Claremont McKenna College | 168 | 56 | 11/15 1/2 | 12/15 2/15 | | |
| Harvey Mudd College | 112 | 45 | 11/15 | 12/15 | | |
| Hope International University | | | 2/1 | | 1/15 | |
| Life Pacific College | | | | | 5/1 | |

| Institution | Early Applicants | | Early Decision | | Early Action | |
| --- | --- | --- | --- | --- | --- | --- |
| | Number applied | Number admitted | Apply by | Notified by | Apply by | Notified by |
| Loyola Marymount University | 2384 | 1115 | 11/1 | 12/20 | 11/1 | 12/20 |
| Menlo College | | | | | 12/1 | 12/15 |
| Mills College | 230 | 155 | | | 11/15 | 12/15 |
| Mount St. Mary's College | | | | | 12/1 | 1/1 |
| Northwestern Polytechnic University | | | | | | |
| Notre Dame de Namur University | | | | | 12/1 | 12/15 |
| Occidental College | 78 | 38 | 11/15 | 12/15 | | |
| Pitzer College | 94 | 52 | 11/15 | 1/1 | | |
| Point Loma Nazarene University | 1133 | 667 | | | 12/1 | 1/15 |
| Pomona College | 637 | 132 | 11/1<br>12/28 | 12/15<br>2/15 | | |
| San Francisco Art Institute | | | | | 11/15 | 12/15 |
| Santa Clara University | 2068 | 1509 | | | 11/1 | 12/31 |
| Scripps College | 84 | 50 | 11/1<br>1/1 | 12/15<br>2/15 | | |
| Soka University of America | 61 | 29 | | | 10/15 | 12/1 |
| St. Mary's College of California | | | | | 11/1 | 12/20 |
| Stanford University | 4636 | 749 | | | 11/1 | 12/15 |
| The Master's College | 292 | 180 | | | 11/15 | 12/22 |
| University of San Diego | | | | | 11/15 | 1/31 |
| University of San Francisco | 1782 | 1093 | | | 11/15 | 1/16 |
| University of the Pacific | | | | | 11/15 | 1/15 |
| University of the West | | | 3/1 | | | |
| Vanguard University of Southern California | | | | | 12/1 | 1/15 |
| Westmont College | 943 | 789 | | | 11/1 | 12/20 |
| Whittier College | | | | | 12/1 | 12/30 |

## Colorado

| Institution | Number applied | Number admitted | Apply by | Notified by | Apply by | Notified by |
| --- | --- | --- | --- | --- | --- | --- |
| CollegeAmerica: Fort Collins | | | | | | |
| Colorado College | 662 | 284 | 11/15<br>1/1 | 12/20<br>2/10 | 11/15 | 1/15 |
| University of Denver | 1677 | 1281 | | | 11/1 | 1/15 |

## Connecticut

| Institution | Number applied | Number admitted | Apply by | Notified by | Apply by | Notified by |
| --- | --- | --- | --- | --- | --- | --- |
| Fairfield University | 4073 | 2368 | | | 11/15 | 1/1 |
| Mitchell College | | | 11/15 | 12/15 | | |
| Post University | 10 | 6 | | | 11/1 | 12/1 |
| Sacred Heart University | 359 | 168 | 11/15 | 12/15 | | |
| Trinity College | 412 | 285 | 11/15<br>1/1 | 12/15<br>2/15 | | |
| United States Coast Guard Academy | 724 | 205 | | | 11/1 | 12/15 |
| University of Connecticut | 11241 | 7076 | | | 12/1 | 2/1 |
| University of Hartford | | | | | 11/15 | 12/1 |
| Wesleyan University | 665 | 288 | 11/15<br>1/1 | 12/15<br>2/15 | | |
| Yale University | | | | | 11/1 | 12/15 |

## District of Columbia

| Institution | Number applied | Number admitted | Apply by | Notified by | Apply by | Notified by |
| --- | --- | --- | --- | --- | --- | --- |
| American University | 370 | 203 | 11/15 | 12/31 | | |
| Catholic University of America | | | | | 11/15 | 12/15 |
| George Washington University | | | 11/10<br>1/10 | 12/15<br>2/15 | | |
| Georgetown University | 4572 | 920 | | | 11/1 | 12/15 |
| Howard University | | | 11/1 | 12/24 | 11/1 | 12/15 |

| Institution | Early Applicants | | Early Decision | | Early Action | |
|---|---|---|---|---|---|---|
| | Number applied | Number admitted | Apply by | Notified by | Apply by | Notified by |
| Trinity Washington University | | | | | 12/1 | 1/1 |
| **Florida** | | | | | | |
| Ave Maria University | 45 | 43 | | | 11/15 | 11/15 |
| Flagler College | 634 | 371 | 12/1 1/15 | 12/15 2/1 | | |
| Florida Southern College | 82 | 61 | 12/1 | 12/15 | | |
| Jacksonville University | | | | | 12/1 | 12/15 |
| Palm Beach Atlantic University | | | | | 12/1 | 12/15 |
| Rollins College | 278 | 190 | 11/15 | 12/15 | 12/1 | 2/1 |
| Stetson University | 24 | 21 | 11/1 | 11/25 | | |
| University of Miami | 7643 | 3864 | 11/1 | 12/15 | 11/1 | 2/1 |
| University of Tampa | | | | | 11/15 | 12/15 |
| **Georgia** | | | | | | |
| Agnes Scott College | | | 11/15 | 12/15 | | |
| Emory University | 1577 | 481 | 11/1 1/1 | 12/15 2/1 | | |
| Georgia College and State University | 1906 | 606 | | | 11/1 | 12/1 |
| Georgia Southwestern State University | | | 12/15 | 1/15 | | |
| Mercer University | 732 | 610 | | | 11/1 | 11/15 |
| Morehouse College | | | | | 11/1 | 12/15 |
| Oglethorpe University | | | | | 12/1 | 1/1 |
| Oxford College of Emory University | 513 | 335 | | | 11/1 | 12/15 |
| Spelman College | | | 11/1 | 12/15 | 11/15 | 12/31 |
| University of Georgia | | | | | 10/15 | 12/15 |
| Wesleyan College | | | 11/15 1/15 | 12/15 2/15 | 2/15 | 3/15 |
| **Idaho** | | | | | | |
| College of Idaho | 255 | 191 | | | 12/15 | |
| Northwest Nazarene University | | | | | 12/15 | 1/15 |
| **Illinois** | | | | | | |
| DePaul University | 4787 | 4208 | | * | 11/15 | 1/1 |
| Knox College | | | | | 12/1 | 12/31 |
| Lake Forest College | | | 12/1 | 12/20 | 12/1 | 12/20 |
| Moody Bible Institute | | | 12/1 | 1/15 | 12/1 | 1/15 |
| Northwestern University | 1296 | 567 | 11/1 | 12/15 | | |
| Principia College | | | | | 11/15 | 12/1 |
| School of the Art Institute of Chicago | | | | | 1/2 | 2/15 |
| Trinity College of Nursing and Health Sciences | | | 12/1 | 12/15 | | |
| University of Chicago | 3054 | 1222 | | | 11/1 | 12/15 |
| University of Illinois at Urbana-Champaign | 17038 | 8008 | | | 11/10 | 12/14 |
| Wheaton College | 1043 | 512 | | | 11/1 | 12/31 |
| **Indiana** | | | | | | |
| Butler University | 3123 | 2744 | | | 12/1 | 12/20 |
| DePauw University | | | 11/1 | 1/1 | 12/1 | 2/15 |
| Earlham College | 674 | 617 | 12/1 | 12/15 | 1/1 | 2/1 |
| Grace College | | | | | 12/1 | 12/20 |
| Hanover College | 1223 | 896 | | | 12/1 | 12/20 |

| Institution | Early Applicants | | Early Decision | | Early Action | |
| --- | --- | --- | --- | --- | --- | --- |
| | Number applied | Number admitted | Apply by | Notified by | Apply by | Notified by |
| Saint Mary's College | 96 | 82 | 11/15 | 12/15 | | |
| Taylor University | | | | | 12/1 | 12/20 |
| University of Evansville | 2131 | 1957 | | | 12/1 | 12/15 |
| University of Notre Dame | 3633 | 1500 | | | 11/1 | 12/20 |
| Valparaiso University | 1786 | 1669 | | | 11/1 | 12/1 |
| Wabash College | | | 11/15 | 12/15 | 12/15 | 1/31 |

## Iowa

| Institution | Number applied | Number admitted | Apply by | Notified by | Apply by | Notified by |
| --- | --- | --- | --- | --- | --- | --- |
| Coe College | | | | | 12/10 | 1/20 |
| Cornell College | 1247 | 565 | 11/1 2/1 | 1/15 4/1 | 12/1 | 5/1 |
| Grinnell College | 164 | 127 | 11/20 1/1 | 12/20 2/1 | | |
| Wartburg College | | | | | 12/1 | |

## Kansas

| Institution | Number applied | Number admitted | Apply by | Notified by | Apply by | Notified by |
| --- | --- | --- | --- | --- | --- | --- |
| Sterling College | | | | | 11/15 | 12/15 |
| Tabor College | 456 | 171 | 12/31 4/1 | | | |

## Kentucky

| Institution | Number applied | Number admitted | Apply by | Notified by | Apply by | Notified by |
| --- | --- | --- | --- | --- | --- | --- |
| Bellarmine University | | | | | 11/1 | 11/15 |
| Centre College | | | | | 12/1 | 1/15 |
| Transylvania University | 646 | 601 | | | 12/1 | 1/15 |

## Louisiana

| Institution | Number applied | Number admitted | Apply by | Notified by | Apply by | Notified by |
| --- | --- | --- | --- | --- | --- | --- |
| Centenary College of Louisiana | | | 12/1 | 12/15 | 1/15 | 1/15 |
| Dillard University | | | | | 12/1 | 12/30 |
| Tulane University | 175 | 56 | 11/1 | 12/15 | 11/1 | 12/15 |
| Xavier University of Louisiana | | | | | 1/15 | 2/15 |

## Maine

| Institution | Number applied | Number admitted | Apply by | Notified by | Apply by | Notified by |
| --- | --- | --- | --- | --- | --- | --- |
| Bates College | 433 | 180 | 11/15 1/1 | 12/20 2/15 | | |
| Bowdoin College | 710 | 211 | 11/15 1/1 | 12/31 2/15 | | |
| Colby College | 453 | 192 | 11/15 1/1 | 12/15 2/1 | | |
| College of the Atlantic | 40 | 37 | 12/1 1/10 | 12/15 1/25 | | |
| Maine Maritime Academy | | | 12/20 | 1/1 | | |
| St. Joseph's College | | | | | 11/15 | 12/15 |
| Thomas College | | | | | 12/15 | 12/31 |
| University of Maine | | | | | 12/15 | 1/31 |
| University of Maine at Farmington | 420 | 410 | | | 11/15 | 1/15 |
| University of Maine at Machias | | | | | 12/15 | 12/31 |

## Maryland

| Institution | Number applied | Number admitted | Apply by | Notified by | Apply by | Notified by |
| --- | --- | --- | --- | --- | --- | --- |
| Baltimore International College | | | | | 12/15 | 2/15 |
| Goucher College | 1048 | 798 | | | 12/1 | 2/15 |
| Hood College | 189 | 118 | | | 12/1 | 12/15 |
| Johns Hopkins University | 997 | 446 | 11/1 | 12/15 | | |
| Loyola College in Maryland | | | | | 11/15 | 1/15 |
| Maryland Institute College of Art | | 43 | 11/15 | 12/15 | | |
| McDaniel College | 1135 | 886 | | | 12/1 | 1/1 |
| Mount St. Mary's University | 477 | 423 | | | 12/1 | 12/15 |

| Institution | Early Applicants | | Early Decision | | Early Action | |
|---|---|---|---|---|---|---|
| | Number applied | Number admitted | Apply by | Notified by | Apply by | Notified by |
| Salisbury University | | | | | 12/1 | 1/15 |
| St. Mary's College of Maryland | 307 | 144 | 12/1 1/15 | 1/1 2/15 | | |
| University of Maryland: Baltimore County | | | | | 11/1 | 12/15 |
| University of Maryland: College Park | | | | | 12/1 | 2/15 |
| University of Maryland: Eastern Shore | | | | | 11/15 | 12/1 |
| Washington College | | | 11/15 | 12/15 | 12/1 | 12/20 |

**Massachusetts**

| Institution | Number applied | Number admitted | Apply by | Notified by | Apply by | Notified by |
|---|---|---|---|---|---|---|
| Amherst College | 350 | 135 | 11/15 | 12/15 | | |
| Assumption College | 853 | 754 | | | 11/15 | 12/15 |
| Babson College | 235 | 129 | 11/15 | 12/15 | 11/15 | 1/1 |
| Bay Path College | 357 | 296 | | | 12/15 | 1/2 |
| Bentley College | 2390 | 1230 | 11/15 | 12/15 | 11/15 | 1/15 |
| Berklee College of Music | | | | | 11/1 | 1/31 |
| Boston College | 6056 | 2027 | | | 11/1 | 12/25 |
| Boston University | 1074 | 400 | 11/1 | 12/15 | | |
| Brandeis University | 359 | 204 | 11/15 1/1 | 12/15 2/1 | | |
| Bridgewater State College | | | | | 11/15 | 12/15 |
| Clark University | 90 | 76 | 11/15 | 12/15 | | |
| College of the Holy Cross | 469 | 251 | 12/15 | 1/15 | | |
| Curry College | 127 | 55 | 12/1 | 12/15 | | |
| Emerson College | 1256 | 744 | | | 11/1 | 12/15 |
| Emmanuel College | | | 11/1 | 12/1 | | |
| Framingham State College | 289 | 235 | | | 11/15 | 12/15 |
| Gordon College | 550 | 506 | 11/15 | 12/15 | 12/1 | 1/1 |
| Hampshire College | 74 | 53 | 11/15 | 12/15 | 12/1 | 2/1 |
| Lesley University | | | | | 12/1 | 12/31 |
| Massachusetts College of Art | 91 | 70 | | | 12/1 | 1/5 |
| Massachusetts College of Liberal Arts | 231 | 160 | | | 12/1 | 12/15 |
| Massachusetts College of Pharmacy and Health Sciences | 556 | 377 | | | 11/15 | 12/15 |
| Massachusetts Institute of Technology | 3348 | 390 | | | 11/1 | 12/15 |
| Massachusetts Maritime Academy | | | | | 11/1 | 12/15 |
| Merrimack College | 773 | 549 | | | 11/15 | 12/15 |
| Mount Holyoke College | 225 | 119 | 11/15 1/1 | 1/1 2/1 | | |
| Newbury College | | | | | 12/1 | 1/1 |
| Northeastern University | 8134 | 4094 | | | 11/15 | 12/31 |
| Simmons College | | | | | 12/1 | 1/20 |
| Smith College | 227 | 147 | 11/15 1/2 | 12/15 2/2 | | |
| Springfield College | | | 12/1 | 2/1 | | |
| Stonehill College | 43 | 28 | 11/1 | 12/15 | 11/1 | 1/15 |
| Suffolk University | 1200 | 689 | | | 11/20 | 12/20 |
| Tufts University | 1293 | 425 | 11/1 1/1 | 12/15 2/1 | | |
| University of Massachusetts Amherst | 4797 | 3808 | | | 11/1 | 12/15 |
| University of Massachusetts Dartmouth | 93 | 64 | 11/15 | 12/15 | | |

| Institution | Early Applicants | | Early Decision | | Early Action | |
|---|---|---|---|---|---|---|
| | Number applied | Number admitted | Apply by | Notified by | Apply by | Notified by |
| Wellesley College | 206 | 136 | 11/1 | 12/15 | | |
| Wheaton College | 259 | 171 | 11/1 1/15 | 12/15 2/15 | | |
| Wheelock College | 192 | 167 | | | 12/1 | 12/20 |
| Williams College | 537 | 215 | 11/10 | 12/15 | | |
| Worcester Polytechnic Institute | 1641 | 1347 | | | 11/15 | 12/15 |

## Michigan

| Institution | Early Applicants | | Early Decision | | Early Action | |
|---|---|---|---|---|---|---|
| Albion College | | | | | 12/1 | 1/1 |
| Cleary University | | | | | | |
| Hillsdale College | 1010 | 668 | 11/15 | 12/1 | 1/1 | 1/20 |
| Kalamazoo College | | | 11/15 | 12/1 | 12/1 | 12/20 |
| Olivet College | | | | | 12/1 | 1/15 |
| University of Michigan | | | | | 10/31 | 12/21 |

## Minnesota

| Institution | Early Applicants | | Early Decision | | Early Action | |
|---|---|---|---|---|---|---|
| Bethel University | 1178 | 973 | | | 11/1 | 12/15 |
| Carleton College | 414 | 182 | 11/15 1/15 | 12/15 2/15 | | |
| College of St. Benedict | 1308 | 958 | | | 12/15 | 1/15 |
| Gustavus Adolphus College | 705 | 623 | | | 11/1 | 11/20 |
| Hamline University | 942 | 835 | | | 12/1 | 12/20 |
| Macalester College | 250 | 114 | 11/15 1/2 | 12/15 2/7 | | |
| St. John's University | 1084 | 770 | | | 12/15 | 1/15 |
| St. Olaf College | | | 11/1 | 12/1 | 12/1 | 2/1 |

## Mississippi

| Institution | Early Applicants | | Early Decision | | Early Action | |
|---|---|---|---|---|---|---|
| Millsaps College | 822 | 712 | | | 1/8 | |
| Mississippi College | | | 12/1 | 12/15 | | |

## Missouri

| Institution | Early Applicants | | Early Decision | | Early Action | |
|---|---|---|---|---|---|---|
| Washington University in St. Louis | | | 11/15 | 12/15 | | |

## Montana

| Institution | Early Applicants | | Early Decision | | Early Action | |
|---|---|---|---|---|---|---|
| University of Great Falls | | | | | 6/1 | 6/15 |

## Nebraska

| Institution | Early Applicants | | Early Decision | | Early Action | |
|---|---|---|---|---|---|---|
| Nebraska Wesleyan University | 542 | 492 | | | 11/15 | 12/15 |

## New Hampshire

| Institution | Early Applicants | | Early Decision | | Early Action | |
|---|---|---|---|---|---|---|
| Colby-Sawyer College | 25 | 22 | 12/1 | 12/15 | | |
| Daniel Webster College | 21 | 20 | 11/15 | | | |
| Dartmouth College | 1285 | 379 | 11/1 | 12/15 | | |
| Magdalen College | | | 1/1 | 1/15 | | |
| Rivier College | | | | | 11/15 | 12/1 |
| Southern New Hampshire University | | | | | 11/15 | 12/15 |
| St. Anselm College | 102 | 76 | 11/15 | 12/1 | | |
| University of New Hampshire | | | | | 11/15 | 1/15 |

## New Jersey

| Institution | Early Applicants | | Early Decision | | Early Action | |
|---|---|---|---|---|---|---|
| Bloomfield College | | | | | 1/7 | 1/21 |
| Caldwell College | | | | | 1/1 | 1/15 |
| Drew University | 36 | 31 | 12/1 1/15 | 12/24 2/15 | | |
| Georgian Court University | | | | | 11/15 | 12/30 |

| Institution | Early Applicants | | Early Decision | | Early Action | |
|---|---|---|---|---|---|---|
| | Number applied | Number admitted | Apply by | Notified by | Apply by | Notified by |
| Monmouth University | 2351 | 1897 | | | 12/1 | 1/15 |
| Ramapo College of New Jersey | | | | | 11/15 | 12/15 |
| Richard Stockton College of New Jersey | | | | | 2/1 | 2/15 |
| Rider University | | | 11/15 | 12/15 | 12/15 | 1/15 |
| Stevens Institute of Technology | 287 | 223 | 11/15 1/15 | 12/15 2/15 | | |
| The College of New Jersey | 532 | 225 | 11/15 | 12/15 | | |
| **New York** | | | | | | |
| Adelphi University | 1198 | 1008 | | | 12/1 | 12/31 |
| Albany College of Pharmacy | 176 | 137 | 11/1 | 12/15 | | |
| Alfred University | | | 12/1 | 12/15 | | |
| Bard College | 417 | 125 | | | 11/1 | 1/1 |
| Barnard College | 432 | 181 | 11/15 | 12/15 | | |
| City University of New York: Baruch College | | | 12/13 | 1/7 | | |
| Clarkson University | 98 | 95 | 12/1 | 1/1 | | |
| Colgate University | | | 11/15 1/15 | 12/15 | | |
| College of Mount St. Vincent | | | | | 11/1 | 12/1 |
| College of New Rochelle | | | 11/1 | 12/15 | | |
| College of Saint Rose | | | | | 12/1 | 12/15 |
| Columbia University | 2438 | 599 | 11/1 | 12/15 | | |
| Columbia University: School of General Studies | | | | | 3/1 | |
| Concordia College | 28 | 26 | | | 11/15 | 12/15 |
| Cooper Union for the Advancement of Science and Art | 380 | 76 | 12/1 12/1 | 12/23 2/1 | | |
| Cornell University | 3015 | 1101 | 11/1 | | | |
| Elmira College | | | 11/15 1/15 | 12/15 1/31 | | |
| Eugene Lang College The New School for Liberal Arts | | | 11/15 | 12/15 | | |
| Fashion Institute of Technology | 1040 | 541 | | | 11/15 | 1/31 |
| Five Towns College | 12 | 8 | 12/15 | 1/15 | | |
| Fordham University | | | | | 11/1 | 12/25 |
| Hamilton College | 640 | 232 | 11/15 1/1 | 12/15 2/15 | | |
| Hartwick College | 129 | 118 | 11/15 1/15 | 12/10 1/24 | | |
| Hobart and William Smith Colleges | 277 | 192 | 11/15 1/1 | 12/15 2/1 | | |
| Hofstra University | 8006 | 3663 | | | 12/15 | 1/15 |
| Houghton College | | | | | 11/15 | 1/1 |
| Iona College | | | | | 12/1 | 12/21 |
| Jewish Theological Seminary of America | | | 11/15 1/15 | 12/15 2/15 | | |
| King's College | | | | | 11/15 | 12/15 |
| Laboratory Institute of Merchandising | 16 | 15 | | | 11/15 | 12/15 |
| Le Moyne College | 51 | 43 | 12/1 | 12/15 | | |
| Manhattan College | | | 11/15 | 12/15 | | |
| Manhattanville College | | | 12/1 | 12/31 | | |
| Marist College | 3479 | 2107 | 11/15 | 12/15 | 12/1 | 1/30 |
| Molloy College | | | | | 12/1 | 1/15 |

| Institution | Early Applicants | | Early Decision | | Early Action | |
|---|---|---|---|---|---|---|
| | Number applied | Number admitted | Apply by | Notified by | Apply by | Notified by |
| Nazareth College of Rochester | 33 | 31 | 11/15 | 12/15 | 12/15 | 1/15 |
| New York University | 2990 | 1042 | 11/1 | 12/15 | | |
| Niagara University | 1919 | 1094 | | | 10/1 | 12/1 |
| North Country Community College | | | 11/15 | 12/15 | | |
| Pace University | 1879 | 1527 | | | 11/30 | 1/1 |
| Pratt Institute | | | | | 11/1 | 12/22 |
| Rensselaer Polytechnic Institute | 326 | 185 | 11/1 1/1 | 12/7 2/1 | | |
| Rochester Institute of Technology | 1130 | 783 | 12/1 | 1/15 | | |
| Russell Sage College | 15 | 13 | 12/1 | 12/15 | | |
| Sarah Lawrence College | 125 | 79 | 11/15 1/1 | 12/15 2/15 | | |
| School of Visual Arts | 270 | 169 | | | 12/1 | 1/15 |
| Siena College | 130 | 43 | 12/1 | 12/15 | 12/1 | 1/1 |
| Skidmore College | 418 | 269 | 11/15 1/15 | 12/15 2/15 | | |
| St. John Fisher College | | | 12/1 | 12/15 | | |
| St. Joseph's College of Nursing | | | 11/15 | 12/15 | | |
| St. Lawrence University | 209 | 165 | 11/15 1/15 | 12/15 2/10 | | |
| St. Thomas Aquinas College | | | 12/15 | 3/1 | | |
| State University of New York College at Buffalo | | | 11/15 | 12/15 | | |
| State University of New York College at Cortland | | | 11/15 | 12/15 | | |
| State University of New York College at Fredonia | 68 | 31 | 11/1 | 12/1 | | |
| State University of New York College at Geneseo | 323 | 137 | 11/15 | 12/15 | | |
| State University of New York College at Old Westbury | | | 11/1 | 12/15 | | |
| State University of New York College at Oneonta | 2569 | 1393 | | | 11/15 | 12/15 |
| State University of New York College at Plattsburgh | 70 | 44 | 11/15 | 12/15 | | |
| State University of New York College of Environmental Science and Forestry | 275 | 227 | | | 11/15 | 1/2 |
| State University of New York Institute of Technology at Utica/Rome | 35 | 20 | 11/1 | 12/1 | | |
| State University of New York Maritime College | | | 11/15 | 12/15 | | |
| State University of New York at Albany | | | | | 11/15 | 1/1 |
| State University of New York at Binghamton | 4925 | 2592 | | | 11/15 | 1/1 |
| State University of New York at Buffalo | 512 | 353 | 11/1 | 12/15 | | |
| State University of New York at New Paltz | | | | | 11/15 | 1/1 |
| State University of New York at Oswego | 160 | 84 | 11/15 | 12/15 | | |
| State University of New York at Purchase | 33 | 22 | 11/1 | 12/5 | | |
| State University of New York at Stony Brook | 3418 | 2689 | | | 11/15 | 1/1 |
| Syracuse University | 757 | 607 | 11/15 | 12/15 | | |
| Union College | 259 | 214 | 11/15 1/15 | 12/15 2/1 | | |

| Institution | Early Applicants | | Early Decision | | Early Action | |
|---|---|---|---|---|---|---|
| | Number applied | Number admitted | Apply by | Notified by | Apply by | Notified by |
| University of Rochester | 652 | 266 | 11/1 | 12/15 | | |
| Vassar College | 534 | 256 | 11/15 1/1 | 12/15 2/1 | | |
| Wagner College | 111 | 69 | 12/1 1/1 | 12/15 | | |
| Webb Institute | 29 | 6 | 10/15 | 12/15 | | |
| Wells College | 547 | 436 | 12/15 | 1/15 | 12/15 | 2/1 |
| **North Carolina** | | | | | | |
| Carolinas College of Health Sciences | | | 12/1 | 1/15 | | |
| Davidson College | 384 | 189 | 11/15 1/2 | 12/15 2/1 | | |
| Duke University | 1159 | 475 | 11/1 | 12/15 | | |
| Elon University | 4980 | 2521 | 11/1 | 12/1 | 11/10 | 12/20 |
| Greensboro College | | | | | 12/15 | 1/15 |
| Guilford College | 2706 | 1629 | | | 1/15 | 2/15 |
| High Point University | 1085 | 948 | 11/3 | 11/25 | 11/10 | 12/12 |
| Lenoir-Rhyne College | 437 | 393 | | | 8/1 | 5/15 |
| Meredith College | 119 | 83 | 10/15 | 11/1 | | |
| North Carolina State University | 8484 | 6112 | | | 11/1 | 1/31 |
| Piedmont Baptist College | | | 11/1 | 12/1 | 11/1 | 12/1 |
| University of North Carolina at Asheville | | | | | 11/10 | 12/23 |
| University of North Carolina at Chapel Hill | | | | | 11/1 | 1/15 |
| University of North Carolina at Charlotte | | | | | 10/15 | 12/1 |
| University of North Carolina at Greensboro | | | | | 1/15 | |
| University of North Carolina at Wilmington | 5000 | 2500 | | | 11/1 | 1/20 |
| Wake Forest University | | | 11/15 | 12/15 | | |
| Warren Wilson College | | | 11/15 | 12/1 | | |
| Western Carolina University | | | | | 10/15 | 12/14 |
| **Ohio** | | | | | | |
| Case Western Reserve University | 1642 | 1370 | | | 11/1 | 1/1 |
| College of Wooster | | | 12/1 1/15 | 12/15 2/1 | | |
| Denison University | 120 | 84 | 12/1 | 1/1 | | |
| Kenyon College | 347 | 185 | 11/15 1/15 | 12/15 2/1 | | |
| Miami University: Oxford Campus | | | 11/1 | 12/15 | 12/1 | 2/1 |
| Oberlin College | 342 | 204 | 11/15 1/2 | 12/20 2/1 | | |
| Ohio Wesleyan University | | | 12/1 | 12/15 | 12/15 | 1/15 |
| School of Advertising Art | | | | | | |
| University of Akron | 3110 | 1410 | | | 11/1 | 12/15 |
| Ursuline College | 134 | 124 | | | 11/15 | 2/15 |
| Wittenberg University | 1549 | 1360 | 11/15 | 1/1 | 12/1 | 1/1 |
| Xavier University | 3555 | 2882 | | | 12/1 | 1/15 |
| **Oklahoma** | | | | | | |
| Oral Roberts University | 732 | 240 | | | 11/15 | 11/15 |
| **Oregon** | | | | | | |
| Eastern Oregon University | | | | | 12/1 | 1/15 |

| Institution | Early Applicants | | Early Decision | | Early Action | |
|---|---|---|---|---|---|---|
| | Number applied | Number admitted | Apply by | Notified by | Apply by | Notified by |
| George Fox University | 305 | 300 | | | 12/1 | 12/15 |
| Lewis & Clark College | 1239 | 856 | | | 11/1 | 1/15 |
| Linfield College | 403 | 393 | | | 11/15 | 1/15 |
| Oregon State University | | | | | 11/1 | 12/15 |
| Reed College | 214 | 121 | 11/15 1/2 | 12/15 2/1 | | |
| University of Oregon | | | | | 11/1 | 12/15 |
| Willamette University | 541 | 490 | | | 12/1 | 1/15 |

## Pennsylvania

| Institution | Early Applicants | | Early Decision | | Early Action | |
|---|---|---|---|---|---|---|
| | Number applied | Number admitted | Apply by | Notified by | Apply by | Notified by |
| Allegheny College | 180 | 128 | 11/15 | 12/15 | | |
| Bloomsburg University of Pennsylvania | 141 | 141 | 11/15 | 12/15 | | 5/1 |
| Bryn Mawr College | 99 | 76 | 11/15 1/1 | 12/15 2/1 | | |
| Bucknell University | 639 | 355 | 11/15 1/15 | 12/15 2/1 | | |
| Carlow University | | | | | 9/30 | 10/30 |
| Carnegie Mellon University | | | 11/1 12/1 | 12/15 1/15 | | |
| Chestnut Hill College | | | 12/1 | 12/15 | | |
| Dickinson College | 1935 | 1085 | 11/15 1/15 | 12/15 2/15 | 12/1 | 1/15 |
| Duquesne University | 1364 | 802 | 11/1 | 12/15 | 12/1 | 1/15 |
| Franklin & Marshall College | 471 | 321 | 11/15 1/15 | 12/15 2/15 | | |
| Gettysburg College | 484 | 315 | 11/15 1/15 | 12/15 2/15 | | |
| Grove City College | 630 | 316 | 11/15 | 12/15 | | |
| Haverford College | 254 | 103 | 11/15 | 12/15 | | |
| Juniata College | 66 | 62 | 12/1 | 12/31 | 1/1 | 1/30 |
| Kaplan Career Institute: Harrisburg | | | | | | |
| La Salle University | | | | | 11/15 | 12/15 |
| Lafayette College | 418 | 255 | 2/15 | | | |
| Lehigh University | 827 | 481 | 11/15 1/15 | 12/15 2/15 | | |
| Lincoln Technical Institute: Allentown | | | | | | |
| Moravian College | 210 | 164 | 2/1 | 12/15 | | |
| Muhlenberg College | 420 | 283 | 2/1 | 12/1 | | |
| Saint Joseph's University | | | | | 11/15 | 1/15 |
| Susquehanna University | 190 | 132 | 11/15 1/1 | 12/1 1/15 | | |
| Swarthmore College | 424 | 151 | 11/15 1/2 | 12/15 2/15 | | |
| University of Pennsylvania | 4001 | 1178 | 11/1 | 12/15 | | |
| University of Scranton | 2851 | 2317 | | | 11/15 | 12/15 |
| Ursinus College | 232 | 138 | 1/15 | 2/1 | 12/1 | 1/15 |
| Villanova University | 4764 | 1930 | | | 11/1 | 12/20 |
| Washington & Jefferson College | 7057 | 2449 | 12/1 | 12/15 | 1/1 | 1/15 |
| Westminster College | | | | | 11/15 | 12/1 |

## Puerto Rico

| Institution | Early Applicants | | Early Decision | | Early Action | |
|---|---|---|---|---|---|---|
| | Number applied | Number admitted | Apply by | Notified by | Apply by | Notified by |
| University of Puerto Rico: Aguadilla | | | | | 1/15 | 1/30 |
| University of Puerto Rico: Mayaguez | | | | | 1/30 | 2/15 |

| Institution | Early Applicants | | Early Decision | | Early Action | |
|---|---|---|---|---|---|---|
| | Number applied | Number admitted | Apply by | Notified by | Apply by | Notified by |
| **Rhode Island** | | | | | | |
| Brown University | 2324 | 525 | 11/1 | 12/15 | | |
| Bryant University | 190 | 105 | 11/15 | 12/15 | | |
| Providence College | 3181 | 1424 | | | 11/1 | 1/1 |
| Rhode Island School of Design | | | | | 12/15 | 1/31 |
| Roger Williams University | | | 11/1 | 12/15 | 11/15 | 1/15 |
| Salve Regina University | 1271 | 758 | | | 11/1 | 12/15 |
| University of Rhode Island | 8545 | 5472 | | | 12/15 | 1/31 |
| **South Carolina** | | | | | | |
| College of Charleston | | | | | 11/1 | 12/20 |
| Furman University | 634 | 437 | 11/15 | 12/15 | | |
| Presbyterian College | 44 | 37 | 11/1 | 12/1 | 11/15 | 12/15 |
| The Citadel | | | 10/26 | | | |
| University of South Carolina | | | | | 10/1 | 12/20 |
| Wofford College | 523 | 455 | 11/15 | 12/1 | | |
| **Tennessee** | | | | | | |
| Maryville College | 310 | 198 | 11/15 | 12/1 | 10/1 | 10/15 |
| Rhodes College | 140 | 67 | 11/1 1/1 | 12/1 2/1 | | |
| University of the South | 221 | 110 | 11/15 1/2 | 12/17 2/8 | | |
| Vanderbilt University | | | 11/1 1/3 | 12/15 2/15 | | |
| **Texas** | | | | | | |
| Austin College | 1015 | 785 | | | 1/15 | 3/1 |
| Baylor University | | | | | 11/1 | 1/15 |
| Rice University | 520 | 156 | 11/1 | 12/15 | | |
| Southern Methodist University | | | | | 11/1 | 12/31 |
| Southwestern University | 72 | 63 | 11/1 | 12/1 | | |
| Tarleton State University | | | | | 11/30 | |
| Texas Christian University | | | | | 11/15 | 1/1 |
| Trinity University | 45 | 29 | 11/1 | 12/15 | 11/1 | 12/15 |
| University of Dallas | 272 | 237 | | | 12/1 | 1/15 |
| **Vermont** | | | | | | |
| Bennington College | 73 | 53 | 11/15 1/3 | 12/15 2/15 | | |
| Champlain College | 366 | 222 | 11/15 1/15 | 12/15 2/15 | | |
| Lyndon State College | | | | | 11/1 | 12/1 |
| Marlboro College | | | 12/1 | 12/15 | 2/1 | 2/15 |
| Middlebury College | 1011 | 253 | 11/1 12/15 | 12/15 2/15 | | |
| Norwich University | | | 11/15 | 12/31 | | |
| St. Michael's College | 1616 | 1224 | | | 11/1 | 1/1 |
| Sterling College | 23 | 21 | | | 12/15 | 1/15 |
| University of Vermont | 4173 | 2929 | | | 11/1 | 12/15 |
| **Virginia** | | | | | | |
| Christendom College | 136 | 118 | | | 12/1 | 12/15 |
| Christopher Newport University | | | | | 12/1 | 1/1 |
| College of William and Mary | | | 11/1 | 12/1 | | |

| Institution | Early Applicants | | Early Decision | | Early Action | |
|---|---|---|---|---|---|---|
| | Number applied | Number admitted | Apply by | Notified by | Apply by | Notified by |
| Emory & Henry College | | | 11/1 | 12/15 | | |
| George Mason University | 1835 | 1389 | | | 11/1 | 12/20 |
| Hampden-Sydney College | 308 | 247 | 11/15 | 12/15 | 1/15 | 2/15 |
| Hampton University | | | | | 12/1 | 12/15 |
| Hollins University | | | 12/1 | 12/15 | | |
| James Madison University | 5438 | 3988 | | | 11/1 | 1/15 |
| Longwood University | 1524 | 1131 | | | 12/1 | 1/15 |
| Lynchburg College | | | 11/15 | 12/15 | | |
| Mary Baldwin College | | | 11/15 | 12/1 | | |
| Old Dominion University | 4231 | 3728 | | | 12/1 | 1/15 |
| Radford University | 4344 | 2315 | | | 12/15 | 1/9 |
| Randolph College | 15 | 11 | 11/15 | 12/15 | | |
| Randolph-Macon College | 290 | 236 | | | 11/15 | 1/1 |
| Roanoke College | 104 | 34 | 12/1 | 12/15 | | |
| Sweet Briar College | 76 | 69 | 12/1 | 12/15 | | |
| University of Mary Washington | | | | | 1/15 | |
| University of Richmond | 288 | 164 | 11/15 1/15 | 12/15 2/15 | | |
| University of Virginia's College at Wise | | | | | 12/1 | 12/15 |
| Virginia Military Institute | 249 | 166 | 11/15 | 12/15 | | |
| Virginia Polytechnic Institute and State University | 2479 | 1239 | 11/1 | 12/15 | | |
| Washington and Lee University | 427 | 164 | 11/15 1/3 | 12/22 2/1 | | |

## Washington

| Institution | Early Applicants | | Early Decision | | Early Action | |
|---|---|---|---|---|---|---|
| Gonzaga University | 2067 | 1544 | | | 11/15 | 1/15 |
| Seattle Pacific University | 936 | 875 | | | 11/15 | 1/6 |
| Seattle University | | | | | 11/15 | 12/22 |
| University of Puget Sound | 128 | 114 | 11/15 12/15 | 12/15 1/15 | | |
| Walla Walla University | | | | | | |
| Whitman College | 160 | 116 | 11/15 1/1 | 12/21 1/21 | | |
| Whitworth University | | | | | 12/1 | 12/20 |

## West Virginia

| Institution | Early Applicants | | Early Decision | | Early Action | |
|---|---|---|---|---|---|---|
| Shepherd University | | | | | 11/15 | 12/15 |

## Wisconsin

| Institution | Early Applicants | | Early Decision | | Early Action | |
|---|---|---|---|---|---|---|
| Beloit College | 556 | 496 | | | 12/1 | 1/1 |
| Lawrence University | 725 | 485 | 11/15 | 12/1 | 12/1 | 1/15 |

## Egypt

| Institution | Early Applicants | | Early Decision | | Early Action | |
|---|---|---|---|---|---|---|
| American University in Cairo | 949 | 530 | | | 3/15 | 3/31 |

## Germany

| Institution | Early Applicants | | Early Decision | | Early Action | |
|---|---|---|---|---|---|---|
| University of Karlsruhe | 4 | 4 | 3/15 | 5/1 | 3/15 | 5/1 |

## Lebanon

| Institution | Early Applicants | | Early Decision | | Early Action | |
|---|---|---|---|---|---|---|
| American University of Beirut | | | | | 11/30 | 1/15 |

## Mexico

| Institution | Early Applicants | | Early Decision | | Early Action | |
|---|---|---|---|---|---|---|
| Universidad de Monterrey | | | | | | |

| Institution | Early Applicants | | Early Decision | | Early Action | |
|---|---|---|---|---|---|---|
| | Number applied | Number admitted | Apply by | Notified by | Apply by | Notified by |
| **Monaco** | | | | | | |
| International University of Monaco | | | 1/2 | | | |
| **Switzerland** | | | | | | |
| Franklin College: Switzerland | 250 | 221 | | | 12/1 | 1/15 |

# Wait list table

Students who are wait listed have met a college's admission requirements, but will only be offered a place in the freshman class if space becomes available. The table that follows shows wait list outcomes for students who applied for admission to the freshman class of 2007-2008 at 295 colleges, which are listed alphabetically by state.

| Institution | Total applied | Number placed on wait list | Number accepting place on wait list | Number on wait list admitted |
|---|---|---|---|---|
| **Alabama** | | | | |
| Tuskegee University | 3092 | 0 | | |
| **Arkansas** | | | | |
| Hendrix College | 1323 | 31 | 31 | 12 |
| **California** | | | | |
| Azusa Pacific University | 3229 | 0 | | |
| California Institute of Technology | 3597 | 315 | 164 | 30 |
| Chapman University | 4861 | 360 | 128 | 74 |
| Charles R. Drew University of Medicine and Science | 300 | 22 | 22 | 5 |
| Claremont McKenna College | 3778 | 852 | 344 | 0 |
| Deep Springs College | 155 | 3 | 3 | 3 |
| Occidental College | 5272 | 600 | 234 | 26 |
| Pepperdine University | 6661 | 868 | 389 | 13 |
| Point Loma Nazarene University | 1757 | 420 | 420 | 238 |
| Pomona College | 5908 | | | 22 |
| Santa Clara University | 9459 | 2035 | 811 | 171 |
| Soka University of America | 378 | 7 | 6 | 4 |
| St. Mary's College of California | 3929 | 158 | 64 | 53 |
| Stanford University | 23958 | 1478 | 967 | 0 |
| Thomas Aquinas College | 222 | 77 | 77 | 32 |
| University of San Diego | 10048 | 1183 | 373 | 250 |
| Westmont College | 1651 | 133 | 103 | 2 |
| **Colorado** | | | | |
| Colorado College | 4826 | 785 | 342 | 42 |
| University of Colorado at Boulder | 19857 | 1542 | 471 | 302 |
| University of Denver | 5072 | 466 | 279 | 92 |
| **Connecticut** | | | | |
| Connecticut College | 4742 | 1169 | 433 | 30 |
| Eastern Connecticut State University | 3740 | 297 | 188 | 61 |
| Fairfield University | 8557 | 2763 | 1196 | 91 |
| Post University | 1344 | 68 | 60 | 60 |
| Quinnipiac University | 12060 | 1513 | 562 | 58 |
| Trinity College | 5950 | 1806 | 460 | 168 |
| University of Connecticut | 21105 | 2753 | 1373 | 370 |
| Wesleyan University | 7750 | 1236 | 441 | 97 |
| **Delaware** | | | | |
| University of Delaware | 20615 | 2211 | 909 | 31 |

| Institution | Total applied | Number placed on wait list | Number accepting place on wait list | Number on wait list admitted |
|---|---|---|---|---|
| **District of Columbia** | | | | |
| George Washington University | 19606 | 2193 | 702 | 155 |
| Georgetown University | 16163 | 1784 | 1035 | 45 |
| **Florida** | | | | |
| Eckerd College | 3118 | | | 35 |
| Flagler College | 2377 | 534 | 181 | 18 |
| New College of Florida | 1029 | 72 | 69 | 10 |
| Rollins College | 2900 | 450 | 374 | 71 |
| University of Central Florida | 26312 | 1097 | 498 | 43 |
| University of Tampa | 7885 | 549 | 397 | 82 |
| **Georgia** | | | | |
| Agnes Scott College | 1595 | 35 | 4 | 2 |
| Emory University | 15366 | 1500 | 800 | 113 |
| Georgia Institute of Technology | 9664 | 177 | 118 | 3 |
| University of Georgia | 16871 | 502 | 342 | 175 |
| **Illinois** | | | | |
| Aurora University | 1420 | 40 | 40 | 10 |
| Bradley University | 4612 | 156 | 36 | 19 |
| Illinois State University | 12550 | 360 | 109 | 109 |
| Illinois Wesleyan University | 3017 | 340 | 63 | 15 |
| Knox College | 2419 | 311 | 108 | 63 |
| Lake Forest College | 2201 | 116 | 33 | 16 |
| Northern Illinois University | 16769 | | 958 | 610 |
| Northwestern University | 21930 | 2734 | 1274 | 471 |
| Trinity College of Nursing and Health Sciences | | 30 | 30 | 10 |
| University of Chicago | 10362 | 1601 | 1031 | 3 |
| University of Illinois at Urbana-Champaign | 21645 | 1189 | 633 | 605 |
| University of Illinois: Springfield | 1112 | 0 | 0 | 0 |
| Wheaton College | 2160 | 438 | 169 | 91 |
| **Indiana** | | | | |
| DePauw University | 3624 | 111 | 30 | 0 |
| Earlham College | 1748 | 81 | 44 | 25 |
| University of Notre Dame | 14503 | 1029 | 619 | 181 |
| Vincennes University | 5692 | 34 | 34 | 34 |
| Wabash College | 1419 | 58 | 49 | 11 |
| **Iowa** | | | | |
| Allen College | 88 | 19 | 19 | 6 |
| Cornell College | 2659 | 131 | 131 | 46 |
| Grinnell College | 3077 | 740 | 279 | 16 |
| Hawkeye Community College | | 180 | 180 | 49 |
| Northeast Iowa Community College | | 301 | 301 | 301 |
| **Kansas** | | | | |
| Colby Community College | 988 | 0 | 0 | 0 |
| **Kentucky** | | | | |
| Alice Lloyd College | 1254 | 140 | 140 | 97 |
| Asbury College | 1364 | 0 | | |
| Centre College | 2159 | 186 | 35 | 19 |

| Institution | Total applied | Number placed on wait list | Number accepting place on wait list | Number on wait list admitted |
|---|---|---|---|---|
| **Louisiana** | | | | |
| Tulane University | 16967 | 586 | 264 | 22 |
| Xavier University of Louisiana | 3074 | 0 | | |
| **Maine** | | | | |
| Colby College | 4679 | 893 | 397 | 45 |
| College of the Atlantic | 305 | 0 | 0 | 0 |
| Husson College | 1175 | 15 | 9 | 7 |
| Unity College | 563 | 7 | 5 | 4 |
| University of Maine | 6958 | 78 | 36 | 23 |
| **Maryland** | | | | |
| Goucher College | 3563 | | | 49 |
| Johns Hopkins University | 14848 | 3069 | 1319 | 46 |
| Loyola College in Maryland | 8594 | 1687 | 791 | 11 |
| McDaniel College | 2742 | 111 | 36 | 23 |
| St. Mary's College of Maryland | 2351 | 243 | 132 | 10 |
| Towson University | 15464 | 2678 | 2678 | 700 |
| University of Maryland: Baltimore County | 5836 | 263 | 263 | 126 |
| **Massachusetts** | | | | |
| Amherst College | 6680 | 1462 | 574 | 0 |
| Assumption College | 3899 | 412 | 240 | 167 |
| Babson College | 3530 | 370 | 159 | 20 |
| Bard College at Simon's Rock | | 0 | | |
| Bentley College | 6689 | 965 | 425 | 1 |
| Berklee College of Music | 2939 | 233 | 165 | 131 |
| Boston College | 28850 | 5000 | 2000 | 100 |
| Boston University | 33930 | 3590 | 1944 | 1146 |
| Brandeis University | 7562 | 1125 | 414 | 105 |
| College of the Holy Cross | 7066 | 1218 | 296 | 43 |
| Curry College | 3739 | 38 | 35 | 0 |
| Emerson College | 4981 | 876 | 281 | 4 |
| Endicott College | 3549 | 410 | 167 | 20 |
| Franklin W. Olin College of Engineering | 1054 | 30 | 20 | 11 |
| Hampshire College | 2571 | 280 | 103 | 23 |
| Lesley University | 1568 | 50 | 33 | 6 |
| Massachusetts Institute of Technology | 12445 | 499 | 443 | 20 |
| New England Conservatory of Music | 1058 | 129 | 91 | 3 |
| Northeastern University | 30349 | 5760 | 1342 | 27 |
| Quinsigamond Community College | 3396 | 734 | 734 | 50 |
| Simmons College | 2937 | 81 | 22 | 1 |
| Smith College | 3329 | 440 | 240 | 7 |
| Stonehill College | 5704 | 957 | 496 | 26 |
| Suffolk University | 8044 | 391 | 391 | 99 |
| University of Massachusetts Amherst | 27138 | 2881 | 426. | 228 |
| Wellesley College | 4017 | 719 | 381 | 0 |
| Wheaton College | 3833 | 828 | 283 | 16 |
| Williams College | 6478 | 1553 | 682 | 67 |
| Worcester Polytechnic Institute | 5658 | 724 | 237 | 40 |
| Worcester State College | 3810 | 86 | 57 | 0 |
| **Michigan** | | | | |
| Central Michigan University | 15220 | 0 | | |

| Institution | Total applied | Number placed on wait list | Number accepting place on wait list | Number on wait list admitted |
|---|---|---|---|---|
| Hillsdale College | 1401 | 45 | 35 | 5 |
| Hope College | 2748 | 234 | 105 | 50 |
| Kalamazoo College | 2092 | 186 | 130 | 28 |
| University of Michigan | 27474 | 5662 | 2067 | 0 |
| **Minnesota** | | | | |
| Bethel University | 1643 | 45 | 38 | 6 |
| Carleton College | 4840 | 1368 | 306 | 5 |
| College of St. Benedict | 1677 | 93 | 92 | 2 |
| Gustavus Adolphus College | 2208 | 69 | 30 | 17 |
| Hamline University | 2018 | 0 | | |
| Macalester College | 4967 | 403 | 177 | 33 |
| St. Cloud Technical College | | 598 | 598 | 555 |
| St. John's University | 1527 | 64 | 64 | 4 |
| St. Olaf College | 4058 | 812 | 352 | 14 |
| **Missouri** | | | | |
| College of the Ozarks | 2709 | 425 | 425 | 15 |
| Metro Business College: Jefferson City | 60 | 6 | 4 | 2 |
| Missouri University of Science and Technology | 2317 | 3 | 0 | 0 |
| **Nebraska** | | | | |
| College of Saint Mary | 650 | 0 | | |
| Creighton University | 4274 | 101 | 101 | 17 |
| Northeast Community College | 1288 | 210 | 210 | 100 |
| **New Hampshire** | | | | |
| Dartmouth College | 14176 | 1381 | 797 | 0 |
| St. Anselm College | 3521 | 404 | 368 | 0 |
| **New Jersey** | | | | |
| Princeton University | 18942 | 792 | 483 | 47 |
| Ramapo College of New Jersey | 4983 | 432 | 198 | 172 |
| Rider University | 6213 | 260 | 93 | 11 |
| Rowan University | 8088 | | 140 | 70 |
| The College of New Jersey | 8607 | 1349 | 547 | 148 |
| **New Mexico** | | | | |
| St. John's College | 344 | 4 | 4 | 2 |
| **New York** | | | | |
| Albany College of Pharmacy | 1050 | 124 | 92 | 0 |
| Bard College | 4980 | 490 | 279 | 23 |
| Barnard College | 4574 | 742 | 457 | 15 |
| Clarkson University | 2983 | 63 | 23 | 19 |
| Cochran School of Nursing-St. John's Riverside Hospital | | 9 | 7 | 4 |
| Colgate University | 8759 | 1136 | 469 | 44 |
| College of Mount St. Vincent | 2092 | 70 | 70 | 13 |
| Columbia University | 21343 | | | 45 |
| Cooper Union for the Advancement of Science and Art | 2551 | 67 | 60 | 3 |
| Cornell University | 30383 | 3213 | 1976 | 279 |
| Daemen College | 1780 | 30 | 30 | 29 |
| Dominican College of Blauvelt | 1474 | 52 | 52 | 0 |

| Institution | Total applied | Number placed on wait list | Number accepting place on wait list | Number on wait list admitted |
|---|---|---|---|---|
| Eugene Lang College The New School for Liberal Arts | 1670 | 107 | 39 | 14 |
| Fordham University | 22035 | 3980 | 1187 | 104 |
| Hamilton College | 4962 | 773 | 248 | 25 |
| Hartwick College | 2422 | 170 | 138 | 11 |
| Hobart and William Smith Colleges | 4165 | 635 | 215 | 24 |
| Hofstra University | 18471 | 2228 | 752 | 176 |
| Iona College | 6017 | 600 | 187 | 79 |
| Juilliard School | 2311 | 35 | 30 | 9 |
| Laboratory Institute of Merchandising | 837 | 0 | | |
| Le Moyne College | 3968 | 132 | 57 | 39 |
| Manhattan College | 5166 | 246 | 183 | 8 |
| Manhattan School of Music | 945 | 0 | | |
| Mannes College The New School for Music | 473 | 17 | 9 | 0 |
| Maria College | 245 | 20 | 20 | 7 |
| Marist College | 8328 | 2247 | 731 | 60 |
| Mohawk Valley Community College | 3708 | 9 | 9 | 0 |
| Monroe College | 2463 | 125 | 63 | 38 |
| Phillips Beth Israel School of Nursing | 60 | 30 | 25 | 10 |
| Pratt Institute | 4341 | 264 | 239 | 13 |
| Rensselaer Polytechnic Institute | 10162 | 2393 | 811 | 45 |
| Rochester Institute of Technology | 11012 | 268 | 174 | 62 |
| Saint Bonaventure University | 1760 | 0 | | |
| Sarah Lawrence College | 2801 | 594 | 271 | 31 |
| School of Visual Arts | 2565 | 10 | 0 | |
| Siena College | 5792 | 1013 | 318 | 17 |
| Skidmore College | 6768 | 1584 | 522 | 59 |
| St. John's University | 27754 | 173 | 63 | 0 |
| St. Joseph's College of Nursing | 72 | 0 | | |
| St. Lawrence University | 4645 | 409 | 151 | 0 |
| State University of New York College at Geneseo | 10274 | 980 | 320 | 0 |
| State University of New York College at Oneonta | 12540 | 264 | 230 | 0 |
| State University of New York College at Plattsburgh | 7136 | 637 | 258 | 103 |
| State University of New York College at Potsdam | 4112 | 50 | 50 | 24 |
| State University of New York College of Environmental Science and Forestry | 1349 | 48 | 40 | 5 |
| State University of New York College of Technology at Canton | 2125 | 18 | 18 | 10 |
| State University of New York at Binghamton | 25242 | 763 | 664 | 97 |
| State University of New York at Buffalo | 19831 | 727 | 344 | 80 |
| State University of New York at New Paltz | 12543 | 417 | 135 | 17 |
| State University of New York at Stony Brook | 24060 | 804 | 309 | 37 |
| Syracuse University | 21219 | 3910 | 1761 | 197 |
| Union College | 4837 | 680 | 183 | 42 |
| Utica College | 2541 | 0 | | |
| Vassar College | 6393 | 976 | 430 | 0 |
| Wagner College | 2842 | 101 | 72 | 3 |

## North Carolina

| Institution | Total applied | Number placed on wait list | Number accepting place on wait list | Number on wait list admitted |
|---|---|---|---|---|
| Appalachian State University | 11468 | 1600 | 360 | 0 |

| Institution | Total applied | Number placed on wait list | Number accepting place on wait list | Number on wait list admitted |
|---|---|---|---|---|
| Duke University | 17748 | | | 252 |
| Elon University | 9380 | 3016 | 1211 | 39 |
| Guilford College | 3486 | 172 | 172 | 28 |
| North Carolina School of the Arts | 679 | 13 | 13 | 4 |
| University of North Carolina at Chapel Hill | 20090 | 2063 | 1240 | 226 |
| University of North Carolina at Wilmington | 8740 | | | 35 |
| Western Carolina University | 4792 | 0 | | |

## Ohio

| Institution | Total applied | Number placed on wait list | Number accepting place on wait list | Number on wait list admitted |
|---|---|---|---|---|
| Case Western Reserve University | 7297 | 284 | 101 | 0 |
| Denison University | 5196 | 497 | 347 | 33 |
| Franciscan University of Steubenville | 1273 | 62 | 56 | 12 |
| Kent State University | 12364 | 932 | 932 | 563 |
| Kenyon College | 4626 | 1115 | 378 | 10 |
| Mercy College of Northwest Ohio | 208 | 57 | 57 | 51 |
| Oberlin College | 7014 | 906 | 666 | 18 |
| Ohio Wesleyan University | 3814 | 24 | 12 | 6 |
| University of Dayton | 8742 | 0 | 0 | 0 |
| Xavier University | 5649 | 383 | 112 | 19 |

## Oklahoma

| Institution | Total applied | Number placed on wait list | Number accepting place on wait list | Number on wait list admitted |
|---|---|---|---|---|
| University of Oklahoma | 8768 | 1331 | 1331 | 1200 |
| University of Tulsa | 3804 | 150 | 150 | 80 |

## Oregon

| Institution | Total applied | Number placed on wait list | Number accepting place on wait list | Number on wait list admitted |
|---|---|---|---|---|
| Lewis & Clark College | 5351 | 759 | 230 | 32 |
| Linfield College | 2050 | 0 | | |
| Reed College | 3365 | 43 | 43 | 27 |
| University of Portland | 7139 | 721 | 721 | 51 |
| Willamette University | 2983 | 169 | 136 | 12 |

## Pennsylvania

| Institution | Total applied | Number placed on wait list | Number accepting place on wait list | Number on wait list admitted |
|---|---|---|---|---|
| Allegheny College | 4354 | 509 | 509 | 18 |
| Antonelli Institute of Art and Photography | 223 | 21 | 21 | 12 |
| Arcadia University | 3767 | 0 | | |
| Bryn Mawr College | 2106 | 322 | 200 | 20 |
| Bucknell University | 8943 | 2186 | 1046 | 14 |
| Cabrini College | 4015 | 25 | 25 | 25 |
| Carnegie Mellon University | 22356 | 2898 | 290 | 82 |
| Curtis Institute of Music | 224 | 5 | 5 | 1 |
| Elizabethtown College | 3370 | 172 | 56 | 25 |
| Franklin & Marshall College | 5018 | 1854 | 511 | 52 |
| Grove City College | 1916 | 677 | 236 | 17 |
| Haverford College | 3492 | 732 | 305 | 10 |
| Hussian School of Art | 108 | 1 | 1 | 0 |
| Johnson College | 319 | 10 | 10 | 10 |
| Lackawanna College | | 36 | 28 | 11 |
| Lafayette College | 6364 | 1694 | 620 | 69 |
| Lehigh University | 12155 | 2716 | 1096 | 72 |
| Manor College | 565 | 10 | 10 | 5 |
| Mansfield University of Pennsylvania | 3367 | 13 | 13 | 10 |
| Millersville University of Pennsylvania | 6723 | 1119 | 536 | 61 |
| Misericordia University | 1289 | 30 | 30 | 6 |
| Moravian College | 2189 | 221 | 122 | 30 |

| Institution | Total applied | Number placed on wait list | Number accepting place on wait list | Number on wait list admitted |
|---|---|---|---|---|
| Muhlenberg College | 4703 | 1669 | 541 | 41 |
| Penn State University Park | 39551 | 1828 | 1704 | 1356 |
| Pennsylvania College of Technology | 3066 | 445 | 445 | 366 |
| Philadelphia University | 4015 | 160 | 151 | 69 |
| Saint Joseph's University | 8779 | 2446 | 683 | 251 |
| Slippery Rock University of Pennsylvania | 4736 | 1744 | 533 | 462 |
| St. Vincent College | 1855 | 213 | 59 | 54 |
| Susquehanna University | 2373 | 307 | 68 | 14 |
| Temple University | 16659 | 400 | 250 | 10 |
| University of Pennsylvania | 22645 | 1911 | 1494 | 37 |
| University of Pittsburgh | 19056 | 762 | 310 | 38 |
| University of Pittsburgh at Bradford | 737 | 5 | 5 | 5 |
| University of Scranton | 7609 | 1207 | 481 | 21 |
| University of the Sciences in Philadelphia | 3963 | 700 | 650 | 80 |
| Ursinus College | 5141 | 400 | 210 | 60 |
| Villanova University | 13760 | 4817 | 2077 | 210 |
| Washington & Jefferson College | 7377 | 287 | 98 | 27 |
| Widener University | 4394 | 172 | 172 | 28 |

## Rhode Island

| Institution | Total applied | Number placed on wait list | Number accepting place on wait list | Number on wait list admitted |
|---|---|---|---|---|
| Brown University | 19097 | 1400 | 450 | 73 |
| Bryant University | 5649 | 1167 | 563 | 66 |
| Providence College | 9802 | 2661 | 879 | 118 |
| Salve Regina University | 5801 | 759 | 225 | 34 |

## South Carolina

| Institution | Total applied | Number placed on wait list | Number accepting place on wait list | Number on wait list admitted |
|---|---|---|---|---|
| Charleston Southern University | 2941 | 304 | 304 | 25 |
| College of Charleston | 8941 | 290 | 256 | 79 |
| Furman University | 3879 | 408 | 146 | 21 |
| University of South Carolina | 14994 | 270 | 70 | 34 |
| Wofford College | 2354 | 127 | 58 | 3 |

## South Dakota

| Institution | Total applied | Number placed on wait list | Number accepting place on wait list | Number on wait list admitted |
|---|---|---|---|---|
| Mitchell Technical Institute | 402 | 21 | 16 | 10 |

## Tennessee

| Institution | Total applied | Number placed on wait list | Number accepting place on wait list | Number on wait list admitted |
|---|---|---|---|---|
| University of the South | 2424 | 265 | 32 | 29 |
| Vanderbilt University | 12911 | 1510 | 719 | 3 |

## Texas

| Institution | Total applied | Number placed on wait list | Number accepting place on wait list | Number on wait list admitted |
|---|---|---|---|---|
| Austin College | 1678 | 44 | 27 | 19 |
| Rice University | 8968 | | 564 | 8 |
| Southern Methodist University | 8253 | 941 | 390 | 124 |
| Southwestern University | 1916 | 62 | 16 | 7 |
| St. Edward's University | 2372 | 315 | 41 | 14 |
| Texas A&M University | 18817 | 1808 | | 689 |
| Texas Christian University | 11888 | 1090 | 547 | 210 |

## Vermont

| Institution | Total applied | Number placed on wait list | Number accepting place on wait list | Number on wait list admitted |
|---|---|---|---|---|
| Bennington College | 1011 | 10 | 10 | 0 |
| Middlebury College | 7180 | 1231 | 603 | 0 |
| St. Michael's College | 3504 | 457 | 203 | 34 |
| University of Vermont | 18814 | 2486 | 1261 | 5 |
| Vermont Technical College | 920 | 138 | 138 | 53 |

| Institution | Total applied | Number placed on wait list | Number accepting place on wait list | Number on wait list admitted |
|---|---|---|---|---|
| **Virginia** | | | | |
| Christendom College | 254 | 5 | 3 | 1 |
| Christopher Newport University | 6694 | 739 | 291 | 14 |
| College of William and Mary | 10853 | 2402 | 1101 | 62 |
| Hollins University | 632 | 26 | 10 | 1 |
| James Madison University | 18352 | 1863 | 845 | 258 |
| Jefferson College of Health Sciences | 554 | 95 | 86 | 6 |
| Radford University | 7046 | 70 | 70 | 30 |
| Randolph-Macon College | 3177 | 281 | 127 | 32 |
| Roanoke College | 3258 | 20 | 6 | 3 |
| University of Mary Washington | 4475 | 622 | 235 | 197 |
| University of Richmond | 6649 | 1776 | 710 | 66 |
| University of Virginia | 17798 | 4130 | 2426 | 159 |
| Virginia Military Institute | 1704 | 158 | 41 | 1 |
| Virginia Polytechnic Institute and State University | 19429 | 1444 | 1444 | 52 |
| Washington and Lee University | 3719 | 872 | 282 | 31 |
| **Washington** | | | | |
| Gonzaga University | 5744 | 419 | 200 | 169 |
| Pacific Lutheran University | 2236 | 10 | 7 | 7 |
| Seattle Pacific University | 2055 | 232 | 232 | 97 |
| University of Puget Sound | 5273 | 425 | 75 | 29 |
| University of Washington | 17877 | 1468 | 773 | 332 |
| Western Washington University | 8850 | 372 | 193 | 193 |
| Whitman College | 2892 | 453 | 116 | 22 |
| **Wisconsin** | | | | |
| Beloit College | 2157 | 207 | 85 | 5 |
| Lawrence University | 2599 | 264 | 101 | 35 |
| Marquette University | 13375 | 1912 | 687 | 568 |
| University of Wisconsin-Eau Claire | 7446 | 17 | 13 | 12 |
| University of Wisconsin-Green Bay | 3452 | 171 | 171 | 168 |
| **Canada** | | | | |
| McGill University | 20391 | 400 | 300 | 150 |
| **United Kingdom** | | | | |
| Richmond, The American International University in London | | 7 | 7 | 5 |

# Indexes

## College type

### Liberal arts colleges

#### Four-year

**Alabama**

Andrew Jackson University
Birmingham-Southern College
Concordia College
Faulkner University
Huntingdon College
Judson College
Miles College
Oakwood College
Spring Hill College
Stillman College
Talladega College
Tuskegee University
University of Mobile
University of Montevallo

**Alaska**

Alaska Pacific University
University of Alaska
Southeast

**Arizona**

Art Institute of Tucson
College of the Humanities and
Sciences
Prescott College

**Arkansas**

Arkansas Baptist College
Arkansas Tech University
Ecclesia College
Henderson State University
Hendrix College
John Brown University
Lyon College
Ouachita Baptist University
Philander Smith College
University of the Ozarks
Williams Baptist College

**California**

American Jewish University
Antioch Southern California
Antioch University Los
Angeles
Antioch University Santa
Barbara
Bethany University
California Baptist University
California Institute of Integral
Studies
California Lutheran University
California State University
Bakersfield
Chico
Monterey Bay
San Bernardino
Stanislaus
Chapman University

Claremont McKenna College
Concordia University
Dominican University of
California
Fresno Pacific University
Harvey Mudd College
Hope International University
Humboldt State University
Humphreys College
John F. Kennedy University
The Master's College
Menlo College
Mifls College
Monterey Institute of
International Studies
Mount St. Mary's College
NewSchool of Architecture &
Design
Notre Dame de Namur University
Occidental College
Pacific Union College
Patten University
Pepperdine University
Pitzer College
Point Loma Nazarene University
Pomona College
St. Mary's College of California
San Diego Christian College
San Jose State University
Scripps College
Simpson University
Soka University of America
Sonoma State University
Thomas Aquinas College
University of La Verne
University of Redlands
University of the West
Vanguard University of Southern
California
Westmont College
Whittier College
William Jessup University

**Colorado**

Adams State College
Colorado Christian University
Colorado College
Fort Lewis College
Mesa State College
Metropolitan State College of
Denver
Naropa University
Regis University
Teikyo Loretto Heights University
Western State College of
Colorado

**Connecticut**

Albertus Magnus College
Charter Oak State College
Connecticut College
Eastern Connecticut State
University
Holy Apostles College and
Seminary
Mitchell College
Sacred Heart University

St. Joseph College
Trinity College
Wesleyan University

**Delaware**

Wesley College
Wilmington University

**District of Columbia**

Gallaudet University
Southeastern University
Trinity Washington University
University of the District of
Columbia

**Florida**

Ave Maria University
Beacon College
Bethune-Cookman University
Clearwater Christian College
Eckerd College
Edison College
Edward Waters College
Flagler College
Florida College
Florida Memorial University
Florida Southern College
Jacksonville University
New College of Florida
Palm Beach Atlantic University
Rollins College
St. John Vianney College
Seminary
Southeastern University
University of Tampa
Warner Southern College

**Georgia**

Agnes Scott College
Albany State University
Atlanta Christian College
Augusta State University
Berry College
Brenau University
Brewton-Parker College
Clayton State University
Columbus State University
Covenant College
Dalton State College
Emmanuel College
Fort Valley State University
Georgia College and State
University
Georgia Southwestern State
University
LaGrange College
Morehouse College
Oglethorpe University
Paine College
Piedmont College
Savannah State University
Shorter College
Spelman College
Thomas University
Toccoa Falls College
Truett-McConnell College
Wesleyan College

**Hawaii**

Brigham Young
University-Hawaii
Hawaii Pacific University
University of Hawaii
West Oahu

**Idaho**

College of Idaho
Lewis-Clark State College

**Illinois**

Augustana College
Benedictine University
Blackburn College
Columbia College Chicago
Dominican University
Elmhurst College
Eureka College
Greenville College
Illinois College

Illinois Wesleyan University
Judson University
Knox College
Lake Forest College
MacMurray College
McKendree University
Monmouth College
North Central College
North Park University
Olivet Nazarene University
Principia College
Quincy University
Rockford College
St. Augustine College
Shimer College
Trinity Christian College
Trinity International University
University of Chicago
University of Illinois
Springfield
University of St. Francis
Wheaton College

**Indiana**

Anderson University
Bethel College
Calumet College of St. Joseph
DePauw University
Earlham College
Franklin College
Goshen College
Grace College
Hanover College
Holy Cross College
Huntington University
Indiana Wesleyan University
Manchester College
Marian College
Martin University
Oakland City University
Saint Joseph's College
Saint Mary's College
St. Mary-of-the-Woods College
Taylor University
Taylor University Fort Wayne
University of Evansville
University of Indianapolis
University of St. Francis
University of Southern Indiana
Wabash College

**Iowa**

Briar Cliff University
Buena Vista University
Central College
Clarke College
Coe College
Cornell College
Divine Word College
Dordt College
Graceland University
Grand View College
Grinnell College
Iowa Wesleyan College
Loras College
Luther College
Maharishi University of
Management
Morningside College
Mount Mercy College
Northwestern College
St. Ambrose University
Simpson College
Waldorf College
Wartburg College
William Penn University

**Kansas**

Baker University
Benedictine College
Bethany College
Bethel College
Central Christian College of
Kansas
Friends University
Kansas Wesleyan University
McPherson College

MidAmerica Nazarene University
Newman University
Ottawa University
Southwestern College
Sterling College
Tabor College

**Kentucky**

Alice Lloyd College
Asbury College
Bellarmine University
Berea College
Brescia University
Centre College
Georgetown College
Kentucky Christian University
Kentucky State University
Kentucky Wesleyan College
Lindsey Wilson College
Mid-Continent University
Midway College
Pikeville College
St. Catharine College
Thomas More College
Transylvania University
Union College
University of the Cumberlands

**Louisiana**

Centenary College of Louisiana
Dillard University
Louisiana College
Loyola University New Orleans
Our Lady of Holy Cross College
St. Joseph Seminary College

**Maine**

Bates College
Bowdoin College
Colby College
College of the Atlantic
St. Joseph's College
Thomas College
Unity College
University of Maine
Farmington
Machias
University of Southern Maine

**Maryland**

College of Notre Dame of
Maryland
Columbia Union College
Coppin State University
Goucher College
Hood College
Loyola College in Maryland
McDaniel College
Morgan State University
Mount St. Mary's University
National Labor College
St. John's College
St. Mary's College of Maryland
Salisbury University
Sojourner-Douglass College
University of Baltimore
Villa Julie College
Washington College

**Massachusetts**

American International College
Amherst College
Anna Maria College
Assumption College
Atlantic Union College
Bard College at Simon's Rock
Becker College
Bridgewater State College
Cambridge College
Clark University
College of the Holy Cross
Curry College
Eastern Nazarene College
Elms College
Emmanuel College
Endicott College
Fitchburg State College
Framingham State College

Gordon College
Hampshire College
Hellenic College/Holy Cross
Lasell College
Lesley University
Massachusetts College of Liberal
Arts
Merrimack College
Mount Holyoke College
Mount Ida College
Newbury College
Nichols College
Pine Manor College
Regis College
Simmons College
Smith College
Springfield College
Stonehill College
Wellesley College
Westfield State College
Wheaton College
Wheelock College
Williams College
Worcester State College

**Michigan**
Adrian College
Albion College
Alma College
Aquinas College
Calvin College
Concordia University
Cornerstone University
Finlandia University
Grace Bible College
Hillsdale College
Hope College
Kalamazoo College
Madonna University
Marygrove College
Michigan Jewish Institute
Olivet College
Rochester College
Spring Arbor University

**Minnesota**
Augsburg College
Bethany Lutheran College
Bethel University
Brown College
Carleton College
College of St. Benedict
College of St. Catherine
College of St. Scholastica
Concordia College: Moorhead
Crown College
Gustavus Adolphus College
Hamline University
Macalester College
Northwestern College
St. John's University
St. Olaf College
Southwest Minnesota State
University
University of Minnesota
Morris
University of St. Thomas

**Mississippi**
Belhaven College
Blue Mountain College
Millsaps College
Mississippi University for Women
Mississippi Valley State
University
Rust College
Tougaloo College
William Carey University

**Missouri**
Avila University
Central Methodist University
College of the Ozarks
Columbia College
Culver-Stockton College
Drury University
Evangel University
Fontbonne University

Hannibal-LaGrange College
Lincoln University
Lindenwood University
Missouri Baptist University
Missouri Southern State
University
Missouri Valley College
Missouri Western State University
Rockhurst University
Stephens College
Truman State University
Westminster College
William Jewell College
William Woods University

**Montana**
Carroll College
Montana State University
Northern
Rocky Mountain College
Salish Kootenai College
University of Great Falls
University of Montana: Missoula
University of Montana: Western

**Nebraska**
Chadron State College
College of Saint Mary
Dana College
Doane College
Hastings College
Midland Lutheran College
Nebraska Wesleyan University
Peru State College
Union College
Wayne State College
York College

**Nevada**
Nevada State College
Sierra Nevada College

**New Hampshire**
Chester College of New England
Colby-Sawyer College
Dartmouth College
Franklin Pierce University
Granite State College
Keene State College
Magdalen College
New England College
Rivier College
St. Anselm College
Thomas More College of Liberal
Arts
University of New Hampshire at
Manchester

**New Jersey**
Bloomfield College
Caldwell College
Centenary College
The College of New Jersey
College of St. Elizabeth
Drew University
Felician College
Georgian Court University
Kean University
Ramapo College of New Jersey
Richard Stockton College of New
Jersey
Rowan University
Saint Peter's College
Thomas Edison State College
William Paterson University of
New Jersey

**New Mexico**
College of Santa Fe
College of the Southwest
New Mexico Institute of Mining
and Technology
St. John's College

**New York**
Bard College
Barnard College
Boricua College
Canisius College

Cazenovia College
City University of New York
Baruch College
Brooklyn College
College of Staten Island
Hunter College
Lehman College
Medgar Evers College
Queens College
York College
Colgate University
College of Mount St. Vincent
College of New Rochelle
College of Saint Rose
Columbia University
School of General Studies
Concordia College
D'Youville College
Daemen College
Dominican College of Blauvelt
Dowling College
Elmira College
Eugene Lang College The New
School for Liberal Arts
Excelsior College
Five Towns College
Hamilton College
Hartwick College
Hilbert College
Hobart and William Smith
Colleges
Houghton College
Iona College
Ithaca College
Keuka College
King's College
Le Moyne College
Long Island University
C. W. Post Campus
Manhattan College
Manhattanville College
Marist College
Marymount Manhattan College
Medaille College
Medaille College: Amherst
Medaille College: Rochester
Mercy College
Metropolitan College of New
York
Molloy College
Mount St. Mary College
Nazareth College of Rochester
Nyack College
Paul Smith's College
Roberts Wesleyan College
Russell Sage College
Sage College of Albany
St. Francis College
St. John Fisher College
St. Joseph's College
St. Joseph's College: Suffolk
Campus
St. Lawrence University
St. Thomas Aquinas College
Sarah Lawrence College
Siena College
Skidmore College
State University of New York
College at Brockport
College at Buffalo
College at Cortland
College at Fredonia
College at Geneseo
College at Old Westbury
College at Oneonta
College at Plattsburgh
College at Potsdam
College of Environmental
Science and Forestry
Empire State College
New Paltz
Purchase
Touro College
Union College
Vassar College
Wagner College
Wells College

Yeshiva University

**North Carolina**
Barton College
Belmont Abbey College
Bennett College
Brevard College
Campbell University
Catawba College
Chowan University
Davidson College
Elizabeth City State University
Elon University
Gardner-Webb University
Greensboro College
Guilford College
Johnson C. Smith University
Lees-McRae College
Lenoir-Rhyne College
Livingstone College
Mars Hill College
Meredith College
Methodist University
Montreat College
Mount Olive College
North Carolina Wesleyan College
Peace College
Pfeiffer University
St. Andrews Presbyterian College
St. Augustine's College
Salem College
Shaw University
University of North Carolina
Asheville
Pembroke
Warren Wilson College
Wingate University

**North Dakota**
Jamestown College
Minot State University
Valley City State University

**Ohio**
Antioch University McGregor
Ashland University
Baldwin-Wallace College
Bluffton University
Cedarville University
Central State University
College of Mount St. Joseph
College of Wooster
Defiance College
Denison University
Heidelberg College
Hiram College
John Carroll University
Kenyon College
Lake Erie College
Laura and Alvin Siegal College of
Judaic Studies
Lourdes College
Malone College
Marietta College
Mount Union College
Muskingum College
Notre Dame College
Oberlin College
Ohio Dominican University
Ohio Wesleyan University
Otterbein College
Pontifical College Josephinum
Union Institute & University
University of Rio Grande
Urbana University
Ursuline College
Walsh University
Wilberforce University
Wilmington College
Wittenberg University

**Oklahoma**
Bacone College
Cameron University
Langston University
Mid-America Christian University
Oklahoma Baptist University
Oklahoma Christian University

Oklahoma City University
Oklahoma Panhandle State
University
Oklahoma Wesleyan University
Oral Roberts University
St. Gregory's University
Southeastern Oklahoma State
University
Southern Nazarene University
University of Science and Arts of
Oklahoma

**Oregon**
Art Institute of Portland
Cascade College
Concordia University
Corban College
Eastern Oregon University
Lewis & Clark College
Linfield College
Marylhurst University
Northwest Christian College
Reed College
Southern Oregon University
Warner Pacific College
Western Oregon University
Willamette University

**Pennsylvania**
Albright College
Allegheny College
Alvernia College
Bloomsburg University of
Pennsylvania
Bryn Athyn College of the New
Church
Bryn Mawr College
Cabrini College
Carlow University
Cedar Crest College
Chatham University
Chestnut Hill College
Delaware Valley College
Dickinson College
Edinboro University of
Pennsylvania
Elizabethtown College
Franklin & Marshall College
Geneva College
Gettysburg College
Grove City College
Gwynedd-Mercy College
Haverford College
Holy Family University
Immaculata University
Juniata College
Keystone College
King's College
La Roche College
La Salle University
Lafayette College
Lebanon Valley College
Lincoln University
Lock Haven University of
Pennsylvania
Lycoming College
Mansfield University of
Pennsylvania
Mercyhurst College
Messiah College
Millersville University of
Pennsylvania
Misericordia University
Moravian College
Mount Aloysius College
Muhlenberg College
Neumann College
Rosemont College
St. Francis University
St. Vincent College
Seton Hill University
Susquehanna University
Swarthmore College
Thiel College
University of Pittsburgh
Greensburg
Johnstown

University of Scranton
Ursinus College
Valley Forge Christian College
Washington & Jefferson College
Waynesburg University
Westminster College
Wilson College
York College of Pennsylvania

**Puerto Rico**
Atlantic College
Caribbean University
Inter American University of
Puerto Rico
  Aguadilla Campus
  Arecibo Campus
Turabo University
Universidad Adventista de las
  Antillas
Universidad del Este
Universidad Metropolitana
University of Puerto Rico
  Aguadilla
  Cayey University College
  Humacao
University of the Sacred Heart

**Rhode Island**
Brown University
Bryant University
Providence College
Rhode Island College
Roger Williams University
Salve Regina University

**South Carolina**
Allen University
Anderson University
Benedict College
Charleston Southern University
Claflin University
Coker College
College of Charleston
Columbia College
Converse College
Erskine College
Francis Marion University
Furman University
Lander University
Limestone College
Morris College
Newberry College
North Greenville University
Presbyterian College
Southern Wesleyan University
University of South Carolina
  Aiken
  Beaufort
Voorhees College
Wofford College

**South Dakota**
Augustana College
Black Hills State University
Dakota Wesleyan University
Mount Marty College
Northern State University
Oglala Lakota College
Sinte Gleska University
University of Sioux Falls

**Tennessee**
Aquinas College
Austin Peay State University
Bethel College
Bryan College
Carson-Newman College
Crichton College
Cumberland University
Fisk University
Freed-Hardeman University
King College
Lambuth University
Lane College
Lee University
LeMoyne-Owen College
Lincoln Memorial University
Lipscomb University
Martin Methodist College

Maryville College
Milligan College
Rhodes College
South College
Southern Adventist University
Tennessee Wesleyan College
Trevecca Nazarene University
Tusculum College
Union University
Williamson Christian College

**Texas**
Austin College
College of Saint Thomas More
Concordia University at Austin
East Texas Baptist University
Houston Baptist University
Howard Payne University
Huston-Tillotson University
Jarvis Christian College
Lubbock Christian University
McMurry University
Midwestern State University
Paul Quinn College
St. Edward's University
Schreiner University
Southwestern Adventist
  University
Southwestern Christian College
Southwestern University
Texas College
Texas Lutheran University
Trinity University
University of Dallas
University of North Texas
University of St. Thomas
University of the Incarnate Word
Wayland Baptist University
Wiley College

**Utah**
Stevens-Henager College: Ogden
Westminster College

**Vermont**
Bennington College
Burlington College
Castleton State College
Champlain College
College of St. Joseph in Vermont
Goddard College
Green Mountain College
Johnson State College
Lyndon State College
Marlboro College
Middlebury College
St. Michael's College
Southern Vermont College
Sterling College

**Virginia**
Averett University
Bluefield College
Bridgewater College
Christendom College
Christopher Newport University
Eastern Mennonite University
Emory & Henry College
Ferrum College
Hampden-Sydney College
Hollins University
Lynchburg College
Mary Baldwin College
Randolph College
Randolph-Macon College
Roanoke College
St. Paul's College
Southern Virginia University
Sweet Briar College
University of Mary Washington
University of Richmond
University of Virginia's College
  at Wise
Virginia Intermont College
Virginia Military Institute
Virginia Union University
Virginia Wesleyan College
Washington and Lee University

**Washington**
Antioch University Seattle
Gonzaga University
Heritage University
Northwest University
Saint Martin's University
Trinity Lutheran College
University of Puget Sound
Walla Walla University
Whitman College
Whitworth University

**West Virginia**
Alderson-Broaddus College
American Public University
  System
Bethany College
Bluefield State College
Davis and Elkins College
Glenville State College
Ohio Valley University
Salem International University
University of Charleston
West Liberty State College
West Virginia State University
West Virginia Wesleyan College
Wheeling Jesuit University

**Wisconsin**
Alverno College
Beloit College
Carroll College
Carthage College
Concordia University Wisconsin
Edgewood College
Lakeland College
Lawrence University
Marian College of Fond du Lac
Mount Mary College
Northland College
Ripon College
St. Norbert College
Silver Lake College
University of Wisconsin
  Green Bay
  River Falls
  Superior
Viterbo University
Wisconsin Lutheran College

**France**
American University of Paris

**Switzerland**
Franklin College: Switzerland

**United Kingdom**
Richmond, The American
  International University in
  London

*Two-year*

**Arkansas**
Arkansas State University:
  Newport
National Park Community
  College

**California**
Deep Springs College
Feather River College
Fresno City College
Marymount College

**Colorado**
Colorado Mountain College

**Georgia**
Andrew College
Georgia Highlands College
Georgia Perimeter College
Oxford College of Emory
  University
Waycross College
Young Harris College

**Hawaii**
Hawaii Tokai International
  College

TransPacific Hawaii College

**Illinois**
Springfield College in Illinois

**Indiana**
Ancilla College

**Kansas**
Donnelly College

**Massachusetts**
Dean College
Fisher College

**Michigan**
Montcalm Community College
Wayne County Community
  College

**Minnesota**
Itasca Community College
White Earth Tribal and
  Community College

**Missouri**
Cottey College
Crowder College
Patricia Stevens College

**New Jersey**
Assumption College for Sisters

**New York**
State University of New York
  College of Technology at
  Alfred
Villa Maria College of Buffalo

**Ohio**
Chatfield College

**Pennsylvania**
University of Pittsburgh
  Titusville

**Puerto Rico**
Colegio de las Ciencias Artes y
  Television

**South Carolina**
Spartanburg Methodist College

**Tennessee**
Hiwassee College

**Texas**
Alvin Community College
Eastfield College
Jacksonville College
Lamar State College at Orange
Lon Morris College
North Lake College
Tarrant County College

**Vermont**
Landmark College

**Virginia**
Richard Bland College

**Washington**
Olympic College

**Wisconsin**
University of Wisconsin
  Baraboo/Sauk County
  Fox Valley
  Manitowoc
  Marinette
  Richland
  Rock County
  Washington County

**Northern Mariana Islands**
Northern Marianas College

**Upper-division colleges**

**Alabama**
Athens State University
United States Sports Academy

**Arizona**
Midwestern University: Glendale

**California**
Alliant International University
Antioch Southern California
  Antioch University Los
    Angeles
  Antioch University Santa
    Barbara
California Institute of Integral
  Studies
Dominican School of Philosophy
  and Theology
International Technological
  University
Monterey Institute of
  International Studies
Pacific Oaks College
Samuel Merritt College

**Georgia**
Medical College of Georgia

**Illinois**
Governors State University
Lakeview College of Nursing
Rosalind Franklin University of
  Medicine and Science
Rush University
Saint Anthony College of Nursing
St. Francis Medical Center
  College of Nursing
St. John's College
West Suburban College of
  Nursing
Western Illinois University: Quad
  Cities

**Kansas**
University of Kansas Medical
  Center

**Louisiana**
Louisiana State University Health
  Sciences Center

**Maryland**
University of Maryland
  Baltimore

**Michigan**
Walsh College of Accountancy
  and Business Administration

**Minnesota**
Northwestern Health Sciences
  University
Walden University

**Mississippi**
University of Mississippi Medical
  Center

**Missouri**
St. Luke's College

**Nebraska**
University of Nebraska
  Medical Center

**Nevada**
University of Southern Nevada

**New Jersey**
University of Medicine and
  Dentistry of New Jersey
  School of Health Related
  Professions

**New York**
State University of New York
  Downstate Medical Center
  Upstate Medical University

**North Dakota**
Medcenter One College of
  Nursing

**Pennsylvania**
Penn State
  Shenango

Tables and Indexes

2077

Thomas Jefferson University:
College of Health Professions

**Puerto Rico**

Carlos Albizu University: San
Juan

**South Carolina**

Medical University of South
Carolina

**Tennessee**

University of Tennessee Health
Science Center

**Texas**

Austin Graduate School of
Theology
Texas A&M University
Baylor College of Dentistry
Texarkana
Texas Tech University Health
Sciences Center
University of Houston
Clear Lake
Victoria
University of Texas
Health Science Center at
Houston
Health Science Center at San
Antonio
Medical Branch at Galveston
Southwestern Medical
Center at Dallas

**Virginia**

Catholic Distance University

**Washington**

Antioch University Seattle
Bastyr University
City University of Seattle

---

**Agricultural and
technical colleges**

*Four-year*

Alabama Agricultural and
Mechanical University, AL
Alcorn State University, MS
Art Institute
of Colorado, CO
of Pittsburgh, PA
Art Institute of Fort Lauderdale,
FL
Art Institute of Seattle, WA
Art Institute of Tucson, AZ
Baker College
of Auburn Hills, MI
of Clinton Township, MI
of Flint, MI
of Jackson, MI
of Muskegon, MI
of Owosso, MI
of Port Huron, MI
Bluefield State College, WV
Boise State University, ID
Briarcliffe College, NY
California Design College, CA
Central Pennsylvania College, PA
Charter College, AK
City College: Fort Lauderdale, FL
City University of New York
New York City College of
Technology, NY
Clayton State University, GA
Coleman College, CA
CollegeAmerica
Colorado Springs, CO
Fort Collins, CO
Collins College, AZ
Colorado Technical University,
CO
Columbia Centro Universitario:
Caguas, PR
Delaware Valley College, PA
Design Institute of San Diego, CA

DeVry Institute of Technology
New York, NY
DeVry University: Memphis, TN
Dixie State College of Utah, UT
ECPI College of Technology:
Newport News, VA
ECPI College of Technology:
Virginia Beach, VA
ECPI Technical College
Glen Allen, VA
Electronic Data Processing
College of Puerto Rico, PR
Ex'pression College for Digital
Arts, CA
Fairmont State University, WV
Gibbs College: Vienna, VA
Hamilton Technical College, IA
Herzing College, LA
Herzing College, AL
Herzing College, GA
Herzing College, WI
Hickey College, MO
International Academy of Design
and Technology: Chicago, IL
International Academy of Design
and Technology: Detroit, MI
International Academy of Design
and Technology: Henderson,
NV
International Academy of Design
and Technology: Schaumburg,
IL
International Academy of Design
and Technology: Tampa, FL
Kansas State University, KS
LA College International, CA
Lewis-Clark State College, ID
Louisiana State University and
Agricultural and Mechanical
College, LA
Miller-Motte Technical College,
NC
Minnesota School of Business,
MN
Minnesota School of Business:
Plymouth, MN
Minnesota School of Business: St.
Cloud, MN
Minnesota School of Business:
Shakopee, MN
Missouri Technical School, MO
Montana State University
Billings, MT
Montana Tech of the University of
Montana, MT
Mt. Sierra College, CA
National American University
Rapid City, SD
National Education Center
Spartan College of
Aeronautics and
Technology, OK
Neumont University, UT
New England Institute of Art, MA
New England Institute of
Technology, RI
Oklahoma Panhandle State
University, OK
Oregon Institute of Technology,
OR
Peirce College, PA
Pennsylvania College of
Technology, PA
Pioneer Pacific College, OR
Platt College
Aurora, CO
Ontario, CA
San Diego, CA
Rasmussen College: Ocala, FL
Remington College: Largo, FL
Remington College: Tampa, FL
Silicon Valley College
Western Career College:
Emeryville, CA
Silicon Valley University, CA
Southern California Institute of
Architecture, CA

Southwest Minnesota State
University, MN
State University of New York
College of Technology at
Canton, NY
Farmingdale, NY
Sterling College, VT
Stevens-Henager College: Logan,
UT
University College of San Juan,
PR
University of Advancing
Technology, AZ
University of Arkansas
Monticello, AR
University of Puerto Rico
Aguadilla, PR
Bayamon University
College, PR
Utuado, PR
Utah Career College, UT
Utah Valley State College, UT
Vaughn College of Aeronautics
and Technology, NY
Vermont Technical College, VT
Virginia College, AL
Virginia College at Huntsville, AL
Wentworth Institute of
Technology, MA
West Virginia University Institute
of Technology, WV
Westwood College of Technology
Westwood College: Denver
South, CO
Westwood College: Inland
Empire, CA
Westwood College: O'Hare
Airport, IL
Westwood College: Anaheim, CA
Westwood College: Atlanta
Midtown, GA
Westwood College: Chicago
Loop, IL
Westwood College: Denver
North, CO
Westwood College: DuPage, IL
Westwood College: Northlake,
GA
Westwood College: South Bay,
CA
Williamson Free School of
Mechanical Trades, PA
Woodbury College, VT
World College, VA

*Two-year*

Abraham Baldwin Agricultural
College, GA
Academy of Court Reporting:
Cleveland, OH
Advanced Technology Institute,
VA
Aiken Technical College, SC
Akron Institute, OH
Albany Technical College, GA
Alexandria Technical College,
MN
Allied Medical and Technical
Institute, PA
Anoka Technical College, MN
Antonelli College, OH
Antonelli College
Hattiesburg, MS
Jackson, MS
Arizona Automotive Institute, AZ
Arkansas State University
Mountain Home, AR
Art Institute
of New York City, NY
Art Institute of Ohio: Cincinnati,
OH
Art Institute of York, PA
Asheville-Buncombe Technical
Community College, NC
Asnuntuck Community College,
CT
Athens Technical College, GA

ATI Career Training Center
Dallas, TX
Ft. Lauderdale, FL
Oakland Park, FL
ATI College of Health, FL
Atlanta Technical College, GA
ATS Institute of Technology, OH
Augusta Technical College, GA
Austin Business College, TX
Aviation Institute of Maintenance:
Indianapolis, IN
Aviation Institute of Maintenance:
Kansas City, MO
Aviation Institute of Maintenance:
Virginia Beach, VA
Bainbridge College, GA
Bates Technical College, WA
Baton Rouge School of
Computers, LA
Bel-Rea Institute of Animal
Technology, CO
Bellingham Technical College,
WA
Belmont Technical College, OH
Benjamin Franklin Institute of
Technology, MA
Berean Institute, PA
Berks Technical Institute, PA
Big Sandy Community and
Technical College, KY
Black River Technical College,
AR
Blackhawk Technical College, WI
Blue Cliff College: Gulfport, MS
Blue Cliff College: Houma, LA
Blue Cliff College: Lafayette, LA
Blue Cliff College: Metairie, LA
Blue Cliff College: Shreveport,
LA
Blue Ridge Community and
Technical College, WV
Bluegrass Community and
Technical College, KY
Bolivar Technical College, MO
Bradford School, OH
Bradford School of Business, TX
Bramson ORT College, NY
Brooks College, CA
Brooks College: Sunnyvale, CA
Brown Mackie College: Atlanta,
GA
Brown Mackie College:
Louisville, KY
Brown Mackie College: South
Bend, IN
Bryan College: Los Angeles, CA
Bryan College: Sacramento, CA
Bryant & Stratton College:
Cleveland, OH
Business Institute of
Pennsylvania, PA
Caldwell Community College and
Technical Institute, NC
Cambria-Rowe Business College:
Indiana, PA
Cambridge College, CO
Camelot College, LA
Capital Community College, CT
Career College of Northern
Nevada, NV
Carteret Community College, NC
CEI College
Maric College: Panorama
City, CA
Central Carolina Technical
College, SC
Central Community College, NE
Central Florida College, FL
Central Georgia Technical
College, GA
Central Lakes College, MN
Central Maine Community
College, ME
Central New Mexico Community
College, NM
Central Ohio Technical College,
OH

Central Texas College, TX
Century Community and
Technical College, MN
Chattahoochee Technical College,
GA
Chattanooga State Technical
Community College, TN
CHI Institute: Broomall, PA
CHI Institute: Franklin Mills, PA
Chippewa Valley Technical
College, WI
Cincinnati State Technical and
Community College, OH
Cleveland Institute of Electronics,
OH
Clover Park Technical College,
WA
Colegio de las Ciencias Artes y
Television, PR
Coleman College
San Marcos, CA
College of Business and
Technology: Flagler, FL
College of Business and
Technology: Hialeah, FL
College of Court Reporting, IN
College of the Mainland, TX
College of the Sequoias, CA
CollegeAmerica
Denver, CO
Colorado School of Trades, CO
Columbus State Community
College, OH
Columbus Technical College, GA
Commonwealth Technical
Institute, PA
Community College of the Air
Force, AL
Concorde Career College
Garden Grove, CA
Concorde Career College: San
Bernardino, CA
Court Reporting Institute of
Dallas, TX
Court Reporting Institute of
Houston, TX
Cowley County Community
College, KS
Dakota County Technical College,
MN
Daytona Beach Community
College, FL
Dean Institute of Technology, PA
DeKalb Technical College, GA
Delaware Technical and
Community College
Owens, DE
Stanton/Wilmington, DE
Terry, DE
Delta College of Arts &
Technology, LA
Delta School of Business &
Technology, LA
Denmark Technical College, SC
Dodge City Community College,
KS
DuBois Business College, PA
Dunwoody College of
Technology, MN
Durham Technical Community
College, NC
Eagle Gate College: Layton, UT
Eagle Gate College: Murray, UT
Eagle Gate College: Salt Lake
City, UT
Eastern Idaho Technical College,
ID
Eastern Maine Community
College, ME
Eastern West Virginia Community
and Technical College, WV
ECPI Technical College
Richmond, VA
ECPI Technical College:
Roanoke, VA
EDIC College, PR

Electronic Computer Programming College, TN
Elizabethtown Community and Technical College, KY
Elmira Business Institute, NY
Elmira Business Institute: Vestal, NY
Erie Institute of Technology, PA
ETI Technical College of Niles, OH
Everest College Phoenix, AZ
Everest College: Arlington, TX
Everest College: Aurora, CO
Fayetteville Technical Community College, NC
Florence-Darlington Technical College, SC
Florida Career College: Hialeah, FL
Florida Career College: Lauderdale Lakes, FL
Florida Career College: Miami, FL
Florida Career College: Pembroke Pines, FL
Florida Career College: West Palm Beach, FL
Florida Technical College Deland, FL
Jacksonville, FL
Orlando, FL
Forsyth Technical Community College, NC
Fountainhead College of Technology, TN
Fox College, IL
Fox Valley Technical College, WI
Full Sail University, FL
Fullerton College, CA
Gadsden State Community College, AL
Gallipolis Career College, OH
Gateway Community College, AZ
Gateway Technical College, WI
George C. Wallace State Community College Selma, AL
Grayson County College, TX
Great Bay Community College, NH
Greenville Technical College, SC
Gretna Career College, LA
Griffin Technical College, GA
Guam Community College, GU
Gulf Coast College, FL
Gupton Jones College of Funeral Service, GA
Gwinnett Technical College, GA
Hallmark College of Aeronautics, TX
Hallmark College of Technology, TX
Hawkeye Community College, IA
Haywood Community College, NC
Hazard Community College, KY
Heald College Fresno, CA
Hayward, CA
Honolulu, HI
Rancho Cordova, CA
Heald College: Portland, OR
Helena College of Technology of the University of Montana, MT
Hennepin Technical College, MN
Heritage College: Kansas City, MO
Heritage Institute: Fort Myers, FL
Heritage Institute: Manassas, VA
Herzing College Minneapolis Drafting School Division of, MN
Hibbing Community College, MN
High-Tech Institute, CA
High-Tech Institute, GA
High-Tech Institute, TN

High-Tech Institute, FL
High-Tech Institute, MO
High-Tech Institute, NV
High-Tech Institute, MN
High-Tech Institute, AZ
Hocking College, OH
Hondros College, OH
Horry-Georgetown Technical College, SC
Huertas Junior College, PR
Hussian School of Art, PA
Institute of Business & Medical Careers, CO
Institute of Design and Construction, NY
IntelliTec College, CO
IntelliTec College: Grand Junction, CO
International College of Broadcasting, OH
International Junior College of Business and Technology, PR
Iowa Western Community College, IA
Island Drafting and Technical Institute, NY
Itawamba Community College, MS
ITI Technical College, LA
J. F. Drake State Technical College, AL
James A. Rhodes State College, OH
Jefferson College, MO
Jefferson Community and Technical College, KY
Jefferson Community College, OH
JNA Institute of Culinary Arts, PA
Johnson College, PA
Johnston Community College, NC
Kaplan Career Institute: Harrisburg, PA
Kaplan College: Denver, CO
Kaplan College: Hammond, IN
Kaplan College: Merrillville, IN
Kennebec Valley Community College, ME
Key College, FL
Keystone Technical Institute, PA
Lake Area Technical Institute, SD
Lake Region State College, ND
Lake Superior College, MN
Lake Washington Technical College, WA
Lakes Region Community College, NH
Lakeshore Technical College, WI
Lamar Institute of Technology, TX
Lamar State College at Port Arthur, TX
Lamson College, AZ
Laurel Business Institute, PA
Le Cordon Bleu College of Culinary Arts, GA
Le Cordon Bleu College of Culinary Arts, MN
Lincoln College of Technology: Denver, CO
Lincoln College of Technology: Indianapolis, IN
Lincoln College of Technology: West Palm Beach, FL
Lincoln Technical Institute: Allentown, PA
Lincoln Technical Institute: Northeast Philadelphia, PA
Lincoln Technical Institute: Philadelphia, PA
Lincoln Technical Institute: Plymouth Meeting, PA
Linn State Technical College, MO
Long Technical College, AZ
Los Angeles Trade and Technical College, CA

Louisville Technical Institute, KY
Luna Community College, NM
Madison Area Technical College, WI
Manchester Community College, NH
Manhattan Area Technical College, KS
Maric College Vista, CA
Maric College: Palm Springs, CA
Maric College: Sacramento, CA
Maric College: Salida, CA
Marion Technical College, OH
Martin Community College, NC
Maysville Community and Technical College, KY
McCann School of Business and Technology: Pottsville, PA
and Technology: Sunbury, PA
McCann School of Business and Technology: Scranton, PA
McDowell Technical Community College, NC
Mesabi Range Community and Technical College, MN
Mesalands Community College, NM
Metropolitan Career Center Computer Technology Institute, PA
Metropolitan Community College, NE
Mid-Plains Community College Area, NE
Mid-State Technical College, WI
Middle Georgia Technical College, GA
Midlands Technical College, SC
Miller-Motte Technical College, SC
Miller-Motte Technical College: Cary, NC
Miller-Motte Technical College: Chattanooga, TN
Miller-Motte Technical College: Lynchburg, VA
Milwaukee Area Technical College, WI
Minneapolis Business College, MN
Minneapolis Community and Technical College, MN
Minnesota State College - Southeast Technical, MN
Minnesota State Community and Technical College: Fergus Falls, MN
Minnesota West Community and Technical College, MN
Missouri College, MO
Mitchell Technical Institute, SD
Montana State University College of Technology: Great Falls, MT
Moraine Park Technical College, WI
Morrison Institute of Technology, IL
Mountain State College, WV
MTI College, CA
Nashua Community College, NH
Nashville Auto-Diesel College, TN
Nashville State Community College, TN
National College Dayton, OH
Knoxville, TN
Nashville, TN
National College of Business and Technology: Arecibo, PR
National College of Business and Technology: Bayamon, PR

National College of Business and Technology: Rio Grande, PR
National Institute of Technology, OH
National Park Community College, AR
National Polytechnic College of Science, CA
Naugatuck Valley Community College, CT
Navajo Technical College, NM
Nebraska College of Technical Agriculture, NE
New Castle School of Trades, PA
New Hampshire Technical Institute, NH
New Mexico Junior College, NM
New River Community and Technical College, WV
Nicolet Area Technical College, WI
North Arkansas College, AR
North Central Kansas Technical College, KS
North Central State College, OH
North Dakota State College of Science, ND
North Georgia Technical College, GA
North Metro Technical College, GA
Northcentral Technical College, WI
Northeast State Technical Community College, TN
Northeast Wisconsin Technical College, WI
Northeastern Technical College, SC
Northern Maine Community College, ME
Northland Community & Technical College, MN
Northland Pioneer College, AZ
Northwest Aviation College, WA
Northwest School of Wooden Boatbuilding, WA
Northwest State Community College, OH
Northwest Technical College, MN
Northwest Technical Institute, MN
Northwest-Shoals Community College, AL
Northwestern Business College, IL
Northwestern Connecticut Community College, CT
Northwestern Technical College, GA
Norwalk Community College, CT
Nossi College of Art, TN
Nunez Community College, LA
Ohio Institute of Photography and Technology, OH
Ohio State University Agricultural Technical Institute, OH
Ohio Technical College, OH
Ohio Valley College of Technology, OH
Oklahoma State University Oklahoma City, OK
Okmulgee, OK
Orangeburg-Calhoun Technical College, SC
Orleans Technical Institute - Center City Campus, PA
Ouachita Technical College, AR
Owensboro Community and Technical College, KY
Ozarka College, AR
Ozarks Technical Community College, MO
Paducah Technical College, KY
Palau Community College, PW

Pellissippi State Technical Community College, TN
Penn Commercial Business and Technical School, PA
Pennco Tech, PA
Pennsylvania Culinary Institute, PA
Pennsylvania Institute of Technology, PA
Pennsylvania School of Business, PA
Piedmont Technical College, SC
Pima Community College, AZ
Pine Technical College, MN
Pinnacle Career Institute: Kansas City, MO
Pioneer Pacific College: Springfield, OR
Pitt Community College, NC
Pittsburgh Institute of Aeronautics, PA
Pittsburgh Institute of Mortuary Science, PA
Pittsburgh Technical Institute, PA
Platt College Huntington Beach, CA
Los Angeles, CA
Pratt Community College, KS
Prince Institute of Professional Studies, AL
Puerto Rico Tech Junior College, PR
Pulaski Technical College, AR
Quinebaug Valley Community College, CT
Rainy River Community College, MN
Ramirez College of Business and Technology, PR
Randolph Community College, NC
Ranken Technical College, MO
Redstone College, CO
Refrigeration School, AZ
Remington College Baton Rouge, LA
Cleveland, OH
Colorado Springs, CO
Dallas, TX
Fort Worth, TX
Houston, TX
Little Rock, AR
Memphis, TN
Mobile, AL
Remington College: Cleveland West, OH
Remington College: Nashville, TN
Remington College: North Houston, TX
Renton Technical College, WA
RETS Tech Center, OH
Ridgewater College, MN
River Valley Community College, NH
Riverland Community College, MN
Robeson Community College, NC
Rochester Community and Technical College, MN
Rockford Business College, IL
Rosedale Technical Institute, PA
Rowan-Cabarrus Community College, NC
Sage College, CA
St. Cloud Technical College, MN
St. Paul College, MN
Salt Lake Community College, UT
San Jacinto College, TX
Sanford-Brown College Colorado Technical University: North Kansas City, MO
Hazelwood, MO
Savannah River College, GA
Savannah Technical College, GA

School of Advertising Art, OH
Scottsdale Culinary Institute, AZ
Shelton State Community College, AL
Silicon Valley College
    Western Career College: San Jose, CA
Sisseton Wahpeton College, SD
Somerset Community College, KY
South Central College, MN
South College, NC
South Florida Community College, FL
South Hills School of Business & Technology, PA
South Hills School of Business & Technology, PA
South Texas College, TX
Southeast Arkansas College, AR
Southeast Kentucky Community and Technical College, KY
Southeast Technical Institute, SD
Southeastern Business College: Lancaster, OH
Southeastern Technical College, GA
Southern Arkansas University Tech, AR
Southern Maine Community College, ME
Southern Union State Community College, AL
Southwest Georgia Technical College, GA
Southwest Institute of Technology, TX
Southwest Tennessee Community College, TN
Southwest Wisconsin Technical College, WI
Southwestern College of Business
    Southwestern College: Franklin, OH
Southwestern Indian Polytechnic Institute, NM
Spartanburg Community College, SC
Spencerian College: Lexington, KY
Springfield Technical Community College, MA
Stark State College of Technology, OH
State University of New York
    College of Agriculture and Technology at Cobleskill, NY
    College of Agriculture and Technology at Morrisville, NY
    College of Technology at Alfred, NY
Stautzenberger College, OH
Stenotype Institute: Orlando, FL
Stevens-Henager College: Boise, ID
Technical Career Institutes, NY
Technical College of the Lowcountry, SC
Technology Education College, OH
Terra State Community College, OH
TESST College of Technology
    Baltimore, MD
    Beltsville, MD
TESST College of Technology: Alexandria, VA
TESST College of Technology: Towson, MD
Texas County Technical Institute, MO
Texas Culinary Academy, TX

Texas State Technical College
    Harlingen, TX
    Sweetwater, TX
    Waco, TX
Texas State Technical College: Marshall, TX
Thaddeus Stevens College of Technology, PA
Three Rivers Community College, CT
Tidewater Tech
    Virginia Beach, VA
Tidewater Tech: Newport News, VA
Tri-County Technical College, SC
Triangle Tech
    DuBois, PA
    Erie, PA
    Greensburg, PA
    Pittsburgh, PA
Triangle Tech: Bethlehem, PA
Triangle Tech: Sunbury, PA
Trident Technical College, SC
Truckee Meadows Community College, NV
Tulsa Welding School, OK
United Tribes Technical College, ND
Universal Technical Institute, AZ
University of Arkansas
    Community College at Hope, AR
University of Hawaii
    Honolulu Community College, HI
University of Northwestern Ohio, OH
Vatterott College, MO
Vatterott College, IA
Vatterott College
    Tulsa, OK
Vatterott College: Cleveland, OH
Vatterott College: Joplin, MO
Vatterott College: Kansas City, MO
Vatterott College: Memphis, TN
Vatterott College: O'Fallon, MO
Vatterott College: Quincy, IL
Vatterott College: St. Joseph, MO
Vatterott College: Spring Valley, NE
Vatterott College: Springfield, MO
Vatterott College: Sunset Hills, MO
Vermilion Community College, MN
Vet Tech Institute, PA
Vincennes University, IN
Virginia College at Austin, TX
Virginia College at Mobile, AL
Wake Technical Community College, NC
Walla Walla Community College, WA
Washington County Community College, ME
Waukesha County Technical College, WI
West Central Technical College, GA
West Georgia Technical College, GA
West Kentucky Community and Technical College, KY
West Virginia Business College, WV
West Virginia Junior College: Charleston, WV
West Virginia State Community and Technical College, WV
Western Career College
    Pleasant Hill, CA
    San Leandro, CA
Western Career College: Antioch, CA

Western Career College: Sacramento, CA
Western Career College: Stockton, CA
Western Dakota Technical Institute, SD
Western School of Health and Business Careers, PA
Western Technical College, TX
Western Technical College, WI
Western Technical College: Diana Drive, TX
Westwood College of Technology
    Westwood College: Los Angeles, CA
Westwood College: Dallas, TX
Westwood College: Fort Worth, TX
Westwood College: Houston South, TX
White Mountains Community College, NH
Williamsburg Technical College, SC
Wisconsin Indianhead Technical College, WI
WyoTech: Fremont, CA
WyoTech: Laramie, WY
WyoTech: Long Beach, CA
York County Community College, ME
York Technical College, SC
Youngstown College of Massotherapy, OH
YTI Career Institute: Lancaster, PA
Zane State College, OH

## Arts/music colleges

### Four-year
Academy of Art University, CA
American Academy of Art, IL
Art Academy of Cincinnati, OH
Art Center College of Design, CA
Art Center Design College, NM
Art Center Design College, AZ
Art Institute
    of Atlanta, GA
    of California: Orange County, CA
    of California: San Diego, CA
    of Charlotte, NC
    of Colorado, CO
    of Dallas, TX
    of Houston, TX
    of Las Vegas, NV
    of Philadelphia, PA
    of Phoenix, AZ
    of Pittsburgh, PA
    of Washington, VA
Art Institute of Boston at Lesley University, MA
Art Institute of California: San Francisco, CA
Art Institute of Fort Lauderdale, FL
Art Institute of Portland, OR
Art Institute of Seattle, WA
Art Institutes International Minnesota, MN
Atlantic College, PR
Berklee College of Music, MA
Boston Conservatory, MA
Brooks Institute, CA
Brooks Institute: Ventura, CA
California College of the Arts, CA
California Design College, CA
California Institute of the Arts, CA
Chester College of New England, NH
Cleveland Institute of Art, OH
Cleveland Institute of Music, OH

Cogswell Polytechnical College, CA
College for Creative Studies, MI
College of Visual Arts, MN
Collins College, AZ
Columbia College Chicago, IL
Columbia College: Hollywood, CA
Columbus College of Art and Design, OH
Conservatory of Music of Puerto Rico, PR
Converse College, SC
Cooper Union for the Advancement of Science and Art, NY
Corcoran College of Art and Design, DC
Cornish College of the Arts, WA
Creative Center, NE
Curtis Institute of Music, PA
DePauw University, IN
DigiPen Institute of Technology, WA
Eastman School of Music of the University of Rochester, NY
Escuela de Artes Plasticas de Puerto Rico, PR
Ex'pression College for Digital Arts, CA
Fashion Institute of Technology, NY
Five Towns College, NY
Harrington College of Design, IL
Illinois Institute of Art: Chicago, IL
Illinois Institute of Art: Schaumburg, IL
Institute of American Indian Arts, NM
Interior Designers Institute, CA
International Academy of Design and Technology: Chicago, IL
International Academy of Design and Technology: Detroit, MI
International Academy of Design and Technology: Henderson, NV
International Academy of Design and Technology: Nashville, TN
International Academy of Design and Technology: Schaumburg, IL
International Academy of Design and Technology: Tampa, FL
Johns Hopkins University: Peabody Conservatory of Music, MD
Juilliard School, NY
Kansas City Art Institute, MO
Kendall College of Art and Design of Ferris State University, MI
Laguna College of Art and Design, CA
Lawrence University, WI
Lyme Academy College of Fine Arts, CT
Maine College of Art, ME
Manhattan School of Music, NY
Mannes College The New School for Music, NY
Maryland Institute College of Art, MD
Massachusetts College of Art, MA
Memphis College of Art, TN
Miami International University of Art and Design, FL
Milwaukee Institute of Art & Design, WI
Minneapolis College of Art and Design, MN
Montserrat College of Art, MA
Moore College of Art and Design, PA

New England Conservatory of Music, MA
New England Institute of Art, MA
New York School of Interior Design, NY
NewSchool of Architecture & Design, CA
North Carolina School of the Arts, NC
Northwest College of Art, WA
O'More College of Design, TN
Oberlin College, OH
Oregon College of Art & Craft, OR
Otis College of Art and Design, CA
Pacific Northwest College of Art, OR
Paier College of Art, CT
Parsons Paris School of Design, FR
Parsons The New School for Design, NY
Pennsylvania College of Art and Design, PA
Platt College
    Aurora, CO
    San Diego, CA
Pratt Institute, NY
Rhode Island School of Design, RI
Rhodec International, MA
Ringling College of Art and Design, FL
Rocky Mountain College of Art & Design, CO
San Francisco Art Institute, CA
San Francisco Conservatory of Music, CA
Savannah College of Art and Design, GA
School of the Art Institute of Chicago, IL
School of the Museum of Fine Arts, MA
School of Visual Arts, NY
Southern California Institute of Architecture, CA
State University of New York Purchase, NY
University of the Arts, PA
VanderCook College of Music, IL
Westminster Choir College of Rider University, NJ
Westwood College: Northlake, GA

### Two-year
American Academy of Dramatic Arts, NY
American Academy of Dramatic Arts: West, CA
Antonelli College, OH
Antonelli Institute of Art and Photography, PA
Art Institute
    of California: Los Angeles, CA
Art Institute of Cincinnati, OH
Art Institute of Ohio: Cincinnati, OH
Art Institute of York, PA
Delaware College of Art and Design, DE
Delta College of Arts & Technology, LA
Douglas Education Center, PA
Fashion Institute of Design and Merchandising
    Los Angeles, CA
    San Diego, CA
    San Francisco, CA
Full Sail University, FL
Hussian School of Art, PA
Madison Media Institute, WI
Nossi College of Art, TN
Oakbridge Academy of Arts, PA

Platt College
    Huntington Beach, CA
    Los Angeles, CA
School of Advertising Art, OH
Villa Maria College of Buffalo, NY
Virginia Marti College of Art and Design, OH

## Bible colleges

### Four-year

Alaska Bible College, AK
Allegheny Wesleyan College, OH
American Baptist College of ABT Seminary, TN
American Indian College of the Assemblies of God, AZ
Appalachian Bible College, WV
Arlington Baptist College, TX
Atlanta Christian College, GA
Austin Graduate School of Theology, TX
Baptist Bible College, MO
Baptist Bible College of Pennsylvania, PA
Baptist College of Florida, FL
Baptist Missionary Association Theological Seminary, TX
Baptist University of the Americas, TX
Barclay College, KS
Bethany University, CA
Bethesda Christian University, CA
Beulah Heights University, GA
Biola University, CA
Boise Bible College, ID
Calvary Bible College and Theological Seminary, MO
Carolina Christian College, NC
Carver Bible College, GA
Central Baptist College, AR
Central Bible College, MO
Central Christian College of the Bible, MO
Clear Creek Baptist Bible College, KY
Colegio Biblico Pentecostal, PR
Colegio Pentecostal Mizpa, PR
College of Biblical Studies-Houston, TX
Columbia International University, SC
Criswell College, TX
Crossroads College, MN
Crown College, MN
Dallas Christian College, TX
Davis College, NY
Emmaus Bible College, IA
Eugene Bible College, OR
Faith Baptist Bible College and Theological Seminary, IA
Family of Faith College, OK
Florida Christian College, FL
Free Will Baptist Bible College, TN
Global University, MO
God's Bible School and College, OH
Grace Bible College, MI
Grace University, NE
Great Lakes Christian College, MI
Griggs University, MD
Heritage Christian University, AL
Hobe Sound Bible College, FL
Huntsville Bible College, AL
John Wesley College, NC
Johnson Bible College, TN
Kaplan University
    Cedar Rapids, IA
Kentucky Christian University, KY
Kentucky Mountain Bible College, KY

The King's College and Seminary, CA
Kuyper College, MI
Lancaster Bible College, PA
Life Pacific College, CA
Lincoln Christian College and Seminary, IL
Lipscomb University, TN
Magnolia Bible College, MS
Manhattan Christian College, KS
Maranatha Baptist Bible College, WI
Mid-Continent University, KY
Moody Bible Institute, IL
Multnomah Bible College, OR
Nazarene Bible College, CO
Nebraska Christian College, NE
New Orleans Baptist Theological Seminary: Leavell College, LA
North Central University, MN
Northwestern College, MN
Oak Hills Christian College, MN
Ohio Christian University, OH
Ozark Christian College, MO
Philadelphia Biblical University, PA
Piedmont Baptist College, NC
Pillsbury Baptist Bible College, MN
Roanoke Bible College, NC
St. Louis Christian College, MO
School of Urban Missions: New Orleans, LA
School of Urban Missions: Oakland, CA
Somerset Christian College, NJ
Southeastern Baptist College, MS
Southeastern Baptist Theological Seminary, NC
Southeastern Bible College, AL
Southwestern Assemblies of God University, TX
Southwestern Christian College, TX
Southwestern Christian University, OK
Southwestern College, AZ
Tennessee Temple University, TN
Toccoa Falls College, GA
Tri-State Bible College, OH
Trinity Bible College, ND
Trinity College of Florida, FL
Trinity Lutheran College, WA
Universidad FLET, FL
Vennard College, IA
W.L. Bonner Bible College, SC
Washington Bible College, MD
Wesley College, MS
William Jessup University, CA
World Mission University, CA
Zion Bible College, RI

### Two-year

Rosedale Bible College, OH

## Business colleges

### Four-year

American University of Puerto Rico, PR
Angley College, FL
Aspen University, CO
Athens State University, AL
Atlantic College, PR
Babson College, MA
Baker College
    of Auburn Hills, MI
    of Cadillac, MI
    of Clinton Township, MI
    of Flint, MI
    of Jackson, MI
    of Muskegon, MI
    of Owosso, MI
    of Port Huron, MI
Baker College of Allen Park, MI

Baltimore International College, MD
Bay Path College, MA
Beckfield College, KY
Bellevue University, NE
Bentley College, MA
Berkeley College, NY
Berkeley College, NJ
Berkeley College of New York City, NY
Briarcliffe College, NY
Brown College, MN
Bryant & Stratton College Willoughby Hills, OH
Bryant University, RI
California College San Diego, CA
California National University for Advanced Studies, CA
California State University Stanislaus, CA
California University of Management and Sciences, CA
Capitol College, MD
Central Pennsylvania College, PA
Chadron State College, NE
Champlain College, VT
City College
    Miami, FL
City College: Fort Lauderdale, FL
City University of New York
    Baruch College, NY
    Medgar Evers College, NY
Clarion University of Pennsylvania, PA
Cleary University, MI
CollegeAmerica
    Fort Collins, CO
Columbia Centro Universitario: Caguas, PR
Columbia Southern University, AL
Crown College, WA
Davenport University, MI
DeVry Institute of Technology New York, NY
DeVry University: Memphis, TN
ECPI College of Technology: Newport News, VA
Electronic Data Processing College of Puerto Rico, PR
Electronic Data Processing College: San Sebastian, PR
Everest University: Brandon, FL
Everest University: North Orlando, FL
Everest University: Pinellas, FL
Everest University: Pompano Beach, FL
Everest University: South Orlando, FL
Everest University: Tampa, FL
Fashion Institute of Technology, NY
Franklin University, OH
Friends University, KS
Gibbs College: Vienna, VA
Globe Institute of Technology, NY
Globe University, MN
Goldey-Beacom College, DE
Herzing College, AL
Herzing College, GA
Herzing College, WI
Hesser College, NH
Hickey College, MO
Hodges University, FL
Humphreys College, CA
Husson College, ME
Huston-Tillotson University, TX
Indiana Institute of Technology, IN
Instituto Tecnologico Autonomo de Mexico, MX
Instituto Tecnologico y de Estudios Superiores de Occidente, MX
International Business College, IN

International Import-Export Institute, AZ
International University of Monaco, MC
Iona College, NY
John F. Kennedy University, CA
Jones College, FL
Jones College: Miami, FL
Keiser University, FL
Kendall College, IL
King's College, PA
LA College International, CA
Lasell College, MA
Linfield College, OR
Loyola College in Maryland, MD
Macon State College, GA
Maine Maritime Academy, ME
Mayville State University, ND
Menlo College, CA
Merrimack College, MA
Metropolitan College of New York, NY
Michigan Jewish Institute, MI
Midstate College, IL
Millsaps College, MS
Minnesota School of Business, MN
Minnesota School of Business: Blaine, MN
Minnesota School of Business: Plymouth, MN
Minnesota School of Business: St. Cloud, MN
Minnesota School of Business: Shakopee, MN
Missouri Western State University, MO
Monroe College, NY
Morrison University, NV
Mount Ida College, MA
National American University Rapid City, SD
    St. Paul, MN
National American University: Rio Rancho, NM
National College Roanoke Valley, VA
New England College, NH
Newbury College, MA
Nichols College, MA
Northwestern Polytechnic University, CA
Northwood University Florida, FL
Northwood University: Michigan, MI
Northwood University: Texas, TX
Okaloosa-Walton College, FL
Parsons Paris School of Design, FR
Peirce College, PA
Post University, CT
Potomac College, VA
Potomac College, DC
Presentation College, SD
Rasmussen College Eagan, MN
Rasmussen College: Brooklyn Park, MN
Rasmussen College: Ocala, FL
Rasmussen College: Pasco County, FL
Reinhardt College, GA
Restaurant School, PA
Rockhurst University, MO
Sage College of Albany, NY
Sanford-Brown College: Milwaukee, WI
Savannah State University, GA
Silicon Valley University, CA
Silver Lake College, WI
South University, GA
South University, AL
South University: West Palm Beach Campus, FL
Southeastern University, DC

Southern California Institute of Technology, CA
State University of New York College at Old Westbury, NY
    Institute of Technology at Utica/Rome, NY
    Purchase, NY
Stevens-Henager College Murray, UT
Stevens-Henager College: Logan, UT
Stevens-Henager College: Orem, UT
Stonehill College, MA
Strayer University, DC
Teikyo Loretto Heights University, CO
Thomas College, ME
Tiffin University, OH
Universidad Privada Boliviana, BO
University of Baltimore, MD
University of Management and Technology, VA
University of Northern Virginia, VA
Virginia College at Huntsville, AL
Walsh College of Accountancy and Business Administration, MI
Webber International University, FL
Western International University, AZ
Westwood College of Technology Westwood College: Inland Empire, CA
Yeshiva University, NY

### Two-year

Academy of Court Reporting: Cincinnati, OH
AEC Southern Ohio College Brown Mackie College: Akron, OH
    Brown Mackie College: Findlay, OH
AIB College of Business, IA
American School of Business, LA
Andover College, ME
Austin Business College, TX
Berean Institute, PA
Berks Technical Institute, PA
Beta Tech: Richmond South, VA
Beta Tech: Richmond West, VA
Bidwell Training Center, PA
Bohecker College, OH
Bradford School, OH
Brown Mackie College: Atlanta, GA
Brown Mackie College: Cincinnati, OH
Brown Mackie College: Fort Wayne, IN
Brown Mackie College: Hopkinsville, KY
Brown Mackie College: Merrillville, IN
Brown Mackie College: Miami, FL
Bryant & Stratton Business Institute
    Bryant & Stratton College: Albany, NY
    Bryant & Stratton College: Amherst, NY
    Bryant & Stratton College: Buffalo, NY
    Bryant & Stratton College: Rochester, NY
    Bryant & Stratton College: Southtowns, NY
    Bryant & Stratton College: Syracuse, NY
Bryant & Stratton College: Henrietta, NY

Bryant & Stratton College: Milwaukee, WI
Bryant & Stratton College: Syracuse North, NY
Bryant & Stratton College: Virginia Beach, VA
Business Informatics Center, NY
Business Institute of Pennsylvania, PA
Cambria-Rowe Business College, PA
Cambria-Rowe Business College: Indiana, PA
Career College of Northern Nevada, NV
City College
  Gainesville, FL
Clemens College, CT
College of Business and Technology: Hialeah, FL
College of Court Reporting, IN
College of Office Technology, IL
College of Westchester, NY
Columbia College
  Columbia Centro Universitario: Yauco, PR
Concorde Career College: Kansas City, MO
Consolidated School of Business
  Lancaster, PA
  York, PA
Daymar College
  Louisville, KY
  Owensboro, KY
Delta School of Business & Technology, LA
Douglas Education Center, PA
Draughons Junior College: Clarksville, TN
Draughons Junior College: Nashville, TN
DuBois Business College, PA
DuBois Business College
  Huntingdon, PA
  Oil City, PA
Duluth Business University, MN
Eagle Gate College: Layton, UT
Eagle Gate College: Murray, UT
Eagle Gate College: Salt Lake City, UT
Elmira Business Institute, NY
Elmira Business Institute: Vestal, NY
Empire College, CA
Erie Business Center, PA
Erie Business Center South, PA
Everest College
  Phoenix, AZ
Everest College: Arlington, TX
Everest College: Colorado Springs, CO
Fashion Careers College, CA
Fashion Institute of Design and Merchandising
  Los Angeles, CA
  San Diego, CA
  San Francisco, CA
Florida Career College: Miami, FL
Florida Career College: Pembroke Pines, FL
Florida Technical College
  Auburndale, FL
Gallipolis Career College, OH
Hallmark College of Technology, TX
Heald College
  Concord, CA
  Fresno, CA
  Honolulu, HI
  Roseville, CA
  Salinas, CA
  San Francisco, CA
  San Jose, CA
  Stockton, CA
Heald College: Portland, OR
Herzing College, FL

Hondros College, OH
Humacao Community College, PR
ICPR Junior College, PR
Indiana Business College
  Anderson, IN
  Columbus, IN
  Evansville, IN
  Fort Wayne, IN
  Indianapolis, IN
  Lafayette, IN
  Marion, IN
  Muncie, IN
  Terre Haute, IN
Indiana Business College: Indianapolis Northwest, IN
Institute of Business & Medical Careers, WY
International Business College: Indianapolis, IN
International Junior College of Business and Technology, PR
Jamestown Business College, NY
Kaplan Career Institute: Pittsburgh, PA
Kaplan College: Hagerstown, MD
Kaplan College: Hammond, IN
Kaplan College: Indianapolis, IN
Keiser Career College: Greenacres, FL
Keiser Career College: Miami Lakes, FL
Keiser Career College: Port St. Lucie, FL
Key College, FL
Las Vegas College, NV
LDS Business College, UT
Long Island Business Institute, NY
Long Island Business Institute: Flushing, NY
Maric College, CA
Maric College: Sacramento, CA
McCann School of Business and Technology: Hazleton, PA
McCann School of Business and Technology: Scranton, PA
Metro Business College, MO
Metro Business College
  Jefferson City, MO
  Rolla, MO
Mildred Elley, NY
Miller-Motte Technical College: Clarksville, TN
Minneapolis Business College, MN
Minnesota School of Business: Brooklyn Center, MN
Mountain State College, WV
MTI College, CA
National College
  Bluefield, VA
  Charlottesville, VA
  Danville, VA
  Danville, KY
  Dayton, OH
  Florence, KY
  Harrisonburg, VA
  Knoxville, TN
  Lexington, KY
  Louisville, KY
  Lynchburg, VA
  Martinsville, VA
  Nashville, TN
  Pikeville, KY
  Richmond, KY
National College of Business & Technology
  National College: Bristol, TN
National College of Business and Technology: Arecibo, PR
National College of Business and Technology: Bayamon, PR
National College of Business and Technology: Rio Grande, PR

New England College of Finance, MA
New England Culinary Institute
  Essex Junction, VT
Newport Business Institute: Lower Burrell, PA
Newport Business Institute: Williamsport, PA
North Florida Institute: Orange Park, FL
Ohio Business College, OH
Ohio Business College: Sandusky, OH
Ohio Valley College of Technology, OH
Olean Business Institute, NY
Penn Commercial Business and Technical School, PA
Pennsylvania School of Business, PA
PJA School, PA
Plaza College, NY
Professional Business College, NY
Ramirez College of Business and Technology, PR
Rasmussen College
  Eden Prairie, MN
  Mankato, MN
Remington College
  Memphis, TN
Rockford Business College, IL
Samuel Stephen College, OH
Sanford-Brown College, MO
Sanford-Brown College
  Hazelwood, MO
Santa Barbara Business College
  Bakersfield, CA
  Santa Maria, CA
Santa Barbara Business College: Ventura, CA
South Coast College, CA
South Hills School of Business & Technology, PA
South Hills School of Business & Technology, PA
Southeastern Business College: Jackson, OH
Southeastern Business College: Lancaster, OH
Southeastern Business College: New Boston, OH
Southern Ohio College
  Brown Mackie College: North Kentucky, KY
Southwestern College of Business
  Southwestern College: Vine Street Campus, OH
Southwestern College: Dayton, OH
Stautzenberger College, OH
Stenotype Institute: Jacksonville, FL
Taylor Business Institute, IL
Technology Education College, OH
Tidewater Tech: Chesapeake, VA
Tidewater Tech: Newport News, VA
Tri-State Business Institute, PA
Trumbull Business College, OH
University of Northwestern Ohio, OH
Utica School of Commerce, NY
Utica School of Commerce: Canastota, NY
Utica School of Commerce: Oneonta, NY
Valley College of Technology, WV
Virginia College at Austin, TX
Virginia College at Pensacola, FL
Virginia College Gulf Coast, MS
Virginia Marti College of Art and Design, OH
West Central Technical College, GA

West Tennessee Business College, TN
West Virginia Business College, WV
West Virginia Business College, WV
West Virginia Career Institute, PA
West Virginia Junior College: Bridgeport, WV
Western School of Health and Business Careers
  Monroeville, PA
Yorktowne Business Institute, PA
YTI Career Institute: Lancaster, PA

## Culinary schools

### Four-year
Art Institute
  of California: Orange County, CA
  of Houston, TX
  of Las Vegas, NV
  of Phoenix, AZ
  of Washington, VA
Art Institutes International Minnesota, MN
Baltimore International College, MD
Culinary Institute of America, NY
Kendall College, IL
Restaurant School, PA

### Two-year
Art Institute
  of New York City, NY
Art Institute of Ohio: Cincinnati, OH
Atlantic Cape Community College, NJ
California Culinary Academy, CA
California School of Culinary Arts, CA
Clemens College, CT
Cooking & Hospitality Institute of Chicago, IL
L'Ecole Culinaire, MO
Le Cordon Bleu College of Culinary Arts, NV
Le Cordon Bleu College of Culinary Arts, MN
Le Cordon Bleu College of Culinary Arts: Miami, FL
Mitchell Technical Institute, SD
New England Culinary Institute, VT
New England Culinary Institute
  Essex Junction, VT
Orlando Culinary Academy, FL
Pennsylvania Culinary Institute, PA
Scottsdale Culinary Institute, AZ
Southwestern Oregon Community College, OR
Walters State Community College, TN

## Engineering colleges

### Four-year
California National University for Advanced Studies, CA
Capitol College, MD
Cogswell Polytechnical College, CA
Colorado School of Mines, CO
Columbia University, NY
Cooper Union for the Advancement of Science and Art, NY
DigiPen Institute of Technology, WA

Franklin W. Olin College of Engineering, MA
Harvey Mudd College, CA
Illinois Institute of Technology, IL
Indiana Institute of Technology, IN
Instituto Tecnologico Autonomo de Mexico, MX
Instituto Tecnologico y de Estudios Superiores de Occidente, MX
Inter American University of Puerto Rico
  Bayamon Campus, PR
International Technological University, CA
Kettering University, MI
Lafayette College, PA
Maine Maritime Academy, ME
Manhattan College, NY
Missouri Technical School, MO
Montana Tech of the University of Montana, MT
Neumont University, UT
New Mexico Institute of Mining and Technology, NM
Northwestern Polytechnic University, CA
Oregon Institute of Technology, OR
Rose-Hulman Institute of Technology, IN
South Dakota School of Mines and Technology, SD
Southern California Institute of Technology, CA
Southern Polytechnic State University, GA
Stevens Institute of Technology, NJ
Tri-State University, IN
Union College, NY
United States Coast Guard Academy, CT
United States Merchant Marine Academy, NY
United States Military Academy, NY
Universidad del Valle de Guatemala, GT
Universidad Politecnica de Puerto Rico, PR
Universidad Privada Boliviana, BO
University of Management and Technology, VA
University of Missouri
  Missouri University of Science and Technology, MO
University of Pittsburgh
  Johnstown, PA
Vaughn College of Aeronautics and Technology, NY
Webb Institute, NY
Wentworth Institute of Technology, MA
West Virginia University Institute of Technology, WV

## Maritime colleges

### Four-year
California Maritime Academy, CA
Maine Maritime Academy, ME
Massachusetts Maritime Academy, MA
State University of New York Maritime College, NY
United States Coast Guard Academy, CT
United States Merchant Marine Academy, NY
Webb Institute, NY

**Two-year**

National Polytechnic College of Science, CA

Northwest School of Wooden Boatbuilding, WA

Northwestern Michigan College, MI

## Military colleges

**Four-year**

The Citadel, SC

Massachusetts Maritime Academy, MA

North Georgia College & State University, GA

Norwich University, VT

United States Air Force Academy, CO

United States Coast Guard Academy, CT

United States Merchant Marine Academy, NY

United States Military Academy, NY

United States Naval Academy, MD

Virginia Military Institute, VA

**Two-year**

Georgia Military College, GA

Marion Military Institute, AL

New Mexico Military Institute, NM

Valley Forge Military College, PA

Wentworth Military Junior College, MO

## Nursing and health science colleges

**Four-year**

Albany College of Pharmacy, NY

Allen College, IA

Angley College, FL

Aquinas College, TN

Baker College of Cadillac, MI

Baker College of Allen Park, MI

Baptist College of Health Sciences, TN

Bastyr University, WA

Beckfield College, KY

Bellin College of Nursing, WI

Blessing-Rieman College of Nursing, IL

Bryant & Stratton College Parma, OH

Cabarrus College of Health Sciences, NC

California College San Diego, CA

California University of Management and Sciences, CA

Caribbean University, PR

Chamberlain College of Nursing, MO

Charles R. Drew University of Medicine and Science, CA

City College Miami, FL

Clarkson College, NE

College of New Rochelle, NY

College of St. Catherine, MN

College of Saint Mary, NE

CollegeAmerica Fort Collins, CO

Columbia College of Nursing, WI

Coppin State University, MD

Curry College, MA

D'Youville College, NY

Dominican College of Blauvelt, NY

ECPI College of Technology: Virginia Beach, VA

Electronic Data Processing College: San Sebastian, PR

Florida Hospital College of Health Sciences, FL

Globe University, MN

Goldfarb School of Nursing at Barnes-Jewish College, MO

Gwynedd-Mercy College, PA

Husson College, ME

Independence University, UT

International Institute of the Americas Phoenix, AZ

Ithaca College, NY

Jefferson College of Health Sciences, VA

Keiser University, FL

Kettering College of Medical Arts, OH

King College, TN

Lakeview College of Nursing, IL

Lester L. Cox College of Nursing and Health Sciences, MO

Lincoln University, CA

Loma Linda University, CA

Louisiana State University Health Sciences Center, LA

Macon State College, GA

Massachusetts College of Pharmacy and Health Sciences, MA

Medcenter One College of Nursing, ND

MedCentral College of Nursing, OH

Medical College of Georgia, GA

Medical University of South Carolina, SC

Mercy College of Health Sciences, IA

Mercy College of Northwest Ohio, OH

Minnesota School of Business: St. Cloud, MN

Misericordia University, PA

Monroe College, NY

Mount Carmel College of Nursing, OH

Mountain State University, WV

National University of Health Sciences, IL

Nebraska Methodist College of Nursing and Allied Health, NE

Nevada State College, NV

New York Institute of Technology, NY

Northwestern Health Sciences University, MN

Oregon Health & Science University, OR

Oregon Institute of Technology, OR

Our Lady of the Lake College, LA

Presentation College, SD

Rasmussen College: Ocala, FL

Regis College, MA

Research College of Nursing, MO

Rosalind Franklin University of Medicine and Science, IL

Rush University, IL

St. Anselm College, NH

Saint Anthony College of Nursing, IL

St. Catharine College, KY

St. Francis Medical Center College of Nursing, IL

St. John's College, IL

St. Luke's College, MO

Samuel Merritt College, CA

Sanford-Brown College: Milwaukee, WI

South University, GA

South University, AL

South University: West Palm Beach Campus, FL

Springfield College, MA

State University of New York Downstate Medical Center, NY

Institute of Technology at Utica/Rome, NY

Upstate Medical University, NY

Stevens-Henager College Murray, UT

Stevens-Henager College: Orem, UT

Texas A&M University Baylor College of Dentistry, TX

Thomas Jefferson University: College of Health Professions, PA

Trinity College of Nursing and Health Sciences, IL

University of Arkansas for Medical Sciences, AR

University of Findlay, OH

University of Kansas Medical Center, KS

University of Maryland Baltimore, MD

University of Medicine and Dentistry of New Jersey School of Health Related Professions, NJ

School of Nursing, NJ

University of Mississippi Medical Center, MS

University of Nebraska Medical Center, NE

University of Tennessee Health Science Center, TN

University of Texas Health Science Center at Houston, TX

Health Science Center at San Antonio, TX

Medical Branch at Galveston, TX

Southwestern Medical Center at Dallas, TX

University of the Sciences in Philadelphia, PA

West Coast University, CA

West Suburban College of Nursing, IL

Winston-Salem State University, NC

**Two-year**

ATI College of Health, FL

ATS Institute of Technology, OH

Aultman College of Nursing and Health Sciences, OH

Beta Tech: Richmond South, VA

Beta Tech: Richmond West, VA

Bidwell Training Center, PA

Blue Cliff College: Lafayette, LA

Bolivar Technical College, MO

Boulder College of Massage Therapy, CO

Brown Mackie College: Atlanta, GA

Brown Mackie College: Cincinnati, OH

Bryman School, AZ

Camelot College, LA

Career College of Northern Nevada, NV

Careers Unlimited, UT

Caritas Laboure College, MA

Carolinas College of Health Sciences, NC

Central Maine Medical Center College of Nursing and Health Professions, ME

Centro de Estudios Multidisciplinarios, PR

City College Gainesville, FL

Cochran School of Nursing-St. John's Riverside Hospital, NY

College of Business and Technology: Kendall, FL

Colorado School of Healing Arts, CO

Columbia College Columbia Centro Universitario: Yauco, PR

Concorde Career College Garden Grove, CA

Concorde Career College: Aurora, CO

Concorde Career College: Kansas City, MO

Concorde Career College: North Hollywood, CA

Concorde Career College: San Diego, CA

EDIC College, PR

Everest Institute, GA

Florida College of Natural Health Bradenton, FL

Maitland, FL

Fremont College, CA

Good Samaritan College of Nursing and Health Science, OH

Goodwin College, CT

Helene Fuld College of Nursing, NY

Heritage College: Denver, CO

Heritage College: Kansas City, MO

Heritage Institute: Fort Myers, FL

Heritage Institute: Jacksonville, FL

Heritage Institute: Manassas, VA

Herzing College, FL

High-Tech Institute, FL

Hondros College, OH

Huntington College of Health Sciences, TN

Indiana Business College Anderson, IN

Columbus, IN

Evansville, IN

Fort Wayne, IN

Indianapolis, IN

Lafayette, IN

Marion, IN

Medical, IN

Muncie, IN

Terre Haute, IN

Indiana Business College: Indianapolis Northwest, IN

Institute of Business & Medical Careers, WY

Jefferson Davis Community College, AL

Kaplan Career Institute: Harrisburg, PA

Kaplan Career Institute: Pittsburgh, PA

Kaplan College: Indianapolis, IN

Keiser Career College: Greenacres, FL

Keiser Career College: Miami Lakes, FL

Keiser Career College: Port St. Lucie, FL

Keystone Technical Institute, PA

Lakeland Academy Division of Herzing College, MN

Las Vegas College, NV

Long Island College Hospital School of Nursing, NY

Los Angeles County College of Nursing and Allied Health, CA

Maric College, CA

Maric College: Palm Springs, CA

Maric College: Salida, CA

Metro Business College Jefferson City, MO

Miller-Motte Technical College: Clarksville, TN

Minnesota State College - Southeast Technical, MN

Myotherapy Institute, NE

National Institute of Technology, OH

North Florida Institute: Orange Park, FL

Ohio College of Massotherapy, OH

Ohio Institute of Health Careers: Columbus, OH

Ohio Institute of Health Careers: Elyria, OH

Phillips Beth Israel School of Nursing, NY

Platt College Tulsa, OK

Platt College: Oklahoma City Central, OK

Ponce Paramedical College, PR

Remington College: Nashville, TN

Remington College: North Houston, TX

St. Elizabeth College of Nursing, NY

St. Joseph's College of Nursing, NY

St. Luke's College, IA

St. Vincent Catholic Medical Centers, NY

St. Vincent's College, CT

Sanford-Brown College, MO

Sanford-Brown College Colorado Technical University: North Kansas City, MO

Sanford-Brown Institute: Tampa, FL

South College, NC

Southeast Missouri Hospital College of Nursing and Health Sciences, MO

Southern Ohio College Brown Mackie College: North Kentucky, KY

Southwestern College of Business Southwestern College: Vine Street Campus, OH

Southwestern College: Florence, KY

Spencerian College, KY

Swedish Institute, NY

Technology Education College, OH

Texas County Technical Institute, MO

Tidewater Tech: Chesapeake, VA

Ultrasound Diagnostic School Sanford-Brown Institute: Jacksonville, FL

Universal Technology College of Puerto Rico, PR

Vatterott College, IA

Vet Tech Institute, PA

Virginia College at Pensacola, FL

Virginia College Gulf Coast, MS

Wallace State Community College at Hanceville, AL

West Tennessee Business College, TN

West Virginia Junior College: Bridgeport, WV

Western Career College Pleasant Hill, CA

San Leandro, CA

Western Career College: Sacramento, CA

Western Career College: Stockton, CA

Western School of Health and Business Careers Monroeville, PA

Westwood College: Fort Worth, TX

White Earth Tribal and Community College, MN

WyoTech: Long Beach, CA

Yorktowne Business Institute, PA

Youngstown College of
Massotherapy, OH

## Schools of mortuary science

### Four-year
Cincinnati College of Mortuary
Science, OH

### Two-year
American Academy McAllister
Institute of Funeral Service, NY
Commonwealth Institute of
Funeral Service, TX
Dallas Institute of Funeral
Service, TX
John A. Gupton College, TN
Mid-America College of Funeral
Service, IN

## Seminary/rabbinical colleges

### Four-year
Amridge University, AL
Austin Graduate School of
Theology, TX
Baptist Bible College, MO
Baptist Bible College of
Pennsylvania, PA
Baptist Missionary Association
Theological Seminary, TX
Beis Medrash Heichal Dovid, NY
Beth Hamedrash Shaarei Yosher
Institute, NY
Beth Hatalmud Rabbinical
College, NY
Beth Medrash Govoha, NJ
Calvary Bible College and
Theological Seminary, MO
Central Yeshiva Tomchei
Tmimim-Lubavitch, NY
Colegio Biblico Pentecostal, PR
Conception Seminary College,
MO
Criswell College, TX
Darkei Noam Rabbinical College,
NY
Divine Word College, IA
Dominican School of Philosophy
and Theology, CA
Earlham College, IN
Erskine College, SC
Faith Baptist Bible College and
Theological Seminary, IA
George Fox University, OR
Global University, MO
Hebrew Theological College, IL
Hellenic College/Holy Cross, MA
Holy Apostles College and
Seminary, CT
Holy Trinity Orthodox Seminary,
NY
Jewish Theological Seminary of
America, NY
Kehilath Yakov Rabbinical
Seminary, NY
The King's College and
Seminary, CA
Liberty University, VA
Lincoln Christian College and
Seminary, IL
Machzikei Hadath Rabbinical
College, NY
The Master's College, CA
Mesivta Torah Vodaath Seminary,
NY
Michigan Theological Seminary,
MI
Mirrer Yeshiva Central Institute,
NY
Mount Angel Seminary, OR
Multnomah Bible College, OR

Ner Israel Rabbinical College,
MD
New Orleans Baptist Theological
Seminary: Leavell College, LA
Ohr Somayach Tanenbaum
Education Center, NY
Piedmont Baptist College, NC
Pontifical College Josephinum,
OH
Rabbi Jacob Joseph School, NJ
Rabbinical Academy Mesivta
Rabbi Chaim Berlin, NY
Rabbinical College Beth Shraga,
NY
Rabbinical College Bobover
Yeshiva B'nei Zion, NY
Rabbinical College Ch'san Sofer
of New York, NY
Rabbinical College of America,
NJ
Rabbinical College of Long
Island, NY
Rabbinical College of Ohr
Shimon Yisroel, NY
Rabbinical College of Telshe, OH
Rabbinical Seminary Adas
Yereim, NY
Rabbinical Seminary of America,
NY
Sacred Heart Major Seminary, MI
St. Charles Borromeo Seminary -
Overbrook, PA
St. John Vianney College
Seminary, FL
St. Joseph Seminary College, LA
Shor Yoshuv Rabbinical College,
NY
Southeastern Baptist Theological
Seminary, NC
Talmudic College of Florida, FL
Talmudical Academy of New
Jersey, NJ
Talmudical Institute of Upstate
New York, NY
Talmudical Seminary Oholei
Torah, NY
Talmudical Yeshiva of
Philadelphia, PA
Telshe Yeshiva-Chicago, IL
Torah Teminah Talmudical
Seminary, NY
U.T.A. Mesivta-Kiryas Jocl, NY
United Talmudical Seminary, NY
University of Dubuque, IA
Washington Bible College, MD
World Mission University, CA
Yeshiva and Kolel Bais Medrash
Elyon, NY
Yeshiva and Kollel Harbotzas
Torah, NY
Yeshiva Beth Yehuda-Yeshiva
Gedolah of Greater Detroit, MI
Yeshiva College of the Nations
Capital, MD
Yeshiva D'Monsey Rabbinical
College, NY
Yeshiva Derech Chaim, NY
Yeshiva Gedolah Imrei Yosef
D'Spinka, NY
Yeshiva Gedolah Rabbinical
College, FL
Yeshiva Gedolah Zichron Moshe,
NY
Yeshiva Karlin Stolin, NY
Yeshiva Mikdash Melech, NY
Yeshiva of Nitra, NY
Yeshiva of the Telshe Alumni, NY
Yeshiva Ohr Elchonon
Chabad/West Coast Talmudical
Seminary, CA
Yeshiva Shaar Hatorah, NY
Yeshiva Shaarei Torah of
Rockland, NY
Yeshiva Toras Chaim Talmudical
Seminary, CO
Yeshivas Novominsk, NY
Yeshivath Beth Moshe, PA

Yeshivath Viznitz, NY

### Two-year
Salvation Army College for
Officer Training at Crestmont,
CA

## Teacher's colleges

### Four-year
American Indian College of the
Assemblies of God, AZ
Anderson University, SC
Arlington Baptist College, TX
Athens State University, AL
Augusta State University, GA
Austin College, TX
Baker University, KS
Baltimore Hebrew University,
MD
Baptist College of Florida, FL
Black Hills State University, SD
Bloomfield College, NJ
Bridgewater State College, MA
California State University
Monterey Bay, CA
Cambridge College, MA
Canisius College, NY
Chadron State College, NE
City University of New York
Queens College, NY
Clarion University of
Pennsylvania, PA
College of St. Joseph in Vermont,
VT
College of Saint Mary, NE
College of Saint Rose, NY
College of the Southwest, NM
Concordia University, IL
Concordia University, MI
Dalton State College, GA
Eastern Illinois University, IL
Edinboro University of
Pennsylvania, PA
Emporia State University, KS
Fitchburg State College, MA
Florida Christian College, FL
Fort Valley State University, GA
Framingham State College, MA
Free Will Baptist Bible College,
TN
Frostburg State University, MD
Glenville State College, WV
Great Basin College, NV
Heritage University, WA
Howard Payne University, TX
Jarvis Christian College, TX
Jones College, FL
Keene State College, NH
Kendall College, IL
Lander University, SC
Laura and Alvin Siegal College of
Judaic Studies, OH
Lesley University, MA
Lyndon State College, VT
Manhattanville College, NY
Mayville State University, ND
National-Louis University, IL
Nevada State College, NV
New England College, NH
Northwestern Oklahoma State
University, OK
Oglala Lakota College, SD
Pacific Oaks College, CA
Peru State College, NE
Piedmont College, GA
Plymouth State University, NH
Rabbinical College of Long
Island, NY
Rabbinical College of Telshe, OH
Reinhardt College, GA
Rivier College, NH
St. Joseph's College, NY
Southeastern Oklahoma State
University, OK
Southeastern University, FL

State University of New York
College at Buffalo, NY
College at Cortland, NY
College at Plattsburgh, NY
College at Potsdam, NY
Tennessee Wesleyan College, TN
Union College, KY
University of Hawaii
West Oahu, HI
University of Maine
Farmington, ME
University of Montana: Western,
MT
Valley City State University, ND
VanderCook College of Music, IL
Wayne State College, NE
West Virginia State University,
WV
Western Oregon University, OR
Westfield State College, MA
Wheelock College, MA
Worcester State College, MA
York College, NE

### Two-year
Northern New Mexico College,
NM
White Earth Tribal and
Community College, MN

# Special characteristics

## Colleges for men

### Four-year
Beth Medrash Govoha, NJ
Conception Seminary College, MO
Divine Word College, IA
Hampden-Sydney College, VA
Holy Trinity Orthodox Seminary, NY
Morehouse College, GA
Mount Angel Seminary, OR
Ner Israel Rabbinical College, MD
Pontifical College Josephinum, OH
St. Charles Borromeo Seminary - Overbrook, PA
St. John Vianney College Seminary, FL
St. John's University, MN
St. Joseph Seminary College, LA
Talmudical Yeshiva of Philadelphia, PA
Wabash College, IN
Williamson Free School of Mechanical Trades, PA
Yeshiva College of the Nations Capital, MD
Yeshiva Mikdash Melech, NY
Yeshivath Beth Moshe, PA

### Two-year
Deep Springs College, CA

## Colleges for women

### Four-year
Agnes Scott College, GA
Alverno College, WI
Barnard College, NY
Bay Path College, MA
Bennett College, NC
Brenau University, GA
Bryn Mawr College, PA
Carlow University, PA
Cedar Crest College, PA
Chatham University, PA
College of New Rochelle, NY
College of Notre Dame of Maryland, MD
College of St. Benedict, MN
College of St. Catherine, MN
College of St. Elizabeth, NJ
College of Saint Mary, NE
Columbia College, SC
Converse College, SC
Georgian Court University, NJ
Hollins University, VA
Judson College, AL
Lexington College, IL
Mary Baldwin College, VA
Meredith College, NC
Midway College, KY
Mills College, CA
Moore College of Art and Design, PA
Mount Holyoke College, MA
Mount Mary College, WI
Peace College, NC
Pine Manor College, MA
Rosemont College, PA
Russell Sage College, NY

St. Joseph College, CT
Saint Mary's College, IN
St. Mary-of-the-Woods College, IN
Salem College, NC
Scripps College, CA
Simmons College, MA
Smith College, MA
Spelman College, GA
Stephens College, MO
Sweet Briar College, VA
Trinity Washington University, DC
Ursuline College, OH
Wellesley College, MA
Wesleyan College, GA
Wilson College, PA

### Two-year
Assumption College for Sisters, NJ
Cottey College, MO

## Affiliated with a religion

### African Methodist Episcopal Church

#### Four-year
Allen University, SC
Edward Waters College, FL
Wilberforce University, OH

### African Methodist Episcopal Zion Church

#### Four-year
Livingstone College, NC

### American Baptist Churches in the USA

#### Four-year
Alderson-Broaddus College, WV
Arkansas Baptist College, AR
Bacone College, OK
Benedict College, SC
Eastern University, PA
Florida Memorial University, FL
Franklin College, IN
Judson University, IL
Keuka College, NY
Linfield College, OR
Ottawa University, KS
University of Sioux Falls, SD

### Assemblies of God

#### Four-year
Bethany University, CA
Central Bible College, MO
Evangel University, MO
Global University, MO
North Central University, MN
Northwest University, WA
School of Urban Missions: Oakland, CA
Southeastern University, FL
Southwestern Assemblies of God University, TX
Trinity Bible College, ND
Valley Forge Christian College, PA
Vanguard University of Southern California, CA
Zion Bible College, RI

### Baptist faith

#### Four-year
American Baptist College of ABT Seminary, TN
Arlington Baptist College, TX
Baptist Bible College, MO
Baptist Bible College of Pennsylvania, PA

Baptist College of Health Sciences, TN
Baylor University, TX
Bluefield College, VA
Campbellsville University, KY
Cedarville University, OH
Central Baptist College, AR
Corban College, OR
Cornerstone University, MI
Dallas Baptist University, TX
East Texas Baptist University, TX
Hardin-Simmons University, TX
Houston Baptist University, TX
Howard Payne University, TX
Judson College, AL
Liberty University, VA
Maranatha Baptist Bible College, WI
Mars Hill College, NC
Mercer University, GA
Missouri Baptist University, MO
Morris College, SC
Piedmont Baptist College, NC
Pillsbury Baptist Bible College, MN
Shaw University, NC
Southwestern College, AZ
Tennessee Temple University, TN
University of Mary Hardin-Baylor, TX
University of Mobile, AL
University of the Cumberlands, KY
Virginia Intermont College, VA
Virginia Union University, VA
William Carey University, MS
Wingate University, NC

#### Two-year
Jacksonville College, TX

### Baptist General Conference

#### Four-year
Bethel University, MN
Oakland City University, IN

### Brethren Church

#### Four-year
Ashland University, OH
Emmaus Bible College, IA
Grace College, IN

### Christian and Missionary Alliance

#### Four-year
Crown College, MN
Nyack College, NY
Simpson University, CA
Toccoa Falls College, GA

### Christian Church

#### Four-year
Bethesda Christian University, CA
Crossroads College, MN
Johnson Bible College, TN
Manhattan Christian College, KS
The Master's College, CA
St. Louis Christian College, MO
Taylor University Fort Wayne, IN
William Jewell College, MO

### Christian Church (Disciples of Christ)

#### Four-year
Barton College, NC
Bethany College, WV
Chapman University, CA
Columbia College, MO
Culver-Stockton College, MO
Eureka College, IL
Hiram College, OH

Jarvis Christian College, TX
Lynchburg College, VA
Midway College, KY
Northwest Christian College, OR
Texas Christian University, TX
Transylvania University, KY
William Woods University, MO

### Christian Methodist Episcopal Church

#### Four-year
Lane College, TN
Miles College, AL
Texas College, TX

### Christian Reformed Church

#### Four-year
Calvin College, MI
Dordt College, IA

### Church of Christ

#### Four-year
Abilene Christian University, TX
Amridge University, AL
Carolina Christian College, NC
Cascade College, OR
Faulkner University, AL
Freed-Hardeman University, TN
Harding University, AR
Heritage Christian University, AL
Lincoln Christian College and Seminary, IL
Lipscomb University, TN
Lubbock Christian University, TX
Magnolia Bible College, MS
Ohio Valley University, WV
Oklahoma Christian University, OK
Pepperdine University, CA
Roanoke Bible College, NC
Rochester College, MI
York College, NE

#### Two-year
Crowley's Ridge College, AR

### Church of God

#### Four-year
Anderson University, IN
Lee University, TN
Mid-America Christian University, OK
University of Findlay, OH
Warner Pacific College, OR
Warner Southern College, FL

### Church of Jesus Christ of Latter-day Saints

#### Four-year
Brigham Young University, UT
Brigham Young University-Hawaii, HI
Brigham Young University-Idaho, ID
Southern Virginia University, VA

#### Two-year
LDS Business College, UT

### Church of the Brethren

#### Four-year
Bridgewater College, VA
Elizabethtown College, PA
Manchester College, IN
McPherson College, KS

### Church of the Nazarene

#### Four-year
Eastern Nazarene College, MA
MidAmerica Nazarene University, KS

Mount Vernon Nazarene University, OH
Nazarene Bible College, CO
Northwest Nazarene University, ID
Olivet Nazarene University, IL
Point Loma Nazarene University, CA
Southern Nazarene University, OK
Trevecca Nazarene University, TN

### Episcopal Church

#### Four-year
Bard College, NY
Clarkson College, NE
St. Augustine's College, NC
St. Luke's College, MO
St. Paul's College, VA
University of the South, TN
Voorhees College, SC

### Evangelical Free Church of America

#### Four-year
Trinity International University, IL

### Evangelical Lutheran Church in America

#### Four-year
Augsburg College, MN
Augustana College, IL
Augustana College, SD
Bethany College, KS
California Lutheran University, CA
Capital University, OH
Carthage College, WI
Concordia College: Moorhead, MN
Dana College, NE
Finlandia University, MI
Grand View College, IA
Gustavus Adolphus College, MN
Lenoir-Rhyne College, NC
Luther College, IA
Midland Lutheran College, NE
Muhlenberg College, PA
Newberry College, SC
Pacific Lutheran University, WA
Roanoke College, VA
St. Olaf College, MN
Susquehanna University, PA
Texas Lutheran University, TX
Thiel College, PA
Waldorf College, IA
Wartburg College, IA
Wittenberg University, OH

### Evangelical Lutheran Synod

#### Four-year
Bethany Lutheran College, MN

### Free Methodist Church of North America

#### Four-year
Central Christian College of Kansas, KS
Greenville College, IL
Roberts Wesleyan College, NY
Seattle Pacific University, WA
Spring Arbor University, MI

### Free Will Baptists

#### Four-year
Free Will Baptist Bible College, TN
Mount Olive College, NC

2085

## General Association of Regular Baptist Churches

### Four-year

Faith Baptist Bible College and Theological Seminary, IA

## Interdenominational tradition

### Four-year

Asbury College, KY
Azusa Pacific University, CA
Biola University, CA
Bryan College, TN
Ecclesia College, AR
Grace University, NE
Heritage University, WA
Hobe Sound Bible College, FL
John Brown University, AR
John Wesley College, NC
Messiah College, PA
Moody Bible Institute, IL
Multnomah Bible College, OR
Oak Hills Christian College, MN
Patten University, CA
Regent University, VA
Taylor University, IN
Trinity College of Florida, FL
Vennard College, IA
Williamson Christian College, TN

## Jewish faith

### Four-year

American Jewish University, CA
Beth Medrash Govoha, NJ
Gratz College, PA
Jewish Theological Seminary of America, NY
Laura and Alvin Siegal College of Judaic Studies, OH
Michigan Jewish Institute, MI
Ner Israel Rabbinical College, MD
Talmudical Yeshiva of Philadelphia, PA
Yeshiva College of the Nations Capital, MD
Yeshiva Mikdash Melech, NY
Yeshivath Beth Moshe, PA

## Lutheran Church

### Four-year

Trinity Lutheran College, WA
Valparaiso University, IN

## Lutheran Church - Missouri Synod

### Four-year

Concordia College, NY
Concordia College, AL
Concordia University, IL
Concordia University, CA
Concordia University, MI
Concordia University, NE
Concordia University, OR
Concordia University at Austin, TX
Concordia University Wisconsin, WI
Concordia University: St. Paul, MN

## Lutheran Church in America

### Four-year

Wagner College, NY

## Mennonite Brethren Church

### Four-year

Fresno Pacific University, CA

---

Tabor College, KS

## Mennonite Church

### Four-year

Bethel College, KS
Bluffton University, OH
Eastern Mennonite University, VA
Goshen College, IN

### Two-year

Hesston College, KS
Rosedale Bible College, OH

## Missionary Church

### Four-year

Bethel College, IN

## Moravian Church in America

### Four-year

Moravian College, PA
Salem College, NC

## Nondenominational tradition

### Four-year

Alaska Bible College, AK
Amberton University, TX
Appalachian Bible College, WV
Boise Bible College, ID
Calvary Bible College and Theological Seminary, MO
Clearwater Christian College, FL
Colorado Christian University, CO
Crichton College, TN
Dallas Christian College, TX
Davis College, NY
Friends University, KS
Gordon College, MA
King's College, NY
The King's College and Seminary, CA
Lancaster Bible College, PA
LeTourneau University, TX
Northwestern College, MN
Occidental College, CA
Oral Roberts University, OK
Ozark Christian College, MO
Palm Beach Atlantic University, FL
San Diego Christian College, CA
Southeastern Bible College, AL
Washington Bible College, MD
Westmont College, CA
Wheaton College, IL
William Jessup University, CA
Williamson Free School of Mechanical Trades, PA

## Pentecostal Holiness Church

### Four-year

Emmanuel College, GA
Southwestern Christian University, OK

## Presbyterian Church (USA)

### Four-year

Agnes Scott College, GA
Alma College, MI
Arcadia University, PA
Austin College, TX
Belhaven College, MS
Bethel College, TN
Blackburn College, IL
Bloomfield College, NJ
Buena Vista University, IA
Carroll College, WI
Centre College, KY
Coe College, IA
College of the Ozarks, MO

---

Davidson College, NC
Davis and Elkins College, WV
Eckerd College, FL
Grove City College, PA
Hampden-Sydney College, VA
Hanover College, IN
Hastings College, NE
Jamestown College, ND
King College, TN
Lafayette College, PA
Lake Forest College, IL
Lees-McRae College, NC
Lindenwood University, MO
Lyon College, AR
Macalester College, MN
Mary Baldwin College, VA
Maryville College, TN
Millikin University, IL
Missouri Valley College, MO
Monmouth College, IL
Montreat College, NC
Muskingum College, OH
Peace College, NC
Pikeville College, KY
Presbyterian College, SC
Queens University of Charlotte, NC
Rhodes College, TN
St. Andrews Presbyterian College, NC
Schreiner University, TX
Sterling College, KS
Stillman College, AL
Trinity University, TX
Tusculum College, TN
University of Dubuque, IA
University of the Ozarks, AR
University of Tulsa, OK
Warren Wilson College, NC
Waynesburg University, PA
Westminster College, MO
Westminster College, PA
Whitworth University, WA
Wilson College, PA

## Reformed Church in America

### Four-year

Central College, IA
Hope College, MI
Northwestern College, IA

## Reformed Presbyterian Church of North America

### Four-year

Geneva College, PA

## Roman Catholic Church

### Four-year

Albertus Magnus College, CT
Alvernia College, PA
Alverno College, WI
Anna Maria College, MA
Aquinas College, MI
Aquinas College, TN
Assumption College, MA
Ave Maria University, FL
Avila University, MO
Barry University, FL
Bayamon Central University, PR
Bellarmine University, KY
Belmont Abbey College, NC
Benedictine College, KS
Benedictine University, IL
Boston College, MA
Brescia University, KY
Briar Cliff University, IA
Cabrini College, PA
Caldwell College, NJ
Calumet College of St. Joseph, IN
Canisius College, NY
Cardinal Stritch University, WI
Carlow University, PA

---

Carroll College, MT
Catholic University of America, DC
Chaminade University of Honolulu, HI
Chestnut Hill College, PA
Christendom College, VA
Christian Brothers University, TN
Clarke College, IA
College of Mount St. Joseph, OH
College of Mount St. Vincent, NY
College of New Rochelle, NY
College of Notre Dame of Maryland, MD
College of St. Benedict, MN
College of St. Catherine, MN
College of St. Elizabeth, NJ
College of St. Joseph in Vermont, VT
College of Saint Mary, NE
College of Saint Rose, NY
College of St. Scholastica, MN
College of Saint Thomas More, TX
College of the Holy Cross, MA
Conception Seminary College, MO
Creighton University, NE
DePaul University, IL
DeSales University, PA
Divine Word College, IA
Dominican School of Philosophy and Theology, CA
Dominican University, IL
Duquesne University, PA
Edgewood College, WI
Elms College, MA
Emmanuel College, MA
Fairfield University, CT
Felician College, NJ
Fontbonne University, MO
Fordham University, NY
Franciscan University of Steubenville, OH
Gannon University, PA
Georgetown University, DC
Georgian Court University, NJ
Gonzaga University, WA
Gwynedd-Mercy College, PA
Hilbert College, NY
Holy Apostles College and Seminary, CT
Holy Cross College, IN
Holy Family University, PA
Holy Names University, CA
Immaculata University, PA
Iona College, NY
John Carroll University, OH
King's College, PA
La Roche College, PA
La Salle University, PA
Le Moyne College, NY
Lewis University, IL
Lexington College, IL
Loras College, IA
Lourdes College, OH
Loyola College in Maryland, MD
Loyola Marymount University, CA
Loyola University Chicago, IL
Loyola University New Orleans, LA
Madonna University, MI
Magdalen College, NH
Manhattan College, NY
Marian College, IN
Marian College of Fond du Lac, WI
Marquette University, WI
Marygrove College, MI
Marylhurst University, OR
Marymount University, VA
Marywood University, PA
Mercy College of Health Sciences, IA
Mercy College of Northwest Ohio, OH

---

Mercyhurst College, PA
Merrimack College, MA
Misericordia University, PA
Molloy College, NY
Mount Aloysius College, PA
Mount Angel Seminary, OR
Mount Marty College, SD
Mount Mary College, WI
Mount Mercy College, IA
Mount St. Mary's College, CA
Mount St. Mary's University, MD
Neumann College, PA
Newman University, KS
Niagara University, NY
Notre Dame College, OH
Notre Dame de Namur University, CA
Ohio Dominican University, OH
Our Lady of the Lake College, LA
Our Lady of the Lake University of San Antonio, TX
Pontifical Catholic University of Puerto Rico, PR
Pontifical College Josephinum, OH
Presentation College, SD
Providence College, RI
Quincy University, IL
Regis College, MA
Regis University, CO
Rivier College, NH
Rockhurst University, MO
Rosemont College, PA
Sacred Heart Major Seminary, MI
Sacred Heart University, CT
St. Ambrose University, IA
St. Anselm College, NH
Saint Bonaventure University, NY
St. Catharine College, KY
St. Charles Borromeo Seminary - Overbrook, PA
St. Edward's University, TX
St. Francis College, NY
St. Francis Medical Center College of Nursing, IL
St. Francis University, PA
St. Gregory's University, OK
St. John Fisher College, NY
St. John Vianney College Seminary, FL
St. John's College, IL
St. John's University, NY
St. John's University, MN
St. Joseph College, CT
St. Joseph Seminary College, LA
St. Joseph's College, ME
Saint Joseph's College, IN
Saint Joseph's University, PA
St. Leo University, FL
Saint Louis University, MO
Saint Martin's University, WA
Saint Mary's College, IN
St. Mary's College of California, CA
St. Mary's University, TX
St. Mary's University of Minnesota, MN
St. Mary-of-the-Woods College, IN
St. Michael's College, VT
St. Norbert College, WI
Saint Peter's College, NJ
Saint Thomas University, FL
St. Vincent College, PA
St. Xavier University, IL
Salve Regina University, RI
Santa Clara University, CA
Seattle University, WA
Seton Hall University, NJ
Seton Hill University, PA
Siena College, NY
Siena Heights University, MI
Silver Lake College, WI
Spring Hill College, AL
Stonehill College, MA
Thomas Aquinas College, CA

Thomas More College, KY
Thomas More College of Liberal
Arts, NH
Trinity Washington University,
DC
Universidad de Monterrey, MX
University of Dallas, TX
University of Dayton, OH
University of Detroit Mercy, MI
University of Great Falls, MT
University of Mary, ND
University of Notre Dame, IN
University of Portland, OR
University of St. Francis, IN
University of St. Francis, IL
University of St. Mary, KS
University of St. Thomas, TX
University of St. Thomas, MN
University of San Diego, CA
University of San Francisco, CA
University of Scranton, PA
University of the Incarnate Word,
TX
University of the Sacred Heart,
PR
Ursuline College, OH
Villanova University, PA
Viterbo University, WI
Walsh University, OH
West Suburban College of
Nursing, IL
Wheeling Jesuit University, WV
Xavier University, OH
Xavier University of Louisiana,
LA

**Two-year**

Ancilla College, IN
Assumption College for Sisters,
NJ
Caritas Laboure College, MA
Chatfield College, OH
Donnelly College, KS
Marian Court College, MA
Marymount College, CA
St. Elizabeth College of Nursing,
NY
St. Joseph's College of Nursing,
NY
St. Vincent Catholic Medical
Centers, NY
Springfield College in Illinois, IL
Trocaire College, NY
Villa Maria College of Buffalo,
NY

### Seventh-day Adventists

**Four-year**

Andrews University, MI
Atlantic Union College, MA
Columbia Union College, MD
Florida Hospital College of
Health Sciences, FL
Griggs University, MD
Kettering College of Medical
Arts, OH
La Sierra University, CA
Loma Linda University, CA
Oakwood College, AL
Pacific Union College, CA
Southern Adventist University,
TN
Southwestern Adventist
University, TX
Union College, NE
Universidad Adventista de las
Antillas, PR
Walla Walla University, WA

### Society of Friends (Quaker)

**Four-year**

Earlham College, IN
George Fox University, OR
Guilford College, NC
William Penn University, IA

Wilmington College, OH

### Southern Baptist Convention

**Four-year**

Anderson University, SC
Baptist College of Florida, FL
Blue Mountain College, MS
Brewton-Parker College, GA
California Baptist University, CA
Carson-Newman College, TN
Charleston Southern University,
SC
Chowan University, NC
Clear Creek Baptist Bible
College, KY
Criswell College, TX
Gardner-Webb University, NC
Georgetown College, KY
Hannibal-LaGrange College, MO
Louisiana College, LA
Mid-Continent University, KY
Mississippi College, MS
North Greenville University, SC
Oklahoma Baptist University, OK
Ouachita Baptist University, AR
Samford University, AL
Shorter College, GA
Southwest Baptist University, MO
Truett-McConnell College, GA
Union University, TN
Wayland Baptist University, TX
Williams Baptist College, AR

### Ukrainian Catholic Church

**Two-year**

Manor College, PA

### United Brethren in Christ

**Four-year**

Huntington University, IN

### United Church of Christ

**Four-year**

Catawba College, NC
Defiance College, OH
Doane College, NE
Elmhurst College, IL
Elon University, NC
Heidelberg College, OH
Lakeland College, WI
Northland College, WI
Pacific University, OR
Williams College, MA

### United Methodist Church

**Four-year**

Adrian College, MI
Albion College, MI
Albright College, PA
Allegheny College, PA
American University, DC
Baker University, KS
Baldwin-Wallace College, OH
Bennett College, NC
Bethune-Cookman University, FL
Birmingham-Southern College,
AL
Brevard College, NC
Centenary College, NJ
Centenary College of Louisiana,
LA
Central Methodist University, MO
Claflin University, SC
Clark Atlanta University, GA
Columbia College, SC
Cornell College, IA
Dakota Wesleyan University, SD
DePauw University, IN
Drew University, NJ

Duke University, NC
Emory & Henry College, VA
Emory University, GA
Ferrum College, VA
Florida Southern College, FL
Green Mountain College, VT
Greensboro College, NC
Hamline University, MN
Hendrix College, AR
High Point University, NC
Huntingdon College, AL
Iowa Wesleyan College, IA
Kansas Wesleyan University, KS
Kentucky Wesleyan College, KY
LaGrange College, GA
Lambuth University, TN
Lebanon Valley College, PA
Lindsey Wilson College, KY
Lycoming College, PA
MacMurray College, IL
Martin Methodist College, TN
McKendree University, IL
McMurry University, TX
Methodist University, NC
Millsaps College, MS
Morningside College, IA
Mount Union College, OH
Nebraska Methodist College of
Nursing and Allied Health, NE
Nebraska Wesleyan University,
NE
North Carolina Wesleyan College,
NC
North Central College, IL
Ohio Northern University, OH
Ohio Wesleyan University, OH
Oklahoma City University, OK
Otterbein College, OH
Pfeiffer University, NC
Philander Smith College, AR
Randolph College, VA
Randolph-Macon College, VA
Reinhardt College, GA
Rust College, MS
Shenandoah University, VA
Simpson College, IA
Southern Methodist University,
TX
Southwestern College, KS
Southwestern University, TX
Tennessee Wesleyan College, TN
Texas Wesleyan University, TX
Union College, KY
University of Denver, CO
University of Evansville, IN
University of Indianapolis, IN
Virginia Wesleyan College, VA
Wesley College, DE
Wesleyan College, GA
West Virginia Wesleyan College,
WV
Wiley College, TX
Willamette University, OR
Wofford College, SC

**Two-year**

Andrew College, GA
Hiwassee College, TN
Lon Morris College, TX
Louisburg College, NC
Oxford College of Emory
University, GA
Spartanburg Methodist College,
SC
Young Harris College, GA

### Wesleyan Church

**Four-year**

Houghton College, NY
Indiana Wesleyan University, IN
Oklahoma Wesleyan University,
OK
Southern Wesleyan University,
SC

### Wisconsin Evangelical Lutheran Synod

**Four-year**

Martin Luther College, MN
Wisconsin Lutheran College, WI

---

### Historically Black colleges

### Four-year

Alabama Agricultural and
Mechanical University, AL
Alabama State University, AL
Albany State University, GA
Alcorn State University, MS
Allen University, SC
Arkansas Baptist College, AR
Benedict College, SC
Bennett College, NC
Bluefield State College, WV
Bowie State University, MD
Central State University, OH
Cheyney University of
Pennsylvania, PA
Claflin University, SC
Clark Atlanta University, GA
Concordia College, AL
Coppin State University, MD
Delaware State University, DE
Dillard University, LA
Edward Waters College, FL
Elizabeth City State University,
NC
Florida Agricultural and
Mechanical University, FL
Florida Memorial University, FL
Fort Valley State University, GA
Grambling State University, LA
Hampton University, VA
Harris-Stowe State University,
MO
Howard University, DC
Huston-Tillotson University, TX
Jackson State University, MS
Jarvis Christian College, TX
Johnson C. Smith University, NC
Kentucky State University, KY
Lane College, TN
Langston University, OK
LeMoyne-Owen College, TN
Lincoln University, PA
Lincoln University, MO
Livingstone College, NC
Miles College, AL
Mississippi Valley State
University, MS
Morehouse College, GA
Morgan State University, MD
Morris College, SC
Norfolk State University, VA
North Carolina Agricultural and
Technical State University, NC
North Carolina Central
University, NC
Oakwood College, AL
Paine College, GA
Philander Smith College, AR
Prairie View A&M University, TX
Rust College, MS
St. Augustine's College, NC
St. Paul's College, VA
Savannah State University, GA
Shaw University, NC
South Carolina State University,
SC
Southern University
New Orleans, LA
Southern University and
Agricultural and Mechanical
College, LA
Spelman College, GA
Stillman College, AL
Tennessee State University, TN
Texas College, TX
Texas Southern University, TX

Tougaloo College, MS
Tuskegee University, AL
University of Arkansas
Pine Bluff, AR
University of Maryland
Eastern Shore, MD
University of the District of
Columbia, DC
University of the Virgin Islands,
VI
Virginia State University, VA
Voorhees College, SC
Wilberforce University, OH
Wiley College, TX
Winston-Salem State University,
NC
Xavier University of Louisiana,
LA

### Two-year

Bishop State Community College,
AL
Coahoma Community College,
MS
Denmark Technical College, SC
Hinds Community College, MS
J. F. Drake State Technical
College, AL
Lawson State Community
College, AL
St. Philip's College, TX
Southern University
Shreveport, LA

---

### Hispanic serving colleges

### Four-year

Adams State College, CO
American University of Puerto
Rico, PR
Atlantic College, PR
Barry University, FL
Bayamon Central University, PR
Boricua College, NY
California State University
Bakersfield, CA
Dominguez Hills, CA
Fresno, CA
Los Angeles, CA
Monterey Bay, CA
Northridge, CA
San Bernardino, CA
Stanislaus, CA
Caribbean University, PR
Carlos Albizu University, FL
City University of New York
City College, NY
John Jay College of
Criminal Justice, NY
Lehman College, NY
New York City College of
Technology, NY
College of Santa Fe, NM
Conservatory of Music of Puerto
Rico, PR
Dominican School of Philosophy
and Theology, CA
Escuela de Artes Plasticas de
Puerto Rico, PR
Florida International University,
FL
Heritage University, WA
Inter American University of
Puerto Rico
Aguadilla Campus, PR
Arecibo Campus, PR
Barranquitas Campus, PR
Bayamon Campus, PR
Fajardo Campus, PR
Guayama Campus, PR
Metropolitan Campus, PR
Ponce Campus, PR
San German Campus, PR
Lexington College, IL
Mercy College, NY

**Tables and Indexes**

Mount Angel Seminary, OR
Mount St. Mary's College, CA
New Jersey City University, NJ
New Mexico State University,
NM
Occidental College, CA
Our Lady of the Lake University
of San Antonio, TX
Pontifical Catholic University of
Puerto Rico, PR
Robert Morris College: Chicago,
IL
St. Edward's University, TX
St. John Vianney College
Seminary, FL
St. Mary's University, TX
Saint Peter's College, NJ
Saint Thomas University, FL
San Diego State University, CA
Sul Ross State University, TX
Texas A&M International
University, TX
Texas A&M University
Kingsville, TX
Turabo University, PR
Universidad Adventista de las
Antillas, PR
Universidad del Este, PR
Universidad Metropolitana, PR
Universidad Politecnica de Puerto
Rico, PR
University College of San Juan,
PR
University of Houston
Downtown, TX
University of La Verne, CA
University of Miami, FL
University of New Mexico, NM
University of Puerto Rico
Aguadilla, PR
Arecibo, PR
Bayamon University
College, PR
Carolina Regional College,
PR
Cayey University College,
PR
Humacao, PR
Mayaguez, PR
Medical Sciences, PR
Ponce, PR
Rio Piedras, PR
Utuado, PR
University of Texas
Brownsville, TX
El Paso, TX
Health Science Center at San
Antonio, TX
Pan American, TX
San Antonio, TX
of the Permian Basin, TX
University of the Incarnate Word,
TX
University of the Sacred Heart,
PR
Vaughn College of Aeronautics
and Technology, NY
Western New Mexico University,
NM
Whittier College, CA
Woodbury University, CA

### Two-year
Allan Hancock College, CA
Arizona Western College, AZ
Bakersfield College, CA
Central Arizona College, AZ
Central New Mexico Community
College, NM
Cerritos College, CA
Chaffey College, CA
Citrus College, CA
City Colleges of Chicago
Harry S. Truman College, IL
Malcolm X College, IL
Richard J. Daley College, IL
Wright College, IL

City University of New York
Borough of Manhattan
Community College, NY
Bronx Community College,
NY
Hostos Community College,
NY
LaGuardia Community
College, NY
Coastal Bend College, TX
Cochise College, AZ
College of the Desert, CA
College of the Sequoias, CA
Community College of Denver,
CO
Del Mar College, TX
Dodge City Community College,
KS
Dona Ana Branch Community
College of New Mexico State
University, NM
East Los Angeles College, CA
Eastern New Mexico University:
Roswell Campus, NM
El Camino College, CA
El Camino College: Compton
Center, CA
El Paso Community College, TX
Evergreen Valley College, CA
Fresno City College, CA
Fullerton College, CA
Gavilan College, CA
Hartnell College, CA
Heald College
Fresno, CA
Salinas, CA
San Jose, CA
Stockton, CA
Hudson County Community
College, NJ
Humacao Community College,
PR
Imperial Valley College, CA
Laredo Community College, TX
Long Beach City College, CA
Los Angeles City College, CA
Los Angeles Harbor College, CA
Los Angeles Mission College, CA
Los Angeles Trade and Technical
College, CA
Los Angeles Valley College, CA
MacCormac College, IL
Merced College, CA
Miami Dade College, FL
Morton College, IL
Mount San Antonio College, CA
Mountain View College, TX
New Mexico Junior College, NM
Northern New Mexico College,
NM
Odessa College, TX
Otero Junior College, CO
Oxnard College, CA
Palo Alto College, TX
Palo Verde College, CA
Pasadena City College, CA
Passaic County Community
College, NJ
Phoenix College, AZ
Pima Community College, AZ
Porterville College, CA
Pueblo Community College, CO
Reedley College, CA
Rio Hondo College, CA
Riverside Community College,
CA
St. Philip's College, TX
San Antonio College, TX
San Bernardino Valley College,
CA
San Jose City College, CA
Santa Ana College, CA
Santa Fe Community College,
NM
South Mountain Community
College, AZ
South Plains College, TX

Southwestern College, CA
Texas Southmost College, TX
Texas State Technical College
Harlingen, TX
Trinidad State Junior College, CO
Ventura College, CA
Victoria College, TX
Waubonsee Community College,
IL
West Hills College: Coalinga, CA

## Tribal colleges

### Four-year
Haskell Indian Nations
University, KS
Institute of American Indian Arts,
NM
Oglala Lakota College, SD

### Two-year
Bay Mills Community College,
MI
Blackfeet Community College,
MT
Chief Dull Knife College, MT
College of Menominee Nation,
WI
Dine College, AZ
Fort Belknap College, MT
Fort Berthold Community
College, ND
Fort Peck Community College,
MT
Lac Courte Oreilles Ojibwa
Community College, WI
Little Priest Tribal College, NE
Nebraska Indian Community
College, NE
Sisseton Wahpeton College, SD
Sitting Bull College, ND
Southwestern Indian Polytechnic
Institute, NM
Stone Child College, MT
Turtle Mountain Community
College, ND
United Tribes Technical College,
ND

# Undergraduate enrollment size

## Four-year

### Alabama
Amridge University
Andrew Jackson University
Concordia College
Heritage Christian University
Judson College
South University
Southeastern Bible College
United States Sports Academy

### Alaska
Alaska Bible College
Alaska Pacific University

### Arizona
Arizona Institute of Business and Technology
    International Institute of the Americas: Mesa
Art Center Design College
Brown Mackie College: Tucson
International Import-Export Institute
International Institute of the Americas
    Phoenix
    Tucson
Midwestern University: Glendale
Northcentral University
Prescott College
Southwestern College

### Arkansas
Arkansas Baptist College
Central Baptist College
Lyon College
Philander Smith College
University of the Ozarks
Williams Baptist College

### California
Alliant International University
American Jewish University
Antioch Southern California
    Antioch University Los Angeles
Bethany University
Bethesda Christian University
California College San Diego
California Institute of Integral Studies
California National University for Advanced Studies
California University of Management and Sciences
Charles R. Drew University of Medicine and Science
Cogswell Polytechnical College
Coleman College
Columbia College: Hollywood
Design Institute of San Diego
DeVry University
    Sherman Oaks
Dominican School of Philosophy and Theology
Golden Gate University
Harvey Mudd College
Holy Names University
Hope International University
Humphreys College
John F. Kennedy University

Life Pacific College
Lincoln University
Menlo College
National Hispanic University
NewSchool of Architecture & Design
Northwestern Polytechnic University
Notre Dame de Namur University
Pacific Oaks College
Pacific States University
Platt College
    Ontario
    San Diego
Samuel Merritt College
San Diego Christian College
San Francisco Art Institute
San Francisco Conservatory of Music
School of Urban Missions: Oakland
Soka University of America
Southern California Institute of Architecture
Thomas Aquinas College
Westwood College: South Bay
William Jessup University
World Mission University

### Colorado
American Sentinel University
Aspen University
CollegeAmerica
    Fort Collins
DeVry University
    Westminster
Jones International University
Naropa University
National American University
    Denver
Rocky Mountain College of Art & Design
Teikyo Loretto Heights University
Westwood College of Technology
    Westwood College: Denver South

### Connecticut
Briarwood College
Holy Apostles College and Seminary
Lyme Academy College of Fine Arts
Paier College of Art

### District of Columbia
Corcoran College of Art and Design
Potomac College
Southeastern University

### Florida
Angley College
Baptist College of Florida
Beacon College
Carlos Albizu University
City College
    Miami
City College: Fort Lauderdale
Clearwater Christian College
Florida Christian College
Florida College
Jones College
Jones College: Miami
Northwood University
    Florida
Rasmussen College: Ocala
Remington College: Largo
Remington College: Tampa
St. John Vianney College Seminary
Trinity College of Florida
Universidad FLET
Webber International University

### Georgia
Beulah Heights University
Carver Bible College

DeVry University
    Alpharetta
Emmanuel College
Herzing College
Life University
Medical College of Georgia
Thomas University
Truett-McConnell College
Wesleyan College

### Idaho
Boise Bible College

### Illinois
Blackburn College
Blessing-Rieman College of Nursing
Lakeview College of Nursing
Lexington College
Lincoln Christian College and Seminary
Midstate College
National University of Health Sciences
Rosalind Franklin University of Medicine and Science
Rush University
St. Francis Medical Center College of Nursing
St. John's College
Shimer College
VanderCook College of Music
West Suburban College of Nursing
Western Illinois University: Quad Cities
Westwood College of Technology
    Westwood College: O'Hare Airport
    Westwood College: River Oaks
Westwood College: DuPage

### Indiana
DeVry University: Indianapolis
Holy Cross College
Taylor University Fort Wayne

### Iowa
Allen College
Emmaus Bible College
Faith Baptist Bible College and Theological Seminary
Kaplan University
    Cedar Rapids
    Des Moines
    Mason City
Maharishi University of Management
Mercy College of Health Sciences
Upper Iowa University
Vennard College
Waldorf College

### Kansas
Barclay College
Bethany College
Bethel College
Central Christian College of Kansas
Manhattan Christian College
McPherson College
Sterling College
Tabor College
University of Kansas Medical Center
University of St. Mary

### Kentucky
Alice Lloyd College
Beckfield College
Brescia University
Clear Creek Baptist Bible College
Kentucky Christian University
Kentucky Mountain Bible College
St. Catharine College
Union College

### Louisiana
Louisiana State University Health Sciences Center
St. Joseph Seminary College
School of Urban Missions: New Orleans

### Maine
College of the Atlantic
Maine College of Art
New England School of Communications
Thomas College
Unity College
University of Maine Machias

### Maryland
Baltimore International College
Capitol College
DeVry University: Bethesda
Johns Hopkins University: Peabody Conservatory of Music
Ner Israel Rabbinical College
St. John's College
Washington Bible College

### Massachusetts
Atlantic Union College
Bard College at Simon's Rock
Boston Architectural College
Boston Conservatory
Eastern Nazarene College
Franklin W. Olin College of Engineering
Hellenic College/Holy Cross
New England Conservatory of Music
Pine Manor College
Rhodec International
School of the Museum of Fine Arts

### Michigan
Cleary University
Concordia University
Finlandia University
Grace Bible College
Great Lakes Christian College
Kuyper College
Michigan Jewish Institute
Michigan Theological Seminary
Sacred Heart Major Seminary

### Minnesota
Academy College
Bethany Lutheran College
College of Visual Arts
DeVry University
    Edina
Martin Luther College
Minneapolis College of Art and Design
Minnesota School of Business: Plymouth
Minnesota School of Business: Rochester
Minnesota School of Business: Shakopee
Northwestern Health Sciences University
Oak Hills Christian College
Pillsbury Baptist Bible College
Rasmussen College
    Eagan

### Mississippi
Blue Mountain College
Magnolia Bible College
University of Mississippi Medical Center
Wesley College

### Missouri
Baptist Bible College
Calvary Bible College and Theological Seminary
Central Bible College
Conception Seminary College

Goldfarb School of Nursing at Barnes-Jewish College
Kansas City Art Institute
Ozark Christian College
Research College of Nursing
St. Louis Christian College

### Montana
University of Great Falls

### Nebraska
Clarkson College
Creative Center
Dana College
Grace University
Nebraska Methodist College of Nursing and Allied Health
York College

### Nevada
DeVry University: Henderson
International Academy of Design and Technology: Henderson
Sierra Nevada College
University of Southern Nevada

### New Hampshire
Chester College of New England
Daniel Webster College
Magdalen College
Thomas More College of Liberal Arts

### New Jersey
Somerset Christian College

### New Mexico
Art Center Design College
College of Santa Fe
College of the Southwest
Institute of American Indian Arts
International Institute of the Americas: Albuquerque
National American University: Rio Rancho
St. John's College

### New York
Berkeley College
City University of New York: CUNY Online
Concordia College
Davis College
Eastman School of Music of the University of Rochester
Holy Trinity Orthodox Seminary
Jewish Theological Seminary of America
Juilliard School
King's College
Manhattan School of Music
Mannes College The New School for Music
Metropolitan College of New York
New York School of Interior Design
Russell Sage College
State University of New York
    Downstate Medical Center
    Upstate Medical University
Webb Institute
Wells College
Yeshiva Mikdash Melech

### North Carolina
Bennett College
Brevard College
Cabarrus College of Health Sciences
DeVry University: Charlotte
John Wesley College
North Carolina School of the Arts
Peace College
Piedmont Baptist College
Roanoke Bible College
St. Andrews Presbyterian College
Salem College

## North Dakota

Medcenter One College of
Nursing
Rasmussen College: Fargo
Trinity Bible College

## Ohio

Art Academy of Cincinnati
Bryant & Stratton College
Parma
Willoughby Hills
Cincinnati College of Mortuary
Science
Cleveland Institute of Art
Cleveland Institute of Music
Kettering College of Medical Arts
Laura and Alvin Siegal College of
Judaic Studies
MedCentral College of Nursing
Mount Carmel College of Nursing
Ohio Christian University
Pontifical College Josephinum

## Oklahoma

DeVry University: Oklahoma City
Center
St. Gregory's University
Southwestern Christian University

## Oregon

Cascade College
DeVry University: Portland
Eugene Bible College
Mount Angel Seminary
Multnomah Bible College
Northwest Christian College
Oregon Health & Science
University
Pacific Northwest College of Art
Pioneer Pacific College
Warner Pacific College

## Pennsylvania

Baptist Bible College of
Pennsylvania
Bryn Athyn College of the New
Church
Chatham University
Curtis Institute of Music
Gratz College
Lancaster Bible College
Moore College of Art and Design
Penn State
Beaver
Dubois
Greater Allegheny
Lehigh Valley
New Kensington
Shenango
Wilkes-Barre
Pennsylvania College of Art and
Design
Rosemont College
St. Charles Borromeo Seminary -
Overbrook
Talmudical Yeshiva of
Philadelphia
Williamson Free School of
Mechanical Trades
Wilson College

## Puerto Rico

Carlos Albizu University: San
Juan
Colegio Pentecostal Mizpa
Conservatory of Music of Puerto
Rico
Escuela de Artes Plasticas de
Puerto Rico
Universidad Adventista de las
Antillas
University of Puerto Rico
Medical Sciences

## Rhode Island

Zion Bible College

## South Carolina

Allen University
Columbia International University
Converse College
Erskine College
South University
Voorhees College

## South Dakota

National American University
Rapid City

## Tennessee

American Baptist College of ABT
Seminary
DeVry University: Memphis
Free Will Baptist Bible College
Lambuth University
LeMoyne-Owen College
Martin Methodist College
Memphis College of Art
Tennessee Temple University
University of Tennessee Health
Science Center

## Texas

Amberton University
Arlington Baptist College
Baptist University of the
Americas
College of Saint Thomas More
Criswell College
Dallas Christian College
Huston-Tillotson University
Jarvis Christian College
Northwood University: Texas
Texas A&M University
Baylor College of Dentistry
Texas College
Texas Tech University Health
Sciences Center
University of Texas
Health Science Center at San
Antonio
Medical Branch at Galveston
Southwestern Medical
Center at Dallas

## Utah

DeVry University: Sandy
Stevens-Henager College
Murray
Stevens-Henager College: Ogden

## Vermont

Bennington College
Burlington College
College of St. Joseph in Vermont
Goddard College
Marlboro College
Southern Vermont College
Sterling College
Woodbury College

## Virginia

Christendom College
DeVry University
Arlington
ECPI Technical College
Glen Allen
Randolph College
St. Paul's College
Southern Virginia University
Sweet Briar College
University of Northern Virginia
Virginia Intermont College
World College

## Washington

Antioch University Seattle
Bastyr University
DeVry University
Federal Way
Northwest College of Art
Trinity Lutheran College

## West Virginia

Alderson-Broaddus College
Appalachian Bible College
Davis and Elkins College
Ohio Valley University
Salem International University

## Wisconsin

Bellin College of Nursing
Columbia College of Nursing
DeVry University: Milwaukee
Milwaukee Institute of Art &
Design
Northland College
Silver Lake College

## France

American University of Paris
Parsons Paris School of Design

## Monaco

International University of
Monaco

## Switzerland

Franklin College: Switzerland

## United Kingdom

Richmond, The American
International University in
London

## *Two-year*

## Alabama

J. F. Drake State Technical
College
Marion Military Institute
Remington College
Mobile

## Arizona

Arizona Automotive Institute
Golf Academy of Arizona
Long Technical College
Paralegal Institute
Tohono O'odham Community
College

## Arkansas

Crowley's Ridge College

## California

American Academy of Dramatic
Arts: West
Brooks College
California Culinary Academy
Coleman College
San Marcos
Concorde Career College: North
Hollywood
Deep Springs College
Empire College
Fashion Careers College
Fashion Institute of Design and
Merchandising
San Diego
High-Tech Institute
Marymount College
National Polytechnic College of
Science
Professional Golfers Career
College
Santa Barbara Business College
Bakersfield
Western Career College: Stockton

## Colorado

Bel-Rea Institute of Animal
Technology
Cambridge College
CollegeAmerica
Denver
Colorado School of Healing Arts
Colorado School of Trades
Denver Academy of Court
Reporting
Everest College: Aurora
Everest College: Colorado
Springs
Institute of Business & Medical
Careers
IntelliTec College
Kaplan College: Denver
Redstone College
Remington College
Colorado Springs

## Connecticut

Clemens College
St. Vincent's College

## Florida

Brown Mackie College: Miami
Central Florida College
City College
Gainesville
City College: Casselberry
College of Business and
Technology: Flagler
College of Business and
Technology: Kendall
Florida College of Natural Health
Bradenton
Florida Technical College
Deland
Orlando
Key College
North Florida Institute: Orange
Park
Professional Golfers Career
College: Orlando
Ultrasound Diagnostic School
Sanford-Brown Institute:
Jacksonville
Virginia College at Pensacola

## Georgia

Everest Institute
Gupton Jones College of Funeral
Service
Oxford College of Emory
University
Savannah River College
Young Harris College

## Hawaii

Hawaii Tokai International
College
Remington College
Honolulu
TransPacific Hawaii College
University of Hawaii
Kauai Community College

## Idaho

Eastern Idaho Technical College
Stevens-Henager College: Boise

## Illinois

College of Office Technology
Fox College
MacCormac College
Morrison Institute of Technology
Rockford Business College
Springfield College in Illinois

## Indiana

Ancilla College
Brown Mackie College: South
Bend
College of Court Reporting
Indiana Business College
Anderson
Columbus
Evansville
Fort Wayne
Lafayette
Marion
Medical
Muncie
Terre Haute
Indiana Business College:
Indianapolis Northwest
Kaplan College: Hammond
Kaplan College: Indianapolis
Kaplan College: Merrillville

## Iowa

St. Luke's College

## Kansas

Brown Mackie College
Salina
Colby Community College
Hesston College

## Kentucky

Brown Mackie College:
Louisville
Daymar College
Louisville
Draughons Junior College
Louisville Technical Institute
Paducah Technical College
Southern Ohio College
Brown Mackie College:
North Kentucky
Southwestern College: Florence
Spencerian College: Lexington

## Louisiana

Blue Cliff College: Lafayette
ITI Technical College
Remington College
Baton Rouge
Lafayette

## Maine

Beal College
Central Maine Medical Center
College of Nursing and Health
Professions
Washington County Community
College

## Maryland

Kaplan College: Hagerstown

## Massachusetts

Benjamin Franklin Institute of
Technology
Caritas Laboure College
Fisher College
Marian Court College
New England College of Finance
Urban College of Boston

## Michigan

Bay Mills Community College
Saginaw Chippewa Tribal College

## Minnesota

Duluth Business University
Herzing College
Minneapolis Drafting School
Division of
Le Cordon Bleu College of
Culinary Arts
Leech Lake Tribal College
Minneapolis Business College
Northwest Technical Institute
Rasmussen College
Mankato
Vermilion Community College
White Earth Tribal and
Community College

## Mississippi

Antonelli College
Hattiesburg
Jackson
Blue Cliff College: Gulfport

## Missouri

Bolivar Technical College
Cottey College
Metro Business College
Jefferson City
Patricia Stevens College
Vatterott College: St. Joseph
Wentworth Military Junior
College

## Montana

Blackfeet Community College
Dawson Community College
Fort Belknap College
Miles Community College
Stone Child College

## Nebraska

Kaplan University
Lincoln
Little Priest Tribal College
Nebraska College of Technical
Agriculture

Vatterott College: Spring Valley

**Nevada**
Career College of Northern Nevada
Heritage College: Las Vegas
Le Cordon Bleu College of Culinary Arts

**New Jersey**
Assumption College for Sisters

**New Mexico**
Mesalands Community College
Navajo Technical College
New Mexico Military Institute
Southwestern Indian Polytechnic Institute

**New York**
American Academy McAllister Institute of Funeral Service
Bryant & Stratton Business Institute
  Bryant & Stratton College: Albany
  Bryant & Stratton College: Buffalo
  Bryant & Stratton College: Rochester
  Bryant & Stratton College: Southtowns
Bryant & Stratton College: Henrietta
Bryant & Stratton College: Syracuse North
Cochran School of Nursing-St. John's Riverside Hospital
Elmira Business Institute
Elmira Business Institute: Vestal
Helene Fuld College of Nursing
Institute of Design and Construction
Island Drafting and Technical Institute
Jamestown Business College
Long Island Business Institute
Long Island College Hospital School of Nursing
Maria College
Mildred Elley
New York Career Institute
Olean Business Institute
Phillips Beth Israel School of Nursing
Plaza College
St. Elizabeth College of Nursing
St. Joseph's College of Nursing
St. Vincent Catholic Medical Centers
Swedish Institute
Utica School of Commerce
Villa Maria College of Buffalo

**North Carolina**
King's College
Louisburg College
Miller-Motte Technical College: Cary
Pamlico Community College
South College

**North Dakota**
Fort Berthold Community College
Minot State University: Bottineau Campus
Rasmussen College: Bismarck
United Tribes Technical College
Williston State College

**Ohio**
AEC Southern Ohio College
  Brown Mackie College: Findlay
Art Institute of Cincinnati
Art Institute of Ohio: Cincinnati
Bradford School
Bryant & Stratton College: Cleveland

Chatfield College
Davis College
ETI Technical College of Niles
Gallipolis Career College
Good Samaritan College of Nursing and Health Science
Hondros College
Ohio Business College
Ohio College of Massotherapy
Ohio Institute of Health Careers: Columbus
Ohio Institute of Photography and Technology
Ohio State University Agricultural Technical Institute
Ohio Valley College of Technology
Remington College: Cleveland West
Samuel Stephen College
School of Advertising Art
Southeastern Business College: New Boston
Southwestern College of Business Southwestern College: Vine Street Campus
Stautzenberger College: Strongsville
Technology Education College
Wright State University: Lake Campus

**Oklahoma**
Platt College Tulsa
Platt College: Oklahoma City Central
Tulsa Welding School

**Oregon**
Pioneer Pacific College: Springfield

**Pennsylvania**
Antonelli Institute of Art and Photography
Art Institute of York
Berean Institute
Bradford School: Pittsburgh
Business Institute of Pennsylvania
Cambria-Rowe Business College
Cambria-Rowe Business College: Indiana
Career Training Academy
Career Training Academy: Monroeville
Career Training Academy: Pittsburgh
CHI Institute: Franklin Mills
Commonwealth Technical Institute
Consolidated School of Business Lancaster York
Dean Institute of Technology
Douglas Education Center
DuBois Business College
DuBois Business College Huntingdon Oil City
Erie Business Center
Erie Business Center South
Erie Institute of Technology
Hussian School of Art
JNA Institute of Culinary Arts
Johnson College
Kaplan Career Institute: Harrisburg
Lansdale School of Business
Laurel Business Institute
Lincoln Technical Institute: Allentown
Lincoln Technical Institute: Northeast Philadelphia
Lincoln Technical Institute: Philadelphia
New Castle School of Trades

Newport Business Institute: Lower Burrell
Newport Business Institute: Williamsport
Oakbridge Academy of Arts
Orleans Technical Institute - Center City Campus
Pace Institute
Penn Commercial Business and Technical School
Pennco Tech
Pennsylvania Institute of Technology
Pittsburgh Institute of Aeronautics
Pittsburgh Institute of Mortuary Science
PJA School
South Hills School of Business & Technology
South Hills School of Business & Technology
Tri-State Business Institute
Triangle Tech
  DuBois
  Erie
  Greensburg
  Pittsburgh
Triangle Tech: Bethlehem
Triangle Tech: Sunbury
University of Pittsburgh Titusville
Valley Forge Military College
Vet Tech Institute
West Virginia Career Institute

**Puerto Rico**
Columbia College
  Columbia Centro Universitario: Yauco
Humacao Community College
Ramirez College of Business and Technology

**South Carolina**
Forrest Junior College
Miller-Motte Technical College
University of South Carolina Union
Williamsburg Technical College

**South Dakota**
Kilian Community College
Mitchell Technical Institute
Sisseton Wahpeton College

**Tennessee**
Draughons Junior College: Clarksville
Draughons Junior College: Murfreesboro
Draughons Junior College: Nashville
Fountainhead College of Technology
Hiwassee College
Huntington College of Health Sciences
John A. Gupton College
National College of Business & Technology
  National College: Bristol
Nossi College of Art
Vatterott College: Memphis

**Texas**
Commonwealth Institute of Funeral Service
Court Reporting Institute of Houston
Dallas Institute of Funeral Service
Everest College: Arlington
Frank Phillips College
Hallmark College of Aeronautics
Hallmark College of Technology
Jacksonville College
Lon Morris College
Remington College
  Fort Worth
  Houston

Southwest Institute of Technology
Texas State Technical College: Marshall
Western Technical College
Westwood College: Houston South

**Utah**
Careers Unlimited

**Vermont**
Landmark College
New England Culinary Institute

**Virginia**
Aviation Institute of Maintenance: Virginia Beach
Beta Tech: Richmond South
Beta Tech: Richmond West
Bryant & Stratton College Richmond
Bryant & Stratton College: Virginia Beach
ECPI Technical College Richmond
ECPI Technical College: Roanoke
Miller-Motte Technical College: Lynchburg
Tidewater Tech Virginia Beach
Tidewater Tech: Chesapeake

**Washington**
Grays Harbor College

**West Virginia**
Eastern West Virginia Community and Technical College
Valley College of Technology
West Virginia Business College
West Virginia Junior College: Bridgeport

**Wisconsin**
College of Menominee Nation
Lac Courte Oreilles Ojibwa Community College
University of Wisconsin
  Baraboo/Sauk County
  Fond du Lac
  Manitowoc
  Richland

**Wyoming**
Eastern Wyoming College

**Palau**
Palau Community College

*Four-year*

**Alabama**
Birmingham-Southern College
Huntingdon College
Miles College
Oakwood College
Spring Hill College
Stillman College
University of Mobile
Virginia College at Huntsville

**Alaska**
University of Alaska Southeast

**Arizona**
Art Institute of Phoenix
DeVry University Phoenix
Embry-Riddle Aeronautical University: Prescott Campus
University of Advancing Technology

**Arkansas**
Hendrix College
John Brown University

Ouachita Baptist University

**California**
Art Institute of California: Orange County
Art Institute of California: San Francisco
California College of the Arts
California Design College
California Institute of Technology
California Institute of the Arts
California Maritime Academy
Claremont McKenna College
Concordia University
DeVry University
  Fremont
  Long Beach
  Pomona
Dominican University of California
Fresno Pacific University
La Sierra University
Loma Linda University
The Master's College
Mills College
Mount St. Mary's College
Occidental College
Otis College of Art and Design
Pacific Union College
Pitzer College
Pomona College
Scripps College
Simpson University
University of California: Merced
University of La Verne
Vanguard University of Southern California
Westmont College
Westwood College of Technology
  Westwood College: Inland Empire
Whittier College
Woodbury University

**Colorado**
Colorado Christian University
Colorado Technical University
Johnson & Wales University: Denver
Nazarene Bible College
Regis University

**Connecticut**
Albertus Magnus College
Charter Oak State College
Connecticut College
Mitchell College
Post University
St. Joseph College
United States Coast Guard Academy
University of Bridgeport

**Delaware**
Goldey-Beacom College

**District of Columbia**
Trinity Washington University

**Florida**
DeVry University
  Miramar
  Orlando
Eckerd College
Edward Waters College
Everest University: Brandon
Everest University: Tampa
Florida Memorial University
Florida Southern College
Hodges University
Johnson & Wales University: North Miami
Keiser University
Miami International University of Art and Design
New College of Florida
Ringling College of Art and Design

Tables and Indexes

Rollins College
St. Leo University
Saint Thomas University
Warner Southern College

**Georgia**
Agnes Scott College
American InterContinental
   University
Bauder College
Berry College
Brenau University
Brewton-Parker College
Covenant College
LaGrange College
Oglethorpe University
Paine College
Piedmont College
Reinhardt College
Shorter College
Toccoa Falls College

**Hawaii**
University of Hawaii
   West Oahu

**Idaho**
College of Idaho
Northwest Nazarene University

**Illinois**
Concordia University
DeVry University
   Addison
   Chicago
   Tinley Park
Dominican University
East-West University
Greenville College
Illinois College
Illinois Institute of Art:
   Schaumburg
Judson University
Knox College
Lake Forest College
Monmouth College
Quincy University
Rockford College
Trinity Christian College
Trinity International University
University of St. Francis
Westwood College: Chicago Loop

**Indiana**
Calumet College of St. Joseph
Earlham College
Franklin College
Goshen College
Grace College
Hanover College
Huntington University
Indiana University
   East
International Business College
Manchester College
Marian College
Oakland City University
Rose-Hulman Institute of
   Technology
Saint Joseph's College
Saint Mary's College
St. Mary-of-the-Woods College
Taylor University
Tri-State University
University of St. Francis
Wabash College

**Iowa**
Briar Cliff University
Buena Vista University
Central College
Clarke College
Coe College
Cornell College
Dordt College
Graceland University
Grand View College
Grinnell College
Iowa Wesleyan College

Loras College
Morningside College
Mount Mercy College
Northwestern College
Simpson College
University of Dubuque
Wartburg College
William Penn University

**Kansas**
Baker University
Benedictine College
MidAmerica Nazarene University
Newman University
Southwestern College

**Kentucky**
Asbury College
Berea College
Campbellsville University
Centre College
Georgetown College
Kentucky Wesleyan College
Lindsey Wilson College
Mid-Continent University
Midway College
Pikeville College
Thomas More College
Transylvania University
University of the Cumberlands

**Louisiana**
Centenary College of Louisiana
Dillard University
Louisiana College
Our Lady of the Lake College

**Maine**
Bates College
Bowdoin College
Colby College
Husson College
Maine Maritime Academy
St. Joseph's College
University of Maine
   Fort Kent
University of New England

**Maryland**
Columbia Union College
Goucher College
Hood College
Maryland Institute College of Art
McDaniel College
Mount St. Mary's University
St. Mary's College of Maryland
Sojourner-Douglass College
University of Maryland
   Baltimore
Washington College

**Massachusetts**
American International College
Amherst College
Anna Maria College
Babson College
Bay Path College
Becker College
Cambridge College
Elms College
Gordon College
Hampshire College
Lasell College
Lesley University
Massachusetts College of Art
Massachusetts College of Liberal
   Arts
Massachusetts Maritime Academy
New England Institute of Art
Nichols College
Regis College
Wheaton College
Wheelock College
Williams College

**Michigan**
Adrian College
Albion College
Alma College

Andrews University
Aquinas College
College for Creative Studies
Cornerstone University
Hillsdale College
Kalamazoo College
Kendall College of Art and
   Design of Ferris State
   University
Marygrove College
Northwood University: Michigan
Olivet College
Rochester College
Siena Heights University
Walsh College of Accountancy
   and Business Administration

**Minnesota**
Art Institutes International
   Minnesota
Brown College
Carleton College
College of St. Scholastica
Concordia University: St. Paul
Crown College
Hamline University
Macalester College
Minnesota School of Business: St.
   Cloud
North Central University
Northwestern College
St. John's University
St. Mary's University of
   Minnesota
University of Minnesota
   Crookston
   Morris
Walden University

**Mississippi**
Millsaps College
Rust College
Tougaloo College
William Carey University

**Missouri**
Avila University
Central Methodist University
College of the Ozarks
Columbia College
Culver-Stockton College
DeVry University
   Kansas City
Drury University
Evangel University
Fontbonne University
Hannibal-LaGrange College
Harris-Stowe State University
Missouri Baptist University
Missouri Valley College
Rockhurst University
Stephens College
Westminster College
William Jewell College
William Woods University

**Montana**
Carroll College
Montana State University
   Northern
Rocky Mountain College
University of Montana: Western

**Nebraska**
College of Saint Mary
Concordia University
Doane College
Hastings College
Midland Lutheran College
Nebraska Wesleyan University
Union College
University of Nebraska
   Medical Center

**Nevada**
Art Institute
   of Las Vegas
Nevada State College

**New Hampshire**
Colby-Sawyer College
Franklin Pierce University
Granite State College
New England College
Rivier College
St. Anselm College
Southern New Hampshire
   University
University of New Hampshire at
   Manchester

**New Jersey**
Caldwell College
College of St. Elizabeth
DeVry University: North
   Brunswick
Drew University
Felician College
Georgian Court University

**New Mexico**
New Mexico Highlands
   University
New Mexico Institute of Mining
   and Technology
Western New Mexico University

**New York**
Albany College of Pharmacy
Bard College
Boricua College
Briarcliffe College
Cazenovia College
College of Mount St. Vincent
College of New Rochelle
Columbia University
   School of General Studies
Cooper Union for the
   Advancement of Science and
   Art
D'Youville College
Daemen College
DeVry Institute of Technology
   New York
Dominican College of Blauvelt
Elmira College
Eugene Lang College The New
   School for Liberal Arts
Five Towns College
Hamilton College
Hartwick College
Hilbert College
Hobart and William Smith
   Colleges
Houghton College
Keuka College
Laboratory Institute of
   Merchandising
Manhattanville College
Marymount Manhattan College
Medaille College
Paul Smith's College
Polytechnic University
Roberts Wesleyan College
Sage College of Albany
Saint Bonaventure University
St. Joseph's College
St. Thomas Aquinas College
Sarah Lawrence College
State University of New York
   College of Environmental
   Science and Forestry
   Institute of Technology at
   Utica/Rome
   Maritime College
United States Merchant Marine
   Academy
Vaughn College of Aeronautics
   and Technology
Wagner College

**North Carolina**
Art Institute
   of Charlotte
Barton College
Belmont Abbey College
Catawba College

Chowan University
Davidson College
Greensboro College
Johnson C. Smith University
Lees-McRae College
Lenoir-Rhyne College
Livingstone College
Meredith College
Methodist University
Montreat College
North Carolina Wesleyan College
Pfeiffer University
Queens University of Charlotte
St. Augustine's College
Warren Wilson College
Wingate University

**North Dakota**
Jamestown College
Mayville State University
Valley City State University

**Ohio**
Bluffton University
Central State University
Cincinnati Christian University
College of Mount St. Joseph
College of Wooster
Columbus College of Art and
   Design
Defiance College
Franciscan University of
   Steubenville
Heidelberg College
Hiram College
Kenyon College
Lake Erie College
Lourdes College
Malone College
Marietta College
Mercy College of Northwest Ohio
Muskingum College
Ohio State University
   Lima Campus
   Mansfield Campus
   Marion Campus
Ohio University
   Chillicothe Campus
   Lancaster Campus
   Southern Campus at Ironton
   Zanesville Campus
Ohio Wesleyan University
Tiffin University
Union Institute & University
University of Rio Grande
Ursuline College
Wilmington College
Wittenberg University

**Oklahoma**
Bacone College
Mid-America Christian University
National Education Center
   Spartan College of
   Aeronautics and
   Technology
Northwestern Oklahoma State
   University
Oklahoma Baptist University
Oklahoma Christian University
Oklahoma Panhandle State
   University
Oklahoma Wesleyan University
Southern Nazarene University
University of Science and Arts of
   Oklahoma

**Oregon**
Art Institute of Portland
Concordia University
Corban College
George Fox University
Lewis & Clark College
Linfield College
Marylhurst University
Pacific University
Reed College
Willamette University

## Pennsylvania

Alvernia College
Bryn Mawr College
Cabrini College
Carlow University
Cedar Crest College
Central Pennsylvania College
Chestnut Hill College
Cheyney University of
 Pennsylvania
Delaware Valley College
DeVry University
 Fort Washington
Geneva College
Gwynedd-Mercy College
Haverford College
Juniata College
Keystone College
La Roche College
Lebanon Valley College
Lincoln University
Lycoming College
Marywood University
Moravian College
Mount Aloysius College
Penn State
 Brandywine
 Fayette, The Eberly Campus
 Hazleton
 Mont Alto
 Schuylkill
 Worthington Scranton
 York
Philadelphia Biblical University
St. Francis University
St. Vincent College
Seton Hill University
Susquehanna University
Swarthmore College
Thiel College
Thomas Jefferson University:
 College of Health Professions
University of Pittsburgh
 Bradford
 Greensburg
Ursinus College
Valley Forge Christian College
Washington & Jefferson College
Waynesburg University
Westminster College

## Puerto Rico

Atlantic College
Columbia Centro Universitario:
 Caguas
University College of San Juan
University of Puerto Rico
 Utuado

## Rhode Island

Rhode Island School of Design

## South Carolina

Anderson University
Claflin University
Columbia College
Limestone College
Morris College
Newberry College
North Greenville University
Presbyterian College
Southern Wesleyan University
University of South Carolina
 Beaufort
Wofford College

## South Dakota

Augustana College
Dakota State University
Dakota Wesleyan University
Mount Marty College
Northern State University
Oglala Lakota College
Presentation College
South Dakota School of Mines
 and Technology
University of Sioux Falls

## Tennessee

Aquinas College
Baptist College of Health
 Sciences
Bethel College
Bryan College
Carson-Newman College
Christian Brothers University
Crichton College
Cumberland University
Freed-Hardeman University
King College
Lane College
Lincoln Memorial University
Maryville College
Milligan College
Rhodes College
Tennessee Wesleyan College
Trevecca Nazarene University
University of the South

## Texas

Art Institute
 of Dallas
 of Houston
Austin College
College of Biblical
 Studies-Houston
Concordia University at Austin
DeVry University
 Irving
DeVry University: Houston
East Texas Baptist University
Hardin-Simmons University
Houston Baptist University
Howard Payne University
Lubbock Christian University
McMurry University
Our Lady of the Lake University
 of San Antonio
Schreiner University
Southwestern Adventist
 University
Southwestern Assemblies of God
 University
Southwestern University
Sul Ross State University
Texas A&M University
 Galveston
 Texarkana
Texas Lutheran University
Texas Wesleyan University
University of Dallas
University of Houston
 Victoria
University of St. Thomas
Wayland Baptist University
Wiley College

## Vermont

Castleton State College
Green Mountain College
Johnson State College
Lyndon State College
St. Michael's College
Vermont Technical College

## Virginia

Art Institute
 of Washington
Averett University
Bluefield College
Bridgewater College
Eastern Mennonite University
Emory & Henry College
Ferrum College
Hampden-Sydney College
Hollins University
Jefferson College of Health
 Sciences
Mary Baldwin College
Randolph-Macon College
Regent University
Roanoke College
Shenandoah University
University of Virginia's College
 at Wise
Virginia Military Institute

Virginia Union University
Virginia Wesleyan College
Washington and Lee University

## Washington

City University of Seattle
Cornish College of the Arts
DigiPen Institute of Technology
Heritage University
Northwest University
Saint Martin's University
Walla Walla University
Whitman College

## West Virginia

Bethany College
Bluefield State College
Glenville State College
University of Charleston
West Virginia Wesleyan College
Wheeling Jesuit University

## Wisconsin

Beloit College
Edgewood College
Lawrence University
Maranatha Baptist Bible College
Marian College of Fond du Lac
Mount Mary College
Ripon College
Viterbo University

## *Two-year*

## Alabama

Chattahoochee Valley Community
 College
Jefferson Davis Community
 College
Lurleen B. Wallace Community
 College

## Arizona

Chandler-Gilbert Community
 College
 Pecos
Dine College
Universal Technical Institute

## Arkansas

Arkansas Northeastern College
Arkansas State University
 Mountain Home
Arkansas State University:
 Newport
Black River Technical College
East Arkansas Community
 College
Mid-South Community College
Ouachita Technical College
Ozarka College
Rich Mountain Community
 College
South Arkansas Community
 College
Southeast Arkansas College
Southern Arkansas University
 Tech
University of Arkansas
 Community College at Hope
University of Arkansas
 Community College at
 Morrilton

## California

California School of Culinary Arts
College of the Siskiyous
Copper Mountain College
Fashion Institute of Design and
 Merchandising
 San Francisco
Feather River College
Lassen College
Maric College: Salida
Mendocino College
San Joaquin Valley College
West Hills College: Coalinga

## Colorado

Lamar Community College

Morgan Community College
Northeastern Junior College
Otero Junior College

## Connecticut

Goodwin College
Middlesex Community College
Northwestern Connecticut
 Community College
Quinebaug Valley Community
 College

## Florida

Florida Keys Community College
North Florida Community
 College
South Florida Community
 College
Southwest Florida College

## Georgia

Atlanta Metropolitan College
Le Cordon Bleu College of
 Culinary Arts
North Georgia Technical College
Northwestern Technical College
South Georgia College
Southwest Georgia Technical
 College
West Georgia Technical College

## Hawaii

University of Hawaii
 Windward Community
 College

## Illinois

Black Hawk College: East
 Campus
Cooking & Hospitality Institute of
 Chicago
Highland Community College
Illinois Eastern Community
 Colleges
 Lincoln Trail College
 Olney Central College
 Wabash Valley College
John Wood Community College
Lincoln College
Northwestern Business College
Sauk Valley Community College

## Indiana

Brown Mackie College: Fort
 Wayne
Indiana Business College
 Indianapolis
Ivy Tech Community College:
 Richmond
Ivy Tech State College
 Ivy Tech Community
 College: Southeast

## Iowa

AIB College of Business
Clinton Community College
Iowa Lakes Community College
Muscatine Community College
Southwestern Community
 College

## Kansas

Coffeyville Community College
Highland Community College
Independence Community
 College
Labette Community College
Neosho County Community
 College
Pratt Community College
Seward County Community
 College

## Kentucky

Spencerian College

## Louisiana

Nunez Community College
River Parishes Community
 College

## Maine

Andover College
Central Maine Community
 College
Eastern Maine Community
 College
Northern Maine Community
 College
York County Community College

## Maryland

Cecil College
Garrett College
TESST College of Technology
 Baltimore

## Massachusetts

Bay State College
Berkshire Community College
Dean College
Greenfield Community College

## Michigan

Bay de Noc Community College
Glen Oaks Community College
Gogebic Community College
Kirtland Community College
West Shore Community College

## Minnesota

Anoka Technical College
Dunwoody College of Technology
Hibbing Community College
Itasca Community College
Mesabi Range Community and
 Technical College
Minnesota State College -
 Southeast Technical
Northland Community &
 Technical College
Northwest Technical College
Pine Technical College
Rasmussen College
 Eden Prairie

## Mississippi

Southwest Mississippi
 Community College

## Missouri

Linn State Technical College
Missouri State University: West
 Plains
North Central Missouri College
Ranken Technical College

## Montana

Flathead Valley Community
 College
Montana State University
 College of Technology:
 Great Falls

## Nebraska

Western Nebraska Community
 College

## New Hampshire

Lakes Region Community
 College
Nashua Community College
River Valley Community College
White Mountains Community
 College

## New Jersey

Salem Community College
Warren County Community
 College

## New Mexico

Clovis Community College

## New York

Art Institute
 of New York City
College of Westchester
Columbia-Greene Community
 College
Fulton-Montgomery Community
 College

North Country Community
  College
Sullivan County Community
  College
Trocaire College

## North Carolina

Beaufort County Community
  College
Bladen Community College
Carteret Community College
College of the Albemarle
Isothermal Community College
James Sprunt Community College
Martin Community College
Mayland Community College
McDowell Technical Community
  College
Rockingham Community College
Sampson Community College
Southeastern Community College
Wilson Community College

## North Dakota

Lake Region State College
Turtle Mountain Community
  College

## Ohio

Belmont Technical College
Brown Mackie College:
  Cincinnati
Brown Mackie College: North
  Canton
Jefferson Community College
Kent State University
  Ashtabula
  East Liverpool
  Salem
  Trumbull
  Tuscarawas
Kent State University: Geauga
Miami University
  Middletown Campus
University of Akron: Wayne
  College
Zane State College

## Oklahoma

Connors State College
Murray State College
Northeastern Oklahoma
  Agricultural and Mechanical
  College
Western Oklahoma State College

## Oregon

Clatsop Community College
Klamath Community College
Treasure Valley Community
  College
Umpqua Community College

## Pennsylvania

Community College of Beaver
  County
Harcum College
Kaplan Career Institute:
  Pittsburgh
Lackawanna College
Manor College
Pennsylvania Culinary Institute
Pennsylvania Highlands
  Community College
Thaddeus Stevens College of
  Technology
YTI Career Institute: York

## Puerto Rico

Huertas Junior College
ICPR Junior College
Universal Technology College of
  Puerto Rico

## South Carolina

Denmark Technical College
Northeastern Technical College
Spartanburg Methodist College
Technical College of the
  Lowcountry

University of South Carolina
  Lancaster
  Salkehatchie Regional
    Campus
  Sumter

## South Dakota

Western Dakota Technical
  Institute

## Texas

Clarendon College
Lamar State College at Orange
Panola College
Texas Culinary Academy
Texas State Technical College
  Sweetwater
Western Texas College

## Virginia

Dabney S. Lancaster Community
  College
Eastern Shore Community
  College
Paul D. Camp Community
  College
Richard Bland College

## Washington

Big Bend Community College
Lower Columbia College
Northwest Indian College
Peninsula College
Renton Technical College

## West Virginia

Blue Ridge Community and
  Technical College
Potomac State College of West
  Virginia University
West Virginia State Community
  and Technical College

## Wisconsin

Nicolet Area Technical College
University of Wisconsin
  Fox Valley
  Rock County
  Washington County
  Waukesha

## Wyoming

Central Wyoming College
Northwest College
Sheridan College

## American Samoa

American Samoa Community
  College

## Guam

Guam Community College

---

### Medium to large (2,000-7,499)

## *Four-year*

## Alabama

Alabama Agricultural and
  Mechanical University
Alabama State University
Athens State University
Auburn University at
  Montgomery
Faulkner University
Jacksonville State University
Samford University
Tuskegee University
University of Alabama
  Huntsville
University of Montevallo
University of North Alabama
University of West Alabama

## Alaska

University of Alaska
  Fairbanks

## Arizona

Arizona State University West
Grand Canyon University
Western International University

## Arkansas

Arkansas Tech University
Harding University
Henderson State University
Southern Arkansas University
University of Arkansas
  Fort Smith
  Monticello
  Pine Bluff

## California

Azusa Pacific University
Biola University
California Baptist University
California Lutheran University
California State University
  Bakersfield
  Monterey Bay
  Stanislaus
California State University:
  Channel Islands
Chapman University
Humboldt State University
Loyola Marymount University
National University
Pepperdine University
Point Loma Nazarene University
St. Mary's College of California
Santa Clara University
Stanford University
University of Redlands
University of San Diego
University of San Francisco
University of the Pacific

## Colorado

Adams State College
Art Institute
  of Colorado
Colorado College
Colorado School of Mines
Colorado State University
  Pueblo
Fort Lewis College
Mesa State College
United States Air Force Academy
University of Colorado
  Colorado Springs
University of Denver
Western State College of
  Colorado

## Connecticut

Eastern Connecticut State
  University
Fairfield University
Quinnipiac University
Sacred Heart University
Trinity College
University of Hartford
University of New Haven
Wesleyan University
Western Connecticut State
  University
Yale University

## Delaware

Delaware State University
Wesley College
Wilmington University

## District of Columbia

American University
Catholic University of America
Georgetown University
Howard University
University of the District of
  Columbia

## Florida

Art Institute of Fort Lauderdale
Barry University
Bethune-Cookman University
Chipola Junior College

Embry-Riddle Aeronautical
  University
Flagler College
Florida Hospital College of
  Health Sciences
Florida Institute of Technology
Jacksonville University
Lynn University
Nova Southeastern University
Palm Beach Atlantic University
Southeastern University
Stetson University
University of Tampa

## Georgia

Albany State University
Armstrong Atlantic State
  University
Art Institute
  of Atlanta
Ashworth University
Augusta State University
Clark Atlanta University
Clayton State University
Columbus State University
Dalton State College
DeVry University
  Decatur
Emory University
Georgia College and State
  University
Georgia Southwestern State
  University
Macon State College
Mercer University
Morehouse College
North Georgia College & State
  University
Savannah College of Art and
  Design
Savannah State University
Southern Polytechnic State
  University
Spelman College

## Hawaii

Brigham Young
  University-Hawaii
Hawaii Pacific University
University of Hawaii
  Hilo

## Idaho

Lewis-Clark State College

## Illinois

Augustana College
Aurora University
Benedictine University
Bradley University
Chicago State University
Elmhurst College
Governors State University
Illinois Institute of Art: Chicago
Illinois Institute of Technology
Illinois Wesleyan University
Lewis University
McKendree University
Millikin University
North Central College
North Park University
Olivet Nazarene University
Robert Morris College: Chicago
Roosevelt University
St. Xavier University
School of the Art Institute of
  Chicago
University of Chicago
University of Illinois
  Springfield
Wheaton College

## Indiana

Anderson University
Bethel College
Butler University
DePauw University
Indiana Institute of Technology

Indiana University
  Kokomo
  Northwest
  South Bend
  Southeast
Indiana Wesleyan University
Purdue University
  North Central
University of Evansville
University of Indianapolis
Valparaiso University

## Iowa

Drake University
Luther College
St. Ambrose University

## Kansas

Emporia State University
Friends University
Pittsburg State University
Washburn University

## Kentucky

Bellarmine University
Kentucky State University
Morehead State University
Sullivan University

## Louisiana

Grambling State University
Louisiana State University
  Alexandria
  Shreveport
Loyola University New Orleans
McNeese State University
Nicholls State University
Southern University
  New Orleans
Southern University and
  Agricultural and Mechanical
  College
Tulane University
University of Louisiana at
  Monroe
Xavier University of Louisiana

## Maine

University of Maine
  Augusta
  Farmington
University of Southern Maine

## Maryland

Bowie State University
College of Notre Dame of
  Maryland
Coppin State University
Frostburg State University
Johns Hopkins University
Loyola College in Maryland
Salisbury University
United States Naval Academy
University of Baltimore
University of Maryland
  Eastern Shore
Villa Julie College

## Massachusetts

Assumption College
Bentley College
Berklee College of Music
Brandeis University
Clark University
College of the Holy Cross
Curry College
Emerson College
Emmanuel College
Endicott College
Fitchburg State College
Framingham State College
Harvard University
Massachusetts College of
  Pharmacy and Health Sciences
Massachusetts Institute of
  Technology
Merrimack College
Mount Holyoke College
Salem State College

Simmons College
Smith College
Springfield College
Stonehill College
Suffolk University
Tufts University
Wellesley College
Wentworth Institute of
  Technology
Western New England College
Westfield State College
Worcester Polytechnic Institute
Worcester State College

### Michigan
Calvin College
Hope College
Kettering University
Lake Superior State University
Lawrence Technological
  University
Madonna University
Michigan Technological
  University
Spring Arbor University
University of Detroit Mercy
University of Michigan
  Dearborn
  Flint

### Minnesota
Augsburg College
Bemidji State University
Bethel University
College of St. Benedict
College of St. Catherine
Concordia College: Moorhead
Gustavus Adolphus College
Metropolitan State University
St. Olaf College
Southwest Minnesota State
  University
University of St. Thomas
Winona State University

### Mississippi
Alcorn State University
Belhaven College
Delta State University
Jackson State University
Mississippi College
Mississippi University for Women
Mississippi Valley State
  University

### Missouri
Global University
Lincoln University
Lindenwood University
Maryville University of Saint
  Louis
Missouri Southern State
  University
Northwest Missouri State
  University
Saint Louis University
Southwest Baptist University
Truman State University
University of Missouri
  Kansas City
  Missouri University of
    Science and Technology
Washington University in St.
  Louis
Webster University

### Montana
Montana State University
  Billings
Montana Tech of the University of
  Montana

### Nebraska
Bellevue University
Chadron State College
Creighton University
University of Nebraska
  Kearney
Wayne State College

### New Hampshire
Dartmouth College
Hesser College
Keene State College
Plymouth State University

### New Jersey
Berkeley College
Bloomfield College
Centenary College
The College of New Jersey
Fairleigh Dickinson University
  College at Florham
  Metropolitan Campus
Monmouth University
New Jersey City University
New Jersey Institute of
  Technology
Princeton University
Ramapo College of New Jersey
Richard Stockton College of New
  Jersey
Rider University
Rutgers, The State University of
  New Jersey
  Camden Regional Campus
  Newark Regional Campus
Saint Peter's College
Seton Hall University
Stevens Institute of Technology

### New Mexico
Eastern New Mexico University

### New York
Adelphi University
Alfred University
Barnard College
Berkeley College of New York
  City
Canisius College
City University of New York
  Medgar Evers College
  York College
Clarkson University
Colgate University
College of Saint Rose
Columbia University
Culinary Institute of America
Dowling College
Globe Institute of Technology
Iona College
Ithaca College
Le Moyne College
Long Island University
  Brooklyn Campus
  C. W. Post Campus
Manhattan College
Marist College
Mercy College
Molloy College
Monroe College
Mount St. Mary College
Nazareth College of Rochester
New York Institute of Technology
Niagara University
Pace University
Parsons The New School for
  Design
Pratt Institute
Rensselaer Polytechnic Institute
St. Francis College
St. John Fisher College
St. Joseph's College: Suffolk
  Campus
St. Lawrence University
School of Visual Arts
Siena College
Skidmore College

State University of New York
  College at Brockport
  College at Cortland
  College at Fredonia
  College at Geneseo
  College at Old Westbury
  College at Oneonta
  College at Plattsburgh
  College at Potsdam
  College of Technology at
    Canton
  Farmingdale
  New Paltz
  Oswego
  Purchase
Union College
United States Military Academy
University of Rochester
Utica College
Vassar College

### North Carolina
Campbell University
Duke University
Elizabeth City State University
Elon University
Fayetteville State University
Gardner-Webb University
Guilford College
High Point University
Johnson & Wales University:
  Charlotte
Mount Olive College
North Carolina Central University
Shaw University
University of North Carolina
  Asheville
  Pembroke
Wake Forest University
Western Carolina University
Winston-Salem State University

### North Dakota
Dickinson State University
Minot State University
University of Mary

### Ohio
Ashland University
Baldwin-Wallace College
Capital University
Case Western Reserve University
Cedarville University
Denison University
DeVry University
  Columbus
John Carroll University
Mount Union College
Mount Vernon Nazarene
  University
Oberlin College
Ohio Dominican University
Ohio Northern University
Ohio State University
  Newark Campus
Otterbein College
Shawnee State University
University of Dayton
University of Findlay
Walsh University
Xavier University

### Oklahoma
Cameron University
East Central University
Langston University
Oklahoma City University
Oral Roberts University
Rogers State University
Southeastern Oklahoma State
  University
Southwestern Oklahoma State
  University
University of Tulsa

### Oregon
Eastern Oregon University
Oregon Institute of Technology
Southern Oregon University

University of Portland
Western Oregon University

### Pennsylvania
Albright College
Allegheny College
Arcadia University
Art Institute
  of Philadelphia
Bucknell University
California University of
  Pennsylvania
Carnegie Mellon University
Clarion University of
  Pennsylvania
DeSales University
Dickinson College
Duquesne University
East Stroudsburg University of
  Pennsylvania
Eastern University
Edinboro University of
  Pennsylvania
Elizabethtown College
Franklin & Marshall College
Gannon University
Gettysburg College
Grove City College
Holy Family University
Immaculata University
King's College
La Salle University
Lafayette College
Lehigh University
Lock Haven University of
  Pennsylvania
Mansfield University of
  Pennsylvania
Mercyhurst College
Messiah College
Millersville University of
  Pennsylvania
Misericordia University
Muhlenberg College
Neumann College
Peirce College
Penn State
  Abington
  Altoona
  Berks
  Erie, The Behrend College
  Harrisburg
Pennsylvania College of
  Technology
Philadelphia University
Point Park University
Robert Morris University
Saint Joseph's University
Shippensburg University of
  Pennsylvania
University of Pittsburgh
  Johnstown
University of Scranton
University of the Arts
University of the Sciences in
  Philadelphia
Villanova University
Widener University
Wilkes University
York College of Pennsylvania

### Puerto Rico
American University of Puerto
  Rico
Caribbean University
Inter American University of
  Puerto Rico
  Aguadilla Campus
  Barranquitas Campus
  Bayamon Campus
  Fajardo Campus
  Guayama Campus
  Metropolitan Campus
  Ponce Campus
  San German Campus
Pontifical Catholic University of
  Puerto Rico

Universidad Politecnica de Puerto
  Rico
University of Puerto Rico
  Aguadilla
  Arecibo
  Bayamon University College
  Carolina Regional College
  Cayey University College
  Humacao
  Ponce
University of the Sacred Heart

### Rhode Island
Brown University
Bryant University
New England Institute of
  Technology
Providence College
Rhode Island College
Roger Williams University
Salve Regina University

### South Carolina
Benedict College
Charleston Southern University
The Citadel
Coastal Carolina University
Francis Marion University
Furman University
Lander University
South Carolina State University
University of South Carolina
  Aiken
  Upstate
Winthrop University

### South Dakota
Black Hills State University
University of South Dakota

### Tennessee
Belmont University
Lee University
Lipscomb University
Southern Adventist University
Tennessee State University
Tusculum College
Union University
University of Tennessee
  Martin
Vanderbilt University

### Texas
Abilene Christian University
Angelo State University
Dallas Baptist University
LeTourneau University
Midwestern State University
Prairie View A&M University
Rice University
St. Edward's University
St. Mary's University
Southern Methodist University
Texas A&M International
  University
Texas A&M University
  Commerce
  Kingsville
Texas Christian University
Texas Woman's University
Trinity University
University of Houston
  Clear Lake
University of Mary Hardin-Baylor
University of Texas
  Tyler
  of the Permian Basin
University of the Incarnate Word
West Texas A&M University

### Utah
Dixie State College of Utah
Southern Utah University
Westminster College

### Vermont
Champlain College
Middlebury College

## Virginia

Christopher Newport University
College of William and Mary
ECPI College of Technology:
   Virginia Beach
Hampton University
Longwood University
Lynchburg College
Marymount University
Norfolk State University
University of Mary Washington
University of Richmond
Virginia State University

## Washington

Art Institute of Seattle
Evergreen State College
Gonzaga University
Pacific Lutheran University
Seattle Pacific University
Seattle University
University of Puget Sound
Whitworth University

## West Virginia

Concord University
Fairmont State University
Mountain State University
Shepherd University
West Liberty State College
West Virginia University at
   Parkersburg

## Wisconsin

Alverno College
Cardinal Stritch University
Carroll College
Carthage College
Concordia University Wisconsin
Lakeland College
Milwaukee School of Engineering
St. Norbert College
University of Wisconsin
   Green Bay
   Parkside
   Platteville
   River Falls
   Stout
   Superior

## Guam

University of Guam

## Virgin Islands, U.S.

University of the Virgin Islands

## Egypt

American University in Cairo

## Lebanon

American University of Beirut

## Mexico

Universidad de Monterrey

## Singapore

Singapore Management
University

## United Arab Emirates

American University in Dubai -
   United Arab Emirates

## *Two-year*

## Alabama

Bevill State Community College
Bishop State Community College
Central Alabama Community
   College
Faulkner State Community
   College
Gadsden State Community
   College
George C. Wallace State
   Community College
   George C. Wallace
      Community College at
      Dothan
Jefferson State Community
   College

Lawson State Community College
Northeast Alabama Community
   College
Northwest-Shoals Community
   College
Snead State Community College
Southern Union State Community
   College

## Arizona

Arizona Western College
Central Arizona College
Cochise College
Coconino County Community
   College
Eastern Arizona College
Estrella Mountain Community
   College
Everest College
   Phoenix
Glendale Community College
Mohave Community College
Northland Pioneer College
Yavapai College

## Arkansas

Arkansas State University
   Beebe
National Park Community
   College
North Arkansas College
Northwest Arkansas Community
   College
Phillips Community College of
   the University of Arkansas

## California

Art Institute
   of California: Los Angeles
Barstow Community College
Berkeley City College
Canada College
Cerro Coso Community College
College of Alameda
College of Marin: Kentfield
College of the Redwoods
Columbia College
Crafton Hills College
El Camino College: Compton
   Center
Fashion Institute of Design and
   Merchandising
      Los Angeles
Gavilan College
Lake Tahoe Community College
Los Angeles City College
Los Angeles Southwest College
Merritt College
Napa Valley College
Oxnard College
Palo Verde College
Porterville College
West Hills College: Lemoore

## Colorado

Aims Community College
Arapahoe Community College
Colorado Northwestern
   Community College
Community College of Aurora
Community College of Denver
Pueblo Community College
Red Rocks Community College

## Connecticut

Capital Community College
Gateway Community College
Housatonic Community College
Manchester Community College
Naugatuck Valley Community
   College
Norwalk Community College
Three Rivers Community College
Tunxis Community College

## Florida

Central Florida Community
   College
Florida National College

Full Sail University
Gulf Coast Community College
Lake City Community College
Lake-Sumter Community College
Pensacola Junior College
Polk Community College
Saint Johns River Community
   College

## Georgia

Albany Technical College
Athens Technical College
Atlanta Technical College
Augusta Technical College
Bainbridge College
Central Georgia Technical
   College
Chattahoochee Technical College
Coastal Georgia Community
   College
Columbus Technical College
Darton College
DeKalb Technical College
Gainesville State College
Georgia Highlands College
Georgia Military College
Gordon College
Griffin Technical College
Gwinnett Technical College
Middle Georgia College
Middle Georgia Technical College
North Metro Technical College
Savannah Technical College
West Central Technical College

## Hawaii

University of Hawaii
   Honolulu Community
      College
   Kapiolani Community
      College
   Maui Community College

## Idaho

College of Southern Idaho
North Idaho College

## Illinois

Black Hawk College
Carl Sandburg College
Danville Area Community
   College
Elgin Community College
Heartland Community College
Illinois Eastern Community
   Colleges
      Frontier Community College
Illinois Valley Community
   College
John A. Logan College
Kankakee Community College
Kaskaskia College
Kishwaukee College
Lake Land College
Lincoln Land Community College
Morton College
Prairie State College
Richland Community College
Shawnee Community College
Southeastern Illinois College
Spoon River College
Waubonsee Community College

## Indiana

Ivy Tech State College
   Ivy Tech Community
      College: Bloomington
   Ivy Tech Community
      College: Columbus
   Ivy Tech Community
      College: East Central
   Ivy Tech Community
      College: Kokomo
   Ivy Tech Community
      College: Lafayette
   Ivy Tech Community
      College: North Central
   Ivy Tech Community
      College: Northeast
   Ivy Tech Community
      College: Northwest
   Ivy Tech Community
      College: South Central
   Ivy Tech Community
      College: Southwest
   Ivy Tech Community
      College: Wabash Valley

## Iowa

Hawkeye Community College
Indian Hills Community College
Iowa Central Community College
Iowa Western Community
   College
North Iowa Area Community
   College
Northeast Iowa Community
   College
Scott Community College
Southeastern Community College
   North Campus
Western Iowa Tech Community
   College

## Kansas

Allen County Community College
Barton County Community
   College
Butler County Community
   College
Cloud County Community
   College
Cowley County Community
   College
Hutchinson Community College
Kansas City Kansas Community
   College

## Kentucky

Henderson Community College
Hopkinsville Community College
Madisonville Community College
Owensboro Community and
   Technical College
Southeast Kentucky Community
   and Technical College

## Louisiana

Baton Rouge Community College
Bossier Parish Community
   College
Louisiana State University
   Eunice
South Louisiana Community
   College
Southern University
   Shreveport

## Maine

Kennebec Valley Community
   College
Southern Maine Community
   College

## Maryland

Allegany College of Maryland
Baltimore City Community
   College
Carroll Community College
Chesapeake College
College of Southern Maryland
Frederick Community College

Hagerstown Community College
Harford Community College
Howard Community College
Wor-Wic Community College

## Massachusetts

Bristol Community College
Cape Cod Community College
Holyoke Community College
Massachusetts Bay Community
   College
Mount Wachusett Community
   College
North Shore Community College
Northern Essex Community
   College
Quincy College
Quinsigamond Community
   College
Roxbury Community College
Springfield Technical Community
   College

## Michigan

Jackson Community College
Kellogg Community College
Lake Michigan College
Mid Michigan Community
   College
Monroe County Community
   College
Montcalm Community College
Mott Community College
Muskegon Community College
North Central Michigan College
Northwestern Michigan College
St. Clair County Community
   College
Southwestern Michigan College

## Minnesota

Alexandria Technical College
Central Lakes College
Dakota County Technical College
Inver Hills Community College
Lake Superior College
Minnesota State Community and
   Technical College: Fergus Falls
North Hennepin Community
   College
Ridgewater College
Riverland Community College
Rochester Community and
   Technical College
St. Cloud Technical College
St. Paul College
South Central College

## Mississippi

Coahoma Community College
Copiah-Lincoln Community
   College
East Central Community College
East Mississippi Community
   College
Itawamba Community College
Meridian Community College
Northeast Mississippi Community
   College
Northwest Mississippi
   Community College
Pearl River Community College

## Missouri

Crowder College
East Central College
Jefferson College
Metropolitan Community
   College: Blue River
Metropolitan Community
   College: Longview
Metropolitan Community
   College: Maple Woods
Metropolitan Community
   College: Penn Valley
Moberly Area Community
   College
St. Charles Community College

St. Louis Community College
Florissant Valley
State Fair Community College
Three Rivers Community College

**Nebraska**

Central Community College
Metropolitan Community College
Northeast Community College

**Nevada**

Western Nevada College

**New Hampshire**

Great Bay Community College
Manchester Community College

**New Jersey**

Atlantic Cape Community
College
Burlington County College
Cumberland County College
Gloucester County College
Hudson County Community
College
Raritan Valley Community
College
Sussex County Community
College

**New Mexico**

Eastern New Mexico University:
Roswell Campus
Northern New Mexico College
San Juan College
Santa Fe Community College

**New York**

Adirondack Community College
ASA Institute of Business and
Computer Technology
Broome Community College
Cayuga County Community
College
City University of New York
Hostos Community College
Clinton Community College
Corning Community College
Erie Community College
City Campus
North Campus
South Campus
Finger Lakes Community College
Genesee Community College
Herkimer County Community
College
Jamestown Community College
Jefferson Community College
Mohawk Valley Community
College
Niagara County Community
College
Onondaga Community College
Orange County Community
College
Rockland Community College
Schenectady County Community
College
State University of New York
College of Agriculture and
Technology at Cobleskill
College of Agriculture and
Technology at Morrisville
College of Technology at
Alfred
College of Technology at
Delhi
Technical Career Institutes
Tompkins-Cortland Community
College
Ulster County Community
College

**North Carolina**

Alamance Community College
Asheville-Buncombe Technical
Community College
Blue Ridge Community College

Caldwell Community College and
Technical Institute
Catawba Valley Community
College
Cleveland Community College
Coastal Carolina Community
College
Craven Community College
Edgecombe Community College
Forsyth Technical Community
College
Gaston College
Haywood Community College
Johnston Community College
Lenoir Community College
Piedmont Community College
Pitt Community College
Randolph Community College
Rowan-Cabarrus Community
College
Sandhills Community College
South Piedmont Community
College
Southwestern Community
College
Stanly Community College
Surry Community College
Vance-Granville Community
College
Wayne Community College
Western Piedmont Community
College

**North Dakota**

Bismarck State College
North Dakota State College of
Science

**Ohio**

Bowling Green State University:
Firelands College
Central Ohio Technical College
Cincinnati State Technical and
Community College
Clark State Community College
Cleveland Institute of Electronics
Edison State Community College
Hocking College
James A. Rhodes State College
Kent State University
Stark
Marion Technical College
Miami University
Hamilton Campus
North Central State College
Northwest State Community
College
Southern State Community
College
University of Cincinnati
Clermont College
University of Northwestern Ohio
Washington State Community
College

**Oklahoma**

Oklahoma State University
Oklahoma City
Okmulgee
Redlands Community College
Rose State College
Seminole State College

**Oregon**

Blue Mountain Community
College
Central Oregon Community
College
Chemeketa Community College
Clackamas Community College
Linn-Benton Community College
Mt. Hood Community College
Rogue Community College
Southwestern Oregon Community
College

**Pennsylvania**

Butler County Community
College

Lehigh Carbon Community
College
Luzerne County Community
College
Pittsburgh Technical Institute
Reading Area Community
College
Westmoreland County
Community College

**Puerto Rico**

Ponce Paramedical College

**South Carolina**

Aiken Technical College
Central Carolina Technical
College
Florence-Darlington Technical
College
Horry-Georgetown Technical
College
Orangeburg-Calhoun Technical
College
Piedmont Technical College
Spartanburg Community College
Tri-County Technical College
York Technical College

**South Dakota**

Southeast Technical Institute

**Tennessee**

Cleveland State Community
College
Dyersburg State Community
College
Jackson State Community College
Motlow State Community College
Nashville State Community
College
Northeast State Technical
Community College
Roane State Community College
Volunteer State Community
College
Walters State Community College

**Texas**

Alvin Community College
Angelina College
Cedar Valley College
Cisco Junior College
Coastal Bend College
College of the Mainland
Eastfield College
El Centro College
Galveston College
Grayson County College
Hill College
Howard College
Kilgore College
Lamar Institute of Technology
Lamar State College at Port
Arthur
Laredo Community College
Lee College
Midland College
Mountain View College
Northeast Texas Community
College
Odessa College
Paris Junior College
Temple College
Texarkana College
Texas State Technical College
Harlingen
Trinity Valley Community
College
Vernon College
Victoria College
Weatherford College
Wharton County Junior College

**Utah**

College of Eastern Utah
Snow College

**Vermont**

Community College of Vermont

**Virginia**

Blue Ridge Community College
Central Virginia Community
College
Danville Community College
Germanna Community College
John Tyler Community College
Lord Fairfax Community College
Mountain Empire Community
College
New River Community College
Piedmont Virginia Community
College
Rappahannock Community
College
Southside Virginia Community
College
Southwest Virginia Community
College
Virginia Highlands Community
College
Wytheville Community College

**Washington**

Bellingham Technical College
Cascadia Community College
Centralia College
Edmonds Community College
Everett Community College
Green River Community College
Lake Washington Technical
College
North Seattle Community College
Olympic College
South Puget Sound Community
College
Spokane Community College
Spokane Falls Community
College
Tacoma Community College
Walla Walla Community College
Wenatchee Valley College
Whatcom Community College
Yakima Valley Community
College

**West Virginia**

New River Community and
Technical College
Southern West Virginia
Community and Technical
College

**Wisconsin**

Blackhawk Technical College
Chippewa Valley Technical
College
Fox Valley Technical College
Gateway Technical College
Lakeshore Technical College
Mid-State Technical College
Moraine Park Technical College
Northcentral Technical College
Northeast Wisconsin Technical
College
Waukesha County Technical
College
Western Technical College
Wisconsin Indianhead Technical
College

**Wyoming**

Casper College
Laramie County Community
College
Western Wyoming Community
College

**Micronesia**

College of Micronesia-FSM

### Large (7,500-14,499)

*Four-year*

**Alabama**

University of Alabama
Birmingham

University of South Alabama

**Alaska**

University of Alaska
Anchorage

**Arkansas**

Arkansas State University
University of Arkansas
University of Arkansas
Little Rock
University of Central Arkansas

**California**

Academy of Art University
California State University
Dominguez Hills
East Bay
San Bernardino
San Marcos
Sonoma State University
University of California
Riverside
Santa Cruz

**Colorado**

University of Colorado
Denver
University of Northern Colorado

**Connecticut**

Central Connecticut State
University
Southern Connecticut State
University

**District of Columbia**

George Washington University

**Florida**

Embry-Riddle Aeronautical
University: Worldwide Campus
Florida Agricultural and
Mechanical University
Florida Gulf Coast University
Okaloosa-Walton College
University of Miami
University of North Florida
University of West Florida

**Georgia**

Georgia Institute of Technology
Georgia Southern University
University of West Georgia
Valdosta State University

**Hawaii**

University of Hawaii
Manoa

**Idaho**

Brigham Young University-Idaho
Idaho State University
University of Idaho

**Illinois**

Columbia College Chicago
DePaul University
DeVry University: Online
Eastern Illinois University
Loyola University Chicago
Northeastern Illinois University
Northwestern University
Southern Illinois University
Edwardsville
Western Illinois University

**Indiana**

Indiana State University
Indiana University-Purdue
University Fort Wayne
Purdue University
Calumet
University of Notre Dame
University of Southern Indiana

**Iowa**

Ashford University
University of Northern Iowa

**Kansas**

Fort Hays State University

Wichita State University

**Kentucky**
Eastern Kentucky University
Murray State University
Northern Kentucky University
University of Louisville

**Louisiana**
Louisiana Tech University
Northwestern State University
Southeastern Louisiana University
University of Louisiana at
  Lafayette
University of New Orleans

**Maine**
University of Maine

**Maryland**
University of Maryland
  Baltimore County

**Massachusetts**
Boston College
Bridgewater State College
University of Massachusetts
  Boston
  Dartmouth
  Lowell

**Michigan**
Davenport University
Ferris State University
Northern Michigan University
Oakland University
Saginaw Valley State University

**Minnesota**
Minnesota State University
  Mankato
Saint Cloud State University
University of Minnesota
  Duluth

**Mississippi**
Mississippi State University
University of Mississippi
University of Southern
  Mississippi

**Missouri**
Grantham University
Missouri State University
Park University
Southeast Missouri State
  University
University of Central Missouri
University of Missouri
  St. Louis

**Montana**
Montana State University
  Bozeman
University of Montana: Missoula

**Nebraska**
University of Nebraska
  Omaha

**Nevada**
University of Nevada
  Reno

**New Hampshire**
University of New Hampshire

**New Jersey**
Kean University
Montclair State University
Rowan University
William Paterson University of
  New Jersey

**New Mexico**
New Mexico State University

**New York**
City University of New York
  Baruch College
  Brooklyn College
  City College
  College of Staten Island
  Hunter College
  John Jay College of
    Criminal Justice
  Lehman College
  New York City College of
    Technology
  Queens College
Cornell University
Fashion Institute of Technology
Fordham University
Hofstra University
Rochester Institute of Technology
St. John's University
State University of New York
  Albany
  Binghamton
  College at Buffalo
  Empire State College
Syracuse University

**North Carolina**
Appalachian State University
North Carolina Agricultural and
  Technical State University
University of North Carolina
  Greensboro
  Wilmington

**North Dakota**
North Dakota State University
University of North Dakota

**Ohio**
Cleveland State University
Miami University
  Oxford Campus
Wright State University
Youngstown State University

**Oklahoma**
Northeastern State University
University of Central Oklahoma

**Pennsylvania**
Art Institute
  Online
Bloomsburg University of
  Pennsylvania
Drexel University
Indiana University of
  Pennsylvania
Kutztown University of
  Pennsylvania
Slippery Rock University of
  Pennsylvania
University of Pennsylvania
West Chester University of
  Pennsylvania

**Puerto Rico**
Turabo University
Universidad del Este
Universidad Metropolitana
University of Puerto Rico
  Mayaguez

**Rhode Island**
Johnson & Wales University:
  Providence
University of Rhode Island

**South Carolina**
Clemson University
College of Charleston

**South Dakota**
South Dakota State University

**Tennessee**
Austin Peay State University
East Tennessee State University
Tennessee Technological
  University

University of Tennessee
  Chattanooga

**Texas**
Baylor University
Lamar University
Sam Houston State University
Stephen F. Austin State University
Tarleton State University
Texas Southern University
University of Houston
  Downtown
University of Texas
  Brownsville
  Dallas
  Pan American

**Utah**
Utah State University

**Vermont**
University of Vermont

**Virginia**
Radford University
University of Virginia

**Washington**
Central Washington University
South Seattle Community College
Western Washington University

**West Virginia**
Marshall University

**Wisconsin**
Marquette University
University of Wisconsin
  Eau Claire
  La Crosse
  Oshkosh
  Stevens Point
  Whitewater

**Wyoming**
University of Wyoming

**Canada**
Memorial University of
  Newfoundland

## *Two-year*

**Alabama**
Calhoun Community College

**Arizona**
Paradise Valley Community
  College
Phoenix College
Scottsdale Community College

**Arkansas**
Pulaski Technical College

**California**
Antelope Valley College
Butte College
Chabot College
Citrus College
Coastline Community College
College of San Mateo
College of the Desert
College of the Sequoias
Contra Costa College
Cosumnes River College
Cuesta College
Cuyamaca College
Cypress College
Evergreen Valley College
Folsom Lake College
Golden West College
Hartnell College
Imperial Valley College
Irvine Valley College
Laney College
Las Positas College
Los Angeles Harbor College
Los Angeles Mission College
Los Angeles Trade and Technical
  College

Los Medanos College
Merced College
MiraCosta College
Mission College
Monterey Peninsula College
Moorpark College
Ohlone College
Reedley College
San Bernardino Valley College
San Diego Miramar College
San Jose City College
Santa Barbara City College
Santiago Canyon College
Shasta College
Skyline College
Solano Community College
Taft College
Ventura College
Victor Valley College
West Los Angeles College
West Valley College
Yuba Community College District

**Colorado**
Colorado Mountain College
Front Range Community College
Pikes Peak Community College

**Florida**
Brevard Community College
Indian River Community College
Manatee Community College
Palm Beach Community College
Seminole Community College
Tallahassee Community College

**Illinois**
College of Lake County
Harper College
Illinois Central College
Joliet Junior College
Lewis and Clark Community
  College
Moraine Valley Community
  College
Parkland College
Triton College

**Indiana**
Ivy Tech State College
  Ivy Tech Community
    College: Central Indiana
Vincennes University

**Kentucky**
Bluegrass Community and
  Technical College
Jefferson Community and
  Technical College

**Louisiana**
Delgado Community College

**Maryland**
Anne Arundel Community
  College
Prince George's Community
  College

**Massachusetts**
Bunker Hill Community College
Middlesex Community College

**Michigan**
Delta College
Grand Rapids Community
  College
Henry Ford Community College
Kalamazoo Valley Community
  College
Lansing Community College
Macomb Community College
Oakland Community College
Schoolcraft College
Washtenaw Community College

**Minnesota**
Anoka-Ramsey Community
  College

Century Community and
  Technical College
Hennepin Technical College
Normandale Community College

**Mississippi**
Hinds Community College
Mississippi Gulf Coast
  Community College
    Jefferson Davis Campus

**Missouri**
Ozarks Technical Community
  College

**Nebraska**
Southeast Community College

**Nevada**
Truckee Meadows Community
  College

**New Jersey**
Bergen Community College
Brookdale Community College
Camden County College
County College of Morris
Essex County College
Mercer County Community
  College
Ocean County College
Union County College

**New Mexico**
Dona Ana Branch Community
  College of New Mexico State
  University

**New York**
City University of New York
  Bronx Community College
  Kingsborough Community
    College
  LaGuardia Community
    College
  Queensborough Community
    College
Dutchess Community College
Hudson Valley Community
  College
Westchester Community College

**North Carolina**
Fayetteville Technical
  Community College
Guilford Technical Community
  College
Wake Technical Community
  College

**Ohio**
Cuyahoga Community College
  Metropolitan Campus
Lakeland Community College
Lorain County Community
  College
Owens Community College
  Toledo

**Oklahoma**
Oklahoma City Community
  College
Tulsa Community College

**Oregon**
Lane Community College

**Pennsylvania**
Bucks County Community
  College
Harrisburg Area Community
  College
Montgomery County Community
  College
Northampton Community College

**South Carolina**
Greenville Technical College
Midlands Technical College
Trident Technical College

**Tennessee**
Chattanooga State Technical
  Community College
Southwest Tennessee Community
  College

**Texas**
Blinn College
Brookhaven College
Del Mar College
McLennan Community College
Navarro College
North Lake College
Northwest Vista College
Palo Alto College
Richland College
St. Philip's College
South Plains College
Texas Southmost College
Tyler Junior College

**Virginia**
J. Sargeant Reynolds Community
  College
Thomas Nelson Community
  College
Virginia Western Community
  College

**Washington**
Bates Technical College
Bellevue Community College

**Wisconsin**
Madison Area Technical College
Milwaukee Area Technical
  College

### Very large (15,000 or more)

*Four-year*

**Alabama**
Auburn University
Troy University
University of Alabama

**Arizona**
Arizona State University
Northern Arizona University
University of Arizona
University of Phoenix

**California**
California Polytechnic State
  University: San Luis Obispo
California State Polytechnic
  University: Pomona
California State University
  Chico
  Fresno
  Fullerton
  Long Beach
  Los Angeles
  Northridge
  Sacramento
San Diego State University
San Francisco State University
San Jose State University
University of California
  Berkeley
  Davis
  Irvine
  Los Angeles
  San Diego
  Santa Barbara
University of Southern California

**Colorado**
Colorado State University
Metropolitan State College of
  Denver
University of Colorado
  Boulder

**Connecticut**
University of Connecticut

**Delaware**
University of Delaware

**Florida**
Florida Atlantic University
Florida International University
Florida State University
St. Petersburg College
University of Central Florida
University of Florida
University of South Florida

**Georgia**
Georgia State University
Kennesaw State University
University of Georgia

**Idaho**
Boise State University

**Illinois**
Illinois State University
Northern Illinois University
Southern Illinois University
  Carbondale
University of Illinois
  Chicago
  Urbana-Champaign

**Indiana**
Ball State University
Indiana University
  Bloomington
Indiana University-Purdue
  University Indianapolis
Purdue University

**Iowa**
Iowa State University
University of Iowa

**Kansas**
Kansas State University
University of Kansas

**Kentucky**
University of Kentucky
Western Kentucky University

**Louisiana**
Louisiana State University and
  Agricultural and Mechanical
  College

**Maryland**
Towson University
University of Maryland
  College Park
  University College

**Massachusetts**
Boston University
Northeastern University
University of Massachusetts
  Amherst

**Michigan**
Central Michigan University
Eastern Michigan University
Grand Valley State University
Michigan State University
University of Michigan
Wayne State University
Western Michigan University

**Minnesota**
University of Minnesota
  Twin Cities

**Missouri**
University of Missouri
  Columbia

**Nebraska**
University of Nebraska
  Lincoln

**Nevada**
University of Nevada
  Las Vegas

**New Jersey**
Rutgers, The State University of
  New Jersey
  New Brunswick/Piscataway
    Campus
Thomas Edison State College

**New York**
Excelsior College
New York University
State University of New York
  Buffalo
  Stony Brook

**North Carolina**
East Carolina University
North Carolina State University
University of North Carolina
  Chapel Hill
  Charlotte

**Ohio**
Bowling Green State University
Kent State University
Ohio State University
  Columbus Campus
Ohio University
University of Akron
University of Cincinnati
University of Toledo

**Oklahoma**
Oklahoma State University
University of Oklahoma

**Oregon**
Oregon State University
Portland State University
University of Oregon

**Pennsylvania**
Art Institute
  of Pittsburgh
Penn State
  University Park
Temple University
University of Pittsburgh

**Puerto Rico**
University of Puerto Rico
  Rio Piedras

**South Carolina**
University of South Carolina

**Tennessee**
Middle Tennessee State
  University
University of Memphis
University of Tennessee
  Knoxville

**Texas**
Texas A&M University
Texas State University: San
  Marcos
Texas Tech University
University of Houston
University of North Texas
University of Texas
  Arlington
  Austin
  El Paso
  San Antonio

**Utah**
Brigham Young University
University of Utah
Utah Valley State College
Weber State University

**Virginia**
George Mason University
James Madison University
Liberty University
Old Dominion University
Virginia Commonwealth
  University
Virginia Polytechnic Institute and
  State University

**Washington**
University of Washington
Washington State University

**West Virginia**
American Public University
  System
West Virginia University

**Wisconsin**
University of Wisconsin
  Madison
  Milwaukee

**Canada**
McGill University
Simon Fraser University
University of Alberta
University of British Columbia
University of Manitoba
University of Toronto

**Germany**
University of Karlsruhe

**Republic of Korea**
Yonsei University

*Two-year*

**Alabama**
Community College of the Air
  Force

**Arizona**
Penn Foster College
Pima Community College
Rio Salado College

**California**
Allan Hancock College
American River College
Bakersfield College
Cabrillo College
Cerritos College
Chaffey College
City College of San Francisco
College of the Canyons
De Anza College
Diablo Valley College
East Los Angeles College
El Camino College
Foothill College
Fresno City College
Fullerton College
Glendale Community College
Grossmont College
Long Beach City College
Los Angeles Pierce College
Los Angeles Valley College
Modesto Junior College
Mount San Antonio College
Mount San Jacinto College
Orange Coast College
Palomar College
Pasadena City College
Rio Hondo College
Riverside Community College
Sacramento City College
Saddleback College
San Diego City College
San Diego Mesa College
San Joaquin Delta College
Santa Ana College
Santa Monica College
Santa Rosa Junior College
Sierra College
Southwestern College

**Florida**
Broward Community College
Florida Community College at
  Jacksonville
Hillsborough Community College
Miami Dade College
Santa Fe Community College
Valencia Community College

**Georgia**
Georgia Perimeter College

**Illinois**
College of DuPage

**Iowa**
Des Moines Area Community
  College
Kirkwood Community College

**Kansas**
Johnson County Community
  College

**Maryland**
Community College of Baltimore
  County
Montgomery College

**Michigan**
Wayne County Community
  College

**Missouri**
St. Louis Community College
  Meramec

**Nevada**
College of Southern Nevada

**New Mexico**
Central New Mexico Community
  College

**New York**
City University of New York
  Borough of Manhattan
    Community College
Monroe Community College
Nassau Community College
Suffolk County Community
  College

**North Carolina**
Central Piedmont Community
  College

**Ohio**
Columbus State Community
  College
Sinclair Community College

**Oregon**
Portland Community College

**Pennsylvania**
Community College of Allegheny
  County
Community College of
  Philadelphia

**Rhode Island**
Community College of Rhode
  Island

**Texas**
Austin Community College
Central Texas College
Collin County Community
  College District
Houston Community College
  System
North Harris Montgomery
  Community College
San Antonio College
San Jacinto College
South Texas College
Tarrant County College

**Utah**
Salt Lake Community College

**Virginia**
Northern Virginia Community
  College
Tidewater Community College

# Admission selectivity

**Admit under 50% of applicants**

## *Four-year*

**Alabama**

Alabama Agricultural and
    Mechanical University
Alabama State University
Stillman College

**Arizona**

Southwestern College

**Arkansas**

Philander Smith College
University of Central Arkansas

**California**

Art Institute
    of California: Orange
    County
Art Institute of California: San
    Francisco
California Institute of Technology
California Institute of the Arts
California Polytechnic State
    University: San Luis Obispo
California State University
    Long Beach
Chapman University
Charles R. Drew University of
    Medicine and Science
Claremont McKenna College
Harvey Mudd College
Holy Names University
La Sierra University
Menlo College
Occidental College
Otis College of Art and Design
Pepperdine University
Pitzer College
Pomona College
San Diego Christian College
San Diego State University
San Francisco Art Institute
Scripps College
Stanford University
University of California
    Berkeley
    Los Angeles
    San Diego
University of San Diego
University of Southern California

**Colorado**

Colorado College
United States Air Force Academy

**Connecticut**

Connecticut College
Quinnipiac University
Southern Connecticut State
    University
Trinity College
United States Coast Guard
    Academy
University of Connecticut
Wesleyan University
Yale University

**Delaware**

Delaware State University

**District of Columbia**

George Washington University
Georgetown University

**Florida**

Flagler College
Florida International University
Jacksonville University
University of Florida
University of Miami
University of South Florida
University of Tampa

**Georgia**

Agnes Scott College
Albany State University
Art Institute
    of Atlanta
Brenau University
Clayton State University
Emmanuel College
Emory University
Fort Valley State University
Georgia Southern University
Life University
Paine College
Piedmont College
Spelman College
Truett-McConnell College
Wesleyan College

**Hawaii**

Brigham Young
    University-Hawaii

**Illinois**

Lexington College
Northwestern University
Roosevelt University
University of Chicago

**Indiana**

Calumet College of St. Joseph
University of Notre Dame
Wabash College

**Iowa**

Cornell College
Grinnell College

**Kansas**

Central Christian College of
    Kansas

**Kentucky**

Alice Lloyd College
Berea College
Kentucky Mountain Bible College
Kentucky State University
University of the Cumberlands

**Louisiana**

Dillard University
Tulane University

**Maine**

Bates College
Bowdoin College
Colby College

**Maryland**

Bowie State University
Columbia Union College
Coppin State University
Johns Hopkins University
Maryland Institute College of Art
Morgan State University
United States Naval Academy
University of Baltimore
University of Maryland
    College Park

**Massachusetts**

Amherst College
Atlantic Union College
Babson College
Bentley College
Berklee College of Music
Boston College
Boston Conservatory
Brandeis University
College of the Holy Cross
Emerson College
Endicott College

Franklin W. Olin College of
    Engineering
Harvard College
Massachusetts Institute of
    Technology
Massachusetts Maritime Academy
New England Conservatory of
    Music
New England Institute of Art
Northeastern University
Tufts University
Wellesley College
Wheaton College
Williams College

**Michigan**

College for Creative Studies
Kuyper College

**Minnesota**

Carleton College
Macalester College

**Mississippi**

Delta State University
Jackson State University
Mississippi University for Women
Mississippi Valley State
    University
Rust College
Wesley College

**Missouri**

College of the Ozarks
St. Louis Christian College
University of Missouri
    St. Louis
Washington University in St.
    Louis

**Nebraska**

College of Saint Mary
Union College

**New Hampshire**

Dartmouth College
Thomas More College of Liberal
    Arts

**New Jersey**

Bloomfield College
The College of New Jersey
Fairleigh Dickinson University
    Metropolitan Campus
New Jersey City University
Princeton University
Ramapo College of New Jersey
Rutgers, The State University of
    New Jersey
    Newark Regional Campus

**New York**

Bard College
Barnard College
Boricua College
City University of New York
    Baruch College
    Brooklyn College
    City College
    Hunter College
    Lehman College
    Queens College
Colgate University
College of New Rochelle
Columbia University
    School of General Studies
Cooper Union for the
    Advancement of Science and
    Art
Cornell University
Fashion Institute of Technology
Fordham University
Hamilton College
Juilliard School
Manhattan School of Music
Manhattanville College
Mannes College The New School
    for Music
Marist College
Mercy College

Metropolitan College of New
    York
New York School of Interior
    Design
New York University
Pratt Institute
Rensselaer Polytechnic Institute
St. Lawrence University
Sarah Lawrence College
Skidmore College
State University of New York
    Binghamton
    College at Brockport
    College at Buffalo
    College at Cortland
    College at Geneseo
    College at Oneonta
    College at Plattsburgh
    Institute of Technology at
        Utica/Rome
    New Paltz
    Purchase
    Stony Brook
Union College
United States Merchant Marine
    Academy
United States Military Academy
University of Rochester
Vassar College
Webb Institute

**North Carolina**

Bennett College
Davidson College
Duke University
Elon University
Johnson C. Smith University
North Carolina School of the Arts
Shaw University
University of North Carolina
    Chapel Hill
Wake Forest University

**Ohio**

Art Academy of Cincinnati
Central State University
Cleveland Institute of Music
Denison University
Kenyon College
Kettering College of Medical Arts
Oberlin College

**Oklahoma**

Oklahoma Wesleyan University

**Oregon**

Eugene Bible College
Northwest Christian College
Reed College

**Pennsylvania**

Bryn Mawr College
Bucknell University
Carnegie Mellon University
Cheyney University of
    Pennsylvania
Curtis Institute of Music
Dickinson College
Franklin & Marshall College
Gettysburg College
Gwynedd-Mercy College
Haverford College
Lafayette College
Lehigh University
Lincoln University
Muhlenberg College
Swarthmore College
University of Pennsylvania
University of the Arts
Villanova University
Washington & Jefferson College
West Chester University of
    Pennsylvania
Williamson Free School of
    Mechanical Trades
Wilson College

**Puerto Rico**

Inter American University of
    Puerto Rico
    Bayamon Campus
    Fajardo Campus
    Metropolitan Campus
Universidad Metropolitana
University of Puerto Rico
    Arecibo
    Bayamon University College
    Carolina Regional College
    Cayey University College
    Humacao
    Ponce
    Rio Piedras

**Rhode Island**

Brown University
Bryant University
Providence College
Rhode Island School of Design

**South Carolina**

Claflin University

**Tennessee**

Baptist College of Health
    Sciences
King College
Lambuth University
Lane College
Memphis College of Art
Middle Tennessee State
    University
O'More College of Design
Tennessee Temple University
Vanderbilt University

**Texas**

Abilene Christian University
Dallas Christian College
Hardin-Simmons University
Houston Baptist University
Huston-Tillotson University
Our Lady of the Lake University
    of San Antonio
Prairie View A&M University
Rice University
Southwestern Adventist
    University
Texas Christian University
University of Texas
    of the Permian Basin

**Vermont**

Middlebury College

**Virginia**

College of William and Mary
Hampton University
Jefferson College of Health
    Sciences
University of Richmond
University of Virginia
Washington and Lee University

**Washington**

Whitman College
Whitworth University

**Wisconsin**

Bellin College of Nursing

**Republic of Korea**

Yonsei University

**Singapore**

Singapore Management
    University

**United Arab Emirates**

American University in Dubai -
    United Arab Emirates

## *Two-year*

**Alabama**

Marion Military Institute

## California

American Academy of Dramatic
Arts: West
Art Institute
of California: Los Angeles
Deep Springs College

## Georgia

Atlanta Metropolitan College

## Iowa

St. Luke's College

## Maine

Central Maine Medical Center
College of Nursing and Health
Professions

## New York

American Academy of Dramatic
Arts
Phillips Beth Israel School of
Nursing
St. Elizabeth College of Nursing
St. Joseph's College of Nursing

## North Carolina

Carolinas College of Health
Sciences

## Pennsylvania

Manor College

---

## Admit 50 to 75% of applicants

### *Four-year*

## Alabama

Auburn University
Birmingham-Southern College
Faulkner University
Heritage Christian University
Huntingdon College
Oakwood College
Spring Hill College
Troy University
Tuskegee University
University of Alabama

## Arkansas

Central Baptist College
Henderson State University
Lyon College
Ouachita Baptist University
Southern Arkansas University
University of Arkansas
University of Arkansas
Pine Bluff
Williams Baptist College

## California

American Jewish University
Azusa Pacific University
Bethany University
California Baptist University
California Lutheran University
California State Polytechnic
University: Pomona
California State University
Bakersfield
Dominguez Hills
East Bay
Fresno
Fullerton
Los Angeles
Monterey Bay
Northridge
Sacramento
San Bernardino
California State University:
Channel Islands
Cogswell Polytechnical College
Concordia University
Dominican University of
California
Fresno Pacific University
Hope International University
Laguna College of Art and Design

Loyola Marymount University
Mills College
National Hispanic University
Point Loma Nazarene University
San Francisco State University
San Jose State University
Santa Clara University
Simpson University
Soka University of America
Sonoma State University
Southern California Institute of
Architecture
Thomas Aquinas College
University of California
Davis
Irvine
Santa Barbara
University of La Verne
University of Redlands
University of San Francisco
University of the Pacific
Westmont College
Whittier College
William Jessup University

## Colorado

Adams State College
Colorado Christian University
Fort Lewis College
Regis University
University of Colorado
Colorado Springs
Denver
University of Denver

## Connecticut

Central Connecticut State
University
Eastern Connecticut State
University
Fairfield University
Paier College of Art
Post University
Sacred Heart University
University of Bridgeport
University of Hartford
University of New Haven
Western Connecticut State
University

## Delaware

University of Delaware

## District of Columbia

American University
Corcoran College of Art and
Design
Gallaudet University
Howard University

## Florida

Ave Maria University
Baptist College of Florida
Barry University
Beacon College
Bethune-Cookman University
Eckerd College
Florida Agricultural and
Mechanical University
Florida Atlantic University
Florida Southern College
Florida State University
Johnson & Wales University:
North Miami
Lynn University
New College of Florida
Northwood University
Florida
Nova Southeastern University
Ringling College of Art and
Design
Rollins College
St. Leo University
Saint Thomas University
Stetson University
Trinity College of Florida
University of Central Florida
University of North Florida
University of West Florida

Warner Southern College
Webber International University

## Georgia

Armstrong Atlantic State
University
Augusta State University
Berry College
Clark Atlanta University
Columbus State University
Covenant College
Dalton State College
Georgia College and State
University
Georgia Institute of Technology
Georgia State University
Kennesaw State University
LaGrange College
Macon State College
Mercer University
Morehouse College
North Georgia College & State
University
Savannah College of Art and
Design
Shorter College
Southern Polytechnic State
University
Toccoa Falls College
University of Georgia
University of West Georgia
Valdosta State University

## Hawaii

University of Hawaii
Hilo
Manoa
West Oahu

## Idaho

Boise Bible College
Lewis-Clark State College
Northwest Nazarene University

## Illinois

Augustana College
Aurora University
Blackburn College
Chicago State University
DePaul University
Eastern Illinois University
Eureka College
Illinois Institute of Technology
Illinois State University
Illinois Wesleyan University
Judson University
Knox College
Lake Forest College
Lewis University
Loyola University Chicago
MacMurray College
McKendree University
Millikin University
North Central College
North Park University
Northeastern Illinois University
Northern Illinois University
Shimer College
Southern Illinois University
Carbondale
University of Illinois
Chicago
Springfield
Urbana-Champaign
University of St. Francis
Western Illinois University
Westwood College of Technology
Westwood College: O'Hare
Airport
Westwood College: River
Oaks
Wheaton College

## Indiana

Anderson University
Ball State University
DePauw University
Earlham College
Franklin College

Goshen College
Grace College
Hanover College
Indiana Institute of Technology
Indiana State University
Indiana University
Bloomington
Indiana University-Purdue
University Indianapolis
Manchester College
Marian College
Rose-Hulman Institute of
Technology
Taylor University Fort Wayne
Tri-State University

## Iowa

Briar Cliff University
Buena Vista University
Clarke College
Coe College
Graceland University
Iowa Wesleyan College
Loras College
Mount Mercy College
St. Ambrose University
University of Dubuque
Upper Iowa University
Vennard College
Waldorf College
William Penn University

## Kansas

Baker University
Benedictine College
Bethany College
Newman University
Ottawa University
Sterling College
University of St. Mary

## Kentucky

Asbury College
Bellarmine University
Campbellsville University
Centre College
Eastern Kentucky University
Kentucky Christian University
Morehead State University
Union College
University of Louisville

## Louisiana

Centenary College of Louisiana
Louisiana State University and
Agricultural and Mechanical
College
Loyola University New Orleans
School of Urban Missions: New
Orleans
Southern University and
Agricultural and Mechanical
College
University of Louisiana at
Lafayette
Xavier University of Louisiana

## Maine

Maine Maritime Academy
New England School of
Communications
University of Maine
Farmington

## Maryland

Baltimore International College
College of Notre Dame of
Maryland
Frostburg State University
Goucher College
Hood College
Johns Hopkins University:
Peabody Conservatory of Music
Loyola College in Maryland
McDaniel College
Ner Israel Rabbinical College
St. Mary's College of Maryland
Salisbury University
Towson University

University of Maryland
Baltimore County
Eastern Shore
Washington College

## Massachusetts

Assumption College
Boston University
Bridgewater State College
Clark University
Curry College
Eastern Nazarene College
Emmanuel College
Fitchburg State College
Framingham State College
Gordon College
Hampshire College
Lasell College
Massachusetts College of Art
Massachusetts College of Liberal
Arts
Massachusetts College of
Pharmacy and Health Sciences
Merrimack College
Mount Holyoke College
Pine Manor College
Salem State College
Simmons College
Smith College
Springfield College
Stonehill College
University of Massachusetts
Amherst
Boston
Dartmouth
Lowell
Western New England College
Westfield State College
Wheelock College
Worcester Polytechnic Institute

## Michigan

Adrian College
Andrews University
Central Michigan University
Concordia University
Cornerstone University
Eastern Michigan University
Finlandia University
Grace Bible College
Grand Valley State University
Hillsdale College
Kalamazoo College
Kettering University
Lawrence Technological
University
Michigan State University
Olivet College
University of Detroit Mercy
University of Michigan
University of Michigan
Dearborn

## Minnesota

Augsburg College
Concordia University: St. Paul
Crossroads College
Metropolitan State University
Minneapolis College of Art and
Design
St. John's University
St. Olaf College
University of Minnesota
Duluth
Twin Cities

## Mississippi

Alcorn State University
Belhaven College
Blue Mountain College
Mississippi College
Mississippi State University
University of Southern
Mississippi

## Missouri

Avila University
Central Methodist University
Columbia College

Kansas City Art Institute
Lindenwood University
Maryville University of Saint Louis
Missouri Baptist University
Missouri State University
Missouri Valley College
Northwest Missouri State University
Park University
Research College of Nursing
Southwest Baptist University
Stephens College
University of Missouri
   Kansas City
   Missouri University of Science and Technology
Webster University

**Montana**
Montana State University Bozeman
Rocky Mountain College
University of Great Falls

**Nebraska**
Dana College
University of Nebraska Lincoln

**Nevada**
University of Nevada Las Vegas

**New Hampshire**
Chester College of New England
Franklin Pierce University
Keene State College
New England College
Plymouth State University
St. Anselm College
Southern New Hampshire University
University of New Hampshire
University of New Hampshire at Manchester

**New Jersey**
Caldwell College
Centenary College
Fairleigh Dickinson University College at Florham
Felician College
Kean University
Monmouth University
Montclair State University
New Jersey Institute of Technology
Richard Stockton College of New Jersey
Rowan University
Rutgers, The State University of New Jersey
  Camden Regional Campus
  New Brunswick/Piscataway Campus
Saint Peter's College
Seton Hall University
Stevens Institute of Technology
William Paterson University of New Jersey

**New Mexico**
Eastern New Mexico University
New Mexico Institute of Mining and Technology

**New York**
Adelphi University
Albany College of Pharmacy
Alfred University
Berkeley College of New York City
College of Mount St. Vincent
College of Saint Rose
Concordia College
Culinary Institute of America
D'Youville College
Daemen College

Eugene Lang College The New School for Liberal Arts
Five Towns College
Hobart and William Smith Colleges
Hofstra University
Iona College
Ithaca College
Jewish Theological Seminary of America
Keuka College
Laboratory Institute of Merchandising
Le Moyne College
Manhattan College
Marymount Manhattan College
Molloy College
Monroe College
Nazareth College of Rochester
New York Institute of Technology
Parsons The New School for Design
Polytechnic University
Roberts Wesleyan College
Rochester Institute of Technology
Sage College of Albany
St. John Fisher College
St. John's University
School of Visual Arts
Siena College
State University of New York
  Albany
  Buffalo
  College at Fredonia
  College at Old Westbury
  College at Potsdam
  College of Environmental Science and Forestry
  Farmingdale
  Maritime College
  Oswego
Syracuse University
Wagner College
Wells College
Yeshiva University

**North Carolina**
Appalachian State University
Barton College
Belmont Abbey College
Brevard College
Cabarrus College of Health Sciences
Campbell University
Chowan University
Elizabeth City State University
Gardner-Webb University
Greensboro College
Guilford College
High Point University
John Wesley College
Johnson & Wales University: Charlotte
Lees-McRae College
Mars Hill College
Methodist University
Montreat College
North Carolina Agricultural and Technical State University
North Carolina Central University
North Carolina State University
North Carolina Wesleyan College
Peace College
Roanoke Bible College
St. Andrews Presbyterian College
Salem College
University of North Carolina
  Greensboro
  Wilmington
Western Carolina University
Wingate University
Winston-Salem State University

**North Dakota**
University of North Dakota

**Ohio**
Baldwin-Wallace College

Bluffton University
Capital University
Case Western Reserve University
Cleveland Institute of Art
College of Mount St. Joseph
College of Wooster
Heidelberg College
Lake Erie College
MedCentral College of Nursing
Mount Carmel College of Nursing
Notre Dame College
Ohio Dominican University
Ohio State University
  Columbus Campus
Ohio Wesleyan University
Tiffin University
University of Cincinnati
University of Findlay
Ursuline College
Wilberforce University
Wittenberg University
Xavier University

**Oklahoma**
Bacone College
Northeastern State University
St. Gregory's University
Southeastern Oklahoma State University
University of Central Oklahoma
University of Tulsa

**Oregon**
Art Institute of Portland
Concordia University
Eastern Oregon University
Lewis & Clark College
Pacific Northwest College of Art
University of Portland

**Pennsylvania**
Allegheny College
Bloomsburg University of Pennsylvania
California University of Pennsylvania
Carlow University
Cedar Crest College
Chestnut Hill College
Clarion University of Pennsylvania
Delaware Valley College
Drexel University
Duquesne University
East Stroudsburg University of Pennsylvania
Eastern University
Elizabethtown College
Grove City College
Holy Family University
Indiana University of Pennsylvania
Juniata College
Kutztown University of Pennsylvania
La Roche College
La Salle University
Lebanon Valley College
Lock Haven University of Pennsylvania
Mansfield University of Pennsylvania
Marywood University
Mercyhurst College
Millersville University of Pennsylvania
Misericordia University
Moore College of Art and Design
Moravian College
Penn State
  Altoona
  Harrisburg
  University Park
Pennsylvania College of Art and Design
Philadelphia University
Rosemont College
Saint Joseph's University

St. Vincent College
Seton Hill University
Slippery Rock University of Pennsylvania
Temple University
University of Pittsburgh
University of Scranton
University of the Sciences in Philadelphia
Ursinus College
Valley Forge Christian College
Waynesburg University
Westminster College
Widener University
York College of Pennsylvania

**Puerto Rico**
Colegio Pentecostal Mizpa
Conservatory of Music of Puerto Rico
Escuela de Artes Plasticas de Puerto Rico
Inter American University of Puerto Rico
  Ponce Campus
University of Puerto Rico Utuado

**Rhode Island**
Johnson & Wales University: Providence
Rhode Island College
Roger Williams University
Salve Regina University

**South Carolina**
Charleston Southern University
Clemson University
Coastal Carolina University
Coker College
College of Charleston
Columbia College
Columbia International University
Converse College
Erskine College
Francis Marion University
Furman University
Limestone College
Presbyterian College
University of South Carolina
University of South Carolina
  Aiken
  Beaufort
  Upstate
Winthrop University
Wofford College

**South Dakota**
Dakota Wesleyan University
Mount Marty College

**Tennessee**
Aquinas College
Belmont University
Bethel College
Bryan College
Carson-Newman College
Christian Brothers University
Cumberland University
LeMoyne-Owen College
Lincoln Memorial University
Lipscomb University
Rhodes College
Southern Adventist University
Tennessee State University
Trevecca Nazarene University
Tusculum College
University of Memphis
University of Tennessee Knoxville
University of the South

**Texas**
Austin College
Baylor University
Concordia University at Austin
Dallas Baptist University
East Texas Baptist University
Howard Payne University

Lamar University
LeTourneau University
Lubbock Christian University
McMurry University
Midwestern State University
Northwood University: Texas
St. Edward's University
St. Mary's University
Schreiner University
Southern Methodist University
Southwestern University
Stephen F. Austin State University
Tarleton State University
Texas A&M International University
Texas A&M University Commerce
Texas Lutheran University
Texas State University: San Marcos
Texas Wesleyan University
Trinity University
University of Dallas
University of North Texas
University of Texas
  Austin
  Dallas
  Pan American
West Texas A&M University

**Utah**
Brigham Young University

**Vermont**
Bennington College
Burlington College
Castleton State College
Champlain College
Marlboro College
Norwich University
St. Michael's College
Southern Vermont College
University of Vermont
Vermont Technical College

**Virginia**
Bluefield College
Christopher Newport University
Eastern Mennonite University
Emory & Henry College
George Mason University
Hampden-Sydney College
James Madison University
Longwood University
Lynchburg College
Mary Baldwin College
Norfolk State University
Old Dominion University
Randolph-Macon College
Regent University
Roanoke College
Virginia Commonwealth University
Virginia Intermont College
Virginia Military Institute
Virginia Polytechnic Institute and State University
Virginia State University

**Washington**
Gonzaga University
Seattle University
University of Puget Sound
University of Washington
Western Washington University

**West Virginia**
Alderson-Broaddus College
Appalachian Bible College
Bethany College
Concord University
Ohio Valley University
University of Charleston
Wheeling Jesuit University

**Wisconsin**
Beloit College
Carroll College
Concordia University Wisconsin

Lakeland College
Lawrence University
Maranatha Baptist Bible College
Marquette University
Milwaukee School of Engineering
Mount Mary College
Northland College
Silver Lake College
University of Wisconsin
    Eau Claire
    Green Bay
    La Crosse
    Madison
    Stevens Point
    Superior

### Canada
McGill University
University of British Columbia
University of Toronto

### Egypt
American University in Cairo

### France
American University of Paris

### Lebanon
American University of Beirut

### Switzerland
Franklin College: Switzerland

*Two-year*

### California
Marymount College

### Connecticut
Clemens College

### Georgia
Georgia Perimeter College
Oxford College of Emory
  University
Young Harris College

### Illinois
Northwestern Business College
Springfield College in Illinois

### Massachusetts
Dean College
Fisher College

### Minnesota
Dunwoody College of Technology

### Missouri
Cottey College

### New Mexico
New Mexico Military Institute

### New York
Maria College
State University of New York
  College of Technology at
  Alfred

### North Carolina
Louisburg College

### Ohio
Bradford School

### Pennsylvania
Harcum College

### South Carolina
University of South Carolina
  Sumter

### Tennessee
Hiwassee College
Nossi College of Art

### Vermont
Landmark College
New England Culinary Institute

*Four-year*

### Alabama
Auburn University at
  Montgomery
Concordia College
Jacksonville State University
Judson College
Samford University
Southeastern Bible College
University of Alabama
  Birmingham
  Huntsville
University of Mobile
University of Montevallo
University of North Alabama
University of South Alabama
University of West Alabama

### Alaska
Alaska Pacific University
University of Alaska
  Fairbanks

### Arizona
Arizona State University
Arizona State University West
Embry-Riddle Aeronautical
  University: Prescott Campus
Prescott College
University of Arizona
Western International University

### Arkansas
Arkansas State University
Arkansas Tech University
Harding University
Hendrix College
University of the Ozarks

### California
Biola University
California College of the Arts
California State University
  Chico
California University of
  Management and Sciences
Design Institute of San Diego
Humboldt State University
Life Pacific College
Lincoln University
The Master's College
Mt. Sierra College
NewSchool of Architecture &
  Design
Northwestern Polytechnic
  University
Notre Dame de Namur University
Pacific Union College
St. Mary's College of California
School of Urban Missions:
  Oakland
University of California
  Riverside
  Santa Cruz
University of California: Merced
Vanguard University of Southern
  California
Woodbury University

### Colorado
Colorado School of Mines
Colorado State University
Colorado State University
  Pueblo
Johnson & Wales University:
  Denver
Mesa State College
Naropa University
Rocky Mountain College of Art &
  Design
University of Colorado
  Boulder
University of Northern Colorado

Westwood College of Technology
  Westwood College: Denver
  South

### Connecticut
Albertus Magnus College
Holy Apostles College and
  Seminary
Lyme Academy College of Fine
  Arts
St. Joseph College

### District of Columbia
Catholic University of America
Trinity Washington University

### Florida
Clearwater Christian College
Embry-Riddle Aeronautical
  University
Florida College
Florida Gulf Coast University
Florida Institute of Technology
Hodges University
Palm Beach Atlantic University
St. John Vianney College
  Seminary

### Georgia
American InterContinental
  University
Brewton-Parker College
Georgia Southwestern State
  University
Herzing College

### Hawaii
Chaminade University of
  Honolulu
Hawaii Pacific University

### Idaho
Boise State University
College of Idaho
Idaho State University
University of Idaho

### Illinois
Benedictine University
Blessing-Rieman College of
  Nursing
Bradley University
Concordia University
Dominican University
Greenville College
Illinois College
Lincoln Christian College and
  Seminary
Monmouth College
National-Louis University
Olivet Nazarene University
Principia College
Quincy University
Robert Morris College: Chicago
St. Xavier University
School of the Art Institute of
  Chicago
Southern Illinois University
  Edwardsville
Trinity Christian College
Trinity International University
VanderCook College of Music
Westwood College: Chicago Loop

### Indiana
Bethel College
Butler University
Huntington University
Indiana University
  Kokomo
  Northwest
  South Bend
  Southeast
Indiana University-Purdue
  University Fort Wayne
Indiana Wesleyan University
Purdue University
Purdue University
  Calumet
  North Central

Saint Joseph's College
Saint Mary's College
St. Mary-of-the-Woods College
Taylor University
University of Evansville
University of Indianapolis
University of Southern Indiana
Valparaiso University

### Iowa
Allen College
Central College
Divine Word College
Dordt College
Drake University
Faith Baptist Bible College and
  Theological Seminary
Grand View College
Iowa State University
Luther College
Mercy College of Health Sciences
Morningside College
Northwestern College
Simpson College
University of Iowa
University of Northern Iowa
Wartburg College

### Kansas
Barclay College
Bethel College
Emporia State University
Fort Hays State University
Kansas State University
McPherson College
MidAmerica Nazarene University
Pittsburg State University
Southwestern College
University of Kansas
Wichita State University

### Kentucky
Brescia University
Georgetown College
Kentucky Wesleyan College
Mid-Continent University
Murray State University
Northern Kentucky University
Thomas More College
Transylvania University
University of Kentucky

### Louisiana
Louisiana College
Louisiana State University
  Shreveport
Nicholls State University
Northwestern State University
Our Lady of the Lake College
St. Joseph Seminary College
Southeastern Louisiana University
University of Louisiana at
  Monroe
University of New Orleans

### Maine
College of the Atlantic
Husson College
Maine College of Art
St. Joseph's College
Thomas College
Unity College
University of Maine
University of Maine
  Machias
University of New England
University of Southern Maine

### Maryland
Mount St. Mary's University
St. John's College
Villa Julie College

### Massachusetts
American International College
Anna Maria College
Bay Path College
Becker College
Elms College

Hellenic College/Holy Cross
Lesley University
Mount Ida College
Newbury College
Nichols College
Regis College
School of the Museum of Fine
  Arts
Suffolk University
Wentworth Institute of
  Technology

### Michigan
Albion College
Alma College
Aquinas College
Calvin College
Cleary University
Davenport University
Hope College
Kendall College of Art and
  Design of Ferris State
  University
Lake Superior State University
Madonna University
Michigan Technological
  University
Northern Michigan University
Northwood University: Michigan
Oakland University
Rochester College
Sacred Heart Major Seminary
Saginaw Valley State University
Spring Arbor University
University of Michigan
  Flint
Wayne State University
Western Michigan University

### Minnesota
Bemidji State University
Bethany Lutheran College
Bethel University
College of St. Benedict
College of St. Catherine
College of St. Scholastica
College of Visual Arts
Concordia College: Moorhead
Gustavus Adolphus College
Hamline University
Martin Luther College
Minnesota School of Business:
  Shakopee
Minnesota State University
  Mankato
  Moorhead
North Central University
Northwestern College
Oak Hills Christian College
Saint Cloud State University
St. Mary's University of
  Minnesota
University of Minnesota
  Crookston
  Morris
University of St. Thomas
Winona State University

### Mississippi
Millsaps College
Tougaloo College
University of Mississippi
William Carey University

### Missouri
Central Bible College
Conception Seminary College
Culver-Stockton College
Drury University
Evangel University
Fontbonne University
Hannibal-LaGrange College
Harris-Stowe State University
Missouri Southern State
  University
Ozark Christian College
Rockhurst University
Saint Louis University

Virginia Marti College of Art and
Design

## Oklahoma
Rose State College

## Pennsylvania
Antonelli Institute of Art and
Photography
Art Institute of York
Business Institute of Pennsylvania
Hussian School of Art
Keystone Technical Institute
Laurel Business Institute
New Castle School of Trades
Oakbridge Academy of Arts
Triangle Tech: Bethlehem
Triangle Tech: Sunbury
University of Pittsburgh
Titusville

## South Carolina
Spartanburg Methodist College

## Texas
Commonwealth Institute of
Funeral Service

## Virginia
Richard Bland College

## Wisconsin
University of Wisconsin
Fond du Lac
Rock County

## Open admission

### *Four-year*

#### Alabama
Amridge University
Andrew Jackson University
Columbia Southern University
Miles College
Virginia College at Huntsville

#### Alaska
Alaska Bible College
University of Alaska
Anchorage
Southeast

#### Arizona
Arizona Institute of Business and
Technology
International Institute of the
Americas: Mesa
Brown Mackie College: Tucson
Grand Canyon University
International Import-Export
Institute
International Institute of the
Americas
Phoenix
Tucson
Northern Arizona University
University of Phoenix

#### Arkansas
Arkansas Baptist College
Ecclesia College
University of Arkansas
Fort Smith
Monticello

#### California
Academy of Art University
Bethesda Christian University
California Coast University
California College San Diego
Coleman College
Columbia College: Hollywood
Humphreys College
Interior Designers Institute
LA College International
National University
Pacific States University
Platt College
San Diego

Southern California Institute of
Technology
University of the West
West Coast University

## Colorado
American Sentinel University
Aspen University
CollegeAmerica
Fort Collins
National American University
Denver
Nazarene Bible College

## Connecticut
Briarwood College

## Delaware
Wilmington University

## District of Columbia
Potomac College
Southeastern University
University of the District of
Columbia

## Florida
Carlos Albizu University
Chipola Junior College
City College: Fort Lauderdale
Edward Waters College
Everest University: Brandon
Everest University: Tampa
International Academy of Design
and Technology: Orlando
International Academy of Design
and Technology: Tampa
Jones College
Jones College: Miami
Okaloosa-Walton College
Rasmussen College: Ocala
Remington College: Largo
Remington College: Tampa
St. Petersburg College
Schiller International University
Southeastern University
Universidad FLET

## Georgia
Ashworth University
Bauder College
Beulah Heights University
Thomas University

## Illinois
Columbia College Chicago
East-West University
Governors State University
Illinois Institute of Art:
Schaumburg
International Academy of Design
and Technology: Chicago
International Academy of Design
and Technology: Schaumburg
Lakeview College of Nursing
Midstate College

## Indiana
Indiana University
East
International Business College
Martin University
Oakland City University

## Iowa
Hamilton Technical College
Kaplan University
Cedar Falls
Cedar Rapids
Davenport
Des Moines
Mason City

## Kansas
University of Kansas Medical
Center
Washburn University

## Kentucky
Beckfield College
Clear Creek Baptist Bible College

Lindsey Wilson College
Midway College
Pikeville College
St. Catharine College
Western Kentucky University

## Louisiana
Grambling State University
Louisiana State University
Alexandria
Southern University
New Orleans
Southwest University

## Maine
University of Maine
Augusta
Fort Kent

## Maryland
University of Maryland
University College

## Massachusetts
Boston Architectural College
Cambridge College
Rhodec International
Worcester State College

## Michigan
Baker College
of Auburn Hills
of Cadillac
of Clinton Township
of Flint
of Jackson
of Muskegon
of Owosso
of Port Huron
Baker College of Allen Park
International Academy of Design
and Technology: Detroit

## Minnesota
Academy College
Art Institutes International
Minnesota
Brown College
Globe University
Rasmussen College
Eagan

## Mississippi
Magnolia Bible College
University of Mississippi Medical
Center

## Missouri
Calvary Bible College and
Theological Seminary
Global University
Grantham University
Lincoln University
Missouri Western State University

## Montana
University of Montana: Western

## Nebraska
Bellevue University
Chadron State College
Clarkson College
Peru State College
Wayne State College

## Nevada
Art Institute
of Las Vegas
International Academy of Design
and Technology: Henderson

## New Hampshire
Granite State College

## New Jersey
Thomas Edison State College

## New Mexico
College of the Southwest
International Institute of the
Americas: Albuquerque

National American University:
Rio Rancho
New Mexico Highlands
University
Western New Mexico University

## New York
City University of New York
Medgar Evers College
New York City College of
Technology
City University of New York:
CUNY Online
Excelsior College
Globe Institute of Technology

## North Carolina
Miller-Motte Technical College
Mount Olive College

## North Dakota
Dickinson State University
Mayville State University
Rasmussen College: Fargo

## Ohio
Allegheny Wesleyan College
Bryant & Stratton College
Parma
Willoughby Hills
Cincinnati College of Mortuary
Science
Cleveland State University
Ohio Christian University
Ohio State University
Lima Campus
Mansfield Campus
Marion Campus
Newark Campus
Ohio University
Chillicothe Campus
Lancaster Campus
Southern Campus at Ironton
Zanesville Campus
Shawnee State University
University of Akron
University of Rio Grande
University of Toledo
Wright State University
Youngstown State University

## Oklahoma
Cameron University
Langston University
Oklahoma Christian University
Rogers State University
Southern Nazarene University
Vatterott College

## Oregon
Cascade College
Marylhurst University
Pioneer Pacific College
Warner Pacific College

## Pennsylvania
Art Institute
of Philadelphia
Central Pennsylvania College
Peirce College
Pennsylvania College of
Technology
Yeshivath Beth Moshe

## Puerto Rico
American University of Puerto
Rico
Atlantic College
Bayamon Central University
Caribbean University
Columbia Centro Universitario:
Caguas
Turabo University
Universidad Adventista de las
Antillas
Universidad del Este

## Rhode Island
New England Institute of
Technology

## South Carolina
Allen University
South University

## South Dakota
National American University
Rapid City
Oglala Lakota College

## Tennessee
American Baptist College of ABT
Seminary
Free Will Baptist Bible College
International Academy of Design
and Technology: Nashville
Lee University
Martin Methodist College
Williamson Christian College

## Texas
Arlington Baptist College
Art Institute
of Dallas
Baptist University of the
Americas
College of Biblical
Studies-Houston
Jarvis Christian College
Texas A&M University
Kingsville
Texas College
Texas Southern University
University of Houston
Downtown
University of Texas
Brownsville
Wiley College

## Utah
Dixie State College of Utah
Neumont University
Stevens-Henager College
Murray
Stevens-Henager College: Ogden
Utah Career College
Utah Valley State College
Weber State University

## Vermont
Goddard College
Woodbury College

## Virginia
National College
Roanoke Valley
Potomac College
World College

## Washington
City University of Seattle
Heritage University
South Seattle Community College

## West Virginia
American Public University
System
Fairmont State University
Glenville State College
Marshall University
Mountain State University
West Virginia University at
Parkersburg

## Wisconsin
Herzing College

## Guam
University of Guam

## Canada
University of Manitoba

## Mexico
Instituto Tecnologico Autonomo
de Mexico

## United Kingdom
Richmond, The American
International University in
London

## Two-year

### Alabama

Bevill State Community College
Bishop State Community College
Calhoun Community College
Central Alabama Community
College
Chattahoochee Valley Community
College
Community College of the Air
Force
Faulkner State Community
College
Gadsden State Community
College
George C. Wallace State
Community College
George C. Wallace
Community College at
Dothan
J. F. Drake State Technical
College
Jefferson Davis Community
College
Jefferson State Community
College
Lawson State Community College
Lurleen B. Wallace Community
College
Northeast Alabama Community
College
Northwest-Shoals Community
College
Remington College
Mobile
Shelton State Community College
Snead State Community College
Southern Union State Community
College

### Alaska

Ilisagvik College
Prince William Sound
Community College

### Arizona

Arizona Automotive Institute
Arizona Western College
Central Arizona College
Chandler-Gilbert Community
College
Pecos
Cochise College
Coconino County Community
College
Dine College
Eastern Arizona College
Estrella Mountain Community
College
Gateway Community College
Glendale Community College
Golf Academy of Arizona
Long Technical College
Mesa Community College
Mohave Community College
Northland Pioneer College
Paradise Valley Community
College
Paralegal Institute
Penn Foster College
Phoenix College
Pima Community College
Refrigeration School
Rio Salado College
Scottsdale Community College
South Mountain Community
College
Tohono O'odham Community
College
Universal Technical Institute
Yavapai College

### Arkansas

Arkansas Northeastern College

Arkansas State University
Beebe
Mountain Home
Arkansas State University:
Newport
Crowley's Ridge College
East Arkansas Community
College
Mid-South Community College
National Park Community
College
North Arkansas College
Northwest Arkansas Community
College
Ouachita Technical College
Ozarka College
Phillips Community College of
the University of Arkansas
Pulaski Technical College
Rich Mountain Community
College
South Arkansas Community
College
Southeast Arkansas College
Southern Arkansas University
Tech
University of Arkansas
Community College at Hope
University of Arkansas
Community College at
Morrilton

### California

Allan Hancock College
American River College
Antelope Valley College
Bakersfield College
Barstow Community College
Berkeley City College
Brooks College
Bryan College: Los Angeles
Butte College
Cabrillo College
California School of Culinary Arts
Canada College
CEI College
Maric College: Panorama
City
Cerritos College
Cerro Coso Community College
Chabot College
Chaffey College
Citrus College
City College of San Francisco
Coastline Community College
College of Alameda
College of Marin: Kentfield
College of San Mateo
College of the Canyons
College of the Desert
College of the Redwoods
College of the Sequoias
College of the Siskiyous
Columbia College
Contra Costa College
Copper Mountain College
Cosumnes River College
Crafton Hills College
Cuesta College
Cuyamaca College
Cypress College
De Anza College
Diablo Valley College
East Los Angeles College
El Camino College
El Camino College: Compton
Center
Empire College
Evergreen Valley College
Fashion Institute of Design and
Merchandising
Los Angeles
San Diego
San Francisco
Feather River College
Folsom Lake College
Foothill College

Fremont College
Fresno City College
Fullerton College
Gavilan College
Glendale Community College
Golden West College
Grossmont College
Hartnell College
Heald College
Stockton
High-Tech Institute
Imperial Valley College
Irvine Valley College
Lake Tahoe Community College
Laney College
Las Positas College
Lassen College
Long Beach City College
Los Angeles City College
Los Angeles Harbor College
Los Angeles Mission College
Los Angeles Pierce College
Los Angeles Southwest College
Los Angeles Trade and Technical
College
Los Angeles Valley College
Los Medanos College
Maric College: Salida
Mendocino College
Merced College
Merritt College
MiraCosta College
Mission College
Modesto Junior College
Monterey Peninsula College
Moorpark College
Mount San Antonio College
Mount San Jacinto College
Napa Valley College
Ohlone College
Orange Coast College
Oxnard College
Palo Verde College
Palomar College
Pasadena City College
Porterville College
Reedley College
Rio Hondo College
Riverside Community College
Sacramento City College
Saddleback College
San Bernardino Valley College
San Diego City College
San Diego Mesa College
San Diego Miramar College
San Joaquin Delta College
San Joaquin Valley College
San Jose City College
Santa Ana College
Santa Barbara City College
Santa Monica College
Santa Rosa Junior College
Santiago Canyon College
Shasta College
Sierra College
Skyline College
Solano Community College
Southwestern College
Taft College
Ventura College
Victor Valley College
West Hills College: Coalinga
West Hills College: Lemoore
West Los Angeles College
West Valley College
Westwood College of Technology
Westwood College: Los
Angeles
Yuba Community College District

### Colorado

Aims Community College
Arapahoe Community College
CollegeAmerica
Denver
Colorado Mountain College

Colorado Northwestern
Community College
Colorado School of Healing Arts
Colorado School of Trades
Community College of Aurora
Community College of Denver
Denver Academy of Court
Reporting
Everest College: Aurora
Front Range Community College
Institute of Business & Medical
Careers
IntelliTec College
IntelliTec College: Grand
Junction
Kaplan College: Denver
Lamar Community College
Morgan Community College
Northeastern Junior College
Otero Junior College
Pikes Peak Community College
Pueblo Community College
Red Rocks Community College
Redstone College
Remington College
Colorado Springs
Trinidad State Junior College

### Connecticut

Asnuntuck Community College
Capital Community College
Gateway Community College
Goodwin College
Housatonic Community College
Manchester Community College
Middlesex Community College
Naugatuck Valley Community
College
Northwestern Connecticut
Community College
Norwalk Community College
Quinebaug Valley Community
College
Three Rivers Community College
Tunxis Community College

### Florida

Brevard Community College
Broward Community College
Brown Mackie College: Miami
Central Florida College
Central Florida Community
College
City College
Gainesville
College of Business and
Technology: Flagler
College of Business and
Technology: Kendall
Daytona Beach Community
College
Florida Career College: Hialeah
Florida Career College: Miami
Florida Career College: Pembroke
Pines
Florida Career College: West
Palm Beach
Florida College of Natural Health
Bradenton
Florida Community College at
Jacksonville
Florida Keys Community College
Florida National College
Florida Technical College
Deland
Orlando
Full Sail University
Gulf Coast Community College
Heritage Institute: Jacksonville
Hillsborough Community College
Indian River Community College
Key College
Lake City Community College
Lake-Sumter Community College
Manatee Community College
Miami Dade College

North Florida Community
College
Palm Beach Community College
Pasco-Hernando Community
College
Pensacola Junior College
Polk Community College
Saint Johns River Community
College
Santa Fe Community College
Seminole Community College
South Florida Community
College
Southwest Florida College
Tallahassee Community College
Valencia Community College
Virginia College at Pensacola

### Georgia

Albany Technical College
Athens Technical College
Atlanta Technical College
Augusta Technical College
Brown Mackie College: Atlanta
Central Georgia Technical
College
Chattahoochee Technical College
Coastal Georgia Community
College
Columbus Technical College
DeKalb Technical College
Georgia Military College
Griffin Technical College
Gupton Jones College of Funeral
Service
Gwinnett College
Gwinnett Technical College
Le Cordon Bleu College of
Culinary Arts
Middle Georgia Technical College
North Georgia Technical College
North Metro Technical College
Northwestern Technical College
Savannah Technical College
South Georgia College
Southeastern Technical College
Southwest Georgia Technical
College
West Central Technical College
West Georgia Technical College

### Hawaii

Heald College
Honolulu
University of Hawaii
Hawaii Community College
Honolulu Community
College
Kapiolani Community
College
Kauai Community College
Maui Community College
Windward Community
College

### Idaho

College of Southern Idaho
Eastern Idaho Technical College
North Idaho College
Stevens-Henager College: Boise

### Illinois

Black Hawk College
Black Hawk College: East
Campus
Carl Sandburg College
City Colleges of Chicago
Harold Washington College
Harry S. Truman College
Kennedy-King College
Malcolm X College
Olive-Harvey College
Richard J. Daley College
Wright College
College of DuPage
College of Lake County
College of Office Technology
Cooking & Hospitality Institute of
Chicago

St. Louis Community College
  Florissant Valley
  Meramec
Sanford-Brown College
  Hazelwood
  St. Peters
Southeast Missouri Hospital
  College of Nursing and Health
  Sciences
State Fair Community College
Three Rivers Community College
Vatterott College
Vatterott College: St. Joseph
Wentworth Military Junior
  College

### Montana

Blackfeet Community College
Chief Dull Knife College
Dawson Community College
Fort Belknap College
Fort Peck Community College
Helena College of Technology of
  the University of Montana
Miles Community College
Montana State University
  College of Technology:
    Great Falls
Stone Child College

### Nebraska

Central Community College
Kaplan University: Omaha
Little Priest Tribal College
Metropolitan Community College
Mid-Plains Community College
  Area
Nebraska College of Technical
  Agriculture
Nebraska Indian Community
  College
Northeast Community College
Southeast Community College
Western Nebraska Community
  College

### Nevada

Career College of Northern
  Nevada
College of Southern Nevada
Le Cordon Bleu College of
  Culinary Arts
Truckee Meadows Community
  College
Western Nevada College

### New Hampshire

Great Bay Community College
Lakes Region Community
  College
Manchester Community College
Nashua Community College
River Valley Community College

### New Jersey

Atlantic Cape Community
  College
Bergen Community College
Brookdale Community College
Burlington County College
Camden County College
County College of Morris
Cumberland County College
Essex County College
Gloucester County College
Hudson County Community
  College
Mercer County Community
  College
Ocean County College
Passaic County Community
  College
Raritan Valley Community
  College
Salem Community College
Sussex County Community
  College

Union County College
Warren County Community
  College

### New Mexico

Central New Mexico Community
  College
Clovis Community College
Dona Ana Branch Community
  College of New Mexico State
  University
Eastern New Mexico University:
  Roswell Campus
Mesalands Community College
Navajo Technical College
New Mexico Junior College
New Mexico State University
  Alamogordo
Northern New Mexico College
San Juan College
Santa Fe Community College
Southwestern Indian Polytechnic
  Institute

### New York

Adirondack Community College
American Academy McAllister
  Institute of Funeral Service
Art Institute
  of New York City
Broome Community College
Bryant & Stratton Business
  Institute
    Bryant & Stratton College:
      Buffalo
    Bryant & Stratton College:
      Rochester
    Bryant & Stratton College:
      Southtowns
    Bryant & Stratton College:
      Syracuse
Bryant & Stratton College:
  Syracuse North
Business Informatics Center
Cayuga County Community
  College
City University of New York
  Borough of Manhattan
    Community College
  Bronx Community College
  Hostos Community College
  Kingsborough Community
    College
  LaGuardia Community
    College
  Queensborough Community
    College
Clinton Community College
Columbia-Greene Community
  College
Corning Community College
Dutchess Community College
Elmira Business Institute
Elmira Business Institute: Vestal
Erie Community College
  City Campus
  North Campus
  South Campus
Finger Lakes Community College
Fulton-Montgomery Community
  College
Genesee Community College
Herkimer County Community
  College
Hudson Valley Community
  College
Institute of Design and
  Construction
Island Drafting and Technical
  Institute
Jamestown Community College
Jefferson Community College
Long Island Business Institute
Mildred Elley
Mohawk Valley Community
  College
Monroe Community College

Nassau Community College
Niagara County Community
  College
North Country Community
  College
Olean Business Institute
Onondaga Community College
Orange County Community
  College
Rockland Community College
Schenectady County Community
  College
State University of New York
  College of Technology at
    Delhi
Suffolk County Community
  College
Sullivan County Community
  College
Technical Career Institutes
Tompkins-Cortland Community
  College
Trocaire College
Ulster County Community
  College
Utica School of Commerce
Villa Maria College of Buffalo
Westchester Community College

### North Carolina

Alamance Community College
Asheville-Buncombe Technical
  Community College
Beaufort County Community
  College
Bladen Community College
Blue Ridge Community College
Brunswick Community College
Caldwell Community College and
  Technical Institute
Carteret Community College
Catawba Valley Community
  College
Central Carolina Community
  College
Central Piedmont Community
  College
Cleveland Community College
Coastal Carolina Community
  College
College of the Albemarle
Craven Community College
Davidson County Community
  College
Durham Technical Community
  College
Edgecombe Community College
Fayetteville Technical
  Community College
Forsyth Technical Community
  College
Gaston College
Guilford Technical Community
  College
Halifax Community College
Haywood Community College
Isothermal Community College
James Sprunt Community College
Johnston Community College
Lenoir Community College
Martin Community College
Mayland Community College
McDowell Technical Community
  College
Mitchell Community College
Montgomery Community College
Nash Community College
Pamlico Community College
Piedmont Community College
Pitt Community College
Randolph Community College
Richmond Community College
Roanoke-Chowan Community
  College
Robeson Community College
Rockingham Community College

Rowan-Cabarrus Community
  College
Sampson Community College
Sandhills Community College
South College
South Piedmont Community
  College
Southeastern Community College
Southwestern Community
  College
Stanly Community College
Surry Community College
Tri-County Community College
Vance-Granville Community
  College
Wake Technical Community
  College
Wayne Community College
Western Piedmont Community
  College
Wilkes Community College
Wilson Community College

### North Dakota

Bismarck State College
Fort Berthold Community College
Lake Region State College
Minot State University: Bottineau
  Campus
North Dakota State College of
  Science
Rasmussen College: Bismarck
Sitting Bull College
Turtle Mountain Community
  College
United Tribes Technical College
Williston State College

### Ohio

AEC Southern Ohio College
  Brown Mackie College:
    Findlay
Art Institute of Ohio: Cincinnati
Belmont Technical College
Bowling Green State University:
  Firelands College
Brown Mackie College:
  Cincinnati
Brown Mackie College: North
  Canton
Central Ohio Technical College
Chatfield College
Cincinnati State Technical and
  Community College
Clark State Community College
Cleveland Institute of Electronics
Columbus State Community
  College
Cuyahoga Community College
  Metropolitan Campus
Edison State Community College
ETI Technical College of Niles
Gallipolis Career College
Hocking College
Hondros College
International College of
  Broadcasting
James A. Rhodes State College
Jefferson Community College
Kent State University
  Ashtabula
  East Liverpool
  Salem
  Stark
  Trumbull
  Tuscarawas
Kent State University: Geauga
Lakeland Community College
Lorain County Community
  College
Marion Technical College
Miami University
  Hamilton Campus
  Middletown Campus
National College
  Dayton
North Central State College

Northwest State Community
  College
Ohio Business College
Ohio Business College: Sandusky
Ohio College of Massotherapy
Ohio Institute of Health Careers:
  Columbus
Ohio Institute of Health Careers:
  Elyria
Ohio Institute of Photography and
  Technology
Ohio State University
  Agricultural Technical
    Institute
Owens Community College
  Toledo
Samuel Stephen College
Sinclair Community College
Southeastern Business College:
  New Boston
Southern State Community
  College
Southwestern College of Business
  Southwestern College:
    Tri-County
  Southwestern College: Vine
    Street Campus
Stark State College of Technology
Stautzenberger College
Stautzenberger College:
  Strongsville
Technology Education College
Terra State Community College
Trumbull Business College
University of Akron: Wayne
  College
University of Cincinnati
  Clermont College
Washington State Community
  College
Wright State University: Lake
  Campus
Zane State College

### Oklahoma

Carl Albert State College
Connors State College
Murray State College
Northeastern Oklahoma
  Agricultural and Mechanical
  College
Oklahoma City Community
  College
Oklahoma State University
  Oklahoma City
  Okmulgee
Platt College
  Tulsa
Platt College: Oklahoma City
  Central
Redlands Community College
Seminole State College
Tulsa Community College
Tulsa Welding School
Western Oklahoma State College

### Oregon

Blue Mountain Community
  College
Central Oregon Community
  College
Chemeketa Community College
Clackamas Community College
Clatsop Community College
Heald College: Portland
Klamath Community College
Lane Community College
Linn-Benton Community College
Mt. Hood Community College
Pioneer Pacific College:
  Springfield
Portland Community College
Rogue Community College
Southwestern Oregon Community
  College

Treasure Valley Community
College
Umpqua Community College

## Pennsylvania

Berean Institute
Bucks County Community
College
Butler County Community
College
Cambria-Rowe Business College:
Indiana
Career Training Academy
Career Training Academy:
Monroeville
Career Training Academy:
Pittsburgh
CHI Institute: Broomall
CHI Institute: Franklin Mills
Commonwealth Technical
Institute
Community College of Allegheny
County
Community College of Beaver
County
Community College of
Philadelphia
Consolidated School of Business
Lancaster
York
Dean Institute of Technology
Douglas Education Center
DuBois Business College
DuBois Business College
Huntingdon
Oil City
Erie Business Center
Erie Business Center South
Erie Institute of Technology
Harrisburg Area Community
College
JNA Institute of Culinary Arts
Johnson College
Kaplan Career Institute:
Harrisburg
Lackawanna College
Lansdale School of Business
Lehigh Carbon Community
College
Lincoln Technical Institute:
Allentown
Lincoln Technical Institute:
Northeast Philadelphia
Lincoln Technical Institute:
Philadelphia
Luzerne County Community
College
Montgomery County Community
College
Newport Business Institute:
Lower Burrell
Newport Business Institute:
Williamsport
Northampton Community College
Orleans Technical Institute -
Center City Campus
Pace Institute
Penn Commercial Business and
Technical School
Pennsylvania Highlands
Community College
Pennsylvania Institute of
Technology
Pittsburgh Institute of Aeronautics
Pittsburgh Institute of Mortuary
Science
Pittsburgh Technical Institute
Reading Area Community
College
South Hills School of Business &
Technology
South Hills School of Business &
Technology
Tri-State Business Institute

Triangle Tech
DuBois
Erie
Greensburg
Pittsburgh
West Virginia Career Institute
Westmoreland County
Community College
YTI Career Institute: Lancaster
YTI Career Institute: York

## Puerto Rico

Columbia College
Columbia Centro
Universitario: Yauco
Huertas Junior College
Humacao Community College
ICPR Junior College
National College of Business and
Technology: Arecibo
National College of Business and
Technology: Bayamon
National College of Business and
Technology: Rio Grande
Ponce Paramedical College
Universal Technology College of
Puerto Rico

## Rhode Island

Community College of Rhode
Island

## South Carolina

Aiken Technical College
Central Carolina Technical
College
Denmark Technical College
Florence-Darlington Technical
College
Forrest Junior College
Greenville Technical College
Horry-Georgetown Technical
College
Midlands Technical College
Northeastern Technical College
Orangeburg-Calhoun Technical
College
Piedmont Technical College
Spartanburg Community College
Technical College of the
Lowcountry
Tri-County Technical College
Trident Technical College
University of South Carolina
Lancaster
Williamsburg Technical College
York Technical College

## South Dakota

Kilian Community College
Mitchell Technical Institute
Sisseton Wahpeton College
Southeast Technical Institute
Western Dakota Technical
Institute

## Tennessee

Chattanooga State Technical
Community College
Cleveland State Community
College
Columbia State Community
College
Draughons Junior College:
Clarksville
Draughons Junior College:
Murfreesboro
Draughons Junior College:
Nashville
Dyersburg State Community
College
Fountainhead College of
Technology
Huntington College of Health
Sciences
Jackson State Community College

Miller-Motte Technical College:
Clarksville
Motlow State Community College
Nashville State Community
College
National College
Knoxville
Nashville
National College of Business &
Technology
National College: Bristol
Northeast State Technical
Community College
Pellissippi State Technical
Community College
Roane State Community College
Southwest Tennessee Community
College
Vatterott College: Memphis
Volunteer State Community
College
Walters State Community College

## Texas

Alvin Community College
Angelina College
Austin Community College
Blinn College
Brookhaven College
Cedar Valley College
Central Texas College
Cisco Junior College
Clarendon College
Coastal Bend College
College of the Mainland
Collin County Community
College District
Court Reporting Institute of
Houston
Dallas Institute of Funeral Service
Del Mar College
Eastfield College
El Centro College
El Paso Community College
Everest College: Arlington
Frank Phillips College
Galveston College
Grayson County College
Hill College
Houston Community College
System
Howard College
Jacksonville College
Kilgore College
Lamar Institute of Technology
Lamar State College at Orange
Lamar State College at Port
Arthur
Laredo Community College
Lee College
McLennan Community College
Midland College
Mountain View College
Navarro College
North Central Texas College
North Harris Montgomery
Community College
North Lake College
Northeast Texas Community
College
Northwest Vista College
Odessa College
Palo Alto College
Panola College
Paris Junior College
Ranger College
Remington College
Houston
Richland College
St. Philip's College
San Antonio College
San Jacinto College
South Plains College
South Texas College
Southwest Institute of Technology
Tarrant County College

Temple College
Texarkana College
Texas Southmost College
Texas State Technical College
Harlingen
Sweetwater
Waco
Texas State Technical College:
Marshall
Trinity Valley Community
College
Tyler Junior College
Vernon College
Victoria College
Weatherford College
Western Technical College
Western Texas College
Wharton County Junior College

## Utah

Careers Unlimited
College of Eastern Utah
LDS Business College
Salt Lake Community College
Snow College

## Vermont

Community College of Vermont

## Virginia

Beta Tech: Richmond South
Beta Tech: Richmond West
Blue Ridge Community College
Bryant & Stratton College
Richmond
Bryant & Stratton College:
Virginia Beach
Central Virginia Community
College
Dabney S. Lancaster Community
College
Danville Community College
Eastern Shore Community
College
Germanna Community College
J. Sargeant Reynolds Community
College
John Tyler Community College
Lord Fairfax Community College
Miller-Motte Technical College:
Lynchburg
Mountain Empire Community
College
National College
Bluefield
Charlottesville
Danville
Harrisonburg
Lynchburg
Martinsville
New River Community College
Northern Virginia Community
College
Patrick Henry Community
College
Paul D. Camp Community
College
Piedmont Virginia Community
College
Rappahannock Community
College
Southside Virginia Community
College
Southwest Virginia Community
College
Thomas Nelson Community
College
Tidewater Community College
Tidewater Tech
Virginia Beach
Tidewater Tech: Chesapeake
Tidewater Tech: Newport News
Tidewater Tech: Norfolk
Virginia Highlands Community
College
Virginia Western Community
College

Wytheville Community College

## Washington

Bates Technical College
Bellevue Community College
Bellingham Technical College
Big Bend Community College
Cascadia Community College
Centralia College
Clark College
Clover Park Technical College
Columbia Basin College
Edmonds Community College
Everett Community College
Grays Harbor College
Green River Community College
Highline Community College
Lake Washington Technical
College
Lower Columbia College
North Seattle Community College
Olympic College
Peninsula College
Renton Technical College
South Puget Sound Community
College
Spokane Community College
Spokane Falls Community
College
Tacoma Community College
Walla Walla Community College
Wenatchee Valley College
Whatcom Community College
Yakima Valley Community
College

## West Virginia

Blue Ridge Community and
Technical College
Eastern West Virginia Community
and Technical College
New River Community and
Technical College
Potomac State College of West
Virginia University
Southern West Virginia
Community and Technical
College
West Virginia Business College
West Virginia Business College
West Virginia Junior College:
Bridgeport
West Virginia State Community
and Technical College

## Wisconsin

Blackhawk Technical College
Chippewa Valley Technical
College
College of Menominee Nation
Fox Valley Technical College
Gateway Technical College
Lac Courte Oreilles Ojibwa
Community College
Lakeshore Technical College
Madison Area Technical College
Madison Media Institute
Mid-State Technical College
Milwaukee Area Technical
College
Moraine Park Technical College
Nicolet Area Technical College
Northcentral Technical College
Northeast Wisconsin Technical
College
University of Wisconsin
Washington County
Waukesha County Technical
College
Western Technical College
Wisconsin Indianhead Technical
College

Tables and Indexes

## Wyoming

Casper College
Central Wyoming College
Eastern Wyoming College
Laramie County Community
  College
Northwest College
Sheridan College
Western Wyoming Community
  College
WyoTech: Laramie

## American Samoa

American Samoa Community
  College

## Guam

Guam Community College

## Palau

Palau Community College

## Bermuda

Bermuda College

# Admission/ placement policies

*Four-year*

### Alabama

Amridge University
Andrew Jackson University
Athens State University
Auburn University at
    Montgomery
Birmingham-Southern College
Columbia Southern University
Faulkner University
Heritage Christian University
Jacksonville State University
Judson College
Oakwood College
Samford University
South University
Stillman College
Troy University
United States Sports Academy
University of Alabama
University of Mobile
University of North Alabama
University of West Alabama
Virginia College at Huntsville

### Alaska

University of Alaska
    Southeast

### Arizona

Arizona Institute of Business and
    Technology
        International Institute of the
        Americas: Mesa
Arizona State University
Arizona State University West
Art Center Design College
Brown Mackie College: Tucson
DeVry University
    Phoenix
Embry-Riddle Aeronautical
    University: Prescott Campus
Grand Canyon University
International Import-Export
    Institute
International Institute of the
    Americas
        Phoenix
        Tucson
Northcentral University
Northern Arizona University
University of Advancing
    Technology
University of Phoenix
Western International University

### Arkansas

Arkansas Baptist College
Arkansas Tech University
Harding University
Henderson State University
John Brown University
Lyon College
Ouachita Baptist University
Philander Smith College

University of Arkansas
    Fort Smith
    Little Rock
    Monticello
    Pine Bluff
University of Central Arkansas
University of the Ozarks
Williams Baptist College

### California

Academy of Art University
Alliant International University
Antioch Southern California
        Antioch University Los
        Angeles
        Antioch University Santa
        Barbara
Art Center College of Design
Art Institute
    of California: Orange
        County
    of California: San Diego
Art Institute of California: San
    Francisco
Bethesda Christian University
Brooks Institute
California Baptist University
California Coast University
California College of the Arts
California College San Diego
California Design College
California Institute of Integral
    Studies
California Maritime Academy
California National University for
    Advanced Studies
California State University
    Bakersfield
    Dominguez Hills
    San Bernardino
Coleman College
Concordia University
Design Institute of San Diego
DeVry University
    Fremont
    Long Beach
    Pomona
    Sherman Oaks
Dominican School of Philosophy
    and Theology
Dominican University of
    California
Golden Gate University
Hope International University
Humphreys College
Interior Designers Institute
John F. Kennedy University
The King's College and Seminary
LA College International
La Sierra University
Laguna College of Art and Design
Lincoln University
Loma Linda University
Loyola Marymount University
The Master's College
Menlo College
Mt. Sierra College
National Hispanic University
National University
NewSchool of Architecture &
    Design
Notre Dame de Namur University
Otis College of Art and Design
Pacific States University
Pacific Union College
Platt College
    Ontario
    San Diego
Samuel Merritt College
San Francisco Art Institute
Simpson University
Southern California Institute of
    Technology
Thomas Aquinas College
University of La Verne
University of San Francisco

Vanguard University of Southern
    California
West Coast University
Westmont College
Westwood College: South Bay
Whittier College
Woodbury University
World Mission University

### Colorado

Adams State College
American Sentinel University
Art Institute
    of Colorado
Aspen University
CollegeAmerica
    Fort Collins
Colorado Technical University
DeVry University
    Westminster
Johnson & Wales University:
    Denver
Jones International University
Mesa State College
Naropa University
National American University
    Denver
Nazarene Bible College
Platt College
    Aurora
Rocky Mountain College of Art &
    Design
Teikyo Loretto Heights University
University of Northern Colorado
Westwood College of Technology
    Westwood College: Denver
    South

### Connecticut

Albertus Magnus College
Briarwood College
Charter Oak State College
Eastern Connecticut State
    University
Holy Apostles College and
    Seminary
Lyme Academy College of Fine
    Arts
Mitchell College
Paier College of Art
Post University
Sacred Heart University
St. Joseph College
University of Bridgeport
University of Hartford
University of New Haven
Western Connecticut State
    University

### Delaware

Delaware State University
Goldey-Beacom College
Wesley College
Wilmington University

### District of Columbia

Corcoran College of Art and
    Design
Gallaudet University
Potomac College
Southeastern University

### Florida

Angley College
Art Institute of Fort Lauderdale
Ave Maria University
Barry University
Bethune-Cookman University
Carlos Albizu University
Chipola Junior College
City College
    Miami
City College: Fort Lauderdale
DeVry University
    Miramar
    Orlando
Eckerd College
Edward Waters College

Embry-Riddle Aeronautical
    University
Embry-Riddle Aeronautical
    University: Worldwide Campus
Everest University: Brandon
Everest University: Lakeland
Everest University: Pompano
    Beach
Everest University: South
    Orlando
Everest University: Tampa
Florida Institute of Technology
Florida International University
Florida Memorial University
Hodges University
International Academy of Design
    and Technology: Orlando
International Academy of Design
    and Technology: Tampa
Jacksonville University
Johnson & Wales University:
    North Miami
Jones College
Jones College: Miami
Keiser University
Lynn University
Miami International University of
    Art and Design
Northwood University
    Florida
Nova Southeastern University
Okaloosa-Walton College
Palm Beach Atlantic University
Rasmussen College: Ocala
Remington College: Largo
Remington College: Tampa
Ringling College of Art and
    Design
St. Petersburg College
Saint Thomas University
Schiller International University
South University: West Palm
    Beach Campus
Stetson University
Universidad FLET
Warner Southern College

### Georgia

American InterContinental
    University
Art Institute
    of Atlanta
Augusta State University
Bauder College
Beulah Heights University
Brenau University
Brewton-Parker College
Carver Bible College
Clayton State University
Covenant College
Dalton State College
DeVry University
    Alpharetta
    Decatur
Fort Valley State University
Herzing College
LaGrange College
Oglethorpe University
Reinhardt College
Savannah College of Art and
    Design
South University
Thomas University

### Hawaii

Chaminade University of
    Honolulu
Hawaii Pacific University

### Idaho

Idaho State University
Lewis-Clark State College

### Illinois

Augustana College
Benedictine University
Blackburn College

Blessing-Rieman College of
    Nursing
Chicago State University
Columbia College Chicago
Concordia University
DePaul University
DeVry University
    Addison
    Chicago
    Tinley Park
DeVry University: Online
Dominican University
East-West University
Eastern Illinois University
Elmhurst College
Governors State University
Illinois Institute of Art: Chicago
Illinois Institute of Art:
    Schaumburg
Illinois Wesleyan University
International Academy of Design
    and Technology: Chicago
Judson University
Lake Forest College
Lewis University
Lexington College
Lincoln Christian College and
    Seminary
Loyola University Chicago
MacMurray College
McKendree University
Midstate College
Millikin University
Monmouth College
National-Louis University
North Central College
Quincy University
Robert Morris College: Chicago
St. Xavier University
Shimer College
Southern Illinois University
    Carbondale
Trinity Christian College
Trinity International University
University of Illinois
    Springfield
VanderCook College of Music
Western Illinois University
Western Illinois University: Quad
    Cities
Westwood College of Technology
    Westwood College: O'Hare
    Airport
    Westwood College: River
    Oaks
Westwood College: DuPage

### Indiana

Calumet College of St. Joseph
DeVry University: Indianapolis
Franklin College
Indiana Institute of Technology
Indiana University
    Bloomington
    East
    Kokomo
    Northwest
    South Bend
    Southeast
International Business College
Manchester College
Martin University
Purdue University
Purdue University
    Calumet
    North Central
Saint Joseph's College
Saint Mary's College
Taylor University
Taylor University Fort Wayne
University of Indianapolis
University of St. Francis
Wabash College

### Iowa

Ashford University
Briar Cliff University

Buena Vista University
Central College
Clarke College
Drake University
Emmaus Bible College
Graceland University
Hamilton Technical College
Iowa Wesleyan College
Kaplan University
Cedar Falls
Cedar Rapids
Davenport
Des Moines
Mason City
Loras College
Luther College
Maharishi University of
Management
Morningside College
Northwestern College
St. Ambrose University
Simpson College
University of Dubuque
Upper Iowa University
Vennard College
Waldorf College
Wartburg College
William Penn University

## Kansas

Baker University
Benedictine College
Bethel College
Emporia State University
Fort Hays State University
Friends University
Kansas State University
Kansas Wesleyan University
McPherson College
Newman University
Ottawa University
Pittsburg State University
Sterling College
Tabor College
University of Kansas Medical
Center
University of St. Mary
Wichita State University

## Kentucky

Alice Lloyd College
Asbury College
Beckfield College
Bellarmine University
Brescia University
Campbellsville University
Kentucky Christian University
Kentucky Mountain Bible College
Kentucky State University
Kentucky Wesleyan College
Lindsey Wilson College
Mid-Continent University
Midway College
Morehead State University
St. Catharine College
Sullivan University
Union College

## Louisiana

Louisiana State University
Alexandria
Louisiana Tech University
Loyola University New Orleans
McNeese State University
Nicholls State University
St. Joseph Seminary College
Southwest University
University of Louisiana at
Lafayette
University of Louisiana at
Monroe

## Maine

Maine College of Art
New England School of
Communications
St. Joseph's College
Thomas College

Unity College
University of Maine
University of Maine
Farmington
Fort Kent
University of Southern Maine

## Maryland

Baltimore International College
Bowie State University
Capitol College
College of Notre Dame of
Maryland
DeVry University: Bethesda
Frostburg State University
Griggs University
Hood College
Morgan State University
Mount St. Mary's University
National Labor College
Ner Israel Rabbinical College
St. John's College
Sojourner-Douglass College
University of Maryland
University College
Villa Julie College

## Massachusetts

American International College
Anna Maria College
Bay Path College
Becker College
Bridgewater State College
Cambridge College
Eastern Nazarene College
Elms College
Fitchburg State College
Gordon College
Lasell College
Lesley University
Massachusetts College of Liberal
Arts
Massachusetts Maritime Academy
Mount Ida College
New England Conservatory of
Music
New England Institute of Art
Newbury College
Nichols College
Pine Manor College
Regis College
Rhodec International
Salem State College
School of the Museum of Fine
Arts
University of Massachusetts
Dartmouth
Lowell
Wentworth Institute of
Technology
Western New England College
Wheelock College

## Michigan

Alma College
Andrews University
Aquinas College
Baker College
of Auburn Hills
of Cadillac
of Clinton Township
of Flint
of Jackson
of Muskegon
of Owosso
of Port Huron
Baker College of Allen Park
Central Michigan University
Concordia University
Cornerstone University
Davenport University
Eastern Michigan University
Great Lakes Christian College
Hope College
International Academy of Design
and Technology: Detroit

Kendall College of Art and
Design of Ferris State
University
Kettering University
Kuyper College
Lake Superior State University
Lawrence Technological
University
Madonna University
Michigan Jewish Institute
Michigan State University
Michigan Technological
University
Michigan Theological Seminary
Northern Michigan University
Northwood University: Michigan
Oakland University
Olivet College
Rochester College
Saginaw Valley State University
Siena Heights University
University of Michigan
Dearborn
Flint
Walsh College of Accountancy
and Business Administration
Western Michigan University

## Minnesota

Academy College
Art Institutes International
Minnesota
Bemidji State University
Bethel University
Brown College
College of St. Benedict
College of St. Catherine
College of St. Scholastica
College of Visual Arts
Concordia College: Moorhead
DeVry University
Edina
Globe University
Hamline University
Minnesota School of Business: St.
Cloud
Minnesota School of Business:
Shakopee
Northwestern Health Sciences
University
Oak Hills Christian College
Pillsbury Baptist Bible College
Rasmussen College
Eagan
St. John's University
St. Olaf College
University of Minnesota
Crookston
Twin Cities
University of St. Thomas
Walden University

## Mississippi

Alcorn State University
Belhaven College
Blue Mountain College
Jackson State University
Magnolia Bible College
Millsaps College
Mississippi College
Mississippi State University
Mississippi University for Women
Rust College
Tougaloo College
University of Southern
Mississippi
William Carey University

## Missouri

Avila University
Baptist Bible College
Central Bible College
Central Methodist University
Columbia College
Culver-Stockton College
DeVry University
Kansas City
Global University

Goldfarb School of Nursing at
Barnes-Jewish College
Grantham University
Harris-Stowe State University
Kansas City Art Institute
Lindenwood University
Missouri Baptist University
Missouri Southern State
University
Missouri Valley College
Northwest Missouri State
University
Research College of Nursing
Rockhurst University
Southwest Baptist University
Stephens College
University of Central Missouri
University of Missouri
Columbia
Kansas City
Westminster College
William Woods University

## Montana

Montana State University
Billings
Bozeman
Northern
Montana Tech of the University of
Montana
University of Montana: Missoula
University of Montana: Western

## Nebraska

Bellevue University
Chadron State College
Clarkson College
College of Saint Mary
Creative Center
Dana College
Doane College
Grace University
Hastings College
Midland Lutheran College
Peru State College
Union College
University of Nebraska
Kearney

## Nevada

Art Institute
of Las Vegas
DeVry University: Henderson
International Academy of Design
and Technology: Henderson
Nevada State College
Sierra Nevada College
University of Nevada
Reno

## New Hampshire

Chester College of New England
Colby-Sawyer College
Daniel Webster College
Franklin Pierce University
Granite State College
Hesser College
New England College
Rivier College
St. Anselm College
Southern New Hampshire
University
Thomas More College of Liberal
Arts

## New Jersey

Berkeley College
Caldwell College
Centenary College
DeVry University: North
Brunswick
Fairleigh Dickinson University
College at Florham
Metropolitan Campus
Felician College
Rider University
Rutgers, The State University of
New Jersey
Newark Regional Campus

Saint Peter's College
Seton Hall University
Thomas Edison State College
University of Medicine and
Dentistry of New Jersey
School of Health Related
Professions

## New Mexico

Art Center Design College
College of Santa Fe
College of the Southwest
Eastern New Mexico University
International Institute of the
Americas: Albuquerque
National American University:
Rio Rancho
New Mexico Highlands
University
New Mexico State University
St. John's College
Western New Mexico University

## New York

Adelphi University
Alfred University
Berkeley College
Berkeley College of New York
City
Boricua College
Briarcliffe College
Cazenovia College
City University of New York
City College
College of Staten Island
Medgar Evers College
New York City College of
Technology
Queens College
York College
College of Mount St. Vincent
College of New Rochelle
Culinary Institute of America
D'Youville College
Daemen College
Davis College
DeVry Institute of Technology
New York
Dominican College of Blauvelt
Dowling College
Excelsior College
Five Towns College
Globe Institute of Technology
Hofstra University
Houghton College
Keuka College
Laboratory Institute of
Merchandising
Le Moyne College
Long Island University
Brooklyn Campus
C. W. Post Campus
Marymount Manhattan College
Medaille College
Mercy College
Metropolitan College of New
York
Molloy College
Monroe College
Mount St. Mary College
New York Institute of Technology
New York School of Interior
Design
Nyack College
Paul Smith's College
Polytechnic University
Rochester Institute of Technology
Russell Sage College
Sage College of Albany
St. Francis College
St. John Fisher College
St. John's University
St. Joseph's College
St. Joseph's College: Suffolk
Campus
St. Thomas Aquinas College
School of Visual Arts

Northwestern Connecticut
Community College
Norwalk Community College
Quinebaug Valley Community
College
Three Rivers Community College
Tunxis Community College

## Florida

Broward Community College
Central Florida College
City College: Casselberry
College of Business and
Technology: Flagler
Daytona Beach Community
College
Florida Career College: Hialeah
Florida Career College: Miami
Florida Career College: Pembroke
Pines
Florida Career College: West
Palm Beach
Florida College of Natural Health
Bradenton
Florida Community College at
Jacksonville
Florida Keys Community College
Florida National College
Florida Technical College
Deland
Orlando
Full Sail University
Gulf Coast Community College
Heritage Institute: Jacksonville
Hillsborough Community College
Indian River Community College
Key College
Lake City Community College
Lake-Sumter Community College
Manatee Community College
Miami Dade College
North Florida Community
College
Pasco-Hernando Community
College
Pensacola Junior College
Polk Community College
Professional Golfers Career
College: Orlando
Saint Johns River Community
College
Santa Fe Community College
South Florida Community
College
Southwest Florida College
Ultrasound Diagnostic School
Sanford-Brown Institute:
Jacksonville

## Georgia

Abraham Baldwin Agricultural
College
Athens Technical College
Atlanta Metropolitan College
Augusta Technical College
Chattahoochee Technical College
Coastal Georgia Community
College
Darton College
East Georgia College
Georgia Highlands College
Gordon College
Griffin Technical College
Gupton Jones College of Funeral
Service
Gwinnett College
Le Cordon Bleu College of
Culinary Arts
Middle Georgia Technical College
North Georgia Technical College
North Metro Technical College
Northwestern Technical College
Oxford College of Emory
University
Savannah River College
Savannah Technical College
South Georgia College

Southwest Georgia Technical
College
Waycross College
West Central Technical College
West Georgia Technical College
Young Harris College

## Hawaii

Heald College
Honolulu
Remington College
Honolulu
University of Hawaii
Honolulu Community
College
Kauai Community College
Maui Community College
Windward Community
College

## Idaho

College of Southern Idaho
North Idaho College
Stevens-Henager College: Boise

## Illinois

Black Hawk College
Black Hawk College: East
Campus
Carl Sandburg College
City Colleges of Chicago
Harold Washington College
Harry S. Truman College
Kennedy-King College
Malcolm X College
Olive-Harvey College
Richard J. Daley College
Wright College
College of DuPage
College of Lake County
College of Office Technology
Cooking & Hospitality Institute of
Chicago
Danville Area Community
College
Elgin Community College
Fox College
Harper College
Heartland Community College
Highland Community College
Illinois Central College
Illinois Eastern Community
Colleges
Frontier Community College
Lincoln Trail College
Olney Central College
Wabash Valley College
Illinois Valley Community
College
John A. Logan College
John Wood Community College
Joliet Junior College
Kankakee Community College
Kaskaskia College
Kishwaukee College
Lake Land College
Lewis and Clark Community
College
Lincoln Land Community College
MacCormac College
McHenry County College
Moraine Valley Community
College
Morrison Institute of Technology
Morton College
Northwestern Business College
Oakton Community College
Parkland College
Prairie State College
Rend Lake College
Richland Community College
Rock Valley College
Rockford Business College
Sauk Valley Community College
Shawnee Community College
South Suburban College of Cook
County
Southeastern Illinois College

Spoon River College
Springfield College in Illinois
Triton College
Vatterott College: Quincy
Waubonsee Community College

## Indiana

Ancilla College
Brown Mackie College: Fort
Wayne
Brown Mackie College: South
Bend
Indiana Business College
Anderson
Columbus
Evansville
Fort Wayne
Indianapolis
Lafayette
Marion
Medical
Muncie
Terre Haute
Ivy Tech Community College:
Richmond
Ivy Tech State College
Ivy Tech Community
College: Bloomington
Ivy Tech Community
College: Central Indiana
Ivy Tech Community
College: Columbus
Ivy Tech Community
College: East Central
Ivy Tech Community
College: Kokomo
Ivy Tech Community
College: Lafayette
Ivy Tech Community
College: North Central
Ivy Tech Community
College: Northeast
Ivy Tech Community
College: Northwest
Ivy Tech Community
College: South Central
Ivy Tech Community
College: Southeast
Ivy Tech Community
College: Southwest
Ivy Tech Community
College: Wabash Valley
Kaplan College: Hammond
Kaplan College: Indianapolis
Kaplan College: Merrillville
National College: Indianapolis
Vincennes University

## Iowa

Clinton Community College
Des Moines Area Community
College
Ellsworth Community College
Hawkeye Community College
Indian Hills Community College
Iowa Central Community College
Iowa Lakes Community College
Iowa Western Community
College
Kirkwood Community College
Marshalltown Community
College
Muscatine Community College
North Iowa Area Community
College
Northeast Iowa Community
College
Scott Community College
Southeastern Community College
North Campus
Southwestern Community
College
Western Iowa Tech Community
College

## Kansas

Allen County Community College

Barton County Community
College
Brown Mackie College
Salina
Butler County Community
College
Cloud County Community
College
Coffeyville Community College
Colby Community College
Cowley County Community
College
Dodge City Community College
Donnelly College
Fort Scott Community College
Garden City Community College
Hesston College
Highland Community College
Hutchinson Community College
Independence Community
College
Johnson County Community
College
Kansas City Kansas Community
College
Labette Community College
Manhattan Area Technical
College
Neosho County Community
College
North Central Kansas Technical
College
Pratt Community College
Seward County Community
College

## Kentucky

Ashland Community and
Technical College
Bluegrass Community and
Technical College
Brown Mackie College:
Louisville
Daymar College
Louisville
Draughons Junior College
Hazard Community College
Hopkinsville Community College
Jefferson Community and
Technical College
Louisville Technical Institute
Maysville Community and
Technical College
National College
Danville
Florence
Lexington
Louisville
Pikeville
Richmond
Paducah Technical College
Somerset Community College
Southeast Kentucky Community
and Technical College
Southern Ohio College
Brown Mackie College:
North Kentucky
Southwestern College: Florence
Spencerian College
Spencerian College: Lexington
West Kentucky Community and
Technical College

## Louisiana

Baton Rouge Community College
Delgado Community College
Delta School of Business &
Technology
ITI Technical College
Nunez Community College
Remington College
Baton Rouge
Lafayette
River Parishes Community
College
South Louisiana Community
College

Southern University
Shreveport

## Maine

Andover College
Beal College
Central Maine Community
College
Eastern Maine Community
College
Kennebec Valley Community
College
Northern Maine Community
College
Southern Maine Community
College
York County Community College

## Maryland

Allegany College of Maryland
Anne Arundel Community
College
Baltimore City Community
College
Carroll Community College
Cecil College
Chesapeake College
College of Southern Maryland
Community College of Baltimore
County
Frederick Community College
Garrett College
Hagerstown Community College
Harford Community College
Howard Community College
Kaplan College: Hagerstown
Montgomery College
Prince George's Community
College
TESST College of Technology
Baltimore
TESST College of Technology:
Towson
Wor-Wic Community College

## Massachusetts

Bay State College
Benjamin Franklin Institute of
Technology
Berkshire Community College
Bristol Community College
Cape Cod Community College
Caritas Laboure College
Dean College
Fisher College
Greenfield Community College
Holyoke Community College
Marian Court College
Massachusetts Bay Community
College
Middlesex Community College
Mount Wachusett Community
College
New England College of Finance
North Shore Community College
Northern Essex Community
College
Quincy College
Quinsigamond Community
College
Roxbury Community College
Springfield Technical Community
College
Urban College of Boston

## Michigan

Alpena Community College
Delta College
Glen Oaks Community College
Gogebic Community College
Henry Ford Community College
Jackson Community College
Kalamazoo Valley Community
College
Kellogg Community College
Kirtland Community College
Lake Michigan College
Lansing Community College

Bryant & Stratton College:
  Cleveland
Central Ohio Technical College
Chatfield College
Cincinnati State Technical and
  Community College
Clark State Community College
Cleveland Institute of Electronics
Columbus State Community
  College
Cuyahoga Community College
  Metropolitan Campus
Edison State Community College
ETI Technical College of Niles
Gallipolis Career College
Good Samaritan College of
  Nursing and Health Science
Hocking College
Hondros College
International College of
  Broadcasting
James A. Rhodes State College
Jefferson Community College
Kent State University
  Ashtabula
  East Liverpool
  Salem
  Stark
  Trumbull
  Tuscarawas
Kent State University: Geauga
Lakeland Community College
Lorain County Community
  College
Marion Technical College
Miami University
  Hamilton Campus
  Middletown Campus
National College
  Dayton
National College: Cincinnati
National College: Stow
National College: Youngstown
North Central State College
Northwest State Community
  College
Ohio Business College
Ohio Business College: Sandusky
Ohio College of Massotherapy
Ohio Institute of Health Careers:
  Columbus
Ohio Institute of Health Careers:
  Elyria
Ohio Institute of Photography and
  Technology
Ohio Valley College of
  Technology
Owens Community College
  Toledo
Remington College
  Cleveland
Remington College: Cleveland
  West
Rosedale Bible College
School of Advertising Art
Sinclair Community College
Southeastern Business College:
  New Boston
Southern State Community
  College
Southwestern College of Business
  Southwestern College:
    Tri-County
  Southwestern College: Vine
    Street Campus
Stark State College of Technology
Stautzenberger College
Stautzenberger College:
  Strongsville
Technology Education College
Terra State Community College
Trumbull Business College
University of Akron: Wayne
  College
University of Cincinnati
  Clermont College
University of Northwestern Ohio

Virginia Marti College of Art and
  Design
Washington State Community
  College
Wright State University: Lake
  Campus
Zane State College

## Oklahoma

Carl Albert State College
Connors State College
Murray State College
Northeastern Oklahoma
  Agricultural and Mechanical
  College
Oklahoma City Community
  College
Oklahoma State University
  Oklahoma City
  Okmulgee
Platt College
  Tulsa
Platt College: Oklahoma City
  Central
Redlands Community College
Seminole State College
Tulsa Community College
Tulsa Welding School
Western Oklahoma State College

## Oregon

Blue Mountain Community
  College
Central Oregon Community
  College
Chemeketa Community College
Clackamas Community College
Clatsop Community College
Heald College: Portland
Klamath Community College
Lane Community College
Mt. Hood Community College
Pioneer Pacific College:
  Springfield
Portland Community College
Rogue Community College
Southwestern Oregon Community
  College
Treasure Valley Community
  College
Umpqua Community College

## Pennsylvania

Antonelli Institute of Art and
  Photography
Art Institute of York
Business Institute of Pennsylvania
Butler County Community
  College
Cambria-Rowe Business College
Cambria-Rowe Business College:
  Indiana
Career Training Academy
Career Training Academy:
  Monroeville
Career Training Academy:
  Pittsburgh
CHI Institute: Broomall
CHI Institute: Franklin Mills
Commonwealth Technical
  Institute
Community College of Allegheny
  County
Community College of Beaver
  County
Community College of
  Philadelphia
Consolidated School of Business
  Lancaster
  York
Dean Institute of Technology
DuBois Business College
DuBois Business College
  Huntingdon
  Oil City
Erie Business Center
Erie Business Center South
Erie Institute of Technology

Harcum College
Harrisburg Area Community
  College
Hussian School of Art
JNA Institute of Culinary Arts
Kaplan Career Institute:
  Harrisburg
Kaplan Career Institute:
  Pittsburgh
Keystone Technical Institute
Lackawanna College
Lansdale School of Business
Laurel Business Institute
Lehigh Carbon Community
  College
Lincoln Technical Institute:
  Allentown
Lincoln Technical Institute:
  Northeast Philadelphia
Lincoln Technical Institute:
  Philadelphia
Luzerne County Community
  College
Montgomery County Community
  College
New Castle School of Trades
Newport Business Institute:
  Lower Burrell
Newport Business Institute:
  Williamsport
Northampton Community College
Oakbridge Academy of Arts
Orleans Technical Institute -
  Center City Campus
Pace Institute
Penn Commercial Business and
  Technical School
Pennco Tech
Pennsylvania Culinary Institute
Pennsylvania Highlands
  Community College
Pennsylvania Institute of
  Technology
Pittsburgh Institute of Aeronautics
Pittsburgh Institute of Mortuary
  Science
Pittsburgh Technical Institute
PJA School
South Hills School of Business &
  Technology
South Hills School of Business &
  Technology
Tri-State Business Institute
Triangle Tech
  DuBois
  Erie
  Greensburg
  Pittsburgh
Triangle Tech: Bethlehem
Triangle Tech: Sunbury
University of Pittsburgh
  Titusville
Vet Tech Institute
West Virginia Career Institute
Westmoreland County
  Community College
YTI Career Institute: Lancaster
YTI Career Institute: York

## Puerto Rico

Huertas Junior College
Humacao Community College
National College of Business and
  Technology: Arecibo
National College of Business and
  Technology: Bayamon
National College of Business and
  Technology: Rio Grande
Ponce Paramedical College
Ramirez College of Business and
  Technology
Universal Technology College of
  Puerto Rico

## Rhode Island

Community College of Rhode
  Island

## South Carolina

Aiken Technical College
Central Carolina Technical
  College
Denmark Technical College
Forrest Junior College
Greenville Technical College
Horry-Georgetown Technical
  College
Midlands Technical College
Miller-Motte Technical College
Orangeburg-Calhoun Technical
  College
Piedmont Technical College
Spartanburg Community College
Spartanburg Methodist College
Technical College of the
  Lowcountry
Tri-County Technical College
University of South Carolina
  Lancaster
  Salkehatchie Regional
    Campus
  Sumter
  Union
Williamsburg Technical College

## South Dakota

Kilian Community College
Lake Area Technical Institute
Mitchell Technical Institute
Southeast Technical Institute

## Tennessee

Chattanooga State Technical
  Community College
Cleveland State Community
  College
Draughons Junior College:
  Clarksville
Draughons Junior College:
  Murfreesboro
Draughons Junior College:
  Nashville
Dyersburg State Community
  College
Fountainhead College of
  Technology
Hiwassee College
Huntington College of Health
  Sciences
Jackson State Community College
John A. Gupton College
Miller-Motte Technical College:
  Clarksville
Nashville Auto-Diesel College
Nashville State Community
  College
National College
  Knoxville
  Nashville
National College of Business &
  Technology
  National College: Bristol
National College: Bartlett
National College: Madison
National College: Memphis
Northeast State Technical
  Community College
Nossi College of Art
Remington College
  Memphis
Roane State Community College
Southwest Tennessee Community
  College
Vatterott College: Memphis
Walters State Community College

## Texas

Alvin Community College
Angelina College
Austin Community College
Blinn College
Bradford School of Business
Brookhaven College
Cedar Valley College
Central Texas College
Cisco Junior College

Clarendon College
Coastal Bend College
College of the Mainland
Collin County Community
  College District
Court Reporting Institute of
  Houston
Del Mar College
Eastfield College
El Centro College
El Paso Community College
Everest College: Arlington
Frank Phillips College
Galveston College
Grayson County College
Hallmark College of Aeronautics
Hallmark College of Technology
Hill College
Houston Community College
  System
Howard College
Jacksonville College
Kilgore College
Lamar Institute of Technology
Lamar State College at Orange
Lamar State College at Port
  Arthur
Laredo Community College
Lee College
Lon Morris College
McLennan Community College
Midland College
Mountain View College
Navarro College
North Central Texas College
North Harris Montgomery
  Community College
North Lake College
Northeast Texas Community
  College
Odessa College
Palo Alto College
Panola College
Paris Junior College
Ranger College
Remington College
  Fort Worth
  Houston
Richland College
St. Philip's College
San Jacinto College
South Plains College
South Texas College
Southwest Institute of Technology
Tarrant County College
Temple College
Texarkana College
Texas Culinary Academy
Texas Southmost College
Texas State Technical College
  Harlingen
  Sweetwater
  Waco
Texas State Technical College:
  Marshall
Trinity Valley Community
  College
Tyler Junior College
Vernon College
Victoria College
Weatherford College
Western Technical College
Western Texas College
Wharton County Junior College

## Utah

College of Eastern Utah
LDS Business College
Salt Lake Community College
Snow College

## Vermont

Community College of Vermont
Landmark College
New England Culinary Institute

## Virginia

Beta Tech: Richmond South

Beta Tech: Richmond West
Blue Ridge Community College
Bryant & Stratton College
　Richmond
Bryant & Stratton College:
　Virginia Beach
Central Virginia Community
　College
Dabney S. Lancaster Community
　College
Danville Community College
Eastern Shore Community
　College
ECPI Technical College
　Richmond
ECPI Technical College: Roanoke
Germanna Community College
J. Sargeant Reynolds Community
　College
John Tyler Community College
Lord Fairfax Community College
Miller-Motte Technical College:
　Lynchburg
Mountain Empire Community
　College
National College
　Bluefield
　Charlottesville
　Danville
　Harrisonburg
　Lynchburg
　Martinsville
New River Community College
Northern Virginia Community
　College
Patrick Henry Community
　College
Paul D. Camp Community
　College
Piedmont Virginia Community
　College
Rappahannock Community
　College
Southside Virginia Community
　College
Southwest Virginia Community
　College
Thomas Nelson Community
　College
Tidewater Community College
Tidewater Tech
　Virginia Beach
Tidewater Tech: Chesapeake
Tidewater Tech: Newport News
Tidewater Tech: Norfolk
Virginia Highlands Community
　College
Virginia Western Community
　College
Wytheville Community College

**Washington**
Bates Technical College
Bellevue Community College
Bellingham Technical College
Big Bend Community College
Cascadia Community College
Centralia College
Clark College
Clover Park Technical College
Columbia Basin College
Edmonds Community College
Everett Community College
Grays Harbor College
Green River Community College
Highline Community College
Lower Columbia College
North Seattle Community College
Olympic College
Peninsula College
Renton Technical College
South Puget Sound Community
　College
Spokane Community College
Spokane Falls Community
　College
Tacoma Community College

Walla Walla Community College
Wenatchee Valley College
Whatcom Community College
Yakima Valley Community
　College

**West Virginia**
Blue Ridge Community and
　Technical College
Eastern West Virginia Community
　and Technical College
New River Community and
　Technical College
Potomac State College of West
　Virginia University
Southern West Virginia
　Community and Technical
　College
Valley College of Technology
West Virginia Business College
West Virginia Business College
West Virginia State Community
　and Technical College

**Wisconsin**
Blackhawk Technical College
Chippewa Valley Technical
　College
Fox Valley Technical College
Gateway Technical College
Lac Courte Oreilles Ojibwa
　Community College
Lakeshore Technical College
Madison Area Technical College
Madison Media Institute
Mid-State Technical College
Moraine Park Technical College
Northcentral Technical College
Southwest Wisconsin Technical
　College
University of Wisconsin
　Fond du Lac
　Fox Valley
　Manitowoc
　Marathon County
　Marinette
　Rock County
　Sheboygan
　Washington County
　Waukesha
Waukesha County Technical
　College
Western Technical College
Wisconsin Indianhead Technical
　College

**Wyoming**
Central Wyoming College
Eastern Wyoming College
Laramie County Community
　College
Northwest College
Sheridan College
Western Wyoming Community
　College
WyoTech: Laramie

**American Samoa**
American Samoa Community
　College

**Guam**
Guam Community College

*Four-year*

**California**
California Institute of Technology
Fresno Pacific University*
Harvey Mudd College*
Pomona College*

University of California*
　Berkeley
　Davis
　Irvine
　Los Angeles
　Riverside
　San Diego
　Santa Barbara
　Santa Cruz
University of California: Merced

**Connecticut**
Wesleyan University*
Yale University*

**Kansas**
Newman University*

**Massachusetts**
Amherst College*
Boston College*
Boston University
Brandeis University*
Franklin W. Olin College of
　Engineering
Harvard College
Massachusetts Institute of
　Technology
Tufts University*
Wellesley College*
Williams College

**Michigan**
Kendall College of Art and
　Design of Ferris State
　University

**Minnesota**
Winona State University*

**Nebraska**
University of Nebraska*
　Kearney
　Lincoln

**New Hampshire**
Dartmouth College*

**New Jersey**
Princeton University*

**New York**
Barnard College*
Columbia University
Hamilton College*
New York University
State University of New York
　College at Buffalo
Vassar College*
Webb Institute

**North Carolina**
Duke University*
North Carolina Agricultural and
　Technical State University

**Ohio**
Bowling Green State University*

**Pennsylvania**
Bryn Mawr College*
Haverford College
Swarthmore College*
University of Pennsylvania*

**Rhode Island**
Brown University*

**South Carolina**
North Greenville University*

**South Dakota**
University of South Dakota*

**Texas**
Rice University*

**Utah**
University of Utah*

**Vermont**
Middlebury College*

**Virginia**
Washington and Lee University*

**West Virginia**
Alderson-Broaddus College*

**Canada**
University of Toronto

*Four-year*

**California**
Chapman University
Dominican University of
　California
Mills College
Occidental College
Simpson University*
Stanford University
University of the Pacific

**Connecticut**
Trinity College

**Delaware**
University of Delaware

**District of Columbia**
American University
Catholic University of America
George Washington University
Georgetown University
Howard University
Trinity Washington University*

**Illinois**
Northwestern University

**Indiana**
Indiana University
　Bloomington

**Maryland**
Johns Hopkins University

**Massachusetts**
Babson College
Smith College

**Michigan**
Albion College
Calvin College
Hillsdale College
Siena Heights University

**Minnesota**
Carleton College

**Montana**
University of Great Falls

**New York**
City University of New York
　Queens College
Clarkson University
Eastman School of Music of the
　University of Rochester*
Fordham University
Hofstra University
St. Joseph's College: Suffolk
　Campus
Skidmore College
State University of New York
　College at Old Westbury
　Stony Brook
University of Rochester

**North Carolina**
Davidson College*

**Ohio**
Cedarville University*
Oberlin College

**Oregon**
Reed College

**Pennsylvania**
Cheyney University of
　Pennsylvania
Lafayette College

**Puerto Rico**
University of Puerto Rico
　Bayamon University College

**Tennessee**
Vanderbilt University

**Texas**
University of Houston

**Vermont**
Bennington College*

**Virginia**
George Mason University
Hampden-Sydney College
University of Mary Washington
University of Virginia

**Canada**
University of Alberta

**Switzerland**
Franklin College: Switzerland

*Two-year*

**California**
Deep Springs College

**Georgia**
Gordon College

**New York**
St. Elizabeth College of Nursing

# Colleges that offer ROTC

## Air Force ROTC

### Four-year

**Alabama**
Alabama State University
Auburn University
Auburn University at
   Montgomery
Birmingham-Southern College
Faulkner University
Huntingdon College
Miles College
Samford University
Spring Hill College
Stillman College
Troy University
Tuskegee University
University of Alabama
University of Alabama
   Birmingham
University of Mobile
University of Montevallo
University of South Alabama
University of West Alabama

**Alaska**
Alaska Pacific University
University of Alaska
   Anchorage

**Arizona**
Arizona State University
DeVry University
   Phoenix
Embry-Riddle Aeronautical
   University: Prescott Campus
Northern Arizona University
Southwestern College
University of Arizona

**Arkansas**
John Brown University
University of Arkansas
University of Arkansas
   Fort Smith

**California**
Biola University
California Baptist University
California Institute of Technology
California Lutheran University
California State University
   Dominguez Hills
   Fresno
   Los Angeles
   Northridge
   Sacramento
   San Bernardino
   San Marcos
Chapman University
Claremont McKenna College
Harvey Mudd College
Holy Names University
The King's College and Seminary
Loyola Marymount University
National University
Occidental College
Pepperdine University
Pitzer College
Point Loma Nazarene University
Pomona College
St. Mary's College of California
Samuel Merritt College
San Diego Christian College
San Diego State University

San Francisco State University
San Jose State University
Santa Clara University
Scripps College
Sonoma State University
Stanford University
University of California
   Berkeley
   Davis
   Irvine
   Los Angeles
   Riverside
   Santa Cruz
University of Redlands
University of San Diego
University of San Francisco
University of Southern California
University of the Pacific
Vanguard University of Southern
   California
Westmont College
Whittier College

**Colorado**
Colorado Christian University
Colorado School of Mines
Colorado State University
Metropolitan State College of
   Denver
Regis University
University of Colorado
   Boulder
   Denver
University of Denver
University of Northern Colorado

**Connecticut**
Central Connecticut State
   University
Eastern Connecticut State
   University
Fairfield University
Quinnipiac University
Southern Connecticut State
   University
University of Connecticut
University of Hartford
Wesleyan University
Western Connecticut State
   University
Yale University

**Delaware**
Delaware State University
University of Delaware
Wilmington University

**District of Columbia**
American University
Catholic University of America
George Washington University
Georgetown University
Howard University
University of the District of
   Columbia

**Florida**
Barry University
Bethune-Cookman University
Clearwater Christian College
Eckerd College
Embry-Riddle Aeronautical
   University
Florida Agricultural and
   Mechanical University
Florida College
Florida International University
Florida Southern College
Florida State University
Lynn University
St. Leo University
University of Central Florida
University of Miami
University of South Florida
University of Tampa
University of West Florida

**Georgia**
Agnes Scott College

Clark Atlanta University
Clayton State University
Emory University
Georgia Institute of Technology
Georgia State University
Kennesaw State University
Morehouse College
Southern Polytechnic State
   University
Spelman College
University of Georgia
Valdosta State University

**Hawaii**
Brigham Young
   University-Hawaii
Chaminade University of
   Honolulu
Hawaii Pacific University
University of Hawaii
   Manoa
   West Oahu

**Idaho**
Lewis-Clark State College
Northwest Nazarene University
University of Idaho

**Illinois**
Elmhurst College
Governors State University
Illinois Institute of Technology
Judson University
Lewis University
Loyola University Chicago
McKendree University
North Central College
North Park University
Northeastern Illinois University
Northwestern University
St. Xavier University
Southern Illinois University
   Carbondale
Southern Illinois University
   Edwardsville
University of Chicago
University of Illinois
   Chicago
   Urbana-Champaign
Wheaton College

**Indiana**
Bethel College
Butler University
DePauw University
Holy Cross College
Indiana State University
Indiana University
   Bloomington
   South Bend
   Southeast
Indiana University-Purdue
   University Indianapolis
Purdue University
Rose-Hulman Institute of
   Technology
Saint Mary's College
St. Mary-of-the-Woods College
Tri-State University
University of Notre Dame
Valparaiso University

**Iowa**
Coe College
Grand View College
Iowa State University
University of Iowa

**Kansas**
Baker University
Haskell Indian Nations University
Kansas State University
Manhattan Christian College
MidAmerica Nazarene University
University of Kansas
University of St. Mary
Washburn University

**Kentucky**
Asbury College
Bellarmine University
Centre College
Georgetown College
Kentucky State University
Northern Kentucky University
Thomas More College
Transylvania University
University of Kentucky
University of Louisville
Western Kentucky University

**Louisiana**
Dillard University
Louisiana State University and
   Agricultural and Mechanical
   College
Loyola University New Orleans
Northwestern State University
Our Lady of the Lake College
Southern University
   New Orleans
Southern University and
   Agricultural and Mechanical
   College
Tulane University
University of Louisiana at
   Monroe
University of New Orleans
Xavier University of Louisiana

**Maine**
University of Maine
   Augusta
University of Southern Maine

**Maryland**
Bowie State University
Johns Hopkins University
Loyola College in Maryland
Towson University
University of Maryland
   College Park

**Massachusetts**
American International College
Amherst College
Anna Maria College
Assumption College
Babson College
Bay Path College
Becker College
Bentley College
Boston College
Boston University
Brandeis University
Bridgewater State College
Clark University
College of the Holy Cross
Curry College
Eastern Nazarene College
Elms College
Endicott College
Gordon College
Harvard College
Massachusetts Institute of
   Technology
Massachusetts Maritime Academy
Merrimack College
Mount Holyoke College
Northeastern University
Pine Manor College
Salem State College
Smith College
Springfield College
Tufts University
University of Massachusetts
   Amherst
   Lowell
Wellesley College
Western New England College
Westfield State College
Williams College
Worcester Polytechnic Institute
Worcester State College

**Michigan**
Concordia University
Eastern Michigan University
Finlandia University
Lawrence Technological
   University
Michigan State University
Michigan Technological
   University
Oakland University
Spring Arbor University
University of Michigan
University of Michigan
   Dearborn
Wayne State University

**Minnesota**
Augsburg College
College of St. Catherine
College of St. Scholastica
Concordia College: Moorhead
Concordia University: St. Paul
Hamline University
Macalester College
Minnesota State University
   Moorhead
North Central University
Northwestern College
University of Minnesota
   Crookston
   Duluth
   Twin Cities
University of St. Thomas

**Mississippi**
Belhaven College
Mississippi State University
Mississippi University for Women
University of Mississippi
University of Southern
   Mississippi
William Carey University

**Missouri**
Central Bible College
Central Methodist University
Columbia College
Fontbonne University
Harris-Stowe State University
Lincoln University
Saint Louis University
Southeast Missouri State
   University
Stephens College
University of Central Missouri
University of Missouri
   Columbia
   Missouri University of
      Science and Technology
   St. Louis
Washington University in St.
   Louis
Webster University
Westminster College
William Woods University

**Montana**
Montana State University
   Bozeman

**Nebraska**
Bellevue University
Clarkson College
College of Saint Mary
Concordia University
Creighton University
Dana College
Doane College
Grace University
Nebraska Wesleyan University
University of Nebraska
   Lincoln
   Medical Center
   Omaha
York College

**New Hampshire**
Colby-Sawyer College
Daniel Webster College

Franklin Pierce University
Keene State College
New England College
Plymouth State University
Rivier College
St. Anselm College
Southern New Hampshire
University
University of New Hampshire
University of New Hampshire at
Manchester

**New Jersey**
The College of New Jersey
Fairleigh Dickinson University
College at Florham
Metropolitan Campus
Kean University
Monmouth University
Montclair State University
New Jersey Institute of
Technology
Princeton University
Ramapo College of New Jersey
Rutgers, The State University of
New Jersey
Camden Regional Campus
New Brunswick/Piscataway
Campus
Newark Regional Campus
Saint Peter's College
Stevens Institute of Technology
William Paterson University of
New Jersey

**New Mexico**
National American University:
Rio Rancho
New Mexico State University
University of New Mexico

**New York**
Adelphi University
Albany College of Pharmacy
Cazenovia College
Clarkson University
College of Mount St. Vincent
College of Saint Rose
Columbia University
School of General Studies
Cornell University
Dowling College
Elmira College
Fordham University
Globe Institute of Technology
Hamilton College
Iona College
Ithaca College
Jewish Theological Seminary of
America
Le Moyne College
Manhattan College
Molloy College
Nazareth College of Rochester
New York Institute of Technology
Rensselaer Polytechnic Institute
Roberts Wesleyan College
Rochester Institute of Technology
Russell Sage College
Sage College of Albany
St. Francis College
St. John Fisher College
St. Joseph's College: Suffolk
Campus
St. Lawrence University
St. Thomas Aquinas College
Siena College
Skidmore College

State University of New York
Albany
Binghamton
College at Brockport
College at Cortland
College at Geneseo
College at Old Westbury
College at Potsdam
College of Environmental
Science and Forestry
College of Technology at
Canton
Stony Brook
Syracuse University
Union College
University of Rochester
Utica College
Vaughn College of Aeronautics
and Technology
Wells College

**North Carolina**
Belmont Abbey College
Bennett College
Davidson College
Duke University
East Carolina University
Elon University
Fayetteville State University
Gardner-Webb University
Greensboro College
Guilford College
High Point University
Johnson C. Smith University
Meredith College
Methodist University
North Carolina Agricultural and
Technical State University
North Carolina Central University
North Carolina State University
Peace College
Queens University of Charlotte
St. Augustine's College
Shaw University
University of North Carolina
Chapel Hill
Charlotte
Greensboro
Pembroke
Wingate University

**North Dakota**
Mayville State University
North Dakota State University
University of North Dakota

**Ohio**
Ashland University
Baldwin-Wallace College
Bowling Green State University
Capital University
Case Western Reserve University
Cedarville University
Central State University
Cleveland Institute of Art
College of Mount St. Joseph
Heidelberg College
Kent State University
Lourdes College
Malone College
Miami University
Oxford Campus
Mount Union College
Ohio Northern University
Ohio State University
Columbus Campus
Lima Campus
Mansfield Campus
Marion Campus
Newark Campus
Ohio University
Ohio University
Lancaster Campus
Ohio Wesleyan University
Otterbein College
University of Akron
University of Cincinnati
University of Dayton

University of Findlay
University of Toledo
Wilberforce University
Wittenberg University
Wright State University
Xavier University
Youngstown State University

**Oklahoma**
Langston University
Oklahoma Baptist University
Oklahoma Christian University
Oklahoma City University
Oklahoma State University
Oral Roberts University
Rogers State University
St. Gregory's University
Southern Nazarene University
University of Oklahoma
University of Tulsa

**Oregon**
Concordia University
Corban College
George Fox University
Linfield College
Oregon State University
Pacific University
Portland State University
University of Portland
Warner Pacific College
Western Oregon University

**Pennsylvania**
Bloomsburg University of
Pennsylvania
Bryn Mawr College
Cabrini College
California University of
Pennsylvania
Carlow University
Carnegie Mellon University
Chatham University
Drexel University
Duquesne University
East Stroudsburg University of
Pennsylvania
Eastern University
Keystone College
King's College
La Roche College
La Salle University
Marywood University
Misericordia University
Penn State
Abington
Altoona
Brandywine
Hazleton
University Park
Wilkes-Barre
Worthington Scranton
Philadelphia Biblical University
Point Park University
Robert Morris University
Rosemont College
Saint Joseph's University
St. Vincent College
Seton Hill University
Swarthmore College
Temple University
Thomas Jefferson University:
College of Health Professions
University of Pennsylvania
University of Pittsburgh
University of Pittsburgh
Greensburg
University of Scranton
University of the Sciences in
Philadelphia
Villanova University
Washington & Jefferson College
West Chester University of
Pennsylvania
Widener University
Wilkes University

**Puerto Rico**
Bayamon Central University
Inter American University of
Puerto Rico
Aguadilla Campus
Bayamon Campus
Fajardo Campus
Metropolitan Campus
San German Campus
Pontifical Catholic University of
Puerto Rico
Universidad Metropolitana
Universidad Politecnica de Puerto
Rico
University of Puerto Rico
Carolina Regional College
Mayaguez
Rio Piedras

**South Carolina**
Anderson University
Benedict College
Charleston Southern University
The Citadel
Clemson University
College of Charleston
South Carolina State University
Southern Wesleyan University
University of South Carolina

**South Dakota**
Dakota State University
South Dakota State University

**Tennessee**
Austin Peay State University
Carson-Newman College
Christian Brothers University
Free Will Baptist Bible College
LeMoyne-Owen College
Lipscomb University
Rhodes College
Tennessee State University
Tennessee Technological
University
University of Memphis
University of Tennessee
Knoxville
Vanderbilt University

**Texas**
Angelo State University
Baylor University
Concordia University at Austin
Dallas Baptist University
Huston-Tillotson University
Midwestern State University
Our Lady of the Lake University
of San Antonio
Rice University
St. Edward's University
St. Mary's University
Southern Methodist University
Texas A&M University
Texas Christian University
Texas Lutheran University
Texas State University: San
Marcos
Texas Tech University
Texas Wesleyan University
Texas Woman's University
Trinity University
University of Dallas
University of Houston
University of Mary Hardin-Baylor
University of North Texas
University of St. Thomas
University of Texas
Arlington
Austin
Dallas
El Paso
San Antonio
Wayland Baptist University

**Utah**
Brigham Young University
University of Utah

Utah State University
Utah Valley State College
Weber State University
Westminster College

**Vermont**
Lyndon State College
Norwich University
St. Michael's College

**Virginia**
George Mason University
James Madison University
Liberty University
Mary Baldwin College
University of Virginia
Virginia Military Institute
Virginia Polytechnic Institute and
State University

**Washington**
Central Washington University
Saint Martin's University
Seattle Pacific University
Seattle University
University of Washington
Washington State University

**West Virginia**
Fairmont State University
Shepherd University
West Virginia University

**Wisconsin**
Alverno College
Carroll College
Carthage College
Maranatha Baptist Bible College
Marquette University
Milwaukee School of Engineering
University of Wisconsin
Madison
Milwaukee
Superior
Whitewater
Wisconsin Lutheran College

**Wyoming**
University of Wyoming

*Two-year*

**Alabama**
Bishop State Community College
Jefferson State Community
College
Marion Military Institute
Shelton State Community College

**Arizona**
Coconino County Community
College
Estrella Mountain Community
College
Gateway Community College
Mesa Community College
Phoenix College
Pima Community College
Yavapai College

**Arkansas**
Northwest Arkansas Community
College

**California**
Antelope Valley College
Chabot College
College of San Mateo
College of the Sequoias
Cuyamaca College
De Anza College
Foothill College
Fresno City College
Irvine Valley College
Los Angeles City College
Los Angeles Mission College
MiraCosta College
Mission College
Mount San Antonio College
Mount San Jacinto College

Ohlone College
Riverside Community College
Sacramento City College
San Diego City College
Solano Community College
Ventura College
West Valley College

### Colorado
Aims Community College
Arapahoe Community College
Front Range Community College

### Connecticut
Capital Community College
Tunxis Community College

### Florida
Brevard Community College
Broward Community College
Daytona Beach Community
College
Hillsborough Community College
Miami Dade College
Santa Fe Community College
Tallahassee Community College

### Hawaii
University of Hawaii
Honolulu Community
College

### Illinois
John A. Logan College
Lincoln Land Community College
Parkland College
Shawnee Community College

### Indiana
Vincennes University

### Iowa
Hawkeye Community College
Iowa Western Community
College

### Louisiana
Delgado Community College

### Maryland
Prince George's Community
College

### Massachusetts
Holyoke Community College
Middlesex Community College
Quinsigamond Community
College

### Michigan
Lansing Community College

### Minnesota
Anoka-Ramsey Community
College
Century Community and
Technical College
Inver Hills Community College
Normandale Community College

### Mississippi
Northwest Mississippi
Community College

### Missouri
St. Louis Community College
Meramec

### New Jersey
Brookdale Community College
Raritan Valley Community
College
Union County College

### New Mexico
Central New Mexico Community
College
Dona Ana Branch Community
College of New Mexico State
University
New Mexico State University
Alamogordo

### New York
Hudson Valley Community
College
Maria College
Monroe Community College
Onondaga Community College
Schenectady County Community
College

### North Carolina
Guilford Technical Community
College

### Ohio
Columbus State Community
College
Cuyahoga Community College
Metropolitan Campus
Hocking College
Kent State University
Ashtabula
East Liverpool
Salem
Stark
Trumbull
Tuscarawas
Miami University
Hamilton Campus
Middletown Campus
Owens Community College
Toledo
Sinclair Community College
University of Akron: Wayne
College

### Oklahoma
Northeastern Oklahoma
Agricultural and Mechanical
College
Rose State College

### Oregon
Clackamas Community College
Linn-Benton Community College

### Pennsylvania
Lackawanna College
Luzerne County Community
College
Valley Forge Military College

### South Carolina
Midlands Technical College
Tri-County Technical College
University of South Carolina
Salkehatchie Regional
Campus

### Tennessee
Roane State Community College
Southwest Tennessee Community
College

### Texas
Austin Community College
Houston Community College
System
Lon Morris College
McLennan Community College
North Central Texas College
San Antonio College
Tarrant County College
Weatherford College

### Utah
LDS Business College
Salt Lake Community College

### Virginia
Piedmont Virginia Community
College

### Washington
Clark College
Highline Community College
South Puget Sound Community
College
Spokane Community College

### Wyoming
Laramie County Community
College

## *Four-year*

### Alabama
Alabama Agricultural and
Mechanical University
Alabama State University
Auburn University
Auburn University at
Montgomery
Birmingham-Southern College
Faulkner University
Huntingdon College
Jacksonville State University
Judson College
Miles College
Samford University
Spring Hill College
Stillman College
Troy University
Tuskegee University
University of Alabama
University of Alabama
Birmingham
Huntsville
University of Mobile
University of Montevallo
University of North Alabama
University of South Alabama

### Alaska
University of Alaska
Fairbanks

### Arizona
Arizona State University
Embry-Riddle Aeronautical
University: Prescott Campus
Grand Canyon University
Northern Arizona University
University of Arizona

### Arkansas
Arkansas State University
Arkansas Tech University
Central Baptist College
Harding University
Henderson State University
Hendrix College
John Brown University
Ouachita Baptist University
Philander Smith College
University of Arkansas
University of Arkansas
Fort Smith
Little Rock
Monticello
Pine Bluff
University of Central Arkansas
Williams Baptist College

### California
Azusa Pacific University
Biola University
California Baptist University
California Institute of Technology
California Lutheran University
California Polytechnic State
University: San Luis Obispo
California State Polytechnic
University: Pomona
California State University
Dominguez Hills
Fresno
Fullerton
Long Beach
Los Angeles
Northridge
Sacramento
San Bernardino
San Marcos
Chapman University

Claremont McKenna College
Harvey Mudd College
Holy Names University
The King's College and Seminary
Loyola Marymount University
Menlo College
National Hispanic University
National University
Occidental College
Pepperdine University
Pitzer College
Point Loma Nazarene University
Pomona College
St. Mary's College of California
Samuel Merritt College
San Diego Christian College
San Diego State University
San Francisco State University
Santa Clara University
Scripps College
Sonoma State University
Stanford University
University of California
Berkeley
Davis
Irvine
Los Angeles
Riverside
Santa Barbara
Santa Cruz
University of La Verne
University of Redlands
University of San Diego
University of San Francisco
University of Southern California
Vanguard University of Southern
California
Westmont College
Whittier College

### Colorado
Colorado Christian University
Colorado College
Colorado School of Mines
Colorado State University
Colorado State University
Pueblo
Colorado Technical University
Metropolitan State College of
Denver
Regis University
University of Colorado
Boulder
Colorado Springs
Denver
University of Denver
University of Northern Colorado

### Connecticut
Central Connecticut State
University
Eastern Connecticut State
University
Fairfield University
Quinnipiac University
Sacred Heart University
Southern Connecticut State
University
Trinity College
University of Bridgeport
University of Connecticut
University of Hartford
Western Connecticut State
University
Yale University

### Delaware
Delaware State University
University of Delaware
Wesley College
Wilmington University

### District of Columbia
American University
Catholic University of America
George Washington University
Georgetown University
Howard University

Trinity Washington University
University of the District of
Columbia

### Florida
Barry University
Bethune-Cookman University
Clearwater Christian College
Eckerd College
Embry-Riddle Aeronautical
University
Florida Agricultural and
Mechanical University
Florida Atlantic University
Florida College
Florida Institute of Technology
Florida International University
Florida Memorial University
Florida Southern College
Florida State University
Okaloosa-Walton College
St. Leo University
Southeastern University
Stetson University
University of Central Florida
University of Miami
University of South Florida
University of Tampa
University of West Florida

### Georgia
Agnes Scott College
Albany State University
Armstrong Atlantic State
University
Augusta State University
Clark Atlanta University
Clayton State University
Columbus State University
Emory University
Fort Valley State University
Georgia College and State
University
Georgia Institute of Technology
Georgia Southern University
Georgia State University
Kennesaw State University
Mercer University
Morehouse College
North Georgia College & State
University
Paine College
Savannah College of Art and
Design
Savannah State University
Southern Polytechnic State
University
Spelman College
University of Georgia
University of West Georgia

### Hawaii
Brigham Young
University-Hawaii
Chaminade University of
Honolulu
Hawaii Pacific University
University of Hawaii
Manoa
West Oahu

### Idaho
Boise State University
Brigham Young University-Idaho
College of Idaho
Idaho State University
Lewis-Clark State College
Northwest Nazarene University
University of Idaho

### Illinois
Aurora University
Benedictine University
Bradley University
Chicago State University
DePaul University
Eastern Illinois University
Elmhurst College
Governors State University

Illinois Institute of Technology
Illinois State University
Illinois Wesleyan University
Judson University
Lewis University
Loyola University Chicago
McKendree University
Monmouth College
North Central College
Northeastern Illinois University
Northern Illinois University
Northwestern University
Olivet Nazarene University
Robert Morris College: Chicago
Southern Illinois University
   Carbondale
Southern Illinois University
   Edwardsville
University of Chicago
University of Illinois
   Chicago
   Urbana-Champaign
Western Illinois University
Wheaton College

## Indiana

Ball State University
Bethel College
Butler University
DePauw University
Franklin College
Holy Cross College
Indiana State University
Indiana University
   Bloomington
   Kokomo
   Northwest
   South Bend
   Southeast
Indiana University-Purdue
   University Indianapolis
Indiana Wesleyan University
Marian College
Purdue University
Purdue University
   Calumet
Rose-Hulman Institute of
   Technology
Saint Mary's College
St. Mary-of-the-Woods College
University of Indianapolis
University of Notre Dame
University of Southern Indiana
Valparaiso University

## Iowa

Allen College
Clarke College
Coe College
Drake University
Grand View College
Iowa State University
Loras College
University of Dubuque
University of Iowa
University of Northern Iowa

## Kansas

Baker University
Benedictine College
Kansas State University
Manhattan Christian College
MidAmerica Nazarene University
Pittsburg State University
University of Kansas
University of St. Mary
Washburn University

## Kentucky

Asbury College
Bellarmine University
Campbellsville University
Centre College
Eastern Kentucky University
Georgetown College
Kentucky Christian University
Kentucky State University
Kentucky Wesleyan College

Midway College
Morehead State University
Murray State University
Northern Kentucky University
Thomas More College
Transylvania University
Union College
University of Kentucky
University of Louisville
University of the Cumberlands
Western Kentucky University

## Louisiana

Dillard University
Grambling State University
Louisiana College
Louisiana State University
   Alexandria
   Shreveport
Louisiana State University and
   Agricultural and Mechanical
   College
Louisiana Tech University
Loyola University New Orleans
Northwestern State University
Southeastern Louisiana University
Southern University
   New Orleans
Southern University and
   Agricultural and Mechanical
   College
Tulane University
University of Louisiana at
   Lafayette
University of Louisiana at
   Monroe
University of New Orleans
Xavier University of Louisiana

## Maine

Colby College
Husson College
Maine Maritime Academy
New England School of
   Communications
St. Joseph's College
Unity College
University of Maine
University of Maine
   Augusta
University of New England
University of Southern Maine

## Maryland

Bowie State University
Capitol College
College of Notre Dame of
   Maryland
Coppin State University
Goucher College
Hood College
Johns Hopkins University
Loyola College in Maryland
Maryland Institute College of Art
McDaniel College
Morgan State University
Mount St. Mary's University
Salisbury University
Towson University
University of Baltimore
University of Maryland
   Baltimore County
   College Park
Villa Julie College

## Massachusetts

American International College
Assumption College
Babson College
Bay Path College
Becker College
Bentley College
Boston College
Boston University
Brandeis University
Bridgewater State College
Clark University
College of the Holy Cross

Curry College
Eastern Nazarene College
Elms College
Emmanuel College
Endicott College
Fitchburg State College
Framingham State College
Gordon College
Hampshire College
Harvard College
Massachusetts Institute of
   Technology
Massachusetts Maritime Academy
Mount Holyoke College
Nichols College
Northeastern University
Pine Manor College
Salem State College
Simmons College
Smith College
Springfield College
Stonehill College
Suffolk University
Tufts University
University of Massachusetts
   Amherst
   Dartmouth
Wellesley College
Wentworth Institute of
   Technology
Western New England College
Westfield State College
Wheaton College
Worcester Polytechnic Institute
Worcester State College

## Michigan

Alma College
Calvin College
Central Michigan University
Concordia University
Eastern Michigan University
Ferris State University
Finlandia University
Grace Bible College
Kalamazoo College
Lawrence Technological
   University
Michigan State University
Michigan Technological
   University
Northern Michigan University
Spring Arbor University
University of Michigan
University of Michigan
   Dearborn
Western Michigan University

## Minnesota

Augsburg College
Bethany Lutheran College
College of St. Benedict
College of St. Catherine
Concordia College: Moorhead
Concordia University: St. Paul
Gustavus Adolphus College
Minnesota State University
   Mankato
   Moorhead
North Central University
Northwestern College
Saint Cloud State University
St. John's University
St. Mary's University of
   Minnesota
University of Minnesota
   Twin Cities
University of St. Thomas
Winona State University

## Mississippi

Alcorn State University
Belhaven College
Jackson State University
Millsaps College
Mississippi College
Mississippi State University
Mississippi University for Women

Mississippi Valley State
   University
Tougaloo College
University of Mississippi
University of Southern
   Mississippi
William Carey University

## Missouri

Avila University
Calvary Bible College and
   Theological Seminary
Central Bible College
Central Methodist University
College of the Ozarks
Columbia College
Drury University
Evangel University
Fontbonne University
Harris-Stowe State University
Lincoln University
Lindenwood University
Maryville University of Saint
   Louis
Missouri Baptist University
Missouri State University
Missouri Valley College
Missouri Western State University
Northwest Missouri State
   University
Park University
Research College of Nursing
Rockhurst University
Saint Louis University
Southwest Baptist University
Stephens College
Truman State University
University of Central Missouri
University of Missouri
   Columbia
   Kansas City
   Missouri University of
     Science and Technology
   St. Louis
Washington University in St.
   Louis
Webster University
Westminster College
William Woods University

## Montana

Carroll College
Montana State University
   Bozeman
Montana Tech of the University of
   Montana
University of Montana: Missoula

## Nebraska

Bellevue University
Chadron State College
Clarkson College
College of Saint Mary
Concordia University
Creighton University
Dana College
Doane College
Grace University
Nebraska Methodist College of
   Nursing and Allied Health
Nebraska Wesleyan University
University of Nebraska
   Lincoln
   Medical Center
   Omaha
Wayne State College
York College

## Nevada

Sierra Nevada College
University of Nevada
   Las Vegas
   Reno

## New Hampshire

Colby-Sawyer College
Daniel Webster College
Dartmouth College
Franklin Pierce University

Granite State College
New England College
Plymouth State University
Rivier College
St. Anselm College
Southern New Hampshire
   University
University of New Hampshire
University of New Hampshire at
   Manchester

## New Jersey

Bloomfield College
Caldwell College
The College of New Jersey
Fairleigh Dickinson University
   College at Florham
   Metropolitan Campus
Kean University
Montclair State University
New Jersey Institute of
   Technology
Princeton University
Rider University
Rowan University
Rutgers, The State University of
   New Jersey
   Camden Regional Campus
   New Brunswick/Piscataway
     Campus
   Newark Regional Campus
Saint Peter's College
Seton Hall University
Stevens Institute of Technology

## New Mexico

New Mexico State University
University of New Mexico

## New York

Adelphi University
Albany College of Pharmacy
Alfred University
Canisius College
Cazenovia College
City University of New York
   Baruch College
   Lehman College
   Queens College
Clarkson University
Colgate University
College of New Rochelle
College of Saint Rose
Columbia University
   School of General Studies
Cornell University
D'Youville College
Daemen College
Elmira College
Fordham University
Globe Institute of Technology
Hamilton College
Hilbert College
Hofstra University
Houghton College
Iona College
Ithaca College
Jewish Theological Seminary of
   America
Le Moyne College
Long Island University
   Brooklyn Campus
   C. W. Post Campus
Manhattan College
Marist College
Medaille College
Molloy College
Monroe College
Nazareth College of Rochester
New York Institute of Technology
New York University
Niagara University
Pace University
Polytechnic University
Rensselaer Polytechnic Institute
Roberts Wesleyan College
Rochester Institute of Technology
Russell Sage College

Old Dominion University
Radford University
Randolph-Macon College
St. Paul's College
Southern Virginia University
University of Richmond
University of Virginia
Virginia Commonwealth
University
Virginia Military Institute
Virginia Polytechnic Institute and
State University
Virginia State University
Virginia Union University
Virginia Wesleyan College
Washington and Lee University

**Washington**
Central Washington University
DeVry University
Federal Way
Gonzaga University
Northwest University
Pacific Lutheran University
Saint Martin's University
Seattle Pacific University
Seattle University
University of Puget Sound
University of Washington
Washington State University
Whitworth University

**West Virginia**
Fairmont State University
Marshall University
University of Charleston
West Virginia University

**Wisconsin**
Alverno College
Bellin College of Nursing
Carroll College
Carthage College
Maranatha Baptist Bible College
Marian College of Fond du Lac
Marquette University
Milwaukee School of Engineering
Mount Mary College
Ripon College
St. Norbert College
University of Wisconsin
Eau Claire
Green Bay
La Crosse
Madison
Milwaukee
Oshkosh
Parkside
Platteville
River Falls
Stevens Point
Whitewater
Viterbo University
Wisconsin Lutheran College

**Wyoming**
University of Wyoming

**Guam**
University of Guam

**Virgin Islands, U.S.**
University of the Virgin Islands

**Republic of Korea**
Yonsei University

*Two-year*

**Alabama**
Bishop State Community College
Chattahoochee Valley Community
College
Gadsden State Community
College
Jefferson State Community
College
Marion Military Institute
Northwest-Shoals Community
College

Shelton State Community College

**Arizona**
Coconino County Community
College
Gateway Community College
Mesa Community College
Paradise Valley Community
College
Phoenix College
Pima Community College
Yavapai College

**Arkansas**
Northwest Arkansas Community
College
Ouachita Technical College

**California**
Chabot College
City College of San Francisco
College of San Mateo
Cuyamaca College
De Anza College
Diablo Valley College
El Camino College
Foothill College
Fresno City College
Los Angeles City College
Los Angeles Mission College
MiraCosta College
Mount San Jacinto College
Riverside Community College
Sacramento City College
San Diego City College
West Valley College

**Colorado**
Arapahoe Community College
Community College of Denver
Front Range Community College
Red Rocks Community College

**Connecticut**
Capital Community College
Tunxis Community College

**Florida**
Brevard Community College
Broward Community College
Daytona Beach Community
College
Hillsborough Community College
Miami Dade College
Pasco-Hernando Community
College
Pensacola Junior College
Polk Community College
Santa Fe Community College
South Florida Community
College
Tallahassee Community College
Valencia Community College

**Georgia**
Darton College
Georgia Military College

**Hawaii**
University of Hawaii
Honolulu Community
College
Windward Community
College

**Illinois**
Carl Sandburg College
John A. Logan College
Kankakee Community College
Kishwaukee College
Lewis and Clark Community
College
Lincoln Land Community College
Parkland College
Shawnee Community College
Spoon River College
Waubonsee Community College

**Indiana**
Vincennes University

**Iowa**
Hawkeye Community College
Iowa Western Community
College

**Kentucky**
Jefferson Community and
Technical College

**Louisiana**
Delgado Community College

**Maryland**
Allegany College of Maryland
Prince George's Community
College

**Massachusetts**
Holyoke Community College
Quinsigamond Community
College
Roxbury Community College

**Michigan**
Lansing Community College
Washtenaw Community College

**Minnesota**
Anoka-Ramsey Community
College
Lake Superior College
Normandale Community College

**Mississippi**
Hinds Community College

**Missouri**
St. Louis Community College
Florissant Valley
Meramec
State Fair Community College
Wentworth Military Junior
College

**Nevada**
College of Southern Nevada
Truckee Meadows Community
College

**New Jersey**
Brookdale Community College
Raritan Valley Community
College

**New Mexico**
Central New Mexico Community
College
Dona Ana Branch Community
College of New Mexico State
University
New Mexico Military Institute

**New York**
Erie Community College
City Campus
North Campus
South Campus
Finger Lakes Community College
Herkimer County Community
College
Hudson Valley Community
College
Maria College
Mohawk Valley Community
College
Monroe Community College
Nassau Community College
Niagara County Community
College
Onondaga Community College
Orange County Community
College
State University of New York
College of Agriculture and
Technology at Morrisville
College of Technology at
Alfred

**North Carolina**
College of the Albemarle

Guilford Technical Community
College
Pitt Community College

**Ohio**
Cincinnati State Technical and
Community College
Columbus State Community
College
Hocking College
Kent State University
Ashtabula
East Liverpool
Salem
Stark
Trumbull
Tuscarawas
Owens Community College
Toledo
Sinclair Community College
University of Akron: Wayne
College
University of Cincinnati
Clermont College

**Oklahoma**
Rose State College

**Oregon**
Central Oregon Community
College
Linn-Benton Community College

**Pennsylvania**
Community College of
Philadelphia
Harrisburg Area Community
College
Lackawanna College
Lehigh Carbon Community
College
Valley Forge Military College

**Rhode Island**
Community College of Rhode
Island

**South Carolina**
Denmark Technical College
Midlands Technical College
Orangeburg-Calhoun Technical
College
Spartanburg Methodist College
Tri-County Technical College
University of South Carolina
Lancaster
Salkehatchie Regional
Campus
Sumter

**Tennessee**
Jackson State Community College
Pellissippi State Technical
Community College
Roane State Community College
Southwest Tennessee Community
College
Walters State Community College

**Texas**
Angelina College
Austin Community College
Central Texas College
Collin County Community
College District
Del Mar College
El Centro College
El Paso Community College
Houston Community College
System
Laredo Community College
Lon Morris College
Mountain View College
St. Philip's College
San Antonio College
Tarrant County College

**Utah**
LDS Business College
Salt Lake Community College

**Virginia**
J. Sargeant Reynolds Community
College
John Tyler Community College
Piedmont Virginia Community
College
Richard Bland College
Southside Virginia Community
College
Thomas Nelson Community
College

**Washington**
Clark College
Highline Community College
Spokane Community College
Spokane Falls Community
College

**American Samoa**
American Samoa Community
College

**Guam**
Guam Community College

**Naval ROTC**

*Four-year*

**Alabama**
Auburn University
Stillman College

**Arizona**
Southwestern College
University of Arizona

**California**
California Maritime Academy
California State University
San Marcos
The King's College and Seminary
Loyola Marymount University
National Hispanic University
National University
Point Loma Nazarene University
Samuel Merritt College
San Diego State University
San Francisco State University
Sonoma State University
Stanford University
University of California
Berkeley
Davis
Los Angeles
Santa Cruz
University of Redlands
University of San Diego
University of Southern California

**Colorado**
Regis University
University of Colorado
Boulder

**District of Columbia**
Catholic University of America
George Washington University
Georgetown University
University of the District of
Columbia

**Florida**
Clearwater Christian College
Embry-Riddle Aeronautical
University
Florida Agricultural and
Mechanical University
Florida State University
Jacksonville University
University of North Florida
University of South Florida
University of Tampa

**Georgia**
Armstrong Atlantic State
University
Clark Atlanta University

Clayton State University
Emory University
Georgia Institute of Technology
Georgia State University
Morehouse College
Savannah State University
Southern Polytechnic State
    University
Spelman College

**Idaho**
Lewis-Clark State College
University of Idaho

**Illinois**
Illinois Institute of Technology
Judson University
Loyola University Chicago
Northwestern University
University of Illinois
    Chicago
    Urbana-Champaign

**Indiana**
Bethel College
Indiana University
    South Bend
Indiana University-Purdue
    University Indianapolis
Purdue University
Saint Mary's College
University of Notre Dame

**Iowa**
Iowa State University

**Kansas**
University of Kansas
Washburn University

**Louisiana**
Dillard University
Louisiana State University and
    Agricultural and Mechanical
    College
Louisiana Tech University
Loyola University New Orleans
Southern University
    New Orleans
Southern University and
    Agricultural and Mechanical
    College
Tulane University
University of New Orleans
Xavier University of Louisiana

**Maine**
Husson College
Maine Maritime Academy
University of Maine
University of Maine
    Augusta

**Maryland**
University of Maryland
    College Park

**Massachusetts**
Babson College
Becker College
Boston College
Boston University
Clark University
College of the Holy Cross
Harvard College
Massachusetts Institute of
    Technology
Massachusetts Maritime Academy
Northeastern University
Tufts University
Worcester Polytechnic Institute
Worcester State College

**Michigan**
Eastern Michigan University
Finlandia University
Lawrence Technological
    University
University of Michigan

University of Michigan
    Dearborn

**Minnesota**
Augsburg College
Concordia University: St. Paul
Macalester College
University of Minnesota
    Twin Cities
University of St. Thomas

**Mississippi**
Tougaloo College
University of Mississippi

**Missouri**
Columbia College
Lincoln University
Stephens College
University of Missouri
    Columbia
    Missouri University of
        Science and Technology
William Woods University

**Nebraska**
University of Nebraska
    Lincoln
York College

**New Hampshire**
Rivier College

**New Jersey**
Montclair State University

**New Mexico**
National American University:
    Rio Rancho
University of New Mexico

**New York**
Albany College of Pharmacy
City University of New York
    Queens College
College of New Rochelle
College of Saint Rose
Columbia University
Cornell University
Eastman School of Music of the
    University of Rochester
Fordham University
Globe Institute of Technology
Jewish Theological Seminary of
    America
Molloy College
New York University
Rensselaer Polytechnic Institute
Rochester Institute of Technology
Russell Sage College
State University of New York
    College at Brockport
    Maritime College
Union College
University of Rochester

**North Carolina**
Belmont Abbey College
Duke University
Guilford College
Lenoir-Rhyne College
North Carolina State University
Peace College
University of North Carolina
    Chapel Hill

**Ohio**
Cleveland Institute of Art
Cleveland State University
Miami University
    Oxford Campus
Ohio State University
    Columbus Campus
    Lima Campus
    Mansfield Campus
    Marion Campus
    Newark Campus
Ohio University
    Lancaster Campus

**Oklahoma**
University of Oklahoma

**Oregon**
Oregon State University
Warner Pacific College
Western Oregon University

**Pennsylvania**
Carlow University
Carnegie Mellon University
Chatham University
Drexel University
Duquesne University
Penn State
    University Park
Saint Joseph's University
Swarthmore College
Temple University
Thomas Jefferson University:
    College of Health Professions
University of Pennsylvania
University of Pittsburgh
Villanova University
Widener University

**Puerto Rico**
Inter American University of
    Puerto Rico
    Bayamon Campus
    Ponce Campus
Universidad Metropolitana

**South Carolina**
The Citadel
University of South Carolina

**Tennessee**
Belmont University
Christian Brothers University
University of Memphis
Vanderbilt University

**Texas**
Houston Baptist University
Huston-Tillotson University
Prairie View A&M University
Rice University
Texas A&M University
Texas A&M University
    Galveston
University of Houston
University of Texas
    Austin

**Utah**
University of Utah
Weber State University
Westminster College

**Vermont**
Norwich University

**Virginia**
Hampton University
Mary Baldwin College
Norfolk State University
Old Dominion University
University of Virginia
Virginia Military Institute
Virginia Polytechnic Institute and
    State University

**Washington**
Seattle Pacific University
Seattle University
University of Washington
Washington State University

**Wisconsin**
Marquette University
Milwaukee School of Engineering
Mount Mary College
University of Wisconsin
    Madison
Wisconsin Lutheran College

**Two-year**

**Arizona**
Gateway Community College

Mesa Community College
Pima Community College

**California**
Contra Costa College
Diablo Valley College
Foothill College
Fullerton College
Los Angeles City College
Mission College
Riverside Community College
Sacramento City College

**Connecticut**
Capital Community College
Tunxis Community College

**Florida**
Florida Community College at
    Jacksonville
Pasco-Hernando Community
    College
Santa Fe Community College
Tallahassee Community College

**Hawaii**
University of Hawaii
    Hawaii Community College

**Illinois**
Lincoln Land Community College
Parkland College
Shawnee Community College

**Iowa**
Hawkeye Community College

**Minnesota**
Anoka-Ramsey Community
    College
Lake Superior College
Normandale Community College

**Mississippi**
East Mississippi Community
    College

**New Mexico**
Central New Mexico Community
    College

**New York**
Maria College
Monroe Community College

**North Carolina**
Guilford Technical Community
    College

**Ohio**
Cuyahoga Community College
    Metropolitan Campus
Miami University
    Hamilton Campus
    Middletown Campus

**South Carolina**
Midlands Technical College
University of South Carolina
    Salkehatchie Regional
    Campus

**Texas**
Lon Morris College

**Virginia**
New River Community College

**Washington**
Spokane Community College

# Colleges with NCAA sports

## Baseball Division I

### Alabama

Alabama Agricultural and
  Mechanical University M
Alabama State University M
Auburn University M
Jacksonville State University M
Samford University M
Troy University M
University of Alabama M
University of Alabama
  Birmingham M
University of South Alabama M

### Arizona

Arizona State University M
University of Arizona M

### Arkansas

Arkansas State University M
University of Arkansas M
University of Arkansas
  Little Rock M
  Pine Bluff M

### California

California Polytechnic State
  University: San Luis Obispo M
California State University
  Fresno M
  Fullerton M
  Long Beach M
  Northridge M
  Sacramento M
Loyola Marymount University M
Pepperdine University M
St. Mary's College of California
  M
San Diego State University M
San Jose State University M
Santa Clara University M
Stanford University M
University of California
  Berkeley M
  Davis M
  Irvine M
  Los Angeles M
  Riverside M
  Santa Barbara M
University of San Diego M
University of San Francisco M
University of Southern California
  M
University of the Pacific M

### Colorado

United States Air Force Academy
  M
University of Northern Colorado
  M

### Connecticut

Central Connecticut State
  University M
Fairfield University M
Quinnipiac University M
Sacred Heart University M
University of Connecticut M
University of Hartford M
Yale University M

### Delaware

Delaware State University M
University of Delaware M

### District of Columbia

George Washington University M
Georgetown University M

### Florida

Bethune-Cookman University M
Florida Agricultural and
  Mechanical University M
Florida Atlantic University M
Florida International University
  M
Florida State University M
Jacksonville University M
Stetson University M
University of Central Florida M
University of Florida M
University of Miami M
University of South Florida M

### Georgia

Georgia Institute of Technology
  M
Georgia Southern University M
Georgia State University M
Mercer University M
Savannah State University M
University of Georgia M

### Hawaii

University of Hawaii
  Hilo M
  Manoa M

### Illinois

Bradley University M
Chicago State University M
Eastern Illinois University M
Northern Illinois University M
Northwestern University M
Southern Illinois University
  Carbondale M
University of Illinois
  Chicago M
  Urbana-Champaign M
Western Illinois University M

### Indiana

Ball State University M
Butler University M
Indiana State University M
Indiana University
  Bloomington M
Indiana University-Purdue
  University Fort Wayne M
Purdue University M
University of Evansville M
University of Notre Dame M
Valparaiso University M

### Iowa

University of Iowa M
University of Northern Iowa M

### Kansas

Kansas State University M
University of Kansas M
Wichita State University M

### Kentucky

Eastern Kentucky University M
Morehead State University M
Murray State University M
University of Kentucky M
University of Louisville M
Western Kentucky University M

### Louisiana

Centenary College of Louisiana
  M
Grambling State University M
Louisiana State University and
  Agricultural and Mechanical
  College M
Louisiana Tech University M
McNeese State University M
Nicholls State University M
Northwestern State University M
Southeastern Louisiana University
  M

Southern University and
  Agricultural and Mechanical
  College M
Tulane University M
University of Louisiana at
  Lafayette M
University of Louisiana at
  Monroe M
University of New Orleans M

### Maine

University of Maine M

### Maryland

Coppin State University M
Mount St. Mary's University M
Towson University M
United States Naval Academy M
University of Maryland
  Baltimore County M
  College Park M
  Eastern Shore M

### Massachusetts

Boston College M
College of the Holy Cross M
Harvard College M
Northeastern University M
University of Massachusetts
  Amherst M

### Michigan

Central Michigan University M
Eastern Michigan University M
Michigan State University M
Oakland University M
University of Michigan M
Western Michigan University M

### Minnesota

University of Minnesota
  Twin Cities M

### Mississippi

Alcorn State University M
Jackson State University M
Mississippi State University M
Mississippi Valley State
  University M
University of Mississippi M
University of Southern
  Mississippi M

### Missouri

Saint Louis University M
Southeast Missouri State
  University M
University of Missouri
  Columbia M

### Nebraska

Creighton University M
University of Nebraska
  Lincoln M

### Nevada

University of Nevada
  Las Vegas M
  Reno M

### New Hampshire

Dartmouth College M

### New Jersey

Fairleigh Dickinson University
  Metropolitan Campus M
Monmouth University M
Princeton University M
Rider University M
Rutgers, The State University of
  New Jersey
  New Brunswick/Piscataway
  Campus M
Saint Peter's College M
Seton Hall University M

### New Mexico

New Mexico State University M
University of New Mexico M

### New York

Barnard College M

Canisius College M
Cornell University M
Fordham University M
Hofstra University M
Iona College M
Le Moyne College M
Long Island University
  · Brooklyn Campus M
Manhattan College M
Marist College M
New York Institute of Technology
  M
Niagara University M
Saint Bonaventure University M
St. John's University M
Siena College M
State University of New York
  Albany M
  Binghamton M
  Buffalo M
  Stony Brook M
United States Military Academy
  M
Wagner College M

### North Carolina

Appalachian State University M
Campbell University M
Davidson College M
Duke University M
East Carolina University M
Elon University M
Gardner-Webb University M
High Point University M
North Carolina Agricultural and
  Technical State University M
North Carolina State University
  M
University of North Carolina
  Chapel Hill M
  Charlotte M
  Greensboro M
  Wilmington M
Wake Forest University M
Western Carolina University M

### Ohio

Bowling Green State University
  M
Cleveland State University M
Kent State University M
Miami University
  Oxford Campus M
Ohio State University
  Columbus Campus M
Ohio University M
University of Akron M
University of Cincinnati M
University of Dayton M
University of Toledo M
Wright State University M
Xavier University M
Youngstown State University M

### Oklahoma

Oklahoma State University M
Oral Roberts University M
University of Oklahoma M

### Oregon

Oregon State University M
University of Portland M

### Pennsylvania

Bucknell University M
Duquesne University M
La Salle University M
Lafayette College M
Lehigh University M
Penn State
  University Park M
Saint Joseph's University M
Temple University M
University of Pennsylvania M
University of Pittsburgh M
Villanova University M

### Rhode Island

Brown University M

University of Rhode Island M

### South Carolina

Charleston Southern University M
The Citadel M
Clemson University M
Coastal Carolina University M
College of Charleston M
Furman University M
University of South Carolina M
Winthrop University M
Wofford College M

### Tennessee

Austin Peay State University M
Belmont University M
East Tennessee State University
  M
Lipscomb University M
Middle Tennessee State
  University M
Tennessee Technological
  University M
University of Memphis M
University of Tennessee
  Knoxville M
  Martin M
Vanderbilt University M

### Texas

Baylor University M
Dallas Baptist University M
Lamar University M
Prairie View A&M University M
Rice University M
Sam Houston State University M
Stephen F. Austin State University
  M
Texas A&M University M
Texas Christian University M
Texas Southern University M
Texas State University: San
  Marcos M
Texas Tech University M
University of Houston M
University of Texas
  Arlington M
  Austin M
  Pan American M
  San Antonio M

### Utah

Brigham Young University M
Southern Utah University M
University of Utah M
Utah Valley State College M

### Vermont

University of Vermont M

### Virginia

College of William and Mary M
George Mason University M
James Madison University M
Liberty University M
Longwood University M
Norfolk State University M
Old Dominion University M
Radford University M
University of Richmond M
University of Virginia M
Virginia Commonwealth
  University M
Virginia Military Institute M
Virginia Polytechnic Institute and
  State University M

### Washington

Gonzaga University M
University of Washington M
Washington State University M

### West Virginia

Marshall University M
West Virginia University M

### Wisconsin

University of Wisconsin
  Milwaukee M

## Baseball Division II

### Alabama
Miles College M
Stillman College M
Tuskegee University M
University of Alabama
Huntsville M
University of Montevallo M
University of North Alabama M
University of West Alabama M

### Arizona
Grand Canyon University M

### Arkansas
Arkansas Tech University M
Harding University M
Henderson State University M
Ouachita Baptist University M
Southern Arkansas University M
University of Arkansas
Monticello M
University of Central Arkansas M

### California
California State Polytechnic
University: Pomona M
California State University
Chico M
Dominguez Hills M
Los Angeles M
Monterey Bay M
San Bernardino M
Stanislaus M
San Francisco State University M
Sonoma State University M
University of California
San Diego M

### Colorado
Colorado Christian University M
Colorado School of Mines M
Colorado State University
Pueblo M
Mesa State College M
Metropolitan State College of
Denver M
Regis University M

### Connecticut
Post University M
Southern Connecticut State
University M
University of Bridgeport M
University of New Haven M

### Delaware
Wilmington University M

### Florida
Barry University M
Eckerd College M
Flagler College M
Florida Gulf Coast University M
Florida Institute of Technology M
Florida Southern College M
Lynn University M
Nova Southeastern University M
Palm Beach Atlantic University M
Rollins College M
St. Leo University M
University of North Florida M
University of Tampa M
University of West Florida M

### Georgia
Albany State University M
Armstrong Atlantic State
University M
Augusta State University M
Clark Atlanta University M
Columbus State University M
Georgia College and State
University M
Georgia Southwestern State
University M
Kennesaw State University M
Morehouse College M

North Georgia College & State
University M
Paine College M
University of West Georgia M
Valdosta State University M

### Hawaii
Hawaii Pacific University M

### Idaho
Northwest Nazarene University M

### Illinois
Lewis University M
Quincy University M
Southern Illinois University
Edwardsville M

### Indiana
Oakland City University M
Saint Joseph's College M
University of Indianapolis M
University of Southern Indiana M

### Iowa
Upper Iowa University M

### Kansas
Emporia State University M
Fort Hays State University M
Newman University M
Pittsburg State University M
Washburn University M

### Kentucky
Bellarmine University M
Kentucky State University M
Kentucky Wesleyan College M
Northern Kentucky University M

### Maryland
Columbia Union College M

### Massachusetts
American International College M
Assumption College M
Bentley College M
Merrimack College M
Stonehill College M
University of Massachusetts
Lowell M

### Michigan
Grand Valley State University M
Hillsdale College M
Northwood University: Michigan
M
Saginaw Valley State University
M
Wayne State University M

### Minnesota
Bemidji State University M
Concordia University: St. Paul M
Minnesota State University
Mankato M
Saint Cloud State University M
Southwest Minnesota State
University M
University of Minnesota
Crookston M
Duluth M
Morris M
Winona State University M

### Mississippi
Delta State University M

### Missouri
Drury University M
Lincoln University M
Missouri Southern State
University M
Missouri Western State University
M
Northwest Missouri State
University M
Rockhurst University M
Southwest Baptist University M
Truman State University M
University of Central Missouri M

University of Missouri
Missouri University of
Science and Technology
M
St. Louis M

### Montana
Montana State University
Billings M

### Nebraska
University of Nebraska
Kearney M
Omaha M
Wayne State College M

### New Hampshire
Franklin Pierce University M
St. Anselm College M
Southern New Hampshire
University M

### New Jersey
Bloomfield College M
Caldwell College M
Felician College M
New Jersey Institute of
Technology M

### New Mexico
Eastern New Mexico University
M
New Mexico Highlands
University M

### New York
Adelphi University M
City University of New York
Queens College M
College of Saint Rose M
Concordia College M
Dominican College of Blauvelt M
Dowling College M
Long Island University
C. W. Post Campus M
Mercy College M
Molloy College M
Nyack College M
Pace University M
St. Thomas Aquinas College M

### North Carolina
Barton College M
Belmont Abbey College M
Brevard College M
Catawba College M
Chowan University M
Elizabeth City State University M
Lenoir-Rhyne College M
Mars Hill College M
Mount Olive College M
North Carolina Central University
M
Pfeiffer University M
St. Andrews Presbyterian College
M
St. Augustine's College M
Shaw University M
University of North Carolina
Pembroke M
Wingate University M

### North Dakota
North Dakota State University M
University of Mary M
University of North Dakota M

### Ohio
Ashland University M
Tiffin University M
University of Findlay M

### Oklahoma
Cameron University M
East Central University M
Northeastern State University M
Oklahoma Panhandle State
University M
Southeastern Oklahoma State
University M

Southwestern Oklahoma State
University M
University of Central Oklahoma
M

### Oregon
Western Oregon University M

### Pennsylvania
Bloomsburg University of
Pennsylvania M
California University of
Pennsylvania M
Chestnut Hill College M
Clarion University of
Pennsylvania M
East Stroudsburg University of
Pennsylvania M
Gannon University M
Indiana University of
Pennsylvania M
Kutztown University of
Pennsylvania M
Lock Haven University of
Pennsylvania M
Mansfield University of
Pennsylvania M
Mercyhurst College M
Millersville University of
Pennsylvania M
Philadelphia University M
Seton Hill University M
Shippensburg University of
Pennsylvania M
Slippery Rock University of
Pennsylvania M
University of Pittsburgh
Johnstown M
University of the Sciences in
Philadelphia M
West Chester University of
Pennsylvania M

### Puerto Rico
University of Puerto Rico
Bayamon University College
M
Cayey University College M
Mayaguez M
Rio Piedras M

### Rhode Island
Bryant University M

### South Carolina
Anderson University M
Benedict College M
Claflin University M
Coker College M
Erskine College M
Francis Marion University M
Lander University M
Limestone College M
Newberry College M
North Greenville University M
Presbyterian College M
University of South Carolina
Aiken M
Upstate M

### South Dakota
Augustana College M
Northern State University M
South Dakota State University M

### Tennessee
Carson-Newman College M
Christian Brothers University M
Lane College M
LeMoyne-Owen College M
Lincoln Memorial University M
Tusculum College M

### Texas
Abilene Christian University M
Angelo State University M
St. Edward's University M
St. Mary's University M
Tarleton State University M

Texas A&M University
Kingsville M
University of Texas
of the Permian Basin M
University of the Incarnate Word
M
West Texas A&M University M

### Utah
Dixie State College of Utah M

### Vermont
St. Michael's College M

### Virginia
St. Paul's College M
Virginia State University M

### Washington
Central Washington University M
Saint Martin's University M

### West Virginia
Alderson-Broaddus College M
Bluefield State College M
Concord University M
Davis and Elkins College M
Fairmont State University M
Ohio Valley University M
Salem International University M
Shepherd University M
University of Charleston M
West Liberty State College M
West Virginia Wesleyan College
M
Wheeling Jesuit University M

### Wisconsin
University of Wisconsin
Parkside M

## Baseball Division III

### Alabama
Huntingdon College M

### Arkansas
Hendrix College M
University of the Ozarks M

### California
California Institute of Technology
M
California Lutheran University M
California State University
East Bay M
Chapman University M
Claremont McKenna College M
La Sierra University M
Menlo College M
Occidental College M
Pomona College M
University of La Verne M
University of Redlands M
Whittier College M

### Connecticut
Albertus Magnus College M
Eastern Connecticut State
University M
Mitchell College M
Trinity College M
United States Coast Guard
Academy M
Wesleyan University M
Western Connecticut State
University M

### Delaware
Wesley College M

### District of Columbia
Catholic University of America M
Gallaudet University M

### Georgia
Emory University M
LaGrange College M
Oglethorpe University M
Piedmont College M

## Illinois

Augustana College M
Aurora University M
Benedictine University M
Blackburn College M
Concordia University M
Dominican University M
Elmhurst College M
Eureka College M
Greenville College M
Illinois College M
Illinois Wesleyan University M
Knox College M
MacMurray College M
Millikin University M
Monmouth College M
North Central College M
North Park University M
Principia College M
Rockford College M
University of Chicago M
Wheaton College M

## Indiana

Anderson University M
DePauw University M
Earlham College M
Franklin College M
Hanover College M
Manchester College M
Rose-Hulman Institute of
Technology M
Tri-State University M
Wabash College M

## Iowa

Buena Vista University M
Central College M
Coe College M
Cornell College M
Grinnell College M
Loras College M
Luther College M
Simpson College M
University of Dubuque M
Wartburg College M

## Kentucky

Centre College M
Thomas More College M
Transylvania University M

## Louisiana

Louisiana College M

## Maine

Bates College M
Bowdoin College M
Colby College M
Husson College M
St. Joseph's College M
Thomas College M
University of Maine
Farmington M
University of Southern Maine M

## Maryland

Frostburg State University M
Johns Hopkins University M
McDaniel College M
St. Mary's College of Maryland
M
Salisbury University M
Villa Julie College M
Washington College M

## Massachusetts

Amherst College M
Anna Maria College M
Babson College M
Becker College M
Brandeis University M
Bridgewater State College M
Clark University M
Curry College M
Eastern Nazarene College M
Elms College M
Endicott College M
Fitchburg State College M

Framingham State College M
Gordon College M
Massachusetts College of Liberal
Arts M
Massachusetts Institute of
Technology M
Massachusetts Maritime Academy
M
Newbury College M
Nichols College M
Salem State College M
Springfield College M
Suffolk University M
Tufts University M
University of Massachusetts
Boston M
Dartmouth M
Wentworth Institute of
Technology M
Western New England College M
Westfield State College M
Wheaton College M
Wheelock College M
Williams College M
Worcester Polytechnic Institute M
Worcester State College M

## Michigan

Adrian College M
Albion College M
Alma College M
Calvin College M
Finlandia University M
Hope College M
Kalamazoo College M
Olivet College M

## Minnesota

Augsburg College M
Bethany Lutheran College M
Bethel University M
Carleton College M
College of St. Scholastica M
Concordia College: Moorhead M
Crown College M
Gustavus Adolphus College M
Hamline University M
Macalester College M
Martin Luther College M
North Central University M
Northwestern University M
St. John's University M
St. Mary's University of
Minnesota M
St. Olaf College M
University of St. Thomas M

## Mississippi

Millsaps College M
Mississippi College M
Rust College M

## Missouri

Fontbonne University M
Maryville University of Saint
Louis M
Washington University in St.
Louis M
Webster University M
Westminster College M

## Nebraska

Nebraska Wesleyan University M

## New Hampshire

Colby-Sawyer College M
Daniel Webster College M
Keene State College M
New England College M
Plymouth State University M
Rivier College M

## New Jersey

Centenary College M
The College of New Jersey M
Drew University M
Fairleigh Dickinson University
College at Florham M
Kean University M

Montclair State University M
New Jersey City University M
Ramapo College of New Jersey M
Richard Stockton College of New
Jersey M
Rowan University M
Rutgers, The State University of
New Jersey
Camden Regional Campus
M
Newark Regional Campus M
Stevens Institute of Technology M
William Paterson University of
New Jersey M

## New York

Cazenovia College M
City University of New York
Baruch College M
City College M
College of Staten Island M
John Jay College of
Criminal Justice M
Lehman College M
Clarkson University M
College of Mount St. Vincent M
D'Youville College M
Hamilton College M
Hilbert College M
Ithaca College M
Keuka College M
Manhattanville College M
Medaille College M
Mount St. Mary College M
Polytechnic University M
Rensselaer Polytechnic Institute
M
Rochester Institute of Technology
M
St. John Fisher College M
St. Lawrence University M
Skidmore College M
State University of New York
College at Brockport M
College at Cortland M
College at Fredonia M
College at Old Westbury M
College at Oneonta M
College at Plattsburgh M
Farmingdale M
Maritime College M
New Paltz M
Oswego M
Purchase M
Union College M
United States Merchant Marine
Academy M
University of Rochester M
Utica College M
Vassar College M
Yeshiva University M

## North Carolina

Greensboro College M
Guilford College M
Methodist University M
North Carolina Wesleyan College
M

## Ohio

Baldwin-Wallace College M
Bluffton University M
Capital University M
Case Western Reserve University
M
College of Mount St. Joseph M
College of Wooster M
Defiance College M
Denison University M
Franciscan University of
Steubenville M
Heidelberg College M
Hiram College M
John Carroll University M
Kenyon College M
Lake Erie College M
Marietta College M
Mount Union College M

Muskingum College M
Oberlin College M
Ohio Northern University M
Ohio Wesleyan University M
Otterbein College M
Wilmington College M
Wittenberg University M

## Oregon

George Fox University M
Lewis & Clark College M
Linfield College M
Pacific University M
Willamette University M

## Pennsylvania

Albright College M
Allegheny College M
Alvernia College M
Arcadia University M
Baptist Bible College of
Pennsylvania M
Delaware Valley College M
DeSales University M
Dickinson College M
Eastern University M
Elizabethtown College M
Franklin & Marshall College M
Geneva College M
Gettysburg College M
Grove City College M
Gwynedd-Mercy College M
Haverford College M
Juniata College M
Keystone College M
King's College M
La Roche College M
Lancaster Bible College M
Lebanon Valley College M
Lincoln University M
Marywood University M
Messiah College M
Misericordia University M
Moravian College M
Mount Aloysius College M
Muhlenberg College M
Neumann College M
Penn State
Altoona M
Berks M
Erie, The Behrend College
M
Harrisburg M
Philadelphia Biblical University
M
St. Vincent College M
Susquehanna University M
Swarthmore College M
Thiel College M
University of Pittsburgh
Bradford M
Greensburg M
University of Scranton M
Ursinus College M
Washington & Jefferson College
M
Waynesburg University M
Westminster College M
Widener University M
Wilkes University M
York College of Pennsylvania M

## Rhode Island

Johnson & Wales University:
Providence M
Rhode Island College M
Roger Williams University M
Salve Regina University M

## South Dakota

Presentation College M

## Tennessee

Maryville College M
Rhodes College M
University of the South M

## Texas

Austin College M

Concordia University at Austin M
East Texas Baptist University M
Hardin-Simmons University M
Howard Payne University M
LeTourneau University M
McMurry University M
Schreiner University M
Southwestern University M
Sul Ross State University M
Texas Lutheran University M
Trinity University M
University of Dallas M
University of Mary Hardin-Baylor
M
University of Texas
Dallas M
Tyler M

## Vermont

Castleton State College M
Lyndon State College M
Middlebury College M
Norwich University M
Southern Vermont College M

## Virginia

Averett University M
Bridgewater College M
Christopher Newport University
M
Eastern Mennonite University M
Emory & Henry College M
Ferrum College M
Hampden-Sydney College M
Lynchburg College M
Randolph-Macon College M
Roanoke College M
Shenandoah University M
University of Mary Washington
M
Virginia Wesleyan College M
Washington and Lee University M

## Washington

Pacific Lutheran University M
University of Puget Sound M
Whitman College M
Whitworth University M

## West Virginia

Bethany College M

## Wisconsin

Beloit College M
Carroll College M
Carthage College M
Concordia University Wisconsin
M
Edgewood College M
Lakeland College M
Lawrence University M
Maranatha Baptist Bible College
M
Marian College of Fond du Lac M
Milwaukee School of Engineering
M
Northland College M
Ripon College M
St. Norbert College M
University of Wisconsin
La Crosse M
Oshkosh M
Platteville M
Stevens Point M
Stout M
Superior M
Whitewater M
Wisconsin Lutheran College M

## Alabama

Alabama Agricultural and
Mechanical University
Alabama State University
Auburn University
Birmingham-Southern College W

Jacksonville State University
Samford University
Troy University
University of Alabama
University of Alabama
    Birmingham
University of South Alabama

## Arizona

Arizona State University
Northern Arizona University
University of Arizona

## Arkansas

Arkansas State University
University of Arkansas
University of Arkansas
    Little Rock
    Pine Bluff

## California

California Polytechnic State
    University: San Luis Obispo
California State University
    Fresno
    Fullerton
    Long Beach W
    Northridge
    Sacramento
Loyola Marymount University
Pepperdine University
St. Mary's College of California
San Diego State University
San Jose State University
Santa Clara University
Stanford University
University of California
    Berkeley
    Davis M
    Irvine
    Los Angeles
    Riverside
    Santa Barbara
University of San Diego
University of San Francisco
University of Southern California
University of the Pacific

## Colorado

Colorado State University
United States Air Force Academy
University of Colorado
    Boulder
University of Denver

## Connecticut

Central Connecticut State
    University
Fairfield University
Quinnipiac University
Sacred Heart University
University of Connecticut
University of Hartford
Yale University

## Delaware

Delaware State University
University of Delaware

## District of Columbia

American University
George Washington University
Georgetown University
Howard University

## Florida

Bethune-Cookman University
Florida Agricultural and
    Mechanical University
Florida Atlantic University
Florida International University
Florida State University
Jacksonville University
Stetson University
University of Central Florida
University of Florida
University of Miami
University of South Florida

## Georgia

Georgia Institute of Technology
Georgia Southern University
Georgia State University
Mercer University
Savannah State University
University of Georgia

## Hawaii

University of Hawaii
    Manoa

## Idaho

Boise State University
Idaho State University
University of Idaho

## Illinois

Bradley University
Chicago State University
DePaul University
Eastern Illinois University
Illinois State University
Loyola University Chicago
Northern Illinois University
Northwestern University
Southern Illinois University
    Carbondale
University of Illinois
    Chicago
    Urbana-Champaign
Western Illinois University

## Indiana

Ball State University
Butler University
Indiana State University
Indiana University
    Bloomington
Indiana University-Purdue
    University Fort Wayne
Indiana University-Purdue
    University Indianapolis
Purdue University
University of Evansville
University of Notre Dame
Valparaiso University

## Iowa

Drake University
Iowa State University
University of Iowa
University of Northern Iowa

## Kansas

Kansas State University
University of Kansas
Wichita State University

## Kentucky

Eastern Kentucky University
Morehead State University
Murray State University
University of Kentucky
University of Louisville
Western Kentucky University

## Louisiana

Centenary College of Louisiana
Grambling State University
Louisiana State University and
    Agricultural and Mechanical
    College
Louisiana Tech University
McNeese State University
Nicholls State University
Northwestern State University
Southeastern Louisiana University
Southern University and
    Agricultural and Mechanical
    College
Tulane University
University of Louisiana at
    Lafayette
University of Louisiana at
    Monroe
University of New Orleans

## Maine

University of Maine

## Maryland

Coppin State University
Loyola College in Maryland
Morgan State University
Mount St. Mary's University
Towson University
United States Naval Academy
University of Maryland
    Baltimore County
    College Park
    Eastern Shore

## Massachusetts

Boston College
Boston University
College of the Holy Cross
Harvard College
Northeastern University
University of Massachusetts
    Amherst

## Michigan

Central Michigan University
Eastern Michigan University
Michigan State University
Oakland University
University of Detroit Mercy
University of Michigan
Western Michigan University

## Minnesota

University of Minnesota
    Twin Cities

## Mississippi

Alcorn State University
Jackson State University
Mississippi State University
Mississippi Valley State
    University
University of Mississippi
University of Southern
    Mississippi

## Missouri

Missouri State University
Saint Louis University
Southeast Missouri State
    University
University of Missouri
    Columbia
    Kansas City

## Montana

Montana State University
    Bozeman
University of Montana: Missoula

## Nebraska

Creighton University
University of Nebraska
    Lincoln

## Nevada

University of Nevada
    Las Vegas
    Reno

## New Hampshire

Dartmouth College
University of New Hampshire

## New Jersey

Fairleigh Dickinson University
    Metropolitan Campus
Monmouth University
Princeton University
Rider University
Rutgers, The State University of
    New Jersey
      New Brunswick/Piscataway
      Campus
Saint Peter's College
Seton Hall University

## New Mexico

New Mexico State University
University of New Mexico

## New York

Barnard College M

Canisius College
Colgate University
Cornell University
Fordham University
Hofstra University
Iona College
Long Island University
    Brooklyn Campus
Manhattan College
Marist College
Niagara University
Saint Bonaventure University
St. Francis College
St. John's University
Siena College
State University of New York
    Albany
    Binghamton
    Buffalo
    Stony Brook
Syracuse University
United States Military Academy
Wagner College

## North Carolina

Appalachian State University
Campbell University
Davidson College
Duke University
East Carolina University
Elon University
Gardner-Webb University
High Point University
North Carolina Agricultural and
    Technical State University
North Carolina State University
University of North Carolina
    Asheville
    Chapel Hill
    Charlotte
    Greensboro
    Wilmington
Wake Forest University
Western Carolina University

## Ohio

Bowling Green State University
Cleveland State University
Kent State University
Miami University
    Oxford Campus
Ohio State University
    Columbus Campus
Ohio University
University of Akron
University of Cincinnati
University of Dayton
University of Toledo
Wright State University
Xavier University
Youngstown State University

## Oklahoma

Oklahoma State University
Oral Roberts University
University of Oklahoma
University of Tulsa

## Oregon

Oregon State University
Portland State University
University of Oregon
University of Portland

## Pennsylvania

Bucknell University
Drexel University
Duquesne University
La Salle University
Lafayette College
Lehigh University
Penn State
    University Park
Robert Morris University
St. Francis University
Saint Joseph's University
Temple University
University of Pennsylvania
University of Pittsburgh

Villanova University

## Rhode Island

Brown University
Providence College
University of Rhode Island

## South Carolina

Charleston Southern University
The Citadel M
Clemson University
Coastal Carolina University
College of Charleston
Furman University
South Carolina State University
University of South Carolina
Winthrop University
Wofford College

## Tennessee

Austin Peay State University
Belmont University
East Tennessee State University
Lipscomb University
Middle Tennessee State
    University
Tennessee State University
Tennessee Technological
    University
University of Memphis
University of Tennessee
    Chattanooga
    Knoxville
    Martin
Vanderbilt University

## Texas

Baylor University
Lamar University
Prairie View A&M University
Rice University
Sam Houston State University
Southern Methodist University
Stephen F. Austin State University
Texas A&M University
Texas Christian University
Texas Southern University
Texas State University: San
    Marcos
Texas Tech University
University of Houston
University of North Texas
University of Texas
    Arlington
    Austin
    El Paso
    Pan American
    San Antonio

## Utah

Brigham Young University
Southern Utah University
University of Utah
Utah State University
Utah Valley State College
Weber State University

## Vermont

University of Vermont

## Virginia

College of William and Mary
George Mason University
Hampton University
James Madison University
Liberty University
Longwood University
Norfolk State University
Old Dominion University
Radford University
University of Richmond
University of Virginia
Virginia Commonwealth
    University
Virginia Military Institute M
Virginia Polytechnic Institute and
    State University

## Washington

Gonzaga University

University of Washington
Washington State University

**West Virginia**
Marshall University
West Virginia University

**Wisconsin**
Marquette University
University of Wisconsin
Green Bay
Madison
Milwaukee

**Wyoming**
University of Wyoming

## Basketball Division II

**Alabama**
Miles College
Stillman College
Tuskegee University
University of Alabama
Huntsville
University of Montevallo
University of North Alabama
University of West Alabama

**Alaska**
University of Alaska
Anchorage
Fairbanks

**Arizona**
Grand Canyon University

**Arkansas**
Arkansas Tech University
Harding University
Henderson State University
Ouachita Baptist University
Southern Arkansas University
University of Arkansas
Monticello
University of Central Arkansas

**California**
California State Polytechnic
University: Pomona
California State University
Bakersfield
Chico
Dominguez Hills
Los Angeles
Monterey Bay
San Bernardino
Stanislaus
Humboldt State University
Notre Dame de Namur University
San Francisco State University
Sonoma State University
University of California
San Diego

**Colorado**
Adams State College
Colorado Christian University
Colorado School of Mines
Colorado State University
Pueblo
Fort Lewis College
Mesa State College
Metropolitan State College of
Denver
Regis University
University of Colorado
Colorado Springs
Western State College of
Colorado

**Connecticut**
Post University
Southern Connecticut State
University
University of Bridgeport
University of New Haven

**Delaware**
Goldey-Beacom College
Wilmington University

**District of Columbia**
University of the District of
Columbia

**Florida**
Barry University
Eckerd College
Flagler College
Florida Gulf Coast University
Florida Institute of Technology
Florida Southern College
Lynn University
Nova Southeastern University
Palm Beach Atlantic University
Rollins College
St. Leo University
University of North Florida
University of Tampa
University of West Florida

**Georgia**
Albany State University
Armstrong Atlantic State
University
Augusta State University
Clark Atlanta University
Clayton State University
Columbus State University
Fort Valley State University
Georgia College and State
University
Georgia Southwestern State
University
Kennesaw State University
Morehouse College M
North Georgia College & State
University
Paine College
University of West Georgia
Valdosta State University

**Hawaii**
Brigham Young
University-Hawaii
Chaminade University of
Honolulu
Hawaii Pacific University
University of Hawaii
Hilo

**Idaho**
Northwest Nazarene University

**Illinois**
Lewis University
Quincy University
Southern Illinois University
Edwardsville

**Indiana**
Oakland City University
Saint Joseph's College
University of Indianapolis
University of Southern Indiana

**Iowa**
Upper Iowa University

**Kansas**
Emporia State University
Fort Hays State University
Newman University
Pittsburg State University
Washburn University

**Kentucky**
Bellarmine University
Kentucky State University
Kentucky Wesleyan College
Northern Kentucky University

**Maryland**
Bowie State University
Columbia Union College

**Massachusetts**
American International College

Assumption College
Bentley College
Merrimack College
Stonehill College
University of Massachusetts
Lowell

**Michigan**
Ferris State University
Grand Valley State University
Hillsdale College
Lake Superior State University
Michigan Technological
University
Northern Michigan University
Northwood University: Michigan
Saginaw Valley State University
Wayne State University

**Minnesota**
Bemidji State University
Concordia University: St. Paul
Minnesota State University
Mankato
Moorhead
Saint Cloud State University
Southwest Minnesota State
University
University of Minnesota
Crookston
Duluth
Morris
Winona State University

**Mississippi**
Delta State University

**Missouri**
Drury University
Lincoln University
Missouri Southern State
University
Missouri Western State University
Northwest Missouri State
University
Rockhurst University
Southwest Baptist University
Truman State University
University of Central Missouri
University of Missouri
Missouri University of
Science and Technology
St. Louis

**Montana**
Montana State University
Billings

**Nebraska**
Chadron State College
University of Nebraska
Kearney
Omaha
Wayne State College

**New Hampshire**
Franklin Pierce University
St. Anselm College
Southern New Hampshire
University

**New Jersey**
Bloomfield College
Caldwell College
Felician College
Georgian Court University W
New Jersey Institute of
Technology

**New Mexico**
Eastern New Mexico University
New Mexico Highlands
University
Western New Mexico University

**New York**
Adelphi University
City University of New York
Queens College
College of Saint Rose

Concordia College
Dominican College of Blauvelt
Dowling College
Le Moyne College
Long Island University
C. W. Post Campus M
Mercy College
Molloy College
New York Institute of Technology
Nyack College
Pace University
St. Thomas Aquinas College

**North Carolina**
Barton College
Belmont Abbey College
Brevard College
Catawba College
Chowan University
Elizabeth City State University
Fayetteville State University
Johnson C. Smith University
Lees-McRae College
Lenoir-Rhyne College
Livingstone College
Mars Hill College
Mount Olive College
North Carolina Central University
Pfeiffer University
Queens University of Charlotte
St. Andrews Presbyterian College
St. Augustine's College
Shaw University
University of North Carolina
Pembroke
Wingate University
Winston-Salem State University

**North Dakota**
North Dakota State University
University of Mary
University of North Dakota

**Ohio**
Ashland University
Central State University
Tiffin University
University of Findlay

**Oklahoma**
Cameron University
East Central University
Northeastern State University
Oklahoma Panhandle State
University
Southeastern Oklahoma State
University
Southwestern Oklahoma State
University
University of Central Oklahoma

**Oregon**
Western Oregon University

**Pennsylvania**
Bloomsburg University of
Pennsylvania
California University of
Pennsylvania
Cheyney University of
Pennsylvania
Clarion University of
Pennsylvania
East Stroudsburg University of
Pennsylvania
Edinboro University of
Pennsylvania
Gannon University
Holy Family University
Indiana University of
Pennsylvania
Kutztown University of
Pennsylvania
Lock Haven University of
Pennsylvania
Mansfield University of
Pennsylvania
Mercyhurst College

Millersville University of
Pennsylvania
Philadelphia University
Seton Hill University
Shippensburg University of
Pennsylvania
Slippery Rock University of
Pennsylvania
University of Pittsburgh
Johnstown
University of the Sciences in
Philadelphia
West Chester University of
Pennsylvania

**Puerto Rico**
University of Puerto Rico
Bayamon University College
Cayey University College
Mayaguez
Rio Piedras

**Rhode Island**
Bryant University

**South Carolina**
Anderson University
Benedict College
Claflin University
Coker College
Converse College W
Erskine College
Francis Marion University
Lander University
Limestone College
Newberry College
North Greenville University
Presbyterian College
University of South Carolina
Aiken
Upstate

**South Dakota**
Augustana College
Northern State University
South Dakota State University
University of South Dakota

**Tennessee**
Carson-Newman College
Christian Brothers University
Lane College
LeMoyne-Owen College
Lincoln Memorial University
Tusculum College

**Texas**
Abilene Christian University
Angelo State University
Dallas Baptist University M
Midwestern State University
St. Edward's University
St. Mary's University
Tarleton State University
Texas A&M International
University
Texas A&M University
Commerce
Kingsville
Texas Woman's University W
University of Texas
of the Permian Basin
University of the Incarnate Word
West Texas A&M University

**Utah**
Dixie State College of Utah M

**Vermont**
St. Michael's College

**Virginia**
St. Paul's College
Virginia State University
Virginia Union University

**Washington**
Central Washington University
Saint Martin's University
Seattle Pacific University

Seattle University
Western Washington University

## West Virginia
Alderson-Broaddus College
Bluefield State College
Concord University
Davis and Elkins College
Fairmont State University
Glenville State College
Ohio Valley University
Salem International University
Shepherd University
University of Charleston
West Liberty State College
West Virginia Wesleyan College
Wheeling Jesuit University

## Wisconsin
University of Wisconsin
    Parkside

## Basketball Division III

## Alabama
Huntingdon College

## Arkansas
Hendrix College
University of the Ozarks

## California
California Institute of Technology
California Lutheran University
California State University
    East Bay
Chapman University
Claremont McKenna College
La Sierra University
Menlo College
Occidental College
Pitzer College
Pomona College
University of California
    Santa Cruz
University of La Verne
University of Redlands
Whittier College

## Colorado
Colorado College

## Connecticut
Albertus Magnus College
Connecticut College
Eastern Connecticut State
    University
Mitchell College
St. Joseph College W
Trinity College
United States Coast Guard
    Academy
Wesleyan University
Western Connecticut State
    University

## Delaware
Wesley College

## District of Columbia
Catholic University of America
Gallaudet University
Trinity Washington University W

## Georgia
Agnes Scott College W
Emory University
LaGrange College
Oglethorpe University
Piedmont College
Spelman College W
Wesleyan College W

## Illinois
Augustana College
Aurora University
Benedictine University
Blackburn College
Concordia University

Dominican University
Elmhurst College
Eureka College
Greenville College
Illinois College
Illinois Wesleyan University
Knox College
Lake Forest College
MacMurray College
Millikin University
Monmouth College
North Central College
North Park University
Principia College
Rockford College
University of Chicago
Wheaton College

## Indiana
Anderson University
DePauw University
Earlham College
Franklin College
Hanover College
Manchester College
Rose-Hulman Institute of
    Technology
Saint Mary's College W
Tri-State University
Wabash College M

## Iowa
Buena Vista University
Central College
Coe College
Cornell College
Grinnell College
Loras College
Luther College
Simpson College
University of Dubuque
Wartburg College

## Kentucky
Centre College
Thomas More College
Transylvania University

## Louisiana
Louisiana College

## Maine
Bates College
Bowdoin College
Colby College
Husson College
Maine Maritime Academy
St. Joseph's College
Thomas College
University of Maine
    Farmington
University of New England
University of Southern Maine

## Maryland
College of Notre Dame of
    Maryland W
Frostburg State University
Goucher College
Hood College
Johns Hopkins University
McDaniel College
St. Mary's College of Maryland
Salisbury University
Villa Julie College
Washington College

## Massachusetts
Amherst College
Anna Maria College
Babson College
Bay Path College W
Becker College
Brandeis University
Bridgewater State College
Clark University
Curry College
Eastern Nazarene College
Elms College

Emerson College
Emmanuel College
Endicott College
Fitchburg State College
Framingham State College
Gordon College
Lasell College
Lesley University
Massachusetts College of Liberal
    Arts
Massachusetts Institute of
    Technology
Mount Holyoke College W
Mount Ida College
Newbury College
Nichols College
Pine Manor College W
Regis College W
Salem State College
Simmons College W
Smith College W
Springfield College
Suffolk University
Tufts University
University of Massachusetts
    Boston
    Dartmouth
Wellesley College W
Wentworth Institute of
    Technology
Western New England College
Westfield State College
Wheaton College
Wheelock College W
Williams College
Worcester Polytechnic Institute
Worcester State College

## Michigan
Adrian College
Albion College
Alma College
Calvin College
Finlandia University
Hope College
Kalamazoo College
Olivet College

## Minnesota
Augsburg College
Bethany Lutheran College
Bethel University
Carleton College
College of St. Benedict W
College of St. Catherine W
College of St. Scholastica
Concordia College: Moorhead
Crown College
Gustavus Adolphus College
Hamline University
Macalester College
Martin Luther College
North Central University
Northwestern College
St. John's University M
St. Mary's University of
    Minnesota
St. Olaf College
University of St. Thomas

## Mississippi
Millsaps College
Mississippi College
Rust College

## Missouri
Baptist Bible College W
Fontbonne University
Maryville University of Saint
    Louis
Washington University in St.
    Louis
Webster University
Westminster College

## Nebraska
Nebraska Wesleyan University

## New Hampshire
Colby-Sawyer College
Daniel Webster College
Keene State College
New England College
Plymouth State University
Rivier College

## New Jersey
Centenary College
The College of New Jersey
College of St. Elizabeth W
Drew University
Fairleigh Dickinson University
    College at Florham
Kean University
Montclair State University
New Jersey City University
Ramapo College of New Jersey
Richard Stockton College of New
    Jersey
Rowan University
Rutgers, The State University of
    New Jersey
    Camden Regional Campus
    Newark Regional Campus
Stevens Institute of Technology
William Paterson University of
    New Jersey

## New York
Alfred University
Bard College
Cazenovia College
City University of New York
    Baruch College
    Brooklyn College
    City College
    College of Staten Island W
    Hunter College
    John Jay College of
        Criminal Justice
    Lehman College
    Medgar Evers College
    New York City College of
        Technology
    York College
Clarkson University
College of Mount St. Vincent
College of New Rochelle W
D'Youville College
Elmira College
Hamilton College
Hartwick College
Hilbert College
Hobart and William Smith
    Colleges M
Ithaca College
Keuka College
Manhattanville College
Medaille College
Mount St. Mary College
Nazareth College of Rochester
New York University
Polytechnic University
Rensselaer Polytechnic Institute
Rochester Institute of Technology
Russell Sage College W
St. John Fisher College
St. Joseph's College: Suffolk
    Campus
St. Lawrence University
Skidmore College

State University of New York
    College at Brockport
    College at Buffalo
    College at Cortland
    College at Fredonia
    College at Geneseo
    College at Old Westbury
    College at Oneonta
    College at Plattsburgh
    College at Potsdam
    College of Agriculture and
        Technology at Morrisville
    Farmingdale
    Institute of Technology at
        Utica/Rome
    Maritime College M
    New Paltz
    Oswego
    Purchase
Union College
United States Merchant Marine
    Academy
University of Rochester
Utica College
Vassar College
Yeshiva University M

## North Carolina
Greensboro College
Guilford College
Meredith College W
Methodist University
North Carolina Wesleyan College
Peace College W
Salem College W

## Ohio
Baldwin-Wallace College
Bluffton University
Capital University
Case Western Reserve University
College of Mount St. Joseph
College of Wooster
Defiance College
Denison University
Franciscan University of
    Steubenville W
Heidelberg College
Hiram College
John Carroll University
Kenyon College
Lake Erie College
Marietta College
Mount Union College
Muskingum College
Oberlin College
Ohio Northern University
Ohio Wesleyan University
Otterbein College
Wilmington College
Wittenberg University

## Oregon
George Fox University
Lewis & Clark College
Linfield College
Pacific University
Willamette University

## Pennsylvania
Albright College
Allegheny College
Alvernia College
Arcadia University
Baptist Bible College of
    Pennsylvania M
Bryn Mawr College W
Cabrini College
Carnegie Mellon University
Cedar Crest College W
Chatham University W
Chestnut Hill College
Delaware Valley College
DeSales University
Dickinson College
Eastern University
Elizabethtown College
Franklin & Marshall College

Geneva College W
Gettysburg College
Grove City College
Gwynedd-Mercy College
Haverford College
Immaculata University
Juniata College
Keystone College
King's College
La Roche College
Lancaster Bible College
Lebanon Valley College
Lincoln University
Lycoming College
Marywood University
Messiah College
Misericordia University W
Moravian College
Mount Aloysius College
Muhlenberg College
Neumann College
Penn State
  Altoona
  Berks
  Erie, The Behrend College
  Harrisburg
Philadelphia Biblical University
Rosemont College W
St. Vincent College
Susquehanna University
Swarthmore College
Thiel College
University of Pittsburgh
  Bradford
  Greensburg
University of Scranton
Ursinus College
Washington & Jefferson College
Waynesburg University
Westminster College
Widener University
Wilkes University
Wilson College W
York College of Pennsylvania

**Rhode Island**
Johnson & Wales University:
  Providence
Rhode Island College
Roger Williams University
Salve Regina University

**South Dakota**
Presentation College

**Tennessee**
Maryville College
Rhodes College
University of the South

**Texas**
Austin College
Concordia University at Austin
East Texas Baptist University
Hardin-Simmons University
Howard Payne University
LeTourneau University
McMurry University
Schreiner University
Southwestern University
Sul Ross State University
Texas Lutheran University
Trinity University
University of Dallas
University of Mary Hardin-Baylor
University of Texas
  Dallas
  Tyler

**Vermont**
Castleton State College
Green Mountain College
Johnson State College
Lyndon State College
Middlebury College
Norwich University
Southern Vermont College

**Virginia**
Averett University
Bridgewater College
Christopher Newport University
Eastern Mennonite University
Emory & Henry College
Ferrum College
Hampden-Sydney College M
Hollins University W
Lynchburg College
Mary Baldwin College W
Marymount University
Randolph College W
Randolph-Macon College
Roanoke College
Shenandoah University
University of Mary Washington
Virginia Wesleyan College
Washington and Lee University

**Washington**
Pacific Lutheran University
University of Puget Sound
Whitman College
Whitworth University

**West Virginia**
Bethany College

**Wisconsin**
Alverno College W
Beloit College
Carroll College
Carthage College
Concordia University Wisconsin
Edgewood College
Lakeland College
Lawrence University
Maranatha Baptist Bible College
Marian College of Fond du Lac
Milwaukee School of Engineering
Mount Mary College W
Northland College
Ripon College
St. Norbert College
University of Wisconsin
  Eau Claire
  La Crosse
  Oshkosh
  Platteville
  River Falls
  Stevens Point
  Stout
  Superior
  Whitewater
Wisconsin Lutheran College

## Bowling Division I

**Alabama**
Alabama Agricultural and
  Mechanical University W
Alabama State University W

**Arkansas**
Arkansas State University W
University of Arkansas
  Pine Bluff W

**Connecticut**
Sacred Heart University W

**Delaware**
Delaware State University W

**District of Columbia**
Howard University W

**Florida**
Bethune-Cookman University W
Florida Agricultural and
  Mechanical University W

**Louisiana**
Grambling State University W
Louisiana Tech University W
Southern University and
  Agricultural and Mechanical
  College W

**Maryland**
Coppin State University W
Morgan State University W
University of Maryland
  Eastern Shore W

**Mississippi**
Jackson State University W
Mississippi Valley State
  University W

**Nebraska**
University of Nebraska
  Lincoln W

**New Jersey**
Fairleigh Dickinson University
  Metropolitan Campus W
Saint Peter's College W

**New York**
St. Francis College W

**North Carolina**
North Carolina Agricultural and
  Technical State University W

**South Carolina**
South Carolina State University
  W

**Tennessee**
Vanderbilt University W

**Texas**
Prairie View A&M University W
Texas Southern University W

**Virginia**
Hampton University W
Norfolk State University W

## Bowling Division II

**Illinois**
Elmhurst College W

**Maryland**
Bowie State University W

**Minnesota**
Minnesota State University
  Mankato W

**Missouri**
University of Central Missouri W

**New York**
Adelphi University W

**North Carolina**
Elizabeth City State University W
Fayetteville State University W
Johnson C. Smith University W
Livingstone College W
North Carolina Central University
  W
St. Augustine's College W
Shaw University W
Winston-Salem State University
  W

**Pennsylvania**
Cheyney University of
  Pennsylvania W

**Virginia**
St. Paul's College W
Virginia State University W

## Bowling Division III

**Missouri**
Fontbonne University W

**New Jersey**
New Jersey City University W
New Jersey Institute of
  Technology W

**New York**
Medaille College W
State University of New York
  Institute of Technology at
  Utica/Rome W

**Wisconsin**
University of Wisconsin
  Whitewater W

## Cross-country Division I

**Alabama**
Alabama Agricultural and
  Mechanical University W
Alabama State University
Auburn University
Birmingham-Southern College
Jacksonville State University
Samford University
Troy University
University of Alabama
University of Alabama
  Birmingham W
University of South Alabama

**Arizona**
Arizona State University
Grand Canyon University M
Northern Arizona University
University of Arizona

**Arkansas**
Arkansas State University
Henderson State University M
University of Arkansas
University of Arkansas
  Little Rock
  Pine Bluff W

**California**
California Polytechnic State
  University: San Luis Obispo
California State University
  Fresno W
  Fullerton
  Northridge
  Sacramento
Loyola Marymount University
Pepperdine University
St. Mary's College of California
San Diego State University W
San Jose State University
Santa Clara University
Stanford University
University of California
  Berkeley
  Davis
  Irvine
  Los Angeles
  Riverside
  Santa Barbara
University of San Diego
University of San Francisco
University of Southern California
  W
University of the Pacific W

**Colorado**
Colorado Christian University M
Colorado State University
Metropolitan State College of
  Denver M
United States Air Force Academy
University of Colorado
  Boulder

**Connecticut**
Central Connecticut State
  University
Fairfield University
Quinnipiac University
Sacred Heart University
University of Connecticut
University of Hartford
Yale University

**Delaware**
Delaware State University
University of Delaware

**District of Columbia**
American University
George Washington University
Georgetown University
Howard University

**Florida**
Bethune-Cookman University
Flagler College M
Florida Agricultural and
  Mechanical University
Florida Atlantic University
Florida International University
Florida State University
Jacksonville University
Stetson University
University of Central Florida
University of Florida
University of Miami
University of South Florida

**Georgia**
Georgia Institute of Technology
Georgia Southern University W
Georgia State University
Mercer University
North Georgia College & State
  University M
Savannah State University
University of Georgia
University of West Georgia M

**Hawaii**
University of Hawaii
  Manoa W

**Idaho**
Boise State University
Idaho State University
University of Idaho

**Illinois**
Bradley University
Chicago State University
DePaul University
Eastern Illinois University
Illinois State University
Loyola University Chicago
Northern Illinois University W
Northwestern University W
Southern Illinois University
  Carbondale
University of Illinois
  Chicago
  Urbana-Champaign
Western Illinois University

**Indiana**
Ball State University W
Butler University
Indiana State University
Indiana University
  Bloomington
Indiana University-Purdue
  University Fort Wayne
Indiana University-Purdue
  University Indianapolis
Purdue University
University of Evansville
University of Notre Dame
Valparaiso University

**Iowa**
Drake University
Iowa State University
University of Iowa
University of Northern Iowa

**Kansas**
Kansas State University
Newman University M
University of Kansas
Wichita State University

**Kentucky**
Eastern Kentucky University

Kentucky Wesleyan College M
Morehead State University
Murray State University
University of Kentucky
University of Louisville
Western Kentucky University

**Louisiana**
Centenary College of Louisiana
Grambling State University
Louisiana State University and Agricultural and Mechanical College
Louisiana Tech University
McNeese State University
Nicholls State University
Northwestern State University
Southeastern Louisiana University
Southern University and Agricultural and Mechanical College
Tulane University W
University of Louisiana at Lafayette
University of Louisiana at Monroe

**Maine**
University of Maine

**Maryland**
Coppin State University
Loyola College in Maryland
Morgan State University
Mount St. Mary's University
Towson University W
United States Naval Academy
University of Maryland
  Baltimore County
  College Park
  Eastern Shore

**Massachusetts**
American International College M
Boston College
Boston University
College of the Holy Cross
Harvard College
Northeastern University
University of Massachusetts Amherst

**Michigan**
Central Michigan University
Eastern Michigan University
Michigan State University
Oakland University
University of Detroit Mercy
University of Michigan
Western Michigan University W

**Minnesota**
University of Minnesota Twin Cities

**Mississippi**
Alcorn State University
Jackson State University
Mississippi State University
Mississippi Valley State University
University of Mississippi
University of Southern Mississippi W

**Missouri**
Saint Louis University
Southeast Missouri State University
University of Missouri
  Columbia
  Kansas City

**Montana**
Montana State University Bozeman
University of Montana: Missoula

**Nebraska**
Creighton University

University of Nebraska Lincoln

**Nevada**
University of Nevada
  Las Vegas W
  Reno W

**New Hampshire**
Dartmouth College
University of New Hampshire

**New Jersey**
Fairleigh Dickinson University Metropolitan Campus
Monmouth University
Princeton University
Rider University
Rutgers, The State University of New Jersey
  New Brunswick/Piscataway Campus
Saint Peter's College
Seton Hall University

**New Mexico**
New Mexico State University
University of New Mexico

**New York**
Barnard College
Canisius College
City University of New York Queens College M
Colgate University
Cornell University
Dowling College M
Fordham University
Hofstra University
Iona College
Long Island University Brooklyn Campus
Manhattan College
Marist College
Niagara University
Saint Bonaventure University
St. Francis College
St. John's University W
Siena College
State University of New York
  Albany
  Binghamton
  Buffalo
  Stony Brook
Syracuse University
United States Military Academy
Wagner College

**North Carolina**
Appalachian State University
Brevard College M
Campbell University
Davidson College
Duke University
East Carolina University
Elon University
Gardner-Webb University
High Point University
North Carolina Agricultural and Technical State University
North Carolina State University
University of North Carolina
  Asheville M
  Chapel Hill
  Charlotte
  Greensboro
  Wilmington
Wake Forest University
Western Carolina University

**North Dakota**
University of Mary M

**Ohio**
Bowling Green State University
Cleveland State University W
Kent State University
Miami University
  Oxford Campus

Ohio State University Columbus Campus
Ohio University
University of Akron
University of Cincinnati
University of Dayton
University of Toledo
Wright State University
Xavier University
Youngstown State University

**Oklahoma**
Oklahoma State University
Oral Roberts University
University of Oklahoma
University of Tulsa

**Oregon**
Oregon State University W
Portland State University
University of Oregon
University of Portland

**Pennsylvania**
Bucknell University
Duquesne University
La Salle University
Lafayette College
Lehigh University
Penn State University Park
Robert Morris University
St. Francis University
Saint Joseph's University
Temple University
University of Pennsylvania
University of Pittsburgh
Villanova University

**Rhode Island**
Brown University
Providence College
University of Rhode Island

**South Carolina**
Charleston Southern University
The Citadel
Clemson University
Coastal Carolina University
College of Charleston
Furman University
South Carolina State University
University of South Carolina W
Winthrop University
Wofford College

**Tennessee**
Austin Peay State University
Belmont University
East Tennessee State University
Lipscomb University
Middle Tennessee State University
Tennessee State University
Tennessee Technological University
University of Memphis
University of Tennessee
  Chattanooga
  Knoxville
  Martin
Vanderbilt University

**Texas**
Baylor University
Lamar University
Prairie View A&M University
Rice University
Sam Houston State University
Southern Methodist University W
Stephen F. Austin State University
Texas A&M University
Texas Christian University
Texas State University: San Marcos
Texas Tech University
University of Houston
University of North Texas

University of Texas
  Arlington
  Austin
  El Paso
  of the Permian Basin M
  Pan American
  San Antonio

**Utah**
Brigham Young University
Dixie State College of Utah M
Southern Utah University
University of Utah W
Utah State University
Utah Valley State College
Weber State University

**Vermont**
University of Vermont

**Virginia**
College of William and Mary
George Mason University
Hampton University
James Madison University W
Liberty University
Longwood University
Norfolk State University
Radford University
University of Richmond
University of Virginia
Virginia Commonwealth University
Virginia Military Institute
Virginia Polytechnic Institute and State University

**Washington**
Gonzaga University
University of Washington
Washington State University

**West Virginia**
Marshall University
West Virginia University W

**Wisconsin**
Marquette University
University of Wisconsin
  Green Bay
  Madison
  Milwaukee

**Wyoming**
University of Wyoming

**Cross-country Division II**

**Alabama**
Miles College
Stillman College
Tuskegee University
University of Alabama Huntsville
University of Montevallo W
University of North Alabama
University of West Alabama

**Alaska**
University of Alaska
  Anchorage
  Fairbanks

**Arizona**
Grand Canyon University W

**Arkansas**
Arkansas Tech University W
Harding University
Henderson State University W
Ouachita Baptist University W
Southern Arkansas University
University of Arkansas Monticello
University of Central Arkansas

**California**
California State Polytechnic University: Pomona

California State University
  Bakersfield W
  Chico
  Dominguez Hills W
  Fresno M
  Los Angeles W
  Monterey Bay
  San Bernardino W
  Stanislaus
Humboldt State University
Notre Dame de Namur University
San Francisco State University
Sonoma State University W
University of California San Diego

**Colorado**
Adams State College
Colorado Christian University W
Colorado School of Mines
Colorado State University Pueblo W
Fort Lewis College
Mesa State College W
Metropolitan State College of Denver W
Regis University
University of Colorado Colorado Springs
Western State College of Colorado

**Connecticut**
Post University
Southern Connecticut State University
University of Bridgeport
University of New Haven

**Delaware**
Goldey-Beacom College
Wilmington University

**District of Columbia**
University of the District of Columbia

**Florida**
Florida Gulf Coast University
Florida Institute of Technology
Florida Southern College
Nova Southeastern University
Palm Beach Atlantic University
Rollins College
St. Leo University
University of North Florida
University of Tampa
University of West Florida

**Georgia**
Albany State University
Augusta State University W
Clark Atlanta University
Clayton State University
Columbus State University
Fort Valley State University
Georgia College and State University
Kennesaw State University
Morehouse College M
North Georgia College & State University W
Paine College
University of West Georgia W
Valdosta State University

**Hawaii**
Brigham Young University-Hawaii
Chaminade University of Honolulu
Hawaii Pacific University
University of Hawaii Hilo

**Idaho**
Northwest Nazarene University

**Illinois**
Lewis University

Tables and Indexes

Southern Illinois University
Edwardsville

**Indiana**
Oakland City University
Saint Joseph's College
University of Indianapolis
University of Southern Indiana

**Kansas**
Emporia State University
Fort Hays State University
Newman University W
Pittsburg State University

**Kentucky**
Bellarmine University
Kentucky State University
Kentucky Wesleyan College W
Northern Kentucky University

**Maryland**
Bowie State University
Columbia Union College

**Massachusetts**
American International College
W
Assumption College
Bentley College
Merrimack College
Stonehill College
University of Massachusetts
Lowell

**Michigan**
Ferris State University
Grand Valley State University
Hillsdale College
Lake Superior State University
Michigan Technological
University
Northern Michigan University W
Northwood University: Michigan
Saginaw Valley State University
Wayne State University

**Minnesota**
Bemidji State University W
Concordia University: St. Paul
Minnesota State University
Mankato
Moorhead
Saint Cloud State University
University of Minnesota
Duluth
Morris W
Winona State University

**Mississippi**
Delta State University W

**Missouri**
Drury University
Lincoln University W
Missouri Southern State
University
Northwest Missouri State
University
Southwest Baptist University
Truman State University
University of Central Missouri
University of Missouri
Missouri University of
Science and Technology

**Montana**
Montana State University
Billings

**Nebraska**
University of Nebraska
Kearney
Omaha W
Wayne State College

**New Hampshire**
Franklin Pierce University W
St. Anselm College
Southern New Hampshire
University

**New Jersey**
Bloomfield College
Caldwell College W
Felician College
Georgian Court University W
New Jersey Institute of
Technology

**New Mexico**
Eastern New Mexico University
New Mexico Highlands
University
Western New Mexico University

**New York**
Adelphi University
City University of New York
Queens College W
College of Saint Rose
Concordia College
Dominican College of Blauvelt W
Dowling College W
Le Moyne College
Long Island University
C. W. Post Campus
Mercy College
Molloy College
New York Institute of Technology
Nyack College
Pace University
St. Thomas Aquinas College

**North Carolina**
Barton College
Belmont Abbey College
Brevard College W
Catawba College
Elizabeth City State University
Fayetteville State University
Johnson C. Smith University
Lees-McRae College
Lenoir-Rhyne College
Livingstone College
Mars Hill College
Mount Olive College
North Carolina Central University
Pfeiffer University
Queens University of Charlotte
St. Andrews Presbyterian College
St. Augustine's College
Shaw University
University of North Carolina
Pembroke
Wingate University
Winston-Salem State University

**North Dakota**
North Dakota State University
University of Mary W
University of North Dakota

**Ohio**
Ashland University
Central State University
Tiffin University
University of Findlay

**Oklahoma**
East Central University
Oklahoma Panhandle State
University
Southeastern Oklahoma State
University W
Southwestern Oklahoma State
University W
University of Central Oklahoma
W

**Oregon**
Western Oregon University

**Pennsylvania**
Bloomsburg University of
Pennsylvania
California University of
Pennsylvania
Cheyney University of
Pennsylvania
Clarion University of
Pennsylvania W

East Stroudsburg University of
Pennsylvania
Eastern University M
Edinboro University of
Pennsylvania
Gannon University
Holy Family University
Indiana University of
Pennsylvania
Kutztown University of
Pennsylvania
Lock Haven University of
Pennsylvania
Mansfield University of
Pennsylvania
Mercyhurst College
Millersville University of
Pennsylvania
Philadelphia University
Seton Hill University
Shippensburg University of
Pennsylvania
Slippery Rock University of
Pennsylvania
University of Pittsburgh
Johnstown W
University of the Sciences in
Philadelphia
West Chester University of
Pennsylvania

**Puerto Rico**
University of Puerto Rico
Bayamon University College
Cayey University College
Mayaguez
Rio Piedras

**Rhode Island**
Bryant University

**South Carolina**
Anderson University
Benedict College
Claflin University
Coker College
Converse College W
Erskine College
Francis Marion University
Lander University W
Limestone College
Newberry College
North Greenville University
Presbyterian College
University of South Carolina
Aiken W
Upstate M

**South Dakota**
Augustana College
Northern State University
South Dakota State University
University of South Dakota

**Tennessee**
Carson-Newman College
Christian Brothers University
Lane College
LeMoyne-Owen College
Lincoln Memorial University
Tusculum College

**Texas**
Abilene Christian University
Angelo State University
Dallas Baptist University
Midwestern State University W
St. Edward's University
St. Mary's University W
Tarleton State University
Texas A&M International
University
Texas A&M University
Commerce
Kingsville
University of Texas
of the Permian Basin W
University of the Incarnate Word
West Texas A&M University

**Utah**
Dixie State College of Utah W

**Vermont**
St. Michael's College

**Virginia**
St. Paul's College
Virginia State University
Virginia Union University

**Washington**
Central Washington University
Saint Martin's University
Seattle Pacific University
Seattle University
Western Washington University

**West Virginia**
Alderson-Broaddus College
Bluefield State College
Concord University
Davis and Elkins College
Fairmont State University
Glenville State College
Ohio Valley University
University of Charleston
West Liberty State College
West Virginia Wesleyan College
Wheeling Jesuit University

**Wisconsin**
University of Wisconsin
Parkside

**Cross-country
Division III**

**Arkansas**
Hendrix College
University of the Ozarks

**California**
California Institute of Technology
California Lutheran University
California State University
East Bay
Chapman University
Claremont McKenna College
Menlo College
Mills College W
Occidental College
Pitzer College
Pomona College
University of California
Santa Cruz W
University of La Verne
University of Redlands
Whittier College

**Colorado**
Colorado College

**Connecticut**
Albertus Magnus College M
Connecticut College
Eastern Connecticut State
University
Mitchell College
St. Joseph College W
Trinity College
United States Coast Guard
Academy
Wesleyan University

**Delaware**
Wesley College

**District of Columbia**
Catholic University of America

**Georgia**
Agnes Scott College W
Emory University
LaGrange College
Oglethorpe University
Piedmont College
Spelman College W
Wesleyan College W

**Illinois**
Augustana College
Aurora University
Benedictine University
Blackburn College
Concordia University
Dominican University
Elmhurst College
Eureka College M
Greenville College
Illinois College
Illinois Wesleyan University
Knox College
Lake Forest College
Millikin University
Monmouth College
North Central College
North Park University
Principia College
Rockford College
University of Chicago
Wheaton College

**Indiana**
Anderson University
DePauw University
Earlham College
Franklin College
Hanover College
Manchester College
Rose-Hulman Institute of
Technology
Saint Mary's College W
Tri-State University
Wabash College M

**Iowa**
Buena Vista University
Central College
Coe College
Cornell College
Grinnell College
Loras College
Luther College
Simpson College
University of Dubuque
Wartburg College

**Kentucky**
Centre College
Thomas More College
Transylvania University

**Louisiana**
Louisiana College W

**Maine**
Bates College
Bowdoin College
Colby College
Maine Maritime Academy
St. Joseph's College
University of Maine
Farmington
University of New England
University of Southern Maine

**Maryland**
Frostburg State University
Goucher College
Hood College
Johns Hopkins University
McDaniel College
Salisbury University
Villa Julie College

**Massachusetts**
Amherst College
Anna Maria College M
Babson College
Bay Path College W
Brandeis University
Bridgewater State College
Clark University
Curry College W
Eastern Nazarene College
Elms College
Emerson College
Emmanuel College

Endicott College
Fitchburg State College
Framingham State College
Gordon College
Lasell College
Lesley University W
Massachusetts College of Liberal Arts
Massachusetts Institute of Technology
Massachusetts Maritime Academy
Mount Holyoke College W
Mount Ida College W
Newbury College
Pine Manor College W
Salem State College
Smith College W
Springfield College
Suffolk University
Tufts University
University of Massachusetts
  Boston
  Dartmouth
Wellesley College W
Western New England College
Westfield State College
Wheaton College
Williams College
Worcester Polytechnic Institute
Worcester State College

**Michigan**
Adrian College
Albion College
Alma College
Calvin College
Finlandia University
Hope College
Kalamazoo College
Olivet College

**Minnesota**
Augsburg College
Bethel University
Carleton College
College of St. Benedict W
College of St. Catherine W
College of St. Scholastica
Concordia College: Moorhead
Crown College
Gustavus Adolphus College
Hamline University
Macalester College
Martin Luther College
North Central University W
Northwestern College
St. John's University M
St. Mary's University of Minnesota
St. Olaf College
University of St. Thomas

**Mississippi**
Millsaps College
Mississippi College
Rust College

**Missouri**
Fontbonne University
Maryville University of Saint Louis
Washington University in St. Louis
Webster University W
Westminster College W

**Nebraska**
Nebraska Wesleyan University

**New Hampshire**
Daniel Webster College
Keene State College
New England College
Rivier College

**New Jersey**
Centenary College
The College of New Jersey
Drew University

Fairleigh Dickinson University
  College at Florham
Kean University
New Jersey City University
Ramapo College of New Jersey
Richard Stockton College of New Jersey
Rowan University
Rutgers, The State University of New Jersey
  Camden Regional Campus
  Newark Regional Campus W
Stevens Institute of Technology

**New York**
Alfred University
Bard College
Cazenovia College
City University of New York
  Baruch College W
  Brooklyn College
  Hunter College
  John Jay College of Criminal Justice
  Lehman College
  Medgar Evers College
  New York City College of Technology
  York College
Clarkson University
College of Mount St. Vincent
Hamilton College
Hartwick College
Hilbert College
Hobart and William Smith Colleges
Ithaca College
Keuka College
Manhattanville College
Medaille College
Mount St. Mary College M
Nazareth College of Rochester
New York University
Polytechnic University
Rensselaer Polytechnic Institute
Rochester Institute of Technology
St. Joseph's College W
St. Joseph's College: Suffolk Campus M
St. Lawrence University
State University of New York
  College at Brockport
  College at Buffalo
  College at Cortland
  College at Fredonia
  College at Geneseo
  College at Old Westbury
  College at Oneonta
  College at Plattsburgh
  College at Potsdam
  Farmingdale
  Institute of Technology at Utica/Rome
  Maritime College
  New Paltz
  Oswego
  Purchase
Union College
United States Merchant Marine Academy
University of Rochester
Utica College
Vassar College
Wells College W
Yeshiva University M

**North Carolina**
Chowan University W
Greensboro College
Guilford College
Meredith College W
Methodist University
North Carolina Wesleyan College W
Peace College W
Salem College W

**Ohio**
Baldwin-Wallace College
Bluffton University
Capital University
Case Western Reserve University
College of Mount St. Joseph
College of Wooster
Defiance College
Denison University
Heidelberg College
Hiram College
John Carroll University
Kenyon College
Lake Erie College
Marietta College
Mount Union College
Muskingum College
Oberlin College
Ohio Northern University
Ohio Wesleyan University
Otterbein College
Wilmington College
Wittenberg University

**Oregon**
George Fox University
Lewis & Clark College
Linfield College
Pacific University
Willamette University

**Pennsylvania**
Albright College
Allegheny College
Alvernia College
Arcadia University M
Baptist Bible College of Pennsylvania
Bryn Mawr College W
Cabrini College
Carnegie Mellon University
Cedar Crest College W
Chestnut Hill College
Delaware Valley College
DeSales University
Dickinson College
Eastern University W
Elizabethtown College
Franklin & Marshall College
Geneva College
Gettysburg College
Grove City College
Gwynedd-Mercy College
Haverford College
Immaculata University
Juniata College
Keystone College
King's College
La Roche College
Lancaster Bible College
Lebanon Valley College
Lincoln University
Lycoming College
Marywood University
Messiah College
Misericordia University
Moravian College
Mount Aloysius College
Muhlenberg College
Penn State
  Altoona
  Berks
  Erie, The Behrend College
  Harrisburg M
St. Vincent College
Susquehanna University
Swarthmore College
Thiel College
University of Pittsburgh
  Bradford
  Greensburg
University of Scranton
Ursinus College
Washington & Jefferson College
Waynesburg University
Westminster College M
Widener University

York College of Pennsylvania
**Rhode Island**
Johnson & Wales University: Providence
Rhode Island College
Roger Williams University
Salve Regina University

**South Dakota**
Presentation College M

**Tennessee**
Maryville College
Rhodes College
University of the South

**Texas**
Concordia University at Austin
East Texas Baptist University
McMurry University
Schreiner University M
Southwestern University
Sul Ross State University
Texas Lutheran University W
Trinity University
University of Dallas
University of Texas
  Dallas
  Tyler

**Vermont**
Castleton State College
Green Mountain College
Johnson State College
Lyndon State College
Middlebury College
Norwich University
Southern Vermont College

**Virginia**
Averett University
Bridgewater College
Christopher Newport University
Eastern Mennonite University
Emory & Henry College
Ferrum College
Hampden-Sydney College M
Lynchburg College
Mary Baldwin College W
Marymount University
Randolph College W
Roanoke College
Shenandoah University
University of Mary Washington
Virginia Wesleyan College
Washington and Lee University

**Washington**
Pacific Lutheran University
University of Puget Sound
Whitman College
Whitworth University

**West Virginia**
Bethany College

**Wisconsin**
Alverno College W
Beloit College
Carroll College
Carthage College
Concordia University Wisconsin
Edgewood College
Lakeland College
Lawrence University
Maranatha Baptist Bible College
Marian College of Fond du Lac
Milwaukee School of Engineering
Mount Mary College W
Northland College
Ripon College
St. Norbert College

University of Wisconsin
  Eau Claire
  La Crosse
  Oshkosh
  Platteville
  River Falls
  Stevens Point
  Stout
  Superior
  Whitewater
Wisconsin Lutheran College

## Fencing Division I

**Alaska**
University of Alaska
  Anchorage W

**California**
California State University
  Fullerton
Stanford University

**Colorado**
United States Air Force Academy

**Connecticut**
Sacred Heart University
Yale University

**Illinois**
Northwestern University W

**Indiana**
University of Notre Dame

**Massachusetts**
Boston College
Harvard College

**Michigan**
University of Detroit Mercy

**New Jersey**
Fairleigh Dickinson University
  Metropolitan Campus W
Princeton University
Rutgers, The State University of New Jersey
  New Brunswick/Piscataway Campus W

**New York**
Barnard College W
Columbia University M
Cornell University W
St. Francis College W
St. John's University

**North Carolina**
Duke University
University of North Carolina
  Chapel Hill

**Ohio**
Cleveland State University
Ohio State University
  Columbus Campus

**Pennsylvania**
Lafayette College
Penn State
  University Park
Temple University W
University of Pennsylvania

**Rhode Island**
Brown University

## Fencing Division II

**California**
University of California
  San Diego

**Michigan**
Wayne State University

Tables and Indexes

**New Jersey**
New Jersey Institute of Technology
**New York**
City University of New York Queens College W

## Fencing Division III

**California**
California Institute of Technology
**Maryland**
Johns Hopkins University
**Massachusetts**
Brandeis University
Massachusetts Institute of Technology
Tufts University W
Wellesley College W
**New Jersey**
Drew University
Stevens Institute of Technology
**New York**
City University of New York City College W
Hunter College
New York University
Vassar College
Yeshiva University M
**Pennsylvania**
Haverford College
**Wisconsin**
Lawrence University

## Field hockey Division I

**California**
Stanford University W
University of California Berkeley W
University of the Pacific W
**Connecticut**
Fairfield University W
Quinnipiac University W
Sacred Heart University W
University of Connecticut W
Yale University W
**Delaware**
University of Delaware W
**District of Columbia**
American University W
Georgetown University W
**Illinois**
Northwestern University W
**Indiana**
Ball State University W
Indiana University Bloomington W
**Iowa**
University of Iowa W
**Kentucky**
University of Louisville W
**Maine**
University of Maine W
**Maryland**
Towson University W
University of Maryland College Park W
**Massachusetts**
Boston College W
Boston University W
College of the Holy Cross W
Harvard College W

Northeastern University W
University of Massachusetts Amherst W
**Michigan**
Central Michigan University W
Michigan State University W
University of Michigan W
**Missouri**
Missouri State University W
Saint Louis University W
**New Hampshire**
Dartmouth College W
University of New Hampshire W
**New Jersey**
Monmouth University W
Princeton University W
Rider University W
**New York**
Barnard College W
Colgate University W
Cornell University W
Hofstra University W
Siena College W
State University of New York Albany W
Syracuse University W
**North Carolina**
Appalachian State University W
Davidson College W
Duke University W
University of North Carolina Chapel Hill W
Wake Forest University W
**Ohio**
Kent State University W
Miami University Oxford Campus W
Ohio State University Columbus Campus W
Ohio University W
**Pennsylvania**
Bucknell University W
Drexel University W
La Salle University W
Lafayette College W
Lehigh University W
Lock Haven University of Pennsylvania W
Penn State University Park W
Robert Morris University W
St. Francis University W
Saint Joseph's University W
Temple University W
University of Pennsylvania W
Villanova University W
West Chester University of Pennsylvania W
**Rhode Island**
Brown University W
Providence College W
University of Rhode Island W
**Vermont**
University of Vermont W
**Virginia**
College of William and Mary W
James Madison University W
Longwood University W
Old Dominion University W
Radford University W
University of Richmond W
University of Virginia W
Virginia Commonwealth University W

## Field hockey Division II

**Arkansas**
Hendrix College W
**Connecticut**
Southern Connecticut State University W
**Kentucky**
Bellarmine University W
**Massachusetts**
American International College W
Assumption College W
Bentley College W
Merrimack College W
Stonehill College W
University of Massachusetts Lowell W
**New Hampshire**
Franklin Pierce University W
St. Anselm College W
**New York**
Long Island University C. W. Post Campus W
**North Carolina**
Catawba College W
**Pennsylvania**
Bloomsburg University of Pennsylvania W
East Stroudsburg University of Pennsylvania W
Indiana University of Pennsylvania W
Kutztown University of Pennsylvania W
Mansfield University of Pennsylvania W
Mercyhurst College W
Millersville University of Pennsylvania W
Philadelphia University W
Seton Hill University W
Shippensburg University of Pennsylvania W
Slippery Rock University of Pennsylvania W
**Rhode Island**
Bryant University W
**Vermont**
St. Michael's College W

## Field hockey Division III

**Connecticut**
Connecticut College W
Eastern Connecticut State University W
Trinity College W
Wesleyan University W
Western Connecticut State University W
**Delaware**
Wesley College W
**District of Columbia**
Catholic University of America W
**Indiana**
DePauw University W
Earlham College W
**Kentucky**
Centre College W
Transylvania University W
**Maine**
Bates College W
Bowdoin College W

Colby College W
Husson College W
St. Joseph's College W
University of Maine Farmington W
University of New England W
University of Southern Maine W
**Maryland**
College of Notre Dame of Maryland W
Frostburg State University W
Goucher College W
Hood College W
Johns Hopkins University W
McDaniel College W
St. Mary's College of Maryland W
Salisbury University W
Villa Julie College W
Washington College W
**Massachusetts**
Amherst College W
Anna Maria College W
Babson College W
Becker College W
Bridgewater State College W
Clark University W
Elms College W
Endicott College W
Fitchburg State College W
Framingham State College W
Gordon College W
Lasell College W
Massachusetts Institute of Technology W
Mount Holyoke College W
Nichols College W
Regis College W
Salem State College W
Simmons College W
Smith College W
Springfield College W
Tufts University W
University of Massachusetts Dartmouth W
Wellesley College W
Western New England College W
Westfield State College W
Wheaton College W
Wheelock College W
Williams College W
Worcester Polytechnic Institute W
Worcester State College W
**New Hampshire**
Keene State College W
New England College W
Plymouth State University W
**New Jersey**
The College of New Jersey W
Drew University W
Fairleigh Dickinson University College at Florham W
Kean University W
Montclair State University W
Ramapo College of New Jersey W
Richard Stockton College of New Jersey W
Rowan University W
Stevens Institute of Technology W
William Paterson University of New Jersey W
**New York**
Elmira College W
Hamilton College W
Hartwick College W
Hobart and William Smith Colleges W
Ithaca College W
Manhattanville College W
Nazareth College of Rochester W
Rensselaer Polytechnic Institute W

St. Lawrence University W
Skidmore College W
State University of New York
College at Brockport W
College at Cortland W
College at Geneseo W
College at Oneonta W
College of Agriculture and Technology at Morrisville W
New Paltz W
Oswego W
Union College W
University of Rochester W
Utica College W
Vassar College W
Wells College W
Yeshiva University W
**Ohio**
College of Wooster W
Denison University W
Kenyon College W
Oberlin College W
Ohio Wesleyan University W
Wittenberg University W
**Pennsylvania**
Albright College W
Alvernia College W
Arcadia University W
Bryn Mawr College W
Cabrini College W
Cedar Crest College W
Delaware Valley College W
DeSales University W
Dickinson College W
Eastern University W
Elizabethtown College W
Franklin & Marshall College W
Gettysburg College W
Gwynedd-Mercy College W
Haverford College W
Immaculata University W
Juniata College W
King's College W
Lebanon Valley College W
Marywood University W
Messiah College W
Misericordia University W
Moravian College W
Muhlenberg College W
Neumann College W
Philadelphia Biblical University W
Rosemont College W
St. Vincent College W
Susquehanna University W
Swarthmore College W
University of Scranton W
Ursinus College W
Washington & Jefferson College W
Widener University W
Wilkes University W
Wilson College W
York College of Pennsylvania W
**Rhode Island**
Salve Regina University W
**Tennessee**
Rhodes College W
University of the South W
**Vermont**
Castleton State College W
Middlebury College W
**Virginia**
Bridgewater College W
Christopher Newport University W
Eastern Mennonite University W
Lynchburg College W
Randolph-Macon College W
Roanoke College W
Shenandoah University W
Sweet Briar College W

University of Mary Washington
W
Virginia Wesleyan College W
Washington and Lee University
W

### Football (tackle) Division IA

**Alabama**
Auburn University M
Troy University M
University of Alabama M
University of Alabama
  Birmingham M

**Arizona**
Arizona State University M
University of Arizona M

**Arkansas**
Arkansas State University M
University of Arkansas M

**California**
California State University
  Fresno M
San Diego State University M
San Jose State University M
Stanford University M
University of California
  Berkeley M
  Los Angeles M
University of Southern California
  M

**Colorado**
Colorado State University M
United States Air Force Academy
  M
University of Colorado
  Boulder M

**Connecticut**
University of Connecticut M

**Florida**
Florida Atlantic University M
Florida International University
  M
Florida State University M
University of Central Florida M
University of Florida M
University of Miami M
University of South Florida M

**Georgia**
Georgia Institute of Technology
  M
University of Georgia M

**Hawaii**
University of Hawaii
  Manoa M

**Idaho**
Boise State University M
University of Idaho M

**Illinois**
Northern Illinois University M
Northwestern University M
University of Illinois
  Urbana-Champaign M

**Indiana**
Ball State University M
Indiana University
  Bloomington M
Purdue University M
University of Notre Dame M

**Iowa**
Iowa State University M
University of Iowa M

**Kansas**
Kansas State University M
University of Kansas M

**Kentucky**
University of Kentucky M
University of Louisville M

**Louisiana**
Louisiana State University and
  Agricultural and Mechanical
  College M
Louisiana Tech University M
Tulane University M
University of Louisiana at
  Lafayette M
University of Louisiana at
  Monroe M

**Maryland**
United States Naval Academy M
University of Maryland
  College Park M

**Massachusetts**
Boston College M

**Michigan**
Central Michigan University M
Eastern Michigan University M
Michigan State University M
University of Michigan M
Western Michigan University M

**Minnesota**
University of Minnesota
  Twin Cities M

**Mississippi**
Mississippi State University M
University of Mississippi M
University of Southern
  Mississippi M

**Missouri**
University of Missouri
  Columbia M

**Nebraska**
University of Nebraska
  Lincoln M

**Nevada**
University of Nevada
  Las Vegas M
  Reno M

**New Jersey**
Rutgers, The State University of
  New Jersey
  New Brunswick/Piscataway
  Campus M

**New Mexico**
New Mexico State University M
University of New Mexico M

**New York**
Syracuse University M
United States Military Academy
  M

**North Carolina**
Duke University M
East Carolina University M
North Carolina State University
  M
University of North Carolina
  Chapel Hill M
Wake Forest University M

**Ohio**
Bowling Green State University
  M
Kent State University M
Miami University
  Oxford Campus M
Ohio State University
  Columbus Campus M
Ohio University M
University of Akron M
University of Cincinnati M
University of Toledo M

**Oklahoma**
Oklahoma State University M

University of Oklahoma M
University of Tulsa M

**Oregon**
Oregon State University M
University of Oregon M

**Pennsylvania**
Penn State
  University Park M
Temple University M
University of Pittsburgh M

**South Carolina**
Clemson University M
University of South Carolina M

**Tennessee**
Middle Tennessee State
  University M
University of Memphis M
University of Tennessee
  Knoxville M
Vanderbilt University M

**Texas**
Baylor University M
Rice University M
Southern Methodist University M
Texas A&M University M
Texas Christian University M
Texas Tech University M
University of Houston M
University of North Texas M
University of Texas
  Austin M
  El Paso M

**Utah**
Brigham Young University M
University of Utah M
Utah State University M

**Virginia**
University of Virginia M
Virginia Polytechnic Institute and
  State University M

**Washington**
University of Washington M
Washington State University M

**West Virginia**
Marshall University M
West Virginia University M

**Wisconsin**
University of Wisconsin
  Madison M

**Wyoming**
University of Wyoming M

### Football (tackle) Division IAA

**Alabama**
Alabama Agricultural and
  Mechanical University M
Alabama State University M
Jacksonville State University M
Samford University M

**Arizona**
Northern Arizona University M

**Arkansas**
University of Arkansas
  Pine Bluff M

**California**
California Polytechnic State
  University: San Luis Obispo M
California State University
  Sacramento M
University of San Diego M

**Colorado**
University of Northern Colorado
  M

**Connecticut**
Central Connecticut State
  University M
Sacred Heart University M
Yale University M

**Delaware**
Delaware State University M
University of Delaware M

**District of Columbia**
Georgetown University M
Howard University M

**Florida**
Bethune-Cookman University M
Florida Agricultural and
  Mechanical University M
Jacksonville University M

**Georgia**
Georgia Southern University M
Savannah State University M

**Idaho**
Idaho State University M

**Illinois**
Eastern Illinois University M
Illinois State University M
Southern Illinois University
  Carbondale M
Western Illinois University M

**Indiana**
Butler University M
Indiana State University M
Valparaiso University M

**Iowa**
Drake University M
University of Northern Iowa M

**Kentucky**
Eastern Kentucky University M
Morehead State University M
Murray State University M
Western Kentucky University M

**Louisiana**
Grambling State University M
McNeese State University M
Nicholls State University M
Northwestern State University M
Southeastern Louisiana University
  M
Southern University and
  Agricultural and Mechanical
  College M

**Maine**
University of Maine M

**Maryland**
Morgan State University M
Towson University M

**Massachusetts**
College of the Holy Cross M
Harvard College M
Northeastern University M
University of Massachusetts
  Amherst M

**Mississippi**
Alcorn State University M
Jackson State University M
Mississippi Valley State
  University M

**Missouri**
Missouri State University M
Southeast Missouri State
  University M

**Montana**
Montana State University
  Bozeman M
University of Montana: Missoula
  M

**New Hampshire**
Dartmouth College M

University of New Hampshire M

**New Jersey**
Monmouth University M
Princeton University M

**New York**
Barnard College M
Colgate University M
Cornell University M
Fordham University M
Hofstra University M
Iona College M
Marist College M
State University of New York
  Albany M
  Stony Brook M
Wagner College M

**North Carolina**
Appalachian State University M
Davidson College M
Elon University M
Gardner-Webb University M
North Carolina Agricultural and
  Technical State University M
Western Carolina University M

**Ohio**
University of Dayton M
Youngstown State University M

**Oregon**
Portland State University M

**Pennsylvania**
Bucknell University M
Duquesne University M
La Salle University M
Lafayette College M
Lehigh University M
Robert Morris University M
St. Francis University M
University of Pennsylvania M
Villanova University M

**Rhode Island**
Brown University M
University of Rhode Island M'

**South Carolina**
Charleston Southern University M
The Citadel M
Coastal Carolina University M
Furman University M
South Carolina State University
  M
Wofford College M

**Tennessee**
Austin Peay State University M
Tennessee State University M
Tennessee Technological
  University M
University of Tennessee
  Chattanooga M
  Martin M

**Texas**
Prairie View A&M University M
Sam Houston State University M
Stephen F. Austin State University
  M
Texas Southern University M
Texas State University: San
  Marcos M

**Utah**
Southern Utah University M
Weber State University M

**Virginia**
College of William and Mary M
Hampton University M
James Madison University M
Liberty University M
Norfolk State University M
University of Richmond M
Virginia Military Institute M

## Football (tackle) Division II

### Alabama
Miles College M
Stillman College M
Tuskegee University M
University of North Alabama M
University of West Alabama M

### Arkansas
Arkansas Tech University M
Harding University M
Henderson State University M
Ouachita Baptist University M
Southern Arkansas University M
University of Arkansas
    Monticello M
University of Central Arkansas M

### California
Humboldt State University M

### Colorado
Adams State College M
Colorado School of Mines M
Fort Lewis College M
Mesa State College M
Western State College of
    Colorado M

### Connecticut
Southern Connecticut State
    University M

### Georgia
Albany State University M
Clark Atlanta University M
Fort Valley State University M
Morehouse College M
University of West Georgia M
Valdosta State University M

### Illinois
Quincy University M

### Indiana
Saint Joseph's College M
University of Indianapolis M

### Iowa
Upper Iowa University M

### Kansas
Emporia State University M
Fort Hays State University M
Pittsburg State University M
Washburn University M

### Kentucky
Kentucky State University M
Kentucky Wesleyan College M

### Maryland
Bowie State University M

### Massachusetts
American International College M
Assumption College M
Bentley College M
Merrimack College M
Stonehill College M

### Michigan
Ferris State University M
Grand Valley State University M
Hillsdale College M
Michigan Technological
    University M
Northern Michigan University M
Northwood University: Michigan
    M
Saginaw Valley State University
    M
Wayne State University M

### Minnesota
Bemidji State University M
Concordia University: St. Paul M

Minnesota State University
    Mankato M
    Moorhead M
Saint Cloud State University M
Southwest Minnesota State
    University M
University of Minnesota
    Crookston M
    Duluth M
    Morris M
Winona State University M

### Mississippi
Delta State University M

### Missouri
Lincoln University M
Missouri Southern State
    University M
Missouri Western State University
    M
Northwest Missouri State
    University M
Southwest Baptist University M
Truman State University M
University of Central Missouri M
University of Missouri
    Missouri University of
    Science and Technology
    M

### Nebraska
Chadron State College M
University of Nebraska
    Kearney M
    Omaha M
Wayne State College M

### New Hampshire
St. Anselm College M

### New Mexico
Eastern New Mexico University
    M
New Mexico Highlands
    University M
Western New Mexico University
    M

### New York
Long Island University
    C. W. Post Campus M
Pace University M

### North Carolina
Brevard College M
Catawba College M
Chowan University M
Elizabeth City State University M
Fayetteville State University M
Johnson C. Smith University M
Lenoir-Rhyne College M
Livingstone College M
Mars Hill College M
North Carolina Central University
    M
St. Augustine's College M
Shaw University M
University of North Carolina
    Pembroke M
Wingate University M
Winston-Salem State University
    M

### North Dakota
North Dakota State University M
University of Mary M
University of North Dakota M

### Ohio
Ashland University M
Central State University M
Tiffin University M
University of Findlay M

### Oklahoma
East Central University M
Northeastern State University M
Oklahoma Panhandle State
    University M

Southeastern Oklahoma State
    University M
Southwestern Oklahoma State
    University M
University of Central Oklahoma
    M

### Oregon
Western Oregon University M

### Pennsylvania
Bloomsburg University of
    Pennsylvania M
Cheyney University of
    Pennsylvania M
Clarion University of
    Pennsylvania M
East Stroudsburg University of
    Pennsylvania M
Edinboro University of
    Pennsylvania M
Gannon University M
Indiana University of
    Pennsylvania M
Kutztown University of
    Pennsylvania M
Lock Haven University of
    Pennsylvania M
Mercyhurst College M
Millersville University of
    Pennsylvania M
Seton Hill University M
Shippensburg University of
    Pennsylvania M
Slippery Rock University of
    Pennsylvania M
West Chester University of
    Pennsylvania M

### Rhode Island
Bryant University M

### South Carolina
Benedict College M
Newberry College M
North Greenville University M
Presbyterian College M

### South Dakota
Augustana College M
Northern State University M
South Dakota State University M
University of South Dakota M

### Tennessee
Carson-Newman College M
Lane College M
Tusculum College M

### Texas
Abilene Christian University M
Angelo State University M
Midwestern State University M
Tarleton State University M
Texas A&M University
    Commerce M
    Kingsville M
West Texas A&M University M

### Utah
Dixie State College of Utah M

### Virginia
St. Paul's College M
Virginia State University M
Virginia Union University M

### Washington
Central Washington University M
Western Washington University
    M

### West Virginia
Concord University M
Fairmont State University M
Glenville State College M
Shepherd University M
University of Charleston M
West Liberty State College M
West Virginia Wesleyan College
    M

## Football (tackle) Division III

### Alabama
Huntingdon College M

### California
California Lutheran University M
Chapman University M
Claremont McKenna College M
Menlo College M
Occidental College M
Pitzer College M
Pomona College M
University of La Verne M
University of Redlands M
Whittier College M

### Colorado
Colorado College M

### Connecticut
Trinity College M
United States Coast Guard
    Academy M
Wesleyan University M
Western Connecticut State
    University M

### Delaware
Wesley College M

### District of Columbia
Catholic University of America M
Gallaudet University M

### Georgia
LaGrange College M

### Illinois
Augustana College M
Aurora University M
Benedictine University M
Blackburn College M
Concordia University M
Elmhurst College M
Eureka College M
Greenville College M
Illinois College M
Illinois Wesleyan University M
Knox College M
Lake Forest College M
MacMurray College M
Millikin University M
Monmouth College M
North Central College M
North Park University M
Principia College M
Rockford College M
University of Chicago M
Wheaton College M

### Indiana
Anderson University M
DePauw University M
Earlham College M
Franklin College M
Hanover College M
Manchester College M
Rose-Hulman Institute of
    Technology M
Tri-State University M
Wabash College M

### Iowa
Buena Vista University M
Central College M
Coe College M
Cornell College M
Grinnell College M
Loras College M
Luther College M
Simpson College M
University of Dubuque M
Wartburg College M

### Kentucky
Centre College M
Thomas More College M

### Louisiana
Louisiana College M

### Maine
Bates College M
Bowdoin College M
Colby College M
Husson College M
Maine Maritime Academy M

### Maryland
Frostburg State University M
Johns Hopkins University M
McDaniel College M
Salisbury University M

### Massachusetts
Amherst College M
Becker College M
Bridgewater State College M
Curry College M
Endicott College M
Fitchburg State College M
Framingham State College M
Massachusetts Institute of
    Technology M
Massachusetts Maritime Academy
    M
Mount Ida College M
Nichols College M
Springfield College M
Tufts University M
University of Massachusetts
    Dartmouth M
Western New England College M
Westfield State College M
Williams College M
Worcester Polytechnic Institute M
Worcester State College M

### Michigan
Adrian College M
Albion College M
Alma College M
Hope College M
Kalamazoo College M
Olivet College M

### Minnesota
Augsburg College M
Bethel University M
Carleton College M
Concordia College: Moorhead M
Crown College M
Gustavus Adolphus College M
Hamline University M
Macalester College M
Martin Luther College M
Northwestern College M
St. John's University M
St. Olaf College M
University of St. Thomas M

### Mississippi
Millsaps College M
Mississippi College M

### Missouri
Washington University in St.
    Louis M
Westminster College M

### Nebraska
Nebraska Wesleyan University M

### New Hampshire
Plymouth State University M

### New Jersey
The College of New Jersey M
Fairleigh Dickinson University
    Metropolitan Campus M
Kean University M
Montclair State University M
Rowan University M
William Paterson University of
    New Jersey M

### New York
Alfred University M
Hamilton College M

Hartwick College M
Hobart and William Smith
  Colleges M
Ithaca College M
Rensselaer Polytechnic Institute
  M
St. John Fisher College M
St. Lawrence University M
State University of New York
  College at Brockport M
  College at Buffalo M
  College at Cortland M
  College of Agriculture and
    Technology at Morrisville
    M
  Maritime College M
Union College M
United States Merchant Marine
  Academy M
University of Rochester M
Utica College M

### North Carolina

Greensboro College M
Guilford College M
Methodist University M
North Carolina Wesleyan College
  M

### Ohio

Baldwin-Wallace College M
Bluffton University M
Capital University M
Case Western Reserve University
  M
College of Mount St. Joseph M
College of Wooster M
Defiance College M
Denison University M
Heidelberg College M
Hiram College M
John Carroll University M
Kenyon College M
Marietta College M
Mount Union College M
Muskingum College M
Oberlin College M
Ohio Northern University M
Ohio Wesleyan University M
Otterbein College M
Wilmington College M
Wittenberg University M

### Oregon

Lewis & Clark College M
Linfield College M
Willamette University M

### Pennsylvania

Albright College M
Allegheny College M
Carnegie Mellon University M
Delaware Valley College M
Dickinson College M
Franklin & Marshall College M
Geneva College M
Gettysburg College M
Grove City College M
Juniata College M
King's College M
Lebanon Valley College M
Lycoming College M
Moravian College M
Muhlenberg College M
St. Vincent College M
Susquehanna University M
Thiel College M
Ursinus College M
Washington & Jefferson College
  M
Waynesburg University M
Westminster College M
Widener University M
Wilkes University M

### Rhode Island

Salve Regina University M

### Tennessee

Maryville College M
Rhodes College M
University of the South M

### Texas

Austin College M
East Texas Baptist University M
Hardin-Simmons University M
Howard Payne University M
McMurry University M
Sul Ross State University M
Texas Lutheran University M
Trinity University M
University of Mary Hardin-Baylor
  M

### Vermont

Middlebury College M
Norwich University M

### Virginia

Averett University M
Bridgewater College M
Christopher Newport University
  M
Emory & Henry College M
Ferrum College M
Hampden-Sydney College M
Randolph-Macon College M
Shenandoah University M
Washington and Lee University M

### Washington

Pacific Lutheran University M
University of Puget Sound M
Whitworth University M

### West Virginia

Bethany College M

### Wisconsin

Beloit College M
Carroll College M
Carthage College M
Concordia University Wisconsin
  M
Lakeland College M
Lawrence University M
Maranatha Baptist Bible College
  M
Ripon College M
St. Norbert College M
University of Wisconsin
  Eau Claire M
  La Crosse M
  Oshkosh M
  Platteville M
  River Falls M
  Stevens Point M
  Stout M
  Whitewater M
Wisconsin Lutheran College M

## Golf Division I

### Alabama

Alabama Agricultural and
  Mechanical University M
Alabama State University
Auburn University
Birmingham-Southern College
Jacksonville State University
Samford University
Troy University
University of Alabama
University of Alabama
  Birmingham
University of South Alabama

### Arizona

Arizona State University
Northern Arizona University W
University of Arizona

### Arkansas

Arkansas State University
University of Arkansas

University of Arkansas
  Little Rock
  Pine Bluff M

### California

California Polytechnic State
  University: San Luis Obispo
California State University
  Fresno
  Long Beach
  Northridge
  Sacramento
Loyola Marymount University M
Pepperdine University
St. Mary's College of California
  M
San Diego State University
San Jose State University
Santa Clara University
Stanford University
University of California
  Berkeley
  Davis
  Irvine
  Los Angeles
  Riverside
  Santa Barbara M
University of San Diego M
University of San Francisco
University of Southern California
University of the Pacific M

### Colorado

Colorado State University
United States Air Force Academy
  M
University of Colorado
  Boulder
University of Denver

### Connecticut

Central Connecticut State
  University
Fairfield University
Quinnipiac University M
Sacred Heart University
University of Connecticut M
University of Hartford
Yale University

### Delaware

University of Delaware M

### District of Columbia

George Washington University M
Georgetown University

### Florida

Bethune-Cookman University
Florida Agricultural and
  Mechanical University M
Florida Atlantic University
Florida International University
  W
Florida State University
Jacksonville University
Stetson University
University of Central Florida
University of Florida
University of Miami W
University of North Florida M
University of South Florida

### Georgia

Augusta State University
Georgia Institute of Technology
  M
Georgia Southern University M
Georgia State University
Kennesaw State University M
Mercer University
Savannah State University
University of Georgia

### Hawaii

University of Hawaii
  Manoa

### Idaho

Boise State University

Idaho State University
University of Idaho

### Illinois

Bradley University
Chicago State University
DePaul University M
Eastern Illinois University
Illinois State University
Loyola University Chicago
Northern Illinois University
Northwestern University
Southern Illinois University
  Carbondale
University of Illinois
  Urbana-Champaign
Western Illinois University

### Indiana

Ball State University
Butler University
Indiana State University W
Indiana University
  Bloomington
Indiana University-Purdue
  University Fort Wayne
Indiana University-Purdue
  University Indianapolis
Purdue University
University of Evansville
University of Notre Dame

### Iowa

Drake University
Iowa State University
University of Iowa
University of Northern Iowa

### Kansas

Kansas State University
University of Kansas
Wichita State University

### Kentucky

Eastern Kentucky University
Morehead State University M
Murray State University
University of Kentucky
University of Louisville
Western Kentucky University

### Louisiana

Centenary College of Louisiana
Grambling State University
Louisiana State University and
  Agricultural and Mechanical
  College
Louisiana Tech University M
McNeese State University
Nicholls State University
Southeastern Louisiana University
  M
Southern University and
  Agricultural and Mechanical
  College
University of Louisiana at
  Lafayette M
University of Louisiana at
  Monroe
University of New Orleans M

### Maryland

Loyola College in Maryland M
Mount St. Mary's University
Towson University
United States Naval Academy M
University of Maryland
  College Park

### Massachusetts

Boston College
Boston University W
College of the Holy Cross
Harvard College

### Michigan

Eastern Michigan University
Michigan State University
Oakland University
University of Detroit Mercy

University of Michigan
Western Michigan University W

### Minnesota

University of Minnesota
  Twin Cities

### Mississippi

Alcorn State University
Jackson State University
Mississippi State University
Mississippi Valley State
  University
University of Mississippi
University of Southern
  Mississippi

### Missouri

Missouri State University M
University of Missouri
  Columbia
  Kansas City

### Montana

Montana State University
  Bozeman W
University of Montana: Missoula
  W

### Nebraska

Creighton University
University of Nebraska
  Lincoln

### Nevada

University of Nevada
  Las Vegas
  Reno

### New Hampshire

Dartmouth College

### New Jersey

Fairleigh Dickinson University
  Metropolitan Campus
Monmouth University
Princeton University
Rider University M
Rutgers, The State University of
  New Jersey
    New Brunswick/Piscataway
    Campus
Saint Peter's College M
Seton Hall University M

### New Mexico

New Mexico State University
University of New Mexico

### New York

Barnard College
Canisius College M
Colgate University M
Cornell University M
Fordham University M
Hofstra University
Iona College M
Long Island University
  Brooklyn Campus
Manhattan College M
Niagara University M
Saint Bonaventure University M
St. Francis College
St. John's University
Siena College
State University of New York
  Albany W
  Binghamton M
United States Military Academy
  M
Wagner College

### North Carolina

Appalachian State University
Campbell University
Davidson College M
Duke University
East Carolina University
Elon University
Gardner-Webb University
High Point University

North Carolina State University
University of North Carolina
    Chapel Hill
    Charlotte M
    Greensboro
    Wilmington
Wake Forest University
Western Carolina University

**Ohio**
Bowling Green State University
Cleveland State University
Kent State University
Miami University
    Oxford Campus M
Ohio State University
    Columbus Campus
Ohio University
University of Akron M
University of Cincinnati
University of Dayton
University of Toledo
Wright State University M
Xavier University
Youngstown State University

**Oklahoma**
Oklahoma State University
Oral Roberts University
University of Oklahoma
University of Tulsa

**Oregon**
Oregon State University
Portland State University W
University of Oregon
University of Portland

**Pennsylvania**
Bucknell University
Drexel University M
Duquesne University M
La Salle University M
Lafayette College M
Lehigh University
Penn State
    University Park
Robert Morris University
St. Francis University
Saint Joseph's University M
Temple University M
University of Pennsylvania
Villanova University M

**Rhode Island**
Brown University
University of Rhode Island M

**South Carolina**
Charleston Southern University
The Citadel W
Clemson University M
Coastal Carolina University
College of Charleston
Francis Marion University M
Furman University
South Carolina State University
University of South Carolina
Winthrop University
Wofford College

**Tennessee**
Austin Peay State University
Belmont University
East Tennessee State University
Lipscomb University
Middle Tennessee State
    University
Tennessee State University
Tennessee Technological
    University
University of Memphis
University of Tennessee
    Chattanooga M
    Knoxville
    Martin M
Vanderbilt University

**Texas**
Baylor University

Lamar University
Prairie View A&M University
Rice University M
Sam Houston State University
Southern Methodist University
Stephen F. Austin State University
    M
Texas A&M University
Texas Christian University
Texas Southern University
Texas State University: San
    Marcos
Texas Tech University
University of Houston M
University of North Texas
University of Texas
    Arlington M
    Austin
    El Paso
    Pan American
    San Antonio

**Utah**
Brigham Young University
Southern Utah University M
University of Utah M
Utah State University M
Utah Valley State College
Weber State University

**Virginia**
College of William and Mary
George Mason University M
Hampton University
James Madison University
Liberty University M
Longwood University
Old Dominion University
Radford University
University of Richmond
University of Virginia
Virginia Commonwealth
    University M
Virginia Polytechnic Institute and
    State University M

**Washington**
Gonzaga University
University of Washington
Washington State University

**West Virginia**
Marshall University

**Wisconsin**
Marquette University M
University of Wisconsin
    Green Bay M
    Madison

**Wyoming**
University of Wyoming

## Golf Division II

**Alabama**
University of Montevallo
University of North Alabama M

**Arizona**
Grand Canyon University

**Arkansas**
Arkansas Tech University
Harding University
Henderson State University
Ouachita Baptist University M
Southern Arkansas University
University of Arkansas
    Monticello
University of Central Arkansas

**California**
California State University
    Bakersfield
    Chico
    Dominguez Hills M
    Monterey Bay
    San Bernardino M
    Stanislaus M
Notre Dame de Namur University
Sonoma State University
University of California
    San Diego M

**Colorado**
Adams State College W
Colorado Christian University
Colorado School of Mines M
Colorado State University
    Pueblo
Fort Lewis College M
Mesa State College W
Regis University
University of Colorado
    Colorado Springs M
University of Northern Colorado

**Connecticut**
Post University M
University of New Haven M

**Delaware**
Goldey-Beacom College M
Wilmington University M

**Florida**
Barry University
Eckerd College
Flagler College
Florida Gulf Coast University
Florida Institute of Technology
Florida Southern College
Lynn University
Nova Southeastern University
Rollins College
St. Leo University
University of Tampa M
University of West Florida

**Georgia**
Armstrong Atlantic State
    University
Clayton State University M
Columbus State University M
Georgia College and State
    University M
Georgia Southwestern State
    University M
Kennesaw State University W
Morehouse College M
Paine College M
University of West Georgia
Valdosta State University M

**Hawaii**
Brigham Young
    University-Hawaii M
Chaminade University of
    Honolulu M
Hawaii Pacific University M
University of Hawaii
    Hilo

**Idaho**
Northwest Nazarene University M

**Illinois**
Lewis University
Quincy University
Southern Illinois University
    Edwardsville

**Indiana**
Oakland City University
Saint Joseph's College
University of Indianapolis
University of Southern Indiana

**Iowa**
Upper Iowa University

**Kansas**
Fort Hays State University
Newman University
Pittsburg State University M
Washburn University M

**Kentucky**
Bellarmine University
Kentucky State University M
Kentucky Wesleyan College
Northern Kentucky University

**Massachusetts**
American International College M
Assumption College M
Bentley College M
University of Massachusetts
    Lowell M

**Michigan**
Ferris State University
Grand Valley State University
Northern Michigan University M
Northwood University: Michigan
Saginaw Valley State University
    M
Wayne State University M

**Minnesota**
Bemidji State University
Concordia University: St. Paul
Minnesota State University
    Mankato
    Moorhead W
Saint Cloud State University
Southwest Minnesota State
    University W
University of Minnesota
    Crookston
    Morris
Winona State University

**Mississippi**
Delta State University M

**Missouri**
Drury University
Lincoln University M
Missouri Southern State
    University M
Missouri Western State University
Rockhurst University
Southwest Baptist University M
Truman State University
University of Central Missouri M
University of Missouri
    St. Louis

**Montana**
Montana State University
    Billings

**Nebraska**
Chadron State College W
University of Nebraska
    Kearney
    Omaha W
Wayne State College

**New Hampshire**
Franklin Pierce University M
St. Anselm College M
Southern New Hampshire
    University M

**New Jersey**
Caldwell College M
Felician College M

**New Mexico**
Western New Mexico University

**New York**
Adelphi University M
College of Saint Rose M
Dominican College of Blauvelt M
Dowling College M
Le Moyne College M
Nyack College M
Pace University M
St. Thomas Aquinas College M

**North Carolina**
Barton College M
Belmont Abbey College
Brevard College M
Catawba College
Chowan University M
Elizabeth City State University M
Fayetteville State University M
Johnson C. Smith University M
Lees-McRae College M
Lenoir-Rhyne College
Mars Hill College
Mount Olive College
North Carolina Central University
    M
Pfeiffer University
Queens University of Charlotte
St. Andrews Presbyterian College
St. Augustine's College M
University of North Carolina
    Pembroke M
Wingate University
Winston-Salem State University
    M

**North Dakota**
North Dakota State University
University of Mary M
University of North Dakota

**Ohio**
Ashland University
Central State University
Tiffin University
University of Findlay

**Oklahoma**
Cameron University
East Central University M
Northeastern State University
Oklahoma Panhandle State
    University
Southeastern Oklahoma State
    University M
Southwestern Oklahoma State
    University
University of Central Oklahoma

**Pennsylvania**
California University of
    Pennsylvania
Clarion University of
    Pennsylvania M
Gannon University
Holy Family University M
Indiana University of
    Pennsylvania M
Kutztown University of
    Pennsylvania W
Mercyhurst College
Millersville University of
    Pennsylvania M
Philadelphia University M
Seton Hill University
University of Pittsburgh
    Johnstown
University of the Sciences in
    Philadelphia M
West Chester University of
    Pennsylvania

**Rhode Island**
Bryant University M

**South Carolina**
Anderson University
Benedict College
Coker College M
Lander University M
Limestone College
Newberry College
North Greenville University M
Presbyterian College
University of South Carolina
    Aiken M
    Upstate

**South Dakota**
Augustana College

Northern State University
South Dakota State University
University of South Dakota

**Tennessee**
Carson-Newman College M
Christian Brothers University
LeMoyne-Owen College M
Lincoln Memorial University
Tusculum College

**Texas**
Abilene Christian University M
Dallas Baptist University
Midwestern State University M
St. Edward's University
St. Mary's University
Tarleton State University W
Texas A&M International
    University M
Texas A&M University
    Commerce
University of the Incarnate Word
West Texas A&M University

**Utah**
Dixie State College of Utah M

**Vermont**
St. Michael's College M

**Virginia**
St. Paul's College M
Virginia Union University M

**Washington**
Saint Martin's University
Western Washington University

**West Virginia**
Bluefield State College M
Concord University M
Davis and Elkins College M
Fairmont State University
Glenville State College
Ohio Valley University
Salem International University
Shepherd University M
University of Charleston M
West Liberty State College
West Virginia Wesleyan College
    M
Wheeling Jesuit University

**Wisconsin**
University of Wisconsin
    Parkside M

**Golf Division III**

**Alabama**
Huntingdon College M

**Arkansas**
Hendrix College

**California**
California Lutheran University M
California State University
    East Bay
Chapman University M
Claremont McKenna College
La Sierra University M
Menlo College M
Occidental College M
Pitzer College M
Pomona College M
University of California
    Santa Cruz W
University of La Verne M
University of Redlands
Whittier College M

**Connecticut**
Mitchell College M
Trinity College M
Wesleyan University M

**Delaware**
Wesley College M

**Georgia**
Emory University M
LaGrange College M
Oglethorpe University
Piedmont College

**Illinois**
Augustana College
Aurora University
Benedictine University M
Blackburn College M
Elmhurst College
Eureka College M
Illinois College
Illinois Wesleyan University
Knox College
Millikin University
Monmouth College
North Central College
North Park University
Rockford College
Wheaton College

**Indiana**
Anderson University
DePauw University
Franklin College
Hanover College
Manchester College
Rose-Hulman Institute of
    Technology
Saint Mary's College W
Tri-State University
Wabash College M

**Iowa**
Buena Vista University
Central College
Coe College
Cornell College
Grinnell College
Loras College
Luther College
Simpson College
University of Dubuque
Wartburg College

**Kentucky**
Centre College
Thomas More College
Transylvania University

**Louisiana**
Louisiana College M

**Maine**
Bates College
Bowdoin College
Husson College M
Maine Maritime Academy M
St. Joseph's College M
Thomas College M
University of Maine
    Farmington M
University of New England M

**Maryland**
Frostburg State University M
Hood College
McDaniel College
Villa Julie College

**Massachusetts**
Amherst College
Anna Maria College M
Babson College M
Becker College M
Brandeis University M
Elms College M
Endicott College M
Massachusetts College of Liberal
    Arts M
Massachusetts Institute of
    Technology M
Mount Holyoke College W
Newbury College M
Nichols College M
Salem State College M
Springfield College M
Suffolk University M

Tufts University M
University of Massachusetts
    Dartmouth M
Wellesley College W
Wentworth Institute of
    Technology M
Western New England College M
Williams College
Worcester State College M

**Michigan**
Adrian College
Albion College
Alma College
Calvin College
Hope College
Kalamazoo College
Olivet College

**Minnesota**
Augsburg College
Bethany Lutheran College
Bethel University M
Carleton College
College of St. Benedict W
Concordia College: Moorhead
Gustavus Adolphus College
Macalester College
Martin Luther College M
North Central University M
Northwestern College M
St. John's University M
St. Mary's University of
    Minnesota
St. Olaf College
University of St. Thomas

**Mississippi**
Millsaps College
Mississippi College M

**Missouri**
Fontbonne University
Maryville University of Saint
    Louis
Webster University M
Westminster College

**Nebraska**
Nebraska Wesleyan University

**New Jersey**
Centenary College M
Fairleigh Dickinson University
    College at Florham M
Rutgers, The State University of
    New Jersey
        Camden Regional Campus
        M
Stevens Institute of Technology M

**New York**
Cazenovia College M
Clarkson University M
D'Youville College M
Elmira College
Hamilton College M
Hilbert College M
Hobart and William Smith
    Colleges
Keuka College M
Manhattanville College M
Nazareth College of Rochester
New York University
Polytechnic University M
Rensselaer Polytechnic Institute
    M
St. John Fisher College M
St. Joseph's College: Suffolk
    Campus M
St. Lawrence University
Skidmore College M
State University of New York
    College at Cortland W
    College at Potsdam M
    Farmingdale M
    Institute of Technology at
        Utica/Rome M
    Oswego M

United States Merchant Marine
    Academy M
University of Rochester M
Utica College M
Vassar College W
Yeshiva University M

**North Carolina**
Greensboro College M
Guilford College M
Methodist University
North Carolina Wesleyan College
    M

**Ohio**
Baldwin-Wallace College
Capital University
College of Mount St. Joseph
College of Wooster M
Defiance College
Denison University
Heidelberg College M
Hiram College
John Carroll University
Kenyon College M
Lake Erie College M
Mount Union College
Muskingum College
Oberlin College M
Ohio Northern University
Ohio Wesleyan University M
Otterbein College
Wilmington College
Wittenberg University

**Oregon**
George Fox University
Lewis & Clark College
Linfield College
Pacific University
Willamette University

**Pennsylvania**
Albright College M
Allegheny College
Alvernia College M
Arcadia University M
Baptist Bible College of
    Pennsylvania M
Cabrini College M
Carnegie Mellon University M
Chestnut Hill College
Delaware Valley College M
DeSales University M
Dickinson College
Eastern University M
Elizabethtown College M
Franklin & Marshall College
Gettysburg College
Grove City College
Gwynedd-Mercy College M
Immaculata University M
Keystone College M
King's College M
La Roche College M
Lebanon Valley College M
Lycoming College M
Messiah College M
Moravian College M
Mount Aloysius College M
Muhlenberg College M
Neumann College M
Penn State
    Altoona
    Berks M
    Erie, The Behrend College
    Harrisburg M
Philadelphia Biblical University
    M
St. Vincent College
Susquehanna University
Swarthmore College M
Thiel College
University of Pittsburgh
    Bradford
    Greensburg
University of Scranton M
Ursinus College M

Washington & Jefferson College
Waynesburg University
Westminster College
Widener University M
Wilkes University M
York College of Pennsylvania M

**Rhode Island**
Johnson & Wales University:
    Providence M
Rhode Island College M

**South Dakota**
Presentation College

**Tennessee**
Rhodes College
University of the South

**Texas**
Concordia University at Austin M
Hardin-Simmons University
LeTourneau University
McMurry University
Schreiner University
Southwestern University
Texas Lutheran University
Trinity University
University of Dallas M
University of Mary Hardin-Baylor
University of Texas
    Dallas
    Tyler

**Vermont**
Castleton State College M
Green Mountain College M
Middlebury College

**Virginia**
Averett University M
Bridgewater College M
Christopher Newport University
    M
Emory & Henry College M
Ferrum College M
Hampden-Sydney College M
Hollins University W
Lynchburg College M
Marymount University M
Randolph-Macon College M
Roanoke College M
Shenandoah University M
Virginia Wesleyan College M
Washington and Lee University M

**Washington**
Pacific Lutheran University
University of Puget Sound
Whitman College
Whitworth University

**West Virginia**
Bethany College

**Wisconsin**
Beloit College
Carroll College
Carthage College
Concordia University Wisconsin
Edgewood College
Lakeland College
Lawrence University M
Marian College of Fond du Lac
Milwaukee School of Engineering
Ripon College
St. Norbert College
University of Wisconsin
    Eau Claire
    Oshkosh W
    Platteville W
    River Falls W
    Stevens Point W
    Stout M
    Superior W
    Whitewater W
Wisconsin Lutheran College

## Gymnastics Division I

**Alabama**
Auburn University W
University of Alabama W

**Alaska**
University of Alaska
Anchorage W

**Arizona**
Arizona State University W
University of Arizona W

**Arkansas**
University of Arkansas W

**California**
California State University
Fullerton W
Sacramento W
San Jose State University W
Stanford University
University of California
Berkeley
Davis W
Los Angeles W

**Colorado**
United States Air Force Academy
University of Denver W

**Connecticut**
Yale University W

**District of Columbia**
George Washington University W

**Florida**
University of Florida W

**Georgia**
University of Georgia W

**Idaho**
Boise State University W

**Illinois**
Illinois State University W
Northern Illinois University W
University of Illinois
Chicago
Urbana-Champaign

**Indiana**
Ball State University W

**Iowa**
Iowa State University W
University of Iowa

**Kentucky**
University of Kentucky W

**Louisiana**
Centenary College of Louisiana
W
Louisiana State University and
Agricultural and Mechanical
College W

**Maryland**
Towson University W
United States Naval Academy M
University of Maryland
College Park W

**Michigan**
Central Michigan University W
Eastern Michigan University W
Michigan State University W
University of Michigan
Western Michigan University W

**Minnesota**
University of Minnesota
Twin Cities W

**Missouri**
Southeast Missouri State
University W
University of Missouri
Columbia W

**Nebraska**
University of Nebraska
Lincoln

**New Hampshire**
University of New Hampshire W

**New Jersey**
Rutgers, The State University of
New Jersey
New Brunswick/Piscataway
Campus W

**New York**
Cornell University W
United States Military Academy
M

**North Carolina**
North Carolina State University
W
University of North Carolina
Chapel Hill W

**Ohio**
Bowling Green State University
W
Kent State University W
Ohio State University
Columbus Campus

**Oklahoma**
University of Oklahoma

**Oregon**
Oregon State University W

**Pennsylvania**
Penn State
University Park
Temple University
University of Pennsylvania W
University of Pittsburgh W

**Rhode Island**
Brown University W
University of Rhode Island W

**Utah**
Brigham Young University W
Southern Utah University W
University of Utah W
Utah State University W

**Virginia**
College of William and Mary

**Washington**
University of Washington W

**West Virginia**
West Virginia University W

## Gymnastics Division II

**Connecticut**
Southern Connecticut State
University W
University of Bridgeport W

**Pennsylvania**
West Chester University of
Pennsylvania W

**Texas**
Texas Woman's University W

**Washington**
Seattle Pacific University W

## Gymnastics Division III

**Massachusetts**
Massachusetts Institute of
Technology
Springfield College

**Minnesota**
Gustavus Adolphus College W

Hamline University W
Winona State University W

**New York**
Ithaca College W
State University of New York
College at Brockport W
College at Cortland W

**Pennsylvania**
Ursinus College W
Wilson College W

**Rhode Island**
Rhode Island College W

**Wisconsin**
University of Wisconsin
Eau Claire W
La Crosse W
Oshkosh W
Stout W
Whitewater W

## Ice hockey Division I

**Alabama**
University of Alabama
Huntsville M

**Alaska**
University of Alaska
Anchorage M
Fairbanks M

**Colorado**
Colorado College M
United States Air Force Academy
M
University of Denver M

**Connecticut**
Quinnipiac University M
Sacred Heart University M
University of Connecticut M
Yale University M

**Indiana**
University of Notre Dame M

**Maine**
University of Maine M

**Massachusetts**
American International College M
Bentley College M
Boston College M
Boston University M
College of the Holy Cross M
Harvard College M
Merrimack College M
Northeastern University M
University of Massachusetts
Amherst M
Lowell M

**Michigan**
Ferris State University M
Lake Superior State University M
Michigan State University M
Michigan Technological
University M
Northern Michigan University M
University of Michigan M
Wayne State University M
Western Michigan University M

**Minnesota**
Bemidji State University M
Minnesota State University
Mankato M
Saint Cloud State University M
University of Minnesota
Duluth
Twin Cities M

**Nebraska**
University of Nebraska
Omaha M

**New Hampshire**
Dartmouth College M
University of New Hampshire M

**New Jersey**
Princeton University M

**New York**
Canisius College M
Clarkson University M
Colgate University M
Cornell University M
Niagara University M
Rensselaer Polytechnic Institute
M
St. Lawrence University M
Union College M
United States Military Academy
M

**Ohio**
Bowling Green State University
M
Miami University
Oxford Campus M
Ohio State University
Columbus Campus M

**Pennsylvania**
Mercyhurst College M
Robert Morris University M

**Rhode Island**
Brown University M
Providence College M

**Vermont**
University of Vermont M

**Wisconsin**
University of Wisconsin
Madison M

## Ice hockey Division II

**Massachusetts**
Assumption College M
Stonehill College M

**Minnesota**
University of Minnesota
Crookston M

**New Hampshire**
Franklin Pierce University M
St. Anselm College M
Southern New Hampshire
University M

**North Dakota**
University of North Dakota M

**Vermont**
St. Michael's College M

## Ice hockey Division III

**Connecticut**
Connecticut College M
Trinity College M
Wesleyan University M

**Illinois**
Lake Forest College M

**Maine**
Bowdoin College M
Colby College M
University of Southern Maine M

**Massachusetts**
Amherst College M
Babson College M
Becker College M
Curry College M
Fitchburg State College M
Framingham State College M
Massachusetts Institute of
Technology M
Nichols College M

Salem State College M
Suffolk University M
Tufts University M
University of Massachusetts
Boston M
Dartmouth M
Wentworth Institute of
Technology M
Western New England College M
Williams College M
Worcester State College M

**Michigan**
Adrian College M
Finlandia University M

**Minnesota**
Augsburg College M
Bethel University M
College of St. Scholastica M
Concordia College: Moorhead M
Gustavus Adolphus College M
Hamline University M
St. John's University M
St. Mary's University of
Minnesota M
St. Olaf College M
University of St. Thomas M

**New Hampshire**
New England College M
Plymouth State University M

**New York**
Elmira College M
Hamilton College M
Hobart and William Smith
Colleges M
Manhattanville College M
Rochester Institute of Technology
M
Skidmore College M
State University of New York
Buffalo M
College at Brockport M
College at Cortland M
College at Fredonia M
College at Geneseo M
College at Plattsburgh M
College at Potsdam M
College of Agriculture and
Technology at Morrisville
M
Oswego M
Utica College M

**Pennsylvania**
Lebanon Valley College M
Neumann College M
University of Scranton M

**Rhode Island**
Johnson & Wales University:
Providence M
Salve Regina University M

**Vermont**
Castleton State College M
Middlebury College M
Norwich University M

**Wisconsin**
Lawrence University M
Marian College of Fond du Lac M
Milwaukee School of Engineering
M
Northland College M
St. Norbert College M
University of Wisconsin
Eau Claire M
River Falls M
Stevens Point M
Stout M
Superior M

## Lacrosse Division I

### California
St. Mary's College of California W
Stanford University W
University of California
    Berkeley W
    Davis W

### Colorado
United States Air Force Academy M
University of Denver

### Connecticut
Central Connecticut State University W
Fairfield University
Quinnipiac University
Sacred Heart University
University of Connecticut W
University of Hartford M
Yale University

### Delaware
University of Delaware

### District of Columbia
American University W
George Washington University W
Georgetown University
Howard University W

### Florida
Rollins College W

### Illinois
Northwestern University W

### Indiana
University of Notre Dame

### Kentucky
University of Louisville W

### Maryland
Johns Hopkins University
Loyola College in Maryland
Mount St. Mary's University
Towson University
United States Naval Academy
University of Maryland
    Baltimore County
    College Park

### Massachusetts
Boston College W
Boston University W
College of the Holy Cross
Harvard College
University of Massachusetts
    Amherst

### New Hampshire
Dartmouth College
University of New Hampshire W

### New Jersey
Monmouth University W
Princeton University
Rutgers, The State University of New Jersey
    New Brunswick/Piscataway
    Campus

### New York
Barnard College W
Canisius College
Colgate University
Cornell University
Hobart and William Smith
    Colleges M
Hofstra University
Iona College W
Le Moyne College W
Long Island University
    Brooklyn Campus W
Manhattan College
Marist College
Niagara University W

Saint Bonaventure University W
St. John's University M
Siena College
State University of New York
    Albany
    Binghamton
    Stony Brook
Syracuse University
United States Military Academy M
Wagner College

### North Carolina
Davidson College W
Duke University
University of North Carolina
    Chapel Hill

### Ohio
Ohio State University
    Columbus Campus

### Oregon
University of Oregon W

### Pennsylvania
Bucknell University
Drexel University
Duquesne University W
Kutztown University of
    Pennsylvania W
La Salle University W
Lafayette College
Lehigh University
Penn State
    University Park
Robert Morris University
St. Francis University W
Saint Joseph's University
Temple University W
University of Pennsylvania
Villanova University

### Rhode Island
Brown University
Providence College M

### Tennessee
Vanderbilt University W

### Vermont
University of Vermont

### Virginia
College of William and Mary W
George Mason University W
James Madison University W
Longwood University W
Old Dominion University W
University of Richmond W
University of Virginia
Virginia Military Institute M
Virginia Polytechnic Institute and State University W

## Lacrosse Division II

### Arizona
Grand Canyon University M

### California
Notre Dame de Namur University M

### Colorado
Regis University W

### Connecticut
Southern Connecticut State University W
University of New Haven W

### Delaware
Wilmington University W

### Florida
Rollins College M
St. Leo University M

### Massachusetts
American International College

Assumption College
Bentley College
Framingham State College W
Merrimack College
Stonehill College W

### Michigan
Adrian College W

### New Hampshire
Franklin Pierce University
St. Anselm College
Southern New Hampshire University

### New Jersey
Georgian Court University W

### New York
Adelphi University
Dominican College of Blauvelt
Dowling College M
Le Moyne College M
Long Island University
    C. W. Post Campus
Molloy College
New York Institute of Technology M
Pace University M

### North Carolina
Belmont Abbey College
Catawba College M
Lees-McRae College
Mars Hill College M
Pfeiffer University
Queens University of Charlotte
St. Andrews Presbyterian College
Wingate University M

### Pennsylvania
Bloomsburg University of
    Pennsylvania W
East Stroudsburg University of
    Pennsylvania W
Gannon University W
Indiana University of
    Pennsylvania W
Lock Haven University of
    Pennsylvania W
Marywood University W
Mercyhurst College
Millersville University of
    Pennsylvania W
Philadelphia University W
St. Vincent College W
Seton Hill University
Shippensburg University of
    Pennsylvania W
Slippery Rock University of
    Pennsylvania W
Waynesburg University W
West Chester University of
    Pennsylvania W

### Rhode Island
Bryant University

### South Carolina
Limestone College
Presbyterian College

### Tennessee
University of the South W

### Vermont
St. Michael's College

### West Virginia
Wheeling Jesuit University M

## Lacrosse Division III

### California
Claremont McKenna College W
Pitzer College W
Pomona College W
University of Redlands W
Whittier College

### Colorado
Colorado College

### Connecticut
Connecticut College
Eastern Connecticut State University
Mitchell College M
St. Joseph College W
Trinity College
Wesleyan University
Western Connecticut State University

### Delaware
Wesley College

### District of Columbia
Catholic University of America
Trinity Washington University W

### Indiana
Tri-State University W

### Maine
Bates College
Bowdoin College
Colby College
Maine Maritime Academy M
St. Joseph's College M
Thomas College
University of New England
University of Southern Maine

### Maryland
College of Notre Dame of
    Maryland W
Frostburg State University W
Goucher College
Hood College
McDaniel College
St. Mary's College of Maryland
Salisbury University
Villa Julie College
Washington College

### Massachusetts
Amherst College
Babson College
Becker College
Bridgewater State College W
Clark University M
Curry College
Elms College W
Emerson College
Endicott College
Gordon College
Lasell College
Massachusetts Institute of
    Technology
Mount Holyoke College W
Mount Ida College M
Nichols College
Pine Manor College W
Regis College W
Smith College W
Springfield College
Tufts University
University of Massachusetts
    Boston M
    Dartmouth
Wellesley College W
Wentworth Institute of
    Technology M
Western New England College
Westfield State College W
Wheaton College
Williams College
Worcester State College W

### Michigan
Adrian College M

### Missouri
Fontbonne University

### New Hampshire
Colby-Sawyer College W
Daniel Webster College M
Keene State College

New England College
Plymouth State University

### New Jersey
Centenary College
The College of New Jersey W
Drew University
Fairleigh Dickinson University
    College at Florham
Kean University
Montclair State University
Ramapo College of New Jersey W
Richard Stockton College of New
    Jersey M
Rowan University W
Stevens Institute of Technology

### New York
Alfred University
Cazenovia College
Clarkson University
College of Mount St. Vincent
Elmira College
Hamilton College
Hartwick College
Hobart and William Smith
    Colleges W
Ithaca College
Keuka College
Manhattanville College
Medaille College
Nazareth College of Rochester
Rensselaer Polytechnic Institute
Rochester Institute of Technology
St. John Fisher College
St. Lawrence University
St. Thomas Aquinas College W
Skidmore College
State University of New York
    Buffalo W
    College at Brockport
    College at Cortland
    College at Fredonia W
    College at Geneseo
    College at Oneonta
    College at Plattsburgh M
    College at Potsdam
    College of Agriculture and
        Technology at Morrisville
    Farmingdale
    Maritime College
    Oswego
Union College
United States Merchant Marine
    Academy M
University of Rochester W
Utica College
Vassar College
Wells College

### North Carolina
Greensboro College
Guilford College
Methodist University W
North Carolina Wesleyan College W

### Ohio
College of Mount St. Joseph M
College of Wooster
Denison University
Kenyon College
Oberlin College
Ohio Wesleyan University
Wittenberg University

### Oregon
Linfield College W
Pacific University W

### Pennsylvania
Allegheny College W
Alvernia College
Arcadia University W
Bryn Mawr College W
Cabrini College
Cedar Crest College W
Chestnut Hill College W

DeSales University M
Dickinson College
Eastern University
Elizabethtown College
Franklin & Marshall College
Gettysburg College
Gwynedd-Mercy College W
Haverford College
Immaculata University
King's College
Lancaster Bible College W
Lycoming College
Marywood University M
Messiah College
Misericordia University
Moravian College
Muhlenberg College
Neumann College
Rosemont College W
St. Vincent College M
Susquehanna University
Swarthmore College
University of Scranton
Ursinus College
Washington & Jefferson College
Widener University
Wilkes University W
York College of Pennsylvania

**Rhode Island**
Rhode Island College W
Roger Williams University
Salve Regina University

**Texas**
University of Dallas W

**Vermont**
Castleton State College
Johnson State College M
Lyndon State College M
Middlebury College
Norwich University

**Virginia**
Bridgewater College W
Christopher Newport University
Ferrum College W
Hampden-Sydney College M
Hollins University W
Lynchburg College
Marymount University
Randolph-Macon College
Roanoke College
Shenandoah University
Sweet Briar College W
University of Mary Washington
Virginia Wesleyan College
Washington and Lee University

**Washington**
University of Puget Sound W

**Rifle Division I**

**Alabama**
Birmingham-Southern College W
Jacksonville State University M
University of Alabama
Birmingham W

**Colorado**
United States Air Force Academy

**Georgia**
Mercer University

**Kentucky**
Morehead State University
Murray State University M
University of Kentucky

**Maryland**
United States Naval Academy

**Mississippi**
University of Mississippi W

**Missouri**
University of Missouri
Kansas City

**Nebraska**
University of Nebraska
Lincoln W

**Nevada**
University of Nevada
Reno

**New York**
United States Military Academy

**North Carolina**
North Carolina State University

**Ohio**
Ohio State University
Columbus Campus
University of Akron

**South Carolina**
The Citadel
Wofford College

**Tennessee**
Tennessee Technological
University
University of Memphis
University of Tennessee
Martin W

**Texas**
Texas Christian University W
University of Texas
El Paso W

**West Virginia**
West Virginia University

**Rifle Division II**

**Alaska**
University of Alaska
Fairbanks

**Pennsylvania**
University of the Sciences in
Philadelphia W

**Rifle Division III**

**Connecticut**
United States Coast Guard
Academy M

**Indiana**
Rose-Hulman Institute of
Technology

**Massachusetts**
Massachusetts Institute of
Technology
Massachusetts Maritime Academy
Wentworth Institute of
Technology W

**New York**
City University of New York
John Jay College of
Criminal Justice
State University of New York
Maritime College

**Rowing (crew)
Division I**

**Alabama**
University of Alabama W

**California**
California State University
Sacramento W
Loyola Marymount University W
St. Mary's College of California
W

San Diego State University W
Santa Clara University W
Stanford University W
University of California
Berkeley W
Davis W
Irvine W
Los Angeles W
University of San Diego W
University of Southern California
W

**Connecticut**
Fairfield University W
Sacred Heart University W
University of Connecticut W
Yale University W

**Delaware**
University of Delaware W

**District of Columbia**
George Washington University W
Georgetown University W

**Florida**
Jacksonville University W
Stetson University W
University of Central Florida W
University of Miami W

**Indiana**
Indiana University
Bloomington W
University of Notre Dame W

**Iowa**
Drake University W
University of Iowa W

**Kansas**
Kansas State University W
University of Kansas W

**Kentucky**
Murray State University W
University of Louisville W

**Maryland**
Loyola College in Maryland W
United States Naval Academy W

**Massachusetts**
Boston College W
Boston University W
College of the Holy Cross W
Harvard College W
Massachusetts Institute of
Technology W
Northeastern University W
University of Massachusetts
Amherst W

**Michigan**
Eastern Michigan University W
Michigan State University W
University of Michigan W

**Minnesota**
University of Minnesota
Twin Cities W

**Nebraska**
Creighton University W

**New Hampshire**
Dartmouth College W

**New Jersey**
Princeton University W
Rutgers, The State University of
New Jersey
New Brunswick/Piscataway
Campus W

**New York**
Barnard College W
Colgate University W
Cornell University W
Fordham University W
Iona College W
Marist College W

State University of New York
Buffalo W
Syracuse University W

**North Carolina**
Duke University W
University of North Carolina
Chapel Hill W

**Ohio**
Ohio State University
Columbus Campus W
University of Dayton W

**Oklahoma**
University of Tulsa W

**Oregon**
Oregon State University W

**Pennsylvania**
Bucknell University W
Drexel University W
Duquesne University W
La Salle University W
Lehigh University W
Robert Morris University W
Saint Joseph's University W
Temple University W
University of Pennsylvania W
Villanova University W

**Rhode Island**
Brown University W
University of Rhode Island W

**South Carolina**
Clemson University W

**Tennessee**
University of Tennessee
Knoxville W

**Texas**
Southern Methodist University W
University of Texas
Austin W

**Virginia**
George Mason University W
University of Virginia W

**Washington**
Gonzaga University W
University of Washington W
Washington State University W

**West Virginia**
West Virginia University W

**Wisconsin**
University of Wisconsin
Madison W

**Rowing (crew)
Division II**

**California**
Humboldt State University W
University of California
San Diego W

**Florida**
Barry University W
Florida Institute of Technology W
Nova Southeastern University W
Rollins College W
University of Tampa W

**Massachusetts**
Assumption College W

**New Hampshire**
Franklin Pierce University W

**New York**
Dowling College W

**Pennsylvania**
Mercyhurst College W
Philadelphia University W

**Washington**
Seattle Pacific University W
Western Washington University
W

**West Virginia**
University of Charleston W

**Rowing (crew)
Division III**

**California**
Chapman University W
Mills College W

**Connecticut**
Connecticut College W
Trinity College W
United States Coast Guard
Academy W
Wesleyan University W

**Illinois**
North Park University W

**Maine**
Bates College W
Colby College W

**Maryland**
Johns Hopkins University W
Washington College W

**Massachusetts**
Clark University W
Lesley University W
Massachusetts Maritime Academy
W
Mount Holyoke College W
Simmons College W
Smith College W
Tufts University W
Wellesley College W
Williams College W
Worcester Polytechnic Institute W

**New Jersey**
Richard Stockton College of New
Jersey W
Rutgers, The State University of
New Jersey
Camden Regional Campus
W

**New York**
Cazenovia College W
D'Youville College W
Hamilton College W
Hobart and William Smith
Colleges W
Ithaca College W
Rochester Institute of Technology
W
St. Lawrence University W
Skidmore College W
State University of New York
Maritime College W
Union College W
United States Merchant Marine
Academy W
Vassar College W

**Ohio**
Marietta College W

**Oregon**
Lewis & Clark College W
Willamette University W

**Pennsylvania**
Bryn Mawr College W
Franklin & Marshall College W

**Virginia**
University of Mary Washington
W

**Washington**
Pacific Lutheran University W
University of Puget Sound W

## Skiing Division I

**Colorado**
University of Colorado
Boulder
University of Denver

**Massachusetts**
Boston College
Harvard College
University of Massachusetts
Amherst

**Montana**
Montana State University
Bozeman

**Nevada**
University of Nevada
Reno

**New Hampshire**
Dartmouth College
University of New Hampshire

**New Mexico**
University of New Mexico

**Rhode Island**
Brown University W

**Utah**
University of Utah

**Vermont**
University of Vermont

**Wisconsin**
University of Wisconsin
Green Bay

## Skiing Division II

**Alaska**
University of Alaska
Anchorage
Fairbanks

**Colorado**
Western State College of
Colorado

**Michigan**
Michigan Technological
University
Northern Michigan University

**Minnesota**
Saint Cloud State University W

**New Hampshire**
St. Anselm College

**Vermont**
St. Michael's College

## Skiing Division III

**Maine**
Bates College
Bowdoin College
Colby College

**Massachusetts**
Babson College
Massachusetts Institute of
Technology
Smith College W
Wellesley College W
Williams College

**Michigan**
Finlandia University

**Minnesota**
College of St. Benedict W
College of St. Scholastica
Gustavus Adolphus College
St. John's University M
St. Olaf College

**Nebraska**
Clarkson College M

**New Hampshire**
Colby-Sawyer College
Plymouth State University

**New York**
Clarkson University W
St. Lawrence University

**Vermont**
Green Mountain College W
Middlebury College

**Washington**
Whitman College

**Wisconsin**
Northland College

## Soccer Division I

**Alabama**
Alabama Agricultural and
Mechanical University
Alabama State University W
Auburn University W
Birmingham-Southern College
Jacksonville State University W
Samford University W
Troy University W
University of Alabama W
University of Alabama
Birmingham
University of South Alabama W

**Arizona**
Arizona State University W
Northern Arizona University W
University of Arizona W

**Arkansas**
Arkansas State University W
University of Arkansas W
University of Arkansas
Little Rock W
Pine Bluff W

**California**
California Polytechnic State
University: San Luis Obispo
California State University
Fresno W
Fullerton
Long Beach W
Northridge
Sacramento
Loyola Marymount University
Pepperdine University W
St. Mary's College of California
San Diego State University
San Jose State University
Santa Clara University
Stanford University
University of California
Berkeley
Davis
Irvine
Los Angeles
Riverside
Santa Barbara
University of San Diego
University of San Francisco
University of Southern California
W
University of the Pacific W

**Colorado**
Colorado College W
United States Air Force Academy
University of Colorado
Boulder W
University of Denver

**Connecticut**
Central Connecticut State
University
Fairfield University

Quinnipiac University
Sacred Heart University
University of Connecticut
University of Hartford
Yale University

**Delaware**
Delaware State University W
University of Delaware

**District of Columbia**
American University
George Washington University
Georgetown University
Howard University

**Florida**
Florida Atlantic University
Florida International University
Florida State University W
Jacksonville University
Stetson University
University of Central Florida
University of Florida W
University of Miami W
University of South Florida

**Georgia**
Georgia Southern University
Georgia State University
Kennesaw State University W
Mercer University
University of Georgia W

**Hawaii**
University of Hawaii
Manoa W

**Idaho**
Boise State University W
Idaho State University W
University of Idaho W

**Illinois**
Bradley University M
DePaul University
Eastern Illinois University
Illinois State University W
Loyola University Chicago
Northern Illinois University
Northwestern University
University of Illinois
Chicago M
Urbana-Champaign W
Western Illinois University

**Indiana**
Ball State University W
Butler University
Indiana State University W
Indiana University
Bloomington
Indiana University-Purdue
University Fort Wayne
Indiana University-Purdue
University Indianapolis
Purdue University W
University of Evansville
University of Notre Dame
Valparaiso University

**Iowa**
Drake University
Iowa State University W
University of Iowa W
University of Northern Iowa W

**Kansas**
University of Kansas W

**Kentucky**
Eastern Kentucky University W
Morehead State University W
Murray State University W
University of Kentucky
University of Louisville
Western Kentucky University

**Louisiana**
Centenary College of Louisiana
Grambling State University W

Louisiana State University and
Agricultural and Mechanical
College W
Louisiana Tech University W
McNeese State University W
Nicholls State University W
Northwestern State University W
Southeastern Louisiana University
W
Southern University and
Agricultural and Mechanical
College W
University of Louisiana at
Lafayette W
University of Louisiana at
Monroe W

**Maine**
University of Maine

**Maryland**
Loyola College in Maryland
Mount St. Mary's University
Towson University
United States Naval Academy
University of Maryland
Baltimore County
College Park

**Massachusetts**
Boston College
Boston University
College of the Holy Cross
Harvard College
Northeastern University
University of Massachusetts
Amherst

**Michigan**
Central Michigan University W
Eastern Michigan University W
Michigan State University
Oakland University
University of Detroit Mercy
University of Michigan
Western Michigan University

**Minnesota**
University of Minnesota
Twin Cities W

**Mississippi**
Alcorn State University W
Jackson State University W
Mississippi State University W
Mississippi Valley State
University W
University of Mississippi W
University of Southern
Mississippi W

**Missouri**
Missouri State University
Saint Louis University
Southeast Missouri State
University W
University of Missouri
Columbia W
Kansas City M

**Montana**
University of Montana: Missoula
W

**Nebraska**
Creighton University
University of Nebraska
Lincoln W

**Nevada**
University of Nevada
Las Vegas
Reno W

**New Hampshire**
Dartmouth College
University of New Hampshire

**New Jersey**
Fairleigh Dickinson University
Metropolitan Campus

Monmouth University
New Jersey Institute of
Technology
Princeton University
Rider University
Rutgers, The State University of
New Jersey
New Brunswick/Piscataway
Campus
Saint Peter's College
Seton Hall University

**New Mexico**
University of New Mexico

**New York**
Adelphi University M
Barnard College
Canisius College
Colgate University
Cornell University
Fordham University
Hartwick College M
Hofstra University
Iona College
Long Island University
Brooklyn Campus
Manhattan College
Marist College
Niagara University
Saint Bonaventure University
St. Francis College M
St. John's University
Siena College
State University of New York
Albany
Binghamton
Buffalo
College at Oneonta M
Stony Brook
Syracuse University
United States Military Academy
Wagner College W

**North Carolina**
Appalachian State University
Campbell University
Davidson College
Duke University
East Carolina University W
Elon University
Gardner-Webb University
High Point University
North Carolina State University
University of North Carolina
Asheville
Chapel Hill
Charlotte
Greensboro
Wilmington
Wake Forest University
Western Carolina University W

**Ohio**
Bowling Green State University
Cleveland State University
Kent State University W
Miami University
Oxford Campus W
Ohio State University
Columbus Campus
Ohio University W
University of Akron
University of Cincinnati
University of Dayton
University of Toledo W
Wright State University
Xavier University
Youngstown State University W

**Oklahoma**
Oklahoma State University W
Oral Roberts University
University of Oklahoma W
University of Tulsa

**Oregon**
Oregon State University W
Portland State University W

University of Oregon W
University of Portland

**Pennsylvania**
Bucknell University
Drexel University
Duquesne University
La Salle University
Lafayette College
Lehigh University
Penn State
    University Park
Philadelphia University M
Robert Morris University
St. Francis University
Saint Joseph's University
Temple University
University of Pennsylvania
University of Pittsburgh
Villanova University

**Rhode Island**
Brown University
Providence College
University of Rhode Island

**South Carolina**
Charleston Southern University
    W
The Citadel W
Clemson University
Coastal Carolina University
College of Charleston
Furman University
South Carolina State University
    W
University of South Carolina
Winthrop University
Wofford College

**Tennessee**
Austin Peay State University W
Belmont University
East Tennessee State University
    W
Lipscomb University
Middle Tennessee State
    University W
Tennessee Technological
    University W
University of Memphis
University of Tennessee
    Chattanooga W
    Knoxville W
    Martin W
Vanderbilt University W

**Texas**
Baylor University W
Lamar University W
Prairie View A&M University W
Rice University W
Sam Houston State University W
Southern Methodist University
Stephen F. Austin State University
    W
Texas A&M University W
Texas Christian University W
Texas Southern University W
Texas State University: San
    Marcos W
Texas Tech University W
University of Houston W
University of North Texas W
University of Texas
    Austin W
    El Paso W
    San Antonio W

**Utah**
Brigham Young University W
Southern Utah University W
University of Utah W
Utah State University W
Utah Valley State College W
Weber State University W

**Vermont**
University of Vermont

**Virginia**
College of William and Mary
George Mason University
James Madison University
Liberty University
Longwood University
Old Dominion University
Radford University
University of Richmond
University of Virginia
Virginia Commonwealth
    University
Virginia Military Institute
Virginia Polytechnic Institute and
    State University

**Washington**
Gonzaga University
University of Washington
Washington State University W

**West Virginia**
Marshall University
West Virginia University

**Wisconsin**
Marquette University
University of Wisconsin
    Green Bay
    Madison
    Milwaukee

**Wyoming**
University of Wyoming W

---

**Soccer Division II**

**Alabama**
University of Alabama
    Huntsville
University of Montevallo
University of North Alabama W

**Arizona**
Grand Canyon University

**Arkansas**
Harding University
Ouachita Baptist University
University of Central Arkansas

**California**
California State Polytechnic
    University: Pomona
California State University
    Bakersfield
    Chico
    Dominguez Hills
    Los Angeles
    Monterey Bay
    San Bernardino
    Stanislaus
Humboldt State University
Notre Dame de Namur University
San Francisco State University
Sonoma State University
University of California
    San Diego

**Colorado**
Adams State College W
Colorado Christian University
Colorado School of Mines
Colorado State University
    Pueblo
Fort Lewis College
Mesa State College
Metropolitan State College of
    Denver
Regis University
University of Colorado
    Colorado Springs M

**Connecticut**
Post University
Southern Connecticut State
    University
University of Bridgeport
University of New Haven

**Delaware**
Goldey-Beacom College
Wilmington University

**District of Columbia**
University of the District of
    Columbia M

**Florida**
Barry University
Eckerd College
Flagler College W
Florida Gulf Coast University W
Florida Institute of Technology
Florida Southern College
Lynn University
Nova Southeastern University
Palm Beach Atlantic University
Rollins College
St. Leo University
University of North Florida
University of Tampa
University of West Florida

**Georgia**
Armstrong Atlantic State
    University W
Clayton State University
Columbus State University W
Georgia College and State
    University W
Georgia Southwestern State
    University
North Georgia College & State
    University
University of West Georgia W

**Hawaii**
Brigham Young
    University-Hawaii
Chaminade University of
    Honolulu
Hawaii Pacific University
University of Hawaii
    Hilo

**Idaho**
Northwest Nazarene University
    W

**Illinois**
Lewis University
Quincy University
Southern Illinois University
    Edwardsville

**Indiana**
Oakland City University
Saint Joseph's College
University of Indianapolis
University of Southern Indiana

**Iowa**
Upper Iowa University

**Kansas**
Emporia State University W
Newman University
Washburn University W

**Kentucky**
Bellarmine University
Kentucky Wesleyan College
Northern Kentucky University

**Maryland**
Columbia Union College

**Massachusetts**
American International College
Assumption College
Bentley College
Merrimack College
Stonehill College
University of Massachusetts
    Lowell

**Michigan**
Ferris State University W
Grand Valley State University W
Northern Michigan University W

Northwood University: Michigan
Saginaw Valley State University

**Minnesota**
Bemidji State University W
Concordia University: St. Paul W
Minnesota State University
    Mankato W
    Moorhead W
Saint Cloud State University W
Southwest Minnesota State
    University W
University of Minnesota
    Crookston W
    Duluth W
    Morris
Winona State University W

**Mississippi**
Delta State University

**Missouri**
Drury University
Missouri Southern State
    University
Missouri Western State University
    W
Northwest Missouri State
    University W
Rockhurst University
Southwest Baptist University W
Truman State University
University of Central Missouri W
University of Missouri
    Missouri University of
        Science and Technology
    St. Louis M

**Montana**
Montana State University
    Billings

**Nebraska**
University of Nebraska
    Omaha W
Wayne State College W

**New Hampshire**
Franklin Pierce University
St. Anselm College
Southern New Hampshire
    University

**New Jersey**
Bloomfield College
Caldwell College
Felician College
Georgian Court University W

**New Mexico**
Eastern New Mexico University
New Mexico Highlands
    University W

**New York**
Adelphi University W
City University of New York
    Queens College
College of Saint Rose
Concordia College
Dominican College of Blauvelt
Dowling College
Le Moyne College
Long Island University
    C. W. Post Campus
Mercy College
Molloy College
New York Institute of Technology
Nyack College
Pace University W
St. Thomas Aquinas College

**North Carolina**
Barton College
Belmont Abbey College
Brevard College
Catawba College
Chowan University W
Lees-McRae College
Lenoir-Rhyne College

Mars Hill College
Mount Olive College
Pfeiffer University
Queens University of Charlotte
St. Andrews Presbyterian College
University of North Carolina
    Pembroke
Wingate University

**North Dakota**
North Dakota State University W
University of Mary
University of North Dakota W

**Ohio**
Ashland University
Tiffin University
University of Findlay

**Oklahoma**
East Central University W
Northeastern State University
Southwestern Oklahoma State
    University W
University of Central Oklahoma
    W

**Oregon**
Western Oregon University W

**Pennsylvania**
Bloomsburg University of
    Pennsylvania
California University of
    Pennsylvania
Clarion University of
    Pennsylvania W
East Stroudsburg University of
    Pennsylvania
Edinboro University of
    Pennsylvania W
Gannon University
Holy Family University
Indiana University of
    Pennsylvania W
Kutztown University of
    Pennsylvania
Lock Haven University of
    Pennsylvania
Mansfield University of
    Pennsylvania W
Mercyhurst College
Millersville University of
    Pennsylvania
Philadelphia University W
Seton Hill University
Shippensburg University of
    Pennsylvania
Slippery Rock University of
    Pennsylvania
University of Pittsburgh
    Johnstown
West Chester University of
    Pennsylvania

**Puerto Rico**
University of Puerto Rico
    Mayaguez M
    Rio Piedras M

**Rhode Island**
Bryant University

**South Carolina**
Anderson University
Coker College
Converse College W
Erskine College
Francis Marion University
Lander University
Limestone College
Newberry College
North Greenville University
Presbyterian College
University of South Carolina
    Aiken
    Upstate

**South Dakota**
Augustana College W

Northern State University W
South Dakota State University W
University of South Dakota W

**Tennessee**
Carson-Newman College
Christian Brothers University
Lincoln Memorial University
Tusculum College

**Texas**
Abilene Christian University W
Angelo State University W
Dallas Baptist University W
Midwestern State University
St. Edward's University
St. Mary's University
Texas A&M International
University
Texas A&M University
Commerce W
Texas Woman's University W
University of Texas
of the Permian Basin
University of the Incarnate Word
West Texas A&M University

**Utah**
Dixie State College of Utah W

**Vermont**
St. Michael's College

**Washington**
Central Washington University W
Saint Martin's University
Seattle Pacific University
Seattle University
Western Washington University

**West Virginia**
Alderson-Broaddus College M
Concord University W
Davis and Elkins College
Ohio Valley University
Salem International University
Shepherd University
University of Charleston
West Virginia Wesleyan College
Wheeling Jesuit University

**Wisconsin**
University of Wisconsin
Parkside

## Soccer Division III

**Alabama**
Huntingdon College

**Arkansas**
Hendrix College
University of the Ozarks

**California**
California Institute of Technology
M
California Lutheran University
California State University
East Bay
Chapman University
Claremont McKenna College
La Sierra University
Menlo College
Mills College W
Occidental College
Pitzer College W
Pomona College
University of California
Santa Cruz
University of La Verne
University of Redlands
Whittier College

**Colorado**
Colorado College M

**Connecticut**
Albertus Magnus College
Connecticut College

Eastern Connecticut State
University
Mitchell College
St. Joseph College W
Trinity College
United States Coast Guard
Academy
Wesleyan University
Western Connecticut State
University

**Delaware**
Wesley College

**District of Columbia**
Catholic University of America
Gallaudet University
Trinity Washington University W

**Georgia**
Agnes Scott College W
Emory University
LaGrange College
Oglethorpe University
Piedmont College
Spelman College W
Wesleyan College W

**Illinois**
Augustana College
Aurora University
Benedictine University
Blackburn College
Concordia University
Dominican University
Elmhurst College
Eureka College
Greenville College
Illinois College
Illinois Wesleyan University
Knox College
Lake Forest College
MacMurray College
Millikin University
Monmouth College
North Central College
North Park University
Principia College
Rockford College W
University of Chicago
Wheaton College

**Indiana**
Anderson University
DePauw University
Earlham College
Franklin College
Hanover College
Manchester College
Rose-Hulman Institute of
Technology
Saint Mary's College W
Tri-State University
Wabash College M

**Iowa**
Buena Vista University
Central College
Coe College
Cornell College
Grinnell College
Loras College
Luther College
Simpson College
University of Dubuque
Wartburg College

**Kentucky**
Centre College
Thomas More College
Transylvania University

**Louisiana**
Louisiana College

**Maine**
Bates College
Bowdoin College
Colby College
Husson College

Maine Maritime Academy
St. Joseph's College
Thomas College
University of Maine
Farmington
University of New England
University of Southern Maine

**Maryland**
College of Notre Dame of
Maryland W
Frostburg State University
Goucher College
Hood College
Johns Hopkins University
McDaniel College
St. Mary's College of Maryland
Salisbury University
Villa Julie College
Washington College

**Massachusetts**
Amherst College
Anna Maria College
Babson College
Bay Path College W
Becker College
Brandeis University
Bridgewater State College
Clark University
Curry College
Eastern Nazarene College
Elms College
Emerson College
Emmanuel College
Endicott College
Fitchburg State College
Framingham State College
Gordon College
Lasell College
Lesley University
Massachusetts College of Liberal
Arts
Massachusetts Institute of
Technology
Massachusetts Maritime Academy
M
Mount Holyoke College W
Mount Ida College
Newbury College
Nichols College
Pine Manor College W
Regis College W
Salem State College
Simmons College W
Smith College W
Springfield College
Suffolk University
Tufts University
University of Massachusetts
Boston
Dartmouth
Wellesley College W
Wentworth Institute of
Technology
Western New England College
Westfield State College
Wheaton College
Wheelock College W
Williams College
Worcester Polytechnic Institute
Worcester State College

**Michigan**
Adrian College
Albion College
Alma College
Calvin College
Finlandia University
Hope College
Kalamazoo College
Olivet College

**Minnesota**
Augsburg College
Bethany Lutheran College
Bethel University
Carleton College

College of St. Benedict W
College of St. Catherine W
College of St. Scholastica
Concordia College: Moorhead
Crown College
Gustavus Adolphus College
Hamline University
Macalester College
Martin Luther College
North Central University
Northwestern College
St. John's University M
St. Mary's University of
Minnesota
St. Olaf College
University of St. Thomas

**Mississippi**
Millsaps College
Mississippi College
Rust College M

**Missouri**
Baptist Bible College
Fontbonne University
Maryville University of Saint
Louis
Washington University in St.
Louis
Webster University
Westminster College

**Nebraska**
Nebraska Wesleyan University

**New Hampshire**
Colby-Sawyer College
Daniel Webster College
Keene State College
New England College
Plymouth State University
Rivier College

**New Jersey**
Centenary College
The College of New Jersey
College of St. Elizabeth W
Drew University
Fairleigh Dickinson University
College at Florham
Kean University
Montclair State University
New Jersey City University
Ramapo College of New Jersey
Richard Stockton College of New
Jersey
Rowan University
Rutgers, The State University of
New Jersey
Camden Regional Campus
Newark Regional Campus
Stevens Institute of Technology
William Paterson University of
New Jersey

**New York**
Alfred University
Bard College
Cazenovia College
City University of New York
Baruch College M
Brooklyn College M
City College
College of Staten Island
Hunter College M
John Jay College of
Criminal Justice M
Medgar Evers College
New York City College of
Technology M
York College M
Clarkson University
College of Mount St. Vincent
D'Youville College
Elmira College
Hamilton College
Hartwick College W
Hilbert College

Hobart and William Smith
Colleges
Ithaca College
Keuka College
Manhattanville College
Medaille College
Mount St. Mary College
Nazareth College of Rochester
New York University
Polytechnic University
Rensselaer Polytechnic Institute
Rochester Institute of Technology
Russell Sage College W
St. John Fisher College
St. Joseph's College: Suffolk
Campus
St. Lawrence University
Skidmore College
State University of New York
College at Brockport
College at Buffalo
College at Cortland
College at Fredonia
College at Geneseo
College at Old Westbury M
College at Oneonta W
College at Plattsburgh
College at Potsdam
College of Agriculture and
Technology at Morrisville
Farmingdale
Institute of Technology at
Utica/Rome
Maritime College
New Paltz
Oswego
Purchase
Union College
United States Merchant Marine
Academy M
University of Rochester
Utica College
Vassar College
Wells College
Yeshiva University

**North Carolina**
Greensboro College
Guilford College
Meredith College W
Methodist University
North Carolina Wesleyan College
Peace College W
Salem College W

**Ohio**
Baldwin-Wallace College
Bluffton University
Capital University
Case Western Reserve University
College of Mount St. Joseph
College of Wooster
Defiance College
Denison University
Franciscan University of
Steubenville
Heidelberg College
Hiram College
John Carroll University
Kenyon College
Lake Erie College
Marietta College
Mount Union College
Muskingum College
Oberlin College
Ohio Northern University
Ohio Wesleyan University
Otterbein College
Wilmington College
Wittenberg University

**Oregon**
George Fox University
Lewis & Clark College W
Linfield College
Pacific University
Willamette University

## Pennsylvania

Albright College
Allegheny College
Alvernia College
Arcadia University
Bryn Mawr College W
Cabrini College
Carnegie Mellon University
Cedar Crest College W
Chatham University W
Chestnut Hill College
Delaware Valley College
DeSales University
Dickinson College
Eastern University
Elizabethtown College
Franklin & Marshall College
Geneva College
Gettysburg College
Grove City College
Gwynedd-Mercy College
Haverford College
Immaculata University
Juniata College
Keystone College
King's College
La Roche College
Lancaster Bible College M
Lebanon Valley College
Lincoln University
Lycoming College
Marywood University
Messiah College
Misericordia University
Moravian College
Mount Aloysius College
Muhlenberg College
Neumann College
Penn State
    Altoona
    Berks
    Erie, The Behrend College
    Harrisburg W
Philadelphia Biblical University
St. Vincent College
Susquehanna University
Swarthmore College
Thiel College
University of Pittsburgh
    Bradford
    Greensburg
University of Scranton
Ursinus College
Washington & Jefferson College
Waynesburg University
Westminster College
Widener University
Wilkes University
Wilson College W
York College of Pennsylvania

## Rhode Island

Johnson & Wales University:
    Providence
Rhode Island College
Roger Williams University
Salve Regina University

## South Dakota

Presentation College

## Tennessee

Maryville College
Rhodes College
University of the South

## Texas

Austin College
Concordia University at Austin
East Texas Baptist University
Hardin-Simmons University
Howard Payne University
LeTourneau University
McMurry University
Schreiner University
Southwestern University
Texas Lutheran University
Trinity University

University of Dallas
University of Mary Hardin-Baylor
University of Texas
    Dallas
    Tyler

## Vermont

Castleton State College
Green Mountain College
Johnson State College
Lyndon State College
Middlebury College
Norwich University
Southern Vermont College

## Virginia

Averett University
Bridgewater College
Christopher Newport University
Eastern Mennonite University
Emory & Henry College
Ferrum College
Hampden-Sydney College M
Hollins University W
Lynchburg College
Mary Baldwin College W
Marymount University
Randolph College W
Randolph-Macon College
Roanoke College
Shenandoah University
Sweet Briar College W
University of Mary Washington
Virginia Wesleyan College
Washington and Lee University

## Washington

Pacific Lutheran University
University of Puget Sound
Whitman College
Whitworth University

## West Virginia

Bethany College

## Wisconsin

Alverno College W
Beloit College
Carroll College
Carthage College
Concordia University Wisconsin
Edgewood College
Lakeland College
Lawrence University
Maranatha Baptist Bible College
Marian College of Fond du Lac
Milwaukee School of Engineering
Mount Mary College W
Northland College
Ripon College
St. Norbert College
University of Wisconsin
    Eau Claire W
    La Crosse W
    Oshkosh
    Platteville
    River Falls W
    Stevens Point W
    Stout W
    Superior
    Whitewater
Wisconsin Lutheran College

---

## Softball Division I

### Alabama

Alabama Agricultural and
    Mechanical University W
Alabama State University W
Auburn University W
Birmingham-Southern College W
Jacksonville State University W
Samford University W
Troy University W
University of Alabama W
University of Alabama
    Birmingham W

University of South Alabama W

### Arizona

Arizona State University W
University of Arizona W

### Arkansas

University of Arkansas W
University of Arkansas
    Pine Bluff W

### California

California Polytechnic State
    University: San Luis Obispo W
California State University
    Fresno W
    Fullerton W
    Long Beach W
    Northridge W
    Sacramento W
Loyola Marymount University W
St. Mary's College of California
    W
San Diego State University W
San Jose State University W
Santa Clara University W
Stanford University W
University of California
    Berkeley W
    Davis W
    Los Angeles W
    Riverside W
    Santa Barbara W
University of San Diego W
University of the Pacific W

### Colorado

Colorado State University W
University of Northern Colorado
    W

### Connecticut

Central Connecticut State
    University W
Fairfield University W
Quinnipiac University W
Sacred Heart University W
University of Connecticut W
University of Hartford W
Yale University W

### Delaware

Delaware State University W
University of Delaware W

### District of Columbia

George Washington University W
Georgetown University W
Howard University W

### Florida

Bethune-Cookman University W
Florida Agricultural and
    Mechanical University W
Florida Atlantic University W
Florida International University
    W
Florida State University W
Jacksonville University W
Stetson University W
University of Central Florida W
University of Florida W
University of South Florida W

### Georgia

Georgia Institute of Technology
    W
Georgia Southern University W
Georgia State University W
Mercer University W
Savannah State University W
University of Georgia W

### Hawaii

University of Hawaii
    Manoa W

### Idaho

Idaho State University W

### Illinois

Bradley University W
DePaul University W
Eastern Illinois University W
Illinois State University W
Loyola University Chicago W
Northern Illinois University W
Northwestern University W
Southern Illinois University
    Carbondale W
University of Illinois
    Chicago W
    Urbana-Champaign W
Western Illinois University W

### Indiana

Ball State University W
Butler University W
Indiana State University W
Indiana University
    Bloomington W
Indiana University-Purdue
    University Fort Wayne W
Indiana University-Purdue
    University Indianapolis W
Purdue University W
University of Evansville W
University of Notre Dame W
Valparaiso University W

### Iowa

Drake University W
Iowa State University W
University of Iowa W
University of Northern Iowa W

### Kansas

University of Kansas W
Wichita State University W

### Kentucky

Eastern Kentucky University W
Morehead State University W
University of Kentucky W
University of Louisville W
Western Kentucky University W

### Louisiana

Centenary College of Louisiana
    W
Grambling State University W
Louisiana State University and
    Agricultural and Mechanical
    College W
Louisiana Tech University W
McNeese State University W
Nicholls State University W
Northwestern State University W
Southeastern Louisiana University
    W
Southern University and
    Agricultural and Mechanical
    College W
University of Louisiana at
    Lafayette W
University of Louisiana at
    Monroe W

### Maine

University of Maine W

### Maryland

Coppin State University W
Morgan State University W
Mount St. Mary's University W
Towson University W
University of Maryland
    Baltimore County W
    College Park W
    Eastern Shore W

### Massachusetts

Boston College W
Boston University W
College of the Holy Cross W
Harvard College W
University of Massachusetts
    Amherst W

### Michigan

Central Michigan University W
Eastern Michigan University W
Michigan State University W
Oakland University W
University of Detroit Mercy W
University of Michigan W
Western Michigan University W

### Minnesota

University of Minnesota
    Twin Cities W

### Mississippi

Alcorn State University W
Jackson State University W
Mississippi State University W
Mississippi Valley State
    University W
University of Mississippi W
University of Southern
    Mississippi W

### Missouri

Missouri State University W
Saint Louis University W
Southeast Missouri State
    University W
University of Missouri
    Columbia W
    Kansas City W

### Nebraska

Creighton University W
University of Nebraska
    Lincoln W

### Nevada

University of Nevada
    Las Vegas W
    Reno W

### New Hampshire

Dartmouth College W

### New Jersey

Fairleigh Dickinson University
    Metropolitan Campus W
Monmouth University W
Princeton University W
Rider University W
Rutgers, The State University of
    New Jersey
    New Brunswick/Piscataway
        Campus W
Saint Peter's College W
Seton Hall University W

### New Mexico

New Mexico State University W
University of New Mexico W

### New York

Barnard College W
Canisius College W
Colgate University W
Cornell University W
Fordham University W
Hofstra University W
Iona College W
Long Island University
    Brooklyn Campus W
Manhattan College W
Marist College W
Niagara University W
Saint Bonaventure University W
St. John's University W
Siena College W
State University of New York
    Albany W
    Binghamton W
    Buffalo W
    Stony Brook W
Syracuse University W
United States Military Academy
    W
Wagner College W

### North Carolina

Appalachian State University W

Campbell University W
East Carolina University W
Elon University W
Gardner-Webb University W
North Carolina Agricultural and
    Technical State University W
North Carolina State University
    W
University of North Carolina
    Chapel Hill W
    Charlotte W
    Greensboro W
    Wilmington W
Western Carolina University W

**Ohio**
Bowling Green State University
    W
Cleveland State University W
Kent State University W
Miami University
    Oxford Campus W
Ohio State University
    Columbus Campus W
Ohio University W
University of Akron W
University of Dayton W
University of Toledo W
Wright State University W
Youngstown State University W

**Oklahoma**
Oklahoma State University W
University of Oklahoma W
University of Tulsa W

**Oregon**
Oregon State University W
Portland State University W
University of Oregon W

**Pennsylvania**
Bucknell University W
Drexel University W
La Salle University W
Lafayette College W
Lehigh University W
Penn State
    University Park W
Robert Morris University W
St. Francis University W
Saint Joseph's University W
Temple University W
University of Pennsylvania W
University of Pittsburgh W
Villanova University W

**Rhode Island**
Brown University W
Providence College W
University of Rhode Island W

**South Carolina**
Charleston Southern University
    W
Coastal Carolina University W
College of Charleston W
Furman University W
South Carolina State University
    W
University of South Carolina W
Winthrop University W

**Tennessee**
Austin Peay State University W
Belmont University W
East Tennessee State University
    W
Lipscomb University W
Middle Tennessee State
    University W
Tennessee State University W
Tennessee Technological
    University W
University of Tennessee
    Chattanooga W
    Knoxville W
    Martin W

**Texas**
Baylor University W
Prairie View A&M University W
Sam Houston State University W
Stephen F. Austin State University
    W
Texas A&M University W
Texas Southern University W
Texas State University: San
    Marcos W
Texas Tech University W
University of Houston W
University of North Texas W
University of Texas
    Arlington W
    Austin W
    El Paso W
    San Antonio W

**Utah**
Brigham Young University W
Southern Utah University W
University of Utah W
Utah State University W
Utah Valley State College W

**Vermont**
University of Vermont W

**Virginia**
George Mason University W
Hampton University W
James Madison University W
Liberty University W
Longwood University W
Norfolk State University W
Radford University W
University of Virginia W
Virginia Polytechnic Institute and
    State University W

**Washington**
University of Washington W

**West Virginia**
Marshall University W

**Wisconsin**
University of Wisconsin
    Green Bay W
    Madison W

**Alabama**
Miles College W
Stillman College W
Tuskegee University W
University of Alabama
    Huntsville W
University of North Alabama W
University of West Alabama W

**Arizona**
Grand Canyon University W

**Arkansas**
Arkansas Tech University W
Henderson State University W
Ouachita Baptist University W
Southern Arkansas University W
University of Arkansas
    Monticello W
University of Central Arkansas W

**California**
California State University
    Bakersfield W
    Chico W
    Dominguez Hills W
    Monterey Bay W
    San Bernardino W
    Stanislaus W
Humboldt State University W
Notre Dame de Namur University
    W
San Francisco State University W
Sonoma State University W

University of California
    San Diego W

**Colorado**
Adams State College W
Colorado School of Mines W
Colorado State University
    Pueblo W
Fort Lewis College W
Mesa State College W
Metropolitan State College of
    Denver W
Regis University W
University of Colorado
    Colorado Springs W

**Connecticut**
Post University W
Southern Connecticut State
    University W
University of Bridgeport W
University of New Haven W

**Delaware**
Goldey-Beacom College W
Wilmington University W

**Florida**
Barry University W
Eckerd College W
Florida Gulf Coast University W
Florida Institute of Technology W
Florida Southern College W
Lynn University W
Nova Southeastern University W
Palm Beach Atlantic University
    W
Rollins College W
St. Leo University W
University of North Florida W
University of Tampa W
University of West Florida W

**Georgia**
Albany State University W
Armstrong Atlantic State
    University W
Augusta State University W
Clark Atlanta University W
Columbus State University W
Fort Valley State University W
Georgia College and State
    University W
Georgia Southwestern State
    University W
Kennesaw State University W
North Georgia College & State
    University W
Paine College W
University of West Georgia W
Valdosta State University W

**Hawaii**
Brigham Young
    University-Hawaii W
Chaminade University of
    Honolulu W
Hawaii Pacific University W
University of Hawaii
    Hilo W

**Idaho**
Northwest Nazarene University
    W

**Illinois**
Lewis University W
Quincy University W
Southern Illinois University
    Edwardsville W

**Indiana**
Oakland City University W
Saint Joseph's College W
University of Indianapolis W
University of Southern Indiana W

**Iowa**
Upper Iowa University W

**Kansas**
Emporia State University W
Fort Hays State University W
Newman University W
Pittsburg State University W
Washburn University W

**Kentucky**
Bellarmine University W
Kentucky State University W
Kentucky Wesleyan College W
Northern Kentucky University W

**Maryland**
Bowie State University W
Columbia Union College W

**Massachusetts**
American International College
    W
Assumption College W
Bentley College W
Merrimack College W
Stonehill College W
University of Massachusetts
    Lowell W

**Michigan**
Ferris State University W
Grand Valley State University W
Hillsdale College W
Lake Superior State University W
Northwood University: Michigan
    W
Saginaw Valley State University
    W
Wayne State University W

**Minnesota**
Bemidji State University W
Concordia University: St. Paul W
Minnesota State University
    Mankato W
    Moorhead W
Saint Cloud State University W
Southwest Minnesota State
    University W
University of Minnesota
    Crookston W
    Duluth W
    Morris W
Winona State University W

**Mississippi**
Delta State University W

**Missouri**
Drury University W
Lincoln University W
Missouri Southern State
    University W
Missouri Western State University
    W
Northwest Missouri State
    University W
Rockhurst University W
Southwest Baptist University W
Truman State University W
University of Central Missouri W
University of Missouri
    Missouri University of
        Science and Technology
        W
    St. Louis W

**Montana**
Montana State University
    Billings W

**Nebraska**
Chadron State College W
University of Nebraska
    Kearney W
    Omaha W
Wayne State College W

**New Hampshire**
Franklin Pierce University W
St. Anselm College W

Southern New Hampshire
    University W

**New Jersey**
Bloomfield College W
Caldwell College W
Felician College W
Georgian Court University W

**New Mexico**
Eastern New Mexico University
    W
New Mexico Highlands
    University W
Western New Mexico University
    W

**New York**
Adelphi University W
City University of New York
    Queens College W
College of Saint Rose W
Concordia College W
Dominican College of Blauvelt W
Dowling College W
Le Moyne College W
Long Island University
    C. W. Post Campus W
Mercy College W
Molloy College W
New York Institute of Technology
    W
Nyack College W
Pace University W
St. Thomas Aquinas College W

**North Carolina**
Barton College W
Belmont Abbey College W
Brevard College W
Catawba College W
Chowan University W
Elizabeth City State University W
Fayetteville State University W
Johnson C. Smith University W
Lees-McRae College W
Lenoir-Rhyne College W
Livingstone College W
Mars Hill College W
Mount Olive College W
North Carolina Central University
    W
Pfeiffer University W
Queens University of Charlotte W
St. Andrews Presbyterian College
    W
St. Augustine's College W
Shaw University W
University of North Carolina
    Pembroke W
Wingate University W
Winston-Salem State University
    W

**North Dakota**
North Dakota State University W
University of Mary W
University of North Dakota W

**Ohio**
Ashland University W
Tiffin University W
University of Findlay W

**Oklahoma**
Cameron University W
East Central University W
Northeastern State University W
Oklahoma Panhandle State
    University W
Southeastern Oklahoma State
    University W
Southwestern Oklahoma State
    University W
University of Central Oklahoma
    W

**Oregon**
Western Oregon University W

**Pennsylvania**

Bloomsburg University of
  Pennsylvania W
California University of
  Pennsylvania W
Clarion University of
  Pennsylvania W
East Stroudsburg University of
  Pennsylvania W
Edinboro University of
  Pennsylvania W
Gannon University W
Holy Family University W
Indiana University of
  Pennsylvania W
Kutztown University of
  Pennsylvania W
Lincoln University W
Lock Haven University of
  Pennsylvania W
Mansfield University of
  Pennsylvania W
Mercyhurst College W
Millersville University of
  Pennsylvania W
Philadelphia University W
Seton Hill University W
Shippensburg University of
  Pennsylvania W
Slippery Rock University of
  Pennsylvania W
University of the Sciences in
  Philadelphia W
West Chester University of
  Pennsylvania W

**Puerto Rico**

University of Puerto Rico
  Cayey University College W
  Mayaguez W
  Rio Piedras W

**Rhode Island**

Bryant University W

**South Carolina**

Anderson University W
Benedict College W
Claflin University W
Coker College W
Erskine College W
Francis Marion University W
Lander University W
Limestone College W
Newberry College W
North Greenville University W
Presbyterian College W
University of South Carolina
  Aiken W
  Upstate W

**South Dakota**

Augustana College W
Northern State University W
South Dakota State University W
University of South Dakota W

**Tennessee**

Carson-Newman College W
Christian Brothers University W
Lane College W
LeMoyne-Owen University W
Lincoln Memorial University W
Tusculum College W

**Texas**

Abilene Christian University W
Angelo State University W
Midwestern State University W
St. Edward's University W
St. Mary's University W
Tarleton State University W
Texas A&M University
  Kingsville W
Texas Woman's University W
University of Texas
  of the Permian Basin W
University of the Incarnate Word
  W

West Texas A&M University W

**Utah**

Dixie State College of Utah W

**Vermont**

St. Michael's College W

**Virginia**

St. Paul's College W
Virginia State University W
Virginia Union University W

**Washington**

Central Washington University W
Saint Martin's University W
Seattle University W
Western Washington University
  W

**West Virginia**

Alderson-Broaddus College W
Bluefield State College W
Concord University W
Davis and Elkins College W
Fairmont State University W
Glenville State College W
Ohio Valley University W
Salem International University W
Shepherd University W
University of Charleston W
West Liberty State College W
West Virginia Wesleyan College
  W
Wheeling Jesuit University W

**Wisconsin**

University of Wisconsin
  Parkside W

## Softball Division III

**Alabama**

Huntingdon College W

**Arkansas**

Hendrix College W
University of the Ozarks W

**California**

California Lutheran University W
California State University
  East Bay W
Chapman University W
Claremont McKenna College W
La Sierra University W
Menlo College W
Occidental College W
Pitzer College W
Pomona College W
University of La Verne W
University of Redlands W
Whittier College W

**Colorado**

Colorado College W

**Connecticut**

Albertus Magnus College W
Eastern Connecticut State
  University W
Mitchell College W
St. Joseph College W
Trinity College W
United States Coast Guard
  Academy W
Wesleyan University W
Western Connecticut State
  University W

**Delaware**

Wesley College W

**District of Columbia**

Catholic University of America W
Gallaudet University W

**Georgia**

Agnes Scott College W
Emory University W

LaGrange College W
Piedmont College W
Spelman College W
Wesleyan College W

**Illinois**

Augustana College W
Aurora University W
Benedictine University W
Blackburn College W
Concordia University W
Dominican University W
Elmhurst College W
Eureka College W
Greenville College W
Illinois College W
Illinois Wesleyan University W
Knox College W
Lake Forest College W
MacMurray College W
Millikin University W
Monmouth College W
North Central College W
North Park University W
Rockford College W
University of Chicago W
Wheaton College W

**Indiana**

Anderson University W
DePauw University W
Franklin College W
Hanover College W
Manchester College W
Rose-Hulman Institute of
  Technology W
Saint Mary's College W
Tri-State University W

**Iowa**

Buena Vista University W
Central College W
Coe College W
Cornell College W
Grinnell College W
Loras College W
Luther College W
Simpson College W
University of Dubuque W
Wartburg College W

**Kentucky**

Centre College W
Thomas More College W
Transylvania University W

**Louisiana**

Louisiana College W

**Maine**

Bates College W
Bowdoin College W
Colby College W
Husson College W
Maine Maritime Academy W
St. Joseph's College W
Thomas College W
University of Maine
  Farmington W
University of New England W
University of Southern Maine W

**Maryland**

Frostburg State University W
Hood College W
McDaniel College W
Salisbury University W
Villa Julie College W
Washington College W

**Massachusetts**

Amherst College W
Anna Maria College W
Babson College W
Bay Path College W
Becker College W
Brandeis University W
Bridgewater State College W
Clark University W
Curry College W

Eastern Nazarene College W
Elms College W
Emerson College W
Emmanuel College W
Endicott College W
Fitchburg State College W
Framingham State College W
Gordon College W
Lasell College W
Lesley University W
Massachusetts College of Liberal
  Arts W
Massachusetts Institute of
  Technology W
Massachusetts Maritime Academy
  W
Mount Ida College W
Newbury College W
Nichols College W
Pine Manor College W
Regis College W
Salem State College W
Simmons College W
Smith College W
Springfield College W
Suffolk University W
Tufts University W
University of Massachusetts
  Boston W
  Dartmouth W
Wellesley College W
Wentworth Institute of
  Technology W
Western New England College W
Westfield State College W
Wheaton College W
Wheelock College W
Williams College W
Worcester Polytechnic Institute W
Worcester State College W

**Michigan**

Adrian College W
Albion College W
Alma College W
Calvin College W
Finlandia University W
Hope College W
Kalamazoo College W
Olivet College W

**Minnesota**

Augsburg College W
Bethany Lutheran College W
Bethel University W
Carleton College W
College of St. Benedict W
College of St. Catherine W
College of St. Scholastica W
Concordia College: Moorhead W
Crown College W
Gustavus Adolphus College W
Hamline University W
Macalester College W
Martin Luther College W
North Central University W
Northwestern College W
St. Mary's University of
  Minnesota W
St. Olaf College W
University of St. Thomas W

**Mississippi**

Millsaps College W
Mississippi College W
Rust College W

**Missouri**

Fontbonne University W
Maryville University of Saint
  Louis W
Washington University in St.
  Louis W
Webster University W
Westminster College W

**Nebraska**

Nebraska Wesleyan University W

**New Hampshire**

Daniel Webster College W
Keene State College W
New England College W
Plymouth State University W
Rivier College W

**New Jersey**

Centenary College W
The College of New Jersey W
College of St. Elizabeth W
Drew University W
Fairleigh Dickinson University
  College at Florham W
Kean University W
Montclair State University W
New Jersey City University W
Ramapo College of New Jersey
  W
Richard Stockton College of New
  Jersey W
Rowan University W
Rutgers, The State University of
  New Jersey
    Camden Regional Campus
      W
    Newark Regional Campus
      W
William Paterson University of
  New Jersey W

**New York**

Alfred University W
Cazenovia College W
City University of New York
  Baruch College W
  Brooklyn College W
  College of Staten Island W
  Hunter College W
  John Jay College of
    Criminal Justice W
  Lehman College W
  Medgar Evers College W
  New York City College of
    Technology W
  York College W
College of Mount St. Vincent W
College of New Rochelle W
D'Youville College W
Elmira College W
Hamilton College W
Hilbert College W
Ithaca College W
Keuka College W
Manhattanville College W
Medaille College W
Mount St. Mary College W
Nazareth College of Rochester W
Polytechnic University W
Rensselaer Polytechnic Institute
  W
Rochester Institute of Technology
  W
Russell Sage College W
St. John Fisher College W
St. Joseph's College: Suffolk
  Campus W
St. Lawrence University W
Skidmore College W

State University of New York
  College at Brockport W
  College at Buffalo W
  College at Cortland W
  College at Fredonia W
  College at Geneseo W
  College at Old Westbury W
  College at Oneonta W
  College at Plattsburgh W
  College at Potsdam W
  College of Agriculture and
    Technology at Morrisville
    W
  Farmingdale W
  Institute of Technology at
    Utica/Rome W
  Maritime College W
  New Paltz W
  Oswego W
  Purchase W
Union College W
United States Merchant Marine
  Academy W
University of Rochester W
Utica College W
Wells College W

**North Carolina**
Greensboro College W
Guilford College W
Meredith College W
Methodist University W
North Carolina Wesleyan College
  W
Peace College W

**Ohio**
Baldwin-Wallace College W
Bluffton University W
Capital University W
Case Western Reserve University
  W
College of Mount St. Joseph W
College of Wooster W
Defiance College W
Denison University W
Franciscan University of
  Steubenville W
Heidelberg College W
Hiram College W
John Carroll University W
Kenyon College W
Lake Erie College W
Marietta College W
Mount Union College W
Muskingum College W
Oberlin College W
Ohio Northern University W
Ohio Wesleyan University W
Otterbein College W
Wilmington College W
Wittenberg University W

**Oregon**
George Fox University W
Lewis & Clark College W
Linfield College W
Pacific University W
Willamette University W

**Pennsylvania**
Albright College W
Allegheny College W
Alvernia College W
Arcadia University W
Baptist Bible College of
  Pennsylvania W
Cabrini College W
Cedar Crest College W
Chatham University W
Chestnut Hill College W
Delaware Valley College W
DeSales University W
Dickinson College W
Eastern University W
Elizabethtown College W
Franklin & Marshall College W
Geneva College W

Gettysburg College W
Grove City College W
Gwynedd-Mercy College W
Haverford College W
Immaculata University W
Juniata College W
Keystone College W
King's College W
La Roche College W
Lebanon Valley College W
Lycoming College W
Marywood University W
Messiah College W
Misericordia University W
Moravian College W
Mount Aloysius College W
Muhlenberg College W
Neumann College W
Penn State
  Altoona W
  Berks W
  Erie, The Behrend College
    W
Philadelphia Biblical University
  W
Rosemont College W
St. Vincent College W
Susquehanna University W
Swarthmore College W
Thiel College W
University of Pittsburgh
  Bradford W
  Greensburg W
University of Scranton W
Ursinus College W
Washington & Jefferson College
  W
Waynesburg University W
Westminster College W
Widener University W
Wilkes University W
Wilson College W
York College of Pennsylvania W

**Rhode Island**
Johnson & Wales University:
  Providence W
Rhode Island College W
Roger Williams University W
Salve Regina University W

**South Dakota**
Presentation College W

**Tennessee**
Maryville College W
Rhodes College W
University of the South W

**Texas**
Austin College W
Concordia University at Austin W
East Texas Baptist University W
Hardin-Simmons University W
Howard Payne University W
LeTourneau University W
Schreiner University W
Sul Ross State University W
Texas Lutheran University W
Trinity University W
University of Dallas W
University of Mary Hardin-Baylor
  W
University of Texas
  Dallas W
  Tyler W

**Vermont**
Castleton State College W
Johnson State College W
Lyndon State College W
Middlebury College W
Norwich University W
Southern Vermont College W

**Virginia**
Averett University W
Bridgewater College W

Christopher Newport University
  W
Eastern Mennonite University W
Emory & Henry College W
Ferrum College W
Lynchburg College W
Mary Baldwin College W
Randolph College W
Randolph-Macon College W
Roanoke College W
Shenandoah University W
Sweet Briar College W
University of Mary Washington
  W
Virginia Wesleyan College W

**Washington**
Pacific Lutheran University W
University of Puget Sound W
Whitworth University W

**West Virginia**
Bethany College W

**Wisconsin**
Alverno College W
Beloit College W
Carroll College W
Carthage College W
Concordia University Wisconsin
  W
Edgewood College W
Lakeland College W
Lawrence University W
Maranatha Baptist Bible College
  W
Marian College of Fond du Lac W
Milwaukee School of Engineering
  W
Mount Mary College W
Northland College W
Ripon College W
St. Norbert College W
University of Wisconsin
  Eau Claire W
  La Crosse W
  Oshkosh W
  Platteville W
  River Falls W
  Stevens Point W
  Stout W
  Superior W
  Whitewater W
Wisconsin Lutheran College W

## Swimming and diving Division I

**Alabama**
Auburn University
University of Alabama

**Arizona**
Arizona State University
Northern Arizona University W
University of Arizona

**Arkansas**
University of Arkansas W
University of Arkansas
  Little Rock W

**California**
California Polytechnic State
  University: San Luis Obispo
California State University
  Northridge
Loyola Marymount University W
Pepperdine University W
San Diego State University W
San Jose State University W
Stanford University
University of California
  Berkeley
  Davis
  Irvine
  Los Angeles W
  Santa Barbara

University of San Diego W
University of Southern California
University of the Pacific

**Colorado**
Colorado State University W
United States Air Force Academy
University of Denver
University of Northern Colorado
  W

**Connecticut**
Central Connecticut State
  University W
Fairfield University
Sacred Heart University W
University of Connecticut
Yale University

**Delaware**
University of Delaware

**District of Columbia**
American University
George Washington University
Georgetown University
Howard University

**Florida**
Florida Agricultural and
  Mechanical University
Florida Atlantic University
Florida International University
  W
Florida State University
University of Florida
University of Miami
University of North Florida W

**Georgia**
Georgia Institute of Technology
Georgia Southern University W
University of Georgia

**Hawaii**
University of Hawaii
  Manoa

**Idaho**
Boise State University W
University of Idaho W

**Illinois**
Eastern Illinois University
Illinois State University W
Northwestern University
Southern Illinois University
  Carbondale
University of Illinois
  Chicago
  Urbana-Champaign W
Western Illinois University

**Indiana**
Ball State University
Butler University W
Indiana University
  Bloomington
Indiana University-Purdue
  University Indianapolis
Purdue University
University of Evansville
University of Notre Dame
Valparaiso University

**Iowa**
Iowa State University W
University of Iowa
University of Northern Iowa W

**Kansas**
University of Kansas W

**Kentucky**
University of Kentucky
University of Louisville
Western Kentucky University

**Louisiana**
Centenary College of Louisiana

Louisiana State University and
  Agricultural and Mechanical
  College
University of New Orleans W

**Maine**
University of Maine

**Maryland**
Loyola College in Maryland
Mount St. Mary's University W
Towson University
United States Naval Academy
University of Maryland
  Baltimore County
  College Park

**Massachusetts**
Boston College
Boston University
College of the Holy Cross
Harvard College
Northeastern University W
University of Massachusetts
  Amherst

**Michigan**
Eastern Michigan University
Michigan State University
Oakland University
University of Michigan

**Minnesota**
University of Minnesota
  Twin Cities

**Missouri**
Missouri State University M
Saint Louis University
University of Missouri
  Columbia

**Nebraska**
University of Nebraska
  Lincoln W

**Nevada**
University of Nevada
  Las Vegas
  Reno W

**New Hampshire**
Dartmouth College
University of New Hampshire W

**New Jersey**
Princeton University
Rider University
Rutgers, The State University of
  New Jersey
    New Brunswick/Piscataway
    Campus
Saint Peter's College
Seton Hall University

**New Mexico**
New Mexico State University W
University of New Mexico W

**New York**
Barnard College
Canisius College
Colgate University
Cornell University
Fordham University
Iona College
Manhattan College W
Marist College
Niagara University
Saint Bonaventure University
St. Francis College
Siena College W
State University of New York
  Binghamton
  Buffalo
  Stony Brook
Syracuse University
United States Military Academy
Wagner College W

**North Carolina**
Campbell University W

Tables and Indexes

Hamilton College
Hartwick College
Hobart and William Smith
  Colleges W
Ithaca College
Mount St. Mary College
Nazareth College of Rochester
New York University
Rensselaer Polytechnic Institute
Rochester.Institute of Technology
St. Joseph's College W
St. Lawrence University
Skidmore College
State University of New York
  College at Brockport
  College at Buffalo
  College at Cortland
  College at Fredonia
  College at Geneseo
  College at Old Westbury
  College at Oneonta
  College at Potsdam
  College of Agriculture and
    Technology at Morrisville
  Maritime College
  New Paltz
  Oswego
  Purchase W
Union College
United States Merchant Marine
  Academy
University of Rochester
Utica College
Vassar College
Wells College

**North Carolina**
Greensboro College W
Guilford College W
Salem College W

**Ohio**
Baldwin-Wallace College
Case Western Reserve University
College of Wooster
Denison University
Hiram College
John Carroll University
Kenyon College
Mount Union College
Oberlin College
Ohio Northern University
Ohio Wesleyan University
Wilmington College
Wittenberg University

**Oregon**
Lewis & Clark College
Linfield College
Pacific University
Willamette University

**Pennsylvania**
Albright College
Allegheny College
Arcadia University
Bryn Mawr College W
Cabrini College W
Carnegie Mellon University
Chatham University W
Dickinson College
Elizabethtown College
Franklin & Marshall College
Gettysburg College
Grove City College
Juniata College W
King's College
Lebanon Valley College
Lycoming College
Misericordia University
Penn State
  Altoona
  Erie, The Behrend College
St. Vincent College
Susquehanna University
Swarthmore College
University of Pittsburgh
  Bradford

University of Scranton
Ursinus College
Washington & Jefferson College
Westminster College
Widener University
York College of Pennsylvania

**Rhode Island**
Roger Williams University

**Tennessee**
Rhodes College
University of the South

**Texas**
Austin College
McMurry University
Southwestern University
Trinity University

**Vermont**
Middlebury College
Norwich University

**Virginia**
Emory & Henry College W
Hollins University W
Marymount University
Randolph College W
Randolph-Macon College W
Sweet Briar College W
University of Mary Washington
Washington and Lee University

**Washington**
Pacific Lutheran University
University of Puget Sound
Whitman College
Whitworth University

**West Virginia**
Bethany College

**Wisconsin**
Beloit College
Carroll College
Carthage College
Lawrence University
Ripon College
St. Norbert College W
University of Wisconsin
  Eau Claire
  La Crosse
  Oshkosh
  River Falls
  Stevens Point
  Whitewater

---

## Tennis Division I

**Alabama**
Alabama Agricultural and
  Mechanical University
Alabama State University
Auburn University
Birmingham-Southern College
Jacksonville State University
Samford University
Troy University
University of Alabama
University of Alabama
  Birmingham
University of South Alabama

**Arizona**
Arizona State University
Northern Arizona University
University of Arizona

**Arkansas**
Arkansas State University W
University of Arkansas
University of Arkansas
  Little Rock
  Pine Bluff

**California**
California Polytechnic State
  University: San Luis Obispo

California State University
  Fresno
  Fullerton W
  Long Beach W
  Northridge W
  Sacramento
Loyola Marymount University
Pepperdine University
St. Mary's College of California
San Diego State University
San Jose State University W
Santa Clara University
Stanford University
University of California
  Berkeley
  Davis
  Irvine
  Los Angeles
  Riverside
  Santa Barbara
University of San Diego
University of San Francisco
University of Southern California
University of the Pacific

**Colorado**
Colorado State University W
United States Air Force Academy
University of Colorado
  Boulder W
University of Denver
University of Northern Colorado
  W

**Connecticut**
Fairfield University
Quinnipiac University
Sacred Heart University
University of Connecticut
University of Hartford
Yale University

**Delaware**
Delaware State University
University of Delaware

**District of Columbia**
George Washington University
Georgetown University
Howard University

**Florida**
Bethune-Cookman University
Florida Agricultural and
  Mechanical University
Florida Atlantic University
Florida International University
  W
Florida State University
Jacksonville University
Stetson University
University of Central Florida
University of Florida
University of Miami
University of South Florida

**Georgia**
Georgia Institute of Technology
Georgia Southern University
Georgia State University
Mercer University
Savannah State University W
University of Georgia

**Hawaii**
University of Hawaii
  Manoa

**Idaho**
Boise State University
Idaho State University
University of Idaho

**Illinois**
Bradley University
Chicago State University
DePaul University
Eastern Illinois University
Illinois State University
Northern Illinois University

Northwestern University
Southern Illinois University
  Carbondale
University of Illinois
  Chicago
  Urbana-Champaign
Western Illinois University

**Indiana**
Ball State University
Butler University
Indiana State University
Indiana University
  Bloomington
Indiana University-Purdue
  University Fort Wayne
Indiana University-Purdue
  University Indianapolis
Purdue University
University of Evansville W
University of Notre Dame
Valparaiso University

**Iowa**
Drake University
Iowa State University W
University of Iowa
University of Northern Iowa W

**Kansas**
Kansas State University W
University of Kansas W
Wichita State University

**Kentucky**
Eastern Kentucky University
Morehead State University
Murray State University
University of Kentucky
University of Louisville
Western Kentucky University

**Louisiana**
Centenary College of Louisiana
Grambling State University
Louisiana State University and
  Agricultural and Mechanical
  College
Louisiana Tech University W
McNeese State University W
Nicholls State University
Northwestern State University W
Southeastern Louisiana University
Southern University and
  Agricultural and Mechanical
  College
University of Louisiana at
  Lafayette
University of Louisiana at
  Monroe W

**Maryland**
Coppin State University
Loyola College in Maryland
Morgan State University
Mount St. Mary's University
Towson University W
United States Naval Academy M
University of Maryland
  Baltimore County
  College Park
  Eastern Shore

**Massachusetts**
Boston College
Boston University
College of the Holy Cross
Harvard College
University of Massachusetts
  Amherst W

**Michigan**
Eastern Michigan University W
Michigan State University
Oakland University W
University of Detroit Mercy W
University of Michigan
Western Michigan University

**Minnesota**
University of Minnesota
  Twin Cities

**Mississippi**
Alcorn State University
Jackson State University
Mississippi State University
Mississippi Valley State
  University
University of Mississippi
University of Southern
  Mississippi

**Missouri**
Saint Louis University
Southeast Missouri State
  University W
University of Missouri
  Columbia W
  Kansas City

**Montana**
Montana State University
  Bozeman
University of Montana: Missoula

**Nebraska**
Creighton University
University of Nebraska
  Lincoln

**Nevada**
University of Nevada
  Las Vegas
  Reno

**New Hampshire**
Dartmouth College

**New Jersey**
Fairleigh Dickinson University
  Metropolitan Campus
Monmouth University
Princeton University
Rider University
Rutgers, The State University of
  New Jersey
    New Brunswick/Piscataway
      Campus W
Saint Peter's College
Seton Hall University W

**New Mexico**
New Mexico State University
University of New Mexico

**New York**
Barnard College W
Colgate University
Columbia University M
Cornell University
Fordham University
Hofstra University
Long Island University
  Brooklyn Campus W
Manhattan College
Marist College
Niagara University
Saint Bonaventure University
St. Francis College
St. John's University
Siena College
State University of New York
  Albany W
  Binghamton
  Buffalo
  Stony Brook
Syracuse University W
United States Military Academy
Wagner College

**North Carolina**
Appalachian State University
Campbell University
Davidson College W
Duke University
East Carolina University
Elon University
Gardner-Webb University

High Point University
North Carolina Agricultural and Technical State University W
North Carolina State University
University of North Carolina
  Asheville
  Chapel Hill
  Charlotte
  Greensboro
  Wilmington
Wake Forest University
Western Carolina University W

## Ohio

Bowling Green State University W
Cleveland State University
Miami University
  Oxford Campus W
Ohio State University
  Columbus Campus
University of Akron W
University of Cincinnati W
University of Dayton
University of Toledo
Wright State University
Xavier University
Youngstown State University

## Oklahoma

Oklahoma State University
Oral Roberts University
University of Oklahoma
University of Tulsa

## Oregon

University of Oregon
University of Portland

## Pennsylvania

Bucknell University
Drexel University
Duquesne University
La Salle University
Lafayette College
Lehigh University
Penn State
  University Park
Robert Morris University
St. Francis University
Saint Joseph's University
Temple University
University of Pennsylvania
University of Pittsburgh W
Villanova University

## Rhode Island

Brown University
Providence College W
University of Rhode Island

## South Carolina

Charleston Southern University
The Citadel M
Clemson University
Coastal Carolina University
College of Charleston
Furman University
South Carolina State University
University of South Carolina
Winthrop University
Wofford College

## Tennessee

Austin Peay State University
Belmont University
East Tennessee State University
Lipscomb University
Middle Tennessee State University
Tennessee State University
Tennessee Technological University
University of Memphis
University of Tennessee
  Chattanooga
  Knoxville
  Martin
Vanderbilt University

## Texas

Baylor University
Lamar University
Prairie View A&M University
Rice University
Sam Houston State University W
Southern Methodist University
Stephen F. Austin State University W
Texas A&M University
Texas Christian University
Texas Southern University W
Texas State University: San Marcos W
Texas Tech University
University of Houston W
University of North Texas W
University of Texas
  Arlington
  Austin
  El Paso W
  Pan American
  San Antonio

## Utah

Brigham Young University
Southern Utah University W
University of Utah
Utah State University
Weber State University

## Virginia

College of William and Mary
George Mason University
Hampton University
James Madison University
Liberty University
Longwood University
Norfolk State University
Old Dominion University
Radford University
University of Richmond
University of Virginia
Virginia Commonwealth University
Virginia Polytechnic Institute and State University

## Washington

Gonzaga University
University of Washington
Washington State University W

## West Virginia

Marshall University W
University of Charleston M
West Virginia University W

## Wisconsin

Marquette University
University of Wisconsin
  Green Bay
  Madison
  Milwaukee W

## Wyoming

University of Wyoming W

# Tennis Division II

## Alabama

Stillman College
Tuskegee University
University of Alabama
  Huntsville
University of Montevallo W
University of North Alabama
University of West Alabama

## Arizona

Grand Canyon University W

## Arkansas

Arkansas Tech University W
Harding University
Henderson State University W
Ouachita Baptist University
Southern Arkansas University W

University of Central Arkansas W

## California

California State Polytechnic University: Pomona
California State University
  Bakersfield W
  Los Angeles W
  San Bernardino W
Notre Dame de Namur University W
Sonoma State University
University of California
  San Diego

## Colorado

Colorado Christian University
Colorado State University
  Pueblo
Mesa State College
Metropolitan State College of Denver

## Connecticut

Post University
University of New Haven W

## Delaware

Goldey-Beacom College W

## District of Columbia

University of the District of Columbia

## Florida

Barry University
Eckerd College
Flagler College
Florida Gulf Coast University
Florida Institute of Technology
Florida Southern College
Lynn University
Nova Southeastern University W
Palm Beach Atlantic University
Rollins College
St. Leo University
University of North Florida
University of Tampa W
University of West Florida

## Georgia

Albany State University W
Armstrong Atlantic State University
Augusta State University
Clark Atlanta University W
Clayton State University W
Columbus State University
Fort Valley State University
Georgia College and State University
Georgia Southwestern State University
Kennesaw State University
Morehouse College M
North Georgia College & State University
Valdosta State University

## Hawaii

Brigham Young University-Hawaii
Chaminade University of Honolulu W
Hawaii Pacific University
University of Hawaii
  Hilo

## Illinois

Lewis University
Quincy University
Southern Illinois University
  Edwardsville

## Indiana

Oakland City University
Saint Joseph's College
University of Indianapolis
University of Southern Indiana

## Iowa

Upper Iowa University W

## Kansas

Emporia State University
Fort Hays State University W
Newman University
Washburn University

## Kentucky

Bellarmine University
Kentucky Wesleyan College W
Northern Kentucky University

## Maryland

Bowie State University W

## Massachusetts

American International College
Assumption College
Bentley College
Merrimack College
Stonehill College

## Michigan

Ferris State University
Grand Valley State University
Lake Superior State University
Michigan Technological University
Northwood University: Michigan
Saginaw Valley State University W
Wayne State University

## Minnesota

Bemidji State University W
Minnesota State University
  Mankato
  Moorhead W
Saint Cloud State University
Southwest Minnesota State University W
University of Minnesota
  Crookston W
  Duluth W
  Morris
Winona State University

## Mississippi

Delta State University

## Missouri

Drury University
Lincoln University W
Missouri Southern State University W
Missouri Western State University W
Northwest Missouri State University
Rockhurst University
Southwest Baptist University
Truman State University
University of Missouri
  St. Louis

## Montana

Montana State University
  Billings

## Nebraska

University of Nebraska
  Kearney
  Omaha W

## New Hampshire

Franklin Pierce University
St. Anselm College
Southern New Hampshire University

## New Jersey

Bloomfield College M
Caldwell College
Georgian Court University W
New Jersey Institute of Technology

## New Mexico

Eastern New Mexico University W
Western New Mexico University

## New York

Adelphi University
City University of New York
  Queens College
College of Saint Rose W
Concordia College
Dowling College
Le Moyne College
Long Island University
  C. W. Post Campus W
Mercy College M
Molloy College W
Pace University
St. Thomas Aquinas College

## North Carolina

Barton College
Brevard College
Catawba College
Chowan University
Elizabeth City State University W
Fayetteville State University W
Johnson C. Smith University
Lees-McRae College
Lenoir-Rhyne College W
Livingstone College W
Mars Hill College
Mount Olive College
North Carolina Central University
Pfeiffer University
Queens University of Charlotte
St. Andrews Presbyterian College
St. Augustine's College
Shaw University
University of North Carolina
  Pembroke W
Wingate University
Winston-Salem State University

## North Dakota

University of Mary
University of North Dakota W

## Ohio

Ashland University W
Central State University
Tiffin University
University of Findlay

## Oklahoma

Cameron University
East Central University
Northeastern State University W
Southeastern Oklahoma State University
University of Central Oklahoma W

## Pennsylvania

Bloomsburg University of Pennsylvania
California University of Pennsylvania W
Cheyney University of Pennsylvania W
Clarion University of Pennsylvania W
East Stroudsburg University of Pennsylvania
Holy Family University W
Indiana University of Pennsylvania W
Kutztown University of Pennsylvania
Mercyhurst College
Millersville University of Pennsylvania
Philadelphia University
Seton Hill University
Shippensburg University of Pennsylvania W
Slippery Rock University of Pennsylvania W

University of the Sciences in
  Philadelphia
West Chester University of
  Pennsylvania

**Puerto Rico**

University of Puerto Rico
  Bayamon University College
  Cayey University College
  Mayaguez
  . Rio Piedras

**Rhode Island**

Bryant University

**South Carolina**

Anderson University
Benedict College
Coker College
Converse College W
Erskine College
Francis Marion University
Lander University
Limestone College
Newberry College
North Greenville University
Presbyterian College
University of South Carolina
  Aiken
  Upstate

**South Dakota**

Augustana College
South Dakota State University
University of South Dakota W

**Tennessee**

Carson-Newman College
Christian Brothers University
Lane College
LeMoyne-Owen College
Lincoln Memorial University
Tusculum College

**Texas**

Abilene Christian University
Dallas Baptist University
Midwestern State University
St. Edward's University
St. Mary's University
Tarleton State University W
University of the Incarnate Word

**Utah**

Dixie State College of Utah W

**Vermont**

St. Michael's College

**Virginia**

St. Paul's College
Virginia State University
Virginia Union University

**West Virginia**

Bluefield State College
Concord University
Fairmont State University
Salem International University M
Shepherd University
University of Charleston W
West Liberty State College
West Virginia Wesleyan College

**Tennis Division III**

**Alabama**

Huntingdon College

**Arkansas**

Hendrix College
University of the Ozarks

**California**

California Institute of Technology
California Lutheran University
Chapman University
Claremont McKenna College
La Sierra University
Mills College W

Occidental College
Pitzer College M
Pomona College
University of California
  Santa Cruz
University of La Verne
University of Redlands
Whittier College

**Colorado**

Colorado College

**Connecticut**

Albertus Magnus College
Connecticut College
Mitchell College
St. Joseph College W
Trinity College
United States Coast Guard
  Academy M
Wesleyan University
Western Connecticut State
  University

**Delaware**

Wesley College

**District of Columbia**

Catholic University of America
Trinity Washington University W

**Georgia**

Agnes Scott College W
Emory University
LaGrange College
Oglethorpe University
Piedmont College
Spelman College W
Wesleyan College W

**Illinois**

Augustana College
Aurora University
Benedictine University W
Blackburn College W
Concordia University
Dominican University
Elmhurst College
Eureka College
Greenville College
Illinois College
Illinois Wesleyan University
Knox College
Lake Forest College
Millikin University W
Monmouth College
North Central College
Principia College
Rockford College
University of Chicago
Wheaton College

**Indiana**

Anderson University
DePauw University
Earlham College
Franklin College
Hanover College
Manchester College
Rose-Hulman Institute of
  Technology
Saint Mary's College W
Tri-State University
Wabash College M

**Iowa**

Buena Vista University
Central College
Coe College
Cornell College
Grinnell College
Loras College
Luther College
Simpson College
University of Dubuque
Wartburg College

**Kentucky**

Centre College
Thomas More College

Transylvania University

**Louisiana**

Louisiana College

**Maine**

Bates College
Bowdoin College
Colby College
Thomas College M
University of Southern Maine

**Maryland**

College of Notre Dame of
  Maryland W
Frostburg State University
Goucher College
Hood College
Johns Hopkins University
McDaniel College
St. Mary's College of Maryland
Salisbury University
Villa Julie College
Washington College

**Massachusetts**

Amherst College
Babson College
Bay Path College W
Becker College
Brandeis University
Bridgewater State College
Clark University
Curry College
Eastern Nazarene College
Emerson College
Emmanuel College W
Endicott College
Gordon College
Massachusetts College of Liberal
  Arts W
Massachusetts Institute of
  Technology
Mount Holyoke College W
Newbury College
Nichols College
Pine Manor College W
Regis College W
Salem State College
Simmons College W
Smith College W
Springfield College
Suffolk University
Tufts University
University of Massachusetts
  Boston
  Dartmouth
Wellesley College W
Wentworth Institute of
  Technology
Western New England College
Wheaton College
Williams College
Worcester State College W

**Michigan**

Adrian College
Albion College
Alma College
Calvin College
Hope College
Kalamazoo College
Olivet College W

**Minnesota**

Bethany Lutheran College
Bethel University
Carleton College
College of St. Benedict W
College of St. Catherine W
College of St. Scholastica
Concordia College: Moorhead
Gustavus Adolphus College
Hamline University
Macalester College
Martin Luther College
Northwestern College
St. John's University M

St. Mary's University of
  Minnesota
St. Olaf College
University of St. Thomas

**Mississippi**

Millsaps College
Mississippi College
Rust College

**Missouri**

Fontbonne University
Maryville University of Saint
  Louis
Washington University in St.
  Louis
Webster University
Westminster College

**Nebraska**

Nebraska Wesleyan University

**New Hampshire**

Colby-Sawyer College
Plymouth State University W

**New Jersey**

The College of New Jersey
College of St. Elizabeth W
Drew University
Fairleigh Dickinson University
  College at Florham
Kean University W
Ramapo College of New Jersey
Richard Stockton College of New
  Jersey W
Rutgers, The State University of
  New Jersey
  Newark Regional Campus
Stevens Institute of Technology
William Paterson University of
  New Jersey W

**New York**

Alfred University
Bard College
City University of New York
  Baruch College
  Brooklyn College
  City College
  College of Staten Island
  Hunter College
  John Jay College of
    Criminal Justice
  Lehman College
  Medgar Evers College W
  New York City College of
    Technology
  York College M
College of Mount St. Vincent
College of New Rochelle W
Elmira College
Hamilton College
Hartwick College
Hobart and William Smith
  Colleges
Ithaca College
Keuka College
Manhattanville College
Mount St. Mary College
Nazareth College of Rochester
New York University
Polytechnic University
Rensselaer Polytechnic Institute
Rochester Institute of Technology
Russell Sage College W
St. John Fisher College
St. Joseph's College M
St. Joseph's College: Suffolk
  Campus W
St. Lawrence University
Skidmore College

State University of New York
  College at Brockport W
  College at Cortland W
  College at Fredonia W
  College at Geneseo W
  College at Oneonta
  College at Plattsburgh W
  College at Potsdam W
  Farmingdale
  New Paltz W
  Oswego
  Purchase
Union College
United States Merchant Marine
  Academy M
University of Rochester
Utica College
Vassar College
Wells College W
Yeshiva University M

**North Carolina**

Greensboro College
Guilford College
Meredith College W
Methodist University
North Carolina Wesleyan College
Peace College W
Salem College W

**Ohio**

Baldwin-Wallace College
Bluffton University
Capital University
Case Western Reserve University
College of Mount St. Joseph
College of Wooster
Defiance College
Denison University
Heidelberg College
Hiram College
John Carroll University
Kenyon College
Marietta College
Mount Union College
Muskingum College
Oberlin College
Ohio Northern University
Ohio Wesleyan University
Otterbein College
Wilmington College
Wittenberg University

**Oregon**

George Fox University
Lewis & Clark College
Linfield College
Pacific University
Willamette University

**Pennsylvania**

Albright College
Allegheny College
Alvernia College
Arcadia University
Baptist Bible College of
  Pennsylvania W
Bryn Mawr College W
Cabrini College
Carnegie Mellon University
Cedar Crest College W
Chatham University W
Chestnut Hill College
DeSales University
Dickinson College
Eastern University
Elizabethtown College
Franklin & Marshall College
Geneva College W
Gettysburg College
Grove City College
Gwynedd-Mercy College
Haverford College
Immaculata University
Juniata College
Keystone College
King's College
Lebanon Valley College

Lincoln University
Lycoming College
Marywood University
Messiah College
Misericordia University
Moravian College
Muhlenberg College
Neumann College
Penn State
  Altoona
  Berks
  Erie, The Behrend College
  Harrisburg
Philadelphia Biblical University
Rosemont College W
St. Vincent College
Susquehanna University
Swarthmore College
University of Pittsburgh
  Greensburg M
University of Scranton
Ursinus College
Washington & Jefferson College
Waynesburg University
Westminster College
Wilkes University
York College of Pennsylvania

**Rhode Island**
Johnson & Wales University:
  Providence
Rhode Island College
Roger Williams University
Salve Regina University

**Tennessee**
Maryville College
Rhodes College
University of the South

**Texas**
Austin College
Concordia University at Austin
Hardin-Simmons University
Howard Payne University
LeTourneau University
McMurry University
Schreiner University
Southwestern University
Sul Ross State University
Texas Lutheran University
Trinity University
University of Mary Hardin-Baylor
University of Texas
  Dallas
  Tyler

**Vermont**
Castleton State College
Johnson State College
Lyndon State College W
Middlebury College
Norwich University M

**Virginia**
Averett University
Bridgewater College
Christopher Newport University
Emory & Henry College
Ferrum College
Hampden-Sydney College M
Hollins University W
Lynchburg College
Mary Baldwin College W
Randolph College W
Randolph-Macon College
Roanoke College
Shenandoah University
Sweet Briar College W
University of Mary Washington
Virginia Wesleyan College
Washington and Lee University

**Washington**
Pacific Lutheran University
University of Puget Sound
Whitman College
Whitworth University

**West Virginia**
Bethany College

**Wisconsin**
Beloit College
Carroll College
Carthage College
Concordia University Wisconsin
Edgewood College W
Lakeland College
Lawrence University
Marian College of Fond du Lac
Milwaukee School of Engineering
Mount Mary College W
Ripon College
St. Norbert College
University of Wisconsin
  Eau Claire
  La Crosse
  Oshkosh
  River Falls W
  Stevens Point W
  Stout W
  Whitewater
Wisconsin Lutheran College W

## Track, indoor Division I

**Alabama**
Alabama State University
Auburn University
Jacksonville State University W
Samford University
Troy University W
University of Alabama
University of Alabama
  Birmingham W
University of South Alabama

**Arizona**
Arizona State University
Northern Arizona University
University of Arizona

**Arkansas**
Arkansas State University
University of Arkansas
University of Arkansas
  Little Rock
  Pine Bluff W

**California**
California Polytechnic State
  University: San Luis Obispo W
California State University
  Fresno W
  Fullerton W
  Long Beach
  Northridge
  Sacramento
San Diego State University W
Stanford University
University of California
  Berkeley
  Davis
  Irvine W
  Los Angeles
  Riverside
University of Southern California
  W

**Colorado**
Colorado State University
United States Air Force Academy
University of Colorado
  Boulder
University of Northern Colorado

**Connecticut**
Central Connecticut State
  University
Quinnipiac University
Sacred Heart University
University of Connecticut
University of Hartford
Yale University

**Delaware**
Delaware State University
University of Delaware

**District of Columbia**
American University
Georgetown University
Howard University

**Florida**
Bethune-Cookman University
Florida Agricultural and
  Mechanical University
Florida Atlantic University W
Florida International University
Florida State University
Jacksonville University W
University of Central Florida W
University of Florida
University of Miami
University of South Florida W

**Georgia**
Georgia Institute of Technology
Georgia Southern University W
Georgia State University W
Savannah State University
University of Georgia

**Hawaii**
University of Hawaii
  Manoa W

**Idaho**
Boise State University
Idaho State University
University of Idaho

**Illinois**
Bradley University W
Chicago State University
DePaul University
Eastern Illinois University
Illinois State University
Loyola University Chicago
Northern Illinois University W
Southern Illinois University
  Carbondale
University of Illinois
  Chicago
  Urbana-Champaign
Western Illinois University

**Indiana**
Ball State University W
Butler University
Indiana State University
Indiana University
  Bloomington
Indiana University-Purdue
  University Fort Wayne W
Purdue University
University of Notre Dame
Valparaiso University

**Iowa**
Drake University
Iowa State University
University of Iowa
University of Northern Iowa

**Kansas**
Kansas State University
University of Kansas
Wichita State University

**Kentucky**
Eastern Kentucky University
Morehead State University
Murray State University W
University of Kentucky
University of Louisville
Western Kentucky University

**Louisiana**
Grambling State University
Louisiana State University and
  Agricultural and Mechanical
  College
Louisiana Tech University
McNeese State University

Nicholls State University W
Northwestern State University
Southeastern Louisiana University
Southern University and
  Agricultural and Mechanical
  College
Tulane University W
University of Louisiana at
  Lafayette
University of Louisiana at
  Monroe

**Maine**
University of Maine

**Maryland**
Coppin State University
Loyola College in Maryland W
Morgan State University
Mount St. Mary's University
Towson University W
United States Naval Academy
University of Maryland
  Baltimore County
  College Park
  Eastern Shore

**Massachusetts**
Boston College
Boston University
College of the Holy Cross
Harvard College
Northeastern University
University of Massachusetts
  Amherst

**Michigan**
Central Michigan University
Eastern Michigan University
Michigan State University
Oakland University W
University of Detroit Mercy
University of Michigan
Western Michigan University W

**Minnesota**
University of Minnesota
  Twin Cities

**Mississippi**
Jackson State University
Mississippi State University W
Mississippi Valley State
  University
University of Mississippi M
University of Southern
  Mississippi

**Missouri**
Missouri State University W
Saint Louis University
Southeast Missouri State
  University
University of Missouri
  Columbia
  Kansas City

**Montana**
Montana State University
  Bozeman
University of Montana: Missoula

**Nebraska**
University of Nebraska
  Lincoln

**Nevada**
University of Nevada
  Las Vegas W
  Reno W

**New Hampshire**
Dartmouth College
University of New Hampshire

**New Jersey**
Fairleigh Dickinson University
  Metropolitan Campus
Monmouth University
Princeton University
Rider University

Rutgers, The State University of
  New Jersey
    New Brunswick/Piscataway
    Campus
Saint Peter's College
Seton Hall University

**New Mexico**
New Mexico State University W
University of New Mexico

**New York**
Barnard College
Colgate University
Cornell University
Fordham University
Iona College
Long Island University
  Brooklyn Campus
Manhattan College
Marist College
St. Francis College
St. John's University W
State University of New York
  Albany
  Binghamton
  Buffalo
  Stony Brook
Syracuse University
United States Military Academy
Wagner College

**North Carolina**
Appalachian State University
Campbell University
Davidson College
Duke University
East Carolina University
Elon University W
Gardner-Webb University
High Point University
North Carolina Agricultural and
  Technical State University
North Carolina State University
University of North Carolina
  Asheville
  Chapel Hill
  Charlotte
  Wilmington
Wake Forest University
Western Carolina University

**Ohio**
Bowling Green State University
  W
Kent State University
Miami University
  Oxford Campus W
Ohio State University
  Columbus Campus
Ohio University W
University of Akron
University of Cincinnati W
University of Dayton W
University of Toledo W
Wright State University W
Xavier University
Youngstown State University

**Oklahoma**
Oklahoma State University
Oral Roberts University
University of Oklahoma
University of Tulsa

**Oregon**
Portland State University
University of Oregon
University of Portland

**Pennsylvania**
Bucknell University
Duquesne University W
La Salle University
Lafayette College
Lehigh University
Penn State
  University Park
Robert Morris University

St. Francis University
Saint Joseph's University
Temple University
University of Pennsylvania
University of Pittsburgh
Villanova University

**Rhode Island**

Brown University
Providence College
University of Rhode Island

**South Carolina**

Charleston Southern University
The Citadel
Clemson University
Coastal Carolina University W
College of Charleston W
Furman University
South Carolina State University
University of South Carolina
Winthrop University
Wofford College

**Tennessee**

Austin Peay State University W
Belmont University
East Tennessee State University
Lipscomb University
Middle Tennessee State
   University
Tennessee State University
Tennessee Technological
   University W
University of Memphis
University of Tennessee
   Chattanooga
   Knoxville
Vanderbilt University W

**Texas**

Baylor University
Lamar University
Prairie View A&M University
Rice University
Sam Houston State University
Southern Methodist University W
Stephen F. Austin State University
Texas A&M University
Texas Christian University
Texas Southern University
Texas State University: San
   Marcos
Texas Tech University
University of Houston
University of North Texas
University of Texas
   Arlington
   Austin
   El Paso
   Pan American
   San Antonio

**Utah**

Brigham Young University
Southern Utah University
University of Utah W
Utah State University
Utah Valley State College
Weber State University

**Vermont**

University of Vermont

**Virginia**

College of William and Mary
George Mason University
Hampton University
James Madison University W
Liberty University
Norfolk State University
Radford University
University of Richmond
University of Virginia
Virginia Commonwealth
   University
Virginia Military Institute
Virginia Polytechnic Institute and
   State University

**Washington**

University of Washington
Washington State University

**West Virginia**

Marshall University W
West Virginia University W

**Wisconsin**

Marquette University
University of Wisconsin
   Madison
   Milwaukee

**Wyoming**

University of Wyoming

## Track, indoor Division II

**Alabama**

University of Alabama
   Huntsville

**Arkansas**

Harding University
University of Central Arkansas

**California**

California State University
   Bakersfield
   Dominguez Hills W
   Los Angeles W
   Stanislaus W
San Francisco State University W

**Colorado**

Adams State College
Colorado School of Mines
Mesa State College W
Metropolitan State College of
   Denver
University of Colorado
   Colorado Springs
Western State College of
   Colorado

**Connecticut**

Southern Connecticut State
   University
University of New Haven

**District of Columbia**

University of the District of
   Columbia W

**Florida**

University of North Florida

**Georgia**

American InterContinental
   University M
Clayton State University
Kennesaw State University
Morehouse College M

**Idaho**

Northwest Nazarene University

**Illinois**

Lewis University
Southern Illinois University
   Edwardsville

**Indiana**

Saint Joseph's College
University of Indianapolis
University of Southern Indiana

**Kansas**

Emporia State University
Fort Hays State University
Pittsburg State University

**Kentucky**

Bellarmine University
Kentucky State University
Northern Kentucky University

**Maryland**

Bowie State University

**Massachusetts**

American International College
   W
Assumption College
Bentley College
Stonehill College
University of Massachusetts
   Lowell

**Michigan**

Ferris State University
Grand Valley State University
Hillsdale College
Lake Superior State University
Northern Michigan University W
Northwood University: Michigan
Saginaw Valley State University

**Minnesota**

Bemidji State University
Concordia University: St. Paul
Minnesota State University
   Mankato
   Moorhead
Saint Cloud State University
University of Minnesota
   Duluth
   Morris
Winona State University W

**Missouri**

Lincoln University
Missouri Southern State
   University
Northwest Missouri State
   University
Southwest Baptist University
Truman State University
University of Central Missouri
University of Missouri
   Missouri University of
   Science and Technology

**Montana**

Montana State University
   Billings

**Nebraska**

Chadron State College
College of Saint Mary W
University of Nebraska
   Kearney
   Omaha W
Wayne State College

**New Jersey**

New Jersey Institute of
   Technology

**New Mexico**

New Mexico Highlands
   University W

**New York**

City University of New York
   Queens College
College of Saint Rose M
Long Island University
   C. W. Post Campus
Mercy College
St. Thomas Aquinas College

**North Carolina**

Lees-McRae College
Livingstone College
North Carolina Central University
St. Augustine's College
Winston-Salem State University

**North Dakota**

North Dakota State University
University of Mary W
University of North Dakota

**Ohio**

Ashland University
Central State University
Tiffin University
University of Findlay

**Oregon**

Western Oregon University

**Pennsylvania**

Bloomsburg University of
   Pennsylvania
California University of
   Pennsylvania
Cheyney University of
   Pennsylvania
Clarion University of
   Pennsylvania W
East Stroudsburg University of
   Pennsylvania
Edinboro University of
   Pennsylvania W
Indiana University of
   Pennsylvania
Kutztown University of
   Pennsylvania
Lock Haven University of
   Pennsylvania
Mansfield University of
   Pennsylvania
Millersville University of
   Pennsylvania
Seton Hill University W
Shippensburg University of
   Pennsylvania
Slippery Rock University of
   Pennsylvania
University of Pittsburgh
   Johnstown W
West Chester University of
   Pennsylvania

**Rhode Island**

Bryant University

**South Carolina**

Anderson University
Claflin University

**South Dakota**

Augustana College
Northern State University
South Dakota State University
University of South Dakota

**Tennessee**

Carson-Newman College

**Texas**

Abilene Christian University
Dallas Baptist University
Texas A&M University
   Kingsville

**Virginia**

St. Paul's College
Virginia State University
Virginia Union University

**Washington**

Central Washington University
Saint Martin's University
Seattle Pacific University
Seattle University
Western Washington University

**West Virginia**

Alderson-Broaddus College
Concord University
Wheeling Jesuit University

**Wisconsin**

University of Wisconsin
   Parkside

## Track, indoor Division III

**California**

California Lutheran University W
Occidental College
Pomona College M
University of La Verne

**Colorado**

Colorado College W

**Connecticut**

Connecticut College
Eastern Connecticut State
   University
Trinity College
United States Coast Guard
   Academy
Wesleyan University

**Delaware**

Wesley College

**District of Columbia**

Catholic University of America

**Georgia**

Emory University

**Illinois**

Augustana College
Aurora University
Benedictine University
Concordia University
Elmhurst College
Greenville College
Illinois College
Illinois Wesleyan University
Knox College
Millikin University
Monmouth College
North Central College
North Park University
Principia College
Rockford College
University of Chicago
Wheaton College

**Indiana**

Anderson University
DePauw University
Earlham College
Hanover College
Manchester College
Rose-Hulman Institute of
   Technology
Tri-State University
Wabash College M

**Iowa**

Buena Vista University
Central College
Clarke College M
Coe College
Cornell College
Grinnell College
Loras College
Luther College
Northwestern College W
Simpson College
University of Dubuque
Wartburg College

**Kentucky**

Centre College W

**Maine**

Bates College
Bowdoin College
Colby College
University of Southern Maine

**Maryland**

Frostburg State University
Goucher College
Johns Hopkins University
McDaniel College
Salisbury University

**Massachusetts**

Amherst College
Brandeis University
Bridgewater State College
Emerson College W
Emmanuel College
Fitchburg State College
Gordon College
Massachusetts Institute of
   Technology
Mount Holyoke College W
Regis College W

Salem State College
Smith College W
Springfield College
Tufts University
University of Massachusetts
   Boston W
   Dartmouth
Wellesley College W
Westfield State College
Wheaton College
Williams College
Worcester Polytechnic Institute
Worcester State College

## Michigan

Adrian College
Albion College
Calvin College

## Minnesota

Augsburg College
Bethel University
Carleton College
College of St. Benedict W
College of St. Catherine W
College of St. Scholastica
Concordia College: Moorhead
Gustavus Adolphus College
Hamline University
Macalester College
North Central University
Northwestern College M
St. John's University M
St. Mary's University of
   Minnesota
St. Olaf College
University of St. Thomas

## Mississippi

Mississippi College

## Missouri

Washington University in St.
   Louis

## Nebraska

Nebraska Wesleyan University

## New Hampshire

Keene State College

## New Jersey

The College of New Jersey
Kean University
Montclair State University
New Jersey City University
Ramapo College of New Jersey
Richard Stockton College of New
   Jersey
Rowan University
Rutgers, The State University of
   New Jersey
      Camden Regional Campus
      Newark Regional Campus
      W
Stevens Institute of Technology

## New York

Alfred University
City University of New York
   City College
   Hunter College
   Lehman College
   Medgar Evers College
   New York City College of
      Technology
   York College
Hamilton College
Ithaca College
Nazareth College of Rochester
New York University
Rensselaer Polytechnic Institute
Rochester Institute of Technology
St. Joseph's College: Suffolk
   Campus
St. Lawrence University

State University of New York
   College at Brockport
   College at Buffalo
   College at Cortland
   College at Fredonia
   College at Geneseo
   College at Oneonta
   College at Plattsburgh
   Farmingdale
   Oswego
Union College
United States Merchant Marine
   Academy
University of Rochester

## North Carolina

Methodist University

## Ohio

Baldwin-Wallace College
Bluffton University
Capital University
Case Western Reserve University
College of Mount St. Joseph
College of Wooster
Defiance College
Denison University
Heidelberg College
Hiram College
John Carroll University
Kenyon College
Marietta College
Mount Union College
Muskingum College
Oberlin College
Ohio Northern University
Ohio Wesleyan University
Otterbein College
Wilmington College
Wittenberg University

## Oregon

Lewis & Clark College
Linfield College
Willamette University

## Pennsylvania

Albright College
Allegheny College
Bryn Mawr College W
Cabrini College
Carnegie Mellon University
Delaware Valley College
DeSales University
Dickinson College
Elizabethtown College
Franklin & Marshall College
Geneva College
Gettysburg College
Gwynedd-Mercy College
Haverford College
Juniata College
Keystone College
Lebanon Valley College
Lincoln University
Messiah College
Misericordia University
Moravian College
Muhlenberg College
Penn State
   Erie, The Behrend College
Susquehanna University
Swarthmore College
Thiel College
Ursinus College
Washington & Jefferson College
Westminster College
Widener University

## Rhode Island

Rhode Island College

## Tennessee

Rhodes College
University of the South

## Texas

Howard Payne University
McMurry University

Texas Lutheran University W
Trinity University

## Vermont

Middlebury College

## Virginia

Bridgewater College
Christopher Newport University
Eastern Mennonite University
Lynchburg College
Roanoke College
University of Mary Washington
Virginia Wesleyan College
Washington and Lee University

## Washington

Pacific Lutheran University
University of Puget Sound
Whitworth University

## West Virginia

Bethany College

## Wisconsin

Beloit College
Carroll College
Carthage College
Concordia University Wisconsin
Edgewood College
Lawrence University
Milwaukee School of Engineering
Ripon College
St. Norbert College
University of Wisconsin
   Eau Claire
   La Crosse
   Oshkosh
   Platteville
   River Falls
   Stevens Point
   Stout
   Superior
   Whitewater
Wisconsin Lutheran College

## Track, outdoor Division I

## Alabama

Alabama Agricultural and
   Mechanical University
Alabama State University
Auburn University
Jacksonville State University W
Samford University
Troy University
University of Alabama
University of Alabama
   Birmingham W
University of South Alabama

## Arizona

Arizona State University
Northern Arizona University
University of Arizona

## Arkansas

Arkansas State University
University of Arkansas
University of Arkansas
   Little Rock
   Pine Bluff

## California

California Polytechnic State
   University: San Luis Obispo
California State University
   Fresno
   Fullerton
   Long Beach M
   Northridge
   Sacramento
Loyola Marymount University
Pepperdine University
San Diego State University W
Santa Clara University
Stanford University

University of California
   Berkeley
   Davis W
   Irvine
   Los Angeles
   Riverside
   Santa Barbara
University of San Diego W
University of San Francisco
University of Southern California

## Colorado

Colorado State University
United States Air Force Academy
University of Colorado
   Boulder
University of Northern Colorado
   M

## Connecticut

Central Connecticut State
   University
Quinnipiac University
Sacred Heart University
University of Connecticut
University of Hartford
Yale University

## Delaware

Delaware State University
University of Delaware

## District of Columbia

American University
Georgetown University
Howard University

## Florida

Bethune-Cookman University
Florida Agricultural and
   Mechanical University
Florida Atlantic University W
Florida International University
Florida State University
Jacksonville University W
University of Central Florida W
University of Florida
University of Miami
University of South Florida

## Georgia

Georgia Institute of Technology
Georgia Southern University W
Georgia State University
Savannah State University
University of Georgia

## Hawaii

University of Hawaii
   Manoa W

## Idaho

Boise State University
Idaho State University
University of Idaho

## Illinois

Bradley University W
Chicago State University
DePaul University
Eastern Illinois University
Illinois State University
Loyola University Chicago
Northern Illinois University W
Southern Illinois University
   Carbondale
University of Illinois
   Chicago
   Urbana-Champaign
Western Illinois University

## Indiana

Ball State University W
Butler University
Indiana State University
Indiana University
   Bloomington
Indiana University-Purdue
   University Fort Wayne W
Purdue University

University of Notre Dame
Valparaiso University

## Iowa

Drake University
Iowa State University
University of Iowa
University of Northern Iowa

## Kansas

Kansas State University
University of Kansas
Wichita State University

## Kentucky

Eastern Kentucky University
Morehead State University
Murray State University W
University of Kentucky
University of Louisville
Western Kentucky University

## Louisiana

Grambling State University
Louisiana State University and
   Agricultural and Mechanical
   College
Louisiana Tech University
McNeese State University
Nicholls State University W
Northwestern State University
Southeastern Louisiana University
Southern University and
   Agricultural and Mechanical
   College
Tulane University W
University of Louisiana at
   Lafayette
University of Louisiana at
   Monroe

## Maine

University of Maine

## Maryland

Coppin State University
Loyola College in Maryland W
Morgan State University
Mount St. Mary's University
Towson University W
United States Naval Academy
University of Maryland
   Baltimore County
   College Park
   Eastern Shore

## Massachusetts

Boston College
Boston University
College of the Holy Cross
Harvard College
Northeastern University
University of Massachusetts
   Amherst

## Michigan

Central Michigan University
Eastern Michigan University
Michigan State University
Oakland University
University of Detroit Mercy
University of Michigan
Western Michigan University W

## Minnesota

University of Minnesota
   Twin Cities

## Mississippi

Alcorn State University
Jackson State University
Mississippi State University
Mississippi Valley State
   University
University of Mississippi
University of Southern
   Mississippi

## Missouri

Missouri State University W
Saint Louis University M

Southeast Missouri State
University
University of Missouri
Columbia
Kansas City

**Montana**
Montana State University
Bozeman
University of Montana: Missoula

**Nebraska**
University of Nebraska
Lincoln

**Nevada**
University of Nevada
Las Vegas W
Reno W

**New Hampshire**
Dartmouth College
University of New Hampshire

**New Jersey**
Fairleigh Dickinson University
Metropolitan Campus
Monmouth University
Princeton University
Rider University
Rutgers, The State University of
New Jersey
New Brunswick/Piscataway
Campus
Saint Peter's College
Seton Hall University

**New Mexico**
New Mexico State University W
University of New Mexico

**New York**
Barnard College W
Colgate University
Columbia University M
Cornell University
Fordham University
Iona College
Long Island University
Brooklyn Campus
Manhattan College
Marist College
St. Francis College
St. John's University W
State University of New York
Albany
Binghamton
Buffalo
Stony Brook
Syracuse University
United States Military Academy
Wagner College

**North Carolina**
Appalachian State University
Campbell University
Davidson College
Duke University
East Carolina University
Elon University W
Gardner-Webb University
High Point University
North Carolina Agricultural and
Technical State University
North Carolina State University
University of North Carolina
Asheville
Chapel Hill
Charlotte
Greensboro
Wilmington
Wake Forest University
Western Carolina University

**Ohio**
Bowling Green State University
W
Kent State University
Miami University
Oxford Campus

Ohio State University
Columbus Campus
Ohio University W
University of Akron
University of Cincinnati
University of Dayton W
University of Toledo W
Wright State University
Xavier University
Youngstown State University

**Oklahoma**
Oklahoma State University
Oral Roberts University
University of Oklahoma
University of Tulsa

**Oregon**
Oregon State University W
Portland State University
University of Oregon
University of Portland

**Pennsylvania**
Bucknell University
Duquesne University
La Salle University
Lafayette College
Lehigh University
Penn State
University Park
Robert Morris University
St. Francis University
Saint Joseph's University
Temple University
University of Pennsylvania
University of Pittsburgh
Villanova University

**Rhode Island**
Brown University
Providence College
University of Rhode Island

**South Carolina**
Charleston Southern University
The Citadel
Clemson University
Coastal Carolina University
College of Charleston W
Furman University
South Carolina State University
University of South Carolina
Winthrop University
Wofford College

**Tennessee**
Austin Peay State University W
Belmont University
East Tennessee State University
Lipscomb University
Middle Tennessee State
University
Tennessee State University
Tennessee Technological
University W
University of Memphis
University of Tennessee
Chattanooga
Knoxville
Vanderbilt University W

**Texas**
Baylor University
Lamar University
Prairie View A&M University
Rice University
Sam Houston State University
Southern Methodist University W
Stephen F. Austin State University
Texas A&M University
Texas Christian University
Texas Southern University
Texas State University: San
Marcos
Texas Tech University
University of Houston
University of North Texas

University of Texas
Arlington
Austin
El Paso
Pan American
San Antonio

**Utah**
Brigham Young University
Southern Utah University
University of Utah W
Utah State University
Utah Valley State College
Weber State University

**Vermont**
University of Vermont

**Virginia**
College of William and Mary
George Mason University
Hampton University
James Madison University W
Liberty University
Norfolk State University
Radford University
University of Richmond
University of Virginia
Virginia Commonwealth
University
Virginia Military Institute
Virginia Polytechnic Institute and
State University

**Washington**
Gonzaga University
University of Washington
Washington State University

**West Virginia**
Marshall University W
West Virginia University W

**Wisconsin**
Marquette University
University of Wisconsin
Madison
Milwaukee

**Wyoming**
University of Wyoming

## Track, outdoor Division II

**Alabama**
Miles College
Stillman College
Tuskegee University
University of Alabama
Huntsville

**Alaska**
University of Alaska
Anchorage

**Arkansas**
Harding University
Southern Arkansas University
University of Central Arkansas W

**California**
California State Polytechnic
University: Pomona
California State University
Bakersfield
Chico
Dominguez Hills W
Los Angeles
Stanislaus
Humboldt State University
San Francisco State University W
University of California
Davis M
San Diego

**Colorado**
Adams State College
Colorado School of Mines
Mesa State College W

Metropolitan State College of
Denver
University of Colorado
Colorado Springs
Western State College of
Colorado

**Connecticut**
Southern Connecticut State
University
University of New Haven

**District of Columbia**
University of the District of
Columbia W

**Florida**
Florida Southern College
Nova Southeastern University
University of North Florida
University of Tampa
University of West Florida

**Georgia**
Albany State University
Clark Atlanta University
Clayton State University
Fort Valley State University
Kennesaw State University
Morehouse College M
Paine College

**Idaho**
Northwest Nazarene University

**Illinois**
Lewis University
Southern Illinois University
Edwardsville

**Indiana**
Anderson University W
Saint Joseph's College
University of Indianapolis
University of Southern Indiana

**Kansas**
Emporia State University
Fort Hays State University
Pittsburg State University

**Kentucky**
Bellarmine University
Kentucky State University
Northern Kentucky University

**Maryland**
Bowie State University
Columbia Union College

**Massachusetts**
American International College
Assumption College
Bentley College
Stonehill College
University of Massachusetts
Lowell

**Michigan**
Ferris State University
Grand Valley State University
Hillsdale College
Lake Superior State University
Michigan Technological
University
Northern Michigan University W
Northwood University: Michigan
Saginaw Valley State University

**Minnesota**
Bemidji State University
Concordia University: St. Paul
Minnesota State University
Mankato
Moorhead
Saint Cloud State University
University of Minnesota
Duluth
Morris
Winona State University W

**Missouri**
Drury University
Lincoln University
Missouri Southern State
University
Northwest Missouri State
University
Southwest Baptist University
Truman State University
University of Central Missouri
University of Missouri
Missouri University of
Science and Technology

**Nebraska**
Chadron State College
University of Nebraska
Kearney
Omaha W
Wayne State College

**New Jersey**
New Jersey Institute of
Technology

**New Mexico**
Eastern New Mexico University
New Mexico Highlands
University W

**New York**
City University of New York
Queens College
College of Saint Rose
Dominican College of Blauvelt W
Long Island University
C. W. Post Campus
Mercy College
Pace University
St. Thomas Aquinas College

**North Carolina**
Brevard College
Johnson C. Smith University
Lees-McRae College
Lenoir-Rhyne College
Livingstone College
Mars Hill College
North Carolina Central University
Queens University of Charlotte
St. Andrews Presbyterian College
St. Augustine's College
Shaw University
University of North Carolina
Pembroke
Winston-Salem State University

**North Dakota**
North Dakota State University
University of Mary
University of North Dakota

**Ohio**
Ashland University
Central State University
Tiffin University
University of Findlay

**Oregon**
Western Oregon University

**Pennsylvania**
Bloomsburg University of
Pennsylvania
California University of
Pennsylvania
Cheyney University of
Pennsylvania
Clarion University of
Pennsylvania W
East Stroudsburg University of
Pennsylvania
Edinboro University of
Pennsylvania
Indiana University of
Pennsylvania
Kutztown University of
Pennsylvania
Lock Haven University of
Pennsylvania

Mansfield University of
Pennsylvania
Millersville University of
Pennsylvania
Seton Hill University
Shippensburg University of
Pennsylvania
Slippery Rock University of
Pennsylvania
University of Pittsburgh
Johnstown W
West Chester University of
Pennsylvania

**Puerto Rico**
University of Puerto Rico
Bayamon University College
Cayey University College M
Mayaguez
Rio Piedras

**Rhode Island**
Bryant University

**South Carolina**
Anderson University M
Benedict College
Claflin University
Francis Marion University
University of South Carolina
Upstate W

**South Dakota**
Augustana College
Northern State University
South Dakota State University
University of South Dakota

**Tennessee**
Carson-Newman College
Lane College

**Texas**
Abilene Christian University
Angelo State University
Dallas Baptist University
Tarleton State University
Texas A&M University
Commerce
Kingsville
University of Texas
of the Permian Basin
University of the Incarnate Word

**Virginia**
St. Paul's College
Virginia State University
Virginia Union University

**Washington**
Central Washington University
Saint Martin's University
Seattle Pacific University
Seattle University
Western Washington University

**West Virginia**
Alderson-Broaddus College
Concord University
Glenville State College
University of Charleston
West Liberty State College
West Virginia Wesleyan College
Wheeling Jesuit University

**Wisconsin**
University of Wisconsin
Parkside

**Track, outdoor
Division III**

**Arkansas**
Hendrix College

**California**
California Institute of Technology
California Lutheran University
California State University
East Bay

Chapman University W
Claremont McKenna College
Mills College W
Occidental College
Pitzer College M
Pomona College
University of La Verne
University of Redlands
Whittier College

**Colorado**
Colorado College

**Connecticut**
Connecticut College
Eastern Connecticut State
University
Trinity College
United States Coast Guard
Academy
Wesleyan University

**Delaware**
Wesley College

**District of Columbia**
Catholic University of America
Gallaudet University

**Georgia**
Emory University
Oglethorpe University

**Illinois**
Augustana College
Aurora University
Benedictine University
Concordia University
Elmhurst College
Eureka College
Greenville College
Illinois College
Illinois Wesleyan University
Knox College
Millikin University
Monmouth College
North Central College
North Park University
Principia College
Rockford College
University of Chicago
Wheaton College

**Indiana**
Anderson University M
DePauw University
Earlham College
Franklin College
Hanover College
Manchester College
Rose-Hulman Institute of
Technology
Tri-State University
Wabash College M

**Iowa**
Buena Vista University
Central College
Clarke College M
Coe College
Cornell College
Grinnell College
Loras College
Luther College
Simpson College
University of Dubuque
Wartburg College

**Kentucky**
Centre College

**Maine**
Bates College
Bowdoin College
Colby College
University of Southern Maine

**Maryland**
Frostburg State University
Goucher College
Hood College

Johns Hopkins University
McDaniel College
Salisbury University

**Massachusetts**
Amherst College
Babson College
Brandeis University
Bridgewater State College
Emmanuel College
Fitchburg State College
Gordon College
Massachusetts Institute of
Technology
Massachusetts Maritime Academy
W
Mount Holyoke College W
Regis College W
Salem State College
Smith College W
Springfield College
Tufts University
University of Massachusetts
Boston
Dartmouth
Wellesley College W
Westfield State College
Wheaton College
Williams College
Worcester Polytechnic Institute
Worcester State College

**Michigan**
Adrian College
Albion College
Alma College
Calvin College
Hope College
Olivet College

**Minnesota**
Augsburg College
Bethel University
Carleton College
College of St. Benedict W
College of St. Catherine W
College of St. Scholastica
Concordia College: Moorhead
Gustavus Adolphus College
Hamline University
Macalester College
Martin Luther College
North Central University
Northwestern College
St. John's University M
St. Mary's University of
Minnesota
St. Olaf College
University of St. Thomas

**Mississippi**
Mississippi College
Rust College

**Missouri**
Fontbonne University
Washington University in St.
Louis

**Nebraska**
Nebraska Wesleyan University

**New Hampshire**
Colby-Sawyer College
Keene State College

**New Jersey**
The College of New Jersey
Kean University
Montclair State University
New Jersey City University
Ramapo College of New Jersey
Richard Stockton College of New
Jersey
Rowan University
Rutgers, The State University of
New Jersey
Camden Regional Campus
Newark Regional Campus
W

Stevens Institute of Technology

**New York**
Alfred University
City University of New York
City College
Hunter College
Lehman College
Medgar Evers College
New York City College of
Technology W
York College
Hamilton College
Ithaca College
Nazareth College of Rochester
New York University
Rensselaer Polytechnic Institute
Rochester Institute of Technology
St. Joseph's College: Suffolk
Campus
St. Lawrence University
State University of New York
College at Brockport
College at Buffalo
College at Cortland
College at Fredonia
College at Geneseo
College at Oneonta
College at Plattsburgh
Farmingdale
Oswego
Union College
United States Merchant Marine
Academy
University of Rochester
Vassar College

**North Carolina**
Methodist University

**Ohio**
Baldwin-Wallace College
Bluffton University
Capital University
Case Western Reserve University
College of Mount St. Joseph
College of Wooster
Defiance College
Denison University
Franciscan University of
Steubenville W
Heidelberg College
Hiram College
John Carroll University
Kenyon College
Marietta College
Mount Union College
Muskingum College
Oberlin College
Ohio Northern University
Ohio Wesleyan University
Otterbein College
Wilmington College
Wittenberg University

**Oregon**
George Fox University
Lewis & Clark College
Linfield College
Pacific University
Willamette University

**Pennsylvania**
Albright College
Allegheny College
Bryn Mawr College W
Cabrini College
Carnegie Mellon University
Delaware Valley College
DeSales University
Dickinson College
Elizabethtown College
Franklin & Marshall College
Geneva College W
Gettysburg College
Grove City College
Gwynedd-Mercy College
Haverford College
Juniata College

Keystone College
Lebanon Valley College
Lincoln University
Messiah College
Misericordia University
Moravian College
Muhlenberg College
Penn State
Erie, The Behrend College
St. Vincent College M
Susquehanna University
Swarthmore College
Thiel College
Ursinus College
Washington & Jefferson College
Waynesburg University
Westminster College
Widener University
York College of Pennsylvania

**Rhode Island**
Rhode Island College
Salve Regina University W

**South Carolina**
Anderson University W

**Tennessee**
Rhodes College
University of the South

**Texas**
Howard Payne University
McMurry University
Southwestern University
Sul Ross State University
Texas Lutheran University W
Trinity University
University of Dallas
University of Texas
Tyler M

**Vermont**
Middlebury College

**Virginia**
Bridgewater College
Christopher Newport University
Eastern Mennonite University
Lynchburg College
Roanoke College
University of Mary Washington
Virginia Wesleyan College
Washington and Lee University

**Washington**
Pacific Lutheran University
University of Puget Sound
Whitworth University

**West Virginia**
Bethany College

**Wisconsin**
Beloit College
Carroll College
Carthage College
Concordia University Wisconsin
Edgewood College
Lakeland College
Lawrence University
Milwaukee School of Engineering
Ripon College
St. Norbert College
University of Wisconsin
Eau Claire
La Crosse
Oshkosh
Platteville
River Falls
Stevens Point
Stout
Superior
Whitewater
Wisconsin Lutheran College

## Volleyball Division I

### Alabama

Alabama Agricultural and
  Mechanical University W
Alabama State University W
Auburn University W
Birmingham-Southern College W
Jacksonville State University W
Samford University W
Troy University W
University of Alabama W
University of Alabama
  Birmingham W
University of South Alabama W

### Arizona

Arizona State University W
Northern Arizona University W
University of Arizona W

### Arkansas

Arkansas State University W
University of Arkansas W
University of Arkansas
  Little Rock W
  Pine Bluff W

### California

California Polytechnic State
  University: San Luis Obispo W
California State University
  Fresno W
  Fullerton W
  Long Beach W
  Northridge W
  Sacramento W
Loyola Marymount University W
Pepperdine University W
St. Mary's College of California
  W
San Diego State University W
San Jose State University W
Santa Clara University W
Stanford University W
University of California
  Berkeley W
  Davis W
  Irvine W
  Los Angeles W
  Riverside W
  Santa Barbara W
University of San Diego W
University of San Francisco W
University of Southern California
  W
University of the Pacific W

### Colorado

Colorado State University W
United States Air Force Academy
  W
University of Colorado
  Boulder W
University of Denver W
University of Northern Colorado
  W

### Connecticut

Central Connecticut State
  University W
Fairfield University W
Quinnipiac University W
Sacred Heart University W
University of Connecticut W
University of Hartford W
Yale University W

### Delaware

Delaware State University W
University of Delaware W

### District of Columbia

American University W
George Washington University W
Georgetown University W
Howard University W

### Florida

Bethune-Cookman University W
Florida Agricultural and
  Mechanical University W
Florida Atlantic University W
Florida International University
  W
Florida State University W
Jacksonville University W
Stetson University W
University of Central Florida W
University of Florida W
University of Miami W
University of South Florida W

### Georgia

Georgia Institute of Technology
  W
Georgia Southern University W
Georgia State University W
Mercer University W
Savannah State University W
University of Georgia W

### Hawaii

University of Hawaii
  Manoa W

### Idaho

Boise State University W
Idaho State University W
University of Idaho W

### Illinois

Bradley University W
Chicago State University W
DePaul University W
Eastern Illinois University W
Illinois State University W
Loyola University Chicago W
Northern Illinois University W
Northwestern University W
Southern Illinois University
  Carbondale W
University of Illinois
  Chicago W
  Urbana-Champaign W
Western Illinois University W

### Indiana

Ball State University W
Butler University W
Indiana State University W
Indiana University
  Bloomington W
Indiana University-Purdue
  University Fort Wayne W
Indiana University-Purdue
  University Indianapolis W
Purdue University W
University of Evansville W
University of Notre Dame W
Valparaiso University W

### Iowa

Drake University W
Iowa State University W
University of Iowa W
University of Northern Iowa W

### Kansas

Kansas State University W
University of Kansas W
Wichita State University W

### Kentucky

Eastern Kentucky University W
Morehead State University W
Murray State University W
University of Kentucky W
University of Louisville W
Western Kentucky University W

### Louisiana

Centenary College of Louisiana
  W
Grambling State University W
Louisiana State University and
  Agricultural and Mechanical
  College W

Louisiana Tech University W
McNeese State University W
Nicholls State University W
Northwestern State University W
Southeastern Louisiana University
  W
Southern University and
  Agricultural and Mechanical
  College W
Tulane University W
University of Louisiana at
  Lafayette W
University of Louisiana at
  Monroe W
University of New Orleans W

### Maine

University of Maine W

### Maryland

Coppin State University W
Loyola College in Maryland W
Morgan State University W
Towson University W
United States Naval Academy W
University of Maryland
  Baltimore County W
  College Park W
  Eastern Shore W

### Massachusetts

Boston College W
College of the Holy Cross W
Harvard College W
Northeastern University W

### Michigan

Central Michigan University W
Eastern Michigan University W
Michigan State University W
Oakland University W
University of Michigan W
Western Michigan University W

### Minnesota

University of Minnesota
  Twin Cities W

### Mississippi

Alcorn State University W
Jackson State University W
Mississippi State University W
Mississippi Valley State
  University W
University of Mississippi W
University of Southern
  Mississippi W

### Missouri

Missouri State University W
Saint Louis University W
Southeast Missouri State
  University W
University of Missouri
  Columbia W
  Kansas City W

### Montana

Montana State University
  Bozeman W
University of Montana: Missoula
  W

### Nebraska

Creighton University W
University of Nebraska
  Lincoln W

### Nevada

University of Nevada
  Las Vegas W
  Reno W

### New Hampshire

Dartmouth College W
University of New Hampshire W

### New Jersey

Fairleigh Dickinson University
  Metropolitan Campus W
Princeton University W

Rider University W
Rutgers, The State University of
  New Jersey
  New Brunswick/Piscataway
    Campus W
Saint Peter's College W
Seton Hall University W

### New Mexico

New Mexico State University W
University of New Mexico W

### New York

Canisius College W
Colgate University W
Cornell University W
Fordham University W
Hofstra University W
Iona College W
Long Island University
  Brooklyn Campus W
Manhattan College W
Marist College W
Niagara University W
St. Francis College W
St. John's University W
Siena College W
State University of New York
  Albany W
  Binghamton W
  Buffalo W
  Stony Brook W
Syracuse University W
United States Military Academy
  W
Wagner College W

### North Carolina

Appalachian State University W
Campbell University W
Davidson College W
Duke University W
East Carolina University W
Elon University W
Gardner-Webb University W
High Point University W
North Carolina Agricultural and
  Technical State University W
North Carolina State University
  W
University of North Carolina
  Asheville W
  Chapel Hill W
  Charlotte W
  Greensboro W
  Wilmington W
Wake Forest University W
Western Carolina University W

### North Dakota

North Dakota State University W

### Ohio

Bowling Green State University
  W
Cleveland State University W
Kent State University W
Miami University
  Oxford Campus W
Ohio State University
  Columbus Campus W
Ohio University W
University of Akron W
University of Cincinnati W
University of Dayton W
University of Toledo W
Wright State University W
Xavier University W
Youngstown State University W

### Oklahoma

Oral Roberts University W
University of Oklahoma W
University of Tulsa W

### Oregon

Oregon State University W
Portland State University W
University of Oregon W

University of Portland W

### Pennsylvania

Bucknell University W
Duquesne University W
La Salle University W
Lafayette College W
Lehigh University W
Penn State
  University Park W
Robert Morris University W
St. Francis University W
Temple University W
University of Pennsylvania W
University of Pittsburgh W
Villanova University W

### Rhode Island

Brown University W
Providence College W
University of Rhode Island W

### South Carolina

Charleston Southern University
  W
The Citadel W
Clemson University W
Coastal Carolina University W
College of Charleston W
Furman University W
South Carolina State University
  W
University of South Carolina W
Winthrop University W
Wofford College W

### South Dakota

South Dakota State University W

### Tennessee

Austin Peay State University W
Belmont University W
East Tennessee State University
  W
Lipscomb University W
Middle Tennessee State
  University W
Tennessee State University W
Tennessee Technological
  University W
University of Memphis W
University of Tennessee
  Chattanooga W
  Knoxville W
  Martin W

### Texas

Baylor University W
Lamar University W
Prairie View A&M University W
Rice University W
Sam Houston State University W
Southern Methodist University W
Stephen F. Austin State University
  W
Texas A&M University W
Texas Christian University W
Texas Southern University W
Texas State University: San
  Marcos W
Texas Tech University W
University of Houston W
University of North Texas W
University of Texas
  Arlington W
  Austin W
  El Paso W
  Pan American W
  San Antonio W

### Utah

Brigham Young University W
University of Utah W
Utah State University W
Utah Valley State College W
Weber State University W

### Virginia

College of William and Mary W
George Mason University W

Hampton University W
James Madison University W
Liberty University W
Norfolk State University W
Radford University W
University of Virginia W
Virginia Commonwealth
University W
Virginia Polytechnic Institute and
State University W

**Washington**
Gonzaga University W
University of Washington W
Washington State University W

**West Virginia**
Marshall University W
West Virginia University W

**Wisconsin**
Marquette University W
University of Wisconsin
Green Bay W
Madison W
Milwaukee W

**Wyoming**
University of Wyoming W

## Volleyball Division II

**Alabama**
Miles College W
Stillman College W
Tuskegee University W
University of Alabama
Huntsville W
University of Montevallo W
University of North Alabama W
University of West Alabama W

**Alaska**
University of Alaska
Anchorage W
Fairbanks W

**Arizona**
Grand Canyon University W

**Arkansas**
Arkansas Tech University W
Harding University W
Henderson State University W
Ouachita Baptist University W
Southern Arkansas University W
University of Arkansas
Monticello W
University of Central Arkansas W

**California**
California State Polytechnic
University: Pomona W
California State University
Bakersfield W
Chico W
Dominguez Hills W
Los Angeles W
Monterey Bay W
San Bernardino W
Stanislaus W
Humboldt State University W
Notre Dame de Namur University
W
Sonoma State University W
University of California
San Diego W

**Colorado**
Adams State College W
Colorado Christian University W
Colorado School of Mines W
Colorado State University
Pueblo W
Fort Lewis College W
Mesa State College W
Metropolitan State College of
Denver W
Regis University W

University of Colorado
Colorado Springs W
Western State College of
Colorado W

**Connecticut**
Post University W
Southern Connecticut State
University W
University of Bridgeport W
University of New Haven W

**Delaware**
Goldey-Beacom College W
Wilmington University W

**District of Columbia**
University of the District of
Columbia W

**Florida**
Barry University W
Eckerd College W
Florida Gulf Coast University W
Florida Institute of Technology W
Florida Southern College W
Lynn University W
Nova Southeastern University W
Palm Beach Atlantic University
W
Rollins College W
St. Leo University W
University of North Florida W
University of Tampa W
University of West Florida W

**Georgia**
Albany State University W
Armstrong Atlantic State
University W
Augusta State University W
Clark Atlanta University W
Fort Valley State University W
Kennesaw State University W
Paine College W
University of West Georgia W
Valdosta State University W

**Hawaii**
Brigham Young
University-Hawaii W
Chaminade University of
Honolulu W
Hawaii Pacific University W
University of Hawaii
Hilo W

**Idaho**
Northwest Nazarene University
W

**Illinois**
Lewis University W
Quincy University W
Southern Illinois University
Edwardsville W

**Indiana**
Oakland City University W
Saint Joseph's College W
University of Indianapolis W
University of Southern Indiana W

**Iowa**
Upper Iowa University W

**Kansas**
Emporia State University W
Fort Hays State University W
Newman University W
Pittsburg State University W
Washburn University W

**Kentucky**
Bellarmine University W
Kentucky State University W
Kentucky Wesleyan College W
Northern Kentucky University W

**Maryland**
Bowie State University W

**Massachusetts**
American International College
W
Assumption College W
Bentley College W
Merrimack College W
Stonehill College W
University of Massachusetts
Lowell W

**Michigan**
Ferris State University W
Grand Valley State University W
Hillsdale College W
Lake Superior State University W
Michigan Technological
University W
Northern Michigan University W
Northwood University: Michigan
W
Saginaw Valley State University
W
Wayne State University W

**Minnesota**
Bemidji State University W
Concordia University: St. Paul W
Minnesota State University
Mankato W
Moorhead W
Saint Cloud State University W
Southwest Minnesota State
University W
University of Minnesota
Crookston W
Duluth W
Morris W
Winona State University W

**Missouri**
Drury University W
Missouri Southern State
University W
Missouri Western State University
W
Northwest Missouri State
University W
Rockhurst University W
Southwest Baptist University W
Truman State University W
University of Central Missouri W
University of Missouri
St. Louis W

**Montana**
Montana State University
Billings W

**Nebraska**
Chadron State College W
University of Nebraska
Kearney W
Omaha W
Wayne State College W

**New Hampshire**
Franklin Pierce University W
St. Anselm College W
Southern New Hampshire
University W

**New Jersey**
Bloomfield College W
Caldwell College W
Felician College W
Georgian Court University W
New Jersey Institute of
Technology W

**New Mexico**
Eastern New Mexico University
W
New Mexico Highlands
University W
Western New Mexico University
W

**New York**
Adelphi University W

City University of New York
Queens College W
College of Saint Rose W
Concordia College W
Dominican College of Blauvelt W
Dowling College W
Le Moyne College W
Long Island University
C. W. Post Campus W
Mercy College W
Molloy College W
New York Institute of Technology
W
Nyack College W
Pace University W

**North Carolina**
Barton College W
Belmont Abbey College W
Brevard College W
Catawba College W
Elizabeth City State University W
Fayetteville State University W
Johnson C. Smith University W
Lees-McRae College W
Lenoir-Rhyne College W
Livingstone College W
Mars Hill College W
Mount Olive College W
North Carolina Central University
W
Pfeiffer University W
Queens University of Charlotte W
St. Andrews Presbyterian College
W
St. Augustine's College W
Shaw University W
University of North Carolina
Pembroke W
Wingate University W
Winston-Salem State University
W

**North Dakota**
University of Mary W
University of North Dakota W

**Ohio**
Ashland University W
Central State University W
Tiffin University W
University of Findlay W

**Oklahoma**
Cameron University W
Oklahoma Panhandle State
University W
Southeastern Oklahoma State
University W
Southwestern Oklahoma State
University W
University of Central Oklahoma
W

**Oregon**
Western Oregon University W

**Pennsylvania**
California University of
Pennsylvania W
Cheyney University of
Pennsylvania W
Clarion University of
Pennsylvania W
East Stroudsburg University of
Pennsylvania W
Edinboro University of
Pennsylvania W
Gannon University W
Holy Family University W
Indiana University of
Pennsylvania W
Kutztown University of
Pennsylvania W
Lock Haven University of
Pennsylvania W
Mercyhurst College W
Millersville University of
Pennsylvania W

Philadelphia University W
Seton Hill University W
Shippensburg University of
Pennsylvania W
Slippery Rock University of
Pennsylvania W
University of Pittsburgh
Johnstown W
University of the Sciences in
Philadelphia W
West Chester University of
Pennsylvania W

**Puerto Rico**
University of Puerto Rico
Bayamon University College
W
Cayey University College W
Mayaguez W
Rio Piedras W

**Rhode Island**
Bryant University W

**South Carolina**
Anderson University W
Benedict College W
Claflin University W
Coker College W
Converse College W
Francis Marion University W
Lander University W
Limestone College W
Newberry College W
North Greenville University W
Presbyterian College W
University of South Carolina
Aiken W
Upstate W

**South Dakota**
Augustana College W
Northern State University W
University of South Dakota W

**Tennessee**
Carson-Newman College W
Christian Brothers University W
Lane College W
LeMoyne-Owen College W
Lincoln Memorial University W
Tusculum College W

**Texas**
Abilene Christian University W
Angelo State University W
Dallas Baptist University W
Midwestern State University W
St. Edward's University W
St. Mary's University W
Tarleton State University W
Texas A&M International
University W
Texas A&M University
Commerce W
Kingsville W
Texas Woman's University W
University of Texas
of the Permian Basin W
University of the Incarnate Word
W
West Texas A&M University W

**Utah**
Dixie State College of Utah W

**Vermont**
St. Michael's College W

**Virginia**
St. Paul's College W
Virginia State University W
Virginia Union University W

**Washington**
Central Washington University W
Saint Martin's University W
Seattle Pacific University W
Seattle University W

Western Washington University W

## West Virginia

Alderson-Broaddus College W
Bluefield State College W
Concord University W
Davis and Elkins College W
Fairmont State University W
Glenville State College W
Ohio Valley University W
Salem International University W
Shepherd University W
University of Charleston W
West Liberty State College W
West Virginia Wesleyan College W
Wheeling Jesuit University W

## Wisconsin

University of Wisconsin Parkside W

### Volleyball Division III

## Alabama

Huntingdon College W

## Arkansas

Hendrix College W

## California

California Institute of Technology W
California Lutheran University W
California State University East Bay W
Chapman University W
Claremont McKenna College W
La Sierra University W
Menlo College W
Mills College W
Occidental College W
Pomona College W
University of California Santa Cruz W
University of La Verne W
University of Redlands W
Whittier College W

## Colorado

Colorado College W

## Connecticut

Albertus Magnus College W
Connecticut College W
Eastern Connecticut State University W
Mitchell College W
St. Joseph College W
Trinity College W
United States Coast Guard Academy W
Wesleyan University W
Western Connecticut State University W

## Delaware

Wesley College W

## District of Columbia

Catholic University of America W
Gallaudet University W
Trinity Washington University W

## Georgia

Agnes Scott College W
Emory University W
LaGrange College W
Oglethorpe University W
Piedmont College W
Spelman College W

## Illinois

Augustana College W
Aurora University W
Benedictine University W
Blackburn College W
Concordia University W

Dominican University W
Elmhurst College W
Eureka College W
Greenville College W
Illinois College W
Illinois Wesleyan University W
Knox College W
Lake Forest College W
MacMurray College W
Millikin University W
Monmouth College W
North Central College W
North Park University W
Principia College W
Rockford College W
University of Chicago W
Wheaton College W

## Indiana

Anderson University W
DePauw University W
Earlham College W
Franklin College W
Hanover College W
Manchester College W
Rose-Hulman Institute of Technology W
Saint Mary's College W
Tri-State University W

## Iowa

Buena Vista University W
Central College W
Coe College W
Cornell College W
Grinnell College W
Loras College W
Luther College W
Simpson College W
University of Dubuque W
Wartburg College W

## Kentucky

Centre College W
Thomas More College W
Transylvania University W

## Maine

Bates College W
Bowdoin College W
Colby College W
Husson College W
Maine Maritime Academy W
St. Joseph's College W
Thomas College W
University of Maine Farmington W
University of New England W

## Maryland

College of Notre Dame of Maryland W
Frostburg State University W
Goucher College W
Hood College W
Johns Hopkins University W
McDaniel College W
St. Mary's College of Maryland W
Salisbury University W
Villa Julie College W
Washington College W

## Massachusetts

Amherst College W
Anna Maria College W
Babson College W
Bay Path College W
Becker College W
Brandeis University W
Bridgewater State College W
Clark University W
Eastern Nazarene College W
Elms College W
Emerson College W
Emmanuel College W
Endicott College W
Framingham State College W
Gordon College W

Lasell College W
Lesley University W
Massachusetts College of Liberal Arts W
Massachusetts Institute of Technology W
Massachusetts Maritime Academy W
Mount Holyoke College W
Mount Ida College W
Newbury College W
Pine Manor College W
Regis College W
Salem State College W
Simmons College W
Smith College W
Springfield College W
Suffolk University W
Tufts University W
University of Massachusetts Boston W
Dartmouth W
Wellesley College W
Wentworth Institute of Technology W
Western New England College W
Westfield State College W
Wheaton College W
Williams College W
Worcester Polytechnic Institute W
Worcester State College W

## Michigan

Adrian College W
Albion College W
Alma College W
Calvin College W
Finlandia University W
Hope College W
Kalamazoo College W
Olivet College W

## Minnesota

Augsburg College W
Bethany Lutheran College W
Bethel University W
Carleton College W
College of St. Benedict W
College of St. Catherine W
College of St. Scholastica W
Concordia College: Moorhead W
Crown College W
Gustavus Adolphus College W
Hamline University W
Macalester College W
Martin Luther College W
North Central University W
Northwestern College W
St. Mary's University of Minnesota W
St. Olaf College W
University of St. Thomas W

## Mississippi

Millsaps College W
Mississippi College W
Rust College W

## Missouri

Fontbonne University W
Maryville University of Saint Louis W
Washington University in St. Louis W
Webster University W
Westminster College W

## Nebraska

Nebraska Wesleyan University W

## New Hampshire

Colby-Sawyer College W
Daniel Webster College W
Keene State College W
Plymouth State University W
Rivier College W

## New Jersey

Centenary College W

College of St. Elizabeth W
Fairleigh Dickinson University College at Florham W
Kean University W
Montclair State University W
New Jersey City University W
Ramapo College of New Jersey W
Richard Stockton College of New Jersey W
Rowan University W
Rutgers, The State University of New Jersey
   Camden Regional Campus W
   Newark Regional Campus W
Stevens Institute of Technology W
William Paterson University of New Jersey W

## New York

Alfred University W
Bard College W
Cazenovia College W
City University of New York
   Baruch College W
   Brooklyn College W
   City College W
   Hunter College W
   John Jay College of Criminal Justice W
   Lehman College W
   Medgar Evers College W
   New York City College of Technology W
   York College W
Clarkson University W
College of Mount St. Vincent W
College of New Rochelle W
Elmira College W
Hamilton College W
Hartwick College W
Hilbert College W
Ithaca College W
Keuka College W
Medaille College W
Mount St. Mary College W
Nazareth College of Rochester W
New York University W
Polytechnic University W
Rochester Institute of Technology W
Russell Sage College W
St. John Fisher College W
St. Joseph's College: Suffolk Campus W
St. Lawrence University W
Skidmore College W
State University of New York
   College at Brockport W
   College at Buffalo W
   College at Cortland W
   College at Fredonia W
   College at Geneseo W
   College at Old Westbury W
   College at Oneonta W
   College at Plattsburgh W
   College at Potsdam W
   College of Agriculture and Technology at Morrisville W
   Farmingdale W
   Institute of Technology at Utica/Rome W
   Maritime College W
   New Paltz W
   Oswego W
   Purchase W
Union College W
United States Merchant Marine Academy W
University of Rochester W
Utica College W
Vassar College W

## North Carolina

Greensboro College W
Guilford College W
Meredith College W
Methodist University W
North Carolina Wesleyan College W
Peace College W
Salem College W

## Ohio

Baldwin-Wallace College W
Bluffton University W
Capital University W
Case Western Reserve University W
College of Mount St. Joseph W
College of Wooster W
Defiance College W
Denison University W
Heidelberg College W
Hiram College W
John Carroll University W
Kenyon College W
Lake Erie College W
Marietta College W
Mount Union College W
Muskingum College W
Oberlin College W
Ohio Northern University W
Ohio Wesleyan University W
Otterbein College W
Wilmington College W
Wittenberg University W

## Oregon

George Fox University W
Lewis & Clark College W
Linfield College W
Pacific University W
Willamette University W

## Pennsylvania

Albright College W
Allegheny College W
Alvernia College W
Arcadia University W
Baptist Bible College of Pennsylvania W
Bryn Mawr College W
Cabrini College W
Carnegie Mellon University W
Cedar Crest College W
Chatham University W
Chestnut Hill College W
Delaware Valley College W
DeSales University W
Dickinson College W
Eastern University W
Elizabethtown College W
Franklin & Marshall College W
Geneva College W
Gettysburg College W
Grove City College W
Gwynedd-Mercy College W
Haverford College W
Immaculata University W
Juniata College W
King's College W
La Roche College W
Lancaster Bible College W
Lebanon Valley College W
Lincoln University W
Lycoming College W
Marywood University W
Messiah College W
Misericordia University W
Moravian College W
Mount Aloysius College W
Muhlenberg College W
Neumann College W
Penn State
   Altoona W
   Berks W
   Erie, The Behrend College W
Philadelphia Biblical University

Rosemont College W
Susquehanna University W
Swarthmore College W
Thiel College W
University of Pittsburgh
    Bradford W
    Greensburg W
University of Scranton W
Ursinus College W
Washington & Jefferson College
    W
Waynesburg University W
Westminster College W
Widener University W
Wilkes University W
York College of Pennsylvania W

**Rhode Island**
Johnson & Wales University:
    Providence W
Rhode Island College W
Roger Williams University W
Salve Regina University W

**South Dakota**
Presentation College W

**Tennessee**
Maryville College W
Rhodes College W
University of the South W

**Texas**
Austin College W
Concordia University at Austin W
East Texas Baptist University W
Hardin-Simmons University W
Howard Payne University W
LeTourneau University W
McMurry University W
Schreiner University W
Southwestern University W
Sul Ross State University W
Texas Lutheran University W
Trinity University W
University of Dallas W
University of Mary Hardin-Baylor
    W
University of Texas
    Dallas W
    Tyler W

**Vermont**
Castleton State College W
Green Mountain College W
Lyndon State College W
Middlebury College W
Norwich University W
Southern Vermont College W

**Virginia**
Averett University W
Bridgewater College W
Christopher Newport University
    W
Eastern Mennonite University W
Emory & Henry College W
Ferrum College W
Lynchburg College W
Mary Baldwin College W
Marymount University W
Randolph College W
Randolph-Macon College W
Roanoke College W
Shenandoah University W
Sweet Briar College W
University of Mary Washington
    W
Virginia Wesleyan College W
Washington and Lee University
    W

**Washington**
Pacific Lutheran University W
University of Puget Sound W
Whitman College W
Whitworth University W

**West Virginia**
Bethany College W

**Wisconsin**
Alverno College W
Beloit College W
Carroll College W
Carthage College W
Concordia University Wisconsin
    W
Edgewood College W
Lakeland College W
Lawrence University W
Maranatha Baptist Bible College
    W
Marian College of Fond du Lac W
Milwaukee School of Engineering
    W
Mount Mary College W
Northland College W
Ripon College W
St. Norbert College W
University of Wisconsin
    Eau Claire W
    La Crosse W
    Oshkosh W
    Platteville W
    River Falls W
    Stevens Point W
    Stout W
    Superior W
    Whitewater W
Wisconsin Lutheran College W

## Water polo Division I

**Arizona**
Arizona State University W

**California**
California State University
    Long Beach W
    Northridge W
Loyola Marymount University W
Pepperdine University M
San Diego State University W
San Jose State University W
Santa Clara University W
Stanford University W
University of California
    Berkeley W
    Davis W
    Irvine W
    Los Angeles W
    Santa Barbara W
University of Southern California
    W
University of the Pacific W

**Colorado**
Colorado State University W
United States Air Force Academy
    M

**District of Columbia**
George Washington University W

**Hawaii**
University of Hawaii
    Manoa W

**Indiana**
Indiana University
    Bloomington W

**Maryland**
United States Naval Academy M
University of Maryland
    College Park W

**Massachusetts**
Harvard College W

**Michigan**
University of Michigan W

**New Jersey**
Princeton University W

**New York**
Fordham University M
Hartwick College W

Iona College W
Marist College W
St. Francis College W
Siena College W
Wagner College W

**Pennsylvania**
Bucknell University W
Villanova University W

**Rhode Island**
Brown University W

## Water polo Division II

**Arizona**
Arizona State University W

**California**
California State University
    Long Beach W
    Northridge W
Loyola Marymount University W
San Diego State University W
San Jose State University W
Santa Clara University W
Stanford University W
University of California
    Berkeley W
    Davis W
    Irvine W
    Los Angeles W
    San Diego M
    Santa Barbara W
University of Southern California
    W
University of the Pacific W

**Colorado**
Colorado State University W

**District of Columbia**
George Washington University W

**Hawaii**
University of Hawaii
    Manoa W

**Indiana**
Indiana University
    Bloomington W

**Maryland**
University of Maryland
    College Park W

**Massachusetts**
Harvard College W

**Michigan**
University of Michigan W

**New Jersey**
Princeton University W

**New York**
City University of New York
    Queens College M
Hartwick College W
Iona College W
Marist College W
St. Francis College W
Siena College W
Wagner College W

**Pennsylvania**
Bucknell University W
Gannon University M
Mercyhurst College M
Villanova University W

**Rhode Island**
Brown University W

**West Virginia**
Salem International University M

## Water polo Division III

**Arizona**
Arizona State University W

**California**
California Institute of Technology
    M
California Lutheran University M
California State University
    Long Beach W
    Northridge W
Chapman University M
Claremont McKenna College M
Loyola Marymount University W
Occidental College M
Pitzer College M
Pomona College M
San Diego State University W
San Jose State University W
Santa Clara University W
Stanford University W
University of California
    Berkeley W
    Davis W
    Irvine W
    Los Angeles W
    Santa Barbara W
    Santa Cruz M
University of La Verne M
University of Redlands M
University of Southern California
    W
University of the Pacific W
Whittier College M

**Colorado**
Colorado State University W

**Connecticut**
Connecticut College M

**District of Columbia**
George Washington University W

**Hawaii**
University of Hawaii
    Manoa W

**Indiana**
Indiana University
    Bloomington W

**Maryland**
Johns Hopkins University M
University of Maryland
    College Park W

**Massachusetts**
Harvard College W
Massachusetts Institute of
    Technology M

**Michigan**
University of Michigan W

**New Jersey**
Princeton University W

**New York**
Hartwick College W
Iona College W
Marist College W
St. Francis College W
Siena College W
Wagner College W

**Pennsylvania**
Bucknell University W
Penn State
    Erie, The Behrend College
    M
Villanova University W
Washington & Jefferson College
    M

**Rhode Island**
Brown University W

## Wrestling Division I

**Arizona**
Arizona State University M
Grand Canyon University M

**California**
California Polytechnic State
    University: San Luis Obispo M
California State University
    Bakersfield M
    Fullerton M
Stanford University M
University of California
    Davis M

**Colorado**
United States Air Force Academy
    M
University of Northern Colorado
    M

**Connecticut**
Sacred Heart University M

**Delaware**
Delaware State University M

**District of Columbia**
American University M

**Idaho**
Boise State University M

**Illinois**
Northern Illinois University M
Northwestern University M
University of Illinois
    Urbana-Champaign M

**Indiana**
Indiana University
    Bloomington M
Purdue University M

**Iowa**
Iowa State University M
University of Iowa M
University of Northern Iowa M

**Maryland**
United States Naval Academy M
University of Maryland
    College Park M

**Massachusetts**
Boston University M
Harvard College M

**Michigan**
Central Michigan University M
Eastern Michigan University M
Michigan State University M
University of Michigan M

**Minnesota**
University of Minnesota
    Twin Cities M

**Missouri**
University of Missouri
    Columbia M

**Nebraska**
University of Nebraska
    Lincoln M

**New Jersey**
Princeton University M
Rider University M
Rutgers, The State University of
    New Jersey
    New Brunswick/Piscataway
    Campus M

**New York**
Columbia University M
Cornell University M
Hofstra University M
State University of New York
    Binghamton M
    Buffalo M

United States Military Academy M

Wagner College M

**North Carolina**

Appalachian State University M

Campbell University M

Davidson College M

Duke University M

Gardner-Webb University M

North Carolina State University M

University of North Carolina
Chapel Hill M
Greensboro M

**North Dakota**

North Dakota State University M

**Ohio**

Cleveland State University M

Kent State University M

Ohio State University
Columbus Campus M

Ohio University M

**Oklahoma**

Oklahoma State University M

University of Oklahoma M

**Oregon**

Oregon State University M

Portland State University M

University of Oregon M

**Pennsylvania**

Bloomsburg University of
Pennsylvania M

Bucknell University M

Clarion University of
Pennsylvania M

Drexel University M

Duquesne University M

East Stroudsburg University of
Pennsylvania M

Edinboro University of
Pennsylvania M

Franklin & Marshall College M

Lehigh University M

Lock Haven University of
Pennsylvania M

Millersville University of
Pennsylvania M

Penn State
University Park M

University of Pennsylvania M

University of Pittsburgh M

**Rhode Island**

Brown University M

**South Carolina**

The Citadel M

**South Dakota**

South Dakota State University M

**Tennessee**

University of Tennessee
Chattanooga M

**Utah**

Utah Valley State College M

**Virginia**

George Mason University M

Liberty University M

Old Dominion University M

University of Virginia M

Virginia Military Institute M

Virginia Polytechnic Institute and
State University M

**West Virginia**

West Virginia University M

**Wisconsin**

University of Wisconsin
Madison M

**Wyoming**

University of Wyoming M

## Wrestling Division II

**California**

San Francisco State University M

**Colorado**

Adams State College M

Colorado School of Mines M

Mesa State College M

Western State College of
Colorado M

**Illinois**

Southern Illinois University
Edwardsville M

**Indiana**

University of Indianapolis M

**Iowa**

Upper Iowa University M

**Kansas**

Fort Hays State University M

Newman University M

**Massachusetts**

American International College M

**Minnesota**

Minnesota State University
Mankato M
Moorhead M

Saint Cloud State University M

Southwest Minnesota State
University M

**Missouri**

Truman State University M

University of Central Missouri M

**Nebraska**

Chadron State College M

University of Nebraska
Kearney M
Omaha M

**New Mexico**

New Mexico Highlands
University M

**North Carolina**

Belmont Abbey College M

St. Andrews Presbyterian College
M

University of North Carolina
Pembroke M

**North Dakota**

University of Mary M

**Ohio**

Ashland University M

University of Findlay M

**Oklahoma**

University of Central Oklahoma
M

**Pennsylvania**

Gannon University M

Kutztown University of
Pennsylvania M

Mercyhurst College M

Seton Hill University M

Shippensburg University of
Pennsylvania M

University of Pittsburgh
Johnstown M

**Puerto Rico**

University of Puerto Rico
Bayamon University College
M
Mayaguez M
Rio Piedras M

**South Carolina**

Anderson University M

Limestone College M

Newberry College M

**South Dakota**

Augustana College M

Northern State University M

**Tennessee**

Carson-Newman College M

**West Virginia**

West Liberty State College M

**Wisconsin**

University of Wisconsin
Parkside M

## Wrestling Division III

**California**

Menlo College M

**Connecticut**

Trinity College M

United States Coast Guard
Academy M

Wesleyan University M

**Illinois**

Augustana College M

Elmhurst College M

Knox College M

Millikin University M

North Central College M

University of Chicago M

Wheaton College M

**Indiana**

Manchester College M

Rose-Hulman Institute of
Technology M

Tri-State University M

Wabash College M

**Iowa**

Buena Vista University M

Central College M

Coe College M

Cornell College M

Loras College M

Luther College M

Simpson College M

University of Dubuque M

Wartburg College M

**Maine**

University of Southern Maine M

**Maryland**

Johns Hopkins University M

McDaniel College M

**Massachusetts**

Bridgewater State College M

Massachusetts Institute of
Technology M

Springfield College M

Western New England College M

Williams College M

Worcester Polytechnic Institute M

**Michigan**

Olivet College M

**Minnesota**

Augsburg College M

Concordia College: Moorhead M

St. John's University M

St. Olaf College M

**New Hampshire**

Plymouth State University M

**New Jersey**

Centenary College M

The College of New Jersey M

Stevens Institute of Technology M

**New York**

City University of New York
Hunter College M

Ithaca College M

New York University M

Rochester Institute of Technology
M

State University of New York
College at Brockport M
College at Cortland M
College at Oneonta M
Oswego M

United States Merchant Marine
Academy M

Yeshiva University M

**Ohio**

Baldwin-Wallace College M

Case Western Reserve University
M

College of Mount St. Joseph M

Heidelberg College M

John Carroll University M

Mount Union College M

Muskingum College M

Ohio Northern University M

Wilmington College M

**Oregon**

Pacific University M

**Pennsylvania**

Delaware Valley College M

Elizabethtown College M

Gettysburg College M

King's College M

Lycoming College M

Messiah College M

Muhlenberg College M

Thiel College M

University of Scranton M

Ursinus College M

Washington & Jefferson College
M

Waynesburg University M

Wilkes University M

York College of Pennsylvania M

**Rhode Island**

Johnson & Wales University:
Providence M

Rhode Island College M

Roger Williams University M

**Vermont**

Norwich University M

**Virginia**

Washington and Lee University M

**Wisconsin**

Concordia University Wisconsin
M

Lakeland College M

Lawrence University M

Maranatha Baptist Bible College
M

Milwaukee School of Engineering
M

University of Wisconsin
Eau Claire M
La Crosse M
Oshkosh M
Platteville M
Stevens Point M
Whitewater M

# Alphabetical index of colleges

Tables and Indexes

# Also Available
# from the College Board

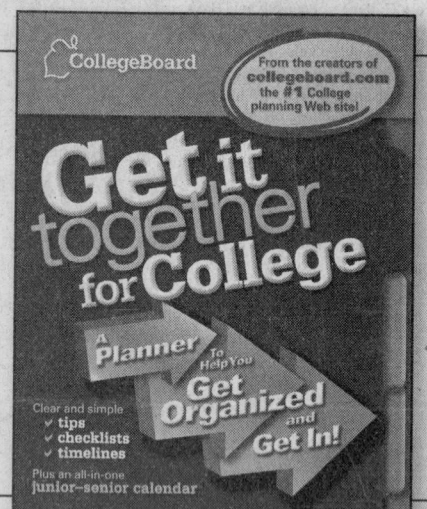

## Get It Together for College

Applying to college? Don't get overwhelmed—get organized with expert tips from the #1 college planning Web site, www.collegeboard.com. This easy-to-use planner will walk you through the forms, tests, and applications and keep you on track for each deadline. Includes insider tips, tracking charts, checklists, easy-to-follow timelines, and a junior–senior year calendar that pulls it all together.

*224 pages, paperbound*
ISBN 978-0-87447-829-7
**$14.9**

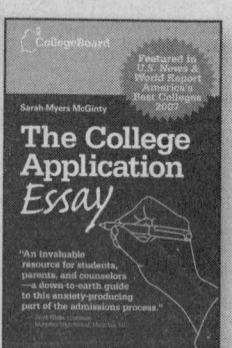

## The College Applica... Essay, Revised Editi...
### by Sarah Myers McGinty

Trying to find a topic for you... application essay? Former a... dean Sarah Myers McGinty shares strategies that will help you stand out from the crowd. Includes critiqued sample essays written by real students, jump starts for writer's block, and a chapter for your parents that explains their role in the process.

*176 pages, paperbound*
ISBN 978-0-87447-711-5
**$15.95**

## ...Majors 2009

...e major for you? Where can ...it? In this book, 190 college ...describe the majors they ...t you'll study, careers the ...major can lead to, and how to prepare for the major in high school. Includes listings showing which colleges offer each of 900 majors, and at what degree level.

*1,328 pages, paperbound*
ISBN 978-0-87447-824-2
**$2.95**

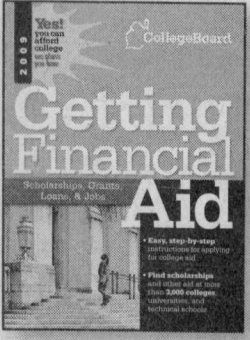

## Getting Financial Aid 2009

This step-by-step guide tells you how to get aid, when to apply, and what kinds of aid to expect from colleges. Includes a planning calendar, tips from college financial aid officers, and indexes showing which colleges offer merit scholarships for your interests.

*1,008 pages, paperbound*
ISBN 978-0-87447-825-9
**$19.95**

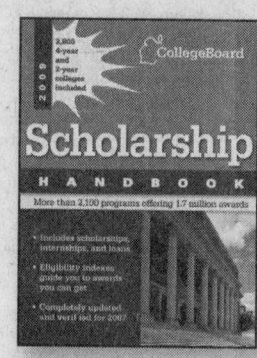

## Scholarship Handbook 2009

This no-nonsense guide speeds you straight to scholarships targeted to who you are, where you live, and what you want to study. Includes detailed profiles of more than 2,100 scholarship, internship, and loan programs.

*632 pages, paperbound*
ISBN 978-0-87447-827-3
**$27.95**

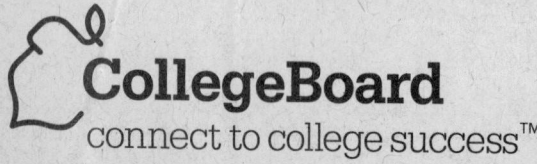

## CollegeBoard
### connect to college success™

Available wherever books are sold.
Distributed by Macmillan